Stanl   ons
Simplified Catalogue

Stamps of the World

Stanley Gibbons Simplified Catalogue

Stamps of the World 3

2011 Edition

Countries **German Commands – Jasdan**

Stanley Gibbons Ltd
London and Ringwood

By Appointment to
Her Majesty the Queen
Stanley Gibbons Limited
London
Philatelists

76th Edition
Published in Great Britain by
Stanley Gibbons Ltd
Publications Editorial, Sales Offices and Distribution Centre
7, Parkside, Christchurch Road,
Ringwood, Hampshire BH24 3SH
Telephone +44 (0) 1425 472363

British Library Cataloguing in
Publication Data.
A catalogue record for this book is available
from the British Library.

ISBN 10: 0-85259-789-4
ISBN 13: 978-0-85259-789-7
(Six volume set)

Published as Stanley Gibbons Simplified Catalogue from 1934 to 1970, renamed Stamps of the World in 1971, and produced in two (1982-88), three (1989-2001), four (2002-2005), five (from 2006) and six volumes from 2011 as Stanley Gibbons Simplified Catalogue of Stamps of the World.

Item No. 2881– Set 11

Printed and bound in Italy by Lego SpA

Contents – Volume 3

Est 1856
STANLEY GIBBONS

About Us

Our History

Edward Stanley Gibbons started trading postage stamps in his father's chemist shop in 1856. Since then we have been at the forefront of stamp collecting for over 150 years. We hold the Royal Warrant, offer unsurpassed expertise and quality and provide collectors with the peace of mind of a certificate of authenticity on all of our stamps. If you think of stamp collecting, you think of Stanley Gibbons and we are proud to uphold that tradition for you.

399 Strand

Our world famous stamp shop is a collector's paradise, with all of our latest catalogues, albums and accessories and, of course, our unrivalled stockholding of postage stamps.

www.stanleygibbons.com shop@stanleygibbons.co.uk +44 (0)20 7836 8444

Specialist Stamp Sales

For the collector that appreciates the value of collecting the highest quality examples, Stanley Gibbons is the only choice. Our extensive range is unrivalled in terms of quality and quantity, with specialist stamps available from all over the world.

www.stanleygibbons.com/stamps shop@stanleygibbons.co.uk +44 (0)20 7836 8444

Stanley Gibbons Auctions and Valuations

Sell your collection or individual rare items through our prestigious public auctions or our regular postal auctions and benefit from the excellent prices being realised at auction currently. We also provide an unparalleled valuation service.

www.stanleygibbons.com/auctions auctions@stanleygibbons.co.uk +44 (0)20 7836 8444

Stanley Gibbons Publications

The world's first stamp catalogue was printed by Stanley Gibbons in 1865 and we haven't looked back since! Our catalogues are trusted worldwide as the industry standard and we print countless titles each year. We also publish consumer and trade magazines, Gibbons Stamp Monthly and Philatelic Exporter to bring you news, views and insights into all things philatelic. Never miss an issue by subscribing today and benefit from exclusive subscriber offers each month.

www.stanleygibbons.com/shop orders@stanleygibbons.co.uk +44 (0)1425 472 363

Stanley Gibbons Investments

The Stanley Gibbons Investment Department offers a unique range of investment propositions that have consistently outperformed more traditional forms of investment, from capital protected products with unlimited upside to portfolios made up of the world's rarest stamps and autographs.

www.stanleygibbons.com/investment investment@stanleygibbons.co.uk +44 (0)1481 708 270

Fraser's Autographs

Autographs, manuscripts and memorabilia from Henry VIII to current day. We have over 60,000 items in stock, including movie stars, musicians, sport stars, historical figures and royalty. Fraser's is the UK's market leading autograph dealer and has been dealing in high quality autographed material since 1978.

www.frasersautographs.com sales@frasersautographs.co.uk +44 (0)20 7557 4404

stanleygibbons.com

Our website offers the complete philatelic service. Whether you are looking to buy stamps, invest, read news articles, browse our online stamp catalogue or find new issues, you are just one click away from anything you desire in the world of stamp collecting at stanleygibbons.com. Happy browsing!

www.stanleygibbons.com

Introduction

The ultimate reference work for all stamps issued around the world since the very first Penny Black of 1840, now with an improved layout.

Stamps of the World provides a comprehensive, illustrated, priced guide to postage stamps, and is the standard reference tool for every collector. It will help you to identify those elusive stamps, to value your collection, and to learn more about the background to issues. *Stamps of the World* was first published in 1934 and has been updated every year since 1950.

New for this year is a section 'Putting on a Good Show' which provides expert advice on starting and developing a collection, then making the most of its presentation. Also included is a guide to stamp identification so that you can easily discover which country issued your stamp.

Newly re-designed this year to provide more colourful, clearer, and easy-to-navigate listings, these volumes continue to present you with a wealth of information to enhance your enjoyment of stamp collecting.

Features:

- Current values for every stamp in the world from the experts
- Easy-to-use simplified listings
- World-recognised Stanley Gibbons catalogue numbers
- A wealth of historical, geographical and currency information
- Indexing and cross-referencing throughout the volumes
- Worldwide miniature sheets listed and priced
- Thousands of new issues since the last edition

For this edition, prices have been thoroughly reviewed for Great Britain up to date, and all Commonwealth countries up to 1970, with further updates for Commonwealth countries which have appeared in our recently-published or forthcoming comprehensive catalogues under the titles *Channel Islands and the Isle of Man, Australia, Bangladesh, Pakistan and Sri Lanka, Northern Caribbean, Falkland Islands, Brunei, Malaysia and Singapore, Hong Kong, India, East Africa.* Other countries with complete price updates from the following comprehensive catalogues are: *Austria and Hungary, Benelux, Balkans, France, Italy and Switzerland*. New issues received from all other countries have been listed and priced. The first *Gibbons Stamp Monthly* Catalogue Supplement to this edition is September 2010.

Information for users

Scope of the Catalogue

Stamps of the World contains listings of postage stamps only. Apart from the ordinary definitive, commemorative and air-mail stamps of each country there are sections for the following, where appropriate. Noted below are the Prefixes used for each section (see Guide to Entries for further information):

postage due stamps –	Prefix in listing D
parcel post or postcard stamps –	Prefix P
official stamps –	Prefix O
express and special delivery stamps -	Prefix E
frank stamps –	Prefix F
charity tax stamps –	Prefix J
newspaper and journal stamps –	Prefix N
printed matter stamps –	Prefix
registration stamps -	Prefix R
acknowledgement of receipt stamps –	Prefix AR
late fee and too late stamps –	Prefix L
military post stamps-	Prefix M
recorded message stamps –	Prefix RM
personal delivery stamps –	Prefix P
concessional letter post –	Prefix CL
concessional parcel post –	Prefix CP
pneumatic post stamps –	Prefix PE
publicity envelope stamps –	Prefix B
bulk mail stamps –	Prefix BP
telegraph used for postage –	Prefix PT
telegraph (Commonwealth Countries) –	Prefix T
obligatory tax –	Prefix T
Frama Labels and Royal Mail Postage Labels	No Prefix-

As this is a simplified listing, the following are NOT included:
Fiscal or revenue stamps: stamps used solely in collecting taxes or fees for non-postal purposes. For example, stamps which pay a tax on a receipt, represent the stamp duty on a contract, or frank a customs document. Common inscriptions found include: Documentary, Proprietary, Inter. Revenue and Contract Note.
Local stamps: postage stamps whose validity and use are limited in area to a prescribed district, town or country, or on certain routes where there is no government postal service. They may be issued by private carriers and freight companies, municipal authorities or private individuals.
Local carriage labels and Private local issues: many labels exist ostensibly to cover the cost of ferrying mail from one of Great Britain's offshore islands to the nearest mainland post office. They are not recognised as valid for national or international mail. Examples: Calf of Man, Davaar, Herm, Lundy, Pabay, Stroma.
Telegraph stamps: stamps intended solely for the prepayment of telegraphic communication.
Bogus or "phantom" stamps: labels from mythical places or non-existent administrations. Examples in the classical period were Sedang, Counani, Clipperton Island and in modern times Thomond and Monte Bello Islands. Numerous labels have also appeared since the War from dissident groups as propaganda for their claims and without authority from the home governments. Common examples are the numerous issues for Nagaland.
Railway letter fee stamps: special stamps issued by railway companies for the conveyance of letters by rail. Example: Talyllyn Railway. Similar services are now offered by some bus companies and the labels they issue likewise do not qualify for inclusion in the catalogue.
Perfins ("perforated initials"): stamps perforated with the initials or emblems of firms as a security measure to prevent pilferage by office staff.
Labels: Slips of paper with an adhesive backing. Collectors tend to make a distinction between stamps, which have postal validity and anything else, which has not.

However, Frama Labels and Royal Mail Postage Labels are both classified as postage stamps and are therefore listed in this catalogue.
Cut-outs: Embossed or impressed stamps found on postal stationery, which are cut out if the stationery has been ruined and re-used as adhesives.

Further information on a wealth of terms is in *Philatelic Terms Illustrated*, published by Stanley Gibbons, details are listed under Stanley Gibbons Publications. There is also a priced listing of the postal fiscals of Great Britain in our *Commonwealth & British Empire Stamps 1840-1970* Catalogue and in Volume 1 of the *Great Britain Specialised Catalogue* (5th and later editions). Again, further details are listed under the Stanley Gibbons Publications section (see p.xii).

Organisation of the Catalogue

The catalogue lists countries in alphabetical order with country headers on each page and extra introductory information such as philatelic historical background at the beginning of each section. The Contents list provides a detailed guide to each volume, and the Index has full cross-referencing to locate each country in each volume.

Each country lists postage stamps in order of date of issue, from earliest to most recent, followed by separate sections for categories such as postage due stamps, express stamps, official stamps, and so on (see above for a complete listing).

"Appendix" Countries

Since 1968 Stanley Gibbons has listed in an appendix stamps which are judged to be in excess of true postal needs. The appendix also contains stamps which have not fulfilled all the normal conditions for full catalogue listing. Full catalogue listing requires a stamp to be:

- issued by a legitimate postal authority
- recognised by the government concerned
- adhesive
- valid for proper postal use in the class of service for which they are inscribed
- available to the general public at face value with no artificial restrictions being imposed on their distribution (with the exception of categories as postage dues and officials)

Only stamps issued from component parts of otherwise united territories which represent a genuine political, historical or postal division within the country concerned have a full catalogue listing. Any such issues which do not fulfil this stipulation will be recorded in the Catalogue Appendix only.

Stamps listed in the Appendix are constantly under review in light of newly acquired information about them. If we are satisfied that a stamp qualifies for proper listing in the body of the catalogue it will be moved in the next edition.

"Undesirable Issues"

The rules governing many competitive exhibitions are set by the Federation Internationale de Philatelie and stipulate a downgrading of marks for stamps classed as "undesirable issues".

This catalogue can be taken as a guide to status. All stamps in the main listings are acceptable. Stamps in the Appendix are considered, "undesirable issues" and should not be entered for competition.

Correspondence

We welcome information and suggestions but we must ask correspondents to include the cost of postage for the return of any materials, plus registration where appropriate. Letters and emails should be addressed to Michelle Briggs, 7 Parkside, Christchurch Road, Ringwood, Hampshire BH24 3SH, UK. mrbriggs@stanleygibbons.co.uk. Where information is solicited purely for the benefit of the enquirer we regret we are seldom able to reply.

Identification of Stamps

We regret we do not give opinion on the authenticity of stamps, nor do we identify stamps or number them by our Catalogue.

Thematic Collectors

Stanley Gibbons publishes a range of thematic catalogues (see page xxxix for details) and *Stamps of the World* is ideal to use with these titles, as it supplements those listings with extra information.

Type numbers

Type numbers (in bold) refer to illustrations, and are not the Stanley Gibbons Catalogue numbers.

A brief description of the stamp design subject is given below or beside the illustrations, or close by in the entry, where needed. Where a design is not illustrated, it is usually the same shape and size as a related design, unless otherwise indicated.

Watermarks

Watermarks are not covered in this catalogue. Stamps of the same issue with differing watermarks are not listed separately.

Perforations

Perforations – all stamps are perforated unless otherwise stated. No distinction is made between the various gauges of perforation but early stamp issues which exist both imperforate and perforated are usually listed separately. Where a heading states, "Imperf or perf"or "Perf. or rouletted" this does not necessarily mean that all values of the issue are found in both conditions

Se-tenant Pairs

Se-tenant Pairs - Many modern issues are printed in sheets containing different designs or face values. Such pairs, blocks, strips or sheets are described as being "se-tenant" and they are outside the scope of this catalogue, although reference to them may occur in instances where they form a composite design.

Miniature Sheets are now fully listed.

Guide to Entries

Ⓐ Country of Issue

Ⓑ Part Number – shows where to find more detailed listings in the Stanley Gibbons Comprehensive Catalogue. Part 6 refers to France and so on – see p. xli for further information on the breakdown of the Catalogue.

Ⓒ Country Information – Brief geographical and historical details for the issuing country.

Ⓓ Currency – Details of the currency, and dates of earliest use where applicable, on the face value of the stamps. Where a Colony has the same currency as the Mother Country, see the details given in that country.

Ⓔ Year Date – When a set of definitive stamps has been issued over several years the Year Date given is for the earliest issue, commeorative sets are listed in chronological order. As stamps of the same design or issue are usually grouped together a list of King George VI stamps, for example, headed "1938" may include stamps issued from 1938 to the end of the reign.

Ⓕ Stanley Gibbons Catalogue number – This is a unique number for each stamp to help the collector identify stamps in the listing. The Stanley Gibbons numbering system is universally recognized as definitive. The majority of listings are in chronological order, but where a definitive set of stamps has been re-issued with a new watermark, perforation change or imprint date, the cheapest example is given; in such cases catalogue numbers may not be in numerical order.

Where insufficient numbers have been left to provide for additional stamps to a listing, some stamps will have a suffix letter after the catalogue number. If numbers have been left for additions to a set and not used they will be left vacant.

The separate type numbers (in bold) refer to illustrations (see **M**).

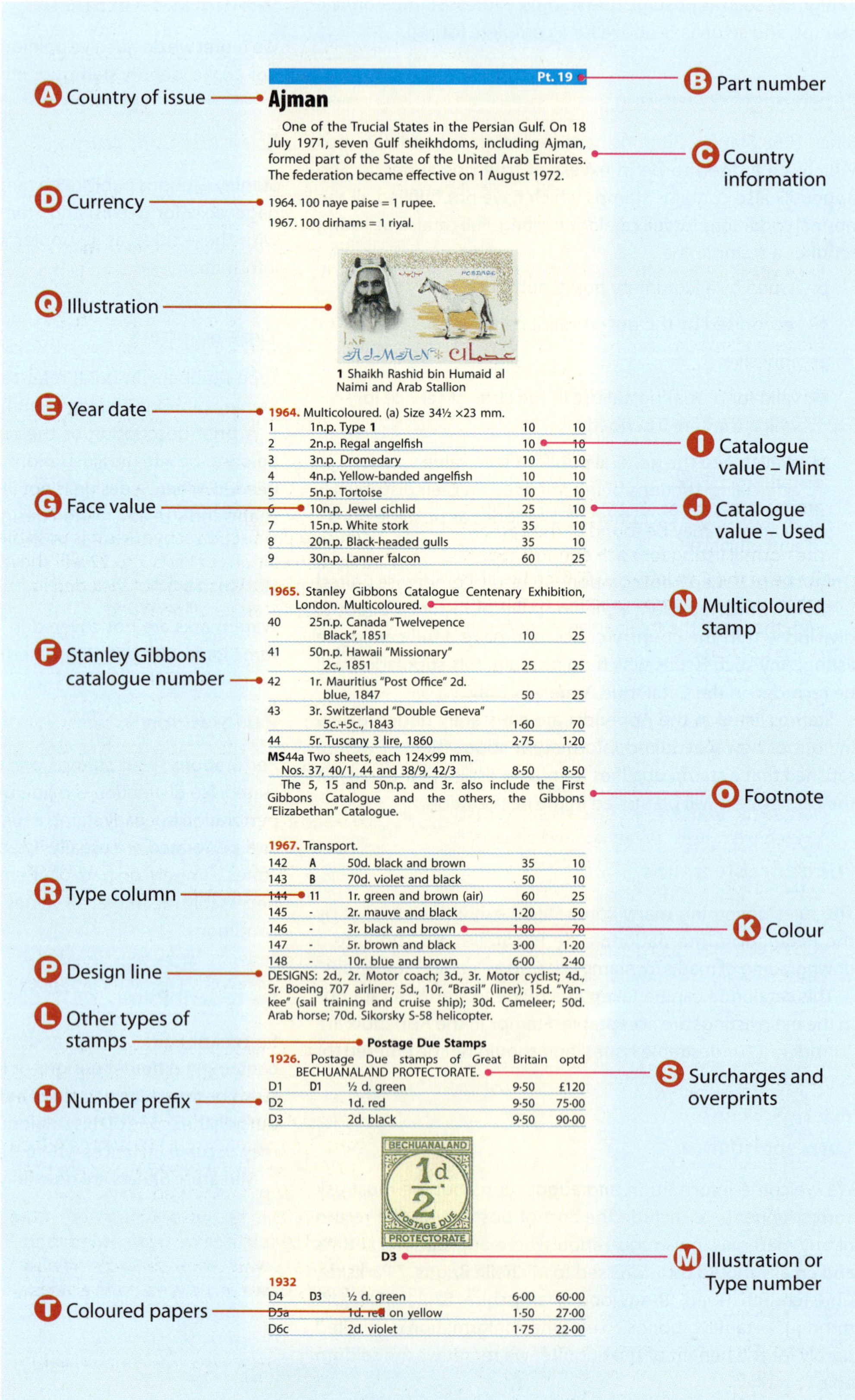

462 Canadian Maple Leaf Emblem

1981

1030a **462** A (30c.) red 20 40

No. 1030a was printed before a new first class domestic letter rate had been agreed, "A" representing the face value of the stamp, later decided to be 30c.

G Face value – This refers to the value of each stamp and is the price it was sold for at the Post Office when issued. Some modern stamps do not have their values in figures but instead shown as a letter, see for example the entry above for Canada 1030a/Illustration 462.

H Number Prefix – Stamps other than definitives and commemoratives have a prefix letter before the catalogue number. Such stamps may be found at the end of the normal listing for each country. (See Scope of the Catalogue p.viii for a list of other types of stamps covered, together with the list of the main abbreviations used in the Catalogue).

Other prefixes are also used in the Catalogue. Their use is explained in the text: some examples are A for airmail, E for East Germany or Express Delivery stamps.

I Catalogue Value – Mint/Unused. Prices quoted for pre-1945 stamps are for lightly hinged examples. Prices quoted of unused King Edward VIII to Queen Elizabeth II issues are for unmounted mint.

J Catalogue Value – Used. Prices generally refer to fine postally used examples. For certain issues they are for cancelled-to-order.

Prices

Prices are given in pence and pounds. Stamps worth £100 and over are shown in whole pounds:

Shown in Catalogue as	Explanation
10	10 pence
1.75	£1.75
15.00	£15
£150	£150
£2300	£2300

Prices assume stamps are in 'fine condition'; we may ask more for superb and less for those of lower quality. The minimum catalogue price quoted is 10p and is intended as a guide for catalogue users. The lowest price for individual stamps purchased from Stanley Gibbons is £1.

Prices quoted are for the cheapest variety of that particular stamp. Differences of watermark, perforation, or other details, outside the scope of this catalogue, often increase the value. Prices quoted for mint issues are for single examples. Those in *se-tenant* pairs, strips, blocks or sheets may be worth more. Where no prices are listed it is either because the stamps are not known to exist in that particular condition, or, more usually, because there is no reliable information on which to base their value.

All prices are subject to change without prior notice and we cannot guarantee to supply all stamps as priced. Prices quoted in advertisements are also subject to change without prior notice. Due to differing production schedules it is possible that new editions of Parts 2 to 22 will show revised prices which are not included in that year's Stamps of the World.

K Colour – Colour of stamp (if fewer than four colours, otherwise noted as "multicoloured"– see N below). Colour descriptions are simple in this catalogue, and only expanded to aid identification – see other more comprehensive Stanley Gibbons catalogues for more detailed colour descriptions (see p.xxxix).

Where stamps are printed in two or more colours, the central portion of the design is the first colour given, unless otherwise stated.

L Other Types of Stamps – See Scope of the Catalogue p.viii for a list of the types of stamps included.

M Illustration or Type Number – These numbers are used to help identify stamps, either in the listing, type column, design line or footnote, usually the first value in a set. These type numbers are in a bold type face – **123**; when bracketed (**123**) an overprint or a surcharge is indicated. Some type numbers include a lower-case letter – **123a**, this indicates they have been added to an existing set. New cross references are also normally shown in bold, as in the example below.

1990. Small Craft of Canada (2nd series). Early Work Boats. As T **563**. Multicoloured.

N Multicoloured – Nearly all modern stamps are multicoloured; this is indicated in the heading, with a description of the stamp given in the listing.

O Footnote – further information on background or key facts on issues

P Design line – Further details on design variations

Q Illustration – Generally, the first stamp in the set. Stamp illustrations are reduced to 75%, with overprints and surcharges shown actual size.

R Key Type – indicates a design type (see p. xii for further details) on which the stamp is based. These are the bold figures found below each illustration. The type numbers are also given in bold in the second column of figures alongside the stamp description to indicate the design of each stamp. Where an issue comprises stamps of similar design, the corresponding type number should be taken as indicating the general design. Where there are blanks in the type number column it means that the type of the corresponding stamp is that shown by the number in the type column of the same issue. A dash (–) in the type column means that the stamp is not illustrated. Where type numbers refer to stamps of another country, e.g. where stamps of one country are overprinted for use in another, this is always made clear in the text.

S Surcharges and Overprints – usually described in the headings. Any actual wordings are shown in bold type. Descriptions clarify words and figures used in the overprint. Stamps with the same overprints in different colours are not listed separately. Numbers in brackets after the descriptions are the catalogue numbers of the non-overprinted stamps. The words "inscribed" or "inscription" refer to the wording incorporated in the design of a stamp and not surcharges or overprints.

T Coloured Papers – stamps printed on coloured paper are shown – e.g. "brn on yell" indicates brown printed on yellow paper. No information on the texture of paper, e.g. laid or wove, is provided in this catalogue.

Key-Types

Standard designs frequently occuring on the stamps of the French, German, Portuguese and Spanish colonies are illustrated below together with the descriptive names and letters by which they are referred to in the lists to avoid repetition. Please see the Guide to Entries for further information.

French Group

A "Blanc"

B "Mouchon"

C "Merson"

D "Tablet"

INTERNATIONAL COLONIAL EXHIBITION

E

F "

G

H

I "Faidherbe"

J "Palms"

K "Balay"

L "Natives"

M "Figure"

German Group

N "Yacht"

O "Yacht"

Spanish Group

X "Alfonso XII"

Y "Baby"

Z "Curly Head"

Portuguese Group

P "Crown"

Q "Embossed"

R "Figures"

S "Carlos"

T "Manoel"

U Ceres"

V "Newspaper"

W "Due"

Pt. 7

GERMAN COMMANDS

100 pfennig = 1 mark.

EASTERN COMMAND

German occupation of Estonia, Latvia and Lithuania during the war of 1914–18.

1916. Stamps of Germany inscr "DEUTSCHES REICH" optd Postgebiet Ob. Ost.

1	**24**	2½pf. grey	55	1·80
2	**10**	3pf. brown	20	60
3	**10**	5pf. green	80	1·90
4	**24**	7½pf. orange	55	1·90
5	**10**	10pf. red	1·20	1·90
6	**24**	15pf. brown	3·50	4·00
7	**24**	15pf. violet	90	2·20
8	**10**	20pf. blue	2·75	1·90
9	**10**	25pf. black & red on yellow	25	90
10	**10**	40pf. black and red	2·75	7·00
11	**10**	50pf. black & pur on buff	1·80	3·00
12a	**12**	1m. red	10·50	4·50

WESTERN COMMAND

For Forces in Belgium and Northern France.

1916. Stamps of Germany surch with new values as 2 Cent., 1F. or 1F.25 Cent.

1	**10**	3c. on 3pf. brown	45	1·10
2	**10**	5c. on 5pf. green	1·30	2·10
3	**24**	8c. on 7½pf. orange	90	2·10
4	**10**	10c. on 10pf. red	1·90	4·50
5	**24**	15c. on 15pf. brown	45	1·10
6	**10**	25c. on 20pf. blue	1·10	3·00
7	**10**	40c. on 30pf. black and orange on buff	1·10	1·80
8	**10**	50c. on 40pf. black and red	1·10	1·80
9	**10**	75c. on 60pf. purple	6·25	11·50
10	**10**	1f. on 80pf. black and red on red	3·50	8·75
11a	**12**	1f.25 on 1m. red	22·00	31·00
12	**13**	2f.50 on 2m. blue	22·00	19·00

Pt. 7

GERMAN EAST AFRICA

A German colony on the east coast of Africa. Placed under British mandate after the First World War.

1893. 64 pesa = 1 rupee.
1905. 100 heller = 1 rupee.

1893. Stamps of Germany surch with value in "PESA".

1	**8**	2p. on 3pf. brown	50·00	60·00
2	**8**	3p. on 5pf. green	60·00	60·00
4	**9**	5p. on 10pf. red	50·00	30·00
5	**9**	10p. on 20pf. blue	36·00	17·00
6	**9**	25p. on 50pf. brown	50·00	34·00

1896. Stamps of Germany surch Deutsch-Ostafrika and value in "Pesa".

7	**8**	2p. on 3pf. brown	13·00	12·00
10	**8**	3p. on 5pf. green	2·75	4·75
11	**9**	5p. on 10pf. red	2·75	4·75
13	**9**	10p. on 20pf. blue	6·00	5·50
14	**9**	25p. on 50pf. brown	26·00	29·00

1901. "Yacht", key-type inscr "DEUTSCH-OSTAFRIKA". Currency in pesa and rupees.

15	**N**	2p. brown	3·25	1·70
16	**N**	3p. green	3·25	2·00
17	**N**	5p. red	3·75	2·50
18	**N**	10p. blue	6·00	5·00
19	**N**	15p. black and orange on buff	6·00	6·75
20	**N**	20p. black and red	8·25	15·00
21	**N**	25p. black and purple on buff	8·25	15·00
22	**N**	40p. black and red on rose	10·00	24·00
23	**O**	1r. red	22·00	60·00
24	**O**	2r. green	11·00	95·00
44	**O**	3r. black and red	55·00	

1905. "Yacht" key-types inscr "DEUTSCH-OSTAFRIKA". Currency in heller.

33	**N**	60h. black and red on rose	41·00	£100
34	**N**	2½h. brown	1·10	1·00
35	**N**	4h. green	1·10	70
36	**N**	7½h. red	1·30	1·70
37	**N**	15h. blue	2·50	1·50
38	**N**	20h. black and red on yellow	2·75	21·00
39	**N**	30h. black and red	3·00	8·50
40	**N**	45h. black and mauve	6·50	60·00

For stamps issued for this territory under British auspices since 1915 see under Tanganyika in Volume 4.

Pt. 7

GERMAN NEW GUINEA

A German colony, part of the island of New Guinea.

100 pfennig = 1 mark.

1897. Stamps of Germany optd Deutsch-Neu-Guinea.

1a	**8**	3pf. brown	9·00	10·00
2	**8**	5pf. green	4·50	6·00
3	**9**	10pf. red	7·25	9·25
4	**9**	20pf. blue	10·00	14·50
5	**9**	25pf. orange	32·00	55·00
6	**9**	50pf. brown	36·00	50·00

1901. "Yacht" key-types inscr "DEUTSCH-NEU-GUINEA".

7	**N**	3pf. brown	1·40	1·30
8	**N**	5pf. green	8·25	1·30
9	**N**	10pf. red	27·00	3·00
10	**N**	20pf. blue	1·60	3·00
11	**N**	25pf. black and red on yellow	1·60	17·00
12	**N**	30pf. black & orange on buff	1·60	21·00
13	**N**	40pf. black and red	1·60	24·00
14	**N**	50pf. black & purple on buff	2·30	20·00
15	**N**	80pf. black and red on rose	4·00	29·00
16	**O**	1m. red	4·50	55·00
17	**O**	2m. blue	6·75	80·00
18	**O**	3m. black	8·25	£160
19	**O**	5m. red and black	£180	£500

Australian forces occupied German New Guinea in 1914 and it was administered as a League of Nations mandate from 1920. For stamps issued since 1914 see under New Guinea.

Pt. 7

GERMAN OCCUPATION OF ALSACE

100 pfennig = 1 mark.

1940. Stamps of Germany optd Elsaß.

1	**94**	3pf. brown	25	40
2	**94**	4pf. slate	55	85
3	**94**	5pf. green	25	40
4	**94**	6pf. green	25	40
5	**94**	8pf. orange	25	40
6	**94**	10pf. brown	25	85
7	**94**	12pf. red	25	50
8	**94**	15pf. red	55	85
9	**94**	20pf. blue	55	85
10	**94**	25pf. blue	80	1·30
11	**94**	30pf. olive	1·10	1·40
12	**94**	40pf. mauve	1·10	1·40
13	**94**	50pf. black and green	1·10	1·70
14	**94**	60pf. black and red	1·80	2·50
15	**94**	80pf. black and blue	2·75	4·25
16	**94**	100pf. black and yellow	3·75	3·50

Pt. 4

GERMAN OCCUPATION OF BELGIUM

German occupation of E. Belgium during the war of 1914–18.

100 centimes = 1 franc.

Stamps of Germany inscr "DEUTSCHES REICH" surcharged

1914. Surch Belgien and value thus: 3 Centimes, 1Franc or 1Fr.25C.

1	**10**	3c. on 3pf. brown	40	35
2	**10**	5c. on 5pf. green	40	35
3	**10**	10c. on 10pf. red	40	35
4	**10**	25c. on 20pf. blue	1·10	1·10
5	**10**	50c. on 40pf. black and red	5·25	5·25
6	**10**	75c. on 60pf. purple	2·00	2·00
7	**10**	1f. on 80pf. black and red on rose	5·75	5·75
8	**12**	1f.25 on 1m. red	46·00	46·00
9	**13**	2f.50 on 2m. blue	44·00	44·00

1916. Surch Belgien and value, thus: 2 Cent.,1F., or 1F.25Cent.

10	**24**	2c. on 2pf. grey	25	25
11	**10**	3c. on 3pf. brown	25	25
12	**10**	5c. on 5pf. green	25	25
13	**24**	8c. on 7½pf. orange	25	25
14	**10**	10c. on 10pf. red	25	25
15	**24**	15c. on 15pf. brown	25	25
16	**24**	15c. on 15pf. violet	25	25
17	**10**	20c. on 25pf. black and red on yellow	30	30
18	**10**	25c. on 20pf. blue	35	40
19	**10**	40c. on 30pf. black and orange on buff	30	30
20	**10**	50c. on 40pf. black and red	50	55
21	**10**	75c. on 60pf. mauve	5·00	5·25
22	**10**	1f. on 80f. black and red on rose	3·75	4·00
23a	**12**	1f.25 on 1m. red	6·00	6·50
24	**13**	2f.50 on 2m. blue	65·00	70·00
25	**15**	6f.25 on 5m. red and black	95·00	£100

Pt. 3

GERMAN OCCUPATION OF DALMATIA

Area formerly under Italian control which were occupied by the Germans in 1943

100 centesimi = 1 lira.

A. ZARA (Zadar)

1943. Imperial series of Italy, 1929, optd Deutsche Besetzung Zara.

1	**98**	5c. brown	47·00	£150
2	-	10c. brown	4·00	12·00
3	-	15c. green	6·75	21·00
4	**99**	20c. red	4·00	14·50
5	-	25c. green	4·00	14·50
6	**103**	30c. brown	4·00	14·50
7	-	35c. blue	£275	£500
8	-	75c. red	13·00	34·00
9	**99**	1l. violet	4·25	14·50
10	**99**	1l.25 blue	5·75	21·00
11	**99**	1l.75 red	18·00	55·00
12	-	2l. red	42·00	85·00
13	**98**	2l.55 green	£225	£550
14	**98**	3l.70 violet	£1400	£2250
15	**98**	5l. red	34·00	85·00
16	-	10l. violet	£950	£1700
17	**99**	20l. green	£11000	£16000
18	-	25l. black	£24000	£34000
19	-	50l. violet	£19000	£21000

1943. War Propaganda stamps of Italy (Nos. 571/4) optd Deutsche Besetzung Zara on stamp and label.

20	**103**	50c. violet (Navy)	10·50	25·00
21	**103**	50c. violet (Army)	10·50	25·00
22	**103**	50c. violet (Air Force)	10·50	25·00
23	**103**	50c. violet (Militia)	10·50	25·00

1943. Air. Nos. 270/7 of Italy optd Deutsche Besetzung Zara.

26	-	25c. green	6·25	20·00
27	**110**	50c. brown	5·25	19·00
28	-	75c. brown	£275	£500
29	-	80c. red	26·00	70·00
30	-	1l. violet	8·00	20·00
31	**113**	2l. blue	18·00	42·00
32	**110**	5l. green	£5500	£7500
33	**110**	10l. red	£16000	£24000

1943. Imperial series of Italy, 1929, optd ZARA within pattern of bars.

46	**103**	50c. violet	4·25	17·00
47	-	75c. red	5·25	20·00
48	-	1l.25 blue	40·00	£140

1943. War Propaganda stamps of Italy (Nos. 563/70) optd ZARA within pattern of bars on stamp and label.

49		25c. green (Navy)	9·00	25·00
50		25c. green (Army)	9·00	25·00
51		25c. green (Air Force)	9·00	25·00
52		25c. green (Militia)	9·00	25·00
53	**103**	30c. brown (Navy)	9·00	22·00
54	**103**	30c. brown (Army)	9·00	22·00
55	**103**	30c. brown (Air Force)	9·00	22·00
56	**103**	30c. brown (Militia)	9·00	22·00

EXPRESS LETTER STAMPS

1943. Nos. E350/1 of Italy optd Deutsche Besetzung Zara.

E24	**E132**	1l.25 green	10·50	30·00
E25	**E132**	2l.50 orange	80·00	£140

1943. Air. No. E370 of Italy optd Deutsche Besetzung Zara.

E34	**E133**	2l. black	19·00	42·00

1943. Nos. E350/1 of Italy optd ZARA within pattern of bars, twice.

E57	**E132**	1l.25 green	10·50	34·00
E58	**E132**	2l.50 orange	80·00	£225

POSTAGE DUE STAMPS

1943. Italian Postage Due stamps optd Deutsche Besetzung Zara.

D35	**D141**	5c. brown	21·00	85·00
D36	**D141**	10c. blue	21·00	85·00
D37	**D141**	20c. red	19·00	85·00
D38	**D141**	25c. green	£550	£1000
D39	**D141**	30c. red	20·00	85·00
D40	**D141**	40c. brown	20·00	85·00
D41	**D141**	50c. violet	20·00	85·00
D42	**D141**	60c. blue	£550	£1000
D43	**D142**	1l. orange	£475	£1000
D44	**D142**	2l. green	£650	£1000
D45	**D142**	5l. violet	£475	£950

B. GULF OF KOTOR

Italian and German currency.

1944. Imperial series of Italy, 1929, surch Deutsche Militar-verwaltung Kotor and new value in lire.

1	-	0.50LIT. on 10c. brown	47·00	£150
2	-	1LIT. on 25c. green	4·00	12·00
3	**103**	1.50LIT. on 50c. violet	6·75	21·00
4	**103**	3LIT. on 30c. brown	4·00	14·50
5	**99**	4LIT. on 20c. red	4·00	14·50
6	**99**	10LIT. on 20c. red	4·00	14·50

1944. Nos. 419/20 of Yugoslavia (King Petar II) surch Boka Kotorska and new value in Reichsmarks.

7	0,10R.M. on 3d. brown	£275	£500
8	0,15R.M. on 3d. brown	13·00	34·00
9	0,25R.M. on 4d. blue	4·25	14·50
10	0,50R.M. on 4d. blue	5·75	21·00

Pt. 10

GERMAN OCCUPATION OF ESTONIA

100 kopeks = 1 rouble.

2

1941. Tartu issue.

3A	**2**	15(k.) brown	10·50	17·00
4A	**2**	20(k.) green	8·00	12·50
5A	**2**	30(k.) blue	8·00	12·50

Originally issued for local use, the above were made available for use throughout Estonia from 29.9.41 to 30.4.42. However, not many were used since the German **OSTLAND** stamps were used from 1 December 1941.

3 "Long Hermann" Tower, Reval (Tallinn)

1941. Reconstruction Fund.

6	**3**	15+15(k.) sepia and brown	35	5·00
7	-	20+20(k.) purple and brown	35	5·00
8	-	30+30(k.) blue and brown	35	5·00
9	-	50+50(k.) green and brown	35	10·00
10	-	60+60(k.) red and brown	35	8·50
11	-	100+100(k.) slate and brown	65	10·00

DESIGNS—HORIZ: 20k. Stone Bridge, Tartu; 30k. Two Narva Castles; 50k. Reval of Tallinn. VERT: 60k. Tartu University; 100k. Hermann Castle, Narva.

German stamps optd **OSTLAND** (see German Occupation of Russia, Nos. 1/20) were used from 1 December 1941 until the Russian re-occupation of Estonia in 1944. Since then Russian stamps have been in use, and since 1991 Estonia have issued their own stamps.

Pt. 10

GERMAN OCCUPATION OF LATVIA

100 kopeks = 1 rouble.

1941. Russian stamps of 1936–39 optd LATVIJA 1941. 1. VII.

1	5k. red (No. 847a)	80	4·25
2	10k. blue (No. 727f)	80	4·25
3	15k. green (No. 847c)	26·00	70·00
4	20k. green (No. 727h)	80	4·25
5	30k. blue (No. 847d)	80	4·25
6	50k. brown on buff (No. 727m)	3·25	10·00

German stamps optd **OSTLAND** (see German Occupation of Russia, Nos. 1/20) were used from 4th November, 1941, until the Russian re-occupation of Latvia in 1944–45. Since then Russian stamps have been in use, and since 1991 Latvia have issued their own stamps.

Pt. 10

GERMAN OCCUPATION OF LITHUANIA

100 kopeks = 1 rouble.

1941. Russian stamps of 1936–40 optd NEPRIKLAUSOMA LIETUVA 1941-VI-23.

1	2k. green (No. 542)	24·00	£150
2	5k. red (No. 847a)	1·60	12·50
3	10k. blue (No. 727f)	1·60	12·50
4	15k. green (No. 847c)	1·60	12·50
5	20k. green (No. 727h)	1·60	12·50
6	30k. blue (No. 847d)	1·60	12·50
7	50k. brown on buff (No. 727m)	5·25	25·00
8	60k. red (No. 847f)	10·50	50·00
9	80k. blue (No. 905)	10·50	50·00

1941. Issue for Vilnius and South Lithuania. Russian stamps of 1936–39 optd VILNIUS.

10	5k. red (No. 847a)	1·10	3·50
11	10k. blue (No. 727f)	1·30	3·50
12	15k. green (No. 847c)	1·30	3·50
13	20k. green (No. 727h)	4·25	12·50
14	30k. blue (No. 847d)	3·75	8·50
15	50k. brown on buff (No. 727m)	4·25	8·50
16	60k. red (No. 847f)	4·25	10·00
17	80k. red and deep red (No. 772)	£200	£250
18	1r. black and red (No. 779)	£650	£600

German stamps optd **OSTLAND** (see German Occupation of Russia, Nos. 1/20) were used from 4th November, 1941, till the Russian re-occupation of Lithuania in 1944. Since then Russian stamps have been in use.

Pt. 7

GERMAN OCCUPATION OF LORRAINE

100 pfennig = 1 mark.

1940. Stamps of Germany optd Lothringen.

1	**94**	3pf. brown	40	70
2	**94**	4pf. slate	40	70
3	**94**	5pf. green	40	70
4	**94**	6pf. green	40	35
5	**94**	8pf. orange	40	70
6	**94**	10pf. brown	40	50
7	**94**	12pf. red	40	50
8	**94**	15pf. lake	40	1·00
9	**94**	20pf. blue	65	1·00
10	**94**	25pf. blue	80	1·30
11	**94**	30pf. olive	95	1·50
12	**94**	40pf. mauve	95	1·50
13	**94**	50pf. black and green	1·60	2·50
14	**94**	60pf. black and red	1·60	3·00
15	**94**	80pf. black and blue	1·80	3·50
16	**94**	100pf. black and yellow	6·25	6·00

Pt. 5

GERMAN OCCUPATION OF POLAND

German Occupation of Poland, 1915 - 18.

100 pfennig = 1 mark.

1915. Stamps of Germany inscr "DEUTSCHES REICH" optd Russisch-Polen.

1	**10**	3pf. brown	45	35
2	**10**	5pf. green	90	35
3	**10**	10pf. red	1·10	55
4	**10**	20pf. blue	1·80	55
5	**10**	40pf. black and red	5·25	2·30

1916. Stamps of Germany inscr "DEUTSCHES REICH" optd Gen.-Gouv. Warschau.

6	**24**	2½pf. grey	80	1·80
7	**10**	3pf. brown	80	2·50
8	**10**	5pf. green	80	3·00
9	**24**	7½pf. orange	1·10	1·90
10	**10**	10pf. red	1·80	1·90
11	**24**	15pf. brown	2·75	2·75
12	**24**	15pf. violet	90	1·90
13	**10**	20pf. blue	1·10	2·20
14	**10**	30pf. black & orange on buff	6·25	11·50
15	**10**	40pf. black and red	1·80	1·90
16	**10**	60pf. purple	2·75	2·50

Pt. 3

GERMAN OCCUPATION OF ROMANIA

German Occupation of Romania, 1917 - 18.

100 bani = 1 leu.

Stamsp of Germany inscr "DEUTSCHES REICH".

1917. Surch M.V.i.R. in frame and value in "Bani".

1	**24**	15b. on 15pf. violet	55	1·10
2	**10**	25b. on 20pf. blue	90	1·10
3	**10**	40b. on 30pf. black and orange on buff	17·00	29·00

1917. Surch M.V.i.R. (not in frame) and value in "Bani".

4		10b. on 10pf. red	1·20	1·80
5	**24**	15b. on 15pf. violet	6·25	4·75
6	**10**	25b. on 20pf. blue	3·50	4·50
7	**10**	40b. on 30pf. black and orange on buff	1·20	2·20

1918. Surch Rumanien and value in "Bani".

8		5b. on 5pf. green	70	2·10
9		10b. on 10pf. red	70	1·90
10	**24**	15b. on 15pf. violet	20	55
11	**10**	25b. on 20pf. blue	70	1·90
12	**10**	40b. on 30pf. black and orange on buff	25	45

1918. Stamps of Germany inscr "DEUTSCHES REICH" optd Gultig 9. Armee in frame.

13		10pf. red	9·75	48·00
14	**24**	15pf. violet	14·00	44·00
15	**10**	20pf. blue	1·30	2·20
16	**10**	30pf. black & orange on buff	14·00	26·00

POSTAGE DUE STAMPS

1918. Postage Due stamps of Rumania optd M.V.i.R. in frame.

D1B	**D38**	5b. blue on green	8·75	13·00
D2B	**D38**	10b. blue on green	8·75	13·00
D3B	**D38**	20b. blue on green	3·50	3·50
D4B	**D38**	30b. blue on green	3·50	3·50
D5B	**D38**	50b. blue on green	3·50	3·50

Pt. 10

GERMAN OCCUPATION OF RUSSIA

100 pfennig = 1 reichsmark.

1941. Issue for Ostland. Stamps of Germany of 1941 optd OSTLAND.

1	**173**	1pf. grey	10	25
2	**173**	3pf. brown	10	25
3	**173**	4pf. slate	10	25
4	**173**	5pf. green	10	25
5	**173**	6pf. violet	10	25
6	**173**	8pf. red	10	25
7	**173**	10pf. brown	85	1·50
10	**173**	12pf. red	40	3·00
11	**173**	15pf. lake	10	25
12	**173**	16pf. green	15	25
13	**173**	20pf. blue	10	25
14	**173**	24pf. brown	10	25
15	**173**	25pf. blue	10	25
16	**173**	30pf. olive	10	25
17	**173**	40pf. mauve	10	25
18	**173**	50pf. green	10	25
19	**173**	60pf. brown	10	25
20	**173**	80pf. blue	10	70

1941. Issue for Ukraine. Stamps of Germany of 1941 optd UKRAINE.

21	1pf. grey	10	15
22	3pf. brown	10	15
23	4pf. slate	10	15
24	5pf. green	10	15
25	6pf. violet	10	15
26	8pf. red	10	15
27	10pf. brown	70	1·70
29	12pf. red	70	1·70
31	15pf. lake	10	15
32	16pf. green	10	25
33	20pf. blue	10	15
34	24pf. brown	10	25
35	25pf. blue	10	15
36	30pf. olive	10	15
37	40pf. mauve	10	25
38	50pf. green	10	15
39	60pf. brown	10	15
40	80pf. blue	10	25

Pt. 3

GERMAN OCCUPATION OF ZANTE

German occupation of Ionian Islands, 1943–44.

100 centesimi = 1 lira = 8 drachma.

(1)

1943. Stamps of Italian Occupation of Ionian Islands further optd with T 1.

1	-	25c. green (postage)	31·00	46·00
2	**103**	50c. violet	31·00	46·00
3	**110**	50c. brown (air)	44·00	50·00

Pt. 7

GERMAN POST OFFICES IN CHINA

German Post Offices in China, now closed.

1898. 100 pfennig = 1 mark.
1905. 100 cents = 1 dollar.

1898. Stamps of Germany optd China.

4	**9**	20pf. blue	16·00	12·00
7	**8**	3pf. brown	7·25	6·75
8	**8**	5pf. green	3·25	3·00
9	**9**	10pf. red	6·50	6·75
11	**9**	25pf. orange	34·00	39·00
12	**9**	50pf. brown	17·00	14·50

1901. Stamps of Germany inscr "REICHSPOST" optd China.

22	**10**	3pf. brown	1·70	1·70
23	**10**	5pf. green	1·70	1·30
24	**10**	10pf. red	2·75	1·30
25	**10**	20pf. blue	3·50	1·70
26	**10**	25pf. black & red on yellow	11·50	19·00
27	**10**	30pf. black & orge on pink	11·50	17·00
28	**10**	40pf. black and red	11·50	10·50
29	**10**	50pf. black & pur on pink	11·50	10·50
30	**10**	80pf. black and red on pink	13·00	13·00
31	**12**	1m. red	34·00	42·00
32	**13**	2m. blue	32·00	31·00
33	**14**	3m. black	55·00	70·00
35b	**15**	5m. red and black	£225	£350

1905. Stamps of Germany inscr "DEUTSCHES REICH" surch China and new value.

39	**10**	10c. on 20pf. blue	3·75	2·10
42	**12**	½d. on 1m. red	20·00	22·00
43	**13**	1d. on 2m. blue	20·00	26·00
44a	**14**	1½d. on 3m. black	20·00	55·00
46	**10**	1c. on 3pf. brown	50	1·70
47	**10**	2c. on 5pf. green	50	1·70
48	**10**	4c. on 10pf. red	50	1·70
50	**10**	20c. on 40pf. black and red	1·20	4·25
51	**10**	40c. on 80pf. black and red on rose	1·30	60·00
55	**15**	2½d. on 5m. red and black	£160	£160

Pt. 7

GERMAN POST OFFICES IN MOROCCO

German Post Offices in Morocco, now closed.

100 centimos = 1 peseta.

Stamps of Germany surcharged Marocco (or Marokko) and new value.

1889. Spelt Marocco.

1	**8**	3c. on 3pf. brown	3·50	2·40
2	**8**	5c. on 5pf. green	3·50	2·75
3	**9**	10c. on 10pf. red	9·00	6·75
4	**9**	25c. on 20pf. blue	22·00	16·00
5	**9**	30c. on 25pf. orange	32·00	35·00
6	**9**	60c. on 50pf. brown	27·00	42·00

1900. Inscr "REICHSPOST" surch Marocco (3c. to 1p.) or Marocco Marocco (others).

7	**10**	3c. on 3pf. brown	1·50	2·00
8	**10**	5c. on 5pf. green	1·80	1·20
9	**10**	10c. on 10pf. red	2·20	1·20
10	**10**	25c. on 20pf. blue	3·00	3·00
11	**10**	30c. on 25pf. black and red on yellow	11·00	16·00
12	**10**	35c. on 30pf. black and orange on rose	8·25	6·75
13	**10**	50c. on 40pf. black and red	8·25	6·75
14	**10**	60c. on 50pf. black and purple on rose	16·00	32·00
15	**10**	1p. on 80pf. black and red on rose	36·00	50·00
16	**12**	1p.25 on 1m. red	41·00	50·00
17	**13**	2p.50 on 2m. blue	36·00	60·00
18	**14**	3p.75 on 3m. black	55·00	70·00
19b	**15**	6p.25 on 5m. red and black	£375	£600

1905. Inscr "DEUTSCHES REICH" surch Marocco (3c. to 1p.) or Marocco Marocco (others).

26	**10**	3c. on 3pf. brown	3·00	2·75
27	**10**	5c. on 5pf. green	5·50	1·20
28	**10**	10c. on 10pf. red	10·00	1·20
30	**10**	30c. on 25pf. black and red on yellow	7·25	5·50
31	**10**	35c. on 30pf. black and orange on buff	11·00	5·50
32	**10**	50c. on 40pf. black and red	11·00	8·50
33	**10**	60c. on 50pf. black and purple on buff	24·00	25·00
34	**10**	1p. on 80pf. black and red on rose	24·00	20·00
35a	**12**	1p.25 on 1m. red	50·00	60·00
36	**13**	2p.50 on 2m. blue	£120	£150
37a	**14**	3p.75 on 3m. black	50·00	60·00
38	**15**	6p.25 on 5m. red & black	£180	£225
42	**10**	25c. on 20pf. blue	18·00	7·50

1911. Inscr "DEUTSCHES REICH". Spelt Marokko.

51	3c. on 3pf. brown	65	75
52	5c. on 5pf. green	65	75
53	10c. on 10pf. red	65	1·20
54	25c. on 20pf. blue	75	1·40
55	30c. on 25pf. black and red on yellow	1·80	17·00
56	35c. on 30pf. black and orange on buff	1·80	9·25
57	50c. on 40pf. black and red	1·50	5·50
58	60c. on 50pf. black and purple on buff	3·00	38·00
59	1p. on 80pf. black and red on rose	1·80	25·00

60	**12**	1p.25 on 1m. red	4·50	11·00
61	**13**	2p.50 on 2m. blue	6·00	50·00
62	**14**	3p.75 on 3m. black	13·00	£250
63	**15**	6p.25 on 5m. red & black	22·00	£350

Pt. 7

GERMAN POST OFFICES IN TURKISH EMPIRE

German Post Offices in the Turkish Empire, now closed.

1884. 40 para = 1 piastre.
1908. 100 centimes = 1 franc.

1884. Stamps of Germany inscr "DEUTSCHE REICHS-POST" and "PFENNIG" without final "E" surch with new value.

1	**5**	10pa. on 5pf. mauve	65·00	35·00
2	**6**	20pa. on 10pf. red	90·00	95·00
3	**6**	1pi. on 20pf. blue	75·00	5·50
4	**6**	1¼pi. on 25pf. brown	£150	£350
6	**6**	2½pi. on 50pf. green	£120	90·00

1889. Stamps of Germany inscr "REICHSPOST" surch.

10	**8**	10pa. on 5pf. green	4·25	4·25
11	**9**	20pa. on 10pf. red	9·25	2·75
12	**9**	1pi. on 20pf. blue	6·50	2·50
14	**9**	1¼pi. on 25pf. orange	41·00	26·00
16	**9**	2½pi. on 50pf. brown	42·00	36·00

1900. Stamps of Germany inscr "REICHSPOST" surch in PARA or PIASTER.

17	**10**	10pa. on 5pf. green	2·00	2·00
18	**10**	20pa. on 10pf. red	2·50	2·40
19	**10**	1pi. on 20pf. blue	5·50	2·30
20	**10**	1¼pi. on 25pf. black and red on yellow	7·25	4·75
21	**10**	1½pi. on 30pf. black and orange on buff	7·25	5·00
22	**10**	2pi. on 40pf. black and red	7·25	5·00
23	**10**	2½pi. on 50pf. black and purple on buff	14·00	14·50
24	**10**	4pi. on 80pf. black and red on rose	17·00	14·50
25	**12**	5pi. on 1m. red	41·00	45·00
26	**13**	10pi. on 2m. blue	37·00	46·00
27	**14**	15pi. on 3m. black	55·00	£120
28a	**15**	25pi. on 5m. red and black	£200	£550

1905. Stamps of Germany inscr "DEUTSCHES REICH" surch in Para or Piaster.

38	**10**	1¼pi. on 25pf. black and red on yellow	11·50	8·50
45	**14**	15pi. on 3m. black	60·00	60·00
47	**10**	10pa. on 5pf. green	2·75	70
48	**10**	20pa. on 10pf. red	5·50	75

49	10	1pi. on 20pf. blue	5·50	75
51	10	1½pi. on 30pf. black and orange on buff	14·50	11·50
52	10	2pi. on 40pf. black and red	6·00	1·90
53	10	2½pi. on 50pf. black and purple on buff	11·50	19·00
54	10	4pi. on 80pf. black and red on pink	18·00	24·00
55	12	5pi. on 1m. red	41·00	34·00
56	13	10pi. on 2m. blue	41·00	50·00
58	15	25pi. on 5m. red and black	36·00	85·00

1908. Stamps of Germany inscr "DEUTSCHES REICH", surch in Centimes.

60	10	5c. on 5pf. green	1·80	3·00
61	10	10c. on 10pf. red	3·75	5·25
62	10	25c. on 20pf. blue	9·00	33·00
63	10	50c. on 40pf. black and red	39·00	75·00
64	10	100c. on 80pf. black and red on rose	80·00	85·00

Pt. 7

GERMAN SOUTH WEST AFRICA

A German colony in S.W. Africa.

100 pfennig = 1 mark.

1897. Stamps of Germany optd. (a) Deutsch-Sudwest-Afrika.

1	8	3pf. brown	9·00	12·00
2	8	5pf. green	5·00	4·25
3	9	10pf. red	24·00	17·00
4	9	20pf. blue	6·50	5·50

(b) Deutsch-Sudwestafrika.

5	8	3pf. brown	4·50	22·00
6	8	5pf. green	3·75	2·75
7	9	10pf. red	3·75	3·50
8	9	20pf. blue	13·00	15·00
9	9	25pf. orange	£375	£425
10	9	50pf. brown	13·00	11·00

1901. "Yacht" key-types inscr "DEUTSCH-SUDWESTAFRIKA".

15	N	25pf. black and red on yellow	1·60	5·50
16	N	30pf. black & orange on buff	65·00	2·75
17	N	40pf. black and red	2·00	3·50
18	N	50pf. black & purple on buff	2·40	6·75
19	N	80pf. black and red on rose	2·40	6·75
22	O	3m. black	36·00	50·00
24	N	3pf. brown	90	3·75
25	N	5pf. green	90	1·40
26	N	10pf. red	1·10	1·40
27	N	20pf. blue	1·10	3·75
29	O	1m. red	13·50	70·00
30	O	2m. blue	13·50	70·00
32	O	5m. red and black	36·00	£300

South Africa occupied the colony in 1914 and administered the territory under a League of Nations mandate from 1920. For stamps issued from 1923 see under South West Africa in Volume 4.

Pt. 7

GERMANY

A country in Northern Central Europe. A federation of states forming the German Reich. An empire till November 1918 and then a republic until the collapse of Germany in 1945. Until 1949 under Allied Military Control when the German Federal Republic was set up for W. Germany and the German Democratic Republic for E. Germany. See also notes before No. 899.

Germany.
1872. Northern areas including Alsace and Lorraine: 30 groschen = 1 thaler. Southern areas: 90 kreuzer = 1 gulden.
1875. Throughout Germany: 100 pfennig = 1 mark.
1923. 100 renten-pfennig = 1 rentenmark (gold currency).
1928. 100 pfennig = 1 reichsmark

Allied Occupation.
100 pfennige = 1 Reichsmark.
21.6.48. 100 pfennige = 1 Deutsche Mark (West).
24.6.48. 100 pfennige = 1 Deutsche Mark (East).

German Federal Republic.
1949. 100 pfennig = 1 Deutsche Mark (West).
2002. 100 cents = 1 euro.

West Berlin.
1948. 100 pfennig = 1 Deutsche Mark (East).
1949. 100 pfennig = 1 Deutsche Mark (West).

German Democratic Republic (East Germany).
1949. 100 pfennig = 1 Deutsche Mark (East).
1990. 100 pfennig = 1 Deutsche Mark (West).

I. GERMANY 1871–1945

1

A

1872. Arms embossed as Type A.

1	1	¼g. violet	£225	£110
2	1	⅓g. green	£550	44·00
3	1	½g. red	£1100	48·00
4	1	½g. yellow	£1300	55·00
5	1	1g. red	£325	6·25
6	1	2g. blue	£1900	18·00
7	1	5g. bistre	£1100	£110
8	1	1k. green	£750	60·00
9	1	2k. red	£650	£350
10	1	2k. yellow	44·00	£190
11	1	3k. red	£2000	15·00
12	1	7k. blue	£2750	£130
13	1	18k. bistre	£550	£450

2

B

1872

14	2	10g. grey	60·00	£1600
15	-	30g. blue	£120	£3000
38d	2	2m. purple	75·00	4·00

On the 30g. the figures are in a rectangular frame.

1872. Arms embossed as Type B.

16	1	¼g. purple	80·00	£110
17	1	⅓g. green	40·00	18·00
18	1	½g. orange	44·00	9·75
19	1	1g. red	80·00	4·50
20	1	2g. blue	26·00	6·25
21	1	2½g. brown	£2250	80·00
22	1	5g. olive	32·00	35·00
23	1	1k. green	40·00	35·00
24	1	2k. orange	£550	£2750
25	1	3k. red	25·00	5·25
26	1	7k. blue	35·00	80·00
27	1	9k. brown	£550	£475
28	1	18k. olive	40·00	£2500

1874. Surch with bold figures over arms.

29		"2½" on 2½g. brown	44·00	48·00
30		"9" on 9k. brown	80·00	£550

5

6

1875. "PFENNIGE" with final "E".

31	5	3pf. green	65·00	6·25
32	5	5pf. mauve	£110	4·00
33	6	10pf. red	48·00	1·80
34a	6	20pf. blue	£600	1·80
35	6	25pf. brown	£550	21·00
36a	6	50pf. grey	£2750	£400
37	6	50pf. green	£1900	15·00

1880. "PFENNIG" without final "E".

39a	5	3pf. green	3·50	1·60
40a	5	5pf. purple	1·80	1·60
41b	6	10pf. red	18·00	1·80
42a	6	20pf. blue	7·00	1·80
43b	6	25pf. brown	18·00	6·25
44a	6	50pf. green	8·75	1·40

8

9

1889

45	8	2pf. grey	60	90
46	8	3pf. brown	1·90	1·30
47a	8	5pf. green	1·50	1·30
48b	9	10pf. red	1·90	1·30
49	9	20pf. blue	8·75	1·30
50b	9	25pf. yellow	35·00	1·80
51b	9	50pf. brown	31·00	1·30

10 "Germania"

12 General Post Office, Berlin

13 Allegory of Union of N. and S. Germany (after Anton von Werner)

14 Unveiling of Kaiser Wilhelm I Memorial in Berlin (after W. Pape)

15 25th Anniv of German Empire Address by Wilhelm II (after W. Pape)

1899. Types 10 to 15 inscr "REICHSPOST".

52	10	2pf. grey	95	60
53	10	3pf. brown	95	1·20
54	10	5pf. green	1·20	60
55	10	10pf. red	2·20	90
56	10	20pf. blue	8·75	60
57a	10	25pf. black & red on yellow	16·00	4·75
58a	10	30pf. black & orge on rose	26·00	1·40
59a	10	40pf. black and red	26·00	1·40
60a	10	50pf. black & pur on rose	26·00	1·10
61a	10	80pf. black and red on rose	44·00	2·75
62	12	1m. red	£120	2·20
63	13	2m. blue	90·00	8·00
64	14	3m. black	£110	55·00
65b	15	5m. red and black	£400	£450

1902. T 10 to 15 inscr "DEUTSCHES REICH".

67	10	2pf. grey	1·80	60
83a	10	3pf. brown	95	70
84a	10	5pf. green	70	1·60
85a	10	10pf. red	12·50	1·60
86d	10	20pf. blue	90	1·60
87	10	25pf. black & red on yellow	44·00	2·50
88a	10	30pf. black & orge on buff	70	1·60
89a	10	40pf. black and red	1·10	1·60
90a	10	50pf. black & pur on buff	70	1·60
91a	10	60pf. purple	1·80	1·60
92a	10	80pf. black and red on rose	1·30	2·20
93B	12	1m. red	2·75	2·75
94B	13	2m. blue	6·25	5·75
95B	14	3m. black	2·75	4·75
96B	15	5m. red and black	2·20	5·75

No. 93 has three pedestrians in front of the carriage in the right foreground and has no tram in the background. See No. 113 for redrawn design.

24 Unshaded background

26

27

28

1916. Inscr "DEUTSCHES REICH".

97	24	2pf. grey	20	3·50
98	24	2½pf. grey	20	1·80
99a	24	7½pf. yellow	35	2·20
100	24	15pf. brown	3·50	2·20
101	24	15pf. violet	15	1·80
102	24	15pf. purple	3·50	3·25
103	24	35pf. brown	25	2·20
104	10	75pf. black and green	25	2·20
113	12	1m. red	2·20	2·75
114	12	1m.25 green	1·80	6·25
115	12	1m.50 brown	25	2·10
116a	13	2m.50 red	25	2·20
140	10	5pf. brown	25	1·80
141	10	10pf. orange	15	1·80
142	10	20pf. green	25	2·20
143a	10	30pf. blue	20	1·80
144a	10	40pf. red	20	1·80
145a	10	50pf. purple	70	1·80
146	10	60pf. olive	70	2·20
147a	10	75pf. purple	70	1·80
148a	10	80pf. blue	25	2·20
149	10	1m. green and violet	20	2·50
150	10	1¼m. purple and red	20	1·80
151	10	2m. blue and red	70	1·80
152	10	4m. red and black	20	2·75

No. 113 has one pedestrian behind the carriage in the right foreground and a tram in the background.

1919. War Wounded Fund. Surch 5 Pf. fur Kriegs=beschadigte.

105		10pf.+5pf. (No. 85a)	55	4·75
106	24	15pf.+5pf. (No. 101)	55	5·25

1919. National Assembly, Weimar.

107	26	10pf. red	15	1·80
108	27	15pf. blue and brown	15	1·80
109	28	25pf. red and green	15	1·80
110	28	30pf. red and purple	20	2·20

29

30 L.V.G. Schneider Biplane

1919. Air.

111	29	10pf. orange	15	2·75
112	30	40pf. green	15	3·50

1920. Stamps of Bavaria optd Deutsches Reich.

117	26	5pf. green	20	1·80
118	26	10pf. orange	20	1·80
119	26	15pf. red	20	1·80
120	27	20pf. purple	20	1·80
121	27	30pf. blue	20	1·80
122	27	40pf. brown	20	1·80
123	28	50pf. red	20	2·75
124	28	60pf. green	20	1·60
125	28	75pf. purple	45	5·75
126	28	80pf. blue	35	3·00
127	29	1m. red and grey	45	3·00
128	29	1¼m. blue and bistre	45	3·00
129	29	1½m. green and grey	55	4·00

130	**29**	2m. violet and bistre	90	4·50
131	**29**	2½m. black and grey	20	3·00
132	**30**	3m. blue	3·00	9·75
133	**30**	4m. red	3·50	11·50
134	**30**	5m. yellow	3·00	10·50
135	**30**	10m. green	5·75	18·00
136	**30**	20m. black	6·50	14·00

1920. Surch with new value and stars.

137	**12**	1m.25 on 1m. green	45	7·00
138	**12**	1m.50 on 1m. brown	35	8·00
139	**13**	2m.50 on 2m. purple	10·50	£225

35

36 Blacksmiths

37 Miners

38 Reapers

40

41 Ploughman

1921

153	**35**	5pf. red	10	1·80
154	**35**	10pf. olive	15	1·80
155	**35**	15pf. blue	10	1·60
156	**35**	25pf. brown	10	1·60
157	**35**	30pf. green	90	1·60
158	**35**	40pf. orange	10	1·60
160	**36**	60pf. red	10	1·60
161	**36**	80pf. red	10	6·25
163	**37**	120pf. blue	10	1·80
165	**38**	160pf. green	10	12·50
170	**40**	10m. red	55	3·00
182	**35**	50pf. purple	25	1·80
184	**35**	75pf. blue	10	3·25
186	**37**	100pf. green	20	1·80
188	**38**	150pf. orange	10	1·10
193	**40**	5m. orange	35	1·60
195	**41**	20m. blue and green	20	3·00

1921. 1902 stamps surch.

172	**10**	1m.60 on 5pf. brown	20	2·20
173	**10**	3m. on 1¼m. purple and red	15	2·75
174	**10**	5m. on 75pf. purple	25	2·20
175	**10**	10m. on 75pf. purple	45	2·20

39 Posthorn

1921

190	**39**	2m. violet and pink	10	1·60
191	**39**	3m. red and yellow	90	1·60
192	**39**	4m. green and light green	10	1·60
204	**39**	2m. purple	25	1·80
205	**39**	3m. red	10	1·80
206	**39**	4m. green	25	1·80
207	**39**	5m. orange and yellow	20	2·50
208	**39**	5m. orange	25	1·80
209	**39**	6m. blue	25	1·80
210	**39**	8m. green	25	1·80
211	**39**	10m. red and pink	20	1·80
212	**39**	20m. violet and red	45	1·80
213	**39**	20m. violet	25	1·80
214	**39**	30m. brown and yellow	20	1·80
215	**39**	30m. brown	25	8·00
216	**39**	40m. green	25	2·20
217	**39**	50m. green and purple	20	1·80

47 Arms of Munich

1922. Munich Exhibition.

198	**47**	1¼m. red	25	2·20
199	**47**	2m. violet	25	2·20
200	**47**	3m. red	20	2·20
201	**47**	4m. blue	20	2·20
202	**47**	10m. brown on buff	70	3·00
203	**47**	20m. red on rose	4·50	13·00

48

1922. Air.

218	**48**	25pf. brown	55	21·00
219	**48**	40pf. orange	45	28·00
220	**48**	50pf. purple	25	9·75
221	**48**	60pf. red	60	23·00
222	**48**	80pf. green	45	23·00
223	-	1m. green	20	4·50
224	-	2m. red and grey	20	4·50
225	-	3m. blue and grey	25	5·25
226	-	5m. orange and yellow	20	4·50
227	-	10m. purple and red	20	10·50
228	-	25m. brown and yellow	20	9·75
229	-	100m. olive and red	20	8·00

The mark values are larger (21×27 mm).
See also Nos. 269/73 and 358/64.

1922. New values.

230	**40**	100m. purple on buff	25	1·60
231	**40**	200m. red on buff	20	1·60
235	**40**	50m. black	25	1·80
238	**40**	300m. green on buff	10	1·60
239	**40**	400m. brown on buff	10	1·60
240	**40**	500m. orange on buff	10	1·60
241	**40**	1000m. grey	10	1·60
242	**40**	2000m. blue	35	2·20
243	**40**	3000m. brown	20	1·80
244	**40**	4000m. violet	20	1·80
245	**40**	5000m. green	35	1·80
246	**40**	100000m. red	10	1·60

50 Allegory of Charity

1922. Fund for the Old and for Children.

247	**50**	6m.+4m. blue and bistre	20	26·00
248	**50**	12m.+8m. red and lilac	20	26·00

51 Miners

1923

249	**51**	5m. orange	10	14·00
250	**38**	10m. blue	10	1·60
251	**38**	12m. red	10	1·60
252	**51**	20m. purple	20	1·60
253	**38**	25m. bistre	10	1·60
254	**51**	30m. olive	20	25
255	**38**	40m. green	25	1·60
256	**51**	50m. blue	45	£130

1923. Relief Fund for Sufferers in the Rhine and Ruhr Occupation Districts. Surch Rhein=Ruhr=Hilfe and premium.

257		5+100m. orange	15	10·50
258	**38**	25+500m. bistre	15	26·00
259	**41**	20+1000m. blue and green	2·30	95·00

54

1923. T = Tausend (thousand).

261	**54**	100m. purple	25	1·80
262	**54**	200m. red	20	1·80
263	**54**	300m. green	10	1·80
264	**54**	400m. brown	10	1·60
265	**54**	500m. red	10	6·50
266	**54**	1000m. grey	10	7·00
312	**54**	5T. blue	10	19·00
313	**54**	50T. brown	10	1·80
314	**54**	75T. purple	10	12·50

55 Wartburg Castle

1923

267	**55**	5000m. blue	25	3·00
268	-	10,000m. olive	35	4·50

DESIGN—VERT: 10,000m. Cologne Cathedral.

1923. Air. As T 48, but larger (21×27 mm).

269		5m. orange	20	48·00
270		10m. purple	20	11·50
271		25m. brown	20	11·50
272		100m. green	20	13·00
273		200m. blue	20	40·00

1923. Surch with new value in Tausend or Millionen (marks). Perf or rouletted.

274	**35**	5T. on 40pf. orange	10	1·90
275a	**35**	8T. on 30pf. green	10	1·80
276	**35**	15T. on 40m. green	25	1·80
277	**38**	20T. on 12m. red	10	1·80
278	**38**	20T. on 25m. brown	10	2·75
279	**54**	20T. on 200m. red	25	2·20
280	**38**	25T. on 25m. brown	10	16·00
281	**38**	30T. on 10m. blue	10	1·60
282	**54**	30T. on 200m. blue	10	1·60
283	**54**	75T. on 300m. green	10	16·00
284	**54**	75T. on 400m. green	25	1·80
285	**54**	75T. on 1000m. green	25	2·20
286	**54**	100T. on 100m. purple	25	2·10
287	**54**	100T. on 400m. green	10	1·60
288	**54**	125T. on 1000m. red	20	2·20
289	**54**	250T. on 200m. red	10	6·25
290	**54**	250T. on 300m. green	10	19·00
291	**54**	250T. on 400m. brown	10	22·00
292	**54**	250T. on 500m. pink	10	1·60
293	**54**	250T. on 500m. orange	10	22·00
294	**35**	800T. on 5pf. green	10	4·75
295	**35**	800T. on 10pf. green	10	5·75
296	**54**	800T. on 200m. red	20	90·00
297	**54**	800T. on 300m. green	10	5·75
298	**54**	800T. on 400m. green	10	14·00
299	**54**	800T. on 400m. brown	10	4·50
300	**54**	800T. on 500m. green	20	£1800
301	**54**	800T. on 1000m. green	25	1·80
302	**54**	2M. on 200m. red	20	2·30
303	**54**	2M. on 300m. green	10	2·50
304	**54**	2M. on 500m. red	10	7·00
305	**54**	2M. on 5T. red	10	10·50
306	**35**	400T. on 15pf. brown	10	5·25
307	**35**	400T. on 25pf. brown	10	5·25
308	**35**	400T. on 30pf. brown	10	5·25
309	**35**	400T. on 40pf. brown	10	5·25

62

1923. Perf or rouletted.

315	**62**	500T. brown	10	3·00
316	**62**	1M. blue	15	1·90
317	**62**	2M. purple	20	23·00
318	**62**	4M. green	20	1·80
319	**62**	5M. red	20	1·80
320	**62**	10M. red	10	1·80
321	**62**	20M. blue	20	2·20
322	**62**	30M. purple	10	10·50
323	**62**	50M. green	25	2·20
324	**62**	100M. grey	10	1·80
325	**62**	200M. brown	20	1·80
326	**62**	500M. olive	20	1·60

1923. As T 62, but value in "Milliarden". Perf or roul.

327		1Md. brown	35	2·20
328		2Md. green and flesh	20	2·20
329		5Md. brown and yellow	20	1·80
330		10Md. green & light green	20	1·80
331		20Md. brown and green	20	2·20
332		50Md. blue	25	40·00

1923. Surch in Milliarden. Perf or roul.

342	**54**	1Md. on 100m. purple	25	33·00
343	**62**	5Md. on 2M. purple	25	£150
344	**62**	5Md. on 4M. green	20	26·00
345	**62**	5Md. on 10M. red	20	3·00
346	**62**	10Md. on 20M. blue	25	5·25
347	**62**	10Md. on 50M. green	20	5·25
348	**62**	10Md. on 100M. grey	20	8·75

1923. As T 62, but without value in words and tablet blank.

352		3pf. brown	45	25
353		5pf. green	45	25
354		10pf. red	45	25
355		20pf. blue	1·30	45
356		50pf. orange	3·00	1·10
357		100pf. purple	9·75	1·30

The values of this and the following issues are expressed on the basis of the gold mark.

1924. Air.

358	**48**	5pf. green	1·50	1·80
359	**48**	10pf. red	1·50	2·10
360	**48**	20pf. blue	8·00	6·25
361	**48**	50pf. orange	13·00	28·00
362	**48**	100pf. purple	35·00	65·00
363	**48**	200pf. blue	65·00	90·00
364	**48**	300pf. grey	£110	£120

65

1924. Welfare Fund.

365	**65**	5+15pf. green	1·30	3·00
366	-	10+30pf. red	1·30	3·00
367	-	20+60pf. blue	7·00	8·75
368	-	50+1m.50 brown	26·00	70·00

DESIGNS: St. Elizabeth feeding the hungry (5pf.); giving drink to the thirsty (10pf.); clothing the naked (20pf.); and caring for the sick (50pf.).

66

1924

369	**66**	3pf. brown	35	45
370	**66**	5pf. green	35	45
371	**66**	10pf. red	45	45
372	**66**	20pf. blue	2·20	45
373	**66**	30pf. red	2·20	55
374	**66**	40pf. olive	15·00	80
375	**66**	50pf. orange	16·00	1·30

67 Rheinstein

1924

376	**67**	1m. green	12·50	2·75
377	-	2m. blue (A)	21·00	2·30
378	-	3m. red	25·00	6·25
379	-	5m. green	40·00	18·00
458	-	2m. blue (B)	31·00	17·00

DESIGNS: 2m. Cologne. (A) inscr "Zwei Mark"; (B) inscr "ZWEI REICHSMARK"; 3m. Marienburg; 5m. Speyer Cathedral.

71 Dr. von Stephan

1924. 50th Anniv of U.P.U.

380	**71**	10pf. green	60	35
381	**71**	20pf. blue	1·40	70
382	-	60pf. brown	4·50	90
383	-	80pf. deep green	11·50	1·80

DESIGN: Nos. 382/3. Similar to Type **71** but with border changed.

73 German Eagle and Rhine

1925. Rhineland Millenary.

384	73	5pf. green	55	45
385	73	10pf. red	1·30	45
386	73	20pf. blue	5·25	1·20

74

1925. Munich Exhibition.

387	74	5pf. green	3·50	6·25
388	74	10pf. red	4·50	11·50

75 Arms of Prussia

1925. Welfare Fund. Arms dated "1925".

389	75	5pf.+5pf. yell, blk & grn	60	2·20
390	-	10pf.+10pf. brn, bl & red	1·30	2·20
391	-	20pf.+20pf. brn, grn & bl	7·00	16·00

ARMS: 10pf. Bavaria; 20pf. Saxony.
See also Nos. 413/16a, 446/50 and 451/5.

76

1926. Air.

392	76	5pf. green	90	1·10
393	76	10pf. red	90	1·10
394	76	15pf. purple	1·90	1·60
395	76	20pf. blue	1·90	2·20
396	76	50pf. orange	21·00	6·25
397	76	1m. red and black	21·00	7·00
398	76	2m. blue and black	21·00	26·00
399	76	3m. olive and black	60·00	95·00

78 Goethe

1926. Portraits.

400	78	3pf. brown	70	25
402	-	5pf. green (Schiller)	1·20	25
404	-	8pf. green (Beethoven)	1·20	25
405	-	10pf. red (Frederick the Great)	1·20	25
406	-	15pf. red (Kant)	2·75	25
407	-	20pf. deep green (Beethoven)	12·50	1·30
408	78	25pf. blue	4·00	1·10
409	-	30pf. olive (Lessing)	7·50	60
410	-	40pf. violet (Leibniz)	13·00	70
411	-	50pf. brown (Bach)	17·00	8·75
412	-	80pf. brown (Durer)	35·00	5·75

1926. Welfare Fund. As T 75. Arms, dated "1926".

413	5pf.+5pf. multicoloured	1·20	2·75
414	10pf.+10pf. red, gold and rose	1·80	3·50
415	25pf.+25pf. blue, yell & red	13·00	22·00
416a	50pf.+50pf. multicoloured	48·00	£110

ARMS: 5pf. Wurttemberg; 10pf. Baden; 25pf. Thuringia; 50pf. Hesse.

79 Pres. von Hindenburg

1927. Welfare Fund. President's 80th Birthday.

417	79	8pf.+7pf. green	1·10	1·80
418	79	15pf.+15pf. red	1·10	1·80
419	79	25pf.+25pf. blue	7·00	25·00
420	79	50pf.+50pf. brown	11·50	28·00

1927. International Labour Office Session, Berlin. Optd I.A.A. 10.–15. 10. 1927.

421	-	8pf. green (No. 404)	19·00	75·00
422	-	15pf. red (No. 406)	19·00	75·00
423	78	25pf. blue	19·00	75·00

81 Pres. Ebert

82 Pres. von Hindenburg

1928

424	81	3pf. brown	25	70
425	82	4pf. blue	90	1·40
426	82	5pf. green	45	70
427	81	6pf. olive	90	80
428	81	8pf. green	25	70
429	81	10pf. red	2·20	2·75
430	81	10pf. purple	1·10	90
431	82	12pf. orange	1·30	80
432	82	15pf. red	70	70
433	81	20pf. deep green	7·50	4·50
434	81	20pf. grey	7·00	90
435	82	25pf. blue	8·75	1·10
436	81	30pf. olive	5·75	1·10
437	82	40pf. violet	15·00	1·10
438	81	45pf. orange	8·00	2·00
439	82	50pf. brown	8·25	1·40
440	81	60pf. brown	10·00	1·90
441	82	80pf. brown	25·00	4·50
442	82	80pf. yellow	9·75	1·10

83 Airship LZ-127 "Graf Zeppelin"

1928. Air.

443	83	1m. red	28·00	40·00
444	83	2m. blue	48·00	55·00
445	83	4m. brown	31·00	40·00

1928. Welfare Fund. As T 75, dated "1928".

446	5pf.+5pf. green, red & yellow	60	4·50
447	8pf.+7pf. multicoloured	60	4·50
448	15pf.+15pf. red, bl & yellow	90	4·50
449	25pf.+25pf. blue, red & yellow	10·50	55·00
450	50pf.+50pf. multicoloured	55·00	£110

ARMS: 5pf. Hamburg; 8pf. Mecklenburg-Schwerin; 15pf. Oldenburg; 25pf. Brunswick; 50pf. Anhalt.

1929. Welfare Fund. As T 75, dated "1929".

451	5pf.+2pf. green, yellow & red	70	1·80
452	8pf.+4pf. yellow, red & green	70	1·80
453	15pf.+5pf. yellow, blk & red	90	1·80
454	25pf.+10pf. multicoloured	13·00	55·00
455	50pf.+40pf. yellow, red & brn	48·00	£110

ARMS: 5pf. Bremen; 8pf. Lippe; 15pf. Lubeck; 25pf. Mecklenburg-Strelitz; 50pf. Schaumburg-Lippe.

1930. Air. LZ-127 "Graf Zeppelin" 1st S. American Flight. T 83 inscr "I. SUDAMERIKA FAHRT".

456	2m. blue	£275	£350
457	4m. brown	£275	£350

1930. Evacuation of Rhineland by Allied Forces. Optd 30. JUNI 1930.

459	81	8pf. green	1·30	1·10
460	82	15pf. red	1·30	1·10

86 Aachen

1930. International Philatelic Exhibition, Berlin.

461	86	8pf.+4pf. green	31·00	£110
462	-	15pf.+5pf. red	31·00	£110
463	-	25pf.+10pf. blue	31·00	£110
464	-	50pf.+40pf. brown	31·00	£110
MS464a		195×148 mm. Nos. 461/4 (sold at 2m.70 in the exhibition)	£450	£1800

DESIGNS: 15p. Berlin; 25pf. Marienwerder; 50pf. Wurzburg.

1930. Welfare Fund.

465	86	8pf.+4pf. green	45	90
466	-	15pf.+5pf. red	55	1·30
467	-	25pf.+10pf. blue	8·75	26·00
468	-	50pf.+40pf. brown	25·00	95·00

DESIGNS: 15pf. Berlin; 25pf. Marienwerder; 50pf. Wurzburg.

1931. Air. LZ-125 "Graf Zeppelin" Polar Flight. Optd POLAR-FAHRT 1931.

469	83	1m. red	£130	£120
470	83	2m. blue	£190	£225
471	83	4m. brown	£475	£800

92 Heidelberg Castle

1931. Welfare Fund.

472	-	8pf.+4pf. green	35	1·10
473	-	15pf.+5pf. red	55	1·10
474	92	25pf.+10pf. blue	8·75	26·00
475	-	50pf.+40pf. brown	35·00	90·00

DESIGNS—VERT: 8pf. The Zwinger, Dresden; 15pf. Town Hall, Breslau; 50pf. The Holstentor, Lubeck.
See also Nos. 485/9.

1932. Welfare Fund. Nos. 472/3 surch.

476	6+4pf. on 8pf.+4pf. green	4·50	11·50
477	12+3pf. on 15pf.+5pf. red	5·25	13·00

94 President von Hindenburg

1932. 85th Birthday of Pres. von Hindenburg.

478	94	4pf. blue	60	70
480	94	12pf. orange	5·25	70
481	94	15pf. red	4·50	11·50
483	94	40pf. violet	21·00	1·80
484	94	50pf. brown	7·00	12·50
496B	94	5pf. green	10	40
503B	94	25pf. blue	55	40

See also Nos. 493/509 and 545/50.

1932. Welfare Fund. As T 92.

485	4pf.+2pf. blue	35	60
486	6pf.+4pf. olive	40	60
487	12pf.+3pf. red	60	1·10
488	25pf.+10pf. blue	8·75	19·00
489	40pf.+40pf. purple	32·00	70·00

CASTLES: 4pf. Wartburg; 6pf. Stolzenfels; 12pf. Nuremberg; 25pf. Lichtenstein; 40pf. Marburg.

96 Frederick the Great (after A. von Menzel)

1933. Opening of Reichstag in Potsdam.

490	96	6pf. green	70	95
491	96	12pf. red	70	95
492	96	25pf. blue	44·00	23·00

1933

493B	94	1pf. black	10	40
494B	94	3pf. brown	10	40
495B	94	4pf. grey	10	40
497B	94	6pf. green	10	40
498B	94	8pf. orange	10	40
499B	94	10pf. brown	10	40
500B	94	12pf. red	10	40
501B	94	15pf. red	35	40
502B	94	20pf. blue	35	40
504B	94	30pf. green	90	40
505B	94	40pf. mauve	90	40
506B	94	50pf. black and green	3·50	40
507B	94	60pf. black and red	90	40
508B	94	80pf. black and blue	2·75	1·30
509B	94	100pf. black and yellow	3·50	1·20

1933. Air. LZ-127 "Graf Zeppelin" Chicago World Exhibition Flight. Optd Chicagofahrt Weltausstellung 1933.

510	83	1m. red	£900	£400
511	83	2m. blue	90·00	£200
512	83	4m. brown	90·00	£200

99 Tannhauser

1933. Welfare Fund. Wagner's Operas.

513	99	3pf.+2pf. brown	2·20	5·25
514	-	4pf.+2pf. blue	1·60	2·10
515	-	5pf.+2pf. green	4·50	6·50
516	-	6pf.+4pf. green	1·60	1·60
517	-	8pf.+4pf. orange	2·30	3·75
518	-	12pf.+3pf. red	2·30	1·90
519a	-	20pf.+10pf. light blue	£120	£110
520	-	25pf.+15pf. blue	28·00	41·00
521	-	40pf.+35pf. mauve	£120	£130

OPERAS: 4pf. "The Flying Dutchman"; 5pf. "Rhinegold"; 6pf. "The Mastersingers"; 8pf. "The Valkyries"; 12pf. "Siegfried"; 20pf. "Tristan and Isolde"; 25pf. "Lohengrin"; 40pf. "Parsifal".

1933. Welfare Fund. Stamps as 1924, issued together in sheets of four, each stamp optd 1923–1933.

522	65	5+15pf. green	90·00	£325
523	-	10+30pf. red	90·00	£325
524	-	20+60pf. blue	90·00	£325
525	-	50pf.+1.50m. brown	90·00	£325
MS525a		210×148 mm. Nos. 522/5	£1600	£11000

100 Golden Eagle, Globe and Swastika

101 Count Zeppelin and Airship LZ-127 "Graf Zeppelin"

1934. Air.

526	100	5pf. green	90	55
527	100	10pf. red	90	80
528	100	15pf. blue	1·30	1·20
529	100	20pf. blue	5·00	1·80
530	100	25pf. brown	4·00	1·60
531	100	40pf. mauve	8·00	1·20
532	100	50pf. green	14·00	80
533	100	80pf. yellow	4·50	4·00
534	100	100pf. black	7·00	2·75
535	-	2m. grey and green	19·00	20·00
536	101	3m. grey and blue	35·00	45·00

DESIGN—As Type **101**: 2m. Otto Lilienthal and Lilienthal biplane glider.

103 Franz A. E. Luderitz

1934. German Colonizers' Jubilee.

537	103	3pf. brown and chocolate	1·80	3·75
538	-	6pf. brown and green	1·30	75
539	-	12pf. brown and red	2·20	1·10
540	-	25pf. brown and blue	10·50	13·00

DESIGNS: 6pf. Gustav Nachtigal; 12pf. Karl Peters; 25pf. Hermann von Wissmann.

104 "Saar Ownership"

1934. Saar Plebiscite.

541	104	6pf. green	3·50	65
542	-	12pf. red	4·50	65

DESIGN: 12pf. Eagle inscribed "Saar" in rays from a swastika-eclipsed sun.

105 Nuremberg Castle

1934. Nuremberg Congress.

543	105	6pf. green	3·50	65
544	105	12pf. red	4·50	65

1934. Hindenburg Memorial. Portrait with black borders.

545	94	3pf. brown	90	50
546	94	5pf. green	90	55
547	94	6pf. green	1·60	50
548	94	8pf. orange	2·75	50
549	94	12pf. red	7·00	50
550	94	25pf. blue	8·00	9·00

106 Blacksmith

1934. Welfare Fund.

551	-	3pf.+2pf. brown	90	1·20

552	106	4pf.+2pf. black	90	1·20
553	-	5pf.+2pf. green	7·00	8·50
554	-	6pf.+4pf. green	55	60
555	-	8pf.+4pf. red	90	1·20
556	-	12pf.+3pf. red	55	60
557	-	20pf.+10pf. green	18·00	24·00
558	-	25pf.+15pf. blue	18·00	24·00
559	-	40pf.+35pf. lilac	55·00	75·00

DESIGNS: 3pf. Merchant; 5pf. Mason; 6pf. Miner; 8pf. Architect; 12pf. Farmer; 20pf. Scientist; 25pf. Sculptor; 40pf. Judge.

107 Friedrich von Schiller

1934. 175th Birth Anniv of Schiller.

560	107	6pf. green	3·00	70
561	107	12pf. red	5·25	70

108 "The Saar comes home"

1935. Saar Restoration.

562	108	3pf. brown	90	1·30
563	108	6pf. green	90	85
564	108	12pf. red	2·75	85
565	108	25pf. blue	9·75	9·25

109 "Steel Helmet"

1935. War Heroes' Day.

566	109	6pf. green	90	1·70
567	109	12pf. red	90	1·70

110 "Victor's Crown"

1935. Apprentices Vocational Contest.

568	110	6pf. green	90	1·50
569	110	12pf. red	1·10	1·50

111 Heinrich Schutz

1935. Musicians' Anniversaries.

570	111	6pf. green	1·20	60
571	-	12pf. red (Bach)	1·80	60
572	-	25pf. blue (Handel)	2·75	1·00

112 Allenstein Castle

1935. International Philatelic Exhibition, Konigsberg. In miniature sheets.

573	112	3pf. brown	40·00	42·00
574	-	6pf. green	40·00	42·00
575	-	12pf. red	40·00	42·00
576	-	25pf. blue	40·00	42·00
MS576a 148×105 mm. Nos. 573/6			£950	£750

DESIGNS: 6pf. Tannenberg Memorial; 12pf. Konigsberg Castle; 25pf. Heilsberg Castle.

113 Stephenson Locomotive "Adler", 1835

1935. German Railway Centenary. Locomotive types inscr "1835–1935".

577	113	6pf. green	1·40	70
578	-	12pf. red	1·40	70
579	-	25pf. blue	8·00	2·00
580	-	40pf. purple	13·00	2·00

DESIGNS: 12pf. Class 03 steam train, 1930s; 25pf. Diesel train "Flying Hamburger"; 40pf. Class 05 streamlined steam locomotive No. 001, 1935.

114 Trumpeter

1935. World Jamboree of "Hitler Youth".

581	114	6pf. green	1·30	2·50
582	114	15pf. red	1·80	3·00

115 Nuremberg

1935. Nuremberg Congress.

583	115	6pf. green	90	40
584	115	12pf. red	2·20	40

116 East Prussia

1935. Welfare Fund. Provincial Costumes.

585	116	3pf.+2pf. brown	20	40
586	-	4pf.+3pf. blue	1·10	1·70
587	-	5pf.+3pf. green	20	85
588	-	6pf.+4pf. green	20	40
589	-	8pf.+4pf. brown	2·75	1·30
590	-	12pf.+6pf. red	25	40
591	-	15pf.+10pf. brown	5·25	6·25
592	-	25pf.+15pf. blue	10·50	6·25
593	-	30pf.+20pf. grey	13·00	22·00
594	-	40pf.+35pf. mauve	11·50	16·00

COSTUMES: 4pf. Silesia; 5pf. Rhineland; 6pf. Lower Saxony; 8pf. Kurmark; 12pf. Black Forest; 15pf. Hesse; 25pf. Upper Bavaria; 30pf. Friesland; 40pf. Franconia.

117 S.A. Man and Feldherrnhalle, Munich

1935. 12th Anniv of 1st Hitler Putsch.

595	117	3pf. brown	35	70
596	117	12pf. red	55	70

118 Skating

1935. Winter Olympic Games, Garmisch-Partenkirchen.

597	118	6pf.+4pf. green	90	60
598	-	12pf.+6pf. red	1·80	1·10
599	-	25pf.+15pf. blue	10·50	8·50

DESIGNS: 12pf. Ski jumping; 25pf. Bobsleighing.

119 Heinkel He 70 Blitz

1936. 10th Anniv of Lufthansa Airways.

600	119	40pf. blue	6·25	3·50

120 Gottlieb Daimler

1936. Berlin Motor Show. 50th Anniv of Invention of First Motor Car.

601	120	6pf. green	55	85
602	120	12pf. red (Carl Benz)	60	85

121 Airship LZ-129 "Hindenburg"

1936. Air.

603	121	50pf. blue	21·00	85
604	121	75pf. green	23·00	1·20

122 Otto von Guericke

1936. 250th Death Anniv of Otto von Guericke (scientist).

605	122	6pf. green	35	50

123 Gymnastics

1936. Summer Olympic Games, Berlin.

606	123	3pf.+2pf. brown	40	35
607	-	4pf.+3pf. blue	40	60
608	-	6pf.+4pf. green	40	35
609	-	8pf.+4pf. red	3·50	1·40
610	-	12pf.+6pf. red	45	35
611	-	15pf.+10pf. red	7·00	3·50
612	-	25pf.+15pf. blue	4·50	4·25
613	-	40pf.+35pf. violet	8·75	8·50
MS613a Two sheets, each 148×105 mm. (a) Nos. 606/8 and 613; (b) Nos. 609/12			55·00	£110

DESIGNS: 4pf. Diver; 6pf. Footballer; 8pf. Javelin thrower; 12pf. Olympic torchbearer; 15pf. Fencer; 25pf. Double scullers; 40pf. Show jumper.

124 Symbolical of Local Government

1936. 6th Int Local Government Congress.

614	124	3pf. brown	35	35
615	124	5pf. green	35	35
616	124	12pf. red	70	70
617	124	25pf. blue	1·50	1·20

125 "Brown Ribbon" Race

1936. "Brown Ribbon of Germany". Single stamp in miniature sheet.

MS618 125 42pf. brown		8·75	15·00

126 "Leisure Time"

1936. Int Recreational Congress, Hamburg.

619	126	6pf. green	45	60
620	126	15pf. red	70	1·10

127 Saluting the Swastika

1936. Nuremberg Congress.

621	127	6pf. green	45	60
622	127	12pf. red	55	70

128 Luitpoldhain Heroes Memorial, Nuremberg

1936. Winter Relief Fund.

623	-	3pf.+2pf. brown	20	35
624	-	4pf.+3pf. black	20	50
625	128	5pf.+3pf. green	20	35
626	-	6pf.+4pf. green	20	35
627	-	8pf.+4pf. brown	90	1·40
628	-	12pf.+6pf. red	20	35
629	-	15pf.+10pf. brown	2·20	3·75
630	-	25pf.+15pf. blue	1·50	4·25
631	-	40pf.+35pf. mauve	3·00	12·50

DESIGNS: 3pf. Munich frontier road; 4pf. Air Ministry, Berlin; 6pf. Bridge over River Saale; 8pf. Deutschlandhalle, Berlin; 12pf. Alpine road; 15pf. Fuhrerhaus, Munich; 25pf. Bridge over River Mangfall; 40pf. German Art Museum, Munich.

129 R(eichs) L(uftschutz) B(und) = Civil Defence Union

1937. 4th Anniv of Civil Defence Union.

632	129	3pf. brown	45	35
633	129	6pf. green	45	35
634	129	12pf. red	1·10	70

130 Adolf Hitler

1937. Hitler's Culture Fund and 48th birthday. Four stamps in miniature sheet (148×105 mm). Perf or Imperf.

MS635 130 6+19pf. green		21·00	12·00

1937. "Brown Ribbon of Germany". No. MS618 optd with German eagle and ornamental border surrounding, "1. AUGUST 1937 MUNCHEN-REIM" in red.

MS637a 125 42pf. (+108pf.) brown		70·00	£110

1937. Nuremberg Congress. Four stamps in miniature sheet, as No. MS637, but optd REICHSPARTEITAG NURNBERG 1937 in panels of stamps.

MS638 130 6+19pf. green		90·00	50·00

131 Fishing Smacks

1937. Winter Relief Fund.

639	-	3pf.+2pf. brown	20	40
640	-	4pf.+3pf. black	1·20	1·30
641	131	5pf.+3pf. green	20	40
642	-	6pf.+4pf. green	20	40
643	-	8pf.+4pf. orange	90	1·30

644	-	12pf.+6pf. red	20	40
645	-	15pf.+10pf. brown	2·30	4·25
646	-	25pf.+15pf. blue	4·50	4·25
647	-	40pf.+35pf. purple	8·75	8·50

DESIGNS: 3pf. "Bremen" (lifeboat), 1931; 4pf. "Burgemeister Oswald" (lightship); 6pf. "Wilhelm Gustloff" (liner); 8pf. "Padua" (barque); 12pf. "Tannenberg" (liner); 15pf. "Schwerin" (train ferry); 25pf. "Hamburg" (liner); 40pf. "Europa" (liner).

132 Hitler Youth

1938. Hitler Culture Fund. 5th Anniv of Hitler's Leadership.

648	132	6pf.+4pf. green	1·10	2·10
649	132	12pf.+8pf. red	1·10	2·10

133 "Unity"

1938. Austrian Plebiscite.

650	133	6pf. green	20	40

134 Adolf Hitler

1938. Hitler's Culture Fund and 49th Birthday.

652	134	12pf.+38pf. red	1·80	2·50

See also No. 660.

135 Breslau Cathedral

1938. 16th German Sports Tournament, Breslau. Inscr as in T 135.

653	135	3pf. brown	35	50
654	-	6pf. green	35	50
655	-	12pf. red	70	50
656	-	15pf. brown	1·10	85

DESIGNS: 6pf. Hermann Goering Stadium; 12pf. Breslau Town Hall; 15pf. Centenary Hall.

136 Airship Gondola and Airship LZ-127 "Graf Zeppelin"

1938. Air. Birth Cent of Count Zeppelin.

657		25pf. blue	2·75	1·40
658	136	50pf. green	4·00	1·40

DESIGN: 25pf. Count Zeppelin and airship LZ-5.

137 Horsewoman

1938. "Brown Ribbon of Germany".

659	137	42pf.+108pf. brown	25·00	50·00

1938. Nuremberg Congress and Hitler's Culture Fund. As No. 652, but inscr "Reichsparteitag 1938".

660	134	6pf.+19pf. green	2·75	4·25

138 Saarpfalz Gautheater, Saarbrucken

1938. Opening of Gautheater and Hitler's Culture Fund.

661	138	6pf.+4pf. green	1·10	2·10
662	138	12pf.+8pf. red	2·20	3·00

139 Forchtenstein Castle, Burgenland

1938. Winter Relief.

663	139	3pf.+2pf. brown	25	35
664	-	4pf.+3pf. blue	1·90	1·30
665	-	5pf.+3pf. green	15	40
666	-	6pf.+4pf. green	1·60	1·30
667	-	8pf.+4pf. red	1·90	1·30
668	-	12pf.+6pf. red	20	35
669	-	15pf.+10pf. red	4·50	5·00
670	-	25pf.+15pf. blue	3·75	5·00
671	-	40pf.+35pf. mauve	7·75	8·50

DESIGNS: 4pf. Flexenstrasse; 5pf. Zell am See; 6pf. Grossglockner; 8pf. Augstein Castle, Wachau; 12pf. Wien (Prince Eugene Statue, Vienna); 15pf. Erzberg, Steiermark; 25pf. Hall-in-Tirol; 40pf. Braunau.

140 Sudeten Miner and Wife

1938. Acquisition of Sudetenland and Hitler's Culture Fund.

672	140	6pf.+4pf. green	1·30	3·00
673	140	12pf.+8pf. red	2·75	3·50

141 Racing Cars

1939. Int Motor Show, Berlin, and Hitler's Culture Fund.

674	-	6pf.+4pf. green	3·00	3·75
675	141	12pf.+8pf. red	3·00	3·75
676	-	25pf.+10pf. blue	8·75	6·75

DESIGNS: 6pf. Early Benz and Daimler cars; 25pf. Volkswagen car.

142 Eagle and Laurel Wreath

1939. Apprentices' Vocational Contest.

677	142	6pf. green	1·30	4·25
678	142	12pf. red	1·80	4·25

143 Adolf Hitler in Braunau

1939. Hitler's 50th Birthday and Culture Fund.

679	143	12pf.+38pf. red	1·80	4·75

144 Horticultural Exhibition Entrance and Arms of Stuttgart

1939. Stuttgart Horticultural Exhibition and Hitler's Culture Fund.

680	144	6pf.+4pf. green	1·20	2·10
681	144	15pf.+5pf. red	1·20	2·10

145 Adolf Hitler Speaking

1939. National Labour Day and Hitler's Culture Fund.

682	145	6pf.+19pf. brown	2·10	4·75

See also No. 689.

1939. Nurburgring Races and Hitler's Culture Fund. Nos. 674/6 optd Nurburgring-Rennen.

683	-	6pf.+4pf. green	33·00	32·00
684	141	12pf.+8pf. red	33·00	32·00
685	-	25pf.+10pf. blue	33·00	32·00

147 "Investment" and Jockey

1939. 70th Anniv of German Derby.

686	147	25pf.+50pf. blue	18·00	17·00

148 Training Thoroughbred Horses

1939. "Brown Ribbon of Germany" and Hitler's Culture Fund.

687	148	42pf.+108pf. brown	18·00	27·00

149 "Young Venetian Woman" after Durer

1939. German Art Day.

688	149	6pf.+19pf. green	6·25	11·00

1939. Nuremberg Congress and Hitler's Culture Fund. As T 145, but inscr "REICHS-PARTEITAG 1939".

689		6pf.+19pf. brown	4·00	10·00

150 Mechanics at Work and Play

1939. Postal Employees' and Hitler's Culture Funds. Inscr "Kameradschaftsblock der Deutschen Reichspost".

690	-	3pf.+2pf. brown	2·50	6·00
691	-	4pf.+3pf. blue	2·50	6·00
692	150	5pf.+3pf. green	90	1·70
693	-	6pf.+4pf. green	90	1·40
694	-	8pf.+4pf. orange	90	1·70
695	-	10pf.+5pf. brown	90	2·20
696	-	12pf.+6pf. red	95	2·20
697	-	15pf.+10pf. red	90	2·20
698	-	16pf.+10pf. green	90	2·20
699	-	20pf.+10pf. blue	1·10	2·20
700	-	24pf.+10pf. olive	2·75	4·25
701	-	25pf.+15pf. blue	2·75	3·50

DESIGNS: 3pf. Postal employees' rally; 4pf. Review in Vienna; 6pf. Youths on parade; 8pf. Flag bearers; 10pf. Distributing prizes; 12pf. Motor race; 15pf. Women athletes; 16pf. Postal police; 20pf. Glider workshop; 24pf. Mail coach; 25pf. Sanatorium, Konigstein.

See also Nos. 761/6 and 876/81.

151 St. Mary's Church, Danzig

1939. Occupation of Danzig. Inscr "DANZIG IST DEUTSCH".

702	151	6pf. green	20	70
703	-	12pf. red (Crane Gate)	35	85

1939. Stamps of Danzig surch Deutsches Reich and new values.

704	28	Rpf. on 3pf. brown	85	2·40
705	28	4Rpf. on 35pf. blue	75	2·20
706	28	Rpf. on 5pf. orange	75	2·75
707	28	Rpf. on 8pf. green	1·30	4·25
708	28	Rpf. on 10pf. green	2·40	4·25
709	28	12Rpf. on 7pf. green	1·50	2·20
710	28	Rpf. on 15pf. red	5·25	12·00
711	28	Rpf. on 20pf. grey	3·25	8·00
712	28	Rpf. on 25pf. red	2·75	11·00
713	28	Rpf. on 30pf. purple	2·20	4·75
714	28	Rpf. on 40pf. blue	2·40	6·00
715	28	Rpf. on 50pf. red and blue	2·75	7·25
716	42	1Rm on 1g. black & orge	8·75	60·00
717	-	2Rm on 2g. black and red (No. 206)	12·50	60·00

155 Elbogen Castle

1939. Winter Relief Fund.

718	155	3pf.+2pf. brown	20	50
719	-	4pf.+3pf. black	1·80	2·10
720	-	5pf.+3pf. green	20	60
721	-	6pf.+4pf. green	20	40
722	-	8pf.+4pf. red	1·80	1·90
723	-	12pf.+6pf. red	30	40
724	-	15pf.+10pf. brown	2·50	5·00
725	-	25pf.+15pf. blue	3·00	5·00
726	-	40pf.+35pf. purple	3·25	6·75

DESIGNS: 4pf. Drachenfels; 5pf. Goslar Castle; 6pf. Clocktower, Graz; 8pf. The Romer, Frankfurt; 12pf. City Hall, Klagenfurt; 15pf. Ruins of Schreckenstein Castle; 25pf. Salzburg Fortress; 40pf. Hohentwiel Castle.

156 Leipzig Library and Gutenberg

1940. Leipzig Fair.

727	156	3pf. brown	35	40
728	-	6pf. green	35	40
729	-	12pf. red	35	40
730	-	25pf. blue	70	1·30

DESIGNS: 6pf. Augustusplatz; 12pf. Old Town Hall; 25pf. View of Fair.

157 Courtyard of Chancellery, Berlin

1940. 2nd Berlin Philatelic Exhibition.

731	157	24pf.+76pf. green	7·00	19·00

158 Hitler and Child

1940. Hitler's 51st Birthday.

732	**158**	12pf.+38pf. red	1·80	6·25

159 Wehrmacht Symbol

1940. National Fete Day and Hitler's Culture Fund.

733	**159**	6pf.+4pf. green	35	1·40

160 Horseman

1940. Hamburg Derby and Hitler's Culture Fund.

734	**160**	25pf.+100pf. blue	4·00	12·00

161 Chariot

1940. Hitler's Culture Fund and "Brown Ribbon" Race.

735	**161**	42pf.+108pf. brown	26·00	30·00

162 Malmedy

1940. Eupen and Malmedy reincorporated in Germany, and Hitler's Culture Fund. Inscr "Eupen-Malmedy wieder Deutsch".

736	**162**	6pf.+4pf. green	80	3·25
737	-	12pf.+8pf. red	80	3·25

DESIGNS: 12pf. View of Eupen.

163 Heligoland

1940. 50th Anniv of Cession of Heligoland to Germany and Hitler's Culture Fund.

738	**163**	6pf.+94pf. red and green	4·75	12·50

164 Artushof, Danzig

1940. Winter Relief Fund.

739	**164**	3pf.+2pf. brown	10	40
740	-	4pf.+3pf. blue	55	85
741	-	5pf.+3pf. green	25	50
742	-	6pf.+4pf. green	25	40
743	-	8pf.+4pf. orange	90	95
744	-	12pf.+6pf. red	25	40
745	-	15pf.+10pf. brown	1·10	3·00
746	-	25pf.+15pf. blue	1·50	3·00
747	-	40pf.+35pf. purple	2·50	6·75

DESIGNS: 4pf. Town Hall, Thorn; 5pf. Kaub Castle; 6pf. City Theatre, Posen; 8pf. Heidelberg Castle; 12pf. Porta Nigra, Trier; 15pf. New Theatre, Prague; 25pf. Town Hall, Bremen; 40pf. Town Hall, Munster.

165 Emil von Behring (bacteriologist)

1940. 50th Anniv of Development of Diphtheria Antitoxin.

748	**165**	6pf.+4pf. green	55	1·70
749	**165**	25pf.+10pf. blue	1·10	2·50

166 Postilion and Globe

1941. Stamp Day.

750	**166**	6pf.+24pf. green	90	2·50

167 Mussolini and Hitler

1941. Hitler's Culture Fund.

751	**167**	12pf.+38pf. red	60	3·00

168 House of Nations, Leipzig

1941. Leipzig Fair. Buildings. Inscr "REICHSMESSE LEIPZIG 1941".

752	**168**	3pf. brown	30	85
753	-	6pf. green	30	85
754	-	12pf. red	35	1·00
755	-	25pf. blue	75	1·70

DESIGNS: 6pf. Cloth Hall; 12pf. Exhibition Building; 25pf. Railway Station.

169 Dancer

1941. Vienna Fair.

756	**169**	3pf. brown	30	60
757	-	6pf. green	35	60
758	-	12pf. red	35	70
759	-	25pf. blue	85	1·70

DESIGNS: 6pf. Arms and Exhibition Building; 12pf. Allegory and Municipal Theatre; 25pf. Prince Eugene's Equestrian Monument.

170 Adolf Hitler

1941. Hitler's 52nd Birthday and Culture Fund.

760	**170**	12pf.+38pf. red	1·30	3·50

1941. Postal Employees' and Hitler's Culture Funds. Inscr "Kameradschaftsblock der Deutschen Reichspost" as Nos. 693/4, 696 and 698/700, but premium values and colours changed.

761		6pf.+9pf. green	70	2·50
762		8pf.+12pf. red	85	1·70
763		12pf.+18pf. red	85	1·70
764		16pf.+24pf. black	85	4·25
765		20pf.+30pf. blue	85	4·25
766		24pf.+36pf. violet	5·25	12·50

171 Racehorse

1941. 72nd Anniv of Hamburg Derby.

767	**171**	25pf.+100pf. blue	3·25	8·50

172 Two Amazons

1941. "Brown Ribbon of Germany".

768	**172**	42pf.+108pf. brown	2·10	5·00

173 Adolf Hitler

1941

769	**173**	1pf. grey	10	10
770	**173**	3pf. brown	10	10
771	**173**	4pf. slate	10	10
772	**173**	5pf. green	10	10
773	**173**	6pf. violet	10	10
774	**173**	8pf. red	10	10
776	**173**	12pf. red	20	50
777	**173**	10pf. brown	35	35
779	**173**	15pf. lake	10	40
780	**173**	16pf. green	10	1·70
781	**173**	20pf. blue	10	50
782	**173**	24pf. brown	10	1·70
783	**173**	25pf. blue	10	50
784	**173**	30pf. olive	10	50
785	**173**	40pf. mauve	10	50
786	**173**	50pf. green	10	50
787	**173**	60pf. brown	10	50
788	**173**	80pf. blue	10	50

Nos. 783/8 are larger (21½×26 mm).

174 Brandenburg Gate, Berlin

1941. Berlin Grand Prix and Hitler's Culture Fund.

789	**174**	25pf.+50pf. blue	2·10	6·00

175 Belvedere Palace, Vienna

176 Belvedere Gardens, Vienna

1941. Vienna Fair and Hitler's Culture Fund.

790	**175**	12pf.+8pf. red	80	2·50
791	**176**	15pf.+10pf. violet	80	3·00

177 Marburg

178 Veldes

1941. Annexation of Northern Slovenia, and Hitler's Culture Fund.

792	**177**	3pf.+7pf. brown	80	2·50
793	**178**	6pf.+9pf. violet	70	2·50
794	-	12pf.+13pf. red	90	3·00
795	-	25pf.+15pf. blue	1·60	2·10

DESIGNS: 12pf. Pettau; 25pf. Triglav.

179 Mozart

1941. 150th Death Anniv of Mozart and Hitler's Culture Fund.

796	**179**	6pf.+4pf. purple	20	70

180 Philatelist

1942. Stamp Day and Hitler's Culture Fund.

797	**180**	6pf.+24pf. violet	60	3·25

181 Symbolical of Heroism

1942. Heroes' Remembrance Day and Hitler's Culture Fund.

798	**181**	12pf.+38pf. slate	35	1·70

182 Adolf Hitler

1942

799a	**182**	1m. green	35	6·00
800	**182**	2m. violet	1·50	6·75
801	**182**	3m. red	1·80	17·00
802a	**182**	5m. blue	1·30	55·00

183 Adolf Hitler

1942. Hitler's 53rd Birthday and Culture Fund.

803	**183**	12pf.+38pf. red	3·00	24·00

184 Jockey and Three-year-old Horse

1942. Hamburg Derby and Hitler's Culture Fund.

804	**184**	25pf.+100pf. blue	5·25	12·50

185 Equine Trio

1942. "Brown Ribbon of Germany" and Hitler's Culture Fund.

805	**185**	42pf.+108pf. brown	1·80	6·00

186 Cream Jug and Loving Cup

1942. 10th Anniv of National Goldsmiths' Institution.

806	**186**	6pf.+4pf. red	25	1·70
807	**186**	12pf.+88pf. green	60	2·50

187 Badge of Armed S.A.

1942. S.A. Military Training Month.

808	**187**	6pf. violet	20	85

188 Peter Henlein

1942. 400th Death Anniv of Henlein (inventor of the watch).

809	**188**	6pf.+24pf. violet	55	1·70

189 Mounted Postilion

1942. European Postal Congress, Vienna.

810	-	3pf.+7pf. blue	35	1·70
811	-	6pf.+14pf. brown & blue	55	1·70
812	**189**	12pf.+38pf. brown & red	75	3·00

DESIGNS—HORIZ: 3pf. Postilion and map of Europe. VERT: 6pf. Mounted postilion and globe.

1942. Signing of European Postal Union Agreement. Nos. 810/2 optd 19.Okt.1942.

813	-	3pf.+7pf. blue	90	3·00
814	-	6pf.+14pf. brown & blue	90	3·00
815	**189**	12pf.+38pf. brown & red	1·20	5·00

191 Mail Coach

1943. Stamp Day and Hitler's Culture Fund.

816	**191**	6pf.+24pf. brn, yell & bl	20	1·00

192 Brandenburg Gate and Torchlight Parade

1943. 10th Anniv of Third Reich.

817	**192**	54pf.+96pf. red	55	2·50

193

1943. Philatelic Cancellation Premium.

818	**193**	3pf.+2pf. bistre	20	1·00

194 Machine Gunners

1943. Armed Forces' and Heroes' Day.

819	-	3pf.+2pf. brown	45	1·40
820	**194**	4pf.+3pf. brown	45	1·40
821	-	5pf.+4pf. green	45	1·40
822	-	6pf.+9pf. violet	45	1·40
823	-	8pf.+7pf. red	50	1·40
824	-	12pf.+8pf. red	50	1·40
825	-	15pf.+10pf. purple	50	1·40
826	-	20pf.+14pf. blue	50	1·40
827	-	25pf.+15pf. blue	50	1·40
828	-	30pf.+30pf. green	75	2·10
829	-	40pf.+40pf. purple	75	2·10
830	-	50pf.+50pf. green	1·10	3·50

DESIGNS: 3pf. U-boat Type VIIA (submarine); 5pf. Armed motor cyclists; 6pf. Wireless operators; 8pf. Engineers making pontoon; 12pf. Grenade thrower; 15pf. Heavy artillery; 20pf. Anti-aircraft gunners; 25pf. Junkers Ju 87B "Stuka" dive bombers; 30pf. Parachutists; 40pf. Tank; 50pf. "S-22" (motor torpedo-boat).

195 Hitler Youth

1943. Youth Dedication Day.

831	**195**	6pf.+4pf. green	25	1·00

196 Adolf Hitler

1943. Hitler's 54th Birthday and Culture Fund.

832	**196**	3pf.+7pf. black	55	1·70
833	**196**	6pf.+14pf. green	55	1·70
834	**196**	8pf.+22pf. blue	55	1·70
835	**196**	12pf.+38pf. red	55	1·70
836	**196**	24pf.+76pf. purple	90	3·75
837	**196**	40pf.+160pf. olive	90	3·75

197 Attestation

1943. Labour Corps.

838	**197**	3pf.+7pf. brown	10	85
839	-	5pf.+10pf. green	10	60
840	-	6pf.+14pf. blue	10	60
841	-	12pf.+18pf. red	25	1·50

DESIGNS: 5pf. Harvester sharpening scythe; 6pf. Labourer wielding sledge-hammer; 12pf. "Pick and shovel fatigue".

198 Huntsman

1943. "Brown Ribbon of Germany".

842	**198**	42pf.+108pf. brown	25	1·40

199 Birthplace of Peter Rosegger

200 Peter Rosegger

1943. Birth Cent of Peter Rosegger (poet).

843	**199**	6pf.+4pf. green	15	1·00
844	**200**	12pf.+8pf. red	20	1·00

201 Racehorse

1943. Grand Prix, Vienna.

845	**201**	6pf.+4pf. violet	20	1·40
846	**201**	12pf.+88pf. red	20	1·40

202 Mother and Children

1943. 10th Anniv of Winter Relief Fund.

847	**202**	12pf.+38pf. red	25	1·40

203 St George and the Dragon

1943. 11th Anniv of National Goldsmiths' Institution.

848	**203**	6pf.+4pf. green	20	85
849	**203**	12pf.+88pf. purple	20	1·30

204 Lubeck

1943. 800th Anniv of Lubeck.

850	**204**	12pf.+8pf. red	20	1·30

205

1943. 20th Anniv of Munich Rising.

851	**205**	24pf.+26pf. red	20	1·30

206 Dr. Robert Koch

1944. Birth Centenary of Dr. Robert Koch (bacteriologist).

852	**206**	12pf.+38pf. sepia	20	1·30

207 Adolf Hitler

1944. 11th Anniv of Third Reich.

853	**207**	54pf.+96pf. brown	25	1·40

208 Focke Wulf Fw 200 Condor over Tempelhof Airport

209 Dornier Do-26 Flying Boat

1944. 25th Anniv of Air Mail Services.

854	**208**	6pf.+4pf. green	15	1·30
855	**209**	12pf.+8pf. purple	15	1·30
856	-	42pf.+108pf. blue	40	2·50

DESIGNS—VERT: 42pf. Junkers Ju 90B airplane seen from above.

210 Day Nursery

211 "Mothers' Help"

1944. 10th Anniv of "Mother and Child" Organization.

857	**210**	3pf.+2pf. brown	10	60
858	**211**	6pf.+4pf. green	10	60
859	-	12pf.+8pf. red	10	60
860	-	15pf.+10pf. purple	15	75

DESIGNS: 12pf. Child auscultation; 15pf. Mothers at convalescent home.

212 Landing Craft

1944. Armed Forces' and Heroes' Day.

861	**212**	3pf.+2pf. brown	40	1·30
862	-	4pf.+3pf. blue	40	1·30
863	-	5pf.+3pf. green	20	60
864	-	6pf.+4pf. violet	20	60
865	-	8pf.+4pf. red	20	70
866	-	10pf.+5pf. brown	20	60
867	-	12pf.+6pf. red	20	60
868	-	15pf.+10pf. purple	20	85
869	-	16pf.+10pf. green	35	1·40
870	-	20pf.+10pf. blue	45	2·10
871	-	24pf.+10pf. brown	45	2·10
872	-	25pf.+15pf. blue	90	4·25
873	-	30pf.+20pf. olive	90	4·25

DESIGNS: 4pf. Caterpillar tricar; 5pf. Parachutists; 6pf. Submarine officer; 8pf. Mortar-firing party; 10pf. Searchlight unit; 12pf. Machine gunners; 15pf. Tank; 16pf. "S-128" (motor torpedo-boat); 20pf. Arado Ar 196A seaplane; 24pf. Railway gun; 25pf. Rocket projectiles; 30pf. Alpine trooper.

213 Fulda Monument

1944. 1200th Anniv of Fulda.

874	**213**	12pf.+38pf. brown	20	1·00

214 Adolf Hitler

1944. Hitler's 55th Birthday.

875	**214**	54pf.+96pf. red	35	2·00

215 Postwoman

1944. Postal Employees' and Hitler's Culture Funds. Inscr "Kameradschaftsblock der Deutschen Reichspost".

876	**215**	6pf.+9pf. blue	15	85
877	-	8pf.+12pf. grey	15	85
878	-	12pf.+18pf. mauve	15	85
879	-	16pf.+24pf. green	15	85
880	-	20pf.+30pf. blue	15	1·50
881	-	24pf.+36pf. violet	25	1·50

DESIGNS—As Type **150**: 8pf. Mail coach; 16pf. Motor-car race; 20pf. Postal police march; 24pf. Glider workshop. As Type **215**: 12pf. The Field Post on Eastern Front.

216 Girl Worker

217 Labourer

1944. Labour Corps.

882	**216**	6pf.+4pf. green	20	75
883	**217**	12pf.+8pf. red	20	75

218 Riflemen

1944. 7th Innsbruck Shooting Competition.

884	**218**	6pf.+4pf. green	20	95
885	**218**	12pf.+8pf. red	20	95

219 Duke Albrecht

1944. 400th Anniv of Albert University, Konigsberg.

886	**219**	6pf.+4pf. green	25	1·40

220 Racehorse and Foal

1944. "Brown Ribbon of Germany".

887	**220**	42pf.+108pf. brown	25	2·30

221 Racehorse and Laurel Wreath

1944. Vienna Grand Prix.

888	**221**	6pf.+4pf. green	20	1·20
889	**221**	12pf.+88pf. red	20	1·20

222 Chambered Nautilus Beaker

1944. National Goldsmiths' Institution.

890	**222**	6pf.+4pf. green	20	1·20
891	**222**	12pf.+88pf. red	20	1·20

223 Posthorn

1944. Stamp Day.

892	**223**	6pf.+24pf. green	20	1·40

224 Eagle and Dragon

1944. 21st Anniv of Munich Rising.

893	**224**	12pf.+8pf. red	20	1·40

225 Adolf Hitler

1944

894	**225**	42pf. green	20	50

226 Count Anton Gunther

1945. 600th Anniv of Oldenburg.

895	**226**	6pf.+14pf. purple	20	1·40

227 "Home Guard"

1945. Mobilization of "Home Guard".

896	**227**	12pf.+8pf. red	35	2·50

228 S.S. Troopers

1945. 12th Anniv of Third Reich.

897	**228**	12pf.+38pf. red	8·75	65·00
898	-	12pf.+38pf. red	8·75	65·00

DESIGN: No. 898, S.A. man with torch.

For Nos. 899 onwards see section B of Allied Occupation.

MILITARY FIELDPOST STAMPS

M184 Junkers Ju 52/3m

1942. Air. No value indicated. Perf. or roul.

M804	**M184**	(-) blue	35	50

M185

1942. Parcel Post. Size 28×23 mm. No value indicated. Perf or roul.

M805	**M185**	(-) brown	25	12·50

Nos. M804/5 also exist overprinted **INSELPOST** in various types for use in Crete and the Aegean Islands and there are various other local fieldpost issues.

1944. Christmas Parcel Post. Size 22½×18 mm. No value indicated. Perf.

M895		(-) green	65	3·75

1944. For 2 kilo parcels. No value indicated. No. 785 optd FELDPOST 2kg.

M896	**173**	(-) on 40pf. mauve	65	2·50

NEWSPAPER STAMPS

N156 Newspaper Messenger and Globe

1939

N727	**N156**	5pf. green	70	6·00
N728	**N156**	10pf. brown	70	6·00

OFFICIAL STAMPS

O23

1903

O82	**O23**	2pf. grey	1·10	4·50
O83	**O23**	3pf. brown	1·10	4·50
O84	**O23**	5pf. green	25	60
O85	**O23**	10pf. red	25	45
O86	**O23**	20pf. blue	25	45
O87	**O23**	25pf. black and red on yellow	25	1·90
O88	**O23**	40pf. black and red	45	2·30
O89	**O23**	50pf. blk & pur on buff	45	2·20

O24

1905

O90	**O24**	2pf. grey	60·00	90·00
O91	**O24**	3pf. brown	7·00	12·50
O92	**O24**	5pf. green	4·75	8·75
O93	**O24**	10pf. red	90	2·50
O94	**O24**	20pf. blue	1·80	3·50
O95	**O24**	25pf. black and red on yellow	35·00	60·00

O31

O32

1920. Numeral designs as Types O 31 and O 32.

O117	5pf. green	25	3·50
O118	10pf. red	90	1·80
O119	15pf. brown	20	1·80
O120	20pf. blue	20	1·60
O121	30pf. orange on pink	20	1·60
O122	50pf. violet on pink	35	1·80
O123	1m. red on pink	9·75	4·50

1920. Similar designs but without figures "21".

O124	5pf. brown on yellow	1·10	16·00
O125	10pf. red	20	1·90
O126	10pf. orange	60	£550
O127	15pf. purple	20	2·75
O128	20pf. blue	20	2·20
O129	30pf. orange on pink	20	2·20
O130	40pf. red	20	2·20
O131	50pf. violet on pink	20	2·20
O132	60pf. brown	20	1·60
O133	1m. red on pink	20	2·20
O134	1m.25 blue on yellow	20	2·75
O135a	2m. blue	10	1·60
O136	5m. brown on yellow	4·75	3·50

1920. Official stamps of Bavaria optd Deutsches Reich.

O137	**O31**	5pf. green	10	3·50
O138	**O31**	10pf. orange	10	2·10
O139	**O31**	15pf. red	10	2·20
O140	**O31**	20pf. purple	10	1·80
O141	**O31**	30pf. blue	10	1·60
O142	**O31**	40pf. brown	10	1·60
O143	**O32**	50pf. red	10	1·60
O144	**O32**	60pf. green	20	1·60
O145	**O32**	70pf. violet	2·20	3·00
O146	**O32**	75pf. red	35	1·60
O147	**O32**	80pf. blue	20	1·60
O148	**O32**	90pf. olive	1·80	3·50
O149	**O33**	1m. brown	20	1·60
O150	**O33**	1¼m. green	20	1·60
O151	**O33**	1½m. red	20	1·60
O152	**O33**	2½m. blue	20	1·60
O153	**O33**	3m. red	20	1·60
O154	**O33**	5m. black	9·75	28·00

1920. Municipal Service stamps of Wurttemberg optd Deutsches Reich.

O155	**M5**	5pf. green	4·50	11·50
O156	**M5**	10pf. red	2·75	5·25
O157	**M5**	15pf. violet	2·75	9·75
O158	**M5**	20pf. blue	4·50	9·75
O159	**M5**	50pf. purple	5·25	19·00

1920. Official stamps of Wurttemberg optd Deutsches Reich.

O160	**O5**	5pf. green	2·75	4·50
O161	**O5**	10pf. red	1·80	3·50
O162	**O5**	15pf. purple	1·80	3·50
O163	**O5**	20pf. blue	1·80	1·60
O164	**O5**	30pf. black and orange	1·80	4·50
O165	**O5**	40pf. black and red	1·80	3·50
O166	**O5**	50pf. purple	1·80	4·50
O167	**O5**	1m. black and grey	2·75	8·75

O48

O50

1922. Figure designs.

O247	-	3m. brown on red	20	1·60
O248	**O50**	10m. green on red	20	1·60
O249	**O48**	75pf. blue	20	8·75
O251	**O50**	20m. blue on red	10	1·60
O252	**O50**	50m. violet on red	10	1·60
O253	**O50**	100m. red on rose	10	1·60

1923. Postage stamps optd Dienstmarke.

O274	**51**	20m. purple	20	8·75
O275	**51**	30m. olive	10	40·00
O276	**38**	40m. green	20	3·50
O277	**54**	200m. red	10	1·60
O278	**54**	300m. green	10	1·60
O279	**54**	400m. brown	10	1·60
O280	**54**	500m. orange	20	1·60
O342	**62**	100M. grey	20	£180
O343	**62**	200M. brown	20	£180
O344	**62**	2Md. green and pink	20	£130
O345	**62**	5Md. brown and yellow	20	95·00
O346	**62**	10Md. green and light green	3·50	£160
O347	**62**	20Md. brown and green	4·50	£180
O348	**62**	50Md. blue	2·20	£225

1923. Official stamps of 1920 and 1922 surch Tausend or Millionen and figure.

O312	-	5T. on 5m. brown on yellow	10	3·50
O313	-	20T. on 30pf. orange on rose (No. O129)	10	3·50
O314	-	100T. on 15pf. purple	10	3·50
O315	-	250T. on 10pf. red (No. O125)	10	3·50
O317	**O50**	75T. on 50m. violet on rose	10	3·50
O318	-	400T. on 15pf. purple	10	32·00
O319	-	800T. on 30pf. orge on rose (No. O129)	20	5·25
O320	**O48**	1M. on 75pf. blue	10	44·00
O321	-	2M. on 10pf. red (No. O125)	20	4·50
O322	**O50**	5M. on 100m. red on rose	10	6·50

1923. Nos. 352/7 optd Dienstmarke.

O358	**64**	3pf. brown	25	90
O359	**64**	5pf. green	25	90
O360	**64**	10pf. red	25	90
O361	**64**	20pf. blue	70	1·30
O362	**64**	50pf. orange	70	1·80
O363	**64**	100pf. purple	4·50	8·75

1924. Optd Dienstmarke.

O376	**66**	3pf. brown	45	2·75
O377	**66**	5pf. green	25	90
O378	**66**	10pf. red	25	90
O379	**66**	20pf. blue	25	90
O380	**66**	30pf. red	90	90
O381	**66**	40pf. olive	90	90
O382	**66**	50pf. orange	8·00	4·50
O384	**72**	60pf. brown	1·80	4·50
O385	**72**	80pf. grey	8·00	37·00

O81

1927

O424	**O81**	3pf. brown	35	90
O425	**O81**	4pf. blue	60	1·10
O427	**O81**	5pf. green	20	90
O428	**O81**	6pf. green	90	1·10
O429	**O81**	8pf. green	35	90
O430	**O81**	10pf. red	8·75	7·00
O432	**O81**	10pf. mauve	35	1·10
O433	**O81**	10pf. brown	3·00	10·50

O434	O81	12pf. orange	60	1·10
O436	O81	15pf. red	55	1·10
O437	O81	20pf. green	8·75	3·50
O438	O81	20pf. grey	2·75	1·30
O439	O81	30pf. green	1·10	1·10
O440	O81	40pf. violet	90	1·10
O441	O81	60pf. brown	1·30	2·20

O100

1934

O528	O100	5pf. green	20	1·20
O529	O100	6pf. green	20	95
O531	O100	10pf. brown	35	8·00
O533	O100	15pf. red	1·10	9·75
O534	O100	20pf. blue	55	1·60
O535	O100	30pf. green	1·10	1·60
O536	O100	40pf. mauve	1·10	1·60
O537	O100	50pf. yellow	1·60	4·00
O809	O100	3pf. brown	25	1·30
O810	O100	4pf. blue	20	3·50
O812	O100	6pf. violet	25	1·30
O813	O100	8pf. red	25	1·30
O815	O100	12pf. red	30	4·25
O820	O100	50pf. green	4·00	21·00

SPECIAL STAMPS FOR USE BY OFFICIALS OF THE NATIONAL SOCIALIST GERMAN WORKERS' PARTY

P132 Party Badge

1938

O648	P132	1pf. black	85	3·50
O651	P132	5pf. green	90	1·70
O652	P132	6pf. green	90	1·70
O655	P132	16pf. grey	2·20	10·00
O656	P132	24pf. green	2·75	5·50
O799	P132	3pf. brown	20	1·20
O800	P132	4pf. blue	90	3·50
O802	P132	6pf. violet	20	6·75
O803	P132	8pf. red	30	2·50
O804	P132	12pf. red	30	1·30
O805	P132	16pf. blue	1·80	85·00
O806	P132	24pf. brown	55	34·00
O807	P132	30pf. green	70	25
O808	P132	40pf. mauve	80	50

II. ALLIED OCCUPATION

A. Allied Military Post (British and American Zones)

The defeat of Germany in May 1945 resulted in the division of the country into four zones of occupation (British, American, French and Russian), while Berlin was placed under joint allied control. Allied Military Post Stamps came into use in the British and American zones, the French issued special stamps in their zone and in the Russian zone the first issues were made by local administrations.

The territory occupied by the Anglo-American and French Zones subsequently became the German Federal Republic (West Germany) which was set up in September 1949. By the Nine Power Agreement of 3 October 1954, the occupation of West Germany was ended and full sovereignty was granted to the German Federal Government as from 5 May 1955 (see Section III).

The territory in the Russian Zone became the German Democratic Republic (East Germany) which was set up on 7 October 1949 (see Section V).

Separate issues for the Western Sectors of Berlin came into being in 1948 (see Section IV). The Russian Zone issues inscribed "STADT BERLIN" were for use in the Russian sector of the city and Brandenburg and these were superseded first by the General Issues of the Russian Zone and then by the stamps of East Germany.

A1

1945

A1	A1	3pf. violet	25	1·80
A5	A1	8pf. orange	25	45
A6	A1	10pf. brown	25	45
A16	A1	1pf. black	25	5·75
A18	A1	4pf. grey	25	1·80
A19a	A1	5pf. green	25	4·75
A20	A1	6pf. yellow	25	1·30
A23	A1	12pf. purple	25	40
A24	A1	15pf. red	25	3·50
A25	A1	16pf. green	25	16·00
A26	A1	20pf. blue	25	3·50
A27a	A1	24pf. brown	35	14·00
A28	A1	25pf. blue	35	3·00
A29	A1	30pf. olive	35	2·20
A30	A1	40pf. mauve	60	3·00
A31	A1	42pf. green	35	1·80
A32	A1	50pf. slate	25	18·00
A33	A1	60pf. plum	90	22·00
A34b	A1	80pf. blue	35·00	£350
A35	A1	1m. green	6·25	£550

Values 30pf. to 80pf. are size 22×25 mm and 1m. is size 25×29½ mm.
Nos. A36 etc continue in Section C.
Used prices are for cancelled-to-order.

B. American, British and Russian Zones 1946–48

From February 1946 to June 1948 these zones used the same stamps (Nos. 899/956). It had been intended that they should be used throughout all four zones but until the creation of the German Federal Republic, in September 1949, the French Zone always had its own stamps, while after the revaluation of the currency in June 1948 separate stamps were again issued for the Russian Zone.

229 Numeral

1946

899	229	1pf. black	20	3·50
900	229	2pf. black	20	25
901	229	3pf. brown	20	4·00
902	229	4pf. blue	20	5·25
903	229	5pf. green	20	70
904	229	6pf. violet	20	20
905	229	8pf. red	20	25
906	229	10pf. brown	20	25
907	229	12pf. red	20	25
908	229	12pf. grey	20	25
909	229	15pf. red	20	8·00
910	229	15pf. green	20	25
911	229	16pf. green	20	25
912	229	20pf. blue	20	25
913	229	24pf. brown	20	25
914	229	25pf. blue	20	7·00
915	229	25pf. orange	20	1·30
916	229	30pf. green	20	25
917	229	40pf. purple	20	25
918	229	42pf. green	2·75	35·00
919	229	45pf. red	20	35
920	229	50pf. green	20	25
921	229	60pf. red	20	25
922	229	75pf. blue	20	25
923	229	80pf. blue	20	25
924	229	84pf. green	20	25
925	229	1m. green (24×30 mm)	20	25
MS925a		107×51 mm. Nos. 912/13 and 917 (sold at 5m.)	90·00	£275

231 1160: Leipzig obtains Charter

1947. Leipzig Spring Fair. Inscr "LEIPZIGER MESSE 1947".

926	231	24pf.+26pf. brown	1·00	5·25
927	-	60pf.+40pf. blue	1·00	5·25

DESIGN: 60pf. 1268: Foreign merchants at Leipzig Fair.
See also Nos. 951/4.

233 Gardener

237 "Dove of Peace"

1947

928	233	2pf. black	20	45
929	233	6pf. violet	20	25
930	A	8pf. red	20	45
931	A	10pf. green	20	45
932	B	12pf. grey	20	25
933	233	15pf. brown	35	2·75
934	C	16pf. green	20	45
935	A	20pf. blue	20	90
936	C	24pf. brown	20	45
937	233	25pf. orange	20	45
938	B	30pf. red	35	1·80
939	A	40pf. mauve	20	45
940	C	50pf. blue	35	1·50
941	B	60pf. red	20	55
942	B	60pf. brown	20	90
943	B	80pf. blue	20	1·10
944	C	84pf. green	45	1·80
945	237	1m. green	20	70
946	237	2m. violet	20	90
947	237	3m. lake	20	18·00
948	237	5m. blue	2·20	70·00

DESIGNS: A, Sower; B, Labourer; C, Bricklayer and reaper.

238 Dr. von Stephan

1947. 50th Death Anniv of Von Stephan.

949	238	24pf. brown	25	1·30
950	238	75pf. blue	25	1·80

1947. Leipzig Autumn Fair. As T 231.

951		12pf. red	25	1·80
952		75pf. blue	25	2·75

DESIGNS: 12pf. 1497: Maximilian I granting Charter; 75pf. 1365: Assessment and Collection of Ground Rents.

1948. Leipzig Spring Fair. As T 231 but dated "1948".

953		50pf. blue	25	1·30
954		84pf. green	25	2·20

DESIGNS: 50pf. 1388: At the customs barrier; 84pf. 1433: Bringing merchandise.

For similar types, dated "1948", "1949" or "1950", but with premium values, see Nos. R31/2, R51/2, R60/1 of Russian Zone and E7/8 of East Germany.

239 Weighing Goods

1948. Hanover Trade Fair.

955	239	24pf. red	35	1·50
956	239	50pf. blue	35	2·40

C. British and American Zones 1948–49

(A 2)

1948. Currency Reform. (a) On Pictorial issue of 1947, Nos. 928/44. (i) Optd with Type A 2.

A36	2pf. black	20	25
A37	6pf. violet	20	25
A38	8pf. red	20	25
A39	10pf. green	25	35
A40	12pf. grey	25	20
A41	15pf. brown	8·25	19·00
A42	16pf. green	1·60	3·00
A43	20pf. blue	70	1·10
A44	24pf. brown	25	20
A45	25pf. orange	45	55
A46	30pf. red	2·75	6·25
A47	40pf. mauve	80	1·20
A48	50pf. blue	95	1·10
A49	60pf. brown	80	1·10
A50	60pf. red	55·00	£250
A51	80pf. blue	1·30	2·75
A52	84pf. green	4·50	7·00

(ii) Optd with multiple posthorns over whole stamp.

A53	2pf. black	95	1·60
A54	6pf. violet	95	1·60
A55	8pf. red	95	1·60
A56	10pf. green	25	35
A57	12pf. grey	1·10	1·80
A58	15pf. brown	25	80
A59	16pf. green	40	55
A60	20pf. blue	25	45
A61	24pf. brown	70	1·80
A62	25pf. orange	8·75	18·00
A63	30pf. red	35	80
A64	40pf. mauve	35	70
A65	50pf. blue	45	70
A66	60pf. brown	45	75
A67	60pf. red	2·75	6·25
A68	80pf. blue	50	75
A69	84pf. green	1·10	1·60

(b) On Numeral issue of 1946, Nos. 900 to 924. (i) Optd with Type A 2.

A70	229	2pf. black	5·75	33·00
A71	229	8pf. red	12·00	70·00
A72	229	10pf. brown	1·20	5·00
A73	229	12pf. red	8·25	55·00
A74	229	12pf. grey	£150	£600
A75	229	15pf. red	8·25	60·00
A76	229	15pf. green	2·75	17·00
A77	229	16pf. green	48·00	£225
A78	229	24pf. brown	90·00	£250
A79	229	25pf. blue	17·00	70·00
A80	229	25pf. orange	1·80	8·50
A81	229	30pf. olive	1·80	8·50
A82	229	40pf. purple	70·00	£250
A83	229	45pf. red	2·75	8·50
A84	229	50pf. green	2·75	8·50
A85	229	75pf. blue	5·75	25·00
A86	229	84pf. green	5·75	25·00

(ii) Optd with multiple posthorns over whole stamp.

A87	2pf. black	26·00	80·00
A88	8pf. red	40·00	£140
A89	10pf. brown	39·00	£140
A90	12pf. red	13·00	70·00
A91	12pf. grey	£300	£1200
A92	15pf. red	13·00	55·00
A93	15pf. green	1·10	8·75
A94	16pf. green	44·00	£180
A95	24pf. brown	48·00	£225
A96	25pf. blue	14·50	65·00
A97	25pf. orange	44·00	£200
A98	30pf. olive	2·00	7·00
A99	40pf. purple	70·00	£275
A100	45pf. red	2·75	13·50
A101	50pf. green	2·75	13·50
A102	75pf. blue	2·75	13·50
A103	84pf. green	3·50	14·50

A4 Crowned Head

A7 Cologne Cathedral

1948. 700th Anniv of Cologne Cathedral and Restoration Fund.

A104	A4	6pf.+4pf. brown	70	75
A105	-	12pf.+8pf. blue	1·60	2·10
A106	-	24pf.+16pf. red	2·75	3·75
A107	A7	50pf.+50pf. blue	6·50	9·75

DESIGNS—As Type A 4: 12pf. The Three Wise Men; 24pf. Cologne Cathedral.

A9 The Romer, Frankfurt am Main

A10 Frauenkirche, Munich

A13 Holstentor Lubeck

1948. Various designs.

A108	A9	2pf. black	25	20
A109	A10	4pf. brown	25	20
A110a	A	5pf. blue	35	55
A111	A10	6pf. brown	25	45
A112	A10	6pf. orange	30	20
A113	A9	8pf. yellow	35	35
A114	A10	8pf. slate	25	20
A115a	A	10pf. green	35	25
A116	A10	15pf. orange	2·10	5·50
A117	A9	15pf. violet	1·20	20
A118	A9	16pf. green	70	60
A119	A9	20pf. blue	1·00	2·75
A120	B	20pf. red	75	20
A121	B	24pf. red	35	25
A122	A	25pf. red	1·00	20
A123	B	30pf. blue	1·20	30
A124	A10	30pf. red	2·75	5·75
A125	A	40pf. mauve	1·60	35
A126	B	50pf. blue	1·20	2·20
A127	A10	50pf. green	1·70	25
A128a	A	60pf. purple	2·75	25
A129	B	80pf. mauve	3·00	25
A130	A10	84pf. purple	2·00	6·25
A131	A	90pf. mauve	3·00	25
A132	A13	1Dm. green	33·00	70
A133	A13	2Dm. violet	29·00	70
A134	A13	3Dm. mauve	33·00	3·00
A135	A13	5Dm. blue	44·00	25·00

DESIGNS—As Type A 9/10: A, Cologne Cathedral; B, Brandenburg Gate.

A15 Brandenburg Gate, Berlin

1948. Aid to Berlin.

A140	**A15**	10pf.+5pf. green	7·00	8·00
A141	**A15**	20pf.+10pf. red	7·00	8·00

A16 Herman Hillebrant Wedigh (after Holbein)

1949. Hanover Trade Fair.

A142	**A16**	10pf. green	2·75	2·50
A143	**A16**	20pf. red	2·75	2·50
A144	**A16**	30pf. blue	3·75	3·25

MSA145 110×65 mm. Nos. A142/4 (sold at 1Dm.) 95·00 £225

A17 Racing Cyclists

1949. Trans-Germany Cycle Race.

A146	**A17**	10pf.+5pf. green	4·75	5·75
A147	**A17**	20pf.+10pf. brown	13·00	18·00

A18 Goethe in Italy

A19 Goethe

1949. Birth Bicentenary of Goethe (poet).

A148	**A18**	10pf.+5pf. green	3·25	3·25
A149	**A19**	20pf.+10pf. red	5·75	5·75
A150	-	30pf.+15pf. blue	26·00	26·00

DESIGN—VERT: 30pf. Profile portrait.

OBLIGATORY TAX STAMPS

AT14

1948. Aid for Berlin. Perf or imperf.

AT136	**AT14**	2pf. blue	45	25

D. French Zone.

(a) General Issues, 1945–46.

F1 Arms of the Palatinate

F2 Goethe

1945. (a) Arms.

F1	**F1**	1pf. green, black & yellow	20	25
F2	-	3pf. yellow, black and red	25	20
F3	-	5pf. black, yellow & brn	20	20
F4	-	8pf. red, yellow and brown	20	20
F5	**F1**	10pf. green, brown & yell	10·00	60·00
F6	-	12pf. yellow, black & red	20	20
F7	-	15pf. blue, black and red	20	25
F8	-	20pf. black, yellow & red	20	25
F9	-	24pf. blue, black and red	20	25
F10	-	30pf. red, yellow & black	20	25

ARMS: 3, 12pf. Rhineland; 5, 20pf. Wurttemberg; 8, 30pf. Baden; 15, 24pf. Saar.

(b) Poets.

F11	**2**	1m. brown	2·75	22·00
F12	-	2m. blue (Schiller)	1·80	65·00
F13	-	5m. red (Heine)	2·20	75·00

(b) Baden, 1947–49.

FB1 J. P. Hebel

FB2 Rastatt Castle

FB3 Hollental Black Forest

FB4 Freiburg Cathedral

1947. Inscr "BADEN".

FB1	**FB1**	2pf. grey	20	35
FB2	-	3pf. brown	20	35
FB3	-	10pf. blue	20	35
FB4	**FB1**	12pf. green	20	35
FB5	-	15pf. violet	20	45
FB6	**FB2**	16pf. green	25	1·80
FB7	-	20pf. blue	20	35
FB8	**FB2**	24pf. red	20	35
FB9	-	45pf. mauve	20	1·10
FB10	**FB1**	60pf. orange	20	3·75
FB11	-	75pf. blue	25	2·10
FB12	**FB3**	84pf. green	25	2·30
FB13	**FB4**	1m. brown	25	1·00

DESIGNS—18×23 mm: 3, 15, 45pf. Badensian girl and yachts; 10, 20, 75pf. Hans Baldung Grien.

1948. Currency Reform. As 1947 issue. (a) Value in "PF".

FB14	**FB1**	2pf. orange	25	35
FB15	-	6pf. brown	25	25
FB16	-	10pf. brown	45	3·75
FB17	**FB1**	12pf. red	40	25
FB18	-	15pf. blue	50	70
FB19	**FB2**	24pf. green	65	35
FB20	-	30pf. mauve	1·30	1·40
FB21	-	50pf. blue	1·40	35

(b) New currency. Value in "D.PF" or "D.M." (="Deutschpfennig" or "Deutschmark").

FB22		8dpf. green	70	1·40
FB23	**FB2**	16dpf. violet	1·10	2·30
FB24	-	20dpf. brown	5·00	1·20
FB25	**FB1**	60dpf. grey	6·50	75
FB26	**FB3**	84dpf. red	7·25	5·50
FB27	**FB4**	1dm. blue	7·25	5·50

DESIGNS—As Types FB **1/2**: 6, 15pf. Badensian girl and yachts; 10pf., 20dpf. Hans Baldung Grien; 8dpf., 30pf. Black Forest girl in festive headdress; 50pf. Grand-Duchess Stephanie of Baden.

Nos. FB14/21 were sold on the new currency basis though not inscribed "D.PF.".

1948. As 1947 issue, but "PF" omitted.

FB28	**FB1**	2pf. orange	1·10	75
FB29	-	4pf. violet	90	55
FB30	-	5pf. blue	1·40	80
FB31	-	6pf. brown	32·00	18·00
FB32	-	8pf. brown	1·40	1·40
FB33	-	10pf. green	1·80	1·40
FB34	-	20pf. mauve	1·80	45
FB35	-	40pf. brown	70·00	95·00
FB36	**FB1**	80pf. red	13·00	8·75
FB37	**FB3**	90pf. red	80·00	£100

DESIGNS—18×23 mm: 4pf., 40pf. Rastatt; 5pf., 6pf. Badensian girl and yachts; 8pf. Black Forest girl in festive headdress; 10pf., 20pf. Portrait of Hans Baldung Grien.

FB5 Cornhouse, Freiburg

1949. Freiburg Rebuilding Fund.

FB38	**FB5**	4pf.+16pf. violet	14·50	46·00
FB39	-	10pf.+20pf. green	14·50	46·00
FB40	-	20pf.+30pf. red	14·50	46·00
FB41	-	30pf.+50pf. blue	18·00	55·00

MSFB41a 65×78 mm. Nos. FB38/41 65·00 £300

MSFB41b Ditto but imperf 65·00 £300

DESIGNS: 10pf. Freiburg Cathedral; 20pf. Trumpeting angel, Freiburg; 30pf. "Fischbrunnen," Freiburg.

FB6 Arms of Baden

1949. Red Cross Fund.

FB42	**FB6**	10pf.+20pf. green	23·00	95·00
FB43	**FB6**	20pf.+40pf. lilac	23·00	95·00
FB44	**FB6**	30pf.+60pf. blue	23·00	95·00
FB45	**FB6**	40pf.+80pf. grey	23·00	95·00

MSFB45a 90×100 mm. Nos. FB42/5 £110 £1400

FB7 Seehof Hotel, Constance

1949. Engineers' Congress, Constance.

FB46	**FB7**	30pf. blue	24·00	80·00

FB8 Goethe

1949. Birth Bicentenary of Goethe (poet).

FB47	**FB8**	10pf.+5pf. green	10·00	23·00
FB48	-	20pf.+10pf. red	10·00	23·00
FB49	-	30pf.+15pf. blue	13·50	55·00

FB9 Carl Schurz and Revolutionary Scene

1949. Cent of Rastatt Insurrection.

FB50	**FB9**	10pf.+5pf. green	11·50	35·00
FB51	**FB9**	20pf.+10pf. mauve	11·50	35·00
FB52	**FB9**	30pf.+15pf. blue	13·00	35·00

FB10 Conradin Kreutzer

1949. Death Centenary of Conradin Kreutzer (composer).

FB53	**FB10**	10pf. green	3·75	10·00

FB11 1849 Mail Coach

1949. German Stamp Centenary.

FB54	**FB11**	10pf. green	5·75	13·00
FB55	-	20pf. brown	5·75	13·00

DESIGN: 20pf. Postal motor-coach with trailer and Douglas DC-4 airliner.

FB12 Posthorn and Globe

1949. 75th Anniv of U.P.U.

FB56	**FB12**	20pf. red	6·75	14·50
FB57	**FB12**	30pf. blue	6·75	11·50

(C) Rhineland Palatinate, 1947–49.

FR1 "Porta Nigra", Trier

FR2 Karl Marx

FR4 Statue of Charlemagne

1947. Inscr "RHEINLAND-PFALZ".

FR1	-	2pf. grey	20	25
FR2	-	3pf. brown	20	25
FR3	-	10pf. blue	20	25
FR4	**FR1**	12pf. green	20	25
FR5	**FR2**	15pf. violet	20	25
FR6	-	16pf. green	20	1·00
FR7	-	20pf. blue	20	25
FR8	-	24pf. red	20	25
FR9	-	30pf. mauve	20	2·30
FR10	-	45pf. mauve	20	65
FR11	-	50pf. blue	20	2·30
FR12	-	60pf. orange	20	25
FR13	-	75pf. blue	20	65
FR14	-	84pf. green	25	1·50
FR15	**FR4**	1m. brown	25	90

DESIGNS—SMALL SIZE: 2pf., 60pf. Beethoven's death mask; 3pf. Baron von Ketteler, Bishop of Mainz; 10pf. Girl vintager; 16pf. Rocks at Arnweiler; 20pf. Palatinate village house; 24pf. Worms Cathedral; 30pf., 75pf. Gutenberg (printer); 45pf., 50pf. Mainz Cathedral. LARGE SIZE—HORIZ: 84pf. Gutenfels Castle and Rhine.

1948. Currency Reform. As 1947 issue. (a) Value in "PF".

FR16	-	2pf. orange	25	30
FR17	-	6pf. brown	25	30
FR18	-	10pf. brown	50	30
FR19	**FR1**	12pf. red	45	25
FR20	**FR2**	15pf. blue	1·30	75
FR21	-	24pf. green	50	25
FR22	-	30pf. mauve	1·10	45
FR23	-	50pf. blue	1·60	45

(b) New currency. Value in "D.PF." or "D.M." (= "Deutschpfennig" or "Deutschmark").

FR24	**FR1**	8dpf. green	50	1·40
FR25	-	16dpf. violet	70	1·60
FR26	-	20dpf. brown	3·50	75
FR27	-	60dpf. grey	10·00	45
FR28	-	84dpf. red	5·25	6·75
FR29	**FR4**	1dm. blue	6·25	6·75

DESIGNS—SMALL SIZE: 6pf. Baron von Ketteler; 30pf. Mainz Cathedral; 50pf. Gutenberg (printer). Others as 1947 issue.

Nos. FR16/23 were sold on the new currency basis though not inscribed "D.PF.".

FR5 St. Martin

1948. Ludwigshafen Explosion Relief Fund.

FR30	**FR5**	20pf.+30pf. mauve	1·60	70·00
FR31	-	30pf.+50pf. blue	1·60	70·00

DESIGN: 30pf. St. Christopher.

1948. Inscr "RHEINLAND-PFALZ". As 1947 issue, but "PF" omitted.

FR32		2pf. orange	90	45
FR33		4pf. violet	90	45
FR34	**FR2**	5pf. blue	90	75
FR35	-	6pf. brown	30·00	18·00
FR36	**FR1**	8pf. red	90·00	£400
FR37	-	10pf. green	1·10	45
FR38	-	20pf. mauve	1·10	45
FR39	-	40pf. brown	4·00	5·25
FR40	**FR1**	80pf. red	5·00	5·50
FR41	-	90pf. red	5·50	18·00

DESIGNS—SMALL SIZE: 4pf. Rocks at Arnweiler; 40pf. Worms Cathedral. LARGE SIZE—HORIZ: 90pf. Gutenfels Castle and Rhine. Others as 1947–48 issues.

1949. Red Cross Fund. As Type FB 6 of Baden, but Arms of Rhineland and inscr "RHEINLANDPFALZ".

FR42	10pf.+20pf. green	20·00	£100
FR43	20pf.+40pf. lilac	20·00	£100
FR44	30pf.+60pf. blue	20·00	£100
FR45	40pf.+80pf. grey	20·00	£100

MSFR45a 90×100 mm. Nos. FR42/5 £100 £1300

1949. Birth Bicentenary of Goethe. As Nos. FB47/9 of Baden.

FR46	10pf.+5pf. green	7·25	22·00
FR47	20pf.+10pf. mauve	7·25	22·00
FR48	30pf.+15pf. blue	13·00	50·00

1949. Centenary of German Postage Stamp. As Nos. FB54/5 of Baden.

FR49	10pf. green	10·00	23·00
FR50	20pf. brown	10·00	23·00

1949. 75th Anniv of U.P.U. As Nos. FB56/7 of Baden.

FR51	20pf. red	6·50	13·50
FR52	30pf. blue	6·50	12·00

FW1 Fr. von Schiller **FW2** Bebenhausen Monastery **FW3** Lichtenstein Castle

1947. Inscr "WURTTEMBERG".

FW1	FW1	2pf. grey	20	65
FW2	-	3pf. brown	20	25
FW3	-	10pf. blue	20	30
FW4	FW1	12pf. green	20	25
FW5	-	15pf. violet	20	45
FW6	FW2	16pf. green	20	1·10
FW7	-	20pf. blue	20	1·10
FW8	FW2	24pf. red	20	25
FW9	-	45pf. mauve	20	1·10
FW10	FW1	60pf. orange	20	80
FW11	-	75pf. blue	25	1·40
FW12	FW3	84pf. green	25	1·60
FW13	-	1m. brown	35	1·40

DESIGNS—SMALL SIZE: 3pf., 15pf., 45pf. Holderlin (poet); 10pf., 20pf., 75pf. Wangen Gate. LARGE SIZE—VERT: 1m. Zwiefalten Monastery Church.

1948. Currency Reform. As 1947 issue. (a) Value in "PF".

FW14	FW1	2pf. orange	25	45
FW15	-	6pf. brown	25	35
FW16	-	10pf. brown	25	45
FW17	FW1	12pf. red	25	35
FW18	-	15pf. blue	75	45
FW19	FW2	24pf. green	1·10	75
FW20	-	30pf. mauve	1·40	75
FW21	-	50pf. blue	2·75	75

(b) Value in "D.PF" (= Deutsch Pfennig) or "D.M." (= Deutsch Mark).

FW22		8dpf. green	1·10	1·30
FW23	FW2	16dpf. violet	90	1·80
FW24	-	20dpf. brown	2·30	90
FW25	FW1	60dpf. grey	13·50	75
FW26	FW3	84dpf. red	4·00	4·50
FW27	-	1dm. blue	4·00	4·50

DESIGNS—SMALL SIZE: 6pf., 15pf. Fr. Holderlin (poet); 8 dpf., 30pf. Waldsee Castle; 50pf. Ludwig Uhland (poet). Others as 1947 issue.

Nos. FW14/21 were sold on the new currency basis though not inscribed "D.PF.".

1948. Inscr "WURTTEMBERG". As 1947 issue, but "PF" omitted.

FW28	FW1	2pf. orange	1·30	75
FW29	FW2	4pf. violet	3·00	45
FW30	-	5pf. blue	7·25	2·75
FW31	-	6pf. brown	9·25	6·50
FW32	-	8pf. red	9·25	2·75
FW33	-	10pf. green	9·00	35
FW34	-	20pf. mauve	9·25	35
FW35	FW2	40pf. brown	23·00	47·00
FW36	FW1	80pf. red	50·00	47·00
FW37	FW3	90pf. red	80·00	£120

DESIGNS—SMALL SIZE: 5pf., 6pf. Holderlin. Others as 1947 and 1948 issues.

FW4 Isny and Coat of Arms

1949. Ski Championships (Northern Combination) at Isny/Allgau.

FW38	FW4	10pf.+4pf. green	7·75	26·00
FW39	-	20pf.+6pf. lake	7·75	26·00

DESIGN: 20pf. Skier and view of Isny.

1949. Red Cross Fund. As Type FB 6 of Baden, but Arms of Wurttemberg and inscr "WURTTEMBERG".

FW40	10pf.+20pf. green	36·00	£110
FW41	20pf.+40pf. lilac	36·00	£110
FW42	30pf.+60pf. blue	36·00	£110
FW43	40pf.+80pf. grey	36·00	£110
MSFW43a	90×100 mm. Nos. FW40/3	£140	£1600

1949. Birth Bicentenary of Goethe. As Nos. FB47/9 of Baden.

FW44	10pf.+5pf. green	8·50	23·00
FW45	20pf.+10pf. mauve	12·50	32·00
FW46	30pf.+15pf. blue	12·50	46·00

FW5 Gustav Werner

1949. Centenary of Christian Institution "Zum Bruderhaus".

FW47	FW5	10pf.+5pf. green	5·75	15·00
FW48	FW5	20pf.+10pf. purple	5·75	15·00

1949. German Stamp Centenary. As Nos. FB54/5 of Baden.

FW49	10pf. green	7·00	16·00
FW50	20pf. brown	7·00	16·00

1949. 75th Anniv of U.P.U. As Nos. FB56/7 of Baden.

FW51	20pf. red	6·25	14·50
FW52	30pf. blue	6·25	12·00

E. Russian Zone.

For a list of the stamps issued by the Russian Zone Provincial Administrations of Berlin (Brandenburg), Mecklenburg-Vorpommern, Saxony (Halle, Leipzig and Dresden) and Thurningia, see Stanley Gibbons Part 7 Catalogue.

In February 1946, the Provincial Issues were replaced by the General Issues, Nos. 899/956, until the revaluation of the currency in June 1948, when Nos. 928/44 were brought into use handstamped with District names and numbers as a control measure pending the introduction of the following overprinted stamps on 3rd July. There are over 1,900 different types of district handstamp.

1948. Optd Sowjetische Besatzungs Zone. (a) On Pictorial issue of 1947, Nos. 928/44.

R1	2pf. black	35	35
R2	6pf. violet	35	35
R3	8pf. red	35	35
R4	10pf. green	35	35
R5	12pf. grey	35	35
R6	15pf. brown	45	35
R7	16pf. green	35	55
R8	20pf. blue	35	45
R9	24pf. brown	35	35
R10	25pf. orange	35	45
R11	30pf. red	75	55
R12	40pf. mauve	45	55
R13	50pf. blue	75	1·10
R14	60pf. brown	90	1·10
R15	60pf. red	65·00	£120
R16	80pf. blue	2·50	1·20
R17	84pf. green	2·50	1·80

(b) On Numerical issue of 1946, Nos. 903, etc.

R18	229	5pf. green	70	1·60
R19	229	30pf. olive	1·20	3·75
R20	229	45pf. red	50	1·50
R21	229	75pf. blue	50	1·50
R22	229	84pf. green	1·50	3·50

Sowjetische Besatzungs Zone
(R1)

(c) On stamps inscr "STADT BERLIN".

R23	R1	5pf. green	40	1·50
R25	-	6pf. violet	40	1·50
R26	-	8pf. orange	40	1·50
R27	-	10pf. brown	40	1·50
R28	-	12pf. red	75	4·50
R29	-	20pf. blue	60	1·60
R30	-	30pf. olive	60	6·75

DESIGNS: 6pf. Bear with spade; 8pf. Bear on shield; 10pf. Bear holding brick; 12pf. Bear carrying plank; 20pf. Bear on small shield; 30pf. Oak sapling amid ruins.

1948. Leipzig Autumn Fair. As T 231 but dated "1948".

R31	16pf.+9pf. purple	50	70
R32	50pf.+25pf. blue	50	70

DESIGNS: 16pf. 1459: The first Spring Fair; 50pf. 1469: Foreign merchants displaying cloth.

R3 Kathe Kollwitz

1948. Politicians, Artists and Scientists.

R33	R3	2pf. grey	1·70	1·70
R34	-	6pf. violet	1·70	1·70
R35	-	8pf. red	1·70	1·70
R36	-	10pf. green	1·70	1·30
R37	-	12pf. blue	5·00	80
R38	-	15pf. brown	1·30	2·50
R39	-	16pf. blue	2·30	1·70
R40	R3	20pf. purple	1·70	1·50
R41	-	24pf. red	4·50	80
R42	-	25pf. olive	1·70	2·20
R43	-	30pf. red	4·00	2·20
R44	-	40pf. purple	9·00	2·00
R45	-	50pf. blue	1·70	2·00
R46	-	60pf. green	8·00	1·70
R47	-	80pf. blue	1·70	1·70
R48	-	84pf. brown	2·75	5·25
E95	-	80pf. red	14·00	8·50

PORTRAITS: 6, 40pf. Gerhart Hauptmann; 8, 50pf. Karl Marx; 10, 84pf. August Bebel; 12, 30pf. Friedrich Engels; 15, 60pf. G. F. W. Hegel; 16, 25pf. Rudolf Virchow; 24, 80pf. Ernst Thalmann.

R4

1948. Stamp Day.

R49	R4	12pf.+3pf. red	45	65

R5 Liebknecht and Rosa Luxemburg

1949. 30th Death Anniv of Karl Liebknecht and Rosa Luxemburg (revolutionaries).

R50	R5	24pf. red	45	85

1949. Leipzig Spring Fair. As T 231 but dated "1949".

R51	30pf.+15pf. red	3·75	4·75
R52	50pf.+25pf. blue	4·00	5·75

DESIGNS: 30pf. 1st Neubau Town Hall bazaar, 1556; 50pf. Italian merchants at Leipzig, 1536.

R6 Dove

1949. 3rd German Peoples' Congress.

R53	R6	24pf. red	1·30	2·40

1949. Optd 3. Deutscher Volkskongreß 29.-30 Mai 1949.

R54	24pf. red	2·10	3·25

R8 Goethe

1949. Birth Bicent of Goethe. Portraits of Goethe.

R55	R8	6pf.+4pf. violet	3·00	3·50
R56	-	12pf.+8pf. brown	3·00	3·50
R57	-	24pf.+16pf. lake	2·50	3·00
R58	-	50pf.+25pf. blue	2·50	3·00
R59	-	84pf.+36pf. grey	4·50	5·50

1949. Goethe Festival Week, Weimar. Sheet 106×104 mm.

MSR59a	R 9 50pf. (+Dm. 4.50) blue	£200	£275

1949. Leipzig Autumn Fair. As T 231 but dated "1949".

R60	12pf.+8pf. slate	4·50	7·25
R61	24pf.+16pf. lake	6·50	9·00

DESIGNS: 12pf. Russian merchants, 1650; 24pf. Goethe at Fair, 1765.

The Russian Zonee was incorporated in East Germany in October 1949.

III. GERMAN FEDERAL REPUBLIC

The Federal Republic was set up on 23 May 1949.Until October 1990 it comprised the territory whixh formerly came under the British, American and French Zones. On 3 October 1990 the former territory of East Germany (German Democratic Republic) was absorbed into the Federal Republic.

257 Constructing Parliament Building

1949. Opening of West German Parliament, Bonn.

1033	257	10pf. green	50·00	25·00
1034	257	20pf. red	60·00	28·00

258 Reproduction of T **1** of Bavaria

1949. Centenary of 1st German Stamps.

1035	258	10pf.+2pf. black & grn	16·00	26·00
1036	-	20pf. blue and red	41·00	44·00
1037	-	30pf. brown and blue	55·00	70·00

DESIGN: 20pf., 30pf. Reproductions of T **2** of Bavaria.

259 Dr. von Stephan, Old G.P.O., Berlin and Standehaus, Berne

1949. 75th Anniv of U.P.U.

1038	259	30pf. blue	75·00	44·00

260 St. Elisabeth of Thuringia

1949. Refugees' Relief Fund. Inscr as in T 260.

1039	260	8pf.+2pf. purple	23·00	26·00
1040	-	10pf.+5pf. green	21·00	14·00
1041	-	20pf.+10pf. red	21·00	14·00
1042	-	30pf.+15pf. blue	£100	£120

PORTRAITS: 10pf. Paracelsus von Hohenheim; 20pf. F. W. A. Froebel; 30pf. J. H. Wichern.

261 J. S. Bach's Seal

1950. Death Bicent of Bach (composer).

1043	261	10pf.+2pf. green	70·00	48·00
1044	261	20pf.+3pf. red	80·00	55·00

262 Numeral and Posthorn

1951

1045	262	2pf. green	5·50	1·10
1046	262	4pf. brown	3·75	35
1047	262	5pf. purple	11·00	35
1048	262	6pf. orange	23·00	3·50
1049	262	8pf. grey	25·00	10·50
1050	262	10pf. green	7·25	35
1051	262	15pf. violet	46·00	1·10
1052	262	20pf. red	5·50	35
1053	262	25pf. plum	£110	5·75
1054	262	30pf. blue	60·00	55
1055	262	40pf. purple	£170	55
1056	262	50pf. grey	£200	55
1057	262	60pf. brown	£150	55
1058	262	70pf. yellow	£500	17·00
1059	262	80pf. red	£550	2·20
1060	262	90pf. green	£600	2·75

The 30pf. to 90pf. are 20×24½ mm.

264 Figures

1951. 700th Anniv of St. Mary's Church, Lubeck.

1065	**264**	10pf.+5pf. black & grn	£100	80·00
1066	**264**	20pf.+5pf. black & red	£120	£110

265 Stamps under Magnifier

1951. National Philatelic Exn, Wuppertal.

1067	**265**	10pf.+2pf. yellow, black and green	50·00	55·00
1068	**265**	20pf.+3pf. yellow, black and red	50·00	55·00

266 St. Vincent de Paul

1951. Humanitarian Relief Fund.

1069	**266**	4pf.+2pf. brown	11·00	12·50
1070	-	10pf.+3pf. green	16·00	10·50
1071	-	20pf.+5pf. red	16·00	10·50
1072	-	30pf.+10pf. blue	£120	£140

PORTRAITS: 10pf. F. Von Bodelschwingh; 20pf. Elsa Brandstrom; 30pf. J. H. Pestalozzi.

267 W. C. Rontgen (physicist)

1951. 50th Anniv of Award to Rontgen of 1st Nobel Prize for Physics.

1073	**267**	30pf. blue	85·00	21·00

268 Mona Lisa

1952. 500th Birth Anniv of Leonardo da Vinci.

1074	**268**	5pf. multicoloured	1·30	1·20

269 Martin Luther

1952. Lutheran World Federation Assembly, Hanover.

1075	**269**	10pf. green	16·00	5·75

270 A. N. Otto and Diagram

1952. 75th Anniv of Otto Gas Engine.

1076	**270**	30pf. blue	35·00	18·00

271 Nuremberg Madonna

1952. Centenary of German National Museum, Nuremberg.

1077	**271**	10pf.+5pf. green	18·00	21·00

272 Trawler "Senator Schaffer" off Heligoland

1952. Rehabilitation of Heligoland.

1078	**272**	20pf. red	18·00	6·50

273 Carl Schurz

1952. Centenary of Arrival of Schurz in America.

1079	**273**	20pf. pink, black and blue	23·00	8·75

274 Boy Hikers

1952. Youth Hostels Fund. Inscr "JUGENDMARKE 1952".

1080	**274**	10pf.+2pf. green	23·00	25·00
1081	-	20pf.+3pf. red	23·00	25·00

DESIGN: 20pf. Girl hikers.

275 Elizabeth Fry

1952. Humanitarian Relief Fund.

1082	**275**	4pf.+2pf. brown	9·00	7·00
1083	-	10pf.+5pf. green	9·00	7·00
1084	-	20pf.+10pf. lake	18·00	14·00
1085	-	30pf.+10pf. blue	90·00	£110

PORTRAITS: 10pf. Dr. C. Sonnenschein; 20pf. T. Fliedner; 30pf. H. Dunant.

276 Postman, 1852

1952. Thurn and Taxis Stamp Centenary.

1086	**276**	10pf. multicoloured	9·00	2·30

277 P. Reis

1952. 75th Anniv of German Telephone Service.

1087	**277**	30pf. blue	55·00	18·00

278 Road Accident Victim

1953. Road Safety Campaign.

1088	**278**	20pf. multicoloured	20·00	5·25

279

1953. 50th Anniv of Science Museum, Munich.

1089	**279**	10pf.+5pf. green	32·00	35·00

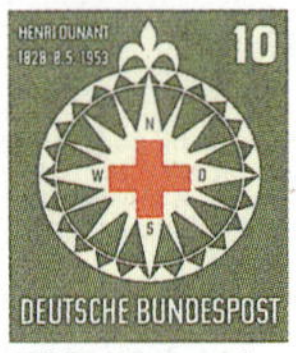

280 Red Cross and Compass

1953. 125th Birth Anniv of Henri Dunant (founder of Red Cross).

1090	**280**	10pf. red and green	24·00	8·00

281 Prisoner of War

1953. Commemorating Prisoners of War.

1091	**281**	10pf. black and grey	7·25	45

282 J. von Liebig

1953. 150th Birth Anniv of Liebig (chemist).

1092	**282**	30pf. blue	55·00	26·00

283 "Rail Transport"

1953. Transport Exn, Munich. Inscr as in T 283.

1093	**283**	4pf. brown	6·75	4·50
1094	-	10pf. green	13·50	7·00
1095	-	20pf. red	27·00	11·50
1096	-	30pf. blue	55·00	26·00

DESIGNS: 10pf. "Air" (dove and aeroplanes); 20pf. "Road" (traffic lights and cars); 30pf. "Sea" (buoy and ships).

284 Gateway, Thurn and Taxis Palace

1953. International Philatelic Exhibition, Frankfurt am Main. Inscr "IFRABA 1953".

1097	**284**	10pf.+2pf. brown, black and green	27·00	31·00
1098	-	20pf.+3pf. grey, blue and red	27·00	31·00

DESIGN: 20pf. Telecommunications Buildings, Frankfurt am Main.

285 A. H. Francke

1953. Humanitarian Relief Fund.

1099	**285**	4pf.+2pf. brown	5·50	8·75
1100	-	10pf.+5pf. green	9·00	8·75
1101	-	20pf.+10pf. red	16·00	13·00
1102	-	30pf.+10pf. blue	65·00	80·00

PORTRAITS: 10pf. S. Kneipp; 20pf. J. C. Senckenberg; 30pf. F. Nansen.

286 Pres. Heuss

1954. (a) Size 18½×22½ mm or 18×22 mm.

1103	**286**	2pf. green	25	25
1104	**286**	4pf. brown	25	25
1105	**286**	5pf. mauve	25	25
1106	**286**	6pf. brown	25	90
1107	**286**	7pf. green	25	35
1108	**286**	8pf. grey	25	70
1109	**286**	10pf. green	25	25
1110	**286**	15pf. blue	70	55
1111	**286**	20pf. red	25	25
1112	**286**	25pf. purple	90	70
1122a	**286**	30pf. green	45	75
1122c	**286**	40pf. blue	2·75	35
1122e	**286**	50pf. olive	1·20	35
1122f	**286**	60pf. brown	4·00	55
1122g	**286**	70pf. violet	14·00	55
1122h	**286**	80pf. orange	7·25	2·40
1122i	**286**	90pf. green	22·00	1·10

(b) Size 20×24 mm.

1113	30pf. blue	17·00	5·50
1114	40pf. purple	6·50	35
1115	50pf. slate	£225	65
1116	60pf. brown	46·00	70
1117	70pf. olive	17·00	2·20
1118	80pf. red	3·50	5·25
1119	90pf. green	17·00	2·75

(c) Size 25×30 mm.

1120	1Dm. olive	1·70	35
1121	2Dm. lavender	3·50	1·30
1122	3Dm. purple	8·75	2·75

287 P. Ehrlich and E. von Behring

1954. Birth Centenaries of Ehrlich and Von Behring (bacteriologists).

1123	**287**	10pf. green	13·00	4·50

288 Gutenburg and Printing-press

1954. 500th Anniv of Gutenberg Bible.

1124	**288**	4pf. brown	1·30	70

289 Sword-pierced Mitre

1954. 1,200th Anniv of Martyrdom of St. Boniface.

1125	**289**	20pf. red and brown	9·00	5·25

290 Kathe Kollwitz

1954. Humanitarian Relief Fund.

1126 **290** 7pf.+3pf. brown 3·75 3·50
1127 - 10pf.+5pf. green 1·80 1·80
1128 - 20pf.+10pf. red 10·50 5·25
1129 - 40pf.+10pf. blue 41·00 48·00

PORTRAITS: 10pf. L. Werthmann; 20pf. J. F. Oberlin; 40pf. Bertha Pappenheim.

291 C. F. Gauss

1955. Death Cent of Gauss (mathematician).

1130 **291** 10pf. green 6·00 70

292 "Flight"

1955. Re-establishment of "Lufthansa" Airways.

1131 **292** 5pf. mauve and black 1·20 90
1132 **292** 10pf. green and black 1·50 1·30
1133 **292** 15pf. blue and black 9·00 6·50
1134 **292** 20pf. red and black 26·00 8·75

293 O. von Miller

1955. Birth Centenary of Von Miller (electrical engineer).

1135 **293** 10f. green 6·00 1·80

295 Schiller

1955. 150th Death Anniv of Schiller (poet).

1136 **295** 40pf. blue 20·00 6·50

296 Motor-coach, 1906

1955. 50th Anniv of Postal Motor Transport.

1137 **296** 20pf. black and red 13·00 5·75

297 Arms of Baden-Wurttemburg

1955. Baden-Wurttemberg Agricultural Exhibition, Stuttgart.

1138 **297** 7pf. black, brn & bistre 5·00 5·25
1139 **297** 10pf. black, grn & bistre 7·75 3·00

298 "Earth and Atom"

1955. Cosmic Research.

1140 **298** 20pf. lake 13·00 1·40

299 Refugees

1955. 10th Anniv of Expulsion of Germans from beyond the Oder–Neisse Line.

1141 **299** 20pf. red 4·50 75

See also No. 1400.

300 Orb, Arrows and Waves

1955. Millenary of Battle of Lechfeld.

1142 **300** 20pf. purple 11·00 4·50

301 Magnifying Glass and Carrier Pigeon

1955. West European Postage Stamp Exn.

1143 **301** 10pf.+2pf. green 5·50 6·50
1144 - 20pf.+3pf. red 13·00 16·00

DESIGN: 20pf. Tweezers and posthorn.

302 Railway Signal

1955. Railway Timetable Conference.

1145 **302** 20pf. black and red 11·00 3·00

303 Stifter Monument

1955. 150th Birth Anniv of Stifter (Austrian poet).

1146 **303** 10pf. green 4·50 3·00

304 U.N. Emblem

1955. U.N. Day.

1147 **304** 10pf. green and brown 4·50 5·25

305 Amalie Sieveking

1955. Humanitarian Relief Fund.

1148 **305** 7pf.+3pf. brown 3·75 4·25
1149 - 10pf.+5pf. green 2·75 2·20
1150 - 20pf.+10pf. red 2·75 2·20
1151 - 40pf.+10pf. blue 38·00 44·00

PORTRAITS: 10pf. A. Kolping; 20pf. Dr. S. Hahnemann; 40pf. Florence Nightingale.

306

1955

1152 **306** 1pf. grey 25 45

307 Von Stephan's Signature

1955. 125th Birth Anniv of H. von Stephan.

1153 **307** 20pf. red 8·25 3·00

308 Spinet and Opening Bars of Minuet

1956. Birth Bicent of Mozart (composer).

1154 **308** 10pf. black and lilac 90 45

309 Heinrich Heine

1956. Death Centenary of Heine (poet).

1155 **309** 10pf. green and black 3·50 3·50

310 Old Houses and Crane

1956. Millenary of Luneburg.

1156 **310** 20pf. red 9·00 9·75

311

1956. Olympic Year.

1157 **311** 10pf. green 90 75

312 Boy and Dove

1956. Youth Hostels' Fund. Inscr "JUGEND".

1158 **312** 7pf.+3pf. grey, black and brown 2·50 4·00
1159 - 10pf.+5pf. grey black and green 8·50 10·00

DESIGN: 10pf. Girl playing flute and flowers.

313 Robert Schumann

1956. Death Centenary of Schumann (composer).

1160 **313** 10pf. black, red & bistre 80 55

314

1956. Evangelical Church Convention, Frankfurt am Main.

1161 **314** 10pf. green 4·50 4·50
1162 **314** 20pf. red 5·50 6·25

315 T. Mann (author)

1956. Thomas Mann Commemoration.

1163 **315** 20pf. red 3·75 2·50

316

1956. 800th Anniv of Maria Laach Abbey.

1164 **316** 20pf. grey and red 2·75 2·30

317 Ground Plan of Cologne Cathedral and Hand

1956. 77th Meeting of German Catholics, Cologne.

1165 **317** 10pf. green and brown 3·25 3·00

318

1956. International Police Exhibition, Essen.

1166 **318** 20pf. green, orange & blk 3·75 3·00

1956. Europa. As Nos. 1582/3 of Belgium.

1167 10pf. green 1·60 25
1168 40pf. blue 8·75 1·30

320 Midwife and Baby

1956. Humanitarian Relief Fund. Centres in black.

1169 **320** 7pf.+3pf. brown 1·80 2·75
1170 - 10pf.+5pf. green 1·40 90
1171 - 20pf.+10pf. red 1·40 90
1172 - 40pf.+10pf. blue 20·00 18·00

DESIGNS: 10pf. I. P. Semmelweis and cot; 20pf. Mother, and baby in cradle; 40f. Nurse maid and children.

321 Carrier Pigeon

1956. Stamp Day.
1173 **321** 10pf. green 1·80 85

322 "Military Graves"

1956. War Graves Commission.
1174 **322** 10pf. green 1·80 85

323 Arms

1957. Return of the Saar to West Germany.
1175 **323** 10pf. brown and green 60 55

324 Children with Luggage

1957. Berlin Children's Holiday Fund.
1176 **324** 10pf.+5pf. orange and green 1·60 2·40
1177 - 20pf.+10pf. blue and orange 3·75 4·75
DESIGN: 20pf. Girl returning from holiday.

325 Heinrich Hertz

1957. Birth Cent of Hertz (physicist).
1178 **325** 10pf. black and green 1·60 70

326 Paul Gerhardt

1957. 350th Birth Anniv of Paul Gerhardt (hymn-writer).
1179 **326** 20pf. red 65 60

327 "Flora and Philately"

1957. Exhibition and 8th Congress of Int Federation of "Constructive Philately".
1180 **327** 20pf. orange 65 60

328 Emblem of Aschaffenburg

1957. Millenary of Aschaffenburg.
1181 **328** 20pf. red and black 65 60

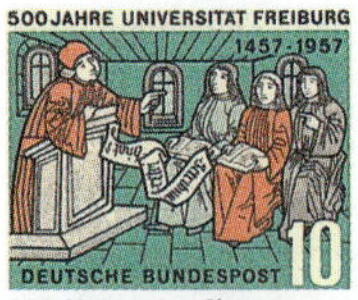

329 University Class

1957. 500th Anniv of Freiburg University.
1182 **329** 10pf. black, red & green 45 45

330 "Bayernstein" (freighter)

1957. German Merchant Shipping Day.
1183 **330** 15pf. black, red and blue 1·40 1·20

331 Justus Liebig University

1957. 350th Anniv of Justus Liebig University, Giessen.
1184 **331** 10pf. green 50 55

332 Albert Ballin

1957. Birth Centenary of Albert Ballin (director of Hamburg-America Shipping Line).
1185 **332** 20pf. black and red 1·60 55

333 Television Screen

1957. Publicizing West German Television Service.
1186 **333** 10pf. green and blue 45 55

334 "Europa" Tree

1957. Europa.
1187 **334** 10pf. green and blue 55 20
1188 **334** 40pf. blue 5·50 45

335 Young Miner

1957. Humanitarian Relief Fund.
1189 **335** 7pf.+3pf. black & brn 1·60 2·00
1190 - 10pf.+5pf. black & grn 1·10 1·10
1191 - 20pf.+10pf. black & red 1·60 1·10
1192 - 40pf.+10pf. black & bl 20·00 22·00
DESIGNS: 10pf. Miner drilling coal-face; 20pf. Miner with coal-cutting machine; 40pf. Operator at mine lift-shaft.

336 Water Lily

1957. Nature Protection Day.
1193 **336** 10pf. orange, yell & grn 50 55
1194 - 20pf. multicoloured 70 65

DESIGN—VERT: 20pf. European robin.

337 Carrier Pigeons

1957. International Correspondence Week.
1195 **337** 20pf. black and red 1·00 60

338 Baron von Stein

1957. Birth Bicentenary of Baron von Stein (statesman).
1196 **338** 20pf. red 1·80 80

339 Dr Leo Baeck (philosopher)

1957. 1st Death Anniv of Dr. Leo Baeck.
1197 **339** 20pf. red 1·80 75

340 Wurttemberg Parliament House

1957. 500th Anniv of First Wurttemberg Parliament.
1198 **340** 10pf. olive and green 1·00 60

341 Stage Coach

1957. Death Centenary of Joseph von Eichendorff (novelist).
1199 **341** 10pf. green 90 60

342 "Max and Moritz" (cartoon characters)

1958. 50th Death Anniv of Wilhelm Busch (writer and illustrator).
1200 **342** 10pf. olive and black 30 20
1201 - 20pf. red and black 1·00 70
DESIGN: 20pf. Wilhelm Busch.

343 "Prevent Forest Fires"

1958. Forest Fires Prevention Campaign.
1202 **343** 20pf. black and red 80 60

344 Rudolf Diesel and First Oil Engine

1958. Birth Centenary of Rudolf Diesel (engineer).
1203 **344** 10pf. myrtle 45 45

345 "The Fox who stole the Goose"

1958. Berlin Students' Fund. Inscr "Fur die Jugend".
1204 **345** 10pf.+5pf. red, black and green 2·10 2·75
1205 - 20pf.+10pf. brown, green and red 4·00 4·50
DESIGN: 20pf. "A hunter from the Palatinate" (horseman).

346 Giraffe and Lion

1958. Centenary of Frankfurt am Main Zoo.
1206 **346** 10pf. black and green 65 50

347 Old Munich

1958. 800th Anniv of Munich.
1207 **347** 20pf. red 65 50

348 Trier and Market Cross

1958. Millenary of Trier Market.
1208 **348** 20pf. red and black 65 50

349 Deutsche Mark (coin)

1958. 10th Anniv of Currency Reform.
1209 **349** 20pf. black and orange 75 90

350 Emblem of Gymnastics

1958. 150th Anniv of German Gymnastics.
1210 **350** 10pf. black, green & grey 45 55

351 H. Schulze-Delitzsch

1958. 150th Birth Anniv of Schulze-Delitzsch (pioneer of German co-operative movement).
1211 **351** 10pf. green 55 35

1958. Europa. As No. 643 of Luxembourg, size 24½×30 mm.
1212 10pf. blue and green 45 25
1213 40pf. red and blue 4·00 55

352 Friedrich Raiffeisen (philanthropist)

353 Dairymaid

1958. Humanitarian Relief and Welfare Funds.

1214	**352**	7pf.+3pf. brown, deep brown and chestnut	55	55
1215	**353**	10pf.+5pf. red, yellow and green	55	55
1216	-	20pf.+10pf. blue, green and red	55	55
1217	-	40pf.+10pf. yellow, orange and blue	7·25	8·00

DESIGNS— As Type **353**: 20pf. Vine-dresser; 40pf. Farm labourer.

354 Cardinal Nicholas of Cues (founder)

1958. 500th Anniv of Hospice of St. Nicholas.

1218	**354**	20pf. black and mauve	55	45

1959. As Type B 53 of West Berlin but without "BERLIN".

1219	7pf. green	30	25
1220	10pf. green	50	25
1221	20pf. red	50	25
1222	40pf. blue	16·00	1·10
1223	70pf. violet	5·00	90

355 Jakob Fugger (merchant prince)

1959. 500th Birth Anniv of Jakob Fugger.

1224	**355**	20pf. black and red	45	55

356 Adam Riese (mathematician)

1959. 400th Death Anniv of Adam Riese.

1225	**356**	10pf. black and green	45	55

357 A. von Humboldt (naturalist)

1959. Death Cent of Alexander von Humboldt.

1226	**357**	40pf. blue	2·00	1·60

358 First Hamburg Stamp of 1859

1959. International Stamp Exhibition, Hamburg, and Centenary of First Stamps of Hamburg and Lubeck.

1228	**358**	10pf.+5pf. brown & grn	25	70
1230	-	20pf.+10pf. brn & red	25	80

DESIGN: 20pf. First Lubeck stamp of 1859.

359 Buxtehude

1959. Millenary of Buxtehude.

1231	**359**	20pf. red, black and blue	45	45

360 Holy Tunic of Trier

1959. Holy Tunic of Trier Exhibition.

1232	**360**	20pf. black, buff & purple	45	45

361 Congress Emblem

1959. German Evangelical Church Day and Congress, Munich.

1233	**361**	10pf. violet, green & blk	35	35

1959. Inauguration of Beethoven Hall, Bonn. T 361a and similar horiz designs in sheet 148×104 mm with extract from Beethoven's music notebooks.

MS1233a 10pf. green (Handell); 15pf. blue (Spohr); 20pf. red (T **361a**); 25pf. brown (Haydn); 40pf. blue (Mendelssohn) 29·00 55·00

1959. Europa. As Nos. 659/60 of Luxembourg, but size 24½×30 mm.

1234	10pf. green	35	20
1235	40pf. blue	1·50	55

362 "Feeding the Poor"

1959. Humanitarian Relief and Welfare Funds.

1236	**362**	7pf.+3pf. sepia & yellow	25	45
1237	-	10pf.+5pf. green & yell	25	45
1238	-	20pf.+10pf. red & yell	35	45
1239	-	40pf.+10pf. mult	3·75	4·75

DESIGNS: 10pf. "Clothing the Naked"; 20pf. "Bounty from Heaven" (scenes from the Brothers Grimm story "The Star Thaler"); 40pf. The Brothers Grimm.

363 "Uprooted Tree"

1960. World Refugee Year.

1240	**363**	10pf. black, purple & grn	25	25
1241	**363**	40pf. black, red and blue	2·50	2·50

364 P. Melanchthon

1960. 400th Death Anniv of Philip Melanchthon (Protestant reformer).

1242	**364**	20pf. black and red	1·60	1·30

365 Cross and Symbols of the Crucifixion

1960. Oberammergau Passion Play.

1243	**365**	10pf. grey, ochre and blue	35	35

366

1960. 37th World Eucharistic Congress, Munich.

1244	**366**	10pf. green	70	55
1245	**366**	20pf. red	90	90

367 Wrestling

1960. Olympic Year. Inscr as in T 367.

1246	**367**	7pf. brown	25	20
1247	-	10pf. green	45	20
1248	-	20pf. red	45	20
1249	-	40pf. blue	1·60	1·50

DESIGNS: 10pf. Running; 20pf. Javelin and discus-throwing; 40pf. Chariot-racing.

368 Hildesheim Cathedral

1960. Birth Millenary of Bishops St. Bernward and St. Godehard.

1250	**368**	20pf. purple	90	60

368a Conference Emblem

1960. Europa.

1251	**368a**	10pf. green and olive	25	25
1252	**368a**	20pf. vermilion and red	75	35
1253	**368a**	40pf. light blue and blue	1·60	1·30

369 Little Red Riding Hood meeting Wolf

1960. Humanitarian Relief and Welfare Funds.

1254	**369**	7pf.+3pf. black, red and bistre	55	55
1255	-	10pf.+5pf. black, red and green	55	45
1256	-	20pf.+10pf. black, green and red	55	45
1257	-	40pf.+20pf. black, red and blue	2·75	4·50

DESIGNS: 10pf. Red Riding Hood and wolf disguised as grandmother; 20pf. Woodcutter and dead wolf; 40pf. Red Riding Hood with grandmother.

1960. 1st Death Anniv of Gen. George C. Marshall. Portrait as T 364.

1258	40pf. black and blue	3·00	2·50

371 "Adler", 1835

1960. 125th Anniv of German Railway.

1259	**371**	10pf. black and bistre	35	45

372 St. George and the Dragon

1961. Pathfinders (German Boy Scouts) Commemoration.

1260	**372**	10pf. green	25	30

1961. Famous Germans. As Nos. B194, etc of West Berlin but without "BERLIN".

1261	5pf. olive	20	20
1262	7pf. brown	20	20
1263	8pf. violet	20	25
1264	10pf. green	20	25
1265	15pf. blue	45	1·10
1266	20pf. red	45	35
1267	25pf. brown	20	30
1268	30pf. sepia	20	25
1269	40pf. blue	25	25
1270	50pf. brown	45	35
1271	60pf. red	35	25
1272	70pf. green	25	25
1273	80pf. brown	45	45
1274	90pf. bistre	35	25
1275	1Dm. violet	65	25
1276	2Dm. green	3·75	65

PORTRAIT: 90pf. Franz Oppenheimer (economist).

373 Early Daimler Motor Car

1961. 75th Anniv of Daimler-Benz Patent.

1277	**373**	10pf. green and black	20	20
1278	-	20pf. red and black	45	45

DESIGN: 20pf. Early Benz motor car.

374 Nuremberg Messenger of 1700

1961. "The Letter during Five Centuries" Exhibition, Nuremberg.

1279	**374**	7pf. black and red	25	35

375 Speyer Cathedral

1961. 900th Anniv of Speyer Cathedral.

1280	**375**	20pf. red	35	55

376 Doves

1961. Europa.

1281	**376**	10pf. green	25	25
1282	**376**	40pf. blue	45	60

377 Hansel and Gretel in the Wood

1961. Humanitarian Relief and Welfare Funds. Multicoloured.

1283	7pf.+3pf. Type **377**	20	35
1284	10pf.+5pf. Hansel, Gretel and the Witch	20	35
1285	20pf.+10pf. Hansel in the Witch's cage	20	35

1286		40pf.+20pf. Hansel and Gretel reunited with their father	1·40	2·20

378 Telephone Apparatus

1961. Centenary of Philipp Reis's Telephone.

1287	**378**	10pf. green	35	45

379 Baron W. E. von Ketteler

1961. 150th Birth Anniv of Baron W. E. von Ketteler (Catholic leader).

1288	**379**	10pf. black and green	35	45

380 Drusus Stone

1962. Bimillenary of Mainz.

1289	**380**	20pf. purple	35	45

381 Apollo

1962. Child Welfare. Butterflies. Mult.

1290		7pf.+3pf. Type **381**	45	60
1291		10pf.+5pf. Camberwell beauty	45	60
1292		20pf.+10pf. Small tortoiseshell	90	1·30
1293		40pf.+20pf. Scarce swallowtail	1·40	2·40

382 Part of "In Dulci Jubilo", from "Musae Sioniae" (M. Praetorius)

1962. "Song and Choir" (Summer Music Festivals).

1294	**382**	20pf. red and black	35	55

383 "Belief, Thanksgiving and Service"

1962. Catholics' Day.

1295	**383**	20pf. mauve	35	55

384 Open Bible

1962. 150th Anniv of Wurttembergische Bibelanstalt (Bible publishers).

1296	**384**	20pf. black and red	35	55

385 Europa "Tree"

1962. Europa.

1297	**385**	10pf. green	25	25
1298	**385**	40pf. blue	55	60

386 Snow White and the Seven Dwarfs

1962. Humanitarian Relief and Welfare Funds. Scenes from "Snow White and the Seven Dwarfs" (Brothers Grimm). Multicoloured.

1299		7pf.+3pf. The "Magic Mirror"	20	25
1300		10pf.+5pf. Type **386**	20	25
1301		20pf.+10pf. "The Poisoned Apple"	20	25
1302		40pf.+20pf. Snow White and Prince Charming	1·10	1·60

387 "Bread for the World"

1963. Freedom from Hunger.

1303	**387**	20pf. brown and black	35	55

388 Relief Distribution

1963. CRALOG and CARE Relief Organizations.

1304	**388**	20pf. red	25	45

389 Ears of Wheat, Cross and Globe

1963. Freedom from Hunger.

1305	**389**	20pf. black, red and grey	25	45

390 Snake's Head Lily

1963. "Flora and Philately" Exhibition, Hamburg. Multicoloured.

1306		10pf. Type **390**	25	20
1307		15pf. Lady's slipper orchid	25	20
1308		20pf. Columbine	25	20
1309		40pf. Sea holly	45	55

391 "Heidelberger Catechismus"

1963. 400th Anniv of Heidelberg Catechism.

1310	**391**	20pf. black, red and orange	35	45

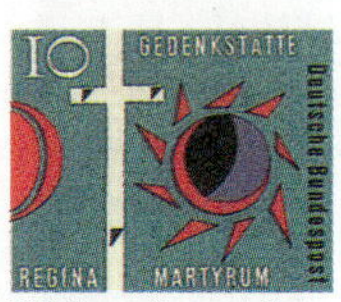

392 Cross, Sun and Moon

1963. Consecration of Regina Martyrum Church, Berlin.

1311	**392**	10pf. multicoloured	25	35

393 Emblems of Conference Participating Countries

1963. Centenary of Paris Postal Conference.

1312	**393**	40pf. blue	50	60

394 Map and Flags

1963. Opening of Denmark–Germany Railway ("Vogelfluglinie").

1313	**394**	20pf. multicoloured	35	35

395 Red Cross Emblem

1963. Red Cross Centenary.

1314	**395**	20pf. red, purple & yell	25	35

396 Hoopoe

1963. Child Welfare. Bird designs inscr "FUR DIE JUGEND 1963". Multicoloured.

1315		10pf.+5pf. Type **396**	55	70
1316		15pf.+5pf. Golden oriole	45	75
1317		20pf.+10pf. Northern bullfinch	45	75
1318		40pf.+20pf. River kingfisher	2·00	3·00

397 Congress Emblem

1963. German Evangelical Church Day and Congress, Dortmund.

1319	**397**	20pf. black and brown	35	45

398 "Co-operation"

1963. Europa.

1320	**398**	15pf. green	25	35
1321	**398**	20pf. red	25	25

399 Mother Goat warning kids

1963. Humanitarian Relief and Welfare Funds.

1322	**399**	10pf.+5pf. mult	20	25
1323	-	15pf.+5pf. mult	20	25
1324	-	20pf.+10pf. mult	20	25
1325	-	40pf.+20pf. mult	80	1·30

DESIGNS: 15pf. Wolf entering house; 20pf. Wolf in house, threatening kids; 40pf. Mother Goat and Kids dancing round wolf in well. From Grimm's "Wolf and the Seven Kids".

400 Atlantic Herring

1964. Child Welfare. Fish designs inscr "Fur die Jugend 1964". Multicoloured.

1326		10pf.+5pf. Type **400**	25	45
1327		15pf.+5pf. Redfish	25	35
1328		20pf.+10pf. Mirror carp	45	55
1329		40pf.+20pf. Atlantic cod	1·20	2·20

401 Old Town Hall, Hanover

1964. Capitals of the Federal Lands. Mult.

1330		20pf. Type **401**	25	30
1331		20pf. Hamburg	25	30
1332		20pf. Kiel	25	30
1333		20pf. Munich	25	30
1334		20pf. Wiesbaden	25	30
1335		20pf. Berlin	25	30
1336		20pf. Mainz	25	30
1337		20pf. Dusseldorf	25	30
1338		20pf. Bonn	25	30
1339		20pf. Bremen	25	30
1340		20pf. Stuttgart	25	30
1340a		20pf. Saarbrucken	25	30

DESIGNS: No. 1331, Liner "Lichtenfels" and St. Michael's Church (775th anniv); 1332, Ferry "Kronprinz Harald"; 1333, National Theatre; 1334, Kurhaus; 1335, Reichstag; 1336, Gutenberg Museum; 1337, Jan Wellen's Monument and Town Hall; 1338, Town Hall; 1339, Market Hall; 1340, Town view; 1340a, Ludwig's Church.

402 Ottobeuren Abbey

1964. 1200th Anniv of Benedictine Abbey, Ottobeuren.

1341	**402**	20pf. black, red and pink	25	35

1964. Re-election of Pres. Lubke. As Type B 67 of West Berlin, inscr "DEUTSCHE BUNDESPOST" only.

1342		20pf. red	20	25
1343		40pf. blue	25	30

402b Sophie Scholl

1964. 20th Anniv of Attempt on Hitler's Life. Anti-Hitlerite Martyrs. Each black and grey.

1343a		20pf. Type **402b**	75	1·30
1343b		20pf. Ludwig Beck	75	1·30
1343c		20pf. Dietrich Bonhoeffer	75	1·30
1343d		20pf. Alfred Delp	75	1·30
1343e		20pf. Karl Friedrich Goerdeler	75	1·30
1343f		20pf. Wilhelm Leuschner	75	1·30
1343g		20pf. Helmuth James (Von Moltke)	75	1·30
1343h		20pf. Claus Schenk (Von Stauffenberg)	75	1·30

403 Calvin

1964. World Council of Reformed Churches.

1344	**403**	20pf. black and red	25	35

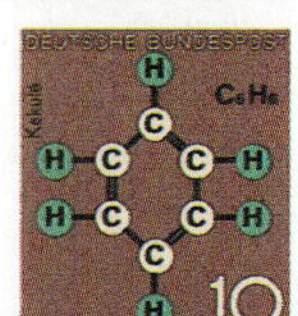

404 Diagram of Benzene Formula

1964. Scientific Anniversaries (1st series).

1345		10pf. green, black and brown	20	20
1346		15pf. multicoloured	20	20
1347		20pf. green, black and red	20	20

DESIGNS: 10pf. Type **404** (centenary of publication of Kekule's benzene formula); 15pf. Diagram of nuclear reaction (25th anniv of publication of Hahn-Strassman treatise on splitting the nucleus of the atom); 20pf. Gas engine (centenary of Otto-Langen internal-combustion engine).

See also Nos. 1426/7 and 1451/3.

405 F. Lassalle

1964. Death Centenary of Ferdinand Lassalle (Socialist founder and leader).

1348	**405**	20pf. black and blue	25	35

406 "The Sun"

1964. 80th Catholics' Day.

1349	**406**	20pf. red and blue	25	35

407 Europa "Flower"

1964. Europa.

1350	**407**	15pf. violet and green	20	20
1351	**407**	20pf. violet and red	20	20

408 "The Sleeping Beauty"

1964. Humanitarian Relief and Welfare Funds.

1352	**408**	10pf.+5pf. mult	20	25
1353	-	15pf.+5pf. mult	20	25
1354	-	20pf.+10pf. mult	20	25
1355	-	40pf.+20pf. mult	55	1·20

DESIGNS: 15pf., 20pf., 40pf. Various scenes from Grimm's "The Sleeping Beauty".

409 Judo

1964. "Olympic Year".

1356	**409**	20pf. multicoloured	25	35

410 Prussian Eagle

1964. 250th Anniv of German Court of Accounts.

1357	**410**	20pf. orange and black	25	35

411 Pres. Kennedy

1964. Pres. Kennedy Commemoration.

1358	**411**	40pf. blue	30	35

412 Castle Gateway, Ellwangen (Jagst)

1964. Twelve Centuries of German Architecture. (a) Size 18½×22 mm. Plain background.

1359	-	10pf. brown	25	25
1360	-	15pf. green	25	25
1361	-	20pf. brown	30	25
1362	-	40pf. blue	25	25
1363	**412**	50pf. brown	45	25
1364	-	60pf. red	1·20	55
1365	-	70pf. green	1·50	55
1366	-	80pf. brown	1·20	45

(b) Size 19½×24 mm. Coloured background.

1367	5pf. brown	20	15
1368	10pf. brown	20	15
1369	20pf. green	25	15
1370	30pf. green	25	15
1371	30pf. red	25	15
1372	40pf. brown	45	25
1373	50pf. blue	55	20
1374	60pf. orange	3·25	1·80
1375	70pf. green	1·40	25
1376	80pf. brown	2·50	1·80
1377	90pf. black	1·10	45
1378	1Dm. blue	90	25
1379	1Dm.10 brown	1·10	55
1380	1Dm.30 green	2·50	1·60
1381	2Dm. purple	2·50	70

BUILDINGS: 5pf. Berlin Gate, Stettin; 10pf. Zwinger pavilion, Dresden; 15pf. Tegel Castle, Berlin; 20pf. Monastery Gate, Lorsch; 30pf. North Gate, Flensburg; 40pf. Trifels Castle (Palatinate); 60pf. Treptow Portal, Neubrandenburg; 70pf. Osthofen Gate, Soest; 80pf. Ellingen Portal, Weissenburg (Bavaria); 90pf. Zschokk's Convent, Konigsberg; 1Dm. Melanchthon House, Wittenberg; 1Dm.10, Trinity Hospital, Hildesheim; 1Dm.30, Tegel Castle, Berlin (diff); 2Dm. Burghers' Hall, Lowenberg Town Hall (Silesia).

413 Owl, Hat, Walking-stick and Satchel

1965. 150th Death Anniv of Matthias Claudius (poet).

1383	**413**	20pf. black and red on grey	25	35

414 Eurasian Woodcock

1965. Child Welfare. Inscr "FUR DIE JUGEND 1965". Multicoloured.

1384	10pf.+5pf. Type **414**	25	35
1385	15pf.+5pf. Common pheasant	25	35
1386	20pf.+10pf. Black grouse	25	35
1387	40pf.+20pf. Western capercaillie	35	1·10

415 Bismarck (statesman)

1965. 150th Birth Anniv of Otto von Bismarck.

1388	**415**	20pf. black and red	25	35

416 Boeing 727-100 Airliner and Space Capsule

1965. Int Transport Exn, Munich. Mult.

1389	5pf. Traffic lights and road signs	25	30
1390	10pf. "Syncom" satellite and tracking station	25	30
1391	15pf. Old and modern postal buses	25	30
1392	20pf. Old semaphore station and modern signal tower	25	30
1393	40pf. Locomotive "Adler" (1835) and Class E.10.12 electric locomotive (1960s)	25	30
1394	60pf. Type **416**	35	35
1395	70pf. "Bremen" (liner) and "Hammonia" (19th-century steamship)	45	45

No. 1394 was also issued to mark the 10th anniv of Lufthansa's renewed air services.

417 Bouquet

1965. 75th Anniv of "May 1st" (Labour Day).

1396	**417**	15pf. multicoloured	25	30

418 I.T.U. Emblem

1965. Centenary of I.T.U.

1397	**418**	40pf. black and blue	35	45

419 A. Kopling

1965. Death Centenary of Adolf Kolping (miners' padre).

1398	**419**	20pf. black, red and grey	25	35

420 Rescue Vessel "Theodor Heuss"

1965. Cent of German Sea-rescue Service.

1399	**420**	20pf. violet, black & red	25	35

1965. 20th Anniv of Influx of East German Refugees. As T 299 but inscr "ZWANZIG JAHRE VERTREIBUNG 1945 1965".

1400	20pf. purple	25	35

421 Evangelical Church Emblem

1965. German Evangelical Church Day and Synod, Cologne.

1401	**421**	20pf. black, turq & bl	25	35

422 Radio Tower

1965. Radio Exhibition, Stuttgart.

1402	**422**	20pf. black, blue & mve	25	35

423 Thurn and Taxis 1, 2 and 5sgr. Stamps of 1852

1965. 125th Anniv of 1st Postage Stamp.

1403	**423**	20pf. multicoloured	25	35

424 Europa "Sprig"

1965. Europa.

1404	**424**	15pf. green	25	25
1405	**424**	20pf. red	25	25

425 Cinderella with Birds

1965. Humanitarian Relief Funds. Mult.

1406	10pf.+5pf. Type **425**	20	25
1407	15pf.+5pf. Cinderella and birds with dress	20	25
1408	20pf.+10pf. Prince offering slipper to Cinderella	20	25
1409	40pf.+20pf. Cinderella and Prince on horse	65	90

426 N. Soderblom

1966. Birth Centenary of Nathan Soderblom (Archbishop of Uppsala).

1410	**426**	20pf. black and lilac	25	35

427 Cardinal von Galen

1966. 20th Death Anniv of Cardinal Clemens von Galen.

1411	**427**	20pf. red, mauve & black	25	35

428 Brandenburg Gate, Berlin

1966

1412	**428**	10pf. brown	25	20
1413	**428**	20pf. green	45	25
1414	**428**	30pf. red	45	25
1415	**428**	50pf. blue	1·80	45
1415a	**428**	100pf. blue	12·00	70

429 Roe deer

1966. Child Welfare. Multicoloured.

1416	10pf.+5pf. Type **429**	25	25
1417	20pf.+10pf. Chamois	25	25
1418	30pf.+15pf. Fallow deer	25	25
1419	50pf.+25pf. Red deer	75	1·20

430 Christ and Fishermen (Miracle of the Fishes)

1966. Catholics' Day.

1420	**430**	30pf. black and salmon	25	35

431 19th-cent Postman

1966. F.I.P. Meeting, Munich. Multicoloured.

1421		30pf.+15pf. Bavarian mail coach	45	90
1422		50pf.+25pf. Type **431**	70	90

432 G. W. Leibniz

1966. 250th Death Anniv of Gottfried Leibniz (scientist).

1423	**432**	30pf. black and mauve	25	35

433 Europa "Ship"

1966. Europa.

1424	**433**	20pf. multicoloured	25	35
1425	**433**	30pf. multicoloured	25	20

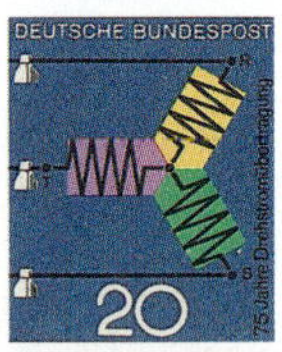

434 Diagram of A.C. Transmission (75th Anniv)

1966. Scientific Annivs (2nd series). Mult.

1426		20pf. Type **434**	20	25
1427		30pf. Diagram of electric dynamo (cent)	25	25

435 Princess and Frog

1966. Humanitarian Relief Funds. Mult.

1428		10pf.+5pf. Type **435**	20	25
1429		20pf.+10pf. Frog dining with Princess	20	25
1430		30pf.+15pf. Prince and Princess	20	25
1431		50pf.+25pf. In coach	55	1·20

Designs from Grimm's "The Frog Prince".

436 UNICEF Emblem

1966. Award of Nobel Peace Prize to United Nations Children's Fund.

1432	**436**	30pf. sepia, black and red	25	35

437 W. von Siemens (electrical engineer)

1966. 150th Birth Anniv of Werner von Siemens (electrical engineer).

1433	**437**	30pf. red	25	35

438 Common Rabbit

1967. Child Welfare. Multicoloured.

1434		10pf.+5pf. Type **438**	20	35
1435		20pf.+10pf. Stoat	30	35
1436		30pf.+15pf. Common hamster	55	70
1437		50pf.+25pf. Red fox	1·20	1·80

See also Nos. 1454/7.

439 Cogwheels

1967. Europa.

1438	**439**	20pf. multicoloured	35	35
1439	**439**	30pf. multicoloured	25	25

440 Francis of Taxis

1967. 450th Death Anniv of Francis of Taxis.

1440	**440**	30pf. black and orange	35	35

441 Evangelical Symbols

1967. 13th German Evangelical Churches Day.

1441	**441**	30pf. black and mauve	25	35

442 Friedrich von Bodelschwingh (Head of Hospital 1910–46)

1967. Cent of Bethel Hospital, Bielefeld.

1442	**442**	30pf. black and brown	25	35

443 Frau Holle at Spinning-wheel

1967. Humanitarian Relief Funds. Mult.

1443		10pf.+5pf. Type **443**	25	25
1444		20pf.+10pf. In the clouds	25	25
1445		30pf.+15pf. With shopping-basket and cockerel	25	25
1446		50pf.+25pf. Covered with soot	75	1·30

Designs from Grimm's "Frau Holle" ("Mother Carey").

1967. Re-election of Pres. Lubke. As Type B 67 of West Berlin, but inscr "DEUTSCHE BUNDESPOST".

1447		30pf. red	25	35
1448		50pf. blue	45	45

444 Wartburg (castle), Eisenach

1967. 450th Anniv of Luther's "Theses" and the Reformation.

1449	**444**	30pf. red	35	45

445 Cross on South American Map

1967. "Adveniat" (Aid for Catholic Church in Latin America).

1450	**445**	30pf. multicoloured	25	35

446 Koenig's Printing Machine

1968. Scientific Anniv (3rd series). Mult.

1451		10pf. Type **446**	15	15
1452		20pf. Ore Crystals	15	15
1453		30pf. Lens Refraction	25	20

ANNIVS: 10pf. 150th anniv; 20pf. Millenary of ore mining in Harz Mountains; 30pf. Centenary of Abbe-Zeiss Scientific Microscope.

1968. Child Welfare. As T 438 but inscr "1968". Multicoloured.

1454		10pf.+5pf. Wildcat	25	55
1455		20pf.+10pf. European otter	45	90
1456		30pf.+15pf. Eurasian badger	70	1·20
1457		50pf.+25pf. Eurasian beaver	2·30	3·50

447 Trade Symbols

1968. German Crafts and Trades.

1458	**447**	30pf. multicoloured	35	45

448 Dr. Adenauer

1968. Adenauer Commemoration (1st issue). T 448 and similar horiz designs in sheet 149×106 mm.

MS1459		10pf. brown and black; 20pf. green and black; 30pf. red and black; 50pf. blue and black	2·75	2·75

DESIGNS: 10pf. Sir Winston Churchill; 20pf. Alcide de Gasperi; 30pf. Robert Schuman.

See also No. 1469.

449 Europa "Key"

1968. Europa.

1460	**449**	20pf. yellow, brn & grn	25	35
1461	**449**	30pf. yellow, brn & red	25	20

450 Karl Marx

1968. 150th Birth Anniv of Karl Marx.

1462	**450**	30pf. red, black & grey	25	35

451 F. von Langen (horseman)

1968. Olympic Games (1972) Promotion Fund (1st series).

1463	**451**	10pf.+5pf. black & grn	35	30
1464	-	20pf.+10pf. black & grn	35	30
1465	-	30pf. black and lilac	30	25
1466	-	30pf.+15pf. black & red	70	60
1467	-	50pf.+25pf. black & bl	1·10	1·10

DESIGN: 20pf. R. Harbig (runner); 30pf. (No. 1465) Pierre de Coubertin (founder of Olympics); 30pf. (No. 1466) Helene Mayer (fencer); 50pf. Carl Diem (sports organiser).

See also Nos. 1493/6, 1524/7, 1589/92, 1621/4, **MS**1625 and 1629/32.

452 Opening Bars of "The Mastersingers"

1968. Centenary of 1st Performance of Richard Wagner's Opera "The Mastersingers".

1468	**452**	30pf. multicoloured	25	35

453 Dr. Adenauer

1968. Adenauer Commemoration (2nd issue).

1469	**453**	30pf. black and orange	35	35

454 Cross, Dove and "The Universe"

1968. Catholics' Day.

1470	**454**	20pf. violet, yellow & grn	25	35

455 Northern District 1g. and Southern District 7k. stamps of 1868

1968. Cent of North German Postal Confederation and First Stamps.

1471	**455**	30pf. red, blue and black	25	35

456 Arrows

1968. Cent of German Trade Unions.

1472	**456**	30pf. multicoloured	25	35

457 Doll of 1878

1968. Humanitarian Relief Funds. Mult.

1473	10pf.+5pf. Type **457**	25	25
1474	20pf.+10pf. Doll of 1850	25	25
1475	30pf.+15pf. Doll of 1870	25	25
1476	50pf.+25pf. Doll of 1885	75	1·10

458 Human Rights Emblem

1968. Human Rights Year.

1477	**458**	30pf. multicoloured	25	35

459 Pony

1969. Child Welfare.

1478	**459**	10pf.+5pf. brown, black and yellow	35	45
1479	-	20pf.+10pf. brown, black and buff	35	45
1480	-	30pf.+15pf. brown, black and red	80	90
1481	-	50pf.+25pf. mult	2·00	1·80

HORSES: 20pf. Draught-horse; 30pf. Saddle-horse; 50pf. Thoroughbred.

460 Junkers Ju 52/3m "Boelke"

1969. 50th Anniv of German Airmail Services. Multicoloured.

1482	20pf. Type **460**	45	25
1483	30pf. Boeing 707 airliner	75	25

461 Colonnade

1969. Europa.

1484	**461**	20pf. yellow, grn & bl	40	25
1485	**461**	30pf. yellow, red & violet	45	25

462 "The Five Continents"

1969. 50th Anniv of I.L.O.

1486	**462**	30pf. multicoloured	55	35

463 Eagle Emblems of Weimar and Federal Republics

1969. 20th Anniv of German Federal Republic.

1487	**463**	30pf. black, gold and red	1·20	55

464 "War Graves"

1969. 50th Anniv of German War Graves Commission.

1488	**464**	30pf. blue and yellow	55	35

465 Lakeside Landscape

1969. Nature Protection. Multicoloured.

1489	10pf. Type **465**	25	25
1490	20pf. Highland landscape	75	45
1491	30pf. Alpine landscape	35	25
1492	50pf. River landscape	1·10	65

466 "Running Track"

1969. Olympic Games (1972). Promotion Fund (2nd series). Multicoloured.

1493	10pf.+5pf. Type **466**	20	25
1494	20pf.+10pf. "Hockey"	45	35
1495	30pf.+15pf. "Shooting target"	65	55
1496	50pf.+25pf. "Sailing"	1·40	1·10

467 "Longing for Justice"

1969. 14th German Protestant Congress, Stuttgart.

1497	**467**	30pf. multicoloured	55	35

468 "Electromagnetic Field"

1969. German Radio Exhibition, Stuttgart.

1498	**468**	30pf. multicoloured	55	35

469 Marie Juchacz

1969. "Fifty Years of German Women's Suffrage". Sheet 102×61 mm containing T 469 and similar vert portraits of women politicians.

MS1499 10pf. olive; 20pf. green; 30pf. red — 1·10 — 80

DESIGNS: 20pf. Marie-Elizabeth Luders; 30pf. Helene Weber.

470 Maltese Cross Symbol

1969. "Malteser Hilfsdienst" (welfare organization).

1500	**470**	30pf. red and black	55	35

471 Bavaria 3k. Stamp of 1867

1969. German Philatelic Federation Congress and Exn, Garmisch-Partenkirchen.

1501	**471**	30pf. red and slate	55	35

472 Map of Pipeline

1969. 350th Anniv of Bad Reichenhall–Traunstein Brine Pipeline.

1502	**472**	20pf. multicoloured	55	35

473 Rothenburg ob der Tauber

1969. Tourism.

1503	**473**	30pf. black and red	55	35

See also Nos. 1523, 1558, 1564, 1587, 1606, 1641/2, 1655/6 and 1680/2.

474 Mahatma Gandhi

1969. Birth Centenary of Mahatma Gandhi.

1504	**474**	20pf. black and green	35	35

475 Pope John XXIII

1969. Pope John XXIII Commemoration.

1505	**475**	30pf. red	45	35

476 "Adler" (1835)

1969. Humanitarian Relief Funds. Pewter Figurines. Mult.
(a) Inscr. "WOHLFAHRTSMARKE".

1506	10pf.+5pf. Type **476**	20	20
1507	20pf.+10pf. Woman watering flowers (1780)	25	25
1508	30pf.+15pf. Bird salesman (1850)	40	40
1509	50pf.+25pf. Mounted dignitary (1840)	1·10	1·30

(b) Christmas. Inscr "WEIHNACHTSMARKE".

1510	10pf.+5pf. "Child Jesus in crib" (1850)	35	35

477 E. M. Arndt

1969. Birth Bicent of Ernst Arndt (writer).

1511	**477**	30pf. lake and bistre	45	35

478 "H. von Rugge"

1970. Child Welfare. Minnesinger Themes. Multicoloured.

1512	10pf.+5pf. Type **478**	45	35
1513	20pf.+10pf. "W. von Eschenbach"	75	45
1514	30pf.+15pf. "W. von Metz"	90	70
1515	50pf.+25pf. "W. von der Vogelweide"	2·10	1·80

479 Beethoven

1970. Birth Bicentenaries.

1516	**479**	10pf. black and blue	90	25
1517	-	20pf. black and olive	45	20
1518	-	30pf. black and pink	45	20

DESIGNS: 20pf. G. W. Hegel (philosopher); 30pf. F. Holderlin (poet).

480 Saar 1m. Stamp of 1947

1970. "Sabria 70" Stamp Exn, Saarbrucken.

1519	**480**	30pf. green, black and red	45	35

481 "Flaming Sun"

1970. Europa.

1520	**481**	20pf. green	40	25
1521	**481**	30pf. red	45	25

482 Von Munchhausen on Severed Horse

1970. 250th Birth Anniv of Baron H. von Munchhausen.

1522	**482**	20pf. multicoloured	45	35

1970. Tourism. As T 473, but with view of Oberammergau.

1523	30pf. black and orange	45	35

483 Royal Palace

1970. Olympic Games (1972). Promotion Fund (3rd series).

1524	**483**	10pf.+5pf. brown	25	20
1525	-	20pf.+10pf. turquoise	55	35
1526	-	30pf.+15pf. red	75	55
1527	-	50pf.+25pf. blue	1·30	1·10

DESIGNS (Munich buildings): 20pf. Propylaea; 30pf. Glyptothek; 50pf. "Bavaria" (statue and colonnade).

484 Liner "Kungsholm IV" and Road-tunnel

1970. 75th Anniv of Kiel Canal.

1528	**484**	20pf. multicoloured	45	35

485 Nurse with Invalid

1970. Voluntary Relief Services. Mult.

1529	5pf. Oxygen-lance operator	20	25
1530	10pf. Mountain rescue	25	25
1531	20pf. Type **485**	35	25
1532	30pf. Fireman with hose	90	25
1533	50pf. Road-accident casualty	90	55
1534	70pf. Rescue from drowning	1·10	90

486 President Heinemann

1970

1535	**486**	5pf. black	25	25
1536	**486**	10pf. brown	25	25
1537	**486**	20pf. green	25	25
1538	**486**	25pf. green	35	25
1539	**486**	30pf. brown	35	25
1540	**486**	40pf. orange	35	25
1541	**486**	50pf. blue	1·60	25
1542	**486**	60pf. blue	65	25
1543	**486**	70pf. brown	90	35
1544	**486**	80pf. green	90	35
1545	**486**	90pf. red	1·60	1·50
1546	**486**	1Dm. green	1·10	45
1547	**486**	110pf. grey	1·30	70
1548	**486**	120pf. brown	1·40	90
1549	**486**	130pf. brown	1·60	90
1550	**486**	140pf. green	1·70	1·10
1551	**486**	150pf. red	1·70	70
1552	**486**	160pf. orange	2·40	1·20
1553	**486**	170pf. orange	2·00	70
1554	**486**	190pf. purple	2·75	90
1555	**486**	2Dm. violet	2·30	45

487 Illuminated Cross

1970. Catholic Church World Mission.

1556	**487**	20pf. yellow and green	35	25

488 Stylized Cross

1970. Catholics Day and 83rd German Catholic Congress, Trier.

1557	**488**	20pf. multicoloured	35	25

1970. Tourism. As T 473.

1558	20pf. black and green	55	35

DESIGN: 20pf. View of Cochem.

489 "Jester"

1970. Humanitarian Relief Funds. Puppets. Multicoloured. (a) Relief Funds.

1559	10pf.+5pf. Type **489**	25	25
1560	20pf.+10pf. "Buffoon"	25	35
1561	30pf.+15pf. "Clown"	45	45
1562	50pf.+25pf. "Harlequin"	1·20	1·10

(b) Christmas.

1563	10pf.+5pf. "Angel"	35	25

1970. Tourism. As T 473, but with view of Freiburg im Breisgau.

1564	20pf. brown and green	55	35

490 A. J. Comenius (scholar)

1970. Int Education Year and 300th Death Anniv of Comenius (Jan Komensky).

1565	**490**	30pf. red and black	55	35

491 Engels as Young Man

1970. 150th Birth Anniv of Friedrich Engels.

1566	**491**	50pf. blue and red	1·60	90

492 German Eagle

1971. Centenary of German Unification.

1567	**492**	30pf. black, red & orange	1·60	35

493 "Ebert" Stamp of 1928 and inscr "To the German People"

1971. Birth Centenary of Friedrich Ebert (Chancellor 1918 and President 1919–25).

1568	**493**	30pf. green, black and red	1·60	35

494 "King of Blackamoors"

1971. Child Welfare. Children's Drawings. Multicoloured.

1569	10pf.+5pf. Type **494**	35	35
1570	20pf.+10pf. "Flea"	45	45
1571	30pf.+15pf. "Puss-in-Boots"	75	70
1572	50pf.+25pf. "Serpent"	1·30	1·20

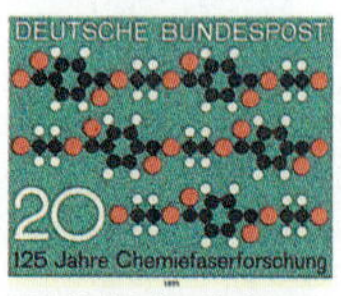

495 Molecular Chain

1971. 125 Years of Chemical Fibre Research.

1573	**495**	20pf. black, red & green	35	25

496 Road-crossing Patrol

1971. New Road Traffic Regulations (1st series).

1574	**496**	10pf. black, blue and red	20	20
1575	-	20pf. black, red & green	40	25
1576	-	30pf. red, black and grey	55	25
1577	-	50pf. black, blue and red	90	65

ROAD SIGNS: 20pf. "Right-of-way across junction"; 30pf. "STOP"; 50pf. "Pedestrian Crossing".

See also Nos. 1579/82.

497 Luther before Charles V

1971. 450th Anniv of Diet of Worms.

1578	**497**	30pf. black and red	75	35

1971. New Traffic Regulations (2nd series). Horiz designs similar to T 496.

1579	5pf. red, black and blue	20	20
1580	10pf. multicoloured	25	20
1581	20pf. red, black and green	45	20
1582	30pf. yellow, black and red	80	20

NEW HIGHWAY CODE: 5pf. Overtaking; 10pf. Warning of obstruction; 20pf. Lane discipline; 30pf. Pedestrian Crossing.

498 Europa Chain

1971. Europa.

1583	**498**	20pf. gold, green & black	35	25
1584	**498**	30pf. gold, red and black	45	25

499 Thomas a Kempis writing "The Imitation of Christ"

1971. 500th Death Anniv of Thomas a Kempis (devotional writer).

1585	**499**	30pf. black and red	65	35

500 Durer's Monogram

1971. 500th Birth Anniv of Albrecht Durer.

1586	**500**	30pf. brown & red	1·50	35

1971. Tourism. As T 473, but with view of Nuremburg.

1587	30pf. black and red	55	35

501 Meeting Emblem

1971. Whitsun Ecumenical Meeting, Augsburg.

1588	**501**	30pf. black, orange & red	55	35

502 Ski Jumping

1971. Olympic Games (1972). Promotion Fund (4th series). Winter Games, Sapporo.

1589	**502**	10pf.+5pf. black & brn	25	20
1590	-	20pf.+10pf. black & grn	55	40
1591	-	30pf.+15pf. black & red	1·00	75
1592	-	50pf.+25pf. black & bl	1·80	1·50
MS1593		112×66 mm. Nos. 1589/92	3·75	3·00

DESIGNS: 20pf. Ice dancing; 30pf. Skiing start; 50pf. Ice hockey.

503 Astronomical Calculus

1971. 400th Birth Anniv of Johann Kepler (astronomer).

1594	**503**	30pf. gold, red and black	65	35

504 Dante

1971. 650th Death Anniv of Dante Alighieri.

1595	**504**	10pf. black	25	25

505 Alcohol and front of Car ("Don't Drink and Drive")

1971. Accident Prevention.

1596	-	5pf. orange	25	20
1597	-	10pf. brown	25	20
1598	-	20pf. violet	35	20
1599	**505**	25pf. green	45	20
1600	-	30pf. red	45	20
1601	-	40pf. mauve	45	20
1602	-	50pf. blue	2·50	20
1603	-	60pf. blue	1·80	55
1603a	-	70pf. blue and green	1·40	35
1604	-	1Dm. green	2·30	25
1605	-	1Dm.50 brown	6·50	1·30

DESIGNS: 5pf. Man within flame, and spent match ("Fire Prevention"); 10pf. Fall from ladder; 20pf. Unguarded machinery ("Factory Safety"); 30pf. Falling brick and protective helmet; 40pf. Faulty electric plug; 50pf. Protruding nail in plank; 60pf., 70pf. Ball in front of car ("Child Road Safety"); 1Dm. Crate on hoist; 1Dm.50, Open manhole.

1971. Tourism. As T 473 but with view of Goslar.

1606	20pf. black and green	55	45

506 Women churning Butter

1971. Humanitarian Relief Funds. Wooden Toys. Mult. (a) Inscr. "WOHLFAHRTSMARKE".

1607	20pf.+10pf. Type **506**	25	20
1608	25pf.+10pf. Horseman on wheels	25	20
1609	30pf.+15pf. Nutcracker man	55	55
1610	60pf.+30pf. Dovecote	1·50	1·40

(b) Christmas. Inscr "WEIHNACHTSMARKE".

1611	20pf.+10pf. Angel with three candles	55	45

507 Deaconess and Nurse

1972. Death Cent of Johann Wilhelm Lohe (founder of Deaconesses Mission, Neuendettelsau).

1612	**507**	25pf. slate, black & green	55	35

508 Ducks crossing Road

1972. Child Welfare. Annimal Protection. Multicoloured.

1613	20pf.+10pf. Type **508**	70	55
1614	25pf.+10pf. Hunter scaring deer	45	35
1615	30pf.+15pf. Child protecting bird from cat	90	90
1616	60pf.+30pf. Boy annoying mute swans	1·80	1·90

509 Senefelder's Press

1972. "175 Years of Offset Lithography".

1617	**509**	25pf. multicoloured	55	35

510 "Communica-tions"

1972. Europa.

1618	**510**	25pf. multicoloured	45	20
1619	**510**	30pf. multicoloured	55	25

511 Lucas Cranach

1972. 500th Birth Anniv of Lucas Cranach the Elder (painter).

1620	**511**	25pf. black, stone & grn	65	35

512 Wrestling

1972. Olympic Games, Munich (5th series). Multicoloured.

1621	20pf.+10pf. Type **512**	55	45
1622	25pf.+10pf. Sailing	55	45
1623	30pf.+15pf. Gymnastics	55	45
1624	60pf.+30pf. Swimming	2·00	1·80

See also Nos. 1629/32.

513 Gymnastics Stadium

1972. Olympic Games, Munich (6th series). Sheet 148×105 mm containing T 513 and similar multicoloured designs.

MS1625 25pf.+10pf. Type **513**; 30pf.+15pf. Athletics stadium; 40pf.+20pf. Tented area; 70pf.+35pf. TV tower 5·50 5·25

514 Invalid Archer

1972. 21st Int Games for the Paralysed, Heidelberg.

1626	**514**	40pf. red, black & yellow	75	35

515 Posthorn and Decree

1972. Cent of German Postal Museum.

1627	**515**	40pf. multicoloured	1·00	35

516 K. Schumacher

1972. 20th Death Anniv of Kurt Schumacher (politician).

1628	**516**	40pf. black and red	1·50	35

1972. Olympic Games, Munich (7th series). As Type 512. Multicoloured.

1629	25pf.+5pf. Long jumping	55	55
1630	30pf.+10pf. Basketball	1·50	1·40
1631	40pf.+10pf. Throwing the discus	2·00	1·90
1632	70pf.+10pf. Canoeing	1·00	95
MS1633	111×66 mm. Nos. 1629/32	5·50	5·25

517 Open Book

1972. International Book Year.

1634	**517**	40pf. multicoloured	75	35

518 Music and Signature

1972. 300th Death Anniv of Heinrich Schutz (composer).

1635	**518**	40pf. multicoloured	90	35

519 Knight

1972. Humanitarian Relief Funds. Mult. (a) 19th-century Faience Chessmen. Inscr "WOHLFAHRTSMARKE".

1636	25pf.+10pf. Type **519**	35	35
1637	30pf.+15pf. Rook	35	25
1638	40pf.+20pf. Queen	65	25
1639	70pf.+35pf. King	2·30	2·20

(b) Christmas. Inscr "WEIHNACHTSMARKE".

1640	30pf.+15pf. "The Three Wise Men" (horiz)	80	55

1972. Tourism. As T 473.

1641	30pf. black and green	55	25
1642	40pf. black and orange	65	25

VIEWS: 30pf. Heligoland; 40pf. Heidelberg.

520 Revellers

1972. 150th Anniv of Cologne Carnival.

1643	**520**	40pf. multicoloured	1·10	35

521 H. Heine

1972. 175th Birth Anniv of Heinrich Heine (poet).

1644	**521**	40pf. black, red and pink	1·10	35

522 "Brot fur die Welt"

1972. Freedom from Hunger Campaign.

1645	**522**	30pf. red and green	55	55

523 Wurzburg Cathedral (seal)

1972. Catholic Synod '72.

1646	**523**	40pf. black, purple & red	65	35

524 National Colours of France and Germany

1973. 10th Anniv of Franco-German Treaty.

1647	**524**	40pf. multicoloured	1·50	35

525 Osprey

1973. Youth Welfare. Birds of Prey. Multicoloured.

1648	25pf.+10pf. Type **525**	1·10	90
1649	30pf.+15pf. Common buzzard	1·40	1·10
1650	40pf.+20pf. Red kite	2·00	1·80
1651	70pf.+35pf. Montagu's harrier	4·50	4·00

526 Copernicus

1973. 500th Birth Anniv of Copernicus.

1652	**526**	40pf. black and red	1·50	35

527 Radio Mast and Transmission

1973. 50th Anniv of Interpol.

1653	**527**	40pf. black, red and grey	60	35

528 Weather Chart

1973. Cent of Int Meteorological Organization.

1654	**528**	30pf. multicoloured	50	35

1973. Tourism. As T 473.

1655	40pf. black and red	1·10	25
1656	40pf. black and orange	90	25

VIEWS: No. 1655, Hamburg; 1656, Rudesheim.

529 "Gymnast" (poster)

1973. Gymnastics Festival, Stuttgart.

1657	**529**	40pf. multicoloured	55	35

530 Kassel (Hesse) Sign

1973. "I.B.R.A. Munchen 73" International Stamp Exhibition, Munich. F.I.P. Congress. Post-house Signs. Multicoloured.

1658	40pf.+20pf. Type **530**	90	90
1659	70pf.+35pf. Prussia	1·60	1·50
MS1660	74×105 mm. 40pf.+20pf. Wurttemberg; 70pf.+35pf. Kurpfalz (Bavaria) (sold at 2.20Dm.)	4·25	4·75

531 Europa "Posthorn"

1973. Europa.

1661	**531**	30pf. yell, myrtle & grn	65	25
1662	**531**	40pf. yellow, lake & pink	70	25

532 "R" Motif

1973. 1000th Death Anniv of Roswitha von Gandersheim (poetess).

1663	**532**	40pf. yellow, black & red	65	35

533 M. Kolbe

1973. Father Maximilian Kolbe (Concentration camp victim) Commemoration.

1664	**533**	40pf. red, brown & black	65	35

534 "Profile" (from poster)

1973. 15th German Protestant Church Conference.

1665	**534**	30pf. multicoloured	45	25

535 Environmental Conference Emblem and Waste

1973. "Protection of the Environment". Multicoloured.
1666 25pf. Type **535** 45 25
1667 30pf. Emblem and "Water" 45 25
1668 40pf. Emblem and "Noise" 90 25
1669 70pf. Emblem and "Air" 1·60 80

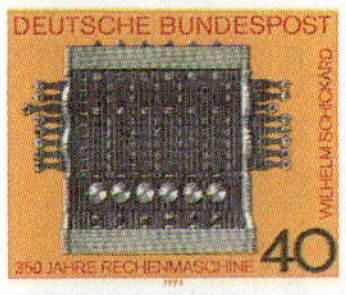

536 Schickard's Calculating Machine

1973. 350th Anniv of Schickard's Calculating Machine.
1670 **536** 40pf. black, red and orange 55 50

537 Otto Wels

1973. Birth Centenary of Otto Wels (Social Democratic Party leader).
1671 **537** 40pf. purple and lilac 65 35

538 Lubeck Cathedral

1973. 800th Anniv of Lubeck Cathedral.
1672 **538** 40pf. multicoloured 1·10 35

539 U.N. and German Eagle Emblems

1973. Admission of German Federal Republic to U.N. Organization.
1673 **539** 40pf. multicoloured 1·60 35

540 French Horn

1973. Humanitarian Relief Funds. Multicoloured. (a) Musical Instruments. Inscr "WOHLFAHRTSMARKE".
1674 25pf.+10pf. Type **540** 70 35
1675 30pf.+15pf. Grand piano 75 35
1676 40pf.+20pf. Violin 90 60
1677 70pf.+70pf. Harp 2·30 1·80

(b) Christmas. Inscr "WEIHNACHTSMARKE".
1678 30pf.+15pf. Christmas star 75 55

541 Radio set of 1923

1973. "50 Years of German Broadcasting".
1679 **541** 30pf. multicoloured 45 25

1974. Tourism. As Type 473.
1680 30pf. black and green 75 22·00
1681 40pf. black and red 75 20
1682 40pf. black and red 75 20
VIEWS: No. 1680, Saarbrucken; 1681, Aachen; 1682, Bremen.

542 Louise Otto-Peters

1974. Women in German Politics. Each black and orange.
1683 40pf. Type **542** 75 55
1684 40pf. Helene Lange 75 55
1685 40pf. Rosa Luxemburg 75 55
1686 40pf. Gertrud Baumer 75 55

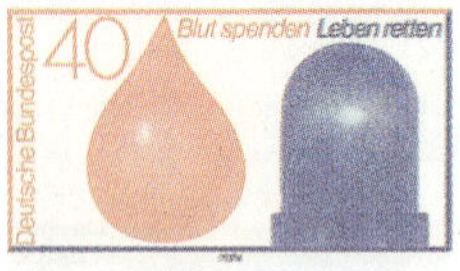

543 Drop of Blood and Emergency Light

1974. Blood Donor and Accident/Rescue Services.
1687 **543** 40pf. red and blue 1·00 35

544 "Deer in Red" (Franz Marc)

1974. German Expressionist Paintings. Mult.
1688 30pf. Type **544** 50 25
1689 30pf. "Girls under Trees" (A. Macke) 75 30
1690 40pf. "Portrait in Blue" (A. von Jawiensky) (vert) 75 25
1691 50pf. "Pechstein asleep" (E. Heckel) (vert) 80 30
1692 70pf. "Still Life with Telescope" (Max Beckmann) 1·10 95
1693 120pf. "Old Peasant" (L. Kirchner) (vert) 2·20 2·00

545 St. Thomas teaching Pupils

1974. 700th Death Anniv of St. Thomas Aquinas.
1694 **545** 40pf. black and red 65 35

546 Disabled Persons in Outline

1974. Rehabilitation of the Handicapped.
1695 **546** 40pf. red and black 1·00 35

547 Construction (Bricklayer)

1974. Youth Welfare. Youth Activities. Multicoloured.
1696 25pf.+10pf. Type **547** 65 55
1697 30pf.+15pf. Folk dancing 1·10 90
1698 40pf.+20pf. Study 1·80 1·60
1699 70pf.+35pf. Research 3·25 3·25

548 "Ascending Youth" (W. Lehmbruck)

1974. Europa.
1700 **548** 30pf. black, green & sil 65 25
1701 - 40pf. black, red and lilac 70 25
DESIGN: 40pf. "Kneeling Woman" (W. Lehmbruck).

549 Immanuel Kant

1974. 250th Birth Anniv of Immanuel Kant (philosopher).
1702 **549** 90pf. red 2·30 55

550 Federal Arms and National Colours

1974. 25th Anniv of Formation of Federal Republic. Sheet 94×64 mm.
MS1703 **550** 40pf. multicoloured 1·50 1·80

551 Country Road

1974. Rambling, and Birth Centenaries of Richard Schirrman and Wilhelm Munker (founders of Youth Hostelling Assn).
1704 **551** 30pf. multicoloured 50 35

552 Friedrich Klopstock

1974. 250th Birth Anniv of Friedrich Gottlieb Klopstock (poet).
1705 **552** 40pf. black and red 65 25

553 "Crowned Cross" Symbol

1974. 125th Anniv of German Protestant Church Diaconal Association (charitable organization).
1706 **553** 40p. multicoloured 60 35

554 Goalkeeper saving Goal

1974. World Cup Football Championship. Multicoloured.
1707 30pf. Type **554** 1·00 25
1708 40pf. Mid-field melee 2·00 25

555 Hans Holbein (self-portrait)

1974. 450th Death Anniv of Hans Holbein the Elder (painter).
1709 **555** 50pf. black and red 90 35

556 Broken Bars of Prison Window

1974. Amnesty International Commemoration.
1710 **556** 70pf. black and blue 1·20 55

557 "Man and Woman looking at the Moon"

1974. Birth Bicentenary of Caspar David Friedrich (artist).
1711 **557** 50pf. multicoloured 1·20 35

558 Campion

1974. Humanitarian Relief Funds. Flowers. Multicoloured. (a) 25th Anniv of Welfare Stamps. Inscr "25 JAHRE WOHLFAHRTSMARKE".
1712 30pf.+15pf. Type **558** 35 35
1713 40pf.+20pf. Foxglove 45 35
1714 50pf.+25pf. Mallow 55 45
1715 70pf.+35pf. Campanula 1·60 1·50

(b) Christmas. Inscr "WEIHNACHTSMARKE".
1716 40pf.+20pf. Poinsettia 90 70

559 Early German Post-boxes

1974. Cent of Universal Postal Union.
1717 **559** 50pf. multicoloured 1·50 45

560 Annette Kolb

1975. International Women's Year. Women Writers.
1718 30pf. Type **560** 75 35
1719 40pf. Ricarda Huch 65 35
1720 50pf. Else Lasker-Schuler 65 35
1721 70pf. Gertrud von le Fort 1·10 1·10

561 Hans Bockler (Trade Union leader)

1975. Birth Centenaries.

1722	**561**	40pf. black and green	80	35
1723	-	50pf. black and red	75	35
1724	-	70pf. black and blue	2·30	90

DESIGNS: 50pf. Matthias Erzberger (statesman); 70pf. Albert Schweitzer (medical missionary).

562 Mother and Child and Emblem

1975. 25th Anniv of Organization for the Rest and Recuperation of Mothers.

1725	**562**	50pf. multicoloured	80	35

563 Detail of Ceiling Painting, Sistine Chapel

1975. 500th Birth Anniv of Michelangelo.

1726	**563**	70pf. black and blue	1·70	1·40

564 Plan of St. Peter's, Rome within a cross

1975. "Holy Year (Year of Reconcillation)".

1727	**564**	50pf. multicoloured	80	35

565 Ice Hockey

1975. World Ice Hockey Championships, Munich and Dusseldorf.

1728	**565**	50pf. multicoloured	1·20	35

566 Class 218 Diesel Locomotive

1975. Youth Welfare. Railway Locomotives. Multicoloured.

1729	30pf.+15pf. Type **566**	55	45
1730	40pf.+20pf. Class 103 electric locomotive	80	75
1731	50pf.+25pf. Class 403 electric railcar	1·20	1·10
1732	70pf.+35pf. Transrapid Maglev train (model)	2·10	1·80

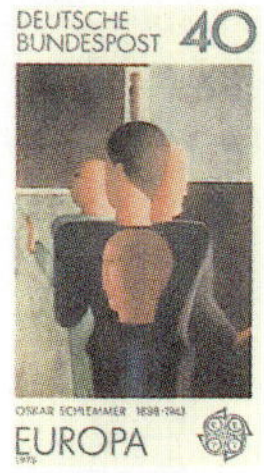

567 "Concentric Group"

1975. Europa. Paintings by Oskar Schlemmer. Multicoloured.

1733	40pf. Type **567**	65	25
1734	50pf. "Bauhaus Staircase"	80	25

568 Morike's Silhouette and Signature

1975. Death Cent of Eduard Morike (writer).

1735	**568**	40pf. multicoloured	60	25

569 "Nuis" (woodcarving)

1975. 500th Anniv of Siege of Neuss.

1736	**569**	50pf. multicoloured	90	35

570 Jousting Contest

1975. 500th Anniv of "Landshut Wedding" (festival).

1737	**570**	50pf. multicoloured	1·10	35

571 Mainz Cathedral

1975. Millenary of Mainz Cathedral.

1738	**571**	40pf. multicoloured	1·10	35

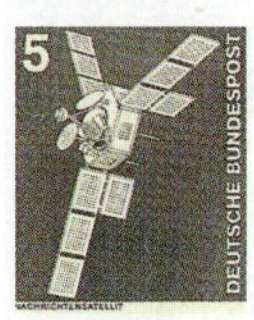

572 Tele-communica-tion Satellite

1975. Industry and Technology.

1739	**572**	5pf. green	15	15
1740	-	10pf. mauve	15	15
1741	-	20pf. red	20	15
1742	-	30pf. lilac	25	15
1743	-	40pf. green	35	20
1744	-	50pf. mauve	45	20
1745	-	60pf. red	65	25
1746	-	70pf. blue	80	25
1747	-	80pf. green	90	25
1748	-	100pf. brown	1·00	25
1748a	-	110pf. purple	1·80	70
1749	-	120pf. blue	1·30	45
1749a	-	130pf. red	2·30	70
1750	-	140pf. red	1·40	45
1751	-	150pf. red	3·00	90
1752	-	160pf. green	2·00	70
1753	-	180pf. brown	2·30	90
1753a	-	190pf. brown	2·75	70
1754	-	200pf. purple	2·00	35
1754a	-	230pf. purple	3·25	1·10
1754b	-	250pf. green	4·00	1·70
1754c	-	300pf. green	4·50	1·70
1755	-	500pf. black	5·50	1·30

DESIGNS: 10pf. Electric train; 20pf. Modern lighthouse; 30pf. MBB-Bolkow Bo 105C rescue helicopter; 40pf. Space laboratory; 50pf. Dish aerial; 60pf. X-ray apparatus; 70pf. Ship-building; 80pf. Farm tractor; 100pf. Lignite excavator; 110pf. Colour television camera; 120pf. Chemical plant; 130pf. Brewery plant; 140pf. Power station; 150, 190pf. Mechanical shovel; 160pf. Blast furnace; 180pf. Wheel loader; 200pf. Marine drilling platform; 230, 250pf. Frankfurt Airport; 300pf. Electromagnetic monorail; 500pf. Radio telescope.

573 Town Hall and Market, Alsfeld

1975. European Architectural Heritage Year. German Buildings. Multicoloured.

1756	50pf. Type **573**	90	65
1757	50pf. Plonlein corner, Siebers tower and Kobelzeller gate, Rothenburg-on-Tauber	90	65
1758	50pf. Town Hall ("The Steipe") Trier	90	65
1759	50pf. View of Xanten	90	65

574 Effects of Drug-taking

1975. Campaign to Fight the Abuse of Drugs and Intoxicants.

1760	**574**	40pf. multicoloured	50	35

575 Posthouse Sign, Royal Prussian Establishment for Transport 1776

1975. Stamp Day.

1761	**575**	10pf. multicoloured	45	25

576 Edelweiss

1975. Humanitarian Relief Funds. Alpine Flowers. Multicoloured. (a) Inscr "Wohlfartsmarke 1975".

1762	30pf.+15pf. Type **576**	45	35
1763	40pf.+20pf. Trollflower	45	35
1764	50pf.+25pf. Alpine rose	75	55
1765	70pf.+35pf. Pasque-flower	1·80	1·60

(b) Inscr "Weihnachtsmarke 1975".

1766	40pf.+20pf. Christmas rose	1·10	95

See also Nos. 1796/9, 1839/42, 1873/6 and 1905/8.

577 Gustav Stresemann (statesman)

1975. German Nobel Peace Prize Winners. Sheet 100×70 mm containing T 577 and similar vert designs in black.

MS1767 50pf. Type **577**; 50pf. Ludwig Quidde (Reichstag deputy); 50pf. Carl von Ossietzky (journalist)	2·30	2·20

578 Stylized Ski-runners

1976. Winter Olympic Games, Innsbruck.

1768	**578**	50pf. multicoloured	1·10	35

579 Konrad Adenauer

1976. Birth Centenary of Konrad Adenauer (Chancellor 1949–63).

1769	**579**	50pf. green	2·20	35

580 Cover Pages from Hans Sachs' Books

1976. 400th Death Anniv of Hans Sachs (poet and composer).

1770	**580**	40pf. multicoloured	75	35

581 Junkers F-13 "Herta"

1976. 50th Anniv of Lufthansa (German civil airline).

1771	**581**	50pf. multicoloured	1·10	35

582 Emblem and Commemorative Inscription

1976. 25th Anniv of Federal Constitutional Court.

1772	**582**	50pf. multicoloured	90	35

583 Letters "E G" representing Steel Girders

1976. 25th Anniv of European Coal and Steel Community.

1773	**583**	40pf. multicoloured	90	35

584 Monorail Train

1976. 75th Anniv of Wuppertal Monorailway.

1774	**584**	50pf. multicoloured	90	35

585 Basketball

1976. Youth Welfare. Training for the Olympics. Multicoloured.

1775	30pf.+15pf. Type **585**	55	35
1776	40pf.+20pf. Rowing	1·00	70
1777	50pf.+25pf. Gymnastics	1·30	1·10
1778	70pf.+35pf. Volleyball	1·70	1·50

586 Swimming

1976. Olympic Games, Montreal. Mult.

1779	40pf.+25pf. Type **586**	90	65
1780	50pf.+25pf. High jumping	1·30	95

MS1781 110×70 mm. 30pf.+15pf. black, orange-red and pale yellow; 70pf. + 35pf. black, new blue and pale blue 2·20 1·80

DESIGNS: 30pf. Hockey; 50pf. High jumping; 70pf. Rowing four.

587 Girl selling Trinkets and Copperplate Prints

1976. Europa. Ludwigsburg China Figures. Multicoloured.

1782	40pf. Type **587**	65	25
1783	50pf. Boy selling copperplate prints	70	25

588 Carl Sonnenschein

1976. Birthday Centenary of Dr. Carl Sonnenschein (clergyman).

1784	**588**	50pf. multicoloured	75	35

589 Opening bars of Hymn "Entrust Yourself to God"

1976. 300th Birth Anniv of Paul Gerhardt (composer).

1785	**589**	40pf. multicoloured	50	25

590 Carl Maria von Weber conducting

1976. 150th Death Anniv of Carl Maria von Weber (composer).

1786	**590**	50pf. black and brown	90	35

591 Carl Schurz

1976. Bicent of American Revolution.

1787	**591**	70pf. multicoloured	1·20	45

592 Wagnerian Stage

1976. Centenary of Bayreuth Festival.

1788	**592**	50pf. multicoloured	1·50	35

593 Bronze Ritual Chariot

1976. Archaeological Heritage. Mult.

1789	30pf. Type **593**	45	35
1790	40pf. Gold-ornamental bowl	65	35
1791	50pf. Silver necklet	90	55
1792	120pf. Roman gold goblet	2·10	1·90

594 Golden Plover

1976. Bird Protection.

1793	**594**	50pf. multicoloured	1·30	35

595 Mythical Creature

1976. 300th Death Anniv of J. J. C. von Grimmelshausen (writer).

1794	**595**	40pf. multicoloured	1·30	35

596 18th-century Posthouse Sign, Hochst-am-Main

1976. Stamp Day.

1795	**596**	10pf. multicoloured	35	25

1976. Humanitarian Relief Funds. Garden Flowers. Designs similar to T 576. Multicoloured.

1796	30pf.+15pf. Phlox	55	45
1797	40pf.+20pf. Marigolds	75	60
1798	50pf.+25pf. Dahlias	80	70
1799	70pf.+35pf. Pansies	1·40	1·30

597 Sophie Schroder ("Sappho")

1976. Famous German Actresses. Mult.

1800	30pf. Carolin Neuber ("Medea")	55	25
1801	40pf. Type **597**	55	25
1802	50pf. Louise Dumont ("Hedda Gabler")	80	45
1803	70pf. Hermine Korner ("Macbeth")	1·40	1·10

598 "Madonna and Child" ("Marienfenster" window, Frauenkirche, Esslingen)

1976. Christmas. Sheet 71×101 mm.

MS1804 **598** 50pf.+25pf. multicoloured 1·10 90

599 Eltz Castle

1977. German Castles.

1805	-	10pf. blue	20	15
1805c	-	20pf. orange	20	15
1805d	-	25pf. red	45	25
1806	-	30pf. bistre	45	20
1806c	-	35pf. red	65	35
1807	**599**	40pf. green	55	15
1807a	-	40pf. brown	55	25
1808	-	50pf. red	70	20
1808b	-	50pf. green	75	25
1809	-	60pf. brown	1·10	20
1809a	-	60pf. red	75	35
1810	-	70pf. blue	1·10	35
1810a	-	80pf. green	1·20	25
1810c	-	90pf. blue	1·40	45
1810d	-	120pf. violet	1·80	60
1811	-	190pf. red	2·30	95
1812	-	200pf. green	3·00	95
1812a	-	210pf. brown	3·75	1·30
1812b	-	230pf. green	3·75	1·30
1812c	-	280pf. blue	3·75	60
1812d	-	300pf. orange	4·50	45

DESIGNS: 10pf. Glucksburg; 20, 190pf. Pfaueninsel, Berlin; 25pf. Gemen; 30pf. Ludwigstein, Werratal; 35pf. Lichtenstein; 40pf. (1807a) Wolfsburg; 50pf. (1808) Neuschwanstein; 50pf. (1808b) Inzlingen; 60pf. (1809) Marksburg; 60pf. (1809a) Rheydt; 70pf. Mespelbrunn; 80pf. Wilhelmsthal; 90pf. Vischering; 120pf. Charlottenburg, Berlin; 200pf. Burresheim; 210pf. Schwanenburg; 230pf. Lichtenberg; 280pf. Ahrensburg; 300pf. Herrenhausen, Hanover.

600 Palais de l'Europe

1977. Inauguration of Palais de l'Europe (Council of Europe buildings), Strasbourg.

1813	**600**	140pf. green and black	2·10	65

601 Book Illustrations

1977. "Till Eulenspiegel" (popular fable).

1814	**601**	50pf. multicoloured	70	35

602 Floral Ornament

1977. German "Nouveau" Art. Sheet 116×86 mm containing T 602 and similar vert designs. Multicoloured.

MS1815 30pf. Type **602**; 70pf. Woman's head; 90pf. Chair 2·50 1·80

603 Jean Monnet

1977. Award of "Citizen of Europe" honour to Jean Monnet (French statesman).

1816	**603**	50pf. black, grey & yell	75	35

604 "Flower"

1977. 25th Anniv of Federal Horticultural Show.

1817	**604**	50pf. multicoloured	1·00	35

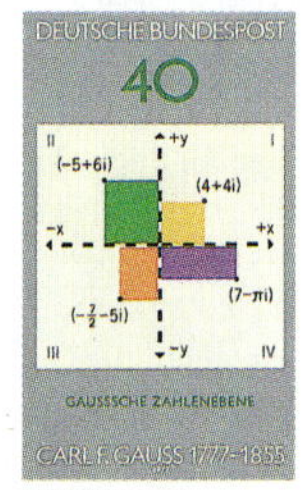

605 Plane of Complex Numbers

1977. Birth Bicentenary of Carl Friedrich Gauss (mathematician).

1818	**605**	40pf. multicoloured	1·50	35

606 "Wappen von Hamburg" (warship)

1977. Youth Welfare. Ships. Multicoloured.

1819	30pf.+15pf. Type **606**	65	60
1820	40pf.+20pf. "Preussen" (full-rigged sailing ship)	80	70
1821	50pf.+25pf. "Bremen" (liner)	1·10	95
1822	70pf.+35pf. "Sturmfels" (container ship)	1·60	1·50

607 Head of Barbarossa

1977. Staufer Year, Baden-Wurttemberg.

1823	**607**	40pf. multicoloured	1·50	35

608 Rhon Autobahn

1977. Europa.

1824	**608**	40pf. black and green	75	25
1825	-	50pf. black and red	80	25

DESIGN: 50pf. Rhine landscape.

609 "Self-Portrait" (Rubens)

1977. 400th Birth Anniv of Peter Paul Rubens.

1826	**609**	30pf. black	1·00	35

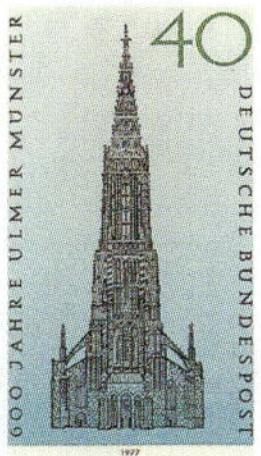

610 Ulm Cathedral

1977. 600th Anniv of Ulm Cathedral.

1827	**610**	40pf. brown, green & bl	80	35

611 Rector's Seal, Mainz University (500th Anniv)

1977. University Anniversaries.

1828	**611**	50pf. black and red	90	35
1829	-	50pf. black and red	1·00	35
1830	-	50pf. black and red	1·20	35

DESIGNS: No. 1829, Great Seal, Marburg University (450th anniv); No. 1830, Great Seal, Tubingen University (500th anniv).

612 "Morning"

1977. Birth Bicentenary of Phillipp Otto Runge (artist).

1831	**612**	60pf. multicoloured	1·00	45

613 Ketteler's Coat of Arms

1977. Death Centenary of Bishop Wilhelm Emmanuel von Ketteler.

1832	**613**	50pf. multicoloured	80	35

614 Fritz von Bodelschwingh

1977. Birth Centenary of Pastor Fritz von Bodelschwingh (pioneer of welfare work for the disabled).

1833	**614**	50pf. multicoloured	90	35

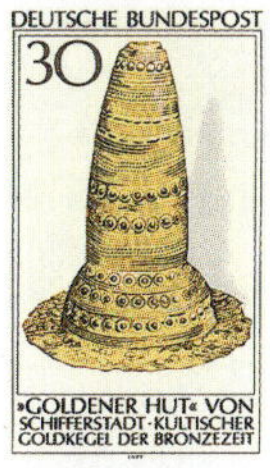

615 Golden Hat

1977. Archaeological Heritage. Multicoloured.

1834		30pf. Type **615**	45	35
1835		120pf. Gilt helmet	1·80	1·30
1836		200pf. Bronze centaur head	2·50	2·20

616 Operator and Switchboard

1977. Centenary of Telephone in Germany.

1837	**616**	50pf. multicoloured	1·30	35

617 19th-century Posthouse Sign, Hamburg

1977. Stamp Day.

1838	**617**	10pf. multicoloured	50	25

1977. Humanitarian Relief Funds. Meadow Flowers. As T 576. Multicoloured.

1839		30pf.+15pf. Caraway	45	35
1840		40pf.+20pf. Dandelion	55	45
1841		50pf.+25pf. Red clover	70	65
1842		70pf.+35pf. Meadow sage	1·40	1·30

618 Travelling Surgeon

1977. 250th Death Anniv of Dr. Johann Andreas Eisenbarth.

1843	**618**	50pf. multicoloured	90	35

619 Wilhelm Hauff

1977. 150th Death Anniv of Wilhelm Hauff (poet and novelist).

1844	**619**	40pf. multicoloured	55	25

620 "King presenting Gift" (stained glass window, Basilica of St. Gereon, Cologne)

1977. Christmas. Sheet 70×105 mm.

MS1845	**620**	50pf.+25pf. multicoloured	1·00	95

621 Book Cover Designs

1978. Birth Centenary of Rudolph Alexander Schroder (writer).

1846	**621**	50pf. multicoloured	75	35

622 Refugees

1978. 20th Anniv of Friedland Aid Society.

1847	**622**	50pf. multicoloured	75	35

623 Skiing

1978. Sport Promotion Fund. Multicoloured.

1848		50pf.+25pf. Type **623**	1·60	1·30
1849		70pf.+35pf. Show jumping	3·50	3·00

624 Gerhart Hauptmann

1978. German Winners of Nobel Prize for Literature. Multicoloured.

1850		30pf. Type **624**	45	20
1851		50pf. Hermann Hesse	65	35
1852		70pf. Thomas Mann	90	60
MS1853		120×70 mm. Nos. 1850/2	2·20	1·60

625 Martin Buber

1978. Birth Centenary of Martin Buber (religious philosopher).

1854	**625**	50pf. multicoloured	75	35

626 Museum Tower and Cupola

1978. 75th Anniv of German Scientific and Technical Museum, Munich.

1855	**626**	50pf. black, yellow & red	75	35

627 Wilhelmine Reichart's Balloon, Munich October Festival, 1820

1978. Youth Welfare. Aviation History (1st series). Multicoloured.

1856		30pf.+15pf. Type **627**	65	55
1857		40pf.+20pf. Airship LZ-1, 1900	80	70
1858		50pf.+25pf. Bleriot XI mono-plane, 1909	1·10	95
1859		70pf.+35pf. Hans Grade's mono-plane, 1909	1·40	1·30

See also Nos. 1886/9 and 1918/21.

628 Old Town Hall, Bamberg

1978. Europa. Multicoloured.

1860		40pf. Type **628**	75	25
1861		50pf. Old Town Hall, Regens-burg	1·10	25
1862		70pf. Old Town Hall, Esslingen am Neckar	1·40	90

629 Piper and Children

1978. Pied Piper of Hamelin.

1863	**629**	50pf. multicoloured	1·00	35

630 Janusz Korczak

1978. Birth Centenary of Janusz Korczak (educational reformer).

1864	**630**	90pf. multicoloured	1·30	60

631 Fossil Bat

1978. Archaeological Heritage, Fossils. Mult.

1865		80pf. Type **631**	1·80	1·60
1866		200pf. Horse ("eohippus") skeleton	2·10	2·00

632 Parliament Building, Bonn

1978. 65th Interparliamentary Union Conference, Bonn.

1867	**632**	70pf. multicoloured	1·30	45

633 Rose Window, Freiburg Minster

1978. 85th Conference of German Catholics, Freiburg.

1868	**633**	40pf. multicoloured	50	35

634 Silhouette

1978. Birth Bicent of Clemens Brentano (poet).

1869	**634**	30pf. multicoloured	45	35

635 Text

1978. 25th Anniv of European Convention for the Protection of Human Rights.
1870 **635** 50pf. multicoloured 1·00 35

636 Baden Post-house Sign

1978. Stamp Day and World Philatelic Movement. Multicoloured.
1871 40pf. Type **636** 50 25
1872 50pf. 1850 3pf. stamp of Saxony 50 25

1978. Humanitarian Relief Funds. Woodland Flowers. As T 576. Multicoloured.
1873 30pf.+15pf. Arum 45 35
1874 40pf.+20pf. Weasel-snout 65 55
1875 50pf.+25pf. Turk's-cap lily 90 90
1876 70pf.+35pf. Liverwort 1·20 1·10

1978. Impressionist Paintings. Multicoloured.
1877 50pf. Type **637** 70 55
1878 70pf. "Horseman on the Shore turning Left" (Max Liebermann) (vert) 1·10 75
1879 120pf. "Lady with a Cat" (Max Slevogt) (vert) 1·80 1·80

638 "Christ Child" (stained glass window, Frauenkirche, Munich)

1978. Christmas. Sheet 65×93 mm.
MS1880 **638** 50pf.+25pf. multicoloured 90 90

639 Child

1979. International Year of the Child.
1881 **639** 60pf. multicoloured 1·10 35

640 Agnes Miegel

1979. Birth Cent of Agnes Miegel (poet).
1882 **640** 60pf. multicoloured 80 35

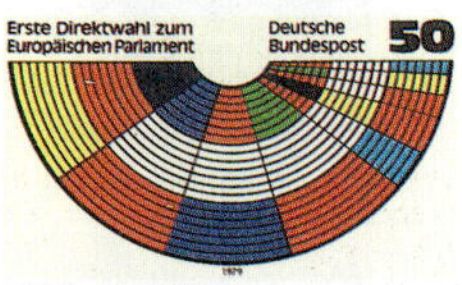

641 Seating Plan

1979. First Direct Elections to European Parliament.
1883 **641** 50pf. multicoloured 1·10 35

642 Film

1979. 25th West German Short Film Festival.
1884 **642** 50pf. black and turquoise 1·00 35

643 Rescue Services Emblems

1979. Rescue Services on the Road.
1885 **643** 50pf. multicoloured 1·00 35

1979. Youth Welfare. History of Aviation (2nd series). As T 627. Multicoloured.
1886 40pf.+20pf. Dornier Do-J Wal flying boat, 1922 65 60
1887 50pf.+25pf. Heinkel He 70 Blitz, 1932 90 90
1888 60pf.+30pf. Junkers W.33 "Bremen", 1928 1·10 1·10
1889 90pf.+45pf. Focke Achgelis Fa 61 helicopter, 1936 1·60 1·40

644 Handball

1979. Sport Promotion Fund. Multicoloured.
1890 60pf.+30pf. Type **644** 1·10 95
1891 90pf.+45pf. Canoeing 1·60 1·40

645 Telegraph Office, 1863

1979. Europa. Multicoloured.
1892 50pf. Type **645** 75 25
1893 60pf. Post Office counter, 1854 1·00 25

646 Anne Frank

1979. 50th Birth Anniv of Anne Frank (concentration camp victim and diary writer).
1894 **646** 60pf. black, grey and red 1·00 35

647 Werner von Siemens's Electric Railway, 1879

1979. International Transport Exhibition. Hamburg.
1895 **647** 60pf. multicoloured 1·10 35

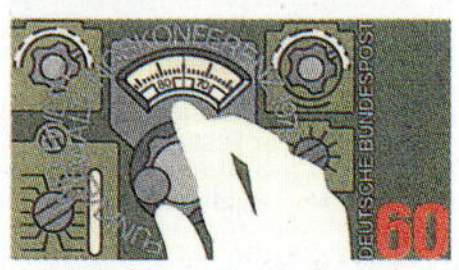

648 Hand operating Radio Dial

1979. World Administrative Radio Conference, Geneva.
1896 **648** 60f. multicoloured 1·00 35

649 "Moses receiving the Tablets of the Law" (woodcut, Cranach the Elder)

1979. 450th Anniv of Publication of Martin Luther's Catechisms.
1897 **649** 50pf. black and green 1·20 35

650 Cross and Orb

1979. Pilgrimage to Aachen.
1898 **650** 50pf. multicoloured 75 35

651 Hildegard von Bingen

1979. 800th Death Anniv of Hildegard von Bingen (writer and mystic).
1899 **651** 110pf. multicoloured 1·30 60

652 Photo-electric Effect

1979. Birth Centenaries of Nobel Prize Winners. Multicoloured.
1900 60pf. Type **652** (Albert Einstein, Physics, 1921) 1·00 45
1901 60pf. Splitting of uranium nucleus (Otto Hahn, Chemistry, 1944) 1·80 45
1902 60pf. Diffraction pattern of X-rays passed through crystal (Max von Laue, Physics, 1914) 1·00 45

653 Pilot and Helmsman

1979. 300th Anniv of 1st Pilotage Regulations.
1903 **653** 60pf. brown and claret 75 35

654 Posthouse Sign, Altheim, Saar (German side), 1754

1979. Stamp Day.
1904 **654** 60pf.+30pf. mult 1·30 1·20

1979. Humanitarian Relief Funds. Woodland Flowers and Fruit. As T 576. Multicoloured.
1905 40pf.+20pf. Red beech (horiz) 55 55
1906 50pf.+25pf. English oak (horiz) 75 70
1907 60pf.+30pf. Hawthorn (horiz) 80 80
1908 90pf.+45pf. Mountain pine (horiz) 1·40 1·30

656 "Bird Garden"

1979. Birth Cent of Paul Klee (artist).
1909 **656** 90pf. multicoloured 1·10 60

657 Faust and Mephistopheles

1979. Doctor Johannes Faust.
1910 **657** 60pf. multicoloured 1·40 35

658 Lightbulb

1979. "Save Energy".
1911 **658** 40pf. multicoloured 75 35

659 "Nativity" (Altenberg medieval manuscript)

1979. Christmas.
1912 **659** 60pf.+30pf. mult 1·10 1·10

660 "Iphigenia"

1980. Death Centenary of Anselm Feuerbach (artist).
1913 **660** 50pf. multicoloured 1·30 35

661 Flags of NATO Members

1980. 25th Anniv of NATO Membership.
1914 **661** 100pf. multicoloured 2·00 90

662 Town Hall, St. Mary's Church, and St Peter's Cathedral

1980. 1200th Anniv of Osnabruck Town and Bishopric.
1915 **662** 60pf. multicoloured 1·00 35

663 "Gotz von Berlichingen" (glass picture)

1980. 500th Birth Anniv of Gotz von Berlichingen (Frankish knight).
1916 **663** 60pf. multicoloured 1·00 35

664 Texts from 1880 and 1980 Duden Dictionaries

1980. Centenary of Konrad Duden's 1st Dictionary.
1917 **664** 60pf. multicoloured 90 35

1980. Youth Welfare. Aviation History (3rd series). As T 627. Multicoloured.
1918 40pf.+20pf. Phoenix FS 24 glider, 1957 45 45
1919 50pf.+25pf. Lockheed L.1049G Super Constellation 75 70
1920 60pf.+30pf. Airbus Industrie A300B2, 1972 1·10 95
1921 90pf.+45pf. Boeing 747-100, 1969 1·70 1·40
No. 1919 is incorrectly dated "1950".

665 Emblems of Association Members

1980. Centenary of German Association of Welfare Societies.
1922 **665** 60pf. blue, red and black 1·00 35

666 "Frederick I with his sons" (Welf Chronicle)

1980. 800th Anniv of Imperial Diet of Gelnhausen.
1923 **666** 60pf. multicoloured 1·20 35

667 Football

1980. Sport Promotion Fund. Multicoloured.
1924 50pf.+25pf. Type **667** 65 55
1925 60pf.+30pf. Dressage 90 70
1926 90pf.+45pf. Skiing 1·60 1·60

668 Albertus Magnus (scholar)

1980. Europa. Multicoloured.
1927 50pf. Type **668** 1·10 25
1928 60pf. Gottfried Leibniz (philosopher) 1·10 25

669 Reading the Augsburg Confession (engraving, G Kohler)

1980. 450th Anniv of Augsburg Confession.
1929 **669** 50pf. black, yellow & grn 80 35

670 Nature Reserve

1980. Nature Conservation.
1930 **670** 40pf. multicoloured 1·20 35

671 Ear and Oscillogram Pulses

1980. International Congress for the Training and Education of the Hard of Hearing, Hamburg.
1931 **671** 90pf. multicoloured 1·40 45

672 First Book of Daily Bible Readings, 1731

1980. 250th Anniv of Moravian Brethren's Book of Daily Bible Readings.
1932 **672** 50pf. multicoloured 85 35

673 St. Benedict

1980. 1500th Birth Anniv of St. Benedict of Nursia (founder of Benedictine Order).
1933 **673** 50pf. multicoloured 75 35

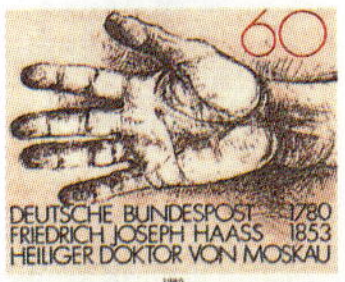

674 Helping Hand

1980. Birth Bicentenary of Friedrich Joseph Haass (philanthropist).
1934 **674** 60pf. multicoloured 90 35

675 Marie von Ebner-Eschenbach

1980. 150th Birth Anniv of Marie von Ebner-Eschenbach (novelist).
1935 **675** 60pf. buff, black & orge 90 35

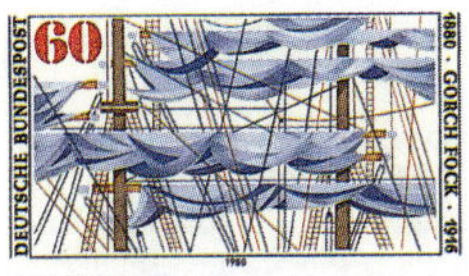

676 Rigging

1980. Birth Centenary of Johan Kinau ("Gorch Fock") (poet).
1936 **676** 60pf. multicoloured 1·80 35

677 Positioning Keystone of South Tower Finial (engraving)

1980. Centenary of Completion of Cologne Cathedral.
1937 **677** 60pf. multicoloured 1·80 35

678 "Ceratocephalus falcatus"

1980. Humanitarian Relief Funds. Endangered Wildflowers. Multicoloured.
1938 40pf.+20pf. Type **678** 65 60
1939 50pf.+25pf. Yellow Vetchling 80 80
1940 60pf.+30pf. Corn Cockle 90 90
1941 90pf.+45pf. Tassel Hyacinth 1·60 1·50
See also Nos. 1972/5.

679 Wine-making (woodcuts)

1980. Bimillenary of Vine Growing in Central Europe.
1942 **679** 50pf. multicoloured 90 35

680 Posthouse Sign, Altheim, Saar, 1754 (French side)

1980. 49th International Philatelic Federation Congress, Essen.
1943 **680** 60pf.+30pf. mult 90 80

681 "Nativity" (Altomunster manuscript)

1980. Christmas.
1944 **681** 60pf.+30pf. mult 1·20 1·10

682 "Landscape with Two Fir Trees" (etching)

1980. 500th Birth Anniv of Albrecht Altdorfer (painter, engraver and architect).
1945 **682** 40pf. lt brown, blk & brn 75 35

683 Elly Heuss-Knapp

1981. Birth Centenary of Elly Heuss-Knapp (social reformer).
1946 **683** 60pf. multicoloured 90 35

684 Society accepting the Handicapped

1981. International Year of Disabled Persons.
1947 **684** 60pf. multicoloured 1·00 35

685 Old Town Houses

1981. European Campaign for Urban Renaissance.
1948 **685** 60pf. multicoloured 1·00 35

686 Telemann and Title Page of "Singet dem Herrn"

1981. 300th Birth Anniv of Georg Philipp Telemann (composer).
1949 **686** 60pf. multicoloured 90 35

687 Visiting a Foreign Family

1981. Integration of Guest Worker Families.
1950 **687** 50pf. multicoloured 1·00 35

688 Polluted Butterfly, Fish and Plant

1981. Preservation of the Environment.
1951 **688** 60pf. multicoloured 1·50 35

689 Patent Office Emblem and Scientific Signs

1981. Establishment of European Patent Office, Munich.
1952 **689** 60pf. grey, red and black 90 35

690 Scintigram showing Distribution of Radioactive Isotope

1981. Cancer Prevention through Medical Check-ups.
1953 **690** 40pf. multicoloured 75 35

691 Borda Circle, 1800

1981. Youth Welfare. Optical Instruments. Multicoloured.
1954 40pf.+20pf. Type **691** 65 45
1955 50pf.+25pf. Reflecting telescope, 1770 1·10 90
1956 60pf.+30pf. Binocular microscope, 1860 1·10 90
1957 90pf.+45pf. Octant, 1775 1·60 1·50

692 Rowing

1981. Sport Promotion Fund. Multicoloured.

1958		60pf.+30pf. Type **692**	1·10	90
1959		90pf.+45pf. Gliding	1·60	1·40

693 South German Dancers

1981. Europa. Multicoloured.

1960		50pf. Type **693**	90	25
1961		60pf. North German dancers	90	25

694 Convention Cross

1981. 19th German Protestant Convention, Hamburg.

1962	**694**	50pf. multicoloured	90	35

695 Group from Crucifixion Altar

1981. 450th Death Anniv of Tilman Riemenschneider (woodcarver).

1963	**695**	60pf. multicoloured	90	35

696 Georg von Neumayer Antarctic Research Station

1981. Polar Research.

1964	**696**	110pf. multicoloured	2·00	55

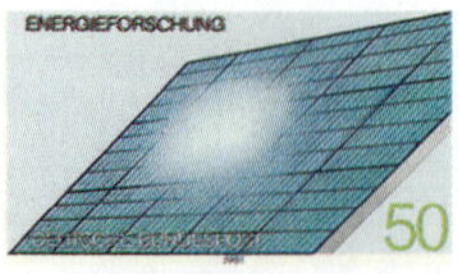

697 Solar Generator

1981. Energy Research.

1965	**697**	50pf. multicoloured	1·20	35

698 Hand holding Baby Black Coot

1981. Animal Protection.

1966	**698**	60pf. multicoloured	1·50	35

699 Arms of different Races forming Square

1981. Co-operation with Developing Countries.

1967	**699**	90pf. multicoloured	1·50	55

700 Wilhelm Raabe

1981. 150th Birth Anniv of Wilhelm Raabe (poet).

1968	**700**	50pf. light green & green	90	35

701 Constitutional Freedom

1981. Fundamental Concepts of Democracy. Article 20 of the Basic Law. Multicoloured.

1969		40pf. Type **701**	1·00	25
1970		50pf. Separation of Powers	1·00	25
1971		60pf. Sovereignty of the People	1·50	25

1981. Humanitarian Relief Funds. Endangered Wildflowers. As T 678. Multicoloured.

1972		40pf.+20pf. Water nut	55	45
1973		50pf.+25pf. Floating Heart	75	60
1974		60pf.+30pf. Water gilly-flower	90	90
1975		90pf.+45pf. Water lobelia	1·80	1·60

702 Posthouse Scene c. 1855

1981. Stamp Day.

1976	**702**	60pf. multicoloured	1·50	35

703 "Nativity" (glass painting)

1981. Christmas.

1977	**703**	60pf.+30pf. mult	1·20	95

704 St. Elisabeth

1981. 750th Death Anniv of St. Elisabeth of Thuringia.

1978	**704**	50pf. multicoloured	1·20	35

705 Clausewitz (after W. Wach)

1981. 150th Death Anniv of General Carl von Clausewitz (military writer).

1979	**705**	60pf. multicoloured	1·20	35

706 People forming Figure "100"

1981. Cent of Social Insurance.

1980	**706**	60pf. multicoloured	1·00	35

707 Map of Antarctica

1981. 20th Anniv of Antarctic Treaty.

1981	**707**	100pf. blue, lt blue & blk	1·60	55

708 Pot with Lid

1982. 300th Birth Anniv of Johann Friedrich Bottger (founder of Meissen China Works).

1982	**708**	60pf. multicoloured	1·00	35

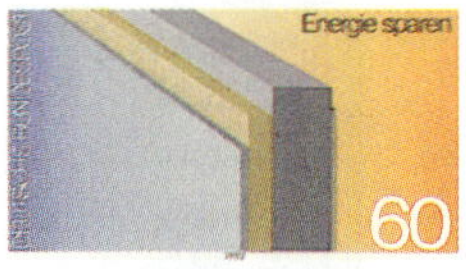

709 Insulated Wall

1982. Energy Conservation.

1983	**709**	60pf. multicoloured	1·00	35

710 Silhouette (Dora Brandenburg-Polster)

1982. "The Town Band of Bremen" (German fairy tale).

1984	**710**	40pf. black and red	75	35

711 Goethe (after Georg Melchior Kraus)

1982. 150th Death Anniv of Johann Wolfgang von Goethe (writer).

1985	**711**	60pf. multicoloured	2·75	35

712 Robert Koch

1982. Centenary of Discovery of Tubercle Bacillus.

1986	**712**	50pf. multicoloured	3·25	35

713 Benz Patent "Motorwagen", 1886

1982. Youth Welfare. Motor Cars. Mult.

1987		40pf.+20pf. Type **713**	65	55
1988		50pf.+25pf. Mercedes "Tourenwagen", 1913	90	70
1989		60pf.+30pf. Hannomag "Kommissbrot", 1925	1·10	90
1990		90pf.+45pf. Opel "Olympia", 1937	1·80	1·90

714 Jogging

1982. Sport Promotion Fund. Multicoloured.

1991		60pf.+30pf. Type **714**	1·10	95
1992		90pf.+45pf. Disabled archers	1·70	1·50

715 "Good Helene"

1982. 150th Birth Anniv of Wilhelm Busch (writer and illustrator).

1993	**715**	50pf. black, green & yell	1·20	35

716 "Procession to Hambach Castle, 1832" (wood engraving)

1982. Europa.

1994	**716**	50pf. black, yellow & red	1·20	25
1995	-	60pf. multicoloured	1·80	25

DESIGN: 60pf. Excerpt from Treaty of Rome (instituting European Economic Community), 1957, and flags.

717 Racing Yachts

1982. Centenary of Kiel Regatta Week.

1996	**717**	60pf. multicoloured	1·20	35

718 Young Couple

1982. Centenary of Young Men's Christian Association in Germany.

1997	**718**	50pf. multicoloured	90	35

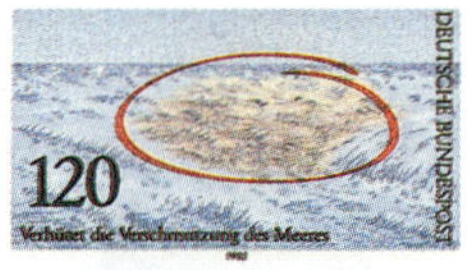

719 Polluted Sea

1982. "Prevent the Pollution of the Sea".

1998	**719**	120pf. multicoloured	3·00	45

720 Battered Licence Plate

1982. "Don't Drink and Drive".

1999	**720**	80pf. multicoloured	1·20	35

721 Doctor examining Leper

1982. 25th Anniv of German Lepers' Welfare Organization.

2000	**721**	80pf. multicoloured	1·20	35

722 Franck and Born

1982. Birth Centenaries of James Franck and Max Born (physicists and Nobel Prize Winners).

2001	**722**	80pf. grey, black and red	1·50	35

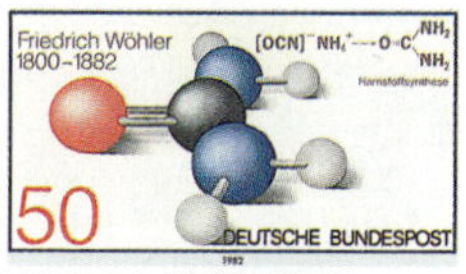

723 Atomic Model of Urea

1982. Death Centenary of Friedrich Wohler (chemist).

2002	**723**	50pf. multicoloured	1·10	35

724 "St. Francis preaching to the Birds" (fresco by Giotto)

1982. 87th German Catholics' Congress, Dusseldorf and 800th Birth Anniv of St. Francis of Assisi.

2003	**724**	60pf. multicoloured	1·10	35

725 Hybrid Tea Rose

1982. Humanitarian Relief Funds. Roses. Multicoloured.

2004	50pf.+20pf. Type **725**	65	55
2005	60pf.+30pf. Floribunda	90	70
2006	80pf.+40pf. Bourbon	1·30	1·20
2007	120pf.+60pf. Polyantha hybrid	1·80	1·60

726 Letters on Desk

1982. Stamp Day.

2008	**726**	80pf. multicoloured	1·60	35

727 Gregorian Calendar by Johannes Rasch, 1586

1982. 400th Anniv of Gregorian Calendar.

2009	**727**	60pf. multicoloured	1·10	35

728 Theodor Heuss

1982. Presidents of the Federal Republic. Sheet 130×100 mm containing T 728 and similar horiz designs. Multicoloured.

MS2010 80pf. Type **728**; 80pf. Heinrich Lubke; 80pf. Gustav Heinemann; 80pf. Walter Scheel; 80pf. Karl Carstens 6·00 5·25

729 "Nativity" (detail from St. Peter Altar by Master Bertram)

1982. Christmas.

2011	**729**	80pf.+40pf. mult	1·80	1·20

730 Edith Stein

1983. 40th Death Anniv (1982) of Edith Stein (philosopher).

2012	**730**	80pf. lt grey, grey & blk	1·80	55

731 White Rose and Barbed Wire

1983. Persecution and Resistance 1933–45.

2013	**731**	80pf. multicoloured	1·80	55

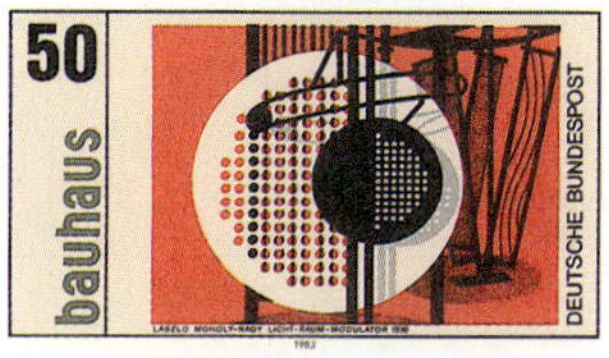

732 "Light Space Modulator" (Laszlo Moholy-Nagy)

1983. Birth Cent of Walter Gropius (founder of Bauhaus School of Art, Weimar). Bauhaus Art. Multicoloured.

2014	50pf. Type **732**	90	35
2015	60pf. "Sanctuary" (lithograph by Josef Albers)	1·30	35
2016	80pf. Skylights from Bauhaus Archives, Berlin (Walter Gropius)	1·50	40

733 Federahannes (Rottweil carnival figure)

1983. Carnival.

2017	**733**	60pf. multicoloured	1·20	35

734 Daimler-Maybach, 1885

1983. Youth Welfare. Motor Cycles. Mult.

2018	50pf.+20pf. Type **734**	65	55
2019	60pf.+30pf. N.S.U., 1901	90	70
2020	80pf.+40pf. Megola "Sport", 1922	1·50	1·30
2021	120pf.+60pf. B.M.W. world record holder, 1936	2·30	2·00

735 Gymnastics (German Festival, Frankfurt am Main)

1983. Sports Promotion Fund. Multicoloured.

2022	80pf.+40pf. Type **735**	1·40	1·10
2023	120pf.+60pf. Modern pentathlon (world championships, Warendorf)	2·20	1·90

736 Stylized Flower

1983. 4th International Horticultural Show. Munich.

2024	**736**	60pf. multicoloured	1·20	35

737 Modern Type and Gutenberg Letters

1983. Europa. Multicoloured.

2025	60pf. Type **737**	2·50	55
2026	80pf. Resonant circuit and electric flux lines	1·60	55

738 Johannes Brahms

1983. 150th Birth Anniv of Johannes Brahms (composer).

2027	**738**	80pf. multicoloured	1·80	55

739 Kafka's Signature and Teyn Church, Prague

1983. Birth Cent of Franz Kafka (writer).

2028	**739**	80pf. multicoloured	1·80	55

740 Brewing (frontispiece of 1677 treatise)

1983. 450th Anniv of Beer Purity Law.

2029	**740**	80pf. multicoloured	1·80	55

741 "Concord"

1983. 300th Anniv of First German Settlers in America.

2030	**741**	80pf. multicoloured	2·00	55

742 Children crossing Road

1983. Children and Road Traffic.

2031	**742**	80pf. multicoloured	1·80	55

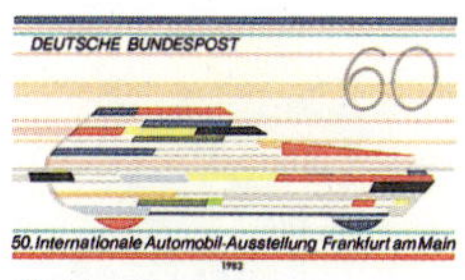

743 Flags forming Car

1983. 50th International Motor Show, Frankfurt-on-Main.

2032	**743**	60pf. multicoloured	90	35

744 Warburg (after Oberland)

1983. Birth Centenary of Otto Warburg. (physiologist and chemist).

2033	**744**	50pf. multicoloured	1·10	55

745 Wieland (after G. B. Bosio)

1983. 250th Birth Anniv of Cristoph Martin Wieland (writer).

2034	**745**	80pf. multicoloured	1·50	55

746 Rosette in National Colours

1983. 10th Anniv of U.N. Membership.

2035	**746**	80pf. multicoloured	2·00	55

747 "Das Rauhe Haus" and Children

1983. 150th Anniv of "Das Rauhe Haus" (children's home, Hamburg).

2036	**747**	80pf. multicoloured	1·60	55

748 Surveying Maps

1983. International Geodesy and Geophysics Union General Assembly, Hamburg.

2037	**748**	120pf. multicoloured	2·00	65

749 Swiss Androsace

1983. Humanitarian Relief Funds. Endangered Alpine Flowers. Multicoloured.

2038	50pf.+20pf. Type **749**	75	55
2039	60pf.+30pf. Krain groundsel	1·00	80
2040	80pf.+40pf. Fleischer's willow herb	1·50	1·30
2041	120pf.+60pf. Alpine sow-thistle	2·30	2·00

750 Horseman with Posthorn

1983. Stamp Day.

2042	**750**	80pf. multicoloured	1·60	55

751 Luther (engraving by G. Konig after Cranach)

1983. 500th Birth Anniv of Martin Luther (Protestant reformer).

2043	**751**	80pf. multicoloured	2·75	55

752 Interwoven National Colours

1983. Federation, Lander and Communities Co-operation.

2044	**752**	80pf. multicoloured	2·00	55

753 Customs Stamps

1983. 150th Anniv of German Customs Union.

2045	**753**	60pf. multicoloured	2·00	35

754 Epiphany Carol Singers

1983. Christmas.

2046	**754**	80pf.+40pf. mult	2·00	1·40

755 Black Gate, Trier

1984. 2000th Anniv of Trier.

2047	**755**	80pf. multicoloured	2·10	55

756 Reis and Telephone Apparatus

1984. 150th Birth Anniv of Philipp Reis (telephone pioneer).

2048	**756**	80pf. multicoloured	2·00	55

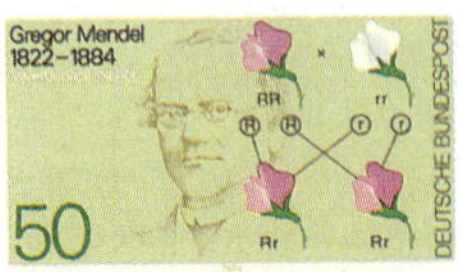

757 Mendel and Genetic Diagram

1984. Death Cent of Gregor Mendel (geneticist).

2049	**757**	50pf. multicoloured	1·20	35

758 Town Hall

1984. 500th Anniv of Michelstadt Town Hall.

2050	**758**	60pf. multicoloured	1·20	35

759 Cloth draped on Cross

1984. 350th Anniv of Oberammergau Passion Play.

2051	**759**	60pf. multicoloured	1·20	35

760 Bee-eating Beetle

1984. Youth Welfare. Pollinating Insects. Multicoloured.

2052	50pf.+20pf. Type **760**	75	60
2053	60pf.+30pf. Red admiral	1·30	1·10
2054	80pf.+40pf. Honey bee	1·60	1·50
2055	120pf.+60pf. "Chrysotoxum festivium" (hover fly)	2·50	2·50

761 Throwing the Discus

1984. Sport Promotion Fund. Multicoloured.

2056	60pf.+30pf. Type **761**	1·30	90
2057	80pf.+40pf. Rhythmic gymnastics	1·60	1·40
2058	120pf.+60pf. Windsurfing	3·50	3·00

762 Parliament Emblem

1984. 2nd Direct Elections to European Parliament.

2059	**762**	80pf. yellow, blue and light blue	2·20	60

763 Bridge

1984. Europa. 25th Anniv of European Post and Telecommunications Conference.

2060	**763**	60pf. blue, lt blue & blk	1·50	45
2061	**763**	80pf. purple, red & black	1·50	45

764 St. Norbert (sculpture)

1984. 850th Death Anniv of St. Norbert von Xanten.

2062	**764**	80pf. green & deep green	1·50	55

765 Nursery Rhyme Illustration

1984. Death Centenary of Ludwig Richter (illustrator).

2063	**765**	60pf. black and brown	90	35

766 Cross and Shadow

1984. 50th Anniv of Protestant Churches' Barmen Theological Declaration.

2064	**766**	80pf. multicoloured	1·50	55

767 Letter sorting, 1800s

1984. 19th Universal Postal Union Congress, Hamburg. Sheet 138×104 mm containing T 767 and similar square designs.

MS2065 60pf. brown and black; 80pf. multicoloured; 120pf. green, black and grey	3·75	3·25

DESIGNS: 80pf. Modern automatic letter sorting machine scanning device; 120pf. Heinrich von Stephan (founder of U.P.U.).

768 Groom leading Horse (detail from tomb of Oclatius)

1984. 2000th Anniv of Neuss.

2066	**768**	80pf. multicoloured	1·50	55

769 Bessel

1984. Birth Bicentenary of Friedrich Wilhelm Bessel (astronomer and mathematician).

2067	**769**	80pf. grey, black and red	1·50	55

770 Eugenio Pacelli (Pope Pius XII)

1984. 88th German Catholics' Congress, Munich.

2068	**770**	60pf. multicoloured	1·20	35

771 Town Hall

1984. 750th Anniv of Duderstadt Town Hall.

2069	**771**	60pf. multicoloured	1·10	35

772 Medieval Document and Visual Display Unit

1984. 10th International Archives Congress, Bonn.

2070	**772**	70pf. multicoloured	1·50	55

773 Knoop Lock

1984. Bicent of Schleswig-Holstein Canal.

2071	**773**	80pf. multicoloured	1·80	55

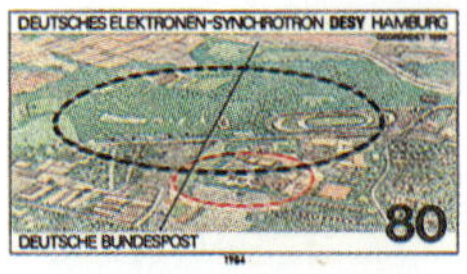

774 Research Centre and Storage Rings

1984. 25th Anniv of German Electron Synchrotron (physics research centre), Hamburg-Bahrenfeld.

2072	**774**	80pf. multicoloured	2·10	55

775 "Aceras anthropophorum"

1984. Humanitarian Relief Funds. Orchids. Multicoloured.

2073	50pf.+20pf. Type **775**	90	80
2074	60pf.+30pf. "Orchis ustulata"	90	80
2075	80pf.+40pf. "Limodorum abortivum"	1·40	1·20
2076	120pf.+60pf. "Dactylorhiza sambucina"	2·75	2·75

776 Taxis Posthouse, Augsburg

1984. Stamp Day.

2077	**776**	80pf. multicoloured	2·10	55

777 Burning Match

1984. Anti-smoking Campaign.

2078	**777**	60pf. multicoloured	1·30	35

778 Male and Female Symbols

1984. Equal Rights for Men and Women.

2079	**778**	80pf. black, mauve & bl	1·80	55

779 Ballot Slip

1984. For Peace and Understanding.

2080	**779**	80pf. grey, black & blue	1·50	55

780 St. Martin giving Cloak to Beggar

1984. Christmas.

2081	**780**	80pf.+40pf. mult	1·60	1·40

781 Emperor Augustus (bust), Buildings and Arms

1985. 2000th Anniv of Augsburg.

2082	**781**	80pf. multicoloured	1·80	45

782 Spener (engraving by Bartholome Kilian after Johann Georg Wagner)

1985. 350th Birth Anniv of Philipp Jakob Spener (church reformer).
2083 **782** 80pf. black and green 1·50 55

783 Grimm Brothers (engraving by Lazarus Sichling)

1985. Birth Bicentenaries of Grimm Brothers (folklorists) and 7th International Union for German Linguistics and Literature Congress, Gottingen.
2084 **783** 80pf. black, grey and red 2·00 55

784 Romano Guardini

1985. Birth Centenary of Romano Guardini (theologian).
2085 **784** 80pf. multicoloured 1·50 55

785 Verden

1985. Millenary of Market and Coinage Rights in Verden.
2086 **785** 60pf. multicoloured 2·00 35

786 Flags and German–Danish Border

1985. 30th Anniv of Bonn–Copenhagen Declarations.
2087 **786** 80pf. multicoloured 2·20 70

787 Bowling

1985. Sport Promotion Fund. Multicoloured.
2088 80pf.+40pf. Type **787** (cent. of German Nine-pin Bowling Association) 1·60 1·50
2089 120pf.+60pf. Kayak (world rapid-river and slalom canoeing championships) 2·40 2·10

788 Kisch

1985. Birth Centenary of Egon Erwin Kisch (journalist).
2090 **788** 60pf. multicoloured 1·20 35

789 "Hebel and the Margravine"

1985. 225th Birth Anniv of Johann Peter Hebel (poet).
2091 **789** 80pf. multicoloured 1·50 55

790 Draisienne Bicycle, 1817

1985. Youth Welfare International Youth Year. Cycles. Multicoloured.
2092 50pf.+20pf. Type **790** 90 90
2093 60pf.+30pf. NSU Germania "ordinary", 1866 1·10 1·10
2094 80pf.+40pf. Cross-frame low bicycle, 1887 1·50 1·40
2095 120pf.+60pf. Adler tricycle, 1888 3·00 2·75

791 Handel

1985. Europa. Composers' 300th Birth Anniversaries. Multicoloured.
2096 60pf. Type **791** 2·30 45
2097 80pf. Bach 2·30 45

792 Saint George's Cathedral

1985. 750th Anniv of Limburg Cathedral.
2098 **792** 60pf. multicoloured 1·20 55

793 Capital (presbytery, "Wies" Church)

1985. 300th Birth Anniv of Dominikus Zimmermann (architect).
2099 **793** 70pf. multicoloured 1·40 55

794 Josef Kentenich

1985. Birth Centenary of Father Josef Kentenich (founder of International Schonstatt (Catholic laymen's) Movement).
2100 **794** 80pf. multicoloured 1·50 55

795 Clock and Forest

1985. Save the Forests.
2101 **795** 80pf. multicoloured 2·10 55

796 Tug of War and Scouting Emblem

1985. 30th World Scouts Conference, Munich.
2102 **796** 60pf. multicoloured 1·30 55

797 "Sunday Walk"

1985. Death Cent of Carl Spitzweg (artist).
2103 **797** 60pf. multicoloured 2·00 55

798 Horses and Postilion

1985. "Mophila 1985" Stamp Exhibition, Hamburg. Multicoloured.
2104 60pf.+20pf. Type **798** 2·75 2·20
2105 80pf.+20pf. Mail coach 2·75 2·20
Nos. 2104/5 were printed se-tenant, forming a composite design.

799 Stock Exchange

1985. 400th Anniv of Frankfurt Stock Exchange.
2106 **799** 80pf. black, red and grey 1·80 55

800 Flowers and Butterfly

1985. Humanitarian Relief Funds. Designs depict motifs from borders of medieval prayer book. Multicoloured.
2107 50pf.+20pf. Type **800** 80 70
2108 60pf.+30pf. Flowers, bird and butterfly 1·00 90
2109 80pf.+40pf. Flowers, berries and snail 1·40 1·10
2110 120pf.+60pf. Flowers, snail and butterfly 2·30 2·20

801 Fritz Reuter

1985. 175th Death Anniv of Fritz Reuter (writer).
2111 **801** 80pf. black, grey and blue 2·20 55

802 "Inauguration of First German Railway" (Heim)

1985. 150th Anniv of German Railways and Birth Bicent. of Johannes Scharrer (joint founder).
2112 **802** 80pf. multicoloured 2·20 55

803 Carpentry Joint in National Colours

1985. 40th Anniv of Integration of Refugees.
2113 **803** 80pf. multicoloured 2·10 55

804 Iron Cross and National Colours

1985. 30th Anniv of Federal Armed Forces.
2114 **804** 80pf. red, black & yellow 3·25 55

805 "Nativity" (detail, High Altar, Freiburg)

1985. Christmas. 500th Birth Anniversary of Hans Baldung Grien (artist).
2115 **805** 80pf.+40pf. mult 1·70 1·70

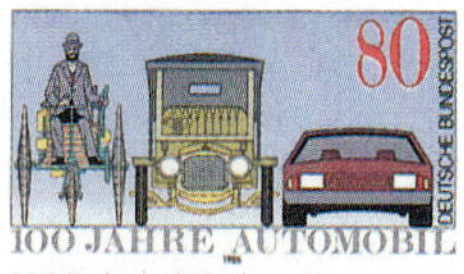

806 Early and Modern Cars

1986. Centenary of Motor Car.
2116 **806** 80pf. multicoloured 2·20 55

807 Town Buildings

1986. 1250th Anniv of Bad Hersfeld.
2117 **807** 60pf. multicoloured 1·50 55

808 "Self-portrait"

1986. Birth Centenary of Oskar Kokoschka (artist and writer).
2118 **808** 80pf. black, grey and red 1·50 55

809 Comet and "Giotto" Space Probe

1986. Appearance of Halley's Comet.
2119 **809** 80pf. multicoloured 2·20 60

810 Running

1986. Sport Promotion Fund. Multicoloured.
2120 80pf.+40pf. Type **810** (European Athletics Championships, Stuttgart) 1·80 1·80
2121 120pf.+55pf. Bobsleigh (World Championships, Konigsee) 2·75 2·75

811 Optician

1986. Youth Welfare. Trades (1st series). Multicoloured.
2122 50pf.+25pf. Type **811** 1·20 1·10
2123 60pf.+30pf. Bricklayer 1·40 1·20
2124 70pf.+35pf. Hairdresser 1·60 1·40
2125 80pf.+40pf. Baker 2·30 2·00
See also Nos. 2179/82.

812 Walsrode Monastery

1986. Millenary of Walsrode.
2126 **812** 60pf. multicoloured 1·50 55

813 Ludwig and Neuschwanstein Castle

1986. Death Centenary of King Ludwig II of Bavaria.
2127 **813** 60pf. multicoloured 2·50 55

814 Mouth

1986. Europa. Details of "David" (sculpture) by Michelangelo. Multicoloured.
2128 60pf. Type **814** 1·60 45
2129 80pf. Nose 1·60 45

815 Karl Barth

1986. Birth Centenary of Karl Barth (theologian).
2130 **815** 80pf. black, red & purple 1·60 55

816 Ribbons

1986. Union of German Catholic Students' Societies 100th Assembly, Frankfurt am Main.
2131 **816** 80pf. multicoloured 1·60 55

817 Weber and Score of "Gloria"

1986. Birth Bicentenary of Carl Maria von Weber (composer).
2132 **817** 80pf. brown, black & red 2·10 55

818 "TV-Sat" and Earth

1986. Launch of German "TV-Sat" and French "TDF-1" Broadcasting Satellites.
2133 **818** 80pf. multicoloured 2·30 60

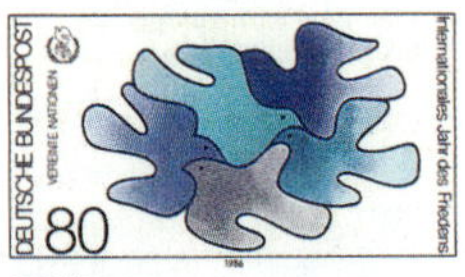

819 Doves

1986. International Peace Year.
2134 **819** 80pf. multicoloured 2·00 55

820 Liszt

1986. Death Centenary of Franz Liszt (composer).
2135 **820** 80pf. blue and orange 2·10 55

821 Reichstag, Berlin

1986. Important Buildings in West German History. Sheet 100×130 mm containing T 821 and similar horiz designs. Multicoloured.
MS2136 80pf. Type **821**; 80pf. Koenig Museum, Bonn (venue of 1948–49 Parliamentary Council); 80pf. Bundeshaus, Bonn (parliamentary building) 4·50 4·00

822 Pollution Damage of Stained Glass Window

1986. Protection of Monuments.
2137 **822** 80pf. multicoloured 2·30 55

823 Frederick the Great (after Anton Graff)

1986. Death Bicentenary of Frederick the Great.
2138 **823** 80pf. multicoloured 3·00 55

824 Congress Card

1986. Centenary of First German Skat Congress and 24th Congress, Cologne.
2139 **824** 80pf. multicoloured 2·10 55

825 Opposing Arrows

1986. 25th Anniv of Organization for Economic Co-operation and Development.
2140 **825** 80pf. multicoloured 1·60 55

826 Old University

1986. 600th Anniv of Heidelberg University.
2141 **826** 80pf. multicoloured 2·00 55

827 Fan of Stamps behind Stagecoach

1986. 50th Anniv of Stamp Day.
2142 **827** 80pf. multicoloured 2·00 55

828 Ornamental Flask, 300 A.D.

1986. Humanitarian Relief Funds. Glassware. Multicoloured.
2143 50pf.+25pf. Type **828** 80 70
2144 60pf.+30pf. Goblet with decorated stem, 1650 1·10 95
2145 70pf.+35pf. Imperial Eagle tankard, 1662 1·30 1·10
2146 80pf.+40pf. Engraved goblet, 1720 1·50 1·30

829 "Dance in Silence" from "Autumnal Dances"

1986. Birth Centenary of Mary Wigman (dancer).
2147 **829** 70pf. multicoloured 1·20 55

830 Cross over Map

1986. 25th Anniv of Adveniat (Advent collection for Latin America).
2148 **830** 80pf. green, blue & blk 1·20 60

831 "Adoration of the Infant Jesus" (Ortenberg altarpiece)

1986. Christmas.
2149 **831** 80pf.+40pf. mult 1·60 1·50

832 Christine Teusch (politician)

1986. Famous German Women. Inscr "Deutsche Bundespost".

2150	-	5pf. brown and grey	25	25
2151	-	10pf. brown and violet	35	25
2152	-	20pf. blue and red	90	45
2152a	-	30pf. bistre and purple	45	35
2153	-	40pf. red and blue	90	25
2154	**832**	50pf. green and brown	90	25
2155	-	60pf. lilac and green	1·10	25
2155a	-	70pf. green and red	1·40	70
2156	-	80pf. brown and green	1·10	25
2156a	-	80pf. brown and blue	1·00	55
2157	-	100pf. grey and red	1·40	45
2157a	-	100pf. bistre and lilac	1·00	55
2158	-	120pf. green and brown	1·80	1·10
2159	-	130pf. violet and blue	2·75	90
2160	-	140pf. ochre and blue	3·25	1·60
2161	-	150pf. blue and red	3·75	1·60
2162	-	170pf. purple and green	2·30	1·30
2163	-	180pf. purple and blue	2·75	1·30
2164	-	200pf. red and brown	2·30	90
2165	-	240pf. brown and green	3·25	2·20
2166	-	250pf. blue and mauve	4·50	2·20
2167	-	300pf. green and purple	2·75	1·30
2168	-	350pf. brown and black	5·00	2·75
2168a	-	400pf. black and red	5·50	4·00
2168b	-	450pf. ultramarine & bl	6·00	4·50
2169	-	500pf. red and green	6·00	3·50

DESIGNS: 5pf. Emma Ihrer (politician and trade unionist); 10pf. Paula Modersohn-Becker (painter); 20pf. Cilly Aussem (tennis player); 30pf. Kathe Kollwitz (artist); 40pf. Maria Sibylla Merian (artist and naturalist); 60pf. Dorothea Erxleben (first German woman Doctor of Medicine); 70pf. Elisabet Boehm (founder of Agricultural Association of Housewives); 80pf. (2156), Clara Schumann (pianist and composer); 80pf. (2156a), Rahel Varnhagen von Ense (humanist) (after Wilhelm Hensel); 100pf. (2157), Therese Giehse (actress); 100pf. (2157a), Luise Henriette of Orange (mother of King Friedrich I of Prussia) (after Gerhard von Honthorst); 120pf. Elisabeth Selbert (politician); 130pf. Lise Meitner (physicist); 140pf. Cecile Vogt (medical researcher); 150pf. Sophie Scholl (resistance member); 170pf. Hannah Arendt (sociologist); 180pf. Lotte Lehmann (opera singer); 200pf. Bertha von Suttner (novelist and pacifist); 240pf. Mathilda Franziska Anneke (women's rights activist); 250pf. Queen Louise of Prussia; 300pf. Fanny Hensel (composer) (after Eduard Magnus); 350pf. Hedwig Dransfeld (politician); 400pf. Charlotte von Stein (friend of Goethe); 450pf. Hedwig Courths-Mahler (novelist); 500pf. Alice Salomon (women's rights activist).

For similar designs inscribed "Deutschland", see Nos. 2785/95.

833 Berlin Landmarks

1987. 750th Anniv of Berlin.
2170 **833** 80pf. multicoloured 2·40 70

834 Staircase, Residenz Palace, Wurzburg

1987. 300th Birth Anniv of Balthasar Neumann (architect).
2171 **834** 80pf. grey, black and red 1·80 55

835 Erhard

1987. 90th Birth Anniv of Ludwig Erhard (former Chancellor).
2172 **835** 80pf. multicoloured 2·10 45

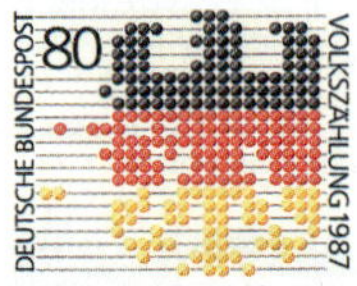

836 Abacus Beads forming Eagle

1987. Census.
2173 **836** 80pf. multicoloured 2·00 55

837 Clemenswerth Castle

1987. 250th Anniv of Clemenswerth Castle.
2174 **837** 60pf. multicoloured 1·60 55

838 Chief Winnetou (from book cover)

1987. 75th Death Anniv of Karl May (writer).
2175 **838** 80pf. multicoloured 1·70 55

839 Solar Spectrum

1987. Birth Bicentenary of Joseph von Fraunhofer (optician and physicist).
2176 **839** 80pf. multicoloured 1·60 55

840 World Sailing Championships, Kiel

1987. Sport Promotion Fund. Multicoloured.
2177 80pf.+40pf. Type **840** 1·60 1·60
2178 120pf.+55pf. World Nordic Skiing Championships, Oberstdorf 2·50 2·50

1987. Youth Welfare. Trades (2nd series). As T 811. Multicoloured.
2179 50pf.+25pf. Plumber 1·40 1·20
2180 60pf.+30pf. Dental technician 1·60 1·50
2181 70pf.+35pf. Butcher 1·80 1·60
2182 80pf.+40pf. Bookbinder 2·50 2·30

841 Clefs, Notes and Leaves

1987. 125th Anniv of German Choir Association.
2183 **841** 80pf. multicoloured 1·70 55

842 Pope's Arms, Madonna and Child and Kevelaer

1987. Visit of Pope John Paul II to Kevelaer (venue for 17th Marian and 10th Mariological Congresses).
2184 **842** 80pf. multicoloured 2·00 55

843 Dulmen's Wild Horses

1987. European Environment Year.
2185 **843** 60pf. multicoloured 2·00 55

844 German Pavilion, International Exhibition, Barcelona, 1929 (Ludwig Mies van der Rohe)

1987. Europa. Architecture. Multicoloured.
2186 60pf. Type **844** 1·50 55
2187 80pf. Kohlbrand Bridge, Hamburg (Thyssen Engineering) 1·80 55

845 Emblem and Globe

1987. Rotary International Convention, Munich.
2188 **845** 70pf. ultram, yell & bl 1·60 55

846 "Without Title (With an Early Portrait)"

1987. Birth Centenary of Kurt Schwitters (artist and writer).
2189 **846** 80pf. multicoloured 1·60 55

847 Organ Pipes and Signature

1987. 350th Birth Anniv of Dietrich Buxtehude (composer).
2190 **847** 80pf. black, stone and red 1·20 55

848 Bengal

1987. 300th Birth Anniv of Johann Albrecht Bengel (theologian).
2191 **848** 80pf. brown, ochre & blk 1·60 55

849 Wilhelm Kaisen

1987. Birth Centenary of Wilhelm Kaisen (Senate president and Mayor of Bremen).
2192 **849** 80pf. multicoloured 1·60 55

850 Charlemagne, Bishop Willehad, Bremen Cathedral and City Arms (after mural)

1987. 1200th Anniv of Bremen Bishopric.
2193 **850** 80pf. multicoloured 1·50 55

851 Target, Crossed Rifles and Wreath

1987. 7th European Riflemen's Festival, Lippstadt.
2194 **851** 80pf. multicoloured 1·50 55

852 4th-century Roman Bracelet

1987. Humanitarian Relief Funds. Precious Metal Work. Multicoloured.
2195 50pf.+25pf. Type **852** 1·40 1·30
2196 60pf.+30pf. 6th-century East Gothic buckle 1·40 1·30
2197 70pf.+35pf. 7th-century Merovingian disc fibula 1·40 1·30
2198 80pf.+40pf. 8th-century reliquary 1·80 1·80

853 Loading and Unloading Mail Train, 1897

1987. Stamp Day.
2199 **853** 80pf. multicoloured 1·50 95

854 Corner Tower, Celle Castle

1987. Tourist Sights. Inscr "DEUTSCHE BUNDESPOST".

2200	-	5pf. blue and grey	25	25
2201	-	10pf. blue and indigo	55	20
2202	-	20pf. pink and blue	35	20
2203	**854**	30pf. brown and green	65	25
2204	-	33pf. green and red	55	35
2205	-	38pf. grey and blue	90	55
2206	-	40pf. brown, red & blue	80	35
2206a	-	41pf. grey and yellow	65	45
2207	-	45pf. pink and blue	55	45
2208	-	50pf. brown and blue	65	25
2209	-	60pf. green and black	90	25
2210	-	70pf. pink and blue	1·00	25
2210a	-	70pf. brown and blue	55	35
2211	-	80pf. grey and green	90	25
2212	-	90pf. bistre and yellow	1·60	1·80
2213	-	100pf. green and orange	1·80	35
2214	-	120pf. green and red	2·00	80
2215	-	140pf. bistre and yellow	2·20	70
2216	-	170pf. grey and yellow	2·40	90
2216a	-	200pf. blue and brown	1·80	80
2217	-	280pf. grey and blue	4·50	2·30
2218	-	300pf. pink and brown	3·75	55
2219	-	350pf. grey and blue	3·75	70
2220	-	400pf. red and brown	4·00	70
2220a	-	450pf. blue and brown	4·50	1·30
2220b	-	500pf. stone and purple	5·00	1·60
2220c	-	550pf. brown and blue	5·50	2·50
2220d	-	700pf. green and yellow	7·25	2·75

DESIGNS: 5pf. Brunswick Lion; 10pf. Frankfurt airport; 20, 70 (2210) pf. Head of Nefertiti, Berlin Museum; 33, 120pf. Schleswig Cathedral; 38, 280pf. Statue of Roland, Bremen; 40pf. Chile House, Hamburg; 41, 170pf. Russian Church, Wiesbaden; 45pf. Rastatt Castle; 50pf. Freiburg Cathedral; 60pf. "Bavaria" (bronze statue), Munich; 70pf. (2210a) Heligoland; 80pf. Zollern II Dortmund Mine Industrial Museum, Westphalia; 90, 140pf. Bronze flagon, Reinheim; 100pf. Pilgrimage Chapel, Altotting; 200pf. Magdeburg Cathedral; 300pf. Hambach Castle; 350pf. Externsteine (rock formation), Horn-Bad Meinberg; 400pf. Dresden Opera House; 450pf. New Gate, Neubrandenburg; 500pf. Cottbus State Theatre; 550pf. Suhl-Heinrichs Town Hall, Thuringia; 700pf. National Theatre, Berlin.

The 10, 60, 80 and 100pf. also exist imperforate and self-adhesive from booklets.

For similar designs inscribed "DEUTSCHLAND", see Nos. 2654/66.

855 Gluck and Score of "Armide"

1987. Death Bicentenary of Christoph Willibald Gluck (composer).
2221 **855** 60pf. black, grey and red 1·20 45

856 Poster by Emil Orlik for "The Weavers"

1987. 125th Birth Anniv of Gerhart Hauptmann (playwright).
2222 **856** 80pf. lt red, black & red 1·80 55

857 Paddy Field

1987. 25th Anniv of German Famine Aid.
2223 **857** 80pf. multicoloured 1·80 55

858 "Birth of Christ" (13th-century Book of Psalms)

1987. Christmas.
2224 **858** 80pf.+40pf. mult 1·80 1·60

859 Jester

1988. 150th Anniv of Mainz Carnival.
2225 **859** 60pf. multicoloured 1·30 55

860 Kaiser

1988. Birth Centenary of Jakob Kaiser (trade unionist and politician).
2226 **860** 80pf. black and grey 1·20 55

861 Stein and Mayer

1988. Beatification of Edith Stein and Father Rupert Mayer.
2227 **861** 80pf. multicoloured 1·50 55

862 Dr Konrad Adenauer (West German Chancellor) and Charles de Gaulle (French President)

1988. 25th Anniv of Franco-German Co-operation Treaty.
2228 **862** 80pf. purple and black 2·00 70

863 "Solitude of the Green Woods" (woodcut of poem, Ludwig Richter)

1988. Birth Bicentenary of Joseph von Eichendorff (writer).
2229 **863** 60pf. multicoloured 1·50 55

864 Raiffeisen and Ploughed Field

1988. Death Centenary of Friedrich Wilhelm Raiffeisen (philanthropist and agricultural co-operative founder).
2230 **864** 80pf. green and black 2·00 55

865 Schopenhauer

1988. Birth Bicentenary of Arthur Schopenhauer (philosopher).

2231	**865**	80pf. brown and black	1·80	55

866 Football (European Championship)

1988. Sport Promotion Fund. Multicoloured.

2232		60pf.+30pf. Type **866**	1·40	1·10
2233		80pf.+40pf. Tennis (Olympic Games)	2·30	1·80
2234		120pf.+55pf. Diving (Olympic Games)	2·75	2·20

867 Buddy Holly

1988. Youth Welfare. Pop Music. Mult.

2235		50pf.+25pf. Type **867**	1·40	1·60
2236		60pf.+30pf. Elvis Presley	3·25	2·75
2237		70pf.+35pf. Jim Morrison	1·80	1·80
2238		80pf.+40pf. John Lennon	3·00	2·50

868 Hutten (wood engraving from "Conquestiones")

1988. 500th Birth Anniv of Ulrich von Hutten (writer).

2239	**868**	80pf. multicoloured	1·50	60

869 City Buildings and Jan Wellem Monument

1988. 700th Anniv of Dusseldorf.

2240	**869**	60pf. multicoloured	1·50	55

870 Airbus Industrie A320 and Manufacturing Nations' Flag

1988. Europa. Transport and Communications. Multicoloured.

2241		60pf. Type **870**	1·40	55
2242		80pf. Diagram of Integrated Services Digital Network	1·40	55

871 University Buildings and City Landmarks

1988. 600th Anniv of Cologne University.

2243	**871**	80pf. multicoloured	1·50	55

872 Monnet

1988. Birth Centenary of Jean Monnet (statesman).

2244	**872**	80pf. multicoloured	1·50	55

873 Storm

1988. Death Centenary of Theodor Storm (writer).

2245	**873**	80pf. multicoloured	1·50	55

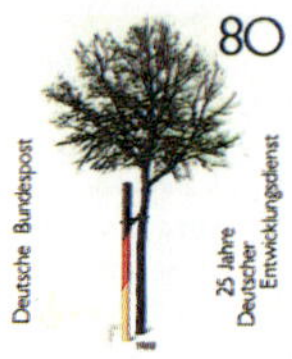

874 Tree supported by Stake in National Colours

1988. 25th Anniv of German Volunteer Service.

2246	**874**	80pf. multicoloured	1·50	55

875 Meersburg

1988. Millenary of Meersburg.

2247	**875**	60pf. multicoloured	1·10	55

876 Gmelin

1988. Birth Bicentenary of Leopold Gmelin (chemist).

2248	**876**	80pf. multicoloured	1·20	55

877 Vernier Caliper Rule in National Colours

1988. "Made in Germany".

2249	**877**	140pf. multicoloured	2·30	1·10

878 Bebel

1988. 75th Death Anniv of August Bebel (Social Democratic Labour Party co-founder).

2250	**878**	80pf. mauve, blue & sil	1·80	55

879 Carrier Pigeon

1988. Stamp Day.

2251	**879**	20pf. multicoloured	75	45

880 13th-century Rock Crystal Reliquary

1988. Humanitarian Relief Funds. Precious Metal Work. Multicoloured.

2252		50pf.+25pf. Type **880**	75	70
2253		60pf.+30pf. 14th-century bust of Charlemagne	1·10	1·10
2254		70pf.+35pf. 10th-cent. crown of Otto III	1·20	1·10
2255		80pf.+40pf. 17th-cent. jewelled flowers	1·60	1·60

881 Red Cross

1988. 125th Anniv of Red Cross.

2256	**881**	80pf. red and black	1·60	55

882 Burning Synagogue, Baden-Baden

1988. 50th Anniv of "Kristallnacht" (Nazi pogrom).

2257	**882**	80pf. purple and black	1·20	55

883 Cancelled Postage Stamps

1988. Centenary of Collection of Used Stamps for the Bethel Charity.

2258	**883**	60pf. multicoloured	1·40	55

884 Linked Arms

1988. Centenary of Samaritan Workers' (first aid) Association.

2259	**884**	80pf. multicoloured	1·40	55

885 "Adoration of the Magi" (illus from Henry the Lion's Gospel Book)

1988. Christmas.

2260	**885**	80pf.+40pf. mult	1·60	1·40

886 "Bluxao I"

1989. Birth Centenary of Willi Baumeister (painter).

2261	**886**	60pf. multicoloured	1·20	55

887 Bonn

1988. 2000th Anniv of Bonn.

2262	**887**	80pf. multicoloured	1·80	80

888 Grass growing from Dry, Cracked Earth

1989. 30th Anniversaries of Misereor and Bread for the World (Third World relief organizations).

2263	**888**	80pf. multicoloured	1·40	55

889 "Cats in the Attic" (woodcut)

1989. Birth Cent of Gerhard Marcks (artist).

2264	**889**	60pf. black, stone and red	1·20	55

890 Table Tennis (World Championships)

1989. Sport Promotion Fund. Multicoloured.

2265		100pf.+50pf. Type **890**	2·30	2·00
2266		140pf.+60pf. Gymnastics (World Championships)	3·25	3·00

891 Elephants

1989. Youth Welfare. Circus. Multicoloured.

2267		60pf.+30pf. Type **891**	1·80	1·80
2268		70pf.+30pf. Acrobat on horseback	2·30	2·20
2269		80pf.+35pf. Clown	3·25	2·75
2270		100pf.+50pf. Caravans and Big Top	4·50	3·00

892 Posthorn and Book of Stamps

1989. "IPHLA '89" International Philatelic Literature Exhibition, Frankfurt.

2271	**892**	100pf.+50pf. mult	3·25	2·75

893 European and Members' Flags

1989. 3rd Direct Elections to European Parliament.

2272	**893**	100pf. multicoloured	2·40	1·10

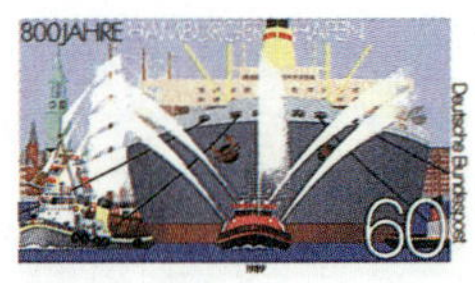

894 Shipping

1989. 800th Anniv of Hamburg Harbour.

2273	**894**	60pf. multicoloured	1·60	55

895 Asam (detail of fresco, Weltenburg Abbey)

1989. 250th Death Anniv of Cosmas Damian Asam (painter and architect).
2274 **895** 60pf. multicoloured 90 55

896 Kites

1989. Europa. Children's Toys. Multicoloured.
2275 60pf. Type **896** 1·40 45
2276 100pf. Puppet show 2·30 45

897 Emblem, National Colours and Presidents' Signatures

1989. 40th Anniv of German Federal Republic.
2277 **897** 100pf. multicoloured 2·20 80

898 Council Assembly and Stars

1989. 40th Anniv of Council of Europe.
2278 **898** 100pf. blue and gold 2·00 90

899 Gabelsberger and Shorthand

1989. Birth Bicentenary of Franz Xaver Gabelsberger (shorthand pioneer).
2279 **899** 100pf. multicoloured 2·00 70

900 Score of "Lorelei" and Silhouette of Silcher

1989. Birth Bicentenary of Friedrich Silcher (composer).
2280 **900** 80pf. multicoloured 1·20 55

901 Saints Kilian, Totnan and Colman (from 12th-century German manuscript)

1989. 1300th Death Anniversaries of Saints Kilian, Colman and Totnan (Irish missionaries to Franconia).
2281 **901** 100pf. multicoloured 1·80 70

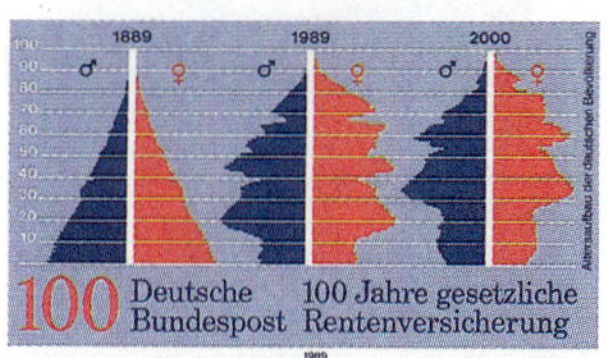

902 Age Graphs of Men and Women

1989. Centenary of National Insurance.
2282 **902** 100p. blue, red & lt blue 1·80 60

903 "Summer Evening" (Heinrich Vogler)

1989. Cent of Worpswede Artists' Village.
2283 **903** 60pf. multicoloured 1·00 55

904 Schneider

1989. 50th Death Anniv of Reverend Paul Schneider (concentration camp victim).
2284 **904** 100pf. blk, lt grey & grey 1·40 60

905 List (after Kriehuber) and Train

1989. Birth Bicentenary of Friedrich List (economist).
2285 **905** 170pf. black and red 2·75 1·10

906 Cathedral

1989. 750th Anniv of Frankfurt Cathedral.
2286 **906** 60pf. multicoloured 1·50 55

907 Children building House

1989. "Don't Forget the Children".
2287 **907** 100pf. multicoloured 1·60 60

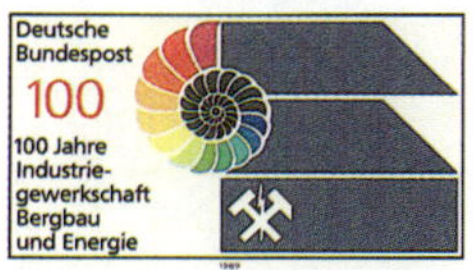

908 Ammonite and Union Emblem

1989. Centenary of Mining and Power Industries Trade Union.
2288 **908** 100pf. multicoloured 1·50 60

909 18th-century Mounted Courier, Thurn and Taxis

1989. Humanitarian Relief Funds. Postal Deliveries. Multicoloured.
2289 60pf.+30pf. Type **909** 1·40 1·20
2290 80pf.+35pf. Hamburg postal messenger, 1808 2·30 1·80
2291 100pf.+50pf. Bavarian mail coach, 1900 3·00 2·75

910 Maier

1989. Birth Centenary of Reinhold Maier (politician).
2292 **910** 100pf. multicoloured 1·60 60

911 Organ Pipes

1989. 300th Anniv of Arp Schnitger Organ, St. James's Church, Hamburg.
2293 **911** 60pf. multicoloured 1·50 55

912 Angel

1989. Christmas. 16th-century Carvings by Veit Stoss, St. Lawrence's Church, Nuremberg. Multicoloured.
2294 60pf.+30pf. Type **912** 1·50 1·20
2295 100pf.+50pf. "Nativity" 1·80 1·80

913 Speyer

1990. 2000th Anniv of Speyer.
2296 **913** 60pf. multicoloured 1·50 55

914 "Courier" (Albrecht Durer)

1990. 500th Anniv of Regular European Postal Services.
2297 **914** 100pf. deep brown, light brown and brown 2·40 70

915 Vine forming Initial "R"

1990. 500 Years of Riesling Grape Cultivation.
2298 **915** 100pf. multicoloured 1·50 70

916 Old Lubeck

1990. UNESCO World Heritage Site, Old Lubeck.
2299 **916** 100pf. multicoloured 1·50 70

917 15th-century Seal and Grand Master's Arms

1990. 800th Anniv of Teutonic Order.
2300 **917** 100pf. multicoloured 1·80 70

918 Frederick II's Seal and Fair Entrance Hall

1990. 750th Anniv of Granting of Fair Privileges to Frankfurt.
2301 **918** 100pf. multicoloured 1·80 70

919 Maze

1990. 25th Anniv of Youth Research Science Competition.
2302 **919** 100pf. multicoloured 1·80 70

920 Wildlife

1990. North Sea Protection.
2303 **920** 100pf. multicoloured 2·00 70

921 Handball

1990. Sport Promotion Fund. Multicoloured.
2304 100pf.+50pf. Type **921** 3·00 1·80
2305 140pf.+60pf. Keep-fit 3·50 2·75

922 Widow Bolte

1990. Youth Welfare. 125th Anniv of Max and Moritz (characters from books by Wilhelm Busch). Multicoloured.
2306 60pf.+30pf. Type **922** 1·00 95
2307 70pf.+30pf. Max asleep 1·50 1·40
2308 80pf.+35pf. Moritz watching Max sawing through bridge 2·00 1·50
2309 100pf.+50pf. Max and Moritz 2·40 2·00

923 "1.MAI" and Factory Silhouette

1990. Centenary of Labour Day.
2310 **923** 100pf. red and black 1·50 70

924 Woman's Face

1990. 75th Anniv of German Association of Housewives.
2311 **924** 100pf. multicoloured 1·50 70

925 Collection Box

1990. 125th Anniv of German Lifeboat Institution.
2312 **925** 60pf. multicoloured 1·50 60

926 Thurn and Taxis Palace, Frankfurt

1990. Europa. Post Office Buildings. Mult.
2313 60pf. Type **926** 1·50 70
2314 100pf. Postal Giro Office, Frankfurt 2·10 70

927 St Philip's Church, Protestant Church Flag and Candle Flames

1990. Centenary of Rummelsberg Diaconal Institution.
2315 **927** 100pf. multicoloured 1·50 70

928 Leuschner

1990. Birth Centenary of Wilhelm Leuschner (trade unionist and member of anti-Hitler Resistance).
2316 **928** 100pf. black and lilac 1·80 70

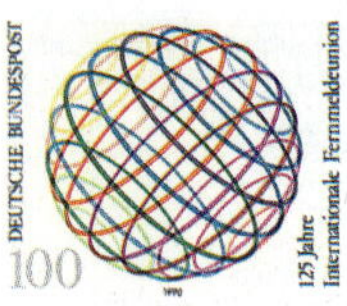

929 Globe

1990. 125th Anniv of I.T.U.
2317 **929** 100pf. multicoloured 1·50 70

930 National Colours and Students

1990. 175th Anniv of German Students' Fraternity and of their Colours (now national colours).
2318 **930** 100pf. multicoloured 1·80 70

931 Hands exchanging Money and Goods

1990. 30th World Congress of International Chamber of Commerce, Hamburg.
2319 **931** 80pf. multicoloured 1·50 90

932 Closing Sentence of Charter

1990. 40th Anniv of Expelled Germans Charter.
2320 **932** 100pf. multicoloured 1·80 60

933 Children of Different Races

1990. 10th International Youth Philatelic Exhibition, Dusseldorf. Sheet 165×101 mm.
MS2321 **933** 6×100pf.+50pf. multicoloured 20·00 22·00

934 Claudius

1990. 250th Birth Anniv of Matthias Claudius (writer).
2322 **934** 100pf. blue, black and red 1·60 60

935 Mail Motor Wagon, 1900

1990. Humanitarian Relief Funds. Posts and Telecommunications. Multicoloured.
2323 60pf.+30pf. Type **935** 1·10 1·10
2324 80pf.+35pf. Telephone exchange, 1890 1·80 1·80
2325 100pf.+50pf. Parcel sorting office, 1900 2·40 2·30

936 "German Unity" and National Colours

1990. Reunification of Germany.
2326 **936** 50pf. black, red & yellow 1·40 50
2327 **936** 100pf. black, red & yell 1·80 65

937 Schliemann and Lion Gate, Mycenae

1990. Death Centenary of Heinrich Schliemann (archaeologist).
2328 **937** 60pf. multicoloured 1·50 55

938 Penny Black, Bavaria 1k. and West Germany 1989 100pf. Stamps

1990. Stamp Day. 150th Anniv of the Penny Black.
2329 **938** 100pf. multicoloured 1·60 55

939 National Colours spanning Breach in Wall

1990. 1st Anniv of Opening of Berlin Wall.
2330 50pf. Type **939** 1·40 80
2331 100pf. Brandenburg Gate and crowd 1·80 80
MS2332 146×100 mm. As Nos. 2330/1 3·75 3·75

940 Angel with Candles

1990. Christmas. Multicoloured.
2333 50pf.+20pf. Type **940** 90 90
2334 60pf.+30pf. Figure of man smoking 1·10 1·10
2335 70pf.+30pf. "Soldier" nutcrackers 1·50 1·40
2336 100pf.+50pf. Tinsel angel 2·30 2·20

941 Kathe Dorsch in "Mrs Warren's Profession"

1990. Birth Centenary of Kathe Dorsch (actress).
2337 **941** 100pf. violet and red 1·60 70

942 View of City

1991. 750th Anniv of Hanover.
2338 **942** 60pf. multicoloured 1·50 55

943 "Three Golden Circles with a Full Circle in Blue" (relief in wood)

1991. Birth Centenary of Erich Buchholz (artist).
2339 **943** 60pf. multicoloured 1·20 55

944 Miniature from 13th-century French Code

1991. 750th Anniv of Promulgation of Pharmaceutical Ethics in Germany.
2340 **944** 100pf. multicoloured 1·80 70

945 Brandenburg Gate (from "Old Engravings of Berlin")

1991. Bicentenary of Brandenburg Gate.
2341 **945** 100pf. black, red and grey 2·10 55

946 Eucken

1991. Birth Centenary of Walter Eucken (economist).
2342 **946** 100pf. multicoloured 1·60 70

947 Globe and "25" (poster)

1991. 25th International Tourism Fair, Berlin.
2343 **947** 100pf. multicoloured 1·60 55

948 Two-man Bobsleigh

1991. World Bobsleigh Championships, Altenberg. Sheet 55×80 mm.
MS2344 **948** 100pf. multicoloured 2·20 2·75

949 Weightlifting (World Championships)

1991. Sport Promotion Fund. Multicoloured.
2345 70pf.+30pf. Type **949** 1·60 1·50
2346 100pf.+50pf. Cycling (world championships) 1·80 1·80
2347 140pf.+60pf. Basketball (centenary) 2·50 2·40
2348 170pf.+80pf. Wrestling (European championships) 2·75 2·75

950 Title Page of "Cautio Criminalis" (tract against witch trials), Langenfeld and Score of "Trutz-Nachtigall"

1991. 400th Birth Anniv of Friedrich Spee von Langenfeld (poet and human rights pioneer).
2349 **950** 100pf. multicoloured 1·60 55

951 Androsace

1991. Plants in Rennsteiggarten (botanical garden), Oberhof. Multicoloured.
2350 30pf. Type **951** 45 45
2351 50pf. Primula 70 60
2352 80pf. Gentian 1·10 45
2353 100pf. Cranberry 1·80 65
2354 350pf. Edelweiss 5·50 3·50

952 Werth (attr Wenzel Hollar)

1991. 400th Birth Anniv of Jan von Werth (military commander).
2355 **952** 60pf. multicoloured 1·20 55

953 Windthorst

1991. Death Centenary of Ludwig Windthorst (politician).
2356 **953** 100pf. multicoloured 1·60 55

954 Junkers F-13, 1930

1991. Historic Mail Aircraft. Multicoloured.
2357 30pf. Type **954** 45 45
2358 50pf. Hans Grade's monoplane, 1909 70 35
2359 100pf. Fokker F.III, 1922 1·80 45
2360 165pf. Airship LZ-127 "Graf Zeppelin", 1928 3·00 2·75

955 Mountain Clouded Yellow

1991. Youth Welfare. Endangered Butterflies. Multicoloured.

2361	30pf.+15pf. Type **955**	45	45
2362	50pf.+25pf. Poplar admiral	60	55
2363	60pf.+30pf. Purple emperor	1·10	1·10
2364	70pf.+30pf. Violet copper	1·20	1·10
2365	80pf.+35pf. Swallowtail	1·50	1·40
2366	90pf.+45pf. Small apollo	1·80	1·80
2367	100pf.+50pf. Moorland clouded yellow	2·30	2·20
2368	140pf.+60pf. Large copper	2·75	2·75

See also Nos. 2449/53.

956 Academy Building, 1830

1991. Bicentenary of Choral Academy, Berlin.

2369	**956**	100pf. multicoloured	1·60	70

957 Typesetting School, 1875

1991. 125th Anniv of Lette Foundation (institute for professional training of women).

2370	**957**	100pf. multicoloured	1·60	55

958 Battle (detail of miniature, Schlackenwerth Codex, 1350)

1991. 750th Anniv of Battle of Legnica.

2371	**958**	100pf. multicoloured	1·80	1·10

959 Arms

1991. 700th Anniv of Granting of Charters to Six Towns of Trier.

2372	**959**	60pf. multicoloured	1·20	55

960 Speeding Train

1991. Inauguration of Inter-City Express (ICE) Railway Service.

2373	**960**	60pf. multicoloured	1·20	55

961 "ERS-1" European Remote Sensing Satellite

1991. Europa. Europe in Space. Mult.

2374	60pf. Type **961**	1·60	60
2375	100pf. "Kopernikus" telecommunications satellite	2·50	60

962 Reger and Organ Pipes

1991. 75th Death Anniv of Max Reger (composer).

2376	**962**	100pf. multicoloured	1·80	80

963 Ruffs

1991. Seabirds. Multicoloured.

2390	60pf. Type **963**	90	55
2391	80pf. Little terns	1·40	90
2392	100pf. Brent geese	1·40	90
2393	140pf. White-tailed sea eagles	2·50	2·00

964 Wilhelm August Lampadius (gas pioneer)

1991. 18th World Gas Congress, Berlin. Each black and blue.

2394	60pf. Type **964**	90	35
2395	100pf. Gas street lamp, Berlin	1·40	55

965 Wallot (after Franz Wurbel) and Reichstag Building, Berlin

1991. 150th Birth Anniv of Paul Wallot (architect).

2396	**965**	100pf. multicoloured	1·90	55

966 "Libellula depressa"

1991. Dragonflies. Multicoloured.

2397	50pf. Type **966**	75	55
2398	60pf. Type **966**	1·40	90
2399	60pf. "Sympetrum sanguineum"	1·40	90
2400	60pf. "Cordulegaster boltonii"	1·40	90
2401	60pf. "Aeshna viridis"	1·40	90
2402	70pf. As No. 2399	1·40	1·10
2403	80pf. As No. 2400	1·40	90
2404	100pf. As No. 2401	1·40	90

967 Hand clutching Cloak

1991. 40th Anniv of Geneva Convention on Refugees.

2405	**967**	100pf. lilac and black	1·70	55

968 Radio Waves and Mast

1991. International Radio Exhibition, Berlin.

2406	**968**	100pf. multicoloured	1·70	55

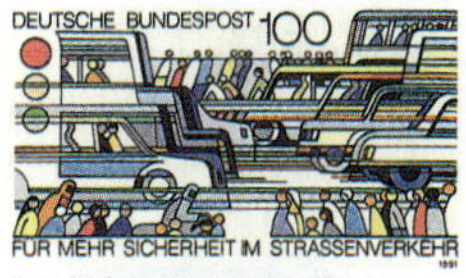

969 Pedestrians and Traffic

1991. Road Safety Campaign.

2407	**969**	100pf. multicoloured	1·80	70

970 Lilienthal

1991. Centenary of First Heavier-than-Air Manned Flight by Otto Lilienthal and "Lilienthal '91" European Airmail Exhibition, Dresden. Sheet 57×82 mm.

MS2408	**970** 100pf.+50pf. brown, blue and red	3·75	3·50

971 August Heinrich Hoffmann von Fallersleben (lyricist) and Third Verse

1991. 150th Anniv of "Song of the Germans" (national anthem).

2409	**971**	100pf. red, black & green	1·70	55

972 Thadden-Trieglaff

1991. Birth Cent of Reinold von Thadden-Trieglaff (founder of German Protestant Convention).

2410	**972**	100pf. multicoloured	1·60	55

973 Transmission Test between Lauffen am Neckar and Frankfurt am Main

1991. Centenary of Three-phase Energy Transmission.

2411	**973**	170pf. multicoloured	2·75	1·30

974 Quill, Pen and Sword

1991. Birth Bicentenary of Theodor Korner (poet). Sheet 55×80 mm containing T 974 and similar vert designs. Multicoloured.

MS2412	60pf. Type **974**; 100pf. Korner	2·75	3·00

975 Albers in "The Winner"

1991. Birth Centenary of Hans Albers (actor).

2413	**975**	100pf. multicoloured	2·40	55

976 Harbour

1991. 275th Anniv of Rhine-Ruhr Port, Duisburg.

2414	**976**	100pf. multicoloured	1·70	55

977 Bethel Post Office

1991. Humanitarian Relief Funds. Postal Buildings. Multicoloured.

2415	30pf.+15pf. Type **977**	55	55
2416	60pf.+30pf. Budingen post station	1·10	1·10
2417	70pf.+30pf. Stralsund post office	1·40	1·30
2418	80pf.+35pf. Lauscha post office	1·70	1·60
2419	100pf.+50pf. Bonn post office	2·20	2·10
2420	140pf.+60pf. Weilburg post office	2·75	2·75

978 Postal Delivery in Spreewald Region

1991. Stamp Day.

2421	**978**	100pf. multicoloured	1·60	55

979 "Bird Monument" (detail)

1991. Birth Centenary of Max Ernst (painter).

2422	**979**	100pf. multicoloured	1·70	55

980 "Portrait of the Dancer Anita Berber"

1991. Birth Cent of Otto Dix (painter). Mult.

2423	60pf. Type **980**	90	55
2424	100pf. "Self-portrait in Right Profile"	1·80	60

981 "The Violinist and the Water Sprite"

1991. Sorbian Legends. Multicoloured.

2425	60pf. Type **981**	1·10	55
2426	100pf. "The Midday Woman and the Woman from Nochten"	1·60	60

982 Angel (detail of "The Annunciation")

1991. Christmas. Works by Martin Schongauer. Multicoloured.

2427	60pf.+30pf. Type **982**	1·20	1·10
2428	70pf.+30pf. Virgin Mary (detail of "The Annunciation")	1·50	1·30
2429	80pf.+35pf. Angel (detail of "Madonna in a Rose Garden")	3·00	2·50
2430	100pf.+50pf. "Nativity"	3·75	3·00

983 Leber

1991. Birth Cent of Julius Leber (politician).
2431 **983** 100pf. multicoloured 1·60 55

984 Nelly Sachs

1991. Birth Centenary of Nelly Sachs (writer).
2432 **984** 100pf. dp violet & violet 1·70 55

985 Mozart

1991. Death Bicentenary of Wolfgang Amadeus Mozart (composer). Sheet 82×56 mm.
MS2433 **985** 100pf. lilac and brown 2·75 3·00

986 Base of William I Monument and City Silhouette

1992. 2000th Anniv of Koblenz.
2434 **986** 60pf. multicoloured 1·80 60

987 Niemoller

1992. Birth Centenary of Martin Niemoller (theologian).
2435 **987** 100pf. multicoloured 1·40 55

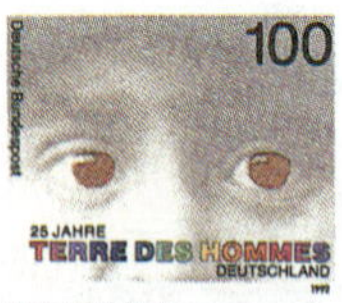

988 Child's Eyes

1992. 25th Anniv of Terre des Hommes (child welfare organization) in Germany.
2436 **988** 100pf. multicoloured 1·80 70

989 Arms of Baden-Wurttemberg

1992. Lander of the Federal Republic.
2437 **989** 100pf. multicoloured 1·70 80

See also Nos. 2448, 2465, 2470, 2474, 2479, 2506, 2526, 2527, 2534, 2539, 2556, 2567, 2580, 2584 and 2597.

990 Fencing

1992. Sport Promotion Fund. Olympic Games, Albertville and Barcelona. Multicoloured.
2438 60pf.+30pf. Type **990** 1·10 1·10
2439 80pf.+40pf. Rowing eight 1·30 1·20
2440 100pf.+50pf. Dressage 2·75 2·75
2441 170pf.+80pf. Skiing (slalom) 4·50 4·25

991 Honegger and Score of Ballet "Semiramis"

1992. Birth Centenary of Arthur Honegger (composer).
2442 **991** 100pf. black and brown 1·80 80

992 Zeppelin and LZ-127 "Graf Zeppelin"

1992. 75th Death Anniv of Ferdinand von Zeppelin (airship manufacturer).
2443 **992** 165pf. multicoloured 2·75 1·40

993 Kiel City and Harbour

1992. 750th Anniv of Kiel.
2444 **993** 60pf. multicoloured 1·30 60

994 Andreas Marggraf, Beet, Franz Achard and Carl Scheibler

1992. 125th Anniv of Berlin Sugar Institute.
2445 **994** 100pf. multicoloured 1·70 80

The stamp depicts the discoverer of beet sugar, the founder of the beet sugar industry and the founder of the Institute respectively.

995 Horses and Renz

1992. Death Centenary of Ernst Jakob Renz (circus director).
2446 **995** 100pf. multicoloured 1·60 60

996 Adenauer

1992. 25th Death Anniv of Konrad Adenauer (Chancellor, 1949–63).
2447 **996** 100pf. brn & cinnamon 2·10 60

1992. Lander of the Federal Republic. As T **989**. Multicoloured.
2448 100pf. Bavaria 1·70 80

1992. Youth Welfare. Endangered Moths. As T **955**. Multicoloured.
2449 60pf.+30pf. Purple tiger moth 1·60 1·60
2450 70pf.+30pf. Hawk moth 1·80 1·80
2451 80pf.+40pf. "Noctuidae sp." 2·40 2·30
2452 100pf.+50pf. Tiger moth 2·50 2·50
2453 170pf.+80pf. "Arichanna melanaria" 3·00 2·75

997 Schall

1992. 400th Birth Anniv of Adam Schall von Bell (missionary astronomer).
2454 **997** 140pf. black, yellow & bl 2·40 1·10

998 Cathedral and St. Severus's Church

1992. 1250th Anniv of Erfurt.
2455 **998** 60pf. multicoloured 1·30 60

999 Woodcut from 1493 Edition of Columbus's Letters

1992. Europa. 500th Anniv of Discovery of America by Columbus. Multicoloured.
2456 60pf. Type **999** 1·40 60
2457 100pf. "Rene de Laudonniere and Chief Athore" (Jacques le Moyne de Morgues, 1564) 1·80 60

1000 "Consecration of St. Ludgerus" (from "Vita Liudgeri" by Altfridus)

1992. 1250th Birth Anniv of St. Ludgerus (first Bishop of Munster).
2458 **1000** 100pf. multicoloured 1·60 70

1001 Arithmetic Sum

1992. 500th Birth Anniv of Adam Riese (mathematician).
2459 **1001** 100pf. multicoloured 1·80 60

1002 Order of Merit

1992. 150th Anniv of Civil Class of Order of Merit (for scientific or artistic achievement).
2460 **1002** 100pf. multicoloured 1·60 60

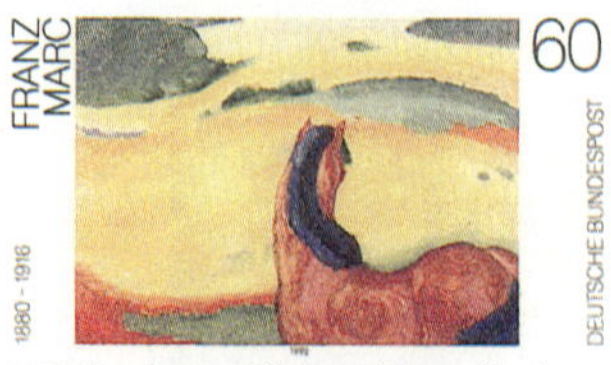

1003 "Landscape with Horse" (Franz Marc)

1992. 20th-century German Paintings (1st series). Multicoloured.
2461 60pf. Type **1003** 90 70
2462 100pf. "Fashion Shop" (August Macke) 1·40 70
2463 170pf. "Murnau with Rainbow" (Wassily Kandinsky) 2·50 1·90

See also Nos. 2507/9, 2590/2, 2615/17 and 2704/6.

1004 Lichtenberg

1992. 250th Birth Anniv of Georg Christoph Lichtenberg (physicist and essayist).
2464 **1004** 100pf. multicoloured 1·60 70

1992. Lander of the Federal Republic. As T **989**. Multicoloured.
2465 100pf. Berlin 1·70 80

1005 Rainforest

1992. "Save the Tropical Rain Forest".
2466 **1005** 100pf.+50pf. mult 2·20 2·10

The premium was for the benefit of environmental projects.

1006 Garden

1992. Leipzig Botanical Garden.
2467 **1006** 60pf. multicoloured 1·20 60

1007 Stylized House and Globe

1992. 17th International Home Economics Congress, Hanover.
2468 **1007** 100pf. multicoloured 1·80 70

1008 Family

1992. Family Life.
2469 **1008** 100pf. multicoloured 1·80 60

1992. Lander of the Federal Republic. As T **989**. Multicoloured.
2470 100pf. Brandenburg 1·70 80

1009 "Assumption of the Virgin Mary" (Rohr Monastery Church)

1992. 300th Birth Anniv of Egid Quirin Asam (sculptor).
2471 **1009** 60pf. multicoloured 1·20 60

1010 Opera House (Georg von Knobelsdorff)

1992. 250th Anniv of German State Opera House, Berlin.
2472 **1010** 80pf. multicoloured 1·60 60

1011 Masked Actors

1992. Centenary of German Amateur Theatres Federation.
2473 **1011** 100pf. multicoloured 1·80 60

1992. Lander of the Federal Republic. As T 989. Multicoloured.
2474 100pf. Bremen 1·70 80

1012 Globe

1992. 500th Anniv of Martin Behaim's Terrestrial Globe.
2475 **1012** 60pf. multicoloured 1·50 60

1013 1890 Pendant and 1990 Clock

1992. 225th Anniv of Jewellery and Watch-making in Pforzheim.
2476 **1013** 100pf. multicoloured 1·60 60

1014 Bergengruen (after Hanni Fries)

1992. Birth Centenary of Werner Bergengruen (writer).
2477 **1014** 100pf. grey, blue & blk 1·60 60

1015 Neue Holzbrucke Bridge, nr Essing

1992. Inauguration of Main–Donau Canal.
2478 **1015** 100pf. multicoloured 1·60 60

1992. Lander of the Federal Republic. As T 989. Multicoloured.
2479 100pf. Hamburg 1·70 80

1016 Turret Clock, 1400

1992. Humanitarian Relief Funds. Clocks. Multicoloured.
2480 60pf.+30pf. Type **1016** 1·30 1·20
2481 70pf.+30pf. Astronomical mantel clock, 1738 1·50 1·40
2482 80pf.+40pf. Flute clock, 1790 1·60 1·60
2483 100pf.+50pf. Figurine clock, 1580 2·00 1·90
2484 170pf.+80pf. Table clock, 1550 3·00 2·75

1017 Distler and Score of "We Praise Our Lord Jesus Christ"

1992. 50th Death Anniv of Hugo Distler (composer).
2485 **1017** 100pf. black and violet 1·80 60

1018 Balloon Post

1992. Stamp Day.
2486 **1018** 100pf. multicoloured 1·80 70

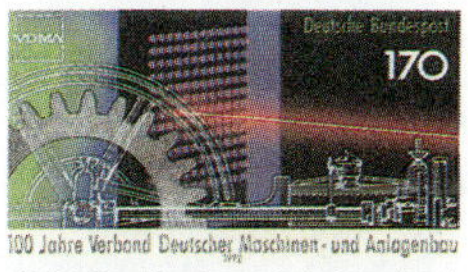

1019 Otto Engine, 1892, Cogwheel and Laser Beam

1992. Centenary of German Plant and Machine Builders Association.
2487 **1019** 170pf. multicoloured 2·20 1·20

1020 "Adoration of the Magi"

1992. Christmas. Carvings by Franz Maidburg, St. Anne's Church, Annaberg-Buchholz. Mult.
2488 60pf.+30pf. Type **1020** 1·30 1·20
2489 100pf.+50pf. "Birth of Christ" 1·80 1·80

1021 Blucher (after Simon Meister)

1992. 250th Birth Anniv of Field Marshal Gebhard Leberecht von Blucher.
2490 **1021** 100pf. multicoloured 1·80 60

1022 Werner von Siemens

1992. Death Centenary of Werner von Siemens (electrical engineer).
2491 **1022** 100pf. brown & dp brn 1·80 60

1023 Klepper

1992. 50th Death Anniv of Jochen Klepper (writer).
2492 **1023** 100pf. multicoloured 1·80 60

1024 Star in German Colours

1992. European Single Market.
2493 **1024** 100pf. multicoloured 2·20 70

1025 Cathedral and Uberwasser Church

1993. 1200th Anniv of Munster.
2494 **1025** 60pf. multicoloured 1·20 60

1026 Newton, Sketch of Refraction of Light and Formula

1993. 350th Birth Anniv of Sir Isaac Newton (scientist).
2495 **1026** 100pf. multicoloured 1·50 60

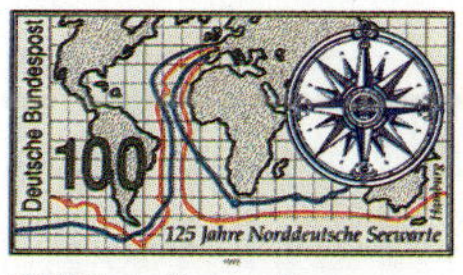

1027 Route Map and Compass Rose

1993. 125th Anniv of North German Naval Observatory, Hamburg.
2496 **1027** 100pf. multicoloured 1·50 60

1028 Emblem and Safety Stripes

1993. European Year of Health, Hygiene and Safety in the Workplace.
2497 **1028** 100pf. blue, yell & blk 1·50 60

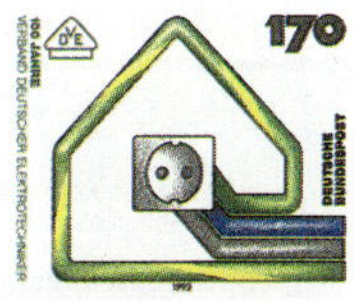

1029 Wires and Wall Socket forming House

1993. Centenary of German Association of Electrical Engineers.
2498 **1029** 170pf. multicoloured 2·20 1·20

1030 Ski-jumping Hill, Garmisch-Partenkirchen

1993. Sport Promotion Fund. German Olympic Venues. Multicoloured.
2499 60pf.+30pf. Type **1030** 1·80 1·60
2500 80pf.+40pf. Olympia-park, Munich 2·40 2·10
2501 100pf.+50pf. Olympic Stadium, Berlin 3·00 2·75
2502 170pf.+80pf. Olympic Harbour, Kiel 3·75 3·25

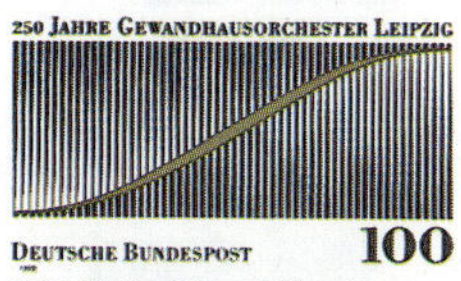

1031 Stylised Sound Vibration

1993. 250th Anniv of Leipzig Gewandhaus Orchestra.
2503 **1031** 100pf. gold and black 1·50 60

1032 Statue of St. John and Charles Bridge, Prague

1993. 600th Death Anniv of St. John of Nepomuk.
2504 **1032** 100pf. multicoloured 1·50 60

1033 Diagram explaining New Postcodes

1993. Introduction of Five-digit Postcode System.
2505 **1033** 100pf. multicoloured 1·80 60

1993. Lander of the Federal Republic. As T 989. Multicoloured.
2506 100pf. Hesse 1·60 80

1993. 20th-century German Paintings (2nd series). As T 1003. Multicoloured.
2507 100pf. multicoloured 1·60 90
2508 100pf. black, grey and mauve 1·60 90
2509 100pf. multicoloured 1·60 90
DESIGNS: No. 2507, "Cafe" (George Grosz); 2508. "Sea and Sun" (Otto Pankok); 2509, "Audience" (Andreas Paul Weber).

1034 Abbeys

1993. 900th Anniversaries of Maria Laach and Bursfelde Benedictine Abbeys.
2510 **1034** 80pf. multicoloured 1·50 60

1035 Alpine Longhorn Beetle

1993. Youth Welfare. Endangered Beetles. Multicoloured.
2511 80pf.+40f. Type **1035** 1·80 1·80
2512 80pf.+40pf. Rose chafer 1·80 1·80
2513 100pf.+50pf. Stag beetle 2·20 2·10
2514 100pf.+50pf. Tiger beetle 2·20 2·10
2515 200pf.+50pf. Cockchafer 3·50 3·25

1036 Plants

1993. 5th International Horticultural Show, Stuttgart.
2516 **1036** 100pf. multicoloured 1·50 60

1037 Horse Race

1993. 125th Anniv of Hoppegarten Racecourse.
2517 **1037** 80pf. multicoloured 1·20 70

1038 "Storage Place" (Joseph Beuys)

1993. Europa. Contemporary Art. Mult.
2518 80pf. Type **1038** 1·50 90
2519 100pf. "Homage to the Square" (Josef Albers) 1·50 90

1039 Church and Pupils

1993. 450th Anniv of Pforta School.
2520 **1039** 100pf. multicoloured 1·50 60

1040 Students, Flag, City Hall and Castle

1993. 125th Anniv of Coburg Association of University Student Unions.
2521 **1040** 100pf. black, grn & red 1·50 60

1041 "Hohentwiel" (lake steamer) and Flags

1993. Lake Constance European Region.
2522 **1041** 100pf. multicoloured 1·60 60

1042 "Old Market—View of St. Nicholas's Church" (detail, Ferdinand von Arnim)

1993. Millenary of Potsdam.
2523 **1042** 80pf. multicoloured 1·60 60

1043 Holderlin (after Franz Hiemer)

1993. 150th Death Anniv of Friedrich Holderlin (poet).
2524 **1043** 100pf. multicoloured 1·60 60

1044 "If People can fly to the Moon, why can't they do anything about so many Children dying?"

1993. 40th Anniv of German United Nations Children's Fund Committee.
2525 **1044** 100pf. multicoloured 1·50 60

1993. Lander of the Federal Republic. As T 989. Multicoloured.
2526 100pf. Mecklenburg-Vorpommern 1·60 80

1993. Lander of the Federal Republic. As T 989. Multicoloured.
2527 100pf. Lower Saxony 1·60 80

1045 Fallada (after E. O. Plauen)

1993. Birth Centenary of Hans Fallada (writer).
2528 **1045** 100pf. green, brn & red 1·50 60

1046 Harz Mountain Range

1993. Landscapes (1st series). Multicoloured.
2529 100pf. Type **1046** 1·40 80
2530 100pf. Rugen 1·40 80
2531 100pf. Hohe Rhon 1·40 80
See also Nos. 2585/8, 2646/9, 2709/12 and 2806/8.

1047 Stages of Manufacture

1993. 250th Death Anniv of Mathias Klotz (violin maker).
2532 **1047** 80pf. multicoloured 1·20 55

1048 George as Gotz von Berlichingen in Goethe's "Urgotz"

1993. Birth Centenary of Heinrich George (actor).
2533 **1048** 100pf. multicoloured 1·50 60

1993. Lander of the Federal Republic. As T 989. Multicoloured.
2534 100pf. Nordrhein-Westfalen 1·60 80

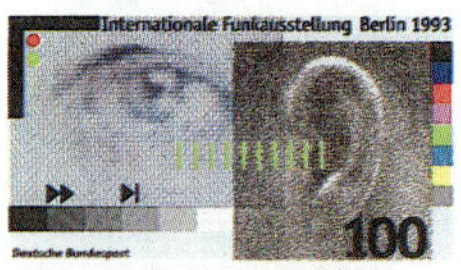

1049 Digitalised Eye and Ear

1993. International Radio Exhibition, Berlin.
2535 **1049** 100pf. multicoloured 1·50 60

1050 Swedish Flag, Heart and Cross

1993. Birth Centenary of Birger Forell (founder of Espelkamp (town for war refugees)).
2536 **1050** 100pf. yell, ultram & bl 1·80 60

1051 "Tuledu Bridge" (engraving)

1993. Birth Centenary of Hans Leip (writer and artist).
2537 **1051** 100pf. black, red & blue 1·80 60

1052 Singing Clown

1993. "For Us Children". Sheet 49×83 mm.
MS2538 **1052** 100pf. multicoloured 1·80 1·90

1993. Lander of the Federal Republic. As T 989. Multicoloured.
2539 100pf. Rheinland-Pfalz 1·60 80

1053 Postman delivering Letter

1993. Stamp Day.
2540 **1053** 100pf.+50pf. mult 1·80 1·80

1054 "Swan Lake"

1993. Death Centenary of Pyotr Tchaikovsky (composer).
2541 **1054** 80pf. multicoloured 1·60 60

1055 Fohr, Schleswig-Holstein

1993. Humanitarian Relief Funds. Traditional Costumes (1st series). Multicoloured.
2542 80pf.+40pf. Type **1055** 1·60 1·50
2543 80pf.+40pf. Rugen, Mecklenburg-Vorpommern 1·60 1·50
2544 100pf.+50pf. Oberndorf, Bavaria 1·80 1·80
2545 100pf.+50pf. Schwalm, Hesse 1·80 1·80
2546 200pf.+40pf. Ernstroda, Thuringia 3·50 3·25
See also Nos. 2598/2602.

1056 St. Jadwiga (miniature, Schlackenwerther Codex)

1993. 750th Death Anniv of St. Jadwiga of Silesia.
2547 **1056** 100pf. multicoloured 1·80 60

1057 Reinhardt on Stage

1993. 50th Death Anniv of Max Reinhardt (theatrical producer).
2548 **1057** 100pf. black, brn & red 1·80 60

1058 Brandt

1993. 80th Birth Anniv of Willy Brandt (statesman).
2549 **1058** 100pf. multicoloured 2·20 1·10

1059 Monteverdi

1993. 350th Death Anniv of Claudio Monteverdi (composer).
2550 **1059** 100pf. multicoloured 1·80 60

1060 Paracelsus (after Augustin Hirschvogel)

1993. 500th Birth Anniv of Paracelsus (physician and philosopher).
2551 **1060** 100pf. ochre, brown and green 1·80 60

1061 "Adoration of the Magi"

1993. Christmas. Carvings from Altar Triptych, Blaubeuren Minster. Multicoloured.
2552 80pf.+40pf. Type **1061** 1·10 1·10
2553 100pf.+50pf. "Birth of Christ" 2·00 1·90

1062 Quayside Buildings, Town Hall and St. Cosmas's Church

1994. Millenary of Stade.
2554 **1062** 80pf. red, brown & blue 1·20 60

1063 "FAMILIE"

1994. International Year of the Family.
2555 **1063** 100pf. multicoloured 1·50 80

1994. Lander of the Federal Republic. As T 989. Multicoloured.
2556 100pf. Saarland 1·60 80

1064 Hertz and Electromagnetic Waves

1994. Death Centenary of Heinrich Hertz (physicist).
2557 **1064** 200pf. black, red and drab 2·75 1·20

1065 Frankfurt am Main

1994. 1200th Anniv of Frankfurt am Main.
2558 **1065** 80pf. multicoloured 1·20 60

1066 Ice Skating

1994. Sport Promotion Fund. Sporting Events and Anniversaries. Multicoloured.
2559 80pf.+40pf. Type **1066** (Winter Olympic Games, Lillehammer, Norway) 1·70 1·60
2560 100pf.+50pf. Football and trophy (World Cup Football Championship, U.S.A.) 2·00 1·80
2561 100pf.+50pf. Flame (cent of International Olympic Committee) 2·00 1·80

2562 200pf.+80pf. Skier (Winter Paralympic Games, Lillehammer) 3·50 3·25

1067 Cathedral, St. Michael's Church and Castle

1994. 1250th Anniv of Fulda.
2563 **1067** 80pf. multicoloured 1·20 60

1068 Council Emblem

1994. Cent of Federation of German Women's Associations—German Women's Council.
2564 **1068** 100pf. black, red & yell 1·50 70

1069 Members' Flags as Stars

1994. 4th Direct Elections to European Parliament.
2565 **1069** 100pf. multicoloured 1·80 80

1070 People holding Banner

1994. "Living Together" (integration of foreign workers in Germany).
2566 **1070** 100pf. multicoloured 1·80 80

1994. Lander of the Federal Republic. As T 989. Multicoloured.
2567 100pf. Saxony 1·60 80

1071 Johnny Head-in-the-Air

1994. Youth Welfare. Death Centenary of Heinrich Hoffmann (writer). Designs illustrating characters from "Slovenly Peter". Multicoloured.
2568 80pf.+40pf. Type **1071** 1·50 1·40
2569 80pf.+40pf. Little Pauline 1·50 1·40
2570 100pf.+50pf. Naughty Friederich 1·60 1·60
2571 100pf.+50pf. Slovenly Peter 1·60 1·60
2572 200pf.+80pf. Fidget-Philipp 3·25 3·00

1072 Frauenkirche

1994. 500th Anniv of Frauenkirche, Munich.
2573 **1072** 100pf. multicoloured 1·80 90

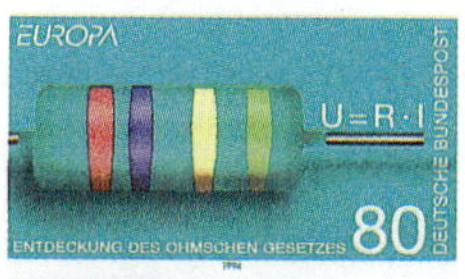

1073 Resistor and Formula

1994. Europa. Discoveries. Multicoloured.
2574 80pf. Type **1073** (Ohm's Law) 1·30 60
2575 100pf. Radiation from black body and formula (Max Planck's Quantum Theory) 1·50 60

1074 Pfitzner (after Emil Orlik)

1994. 125th Birth Anniv of Hans Pfitzner (composer).
2576 **1074** 100pf. deep blue, blue and red 1·50 70

1075 Hegenbeck and Animals

1994. 150th Anniversaries. Sheet 77×108 mm containing T 1075 and similar horiz design. Multicoloured.
MS2577 100pf. Type **1075** (birth anniv of Carl Hagenbeck (circus owner and founder of first zoo without bars)); 200pf. Animals and entrance to Berlin Zoo 3·75 4·75

1076 Spandau Castle

1994. 400th Anniv of Spandau Castle.
2578 **1076** 80pf. multicoloured 1·20 60

1077 Village Sign showing Society Emblem

1994. Centenary of Herzogsagmuhle (Society for the Domestic Missions welfare village).
2579 **1077** 100pf. multicoloured 1·50 70

1994. Lander of the Federal Republic. As T 989. Multicoloured.
2580 100pf. Saxony-Anhalt 1·60 80

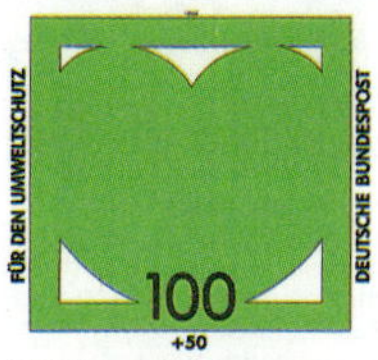

1078 Heart inside Square

1994. Environmental Protection.
2581 **1078** 100pf.+50pf. green and black 1·80 1·80

1079 Friedrich II (13th-century miniature, "Book of Falcons")

1994. 800th Birth Anniv of Emperor Friedrich II.
2582 **1079** 400pf. multicoloured 5·00 4·00

1080 "20 JULY 1944" behind Bars

1994. 50th Anniv of Attempt to Assassinate Hitler. Sheet 105×70 mm.
MS2583 **1080** 100pf. black, yellow and red 1·80 1·80

1994. Lander of the Federal Republic. As T 989. Multicoloured.
2584 100pf. Schleswig-Holstein 1·60 80

1994. Landscapes (2nd series). As T 1046. Multicoloured.
2585 100pf. The Alps 1·30 90
2586 100pf. Erzgebirge 1·30 90
2587 100pf. Main valley 1·30 90
2588 100pf. Mecklenburg lakes 1·30 90

1081 Herder (after Anton Graff)

1994. 250th Birth Anniv of Johann Gottfried Herder (philosopher).
2589 **1081** 80pf. multicoloured 1·20 60

1994. 20th-century German Paintings (3rd series). As T 1003. Multicoloured.
2590 100pf. "Maika" (Christian Schad) 1·10 70
2591 200pf. "Dresden Landscape" (Erich Heckel) 2·20 1·80
2592 300pf. "Aleksei Javlensky and Marianne Werefkin" (Gabriele Munter) 3·25 2·75

1082 Early 20th-century Makonde Mask (Tanzania)

1994. 125th Anniv of Leipzig Ethnology Museum.
2593 **1082** 80pf. multicoloured 1·20 60

1083 Helmholtz, Eye and Colour Triangle

1994. Death Centenary of Hermann von Helmholtz (physicist).
2594 **1083** 100pf. multicoloured 1·50 60

1084 Richter

1994. Birth Cent of Willi Richter (President of Confederation of German Trade Unions).
2595 **1084** 100pf. brown, purple and black 1·50 60

1085 "Flying on Dragon"

1994. "For Us Children". Sheet 106×61 mm.
MS2596 **1085** 100pf. multicoloured 1·80 1·90

1994. Lander of the Federal Republic. As T 989. Multicoloured.
2597 100pf. Thuringia 1·60 80

1994. Humanitarian Relief Funds. Traditional Costumes (2nd series). As T 1055. Multicoloured.
2598 80pf.+40pf. Buckeburg 1·40 1·30
2599 80pf.+40pf. Halle an der Saale 1·40 1·30
2600 100pf.+50pf. Minden 1·80 1·80
2601 100pf.+50pf. Hoyerswerda 1·80 1·80
2602 200pf.+70pf. Betzingen 3·00 2·75

1086 St. Wolfgang with Church Model (woodcut)

1994. Death Millenary of St. Wolfgang, Bishop of Regensburg.
2603 **1086** 100pf. gold, cream and black 1·50 70

1087 Sachs

1994. 500th Birth Anniv of Hans Sachs (mastersinger and poet).
2604 **1087** 100pf. purple and green on greyish 1·50 70

1088 Spreewald Postman, 1900

1994. Stamp Day.
2605 **1088** 100pf. multicoloured 1·50 70

1089 Quedlinburg

1994. Millenary of Quedlinburg.
2606 **1089** 80pf. multicoloured 1·20 60

1090 "Adoration of the Magi"

1994. Christmas. 500th Death Anniv of Hans Memling (painter). Details of his triptych in St. John's Hospice, Bruges. Multicoloured.
2607 80pf.+40pf. Type **1090** 1·50 1·60
2608 100pf.+50pf. "Nativity" 2·00 1·80

1091 Steuben and "Surrender of Cornwallis at Yorktown" (detail, John Trumbull)

1994. Death Bicentenary of Gen. Friedrich Wilhelm von Steuben (Inspector General of Washington's Army).
2609 **1091** 100pf. multicoloured 1·50 70

1092 Cemetery

1994. 75th Anniv of National Assn for the Preservation of German Graves Abroad.
2610 **1092** 100pf. black and red 1·50 70

1093 Obersuhl Checkpoint, 11 November 1989

1994. 5th Anniv of Opening of Borders between East and West Germany.
2611 **1093** 100pf. multicoloured 1·50 70

1094 Fontane (after Max Liebermann) and Lines from "Prussian Song"

1994. 175th Birth Anniv of Theodor Fontane (writer).
2612 **1094** 100pf. green, black and mauve 1·50 70

1095 Simson Fountain, Town Hall and St. Mary's and St Salvator's Churches

1995. Millenary of Gera.
2613 **1095** 80pf. multicoloured 1·10 60

1096 Emperor Friedrich III, First Page of "Libellus" and Zur Munze (venue)

1995. 500th Anniv of Diet of Worms.
2614 **1096** 100pf. black and red 1·20 70

1995. 20th-century German Paintings (4th series). As T 1003. Multicoloured.
2615 100pf. "The Water Tower, Bremen" (Franz Radziwill) 1·10 70
2616 200pf. "Still Life with Cat" (Georg Schrimpf) 2·30 2·20
2617 300pf. "Estate in Dangast" (Karl Schmidt-Rottluff) 3·25 2·75

1097 Canoeing

1995. Sport Promotion Fund. Multicoloured.
2618 80pf.+40pf. Type **1097** (27th World Canoeing Championships, Duisburg) 1·40 1·30
2619 100pf.+50pf. Hoop exercises (10th Int Gymnastics Festival, Berlin) 1·40 1·30
2620 100pf.+50pf. Boxing (8th World Amateur Boxing Championships, Berlin) 1·40 1·30
2621 200pf.+80pf. Volleyball (centenary) 3·25 3·00

1098 Friedrich Wilhelm (after A. Romandon)

1995. 375th Birth Anniv of Friedrich Wilhelm of Brandenburg, The Great Elector.
2622 **1098** 300pf. multicoloured 3·75 2·75

1099 Deed of Donation (995) and Arms of Mecklenburg-Vorpommern

1995. Millenary of Mecklenburg.
2623 **1099** 100pf. multicoloured 1·20 70

1100 Computer Image of Terminal and Lion

1995. 250th Anniv of Carolo-Wilhelmina Technical University, Braunschweig.
2624 **1100** 100pf. multicoloured 1·20 70

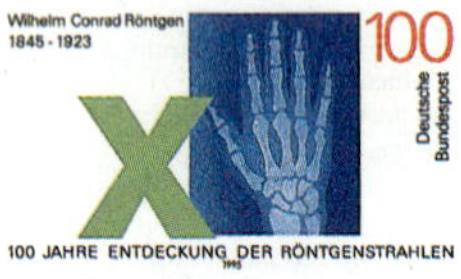

1101 X-ray of Hand

1995. 150th Birth Anniv of Wilhelm Rontgen and Centenary of his Discovery of X-rays.
2625 **1101** 100pf. multicoloured 1·20 70

1102 Globe and Rainbow

1995. 1st Conference of Signatories to General Convention on Climate, Berlin.
2626 **1102** 100pf. multicoloured 1·20 70

1103 Old Town Hall Reliefs

1995. 750th Anniv of Regensburg.
2627 **1103** 80pf. multicoloured 1·00 60

1104 Bonhoeffer

1995. 50th Death Anniv of Dietrich Bonhoeffer (theologian).
2628 **1104** 100pf. black, bl & grey 1·20 70

1105 Symbols of Speech, Writing and Pictures

1995. Freedom of Expression.
2629 **1105** 100pf. multicoloured 1·20 70

1106 St. Clement's Church, Munster

1995. 300th Birth Anniv of Johann Conrad Schlaun (architect).
2630 **1106** 200pf. multicoloured 2·30 1·90

1107 Friedrich Schiller, Signature and Schiller Museum, Marbach

1995. Centenary of German Schiller Society.
2631 **1107** 100pf. multicoloured 1·20 70

1108 St. Vincent de Paul

1995. 150th Anniv of Vincent Conferences (charitable organization) in Germany.
2632 **1108** 100pf. multicoloured 1·20 80

1109 Number on Cloth and Barbed Wire

1995. 50th Anniv of Liberation of Concentration Camps. Sheet 105×70 mm.
MS2633 **1109** 100pf. grey, blue and black 1·50 1·80

1110 City Ruins

1995. 50th Anniv of End of Second World War. Sheet 104×70 mm containing T 1110 and similar square design. Multicoloured.
MS2634 100pf. Type **1110**; 100pf. Refugees 2·50 2·75

1111 Returning Soldiers ("End of War")

1995. Europa. Peace and Freedom.
2635 **1111** 100pf. black and red 1·10 80
2636 - 200pf. blue, yell & blk 2·20 2·00
DESIGN: 200pf. Emblem of European Community ("Moving towards Europe").

1112 Shipping Routes before and after 1895

1995. Centenary of Kiel Canal.
2637 **1112** 80pf. multicoloured 1·00 60

1113 Guglielmo Marconi and Wireless Equipment

1995. 100 Years of Radio.
2638 **1113** 100pf. multicoloured 1·50 95

1114 U.N. Emblem

1995. 50th Anniv of U.N.O.
2639 **1114** 100pf. lilac, gold and grey 1·20 70

1115 Munsterlander

1995. Youth Welfare. Dogs (1st series). Mult.
2640 80pf.+40pf. Type **1115** 1·40 1·30
2641 80pf.+40pf. Giant schnauzer 1·40 1·30
2642 100pf.+50pf. Wire-haired dachshund 1·60 1·50
2643 100pf.+50pf. German shepherd 1·60 1·50
2644 200pf.+80pf. Keeshund 3·00 2·75
See also Nos. 2696/2700.

1116 Opening Bars of "Carmina Burana" and Characters

1995. Birth Centenary of Carl Orff (composer).
2645 **1116** 100pf. multicoloured 1·20 70

1995. Landscapes (3rd series). As T 1046. Multicoloured.
2646 100pf. Franconian Switzerland 1·10 90
2647 100pf. River Havel, Berlin 1·10 90
2648 100pf. Oberlausitz 1·10 90
2649 100pf. Sauerland 1·10 90

1117 Lion (from 12th-century coin)

1995. 800th Death Anniv of Henry the Lion, Duke of Saxony and Bavaria.
2650 **1117** 400pf. multicoloured 4·00 3·75

1118 Kaiser Wilhelm Memorial Church

1995. Centenary of Kaiser Wilhelm Memorial Church, Berlin.
2651 **1118** 100pf. multicoloured 1·20 70

1119 Werfel and Signature

1995. 50th Death Anniv of Franz Werfel (writer).
2652 **1119** 100pf. mauve, bl & blk 1·20 70

1995. Tourist Sights. As T 854 but inscr "DEUTSCHLAND".

2654	47pf. green and black	65	55
2656	100pf. blue and black	90	90
2657	110pf. cinnamon and brown	1·00	45
2658	110pf. orange and blue	1·10	60
2659	220pf. green and black	1·80	90
2661	440pf. orange and blue	4·50	4·00
2663	510pf. red and blue	4·50	4·50
2665	640pf. blue and brown	6·50	3·50
2666	690pf. black and green	6·75	4·50

DESIGNS: 47pf. Berus Monument, Uberherrn; 100pf. Goethe-Schiller Monument, Weimar; 110pf. (2657) Bellevue Castle, Berlin; 110pf. (2658) Emblem of "Expo 2000" World's Fair, Hanover; 220pf. Bruhl's Terrace, Dresden; 440pf. Town Hall, Bremen; 510pf. Holsten Gate, Lubeck; 640pf. Speyer Cathedral; 690pf. St. Michael's Church, Hamburg.

1120 Strauss

1995. 80th Birth Anniv of Franz Josef Strauss (politician).
2675 **1120** 100pf. multicoloured 1·40 90

1121 Postwoman

1995. Stamp Day.
2676 **1121** 200pf.+100pf. mult 3·00 3·00

1122 "Metropolis" (dir. Fritz Lang)

1995. Centenary of Motion Pictures. Sheet 100×130 mm containing T 1122 and similar horiz designs showing frames from films. Multicoloured.
MS2677 80pf. Type **1122**; 100pf. "Little Superman" (dir. Wolfgang Staudte); 200pf. "The Sky over Berlin" (dir. Wim Wenders) 4·50 5·75

1123 Eifel

1995. Humanitarian Relief Funds. Farmhouses (1st series). Multicoloured.

2678	80pf.+40pf. Type **1123**	1·40	1·30
2679	80pf.+40pf. Saxony	1·40	1·30
2680	100pf.+50pf. Lower Germany	1·60	1·50
2681	100pf.+50pf. Upper Bavaria	1·60	1·50
2682	200pf.+70pf. Mecklenburg	3·00	2·75

See also Nos. 2742/6.

1124 Schumacher

1995. Birth Centenary of Kurt Schumacher (politician).
2683 **1124** 100pf. multicoloured 1·20 70

1125 Animals gathered on Hill

1995. "For Us Children". Sheet 110×60 mm.
MS2684 **1125** 80pf. multicoloured 1·50 1·80

1126 Ranke

1995. Birth Bicentenary of Leopold von Ranke (historian).
2685 **1126** 80pf. multicoloured 90 60

1127 Hindemith

1995. Birth Centenary of Paul Hindemith (composer).
2686 **1127** 100pf. multicoloured 1·20 70

1128 Alfred Nobel and Will

1995. Centenary of Nobel Prize Trust Fund.
2687 **1128** 100pf. multicoloured 1·50 1·10

1129 "CARE" in American Colours

1995. 50th Anniv of CARE (Co-operative for Assistance and Remittances Overseas).
2688 **1129** 100pf. multicoloured 1·20 70

1130 Berlin Wall

1995. Commemorating Victims of Political Oppression, 1945–89.
2689 **1130** 100pf. multicoloured 1·20 70

1131 "The Annunciation"

1995. Christmas. Stained Glass Windows in Augsburg Cathedral. Multicoloured.

2690	80pf.+40pf. Type **1131**	1·40	1·30
2691	100pf.+50pf. "Nativity"	1·80	1·80

1132 Dribbling

1995. Borussia Dortmund, German Football Champions.
2692 **1132** 100pf. multicoloured 1·50 90

1133 Auguste von Sartorius (founder)

1996. 150th Anniv of German Institute for Children's Missionary Work.
2693 **1133** 100pf. multicoloured 1·10 80

1134 Bodelschwingh

1996. 50th Death Anniv of Friedrich von Bodelschwingh (theologian).
2694 **1134** 100pf. black and red 1·10 80

1135 Luther (after Lucas Cranach)

1996. 450th Death Anniv of Martin Luther (Protestant reformer).
2695 **1135** 100pf. multicoloured 1·20 95

1996. Youth Welfare. Dogs (2nd series). As T 1115. Multicoloured.

2696	80pf.+40pf. Borzoi	1·50	1·50
2697	80pf.+40pf. Chow chow	1·50	1·50
2698	100pf.+50pf. St. Bernard	1·80	1·80
2699	100pf.+50pf. Rough collie	1·80	1·80
2700	200pf.+80pf. Briard	2·75	2·75

1136 Siebold

1996. Birth Bicentenary of Philipp Franz von Siebold (physician and Japanologist).
2701 **1136** 100pf. multicoloured 1·20 95

1137 Cathedral Square

1996. Millenary of Cathedral Square, Halberstadt.
2702 **1137** 80pf. multicoloured 80 55

1138 Galen

1996. 50th Death Anniv of Cardinal Count Clemens von Galen, Bishop of Munster.
2703 **1138** 100pf. grey, blue & gold 1·10 70

1996. 20th-century German Paintings (5th series). As T 1003. Multicoloured.

2704	100pf. "Seated Female Nude" (Max Pechstein)	1·10	1·10
2705	200pf. "For Wilhelm Runge" (Georg Muche)	2·20	1·90
2706	300pf. "Still Life with Guitar, Book and Vase" (Helmut Kolle)	3·00	3·00

1139 Detail of Ceiling Fresco, Prince-bishop's Residence, Wurzburg

1996. 300th Birth Anniv of Giovanni Battista Tiepolo (artist).
2707 **1139** 200pf. multicoloured 2·00 1·80

1140 Post Runner

1996. "For Us Children". Sheet 83×67 mm.
MS2708 **1140** 100pf. multicoloured 1·20 1·60

1996. Landscapes (4th series). As T 1046. Multicoloured.

2709	100pf. Eifel	1·10	90
2710	100pf. Holstein Switzerland	1·10	90
2711	100pf. Saale	1·10	90
2712	100pf. Spreewald	1·10	90

1141 Paula Modersohn-Becker (self-portrait)

1996. Europa. Famous Women.

2713	**1141**	80pf. multicoloured	1·20	55
2714	-	100pf. black, grey and mauve	1·20	90

DESIGN: 100pf. Kathe Kollwitz (self-portrait).

1142 Opening Lines of Document and Town (1642 engraving, Matthaeus Merian)

1996. Millenary of Granting to Freising the Right to hold Markets.
2715 **1142** 100pf. multicoloured 1·10 80

1143 Borchert

1996. 75th Birth Anniv of Wolfgang Borchert (writer).
2716 **1143** 100pf. multicoloured 1·10 80

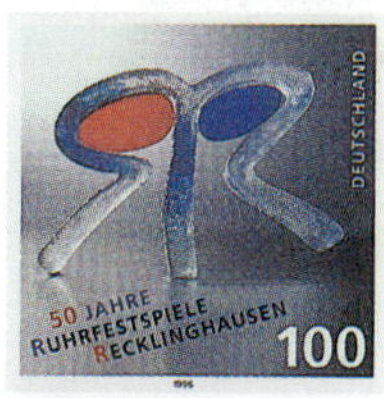

1144 Emblem

1996. 50th Anniv of Ruhr Festival, Recklinghausen.
2717 **1144** 100pf. multicoloured 1·10 80

1145 Ticket and Stage Curtain

1996. 150th Anniv of German Theatre Assn.
2718 **1145** 200pf. multicoloured 2·00 1·50

1146 Leibniz and Mathematical Diagram

1996. 350th Birth Anniv of Gottfried Leibniz.
2719 **1146** 100pf. red and black 1·10 80

1147 Kneeling Figure and Motto forming "A"

1996. 300th Anniv of Berlin Academy of Arts.

2720	**1147**	100pf. multicoloured	1·10	80

1148 Carl Schuhmann (wrestling, equestrian sports and gymnastics, 1896)

1996. Sport Promotion Fund. Centenary of Modern Olympic Games. German Olympic Champions. Multicoloured.

2721	80pf.+40pf. Type **1148**	2·30	1·80
2722	100pf.+50pf. Josef Neckermann (dressage, 1964 and 1968)	2·75	2·10
2723	100pf.+50pf. Annie Hubler-Horn (ice skating, 1908)	2·75	2·10
2724	200pf.+80pf. Alfred and Gustav Flatow (gymnastics, 1896)	4·00	3·00

1149 Townscape

1996. 800th Anniv of Heidelberg.

2725	**1149**	100pf. multicoloured	1·10	80

1150 Children's Handprints

1996. 50th Anniv of UNICEF.

2726	**1150**	100pf. multicoloured	1·10	80

1151 "Wedding" (illustration by Bruno Paul)

1996. 75th Death Anniv of Ludwig Thoma (satirist).

2727	**1151**	100pf. multicoloured	1·10	80

1152 Beach

1996. Western Pomerania National Park. Sheet 166×111 mm containing T 1152 and similar horiz designs showing Park landscapes. Multicoloured.

MS2728	100pf. Type **1152**; 200pf. Mudflat; 300pf. Sea inlet	7·25	7·00

1153 Map and Tropical Wildlife

1996. Environmental Protection. Preservation of Tropical Habitats.

2729	**1153**	100pf.+50pf. mult	1·60	1·70

1154 Volklingen Blast Furnace

1996. UNESCO World Heritage Sites.

2730	**1154**	100pf. multicoloured	1·10	80

1155 Lincke

1996. 50th Death Anniv of Paul Lincke (composer and conductor).

2731	**1155**	100pf. multicoloured	1·10	80

1156 Gendarmenmarkt, Berlin

1996. Images of Germany.

2732	**1156**	100pf. multicoloured	1·10	80

1157 "50" comprising Stamp under Magnifying Glass

1996. Stamp Day. 50th Anniv of Association of German Philatelists.

2733	**1157**	100pf. multicoloured	1·10	80

1158 Book

1996. Centenary of German Civil Code.

2734	**1158**	300pf. multicoloured	3·00	2·75

1159 Players

1996. Borussia Dortmund, German Football Champions.

2735	**1159**	100pf. multicoloured	1·10	80

1160 Bamburg Old Town

1996. UNESCO World Heritage Sites.

2736	**1160**	100pf. multicoloured	1·10	80

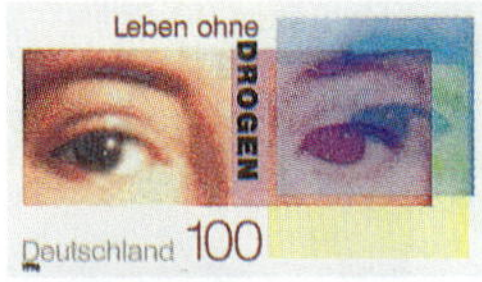

1161 Eyes

1996. "Life without Drugs".

2737	**1161**	100pf. multicoloured	1·10	80

1162 "Like will Cure Like" and Samuel Hahnemann (developer of principle)

1996. Bicentenary of Homeopathy.

2738	**1162**	400pf. multicoloured	3·75	3·75

1163 Bruckner and Symphony No. III

1996. Death Centenary of Anton Bruckner (composer).

2739	**1163**	100pf. multicoloured	1·10	80

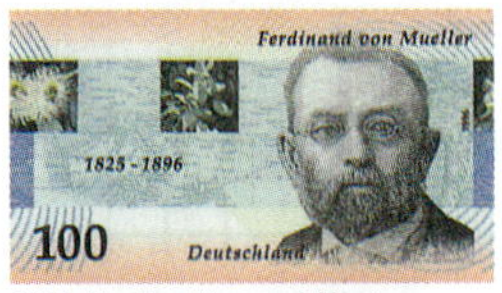

1164 Mueller, Map and Plants

1996. Death Centenary of Ferdinand von Mueller (botanist).

2740	**1164**	100pf. multicoloured	1·10	80

1165 Score by John Cage

1996. 75th Anniv of Donaueschingen Music Festival.

2741	**1165**	100pf. blue, blk & mve	1·10	80

1996. Humanitarian Relief Funds. Farmhouses (2nd series). As T 1123. Multicoloured.

2742	80pf.+40pf. Spree Forest	1·10	1·10
2743	80pf.+40pf. Thuringia	1·10	1·10
2744	100pf.+50pf. Black Forest	1·50	1·50
2745	100pf.+50pf. Westphalia	1·50	1·50
2746	200pf.+70pf. Schleswig-Holstein	3·00	3·00

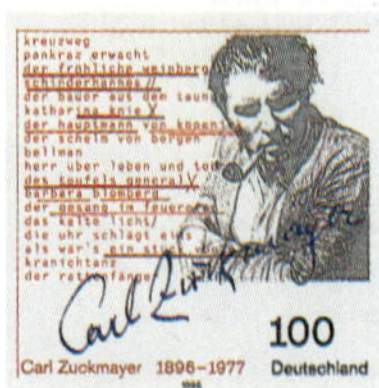

1166 Titles of Plays and Zuckmayer

1996. Birth Centenary of Carl Zuckmayer (dramatist).

2747	**1166**	100pf. multicoloured	1·10	80

1167 "Adoration of the Magi"

1996. Christmas. Illustrations from Henry II's "Book of Pericopes" (illuminated manuscript of readings from the Gospels). Multicoloured.

2748	80pf.+40pf. Type **1167**	1·40	1·40
2749	100pf.+50pf. "Nativity"	1·60	1·80

1168 Schmid

1996. Birth Centenary of Carlo Schmid (politician and writer).

2750	**1168**	100pf. multicoloured	1·10	80

1169 "Friends of Schubert in Afzenbrugg" (detail, L. Kupelwieser)

1997. Birth Bicentenary of Franz Schubert (composer).

2751	**1169**	100pf. multicoloured	1·10	80

1170 Pitch, Player and Herberger

1997. Birth Centenary of Sepp Herberger (national football team coach, 1936–64).

2752	**1170**	100pf. green, red & blk	1·10	80

1171 Motor Cars

1997. "More Safety for Children" (road safety campaign).

2752a	**1171**	10pf. multicoloured	30	25
2753	**1171**	100pf. multicoloured	1·10	80

1172 Melanchthon (after Lucas Cranach the younger)

1997. 500th Birth Anniv of Philipp Melanchthon (religious reformer).

2754	**1172**	100pf. multicoloured	1·10	80

1173 Revellers "Wiggling"

1997. 175th Anniv of Cologne Carnival.

2755	**1173**	100pf. multicoloured	1·10	80

1174 Erhard

1997. Birth Centenary of Ludwig Erhard (Chancellor, 1963–66).
2756 **1174** 100pf. black and red 1·10 80

1175 Aerobics

1997. Sport Promotion Fund. Fun Sports. Multicoloured.

2757	80pf.+40pf. Type **1175**	1·30	1·20
2758	100pf.+50pf. Inline skating	1·60	1·60
2759	100pf.+50pf. Streetball	1·60	1·60
2760	200pf.+80pf. Freeclimbing	3·00	2·75

1176 New Pavilion

1997. 500th Anniv of Granting of Imperial Fair Rights to Leipzig.
2761 **1176** 100pf. silver, red & blue 1·10 80

1177 Philharmonic, Berlin (Hans Scharoun)

1997. Post-1945 German Architecture. Sheet 137×101 mm containing T 1177 and similar square designs. Multicoloured.
MS2762 100pf. Type **1177**; 100pf. National Gallery, Berlin (Ludwig Miles van der Rohe); 100pf. St. Mary, Queen of Peace Pilgrimage Church, Neviges (Gottfried Bohm); 100pf. German Pavilion, 1967 World's Trade Fair, Montreal (Frei Otto) 4·25 4·50

1178 Straubing

1997. 1100th Anniv of Straubing.
2763 **1178** 100pf. multicoloured 1·10 80

1179 Stephan, Telephone and Postcards

1997. Death Centenary of Heinrich von Stephan (founder of U.P.U.).
2764 **1179** 100pf. multicoloured 1·10 80

1180 Augustusburg and Falkenlust Castles

1997. UNESCO World Heritage Sites.
2765 **1180** 100pf. multicoloured 1·10 80

1181 Diamonds

1997. 500th Anniv of Idar-Oberstein Region Gem Industry.
2766 **1181** 300pf. multicoloured 3·25 2·75

1182 St. Adalbert

1997. Death Millenary of St. Adalbert (Bishop of Prague).
2767 **1182** 100pf. lilac 1·10 80

1183 "The Fisherman and His Wife" (Brothers Grimm)

1997. Europa. Tales and Legends. Mult.

2768	80pf. Type **1183**	1·10	70
2769	100pf. "Rubezahl"	1·10	90

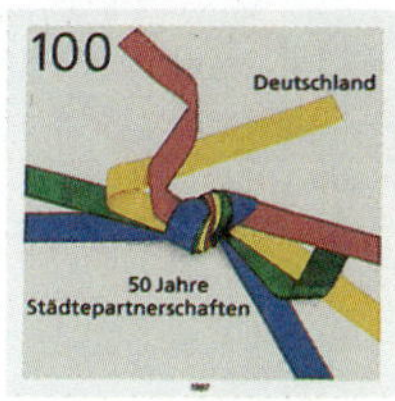

1184 Knotted Ribbons

1997. 50th Anniv of Town Twinning Movement.
2770 **1184** 100pf. multicoloured 1·10 80

1185 Deciduous Trees

1997. 50th Anniv of Society for the Protection of the German Forest. Sheet 105×70 mm containing T 1185 and similar square design. Multicoloured.
MS2771 100pf. Type **1185**; 200pf. Evergreen trees 3·75 3·50

1186 Kneipp

1997. Death Cent of Father Sebastian Kneipp (developer of naturopathic treatments).
2772 **1186** 100pf. multicoloured 1·10 80

1187 United States Flag, George Marshall and Bomb Site

1997. 50th Anniv of Marshall Plan (European Recovery Program).
2773 **1187** 100pf. multicoloured 1·10 80

1188 Rheno-German Heavy Horse

1997. Youth Welfare. Horses. Multicoloured.

2774	80pf.+40pf. Type **1188**	1·30	1·20
2775	80pf.+40pf. Shetland ponies	1·30	1·20
2776	100pf.+50pf. Frisian	1·50	1·40
2777	100pf.+50pf. Haflinger	1·50	1·40
2778	200pf.+80pf. Hanoverian with foal	2·75	2·75

1189 Train on Bridge

1997. Centenary of Mungsten Railway Bridge.
2779 **1189** 100pf. multicoloured 1·10 80

1190 "Composition" (Fritz Winter)

1997. 10th "Documenta" Modern Art Exhibition, Kassel. Sheet 137×97 mm containing T 1190 and similar horiz designs. Multicoloured.
MS2780 100pf. Type **1190**; 100pf. "Mouth No. 15" (Tom Wesselmann); 100pf. "Quathlamba" (Frank Stella); 100pf. "Beuys/Bois" (Nam June Paik) 4·50 4·50

1191 Children holding Envelopes

1997. "For Us Children". Sheet 70×105 mm.
MS2781 **1191** 100pf. multicoloured 1·40 1·60

1997. Famous Women. As T 832 but inscr "Deutschland".

2785	100pf. brown and green	1·20	90
2786	110pf. drab and violet	1·20	90
2790	220pf. ultramarine and blue	2·30	2·10
2792	300pf. brown and blue	2·75	2·40
2795	440pf. brown and violet	5·00	4·75

DESIGNS: 100pf. Elisabeth Schwarzhaupt (politician); 110pf. Marlene Dietrich (actress); 220pf. Marie-Elisabeth Luders (politician); 300pf. Maria Probst (social reformer and politician); 440pf. Gret Palucca (dancer).

1192 Arms of Brandenburg

1997. Flood Relief Funds.
2805 **1192** 110pf.+90pf. mult 1·90 1·90

1997. Landscapes (5th series). As T 1046. Multicoloured.

2806	110pf. Bavarian Forest	1·20	1·10
2807	110pf. North German Moors	1·20	1·10
2808	110pf. Luneburg Heath	1·20	1·10

1193 Rudolf Diesel and First Oil Engine

1997. Centenary of Diesel Engine.
2809 **1193** 300pf. black and blue 3·00 2·75

1194 Potato Plant and Cultivation

1997. 350th Anniv of Introduction of the Potato to Germany.
2810 **1194** 300pf. multicoloured 3·00 2·75

1195 Biplane and Motorized Tricycle

1997. Stamp Day. Sheet 70×105 mm.
MS2811 **1195** 440pf.+220pf. multi-coloured 6·50 7·00

1196 Mendelssohn-Bartholdy and Music Score

1997. 150th Death Anniv of Felix Mendelssohn-Bartholdy (composer).
2813 **1196** 110pf. green, olive & yell 1·10 90

1197 Watermill, Black Forest

1997. Humanitarian Relief Funds. Mills. Multicoloured.

2814	100pf.+50pf. Type **1197**	2·20	2·10
2815	110pf.+50pf. Watermill, Hesse	2·40	2·30
2816	110pf.+50pf. Post mill, Lower Rhine	2·40	2·30
2817	110pf.+50pf. Scoop windmill, Schleswig-Holstein	2·40	2·30
2818	220pf.+80pf. Dutch windmill	3·75	3·50

1198 Emblem

1997. Saar–Lor–Lux European Region.
2819 **1198** 110pf. multicoloured 1·30 90

1199 Team celebrating

1997. Bayern Munchen, German Football Champions.
2820 **1199** 110pf. multicoloured 1·30 90

1200 Dehler

1997. Birth Centenary of Thomas Dehler (politician).

2821 **1200** 110pf. multicoloured 1·10 90

1201 Heine (after Wilhelm Hensel)

1997. Birth Bicentenary of Heinrich Heine (journalist and poet).

2822 **1201** 110pf. multicoloured 1·10 90

1202 Tree and Title of Hymn

1997. 300th Birth Anniv of Gerhard Tersteegen (religious reformer).

2823 **1202** 110pf. brown, grey and black 1·10 90

1203 Emblem

1997. Cent of Deutscher Caritas Verband (Catholic charitable association).

2824 **1203** 110pf. multicoloured 1·10 90

1204 Three Kings

1997. Christmas. Multicoloured.

2825 100pf.+50pf. Type **1204** 1·50 1·40

2826 110pf.+50pf. Nativity 1·70 1·70

The premium was for the benefit of the Federal Association of Free Welfare Work, Bonn.

1205 Monastery Plan and Church

1998. UNESCO World Heritage Site. Maulbronn Monastery.

2827 **1205** 100pf. multicoloured 1·10 90

1206 Walled City

1998. 1100th Anniv of Nordlingen.

2828 **1206** 110pf. multicoloured 1·10 90

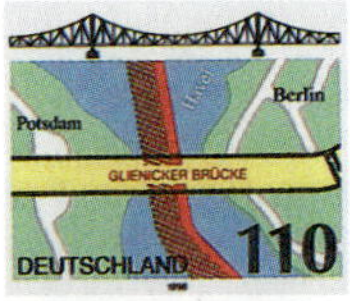

1207 Glienicke Bridge, Potsdam–Berlin

1998. Bridges. (1st series).

2829 **1207** 110pf. multicoloured 1·10 90

See also Nos. 2931, 2956 and 3046.

1208 Football

1998. Sport Promotion Fund. International Championships. Multicoloured.

2830 100pf.+50pf. Type **1208** (World Cup Football Championship, France) 1·80 1·80

2831 110pf.+50pf. Ski jumping (Winter Olympic Games, Nagano, Japan) 2·20 2·10

2832 110pf.+50pf. Rowing (World Rowing Championships, Cologne) 2·20 2·10

2833 300pf.+100pf. Disabled skier (Winter Paralympic Games, Nagano) 5·00 4·75

1209 Characters in Brecht's Head

1998. Birth Centenary of Bertolt Brecht (dramatist).

2834 **1209** 110pf. multicoloured 1·10 90

1210 X-ray Photographs of Moon, Ionic Lattice Structure and Nerve of Goldfish and Founding Assembly

1998. 50th Anniv of Max Planck Society for the Advancement of Science.

2835 **1210** 110pf. multicoloured 1·10 90

1211 Bad Frankenhausen

1998. Millenary of First Documentary Mention of Bad Frankenhausen.

2836 **1211** 110pf. multicoloured 1·10 90

1212 Signatories

1998. 350th Anniv of Peace of Westphalia (settlements ending Thirty Years' War).

2837 **1212** 110pf. blk, grey & mve 1·10 90

1213 Baden-Wurttemberg (Kurt Viertel)

1998. Federal State Parliament Buildings (1st series). Multicoloured.

2838 110pf. Type **1213** 1·20 90

2839 110pf. Bavaria (designed Friedrich Burklein) 1·20 90

2840 110pf. Chamber of Deputies, Berlin (Friedrich Schulze) 1·20 90

2841 110pf. Brandenburg (Franz Schwechten) 1·20 90

See also Nos. 2885, 2893/4, 2897, 2953, 2957, 2978, 3025, 3043, 3052, 3064 and 3071.

1214 Hildegard's Vision of Life Cycle

1998. 900th Birth Anniv of Hildegard of Bingen (writer and mystic).

2842 **1214** 100pf. multicoloured 1·10 90

1215 Marine Life

1998. "For Us Children". Sheet 110×66 mm.

MS2843 **1215** 110pf. multicoloured 1·30 1·40

1216 St. Marienstern Abbey

1998. 750th Anniv of St. Marienstern Abbey, Panschwitz-Kuckau.

2844 **1216** 110pf. multicoloured 1·10 90

1217 Auditorium

1998. 250th Anniv of Bayreuth Opera House.

2845 **1217** 300pf. multicoloured 3·00 2·75

1218 Junger

1998. Ernst Junger (writer) Commemoration.

2846 **1218** 110pf. multicoloured 1·10 90

1219 Doves and Tree (German Unification Day)

1998. Europa. National Festivals.

2847 **1219** 110pf. multicoloured 1·40 90

1220 Association Manifesto

1998. 50th Anniv of German Rural Women's Association.

2848 **1220** 110pf. grn, emer & blk 1·10 90

1221 Opening Session of Parliamentary Council, 1948

1998. Parliamentary Anniversaries. Sheet 105×70 mm containing T 1221 and similar square design. Multicoloured.

MS2849 110pf. Type **1221**; 220pf. First German National Assembly, St. Paul's Church, Frankfurt, 1848 3·75 3·50

1222 Coast and Ocean

1998. Environmental Protection.

2850 **1222** 110pf.+50pf. mult 1·60 1·80

1223 "The Mouse"

1998. Youth Welfare. Children's Cartoons. Multicoloured.

2851 100pf.+50pf. Type **1223** 1·50 1·40

2852 100pf.+50pf. "The Sandman" 1·50 1·40

2853 110pf.+50pf. "Maja the Bee" 1·60 1·60

2854 110pf.+50pf. "Captain Bluebear" 1·60 1·60

2855 220pf.+80pf. "Pumuckl" 3·25 3·00

1224 Crowds of People and Cross

1998. 150th Anniv of First Congress of German Catholics.

2856 **1224** 110pf. multicoloured 1·10 80

1225 One Deutschmark Coin

1998. 50th Anniv of the Deutschmark.
2857 **1225** 110pf. multicoloured 1·60 1·10

1226 Harvesting Hops

1998. 1100 Years of Hop Cultivation in Germany.
2858 **1226** 110pf. multicoloured 1·10 90

1227 Euro Banknotes forming "EZB"

1998. Inauguration of European Central Bank, Frankfurt am Main.
2859 **1227** 110pf. multicoloured 1·10 80

1228 Rock Face, Elbe Sandstone Mountains

1998. Saxon Switzerland National Park. Sheet 105×70 mm containing T 1228 and similar square design. Multicoloured.
MS2860 110pf. Type **1228**; 220pf. Elbe Sandstone Mountains 3·75 3·50

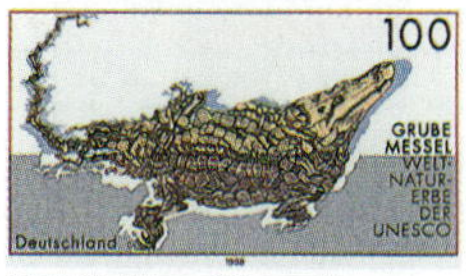

1229 Skeleton of Crocodile

1998. UNESCO World Heritage Sites. Grube Messel Fossil Deposits.
2861 **1229** 100pf. multicoloured 1·10 80

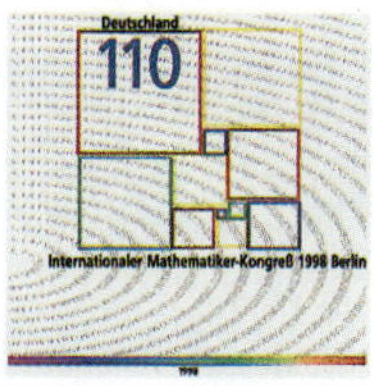

1230 Coloured Squares and Ludolphian Number

1998. 23rd International Congress of Mathematicians, Berlin.
2862 **1230** 110pf. multicoloured 1·10 90

1231 Wurzburg Palace

1998. UNESCO World Heritage Sites. Multicoloured.
2863 110pf. Type **1231** 1·10 80
2864 110pf. Puning Temple, Chengde, China 1·10 80

1232 Glasses (Peter Behrens)

1998. Contemporary Design (1st series). Sheet 138×97 mm containing T 1232 and similar horiz designs. Multicoloured.
MS2865 110pf. Type **1232**; 110pf. Teapot (Marianne Brandt); 110pf. Table lamp (Wilhelm Wagenfeld); 110pf. "Wassily" chair (Marcel Breuer) 4·50 4·50
See also No. **MS**2922.

1233 Players, Ball and Pitch

1998. 1st FC Kaiserslautern, National Football Champions, 1998.
2866 **1233** 110pf. multicoloured 1·30 90

1234 Main Building

1998. 300th Anniv of Francke Charitable Institutions, Halle.
2867 **1234** 110pf. multicoloured 1·10 90

1235 Hausmann and Book Cover

1998. Birth Centenary of Manfred Hausmann (writer).
2868 **1235** 100pf. multicoloured 1·10 90

1236 Hands on T-shirt

1998. Child Protection.
2869 **1236** 110pf. red and black 1·10 90

1237 Hen Harriers and Chicks

1998. Humanitarian Relief Funds. Birds. Multicoloured.
2870 100pf.+50pf. Type **1237** 1·50 1·40
2871 110pf.+50pf. Great bustards 1·60 1·60
2872 110pf.+50pf. Ferruginous ducks 1·60 1·60
2873 110pf.+50pf. Aquatic warblers on reeds 1·60 1·60
2874 220pf.+80pf. Woodchat shrike 3·25 3·00

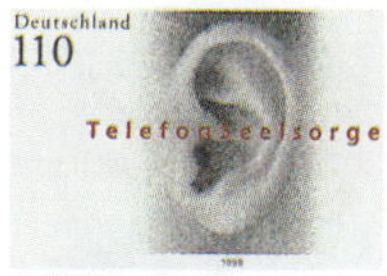

1238 Ear

1998. Telephone Help Lines.
2875 **1238** 110pf. black and orange 1·10 90

1239 "Hiorten" (sailing packet), 1692

1998. Stamp Day.
2876 **1239** 110pf. multicoloured 1·10 90

1240 Ramin

1998. Birth Centenary of Gunther Ramin (choir leader and organist).
2877 **1240** 300pf. multicoloured 3·00 2·75

1241 Shepherds following Star

1998. Christmas. Multicoloured.
2878 100pf.+50pf. Type **1241** 1·50 1·40
2879 110pf.+50pf. Baby Jesus 1·60 1·60

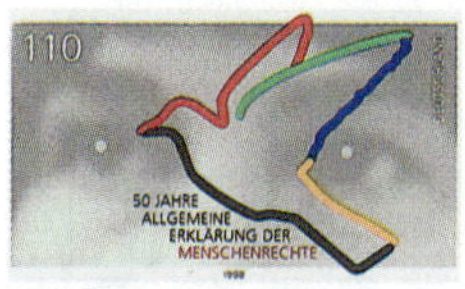

1242 Dove

1998. 50th Anniv of Declaration of Human Rights.
2880 **1242** 110pf. multicoloured 1·10 90
For charity stamp for Kosovo Relief Fund in similar design see No. 2899.

1243 Conductor's Hands and Baton

1998. 450th Anniv of Saxony State Orchestra, Dresden.
2881 **1243** 300pf. multicoloured 3·00 2·75

1244 National Theatre, Schiller, Goethe, Wieland and Herder

1999. 1100th Anniv of Weimar, European City of Culture.
2882 **1244** 100pf. multicoloured 1·10 95

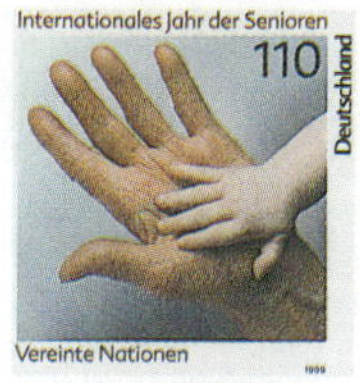

1245 Hands of Elderly Person and Child

1999. International Year of the Elderly.
2883 **1245** 110pf. multicoloured 1·20 95

1246 Katharina von Bora

1999. 500th Birth Anniv of Katharina von Bora (wife of Martin Luther).
2884 **1246** 110pf. multicoloured 1·20 95

1999. Federal State Parliament Buildings (2nd series). As T 1213.
2885 110pf. Hesse (Richard Goerz) (former palace of Dukes of Hesse) 1·20 95

1247 Cycle Racing

1999. Sport Promotion Fund. Multicoloured.
2886 100pf.+50pf. Type **1247** 1·50 1·40
2887 110pf.+50pf. Horse racing 1·60 1·60
2888 110pf.+50pf. Motor racing 1·60 1·60
2889 300pf.+100pf. Motor cycle racing 4·00 4·00

1248 Cover Illustration (by Walter Trier) of "Emil and the Detectives" (novel)

1999. Birth Centenary of Erich Kastner (writer).
2890 **1248** 300pf. multicoloured 3·00 2·75

1249 Coloured Diodes

1999. 50th Anniv of Fraunhofer Society (for applied research).
2891 **1249** 110pf. multicoloured 1·20 95

1250 Emblem and Initials

1999. 50th Anniv of North Atlantic Treaty Organization.
2892 **1250** 110pf. multicoloured 1·20 95

1999. Federal State Parliament Buildings (3rd series). As T 1213. Multicoloured.
2893 110pf. City Parliament of Hamburg 1·20 95
2894 110pf. Mecklenburg-Western Pomerania (Schwerin Castle, rebuilt by Georg Demmler and Friedrich Stuler) 1·20 95

1251 Maybach Cabriolet of 1936 and Club Emblem

1999. Centenary of German Automobile Club.

2895 **1251** 110pf. multicoloured 1·20 95

1252 Emblem

1999. 25th Anniv of German Cancer Relief.

2896 **1252** 110pf. multicoloured 1·20 95

1999. Federal State Parliament Buildings (4th series). As T 1213.

2897 110pf. Bremen (Wassili Luckhardt) 1·20 95

1253 "Man, Nature, Technology"

1999. "EXPO 2000" World's Fair, Hanover (1st issue).

2898 **1253** 110pf. multicoloured 1·20 95

See also Nos. 2936, 2959 and 2979.

1999. Kosovo Relief Fund. As T 1242 but with inscription changed to "KOSOVO–HILFE 1999".

2899 110pf.+100pf. multicoloured 2·30 2·20

1254 Bavaria 1849 1k. and Saxony 1850 3pf. Stamps

1999. "IBRA'99" International Stamp Exhibition, Nuremberg. Sheet 140×100 mm.

MS2900 **1254** 300pf.+110pf. black, red and gold/cream 4·50 4·50

1255 Berchtesgaden National Park

1999. Europa. Parks and Gardens. Sheet 110×66 mm.

MS2901 **1255** 110pf. multicoloured 1·60 1·80

1256 Cross of St. John

1999. 900th Anniv of Order of Knights of St. John of Jerusalem.

2902 **1256** 110pf. multicoloured 1·20 95

1257 Flags and Children

1999. 50th Anniv of Berlin Airlift of 1948–49.

2903 **1257** 110pf. multicoloured 1·20 95

1258 Emblem

1999. 50th Anniv of Council of Europe.

2904 **1258** 110pf. multicoloured 1·40 95

1259 State Arms and Article 1

1999. 50th Anniv of German Basic Law. Sheet 110×66 mm.

MS2905 **1259** 110pf. multicoloured 1·20 1·40

1260 Politicians and New Parliament Chamber, Berlin

1999. 50th Anniv of Federal Republic of Germany. Sheet 138×97 mm containing T 1260 and similar horiz designs. Multicoloured.

MS2906 110pf. Type **1260**; 110pf. Child playing in rubble and child among flowers; 110pf. Berlin Wall and its fall; 110pf. Soldiers confronting civilians and debating chamber 4·50 4·75

1261 Lars, the Little Polar Bear

1999. Youth Welfare. Cartoon Characters. Mult.

2907 100pf.+50pf. Type **1261**	1·60	1·50
2908 100pf.+50pf. Rudi the Crow	1·60	1·50
2909 110pf.+50pf. Twipsy (mascot of "Expo 2000" World's Fair, Hanover)	1·80	1·80
2910 110pf.+50pf. Mecki (hedgehog)	1·80	1·80
2911 220pf.+80pf. Tabaluga (dragon)	3·25	3·00

1262 Cross Clasp, Altar, Cathedral Spire and Time-line

1999. 1200th Anniv of Paderborn Diocese.

2912 **1262** 110pf. multicoloured 1·20 90

1263 House (child's painting)

1999. 50th Anniv of S.O.S. Children's Villages.

2913 **1263** 110pf. multicoloured 1·20 90

1264 "Ball at the Viennese Hofburg" and Score

1999. Death Centenary of Johann Strauss the younger (composer).

2914 **1264** 300pf. multicoloured 3·00 2·75

1265 Children at Desks (tapestry)

1999. 115th Anniv of Dominikus-Ringeisen Institute for Disabled People, Ursberg.

2915 **1265** 110pf. multicoloured 1·20 90

1266 Heinemann

1999. Birth Centenary of Gustav Heinemann (President 1969–74).

2916 **1266** 110pf. grey and red 1·20 90

1267 "Old Woman laughing" (Ernst Barlach)

1999. Cultural Foundation of the Federal States (1st series). Sculptures. Multicoloured.

2917 110pf. Type **1267** 1·20 90

2918 220pf. "Bust of a Thinker" (Wilhelm Lehmbruck) 2·00 1·80

See also Nos. 2960/1.

1268 Participating Countries and Dove

1999. Centenary of First Peace Conference, The Hague.

2919 **1268** 300pf. grey, red and blue 3·00 2·75

1269 Goethe (after J. K. Stieler)

1999. 250th Birth Anniv of Johann Wolfgang von Goethe (poet and playwright).

2920 **1269** 110pf. multicoloured 1·20 90

1270 Mouse carrying Letter

1999. "For Us Children". Sheet 105×71 mm.

MS2921 **1270** 110pf. multicoloured 1·20 1·20

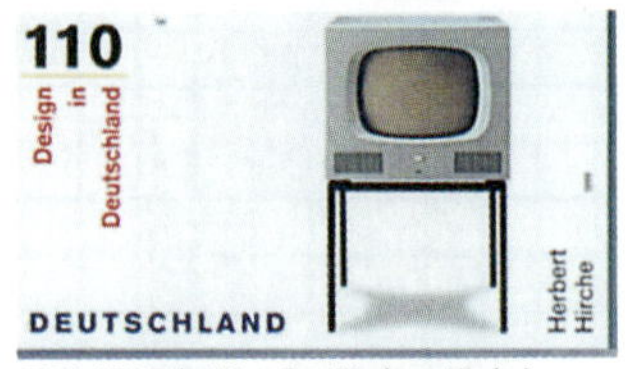

1271 HF1 Television Set (Herbert Hirche)

1999. Contemporary Design (2nd series). Sheet 138×97 mm containing T 1271 and similar horiz designs. Multicoloured.

MS2922 110pf. Type **1271**; 110pf. "Mono-a" cutlery (Peter Raacke); 110pf. Pearl bottles (Gunter Kupetz); 110pf. Transrapid Maglev train (Alexander Neumeister) 4·50 4·50

1272 Player

1999. FC Bayern Munich, National Football Champions.

2923 **1272** 110pf. multicoloured 1·20 95

1273 Book and Bookmark

1999. 50th Anniv of Federal Association of German Book Traders' Peace Prize.

2924 **1273** 110pf. multicoloured 1·20 95

1274 Strauss and Poster from "Salome" (opera)

1999. 50th Death Anniv of Richard Strauss (composer).

2925 **1274** 300pf. multicoloured 3·00 2·75

1275 Andromeda Galaxy

1999. Humanitarian Relief Funds. Outer Space. Multicoloured.

2926 100pf.+50pf. Type **1275**	1·50	1·40
2927 100pf.+50pf. Swan constellation	1·50	1·40
2928 110pf.+50pf. X-ray image of exploding star	1·60	1·60
2929 110pf.+50pf. Comet colliding with Jupiter	1·60	1·60
2930 300pf.+100pf. Gamma ray image of sky	4·00	4·00

1276 Goltzsch Valley Railway Bridge

1999. Bridges (2nd series).
2931 **1276** 110pf. multicoloured 1·20 95

1277 "DGB"

1999. 50th Anniv of German Federation of Trade Unions.
2932 **1277** 110pf. black and bright red 1·20 95

1278 Greater Horseshoe Bats

1999. Endangered Species.
2933 **1278** 100pf. multicoloured 1·10 95

1279 The Annunciation

1999. Christmas. Multicoloured.
2934 100pf.+50pf. Type **1279** 1·50 1·40
2935 110pf.+50pf. Nativity 1·60 1·50

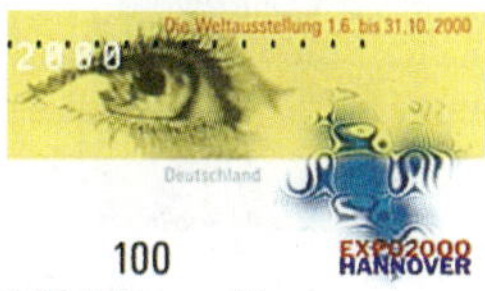

1280 Emblem and Eye

2000. "EXPO 2000" World's Fair, Hanover (2nd issue).
2936 **1280** 100pf. multicoloured 1·10 95

1281 Emblem

2000. Holy Year 2000.
2937 **1281** 110pf. multicoloured 1·20 95

1282 Charlemagne and Plan of Palace Chapel

2000. 1200th Anniv of Aachen Cathedral.
2938 **1282** 110pf. multicoloured 1·20 95

1283 Schweitzer and Signature

2000. 125th Birth Anniv of Albert Schweitzer (missionary doctor).
2939 **1283** 110pf. multicoloured 1·40 95

1284 Football

2000. Centenary of German Football Association.
2940 **1284** 110pf. multicoloured 1·20 95

1285 Wehner

2000. 10th Death Anniv of Herbert Wehner (politician).
2941 **1285** 110pf. multicoloured 1·20 95

1286 Woman

2000. Prevention of Violence Against Women.
2942 **1286** 110pf. red, grey and black 1·20 95

1287 "2000" in Moving Film Sequence

2000. 50th Berlin International Film Festival.
2943 **1287** 100pf. multicoloured 1·10 95

1288 Boxing

2000. Sport Promotion Fund. Multicoloured.
2944 100pf.+50pf. Type **1288** (fair play) 1·50 1·40
2945 110pf.+50pf. Rhythmic gymnastics (beauty) 1·60 1·60
2946 110pf.+50pf. Running (competition) 1·60 1·60
2947 300pf.+100pf. Raised hands (culture of interaction) 4·00 4·00

1289 Gutenberg (after engraving by A. Thevet) and Letters from Gutenberg Bible

2000. 600th Birth Anniv of Johannes Gutenberg (inventor of printing press).
2948 **1289** 110pf. black and red 1·20 95

1290 Jester

2000. 175th Anniv of First Dusseldorf Carnival.
2949 **1290** 110pf. multicoloured 1·30 95

1291 Ebert

2000. 75th Death Anniv of Friedrich Ebert (President, 1919–25).
2950 **1291** 110pf. multicoloured 1·20 95

1292 Weill at Rehearsal of "One Touch of Venus" (musical), 1943

2000. Birth Centenary of Kurt Weill (composer).
2951 **1292** 300pf. blk, stone & red 3·00 2·75

1293 Passau

2000. Images of Germany.
2952 **1293** 110pf. multicoloured 1·20 95

2000. Federal State Parliament Buildings (5th series). As T 1213. Multicoloured.
2953 110pf. Leine Palace, Lower Saxony 1·20 95

1294 Trees

2000. Hainich National Park. Sheet 105×70 mm.
MS2954 **1294** 110pf. multicoloured 1·20 1·20

1295 Toy Windmill and "Post!"

2000
2955 **1295** 110pf. multicoloured 1·20 95

1296 "Blue Wonder" Bridge, Dresden

2000. Bridges (3rd series).
2956 **1296** 100pf. multicoloured 1·10 90

2000. Federal State Parliament Buildings (6th series). As T 1213. Multicoloured.
2957 110pf. North-Rhine/Westphalia (Fritz Eller) 1·20 95

1297 City Buildings

2000. 750th Anniv of Greifswald.
2958 **1297** 110pf. multicoloured 1·20 95

2000. "EXPO 2000" World's Fair, Hanover (3rd issue). As No. 2898 but self-adhesive.
2959 **1253** 110pf. multicoloured 5·00 4·50

1298 "Expulsion from Paradise" (Leonhard Kern)

2000. Cultural Foundation of the Federal States. Sculptures. Multicoloured.
2960 110pf. Type **1298** 1·10 90
2961 220pf. Silver table fountain (Melchior Gelb) 2·00 1·90

1299 "Building Europe"

2000. Europa. Ordinary or self-adhesive gum.
2962 **1299** 110pf. multicoloured 1·40 95

1300 Von Zinzendorf and Natives

2000. 300th Birth Anniv of Nikolaus Ludwig von Zinzendorf (leader of Moravian Brethren).
2964 **1300** 110pf. multicoloured 1·20 90

1301 Countryside

2000. Environmental Protection.
2965 **1301** 110pf.+50pf. mult 1·60 1·60

1302 Crowd at Music Festival

2000. Youth Welfare. "EXPO 2000" World's Fair, Hanover (4th issue). Multicoloured.
2966 100pf.+50pf. Type **1302** 1·50 1·40
2967 100pf.+50pf. Back-packers 1·50 1·40
2968 110pf.+50pf. Map of Africa and text 1·60 1·60
2969 110pf.+50pf. Eye of Buddha 1·60 1·60
2970 110pf.+50pf. Chinese calligraphy 1·60 1·60
2971 300pf.+100pf. Psychedelic swirl 3·75 3·50

1303 Front Page of Issue 17, 1650, and Modern Pages of Newspaper

2000. 350th Anniv of Einkommende Zeitungen (first German daily newspaper).
2972 **1303** 110pf. multicoloured 1·30 95

1304 Emblem

2000. Centenary of Chambers of Handicrafts.

2973	**1304**	300pf. orange and black	3·00	2·75

1305 Meteorological Station

2000. Centenary of the Zugspitze Meteorological Station.

2974	**1305**	100pf. multicoloured	1·30	95

1306 Road Sign and Flashing Light

2000. 50th Anniv of Technisches Hilfwerk (Federal disaster relief organization).

2975	**1306**	110pf. multicoloured	1·40	95

1307 Bach

2000. 250th Death Anniv of Johann Sebastian Bach (composer).

2976	**1307**	110pf. multicoloured	1·40	95

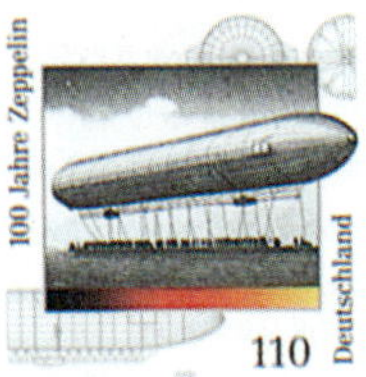

1308 LZ-1

2000. Centenary of Inaugural Flight of LZ-1 (Zeppelin airship), 1900.

2977	**1308**	110pf. multicoloured	1·30	95

2000. Federal State Parliament Buildings (7th series). As T 1213. Multicoloured.

2978	110pf. Rhineland-Palatinate, Mainz	1·20	95

1309 Emblem, Globe and Fingerprint

2000. "EXPO 2000" World's Fair, Hanover (5th issue).

2979	**1309**	110pf. multicoloured	1·20	95

1310 Wiechert

2000. 50th Death Anniv of Ernst Wiechert (writer).

2980	**1310**	110pf. multicoloured	1·20	95

1311 Nietzsche (Edvard Munch)

2000. Death Centenary of Friedrich Nietzsche (philosopher).

2981	**1311**	110pf. multicoloured	1·30	95

1312 "For You"

2000. Greetings Stamp.

2982	**1312**	100pf. multicoloured	1·10	95

1313 Saar River, Mettlach

2000. Images of Germany.

2983	**1313**	110pf. multicoloured	1·20	95

1314 Adolph Kopling

2000. 150th Anniv of Kopling Society (voluntary organization).

2984	**1314**	110pf. multicoloured	1·20	95

1315 Building

2000. 50th Anniv of Federal Court of Justice.

2985	**1315**	110pf. multicoloured	1·10	95

1316 Clown's Face

2000. "For Us Children". Sheet 55×82 mm.

MS2986	**1316**	110pf. multicoloured	1·20	1·10

1317 Nocht (founder), World Map and Microscope Images of Pathogens

2000. Centenary of Bernard Nocht Institute for Tropical Medicine.

2987	**1317**	300pf. multicoloured	3·25	3·00

1318 Town Hall, Wernigerode

2000. Tourist Sights. Showing face values in German currency and euros.

2988	**1318**	10pf. grey, orge & slate	55	20
2989	-	20pf. orange and black	55	45
2990	-	47pf. mauve and green	55	55
2991	-	50pf. brown and red	90	60
2992	-	80pf. green and brown	80	70
2993	-	100pf. blue and brown	1·40	1·30
2994	-	110pf. pur, brn & orge	1·30	90
2997	-	220pf. blue and brown	2·30	2·20
3000	-	300pf. brown and blue	2·75	2·50
3001	-	400pf. brown and red	3·75	3·00
3002	-	440pf. black and grey	4·00	3·50
3003	-	510pf. pink and red	5·00	4·50
3004	-	720pf. purple & mauve	6·75	6·25

DESIGNS: 20pf. Bottcherstrasse, Bremen; 47pf. Wilhelmshohe Park, Kassel; 50pf. Ceiling decoration, Kircheim Castle; 80pf. St. Reinoldi Church, Dortmund; 100pf. Schwerin Castle, Mecklenberg; 110pf. Stone bridge, Regensburg; 220pf. St. Nikolai Cathedral, Greifswald; 300pf. Town Hall Grimma; 400pf. Wartburg Castle, Eisenach; 440pf. Cologne Cathedral; 510pf. Heidelberg Castle; 720pf. Town Hall, Hildesheim.

Nos. 2988, 2993/4 also come self-adhesive.

1319 National Colours

2000. 10th Anniv of Reunification of Germany.

3010	**1319**	110pf. black, red & yell	1·10	95

1320 Curd Jurgens

2000. Humanitarian Relief Funds. Actors. Mult.

3011	100pf.+50pf. Type **1320**	1·60	1·60
3012	100pf.+50pf. Lilli Palmer	1·60	1·60
3013	110pf.+50pf. Heinz Ruhmann	1·80	1·80
3014	110pf.+50pf. Romy Schneider	1·80	1·80
3015	300pf.+100pf. Gert Frobe	3·75	3·50

1321 Pens, Envelope and 1999 110pf. Stamp

2000. Stamp Day.

3016	**1321**	110pf. multicoloured	1·10	95

1322 Grethe Weiser (actress and singer)

2000. Famous German Women.

3017	**1322**	100pf. green and brown	1·00	90
3018	-	110pf. red and green	1·10	90
3019	-	220pf. brown and green	2·00	1·90
3020	-	300pf. purple and brown	2·50	2·50

DESIGNS: 110pf. Kate Strobel (politician); 200pf. Marieluise Fleisser (writer); 300pf. Nelly Sachs (writer).

2000. Federal State Parliament Buildings (8th series). As T 1213. Multicoloured.

3025	110pf. Saarland	1·10	95

1323 Book Cover

2000. 125th Birth Anniv of Rainer Maria Rilke (poet).

3026	**1323**	110pf. multicoloured	1·10	95

1324 Bode

2000. Birth Centenary of Arnold Bode (artist).

3027	**1324**	110pf. black and red	1·10	95

1325 "Birth of Christ" (Conrad von Soest)

2000. Christmas. Multicoloured.

3028	100pf.+50pf. Type **1325**	1·50	1·30
3029	110pf.+50pf. Nativity	1·60	1·40

1326 Indian Pepper (illustration from *New Book of Herbs*)

2001. 500th Birth Anniv of Leonhart Fuchs (physician and botanist).

3030	**1326**	100pf. multicoloured	90	80

1327 "VdK"

2001. 50th Anniv (2000) of Disabled War Veterans' Association.

3031	**1327**	110pf. multicoloured	1·00	90

1328 Prussian Eagle

2001. 300th Anniv of the Kingdom of Prussia.

3032	**1328**	110pf. multicoloured	1·00	90

1329 Lortzing and Music Score

2001. Birth Bicent of Albert Lortzing (composer).

3033	**1329**	110pf. multicoloured	1·00	90

1330 Telephone Handset and Number

2001. National Federation of Child and Youth Telephone Helplines.
3034 **1330** 110pf. yellow, red & blk 1·00 90

1331 Bucer

2001. 450th Death Anniv of Martin Bucer (teacher and Protestant reformer).
3035 **1331** 110pf. multicoloured 1·10 90

1332 Children running

2001. Sport Promotion Fund. Multicoloured.
3036 100pf.+50pf. Type **1332** 1·40 1·30
3037 110pf.+50pf. Disabled and able-bodied athletes 1·50 1·50
3038 110pf.+50pf. Adult and children skating 1·50 1·50
3039 300pf.+100pf. Men playing basketball 3·75 3·50

1333 Hand holding Quill

2001. 250th Birth Anniv of Johann Heinrich Voss (writer and translator). (a) Ordinary gum.
3040 **1333** 300pf. multicoloured 3·00 2·75

(b) Self-adhesive gum.
3040a €1.53 multicoloured 3·75 3·00

1334 Ollenhauer

2001. Birth Centenary of Erich Ollenhauer (politician).
3041 **1334** 110pf. red, black & sil 1·00 90

1335 Arnold

2001. Birth Centenary of Karl Arnold (politician).
3042 **1335** 110pf. black, green & red 1·00 90

2001. Federal State Parliament Buildings (9th series). As T 1213. Multicoloured.
3043 110pf. Saxony 1·00 90

1336 Badge

2001. 50th Anniv of Federal Border Police.
3044 **1336** 110pf. multicoloured 1·00 90

1337 Suspension Railway

2001. Centenary of Suspension Railway, Wuppertal.
3045 **1338** 110pf.+50pf. mult 1·60 1·40

1338 Rendsberg Railway Viaduct

2001. Bridges (4th series).
3046 100pf. multicoloured 1·00 80

1339 "Post!"

2001
3047 **1339** 110pf. multicoloured 1·00 90

1340 Accordion

2001. Folk Music.
3048 **1340** 110pf. multicoloured 1·00 90

1341 World Map

2001. 50th Anniv of Goethe Institute.
3049 **1341** 300pf. multicoloured 2·75 2·75

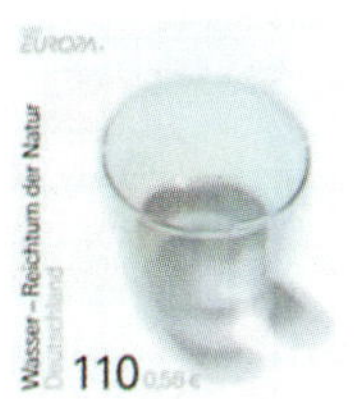

1342 Glass of Water

2001. Europa. Water Resources.
3050 **1342** 110pf. multicoloured 1·40 90

1343 Egk

2001. Birth Centenary of Werner Egk (composer and conductor).
3051 **1343** 110pf. multicoloured 1·00 90

2001. Federal State Parliament Buildings (10th series). As T 1213. Multicoloured.
3052 110pf. Saxony-Anhalt 1·00 90

1344 Mountain Gorilla with Young

2001. Endangered Species. Multicoloured. Ordinary or self-adhesive gum.
3053 110pf. Type **1344** 1·70 95
3054 110pf. Indian rhinoceros with young 1·70 95

1345 Pinocchio

2001. Youth Welfare. Characters from Children's Stories. Multicoloured.
3057 100pf.+50pf. Type **1345** 1·40 1·30
3058 100pf.+50pf. Pippi Longstocking 1·40 1·30
3059 110pf.+50pf. Heidi and Peter 1·60 1·60
3060 110pf.+50pf. Jim Knopf 1·60 1·60
3061 300pf.+100pf. Tom Sawyer and Huckleberry Finn 3·75 3·50

1346 St. Catherine's Monastery and Oceanographic Chart

2001. 750th Anniv of St. Catherine's Monastery and 50th Anniv of German Oceanographic Museum, Stralsund.
3062 **1346** 110pf. multicoloured 1·00 90

1347 Church Exterior and Plan

2001. 250th Anniv of Catholic Court Church, Dresden.
3063 **1347** 110pf. multicoloured 1·00 90

2001. Federal State Parliament Buildings (11th series). As T 1213. Multicoloured.
3064 110pf. Schleswig-Holstein 1·00 90

1348 Church Bell Tower, Canzow

2001
3065 **1348** 110pf. black, blue and mauve 1·00 90

1349 Hand (circulatory disease)

2001. Health Awareness Campaign. Sheet 138×110 mm containing T 1349 and similar horiz designs. Multicoloured.
MS3066 110pf. Type **1349**; 110pf. Torso (cancer); 110pf. Lower body (infectious diseases); 110pf. Man holding head (depression) 6·00 4·75

1350 Emblem

2001. Dragon Lancing Festival, Furth im Wald.
3067 **1350** 100pf. multicoloured 90 80

1351 Lime Tree, Himmelsberg

2001. Natural Heritage. Ordinary or self-adhesive gum.
3068 **1351** 110pf. multicoloured 1·00 90

1352 "Schoolmaster Lampel" (Wilhelm Busch) and Text

2001. Lifelong Learning.
3070 **1352** 110pf. multicoloured 1·00 90

1353 Felix standing on Cat

2001. "For Us Children". Sheet 110×66 mm.
MS3071 **1353** 110pf. multicoloured 1·20 1·10

2001. Federal State Parliament Buildings (12th series). As T 1213. Multicoloured.
3072 110pf. Thuringia 1·00 90

1354 "Justice" (sculpture)

2001. 50th Anniv of Federal Constitutional Court.
3073 **1354** 110pf. multicoloured 1·00 90

1355 Members' Flags

2001. 1st Union Network International World Congress, Berlin.
3074 **1355** 110pf. multicoloured 1·00 90

1356 Museum Floor Plan

2001. Jewish Museum, Berlin.
3075 **1356** 110pf. multicoloured 1·00 90

1357 Marilyn Monroe

2001. Humanitarian Relief Funds. Film Industry. Multicoloured.

3076 100pf.+50pf. Type **1357** 1·50 1·40
3077 100pf.+50pf. Charlie Chaplin 1·50 1·40
3078 110pf.+50pf. Greta Garbo 1·60 1·60
3079 110pf.+50pf. Film reel 1·60 1·60
3080 300pf.+100pf. Jean Gabin 3·75 3·50
MS3080a 205×156 mm. As Nos. 3076/80 13·00 12·50

1358 Ribbon and "fur Dich"

2001. Greetings Stamp.
3081 **1358** 110pf. red and black 1·00 90

1359 "Virgin and Child" (Alfredo Roldan)

2001. Christmas. Religious Paintings. Mult.
3082 100pf.+50pf. Type **1359** 1·50 1·40
3083 110pf.+50pf. "The Shepherd's Adoration" (Jusepe de Ribera) 1·60 1·60
MS3083a 106×133 mm. Nos. 3082/3 and 3788/9 of Spain 13·00 12·50

1360 *Gauss* (survey barquentine)

2001. Centenary of German Antarctic Research. Sheet 135×105 mm containing T 1360 and similar horiz design. Multicoloured.
MS3084 110pf. Type **1360**; 220pf. *Polarstern* (exploration ship) 3·75 3·50

1361 Heisenberg

2001. Birth Centenary of Werner Heisenberg (physicist).
3085 **1361** 300pf. black and blue 3·25 2·75

1362 Bautzen

2002. Millenary of Bautzen. Ordinary or self-adhesive gum.
3086 **1362** 56c. multicoloured 1·00 90

1363 Von Dohnanyi

2002. Birth Centenary of Hans von Dohnanyi (German resistance co-ordinator).
3087 **1363** 56c. multicoloured 1·00 90

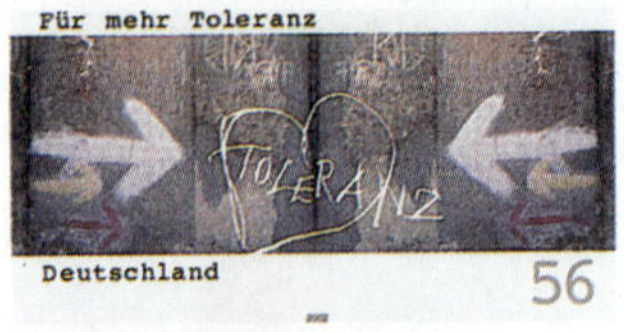

1364 Graffiti

2002. "Tolerance".
3088 **1364** 56c. multicoloured 1·00 90

1365 " € "

2002. New Currency. Ordinary or self-adhesive gum.
3089 **1365** 56c. yellow and blue 1·30 1·20

1366 Mountains

2002. International Year of Mountains.
3091 **1366** 56c.+26c. multicoloured 1·60 1·40

No. 3091 was sold with a premium towards environmental protection.

1367 Cross-country Skier (biathlon)

2002. Winter Olympic Games, Salt Lake City, U.S.A. Multicoloured.
3092 51c.+26c. Type **1367** 1·50 1·40
3093 56c.+26c. Ice skater (speed skating) 1·60 1·50
3094 56c.+26c. Skier (ski jumping) 1·60 1·50
3095 153c.+51c. Man in helmet (luge) 4·00 3·75
MS3096 142×98 mm. As Nos. 3092/5 11·00 10·50

Nos. 3092/**MS**3096 were sold with a premium towards "Foundation for the Promotion of Sport in Germany".

1368 Knigge and Books

2002. 250th Birth Anniv of Adolf Freiherr Knigge (author of Uber den Umgang mit Menschen (book on etiquette)).
3097 **1368** 56c. multicoloured 1·00 90

1369 Front of Train Carriage

2002. Centenary of Berlin Subway.
3098 **1369** 56c. multicoloured 1·00 90

1370 Deggendorf

2002. Millenary of Deggendorf.
3099 **1370** 56c. multicoloured 1·00 90

1371 Mechanical Calculator (Johann Christoph Schuster)

2002. Cultural Foundation of the Federal States.
3100 **1371** 56c. multicoloured 1·00 90

1372 Ecksberg Pilgrimage Church

2002. 150th Anniv of Ecksberg Foundation (for people with disabilities).
3101 **1372** 56c. multicoloured 1·00 90

1373 Exhibits and Building

2002. Centenary of Freemason's Museum, Bayreuth.
3102 **1373** 56c. multicoloured 1·00 90

1374 Armorial Lions

2002. 50th Anniv of Baden-Württenberg State.
3103 **1374** 56c. black, gold and yellow 1·00 90

1375 "post"

2002
3104 **1375** 56c. multicoloured 1·00 90

1376 Emblem

2002. 50th Anniv of Federal Employment Services.
3105 **1376** €1.53 red and black 3·00 2·75

1377 Modern Student and Elector Friedrich the Wise (founder of Wittenberg University)

2002. 500th Anniv of Martin Luther University, Halle-Wittenberg.
3106 **1377** 56c. grey, blue and mauve 1·00 90

1378 "KINDERGOTTESDIENST!"

2002. 150th Anniv of Children's Church Services.
3107 **1378** 56c. multicoloured 1·00 90

1379 "Documenta11"

2002. 11th "Documenta" Modern Art Exhibition, Kassel. Sheet 100×70 mm.
MS3108 **1379** 56c. ultramarine, lilac and blue 1·20 1·10

1380 Flags of Championship Winners and Football

2002. 20th-century World Cup Football Champions. Multicoloured.
3109 56c. Type **1380** 1·10 1·10
3110 56c. German Footballer 1·10 1·10

1381 Clown

2002. Europa. Circus. Ordinary or self-adhesive gum.
3111 **1381** 56c. black, red and green 1·00 90

1382 Dessau-Worlitz

2002. UNESCO World Heritage Site. Dessau-Worlitz Gardens. Ordinary or self-adhesive gum.
3113 **1382** 56c. multicoloured 1·00 90

1383 Thaer

2002. 250th Birth Anniv of Albrecht Daniel Thaer (agronomist).
3115 **1383** €2.25 multicoloured 4·25 4·25

1384 Desmoulin's Whorl Snail

2002. Endangered Species. Molluscs. Multicoloured.
3116 51c. Type **1384** 90 90
3117 56c. Freshwater pearl mussel 1·00 95

1385 Chess Pieces

2002. Youth Welfare. Toys. Multicoloured.

3118	51c.+26c. Type **1385**	1·40	1·30
3119	51c.+26c. Wooden crane	1·40	1·30
3120	56c.+26c. Doll	1·50	1·50
3121	56c.+26c. Teddy bear	1·50	1·50
3122	153c.+51c. Electric train	3·75	3·50

1386 "Yellow Feather in Red"

2002. Birth Centenary of Ernst Wilhelm Nay (artist).
3123 **1386** 56c. multicoloured 1·20 90

1387 Leaves and Silhouettes

2002. 40th Anniv of "Deutsche Welthungerhilfe" (humanitarian aid organization).
3124 **1387** 51c. multicoloured 1·20 90

1388 "Way of Human Rights" (sculpture, Danni Karavan)

2002. 150th Anniv of National Museum of German Art and Culture, Nuremberg.
3125 **1388** 56c. multicoloured 1·30 90

1389 Hesse

2002. 125th Birth Anniv of Hermann Hesse (writer).
3126 **1389** 56c. blue and yellow 1·30 90

1390 Trees and Rocks

2002. Hochharz National Park. Sheet 110×66 mm.
MS3127 **1390** 56c. multicoloured 1·30 1·10

1391 Felder

2002. 2nd Death Anniv of Josef Felder (politician and journalist).
3128 **1391** 56c. multicoloured 1·30 90

1392 Museum Buildings

2002. UNESCO World Heritage Site. Museum Island, Berlin.
3129 **1392** 56c. black and green 1·30 90

1393 Firemen fighting Fire

2002. Voluntary Fire Brigades.
3130 **1393** 56c. multicoloured 1·30 90

1394 Building Facade

2002. 130th Anniv of Communications Museum, Berlin.
3131 **1394** 153c. multicoloured 3·25 2·75

2002. Flood Relief. As T 1222 but with "HOCHWASSERHILFE 2002" inscribed at left and new face value.
3132 56c.+44c. multicoloured 2·10 1·60

1395 Walls of Roman Bathhouse, Wurmlingen (illustration from *Die Alamannen* by Konrad Theiss)

2002. Archaeology.
3133 **1395** 51c. multicoloured 1·20 95

1396 Face painted on Child's Toe

2002. "For Us Children". Sheet 110×66 mm.
MS3134 **1396** 56c. multicoloured 1·40 1·10

1397 "Rotes Elisabeth-Ufer" (painting, Ernst Ludwig Kirchner)

2002
3135 **1397** 112c. multicoloured 2·40 1·90

1398 Von Kleist (miniature, Peter Friedel)

2002. 225th Birth Anniv of Heinrich von Kleist (writer).
3136 **1398** 56c. multicoloured 1·40 90

1399 Jochum rehearsing

2002. Birth Centenary of Eugen Jochum (conductor).
3137 **1399** 56c. multicoloured 1·40 90

1400 Diagram of Planets (Copernicus), Horsemen and Sphere

2002. 400th Birth Anniv of Otto von Guericke (engineer and physicist).
3138 **1400** 153c. multicoloured 3·50 2·75

1401 Angel (detail, "The Annunciation")

2002. Christmas. Paintings by Rogier van der Weyden. Multicoloured.

3139	51c.+26c. Type **1401**	1·80	1·50
3140	56c.+26c. The Holy Family (detail, Miraflores alterpiece)	1·90	1·60

1402 Arrows

2002. 50th Anniv of Federal Agency for Civic Education.
3141 **1402** 56c. black, red and yellow 1·40 90

1403 Clock and Eye

2002. 50th Anniv of German Television.
3142 **1403** 56c. multicoloured 1·40 90

1404 BMW Isetta 300

2002. Cars. Multicoloured.

3144	45c.+20c. Type **1404**	1·40	1·20
3145	55c.+25c. Volkswagen Beetle	1·70	1·50
3146	55c.+25c. Mercedes Benz 300 SL	1·70	1·50
3147	55c.+25c. VEB Sachsenring Trabant P50	1·70	1·50
3148	144c.+56c. Borgward Isabella Coupe	4·25	3·75

See also Nos. 3238/42.

1405 "Halle Market Church" (Lyonel Feininger)

3149 **1405** 55c. multicoloured 1·40 90

2002. Tourist Sights. As T 1318 but with face value in new currency.

3150	5c. brown and green	20	20
3151	25c. olive and violet	55	45
3153	40c. multicoloured	85	70
3154	44c. yellow and black	1·10	90
3155	45c. pink and black	1·10	90
3156	55c. yellow and black	1·30	1·10
3157	€1 grey and black	2·30	1·80
3158	€1.44 pink and green	3·25	2·75
3159	€1.60 grey, black and orange	3·50	3·00
3160	€1.80 green and chestnut	4·00	3·25
3161	€2 red and green	4·50	3·75
3162	€2.20 blue and black	5·00	4·00
3163	€2.60 blue and red	5·50	4·50
3164	€4.10 purple and blue	8·75	7·00

DESIGNS: 5c. Erfuster Cathedral; 25c. Schloss Arolsen; 40c. J.S. Bach (statue), Leipzig; 44c. Philharmonic Hall, Berlin; 45c. Canal warehouse, Tonning; 55c. Old Opera House, Frankfurt; €1 Porta Niga (black gate), Trier; €1.44 Beethoven's birthplace, Bonn; €1.60 Bauhaus, Dessau; €1.80 Staatsgalerie, Stuttgart; €2 Bamberger Reister (statue); €2.20 Theodor Fontane monument, Neuruppin; €2.60 *Seute Dern* (four-mast barque), Maritime Museum, Bremerhaven; €4.10 Houses, Wismar.

Nos. 3151 and 3155/6 also come self-adhesive.

2002. Famous German Women. As T 1322 but with face value in new currency.

3190	45c. green and blue	1·10	90
3191	55c. red and black	1·30	1·10
3192	€1 purple and blue	2·30	1·80
3193	€1.44 brown and blue	3·00	2·75

DESIGNS: 45c. Annette von Droste-Hulshoff (writer); 55c. Hildegard Knef (actress); €1 Marie Juchacz (politician); €1.44 Esther von Kirchbach (writer).

1406 Town Buildings

2003. Millenary of Kronach.
3194 **1406** 45c. multicoloured 1·10 90

1407 Georg Elser

2003. Birth Centenary of Georg Elser (attempted assassination of Adolf Hitler).
3195 **1407** 55c. multicoloured 1·30 1·10

1408 Bridge joined by Heart

2003. 40th Anniv of German–French Co-operation Treaty.
3196 **1408** 55c. multicoloured 1·30 1·10

1409 Hand and Page

2003. Year of the Bible.
3197 **1409** 55c. multicoloured 1·30 1·10

1410 "Proun 30t" (El Lissitzky)

2003. Cultural Foundation of the Federal States.
3198 **1410** €1.44 multicoloured 3·50 2·75

1411 St. Thomas Church Choir, Leipzig

2003. Boys' Choirs. Sheet 172×77 mm containing T 1411 and similar horiz designs. Multicoloured.
MS3199 45c. Type **1411**; 55c. Dresden Church choir; 100c. St. Peter's Cathedral choir, Regensburg 5·00 4·75

1412 Rose

2003. Greetings Stamp. Ordinary or self-adhesive gum.
3200 **1412** 55c. multicoloured 1·30 1·10

1413 "Junger Argentier" (Max Beckman)

2003. Artists' Anniversaries. Multicoloured.
3202 55c. Type **1413** (53rd death anniv) 1·40 1·10
3203 €1 "Komposition" (Adolf Holzel) (150th birth anniv) 2·40 2·00

1414 Footballer

2003. Sports Promotion Fund. World Cup Football Championship (2006), Germany. Multicoloured.
3204 45c.+20c. Type **1414** 1·60 1·40
3205 55c.+25c. Boys playing football 1·80 1·60
3206 55c.+25c. Fan with arms raised 1·80 1·60
3207 55c.+25c. Young player heading ball 1·80 1·60
3208 €1.44+56c. Boy kicking ball to older man 4·25 4·00

1415 Building Facade

2003. UNESCO World Heritage Sites. Cologne Cathedral. Ordinary or self-adhesive gum.
3209 **1415** 55c. grey, red and black 1·30 1·10

1416 Flower

2003. International Horticultural Exhibition, Rostock.
3211 **1416** 45c. multicoloured 1·10 85

1417 Oskar von Miller (founder) and Technological Symbols

2003. Centenary of Deutsches Museum, Munich.
3212 **1417** 55c. multicoloured 1·30 1·10

1418 Cut-out Figures

2003. 50th Anniv of Deutscher Kinderschutzbund (children's organization).
3213 **1418** 55c. multicoloured 1·30 1·10

1419 Map and Representation of Radio Waves

2003. 50th Anniv of Deutsche Welle (radio station).
3214 **1419** 55c. multicoloured 1·30 1·10

1420 Aviators and Junkers W.33 Bremen

2003. 75th Anniv East–West North Atlantic Flight.
3215 **1420** 144c.+56c. multicoloured 5·00 4·25

1421 1960s Posters

2003. Europa. Poster Art.
3216 **1421** 55c. multicoloured 1·40 1·20

1422 Justus von Liebig

2003. Birth Bicentenary of Justus von Liebig (chemist).
3217 **1422** 55c. multicoloured 1·40 1·20

1423 Reinhold Schneider and Text

2003. Birth Centenary of Reinhold Schneider (writer).
3218 **1423** 55c. multicoloured 1·40 1·20

1424 Eurocopter EC135 and Patrol Vehicle

2003. Centenary of ADAC (automobile association).
3219 **1424** 55c. multicoloured 1·40 1·20

1425 Rainbow

2003. Ecumenical Church Conference, Berlin.
3220 **1425** 55c. multicoloured 1·40 1·20

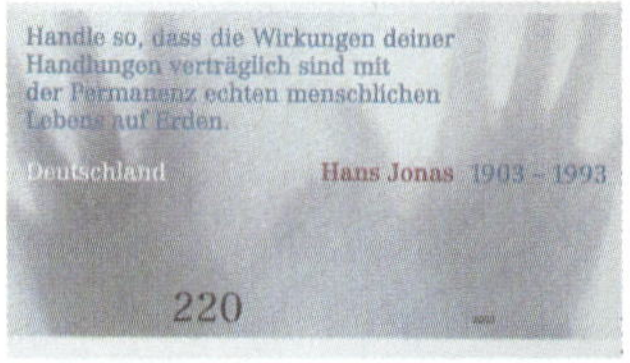

1426 Hands and Text

2003. Birth Centenary of Hans Jonas (philosopher).
3221 **1426** 220c. multicoloured 5·50 4·75

1427 Hand with Face and Feet

2003. 10th Anniv of Postal Codes.
3222 **1427** 55c. multicoloured 1·40 1·20

1428 Bridge over Salzach River

2003. Centenary of Oberndorf–Laufen Bridge. Ordinary or self-adhesive gum.
3223 **1428** 55c. multicoloured 1·40 1·20
A stamp of the same design was issued by Austria.

1429 Lake, Trees and Islands

2003. Unteres Odertal National Park. Sheet 111×66 mm.
MS3225 **1429** 55c. multicoloured 1·10 1·10

1430 Protesters and Tanks

2003. 50th Anniv of Uprising in East Berlin.
3226 **1430** 55c.+25c. multicoloured 2·10 1·70

1431 Musical Notations

2003. 50th Anniv of Deutscher Musikrat (music association). Ordinary or self-adhesive gum.
3227 **1431** €1.44 silver and blue 3·75 3·00

1432 Father chasing Son

2003. "For Us Children". "Father and Son" (cartoon by E.O. Plauen (Erich Ohser)). Sheet 111×191 mm containing T 1432 and similar horiz designs. Multicoloured.
MS3228 45c.+20c. Type **1432**; 55c.+25c. Father and son falling; 55c.+25c. Father looking over shoulder at son running away; 55c.+25c. Father chasing son in a circle; €1.44+56c. Father and son sliding 12·00 11·00

1433 Winding Gear and Trees

2003. Ruhr District Industrial Landscape.
3229 **1433** 55c. multicoloured 1·40 1·20

1434 Andres Hermes

2003. 125th Birth Anniv of Andreas Hermes (politician).
3230 **1434** 55c. multicoloured 1·40 1·20

1435 Market Stalls, Munich

2003. German Cities. Multicoloured.
3231 45c. Type **1435** 1·20 95
3232 55c. Building facades, Altstadt Gorlitz 1·40 1·20
No. 3231 also comes self-adhesive.

1436 Petrified Forest, Chemnitz

2003
3234 **1436** 144c. multicoloured 3·75 3·25

1437 Viaduct and Enz River

2003. 150th Anniv of Enztal Viaduct (railway).
3235 **1437** 55c. multicoloured 1·70 1·30

1438 Theodor Adorno and Manuscript

2003. Birth Centenary of Theodor Adorno (philosopher and sociologist).
3236 **1438** 55c. multicoloured 1·70 1·30

1439 Elephant and Bird

2003. "For Us Children". Sheet 111×65 mm.
MS3237 **1439** 55c. multicoloured 1·90 1·70

2003. Cars. As T 1404. Multicoloured.
3238 45c.+20c. Wartburg 311 Coupe 1·90 1·50
3239 55c.+25c. Ford Taunus 17 M P3 2·40 1·80
3240 55c.+25c. Porsche 356 B Coupe 2·40 1·80
3241 55c.+25c. Opel Olympia Rekord P1 2·40 1·80
3242 144c.+56c. Auto Union 1000 S 5·25 4·50

1440 Letter Box

2003. Post.
3243 **1440** 55c. multicoloured 1·70 1·30

1441 Lifeguards

2003. 90th Anniv of DLRG (safety organization).
3244 **1441** 144c. multicoloured 4·50 3·50

1442 Nativity Figures (19th-century)

2003. Christmas. Multicoloured.
3245 45c.+20c. Type **1442** 2·10 1·60
3246 55c.+25c. Holy Family 2·50 2·00

1443 Dresden Opera House

2003. Birth Bicentenary of Gottfried Semper (architect).
3247 **1443** 55c. multicoloured 1·70 1·30

1444 Hands and Women

2003. Centenary of German Catholic Women's Federation.
3248 **1444** 55c. multicoloured 1·70 1·30

1445 Stars

2003. 10th Anniv of Maastricht Treaty.
3249 **1445** 55c. blue and yellow 1·70 1·30

1446 St. Martin's Church

2004. 800th Anniv of Landshut.
3250 **1446** 45c. multicoloured 1·50 1·10

1447 Cathedral and Images of Schleswig

2004. 1200th Anniv of Schleswig.
3251 **1447** 55c. multicoloured 1·90 1·50

1448 Clouds, Sun and Trees

2004. Environmental Protection and Renewable Energy.
3252 **1448** 55c.+25c. multicoloured 2·50 2·00

1449 Football Players

2004. Sport Promotion Fund. Multicoloured.
3253 45c.+20c. Type **1449** (European Football Championship) 2·10 1·60
3254 55c.+25c. Wheelchair athlete (Paralympics) 2·50 2·00
3255 55c.+25c. Runner (Olympic Games, Greece) 2·50 2·00
3256 55c.+25c. Footballer (50th anniv of Germany winning World Cup) 2·50 2·00
3257 144c.+56c. Hands holding trophy (Centenary of FIFA) 6·25 5·00

1450 Paper Airplanes

2004. Post.
3258 **1450** 55c. multicoloured 1·80 1·40

1451 Buildings

2004. 1300th Anniv of Arnstadt.
3259 **1451** 55c. multicoloured 1·80 1·40

1452 Shadow of Boy, Apple and Arrow

2004. Classic Theatre. Sheet 102×73 mm containing T 1452 and similar square design. Multicoloured.
MS3260 45c. Type **1452** (William Tell (Friedrich von Schiller) (200th anniv)); 100c. Faust and the devil (Faust II (Johann Wolfgang von Goethe) (150th anniv)) 4·75 3·50

1453 Joseph Schmidt

2004. Birth Centenary of Joseph Schmidt (singer).
3261 **1453** 55c. brown 1·80 1·40

1454 Paul Ehrlich (chemistry) and Emil von Behring (medicine)

2004. 150th Birth Anniv of Nobel Prize Winners.
3262 **1454** 144c. multicoloured 4·25 3·50

1455 White Stork in Flight

2004. Endangered Species. White Stork (Circona circona).
3263 **1455** 55c. black, blue and red 1·80 1·40

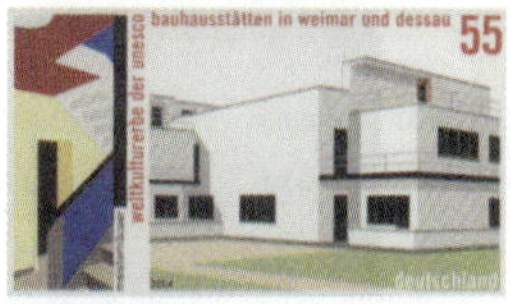

1456 Master House, Dessau

2004. Bauhaus (design group).
3264 **1456** 55c. multicoloured 1·80 1·40

1457 Kurt Kiesinger

2004. Birth Centenary of Kurt Georg Kiesinger (politician).
3265 **1457** 55c. multicoloured 1·80 1·40

1458 Early and Modern Light Bulbs

2004. 150th Anniv of Electric Light Bulb.
3266 **1458** 220c. multicoloured 6·50 5·50

1459 Sunflower and Holiday Symbols

2004. Europa. Holidays.
3267 **1459** 45c. multicoloured 1·50 1·10

1460 New Members' Flags as Cones

2004. Enlargement of European Union.
3268 **1460** 55c. multicoloured 1·80 1·40

1461 Reinhard Schwarz-Schilling

2004. Birth Centenary of Reinhard Schwarz-Schilling (composer).
3269 **1461** 55c. sepia 1·80 1·40

1462 St. Boniface under Attack

2004. 350th Anniv of Martyrdom of St. Boniface (papal envoy to Germany).
3270 **1462** 55c. multicoloured 1·80 1·40

1463 Schloss Ludwigsburg

2004. 300th Anniv of Schloss Ludwigsburg.
3271 **1463** €1.44 multicoloured 4·25 3·50

1464 Two Kittens playing with String

2004. "For Us Children". Cats. Multicoloured.
3272 45c.+20c. Type **1464** 2·20 1·70
3273 55c.+25c. Three kittens playing with ball 2·30 1·80
3274 55c.+25c. Mother and kitten 2·30 1·80
3275 55c.+25c. Cat washing paw 2·30 1·80
3276 €1.44+56c. Two kittens asleep 6·50 5·00

1465 Sea and Sand

2004. Wattenmeer National Park.
3277 **1465** 55c. multicoloured 1·80 1·40

1466 National Flags as Heart-shaped Kite

2004. 21st-century German—Russian Youth Forum.
3278 **1466** 55c. multicoloured 1·80 1·40

1467 Greifswalder Oie, Baltic Sea

2004. Lighthouses. Multicoloured. (a) Ordinary gum.
3279 45c. Type **1467** 1·50 1·10
3280 55c. Roter Sands 1·80 1·40

(b) Self-adhesive gum.
3281 55c. As No. 3280 (35×35 mm) 1·80 1·40

1468 *Bremen* (passenger ship) and New York Harbour

2004. Bremen—1929 Winner of Blue Ribbon (Europe to America speed record). Ordinary or self-adhesive gum.
3282 **1468** 55c. multicoloured 1·80 1·40

1469 Ludwig Fuerbach

2004. Birth Bicentenary of Ludwig Fuerbach (philosopher).
3284 **1469** 144c. rosine and black 4·25 3·50

1470 Camellia

2004. Greetings Stamp. Ordinary or Self-adhesive gum.
3285 **1470** 55c. multicoloured 1·80 1·40

1471 Church Facade

2004. Centenary of Protestant Regional Church, Speyer.
3287 **1471** 55c. multicoloured 1·80 1·40

1472 Scene from "Hansel and Gretel" and Engelbert Humperdinck

2004. 150th Birth Anniv of Engelbert Humperdinck (composer).
3288 **1472** 45c. multicoloured 1·50 1·10

1473 Ink Pot, Quill Pen, Manuscript and Glasses

2004. Birth Bicentenary of Eduard Morike (writer).
3289 **1473** 55c. multicoloured 1·80 1·40

1474 Feet and Hand Prints forming Face

2004. "For Us Children".
3290 **1474** 55c. multicoloured 1·80 1·40

1475 Kaiser Wilhelm Cathedral church, Berlin and Egon Eiermann

2004. Birth Centenary of Egon Eiermann (architect).
3291 **1475** 100c. multicoloured 3·25 2·50

1476 Court Seal

2004. 50th Anniv of Federal Social Court.
3292 **1476** 144c. multicoloured 4·25 3·50

1477 Iceberg, Greenland

2004. Climate Zones. Multicoloured.
3293 45c.+20c. Type **1477** (arctic) 2·20 1·70
3294 55c.+25c. Mountains, Tibet (alpine) 2·75 2·00
3295 55c.+25c. River and grazing animals, Mecklenburg-Vorpommern (temperate) 2·75 2·00
3296 55c.+25c. Dunes, Sahara (desert) 2·75 2·00
3297 144c.+56c. Rainforest, Galapagos Islands (tropics) 6·25 5·00

1478 Flying Boat Dornier Do-X (1930)

2004. Stamp Day.
3298 **1478** 55c. ultramarine and vermilion 2·00 1·50

1479 "Flight into Egypt"

2004. Christmas. Paintings by Peter Paul Rubens. Multicoloured.
3299 45c.+20c. Type **1479** 2·20 1·70
3300 55c.+25c. "Adoration of the Magi" 2·75 2·00
Stamps of the same design were issued by Belgium.

1480 Snow-covered Avenue

2004. Post.
3301 **1480** 55c. multicoloured 1·80 1·40

1481 "Das Geheimnis"

2004. Birth Centenary of Felix Nussbaum (artist).
3302 **1481** 55c. multicoloured 2·00 1·50

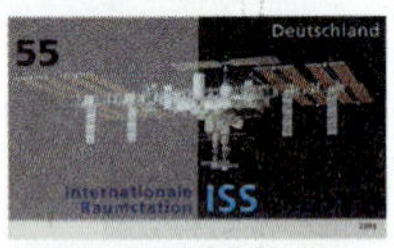
1482 International Space Station

2004
3303 **1482** 55c. multicoloured 1·80 1·40

1483 City Hall

2005. 1200th Anniv of Forchheim.
3304 **1483** 45c. multicoloured 1·50 1·10

1484 Three Kings (board painting, Cologne (c. 1350))

2005. Art.
3305 **1484** 55c. multicoloured 2·00 1·50

1485 Sunflower

2005. Flowers. Multicoloured. (a) Ordinary gum.
3306 5c. Crocus 30 25
3306a 10c. Tulip 30 25
3307 20c. Tagetes 60 45
3307a 25c. Carnation 1·20 95
3308 25c. Mallow 80 60
3308a 35c. Dahlia 1·10 85
3308b 40c. Blue flower 1·20 95
3310 45c. Daisy 1·20 95
3311 50c. Aster 1·40 1·10
3312 55c. Poppy 1·60 1·20
3313 55c. Red rose 2·40 1·80
3314 65c. Rudbeckia 1·90 1·40
3315 70c. Pink flower 2·00 1·50
3318 90c. Narcissus 2·75 2·00
3320 95c. Type **1485** 2·75 2·10
3320a 100c. *Dicentra spectabilis* 2·75 2·10
3320b 145c. Iris 4·00 3·00
3320c 200c. *Eschscholzia californica* 5·50 4·25
3320d 220c. Edlweiss 6·25 4·75
3320e 390c. Lily 12·00 9·00
3320f €4.10 Ladies slipper 20·00 18·00
3321 €4.30 Larkspur 12·50 9·50

(b) Self-adhesive.
3324 35c. Dahlia 1·10 85
3325 55c. Poppy 1·60 1·20
3326 55c. Red rose 2·40 1·80
3327 65c. As No. 3314 2·40 1·80
3328 70c. As No. 3315 2·40 1·80
3330 90c. As No. 3318 (Narcissus) 2·75 2·00

1486 Celtic Statue, Glauberg

2005. Archaeology.
3335 **1486** €1.44 multicoloured 4·75 3·50

1487 Championship Mascot (2/3-size illustration)

2005. Sport Promotion Fund. Multicoloured.
3336 45c.+20c. Type **1487** (World Cup Football Championship, Germany 2006) 2·20 1·70
3337 55c.+25c. Footballers (World Cup Football Championships, Germany 2006) 2·75 2·00
3338 55c.+25c. Skier (Nordic World Ski Championships, Oberstdorf) 2·75 2·00
3339 55c.+25c. Gymnasts (International German Gymnastics Festival, Berlin) 2·75 2·00
3340 144c.+56c. Fencers (Fencing World Championships, Leipzig) 6·50 5·00

1488 Pillar

2005. 150th Anniv of Advertisement Pillars.
3341 **1488** 55c. multicoloured 2·00 1·50

1489 Cathedral Facade

2005. Centenary of Berlin Cathedral. Ordinary or self-adhesive gum.
3342 **1489** 95c. multicoloured 3·00 2·40

1490 Postman walking in Mountains

2005. Postal Service (1st series). Multicoloured.
3344 55c. Type **1490** 1·80 1·40
3345 55c. Postman cycling 1·80 1·40
See also Nos. 3370/1.

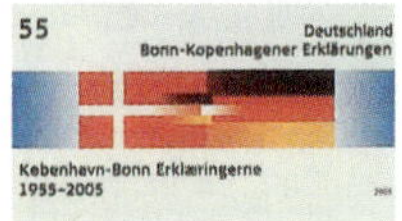
1491 Danish and German Flags

2005. 50th Anniv of Germany—Denmark Relations.
3346 **1491** 55c. multicoloured 2·00 1·50
A stamp of the same design was issued by Denmark.

1492 Lockheed L-1049 Super Constellation

2005. 50th Anniv of Resumption of German Air Traffic.
3347 **1492** 155c. multicoloured 5·00 3·75

1493 Aquaduct

2005. Centenary of Mittelland Canal.
3348 **1493** 45c. multicoloured 1·50 1·10

1494 Rock, Ferns and Tree

2005. National Parks. Bavarian Forest.
3349 **1494** 55c. multicoloured 1·80 1·40

1495 Silhouettes of Characters

2005. Birth Bicentenary of Hans Christian Andersen (writer). Ordinary or self-adhesive gum.
3350 **1495** 144c. light orange, orange and black 4·25 3·50

1496 Book Bindings and Signature

2005. Birth Bicentenary of Friedrich Schiller (poet). Schiller Year.
3352 **1496** 55c. multicoloured 1·80 1·40

1497 Signatories.

2005. 50th Anniv of Paris Agreements (establishing Federal Democratic Republic of Germany in Western European Union (WEU) and North Atlantic Treaty Organization (NATO).
3353 **1497** 55c. black and vermilion 1·80 1·40

1498 "Sitzende Franzi" (woodcut) (Erich Heikel)

2005. Centenary of Die Brucke (The Bridge) (group of Expressionist artists).

3354 **1498** 55c. black, vermilion and stone 1·80 1·40

1499 Wine Glass, Wine Bottle, Candle and Cup

2005. Europa. Gastronomy.

3355 **1499** 55c. chocolate, orange and rose 1·80 1·40

1500 Pope John Paul II

2005. Pope John Paul II Commemoration.

3356 **1500** 55c. multicoloured 1·80 1·40

1501 Kraftpost Omnibus

2005. Stamp Day. Centenary of Post Bus.

3357 **1501** 55c.+25c. multicoloured 2·75 2·00

1502 *Greif* ("Reach") (training ship)

2005. Youth Welfare. Ships. Multicoloured.

3358 45c.+20c. Type **1502** 2·20 1·70

3359 55c.+25c. *Passat* ("Trade Wind") (four-mast bark) 2·75 2·00

3360 55c.+25c. *Rickmer Rickmers* (cargo ship) 2·75 2·00

3361 55c.+25c. *Grand Duchess Elizabeth* (schooner) 2·75 2·00

3362 144c.+56c. *Deutschland* (training ship) 6·50 5·00

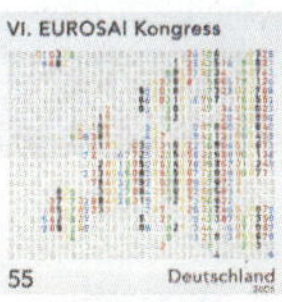
1503 Numbers as Map of Europe

2005. EUROSAI (European Organization of Supreme Audit Institutions) Conference, Bonn.

3363 **1503** 55c. multicoloured 1·90 1·40

1504 Cross and Globe

2005. World Youth Day.

3364 **1504** 55c. multicoloured 1·90 1·40

A stamp of the same design was issued by Vatican City.

1505 Brunsbuttel Lighthouse

2005. Lighthouses. Multicoloured. Ordinary or self-adhesive gum.

3365 45c. Type **1505** 1·50 1·10

3366 55c. Westerheversand 1·80 1·40

See also Nos. 3429/30.

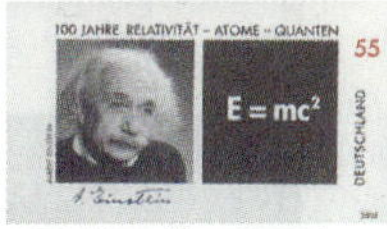
1506 Albert Einstein and "E=mc²"

2005. Centenary of Special Theory of Relativity by Albert Einstein (physicist).

3368 **1506** 55c. black and scarlet 1·90 1·40

1507 New Palace, Sanssouci Park, Potsdam

2005. Prussian Schlosses. Sheet 98×70 mm.

MS3369 **1507** 220c. multicoloured 7·00 6·50

2005. Postal Service (2nd issue). As T 1490. Multicoloured.

3370 55c. Postman with trolley 1·90 1·40

3371 55c. Postman in boat 1·90 1·40

1508 Tree and Figure

2005. Centenary of NaturFreunde Deutschlands (conservation organization).

3372 **1508** 144c. green and rose 4·75 3·50

1509 Chickens

2005. "For us Children".

3373 **1509** 55c. multicoloured 1·90 1·40

1510 City from River (15th-century woodcut)

2005. 1200th Anniv of Magdeburg.

3374 **1510** 55c. multicoloured 1·90 1·40

1511 Angel

2005. 450th Anniv of Religious Freedom.

3375 **1511** 55c. multicoloured 1·90 1·40

1512 Max Schmeling

2005. Birth Centenary of Max Schmeling (boxer).

3376 **1512** 100c. black and vermilion 1·90 1·40

1513 Church

2005. Completion of Reconstruction of Frauenkirche (Church of our Lady) Dresden (2004).

3377 **1513** 55c. multicoloured 1·90 1·40

1514 Script and Pen Nib

2005. Birth Bicentenary of Adalbert Stifter (writer).

3378 **1514** 55c. multicoloured 3·25 2·50

1515 Horse-drawn Procession

2005. 150th Anniv of Bad Tolz Leonhardifahrt (festival).

3379 **1515** 45c. multicoloured 1·60 1·20

1516 "Adoration of the Child Jesus"

2005. Christmas. Paintings by Stefan Lochner. Multicoloured.

3380 45c.+20c. Type **1516** 2·00 1·70

3381 55c.+25c. "Madonna of the Rose Bush" 2·50 2·00

1517 Israeli and German Flags

2005. 40th Anniv of Diplomatic Relations with Israel.

3382 **1517** 55c. multicoloured 1·90 1·40

1518 Bertha von Suttner and "Die Waffen nieder"

2005. Centenary of Bertha von Suttner's Nobel Peace Prize.

3383 **1518** 55c. multicoloured 1·90 1·40

1519 "50 JAHRE BUNDES WEHR"

2005. 50th Anniv of German Federal Armed Forces.

3384 **1519** 55c. multicoloured 1·90 1·40

1520 Robert Koch and Microscope

2005. Centenary of Robert Koch's Nobel Prize for Physiology and Medicine.

3385 **1520** 55c. multicoloured 4·50 3·50

2005. Prussian Schlosses. New Palace, Sansouci Park, Potsdam (2nd issue). Self-adhesive Stamp.

3386 **1507** 220c. multicoloured 7·00 6·00

1521 *Gonepteryx rhamni*

2005. Butterflies and Moths. Multicoloured Ordinary gum.

3387 45c.+20c. Type **1521** 2·20 1·70

3388 55c.+25c. *Panaxia quadripunctaria* 2·75 2·00

3389 55c.+25c. *Inachis io* 2·75 2·00

3390 145c.+55c. *Brintesia circe* 6·50 5·00

(b) Self-adhesive.

3391 55c.+25c. As No. 3389 2·75 2·40

1522 Sights of Halle

2006. 1200th Anniv of Halle.

3392 **1522** 45c. multicoloured 1·60 1·20

1523 Wolfgang Mozart

2006. 250th Birth Anniv of Wolfgang Amadeus Mozart (composer).

3393 **1523** 55c. multicoloured 1·90 1·40

1524 Snow-covered Tree

2006. Winter.

3394 **1524** 55c. multicoloured 1·90 1·40

1525 Clouds over Earth

2006. Climate Protection Awareness.

3395 **1525** 55c.+25c. multicoloured 2·75 2·10

1526 Bull (detail) and Charles IV's Seal

2006. 650th Anniv of Charles IV's Golden Bull (document creating constitutional structure). (a) Ordinary or Self-adhesive gum.

3396 **1526** 145c. multicoloured 4·75 3·50

1527 German Flags

2006. Sport Promotion Fund. World Cup Football Championship, Germany. Multicoloured.

3398	45c.+20c. Type **1527**	2·00	1·70
3399	55c.+25c. Horse and rider (World Equestrian Games, Aachen 2006)	2·50	2·00
3400	55c.+25c. Stadium lights (opening game)	2·50	2·00
3401	55c.+25c. Pitch (final)	2·50	2·00
3402	145c.+56c. Fireworks and emblem	6·25	5·00

1528 Rooftops

2006. 850th Anniv of Michaelskirche, Schwäbisch Hall.
3403 **1528** 55c. multicoloured 1·90 1·40

1529 "Fraiske Räid"

2006. 50th Anniv of Friesenrat (Frisian council).
3404 **1529** 90c. multicoloured 2·75 2·20

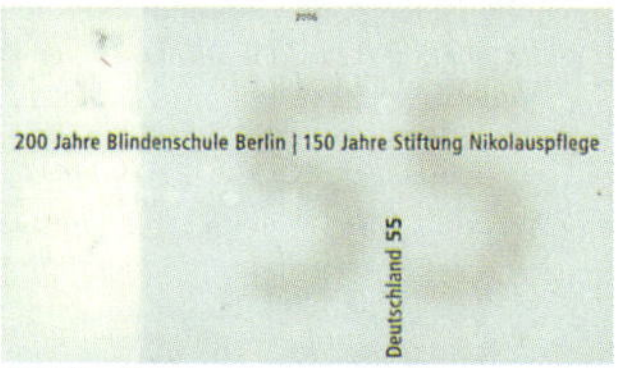

1530 Braille

2006. Bicentenary of Blind School, Berlin. 150th Anniv of Nikolauspflege (charitable organization).
3405 **1530** 55c. black and grey 1·90 1·40

1531 Early Town and Map

2006. 1200th Anniv of Ingolstadt.
3406 **1531** 55c. multicoloured 1·90 1·40

1532 Altes Museum, Lustgarten

2006. 225th Birth Anniv of Karl Friedrich Schinkel (architect). Ordinary or self-adhesive gum.
3407 **1532** 55c. multicoloured 1·90 1·40

1533 Johannes Rau

2006. Johannes Rau (president 1999—2004) Commemoration.
3408 **1533** 55c. multicoloured 1·90 1·40

1534 Emblem

2006. 500th Anniv of European University Viadrina Frankfurt (Oder).
3409 **1534** 55c. blue and black 1·90 1·40

1535 Blossom-covered Trees

2006. Spring.
3410 **1535** 55c. multicoloured 1·90 1·40

1536 Self-Portrait (Albrecht Durer)

2006. Art.
3411 **1536** 145c. blue and black 4·75 3·50

2006. World Cup Football Championship, Germany. Sheet 130×180 mm containing T 1527 and similar horiz designs. Multicoloured.
MS3412 130×180 mm. Nos. 3398, 3400/2 13·50 12·00

1537 "Integration" on Jacket

2006. Europa. Integration.
3413 **1537** 55c. multicoloured 1·90 1·40

1538 Rhine Valley

2006. Upper Central Rhine Valley (Oberes Mittelrheintal). World Heritage Site. Ordinary or self-adhesive gum.
3414 **1538** 55c. multicoloured 1·90 1·40

1539 Gerd Bucerius

2006. Birth Centenary of Gerd Bucerius (politician).
3416 **1539** 85c. multicoloured 2·75 2·10

1540 Pine Marten

2006. Youth Welfare. Animals. Multicoloured.

3417	45c.+20c. Type **1540**	2·00	1·70
3418	55c.+25c. Hares	2·50	2·00
3419	55c.+25c. Red squirrel	2·50	2·00
3420	55c.+25c. Roe deer and fawn	2·50	2·00
3421	145c.+55c. Wild boar and young	6·25	5·00

1541 Stripes

2006. Birth Centenary of Stefan Andres (writer).
3422 **1541** 55c. multicoloured 1·90 1·40

1542 Brooklyn Bridge, New York

2006. Birth Bicentenary of Johan August Robling (architect).
3423 **1542** 145c. multicoloured 4·75 3·50

1543 Car Number Plates

2006. Centenary of First Number Plates.
3424 **1543** 45c. multicoloured 1·60 1·20

1544 Berghauser Castle, Burganlage

2006
3425 **1544** 55c. multicoloured 1·90 1·40

1545 Flowering Rapeseed

2006. Summer.
3426 **1545** 55c. multicoloured 1·90 1·40

1546 "Saskia van Uylenburgh"

2006. 400th Birth Anniv of Rembrandt Harmenszoon van Rijn (Rembrandt) (artist).
3427 **1546** 55c. multicoloured 2·40 1·90

2006. Lighthouses. As T 1505. Multicoloured.

3429	45c. Neuland	1·50	1·20
3430	55c. Hohe Weg	1·80	1·40

1547 Valley

2006. Tourism. Schwarzwald. Sheet 145×70 mm.
MS3432 **1547** 55c. multicoloured 1·90 1·40

1548 Valley and Skull

2006. 150th Anniv of Discovery of Neanderthal Skull.
3433 **1548** 220c. multicoloured 7·00 6·00

1549 Cat and Envelopes

2006. For us Children
3434 **1549** 55c. multicoloured 1·90 1·40

1550 Hauptmann von Kopenick

2006. Centenary of Hauptmann von Kopenick (fraudulent identity of William Voigt) Affair.
3435 **1550** 55c. multicoloured 1·90 1·40

1551 Shipping and Trade

2006. 650th Anniv of Hanseatic league (Stadtehanse).
3436 **1551** 70c. multicoloured 2·40 1·80

1552 Fliegender Hamburger VT 877

2006. Welfare. Trains. Multicoloured. (a) Ordinary gum.

3437	45c.+20c. Type **1552**	2·00	1·70
3438	55c.+25c. Intercity Express ET 403	2·50	2·00
3439	55c.+25c. Trans Europe Express VT 11.5	2·50	2·00
3440	145c.+55c. Henschel-Wegmann-Zug 61 001	6·25	5·00

(b) Self-adhesive.
3441 55c.+25c. As No. 3438 2·50 2·00

1553 Postcard, 1896

2006. Stamp Day.
3442 **1553** 55c. multicoloured 1·90 1·40

1554 Woodland

2006. Autumn.
3443 **1554** 55c. multicoloured 1·90 1·40

1555 Hannah Arendt

2006. Birth Centenary of Hannah Arendt (political theorist and philosopher).
3444 **1555** 145c. multicoloured 4·50 3·50

1556 Eugen Bolz

2006. 125th Birth Anniv of Eugen Anton Bolz (Catholic politician).
3445 **1556** 45c. blue and yellow 1·60 1·20

1557 The Nativity

2006. Christmas. Paintings by Meister Franke. Multicoloured.

3446	45c.+20c. Type **1557**	2·00	1·70
3447	55c.+25c. Three Kings	2·50	2·00

1558 Cardinal Hoffner

2006. Birth Centenary of Cardinal Joseph Hoffner (Bishop of Munster and Archbishop of Cologne).
3448 **1558** 55c. multicoloured 1·90 1·40

2006. Seasons. As T 1524. Multicoloured. Self-adhesive.

3449	55c. As Type **1535**	1·90	1·40
3450	55c. As Type **1545**	1·90	1·40
3451	55c. As Type **1554**	1·90	1·40
3452	55c. As Type **1524**	1·90	1·40

1559 Werner Forbmann

2006. 50th Anniv of Werner Forbmann's (surgeon and inventor of the heart catheter) Nobel Prize for Medicine.
3453 **1559** 90c. multicoloured 3·00 2·20

1560 Street

2007. Furth Millenary. (a) Ordinary or self-adhesive gum.
3454 **1560** 45c. multicoloured 1·60 1·20

1561 Stars

2007. Germany's Presidency of European Union.
3456 **1561** 55c. black, vermilion and yellow 1·90 1·40

1562 Imperial Cathedral Facade

2007. Bamberg Diocese Millenary.
3457 **1562** 55c. rosine, blue and gold 1·90 1·40

1563 Symbols of Saarland

2007. 50th Anniv of Federal Republic of Saarland. (a) Ordinary or self-adhesive gum.
3458 **1563** 55c. multicoloured 1·90 1·40

1564 Ball and Hands

2007. Sport Promotion Fund (1st issue). World Handball Championship, Germany.
3460 **1564** 55c.+25c. multicoloured 2·50 1·90
See also Nos. 3462/4.

1565 Engine Diagram and NSU Ro80

2007. 50th Anniv of Rotary Engine designed by Felix Wankel.
3461 **1565** 145c. multicoloured 4·50 3·50

2007. Sport Promotion Fund (2nd issue). As T 1564. Multicoloured.
3462 45c.+20c. Canoeing (world championships, Wedau Park) 2·00 1·50
3463 55c.+25c. Gymnastics (world championships, Stuttgart) 2·50 1·90
3464 145c.+55c. Swimming (world pentathlon championships, Berlin) 4·75 3·50

1566 Johann Senckenberg and Institute Building

2007. 300th Birth Anniv of Johann Christian Senckenberg (physician and health reformer).
3465 **1566** 90c. multicoloured 3·00 2·40

1567 Claus Schenk Graf von Stauffenberg and Helmuth James Graf von Moltke

2007. Birth Centenaries.
3466 **1567** 55c. vermilion and black 1·90 1·40

1568 Star of David

2007. Jewish Centre, Munich.
3467 **1568** 55c. multicoloured 1·90 1·40

1569 "Die Ausgrabung der Kreuze" (Adam Elsheimer)

2007
3468 **1569** 55c. multicoloured 1·90 1·40

1570 Signatories

2007. 50th Anniv of Treaty of Rome.
3469 **1570** 55c. multicoloured 1·90 1·40

1571 Paul Gerhardt and Score

2007. 400th Birth Anniv of Paul Gerhardt.
3470 **1571** 55c. multicoloured 1·90 1·40

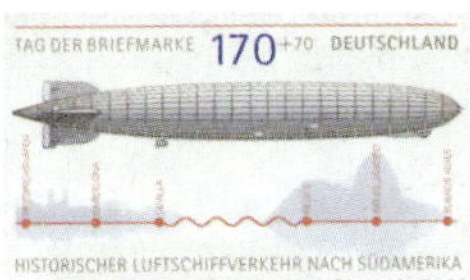

1572 LZ 127 *Graf Zeppelin*

2007. Stamp Day. Sheet 105×70 mm.
MS3471 **1572** 170c.+70c. mult 7·50 7·00

1573 Writing a Letter

2007. Post. Each yellow, black and vermilion.
3472 55c. Type **1573** 1·70 1·40
3473 55c. Posting letter 1·70 1·40

1574 Pope Benedict XVI

2007. 80th Birthday of Pope Benedict XVI.
3474 **1574** 55c. multicoloured 1·90 1·40

1575 "Universalis Cosmographia"

2007. 500th Anniv of World Map drawn by Martin Waldseemüller.
3475 **1575** €2.20 multicoloured 7·00 6·50

1576 Scouts

2007. Europa. Centenary of Scouting.
3476 **1576** 45c. multicoloured 1·60 1·20

2007. 40th Anniv of Sport Promotion Fund. As T 1564. Multicoloured.
MS3477 45c.+20c. As No. 3462; 55c.+25c. As No. 3460; 55c.+25c. As No. 3463; 145c.+55c. As No. 3464 12·00 10·50

1577 Schloss

2007. Bellevue Schloss. Ordinary or self-adhesive gum.
3478 **1577** 55c. multicoloured 1·90 1·40

1578 Schloss and Sculptures

2007. 700th Anniv of Moyland Schloss.
3480 **1578** 85c. multicoloured 2·75 2·10

1579 Early Festival Goers

2007. 175th Anniv of Hambacher Fest (democratic festival). (a) Ordinary or Self-adhesive gum.
3481 **1579** 145c. multicoloured 4·50 3·50

1580 Sawing legs from Chair

2007. 125th Birth Anniv of Valentin Ludwig Fey (Karl Valentin) (comedian and writer).
3483 **1580** 45c. multicoloured 1·60 1·20

1581 'Nichts Schonres gab's fur Tante Lotte Als Schwarze-Heidel-beer-Kompotte' (Behold Aunt Lotte's choicest snack: Blueberry compote, sweet and black)

2007. For the Young. 175th Birth Anniv of Wilhelm Busch (poet and cartoonist). Sheet 165×75 mm containing T 1581 and similar square designs showing scenes from illustrated poem Hans Huckebein-der Unglucksrabe (the unlucky raven) by Wilhelm Busch. Multicoloured.
MS3484 45c.+20c. Type **1581**; 55c.+25c. Doch Huckebein ver-schleudert nur Die schone Gabe der Natur (But Huckebein, unused to thrift, Just squanders nature's precious gift); 55c.+25c. Die Tante naht voll Zorn und Schrecken; Hans Huckebein verläßt das Becken (The aunt descends in shock and wrath. Hans Huckebein deserts his bath); 145c.+55c. Und schnell betritt er, angstbeflugelt, Die Wasche, welche frisch gebugelt (And tramples, on the wings of fright, The ironed laundry, clean and white) 12·00 10·50

1582 Paul Klinger and Nadia Grey (poster for film 'Hengst Maestoso Austria')

2007. Birth Centenary of Paul Karl Heinrich Klinksik (Paul Klinger) (actor).
3485 **1582** 55c. multicoloured 2·00 1·50

2007. Lighthouses. As T 1467. Multicoloured.
3486 45c. Bremerhaven Oberfeuer 1·60 1·20
3487 55c. Hornum 1·70 1·40

1583 House of Blackheads, Riga

2007. World Heritage Sites, Riga and Wismar. Multicoloured.
3488 65c. Type **1583** 2·20 1·70
3489 70c. City Hall and St. George's Church, Wismar 2·30 1·80
Stamps of a similar design were issued by Latvia.

1584 Banknotes and Coins from Various Currency Epochs

2007. 50th Anniv of German Bundesbank (Federal bank).
3490 **1584** 55c. multicoloured 2·00 1·50

1585 Saale River Plain

2007. 75th Anniv of Saaletalsperre Bleiloch (dam across Saale valley).
3491 **1585** 55c. multicoloured 2·00 1·50

1586 Kaiser Wilhelm Bridge

2007. Centenary of Kaiser Wilhelm Bridge, Wilhelmshaven.
3492 **1586** 145c. multicoloured 4·75 3·50

1587 Hedgehog and Hearts

2007. For us Children
3493 **1587** 55c. multicoloured 2·00 1·50

1588 Receiving a Letter

2007. Post. Multicoloured.
3494 55c. Type **1588** 1·90 1·40
3495 55c. Reading letter 1·90 1·40

1589 Symbols of Science

2007. 50th Anniv of Wissenschaftsrat (government scientific advisors).
3496 **1589** 90c. multicoloured 3·25 2·50

1590 Stylized Building

2007. Centenary of Deutscher Werkbund (artistic design group).

3497	**1590**	55c. multicoloured	1·90	1·40

1591 Section of 'Limes' and Watch Towers

2007. World Heritage Site. 'The Roman Limes' (Roman camp, castle and walls). Sheet 105×70 mm.

MS3498	55c. multicoloured	1·90	1·40

1592 Karl Freiherr Vom Stein

2007. 250th Birth Anniv of Heinrich Friedrich Carl Freiherr Vom und Zum Stein (statesman and reformer).

3499	**1592**	145c. multicoloured	4·75	3·50

1593 Three Kings

2007. Christmas. Multicoloured.

3500	45c+20c. Type **1593**	2·00	1·70
3501	55c.+25c. Virgin and Child	2·50	2·00

1594 St. Elizabeth feeding Invalid

2007. 800th Birth Anniv of St. Elizabeth von Thuringen.

3502	**1594**	55c. multicoloured	1·90	1·40

1595 Astrid Lindgren and Emil from Lönneberga (character from book)

2007. Birth Centenary of Astrid Lindgren (children's author).

3503	**1595**	100c. multicoloured	1·90	1·40

A stamp of the same design was issued by Sweden.

1596 Brandenburg Gate, Berlin

2007. 275th Birth Anniv of Carl Gotthard Langhans (architect). Ordinary or self-adhesive gum.

3504	**1596**	55c. multicoloured	1·90	1·40

1597 Guinea Pigs

2007. Welfare. Pets. Showing animals and young. Multicoloured. (a) Ordinary gum.

3506	45c.+20c. Type **1597**	2·00	1·70
3507	55c.+25c. Dogs	2·50	2·00
3508	55c.+25c. Horses	2·50	2·00
3509	145c.+55c. Rabbits	6·25	5·00

(b) Self-adhesive.

3510	55c.+25c. As No. 3508	2·50	2·00

1598 Liturgical Book and Gothic Wall Painting (detail), Reichenau Abbey

2008. World Heritage Site. Ordinary or self-adhesive gum.

3511	**1598**	45c. multicoloured	1·60	1·20

1599 *Old Berlin Distillery*

2008. 150th Birth Anniv of Heinrich Zille (artist).

3513	**1599**	55c. multicoloured	1·90	1·40

1600 '50 Jahre Bundeskartellamt'

2008. 50th Anniv of Bundeskartellamt (monopolies commission).

3514	**1600**	90c. multicoloured	1·90	1·40

1601 Cathedral Square

2008. 1100th Anniv of Eichstatt. Ordinary or self-adhesive gum.

3515	**1601**	145c. multicoloured	4·50	3·50

1602 Decorative Pot with Shell Insert

2008. 500th Birth Anniv of Wenzel Jamnitzer (goldsmith).

3517	**1602**	220c. multicoloured	7·00	6·50

1603 *Der Arme Poet*

2008. Birth Bicentenary of Carl Spitzweg (artist). Ordinary or self-adhesive gum.

3518	**1603**	55c. multicoloured	1·90	1·40

1604 Fish and Heart ('Herzlichen Gluckwunsch') (Congratulations)

2008. Post

3519	55c. Type **1604**	1·90	1·40
3520	55c. Cats ('Alles Gute') (All Good)	1·90	1·40

1605 Church Facade

2008. Millenary of Bochum-Stiepel Village Church.

3521	**1605**	145c. multicoloured	4·50	3·50

1606 Glider World Championships, Lusse

2008. Sports Promotion Fund. Multicoloured.

3522	45c.+20c. Type **1606**	2·00	1·70
3523	55c.+25c. European Football Championships, Austria and Switzerland	2·50	2·00
3524	55c.+25c. Chess Olympiad, Dresden	2·50	2·00
3525	145c.+55c. Olympic Games, Beijing	6·25	5·00

1607 Helmut Kautner

2008. Birth Centenary of Helmut Kautner (film director).

3526	**1607**	55c. multicoloured	1·90	1·40

1608 Gnu Herd

2008. 150th Anniv of Frankfurt Zoological Society.

3527	**1608**	65c. multicoloured	2·20	1·70

2008. 50th Anniv of Bundeskartellamt (monopolies commission) (2nd issue). Self adhesive.

3528	**1600**	90c. multicoloured	2·40	1·90

1609 Birds

2008. Centenary of State Bird Sanctuary, Seebach.

3529	**1609**	45c. multicoloured	1·60	1·20

1610 Max Planck

2008. 150th Birth Anniv of Max Planck (physicist, Nobel Prize Winner–1918).

3530	**1610**	55c. multicoloured	1·90	1·40

1611 Johann Wichern

2008. Birth Bicentenary of Johann Hinrich Wichern (theologian).

3531	**1611**	55c. multicoloured	1·90	1·40

1612 Knut (hand reared polar bear cub)

2008. Environmental Protection.

3532	**1612**	55c.+25c. multicoloured	3·25	2·60

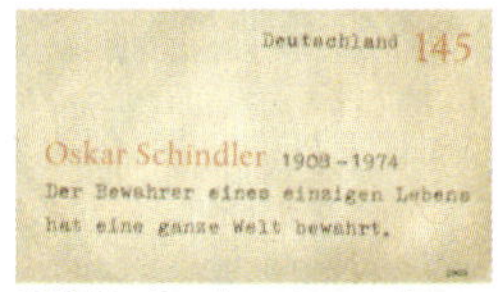

1613 'Der Bewahrer eines einzigen Lebens hat eine ganze Welt bewahrt' ((he who saves a single life saves the whole world) (translation of Hebrew engraving on Oskar Schindler's ring, gift of farewell from rescuee on 8 May 1945))

2008. Birth Centenary of Oskar Schindler (industrialist who saved Jews during WWII).

3533	**1613**	145c. multicoloured	4·50	3·50

1614 Photograph of German Players (5 April 1908) and Parts of Original Poster

2008. Centenary of German Soccer Internationals.

3534	**1614**	170c. multicoloured	4·75	3·75

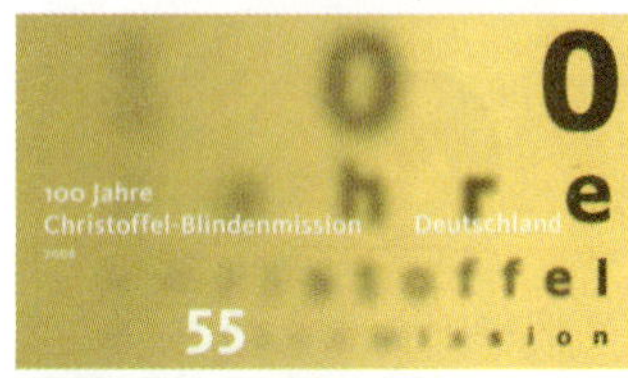

1615 Blurred Script

2008. Centenary of Christoffel Blind Mission. (Christoffel Blindoffmission) (charity founded by pastor Ernst Jakob Christoffel for sopport of the blind worldwide.

3535	**1615**	55c. multicoloured	2·25	1·80

1616 Sun and Moon ('Herzliche Grube (cordial greetings)')

2008. Greetings Stamps. Europa. The Letter (3536/8). Multicoloured. (a) Ordinary gum.

3536	55c. Type **1616**	2·00	1·60
3537	55c. Hands holding bird and flower ('Danke' (thank you))	2·00	1·60

(b) Self-adhesive.

3538 55c. As Type **1616** 2·00 1·60
3539 55c. As No. 3520 2·00 1·60
3540 55c. As No. 3519 2·00 1·60
3541 55c. As No. 3537 2·00 1·60

1617 Dornier Do J *Wal*

2008. Welfare. Aircraft. Multicoloured. (a) Ordinary gum.
3542 45c.+20c. Type **1617** 2·50 2·00
3543 55c.+25c. A380 Airbus 3·50 2·75
3544 55c.+25c. Junkers Ju 52 3·50 2·75
3545 145c.+55c. Messerschmitt-Bolkow-Blohm (MBB) BO 105 6·50 5·25

(b) Self-adhesive.

3546 55c.+25c. As No. 3543 3·50 2·75

1618 Faces

2008. Community Service.
3547 **1618** 55c. multicoloured 2·00 1·60

1619 Steam Locomotive, Early Station and Passengers

2008. 125th Anniv of Drachenfels Railway (Drachenfelsbahn) (rack railway line from Konigswinter to summit of Drachenfels).
3548 **1619** 45c. multicoloured 2·00 1·60

1620 Warnemunde

2008. Lighthouses. Multicoloured. (a) Ordinary gum.
3549 45c. Type **1620** 2·00 1·60
3550 55c. Amrum 2·30 1·90

(b) Self-adhesive.

3551 55c. Hornum 2·40 1·90
3552 55c. As No. 3550 2·40 1·90

1621 Man at Table (drawing by Franz Kafka)

2008. 125th Birth Anniv of Franz Kafka (Czech writer).
3553 **1621** 55c. black 2·20 1·80

1622 *Selbstportrat mit Ruckenakt* and *Morgensonne*

2008. 150th Birth Anniv of Lovis Corinth (artist).
3554 **1622** 145c. multicoloured 6·00 4·75

1623 *Gorch Fock*

2008. 50th Anniv of Gorch Fock (sail training ship).
3555 **1623** 55c. multicoloured 2·50 2·00

1624 Silhouette *Ringelnatz* (Ernst Moritz Engert)

2008. 125th Birth Anniv of Joachim Ringelnatz (writer and artist).
3556 **1624** 85c. blue and black 3·75 3·00

1625 Herman Schulze-Delitzsch

2008. Birth Bicentenary of Herman Schulze-Delitzsch (politician and founder of German cooperative system).
3557 **1625** 90c. multicoloured 4·00 3·25

1626 Triceratops

2008. Youth Stamp. Dinosaurs. Sheet 190×110 mm containing T 1626 and similar horiz designs. Multicoloured.
MS3558 45c.+20c. Type **1626**; 55c.+25c. Tyrannosaurus; 55c.+25c. Diplodocus; 145c.+55c. Plateosaurus 17·00 17·00

1627 Arrival of First Mail Coach in Ohrdruff

2008. Stamp Day. Philatelic Treasures.
3559 **1627** 55c. multicoloured 2·50 2·00

1628 Ronald, Gunni and Jenny the Rat riding Blue Horse

2008. For us Children
3560 **1628** 55c. multicoloured 2·50 2·00

1629 Old Bridge, Bad Sackingen–Stein/Aargau

2008. Bridges.
3561 **1629** 70c. multicoloured 3·00 2·40

A stamp of a similar design was issued by Switzerland.

1630 Livestock Market

2008. 500th Anniv of Gallimarkt (annual fair), Leer.
3562 **1630** 45c. multicoloured 2·00 1·60

1631 Disc and Two Bronze Swords

2008. Archaeology. Sky Disc of Nebra (bronze plate with apparent astronomical phenomena and religious themes).
3563 **1631** 55c. multicoloured 2·50 2·00

1632 Lorenz Werthmann

2008. 150th Birth Anniv of Lorenz Werthmann (founder and first president of the German Caritas association).
3564 **1632** 55c. multicoloured 2·50 2·00

1633 Aircraft in Flight

2008. Centenary of Hans Grade's First Powered Flight in Germany.
3565 **1633** 145c. multicoloured 6·00 4·75

2008. Winter. 450th Anniv (2005) of the 'Peace of Augsburg' (treaty marking the beginning of peaceful cohabitation of Catholics and Protestants) (3566). As Types 1484 and 1511. Multicoloured. Self-adhesive.
3566 55c. As Type **1484** 2·50 2·00
3567 55c. As Type **1511** 2·50 2·00

Type **1634** is vacant.

See also Nos. 3305 and 3375.

1635 *The Nativity* (Albrecht Durer)

2008. Christmas. Multicoloured.
3568 45c.+20c. Type **1635** 2·50 2·00
3569 55c.+25c. *The Nativity* (Raffaello Santi) (horiz) 3·50 2·75

1636 Association Emblem

2008. 30th Anniv of 'Heart for Children' Association (children's charity).
3570 **1636** 55c. vermilion and black 2·50 2·00

1637 'Leben'

2008. 50th Anniv of Federal Association of Life (intellectual diasablities charity).
3571 **1637** 55c. multicoloured 2·50 2·00

1638 *Nils Holgersson with Ganz* (book illustration by Wilhelm Schultz)

2008. 150th Birth Anniv of Selma Ottilia Lovisz Lagerlof (winner of Nobel Prize for Literature–1909).
3572 **1638** 100c. multicoloured 4·50 3·75

1639 Building Facade

2009. 500th Anniv of Frankenberg Hall. Multicoloured. Ordinary or self-adhesive gum.
3573 45c. Type **1639** 2·25 1·80

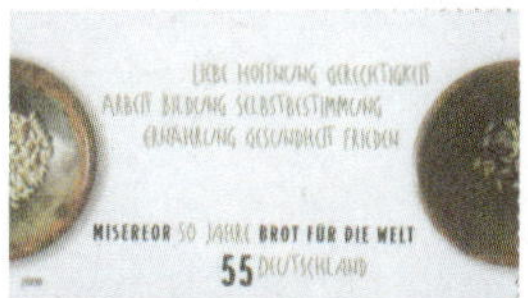

1640 Plates with Cereal Grains

2009. 50th Anniv of MISEREOR and Bread for the World (church charities).
3575 **1640** 55c. multicoloured 2·75 2·20

1641 Rainbow

2009. Welfare Stamps. Celestial Phenomena. Multicoloured. (a) Ordinary gum.
3576 45c.+20c. Type **1641** 2·30 1·90
3577 55c.+25c. Aurora borealis 4·00 3·25
3578 55c.+25c. Sunset 4·00 3·25
3579 145c.+55c. Lightning 9·75 7·75

(b) Self-adhesive.

3580 55c.+25c. As No. 3678 4·00 3·25

1642 Tangermunde Castle

2009. Tangermunde Castle Millennary.
3581 **1642** 90c. multicoloured 4·50 3·75

1643 Theodor Heuss

2009. 125th Birth Anniv of Theodor Heuss (politician, writer and first FDR Head of State).

3582	**1643**	145c. multicoloured	7·00	5·50

1644 Heinz Erhardt

2009. Birth Centenary of Heinz Erhardt (comedian).

3583	**1644**	55c. multicoloured	2·75	2·20

1645 Felix Mendelssohn

2009. Birth Bicentenary of Jakob Ludwig Felix Mendelssohn Bartholdy (composer).

3584	**1645**	65c. multicoloured	3·00	2·40

1646 *The Propylaea in Munich*

2009. 225th Birth Anniv of Leo von Klenze (architect).

3585	**1646**	70c. multicoloured	3·25	2·60

1647 *The Firebird*

2009. Birth Centenary of Helmut Andreas Paul (HAP) Grieshaber (artist).

3586	**1647**	165c. multicoloured	7·50	4·00

1648 Golo Mann

2009. Birth Centenary of Angelus Gottfried Thomas Mann (Golo) Mann (historian and writer).

3587	**1648**	45c. multicoloured	2·25	1·80

1649 Applying Stamp

2009. Post. Multicoloured.

3588	55c. Type **1649**	2·60	2·10
3589	55c. Post Office	2·60	2·10

1650 Stahlradwagen

2009. 175th Birth Anniv of Gottlieb Wilhelm Daimler (engineer and motor vehicle pioneer).

3590	**1650**	170c. multicoloured	8·00	6·50
3591	**1650**	45c. + 27c. multicoloured	2·30	1·90

1651 Hurdler

2009. Sports Promotion Fund. International Association of Athletics Federations World Championship—Berlin 2009. Multicoloured.

3591	45c.+20c. Type **1651**	2·30	1·90
3592	55c.+25c. Pole vaulter	4·00	3·25
3593	55c.+25c. Runners	4·00	3·25
3594	145c.+55c. Discus	9·75	7·75

1652 Bernhard Grzimek

2009. Birth Centenary of Bernhard Grzimek (film maker).

3595	**1652**	55c. multicoloured	2·75	2·20

1653 Planets

2009. Europa. Astronomy. 400th Anniv of Kepler's Laws.

3596	**1653**	55c. multicoloured	2·75	2·20

2009. Post. As T 1649. Multicoloured.

3597	55c. Transport	2·75	2·20
3598	55c. Delivery	2·75	2·20

1654 Eichstatt Letter (showing first German stamps, franked 1849)

2009. Stamp Day.

3599	**1654**	55c.+25c. multicoloured	5·00	4·50

1655 Luther Memorials, Eisleben and Wittenberg

2009. World Heritage Sites.

3600	**1655**	145c. multicoloured	6·50	5·25

1656 First Exhibition Poster, Frankfurt 1909

2009. Centenary of International Areospace Exhibition.

3601	**1656**	55c. multicoloured	2·75	2·20

1657 *Mask* (Christian Grovermann), *Emperor Agustus* (Jochen Hahnel), Hermann Monument, Teutoburg Forest and *Forest* (Thomas Serres)

2009. Bimillennary of Varus (Teutoburg Forest) Battle. Multicoloured. Ordinary or self-adhesive gum.

3602	55c. Type **1657**	1·30	1·00

1658 Illustration from *Struwwelpeter*

2009. Birth Bicentenary of Heinrich Hoffman (children's author and politician).

3604	**1658**	85c. multicoloured	3·75	3·00

1659 Eifel National Park

2009. Sheet 105×70 mm.

MS3605	multicoloured	9·50	9·50

1660 Norderney

2009. Lighthouses. Multicoloured.

3606	45c. Type **1660**	2·25	1·10
3607	55c. Dornbusch	2·75	2·20

1661 Early Campus

2009. 600th Anniv of Leipzig University. Multicoloured.

(a) Ordinary gum.

3608	55c. Type **1661**	1·30	1·00

(b) Size 38×22 mm. Self-adhesive.

3609	55c. As Type **1661**	1·30	1·00

1662 John Calvin

2009. 500th Birth Anniv of John Calvin (religious reformer).

3610	**1662**	70c. black	3·25	2·60

1663 Loading

2009. Centenary of Sassnitz to Trelleborg Ferry.

3611	**1663**	145c. multicoloured	7·00	5·50

1664 Baltic Sea Beach

2009. Youth Stamps. 50th Anniv of Unser Sandmannchen (children's television programme). Multicoloured.

3612	45c.+20c. Type **1664**	2·30	1·90
3613	55c.+25c. Flying machine	4·00	3·25
3614	55c.+25c. Harz narrow-gauge railway	4·00	3·25
3615	145c.+55c. Planet Gugel	9·75	7·75

1665 Houses and Young People

2009. Centenary of Jugendherbergen (youth hostels).

3616	**1665**	55c. multicoloured	2·75	2·20

2009. Centenary of International Aerospace Exhibition. Self-adhesive.

3616a	**1656**	55c. multicoloured	2·75	2·20

1666 Early Race Cars

2009. Historic Motorsport. 115th Anniv of First Automobile Race between Paris and Rouen in France. Sheet 105×70 mm.

MS3617	multicoloured	4·00	3·25

1667 Cathedral

2009. Millenary of Mainz Cathedral (Mainzer Dom) Consecration.

3618	**1667**	90c. multicoloured	4·50	3·75

1668 Cowboy and Indian

2009. For us Children

3619	**1668**	55c. multicoloured	2·75	2·20

1669 Celebration

2009. 60th Anniv of Basic Law and 20th Anniv of Fall of Berlin Wall.

3620	**1669**	55c. multicoloured	2·75	2·20

1670 Bundestag, Reichstag Building (parliament)

2009. Government. Sheet 130×90 mm containing T 1670 and similar horiz design. Multicoloured.

MS3621		55c. Type **1670**; 90c. Bundesrat, Prussian Manor, Berlin (federal council)	7·00	5·50

1671 '20'

2009. 20th Anniv of Opening of Border between Austria and Hungary.

3622	**1671**	70c. multicoloured	3·35	2·60

A stamp of a similar design was issued by Austria and Hungary.

1672 *Still Life with Cherries* (Georg Flegel)

2009. Art.

3623	**1672**	45c. multicoloured	2·25	1·80

1673 Crowd and Nikolai Church, Leipzig

2009. 20th Anniv of Peaceful Revolution.

3624	**1673**	55c. multicoloured	2·75	2·20

1674 Adoration of the Magi

2009. Christmas. The Hoya Missal. Multicoloured.

3625		45c.+20c. Type **1674**	2·30	1·80
3626		55c.+25c. Holy Family	4·00	3·25

1675 Badger

2009. Animal of the Year.

3627	**1675**	55c. multicoloured	2·75	2·20

1676 Marion Grafin Donhoff

2009. Birth Centenary of Marion Grafin Donhoff (political Journalist).

3628	**1676**	55c. multicoloured	2·75	2·20

1677 'Die Kunste ist eine Tochter der Freiheit'

2009. Birth Bicentenary of Johann Christoph Friedrich von Schiller.

3629	**1677**	145c. black, ultramarine and brownish grey	7·00	5·50

1678 Exhibits

2010. Bicentenary of Natural History Museum, Berlin. Ordinary or self-adhesive gum.

3630	**1678**	45c. multicoloured	2·25	1·80

1679 *Malus domestica* (apple)

2010. Welfare Stamps. Fruit. Multicoloured. (a) Ordinary gum.

3632		45c.+20c. Type **1679**	2·30	1·90
3633		55c.+25c. *Citrus limon* (lemon)	4·00	3·25
3634		55c.+25c. *Fragaria ananassa* (strawberry)	4·00	3·25
3635		145c.+55c. *Vaccinium myrtillus* (bilberry)	7·00	5·50

(b) Self-adhesive.

3636		55c.+25c. As No. 3634 (strawberry)	4·00	3·25

1680 'Ruhr 2010'

2010. Ruhr–European Capital of Culture, 2010.

3637	**1680**	55c. multicoloured	2·75	2·25

1681 *Limburg an der Lahn* (George Clarkson Stanfield)

2010. 1100th Anniv of Limburg an der Lahn. Ordinary or self-adhesive gum.

3638	**1681**	145c. multicoloured	7·25	5·75

1682 St Michael's Church, Hildesheim

2010. Millennary of St Michael's Church, Hildesheim. UNESCO World Heritage Site. Ordinary or self-adhesive gum.

3640	**1682**	220c. multicoloured	5·50	4·50

1683 Disabled Athlete

2010. Sports Promotion Fund. Winter Paralympics (45c.+20c.) or Winter Olympic Games, Vancouver (55c.+25c.). Multicoloured.

3642		45c.+20c. Type **1683**	2·30	1·90
3643		55c.+25c. Skier	4·00	3·25

1684 Family playing

2010. Mensch argere dich nicht (board game designed by Joseph Friedrich Schmidt).

3644	**1684**	55c. multicoloured	2·75	2·25

1685 Ring

2010. 14th-century Jewish Wedding Ring found at Erfurt.

3645	**1685**	90c. multicoloured	4·50	3·75

1686 Ship

2010. Post. Greeting Stamps (1st issue). Multicoloured.

3646		55c. Type **1686**	2·75	2·25
3647		55c. Rainbow	2·75	2·25

1687 *Ariadne abandoned by Theseus*

2010. Art. Painting by Maria Anna Catharina Angelica (Angelica) Kauffmann.

3648	**1687**	260c. multicoloured	13·00	11·00

2010. Post. Greeting Stamps (2nd issue). As T 1686. Multicoloured.

3649		55c. Dove	2·75	2·25
3650		55c. Angel carrying heart	2·75	2·25

1688 Footballers

2010. Sports Promotion Fund. Football World Cup Championships, South Africa (55c.+25c) or 2010 Ice Hockey World Cup, Germany (145c.+55c.). Multicoloured.

3651		55c.+25c. Type **1688**	4·00	3·25
3652		145c.+55c. Ice hockey players	9·75	7·75

IV. WEST BERLIN

The Russian Government withdrew from the four-power control of Berlin on 1 July 1948, with the Western Sectors remaining under American, British and French control. West Berlin was constituted a "Land" of the Federal Republic on 1 September 1950. The Russian Zone issues inscribed "STADT BERLIN" (which we do not list unoverprinted in this Catalogue), were not intended for use throughout Berlin, but were for the Russian sector of the city and for Brandenburg.

The first stamps to be used in the Western Sectors were Nos. A4/5 and A7 of the Anglo-American Zones, followed by Nos. A36/52, which were on sale from 24 June to 31 August 1948, and remained valid until 19 September 1948.

1948. Pictorial issue of 1947 (Nos. 928/48) optd BERLIN.

B2		6pf. violet	1·10	5·50
B3		8pf. red	1·10	5·75
B4		10pf. green	1·10	1·60
B5		12pf. grey	1·10	1·40
B7		16pf. green	4·00	2·00
B9		24pf. brown	1·10	60
B10		25pf. orange	26·00	65·00
B11		30pf. red	4·50	9·25
B12		40pf. mauve	7·00	9·25
B13		50pf. blue	10·50	38·00
B14		60pf. brown	3·00	55
B15		80pf. blue	11·00	30·00
B16		84pf. green	21·00	£120
B17		1m. olive	70·00	£180
B18		2m. violet	75·00	£650
B19		3m. red	£100	£900
B20		5m. blue	£130	£900
B21		2pf. black	2·75	2·10
B25		15pf. brown	10·50	2·40
B26		20pf. blue	3·25	85

B2 Schoneberg

1949. Inscr "DEUTSCHE POST". Berlin Views. (a) Small size.

B35	-	1pf. grey	35	25
B36	**B2**	4pf. brown	1·70	1·90
B36c	-	4pf. brown	7·50	6·25
B37	-	5pf. green	1·20	30
B38	-	6pf. purple	2·30	1·30
B39	**B2**	8pf. orange	2·30	1·70
B40	-	10pf. green	1·10	20
B41	**B3**	15pf. brown	20·00	1·00
B42	-	20pf. red	6·25	35
B42b	-	20pf. red	90·00	2·10
B43	-	25pf. yellow	34·00	1·30
B44	-	30pf. blue	18·00	1·50
B45	**B2**	40pf. lake	26·00	1·40
B46	-	50pf. olive	26·00	40
B47	-	60pf. red	90·00	40
B48	-	80pf. blue	22·00	1·50
B49	-	90pf. green	25·00	1·80

B3 Douglas C-54 over Tempelhof Airport

(b) Large size.

B50	**B3**	1Dm. olive	34·00	1·50
B51	-	2Dm. purple	95·00	1·80
B52	-	3Dm. red	£375	18·00
B53	-	5Dm. blue	£180	18·00

DESIGNS—As Type B **2**: 1pf. Brandenburg Gate; 4pf. (B36c) Exhibition Building; 5, 25pf. "Tegel Schloss". 6, 50pf. Reichstag Building. 10, 30pf. "Kleistpark". 20 (B42), 80, 90pf. Technical High School; 20pf. (B42b) Olympia Stadium; 60pf. National Gallery. As Type B **3**: 2Dm. "Gendarmenmarkt"; 3Dm. Brandenburg Gate; 5Dm. "Tegel Schloss".

For similar views inscribed "DEUTSCHE POST BERLIN" see Nos. B118/19.

B4 Stephan Monument and Globe

B5 Heinrich von Stephan Monument

1949. 75th Anniv of U.P.U.

B54	**B4**	12pf. grey	38·00	9·25
B55	**B4**	16pf. green	55·00	21·00
B56	**B4**	24pf. orange	40·00	1·00
B57	**B4**	50pf. olive	£200	50·00
B58	**B4**	60pf. brown	£250	44·00
B59	**B5**	1Dm. olive	£170	£160
B60	**B5**	2Dm. purple	£170	95·00

B6 Goethe and Scene from "Iphigenie"

1949. Birth Bicent of Goethe (poet). Portraits of Goethe and scenes from his works.

B61	**B6**	10pf. green	£190	85·00
B62	-	20pf. red	£190	95·00
B63	-	30pf. blue	40·00	65·00

DESIGNS—Scenes from: 20pf. "Reineke Fuchs"; 30pf. "Faust".

1949. Numeral and pictorial issues of 1946/7 surch BERLIN and bold figures.

B64	**229**	5pf. on 45pf. red	4·50	30
B65	**C**	10pf. on 24pf. brown	19·00	30
B66	**B**	20pf. on 80pf. blue	90·00	20·00
B67	**237**	1m. on 3m. lake	£225	21·00

B9 Alms Bowl and Bear

1949. Berlin Relief Fund.

B68	**B9**	10pf.+5pf. green	£130	£200
B69	**B9**	20pf.+5pf. red	£160	£200
B70	**B9**	30pf.+5pf. blue	£160	£300
MSB70a 111×65 mm. Nos. B68/70 (sold at 1Dm.)			£1000	£2750

B10

1950. European Recovery Programme.

B71	**B10**	20pf. red	£110	44·00

B11 Harp

1950. Restablishment of Berlin Philharmonic Orchestra.

B72	**B11**	10pf.+5pf. green	65·00	44·00
B73	-	30pf.+5pf. blue	£130	£110

DESIGN: 30pf. "Singing Angels" (after H. and J. van Eyck).

B13 G. A. Lortzing

1951. Death Cent of Lortzing (composer).

B74	**B13**	20pf. brown	70·00	65·00

B14 Freedom Bell

1951. (a) Clapper at left.

B75	**B14**	5pf. brown	2·50	8·75
B76	**B14**	10pf. green	22·00	28·00
B77	**B14**	20pf. red	10·50	25·00
B78	**B14**	30pf. blue	80·00	90·00
B79	**B14**	40pf. purple	16·00	45·00

(b) Clapper at right.

B82	5pf. green	2·40	2·00
B83	10pf. green	7·75	4·50
B84	20pf. red	29·00	22·00
B85	30pf. blue	75·00	60·00
B86	40pf. red	29·00	18·00

(c) Clapper in centre.

B101	5pf. brown	1·00	95
B102	10pf. green	2·20	1·60
B103	20pf. red	8·25	3·75
B104	30pf. blue	17·00	16·00
B105	40pf. violet	75·00	42·00

B15 Boy Stamp Collectors

1951. Stamp Day.

B80	**B15**	10pf.+3pf. green	36·00	38·00
B81	**B15**	20pf.+2pf. red	41·00	44·00

B16 Mask of Beethoven (taken from life, 1812)

1952. 125th Death Anniv of Beethoven (composer).

B87	**B16**	30pf. blue	50·00	37·00

B17 Olympic Torch

1952. Olympic Games Festival, Berlin.

B88	**B17**	4pf. brown	1·00	2·00
B89	**B17**	10pf. green	14·50	20·00
B90	**B17**	20pf. red	22·00	28·00

B18 W. von Siemens (electrical engineer)

1952. Famous Berliners.

B91	-	4pf. brown	50	50
B92	-	5pf. blue	1·30	50
B93	-	6pf. purple	7·50	12·00
B94	-	8pf. brown	2·50	2·75
B95	-	10pf. green	3·50	70
B96	-	15pf. lilac	21·00	20·00
B97	**B18**	20pf. red	2·75	90
B98	-	25pf. green	65·00	6·75
B99	-	30pf. purple	22·00	11·00
B100	-	40pf. black	39·00	3·50

PORTRAITS: 4pf. Zelter (musician); 5pf. Lilienthal (aviator); 6pf. Rathenau (statesman); 8pf. Fontane (writer); 10pf. Von Menzel (artist); 15pf. Virchow (pathologist); 25pf. Schinkel (architect); 30pf. Planck (physicist); 40pf. W. von Humboldt (philologist).

B19 Church before Bombing

1953. Kaiser Wilhelm Memorial Church Reconstruction Fund.

B106	**B19**	4pf.+1pf. brown	50	17·00
B107	**B19**	10pf.+5pf. green	1·60	50·00
B108	-	20pf.+10pf. red	4·50	50·00
B109	-	30pf.+15pf. blue	23·00	£120

DESIGN: 20pf., 30pf. Church after bombing.

B20 Chainbreaker

1953. East German Uprising. Inscr "17. JUNI 1953".

B110	**B20**	20pf. black	5·50	2·00
B111	-	30pf. red	39·00	33·00

DESIGN: 30pf. Brandenburg Gate.

B21 Ernst Reuter

1954. Death of Ernst Reuter (Mayor of West Berlin).

B112	**B21**	20pf. brown	9·50	2·30

B22 Conference Buildings

1954. Four-Power Conference, Berlin.

B113	**B22**	20pf. red	10·00	5·25

B23 O. Mergenthaler and Linotype Machine

1954. Birth Cent of Mergenthaler (inventor).

B114	**B23**	10pf. green	3·25	3·00

1954. West German Presidential Election. No. B103 optd Wahl des Bundespräsidenten in Berlin 17. Juli 1954.

B115	**B14**	20pf. red	5·00	6·00

B25 "Germany in Bondage"

1954. 10th Anniv of Attempt on Hitler's Life.

B116	**B25**	20pf. grey and red	6·25	5·50

B26 Prussian Postilion, 1827

1954. National Stamp Exhibition.

B117	**B26**	20pf.+10pf. mult	17·00	36·00

1954. Berlin Views. As Type B 2 but inscr "DEUTSCHE POST BERLIN".

B118	7pf. green	7·50	1·00
B119	70pf. olive	£130	25·00

DESIGNS: 7pf. Exhibition building; 70pf. Grunewald hunting lodge.

B27 Memorial Library

1954

B120	**B27**	40pf. purple	12·50	3·50

B28 Richard Strauss

1954. 5th Death Anniv of Strauss (composer).

B121	**B28**	40pf. blue	13·50	4·50

B29 Blacksmiths forging Rail

1954. Death Cent of A. Borsig (industrialist).

B122	**B29**	20pf. brown	10·00	2·30

B30 "Berlin" (liner)

1955

B123	**B30**	10pf. green	1·70	50
B124	**B30**	25pf. blue	9·00	4·75

B31 Wilhelm Furtwangler (conductor)

1955. 1st Death Anniv of Furtwangler.

B125	**B31**	40pf. blue	26·00	23·00

B32

1955. Federal Parliament Session, Berlin.

B126	**B32**	10pf. black, yell & red	50	60
B127	**B32**	20pf. black, yell & red	6·75	10·50

B33 Prussian Rural Postilion, 1760

1955. Stamp Day and Philatelic Fund.

B128	**B33**	25pf.+10pf. mult	7·75	16·00

B34 St. Otto

1955. 25th Anniv of Berlin Bishopric.

B129	**B34**	7pf.+3pf. brown	1·00	3·25
B130	-	10pf.+5pf. green	1·50	3·75
B131	-	20pf.+10pf. mauve	2·50	5·00

DESIGNS: 10pf. St. Hedwig; 20pf. St. Peter.

B35 Radio Tower and Exhibition Hall

1956. Berlin Buildings and Monuments.

B132	**B35**	7pf. turquoise (A)	9·50	3·00
B133	-	1pf. grey	20	15
B133b	-	3pf. violet	35	25
B134	-	5pf. mauve	20	15
B135	-	7pf. turquoise (B)	20	15
B136	-	8pf. grey	55	45
B136a	-	8pf. red	35	35
B137	-	10pf. green	20	15
B138	-	15pf. blue	50	25
B139	-	20pf. red	50	15
B140	-	25pf. brown	55	50
B141	-	30pf. green	1·00	95
B142	-	40pf. blue	13·50	8·25
B143	-	50pf. green	1·00	95
B144	-	60pf. brown	1·20	1·10
B145	-	70pf. violet	36·00	15·00

B146	-	1Dm. green	2·50	2·50
B146a	-	3Dm. red	7·75	16·00

DESIGNS—As Type B **35** (B)—HORIZ: 1pf., 3pf. Brandenburg Gate; 5pf. P.O. Headquarters; 20pf. Free University; 40pf. Charlottenburg Castle; 60pf. Chamber of Commerce and Bourse; 70pf. Schiller Theatre. VERT: 8pf. Town Hall, Neukollin; 10pf. Kaiser Wilhelm Memorial Church; 15pf. Airlift Monument; 25pf. Lilienthal Monument; 30pf. Pfaueninsel Castle; 50pf. Reuter Power-station. LARGER (24×30 mm): 1Dm. "The Great Elector" (statue, after Schluter). (29½×25 mm): 3Dm. Congress Hall, Berlin.

7pf. (A) Type B **35**. (B) As Type B **35** but with inscription at top.

B37 Eagle and Arms of Berlin

1956. Federal Council Meeting.

B147	**B37**	10pf. black, yell & red	1·50	70
B148	**B37**	25pf. black, yell & red	5·50	5·00

B38

1956. Centenary of German Engineers' Union.

B149	**B38**	10pf. green	2·50	1·70
B150	**B38**	20pf. red	6·25	6·00

1956. Flood Relief Fund. As No. B 77 (colour changed) surch +10 Berlinhilfe fur die Hochwassergeschadigten DEUTSCHE BUNDESPOST-BERLIN and bar.

B151	**B14**	20pf.+10pf. bistre	3·25	3·50

B40 P. Lincke

1956. 10th Death Anniv of Lincke (composer).

B152	**B40**	20pf. red	3·00	3·25

B41 Wireless Transmitter

1956. Industrial Exhibition.

B153	**B41**	25pf. brown	7·50	9·75

B42 Brandenburg Postilion, 1700

1956. Stamp Day and Philatelic Fund.

B154	**B42**	25pf.+10pf. mult	3·25	4·00

B43 Spandau

1957. 725th Anniv of Spandau.

B155	**B43**	20pf. olive and brown	65	80

B44 Model of Hansa District

1957. International Building Exn, Berlin.

B156	**B44**	7pf. brown	20	20
B157	-	20pf. red	1·00	90
B158	-	40pf. blue	2·50	2·50

DESIGNS—HORIZ: 20pf. Aerial view of Exhibition; 40pf. Exhibition Congress Hall.

B45 Friedrich K. von Savigny (jurist)

1957. Portraits as Type B 45.

B159		7pf. brown and green	20	15
B160		8pf. brown and grey	20	20
B161		10pf. brown and green	35	20
B162		15pf. sepia and blue	50	90
B163		20pf.+10pf. sepia and red	1·00	80
B164		20pf. brown and red	20	30
B165		25pf. sepia and lake	1·20	1·10
B166	**B45**	30pf. sepia and green	2·75	3·00
B167	-	40pf. sepia and blue	1·20	1·10
B168	-	50pf. sepia and olive	5·00	8·00

PORTRAITS—VERT: 7pf. T. Mommsen (historian); 8pf. H. Zille (painter); 10pf. E. Reuter (Mayor of Berlin); 15pf. F. Haber (chemist); 20pf. (No. B164), F. Schleiermacher (theologian); 20pf. (B163), L. Heck (zoologist); 25pf. Max Reinhardt (theatrical producer); 40pf. A. von Humboldt (naturalist); 50pf. C. D. Rauch (sculptor).

The premium on No. B163 was for the Berlin Zoo. No. B167 commemorates Humboldt's death centenary.

B46 Uta von Naumburg (statue)

1957. German Cultural Congress.

B169	**B46**	25pf. brown	1·10	1·20

B47 "Unity Justice and Freedom"

1957. 3rd Federal Parliament Assembly.

B170	**B47**	10pf. black, ochre & red	40	90
B171	**B47**	20pf. black, ochre & red	2·75	3·50

B48 Postilion, 1897–1925

1957. Stamp Day.

B172	**B48**	20pf. multicoloured	95	1·00

B49 Torch of Remembrance

1957. 7th World War Veterans Congress.

B173	**B49**	20pf. myrtle, yell & grn	1·00	90

B50 Elly Heuss-Knapp (social worker)

1957. Mothers' Convalescence Fund.

B174	**B50**	20pf.+10pf. red	1·80	2·75

B51 Christ and Symbols of the Cosmos

1958. German Catholics' Day.

B175	**B51**	10pf. black and green	50	60
B176	**B51**	20pf. black and mauve	1·30	1·70

B52 Otto Suhr

1958. 1st Death Anniv of Burgomaster Otto Suhr.

B177	**B52**	20pf. red	1·30	1·80

See also Nos. B187 and B193.

B53 Pres. Heuss

1959

B178	**B53**	7pf. green	20	40
B179	**B53**	10pf. green	35	40
B180	**B53**	20pf. red	70	40
B181	**B53**	40pf. blue	3·25	5·50
B182	**B53**	70pf. violet	11·50	12·50

B54 Symbolic Airlift

1959. 10th Anniv of Berlin Airlift.

B183	**B54**	25pf. black and red	55	50

B55 Brandenburg Gate, Berlin

1959. 14th World Communities Congress, Berlin.

B184	**B55**	20pf. blue, red & lt blue	1·00	45

B56 Schiller

1959. Birth Bicentenary of Schiller (poet).

B185	**B56**	20pf. brown and red	45	50

B57 Robert Koch

1960. 50th Death Anniv of Robert Koch (bacteriologist).

B186	**B57**	20pf. purple	55	60

1960. 4th Death Anniv of Walther Schreiber (Mayor of Berlin, 1951–53). As Type B 52.

B187	20pf. red	65	80

DESIGN: Portrait of Schreiber.

B58 Boy at Window

1960. Berlin Children's Holiday Fund. Inscr "FERIENPLATZE FUR BERLINER KINDER".

B188	**B58**	7pf.+3pf. dp brown, brown & light brown	30	40
B189	-	10pf.+5pf. deep green, olive and green	30	40
B190	-	20pf.+10pf. brown, red and pink	55	70
B191	-	40pf.+20pf. deep blue, blue & light blue	1·60	4·00

DESIGNS: 10pf. Girl in street; 20pf. Girl blowing on Alpine flower; 40pf. Boy on beach.

B59 Hans Boeckler

1961. 10th Anniv of Hans Boeckler (politician).

B192	**B59**	20pf. black and red	40	35

1961. Louise Schroeder Commemoration. As Type B 52.

B193	20pf. brown	45	35

DESIGN: Portrait of Schroeder.

B60 Durer

1961. Famous Germans.

B194	5pf. olive (Magnus)	20	25
B195	7pf. brown (St. Elizabeth of Thuringia)	20	45
B196	8pf. violet (Gutenberg)	20	40
B197	10pf. green (Type B **60**)	20	25
B198	15pf. blue (Luther)	20	50
B199	20pf. red (Bach)	20	25
B200	25pf. brown (Neumann)	20	45
B201	30pf. brown (Kant)	30	60
B202	40pf. blue (Lessing)	70	90
B203	50pf. brown (Goethe)	50	1·10
B204	60pf. red (Schiller)	50	1·20
B205	70pf. green (Beethoven)	70	1·20
B206	80pf. brown (Kleist)	4·00	9·50
B207	1Dm. violet (Annette von Droste-Hulshoff)	1·80	3·50
B208	2Dm. green (Hauptmann)	2·50	5·75

B61 "Five Crosses" Symbol and St. Mary's Church

1961. 10th Evangelical Churches' Day. Crosses in violet.

B210	**B61**	10pf. green	30	20
B211	-	20pf. purple	35	25

DESIGN: 20pf. "Five Crosses" and Kaiser Wilhelm Memorial Church.

B62 Exhibition Emblem

1961. West Berlin Radio and Television Exn.

B212	**B62**	20pf. brown and red	35	35

B63 "Die Linden" (1650)

1962. "Old Berlin" series.

B213	**B63**	7pf. sepia and brown	20	15
B214	-	10pf. sepia and green	20	15
B215	-	15pf. black and blue	20	15
B216	-	20pf. sepia and brown	20	15
B217	-	25pf. sepia and olive	20	15
B218	-	40pf. black and blue	40	40
B219	-	50pf. sepia and purple	40	45
B220	-	60pf. sepia and mauve	55	60
B221	-	70pf. black and purple	55	60
B222	-	80pf. sepia and red	75	85
B223	-	90pf. sepia and brown	85	90
B224	-	1Dm. sepia and green	1·00	1·30

DESIGNS: 10pf. "Waisenbrucke" (Orphans' Bridge), 1783; 15pf. Mauerstrasse, 1780; 20pf. Berlin Castle, 1703; 25pf. Potsdamer Platz, 1825; 40pf. Bellevue Castle, c. 1800; 50pf. Fischer Bridge, 1830; 60pf. Halle Gate, 1880; 70pf. Parochial Church, 1780; 80pf. University, 1825; 90pf. Opera House, 1780; 1Dm. Grunewald Lake, c. 1790.

B64 Euler Gelberhund Biplane, 1912, and Boeing 707 Airliner

1962. 50th Anniv of German Airmail Transport.

B225	**B64**	60pf. black and blue	60	55

B65 Exhibition Emblem

1963. West Berlin Broadcasting Exn.

B226	**B65**	20pf. ultram, grey & bl	30	30

B66 Town Hall Schoneberg

1964. 700th Anniv of Schoneberg.

B227	**B66**	20pf. brown	30	30

B67 Pres. Lubke

1964. Re-election of Pres. Lubke.

B228	**B67**	20pf. red	20	15
B229	**B67**	40pf. blue	45	40

See also Nos. B308/9.

WEST BERLIN DESIGNS. Except where illustrated the following are the same or similar designs to German Federal Republic additonally inscr "BERLIN".

1964. Capitals of the Federal Lands. As No. 1335.

B230	20pf. multicoloured	40	40

1964. Humanitarian Relief and Welfare Funds. As Nos. 1352/5.

B231	10pf.+5pf. multicoloured	20	20
B232	15pf.+5pf. multicoloured	20	20
B233	20pf.+10pf. multicoloured	45	25
B234	40pf.+20pf. multicoloured	70	1·10

1964. Pres. Kennedy Commem. As Type 411.

B235	40pf. blue	45	45

1964. Twelve Centuries of German Architecture. (a) Size 18½×22½ mm. As Nos. 1359/66. Plain backgrounds.

B236	10pf. brown	20	25
B237	15pf. green	20	25
B238	20pf. red	20	25
B239	40pf. blue	85	1·20
B240	50pf. bistre	1·80	1·80
B241	60pf. red	1·30	1·40
B242	70pf. green	2·50	3·75
B243	80pf. brown	2·50	1·90

(b) Size 19½×24 mm. As Nos. 1367/81. Coloured backgrounds.

B244	5pf. bistre	20	20
B245	8pf. red	20	20
B246	10pf. purple	20	20
B247	20pf. green	20	20
B248	30pf. olive	30	25
B249	30pf. red	30	20
B250	40pf. bistre	70	90
B251	50pf. blue	55	55
B252	60pf. red	1·90	2·30
B253	70pf. bronze	1·10	90
B254	80pf. brown	1·20	2·20
B255	90pf. black	70	90
B256	1Dm. blue	70	90
B257	1Dm.10 brown	1·60	1·60
B258	1Dm.30 green	2·75	2·75
B259	2Dm. purple	2·75	2·30

BUILDINGS: 8pf. Palatine Castle, Kaub. Others as Nos. 1359/81 of German Federal Republic.

1965. Child Welfare. As Nos. 1384/7.

B261	10pf.+5pf. Eurasian woodcock	20	25
B262	15pf.+5pf. Common pheasant	20	25
B263	20pf.+10pf. Black grouse	20	25
B264	40pf.+20pf. Western capercaillie	65	90

B68 Kaiser Wilhelm Memorial Church

1965. "New Berlin". Multicoloured.

B265	10pf. Type B **68**	15	20
B266	15pf. Opera House (horiz)	15	20
B267	20pf. Philharmonic Hall (horiz)	20	20
B268	30pf. Jewish Community Centre (horiz)	20	20
B269	40pf. Regina Martyrum Memorial Church (horiz)	30	25
B270	50pf. Ernst-Reuter Square (horiz)	30	35
B271	60pf. Europa Centre	35	40
B272	70pf. Technical University, Charlottenburg (horiz)	55	50
B273	80pf. City Motorway	55	50
B274	90pf. Planetarium (horiz)	75	80
B275	1Dm. Telecommunications, Tower	85	90
B276	1Dm.10 University Clinic, Steglitz (horiz)	90	1·10

1965. Humanitarian Relief Funds. As Nos. 1406/9.

B277	10pf.+5pf. Type **425**	20	20
B278	15pf.+5pf. Cinderella and birds with dress	20	20
B279	20pf.+10pf. Prince offering slipper to Cinderella	30	20
B280	40pf.+20pf. Cinderella and Prince on horse	55	90

1966. As Nos. 1412/15a.

B281	10pf. brown	20	20
B282	20pf. green	20	20
B283	30pf. red	20	20
B284	50pf. blue	70	50
B284a	100pf. blue	5·50	5·00

1966. Child Welfare. As Nos. 1416/19.

B285	10pf.+5pf. Type **429**	20	25
B286	20pf.+10pf. Chamois	20	25
B287	30pf.+15pf. Fallow deer	30	35
B288	50pf.+25pf. Red deer	75	90

1966. Humanitarian Relief Funds. As Nos. 1428/31.

B289	10pf.+5pf. Type **435**	20	25
B290	20pf.+10pf. Frog dining with Princess	20	25
B291	30pf.+15pf. Frog Prince and Princess	40	30
B292	50pf.+25pf. In coach	55	90

Designs from Grimm's "The Frog Prince".

1967. Child Welfare. As Nos. 1434/7.

B293	10pf.+5pf. Common rabbit	20	30
B294	20pf.+10pf. Stoat	20	30
B295	30pf.+15pf. Common hamster	40	35
B296	50pf.+25pf. Red fox	1·20	1·60

B69 "Bust of a Young Man" (after C. Meit)

1967. Berlin Art Treasures.

B297	**B69**	10pf. sepia and bistre	20	20
B298	-	20pf. olive and blue	20	20
B299	-	30pf. brown and olive	20	20
B300	-	50pf. sepia and grey	40	45
B301	-	1Dm. black and blue	95	95
B302	-	1Dm.10 brn & chest	1·30	1·70

DESIGNS: 20pf. Head of "The Elector of Brandenburg" (statue by Schlüter); 30pf. "St. Mark" (statue by Riemenschneider); 50pf. Head from Quadriga, Brandenburg Gate. 1Dm. "Madonna" (carving by Feuchtmayer). (22½×39 mm) 1Dm.10, "Christ and St. John" (after carving from Upper Swabia, c. 1320).

B70 Broadcasting Tower and T.V. Screen

1967. West Berlin Broadcasting Exn.

B303	**B70**	30pf. multicoloured	35	40

1967. Humanitarian Relief Funds. As Nos. 1443/6.

B304	10pf.+5pf. multicoloured	20	30
B305	20pf.+10pf. multicoloured	20	30
B306	30pf.+15pf. multicoloured	30	45
B307	50pf.+25pf. multicoloured	65	90

1967. Re-election of President Lubke. As Type B 67.

B308	**B67**	30pf. red	20	25
B309	**B67**	50pf. blue	55	45

1968. Child Welfare. As Nos. 1454/7.

B310	10pf.+5pf. Wild cat	30	50
B311	20pf.+10pf. European otter	45	50
B312	30pf.+15pf. Eurasian badger	70	1·00
B313	50pf.+25pf. Eurasian beaver	2·10	2·40

B71 Former Court-house

1968. 500th Anniv of Berlin Magistrates' Court.

B314	**B71**	30pf. black	35	35

B72 Festival Emblems

1968. Athletics Festival, Berlin.

B315	**B72**	20f. red, black and grey	30	25

1968. Humanitarian Relief Funds. As Nos. 1473/6.

B316	10pf.+5pf. Doll of 1878	20	25
B317	20pf.+10pf. Doll of 1850	20	25
B318	30pf.+15pf. Doll of 1870	20	25
B319	50pf.+25pf. Doll of 1885	70	90

B74 "The Newspaper Seller" (C. W. Allers, 1889)

1969. 19th-cent Berliners. Contemporary Art.

B320	-	5pf. black	20	15
B321	**B74**	10pf. purple	20	15
B322	-	10pf. brown	20	15
B323	-	20pf. green	25	25
B324	-	20pf. turquoise	25	25
B325	-	30pf. brown	80	50
B326	-	30pf. brown	80	50
B327	-	50pf. blue	2·10	2·00

DESIGNS—HORIZ: 5pf. "The Cab-driver" (H. Zille, 1875). VERT: 10pf. "The Bus-driver" (C. W. Allers, 1890); 20pf. (No. B323) "The Cobblers Boy" (F. Kruger, 1839); 20pf. (No. B324) "The Cobbler" (A. von Menzel, 1833); 30pf. (No. B325) "The Borsig Forge" (P. Meyerheim, 1878); 30pf. (No. B326) "Three Berlin Ladies" (F. Kurger, 1839); 50pf. "At the Brandenburg Gate" (C. W. Allers, 1889).

1969. Child Welfare. As Nos. 1478/81.

B328	10pf.+5pf. brn, blk & yell	20	25
B329	20pf.+10pf. brown, black and buff	35	40
B330	30pf.+15pf. brn, blk & red	45	60
B331	50pf.+25pf. grey, yellow, black and blue	1·50	1·60

B75 Orang-Utan Family

1969. 125th Anniv of Berlin Zoo. Sheet 99×74 mm containing Type B 75 and similar horiz designs.

MSB332	10pf. black and brown; 20pf. black and green; 30pf. black and purple; 50pf. black and blue (sold for 1Dm.30)	2·50	2·50

DESIGNS: 20pf. Dalmatian pelican family; 30pf. Gaur and calf; 50pf. Common zebra and foal.

B76 Postman

1969. 20th Congress of Post Office Trade Union Federation (I.P.T.T.), Berlin.

B333	**B76**	10pf. olive	20	25
B334	-	20pf. brown and buff	30	25
B335	-	30pf. violet and ochre	60	65
B336	-	50pf. blue and light blue	1·30	1·20

DESIGNS: 20pf. Telephonist; 30pf. Technician; 50pf. Airmail handlers.

B77 J. Joachim (violinist and director, after A. von Menzel)

1969. Anniversaries. Multicoloured.

B337	30pf. Type B **77**	60	50
B338	50pf. Alexander von Humboldt (after J. Stieler)	1·10	1·50

ANNIVERSARIES: 30pf. Centenary of Berlin Academy of Music; 50pf. Birth bicentenary of Humboldt.

B78 Railway Carriage (1835)

1969. Humanitarian Relief Funds. Pewter Models. Multicoloured. (a) Inscr "WOHLFAHRTSMARKE".

B339	10pf.+5pf. Type B **78**	20	20

B340		20pf.+10pf. Woman feeding chicken (1850)	20	20
B341		30pf.+15pf. Market stall (1850)	40	40
B342		50pf.+25pf. Mounted postilion (1860)	1·30	1·20

(b) Christmas. Inscr "WEIHNACHTSMARKE".

B343		10pf.+5pf. "The Three Kings"	45	35

B79 T. Fontane

1970. 150th Birth Anniv of Theodor Fontane (writer).

B344	**B79**	20pf. multicoloured	45	35

B80 Heinrich von Stretlingen

1970. Miniatures of Minnesingers. Mult.

B345		10pf.+5pf. Type B **80**	20	25
B346		20pf.+10pf. Meinloh von Sevelingen	45	50
B347		30pf.+15pf. Burkhart von Hohenfels	65	70
B348		50pf.+25pf. Albrecht von Johannsdorf	1·50	1·70

B81 Film "Title"

1970. 20th International Film Festival, Berlin.

B349	**B81**	30pf. multicoloured	50	55

1970. Pres. Heinemann. As Nos. 1535/55.

B350	**486**	5pf. black	20	15
B351	**486**	8pf. brown	90	1·00
B352	**486**	10pf. brown	20	15
B353	**486**	15pf. bistre	25	25
B354	**486**	20pf. green	20	15
B355	**486**	25pf. green	1·20	65
B356	**486**	30pf. brown	1·30	50
B357	**486**	40pf. orange	70	30
B358	**486**	50pf. blue	50	20
B359	**486**	60pf. blue	1·10	70
B360	**486**	70pf. brown	1·00	70
B361	**486**	80pf. green	1·20	1·10
B362	**486**	90pf. red	2·30	2·75
B363	**486**	1Dm. green	1·20	85
B364	**486**	110pf. grey	1·50	1·40
B365	**486**	120pf. brown	1·50	1·10
B366	**486**	130pf. brown	2·00	1·80
B367	**486**	140pf. green	2·10	1·90
B368	**486**	150pf. red	2·10	1·40
B369	**486**	160pf. orange	2·75	2·40
B370	**486**	170pf. orange	2·10	1·90
B371	**486**	190pf. purple	2·40	2·10
B372	**486**	2Dm. violet	2·50	1·70

B82 Allegory of Folklore

1970. 20th Berlin Folklore Week.

B373	**B82**	30pf. multicoloured	60	55

B83 "Caspar"

1970. Humanitarian Relief Funds. Puppets. Multicoloured. (a) Relief Funds.

B374		10pf.+5pf. Type B **83**	20	20
B375		20pf.+10pf. "Polichinelle"	35	30
B376		30pf.+15pf. "Punch"	55	55
B377		50pf.+25pf. "Pulcinella"	1·20	1·30

(b) Christmas.

B378		10pf.+5pf. "Angel"	35	35

B84 L. von Ranke (after painting by J. Schrader)

1970. 175th Birth Anniv of Leopold von Ranke (historian).

B379	**B84**	30pf. multicoloured	55	45

1971. Centenary of German Unification.

B380	**492**	30pf. black, red & orange	65	65

B85 Class ET 165.8 Electric Train, 1933

1971. Berlin Rail Transport. Multicoloured.

B381		5pf. Class T.12 steam train, 1925	25	20
B382		10pf. Electric tram, 1890	25	20
B383		20pf. Horse tram, 1880	30	30
B384		30pf. Type B **85**	55	45
B385		50pf. Electric tram, 1950	2·10	1·50
B386		1Dm. Underground train No. 2431, 1971	2·30	2·20

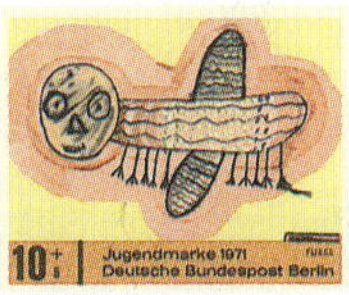

B86 "Fly"

1971. Child Welfare. Children's Drawings. Multicoloured.

B387		10pf.+5pf. Type B **86**	35	40
B388		20pf.+10pf. "Fish"	40	40
B389		30pf.+15pf. "Porcupine"	50	55
B390		50pf.+25pf. "Cockerel"	1·60	1·60

B87 "The Bagpiper" (copper engraving, Durer, c. 1514)

1971. 500th Birth Anniv of Albrecht Durer.

B391	**B87**	10pf. black and brown	50	40

B88 Communications Tower and Dish Aerials

1971. West Berlin Broadcasting Exhibition.

B392	**B88**	30pf. indigo, blue & red	95	70

B89 Bach and part of 2nd Brandenburg Concerto

1971. 250th Anniv of Bach's Brandenburg Concertos.

B393	**B89**	30pf. multicoloured	85	70

B90 H. von Helmholtz (from painting by K. Morell-Kramer)

1971. 150th Anniv of Hermann von Helmholtz (scientist).

B394	**B90**	25pf. multicoloured	60	45

B91 "Opel" Racing-car (1921)

1971. 50th Anniv of Avus Motor-racing Track. Sheet 100×75 mm containing horiz designs as Type B 91. Multicoloured.

MSB395		10pf. Type B **91**; 25pf. "Auto-Union" (1936); 30pf. "Mercedes-Benz SSKL" (1931); 60pf. "Mercedes" racing with "Auto-Union" (1937)	1·80	1·60

1971. Accident Prevention. As Nos. 1596/1605.

B396		5pf. orange	30	35
B397		10pf. brown	30	20
B398		20pf. violet	30	20
B399		25pf. green	50	65
B400		30pf. red	45	50
B401		40pf. mauve	50	50
B402		50pf. blue	2·20	1·30
B403		60pf. blue	2·50	2·75
B404		70pf. blue and green	2·00	1·50
B405		100pf. green	2·20	1·40
B406		150pf. brown	6·25	8·25

B92 Dancing Men

1971. Humanitarian Relief Funds. Wooden Toys. Mult. (a) Inscr "WOHLFAHRTSMARKE".

B407		10pf.+5pf. Type B **92**	20	20
B408		25pf.+10pf. Horseman on wheels	35	40
B409		30pf.+15pf. Acrobat	65	65
B410		60pf.+30pf. Nurse and babies	1·20	1·30

(b) Christmas. Inscr "WEIHNACHTSMARKE".

B411		10pf.+5pf. Angel with two candles	40	35

B93 Microscope

1971. Birth Centenary of Material-testing Laboratory, Berlin.

B412	**B93**	30pf. multicoloured	50	45

B94 F. Gilly (after bust by Schadow)

1972. Birth Bicentenary of Friedrich Gilly (architect).

B413	**B94**	30pf. black and blue	65	45

B95 Boy raiding Bird's-nest

1972. Child Welfare. Animal Protection. Multicoloured.

B414		10pf.+5pf. Type B **95**	25	20
B415		25pf.+10pf. Care of kittens	35	40
B416		30pf.+15pf. Man beating watch-dog	70	65
B417		60pf.+30pf. Animals crossing road at night	1·60	1·50

B96 "Grunewaldsee" (A. von Riesen)

1972. Paintings of Berlin Lakes. Multicoloured.

B418		10pf. Type B **96**	25	20
B419		25pf. "Wannsee" (Max Liebermann)	60	60
B420		30pf. "Schlachtensee" (W. Leistikow)	1·20	75

B97 E. T. A. Hoffman

1972. 150th Death Anniv of E. T. A. Hoffman (poet and musician).

B421	**B97**	60pf. black and violet	1·30	1·10

B98 Max Liebermann (self-portrait)

1972. 125th Birth Anniv of Max Liebermann (painter).

B422	**B98**	40pf. multicoloured	85	55

B99 Stamp Printing-press

1972. Stamp Day.

B423	**B99**	20pf. blue, black & red	50	35

1972. Humanitarian Relief Funds. Multicoloured. (a) 19th-century Faience Chessmen. As Nos. 1636/40 of West Germany. Inscr "WOLHFAHRTSMARKE".

B424		20pf.+10pf. Knight	35	40
B425		30pf.+15pf. Rook	60	60
B426		40pf.+20pf. Queen	1·60	1·40
B427		70pf.+35pf. King	2·20	2·10

(b) Christmas. Inscr "WEIHNACHTSMARKE".

B428		20pf.+10pf. "The Holy Family"	65	55

B100 Prince von Hardenberg (after Tischbein)

1972. 150th Death Anniv of Karl August von Hardenberg (statesman).

B429	**B100**	40pf. multicoloured	75	50

B101 Northern Goshawk

1973. Youth Welfare. Birds of Prey. Mult.

B430	20pf.+10pf. Type B **101**	60	60
B431	30pf.+15pf. Peregrine falcon	90	85
B432	40pf.+20pf. Northern sparrow hawk	1·20	1·10
B433	70pf.+35pf. Golden eagle	2·10	2·00

B102 Horse-bus, 1907

1973. Berlin Buses. Multicoloured.

B434	20pf. Type B **102**	40	30
B435	20pf. Trolley bus, 1933	40	30
B436	30pf. Motor bus, 1919	90	50
B437	30pf. Double-decker, 1970	1·30	50
B438	40pf. Double-decker, 1925	1·60	90
B439	40pf. "Standard" bus, 1973	1·60	90

B103 L. Tieck

1973. Birth Bicentenary of Ludwig Tieck (poet and writer).

B440	**B103**	40pf. multicoloured	85	55

B104 J. J. Quantz

1973. Death Bicentenary of Johann Quantz (composer).

B441	**B104**	40pf. black	90	65

B105 Radio Set, 1926

1973. "50 Years of German Broadcasting". Sheet 148×105 mm containing horiz designs as Type B 105.

MSB442	20pf. black and yellow; 30pf. black and green; 40pf. black and red; 70pf. black and blue (sold at 1.80Dm)	5·00	4·50

DESIGNS: 30pf. Hans Bredow and microphone of 1924; 40pf. Girl with TV and video tape-recorder; 70pf. TV camera.

B106 17th-century Hurdy-Gurdy

1973. Humanitarian Relief Funds. Mult. (a) Musical Instruments. Inscr "WOHLFAHRTSMARKE".

B443	20pf.+10pf. Type B **106**	40	35
B444	30pf.+15pf. 16th century drum	90	80
B445	40pf.+20pf. 18th century lute	1·00	95
B446	70pf.+35pf. 16th century organ	1·70	1·50

(b) Christmas. Inscr "WEIHNACHTSMARKE".

B447	20pf.+10pf. Christmas star	65	60

B107 G. W. Knobelsdorff

1974. 275th Birth Anniv of Georg W. von Knobelsdorff (architect).

B448	**B107**	20pf. brown	45	35

B108 G. R. Kirchoff

1974. 150th Birth Anniv of Gustav R. Kirchhoff (physicist).

B449	**B108**	30pf. green and grey	40	40

B109 A. Slaby

1974. 125th Birth Anniv of Adolf Slaby (radio pioneer).

B450	**B109**	40pf. black and red	65	55

B110 Airlift Memorial

1974. 25th Anniv of Berlin Airlift.

B451	**B110**	90pf. multicoloured	2·50	1·90

B111 Photography

1974. Youth Welfare. Youth Activities. Multicoloured.

B452	20pf.+10pf. Type B **111**	45	50
B453	30pf.+15pf. Athletics	45	50
B454	40pf.+20pf. Music	1·00	1·10
B455	70pf.+35pf. Voluntary service (Nurse)	1·70	1·70

B112 School Seal

1974. 400th Anniv of Evangelical Grammar School, Berlin.

B456	**B112**	50pf. grey, brn & gold	90	60

B113 Spring Bouquet

1974. Humanitarian Relief Funds. Flowers. Multicoloured. (a) 25th Anniv of Humanitarian Relief Stamps. Inscr "25 JAHRE WOHLFAHRTSMARKE".

B457	30pf.+15pf. Type B **113**	40	45
B458	40pf.+20pf. Autumn bouquet	80	80
B459	50pf.+25pf. Bouquet of roses	90	90
B460	70pf.+35pf. Winter bouquet	1·60	1·50

(b) Christmas. Inscr "WEIHNACHTSMARKE".

B461	30pf.+15pf. Christmas bouquet	95	1·00

B114 Tegel Airport

1974. Opening of Tegel Airport. Berlin.

B462	**B114**	50pf. violet, bl & grn	1·20	75

B115 "Venus" (F. E. Meyer)

1974. Berlin Porcelain Figures. Mult.

B463	30pf. Type B **115**	65	50
B464	40pf. "Astronomy" (W. C. Meyer)	75	65
B465	50pf. "Justice" (J. G. Muller)	85	80

B116 Gottfried Schadow

1975. 125th Death Anniv of Gottfried Schadow (sculptor).

B466	**B116**	50pf. brown	90	60

B117 "Prinzess Charlotte"

1975. Berlin Pleasure Boats. Multicoloured.

B467	30pf. Type B **117**	80	40
B468	40pf. "Siegfried"	80	40
B469	50pf. "Sperber"	1·50	90
B470	60pf. "Vaterland"	1·50	90
B471	70pf. "Moby Dick"	1·90	1·70

B118 Steam Locomotive "Drache", 1848

1975. Youth Welfare. Railway Locomotives. Multicoloured.

B472	30pf.+15pf. Type B **118**	90	75
B473	40pf.+20pf. Class 89 tank locomotive	90	90
B474	50pf.+25pf. Class 050 steam locomotive	1·90	1·50
B475	70pf.+35pf. Class 010 steam locomotive	2·75	2·50

B119 Ferdinand Sauerbruch (surgeon)

1975. Birth Cent of Ferdinand Sauerbruch.

B476	**B119**	50pf. dp brn, brn & pk	90	65

B120 Gymnastics Emblem

1975. Gymnaestrada (Gymnastic Games), Berlin.

B477	**B120**	40pf. black, gold and green	65	45

1975. Industry and Technology. As Nos. 1742/55.

B478	-	5pf. green	20	15
B479	-	10pf. purple	20	15
B480	-	20pf. red	30	15
B481	-	30pf. violet	40	20
B482	**572**	40pf. green	65	30
B483	-	50pf. red	65	20
B483a	-	60pf. red	1·10	40
B484	-	70pf. blue	1·10	50
B485	-	80pf. green	1·10	30
B486	-	100pf. brown	1·10	50
B486a	-	110pf. purple	1·60	1·40
B487	-	120pf. blue	1·50	1·00
B487a	-	130pf. red	2·50	1·60
B488	-	140pf. red	1·50	1·50
B488a	-	150pf. red	3·50	1·50
B489	-	160pf. green	3·00	1·50
B489a	-	180pf. brown	3·50	2·30
B489b	-	190pf. brown	3·50	2·75
B490	-	200pf. purple	2·10	90
B490a	-	230pf. purple	2·75	2·30
B490b	-	250pf. green	4·00	2·50
B490c	-	300pf. green	4·50	2·75
B491	-	500pf. black	7·00	4·75

B121 "Lovis Corinth" (self-portrait)

1975. 50th Death Anniv of Lovis Corinth (painter).

B492	**B121**	50pf. multicoloured	90	60

B122 Buildings in Naunynstrasse, Berlin-Kreuzberg

1975. European Architectural Heritage Year.

B493	**B122**	50pf. multicoloured	1·00	70

B123 Yellow Gentian

1975. Humanitarian Relief Funds. Alpine Flowers. Multicoloured.

B494	30pf.+15pf. Type B **123**	65	60
B495	40pf.+20pf. Arnica	65	60
B496	50pf.+25pf. Cyclamen	85	75
B497	70pf.+35pf. Blue gentian	1·30	1·20

1975. Christmas. As Type B 123, inscr "WEIHNACHTSMARKE". Mult.

B498	30pf.+15pf. Snow heather	90	80

See also Nos. B508/11, B540/3 and B557/60.

B124 Paul Lobe

1975. Birth Cent of Paul Lobe (politician).

B499	**B124**	50pf. red	90	65

B125 Ears of Wheat, with inscription "Grune Woche"

1976. "International Agriculture Week", Berlin.

B500	**B125**	70pf. yellow and green	1·00	80

B126 Putting the Shot

1976. Youth Welfare. Training for the Olympics. Multicoloured.

B501	30pf.+15pf. Type B **126**	90	80
B502	40pf.+20pf. Hockey	90	80
B503	50pf.+25pf. Handball	95	90
B504	70pf.+35pf. Swimming	2·00	2·00

B127 Hockey

1976. Women's World Hockey Championships.

B505	**B127**	30pf. green	85	45

B128 Treble Clef

1976. German Choristers' Festival.

B506	**B128**	40pf. multicoloured	90	60

B129 Fire Service Emblem

1976. 125th Anniv of Berlin Fire Service.

B507	**B129**	50pf. multicoloured	1·50	95

1976. Humanitarian Relief Funds. Garden Flowers. As Type B 123. Multicoloured.

B508	30pf.+15pf. Iris	45	45
B509	40pf.+20pf. Wallflower	45	45
B510	50pf.+25pf. Dahlia	85	85
B511	70pf.+35pf. Larkspur	1·30	1·30

B130 Julius Tower, Spandau

1976. Berlin Views (1st series).

B512	-	30pf. black and blue	60	45
B513	**B130**	40pf. black and brown	90	45
B514	-	50pf. black and green	1·00	50

DESIGNS: 30pf. Yacht on the Havel; 50pf. Lake and Victory Column, Tiergarten park.

See also Nos. B562/4, B605/7 and B647/9.

B131 "Annunciation to the Shepherds" (window, Frauenkirche, Esslingen)

1976. Christmas. Sheet 71×101 mm.

MSB515 B **131** 30pf.+15pf. multicoloured	90	80

1977. Coil Stamps. German Castles. As Nos. 1805/12d.

B516	10pf. blue	20	15
B517	20pf. orange	20	20
B517a	25pf. red	55	40
B518	30pf. brown	30	25
B518c	35pf. red	45	40
B519	40pf. green	35	25
B519a	40pf. brown	65	35
B520	50pf. red	60	25
B520b	50pf. green	65	35
B521	60pf. brown	1·20	55
B521a	60pf. red	1·00	50
B522	70pf. blue	1·20	60
B522a	80pf. green	85	35
B522b	90pf. blue	1·20	90
B522c	120pf. violet	1·30	1·00
B523	190pf. red	1·60	1·50
B524	200pf. green	2·20	1·60
B524a	210pf. brown	2·50	1·70
B524b	230pf. green	2·50	1·70
B524c	280pf. blue	4·50	2·75
B524d	300pf. orange	4·50	2·75

B132 "Eugenie d'Alton" (Cristian Rauch)

1977. Birth Bicentenary of Christian Daniel Rauch (sculptor).

B525	**B132**	50pf. black	90	65

B133 "Eduard Gaertner" (self-portrait)

1977. Death Cent of Eduard Gaertner (artist).

B526	**B133**	40pf. black, green and deep green	65	45

B134 Bremen Kogge, 1380

1977. Youth Welfare. Ships. Multicoloured.

B527	30pf.+15pf. Type B **134**	50	50
B528	40pf.+20pf. "Helena Sloman" (steamship), 1850	60	60
B529	50pf.+25pf. "Cap Polonio" (liner), 1914	1·10	1·10
B530	70pf.+35pf. "Widar" (bulk carrier), 1971	1·30	1·30

B135 Female Figure

1977. Birth Cent of Georg Kolbe (sculptor).

B531	**B135**	30pf. green and black	60	45

B136 Crosses and Text

1977. 17th Evangelical Churches Day.

B532	**B136**	40pf. yellow, blk & grn	60	45

B137 Telephones of 1905 and 1977

1977. International Telecommunications Exhibition and Centenary of German Telephone Service.

B533	**B137**	50pf. buff, black & red	2·30	1·20

B138 Imperial German Patent Office, Berlin-Kreuzberg

1977. Centenary of German Patent Office.

B534	**B138**	60pf. black, red & grey	1·80	80

B139 Untitled Painting (G. Grosz)

1977. 15th European Art Exhibition.

B535	**B139**	70pf. multicoloured	1·30	90

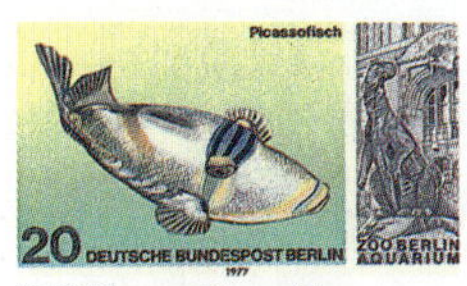

B140 Picasso Triggerfish

1977. 25th Anniv of Reopening of Berlin Aquarium. Multicoloured.

B536	20pf. Type B **140**	60	50
B537	30pf. Paddlefish	85	75
B538	40pf. Radiated tortoise	1·20	90
B539	50pf. Rhinoceros iguana	1·70	1·10

1977. Humanitarian Relief Funds. Meadow Flowers. As Type B 123. Multicoloured.

B540	30pf.+15pf. Daisy	35	40
B541	40pf.+20pf. Marsh marigold	65	60
B542	50pf.+25pf. Sainfoin	90	85
B543	70pf.+35pf. Forget-me-not	1·40	1·30

B141 "Madonna and Child" (stained glass window, Basilica of St. Gereon, Cologne)

1977. Christmas. Sheet 70×105 mm.

MSB544 B **141** 30pf.+15pf. multicoloured	95	85

B142 Walter Kollo

1978. Birth Cent of Walter Kollo (composer).

B545	**B142**	50pf. brown and red	1·20	80

B143 Emblem of U.S. Chamber of Commerce

1978. 75th Anniv of U.S. Chamber of Commerce in Germany.

B546	**B143**	90pf. blue and red	1·50	1·30

1978. Youth Welfare. Aviation History (1st series). As T 627. Multicoloured.

B547	30pf.+15pf. Montgolfier balloon, 1783	45	50
B548	40pf.+20pf. Lilienthal glider, 1891	70	70
B549	50pf.+25pf. Wright Type A biplane	90	90
B550	70pf.+35pf. Etrich/Rumpler Taube, 1910	1·50	1·50

See also Nos. B567/70 and B589/92.

1978. Sport Promotion Fund. As T 623. Multicoloured.

B551	50pf.+25pf. Cycling	1·00	75
B552	70pf.+35pf. Fencing	1·40	1·20

B146 Albrecht von Graefe

1978. 150th Birth Anniv of Albrecht von Graefe (pioneer of medical eye services).

B553	**B146**	30pf. black and brown	70	40

B147 Friedrich Ludwig Jahn

1978. Birth Bicentenary of F. L. Jahn (pioneer of physical education).

B554	**B147**	50pf. red	95	60

B148 Swimming

1978. 3rd World Swimming Championships.

B555	**B148**	40pf. multicoloured	1·20	95

B149 "The Boat" (Karl Hofer)

1978. Birth Centenary of Karl Hofer (Impressionist painter).

B556	**B149**	50pf. multicoloured	95	70

1978. Humanitarian Relief Funds. Woodland Flowers. As Type B 123. Multicoloured.

B557	30pf.+15pf. Solomon's seal	55	45
B558	40pf.+20pf. Wood primrose	70	65
B559	50pf.+25pf. Red helle-borine	90	90
B560	70pf.+35pf. Bugle	1·40	1·40

B150 Prussian State Library

1978. Opening of New Prussian State Library Building.

B561	**B150**	90pf. olive and red	1·60	1·20

1978. Berlin Views (2nd series). As Type B 130.

B562	40pf. black and green	75	45
B563	50pf. black and purple	90	70

B564		60pf. black and brown	1·20	80

DESIGNS: 40pf. Belvedere; 50pf. Landwehr Canal; 60pf. Village church, Lichtenrade.

B151 "Madonna" (stained glass window, Frauenkirche, Munich)

1978. Christmas. Sheet 65×92 mm.

MSB565 B **151** 30pf.+15pf. multicoloured		95	85

B152 Congress Centre

1979. Opening of International Congress Centre, Berlin.

B566	**B152**	60pf. black, blue & red	1·20	85

1979. Youth Welfare. History of Aviation (2nd series). As T 627. Multicoloured.

B567	40pf.+20pf. Vampyr glider, 1921	55	60
B568	50pf.+25pf. Junkers Ju 52/3m D-2202 "Richthofen", 1932	90	90
B569	60pf.+30pf. Messerschmitt Bf 108 D-1010, 1934	1·20	1·20
B570	90pf.+45pf. Douglas DC-3 NC-14988, 1935	1·80	1·80

B153 Relay Runners

1979. Sport Promotion Fund. Multicoloured.

B571	60pf.+30pf. Type B **153**	1·10	1·00
B572	90pf.+45pf. Archers	1·40	1·40

B154 Old and New Arms

1979. Centenary of State Printing Works, Berlin.

B573	**B154**	60pf. multicoloured	1·70	1·20

B155 Arrows and Target

1979. World Archery Championships.

B574	**B155**	50pf. multicoloured	95	65

B156 Television Screen

1979. International Telecommunications Exhibition, Berlin.

B575	**B156**	60pf. black, grey & red	1·30	90

B157 Moses Mendelssohn

1979. 250th Birth Anniv of Moses Mendelssohn (philosopher).

B576	**B157**	90pf. black	1·40	95

B158 Venus Slipper Orchid and Great Tropical House

1979. 300th Anniv of Berlin Botanical Gardens.

B577	**B158**	50pf. multicoloured	95	60

B159 Gas Lamp, Kreuzberg District

1979. 300th Anniv of Street Lighting.

B578	**B159**	10pf. green, bl & grey	45	20
B579	-	40pf. green, bis & grey	90	70
B580	-	50pf. green, brn & grey	1·30	80
B581	-	60pf. green, red & grey	1·40	1·20

DESIGNS: 40pf. Electric carbon-arc lamp, Hardenbergstrasse; 50pf. Gas Lamps, Wittenberg-platz; 60pf. Five-armed chandelier, Charlottenburg.

1979. Humanitarian Relief Funds. Woodland Flowers and Fruit. As Type B 123, but horiz. Multicoloured.

B582	40pf.+20pf. Larch	70	50
B583	50pf.+25pf. Hazelnut	90	80
B584	60pf.+30pf. Horse chestnut	1·40	1·10
B585	90pf.+45pf. Blackthorn	1·60	1·60

B161 Advertisement Pillar

1979. 125th Anniv of Advertisement Pillars.

B586	**B161**	50pf. red and lilac	1·80	95

B162 "Nativity" (Altenberg medieval manuscript)

1979. Christmas.

B587	**B162**	40pf.+20pf. mult	1·10	90

B163 Map showing Wegener's Theory of Continental Drift

1980. Birth Centenary of Alfred Wegener (explorer and geophysicist).

B588	**B163**	60pf. black, orange and blue	1·50	1·20

1980. Youth Welfare. Aviation History (3rd series). As T 627. Multicoloured.

B589	40pf.+20pf. Vickers Viscount 810	85	80
B590	50pf.+25pf. Fokker Friendship "Condor"	90	90
B591	60pf.+30pf. Sud Aviation Caravelle F-BKSZ, 1955	1·20	1·10
B592	90pf.+45pf. Sikorsky S-55 helicopter OO-SHB, 1949	1·70	1·60

Nos. B589/90 are incorrectly dated.

B164 Throwing the Javelin

1980. Sport Promotion Fund. Multicoloured.

B593	50pf.+25pf. Type B **164**	85	85
B594	60pf.+30pf. Weightlifting	90	90
B595	90pf.+45pf. Water polo	1·40	1·40

B165 Cardinal Preysing

1980. 86th German Catholics Congress.

B596	**B165**	50pf. red and black	95	65

B166 "Operatio" (enamel medallion)

1980. 150th Anniv of Prussian Museums. Multicoloured.

B597	40pf. Type B **166**	90	50
B598	60pf. "Monks Reading" (oak sculpture, Ernst Barlach)	1·20	75

B167 Robert Stolz

1980. Birth Centenary of Robert Stolz (composer).

B599	**B167**	60pf. multicoloured	1·30	90

B168 Von Steuben

1980. 250th Birth Anniv of Friedrich Wilhelm von Steuben (American general).

B600	**B168**	40pf. multicoloured	1·20	60

B169 Orlaya grandiflora

1980. Humanitarian Relief Funds. Endangered Wild Flowers. Multicoloured.

B601	40pf.+20pf. Type B **169**	85	85
B602	50pf.+25pf. Yellow gagae	1·00	1·00
B603	60pf.+30pf. Summer pheasant's-eye	1·00	1·00
B604	90p.+45pf. Venus's looking-glass	1·80	1·80

See also Nos. B622/5.

1980. Berlin Views (3rd series). As Type B 130.

B605	40pf. black and green	90	50
B606	50pf. black and brown	1·10	80
B607	60pf. black and blue	1·60	1·00

DESIGNS: 40pf. Lilienthal Monument; 50pf. "Grosse Neugierde"; 60pf. Grunewald Tower.

B170 "Message to the Shepherds" (Altomunster manuscript)

1980. Christmas.

B608	**B170**	40pf.+20pf. mult	1·10	1·00

B171 Von Arnim (after Strohling)

1981. Birth Bicentenary of Achim von Arnim (poet).

B609	**B171**	60pf. green	1·10	70

B172 Von Chamisso (bronze medallion, David d'Angers)

1981. Birth Bicentenary of Adelbert von Chamisso (poet and naturalist).

B610	**B172**	60pf. brown, deep brown and ochre	1·10	70

B173 Von Gontard

1981. 250th Birth Anniv of Karl Phillipp von Gontard (architect).

B611	**B173**	50pf. red, black & grey	1·10	70

B174 Kreuzberg War Memorial

1981. Birth Bicentenary of Karl Friedrich Schinkel (architect).

B612	**B174**	40pf. green and brown	1·30	80

B175 Theodolite, c. 1810

1981. Youth Welfare. Optical Instruments. Multicoloured.

B613	40pf.+20pf. Type B **175**	65	65
B614	50pf.+25pf. Equatorial telescope, 1820	90	90
B615	60pf.+30pf. Microscope, 1790	1·10	1·10
B616	90pf.+45pf. Sextant, 1830	1·80	1·80

B176 Group Gymnastics

1981. Sport Promotion Fund. Multicoloured.

B617	60pf.+30pf. Type B **176**	1·20	90
B618	90pf.+45pf. Cross-country race	1·80	1·50

B177 "Cupid and Psyche"

1981. 150th Birth Anniv of Reinhold Begas (sculptor).
B619 **B177** 50pf. black and blue 95 65

B178 Badge of Order "Pour le Merite"

1981. Prussian Exhibition, Berlin-Kreuzberg.
B620 **B178** 40pf. multicoloured 95 65

B179 Broadcasting House, Charlottenburg

1981. International Telecommunications Exhibition, Berlin.
B621 **B179** 60pf. multicoloured 1·40 90

1981. Humanitarian Relief Funds. Endangered Wild Flowers. As Type B 169. Multicoloured.
B622 40pf.+20pf. Common bistort 90 80
B623 50pf.+25pf. Moor-king 1·00 90
B624 60pf.+30pf. "Gladiolus palustris" 1·20 90
B625 90pf.+45pf. Siberian iris 2·10 1·90

B180 "Three Kings" (glass painting)

1981. Christmas.
B626 **B180** 40pf.+20pf. mult 1·00 85

B181 Peter Beuth

1981. Birth Bicentenary of Peter Beuth (constitutional lawyer).
B627 **B181** 60pf. black and brown 90 80

B182 "Dancer Nijinsky" (Georg Kolbe)

1981. 20th Century Sculptures. Mult.
B628 40pf. Type B **182** 60 45
B629 60pf. "Mother Earth II" (Ernst Barlach) 1·00 70
B630 90pf. "Flora Kneeling" (Richard Scheibe) 1·50 1·20

B183 Arms and View of Spandau, c. 1700

1982. 750th Anniv of Spandau.
B631 **B183** 60pf. multicoloured 1·30 1·10

B184 Daimler Steel-wheeled Car, 1889

1982. Youth Welfare Fund. Motor Cars. Multicoloured.
B632 40pf.+20pf. Type B **184** 90 90
B633 50pf.+25pf. Wanderer "Puppchen", 1911 95 95
B634 60pf.+30p. Adler limousine, 1913 1·20 1·20
B635 90pf.+45pf. DKW "F 1", 1913 1·80 1·80

B185 Sprinting

1982. Sport Promotion Fund. Multicoloured.
B636 60pf.+30pf. Type B **185** 1·20 90
B637 90pf.+45pf. Volleyball 1·70 1·30

B186 Harp

1982. Centenary of Berlin Philharmonic Orchestra.
B638 **B186** 60pf. grey, red & green 1·30 80

B187 "Emigrants reaching Prussian Frontier" (woodcut after drawing by Adolph von Menzel)

1982. 250th Anniv of Salzburg Emigrants' Arrival in Prussia.
B639 **B187** 50pf. stone, deep brown and brown 1·00 65

B188 "Italian Stone Carriers" (Max Pechstein)

1982. Paintings. Multicoloured.
B640 50pf. Type B **188** 1·20 80
B641 80pf. "Two Girls Bathing" (Otto Mueller) 1·60 1·30

B189 Floribunda-Grandiflora

1982. Humanitarian Relief Funds. Roses. Multicoloured.
B642 50pf.+20pf. Type B **189** 1·20 1·00
B643 60pf.+30pf. Hybrid tea 1·30 1·10
B644 80pf.+40pf. Floribunda 1·80 1·60
B645 120pf.+60pf. Miniature rose 3·00 3·00

B190 Castle Theatre, Charlottenburg

1982. 250th Birth Anniv of Carl Gotthard Langhans (architect).
B646 **B190** 80pf. red, grey and black 2·00 1·50

1982. Berlin Views (4th series). As Type B 130.
B647 50pf. black and blue 1·30 80
B648 60pf. black and red 1·40 90
B649 80pf. black and brown 1·80 1·00

DESIGNS: 50pf. Villa Borsig; 60pf. Sts. Peter and Paul Church; 80pf. Villa von der Heydt.

B191 "Adoration of the Kings" (detail from St. Peter altar by Master Bertram)

1982. Christmas.
B650 **B191** 50pf.+20pf. mult 1·20 90

B192 Water Pump, Klausenerplatz

1983. Street Water Pumps. Multicoloured.
B651 50pf. Type B **192** 1·30 90
B652 60pf. Chamissoplatz 1·60 95
B653 80pf. Schloss-strasse 1·90 1·40
B654 120pf. Kuerfurstendamm 2·75 2·30

B193 Royal Prussian Telegraphy Inspectors at St. Anne's Church

1983. 150th Anniv of Berlin–Coblenz Optical-Mechanical Telegraph.
B655 **B193** 80pf. brown 2·20 1·70

B194 Hildebrand & Wolfmuller, 1894

1983. Youth Welfare. Motor Cycles. Mult.
B656 50pf.+20pf. Type B **194** 90 65
B657 60pf.+30pf. Wanderer, 1908 1·40 1·10
B658 80pf.+40pf. D.K.W.-Lomos, 1922 1·60 1·20
B659 120pf.+60pf. Mars, 1925 3·50 2·75

B195 Latin-American Dancing

1983. Sport Promotion Fund. Multicoloured.
B660 80pf.+40pf. Type B **195** 1·90 1·30
B661 120pf.+60pf. Ice hockey 2·75 2·20

B196 "La Barbarina" (painting of Barbara Campanini)

1983. 300th Birth Anniv of Antoine Pesne (artist).
B662 **B196** 50pf. multicoloured 1·20 80

B197 Ringelnatz (silhouette by E. M. Engert)

1983. Birth Centenary of Joachim Ringelnatz (poet and painter).
B663 **B197** 50pf. green, brn & red 1·20 90

B198 Paul Nipkow's Picture Transmission System, 1884

1983. International Broadcasting Exn, Berlin.
B664 **B198** 80pf. multicoloured 2·00 1·50

B199 Mountain Windflower

1983. Humanitarian Relief Funds. Endangered Alpine Flowers. Multicoloured.
B665 50pf.+20pf. Type B **199** 70 70
B666 60pf.+30pf. Alpine auricula 1·20 1·20
B667 80pf.+40pf. Little primrose 2·10 2·10
B668 120pf.+60pf. Einsele's aquilegia 3·00 3·00

B200 Nigerian Yoruba Crib

1983. Christmas.
B669 **B200** 50pf.+20pf. mult 1·10 95

B201 Queen Cleopatra VII (Antikenmuseum)

1984. Art Objects in Berlin Museums. Multicoloured.
B670 30pf. Type B **201** 1·10 90
B671 50pf. Statue of seated couple from Giza Necropolis (Egyptian Museum) 1·60 1·30
B672 60pf. Goddess with pearl turban (Ethnology Museum) 2·00 1·60
B673 80pf. Majolica dish (Applied Arts Museum) 2·50 2·20

B202 "Trichius Fasciatus"

1984. Youth Welfare. Pollinating Insects. Multicoloured.
B674 50pf.+20pf. Type B **202** 1·30 90
B675 60pf.+30pf. "Agrumenia carniolica" 1·30 1·00
B676 80pf.+40pf. "Bombus terrestris" 2·00 1·50
B677 120pf.+60pf. "Eristalis tenax" 2·75 2·50

B203 Hurdling

1984. Sport Promotion Fund. Multicoloured.

B678	60pf.+30pf. Type B **203**	1·80	1·30
B679	80pf.+40pf. Cycling	2·30	1·30
B680	120pf.+60pf. Four-seater kayaks	3·50	3·00

B204 Klausener

1984. 50th Death Anniv of Dr. Erich Klausener (chairman of Catholic Action).

B681	**B204**	80pf. green & dp green	1·20	90

B205 "Electric Power" (K. Sutterlin)

1984. Centenary of Berlin Electricity Supply.

B682	**B205**	50pf. yell, orge & blk	1·00	85

B206 Conference Emblem

1984. 4th European Ministers of Culture Conference, Berlin.

B683	**B206**	60pf. multicoloured	1·30	90

B207 Brehm and White Stork

1984. Death Centenary of Alfred Brehm (zoologist).

B684	**B207**	80pf. multicoloured	2·20	1·50

B208 Heim (bust, Freidrich Tieck)

1984. 150th Death Anniv of Ernst Ludwig Heim (medical pioneer).

B685	**B208**	50pf. black and red	1·20	90

B209 "Listera cordata"

1984. Humanitarian Relief Funds. Orchids. Multicoloured.

B686	50pf.+20pf. Type B **209**	2·00	1·30
B687	60pf.+30pf. "Ophrys insectifera"	2·10	1·30
B688	80pf.+40pf. "Epipactis palustris"	3·00	2·75
B689	120pf.+60pf. "Ophrys coriophora"	5·00	4·50

B210 "Sunflowers on Grey Background"

1984. Birth Centenary of Karl Schmidt-Rottluff (artist).

B690	**B210**	60pf. multicoloured	1·20	90

B211 St. Nicholas

1984. Christmas.

B691	**B211**	50pf.+20pf. mult	1·20	1·10

B212 Bettina von Arnim

1985. Birth Bicentenary of Bettina von Arnim (writer).

B692	**B212**	50pf. black, brn & red	1·10	1·00

B213 Humboldt (statue, Paul Otto)

1985. 50th Death Anniv of Wilhelm von Humboldt (philologist).

B693	**B213**	80pf. black, blue & red	1·80	1·50

B214 Ball in Net

1985. Sport Promotion Fund. Multicoloured.

B694	80pf.+40pf. Type B **214** (50th anniv of basketball in Germany and European championships, Stuttgart)	1·70	1·60
B695	120pf.+60pf. Table tennis (60th anniv of German Table Tennis Association)	2·75	2·50

B215 Stylized Flower

1985. Federal Horticultural Show, Berlin.

B696	**B215**	80pf. multicoloured	1·70	1·20

B216 Bussing Bicycle, 1868

1985. Youth Welfare. International Youth Year. Bicycles. Multicoloured.

B697	50pf.+20pf. Type B **216**	1·40	1·30
B698	60pf.+30pf. Child's tricycle, 1885	1·40	1·30
B699	80pf.+40pf. Jaray bicycle, 1925	1·80	1·80
B700	120pf.+60pf. Opel racing bicycle, 1925	4·25	4·00

B217 Stock Exchange, 1863–1945

1985. 300th Anniv of Berlin Stock Exchange.

B701	**B217**	50pf. multicoloured	1·20	1·00

B218 Otto Klemperer

1985. Birth Centenary of Otto Klemperer (orchestral conductor).

B702	**B218**	60pf. blue	1·60	1·30

B219 Association Emblem

1985. 11th International Gynaecology and Obstetrics Association Congress, Berlin.

B703	**B219**	60pf. multicoloured	1·20	1·00

B220 "FE 3" Television Camera, 1935

1985. International Broadcasting Exn, Berlin.

B704	**B220**	80pf. multicoloured	2·20	1·80

B221 Seal of Brandenburg-Prussia and Preamble of Edict

1985. 300th Anniv of Edict of Potsdam (admitting Huguenots to Prussia).

B705	**B221**	50pf. lilac and black	1·10	80

B222 Flowers, Strawberries and Ladybirds

1985. Humanitarian Relief Funds. Motifs from borders of medieval prayer book. Multicoloured.

B706	50pf.+20pf. Type B **222**	1·40	1·40
B707	60pf.+30pf. Flowers, bird and butterfly	1·80	1·80
B708	80pf.+40pf. Flowers, bee and butterfly	1·80	1·80
B709	120pf.+60pf. Flowers, berries, butterfly and snail	2·75	2·75

B223 "Adoration of the Kings" (detail, Epiphany Altar)

1985. Christmas. 500th Birth Anniv of Hans Baldung Grien (artist).

B710	**B223**	50pf.+20pf. mult	1·40	1·20

B224 Kurt Tucholsky

1985. 50th Death Anniv of Kurt Tucholsky (writer and journalist).

B711	**B224**	80pf. multicoloured	2·00	1·20

B225 Furtwangler and Score

1986. Birth Centenary of Wilhelm Furtwangler (composer and conductor).

B712	**B225**	80pf. multicoloured	2·20	1·80

B226 Rohe and National Gallery

1986. Birth Centenary of Ludwig Mies van der Rohe (architect).

B713	**B226**	50pf. multicoloured	1·40	1·30

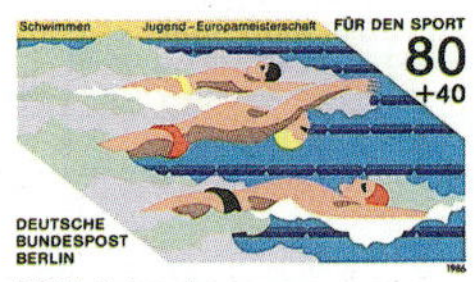

B227 Swimming

1986. Sport Promotion Fund. Multicoloured.

B714	80pf.+40pf. Type B **227** (European Youth Championships, Berlin)	2·00	2·00
B715	120pf.+55pf. Show-jumping (World Championships, Aachen)	2·50	2·50

B228 Glazier

1986. Youth Charity. Trades (1st series). Multicoloured.

B716	50pf.+25pf. Type B **228**	1·30	1·30
B717	60pf.+30pf. Locksmith	1·70	1·70
B718	70pf.+35pf. Tailor	1·70	1·70
B719	80pf.+40pf. Carpenter	2·30	2·30

See also Nos. B765/8.

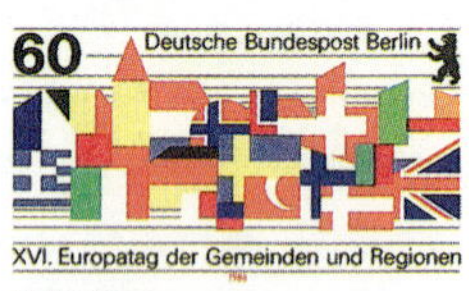

B229 Flags

1986. 16th European Communities Day.

B720	**B229**	60pf. multicoloured	1·20	1·10

B230 Ranke

1986. Death Centenary of Leopold von Ranke (historian).

B721	**B230**	80pf. brown and grey	2·00	1·50

B231 Benn

1986. Birth Centenary of Gottfried Benn (poet).
B722 **B231** 80pf. blue 2·00 1·50

B232 Charlottenburg Gate

1986. Gateways. Multicoloured.
B723 50pf. Type B **232** 1·50 1·50
B724 60pf. Griffin Gate, Glienicke Palace 1·60 1·60
B725 80pf. Elephant Gate, Berlin Zoo 2·00 2·00

B233 "The Flute Concert" (detail, Adolph von Menzel)

1986. Death Bicentenary of Frederick the Great.
B726 **B233** 80pf. multicoloured 1·90 1·50

B234 Cantharus, 1st century A.D.

1986. Humanitarian Relief Funds. Glassware. Multicoloured.
B727 50pf.+25pf. Type B **234** 1·30 1·30
B728 60pf.+30pf. Beaker, 200 A.D. 1·80 1·80
B729 70pf.+35pf. Jug, 3rd century A.D. 1·80 1·80
B730 80pf.+40pf. Diatreta 4th century A.D. 2·50 2·50

B235 "Adoration of the Three Kings" (Ortenberg altarpiece)

1986. Christmas.
B731 **B235** 50pf.+25pf. mult 1·10 1·00

1986. Famous German Women. As Nos. 2149a/54, 2158, 2161, 2166/9a.
B732 5pf. brown and grey 40 2·00
B733 10pf. brown and violet 50 1·90
B734 20pf. blue and red 2·00 4·00
B735 40pf. red and blue 1·50 4·25
B736 50pf. green and brown 2·30 3·25
B737 60pf. lilac and green 1·30 4·25
B738 80pf. brown and green 1·70 3·00
B739 100pf. grey and red 2·30 1·90
B740 130pf. violet and blue 4·50 12·00
B741 140pf. brown and blue 5·25 12·50
B742 170pf. purple and green 3·00 10·50
B743 180pf. purple and blue 4·50 14·50
B744 240pf. brown and blue 4·00 16·00
B745 250pf. blue and mauve 9·25 25·00
B746 300pf. green and plum 9·50 23·00
B747 350pf. brown and black 7·00 18·00
B748 500pf. red and green 10·50 38·00

B236 Berlin, 1650

1987. 750th Anniv of Berlin. (a) As No. 2170.
B760 **833** 80pf. multicoloured 2·10 1·90

(b) Sheet 130×100 mm containing Type B 236 and similar horiz designs. Multicoloured.
MSB761 40pf. Type B **236**; 50pf. Charlottenburg Castle, 1830; 60pf. Turbine Hall; 80pf. Philharmonic and Chamber Music Concert Hall 4·50 4·25

B237 Louise Schroeder

1987. Birth Centenary of Louise Schroeder (Mayor of Berlin).
B762 **B237** 50pf. brown and orange on light brown 1·20 1·20

B238 German Gymnastics Festival, Berlin

1987. Sport Promotion Fund. Multicoloured.
B763 80pf.+40pf. Type B **238** 1·80 1·80
B764 120pf.+55pf. World Judo Championships, Essen 2·75 2·50

1987. Youth Welfare. Trades (2nd series). As Type B 228. Multicoloured.
B765 50pf.+25pf. Cooper 1·30 1·30
B766 60pf.+30pf. Stonemason 1·40 1·40
B767 70pf.+35pf. Furrier 1·80 1·80
B768 80pf.+40pf. Painter/ lacquerer 1·80 1·80

B239 "Bohemian Refugees" (detail of relief, King Friedrich Wilhelm Monument, Berlin-Neukolln)

1987. 250th Anniv of Bohemian Settlement, Rixdorf.
B769 **B239** 50pf. brown and green 1·00 90

B240 New Buildings

1987. International Building Exhibition, Berlin.
B770 **B240** 80pf. silver, black & bl 1·50 1·30

B241 Tree in Arrow Circle

1987. 14th International Botanical Congress, Berlin.
B771 **B241** 60pf. multicoloured 1·00 90

B242 Compact Disc and Gramophone

1987. International Broadcasting Exhibition, Berlin. Centenary of Gramophone Record.
B772 **B242** 80pf. multicoloured 1·40 1·20

B243 5th-century Bonnet Ornament

1987. Humanitarian Relief Funds. Precious Metal Work. Multicoloured.
B773 50pf.+25pf. Type B **243** 90 90
B774 60pf.+30pf. Athene plate, 1st-century B.C. 1·40 1·50
B775 70pf.+35pf. "Armilla" armlet, 1180 1·60 1·70
B776 80pf.+40pf. Snake bracelet, 300 B.C. 2·10 2·20

1987. Tourist Sights. As Nos. 2200/19.
B777 5pf. blue and grey 35 50
B778 10pf. blue and indigo 45 40
B779 20pf. flesh and blue 45 90
B780 30pf. brown and green 1·20 1·10
B781 40pf. brown, red and blue 1·50 2·30
B782 50pf. ochre and blue 1·80 1·30
B783 60pf. green and black 1·60 1·30
B784 70pf. flesh and blue 1·90 3·00
B785 70pf. brown and blue 2·50 5·00
B786 80pf. grey and green 1·70 1·30
B787 100pf. green and orange 1·40 1·60
B788 120pf. green and red 2·75 4·00
B789 140pf. bistre and yellow 2·75 5·00
B790 300pf. flesh and brown 5·50 5·00
B791 350pf. brown and blue 5·75 7·75

B244 "Adoration of the Magi" (13th-century Book of Psalms)

1987. Christmas.
B797 **B244** 50pf.+25pf. mult 1·10 1·00

B245 Heraldic Bear

1988. Berlin, European City of Culture.
B798 **B245** 80pf. multicoloured 2·50 2·30

B246 Old and New Buildings

1988. Centenary of Urania Science Museum.
B799 **B246** 50pf. multicoloured 1·50 1·50

B247 "Large Pure-bred Foal" (bronze)

1988. Birth Centenary of Rene Sintenis (sculptor).
B800 **B247** 60pf. multicoloured 1·10 1·00

B248 Clay-pigeon Shooting

1988. Sport Promotion Fund. Olympic Games. Multicoloured.
B801 60pf.+30pf. Type B **248** 1·80 1·50
B802 80pf.+40pf. Figure skating (pairs) 1·80 1·50
B803 120pf.+55pf. Throwing the hammer 2·30 2·30

B249 Piano, Violin and Cello

1988. Youth Welfare. Music. Multicoloured.
B804 50pf.+25pf. Type B **249** 1·40 1·40
B805 60pf.+30pf. Wind quintet 1·80 1·80
B806 70pf.+35pf. Guitar, recorder and mandolin 1·80 1·80
B807 80pf.+40pf. Children's choir 2·50 2·50

B250 Great Elector and Family in Berlin Castle Gardens

1988. 300th Death Anniv of Friedrich Wilhelm, Great Elector of Brandenburg.
B808 **B250** 50pf. multicoloured 1·30 1·20

B251 Globe

1988. International Monetary Fund and World Bank Boards of Governors Annual Meetings, Berlin.
B809 **B251** 70pf. multicoloured 1·40 1·10

B252 First Train leaving Potsdam Station

1988. 150th Anniv of Berlin–Potsdam Railway.
B810 **B252** 10pf. multicoloured 60 50

B253 "The Collector" (bronze statue)

1988. 50th Death Anniv of Ernst Barlach (artist).
B811 **B253** 40pf. multicoloured 85 60

B254 18th-century Breast Ornament

1988. Humanitarian Relief Funds. Precious Metal Work. Multicoloured.
B812 50pf.+25pf. Type B **254** 1·20 1·20
B813 60pf.+30pf. 16th-century lion-shaped jug 1·50 1·50
B814 70pf.+35pf. 16th-century goblet 1·60 1·60
B815 80pf.+40pf. 15th-century cope clasp 1·90 1·90

B255 "Annunciation to the Shepherds" (illus from Henry the Lion's Gospel Book)

1988. Christmas.
B816 **B255** 50pf.+25pf. mult 1·40 1·20

B256 Volleyball (European Championships)

1989. Sport Promotion Fund. Multicoloured.
B817 100pf.+50pf. Type B **256** 2·75 2·50
B818 140pf.+60pf. Hockey (Champions Trophy) 3·75 3·50

B257 Tigers and Tamer

1989. Youth Welfare. Circus. Multicoloured.

B819		60pf.+30pf. Type B **257**	1·90	1·90
B820		70pf.+30pf. Trapeze artistes	2·30	2·30
B821		80pf.+35pf. Sealions	3·00	3·00
B822		100pf.+50pf. Jugglers	3·75	3·75

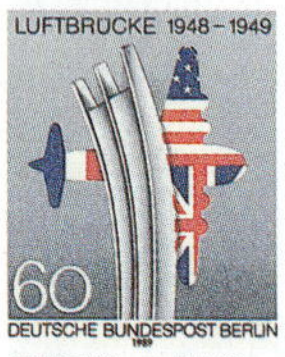

B258 U.S. and U.K. Flags forming Airplane

1989. 40th Anniv of Berlin Airlift.

B823	**B258**	60pf. multicoloured	1·40	1·30

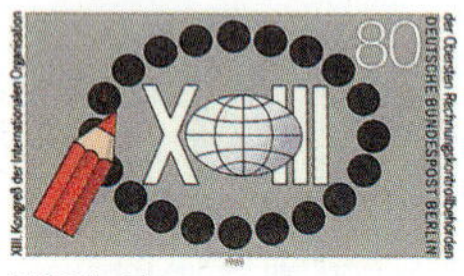

B259 Emblem

1989. 13th International Organization of Chief Accountants Congress.

B824	**B259**	80pf. multicoloured	1·50	1·50

B260 Reuter

1989. Birth Centenary of Ernst Reuter (politician and Mayor of Berlin).

B825	**B260**	100pf. multicoloured	2·00	1·90

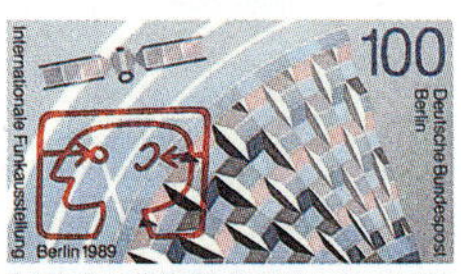

B261 Satellite Radio Waves and T.V. Screen

1989. International Broadcasting Exn, Berlin.

B826	**B261**	100pf. multicoloured	1·80	1·50

B262 Plan of Berlin Zoo and Lenne

1989. Birth Bicentenary of Peter Joseph Lenne (landscape designer).

B827	**B262**	60pf. multicoloured	1·80	1·30

B263 Ossietzky and Masthead of "Die Weltbühne"

1989. Birth Centenary of Carl von Ossietzky (journalist and peace activist).

B828	**B263**	100pf. multicoloured	2·00	1·80

B264 Former School Building

1989. 300th Anniv of Berlin Lycee Francais.

B829	**B264**	40pf. multicoloured	1·00	90

B265 St. Nicholas's Church, Berlin-Spandau

1989. 450th Anniv of Reformation.

B830	**B265**	60pf. multicoloured	1·10	1·00

B266 15th-century Letter Messenger

1989. Humanitarian Relief Funds. Postal Deliveries. Multicoloured.

B831		60pf.+30pf. Type B **266**	2·50	2·50
B832		80pf.+35pf. Brandenburg mail coach, 1700	3·75	3·25
B833		100pf.+50pf. 19th-century Prussian postal messengers	4·50	4·25

B267 "Journalists"

1989. Birth Centenary of Hannah Hoch (painter).

B834	**B267**	100pf. multicoloured	2·20	1·80

B268 Angel

1989. Christmas. 16th-century Carvings by Veit Stoss, St. Lawrence's Church, Nuremberg. Multicoloured.

B835		40pf.+20pf. Type B **268**	1·20	1·20
B836		60pf.+30pf. "Adoration of the Magi"	2·30	2·30

B269 Horse-drawn Passenger Vehicle

1990. 250th Anniv of Public Transport in Berlin.

B837	**B269**	60pf. multicoloured	2·30	1·60

B270 Rudorff

1990. 150th Birth Anniv of Ernst Rudorff (founder of conservation movement).

B838	**B270**	60pf. multicoloured	2·30	1·60

1990. 500th Anniv of Regular European Postal Services. As No. 2297.

B839	**914**	100pf. deep brown, light brown and brown	2·75	2·50

B271 Curtain and Theatre

1990. Cent of National Free Theatre, Berlin.

B840	**B271**	100pf. multicoloured	2·20	2·00

B272 Facade

1990. 40th Anniv of Bundeshaus, Berlin.

B841	**B272**	100pf. multicoloured	3·25	2·20

B273 Water Polo

1990. Sport Promotion Fund. Multicoloured.

B842		100pf.+50pf. Type B **273**	3·75	4·00
B843		140pf.+60pf. Wheelchair basketball	6·00	6·50

B274 Moritz filling Pipe with Gunpowder

1990. Youth Welfare. 125th Anniv of Max and Moritz (characters from books by Wilhelm Busch). Multicoloured.

B844		60pf.+30pf. Type B **274**	1·80	1·80
B845		70pf.+30pf. Max and Moritz running off	2·50	2·50
B846		80pf.+35pf. Moritz slashing sack open	2·75	2·75
B847		100pf.+50pf. Insect on Uncle Fritz's nose	3·25	3·25

B275 Poster

1990. 90th German Catholic Day.

B848	**B275**	60pf. multicoloured	2·00	1·80

B276 "Street Singer" (etching, Ludwig Knaus)

1990. Bicentenary of Barrel-organ.

B849	**B276**	100pf. multicoloured	2·30	2·10

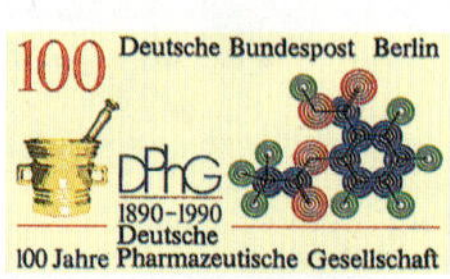

B277 Pestle and Mortar and Diagram of Aspirin Molecule

1990. Centenary of German Pharmaceutical Society.

B850	**B277**	100pf. multicoloured	4·75	3·50

B278 Diesterweg

1990. Birth Bicentenary of Adolph Diesterweg (educationist).

B851	**B278**	60pf. multicoloured	3·00	3·25

B279 Travelling Post Office, 1900

1990. Humanitarian Relief Funds. Posts and Telecommunications. Multicoloured.

B852		60pf.+30pf. Type B **279**	2·50	2·50
B853		80pf.+35pf. Installing telephone lines, 1900	3·25	3·25
B854		100pf.+50pf. Electric parcels van, 1930	4·50	4·50

With the absorption of East Germany into the Federal Republic of Germany on 3 October 1990, separate issues for West Berlin ceased.

GERMAN DEMOCRATIC REPUBLIC (East Germany)

The German Democratic Republic was set up in October 1949 and comprised the former Russian Zone. Its stamps were used in East Berlin.

On 3 October 1990 the territory was absorbed into the German Federal Republic.

E1 Pigeon and Globe

1949. 75th Anniv of U.P.U.

E1	**E1**	50pf. blue and deep blue	14·00	11·00

E2 Postal Workers and Globe

1949. Postal Workers' Congress.

E2	**E2**	12pf. blue	10·50	12·50
E3	**E2**	30pf. red	17·00	21·00

E3 Type **1** of Bavaria and Magnifying Glass

1949. Stamp Day.

E4	**E3**	12pf.+3pf. black	8·50	6·75

E4 Skier

1950. 1st Winter Sports Meeting, Schierke.

E5	**E4**	12pf. violet	8·00	4·25
E6	-	24pf. blue	10·00	7·25

DESIGN: 24pf. Girl skater.

1950. Leipzig Spring Fair. As T 231 but dated "1950".

E7		24pf.+12pf. purple	12·00	10·00
E8		30pf.+14pf. red	14·00	13·50

DESIGNS: 24pf. First Dresden China Fair, 1710; 30pf. First Sample Fair, 1894.

E5 Globe and Sun

1950. 60th Anniv of Labour Day.

E9	**E5**	30pf. red	24·00	18·00

E6 Wilhelm Pieck

E7 Wilhelm Pieck

1950

E12	**E7**	1Dm. green	42·00	5·50
E13	**E7**	2Dm. red	25·00	5·00
E14	**E7**	5Dm. blue	9·50	1·70
E68	**E6**	5pf. green	12·50	3·50
E69	**E6**	12pf. blue	30·00	1·70
E70	**E6**	24pf. brown	28·00	1·40

For 1 and 2Dm. with different portrait of president, see Nos. E320/1 (1953).

E8 Shepherd Playing Pipes

1950. Death Bicentenary of J. S. Bach (composer).

E15	**E8**	12pf.+4pf. green	8·00	5·50
E16	-	24pf.+6pf. olive	8·00	5·50
E17	-	30pf.+8pf. red	15·00	12·50
E18	-	50pf.+16pf. blue	24·00	19·00

DESIGNS: 24pf. Girl playing hand-organ; 30pf. Bach; 50pf. Three singers.

E9 Dove, Globe and Stamp

1950. Philatelic Exhibition (DEBRIA), Leipzig.

E19	**E9**	84pf.+41pf. red	55·00	13·50

E10 L. Euler

1950. 250th Anniv of Academy of Science, Berlin.

E20	**E10**	1pf. grey	5·75	1·70
E21	-	5pf. green	7·00	5·00
E22	-	6pf. violet	13·50	5·00
E23	-	8pf. brown	22·00	12·00
E24	-	10pf. green	20·00	12·00
E25	-	12pf. blue	17·00	3·50
E26	-	16pf. blue	23·00	20·00
E27	-	20pf. purple	21·00	17·00
E28	-	24pf. red	23·00	3·50
E29	-	50pf. blue	35·00	22·00

PORTRAITS: 5pf. A. von Humboldt; 6pf. T. Mommsen; 8pf. W. von Humboldt; 10pf. H. von Helmholtz; 12pf. M. Planck; 16pf. J. Grimm; 20pf. W. Nernst; 24pf. G. W. Leibniz; 50pf. A. von Harnack.

1950. German Stamp Exhibition, "DEBRIA". Sheet 92×52 mm.

MSE29a	Nos. E4 and E19	£190	£170

E11 Miner

1950. 750th Anniv of Mansfeld Copper Mines.

E30	**E11**	12pf. blue	7·50	8·50
E31	-	24pf. red	11·50	9·25

DESIGN: 24pf. Copper smelting.

E12 Ballot Box

1950. East German Elections.

E32	**E12**	24pf. brown	19·00	5·00

E13 Hand, Dove and Burning Buildings

1950. Peace Propaganda. Inscr "ERKAMPFT DEN FRIEDEN".

E33	-	6pf. blue	5·25	3·75
E34	**E13**	8pf. brown	5·25	1·70
E35	-	12pf. blue	7·25	3·75
E36	-	24pf. red	7·25	1·70

DESIGNS (all include hand and dove): 6pf. Tank; 12pf. Atom bomb explosion; 24pf. Rows of gravestones.

E14 Tobogganing

1951. 2nd Winter Sports Meeting, Oberhof.

E37	**E14**	12pf. blue	11·50	8·50
E38	-	24f. red (ski jumper)	14·00	10·00

E15

1951. Leipzig Spring Fair.

E39	**E15**	24pf. red	22·00	17·00
E40	**E15**	50pf. blue	22·00	17·00

E16 Presidents Pieck and Bierut

1951. Visit of Polish President to Berlin.

E41	**E16**	24pf. red	26·00	20·00
E42	**E16**	50pf. blue	26·00	20·00

E17 Mao Tse-tung

E18 Chinese Land Reform

1951. Friendship with China.

E43	**E17**	12pf. green	£110	25·00
E44	**E18**	24pf. red	£130	32·00
E45	**E17**	50pf. blue	£110	30·00

E19 Youth Hoisting Flag

1951. 3rd World Youth Festival. Inscr as in Type E 19. On coloured papers.

E46	**E19**	12pf. brown	14·00	6·75
E47	-	24pf. green and red	14·00	4·25
E48	**E19**	30pf. buff and green	17·00	8·50
E49	-	50pf. red and blue	17·00	8·50

DESIGN: 24pf., 50pf. Three girls dancing.

E20 Symbols of Agriculture & Industry

1951. Five Year Plan.

E50	**E20**	24pf. multicoloured	5·75	2·20

E21 K. Liebknecht

1951. 80th Birth Anniv of Liebknecht (revolutionary).

E51	**E21**	24pf. slate and red	6·00	2·50

E22 Instructing Young Collectors

1951. Stamp Day.

E52	**E22**	12pf. blue	6·25	2·50

E23 P. Bykow and E. Wirth

1951. German–Soviet Friendship.

E53	**E23**	12pf. blue	6·25	4·25
E54	-	24pf. red	6·25	6·00

DESIGN: 24pf. Stalin and Pres. Pieck.

E24 Skier

1952. 3rd Winter Sports Meeting. Oberhof.

E55	**E24**	12pf. green	7·50	4·25
E56	-	24pf. blue	7·50	4·25

DESIGN: 24pf. Ski jumper.

E25 Beethoven

1952. 125th Death Anniv of Beethoven (composer).

E57		12pf. blue and light blue	2·75	70
E58	**E25**	24pf. brown and grey	3·75	1·00

DESIGN: 12pf. Full face portrait.

E26 President Gottwald

1952. Czechoslovak–German Friendship.

E59	**E26**	24pf. blue	3·50	2·00

E27 Bricklayers

1952. National Reconstruction Fund.

E60	-	12pf.+3pf. violet	2·10	50
E61	**E27**	24pf.+6pf. red	1·90	70
E62	-	30pf.+10pf. green	2·30	85
E63	-	50pf.+10pf. blue	2·75	1·70

DESIGNS: 12pf. Workers clearing debris; 30pf. Carpenters; 50pf. Architect and workmen.

E28 Cyclists

1952. 5th Warsaw–Berlin–Prague Cycle Race.

E64	**E28**	12pf. blue	4·25	1·50

E29 Handel

1952. Handel Festival, Halle.

E65	**E29**	6pf. brown	2·75	1·70
E66	-	8pf. red	3·75	3·00
E67	-	50pf. blue	3·75	3·50

COMPOSERS: 8pf. Lortzing; 50pf. Weber.

E31 Victor Hugo

1952. Cultural Anniversaries.

E73	**E31**	12pf. brown	3·75	5·50
E74	-	20pf. green	3·75	5·50
E75	-	24pf. red	3·75	5·50
E76	-	35pf. blue	5·75	7·25

PORTRAITS: 20pf. Leonardo da Vinci; 24pf. N. Gogol; 35pf. Avicenna.

E32 Machinery, Dove and Globe

1952. Leipzig Autumn Fair.

E77	**E32**	24pf. red	2·75	1·30
E78	**E32**	35pf. blue	2·75	2·10

E33 F. L. Jahn

1952. Death Centenary of Jahn (patriot).

E79	**E33**	12pf. blue	2·50	1·30

E34 University Building

1952. 450th Anniv of Halle-Wittenberg University.

E80	**E34**	24pf. green	2·50	1·20

E35 Dove, Stamp and Flags

1952. Stamp Day.

E81	**E35**	24pf. brown	3·25	1·30

E36 Dove, Globe and St. Stephen's Cathedral, Vienna

1952. Vienna Peace Congress.

E97	**E36**	24pf. red	1·90	2·50
E98	**E36**	35pf. blue	1·90	4·50

E37 President Pieck

1953. President's Birthday.

E320	**E37**	1Dm. olive	1·80	40
E321	**E37**	2Dm. brown	1·80	45

E38 Karl Marx

1953. 70th Death Anniv of Marx.

E102	-	6pf. red and green	1·90	70
E103	-	10pf. brown and green	5·25	1·00
E104	-	12pf. red and green	1·40	70
E105	-	16pf. blue and red	3·75	2·10
E106	-	20pf. brown and yellow	1·90	1·30
E107	**E38**	24pf. brown and red	3·75	85
E108	-	35pf. yellow and purple	3·75	3·25
E109	-	48pf. brown and green	2·75	85
E110	-	60pf. red and brown	4·75	3·00
E111	-	84pf. brown and blue	4·25	2·10

MSE111a Two sheets, each 148×104 mm. (a) the six vert, and (b) the four horiz designs Set of 2 sheets £225 £300

DESIGNS—VERT: 6pf. Flag and foundry; 12pf. Flag and Spassky Tower, Kremlin; 20pf. Marx reading from "Das Kapital"; 35pf. Marx addressing meeting; 48pf. Marx and Engels. HORIZ: 10pf. Marx, Engels and "Communist Manifesto"; 16pf. Marching crowd; 60pf. Flag and workers; 84pf. Marx in medallion and Stalin Avenue, Berlin.

In each case the flag shows heads of Marx, Engels, Lenin and Stalin.

E39 Gorky

1953. 85th Birth Anniv of Maksim Gorky (writer).

E112	**E39**	35pf. brown	45	40

E40 Cyclists

1953. 6th International Cycle Race.

E113	**E40**	24pf. green	2·75	2·50
E114	-	35pf. blue	1·40	1·30
E115	-	60pf. brown	1·90	1·90

DESIGNS—VERT: 35pf. Cyclists and countryside; 60pf. Cyclists in town.

E41 H. Von Kleist

1953. 700th Anniv of Frankfurt-on-Oder.

E116	**E41**	16pf. brown	1·90	2·30
E117	-	20pf. green	1·10	1·70
E118	-	24pf. red	1·90	2·30
E119	-	35pf. blue	1·90	2·50

DESIGNS—HORIZ: 20pf. St. Mary's Church; 24pf. Frankfurt from R. Oder; 35pf. Frankfurt Town Hall and coat of arms.

E42 Miner

1953. Five Year Plan. (a) Design in minute dots.

E120	**E42**	1pf. black	1·90	60
E121	-	5pf. green	2·40	1·00
E122	-	6pf. violet	2·40	80
E123	-	8pf. brown	3·25	1·00
E124	-	10pf. blue	2·40	80
E125	-	12pf. blue	2·40	85
E126	-	15pf. violet	3·75	1·80
E127	-	16pf. violet	6·25	2·30
E128	-	20pf. green	5·75	2·30
E129	-	24pf. red	10·50	1·00
E130	-	25pf. green	7·50	3·00
E131	-	30pf. red	7·50	3·50
E132	-	35pf. blue	19·00	3·50
E133	-	40pf. red	19·00	2·75
E134	-	48pf. mauve	19·00	2·30
E135	-	60pf. blue	19·00	5·25
E136	-	80pf. turquoise	19·00	4·75
E137	-	84pf. brown	19·00	13·00

(b) Design in lines.

E153	**E42**	1pf. black	90	20
E155	-	6pf. violet	3·50	45
E156	-	8pf. brown	3·75	40
E159	-	12pf. turquoise	3·50	40
E160	-	15pf. lilac	23·00	60
E162	-	16pf. violet	4·50	90
E163	-	20pf. green	95·00	90
E165	-	24pf. red	7·00	40
E168	-	35pf. blue	6·25	1·10
E169	-	40pf. red	13·00	1·10
E171	-	48pf. mauve	12·50	1·60
E173	-	60pf. blue	19·00	1·80
E175	-	80pf. turquoise	4·50	1·80
E176	-	84pf. brown	22·00	1·80
E310A	-	5pf. green	35	20
E311A	-	10pf. blue	6·25	20
E312A	-	10pf. green	60	45
E313A	-	15pf. violet	35	20
E314A	-	20pf. red	35	20
E315A	-	25pf. green	35	30
E316A	-	30pf. red	80	30
E317A	-	40pf. mauve	1·10	30
E318A	-	50pf. blue	1·80	30
E319A	-	70pf. brown	2·75	30

DESIGNS—VERT: 5pf. Woman turning wheel; 6pf. Workmen shaking hands; 8pf. Students; 10pf. grn Engineers; 10pf. bl and 12pf. Agricultural and industrial workers; 15pf. mve Tele-typist; 15pf. vio and 16pf. Foundry worker; 20pf. grn Workers' health centre, Elster; 20pf. red and 24pf. Stalin Avenue, Berlin; 25pf. Locomotive construction workers; 30pf. Folk dancers; 35pf. Stadium; 40pf. red, Scientist; 40pf. mve, 48pf. Zwinger, Dresden; 50pf., 60pf. Launching ship; 80pf. Farm workers; 70pf., 84pf. Workman and family.

E43 Mechanical Grab

1953. Leipzig Autumn Fair.

E138	**E43**	24pf. brown	3·00	2·40
E139	-	35pf. green	4·00	2·75

DESIGN: 35pf. Potato-harvester.

E44 G. W. von Knobelsdorff and Opera House, Berlin

1953. German Architects.

E140	**E44**	24pf. mauve	1·80	1·20
E141	-	35pf. slate	2·20	1·90

DESIGN: 35pf. B. Neumann and Wurzburg Palace.

E45 Lucas Cranach

1953. 400th Death Anniv of Cranach (painter).

E142	**E45**	24pf. brown	3·50	1·50

E46 Nurse and Patient

1953. Red Cross.

E143	**E46**	24pf. red and brown	3·00	2·75

E47 Postman delivering Letters

1953. Stamp Day.

E144	**E47**	24pf. blue	2·75	85

E48 Lion

1953. 75th Anniv of Leipzig Zoo.

E145	**E48**	24pf. brown	2·20	85

E49 Muntzer and Peasants

1953. German Patriots.

E146	**E49**	12pf. brown	1·60	80
E147	-	16pf. brown	1·60	80
E148	-	20pf. red	1·60	50
E149	-	24pf. blue	1·60	50
E150	-	35pf. green	2·75	2·20
E151	-	48pf. sepia	2·75	1·60

DESIGNS: 16pf. Baron vom Stein and scroll; 20pf. Von Schill and cavalry; 24pf. Blucher and infantry; 35pf. Students marching; 48pf. Barricade, 1848 Revolution.

E50 Franz Schubert

1953. 125th Death Anniv of Schubert.

E152	**E50**	48pf. brown	3·00	1·80

E52 G. E. Lessing (writer)

1954. 225th Birth Anniv of Lessing.

E177	**E52**	20pf. green	2·30	1·10

E53 Conference Table and Crowd

1954. Four-Power Conference, Berlin.

E178	**E53**	12pf. blue	1·90	95

E54 Stalin

1954. 1st Death Anniv of Stalin.

E179	**E54**	20pf. brown, orange and grey	3·00	95

E55 Racing Cyclists

1954. 7th International Cycle Race.

E180	**E55**	12pf. brown	1·50	95
E181	-	24pf. green	2·40	1·60

DESIGN: 24pf. Cyclists racing through countryside.

E56 Folk Dancing

1954. 2nd German Youth Assembly.

E182	**E56**	12pf. green	1·30	1·10
E183	-	24pf. red	1·30	1·10

DESIGN: 24pf. Young people and flag.

E57 F. Reuter

1954. 80th Death Anniv of Reuter (author).

E184	**E57**	24pf. brown	2·00	1·30

E58 Dam and Forest

1954. Flood Relief Fund.

E185	**E58**	24pf.+6pf. green	80	1·00

E59 E. Thalmann

1954. 10th Death Anniv of Thalmann (politician).

E186	**E59**	24pf. brown, bl & orge	1·20	1·00

E60 Exhibition Buildings

1954. Leipzig Autumn Fair.

E187	**E60**	24pf. red	95	55
E188	**E60**	35pf. blue	95	75

1954. (a) Nos. E155, etc surch in figures.

E189	5pf. on 6pf. violet	1·10	40
E190	5pf. on 8pf. brown	1·60	40
E191	10pf. on 12pf. turquoise	1·30	40
E192	15pf. on 16pf. lilac	1·10	40
E194	20pf. on 24pf. red	2·10	55
E195	40pf. on 48pf. mauve	3·50	90
E196	50pf. on 60pf. blue	3·50	90
E197	70pf. on 84pf. brown	11·50	90

(b) No. E129 similarly surch.

E193a	20pf. on 24pf. red	1·20	55

E62 President Pieck

1954. 5th Anniv of German Democratic Republic.
E198 **E62** 20pf. brown 3·00 1·10
E199 **E62** 35pf. blue 3·00 1·30

E63 Stamp of 1953

1954. Stamp Day.
E200 **E63** 20pf. mauve 1·90 95
MSE200b 60×80 mm. No. E200 imperf (sold at Dm.30) 55·00 55·00

E64 Russian Pavilion

1955. Leipzig Spring Fair.
E201 **E64** 20pf. purple 1·10 95
E202 - 35pf. blue (Chinese Pavilion) 2·00 1·90

1955. Flood Relief Fund. Surch in figures.
E203 **E58** 20+5pf. on 24pf.+6pf. green 90 70

E66 "Women of All Nations"

1955. 45th Anniv of International Women's Day.
E204 **E66** 10pf. green 1·40 65
E205 **E66** 20pf. red 1·40 65

E67 Parade of Workers

1955. International Conference of Municipal Workers, Vienna.
E206 **E67** 10pf. black and red 1·20 1·20

E68 Monument to Fascist Victims, Brandenburg

1955. International Liberation Day.
E207 **E68** 10pf. blue 1·20 1·30
E208 **E68** 20pf. mauve 1·40 1·50
MSE208a 73×99 mm. Nos. E207/8 21·00 33·00

E69 Monument to Russian Soldiers, Treptow

1955. 10th Anniv of Liberation.
E209 **E69** 20pf. mauve 1·50 95

E70 Schiller (poet)

1955. 150th Death Anniv of Schiller.
E210 **E70** 5pf. green 3·00 2·75
E211 - 10pf. blue 45 30
E212 - 20pf. brown 45 30
MSE212a 73×100 mm. Nos. E210/12 (+15pf.) 25·00 38·00
PORTRAITS OF SCHILLER: 10pf. Full-face; 20pf. Facing left.

E71 Cyclists

1955. 8th International Cycle Race.
E213 **E71** 10pf. turquoise 65 60
E214 **E71** 20pf. red 90 75

E72 Karl Liebknecht

1955. German Labour Leaders.
E215 **E72** 5pf. green 35 25
E216 - 10pf. blue 55 30
E217 - 15pf. violet 7·50 6·00
E218 - 20pf. red 55 30
E219 - 25pf. blue 55 30
E220 - 40pf. red 2·75 30
E221 - 60pf. brown 55 30
PORTRAITS: 10pf. A. Bebel; 15pf. F. Mehring; 20pf. E. Thalmann; 25pf. Clara Zetkin; 40pf. Wilhelm Liebknecht; 60pf. Rosa Luxemburg.

E73 Pottery

1955. Leipzig Autumn Fair.
E222 - 10pf. blue 75 50
E223 **E73** 20pf. green 75 50
DESIGN: 10pf. Camera and microscope.

E74 Workers and Charter

1955. 10th Anniv of Land Reform.
E224 **E74** 5pf. green 6·25 5·75
E225 - 10pf. blue 90 35
E226 - 20pf. red 90 45
DESIGNS—VERT: 10pf. Bricklayers at work. HORIZ: 20pf. Combine-harvesters.

E75 "Solidarity"

1955. 10th Anniv of People's Solidarity Movement.
E227 **E75** 10pf. blue 80 50

E76 Engels Speaking

1955. 135th Birth Anniv of Engels.
E228 **E76** 5pf. blue and yellow 35 25
E229 - 10pf. violet and yellow 75 25
E230 - 15pf. green and yellow 75 25
E231 - 20pf. brown and orange 1·50 25
E232 - 30pf. brown and grey 9·75 11·00
E233 - 70pf. green and red 2·75 40
MSE233a 148×105 mm. Nos. E228/33 70·00 95·00
DESIGNS: 10pf. Engels and Marx; 15pf. Engels and newspaper; 20pf. Portrait facing right; 30pf. Portrait facing left; 70pf. 1848 Revolution scene.

E77 Magdeburg Cathedral

1955. Historic Buildings.
E234 **E77** 5pf. sepia 80 55
E235 - 10pf. green 80 55
E236 - 15pf. purple 80 5·75
E237 - 20pf. red 80 95
E238 - 30pf. brown 13·50 17·00
E239 - 40pf. blue 1·80 95
DESIGNS: 10pf. State Opera House, Berlin; 15pf. Old Town Hall, Leipzig; 20pf. Town Hall, Berlin; 30pf. Erfurt Cathedral; 40pf. Zwinger, Dresden.

E78 Georg Agricola

1955. 400th Death Anniv of Agricola (scholar).
E240 **E78** 10pf. brown 80 65

E79 "Portrait of a Young Man" (Durer)

1955. Dresden Gallery Paintings. (1st series).
E241 **E79** 5pf. brown 70 25
E242 - 10pf. brown 70 25
E243 - 15pf. purple 33·00 30·00
E244 - 20pf. sepia 70 25
E245 - 40pf. green 70 45
E246 - 70pf. blue 1·80 95
PAINTINGS: 10pf. "The Chocolate Girl" (Liotard); 15pf. "Portrait of a Boy" (Pinturicchio); 20pf. "Self-portrait with Saskia" (Rembrandt); 40pf. "Maiden with Letter" (Vermeer); 70pf. "Sistine Madonna" (Raphael).
See also Nos. E325/30 and E427/31.

E80 Mozart

1956. Birth Bicent of Mozart (composer).
E247 **E80** 10pf. green 13·00 12·00
E248 - 20pf. brown 4·00 1·90
PORTRAIT: 20pf. Facing left.

E81 Ilyushin Il-14P DDR-ABA

1956. Establishment of East German Lufthansa Airways.
E249 - 5pf. multicoloured 14·50 12·00
E250 **E81** 10pf. green 90 25
E251 - 15pf. blue 90 25
E252 - 20pf. red 90 25
DESIGNS: 5pf. Lufthansa flag; 15pf. View of Ilyushin Il-14P DDR-ABF airplane from below; 20pf. Ilyushin Il-14P DDR-ABA airplane facing left.

E82 Heinrich Heine (poet)

1956. Death Centenary of Heine.
E253 **E82** 10pf. green 14·00 7·25
E254 - 20pf. red 2·75 80
PORTRAIT: 20pf. Full-face.

E83 Mobile Cranes

1956. Leipzig Spring Fair.
E255 **E83** 20pf. red 75 45
E256 **E83** 35pf. blue 1·30 1·10

E84 E Thalmann

1956. 70th Birth Anniv of Thalmann (communist leader).
E257 **E84** 20pf. black, brn & red 60 45
MSE257a 73×100 mm. No. E257 10·50 30·00

E85 Hand, Laurels and Cycle Wheel

1956. 9th International Cycle Race.
E258 **E85** 10pf. green 75 45
E259 - 20pf. red 75 45
DESIGN: 20pf. Arms of Warsaw, Berlin and Prague and cycle wheel.

E86 New Buildings, Old Market-place

1956. 750th Anniv of Dresden.
E260 **E86** 10pf. green 25 20
E261 - 20pf. red 25 20
E262 - 40pf. violet 2·10 2·50
DESIGNS: 20pf. Elbe Bridge; 40pf. Technical High School.

E87 Workman

1956. 10th Anniv of Industrial Reforms.
E263 **E87** 20pf. red 50 30

E88 Robert Schumann

1956. Death Centenary of Schumann (composer). (a) Type E 88 (wrong music).

E264	**E88**	10pf. green	2·75	2·00
E265	**E88**	20pf. red	1·10	20

E88a Robert Schumann

(b) Type E 88a (correct music).

E266	**E88a**	10pf. green	6·50	2·50
E267	**E88a**	20pf. red	3·50	45

E89 Footballers

1956. 2nd Sports Festival, Leipzig.

E268	**E89**	5pf. green	25	15
E269	-	10pf. blue	25	15
E270	-	15pf. purple	2·75	1·40
E271	-	20pf. red	25	15

DESIGNS: 10pf. Javelin thrower; 15pf. Hurdlers; 20pf. Gymnast.

E90 T. Mann (author)

1956. 1st Death Anniv of Thomas Mann.

E272	**E90**	20pf. black	1·20	70

E91 J. B. Cisinski

1956. Birth Centenary of Cisinski (poet).

E273	**E91**	50pf. brown	1·10	70

E92 Lace

1956. Leipzig Autumn Fair.

E274	**E92**	10pf. green and black	40	40
E275	-	20pf. pink and black (Sailing dinghy)	40	40

E93 Buchenwald Memorial

1956. Concentration Camp Memorials Fund.

E276	**E93**	20pf.+80pf. red	1·30	4·75

For similar stamp see No. E390.

E94 Torch and Olympic Rings

1956. Olympic Games.

E277	**E94**	20pf. brown	45	30
E278	-	35pf. slate	90	50

DESIGN: 35pf. Greek athlete.

E95

1956. 500th Anniv of Greifswald University.

E279	**E95**	20pf. red	55	40

E96 Postal Carrier, 1450

1956. Stamp Day.

E280	**E96**	20pf. red	55	40

E97 E. Abbe

1956. 110th Anniv of Zeiss Factory, Jena.

E281	**E97**	10pf. green	20	15
E282	-	20pf. brown	20	15
E283	-	25pf. blue	50	40

DESIGNS—HORIZ: 20pf. Factory buildings; 25pf. Carl Zeiss.

E98 "Negro"

1956. Human Rights Day.

E284		5pf. green on olive	1·70	1·50
E285	**E98**	10pf. brown on pink	25	25
E286	-	25pf. blue on lavender	25	25

DESIGNS: 5pf. "Chinese"; 25pf. "European".

E99 Indian Elephants

1956. Berlin Zoological Gardens. Centres in grey.

E287	**E99**	5pf. black	25	20
E288	-	10pf. green	25	20
E289	-	15pf. purple	5·25	3·75
E290	-	20pf. red	30	20
E291	-	25pf. brown	35	20
E292	-	30pf. blue	45	20

DESIGNS: 10pf. Greater flamingos; 15pf. Black rhinoceros; 20pf. Mouflon; 25pf. European bison; 30pf. Polar bear.

1956. Egyptian Relief Fund. No. E237 surch HELFT AGYPTEN +10.

E293	20pf.+10pf. red	55	45

1956. Hungarian Socialists' Relief Fund. No. E237 surch HELFT DEM SOZIALISTISCHEN UNGARN +10.

E294	20pf.+10pf. red	55	45

E103 "Frieden" (freighter)

1957. Leipzig Spring Fair.

E295	**E103**	20pf. red	30	25
E296	-	25pf. blue	30	25

DESIGN: 25pf. Class E251 electric locomotive.

E104 Silver Thistle

1957. Nature Protection Week.

E297	**E104**	5pf. brown	20	15
E298	-	10pf. green	2·75	2·75
E299	-	20pf. brown	30	15

DESIGNS: 10pf. Green lizard; 20pf. Lady's slipper orchid.

E105 Friedrich Froebel and Children

1957. 175th Birth Anniv of Froebel (educator).

E300		10pf. black and green	1·60	1·30
E301	**E105**	20pf. black and brown	20	15

DESIGN: 10pf. Children at play.

E106 Ravensbruck Memorial

1957. Concentration Camp Memorials Fund.

E302	**E106**	5pf.+5pf. green	20	30
E303	-	20pf.+10pf. red	40	60

DESIGN—HORIZ: 20pf. Memorial and environs.

For similar stamp to No. E303 see No. E453.

E107 Cycle Race Route

1957. 10th International Cycle Race.

E304	**E107**	5pf. orange	45	40

E108 Miner

1957. Coal Mining Industry.

E305	-	10pf. green	25	20
E306	-	20pf. brown	25	20
E307	**E108**	25pf. blue	2·75	1·20

DESIGNS (39×21 mm): 10pf. Mechanical shovel and coal trucks; 20pf. Gantry.

E109 Henri Dunant and Globe

1957. Int Red Cross Day. Cross in red.

E308	**E109**	10pf. brown and green	25	30
E309	-	25pf. brown and blue	25	30

DESIGN: 25pf. H. Dunant wearing hat, and globe.

E110 Joachim Jungius (botanist)

1957. Scientists' Anniversaries.

E322	**E110**	5pf. brown	1·80	1·10
E323	-	10pf. green	25	20
E324	-	20pf. brown	25	20

PORTRAITS: 10pf. L. Euler (mathematician); 20pf. H. Hertz (physicist).

1957. Dresden Gallery Paintings (2nd series). As Type E 79.

E325	5pf. sepia	35	20
E326	10pf. green	35	20
E327	15pf. brown	35	20
E328	20pf. red	35	20
E329	25pf. purple	35	20
E330	40pf. grey	5·25	2·50

PAINTINGS—VERT: 5pf. "The Holy Family" (Mantegna); 10pf. "The Dancer, Barbarina Campani" (Carriera); 15pf. "Portrait of Morette" (Holbein the Younger); 20pf. "The Tribute Money" (Titian); 25pf. "Saskia with a Red Flower" (Rembrandt); 40pf. "A Young Standard-bearer" (Piazetta).

E111 Clara Zetkin and Flower

1957. Birth Cent of Clara Zetkin (patriot).

E331	**E111**	10pf. green and red	80	40

E112 Bertolt Brecht (dramatist)

1957. 1st Death Anniv of Bertolt Brecht.

E332	**E112**	10pf. green	35	30
E333	**E112**	25pf. blue	80	30

E113 Congress Emblem

1957. 4th World Trade Unions Congress.

E334	**E113**	20pf. black and red	70	45

E114 Fair Emblem

1957. Leipzig Autumn Fair.

E335	**E114**	20pf. red	30	25
E336	**E114**	25pf. blue	40	25

E115 Savings Bank Book

1957. Savings Week.

E337	**E115**	10pf. black and green on grey	95	90
E338	**E115**	20pf. black and mauve on grey	35	40

E116 Postrider of 1563

1957. Stamp Day.

E339	**E116**	5pf. blue on brown	65	30

E117 Revolutionary's Rifle and Red Flag

1957. 40th Anniv of Russian Revolution.

E340	**E117**	10pf. green and red	25	25
E341	**E117**	25pf. blue and red	25	35

E118 Artificial Satellite

1957. International Geophysical Year.

E342	**E118**	10pf. blue	50	40
E343	-	20pf. red	60	25
E344	-	25pf. blue	2·40	1·80

DESIGNS: 20pf. Stratosphere balloon; 25pf. Ship using echo-sounder.

E119 Professor Ramin

1957. "National Prize" Composers.

E345	**E119**	10pf. black and green	1·10	1·20
E346	-	20pf. black and orange	25	20

PORTRAIT: 20pf. Professor Abendroth.

E120 Ernst Thalmann

1957. National Memorials Fund. East German War Victims. Portraits in grey.

E347	**E120**	20pf.+10pf. mauve	20	20
E348	-	25pf.+15pf. blue	20	20
E349	-	40pf.+20pf. violet	45	55
MSE349a 140×95 mm. Nos. E347/9 (+20pf.)			60·00	£120

PORTRAITS: 25pf. R. Breitscheid; 40pf. Father P. Schneider.
For other stamps as Type E **120** see Nos. E374/8, E448/52, E485/7, E496/500, E540/4 and E588/92.

E121

E122

1957. Air.

E350	**E121**	5pf. black and grey	2·75	20
E351	**E121**	20pf. black and red	25	20
E352	**E121**	35pf. black and violet	25	20
E353	**E121**	50pf. black and brown	45	20
E354	**E122**	1Dm. olive and yellow	1·30	20
E355	**E122**	3Dm. brown & yellow	2·20	45
E356	**E122**	5Dm. blue and yellow	5·25	85

E123 Fair Emblem

1958. Leipzig Spring Fair.

E357	**E123**	20pf. red	30	20
E358	**E123**	25pf. blue	45	30

E124 Transmitting Aerial and Posthorn

1958. Communist Postal Conf, Moscow.

E359	**E124**	5pf. black and grey	1·00	80
E360	-	20pf. red	45	25

DESIGN—HORIZ: 20pf. Aerial as in 5pf. but posthorn above figures of value.

E125 "Zille at play"

1958. Birth Cent of Heinrich Zille (painter).

E361	**E125**	10pf. drab and green	3·00	1·90
E362	-	20pf. drab and red	75	30

DESIGN—VERT: 20pf. Self-portrait of Zille.

E126 Max Planck

1958. Birth Cent of Max Planck (physicist).

E363		10pf. olive	1·70	1·50
E364	**E126**	20pf. mauve	45	25

DESIGN—VERT: 10pf. "h" (symbol of Planck's Constant).

E127 Breeding Cow

1958. 6th Markkleeberg Agricultural Exn. Inscr "6 Landwirtschaftausstellung der DDR in Markkleeberg".

E365	**E127**	5pf. grey	2·75	1·90
E366	-	10pf. green	45	25
E367	-	20pf. red	45	25

DESIGNS (39×22½ mm): 10pf. Chaff-cutter; 20pf. Beet-harvester.

E128 Charles Darwin

1958. Centenary of Darwin's Theory of Evolution and Bicentenary of Linnaeus's Plant Classification System. Portraits in black.

E368	**E128**	10pf. green	1·60	1·60
E369	-	20pf. red	25	20

PORTRAIT—HORIZ: 20pf. Linnaeus (Carl von Linne) inscr "200 JAHRE SYSTEMA NATURAE".

E129 Congress Emblem

1958. 5th German Socialist Unity Party Congress.

E370	**E129**	10pf. red	45	40

E130 "The Seven Towers of Rostock", Liner and Freighters

1958. Rostock Port Reconstruction.

E371	-	10pf. green	20	15
E372	**E130**	20pf. orange	55	40
E373	-	25pf. blue	1·30	1·40

DESIGNS: 10pf. "Freundschaft" (freighter) at quayside; 25pf. "Frieden" (freighter) in Rostock harbour.

1958. "Resistance Fighters". As Type E 120. Portraits in grey.

E374		5pf.+5pf. brown	25	95
E375		10pf.+5pf. green	20	95
E376		15pf.+10pf. violet	20	3·75
E377		20pf.+10pf. brown	20	95
E378		25pf.+15pf. black	75	14·00

PORTRAITS—VERT: 5pf. A. Kuntz; 10pf. R. Arndt; 15pf. Dr. K. Adams; 20pf. R. Renner; 25pf. W. Stoecker.

E131 Mare and Foal

1958. "Grand Prix of the D.D.R." Horse Show.

E379	**E131**	5pf. sepia	2·75	3·00
E380	-	10pf. green	25	25
E381	-	20pf. brown	25	25

DESIGNS: 10pf. Horse-trotting; 20pf. Racing horses.

E132 J. A. Komensky ("Comenius")

1958. Komensky Commem. Centres in black.

E382	**E132**	10pf. green	1·80	1·50
E383	-	20pf. brown	25	25

DESIGN: 20pf. Komensky with pupils (from an old engraving).

E133 Camp Bugler

1958. 10th Anniv of East German "Pioneer" Organization.

E384	**E133**	10pf.+5pf. green	35	35
E385	-	20pf.+10pf. red	45	35

DESIGN—VERT: 20pf. Young Pioneer saluting.

E134 University Seal

1958. 400th Anniv of Friedrich Schiller University, Jena.

E386	**E134**	5pf. black and grey	1·80	1·40
E387	-	20pf. grey and red	35	25

DESIGN: 20pf. University building.

E135 Model with Hamster-lined Coat, and Leipzig Central Railway Station

1958. Leipzig Autumn Fair.

E388	**E135**	10pf. brown and green	25	25
E389	-	25pf. black and blue	35	30

DESIGN: 25pf. Model with Karakul fur coat, and Leipzig Old Town Hall.

1958. Concentration Camp Memorials Fund. As Type E 93 but additionally inscr "14. SEPTEMBER 1958" in black.

E390		20pf.+20pf. red	60	60

E136 Soldier climbing Wall

1958. 1st Summer Military Games, Leipzig.

E391	**E136**	10pf. brown and green	1·80	1·40
E392	-	20pf. yellow and brown	20	20
E393	-	25pf. red and blue	20	1·90

DESIGNS: 20pf. Games emblem; 25pf. Marching athletes with banner.

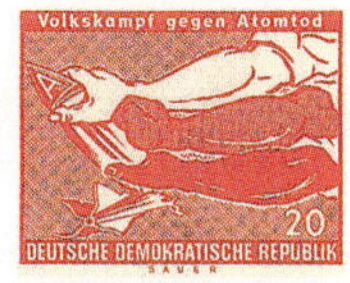

E137 Warding off the Atomic Bomb

1958. Campaign Against Atomic Warfare.

E394	**E137**	20pf. red	20	20
E395	**E137**	25pf. blue	55	30

E138 17th-century Mail Cart

1958. Stamp Day.

E396	**E138**	10pf. green	2·75	1·70
E397	-	20pf. red	45	20

DESIGN: 20pf. Modern postal sorting train and Baade-Bonin 152 jetliner.

E139 Revolutionary and Soldier

1958. 40th Anniv of November Revolution.

E398	**E139**	20pf. purple and red	11·50	19·00

E140 Brandenburg Gate, Berlin

1958. Brandenburg Gate Commemoration.

E399	**E140**	20pf. red	55	25
E400	**E140**	25pf. blue	3·00	2·00

E141 "Girl's Head" (bas-relief)

1958. Antique Art Treasures.

E401	**E141**	10pf. black and green	1·80	1·60
E402	-	20pf. black and red	25	20

DESIGN: 20pf. "Large Head" (from Pergamon frieze).
See also Nos. E475/8.

E142 Negro and European Youths

1958. 10th Anniv of Declaration of Human Rights.
E403 **E142** 10pf. black and green 25 15
E404 - 25pf. black and blue 2·20 1·50
DESIGN: 25pf. Chinese and European girls.

E143 O. Nuschke

1958. 1st Death Anniv of Vice-Premier Otto Nuschke.
E405 **E143** 20pf. red 40 35

E144 "The Red Flag" (Party Newspaper)

1958. 40th Anniv of German Communist Party.
E406 **E144** 20pf. red 50 40

E145 Pres. Pieck

1959. Pres. Pieck's 83rd Birthday.
E407 **E145** 20pf. red 55 30
For 20pf. black see No. E517.

E146 Rosa Luxemburg (revolutionary)

1959. 40th Death Anniv of Rosa Luxemburg and Karl Liebknecht. Centres in black.
E408 **E146** 10pf. green 2·30 1·80
E409 - 20pf. red 25 25
DESIGN—HORIZ: 20pf. Liebknecht-(revolutionary).

E147 Concert Hall, Leipzig

1959. 150th Birth Anniv of Felix Mendelssohn-Bartholdy (composer).
E410 **E147** 10pf. green on green 90 95
E411 - 25pf. blue on blue 1·80 3·25
DESIGN—HORIZ: 25pf. Opening theme of Symphony in A Major ("The Italian").

E148 "Schwarze Pumpe" plant

1959. Leipzig Spring Fair. Inscr as in Type E 148.
E412 **E148** 20pf. red 20 20
E413 - 25pf. blue 50 30
DESIGN—HORIZ: 25pf. Various cameras.

E149 Boy holding Book for Girl

1959. 5th Anniv of "Youth Consecration".
E414 **E149** 10pf. black on green 2·00 1·30
E415 - 20pf. black on salmon 25 20
DESIGN: 20pf. Girl holding book for boy.

E150 Handel's Statue, Oboe and Arms of Halle

1959. Death Bicentenary of Handel. Centre in black.
E416 **E150** 10pf. green 2·00 1·50
E417 - 20pf. red 25 20
DESIGN: 20pf. Portrait of Handel (after oil painting by Thomas Hudson).

E151 A. von Humboldt and Jungle Scene

1959. Death Centenary of Alexander von Humboldt (naturalist).
E418 **E151** 10pf. green 1·90 1·60
E419 - 20pf. red 35 25
DESIGN: 20pf. As Type E **151** but with view of sleigh in forest.

E152 Posthorn

1959. Socialist Countries' Postal Ministers Conference, Berlin.
E420 **E152** 20pf. black, yell & red 25 25
E421 **E152** 25pf. black, yell & bl 1·00 1·10

E153 Grey Heron

1959. Nature Preservation.
E422 **E153** 5pf. lilac, black & blue 20 15
E423 - 10pf. brn, sep & turq 20 15
E424 - 20pf. multicoloured 20 15
E425 - 25pf. multicoloured 45 25
E426 - 40pf. yell, blk & grey 7·00 4·25
DESIGNS: 10pf. Eurasian bittern; 20pf. Lily of the valley and "Inachis io" (butterfly); 25pf. Eurasian beaver; 40pf. "Apis mellifera" (bee) and willow catkin.

1959. Dresden Gallery Paintings as Type E 79 (3rd series).
E427 5pf. olive 20 20
E428 10pf. green 20 20
E429 20pf. orange 20 20
E430 25pf. brown 45 30
E431 40pf. red 6·50 3·75
PAINTINGS—VERT: 5pf. "The Vestal Virgin" (Kauffman); 10pf. "The Needlewoman" (Metsu); 20pf. "Mlle. Lavergne reading a letter" (Liotard); 25pf. "Old woman with a brazier" (Rubens); 40pf. "Young man in black coat" (Hals).

E154 Great Cormorant

1959. "Birds of the Homeland". Centres and inscriptions in black.
E432 **E154** 5pf. yellow 20 25
E433 - 10pf. green 20 25
E434 - 15pf. violet 6·00 3·75
E435 - 20pf. pink 30 25
E436 - 25pf. blue 30 25
E437 - 40pf. red 35 25
BIRDS: 10pf. Black Stork; 15pf. Eagle Owl; 20pf. Black Grouse; 25pf. Hoopoe; 40pf. Peregrine Falcon.

E155

1959. 7th World Youth Festival, Vienna.
E438 **E155** 20pf. red 20 20
E439 - 25pf. blue 90 75
DESIGN—HORIZ: 25pf. White girl embracing negro girl.

E156 Hoop Exercises

1959. 3rd German Gymnastic and Sports Festival, Leipzig.
E440 **E156** 5pf.+5pf. brown 20 20
E441 - 10pf.+5pf. green 20 20
E442 - 20pf.+10pf. red 20 20
E443 - 25pf.+10pf. blue 25 20
E444 - 40pf.+20pf. purple 2·40 1·00
DESIGNS: 10pf. High jumping; 20pf. Vaulting; 25pf. Club exercises; 40pf. Fireworks over Leipzig Stadium.

E157 Modern Leipzig Building

1959. Leipzig Autumn Fair.
E445 **E157** 20pf. grey and red 45 40
See also Nos. E483/4.

E158 Glass Tea-set

1959. 75 Years of Jena Glassware.
E446 **E158** 10pf. turquoise 20 20
E447 - 25pf. blue 2·30 1·40
DESIGN—VERT: 25pf. Laboratory retorts.

1959. Ravensbruck Concentration Camp Victims. As Type E 120. Portraits in black.
E448 5pf.+5pf. brown 20 20
E449 10pf.+5pf. green 20 20
E450 15pf.+10pf. violet 20 20
E451 20pf.+10pf. mauve 20 20
E452 25pf.+15pf. blue 70 1·50
PORTRAITS: 5pf. T. Klose; 10pf. K. Niederkirchner; 15pf. C. Eisenblatter; 20pf. O. Benario-Prestes; 25pf. M. Grollmuss.

1959. Concentration Camp Memorials Fund. As No. E303 but inscr "12. SEPTEMBER 1959" in black.
E453 20pf.+10pf. red 60 40

E159 "Russian Pennant on the Moon"

1959. Landing of Russian Rocket on the Moon.
E454 **E159** 20pf. red 80 45

E160 E. German Flag and Combine-harvester

1959. 10th Anniv of German Democratic Republic. Designs as Type E 160 showing E. German flag in black, red and yellow. Inscriptions in black and red on coloured paper.
E455 **E160** 5pf. buff 20 20
E456 - 10pf. grey 20 20
E457 - 15pf. pale yellow 20 20
E458 - 20pf. lilac 20 20
E459 - 25pf. pale olive 20 20
E460 - 40pf. yellow 20 20
E461 - 50pf. salmon 20 20
E462 - 60pf. turquoise 20 20
E463 - 70pf. pale green 20 20
E464 - 1Dm. brown 45 40
DESIGNS—East German flag and: 10pf. "Fritz Heckert" convalescent home; 15pf. Zwinger Palace, Dresden; 20pf. Steel worker; 25pf. Industrial chemist; 40pf. Leipzig Stadium; 50pf. Woman tractor-driver; 60pf. Ilyushin Il-14M airplane; 70pf. Shipbuilding; 1Dm. East Germany's first atomic reactor.

E161 J. R. Becher

1959. 1st Death Anniv of Becher (poet).
E465 **E161** 20pf. slate and red 1·60 30

E162 Schiller

1959. Birth Bicentenary of Schiller (poet).
E466 - 10pf. green on green 1·80 1·60
E467 **E162** 20pf. lake on pink 65 1·90
DESIGN: 10pf. Schiller's house, Weimar.

E163 18th-century Courier and Milestone

1959. Stamp Day.
E468 **E163** 10pf. green 1·50 1·50
E469 - 20pf. lake 20 20
DESIGN: 20pf. Postwoman on motor cycle.

E164 Eurasian Red Squirrels

1959. Forest Animals.
E470 **E164** 5pf. red, brown & grey 45 20
E471 - 10pf. lt brn, brn & grn 55 20
E472 - 20pf. multicoloured 55 20
E473 - 25pf. multicoloured 65 25
E474 - 40pf. yellow, brown and blue 11·00 4·25
ANIMALS: 10pf. Brown hares; 20pf. Roe deer; 25pf. Red deer; 40pf. Lynx.

1959. Antique Art Treasures (2nd series). As Type E 141.
E475 5pf. black and yellow 20 20
E476 10pf. black and green 20 20
E477 20pf. black and red 20 20
E478 25pf. black and blue 1·30 95
DESIGNS: 5pf. Attic goddess (about 580 B.C.); 10pf. Princess of Tell el-Amarna (about 1360 B.C.); 20pf. Bronze horse of Toprak-Kale, Armenia (7th-century B.C.). HORIZ: (49×28 mm): 25pf. Altar of Zeus, Pergamon (about 160 B.C.).

E165 Boxing

1960. Olympic Games. As Type E 165 inscr "OLYMPISCHE SOMMERSPIELE 1960" or "WINTERSPIELE" etc (20pf.). Centres and inscriptions in bistre.
E479 **E165** 5pf. brown 5·25 3·00
E480 - 10pf. green 20 20
E481 - 20pf. red 20 20
E482 - 25pf. blue 25 20
DESIGNS: 10pf. Running; 20pf. Ski jumping; 25pf. Sailing.

1960. Leipzig Spring Fair. As Type E 157 but inscr "LEIPZIGER FRUHJAHRSMESSE 1960".
E483 20pf. grey and red 20 20
E484 25pf. grey and blue 35 20

DESIGNS: 20pf. Northern Entrance, Technical Fair; 25pf. Ring Fair Building.

1960. Sachsenhausen Concentration Camp Victims (1st issue). As Type E 120. Portraits in black.

E485		5pf.+5pf. drab	25	20
E486		10pf.+5pf. myrtle	25	20
E487		20pf.+10pf. purple	25	20

PORTRAITS: 5pf. L. Erdmann; 10pf. E. Schneller; 20pf. L. Horn.

See also Nos. E496/500.

E166 Purple Foxglove

1960. Medicinal Flowers. Background in pale drab.

E488	**E166**	5pf. red and green	25	20
E489	-	10pf. olive and green	25	20
E490	-	15pf. red and green	25	20
E491	-	20pf. violet & turq	25	20
E492	-	40pf. red, green & brn	6·50	3·00

FLOWERS: 10pf. Camomile; 15pf. Peppermint; 20pf. Poppy; 40pf. Wild Rose.

E167 Lenin

1960. 90th Birth Anniv of Lenin.

E493	**E167**	20pf. red	45	30

1960. Re-opening of Rostock Port. No. E371 optd Inbetriebnahme des Hochsee-hafens 1. Mai 1960.

E494		10pf. green	55	45

E169 Russian Soldier and Liberated Prisoner

1960. 15th Anniv of Liberation.

E495	**E169**	20pf. red	45	40

1960. Sachsenhausen Concentration Camp Victims (2nd issue). As Type E 120. Portraits in black.

E496		10pf.+5pf. green	20	20
E497		15pf.+5pf. violet	1·20	95
E498		20pf.+10pf. lake	20	20
E499		25pf.+10pf. blue	25	30
E500		40pf.+20pf. brown	2·40	2·10

PORTRAITS: 10pf. M. Lademann; 15pf. L. Breunig; 20pf. M. Thesen; 25pf. G. Sandtner; 40pf. H. Rothbarth.

E170 Model and Plan of "Fritz Heckert" (Liner)

1960. Launching of Cruise Liner "Fritz Heckert".

E501	**E170**	5pf. slate, red & yell	20	20
E502	-	10pf.+5pf. black, red and yellow	20	20
E503	-	20pf.+10pf. black, red and blue	25	20
E504	-	25pf. black, yellow and blue	5·25	5·75

DESIGNS: 10pf. Liner under construction at Wismar; 20pf. Liner off Stubbenkammer; 25pf. Liner and Russian cruiser "Aurora" at Leningrad.

E171 Lenin Statue, Eisleben

1960. Lenin-Thalmann Statues.

E505	**E171**	10pf. green	30	35
E506	-	20pf. red	30	35

DESIGN: 20pf. Thalmann statue, Pushkin, U.S.S.R.

E172 Masked Dancer (statuette)

1960. 250th Anniv of Porcelain Industry, Meissen. Centres and inscriptions in blue. Figures in colours given.

E507	**E172**	5pf. orange	25	20
E508	-	10pf. green	25	20
E509	-	15pf. purple	4·25	4·25
E510	-	20pf. red	25	25
E511	-	25pf. olive	25	25

DESIGNS: 10pf. Dish inscr with swords and years "1710 1960"; 15pf. Otter; 20pf. Potter; 25pf. Coffee-pot.

E173 Racing Cyclist

1960. World Cycling Championships.

E512	**E173**	20pf.+10pf. mult	25	30
E513	-	25pf.+10pf. brown, drab and blue	1·80	3·25

DESIGN (38½×21 mm): 25pf. Racing cyclists on track.

E174 Opera House, Leipzig

1960. Leipzig Autumn Fair.

E514	**E174**	20pf. grey and red	30	20
E515	-	25pf. brown and blue	45	40

DESIGN: 25pf. Export goods.

E175 Sachsenhausen Memorial

1960. Concentration Camp Memorials Fund.

E516	**E175**	20pf.+10pf. red	45	40

1960. President Pieck Mourning issue.

E517	**E145**	20pf. black	55	40
MSE517a		88×108 mm. No. E517. Imperf	1·60	2·75

E176 18th-century Rook

1960. 14th Chess Olympiad, Leipzig. German Chessmen.

E518	**E176**	10pf.+5pf. green	20	20
E519	-	20pf.+10pf. purple	20	20
E520	-	25pf.+10pf. blue	1·20	3·50

DESIGNS: 20pf. 18th-century knight; 25pf. 14th-century knight.

E177 Mail Vans

1960. Stamp Day.

E521	**E177**	20pf. yell, blk & mve	25	25
E522	-	25pf. mauve, blk & bl	3·25	2·10

DESIGN: 25pf. 19th-century railway mail coach.

E178 Medal of 1518 showing Hans Burgkmair (painter)

1960. 400th Anniv of Dresden Art Collections.

E523	**E178**	20pf. ochre, green and buff	20	25
E524	-	25pf. black and blue	1·80	2·40

DESIGN: 25pf. "Dancing Peasants" (after Durer).

E179 Count N. von Gneisenau

1960. Birth Bicent of Count N. von Gneisenau.

E525	**E179**	20pf. black and red	20	25
E526	-	25pf. blue	1·60	1·80

DESIGN: 25pf. Similar portrait but vert.

E180 R. Virchow

1960. 250th Anniv of Berlin Charity and 150th Anniv of Humboldt University, Berlin. Centres in black.

E527	**E180**	5pf. ochre	20	15
E528	-	10pf. green	20	15
E529	-	20pf. brown	20	15
E530	-	25pf. blue	20	15
E531	-	40pf. red	2·75	2·00

DESIGNS—As Type E **180** (Berlin Charity); 10pf. Robert Koch; 40pf. W. Griesinger. (Humboldt University); 20pf. University building and statues of William and Alexander von Humboldt; 25pf. Plaque with profiles of Von Humboldt brothers.

E181 Scientist with Notebook

1960. Chemical Workers' Day.

E532	**E181**	5pf. grey and red	20	15
E533	-	10pf. green and orange	20	15
E534	-	20pf. red and blue	20	15
E535	-	25pf. blue and yellow	2·20	2·75

DESIGNS: 10pf. Chemical worker with fertiliser; 20pf. Girl worker with jar, and Trabant car; 25pf. Laboratory assistant and synthetic dress.

E182 "Young Socialists' Express" (double-deck train)

1960. 125th Anniv of German Railways.

E536	**E182**	10pf. black and green	25	30
E537	-	20pf. black and red	25	30
E538	-	25pf. black and blue	5·25	5·75

DESIGNS—As Type E **182**: 25pf. Stephenson locomotive "Adler" (1835) and Class V180 diesel locomotive. (43×25½ mm): 20pf. Sassnitz Harbour station and train ferry "Sassnitz".

E183 President Pieck

1961. 85th Birth Anniv of President Pieck.

E539	**E183**	20pf. red and black	45	40

1961. Concentration Camp Victims. As Type E 120. Portraits in black.

E540		5pf.+5pf. green	20	20
E541		10pf.+5pf. green	20	20
E542		15pf.+5pf. violet	1·70	3·00
E543		20pf.+10pf. red	20	20
E544		25pf.+10pf. blue	20	20

PORTRAITS: 5pf. W. Kube; 10pf. H. Gunther; 15pf. Elvira Eisenschneider; 20pf. Hertha Lindner; 25pf. H. Tschape.

E184 High-voltage Switchgear

1961. Leipzig Spring Fair. Inscr as in Type E 184.

E545	**E184**	10pf. slate and green	35	25
E546	-	25pf. slate and blue	55	35

DESIGN: 25pf. Ilyushin Il-12 over Fair Press Centre.

E185 Lilienstein Saxony

1961. Landscapes and Historical Buildings.

E547		5pf. grey	20	20
E548		10pf. green	20	20
E549	**E185**	20pf. brown	20	30
E550	-	20pf. red	20	20
E551	-	25pf. blue	20	30

DESIGNS—VERT: 5pf. Ruins of Rudelsburg; 10pf. Wartburg; 20pf. (No. E550), Town Hall, Wernigerode. HORIZ: 25pf. Brocken, Oberharz.

E186 "Ros" (Trawler)

1961. Deep Sea Fishing Industry.

E552	**E186**	10pf. green	20	15
E553	-	20pf. purple	20	15
E554	-	25pf. blue	20	15
E555	-	40pf. violet	2·75	2·10

DESIGNS: 20pf. Hauling nets; 25pf. "Robert Koch" (trawler); 40pf. Processing Atlantic cod.

E187 Cosmonaut in Capsule

1961. 1st Manned Space Flight. Inscr "12.4.1961".

E556		10pf. red and green	1·30	95
E557	**E187**	20pf. red	1·30	95
E558	-	25pf. blue	5·25	6·25

DESIGNS: 10pf. Space rocket leaving globe; 25pf. Capsule's parachute descent.

E188 Marx, Engels, Lenin and Demonstrators

1961. 15th Anniv of German Socialist Unity Party.

E559	E188	20pf. red	55	40

E189 Common Zebra

1961. Centenary of Dresden Zoo.

E560	E189	10pf. black and green	5·75	5·75
E561	-	20pf. black and mauve	90	45

DESIGN: 20pf. Eastern black-and-white colobus.

E190 Pioneers playing Volleyball

1961. Pioneers Meeting, Erfurt. Mult.

E562	10pf.+5pf. Type E **190**	20	15
E563	20pf.+10pf. Folk dancing	20	15
E564	25pf.+10pf. Model airplane construction	3·50	3·25

E191 High Jump

1961. 3rd European Women's Gymnastic Championships, Leipzig.

E565	E191	10pf. green	20	15
E566	-	20pf. mauve	20	15
E567	-	25pf. blue	6·25	6·25

DESIGNS—VERT: 20pf. Gymnast. HORIZ: 25pf. Exercise on parallel bars.

E192 Salt Miners and Castle

1961. Halle (Saale) Millenary.

E568	E192	10pf. black, yell & grn	2·75	1·70
E569	-	20pf. black, yell & red	20	20

DESIGN: 20pf. Scientist and Five Towers of Halle.

E193 Canadian Canoe

1961. World Canoeing Championships.

E570		5pf. blue and grey	3·25	3·50
E571	E 193	10pf. green and grey	20	15
E572	-	20pf. purple and grey	20	15

DESIGNS: 5pf. Folding canoe; 20pf. Canadian two-seater canoe.

E194 Line-casting

1961. World Angling Championships.

E573	E194	10pf. green and blue	2·75	2·75
E574	-	20pf. lake and blue	45	20

DESIGN: 20pf. River-fishing.

E195 Old Weigh-house, Leipzig

1961. Leipzig Autumn Fair.

E575	E195	10pf. olive and green	20	15
E576	-	25pf. blue & ultram	1·20	40

DESIGN: 25pf. Old Stock Exchange, Leipzig.
See also Nos. E612/14.

E196 Walter Ulbricht

1961. Type E 196 or larger, 24×29 mm (Dm. values).

E577	5pf. blue	25	20
E578	10pf. green	35	30
E579	15pf. purple	55	20
E580	20pf. red	75	60
E581	25pf. turquoise	35	20
E582	30pf. red	20	20
E582a	35pf. green	55	60
E583	40pf. violet	25	20
E584	50pf. blue	30	20
E584a	60pf. green	35	30
E585	70pf. brown	35	20
E585a	80pf. blue	55	45
E586	1Dm. green	90	65
E587	2Dm. brown	1·80	65

See also Nos. E805/6, E1197/8 and E1255.

1961. Concentration Camps Memorials Fund. As Type E 120. Portraits in grey and black.

E588	5pf.+5pf. green	20	30
E589	10pf.+5pf. green	20	30
E590	20pf.+10pf. mauve	20	30
E591	25pf.+10pf. blue	20	30
E592	40pf.+20pf. lake	2·30	7·00

PORTRAITS: 5pf. C. Schonhaar; 10pf. H. Baum; 20pf. Liselotte Herrmann. HORIZ: (41×32½ mm): 25pf. Sophie and Hans Scholl; 40pf. Hilde and Hans Coppi.

E197 Dahlia

1961. International Horticultural Exn.

E593	-	10pf. red, yellow & grn	35	30
E594	E197	20pf. red, yellow & brn	35	30
E595	-	40pf. red, yellow & bl	8·75	10·50

FLOWERS: 10pf. Tulip. 40pf. Rose.

E198 Liszt and Berlioz (after Von Kaulbach and Prinzhofer)

1961. 150th Birth Anniv of Liszt (composer).

E596	E198	5pf. black	25	20
E597	-	10pf. green	2·50	2·75
E598	-	20pf. red	25	20
E599	-	25pf. blue	3·00	3·25

DESIGNS: 10pf. Young hand of Liszt (from French sculpture, Liszt Museum, Budapest); 20pf. Liszt (after Rietschel); 25pf. Liszt and Chopin (after Bartolini and Bovy).

E199 TV Camera and Screen

1961. Stamp Day.

E600	E199	10pf. black and green	1·90	3·25
E601	-	20pf. black and red	20	30

DESIGNS: 20pf. Studio microphone and radio tuning-scale.

E200 G. S. Titov with Young Pioneers

1961. 2nd Russian Manned Space Flight.

E602	E200	5pf. violet and red	25	20
E603	-	10pf. green and red	25	20
E604	-	15pf. mauve and blue	8·75	10·50
E605	-	20pf. red and blue	25	25
E606	-	25pf. blue and red	25	25
E607	-	40pf. blue and red	1·60	1·40

DESIGNS—HORIZ: 15pf. Titov in space-suit; 20pf. Titov receiving Karl Marx Order from Ulbricht; 25pf. "Vostok 2" rocket in flight; 40pf. Titov and Ulbricht in Berlin. VERT: 10pf. Titov in Leipzig.

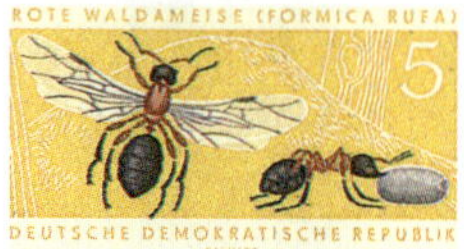

E201 "Formica ruta" (Ant)

1962. Fauna Protection Campaign (1st series).

E608	E201	5pf. yellow, brn & blk	4·00	7·00
E609	-	10pf. brown and green	20	15
E610	-	20pf. brown and red	20	15
E611	-	40pf. yellow, blk & vio	65	45

DESIGNS: 10pf. Weasels; 20pf. Eurasian common shrews; 40pf. Common long-eared bat.
See also Nos. E699/703.

1962. Leipzig Spring Fair. As Type E 195.

E612	10pf. sepia and green	20	20
E613	20pf. black and red	35	20
E614	25pf. purple and blue	1·00	1·10

BUILDINGS: 10pf. Zum Kaffeebaum; 20pf. Gobliser Schlosschen; 25pf. Romanus-Haus.

E203 Pilot and Mikoyan Gurevich MiG-17 Jet Fighters

1962. 6th Anniv of East German People's Army.

E615	E203	5pf. blue	20	15
E616	-	10pf. green	20	15
E617	-	20pf. red	20	15
E618	-	25pf. blue	30	45
E619	-	40pf. brown	2·00	1·80

DESIGNS: 10pf. Soldier and armoured car; 20pf. Factory guard; 25pf. Sailor and Habich I class minesweeper; 40pf. Tank and driver.

E204 Danielle Casanova

1962. Concentration Camps Memorial Fund. Camp Victims.

E620	E204	5pf.+5pf. black	20	15
E621	-	10pf.+5pf. green	20	15
E622	-	20pf.+10pf. purple	20	15
E623	-	25pf.+10pf. blue	25	20
E624	-	40pf.+20pf. purple	2·00	3·00

PORTRAITS: 10pf. Julius Fucik; 20pf. Johanna J. Schaft; 25pf. Pawel Finder; 40pf. Soja A. Kosmodemjanskaja.

E205 Racing Cyclists and Prague Castle

1962. 15th Int Peace Cycle Race. Mult.

E625	10pf. Type E **205**	20	15
E626	20pf.+10pf. Cyclists and Palace of Culture and Science, Warsaw	20	25
E627	25pf. Cyclist and Town Hall, East Berlin	1·70	1·80

E206 Johann Fichte

1962. Birth Bicent of Fichte (philosopher).

E628	-	10pf. green and black	1·70	2·50
E629	E206	20pf. red and black	25	30

DESIGN: 10pf. Fichte's birthplace, Ramenau.

E207 Cross of Lidice

1962. 20th Anniv of Destruction of Lidice.

E630	E207	20pf. red and black	20	20
E631	E207	25pf. blue and black	1·10	1·50

E208 Dimitrov at Leipzig

1962. 80th Birth Anniv of G. Dimitrov (Bulgarian statesman).

E632	E208	5pf. black & turquoise	65	70
E633	-	20pf. black and red	20	25

DESIGN: 20pf. Dimitrov as Premier of Bulgaria.

E209 Maize-planting machine

1962. 10th D.D.R. Agricultural Exhibition, Markkleeberg. Multicoloured.

E634	10pf. Type E **209**	20	15
E635	20pf. Milking shed	20	15
E636	40pf. Combine-harvester	2·00	2·00

E210 "Frieden" (freighter)

1962. 5th Baltic Sea Week, Rostock.

E637	-	10pf. turquoise & blue	20	15
E638	-	20pf. red and yellow	20	15
E639	E210	25pf. bistre and blue	2·40	2·50

DESIGNS—HORIZ: 10pf. Map of Baltic Sea inscr "Meer des Friedens" ("Sea of Peace"). VERT: 20pf. Hochhaus, Rostock.

E211/E212 Brandenburg Gate, Berlin and Youth of Three Races

E213-E214 Folk Dancers and Youth of Three Nations

1962. World Youth Festival Games, Helsinki. Multicoloured.

E640		5pf. Type E **211**	2·20	2·75
E641		5pf. Type E **212**	2·20	2·75
E642		10pf.+5pf. Type E **213**	45	25
E643		15pf.+5pf. Type E **214**	45	25
E644		20pf. Dove	2·20	2·75
E645		20pf. National Theatre, Helsinki	2·20	2·75

Nos. 640/11 and 644/5 were issued together as a se-tenant block of four and Nos. 642/3 in horizontal pairs, both forming composite designs.

E217 Free-style Swimming

1962. 10th European Swimming Championships, Leipzig. Design in blue: value colours given.

E646	**E217**	5pf. orange	20	15
E647	-	10pf. blue	20	15
E648	-	20pf.+10pf. mauve	20	15
E649	-	25pf. blue	20	15
E650	-	40pf. violet	1·30	1·40
E651	-	70pf. brown	20	15

DESIGNS: 10pf. Back stroke; 20pf. High diving; 25pf. Butterfly stroke; 40pf. Breast stroke; 70pf. Water-polo.

On Nos. E649/51 the value, etc, appears at the foot of the design.

E218 Municipal Store, Leipzig

1962. Leipzig Autumn Fair.

E652	**E218**	10pf. black and green	20	20
E653	-	20pf. black and red	35	25
E654	-	25pf. black and blue	1·10	95

DESIGNS: 20pf. Madler Arcade, Leipzig; 25pf. Leipzig Airport and Ilyushin Il-14M airplane.

E219 "Transport and Communications"

1962. 10th Anniv of "Friedrich List" Transport High School, Dresden.

E655	**E219**	5pf. black and blue	45	25

E219a P. Popovich and A. Nikolaev

1962. "Vostok 3" and "Vostok 4" Space Flights. Sheet 89×108 mm.

MSE655a	E **219a**	70pf. green, blue and yellow	2·40	5·50

E220 Rene Blieck

1962. Concentration Camp Victims. Memorials Fund.

E656	**E220**	5pf.+5pf. blue	20	15
E657	-	10pf.+5pf. green	20	15
E658	-	15pf.+5pf. violet	20	15
E659	-	20pf.+10pf. purple	25	25
E660	-	70pf.+30pf. brown	2·20	3·25

PORTRAITS—As Type E **220**: 10pf. Dr. A. Klahr; 15pf. J. Diaz; 20pf. J. Alpari. HORIZ: (39×21 mm): 70pf. Seven Cervi brothers.

E221 Television Screen and Call-sign

1962. Stamp Day and 10th Anniv of German Television.

E661	**E221**	20pf. purple and green	20	20
E662	-	40pf. purple & mauve	1·90	2·40

DESIGN: 40pf. Children with stamp album (inscr "TAG DER BRIEFMARKE 1962").

E222 G. Hauptmann

1962. Birth Centenary of Gerhart Hauptmann (author).

E663	**E222**	20pf. black and red	55	25

E222a Gagarin and "Vostok 1"

1962. Five Years of Russian Space Flights. Sheet 127×108 mm. Multicoloured.

MSE663a		5pf. Dogs "Belka" and "Strelka", 10pf. Type **E222a**; 15pf. "Sputniks 1, 2 and 3"; 20pf. Titov and "Vostok 2"; 25pf. "Luniks 1 and 2"; 30pf. Nikolaev and Popovich; 40pf. Interplanetary station and spacecraft; 50pf. "Lunik 3"	35·00	55·00

E223 Pierre de Coubertin

1963. Birth Centenary of Pierre de Coubertin (reviver of Olympic Games).

E664	**E223**	20pf. red and grey	20	20
E665	-	25pf. blue and ochre	1·90	3·00

DESIGN: 25pf. Stadium.

E224 Party Flag

1963. 6th Socialists Unity Party Day.

E666	**E224**	10pf. red, black & yell	35	25

E225 Insecticide Sprayer

1963. Malaria Eradication.

E667	**E225**	20pf. black, red & orge	20	20
E668	-	25pf. multicoloured	20	20
E669	-	50pf. multicoloured	1·50	1·90

DESIGNS: 25pf. Rod of Aesculapius; 50pf. Mosquito. Map is common to all values.

E226 Red Fox (Silver Fox race)

1963. International Fur Auctions, Leipzig.

E670	**E226**	20pf. blue and red	25	25
E671	-	25pf. indigo and blue	1·80	2·75

DESIGN: 25pf. Karakul lamb.

E227 Barthels Hof, Leipzig (1748–1872)

1963. Leipzig Spring Fair.

E672	**E227**	10pf. black and yellow	25	25
E673	-	20pf. black and brown	35	30
E674	-	25pf. black and blue	1·30	1·50

LEIPZIG BUILDINGS: 20pf. New Town Hall; 25pf. Clock-tower, Karl-Marx Square.

E227a Laboratory Worker and Apparatus

1963. "Chemistry for Freedom and Socialism". Sheet 105×74 mm with Type E 227a and similar horiz design. Imperf. No gum.

MSE674a		50pf. blue and black (E **227a**); 70pf. blue and grey (oil refinery)	4·50	24·00

E228 J. G. Seume (poet) and Scene from "Syracuse Walk" (Birth Bicent)

1963. Cultural Anniversaries. Design and portrait in black.

E675	**E228**	5pf. yellow	20	20
E676	-	10pf. turquoise	20	20
E677	-	20pf. orange	20	20
E678	-	25pf. blue	2·10	2·20

DESIGNS: 10pf. F. Hebbel (poet) and scene from "Mary Magdalene" (150th birth anniv); 20pf. G. Buchner (poet) and scene from "Woyzeck" (150th birth anniv); 25pf. R. Wagner (composer) and scene from "The Flying Dutchman" (150th birth anniv).

E229 Nurse bandaging Patient

1963. Centenary of Red Cross.

E679	**E229**	10pf. multicoloured	1·30	1·40
E680	-	20pf. black, grey and red	20	20

DESIGN: 20pf. Barkas type "B 1000" ambulance.

E230 W. Bohne (runner)

1963. Concentration Camps Memorial Fund. Sportsmen Victims (1st series). Designs in black.

E681	**E230**	5pf.+5pf. yellow	20	20
E682	-	10pf.+5pf. green	20	20
E683	-	15pf.+5pf. mauve	20	20
E684	-	20pf.+10pf. pink	20	25
E685	-	25pf.+10pf. blue	2·40	9·50

SPORTSMEN: 10pf. W. Seelenbinder (wrestler); 15pf. A. Richter (cyclist); 20pf. H. Steyer (footballer); 25pf. K. Schlosser (mountaineer).

See also Nos. E704/8.

E231 Gymnastics

1963. 4th East German Gymnastics and Sports Festival, Leipzig. Inscr in black.

E686	**E231**	10pf.+5pf. yellow and green	20	15
E687	-	20pf.+10pf. violet and red	20	15
E688	-	25pf.+10pf. green and blue	4·00	4·00

DESIGNS: 20pf. Dederon kerchief exercises; 25pf. Relay-racing.

E232 E. Pottier (lyricist) and Opening Bars of the "Internationale"

1963. 75th Anniv of "Internationale" (song).

E689	**E232**	20pf. black and red	20	20
E690	-	25pf. black and blue	1·20	1·70

DESIGN: 25pf. As 20pf. but portrait of P.-C. Degeyter.

E 233 V. Tereshkova and "Vostok 6"
E 234 V. Bykovsky and "Vostok 5"

1963. 2nd "Team" Manned Space Flights.

E691	**E233**	20pf. black, grey & bl	90	20
E692	**E234**	20pf. black, grey & bl	90	20

Nos. E691/2 were printed together, se-tenant, forming a composite design.

E235 Motor Cyclist competing in "Motocross", Apolda

1963. World Motor Cycle Racing Championships.

E693	**E235**	10pf. emerald & green	4·00	4·50
E694	-	20pf. red and pink	25	25
E695	-	25pf. blue & light blue	25	25

DESIGNS—HORIZ (39×22 mm): 20pf. Motor cyclist; 25pf. Two motor cyclists cornering.

E236 Treblinka Memorial

1963. Erection of Treblinka Memorial, Poland.

E696	**E236**	20pf. blue and red	35	30

E237/E238 Transport

1963. Leipzig Autumn Fair.

E697	**E237**	10pf. multicoloured	90	15
E698	**E238**	10pf. multicoloured	90	15

Nos. E697/8 were printed together, se-tenant, forming a composite design.

1963. Fauna Protection Campaign (2nd series). As Type E 201. Fauna in natural colours, background colours given.

E699	10pf. green	20	15
E700	20pf. red	20	15
E701	30pf. red	25	25
E702	50pf. blue	4·00	4·00
E703	70pf. brown	65	70

DESIGNS: 10pf. Stag-beetle; 20pf. Salamander; 30pf. European pond tortoise; 50pf. Green toad; 70pf. West European hedgehogs.

1963. Concentration Camps Memorial Fund. Sportsmen Victims (2nd series). As Type E 230. Designs in black.

E704	5pf.+5pf. yellow	20	20
E705	10pf.+5pf. green	20	20
E706	15pf.+5pf. violet	20	20
E707	20pf. 10pf. red	20	20
E708	40pf.+20pf. blue	3·75	5·75

SPORTSMEN: 5pf. H. Tops (Gymnast); 10pf. Kate Tucholla (hockey-player); 15pf. R. Seiffert (swimmer); 20pf. E. Grube (athlete); 40pf. K. Biedermann (canoeist).

E239 N. von Gneisenau and G. L. von Blucher

1963. 150th Anniv of German War of Liberation.

E709	**E239**	5pf. black, buff & yell	20	15
E710	-	10pf. black, buff & grn	20	15
E711	-	20pf. blk, buff & orge	25	15
E712	-	25pf. black, buff & bl	25	15
E713	-	40pf. black, buff & red	2·50	1·30

DESIGNS: 10pf. "Cossacks and (German) Soldiers in Berlin" (Ludwig Wolf); 20pf. E. M. Arndt and Baron vom Stein; 25pf. Lutzow corps in battle order (detail from painting by Hans Kohlschein); 40pf. G. von Scharnhorst and Prince Kutuzov.

E240 V. Tereshkova

1963. Visit of Soviet Cosmonauts to East Berlin.

E714	**E240**	10pf. green and blue	20	15
E715	-	20pf. black, red & buff	25	15
E716	-	20pf. green, red & buff	25	15
E717	-	25pf. orange and blue	4·50	3·00

DESIGNS—SQUARE: No. E717, Tereshkova in capsule. VERT: (24×32 mm). No. E715, Tereshkova with bouquet; No. E716, Gagarin (visit to Berlin).

E241 Synagogue aflame

1963. 25th Anniv of "Kristallnacht" (Nazi pogrom).

E718	**E241**	10pf. multicoloured	35	40

E242 Letter-sorting Machine

1963. Stamp Day. Multicoloured.

E719	10pf. Type E **242**	2·00	2·75
E720	20pf. Fork-lift truck loading mail train	25	25

E243 Ski Jumper commencing Run

1963. Winter Olympic Games, Innsbruck, 1964. Rings in different colours; skier in black.

E721	**E243**	5pf. yellow	20	15
E722	-	10pf. green	20	15
E723	-	20pf.+10pf. red	20	15
E724	-	25pf. blue	2·40	2·75

DESIGNS: Ski jumper—10pf. Taking-off; 20pf. In mid-air; 25pf. Landing.

E244 "Vanessa atlanta"

1964. Butterflies. Butterflies in natural colours; inscr in black.

E725	**E244**	10pf. olive	45	20
E726	-	15pf. lilac	45	20
E727	-	20pf. orange	45	20
E728	-	25pf. blue	45	25
E729	-	40pf. blue	6·50	2·75

BUTTERFLIES: 15pf. "Parnassius phoebus"; 20pf. "Papilio machaon"; 25pf. "Colius croceus"; 40pf. "Nymphalis polychloros".

E245 Shakespeare (b. 1564)

1964. Cultural Anniversaries.

E730		20pf. blue and pink	25	20
E731		25pf. purple and blue	25	20
E732	**E245**	40pf. blue and lilac	1·60	1·40

DESIGNS: 20pf. Quadriga, Brandenburg Gate (J. G. Schadow, sculptor, b. 1764); 25pf. Portal keystone, German Historical Museum (A. Schluter, sculptor, b. 1664).

E246 "Elektrotecknik" Hall

1964. Leipzig Spring Fair.

E733	**E246**	10pf. black and green	3·25	30
E734	-	20pf. black and red	3·25	30

DESIGN: 20pf. Braunigkes Hof, c. 1700.

E247 A. Saefkow

1964. Concentration Camp Victims. Memorials Fund.

E735	**E247**	5pf.+5pf. brown & bl	25	15
E736	-	10pf.+5pf. brn & ol	25	15
E737	-	15pf.+5pf. brn & vio	25	15
E738	-	20pf.+5pf. olive and red	25	20
E739	-	25pf.+10pf. blue & ol	45	30
E740	-	40pf.+10pf. ol & brn	1·60	2·10

PORTRAITS—As Type E **247**: 10pf. F. Jacob; 15pf. B. Bastlein; 20pf. H. Schulze-Boysen; 25pf. Dr. A. Kuckhoff. (49×27½ mm): 40pf. Dr. A. and Mildred Harnack.

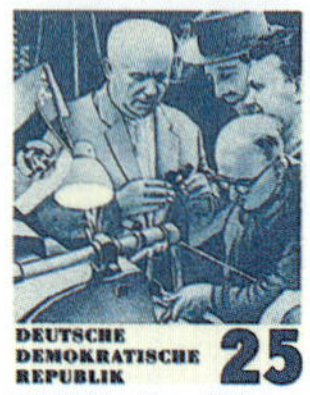

E248 Mr. Khrushchev with East German Officials

1964. Mr. Khrushchev's 70th Birthday.

E741	**E248**	25pf. blue	25	20
E742	-	40pf. black and purple	3·25	2·75

DESIGN: 40pf. Mr. Khrushchev with cosmonauts Tereshkova and Gagarin.

E249 Boys and Girls

1964. German Youth Meeting, Berlin. Multicoloured.

E743	10pf. Type E **249**	20	15
E744	20pf. Young gymnasts	20	15
E745	25pf. Youth with accordion and girl with flowers	1·90	1·20

E250 Flax, Krumel and Struppi, the dog

1964. Children's Day. Multicoloured.

E746	5pf. Type E **250**	20	15
E747	10pf. Master Nadelohr	20	15
E748	15pf. Pittiplatsch	20	15
E749	20pf. Sandmannschen (sand-man)	20	15
E750	40pf. Bummi (teddy bear) and Schnatterinchen (duckling)	2·10	2·20

The designs show characters from children's T.V. programmes.

E251 Governess and Child (with portrait of Jenny Marx)

1964. East German Women's Congress. Mult.

E751	20pf. Type E **251**	35	10
E752	25pf. Switchboard technicians	1·40	1·20
E753	70pf. Farm girls	35	10

E252 Cycling

1964. Olympic Games, Tokyo. Multicoloured. (a) 1st Series. As Type E 252.

E754	5pf. Type E **252**	20	20
E755	10pf. Volleyball	20	20
E756	20pf. Judo	20	20
E757	25pf. Diving	20	20
E758	40pf.+20pf. Running	35	25
E759	70pf. Horse-jumping	2·30	2·00

E253 Diving

(b) 2nd Series. As Type E 253.

E760	10pf. Type E **253**	3·25	3·75
E761	10pf.+5pf. Horse-jumping	3·25	3·75
E762	10pf. Volleyball	3·25	3·75
E763	10pf. Cycling	3·25	3·75
E764	10pf.+5pf. Running	3·25	3·75
E765	10pf. Judo	3·25	3·75

Nos. E760/5 were printed together in se-tenant blocks of six (3×2) within sheets of 60 (6×10), and with an overall pattern of the five Olympic "rings" in each block.

E254 Young Artists

1964. 5th Young Pioneers' Meeting, East Berlin. Multicoloured.

E766	10pf.+5pf. Type E **254**	1·10	25
E767	20pf.+10pf. Planting tree	1·10	25
E768	25pf.+10pf. Playing with ball	3·75	4·25

E255 Leningrad Memorial

1964. Victims of Leningrad Siege Commem.

E769	**E255**	25pf. black, yellow and blue	1·20	30

E256 F. Joliot-Curie

1964. "World Peace".

E770	**E256**	20pf. sepia and red	25	20
E771	-	25pf. black and blue	25	20
E772	-	50pf. black and lilac	1·70	1·20

PORTRAITS (Campaigners for "World Peace"): 25pf. B. von Suttner; 50pf. C. von Ossietzky.

E257 Ancient Glazier's Shop

1964. Leipzig Autumn Fair. Multicoloured.

E773	10pf. Type E **257**	80	20
E774	15pf. Jena glass factory	80	20

E258 I.W.M.A. Cachet

1964. Centenary of "First International".

E775	**E258**	20pf. black and red	20	15
E776	**E258**	25pf. black and blue	80	75

E259 "Rostock Port" Stamp of 1958

1964. National Stamp Exn, East Berlin.

E777	**E259**	10pf.+5pf. green and orange	25	20
E778	-	20pf.+10pf. blue and purple	35	30
E779	-	50pf. brown and grey	2·50	1·90

DESIGNS: 20pf., 12pf. "Peace" stamp of 1950; 50pf., 5pf. "Dresden Paintings" stamp of 1955.

E260 Modern Buildings and Flag ("Reconstruction")

1964. 15th Anniv of German Democratic Republic. Multicoloured.

E780	10pf. Type E **260**	35	25
E781	10pf. Surveyor and conveyor ("Coal")	35	25
E782	10pf. Scientist and chemical works ("Chemical Industry")	35	25
E783	10pf. Guard and chemical works ("Chemical Industry")	35	25
E784	10pf. Milkmaid and dairy pen ("Agriculture")	35	25
E785	10pf. Furnaceman and mills ("Steel")	35	25
E786	10pf. Student with microscope, and lecture hall ("Education")	35	25
E787	10pf. Operator and lathe ("Engineering")	35	25
E788	10pf. Scientist and planetarium ("Optics")	35	25
E789	10pf. Girl with cloth, and loom ("Textiles")	35	25
E790	10pf. Docker and ship at quayside ("Shipping")	35	25
E791	10pf. Leipzig buildings and "businessmen" formed of Fair emblem ("Exports")	35	25
E792	10pf. Building worker and flats ("New Construction")	35	25
E793	10pf. Sculptor modelling and Dresden gateway ("Culture")	35	25
E794	10pf. Girl skier and holiday resort ("Recreation")	35	25
MSE794a 210×285 mm. Nos. E780/94		60·00	85·00

E261 Monchgut (Rugen) Costume

1964. Provincial Costumes (1st series). Mult.

E795	5pf. Type E **261**	13·50	9·50
E796	5pf. Monchgut (male)	13·50	9·50
E797	10pf. Spreewald (female)	45	35
E798	10pf. Spreewald (male)	45	35
E799	20pf. Thuringen (female)	45	35
E800	20pf. Thuringen (male)	45	35

See Nos. E932/7 and E1073/6.

E261a Observation of Sun's Activity

1964. Quiet Sun Year. Three sheets, each 108×90 mm incorporating stamp as Type E 261a. Multicoloured.

MSE801 (a) 25pf. Rocket over part of Earth. (b) 40pf. Type E **261a**. (c) 70pf. Earth and rocket routes	10·00	14·00

E262 Dr. Schweitzer and Lambarene River

1965. 90th Birthday of Dr. Albert Schweitzer.

E802	**E262**	10pf. yellow, blk & grn	45	15
E803	-	20pf. yellow, blk & red	45	15
E804	-	25pf. yellow, blk & bl	3·75	2·75

DESIGNS: 20pf. Schweitzer and "nuclear disarmament" marchers; 25pf. Schweitzer and part of a Bach organ prelude.

1965. As Nos. E586/7 but values expressed in "MDN" (Deutschen Notenbank Marks) instead of "DM".

E805	1MDN. green	65	75
E806	2MDN. brown	75	95

E263 A. Bebel

1965. 125th Birth Anniv of August Bebel (founder of Social Democratic Party).

E807	**E263**	20pf. yellow, brn & red	50	25

See also Nos. E814/15, E839, E842 and E871.

E264 Fair Medal (obverse)

1965. Leipzig Spring Fair and 800th Anniv of Leipzig Fair.

E808	**E264**	10pf. gold and mauve	25	15
E809	-	15pf. gold and mauve	25	15
E810	-	25pf. multicoloured	70	30

DESIGNS: 15pf. Fair medal (reverse); 25pf. Chemical Works.

E265 Giraffe

1965. 10th Anniv of East Berlin Zoo.

E811	**E265**	10pf. grey and green	20	15
E812	-	25pf. grey and blue	30	20
E813	-	30pf. grey and sepia	2·75	1·90

ANIMALS—HORIZ: 25pf. Iguana; 30pf. Black wildebeest.

1965. 120th Birth Anniv of W. C. Rontgen (physicist). As Type E 263 but portrait of Rontgen.

E814	10pf. yellow, brown and green	60	25

1985. 700th Birth Anniv of Dante. As Type E 263 but portrait of Dante.

E815	50pf. yellow, brown & lemon	1·80	30

E266 Belyaev and Leonov

1965. Space Flight of "Voskhod 2".

E816	**E266**	10pf. red	35	25
E817	-	25pf. blue	2·50	2·20

DESIGN: 25pf. Leonov in space.

E267 Boxing Gloves

1965. European Boxing Championships, Berlin.

E818	**E267**	10pf.+5pf. mult	25	15
E819	-	20pf. gold, black and red	90	85

DESIGN: 20pf. Boxing glove.

E268 Dimitrov denouncing Fascism

1965. 20th Anniv of Liberation. Multicoloured.

E820	5pf.+5pf. Type E **268**	25	15
E821	10pf.+5pf. Distributing "Communist Manifesto"	25	15
E822	15pf.+5pf. Soldiers of International Brigade fighting in Spain	25	15
E823	20pf.+10pf. "Freedom for Ernst Thalmann" demonstration	25	15
E824	25pf.+10pf. Founding of "Free Germany" National Committee (Moscow)	25	15
E825	40pf. Ulbricht and Weinert distributing "Manifesto" on Eastern Front	25	15
E826	50pf. Liberation of concentration camps	25	15
E827	60pf. Hoisting Red Flag on Reichstag	2·75	2·75
E828	70pf. Bilateral demonstration of Communist and Socialist parties	25	20

E269 Transmitter Aerial and Globe

1965. 20th Anniv of East German Broadcasting Service.

E829	**E269**	20pf. black, red and cerise	35	15
E830	-	40pf. black and blue	1·80	60

DESIGN: 40pf. Radio workers.

E270 I.T.U. Emblem and Radio Circuit Diagram

1965. Centenary of I.T.U.

E831	**E270**	20pf. black, yell & ol	45	15
E832	-	25pf. black, mve & vio	2·75	60

DESIGN: 25pf. I.T.U. emblem and switch diagram.

E271 F.D.G.B. Emblem

1965. 20th Anniv of Free German (F.D.G.B.) and World Trade Unions.

E833	**E271**	20pf. gold and red	35	15
E834	-	25pf. black, bl & gold	1·40	50

DESIGN—HORIZ (39×21½ mm): 25pf. Workers of "two hemispheres" (inscr "20 JAHRE WELTGEWERKSCHAFTSBUND").

E272 Industrial Machine

1965. 800th Anniv of Karl-Marx-Stadt (formerly Chemnitz).

E835	**E272**	10pf. green and gold	25	15
E836	-	20pf. red and gold	25	15
E837	-	25pf. blue and gold	1·60	55

DESIGNS: 20pf. Red Tower, Chemnitz; 25pf. Town Hall, Chemnitz.

E273 Marx and Lenin

1965. Socialist Countries' Postal Ministers Conference, Peking.

E838	**E273**	20pf. black, yell & red	50	25

1965. 90th Birth Anniv of Dr. Wilhelm Kulz (politician). As Type E 263 but portrait of Kulz.

E839	25pf. yellow, brown and blue	1·20	25

E274 Congress Emblem

1965. World Peace Congress, Helsinki.

E840	**E274**	10pf.+5pf. green and blue	20	15
E841	**E274**	20pf.+5pf. blue and red	65	45

1965. 75th Birth Anniv of Erich Weinert (poet). As Type E 263, but portrait of Weinert.

E842	40pf. yellow, brown and red	60	25

1965. "Help for Vietnam". Surch Hilfe fur VIETNAM +10.

E843	**E260**	10pf.+10pf. mult	50	25

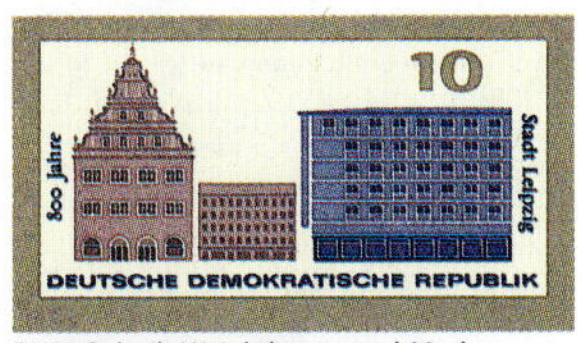

E276 Rebuilt Weigh-house and Modern Buildings, Katharinenstrasse

1965. 800th Anniv of Leipzig.

E844	**E276**	10pf. purple, bl & gold	20	15
E845	-	25pf. orge, sep & gold	20	15
E846	-	40pf. multicoloured	25	15
E847	-	70pf. blue and gold	2·40	1·00

DESIGNS: 25pf. Old Town Hall; 40pf. Opera House and new G.P.O.; 70pf. "Stadt Leipzig" Hotel.

E277 "Praktica" and "Praktisix" Cameras

1965. Leipzig Autumn Fair.

E848	**E277**	10pf. blk, gold & grn	25	20
E849	-	15pf. multicoloured	25	20
E850	-	25pf. multicoloured	80	30

DESIGNS: 15pf. Clavichord and electric guitar; 25pf. "Zeiss" microscope.

1965. Leipzig Philatelic Exhibition, "INTERMESS III". Nos. E844/7 in two miniature sheets each 137×99 mm.

MSE851	(a) Nos. E844 and E847. (b) Nos. E845/6 (sold for 1 MDN.75)	5·75	5·75

E278 Show Jumping

1965. World Modern Pentathlon Championships, Leipzig. Multicoloured.

E852	10pf. Type E **278**	25	15
E853	10pf. Swimming	25	15
E854	10pf. Running	3·25	3·25
E855	10pf.+5pf. Fencing	25	15
E856	10pf.+5pf. Pistol-shooting	25	15

E279 E. Leonov

1965. Soviet Cosmonauts Visit to East Germany.

E857	**E279**	20pf. blue, silver & red	70	80
E858	-	20pf. blue, silver & red	70	80
E859	-	25pf. multicoloured	70	80

DESIGNS—As Type E **275**. No. E858, Belyaev. HORIZ (48×29 mm): No. E859, "Voskhod 2" and Leonov in space.

E280 Memorial at Putten, Netherlands

1965. Putten War Victims Commem.

E860	**E280**	25pf. black, yell & bl	80	25

E281 Stoking Furnace (from old engraving)

1965. Bicent of Mining School, Freiberg. Multicoloured.

E861	10pf. Type E **281**	25	20
E862	15pf. Mining ore (old engraving)	80	95
E863	20pf. Ore	25	20
E864	25pf. Sulphur	25	20

E282 Red Kite

1965. Birds of Prey. Multicoloured.

E865	5pf. Type E **282**	20	15
E866	10pf. Lammergeier	20	15
E867	20pf. Common Buzzard	25	15
E868	25pf. Common Kestrel	25	15
E869	40pf. Northern Goshawk	45	25
E870	70pf. Golden Eagle	5·00	3·25

1965. 150th Birth Anniv of A. von Menzel (painter). As Type E 263 but portrait of Menzel.

E871	10pf. yellow, brown and red	80	25

E283 Otto Grotewohl

1965. Grotewohl Commemoration.

E872	**E283**	20f. black	80	25

E284 Extract from Newsletter

1966. 50th Anniv of Spartacus Group Conference. Miniature sheet 138×98 mm. Type E 284 and similar horiz design.

MSE873	20pf. black and red (Type E **284**); 50pf. black and red (Karl Liebknecht and Rosa Luxemburg)	2·30	6·50

E285 Ladies' Single-seater

1966. World Tobogganing Championships, Friedrichroda.

E874	**E285**	10pf. green and olive	20	15
E875	-	20pf. blue and red	20	15
E876	-	25pf. indigo and blue	1·60	1·10

DESIGNS: 20pf. Men's double-seater; 25pf. Men's single seater.

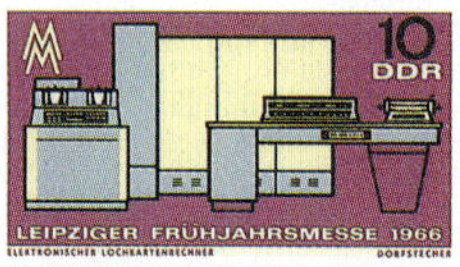

E286 Electronic Punch-card Computer

1966. Leipzig Spring Fair. Multicoloured.

E877	10pf. Type E **286**	25	15
E878	15pf. Drilling and milling plant	1·10	30

E287 Soldier and National Gallery, Berlin

1966. 10th Anniv of National People's Army.

E879	**E287**	5pf. black, olive & yell	20	15
E880	-	10pf. black, ol & yell	20	15
E881	-	20pf. black, ol & yell	20	15
E882	-	25pf. black, ol & yell	1·60	1·10

DESIGNS: Soldier and—10pf. Brandenburg Gate; 20pf. Industrial plant; 25pf. Combine-harvester.

E288 J. A. Smoler (Sorb patriot and savant)

1966. 150th Birth Anniv of Jan Smoler.

E883	**E288**	20pf. black, red & blue	20	15
E884	-	25pf. black, red & blue	70	60

DESIGN: 25pf. House of the Sorbs, Bautzen.

E289 "Good Knowledge" Badge

1966. 20th Anniv of "Freie Deutsche Jugend" (Socialist Youth Movement).

E885	**E289**	20pf. multicoloured	70	25

E290 "Luna 9" on Moon

1966. Moon Landing of "Luna 9".

E886	**E290**	20pf. multicoloured	2·75	45

E291 Road Signs

1966. Road Safety.

E887	**E291**	10pf. red, bl & ultram	20	15
E888	-	15pf. black, yell & grn	20	15
E889	-	25pf. black, blue & bis	20	15
E890	-	50pf. black, yell & red	1·40	95

DESIGNS: 15pf. Child on scooter crossing in front of car; 25pf. Cyclist and hand-signal; 50pf. Motor cyclist, glass of beer and ambulance.

E292 Marx and Lenin Banner

1966. 20th Anniv of Socialist Unity Party (S.E.D.).

E891		5pf. multicoloured	20	15
E892	**E292**	10pf. yellow, blk & red	20	15
E893	-	15pf. black and green	20	15
E894	-	20pf. black and red	25	15
E895	-	25pf. black, yell & red	2·10	1·40

DESIGNS—VERT: 5pf. Party badge and demonstrators; 15pf. Marx, Engels and manifesto; 20pf. Pieck and Grotewohl. HORIZ: 25pf. Workers greeting Ulbricht.

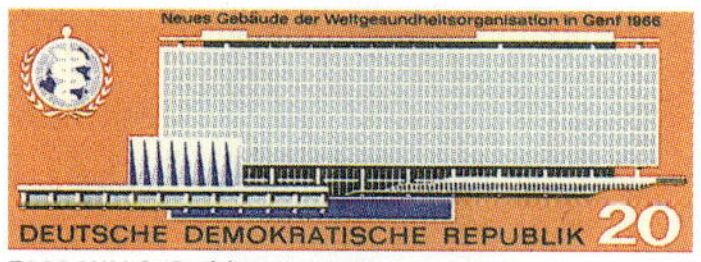

E293 W.H.O. Building

1966. Inaug of W.H.O. Headquarters, Geneva.

E896	**E293**	20pf. multicoloured	45	40

E294 Spreewald

1966. National Parks. Multicoloured.

E897	10pf. Type E **294**	20	15
E898	15pf. Konigsstuhl (Isle of Rugen)	20	15
E899	20pf. Sachsische Schweiz	20	15
E900	25pf. Westdarss	25	15
E901	30pf. Teufelsmauer	25	20
E902	50pf. Feldberg Lakes	2·30	1·30

E295 Lace "Flower"

1966. Plauen Lace. Floral Patterns as Type E 295.

E903	**E295**	10pf. myrtle and green	20	15
E904	-	20pf. indigo and blue	20	15
E905	-	25pf. red and rose	25	20
E906	-	50pf. violet and lilac	2·75	1·50

E296 Lily of the Valley

1966. Int Horticultural Show, Erfurt. Mult.

E907	20pf. Type E **296**	20	15
E908	25pf. Rhododendrons	25	20
E909	40pf. Dahlias	35	35
E910	50pf. Cyclamen	4·50	4·25

E297 Parachutist on Target

1966. 8th World Parachute Jumping Championships, Leipzig.

E911	**E297**	10pf. blue, black & bis	20	15
E912	-	15pf. multicoloured	80	80
E913	-	20pf. black, bistre & bl	25	15

DESIGNS: 15pf. Group descent; 20pf. Free fall.

E298 Hans Kahle and Music of "The Thalmann Column"

1966. 30th Anniv of International Brigade in Spain. Multicoloured.

E914	5pf. Type E **298**	25	15
E915	10pf.+5pf. W. Bredel and open-air class	25	15
E916	15pf. H. Beimler and Madrid street-fighting	25	15
E917	20pf.+10pf. H. Rau and march-past after Battle of Brunete	25	15
E918	25pf.+10pf. H. Marchwitza and soldiers	25	15
E919	40pf.+10pf. A. Becker and Ebro battle	1·80	1·20

E299 Canoeing

1966. World Canoeing Championships, Berlin. Multicoloured.

E920	10pf.+5pf. Type E **299**	25	15
E921	15pf. Kayak doubles	1·50	1·30

E300 Television Set

1966. Leipzig Autumn Fair. Multicoloured.

E922	10pf. Type E **300**	75	20
E923	15pf. Electric typewriter	1·60	30

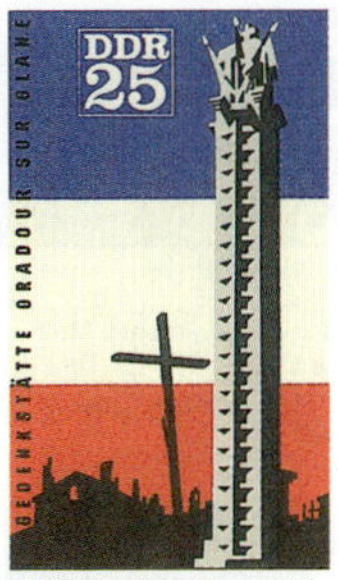

E301 Oradour Memorial

1966. Oradour-sur-Glane War Victims Commem.

E924	**E301**	25pf. black, blue & red	45	30

E302 "Blood Donors"

1966. International Health Co-operation.

E925	**E302**	5pf. red and green	25	20
E926	-	20pf.+10pf. red and violet	45	20
E927	-	40pf. red and blue	2·00	70

DESIGNS—HORIZ: 20pf. I.C.Y. emblem. VERT: 40pf. Health symbol.

E303 Weightlifting ("snatch")

1966. World and European Weightlifting Championships, Berlin.

E928	**E303**	15pf. black and brown	1·80	1·80
E929	-	20pf.+5pf. black and blue	45	25

DESIGN: 20pf. Weightlifting ("jerk").

E304 Congress Hall

1966. 6th Int Journalists' Congress, Berlin.

E930	**E304**	10pf. multicoloured	55	45
E931	-	20pf. yellow and blue	25	15

DESIGN—VERT: 20pf. Emblem of Int Organization of Journalists.

1966. Provincial Costumes (2nd series). As Type E 261. Multicoloured.

E932	5pf. Altenburg (female)	45	25
E933	10pf. Altenburg (male)	45	25
E934	10pf. Mecklenburg (female)	45	25
E935	15pf. Mecklenburg (male)	45	25
E936	20pf. Magdeburger Borde (female)	2·30	2·40
E937	30pf. Magdeburger Borde (male)	2·30	2·40

E305 "Vietnam is Invincible"

1966. Aid for Vietnam.

E938	**E305**	20pf.+5pf. black and pink	45	30

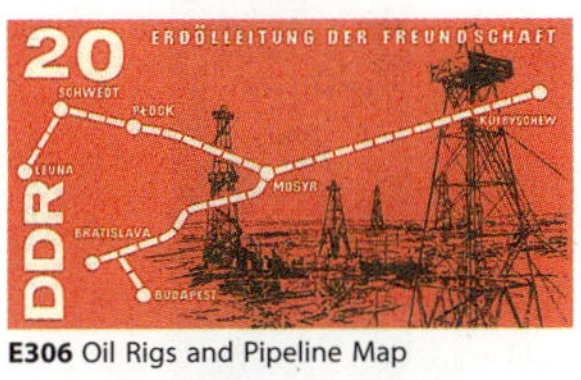

E306 Oil Rigs and Pipeline Map

1966. Inaug of Int "Friendship" Oil Pipeline.

E939	**E306**	20pf. black and red	25	20
E940	-	25pf. black and blue	1·10	45

DESIGN: 25pf. "Walter Ulbricht" Oil Works, Leuna and pipeline map.

E307 Black Phantom Tetra

1966. Aquarium Fishes. Multicoloured.

E941	5pf. Type E **307**	20	15
E942	10pf. Cardinal tetra	20	15
E943	15pf. Rio Grande cichlid	3·00	2·50
E944	20pf. Blue gularis	20	15
E945	25pf. Ramirez's dwarf cichlid	25	20
E946	40pf. Honey gourami	35	25

E308 "Horse" (detail from Ishtar Gate)

1966. Babylonian Art Treasures, Vorderasiatisches Museum, Berlin. Multicoloured.

E947	10pf. Type E **308**	20	15
E948	20pf. Mythological animal, Ishtar Gate	20	15
E949	25pf. Lion facing right (vert)	25	20
E950	50pf. Lion facing left (vert)	80	1·30

E309 The Wartburg from the East

1966. 900th Anniv of Wartburg Castle.

E951	**E309**	10pf.+5pf. slate	20	15
E952	-	20pf. green	25	15
E953	-	25pf. purple	75	50

DESIGNS: 20pf. Castle bailiwick; 25pf. Residence.

E310 "Gentiana pneumonanthe"

1966. Protected Plants (1st series). Mult.

E954	10pf. Type E **310**	20	15
E955	20pf. "Cephalanthera rubra"	25	15
E956	25pf. "Arnica montana"	1·80	1·20

See also Nos. E1177/82 and E1284/9.

E311 Son leaves Home

1966. Fairy Tales (1st series). "The Wishing Table". Multicoloured.

E957	5pf. Type E **311**	25	30
E958	10pf. Setting the table	25	30
E959	20pf. The thieving inn-keeper	80	80
E960	25pf. The magic donkey	80	80
E961	30pf. The cudgel in the sack	25	30
E962	50pf. Return of the son	25	30

See also Nos. E1045/50, E1147/52, E1171/6, E1266/71, E1437/42, E1525/30, E1623/8, E1711/16, E1811/13, E1902/7, E1996/2001 and E2092/7.

E312 Worlitz Castle

1967. Principal East German Buildings. (1st series). Multicoloured.

E964	5pf. Type E **312**	20	15
E965	10pf. Stralsund Town Hall (vert)	20	15
E966	15pf. Chorin Monastery (vert)	25	15
E967	20pf. Ribbeck House, Berlin	25	15
E968	25pf. Moritzburg, Zeitz (vert)	25	15
E969	40pf. Old Town Hall, Potsdam (vert)	1·80	1·20

See also Nos. E1100/3 and E1155/60.

E313 Rifle-shooting

1967. World Biathlon Championships, Altenburg.

E970	**E313**	10pf. blue, drab & mve	20	15
E971	-	20pf. olive, blue & grn	20	15
E972	-	25pf. green, blue & ol	1·00	70

DESIGNS: 20pf. Shooting on skis; 25pf. Riflemen racing on skis.

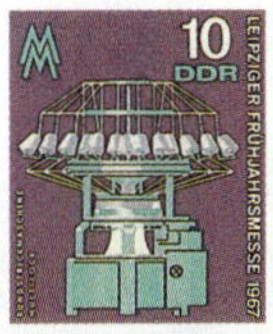

E314 "Multilock" Loom

1967. Leipzig Spring Fair.

E973	**E314**	10pf. green, grey & pur	25	15
E974	-	15pf. bistre & blue	1·10	30

DESIGN: 15pf. Zeiss tracking telescope.

E315 Mother and Child

1967. 20th Anniv of German Democratic Women's Federation.

E975	**E315**	20pf. grey, red and purple	25	25
E976	-	25pf. brown, turquoise and brown	85	90

DESIGN: 25pf. Professional woman.

E316 Industrial Control Desk

1967. Socialist Party Rally. Multicoloured.(a) 1st series.

E977	10pf. Type E **316**	20	15
E978	20pf. Ulbricht meeting workers	20	15
E979	25pf. Servicemen guarding industrial plants	20	15
E980	40pf. Agricultural workers and harvesters	80	85

Each with inset portraits of Marx, Engels and Lenin.

(b) 2nd series. As Type E 316 but vert.

E981	5pf. Agricultural worker	20	20
E982	10pf. Teacher and pupil	20	20
E983	15pf. Socialist family	45	45
E984	20pf. Servicemen	20	20

Each with inset portraits as above.

E317 "Portrait of a Girl" (after F Hodler)

1967. Dresden Gallery Paintings (1st series). Multicoloured.

E985	20pf. Type E **317**	20	15
E986	25pf. "Peter at the Zoo" (H. Hakenbeck)	20	15
E987	30pf. "Venetian Episode" (R. Bergander)	20	15
E988	40pf. "Tahitian Women" (Gauguin) (horiz)	25	20
E989	50pf. "The Grandchild" (J. Scholtz)	2·50	2·10
E990	70pf. "Cairn in the Snow" (C. D. Friedrich) (horiz)	35	30

See also Nos. E1114/19 and E1249/54.

E318 Barn Owl

1967. Protected Birds. Multicoloured.

E991	5pf. Type E **318**	20	15
E992	10pf. Common Crane	20	15
E993	20pf. Peregrine Falcon	25	15
E994	25pf. Northern bullfinches	25	15
E995	30pf. River kingfisher	4·50	3·25
E996	40pf. European roller	45	20

E319 Cycle Wheels

1967. 20th Warsaw–Berlin–Prague Cycle Race.

E997	**E319**	10pf. violet, black and yellow	15	15
E998	-	25pf. red and blue	55	45

DESIGN: 25pf. Racing cyclists.

E320 "Tom Cat"

1967. Int Children's Day. Multicoloured.

E999	5pf. Type E **320**	20	15
E1000	10pf. "Snow White"	20	15
E1001	15pf. "Fire Brigade"	25	15
E1002	20pf. "Cockerel"	25	15
E1003	25pf. "Vase of Flowers"	25	20
E1004	30pf. "Children Playing with Ball"	1·30	95

E321 "Girl with Grapes" (Gerard Dou)

1967. Paintings Missing from German National Galleries (after World War II).

E1005	**E321**	5pf. blue	20	15
E1006	-	10pf. brown	20	15
E1007	-	20pf. green	20	20
E1008	-	25pf. purple	25	20

E1009 - 40pf. olive 25 20
E1010 - 50pf. sepia 2·10 1·80
DESIGNS—VERT: 25pf. "Portrait of W Schroeder-Devrient" (after K. Begas); 40pf. "Young Girl in Straw Hat" (after S. Bray); 50pf. "The Four Evangelists" (after Jordaens). HORIZ: 5pf. "Three Horsemen" (after Rubens); 20pf. "Spring Idyll" (after H. Thoma).

E322 Exhibition Emblem

1967. 15th Agricultural Exn, Markkleeberg.
E1011 **E322** 20pf. red, green and yellow 35 30

E323 Marie Curie (Birth Cent)

1967. Birth Anniversaries.
E1012 - 5pf. brown 25 15
E1013 **E323** 10pf. blue 25 15
E1014 - 20pf. red 25 15
E1015 - 25pf. sepia 25 15
E1016 - 40pf. green 1·10 85
PORTRAITS: 5pf. G. Herwegh (poet—150th); 20pf. Kathe Kollwitz (artist—cent); 25pf. J. J. Winckelmann (archaeologist—250th); 40pf. T. Storm (poet—150th).

E324 Jack of Diamonds

1967. German Playing-cards. Multicoloured.
E1017 5pf. Type E **324** 20 15
E1018 10pf. Jack of Hearts 20 15
E1019 20pf. Jack of Spades 25 15
E1020 25pf. Jack of Clubs 6·50 3·50

E325 Mare and Filly

1967. Thoroughbred Horse Meeting, Berlin. Multicoloured.
E1021 5pf. Type E **325** 25 15
E1022 10pf. Stallion 25 15
E1023 20pf. Horse-racing 30 20
E1024 50pf. Two fillies (vert) 3·75 2·75

E326 Kitchen Equipment

1967. Leipzig Autumn Fair. Multicoloured.
E1025 10pf. Type E **326** 45 20
E1026 15pf. Fur coat and "Interpelz" brand-mark 1·30 50

E327 Max Reichpietsch and "Friedrich der Grosse" (battleship), 1914–18

1967. 50th Anniv of Revolutionary Sailors' Movement. Multicoloured.
E1027 10pf. Type E **327** 25 15
E1028 15pf. Albin Kobis and "Prinzregent Luitpold" (battleship), 1914–18 1·60 70
E1029 20pf. Sailors' demonstration and "Seydlitz" (battle cruiser), 1914–18 45 15

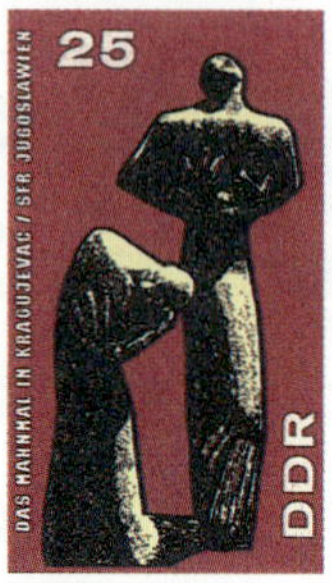

E328 Kragujevac Memorial

1967. Victims of Kragujevac (Yugoslavia) Massacre.
E1030 **E328** 25pf. black, yellow and red 95 40

E329 Worker and Dam ("Electrification")

1967. 50th Anniv of October Revolution.
E1031 - 5pf. black, orange and red 20 15
E1032 **E 329** 10pf. black, red and bistre 20 15
E1033 - 15pf. black, red and grey 20 15
E1034 - 20pf. black, red and orange 35 15
E1035 - 40pf. black, red and orange 3·50 2·50
MSE1036 127×83 mm. Nos. E1034/5. Imperf (sold for 85pf.) 1·40 4·50
DESIGNS: 5pf. Worker and newspaper headline "Hands off Soviet Russia!"; 15pf. Treptow Memorial ("Victory over Fascism"); 20pf. German and Soviet soldiers ("Friendship"); 40pf. Lenin and "Aurora" (Russian cruiser) . Each with hammer and sickle.

E330 Martin Luther (from engraving by Lucas Cranach the Elder)

1967. 450th Anniv of Reformation.
E1037 **E330** 20pf. black & mauve 25 15
E1038 - 25pf. black and blue 25 15
E1039 - 40pf. black and bistre 2·50 1·30
DESIGNS—HORIZ: 25pf. Luther's house, Wittenberg. VERT: 40pf. Castle church, Wittenberg.

E331 Young Workers

1967. 10th "Masters of Tomorrow" Fair, Leipzig.
E1040 **E 331** 20pf. black, gold and blue 55 55
E1041 - 20pf. black, gold and blue 55 55
E1042 - 25pf. multicoloured 55 55
DESIGNS—VERT: No. E1041, Young man and woman. HORIZ: (51×29 mm): No. E1042, Presentation of awards.

E332 Goethe's House, Weimar

1967. Cultural Places.
E1043 **E332** 20pf. blk, brn & grey 30 15
E1044 - 25pf. olive, brn & yell 2·10 80
DESIGN: 25pf. Schiller's House, Weimar.

E333 Queen and Courtiers

1967. Fairy Tales (2nd series). "King Thrushbeard". Designs showing different scenes.
E1045 **E333** 5pf. multicoloured 25 25
E1046 - 10pf. multicoloured 25 25
E1047 - 15pf. multicoloured 90 95
E1048 - 20pf. multicoloured 90 95
E1049 - 25pf. multicoloured 25 25
E1050 - 30pf. multicoloured 25 25

E334 Peasants and Modern Farm Buildings

1967. 15th Anniv of Agricultural Co-operatives.
E1052 **E334** 10pf. sepia, green and olive 35 25

E335 Nutcracker and Two "Smokers"

1967. Popular Art of the Erzgebirge. Multicoloured.
E1053 10pf. Type E **335** 90 55
E1054 20pf. "Angel" and miner with candles (carved figures) 25 15

E336 Ice Skating

1968. Winter Olympic Games, Grenoble.
E1055 **E336** 5pf. blue, red and light blue 25 15
E1056 - 10pf.+5pf. blue, red and turquoise 25 15
E1057 - 15pf. multicoloured 25 15
E1058 - 20pf. ultramarine, red and blue 25 15
E1059 - 25pf. multicoloured 25 15
E1060 - 30pf. ultramarine, red and blue 4·00 1·80
DESIGNS: 10pf. Tobogganning; 15pf. Slalom; 20pf. Ice hockey; 25pf. Figure skating (pairs); 30pf. Cross-country skiing.

E337 Actinometer

1968. 75th Anniv of Potsdam Meteorological Observatory and World Meteorological Day (23 March).
E1061 **E337** 10pf. blk, red & pur 45 45
E1062 - 20pf. multicoloured 45 45
E1063 - 25pf. blk, yell & grn 45 45
DESIGNS—VERT: 25pf. Cornfield by day and night. HORIZ—(50×28 mm): 20pf. Satellite picture of clouds.

E338 "Venus 4"

1968. Soviet Space Achievements. Mult.
E1064 20pf. Type E **338** 25 15
E1065 25pf. Coupled satellites "Cosmos 186" and "188" 1·30 65

E339 "Illegal Struggle" (man, wife and child)

1968. Stained-glass Windows, Sachsenhausen National Memorial Museum. Multicoloured.
E1066 10pf. Type E **339** 20 15
E1067 20pf. "Liberation" 20 15
E1068 25pf. "Partisans' Struggle" 65 45

E340 Type DE1 Diesel-electric Locomotive (built for Brazil)

1968. Leipzig Spring Fair. Multicoloured.
E1069 10pf. Type E **340** 35 25
E1070 15pf. Deep sea trawler 1·30 45

E341 Gorky

1968. Birth Cent of Maxim Gorky (writer).
E1071 **E341** 20pf. purple and red 25 25
E1072 - 25pf. purple and red 85 45
DESIGN: 25pf. Fulmar (from "Song of the Stormy Petrel"—poem).

1968. Provincial Costumes (3rd series). As Type E 261. Multicoloured.
E1073 10pf. Hoyerswerda (female) 20 15
E1074 20pf. Schleife (female) 25 15
E1075 40pf. Crostwitz (female) 30 25
E1076 50pf. Spreewald (female) 3·25 1·40

E342 Common Pheasants

1968. Small Game. Multicoloured.
E1077 10pf. Type E **342** 20 20
E1078 15pf. Grey Partridges 25 20
E1079 20pf. Mallards 25 20
E1080 25pf. Greylag Geese 25 20
E1081 30pf. Wood Pigeon 25 20
E1082 40pf. Brown hares 4·00 6·50

E343 Karl Marx

1968. 150th Birth Anniv of Karl Marx.
E1083 - 10pf. black and green 30 35

E1084 **E343** 20pf. black, yell & red 30 35
E1085 - 25pf. blk, brn & yell 30 35
MSE1086 126×86 mm. Nos. E1083/5. Imperf 1·30 3·75
DESIGNS: 10pf. Title-page of "Communist Manifesto"; 25pf. Title-page of "Das Kapital".

E344 "Fritz Heckert" (after E. Hering)

1968. 7th Confederation of Free German Trade Unions Congress. Multicoloured.
E1087 10pf. Type E **344** 20 20
E1088 20pf. Young workers and new tenements 35 40

E345 Hammer and Anvil ("The right to work")

1968. Human Rights Year.
E1089 **E345** 5pf. mauve & purple 20 15
E1090 - 10pf. bistre & brown 20 15
E1091 - 25pf. blue & turq 90 65
DESIGNS: 10pf. Tree and Globe ("The right to live"); 25pf. Dove and Sun ("The right to peace").

E346 Vietnamese Mother and Child

1968. Aid for Vietnam.
E1092 **E346** 10pf.+5pf. mult 25 20

E347 Angling (World Angling Championships, Gustrow)

1968. Sporting Events.
E1093 **E347** 20pf. blue, grn & red 25 15
E1094 - 20pf. blue, turq & grn 25 15
E1095 - 20pf. purple, red & bl 90 95
DESIGNS: No. E1094, Sculling (European Women's Rowing Championships, Berlin); No. E1095, High jumping (2nd European Youth Athletic Competitions).

E348 Brandenburg Gate and Torch

1968. German Youth Sports Day. Mult.
E1096 10pf. Type E **348** 20 15
E1097 25pf. Stadium plan and torch 1·00 75

E349 Festival Emblem

1968. Peace Festival, Sofia.
E1098 **E349** 20pf.+5pf. mult 35 15
E1099 **E349** 25pf. multicoloured 90 60

1968. Principal East German Buildings (2nd series). As Type E 312. Multicoloured.
E1100 10pf. Town Hall, Wernigerode 20 15
E1101 20pf. Moritzburg Castle, Dresden 20 15
E1102 25pf. Town Hall, Greifswald 20 15
E1103 30pf. New Palace, Potsdam 95 1·20
DESIGN SIZES—VERT: 10pf., 25pf. (24×29 mm). HORIZ: 20pf., 30pf. (51½×29½ mm).

E350 Walter Ulbricht

1968. 75th Birthday of Walter Ulbricht (Chairman of Council of State).
E1104 **E350** 20pf. black, red and orange 45 25

E351 Ancient Rostock

1968. 750th Anniv of Rostock. Mult.
E1105 20pf. Type E **351** 20 15
E1106 25pf. Rostock, 1968 70 60

E352 Dr K. Landsteiner (physician and pathologist, birth cent)

1968. Celebrities' Annivs. (1st series).
E1107 **E352** 10pf. grey 20 15
E1108 - 15pf. black 20 15
E1109 - 20pf. brown 25 15
E1110 - 25pf. blue 25 15
E1111 - 40pf. red 1·10 85
DESIGNS: 15pf. Dr. E. Lasker (chess master, birth cent); 20pf. Hans Eisler (composer, 70th birth anniv); 25pf. Ignaz Semmelweis (physician, 150th birth anniv); 40pf. Max von Pettenkofer (hygienist, 150th birth anniv).
See also Nos. E1161/4 and E1256/61.

E353 Zlin Z-226 Trener 6 DM-WKM looping

1968. Aerobatics World Championships, Magdeburg. Multicoloured.
E1112 10pf. Type E **353** 20 15
E1113 25pf. Stunt flying 75 60

E354 "At the Seaside" (Womacka)

1968. Dresden Gallery Paintings (2nd series). Multicoloured.
E1114 10pf. Type E **354** 25 15
E1115 15pf. "Peasants Mowing Mountain Meadow" (Egger-Lienz) 25 15
E1116 20pf. "Portrait of a Farmer's Wife" (Liebl) (vert) 25 15
E1117 40pf. "Portrait of my Daughter" (Venturelli) (vert) 45 25
E1118 50pf. "High-School Girl" (Michaelis) (vert) 45 25
E1119 70pf. "Girl with Guitar" (Castelli) (vert) 2·75 1·80

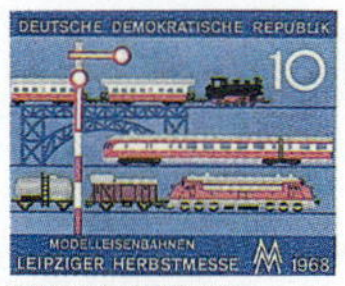

E355 Model Trains

1968. Leipzig Autumn Fair.
E1120 **E355** 10pf. multicoloured 35 30

E356 Spremberg Dam

1968. East German Post-War Dams. Multicoloured.
E1121 5pf. Type E **356** 20 15
E1122 10pf. Pohl Dam (vert) 20 15
E1123 15pf. Ohra Valley Dam (vert) 65 75
E1124 20pf. Rappbode Dam 25 30

E357 Sprinting

1968. Olympic Games, Mexico. Multicoloured.
E1125 5pf. Type E **357** 20 15
E1126 10pf.+5pf. Pole-vaulting (vert) 20 15
E1127 20pf.+10pf. Football (vert) 25 15
E1128 25pf. Gymnastics (vert) 25 15
E1129 40pf. Water-polo (vert) 30 25
E1130 70pf. Sculling 1·80 1·70

E358 Breendonk Memorial, Belgium

1968. Breendonk War Victims Commem.
E1131 **E358** 25pf. multicoloured 45 20

E359 "Cicindela campestris"

1968. "Useful Beetles". Multicoloured.
E1132 10pf. Type E **359** 20 15
E1133 15pf. "Cychrus caraboides" 20 15
E1134 20pf. "Adalia bipunctata" 20 15
E1135 25pf. "Carabus arvensis" ("arcensis") 2·75 2·10
E1136 30pf. "Hister bipustulatus" 25 20
E1137 40pf. "Clerus mutillarius" ("Pseudoclerops mutillarius") 30 25

E360 Lenin and Letter to Spartacus Group

1968. 50th Anniv of German November Revolution.
E1138 **E 360** 10pf. black, red and yellow 20 15
E1139 - 20pf. black, red and yellow 20 15
E1140 - 25pf. black, red and yellow 55 45
DESIGNS: 20pf. Revolutionaries and title of Spartacus newspaper "Die Rote Fahne"; 25pf. Karl Liebknecht and Rose Luxemburg.

E361 "Lailio-cattleya alba rubra" ("Maggie Raphaela")

1968. Orchids. Multicoloured.
E1141 5pf. Type E **361** 20 15
E1142 10pf. "Paphiopedilum albertianum" 20 15
E1143 15pf. "Cattleya fabia" 20 15
E1144 20pf. "Cattleya aclaniae" 20 15
E1145 40pf. "Sobralia macrantha" 30 25
E1146 50pf. "Dendrobium alpha" 2·75 1·90

E362 Trying on the Boots

1968. Fairy Tales (3rd series). "Puss in Boots". As Type E 362. Designs showing different scenes.
E1147 5pf. multicoloured 25 25
E1148 10pf. multicoloured 25 25
E1149 15pf. multicoloured 1·10 1·20
E1150 20pf. multicoloured 1·10 1·20
E1151 25pf. multicoloured 25 25
E1152 30pf. multicoloured 25 25

E363 Young Pioneers

1968. 20th Anniv of Ernst Thalmann's "Young Pioneers." Multicoloured.
E1153 10pf. Type E **363** 25 15
E1154 15pf. Young pioneers (diff) 90 40

1969. Principal East German Buildings (3rd series). As Type E 312. Multicoloured.
E1155 5pf. Town Hall, Tangermunde (vert) 20 15
E1156 10pf. State Opera House, Berlin 20 15
E1157 20pf. Rampart Pavilion, Dresden Castle (vert) 20 15
E1158 25pf. Patrician's House, Luckau (vert) 1·40 95
E1159 30pf. Dornburg Castle 25 20
E1160 40pf. "Zum Stockfisch" Inn, Erfurt (vert) 25 20

1969. Celebrities' Annivs. (2nd series). As Type E 352.
E1161 10pf. olive 20 15
E1162 20pf. brown 20 15
E1163 25pf. blue 1·10 45
E1164 40pf. brown 25 15
DESIGNS: 10pf. M. A. Nexo (Danish poet—birth cent.); 20pf. O. Nagel (painter—75th birth anniv); 25pf. A. von Humboldt (naturalist—bicent. of birth); 40pf. T. Fontane (writer—150th birth anniv).

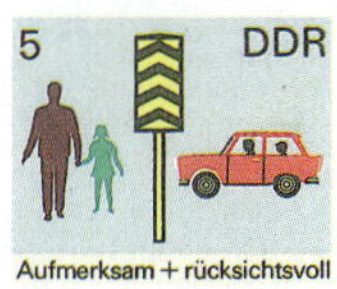

E364 Pedestrian Crossing

1969. Road Safety. Multicoloured.
E1165 5pf. Type E **364** 20 15
E1166 10pf. Traffic lights 20 15
E1167 20pf. Class 103 electric locomotive and railway crossing sign 25 15
E1168 25pf. Motor-vehicle overtaking 70 45

E365 "E-512" Combine- harvester

1969. Leipzig Spring Fair. Multicoloured.
E1169 10pf. Type E **365** 20 15

E1170 15pf. "Planeta-Varianii" lithograph printing-press 30 30

E366 Jorinde and Joringel

1969. Fairy Tales (4th series). "Jorinde and Joringel". As Type E 366, showing different scenes.

E1171 5pf. multicoloured 25 30
E1172 10pf. multicoloured 25 30
E1173 15pf. multicoloured 60 65
E1174 20pf. multicoloured 60 65
E1175 25pf. multicoloured 25 30
E1176 30pf. multicoloured 25 30

E367 Spring Snowflake

1969. Protected Plants (2nd series). Mult.

E1177 5pf. Type E **367** 20 15
E1178 10pf. Yellow pheasant's-eye ("Adonis vernalis") 20 15
E1179 15pf. Globe flower ("Trollius europaeus") 20 15
E1180 20pf. Martagon lily ("Lilium martagon") 25 15
E1181 25pf. Sea holly ("Eryngium maritmum") 3·50 2·20
E1182 30pf. "Dactylorchis latifolia" 35 20

See also Nos. E1284/9.

E368 Plantation of Young Conifers

1969. Forest Fires Prevention. Mult.

E1183 5pf. Type E **368** 25 20
E1184 10pf. Lumber, and resin extraction 25 20
E1185 20pf. Forest stream 25 20
E1186 25pf. Woodland camp 2·10 1·10

E369 Symbols of the Societies

1969. 50th Anniv of League of Red Cross Societies. Multicoloured.

E1187 10pf. Type E **369** 25 20
E1188 15pf. Similar design with symbols in oblong 1·60 55

E370 Erythrite (Schneeberg)

1969. East German Minerals. Multicoloured.

E1189 5pf. Type E **370** 20 15
E1190 10pf. Fluorite (Halsbrucke) 20 15
E1191 15pf. Galena (Neudorf) 20 15
E1192 20pf. Smoky Quartz (Lichtenberg) 20 15
E1193 25pf. Calcite (Niederrabenstein) 1·10 95
E1194 50pf. Silver (Freiberg) 30 20

E371 Women and Symbols

1969. 2nd D.D.R. Women's Congress.

E1195 **E371** 20pf. red and blue 25 15
E1196 - 25pf. blue and red 1·00 45

DESIGN: 25pf. Woman and Symbols (different).

1969. As Nos. E586/7 (Ulbricht), but with face values expressed in "M" (Mark).

E1197 1M. green 45 95
E1198 2M. brown 55 1·40

E372 Badge of D.D.R. Philatelists' Association

1969. 20th Anniv of D.D.R. Stamp Exhibition, Magdeburg (1st issue).

E1199 **E372** 10pf. gold, blue and red 35 25

See also Nos. E1233/4.

E373 Armed Volunteers

1969. Aid for Vietnam.

E1200 **E373** 10pf.+5pf. mult 35 25

E374 "Development of Youth"

1969. Int Peace Meeting, East Berlin. Mult.

E1201 10pf. Type E **374** 80 1·20
E1202 20pf.+5pf. Berlin landmarks (50×28 mm) 80 1·20
E1203 25pf. "Workers of the World" 80 1·20

E375 Inaugural Ceremony

1969. 5th Gymnastics and Athletic Meeting, Leipzig. Multicoloured.

E1204 5pf. Type E **375** 20 15
E1205 10pf.+5pf. Gymnastics 20 15
E1206 15pf. Athletes' parade 25 15
E1207 20pf.+5pf. "Sport" Art Exhibition 25 15
E1208 25pf. Athletic events 2·10 85
E1209 30pf. Presentation of colours 25 15

E376 Pierre de Coubertin (from bust by W. Forster)

1969. 75th Anniv of Pierre de Coubertin's Revival of Olympic Games' Movement.

E1210 **E376** 10pf. sepia, black & bl 20 15
E1211 - 25pf. sepia, blk & red 1·10 80

DESIGN: 25pf. Coubertin monument, Olympia.

E377 Knight

1969. World Sports Championships. Mult.

E1212 **E377** 20pf. gold, red & pur 25 20
E1213 - 20pf. multicoloured 25 20
E1214 - 20pf. multicoloured 25 20

DESIGNS AND EVENTS: No. E1212, 16th World Students' Team Chess Championship, Dresden; No. E1213, Cycle Wheel (World Covered Court Cycling Championships, Erfurt); No. E1214, Ball and net (2nd World Volleyball Cup).

E378 Fair Display Samples

1969. Leipzig Autumn Fair.

E1215 **E378** 10pf. multicoloured 25 30

E379 Rostock

1969. 20th Anniv of German Democratic Republic. (1st issue). Multicoloured.

E1216 10pf. Type E **379** 20 15
E1217 10pf. Neubrandenburg 20 15
E1218 10pf. Potsdam 20 15
E1219 10pf. Eisenhuttenstadt 20 15
E1220 10pf. Hoyerswerda 20 15
E1221 10pf. Magdeburg 20 15
E1222 10pf. Halle-Neustadt 20 15
E1223 10pf. Suhl 20 15
E1224 10pf. Dresden 20 15
E1225 10pf. Leipzig 20 15
E1226 10pf. Karl-Marx Stadt 20 15
E1227 10pf. East Berlin 20 15
MSE1228 88×110 mm. 1m. East Berlin and D.D.R. emblem (30×52 mm) 2·30 3·50

E380 Flags and Rejoicing Crowd (1/2-size illustration)

1969. 20th Anniv of German Democratic Republic (2nd issue). Sheet 110×154 mm.

MSE1229 E **380** 1m. multicoloured 1·80 2·10

E381 T.V. Tower, East Berlin

1969. 20th Anniv of German Democratic Republic (3rd issue). Completion of East Berlin T.V. Tower. Type E 381 and similar vert designs. Multicoloured.

E1230 10pf. Type E **381** 20 15
E1231 20pf. "Globe" of Tower on T.V. screen 30 20
MSE1232 96×115 mm. 1m. T.V. Tower and receiver 1·60 3·25

The design of No. **MS**E1232 is larger, 21½×60½ mm.

E382 O. von Guericke Memorial, Cathedral and Hotel International, Magdeburg

1969. 20th Anniv of D.D.R. Stamp Exhibition, Magdeburg (2nd issue). Multicoloured.

E1233 20pf. Type E **382** 25 15
E1234 40pf.+10pf. Von Guericke's vacuum experiment 1·30 65

E383 Ryvangen Memorial

1969. War Victims' Memorial, Ryvangen (Copenhagen).

E1235 **E383** 25pf. multicoloured 75 25

E384 U.F.I. Emblem

1969. 36th Int Fairs Union (U.F.I.) Congress, Leipzig.

E1236 **E384** 10pf. multicoloured 25 20
E1237 **E384** 15pf. multicoloured 2·10 45

E385 I.L.O. Emblem

1969. 50th Anniv of I.L.O.

E1238 **E385** 20pf. silver and green 25 15
E1239 **E385** 25pf. silver & mauve 1·60 45

E386 University Seal and Building

1969. 550th Anniv of Rostock University. Multicoloured.

E1240 10pf. Type E **386** 25 15
E1241 15pf. Steam-turbine rotor and curve (University emblem) 1·40 35

E387 "Horseman" Pastry-mould

1969. Lausitz Folk Art.

E1242	**E387**	10pf. brn, blk & flesh	1·40	1·40
E1243	-	20pf.+5pf. mult	45	45
E1244	-	50pf. multicoloured	2·30	2·40

DESIGNS: 20pf. Plate; 50pf. Pastry in form of Negro couple.

E388 Antonov An-24B

1969. Interflug Aircraft. Multicoloured.

E1245	20pf. Type E **388**	20	15
E1246	25pf. Ilyushin Il-18	1·60	1·20
E1247	30pf. Tupolev Tu-134	20	20
E1248	50pf. Mil Mi-8 helicopter DM-SPA	25	20

E389 "Siberian Teacher" (Svechnikov)

1969. Dresden Gallery Paintings (3rd series). Multicoloured.

E1249	5pf. Type E **389**	20	15
E1250	10pf. "Steel-worker" (Serov)	20	15
E1251	20pf. "Still Life" (Aslamasjan)	20	15
E1252	25pf. "A Warm Day" (Romas)	1·40	1·30
E1253	40pf. "Springtime Again" (Kabatchek)	25	20
E1254	50pf. "Man by the River" (Makovsky)	25	25

1970. Coil Stamp. As Nos. E577 etc, but value expressed in "M".

E1255	**E196**	1m. olive	90	3·75

1970. Celebrities Annivs. (3rd series). As Type E 352.

E1256	5pf. blue	25	15
E1257	10pf. brown	25	15
E1258	15pf. blue	25	15
E1259	20pf. purple	45	15
E1260	25pf. blue	3·00	75
E1261	40pf. red	60	25

DESIGNS: 5pf. E. Barlach (sculptor and playwright; birth cent); 10pf. J. Gutenberg (printer; 500th death anniv) (1968); 15pf. K. Tucholsky (author; 80th birth anniv); 20pf. Beethoven (birth bicent); 25pf. F. Holderlin (poet; birth bicent); 40 pf G. W. F. Hegel (philosopher; birth bicent).

E390 Red fox

1970. Int Fur Auction, Leipzig. Mult.

E1262	10pf. Rabbit	20	15
E1263	20pf. Type E **390**	25	15
E1264	25pf. European mink	3·75	3·00
E1265	40pf. Common hamster	45	25

E391 "Little Brother and Little Sister"

1970. Fairy Tales (5th series). "Little Brother and Little Sister".

E1266	**E 391**	5pf. multicoloured	25	30
E1267	-	10pf. multicoloured	25	30
E1268	-	15pf. multicoloured	70	70
E1269	-	20pf. multicoloured	70	70
E1270	-	25pf. multicoloured	25	30
E1271	-	30pf. multicoloured	25	30

DESIGNS: 10pf. to 30pf. showing different scenes.

E392 Telephone and Electrical Switchgear

1970. Leipzig Spring Fair. Multicoloured.

E1272	10pf. Type E **392**	20	15
E1273	15pf. High-voltage transformer (vert)	75	30

E393 Horseman's Gravestone (A.D. 700)

1970. Archaeological Discoveries.

E1274	**E393**	10pf. olive, blk & grn	20	20
E1275	-	20pf. black, yell & red	20	20
E1276	-	25pf. grn, blk & yell	1·10	1·50
E1277	-	40pf. chestnut, black and brown	25	20

DESIGNS: 20pf. Helmet (A.D. 500); 25pf. Bronze basin (1000 B.C.); 40pf. Clay drum (2500 B.C.).

E394 Lenin and "Iskra" (= the Spark) press

1970. Birth Centenary of Lenin. Multicoloured.

E1278	10pf. Type E **394**	20	15
E1279	20pf. Lenin and Clara Zetkin	20	15
E1280	25pf. Lenin and "State and Revolution" (book)	2·50	1·30
E1281	40pf. Lenin Monument, Eisleben	20	15
E1282	70pf. Lenin Square, East Berlin	35	25
MSE1283	118×84 mm. 1m. Lenin (vert)	2·10	3·75

1970. Protected Plants (3rd series). Vert designs as Type E 367. Multicoloured.

E1284	10pf. Sea kale ("Crambe maritima")	20	15
E1285	20pf. Pasque flower ("Pulsatilla vulgaris")	20	15
E1286	25pf. Fringed gentian ("Gentiana ciliata")	2·30	2·40
E1287	30pf. Military orchid ("Orchis militaris")	20	20
E1288	40pf. Labrador tea ("Ledum palustre")	25	30
E1289	70pf. Round-leaved wintergreen ("Pyrola rotundifolia")	35	40

E395 Capture of the Reichstag, 1945

1970. 25th Anniv of "Liberation from Fascism". Multicoloured.

E1290	10pf. Type E **395**	25	15
E1291	20pf. Newspaper headline, Kremlin and State Building, East Berlin	25	15
E1292	25pf. C.M.E.A. Building, Moscow and flags	1·50	65
MSE1293	135×105 mm. 70pf. Buchenwald Monument (horiz)	2·10	3·00

E396 Shortwave Aerial

1970. 25th Anniv of D.D.R. Broadcasting Service. Multicoloured.

E1294	10pf. Type E **396**	70	70
E1295	15pf. Radio Station, East Berlin (horiz) (50×28 mm)	1·10	1·20

E397 Globe and Ear of Corn

1970. 5th World Corn and Bread Congress, Dresden. Multicoloured.

E1296	20pf. Type E **397**	1·10	1·20
E1297	25pf. Palace of Culture and ear of corn	1·10	1·20

E398 Fritz Heckert Medal

1970. 25th Annivs of German Confederation of Trade Unions and World Trade Union Federation ("Federation Syndicale Mondiale"). Mult.

E1298	20pf. Type E **398**	20	15
E1299	25pf. F.S.M. Emblem	70	70

E399 Gods Amon, Shu and Tefnut

1970. Sudanese Archaeological Excavations by Humboldt University Expedition. Multicoloured.

E1300	10pf. Type E **399**	20	15
E1301	15pf. King Arnekhamani	20	15
E1302	20pf. Cattle frieze	20	15
E1303	25pf. Prince Arka	1·50	95
E1304	30pf. God Arensnuphis (vert)	20	15
E1305	40pf. War elephants and prisoners	20	15
E1306	50pf. God Apedemak	20	15

The above designs reproduce carvings unearthed at the Lions' Temple, Musawwarat, Sudan.

E400 Road Patrol

1970. 25th Anniv of "Deutsche Volkspolizei" (police force). Multicoloured.

E1307	5pf. Type E **400**	25	15
E1308	10pf. Policewoman with children	25	15
E1309	15pf. Radio patrol car	25	15
E1310	20pf. Railway policeman and Class SVT18.16 diesel-hydraulic locomotive	25	15
E1311	25pf. River police in patrol boat	2·00	45

E401 D.K.B. Emblem

1970. 25th Anniv of "Deutscher Kulturbund" (cultural assn).

E1312	**E401**	10pf. brown, silver and blue	2·75	3·25
E1313	-	25pf. brown, gold and blue	2·75	3·00

DESIGN: 25pf. Johannes Becher medal.

E402 Arms of D.D.R. and Poland

1970. 20th Anniv of Gorlitz Agreement on Oder-Neisse Border.

E1314	**E402**	20pf. multicoloured	35	25

E403 Vaulting

1970. 3rd Children and Young People's Sports Days. Multicoloured.

E1315	10pf. Type E **403**	20	15
E1316	20pf.+5pf. Hurdling	60	20

E404 Boy Pioneer with Neckerchief

1970. 6th Young Pioneers Meeting. Cottbus. Multicoloured.

E1317	10pf.+5pf. Type E **404**	30	45
E1318	25pf.+5pf. Girl pioneer with neckerchief	30	45

Nos. E1317/18 were issued together, se-tenant, forming a composite design.

E405 Cecilienhof Castle

1970. 25th Anniv of Potsdam Agreement.

E1319	**E405**	10pf. yellow, red and black	25	45
E1320	-	20pf. black, red and yellow	25	45
E1321	-	25pf. black and red	25	45

DESIGNS—VERT: 20pf. "Potsdam Agreement" in four languages. HORIZ (77×28 mm): 25pf. Conference delegates around the table.

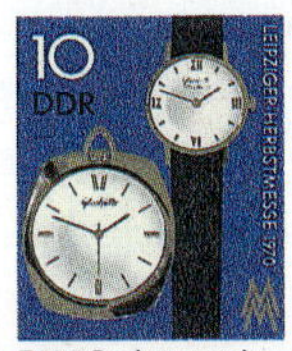

E406 Pocket-watch and Wristwatch

1970. Leipzig Autumn Fair.

E1322	**E406**	10pf. multicoloured	35	25

E407 T. Neubauer and M. Poser

1970. "Anti-Fascist Resistance".

E1323	**E407**	20pf. purple, red & bl	25	25
E1324	-	25pf. olive and red	30	35

DESIGN—VERT: 25pf. "Motherland"—detail from Soviet War Memorial, Treptow, Berlin.

E408 Pres. Ho-Chi-Minh

1970. Aid for Vietnam and Ho-Chi-Minh. Commemoration.

E1325	**E408**	20pf.+5pf. black, red and pink	45	25

E409 Compass and Map

1970. World "Orienteering" Championships. East Germany. Multicoloured.

E1326	10pf. Type E **409**	25	15
E1327	25pf. Runner and three map sections	1·50	45

E410 "Forester Scharf's Birthday" (Nagel)

1970. "The Art of Otto Nagel, Kathe Kollwitz and Ernst Barlach".

E1328	**E410**	10pf. multicoloured	20	15
E1329	-	20pf. multicoloured	20	15
E1330	-	25pf. brown & mauve	1·60	1·70
E1331	-	30pf. black and pink	20	15
E1332	-	40pf. black and yellow	20	15
E1333	-	50pf. black and yellow	25	20

DESIGNS: 20pf. "Portrait of a Young Girl" (Nagel); 25pf. "No More War" (Kollwitz); 30pf. "Mother and Child" (Kollwitz); 40pf. Sculptured head from Gustrow Cenotaph (Barlach); 50pf. "The Flute-player" (Barlach).

E411 "The Little Trumpeter" (Weineck Memorial, Halle)

1970. 2nd National Youth Stamp Exhibition, Karl-Marx-Stadt. Multicoloured.

E1334	10pf. Type E **411**	25	40
E1335	15pf.+5pf. East German 25pf. stamp of 1959	25	40

E412 Flags Emblem

1970. "Comrades-in-Arms". Warsaw Pact Military Manoeuvres.

E1336	**E412**	10pf. multicoloured	20	20
E1337	**E412**	20pf. multicoloured	25	30

E413 Musk Ox

1970. Animals in East Berlin "Tierpark" (Zoo). Multicoloured.

E1338	10pf. Type E **413**	35	20
E1339	15pf. Whale-headed Stork	35	20
E1340	20pf. Addax	70	40
E1341	25pf. Sun bear	6·75	6·25

E414 U.N. Emblem and Headquarters, New York

1970. 25th Anniv of United Nations.

E1342	**E414**	20pf. multicoloured	75	30

E415 Engels

1970. 150th Birth Anniv of Friedrich Engels.

E1343	**E415**	10pf. black, grey and orange	25	15
E1344	-	20pf. blk, grn & orge	25	15
E1345	-	25pf. blk, red & orge	1·70	95

DESIGNS: 20pf. Engels, Marx and "Communist Manifesto"; 25pf. Engels and "Anti-Duhring".

E416 "Epiphyllum hybr"

1970. Cacti Cultivation in D.D.R. Mult.

E1346	5pf. Type E **416**	20	15
E1347	10pf. "Astrophytum myriostigma"	20	15
E1348	15pf. "Echinocereus salmdyckianus"	20	15
E1349	20pf. "Selenicereus grandiflorus"	20	15
E1350	25pf. "Hamatoc setispinus"	2·40	2·20
E1351	30pf. "Mamillaria boolii"	30	15

1970. Birth Bicentenary of Beethoven. As No. E1259, but colour and face value changed, in sheet 81×55 mm.

MSE1352	1m. green	1·80	2·10

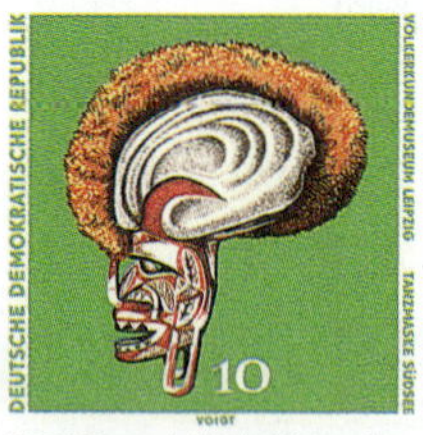

E417 Dancer's Mask, Bismarck Archipelago

1971. Exhibits from the Ethnological Museum, Leipzig.

E1353	**E417**	10pf. multicoloured	20	15
E1354	-	20pf. brown & orange	20	15
E1355	-	25pf. multicoloured	1·20	90
E1356	-	40pf. brown and red	30	15

DESIGNS: 20pf. Bronze head, Benin; 25pf. Tea-pot, Thailand; 40pf. Zapotec earthenware Jaguar-god, Mexico.

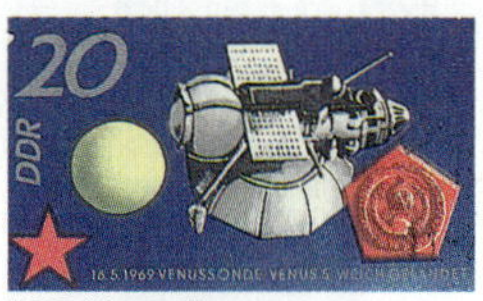

E418 "Venus 5"

1971. Soviet Space Research. Multicoloured.

E1357	20pf. Type E **418**	25	30
E1358	20pf. Orbital space station	25	30
E1359	20pf. "Luna 10" and "Luna 16"	55	55
E1360	20pf. Various "Soyuz" spacecraft	55	55
E1361	20pf. "Proton 1" satellite and "Vostok" rocket	55	55
E1362	20pf. "Molniya 1" communications satellite	55	55
E1363	20pf. Gagarin and "Vostok 1"	30	35
E1364	20pf. Leonov in space	30	35

E419 K. Liebknecht

1971. Birth Centenaries of Karl Liebknecht and Rosa Luxemburg (revolutionaries).

E1365	**E419**	20pf. mauve, gold and black	60	60
E1366	-	25pf. mauve, gold and black	60	60

DESIGN: 25pf. Rosa Luxemburg.

E420 J. R. Becher (poet)

1971. Celebrities' Birth Anniversaries.

E1367	**E420**	5pf. brown	20	15
E1368	-	10pf. blue	20	15
E1369	-	15pf. black	20	15
E1370	-	20pf. purple	20	15
E1371	-	25pf. green	1·00	85
E1372	-	50pf. blue	30	20

DESIGNS: 5pf. (80th birth anniv); 10pf. H. Mann (writer—birth cent); 15pf. J. Heartfield (artist—80th birth anniv); 20pf. W. Bredel (70th birth anniv); 25pf. F. Mehring (politician—125th birth anniv); 50pf. J. Kepler (astronomer—400th birth anniv).

See also Nos. E1427 and E1451/5.

E421 Soldier and Army Badge

1971. 15th Anniv of National People's Army.

E1373	**E421**	20pf. multicoloured	35	25

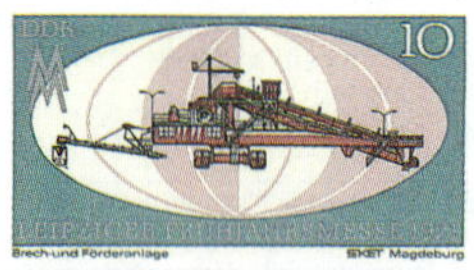

E422 "Sket" Mobile Ore-crusher

1971. Leipzig Spring Fair. Multicoloured.

E1374	10pf. Type E **422**	20	15
E1375	15pf. Dredger "Takraf"	25	15

E423 Proclamation of the Commune

1971. Centenary of Paris Commune.

E1376	**E423**	10pf. black, brown and red	25	15
E1377	-	20pf. black, brown and red	25	15
E1378	-	25pf. black, brown and red	80	75
E1379	-	30pf. black, grey and red	25	15

DESIGNS: 20pf. Women at the Place Blanche barricade; 25pf. Cover of "L'Internationale"; 30pf. Title page of Karl Marx's "The Civil War in France".

E424 "Lunokhod 1" on Moon's Surface

1971. Moon Mission of "Lunokhod 1".

E1380	**E424**	20pf. turquoise, blue and red	65	40

E425 St. Mary's Church

1971. Berlin Buildings. Multicoloured.

E1381	10pf. Type E **425**	20	15
E1382	15pf. Kopenick Castle (horiz)	20	15
E1383	20pf. Old Library (horiz)	20	15
E1384	25pf. Ermeler House	3·50	3·00
E1385	50pf. New Guardhouse (horiz)	25	20
E1386	70pf. National Gallery (horiz)	35	20

E426 "The Discus-thrower"

1971. 20th Anniv of D.D.R. National Olympics Committee.

E1387	**E426**	20pf. multicoloured	85	30

E427 Handclasp and XXV Emblem

1971. 25th Anniv of Socialist Unity Party.

E1388	**E427**	20pf. black, red and gold	35	20

E428 Schleife Costume

1971. Sorbian Dance Costumes. Mult.

E1389	10pf. Type E **428**	20	20
E1390	20pf. Hoyerswerda	20	20
E1391	25pf. Cottbus	90	95
E1392	40pf. Kamenz	25	25

For 10pf. and 20pf. in smaller size, see Nos. E1443/4.

E429 Self-portrait, c. 1500

1971. 500th Birth Anniv of Albrecht Durer. Paintings. Multicoloured.

E1393	10pf. Type E **429**	25	15
E1394	40pf. "The Three Peasants"	35	15
E1395	70pf. "Philipp Melanchthon"	2·10	1·10

E430 Construction Worker

1971. 8th S.E.D. Party Conference.

E1396	**E430**	5pf. multicoloured	20	15
E1397	-	10pf. multicoloured	20	15
E1398	-	20pf. multicoloured	20	15
E1399	-	25pf. multicoloured	55	55
E1400	-	20pf. gold, red and mauve	35	25

DESIGNS: 10pf. Technician; 20pf. (No. E1398) Farm girl; 20pf. (No. E1400) Conference emblem (smaller, 23×29 mm); 25pf. Soldier.

E432 "Internees"

1971. 20th Anniv of International Resistance Federation (F.I.R.). Lithographs from Fritz Cremer's "Buchenwaldzyklus".

E1401	**E432**	20pf. black & yellow	70	70
E1402	-	25pf. black and blue	70	70

DESIGN: 25pf. "Attack on Guard".

E433 Cherry stone with 180 Carved Heads

1971. Art Treasures of Dresden's Green Vaults. Multicoloured.

E1403		5pf. Type E **433**	20	15
E1404		10pf. Insignia of the Golden Fleece, c. 1730	20	15
E1405		15pf. Nuremberg jug, c. 1530	20	15
E1406		20pf. Mounted Moorish drummer figurine, c. 1720	20	15
E1407		25pf. Writing-case, 1562	1·10	1·30
E1408		30pf. St. George medallion, c. 1570	25	15

E434 Mongolian Arms

1971. 50th Anniv of Mongolian People's Republic.

E1409	**E434**	20pf. multicoloured	35	30

E435 Child's Face

1971. 25th Anniv of UNICEF.

E1410	**E435**	20pf. multicoloured	35	25

E436 Servicemen

1971. 10th Anniv of Berlin Wall. Mult.

E1411		20pf. Type E **436**	90	30
E1412		35pf. Brandenburg Gate	1·80	1·50

E437 "Ivan Franko" (liner)

1971. East German Shipbuilding Industry.

E1413	**E437**	10pf. brown	20	15
E1414	-	15pf. blue and brown	20	15
E1415	-	20pf. green	20	15
E1416	-	25pf. blue	1·50	1·40
E1417	-	40pf. brown	25	15
E1418	-	50pf. blue	25	15

DESIGNS: 15pf. "Irkutsk" (freighter); 20pf. "Rostock" freighter, 1966; 25pf. "Junge Welt" (fish-factory ship); 40pf. "Hansel" (container ship); 50pf. "Akademik Kurchatov" (research ship).

E438 Vietnamese Woman and Child

1971. Aid for Vietnam.

E1419	**E438**	10pf.+5pf. mult	35	25

E439 MAG-Butadien Plant

1971. Leipzig Autumn Fair.

E1420	**E439**	10pf. vio, mve & grn	20	15
E1421	-	25pf. violet, grn & bl	35	30

DESIGN: 25pf. SKL reactor plant.

E440 Upraised Arms (motif by J. Heartfield)

1971. Racial Equality Year.

E1422	**E440**	35pf. black, sil & bl	35	25

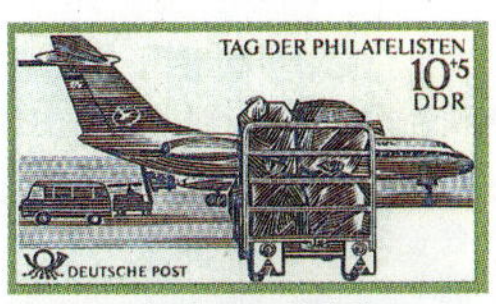

E441 Tupolev Tu-134 Mail Plane at Airport

1971. Philatelists' Day.

E1423	**E441**	10pf.+5pf. blue, red and green	20	15
E1424	-	25pf. red, green & bl	60	55

DESIGN: 25pf. Milestone and Zurner's measuring cart.

E442 Wiltz Memorial, Luxembourg

1971. Monuments. Multicoloured.

E1425		25pf. Type E **442**	25	20
E1426		35pf. Karl Marx monument, Karl-Marx-Stadt	45	20

1971. 150th Birth Anniv of R. Virchow (physician). As Type E 420.

E1427		40pf. plum	45	20

E443 German Violin

1971. Musical Instruments in Markneukirchen Museum. Multicoloured.

E1428		10pf. North African "darbuka"	20	15
E1429		15pf. Mongolian "morin chuur"	20	15
E1430		20pf. Type E **443**	20	15
E1431		25pf. Italian mandolin	20	15
E1432		40pf. Bohemian bagpies	25	25
E1433		50pf. Sudanese "kasso"	1·50	1·50

E444 "Dahlta O 10 A" Theodolite

1971. 125th Anniv of Carl Zeiss Optical Works, Jena.

E1434	**E444**	10pf. black, red & bl	70	70
E1435	-	20pf. black, red & bl	70	70
E1436	-	25pf. blue, yellow and ultramarine	70	70

DESIGNS—VERT: 20pf. "Ergaval" microscope. HORIZ (52×29 mm) 25pf. Planetarium.

E445 Donkey and Windmill

1971. Fairy Tales (6th series). As Type E 445. "The Town Musicians of Bremen".

E1437		5pf. multicoloured	25	30
E1438		10pf. multicoloured	25	30
E1439		15pf. multicoloured	70	95
E1440		20pf. multicoloured	70	95
E1441		25pf. multicoloured	25	30
E1442		30pf. multicoloured	25	30

1971. Sorbian Dance Costumes. As Nos. E1389/90 but smaller, size 23×28 mm.

E1443	**E428**	10pf. multicoloured	25	15
E1444	-	20pf. multicoloured	75	50

E446 Tobogganing

1971. Winter Olympic Games, Sapporo, Japan (1972).

E1445	**E 446**	5pf. black, green and mauve	20	15
E1446	-	10pf.+5pf. blk, bl & mve	20	15
E1447	-	15pf.+5pf. black, grn & bl	25	15
E1448	-	20pf. black, mauve & violet	25	15
E1449	-	25pf. black, violet & mauve	2·10	1·60
E1450	-	70pf. black, blue and violet	35	20

DESIGNS: 10pf. Figure skating; 15pf. Speed skating; 20pf. Cross-country skiing; 25pf. Biathlon; 70pf. Ski jumping.

1972. German Celebrities. As Type E 420.

E1451		10pf. green	20	15
E1452		20pf. mauve	20	15
E1453		25pf. blue	20	15
E1454		35pf. brown	20	15
E1455		50pf. lilac	1·60	1·70

CELEBRITIES: 10pf. J. Tralow (writer); 20pf. L. Frank (writer); 25pf. K. A. Kocor (composer); 35pf. H. Schliemann (archaeologist); 50pf. Caroline Neuber (actress).

E447 Gypsum from Eisleben

1972. Minerals. Multicoloured.

E1456		5pf. Type E **447**	20	15
E1457		10pf. Zinnwaldite, Zinnwald	20	15
E1458		20pf. Malachite, Ullersreuth	20	15
E1459		25pf. Amethyst, Wiesenbad	20	15
E1460		35pf. Halite, Merkers	25	15
E1461		50pf. Proustite, Schneeberg	1·50	1·30

E448 Vietnamese Woman

1972. Aid for Vietnam.

E1462	**E448**	10pf.+5pf. mult	35	20

E449 Soviet Exhibition Hall

1972. Leipzig Spring Fair. Multicoloured.

E1463		10pf. Type E **449**	20	15
E1464		25pf. East German and Soviet flags	25	30

E450 Anemometer of 1896 and Koppen's Chart of 1876

1972. International Meteorologists Meeting, Leipzig. Three sheets, each 85×57 mm. Multicoloured.

MSE1465		20pf. Type E **450**; 35pf. Weather station and clouds; 70pf. Satellite and weather map	2·50	3·25

E451 W.H.O. Emblem

1972. World Health Day.

E1466	**E451**	35pf. ultramarine, silver and blue	35	25

E452 Kamov Ka-26 Helicopter

1972. East German Aircraft. Multicoloured.

E1467	5pf. Type E **452**	20	20
E1468	10pf. Letov Z-37 Cmelak crop-sprayer DM-SMC	20	20
E1469	35pf. Ilyushin Il-62M	25	20
E1470	1m. Ilyushin Il-62M	1·70	1·70

E453 Wrestling

1972. Olympic Games, Munich. Mult.

E1471	5pf. Type E **453**	20	15
E1472	10pf.+5pf. High-diving	20	15
E1473	20pf. Pole-vaulting	20	15
E1474	25pf.+10pf. Rowing	20	20
E1475	35pf. Handball	30	25
E1476	70pf. Gymnastics	3·50	2·40

E454 Soviet and East German Flags

1972. 25th Anniv of German–Soviet Friendship Society. Multicoloured.

E1477	10pf. Type E **454**	1·20	95
E1478	20pf. Brezhnev (U.S.S.R.) and Honecker (D.D.R.)	1·20	95

E455 Steel Workers

1972. Trade Unions Federation Congress.

E1479	**E455**	10pf. pur, orge & brn	25	25
E1480	-	35pf. blue and brown	25	25

DESIGN: 35pf. Students.

E456 "Karneol" Rose

1972. International Rose Exhibition. German Species. Multicoloured.

E1481	5pf. Type E **456**	20	15
E1482	10pf. "Berger's Rose"	20	15
E1483	15pf. "Charme"	2·10	2·20
E1484	20pf. "Izetka Spreeathen"	20	15
E1485	25pf. "Kopernicker Sommer"	20	15
E1486	35pf. "Professor Knoll"	25	15
E1497	10pf. "Berger's Rose"	25	25
E1498	25pf. "Kopernicker Sommer"	1·60	70
E1499	35pf. "Professor Knoll"	1·60	70

Nos. E1497/9 are smaller, size 24×28 mm.

E457 "Portrait of Young Man"

1972. 500th Birth Anniv of Lucas Cranach the Elder. Multicoloured.

E1487	5pf. Type E **457**	20	15
E1488	20pf. "Mother and Child"	20	20
E1489	25pf. "Margarete Luther"	30	45
E1490	70pf. "Nymph" (horiz)	2·50	3·75

E458 Compass and Motor Cyclist

1972. Sports and Technical Sciences Association. Multicoloured.

E1491	5pf. Type E **458**	20	20
E1492	10pf. Light airplane and parachute	20	20
E1493	20pf. Target and obstacle race	20	20
E1494	25pf. Radio set and Morse key	1·00	1·00
E1495	35pf. "Wilhelm Pieck" (brigantine) and propeller	20	20

E459 "Young Worker Reading" (J. Damme)

1972. Int Book Year.

E1496	**E459**	50pf. multicoloured	75	40

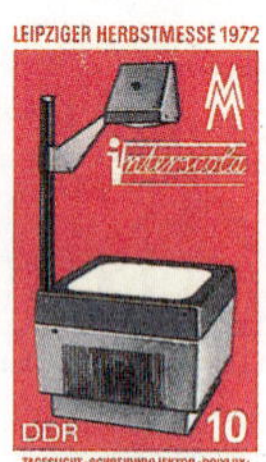

E460 Overhead Projector

1972. Leipzig Autumn Fair.

E1500	**E460**	10pf. black and red	20	15
E1501	-	25pf. black and green	25	30

DESIGN—HORIZ: 25pf. Slide projector.

E461 G. Dimitrov

1972. 90th Birth Anniv of Georgi Dimitrov (Bulgarian statesman).

E1502	**E461**	20pf. black and red	45	30

E462 "Catching Birds" (Egyptian relief painting, c. 2400 B.C.)

1972. "Interartes" Stamp Exhibition, East Berlin. Multicoloured.

E1503	10pf. Type E **462**	20	15
E1504	15pf.+5pf. "Persian Spearman" (glazed tile, c. 500 B.C.)	1·00	1·00
E1505	20pf. Anatolian tapestry c. 1400 B.C	20	15
E1506	35pf.+5pf. "The Grapesellers" (Max Lingner, 1949) (horiz)	25	15

E463 Red Cross Team and Patient

1972. East German Red Cross.

E1507	**E463**	10pf. ultramarine, blue and red	25	30
E1508	-	15pf. ultramarine, blue and red	25	30
E1509	-	35pf. red, blue and ultramarine	25	30

DESIGNS—VERT: 15pf. Sea-rescue launch. HORIZ (50½×28 mm): 35pf. World map on cross, and transport.

E464 Terrestrial Globe (J. Praetorius, 1568)

1972. Terrestrial and Celestial Globes. Mult.

E1510	5pf. Arab celestial globe, 1279	20	15
E1511	10pf. Type E **464**	20	15
E1512	15pf. Globe clock (J. Reinhold and G. Roll, 1586)	3·00	3·00
E1513	20pf. Globe clock (J. Burgi, 1590)	20	20
E1514	25pf. Armillary sphere (J. Moeller, 1687)	25	25
E1515	35pf. Heraldic celestial globe, 1690	30	35

E465 Monument

1972. German–Polish Resistance Memorial, Berlin, Inauguration.

E1516	**E465**	25pf. multicoloured	45	25

E466 Educating Juveniles

1972. Juvenile Inventions Exhibition. Mult.

E1517	10pf. Type E **466**	25	25
E1518	25pf. Youths with welding machine	25	25

E467 "Mauz and Hoppel" (Cat and Hare)

1972. Children's T.V. Characters. Mult.

E1519	5pf. Type E **467**	25	25
E1520	10pf. "Fuchs and Elster" (Fox and Magpie)	25	25
E1521	15pf. "Herr Uhn" (Eagle Owl)	90	95
E1522	20pf. "Frau Igel and Borstel" (Hedgehogs)	90	95
E1523	25pf. "Schuffel and Pieps" (Dog and Mouse)	25	25
E1524	35pf. "Paulchen" (Paul from the children's library)	25	25

E468 "The Snow Queen"

1972. Fairy Tales (7th series). As Type E 468. "The Snow Queen" (Hans Christian Andersen).

E1525	5pf. multicoloured	25	40
E1526	10pf. multicoloured	70	1·20
E1527	15pf. multicoloured	25	40
E1528	20pf. multicoloured	25	40
E1529	25pf. multicoloured	70	1·20
E1530	35pf. multicoloured	25	40

E469 H. Heine

1972. 175th Birth Anniv of Heinrich Heine (poet). Sheet 60×86 mm.

MSE1531	E **469** 1m. black, red and green	2·10	2·10

E470 Arms of U.S.S.R.

1972. 50th Anniv of U.S.S.R.

E1532	**E470**	20pf. multicoloured	45	25

E471 Leninplatz, East Berlin

1973. (a) Size 29×24 mm.

E1533	-	5pf. green	25	25
E1534	-	10pf. green	55	25
E1535	-	15pf. mauve	55	25
E1536	**E471**	20pf. mauve	1·00	40
E1537	-	25pf. green	1·20	25
E1538	-	30pf. orange	25	20
E1539	-	35pf. blue	1·00	40
E1540	-	40pf. violet	70	25
E1541	-	50pf. blue	70	25
E1542	-	60pf. purple	1·00	20
E1543	-	70pf. brown	70	25
E1544	-	80pf. blue	1·10	20
E1545	-	1m. green	1·60	25
E1546	-	2m. red	2·50	25
E1546a	-	3m. mauve	2·75	60

(b) Size 22×18 mm.

No.	Type	Description	Unused	Used
E1548		10pf. green	50	35
E1549a		25pf. green	50	25
E2197		5pf. green	25	15
E2198		10pf. green	40	15
E2199		15pf. mauve	50	30
E2200	**E471**	20pf. mauve	65	15
E2202	-	30pf. orange	55	40
E2203	-	35pf. blue	60	35
E2204	-	40pf. violet	1·10	45
E2205	-	50pf. blue	65	40
E2206	-	60pf. purple	90	40
E2207	-	70pf. brown	80	55
E2208	-	80pf. blue	1·00	45
E2209	-	1m. green	1·10	50
E2210	-	2m. red	2·30	1·10
E2211	-	3m. mauve	3·25	1·20

DESIGNS: 5pf. Eastern white pelican and Alfred Brehm House, Tierpark, Berlin; 10pf. (Nos. E1534, E1548) Neptune Fountain and Rathausstrasse, Berlin; 10pf. (No. E2198) Palace of the Republic, Berlin; 15pf. Apartment Blocks, Fishers' Island, Berlin; 25pf. TV Tower, Alexander Square, Berlin; 30 pf, Workers' Memorial, Halle; 35pf. Karl-Marx-Stadt; 40pf. Brandenburg Gate Berlin; 50pf. New Guardhouse, Berlin; 60pf. Crown Gate and Zwinger, Dresden; 70pf. Old Town Hall, Leipzig; 80pf. Rostock-Warnemunde; 1m. Soviet War Memorial, Treptow; 2, 3m. Arms of East Germany.

E472 M. da Caravaggio

1973. Cultural Anniversaries.

No.	Type	Description	Unused	Used
E1551	**E472**	5pf. brown	1·10	1·10
E1552	-	10pf. green	20	15
E1553	-	20pf. purple	20	15
E1554	-	25pf. blue	20	15
E1555	-	35pf. red	25	20

PORTRAITS AND ANNIVERSARIES: 5pf. (painter, 400th birth anniv); 10pf. Friedrich Wolf (dramatist, 85th birth anniv); 20pf. Max Reger (composer, birth cent.); 25pf. Max Reinhardt (impressario, birth cent.); 35pf. Johannes Dieckmann (politician, 80th birth anniv).

E473 "Lebachia speciosa"

1973. Fossils in Palaeontological Collection, Berlin Natural History Museum. Multicoloured.

No.	Description	Unused	Used
E1556	10pf. Type E **473**	20	15
E1557	15pf. "Spheronopteris hol-landica"	20	15
E1558	20pf. "Pterodactylus kochi"	20	15
E1559	25pf. "Botryopteris"	20	15
E1560	35pf. "Archaeopteryx litho-graphica"	20	15
E1561	70pf. "Odontopleura ovata"	2·10	1·90

E474 Copernicus (image scaled to 63% of original size)

1973. 500th Birth Anniv of Copernicus.

No.	Type	Description	Unused	Used
E1562	**E474**	70pf. multicoloured	90	45

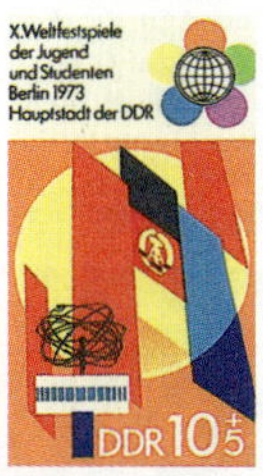
E475 National Flags

1973. 10th World Youth Festival, Berlin (1st issue). Multicoloured.

No.	Description	Unused	Used
E1563	10pf.+5pf. Type E **475**	20	20
E1564	25pf.+5pf. Youths and peace dove	30	30

See also Nos. E1592/6.

E476 Bobsleigh Course

1973. 15th World Bobsleigh Championships, Oberhof.

No.	Type	Description	Unused	Used
E1565	**E476**	35pf. multicoloured	45	40

E477 Combine Harvester

1973. Leipzig Spring Fair. Multicoloured.

No.	Description	Unused	Used
E1566	10pf. Type E **477**	20	20
E1567	25pf. Automatic lathe	35	40

E478 Firecrests

1973. Songbirds. Multicoloured.

No.	Description	Unused	Used
E1568	5pf. Type E **478**	20	20
E1569	10pf. White-winged crossbill	20	20
E1570	15pf. Bohemian waxwing	20	20
E1571	20pf. Bluethroats	20	20
E1572	25pf. Eurasian goldfinch	20	20
E1573	35pf. Golden oriole	25	20
E1574	40pf. Grey wagtail	25	25
E1575	60pf. Wallcreeper	3·25	3·25

E479 Class 211 Electric Locomotive No. 200-3

1973. Railway Rolling Stock. Multicoloured.

No.	Description	Unused	Used
E1576	5pf. Type E **479**	20	15
E1577	10pf. Refrigerator wagon	20	15
E1578	20pf. Long-distance passenger carriage	20	15
E1579	25pf. Tank wagon	20	15
E1580	35pf. Double-deck carriage	20	20
E1581	85pf. Passenger carriage	2·50	2·75

E480 "King Lear" (directed by W. Langhoff)

1973. Famous Theatrical Productions. Mult.

No.	Description	Unused	Used
E1582	10pf. Type E **480**	20	15
E1583	25pf. "A Midsummer Night's Dream" (opera) (Benjamin Britten) (directed by Walter Felsenstein)	20	15
E1584	35pf. "Mother Courage" (directed by Berthold Brecht)	1·00	95

E481 H. Matern

1973. 80th Birth Anniv of Hermann Matern (politician).

No.	Type	Description	Unused	Used
E1585	**E481**	40pf. red	60	30

E482 Goethe and House

1973. Cultural Celebrities and Houses in Weimar. Multicoloured.

No.	Description	Unused	Used
E1586	10pf. Type E **482**	20	15
E1587	15pf. C. M. Wieland (writer)	20	15
E1588	20pf. F. Schiller (writer)	20	15
E1589	25pf. J. G. Herder (writer)	20	15
E1590	35pf. Lucas Cranach the Elder (painter)	20	15
E1591	50pf. Franz Liszt (composer)	2·40	1·80

E483 Firework Display

1973. World Festival of Youth and Students, East Berlin (2nd issue). Multicoloured.

No.	Description	Unused	Used
E1592	5pf. Type E **483**	20	25
E1593	15pf. Students ("Int Solidarity")	20	15
E1594	20pf. Young workers ("Economic Integration")	20	15
E1595	30pf. Students ("Aid for Young Nations")	1·50	75
E1596	35pf. Youth and Students' Emblems	20	15
MSE1597	86×107 mm. 50pf. Emblem and Brandenburg Gate (26.7)	1·30	1·00

E484 W. Ulbricht

1973. Death of Walter Ulbricht.

No.	Type	Description	Unused	Used
E1598	**E484**	20pf. black	80	40

E485 Power Network

1973. 10th Anniv of "Peace" United Energy Supply System.

No.	Type	Description	Unused	Used
E1599	**E485**	35pf. orge, pur & bl	45	40

E486 "Leisure Activities"

1973. Leipzig Autumn Fair. Multicoloured.

No.	Description	Unused	Used
E1600	10pf. Type E **486**	25	15
E1601	25pf. Yacht, guitar and power drill	40	30

E487 Militiaman and Emblem

1973. 20th Anniv of Workers Militia. Mult.

No.	Description	Unused	Used
E1602	10pf. Type E **487**	25	20
E1603	20pf. Militia guard	40	25

No.	Description	Unused	Used
MSE1604	61×87 mm. 50pf. Militiamen (vert)	90	95

E488 Red Flag encircling Globe

1973. 15th Anniv of "Problems of Peace and Socialism".

No.	Type	Description	Unused	Used
E1605	**E488**	20pf. red and gold	55	30

E489 Langenstein-Zwieberge Memorial

1973. Langenstein-Zwieberge Monument.

No.	Type	Description	Unused	Used
E1606	**E489**	25pf. multicoloured	55	30

E490 U.N. H.Q. and Emblems

1973. Admission of German Democratic Republic to United Nations Organization.

No.	Type	Description	Unused	Used
E1607	**E490**	35pf. multicoloured	60	30

E491 "Young Couple" (G. Glombitza)

1973. Philatelists' Day and 3rd Young Philatelists' Stamp Exhibition, Halle.

No.	Type	Description	Unused	Used
E1608	**E491**	20pf.+5pf. mult	35	25

E492 Congress Emblem

1973. 8th World Trade Union Congress, Varna, Bulgaria.

No.	Type	Description	Unused	Used
E1609	**E492**	35pf. multicoloured	45	40

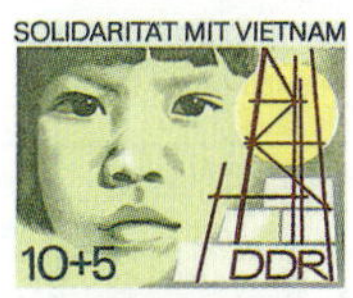
E493 Vietnamese Child

1973. "Solidarity with Vietnam".

No.	Type	Description	Unused	Used
E1610	**E493**	10pf.+5pf. mult	35	25

E494 Launching Rocket

1973. Soviet Science and Technology Days. Multicoloured.

E1611	10pf. Type E **494**	20	15
E1612	20pf. Soviet map and emblem (horiz)	20	15
E1613	25pf. Oil refinery	1·10	1·00

E495 L. Corvalan

1973. Solidarity with the Chilean People. Multicoloured.

E1614	10pf.+5pf. Type E **495**	25	30
E1615	25pf.+5pf. Pres. Allende	55	55

E496 "Child with Doll" (C. L. Vogel)

1973. Paintings by Old Masters. Mult.

E1616	10pf. Type E **496**	20	20
E1617	15pf. "Madonna with Rose" (Parmigianino)	20	20
E1618	20pf. "Woman with Fair Hair" (Rubens)	20	20
E1619	25pf. "Lady in White" (Titian)	20	20
E1620	35pf. "Archimedes" (D. Fetti)	25	20
E1621	70pf. "Flower Arrangement" (Jan D. de Heem)	3·00	2·20

E497 Flame Emblem

1973. 25th Anniv of Declaration of Human Rights.

E1622	**E497**	35pf. multicoloured	55	40

E498 "Catching the Pike"

1973. Fairy Tales (8th series). As Type E 498. "At the Bidding of the Pike".

E1623	5pf. multicoloured	25	30
E1624	10pf. multicoloured	90	1·70
E1625	15pf. multicoloured	25	30
E1626	20pf. multicoloured	25	30
E1627	25pf. multicoloured	90	1·70
E1628	35pf. multicoloured	25	30

E499 E. Hoernle

1974. Socialist Personalities.

E1629	**E499**	10pf. grey	25	20
E1630	-	10pf. lilac	25	20
E1631	-	10pf. blue	25	20
E1632	-	10pf. brown	25	20
E1633	-	10pf. green	25	20
E1634	-	10pf. brown	25	20
E1635	-	10pf. blue	25	20
E1636	-	10pf. brown	25	20

PERSONALITIES: No. E1630, Etkar Andre; E1631, Paul Merker; E1632, Hermann Duncker; E1633, Fritz Heckert; E1634, Otto Grotewohl; E1635, Wilhelm Florin; E1636, Georg Handke.

See also Nos. E1682/4.

E500 Pablo Neruda

1974. Pablo Neruda (Chilean poet) Commem.

E1637	**E500**	20pf. multicoloured	45	30

E501 "Comecon" Emblem

1974. 25th Anniv of Council for Mutual Economic Aid.

E1638	**E501**	20pf. multicoloured	45	25

E502 "Echinopsis multiplex"

1974. Cacti. Multicoloured.

E1639	5pf. Type E **502**	20	15
E1640	10pf. "Lobivia haageana"	20	15
E1641	15pf. "Parodia sanguiniflora"	2·75	2·75
E1642	20pf. "Gymnocal monvillei"	20	20
E1643	25pf. "Neoporteria rapifera"	25	25
E1644	35pf. "Notocactus concinnus"	30	35

E503 Handball Players

1974. 8th Men's World Indoor Handball Championships.

E1645	**E503**	5pf. multicoloured	40	45
E1646	-	10pf. multicoloured	40	45
E1647	-	35pf. multicoloured	40	45

Nos. E1645/7 were issued together, se-tenant, forming a composite design of a handball match.

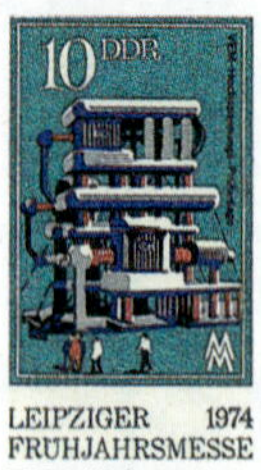

E504 High-tension Testing Plant

1974. Leipzig Spring Fair. Multicoloured.

E1648	10pf. Type E **504**	25	15
E1649	25pf. "Robotron" computer (horiz)	35	30

E505 "Rhodophyllus sinuatus"

1974. Poisonous Fungi. Multicoloured.

E1650	5pf. Type E **505**	20	15
E1651	10pf. "Boletus satanas"	20	15
E1652	15pf. "Amanita pantherina"	20	15
E1653	20pf. "Amanita muscaria"	20	15
E1654	25pf. "Gyromitra esculenta"	25	15
E1655	30pf. "Inocybe patouillardii"	25	25
E1656	35pf. "Amanita phalloides"	30	25
E1657	40pf. "Clitocybe dealbata"	2·30	2·10

E506 Gustav Kirchhoff

1974. Celebrities' Birth Anniversaries.

E1658	**E506**	5pf. black and grey	20	15
E1659	-	10pf. ultram & bl	20	15
E1660	-	20pf. red and pink	20	20
E1661	-	25pf. green & turq	25	20
E1662	-	35pf. choc & brn	85	90

PORTRAITS AND ANNIVERSARIES: 5pf. (physicist, 150th); 10pf. Immanuel Kant (philosopher, 250th); 20pf. Elm Welk (writer, 90th); 25pf. Johann Herder (author, 230th); 35pf. Lion Feuchtwanger (novelist, 90th).

E507 Globe and "PEACE"

1974. 25th Anniv of 1st World Peace Congress.

E1663	**E507**	35pf. multicoloured	50	40

E508 Tractor Driver

1974. 25th Anniv of German Democratic Republic. Multicoloured.

E1664	10pf. Type E **508**	20	15
E1665	20pf. Students	20	15
E1666	25pf. Woman worker	20	20
E1667	35pf. East German family	1·10	1·00

E509 Buk Lighthouse, 1878

1974. Lighthouses (1st series). Multicoloured.

E1668	10pf. Type E **509**	20	15
E1669	15pf. Warnemunde lighthouse, 1898	20	15
E1670	20pf. Darsser Ort lighthouse, 1848	20	15
E1671	35pf. Arkona lighthouse in 1827 and 1902	20	15
E1672	40pf. Greifswalder Oie lighthouse, 1855	1·60	1·20

See also Nos. E1760/4.

E510 "Man and Woman looking at the Moon"

1974. Birth Bicentenary of Caspar Friedrich (painter). Multicoloured.

E1673	10pf. Type E **510**	20	15
E1674	20pf. "The Stages of Life" (seaside scene)	20	15
E1675	25pf. "Heath near Dresden"	2·10	2·00
E1676	35pf. "Trees in the Elbe Valley"	30	20
MSE1677	80×55 mm. E **511** 70pf. sepia	1·70	2·10

E512 Lace Pattern

1974. Plauen Lace.

E1678	**E512**	10pf. black and violet	20	15
E1679	-	20pf. brown, black and bistre	20	15
E1680	-	25pf. black, blue and turquoise	1·60	1·40
E1681	-	35pf. black, mauve and pink	25	20

DESIGNS: Nos. E1679/81, Lace patterns similar to Type E **512**.

1974. Socialist Personalities. As Type E 499.

E1682	10pf. blue	25	20
E1683	10pf. violet	25	20
E1684	10pf. brown	25	20

DESIGNS: No. E1682, R. Breitscheid; No. E1683, K. Burger; No. E1684, C. Moltmann.

E513 Show Jumping

1974. International Horse-breeders' Congress, Berlin. Multicoloured.

E1685	10pf. Type E **513**	20	15
E1686	20pf. Horse & trap (horiz)	20	15
E1687	25pf. Haflinger draught horses (horiz)	1·80	2·40
E1688	35pf. Horse-racing (horiz)	30	25

E514 Crane lifting Diesel Locomotive

1974. Leipzig Autumn Fair. Multicoloured.

E1689	10pf. Type E **514**	20	15
E1690	25pf. Agricultural machine	35	30

E515 "The Porcelain Shop"

1974. "Mon Plaisir". Exhibits in Dolls' Village, Castle Museum, Arnstadt. Mult.

E1691	5pf. Type E **515**	20	15
E1692	10pf. "Fairground Crier"	20	15
E1693	15pf. "Wine-tasting in Cellar"	20	15
E1694	20pf. "Cooper and Apprentice"	20	15
E1695	25pf. "Bagpiper playing for Dancing Bear"	1·90	2·00
E1696	35pf. "Butcher's Wife and Crone"	25	25

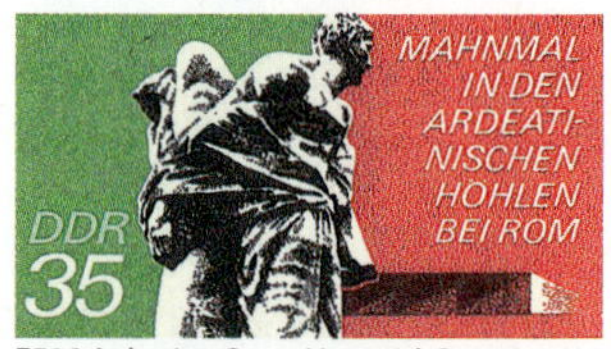

E516 Ardeatine Caves Memorial, Rome

1974. International War Memorials.

E1697	**E516**	35pf. black, grn & red	45	40
E1698	-	35pf. black, bl & red	45	40

DESIGN: No. E1698, Resistance Memorial, Chateaubriant, France.

E517 Arms of East Germany and Family

1974. 25th Anniv of German Democratic Republic. Sheet 90×108 mm.

MSE1699	E **517**	1m. multicoloured	1·80	1·90

E518 "James Watt" (paddle-steamer) and Modern Freighter

1974. Centenary of U.P.U. Multicoloured.

E1700	10pf. Type E **518**	20	15
E1701	20pf. Steam and diesel railway locomotives	20	15
E1702	25pf. Early airliner and Tupolev Tu-134	20	15
E1703	35pf. Early mail coach and modern truck	1·40	1·00

E519 "The Revolutionaries" (E. Rossdeutscher)

1974. "DDR 74" Stamp Exhibition. Sculptures in Karl-Marx-Stadt. Each black, bistre and green.

E1704	10pf.+5pf. Type E **519**	25	25
E1705	20pf. "The Dialectics"	25	25
E1706	25pf. "The Party"	25	25

E520 "The Sun shines for all" (G. Milosch)

1974. Children's Paintings. Multicoloured.

E1707	20pf. Type E **520**	40	45
E1708	20pf. "My Friend Sascha" (B. Ozminski)	40	45
E1709	20pf. "Carsten the Best Swimmer" (M. Kluge)	40	45
E1710	20pf. "Me and the Blackboard" (P. Westphal)	40	45

E521 "The Woodchopper"

1974. Fairy Tales (9th series). "Twittering To and Fro" by A. Tolstoi.

E1711	**E521**	10pf. multicoloured	25	25
E1712	-	15pf. multicoloured	1·10	1·20
E1713	-	20pf. multicoloured	25	25
E1714	-	30pf. multicoloured	25	25
E1715	-	35pf. multicoloured	1·10	1·20
E1716	-	40pf. multicoloured	25	25

DESIGNS: Nos. E1712/16, Scenes from "Twittering To and Fro" fairy tale, similar to Type E **521**.

E522 "Still Life" (R. Paris)

1974. Paintings from Berlin Museums. Mult.

E1717	10pf. Type E **522**	20	15
E1718	15pf. "Girl in Meditation" (W. Lachnit) (vert)	20	15
E1719	20pf. "Fisherman's House" (H. Hakenbeck) (vert)	20	15
E1720	35pf. "Girl in Red" (R. Bergander)	30	15
E1721	70pf. "Parents" (W. Sitte) (vert)	1·90	2·00

E523 Banded Jasper

1974. Gem-stones in Freiberg Mining Academy Collection. Multicoloured.

E1722	10pf. Type E **523**	20	15
E1723	15pf. Smoky quartz	20	15
E1724	20pf. Topaz	20	15
E1725	25pf. Amethyst	20	15
E1726	35pf. Aquamarine	35	15
E1727	70pf. Agate	2·20	2·00

E524 Martha Arendsee

1975. 90th Birth Anniv of Martha Arendsee (Socialist).

E1728	**E524**	10pf. red	35	25

E525 Peasants doing Forced Labour

1975. 450th Anniv of Peasants' War.

E1729	**E525**	5pf. black, green and grey	45	45
E1730	-	10pf. black, brown and grey	45	45
E1731	-	20pf. black, blue and grey	45	45
E1732	-	25pf. black, yellow and grey	65	65
E1733	-	35pf. black, lilac and grey	65	65
E1734	-	50pf. black, grey and light grey	45	45

DESIGNS: 10pf. "Paying Tithe"; 20pf. Thomas Muntzer (leader); 25pf. "Armed Peasants"; 35pf. "Liberty" flag; 50pf. Peasants on trial.

E526 Women and Emblem

1975. International Women's Year.

E1735	**E526**	10pf. multicoloured	25	30
E1736	-	20pf. multicoloured	25	30
E1737	-	25pf. multicoloured	25	30

DESIGNS: 20pf., 25pf. Similar to Type E **526**.

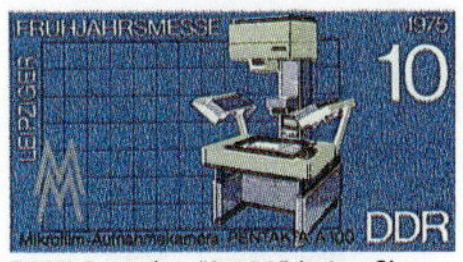

E527 Pentakta "A-100" (microfilm camera)

1975. Leipzig Spring Fair. Multicoloured.

E1738	10pf. Type E **527**	20	15
E1739	25pf. "SKET" (cement works)	35	30

E528 Hans Otto (actor) (1900–33)

1975. Celebrities' Birth Anniversaries.

E1740	**E528**	5pf. blue	20	15
E1741	-	10pf. red	20	15
E1742	-	20pf. green	20	15
E1743	-	25pf. brown	20	15
E1744	-	35pf. blue	1·20	95

PORTRAITS AND ANNIVERSARIES: 10pf. Thomas Mann, author (1875–1955); 20pf. Dr. A. Schweitzer (1875–1965); 25pf. Michelangelo (1475–1564); 35pf. Andre-Marie Ampere, scientist (1775–1836).

E529 Blue and Yellow Macaws

1975. Zoo Animals. Multicoloured.

E1745	5pf. Type E **529**	20	15
E1746	10pf. Orang-utan	20	15
E1747	15pf. Ibex	20	15
E1748	20pf. Indian rhinoceros (horiz)	20	15
E1749	25pf. Pygmy hippopotamus (horiz)	20	15
E1750	30pf. Grey seals (horiz)	20	15
E1751	35pf. Tiger (horiz)	25	15
E1752	50pf. Common zebra	2·30	2·00

E530 Soldiers, "Industry" and "Agriculture"

1975. 20th Anniv of Warsaw Treaty.

E1753	**E530**	20pf. multicoloured	1·20	40

E531 Soviet Memorial, Berlin-Treptow

1975. 30th Anniv of Liberation. Mult.

E1754	10pf. Type E **531**	20	15
E1755	20pf. Detail of Buchenwald memorial	20	15
E1756	25pf. Woman voluntary worker	20	15
E1757	55pf. "Socialist economic integration"	90	95
MSE1758	109×90 mm. 50pf. Soldier planting Red flag on Reichstag. Imperf	85	90

E532 Ribbons with "Komsomol" and "F.D.J." Badges

1975. 3rd Youth Friendship Festival, Halle.

E1759	**E532**	10pf. mult	50	25

1975. Lighthouses (2nd series). As Type E 509. Multicoloured.

E1760	5pf. Trimmendorf lighthouse	20	15
E1761	10pf. Gellen lighthouse	20	15
E1762	20pf. Sassnitz lighthouse	20	15
E1763	25pf. Dornbusch lighthouse	20	15
E1764	35pf. Peenemunde lighthouse	1·30	1·10

E533 Wilhelm Leibknecht and August Bebel

1975. Centenary of Marx's "Programmkritik" and Gotha Unity Congress.

E1765	**E533**	10pf. deep brown, brown and red	25	25
E1766	-	20pf. multicoloured	25	25
E1767	-	25pf. deep brown, brown and red	25	25

DESIGNS: 20pf. Tivoli (meeting place at Gotha) and title-page of Minutes of Unity Congress; 25pf. Karl Marx and Friedrich Engels.

E534 Dove and "Scientific Co-operation between Socialist Countries"

1975. 25th Anniv of Eisenhuettenstadt.

E1768	**E534**	20pf. multicoloured	35	25

E535 Construction Workers

1975. 30th Anniv of Free-German Trade Union Association.

E1769	**E535**	20pf. multicoloured	35	20

E536 Automatic Clock, 1585

1975. Ancient Clocks. Multicoloured.

E1770	5pf. Type E **536**	20	15
E1771	10pf. Astronomical Mantlepiece clock, 1560	20	15
E1772	15pf. Automatic clock, 1600	2·10	2·10
E1773	20pf. Mantlepiece Clock, 1720	20	15
E1774	25pf. Mantlepiece Clock, 1700	20	15
E1775	35pf. Astronomical Clock, 1738	25	25

E537 Jacob and Wilhelm Grimm's German Dictionary

1975. 275th Anniv of Academy of Science.

E1776	**E537**	10pf. black, grn & red	20	15
E1777	-	20pf. black and blue	20	15
E1778	-	25pf. blk, yell & grn	20	15
E1779	-	35pf. multicoloured	1·20	1·30

DESIGNS: 20pf. Karl Schwarzschildt observatory, Tautenberg; 25pf. Electron microscope and chemical plant; 35pf. Intercosmic satellite.

E538 Runner with Torch

1975. 5th National Youth Sports Day.

E1780	**E538**	10pf. black and pink	20	15
E1781	-	20pf. black and yellow	20	15
E1782	-	25pf. black and blue	20	15
E1783	-	35pf. black and green	1·20	1·30

DESIGNS: 20pf. Hurdling; 25pf. Swimming; 35pf. Gymnastics.

E539 Map of Europe

1975. European Security and Co-operation Conference, Helsinki.

E1784	**E539**	20pf. multicoloured	45	30

E540 Asters

1975. Flowers. Multicoloured.

E1785	5pf. Type E **540**	20	15
E1786	10pf. Pelargoniums	20	15
E1787	20pf. Gerberas	20	15
E1788	25pf. Carnation	20	15
E1789	35pf. Chrysanthemum	25	20
E1790	70pf. Pansies	3·00	2·50

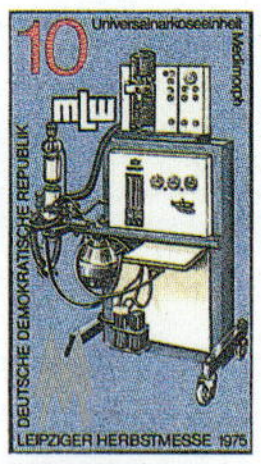

E541 "Medimorph" (Anaesthetizing machine)

1975. Leipzig Autumn Fair. Multicoloured.

E1791	10pf. Type E **541**	25	15
E1792	25pf. Zschopau "TS-250" motor-cycle (horiz)	45	30

E542 School Crossing

1975. Road Safety. Multicoloured.

E1793	10pf. Type E **542**	20	15
E1794	15pf. Policewoman controlling traffic	1·80	1·20
E1795	20pf. Policeman assisting motorist	20	15
E1796	25pf. Car having check-up	25	15
E1797	35pf. Road safety instruction	25	20

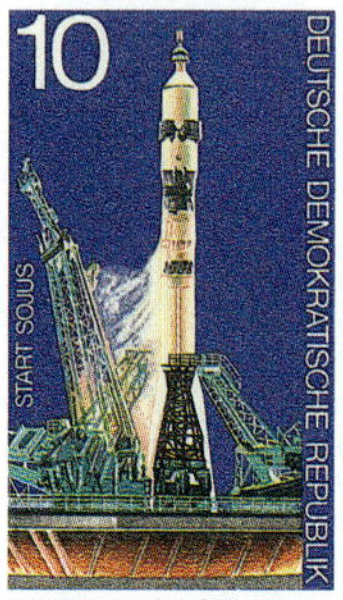

E543 Launch of "Soyuz"

1975. "Apollo"–"Soyuz" Space Link. Mult.

E1798	10pf. Type E **543**	20	15
E1799	20pf. Spaceships in linking manoeuvre	20	15
E1800	70pf. The completed link (88×33 mm)	2·10	2·10

E544 Clenched Fist and Red Star

1975. "International Solidarity".

E1801	**E544**	10pf.+5pf. black, red and olive	35	25

E545 "Weimar in 1650" (Merian)

1975. Millenary of Weimar.

E1802	**E545**	10pf. brown, light green and green	20	15
E1803	-	20pf. multicoloured	20	15
E1804	-	35pf. multicoloured	70	60

DESIGNS:—VERT: 20pf. Buchenwald memorial. HORIZ: 35pf. Weimar buildings (975–1975).

E546 Vienna Memorial (F. Cremer)

1975. Austrian Patriots Monument, Vienna.

E1805	**E546**	35pf. multicoloured	45	25

E547 Louis Braille

1975. International Braille Year. Mult.

E1806	20pf. Type E **547**	20	15
E1807	35pf. Hands reading braille	20	15
E1808	50pf. An eye-ball, eye shade and safety goggles	1·60	1·60

E548 Post Office Gate, Wurzen

1975. National Philatelists' Day. Mult.

E1809	10pf.+5pf. Type E **548**	60	60
E1810	20pf. Post Office, Barenfels	20	20

E549 Hans Christian Andersen and scene from "The Emperor's New Clothes" (image scaled to 73% of original size)

1975. Fairy Tales (10th series). "The Emperor's New Clothes".

E1811	**E549**	20pf. multicoloured	55	55
E1812	-	35pf. multicoloured	90	95
E1813	-	50pf. multicoloured	55	55

DESIGNS: 35, 50pf. Different scenes.

E550 Tobogganing

1975. Winter Olympic Games, Innsbruck (1976). Multicoloured.

E1814	5pf. Type E **550**	20	15
E1815	10pf.+5pf. Bobsleigh track	20	15
E1816	20pf. Speed-skating rink	20	15
E1817	25pf.+5pf. Ski-jump	25	15
E1818	35pf. Skating-rink	25	20
E1819	70pf. Skiing	2·50	2·20
MSE1820	80×55 mm. 1m. Innsbruk (33×28 mm)	2·50	2·10

E551 W. Pieck

1975. Birth Cent of President Pieck (statesman).

E1821	**E551**	10pf. brown & blue	25	20

1976. Members of German Workers' Movement. As Type E 551.

E1822	10pf. brown and red	25	20
E1823	10pf. brown and green	25	20
E1824	10pf. brown and orange	25	20
E1825	10pf. brown and violet	25	20

PORTRAITS: No. E1822, Ernst Thalmann; E1823, Georg Schumann; E1824, Wilhelm Koenen; E1825, John Schehr.

E552 Organ, Rotha

1976. Gottfried Silbermann (organ builder) Commemoration. Multicoloured.

E1826	10pf. Type E **552**	20	15
E1827	20pf. Organ, Freiberg	20	15
E1828	35pf. Organ, Fraureuth	25	20
E1829	50pf. Organ, Dresden	1·50	1·10

E553 Richard Sorge

1976. Dr. Richard Sorge (Soviet agent) Commemoration. Sheet 82×65 mm.

MSE1830	E **553** 1m. black and pale olive-grey	2·10	2·10

E554 Servicemen and Emblem

1976. 20th Anniv of National Forces (N.V.A.). Multicoloured.

E1831	10pf. Type E **554**	25	15
E1832	20pf. N.V.A. equipment	35	30

E555 Telephone and Inscription

1976. Centenary of Telephone.

E1833	**E555**	20pf. blue	35	25

E556 Block of Flats, Leipzig

1976. Leipzig Spring Fair. Multicoloured.

E1834	10pf. Type E **556**	25	15
E1835	25pf. "Prometey" (deep sea trawler) (horiz)	45	30

E557 Palace of the Republic, Berlin

1976. Opening of Palace of Republic, Berlin.

E1836	**E557**	10pf. multicoloured	80	25

E558 Telecommunications Satellite Tracking Radar

1976. "Intersputnik".

E1837	**E558**	20pf. multicoloured	35	20

E559 Marx, Engels, Lenin and Socialist Party Emblem

1976. 9th East German Socialist Party Congress.

E1838	**E559**	10pf. red, gold and deep red	25	20
E1839	-	20pf. multicoloured	35	25
MSE1840 110×91 mm. E 557 1m. multicoloured			1·70	1·80

DESIGN—HORIZ: 20pf. Industrial site, housing complex and emblem.

E560 Cycling

1976. Olympic Games, Montreal. Mult.

E1841		5pf. Type E **560**	20	15
E1842		10pf.+5pf. Modern swimming pool	20	15
E1843		20pf. Modern sports hall	20	15
E1844		25pf. Regatta course	20	15
E1845		35pf.+10pf. Rifle-range	30	20
E1846		70pf. Athletics	3·00	2·50
MSE1847 81×55 mm. 1m. Modern sports stadium (33×28 mm)			1·80	1·90

E561 Intertwined Ribbon and Emblem

1976. 10th Youth Parliament Conference, Berlin. Multicoloured.

E1848		10pf. Type E **561**	20	15
E1849		20pf. Members of Youth Parliament and stylised industrial plant	25	30

E562 "Himantoglossum bircinum"

1976. Flowers. Multicoloured.

E1850		10pf. Type E **562**	20	15
E1851		20pf. "Dactylorhiza incarnata"	20	15
E1852		25pf. "Anacamptis pyramidalis"	25	15
E1853		35pf. "Dactylorhiza sambucina"	25	20
E1854		40pf. "Orchis coriophora"	30	20
E1855		50pf. "Cypripedium calceolus"	3·00	2·30

E563 "Shetland Pony" (H. Drake)

1976. Statuettes from Berlin Museums.

E1856	**E563**	10pf. black and blue	20	15
E1857	-	20pf. black & brown	25	15
E1858	-	25pf. black & orange	25	15
E1859	-	35pf. black and green	25	15
E1860	-	50pf. black and pink	2·30	1·90

STATUETTES—VERT: 20pf. "Tanzpause" (W. Arnold); 25pf. "Am Strand" (L. Englehardt); 35pf. "Herman Duncker" (W. Howard); 50pf. "Das Gesprach" (G. Weidanz).

E564 Marx, Engels, Lenin and Red Flag

1976. European Communist Parties' Conference.

E1861	**E564**	20pf. blue, deep red and red	45	25

E565 State Carriage, 1790

1976. 19th-century Horse-drawn Vehicles. Multicoloured.

E1862		10pf. Type E **565**	20	15
E1863		20pf. Russian trap, 1800	20	15
E1864		25pf. Carriage, 1840	20	15
E1865		35pf. State carriage, 1860	25	20
E1866		40pf. Stagecoach, 1850	25	25
E1867		50pf. Carriage, 1889	2·75	2·75

E566 Gera, c. 1652

1976. National Philatelists' Day, Gera. Mult.

E1868		10pf.+5pf. Type E **566**	25	25
E1869		20pf. Gera buildings	25	25

E567 Boxer

1976. Domestic Dogs. Multicoloured.

E1870		5pf. Type E **567**	20	15
E1871		10pf. Airedale Terrier	20	15
E1872		20pf. Alsatian	20	15
E1873		25pf. Collie	20	20
E1874		35pf. Schnauzer	25	25
E1875		70pf. Great Dane	3·00	3·00

E568 Oil Refinery

1976. Autumn Fair, Leipzig. Multicoloured.

E1876		10pf. Type E **568**	20	15
E1877		25pf. Library, Leipzig	45	30

E569 Templin Lake Railway Bridge

1976. East German Bridges. Multicoloured.

E1878		10pf. Type E **569**	20	15
E1879		15pf. Adlergestell Railway Bridge, Berlin	20	15
E1880		20pf. River Elbe Railway Bridge, Rosslau	20	15
E1881		25pf. Goltzschtal Viaduct	25	15
E1882		35pf. Elbe River Bridge, Magdeburg	25	15
E1883		50pf. Grosser Dreesch Bridge, Schwerin	2·30	2·30

E570 Memorial Figures

1976. Patriots' Memorial, Budapest.

E1884	**E570**	35pf. multicoloured	50	40

E571 Brass Jug, c. 1500

1976. Exhibits from Applied Arts Museum, Kopenick Castle, Berlin. Multicoloured.

E1885		10pf. Type E **571**	20	15
E1886		20pf. Faience covered vase, c. 1710	20	15
E1887		25pf. Porcelain "fruit-seller" table centre, c. 1768	25	15
E1888		35pf. Silver "basket-carrier" statuette, c. 1700	25	15
E1889		70pf. Coloured glass vase, c. 1900	2·30	2·40

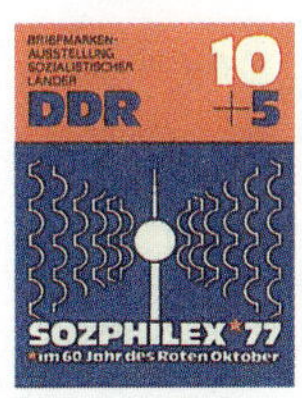

E572 Berlin T.V. Tower

1976. "Sozphilex 77" Stamp Exhibition. East Berlin (1st issue).

E1890	**E572**	10pf.+5pf. blue, black and red	35	25

See also Nos. E1962/3.

E573 Spade-tailed Guppy

1976. Aquarium Fishes – Guppies. Mult.

E1891		10pf. Type E **573**	20	15
E1892		15pf. Lyre-tailed	20	15
E1893		20pf. Flag-tailed	20	15
E1894		25pf. Sword-tailed	25	15
E1895		35pf. Delta	25	15
E1896		70pf. Round-tailed	2·75	2·50

E574 Clay Pots c. 3000 B.C.

1976. Archaeological Discoveries in D.D.R. Multicoloured.

E1897		10pf. Type E **574**	20	15
E1898		20pf. Bronze cult vessel on wheels, c. 1300 B.C.	20	15
E1899		25pf. Roman gold aureus of Tetricus I, A.D. 270–273	25	15
E1900		35pf. Viking cross-shaped pendant, 10th century A.D.	25	15
E1901		70pf. Roman glass beaker, 3rd century A.D.	2·50	2·40

E575 The Miller and the King

1976. Fairy Tales (11th series). "Rumpelstiltskin".

E1902	**E575**	5pf. multicoloured	25	25
E1903	-	10pf. multicoloured	70	70
E1904	-	15pf. multicoloured	25	25
E1905	-	20pf. multicoloured	25	25
E1906	-	25pf. multicoloured	70	70
E1907	-	30pf. multicoloured	25	25

DESIGNS: 10pf. to 30pf. Scenes from the fairy tale.

E576 "The Air" (R. Carriera)

1976. Paintings by Old Masters from the National Art Collection, Dresden. Mult.

E1908		10pf. Type E **576**	20	15
E1909		15pf. "Madonna and Child" (Murillo)	20	15
E1910		20pf. "Viola Player" (B. Strozzi)	20	15
E1911		25pf. "Ariadne Forsaken" (A. Kauffman)	25	15
E1912		35pf. "Old Man in Black Cap" (B. Nazzari)	25	15
E1913		70pf. "Officer reading a Letter" (G. Terborch)	3·00	2·20

E577 Arnold Zweig (author)

1977. German Celebrities.

E1914	**E577**	10pf. black and pink	20	15
E1915	-	20pf. black and grey	20	15
E1916	-	35pf. black and green	25	20
E1917	-	40pf. black and blue	1·20	1·10

DESIGNS: 20pf. Otto von Guericke (scientist); 35pf. Albrecht D. Thaer (agriculturalist); 40pf. Gustav Hertz (physicist).

E578 Spring near Plaue, Thuringia

1977. Natural Phenomena. Multicoloured.

E1918		10pf. Type E **578**	20	15
E1919		20pf. Rock face near Jonsdorf	20	15

E1920	25pf. Oaks near Reuterstadt Stavenhagen	20	15
E1921	35pf. Rocky ledge near Saalburg	25	15
E1922	50pf. Erratic boulder near Furstenwalde/Spree	1·80	1·80

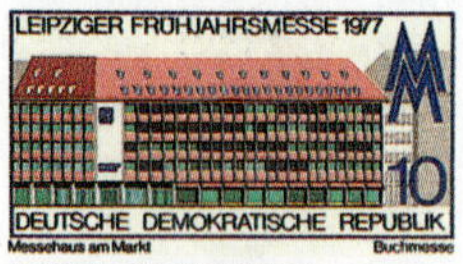

E579 Book Fair Building

1977. Leipzig Spring Fair. Multicoloured.

E1923	10pf. Type E **579**	20	15
E1924	25pf. Aluminium casting machine	35	25

E580 Senftenberg Costume, Zly Komorrow

1977. Sorbian Historical Costumes. Mult.

E1925	10pf. Type E **580**	20	15
E1926	20pf. Bautzen, Budysin	20	15
E1927	25pf. Klitten, Kletno	25	15
E1928	35pf. Nochten, Wochozy	25	15
E1929	70pf. Muskau, Muzakow	2·75	2·10

E581 Carl Friedrich Gauss

1977. Birth Bicentenary of Carl Friedrich Gauss (mathematician).

E1930	**E581** 20pf. black and blue	75	30

E582 Start of Race

1977. 30th International Peace Cycle Race. Multicoloured.

E1931	10pf. Type E **582**	30	35
E1932	20pf. Spurt	30	35
E1933	35pf. Race finish	30	35

E583 Three Flags

1977. 9th Congress of Free German Trade Unions Association.

E1934	**E583** 20pf. multicoloured	35	25

E584 VKM Channel Converter and Filters

1977. World Telecommunications Day.

E1935	**E584** 20pf. black, blue and red	35	25

E585 Shooting

1977. 25th Anniv of Sports and Technical Sciences Association.

E1936	**E585** 10pf. black, grn & red	20	20
E1937	- 20pf. black, bl & mve	20	20
E1938	- 35pf. black, pk & grn	1·10	1·10

DESIGNS: 20pf. Skin diving; 25pf. Radio-controlled model boat.

E586 Accordion, 1900

1977. Old Musical Instruments from Vogtland. Multicoloured.

E1939	10pf. Type E **586**	20	15
E1940	20pf. Treble viola da gamba, 1747	20	15
E1941	25pf. Oboe, 1785, Clarinet, 1830, Flute, 1817	20	15
E1942	35pf. Concert zither, 1891	20	15
E1943	70pf. Trumpet, 1860	2·75	2·50

E587 "Bathsheba at the Fountain"

1977. 400th Birth Anniv of Peter Paul Rubens. Dresden Gallery Paintings. Multicoloured.

E1944	10pf. Type E **587**	20	15
E1945	15pf. "Mercury and Argus" (horiz)	25	15
E1946	20pf. "The Drunk Hercules"	25	15
E1947	25pf. "Diana's Return from Hunting" (horiz)	25	15
E1948	35pf. "The Old Woman with the Brazier"	30	20
E1949	50pf. "Leda with the Swan" (horiz)	3·75	2·75

E588 Soviet and East German Flags

1977. 30th Anniv of German-Soviet Friendship Society. Sheet 80×55 mm.

MSE1950	E **588** 50pf. multicoloured	1·30	1·20

E589 Tractor and Plough

1977. Modern Agricultural Techniques. Multicoloured.

E1951	10pf. Type E **589**	20	15
E1952	20pf. Fertilizer spreader on truck	20	15
E1953	25pf. Potato digger and loader	20	15
E1954	35pf. High pressure collecting press	25	20
E1955	50pf. Milking machine	2·40	2·30

E590 High Jump

1977. 6th Gymnastics and Athletic Meeting and 6th Children and Young People's Sports Days, Leipzig. Multicoloured.

E1956	5pf. Type E **590**	20	15
E1957	10pf.+5pf. Running	20	15
E1958	20pf. Hurdling	20	15
E1959	25pf.+5pf. Gymnastics	20	15
E1960	35pf. Dancing	25	20
E1961	40pf. Torch bearer and flags	2·30	2·40

E591 "Bread for Everybody" (Wolfram Schubert)

1977. "Sozphilex 77" Stamp Exhibition, East Berlin (2nd issue). Multicoloured.

E1962	10pf. Type E **591**	25	20
E1963	25pf. "... when Communists are Dreaming" (Walter Womacka)	55	55
MSE1964	Two sheets, each 77×110 mm. (a) No. E1962 ×4; (b) No. E1963 ×4 Set of 2 sheets	3·75	3·50
MSE1965	85×54 mm. 50pf.+20pf. "World Youth Song" (Lothar Zitzmann) (horiz)	1·60	1·70

E592 "Konsument" Department Store, Leipzig

1977. Leipzig Autumn Fair. Multicoloured.

E1966	10pf. Type E **592**	25	15
E1967	25pf. Carved bowl and Thuringian blown-glass vases	40	30

E593 Bust of Dzerzhinsky and Young Pioneers

1977. Birth Centenary of Feliks E. Dzerzhinsky (founder of Soviet Cheka). Sheet 127×69 mm containing Type E 593 and similar vert design. Multicoloured.

MSE1968	20pf. Type E **593**; 35pf. Portrait	1·70	1·70

E594 Steam Locomotive "Muldenthal", 1861

1977. Transport Museum, Dresden. Mult.

E1969	5pf. Type E **594**	25	20
E1970	10pf. Dresden tram, 1896	25	20
E1971	20pf. Hans Grade's monoplane, 1909	25	20
E1972	25pf. Phanomobil tricar, 1924	25	20
E1973	35pf. River Elbe passenger steamer, 1837	2·75	2·30

E595 "Aurora" (cruiser)

1977. 60th Anniv of October Revolution. Multicoloured.

E1974	10pf. Type E **595**	25	20
E1975	25pf. Assault on Winter Palace	55	55
MSE1976	55×86 mm. 1m. Lenin (vert)	2·50	2·10

E596 Soviet Memorial

1977. Soviet Memorial, Berlin-Schoenholz.

E1977	**E596** 35pf. multicoloured	50	25

E597 Flaming Torch

1977. "Solidarity".

E1978	**E597** 10pf.+5pf. mult	35	25

E598 Ernst Meyer

1977. Socialist Personalities.

E1979	**E598** 10pf. brown	25	20
E1980	- 10pf. red	25	20
E1981	- 10pf. blue	25	20

PERSONALITIES: No. E1980, A. Frolich; No. E1981, G. Eisler.

E599 H. von Kleist

1977. Birth Bicentenary of Heinrich von Kleist (poet). Sheet 82×54 mm.

MSE1982	E **599** 1m. black and red	3·00	2·40

E600 Rocket pointing Right

1977. 20th "Masters of Tomorrow" Fair, Leipzig.

E1983	**E600** 10pf. red, silver and black	20	20
E1984	- 20pf. blue, gold and black	30	35

DESIGN: 20pf. Rocket pointing left.

E601 Mouflon

1977. Hunting. Multicoloured.

E1985	10pf. Type E **601**	20	15

E1986	15pf. Red deer	2·50	2·50
E1987	20pf. Shooting common pheasant	20	15
E1988	25pf. Red fox and mallard	25	15
E1989	35pf. Tractor driver with roe deer fawn	25	15
E1990	70pf. Wild boars	35	30

E602 Firemen with Scaling Ladders

1977. Fire Brigade. Multicoloured.

E1991	10pf. Type E **602**	20	15
E1992	20pf. Children visiting fire brigade (vert)	20	15
E1993	25pf. Fire engines in countryside	20	15
E1994	35pf. Artificial respiration (vert)	20	15
E1995	50pf. Fire-fighting tug	2·50	2·30

E603 Traveller and King

1977. Fairy Tales (12th series). "Six World Travellers" (Brothers Grimm).

E1996	**E603** 5pf. multicoloured	25	25
E1997	- 10pf. multicoloured	1·10	1·20
E1998	- 20pf. multicoloured	25	25
E1999	- 25pf. multicoloured	25	25
E2000	- 35pf. multicoloured	1·10	1·20
E2001	- 60pf. multicoloured	25	25

DESIGNS: 10pf. to 60pf. Scenes from the fairy tale.

E604 Rosehips

1978. Medicinal Plants. Multicoloured.

E2002	10pf. Type E **604**	20	15
E2003	15pf. Birch leaves	20	15
E2004	20pf. Camomile flowers	20	15
E2005	25pf. Coltsfoot	25	15
E2006	35pf. Lime flowers	25	15
E2007	50pf. Elder flowers	2·75	2·40

E605 Amilcar Cabral

1978. Amilcar Cabral (nationalist leader of Guinea-Bissau) Commemoration.

E2008	**E605** 20pf. multicoloured	45	40

E606 Town Hall, Suhl-Heinrichs

1978. Half-timbered Buildings. Multicoloured.

E2009	10pf. Type E **606**	20	15
E2010	20pf. Farmhouse, Niederoderwitz	20	15
E2011	25pf. Farmhouse, Strassen	20	15
E2012	35pf. House, Quedlinburg	25	15
E2013	40pf. House, Eisenach	2·40	2·40

E607 Post Office Van, 1921

1978. Postal Transport. Multicoloured.

E2014	10pf. Type E **607**	25	25
E2015	20pf. Postal truck, 1978	45	45
E2016	25pf. Railway mail coach, 1896	60	60
E2017	35pf. Railway mail coach, 1978	75	75

E608 Ear-pendant, 11th century

1978. Slavonic Treasures. Multicoloured.

E2018	10pf. Type E **608**	20	15
E2019	20pf. Ear-ring, 10th century	20	15
E2020	25pf. Bronze tag, 10th century	20	15
E2021	35pf. Bronze horse, 12th century	25	20
E2022	70pf. Arabian coin, 8th century	2·20	2·00

E609 "Royal House" Market Square, Leipzig

1978. Leipzig Spring Fair.

E2023	**E609** 10pf. yell, blk & red	25	15
E2024	- 25pf. green, blk & red	45	40

DESIGN: 25pf. Universal measuring instrument, UMK 10/1318.

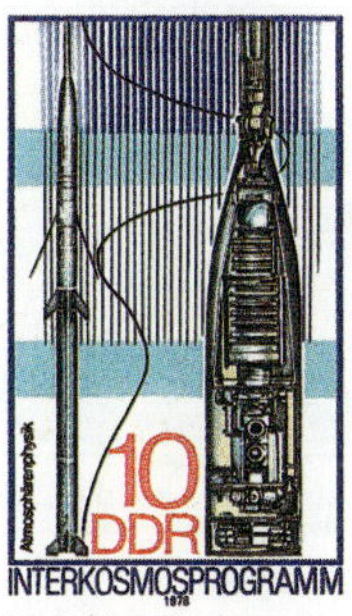

E610 "M-100" Meteorological Rocket

1978. "Interkosmos" Space Programme. Mult.

E2025	10pf. Type E **610**	20	20
E2026	20pf. "Interkosmos 1" satellite	20	20
E2027	35pf. "Meteor" satellite with Fourier spectrometer	1·10	1·10
MSE2028	90×109 mm. 1m. "MKF-6" multispectral camera	3·00	2·50

E611 Samuel Heinicke (founder)

1978. Bicentenary of First National Deaf and Dumb Educational Institution.

E2029	20pf. Type E **611**	20	20
E2030	25pf. Child learning alphabet	80	80

E612 Radio-range Tower, Dequede, and Television Transmission Van

1978. World Telecommunications Day. Mult.

E2031	10pf. Type E **612**	20	20
E2032	20pf. Equipment in Berlin television tower and Dresden television tower	40	45

E613 Saxon miner in Gala Uniform

1978. 19th-Century Gala Uniforms of Mining and Metallurgical Industries. Multicoloured.

E2033	10pf. Type E **613**	20	15
E2034	20pf. Freiberg foundry worker	25	15
E2035	25pf. School of Mining academician	25	15
E2036	35pf. Chief Inspector of Mines	1·60	1·40

E614 Lion Cub

1978. Centenary of Leipzig Zoo. Multicoloured.

E2037	10pf. Type E **614**	20	15
E2038	20pf. Leopard cub	20	15
E2039	35pf. Tiger cub	20	20
E2040	50pf. Snow leopard cub	1·70	1·80

E615 Loading Container

1978. Container Goods Traffic. Multicoloured.

E2041	10pf. Type E **615**	20	15
E2042	20pf. Placing container on truck	20	15
E2043	35pf. Diesel locomotive and container wagons	25	25
E2044	70pf. Placing containers on "Boltenhagen"	2·20	1·90

E616 Clay Ox (Egyptian Museum, Leipzig)

1978. Ancient African Works of Art in Egyptian Museums at Leipzig and Berlin. Multicoloured.

E2045	5pf. Type E **616**	20	15
E2046	10pf. Clay head of woman (Leipzig)	20	15
E2047	20pf. Gold bangle (Berlin) (horiz)	20	15
E2048	25pf. Gold ring plate (Berlin)	20	20
E2049	35pf. Gold signet-ring plate (Berlin)	25	20
E2050	40pf. Necklace (Berlin) (horiz)	1·80	1·80

E617 Justus von Liebig (agricultural chemist, 175th birth anniv)

1978. Celebrities' Birth Anniversaries.

E2051	**E617** 5pf. black and ochre	20	15
E2052	- 10pf. black and blue	20	15
E2053	- 15pf. black and green	20	15
E2054	- 20pf. black and blue	20	15
E2055	- 25pf. black and red	20	15
E2056	- 35pf. black and green	20	15
E2057	- 70pf. black and drab	2·10	1·90

DESIGNS: 10pf. Joseph Dietzgen (writer, 150th); 15pf. Alfred Doblin (novelist, 100th); 20pf. Hans Loch (politician, 80th); 25pf. Theodor Brugsch (scientist, 100th); 35pf. Friedrich Ludwig Jahn (gymnast, 200th); 70pf. Albrecht von Graefe (ophthalmatician, 150th).

E618 Cottbus, 1730

1978. 5th National Youth Stamp Exhibition, Cottbus. Multicoloured.

E2058	10pf.+5pf. Type E **618**	25	30
E2059	20pf. Modern Cottbus	25	30

E619 Havana Buildings and Festival Emblem

1978. 11th World Youth and Students' Festival, Havana. Multicoloured.

E2060	20pf. Type E **619**	45	45
E2061	35pf. Festival emblem and East Berlin buildings	45	45

E620 "Trooper with Halberd" (Hans Schaufelein)

1978. Drawings in Berlin State Museum. Sheet 110×98 mm containing Type E 620 and similar vert designs, each brownish black and stone.

MSE2062	10pf. Type E **620**; 20pf. "Woman reading a Letter" (Jean Antoine Watteau); 25pf. "Seated Boy" (Gabriel Metsu); 30pf. "Young Man cutting a Loaf" (Cornelis Saftleven); 35pf. "St. Anthony in a Landscape" (Matthias Grunewald); 50pf. "Man seated in an Armchair" (Abraham van Diepenbeeck)	4·00	4·00

E621 "Multicar 25" Truck

1978. Leipzig Autumn Fair. Multicoloured.

E2063	10pf. Type E **621**	25	15
E2064	25pf. "Three Kings" Fair building, Petersstrasse	50	40

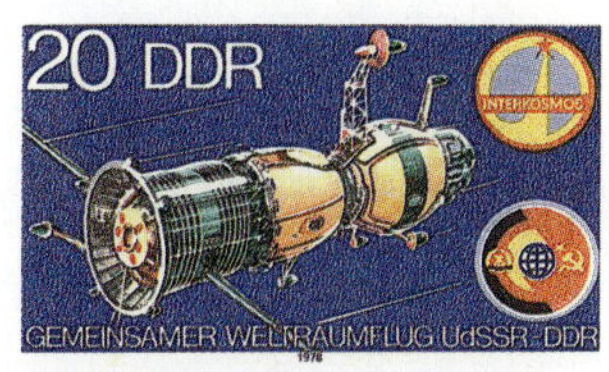

E622 "Soyuz" Spaceship and Emblems

1978. Soviet–East German Space Flight (1st issue).

E2065	**E622** 20pf. multicoloured	45	30

See also Nos. E2069/**MS**2073.

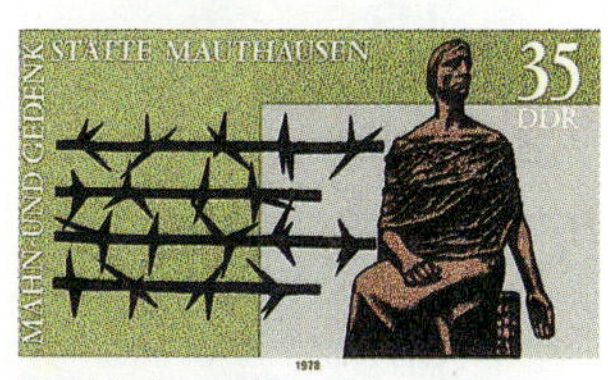

E623 Mauthausen Memorial

1978. War Victims' Memorial, Mauthausen, Austria.

E2066	**E623** 35pf. multicoloured	45	40

E624 W.M.S. Unit on the March

1978. 25th Anniv of Workers' Militia Squads.

E2067	20pf. Type E **624**	40	45
E2068	35pf. Members of Red Army, National People's Army and W.M.S.	40	45

E625 "Soyuz", "MKF 6M" Camera and Space Station

1978. Soviet–East German Space Flight (2nd issue). Multicoloured.

E2069	5pf. Type E **625**	20	15
E2070	10pf. Albert Einstein and "Soyuz"	20	15
E2071	20pf. Sigmund Jahn (first East German cosmonaut) (vert)	20	15
E2072	35pf. "Salyut", "Soyuz" and Lilienthal monoplane glider	1·40	1·20
MSE2073	110×90 mm. 1m. Space station and cosmonauts Valeri Bykovski and Jahn (54×32 mm)	2·20	2·30

E626 Human Pyramid

1978. The Circus. Multicoloured.

E2074	5pf. Type E **626**	35	70
E2075	10pf. Elephant on tricycle	70	1·20
E2076	20pf. Performing horse	1·10	1·90
E2077	35pf. Polar bear kissing girl	2·30	3·75

E627 African behind Barbed Wire

1978. International Anti-Apartheid Year.

E2078	**E627** 20pf. multicoloured	45	25

E628 Construction of Natural Gas Pipe Line

1978. Construction of "Friendship Line" (Drushba-Trasse) by East German Youth.

E2079	**E628** 20pf. multicoloured	45	25

E629 "Parides hahneli" ("Papilio hahneli")

1978. 250th Anniv of Dresden Scientific Museums. Multicoloured.

E2080	10pf. Type E **629**	20	15
E2081	20pf. "Agama lehmanni"	20	15
E2082	25pf. Agate	20	15
E2083	35pf. "Palaeobatrachus diluvianus"	20	15
E2084	40pf. Mantlepiece clock, c. 1720	25	20
E2085	50pf. Table telescope, c. 1750	3·00	2·75

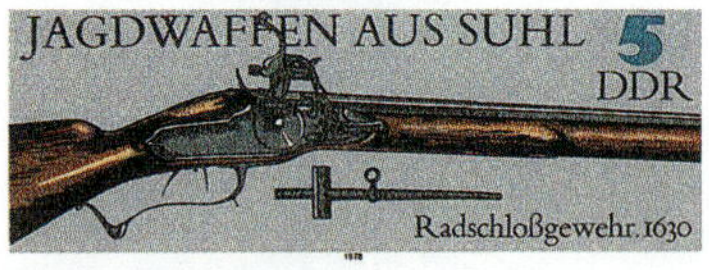

E630 Wheel-lock Gun, 1630

1978. Sporting Guns from Suhl. Multicoloured.

E2086	5pf. Type E **630**	20	20
E2087	10pf. Double-barrelled gun, 1978	20	20
E2088	20pf. Spring-cock gun, 1780	30	35
E2089	25pf. Superimposed double-barrelled gun, 1978	35	40
E2090	35pf. Percussion gun, 1850	55	55
E2091	70pf. Three-barrelled gun, 1978	1·10	1·20

E631 Old Woman and Youth

1978. Fairy Tales. "Rapunzel". Multicoloured.

E2092	10pf. Type E **631**	25	25
E2093	15pf. Old Woman climbing tower on Rapunzel's hair	1·10	1·20
E2094	20pf. Prince calling to Rapunzel	25	25
E2095	25pf. Prince climbing through window	25	25
E2096	35pf. Old woman about to cut Rapunzel's hair	1·10	1·20
E2097	50pf. "Happy ever after"	25	25

E632 Chaffinches

1979. Songbirds. Multicoloured.

E2098	5pf. Type E **632**	20	15
E2099	10pf. Eurasian nuthatch	20	15
E2100	20pf. European robin	20	15
E2101	25pf. Common rosefinch	20	15
E2102	35pf. Blue tit	25	15
E2103	50pf. Linnet	3·00	2·50

E633 Chabo

1979. Poultry. Multicoloured.

E2104	10pf. Type E **633**	20	15
E2105	15pf. Crows head	20	15
E2106	20pf. Porcelain-colour Feather-footed dwarf	20	15
E2107	25pf. Saxonian	20	15
E2108	35pf. Phoenix	25	15
E2109	50pf. Striped Italian	3·00	2·40

E634 Telephone Exchanges in 1900 and 1979

1979. Telephone and Telegraphs Communications. Multicoloured.

E2110	20pf. Type E **634**	20	15
E2111	35pf. Transmitting telegrams in 1800 and 1979	1·10	75

E635 Albert Einstein

1979. Birth Centenary of Albert Einstein (physicist). Sheet 55×86 mm.

MSE2112	E **635** 1m. light brown, deep brown and brown	2·50	2·40

E636 Max Klinger Exhibition House, Leipzig

1979. Leipzig Spring Fair. Multicoloured.

E2113	10pf. Type E **636**	25	15
E2114	25pf. Horizontal drill and milling machine	45	30

E637 Otto Hahn (physicist, centenary)

1979. Celebrities' Birth Anniversaries.

E2115	**E637**	5pf. black and pink	20	15
E2116	-	10pf. black and blue	20	15
E2117	-	20pf. black and yellow	20	15
E2118	-	25pf. black and green	25	15
E2119	-	35pf. black and blue	25	15
E2120	-	70pf. black and pink	2·50	2·10

DESIGNS: 10pf. Max von Laue (physicist, centenary); 20pf. Arthur Scheunert (physiologist, centenary); 25pf. Friedrich August Kekule (chemist, 150th); 35pf. Georg Forster (explorer and writer, 225th); 70pf. Gotth Ephraim Lessing (playwright and essayist, 250th).

E638 "Radebeul" (container ship), "Sturmvogel" (tug) and Shipping Route Map

1979. World Navigation Day.

E2121	**E638**	20pf. multicoloured	45	30

E639 Horch "8", 1911

1979. Zwickau Motor Industry. Multicoloured.

E2122	20pf. Type E **639**	45	45
E2123	35pf. Trabant "601 S de luxe", 1978	80	80

E640 MXA Electric Train

1979. East German Locomotives and Wagons. Multicoloured.

E2124	5pf. Type E **640**	20	15
E2125	10pf. Self-discharging wagon	20	15
E2126	20pf. Diesel locomotive No. 110836.4	20	15
E2127	35pf. Railway car transporter	1·20	1·00

E641 Durga (18th century)

1979. Indian Miniatures. Multicoloured.

E2128	20pf. Type E **641**	20	10
E2129	35pf. Mahavira (15th/16th century)	25	15
E2130	50pf. Todi Ragini (17th century)	30	20
E2131	70pf. Asavari Ragini (17th century)	2·75	2·75

E642 Children Playing

1979. International Year of the Child. Multicoloured.

E2132	10pf. Type E **642**	20	20
E2133	20pf. Overseas aid for children	60	60

E643 Construction Work on Leipziger Strasse Complex

1979. "Berlin Project" of Free German Youth Organization. Multicoloured.

E2134	10pf. Type E **643**	20	15
E2135	20pf. Berlin-Marzahn building site	50	45

E644 Torchlight Procession of Free German Youth, 1949

1979. National Youth Festival. Mult.

E2136	10pf.+5pf. Type E **644**	30	35
E2137	20pf. Youth rally	30	35

E645 Exhibition Symbol

1979. "agra 79" Agricultural Exhibition, Markkleeberg.

E2138	**E645**	10pf. multicoloured	45	25

E646 "Rostock" (train ferry), 1977

1979. 70th Anniv of Sassnitz–Trelleborg Railway Ferry. Multicoloured.

E2139	20pf. Type E **646**	45	45
E2140	35pf. "Rugen" (train ferry)	45	45

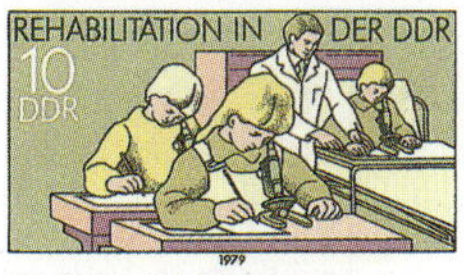

E647 Hospital Classroom

1979. Rehabilitation. Multicoloured.

E2141	10pf. Type E **647**	20	15
E2142	35pf. Wheelchair-bound factory worker	65	65

E648 Cycling

1979. 7th Children's and Young People's Sports Day, Berlin. Multicoloured.

E2143	10pf. Type E **648**	20	15
E2144	20pf. Roller-skating	60	45

E649 Dahlia "Rubens"

1979. "iga" International Garden Exhibition, Erfurt. Dahlias. Multicoloured.

E2145	10pf. Type E **649**	20	15
E2146	20pf. "Rosalie"	20	15
E2147	25pf. "Corinna"	20	15
E2148	35pf. "Enzett-Dolli"	25	15
E2149	50pf. "Enzett-Carola"	30	25
E2150	70pf. "Don Lorenzo"	3·25	3·25

E650 Goose-thief Fountain, Dresden

1979. National Stamp Exhibition, Dresden. Multicoloured.

E2151	10pf.+5pf. Type E **650**	60	50
E2152	20pf. Dandelion fountain, Dresden	20	15
MSE2153	86×55 mm. 1m. Dresden buildings (horiz)	2·50	2·10

E651 World Map and Russian Alphabet

1979. 4th International Congress of Russian Language and Literature Teachers, Berlin.

E2154	**E651** 20pf. multicoloured	35	25

E652 Italian Lira de Gamba, 1592

1979. Musical Instruments in Leipzig Museum. Multicoloured.

E2155	20pf. Type E **652**	20	15
E2156	25pf. French serpent, 17th/18th century	20	15
E2157	40pf. French barrel-lyre, 1750	25	20
E2158	85pf. German tenor flugelhorn, 1850	2·75	2·10

E653 Horseracing

1979. 30th International Congress on Horse-breeding in Socialist Countries, Berlin. Multicoloured.

E2159	10pf. Type E **653**	20	15
E2160	25pf. Dressage (pas de deux)	95	85

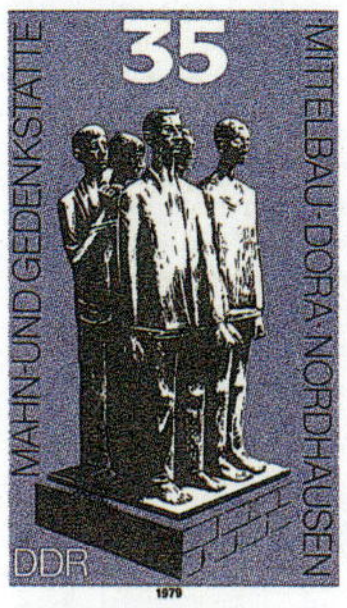

E654 Mittelbau-Dora Memorial

1979. Mittelbau-Dora Memorial, Nordhausen.

E2161	**E654** 35pf. black and violet	60	40

E655 Teddy Bear

1979. Leipzig Autumn Fair. Multicoloured.

E2162	10pf. Type E **655**	20	15
E2163	25pf. Grosser Blumenberg building, Richard Wagner Square	40	20

E656 Philipp Dengel

1979. Socialist Personalities.

E2164	**E656** 10pf. black, green and deep green	25	20
E2165	- 10pf. black, bl & ind	25	20
E2166	- 10pf. blk, stone & bis	25	20
E2167	- 10pf. black, red & brn	25	20

DESIGNS: No. E2165, Otto Buchwitz; No. E2166, Bernard Koenen; No. E2167, Heinrich Rau.

E657 Building Worker and Flats

1979. 30th Anniv of German Democratic Republic. Multicoloured.

E2168	5pf. Type E **657**	20	15
E2169	10pf. Boy and girl	20	15
E2170	15pf. Soldiers	75	50
E2171	20pf. Miner and Soviet soldier	20	15
MSE2172	90×110 mm. 1m. Family and flats (29×51 mm)	2·10	1·70

E658 Girl applying Lipstick (1966/7)

1979. Meissen Porcelain. Multicoloured.

E2173	5pf. Type E **658**	20	20
E2174	10pf. "Altozier" coffee pot (18th cent)	25	25
E2175	15pf. "Gosser Ausschnitt" coffee pot (1973/4)	30	35
E2176	20pf. Vase with lid (18th century)	45	45
E2177	25pf. Parrot with cherry (18th century)	55	55
E2178	35pf. Harlequin with tankard (18th century)	80	80
E2179	50pf. Flower girl (18th century)	1·10	1·10
E2180	70pf. Sake bottle (18th century)	1·60	1·60

E659 Vietnamese Soldier, Mother and Child

1979. "Invincible Vietnam".

E2181	**E659** 10pf.+5pf. black and red	45	40

E660 Rag-doll, 1800

1979. Dolls. Multicoloured.

E2182	10pf. Type E **660**	25	25
E2183	15pf. Ceramic doll, 1960	1·10	1·20
E2184	20pf. Wooden doll, 1780	25	25
E2185	35pf. Straw puppet, 1900	25	25
E2186	50pf. Jointed doll, 1800	1·10	1·20
E2187	70pf. Tumbler-doll, 1820	25	25

E661 "Balance on Ice" (Johanna Starke)

1980. Winter Olympic Games, Lake Placid. Multicoloured.

E2188	10pf. "Bobsleigh Start" (Gunter Rechn) (horiz)	20	20
E2189	20pf. Type E **661**	20	20
E2190	25pf.+10pf. "Ski jumpers" (plastic sculpture, Gunter Schultz)	20	20
E2191	35pf. "Speed Skaters at the Start" (Axel Wunsch)	1·60	1·60
MSE2192	79×55 mm. 1m. "Skiing Girls" (Lothar Zitmann) (29×24 mm)	2·50	2·10

E662 Stille Musik Rock Garden, Grosssedlitz

1980. Baroque Gardens. Multicoloured.

E2193	10pf. Type E **662**	20	15
E2194	20pf. Belvedere Orangery, Weimar	20	15
E2195	50pf. Flower garden, Dornburg Castle	25	15
E2196	70pf. Park, Rheinsberg Castle	2·10	2·10

E663 Cable-laying Machine and Dish Aerial

1980. Post Office Activities. Multicoloured.

E2212	10pf. Type E **663**	20	15
E2213	20pf. T.V. Tower, Berlin, and television	30	30

E664 Johann Wolfgang Dobereiner (chemist, bicent)

1980. Celebrities' Birth Anniversaries.

E2214	**E664** 5pf. black and bistre	20	15
E2215	- 10pf. black and red	20	15
E2216	- 20pf. black and green	20	15
E2217	- 25pf. black and blue	20	15
E2218	- 35pf. black and blue	20	20
E2219	- 70pf. black and red	1·90	1·40

DESIGNS: 10pf. Frederic Joliot-Curie (physicist, and chemist, 80th anniv); 20pf. Johann Friedrich Naumann (zoologist, bicent); 25pf. Alfred Wegener (explorer and geophysicist, cent); 35pf. Carl von Clausewitz (Prussian general, bicent); 70pf. Helene Weigel (actress, 80th anniv).

E665 Karl Marx University, Leipzig

1980. Leipzig Spring Fair. Multicoloured.

E2220	10pf. Type E **665**	25	15
E2221	25pf. "ZT 303" tractor	35	30

E666 Werner Eggerath

1980. 80th Birth Anniv of Werner Eggerath (socialist).

E2222	**E666** 10pf. brown and red	55	40

E667 Cosmonauts and "Interkosmos" Emblem

1980. "Interkosmos" Programme. Sheet 109×89 mm.

MSE2223	E **667** 1m. multicoloured	2·50	2·10

E668 "On the Horizontal Beam" (sculpture, Erich Wurzer)

1980. Olympic Games, Moscow (1st issue). Multicoloured.

E2224	10pf. Type E **668**	25	20
E2225	20pf.+5pf. "Runners before the Winning Post" (Lothar Zitzmann)	25	20

E2226 50pf. "Coxless Four" (Wilfred Falkenthal) 1·50 1·40

See also Nos. E2247/9.

E669 Flags of Member States

1980. 25th Anniv of Warsaw Pact.

E2227	**E669**	20pf. multicoloured	55	25

E670 Co-operative Society Building (W. Gropius)

1980. Bauhaus Architecture. Multicoloured.

E2228	5pf. Type E **670**	25	20
E2229	10pf. Socialists' Memorial Place (M. v. d. Rhode) (horiz)	25	20
E2230	15pf. Monument to the Fallen of March 1922 (W. Gropius)	25	20
E2231	20pf. Steel Building 1926 (G. Muche and R. Paulick) (horiz)	25	20
E2232	50pf. Trade Union school (H. Meyer)	35	20
E2233	70pf. Bauhaus building (W. Gropius) (horiz)	3·00	2·20

E671 Rostock Buildings

1980. 18th Workers' Festival, Rostock. Mult.

E2234	10pf. Type E **671**	25	15
E2235	20pf. Costumed dancers	45	30

E672 Radar Complex, Berlin-Schoenefeld Airport

1980. "Aerosozphilex 1980" International Airmail Exhibition, Berlin. Multicoloured.

E2236	20pf. Type E **672**	45	45
E2237	25pf. Ilyushin Il-62M at Schonefeld Airport	45	45
E2238	35pf. PZL-106A Kruk crop-spraying airplane	70	70
E2239	70pf. Antonov An-2 aerial photography biplane and multispectrum camera	1·40	1·40
MSE2240	64×95 mm. 1m.+10pf. Ilyushin Il-62M jetliner and globe	2·50	2·50

E673 Okapi

1980. Endangered Animals. Multicoloured.

E2241	5pf. Type E **673**	20	15
E2242	10pf. Lesser pandas	20	15
E2243	15pf. Maned wolf	20	15
E2244	20pf. Arabian oryx	20	15
E2245	25pf. White-eared pheasant	25	15
E2246	35pf. Musk oxen	2·30	1·90

1980. Olympic Games, Moscow (2nd issue). As Type E 668. Multicoloured.

E2247	10pf. "Judo" (Erhard Schmidt)	20	15
E2248	20pf.+10pf. "Swimmer" (Willi Sitte) (vert)	20	15
E2249	50pf. "Spurt" (sculpture, Siegfried Schreiber)	1·60	1·40
MSE2250	79×55 mm. 1m. "Spinnakers" (Karl Raetsch) (29×24 mm)	2·50	2·30

E674 Suhl, 1700

1980. 6th National Youth Stamp Exhibition, Suhl. Multicoloured.

E2251	10pf.+5pf. Type E **674**	40	40
E2252	20pf. Modern Suhl	40	40

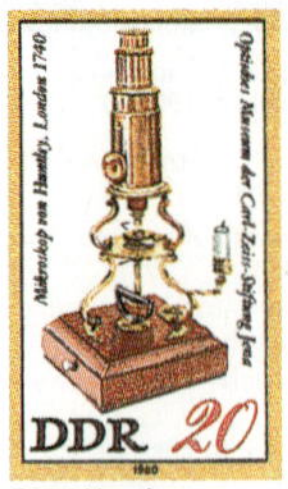

E675 Huntley Microscope

1980. Carl Zeiss Optical Museum, Jena. Mult.

E2253	20pf. Type E **675**	40	40
E2254	25pf. Magny microscope, 1751	45	45
E2255	35pf. Amici microscope, 1845	65	65
E2256	70pf. Zeiss microscope, 1873	1·40	1·40

E676 Majdanek Memorial

1980. War Victims' Memorial, Majdanek, Poland.

E2257	**E676**	35pf. multicoloured	65	40

E677 Information Centre, Leipzig

1980. Leipzig Autumn Fair. Multicoloured.

E2258	10pf. Type E **677**	25	15
E2259	25pf. Carpet-knitting machine	55	30

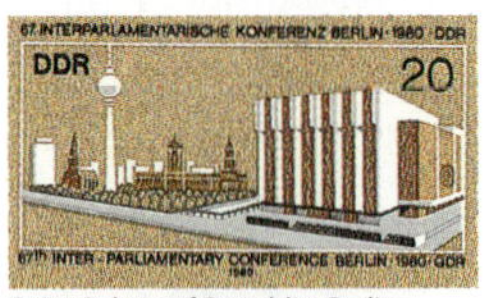

E678 Palace of Republic, Berlin

1980. 67th Interparliamentary Conference, Berlin.

E2260	**E678**	20pf. multicoloured	90	30

E679 "Laughing Boy with Flute"

1980. 400th Anniv of Frans Hals (artist). Multicoloured.

E2261	10pf. Type E **679**	20	15
E2262	20pf. "Portrait of Young Man in Drab Coat"	20	15
E2263	25pf. "The Mulatto"	25	15
E2264	35pf. "Portrait of Young Man in Black Coat"	1·40	1·30
MSE2265	80×55 mm. 1m. brown (Self-portrait) (29×23 mm)	2·75	2·10

E680 Clenched Fist and Star

1980. "Solidarity".

E2266	**E680**	10pf.+5pf. turq & red	45	25

E681 "Leccinum versipelle" ("Leccinum testaceo scabrum")

1980. Edible Mushrooms. Multicoloured.

E2267	5pf. Type E **681**	20	15
E2268	10pf. "Boletus miniatoporus" ("Boletus erythropus")	20	15
E2269	15pf. "Agaricus campestris" ("Agaricus campester")	20	15
E2270	20pf. "Xerocomus badius"	25	15
E2271	35pf. "Boletus edulis"	30	20
E2272	70pf. "Cantharellus cibarius"	2·40	2·30

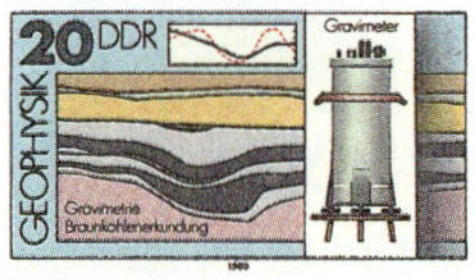

E682 Gravimetry

1980. Geophysics. Multicoloured.

E2273	20pf. Type E **682**	35	25
E2274	25pf. Bore-hole measuring	45	40
E2275	35pf. Seismic prospecting	70	70
E2276	50pf. Seismology	1·00	1·00

E683 Radebeul–Radeburg Steam Locomotive

1980. Narrow-gauge Railways (1st series). Multicoloured.

E2277	20pf. Type E **683**	45	45
E2278	20pf. Bad Doberan–Ostsee-bad Kuhlungsborn steam locomotive	45	45
E2279	25pf. Radebeul–Radeburg passenger carriage	45	45
E2280	35pf. Bad Doberan–Ostseebad Kuhlungsborn passenger carriage	45	45

See also Nos. E2342/5, E2509/12 and E2576/9.

E684 Toy Steam Locomotive, 1850

1980. Historical Toys. Multicoloured.

E2281	10pf. Type E **684**	25	30
E2282	20pf. Aeroplane, 1914	1·10	1·10
E2283	25pf. Steam-roller, 1920	25	30
E2284	35pf. Sailing ship, 1825	25	30
E2285	40pf. Car, 1900	1·10	1·10
E2286	50pf. Balloon, 1920	25	30

E685 Mozart

1981. 225th Birth Anniv of Wolfgang Amadeus Mozart (composer). Sheet 55×80 mm.

MSE2287	E **685**	1m. black, carmine-rose and stone	2·75	2·30

E686 "Malus pumila"

1981. Rare Plants in Berlin Arboretum. Mult.

E2288	5pf. Type E **686**	20	15
E2289	10pf. "Halesia carolina" (horiz)	20	15
E2290	20pf. "Colutea arborescens"	20	15
E2291	25pf. "Paulownia tomentosa"	25	15
E2292	35pf. "Lonicera periclymenum" (horiz)	30	20
E2293	50pf. "Calycanthus floridus"	2·75	2·50

E687 Heinrich von Stephan

1981. 150th Birth Anniv of Heinrich von Stephan (founder of U.P.U.).

E2294	**E687**	10pf. black and yellow	45	30

E688 Soldiers on Parade

1981. 25th Anniv of National People's Army. Multicoloured.

E2295	10pf. Type E **688**	25	20
E2296	20pf. Marching soldiers	35	20

E689 Marx and Lenin

1981. 10th East German Socialist Party Congress (1st series).

E2297	**E689**	10pf. multicoloured	45	20

See Nos. E2309/**MS**2313.

E690 Counter Clerks

1981. Post Office Training. Multicoloured.

E2298	5pf. Type E **690**	20	15
E2299	10pf. Telephone engineers	20	15
E2300	15pf. Radio communications	20	15
E2301	20pf. Rosa Luxemburg Engineering School, Leipzig	25	20
E2302	25pf. Freidrich List Communications School, Dresden	1·50	1·10

E691 Erich Baron

1981. Socialist Personalities.

E2303	**E691**	10pf. black and green	25	20
E2304	-	10pf. black and yellow	25	20
E2305	-	10pf. black and blue	25	20
E2306	-	10pf. black and brown	25	20

DESIGNS: No. E2304, Conrad Blenkle; E2305, Arthur Ewert; E2306, Walter Stoecker.

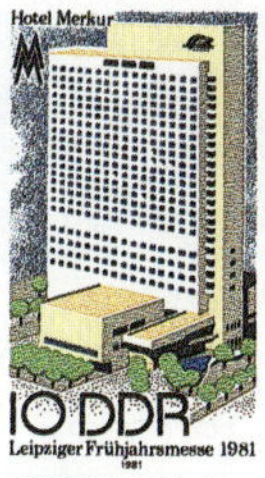

E692 Hotel Merkur Leipzig

1981. Leipzig Spring Fair. Multicoloured.

E2307	10pf. Type E **692**	25	15
E2308	25pf. Open-cast mining machine	45	30

E693 "Ernst Thalmann" (Willi Sitte)

1981. 10th East German Socialist Party Congress (2nd series). Multicoloured.

E2309	10pf. Type E **693**	20	15
E2310	20pf. "Brigadier" (Bernhard Heisig)	20	15
E2311	25pf. "Festival Day" (Rudolf Bergander)	1·10	1·00
E2312	35pf. "Comrades in Arms" (Paul Michaelis)	25	15
MSE2313	108×82 mm. 1m. "When Communists are Dreaming" (Walter Womacka)	2·10	1·60

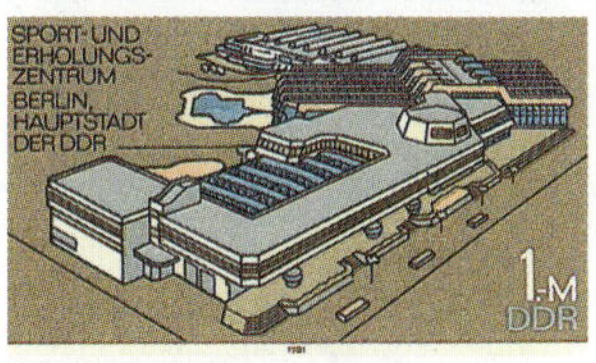

E694 Sports Centre

1981. Sports Centre, Berlin. Sheet 110×90 mm.

MSE2314	E **694** 1m. multicoloured	2·50	2·40

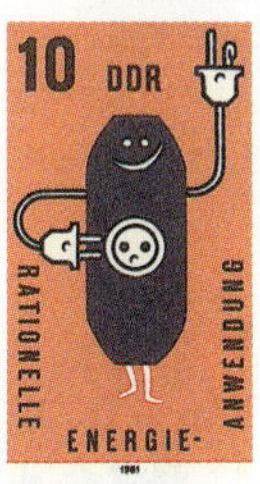

E695 Plugs and Socket

1981. Conservation of Energy.

E2315	**E695** 10pf. black & orange	25	25

E696 Heinrich Barkhausen

1981. Celebrities' Birth Anniversaries.

E2316	**E696** 10pf. black and blue	20	15
E2317	- 20pf. black and red	20	15
E2318	- 25pf. black and brown	2·75	2·00
E2319	- 35pf. black and violet	25	20
E2320	- 50pf. black and green	35	20
E2321	- 70pf. black and brown	55	30

DESIGNS: 10pf. Type E **696** (physicist, birth centenary); 20pf. Johannes R. Becher (writer, 90th birth anniv); 25pf. Richard Dedekind (mathematician, 150th birth anniv); 35pf. Georg Philipp Telemann (composer, 300th anniv); 50pf. Adelbert V. Chamisso (poet and naturalist, bicentenary); 70pf. Wilhelm Raabe (novelist, 150th birth anniv).

E697 Free German Youth Members and Banner

1981. 11th Free German Youth Parliament. Multicoloured.

E2322	10pf. Type E **697**	25	30
E2323	20pf. Free German Youth members instructing foreign students	25	30

E698 Worlitz Park

1981. Landscaped Parks. Multicoloured.

E2324	5pf. Type E **698**	20	15
E2325	10pf. Tiefurt Park, Weimar	20	15
E2326	15pf. Marxwalde	20	15
E2327	20pf. Branitz Park	20	15
E2328	25pf. Treptow Park, Berlin	2·00	1·90
E2329	35pf. Wiesenburg Park	25	30

E699 Children at Play and Sport

1981. 8th Children's and Young People's Sports Days, Berlin. Multicoloured.

E2330	10pf.+5pf. Type E **699**	75	55
E2331	20pf. Artistic gymnastics	30	25

E700 Berlin Theatre

1981. Birth Bicentenary of Karl Friedrich Schinkel (architect).

E2332	**E700** 10pf. stone and black	1·00	15
E2333	- 25pf. stone and black	2·50	1·00

DESIGN: 25pf. Old Museum, Berlin.

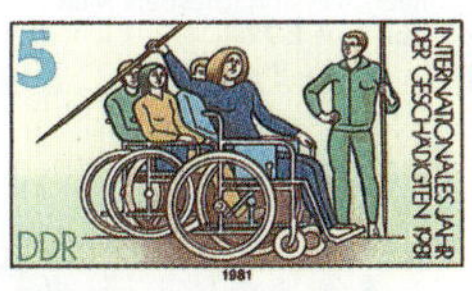

E701 Throwing the Javelin from a Wheel chair

1981. International Year of Disabled Persons. Multicoloured.

E2334	5pf. Type E **701**	25	20
E2335	15pf. Disabled people in art gallery	25	20

E702 House, Zaulsdorf

1981. Half-timbered Buildings. Multicoloured.

E2336	10pf. Type E **702**	20	15
E2337	20pf. "Sugar-loaf" cottage, Gross Zicker (horiz)	20	15
E2338	25pf. Farmhouse, Weckersdorf	25	15
E2339	35pf. House, Pillgram (horiz)	25	20
E2340	50pf. House, Eschenbach	35	30
E2341	70pf. House, Ludersdorf (horiz)	3·75	2·75

1981. Narrow-Gauge Railways (2nd series). As Type E 683. Multicoloured.

E2342	5pf. black and red	25	20
E2343	5pf. black and red	25	20
E2344	15pf. multicoloured	25	20
E2345	20pf. multicoloured	25	20

DESIGNS: Nos. E2342, Freital–Kurort Kipsdorf steam locomotive; E2343, Putbus–Gohren steam locomotive; E2344, Freital–Kurort Kipsdorf luggage van; E2345, Putbus–Gohren passenger carriage.

E703 Chemical Works

1981. Leipzig Autumn Fair. Multicoloured.

E2346	10pf. Type E **703**	25	15
E2347	25pf. New Draper's Hall (horiz)	45	45

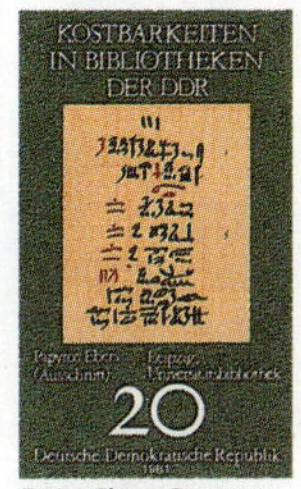

E704 Ebers Papyrus (Leipzig University Library)

1981. Precious Books from East German Libraries. Multicoloured.

E2348	20pf. Type E **704**	20	15
E2349	35pf. Maya manuscript (Dresden Library)	25	15
E2350	50pf. Miniature from "Les six visions Messire Francoys Petrarque" (Berlin State Library)	1·80	1·80

E705 Sassnitz Memorial

1981. Resistance Fighters' Memorial, Sassnitz.

E2351	**E705** 35pf. multicoloured	60	40

E706 Henbane and Incense Burner

1981. Early Medical Equipment in the Karl-Sudhoff Institute, Leipzig. Multicoloured.

E2352	10pf. Type E **706**	20	15
E2353	20pf. Dental instruments	20	15
E2354	25pf. Forceps	20	15
E2355	35pf. Bladder knife and hernia shears	25	20
E2356	50pf. Speculum and gynaecological forceps (vert)	3·25	3·00
E2357	85pf. Triploid elevators (vert)	60	40

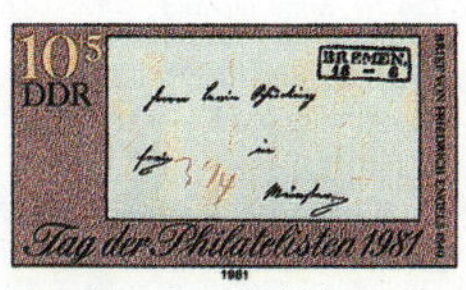

E707 Letter from Friedrich Engels, 1840

1981. Stamp Day. Multicoloured.

E2358	10pf.+5pf. Type E **707**	1·00	65
E2359	20pf. Postcard from Karl Marx, 1878	25	15

E708 African breaking Chains

1981. "Solidarity".

E2360	**E708** 10pf.+5pf. mult	35	20

E709 Tug

1981. Inland Shipping. Multicoloured.

E2361	10pf. Type E **709**	20	15
E2362	20pf. Tug and barges	20	15
E2363	25pf. Diesel-electric paddle-ferry, River Elbe	25	15
E2364	35pf. Ice-breaker in the Oder estuary	25	20
E2365	50pf. "Schonewalde" (motor barge)	35	25
E2366	85pf. Dredger	3·00	3·00

E710 Windmill, Dabel

1981. Windmills. Multicoloured.

E2367	10pf. Type E **710**	20	15
E2368	20pf. Pahrenz	20	15
E2369	25pf. Dresden-Gohlis	25	15
E2370	70pf. Ballstadt	2·10	1·90

E711 Snake, 1850

1981. Historical Toys. Multicoloured.

E2371	10pf. Type E **711**	25	30
E2372	20pf. Teddy bear, 1910	25	30
E2373	25pf. Goldfish, 1935	1·40	1·40
E2374	35pf. Hobby-horse, 1850	1·40	1·40
E2375	40pf. Pull-along duck, 1800	25	30
E2376	70pf. Clockwork frog, 1930	25	30

E712 Coffee Pot, 1715

1982. 300th Birth Anniv of Johann Friedrich Bottger (founder of Meissen China Works). Multicoloured.

E2377	10pf. Type E **712**	25	20
E2378	20pf. Vase decorated with flowers, 1715	45	40
E2379	25pf. "Oberon" (figurine), 1969	60	55
E2380	35pf. Vase "Day and Night", 1979	80	75
MSE2381	89×110 mm. 50pf. Portrait medal; 50pf. Bottger's seal	3·00	2·40

E713 Post Office, Bad Liebenstein

1982. Post Office Building. Multicoloured.

E2382	20pf. Type E **713**	20	15
E2383	25pf. Telecommunications Centre, Berlin	20	15
E2384	35pf. Head Post Office, Erfurt	25	15

E2385 50pf. Head Post Office, Dresden 6 2·10 1·90

E714 Alpine Marmot

1982. International Fur Auction, Leipzig. Multicoloured.

E2386	10pf. Type E **714**	20	15
E2387	20pf. Polecat	20	15
E2388	25pf. European mink	25	20
E2389	35pf. Beech marten	1·60	1·40

E715 Silhouette of Goethe

1982. Johann Wolfgang von Goethe and Friedrich von Schiller (writers) Commemoration. Sheet 110×90 mm containing Type E 715 and similar vert design. Multicoloured.

MSE2390 50pf. Type E **715** (150th death anniv); 50pf. Silhouette of Schiller (175th death (1980) and 225th birth (1984) annivs) 3·25 2·75

E716 West Entrance to Fairground

1982. Leipzig Spring Fair. Multicoloured.

E2391	10pf. Type E **716**	20	15
E2392	25pf. Seamless steel tube plant, Riesa Zeithain	40	30

E717 Dr. Robert Koch

1982. Centenary of Discovery of Tubercle Bacillus. Sheet 80×55 mm.

MSE2393 E **717** 1m. multicoloured 2·50 2·20

E718 Max Fechner

1982. Socialist Personalities.

E2394	**E718**	10pf. brown	20	10
E2395	-	10pf. green	20	10
E2396	-	10pf. lilac	20	10
E2397	-	10pf. blue	20	10
E2398	-	10pf. green	20	10

DESIGNS: No. E2395, Ottomar Geschke; E2396, Helmut Lehmann; E2397, Herbert Warnke; E2398, Otto Winzer.

E719 Meadow Saffron

1982. Poisonous Plants. Multicoloured.

E2399	10pf. Type E **719**	20	20
E2400	15pf. Bog arum	20	20
E2401	20pf. Labrador tea	20	20
E2402	25pf. Bryony	20	20
E2403	35pf. Monkshood	25	20
E2404	50pf. Henbane	1·80	1·70

E720 Decorative Initial "I"

1982. International "Art of the Book" Exhibition, Leipzig.

E2405	**E720**	15pf. multicoloured	55	55
E2406	-	35pf. brn, red & blk	55	55

DESIGN: 35pf. Exhibition emblem.

E721 "Mother with Child" (W. Womacka)

1982. 10th Free German Trade Unions Association Congress, Berlin.

E2407	**E721**	10pf. black, red and yellow	20	15
E2408	-	20pf. multicoloured	25	15
E2409	-	25pf. multicoloured	90	80

DESIGNS—HORIZ: 20pf. "Discussion by Collective of Innovators" (Willi Neubert). VERT: 25pf. "Young Couple" (Karl-Heinz Jakob).

E722 Osprey

1982. Protected Birds. Multicoloured.

E2410	10pf. Type E **722**	25	15
E2411	20pf. White-tailed sea eagle (horiz)	25	15
E2412	25pf. Little owl	25	15
E2413	35pf. Eagle owl	2·10	1·60

E723 Old and Modern Buildings

1982. 19th Workers' Festival, Neubrandenburg. Multicoloured.

E2414	10pf. Type E **723**	25	25
E2415	20pf. Couple in traditional costume	55	45

E724 Memorial Medal

1982. Birth Centenary of Georgi Dimitrov (Bulgarian statesman). Sheet 80×55 mm.

MSE2416 E **724** 1m. multicoloured 3·00 2·75

E725 "Frieden" (freighter)

1982. Ocean-going Ships. Multicoloured.

E2417	5pf. Type E **725**	20	15
E2418	10pf. "Fichtelberg" (roll on roll off freighter)	20	15
E2419	15pf. "Brocken" (heavy cargo carrier)	20	15
E2420	20pf. "Weimar" (container ship)	20	15
E2421	25pf. "Vorwarts" (freighter)	20	15
E2422	35pf. "Berlin" (container ship)	2·10	1·70

E726 Members' Activities

1982. 30th Anniv of Sports and Science Association.

E2423	**E726**	20pf. multicoloured	50	25

E727 Bird Wedding

1982. Sorbian Folk Customs. Multicoloured.

E2424	10pf. Type E **727**	25	15
E2425	20pf. Shrove Tuesday procession	30	25
E2426	25pf. Egg rolling	45	45
E2427	35pf. Painted Easter eggs	70	70
E2428	40pf. St. John's Day riders	80	80
E2429	50pf. Distribution of Christmas gifts to hard-working children	1·00	1·00

E728 Schwerin, 1640

1982. 7th National Youth Stamp Exhibition, Schwerin. Multicoloured.

E2430	10pf.+5pf. Type E **728**	35	40
E2431	20pf. Modern Schwerin	35	40

E729 Flag and Pioneers

1982. 7th Pioneers Meeting, Dresden. Mult.

E2432	10pf.+5pf. Type E **729**	60	60
E2433	20pf. Trumpet and drum	25	15

E730 "Stormy Sea" (Ludolf Backhuysen)

1982. Paintings in Schwerin State Museum. Multicoloured.

E2434	5pf. Type E **730**	20	15
E2435	10pf. "Music making at Home" (Frans van Mieris) (vert)	20	15
E2436	20pf. "The Watchman" (Carel Fabritius) (vert)	20	15
E2437	25pf. "Company of Peasants" (Adriaen Brouwer)	25	20
E2438	35pf. "Breakfast Table with Ham" (Willem Claesz Heda)	30	20
E2439	70pf. "River Landscape" (Jan van Goyen)	2·40	2·30

E731 Karl-Marx-Stadt

1982. 13th Socialist Countries' Postal Ministers Conference, Karl-Marx-Stadt.

E2440	**E731**	10pf. multicoloured	55	40

E732 Stentzlers Hof

1982. Leipzig Autumn Fair. Multicoloured.

E2441	10pf. Type E **732**	20	15
E2442	25pf. Amber box, ring and pendant	40	30

E733 Auschwitz-Birkenau Memorial

1982. War Victims' Memorial, Auschwitz-Birkenau.

E2443	**E733**	35pf. blue, blk & red	45	40

E734 Federation Badge

1982. 9th International Federation of Resistance Fighters Congress, Berlin.

E2444	**E734**	10pf. multicoloured	45	30

E735 "Anemone hupehensis"

1982. Autumn Flowers. Multicoloured.

E2445	5pf. Type E **735**	20	15
E2446	10pf. French marigolds	20	15
E2447	15pf. Gazania	20	15
E2448	20pf. Sunflower	25	15
E2449	25pf. Annual chrysanthemum	25	20
E2450	35pf. Cosmea	2·75	2·00

E736 Palestinian Family

1982. Solidarity with Palestinian People.

E2451	**E736**	10pf.+5pf. mult	50	30

E737 "B 1000" Ambulance

1982. IFA Vehicles. Multicoloured.

E2452	5pf. Type E **737**	20	15
E2453	10pf. Road cleaner	20	15
E2454	20pf. "LD 3000" omnibus	20	15
E2455	25pf. "LD 3000" lorry	25	20
E2456	35pf. "W 50" lorry	30	20
E2457	85pf. "W 50" milk tanker	3·00	2·50

E738 Fair Emblem

1982. 25th "Masters of Tomorrow" Fair, Leipzig.

E2458	**E738**	20pf. multicoloured	35	25

E739 Aircraft and Envelope

1982. Air.

E2459	**E739**	5pf. black and blue	20	20
E2460	**E739**	15pf. black and mauve	20	40
E2461	**E739**	20pf. black and orange	35	20
E2462	**E739**	25pf. black and bistre	45	30
E2463	**E739**	30pf. black and green	25	20
E2464	**E739**	40pf. black and green	35	20
E2465	**E739**	1m. black and blue	1·30	55
E2466	**E739**	3m. black and brown	3·25	1·90
E2467	**E739**	5m. black and red	4·50	1·70

E740 Seal of Eisleben, 1500

1982. 500th Birth Anniv of Martin Luther (Protestant reformer).

E2471	10pf. Type E **740**	25	20
E2472	20pf. Luther as Junker Jog, 1521	30	20
E2473	35pf. Seal of Wittenberg, 1500	55	20
E2474	85pf. Luther (after Cranach)	3·75	2·40

See also No. **MS**2548.

E741 Carpenter

1982. Mechanical Toys. Multicoloured.

E2475	10pf. Type E **741**	25	25
E2476	20pf. Shoemaker	1·40	1·40
E2477	25pf. Baker	25	25
E2478	35pf. Cooper	25	25
E2479	40pf. Tanner	1·40	1·40
E2480	70pf. Wheelwright	25	25

E742 Johannes Brahms

1983. 150th Birth Anniv of Johannes Brahms (composer). Sheet 55×80 mm.

MSE2481	E **742**	1m.15, green, brown and sepia	4·00	2·75

E743 Franz Dahlem

1983. Socialist Personalities.

E2482	**E743**	10pf. brown	20	15
E2483	-	10pf. green	20	15
E2484	-	10pf. green	20	15
E2485	-	10pf. lilac	20	15
E2486	-	10pf. blue	20	15

DESIGN: No. E2483, Karl Maron; E2484, Josef Miller; E2485, Fred Oelssner; E2486, Siegfried Radel.

E744 Telephone Handset and Push-buttons

1983. World Communications Year.

E2487	**E744**	5pf. brown, black and deep brown	20	15
E2488	-	10pf. blue, turquoise and deep blue	20	15
E2489	-	20pf. green, deep green and black	20	15
E2490	-	35pf. multicoloured	1·60	1·20

DESIGNS: 10pf. Aerials and tankers (Rugen Radio); 20pf. Ilyushin Il-62, container ship, letter and parcel; 35pf. Optical fibre cables.

E745 Otto Nuschke

1983. Birth Cent of Otto Nuschke (politician).

E2491	**E745**	20pf. light brown, black and brown	35	35

E746 Stolberg Town Hall

1983. Historic Town Halls. Multicoloured.

E2492	10pf. Type E **746**	20	15
E2493	20pf. Gera (vert)	20	15
E2494	25pf. Possneck (vert)	25	15
E2495	35pf. Berlin	1·70	1·50

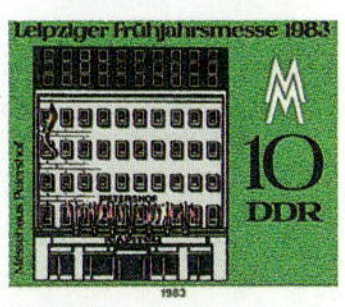

E747 Petershof

1983. Leipzig Spring Fair. Multicoloured.

E2496	10pf. Type E **747**	25	15
E2497	25pf. Robotron micro- elec-tronic calculator	40	30

E748 Paul Robeson

1983. 85th Birth Anniv of Paul Robeson (singer).

E2498	**E748**	20pf. multicoloured	35	35

E749 Harnack, Schulze-Boysen and Sieg

1983. 40th Death Annivs of Arvid Harnack, Harro Schulze-Boysen and John Sieg (Resistance workers). Sheet 80×55 mm.

MSE2499	E **749**	85pf. black and green	1·60	1·70

E750 Karl Marx and Newspaper Mastheads

1983. Death Cent of Karl Marx. Multicoloured.

E2500	10pf. Type E **750**	20	20
E2501	20pf. Marx, Lyons silk weavers and title page of "Deutsche-Franzosische Jahrbucher"	20	20
E2502	35pf. Marx, Engels and "Communist Manifesto"	25	20
E2503	50pf. Marx and German, Russian and French versions of "Das Kapital"	25	25
E2504	70pf. Marx and part of letter to Wilhelm Bracke containing commentary on German Workers' Party Programme	45	30
E2505	85pf. Globe and banner portraying Marx, Engels, Lenin	3·25	3·25
MSE2506	81×56 mm. 1m.15 Karl Marx (26×32 mm)	2·75	2·75

E751 "Athene"

1983. Sculptures in State Museum, Berlin.

E2507	**E751**	10pf. brown, light brown and blue	25	15
E2508	-	20pf. brown, light brown and green	55	30

DESIGN: 20pf. "Amazon".

1983. Narrow-gauge Railways (3rd series). As Type E 683.

E2509	15pf. grey, black and red	55	45
E2510	20pf. multicoloured	55	45
E2511	20pf. grey, black and red	55	45
E2512	50pf. brown, black and grey	55	45

DESIGNS: No. E2509, Wernigerode–Nordhausen steam locomotive; E2510, Wernigerode–Nordhausen passenger carriage; E2511, Zittau–Kurort Oybin/Kurort Jonsdorf steam locomotive; E2512, Zittau–Kurort Oybin/Kurort Jonsdorf luggage van.

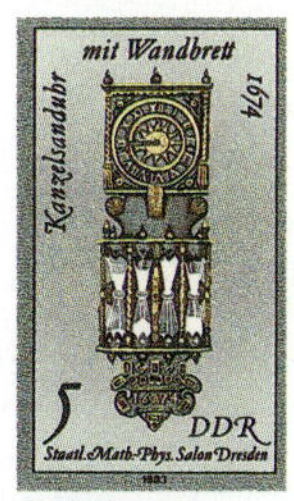

E752 Chancery Hourglass with Wallmount, 1674

1983. Hourglasses and Sundials. Multicoloured.

E2513	5pf. Type E **752**	20	15
E2514	10pf. Chancery hour-glass, 1700	20	15
E2515	20pf. Horizontal table sundial, 1611	25	15
E2516	30pf. Equatorial sundial, 1750	30	25
E2517	50pf. Equatorial sundial, 1760	45	35
E2518	85pf. "Noon Gun" table sundial, 1800	3·25	2·50

E753 "Coryphantha elephantidens"

1983. Cultivated Cacti. Multicoloured.

E2519	5pf. Type E **753**	20	15
E2520	10pf. "Thelocactus schwarzii"	20	15
E2521	20pf. "Leuchtenbergia principis"	20	15
E2522	25pf. "Submatucana madisoniorum"	25	20
E2523	35pf. "Oroya peruviana"	30	20
E2524	50pf. "Copiapoa cinerea"	2·20	2·00

E754 Thimo and Wilhelm

1983. Founders of Naumberg Cathedral. Statues in the West Choir. Multicoloured.

E2525	20pf. Type E **754**	45	45
E2526	25pf. Gepa and Gerburg	55	55
E2527	35pf. Hermann and Reglindis	65	65
E2528	85pf. Eckehard and Uta	1·70	1·60

E755 "Glasewaldt and Zinna defending the Barricade, Berlin, 1848" (Theodor Hosemann)

1983. "Junior Sozphilex 1983" Stamp Exhibition, Berlin.

E2529	**E 755**	10pf.+5pf. brown, black and red	90	65
E2530	-	20pf. multicoloured	25	15

DESIGN—HORIZ: 20pf. "Instruction at Polytechnic" (Harald Metzkes).

E756 Simon Bolivar and Alexander von Humboldt

1983. Birth Bicentenary of Simon Bolivar.

E2531	**E756**	35pf. black, brown and deep brown	75	40

E757 Exercise with Balls

1983. 7th Gymnastics and Sports Festival and 9th Children and Young People's Sports Days, Leipzig. Multicoloured.

E2532	10pf.+5pf. Type E **757**	65	45
E2533	20pf. Volleyball	25	25

E758 Arms of Cottbus

1983. Town Arms (1st series).

E2534	**E758**	50pf. multicoloured	95	95
E2535	-	50pf. multicoloured	95	95
E2536	-	50pf. red, black and silver	95	95
E2537	-	50pf. multicoloured	95	95
E2538	-	50pf. black, red and silver	95	95

DESIGNS: No. E2535, Dresden; E2536, Erfurt; E2537, Frankfurt-on-Oder. (21×39 mm); No. E2538, Berlin.

See also Nos. E2569/73 and E2644/8.

E759 Central Fair Palace

1983. Leipzig Autumn Fair. Multicoloured.

E2539	10pf. Type E **759**	25	15
E2540	25pf. Microchip	55	30

E760 Militiaman

1983. 30th Anniv of Workers' Militia. Sheet 63×86 mm.

MSE2541	E **760** 1m. multicoloured	2·50	2·00

E761 Euler, Formula and Model

1983. Death Bicentenary of Leonhard Euler (mathematician).

E2542	**E761** 20pf. blue and black	55	40

E762 Sanssouci Castle

1983. Public Palaces and Gardens of Potsdam-Sanssouci. Multicoloured.

E2543	10pf. Type E **762**	20	15
E2544	20pf. Chinese tea house	25	20
E2545	40pf. Charlottenhof Palace	55	30
E2546	50pf. Film museum (former stables)	3·25	2·75

E763 "Mother Homeland" (Yevgeni Vuzhetich)

1983. Vologr011 War Memorial.

E2547	**E763** 35pf. blue, blk & grn	75	40

E764 "D.M.L." (Dr. Martin Luther)

1983. 500th Birth Anniv of Martin Luther (Protestant reformer) (2nd issue). Sheet 108×83 mm.

MSE2548	E **764** 1m. multicoloured	3·75	3·00

E765 Learning to Read and Write

1983. "Solidarity with Nicaragua".

E2549	**E765** 10pf.+5pf. mult	45	30

E766 Cockerel

1983. Thuringian Glass. Multicoloured.

E2550	10pf. Type E **766**	25	20
E2551	20pf. Beaker	25	20
E2552	25pf. Vase	25	20
E2553	70pf. Goblet	2·30	2·10

E767 Luge

1983. Winter Olmpic Games, Sarajevo (1984).

E2554	**E767** 10pf.+5pf. multicoloured	20	15
E2555	- 20pf.+10pf. multicoloured	20	15
E2556	- 25pf. multicoloured	25	25
E2557	- 35pf. multicoloured	1·80	1·70
MSE2558	83×57 mm. 85pf. blue and silver	2·10	1·90

DESIGNS: 20pf. Cross-country skiing and ski jumping; 25pf. Cross-country skiing; 35pf. Biathlion; 85pf. Olympic Centre, Sarajevo.

E768 Dove and Greeting in German and English

1983. New Year. Sheet 93×83 mm containing Type E 768 and similar horiz designs, each showing dove and greeting in named languages. Multicoloured.

MSE2559	10pf. Type E **768**; 20pf. German and Russian; 25pf. French and German; 35pf. Spanish and German	2·10	1·90

E769 Dr. Otto Schott (chemist)

1984. Centenary of Jena Glass.

E2560	**E769** 20pf. multicoloured	45	30

E770 Friedrich Ebert

1984. Socialist Personalities.

E2561	**E770** 10pf. black	25	20
E2562	- 10pf. green	25	20
E2563	- 10pf. black	25	20

DESIGNS: No. E2562, Fritz Grosse; E2563, Albert Norden.

E771 Mendelssohn

1984. 175th Birth Anniv of Felix Mendelssohn Bartholdy (composer). Sheet 82×57 mm.

MSE2564	E **771** 85pf. multicoloured	1·30	1·30

E772 Milestones, Muhlau and Oederan

1984. Postal Milestones. Multicoloured.

E2565	10pf. Type E **772**	20	15
E2566	20pf. Milestones, Johanngeorgenstadt and Schonbrunn	35	30
E2567	35pf. Distance column, Freiberg	55	55
E2568	85pf. Distance column, Pegau	1·10	1·10

1984. Town Arms (2nd series). As Type E 758.

E2569	50pf. multicoloured	70	65
E2570	50pf. red, black and silver	70	65
E2571	50pf. multicoloured	70	65
E2572	50pf. multicoloured	70	65
E2573	50pf. multicoloured	70	65

DESIGNS: No. E2569, Gera; E2570, Halle; E2571, Karl-Marx-Stadt; E2572, Leipzig; E2573, Magdeburg.

E773 Old Town Hall, Leipzig

1984. Leipzig Spring Fair. Multicoloured.

E2574	10pf. Type E **773**	25	15
E2575	25pf. Body stamping press	35	30

1984. Narrow-gauge Railways (4th series). As Type E 683.

E2576	30pf. grey, black and red	30	30
E2577	40pf. grey, black and red	40	40
E2578	60pf. multicoloured	55	55
E2579	80pf. multicoloured	80	80

DESIGNS: 30pf. Cranzahl–Kurort Oberwiesenthal steam locomotive; 40pf. Selketalbahn steam locomotive; 60pf. Selketalbahn passenger carriage; 80pf. Cranzahl–Kurort Oberwiesenthal passenger carriage.

E774 Town Hall, Rostock

1984. 7th International Society for Preservation of Monuments General Assembly, Rostock and Dresden. Multicoloured.

E2580	10pf. Type E **774**	20	15
E2581	15pf. Albrecht Castle, Meissen	25	20
E2582	40pf. Gateway, Rostock (vert)	65	55
E2583	85pf. Stables, Dresden	1·40	1·20

E775 Telephone, Letter, Pencil and Headquarters

1984. 25th Meeting of Posts and Telecommunications Commission of Council of Mutual Economic Aid, Cracow.

E2584	**E775** 70pf. multicoloured	80	45

E776 Cast Iron Bowl

1984. Cast Iron from Lauchhammer. Multicoloured.

E2585	20pf. Type E **776**	25	30
E2586	85pf. "Climber" (Fritz Cremer)	1·00	1·30

E777 String Puppet

1984. Puppets. Multicoloured.

E2587	50pf. Type E **777**	70	70
E2588	80pf. Hand puppet	1·20	1·30

E778 Marchers with Flags

1984. National Youth Festival, Berlin. Multicoloured.

E2589	10pf.+5pf. Type E **778**	20	20
E2590	20pf. Young construction workers	25	30

E779 Gera Buildings

1984. 20th Workers' Festival, Gera. Multicoloured.

E2591	10pf. Type E **779**	20	15
E2592	20pf. Couple in traditional costume	35	30

E780 Salt Carrier

1984. National Stamp Exhibition, Halle. Mult.

E2593	10pf.+5pf. Type E **780**	25	20
E2594	20pf. Citizen of Halle with his bride	35	30

E781 Bakers' Seal, Berlin

1984. Historical Seals of 1442. Multicoloured.

E2595	5pf. Type E **781**	35	20
E2596	10pf. Wool weavers, Berlin	70	40
E2597	20pf. Wool weavers, Colln on Spree	1·40	45
E2598	35pf. Shoemakers, Colln on Spree	2·30	1·90

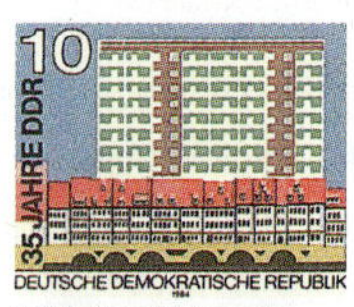

E782 New Flats and Restored Terrace

1984. 35th Anniv of German Democratic Republic (1st issue). Multicoloured.

E2599	10pf. Type E **782**	25	15
E2600	20pf. Surface mining	40	40
MSE2601	80×55 mm. 1m. Privy Council building	1·40	1·40

See also Nos. E2604/**MS**E2607 and E2069/**MS**E2613.

E783 Frege House, Katherine Street

1984. Leipzig Autumn Fair. Multicoloured.

E2602	10pf. Type E **783**	25	15
E2603	25pf. Crystal jar from Olbernhau	35	30

E784 East Ironworks

1984. 35th Anniv of German Democratic Republic (2nd issue). Multicoloured.

E2604	10pf. Type E **784**	20	15
E2605	20pf. Soldiers, Mil Mi-8 helicopter, tank and warship	25	30
E2606	25pf. Petro-chemical complex, Schwedt	50	45
MSE2607	110×90 mm. 1m. bright carmine (Family and new flats) (51×29 mm)	1·40	1·40

E785 "Members of the Resistance" (Arno Wittig)

1984. Resistance Memorial, Georg-Schumann Building, Technical University of Dresden.

E2608	**E785**	35pf. multicoloured	80	40

E786 Construction Workers

1984. 35th Anniv of German Democratic Republic (3rd issue). Multicoloured.

E2609	10pf. Type E **786**	20	15
E2610	20pf. Soldiers	25	20
E2611	25pf. Industrial workers	45	40
E2612	35pf. Agricultural workers	55	45
MSE2613	108×88 mm. 1m. Dove and national arms (vert)	1·40	1·40

E787 Magdeburg, 1551

1984. 8th National Youth Exhibition, Magdeburg. Multicoloured.

E2614	10pf.+5pf. Type E **787**	25	25
E2615	20pf. Modern Magdeburg	25	25

E788 "Spring"

1984. Statuettes by Balthasar Permoser in Green Vault, Dresden. Multicoloured.

E2616	10pf. Type E **788**	20	15
E2617	20pf. "Summer"	30	30
E2618	35pf. "Autumn"	55	55
E2619	70pf. "Winter"	1·10	1·10
MSE2620	144×115 mm. No. E 2617×8	3·00	3·00

E789 Entwined Cable and Red Star

1984. "Solidarity".

E2621	**E789**	10pf.+5pf. mult	45	30

E790 Falkenstein Castle

1984. Castles (1st series). Multicoloured.

E2622	10pf. Type E **790**	20	15
E2623	20pf. Kriebstein Castle	30	30
E2624	35pf. Ranis Castle	70	70
E2625	80pf. Neuenburg	1·40	1·40

See also Nos. E2686/9 and E2742/5.

E791 Queen and Princess

1984. Fairy Tales. "Dead Tsar's Daughter and the Seven Warriors" by Pushkin. Multicoloured.

E2626	5pf. Type E **791**	25	30
E2627	10pf. Princess and dog outside cottage	25	30
E2628	15pf. Princess and seven warriors	3·75	2·40
E2629	20pf. Princess holding poisoned apple	3·75	2·40
E2630	35pf. Princess awakened by Prince	25	30
E2631	50pf. Prince and Princess on horse	25	30

E792 Anton Ackermann

1985. Socialist Personalities.

E2632	**E792**	10pf. black	20	20
E2633	-	10pf. brown	20	20
E2634	-	10pf. purple	20	20

DESIGNS: No. E2633, Alfred Kurella; E2634, Otto Schon.

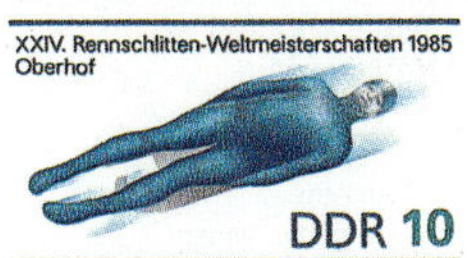

E793 Luge

1985. 24th World Luge Championships, Oberhof.

E2635	**E793**	10pf. multicoloured	35	30

E794 Letter-box, 1850

1984. Letter-boxes.

E2636	**E794**	10pf. brown and black	20	20
E2637	-	20pf. black, brown and red	20	20
E2638	-	35pf. multicoloured	45	45
E2639	-	50pf. brown, black and grey	65	65

DESIGNS: 20pf. Letter-box, 1860; 35pf. Letter-box, 1900; 50pf. Letter-box, 1920.

E795 Semper Opera House, 1985

1985. Re-opening of Semper Opera House, Dresden. Sheet 57×80 mm.

MSE2640	E **795** 85pf. brown, grey and red	1·20	1·20

E796 Bach Statue, Leipzig

1985. Leipzig Spring Fair. Multicoloured.

E2641	10pf. Type E **796**	25	15
E2642	25pf. Meissen porcelain pot	35	30

E797 Johann Sebastian Bach

1985. 300th Birth Annivs of Bach and Handel and 400th Birth Anniv of Schutz (composers). Sheet 90×114 mm containing Type E 797 and similar vert designs, together with se-tenant horiz labels.

MSE2643	10pf. blue and bistre; 20pf. purple and bistre; 85pf. green and bistre	2·20	2·20

DESIGNS: 20pf. Georg Friedrich Handel; 85pf. Heinrich Schutz.

1985. Town Arms (3rd series). As Type E 758. Multicoloured.

E2644	50pf. Neubrandenburg	70	65
E2645	50pf. Potsdam	70	65
E2646	50pf. Rostock	70	65
E2647	50pf. Schwerin	70	65
E2648	50pf. Suhl	70	65

E798 Liberation Monument

1985. Liberation Monument, Seelow Heights.

E2649	**E798**	35pf. multicoloured	55	40

E799 Egon Erwin Kisch

1985. Birth Centenary of Egon Erwin Kisch (journalist).

E2650	**E799**	35pf. multicoloured	55	50

E800 Sigmund Jahn and Valeri Bykovski

1985. 40th Anniv of Defeat of Fascism. Multicoloured.

E2651	10pf. Type E **800**	20	20
E2652	20pf. Adolf Hennecke as miner	25	30
E2653	25pf. Agricultural workers reading paper	35	40
E2654	50pf. Laboratory technicians	80	95
MSE2655	55×81 mm. 1m. Soviet war memorial, Berlin-Treptow (22×40 mm)	1·50	1·40

E801 Flags forming "Frieden" (Peace)

1985. 30th Anniv of Warsaw Pact.

E2656	**E801**	20pf. multicoloured	45	30

E802 Emblem and Berlin Buildings

1985. 12th Free German Youth Parliament, Berlin. Multicoloured.

E2657	10pf.+5pf. Type E **802**	20	20
E2658	20pf. Flags, Ernst Thalmann and emblem	20	20

E803 "Solidarity" and Dove on Globe

1985. "Solidarity".

E2659	**E803**	10pf.+5pf. mult	35	25

E804 Olympic Flag

1985. 90th International Olympic Committee Meeting, Berlin.

E2660	**E804**	35pf. multicoloured	1·00	75

E805 "40" and Emblem

1985. 40th Anniv of Free German Trade Unions Federation.

E2661	**E805**	20pf. multicoloured	35	30

E806 Harpy Eagle

1985. Protected Animals. Multicoloured.

E2662	5pf. Type E **806**	20	15
E2663	10pf. Red-breasted geese (horiz)	20	15
E2664	20pf. Spectacled bear (horiz)	30	30
E2665	50pf. Bantengs (horiz)	70	55
E2666	85pf. Sunda gavial (horiz)	1·60	1·60

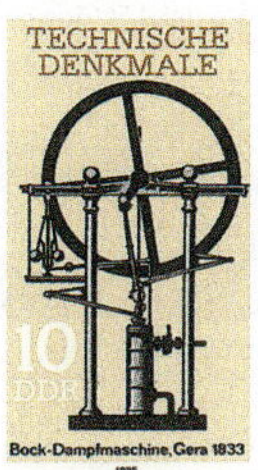

E807 Support Steam-engine, Gera, 1833

1985. Steam Engines. Multicoloured.

E2667	10pf. Type E **807**	25	20
E2668	85pf. Balance steam-engine, Frieberg, 1848	1·40	1·20

E808 Students reading

1985. 12th World Youth and Students' Festival, Moscow. Multicoloured.

E2669	20pf.+5pf. Type E **808**	30	35
E2670	50pf. Students with raised arms	55	55

E809 Diver at Turning Post

1985. Second World Orienteering Diving Championship, Neuglobsow. Multicoloured.

E2671	10pf. Type E **809**	20	20
E2672	70pf. Divers	1·10	1·10

E810 Bose House, Saint Thomas Churchyard

1985. Leipzig Autumn Fair. Multicoloured.

E2673	10pf. Type E **810**	25	15
E2674	25pf. J. Scherzer Bach- trumpet	45	30

E811 Passenger Mail Coach (relief, Hermann Steinemann)

1985. "Sozphilex '85" Stamp Exhibition, Berlin. Multicoloured.

E2675	5pf. Type E **811**	15	15
E2676	20pf.+5pf. Team of horses	25	30

Nos. E2675/6 were printed together, se-tenant, forming a composite design.

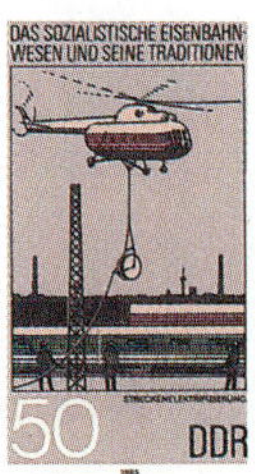

E812 Electrification of Railway

1985. Railways. Multicoloured.

E2677	20pf. Signal box	25	20
E2678	25pf. Andreas Schubert (engineer), his steam locomotive "Saxonia", 1838, and electric locomotive Type BR250	45	30
E2679	50pf. Type E **812**	75	65
E2680	85pf. Leipzig Central Station	1·60	1·60

E813 Gertrauden Bridge

1985. Berlin Bridges. Multicoloured.

E2681	10pf. Type E **813**	20	20
E2682	20pf. Jungfern Bridge	25	30
E2683	35pf. Weidendammer Bridge	55	55
E2684	70pf. Marx-Engels Bridge	1·00	1·00

MSE2685	107×128 mm. No. E2673×8	3·75	3·75

1985. Castles (2nd series). As Type E 790. Mult.

E2686	10pf. Hohnstein Castle	20	20
E2687	20pf. Rochsburg	25	25
E2688	35pf. Schwarzenberg Castle	45	45
E2689	80pf. Stein Castle	1·40	1·40

E814 Humboldt University

1985. Anniversaries. Multicoloured.

E2690	20pf. Type E **814** (175th anniv of Humboldt University, Berlin)	30	35
E2691	85pf. New and old Charite buildings (275th anniv of Berlin Charite (training clinic))	1·30	1·40

E815 Cecilienhof Castle and U.N. Emblem

1985. 40th Anniv of U.N.O.

E2692	**E815** 85pf. multicoloured	1·20	60

E816 Elephants on Balls

1985. Circus. Multicoloured.

E2693	10pf. Type E **816**	30	30
E2694	20pf. Trapeze artiste	55	55
E2695	35pf. Acrobats on monocycles	1·10	1·10
E2696	50pf. Tigers and trainer	1·60	1·60

E817 Grimm Brothers

1985. Birth Bicentenaries of Jacob and Wilhelm Grimm (folklorists). Multicoloured.

E2697	5pf. Type E **817**	25	25
E2698	10pf. "The Valiant Tailor"	25	25
E2699	20pf. "Lucky John"	70	1·10
E2700	25pf. "Puss in Boots"	70	1·10
E2701	35pf. "The Seven Ravens"	25	25
E2702	85pf. "The Sweet Pap"	25	25

E818 Water Pump, Berlin, 1900

1986. Water Supply.

E2703	**E818** 10pf. green and red	20	15
E2704	- 35pf. deep brown, brown and green	45	40
E2705	- 50pf. purple & green	70	65
E2706	- 70pf. blue and brown	1·10	95

DESIGNS: 35pf. Water tower, Berlin-Altglienicke, 1906; 50pf. Waterworks, Berlin-Friedrichshagen, 1893; 70pf. Rappbode dam, 1959.

E819 Saxon Postilion

1986. Postal Uniforms of 1850. Multicoloured.

E2707A	10pf. Type E **819**	25	15
E2708A	20pf. Prussian postman	35	30
E2709A	85pf. Prussian postal official	1·50	1·30
E2710A	1m. Postal official from Mecklenburg region	2·10	2·10

E820 Flag

1986. 40th Anniv of Free German Youth.

E2711	**E820** 20pf. yellow, bl & blk	45	40

E821 Flag

1986. 30th Anniv of National People's Army.

E2712	**E821** 20pf. multicoloured	75	55

E822 Exhibition Hall

1986. Leipzig Spring Fair. Multicoloured.

E2713	35pf. Type E **822**	45	35
E2714	50pf. "Atlantik 488" (factory trawler)	80	45

E823 Yuri Gagarin and "Vostok"

1986. 25th Anniv of Manned Space Flight. Multicoloured.

E2715	40pf. Type E **823** (first man in space)	45	45
E2716	50pf. Cosmonauts Valeri Bykovski and Sigmund Jahn, space station and "Interkosmos" emblem	55	55
E2717	70pf. Space probe "Venera", orbit around Venus and spectrometer	75	75
E2718	85pf. Reconnaissance camera MKF-6, photo, "Soyuz 22" spaceship, airplane and research ship	90	90

E824 Marx, Engels and Lenin

1986. 11th Socialist Unity Party of Germany Day.

E2719	**E824** 10pf. black, red and silver	20	20
E2720	- 20pf. red, black and silver	25	25
E2721	- 50pf. multicoloured	70	70
E2722	- 85pf. black, red and silver	1·40	1·40
MSE2723	80×55 mm. 1m. multicoloured	1·40	1·40

DESIGNS: 20pf. Ernst Thalmann (birth centenary); 50pf. Wilhelm Pieck and Otto Grotewohl, April 1946; 85pf. Family; 1m. Construction worker holding symbolic key.

E825 Memorial

1986. Opening of Ernst Thalmann Park, Berlin.

E2724	**E825** 20pf. multicoloured	45	40

E826 Horse Tram, Dresden, 1886

1986. Trams. Multicoloured.

E2725	10pf. Type E **826**	20	20
E2726	20pf. Leipzig, 1896	25	25
E2727	40pf. Berlin, 1919	70	70
E2728	70pf. Halle, 1928	1·40	1·40

E827 Orang-utan

1986. 125th Anniv of Dresden Zoo. Multicoloured.

E2729	10pf. Type E **827**	25	20
E2730	20pf. Eastern black-and-white colobus	45	40
E2731	50pf. Mandrill	90	90
E2732	70pf. Ring-tailed lemurs	1·60	1·60

E828 City Seal, 1253

1986. 750th Anniv of Berlin (1st issue).

E2733	**E 828** 10pf. deep brown, bistre and brown	25	15
E2734	- 20pf. olive, grn & brn	55	30
E2735	- 50pf. blk, brn & red	1·40	75
E2736	- 70pf. green & brown	2·50	1·90
MSE2737	54×80 mm. 1m. green	1·80	1·70

DESIGNS—HORIZ: 20pf. City map, 1648; 50pf. Oldest City arms. VERT: 70pf. St. Nicolas's Church, 1832; 1m. Cabinet building tower.

See also Nos. E2780/**MS**E2784 and **MS**E2828.

E829 Couple, Tractor and House

1986. 21st Workers' Festival, Magdeburg. Mult.

E2738	20pf. Type E **829**	20	20
E2739	50pf. Port and town of Magdeburg	45	45

E830 Berlin, 1652

1986. 9th Youth Stamp Exhibition, Berlin. Multicoloured.

E2740	10pf.+5pf. Type E **830**	20	20
E2741	20pf. Historic and modern Berlin buildings	25	25

E831 Schwerin Castle

1986. Castles (3rd series). Multicoloured.

E2742	10pf. Type E **831**	20	15
E2743	20pf. Gustrow castle	25	20
E2744	85pf. Rheinsberg castle	1·10	1·00
E2745	1m. Ludwigslust castle	1·60	1·60

E832 Soldiers and Girl before Brandenburg Gate

1986. 25th Anniv of Berlin Wall.

E2746	**E832**	20pf. multicoloured	75	45

E833 Doves flying from Emblem

1986. International Peace Year.

E2747	**E833**	35pf. multicoloured	65	45

E834 Ring-Messe-haus

1986. Leipzig Autumn Fair. Sheet 82×57 mm containing Type E 834 and similar vert design.

MSE2748	25pf. Type E **834**; 85pf. Merchants displaying cloth	1·60	1·60

E835 Rostock, 1637

1986. Coins.

E2749	**E835**	10pf. black, silver and red	20	15
E2750	-	35pf. black, silver and blue	45	45
E2751	-	50pf. multicoloured	70	70
E2752	-	85pf. black, silver and blue	1·10	1·10
E2753	-	1m. black, silver and green	1·40	1·40

DESIGNS: 35pf. Nordhausen, 1660; 50pf. Erfurt, 1633; 85pf. Magdeburg, 1638; 1m. Stralsund, 1622.

E836 Man with Rifle

1986. 44th World Sports Shooting Championships, Suhl.

E2754	**E836**	20pf. black, green and grey	25	20
E2755	-	70pf. black, red and grey	90	85
E2756	-	85pf. black, blue and grey	1·20	1·10

DESIGNS: 70pf. Woman with pistol; 85pf. Man with double-barrelled shotgun.

E837 Guard and Boundary Post

1986. 40th Anniv of Border Guards.

E2757	**E837**	20pf. multicoloured	45	40

E838 Hemispheres and Red Banner

1986. 11th World Trade Unions Congress, Berlin.

E2758	**E838**	70pf. multicoloured	1·10	95

E839 German Members Memorial, Friedrichshain

1986. 50th Anniv of Formation of International Brigades in Spain.

E2759	**E839**	20pf. brown, black and red	45	40

E840 Memorial

1986. 25th Anniv of Sachsenhausen Memorial.

E2760	**E840**	35pf. black, grn & bl	60	40

E841 Double-deck Train Ferry Loading Ramps

1986. Opening of Mukran–Klaipeda Railway Ferry Service. Multicoloured.

E2761	50pf. Type E **841**	55	55
E2762	50pf. "Mukran" (train ferry)	55	55

Nos. E2761/2 were printed together, se-tenant, forming a composite design.

E842 "Help for Developing Countries"

1986. "Solidarity".

E2763	**E842**	10pf.+5pf. mult	40	40

E843 Weber (after F. Jugel)

1986. Birth Bicentenary of Carl Maria von Weber (composer). Sheet 82×57 mm.

MSE2764	E **843**	85pf. multicoloured	1·40	1·30

E844 Indira Gandhi

1986. 2nd Death Anniv of Indira Gandhi (Indian Prime Minister).

E2765	**E844**	10pf. stone & brown	40	30

E845 Candle Holder, 1778

1986. Candle Holders from the Erzgebirge. Multicoloured.

E2766	10pf. Type E **845**	25	25
E2767	20pf. Candle holder, 1796	25	25
E2768	25pf. Candle holder, 1810	70	70
E2769	35pf. Candle holder, 1821	70	70
E2770	40pf. Candle holder, 1830	25	25
E2771	85pf. Candle holder, 1925	25	25

E846 Ronald Statue, Stendal

1987. Statues of Roland (1st series).

E2772	10pf. lt brown, brown & yell	20	15
E2773	20pf. lt brown, brown & bl	30	20
E2774	35pf. lt brown, brown & orge	60	60
E2775	50pf. lt brown, brown & grn	90	90

DESIGNS: Statues at—10pf. Type E **846**; 20pf. Halle; 35pf. Brandenburg; 50pf. Quedlinburg.

See also Nos. E2984/7.

E847 Post Office, Freiberg

1987. Post Offices.

E2776	**E847**	10pf. black, red and blue	20	20
E2777	-	20pf. multicoloured	30	30
E2778	-	70pf. multicoloured	75	75
E2779	-	1m.20 mult	1·80	1·80

DESIGNS: 20pf. Perleberg; 70pf. Weimar; 1m.20, Kirschau.

1987. 750th Anniv of Berlin (2nd issue). As Type E 828.

E2780	20pf. brown and green	25	25
E2781	35pf. green and red	55	55
E2782	70pf. blue and red	85	85
E2783	85pf. olive and green	1·40	1·40
MSE2784	Four sheets, 75×108 mm (a) or 107×75 mm (others). (a) 10pf. As No. E2780; (b) 10pf. ×4, As No. E2781; (c) 20pf. ×4, As No. E2782; (d) 20pf. ×4, As No. E2783	4·75	5·75

DESIGNS—VERT: 20pf. Ephraim Palace. HORIZ: 35pf. New buildings, Alt Marzahn; 70pf. Marx-Engels Forum; 85pf. Friedrichstadtpalast.

E848 Woman with Flower in Hair

1987. 40th Anniv and 12th Congress (Berlin) of German Democratic Women's Federation.

E2785	**E848**	10pf. blue, red & sil	40	40

E849 Fair Hall 20

1987. Leipzig Spring Fair. Multicoloured.

E2786	35pf. Type E **849**	45	45
E2787	50pf. "Traders at Weighbridge, 1804" (Christian Geissler)	80	80

E850 Clara Zetkin

1987. Socialist Personalities. Multicoloured.

E2788	**E850**	10pf. purple	20	15
E2789	-	10pf. black	20	15
E2790	-	10pf. black	20	15
E2791	-	10pf. green	20	15

DESIGNS: No. E2789, Fritz Gabler; E2790, Walter Vesper; E2791, Robert Siewert.

E851 Construction Industry

1987. 11th Federation of Free German Trade Unions Congress, Berlin. Multicoloured.

E2792	20pf. Type E **851**	25	25
E2793	50pf. Communications industry	55	55

E852 Flag, World Map and Doves

1987. 10th German Red Cross Congress, Dresden.

E2794	**E852**	35pf. multicoloured	60	30

E853 Museum and Karl August Lingner (founder) (after Robert Sterl)

1987. 75th Anniv of German Hygiene Museum, Dresden.

E2795	**E853**	85pf. multicoloured	1·20	95

E854 Old and New Farming Methods

1987. 35th Anniv of Agricultural Co-operatives.

E2796	**E854**	20pf. multicoloured	45	40

E855 Ludwig Uhland (poet)

1987. Birth Anniversaries. Multicoloured.

E2797	10pf. Type E **855** (bicent)	20	20

E2798 20pf. Arnold Zweig (writer, centenary) 30 30
E2799 35pf. Gerhart Hauptmann (writer, 125th anniv) 55 55
E2800 50pf. Gustav Hertz (physicist, centenary) 95 95

E856 Bream

1987. Freshwater Fishes. Multicoloured.
E2801 5pf. Type E **856** 20 15
E2802 10pf. Brown trout 20 20
E2803 20pf. Wels 30 20
E2804 35pf. European grayling 45 45
E2805 50pf. Barbel 70 45
E2806 70pf. Northern pike 1·20 1·10

E857 Woman holding Baby

1987. "Solidarity" Anti-Apartheid Campaign.
E2807 **E857** 10pf.+5pf. mult 40 30

E858 Horse-drawn Hand-pumped Fire Engine, 1756

1987. Fire Engines. Multicoloured.
E2808 10pf. Type E **858** 20 20
E2809 25pf. Steam engine, 1903 30 30
E2810 40pf. Model "LF 15", 1919 60 60
E2811 70pf. Model "LF 16-TS 8", 1971 95 95

E859 Ludwig Lazarus Zamenhof (inventor)

1987. Centenary of Esperanto (invented language). Sheet 55×80 mm.
MSE2812 E **859** 85pf. multicoloured 1·20 1·70

E860 Otters

1987. Endangered Animals. European Otter. Multicoloured.
E2813 10pf. Type E **860** 20 15
E2814 25pf. Otter swimming 40 35
E2815 35pf. Otter 60 45
E2816 60pf. Otter's head 1·50 1·30

E861 Tug-of-War

1987. 8th Gymnastics and Sports Festival and 11th Children and Young People's Sports Days, Leipzig. Multicoloured.
E2817 5pf. Type E **861** 20 15
E2818 10pf. Handball 20 15
E2819 20pf.+5pf. Long jumping 30 25
E2820 35pf. Table tennis 45 40
E2821 40pf. Bowling 65 55
E2822 70pf. Running 1·60 1·60

E862 Association Activities

1987. 35th Anniv of Association of Sports and Technical Sciences.
E2823 **E862** 10pf. multicoloured 40 25

E863 Head Post Office, Berlin, 1760

1987. Stamp Day. Multicoloured.
E2824 10pf.+5pf. Type E **863** 25 25
E2825 20pf. Wartenberg Palace 25 25

E864 Market Scene

1987. Leipzig Autumn Fair. Sheet 80×58 mm containing Type E 864 and similar vert design showing "Market Scene" by Christian Geissler.
MSE2826 40pf. multicoloured; 50pf. multicoloured 1·70 1·70

E865 Memorial Statue (Jozsef Somogyi)

1987. War Victims' Memorial, Budapest.
E2827 **E865** 35pf. multicoloured 50 30

E866 Memorial, Ernst Thalmann Park

1987. 750th Anniv of Berlin (3rd issue). Sheet 80×55 mm.
MSE2828 E **866** 1m.35 black, stone and red 2·10 2·10

E867 "Weidendamm Bridge" (Arno Mohr)

1987. 10th Art Exhibition, Dresden. Mult.
E2829 10pf. Type E **867** 20 20
E2830 50pf. "They only wanted to learn Reading and Writing (Nicaragua)" (Willi Sitte) 65 65
E2831 70pf. "Big Mourning Man" (Wieland Forster) 85 85
E2832 1m. Vase (Gerd Lucke) (horiz) 1·90 1·90

E868 Red Flag, Smolny Building (Leningrad), "Aurora" and Lenin

1987. 70th Anniv of Russian Revolution. Multicoloured.
E2833 10pf. Type E **868** 20 15
E2834 20pf. Moscow Kremlin towers 35 20

E869 Youth using Personal Computer

1987. 39th "Masters of Tomorrow" Fair, Leipzig. Multicoloured.
E2835 10pf. Type E **869** 20 15
E2836 20pf. "ZIM 10-S" robot-welder 35 20

E870 Annaberg, 1810

1987. Christmas Pyramids from Erzgebirge. Multicoloured.
E2837 10pf. Type E **870** 30 30
E2838 20pf. Freiberg, 1830 70 70
E2839 25pf. Neustadtel, 1870 30 30
E2840 35pf. Schneeberg, 1870 30 30
E2841 40pf. Lossnitz, 1880 70 70
E2842 85pf. Seiffen, 1910 30 30

E871 Ski Jumping

1988. Winter Olympic Games, Calgary. Mult.
E2843 5pf. Type E **871** 30 20
E2844 10pf. Speed skating 30 20
E2845 20pf.+10pf. Four-man bobsleigh 45 40
E2846 35pf. Biathlon 70 70
MSE2847 80×55 mm. 1m.20 Two-man and single luge (horiz) 2·10 1·70

E872 Berlin-Buch Post Office

1988. Postal Buildings. Multicoloured.
E2848 15pf. Type E **872** 40 25
E2849 20pf. Postal museum 45 25
E2850 50pf. Berlin-Marzahn general post office 1·20 75

E873 Brecht

1988. 90th Birth Anniv of Bertholt Brecht (writer). Sheet 58×82 mm.
MSE2851 E **873** 70pf. grey, black and red 1·30 1·10

E874 "Tillandsia macrochlamys"

1988. Bromeliads. Multicoloured.
E2852 10pf. Type E **874** 20 15
E2853 25pf. "Tillandsia bulbosa" 30 30
E2854 40pf. "Tillandsia kalmbacheri" 55 45
E2855 70pf. "Guzmania blassii" 1·20 1·20

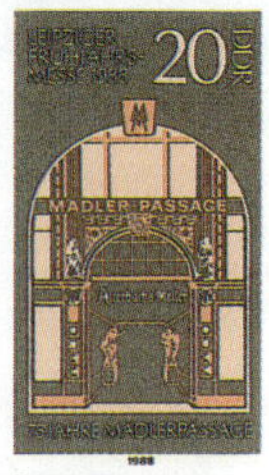

E875 Madler-passage Entrance

1988. Leipzig Spring Fair. 75th Anniv of Madler-passage (fair building). Each brown, orange and pink.
E2856 20pf. Type E **875** 25 20
E2857 70pf. "Faust and Mephistopheles" (bronze statue, Matthieu Molitor) 1·20 95

E876 Eichendorff

1988. Birth Bicentenary of Joseph von Eichendorff (writer). Sheet 82×55 mm.
MSE2858 E **876** 70pf. olive, drab and blue 1·60 1·30

E877 Saddler, Muhlhausen, 1565

1988. Historic Seals. Multicoloured.
E2859 10pf. Type E **877** 20 20
E2860 25pf. Butcher, Dresden, 1564 30 30
E2861 35pf. Smith, Nauen, 16th-century 45 45
E2862 50pf. Clothier, Frankfurt on Oder, 16th-century 65 65

E878 Georg Forster Antarctic Research Station

1988. 12th Anniv of Georg Forster Antarctic Research Station.
E2863 **E878** 35pf. multicoloured 55 30

E879 Wismar

1988. Northern Towns of the Democratic Republic.
E2864 5pf. black, green & turquoise 20 15
E2865 10pf. black, ochre and brown 20 15
E2866 25pf. black, lightt blue & blue 40 30
E2867 60pf. black, pink and red 75 65
E2868 90pf. black, lt green & green 1·00 95
E2869 1m.20 black, brown and red 1·70 1·60

DESIGNS: 5pf. Type E **879**.; 10pf. Anklam; 25pf. Ribnitz-Damgarten; 60pf. Stralsund; 90pf. Bergen; 1m.20, Greifswald.

E880 Hutten

1988. 500th Birth Anniv of Ulrich von Hutten (humanist). Sheet 54×80 mm.

MSE2870 E **880** 70pf. black, yellow and ochre 1·30 1·20

E881 Chorin and Neuzelle Monasteries, Industrial and Agricultural Symbols

1988. 22nd Workers' Arts Festival, Frankfurt-on-Oder. Multicoloured.

E2871 20pf. Type E **881** 25 25

E2872 50pf. Buildings of Frankfurt 55 55

E882 Cosmonauts Sigmund Jahn and Valery Bykovski

1988. 10th Anniv of U.S.S.R.–East German Manned Space Flight (1st issue). Multicoloured.

E2873 5pf. Type E **882** 25 20

E2874 10pf. "MKS-M" multi- channel spectrometer 25 20

E2875 20pf. "Mir"–"Soyuz" space complex 30 30

See also Nos. E2894/6.

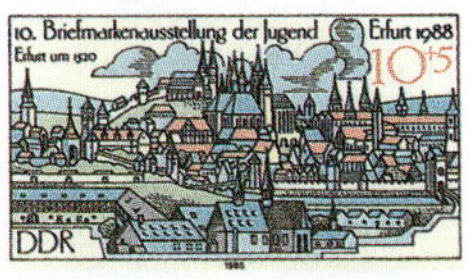

E883 Erfurt, 1520

1988. 10th Youth Stamp Exhibition, Erfurt and Karl-Marx-Stadt. Multicoloured.

E2876 10pf.+5pf. Type E **883** 20 20

E2877 20pf.+5pf. Chemnitz, 1620 30 30

E2878 25pf. Modern view of Erfurt 30 30

E2879 50pf. Modern view of Karl-Marx-Stadt (formerly Chemnitz) 70 65

E884 Swearing-in Ceremony

1988. 35th Anniv of Workers' Militia Squads. Multicoloured.

E2880 5pf. Type E **884** 20 20

E2881 10pf. Tribute to Ernst Thalmann 20 20

E2882 15pf. Parade 40 40

E2883 20pf. Arms distribution 25 25

E885 Balloons and Doves over Karl-Marx-Stadt

1988. 8th Pioneers Meeting, Karl-Marx-Stadt. Multicoloured.

E2884 10pf. Type E **885** 20 20

E2885 10pf.+5pf. Doves, balloons and Pioneers 25 25

E886 Swimming

1988. Olympic Games, Seoul. Multicoloured.

E2886 5pf. Type E **886** 20 20

E2887 10pf. Handball 20 20

E2888 20pf.+10pf. Hurdling 45 45

E2889 25pf. Rowing 40 40

E2890 35pf. Boxing 70 70

E2891 50pf.+20pf. Cycling 85 85

MSE2892 55×80 mm. 85pf. Relay race 2·50 2·20

E887 Examining Fair Goods, 1810

1988. Leipzig Autumn Fair and 175th Anniv of Battle of Leipzig. Sheet 110×90 mm containing Type E 887 and similar vert designs. Multicoloured.

MSE2893 5pf. Type E **887**; 15pf. Battle of Leipzig Monument; 100pf. Fair, 1820 1·70 1·70

1988. 10th Anniv of U.S.S.R.–East German Manned space Flight (2nd issue). As Nos. E2873/5 but values changed. Multicoloured.

E2894 10pf. Type E **882** 30 30

E2895 20pf. As No. E2874 30 30

E2896 35pf. As No. E2875 60 60

E888 Buchenwald Memorial (Fritz Cremer)

1988. War Memorials.

E2897 **E888** 10pf. green, black and brown 30 30

E2898 - 35pf. multicoloured 50 40

DESIGN: 35pf. Resistance Monument, Lake Como, Italy (Gianni Colombo).

E889 "Adolph Friedrich' at Stralsund: Captain C. Leplow" (E. Laschke)

1988. 500th Anniv of Stralsund Shipping Company. Captains' Paintings. Multicoloured.

E2899 5pf. Type E **889** 20 15

E2900 10pf. "'Gartenlaube' of Stralsund: Captain J. F. Kruger" (A. Luschky) 20 15

E2901 70pf. "Brigantina 'Auguste Mathilde' of Stralsund: Captain I. C. Grunwaldt" (Johnsen-Seby Bergen) 1·10 1·10

E2902 1m.20 "Brig 'Hoffnung' of Cologne-on-Rhine: Captain G. A. Luther" (anon) 1·50 1·50

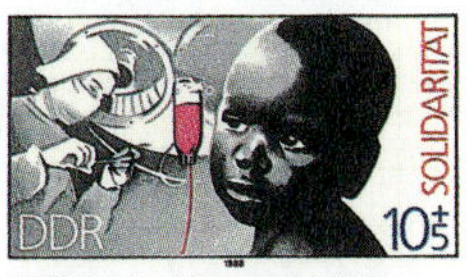

E890 Medical Scene and African Child

1988. "Solidarity".

E2903 **E890** 10pf.+5pf. mult 75 75

E891 Magdeburg Drawbridge

1988. Drawbridges and Ship Lifts. Mult.

E2904 5pf. Type E **891** 20 15

E2905 10pf. Lift, Magdeburg–Rothensee Canal 20 20

E2906 35pf. Lift, Niederfinow 55 55

E2907 70pf. Bridge and lock, Altfriesack 85 85

E2908 90pf. Drawbridge, Rugendamm 1·20 1·20

E892 Menorah

1988. 50th Anniv of "Kristallnacht" (Nazi pogrom).

E2909 **E892** 35pf. purple, yellow and black 55 30

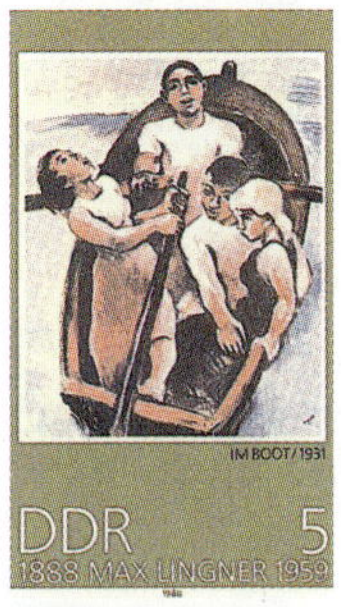

E893 "In the Boat"

1988. Birth Centenary of Max Lingner (artist). Multicoloured.

E2910 5pf. Type E **893** 20 15

E2911 10pf. "Mademoiselle Yvonne" 20 15

E2912 20pf. "Free, Strong and Happy" 30 20

E2913 85pf. "New Harvest" 1·30 1·30

E894 Lace (Regine Wengler)

1988. Bobbin Lace from Erzgebirge. Pieces by lacemakers named. Each black, brown and yellow.

E2914 20pf. Type E **894** 30 30

E2915 25pf. Wally Tilp 70 70

E2916 35pf. Elisabeth Mehnert-Pfabe 30 30

E2917 40pf. Ute Siewert 30 30

E2918 50pf. Regine Siebdraht 70 70

E2919 85pf. Elise Schubert 30 30

E895 W.H.O. Emblem

1988. 40th Anniv of W.H.O.

E2920 **E895** 85pf. silver, bl & grey 1·20 55

E896 Dr. Wolf

1988. Birth Centenary of Dr. Freidrich Wolf (writer). Sheet 87×59 mm.

MSE2921 E**896** 110pf. grey, black and vermilion 1·50 1·50

E897 Members' Flags

1989. 40th Anniv of Council of Mutual Economic Aid.

E2922 **E897** 20pf. multicoloured 40 30

E898 Edith Baumann

1989. Socialist Personalities.

E2923 **E898** 10pf. brown 25 15

E2924 - 10pf. green 25 15

E2925 - 10pf. brown 25 15

E2926 - 10pf. blue 25 15

DESIGNS: No. E2924, Otto Meier; E2925, Alfred Oelssner; E2926, Fritz Selbmann.

E899 Philipp Reis Telephone, 1861

1989. Telephones. Multicoloured.

E2927 10pf. Type E **899** 20 20

E2928 20pf. Siemens & Halske wall telephone, 1882 30 30

E2929 50pf. "OB 03" wall telephone, 1903 70 60

E2930 85pf. "OB 05" desk telephone, 1905 1·20 1·20

E900 Johann Beckmann (technologist, 250th anniv)

1989. Birth Anniversaries. Multicoloured.

E2931 10pf. Type E **900** 25 15

E2932 10pf. Rudolf Mauersberger and church choir (musician, cent) 25 15

E2933 10pf. Carl von Ossietzky and masthead of "Die Weltbuhne" (journalist and peace activist, centenary) 25 15

E2934 10pf. Ludwig Renn and International Brigades flag (writer, centenary) 25 15

E2935 10pf. Adam Scharrer and cover of "Stateless People" (novelist, centenary) 25 15

E901 Handelshof Fair Building

1989. Leipzig Spring Fair. Multicoloured.

E2936 70pf. Type E **901** (80th anniv) 1·20 85

E2937 85pf. Naschmarkt bake-house and bread shop, 1690 1·40 1·10

E902 Muntzer (after Christoph van Stichen and Romeyn de Hooghe)

1989. 500th Birth Anniv of Thomas Muntzer (religious reformer) (1st issue). Sheet 86×66 mm.

MSE2938 E **902** 110pf. black and buff 1·40 1·70

See also Nos. E2967/**MS**2972.

E903 Friedrich List (economist and promoter of railway system)

1989. 150th Anniv of Leipzig–Dresden Railway (first German long-distance service).

E2939	**E903**	15pf. brown, pale brown and green	40	30
E2940	-	20pf. black, green and red	40	20
E2941	-	50pf. black, brown and deep brown	95	95

DESIGNS: 20pf. Dresdner Station, Leipzig, 1839; 50pf. Leipziger Station, Dresden, 1839.

E904 Tea Caddy

1989. Meissen Porcelain. 250th Anniv of Onion Design. Each brown, blue and ultramarine.

E2942A	10pf. Type E **904**	25	15
E2943A	20pf. Vase	25	15
E2944A	35pf. Bread board	75	60
E2945A	70pf. Coffee pot	1·30	1·20

E905 Renaissance Initial "I"

1989. 7th International Typography Exhibition, Leipzig.

E2946	**E905**	20pf. multicoloured	30	20
E2947	-	50pf. black, yellow and green	70	70
E2948	-	1m.35 red, black and grey	1·90	1·90

DESIGNS: 50pf. Art Nouveau initial "B"; 1m.35, Modern initial "A"s.

E906 Chollima Statue, Pyongyang

1989. 13th World Youth and Students' Festival, Pyongyang (E2949) and Free German Youth Whitsun Festival, Berlin (E2950). Multicoloured.

E2949	20pf. Type E **906**	30	30
E2950	20pf.+5pf. Berlin buildings	35	35

E907 "Princess Louise"

1989. 225th Birth Anniv of Johann Gottfried Schadow (sculptor). Details of "Princesses". Multicoloured.

E2951	50pf. Type E **907**	85	55
E2952	85pf. "Princess Friederike"	1·50	1·30

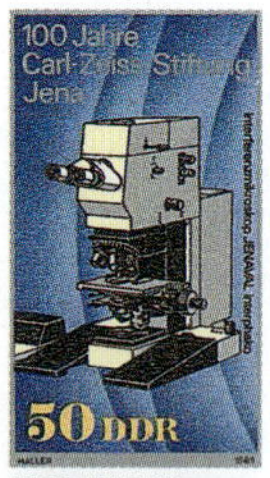

E908 JENEVAL Interference Microscope

1989. Centenary of Carl Zeiss Foundation, Jena. Multicoloured.

E2953	50pf. Type E **908**	60	60
E2954	85pf. "ZKM 01-250 C" bi-coordinate measuring instrument	1·10	1·10

E909 Front Page of Address

1989. Bicentenary of Inaugural Address to University by Friedrich Schiller (writer and philosopher). Each brown, black & grey.

E2955	25pf. Type E **909**	30	30
E2956	85pf. Part of address	1·00	1·00

E910 A. E. Brehm

1989. 160th Birth Anniv of Alfred Edmund Brehm and 125th Death Anniv of Christian Ludwig Brehm (naturalists). Sheet 110×80 mm containing Type E 910 and similar vert design. Multicoloured.

MSE2957	50pf. Type E **910**; 85pf. C. L. Brehm	2·10	12·00

E911 Storming the Bastille

1989. Bicent of French Revolution. Mult.

E2958	5pf. Type E **911**	20	15
E2959	20pf. Sans-culottes	30	20
E2960	90pf. Invading the Tuileries	1·30	1·30

E912 Haflingers

1989. 40th International Horse Breeding in Socialist States Congress, Berlin. Multicoloured.

E2961	10pf. Type E **912**	20	20
E2962	20pf. English thoroughbreds (racehorses)	20	20
E2963	70pf. Heavy horses (plough team)	85	85
E2964	110pf. Thoroughbreds (dressage)	1·50	1·50

E913 Till Eulenspiegel Fountain

1989. National Stamp Exn, Magdeburg. Fountains by Heinrich Apel. Multicoloured.

E2965	20pf. Type E **913**	25	20
E2966	70pf.+5pf. Devil's fountain	1·00	1·00

E914 "Annunciation to the Peasants"

1989. 500th Birth Anniv of Thomas Muntzer (Protestant reformer) (2nd issue). Details of "Early Bourgeois Revolution in Germany" by Werner Tubke. Multicoloured.

E2967	5pf. Type E **914**	20	15
E2968	10pf. "Fountain of Life"	20	20
E2969	20pf. "Muntzer in the Battle"	30	20
E2970	50pf. "Lutheran Cat Battle"	85	70
E2971	85pf. "Justice, Jester"	1·40	1·40
MSE2972	99×142 mm. No. E2609/4	1·30	1·30

E915 New Fair Building

1989. Leipzig Autumn Fair. Sheet 105×75 mm containing Type E 915 and similar horiz design. Multicoloured.

MSE2973	50pf. Type E **915**; 85pf. New fair building (different)	2·10	2·10

E916 African Children

1989. "Solidarity".

E2974	**E916**	10pf.+5pf. mult	30	30

E917 "Mother Group" (Fritz Cremer)

1989. 30th Anniv of Ravensbruck War Victims' Memorial.

E2975	**E917**	35pf. multicoloured	50	40

E918 "Adriana"

1989. Epiphyllums. Multicoloured.

E2976	10pf. Type E **918**	20	15
E2977	35pf. "Fire Magic"	45	40
E2978	50pf. "Franzisko"	95	95

E919 Dove, Flag and Schoolchildren

1989. 40th Anniv of German Democratic Republic. Multicoloured.

E2979	5pf. Type E **919**	20	15
E2980	10pf. Combine harvester and agricultural workers	20	15
E2981	20pf. Political activists working together	40	30
E2982	25pf. Industrial workers	75	65
MSE2983	113×93 mm. 135pf. Construction workers (54×32 mm)	4·75	2·10

1989. Statues of Roland (2nd series). As Type E 846. Multicoloured.

E2984	5pf. Zerbst	20	15
E2985	10pf. Halberstadt	20	15
E2986	20pf. Buch-Altmark	30	30
E2987	50pf. Perleberg	85	85

E920 Nehru

1989. Birth Centenary of Jawaharlal Nehru (Indian statesman).

E2988	**E920**	35pf. brown and black	50	50

E921 Schneeberg, 1860

1989. Chandeliers from the Erzgebirge. Mult.

E2989	10pf. Type E **921**	30	30
E2990	20pf. Schwarzenberg, 1850	70	70
E2991	25pf. Annaberg, 1880	30	30
E2992	35pf. Seiffen, 1900	30	30
E2993	50pf. Seiffen, 1930	70	70
E2994	70pf. Annaberg, 1925	30	30

E922 Bee on Apple Blossom

1990. The Honey Bee. Multicoloured.

E2995	5pf. Type E **922**	20	15
E2996	10pf. Bee on heather	20	15
E2997	20pf. Bee on rape	30	30
E2998	50pf. Bee on clover	1·20	1·10

E923 "Courier" (Albrecht Durer)

1990. 500th Anniv of Regular European Postal Services.

E2999	**E923**	35pf. chocolate, light brown and brown	55	50

E924 Erich Weinert

1990. Socialist Personalities.

E3000	**E924**	10pf. blue	35	30
E3001	-	10pf. brown	35	25

DESIGN: No. E3001, Bruno Leuschner.

E925 19th-century Sign, Blankenburg

1990. Posthouse Signs. Multicoloured.
E3002B 10pf. Type E **925** 25 25
E3003A 20pf. Royal Saxony sign (19th century) 30 20
E3004A 50pf. German Empire sign (1870s) 95 95
E3005A 110pf. German Empire auxiliary station sign (1900s) 1·90 1·90

E926 Bebel

1990. 150th Birth Anniv of August Bebel (politician).
E3006 **E926** 20pf. black, grey and red 50 45

E927 Drawings by Leonardo da Vinci

1990. "Lilienthal '91" European Airmail Exhibition. Historic Flying Machine Designs. Multicoloured.
E3007 20pf. Type E **927** 30 20
E3008 35pf.+5pf. Melchior Bauer's man-powered airplane design, 1764 70 70
E3009 50pf. Albrecht Berblinger's man-powered flying machine, 1811 80 80
E3010 90pf. Otto Lilienthal's design for a monoplane glider 1·50 1·50

E928 St. Nicholas's Church, Leipzig, and Demonstrators

1990. "We Are The People".
E3011 **E928** 35pf.+15pf. mult 75 75

E929 Warrior's Head

1990. Museum of German History, Berlin. Stone Reliefs by Andreas Schluter.
E3012 **E929** 40pf. yell, grn & blk 70 70
E3013 - 70pf. multicoloured 1·20 1·20
DESIGN: 70pf. Warrior's head (different).

E930 Fair Seal, 1268

1990. Leipzig Spring Fair and 825th Anniv of Leipzig. Multicoloured.
E3014 70pf. Type E **930** 1·60 95
E3015 85pf. Fair seal, 1497 1·90 1·40

E931 Kurt Tucholsky (writer, centenary)

1990. Birth Anniversaries.
E3016 **E931** 10pf. black, green and deep green 40 40
E3017 - 10pf. black, brown and red 40 40
DESIGN: No. E3017, Friedrich Adolph Wilhelm Diesterweg (educationist, bicent).

E932 "Solidarity of Labour" (Walter Crane)

1990. Centenary of Labour Day.
E3018 **E932** 10pf. grey, black and red 45 30
E3019 - 20pf. red, grey and black 95 70
DESIGN: 20pf. Red carnation.

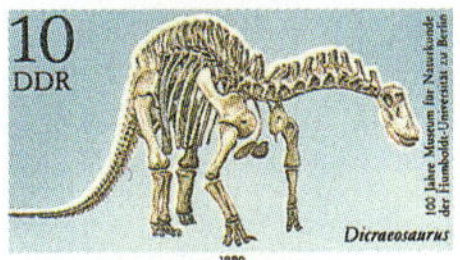

E933 Dicraeosaurus

1990. Centenary of Natural Science Museum, Berlin. Dinosaur Skeletons. Multicoloured.
E3020 10pf. Type E **933** 20 15
E3021 25pf. Kentrurosaurus 40 40
E3022 35pf. Dysalotosaurus 50 50
E3023 50pf. Brachiosaurus (vert) 70 70
E3024 85pf. Skull of brachiosaurus (vert) 1·30 1·30

E934 Penny Black

1990. 150th Anniv of the Penny Black.
E3025 **E934** 20pf. black, mauve and magenta 45 45
E3026 - 35pf.+15pf. red, lilac and black 95 95
E3027 - 110pf. multicoloured 2·50 2·50
DESIGNS: 35pf. Saxony 1850 3pf. stamp; 110pf. First East Germany stamp, 1949.

E935 Edward Hughes and 1855 Printing Telegraph

1990. 125th Anniv of I.T.U. Multicoloured.
E3028 10pf. Type E **935** 20 20
E3029 20pf. Distribution rods from Berlin-Kopenick post office 40 40
E3030 25pf. Transmitting tower and radio control desk 55 55
E3031 50pf. "Molniya" communications satellite and globe 1·20 1·20
MSE3032 82×56 mm. 70pf. Philipp Reis (telephone pioneer) 2·40 2·20

E936 Pope John Paul II

1990. Pope's 70th Birthday.
E3033 **E936** 35pf. multicoloured 65 50

E937 Halle (18th-century)

1990. 11th National Youth Stamp Exhibition, Halle. Multicoloured.
E3034 10pf.+5pf. Type E **937** 35 30
E3035 20pf. Modern Halle 40 35

E938 Rules of Order of Teutonic Knights, 1264

1990. Exhibits in German State Library, Berlin. Multicoloured.
E3036 20pf. Type E **938** 45 30
E3037 25pf. World map from "Rudimentum Novitiorum", 1475 85 45
E3038 50pf. "Chosrou and Schirin" by Nizami (18th century Persian manuscript) 1·30 95
E3039 110pf. Book cover from Amalia musical library 3·25 2·40

WEST GERMAN CURRENCY

On 1 July 1990 the Ostmark was abolished and replaced by the West German Deutsche Mark.

E939 Albrechts Castle and Cathedral, Meissen

1990. Tourist Sights.
E3040 **E939** 10pf. blue 25 20
E3041 - 30pf. green 40 30
E3042 - 50pf. green 55 45
E3043 - 60pf. brown 70 60
E3044 - 70pf. brown 75 85
E3045 - 80pf. red 95 1·20
E3046 - 100pf. red 1·30 95
E3047 - 200pf. violet 2·10 1·90
E3048 - 500pf. green 5·75 4·75
DESIGNS: 30pf. Goethe-Schiller Monument, Weimar; 50pf. Brandenburg Gate, Berlin; 60pf. Kyffhauser Monument; 70pf. Semper Opera House, Dresden; 80pf. Sanssouci Palace, Potsdam; 100pf. Wartburg Castle, Eisenach; 200pf. Magdeburg Cathedral; 500pf. Schwerin Castle.

E940 Different Alphabets

1990. International Literacy Year.
E3049 **E940** 30pf.+5pf. on 10pf.+5pf. mult 1·20 1·60
No. E3049 was not issued without surcharge.

E941 Letter-carrier (from playing card) and Messenger, 1486

1990. 500th Anniv of Regular European Postal Services.
E3050 **E941** 30pf. blk, brn & grn 45 45
E3051 - 50pf. black, red and blue 70 65
E3052 - 70pf. black, brown and red 85 1·20
E3053 - 100pf. black, grn & bl 1·70 1·70
DESIGNS: 50pf. "Courier" (Albrecht Durer) and post rider, 1590; 70pf. Open wagon, 1595, and mail carriage, 1750; 100pf. Travelling post office vans, 1842 and 1900.

E942 Louis Lewandowski (choir conductor)

1990. Reconstruction of New Synagogue, Berlin. Multicoloured.
E3054 30pf. Type E **942** 40 40
E3055 50pf.+15pf. New Synagogue 1·00 1·00

E943 Schliemann and Two-handled Vessel

1990. Death Cent of Heinrich Schliemann (archaeologist). Multicoloured.
E3056 30pf. Type E **943** 45 45
E3057 50pf. Schliemann and double pot (horiz) 95 95

E944 Dresden

1990. 41st International Astronautics Federation Congress, Dresden.
E3058 **E944** 30pf. black and grey 35 35
E3059 - 50pf. multicoloured 70 70
E3060 - 70pf. dp bl, grn & bl 95 1·20
E3061 - 100pf. multicoloured 1·50 1·50
DESIGNS: 50pf. Earth; 70pf. Moon; 100pf. Mars.

On 3 October 1990 the territory of the Democratic Republic was absorbed into the Federal Republic of Germany, whose stamps have been used since then.

OFFICIAL STAMPS

EO58 (Cross-piece projects to left)

1954. (a) Design in minute dots.
EO185 **EO58** 5pf. green 20
EO186 **EO58** 6pf. violet 20
EO187 **EO58** 8pf. brown 10
EO188 **EO58** 10pf. turquoise 10
EO189 **EO58** 12pf. blue 20
EO190 **EO58** 15pf. violet 10
EO191 **EO58** 16pf. violet 10
EO192 **EO58** 20pf. olive 10
EO193 **EO58** 24pf. red 10
EO194 **EO58** 25pf. turquoise 20
EO195 **EO58** 30pf. red 10
EO196 **EO58** 40pf. red 10
EO197 **EO58** 48pf. lilac 1·80
EO198 **EO58** 50pf. lilac 20
EO199 **EO58** 60pf. blue 20
EO200 **EO58** 70pf. brown 20
EO201 **EO58** 84pf. brown 4·00

EO59 (Cross-piece projects to right)

(b) Design in lines.
EO202 **EO59** 5pf. green 25
EO203 **EO59** 10pf. turquoise 25
EO204 **EO59** 12pf. turquoise 25
EO205 **EO59** 15pf. violet 25
EO207 **EO59** 25pf. green 25
EO210 **EO59** 50pf. lilac 25
EO211 **EO59** 70pf. brown 25
EO298 **EO59** 20pf. olive 30

EO299	**EO59**	30pf. red		30
EO300	**EO59**	40pf. red		30

EO84

1956. For internal use.

EO257	**EO84**	5pf. black		30
EO258	**EO84**	10pf. black		30
EO259	**EO84**	20pf. black		30
EO260	**EO84**	40pf. black		30
EO261	**EO84**	70pf. black		55

Nos. EO257/61 were not on sale to the public in unused condition, although specimens of all values are available on the market. The used prices are for cancelled-to-order, with segments across the corners of the stamps. Postally used are worth more.

OFFICIAL CENTRAL COURIER SERVICE STAMPS

These were for use on special postal services for confidential mail between Government officials and state-owned enterprises.

EO95

1956. With or without control figures.

EO303	**EO95**	10pf. black & purple	60	45
EO304	**EO95**	20pf. black & purple	1·80	45
EO305	**EO95**	40pf. black & purple	60	95
EO306	**EO95**	70pf. black & purple	3·00	4·75

EO123

1958. With various control figures. (a) With one bar (thick or thin) each side of figure.

EO357	**EO123**	(10pf.) red & yell	44·00	6·50
EO373	**EO123**	(10pf.) brown & bl	22·00	7·50
EO375	**EO123**	(10pf.) violet and orange	26·00	9·50
EO377	**EO123**	(10pf.) red and green	10·50	11·50

(b) With two bars (thick or thin) each side of figure.

EO358	(20pf.) red & yell	44·00	3·75
EO374	(20pf.) brown & bl	55·00	4·75
EO376	(20pf.) violet and orange	70·00	7·50
EO378	(20pf.) red and green	13·00	5·25

Used prices for Nos. EO357/EO378 are for postally used copies.

EO149

1959. With various control figures. (a) With one bar each side of figure.

EO414	**EO149**	(10pf.) red, violet and green	10·50	7·50
EO416	**EO149**	(10pf.) black & bl	13·00	70·00
EO418	**EO149**	(10pf.) black, brown and blue	44·00	80·00

(b) With two bars each side of figure.

EO415	(20pf.) blue, brown and yellow	16·00	6·50
EO417	(20pf.) green, blue and red	13·00	9·50
EO419	(20pf.) violet, black and brown	31·00	6·50

REGISTRATION STAMPS

SELF=SERVICE POST OFFICE

These registration labels embody a face value to cover the registration fee and have franking value to this extent. They are issued in pairs from automatic machines together with a certificate of posting against a 50pf. coin. The stamps are serially numbered in pairs and inscribed with the name of the town of issue.

The procedure is to affix one label to the letter (already franked with stamps for carriage of the letter) and complete page 1 of the certificate of posting which is then placed in the box provided together with the letter. The duplicate label is affixed to the second page of the certificate and retained for production as evidence in the event of a claim. They are not obtainable over the post office counter.

Unused prices are for pairs.

ER318

1967

ER992	**ER318**	50pf. red and black	4·50

ER319

1968

ER993	**ER319**	50pf. red	1·80

ER345

1968. For Parcel Post.

ER1089	**ER345**	50pf. black	7·25

Pt. 6

GHADAMES

A caravan halting place in the Libyan desert, under French administration from 1943 until 1951 when the area reverted to Libya. From 1943 to 1948 stamps of Fezzan were used.

100 centimes = 1 franc.

1 Cross of Agadem

1949

1	**1**	4f. chestnut & brn (postage)	8·00	20·00
2	**1**	5f. green and blue	8·00	20·00
3	**1**	8f. chestnut and brown	7·75	27·00
4	**1**	10f. blue and black	7·75	27·00
5	**1**	12f. mauve and purple	9·75	50·00
6	**1**	15f. chestnut and brown	10·50	45·00
7	**1**	20f. green and brown	11·00	45·00
8	**1**	25f. blue and brown	11·00	45·00
9	**1**	50f. cerise and purple (air)	11·00	45·00
10	**1**	100f. purple and brown	11·00	45·00

Pt. 1

GHANA

Formerly the British Colony of Gold Coast. Attained Dominion status on 6 March 1957, and became a republic within the British Commonwealth in 1960.

1957. 12 pence = 1 shilling; 20 shillings = 1 pound.
1965. 100 pesewas = 1 cedi.
1967. 100 new pesewas = 1 new cedi.
1972. 100 pesewas = 1 cedi = 0.8 (1967) new cedi.

CANCELLED REMAINDERS. In 1961 remainders of some issues of 1957 to 1960 were put on the market cancelled-to-order in such a way as to be indistinguishable from genuine postally used copies. Our used quotations which are indicated by an asterisk are, therefore, for cancelled-to-order copies.

29 Dr. Kwame Nkrumah, Palm-nut Vulture and Map of Africa

1957. Independence Commemoration.

166	**29**	2d. red*	10	10
167	**29**	2½d. green*	10	15
168	**29**	4d. brown*	10	15
169	**29**	1s.3d. blue*	15	15

1957. Queen Elizabeth stamps of 1952 of Gold Coast optd GHANA INDEPENDENCE 6TH. MARCH, 1957.

170	½d. brown and red*	10	10
171	1d. blue*	10	10
172	1½d. green*	10	10
173	2d. brown	30	30
174	2½d. red	1·00	1·25
175	3d. mauve*	30	10
176	4d. blue	6·50	8·50
177	6d. black and orange*	10	10
178	1s. black and red*	10	10
179	2s. olive and red*	60	10
180	5s. purple and black*	1·50	10
181	10s. black and olive*	1·75	70

31 Viking Ship

1957. Inauguration of Black Star Shipping Line.

182	**31**	2½d. green	30	20
183	-	1s.3d. blue	35	1·25
184	-	5s. purple	45	3·00

DESIGNS—HORIZ: 1s.3d. Galleon; 5s. M.V. "Volta River".

34 Ambassador Hotel, Accra

1958. 1st Anniv of Independence. Flag and Coat of Arms in national colours.

185	**34**	½d. black and red	10	40
186	-	2½d. black, red and yellow	10	10
187	-	1s.3d. black and blue	30	10
188	-	2s. yellow and black	45	50

DESIGNS—HORIZ: 2½d. State Opening of Parliament; 1s.3d. National Monument. VERT: 2s. Ghana Coat of Arms.

38 Map showing the Independent African States

1958. 1st Conference of Independent African States, Accra. Star in black and yellow.

189	**38**	2½d. red and yellow	10	10
190	**38**	3d. green and brown	10	10
191	-	1s. blue, yellow and orange	20	10
192	-	2s.6d. red and purple	40	65

DESIGN—VERT: 1s., 2s.6d. Map of Africa and flaming torch.

40 Palm-nut Vulture over Globe

41 Bristol Britannia

1958. Inauguration of Ghana Airways. Inscr as in T 40/41.

193	**40**	2½d. black, bistre and red	35	10
194	**41**	1s.3d. multicoloured	55	20
195	-	2s. multicoloured	65	55
196	-	2s.6d. black and bistre	65	95

DESIGNS—(As Type **41**): 2s. Boeing Stratocruiser and yellow-nosed albatross. (As Type **40**): 2s.6d. Palm-nut vulture and Vickers VC-10 aircraft.

1958. Prime Minister's Visit to United States and Canada. Optd PRIME MINISTER'S VISIT, U.S.A. AND CANADA.

197	**29**	2d. red	10	40
198	**29**	2½d. green	10	30
199	**29**	4d. brown	10	50
200	**29**	1s.3d. blue	15	25

45

1958. United Nations Day.

201	**45**	2½d. brown, green and black	10	10
202	**45**	1s.3d. brown, blue and black	15	10
203	**45**	2s.6d. brown, violet black	15	35

46 Dr. Nkrumah and Lincoln Statue, Washington

1959. 150th Birth Anniv of Abraham Lincoln.

204	**46**	2½d. pink and purple	10	10
205	**46**	1s.3d. light blue and blue	10	10
206	**46**	2s.6d. yellow and olive	15	35
MS206a		102×77 mm. Nos. 204/6. Imperf	55	2·25

48 Kente Cloth and Traditional Symbols

1959. Independence. Inscr "SECOND ANNIVERSARY OF INDEPENDENCE".

207	**48**	½d. multicoloured	10	10
208	-	2½d. multicoloured	10	10
209	-	1s.3d. multicoloured	15	10
210	-	2s. multicoloured	30	1·25

DESIGNS—HORIZ: 2½d. Talking drums and elephant-horn blower; 2s. Map of Africa, Ghana flag and palms. VERT: 1s.3d. "Symbols of Greeting".

52 Globe and Flags

1959. Africa Freedom Day.

211	**52**	2½d. multicoloured	15	10
212	**52**	8½d. multicoloured	15	20

54 Nkrumah Statue, Accra

55 Ghana Timber

65a Red-fronted Gazelle

1959. Multicoloured.

213	½d. "God's Omnipotence" (postage)	10	10
213a	½d. "Gye Nyame"	30	10
214	1d. Type **54**	10	10
215	1½d. Type **55**	10	10
216	2d. Volta river	10	10
217	2½d. Cocoa bean	40	10
218	3d. "God's Omnipotence"	10	10
218a	3d. "Gye Nyame"	30	10
219	4d. Diamond and mine	4·00	65
220	6d. Red-crowned bishop (bird)	1·00	10
221	11d. Golden-spider lily	25	10
222	1s. Shell ginger	25	10
223	2s.6d. Giant blue turaco	1·75	15
224	5s. Tiger orchid	2·00	65
225	10s. Jewel cichlid	75	70
225a	£1 Type **65a**	2·00	4·75
226	1s.3d. Pennant-winged nightjar (air)	1·75	10
227	2s. Crowned cranes	1·50	10

SIZES—HORIZ (As Type **54**): ½d. (As Type **55**): 2d., 2½d., 3d., 4d., 6d., 1s.3d., 2s.6d. (As Type **65a**): 10s. VERT (As Type **55**): 11d., 1s., 2s., 5s.

The 3d. is a different symbolic design from the ½d.

68 Gold Cup and West African Map

1959. West African Football Competition, 1959. Multicoloured.

228	½d. Type **68***	10	10
229	1d. Footballers (vert)*	10	10
230	3d. Goalkeeper saving ball*	10	10
231	8d. Forward attacking goal*	40	15
232	2s.6d. "Kwame Nkrumah" Gold Cup (vert)*	50	15

73 Duke of Edinburgh and Arms of Ghana

1959. Visit of the Duke of Edinburgh.

233	**73**	3d. black and mauve	30	10

74 Ghana Flag and Talking Drums

1959. U.N. Trusteeship Council. Multicoloured.

234	3d. Type **74***	10	10
235	6d. Ghana flag and U.N. emblem (vert)*	10	10
236	1s.3d. As 6d. but emblem above flag (vert)*	20	15
237	2s.6d. "Totem pole" (vert)*	25	15

78 Eagles in Flight

1960. 3rd Anniv of Independence. Mult.

238	½d. Type **78***	10	10
239	3d. Fireworks*	10	10
240	1s.3d. "Third Anniversary"*	30	10
241	2s. "Ship of State"*	30	15

82 Flags and Map forming letter "A"

1960. African Freedom Day. Multicoloured.

242	3d. Type **82***	10	10
243	6d. Letter "f"*	20	10
244	1s. Letter "d"*	20	10

85 Dr. Nkrumah

1960. Republic Day. Inscr "REPUBLIC DAY 1ST JULY 1960". Multicoloured.

245	3d. Type **85**	10	10
246	1s.3d. Ghana flag	30	10
247	2s. Torch of Freedom	20	20
248	10s. Ghana arms (horiz)	50	80
MS248a	102×77 mm. Nos. 245/8. Imperf	40	1·50

90 Athlete

1960. Olympic Games.

249	-	3d. multicoloured	10	10
250	-	6d. multicoloured	15	10
251	**90**	1s.3d. multicoloured	25	10
252	**90**	2s.6d. multicoloured	35	60

DESIGN—VERT: 3d., 6d. Olympic torch.

91 President Nkrumah

1960. Founder's Day. Inscribed as in T 91.

253	**91**	3d. multicoloured	10	10
254	-	6d. multicoloured	10	15
255	-	1s.3d. multicoloured	20	30

DESIGNS—VERT: 6d. President Nkrumah within star; 1s.3d. Map of Africa and column.

94 U.N. Emblem and Ghana Flag

1960. Human Rights Day.

256	**94**	3d. multicoloured	10	10
257	-	6d. yellow, black and blue	15	15
258	-	1s.3d. multicoloured	25	55

DESIGNS: U.N. Emblem with torch (6d.) or within laurel (1s.3d.).

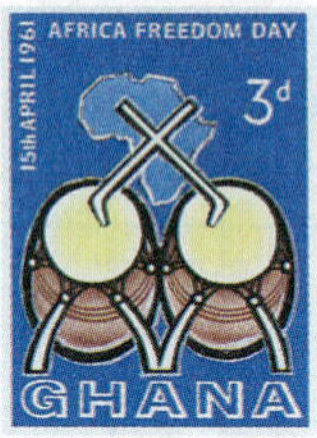

97 Talking Drums

1961. Africa Freedom Day. Inscr "15th APRIL 1961".

259	**97**	3d. multicoloured	10	10
260	-	6d. red, black and green	20	10
261	-	2s. multicoloured	50	45

DESIGNS—VERT: 6d. Map of Africa. HORIZ: 2s. Flags and map.

100 Eagle on Column

1961. 1st Anniv of Republic. Multicoloured.

262	3d. Type **100**	10	10
263	1s.3d. "Flower"	10	10
264	2s. Ghana flags	20	1·25

103 Dove with Olive Branch

1961. Belgrade Conference.

265	**103**	3d. green	10	10
266	-	1s.3d. blue	15	10
267	-	5s. purple	40	1·00

DESIGNS—HORIZ: 1s.3d. World map, chain and olive branch; 5s. Rostrum, Conference room.

106 President Nkrumah and Globe

1961. Founder's Day. Multicoloured.

268	3d. Type **106**	10	10
269	1s.3d. President in Kente cloth (vert)	20	10
270	5s. President in national costume (vert)	65	2·50
MS270a	Three sheets, 106×86 mm (3d.) or 86×106 mm (others), each with Nos. 268/70 in block of four. Imperf Set of three sheets	3·25	14·00

109 Queen Elizabeth II and African Map

1961. Royal Visit.

271	**109**	3d. multicoloured	15	10
272	**109**	1s.3d. multicoloured	30	20
273	**109**	5s. multicoloured	65	3·75
MS273a		106×84 mm. No. 273 in block of 4. Imperf	2·25	8·00

110 Ships in Tema Harbour

1962. Opening of Tema Harbour. Multicoloured.

274	3d. Type **110** (postage)	15	10
275	1s.3d. Douglas DC-8 aircraft and ships at Tema (air)	65	15
276	2s.6d. As No. 275	80	2·50

112 Africa and Peace Dove

1962. 1st Anniv of Casablanca Conference.

277	**112**	3d. multicoloured (postage)	10	10
278	**112**	1s.3d. multicoloured (air)	20	15
279	**112**	2s.6d. multicoloured	30	2·00

113 Compass over Africa

1962. Africa Freedom Day.

280	**113**	3d. sepia, turquoise & pur	10	10
281	**113**	6d. sepia, turquoise & brn	10	15
282	**113**	1s.3d. sepia, turq & red	15	15

115 Atomic Bomb- burst "Skull"

1962. The Accra Assembly.

283	-	3d. black and lake	10	10
284	**115**	6d. black and red	25	35
285	-	1s.3d. turquoise	30	50

DESIGNS: 3d. Ghana Star over "five continents"; 1s.3d. Dove of Peace.

117 Patrice Lumumba

1962. 1st Death Anniv of Lumumba.

286	**117**	3d. black and yellow	10	10
287	**117**	6d. black, green and slate	10	30
288	**117**	1s.3d. black, pink and green	15	35

118 Star over Two Columns

1962. 2nd Anniv of Republic. Inscribed "1st JULY 1962". Multicoloured.

289	3d. Type **118**	10	10
290	6d. Flaming torch	20	20
291	1s.3d. Eagle trailing flag (horiz)	40	40

121 President Nkrumah

1962. Founder's Day.

292	**121**	1d. multicoloured	10	10
293	-	3d. multicoloured	10	10
294	-	1s.3d. black and blue	30	15
295	-	2s. multicoloured	30	1·25

DESIGNS: 3d. Nkrumah medallion; 1s.3d. President and Ghana Star; 2s. Laying "Ghana" brick.

125 Campaign Emblem

1962. Malaria Eradication.

296	**125**	1d. red	10	10
297	**125**	4d. green	20	1·25
298	**125**	6d. bistre	20	30
299	**125**	1s.3d. violet	25	90
MS299a		90×115 mm. Nos. 296/9. Imperf	75	1·50

126 Campaign Emblem

1963. Freedom from Hunger.

300	**126**	1d. multicoloured	15	25
301	-	4d. sepia, yellow and orange	75	1·25
302	-	1s.3d. ochre, black grn	1·60	1·25

DESIGNS—HORIZ: 4d. Emblem in hands; 1s.3d. World map and emblem.

129 Map of Africa

1963. Africa Freedom Day.

303	**129**	1d. gold and red	10	10
304	-	4d. red, black and yellow	10	10
305	-	1s.3d. multicoloured	20	10
306	-	2s.6d. multicoloured	35	1·25

DESIGNS—HORIZ: 4d. Carved stool. VERT: 1s.3d. Map and bowl of fire; 2s.6d. Topi (antelope) and flag.

133 Red Cross

1963. Centenary of Red Cross. Multicoloured.

307	1d. Type **133**	40	15
308	1½d. Centenary emblem (horiz)	55	2·25
309	4d. Nurses and child (horiz)	75	20
310	1s.3d. Emblem, globe and laurel	1·75	2·00
MS310a	102×127 mm. Nos. 307/10. Imperf	2·75	12·00

137 "3rd Anniversary"

1963. 3rd Anniv of Republic. Multicoloured.

311	1d. Type **137**	10	10
312	4d. Three Ghanian flags	10	10
313	1s.3d. Map, flag and star (vert)	20	15
314	2s.6d. Flag and torch (vert)	35	2·25

141 President Nkrumah and Ghana Flag

1963. Founder's Day.

315	**141**	1d. multicoloured	10	10
316	-	4d. multicoloured	15	10
317	-	1s.3d. multicoloured	30	10
318	-	5s. yellow and mauve	65	75

DESIGNS—VERT: 4d. Type **141** but with larger flag behind President Nkrumah. HORIZ: 1s.3d. President Nkrumah and fireworks; 5s. Native symbol of wisdom.

145 Rameses II, Abu Simbel

1963. Preservation of Nubian Monuments. Multicoloured.

319	1d. Type **145**	15	10
320	1½d. Rock paintings (horiz)	20	65
321	2d. Queen Nefertari (horiz)	20	10
322	4d. Sphinx, Sebua	35	15
323	1s.3d. Rock Temple, Abu Simbel (horiz)	80	90

150 Class 248 Steam Locomotive and Diesel-electric Locomotive No. 1401

1963. 60th Anniv of Ghana Railway.

324	**150**	1d. multicoloured	10	10
325	**150**	6d. multicoloured	40	10
326	**150**	1s.3d. multicoloured	45	40
327	**150**	2s.6d. multicoloured	75	1·90

151 Eleanor Roosevelt and "Flame of Freedom"

1963. 5th Anniv of Declaration of Human Rights. Multicoloured.

328		1d. Type **151**	10	10
329		4d. Type **151**	10	30
330		6d. Eleanor Roosevelt	10	10
331		1s.3d. Eleanor Roosevelt and emblems (horiz)	15	15

154 Sun and Globe Emblem

1964. International Quiet Sun Years.

332	**154**	3d. multicoloured	15	10
333	**154**	6d. multicoloured	25	10
334	**154**	1s.3d. multicoloured	25	15

MS334a 90×90 mm. No. 334 in block of 4. Imperf 75 2·50

155 Harvesting Corn on State Farm

1964. 4th Anniv of Republic.

335	**155**	3d. olive, brown and yellow	10	10
336	-	6d. green, brown turq	10	10
337	-	1s.3d. red, brn salmon	10	10
338	-	5s. multicoloured	40	1·25

MS338a 126×100 mm. Nos. 335/8. Imperf 85 2·00

DESIGNS: 6d. Oil refinery, Tema; 1s.3d. "Communal Labour"; 5s. Procession headed by flag.

159 Globe and Dove

1964. 1st Anniv of African Unity Charter.

339	**159**	3d. multicoloured	10	10
340	-	6d. green and red	10	10
341	-	1s.3d. multicoloured	15	10
342	-	5s. multicoloured	45	70

DESIGNS—VERT: 6d. Map of Africa and quill pen; 5s. Planting flower. HORIZ: 1s.3d. Hitched rope on map of Africa.

163 President Nkrumah and Hibiscus Flowers

1964. Founder's Day.

343	**163**	3d. multicoloured	10	10
344	**163**	6d. multicoloured	15	10
345	**163**	1s.3d. multicoloured	25	10
346	**163**	2s.6d. multicoloured	40	1·00

MS346a 90×122 mm. No. 346 in block of 4. Imperf 70 2·50

164 Hurdling

1964. Olympic Games, Tokyo. Multicoloured.

347		1d. Type **164**	10	10
348		2½d. Running	10	1·50
349		3d. Boxing (vert)	10	10
350		4d. Long-jumping (vert)	10	10
351		6d. Football (vert)	15	10
352		1s.3d. Athlete holding Olympic Torch (vert)	20	10
353		5s. Olympic "Rings" and flags	55	3·25

MS353a 128×102 mm. Nos. 351/3. Imperf 75 2·50

171 G. Washington Carver (botanist) and Plant

1964. UNESCO Week.

354	**171**	6d. blue and green	15	10
355	-	1s.3d. purple and blue	30	10
356	**171**	5s. sepia and red	50	4·25

MS356a 127×77 mm. Nos. 354/6. Imperf 75 2·00

DESIGN: 1s.3d. Albert Einstein (scientist) and Atomic symbol.

173 African Elephant

1964. Multicoloured.

357		1d. Type **173**	40	50
358		1½d. Secretary bird (horiz)	60	2·50
359		2½d. Purple wreath (flower)	20	2·50
360		3d. Grey parrot	60	50
361		4d. Blue-naped mousebird (horiz)	60	70
362		6d. African tulip tree (horiz)	20	30
363		1s.3d. Violet starling (horiz)	75	1·25
364		2s.6d. Hippopotamus (horiz)	75	5·50

MS364a Two sheets. (a) 150×86 mm. Nos. 357/9. (b) 150×110 mm. Nos. 360/4. Imperf Set of 2 sheets 3·75 14·00

181 I.C.Y. Emblem

1965. International Co-operation Year.

365	**181**	1d. multicoloured	35	70
366	**181**	4d. multicoloured	1·00	2·00
367	**181**	6d. multicoloured	1·00	70
368	**181**	1s.3d. multicoloured	1·25	2·75

MS368a 100×100 mm. No. 368 in block of 4. Imperf 2·75 5·00

182 I.T.U. Emblem and Symbols

1965. Centenary of I.T.U.

369	**182**	1d. multicoloured	15	15
370	**182**	6d. multicoloured	30	15
371	**182**	1s.3d. multicoloured	55	25
372	**182**	5s. multicoloured	1·25	3·25

MS372a 132×115 mm. Nos. 369/72. Imperf 7·50 10·00

183 Lincoln's Home

1965. Death Centenary of Abraham Lincoln.

373	**183**	6d. multicoloured	10	10
374	-	1s.3d. black, red and blue	15	15
375	-	2s. black, brown and yellow	15	35
376	-	5s. black and red	30	1·75

MS376a 115×115 mm. Nos. 373/6. Imperf 75 3·50

DESIGNS: 1s.3d. Lincoln's inaugural address; 2s. Abraham Lincoln; 5s. Adaption of U.S. 90c. Lincoln stamp of 1869.

187 Obverse (President Nkrumah) and Reverse of 5p. Coin

1965. Introduction of Decimal Currency. Multicoloured designs showing coins expressed in the same denominations as on the stamps.

377		5p. Type **187**	20	10
378		10p. As Type **187**	25	10
379		25p. Size 63×39 mm	55	1·00
380		50p. Size 71×43½ mm	1·00	2·50

1965. Nos. 214/27 surch Ghana New Currency 19th July. 1965. and value. Multicoloured.

381	**54**	1p. on 1d. (postage)	10	10
382	-	2p. on 2d.	10	10
383	-	3p. on 3d. (No. 218a)	1·00	5·50
384	-	4p. on 4d.	5·00	45
385	-	6p. on 6d.	50	10
386	-	11p. on 11d.	25	10
387	-	12p. on 1s.	25	10
388	-	30p. on 2s.6d.	4·75	9·00
389	-	60p. on 5s.	4·50	70
390	-	1c.20 on 10s.	75	2·25
391	**65a**	2c.40 on £1	1·00	6·50
392	-	15p. on 1s.3d. (air)	2·50	70
393	-	24p. on 2s.	2·50	30

189 "OAU" and Flag

1965. O.A.U. Summit Conf, Accra. Mult.

394		1p. Type **189**	15	10
395		2p. "OAU" heads and flag	15	10
396		5p. OAU emblem and flag	20	10
397		6p. African map and flag (horiz) (37½×27½ mm)	20	10
398		15p. "Sunburst" and flag (horiz) (37½×27½ mm)	30	30
399		24p. "O.A.U." on map, and flag (horiz) (37½×27½ mm)	45	60

195 Goalkeeper saving Ball

1965. African Soccer Cup Competition. Mult.

400		6p. Type **195**	25	10
401		15p. Player with ball (vert)	40	30
402		24p. Player, ball and Soccer Cup	45	70

198 President Kennedy and Grave Memorial

1965. 2nd Death Anniv of President Kennedy.

403	**198**	6p. multicoloured	15	10
404	-	15p. violet, red and green	20	35
405	-	24p. black and purple	20	60
406	-	30p. purple and black	25	1·25

MS407 114½×114 mm. Nos. 403/6. Imperf 3·00 6·50

DESIGNS: 15p. President Kennedy and Eternal Flame; 24p. President Kennedy and Memorial Inscription; 30p. President Kennedy.

202 Section of Dam and Generators

1966. Volta River Project.

408	**202**	6p. multicoloured	15	10
409	-	15p. multicoloured	20	15
410	-	24p. multicoloured	25	20
411	-	30p. black and blue	35	50

DESIGNS: 15p. Dam and Lake Volta; 24p. Word "GHANA" as Dam; 30p. "Fertility".

1965. "Black Stars" Victory in African Soccer Cup Competition. Optd Black Stars Retain Africa Cup 21st Nov. 1965.

412	**195**	6p. multicoloured	50	15
413	-	15p. multicoloured	70	30
414	-	24p. multicoloured	75	70

207 W.H.O. Building and Ghana Flag

1966. Inaug of W.H.O. Headquarters, Geneva. Mult.

415		6p. Type **207**	60	10
416		15p. Type **207**	1·40	65
417		24p. W.H.O. Building and emblem	1·50	1·75
418		30p. W.H.O. Building and emblem	1·75	4·00

MS419 120×101 mm. Nos. 415/18. Imperf 23·00 22·00

209 Atlantic Herring

1966. Freedom from Hunger. Multicoloured.

420		6p. Type **209**	25	10
421		15p. Turbot	45	15
422		24p. Spadefish	45	35
423		30p. Red snapper	50	1·25
424		60p. Blue-finned tuna	70	4·75

MS425 126×109 mm. No. 423 in block of 4. Imperf 10·00 13·00

214 African "Links" and Ghana Flag

1966. 3rd Anniv of African Charter. Multicoloured.

426		6p. Type **214**	15	10

427	15p. Flags as "quill" and diamond (horiz)	35	55
428	24p. Ship's wheel, map and cocoa bean (horiz)	40	70

217 Player heading Ball, and Jules Rimet Cup

1966. World Cup Football Championship. Multicoloured.

429	5p. Type **217**	55	20
430	15p. Goalkeeper clearing ball	1·25	30
431	24p. Player and Jules Rimet Cup (replica)	1·50	50
432	30p. Players and Jules Rimet Cup (replica)	1·75	1·75
433	60p. Players with ball	2·50	9·00
MS434	120×102 mm. No. 433 in block of 4. Imperf	24·00	26·00

222 UNESCO Emblem

1966. 20th Anniv of UNESCO.

435	**222**	5p. multicoloured	90	25
436	**222**	15p. multicoloured	2·00	60
437	**222**	24p. multicoloured	2·50	1·25
438	**222**	30p. multicoloured	2·75	3·25
439	**222**	60p. multicoloured	3·50	11·00
MS440		140×115 mm. Nos. 435/9. Imperf	25·00	27·00

223 Fair Emblem and Crates

1967. Ghana Trade Fair, Accra. Multicoloured.

441	5p. Type **223**	10	10
442	15p. Fair emblem and world map	15	20
443	24p. Shipping and flags	25	30
444	36p. Fair emblem and hand-held hoist	40	2·50

1967. New Currency. Nos. 216/26 and 393 surch with new value.

445	1½n.p. on 2d. (postage)	2·00	8·50
446	3½n.p. on 4d.	8·00	4·00
447	5n.p. on 6d.	3·75	2·25
448	9n.p. on 11d.	30	50
449	10n.p. on 1s.	30	1·25
450	25n.p. on 2s.6d.	3·50	7·50
451	1n.c. on 10s.	2·50	15·00
452	2n.c. on £1	5·00	24·00
453	12½n.p. on 1s.3d. (air)	4·00	4·75
454	20n.p. on 24p. on 2s.	6·00	8·00

229 Ghana Eagle and Flag

1967. 1st Anniv of 24 February Revolution.

455	**229**	1n.p. multicoloured	10	90
456	**229**	4n.p. multicoloured	10	10
457	**229**	12½n.p. multicoloured	35	60
458	**229**	25n.p. multicoloured	65	3·50
MS459		89×108 mm. Nos. 455/8. Perf or imperf	5·00	12·00

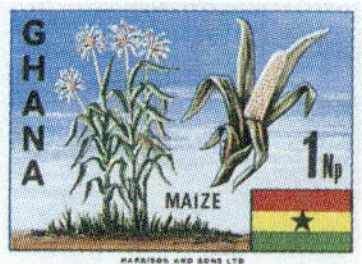

230 Maize

232 The Ghana Mace

1967. Multicoloured.

460	1n.p. Type **230**	10	10
461	1½n.p. Forest kingfisher	1·00	2·75
462	2n.p. Type **232**	10	10
463	2½n.p. Commelina	35	10
464	3n.p. West African lungfish	20	40
465	4n.p. Rufous-crowned roller	1·50	10
466	6n.p. Akosombo Dam	15	2·25
467	8n.p. Adomi Bridge	15	1·00
468	9n.p. Chameleon	75	10
469	10n.p. Tema Harbour	15	10
470	20n.p. Bush hare (blue)	20	10
471	50n.p. Black-winged stilt	9·50	2·75
472	1n.c. Wooden stool	2·00	1·00
473	2n.c. Frangipani	2·00	3·50
474	2n.c.50 Seat of State	1·75	11·00

SIZES—VERT (As Type **230**): 4n.p. (As Type **232**): 1½n.p., 2½n.p., 20n.p., 2n.c., 2n.c.50. HORIZ (as Type **230**): 8n.p. (As Type **232**): 3n.p., 6n.p., 9n.p., 10n.p., 50n.p., 1n.c.

245 Kumasi Fort

1967. Castles and Forts.

475	**245**	4n.p. multicoloured	25	10
476	-	12½n.p. multicoloured	60	1·00
477	-	20n.p. multicoloured	75	2·75
478	-	25n.p. multicoloured	75	3·50

DESIGNS: 12½n.p. Christiansborg Castle and British galleon; 20n.p. Elmina Castle and Portuguese galleon; 25n.p. Cape Coast Castle and Spanish galleon.

249 "Luna 10"

1967. "Peaceful Use of Outer Space". Multicoloured.

479	4n.p. Type **249**	10	10
480	10n.p. "Orbiter 1"	10	45
481	12½n.p. Man in Space	20	80
MS482	140×90 mm. Nos. 479/81. Imperf	1·75	4·50

252 Scouts and Campfire

1967. 50th Anniv of Ghanaian Scout Movement. Multicoloured.

483	4n.p. Type **252**	20	10
484	10n.p. Scout on march	40	50
485	12½n.p. Lord Baden-Powell	50	1·75
MS486	167×95 mm. Nos. 483/5. Imperf	5·00	10·00

255 U.N. Headquarters Building

1967. United Nations Day (24 October).

487	**255**	4n.p. multicoloured	10	10
488	**255**	10n.p. multicoloured	10	15
489	-	50n.p. multicoloured	20	70
490	-	2n.c.50 multicoloured	55	4·00
MS491		76×75 mm. No. 490. Imperf	1·75	9·50

DESIGN: 50n.p., 2n.c.50, General view of U.N. H.Q., Manhattan.

257 Leopard

1967. International Tourist Year. Multicoloured.

492	4n.p. Type **257**	1·00	20
493	12½n.p. "Papilio demodocus" (butterfly)	2·25	1·50
494	20n.p. Carmine bee eater	2·50	3·75
495	50n.p. Waterbuck	2·50	9·00
MS496	126×126 mm. Nos. 492/5. Imperf	18·00	22·00

261 Revolutionaries entering Accra

1968. 2nd Anniv of February Revolution. Mult.

497	4n.p. Type **261**	10	10
498	12½n.p. Marching troops	20	20
499	20n.p. Cheering people	30	40
500	40n.p. Victory celebrations	50	2·75

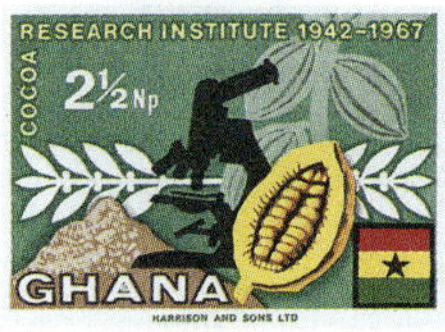

265 Microscope and Cocoa Beans

1968. Cocoa Research.

501	**265**	2½n.p. multicoloured	10	1·25
502	-	4n.p. multicoloured	10	10
503	**265**	10n.p. multicoloured	15	30
504	-	25n.p. multicoloured	60	1·75
MS505		102×102 mm. Nos. 501/4. Imperf	2·25	5·50

DESIGNS: 4n.p. and 25n.p. Microscope and cocoa tree, beans and pods.

267 Kotoka and Flowers

1968. 1st Death Anniv of Lt.-Gen. E. K. Kotoka. Multicoloured.

506	4n.p. Type **267**	10	10
507	12½n.p. Kotoka and wreath	20	30
508	20n.p. Kotoka in civilian clothes	35	75
509	40n.p. Lt.-Gen. Kotoka	50	2·75

271 Tobacco

1968. Flora and Fauna. Multicoloured.

510	4n.p. Type **271**	15	10
511	5n.p. North African crested porcupine	15	1·25
512	12½n.p. Rubber	30	75
513	20n.p. "Cymothoe sangaris" (butterfly)	1·25	2·75
514	40n.p. "Charaxes ameliae" (butterfly)	1·50	5·00
MS515	88×114 mm. Nos. 510 and 512/14. Imperf	3·00	9·00

276 Surgeons, Flag and W.H.O. Emblem

1968. 20th Anniv of W.H.O.

516	**276**	4n.p. multicoloured	20	10
517	**276**	12½n.p. multicoloured	40	40
518	**276**	20n.p. multicoloured	60	1·25
519	**276**	40n.p. multicoloured	1·00	3·75
MS520		132×110 mm. Nos. 516/19. Imperf	2·75	7·00

277 Hurdling

1969. Olympic Games, Mexico (1968). Multicoloured.

521	4n.p. Type **277**	10	10
522	12½n.p. Boxing	20	30
523	20n.p. Torch, Olympic Rings and flags	40	75
524	40n.p. Football	70	3·25
MS525	89×114 mm. Nos. 521/4. Imperf	3·50	8·00

281 U.N. Building

1969. United Nations Day. Multicoloured.

526	4n.p. Type **281**	10	10
527	12½n.p. Native stool, staff and U.N. emblem	15	25
528	20n.p. U.N. building and emblem over Ghanian Flag	20	45
529	40n.p. U.N. emblem encircled by flags	40	2·50
MS530	127×117 mm. Nos. 526/9. Imperf	75	3·50

285 Dr. J. B. Danquah

1969. Human Rights Year. Multicoloured.

531	4n.p. Type **285**	10	10
532	12½n.p. Dr. Martin Luther King	20	35
533	20n.p. As 12½n.p.	35	75
534	40n.p. Type **285**	50	2·75
MS535	116×50 mm. Nos. 531/4. Imperf	80	4·00

287 Constituent Assembly Building

1969. 3rd Anniv of Revolution. Multicoloured.

536	4n.p. Type **287**	10	10
537	12½n.p. Arms of Ghana	10	15
538	20n.p. Type **287**	15	20
539	40n.p. As 12½n.p.	20	75
MS540	114×89 mm. Nos. 536/9. Imperf	70	3·00

1969. New Constitution. Nos. 460/74 optd NEW CONSTITUTION 1969.

541	**230**	1n.p. multicoloured	10	2·25
542	-	1½n.p. multicoloured	2·75	5·50
543	**232**	2n.p. multicoloured	10	4·00
544	-	2½n.p. multicoloured	10	2·50

545	-	3n.p. multicoloured	1·00	2·25
546	-	4n.p. multicoloured	3·00	1·00
547	-	6n.p. multicoloured	15	3·00
548	-	8n.p. multicoloured	15	3·75
549	-	9n.p. multicoloured	15	3·75
550	-	10n.p. multicoloured	1·00	3·50
551	-	20n.p. multicoloured	1·25	2·25
552	-	50n.p. multicoloured	7·00	6·50
553	-	1n.c. multicoloured	1·50	7·50
554	-	2n.c. multicoloured	1·50	9·00
555	-	2n.c.50 multicoloured	1·50	9·50

On Nos. 541, 545, 547/50 and 552/3 the opt is horiz. The rest are vert.

290 Map of Africa and Flags

1969. Inauguration of 2nd Republic. Multicoloured.

556	4n.p. Type **290**	10	10
557	12½n.p. Figure "2", branch and Ghanaian colours	20	10
558	20n.p. Hands receiving egg	35	35
559	40n.p. Type **290**	60	1·50

293 I.L.O. Emblem and Cogwheels

1970. 50th Anniv of I.L.O.

560	**293**	4n.p. multicoloured	10	10
561	**293**	12½n.p. multicoloured	20	55
562	**293**	20n.p. multicoloured	30	1·25
MS563		117×89 mm. Nos. 560/2. Imperf	70	3·00

294 Red Cross and Globe

1970. 50th Anniv of League of Red Cross Societies. Multicoloured.

564	4n.p. Type **294**	20	10
565	12½n.p. Henri Dunant and Red Cross emblem (horiz)	25	25
566	20n.p. Patient receiving medicine (horiz)	30	85
567	40n.p. Patient having arm bandaged (horiz)	35	3·00
MS568	114×89 mm. Nos. 564/7. Imperf	1·50	6·00

298 General Kotoka, Vickers VC-10 and Airport

1970. Inauguration of Kotoka Airport. Mult.

569	4n.p. Type **298**	15	10
570	12½n.p. Control tower and tail of Vickers VC-10	25	15
571	20n.p. Aerial view of airport	40	30
572	40n.p. Airport and flags	75	80

302 Lunar Module landing on Moon

1970. Moon Landing. Multicoloured.

573	4n.p. Type **302**	30	10
574	12½n.p. Astronaut's first step onto the Moon	50	60
575	20n.p. Astronaut with equipment on Moon (horiz)	60	1·40
576	40n.p. Astronauts (horiz)	70	3·25
MS577	142×142 mm. Nos. 573/6. Imperf	2·25	12·00

306 Adult Education

1970. International Education Year. Multicoloured.

578	4n.p. Type **306**	10	10
579	12½n.p. International education	20	20
580	20n.p. "Ntesie" and I.E.Y. symbols	35	30
581	40n.p. Nursery schools	60	1·40

310 Saluting March-Past

1970. 1st Anniv of Second Republic. Multicoloured.

582	4n.p. Type **310**	20	10
583	12½n.p. Busia Declaration	15	15
584	20n.p. Doves symbol	25	30
585	40n.p. Opening of Parliament	50	1·00

314 "Crinum ornatum"

1970. Flora and Fauna. Multicoloured.

586	4n.p. Type **314**	1·75	25
587	12½n.p. Lioness	1·25	85
588	20n.p. "Ansellia africana" (flower)	1·25	1·50
589	40n.p. African elephant	2·00	6·00

315 Kuduo Brass Casket

1970. Monuments and Archaeological Sites in Ghana. Multicoloured.

590	4n.p. Type **315**	15	10
591	12½n.p. Akan traditional house	30	20
592	20n.p. Larabanga Mosque	35	55
593	40n.p. Funerary clay head	50	2·00
MS594	89×71 mm. Nos. 590, 592 and 12½n.p. Basilica of Pompeii, 40n.p. Pistrinum of Pompeii. Imperf	5·50	9·50

316 Trade Fair Building

1971. International Trade Fair, Accra. Multicoloured.

595	4n.p. Type **316**	10	10
596	12½n.p. Cosmetic and pharmaceutical goods	60	20
597	20n.p. Vehicles	65	25
598	40n.p. Construction equipment	95	95
599	50n.p. Transport and packing case (vert)	1·10	1·10

317 Christ on the Cross

1971. Easter. Multicoloured.

600	4n.p. Type **317**	20	10
601	12½n.p. Christ and Disciples	40	70
602	20n.p. Christ blessing Disciples	50	1·40

318 Corn Cob

1971. Freedom from Hunger Campaign.

603	**318**	4n.p. multicoloured	10	10
604	**318**	12½n.p. multicoloured	35	90
605	**318**	20n.p. multicoloured	40	2·00

Remainder stocks of the above stamps were optd on the occasion of the death of Lord Boyd Orr and further surch 12½, 20 and 60n.p.

It is understood that 8070 sets from the agency were overprinted locally and returned to New York. Limited remainders of these stamps (only 330 of 60n.p.) were sold at the G.P.O. We do not list these as they were not freely on sale in Ghana.

319 Guides Emblem and Ghana Flag

1971. Golden Jubilee of Ghana Girl Guides. Each design includes Guides emblem. Mult.

606	4n.p. Type **319**	20	10
607	12½n.p. Mrs E. Ofuatey-Kodjoe (founder) and guides with flags	50	50
608	20n.p. Guides laying stones	70	90
609	40n.p. Camp-fire and tent	1·25	1·75
610	50n.p. Signallers	1·50	2·00
MS611	133×105 mm. Nos. 606/610. Imperf	11·00	13·00
MS611	133×105 mm. Nos. 606/610. Imperf	11·00	13·00

320 Child-care Centre

1971. Y.W.C.A. World Council Meeting, Accra. Multicoloured.

612	4n.p. Type **320**	10	10
613	12½n.p. Council meeting	10	15
614	20n.p. School typing class	15	30
615	40n.p. Building Fund Day	30	1·00
MS616	84×83 mm. Nos. 612/15. Imperf	70	2·00

321 Firework Display

1971. Christmas. Multicoloured.

617	1n.p. Type **321**	10	70
618	3n.p. African Nativity	15	80
619	6n.p. The Flight into Egypt	15	80

322 Weighing Baby

1971. 25th Anniv of UNICEF. Multicoloured.

620	5n.p. Type **322**	10	10
621	15n.p. Mother and child (horiz)	20	30
622	30n.p. Nurse	30	70
623	50n.p. Young boy (horiz)	50	2·25
MS624	111×120 mm. Nos. 620/3. Imperf	1·75	6·50

323 Unity Symbol and Trade Fair Emblem

1972. All African Trade Fair. Multicoloured.

625	5n.p. Type **323**	10	10
626	15n.p. Horn of Plenty	15	30
627	30n.p. Fireworks on map of Africa	20	70
628	60n.p. "Participating Nations"	25	2·00
629	1n.c. As No. 628	40	2·50

On 24 June 1972, on the occasion of the Belgian International Philatelic Exhibition, Nos. 625/9 were issued optd **BELGICA72**. Only very limited supplies were sent to Ghana (we understand not more than 900 sets), and for this reason we do not list them.

324 Books for the Blind

1972. International Book Year. Multicoloured.

630	5p. Type **324**	30	10
631	15p. Children's books	65	50
632	30p. Books for recreation	1·25	1·25
633	50p. Books for students	1·75	3·00
634	1c. Book and flame of knowledge (vert)	2·25	5·00
MS635	99×106 mm. Nos. 630/4. Imperf	7·00	11·00

325 "Hypoxis urceolata"

1972. Flora and Fauna. Multicoloured.

636	5p. Type **325**	30	10
637	15p. Mona monkey	65	65
638	30p. "Crinum ornatum"	3·00	4·00
639	1c. De Winton's tree squirrel	2·00	8·00

326 Football

1972. Olympic Games, Munich. Multicoloured.

640	5p. Type **326**	20	10
641	15p. Running	30	20
642	30p. Boxing	50	65
643	50p. Long-jumping	60	2·25
644	1c. High-jumping	1·10	3·50
MS645	86×43 mm. 40p. as No. 642 se-tenant with 60p. as No. 640	2·50	7·00

327 Senior Scout and Cub

1972. 65th Anniv of Boy Scouts. Multicoloured.

646	5p. Type **327**	30	10
647	15p. Scout and tent	55	45
648	30p. Sea scouts	80	1·25
649	50p. Leader with cubs	90	2·00
650	1c. Training school	1·25	3·50
MS651	110×110 mm. 40p. as 30p.; 60p. as 1c.	3·25	5·50

328 "The Holy Night" (Correggio)

1972. Christmas. Multicoloured.

652	1p. Type **328**	10	10
653	3p. "Adoration of the Kings" (Holbein the Elder)	10	10
654	15p. "Madonna of the Passion" (School of Ricco)	30	30
655	30p. "King Melchior"	60	70
656	60p. "King Gaspar, Mary and Jesus"	80	2·00
657	1c. "King Balthasar"	1·00	3·25
MS658	139×90 mm. Nos. 655/7. Imperf	5·00	9·00

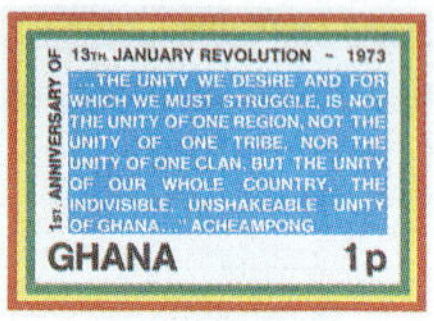

329 Extract from Speech

1973. 1st Anniv of 13 January Revolution. Multicoloured.

659	1p. Type **329**	10	10
660	3p. Market scene	10	10
661	5p. Selling bananas (vert)	10	10
662	15p. Farmer with hoe and produce (vert)	20	25
663	30p. Market traders	30	40
664	1c. Farmer cutting palm-nuts	70	1·40
MS665	90×55 mm. 40p. as 1c. and 60p. Miners	70	2·25

330 Under 5's Clinic

1973. 25th Anniv of W.H.O. Multicoloured.

666	5p. Type **330**	10	10
667	15p. Radiography	15	25
668	30p. Immunisation	25	40
669	50p. Starving child	25	80
670	1c. W.H.O. H.Q., Geneva	25	1·75

1973. World Scouting Conference, Nairobi/Addis Ababa. Nos. 646/50 optd 1st WORLD SCOUTING CONFERENCE IN AFRICA.

671	**327**	5p. multicoloured	10	15
672	-	15p. multicoloured	30	60
673	-	30p. multicoloured	40	1·40
674	-	50p. multicoloured	55	2·00
675	-	1c. multicoloured	70	3·00
MS676		110×110 mm. 40p. as 30p.; 60p. as 1c.	1·75	6·50

332 Poultry Farming

1973. 10th Anniv of World Food Programme. Multicoloured.

677	5p. Type **332**	10	10
678	15p. Mechanisation	15	15
679	50p. Cocoa harvest	40	90
680	1c. F.A.O. H.Q., Rome	60	1·90
MS681	92×104 mm. 40p. as 15p.; 60p. as 1c.	60	2·25

333 "Green Alert"

1973. 50th Anniv of Interpol. Multicoloured.

682	5p. Type **333**	25	10
683	30p. "Red Alert"	90	80
684	50p. "Blue Alert"	1·25	1·75
685	1c. "Black Alert"	2·00	4·00

334 Handshake

1973. 10th Anniv of O.A.U. Multicoloured.

686	5p. Type **334**	10	10
687	30p. Africa Hall, Addis Ababa	15	30
688	50p. O.A.U. emblem	20	1·00
689	1c. "X" in colours of Ghana flag	35	1·50

335 Weather Balloon

1973. Centenary of I.M.O./W.M.O. Multicoloured.

690	5p. Type **335**	10	10
691	15p. Satellite "Tiros"	15	20
692	30p. Computer weather map	30	65
693	1c. Radar screen	60	2·25
MS694	120×95 mm. 40p. as 15p.; 60p. as 30p.	1·25	3·25

336 Epiphany Scene

1973. Christmas. Multicoloured.

695	1p. Type **336**	10	10
696	3p. Madonna and Child	10	10
697	30p. "Madonna and Child" (Murillo)	30	75
698	50p. "Adoration of the Magi" (Tiepolo)	45	1·00
MS699	77×103 mm. Nos. 695/8. Imperf	1·25	3·00

337 "Christ carrying the Cross" (Thomas de Kolozsvar)

1974. Easter.

700	**337**	5p. multicoloured	10	10
701	-	30p. blue, silver and brown	15	35
702	-	50p. red, silver and brown	25	60
703	-	1c. green, silver and brown	35	1·25
MS704		111×106 mm. 15p. as No. 700; 20p. as No. 701; 25p. as No. 702. Imperf	80	1·75

DESIGNS (from 15th-century English carved alabaster): 30p. "The Betrayal"; 50p. "The Deposition"; 1c. "The Risen Christ and Mary Magdalene".

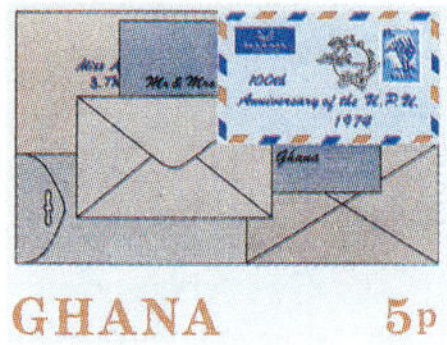

338 Letters

1974. Centenary of U.P.U. Multicoloured.

705	5p. Type **338**	10	10
706	9p. U.P.U. Monument and H.Q.	10	15
707	50p. Airmail letter	35	1·00
708	1c. U.P.U. Monument and Ghana stamp	60	1·75
MS709	108×90 mm. 20p. as No. 705; 30p. as No. 706; 40p. as No. 707; 60p. as No. 708	75	1·60

1974. "Internaba 1974" Stamp Exhibition. As Nos. 705/8 additionally inscr "INTERNABA 1974".

710	5p. multicoloured	10	10
711	9p. multicoloured	10	15
712	50p. multicoloured	30	1·00
713	1c. multicoloured	45	1·75
MS714	108×90 mm. 20p. as No. 710; 30p. as No. 711; 40p. as No. 712; 60p. as No. 713	1·50	4·00

339 Footballers

1974. World Cup Football Championship.

715	**339**	5p. multicoloured	10	10
716	-	30p. multicoloured	20	60
717	-	50p. multicoloured	25	85
718	-	1c. multicoloured	30	1·50
MS719		148×94 mm. 25, 40, 55 and 60p. as Nos. 715/18	1·00	3·25

DESIGNS: As Type **339** showing footballers in action.

340 Roundabout

1974. Change to Driving on the Right.

720	**340**	5p. green, red and black	10	10
721	-	15p. purple, red and black	20	35
722	-	30p. multicoloured	30	40
723	-	50p. multicoloured	40	85
724	-	1c. multicoloured	75	1·75

DESIGNS—HORIZ: 15p. Warning triangle sign. VERT: 30p. Highway arrow and slogan; 50p. Warning hands; 1c. Car on symbolic hands.

1974. West Germany's Victory in World Cup. Nos. 715/18 optd WEST GERMANY WINNERS.

725	5p. multicoloured	10	10
726	30p. multicoloured	20	40
727	50p. multicoloured	35	55
728	1c. multicoloured	45	1·25
MS729	148×94 mm. 25, 40, 55 and 60p. as Nos. 725/8	1·40	2·50

342 "Planned Family"

1974. World Population Year. Multicoloured.

730	5p. Type **342**	10	10
731	30p. Family planning clinic	25	35
732	50p. Immunization	35	60
733	1c. Population census enumeration	60	1·40

343 Angel

1974. Christmas. Multicoloured.

734	5p. Type **343**	10	10
735	7p. The Magi (diamond 47×47 mm)	10	10
736	9p. The Nativity	10	10
737	1c. The Annunciation	60	1·40
MS738	128×128 mm. 15p. Type **343**; 30p. as 7p.; 45p. as 9p.; 60p. as 1c. Imperf	80	2·50

1975. "Apollo"–"Soyuz" Space Link. Nos. 715/18 optd APOLLO SOYUZ JULY 15, 1975.

739	**339**	5p. multicoloured	10	10
740	-	30p. multicoloured	20	25
741	-	50p. multicoloured	30	55
742	-	1c. multicoloured	55	80
MS743		148×94 mm. 25, 40, 55 and 60p. as Nos. 739/42	1·00	2·00

345 Tractor Driver

1975. International Women's Year. Multicoloured.

744	7p. Type **345**	45	10
745	30p. Motor mechanic	1·00	35
746	60p. Factory workers	1·10	80
747	1c. Cocoa research	1·40	1·40
MS748	136×110 mm. 15, 40, 65 and 80p. as Nos. 744/7. Imperf	2·00	6·00

346 Angel

1975. Christmas.

749	**346**	2p. multicoloured	10	10
750	-	5p. yellow and green	10	10
751	-	7p. yellow and green	10	10
752	-	30p. yellow and green	20	20
753	-	1c. yellow and green	50	1·00
MS754		98×87 mm. 15, 40, 65 and 80p. as Nos. 750/3. Imperf	90	3·00

DESIGNS: 5p. Angle with harp; 7p. Angel with lute; 30p. Angel with violin; 1c. Angel with trumpet.

347 Map Reading

1976. 14th World Scout Jamboree, Norway. Multicoloured.

755	7p. Type **347**	20	10
756	30p. Sailing	55	90

757		60p. Hiking	70	2·25
758		1c. Life-saving	80	2·50
MS759		133×99 mm. 15, 40, 65 and 80p. as Nos. 755/8	2·25	6·50

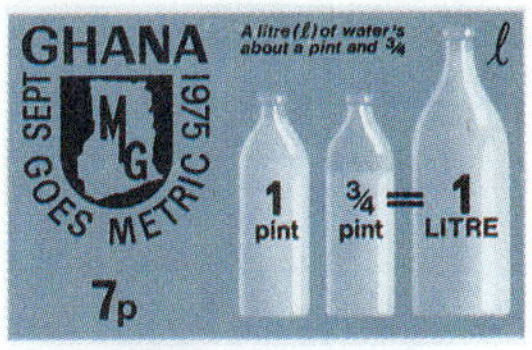

348 Bottles (litre)

1976. Metrication Publicity. Multicoloured.

760		7p. Type **348**	15	10
761		30p. Scales (kilogramme)	20	40
762		60p. Tape measure and bale of cloth (metre)	40	1·00
763		1c. Ice, thermometer and kettle (temperature)	60	1·75

349 Fair Site

1976. International Trade Fair, Accra.

764	**349**	7p. multicoloured	10	10
765	-	30p. multicoloured	15	20
766	-	60p. multicoloured	25	60
767	-	1c. multicoloured	40	1·00

DESIGNS: As Type **349** showing different views of the Fair.

1976. Interphil Stamp Exhibition. Nos. 755/8 optd 'INTERPHIL' 76 BICENTENNIAL EXHIBITION.

768	**347**	7p. multicoloured	15	15
769	-	30p. multicoloured	35	50
770	-	60p. multicoloured	55	75
771	-	1c. multicoloured	80	1·25
MS772		133×99 mm. 15, 40, 65 and 80p. as Nos. 768/71	1·25	2·50

351 Shot-put

1976. Olympic Games, Montreal. Multicoloured.

773		7p. Type **351**	15	10
774		30p. Football	30	25
775		60p. Women's 1500 m	45	50
776		1c. Boxing	60	80
MS777		103×135 mm. 15, 40, 65 and 80p. as Nos. 773/6	1·50	1·50

352 Supreme Court

1976. Centenary of Supreme Court.

778	**352**	8p. multicoloured	10	10
779	-	30p. multicoloured	20	25
780	-	60p. multicoloured	35	50
781	-	1c. multicoloured	60	1·00

DESIGNS: As Type **352** showing different views of the Court Buildings.

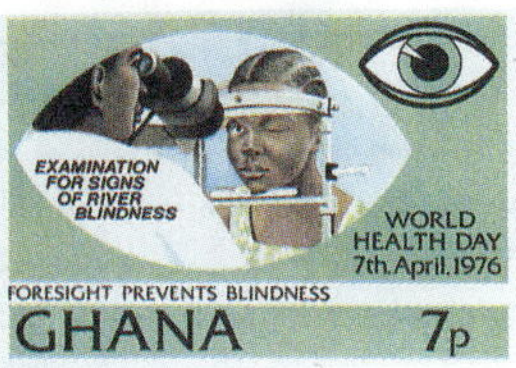

353 Examination for River Blindness

1976. Prevention of Blindness. Multicoloured.

782		7p. Type **353**	65	10
783		30p. Entomologist	1·75	1·40
784		60p. Normal vision	2·75	2·75
785		1c. Blackfly eradication	4·25	4·50

354 Fireworks Party, Christmas Eve

1976. Christmas. Multicoloured.

786		6p. Type **354**	15	10
787		8p. Children and gifts	15	10
788		30p. Christmas feast	35	30
789		1c. As 8p.	75	1·75
MS790		122×98 mm. 15, 40, 65 and 80p. as Nos. 786/9. Imperf	1·10	4·00

355 "Gallows Frame" Telephone and Alexander Graham Bell

1976. Centenary of Telephone. Multicoloured.

791		8p. Type **355**	15	10
792		30p. Bell and 1895 telephone	30	30
793		60p. Bell and 1929 telephone	45	70
794		1c. Bell and 1976 telephone	1·00	1·25
MS795		125×92 mm. 15, 40, 65 and 80p. as Nos. 791/4	1·00	1·40

1977. Olympic Winners. Nos. 773/6 optd WINNERS and country name.

796	**351**	7p. multicoloured	15	15
797	-	30p. multicoloured	20	40
798	-	60p. multicoloured	35	85
799	-	1c. multicoloured	40	1·50
MS800		103×135 mm. 15, 40, 65 and 80p. as Nos. 796/9	2·25	2·50

OPTD: 7p., 30p. **EAST GERMANY**; 60p. **U.S.S.R.**; 1c. **U.S.A.**

357 Dipo Dancers and Drum Ensemble

1977. 2nd World Black and African Festival of Arts and Culture, Nigeria. Multicoloured.

801		8p. Type **357**	15	15
802		30p. Arts and crafts	25	60
803		60p. Acon music and dancing priests	35	1·25
804		1c. African huts	40	2·00
MS805		164×120 mm. 15, 40, 65 and 80p. as Nos. 801/4	1·00	1·50

1977. Prince Charles's Visit to Ghana. Nos. 791/94 optd PRINCE CHARLES VISITS GHANA 17th TO 25th MARCH, 1977.

806		8p. Type **355**	50	55
807		30p. 1895 telephone	1·25	1·00
808		60p. 1929 telephone	1·50	2·00
809		1c. 1976 telephone	2·00	2·50
MS810		125×92 mm. 15, 40, 65 and 80p. as Nos. 806/9	6·50	9·00

359 Olive Colobus Monkey

1977. Wildlife. Multicoloured.

811		8p. Type **359**	45	15
812		20p. Temminck's giant squirrel	1·00	80
813		30p. Hunting dog	1·10	1·25
814		60p. African manatee (sea cow)	2·00	2·75
MS815		140×101 mm. 15, 40, 65 and 80p. as Nos. 811/14	4·00	4·50

360 "Le Chapeau de Paille" (Rubens—400th Birth Anniv)

1977. Painters' Anniversaries. Multicoloured.

816		8p. Type **360**	25	10
817		30p. "Isabella of Portugal" (Titian—500th birth anniv)	40	40
818		60p. "Duke and Duchess of Cumberland" (Gainsborough—250th birth anniv)	55	65
819		1c. "Rubens and Isabella Brandt"	75	1·25
MS820		99×149 mm. 15, 40, 65 and 80p. as Nos. 816/19	2·50	2·25

361 The Magi, Madonna and Child

1977. Christmas. Multicoloured.

821		1p. Type **361**	10	10
822		2p. Choir, St. Andrew's Anglican Church, Abossey Okai	10	10
823		6p. Methodist Church, Wesley, Accra	10	10
824		8p. Madonna and Child	10	10
825		30p. Holy Spirit Cathedral, Accra	30	50
826		1c. Ebenezer Presbyterian Church, Accra	1·00	1·60
MS827		122×97 mm. 15, 40, 65 and 80p. as Nos. 822/3 and 825/6. Imperf	1·25	3·75

1978. Referendum. Nos. 821/26 optd REFERENDUM 1978 VOTE EARLY.

828		1p. Type **361**	10	10
829		2p. Choir, St. Andrew's Anglican Church, Abossey Okai	10	10
830		6p. Methodist Church, Wesley, Accra	10	10
831		8p. Madonna and Child	10	10
832		30p. Holy Spirit Cathedral, Accra	30	50
833		1c. Ebenezer Presbyterian Church, Accra	1·00	1·50
MS834		122×97 mm. 15, 40, 65 and 80p. as Nos. 829/30 and 832/3	27·00	17·00

363 Cutting Bananas

1978. Operation "Feed Yourself". Multicoloured.

835		2p. Type **363**	10	10
836		8p. Home produce	15	10
837		30p. Market	35	35
838		60p. Fishing	70	60
839		1c. Mechanisation	1·25	1·25

364 Wright Flyer III

1978. 75th Anniv of Powered Flight.

840	**364**	8p. black, brown and ochre	20	10
841	-	30p. black, brown and green	30	30
842	-	60p. black, brown and red	40	60
843	-	1c. black, brown and blue	2·75	1·10
MS844		167×100 mm. 15, 40, 65 and 80p. as Nos. 840/3	2·00	1·40

DESIGNS: 30p. Handley Page H.P.42; 60p. De Havilland Comet 1; 1c. Concorde.

1978. "CAPEX 1978" International Stamp Exhibition, Toronto. Nos. 840/3 optd "CAPEX 78 JUNE 9-18 1978".

845	**364**	8p. black, brown and ochre	15	15
846	-	30p. black, brown and green	25	25
847	-	60p. black, brown and red	50	50
848	-	1c. black, brown and blue	1·10	80
MS849		167×100 mm. 15, 40, 65 and 80p. as Nos. 845/8	1·25	1·60

366 Players and African Cup Emblem

1978. Football Championships. Multicoloured.

850		8p. Type **366**	20	15
851		30p. Players and African Cup emblem (different)	25	30
852		60p. Players and World Cup emblem	40	60
853		1c. Goalkeeper and World Cup emblem	55	1·00
MS854		111×105 mm. 15, 40, 65 and 80p. as Nos. 850/3	1·10	1·25

367 "The Betrayal"

1978. Easter. Drawings by Durer.

855	**367**	11p. black and mauve	10	10
856	-	39p. black and flesh	25	30
857	-	60p. black and yellow	35	45
858	-	1c. black and green	40	65

DESIGNS: 39p. "The Crucifixion"; 60p. "The Deposition"; 1c. "The Resurrection".

1978. Football Victories of Ghana and Argentina. Nos. 850/3 and MS854 optd "GHANA WINNERS" (8, 30p.) or "ARGENTINA WINS" (others).

859	**366**	8p. multicoloured	45	15
860	-	30p. multicoloured	45	30
861	-	60p. multicoloured	70	45
862	-	1c. multicoloured	80	75
MS863		111×105 mm. 15, 40, 65 and 80p. as Nos. 859/62 but all optd	1·00	1·10

369 "Bauhinia purpurea"

1978. Flowers. Multicoloured.

864		11p. Type **369**	15	10
865		39p. "Cassia fistula"	20	55
866		60p. "Plumeria acutifolia"	20	70
867		1c. "Jacaranda mimosifolia"	20	1·00

370 Mail Van

1978. 75th Anniv of Ghana Railways. Multicoloured.

868	11p. Type **370**	20	10
869	39p. Pay and bank car	20	65
870	60p. Steam locomotive No. 1 "Amanful", 1922	20	1·00
871	1c. Diesel-electric locomotive No. 1651, 1960	20	1·40

371 "Orbiter" Spacecraft

1979. "Pioneer" Venus Space Project. Multicoloured.

872	11p. Type **371**	15	10
873	39p. "Multiprobe" space craft	15	30
874	60p. "Orbiter" and "Multiprobe" spacecraft in Venus orbit	20	45
875	3c. Radar chart of Venus	30	1·40
MS876	135×94 mm. 15, 40, 65p. and 2c. as Nos. 872/5. Imperf	1·10	1·25

372 "O Come All Ye Faithful"

1979. Christmas. Lines and Scenes from Christmas Carols. Multicoloured.

877	8p. Type **372**	10	10
878	10p. "O Little Town of Bethlehem"	10	10
879	15p. "We Three Kings of Orient Are"	10	10
880	20p. "I Saw Three Ships come Sailing By"	10	10
881	2c. "Away In a Manger"	30	80
882	4c. "Ding Dong Merrily on High"	50	1·40
MS883	110×95 mm. 25, 65p., 1 and 2c. as Nos. 877, 879 and 881/2	75	1·00

373 Dr. J. B. Danquah (lawyer and nationalist)

1980. Famous Ghanaians. Multicoloured.

884	20p. Type **373**	10	10
885	65p. John Mensah Sarbah (nationalist)	10	10
886	80p. Dr J. E. K. Aggrey (educationalist)	15	20
887	2c. Dr. Kwame Nkrumah (nationalist)	20	30
888	4c. G. E. (Paa) Grant (lawyer)	40	80

374 Tribesman ringing Clack Bells

1980. Death Centenary of Sir Rowland Hill (1979). Multicoloured.

889	20p. Type **374**	15	15
890	65p. As 50p.	15	20
891	2c. As 1c.	25	75
892	4c. Chieftain with ivory and gold staff	30	1·50
893	25p. Type **374**	15	40
894	50p. Chieftain with Golden Elephant staff	15	40
895	1c. Signalling with drums	20	85
896	5c. As 4c.	35	3·00
MS897	115×86 mm. Nos. 893/6	75	1·00

375 Children in Classroom

1980. International Year of the Child (1979). Multicoloured.

898	20p. Type **375**	15	15
899	65p. Playing football	25	45
900	2c. Playing in a boat	40	1·00
901	4c. Mother and child	60	1·75
MS902	156×94 mm. 25, 50p., 1 and 3c. as Nos. 898/901	75	1·75

1980. "London 1980" International Stamp Exhibition. Nos. 889/96 optd "LONDON 1980" 6th - 14th May 1980.

903	**374**	20p. multicoloured	15	15
904	-	65p. multicoloured	15	50
905	-	2c. multicoloured	25	1·25
906	-	4c. multicoloured	35	2·25
907	-	25p. multicoloured	1·25	2·75
908	-	50p. multicoloured	1·50	3·00
909	-	1c. multicoloured	2·25	3·50
910	-	5c. multicoloured	4·00	6·00
MS911		115×86 mm. Nos. 907/10	1·00	2·00

1980. Papal Visit. Nos. 898/901 optd "PAPAL VISIT" 8th - 9th May 1980.

912	**375**	20p. multicoloured	55	35
913	-	65p. multicoloured	1·00	60
914	-	2c. multicoloured	1·75	1·40
915	-	4c. multicoloured	2·50	2·50
MS916		156×94 mm. 25, 50p., 1 and 3c. as Nos. 912/15	9·00	7·50

378 Parliament House

1980. 3rd Republic Commemoration. Multicoloured.

917	20p. Type **378**	10	10
918	65p. Supreme Court	20	25
919	2c. The Castle	40	70
MS920	72×113 mm. 25p., 1 and 3c. as Nos. 917/19	60	1·10

379 Boeing 737 Airliner and Map of West Africa

1980. 5th Anniv of Economic Community of West African States. Multicoloured.

921	20p. Type **379**	10	10
922	65p. Antenna and map	15	20
923	80p. Cog-wheels and map	20	25
924	2c. Corn and map	35	50

380 "O.A.U."

1980. 1st Organization of African Unity Economic Summit Conference, Nigeria.

925	**380**	20p. multicoloured	10	10
926	-	65p. multicoloured	15	20
927	-	80p. deep red, red and black	15	25
928	-	2c. multicoloured	20	65

DESIGNS: 65p. Maps of Africa and Ghana and banner; 80p. Map of Africa; 2c. Map of Africa, banner and Ghanaian flag.

381 "The Adoration of the Magi"

1980. Christmas. Paintings by Fra Angelico. Multicoloured.

929	15p. Type **381**	10	10
930	20p. "The Virgin and Child, enthroned with Four Angels"	10	10
931	2c. "The Virgin and Child enthroned with Eight Angels"	35	80
932	4c. "The Annunciation"	60	1·60
MS933	77×112 mm. 25, 50p., 1 and 3c. as Nos. 929/32	75	1·25

382 "Health"

1980. 75th Anniv of Rotary International. Multicoloured.

934	20p. Type **382**	10	10
935	65p. Rotary emblem and motto with maps of World and Ghana	15	30
936	2c. Rotary emblem, globe and outstretched hands	35	85
937	4c. "Eradication of Hunger"	60	1·50
MS938	121×93 mm. 25, 50p., 1 and 3c. as Nos. 934/7	1·10	2·00

383 Narina's Trogon ("Narina Trogon")

1981. Birds. Multicoloured.

939	20p. Type **383**	80	15
940	65p. White-crowned robin chat	1·25	50
941	2c. Swallow-tailed bee eater	1·50	1·75
942	4c. Rose-ringed parakeet	2·00	3·25
MS943	89×121 mm. 25, 50p., 1 and 3c. as Nos. 939/42	5·00	4·00

384 Pope John Paul II, Archbishop of Canterbury and President Limann during Papal Visit

1981. 1st Anniv of Papal Visit.

944	**384**	20p. multicoloured	25	15
945	**384**	65p. multicoloured	45	55
946	**384**	80p. multicoloured	60	70
947	**384**	2c. multicoloured	1·10	2·00

385 Royal Yacht "Britannia"

1981. Royal Wedding. Multicoloured.

948	20p. Prince Charles and Lady Diana Spencer	10	10
949	80p. Prince Charles on visit to Ghana	15	20
950	4c. Type **385**	50	80
MS951	95×85 mm. 7c. St. Paul's Cathedral	70	1·25
952	65p. As 20p.	15	25
953	1c. As 80p.	25	35
954	3c. Type **385**	70	1·10
955	2c. Type **385**	1·00	1·50
956	5c. As 20p.	1·00	2·75

386 Earth Satellite Station

1981. Commissioning of Earth Satellite Station. Mult.

957	20p. Type **386**	10	10
958	65p. Satellites beaming signals to Earth	15	15
959	80p. Satellite	15	20
960	4c. Satellite orbiting Earth	1·00	1·50
MS961	112×100 mm. 25p., 50p., 1c. and 3c. as Nos. 957/60	70	1·40

387 Pounding Fufu

1981. World Food Day. Multicoloured.

962	20p. Type **387**	10	10
963	65p. Plucking cocoa	25	35
964	80p. Preparing banku	35	45
965	2c. Garri processing	75	2·25
MS966	131×99 mm. 25p., 50p., 1c. and 3c. as Nos. 962/5	1·00	1·50

388 "The Betrothal of St. Catherine of Alexandria" (Lucas Cranach)

1981. Christmas. Details from Paintings. Multicoloured.

967	15p. Type **388**	15	10
968	20p. "Angelic Musicians play for Mary and Child" (Aachener Altares)	15	10
969	65p. "Child Jesus embracing his Mother" (Gabriel Metsu)	20	15
970	80p. "Madonna and Child" (Fra Filippo Lippi)	20	20
971	2c. "The Madonna with Infant Jesus" (Barnaba da Modena)	40	70
972	4c. "The Immaculate Conception" (Murillo)	45	1·10
MS973	82×102 mm. 6c. "Madonna and Child with Angels" (Hans Memling)	1·00	2·25

389 Blind Person

1982. International Year for Disabled Persons. Multicoloured.

974	20p. Type **389**	25	10
975	65p. Disabled person with crutches	35	35
976	80p. Blind child reading braille	60	45
977	4c. Disabled people helping one another	1·75	2·25
MS978	109×85 mm. 6c. Group of disabled people	2·75	3·00

390 African Clawless Otter

1982. Flora and Fauna. Multicoloured.

979 20p. Type **390** 25 15
980 65p. Bushbuck 40 40
981 80p. Aardvark 40 50
982 1c. Scarlet bell tree 40 60
983 2c. Glory-lilies 60 1·25
984 4c. Blue-pea 1·00 2·25
MS985 76×100 mm. 5c. Chimpanzee 1·25 5·00

391 "Precis westermanni"

1982. Butterflies. Multicoloured.

986 20p. Type **391** 70 15
987 65p. "Papilio menestheus" 1·25 1·00
988 2c. "Antanartia delius" 2·00 3·50
989 4c. "Charaxes castor" 2·75 4·75
MS990 98×123 mm. 25p., 50p., 1c. and 3c. as Nos. 986/9 7·00 12·00

392 Scouts planting Tree

1982. 75th Anniv of Boy Scout Movement. Multicoloured.

991 20p. Type **392** 25 15
992 65p. Scouts cooking on campfire 70 65
993 80p. Sea Scouts sailing 90 85
994 3c. Scouts observing African elephant 2·25 3·25
MS995 101×71 mm. 5c. Lord Baden-Powell (vert) 2·25 6·50

393 Initial Stages of Construction

1982. Kpong Hydro-Electric Project. Multicoloured.

996 20p. Type **393** 65 10
997 65p. Truck removing rubble 1·25 45
998 80p. Hydro-electric turbines 2·00 65
999 2c. Aerial view of completed plant 2·75 1·60

394 Footballers

1982. World Cup Football Championship, Spain.

1000 **394** 20p. multicoloured 25 10
1001 - 65p. multicoloured 70 35
1002 - 80p. multicoloured (Heading) 80 45
1003 - 4c. multicoloured 1·10 2·00
MS1004 110×90 mm. 6c. multicoloured 3·75 2·75
1005 **394** 30p. multicoloured 65 50
1006 - 80p. multicoloured (Three footballers) 85 75
1007 - 1c. multicoloured 95 90
1008 - 3c. multicoloured 1·40 1·60

DESIGNS: 65p. to 6c. Scenes showing footballers.

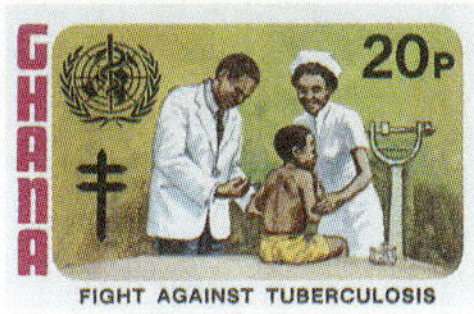

395 The Fight against Tuberculosis

1982. Centenary of Robert Koch's Discovery of Tubercle Bacillus. Multicoloured.

1009 20p. Type **395** 70 20
1010 65p. Robert Koch 1·60 1·25
1011 80p. Robert Koch in Africa 2·00 1·75
1012 1c. Centenary of discovery of Tuberculosis 2·25 2·75
1013 2c. Robert Koch and Nobel Prize, 1905 3·25 4·00

396 The Shepherds worship Jesus

1982. Christmas. Multicoloured.

1014 15p. Type **396** 10 10
1015 20p. Mary, Joseph and baby Jesus 10 10
1016 65p. The Three Kings sight star 20 30
1017 4c. Winged Angel 70 1·75
MS1018 90×110 mm. 6c. The Three Kings with Jesus 1·00 1·75

397 Ghana and Commonwealth Flags with Coat of Arms

1983. Commonwealth Day. Multicoloured.

1019 20p. Type **397** 25 15
1020 55p. Satellite view of Ghana 45 65
1021 80p. Minerals of Ghana 1·00 1·25
1022 3c. African fish eagle 1·50 4·25

1983. Italy's Victory in World Cup Football Championships (1982). Nos. 1000/8 optd WINNER ITALY 3–1.

1023 20p. multicoloured 15 10
1024 65p. multicoloured 25 15
1025 80p. multicoloured 25 20
1026 4c. multicoloured 1·40 1·75
MS1027 110×90 mm. 6c. multicoloured 1·75 1·50
1028 30p. multicoloured 75 90
1029 80p. multicoloured 1·25 1·50
1030 1c. multicoloured 1·50 1·75
1031 3c. multicoloured 2·00 3·75

1983. No. 470 surch C1.

1031a 1c. on 20n.p. Bush hare (blue) 40 40

399 Short-finned Pilot Whale

1983. Coastal Marine Mammals. Multicoloured.

1032 1c. Type **399** 35 1·00
1033 1c.40 Risso's dolphin 40 1·10
1034 2c. False killer whale 45 1·25
1035 3c. Spinner dolphin 50 1·60
1036 4c. Atlantic hump-backed dolphin 50 2·00
MS1037 117×76 mm. 6c. As 4c. 1·25 1·00

400 Banded Jewelfish

1983

1038 **400** 5p. multicoloured 30 20
1039 - 10p. multicoloured 30 20
1040 - 20p. multicoloured 40 20
1041 - 50p. green, orange blk 40 30
1042 - 1c. orange, blue and black 50 20
1043 - 2c. multicoloured 50 30
1044 - 3c. multicoloured 1·25 30
1045 - 4c. multicoloured 40 40
1046 - 5c. multicoloured 50 40
1047 - 10c. multicoloured 1·25 1·00

DESIGNS—HORIZ: 10p. Banded jewelfish (different); 2c. Jet airliner. VERT: 20p. "Haemanthus rupestris"; 50p. Mounted warrior; 1c. Scorpion; 3c. White-collared mangabey; 4c. Demidoff's galago; 5c. "Kaemferia nigerica"; 10c. Grey-backed camaroptera.

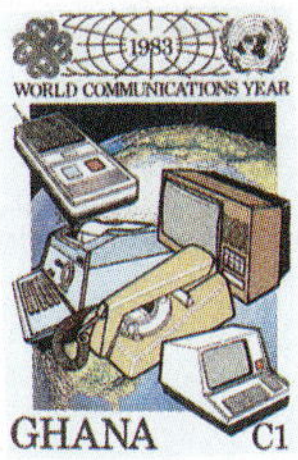

401 Communication Devices

1983. World Communications Year. Multicoloured.

1048 1c. Type **401** 15 25
1049 1c.40 Satellite dish aerial 20 30
1050 2c.30 Cable and "Long Lines" (cable ship) 35 55
1051 3c. Switchboard operators 40 65
1052 5c. Aircraft cockpit and air traffic controllers 55 85
MS1053 95×70 mm. 6c. Space satellite 30 50

402 Children receiving Presents

1983. Christmas. Multicoloured.

1054 70p. Type **402** 15 10
1055 1c. Nativity and Star of Bethlehem (vert) 15 10
1056 1c.40 Children celebrating (vert) 20 55
1057 2c.30 Family praying together (vert) 25 1·00
1058 3c. Dancing to bongo drum 35 1·25
MS1059 70×90 mm. 6c. As 2c.30 30 1·00

403 Soldiers with Rifles

1983. Namibia Day.

1060 **403** 50p. green and black 10 10
1061 - 1c. multicoloured 10 10
1062 - 1c.40 blue, lt blue blk 15 15
1063 - 2c.30 multicoloured 20 25
1064 - 3c. multicoloured 25 30

DESIGNS: 1c. Soldiers supported by tank; 1c.40, Machete cutting chains; 2c.30, Peasant woman; 3c. Soldiers and artillery support.

1984. (a) Nos. 948/50, 952 and 954 surch.

1065 1c. on 20p. Prince Charles and Lady Diana Spencer 2·50 3·00
1066 9c. on 65p. Prince Charles and Lady Diana Spencer 3·00 4·00
1067 9c. on 80p. Prince Charles on visit to Ghana 3·00 4·00
1068 20c. on 3c. Type **385** 3·50 6·00
1069 20c. on 4c. Type **385** 3·50 6·00
MS1070 95×85 mm. 60c on 7c. St. Paul's Cathedral 1·00 3·00

(b) Nos. 991/2 and 994 surch.

1071 10c. on 20p. Type **392** 40 45
1072 19c. on 65p. Scouts cooking on campfire 80 85
1073 30c. on 3c. Scouts observing African elephant 2·00 2·00
MS1074 101×71 mm. 60c. on 5c. Lord Baden-Powell 1·00 3·50

(c) Nos. 1000/3, 1005/6 and 1008 surch.

1075 **394** 1c. on 20p. multicoloured 30 50
1076 - 9c. on 65p. multicoloured 70 70
1077 - 9c. on 3c. multicoloured 70 70
1078 **394** 10c. on 30p. multicoloured 70 70
1079 - 10c. on 80p. multicoloured 70 70
1080 - 20c. on 80p. multicoloured 2·00 2·00
1081 - 20c. on 4c. multicoloured 2·00 2·00
MS1082 110×90 mm. 60c. on 6c. multicoloured 1·00 2·25

(d) Nos. 1019/22 surch.

1083 1c. on 20p. Type **397** 10 10
1084 9c. on 55p. Satellite view of Ghana 50 45
1085 30c. on 80p. Minerals of Ghana 2·25 1·75
1086 50c. on 3c. African fish eagle 3·25 3·50

(e) Nos. 1023/6, 1028/9 and 1031 surch.

1087 **394** 1c. on 20p. multicoloured 20 50
1088 - 9c. on 65p. multicoloured 55 60
1089 - 9c. on 3c. multicoloured 55 60
1090 **394** 10c. on 30p. multicoloured 55 60
1091 - 10c. on 80p. multicoloured 55 60
1092 - 20c. on 80p. multicoloured 90 1·00
1093 - 20c. on 4c. multicoloured 90 1·00
MS1094 110×90 mm. 60c. on 6c. multicoloured 1·00 2·00

1984. Universal Postal Union Congress, Hamburg. Nos. 1035/6 surch 19th U.P.U. CONGRESS - HAMBURG, emblem and new value.

1095 10c. on 3c. Spinner dolphin 40 45
1096 50c. on 5c. Atlantic hump-backed dolphin 2·10 2·25
MS1097 117×76 mm. 60c. on 6c. as No. 1096 2·75 3·50

407 Cross and Crown of Thorns

1984. Easter. Multicoloured.

1098 1c. Type **407** 10 10
1099 1c.40 Christ praying 10 10
1100 2c.30 The Resurrection 10 10
1101 3c. Palm Sunday 10 15
1102 50c. Christ on the road to Emmaus 1·10 2·25
MS1103 102×86 mm. 60c. Type **407** 1·00 2·50

408 Women's 400 Metre Race

1984. Olympic Games, Los Angeles. Multicoloured.

1104 1c. Type **408** 10 10
1105 1c.40 Boxing 15 10
1106 2c.30 Hockey 20 15
1107 3c. Men's 400 metre hurdles race 20 15
1108 50c. Rhythmic gymnastics 1·75 3·50
MS1109 103×78 mm. 70c. Football 2·00 3·50

No. 1108 is inscribed "RYTHMIC" in error.

409 "Amorphophallus johnsonii"

1984. Flowers. Multicoloured.

1110	1c. Type **409**	10	10
1111	1c.40 "Pancratium trianthum"	10	10
1112	2c.30 "Eulophia cucullata"	10	15
1113	3c. "Amorphophallus abyssinicus"	10	15
1114	50c. "Chlorophytum togoense"	1·10	5·00
MS1115	70×96 mm. 60c. Type **409**	1·25	3·50

410 Young Bongo

1984. Endangered Antelopes. Multicoloured.

1116	1c. Type **410**	30	20
1117	2c.30 Bongo bucks fighting	40	55
1118	3c. Bongo family	50	70
1119	20c. Bongo herd in high grass	1·25	3·50
MS1120	Two sheets, each 100×71 mm. (a) 70c. Head of Kob; (b) 70c. Head of Bush buck Set of 2 sheets	10·00	13·00

411 Dipo Girl

1984. Ghanaian Culture. Multicoloured.

1121	1c. Type **411**	10	25
1122	1c.40 Adowa dancer	10	25
1123	2c.30 Agbadza dancer	10	25
1124	3c. Damba dancer	10	25
1125	50c. Dipo dancer	90	3·00
MS1126	70×84 mm. 70c. Mandolin player	1·50	4·00

412 The Three Wise Men bringing Gifts

1984. Christmas. Multicoloured.

1127	70p. Type **412**	10	10
1128	1c. Choir of angels	10	10
1129	1c.40 Mary and shepherds at manger	10	10
1130	2c.30 The flight into Egypt	10	10
1131	3c. Simeon blessing Jesus	10	15
1132	50c. Holy Family and angels	90	3·00
MS1133	70×90 mm. 70c. Type **412**	1·50	2·75

1984. Olympic Winners. Nos. 1104/8 optd.

1134	1c. Type **408** (optd **VALERIE BRISCO-HOOKS U.S.A.**)	10	10
1135	1c.40 Boxing (optd **U.S. WINNERS**)	10	10
1136	2c.30 Hockey (optd **PAKISTAN (FIELD HOCKEY)**)	10	10
1137	3c. Men's 400 metre hurdles race (optd **EDWIN MOSES U.S.A.**)	10	10
1138	50c. Rhythmic gymnastics (optd **LAURI FUNG CANADA**)	1·10	1·60
MS1139	103×78 mm. 70c. Football (optd **FRANCE**)	1·75	2·50

414 The Queen Mother attending Church Service

1985. Life and Times of Queen Elizabeth the Queen Mother. Multicoloured.

1140	5c. Type **414**	10	15
1141	12c. At Ascot Races	25	30
1142	100c. At Clarence House on her 84th birthday	1·75	2·50
MS1143	56×84 mm. 110c. With Prince Charles at Garter ceremony	1·75	3·00

Stamps as Nos. 1140/2 but with face values of 8c., 20c. and 70c. exist from additional sheetlets with changed background colours.

415 Moslems going to Mosque

1985. Islamic Festival of Id-el-Fitr. Multicoloured.

1144	5c. Type **415**	25	20
1145	8c. Moslems at prayer	35	30
1146	12c. Pilgrims visiting the Dome of the Rock	55	45
1147	18c. Preaching the Koran	70	60
1148	50c. Banda Nkwanta Mosque, Accra, and map of Ghana	1·75	1·60

416 Youths clearing Refuse ("Make Ghana Clean")

1985. International Youth Year. Multicoloured.

1149	5c. Type **416**	10	10
1150	8c. Planting sapling ("Make Ghana Green")	15	15
1151	12c. Youth carrying bananas ("Feed Ghana")	20	25
1152	100c. Open-air class ("Educate Ghana")	65	2·25
MS1153	103×78 mm. 110c. as 8c.	1·25	3·00

417 Honda "Interceptor", 1984

1985. Centenary of the Motorcycle. Multicoloured.

1154	5c. Type **417**	40	30
1155	8c. DKW, 1938	50	40
1156	12c. BMW "R 32", 1923	75	70
1157	100c. NSU, 1900	4·00	7·00
MS1158	78×108 mm. 110c. Zündapp, 1973 (vert)	3·50	4·25

418 Fork-tailed Flycatcher

1985. Birth Bicentenary of John J. Audubon (ornithologist). Designs showing original paintings. Multicoloured.

1159	5c. Type **418**	1·25	50
1160	8c. Barred owl	2·25	2·00
1161	12c. Black-throated mango	2·25	2·00
1162	100c. White-crowned pigeon	6·50	9·50
MS1163	85×115 mm. 110c. Downy Woodpecker	6·50	3·50

No. 1159 is inscribed "York-tailed fly catcher" in error.

419 United Nations Building, New York

1985. 40th Anniv of U.N.O. Multicoloured.

1164	5c. Type **419**	10	10
1165	8c. Flags of member nations and U.N. Building	10	15
1166	12c. Dove with olive branch	10	25
1167	18c. General Assembly	15	35
1168	100c. Flags of Ghana and United Nations	90	1·75
MS1169	90×70 mm. 110c. United Nations (New York) 1955 4c. 10th anniv stamp	75	1·75

420 Coffee

1985. 20th Anniv of United Nations Conference on Trade and Development. Designs showing export products. Multicoloured.

1170	5c. Type **420**	10	10
1171	8c. Cocoa	15	15
1172	12c. Timber	25	25
1173	18c. Bauxite	1·25	90
1174	100c. Gold	6·50	8·50
MS1175	104×74 mm. 110c. Agricultural produce and plate of food	1·25	2·50

421 Growth Monitoring

1985. UNICEF Child Survival Campaign. Multicoloured.

1176	5c. Type **421**	30	10
1177	8c. Oral rehydration therapy	50	30
1178	12c. Breast-feeding	70	40
1179	100c. Immunization	2·50	4·50
MS1180	99×69 mm. 110c. Campaign logo	1·75	2·25

422 Airline Stewardess and Boys with Stamp Album

1986. "Ameripex" International Stamp Exhibition, Chicago. Multicoloured.

1181	5c. Type **422**	15	15
1182	25c. Globe and Douglas DC-10 airplane	60	45
1183	100c. Ghana Airways stewardess (vert)	2·25	3·00
MS1184	90×70 mm. 150c. Stamp collecting class	1·50	2·50

423 Kejetia Roundabout, Kumasi

1986. "Inter-Tourism '86" Conference. Mult.

1185	5c. Type **423**	10	10
1186	15c. Fort St. Jago, Elmina	30	30
1187	25c. Tribal warriors	45	45
1188	100c. Chief holding audience	1·75	3·25
MS1189	110×70 mm. 150c. African elephants	3·75	6·00

424 Tackling

1987. World Cup Football Championship, Mexico (1986). Multicoloured.

1190	5c. Type **424**	20	10
1191	15c. Player taking control of ball	30	15
1192	25c. Player kicking ball	50	25
1193	100c. Player with ball	1·50	1·25
MS1194	90×70 mm. 150c. Player kicking ball (different)	1·50	2·00

425 Fertility Doll

1987. Ghanaian Fertility Dolls. Designs showing different dolls.

1195	**425** 5c. multicoloured	10	10
1196	- 15c. multicoloured	15	15
1197	- 25c. multicoloured	25	25
1198	- 100c. multicoloured	90	2·00
MS1199	90×70 mm. **425** 150c. multicoloured	1·50	2·00

426 Children of Different Races, Peace Doves and Sun

1987. International Peace Year (1986). Multicoloured.

1200	5c. Type **426**	15	10
1201	25c. Plough, peace dove and rising sun	75	25
1202	100c. Peace dove, olive branch and globe (vert)	2·50	3·00
MS1203	90×70 mm. 150c. Dove perched on plough (vert)	1·75	2·25

427 Lumber and House under Construction

1987. "Gifex '87" International Forestry Exposition, Accra. Multicoloured.

1204	5c. Type **427**	10	10
1205	15c. Planks and furniture	15	15
1206	25c. Felled trees	25	25
1207	200c. Logs and wood carvings	1·60	2·25

1987. Appearance of Halley's Comet (1986). As T 151a of Gambia. Multicoloured.

1208	5c. Mikhail Lomonosov (scientist) and Chamber of Curiosities, St. Petersburg	20	10
1209	25c. Lunar probe "Surveyor 3", 1966	70	30

1210	200c. Wedgwood plaques for Isaac Newton, 1790 and "Apollo 11" Moon landing, 1968	3·25	2·25
MS1211	100×70 mm. 250c. Halley's Comet	4·75	2·75

428 Demonstrator and Arms breaking Shackles

1987. Solidarity with the People of Southern Africa. Multicoloured.

1212	5c. Type **428**	10	10
1213	15c. Miner and gold bars	40	15
1214	25c. Xhosa warriors	30	25
1215	100c. Nelson Mandela and shackles	1·25	3·00
MS1216	70×90 mm. 150c. Nelson Mandela	1·50	2·00

429 Aerophones

1987. Musical Instruments. Multicoloured.

1217	5c. Type **429**	10	10
1218	15c. Xylophone	15	15
1219	25c. Chordophones	30	25
1220	100c. Membranophones	1·00	1·25
MS1221	90×70 mm. 200c. Idiophones	1·90	2·25

430 Woman filling Water Pot at Pump

1987. Int Year of Shelter for the Homeless. Mult.

1222	5c. Type **430**	10	10
1223	15c. Building house from breeze blocks	15	15
1224	25c. Modern village with stream	20	25
1225	100c. Modern houses with verandahs	75	1·25

431 Ga Women preparing Kpokpoi for Homowo Festival

1988. Ghana Festivals. Multicoloured.

1226	5c. Type **431**	10	10
1227	15c. Efute hunters with deer, Aboakyir festival	15	15
1228	25c. Fanti chief dancing at Odwira festival	25	25
1229	100c. Chief in palanquin, Yam festival	65	1·25

432 Port Installation

1988. 5th Anniv (1987) of 31 December Revolution. Multicoloured.

1230	5c. Type **432**	1·25	40
1231	15c. Repairing railway line	12·00	2·50
1232	25c. Planting cocoa	1·75	55
1233	100c. Miners with ore truck	13·00	14·00

433 Nurse giving Injection

1988. UNICEF Global Immunization Campaign. Multicoloured.

1234	5c. Type **433**	20	10
1235	15c. Girl receiving injection	25	20
1236	25c. Schoolgirl crippled by polio	35	50
1237	100c. Nurse giving oral vaccine to baby	60	2·25

434 Fishing

1988. 10th Anniv of International Fund for Agricultural Development. Multicoloured.

1238	5c. Type **434**	85	30
1239	15c. Women harvesting crops	1·40	40
1240	25c. Cattle	1·75	50
1241	100c. Village granaries	4·00	8·50

435 Akwadjan Men

1988. Tribal Costumes. Multicoloured.

1242	5c. Type **435**	15	10
1243	25c. Banaa man	35	20
1244	250c. Agwasen woman	1·50	2·00

1988. Nos. 460, 464/6, 469/70, 474, 1031a, 1038/42, 1044 and 1046 surch.

1245	-	20c. on 50p. green, orange and black (No. 1041)	30	30
1246	-	20c. on 1c. orange, blue and black (No. 1042)	30	30
1247	-	50c. on 10n.p. mult (No. 469)	2·00	2·00
1248	-	50c. on 20n.p. deep blue and blue (No. 470) (surch **C50**)	10·00	10·00
1249	-	50c. on 20n.p. deep blue and blue (No. 470) (surch **C50.00**)	10·00	10·00
1250	-	50c. on 10p. mult (No. 1039)	1·00	2·00
1251	-	50c. on 1c. on 20n.p. deep blue and blue (No. 1031a) (surch **C50**)	6·00	5·00
1252	-	50c. on 1c. on 20n.p. deep blue and blue (No. 1031a) (surch **C50.00**)	10·00	10·00
1254	-	50c. on 1c. orange, blue and black (No. 1042)	6·00	30
1254b	–	50c. on 2n.c.50 multi-coloured	50	15
1255	**230**	60c. on 1n.p. mult	6·00	60
1256	-	60c. on 4n.p. mult (No. 465)	6·00	1·00
1257	-	60c. on 3c. mult (No. 1044)	1·00	45
1258	**400**	80c. on 5p. multicol-oured	1·00	45
1259	-	80c. on 5c. mult (No. 1046)	10·00	10·00
1260	-	100c. on 3n.p. mult (No. 464)	12·00	12·00
1261	-	100c. on 20n.p. deep blue and blue (No. 470)	10·00	10·00
1262	-	100c. on 20p. mult (No. 1040)	1·00	1·00
1263	-	100c. on 3c. mult (No. 1044)	2·00	2·00
1264	-	200c. on 6n.p. mult (No. 466)	8·00	10·00

440 Boxing

1988. Olympic Games, Seoul. Multicoloured.

1265	20c. Type **440**	20	15
1266	60c. Athletics	45	55
1267	80c. Discus-throwing	50	80
1268	100c. Javelin-throwing	60	1·10
1269	350c. Weightlifting	1·40	3·00
MS1270	75×105 mm. As 80c.	4·00	3·00

441 Nutrition Lecture

1988. 125th Anniv of Int Red Cross. Mult.

1271	20c. Type **441**	40	15
1272	50c. Red Cross volunteer with blind woman	90	90
1273	60c. Distributing flood relief supplies	1·00	1·00
1274	200c. Giving first aid	2·50	3·25

442 Tropical Forest

1988. Christmas. Multicoloured.

1275	20c. Type **442**	15	10
1276	60c. Christ Child (vert)	35	35
1277	80c. Virgin and Child with Star (vert)	50	60
1278	100c. Three Wise Men follow-ing Star	60	70
1279	350c. Symbolic Crucifixion (vert)	2·00	2·50
MS1280	100×70 mm. 500c. Virgin and Child (vert)	2·00	2·75

443 "African Solidarity"

1989. 25th Anniv (1988) of Organization of African Unity. Multicoloured.

1281	20c. Type **443**	10	10
1282	50c. O.A.U. Headquarters Addis Ababa	15	20
1283	60c. Emperor Haile Selassie and Ethiopian flag (horiz)	30	25
1284	200c. Kwame Nkrumah (former Ghanaian President) and flag (horiz)	60	85

444 "Amor"

1989. 500th Birth Anniv of Titian (artist). Multicoloured.

1285	20c. Type **444**	30	15
1286	60c. "The Appeal"	55	45
1287	80c. "Bacchus and Ariadne" (detail)	60	55
1288	100c. "Portrait of a Musician"	70	1·00
1289	350c. "Philip II seated"	1·40	4·00
MS1290	77×115 mm. 500c. "Portrait of a Gentleman"	2·50	2·75

1989. Olympic Medal Winners, Seoul. Nos. 1251/5 optd.

1291	20c. Type **436** (optd **A. ZUELOW DDR 60 KG**)	50	10
1292	60c. Athletics (optd **G. BORDIN ITALY MARATHON**)	65	25
1293	80c. Discus-throwing (optd **J. SCHULT DDR**)	70	30
1294	100c. Javelin-throwing (optd **T. KORJUS FINLAND**)	70	35
1295	350c. Weightlifting (optd **B. GUIDIKOV BULGARIA 75 KG**)	1·75	1·10
MS1296	75×105 mm. 500c. As 80c. (optd **GOLD J. SCHULT DDR SILVER R. OUBARTAS USSR BRONZE R. DANNEBERG W. GERMANY** on sheet margin)	2·40	2·10

1989. Various stamps surch. (a) Nos. 949/50 and 952/4.

1297	80c. on 65p. Prince Charles and Lady Diana Spencer	80	80
1298	100c. on 80p. Prince Charles on visit to Ghana	90	1·00
1299	100c. on 1c. Prince Charles on visit to Ghana	90	1·00
1300	300c. on 3c. Type **385**	2·25	2·75
1301	500c. on 4c. Type **385**	3·50	4·50

(b) Nos. 1048/51 and MS1053.

1302	60c. on 1c. Type **401**	1·10	50
1303	80c. on 1c.40 Satellite dish aerial	1·25	65
1304	200c. on 2c.30 Cable and cable-laying ship	3·00	3·00
1305	300c. on 3c. Switchboard operators	3·25	4·00
MS1306	95×70 mm. 500c. on 6c. Space satellite	5·00	6·00

(c) Nos. 1104/7 and MS1109.

1307	60c. on 1c. Type **408**	30	30
1308	80c. on 1c.40 Boxing	40	40
1309	200c. on 2c.30 Hockey	1·25	1·60
1310	300c. on 3c. Men's 400 metre hurdles race	1·40	1·75
MS1311	103×78 mm. 600c. on 70c. Football	3·00	4·50

(d) Nos. 1134/7 and MS1139.

1312	60c. on 1c. Type **408** (optd **VALERIE BRISCO-HOOKS U.S.A.**)	1·25	1·00
1313	80c. on 1c.40 Boxing (optd **U.S. WINNERS**)	1·50	1·25
1314	200c. on 2c.30 Field hockey (optd **PAKISTAN (FIELD HOCKEY)**)	4·25	4·25
1315	300c. on 3c. Men's 400 metre hurdles race (optd **EDWIN MOSES U.S.A.**)	4·25	4·75
MS1316	103×78 mm. 600c. on 70c. Football (optd **FRANCE**)	5·00	6·00

(e) Nos. 1140/2. and MS1143.

1317	80c. on 5c. Type **414**	35	40
1318	250c. on 12c. At Ascot Races	1·10	1·75
1319	300c. on 100c. At Clarence House on her 84th birthday	1·25	1·75
MS1320	56×84 mm. 500c. on 110c. With Prince Charles at Garter Ceremony	3·25	4·50

(f) Nos. 1159/61 and MS1163.

1321	80c. on 5c. Type **418**	2·50	1·00
1322	100c. on 8c. Barred owl	3·75	2·50
1323	300c. on 12c. Black-throated mango	4·25	4·75
MS1324	85×115 mm. 500c. on 110c. Downy Woodpecker	9·00	9·00

(g) Nos. 1190/2 and MS1194.

1325	60c. on 5c. Type **424**	45	45
1326	200c. on 15c. Player taking control of ball	1·50	2·00
1327	300c. on 25c. Player kicking ball	2·00	2·75
MS1328	90×70 mm. 600c. on 150c. Player kicking ball (different)	7·50	8·50

(h) As Nos. 1190/2 and MS1194 but with unissued opt WINNERS Argentina 3 W.Germany 2.

1329	60c. on 5c. Type **424**	1·00	40
1330	200c. on 15c. Player taking control of ball	2·00	2·50
1331	300c. on 25c. Player kicking ball	2·50	3·00
MS1332	90×70 mm. 600c. on 150c. Player kicking ball (different)	4·00	5·00

(i) Nos. 1208/10.

1333	60c. on 5c. Mikhail Lomonosov (scientist) and Chamber of Curiosities, St. Petersburg	1·10	60
1334	80c. on 25c. Lunar probe "Surveyor 3", 1966	1·50	85
1335	500c. on 200c. Wedgwood plaques for Isaac Newton, 1790, and "Apollo 11" Moon landing, 1968	4·25	6·00
MS1336	100×70 mm. 750c. on 250c. Halley's Comet	4·50	5·50

(j) As Nos. 1208/10 and MS1211 optd HALLEYS COMET 1985 - OFFICIAL - 1996 and emblem.

1337	60c. on 5c. Mikhail Lomonosov (scientist) and Chamber of Curiosities, St. Petersburg	50	40
1338	80c. on 25c. Lunar probe "Surveyor 3", 1966	50	50
1339	500c. on 200c. Wedgwood plaques for Isaac Newton, 1790, and "Apollo 11" Moon landing, 1968	2·75	4·75
MS1340	100×70 mm. 750c. on 250c. Halley's Comet	6·50	8·00

448 French Royal Standard and Field Gun

1989. "Philexfrance 89" International Stamp Exhibition, Paris. Multicoloured.

1341	20c. Type **448**	60	25
1342	60c. Regimental standard, 1789, and French infantry- man	1·25	90
1343	80c. Revolutionary standard, 1789, and pistol	1·50	1·00
1344	350c. Tricolour, 1794, and musket	3·75	5·50
MS1345	77×106 mm. 600c. Street plan of Paris, 1789 (horiz)	3·00	3·50

1989. Japanese Art. Portraits. As T 177a of Gambia. Multicoloured.

1346	20c. "Minamoto-no-Yoritomo" (Fujiwara-no-Takanobu) (vert)	35	20
1347	50c. "Takami Senseki" (Watan- abe Kazan) (vert)	50	30
1348	60c. "Ikkyu Sojun" (study) (Bokusai) (vert)	55	35
1349	75c. "Nakamura Kuranosuka" (Ogata Korin) (vert)	60	40
1350	125c. "Portrait of a Lady" (Kyoto branch, Kano School) (vert)	85	75
1351	150c. "Portrait of Zemmui" (anon, 12th-century) (vert)	85	80
1352	200c. "Ono no Komachi the Poetess" (Hokusai) (vert)	1·00	1·25
1353	500c. "Kobo Daisi as a Child" (anon) (vert)	2·50	3·50
MS1354	Two sheets, each 102×77 mm. (a) 500c. "Kodai-no-Kimi" (attr Fujiwara-no-Nobuzane) (vert). (b) 500c. "Emperor Hanazono" (Fujiwara-no-Goshin) Set of 2 sheets	8·50	8·50

449 Storming the Bastille

1989. Bicentenary of French Revolution. Mult.

1355	20c. Type **449**	55	20
1356	60c. Declaration of Human Rights	1·00	50
1357	80c. Storming the Bastille (horiz)	1·25	75
1358	200c. Revolution monument (horiz)	2·25	2·50
1359	350c. Tree of Liberty (horiz)	3·00	4·25

450 "Collybia fusipes"

1989. Fungi (1st series). Multicoloured.

1360	20c. Type **450**	25	25
1361	50c. "Coprinus comatus"	40	40
1362	60c. "Xerocomus subtomen- tosus"	40	45
1363	80c. "Lepista nuda"	55	55
1364	150c. "Suillus placidus"	80	95
1365	200c. "Lepista nuda" (different)	1·00	1·25
1366	300c. "Marasmius oreades"	1·50	1·75
1367	500c. "Agaricus campestris"	2·25	3·25
MS1368	Two sheets, each 110×80 mm. (a) 600c. "*Boletus rhodoxanthus*". (b) 600c. "*Amanita rubescens*" Set of 2 sheets	7·50	8·00

See also Nos. 1489/96.

451 "The Course of True Love ..."

1989. 425th Birth Anniv of Shakespeare. Verses and scenes from "A Midsummer Night's Dream". Multicoloured.

1369	40c. Type **451**	75	65
1370	40c. "Love looks not with the eye but with the mind"	75	65
1371	40c. "Nature here shows art"	75	65
1372	40c. "Things growing are not ripe till their season"	75	65
1373	40c. "He is defiled that draws a sword on thee"	75	65
1374	40c. "It is not enough to speak, but to speak true"	75	65
1375	40c. "Thou art as wise as thou are beautiful"	75	65
1376	40c. Wildcat in wood (face value at left)	75	65
1377	40c. Man	75	65
1378	40c. Woman with flower	75	65
1379	40c. King and queen	75	65
1380	40c. Bottom	75	65
1381	40c. Wildcat in wood (face value at right)	75	65
1382	40c. Woman	75	65
1383	40c. Leopard	75	65
1384	40c. Tree trunk and man	75	65
1385	40c. Meadow flowers	75	65
1386	40c. Mauve flowers	75	65
1387	40c. Plants	75	65
1388	40c. Lion	75	65
1389	40c. Fern and flowers	75	65

Nos. 1369/89 were printed together, forming a composite design.

451a Bronze Mannikin

1989. Birds. Multicoloured.

1390	20c. Type **451a**	30	10
1391	50c. African pied wagtail	45	30
1392	60c. African pygmy kingfisher (inscr "Halcyon malimbicus")	1·25	1·75
1392a	60c. African pygmy kingfisher (inscr "Ispidina picta")	3·00	3·00
1393	80c. Blue-breasted kingfisher (inscr "Ispidina picta")	1·75	2·25
1393a	80c. Blue-breasted kingfisher (inscr "Halcyon malimbicus")	3·00	3·00
1394	150c. Striped kingfisher (vert)	1·10	1·25
1395	200c. Shikra (vert)	1·25	1·40
1396	300c. Grey parrot (vert)	1·50	1·75
1397	500c. Black kite (vert)	2·50	3·25
MS1398	Two sheets. (a) 128×83 mm. 600c. Cinnamon-breasted rock bunting and barn swallow (horiz). (b) 83×128 mm. 600c. Senegal puff-back flycatcher Set of 2 sheets	14·00	14·00

452 Command Module "Columbia" orbiting Moon

1989. 20th Anniv of First Manned Landing on Moon. Multicoloured.

1399	20c. Type **452**	30	15
1400	80c. Neil Armstrong's footprint on Moon	50	60
1401	200c. Edwin Aldrin on Moon	1·25	1·75
1402	300c. "Apollo 11" capsule on parachutes	1·60	2·00
MS1403	Two sheets, each 100×72 mm. (a) 500c. Launch of "Apollo 11". (b) 500c. Earth seen from Moon Set of 2 sheets	5·50	7·00

453 Desertification of Pasture

1989. World Environment Day. Multicoloured.

1404	20c. Type **453**	50	15
1405	60c. Wildlife fleeing bush fire	90	80
1406	400c. Industrial pollution	2·75	3·50
1407	500c. Erosion	3·00	3·75

454 "Bebearia arcadius"

1990. Butterflies. Multicoloured.

1408	20c. Type **454**	45	20
1409	60c. "Charaxes laodice"	60	40
1410	80c. "Euryphura porphyrion"	70	45
1411	100c. "Neptis nicomedes"	80	50
1412	150c. "Citrinophila erastus"	1·00	90
1413	200c. "Aethiopana honorius	1·40	1·40
1414	300c. "Precis westermanni"	1·75	2·00
1415	500c. "Cymothoe hypatha"	2·25	3·00
MS1416	Two sheets, each 104×72 mm. (a) 600c. "Telipna acraea". (b) 600c. "Pentila abraxas" Set of 2 sheets	9·00	10·00

455 Great Ribbed Cockle

1990. Seashells. Multicoloured.

1417	20c. Type **455**	60	25
1418	60c. Elephant's snout	75	40
1419	80c. Garter cone	85	80
1420	200c. Tankerville's ancilla	2·25	2·50
1421	350c. Coronate prickly-winkle	3·00	4·00

456 Nehru welcoming President Nkrumah of Ghana

1990. Birth Centenary of Jawaharlal Nehru (Indian statesman). Multicoloured.

1422	20c. Type **456**	60	25
1423	60c. Nehru addressing Bandung Conference, 1955	75	30
1424	80c. Nehru with garland and flowers (vert)	80	55
1425	200c. Nehru releasing pigeon (vert)	1·25	1·50
1426	350c. Nehru (vert)	1·75	2·75

457 Wyon Medal, 1838

1990. 150th Anniv of the Penny Black.

1427	**457**	20c. black and violet	40	20
1428	-	60c. black and green	80	30
1429	-	80c. black and violet	1·00	35
1430	-	200c. black and green	1·50	1·25
1431	-	350c. black and green	2·00	2·50
1432	-	400c. black and red	2·50	3·00
MS1433		Two sheets, each 112×83 mm. (a) 600c. brown and black; (b) 600c. brown, buff and black Set of 2 sheets	6·50	8·00

DESIGNS: 60, 600c. (**MS**1433b) Bath mail coach, 1840; 80c. Leeds mail coach, 1840; 200c. Proof of Queen's head engraved by Heath, 1840; 350c. Master die, 1840; 400c. London mail coach, 1840; 600c. (**MS**1433a) Printing the Penny Black.

458 Anniversary Emblem

1990. 10th Anniv (1989) of 4 June Revolution. Multicoloured.

1434	20c. Type **458**	15	15
1435	60c. Foodstuffs	20	20
1436	80c. Cocoa	25	30
1437	200c. Mining	1·50	1·75
1438	350c. Scales of Justice and sword	1·75	2·25

459 Map of Africa and Satellite Network

1990. 25th Anniv of Intelsat Satellite System. Multicoloured.

1439	20c. Type **459**	20	20
1440	60c. Map of Americas	30	30
1441	80c. Map of Asia and Pacific	35	35
1442	200c. Map of South America and Africa	90	1·00
1443	350c. Map of Indian Ocean and Pacific	1·50	2·00

460 Housewife using Telephone

1990. 2nd Anniv of Introduction of International Direct Dialling Service. Multicoloured.

1444	20c. Type **460**	25	20
1445	60c. Businessman using telephone	35	35
1446	80c. Man using phonecard telephone	40	40
1447	200c. Public telephones for internal and IDD services	90	1·00
1448	350c. Satellite station	1·50	2·00

461 Blue Flycatcher

1990. African Tropical Rain Forest. Multicoloured.

1449	40c. Type **461**	90	90
1450	40c. Boomslang (snake)	90	90
1451	40c. Superb sunbird	90	90
1452	40c. Bateleur	90	90
1453	40c. Yellow-casqued hornbill	90	90
1454	40c. "Salamis temora" (butterfly)	90	90
1455	40c. Potto	90	90
1456	40c. Leopard	90	90
1457	40c. Bongo	90	90
1458	40c. Grey parrot	90	90
1459	40c. Okapi	90	90
1460	40c. Gorilla	90	90
1461	40c. Flap-necked chameleon	90	90
1462	40c. West African dwarf crocodile	90	90
1463	40c. Python	90	90
1464	40c. Giant ground pangolin	90	90
1465	40c. "Pseudacraea boisduvali" (butterfly)	90	90
1466	40c. North African crested porcupine	90	90
1467	40c. Rosy-columned aerangis (orchid)	90	90
1468	40c. "Cymothoe sangaris" (butterfly)	90	90
MS1469	100×75 mm. 600c. Head of leopard (vert)	4·50	5·00

Nos. 1449/68 were printed together, se-tenant, forming a composite design.

462 Jupiter

1990. Space Flight of "Voyager 2". Multicoloured.

1470	100c. Type **462**	85	85
1471	100c. Neptune and Triton	85	85
1472	100c. Ariel, moon of Uranus	85	85
1473	100c. Saturn from Mimas	85	85
1474	100c. Saturn	85	85
1475	100c. Rings of Saturn	85	85
1476	100c. Neptune	85	85
1477	100c. Uranus from Miranda	85	85
1478	100c. Volcano on Io	85	85
MS1479	Two sheets. (a) 111×81 mm. 600c. "Voyager 2" spacecraft (vert). (b) 80×111 mm. 600c. Lift off of "Voyager 2" (vert) Set of 2 sheets	4·75	6·00

463 "Eulophia guineensis"

1990. Orchids. Multicoloured.

1480	20c. Type **463**	45	45
1481	40c. "Eurychone roth-schildiana"	60	60
1482	60c. "Bulbophyllum barbigerum"	80	80
1483	80c. "Polystachya galeata"	1·10	1·10
1484	200c. "Diaphananthe kamerunensis"	2·00	1·75
1485	300c. "Podangis dactyloceras"	2·25	2·00
1486	400c. "Ancistrochilus rothschildianus"	2·50	2·00
1487	500c. "Rangaeris muscicola"	2·75	2·00
MS1488	Two sheets, each 101×70 mm. (a) 600c. "Bolusiella imbricata". (b) "Diaphananthe rotila" Set of 2 sheets	13·00	14·00

464 "Coprinus atramentarius"

1990. Fungi (2nd series). Multicoloured.

1489	20c. Type **464**	70	45
1490	50c. "Marasmius oreades"	90	65
1491	60c. "Oudemansiella radicata"	1·00	70
1492	80c. "Boletus edulis" (Cep)	1·25	90
1493	150c. "Hebeloma crustuliniforme"	2·00	1·50
1494	200c. "Coprinus micaceus"	2·25	2·00
1495	300c. "Macrolepiota procera" ("Lepiota procera")	2·50	2·50
1496	500c. "Amanita phalloides"	2·75	3·00
MS1497	Two sheets, each 104×82 mm. (a) Nos. 1489, 1491/2 and 1496. (b) Nos. 1490 and 1493/5 Set of 2 sheets	8·00	9·00

465 Italian and Swedish Players chasing Ball

1990. World Cup Football Championship, Italy. Multicoloured.

1498	20c. Type **465**	45	20
1499	50c. Egyptian player penetrating Irish defence	55	30
1500	60c. Cameroon players celebrating	60	30
1501	80c. Rumanian player beating challenge	70	40
1502	100c. Russian goalkeeper Dassayev	85	65
1503	150c. Roger Milla of Cameroon (vert)	1·40	1·10
1504	400c. South Korean player challenging opponent	2·25	2·50
1505	600c. Klinsman of West Germany celebrating	2·75	3·50
MS1506	Two sheets, each 88×98 mm. (a) 800c. United Arab Emirates player watching ball. (b) 800c. Colombian player Set of 2 sheets	5·50	6·50

1990. 350th Death Anniv of Rubens. As T 195c of Gambia, but vert. Multicoloured.

1507	20c. "Duke of Mantua"	45	20
1508	50c. "Jan Brant"	60	30
1509	60c. "Portraits of a Young Man"	65	30
1510	80c. "Michel Ophovius"	75	40
1511	100c. "Caspar Gevaerts"	85	65
1512	200c. "Head of Warrior" (detail)	1·50	1·50
1513	300c. "Study of a Bearded Man"	2·00	2·50
1514	400c. "Paracelsus"	2·50	3·50
MS1515	Two sheets, each 71×100 mm. (a) 600c. "Warrior with two Pages" (detail). (b) 600c. "Archduke Ferdinand" (detail) Set of 2 sheets	8·00	9·00

466 Manganese Ore

1991. Minerals. Multicoloured.

1516	20c. Type **466**	55	30
1517	60c. Iron ore	70	60
1518	80c. Bauxite ore	90	75
1519	200c. Gold ore	2·00	2·00
1520	350c. Diamond	3·00	4·00
MS1521	70×90 mm. 600c. Uncut and cut diamonds	9·50	10·00

467 Dance Drums

1991. Tribal Drums. Multicoloured.

1522	20c. Type **467**	50	20
1523	60c. Message drums	1·00	40
1524	80c. War drums	1·25	50
1525	200c. Dance drums (different)	2·25	2·50
1526	350c. Ceremonial drums	2·75	4·50
MS1527	70×90 mm. 600c. Drum with carrying strap	7·50	8·50

468 "Amorphophallus dracontioides"

1991. Flowers (1st series). Multicoloured.

1528	20c. Type **468**	85	25
1529	60c. "Anchomanes difformis"	1·25	50
1530	80c. "Kaemferia nigerica"	1·50	70
1531	200c. "Aframomum sceptrum"	2·50	3·00
1532	350c. "Amorphophallus flavovirens"	2·75	4·00
MS1533	70×90 mm. 600c. "Amorphophallus flavovirens" (different)	6·00	6·50

1991. Flowers (2nd series). As T 468 but inscr "GHANA" in capitals. Multicoloured.

1534	20c. "Urginea indica"	55	25
1535	60c. "Hymencallis littoralis"	90	50
1536	80c. "Crinum jagus"	1·75	80
1537	200c. "Dipcadi tacazzeanum"	2·25	3·00
1538	350c. "Haemanthus rupestris"	2·75	4·00
MS1539	70×90 mm. 600c. "Urginea indica" (different)	6·00	6·50

469 Transport and Telecommunication Symbols

1991. 40th Anniv of United Nations Development Programme. Multicoloured.

1540	20c. Type **469**	55	20
1541	60c. Agricultural research	80	40
1542	80c. Literacy	90	55
1543	200c. Advances in agricultural crop growth	1·75	2·00
1544	350c. Industrial symbols	2·75	4·00

470 Drawing of Scout from First Handbook

1991. 50th Death Anniv of Lord Baden-Powell.

1545	**470**	20c. black and buff	90	20
1546	-	50c. grey, blue and black	1·10	40
1547	-	60c. multicoloured	1·10	45
1548	-	80c. black and buff	1·40	55
1549	-	100c. multicoloured	2·00	75
1550	-	200c. multicoloured	2·50	2·00
1551	-	500c. multicoloured	3·50	4·00
1552	-	600c. multicoloured	3·75	5·50
MS1553		Two sheets. (a) 104×75 mm. 800c. multicoloured. (b) 74×105 mm. 800c. multicoloured Set of 2 sheets	10·00	11·00

DESIGNS—VERT: 50c. Lord Baden-Powell; 80c. Handbook illustrations by Norman Rockwell; 500c. Scout at prayer. HORIZ: 60c. Hands holding Boy Scout emblem; 100c. Mafeking Siege 1d. Goodyear stamp and African runner; 200c. Scouts with Blitz victim, London, 1944; 600c. Mafeking Siege 1d. Goodyear stamp; 800c. (**MS**1553a) Scout camp; 800c. (**MS**1553b) Envelope from Mafeking Siege.

471 Women sorting Fish

1991. Chorkor Smoker (fish smoking process). Multicoloured.

1554	20c. Type **471**	30	20
1555	60c. Cleaning the ovens	55	40
1556	80c. Washing fish	65	55
1557	200c. Laying fish on pallets	1·25	1·50
1558	350c. Stacking pallets over ovens	1·75	2·50

472 African Hind

1991. Fishes. Multicoloured.

1559	20c. Type **472**	25	25
1560	50c. Shrew squeaker	40	40
1561	80c. West African triggerfish	55	55
1562	100c. Stonehead	70	70
1563	200c. Lesser pipefish	1·50	1·50
1564	300c. Aba	1·60	1·60
1565	400c. Jewel cichlid	1·75	1·75
1566	500c. Smooth hammerhead	1·90	1·90
MS1567	Two sheets, each 108×81 mm. (a) 800c. Bayad. (b) 800c. Eastern flying gurnard Set of 2 sheets	6·00	7·00

1991. Death Centenary (1990) of Vincent van Gogh (artist). As T 200b of Gambia. Multicoloured.

1568	20c. "Reaper with Sickle"	35	25
1569	50c. "The Thresher"	55	40
1570	60c. "The Sheaf-Binder"	60	50
1571	80c. "The Sheep-Shearers"	70	65
1572	100c. "Peasant Woman cutting Straw"	85	80
1573	200c. "The Sower"	1·60	1·75
1574	500c. "The Plough and the Harrow" (horiz)	2·25	2·50
1575	600c. "The Woodcutter"	2·25	2·50
MS1576	Two sheets, each 117×80 mm. (a) 800c. "Evening: The Watch" (horiz). (b) 800c. "Evening: The End of the Day" (horiz). Imperf Set of 2 sheets	9·00	9·50

473 Gamal Nasser (Egypt) and Conference Hall

1991. 10th Non-Aligned Ministers' Conference, Accra. Statesmen. Multicoloured.

1577	20c. Type **473**	50	30
1578	60c. Josip Tito (Yugoslavia)	55	45
1579	80c. Pandit Nehru (India)	4·00	1·75
1580	200c. Kwame Nkrumah (Ghana)	1·75	2·25
1581	350c. Achmad Sukarno (Indonesia)	1·90	3·50

474 Green-winged Pytila

1991. Birds. As T 474. Multicoloured.

1582-1629	80c.×16, 100c.×32		
MS1630	Three sheets, each 107×86 mm. (a) 800c. Marabou stork. (b) 800c. African fish eagle. (c) 800c. Saddle-bill stork Set of 3 sheets	12·00	13·00

Nos. 1582/1629 were issued together, se-tenant, as three sheetlets of 16 forming composite designs. The 80c. values show Green-winged pytilia, Orange-cheeked waxbill, African paradise flycatcher, Great blue turaco ("Blue plantain-eater"), Red bishop, Splendid glossy starling, Red-faced lovebird, African palm swift, Narina's trogon ("Narina Trogon"), Tawny eagle, Bateleur, Hoopoe, Secretary bird, African white-backed vulture, White-necked bald crow ("Bare-headed rockfowl"), Abyssinian ground hornbill, and the 100c. African open-bill stork, African spoonbill, Pink-backed pelican, Little bittern, Purple swamphen ("King reed-hen"), Saddle-bill stork, Glossy ibis, White-faced whistling duck, Black-headed heron, Hammerkop, African darter, Woolly-necked stork, Yellow-billed stork, Black-winged stilt, Goliath heron, African jacana ("Lily trotter"), Shikra, Abyssinian roller, Carmine bee eater, Pin-tailed whydah, Purple glossy starling, Yellow-mantled whydah, Pel's fishing owl, Crested touraco, Red-cheeked cordon-bleu, Olive-bellied sunbird, Red-billed hornbill, Red-billed quelea, South African crowned crane, Indian blue quail ("Blue Quail"), Egyptian vulture and Helmeted guineafowl.

475 "Nularda" (beetle)

1991. Insects. Multicoloured.

1631	20c. Type **475**	70	20
1632	50c. "Zonocrus" (grasshopper)	85	30
1633	60c. "Gryllotalpa africana" (mole cricket)	95	30
1634	80c. Weevil	1·10	60
1635	100c. "Coenagrion" (dragonfly)	1·40	70
1636	150c. "Sahlbergella" (fly)	1·75	2·25
1637	200c. "Anthia" (ant)	2·00	2·50
1638	350c. "Megacephala" (beetle)	2·50	2·75
MS1639	106×79 mm. 600c. "Lacetus" (lacewing)	10·00	11·00

476 Boti Falls

1991. Multicoloured.

1639a	20c. Oil palm fruit	20	10
1640	50c. Type **476**	40	10
1641	60c. Larabanga Mosque (horiz)	40	10
1642	80c. Fort Sebastian, Shama (horiz)	40	10
1643	100c. Cape Coast Castle (horiz)	1·75	30
1644	200c. White-toothed cowrie (horiz)	3·00	75

1645	400c. True achatina (horiz)	4·00	1·25

1991. Christmas. Religious Paintings. As T 200c of Gambia. Multicoloured.

1646	20c. "Adoration of the Magi" (Bosch)	55	20
1647	50c. "The Annunciation" (Campin)	75	30
1648	60c. "Virgin and Child" (detail) (Bouts)	80	30
1649	80c. "Presentation in the Temple" (Memling)	1·00	50
1650	100c. "Virgin and Child enthroned with Angel and Donor" (Memling)	1·25	65
1651	200c. "Virgin and Child with Saints and Donor" (Van Eyck)	2·00	2·00
1652	400c. "St. Luke painting the Virgin" (Van der Weyden)	3·00	3·75
1653	700c. "Virgin and Child" (Bouts)	4·25	6·00
MS1654	Two sheets, each 103×128 mm. (a) 800c. "Virgin and Child standing in a Niche" (Van der Weyden). (b) 800c. "The Annunciation" (Memling) Set of 2 sheets	7·50	9·00

477 Women collecting Water from Bore Hole

1992. Decade of Revolutionary Progress. Multicoloured.

1655	20c. Type **477**	15	10
1656	50c. Miners	40	15
1657	60c. Wood carver	30	15
1658	80c. Forestry	30	20
1659	200c. Cacao tree	60	75
1660	350c. Village electrification	1·00	1·75

478 Mount Fuji and Flying Fish

1992. "Phila Nippon '91" International Stamp Exhibition, Tokyo. Multicoloured.

1661	20c. Type **478**	65	30
1662	60c. Itsukushima Jingu Shrine	80	40
1663	80c. Geisha	1·00	50
1664	100c. Samurai house	1·40	70
1665	200c. Bonsai tree	2·25	1·75
1666	400c. Olympic Sports Hall	2·75	3·00
1667	500c. Great Buddha (statue)	2·75	3·00
1668	600c. Nagoya Castle	3·00	3·50
MS1669	Two sheets, each 109×80 mm. (a) 800c. Takamatsu Castle. (b) 800c. Heian Shrine Set of 2 sheets	13·00	14·00

479 East and West Germans celebrating

1992. Reunification of Germany. Multicoloured.

1670	20c. Type **479**	30	20
1671	60c. Signing Reunification Treaty	40	40
1672	80c. Chariot on Brandenburg Gate and fireworks	45	45
1673	1000c. Germans with unified currency	8·00	10·00
MS1674	Three sheets. (a) 109×78 mm. 400c. Doves and Brandenburg Gate; 400c. Chancellor Kohl and Prime Minister De Maizière. (b) 125×87 mm. 800c. Chancellor Kohl and members of last German Democratic Republic administration. (c) 130×92 mm. 300c. President Gorbachev (vert); 300c. Chancellor Kohl (vert); 300c. Map of Western Germany (face value in black) (vert); 300c. Map of Eastern Germany (face value in white) (vert) Set of 3 sheets	13·00	13·00

480 Steam Side-tank Locomotive, 1903

1992. Ghanaian Railways. Multicoloured.

1675	20c. Type **480**	55	30
1676	50c. AIA-AIA diesel locomotive	75	40
1677	60c. First class coach, 1931	75	45
1678	80c. Railway inspection coach No. 2212	80	70
1679	100c. Steam locomotive No. 401 on Kumasi turntable	1·10	90
1680	200c. Cocoa wagon, 1921	1·60	1·60
1681	500c. Steam locomotive No. 223 "Prince of Wales"	2·50	3·00
1682	600c. Cattle wagon	2·50	3·00
MS1683	Two sheets. (a) 106×76 mm. 800c. Beyer-Garratt steam locomotive No. 301, 1943. (b) 76×106 mm. 800c. German-built steam locomotive Set of 2 sheets	9·00	9·50

1992. Olympic Games, Albertville and Barcelona. Past Medal Winners. As T 203 of Gambia. Mutlcoloured.

1684	20c. E. Blay (Ghana) (boxing) and windmill	50	20
1685	60c. M. Ahey (Ghana) (athletics) and Catalan coat of arms	70	35
1686	80c. T. Wilson (U.S.A.) (70 m ski jump) and grapes	90	50
1687	100c. Four-man bobsleighing (East Germany) and passport	1·25	75
1688	200c. G. Louganis (U.S.A.) (platform diving) and decorative vase	2·00	1·50
1689	300c. L. Visser (Netherlands) (5000 m speed skating) and wine bottle cork	2·25	2·25
1690	350c. J. Passler (Italy) (biathlon) and lily	2·25	2·50
1691	400c. M. Retton (U.S.A.) (gymnastics) and silhouette of castle	2·50	2·75
1692	500c. J. Hingsen (West Germany) (decathlon) and gold and silver coins	2·50	2·75
1693	600c. R. Neubert (West Germany) (heptathlon) and leather work	2·50	3·00
MS1694	Two sheets. (a) 112×82 mm. 800c. Silhouette of windmill. (b) 82×112 mm. 800c. Silhouette of folk dancer (vert) Set of 2 sheets	12·00	13·00

481 "Angides lugubris"

1992. Reptiles. Multicoloured.

1695	20c. Type **481**	35	20
1696	50c. "Kinixys erosa" (tortoise)	50	30
1697	60c. "Agama agama" (lizard)	50	30
1698	80c. "Chameleo gracilis" (chameleon)	60	40
1699	100c. "Naja melanleuca" (snake)	70	50
1700	200c. "Crocodylus niloticus" (crocodile)	1·25	1·10
1701	400c. "Chelonia mydas" (turtle)	2·00	2·50
1702	500c. "Varanus exanthematicus" (lizard)	2·25	2·75
MS1703	94×66 mm. 600c. Tortoise and snake	3·00	4·00

1992. Easter. Religious Paintings. As T 204a of Gambia but vert designs. Multicoloured.

1704	20c. "The Four Apostles" (detail) (Durer)	40	20
1705	50c. "The Last Judgement" (detail) (Rubens)	60	30
1706	60c. "The Four Apostles" (different detail) (Durer)	60	30
1707	80c. "The Last Judgement" (different detail) (Rubens)	75	40
1708	100c. "Crucifixion" (Rubens)	90	50
1709	200c. "The Last Judgement" (different detail) (Rubens)	1·75	1·50
1710	500c. "Christum Videre" (Rubens)	2·75	3·50
1711	600c. "The Last Judgement" (different detail) (Rubens)	3·00	4·50
MS1712	Two sheets. (a) 69×100 mm. 800c. "Last Communion of St. Francis of Assisi" (detail) (Rubens) (vert). (b) 100×69 mm. 800c. "Scourging the Money Changers from the Temple" (detail) (El Greco) Set of 2 sheets	7·50	8·50

481a "Two Men at Table" (Velazquez)

1992. "Granada '92" International Stamp Exhibition, Spain. Spanish Paintings. Mult.

1713	20c. Type **481a**	40	20
1714	60c. "Christ in the House of Mary and Martha" (detail) (Velazquez)	55	30
1715	80c. "The Supper at Emmaus" (Velazquez)	65	40
1716	100c. "Three Musicians" (Velazquez)	75	50
1717	200c. "Old Woman cooking Eggs" (Velazquez) (vert)	1·50	90
1718	400c. "Old Woman cooking Eggs" (detail) (Velazquez) (vert)	2·50	2·75
1719	500c. "The Surrender of Breda" (detail) (Velazquez) (vert)	2·75	3·00
1720	700c. "The Surrender of Breda" (different detail) (Velazquez) (vert)	3·00	4·25
MS1721	Two sheets. (a) 95×120 mm. 900c. "The Waterseller of Seville" (Velazquez) (86×111 mm). (b) 120×95 mm. 900c. "They still Say that Fish is Expensive" (Joaquín Sorolla y Bastida) (111×86 mm). Imperf Set of 2 sheets	9·00	9·50

482 "Danaus chrysippus"

1992. "Genova '92" International Thematic Stamp Exhibition. Butterflies. Mult.

1722	20c. Type **482**	50	30
1723	60c. "Papilio dardanus"	80	45
1724	80c. "Cynthia cardui"	90	60
1725	100c. "Meneris tulbaghia"	1·00	75
1726	200c. "Salamis temora"	1·50	1·60
1727	400c. "Charaxes jasius"	2·00	2·50
1728	500c. "Precis oenone"	2·25	2·50
1729	700c. "Precis sophia"	2·50	2·75
MS1730	Two sheets, each 100×70 mm. (a) 900c. "Papilio demodocus". (b) 900c. "Precis octavia" Set of 2 sheets	7·50	8·50

1992. Prehistoric Animals. As T 207a of Gambia. Multicoloured.

1731	20c. Iguanodon	35	25
1732	50c. Anchisaurus	50	35
1733	60c. Heterodontosaurus	55	35
1734	80c. Ouranosaurus	60	45
1735	100c. Anatosaurus	75	55
1736	200c. Elaphrosaurus	1·25	1·50
1737	500c. Coelophysis	2·25	2·75
1738	600c. Rhamphorynchus	2·50	3·00
MS1739	Two sheets, each 100×70 mm. (a) 1500c. As 200c. (b) 1500c. As 500c. Set of 2 sheets	9·00	10·00

483 Martin Pinzon and "Pinta"

1992. World Columbian Stamp "Expo '92", Chicago. 500th Anniv of Discovery of America by Columbus. Multicoloured.

1740	200c. Type **483**	90	1·00
1741	200c. Vicente Pinzon and "Nina"	90	1·00
1742	200c. Columbus and Father Marchena at La Rabida	90	1·00
1743	200c. Columbus in his cabin	90	1·00
1744	200c. Fleet sights land	90	1·00
1745	200c. Columbus on Samana Cay	90	1·00
1746	200c. Wreck of "Santa Maria"	90	1·00
1747	200c. Amerindians at Spanish Court	90	1·00
MS1748	122×86 mm. 500c. Columbus and "Santa Maria"	3·75	4·25

484 Olive-grey Ancilla

1992. Shells. Multicoloured.

1749	20c. Type **484**	20	20
1750	20c. Radula cerith	20	20
1751	60c. Rugose donex	30	30
1752	60c. Horned murex	30	30
1753	80c. Concave ear moon	40	40
1754	80c. Triple twella	40	40
1755	200c. "Pila africana"	90	1·00
1756	200c. Rat cowrie	90	1·00
1757	350c. "Thais hiatula"	1·60	1·90
1758	350c. West African helmet	1·60	1·90
MS1759	Two sheets, each 87×117 mm. (a) 600c. Fanel moon ("Natica fanel"). (b) 600c. Giant hairy melongena ("Pugilina moria") Set of 2 sheets	6·00	7·00

485 "Presentation in the Temple" (Master of the Braunschweiti)

1992. Christmas. Religious Paintings. Mult.

1760	20c. Type **485**	50	20
1761	50c. "Presentation in the Temple" (detail) (Master of St. Severin)	70	30
1762	60c. "The Visitation" (Sebastiano del Piombo)	80	30
1763	80c. "The Visitation" (detail) (Giotto)	90	40
1764	100c. "The Circumcision" (detail) (Studio of Bellini)	1·10	50
1765	200c. "The Circumcision" (Studio of Garofalo)	2·00	1·60
1766	500c. "The Visitation" (Studio of Van der Weyden)	3·00	3·25
1767	800c. "The Visitation" (detail) (Studio of Van der Weyden)	3·50	5·50
MS1768	Two sheets, each 77×102 mm. (a) 900c. "Presentation in the Temple" (Bartolo di Fredi). (b) 900c. "The Visitation" (larger detail) (Giotto) Set of 2 sheets	7·50	9·00

486 "Calappa rubroguttata"

1993. Crabs. Multicoloured.

1769	20c. Type **486**	40	20
1770	60c. "Cardisoma amatum"	70	25
1771	80c. "Maia squinado"	80	30
1772	400c. "Ocypoda cursor"	1·75	2·00
1773	800c. "Grapus grapus"	2·50	3·25
MS1774	127×97 mm. Nos. 1769/73	6·50	6·50

487 "Clerodendrum thomsoniae"

1993. Flowers. Multicoloured.

1775	20c. Type **487**	20	15
1776	20c. "Lagerstroemia flos-reginae"	20	15
1777	60c. "Cassia fistula"	35	25
1778	60c. "Spathodea campanulata"	35	25

1779 80c. "Hildegardia barteri" 40 25
1780 80c. "Mellitea ferrugenea" 40 25
1781 200c. "Petrea volubilis" 60 85
1782 200c. "Ipomoea asarifolia" 60 85
1783 350c. "Bryphyllum pinnatum" 90 1·25
1784 350c. "Ritchiea reflexa" 90 1·25
MS1785 Two sheets, each 86×125 mm. (a) 50c. As No. 1777; 100c. As No. 1783; 150c. As No. 1782; 300c. As No. 1779. (b) 50c. As No. 1778; 100c. As No. 1776; 150c. As No. 1780; 300c. As No. 1784 Set of 2 sheets 4·50 5·00

488 Zeppelin LZ-3 entering Floating Hangar, Lake Constance

1993. Anniversaries and Events. Multicoloured.
1786 20c. Type **488** 85 30
1787 100c. Launch of European "Ariane 4" rocket (vert) 1·25 75
1788 200c. Leopard 2·00 1·75
1789 300c. Colosseum and fruit 2·25 2·50
1790 400c. Mozart (vert) 3·75 3·25
1791 600c. Launch of Japanese "H-1" rocket (vert) 3·75 4·25
1792 800c. Zeppelin LZ-10 "Schwaben" 3·75 5·00
MS1793 Four sheets. (a) 106×76 mm. 900c. Count Ferdinand von Zeppelin (vert). (b) 76×106 mm. 900c. Launch of American space shuttle (vert). (c) 106×76 mm. 900c. Bongo. (d) 99×69 mm. 900c. Cherubino from "The Marriage of Figaro" (vert) Set of 4 sheets 17·00 17·00
ANNIVERSARIES AND EVENTS: Nos. 1786, 1792, **MS**1793a, 75th death anniv of Count Ferdinand von Zeppelin; 1787, 1791, **MS**1793b, International Space Year; 1788, **MS**1793c, Earth Summit '92, Rio; 1789, International Conference on Nutrition, Rome; 1790, **MS**1793d, Death bicentenary of Mozart.

1993. Bicentenary of the Louvre, Paris. As T 209b of Gambia. Multicoloured.
1794 200c. "Carnival Minuet" (left detail) (Giovanni Domenico Tiepolo) 85 1·00
1795 200c. "Carnival Minuet" (centre detail) (Giovanni Domenico Tiepolo) 85 1·00
1796 200c. "Carnival Minuet" (right detail) (Giovanni Domenico Tiepolo) 85 1·00
1797 200c. "The Tooth Puller" (left detail) (Giovanni Domenico Tiepolo) 85 1·00
1798 200c. "The Tooth Puller" (right detail) (Giovanni Domenico Tiepolo) 85 1·00
1799 200c. "Rebecca at the Well" (Giovanni Battista Tiepolo) 85 1·00
1800 200c. "Presenting Christ to the People" (left detail) (Giovanni Battista Tiepolo) 85 1·00
1801 200c. "Presenting Christ to the People" (right detail) (Giovanni Battista Tiepolo) 85 1·00
MS1802 100×70 mm. 700c. "Chancellor Seguier" (Charles le Brun) (85×52 mm) 2·75 3·25

489 Energy Foods

1993. Int Conference on Nutrition, Rome. Mult.
1803 20c. Type **489** 30 15
1804 60c. Body-building foods 50 20
1805 80c. Protective foods 55 25
1806 200c. Disease prevention equipment 1·75 1·25
1807 400c. Quality control and preservation of fish products 2·25 3·00

490 Kwame Nkrumah Mausoleum

1993. Proclamation of 4th Republic. Mult.
1808 50c. Type **490** 20 15
1809 100c. Kwame Nkrumah Conference Centre 35 25
1810 200c. Book of Constitution (vert) 80 80
1811 350c. Independence Square (vert) 1·60 2·00
1812 400c. Christiansborg Castle (vert) 1·75 2·00

491 Resurrection Egg

1993. Easter. Faberge Eggs. Multicoloured.
1813 50c. Type **491** 40 15
1814 80c. Imperial Red Cross egg with Resurrection triptych 65 25
1815 100c. Imperial Uspensky Cathedral egg 75 25
1816 150c. Imperial Red Cross egg with portraits 1·10 65
1817 200c. Orange Tree egg 1·25 1·25
1818 250c. Rabbit egg 1·25 1·50
1819 400c. Imperial Coronation egg 2·00 2·50
1820 900c. Silver-gilt enamel Easter egg 3·25 5·00
MS1821 Two sheet. (a) 73×100 mm. 1000c. Renaissance egg. (b) 100×73 mm. 1000c. Egg charms (horiz) Set of 2 sheets 8·00 9·00

491a Mercedes Benz "300 SLR", Mille Miglia, 1955

1993. Centenaries of Henry Ford's First Petrol Engine (Nos. 1823/4) and Karl Benz's First Four-wheeled Car (others). Multicoloured.
1822 150c. Type **491a** 75 50
1823 400c. Ford "Depot Wagon", 1920 1·75 1·75
1824 600c. Ford "Mach 1 Mustang", 1970 2·25 2·75
1825 800c. Mercedes Benz racing car, Monaco Grand Prix, 1937 3·50 4·50
MS1826 Two sheets, each 110×80 mm. (a) 1000c. Mercedes Benz "Type 196" racing car, 1955 (85½×28½ mm). (b) 1000c. Ford "Super T", 1910 (85½×28½ mm) Set of 2 sheets 7·75 8·25

491b Airship "Graf Zeppelin" over Alps

1993. Aviation Anniversaries. Multicoloured.
1827 50c. Type **491b** 50 30
1828 150c. Airship LZ-7 "Deutschland" (horiz) 85 55
1829 400c. Avro Vulcan jet bomber (horiz) 1·75 1·75
1830 400c. U.S. Mail Ford Trimotor (horiz) 1·75 1·75
1831 600c. Nieuport 27 biplane 2·25 2·25
1832 600c. Loading mail on "Graf Zeppelin" 2·25 2·25
1833 800c. Airship LZ-10 "Schwaben" (horiz) 3·50 4·00
MS1834 Three sheets, each 111×80 mm. (a) 1000c. LZ-127 "Graf Zeppelin". (b) 1000c. S.E.5A, 1918. (c) 1000c. Early airmail flight by Walter Edwards between Portland and Vancouver (57×42½ mm) Set of 3 sheets 15·00 15·00
ANNIVERSARIES: Nos. 1827/28, 1833, **MS**1834a, 125th birth anniv of Hugo Eckener (airship commander); 1829, 1831, **MS**1834b, 75th anniv of Royal Air Force; 1830, 1832, **MS**1834c, Bicentenary of first airmail flight.

492 African Buffalo

1993. Wild Animals. Multicoloured.
1835 20c. Type **492** 30 15
1836 50c. Giant forest hog 40 20
1837 60c. Potto 45 25
1838 80c. Bay duiker 60 30
1839 100c. Royal antelope 70 35
1840 200c. Serval 1·25 90
1841 500c. Golden cat 2·00 2·75
1842 800c. "Megaloglossus woermanni" (bat) 3·25 4·00
MS1843 Two sheets, each 68×98 mm. (a) 900c. Dormouse. (b) 900c. White-collared mangabey Set of 2 sheets 8·50 9·00

1993. 40th Anniv of Coronation. Nos. 1549/53 optd 40TH ANNIVERSARY OF CORONATION H.M. ELIZABETH II.
1844 100c. multicoloured 1·25 30
1845 200c. multicoloured 2·00 1·00
1846 500c. multicoloured 4·00 4·00
1847 600c. multicoloured 4·00 4·50
MS1848 Two sheets. (a) 104×75 mm. 800c. multicoloured. (b) 74×105 mm. 800c. multicoloured Set of 2 sheets 12·00 12·00

1993. 35th Anniv of Rotary International and 60th Anniv of Ghana Red Cross Society (1992). Nos. 1562 and 1564/6 optd 35 YEARS OF ROTARY INTERNATIONAL GHANA 1958 (Nos. 1849, 1852, MS1853a) or GHANA RED CROSS SOCIETY FOUNDED 1932 and cross (others).
1849 100c. Stonehead 1·25 30
1850 300c. Aba 3·00 3·00
1851 400c. Jewel cichlid 3·25 3·50
1852 500c. Smooth hammerhead 3·75 4·25
MS1853 Two sheets, each 108×81 mm. (a) 800c. Bayad. (b) 800c. Eastern flying gurnard Set of 2 sheets 10·00 11·00

496 "Cantharellus cibarius"

1993. Mushrooms. Multicoloured.
1854 20c. Type **496** 40 25
1855 50c. "Russula cyanoxantha" 50 30
1856 60c. "Clitocybe rivulosa" 55 30
1857 80c. "Cortinarius elatior" 60 35
1858 80c. "Mycena galericulata" 60 35
1859 200c. "Tricholoma gambosum" 1·00 1·00
1860 200c. "Boletus edulis" 1·00 1·00
1861 200c. "Lepista saeva" 1·00 1·00
1862 250c. "Gyroporus castaneus" 1·10 1·10
1863 300c. "Boletus chrysenteron" 1·25 1·25
1864 350c. "Nolanea sericea" 1·40 1·40
1865 350c. "Hygrophorus punicea" ("Hygrophorus puiceus") 1·40 1·40
1866 500c. "Gomphidius glutinosus" 1·60 1·75
1867 600c. "Russula olivacea" 1·75 2·00
1868 1000c. "Russula aurata" 2·25 2·75
MS1869 Two sheets, each 85×130 mm. (a) 50c. As No. 1856; 100c. As No. 1858; 150c. As No. 1860; 1000c. As No. 1864. (b) 100c. As Type **496**; 150c. As No. 1857; 300c. As No. 1859; 600c. As No. 1865 Set of 2 sheets 9·50 11·00

497 "The Actor" (Picasso)

1993. Anniversaries and Events. Multicoloured.
1870 20c. Type **497** 75 50
1871 20c. Early astronomical equipment 1·25 50
1872 80c. "Portrait of Allan Stein" (Picasso) 85 50
1873 200c. Modern telescope 2·25 1·50
1874 200c. "Tattoo" (Lesek Sobocki) 1·50 1·50
1875 600c. "Prison" (Sasza Blonder) 2·75 3·50
1876 800c. "Seated Male Nude" (Picasso) 3·50 4·00
MS1877 Four sheets. (a) 75×105 mm. 900c. "Guernica" (Picasso). (b) 75×105 mm. 1000c. "Bajika o Czlowieku Szczesliwym" (detail) (Antoni Mickalak) (horiz). (c) 105×75 mm. 1000c. Copernicus (face value at top left). (d) 105×75 mm. 1000c. Copernicus (face value at centre top) Set of 4 sheets 14·00 15·00
ANNIVERSARIES AND EVENTS: Nos. 1870, 1872, 1876, **MS**1877a, 20th death anniv of Picasso (artist); 1871, 1873, **MS**1877c/d, 450th death anniv of Copernicus (astronomer); 1874/5, **MS**1877b, "Polska '93" International Stamp Exhibition, Poznan.

498 Abedi Pele (Ghana)

1993. World Cup Football Championship, U.S.A. (1st issue). Multicoloured.
1878 50c. Type **498** 80 35
1879 80c. Pedro Troglio (Argentina) 90 40
1880 100c. Fernando Alvez (Uruguay) 1·00 40
1881 200c. Franco Baresi (Italy) 2·00 1·25
1882 250c. Gomez (Colombia) and Katanec (Yugoslavia) 2·00 2·75
1883 600c. Diego Maradona (Argentina) 3·50 3·50
1884 800c. Hasek (Czechoslovakia) and Wynalda (U.S.A.) 3·50 4·25
1885 1000c. Lothar Matthaeus (Germany) 4·25 5·00
MS1886 Two sheets, each 70×100 mm. (a) 1200c. Rabie Yassein (Egypt) and Ruud Gullit (Netherlands). (b) 1200c. Giuseppe Giannini (Italy) Set of 2 sheets 12·00 13·00
See also Nos. 2037/43.

499 Common Turkey

1993. Domestic Animals. Multicoloured.
1887 50c. Type **499** 60 25
1888 100c. Goats 80 40
1889 150c. Muscovy ducks 1·25 75
1890 200c. Donkeys 1·50 1·00
1891 250c. Red junglefowl cock 1·50 1·25
1892 300c. Pigs 1·60 1·40
1893 400c. Helmeted guineafowl 1·90 1·75
1894 600c. Dog 2·75 3·00
1895 800c. Red junglefowl hen 3·25 3·75
1896 1000c. Sheep 3·75 4·25
MS1897 Two sheets, each 133×106 mm. (a) 100c. As No. 1888; 250c. No. 1894; 350c. No. 1892; 500c. No. 1896. (b) 100c. No. 1893; 250c. As No. 1891; 350c. No. 1895; 500c. Type **499** Set of 2 sheets 15·00 15·00

1993. Christmas. Religious Paintings. As T 221b of Gambia. Black, yellow and red (Nos. 1898, 1900/1, 1905 and MS1906a) or multicoloured (others).
1898 50c. "Adoration of the Magi" (Durer) 60 20
1899 100c. "The Virgin and Child with St. John and an Angel" (Botticelli) 80 25
1900 150c. "Mary as Queen of Heaven" (Durer) 1·00 45
1901 200c. "Saint Anne" (Durer) 1·25 65
1902 250c. "The Madonna of the Magnificat" (Botticelli) 1·40 75
1903 400c. "The Madonna of the Goldfinch" (Botticelli) 2·25 2·50
1904 600c. "The Virgin and Child with the young St. John the Baptist" (Botticelli) 3·00 3·75
1905 1000c. "Adoration of the Shepherds" (Durer) 4·25 6·50
MS1906 Two sheets, each 102×128 mm. (a) 1000c. "Madonna in a Circle" (detail) (Dürer). (b) 1000c. "Mystic Nativity" (detail) (Botticelli) (horiz) Set of 2 sheets 9·50 12·00

500 Doll

1994. Traditional Crafts. Multicoloured.

1907 50c. Type **500** 40 30
1908 50c. Pot with "head" lid 40 30
1909 200c. Bead necklace 1·00 1·00
1910 200c. Snake charmers (statuette) 1·00 1·00
1911 250c. Hoe 1·00 1·00
1912 250c. Scabbard 1·00 1·00
1913 600c. Pipe 2·25 2·75
1914 600c. Deer (carving) 2·25 2·75
1915 1000c. Mask 3·50 4·00
1916 1000c. Doll (different) 3·50 4·00
MS1917 Two sheets, each 95×128 mm. (a) 100c. As Type **500**; 250c. As No. 1909; 350c. As No. 1911; 500c. As No. 1913. (b) 100c. As No. 1908; 250c. As No. 1910; 350c. As No. 1912; 500c. As No. 1914 Set of 2 sheets 6·00 7·50

1994. "Hong Kong '94" International Stamp Exhibition (1st issue). As T 222a of Gambia. Multicoloured.

1918 200c. Hong Kong 1986 50c. "Expo '86" stamp and tram 1·00 1·25
1919 200c. Ghana 1992 20c. Railways stamp and tram 1·00 1·25

Nos. 1918/19 were printed together, se-tenant, forming a complete design. See also Nos. 1920/25.

1994. "Hong Kong '94" International Stamp Exhibition (2nd issue). Imperial Palace Clocks. As T 222b of Gambia. Multicoloured.

1920 100c. Windmill clock 1·10 1·10
1921 100c. Horse clock 1·10 1·10
1922 100c. Balloon clock 1·10 1·10
1923 100c. Zodiac clock 1·10 1·10
1924 100c. Shar-pei dog clock 1·10 1·10
1925 100c. Cat clock 1·10 1·10

501 Mickey Mouse in "Steamboat Willie", 1928

1994. 65th Anniv (1993) of Mickey Mouse (Walt Disney cartoon character) (1993). Scenes from various cartoon films.

1926 50c. Type **501** 60 15
1927 100c. "The Band Concert", 1935 80 20
1928 150c. "Moose Hunters", 1937 1·10 45
1929 200c. "Brave Little Tailor", 1938 1·25 60
1930 250c. "Fantasia", 1940 1·40 80
1931 400c. "The Nifty Nineties", 1941 2·25 2·75
1932 600c. "Canine Caddy", 1941 2·75 3·25
1933 1000c. "Mickey's Christmas Carol", 1983 3·50 4·25
MS1934 Two sheets, each 127×102 mm. (a) 1200c. "Mickey's Elephant", 1936. (b) 1200c. "Mickey's Amateurs", 1937 Set of 2 sheets 8·00 9·50

No. 1929 is inscribed "TAYLOR" in error. The dates on Nos. 1927 and 1932 are incorrectly shown as "1937" and "1944".

501a Boy Hiker

1994. Easter. Hummel Figurines. Multicoloured.

1935 50c. Type **501a** 35 15
1936 100c. Girl with basket behind back 45 20
1937 150c. Boy with rabbits 65 35
1938 200c. Boy holding basket 75 50
1939 250c. Girl with chicks 80 70
1940 400c. Girl with lamb 1·75 2·00
1941 600c. Girl waving red handkerchief with lamb 2·00 2·25
1942 1000c. Girl with basket and posy 2·75 3·25
MS1943 Two sheets, each 93×126 mm. (a) 50c. As No. 1935; 150c. As No. 1942; 500c. As No. 1936; 1200c. As No. 1938. (b) 200c. As No. 1940; 300c. As No. 1939; 500c. As No. 1941; 1000c. As No. 1937 Set of 2 sheets 7·50 8·00

502 Diana Monkey with Young

1994. Wildlife. Multicoloured.

1944 50c. Type **502** 40 15
1945 100c. Bushbuck (horiz) 40 20
1946 150c. Spotted hyena (horiz) 55 35
1947 200c. Diana monkey on branch facing left 75 50
1948 500c. Diana monkey on branch facing right 1·25 1·50
1949 800c. Head of Diana monkey 1·75 2·00
1950 1000c. Aardvark (horiz) 2·00 2·50
MS1951 Two sheets, each 106×76 mm. (a) 2000c. Leopard. (b) 2000c. Waterbuck Set of 2 sheets 10·00 11·00

Designs of Nos. 1944 and 1947/9 include the W.W.F. Panda emblem.

503 Norwegian Forest Cat

1994. Cats. Multicoloured.

1952 200c. Type **503** 50 50
1953 200c. Blue longhair 50 50
1954 200c. Red self longhair 50 50
1955 200c. Black longhair 50 50
1956 200c. Chinchilla 50 50
1957 200c. Dilute calico longhair 50 50
1958 200c. Blue tabby and white longhair 50 50
1959 200c. Ruby Somali 50 50
1960 200c. Blue smoke longhair 50 50
1961 200c. Calico longhair 50 50
1962 200c. Brown tabby longhair 50 50
1963 200c. Balinese 50 50
1964 200c. Sorrel Abyssinian 50 50
1965 200c. Silver classic tabby 50 50
1966 200c. Chocolate-point Siamese 50 50
1967 200c. Brown tortie Burmese 50 50
1968 200c. Exotic shorthair 50 50
1969 200c. Havana brown 50 50
1970 200c. Devon rex 50 50
1971 200c. Black Manx 50 50
1972 200c. British blue shorthair 50 50
1973 200c. Calico American wirehair 50 50
1974 200c. Spotted oriental Siamese 50 50
1975 200c. Red classic tabby 50 50
MS1976 Two sheets, each 102×89 mm. (a) 2000c. Brown mackerel tabby Scottish fold. (b) 2000c. Seal-point colourpoint Set of 2 sheets 8·50 9·00

No. 1957 is inscribed "Dilut" in error.

504 Red-bellied Paradise Flycatcher

1994. Birds. Multicoloured.

1977 200c. Type **504** 60 60
1978 200c. Many-coloured bush shrike 60 60
1979 200c. Broad-tailed paradise whydah 60 60
1980 200c. White-crowned robin chat 60 60
1981 200c. Violet turaco ("Violet plantain-eater") 60 60
1982 200c. Village weaver 60 60
1983 200c. Red-crowned bishop 60 60
1984 200c. Common shoveler 60 60
1985 200c. Spur-winged goose 60 60
1986 200c. African crake 60 60
1987 200c. Purple swamphen ("King reed-hen") 60 60
1988 200c. White-crested tiger bittern 60 60
1989 200c. Oriole warbler ("Moho") 60 60
1990 200c. Superb sunbird 60 60
1991 200c. Blue-breasted kingfisher 60 60
1992 200c. African blue cuckoo shrike 60 60
1993 200c. Great blue turaco ("Blue plantain-eater") 60 60
1994 200c. Greater flamingo 60 60
1995 200c. African jacana ("Lily-trotter") 60 60
1996 200c. Black-crowned night heron 60 60
1997 200c. Black-winged stilt 60 60
1998 200c. White-spotted crake 60 60
1999 200c. African pygmy goose 60 60
2000 200c. African pitta 60 60
MS2001 Two sheets, each 113×83 mm. (a) 2000c. African spoonbill. (b) 2000c. Goliath heron Set of 2 sheets 8·50 9·50

505 Women at Stand-pipe

1994. 1st Anniv of Fourth Republic. Multicoloured.

2002 50c. Type **505** 25 15
2003 100c. Presenting certificate to farmers 35 20
2004 200c. Village electricity supply 50 35
2005 600c. Bridge 1·75 2·00
2006 800c. National Theatre 1·75 2·25
2007 1000c. Lighting perpetual flame 2·00 2·75

1994. 25th Anniv of First Manned Moon Landing. As T 326 of Antigua showing scientists. Mult.

2008 300c. Sigmund Jahn 1·00 1·00
2009 300c. Ulf Merbold 1·00 1·00
2010 300c. Hans Wilhelm Schegal 1·00 1·00
2011 300c. Ulrich Walter 1·00 1·00
2012 300c. Reinhard Furrer 1·00 1·00
2013 300c. Ernst Messerschmid 1·00 1·00
2014 300c. Mamoru Mohri 1·00 1·00
2015 300c. Klaus-Dietrich Flade 1·00 1·00
2016 300c. Chaiki Naito-Mukai 1·00 1·00
MS2017 130×118 mm. 2000c. Poster for "Frau im Mond" (film) by Fritz Lang 6·50 7·00

1994. Centenary of International Olympic Committee. Gold Medal Winners. As T 227b of Gambia, but vert. Multicoloured.

2018 300c. Dieter Modenburg (Germany) (high jump), 1984 70 75
2019 400c. Ruth Fuchs (Germany) (javelin), 1972 and 1976 90 1·00
MS2020 77×106 mm. 1500c. Jans Weissflog (Germany) (ski jump), 1994 3·75 4·00

1994. 50th Anniv of D-Day. As T 331 of Antigua. Multicoloured.

2021 60c. H.M.S. "Roberts" (monitor) 1·50 60
2022 100c. H.M.S. "Warspite" (battleship) 1·75 1·10
2023 200c. U.S.S. "Augusta" (cruiser) 2·25 2·75
MS2024 107×76 mm. 1500c. U.S.S. "Nevada" (battleship) firing salvo 6·50 6·50

1994. "Philakorea '94" International Stamp Exn, Seoul. As T 227d of Gambia. Mult.

2025 20c. Ch'unghak-dong village elder in traditional costume, (24½×38 mm) 20 15
2026 150c. Stone Pagoda, Punhwangsa (24½×38 mm) 50 40
2027 250c. Character with eggs 50 60
2028 250c. Character with pair of birds on house 50 60
2029 250c. Character with cock 50 60
2030 250c. Character with dragon and pagoda 50 60
2031 250c. Character with orange flowers 50 60
2032 250c. Character with parrot and pagoda 50 60
2033 250c. Character with plant 50 60
2034 250c. Character with fish 50 60
2035 300c. Traditional country house, Andong (24½×34 mm) 60 65
MS2036 100×70 mm. 1500c. Temple judges deliberating (42½×28½ mm) 4·50 5·50

506 Dennis Bergkamp (Netherlands)

1994. World Cup Football Championship, U.S.A. (2nd issue). Multicoloured.

2037 200c. Type **506** 75 80
2038 200c. Lothar Matthaus (Germany) 75 80
2039 200c. Giuseppe Signori (Italy) 75 80
2040 200c. Carlos Valderama (Colombia) 75 80
2041 200c. Jorge Campos (Mexico) 75 80
2042 200c. Tony Meola (U.S.A.) 75 80
MS2043 Two sheets, each 100×70 mm. (a) 1200c. Giants' Stadium, New Jersey (vert). (b) 1200c. Citrus Bowl, Orlando (vert) Set of 2 sheets 6·50 7·50

507 Common ("Crowned") Duiker

1994. Duikers (antelopes). Multicoloured.

2044 50c. Type **507** 30 15
2045 100c. Red-flanked duiker 40 25
2046 200c. Yellow-backed duiker 60 40
2047 400c. Ogilby's duiker 1·00 1·25
2048 600c. Bay duiker 1·25 1·75
2049 800c. Jentink's duiker 1·50 2·00
MS2050 Two sheets, each 106×76 mm. (a) 2000c. Red forest duiker. (b) 2000c. Black duiker Set of 2 sheets 8·00 9·00

1994. Christmas. Religious Paintings. As T 231a of Gambia. Multicoloured.

2051 100c. "Madonna of the Annunciation" (Simone Martini) 60 15
2052 200c. "Madonna and Child" (Niccolo di Pietro Gerini) 90 20
2053 250c. "Virgin and Child on the Throne with Angels and Saints" (Raffaello Botticini) 1·10 60
2054 300c. "Madonna and Child with Saints" (Antonio Fiorentino) 1·40 1·10
2055 400c. "Adoration of the Magi" (Bartolo di Fredi) 1·50 1·50
2056 500c. "The Annunciation" (Cima da Congeliano) 1·75 2·00
2057 600c. "Virgin and Child with the Young St. John the Baptist" (workshop of Botticelli) 2·25 2·75
2058 1000c. "The Holy Family" (Giorgione) 2·75 3·75
MS2059 Two sheets, each 135×95 mm. (a) 2000c. "Adoration of the Kings" (detail showing Holy Family) (Giorgione). (b) 2000c. "Adoration of the Kings" (detail showing King and attendants) (Giorgione) Set of 2 sheets 8·50 9·00

508 Northern Region Dancer

1994. Panafest '94 (2nd Pan-African Historical Theatre Festival). Multicoloured.

2060 50c. Type **508** 20 15
2061 100c. Traditional artefacts 35 25
2062 200c. Chief with courtiers 65 60
2063 400c. Woman in ceremonial costume 1·25 1·25
2064 600c. Cape Coast Castle 2·00 2·50
2065 800c. Clay figurines 2·25 3·25

509 Red Cross Stretcher-bearers

1994. 75th Anniv of Red Cross. Multicoloured.

2066 50c. Type **509** 70 15

2067	200c. Worker with children	1·50	50
2068	600c. Workers erecting tents	2·50	3·50
MS2069	147×99 mm. Nos. 2066/7 and 1000c. As 600c.	5·50	6·00

510 Fertility Doll

1994. Fertility Dolls.

2070	**510**	50c. multicoloured	40	10
2071	-	100c. multicoloured	60	15
2072	-	150c. multicoloured	80	30
2073	-	200c. multicoloured	90	30
2074	-	400c. multicoloured	1·50	1·50
2075	-	600c. multicoloured	1·75	2·00
2076	-	800c. multicoloured	2·00	2·50
2077	-	1000c. multicoloured	2·25	2·75
MS2078		147×99 mm. Nos. 2071, 2074/5 and 250c. As 1000c.	4·50	5·00

DESIGNS: 100c. to 1000c. Different dolls.

511 Ghanaian Family

1994. International Year of the Family. Mult.

2079	50c. Type **511**	35	15
2080	100c. Teaching carpentry	55	15
2081	200c. Child care	90	25
2082	400c. Care for the elderly	1·40	1·40
2083	600c. Learning pottery	1·75	2·00
2084	1000c. Adult education students	2·25	2·75

512 Control Tower and Emblem

1995. 50th Anniv of I.C.A.O. Mult. (a) Inscr "50th Anniversary Of Ghana Civil Aviation Authority".

2085	100c. Type **512**	1·50	
2086	400c. Communications equipment	2·75	
2087	1000c. Airliner taking off	4·00	

(b) Inscr "50th Anniversary Of The International Civil Aviation Organisation (I.C.A.O.)".

2088	100c. Type **512**	40	20
2089	400c. Communications equipment	90	90
2090	1000c. Airliner taking off	2·00	2·50

513 Pluto, Donald Duck and Chip n' Dale around Table

1995. 60th Anniv of Donald Duck. Walt Disney Cartoon Characters at Birthday Party. Mult.

2091	40c. Type **513**	25	15
2092	50c. Mickey Mouse and pup with banner	25	15
2093	60c. Daisy Duck with balloons	25	20
2094	100c. Goofy making cake	35	25
2095	150c. Goofy on roller blades delivering cake	45	40
2096	250c. Donald pinning donkey tail on Goofy	60	60
2097	400c. Ludwig von Drake singing to Pluto	90	90
2098	500c. Grandma Duck giving cake to puppies	1·00	1·00
2099	1000c. Mickey and Minnie Mouse at piano	1·75	2·00
2100	1500c. Pluto with bone and ball	2·50	3·25
MS2101	Two sheets. (a) 117×95 mm. 2000c. Donald blowing out birthday candles (vert). (b) 95×117 mm. 2000c. Donald wearing party hat (vert) Set of 2 sheets	9·00	9·00

514 Fort Appolonia, Beyin

1995. Forts and Castles of Ghana. Multicoloured.

2102	50c. Type **514**	30	10
2103	200c. Fort Patience, Apam	60	25
2104	250c. Fort Amsterdam, Kormantin	65	45
2105	300c. Fort St. Jago, Elmina	75	70
2106	400c. Fort William, Anomabo	90	90
2107	600c. Kumasi Fort	1·50	2·00
MS2108	Two sheets, each 102×72 mm. (a) 800c. Elmina Castle (vert). (b) 1000c. Fort St. Antonio, Axim Set of 2 sheets	4·75	5·50

515 Cochem Castle, Germany

1995. Castles of the World. Multicoloured.

2109	150c. Type **515**	40	30
2110	500c. Windsor Castle, England	70	70
2111	500c. Osaka Castle, Japan	70	70
2112	500c. Vaj Dahunyad Castle, Hungary	70	70
2113	500c. Karlstejn Castle, Czech Republic	70	70
2114	500c. Kronborg Castle, Denmark	70	70
2115	500c. Alcazar of Segovia, Spain	70	70
2116	500c. Chambourd Castle, France	70	70
2117	500c. Linderhof Castle, Germany	70	70
2118	500c. Red Fort, Delhi, India	70	70
2119	600c. Hohenzollern Castle, Germany	80	80
2120	800c. Uwajima Castle, Japan	1·00	1·00
2121	1000c. Hohenschwangau Castle, Germany	1·10	1·10
MS2122	Two sheets, each 102×72 mm. (a) 2500c. Neuschwanstein Castle, Germany. (b) 2500c. Himeji Castle, Japan Set of 2 sheets	9·00	9·00

516 European Pochard ("Eurasian Pochard")

1995. Ducks. Multicoloured.

2123	200c. Type **516**	80	35
2124	400c. African pygmy goose	90	90
2125	400c. Southern pochard	90	90
2126	400c. Cape teal	90	90
2127	400c. Ruddy shelduck	90	90
2128	400c. Fulvous whistling duck	90	90
2129	400c. White-faced whistling duck	90	90
2130	400c. Ferruginous duck ("Ferruginous White-eye")	90	90
2131	400c. Hottentot teal	90	90
2132	400c. African black duck	90	90
2133	400c. African yellow-bill ("Yellow-billed Duck")	90	90
2134	400c. Bahama pintail ("White-checked Pintail Duck")	90	90
2135	400c. Hartlaub's duck	90	90
2136	500c. Maccoa duck	1·00	1·10
2137	800c. Cape shoveler	1·50	1·75
2138	1000c. Red-crested pochard	1·90	2·25
MS2139	Two sheets, each 104×74 mm. (a) 2500c. Roseate tern. (b) 2500c. Northern shoveler Set of 2 sheets	8·50	9·00

Nos. 2124/35 were printed together, se-tenant, forming a composite design.

No. 2128 is inscribed "Wistling" in error.

517 Cycling

1995. Olympic Games, Atlanta (1996) (1st issue). Multicoloured.

2140	300c. Type **517**	1·10	1·00
2141	300c. Archery	1·10	1·00
2142	300c. Diving	1·10	1·00
2143	300c. Swimming	1·10	1·00
2144	300c. Women's gymnastics	1·10	1·00
2145	300c. Fencing	1·10	1·00
2146	300c. Boxing	1·10	1·00
2147	300c. Men's gymnastics	1·10	1·00
2148	300c. Javelin	1·10	1·00
2149	300c. Tennis	1·10	1·00
2150	300c. Football	1·10	1·00
2151	300c. Equestrian	1·10	1·00
2152	500c. Carl Lewis (U.S.A.)	1·25	1·10
2153	800c. Eric Liddell (Great Britain)	1·40	1·60
2154	900c. Jesse Owens (U.S.A.)	1·40	1·60
2155	1000c. Jim Thorpe (U.S.A.)	1·40	1·60
MS2156	Two sheets, each 70×100 mm. (a) 1200c. Pierre de Coubertin (founder of International Olympic Committee). (b) 1200c. John Akii Bua (Uganda) Set of 2 sheets	3·50	4·00

Nos. 2140/51 were printed together, se-tenant, forming a composite design.

See also Nos. 2334/55.

518 "Cymothoe beckeri" (butterfly)

1995. Multicoloured.

2156c	300c. European goldfinch (vert)	15	20
2157	400c. Type **518**	60	20
2158	500c. "Graphium policenes" (butterfly)	25	20
2159	1000c. African long-tailed hawk (vert)	1·25	1·00
2159a	1100c. Kente cloth	90	30
2160	2000c. Swordfish	2·50	1·75
2161	3000c. Guinean fingerfish	1·25	40
2162	5000c. Purple heron (vert)	4·50	5·00

519 Ghanaian Scouts

1995. 18th World Scout Jamboree, Netherlands.

2163	**519**	400c. multicoloured	90	1·00
2164	-	800c. multicoloured	1·25	1·40
2165	-	1000c. multicoloured	1·25	1·40
MS2166		70×100 mm. 1200c. multicoloured	1·90	2·25

DESIGNS: 800c. to 1200c. Ghanaian scouts (different).

1995. 50th Anniv of End of Second World War in Europe. As T 237a of Gambia. Multicoloured.

2167	400c. Winston Churchill	75	75
2168	400c. Gen. Dwight D. Eisenhower	75	75
2169	400c. Air Marshal Sir Arthur Tedder	75	75
2170	400c. Field-Marshal Sir Bernard Montgomery	75	75
2171	400c. Gen. Omar Bradley	75	75
2172	400c. Gen. Charles de Gaulle	75	75
2173	400c. French resistance fighters	75	75
2174	400c. Gen. George S. Patton	75	75
MS2175	104×74 mm. 1200c. "GIVE ME FIVE YEARS & YOU WILL NOT RECOGNISE GERMANY AGAIN" quote by Adolf Hitler in English and German (42×57 mm)	2·75	3·00

520 Trygve Lie (1946–52) and United Nations Building

1995. 50th Anniv of United Nations. Secretary-Generals. Multicoloured.

2176	200c. Type **520**	30	55
2177	300c. Dag Hammarskjold (1953–61)	40	65
2178	400c. U. Thant (1961–71)	50	70
2179	500c. Kurt Waldheim (1972–81)	60	75
2180	600c. Javier Perez de Cuellar (1982–91)	70	90
2181	800c. Boutrous Boutrous-Ghali (1992)	80	1·00
MS2182	104×74 mm. 1200c. U.N. flag (horiz)	1·90	2·50

521 Preserving Fish

1995. 50th Anniv of F.A.O. Multicoloured.

2183	200c. Type **521**	70	15
2184	300c. Fishermen with fish traps	85	40
2185	400c. Ox-drawn plough	95	80
2186	600c. Harvesting bananas	1·25	1·75
2187	800c. Planting saplings	1·50	2·50
MS2188	100×70 mm. 2000c. Canoe and cattle	3·00	3·50

522 National Flag and Rotary Emblem

1995. 90th Anniv of Rotary International. Multicoloured.

2189	600c. Type **522**	1·00	1·25
MS2190	94×65 mm. 1200c. Ghanaian Rotary banner (vert)	1·90	2·25

1995. 95th Birthday of Queen Elizabeth the Queen Mother. As T 239a of Gambia. Multicoloured.

2191	600c. brown, light brown and black	1·75	1·75
2192	600c. multicoloured	1·75	1·75
2193	600c. multicoloured	1·75	1·75
2194	600c. multicoloured	1·75	1·75
MS2195	102×127 mm. 2500c. multicoloured	4·75	4·25

DESIGNS: No. 2191, Queen Elizabeth the Queen Mother (pastel drawing); 2192, Wearing light blue hat and floral dress; 2193, At desk (oil painting); 2194, Wearing red hat and dress; **MS**2195, Wearing pale blue hat and jacket.

1995. 50th Anniv of End of Second World War in the Pacific. Medals. As T 229b of Gambia. Mult.

2196	500c. Navy Cross and Purple Heart, U.S.A.	85	85
2197	500c. Air Force Cross and Distinguished Flying Cross, Great Britain	85	85
2198	500c. Navy and Marine Corps Medal and Distinguished Service Cross, U.S.A.	85	85
2199	500c. Distinguished Service Medal and Distinguished Conduct Medal, Great Britain	85	85
2200	500c. Military Medal and Military Cross, Great Britain	85	85
2201	500c. Distinguished Service Cross and Distinguished Service Order, Great Britain	85	85
MS2202	108×76 mm. 1200c. Congressional Medal of Honor, U.S.A.	2·50	2·50

523 Seismosaurus

1995. "Singapore '95" International Stamp Exhibition. Prehistoric Animals. Multicoloured.

2203	400c. Type **523**	65	65
2204	400c. Supersaurus	65	65
2205	400c. Ultrasaurus	65	65
2206	400c. Saurolophus	65	65
2207	400c. Lambeosaurus	65	65
2208	400c. Parasaurolophus	65	65
2209	400c. Triceratops	65	65
2210	400c. Styracosaurus	65	65
2211	400c. Pachyrhinosaurus	65	65
2212	400c. Peteinosaurus	65	65
2213	400c. Quetzalcoatlus	65	65
2214	400c. Eudimorphodon	65	65
2215	400c. Allosaurus	65	65
2216	400c. Daspletosaurus	65	65
2217	400c. Tarbosaurus bataar	65	65
2218	400c. Velociraptor mongoliensis	65	65
2219	400c. Herrerasaurus	65	65
2220	400c. Coelophysis	65	65
MS2221	Two sheets, each 106×76 mm. (a) 2500c. Tyrannosaurus rex (horiz). (b) 2500c. Albertosaurus (horiz) Set of 2 sheets	8·00	8·50

Nos. 2203/11 and 2212/20 respectively were printed together, se-tenant, forming composite designs.

524 Arms of Otumfuo Opoku Ware II

1995. Silver Jubilee of Otumfuo Opoku Ware II (King of Ashanti). Multicoloured.

2222	50c. Type **524**	30	10
2223	100c. Silver casket	45	10
2224	200c. Golden stool	70	20
2225	400c. Busummuru sword bearer	1·10	75
2226	600c. Otumfuo Opoku Ware II	1·75	1·75
2227	800c. Otumfuo Opoku Ware II under umbrella	2·00	2·25
2228	1000c. Mponponsuo sword bearer	2·25	2·75

525 Nelson Mandela (1993 Peace)

1995. Centenary of Nobel Prize Trust Fund. Past Prize Winners. Multicoloured.

2229	400c. Type **525**	80	80
2230	400c. Albert Schweitzer (1952 Peace)	80	80
2231	400c. Wole Soyinka (1986 Literature)	80	80
2232	400c. Emil Fischer (1902 Chemistry)	80	80
2233	400c. Rudolf Mossbauer (1961 Physics)	80	80
2234	400c. Archbishop Desmond Tutu (1984 Peace)	80	80
2235	400c. Max Born (1954 Physics)	80	80
2236	400c. Max Planck (1918 Physics)	80	80
2237	400c. Hermann Hesse (1946 Literature)	80	80
MS2238	104×75 mm. 1200c. Paul Ehrlich (1908 Medicine) and medal	1·75	2·00

1995. Christmas. Religious Paintings. As T 245a of Gambia. Multicoloured.

2239	50c. "The Child Jesus and the Young St. John" (Murillo)	25	10
2240	80c. "Rest on the Flight into Egypt" (Memling)	30	10
2241	300c. "Holy Family" (Van Dyck)	75	35
2242	600c. "Enthroned Madonna and Child" (Uccello)	1·10	1·40
2243	800c. "Madonna and Child" (Van Eyck)	1·25	1·75
2244	1000c. "Head of Christ" (Rembrandt)	1·40	2·00
MS2245	Two sheets, each 101×127 mm. (a) 2500c. "The Holy Family" (Pulzone). (b) 2500c. "Madonna and Child with Two Saints" (Montagna) Set of 2 sheets	7·75	8·50

526 Ernemann Camera (1903)

1995. Centenary of Cinema. Multicoloured.

2246	400c. Type **526**	1·25	1·00
2247	400c. Charlie Chaplin	1·25	1·00
2248	400c. Rudolph Valentino	1·25	1·00
2249	400c. Will Rogers	1·25	1·00
2250	400c. Greta Garbo	1·25	1·00
2251	400c. Jackie Cooper	1·25	1·00
2252	400c. Bette Davis	1·25	1·00
2253	400c. John Barrymore	1·25	1·00
2254	400c. Shirley Temple	1·25	1·00
MS2255	106×76 mm. 2500c. Laurel and Hardy	5·50	5·50

No. 2246 is inscribed "ERNMANN" in error.

527 John Lennon

1995. John Lennon (musician) Commemoration. Multicoloured.

2256	400c. Type **527**	1·10	1·10
2257	400c. Full face portrait (green background)	1·10	1·10
2258	400c. With guitar	1·10	1·10
2259	400c. Wearing glasses and caftan	1·10	1·10
2260	400c. Full face portrait (red background)	1·10	1·10
2261	400c. Wearing headphones	1·10	1·10
2262	400c. Wearing purple T-shirt	1·10	1·10
2263	400c. Full face portrait (blue background)	1·10	1·10
2264	400c. Facing right	1·10	1·10
2265	400c. As No. 2263, but smaller (24×39 mm)	1·10	1·10
MS2266	102×73 mm. 2000c. John Lennon playing guitar	6·00	6·50

528 Louis Pasteur in Laboratory

1995. Death Centenary of Louis Pasteur (scientist). Multicoloured.

2267	600c. Type **528**	1·60	1·60
2268	600c. Pasteur injecting rabid dog	1·60	1·60
2269	600c. Pasteur and microscope slide	1·60	1·60
2270	600c. Laboratory equipment and birds	1·60	1·60
2271	600c. Yeast vats	1·60	1·60

529 Rat Musicians

1996. Chinese New Year ("Year of the Rat").

2272	**529**	250c. brown, violet and red	60	60
2273	-	250c. brown, violet and red	60	60
2274	-	250c. brown, violet and red	60	60
2275	-	250c. brown, violet and red	60	60
MS2276		142×60 mm. As Nos. 2272/5, but face values and "GHANA" in red instead of white	2·00	2·00
MS2277		106×75 mm. 1000c. red and orange	2·00	2·00

DESIGNS:—VERT: No. 2273, Rats carrying banners; 2274, Rats carrying palanquin; 2275, Rats with offerings. HORIZ: No. **MS**2277, Four rats carrying palanquin.

1996. 125th Anniv of Metropolitan Museum of Art, New York. As T 251 of Gambia. Multicoloured.

2278	400c. "Portrait of a Man" (Van der Goes)	85	85
2279	400c. "Paradise" (detail) (Di Paolo)	85	85
2280	400c. "Portrait of a Young Man" (Messina)	85	85
2281	400c. "Tommaso Portinari" (detail) (Memling)	85	85
2282	400c. "Maria Portinari" (detail) (Memling)	85	85
2283	400c. "Portrait of a Lady" (detail) (Ghirlandaio)	85	85
2284	400c. "St. Christopher and the Infant Christ" (Ghirlandaio)	85	85
2285	400c. "Francesco D'Este" (detail) (Weyden)	85	85
2286	400c. "The Interrupted Sleep" (Boucher)	85	85
2287	400c. "Diana and Cupid" (detail) (Batoni)	85	85
2288	400c. "Boy blowing Bubbles" (Chardin)	85	85
2289	400c. "Ancient Rome" (detail) (Pannini)	85	85
2290	400c. "Modern Rome" (detail) (Pannini)	85	85
2291	400c. "The Calmady Children" (Lawrence)	85	85
2292	400c. "The Triumph of Marius" (detail) (Tiepolo)	85	85
2293	400c. "Garden at Vaucression" (detail) (Vuillard)	85	85
MS2294	Two sheets, each 95×70 mm. (a) 2500c. "The Epiphany" (detail) (Giotto) (80×56 mm). (b) 2500c. "The Calling of Matthew" (detail) (Hemessen) (80×56 mm) Set of 2 sheets	12·00	13·00

530 Toco Toucan

1996. Wildlife of the Rainforest. Multicoloured.

2295	400c. Type **530**	90	90
2296	400c. Two-toed sloth	90	90
2297	400c. Orang-utan	90	90
2298	400c. Crested hawk eagle	90	90
2299	400c. Tiger	90	90
2300	400c. Painted stork	90	90
2301	400c. Green-winged macaw	90	90
2302	400c. Common squirrel-monkey	90	90
2303	400c. Crab-eating macaque	90	90
2304	400c. "Cithaerias menander" and "Ithomiidae" (butterflies)	90	90
2305	400c. "Coryptophanes cristatus" and "Gekkonidae" (lizards)	90	90
2306	400c. Boa constrictor	90	90
2307	400c. Hoatzin	90	90
2308	400c. Western tarsier	90	90
2309	400c. Golden Lion tamarin	90	90
2310	400c. "Pteropus gouldii" (bat)	90	90
2311	400c. Guianan cock of the rock	90	90
2312	400c. Resplendent quetzal	90	90
2313	400c. Tree frog and poison-arrow frog	90	90
2314	400c. Ring-tailed lemur	90	90
2315	400c. Iguana	90	90
2316	400c. "Heliconius burneyi" (butterfly)	90	90
2317	400c. Vervain hummingbird	90	90
2318	400c. Verreauv's sifaka	90	90
MS2319	Two sheets, each 74×104 mm. (a) 3000c. Raggiana bird of paradise. (b) 3000c. King vulture Set of 2 sheets	13·00	13·00

531 Pagoda of Kaiyan Si Temple, Fujian

1996. "CHINA '96" 9th Asian International Stamp Exhibition. Pagodas. Multicoloured.

2320	400c. Type **531**	1·10	1·10
2321	400c. Kaiyuan Si Temple, Hebei	1·10	1·10
2322	400c. Fogong Si Temple, Shanxi	1·10	1·10
2323	400c. Xiangshan, Beijing	1·10	1·10
MS2324	Two sheets. (a) 100×70 mm. 1000c. Baima Si Temple, Henan. (b) 143×98 mm. 1000c. Gold statue (38×50 mm) Set of 2 sheets	4·50	5·00

1996. 70th Birthday of Queen Elizabeth II. As T 255a of Gambia showing different photographs. Multicoloured.

2325	1000c. Queen Elizabeth II	2·00	2·00
2326	1000c. In blue hat and coat	2·00	2·00
2327	1000c. Wearing straw hat and carrying bouquet	2·00	2·00
MS2328	125×103 mm. 2500c. In open carriage at Trooping the Colour (horiz)	4·75	4·75

532 Serafim Todorow (Bulgaria)

1996. 50th Anniv of International Amateur Boxing Association. Multicoloured.

2329	300c. Type **532**	65	55
2330	400c. Oscar de la Hoya (U.S.A.)	80	70
2331	800c. Ariel Hernandez (Cuba)	1·50	1·75
2332	1500c. Arnoldo Mesa (Cuba)	2·50	3·00
MS2333	80×110 mm. 3000c. Tadahiro Sasaki (Japan)	4·75	5·50

533 Ancient Greek Wrestlers

1996. Olympic Games, Atlanta (2nd issue). Previous Medal Winners. Multicoloured.

2334	300c. Type **533**	75	55
2335	400c. Aileen Riggin, 1920 (U.S.A.)	85	85
2336	400c. Pat McCormick, 1952 (U.S.A.)	85	85
2337	400c. Dawn Fraser, 1956 (Australia)	85	85
2338	400c. Chris von Saltza, 1960 (U.S.A.)	85	85
2339	400c. Anita Lonsbrough, 1960 (Great Britain)	85	85
2340	400c. Debbie Meyer, 1968 (U.S.A.)	85	85
2341	400c. Shane Gould, 1972 (Australia)	85	85
2342	400c. Petra Thuemer, 1976 (Germany)	85	85
2343	400c. Marjorie Gestring, 1936 (U.S.A.)	85	85
2344	400c. Abedi Pele (Ghana) (vert)	85	85
2345	400c. Quico Navarez (Spain) (vert)	85	85
2346	400c. Heino Hanson (Denmark) (vert)	85	85
2347	400c. Mostafa Ismail (Egypt) (vert)	85	85

2348	400c. Anthony Yeboah (Ghana) (vert)	85	85
2349	400c. Jurgen Klinsmann (Germany) (vert)	85	85
2350	400c. Cobi Jones (U.S.A.) (vert)	85	85
2351	400c. Franco Baresi (Italy) (vert)	85	85
2352	400c. Igor Dobrovolski (Russia) (vert)	85	85
2353	500c. Wilma Rudolph (U.S.A.) (track and field, 1960)	1·00	1·00
2354	600c. Olympic Stadium, 1960, and Roman landmarks	1·25	1·40
2355	800c. Ladies Kayak pairs, 1960 (Soviet Union)	1·50	1·75
MS2356	Two sheets, each 110×80 mm. (a) 2000c. Tracy Caulkins (U.S.A.) (200m freestyle, 1984). (b) 2000c. Kornelia Ender (Germany) (200m freestyle, 1976) Set of 2 sheets	8·50	8·50

Nos. 2335/43 (swimming and diving), and 2344/52 (football) respectively were printed together, se-tenant, with the backgrounds forming composite designs.

534 E. W. Agyare (35 years service with Ghana Broadcasting)

1996. Local Broadcasting.

2357	**534**	100c. multicoloured	40	40

1996. 50th Anniv of UNICEF. As T 258a of Gambia. Multicoloured.

2358	400c. Ghanaian child	35	35
2359	500c. Mother and child	45	45
2360	600c. Mother and child drinking	55	70
MS2361	74×104 mm. 1000c. Young child	1·40	1·60

534a St. Stephen's Gate and "Jasminum mesyni"

1996. 3000th Anniv of Jerusalem. Multicoloured.

2362	400c. Type **534a**	60	40
2363	600c. The Citadel, Tower of David and "Nerium oleander"	80	80
2364	800c. Chapel of the Ascension and "Romulea bulbocodium"	1·00	1·10
MS2365	65×80 mm. 2000c. Russian Orthodox Church of St. Mary Magdalene (48×30 mm)	2·75	3·00

1996. Centenary of Radio. Entertainers. As T 259a of Gambia. Multicoloured.

2366	500c. Frank Sinatra	45	35
2367	600c. Judy Garland	60	70
2368	600c. Bing Crosby	60	70
2369	800c. Martin and Lewis	80	90
MS2370	81×110 mm. 2000c. Edgar Bergen and Charlie McCarthy	2·25	2·75

1996. 50th Anniv of UNESCO. As T 273a of Gambia. Multicoloured.

2371	400c. The Citadel, Haiti (vert)	50	25
2372	800c. Ait-Ben-Hadou (fortified village), Morocco (vert)	90	1·00
2373	1000c. Spissky Hrad, Slovakia	1·25	1·40
MS2374	106×76 mm. 2000c. Cape Coast Castle, Ghana	2·25	2·75

535 Fiddles

1996. Musical Insruments. Multicoloured.

2375	500c. Type **535**	90	90
2376	500c. Proverbial drum	90	90
2377	500c. Double clapless bell and castanet	90	90
2378	500c. Gourd rattle	90	90
2379	500c. Horns	90	90

536 Ariel, Flounder and Sebastian

1996. Disney Friends. Disney Cartoon Characters. Multicoloured.

2380	60c. Type **536**	30	30
2381	60c. Pinocchio and Jiminy Cricket	30	30
2382	60c. Cogsworth and Lumiere	30	30
2383	60c. Copper and Tod	30	30
2384	60c. Pocahontas, Meeko and Flit	30	30
2385	60c. Bambi, Flower and Thumper	30	30
2386	150c. As No. 2381	50	50
2387	200c. Type **536**	50	50
2388	200c. As No. 2383	50	50
2389	300c. As No. 2385	60	60
2390	350c. As No. 2382	60	60
2391	450c. As No. 2384	65	65
2392	600c. Aladdin and Abu	70	70
2393	700c. Penny and Rufus	75	75
2394	800c. Mowgli and Baloo	80	80
MS2395	Two sheets. (a) 98×124 mm. 3000c. Winnie the Pooh (vert). (b) 133×108 mm. 3000c. Simba and Timon Set of 2 sheets	6·00	6·50

1996. 20th Anniv of Rocky (film). Sheet 143×182 mm, containing vert design as T 266 of Gambia. Multicoloured.

MS2396	2000c.×3 Sylvester Stallone in "Rocky II"	5·50	6·00

537 Herd Boy and Ox

1997. Chinese New Year ("Year of the Ox"). "The Herd Boy and Weaver". Each brown, silver and black.

2397	500c. Type **537**	70	70
2398	500c. Ox and weaver in lake	70	70
2399	500c. Weaver at work	70	70
2400	500c. Herd boy with dying Ox	70	70
2401	500c. Weaver flying out of window	70	70
2402	500c. Herd boy carrying children	70	70
2403	500c. Family separated by "river"	70	70
2404	500c. Petitioning the emperor	70	70
2405	500c. Family reunited	70	70

538 The Tomb of Dr. Hideyo Noguchi

1997. 120th Birth Anniv of Dr. Hideyo Noguchi (bacteriologist). Multicoloured.

2406	1000c. Type **538**	1·25	1·40
2407	1000c. Dr. Hideyo Noguchi	1·25	1·40
2408	1000c. Birthplace of Dr. Noguchi at Sanjogarta	1·25	1·40
2409	1000c. Noguchi Institute, Legon	1·25	1·40
2410	1000c. Noguchi Gardens, Accra	1·25	1·40
MS2411	Two sheets, each 67×97 mm. (a) 3000c. Dr. Noguchi in his laboratory. (b) 3000c. Statue of Dr. Noguchi Set of 2 sheets	6·50	8·00

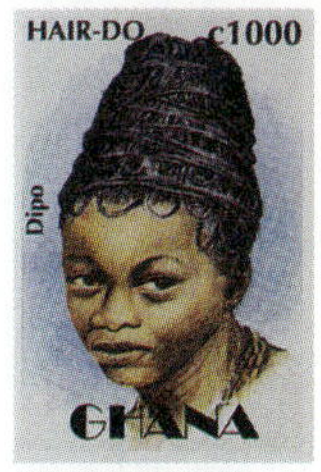

539 Dipo Hairstyle

1997. Ghanaian Women's Hairstyle. Multicoloured.

2412	1000c. Type **539**	75	75
2413	1000c. Oduku with flowers	75	75
2414	1000c. Dansinkran	75	75
2415	1000c. Mbobom	75	75
2416	1000c. Oduku with hair pins	75	75
2417	1000c. African corn row	75	75
2418	1000c. Chinese raster	75	75
2419	1000c. Chinese raster with top knot	75	75
2420	1000c. Corn row	75	75
2421	1000c. Mbakaa	75	75

540 Independence Anniversary Emblem

1997. 40th Anniv of Independence. Multicoloured.

2422	200c. Type **540**	35	25
2423	200c. President J. J. Rawlings (vert)	1·75	1·50
2424	550c. Dr. Kwane Nkrumah (first President) (vert)	75	80
2425	800c. Children in class	1·25	1·50
2426	1100c. Akosombo Dam	1·75	2·00
MS2427	Two sheets. (a) 70×100 mm. 2000c. Dr. Nkrumah proclaiming independence (vert). (b) 101×141 mm. 3000c. United Nations Secretary-General Kofi Annan (37×50 mm) Set of 2 sheets	5·50	6·50

No. 2425 is inscribed "Acheivement" in error.

1997. 10th Anniv of Chernobyl Nuclear Disaster. As T 276b of Gambia. Multicoloured.

2428	800c. Child's face and UNESCO emblem	1·25	1·40
2429	1000c. As No. 2428, but inscribed "CHABAD'S CHILDREN OF CHERNOBYL" at foot	1·40	1·60

541 Deng Xiaoping

1997. Deng Xiaoping (Chinese statesman) Commemoration. Different portraits. Multicoloured.

2430	300c. Type **541**	45	30
2431	500c. Looking thoughtful	60	55
2432	600c. Wearing glasses	70	70
2433	600c. Delivering speech	70	70
2434	800c. As No. 2432	90	1·00
2435	800c. As No. 2433	90	1·00
2436	1000c. Type **541**	1·10	1·25
2437	1000c. As No. 2431	1·10	1·25
MS2438	Two sheets, each 101×70 mm. (a) 3000c. Deng Xiaoping making speech (47×34 mm). (b) 4000c. Deng Xiaoping with hand raised (47×34 mm) Set of 2 sheets	6·00	7·00

1997. 50th Death Anniv of Paul Harris (founder of Rotary International). As T 276c of Gambia. Multicoloured.

2439	2000c. Paul Harris and Egyptian patient receiving polio vaccination	2·25	2·75
MS2440	78×107 mm. 3000c. Paul Harris with Rotary and PolioPlus emblems	2·50	3·00

1997. Golden Wedding of Queen Elizabeth and Prince Philip. As T 276d of Gambia. Multicoloured.

2441	800c. Queen Elizabeth II	90	90
2442	800c. Royal coat of arms	90	90
2443	800c. Queen Elizabeth and Prince Philip waving	90	90
2444	800c. Queen Elizabeth and Prince Philip on official visit	90	90
2445	800c. Queen in Irish State Coach	90	90
2446	800c. Prince Philip in 1947	90	90
MS2447	100×71 mm. 3000c. Princess Elizabeth in 1947	2·25	2·50

1997. "Pacific '97" International Stamp Exhibition, San Francisco. Death Centenary of Heinrich von Stephan (founder of the U.P.U.). As T 276e of Gambia.

2448	1000c. blue	1·00	1·10
2449	1000c. brown	1·00	1·10
2450	1000c. red	1·00	1·10
MS2451	82×119 mm. 3000c. green	2·50	3·00

DESIGNS: No. 2448, Early motor car; 2449, Von Stephan and Mercury; 2450, Blanchard's balloon flight, 1784; **MS**2451, African messenger.

541a "Nihonbashi Bridge and Edobashi Bridge"

1997. Birth Bicentenary of Hiroshige (Japanese painter). "One Hundred Famous Views of Edo". Multicoloured.

2452	600c. Type **541a**	70	70
2453	600c. "View of Nihonbashi Tori 1-chome"	70	70
2454	600c. "Open Garden at Fukagawa Hachiman Shrine"	70	70
2455	600c. "Inari Bridge and Minato Shrine, Teppozu"	70	70
2456	600c. "Bamboo Yards, Kyobashi Bridge"	70	70
2457	600c. "Hall of Thirty-Three Bays, Fukagawa"	70	70
MS2458	Two sheets, each 102×127 mm. (a) 3000c. "Sumiyoshi Festival, Tsukudajima". (b) 3000c. "Teppozu and Tsukjii Honganji Temple" Set of 2 sheets	5·50	6·50

542a *"Amorphophallus flavovirens"*

1997

2458c	200c. Type **542a**	15	10
2458d	550c. Atumpan drums	10	40
2458e	800c. *Cyrestis camillus* (butterfly)	60	15
2458f	800c. *Musa sapientum* (bananas)	20	15
2458g	1000c. *Boletus edulis*	25	20
2458h	1500c. *Bebearia arcadius* (butterfly)	40	30
2458i	6000c. *Spathodea campanulata* (flower)	1·00	1·00

542 Jackie Gleason

1997. Famous Comedians. Multicoloured.

2459	600c. Type **542**	75	75
2460	600c. Danny Kaye	75	75
2461	600c. John Cleese	75	75
2462	600c. Lucille Ball	75	75
2463	600c. Jerry Lewis	75	75
2464	600c. Sidney James	75	75
2465	600c. Louis Defuenes	75	75
2466	600c. Mae West	75	75
2467	600c. Bob Hope	75	75
MS2468	Two sheets. (a) 83×113 mm. 3000c. Groucho Marx. (b) 76×106 mm. 2000c. Professor Ajax Bukana in front of curtain; 2000c. Professor Ajax Bukana (different) (both 28×42 mm) Set of 2 sheets	4·50	5·00

543 "Gelerina calyptrata"

1997. Fungi of the World. Multicoloured.

2469	200c. Type **543**	30	30
2470	300c. "Lepiota ignivolvata"	40	40
2471	400c. "Omphalotus olearius"	50	50
2472	550c. "Amanita phalloides"	60	60
2473	600c. "Entoloma conferendum"	60	60
2474	800c. "Entoloma nitidum"	70	70
2475	800c. "Coprinus picaceus"	70	70
2476	800c. "Stropharia aurantiaca"	70	70
2477	800c. "Cortinarius splendens"	70	70
2478	800c. "Gomphidius roseus"	70	70
2479	800c. "Russula sardonia"	70	70
2480	800c. "Geastrum schmidelia"	70	70
MS2481	Two sheets, each 73×103 mm. (a) 3000c. "Craterellus cornucopioides". (b) 3000c. "Mycena crocata" Set of 2 sheets	5·50	6·00

1997. World Football Championship, France (1998). As T 283a of Gambia. Multicoloured.

2482	200c. Azteca Stadium, Mexico	35	30
2483	300c. The Rose Bowl, U.S.A.	45	40
2484	400c. Stadio Giuseppe Meazza, Italy	60	50
2485	500c. Olympiastadion, Germany	65	55
2486	600c. Patrick Kluivert, Netherlands	70	70
2487	600c. Roy Keane, Republic of Ireland	70	70
2488	600c. Abedi Ayew Pele, Ghana	70	70
2489	600c. Peter Schmeichel, Denmark	70	70
2490	600c. Roberto di Matteo, Italy	70	70
2491	600c. Bebeto, Brazil	70	70
2492	600c. Steve McManaman, England	70	70
2493	600c. George Oppon Weah, Liberia	70	70
2494	1000c. Maracana Stadium, Brazil	1·10	1·25
2495	2000c. Bernabeu Stadium, Spain	1·75	2·00
MS2496	Two sheets. (a) 127×102 mm. 3000c. David Seaman, England. (b) 102×127 mm. 3000c. Juninho, Brazil Set of 2 sheets	6·00	7·00

544 African Pygmy Angelfish

1997. Marine Life. Multicoloured.

2497	400c. Type **544**	50	50
2498	500c. Violet-crested turaco	55	55
2499	500c. Pied avocet	55	55
2500	500c. Bottle-nosed dolphin	55	55
2501	500c. Bottle-nosed dolphin and long-toed lapwing	55	55
2502	500c. Longfinned spadefish	55	55
2503	500c. Imperial angelfish and manta	55	55
2504	500c. Racoon butterflyfish and African pompano	55	55
2505	500c. Silvertip shark	55	55
2506	500c. Longfin banner fish	55	55
2507	500c. Longfin banner fish and manta	55	55
2508	500c. Rust parrotfish	55	55
2509	500c. Coral trout	55	55
2510	600c. Angelfish	60	60
2511	800c. Broomtail wrasse	70	75
2512	1000c. Indian butterflyfish	85	95
MS2513	Two sheets, each 106×76 mm. (a) 3000c. King angelfish. (b) 3000c. Crown butterflyfish Set of 2 sheets	6·00	7·00

Nos. 2498/2509 were printed together, se-tenant, with the backgrounds forming a composite design.

545 Ghanaian Players holding Trophy

1997. J.V.C. Under-17 World Soccer Champions (1995). Multicoloured.

2514	200c.+50c. Type **545**	40	40
2515	550c.+50c. Ghana football team (horiz)	75	75
2516	800c.+50c. Abu Iddrisu	90	90
2517	1000c.+50c. Emmanuel Bentil (captain)	1·10	1·25
2518	1500c.+50c. Basiru Gambo	1·60	1·75

546 "Eurychone rothschildiana"

1997. Flowers of the World. Multicoloured.

2519	200c. Type **546**	40	30
2520	550c. "Bulbophyllum lepidum"	70	60
2521	800c. "Ansellia africana"	80	80
2522	800c. "Strophanthus preusii" (vert)	80	80
2523	800c. "Ancistrochilus rothschildlanus" (vert)	80	80
2524	800c. "Mussaendra arcuata" (vert)	80	80
2525	800c. "Microcoelia guyoniane" (vert)	80	80
2526	800c. "Gloriosa simplex" (vert)	80	80
2527	800c. "Brachycorythis kalbreyeri" (vert)	80	80
2528	800c. "Aframomum sceptrum" (vert)	80	80
2529	800c. "Thunbergia alata" (vert)	80	80
2530	800c. "Clerodendrum thomsoniae" (vert)	80	80
2531	1100c. "Combbretum grandiflorum"	1·25	1·50
MS2532	Two sheets, each 82×77 mm. (a) 3000c. "Kigelia africana" (vert). (b) 3000c. "Spathodea campanulata" (vert) Set of 2 sheets	5·50	5·50

Nos. 2522/30 were printed together, se-tenant, with the backgrounds forming a composite design.

547 Eurasian Goldfinch

1997. Birds of Africa. Multicoloured.

2533	200c. Type **547**	40	30
2534	300c. Cape puff-back flycatcher ("Cape Batis")	55	40
2535	400c. Double-toothed barbet ("Bearded Barbet")	65	50
2536	500c. African white-necked raven ("White-necked Raven")	70	60
2537	600c. Purple grenadier	75	75
2538	800c. Black bustard	80	80
2539	800c. Northern lapwing	80	80
2540	800c. Lichtenstein's sandgrouse ("Sandgrouse")	80	80
2541	800c. Red-crested turaco	80	80
2542	800c. White-browed coucal	80	80
2543	800c. Lilac-breasted roller	80	80
2544	800c. Golden pipit	80	80
2545	800c. Burchell's gonolek ("Crimson-breasted Gonolek")	80	80
2546	800c. Blackcap	80	80
2547	1000c. Zebra waxbill	1·10	1·40
MS2548	Two sheets, each 106×75 mm. (a) 3000c. Shaft-tailed whydah. (b) 3000c. Yellow-tufted malachite sunbird Set of 2 sheets	6·50	6·50

548 Havana Cat

1997. Cats and Dogs. Multicoloured.

2549	20c. Type **548**	25	25
2550	50c. Singapura cat	25	25
2551	80c. Papillon	30	30
2552	100c. Sphinx cat	30	30
2553	150c. British white cat	30	30
2554	200c. Bulldog	30	30
2555	300c. Snowshoe cat	40	40
2556	400c. Shetland sheepdog	50	50
2557	500c. Schnauzer	55	55
2558	600c. Persian cat	60	60
2559	800c. Shih tzu	70	70
2560	1000c. Russian wolfhound	90	90
2561	1000c. Birman cat	90	90
2562	1000c. Basset hound	90	90
2563	1000c. Silver tabby cat	90	90
2564	1000c. Afghan	90	90
2565	1000c. Burmilla cat	90	90
2566	1000c. Abyssinian cat	90	90
2567	1000c. Border terrier	90	90
2568	1000c. Scottish fold cat	90	90
2569	1000c. Boston terrier	90	90
2570	1000c. Oriental cat	90	90
2571	1000c. Keeshond	90	90
2572	2000c. Chow Chow	1·60	1·75
MS2573	Two sheets, each 73×100 mm. (a) 3000c. Alaskan malamute. (b) 3000c. Ragdoll cat Set of 2 sheets	7·00	7·00

549 "Landscape" (Huang Binhong)

1997. Return of Hong Kong to China.

2574	**549**	200c. multicoloured	30	30
2575	-	300c. multicoloured	35	35
2576	-	400c. multicoloured	40	40
2577	-	500c. multicoloured	50	50
2578	-	600c. multicoloured	60	60
2579	-	800c. multicoloured	70	70
2580	-	1000c. multicoloured	90	95
2581	-	2000c. multicoloured	1·60	1·75
MS2582		138×105 mm. (a) 2000c. multicoloured (farm). (b) 2000c. multicoloured (mountains) (each 50×37 mm). P 14×13½	2·50	2·75
MS2583		150×125 mm. (a) 1000c.×2 multicoloured (Lin Tse-Hue). (b) 1000c.×2 multicoloured (Gwen Tian-Pei) (each 63×31 mm)	2·50	2·75

DESIGNS: Nos. 2575/81 and **MS**2582, Landscape paintings by Huang Binhong; **MS**2583, Historical scenes.

1997. Christmas. Paintings. As T 284a of Gambia. Multicoloured.

2584	200c. "Cupid" (Botticelli)	20	10
2585	550c. "Zephyr and Chloris" (Botticelli)	50	25
2586	800c. "Triumphant Cupid" (Caravaggio)	75	65
2587	1100c. "The Seven Works of Mercy" (Caravaggio)	1·25	1·40
2588	1500c. "The Toilet of Venus" (Diego Velazquez)	1·40	1·75
2589	2000c. "Freeing of St. Peter" (Raphael)	1·60	2·00
MS2590	Two sheets. (a) 95×105 mm. 5000c. "The Cavalcanti Annunciation" (Donatello). (b) 105×95 mm. 5000c. Ancient Egyptian painting of Isis and Nephthys Set of 2 sheets	8·00	8·50

550 Diana, Princess of Wales

1997. Diana, Princess of Wales Commemoration. Multicoloured (except Nos. 2591, 2596, 2602).

2591	1200c. Type **550** (red)	80	90
2592	1200c. Wearing blue suit and holding flowers	80	90
2593	1200c. Looking right	80	90
2594	1200c. Sitting crossed-legged	80	90
2595	1200c. With Prince William	80	90
2596	1200c. Wearing spotted scarf (blue and black)	80	90
2597	1200c. Wearing pink shirt	80	90
2598	1200c. Wearing red dress	80	90
2599	1200c. Carrying bouquet	80	90
2600	1200c. Wearing sunglasses	80	90
2601	1200c. With children	80	90
2602	1200c. Wearing hat (brown and black)	80	90
MS2603	Two sheets. (a) 100×70 mm. 3000c. Diana, Princess of Wales. (b) 70×100 mm. 3000c. Diana, Princess of Wales (violet and black) Set of 2 sheets	4·50	5·00

551 Horse

1998. Animals of the Chinese Lunar Calendar. Multicoloured.

2604	400c. Type **551**	30	30
2605	400c. Monkey	30	30
2606	400c. Ram	30	30
2607	400c. Cock	30	30
2608	400c. Dog	30	30
2609	400c. Ox	30	30
2610	400c. Rabbit	30	30
2611	400c. Pig	30	30
2612	400c. Snake	30	30
2613	400c. Dragon	30	30
2614	400c. Tiger	30	30
2615	400c. Rat	30	30

552 Mortie and Ferdie (January)

1998. A Year in the Life of Mickey Mouse and Friends. Walt Disney cartoon characters. Multicoloured.

2616	1000c. Type **552**	1·40	1·40
2617	1000c. Minnie on Valentine's Day (February)	1·40	1·40
2618	1000c. Goofy with kite (March)	1·40	1·40
2619	1000c. Mickey, Minnie and Pluto in rain (April)	1·40	1·40
2620	1000c. Minnie with flowers (May)	1·40	1·40
2621	1000c. Daisy watering garden (June)	1·40	1·40
2622	1000c. Donald at Independance Day celebrations (July)	1·40	1·40
2623	1000c. Donald and Daisy on the beach (August)	1·40	1·40
2624	1000c. Morty and Ferdie returning to school (September)	1·40	1·40
2625	1000c. Hewey, Dewey and Louie at Hallowe'en (October)	1·40	1·40
2626	1000c. Mickey on Thanksgiving Day (November)	1·40	1·40

2627 1000c. Mickey and Minnie at Christmas (December) 1·40 1·40

MS2628 Four sheets, each 132×107 mm. (a) 5000c. Mickey bottle feeding calf (Spring) (horiz). (b) 5000c. Minnie camping (Summer). (c) 5000c. Goofy sweeping leaves (Autumn). (d) 5000c. Daisy and Nephews on ice (Winter) (horiz) Set of 4 sheets 19·00 19·00

553 Union Pacific SD60M diesel Locomotive No. 6331, U.S.A.

1998. Trains of the World. Multicoloured.

2629 300c. Type **553** 20 15
2630 500c. ETR 450 high-speed train, Italy 40 25
2631 800c. X200 high-speed train, Sweden 60 60
2632 800c. SPS steam locomotive, Pakistan 60 60
2633 800c. Class WP steam locomotive, India 60 60
2634 800c. Class QJ steam locomotive, China 60 60
2635 800c. Type 12 steam locomotive, Belgium 60 60
2636 800c. Class P8 steam locomotive, Germany 60 60
2637 800c. Class "Castle" steam locomotive, Great Britain 60 60
2638 800c. Tank locomotive, Austria 60 60
2639 800c. Class P36 steam locomotive, Russia 60 60
2640 800c. Steam locomotive "William Mason", U.S.A. 60 60
2641 800c. AVE high-speed train, Spain 60 60
2642 800c. Diesel locomotive No. 1602, Luxembourg 60 60
2643 800c. "Hikari" express train, Japan 60 60
2644 800c. Santa Fe Railroad GM F7 "Warbonnet" diesel locomotive, U.S.A. 60 60
2645 800c. Class E1500 diesel locomotive, Morocco 60 60
2646 800c. Class "Deltic" diesel locomotive, Great Britain 60 60
2647 800c. XPT high-speed train, Australia 60 60
2648 800c. Channel Tunnel shuttle train, France and Great Britain 60 60
2649 800c. Class 201 diesel locomotive, Ireland 60 60
2650 1000c. TGV Duplex high-speed train, France 70 70
2651 2000c. Class EL diesel locomotive, Australia 1·40 1·60
2652 3000c. Eurostar high-speed train, Great Britain 1·60 1·90

MS2653 Two sheets, each 106×76 mm. (a) 5500c. Class "Duchess" steam locomotive heading the "Irish Mail", Great Britain (56×42 mm). (b) 5500c. TGV express train, France (56×42 mm) Set of 2 sheets 6·00 6·50

554 Maya Angelou

1998. Great Writers of the 20th Century. Mult.

2654 350c. Type **554** 40 40
2655 350c. Alex Haley 40 40
2656 350c. Charles Johnson 40 40
2657 350c. Richard Wright 40 40
2658 350c. Toni Cade Bambara 40 40
2659 350c. Henri Louis Gates Jr 40 40

555 Breguet Br 14 B2, France

1998. History of Aviation. Multicoloured.

2660 800c. Type **555** 70 70
2661 800c. Curtiss BF2C-1 Goshawk, U.S.A. 70 70
2662 800c. Supermarine Spitfire Mk IX, Great Britain 70 70
2663 800c. Fiat G.50, Italy 70 70
2664 800c. Douglas B-18A, U.S.A. 70 70
2665 800c. Boeing FB-5, U.S.A. 70 70
2666 800c. Bristol F2B "Brisfit", Great Britain 70 70
2667 800c. Hawker Fury 1, Great Britain 70 70
2668 800c. Fiat CR-42, Italy 70 70
2669 800c. Messerschmitt Bf 109 E-7, Germany 70 70
2670 800c. Lockheed PV-2 Harpoon, U.S.A. 70 70
2671 800c. Airspeed Oxford Mk 1, Great Britain 70 70
2672 800c. Junkers Ju 87D-1, Germany 70 70
2673 800c. Yakovlev Yak-9D, U.S.S.R. 70 70
2674 800c. North American P-51D Mustang, U.S.A. 70 70
2675 800c. Douglas A-206 Havoc, U.S.A. 70 70
2676 800c. Supermarine Attacker F1, Great Britain 70 70
2677 800c. Mikoyan Gurevich MiG-15, U.S.S.R. 70 70

MS2678 Two sheets, each 106×76 mm. (a) 3000c. Supermarine Spitfires Mk 1 and Mk XIV, Great Britain (58×43 mm). (b) 3000c. Mitsubishi AGM8 Reisen, Japan (58×43 mm) Set of 2 sheets 7·50 8·00

556 "Empress of Ireland" (liner)

1998. Famous Ships. Multicoloured.

2679 800c. Type **556** 70 70
2680 800c. "Transylvania" (liner) 70 70
2681 800c. "Mauretania I" (liner) 70 70
2682 800c. "Reliance" (liner) 70 70
2683 800c. "Aquitania" (liner) 70 70
2684 800c. "Lapland" (liner) 70 70
2685 800c. "Cap Polonio" (liner) 70 70
2686 800c. "France I", 1910 (liner) 70 70
2687 800c. "Imperator" (liner) 70 70
2688 800c. H.M.S. "Rodney" (battleship) 70 70
2689 800c. U.S.S. "Alabama" (battleship) 70 70
2690 800c. H.M.S. "Nelson" (battleship) 70 70
2691 800c. "Ormonde" (camouflaged liner) 70 70
2692 800c. U.S.S. "Radford" (destroyer) 70 70
2693 800c. "Empress of Russia" (camouflaged liner) 70 70
2694 800c. Type XIV U-boat 70 70
2695 800c. Japanese Type A midget submarine 70 70
2696 800c. "Brin" (Italian submarine) 70 70

MS2697 Two sheets, each 100×75 mm. (a) 5500c. "Titanic" (liner) (43×57 mm). (b) 5500c. "Amistad" (slave schooner) (43×57 mm) Set of 2 sheets 7·50 8·00

No. 2681 is inscribed "MAURITANIA" in error.

1998. "Israel 98" International Stamp Exhibition, Tel-Aviv. Nos. 2362/4 optd with Emblem.

2698 400c. St. Stephen's Gate and "Jasminum mesnyi" 65 50
2699 600c. The Citadel, Tower of David and "Nerium oleander" 75 75
2700 800c. Chapel of the Ascension and "Romulea bulbocodium" 1·00 1·00

MS2701 65×80 mm. 2000c. Russian Orthodox Church of St. Mary Magdalene (48×30 mm) 2·25 2·25

No. **MS**2701 is additionally overprinted **ISRAEL 98 – WORLD STAMP EXHIBITION TEL-AVIV 13–21 MAY 1998** on the sheet margin.

558 "Renanthera imschootiana"

1998. Orchids of the World. Multicoloured.

2702 800c. Type **558** 70 70
2703 800c. "Arachnis flos-aeris" 70 70
2704 800c. "Restrepia lansbergi" 70 70
2705 800c. "Paphiopedilum tonsum" 70 70
2706 800c. "Phalaenopsis ebauche" 70 70
2707 800c. "Pleione limprichti" 70 70
2708 800c. "Phragmipedium schroderae" 70 70
2709 800c. "Zygopetalum clayii" 70 70
2710 800c. "Vanda coerulea" 70 70
2711 800c. "Odontonia boussole" 70 70
2712 800c. "Disa uniflora" 70 70
2713 800c. "Dendrobium bigibbum" 70 70

MS2714 Two sheets, each 98×68 mm. (a) 5500c. "Cypripedium calceolus". (b) 5500c. "Sobralia candida" Set of 2 sheets 9·00 10·00

559 Elvis Presley

1998. 30th Anniv of Elvis Presley's "68 Special" Television Programme. Multicoloured.

2715 800c. Type **559** 85 85
2716 800c. Elvis in white suit 85 85
2717 800c. In leather jacket, holding microphone 85 85
2718 800c. Wearing light blue jacket 85 85
2719 800c. Elvis with silhouetted figures in background 85 85
2720 800c. Elvis with guitar and microphone 85 85

560 Crest of Accra Metropolitan Assembly and Surf Boats

1998. Centenary of Accra Metropolitan Assembly. Multicoloured.

2721 200c. Type **560** 20 10
2722 550c. King Tackie Tawiah I 40 20
2723 800c. Achimota School 70 35
2724 1100c. Korle Bu Hospital 90 1·00
2725 1500c. Christianborg Castle 1·40 1·75

561 Tetteh Quarshie (cocoa industry pioneer)

1998. 50th Anniv of Ghana Cocoa Board. Multicoloured.

2726 200c. Type **561** 20 10
2727 550c. Ripe hybrid cocoa pods 50 20
2728 800c. Opening cocoa pods 75 40
2729 1100c. Fermenting cocoa beans 1·00 1·10
2730 1500c. Loading freighter with cocoa 1·50 2·00

562 Bamboo

1998. Oriental Flowers. Multicoloured.

2731 2000c. Type **562** 1·00 1·00
2732 2000c. Cherry blossom 1·00 1·00
2733 2000c. Yellow chrysanthemum 1·00 1·00
2734 2000c. Orchid 1·00 1·00
2735 2000c. Green peony 1·00 1·00
2736 2000c. Red peony 1·00 1·00
2737 2000c. Pink peony 1·00 1·00
2738 2000c. White peony 1·00 1·00

MS2739 Two sheets, each 109×85 mm. (a) 5500c. Cherry blossom (horiz). (b) 5500c. Peonies (horiz) Set of 2 sheets 7·00 7·50

563 Two Dolphins

1998. International Year of the Ocean. Multicoloured.

2740 500c. Type **563** 50 50
2741 500c. Dolphin 50 50
2742 500c. Seagull 50 50
2743 500c. Least tern 50 50
2744 500c. Emperor angelfish 50 50
2745 500c. White ear (juvenile) 50 50
2746 500c. Blue shark and diver 50 50
2747 500c. Parrotfish 50 50
2748 500c. Dottyback 50 50
2749 500c. Blue-spotted stingray 50 50
2750 500c. Masked butterflyfish 50 50
2751 500c. Jackknife-fish 50 50
2752 500c. Octopus 50 50
2753 500c. Lionfish 50 50
2754 500c. Seadragon 50 50
2755 500c. Rock cod 50 50

MS2756 Two sheets. (a) 63×98 mm. 3000c. Great white shark. (b) 98×63 mm. 3000c. Devil ray Set of 2 sheets 6·00 6·50

Nos. 2740/55 were printed together, se-tenant, with the backgrounds forming a composite design.

No. 2745 is inscribed "Whit Ear" in error.

1998. Millennium Series. Famous People of the Twentieth Century. Inventors. As T 289a of Gambia. Multicoloured.

2757 1000c. Thomas Edison 60 60
2758 1000c. Peephole kinetoscope (Edison) (53×38 mm) 60 60
2759 1000c. Tesla coil (53×38 mm) 60 60
2760 1000c. Nikola Tesla 60 60
2761 1000c. Gottlieb Daimler 60 60
2762 1000c. Motorcycle (Daimler) (53×38 mm) 60 60
2763 1000c. Early transmitter circuit (Marconi) and dish aerial (53×38 mm) 60 60
2764 1000c. Guglielmo Marconi 60 60
2765 1000c. Orville and Wilbur Wright 60 60
2766 1000c. "Flyer I" (Wright Brothers) (53×38 mm) 60 60
2767 1000c. Neon lights and signs (Claude) (53×38 mm) 60 60
2768 1000c. Georges Claude 60 60
2769 1000c. Alexander Graham Bell 60 60
2770 1000c. Early telephone transmitter (Bell) (53×38 mm) 60 60
2771 1000c. Uses of lasers (Townes) (53×38 mm) 60 60
2772 1000c. Charles Townes 60 60

MS2773 Two sheets, each 76×106 mm. (a) 5500c. Paul Ehrlich. (b) 5500c. Robert Goddard Set of 2 sheets 7·00 7·50

564 British Colourpoint with Tree Decoration

1998. Christmas. Cats and Dogs. Multicoloured.

2774 500c. Type **564** 45 15
2775 600c. American shorthair kitten with basket 50 20
2776 800c. Peke-faced Persian on piano keys 65 30
2777 1000c. German spitz dog in box 80 40
2778 2000c. British shorthair Blue with antlers 1·40 1·75
2779 3000c. Persian in sleigh 1·60 2·00

MS2780 Two sheets, each 76×106 mm. (a) 5500c. English pointer puppy. (b) 5500c. Manx cat with decoration Set of 2 sheets 7·00 7·50

1999. 25th Death Anniv of Pablo Picasso (painter). As T 293a of Gambia. Multicoloured.

2781 1000c. "Composition with Butterfly" 70 80
2782 1000c. "Mandolin and Clarinet" (vert) 70 80
2783 2000c. "Woman throwing a Stone" 1·40 1·60

MS2784 101×127 mm. 5500c. "Tomato Plant" (vert) 4·25 4·75

564a Lampredi

1999. Birth Centenary of Enzo Ferrari (car manufacturer). Multicoloured.

2785 2000c. Type **564a** 1·40 1·40
2786 2000c. 250 GT Cabriolet 1·40 1·40
2787 2000c. 121 LM 1·40 1·40
MS2788 100×70 mm. 3000c. 365 GTS/4 Spyder (91×34 mm) 3·00 3·50

1999. 19th World Scout Jamboree, Chile. As T 291b of Gambia. Multicoloured (except No. MS2792).

2789 2000c. Scout salute 1·25 1·50
2790 2000c. Scout with backpack 1·25 1·50
2791 2000c. Bowline knot 1·25 1·50
MS2792 55×70 mm. 5000c. Lord Baden-Powell (bistre and black) 2·75 3·00

1999. 50th Death Anniv of Mahatma Gandhi. As T 292 of Gambia. Multicoloured.

2793 2000c. Gandhi, 1931 1·60 1·60
2794 2000c. On Salt March, 1930 (53×38 mm) 1·60 1·60
2795 2000c. Collecting natural salt, 1930 (53×38 mm) 1·60 1·60
2796 2000c. After graduating from high school, 1887 1·60 1·60
MS2797 60×79 mm. 5500c. Mahatma Gandhi seated, 1931 5·00 5·00

1999. 80th Anniv of Royal Air Force. As T 292 of Gambia. Multicoloured.

2798 2000c. C-130 Hercules on tarmac 1·50 1·50
2799 2000c. HC2 Chinook helicopter 1·50 1·50
2800 2000c. C-130 Hercules W2 taking off 1·50 1·50
2801 2000c. Panavia Tornado F3 1·50 1·50
MS2802 Two sheets, each 90×70 mm. (a) 5500c. Chipmunk and EF-2000 Euro-fighter. (b) 5500c. Bristol F2B fighter and merlin (bird) Set of 2 sheets 7·50 7·50

1999. 1st Death Anniv of Diana, Princess of Wales. As T 293a of Gambia.

2803 1000c. multicoloured 1·00 1·00

565 Farmer working

1999. Chinese New Year ("Year of the Rabbit"). "Farmer and the Hare" (Han Fei Tzu). Mult.

2804 1400c. Type **565** 1·00 1·00
2805 1400c. Farmer watching hare hit tree 1·00 1·00
2806 1400c. Farmer with dead hare 1·00 1·00
2807 1400c. Farmer asleep under tree 1·00 1·00

566 Shirley Temple praying

1999. 70th Birthday of Shirley Temple (actress). Showing film scenes from "Curly Top". Multicoloured.

2808 1000c. Type **566** 60 70
2809 1000c. Man looking at painting 60 70
2810 1000c. With butler 60 70
2811 1000c. As old woman in rocking chair 60 70
2812 1000c. With mother (horiz) 60 70
2813 1000c. Wearing brown coat and bowler hat (horiz) 60 70
2814 1000c. With cuddly toys (horiz) 60 70
2815 1000c. Pulling father's tie (horiz) 60 70
2816 1000c. With family (horiz) 60 70
2817 1000c. Watching parents (horiz) 60 70
MS2818 106×76 mm. 5000c. Shirley Temple on piano 3·25 4·25

567 Corythosaurus

1999. Prehistoric Animals. Multicoloured.

2819 400c. Type **567** 60 30
2820 600c. Struthiomimus 70 40
2821 800c. Pterodactylus 75 80
2822 800c. Scelidosaurus 75 80
2823 800c. Pteranodon 75 80
2824 800c. Plateosaurus 75 80
2825 800c. Ornithosuchus 75 80
2826 800c. Kentrosaurus 75 80
2827 800c. Hypsognathus 75 80
2828 800c. Erythrosuchus 75 80
2829 800c. Stegoceras 75 80
2830 800c. Ankylosaurus 75 80
2831 800c. Anatosaurus 75 80
2832 800c. Diplodocus 75 80
2833 800c. Monoclonius 75 80
2834 800c. Tyrannosaurus 75 80
2835 800c. Camptosaurus 75 80
2836 800c. Ornitholestes 75 80
2837 800c. Archaeopteryx 75 80
2838 800c. Allosaurus 75 80
2839 1000c. Lambeosaurus 80 85
2840 2000c. Hesperasuchus 1·40 1·75
MS2841 Two sheets, each 85×110 mm. (a) 5000c. Dimorphodon (vert). (b) 5000c. Apatosaurus Set of 2 sheets 7·00 7·50

Nos. 2821/9 and 2830/8 respectively were printed together, se-tenant, with the backgrounds forming composite designs.

568 Badgers

1999. Endangered Species. Multicoloured.

2842 200c. Type **568** 20 15
2843 400c. Azure-winged magpie 40 20
2844 600c. White stork 55 25
2845 800c. Red fox 60 30
2846 1000c. European bee eater ("Merops apiaster") 70 75
2847 1000c. Hoopoe ("Upupa epops") 70 75
2848 1000c. Red deer 70 75
2849 1000c. Short-toed eagle ("Cycaetus gallicus") 70 75
2850 1000c. Lacerta oceliata (lizard) 70 75
2851 1000c. Lynx 70 75
2852 1000c. Pine martin 70 75
2853 1000c. Tawny owl ("Strix aluco") 70 75
2854 1000c. Wild boar 70 75
2855 1000c. Northern goshawk ("Accipiter gentilis") 70 75
2856 1000c. Garden dormouse 70 75
2857 1000c. Stag beetles 70 75
2858 2000c. Cinereous vulture (vert) 1·25 1·50
2859 3000c. Jay (vert) 1·50 2·00
MS2860 Two sheets, each 85×110 mm. (a) 5000c. Imperial eagle ("Iberian Imperial Eagle"). (b) 5000c. Wolf cub (vert) Set of 2 sheets 7·00 7·00

Nos. 2846/51 and 2852/7 respectively were printed together, se-tenant, with the backgrounds forming composite designs.

569 California Sister Butterfly

1999. "Australia '99" International Stamp Exhibition, Melbourne. Butterflies. Multicoloured.

2861 300c. Type **569** 30 15
2862 500c. Red-splashed sulphur 40 20
2863 600c. Checked white 50 25
2864 800c. Blue emperor 60 30
2865 1000c. Red admiral (vert) 70 75
2866 1000c. Buckeye (vert) 70 75
2867 1000c. Desert chequered skipper (vert) 70 75
2868 1000c. Orange sulphur (vert) 70 75
2869 1000c. Tiger swallowtail (vert) 70 75
2870 1000c. Orange-bordered blue (vert) 70 75
2871 1000c. Gulf fritillary "vanillae") (vert) 70 75
2872 1000c. Monarch (vert) 70 75
2873 1000c. Small tortoiseshell (vert) 70 75
2874 1000c. Brimstone (vert) 70 75
2875 1000c. Camberwell beauty (vert) 70 75
2876 1000c. Marbled white (vert) 70 75
2877 1000c. Purple Emperor (vert) 70 75
2878 1000c. Clouded yellow (vert) 70 75
2879 1000c. Ladoga camilla (vert) 70 75
2880 1000c. Marsh fritillary (vert) 70 75
MS2881 Two sheets, each 106×76 mm. (a) 5000c. Homerus swallowtail (vert). (b) 5000c. Blue copper Set of 2 sheets 7·00 7·00

Nos. 2865/72 and 2873/80 respectively were printed together, se-tenant, with the backgrounds forming composite designs.

No. 2862 is inscribed "Red-splashed Sulfer" and No. 2864 "Blue Emperorl", both in error.

571 ICE 2 (Germany), 1966

1999. Railways of the World. Multicoloured.

2883 400c. Type **571** 30 20
2884 500c. M41 No. 2112 (Hungary), 1982 40 20
2885 600c. DVR No. 2526 (Finland), 1963 50 30
2886 1000c. Class AVE 100 (Spain), 1992 70 40
2887 1300c. Conrail EMD SD80 No. 4110 (U.S.A.), 1993 80 85
2888 1300c. Columbus and Greenville EMD SDP35 No. 701 (U.S.A.), 1964–6 80 85
2889 1300c. Providence and Worcester MLW M420 (U.S.A.), 1973–77 80 85
2890 1300c. Missouri Pacific C36-7 No. 9044 (U.S.A.), 1978–85 80 85
2891 1300c. Virginia and Maryland ALCO C-420 No. 203 (U.S.A.), 1963–68 80 85
2892 1300c. Reading EMD GP30 No. 3615 (U.S.A.), 1961–63 80 85
2893 1300c. Illinois Terminal EMD GP7 No. 1506 (U.S.A.), 1949/54 80 85
2894 1300c. Canadian Pacific EMD SD 38-2 (Canada), 1972–79 80 85
2895 1300c. EMD SD 60M 500 No. 6058 (U.S.A.), 1989–96 80 85
2896 1300c. GE U25C No. 2808 (U.S.A.), 1963–65 80 85
2897 1300c. EMD GP 28 (U.S.A.), 1961–63 80 85
2898 1300c. EMD SD 9 No. 162 (U.S.A.), 1954–59 80 85
MS2899 Two sheets. (a) 85×110 mm. 5000c. Swiss Federal Class RE 6/6 No. 11630, 1972. (b) 110×85 mm. 5000c. AGP44 (U.S.A), 1990–91 Set of 2 sheets 7·00 7·50

1999. "iBRA '99" International Stamp Exhibition, Nuremberg. Multicoloured. As T 298a of Gambia.

2900 500c. "Schomberg" (sailing ship) and Hanover 1850 1 ggr. stamp 50 25
2901 800c. Class P8 railway locomotive and Hamburg 1859 ½s. 70 40
2902 1000c. "Schomberg" (sailing ship) and Lubeck 1859 ½s. 85 70
2903 2000c. Class P8 railway locomotive and Heligoland 1867 ½s. 1·40 1·75
MS2904 134×106 mm. 5000c. Germany 3pf. stamp on 1912 Bork-Bruck flown cover (vert) 3·25 3·50

1999. 150th Death Anniv of Katsushika Hokusai (Japanese artist). Multicoloured as T 298b of Gambia, but horiz.

2905 1300c. "Girl picking Plum Blossoms" 80 85
2906 1300c. "Surveying a Region" 80 85
2907 1300c. "Sumo Wrestler" (bending down) 80 85
2908 1300c. "Sumo Wrestler" (dancing) 80 85
2909 1300c. "Landscape with Seaside Village" 80 85
2910 1300c. "Courtiers crossing a Bridge" 80 85
2911 1300c. "Climbing the Mountain" 80 85
2912 1300c. "Nakahara in Sagami Province" 80 85
2913 1300c. "Sumo Wrestlers" 80 85
2914 1300c. "An Oiran and Maid by a Fence" 80 85
2915 1300c. "Fujiwara Yoshitaka" 80 85
MS2916 Two sheets, each 100×70 mm. (a) 5000c. "Palanquin Bearers on a Steep Hill" (vert). (b) 5000c. "Three Ladies by a Well" (vert) Set of 2 sheets 6·50 7·00

1999. 10th Anniv of United Nations Rights of the Child Convention. Vert designs as T 298c of Gambia. Multicoloured.

2917 3000c. Boy smiling and U.N. Headquarters Building 1·60 1·90
2918 3000c. Dove and Earth 1·60 1·90
2919 3000c. Mother and baby 1·60 1·90
MS2920 110×85 mm. 5000c. Boy and UNICEF emblem 3·25 3·75

Nos. 2917/19 were printed together, se-tenant, forming a composite design.

1999. "PhilexFrance '99" International Stamp Exhibition, France. Railway Locomotives. Two sheets, each 106×76 mm, containing horiz designs as T 299d of Gambia. Multicoloured.

MS2921 Two sheets. (a) 5000c. Western Railway suburban tank locomotive. (b) 5000c. National Railways Class 232-U1 Set of 2 sheets 6·50 7·00

1999. 250th Birth Anniv of Johann von Goethe (German writer). As T 298d of Gambia. Multicoloured.

2922 2000c. Wagner entreats Faust in his study 1·25 1·50
2923 2000c. Von Goethe and Von Schiller 1·25 1·50
2924 2000c. Mephistopheles disguised as the Fool 1·25 1·50
MS2925 106×71 mm. 5000c. Faust attended by Spirits 3·25 3·75

1999. 30th Anniv of First Manned Landing on Moon. T 298e of Gambia. Multicoloured.

2926 1300c. Command module 1·25 1·40
2927 1300c. Lunar module ascending 1·25 1·40
2928 1300c. Giant moon rock 1·25 1·40
2929 1300c. Lunar module's aerials and Earth from Moon 1·25 1·40
2930 1300c. Neil Armstrong 1·25 1·40
2931 1300c. "One small step" (alighting on lunar surface) 1·25 1·40
MS2932 71×106 mm. 5000c. Earth from Moon 3·50 4·00

Nos. 2926/31 were printed together, se-tenant, forming a composite design. No. 2927 is inscribed "LUNAR MODULE ASCENSION" in error.

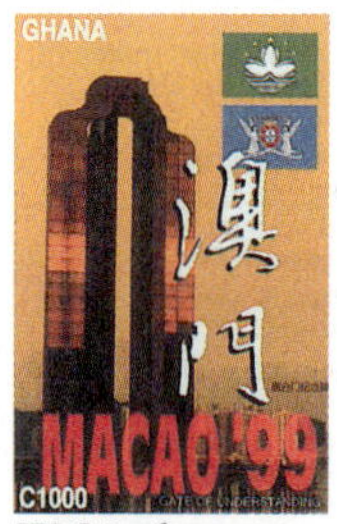

572 Gate of Understanding, Macao

1999. "China '99" World Philatelic Exhibition, Beijing. Return of Macao to China.

2933 **572** 1000c. multicoloured 1·25 1·50

1999. "Queen Elizabeth the Queen Mother's Century". As T 304a of Gambia.

2934 2000c. black and gold 1·75 1·75
2935 2000c. black and gold 1·75 1·75
2936 2000c. multicoloured 1·75 1·75
2937 2000c. multicoloured 1·75 1·75
MS2938 153×157 mm. 5000c. multicoloured 4·00 4·50

DESIGNS: No. 2934, Lady Elizabeth Bowes-Lyon with her brother, David, 1904; 2935, Queen Mother in Rhodesia, 1957; 2936, Queen Mother seated, 1970; 2937, Queen Mother holding bouquet, 1992. (37×50 mm)—**MS**2938, Queen Mother in garden, 1970.

573 Dr. Ephraim Apu

1999. Birth Centenary of Dr. Ephraim Apu (traditional musicologist). Multicoloured.

2939 200c. Type **573** 20 15
2940 800c. Playing Odurugya flute 70 70
2941 1100c. Indigenious flutes 90 1·10

574 Grandma Alice and Village

1999. 25th Anniv of S.O.S. in Ghana (200, 1100c.) and 50th Anniv of S.O.S. Kinderdorf International (children's villages) (others). Multicoloured.

2942	200c. Type **574**	35	15
2943	550c. Kindergarten	80	40
2944	800c. Hermann Gneiner (founder) and Asiakwa S.O.S. building	1·25	90
2945	1100c. Preparing food	1·50	2·00

575 Fishes inside Cloud

1999. Save the Ozone Layer Campaign. Mult.

2946	200c. Type **575**	25	15
2947	550c. African looking at diagram of ozone layer	55	30
2948	800c. Earth weeping	75	65
2949	1100c. Africans shielding Earth	1·00	1·25
2950	1500c. CFC and no-CFC appliances	1·25	1·50

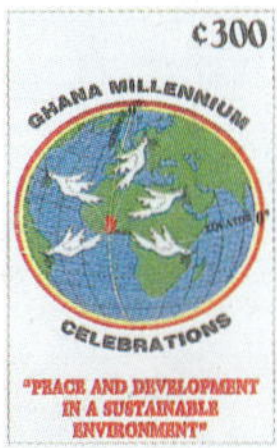

576 Peace Doves flying from Ghana

1999. New Millennium. Multicoloured.

2951	300c. Type **576**	30	20
2952	700c. Kwame Nkrumah (first President) speaking (horiz)	70	70
2953	1200c. Clock tower, University of Ghana	1·10	1·40

577 Liu-Yi meets Daughter of the Dragon King

2000. Chinese New Year ("Year of the Dragon"). Vert designs showing scenes from "Daughter of the Dragon King". Each design brown and silver.

2954	1600c. Type **577**	80	90
2955	1600c. Liu-Yi and Fairy Soldier	80	90
2956	1600c. Liu-Yi and the Dragon King	80	90
2957	1600c. Liu-Yi, Dragon King and Red Dragon	80	90
2958	1600c. Red Dragon and Dragon of Jing River fighting	80	90
2959	1600c. Dragon King with his daughter and brother	80	90
2960	1700c. Dragon King's brother inviting Liu-Yi to marry his niece	80	90
2961	1700c. Liu-Yi bidding farewell to Dragon King	80	90
2962	1700c. Liu-Yi with gifts from Dragon King	80	90
2963	1700c. Liu-Yi with third wife	80	90
2964	1700c. Liu-Yi with third wife and son	80	90
2965	1700c. Liu-Yi realises that third wife is Daughter of the Dragon King	80	90

578 Black-faced Impala

2000. African Wildlife. Multicoloured.

2966	300c. Type **578**	30	10
2967	500c. Cheetah	45	15
2968	1000c. Wildebeest	60	30
2969	1100c. Chimpanzee (vert)	80	85
2970	1100c. Boomslang tree snake (vert)	80	85
2971	1100c. Ruppell's griffon ("Vulture") (vert)	80	85
2972	1100c. Leopard (vert)	80	85
2973	1100c. African rhinoceros (vert)	80	85
2974	1100c. Zebra (vert)	80	85
2975	1100c. South African crowned crane ("Crowned Crane") (vert)	80	85
2976	1100c. Female lesser Kudu (vert)	80	85
2977	1200c. Rufous-crowned roller ("Purple Roller") (vert)	5·75	85
2978	1200c. Eastern white pelican ("Pelicans") (vert)	80	85
2979	1200c. Cattle egret ("Egrets") (vert)	80	85
2980	1200c. Zebra waxbill ("Orange-breasted Waxbill") (vert)	80	85
2981	1200c. Giraffe (vert)	80	85
2982	1200c. African buffalo (vert)	80	85
2983	1200c. Elephant (vert)	80	85
2984	1200c. African lion (vert)	80	85
2985	3000c. Hippopotamus	2·00	2·50
MS2986	Two sheets, each 76×106 mm. (a) 7000c. Ostrich. (b) 7000c. Young waterbuck Set of 2 sheets	6·50	7·00

Nos. 2969/76 and 2977/84 were each printed together, se-tenant, with the backgrounds forming composite designs.

579 Cape Coast Castle

2000. Tourism. Multicoloured.

2987	300c. Type **579**	80	80
2988	300c. Banda Nkwanta Mosque, Accra	80	80
2989	300c. Elephants	80	80
2990	1100c. Tribal chief	1·00	1·40
2991	1200c. Ghanaians with antelope	1·00	1·40
2992	1800c. Tribal chiefs	1·25	1·75

580 Banded ("Zebra") Duiker

2000. Fauna and Flora. Multicoloured.

2993	500c. Type **580**	40	15
2994	600c. Leopard	50	20
2995	1600c. Large spotted genet	90	95
2996	1600c. Tree pangolin	90	95
2997	1600c. Bongo	90	95
2998	1600c. Elephant	90	95
2999	1600c. Flap-necked chameleon	90	95
3000	1600c. West African dwarf crocodile	90	95
3001	1600c. Lowe's monkey	90	95
3002	1600c. Diana monkey	90	95
3003	1600c. Potto	90	95
3004	1600c. Moustached monkey	90	95
3005	1600c. Thomas's galago	90	95
3006	1600c. Chimpanzee	90	95
3007	1600c. Grey parrot	90	95
3008	1600c. Hoopoe	90	95
3009	1600c. European roller	90	95
3010	1600c. European bee-eater	90	95
3011	1600c. Blue-breasted kingfisher	90	95
3012	1600c. White-throated bee eater	90	95
3013	2000c. Bushbuck	1·00	1·25
3014	3000c. African wood owl	2·25	2·50
MS3015	Two sheets. (a) 100×70 mm. 6000c. Hippopotamus (vert). (b) 70×100 mm. 6000c. Great blue turaco (vert) Set of 2 sheets	8·50	9·00

Nos. 2995/3000, 3001/6 and 3007/12 were each printed together, se-tenant, with the backgrounds forming composite designs.

No. 2995 is inscribed "BLOTHED GENET" in error.

581 *Suillus luteus*

2000. African Mushrooms. Multicoloured.

3016	1500c. Type **581**	1·00	1·10
3017	1500c. *Laccaria amethystina*	1·00	1·10
3018	1500c. *Coriolus versicolor*	1·00	1·10
3019	1500c. *Armillaria mellea*	1·00	1·10
3020	1500c. *Lepiota rhacodes*	1·00	1·10
3021	1500c. *Russula queletil*	1·00	1·10
3022	2000c. *Amanita vaginata*	1·10	1·25
3023	2000c. *Lycoperdon perlatum*	1·10	1·25
3024	2000c. *Schizophyllum commune*	1·10	1·25
3025	2000c. *Cantharellus cinereus*	1·10	1·25
3026	2000c. *Coprinus disseminatus*	1·10	1·25
3027	2000c. *Russula cyanoxantaha*	1·10	1·25
MS3028	Two sheets, each 53×81 mm. (a) 5000c. *Aleuria aurantia* (vert). (b) 5000c. *Tylopilus felleus* (vert) Set of 2 sheets	7·50	8·00

582 Cooking Demonstration

2000. 19th International Home Economics Congress, Accra. Multicoloured.

3029	300c. Type **582**	25	15
3030	700c. Student with home economics text book (vert)	65	30
3031	1200c. Mrs. Alberta Ollennu, Ms. Patience Adow and Association logo	1·00	1·10
3032	1800c. Congress logo (vert)	1·50	2·00

2000. 18th Birthday of Prince William. At T 312b of Gambia. Multicoloured.

3033	2000c. In skiing gear	1·75	1·75
3034	2000c. In Eton uniform	1·75	1·75
3035	2000c. With Prince Harry	1·75	1·75
3036	2000c. Prince William (Royal Artillery cap in background)	1·75	1·75
MS3037	100×80 mm. 8000c. Prince William in blue jumper (37×50 mm)	6·00	6·25

582a "Mercury"

2000. "EXPO 2000" World Stamp Exhibition, Anaheim. Manned Spacecraft. Multicoloured.

3038	2000c. Type **582a**	1·40	1·50
3039	2000c. "Gemini"	1·40	1·50
3040	2000c. "Apollo"	1·40	1·50
3041	2000c. "Vostok"	1·40	1·50
3042	2000c. "Voskhod 2"	1·40	1·50
3043	2000c. "Soyuz"	1·40	1·50
MS3044	75×115 mm. 2000c. Space Shuttle *Challenger* mission emblem (vert)	2·00	2·50

Nos. 3038/43 were printed together, se-tenant, with the backgrounds forming a composite design.

582b "Apollo 18"

2000. 25th Anniv of "Apollo"–"Soyuz" Joint Project. Multicoloured.

3045	4000c. Type **582b**	2·25	2·50
3046	4000c. "Apollo 18" and "Soyuz 19" docking	2·25	2·50
3047	4000c. "Soyuz 19"	2·25	2·50
MS3048	105×75 mm. 8000c. "Soyuz 19" and Earth	4·75	5·50

Nos. 3045/7 were printed together, se-tenant, with the backgrounds forming a composite design.

582c *Wetherby*, 1985

2000. 50th Anniv of Berlin Film Festival. Mult.

3049	2000c. Type **582c**	1·25	1·40
3050	2000c. *Die Frau und der Fremde*, 1985	1·25	1·40
3051	2000c. *Hong Gaoliang*, 1988	1·25	1·40
3052	2000c. *Skrivanci na Nitich*, 1990	1·25	1·40
3053	2000c. *Music Box*, 1990	1·25	1·40
3054	2000c. *Terma*, 1987	1·25	1·40
MS3055	95×103 mm. 6000c. *Justice est Faite*, 1951	5·50	6·00

582d Marc Seguin

2000. 175th Anniv of Stockton and Darlington Line (first public railway). Multicoloured.

3056	4000c. Type **582d**	2·50	2·50
3057	4000c. Blenkinsop's locomotive	2·50	2·50
3058	4000c. Pumping station at Dawlish	2·50	2·50

2000. Election of Albert Einstein (mathematical physicist) as Time Magazine "Man of the Century". Sheet 120×90 mm, containing vert portrait as T 312d of Gambia.

MS3059	8000c. multicoloured	4·25	4·50

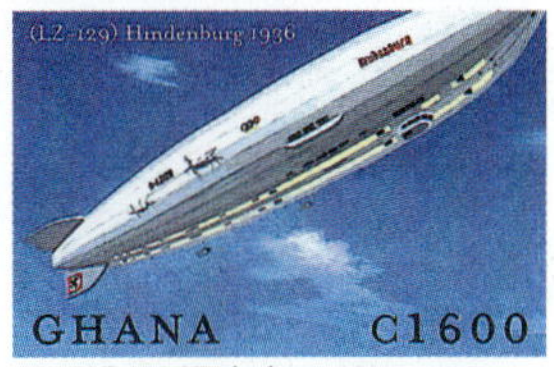

582e LZ-129 *Hindenburg*, 1936

2000. Centenary of First Zeppelin Flight. Mult.

3060	1600c. Type **582e**	1·50	1·60
3061	1600c. LZ-9 *Ersatz Deutschland*, 1911	1·50	1·60
3062	1600c. LZ-4, 1908	1·50	1·60
MS3063	96×65 mm. 5000c. LZ-11 *Viktoria Luise*, 1912	4·25	4·75

Nos. 3060/2 were printed together, se-tenant, with the backgrounds forming a composite design.

582f Gymnast on Parallel Bars, Athens (1896)

2000. Olympic Games, Sydney. Multicoloured.

3064	1300c. Type **582f**	1·10	1·25
3065	1300c. Long jumping	1·10	1·25
3066	1300c. Olympic Stadium, Los Angeles (1984)	1·10	1·25
3067	1300c. Ancient Greek chariot racing	1·10	1·25

583 African Shorthair Cat

2000. Domestic Cats and Dogs. Multicoloured.

3068	1100c. Type **583**	80	60
3069	1200c. Russian blue cat	80	60
3070	1600c. Weimaraner (horiz)	1·00	1·00
3071	1800c. Keeshond (horiz)	1·00	1·00
3072	1800c. Fox terrier (horiz)	1·00	1·00

3073	1800c. Saluki (horiz)	1·00	1·00
3074	1800c. Dalmatian (horiz)	1·00	1·00
3075	1800c. English setter (horiz)	1·00	1·00
3076	1800c. Basenji	1·00	1·00
3077	1800c. Silver Persian (horiz)	1·00	1·00
3078	1800c. Creampoint Himalayan (horiz)	1·00	1·00
3079	1800c. British tortoiseshell shorthair (horiz)	1·00	1·00
3080	1800c. American shorthair tabby (horiz)	1·00	1·00
3081	1800c. Black Persian (horiz)	1·00	1·00
3082	1800c. Turkish van (horiz)	1·00	1·00
3083	2000c. Basset hound	1·25	1·50
MS3084	Two sheets, each 110×85 mm. (a) 8000c. Lilac Persian cat. (b) 8000c. Cocker spaniel Set of 2 sheets	8·50	9·00

584 Xu Xian, White Lady and Xiao Qing

2001. Chinese New Year ("Year of the Snake"). Showing scenes from Tale of the White Snake (traditional Chinese story). Each red and silver.

3085	2500c. Type **584**	1·50	1·50
3086	2500c. White Lady and Xu Xian in pharmacy	1·50	1·50
3087	2500c. Xu Xian with monk Fa Hai	1·50	1·50
3088	2500c. Xu Xian and White Lady drinking wine	1·50	1·50
3089	2500c. Xu Xian having heart attack	1·50	1·50
3090	2500c. White Lady attacked by stork	1·50	1·50
3091	2500c. White Lady, Xiao Qing with swords confront Fa Hai	1·50	1·50
3092	2500c. Xiao Qing and Xu Xian on staircase	1·50	1·50
3093	2500c. Fa Hai entrapping White Lady beneath pagoda	1·50	1·50
3094	2500c. Xiao Qing, Xu Xian praying at pagoda	1·50	1·50
3095	2500c. Xiao Qing attacking Fa Hai	1·50	1·50
3096	2500c. Fa Hai turned into crab	1·50	1·50

585 Walter Gropius (architect)

2001. Twentieth Century Achievements in Architecture, Art and Medicine. Multicoloured.

3097	2500c. Type **585**	1·50	1·50
3098	2500c. Aldo Rossi	1·50	1·50
3099	2500c. Le Corbusier	1·50	1·50
3100	2500c. Antonio Gaudi	1·50	1·50
3101	2500c. Paolo Soleri	1·50	1·50
3102	2500c. Mies van der Rohe	1·50	1·50
3103	2500c. Wassily Kandinsky	1·50	1·50
3104	2500c. Henry Moore	1·50	1·50
3105	2500c. Marc Chagall	1·50	1·50
3106	2500c. Norman Rockwell	1·50	1·50
3107	2500c. Antonio Lopez Garcia	1·50	1·50
3108	2500c. Frida Kahlo	1·50	1·50
MS3109	Three sheets, each 93×64 mm. (a) 14000c. "FRANK LLOYD WRIGHT". (b) 14000c. "Picasso". (c) 14000c. Double helix structure of DNA molecule Set of 3 sheets	22·00	24·00

586 James Cagney

2001. Hollywood Legends. James Cagney and Edward G. Robinson. Designs showing different portraits.

3110	**586**	4000c. green and black	1·75	2·00
3111	-	4000c. green and black	1·75	2·00
3112	-	4000c. blue and black	1·75	2·00
3113	-	4000c. brown and black	1·75	2·00
3114	-	4000c. mauve and black	1·75	2·00
3115	-	4000c. orange and black	1·75	2·00
3116	-	4000c. green and black	1·75	2·00
3117	-	4000c. lilac, purple and black	1·75	2·00
3118	-	4000c. purple and black	1·75	2·00
3119	-	4000c. brown and black	1·75	2·00
3120	-	4000c. brown and black	1·75	2·00
3121	-	4000c. blue and black	1·75	2·00

Nos. 3110/15 (Cagney) and 3116/21 (Robinson) were each printed together, se-tenant, showing a photograph of the actor.

586a Margie Hendrix (shoulder at bottom right)

2001. Famous Girl Pop Groups. The Cookies (Nos. 3122/4), The Ronettes (Nos. 3125/7) and The Supremes (Nos. 3128/30). Multicoloured.

3122	2700c. Type **586a**	1·50	1·75
3123	2700c. Ethel McCrea (with straight hair)	1·50	1·75
3124	2700c. Pat Lyles's head (background at bottom right)	1·50	1·75
3125	2700c. Estelle Bennett (inscr and value clear of portrait)	1·50	1·75
3126	2700c. Veronica Bennett (inscr and value touch portrait)	1·50	1·75
3127	2700c. Nedra Talley (inscr touches, value clear of portrait)	1·50	1·75
3128	2700c. Florence Ballard (left earring)	1·50	1·75
3129	2700c. Mary Wilson (two earrings)	1·50	1·75
3130	2700c. Diana Ross (right earring)	1·50	1·75

Each group forms a horizontal strip with different background colour: The Cookies cobalt, The Ronettes blue and The Supremes yellow and red.

587 Edward "Kid" Ory (trombonist)

2001. Famous American Jazz Musicians. Multicoloured.

3131	4000c. Type **587**	1·75	2·00
3132	4000c. Earl "Fatha" Hines (pianist)	1·75	2·00
3133	4000c. Lil Hardin-Armstrong (pianist)	1·75	2·00
3134	4000c. John Philip Sousa (composer)	1·75	2·00
3135	4000c. James P. Johnson (pianist)	1·75	2·00
3136	4000c. Johnny St. Cyr (banjo/guitar player)	1·75	2·00
3137	4000c. Scott Joplin (composer)	1·75	2·00
3138	4000c. Clarence Williams (pianist)	1·75	2·00
3139	4000c. Sidney Bechet (clarinetist/saxophonist)	1·75	2·00
3140	4000c. Willie "The Lion" Smith (pianist)	1·75	2·00
3141	4000c. Ferdinand "Jelly Roll" Morton (composer)	1·75	2·00
3142	4000c. Coleman "Bean" Hawkins (saxophonist)	1·75	2·00
MS3143	Two sheets, each 60×77 mm. (a) 14000c. Louis "Satchmo" Armstrong (cornet player). (b) 14000c. Joe "King" Oliver (cornet player) Set of 2 sheets	11·00	13·00

588 "Cranes" (Kano Eisen'in Michinobu)

2001. "Philanippon '01" International Stamp Exhibition, Tokyo. Japanese Paintings. Multicoloured.

3144	500c. Type **588**	30	20
3145	800c. "Flowers and Trees in Chen Chun's Style" (Tsubaki Chinzan)	40	25
3146	1200c. "Poetry Contest of 42 Matches" (unsigned)	60	40
3147	2000c. "Cranes" (different detail) (Kano Eisen'in Michinobu)	1·00	75
3148	3000c. "Coming-of-Age Rite" (vert)	1·25	1·25
3149	3000c. "West Wing" (vert)	1·25	1·25
3150	3000c. "Akuta River" (vert)	1·25	1·25
3151	3000c. "Eastbound Trip: Mt. Utsu" (vert)	1·25	1·25
3152	3000c. "Eastbound Trip: Mt. Fuji" (vert)	1·25	1·25
3153	3000c. "Eastbound Trip: Black-headed Gulls" (vert)	1·25	1·25
3154	3000c. "Crossing Kawachi" (vert)	1·25	1·25
3155	3000c. "By Well Wall" (vert)	1·25	1·25
3156	4000c. "Excursion through South Gate" (vert)	1·40	1·40
3157	4000c. "Excursion through East Gate" (vert)	1·40	1·40
3158	4000c. "Excursion through North Gate" (vert)	1·40	1·40
3159	4000c. "Excursion through West Gate" (vert)	1·40	1·40
3160	4000c. "Sakyamuni entering Nirvana" (vert)	1·40	1·40
3161	4000c. "Animals" (vert)	1·40	1·40
3162	5000c. "Poetry Contest of 42 Matches" (different detail) (unsigned)	1·60	1·75
3163	12000c. "Plum Trees" (Tani Buncho)	3·50	4·50
MS3164	Four sheets, each 100×76 mm. (a) 14000c. "Cranes" (Kano Eisen'in Michinobu) ("GHANA" and value in red). (b) 14000c. "Cranes" (Kano Eisen'in Michinobu) ("GHANA" in yellow). (c) 14000c. "Coming-of-Age Rite" (Sumiyoshi Jokei). (d) 14000c. "Musashino Plain" (unknown artist) Set of 4 sheets	24·00	26·00

Nos. 3148/55 ("The Tales of Ise" (Sumiyoshi Jokei)) and 3156/63 ("The Story of Sakyamuni").

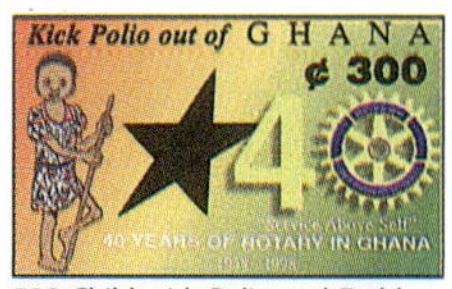

589 Child with Polio and Emblem

2001. 40th Anniv of Rotary in Ghana. Each including the Rotary International symbol. Multicoloured.

3165	300c. Type **589**	50	20
3166	1100c. Boy getting clean water from tap	1·00	1·10
3167	1200c. Paul Harris (founder of Rotary International)	1·00	1·10
3168	1800c. Man giving blood	1·50	2·00

590 Bentley S-Series Convertible (1950)

2001. "Belgica 2001" International Stamp Exhibition, Brussels. Twentieth-century classic Cars. Multicoloured.

3169	2000c. Type **590**	1·00	1·00
3170	3000c. Chrysler Town and Country (1948)	1·25	1·25
3171	4000c. B.M.W. 507 (1956–59)	1·40	1·40
3172	4000c. Bentley English Tourer (1934)	1·40	1·40
3173	4000c. Morris Minor (1948)	1·40	1·40
3174	4000c. Daimler SP-250 Dart (1954)	1·40	1·40
3175	4000c. DeSoto Custom Convertible (1950)	1·40	1·40
3176	4000c. Ford Thunderbird (1955–60)	1·40	1·40
3177	4000c. Porsche 356B (1959–63)	1·40	1·40
3178	4000c. Rolls-Royce Silver Cloud (1962)	1·40	1·40
3179	4000c. Austin Healey Sprite Mk 1 (1958)	1·40	1·40
3180	4000c. Mercedes 300SL (1954–57)	1·40	1·40
3181	4000c. Citroen 2cv (1949)	1·40	1·40
3182	4000c. Cadillac Series-62 (1949)	1·40	1·40
3183	5000c. Lotus Elite (1957)	1·50	1·60
3184	6000c. Corvette Sting Ray (1966)	1·75	1·90
MS3185	Two sheets, each 102×74 mm. (a) 14000c. Mercedes-Benz (1933) (85×28 mm). (b) 14000c. Triumph TR2 (1953–55) (85×28 mm) Set of 2 sheets	9·50	11·00

No. 3172 is inscribed "Bentler" and No. 3181 "Citreon", both in error.

590a Princess Victoria as a Young Girl

2001. Death Centenary of Queen Victoria. Multicoloured.

3186	5000c. Type **590a**	2·00	2·25
3187	5000c. Albert Edward, Prince of Wales	2·00	2·25
3188	5000c. Queen Victoria and Prince of Wales	2·00	2·25
3189	5000c. Queen Victoria and Prince Albert on Wedding Day	2·00	2·25
MS3190	66×96 mm. 12000c. Princess Victoria (The Princess Royal)	5·00	6·00

MS3190 is inscr Princess Victoria in error.

590b Mao in Uniform acknowledging Crowd

2001. 25th Death Anniv of Mao Tse-tung (Chinese leader). Multicoloured.

3191	7000c. Type **590b**	1·75	2·25
3192	7000c. Head and shoulders portrait	1·75	2·25
3193	7000c. Mao in overcoat acknowledging crowd	1·75	2·25
MS3194	116×102 mm. 12000c. Mao as a young man	4·00	5·00

590c "Zaandam"

2001. 75th Death Anniv Claude-Oscar Monet. (French painter). Multicoloured.

3195	5000c. Type **590c**	1·75	2·00
3196	5000c. "On the Seine at Bennecourt"	1·75	2·00
3197	5000c. "The Studio-boat"	1·75	2·00
3198	5000c. "Houses on the Waterfront, Zaandam"	1·75	2·00
MS3199	139×110 mm. 15000c. "Madame Gaudibert" (vert)	5·50	6·50

590d Queen Elizabeth in pink hat

2001. 75th Birthday of Queen Elizabeth II. Multicoloured.

3200	4000c. Type **590d**	1·75	1·75
3201	4000c. Queen Elizabeth in white hat with flowers	1·75	1·75
3202	4000c. In red "trilby"	1·75	1·75
3203	4000c. Wearing tiara	1·75	1·75
3204	4000c. In matching blue and pink hat and coat	1·75	1·75
3205	4000c. Queen Elizabeth in uniform for Trooping the Colour	1·75	1·75
MS3206	85×135 mm. 15000c. Queen Elizabeth with Duke of Edinburgh (horiz)	6·50	7·00

590e Giuseppe Verdi

2001. Death Centenary of Giuseppe Verdi (Italian composer). Multicoloured.

3207	5000c. Type **590e**	2·25	2·25
3208	5000c. Musical scores for *Aida* and *Rigoletto*	2·25	2·25
3209	5000c. Inn at Le Roncole (Verdi's birthplace)	2·25	2·25
3210	5000c. Map of Italy	2·25	2·25
MS3211	76×106 mm. 13000c. Giuseppe Verdi	6·00	6·00

Nos. 3207/11 were printed together, se-tenant, with the backgrounds forming a composite design.

590f "Jane Avril leaving the Moulin Rouge"

2001. Death Centenary of Henri de Toulouse-Lautrec (French painter). Multicoloured.

3212	6700c. Type **590f**	2·00	2·25
3213	6700c. "Jane Avril dancing"	2·00	2·25
3214	6700c. "Jane Avril entering the Moulin Rouge"	2·00	2·25

591 Killer Whale

2001. Whales and Dolphins. Multicoloured.

3215	1000c. Type **591**	80	45
3216	3000c. Narwhal	1·40	1·40
3217	4000c. Humpback whale	1·50	1·50
3218	4000c. Fin whale	1·50	1·50
3219	4000c. Bowhead whale	1·50	1·50
3220	4000c. Grey whale	1·50	1·50
3221	4000c. Narwhal	1·50	1·50
3222	4000c. White whale ("Beluga")	1·50	1·50
3223	4000c. Head of blue whale	1·50	1·50
3224	4000c. Killer whale	1·50	1·50
3225	4000c. Northern bottlenose dolphin	1·50	1·50
3226	4000c. Sperm whale	1·50	1·50
3227	4000c. Southern right whale	1·50	1·50
3228	4000c. Pygmy right whale	1·50	1·50
3229	5000c. White whale ("Beluga")	1·75	1·90
3230	6000c. Bowhead whale	2·00	2·25
MS3231	Two sheets, each 100×85 mm. (a) 14000c. Blue whale adult and calf. (b) 14000c. Head of sperm whale Set of 2 sheets	11·00	12·00

Nos. 3217/22 and 3223/8 were each printed together, se-tenant, the backgrounds forming composite designs.

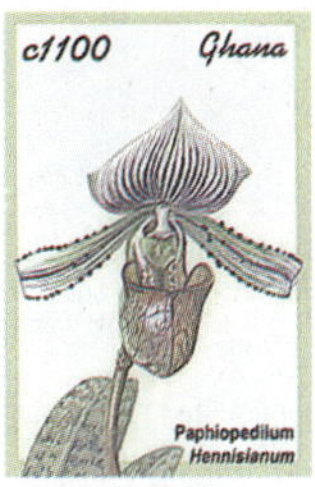

592 *Paphiopedilum hennisianum*

2001. African Orchids. Multicoloured.

3232	1100c. Type **592**	70	40
3233	1200c. *Vuylstekeara cambria Plush*	70	40
3234	1800c. *Cymbidium Ormoulu*	95	70
3235	2000c. *Phalaenopsis Barbara Moler*	1·00	70
3236	4500c. *Odontocidium Tigersun*	1·60	1·60
3237	4500c. *Miltonia Emotion*	1·60	1·60
3238	4500c. *Odontonia sappho Excul*	1·60	1·60
3239	4500c. *Cymbidium Bulbarrow*	1·60	1·60
3240	4500c. *Dendrobium nobile*	1·60	1·60
3241	4500c. *Paphiopedilum insigne*	1·60	1·60
3242	4500c. *Cattleya capra*	1·60	1·60
3243	4500c. *Odontoglossum rossii*	1·60	1·60
3244	4500c. *Epidendrum pseudepidendrum*	1·60	1·60
3245	4500c. *Encyclia cochleata*	1·60	1·60
3246	4500c. *Cymbidium Baldoyle Melbury*	1·60	1·60
3247	4500c. *Phalaenopsis asean*	1·60	1·60
MS3248	Two sheets, each 68×98 mm. (a) 15000c. *Calanthe vestita*. (b) 15000c. *Angraecum eburneum* Set of 2 sheets	12·00	13·00

593 50th Anniversary Logo

2001. 50th Anniv of Kwame Nkrumah University of Science and Technology, Kumasi. Multicoloured.

3249	300c. Type **593**	30	15
3250	700c. Main entrance	50	35
3251	1100c. Milking cows	80	80
3252	1200c. Students in pharmacy department	80	80
3253	1800c. Halls of residence	1·10	1·40
MS3254	120×100 mm. As Nos. 3250/3, but each with a face value of 4000c.	6·50	7·50

594 Bamboo Orchestra

2001. Musical Instruments. Multicoloured.

3255	4000c. Type **594**	1·50	1·50
3256	4000c. Women playing mensuon (wind instruments)	1·50	1·50
3257	4000c. Fontomfrom (drums)	1·50	1·50
3258	4000c. Pati	1·50	1·50

595 George Olah (Chemistry Prize, 1994)

2002. Centenary of Nobel Prizes. Chemistry Prize Winners (except Nos. MS3277d/e). Multicoloured.

3259	4000c. Type **595**	1·40	1·40
3260	4000c. Kary Mullis (1993)	1·40	1·40
3261	4000c. Sir Harold Kroto (1996)	1·40	1·40
3262	4000c. Richard Ernst (1991)	1·40	1·40
3263	4000c. Ahmed Zewail (1999)	1·40	1·40
3264	4000c. Paul Crutzen (1995)	1·40	1·40
3265	4000c. John Walker (1997)	1·40	1·40
3266	4000c. Jens Skou (1997)	1·40	1·40
3267	4000c. Alan MacDiarmid (2000)	1·40	1·40
3268	4000c. Thomas Cech (1989)	1·40	1·40
3269	4000c. John Pople (1998)	1·40	1·40
3270	4000c. Rudolph Marcus (1992)	1·40	1·40
3271	4000c. Walter Kohn (1998)	1·40	1·40
3272	4000c. Frank Rowland (1995)	1·40	1·40
3273	4000c. Mario Molina (1995)	1·40	1·40
3274	4000c. Hideki Shirakawa (2000)	1·40	1·40
3275	4000c. Paul Boyer (1997)	1·40	1·40
3276	4000c. Richard Smalley (1996)	1·40	1·40
MS3277	Five sheets, each 106×77 mm. (a) 15000c. Svante Arrhenius (1903). (b) 15000c. Alfred Werner (1913). (c) 15000c. Peter Debye (1936). (d) 15000c. Wole Soyinka (Literature, 1986). (e) 15000c. Nelson Mandela (Peace, 1993) Set of 5 sheets	23·00	25·00

596 Queen Elizabeth at the Races

2002. Golden Jubilee. Multicoloured.

3278	6500c. Type **596**	2·75	3·00
3279	6500c. Queen Elizabeth on horseback	2·75	3·00
3280	6500c. Queen Elizabeth inspecting horses	2·75	3·00
3281	6500c. Queen Elizabeth in carriage with Duke of Edinburgh, Ascot races	2·75	3·00
MS3282	76×108 mm. 15000c. Princess Elizabeth with Duke of Edinburgh	7·00	8·00

597 Conference Logo

2002. 5th International Copyright Conference, Accra. Multicoloured.

3283	300c. Type **597**	35	15
3284	700c. Girl reading (horiz)	60	35
3285	1100c. Spider on web (horiz)	1·00	1·10
3286	1200c. Woven cloth in shape of Ghana (horiz)	1·00	1·10
3287	1800c. Woman playing drum (horiz)	1·50	2·00

598 Jay Jay Okacha (Nigeria)

2002. World Cup Football Championship, Japan and Korea. Multicoloured.

3288	100c. Type **598**	15	15
3289	150c. South African player	20	15
3290	300c. Pele (Brazil)	30	20
3291	400c. Roger Milla (Cameroun)	35	20
3292	500c. Bobby Charlton (England)	45	25
3293	800c. Michel Platini (France)	50	30
3294	1000c. Franz Beckenbauer (West Germany)	60	35
3295	1500c. Ulsan Munsu Stadium, Korea (horiz)	80	65
3296	2000c. German player	90	75
3297	3000c. Brazilian player	1·25	1·25
3298	4000c. South Korean player	1·40	1·40
3299	5000c. Yokohama International Stadium, Japan (horiz)	1·50	1·60
3300	6000c. Italian player	1·75	2·00
3301	11000c. Publicity poster, Brazil, 1950	3·00	3·75
3302	12000c. Publicity poster, Italy, 1934	3·25	3·75
MS3303	Two sheets. (a) 77×107 mm. 15000c. Geoff Hurst (England), 1966 (43×58 mm). (b) 107×77 mm. 15000c. Gordon Banks (England), 1970 (58×43 mm) Set of 2 sheets	11·00	12·00

599 Girl on Pony

2002. Chinese New Year ("Year of the Horse"). Multicoloured.

3304	4000c. Type **599**	1·25	1·40
3305	4000c. Girl and caparisoned pony	1·25	1·40
3306	4000c. Girl with whip and pony	1·25	1·40
3307	4000c. Girl on hobby horse	1·25	1·40

2002. No. 2159a surch c 1000.

3308	1000c. on 1100c. Kente cloth	4·50	3·50

2002. No. 2458e surch c2,500.

3309	2500c. on 800c. *Cyrestis camillus* (butterfly)	7·00	7·00

602 Crown Prince Willem-Alexander and Princess Maxima of the Netherlands

2002. "Amphilex 2002" International Stamp Exhibition, Amsterdam. Visit of Crown Prince and Princess of the Netherlands. Multicoloured.

3310	6000c. Type **602**	1·50	1·60
3311	6000c. Royal couple on wedding day	1·50	1·60
3312	6000c. Standing by windmill	1·50	1·60
3313	6000c. Serenaded by accordionist on wedding day	1·50	1·60
3314	6000c. Meeting crowds	1·50	1·60
3315	6000c. Kissing on wedding day	1·50	1·60

603 "Trying to retrieve a Ball caught in a Tree"

2002. Japanese Paintings by Katsukawa Shunsho. Multicoloured.

MS3316	170×123 mm. 9000c. Type **603**; 9000c. "Listening to a Cuckoo in the Bedroom"; 9000c. "Holding a Cage filled with Fireflies for a Woman to read a Book"	8·00	9·00
MS3317	170×123 mm. 9000c. "Mother and Child taking a Tub-bath while Woman holds a Revolving Lantern"; 9000c. "Strips of Paper with Wishes and Poems are Tied on a Bamboo"; 9000c. "Women enjoying the Cool Air on a Boat"	8·00	9·00
MS3318	170×123 mm. 9000c. "Celebrating Feast of the Chrysanthemum"; 9000c. "Looking out for Coloured Leaves"; 9000c. "Mother reading Picture Book while sitting at a Foot-warmer"	8·00	9·00
MS3319	Four sheets, each 95×105 mm. (a) 15000c. "Three Women decorating a Gate with Twigs of Holly on the Day before the Setting-in of the Spring". (b) 15000c. Woman looking at flowering plant in pot. (c) 15000c. Woman at writing desk. (d) 15000c. Woman pulling down blind Set of 4 sheets	17·00	19·00

Nos. **MS**3316/19a show details of paintings on silk "Activities of Women in the Twelve Months".

Nos. **MS**3319b/d show details from triptych "Snow, Moonlight and Flowers".

604 Scout hiking

2002. 20th World Scout Jamboree, Thailand. Multicoloured.

MS3320	109×90 mm. 6500c. Type **604**; 6500c. Scout hiking (standing on horizon); 6500c. Campfire and tent; 6500c. Scout tying knot	8·00	8·50
MS3321	99×71 mm. 15000c. Ghanian scout (vert)	4·25	4·50

605 Mt. Tateyama, Japan

2002. International Year of Mountains. Multicoloured.

MS3322 105×90 mm. 6000c. Type **605**; 6000c. Mt. Shivling, India; 6000c. Wong Leng, Hong Kong; 6000c. Mt. Blanc, France 6·00 7·00

MS3323 100×72 mm. 15000c. Mt. Fuji, Japan 4·50 5·00

606 Lindbergh and Ryan NYP Special *Spirit of St. Louis*

2002. 75th Anniv of First Solo Trans-Atlantic Flight. Multicoloured.

MS3324 171×129 mm. 8500c. Type **606**; 8500c. Charles and Anne Lindbergh in *Spirit of St. Louis* 7·50 8·00

MS3325 114×81 mm. 15000c. Charles Lindbergh (vert) 4·50 5·00

607 Variable Sunbird

2002. Year of Eco Tourism. Multicoloured.

MS3326 116×125 mm. 4000c. Type **607**; 4000c. Leopard; 4000c. Kob (antelope); 4000c. African buffalo; 4000c. Chimpanzee; 4000c. Lesser bushbaby 8·00 9·00

MS3327 81×97 mm. 12000c. African elephant 5·00 5·00

2002. Queen Elizabeth the Queen Mother Commemoration. Nos. 2191/5 (95th Birthday) surch C3000.

3328	3000c. on 600c. brown, light brown and black	1·75	1·75
3329	3000c. on 600c. multicoloured	1·75	1·75
3330	3000c. on 600c. multicoloured	1·75	1·75
3331	3000c. on 600c. multicoloured	1·75	1·75

MS3332 102×127 mm. 20000c. on 2500c. multicoloured 8·00 8·50

The sheetlet and miniature sheet margins have black borders and are overprinted **IN MEMORIAM 1900–2002**.

609 Ice Skaters

2002. Winter Olympic Games, Salt Lake City. Multicoloured.

3333	7000c. Type **609**	3·00	3·00
3334	7000c. Skier in aerials competition	3·00	3·00

MS3335 88×119 mm. Nos. 3333/4 6·00 6·00

610 US Flag as Statue of Liberty with Ghana Flag

2002. "United We Stand". Support for Victims of 11 September 2001 Terrorist Attacks.

3336	**610**	7000c. multicoloured	2·50	3·00

611 Malachite Kingfisher

2002. Birds, Butterflies, Insects and Moths. Multicoloured.

MS3337 160×93 mm. 4500c. Type **611**; 4500c. Brown snake eagle ("Brown Harrier-eagle"); 4500c. Heuglin's masked weaver; 4500c. Egyptian plover; 4500c. Swallow-tailed bee eater; 4500c. Black-faced fire-finch 9·00 9·00

MS3338 160×93 mm. 4500c. *Iolaus menas*; 4500c. *Neptis melicerta*; 4500c. *Cymothoe lucas*; 4500c. *Euphaedra francina*; 4500c. Lilac nymph; 4500c. Mocker swallowtail 9·00 9·00

MS3339 160×93 mm. 4500c. *Phymateus viridipes* (bush-hopper); 4500c. *Tomatares citrinus* (ant-lion); 4500c. *Ameg-illa acraensis* (digger-bee); 4500c. *Mesotopus tarandus* (stag-beetle); 4500c. *Pseudocreobotra wahlbergi* (mantis); 4500c. *Phosphorus jansoni* (longhorn beetle) 9·00 9·00

MS3340 160×93 mm. 4500c. *Phiala cunina*; 4500c. *Mazuca strigicincta*; 4500c. Steindachner's emperor moth; 4500c. *Amphicallia pactolicus*; 4500c. Verdant sphinx moth; 4500c. Oleander hawk-moth 9·00 9·00

MS3341 Four sheets, each 83×86 mm. (a) 15000c. Rufous fishing owl. (b) 15000c. Giant blue swallowtail. (c) 15000c. *Pseudocreobotra wahlbergi* (mantis nymph). (d) 15000c. African moon-moth Set of 4 sheets 19·00 21·00

612 Casting of Net

2002. Edina Bakatue Festival. Multicoloured.

3342	1000c. Type **612**	70	30
3343	2000c. Chief in palanquin	1·10	90
3344	2500c. Canoe in regatta	1·25	1·25
3345	3000c. Fishermen in festival boat	1·40	1·40
3346	4000c. Opening ritual	1·50	1·60
3347	5000c. Parade of priestesses	1·75	1·90

MS3348 160×90 mm. 4000c. As No. 3347; 4000c. As No. 3343; 4000c. As No. 3344; 4000c. As No. 3345; 4000c. As No. 3346; 4000c. Type **612** 8·50 9·00

613 Home Economics

2002. 25th Anniv of Japan Overseas Co-operation Volunteers in Ghana. Multicoloured.

3349	1000c. Type **613**	70	50
3350	1000c. Public health administration	70	50
3351	2000c. Education in science and mathematics	1·10	90
3352	2500c. Computer technology	1·25	1·25
3353	3000c. Judo coaching	1·40	1·50

MS3354 172×120 mm. 4000c. As No. 3351; 4000c. As No. 3350; 4000c. As No. 3353; 4000c. As No. 3352; 4000c. Type **613** 8·50 9·00

Stamps from No. **MS**3354 have the white descriptive inscriptions omitted.

614 Kofi Annan with Pres. Kufuor at Nobel Prize Award Ceremony

2002. Kofi Annan (United Nations Secretary-General). Multicoloured.

3355	1000c. Type **614**	55	30
3356	2000c. Kofi Annan holding Citation and Nobel Peace Medal	90	70
3357	2500c. Kofi Annan	1·00	1·00
3358	3000c. In academic procession, Kwame Nkrumah University, Kumasi	1·25	1·50

615 Charlie Chaplin

2003. 25th Death Anniv of Charlie Chaplin (actor and director). Multicoloured.

MS3359 151×126 mm. 6500c. Type **615**; 6500c. Wearing dark jacket; 6500c. Wearing pinstriped dungarees; 6500c. Holding Honorary Academy Award, 1972 9·00 9·00

616 Marlene Dietrich

2003. 10th Death Anniv (2002) of Marlene Dietrich (actress and singer). Sheets containing T 616 and similar vert designs showing different portraits.

MS3360 127×178 mm. 4500c.×6 multicoloured 8·00 9·00

MS3361 76×101 mm. 15000c. Holding cigarette 4·50 5·00

617 Popeye alongside Canal

2003. "Popeye the Sailorman tours Amsterdam". Multicoloured.

MS3362 173×202 mm. 4500c. Type **617**; 4500c. Outside Anne Frank's House; 4500c. At Restaurant Row; 4500c. Downtown, carrying Olive Oyl; 4500c. Scientific Station; 4500c. With telescope, by windmill 7·50 8·50

MS3363 136×93 mm. 15000c. Eating spinach (50×75 mm) 4·00 4·50

618 "Under the Pagoda Tree" (Liu Kui Ling)

2003. Chinese New Year ("Year of the Ram").

MS3364 **618** 141×115 mm. 5000c.×4 multicoloured 7·00 7·50

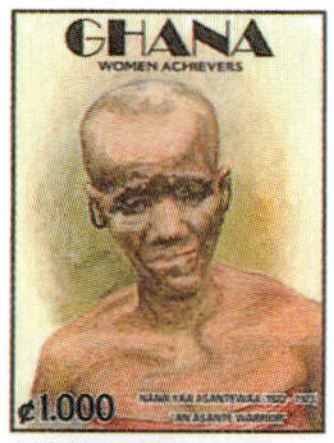

619 Nana Yaa Asantewaa (Asante warrior)

2003. Women Achievers. Multicoloured.

3365	1000c. Type **619**	55	30
3366	2000c. Justice Annie Jiagge (judge)	90	70
3367	2500c. Dr. Esther Ocloo (industrialist)	1·10	1·10
3368	3000c. Dr. Efua T. Sutherland (playwright)	1·25	1·40
3369	5000c. Rebecca Dedei Aryeetay (womens rights activist)	1·75	1·90

620 Children holding Drawings ("tomorrow's leaders")

2003. 60th Anniv of British Council in Ghana. Multicoloured.

3370	1000c. Type **620**	55	30
3371	2000c. Women holding Africa-woman newspapers	90	70
3372	2500c. Singers on stage ("partners in culture")	1·10	1·10
3373	3000c. People reading in library ("window on the world")	1·25	1·40
3374	5000c. Footballers and coach ("leadership through sport")	1·75	1·90

621 Queen Elizabeth II wearing Diadem

2003. 50th Anniv of Coronation. Multicoloured.

MS3375 156×94 mm. 10000c. Type **621**; 10000c. Queen wearing blue dress and hat; 10000c. Wearing Garter robes 10·00 11·00

MS3376 76×106 mm. 20000c. Wearing Garter robes (different) 7·00 8·00

622 Ryan NYP Special *Spirit of St. Louis* (first non-stop solo transatlantic crossing, 1927)

2003. Centenary of Powered Flight. Multicoloured.

MS3377 185×116 mm. 7000c. Type **622**; 7000c. Lockheed Vega V *Winnie Mae* (first solo round-the-world flight, 1933); 7000c. Heinkel He 178 (first turbo-jet aircraft, 1939); 7000c. Bell XS-1 rocket airplane (first manned supersonic flight, 1947) 8·00 9·00

MS3378 106×76 mm. 20000c. Dr. Robert Goddard and first liquid-fuelled rocket 6·50 7·50

623 Romain Maes (1935)

2003. Centenary of Tour de France Cycle Race. Designs showing past winners. Multicoloured.

MS3379 7000c. Type **623**; 7000c. Sylvere Maes (1936); 7000c. Roger Lapebie (1937); 7000c. Gino Bartali (1938) 9·00 9·50

MS3380 107×75 mm. 20000c. Henri Pelissier (1923) 7·00 7·50

624 Cadillac Sixty Special (1941)

2003. Centenary of General Motors Cadillac. Multicoloured.

MS3381 126×176 mm. 7000c. Type **624**; 7000c. Eldorado (1953); 7000c. Eldorado Brougham (1957); 7000c. Eldorado Convertible (1959) 8·00 9·00

MS3382 90×125 mm. 20000c. Early Cadillac 5·50 6·00

625 Corvette (1962)

2003. 50th Anniv of General Motors Chevrolet Corvette. Multicoloured.

MS3383 126×152 mm. 7000c. Type **625**; 7000c. Corvette Stingray (1963); 7000c. Corvette Stingray (1964); 7000c. Corvette (1968) 8·00 9·00

MS3384 126×89 mm. 20000c. Corvette Stingray (1966) 5·50 6·00

626 "Preparation for Christmas" (Kwame Owusu Aduomi)

2003. Christmas. Children's Paintings. Multicoloured.

3385 2000c. Type **626** 1·00 35

3386 4000c. "Typical Christmas Present" (Thomas Kyerematteng) (vert) 1·50 1·75

3387 4500c. "Making Merry at Christmas" (Samuel Baffoe Maison) 1·50 2·00

3388 5000c. "Christmas is Here" (Patrick Annan) 1·75 2·00

627 Female Mandrill

2004. Chinese New Year ("Year of the Monkey"). Multicoloured.

MS3389 137×172 mm. 5000c. Type **627**; 5000c. Mueller's gibbon; 5000c. Red howler monkey 4·00 4·50

628 Richie Jen

2004. Chinese Actors and Singers. Multicoloured.

MS3390 176×126 mm. 5000c. Type **628**; 5000c. Richie Jen wearing black; 5000c.Wearing gold helmet; 5000c. With moustache; 5000c. In Elixir of Love (wearing brown hat); 5000c. Wearing red jacket 5·50 6·50

MS3391 176×126 mm. 5000c. Ray Lui (wearing jacket and tie); 5000c. With shaven head; 5000c. Wearing hood; 5000c. Wearing spotted shirt; 5000c. Wearing pigtail; 5000c. As Xiang Yu in The Great Emperor's Concubine 5·50 6·50

MS3392 176×126 mm. 5000c. Jiang Wen (with head tilted left); 5000c. With copper pot on head; 5000c. Looking to left; 5000c. Wearing brown jacket; 5000c. Wearing black T-shirt; 5000c. Wearing blue T-shirt 5·50 6·50

No. **MS**3390 shows Richie Jen (singer and actor), **MS**3391 Ray Lui (actor) and **MS**3392 Jiang Wen (actor).

629 Edwene Asa

2004. Kente Designs. Multicoloured.

3393 2000c. Type **629** 50 30

3394 4000c. Fatia Fata Nkruma 90 75

3395 4500c. Asam Takra 95 95

3396 5000c. Toku Akra Ntoma 1·00 1·10

3397 6000c. Sika Futuro 1·25 1·50

630 Exodus from Notsie

2004. Festival of Hogbetsotso. Multicoloured.

3398 2000c. Type **630** 50 30

3399 4000c. Misego Dance 90 75

3400 4500c. Royal stools carried in procession 95 95

3401 5000c. Man pouring libation 1·00 1·10

3402 6000c. King carried aloft 1·25 1·50

MS3403 190×145 mm. 3000c. Two men pouring libation; 3000c. Togbe Adeladza II, Paramount Chief of Anlo; 3000c. Display of traditional symbols of wealth; 3000c. Exodus from Notsie; 3000c. Procession of the royalty; 3000c. Royalty at Durbar; 3000c. Ewe cultural dance; 3000c. Woman with symbols of bountiful harvest; 3000c. Royal stools carried in procession (different) 6·50 7·50

631 Girl Scout

2004. 25th Death Anniv of Norman Rockwell (artist). Multicoloured.

MS3404 180×116 mm. 7000c. Type **631**; 7000c. Cub scout (with tartan neckerchief); 7000c. Boy scout; 7000c. Cub scout (with yellow and mauve neckerchief) 6·50 7·50

MS3405 87×94 mm. 20000c. "Good Friends" 4·50 5·00

No. **MS**3404 shows details from Boy Scout calendar of 1971.

632 "Portrait of Anne of Austria as Minerva" (Simon Vouet)

2004. 300th Anniv of St. Petersburg. "Treasures of the Hermitage". Multicoloured.

3406 2000c. Type **632** 50 30

3407 3000c. "Lasciviousness" (Pompeo Girolamo Batoni) 70 45

3408 10000c. "Allegory of Faith" (Moretto da Brescia) 2·25 2·75

MS3409 162×142 mm. 6500c. "Allegory of the Arts" (Bernardo Strozzi); 6500c. "Vulcan's Forge" (Luca Giordano); 6500c. "Daedalus and Icarus" (detail) (Charles Lebrun); 6500c. "The Infant Hercules Strangling Serpents in His Cradle" (Sir Joshua Reynolds) 6·00 7·00

MS3410 Two sheets. (a) 55×78 mm. 20000c. "Cupid Undoing Venus's Belt" (Sir Joshua Reynolds). (b) 78×55 mm. 20000c. "Perseus Liberating Andromeda" (Rubens). Both Imperf. Set of 2 sheets 8·50 9·50

633 "Jacqueline in a Black Scarf"

2004. 30th Death Anniv of Pablo Picasso (artist) (2003). Multicoloured.

MS3411 154×154 mm. 6500c. Type **633**; 6500c. "Portrait of Olga"; 6500c. "Woman in White (Sara Murphy)"; 6500c. "Portrait of Dora Maar" 6·00 7·00

MS3412 45×68 mm. 16000c. "Portrait of the Artist's Sister, Lola". Imperf 4·25 4·50

634 "Head of a Peasant Woman"

2004. Death Centenary of James Whistler (artist) (2003). Multicoloured.

3413 2000c. Type **634** 50 30

3414 4000c. "The Master Smith of Lyme Regis" 85 75

3415 5000c. "The Little Rose of Lyme Regis" 1·10 1·25

3416 6000c. "Arrangement in Grey: Portrait of a Painter (Self-portrait)" 1·25 1·50

MS3417 128×130 mm. 7500c. "Rose and Silver: La Princesse du pays de la porcelaine"; 7500c. "Variations in Flesh Colour and Green, The Balcony"; 7500c. "Caprice in Purple and Gold: The Golden Screen" (detail); 7500c. "Purple and Rose: The Lange Lijzen of the Six Marks" 7·00 8·00

MS3418 82×102 mm. 20000c. "Harmony in Green and Rose: The Music Room" (horiz) 4·50 4·75

634a Polio Vaccination and Rotary Emblems

2004. Centenary of Rotary International (2005) (1st issue). Designs showing Rotary emblem. Multicoloured.

3418a 2000c. Type **634a** 60 25

3418b 4000c. *Anopheles* mosquito and Ghana flag ("Rotarians Against Malaria") (vert) 1·00 85

3418c 4500c. Paul Harris (founder) (vert) 1·00 1·00

3418d 5000c. Jonathan B. Majiyagbe (President 2003–4) and Ghana flag (vert) 1·25 1·40

3418e 6000c. "100 Years", emblem and Ghana flag (vert) 1·40 1·60

See also **MS**3527.

635 Jacques Rogge and Olympic Flame

2004. Olympic Games, Athens. Multicoloured.

3419 500c. Type **635** 20 15

3420 800c. Abedi Ayew Pele (footballer) 30 15

3421 7000c. Margaret Simpson 1·40 1·50

3422 10000c. Athletes in ancient Greek art – 384 meter diaulos (horiz) 1·90 2·25

636 Fleet Admiral Ernest King, US Navy

2004. 60th Anniv of D-Day Landings. Multicoloured.

MS3423 155×108 mm. 8000c. Type **636**; 8000c. General William Lee, US Airborne; 8000c. Lt Commander John Bulkeley, US Naval Reserve; 8000c. Admiral Sir Bertram Ramsey, Royal Navy 7·50 8·00

MS3424 105×77 mm. 20000c. Rear Admiral Alan Kirk, US Navy (horiz) 4·50 5·00

2004. European Football Championship 2004, Portugal. Multicoloured designs as T 407 of Dominica.

MS3425 147×85 mm. 7500c. Gerd Müller; 7500c. Presentation of the European Cup; 7500c. Franz Beckenbauer; 7500c. Heysel Stadium, Brussels 6·00 7·00

MS3426 97×85 mm. 20000c. Germany, 1972 (50×38 mm) 4·00 4·50

2004. 25th Anniv of the Pontificate of Pope John Paul II. Sheet 163×152 mm containing horiz designs as T 408 of Dominica. Multicoloured.

MS3427 6000c. Pope in Ghana, 1980; 6000c. Pope receiving gift, Ghana, 1982; 6000c. Pope in 1991; 6000c. Pope giving blessing, 2000; 6000c. Pope giving blessing to children, 2001 8·50 9·00

637 Martin Luther King

2004. United Nations International Year of Peace. Sheet 137×77 mm containing T 637 and similar horiz designs showing Martin Luther King. Multicoloured.
MS3428 10000c. Type **637**; 10000c. Making speech; 10000c. Martin Luther King (looking to left) 5·50 6·50

638 Deng Xiaoping

2004. Birth Centenary of Deng Xiaoping (Chinese leader). Sheet 98×68 mm.
MS3429 20000c. multicoloured 3·75 4·25

639 Zebra Bullhead Shark

2004. Sharks. Multicoloured.
MS3430 137×108 mm. 7500c. Type **639**; 7500c. Swellshark; 7500c. Port Jackson shark; 7500c. Leopard shark 7·00 7·50
MS3431 95×65 mm. 20000c. California horn shark 4·50 4·75

640 Lion Cubs

2004. Lions. Multicoloured.

3432	5000c. Type **640**	95	1·10
3433	5000c. Lions standing in water	95	1·10
3434	5000c. Male lion	95	1·10
3435	5000c. Lioness with cubs	95	1·10
MS3436	155×125 mm. Nos. 3432/5, each×2	7·00	8·00

641 *Boletus badius*

2004. Mushrooms. Multicoloured.

3437	500c. Type **641**	40	15
3438	3000c. *Clitocybe nebularis*	85	60
3439	5000c. *Amanita muscaria*	1·25	1·25
3440	8000c. *Russula vesca*	1·75	2·00
MS3441	115×135 mm. 7500c. *Boletus parasiticus* (vert); 7500c. *Cortinarius armillatus* (vert); 7500c. *Gymnopilus spectabilis* (vert); 7500c. *Cortinarius flexipes* (vert)	8·00	8·50
MS3442	67×95 mm. 20000c. *Chlorosplenium aeruginosum* (vert)	5·00	5·50

642 Serval

2004. Animals. Multicoloured.

3443	1000c. Type **642**	30	25
3444	1200c. Sable antelope	35	25
3445	2000c. Cheetah	60	60
3446	3000c. Bohor reedbuck	75	1·00
MS3447	115×135 mm. 7500c. White rhinoceros; 7500c. Leopard; 7500c. Burchell's zebra; 7500c. Red river hog (all horiz)	7·50	8·00
MS3448	97×66 mm. 20000c. Hippopotamus (horiz)	5·50	5·50

643 *Oncidium desertorum*

2004. Orchids. Multicoloured.

3449	800c. Type **643**	30	15
3450	3500c. *Oncidium variegatum*	75	75
3451	4000c. *Anguloa uniflora* (vert)	80	80
3452	10000c. *Oncidium gardneri* (vert)	1·75	2·00
MS3453	115×135 mm. 7500c. *Vanda rothschildiana*; 7500c. *Laelia cattleya*; 7500c. *Laelia anceps*; 7500c. *Odontioda dalmar*	6·50	7·00
MS3454	65×95 mm. 20000c. *Renanthera bella* (vert)	5·00	5·50

643a Migrating to Freedom

2005. Akwantukese Festival of New Juaben Area. Multicoloured.

3454a	2000c. State Emblem of Yiadom and Hwedie	50	30
3454b	4000c. Type **643a**	80	75
3454c	4500c. Crossing Suhyien River	85	85
3454d	5000c. Chief at State Durbar	95	1·10
3454e	6000c. Sacrificing at the cave	1·10	1·25
MS3454f	140×115 mm. 4000c. As No. 3454c.; 4000c. Palace guards; 4000c. As No. 3454a; 4000c. As No. 3454d; 4000c. Pouring libation; 4000c. Parading the Royal Treasury	4·50	5·50

2005. Centenary of FIFA (Federation Internationale de Football Association). As T 413 of Dominica. Multicoloured.

MS3455	192×95 mm. 7500c. Roberto Di Matteo (Italy); 7500c. Marcel Desailly (France); 7500c. Osei Kufuor (Germany); 7500c. Eusebio (Portugal)	6·50	7·00
MS3456	107×85 mm.20000c. Johan Cruyff (Holland)	4·50	4·75

644 Talgo Train, Spain

2005. Bicentenary of Steam Locomotives (2004).

3457–3462	5000c.×6 Type **644**; VIA Turbotrain, Canada; Southern Pacific steam locomotive No. 4449; Union Pacific City of Portland; Shinkansen train, Japan; Deltic diesel-electric locomotive, Britain	7·50	8·00
3463–3468	5000c.×6 Stanier Class steam locomotive; Central Pacific steam locomotive Jupiter; RSC3 Class 9401 locomotive, Robe River; BTS trains, Bangkok; Streamlined tank locomotive; ETR450 locomotive	7·50	8·00
3469–3474	5000c.×6 Mogul steam locomotive; Milwaukee Railroad steam locomotive; Shinkansen train at station; Steam locomotive 2101, Reading; HST Inter-City 125 train; Daylight steam train	7·50	8·00
3475–3478	8000c.×4 Baldwin locomotive; Atchison Topeka & Santa Fe "American" steam train; Baldwin locomotive No. 44; Baldwin 3 three-spot locomotive	7·50	8·00
MS3479	Four sheets, each 100×70 mm. (a) 20000c. LMS 5305 steam train. (b) 20000c. City train in station, Chicago. (c) 20000c. Santa Fe train. (d) 20000c. Empire Builder train, USA	16·00	18·00

645 Setra State Transport Coach

2005. Early Vehicles. Multicoloured.

3480	2000c. Type **645**	65	30
3481	4000c. Albium double-decker bus	1·25	70
3482	4500c. Bedford Mummy truck with trailer	1·25	90
3483	5000c. Mail carrier, 1925	1·40	1·00
3484	6000c. Morris truck	1·50	1·10

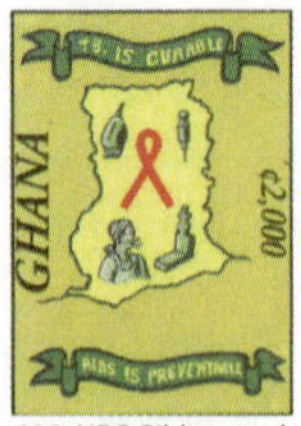

646 AIDS Ribbon and Map of Ghana

2006. "HIV/AIDS is Preventable TB is Curable" Campaign. Multicoloured.

3485	2000c. Type **646**	60	60
3486	2000c. Crowd with placards (horiz)	60	60
3487	2000c. AIDS victims	60	60
3488	3000c. Profile of tuberculosis patient and AIDS ribbon	80	80
3489	4000c. Hands holding map of Africa ("TOGETHER WE FIGHT THE HIV/AIDS AND TB MENACE")	90	90
3490	4500c. Crumbling bricks in man's outline ("HIV/AIDS DESTROYS THE BODY DEFENCE SYSTEM")	95	95
3491	4500c. Nurses and patients enclosed in hand	1·10	1·25
3492	5000c. Globe enclosed in heart	1·25	1·40
3493	5000c. Emaciated man carrying "TB" and "HIV/AIDS" on yoke	1·25	1·40
3494	6000c. Hands holding "HIV/AIDS PREVENT IT" and "TUBERCULOSIS CURE IT" placards	1·40	1·50

647 Elvis Presley

2006. 70th Birth Anniv of Elvis Presley (2005). Designs showing portraits. Multicoloured.

3495–3501	3500c. Type **647**×9 Background colours given: violet (×3); green; yellow and red; green; red and yellow; yellow; emerald and blue	5·50	6·00
3502–3505	8000c.×4 Elvis Presley wearing striped jacket background colours given: mauve; grey; bistre; blue	5·50	6·00
3506–3509	8000c.×4 Elvis Presley wearing black background tint given: mauve; grey; deep grey; blue	5·50	6·00

648 Carlos Arroyo, Detroit Pistons

2006. US National Basketball Association Players. Multicoloured.

3510	3500c. Detroit Pistons emblem	75	80
3511	3500c. Type **648**	75	80
3512	3500c. Carlos Boozer, Utah Jazz	75	80
3513	3500c. Utah Jazz emblem	75	80
3514	3500c. San Antonio Spurs emblem	75	80
3515	3500c. Manu Ginobili, San Antonio Spurs	75	80
3516	3500c. Atlanta Hawks emblem	75	80
3517	3500c. Al Harrington, Atlanta Hawks	75	80
3518	3500c. Los Angeles Clippers emblem	75	80
3519	3500c. Corey Maggette, Los Angeles Clippers	75	80
3520	3500c. Houston Rockets emblem	75	80
3521	3500c. David Wesley, Houston Rockets	75	80

649 Emblem of Ghana Atomic Energy Commission (40th anniv)

2006. International Year of Physics (2005). Multicoloured.

3522	2000c. Type **649**	50	30
3523	4000c. Ghana Research Reactor	80	75
3524	4500c. Albert Einstein (physicist) (50th death anniv)	90	85
3525	5000c. Prof. Francis K. Allotey (Ghanaian physicist)	95	1·00
3526	6000c. Electricity experiment in a physics laboratory	1·10	1·25

650 Women getting Water from Standpipe

2006. Centenary of Rotary International (2005) (2nd issue). Multicoloured.
MS3527 150×88 mm. 10000c.×3 Type **650**; 10000c. Building low-cost shelter; 10000c. Girl guides planting ("Preserve Planet Earth Program") 6·00 7·00

651 Pope John Paul II ("Self Help through Rotary Village Corps")

2006. Pope John Paul II Commemoration.
3528 **651** 12000c. multicoloured 3·25 3·50

2006. 75th Anniv of First World Cup Football Championship, Uruguay (2005). As T 420 of Dominica showing scenes from World Cup, France, 1938. Multicoloured.

3529	8000c. Italian team, 19381	1·40	1·50
3530	8000c. Final between Italy and Hungary	1·40	1·50
3531	8000c. Stade Olympique de Colombes	1·40	1·50
3532	8000c. Silvio Piola (Italy)	1·40	1·50
MS3533	116×90 mm. 20000c. Group photograph of winning Italian team, 1938	3·75	5·00

652 Jules Verne

2006. Death Centenary of Jules Verne (writer) (2005). Multicoloured.

3534	8000c. Type **652**	1·50	1·60
3535	8000c. Hot-air balloon and book illustration from "Five Weeks in a Balloon"	1·50	1·60
3536	8000c. Montgolfier balloon over Paris, 1783	1·50	1·60
3537	8000c. Modern hot air balloon	1·50	1·60
MS3538	100×70 mm. 20000c. Airship LZ-129 *Hindenburg* (1937)	4·00	4·25

653 Friedrich von Schiller

2006. Death Bicentenary (2005) of Friedrich von Schiller (poet and dramatist). Multicoloured.

No.	Description		
3539	11000c. Type **653**	2·25	2·40
3540	11000c. Friedrich von Schiller and birthplace, Marbach	2·25	2·40
3541	11000c. Johannes Brahms (composer)	2·25	2·40
MS3542	60×53 mm. 20000c. Friedrich von Schiller and Johannes Brahms. Imperf	4·50	4·75

2006. Bicentenary of the Battle of Trafalgar (2005). As T 423 of Dominica. Multicoloured.

No.	Description		
3543	2000c. Sir John Jervis, first Earl of St. Vincent and First Lord of the Admiralty, 1801–06 (vert)	75	35
3544	3000c. Ship with broken mast ("Chase and Race in the Summer of 1805") (vert)	1·00	80
3545	5000c. HMS *Goliath* firing on *Guerrier*	2·00	2·25
3546	10000c. Death of Admiral Lord Nelson	3·50	4·00
MS3547	100×71 mm. 20000c. Nelson's flagships HMS *Agamemnon*, *Vanguard*, *Elephant* and *Captain*	7·00	7·50

654 Ghana Black Stars Team

2006. World Cup Football Championship, Germany. Ghana's Qualification for World Cup. Multicoloured.

No.	Description		
3548	2000c. Stephen Appiah in action (vert)	50	50
3549	2000c. Type **654**	50	50
3550	4000c. Exchanging of pennants	95	95
3551	4000c. Five victorious Ghana players ("THE JOY OF SUCCESS")	95	95
3552–3559	4000c.×8 Asamoah Gyan; Sammy Adjei; Matthew Amoah; John Mensah; Emmanuel Pappoe; Mark Daniel Edusei; Abubakari Yakubu; Godwin Attram (all 42×28 mm)	6·00	6·50
3560–3567	4000c.×8 Stephen Appiah; Issah Ahmed; John Paintsil; Laryea Kingston; Michael Essien; Sule Ali Muntari; Joe Tex Frimpong; Ratomir Dujkovic (Ghana coach) (all 42×28 mm)	6·00	6·50
3568	4500c. Franz Beckenbauer (Germany) and World Cup Stadium, Hanover	1·00	1·10
3569	4500c. Michael Essien in action	1·00	1·10
3570	5000c. Ghana team ("THE VICTORY SQUAD")	1·10	1·25
3571	5000c. Ghana v. Burkina Faso World Cup qualifying match	1·10	1·25
3572	6000c. Ghana v. South Africa World Cup qualifying match	1·25	1·40
3573	6000c. Team parading with Ghana flag T-shirts	1·25	1·40

2006. Various stamps surch. (a) Nos. 1944 and 1947/9 surch 2000c.

No.	Description		
3574	2000c. on 50c. Type **502**	15·00	5·00
3575	2000c. on 200c. Diana monkey on branch facing left	15·00	5·00
3576	2000c. on 500c. Diana monkey on branch facing right	15·00	5·00
3577	2000c. on 800c. Head of Diana monkey	15·00	5·00

(b) Nos. 2044/9 surch 3000c.

No.	Description		
3578	3000c. on 50c. Type **507**	1·00	80
3579	3000c. on 100c. Red-flanked duiker	1·00	80
3580	3000c. on 200c. Yellow-backed duiker	1·00	80
3581	3000c. on 400c. Ogilby's duiker	1·00	80
3582	3000c. on 600c. Bay duiker	1·00	80
3583	3000c. on 800c. Jentink's duiker	1·00	80

(c) Nos. 2066/8 surch 4000c.

No.	Description		
3584	4000c. on 50c. Type **509**	1·50	1·00
3585	4000c. on 200c. Worker with children	1·50	1·00
3586	4000c. on 600c. Workers erecting tents	1·50	1·00

(d) Nos. 2070/7 (showing different fertility dolls, background colours given) surch 5000c.

No.	Description		
3587	5000c. on 50c. multicoloured (green)	2·00	1·50
3588	5000c. on 100c. multicoloured (yellow)	2·00	1·50
3589	5000c. on 150c. multicoloured (blue)	2·00	1·50
3590	5000c. on 200c. multicoloured (claret)	2·00	1·50
3591	5000c. on 400c. multicoloured (brown)	2·00	1·50
3592	5000c. on 600c. multicoloured (yellow)	2·00	1·50
3593	5000c. on 800c. multicoloured (yellow)	2·00	1·50
3594	5000c. on 1000c. multicoloured (blue)	2·00	1·50

(e) Nos. 2085/7 surch as T 659.

No.	Description		
3595	4500c. on 100c. Type **512**	1·75	1·25
3596	4500c. on 400c. Communications equipment	1·75	1·25
3597	4500c. on 1000c. Airliner taking off	1·75	1·25

(f) Nos. 2088/90 surch 6000c.

No.	Description		
3598	6000c. on 100c. Type **512**	2·50	2·00
3599	6000c. on 400c. Communications equipment	2·50	2·00
3600	6000c. on 1000c. Airliner taking off	2·50	2·00

(g) Nos. 2183/7 surch 2000c.

No.	Description		
3601	2000c. on 200c. Type **521**	75	35
3602	2000c. on 300c. Fishermen with fish traps	75	35
3603	2000c. on 400c. Ox-drawn plough	75	35
3604	2000c. on 600c. Harvesting bananas	75	35
3605	2000c. on 800c. Planting saplings	75	35

662 Queen Elizabeth II

2007. 80th Birthday (2006) of Queen Elizabeth II. Multicoloured.

No.	Description		
3606	6000c. Type **662**	1·25	1·40
3607	6000c. Wearing purple hat	1·25	1·40
3608	6000c. Wearing pale green	1·25	1·40
3609	6000c. Wearing yellow and pale green	1·25	1·40
MS3610	120×120 mm. 25000c. Wearing tiara	7·25	7·50

663 Soyuz 19

2007. Space Anniversaries. Multicoloured. (a) 30th Anniv (2005) of Apollo-Soyuz Test Project.

No.	Description		
MS3611	100×150 mm. 6500c.×6 Type **663**; Apollo/Soyuz emblem; Tom Stafford (Apollo Commander) and Apollo-Soyuz linkup; Aleksei Leonov (Soyuz Commander); Deke Slayton (astronaut); Vance Brand (astronaut) and Valeri Kubasov (flight engineer)	8·00	8·75

(b) 20th Anniv (2006) of Giotto Comet Probe

No.	Description		
MS3612	150×100 mm. 6500c.×6 *Giotto* Comet Probe in space; *Giotto* and Halley's Comet above Earth's surface; *Giotto* on ground; *Giotto* and Halley's Comet; *Giotto* and diagram of structure; *Giotto* (all vert)	8·50	8·75

(c) 20th Anniv of Luna 9

No.	Description		
MS3613	150×100 mm. 10000c.×4 Luna 9 soft lander approaching Moon; Luna 9 soft lander in space; Luna 9 flight apparatus and Moon; Luna 9	8·00	8·25
MS3614	Three sheets, each 100×70 mm. (a) 20000c. Handshake in space, Apollo-Soyuz, 1975. (b) 20000c. Apollo 11 astronaut Buzz Aldrin, 1969 (vert). (c) 20000c. Viking 1 on Mars, 1976	18·00	19·00

The stamps within **MS**3611 form a composite background design showing Apollo-Soyuz crew and emblem. The two left-hand stamps within **MS**3613 have a composite background of the Moon.

664 Marilyn Monroe

2007. 80th Birth Anniv of Marilyn Monroe (actress). Multicoloured.

No.	Description		
3615	9000c. Type **664**	1·90	2·00
3616	9000c. Wearing dressing gown	1·90	2·00
3617	9000c. Wearing purple dress with single crossover strap	1·90	2·00
3618	9000c. Wearing red jacket with silver collar	1·90	2·00
MS3619	100×70 mm. 20000c. With eyes closed and head on pillow	7·00	7·50

665 Scout saluting

2007. Centenary of World Scouting. Multicoloured.

No.	Description		
3620	12000c. Type **665**	2·40	2·50
3621	12000c. Scout blowing trumpet	2·40	2·50
3622	12000c. Scout carrying sick man	2·40	2·50
MS3623	80×110 mm. 20000c. Scout saluting (horiz)	7·00	7·50

666 50 Logo

2007. 50th Anniv of Independence (1st issue).

No.	Description		
3624	**666** 4000c. multicoloured	90	65

See also Nos. 3625/30, 3631/41 and 3642/52.

667 Sika ne Barima

2007. 50th Anniv of Independence (2nd issue). Kente Designs. Multicoloured.

No.	Description		
3625	4000c. Type **667**	90	95
3626	7300c. Edwene Si So	1·60	1·75
3627	7500c. Dakoro Yesere	1·60	1·75
3628	9000c. Nkatoa Sa	2·00	2·10
3629	9000c. Agyenegyne Nsu	2·00	2·10
3630	10000c. Edwene Asa	2·40	2·50

668 Cocoa Beverages and Spread

2007. 50th Anniv of Independence (3rd issue). Cocoa of Ghana. Multicoloured.

No.	Description		
3631	4000c. Type **668**	90	95
3632	6000c. Finished cocoa products	1·25	1·40
3633	6000c. Cocoa pods (wrongly inscr 'Cocoa Beverages & Spread')	1·25	1·40
3634	6000c. Assorted chocolates	1·25	1·40
3635	6000c. Worker in cocoa processing plant	1·25	1·40
3636	6000c. Cocoa pebbles	1·25	1·40
3637	6000c. Packaging of cocoa products	1·25	1·40
3638	7300c. As No. 3636	1·60	1·75
3639	7500c. As No. 3634	1·60	1·75
3640	9000c. As No. 3635	2·00	2·10
3641	10000c. As No. 3632	2·40	2·50

669 The Bamboo Groves

2007. 50th Anniv of Independence (4th issue). Aburi Botanical Gardens. Multicoloured.

No.	Description		
3642	4000c. Type **669**	90	95
3643	6000c. Royal Palm Walkway	1·25	1·40
3644	6000c. School of Horticulture	1·25	1·40
3645	6000c. The Silk Cotton Tree (oldest tree in gardens)	1·25	1·40
3646	6000c. The Famous Ficus Tree	1·25	1·40
3647	6000c. As Type **669**	1·25	1·40
3648	6000c. The Sanatorium	1·25	1·40
3649	7300c. As No. 3644	1·60	1·75
3650	7500c. As No. 3645 but vert	1·60	1·75
3651	9000c. As No. 3643	2·00	2·10
3652	10000c. As No. 3646	2·40	2·50

670 Chartreux

2007. Cats. Multicoloured.

No.	Description		
3653	6000c. Type **670**	1·25	1·40
3654	7000c. Blue mitted Ragdoll	1·50	1·60
3655	8000c. Blue lynx point Birman (horiz)	1·90	2·00
3656	9000c. Norwegian Forest Cat	2·00	2·10
MS3657	72×100 mm. 20000c. Cinnamon point Siamese	7·25	7·50

671 American Bulldog

2007. Dogs. Multicoloured.

No.	Description		
3658	7500c. Type **671**	1·60	1·75
3659	7500c. Old English Sheepdog	1·60	1·75
3660	7500c. Chinese Shar-pei	1·60	1·75
3661	7500c. Boston Terrier	1·60	1·75

No. **MS**3662 is left for a miniature sheet not yet received.

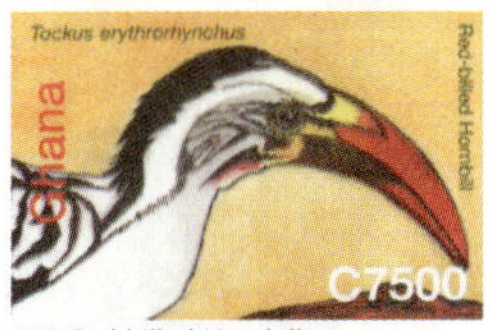

672 Red-billed Hornbill

2007. Birds of Africa. Multicoloured.

No.	Description		
MS3663	133×110 mm. 7500c.×4 Type **672**; Bearded barbet; Hoopoe; Pygmy kingfisher	6·00	6·75
MS3664	70×101 mm. 20000c. Grey crowned-crane (vert)	7·00	7·25

The stamps within **MS**3663 form a composite background design.

673 *Epipactis atrorubens*

2007. Orchids. Multicoloured.

3665	7500c. Type **673**	1·60	1·75
3666	7500c. *Galeandra bicarinata*	1·60	1·75
3667	7500c. *Platanthera tipuloides*	1·60	1·75
3668	7500c. *Platanthera ciliaris*	1·60	1·75
MS3669	96×66 mm. 20000c. *Spathoglottis plicata*	7·00	7·75

674 Philip Gbeho (composer of national anthem)

2007. 50th Anniv of Independence (5th issue). Important Personalities. Multicoloured.

3670	4000c. Type **674**	80	80
3671	4000c. Sir Arko Korsah (first Ghanaian Chief Justice, 1957)	80	80
3672	4000c. Amon Kotei (designer of national coat of arms)	80	80
3673	4500c. Hon. F. K. Buah (educationist and historian)	95	95
3674	6000c. Prof. Albert Abu Boahene (historian and politician)	1·20	1·20
3675	7300c. Leticia Obeng (aquatic biologist and international civil servant)	1·60	1·60
3676	7500c. His Eminence Peter Cardinal Appiah Turkson (first Ghanaian cardinal)	1·60	1·60
3677	9000c. Susanna Alhassan (first woman minister, 1960)	1·80	1·80

675 War Dress of Northern Ghana

2007. 50th Anniv of Independence (6th issue). Costumes. Multicoloured.

3678	4000c. Type **675**	80	80
3679	7300c. Woman in traditional wear	1·60	1·60
3680	7500c. Traditional mourning wear	1·60	1·60
3681	9000c. Traditional smock (batakari)	1·80	1·80
3682	10000c. Costume of the Wulomo	2·00	2·00

676 Gold Ore

2007. 50th Anniv of Independence (7th issue). Minerals of Ghana. Multicoloured.

3683	4000c. Type **676**	1·25	1·00
3684	7300c. Melting gold ore	2·25	2·25
3685	7500c. Woman holding gold bar	2·25	2·25
3686	9000c. Entrance of Obuasi Gold Mines (horiz)	2·75	3·25
3687	10000c. Gold plated chair	2·75	3·25

677 SIC Emblem

2007. SIC State Insurance. Multicoloured.

3688	40Gp. Type **677**	80	80
3689	73Gp. The Pioneering Executive	1·20	1·20
3690	75Gp. New office building	1·60	1·60
3691	90Gp. Boy ('Focused On You')	1·80	1·80
3692	GHc1 3X CIMG award (vert)	2·00	2·00

678 GCB Emblems

2007. GCB Commercial Bank. Multicoloured.

3693	40Gp. Type **678**	80	80
3694	73Gp. Palm-nut vulture and world map ('Fast int money transfer')	1·20	1·20
3695	75Gp. GCB Tower (vert)	1·60	1·60
3696	90Gp. Palm-nut vulture and emblems ('GCB Xpress money transfer') (vert)	1·80	1·80

679 ADB Emblem

2007. Agricultural Development Bank. Multicoloured.

3697	40Gp. Type **679**	80	80
3698	75Gp. Man working abroad and woman at home ('Home link account') (vert)	1·60	1·60
3699	90Gp. Young farmers and produce ('Young farmers programme') (vert)	1·80	1·80
3700	GHc1 Farmer with vehicle ('Gold Drive motor loan') (vert)	2·00	2·00

680 Aircraft on Ground

2007. Antrak Air. Multicoloured.

3701	40Gp. Type **680**	80	80
3702	73Gp. Aircraft in flight	1·20	1·20

Values in Ghana pesewas.

681 Independence Arch

2007. 50th Anniv of Independence (12th issue). Monuments. Multicoloured.

3703	20Gp. Type **681**	40	40
3704	40Gp. Independence Square	80	80
3705	73Gp. Supreme Court Building	1·20	1·20
3706	75Gp. National Theatre	1·20	1·20
3707	90Gp. International Conference Centre	1·80	1·80

682 Dr. Kwame Nkrumah, 1957–66

2007. 50th Anniv of Independence (13th issue). Heads of State of the Republic of Ghana. Multicoloured.

3708	60Gp. Type **682**	1·20	1·20
3709	60Gp. Lt. General J. A. Ankrah, 1966–7	1·20	1·20
3710	60Gp. General A. A. Afrifa, 1967–72	1·20	1·20
3711	60Gp. Dr. Kofi Abrefa Busia, 1969–72	1·20	1·20
3712	60Gp. General I. K. Acheampong, 1972–8	1·20	1·20
3713	60Gp. Lt. General W. A. Akuffo, 1978–9	1·20	1·20
3714	60Gp. Dr. Hilla Limann, 1979–81	1·20	1·20
3715	60Gp. Flt Lt. J. J. Rawlings, 1981–2000	1·20	1·20
3716	60Gp. President J. A. Kufuor, 2001–	1·20	1·20
MS3717	110×80 mm. GHc1 Swearing in with State Sword of Dr. Kwame Nkrumah (1957) and Pres. Kufuor (2001)	2·00	2·00

683 Pope Benedict XVI

2007. 80th Birthday of Pope Benedict XVI.

3718	**683**	4000c. multicoloured	80	80

684 Kenyans in Traditional Dress

2007. 24th UPU Congress, Nairobi. Multicoloured.

3719	40Gp. Type **684**	80	80
3720	73Gp. Akwaaba and Karibu traditional dress (vert)	1·20	1·20
3721	75Gp. UPU emblem in opened box	1·20	1·20
3722	90Gp. UPU emblem, clasped hands and map of Africa (vert)	1·80	1·80
MS3723	192×132 mm. GHc3×3 UPU emblem (left section) and map segments; UPU emblem (right section) and map segments; Map showing Kenya and Nairobi	4·50	4·50

685 Queen Elizabeth II

2008. Diamond Wedding of Queen Elizabeth II and Prince Philip (2007). Multicoloured.

3724	60Gp. Type **685** (inscr in emerald)	1·20	1·20
3725	60Gp. Queen Elizabeth and Prince Philip in Garter robes (inscr in emerald)	1·20	1·20
3726	60Gp. As No. 3720 (inscr in orange)	1·20	1·20
3727	60Gp. Type **684** (inscr in orange)	1·20	1·20
3728	60Gp. Type **684** (inscr in blue)	1·20	1·20
3729	60Gp. As No. 3720 (inscr in blue)	1·20	1·20

686 Lotus (*Lotus and Mandarin Ducks*)

2008. 50th Death Anniv of Qi Baishi (2007). Multicoloured.

MS3730	90Gp.×4 Type **686**; Boats on river (*River Landcape with Boats*); Mandarin ducks (*Lotus and Mandarin Ducks*); Trees and river (*River Landscape with Boats*)	7·25	7·25
MS3731	60×125 mm. GHc3 *Peony in a Dragon Vase* (30×80 mm)	4·50	4·50

687 Boxing

2008. Olympic Games, Beijing. Multicoloured.

3732	40Gp. Type **687**	80	80
3733	40Gp. Relay	80	80
3734	40Gp. Athletics	80	80
3735	40Gp. Football	80	80

688 Pres. George Bush

2008. Visit of US President George Bush to Ghana. Sheet 127×89 mm containing T 688 and similar vert design. Multicoloured.

MS3736	GHc1.25 Type **688**; GHc1.25 Pres. John Agyekum Kufuor of Ghana	2·50	2·50

The stamps and margins of No. **MS**3736 form a composite design showing Presidents Bush and Kufuor at a joint press conference at Osu Castle, Accra, Ghana on 20 February 2008.

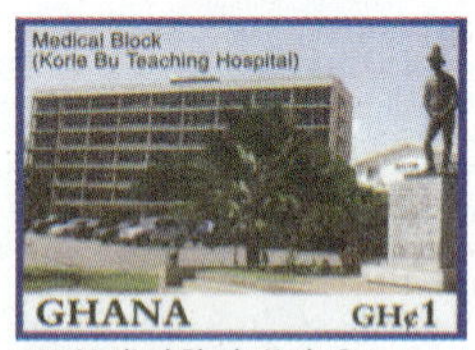

689 Medical Block, Korle Bu Teaching Hospital

2009. Korle Bu Teaching Hospital, Accra. Multicoloured.

3737	GHc1 Type **689**	2·00	2·00
3738	GHc1.10 Cardiothoracic Centre	2·10	2·10
3739	GHc1.10 The New Adminstration Block	2·10	2·10
3740	GHc1.20 Professor Frimpong Boateng (first heart surgeon) (vert)	2·25	2·25

690 Tomatoes

2009. Vegetables of Ghana. Multicoloured.

3741	GHc1 Type **690**	2·00	2·00
3742	GHc1.20 Tomatoes and garden eggs	2·25	2·25
3743	GHc1.30 Garden eggs (scarlet eggplant *Solanum aethiopicum*)	2·50	2·50

691 Aggrey Fynn

2009. Footballers of the 1960s. Multicoloured.

3744	GHc1 Type **691**	2·00	2·00
3745	GHc1 Baba Yara	2·00	2·00
3746	GHc1 Edward Acquah	2·00	2·00
3747	GHc1 Nana Gyamfi II	2·00	2·00
3748	GHc1 Robert Mensah (goal-keeper)	2·00	2·00

692 Administration Block, Tweneboa School

2009. Tweneboa Kodua School, Abuakwa. Multicoloured.

3749	GHc1 Type **692**	2·00	2·00
3750	GHc1.10 Girls Dormitory	2·10	2·10
3751	GHc1.20 Students at ICT Centre	2·25	2·25
3752	GHc1.30 Students playing volleyball	2·50	2·50

693 Arms of Ghana

2009. Personalised Stamps.

3753	**693**	GHc1 blackish-brown and lavender	2·00	2·00

694 Red Peony

2009. China 2009 World Stamp Exhibition, Luoyang. Peonies.

3754	**694**	GHc1 multicoloured	2·00	2·00

POSTAGE DUE STAMPS

1958. Postage Due stamps of Gold Coast optd GHANA and bar.

D9	**D1**	1d. black	10	30
D10	**D1**	2d. black	10	30
D11	**D1**	3d. black	10	30
D12	**D1**	6d. black	15	65
D13	**D1**	1s. black	20	1·50

D3

1958

D14	**D3**	1d. red	10	30
D15	**D3**	2d. green	10	30
D16	**D3**	3d. orange	10	30
D17	**D3**	6d. blue	10	50
D18	**D3**	1s. violet	15	2·00

1965. Surch Ghana New Currency 19th July. 1965. and value.

D19	1p. on 1d.	10	75
D20	2p. on 2d.	10	1·40
D21	3p. on 3d.	10	1·40
D22	6p. on 6d.	10	2·50
D23	12p. on 1s.	15	2·75

1968. Nos. D20/2 additionally surch.

D24	1½n.p. on 2p. on 2d.	5·50	4·25
D25	2½n.p. on 3p. on 3d.	1·00	5·00
D26	5n.p. on 6p. on 6d.	1·75	

1970. Inscr in new currency.

D27	1n.p. red	1·50	5·00
D28	1½n.p. green	1·75	6·00
D29	2½n.p. orange	2·25	7·50
D30	5n.p. blue	2·75	7·50
D31	10n.p. violet	4·00	9·00

1980. Currency described as "p".

D32	2p. orange	1·00	4·25
D33	3p. brown	1·00	4·25

Pt. 1

GIBRALTAR

A British colony at the W. entrance to the Mediterranean.

1886. 12 pence = 1 shilling; 20 shillings = 1 pound.
1971. 100 (new) pence = 1 pound.

1886. Stamps of Bermuda (Queen Victoria) optd GIBRALTAR.

1	9	½d. green	18·00	9·00
2	9	1d. red	75·00	4·25
3	9	2d. purple	£140	80·00
4	9	2½d. blue	£170	3·25
5	9	4d. orange	£180	£100
6	9	6d. lilac	£300	£225
7	9	1s. brown	£450	£375

2

1886. Various frames.

10	2	2d. purple	30·00	26·00
12	2	4d. orange	85·00	80·00
13	2	6d. lilac	£140	£130
14	2	1s. brown	£250	£200
39	2	½d. green	10·00	1·75
40	2	1d. red	10·00	50
42	2	2½d. blue	32·00	50

1889. Surch with new value in CENTIMOS.

15	5c. on ½d. green	7·50	27·00
16	10c. on 1d. red	13·00	15·00
17	25c. on 2d. purple	4·75	10·00
18	25c. on 2½d. blue	23·00	2·25
19	40c. on 4d. orange	55·00	75·00
20	50c. on 6d. lilac	55·00	75·00
21	75c. on 1s. brown	55·00	65·00

7

1889

22	7	5c. green	5·50	80
23	7	10c. red	4·50	50
24	7	20c. green and brown	45·00	22·00
25	7	20c. green	13·00	90·00
26	7	25c. blue	21·00	70
27	7	40c. orange	3·75	3·75
28	7	50c. lilac	3·25	2·00
29	7	75c. green	32·00	32·00
30	7	1p. brown	75·00	20·00
31	7	1p. brown and blue	4·75	7·50
32	7	2p. black and red	11·00	30·00
33	7	5p. grey	42·00	£100

1898. As 1886.

41	2	2d. purple and blue	24·00	1·75
43	2	4d. brown and green	18·00	4·75
44	2	6d. violet and red	42·00	24·00
45	2	1s. brown and red	38·00	11·00

1903

49	8	2½d. purple and black on blue	7·50	60
53	9	4s. purple and green	£120	£200
54	9	8s. purple and black on blue	£160	£180
55	9	£1 purple and black on red	£550	£700
57c	8	1d. purple on red	8·00	85
58a	8	2d. green and red	10·00	10·00
60a	8	6d. purple and violet	32·00	17·00
61a	8	1s. black and red	55·00	19·00
62a	9	2s. green and blue	90·00	£110
66	8	½d. green	9·00	1·75

8

9

1907

67		1d. red	5·50	60
68		2d. grey	8·50	11·00
69		2½d. blue	6·00	1·60
70		6d. purple	£140	£375
71		1s. black on green	23·00	21·00
72	9	2s. purple and blue on blue	50·00	48·00
73	9	4s. black and red	£140	£170
74	9	8s. purple and green	£225	£225

1912. As T 8/9, but portrait of King George V. (3d. A. Inscr "3 PENCE". B. Inscr "THREE PENCE").

79	2½d. blue	9·50	2·00
81	1s. black on green	11·00	3·25
82	2s. purple and blue on blue	26·00	3·50
83	4s. black and red	35·00	55·00
84	8s. purple and green	85·00	£110
85	£1 purple and black on red	£140	£225
89	½d. green	1·50	1·50
90	1d. red	1·75	1·00
91a	1½d. brown	1·75	30
93	2d. grey	1·25	1·25
95a	3d. blue (A)	2·50	1·50
97a	6d. purple	1·60	3·50
102a	1s. olive and black	14·00	17·00
103	2s. brown and black	10·00	35·00
104	2s.6d. green and black	10·00	24·00
105	5s. red and black	16·00	70·00
106	10s. blue and black	32·00	75·00
107	£1 orange and black	£180	£275
108	£5 violet and black	£1500	£5000
109	3d. blue (B)	7·50	2·00

1918. Optd WAR TAX.

86	½d. green (No. 89)	1·00	1·75

13 The Rock of Gibraltar

1931

110	13	1d. red	2·50	2·50
111	13	1½d. brown	1·75	2·25
112	13	2d. grey	6·50	1·75
113	13	3d. blue	6·00	3·00

1935. Silver Jubilee. As T 10a of Gambia.

114	2d. blue and black	1·60	2·50
115	3d. brown and blue	3·25	4·50
116	6d. green and blue	12·00	18·00
117	1s. grey and purple	14·00	18·00

1937. Coronation. As T 10b of Gambia.

118	½d. green	25	50
119	2d. grey	1·75	3·25
120	3d. blue	2·75	3·25

14 King George VI

15 Rock of Gibraltar

1938. King George VI.

121	14	½d. green	10	40
122b	15	1d. brown	50	60
123	15	1½d. red	35·00	1·00
123b	-	1½d. violet	50	1·50
124a	-	2d. grey	4·25	35
124c	-	2d. red	50	60
125b	-	3d. blue	1·25	30
125c	-	5d. orange	1·25	1·25
126b	-	6d. red and violet	6·50	1·75
127b	-	1s. black and green	3·25	4·25
128b	-	2s. black and brown	6·50	6·50
129b	-	5s. black and red	26·00	17·00
130a	-	10s. black and blue	38·00	25·00
131	14	£1 orange	38·00	48·00

DESIGNS—HORIZ: 2d. The Rock (North side); 3d., 5d. Europa Point; 6d. Moorish Castle; 1s. South-port Gate; 2s. Eliott Memorial; 5s. Government House; 10s. Catalan Bay.

1946. Victory. As T 11a of Gambia.

132	½d. green	10	1·25
133	3d. blue	50	1·25

1948. Silver Wedding. As T 11b/11c of Gambia.

134	½d. green	1·50	2·75
135	£1 orange	60·00	75·00

1949. U.P.U. As T 11d/11g of Gambia.

136	2d. red	1·00	1·25
137	3d. blue	2·00	1·50
138	6d. purple	1·25	2·00
139	1s. green	1·00	3·50

1950. Inauguration of Legislative Council. Optd NEW CONSTITUTION 1950.

140	2d. red (No. 124c)	30	1·50
141	3d. blue (No. 125b)	65	1·00
142	6d. red and violet (No. 126b)	75	2·00
143	1s. black and green (No. 127b)	75	2·00

1953. Coronation. As T 11h of Gambia.

144	½d. black and green	50	1·50

24 Cargo and Passenger Wharves

1953

145	24	½d. blue and green	15	30
146	-	1d. green	1·50	65
147	-	1½d. black	1·00	2·00
148	-	2d. brown	1·75	1·00
149a	-	2½d. red	6·00	1·50
150	-	3d. blue	4·25	10
151	-	4d. blue	6·00	3·50
152	-	5d. purple	1·50	1·00
153	-	6d. black and blue	3·50	1·75
154	-	1s. blue and brown	70	1·25
155a	-	2s. orange and violet	26·00	6·50
156	-	5s. brown	38·00	15·00
157	-	10s. brown and blue	45·00	42·00
158	-	£1 red and yellow	50·00	50·00

DESIGNS—HORIZ: 1d. South view from Straits; 1½d. Gibraltar Fish Canneries; 2d. Southport Gate; 2½d. Sailing in the Bay; 3d. Liner; 4d. Coaling wharf; 5d. English Electric Canberra at Gibraltar Airport; 6d. Europa Point; 1s. Straits from Buena Vista; 2s. Rosia Bay and Straits; 5s. Main entrance, Government House. VERT: 10s. Tower of Homage, Moorish Castle; £1 Arms of Gibraltar.

1954. Royal Visit. As No. 150, but inscr "ROYAL VISIT 1954".

159	3d. blue	50	20

38 Gibraltar Candytuft

40 Rock and Badge of Gibraltar Regiment

1960

160	38	½d. purple and green	15	50
161	-	1d. black and green	20	10
162	-	2d. blue and brown	1·00	20
163a	-	2½d. black and blue	1·00	30
164	-	3d. blue and orange	30	10
166	-	6d. brown and green	1·00	70
167	-	7d. blue and red	2·50	1·75
168	-	9d. blue and turquoise	1·00	1·00
169	-	1s. brown and green	1·50	70
170	-	2s. brown and blue	18·00	3·00
171	-	5s. blue and green	8·00	7·00
172	-	10s. yellow and blue	24·00	18·00
173	40	£1 black and brown	18·00	18·00
199	-	4d. brown and turquoise	30	2·25

DESIGNS (As Type **38**):—HORIZ: 1d. Moorish Castle; 2d. St George's Hall; 3d. The Rock by moonlight; 4d. Catalan Bay; 1s. Barbary ape; 2s. Barbary Partridge; 5s. Blue Rock Thrush. VERT: 2½d. The keys; 6d. Map of Gibraltar; 7d. Hawker Siddeley Comet 4 over airport; 9d. American War Memorial; 10s. Rock lily.

1963. Freedom from Hunger. As T 21a of Gambia.

174	40	9d. sepia	3·00	1·50

1963. Centenary of Red Cross. As T 21b of Gambia.

175	1d. red and black	1·00	2·00
176	9d. red and blue	2·50	4·00

1964. 400th Birth Anniv of Shakespeare. As T 35a of Gambia.

177	7d. bistre	60	20

1964. New Constitution. Nos. 164 and 166 optd NEW CONSTITUTION 1964.

178	3d. blue and orange	20	10
179	6d. sepia and green	20	60

45 I.T.U. Emblem

1965. Centenary of I.T.U.

180	45	4d. green and yellow	2·00	50
181	45	2s. green and blue	5·50	3·25

46 I.C.Y. Emblem

1965. I.C.Y.

182	46	½d. green and lavender	20	2·50
183	46	4d. purple and turquoise	70	50

The value of the ½d. stamp is shown as "½".

47 Winston Churchill and St. Paul's Cathedral in Wartime

1966. Churchill Commemoration.

184	47	½d. blue	20	2·25
185	47	1d. green	30	10
186	47	4d. brown	1·25	10
187	47	9d. violet	1·25	2·50

48 Footballer's Legs, Ball and Jules Rimet Cup

1966. World Cup Football Championships.

188	48	2½d. multicoloured	75	1·00
189	48	6d. multicoloured	1·00	50

53 Red Seabream

1966. European Sea Angling Championships. Gibraltar.

190	53	4d. red, blue and black	30	10
191	-	7d. red, green and black	30	70
192	-	1s. brown, green and black	50	30

DESIGNS—HORIZ: 7d. Red scorpionfish. VERT: 1s. Stone bass.

54 W.H.O. Building

1966. Inauguration of W.H.O. Headquarters, Geneva.

193	54	6d. black, green and blue	2·75	1·75
194	54	9d. black, purple and ochre	3·25	2·75

56 "Our Lady of Europa"

1966. Centenary of Re-enthronement of "Our Lady of Europa".

195	**56**	2s. blue and black	30	80

56a "Education"

56b "Science"

56c "Culture"

1966. 20th Anniv of UNESCO.

196	**56a**	2d. multicoloured	50	10
197	**56b**	7d. yellow, violet and olive	2·00	10
198	**56c**	5s. black, purple & orge	4·25	3·00

57 H.M.S. "Victory"

1967. Multicoloured.

200	½d. Type **57**	10	20
201	1d. "Arab" (early steamer)	10	10
202	2d. H.M.S. "Carmania" (merchant cruiser)	15	10
203	2½d. "Mons Calpe" (ferry)	40	30
204	3d. "Canberra" (liner)	20	10
205	4d. H.M.S. "Hood" (battle cruiser)	30	10
205a	5d. "Mirror" (cable ship)	2·00	55
206	6d. Xebec (sailing vessel)	30	50
207	7d. "Amerigo Vespucci" (Italian cadet ship)	30	70
208	9d. "Raffaello" (liner)	30	1·50
209	1s. "Royal Katherine" (galleon)	30	35
210	2s. Fairey Swordfish over H.M.S. "Ark Royal" (aircraft carrier, 1937)	3·50	2·50
211	5s. H.M.S. "Dreadnought" (nuclear submarine)	3·50	7·00
212	10s. "Neuralia" (liner)	14·00	23·00
213	£1 "Mary Celeste" (sailing vessel)	14·00	23·00

58 Aerial Ropeway

1967. International Tourist Year. Multicoloured.

214	7d. Type **58**	15	10
215	9d. Shark fishing (horiz)	15	10
216	1s. Skin-diving (horiz)	20	15

59 Mary, Joseph and Child Jesus

1967. Christmas. Multicoloured.

217	2d. Type **59**	15	10
218	6d. Church window (vert)	15	10

61 General Eliott and Route Map

1967. 250th Birth Anniv of General Eliott. Mult.

219	4d. Type **61**	15	10
220	9d. Heathfield Tower and Monument, Sussex	15	10
221	1s. General Eliott (vert)	15	10
222	2s. Eliott directing rescue operations (55×21 mm)	25	50

65 Lord Baden-Powell

1968. 60th Anniv of Gibraltar Scout Association.

223	**65**	4d. buff and violet	15	10
224	-	7d. ochre and green	15	20
225	-	9d. blue, orange and black	15	30
226	-	1s. yellow and green	15	30

DESIGNS: 7d. Scout flag over the Rock; 9d. Tent, Scouts and salute; 1s. Scout badges.

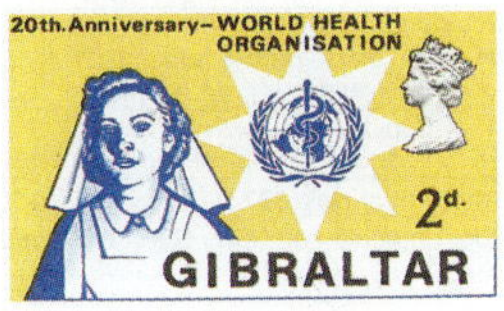

66 Nurse and W.H.O. Emblem

1968. 20th Anniv of W.H.O. Multicoloured.

227	2d. Type **66**	10	15
228	4d. Doctor and W.H.O. emblem	10	10

68 King John signing Magna Carta

1968. Human Rights Year.

229	**68**	1s. orange, brown and gold	15	10
230	-	2s. myrtle and gold	15	20

DESIGN: 2s. "Freedom" and Rock of Gibraltar.

70 Shepherd, Lamb and Star

1968. Christmas. Multicoloured.

231	4d. Type **70**	10	10
232	9d. Mary holding Holy Child	15	20

72 Parliament Houses

1969. Commonwealth Parliamentary Association Conference.

233	**72**	4d. green and gold	10	10
234	-	9d. violet and gold	10	10
235	-	2s. red, gold and blue	15	20

DESIGNS—HORIZ: 9d. Parliamentary emblem and outline of "The Rock". VERT: 2s. Clock Tower, Westminster (Big Ben) and Arms of Gibraltar.

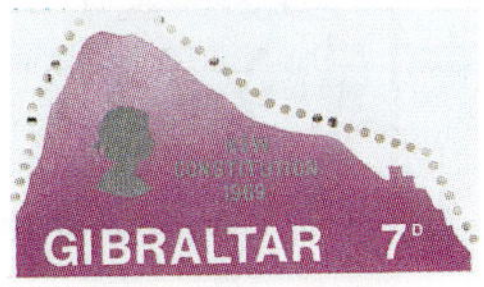

75 Silhouette of Rock and Queen Elizabeth II

1969. New Constitution.

236	**75**	½d. gold and orange	10	10
237	**75**	5d. silver and green	20	10
238	**75**	7d. silver and purple	20	10
239	**75**	5s. silver and blue	65	1·10

77 Soldier and Cap Badge, Royal Anglian Regiment, 1969

1969. Military Uniforms (1st series). Multicoloured.

240	1d. Royal Artillery Officer, 1758, and modern cap badge	15	10
241	6d. Type **77**	20	15
242	9d. Royal Engineers' Artificer, 1786, and modern cap badge	30	15
243	2s. Private, Fox's Marines, 1704, and modern Royal Marines' cap badge	75	70

See also Nos. 248/51, 290/3, 300/303, 313/16, 331/4, 340/3 and 363/6.

80 "Madonna of the Chair" (detail, Raphael)

1969. Christmas. Multicoloured.

244	5d. Type **80**	10	35
245	7d. "Virgin and Child" (detail, Morales)	20	35
246	1s. "The Virgin of the Rocks" (detail, Leonardo da Vinci)	20	40

83 Europa Point

1970. Europa Point.

247	**83**	2s. multicoloured	45	30

1970. Military Uniforms (2nd series). As T 77. Multicoloured.

248	2d. Royal Scots Officer (1839) and cap badge	25	10
249	5d. South Wales Borderers Private (1763) and cap badge	35	10
250	7d. Queen's Royal Regiment Private (1742) and cap badge	35	10
251	2s. Royal Irish Rangers piper (1969) and cap badge	1·00	90

88 Stamp and Rock of Gibraltar

1970. "Philympia 70" Stamp Exhibition, London.

252	**88**	1s. red and green	15	10
253	-	2s. blue and mauve	25	65

DESIGN: 2s. Stamp and Moorish Castle.

The stamps shown in the designs are well-known varieties with values omitted.

90 "The Virgin and Mary" (stained-glass window, Gabriel Loire)

1970. Christmas.

254	**90**	2s. multicoloured	30	60

91 Saluting Battery, Rosia

92 Saluting Battery, Rosia, Modern View

1971. Decimal Currency.

255	**91**	½p. multicoloured	20	30
256	**92**	½p. multicoloured	20	30
257	-	1p. multicoloured	80	30
258	-	1p. multicoloured	80	30
259	-	1½p. multicoloured	20	50
260	-	1½p. multicoloured	20	50
263a	-	2½p. multicoloured	20	50
264	-	2½p. multicoloured	20	50
265	-	3p. multicoloured	20	20
266	-	3p. multicoloured	20	20
269	-	5p. multicoloured	35	35
270	-	5p. multicoloured	35	35
271	-	7p. multicoloured	65	65
272	-	7p. multicoloured	65	65
273	-	8p. multicoloured	70	80
274	-	8p. multicoloured	70	80
275	-	9p. multicoloured	70	80
276	-	9p. multicoloured	70	80
277	-	10p. multicoloured	80	80
278	-	10p. multicoloured	80	80
279	-	12½p. multicoloured	1·00	1·75
280	-	12½p. multicoloured	1·00	1·75
281	-	25p. multicoloured	1·10	1·75
282	-	25p. multicoloured	1·10	1·75
283	-	50p. multicoloured	1·50	2·50
284	-	50p. multicoloured	1·50	2·50
285	-	£1 multicoloured	2·25	4·00
286	-	£1 multicoloured	2·25	4·00
317	-	2p. multicoloured	1·25	2·50
318	-	2p. multicoloured	1·25	2·50
319	-	4p. multicoloured	1·40	2·75
320	-	4p. multicoloured	1·40	2·75

DESIGNS: The two versions of each value show the same Gibraltar view taken from an early 19th-century print (first design) or modern photograph (second design): HORIZ: 1p. Prince George of Cambridge Quarters and Trinity Church; 1½p. The Wellington Bust, Alameda Gardens; 2p. Gibraltar from the North Bastion; 2½p. Catalan Bay; 3p. Convent Garden; 4p. The Exchange and Spanish Chapel; 5p. Commercial Square and Library; 7p. South Barracks and Rosia Magazine; 8p. Moorish Mosque and Castle; 9p. Europa Pass Road; 10p. South Barracks from Rosia Bay; 12½p. Southport Gates; 25p. Trooping the Colour, The Alameda. VERT: 50p. Europa Pass Gorge; £1 Prince Edward's Gate.

93

1971. Coil Stamps.

No.	Type	Description	Unused	Used
287	**93**	½p. orange	15	30
288	**93**	1p. blue	15	30
289	**93**	2p. green	50	1·10

1971. Military Uniforms (3rd series). As T 77. Multicoloured.

No.	Description	Unused	Used
290	1p. The Black Watch (1845)	35	30
291	2p. Royal Regimental of Fusiliers (1971)	55	30
292	4p. King's Own Royal Border Regiment (1704)	75	50
293	10p. Devonshire and Dorset Regiment (1801)	2·75	3·00

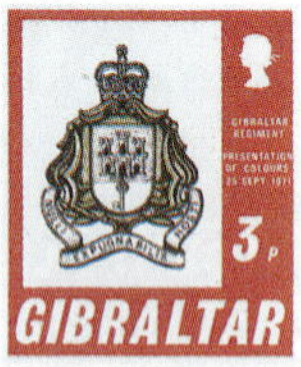

94 Regimental Arms

1971. Presentation of Colours to the Gibraltar Regiment.

No.	Type	Description	Unused	Used
294	**94**	3p. black, gold and red	55	30

95 Nativity Scene

1971. Christmas. Multicoloured.

No.	Description	Unused	Used
295	3p. Type **95**	40	60
296	5p. Mary and Joseph going to Bethlehem	40	65

96 Soldier Artificer, 1773

1972. Bicentenary of Royal Engineers in Gibraltar. Multicoloured.

No.	Description	Unused	Used
297	1p. Type **96**	50	60
298	3p. Modern tunneller	60	80
299	5p. Old and new uniforms and badge (horiz)	70	90

1972. Military Uniforms (4th series). As T 77. Multicoloured.

No.	Description	Unused	Used
300	1p. The Duke of Cornwall's Light Infantry, 1704	50	20
301	3p. King's Royal Rifle Corps, 1830	1·25	40
302	7p. 37th North Hampshire, Officer, 1825	2·00	70
303	10p. Royal Navy, 1972	2·25	1·50

97 "Our Lady of Europa"

1972. Christmas.

No.	Type	Description	Unused	Used
304	**97**	3p. multicoloured	10	20
305	**97**	5p. multicoloured	10	35

98 Keys of Gibraltar and "Narcissus niveus"

1972. Royal Silver Wedding.

No.	Type	Description	Unused	Used
306	**98**	5p. red	25	20
307	**98**	7p. green	25	20

99 Flags of Member Nations and E.E.C. Symbol

1973. Britain's Entry into E.E.C.

No.	Type	Description	Unused	Used
308	**99**	5p. multicoloured	40	50
309	**99**	10p. multicoloured	60	1·00

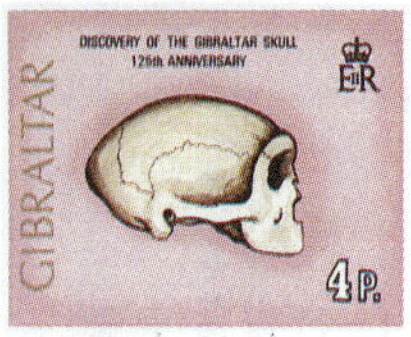

100 Skull

1973. 125th Anniv of Gibraltar Skull Discovery. Multicoloured.

No.	Description	Unused	Used
310	4p. Type **100**	1·25	60
311	6p. Prehistoric man	1·50	1·25
312	10p. Prehistoric family	2·00	2·50

No. 312 is size 40×26 mm.

1973. Military Uniforms (5th series). As T 77. Multicoloured.

No.	Description	Unused	Used
313	1p. King's Own Scottish Borderers, 1770	50	50
314	4p. Royal Welsh Fusiliers, 1800	1·25	80
315	6p. Royal Northumberland Fusiliers, 1736	1·75	1·75
316	10p. Grenadier Guards, 1898	2·50	4·00

101 "Nativity" (Danckerts)

1973. Christmas.

No.	Type	Description	Unused	Used
321	**101**	4p. violet and red	30	15
322	**101**	6p. mauve and blue	40	1·10

101a Princess Anne and Captain Mark Phillips

1973. Royal Wedding.

No.	Type	Description	Unused	Used
323	**101a**	6p. multicoloured	10	10
324	**101a**	14p. multicoloured	20	20

102 Victorian Pillar-box

1974. Centenary of U.P.U. Multicoloured.

No.	Description	Unused	Used
325	2p. Type **102**	15	30
326	6p. Pillar-box of George VI	20	35
327	14p. Pillar-box of Elizabeth II	30	80

Nos. 325/7 also come self-adhesive from booklet panes.

1974. Military Uniforms (6th series). As T 77. Multicoloured.

No.	Description	Unused	Used
331	4p. East Lancashire Regiment, 1742	50	50
332	6p. Somerset Light Infantry, 1833	70	70
333	10p. Royal Sussex Regiment, 1790	1·00	1·40
334	16p. R.A.F. officer, 1974	2·25	4·00

103 "Madonna with the Green Cushion" (Solario)

1974. Christmas. Multicoloured.

No.	Description	Unused	Used
335	4p. Type **103**	40	30
336	6p. "Madonna of the Meadow" (Bellini)	60	95

104 Churchill and Houses of Parliament

1974. Birth Centenary of Sir Winston Churchill. Multicoloured.

No.	Type	Description	Unused	Used
337	**104**	6p. black, purple and lavender	25	15
338	-	20p. black, brown and red	35	45
MS339		114×93 mm. Nos. 337/8	4·50	6·50

DESIGN: 20p. Churchill and "King George V" (battleship).

1975. Military Uniforms (7th series). As T 77. Multicoloured.

No.	Description	Unused	Used
340	4p. East Surrey Regiment, 1846	30	20
341	6p. Highland Light Infantry, 1777	45	40
342	10p. Coldstream Guards, 1704	60	70
343	20p. Gibraltar Regiment, 1974	1·10	2·50

105 Girl Guides' Badge

1975. 50th Anniversary of Gibraltar Girl Guides.

No.	Type	Description	Unused	Used
346	**105**	5p. gold, blue and violet	25	55
347	**105**	7p. gold, brown and light brown	35	60
348	-	15p. silver, black and brown	50	1·25

No. 348 is as Type **105** but shows a different badge.

106 Child at Prayer

1975. Christmas. Multicoloured.

No.	Description	Unused	Used
349	6p. Type **106**	40	60
350	6p. Angel with lute	40	60
351	6p. Child singing carols	40	60
352	6p. Three children	40	60
353	6p. Girl at prayer	40	60
354	6p. Boy and lamb	40	60

107 Bruges Madonna

1975. 500th Birth Anniv of Michelangelo. Multicoloured.

No.	Description	Unused	Used
355	6p. Type **107**	20	25
356	9p. Taddei Madonna	20	40
357	15p. Pieta	30	1·10

Nos. 355/7 also come self-adhesive from booklet panes.

108 Bicentennial Emblem and Arms of Gibraltar

1976. Bicentenary of American Revolution.

No.	Type	Description	Unused	Used
361	**108**	25p. multicoloured	50	50
MS362		85×133 mm. No. 361×4	4·50	7·00

1976. Military Uniforms (8th series). As T 24. Multicoloured.

No.	Description	Unused	Used
363	1p. Suffolk Regiment, 1795	15	20
364	6p. Northamptonshire Regiment, 1779	30	30
365	12p. Lancashire Fusiliers, 1793	40	60
366	25p. Ordnance Corps, 1896	55	1·40

109 The Holy Family

1976. Christmas. Multicoloured.

No.	Description	Unused	Used
367	6p. Type **109**	25	15
368	9p. Madonna and Child	35	25
369	12p. St. Bernard	50	60
370	20p. Archangel Michael	85	1·40

Nos. 367/70 show different stained-glass windows from St. Joseph's Church, Gibraltar.

110 Queen Elizabeth II, Royal Arms and Gibraltar Arms

1977. Silver Jubilee. Multicoloured.

No.	Type	Description	Unused	Used
371	**110**	6p. red	15	20
372	**110**	£1 blue	1·10	2·25
MS373		124×115 mm. Nos. 371/2	1·25	2·25

111 Toothed Orchid

1977. Birds, Flowers, Fish and Butterflies. Multicoloured.

No.	Description	Unused	Used
374	½p. Type **111**	60	2·50
375	1p. Red mullet (horiz)	15	70
376	2p. "Maculinea arion" (butterfly) (horiz)	30	1·75
377	2½p. Sardinian warbler	1·75	2·75
378	3p. Giant squill	20	10
379	4p. Grey wrasse (horiz)	30	10
380	5p. "Vanessa atalanta" (butterfly) (horiz)	50	1·00
381	6p. Black kite	2·25	55
382	9p. Shrubby scorpion-vetch	70	70
383	10p. John dory (fish) (horiz)	40	20
384	12p. "Colias crocea" (butterfly) (horiz)	1·00	35
384b	15p. Winged asparagus pea	1·50	55
385	20p. Audouin's gull	2·00	3·25
386	25p. Barbary nut (iris)	1·25	2·00
387	50p. Swordfish (horiz)	2·00	2·50
388	£1 "Papilio machaon" (butterfly) (horiz)	4·25	5·00
389	£2 Hoopoe	9·00	12·00
389a	£5 Arms of Gibraltar	10·00	12·00

112 "Our Lady of Europa" Stamp

1977. "Amphilex '77" Stamp Exhibition, Amsterdam. Multicoloured.

No.	Description	Unused	Used
390	6p. Type **112**	10	20
391	12p. "Europa Point" stamp	15	30
392	25p. "E.E.C. Entry" stamp	20	50

113 "The Annunciation" (Rubens)

1977. Christmas and 400th Birth Anniv of Rubens. Multicoloured.

No.	Description	Unused	Used
393	3p. Type **113**	10	10
394	9p. "The Adoration of the Magi"	25	25
395	12p. "The Adoration of the Magi" (horiz)	30	50
396	15p. "The Holy Family under the Apple Tree"	30	55
MS397	110×200 mm. Nos. 393/6	2·75	4·00

114 Aerial View of Gibraltar

1978. Gibraltar from Space. Multicoloured.

No.	Description	Unused	Used
398	12p. Type **114**	25	50
MS399	148×108 mm. 25p. Aerial view of Straits of Gibraltar	80	80

115 Holyroodhouse

1978. 25th Anniv of Coronation. Multicoloured.

No.	Description	Unused	Used
400	6p. Type **115**	20	15
401	9p. St. James's Palace	25	15
402	12p. Sandringham	30	30
403	18p. Balmoral	40	85
406	25p. Windsor Castle	1·25	2·00

Nos. 402/3 also exist as self-adhesive stamps from booklet panes, No. 406 only coming in this form.

116 Short S.25 Sunderland, 1938–58

1978. 60th Anniv of Royal Air Force. Multicoloured.

No.	Description	Unused	Used
407	3p. Type **116**	15	10
408	9p. Caudron G-3, 1918	35	40
409	12p. Avro Shackleton M.R.2, 1953–66	40	55
410	16p. Hawker Hunter F.6, 1954–77	45	1·00
411	18p. Hawker Siddeley H.S.801 Nimrod M.R.1, 1969–78	50	1·10

117 "Madonna with Animals"

1978. Christmas. Paintings by Durer. Multicoloured.

No.	Description	Unused	Used
412	5p. Type **117**	20	10
413	9p. "The Nativity"	25	15
414	12p. "Madonna of the Goldfinch"	30	40
415	15p. "Adoration of the Magi"	35	1·00

118 Sir Rowland Hill and 1d. Stamp of 1886

1979. Death Centenary of Sir Rowland Hill.

No.	Type	Description	Unused	Used
416	**118**	3p. multicoloured	10	10
417	-	9p. multicoloured	15	15
418	-	12p. multicoloured	15	20
419	-	25p. black, purple yellow	25	50

DESIGNS: 9p. 1971 1p. coil stamp; 12p. 1840 Post Office Regulations; 25p. "G" cancellation.

119 Posthorn, Dish Antenna and Early Telephone

1979. Europa. Communications.

No.	Type	Description	Unused	Used
420	**119**	3p. green and pale green	15	10
421	**119**	9p. brown and ochre	30	90
422	**119**	12p. blue and violet	35	1·25

120 African Child

1979. Christmas. International Year of the Child. Multicoloured.

No.	Description	Unused	Used
423	12p. Type **120**	25	30
424	12p. Asian child	25	30
425	12p. Polynesian child	25	30
426	12p. American Indian child	25	30
427	12p. Nativity and children of different races	25	30
428	12p. European child	25	30

121 Early Policeman

1980. 150th Anniv of Gibraltar Police Force. Multicoloured.

No.	Description	Unused	Used
429	3p. Type **121**	20	10
430	6p. Policemen of 1895, early 1900s and 1980	20	15
431	12p. Police officer and police ambulance	25	20
432	37p. Policewoman and police motor-cyclist	55	1·25

122 Peter Amigo (Archbishop)

1980. Europa. Personalities. Multicoloured.

No.	Description	Unused	Used
433	12p. Type **122**	20	30
434	12p. Gustavo Bacarisas (artist)	20	30
435	12p. John Mackintosh (philanthropist)	20	30

123 Queen Elizabeth the Queen Mother

1980. 80th Birthday of The Queen Mother.

No.	Type	Description	Unused	Used
436	**123**	15p. multicoloured	30	30

124 "Horatio Nelson" (J. F. Rigaud)

1980. 175th Death Anniv of Nelson. Paintings. Multicoloured.

No.	Description	Unused	Used
437	3p. Type **124**	15	10
438	9p. "H.M.S. Victory' (horiz)	25	25
439	15p. "Horatio Nelson" (Sir William Beechey)	35	35
440	40p. "'H.M.S. Victory' being towed into Gibraltar" (Clarkson Stanfield) (horiz)	80	1·00
MS441	159×99 mm. No. 439	1·00	1·50

125 Three Kings

1980. Christmas.

No.	Type	Description	Unused	Used
442	**125**	15p. brown and yellow	25	35
443	-	15p. brown and yellow	25	35

DESIGN: No. 443, Nativity scene.

126 Hercules creating the Mediterranean

1981. Europa. Multicoloured.

No.	Description	Unused	Used
444	9p. Type **126**	20	15
445	15p. Hercules and Pillars of Hercules	25	35

127 Dining-room

1981. 450th Anniv of The Convent (Governor's Residence). Multicoloured.

No.	Description	Unused	Used
446	4p. Type **127**	10	10
447	14p. King's Chapel	15	15
448	15p. The Convent	15	15
449	55p. Cloister	60	80

128 Prince Charles and Lady Diana Spencer

1981. Royal Wedding.

No.	Type	Description	Unused	Used
450	**128**	£1 multicoloured	1·25	1·25

129

1981

No.	Type	Description	Unused	Used
451	**129**	1p. black	50	60
452	**129**	4p. blue	50	50
453	**129**	15p. green	50	40

130 Paper Airplane

1981. 50th Anniv of Gibraltar Airmail Service. Multicoloured.

No.	Description	Unused	Used
454	14p. Type **130**	15	15
455	15p. Airmail letters, post box and aircraft tail fin	15	15
456	55p. Jet airliner circling globe	60	80

131 Carol Singers

1981. Christmas. Children's Drawings. Multicoloured.

No.	Description	Unused	Used
457	15p. Type **131**	30	15
458	55p. Postbox (vert)	1·00	85

132 I.Y.D.P. Emblem and Stylized Faces

1981. International Year for Disabled Persons.

No.	Type	Description	Unused	Used
459	**132**	14p. multicoloured	30	30

133 Douglas DC-3

1982. Aircraft. Multicoloured.

No.	Description	Unused	Used
460	1p. Type **133**	25	2·00
461	2p. Vickers Viking 1B	30	2·00
462	3p. Airspeed A.S.57 Ambassador G-ALZN	30	1·75

463	4p. Vickers 953 Viscount 800	40	20
464	5p. Boeing 727-100	90	60
465	10p. Vickers Vanguard	1·75	50
466	14p. Short Solent 2	1·75	3·50
467	15p. Fokker F.27 Friendship	2·75	3·50
468	17p. Boeing 737	1·00	75
469	20p. B.A.C. One Eleven 500G-AWYV	1·00	65
470	25p. Lockheed Constellation	4·00	5·00
471	50p. de Havilland Comet 4B	4·00	2·25
472	£1 Saro Windhover G-ABJP "General Godley"	5·50	2·25
473	£2 Hawker Siddeley Trident 2E	6·50	5·00
474	£5 De Havilland D.H.89A Dragon Rapide	8·00	14·00

134 Crest, H.M.S. "Opossum"

1982. Naval Crests (1st series). Multicoloured.

475	½p. Type **134**	10	30
476	15½p. H.M.S. "Norfolk"	40	55
477	17p. H.M.S. "Fearless"	40	60
478	60p. H.M.S. "Rooke"	85	2·75

See also Nos. 493/6, 510/13, 522/5, 541/4, 565/8, 592/5, 616/19 and 651/4.

135 Hawker Hurricane Mk I and Supermarine Spitfires at Gibraltar

1982. Europa. Operation Torch. Multicoloured.

479	14p. Type **135**	25	70
480	17p. General Giraud, General Eisenhower and Gibraltar	35	80

136 Gibraltar Chamber of Commerce Centenary

1982. Anniversaries. Multicoloured.

481	½p. Type **136**	10	65
482	15½p. British Forces Postal Service centenary	45	30
483	60p. 75th anniv of Gibraltar Scout Association	1·25	2·00

137 Printed Circuit forming Map of World

1982. International Direct Dialling.

484	**137** 17p. black, blue and orange	35	35

138 Gibraltar illuminated at Night and Holly

1982. Christmas. Multicoloured.

485	14p. Type **138**	50	30
486	17p. Gibraltar illuminated at night and mistletoe	50	35

139 Yacht Marina

1983. Commonwealth Day. Multicoloured.

487	4p. Type **139**	10	10
488	14p. Scouts and Guides Commonwealth Day Parade	20	15
489	17p. Flag of Gibraltar (vert)	25	20
490	60p. Queen Elizabeth II (from photo by Tim Graham) (vert)	70	1·00

140 St. George's Hall Gallery

1983. Europa.

491	**140** 16p. black and brown	35	50
492	- 19p. black and blue	40	75

DESIGN: 19p. Water catchment slope.

1983. Naval Crests (2nd series). As T 134. Multicoloured.

493	4p. H.M.S. "Faulknor"	30	10
494	14p. H.M.S. "Renown"	70	35
495	17p. H.M.S. "Ark Royal"	75	40
496	60p. H.M.S. "Sheffield"	1·75	1·50

141 Landport Gate, 1729

1983. Fortress Gibraltar in the 18th Century. Multicoloured.

497	4p. Type **141**	15	10
498	17p. Koehler Gun, 1782	35	30
499	77p. King's Bastion, 1779	1·00	1·25
MS500	97×145 mm. Nos. 497/9	2·25	1·50

142 "Adoration of the Magi" (Raphael)

1983. Christmas. 500th Birth Anniv of Raphael. Multicoloured.

501	4p. Type **142**	25	10
502	17p. "Madonna of Foligno" (vert)	70	35
503	60p. "Sistine Madonna" (vert)	1·75	1·40

143 1932 2d. Stamp and Globe

1984. Europa, Posts and Telecommunications. Multicoloured.

504	17p. Type **143**	45	50
505	23p. Circuit board and globe	55	1·00

144 Hockey

1984. Sports. Multicoloured.

506	20p. Type **144**	70	80
507	21p. Basketball	70	80
508	26p. Rowing	70	1·25
509	29p. Football	70	1·50

1984. Naval Crests (3rd series). As T 134. Multicoloured.

510	20p. H.M.S. "Active"	1·75	2·25
511	21p. H.M.S. "Foxhound"	1·75	2·50
512	26p. H.M.S. "Valiant"	2·00	2·50
513	29p. H.M.S. "Hood"	2·00	2·75

145 Mississippi River Boat Float

1984. Christmas. Epiphany Floats. Multicoloured.

514	20p. Type **145**	30	30
515	80p. Roman Temple float	1·40	2·75

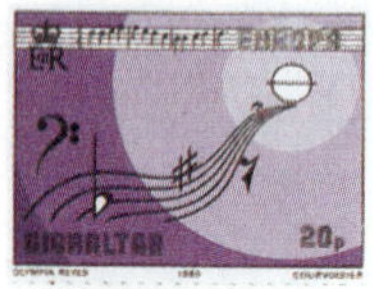

146 Musical Symbols, and Score from Beethoven's 9th (Choral) Symphony

1985. Europa. European Music Year. Multicoloured.

516	**146** 20p. multicoloured	30	30
517	- 29p. multicoloured	40	1·50

DESIGN: The 29p. is as T **146**, but shows different symbols.

147 Globe and Stop Polio Campaign Logo

1985. Stop Polio Campaign.

518	26p. multicoloured (Type **147**)	90	1·40
519	26p. multicoloured ("ST" visible)	90	1·40
520	26p. multicoloured ("STO" visible)	90	1·40
521	26p. multicoloured ("STOP" visible)	90	1·40

Each design differs in the position of the logo across the centre of the globe. On No. 518 only the letter "S" is fully visible, on No. 519 "ST", on No. 520 "STO" and on No. 521 "STOP". Other features of the design also differ, so that the word "Year" moves towards the top of the stamp and on No. 521 the upper logo is omitted.

1985. Naval Crests (4th series). As T 134. Multicoloured.

522	4p. H.M.S. "Duncan"	65	10
523	9p. H.M.S. "Fury"	1·00	50
524	21p. H.M.S. "Firedrake"	2·25	2·00
525	80p. H.M.S. "Malaya"	4·50	6·00

148 I.Y.Y. Logo

1985. International Youth Year. Multicoloured.

526	4p. Type **148**	35	10
527	20p. Hands passing diamond	1·40	1·10
528	80p. 75th anniv logo of Girl Guide Movement	3·25	3·75

149 St. Joseph

1985. Christmas. Centenary of St. Joseph's Parish Church. Multicoloured.

529	4p. Type **149**	65	90
530	4p. St. Joseph's Parish Church	65	90
531	80p. Nativity crib	4·50	4·75

150 "Papilio machaon" (butterfly) and The Convent

1986. Europa. Nature and the Environment. Multicoloured.

532	22p. Type **150**	1·00	50
533	29p. Herring gull and Europa Point	1·50	4·25

151 1887 Queen Victoria 6d. Stamp

1986. Centenary of First Gibraltar Postage Stamps. Designs showing stamps. Multicoloured.

534	4p. Type **151**	30	10
535	22p. 1903 Edward VII 2½d.	1·00	1·00
536	32p. 1912 George V 1d.	1·50	2·00
537	36p. 1938 George VI £1	1·60	2·50
538	44p. 1953 Coronation ½d. (29×46 mm)	2·00	3·00
MS539	102×73 mm. 29p. 1886 "GIBRALTAR" overprinted on Bermuda 1d.	2·50	3·00

152 Queen Elizabeth II in Robes of Order of the Bath

1986. 60th Birthday of Queen Elizabeth II.

540	**152** £1 multicoloured	1·75	3·00

1986. Naval Crests (5th series). As T 134. Multicoloured.

541	22p. H.M.S. "Lightning"	1·75	1·00
542	29p. H.M.S. "Hermione"	2·00	1·75
543	32p. H.M.S. "Laforey"	2·25	3·25
544	44p. H.M.S. "Nelson"	2·75	4·50

153 Prince Andrew and Miss Sarah Ferguson

1986. Royal Wedding. Sheet 115×85 mm.

MS545	**153** 44p. multicoloured	1·40	2·25

154 Three Kings and Cathedral of St. Mary the Crowned

1986. Christmas. International Peace Year. Multicoloured.

546	18p. Type **154**	1·00	50
547	32p. St. Andrew's Church	1·50	3·00

155 Neptune House

1987. Europa. Architecture. Multicoloured.

563	22p. Type **155**	1·50	50
564	29p. Ocean Heights	2·50	4·25

1987. Naval Crests (6th series). As T 134. Multicoloured.

565	18p. H.M.S. "Wishart"	1·60	75
566	22p. H.M.S. "Charybdis"	1·75	1·10
567	32p. H.M.S. "Antelope"	2·50	3·50
568	44p. H.M.S. "Eagle"	3·00	4·50

156 13-inch Mortar, 1783

1987. Guns. Multicoloured.

569	1p. Type **156**	20	70
570	2p. 6-inch coastal gun, 1909	30	70
571	3p. 8-inch howitzer, 1783	40	70
572	4p. Bofors "L40/70" AA gun, 1951	40	10
573	5p. 100 ton rifled muzzle-loader, 1882	40	70
574	10p. 5.25 inch heavy AA gun, 1953	40	70
575	18p. 25-pounder gun-how, 1943	65	1·00
576	19p. 64-pounder rifled muzzle-loader, 1873	70	1·25
577	22p. 12-pounder gun, 1758	70	50
578	50p. 10-inch rifled muzzle-loader, 1870	1·40	3·00
579	£1 Russian 24-pounder gun, 1854	2·50	2·50
580	£3 9.2 inch "Mk 10" coastal gun, 1935	3·00	11·00
581	£5 24-pounder gun, 1779	5·00	14·00

157 Victoria Stadium

1987. Bicentenary of Royal Engineers' Royal Warrant. Multicoloured.

582	18p. Type **157**	1·25	65
583	32p. Freedom of Gibraltar scroll and casket	1·75	3·00
584	44p. Royal Engineers' badge	2·50	4·00

158 The Three Kings

1987. Christmas. Multicoloured.

585	4p. Type **158**	20	10
586	22p. The Holy Family	1·00	1·00
587	44p. The Shepherds	1·90	3·50

159 "Canberra" (liner) passing Gibraltar

1988. Europa. Transport and Communications. Multicoloured.

588	22p. Type **159**	1·50	2·25
589	22p. "Gibline I" (ferry), dish aerial and Boeing 737 airliner	1·50	2·25
590	32p. Horse-drawn carriage and modern coach	2·00	2·75
591	32p. Car, telephone and Rock of Gibraltar	2·00	2·75

1988. Naval Crests (7th series). As T 134.

592	18p. multicoloured	1·50	65
593	22p. black, brown and gold	2·00	1·25
594	32p. multicoloured	2·25	3·50
595	44p. multicoloured	3·00	4·75

DESIGNS: 18p. H.M.S. "Clyde"; 22p. H.M.S. "Foresight"; 32p. H.M.S. "Severn"; 44p. H.M.S. "Rodney".

160 European Bee Eater

1988. Birds. Multicoloured.

596	4p. Type **160**	75	20
597	22p. Atlantic puffin	1·75	90
598	32p. Western honey buzzard ("Honey Buzzard")	2·25	2·50
599	44p. Blue rock thrush	2·75	3·50

161 "Zebu" (brigantine)

1988. Operation Raleigh. Multicoloured.

600	19p. Type **161**	65	60
601	22p. Miniature of Sir Walter Raleigh and logo	75	70
602	32p. "Sir Walter Raleigh" (expedition ship) and world map	1·10	2·00
MS603	135×86 mm. 22p. As No. 601; 44p. "Sir Walter Raleigh" (expedition ship) passing Gibraltar	4·25	5·00

162 "Snowman" (Rebecca Falero)

1988. Christmas. Children's Paintings. Mult.

604	4p. Type **162**	15	10
605	22p. "The Nativity" (Dennis Penalver)	55	60
606	44p. "Father Christmas" (Gavin Key) (23×31 mm)	1·00	2·00

163 Soft Toys and Toy Train

1989. Europa. Children's Toys. Multicoloured.

607	25p. Type **163**	1·25	75
608	32p. Soft toys, toy boat and doll's house	1·75	2·75

164 Port Sergeant with Keys

1989. 50th Anniv of Gibraltar Regiment. Mult.

609	4p. Type **164**	50	10
610	22p. Regimental badge and colours	1·40	1·10
611	32p. Drum major	1·90	3·50
MS612	124×83 mm. 22p. As No. 610; 44p. Former Gibraltar Defence Force badge	3·50	4·25

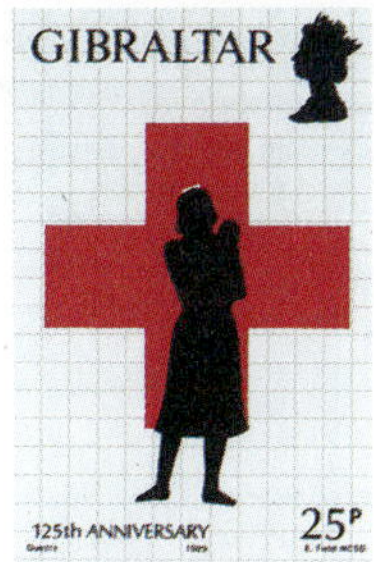

165 Nurse and Baby

1989. 125th Anniv of International Red Cross.

613	**165**	25p. black, red and brown	1·00	60
614	-	32p. black, red and brown	1·25	1·75
615	-	44p. black, red and brown	1·50	3·50

DESIGNS: 32p. Famine victims; 44p. Accident victims.

1989. Naval Crests (8th series). As T 134.

616	22p. multicoloured	1·50	75
617	25p. black and gold	1·50	1·50
618	32p. gold, black and red	2·00	3·25
619	44p. multicoloured	3·00	5·50

DESIGNS: 22p. H.M.S. "Blankney"; 25p. H.M.S. "Deptford"; 32p. H.M.S. "Exmoor"; 44p. H.M.S. "Stork".

166 One Penny Coin

1989. New Coinage. T 166 and similar vert designs in two miniature sheets.

MS620	72×94 mm. 4p. bronze, black and red (Type **166**); 4p. bronze, black and brown (two pence); 4p. silver, black and yellow (ten pence); 4p. silver, black and green (five pence)	1·25	2·00
MS621	100×95 mm. 22p. silver, black and green (fifty pence); 22p. gold, black and blue (five pounds); 22p. gold, black and brown (two pounds); 22p. gold, black and green (one pound); 22p. gold, black and violet (obverse of coin series); 22p. silver, black and blue (twenty pence)	5·50	7·00

167 Father Christmas in Sleigh

1989. Christmas. Multicoloured.

622	4p. Type **167**	20	10
623	22p. Shepherds and sheep	90	70
624	32p. The Nativity	1·40	1·75
625	44p. The Three Wise Men	2·25	4·00

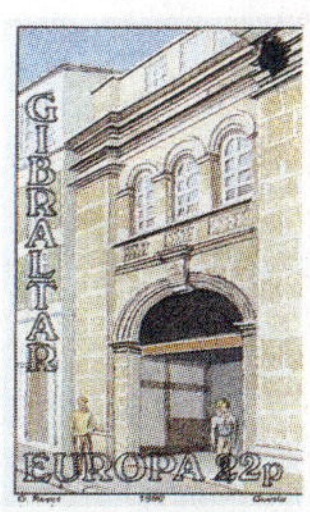

168 General Post Office Entrance

1990. Europa. Post Office Buildings. Multicoloured.

626	22p. Type **168**	1·00	1·50
627	22p. Interior of General Post Office	1·00	1·50
628	32p. Interior of South District Post Office	1·50	2·50
629	32p. South District Post Office	1·50	2·50

169 19th-century Firemen

1990. 125th Anniv of Gibraltar Fire Service. Multicoloured.

630	4p. Type **169**	85	15
631	20p. Early fire engine (horiz)	2·25	1·10
632	42p. Modern fire engine (horiz)	2·75	3·75
633	44p. Modern fireman in breathing apparatus	2·75	3·75

170 Henry Corbould (artist) and Penny Black

1990. 150th Anniv of the Penny Black. Multicoloured.

634	19p. Type **170**	1·10	1·00
635	22p. Bath Royal Mail coach	1·25	1·00
636	32p. Sir Rowland Hill and Penny Black	2·50	4·50
MS637	145×95 mm. 44p. Penny Black with Maltese Cross cancellation	4·50	5·50

1990. Naval Crests (9th series). As T 134. Multicoloured.

638	22p. H.M.S. "Calpe"	1·75	70
639	25p. H.M.S. "Gallant"	1·90	1·75
640	32p. H.M.S. "Wrestler"	2·50	3·25
641	44p. H.M.S. "Greyhound"	3·00	6·50

171 Model of Europort Development

1990. Development Projects. Multicoloured.

642	22p. Type **171**	75	80
643	23p. Construction of building material factory	75	1·50
644	25p. Land reclamation	95	1·50

172 Candle and Holly

1990. Christmas. Multicoloured.

645	4p. Type **172**	15	10
646	22p. Father Christmas	75	65
647	42p. Christmas tree	1·50	2·50
648	44p. Nativity crib	1·50	2·50

173 Space Laboratory and Spaceplane (Columbus Development Programme)

1991. Europa. Europe in Space. Multicoloured.

649	25p. Type **173**	75	75
650	32p. "ERS-1" earth resources remote sensing satellite	1·00	2·25

1991. Naval Crests (10th series). As T 134.

651	4p. black, blue and gold	60	10
652	21p. multicoloured	1·75	1·25
653	22p. multicoloured	1·75	1·25
654	62p. multicoloured	3·75	7·00

DESIGNS: 4p. H.M.S. "Hesperus"; 21p. H.M.S. "Forester"; 22p. H.M.S. "Furious"; 62p. H.M.S. "Scylla".

174 Shag

1991. Endangered Species. Birds. Multicoloured.

655	13p. Type **174**	1·40	1·60
656	13p. Barbary partridge	1·40	1·60
657	13p. Egyptian vulture	1·40	1·60
658	13p. Black stork	1·40	1·60

1991. No. 580 surch £1.05.

659	£1.05 on £3 9.2-inch "Mk.10" coastal gun, 1935	3·50	1·60

176 "North View of Gibraltar" (Gustavo Bacarisas)

1991. Local Paintings. Multicoloured.

660	22p. Type **176**	85	50
661	26p. "Parson's Lodge" (Elena Mifsud)	1·00	1·00
662	32p. "Governor's Parade" (Jacobo Azagury)	1·50	2·25
663	42p. "Waterport Wharf" (Rudesindo Mannia) (vert)	2·25	4·50

177 "Once in Royal David's City"

1991. Christmas. Carols. Multicoloured.

664	4p. Type **177**	40	10
665	24p. "Silent Night"	1·75	70
666	25p. "Angels We Have Heard on High"	1·75	1·25
667	49p. "O Come All Ye Faithful"	2·50	6·00

178 "Danaus chrysippus"

1991. "Phila Nippon '91" International Stamp Exhibition, Tokyo. Sheet 116×91 mm.

MS668	**178** £1.05, multicoloured	3·50	4·50

179 Columbus and "Santa Maria"

1992. Europa. 500th Anniv of Discovery of America by Columbus. Multicoloured.

669	24p. Type **179**	1·25	2·00
670	24p. Map of Old World and "Nina"	1·25	2·00
671	34p. Map of New World and "Pinta"	1·50	2·50
672	34p. Map of Old World and look-out	1·50	2·50

Nos. 669/70 and 671/2 were issued together, se-tenant, each pair forming a composite design.

179a Gibraltar from North

1992. 40th Anniv of Queen Elizabeth II's Accession. Multicoloured.

673	4p. Type **179a**	15	10
674	20p. H.M.S. "Arrow" (frigate) and Gibraltar from south	60	60
675	24p. Southport Gates	75	80
676	44p. Three portraits of Queen Elizabeth	1·25	1·60
677	54p. Queen Elizabeth II	1·60	1·90

180 Compass Rose, Sail, and Atlantic Map

1992. Round the World Yacht Rally. Multicoloured designs, each incorporating compass rose and sail.

678	21p. Type **180**	75	80
679	24p. Map of Indonesian Archipelago (horiz)	95	1·40
680	25p. Map of India Ocean (horiz)	95	1·75
MS681	108×72 mm. 21p. Type **180**; 49p. Map of Mediterranean and Red Sea	2·50	3·50

181 Holy Trinity Cathedral

1992. 150th Anniv of Anglican Diocese of Gibraltar-in-Europe. Multicoloured.

682	4p. Type **181**	20	10
683	24p. Diocesan crest and map (horiz)	1·00	65
684	44p. Construction of Cathedral and Sir George Don (horiz)	1·75	3·00
685	54p. Bishop Tomlinson	2·00	3·50

182 Sacred Heart of Jesus Church

1992. Christmas. Churches. Multicoloured.

686	4p. Type **182**	35	10
687	24p. Cathedral of St. Mary the Crowned	1·50	55
688	34p. St. Andrew's Church of Scotland	2·00	2·50
689	49p. St. Joseph's Church	2·50	5·50

183 "Drama and Music"

1993. Europa. Contemporary Art. Multicoloured.

690	24p. Type **183**	1·50	2·00
691	24p. "Sculpture, Art and Pottery"	1·50	2·00
692	34p. "Architecture"	2·00	2·75
693	34p. "Printing and Photography"	2·00	2·75

184 H.M.S. "Hood" (battle cruiser)

1993. Second World War Warships (1st series). Sheet 120×79 mm, containing T 184 and similar horiz designs. Multicoloured.

MS694	24p. Type **184**; 24p. H.M.S. "Ark Royal" (aircraft carrier, 1937); 24p. H.M.A.S. "Waterhen" (destroyer); 24p. U.S.S. "Gleaves" (destroyer)	9·00	9·00

See also Nos. **MS**724, **MS**748, **MS**779 and **MS**809.

185 Landport Gate

1993. Architectural Heritage. Multicoloured.

695	1p. Type **185**	30	1·25
696	2p. St. Mary the Crowned Church (horiz)	50	1·25
697	3p. Parsons Lodge Battery (horiz)	50	1·25
698	4p. Moorish Castle (horiz)	50	1·25
699	5p. General Post Office	50	30
699a	6p. House of Assembly	1·75	75
699b	7p. Bleak House (horiz)	1·75	75
699c	8p. General Eliott Memorial	1·75	75
699d	9p. Supreme Court Building (horiz)	1·75	75
700	10p. South Barracks (horiz)	50	60
700a	20p. The Convent (horiz)	2·50	75
701	21p. American War Memorial	1·00	80
702	24p. Garrison Library (horiz)	1·10	80
703	25p. Southport Gates	1·10	80
704	26p. Casemates Gate (horiz)	1·10	80
704a	30p. St. Bernard's Hospital	3·50	80
704b	40p. City Hall (horiz)	3·50	1·50
705	50p. Central Police Station (horiz)	2·50	2·25
706	£1 Prince Edward's Gate	2·25	2·75
706a	£2 Church of the Sacred Heart of Jesus	8·00	6·50
707	£3 Lighthouse, Europa Point	10·00	11·00
708	£5 Coat of Arms and fortress keys	10·00	15·00

186 £sd and Decimal British Coins (25th anniv of decimal currency)

1993. Anniversaries. Multicoloured.

709	21p. Type **186**	1·00	65
710	24p. R.A.F. crest with Handley Page 0/400 and Panavia Tornado F Mk 3 (75th anniv)	1·75	75
711	34p. Garrison Library badge and building (bicent)	1·60	2·25
712	49p. Sir Winston Churchill and air raid (50th anniv of visit)	3·50	5·00

187 Mice decorating Christmas Tree

1993. Christmas. Multicoloured.

713	5p. Type **187**	25	10
714	24p. Mice pulling cracker	1·10	70
715	44p. Mice singing carols	2·25	2·75
716	49p. Mice building snowman	2·75	3·25

188 Exploding Atom (Lord Penney)

1994. Europa. Scientific Discoveries. Mult.

717	24p. Type **188**	1·00	1·50
718	24p. Polonium and radium experiment (Marie Curie)	1·00	1·50
719	34p. First oil engine (Rudolph Diesel)	1·25	2·00
720	34p. Early telescope (Galileo)	1·25	2·00

189 World Cup and Map of U.S.A.

1994. World Cup Football Championship, U.S.A. Multicoloured.

721	26p. Type **189**	80	55
722	39p. Players and pitch in shape of U.S.A	1·25	2·00
723	49p. Player's legs (vert)	1·60	2·75

1994. Second World War Warships (2nd series). Sheet 112×72 mm, containing horiz designs as T 184. Multicoloured.

MS724	5p. H.M.S. "Penelope" (cruiser); 25p. H.M.S. "Warspite" (battleship); 44p. U.S.S. "McLanahan" (destroyer); 49p. "Isaac Sweers" (Dutch destroyer)	8·50	10·00

190 Pekingese

1994. "Philakorea '94" International Stamp Exhibition, Seoul. Sheet 102×76 mm.

MS725	**190** £1.05, multicoloured	3·00	4·00

191 Golden Star Coral

1994. Marine Life. Multicoloured.

726	21p. Type **191**	75	45
727	24p. Star fish	90	55
728	34p. Gorgonian sea-fan	1·50	2·25
729	49p. Peacock wrasse ("Turkish wrasse")	2·00	3·50

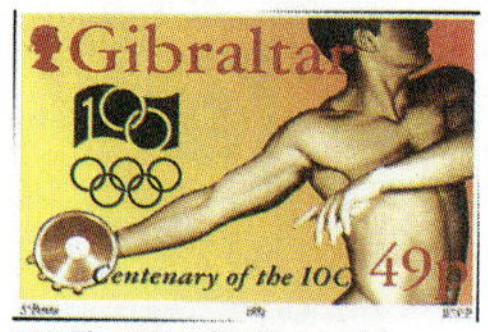

192 Throwing the Discus and Centenary Emblem

1994. Centenary of Int Olympic Committee. Mult.

730	49p. Type **192**	1·75	2·25
731	54p. Javelin throwing and emblem	1·75	2·50

193 Great Tit

1994. Christmas. Songbirds. Multicoloured.

732	5p. Type **193**	70	10
733	24p. European robin (horiz)	2·00	70
734	34p. Blue tit (horiz)	2·25	1·50
735	54p. Eurasian goldfinch ("Goldfinch")	3·00	5·00

194 Austrian Flag, Hand and Star

1995. Expansion of European Union. Multicoloured.

736	24p. Type **194**	60	55
737	26p. Finnish flag, hand and star	60	60
738	34p. Swedish flag, hand and star	90	1·50
739	49p. Flags of new members and European Union emblem	1·60	3·25

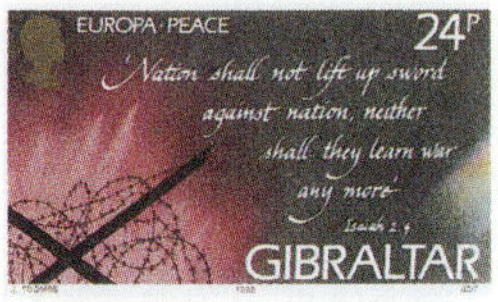

195 Barbed Wire and Quote from Isaiah Ch 2.4

1995. Europa. Peace and Freedom. Multicoloured.

740	24p. Type **195**	1·40	1·60
741	24p. Rainbow and hands releasing peace dove	1·40	1·60
742	34p. Shackles on wall and quote from Isaiah ch 61.1	1·60	2·25
743	34p. Hands and sea birds	1·60	2·25

196 Fairey Swordfish, I Class Destroyer and Rock of Gibraltar

1995. 50th Anniv of End of Second World War. Sheet 101×66 mm.

MS744	**196** £1.05, multicoloured	3·25	4·00

197 Yachting

1995. Island Games '95. Multicoloured.

745	24p. Type **197**	70	60
746	44p. Athlete on starting blocks	1·60	2·50
747	49p. Swimmer at start of race	1·60	2·50

1995. Second World War Warships (3rd series). Sheet 133×85 mm, containing horiz designs as T 184. Multicoloured.

MS748	5p. H.M.S. "Calpe" (destroyer); 24p. H.M.S. "Victorious" (aircraft carrier); 44p. U.S.S. "Weehawken" (attack transport); 49p. "Savorgan de Brazza" (French destroyer)	8·50	9·00

198 Bee Orchid

1995. "Singapore '95" International Stamp Exhibition. Orchids. Multicoloured.

749	22p. Type **198**	1·40	1·60
750	23p. Brown bee orchid	1·40	1·60
751	24p. Pyramidal orchid	1·40	1·60
752	25p. Mirror orchid	1·40	1·60
753	26p. Sawfly orchid	1·40	1·60

199 Handshake and United Nations Emblem

1995. 50th Anniv of United Nations. Multicoloured.

754	34p. Type **199**	1·50	1·10
755	49p. Peace dove and U.N. emblem	1·75	3·00

200 Marilyn Monroe

1995. Centenary of Cinema. T 200 and similar horiz designs showing film stars. Multicoloured.

MS756	Two sheets, each 116×80 mm. (a) 5p. Type **200**; 25p. Romy Schneider; 28p. Yves Montand; 38p. Audrey Hepburn. (b) 24p. Ingrid Bergman; 24p. Vittorio de Sica; 24p. Marlene Dietrich; 24p. Laurence Olivier Set of 2 sheets	4·50	5·50

201 Father Christmas

1995. Christmas. Multicoloured.

757	5p. Type **201**	40	10
758	24p. Toys in sack	1·25	55
759	34p. Reindeer	1·75	1·25
760	54p. Sleigh over houses	3·00	4·50

202 Shih Tzu

1996. Puppies. Multicoloured.

761	5p. Type **202**	40	85
762	21p. Dalmatians	75	95
763	24p. Cocker spaniels	80	1·10
764	25p. West Highland white terriers	80	1·10
765	34p. Labrador	90	1·25
766	35p. Boxer	90	1·25

No. 762 is inscr "Dalmation" in error.

203 Princess Anne

1996. Europa. Famous Women.

767	**203**	24p. black and yellow	1·60	1·60
768	-	24p. black and green	1·60	1·60
769	-	34p. black and red	2·00	2·25
770	-	34p. black and purple	2·00	2·25

DETAILS: Nos. 768, Princess Diana; 769, Queen Elizabeth II; 770, Queen Elizabeth the Queen Mother.

204 West German Player, 1980

1996. European Football Championship, England. Players from previous winning teams. Multicoloured.

771	21p. Type **204**	55	45
772	24p. French player, 1984	65	55
773	34p. Dutch player, 1988	95	1·10
774	£1.20 Danish player, 1992	3·00	4·75
MS775	135×91 mm. As Nos. 771/4	6·50	7·50

205 Ancient Greek Athletes

1996. Centenary of Modern Olympic Games.

776	**205**	34p. black, purple & orge	95	90
777	-	49p. black and brown	1·40	1·75
778	-	£1.05 multicoloured	3·00	4·50

DESIGNS: 49p. Start of early race; £1.05, Start of modern race.

1996. Second World War Warships (4th series). Sheet 118×84 mm, containing horiz designs as T 184. Multicoloured.

MS779	5p. H.M.S. "Starling" (sloop); 25p. H.M.S. "Royalist" (cruiser); 49p. U.S.S. "Philadelphia" (cruiser); 54p. H.M.C.S. "Prescott" (corvette)	6·00	7·50

206 Asian Children

1996. 50th Anniv of UNICEF.

780	**206**	21p. multicoloured	60	80
781	-	24p. multicoloured	70	90
782	-	49p. multicoloured	1·25	2·00
783	-	54p. multicoloured	1·40	2·25

DESIGNS: 24p. to 54p. Children from different continents.

207 Red Kites in Flight

1996. Endangered Species. Red Kite. Multicoloured.

784	34p. Type **207**	1·40	1·75
785	34p. Red kite on ground	1·40	1·75
786	34p. On rock	1·40	1·75
787	34p. Pair at nest	1·40	1·75

208 Christmas Pudding

1996. Christmas. Designs created from "Lego" Blocks. Multicoloured.

788	5p. Type **208**	15	15
789	21p. Snowman face	70	45
790	24p. Present	80	55
791	34p. Father Christmas face	1·10	1·25
792	54p. Candle	1·50	2·75

209 "Mary Celeste" passing Gibraltar

1997. Europa. Tales and Legends. "The Mary Celeste". Multicoloured.

793	28p. Type **209**	1·40	1·40
794	28p. Boarding the "Mary Celeste"	1·40	1·40
795	30p. Crew leaving "Mary Celeste"	1·40	1·60
796	30p. "Mary Celeste" found by "Dei Gratia"	1·40	1·60

210 American Shorthair Silver Tabby

1997. Kittens. Multicoloured.

797	5p. Type **210**	40	1·00
798	24p. Rumpy Manx red tabby	75	1·25
799	26p. Blue point birmans	75	1·25
800	28p. Red self longhair	80	1·25
801	30p. British shorthair tortoiseshell and white	80	1·25
802	35p. British bicolour shorthairs	90	1·40
MS803	132×80 mm. Nos. 797/802 with "HONG KONG '97" International Stamp Exhibition logo at bottom left	7·00	8·00

211 "Anthocharis belia euphenoides"

1997. Butterflies. Multicoloured.

804	23p. Type **211**	70	50
805	26p. "Charaxes jasius"	85	60
806	30p. "Vanessa cardui"	95	90
807	£1.20 "Iphiclides podalirius"	3·25	5·00
MS808	135×90 mm. Nos. 804/7	5·25	6·50

1997. Second World War Warships (5th series). Sheet 117×82 mm, containing horiz designs as T 184. Multicoloured.

MS809	24p. H.M.S. "Enterprise" (cruiser); 26p. H.M.S. "Cleopatra" (cruiser); 38p. U.S.S. "Iowa" (battleship); 50p. "Orkan" (Polish destroyer)	3·75	5·00

212 Queen Elizabeth and Prince Philip at Carriage-driving Trials

1997. Golden Wedding of Queen Elizabeth and Prince Philip. Multicoloured.

810	£1.20 Type **212**	4·50	5·00
811	£1.40 Queen Elizabeth in Trooping the Colour uniform	4·50	5·00

213 Christian Dior Evening Dress

1997. Christian Dior Spring/Summer '97 Collection. Multicoloured.

812	30p. Type **213**	80	1·25
813	35p. Tunic top and skirt	1·10	1·60
814	50p. Ballgown	1·25	1·75
815	62p. Two-piece suit	1·60	2·25
MS816	110×90 mm. £1.20, Ballgown (different)	2·75	3·50

214 "Our Lady and St. Bernard" (St. Joseph's Parish Church)

1997. Christmas. Stained Glass Windows. Mult.

817	5p. Type **214**	25	10
818	26p. "The Epiphany" (Our Lady of Sorrows Church)	1·00	60
819	38p. "St. Joseph" (Our Lady of Sorrows Church)	1·25	95
820	50p. "The Holy Family" (St. Joseph's Parish Church)	1·50	2·25
821	62p. "The Miraculous Medal" (St. Joseph's Parish Church)	1·75	3·25

215 Sir Joshua Hassan

1997. Sir Joshua Hassan (former Chief Minister) Commemoration.

822	**215**	26p. black	1·25	75

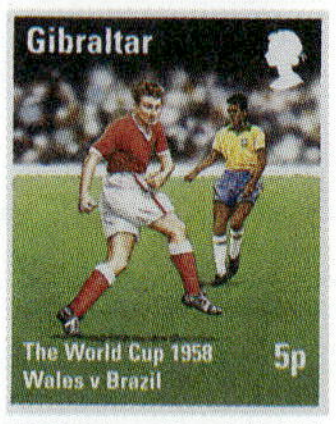

216 Wales v Brazil (1958)

1998. World Football Championship, France (1998). Multicoloured.

823	5p. Type **216**	25	10
824	26p. Northern Ireland v France (1958)	1·00	60
825	38p. Scotland v Holland (1978)	1·25	90
826	£1.20 England v West Germany (1966)	2·75	4·75
MS827	153×96 mm. Nos. 823/6	4·75	6·00

1998. Diana, Princess of Wales Commemoration. Sheet 145×70 mm, containing vert designs as T 177 of Ascension. Multicoloured.

MS828	26p. Wearing jacket with white fur collar, 1988; 26p. Wearing pink checked suit and hat; 38p. Wearing black jacket, 1995; 38p. Wearing blue jacket with gold embroidery, 1987 (sold at £1.28+20p. charity premium)	2·75	3·75

216b Saunders Roe (Saro) London (flying boat)

1998. 80th Anniv of Royal Air Force. Multicoloured.

829	24p. Type **216b**	70	55
830	26p. Fairey Fox	75	60
831	38p. Handley Page Halifax GR.VI	95	1·25
832	50p. Hawker Siddeley Buccaneer S.2B	1·25	2·50
MS833	110×77 mm. 24p. Sopwith Strutter; 26p. Bristol M.IB; 38p. Supermarine Spitfire XII; 50p. Avro York 685 York	3·50	4·50

217 Miss Gibraltar saluting

1998. Europa. Festivals. National Day. Mult.

834	26p. Type **217**	1·10	1·25
835	26p. In black bodice and long red skirt	1·10	1·25
836	38p. In black bodice and short red skirt, with Gibraltar flag	1·40	1·60
837	38p. In Genoese-style costume	1·40	1·60

218 Striped Dolphin

1998. International Year of the Ocean. Sheet 155×64 mm, containing T 218 and similar multicoloured designs.

MS838	5p. Type **218**; 5p. Common dolphin (vert); 26p. Killer whale (vert); £1.20, Blue whale	5·50	6·50

219 Nileus (dog) with Hat and Telescope

1998. Bicentenary of Battle of the Nile. Multicoloured.

839	12p. Type **219**	50	30
840	26p. Rear-Admiral Sir Horatio Nelson	1·00	55
841	28p. Frances Nisbet, Lady Nelson	1·25	75
842	35p. H.M.S. "Vanguard" (ship of the line)	1·50	1·75
843	50p. Battle of the Nile (47×29 mm)	1·75	3·25

220 "Love comforts like Sunshine after Rain" (William Shakespeare)

1998. Famous Quotations. Multicoloured.

844	26p. Type **220**	90	1·00
845	26p. "The price of greatness is responsibility" (Sir Winston Churchill)	90	1·00
846	38p. "Hate the sin, love the sinner" (Mahatma Gandhi)	1·10	1·50
847	38p. "Imagination is more important than knowledge" (Albert Einstein)	1·10	1·50

221 The Nativity

1998. Christmas. Multicoloured.

848	5p. Type **221**	35	10
849	26p. Star and stable	1·25	70
850	30p. King with gold	1·40	75
851	35p. King with myrrh	1·40	1·25
852	50p. King with frankincense	1·75	3·25

222 Barbary Macaque

1999. Europa. Parks and Gardens. Upper Rock Nature Reserve. Multicoloured.

853	30p. Type **222**	1·75	1·50
854	30p. Dartford warbler	1·75	1·50
855	42p. Dusky grouper	2·00	2·25
856	42p. River kingfisher ("Common Kingfisher")	2·00	2·25

223 Queen Elizabeth II

1999. (a) Ordinary gum.

857	**223**	1p. purple	10	50
858	**223**	2p. brown	10	50
859	**223**	4p. blue	20	30
860	**223**	5p. green	20	30
861	**223**	10p. orange	40	30
862	**223**	12p. red	45	40
863	**223**	20p. green	1·00	45
864	**223**	28p. mauve	1·25	60
865	**223**	30p. orange	1·50	65
866	**223**	40p. grey	1·75	85
867	**223**	42p. green	1·75	90
868	**223**	50p. bistre	2·00	1·25
869	**223**	£1 black	3·50	2·75
869a	**223**	£1.20 red	3·50	3·25
869b	**223**	£1.40 blue	4·00	3·75
870	**223**	£3 blue	8·50	10·00

(b) Self-adhesive.

871	(1st) orange	1·00	60

Nos. 868/71 are larger, 22×28 mm.
No. 871 was initially sold at 26p.

224 Roman Marine and Galley

1999. Maritime Heritage. Multicoloured.

872	5p. Type **224**	25	10
873	30p. Arab sailor, medieval galley house and dhow	95	65
874	42p. Marine officer and British ship of the line (1779–83)	1·50	1·50
875	£1.20 Naval rating, Queen Alexandra Dry Dock and H.M.S. "Berwick" (cruiser) (1904)	3·25	4·25
MS876	116×76 mm. Nos. 872/5	5·50	6·50

225 John Lennon (musician)

1999. 30th Wedding Anniv of John Lennon and Yoko Ono. Designs showing John Lennon.

877	-	20p. multicoloured	75	55
878	**225**	30p. black and blue	1·10	90
879	-	40p. multicoloured	1·40	1·60
MS880		Two sheets, each 62×100 mm. (a) £1 black and blue. (b) £1 multicoloured Set of 2 sheets	8·50	8·50

DESIGNS 20p. With flower over left eye; 40p. Wearing orange glasses; £1 (No. **MS**880a), Holding marriage certificate; £1 (No. **MS**880b), Standing on aircraft steps.

226 Postal Van at Dockside, 1930s

1999. 125th Anniv of U.P.U. Multicoloured.

881	5p. Type **226**	25	20
882	30p. Space shuttle and station	75	1·25

227 Eurofighter EF-2000 Typhoon

1999. "Wings of Prey" (1st series). Birds of Prey and R.A.F. Fighter Aircraft. Multicoloured.

883	30p. Type **227**	1·10	1·25
884	30p. Panavia Tornado F.Mk3	1·10	1·25
885	30p. BAe Harrier II GR7	1·10	1·25
886	42p. Lesser kestrel	1·10	1·25
887	42p. Peregrine falcon	1·10	1·25
888	42p. Common kestrel ("Kestrel")	1·10	1·25
MS889	Two sheets, each 105×86 mm. (a) Nos. 883/5. (b) Nos. 886/8 Set of 2 sheets	6·50	7·50

See also Nos. 943/8 and 982/7.

228 Prince Edward and Sophie Rhys-Jones

1999. Royal Wedding. Multicoloured.

890	30p. Type **228**	1·00	65
891	42p. Prince Edward and Sophie Rhys-Jones holding hands (vert)	1·40	90
892	54p. In carriage on wedding day	1·75	2·25
893	66p. On Chapel steps after wedding (vert)	2·00	2·50

229 Football

1999. Local Sporting Centenaries. Multicoloured.

894	30p. Type **229**	75	65
895	42p. Rowing	1·00	90
896	£1.20 Cricket	3·25	4·25

230 "Seasons Greetings"

1999. Christmas. Multicoloured.

897	5p. Type **230**	15	10
898	5p. "Happy Christmas"	15	10
899	30p. "Happy Millennium"	80	80
900	30p. "Happy Christmas" and Santa with reindeer	80	80
901	42p. Santa Claus in chimney	1·25	1·75
902	54p. Santa Claus leaving presents	1·40	2·50

231 "People travelling with Environmentally-friendly Jet-packs" (Colin Grech)

2000. "Stampin' the Future" (children's stamp design competition). Multicoloured.

903	30p. Type **231**	1·50	1·60
904	42p. "Robotic Postman" (Kim Barea)	1·50	1·60
905	54p. "Living on the Moon" (Stephan Williamson-Fa)	1·50	1·60
906	66p. "Jet-powered Cars" (Michael Podesta)	1·50	1·60

232 Dutch Football Player and Flag, 1988

2000. European Football Championship, Belgium and Netherlands. Multicoloured.

907	30p. Type **232**	85	90
908	30p. French player and flag, 1984	85	90
909	42p. German player scoring and flag, 1996	1·10	1·40
910	42p. Danish player and flag, 1992	1·10	1·40
MS911	Two sheets, each 115×85 mm. (a) 54p.×4, English player and flag. (b) Nos. 907/10 Set of 2 sheets	11·00	12·00

233 Fountain of Stars

2000. Europa. Multicoloured.

912	30p. Type **233**	1·00	80

913	40p. Exchanging star	1·25	1·40
914	42p. Stars and airplane	1·25	1·40
915	54p. Stars and end of rainbow	1·75	2·75

234 3000 m Waterfall between Gibraltar and North African Coast, 5 Million B.C.

2000. New Millennium. History of Gibraltar. Multicoloured (except Nos. 926/30).

916	5p. Type **234**	30	50
917	5p. Sabre-tooth tiger, 2 million B.C.	30	50
918	5p. Neanderthal hunting goat, and skull, 30,000 B.C.	30	50
919	5p. Phoenician traders and galley, 700 B.C.	30	50
920	5p. Roman warship, 100 B.C.	30	50
921	5p. Tarik-Ibn-Zayad, ape and Moorish Castle, 711 A.D.	30	50
922	5p. Coat of arms, 1502	30	50
923	5p. Admiral George Rooke and Union Jack, 1704	30	50
924	30p. General Eliott at The Great Siege, 1779–83	80	90
925	30p. H.M.S. *Victory*, 1805	80	90
926	30p. Queen Alexandra in horse-drawn carriage, 1903 (brown, silver and black)	80	90
927	30p. 100 ton gun, 1870s (grey, silver and black)	80	90
928	30p. Evacuees, 1940 (purple, silver and black)	80	90
929	30p. Tank and anti-aircraft gun, 1940s (brown, silver and black)	80	90
930	30p. Queen Elizabeth II in Gibraltar, 1954 (grey, silver and black)	80	90
931	30p. Aerial view of office district, 2000	80	90

235 Princess Diana holding Prince William, 1982

2000. 18th Birthday of Prince William. Multicoloured.

932	30p. Type **235**	90	65
933	42p. Prince William as a toddler	1·25	90
934	54p. Prince William with Prince Charles	1·50	2·00
935	66p. Prince William at 18	1·75	2·75
MS936	115×75 mm. Nos. 932/5	5·00	6·00

236 Lady Elizabeth Bowes-Lyon signing Book

2000. Queen Elizabeth the Queen Mother's 100th Birthday.

937	**236**	30p. black and blue	90	65
938	-	42p. black and brown	1·25	90
939	-	54p. multicoloured	1·50	2·00
940	-	66p. multicoloured	1·75	2·75
MS941		115×75 mm. Nos. 937/40	4·75	6·00

DESIGNS: 42p. Duke and Duchess of York; 54p. Queen Mother with bouquet; 66p. Queen Mother in orange coat and hat.

237 Moorish Castle

2000

942	**237**	£5 black, silver and gold	10·00	10·50

The Queen's head on this stamp is printed in optically variable ink, which changes colour from gold to green when viewed from different angles.

2000. "Wings of Prey" (2nd series). Birds of Prey and R.A.F. Second World War Aircraft. As T 227. Multicoloured.

943	30p. Supermarine Spitfire Mk IIA *Gibraltar*	1·75	1·75
944	30p. Hawker Hurricane Mk IIC	1·75	1·75
945	30p. Avro Lancaster BI-III *City of Lincoln*	1·75	1·75
946	42p. Merlin (male)	2·00	2·00
947	42p. Merlin (female)	2·00	2·00
948	42p. Bonelli's eagle	2·00	2·00
MS949	Two sheets, each 105×85 mm. (a) Nos. 943/5. (b) Nos. 946/8 Set of 2 sheets	10·00	11·00

238 Infant Jesus

2000. Christmas. Multicoloured.

950	5p. Type **238**	25	15
951	30p. Virgin Mary with infant Jesus	85	65
952	30p. Journey to Bethlehem	85	65
953	40p. Mary and Joseph with innkeeper	1·10	1·00
954	42p. The Nativity	1·10	1·25
955	54p. Visit of the Wise Men	1·60	2·25

239 Wedding of Queen Victoria and Prince Albert

2001. Death Centenary of Queen Victoria.

956	**239**	30p. blue, violet and black	1·00	65
957	-	42p. myrtle, green & black	1·40	1·00
958	-	54p. purple, red and black	2·00	2·50
959	-	66p. brown, gold & black	2·25	3·25

DESIGNS: 42p. Victoria as Empress of India; 54p. Queen Victoria in carriage; 66p. Queen Victoria standing by chair.

240 Grass Snake

2001. Snakes. Multicoloured.

960	5p. Type **240**	25	40
961	5p. Ladder snake	25	40
962	5p. Montpellier snake	25	40
963	30p. Viperine snake	85	1·00
964	30p. Southern smooth snake	85	1·00
965	30p. False smooth snake	85	1·00
966	66p. Horseshoe whip snake (30×62 mm)	1·75	2·50
MS967	155×87 mm. Nos. 960/6	7·00	7·50

No. **MS**967 also commemorates the Chinese New Year "Year of the Snake".

No. 962 and **MS**967 are inscribed "MONTPELIER" in error.

241 Long-snouted Seahorse

2001. Europa. Water and Nature. Multicoloured.

968	30p. Type **241**	1·75	65
969	40p. Snapdragon	2·25	1·00
970	42p. Herring gull ("Yellow-legged Gull")	2·75	1·50
971	54p. Goldfish	2·75	4·00

242 Queen Elizabeth II as a Baby

2001. 75th Birthday of Queen Elizabeth II.

972	**242**	30p. black and mauve	85	75
973	-	30p. black and violet	85	75
974	-	42p. black and red	1·25	1·50
975	-	42p. black and violet	1·25	1·50
976	-	54p. multicoloured	1·60	2·25
MS977		101×89 mm. £2 multicoloured	5·50	6·50

DESIGNS—HORIZ: No. 973, Queen Elizabeth as teenager; 974, On wedding day, 1947; 975, After Coronation, 1953; 976, Queen Elizabeth in blue hat. VERT: (35×49 mm)—No. **MS**977, Queen Elizabeth II, 2001 (photo by Fiona Hanson).

No. **MS**977 marks a successful attempt on the record for the fastest produced stamp issue. The miniature sheet was on sale in Gibraltar 10 hours and 24 minutes after the artwork was approved at Buckingham Palace.

243 Battle of Trafalgar, 1805

2001. Bicentenary of The Gibraltar Chronicle (newspaper). Each black.

978	30p. Type **243**	1·50	65
979	42p. Invention of the telephone, 1876	1·25	90
980	54p. Winston Churchill (Victory in Second World War, 1945)	2·50	2·50
981	66p. Footprint on Moon (Moon landing, 1969)	2·50	3·75

2001. "Wings of Prey" (3rd series). Birds of Prey and Modern Military Aircraft. As T 227. Multicoloured.

982	40p. Royal Navy Sea Harrier FA MK.2	1·25	1·50
983	40p. Western marsh harrier ("Marsh Harrier")	1·25	1·50
984	40p. R.A.F. Hawk T MK.1	1·25	1·50
985	40p. Northern sparrowhawk ("Sparrowhawk")	1·25	1·50
986	40p. R.A.F. SEPECAT Jaguar GR1B	1·25	1·50
987	40p. Northern hobby ("Hobby")	1·25	1·50
MS988	Two sheets, each 103×84 mm. (a) Nos. 982, 984 and 986. (b) Nos. 983, 985 and 987 Set of 2 sheets	6·50	7·00

244 Snoopy as Father Christmas with Woodstock

2001. Christmas. Peanuts (cartoon characters by Charles Schulz). Multicoloured.

989	5p. Type **244**	25	15
990	30p. Charlie Brown and Snoopy with Christmas tree	85	65
991	40p. Snoopy asleep in wreath	1·10	1·00
992	42p. Snoopy with plate of biscuits	1·25	1·25
993	54p. Snoopy asleep on kennel	1·75	2·50
MS994	140×85 mm. Nos. 989/93	4·75	5·50

245 One Cent Coin

2002. Introduction of Euro Currency by European Union. Coins. Sheet 165×105 mm, containing T 245 and similar square designs showing coins. Multicoloured.

MS995	5p. Type **245**; 12p. 2 cents; 30p. 5 cents; 35p. 10 cents; 40p. 20 cents; 42p. 50 cents; 54p. 1 Euro; 66p. 2 Euros.	7·00	7·50

2002. Golden Jubilee. As T 219 of Falkland Islands.

996	30p. black, red and gold	1·25	1·40
997	30p. agate, red and gold	1·25	1·40
998	30p. multicoloured	1·25	1·40
999	30p. multicoloured	1·25	1·40
1000	75p. multicoloured	2·25	3·00
MS1001	162×95 mm. Nos. 996/1000	7·00	8·00

DESIGNS—HORIZ: No. 996, Princess Elizabeth and Princess Margaret making radio broadcast, 1940; 997, Princess Elizabeth in Girl Guide uniform, 1942; 998, Queen Elizabeth in evening dress, 1961; 999, Queen Elizabeth in Chelsea, 1993. VERT (38×51 mm): No 1000, Queen Elizabeth after Annigoni.

246 Joshua Grimaldi

2002. Europa. Circus. Famous Clowns. Multicoloured.

1002	30p. Type **246**	90	65
1003	40p. Karl Wettach ("Grock")	1·25	1·25
1004	42p. Nicolai Polakovs ("Coco")	1·25	1·25
1005	54p. Charlie Cairoli	1·75	2·50

247 Bobby Moore holding Jules Rimet Trophy, 1966

2002. World Cup Football Championship, Japan and Korea (2002). England's Victory, 1966. Multicoloured.

1006	30p. Type **247**	1·00	65
1007	42p. Kissing Trophy	1·40	90
1008	54p. Bobby Moore with Queen Elizabeth II	1·75	2·00
1009	66p. Bobby Moore in action	2·00	2·75
MS1010	135×90 mm. Nos. 1006/9	5·50	6·00

248 Barbary Macaque

2002. Wildlife. Multicoloured.

1011	30p. Type **248**	90	80
1012	30p. Red fox (horiz)	90	80
1013	40p. White-toothed shrew (horiz)	1·25	85
1014	£1 Rabbit	2·75	3·50
MS1015	125×100 mm. Nos. 1011/14	5·50	6·50

249 Gibraltar from the North

2002. Views of the Rock of Gibraltar. Multicoloured.

1016	30p. Type **249**	1·25	1·25
1017	30p. View from the south	1·25	1·25
1018	£1 View from the east (50×40 mm)	2·75	3·50
1019	£1 View from the west (50×40 mm)	2·75	3·50

Nos. 1016/19 were printed together, se-tenant, with powdered particles of the Rock sintered to their surface using thermography.

250 Princess Diana holding Prince Harry

2002. 18th Birthday of Prince Harry. Multicoloured.

1020	30p. Type **250**	90	65
1021	42p. Prince Harry waving	1·25	90
1022	54p. Prince Harry skiing	1·50	1·60
1023	66p. Wearing dark suit	1·90	2·75
MS1024	115×75 mm. Nos. 1020/3	5·50	6·50

251 Crib, Cathedral of St. Mary the Crowned

2002. Christmas. Cribs from Gibraltar Cathedrals and Churches. Multicoloured.

1025	5p. Type **251**	35	10
1026	30p. St. Joseph's Parish Church	1·25	65
1027	40p. St. Theresa's Parish Church	1·50	85
1028	42p. Our Lady of Sorrows Church	1·50	90
1029	52p. St. Bernard's Church	1·75	2·50
1030	54p. Cathedral of the Holy Trinity	1·75	2·50

252 Archbishop of Canterbury crowning Queen Elizabeth II

2003. 50th Anniv of the Coronation. Each black, grey and purple.

1031	30p. Type **252**	90	80
1032	30p. Queen Elizabeth II in Coronation robes	90	80
1033	40p. Queen Elizabeth holding the Orb and Sceptre	1·25	85
1034	£1 Queen Elizabeth in Coronation Coach	2·75	3·50
MS1035	116×76 mm. Nos. 1031/4	5·50	6·50

253 Young Prince William with Princess Diana

2003. 21st Birthday of Prince William of Wales. Each black, grey and violet.

1036	30p. Type **253**	1·50	1·00
1037	30p. Prince William at Eton College	1·50	1·00
1038	40p. Prince William	2·00	1·00
1039	£1 Prince William in Operation Raleigh sweatshirt	3·75	4·50
MS1040	115×75 mm. Nos. 1036/9	7·00	7·50

254 Drama Festival Poster

2003. Europa. Poster Art. Multicoloured.

1041	30p. Type **254**	90	65
1042	40p. Spring Festival poster	1·25	1·00
1043	42p. Art Festival poster	1·25	1·00
1044	54p. Dance festival poster	1·75	2·50

255 Wright Brothers' *Flyer I*, 1903

2003. Centenary of Powered Flight. Aircraft.

1045	**255**	30p. multicoloured	90	65
1046	-	40p. black and brown	1·25	1·25
1047	-	40p. black and blue	1·25	1·25
1048	-	42p. black and blue	1·25	1·25
1049	-	44p. multicoloured	1·40	1·40
1050	-	66p. multicoloured	2·00	2·75
MS1051		140×110 mm. Nos. 1045/50	7·25	7·75

DESIGNS—HORIZ: (37×28 mm) 40p. (No. 1046) Charles Lindbergh and *Spirit of St. Louis* (first Transatlantic solo flight, 1927); 40p. (No. 1047) Boeing 314 *Yankee Clipper* flying boat (first Transatlantic scheduled air service, 1939). (77×28 mm)—42p. Saunders Roe (Saro) A21 Windhover (first scheduled air service between Gibraltar and Tangier, 1931); 44p. Aerospatiale/BAe Concorde (first supersonic airliner, 1976). VERT (37×58 mm)—66p. Space shuttle *Columbia* (first shuttle flight in Space orbit, 1981).

256 Flag of St. George

2003. 1700th Death Anniv of St. George. Multicoloured.

1052	30p. Type **256**	1·00	65
1053	40p. Cross of Military Constantinian Order of St. George	1·25	95
1054	£1.20 "St. George and the Dragon" (stained glass window, St. Joseph's Church, Gibraltar) (32×63 mm)	3·50	4·00
MS1055	150×100 mm. Nos. 1052/4	5·25	6·00

257 Big Ben, Swift and Rock of Gibraltar

2003

1056	**257**	(£3) multicoloured†	8·00	8·50

No. 1056 is inscribed "UK express" and was initially sold at £3.

†The Queen's head on this stamp is printed in optically variable ink which changes colour from gold to green when viewed from different angles.

258 Wood Blewit (*Lepista nuda*)

2003. Mushrooms of Gibraltar. Multicoloured.

1057	30p. Type **258**	1·00	1·00
1058	30p. Blue-green funnel-cap (*Clitocybe odora*)	1·00	1·00
1059	30p. Sulphur tuft (*Hypholoma fasciculare*)	1·00	1·00
1060	£1.20 Field mushrooms (*Agaricus campestris*)	3·50	4·00
MS1061	105×90 mm. Nos. 1057/60	6·00	7·00

259 Daisy (Latvia), Cornflower (Estonia) and Rue (Lithuania)

2003. Enlargement of the European Union (2004). Designs showing the national flowers of new member countries. Multicoloured.

1062	30p. Type **259**	1·25	65
1063	40p. Rose (Cyprus) and Maltese Centaury (Malta)	1·50	1·00
1064	42p. Tulip (Hungary), Carnation (Slovenia) and Dog Rose (Slovakia)	1·50	1·00
1065	54p. Corn Poppy (Poland) and Scented Thyme (Czech Republic)	2·25	3·00

260 Baby Jesus Crib Figure, Our Lady of Sorrows Church

2003. Christmas. Multicoloured.

1066	5p. Type **260**	20	10
1067	30p. Children making Crib	90	65
1068	40p. Three Kings Cavalcade	1·25	1·00
1069	42p. Children's provisions for Santa and reindeer	1·25	1·00
1070	54p. Cathedral of St. Mary the Crowned lit for Christmas Eve Midnight Mass	1·75	2·50
MS1071	100×80 mm. £1 Cartoon characters from Peanuts carol singing around Christmas tree (50×40 mm)	3·50	4·00

261 Street Cafe

2004. Europa. Holidays. Multicoloured.

1072	40p. Type **261**	1·25	1·40
1073	40p. St. Michael's Cave	1·25	1·40
1074	54p. Dolphins	1·75	2·25
1075	54p. Harbourside restaurant	1·75	2·25

262 Arms

2004. 300th Anniv of British Gibraltar (1st series). Multicoloured.

1076	8p. Type **262**	65	65
MS1077	144×114 mm. 30p. Royal Katarine flying Red Ensign, 1704; 30p. Landing party, 1704; 30p. Soldiers of 1704; 30p. Arms of Gibraltar on military uniform; 30p. Royal Gibraltar police helmet and red phone box; 30p. Post Office arms and red pillar box; 30p. Graduates and University of Cambridge examination certificate; 30p. Crowd waving Union Jacks and Gibraltar flags; £1.20 Union Jack	12·00	13·00

See also **MS**1095.

263 Queen Elizabeth holding Bouquet

2004. 50th Anniv of Visit of Queen Elizabeth II.

1078	**263**	38p. multicoloured	1·10	85
1079	-	40p. black and yellow	1·10	85
1080	-	47p. multicoloured	1·25	1·25
1081	-	£1 black	2·75	3·50
MS1082		95×110 mm. £1.50 black	3·75	4·50

DESIGNS: 38p. Type **263**; 40p.Queen Elizabeth holding out keys; 47p. Queen and Duke of Edinburgh in car; £1 Queen, Prince Charles and Princess Anne with members of British armed forces; £1.50 Queen waving with Duke of Edinburgh.

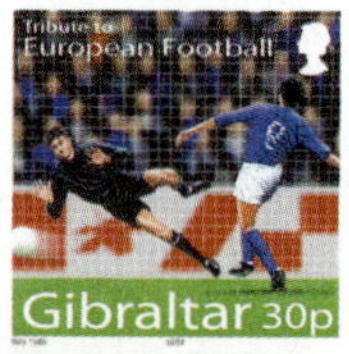

264 Scoring a Goal

2004. European Football Championships 2004, Portugal. Multicoloured.

1083	30p. Type **264**	90	65
1084	40p. Two defenders blocking a goal attempt	1·25	1·25
1085	40p. Overhead kick	1·25	1·25
1086	£1 Player performing header	2·75	3·25
MS1087	Two sheets. (a) 102×77 mm. £1.50 Player celebrating with arms in air (51×39 mm) (b) 105×105 mm (circular). Nos. 1083/6	8·00	8·50

265 Landing at St. Aubin, 1944

2004. 60th Anniv of D-Day Landings. Each black, brown and red.

1088	38p. Type **265**	1·25	85
1089	40p. Cruiser tank Mk VIII Cromwell	1·25	85
1090	47p. Handley Page Halifax plane	1·40	1·40
1091	£1 HMS *Belfast*	2·50	3·00
MS1092	170×100 mm. Nos. 1088/91	5·50	6·00

266 Union Jack Flag

2004. 300th Anniv of British Gibraltar (2nd series). Elton John Tercentenary Concert. Circular sheet 105×105 mm.

MS1093	**266**	£1.20 multicoloured	3·00	3·25

Stamp in No. **MS**1093 is similar in design to the £1.20 stamp in No. **MS**1077.

267 Mallow-leaved Bindweed

2004. Wild Flowers. Multicoloured.

1094	1p. Type **267**	10	10
1095	2p. Gibraltar sea lavender	10	10
1095b	3p. Gibraltar restharrow	10	10
1096	5p. Gibraltar chickweed	15	10
1097	(7p.) Romulea	25	10
1098	10p. Common centaury	30	25
1099	(12p.) Pyramidal orchid	50	50
1099b	15p. Paper-white narcissus	50	50
1100	(28p.) Friars cowl	90	60
1101	(38p.) Corn poppy	1·00	85
1102	(40p.) Giant Tangier fennel	1·10	65
1103	(47p.) Snapdragon	1·50	1·10
1104	50p. Common gladiolus	1·50	1·10
1104b	53p. Gibraltar campion	1·50	1·10
1105	£1 Yellow horned poppy	3·00	2·50
1105b	£1.60 Sea daffodil	3·50	3·00
1106	£3 Gibraltar candytuft	8·00	8·50

Nos. 1097 and 1099/103 are inscribed "G", "G1", "S", "UK", "E" and "U" and were initially sold for 7p., 12p., 28p., 38p., 40p. and 47p. respectively.

268 Father Christmas

2004. Christmas. Decorations. Multicoloured.

1107	7p. Type **268**	30	20
1108	28p. Cherub	1·25	60
1109	38p. Red star	1·40	80
1110	40p. Gold conical tree	1·40	85
1111	47p. Red bauble	1·60	1·25
1112	53p. Gold star	1·90	2·50

269 Ferrari F2003 GA

2004. Ferrari. Multioloured.

1113	5p. Type **269**	30	40
1114	5p. F2004	30	40
1115	30p. F2001	1·00	1·00
1116	30p. F2002	1·00	1·00
1117	75p. F399	2·50	2·75
1118	75p. F1-2000	2·50	2·75
MS1119	161×116 mm. Nos. 1113/18	7·00	7·50

270 Soldier guarding Nelson's Body

2005. Bicentenary of the Battle of Trafalgar. Multicoloured.

1120	38p. Type **270**	1·75	75
1121	40p. HMS *Entreprenante*	1·75	85
1122	47p. Admiral Nelson (vert)	2·00	1·50
1123	£1.60 HMS *Victory*	5·50	7·00
MS1124	120×80 mm. £2 HMS *Victory* (44×44 mm)	9·00	9·50

Nos. 1120/4 contain traces of powdered wood from HMS *Victory*.

271 Spinach Pie

2005. Europa. Gastronomy. Multicoloured.

1125	47p. Type **271**	1·75	1·75
1126	47p. Grilled sea-bass	1·75	1·75
1127	47p. Veal "Birds"	1·75	1·75
1128	47p. Sherry trifle	1·75	1·75

272 Churchill giving Victory Salute

2005. 60th Anniv of VE Day. Multicoloured.

1129	38p. Type **272**	1·40	90
1130	40p. Family with Union Jack flags	1·40	90
1131	47p. VE Day celebrations	1·60	1·50
1132	£1 Returning Gibraltar people on dockside	3·75	4·00
MS1133	150×100 mm. Nos. 1129/32	7·25	7·50

273 *Circassia*

2005. Cruise Ships (1st series). Multicoloured.

1134	38p. Type **273**	1·40	90
1135	40p. *Nevasa*	1·40	90
1136	47p. *Black Prince*	1·60	1·50
1137	£1 *Arcadia*	3·75	4·00
MS1138	150×85 mm. Nos. 1134/7	7·25	7·50

See also Nos. 1180/**MS**1184 and 1207/**MS**1211.

274 Early and Modern Police Officers

2005. Anniversaries. Multicoloured.

1139	38p. Type **274** (175th anniv of Royal Gibraltar Police)	1·40	90
1140	47p. Skull, plate and ceramic horses (75th anniv of Gibraltar Museum)	1·40	90
1141	£1 Charter of Justice (175th anniv)	3·75	4·00

The back of Nos. 1139/41 is printed with a brief description of the subject of the stamp.

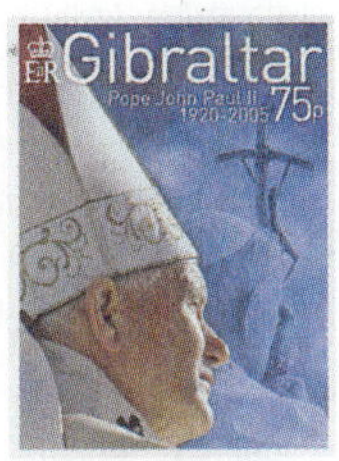

275 Pope John Paul II

2005. Pope John Paul II Commemoration.

1142	**275**	75p. multicoloured	2·50	2·50

276 Map of Europe and 1979 Europa 12p. Stamp

2005. 50th Anniv of Europa Stamps.

1143	**276**	£5 multicoloured	14·00	15·00

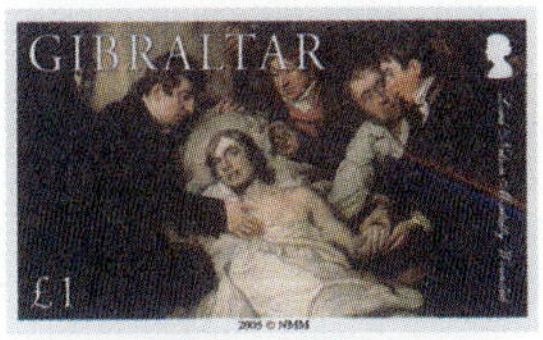

277 "Death of Nelson" (William Devis)

2005. Bicentenary of the Battle of Trafalgar and Death of Admiral Lord Nelson. Multicoloured.

MS1144	120×80 mm. £1 Type **277**	3·25	3·50
MS1145	170×75 mm. £1 As Type **277**, but 50×31 mm together with £1 stamp from Isle of Man No. **MS**1264	6·50	6·50

No. **MS**1145 was also issued by Isle of Man.

278 Two Angels

2005. Christmas. Angels. Multicoloured.

1146	7p. Type **278**	25	20
1147	38p. Angel with children by Christmas tree	1·25	80
1148	40p. Angel with toys	1·25	80
1149	47p. Angel with hymn book and top of Christmas tree	1·75	1·40
1150	53p. Angel with basket of fruit	2·00	2·25
MS1151	168×86 mm. Nos. 1146/50	6·00	6·50

279 Giant Devil Ray

2006. Endangered Species. Giant Devil Ray (Mobula mobular). Multicoloured.

1152	38p. Type **279**	1·25	1·10
1153	40p. Giant devil ray and trail of bubbles	1·40	1·25
1154	47p. Two giant devil rays	1·75	1·60
1155	£1 Upperside of giant devil ray	3·75	4·00

280 Queen Elizabeth II

2006. 80th Birthday of Queen Elizabeth II. Each showing 1950s and more recent photograph. Multicoloured.

1156	38p. Type **280**	1·60	1·25
1157	40p. In evening dress, c. 1955 and wearing purple hat	1·75	1·40
1158	47p. Smelling carnation, c. 1955 and wearing yellow hat	2·00	1·60
1159	£1 Princess Elizabeth, c. 1950 and Queen wearing red and black hat	3·50	4·00
MS1160	Two sheets, each 142×82 mm. (a) Nos. 1156 and 1159. (b) Nos. 1157/8	7·75	8·00

281 Uruguay

2006. World Cup Football Championship, Germany. Showing children with flags painted on faces. Multicoloured.

1161	38p. Type **281**	1·25	1·40
1162	38p. Italy	1·25	1·40
1163	38p. Germany	1·25	1·40
1164	38p. Brazil	1·25	1·40
1165	38p. England	1·25	1·40
1166	38p. Argentina	1·25	1·40
1167	38p. France	1·25	1·40

282 Children making Model Building

2006. Europa. Integration. Multicoloured.

1168	47p. Type **282**	1·40	1·10
1169	47p. Boy and girl	1·40	1·10
1170	47p. Children playing football	1·40	1·10
1171	47p. Children playing music	1·40	1·10

283 *Cornwallis*

2006. Bicentenary of the Gibraltar Packet Agency. Designs showing packet ships of the 1800s. Multicoloured.

1172	8p. Type **283**	40	30
1173	40p. *Meteor*	1·60	90
1174	42p. *Carteret*	1·60	95
1175	68p. *Prince Regent*	2·25	2·75

284 Saunders Roe (Saro) A21 Windhover Flying Boat, 1931

2006. 75th Anniv of Gibraltar Airmail Service. Multicoloured.

1176	8p. Type **284**	50	30
1177	40p. Vickers Vanguard, 1959	1·75	90
1178	49p. Vickers Viscount	2·50	1·40
1179	£1.60 Boeing 737	5·50	6·00

285 *Coral*

2006. Cruise Ships (2nd series). Multicoloured.

1180	40p. Type **285**	1·40	1·25
1181	42p. *Legend of the Seas*	1·50	1·40
1182	66p. *Saga Ruby*	2·50	2·75
1183	78p. *Costa Concordia*	3·00	3·50
MS1184	100×80 mm. Nos. 1180/83	7·75	8·00

286 St. Nicholas and Christmas Tree

2006. Christmas. St. Nicholas. Multicoloured.

1185	8p. Type **286**	35	15
1186	40p. St. Nicholas (in red) carrying presents	1·40	80
1187	42p. St. Nicholas giving present to young girl	1·50	85
1188	49p. St. Nicholas (in green) carrying sack of toys	1·90	1·75
1189	55p. St. Nicholas (in white) carrying sack and small Christmas tree	2·00	2·50
MS1190	165×80 mm. Nos. 1185/8	6·50	7·00

287 Navigational Instruments

2006. 500th Death Anniv of Christopher Columbus. Multicoloured.

1191	40p. Type **287**	1·50	1·25
1192	42p. Columbus writing report of voyage, 1492	1·50	1·25
1193	66p. *Santa Maria*	2·50	2·75
1194	78p. Columbus and Arawak chief	3·00	3·50
MS1195	95×74 mm. £1.60 Columbus' fleet, 1492 (47×47 mm)	5·25	5·50

288 Engagement, 1947

2007. Diamond Wedding of Queen Elizabeth II and Prince Philip. Multicoloured.

1196	40p. Type **288**	1·50	1·25
1197	42p. Wedding photograph, 1947	1·60	1·40
1198	66p. Silver Wedding anniversary, 1972	2·40	2·50
1199	78p. Ruby Anniversary, 1987	2·75	3·00
MS1200	105×105 mm. £1.60 Wedding photograph with bridesmaids and pageboys, 1947 (diamond shape, 84×83 mm)	5·25	5·50

289 Flag of Belgium

2007. 50th Anniv of the Treaty of Rome. Sheet 137×100 mm containing T 289 and similar horiz designs showing national flags. Multicoloured.

MS1201	40p.×6 Type **289**; Germany; France; Italy; Luxembourg; Netherlands	7·75	7·75

290 Princess Diana

2007. 10th Death Anniv of Princess Diana. Multicoloured.

1202	8p. Type **290**	40	25
1203	40p. Seen full-face, eyes looking sideways	1·40	1·40
1204	42p. In half profile, smiling	1·40	1·40
1205	£1.60 Seen full-face, smiling	5·50	5·75
MS1206	165×92 mm. Nos. 1202/4	8·00	8·00

2007. Cruise Ships (3rd series). As T 285. Multicoloured.

1207	40p. *Oriana*	1·40	1·25
1208	42p. *Oceana*	1·50	1·40
1209	66p. *Queen Elizabeth 2*	2·40	2·75
1210	78p. *Queen Mary 2*	2·75	3·25
MS1211	168×67 mm. Nos. 1207/10	7·25	7·75

291 Gibraltar Scout, 1908

2007. Europa. Centenary of World Scouting. Multicoloured.

1212	8p. Type **291**	40	30
1213	40p. Scout, 1950s	1·40	1·25
1214	42p. Sea scout, 1980s	1·50	1·40
1215	£1 Modern scout	3·50	4·00

292 Postcard from Fez, 1907

2007. Gibraltar Postal Anniversaries. Multicoloured.

1216	8p. Type **292** (Cent of Gibraltar relinquishing control of British Postal Service in Morocco)	55	30
1217	40p. Gibraltar date stamp of Packet Agency, 1857 (150th anniv of Gibraltar Post Office)	1·75	1·25
1218	42p. Letter with British postage stamps cancelled 'G' (150th anniv of the introduction of British postage stamps in Gibraltar)	1·90	1·40
1219	£1 Earliest known letter from Morocco via Gibraltar (150th anniv of first British Postal Agency in Morocco)	4·00	4·50

Nos. 1216/19 have information about the anniversaries commemorated printed on the reverse (gummed) side of the stamps.

293 Bear and Cub feeding on Dolphin

2007. Prehistoric Wildlife of Gibraltar. Mult.

1220	8p. Type **293**	40	25
1221	40p. Eagle owl	1·50	1·40
1222	42p. Great auk and eagle	1·60	1·40
1223	55p. Red deer and boar	1·75	2·00
1224	78p. Wolf and vulture feeding on wild horse	2·75	3·00
MS1225	154×100 mm. £2 Ibex	6·50	7·00

294 Stork ('New baby')

2007. YouStamps

1226	(8p.) Type **294**	40	40
1227	(8p.) Lion, sheep and dog wearing party hats ('Let's celebrate')	40	40
1228	(8p.) Crab finding heart written in beach sand ('With love')	40	40
1229	(8p.) Heart enclosed in wedding ring ('Commitment')	40	40
1230	(8p.) Dolphins and Rock of Gibraltar ('Greetings from Gibraltar')	40	40
1231	(40p.) As Type **294**	1·40	1·40
1232	(40p.) As No. 1227	1·40	1·40
1233	(40p.) As No. 1228	1·40	1·40
1234	(40p.) As No. 1229	1·40	1·40
1235	(40p.) As No. 1230	1·40	1·40

Nos. 1226/30 are inscr 'G' and sold for 8p. each.
Nos. 1231/5 are inscr 'E' and sold for 40p. each.

295 Rock of Gibraltar

2007. Panoramic Views of Gibraltar. Multicoloured.

1236	40p. Type **295**	1·30	1·30
1237	42p. Beach and Rock of Gibraltar	1·40	1·40
1238	55p. Rock of Gibraltar at sunset	1·80	1·80
1239	78p. Town and Rock of Gibraltar	2·50	2·50
MS1240	114×67 mm. £1.70 Gibraltar Trinity Lighthouse (52×20 mm)	5·50	5·50

No. 1236 is inscr 'sepac'.

296 Joseph

2007. Christmas. Porcelain Figurines. Multicoloured.

1241	8p. Type **296**	25	25
1242	8p. Baby Jesus	25	25
1243	40p. Mary	1·25	80
1244	42p. King Melchoir	1·40	90
1245	49p. King Balthasar	1·60	1·60
1246	55p. King Gaspar	1·75	2·25
MS1247	124×105 mm. Nos. 1241/6	6·50	6·50

Nos. 1241/6 have biblical quotations printed on the reverse (gummed) side of the stamps.

297 Woodchat Shrike

2008. Birds of the Rock. Multicoloured.

1248	1p. Type **297**	10	10
1249	2p. Balearic shearwater	15	10
1250	5p. Eagle owl	20	15
1251	(8p.) Egyptian vulturel	40	35
1252	10p. Razorbil	50	45
1252a	10p. Black stalk	75	80
1253	(30p.) European bee-eater	90	85
1254	(40p.) Hoopoe	1·25	1·10
1255	(42p.) Bonelli's eagle	1·40	1·25
1256	(49p.) Blue rock thrush	1·50	1·25
1257	50p. Greater flamingo	1·50	1·25
1258	55p. Mediterranean shag	1·60	1·50
1259	£1 Honey buzzard (34×47 mm)	2·50	2·25
1259a	£2 Northern gannett (35×48 mm)	6·00	5·75
1259b	£3 Osprey (35×38 mm)	9·25	9·00
1260	£5 Lesser kestrel (34×47 mm)	12·00	11·00

Nos. 1252 and 1255/8 are inscribed 'S', 'G', 'E', 'U' and 'UK' and were sold for 8p, 30p, 40p, 42p and 49p respectively.

298 Short 184 and Saro London

2008. 90th Anniv of the Royal Air Force. Multicoloured.

1261	40p. Type **298**	1·10	1·00
1262	40p. Spitfire IV and Hurricane IIc	1·10	1·00
1263	42p. Beaufighter II and Lancaster TS III	1·40	1·25
1264	42p. Hunter Mk.6 and Shackleton MR2	1·40	1·25
1265	49p. Vulcan and Mosquito	1·60	1·50
1266	49p. Tornado GR4 and Jaguar GR3	1·60	1·50
MS1267	107×75 mm. £2 Felixstowe F.3 of No. 265 Squadron on anti-submarine patrol, Gibraltar, 1918	6·50	6·50

299 HMS *La Minerve*

2008. 250th Birth Anniv of Admiral Lord Nelson. Multicoloured.

1268	40p. Type **299**	1·40	1·25
1269	40p. HMS *Agamemnon*	1·40	1·25
1270	42p. HMS *Vanguard*	1·40	1·25
1271	42p. HMS *Captain*	1·40	1·25
1272	49p. HMS *Victory*	1·60	1·50
1273	49p. HMS *Amphion*	1·60	1·50
MS1274	120×80 mm. £2 Birthplace at Burnham Thorpe, Norfolk (horiz)	6·50	6·50

300 Sir Winston Churchill

2008. Europa. Writing Letters. Multicoloured.

1275	10p. Type **300**	35	30
1276	42p. Lord Nelson	1·40	1·25
1277	44p. President John F. Kennedy	1·50	1·40
1278	£1 Mahatma Ghandi	3·00	2·75

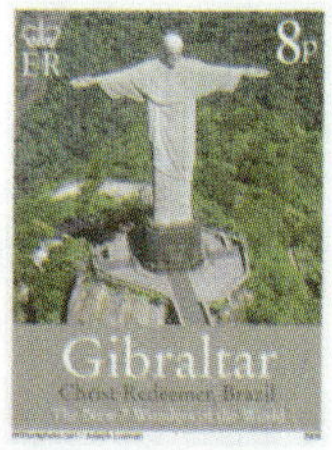

301 Christ the Redeemer Statue, Rio de Janeiro, Brazil

2008. The New Seven Wonders of the World. Multicoloured.

1279	8p. Type **301**	25	20
1280	8p. Colosseum, Rome, Italy	25	20
1281	38p. Petra, Jordan	1·25	1·10
1282	38p. The Great Wall of China	1·25	1·10
1283	40p. Machu Picchu, Peru	1·40	1·25
1284	40p. Chichen Itza	1·40	1·25
1285	66p. Taj Mahal, India	2·25	2·10

2008. Cruise Ships (4th series). As T 285. Multicoloured.

1286	40p. *Century*	1·40	1·25
1287	42p. *Grand Princess*	1·40	1·25
1288	66p. *Queen Victoria*	2·10	2·00
1289	78p. *Costa Mediterranea*	2·75	1·40
MS1290	168×66 mm. Nos. 1286/9	7·50	7·50

302 *Launch of Apollo 11*

2008. 50th Anniv of NASA (US National Aeronautics and Space Administration). Sheet 144×98 mm containing T 302 and similar square designs. Multicoloured.

MS1291	10p. Type **302**; 17p. The Earth seen from the Moon; 42p. Lunar module; £2 US flag on the Moon	8·50	8·50

303 Gibraltar Volunteer Corps, World War I

2008. Royal Gibraltar Regiment. Multicoloured.

1292	10p. Type **303**	20	20
1293	10p. Gibraltar Defence Force, World War II	20	15
1294	10p. Buena Vista Barracks (National Service)	20	15
1295	42p. Thomson's Battery 1958–91 (Gibraltar Regiment)	1·25	1·10
1296	42p. Infantry Company 1958–99 (Gibraltar Regiment)	1·25	1·10
1297	44p. Air Defence Troop 1958–91 (Gibraltar Regiment)	1·40	1·25
1298	44p. 'Guarding the Rock' (Royal Gibraltar Regiment)	1·50	1·25
1299	51p. Training African Peace-keepers (Royal Gibraltar Regiment)	1·75	1·60
1300	51p. Operations in Iraq (Royal Gibraltar Regiment)	1·75	1·60
1301	£2 Operations in Afghanistan (Royal Gibraltar Regiment)	7·00	6·75

304 *When Santa got stuck in a Chimney*

2008. Christmas. Christmas Songs and Carols. Multicoloured.

1302	10p. Type **304**	30	25
1303	42p. *Rudolph the Red-nosed Reindeer*	1·40	1·25
1304	44p. *Oh Christmas Tree*	1·40	1·25

1305	51p. *Away in a Manger*	1·60	1·50
1306	59p. *Jingle Bells*	1·75	1·60

305 Catherine of Aragon

2009. 500th Anniv of the Coronation of King Henry VIII. Multicoloured.

1307	10p. Type **305**	25	15
1308	10p. Anne Boleyn	25	15
1309	42p. Jane Seymour	1·25	1·10
1310	42p. Anne of Cleves	1·25	1·10
1311	44p. Catherine Howard	1·40	1·25
1312	44p. Katherine Parr	1·40	1·25
1313	51p. King Henry VIII	1·75	1·50
1314	51p. *Mary Rose* (galleon)	1·75	1·50
MS1315	120×80 mm. £2 King Henry VIII and Hampton Court Palace	6·25	6·25

306 Virgin and Child (shrine of Our Lady of Europe at Europa Point, Gibraltar)

2009. 700th Anniv of Our Lady of Europe.

1316	**306**	61p. multicoloured	2·00	1·75

Stamps of a similar design were issued by Vatican City.

307 Short S27

2009. Centenary of Naval Aviation. Multicoloured.

1317	42p. Type **307**	1·40	1·25
1318	42p. Morane-Saulnier Type L and Zeppelin LZ 37	1·40	1·25
1319	42p. Short Type 184 seaplane	1·40	1·25
1320	42p. SS Type Non Rigid Airship	1·40	1·25
1321	42p. Caudron Gill	1·40	1·25
1322	42p. Avro 504	1·40	1·25
MS1323	120×80 mm. £2 Short Type 184 seaplane hoisted over stern of First World War seaplane carrier and Hawker Siddeley Sea Harrier on ramp of modern Invincible Class CVS aircraft carrier	6·25	6·25

The stamp within No. **MS**1323 has text printed on the back describing the aircraft and ships depicted on the miniature sheet.

308 Peter Phillips

2009. Queen Elizabeth II's Grandchildren. Multicoloured.

1324	42p. Type **308**	1·40	1·25
1325	42p. Zara Phillips	1·40	1·25
1326	42p. Prince William of Wales	1·40	1·25
1327	42p. Prince Henry of Wales	1·40	1·25
1328	42p. Princess Beatrice of York	1·40	1·25
1329	42p. Princess Eugenie of York	1·40	1·25
1330	42p. Lady Louise Windsor	1·40	1·25
1331	42p. Viscount Severn	1·40	1·25

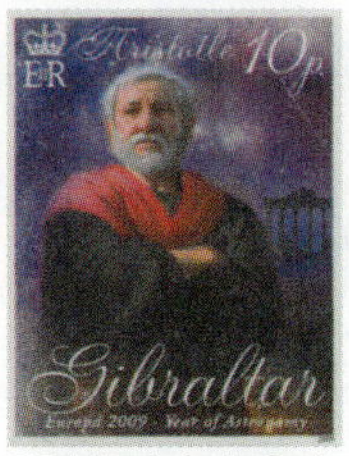

309 Aristotle (early Greek philosopher and scientist)

2009. Europa. International Year of Astronomy. Multicoloured.

1332	10p. Type **309**	30	25
1333	42p. Galileo Galilei (astronomer, mathematician and philosopher)	1·40	1·25
1334	44p. Nicolaus Copernicus (astronomer)	1·75	1·50
1335	£1.50 Sir Isaac Newton (scientist and mathematician)	4·25	4·00

310 Road to the Frontier

2009. Old Views of Gibraltar. Showing scenes from postcards. Multicoloured.

1336	10p. Type **310**	30	25
1337	42p. Catalan Bay village	1·40	1·25
1338	44p. The Rock of Gibraltar	1·40	1·25
1339	51p. The Moorish Castle	1·50	1·40
1340	59p. South Barracks	1·75	1·50
MS1341	163×79 mm. 10p. Garrison Library; 42p. The Piazza; 44p. The Plazza – Casemates; £1 Main Street	6·25	6·25

POSTAGE DUE STAMPS

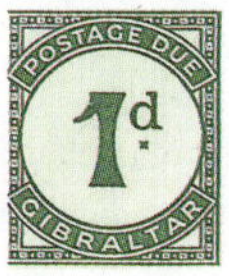

D1

1956

D1	**D1**	1d. green	1·50	4·25
D2	**D1**	2d. brown	1·50	2·75
D3	**D1**	4d. blue	1·75	5·00

1971. As Nos. D1/3, but inscr in decimal currency.

D4	½p. green	25	80
D5	1p. brown	25	70
D6	2p. blue	25	1·00

D2

1976

D7	**D2**	1p. orange	15	60
D8	**D2**	3p. blue	15	75
D9	**D2**	5p. red	20	75
D10	**D2**	7p. violet	20	75
D11	**D2**	10p. green	25	75
D12	**D2**	20p. green	45	1·00

D3 Gibraltar Coat of Arms

1984

D13	**D3**	1p. black	25	50
D14	**D3**	3p. red	35	50
D15	**D3**	5p. blue	40	50
D16	**D3**	10p. blue	50	50
D17	**D3**	25p. mauve	90	1·00
D18	**D3**	50p. orange	1·40	1·75
D19	**D3**	£1 green	2·25	3·00

D4 Water Port Gates

1996. Gibraltar Landmarks.

D20	**D4**	1p. black, emerald and green	15	50
D21	-	10p. black and grey	50	60
D22	-	25p. black, brown and chestnut	80	80
D23	-	50p. black and lilac	1·25	1·40
D24	-	£1 black, brown and chestnut	2·75	3·00
D25	-	£2 black and blue	4·25	4·75

DESIGNS: 10p. Naval Dockyard; 25p. Military Hospital; 50p. Governor's Cottage; £1 Swans on the Laguna; £2 Catalan Bay.

D5 Greenfinch

2002. Gibraltar Finches. Type D 5 Multicoloured.

D26	5p. Type D **5**	10	10
D27	10p. Serin	20	15
D28	20p. Siskin	40	45
D29	50p. Linnet	1·00	1·10
D30	£1 Chaffinch	2·00	2·10
D31	£2 Goldfinch	4·00	4·25

Pt. 1

GILBERT AND ELLICE ISLANDS

A British colony in the South Pacific.

1911. 12 pence = 1 shilling; 20 shillings = 1 pound.
1966. 100 cents = $1 Australian.

1911. Stamps of Fiji (King Edward VII) optd GILBERT & ELLICE PROTECTORATE.

1	**23**	½d. green	5·00	45·00
2	**23**	1d. red	50·00	28·00
3	**23**	2d. grey	14·00	15·00
4	**23**	2½d. blue	15·00	42·00
5	**23**	5d. purple and green	60·00	90·00
6	**23**	6d. purple	24·00	45·00
7	**23**	1s. black on green	24·00	65·00

2 Pandanus Pine

1911

8	**2**	½d. green	4·75	19·00
9	**2**	1d. red	2·00	7·50
10	**2**	2d. grey	1·50	7·00
11	**2**	2½d. blue	5·50	11·00

3

1912

13	**3**	1d. red	2·25	8·00
15	**3**	2½d. blue	1·75	11·00
16	**3**	3d. purple on yellow	2·50	8·50
17	**3**	4d. black and red on yellow	75	6·00
18	**3**	5d. purple and green	1·75	6·00
19	**3**	6d. purple	1·25	6·50
20	**3**	1s. black on green	1·25	4·50
21	**3**	2s. purple and blue on blue	14·00	30·00
22	**3**	2s.6d. black and red on blue	17·00	25·00
23	**3**	5s. green and red on yellow	32·00	65·00
24	**3**	£1 purple and black on red	£550	£1400
27	**3**	½d. green	3·25	3·25
28	**3**	1d. violet	4·50	5·50
29	**3**	1½d. red	4·50	2·50
30	**3**	2d. grey	7·00	32·00
35	**3**	10s. green and red on green	£160	£375

1918. Optd WAR TAX.

26	1d. red	50	6·50

1935. Silver Jubilee. As T 10a of Gambia.

36	1d. blue and black	2·25	12·00
37	1½d. blue and red	1·75	4·00
38	3d. brown and blue	5·50	20·00
39	1s. grey and purple	22·00	20·00

1937. Coronation. As T10b of Gambia.

40	1d. violet	35	65
41	1½d. red	35	65
42	3d. blue	40	70

6 Great Frigate Bird

7 Pandanus Pine

1939

43	**6**	½d. blue and green	60	1·00
44	**7**	1d. green and purple	30	1·50
45	-	1½d. black and red	30	1·25
46	-	2d. brown and black	75	1·00
47	-	2½d. black and green	50	70
48	-	3d. black and blue	50	1·00
49	-	5d. blue and brown	4·75	1·50
50	-	6d. green and violet	60	60
51a	-	1s. black and turquoise	11·00	3·75
52	-	2s. blue and red	10·00	10·00
53	-	2s.6d. blue and green	10·00	11·00
54	-	5s. red and blue	13·00	14·00

DESIGNS: 1½d. Canoe crossing reef; 2d. Canoe and boat-house; 2½d. Native house; 3d. Seascape; 5d. Ellice Is. canoe; 6d. Coconut palms; 1s. Jetty, Ocean Is.; 2s. H.M.C.S. "Nimanoa"; 2s.6d. Gilbert Is. canoe; 5s. Coat of arms.

1946. Victory. As T 11a of Gambia.

55	1d. purple	15	50
56	3d. blue	15	50

1949. Silver Wedding. As T 11b/c of Gambia.

57	1d. violet	50	1·25
58	£1 red	15·00	23·00

1949. U.P.U. As T 11d/g of Gambia.

59	1d. purple	40	1·50
60	2d. black	2·00	3·25
61	3d. blue	50	3·25
62	1s. blue	50	2·25

1953. Coronation. As T 11h of Gambia.

63	2d. black and grey	1·00	2·25

18 Great Frigate Bird

1956. As 1939 issue but with portrait of Queen Elizabeth II as in T 18 and colours changed.

64	**18**	½d. black and blue	65	1·25
65	**7**	1d. olive and violet	60	1·25
67	-	2½d. black and green	50	60
68	-	3d. black and red	50	60
69	-	5d. blue and orange	8·50	2·50
70	-	6d. brown and black	55	2·75
71	-	1s. black and olive	3·00	60
72	-	2s. blue and sepia	6·00	4·00
73	-	2s.6d. red and blue	7·00	4·00
74	-	5s. blue and green	7·00	5·00
75	-	10s. black & turq (as 1½d.)	28·00	8·50
85	-	2d. green and purple	1·00	1·25

19 Loading Phosphate from Cantilever

1960. Diamond Jubilee of Phosphate Discovery at Ocean Is. Inscr "1900 1960".

76	**19**	2d. green and red	80	85
77	-	2½d. black and olive	80	85
78	-	1s. black and turquoise	80	85

DESIGNS: 2½d. Phosphate rock; 1s. Phosphate mining.

1963. Freedom from Hunger. As T 20a of Gambia.

79		10d. blue	75	30

1963. Red Cross Cent. As T 20b of Gambia.

80		2d. red and black	50	1·00
81		10d. red and blue	75	2·50

23 Reef Heron in Flight

1964. First Air Service.

82	-	3d. blue, black and light blue	70	30
83	23	1s. light blue, black and blue	90	30
84	-	3s.7d. green, black & emerald	1·40	1·50

DESIGNS—VERT: 3d. De Havilland Heron 2 and route map; 3s.7d. De Havilland Heron 2 over Tarawa lagoon.

1965. Cent of I.T.U. As T 44 of Gibraltar.

87		3d. orange and green	15	10
88		2s.6d. turquoise and purple	45	20

26 Gilbertese Women's Dance

1965. Multicoloured.

89		½d. Maneaba and Gilbertese man blowing Bu shell (vert)	10	10
90		1d. Ellice Islanders Reef fishing by flare (vert)	10	10
91		2d. Gilbertese girl weaving head-garland (vert)	10	10
92		3d. Gilbertese woman performing Ruoia (vert)	10	10
93		4d. Gilbertese man performing Kamei (vert)	15	10
94		5d. Gilbertese girl drawing water (vert)	20	10
95		6d. Ellice Islander performing a Fatele (vert)	20	10
96		7d. Ellice youths performing spear dance (vert)	25	10
97		1s. Gilbertese girl tending Ikaroa Babai plant (vert)	50	10
98		1s.6d. Ellice Islanders dancing a Fatele (vert)	1·00	1·00
99		2s. Ellice Islanders pounding Pulaka (vert)	1·00	1·40
100		3s.7d. Type **26**	1·75	65
101		5s. Gilbertese boys playing a stick game	1·75	80
102		10s. Ellice youths beating the box for the Fatele	2·50	1·00
103		£1 Coat of arms	3·00	1·75

1965. I.C.Y. As T 45 of Gibraltar.

104		½d. purple and turquoise	10	10
105		3s.7d. green and lavender	50	20

1966. Churchill Commem. As T 46 of Gibraltar.

106		½d. blue	10	10
107		3d. green	20	10
108		3s. brown	40	35
109		3s.7d. violet	45	35

1966. Decimal Currency. Nos. 89/103 surch.

110		1c. on 1d.	10	10
111		2c. on 2d.	10	10
112		3c. on 3d.	10	10
113		4c. on ½d.	10	10
114		5c. on 6d.	15	10
115		6c. on 4d.	15	10
116		8c. on 5d.	15	10
117		10c. on 1s.	15	10
118		15c. on 7d.	60	40
119		20c. on 1s.6d.	30	25
120		25c. on 2s.	30	20
121		35c. on 3s.7d.	1·00	20
122		50c. on 5s.	55	35
123		$1 on 10s.	55	40
124		$2 on £1	1·25	2·50

1966. World Cup Football Championship. As T 47 of Gibraltar.

125		3c. multicoloured	20	10
126		35c. multicoloured	55	20

1966. Inauguration of W.H.O. Headquarters, Geneva. As T 54 of Gibraltar.

127		3c. black, green and blue	20	10
128		12c. black, purple and ochre	45	40

1966. 20th Anniv of UNESCO. As T 56a/c of Gibraltar.

129		5c. multicoloured	25	35
130		10c. yellow, violet and olive	35	10
131		20c. black, purple and orange	60	45

41 H.M.S. "Royalist"

1967. 75th Anniv of Protectorate.

132	41	3c. red, blue and green	30	50
133	-	10c. multicoloured	15	15
134	-	35c. sepia, yellow and green	30	50

DESIGNS: 10c. Trading post; 35c. Island family.

1968. Decimal Currency. As Nos. 89/103, but with values inscr in decimal currency.

135		1c. multicoloured (as 1d.)	10	15
136		2c. multicoloured (as 2d.)	15	10
137		3c. multicoloured (as 3d.)	15	10
138		4c. multicoloured (as ½d.)	15	10
139		5c. multicoloured (as 6d.)	15	10
140		6c. multicoloured (as 4d.)	20	10
141		8c. multicoloured (as 5d.)	20	10
142		10c. multicoloured (as 1s.)	20	10
143		15c. multicoloured (as 7d.)	50	20
144		20c. multicoloured (as 1s.6d.)	65	15
145		25c. multicoloured (as 2s.)	1·25	20
146	26	35c. multicoloured	1·50	20
147	-	50c. multicoloured (as 5s.)	1·50	2·50
148	-	$1 multicoloured (as 10s.)	1·50	3·75
149	-	$2 multicoloured (as £1)	4·00	3·75

45 Map of Tarawa Atoll

1968. 25th Anniversary of Battle of Tarawa.

150		3c. Type **45**	20	30
151		10c. Marines landing	20	20
152		15c. Beach-head assault	20	35
153		35c. Raising U.S. and British flags	25	50

46 Young Pupil against Outline of Abemama Island

1969. End of Inaugural Year of South Pacific University.

154	46	3c. multicoloured	10	25
155	-	10c. multicoloured	10	10
156	-	35c. black, brown and green	15	30

DESIGNS: 10c. Boy and girl students and Tarawa atoll; 35c. University graduate and South Pacific islands.

47 "Virgin and Child" in Pacific Setting

1969. Christmas.

157		2c. multicoloured	15	20
158	47	10c. multicoloured	15	10

DESIGN: 2c. as Type **47**. but with grass foreground instead of sand.

48 "Kiss of Life"

1970. Centenary of British Red Cross.

159	48	10c. multicoloured	20	10
160	-	15c. multicoloured	30	45
161	-	35c. multicoloured	60	90

Nos. 160/1 are as Type **48**, but arranged differently.

49 Foetus and Patients

1970. 25th Anniversary of U.N.

162	49	5c. multicoloured	15	30
163	-	10c. black, grey and red	15	15
164	-	15c. multicoloured	20	30
165	-	35c. blue, green and black	30	45

DESIGNS: 10c. Nurse and surgical instruments; 15c. X-ray plate and technician; 35c. U.N. emblem and map.

53 Map of Gilbert Islands

1970. Centenary of Landing in Gilbert islands by London Missionary Society.

166	53	2c. multicoloured	15	90
167	-	10c. black and green	25	15
168	-	25c. brown and blue	20	20
169	-	35c. blue, black and red	50	70

DESIGNS—VERT: 10c. Sailing-ship "John Williams III"; 25c. Rev. S. J. Whitmee. HORIZ: 35c. M.V. "John Williams VII".

57 "Child with Halo" (T. Collis)

1970. Christmas. Sketches. Multicoloured.

170		2c. Type **57**	10	60
171		10c. "Sanctuary, Tarawa Cathedral" (Mrs A. Burroughs)	10	10
172		35c. "Three Ships inside Star" (Mrs. C. Barnett)	20	20

60 Casting Nets

1971. Multicoloured.

173		1c. Cutting toddy (vert)	10	10
174		2c. Lagoon fishing	15	30
175		3c. Cleaning pandanus leaves	15	15
176		4c. Type **60**	20	25
177		5c. Gilbertese canoe	45	15
178		6c. De-husking coconuts (vert)	30	45
179		8c. Weaving pandanus fronds (vert)	35	15
180		10c. Weaving a basket (vert)	40	15
181		15c. Tiger shark and fishermen (vert)	2·75	1·50
182		20c. Beating rolled pandanus leaf	1·50	90
183		25c. Loading copra	2·00	1·00
184		35c. Fishing at night	2·00	50
185		50c. Local handicrafts (vert)	75	1·50
186		$1 Weaving coconut screens (vert)	1·10	1·25
187		$2 Coat of arms (vert)	1·75	8·00

61 House of Representatives

1971. New Constitution. Multicoloured.

188		3c. Type **61**	10	20
189		10c. Maneaba Betio (Assembly hut)	20	10

62 Pacific Nativity Scene

1971. Christmas.

190	62	3c. black, yellow and blue	10	20
191	-	10c. black, gold and blue	10	10
192	-	35c. black, gold and red	25	35

DESIGNS: 10c. Star and palm leaves; 35c. Outrigger canoe and star.

63 Emblem and Young Boys

1971. 25th Anniv of UNICEF. Multicoloured.

193		3c. Type **63**	10	90
194		10c. Young boy	15	25
195		35c. Young boy's face	45	90

Nos. 193/5 include the UNICEF emblem within each design.

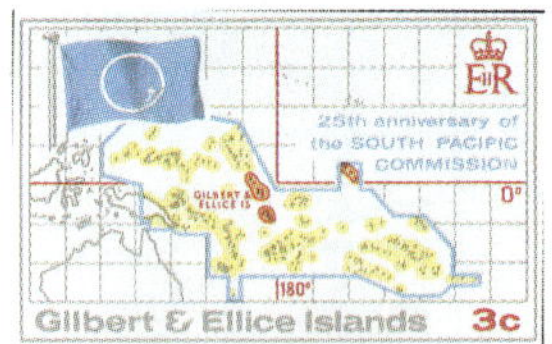

64 Flag and Map of South Pacific

1972. 25th Anniv of South Pacific Commission. Multicoloured.

196		3c. Type **64**	10	80
197		10c. Flag and native boats	15	20
198		35c. Flags of member nations	15	95

65 "Alveopora"

1972. Coral. Multicoloured.

199		3c. Type **65**	25	45
200		10c. "Euphyllia"	30	15
201		15c. "Melithea"	40	35
202		35c. "Spongodes"	80	60

66 Star of Peace

1972. Christmas. Multicoloured.

208		3c. Type **66**	10	10
209		10c. "The Nativity"	10	10

210	35c. Baby in "manger" (horiz)	30	30

1972. Royal Silver Wedding. As T 98 of Gibraltar, but with Floral Headdresses in background.

211	3c. brown	10	15
212	35c. brown	25	15

68 Funafuti ("The Land of Bananas")

1973. Legends of Island Names (1st series). Mult.

213	3c. Type **68**	20	60
214	10c. Butaritari ("The Smell of the Sea")	20	20
215	25c. Tarawa ("The Centre of the World")	35	55
216	35c. Abemama ("The Land of the Moon")	35	65

See also Nos. 252/5.

69 Dancer

1973. Christmas. Multicoloured.

217	3c. Type **69**	10	25
218	10c. Canoe and lagoon	10	10
219	35c. Lagoon at evening	30	15
220	50c. Map of Christmas Island	40	1·60

1973. Royal Wedding. As T 101a of Gibraltar. Multicoloured, background colours given.

221	3c. green	10	15
222	35c. blue	20	15

70 Meteorological Observation

1973. Centenary of I.M.O./W.M.O. Mult.

223	3c. Type **70**	30	30
224	10c. Island observing-station	30	20
225	35c. Wind-finding radar	40	25
226	50c. World weather watch stations	50	1·25

71 Te Mataaua Crest

1974. Canoe Crests. Multicoloured.

227	3c. Type **71**	10	25
228	10c. "Te Nimta-wawa"	15	10
229	35c. "Tara-tara-venei-na"	25	10
230	50c. "Te Bou-uoua"	35	1·60
MS231	154×130 mm. Nos. 227/30	2·00	5·50

72 £1 Stamp of 1924 and Te Koroba (canoe)

1974. Centenary of U.P.U.

232	**72**	4c. multicoloured	20	40
233	-	10c. multicoloured	20	15
234	-	25c. multicoloured	25	30
235	-	35c. multicoloured	30	50

DESIGNS: 10c. 5s. stamp of 1939 and sailing vessel "Kia-kia"; 25c. $2 stamp of 1971 and B.A.C. One Eleven airplane; 35c. U.P.U. emblem.

73 Toy Canoe

1974. Christmas. Multicoloured.

236	4c. Type **73**	10	30
237	10c. Toy windmill	15	15
238	25c. Coconut "ball"	20	40
239	35c. Canoes and constellation Pleiades	25	55

74 North Front Entrance, Blenheim Palace

1974. Birth Cent of Sir Winston Churchill. Mult.

240	4c. Type **74**	10	40
241	10c. Churchill painting	10	15
242	35c. Churchill's statue, London	25	50

75 Barometer Crab

1975. Crabs. Multicoloured.

243	4c. Type **75**	40	1·25
244	10c. "Ranina ranina"	40	25
245	25c. Pelagic swimmming crab	65	90
246	35c. Ghost crab	75	1·75

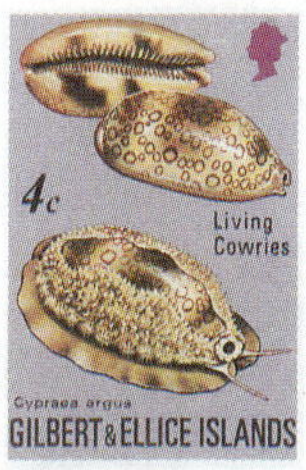

76 Eyed Cowrie

1975. Cowrie Shells. Multicoloured.

247	4c. Type **76**	45	1·25
248	10c. Sieve cowrie	60	30
249	25c. Mole cowrie	80	1·50
250	35c. All-red map cowrie	1·00	2·50
MS251	146×137 mm. Nos. 247/50	14·00	17·00

1975. Legends of Island Names (2nd series). As T 68. Multicoloured.

252	4c. Beru ("The Bud")	10	50
253	10c. Onotoa ("Six Giants")	10	15
254	25c. Abaiang ("Land to the North")	20	40
255	35c. Marakei ("Fish-trap floating on eaves")	30	55

77 "Christ is Born"

1975. Christmas. Multicoloured.

256	4c. Type **77**	15	80
257	10c. Protestant Chapel, Tarawa	20	35
258	25c. Catholic Church, Ocean Island	35	1·00
259	35c. Fishermen and star	40	1·75

POSTAGE DUE STAMPS

D1

1940

D1	**D1**	1d. green	12·00	25·00
D2	**D1**	2d. red	13·00	25·00
D3	**D1**	3d. brown	17·00	26·00
D4	**D1**	5d. blue	19·00	35·00
D5	**D1**	4d. olive	24·00	35·00
D6	**D1**	6d. purple	24·00	35·00
D7	**D1**	1s. violet	26·00	48·00
D8	**D1**	1s.6d. green	50·00	90·00

Pt. 1

GILBERT ISLANDS

On 1 January 1976 the Gilbert Islands and Tuvalu (Ellice) Islands became separate Crown Colonies. The Gilbert Islands became independent on 12 July 1979, under the name of Kiribati.

100 cents = $1.

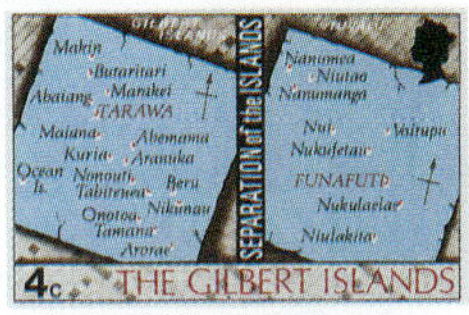

1 Charts of Gilbert Islands and Tuvalu (formerly Ellice) Islands

1976. Separation of the Islands. Multicoloured.

1	4c. Type **1**	45	1·00
2	35c. Maps of Tarawa and Funafuti	80	1·50

1976. Nos. 173/87 of Gilbert and Ellice Islands optd THE GILBERT ISLANDS.

3	1c. Cutting toddy	25	30
5	2c. Lagoon fishing	50	30
7	4c. Type **60**	30	1·25
12	3c. Cleaning pandanus leaves	40	2·25
13	5c. Gilbertese canoe	50	1·00
14	6c. De-husking coconuts	50	1·00
15	8c. Weaving pandanus fronds	50	1·00
16	10c. Weaving a basket	50	1·00
17	15c. Tiger shark	2·25	1·25
18	20c. Beating a pandanus leaf	1·00	2·25
19	25c. Loading copra	1·50	1·25
20	35c. Fishing at night	2·00	1·75
21	50c. Local handicrafts	1·50	2·25
22	$1 Weaving coconut screens	2·75	8·00

3 "Teraaka" (training ship)

1976. Multicoloured.

23	1c. Type **3**	40	70
24	3c. "Tautunu" (inter-island freighter)	60	80
25	4c. Moorish idol (fish)	30	70
26	5c. Hibiscus	30	30
27	6c. Reef heron	1·50	90
28	7c. Catholic Cathedral, Tarawa	20	30
29	8c. Frangipani	20	30
30	10c. Maneaba, Bikenibeu	20	30
31	12c. Betio Harbour	35	45
32	15c. Evening scene	40	45
33	20c. Marakei Atoll	25	35
34	35c. G.I.P.C. Chapel, Tangintebu	25	40
35	40c. Flamboyant tree	40	45
36	50c. "Hypolimnas bolina", (butterfly)	1·25	1·75
37	$1 "Tabakea" (Tarawa Lagoon ferry)	75	2·50
38	$2 National flag	75	2·50

4 Church

1976. Christmas. Children's Drawings. Mult.

39	5c. Type **4**	20	15
40	15c. Feasting (vert)	30	15
41	20c. Maneaba (vert)	30	35
42	35c. Dancing	30	45

5 Porcupine Fish Helmet

1976. Artefacts. Multicoloured.

43	5c. Type **5**	20	15
44	15c. Shark's teeth dagger	30	35
45	20c. Fighting gauntlet	30	40
46	35c. Coconut body armour	45	55
MS47	140×130 mm. Nos. 43/6	4·50	13·00

6 The Queen in Coronation Robes

1977. Silver Jubilee. Multicoloured.

48	8c. Prince Charles' visit, 1970	10	10
49	20c. Prince Philip's visit, 1959	15	15
50	40c. Type **6**	20	35

7 Commodore Bryon and H.M.S. "Dolphin"

1977. Explorers. Multicoloured.

51	5c. Type **7**	45	1·50
52	15c. Capt. Fanning and "Betsey"	55	2·75
53	20c. Admiral Bellingshausen and "Vostok"	55	2·75
54	35c. Capt. Wilkes and U.S.S. "Vincennes"	65	4·00

8 H.M.S. "Resolution" and H.M.S. "Discovery"

1977. Christmas and Bicentenary of Capt. Cook's Discovery of Christmas Is. Mult.

55	8c. Type **8**	30	15
56	15c. Logbook entry (horiz)	30	15
57	20c. Captain Cook	40	20
58	40c. Landing party (horiz)	40	60
MS59	140×140 mm. Nos. 55/8	2·75	9·00

9 Scout Emblem and Island Scene

1977. 50th Anniv of Scouting in the Gilbert Is. Multicoloured.

60	8c. Type **9**	40	15

61	15c. Patrol meeting (horiz)	45	20
62	20c. Scout making mat (horiz)	50	20
63	40c. Canoeing	65	55

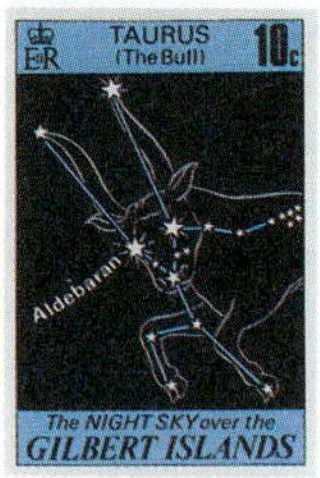

10 Taurus (The Bull)

1978. The Night Sky over the Gilbert Islands.

64	**10**	10c. black and blue	45	35
65	-	20c. black and red	50	50
66	-	25c. black and green	50	55
67	-	45c. black and orange	75	90

DESIGNS: 20c. Canis Major (the Great Dog); 25c. Scorpio (the Scorpion); 45c. Orion (the Giant Warrior).

11 Unicorn of Scotland

1978. 25th Anniv of Coronation.

68	**11**	45c. green, violet and silver	25	40
69	-	45c. multicoloured	25	40
70	-	45c. green, violet and silver	25	40

DESIGNS: No. 69, Queen Elizabeth II. No. 70, Great Frigate Bird.

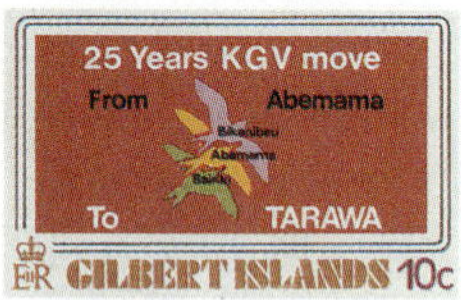

12 Birds in Flight to Tarawa

1978. 25th Anniv of Return of George V School to Tarawa. Multicoloured.

71	10c. Type **12**	10	10
72	20c. Tarawa, Abemama and school badge	20	20
73	25c. Rejoicing islanders	20	20
74	45c. King George V School on Tarawa and Abemama	35	35

13 "Te Kaue ni Maie"

1978. Christmas. Kaue (traditional head decorations). Multicoloured.

75	10c. Type **13**	10	10
76	20c. "Te Itera"	15	15
77	25c. "Te Bau"	20	20
78	45c. "Te Tai"	25	30
MS79	149×99 mm. Nos. 75/8	90	4·50

14 H.M.S. "Endeavour"

1979. Bicent of Captain Cook's Voyages, 1768–79.

80	**14**	10c. multicoloured	20	15
81	-	20c. multicoloured	25	30
82	-	25c. black, lilac and green	25	45
83	-	45c. multicoloured	25	80

DESIGNS: 20c. Green Turtle; 25c. Quadrant; 45c. Flaxman/Wedgwood medallion.

For later issues see **KIRIBATI**.

Pt. 1

GOLD COAST

A British colony on the W. coast of Africa. For later issues after independence in 1957 see under Ghana.

12 pence = 1 shilling; 20 shillings = 1 pound.

1

1875

4	1	½d. yellow	80·00	29·00
5	1	1d. blue	28·00	6·50
6	1	2d. green	£110	9·00
11a	1	½d. green	3·50	1·00
12	1	1d. red	4·00	50
13b	1	2d. grey	9·00	50
14	1	2½d. blue and orange	8·50	70
15a	1	3d. olive	17·00	7·50
16	1	4d. mauve	17·00	3·00
17	1	6d. orange	17·00	5·00
18a	1	1s. mauve	9·50	1·50
19a	1	2s. brown	50·00	15·00

1889. Surch ONE PENNY. and bar.

20	1d. on 6d. orange	£130	50·00

4

1889

22	**4**	5s. mauve and blue	65·00	20·00
23	**4**	10s. mauve and red	90·00	15·00
24	**4**	20s. green and red	£3250	
25	**4**	20s. mauve and black on red	£160	35·00
26	**4**	½d. mauve and green	4·50	1·00
27	**4**	1d. mauve and red	5·00	50
27b	**4**	2d. mauve and red	50·00	£160
28	**4**	2½d. mauve and blue	7·50	7·50
29	**4**	3d. mauve and orange	8·00	3·00
30	**4**	6d. mauve and violet	8·50	2·75
31	**4**	1s. green and black	13·00	26·00
32	**4**	2s. green and red	23·00	27·00
33	**4**	5s. green and mauve	70·00	42·00
34	**4**	10s. green and brown	£160	60·00

1901. Surch ONE PENNY. and bar.

35	1d. on 2½d. mauve and blue	5·50	4·75
36	1d. on 6d. mauve and violet	5·50	3·50

1902. As T 4, but with portrait of King Edward VII.

38	½d. purple and green	1·50	40
39	1d. purple and red	1·50	15
41	2½d. purple and blue	4·50	9·00
42	3d. purple and orange	4·00	1·75
43	6d. purple and violet	4·50	2·00
44	1s. green and black	14·00	3·25
45	2s. green and red	17·00	24·00
46	5s. green and mauve	55·00	£100
47	10s. green and brown	70·00	£130
48	20s. purple and black on red	£160	£200
51	2d. purple and red	8·00	1·00
57	2s.6d. green and yellow	30·00	£120

1907. As last.

59	½d. green	8·00	30
60	1d. red	13·00	40
61	2d. grey	2·25	40
62	2½d. blue	14·00	3·50
63	3d. purple on yellow	8·50	55
64a	6d. purple	4·50	4·00
65	1s. black and green	18·00	50
66	2s. purple and blue on blue	8·00	16·00
67	2s.6d. black and red on blue	38·00	95·00
68	5s. green and red on yellow	60·00	£225

8

1908

69	**8**	1d. red	6·00	10

1913. As T 4 and 8 (1d.) but portraits of King George V.

72	1d. red	1·25	10
76	2½d. blue	10·00	1·00
77b	3d. purple on yellow	1·75	40
78	6d. purple	6·50	2·25
79e	1s. black on green	1·50	50
81	2s.6d. black and red on blue	9·50	13·00
83a	10s. green and red on green	26·00	85·00
84	20s. purple and black on red	£150	£100
86	½d. green	80	50
87	1d. brown	70	10
88	1½d. red	1·75	10
89	2d. grey	1·75	30
90	2½d. orange	1·25	9·50
91	3d. blue	1·75	60
96	2s. purple and blue on blue	3·25	3·25
98	5s. green and red on yellow	18·00	70·00
100a	15s. purple and green	£140	£450
102	£2 green and orange	£500	£1300

1918. Surch WAR TAX ONE PENNY.

85	1d. on red (No. 72)	3·00	1·00

13 King George V and Christiansborg Castle

1928

103	**13**	½d. green	1·00	40
104	**13**	1d. brown	85	10
105	**13**	1½d. red	2·50	1·50
106	**13**	2d. grey	2·50	20
107	**13**	2½d. orange	2·75	3·50
108	**13**	3d. blue	2·50	40
109	**13**	6d. black and purple	3·00	40
110	**13**	1s. black and orange	4·00	75
111	**13**	2s. black and violet	27·00	4·75
112	**13**	5s. red and olive	60·00	50·00

1935. Silver Jubilee. As T 10a of Gambia.

113	1d. blue and black	60	50
114	3d. brown and blue	3·00	6·00
115	6d. green and blue	16·00	23·00
116	1s. grey and purple	5·00	30·00

1937. Coronation. As T 10b of Gambia.

117	1d. brown	1·75	2·50
118	2d. grey	1·75	4·50
119	3d. blue	2·00	2·75

14

15 King George VI and Christiansborg Castle, Accra

1938

120a	**14**	½d. green	40	50
121a	**14**	1d. brown	40	10
122a	**14**	1½d. red	40	50
123a	**14**	2d. slate	40	10
124a	**14**	3d. blue	40	35
125a	**14**	4d. mauve	80	1·25
126a	**14**	6d. purple	80	20
127a	**14**	9d. orange	1·25	55
128a	**15**	1s. black and olive	1·50	65
129	**15**	1s.3d. brown and blue	2·00	50
130a	**15**	2s. blue and violet	5·00	19·00
131a	**15**	5s. olive and red	10·00	22·00
132	**15**	10s. black and violet	7·50	29·00

1946. Victory. As T 11a of Gambia.

133a	2d. violet	10	10
134a	4d. mauve	1·50	3·25

16 Northern Territories Mounted Constabulary

1948

135	**16**	½d. green	20	40
136	-	1d. blue	15	15
137	-	1½d. red	1·25	80
138	-	2d. brown	55	10
139	-	2½d. brown and red	2·00	4·25
140	-	3d. blue	4·00	60
141	-	4d. mauve	3·50	3·75
142	-	6d. black and orange	40	30
143	-	1s. black and red	2·00	30
144	-	2s. olive and red	4·00	3·50
145	-	5s. purple and black	30·00	10·00
146	-	10s. black and olive	14·00	10·00

DESIGNS—HORIZ: 1d. Christiansborg Castle; 1½d. Emblem of Joint Provincial Council; 2½d. Map showing position of Gold Coast; 3d. Nsuba manganese mine; 4d. Lake Bosumtwi; 1s. Breaking cocoa pods; 2s. Gold Coast Regt. trooping the Colour; 5s. Surfboats. VERT: 2d. Talking drums; 6d. Cocoa farmer; 10s. Forest.

1948. Silver Wedding. As T 11b/c of Gambia.

147	1½d. red	30	70
148	10s. olive	29·00	35·00

1949. U.P.U. As T 11d/g of Gambia.

149	2d. brown	25	20
150	2½d. orange	1·50	4·50
151	3d. blue	35	1·75
152	1s. green	35	30

1952. As 1948 but portrait of Queen Elizabeth II. Designs as for corresponding values except where stated.

153	½d. brown and red (as 2½d.)	10	20
154	1d. blue	30	10
155	1½d. green	30	1·50
156	2d. brown	30	10
157	2½d. red (as ½d.)	35	1·50
158	3d. mauve	75	10
159	4d. blue	35	30
160	6d. black and orange	40	15
161	1s. black and red	1·50	15
162	2s. olive and red	12·00	85
163	5s. purple and black	22·00	7·50
164	10s. black and olive	20·00	12·00

1953. Coronation. As T 11h of Gambia.

165	2d. black and brown	1·00	10

POSTAGE DUE STAMPS

D1

1923

D1	**D1**	½d. black	15·00	£120
D2	**D1**	1d. black	75	1·25
D3	**D1**	2d. black	13·00	3·25
D6	**D1**	3d. black	3·75	25·00
D7	**D1**	6d. black	1·75	11·00
D8	**D1**	1s. black	1·75	70·00

For later issues see **GHANA**.

Pt. 1

GREAT BRITAIN

Consisting of England, Wales, Scotland and Northern Ireland, lying to the N.W. of the European continent.

1840. 12 pence = 1 shilling; 20 shillings = 1 pound sterling.
1971. 100 (new) pence = 1 pound sterling.

1

1840. Letters in lower corners. Imperf.

2	1	1d. black	£10000	£275
5	1	2d. blue	£30000	£675

3

1841. Imperf.

8		1d. brown	£500	25·00
14	3	2d. blue	£4250	75·00

In T **3** there are white lines below "POSTAGE" and above "TWO PENCE".

12 10

1847. Imperf.

54	10	1s. green	£16000	£850
57	10	10d. brown	£8000	£1200
59	12	6d. purple	£13000	£900

1854. Perf.

29	1	1d. brown	£200	18·00
34	3	2d. blue	£2250	60·00
40	1	1d. red	45·00	10·00

14 18 19

1855. No letters in corners.

66a	14	4d. red	£1350	£110
70	18	6d. lilac	£1100	95·00
72	19	1s. green	£2500	£260

7 5 8

6

1858. Letters in four corners.

43	5	1d. red	18·00	2·50
45	6	2d. blue	£300	12·00
48	7	½d. red	90·00	18·00
52	8	1½d. red	£500	60·00

21 22 23

24 25

1862. Small white letters in corners.

76	21	3d. red	£2000	£250
82	22	4d. red	£1800	90·00
84	23	6d. lilac	£1700	90·00
87	24	9d. bistre	£3500	£350
90	25	1s. green	£2500	£200

30 32

1865. Designs as 1862 and T 30 and 32, but large white letters in corners.

94	22	4d. red	£450	55·00
97	23	6d. lilac (with hyphen)	£900	80·00
103	21	3d. red	£450	55·00
109	23	6d. lilac (without hyphen)	£550	80·00
111	24	9d. straw	£1900	£250
112	30	10d. brown	£2800	£300
117	25	1s. green	£650	35·00
118	32	2s. blue	£3250	£175
121	32	2s. brown	£20000	£3250

35

38

1867

126	35	5s. red	£8250	£600
128	-	10s. green	£50000	£2800
129	-	£1 brown	£80000	£4000
137	38	£5 orange	£12500	£4500

The 10s. and £1 are as Type **35**, but have different frames.

34

1872. Large white letters in corners.

122b	34	6d. brown	£575	50·00
125	34	6d. grey	£1600	£225

41 46

1873. Large coloured letters in corners.

141	41	2½d. mauve	£425	50·00
143	21	3d. red	£350	45·00
150	25	1s. green	£500	£100
152	22	4d. red	£2400	£425
153	22	4d. green	£1000	£275
156	46	8d. orange	£1500	£300
157	41	2½d. blue	£350	28·00
160	22	4d. brown	£350	60·00
161	34	6d. grey	£350	65·00
163	25	1s. brown	£550	£140

The 3d, 4d. and 1s. are as 1862, and the 6d. as Type **34**, but all with large coloured letters.

52 53

1880. Various frames.

164	52	½d. green	45·00	12·00
166	53	1d. brown	22·00	12·00
167	-	1½d. red	£200	45·00
168	-	2d. red	£275	90·00
169	-	5d. blue	£675	£110
187	52	½d. blue	25·00	8·00

57

1881

174	57	1d. lilac	2·50	1·50

1883. Types, as 1873, surch 3d. or 6d.

159	21	3d. on 3d. lilac	£500	£130
162	34	6d. on 6d. lilac	£550	£130

58

61

1883

178	58	2s.6d. lilac	£500	£140
180	-	5s. red	£950	£200
183	-	10s. blue	£2000	£475
185	61	£1 brown	£30000	£2500
212	61	£1 green	£3600	£750

The 5s. and 10s. are similar to Type **58**, but have different frames.

62 63

1883. Various frames.

188	62	1½d. purple	£110	38·00
189	63	2d. purple	£175	70·00
190	63	2½d. purple	75·00	15·00
191	62	3d. purple	£225	90·00
192	62	4d. green	£450	£185
193	62	5d. green	£450	£185
194	63	6d. green	£475	£200
195	63	9d. green	£950	£400
196	62	1s. green	£1100	£250

71 72 73

74 75 76

77 78 79

80 81 82

1887

197	71	½d. red	1·50	1·00
198	72	1½d. purple and green	15·00	7·00
200	73	2d. green and red	28·00	12·00
201	74	2½d. purple on blue	22·00	3·00
202	75	3d. purple on yellow	22·00	3·25
205	76	4d. green and brown	30·00	13·00
206	77	4½d. green and red	10·00	40·00
207a	78	5d. purple and blue	35·00	11·00
208	79	6d. purple on red	30·00	10·00
209	80	9d. purple and blue	60·00	40·00
210	81	10d. purple and red	45·00	38·00
211	82	1s. green	£200	60·00
213	71	½d. green*	1·75	2·00
214	82	1s. green and red	50·00	£125

*No. 213, in blue, has had the colour changed after issue.

83 90

1902. Designs not shown are as 1887 (2s.6d. to £1 as 1883) but with portrait of King Edward VII.

217	83	½d. green	2·00	1·50
219	83	1d. red	2·00	1·50
221	-	1½d. purple and green	45·00	20·00
231	83	2½d. blue	20·00	10·00
234	-	3d. purple on yellow	40·00	18·00
238	-	4d. green and brown	40·00	18·00
240	-	4d. orange	20·00	15·00
245	83	6d. purple	40·00	20·00
249	90	7d. grey	12·00	20·00
260	-	2s.6d. purple	£225	£140
263	-	5s. red	£350	£200
265	-	10s. blue	£850	£450
266	-	£1 green	£2000	£750
291	-	2d. green and red	28·00	20·00
294	-	5d. purple and blue	30·00	20·00
307	-	9d. purple and blue	60·00	60·00
311	-	10d. purple and red	80·00	60·00
314	-	1s. green and red	55·00	35·00

98 (Hair heavy) 99 (Lion unshaded)

1911

325	98	½d. green	8·00	1·50
327	99	1d. red	4·50	2·50

101 (Hair light) 102 (Lion shaded)

1912

341	102	1d. red	5·00	2·00
344	101	½d. green	7·00	3·00

104 105 106

107 108

109

1912. Lined background.

376	106	3d. violet	9·00	3·00
381	107	5d. brown	15·00	5·00
387	107	7d. green	20·00	10·00
390	107	8d. black on yellow	32·00	11·00
392	108	9d. agate	15·00	6·00
394	108	10d. blue	22·00	20·00
395	108	1s. brown	20·00	4·00
403	109	£1 green	£2800	£1250
418	105	½d. green	1·00	1·00
419	104	1d. red	1·00	1·00
420	105	1½d. brown	1·00	1·00
421	106	2d. orange	2·50	2·50
422	104	2½d. blue	5·00	3·00
424	106	4d. green	12·00	2·50
426a	107	6d. purple	3·00	1·50
427	108	9d. green	12·00	3·50
450	109	2s.6d. brown	80·00	40·00
451	109	5s. red	£175	85·00
452	109	10s. blue	£350	80·00

112

1924. British Empire Exhibition. Dated "1924".

430	**112**	1d. red	10·00	11·00
431	**112**	1½d. brown	15·00	15·00

1925. Dated "1925".

432	1d. red	15·00	15·00
433	1½d. brown	40·00	40·00

113 114 115

116 St. George and the Dragon

1929. 9th U.P.U. Congress, London.

434	**113**	½d. green	2·25	2·25
435	**114**	1d. red	2·25	2·25
436	**114**	1½d. brown	2·25	2·25
437	**115**	2½d. blue	10·00	10·00
438	**116**	£1 black	£750	£750

118 119 120

121

122

1934. Solid background.

439	**118**	½d. green	50	50
440	**119**	1d. red	50	50
441	**118**	1½d. brown	50	50
442	**120**	2d. orange	75	75
443	**119**	2½d. blue	1·50	1·50
444	**120**	3d. violet	1·50	1·50
445	**120**	4d. green	2·00	2·00
446	**121**	5d. brown	6·50	6·50
447	**122**	9d. olive	12·00	12·00
448	**122**	10d. blue	15·00	15·00
449	**122**	1s. brown	15·00	15·00

123

1935. Silver Jubilee.

453	**123**	½d. green	1·00	1·00
454	**123**	1d. red	1·50	1·50
455	**123**	1½d. brown	1·00	1·00
456	**123**	2½d. blue	5·00	5·00

Emblems at right differ.

124 King Edward VIII

1936

457	**124**	½d. green	30	30
458	**124**	1d. red	60	50
459	**124**	1½d. brown	30	30
460	**124**	2½d. blue	30	85

126 King George VI and Queen Elizabeth

1937. Coronation.

461	**126**	1½d. brown	30	30

128

129

130

1937

462	**128**	½d. green	30	25
463	**128**	1d. red	30	25
464	**128**	1½d. brown	30	25
465	**128**	2d. orange	1·20	50
466	**128**	2½d. blue	40	25
468	**129**	4d. green	60	75
469	**129**	5d. brown	3·50	85
470	**129**	6d. purple	1·50	60
471	**130**	7d. green	5·00	60
472	**130**	8d. red	7·50	80
473	**130**	9d. green	6·50	80
474	**130**	10d. blue	7·00	80
474a	**130**	11d. purple	3·00	2·75
475	**130**	1s. brown	9·00	75
490	**128**	3d. violet	2·50	1·00
503	**128**	½d. orange	30	30
504	**128**	1d. blue	30	30
505	**128**	1½d. green	65	60
506	**128**	2d. brown	75	40
507	**128**	2½d. red	60	40
508	**129**	4d. blue	2·00	1·75

131 King George VI

1939

476	**131**	2s.6d. brown	85·00	6·00
476a	**131**	2s.6d. green	15·00	1·50
477	**131**	5s. red	20·00	2·00
478a	-	10s. blue	40·00	5·00
478b	-	£1 brown	25·00	26·00

The 10s. and £1 values have the portrait in the centre in an ornamental frame.

134 Queen Victoria and King George VI

1940. Centenary of First Adhesive Postage Stamps.

479	**134**	½d. green	30	75
480	**134**	1d. red	1·00	75
481	**134**	1½d. brown	50	1·50
482	**134**	2d. orange	1·00	75
483	**134**	2½d. blue	2·25	50
484	**134**	3d. violet	3·00	3·50

135

1946. Victory Commemoration.

491	**135**	2½d. blue	20	20
492	-	3d. violet	20	50

DESIGN—HORIZ: 3d. Symbols of Peace and Reconstruction.

137

138 King George VI and Queen Elizabeth

1948. Royal Silver Wedding.

493	**137**	2½d. blue	35	20
494	**138**	£1 blue	40·00	40·00

139 Globe and Laurel Wreath

140 "Speed"

1948. Olympic Games. Inscr "OLYMPIC GAMES 1948".

495	**139**	2½d. blue	35	10
496	**140**	3d. violet	35	50
497	-	6d. purple	2·50	75
498	-	1s. brown	3·75	2·00

DESIGNS: 6d. Olympic symbol; 1s. Winged Victory.

143 Two Hemispheres

144 U.P.U. Monument, Berne

1949. 75th Anniv of U.P.U. Inscr as in T 143/4.

499	**143**	2½d. blue	25	10
500	**144**	3d. violet	25	50
501	-	6d. purple	50	75
502	-	1s. brown	1·00	1·25

DESIGNS: 6d. Goddess Concordia, globe and points of compass; 1s. Posthorn and globe.

147 H.M.S. "Victory"

1951

509	**147**	2s.6d. green	7·50	1·00
510	-	5s. red	35·00	1·00
511	-	10s. blue	15·00	7·50
512	-	£1 brown	45·00	18·00

DESIGNS: 5s. White Cliffs of Dover; 10s. St. George and Dragon; £1 Royal Coat of Arms.

152 Festival Symbol

1951. Festival of Britain.

513		2½d. red	20	15
514	**152**	4d. blue	30	35

DESIGN: 2½d. Britannia, cornucopia and Mercury.

154

155

157

158

159 Queen Elizabeth II and National Emblems

1952

517	**154**	1½d. green	10	20
519	**155**	2½d. red	15	15
553	**158**	11d. plum	50	1·10
570	**154**	½d. orange	10	10
571	**154**	1d. blue	10	10
573	**154**	2d. brown	10	10
575	**155**	3d. lilac	10	20
576a	**155**	4d. blue	15	15
577	**155**	4½d. brown	10	25
582	**158**	9d. green	60	40
585	**159**	1s.3d. green	45	30
616c	**157**	5d. brown	25	35
617	**157**	6d. purple	30	30
617a	**157**	7d. green	55	50
617b	**158**	8d. mauve	40	45
617d	**158**	10d. blue	70	60
617e	**159**	1s. brown	40	35
618a	**159**	1s.6d. blue	2·00	2·00

The 4d., 4½d. and 1s.3d. values are printed with colour tones reversed.

Stamps with either one or two vertical black lines on the back were issued in 1957 in connection with the Post Office automatic facing machine experiments in the Southampton area. Later the lines were replaced by almost invisible phosphor bands on the face, in the above and later issues. They are listed in the Stanley Gibbons British Commonwealth Catalogue.

For stamps as T **157**, but with face values in decimal currency, see Nos. 2031/3.

161

163

1953. Coronation. Portraits of Queen Elizabeth II.

532	**161**	2½d. red	20	25
533	-	4d. blue	1·10	1·90
534	**163**	1s.3d. green	5·00	3·00
535	-	1s.6d. blue	10·00	4·75

DESIGNS: 4d. Coronation and National Emblems; 1s.6d. Crowns and Sceptres dated "2 JUNE 1953".

166 Carrickfergus Castle

1955

595a	**166**	2s.6d. brown	35	40
597a	-	10s. blue	4·50	4·50
760	-	5s. red	70	75
762	-	£1 black	7·50	4·50

CASTLES: 5s. Caernarvon; 10s. Edinburgh; £1 Windsor.

170 Scout Badge and "Rolling Hitch"

171 "Scouts coming to Britain"

1957. World Scout Jubilee Jamboree.

557	**170**	2½d. red	50	50
558	**171**	4d. blue	75	1·50
559	-	1s.3d. green	4·50	4·50

DESIGN: 1s.3d. Globe within a compass.

1957. Inter-Parliamentary Union Conference. As No. 576a but Inscr "46th PARLIAMENTARY CONFERENCE".

560	4d. blue	1·00	1·00

176 Welsh Dragon

1958. 6th British Empire and Commonwealth Games, Cardiff. Inscr as in T 176.

567	**176**	3d. lilac	20	20
568	-	6d. mauve	40	45
569	-	1s.3d. green	2·25	2·40

DESIGNS: 6d. Flag and Games emblem; 1s.3d. Welsh Dragon.

180 Postboy of 1660

181 Posthorn of 1660

1960. Tercentenary of Establishment of General Letter Office.

619	**180**	3d. lilac	50	50
620	**181**	1s.3d. green	3·75	4·25

182 Conference Emblem

1960. 1st Anniv of European Postal and Telecommunications Conference.

621	**182**	6d. green and purple	2·00	50
622	**182**	1s.6d. brown and blue	9·50	5·00

184 "Growth of Savings"

1961. Centenary of Post Office Savings Bank. Inscr "POST OFFICE SAVINGS BANK".

623A	-	2½d. black and red	25	25
624A	**184**	3d. brown and violet	20	20
625A	-	1s.6d. red and blue	2·50	2·25

DESIGNS—VERT: 2½d. Thrift plant. HORIZ: 1s.6d. Thrift plant.

186 C.E.P.T. Emblem **187** Doves and Emblem

1961. Europa.

No.	Type	Description	Mint	Used
626	**186**	2d. orange, pink and brown	15	10
627	**187**	4d. buff, mauve and blue	15	15
628	-	10d. turquoise, green bl	15	50

DESIGN: 10d. As 4d. but arranged differently.

189 Hammer Beam Roof, Westminster Hall

1961. 7th Commonwealth Parliamentary Conference.

No.	Type	Description	Mint	Used
629	**189**	6d. purple and gold	25	25
630	-	1s.3d. green and blue	2·50	2·75

DESIGN—VERT: 1s.3d. Palace of Westminster.

191 "Units of Productivity"

1962. National Productivity Year.

No.	Type	Description	Mint	Used
631	**191**	2½d. green and red	20	20
632	-	3d. blue and violet	50	25
633	-	1s.3d. red, blue and green	1·50	1·75

DESIGNS: 3d. Arrows over map; 1s.3d. Arrows in formation.

194 Campaign Emblem and Family

1963. Freedom from Hunger.

No.	Type	Description	Mint	Used
634	**194**	2½d. red and pink	25	10
635	-	1s.3d. brown and yellow	1·90	1·90

DESIGN: 1s.3d. Children of Three Races.

196 "Paris Conference"

1963. Centenary of Paris Postal Conference.

No.	Type	Description	Mint	Used
636	**196**	6d. green and mauve	50	50

197 Posy of Flowers

1963. National Nature Week. Multicoloured.

No.	Type	Description	Mint	Used
637		3d. Type **197**	15	15
638		4½d. Woodland life	35	35

199 Westland Widgeon III (Rescue at Sea)

1963. 9th International Lifeboat Conference, Edinburgh. Multicoloured.

No.	Type	Description	Mint	Used
639		2½d. Type **199**	25	25
640		4d. 19th-century lifeboat	50	50
641		1s.6d. Lifeboatmen	3·00	3·25

202 Red Cross

1963. Red Cross Centenary Congress.

No.	Type	Description	Mint	Used
642	**202**	3d. red and lilac	25	25
643	-	1s.3d. red, blue and grey	3·00	3·00
644	-	1s.6d. red, blue and bistre	3·00	3·00

DESIGNS: Nos. 643/4 are as Type **202** but differently arranged.

205 Commonwealth Cable

1963. COMPAC (Trans-Pacific Telephone Cable) Opening.

No.	Type	Description	Mint	Used
645	**205**	1s.6d. blue and black	2·75	2·50

206 Puck and Bottom (*"A Midsummer Night's Dream"*) **210** Hamlet contemplating Yorick's Skull (*"Hamlet"*) and Queen Elizabeth II

1964. Shakespeare Festival.

No.	Type	Description	Mint	Used
646	**206**	3d. multicoloured	15	15
647	-	6d. multicoloured	30	30
648	-	1s.3d. multicoloured	75	1·00
649	-	1s.6d. multicoloured	1·00	85
650	**210**	2s.6d. slate-purple	2·75	2·75

DESIGNS—As Type **206**: 6d. Feste (*"Twelfth Night"*); 1s.3d. Balcony scene (*"Romeo and Juliet"*); 1s.6d. "Eve of Agincourt" (*"Henry V"*).

211 Flats near Richmond Park

1964. 20th Int Geographical Congress, London. Multicoloured.

No.	Type	Description	Mint	Used
651		2½d. Type **211**	10	10
652		4d. Shipbuilding yards, Belfast	30	30
653		8d. Beddgelert Forest Park, Snowdonia	75	85
654		1s.6d. Nuclear reactor, Dounreay	3·50	3·50

The designs represent "Urban development", "Industrial activity", "Forestry" and "Technological development" respectively.

215 Spring Gentian

1964. 10th Int Botanical Congress, Edinburgh. Multicoloured.

No.	Type	Description	Mint	Used
655		3d. Type **215**	25	25
656		6d. Dog rose	50	50
657		9d. Honeysuckle	1·75	2·25
658		1s.3d. Fringed water lily	2·50	2·50

219 Forth Road Bridge

1964. Opening of Forth Road Bridge.

No.	Type	Description	Mint	Used
659	**219**	3d. black, blue and violet	10	10
660	-	6d. lilac, blue and red	40	40

DESIGN: 6d. Forth Road and Railway Bridges.

221 Sir Winston Churchill

1965. Churchill Commemoration.

No.	Type	Description	Mint	Used
661	**221**	4d. black and drab	10	10
662	-	1s.3d. black and grey	30	40

The 1s.3d. shows a closer view of Churchill's head.

222 Simon de Montfort's Seal

1965. 700th Anniv of Simon de Montfort's Parliament.

No.	Type	Description	Mint	Used
663	**222**	6d. olive	20	20
664	-	2s.6d. black, grey and drab	80	1·50

DESIGN—(58½×21½ mm): 2s.6d. Parliament buildings (after engraving by Hollar, 1647).

224 Bandsmen and Banner

1965. Centenary of Salvation Army. Mult.

No.	Type	Description	Mint	Used
665		3d. Type **224**	25	25
666		1s.6d. Three Salvationists	1·00	1·50

226 Lister's Carbolic Spray

1965. Centenary of Joseph Lister's Discovery of Antiseptic Surgery.

No.	Type	Description	Mint	Used
667	**226**	4d. blue, brown and grey	25	15
668	-	1s. black, purple and blue	1·00	1·10

DESIGN: 1s. Lister and chemical symbols.

228 Trinidad Carnival Dancers

1965. Commonwealth Arts Festival.

No.	Type	Description	Mint	Used
669	**228**	6d. black and orange	20	20
670	-	1s.6d. black and violet	80	1·10

DESIGN: 1s.6d. Canadian folk-dancers.

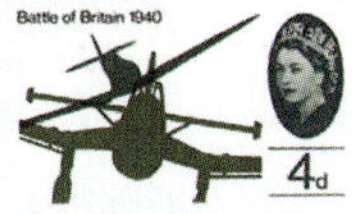

230 Flight of Supermarine Spitfires **234** Supermarine Spitfire attacking Junkers Ju 878 "Stuka"

1965. 25th Anniv of Battle of Britain. Inscr "Battle of Britain 1940".

No.	Type	Description	Mint	Used
671	**230**	4d. olive and black	25	25
672	-	4d. olive and black	25	25
673	-	4d. multicoloured	25	25
674	-	4d. olive and black	25	25
675	**234**	4d. olive and black	25	25
676	-	4d. multicoloured	25	25
677	-	9d. violet, orange and purple	1·75	1·75
678	-	1s.3d. grey, black and blue	1·75	1·75

DESIGNS: No. 672, Pilot in Hawker Hurricane Mk I; 673, Wingtips of Supermarine Spitfire and Messerschmitt BF 109; 674, Supermarine Spitfires attacking Heinkel HE 111H bomber; 676, Hawker Hurricanes Mk 1 over wreck of Dornier DO-17Z bomber; 9d. Anti-aircraft artillery in action; 1s.3d. Air battle over St. Paul's Cathedral.

239 Tower and "Nash" Terrace, Regent's Park

1965. Opening of Post Office Tower.

No.	Type	Description	Mint	Used
679		3d. yellow, blue and green	10	15
680p	**239**	1s.3d. green and blue	30	50

DESIGN—VERT: 3d. Tower and Georgian build-ings.

240 U.N. Emblem

1965. 20th Anniv of U.N.O. and International Co-operation Year.

No.	Type	Description	Mint	Used
681	**240**	3d. black, orange and blue	25	20
682	-	1s.6d. black, purple blue	1·00	80

DESIGN: 1s.6d. I.C.Y. Emblem.

242 Telecommunications Network

1965. Centenary of I.T.U. Multicoloured.

No.	Type	Description	Mint	Used
683		9d. Type **242**	50	40
684		1s.6d. Radio waves and switchboard	1·50	1·25

244 Robert Burns (after Skirving chalk drawing)

1966. Burns Commemoration.

No.	Type	Description	Mint	Used
685	**244**	4d. black, indigo and blue	15	15
686	-	1s.3d. black, blue orange	40	70

DESIGN: 1s.3d. Robert Burns (after Nasmyth portrait).

246 Westminster Abbey

1966. 900th Anniv of Westminster Abbey.

No.	Type	Description	Mint	Used
687	**246**	3d. black, brown and blue	15	20
688	-	2s.6d. black	55	80

DESIGN: 2s.6d. Fan vaulting, Henry VII Chapel.

248 View near Hassocks, Sussex

1966. Landscapes.

No.	Type	Description	Mint	Used
689	**248**	4d. black, green and blue	10	15
690	-	6d. black, green and blue	15	20
691	-	1s.3d. black, yellow & bl	25	35
692	-	1s.6d. black, orange & blue	40	35

VIEWS: 6d. Antrim, Northern Ireland; 1s.3d. Harlech Castle, Wales; 1s.6d. Cairngorm Mountains, Scotland.

253 Goalmouth Melee

1966. World Cup Football Championship. Multicoloured.

No.	Type	Description	Mint	Used
693		4d. Players with ball (*vert*)	10	25
694		6d. Type **253**	15	25
695		1s.3d. Goalkeeper saving goal	50	1·00

255 Black-headed Gull

1966. British Birds. Multicoloured.

No.	Type	Description	Mint	Used
696		4d. Type **255**	20	20
697		4d. Blue tit	20	20
698		4d. European robin	20	20
699		4d. Blackbird	20	20

1966. England's World Cup Football Victory. As No. 693 but inscr "ENGLAND WINNERS".

No.	Type	Description	Mint	Used
700		4d. multicoloured	30	30

260 Jodrell Bank Radio Telescope

1966. British Technology.

No.	Type	Description	Mint	Used
701p	**260**	4d. black and lemon	10	10
702p	-	6d. red, blue and orange	15	25
703p	-	1s.3d. multicoloured	35	40
704	-	1s.6d. multicoloured	50	60

DESIGN: 6d. British motor-cars; 1s.3d. SRN 6 Hovercraft; 1s.6d. Windscale reactor.

264 **265**

1966. 900th Anniv of Battle of Hastings. Mult.

No.	Type	Description	Mint	Used
705		4d. Type **264**	10	10
706		4d. Type **265**	10	10
707		4d. "Yellow" horse	10	10
708		4d. "Blue" horse	10	10
709		4d. "Purple" horse	10	10
710		4d. "Grey" horse	10	10

711	6d. Norman horsemen	10	10
712	1s.3d. Norman horsemen attacking Harold's troops (59×22½ mm)	20	75

272 King of the Orient

1966. Christmas. Multicoloured.

713	3d. Type **272**	10	25
714	1s.6d. Snowman	30	50

274 Sea Freight

1967. European Free Trade Assn (EFTA).

715	9d. Type **274**	25	20
716p	1s.6d. Armstrong Whitworth A.W.650 Argosy (Air freight)	25	40

276 Hawthorn and Bramble

1967. British Wild Flowers. Multicoloured.

717p	4d. Type **276**	10	15
718p	4d. Larger bindweed and viper's bugloss	10	15
719p	4d. Ox-eye daisy, coltsfoot and buttercup	10	15
720p	4d. Bluebell, red campion and wood anemone	10	15
721p	9d. Dog violet	15	25
722p	1s.9d. Primroses	20	30

282

1967

723	282	½d. brown	10	20
724	282	1d. olive	10	10
726	282	2d. brown	10	15
729	282	3d. violet	15	10
731	282	4d. sepia	10	10
733	282	4d. red	10	10
735	282	5d. blue	10	10
736	282	6d. purple	20	25
737	282	7d. green	40	35
738	282	8d. red	20	45
739	282	8d. turquoise	50	60
740	282	9d. green	40	25
741	282	10d. drab	50	50
742	282	1s. violet	45	25
743	282	1s.6d. blue and indigo	50	50
744	282	1s.9d. orange and black	50	45

For decimal issue, see Nos. X841 etc.

284 "Mares and Foals in a Landscape" (George Stubbs)

1967. British Paintings.

748	-	4d. multicoloured	10	10
749	284	9d. multicoloured	15	15
750	-	1s.6d. multicoloured	25	35

PAINTINGS—VERT: 4d. "Master Lambton" (Sir Thomas Lawrence). HORIZ: 1s.6d. "Children Coming Out of School" (L. S. Lowry).

286 *"Gipsy Moth IV"*

1967. Sir Francis Chichester's World Voyage.

751	286	1s.9d. multicoloured	20	20

287 Radar Screen

1967. British Discovery and Invention. Mult.

752	4d. Type **287**	10	10
753	1s. *"Penicillium notatum"*	10	20
754	1s.6d. Vickers VC-10 jet engines and Gloster Whittle E28/39	20	25
755	1s.9d. Television equipment	20	30

292 "Madonna and Child" (Murillo)

1967. Christmas.

756	-	3d. multicoloured	10	15
757	292	4d. multicoloured	10	15
758	-	1s.6d. multicoloured	15	15

PAINTINGS—VERT: 3d. "The Adoration of the Shepherds" (School of Seville). HORIZ: 1s.6d. "The Adoration of the Shepherds" (Louis le Nain).

294 Tarr Steps, Exmoor

1968. British Bridges. Multicoloured.

763	4d. Type **294**	10	10
764	9d. Aberfeldy Bridge	10	15
765	1s.6d. Menai Bridge	15	25
766	1s.9d. M4 viaduct	20	30

298 "T U C" and Trades Unionists

1968. British Annivs. Events described on stamps.

767	298	4d. multicoloured	10	10
768	-	9d. violet, grey and black	10	15
769	-	1s. multicoloured	15	15
770	-	1s.9d. ochre and brown	35	35

DESIGNS: 9d. Mrs. Emmeline Pankhurst (statue); 1s. Sopwith Camel and English Electric Lightning fighters; 1s.9d. Captain Cook's "Endeavour" and signature.

302 "Queen Elizabeth I" (unknown artist)

1968. British Paintings.

771	302	4d. multicoloured	10	10
772	-	1s. multicoloured	10	20
773	-	1s.6d. multicoloured	20	25
774	-	1s.9d. multicoloured	25	40

PAINTINGS—VERT: 1s. "Pinkie" (Lawrence); 1s.6d. "Ruins of St. Mary Le Port" (Piper). HORIZ: 1s.9d. "The Hay Wain" (Constable).

306 Boy and Girl with Rocking Horse

1968. Christmas. Multicoloured.

775	4d. Type **306**	10	15
776	9d. Girl with doll's house (*vert*)	15	25
777	1s.6d. Boy with train set (*vert*)	15	50

310 Elizabethan Galleon

1969. British Ships. Multicoloured.

778	5d. *"Queen Elizabeth 2"*	10	15
779	9d. Type **310**	10	25
780	9d. East Indiaman	10	25
781	9d. *"Cutty Sark"*	10	25
782	1s. *"Great Britain"*	40	35
783	1s. *"Mauretania I"*	40	35

Nos. 778 and 782/3 are 58×23 mm.

315 Concorde in Flight

1969. 1st Flight of Concorde.

784	315	4d. multicoloured	25	25
785	-	9d. multicoloured	55	75
786	-	1s.6d. indigo, grey and blue	75	1·00

DESIGNS: 9d. Plan and elevation views; 1s.6d. Concorde's nose and tail.

318 Queen Elizabeth II

1969

787	318	2s.6d. brown	35	30
788	318	5s. lake	1·75	60
789	318	10s. blue	6·00	7·00
790	318	£1 black	3·25	1·50

For decimal issues see Nos. 829/31b.

No. 790 has an italic "£". For larger version with roman "£" see No. 831b.

319 Page from "Daily Mail", and Vickers FB-27 Vimy Biplane

1969. Anniversary Events described on stamps.

791	319	5d. multicoloured	10	15
792	-	9d. multicoloured	15	25
793	-	1s. claret, red and blue	15	25
794	-	1s.6d. multicoloured	15	30
795	-	1s.9d. turquoise, yell & sepia	20	40

DESIGNS: 9d. Europa and C.E.P.T. emblems; 1s. I.L.O. emblem; 1s.6d. Flags of N.A.T.O. countries; 1s.9d. Vickers FB-27 Vimy G-EAOU and globe showing flight route.

324 Durham Cathedral

1969. British Architecture (Cathedrals). Mult.

796	5d. Type **324**	10	10
797	5d. York Minster	10	10
798	5d. St. Giles' Cathedral, Edinburgh	10	10
799	5d. Canterbury Cathedral	10	10
800	9d. St. Paul's Cathedral	25	30
801	1s.6d. Liverpool Metropolitan Cathedral	25	35

332 Queen Eleanor's Gate, Caernarvon Castle

1969. Investiture of H.R.H. The Prince of Wales.

802	-	5d. multicoloured	10	15
803	-	5d. multicoloured	10	15
804	332	5d. multicoloured	10	15
805	-	9d. multicoloured	15	30
806	-	1s. black and gold	15	30

DESIGNS: No. 802, The King's Gate, Caernarvon Castle; No. 803, The Eagle Tower, Caernarvon Castle; No. 805, Celtic Cross, Margam Abbey; No. 806, H.R.H. The Prince of Wales.

335 Mahatma Gandhi

1969. Gandhi Centenary Year.

807	335	1s.6d. multicoloured	30	30

336 National Giro "G" Symbol

1969. Post Office Technology Commemoration.

808	336	5d. multicoloured	10	10
809	-	9d. green, blue and black	20	25
810	-	1s. green, lavender & black	20	25
811	-	1s.6d. purple, blue & black	25	50

DESIGNS: 9d. International subscriber dialling (Telecommunications); 1s. Pulse code modulations (Telecommunications); 1s 6d. Automatic sorting (Postal Mechanisation).

340 Herald Angel

1969. Christmas. Multicoloured.

812	4d. Type **340**	10	10
813	5d. The Three Shepherds	15	15
814	1s.6d. The Three Kings	20	20

343 Fife Harling

1970. British Rural Architecture. Multicoloured.

815	5d. Type **343**	10	10
816	9d. Cotswold limestone	10	25
817	1s. Welsh stucco	15	25
818	1s.6d. Ulster thatch	20	40

The 1s. and 1s.6d. are larger (38×27 mm).

347 Signing the Declaration of Arbroath

1970. Anniversaries. Events described on stamps. Multicoloured.

819	5d. Type **347**	10	10
820	9d. Florence Nightingale attending patients	15	15
821	1s. Signing of International Co-operative Alliance	20	25
822	1s.6d. Pilgrims and *"Mayflower"*	20	30
823	1s.9d. Sir William and Sir John Herschel, Francis Baily and Telescope	25	30

352 Mr Pickwick and Sam (*"Pickwick Papers"*)

1970. Literary Annivs. Death Cent of Charles Dickens (novelist) (824/7) and Birth Bicent of William Wordsworth (poet) (828). Mult.

824	5d. Type **352**	10	25
825	5d. Mr. and Mrs. Micawber (*"David Copperfield"*)	10	25
826	5d. David Copperfield and Betsy Trotwood (*"David Copperfield"*)	10	25
827	5d. "Oliver asking for more" (*"Oliver Twist"*)	10	25
828	1s.6d. "Grasmere" (from engraving by J. Farrington, R.A.)	25	50

357 Queen Elizabeth II

1970. Decimal Currency. Designs as T 318 but inscr in decimal currency as T 357.

829	**357**	10p. red	50	75
830	**357**	20p. green	60	25
831	**357**	50p. blue	1·50	40
831b	**357**	£1 black	3·50	80

On No. 831b the "£" is in roman type.

360 Cyclists

1970. 9th British Commonwealth Games. Mult.

832	5d. Runners	25	25
833	1s.6d. Swimmers	50	50
834	1s.9d. Type **360**	50	50

361 1d. Black (1840)

1970. "Philympia 70" Stamp Exhibition. Mult.

835	5d. Type **361**	25	10
836	9d.1s. green (1847)	25	30
837	1s.6d. 4d. red (1855)	25	45

364 Shepherds and Apparition of the Angel

1970. Christmas. Multicoloured.

838	4d. Type **364**	15	10
839	5d. Mary, Joseph, and Christ in the manger	15	15
840	1s.6d. The Wise Men bearing gifts	25	30

367

1971. Decimal currency. As Nos. 723, etc. but new colours and with decimal figures of value as in T 367.

X670	6p. light emerald	25	20
X841	½p. turquoise-blue	10	10
X844	1p. crimson	10	15
X848	1½p. black	15	25
X849	2p. myrtle-green	15	20
X851	2½p. magenta	20	15
X855	10p. orange-brown and chestnut	20	25
X856	3p. ultramarine	15	20
X858	3½p. olive-grey	25	30
X861	4p. ochre-brown	20	25
X865	4½p. grey-blue	25	30
X866	5p. pale violet	20	20
X868	5½p. violet	25	30
X872	6½p. greenish-blue	25	20
X875	7p. purple-brown	25	30
X877	7½p. pale chestnut	25	35
X878	8p. rosine	30	30
X881	8½p. light yellowish green	30	30
X882	9p. yellow-orange and black	45	55
X883	9p. deep violet	35	30
X884	9½p. purple	35	45
X888	10p. orange-brown	35	25
X890	10½p. yellow	40	45
X891	10½p. deep dull blue	45	50
X892	11p. brown-red	40	30
X893	11½p. drab	40	35
X895	12p. yellowish green	45	45
X896	12p. bright emerald	45	45
X898	12½p. light emerald	45	40
X900	13p. pale chestnut	40	40
X903	14p. deep blue	45	50
X905	15p. bright blue	65	65
X909	17p. grey-blue	60	60
X913	18p. bright green	60	60
X927	2p. deep green	20	20
X929	2½p. rose-red	15	20
X930	3p. bright magenta	20	25
X931	3½p. purple-brown	50	60
X932	4p. greenish blue	25	40
X933	4p. new blue	20	25
X937	7p. brownish-red	1·10	1·25
X938	8½p. yellowish green	40	50
X942	11½p. ochre-brown	55	55
X944	13p. olive-grey	45	50
X945	13½p. purple-brown	60	60
X946	14p. grey-blue	50	50
X947	15p. ultramarine	60	60
X948	15½p. pale violet	60	50
X949	16p. olive-drab	55	55
X950	16½p. pale chestnut	80	80
X951	17p. light emerald	60	60
X953	17½. Pale chestnut	70	75
X954	18p. deep violet	70	70
X955	18p. deep olive-grey	75	60
X956	19p. bright orange-red	80	60
X957	19½p. olive-grey	2·00	2·00
X958	20p. dull purple	1·00	75
X959	20p. turquoise-green	75	70
X960	20p. brownish black	1·00	1·00
X961	20½p. ultramarine	1·25	1·25
X962	22p. blue	90	75
X963	22p. yellow-green	90	80
X964	22p. bright orange-red	90	80
X965	23p. brown-red	1·25	1·10
X966	23p. bright green	1·10	1·10
X967	24p. violet	1·40	1·50
X968	24p. Indian red	2·00	1·60
X969	24p. chestnut	80	80
X970	25p. purple	1·00	1·00
X971	26p. rosine	1·10	80
X972	26p. drab	1·50	1·25
X973	27p. chestnut	1·25	1·25
X974	27p. violet	1·50	1·25
X975	28p. deep violet	1·25	1·25
X976	28p. ochre	1·40	1·25
X977	28p. deep bluish grey	1·40	1·25
X978	29p. ochre-brown	1·75	1·75
X979	29p. deep mauve	1·75	1·75
X981	31p. purple	1·25	1·25
X983	32p. greenish blue	1·90	1·75
X985	34p. ochre-brown	1·75	1·75
X986	34p. deep bluish grey	2·00	1·90
X987	34p. deep mauve	1·75	1·75
X992	50p. ochre-brown	1·75	70
X993	75p. grey-black	3·25	1·50
X1000	2p. emerald-green	20	25
X1001	2p. bright green and deep green	75	70
X1003	5p. light violet	40	40
X1004	5p. claret	50	50
X1008	17p. deep blue	80	80
X1021	34p. bistre-brown	7·50	7·50
X1022	39p. bright mauve	1·50	1·60
X1023	75p. black	3·00	1·50
X1024	75p. brownish grey and black	9·00	8·50
X1056	31p. ultramarine	1·40	1·40
X1057	33p. light emerald	1·25	1·25

1998

Y1473t	5p. red-brown	70	70
Y1473t	5p. red-brown	70	70
Y1670	5p. dull red-brown	25	25
Y1671	6p. yellow-olive	25	30
Y1672	7p. grey	25	25
Y1673	7p. bright magenta	25	25
Y1674	8p. yellow	35	35
Y1675	9p. yellow-orange	15	20
Y1676	10p. dull orange	35	35
Y1676b	12p. greenish blue	20	25
Y1676c	14p. rose-red	20	25
Y1676d	15p. bright magenta	35	35
Y1676e	16p. pale cerise	35	35
Y1676f	17p. brown-olive	50	50
Y1677	19p. bistre	75	75
Y1680	20p. bright green	70	70
Y1682b	22p. drab	50	50
Y1683	25p. rose-red	1·10	1·10
Y1685	26p. red-brown	1·10	1·10
Y1686	26p. gold	1·10	1·10
Y1687	29p. grey	1·25	1·25
Y1688	30p. olive-grey	1·10	1·10
Y1689	31p. deep mauve	1·20	1·20
Y1690	33p. grey-green	1·50	1·50
Y1691	34p. yellow-olive	1·25	1·00
Y1692	35p. yellow	1·50	1·50
Y1694	35p. sepia	1·10	1·10
Y1695	35p. yellow-olive	50	55
Y1696	36p. bright ultramarine	1·50	1·50
Y1697	37p. bright mauve	1·40	1·40
Y1698	37p. grey-black	1·40	1·40
Y1699	37p. brown-olive	90	90
Y1700	38p. rosine	1·50	1·50
Y1701	38p. ultramarine	2·00	2·00
Y1702	39p. bright magenta	1·50	1·50
Y1703	39p. grey	1·20	1·20
Y1704	40p. deep azure	1·40	1·40
Y1705	40p. turquoise-blue	1·30	1·30
Y1706	41p. grey-brown	1·75	1·75
Y1708	41p. rosine	1·40	1·40
Y1709	42p. deep olive-grey	1·40	1·40
Y1710	43p. deep olive-brown	1·75	1·75
Y1711	43p. sepia	2·50	2·50
Y1712	43p. emerald	1·40	1·40
Y1713	44p. grey-brown	5·00	5·00
Y1714	44p. deep bright blue	1·00	1·00
Y1715	45p. bright mauve	1·50	1·50
Y1716	46p. yellow	1·00	1·00
Y1717	47p. turquoise-green	1·75	1·75
Y1717a	48p. mauve	1·00	1·00
Y1718	49p. red-brown	1·00	1·00
Y1719	50p. ochre	1·75	1·75
Y1719b	50p. grey	1·00	1·00
Y1719c	54p. red-brown	1·10	1·10
Y1719d	56p. yellow-olive	1·10	1·10
Y1719e	60p. light emerald	1·00	1·00
Y1719f	62p. rosine	2·00	2·00
Y1720	63p. light emerald	2·00	2·00
Y1721	64p. turquoise-green	2·25	2·25
Y1722	65p. greenish blue	2·10	2·10
Y1722a	67p. bright mauve	2·10	2·10
Y1723	68p. grey-brown	2·10	2·10
Y1724	72p. rosine	1·50	1·50
Y1724a	78p. emerald	1·50	1·50
Y1724b	81p. turquoise-green	1·50	1·50
Y1724c	88p. bright magenta	1·50	1·50
Y1724d	90p. ultramarine	1·40	1·40
Y1724e	97p. violet	3·00	2·75
Y1725	£1 bluish violet	3·25	3·00
Y1725b	£1 magenta	2·00	2·00
Y1725c	£1.46 greenish blue	2·25	2·25
Y1726	£1.50 brown-red	4·00	4·00
Y1727	£2 deep blue-green	5·50	5·50
Y1728	£3 deep mauve	8·00	8·00
Y1729	£5 azure	14·00	14·00
Y1743	1p. lake	40	40
Y1743n	1p. reddish purple	1·00	1·00
Y1749n	17p. bistre	1·00	1·00
Y1751	20p. bright yellow-green	2·25	2·25
Y1751m	20p. light green	2·25	2·25
Y1751n	22p. olive-brown	2·50	2·50
Y1752	25p. red	1·10	1·10
Y1753	26p. chestnut	1·00	1·00
Y1757	41p. drab	1·75	1·75
Y1757f	48p. bright mauve	2·25	2·25
Y1757j	54p. chestnut	1·50	1·50
Y1758	60p. dull blue-grey	2·50	2·50
Y1758a	60p. yellow	2·50	2·50
Y1760	90p. bright blue	2·25	2·25
Y1800	£1.50 red	4·50	2·00
Y1801	£2 dull blue	6·00	2·25
Y1802	£3 dull violet	9·00	3·00
Y1803	£5 brown	15·50	5·00

For stamps in this design but with face values expressed as 2nd, 1st or E see Nos. 1447 (1979) and 1668/71 (1989).

374 Servicemen and Nurse of 1921

1971. British Anniversaries Events described on stamps. Multicoloured.

887	3p. Type **374**	25	25
888	7½p. Roman centurion	50	50
889	9p. Rugby football, 1871	50	50

DESIGNS AND ANNIVERSARIES: 5p. Thomas Gray (death bicentenary); 7½p. Sir Walter Scott (birth bicentenary).

377 Physical Sciences Building, University College of Wales, Aberystwyth

1971. British Architecture. Modern University Buildings.

890	**377**	3p. multicoloured	10	10
891	-	5p. multicoloured	25	20
892	-	7½p. ochre, black and brown	45	55
893	-	9p. multicoloured	75	80

DESIGNS: 5p. Faraday Building, Southampton University; 7½p. Engineering Department, Leicester University; 9p. Hexagon Restaurant, Essex University.

381 "Dream of the Wise Men"

1971. Christmas. Multicoloured.

894	2½p. Type **381**	10	10
895	3p. "Adoration of the Magi"	10	10
896	7½p. "Ride of the Magi"	55	75

384 Sir James Clark Ross

1972. British Polar Explorers. Multicoloured.

897	3p. Type **384**	10	10
898	5p. Sir Martin Frobisher	15	15
899	7½p. Henry Hudson	45	50
900	9p. Capt. Robert Scott	70	85

See also Nos. 923/7.

368 "A Mountain Road" (T. P. Flanagan)

1971. "Ulster '71" Festival. Paintings. Mult.

881	3p. Type **368**	25	25
882	7½p. "Deer's Meadow" (Tom Carr)	50	50
883	9p. "Slieve na brock" (Colin Middleton)	50	50

371 John Keats (150th Death Anniv)

1971. Literary Anniversaries.

884	**371**	3p. black, gold and blue	25	10
885	-	5p. black, gold and green	45	50
886	-	7½p. black, gold and brown	45	45

388 Statuette of Tutankhamun

1972. General Anniversaries. Multicoloured.

901	3p. Type **388**	25	25
902	7½p. 19th-century Coastguard	50	50
903	9p. Ralph Vaughan Williams (composer) and score	50	50

ANNIVERSARIES: 3p. 50th anniversary of discovery of Tutankhamun's tomb; 7½p. 150th anniversary of Formation of H.M. Coastguard: 9p. Birth centenary.

391 St. Andrew's Greensted-juxta-Ongar, Essex

1972. British Architecture. Village Churches. Multicoloured.

904	3p. Type **391**	10	10
905	4p. All Saints, Earls Barton, Northants	10	20

906		5p. St. Andrew's, Letheringsett, Norfolk	15	20
907		7½p. St. Andrew's, Helpringham, Lincs	50	75
908		9p. St. Mary the Virgin, Huish Episcopi, Somerset	50	80

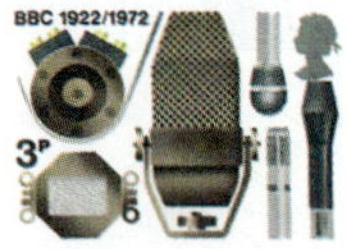

396 Microphones, 1924–69

1972. Broadcasting Anniversaries Multicoloured.

909		3p. Type **396**	10	10
910		5p. Horn loudspeaker	10	20
911		7½p. T.V. camera, 1972	45	50
912		9p. Oscillator and spark transmitter, 1897	50	50

ANNIVERSARIES: Nos. 909/11, 50th anniversary of daily broadcasting by the B.B.C.; No. 912, 75th anniversary of Marconi and Kemp's radio experiments.

400 Angel holding Trumpet

1972. Christmas. Multicoloured.

913		2½p. Type **400**	10	10
914		3p. Angel playing lute	10	10
915		7½p. Angel playing harp	50	45

403 Queen Elizabeth and Duke of Edinburgh

1972. Royal Silver Wedding.

916	**403**	3p. black, blue and silver	25	25
917	**403**	20p. black, purple & silver	1·00	1·00

404 "Europe"

1973. Britain's Entry into European Communities.

919	**404**	3p. multicoloured	25	25
920	**404**	5p. mult (blue jigsaw)	25	50
921	**404**	5p. mult (green jigsaw)	25	50

405 Oak Tree

1973. Tree Planting Year. British Trees (1st issue).

922	**405**	9p. multicoloured	35	40

See also No. 949.

1973. British Explorers. As T 384. Mult.

923		3p. David Livingstone	40	25
924		3p. H. M. Stanley	40	25
925		5p. Sir Francis Drake	40	50
926		7½p. Sir Walter Raleigh	40	50
927		9p. Charles Sturt	40	75

411 W. G. Grace

1973. County Cricket 1873–1973. Designs as T 411 showing caricatures of W. G. Grace by Harry Furniss.

928	**411**	3p. black, brown and gold	25	25
929	-	7½p. black, green and gold	75	75
930	-	9p. black, blue and gold	1·25	1·00

414 "Self-portrait" (Reynolds)

1973. British Paintings. 250th Birth Anniv of Sir Joshua Reynolds, and 150th Death Anniv of Sir Henry Raeburn. Multicoloured.

931		3p. Type **414**	10	10
932		5p. "Self-portrait" (Raeburn)	30	30
933		7½p. "Nelly O' Brien" (Reynolds)	30	30
934		9p. "Rev. R. Walker (The Skater)" (Raeburn)	60	60

418 Court Masque Costumes

1973. 400th Birth Anniv of Inigo Jones (architect and designer). Multicoloured.

935		3p. Type **418**	10	25
936		3p. St. Paul's Church, Covent Garden	10	25
937		5p. Prince's Lodging, Newmarket	35	50
938		5p. Court Masque stage scene	35	50

422 Palace of Westminster, seen from Whitehall

1973. 19th Commonwealth Parliamentary Conference.

939	**422**	8p. black, grey and stone	45	50
940	-	10p. gold and black	45	40

DESIGN: 10p. Palace of Westminster, seen from Millbank.

424 Princess Anne and Capt. Mark Phillips

1973. Royal Wedding.

941	**424**	3½p. violet and silver	25	25
942	**424**	20p. brown and silver	1·00	75

425 "Good King Wenceslas looked out."

1973. Christmas. Multicoloured.

943		3p. Type **425**	20	25
944		3p. King and page at window	20	25
945		3p. Leaving the palace	20	25
946		3p. Struggling against the wind	20	25
947		3p. Delivering gifts	20	25
948		3½p. King, page and peasant	20	25

431 Horse Chestnut

1974. British Trees (2nd issue).

949	**431**	10p. multicoloured	40	35

432 First Motor Fire-engine, 1904

1974. Bicentenary of Fire Prevention (Metropolis) Act. Multicoloured.

950		3½p. Type **432**	25	10
951		5½p. Prize-winning fire-engine, 1863	25	30
952		8p. First steam fire-engine, 1830	50	50
953		10p. Fire-engine. 1766	50	50

436 P&O. Packet "*Peninsular*", 1888

1974. Cent of Universal Postal Union. Mult.

954		3½p. Type **436**	25	10
955		5½p. Farman H.F.III biplane, 1911	25	30
956		8p. Airmail—blue van and postbox, 1930	25	35
957		10p. Imperial Airways Short S.21 flying boat "*Maia*", 1937	50	40

440 Robert the Bruce

1974. Medieval Warriors. Multicoloured.

958		4½p. Type **440**	25	10
959		5½p. Owain Glyndwr	25	35
960		8p. Henry the Fifth	50	50
961		10p. The Black Prince	50	50

444 Churchill in Royal Yacht Squadron Uniform

1974. Birth Centenary of Sir Winston Churchill.

962	**444**	4½p. silver, blue and green	20	15
963	-	5½p. silver, brown and grey	35	35
964	-	8p. silver, red and pink	60	50
965	-	10p. silver, brown and stone	60	50

DESIGNS: 5½p. Prime Minister, 1940; 8p. Secretary for War and Air, 1919; 10p. War correspondent, South Africa, 1899.

448 "Adoration of the Magi" (York Minster, *c.* 1355)

1974. Christmas. Church Roof Bosses. Multicoloured.

966		3½p. Type **448**	10	10
967		4½p. "The Nativity" (St. Helen's Church, Norwich, *c.* 1480)	10	10
968		8p. "Virgin and Child" (Ottery St. Mary Church, *c.* 1350)	25	50
969		10p. "Virgin and Child" (Worcester Cathedral, *c.* 1224)	50	50

452 Invalid in Wheelchair

1975. Health and Handicap Funds.

970	**452**	4½p.+1½p. blue and azure	25	25

453 "Peace–Burial at Sea"

1975. Birth Bicentenary of J. M. W. Turner (painter). Multicoloured.

971		4½p. Type **453**	25	25
972		5½p. "Snowstorm–Steamer off a Harbour's Mouth"	25	25
973		8p. "The Arsenal, Venice"	25	50
974		10p. "St. Laurent"	50	50

457 Charlotte Square, Edinburgh

1975. European Architectural Heritage Year. Multicoloured.

975		7p. Type **457**	15	15
976		7p. The Rows, Chester	15	15
977		8p. Royal Observatory, Greenwich	40	30
978		10p. St. George's Chapel, Windsor	40	30
979		12p. National Theatre, London	40	35

462 Sailing Dinghies

1975. Sailing. Multicoloured.

980		7p. Type **462**	25	20
981		8p. Racing keel yachts	35	40
982		10p. Cruising yachts	35	45
983		12p. Multihulls	50	50

466 Stephenson's "Locomotion", 1825

1975. 150th Anniv of Public Railways. Mult.

984		7p. Type **466**	25	25
985		8p. "*Abbotsford*", 1876	50	50
986		10p. "*Caerphilly Castle*", 1923	50	50
987		12p. High Speed Train, 1975	40	50

470 Palace of Westminster

1975. 62nd Inter-Parliamentary Union Conference.

988	**470**	12p. multicoloured	50	40

471 Emma and Mr. Woodhouse ("*Emma*")

1975. Birth Bicentenary of Jane Austen (novelist). Multicoloured.

989		8½p. Type **471**	25	20
990		10p. Catherine Morland ("*Northanger Abbey*")	45	45
991		11p. Mr. Darcy ("*Pride and Prejudice*")	45	45
992		13p. Mary and Henry Crawford ("*Mansfield Park*")	50	50

475 Angels with Harp and Lute

1975. Christmas. Multicoloured.

993	6½p. Type **475**	25	25
994	8½p. Angel with mandolin	25	40
995	11p. Angel with horn	50	45
996	13p. Angel with trumpet	50	45

479 Housewife

1976. Centenary of Telephone. Multicoloured.

997	8½p. Type **479**	25	20
998	10p. Policeman	40	40
999	11p. District nurse	50	50
1000	13p. Industrialist	60	60

483 Hewing Coal (Thomas Hepburn)

1976. Social Reformers. Multicoloured.

1001	8½p. Type **483**	25	20
1002	10p. Machinery (Robert Owen)	40	40
1003	11p. Chimney cleaning (Lord Shaftesbury)	50	50
1004	13p. Hands clutching prison bars (Elizabeth Fry)	60	60

487 Benjamin Franklin (bust by Jean-Jacques Caffieri)

1976. Bicentenary of American Revolution.

1005	**487**	11p. multicoloured	50	50

488 "Elizabeth of Glamis"

1976. Centenary of Royal National Rose Society. Multicoloured.

1006	8½p. Type **488**	15	10
1007	10p. "Grandpa Dickson"	40	40
1008	11p. "*Rosa Mundi*"	50	50
1009	13p. "Sweet Briar"	65	65

492 Archdruid

1976. British Cultural Traditions. Multicoloured.

1010	8½p. Type **492**	25	20
1011	10p. Morris dancing	40	40
1012	11p. Scots piper	45	45
1013	13p. Welsh harpist	60	60

The 8½p. and 13p. commemorate the 800th Anniv of the Royal National Eisteddfod.

496 Woodcut from *"The Canterbury Tales"*

1976. 500th Anniv of British Printing. Multicoloured.

1014	8½p. Type **496**	25	20
1015	10p. Extract from *"The Tretyse of Love"*	40	40
1016	11p. Woodcut from *"The Game and Playe of Chesse"* by William Caxton	45	45
1017	13p. Early printing press	60	60

500 Virgin and Child

1976. Christmas. English Medieval Embroidery. Multicoloured.

1018	6½p. Type **500**	25	25
1019	8½p. Angel with crown	35	25
1020	11p. Angel appearing to Shepherds	40	45
1021	13p. The Three Kings	45	50

504 Lawn Tennis

1977. Racket Sports. Multicoloured.

1022	8½p. Type **504**	25	20
1023	10p. Table tennis	40	40
1024	11p. Squash	45	40
1025	13p. Badminton	45	50

508

1977

1026	**508**	£1 green and olive	3·00	25
1026b	**508**	£1.30 brown and blue	5·50	6·00
1026c	**508**	£1.33 mauve and black	7·50	7·00
1026d	**508**	£1.41 brown and blue	8·50	8·50
1026e	**508**	£1.50 olive and black	6·00	5·00
1026f	**508**	£1.60 brown and blue	6·50	7·00
1027	**508**	£2 green and brown	9·00	50
1028	**508**	£5 pink and blue	22·00	3·00

509 Steroids—Conformational Analysis

1977. Centenary of Royal Insitute of Chemistry. Multicoloured.

1029	8½p. Type **509**	25	20
1030	10p. Vitamin C—synthesis	45	45
1031	11p. Starch—chromatography	45	45
1032	13p. Salt—crystallography	45	45

513

1977. Silver Jubilee. Multicoloured.

1033	8½p. Type **513**	25	25
1034	9p. Type **513**	35	35
1035	10p. "Leaf" initials	25	25
1036	11p. "Star" initials	50	50
1037	13p. "Oak" initials	50	50

517 "Gathering of Nations"

1977. Commonwealth Heads of Government Meeting, London.

1038	**517**	13p. multicoloured	50	50

518 West European Hedgehog

1977. British Wildlife. Multicoloured.

1039	9p. Type **518**	25	20
1040	9p. Brown hare	25	20
1041	9p. Eurasian red squirrel	25	20
1042	9p. European otter	25	20
1043	9p. Eurasian badger	25	20

523 "Three French Hens, Two Turtle Doves and a Partridge in a Pear Tree"

1977. Christmas. "The Twelve Days of Christmas". Multicoloured.

1044	7p. Type **523**	20	15
1045	7p. "Six Geese a-laying, Five Gold Rings, Four Colly Birds"	20	15
1046	7p. "Eight Maids a-milking, Seven Swans a-Swimming"	20	15
1047	7p. "Ten Pipers piping, Nine Drummers drumming"	20	15
1048	7p. "Twelve Lords a-leaping, Eleven Ladies dancing"	20	15
1049	9p. "A Partridge in a Pear Tree"	35	30

529 Oil–North Sea Production Platform

1978. Energy Resources. Multicoloured.

1050	9p. Type **529**	25	25
1051	10½p. Coal–modern pithead	25	25
1052	11p. Natural gas–flame rising from sea	50	50
1053	13p. Electricity–nuclear power station and uranium atom	50	50

533 The Tower of London

1978. British Architecture. Historic Buildings. Multicoloured.

1054	9p. Type **533**	25	20
1055	10½p. Holyrood House	25	40
1056	11p. Caernarvon Castle	60	40
1057	13p. Hampton Court Palace	60	40
MS1058	121×89 mm. Nos. 1054/7	1·50	1·75

537 State Coach

1978. 25th Anniv of Queen's Coronation.

1059	**537**	9p. gold and blue	35	25
1060	-	10½p. gold and red	45	45
1061	-	11p. gold and green	45	45
1062	-	13p. gold and violet	50	50

DESIGNS: 10½p. St. Edward's Crown; 11p. The Sovereign's Orb; 13p. Imperial State Crown.

541 Shire Horse

1978. Horses. Multicoloured.

1063	9p. Type **541**	20	10
1064	10½p. Shetland pony	35	40
1065	11p. Welsh pony	35	45
1066	13p. Thoroughbred	45	50

545 "Pennyfarthing" and 1884 Safety Bicycle

1978. Centenaries of Cyclists' Touring Club and British Cycling Federation. Multicoloured.

1067	9p. Type **545**	25	20
1068	10½p. 1920 Touring bicycles	35	40
1069	11p. Modern small-wheeled bicycles	40	40
1070	13p. 1978 Road-racers	50	50

549 Singing Carols round the Christmas Tree

1978. Christmas. Carol-singing. Mult.

1071	7p. Type **549**	25	25
1072	9p. The Waits	25	25
1073	11p. 18th-century carol singers	50	50
1074	13p. "The Boar's Head Carol"	50	50

553 Old English Sheepdog

1979. Dogs. Multicoloured.

1075	9p. Type **553**	25	20
1076	10½p. Welsh springer spaniel	40	40
1077	11p. West Highland terrier	40	40
1078	13p. Irish setter	40	50

557 Primrose

1979. Spring Wild Flowers. Multicoloured.

1079	9p. Type **557**	25	20
1080	10½p. Daffodil	25	45
1081	11p. Bluebell	50	45
1082	13p. Snowdrop	50	40

561 Hands placing National Flags into Ballot Boxes

1979. First Direct Elections to European Assembly.

1083	**561**	9p. multicoloured	25	20
1084	-	10½p. multicoloured	35	35
1085	-	11p. multicoloured	40	40
1086	-	13p. multicoloured	45	40

DESIGNS: Nos. 1084/6 differ from Type **561** in the position of the hands and flags.

565 "Saddling 'Mahmoud' for the Derby, 1936" (Sir Alfred Munnings)

1979. Horse-racing Paintings. Bicentenary of the Derby (9p). Multicoloured.

1087	9p. Type **565**	25	25
1088	10½p. "The Liverpool Great National Steeple Chase, 1839" (aquatint, F. C. Turner)	25	25
1089	11p. "The First Spring Meeting, Newmarket, 1793" (J. N. Sartorius)	50	50
1090	13p. "Racing at Dorsett Ferry, Windsor, 1684" (Francis Barlow)	50	50

569 *"The Tale of Peter Rabbit"* (Beatrix Potter)

1979. International Year of the Child. Multicoloured.

1091	9p. Type **569**	30	25
1092	10½p. *"The Wind in the Willows"* (Kenneth Grahame)	35	35
1093	11p. *"Winnie-the-Pooh"* (A. A. Milne)	40	40
1094	13p. *"Alice's Adventures in Wonderland"* (Lewis Carroll)	60	60

573 Sir Rowland Hill

1979. Death Cent of Sir Rowland Hill. Mult.

1095	10p. Type **573**	25	20
1096	11½p. Postman, c. 1839	25	35
1097	13p. London postman, c. 1839	50	45
1098	15p. Woman and young girl with letters, 1840	75	50
MS1099	82×121 mm. Nos. 1095/8	1·25	1·50

577 Policeman on the Beat

1979. 150th Anniv of Metropolitan Police. Mult.

1100	10p. Type **577**	30	20
1101	11½p. Policeman directing traffic	35	35
1102	13p. Mounted policewoman	40	55
1103	15p. River patrol boat	60	55

581 The Three Kings

1979. Christmas. Multicoloured.

1104	8p. Type **581**	25	20
1105	10p. Angel appearing to the Shepherds	25	25
1106	11½p. The Nativity	25	35
1107	13p. Mary and Joseph travelling to Bethlehem	50	50
1108	15p. The Annunciation	50	50

586 River Kingfisher ("Kingfisher")

1980. Cent of Wild Bird Protection Act. Mult.

1109	10p. Type **586**	20	10
1110	11½p. White-throated dipper ("Dipper")	40	35
1111	13p. Moorhen	50	55
1112	15p. Yellow wagtails	50	55

590 *"Rocket"* approaching Moorish Arch, Liverpool

1980. 150th Anniv of Liverpool and Manchester Railway. Multicoloured.

1113	12p. Type **590**	20	15
1114	12p. First and Second Class carriages passing through Olive Mount cutting	20	15
1115	12p. Third Class carriage and sheep truck crossing Chat Moss	20	15
1116	12p. Horsebox and carriage truck near Bridgewater Canal	20	15
1117	12p. Truck and mail coach at Manchester	20	15

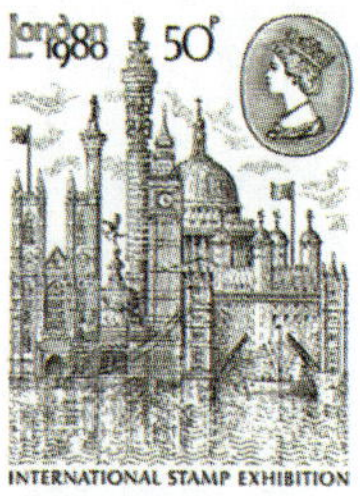

595 Montage of London Buildings

1980. "London 1980" International Stamp Exn.

1118	**595** 50p. brown	1·50	1·50
MS1119	90×123 mm. No. 1118 (sold at 75p.)	1·50	1·75

596 Buckingham Palace

1980. London Landmarks. Multicoloured.

1120	10½p. Type **596**	25	10
1121	12p. The Albert Memorial	25	15
1122	13½p. Royal Opera House	40	50
1123	15p. Hampton Court	50	75
1124	17½p. Kensington Palace	75	75

601 Charlotte Bronte (*"Jane Eyre"*)

1980. Famous Authoresses. Multicoloured.

1125	12p. Type **601**	35	20
1126	13½p. George Eliot (*"The Mill on the Floss"*)	40	45
1127	15p. Emily Bronte (*"Wuthering Heights"*)	40	45
1128	17½p. Elizabeth Gaskell (*"North and South"*)	50	50

605 Queen Elizabeth the Queen Mother

1980. 80th Birthday of The Queen Mother.

1129	**605** 12p. multicoloured	75	75

606 Sir Henry Wood

1980. British Conductors. Multicoloured.

1130	12p. Type **606**	30	10
1131	13½p. Sir Thomas Beecham	45	40
1132	15p. Sir Malcolm Sargent	50	55
1133	17½p. Sir John Barbirolli	50	55

610 Running

1980. Sport Centenaries. Multicoloured.

1134	12p. Type **610**	25	20
1135	13½p. Rugby	50	50
1136	15p. Boxing	50	45
1137	17½p. Cricket	50	50

CENTENARIES: 12p. Amateur Athletics Association; 13½p. Welsh Rugby Union; 15p. Amateur Boxing Association; 17½p. First England–Australia Test Match.

614 Christmas Tree

1980. Christmas. Multicoloured.

1138	10p. Type **614**	20	10
1139	12p. Candles	20	20
1140	13½p. Mistletoe and apples	40	40
1141	15p. Crown, chains and bell	55	50
1142	17½p. Holly wreath	55	50

619 St. Valentine's Day

1981. Folklore. Multicoloured.

1143	14p. Type **619**	25	25
1144	18p. Morris dancers	50	50
1145	22p. Lammastide	75	80
1146	25p. Medieval mummers	1·00	1·10

623 Blind Man with Guide Dog

1981. Int Year of Disabled Persons. Mult.

1147	14p. Type **623**	50	25
1148	18p. Hands spelling "Deaf" in sign language	50	50
1149	22p. Disabled man in wheelchair	75	85
1150	25p. Disabled artist painting with foot	1·00	1·00

627 *"Aglais urticae"*

1981. Butterflies. Multicoloured.

1151	14p. Type **627**	25	20
1152	18p. *"Maculinea arion"*	75	70
1153	22p. *"Inachis io"*	70	85
1154	25p. *"Carterocephalus palaemon"*	75	85

631 Glenfinnan, Scotland

1981. 50th Anniv of National Trust for Scotland. British Landscapes. Multicoloured.

1155	14p. Type **631**	15	25
1156	18p. Derwentwater, England	45	50
1157	20p. Stackpole Head, Wales	70	75
1158	22p. Giant's Causeway, Northern Ireland	75	1·00
1159	25p. St. Kilda, Scotland	90	1·00

636 Prince Charles and Lady Diana Spencer

1981. Royal Wedding.

1160	**636** 14p. multicoloured	75	25
1161	**636** 25p. multicoloured	1·50	1·50

637 "Expeditions"

1981. 25th Anniv of Duke of Edinburgh Award Scheme. Multicoloured.

1162	14p. Type **637**	25	20
1163	18p. "Skills"	45	50
1164	22p. "Service"	80	80
1165	25p. "Recreation"	90	1·00

641 Cockle-dredging from *"Linsey II"*

1981. Fishing Industry. Multicoloured.

1166	14p. Type **641**	25	25
1167	18p. Hauling in trawl net	50	50
1168	22p. Lobster potting	85	85
1169	25p. Hoisting seine net	85	85

645 Father Christmas

1981. Christmas. Children's Pictures. Mult.

1170	11½p. Type **645**	25	20
1171	14p. Jesus Christ	35	20
1172	18p. Flying angel	50	60
1173	22p. Joseph and Mary arriving at Bethlehem	75	75
1174	25p. Three Kings approaching Bethlehem	85	85

650 Charles Darwin and Giant Tortoises

1982. Death Cent of Charles Darwin. Mult.

1175	15½p. Type **650**	50	20
1176	19½p. Darwin and Marine iguanas	50	60
1177	26p. Darwin and cactus ground finch and large ground finch	75	85
1178	29p. Darwin and prehistoric skulls	95	90

654 Boys' Brigade

1982. Youth Organizations. Multicoloured.

1179	15½p. Type **654**	25	15
1180	19½p. Girls' Brigade	50	50
1181	26p. Boy Scout Movement	85	85
1182	29p. Girl Guide Movement	1·00	1·10

658 Ballerina

1982. Europa. British Theatre. Multicoloured.

1183	15½p. Type **658**	25	15
1184	19½p. Harlequin	50	50
1185	26p. Hamlet	1·25	1·00
1186	29p. Opera singer	1·50	1·00

662 Henry VIII and "*Mary Rose*"

1982. Maritime Heritage. Multicoloured.

1187	15½p. Type **662**	35	25
1188	19½p. Admiral Blake and "*Triumph*"	50	50
1189	24p. Lord Nelson and H.M.S. "*Victory*"	75	85
1190	26p. Lord Fisher and H.M.S. "*Dreadnought*"	75	85
1191	29p. Viscount Cunningham and H.M.S. "*Warspite*"	1·00	1·00

667 "Strawberry Thief" (William Morris)

1982. British Textiles. Multicoloured.

1192	15½p. Type **667**	25	25
1193	19½p. Untitled (Steiner and Co.)	75	75
1194	26p. "Cherry Orchard" (Paul Nash)	75	1·00
1195	29p. "Chevron" (Andrew Foster)	1·00	1·25

671x Development of Communications (image scaled to 68% of original size)

1982. Information Technology. Multicoloured.

1196	15½p. Type **671**	50	25
1197	26p. Modern technological aids	75	1·00

673 Austin "Seven" and "Metro"

1982. British Motor Industry. Multicoloured.

1198	15½p. Type **673**	50	25
1199	19½p. Ford "Model T" and "Escort"	75	75
1200	26p. Jaguar "SS1" and "XJ6"	75	75
1201	29p. Rolls-Royce "Silver Ghost" and "Silver Spirit"	1·00	1·00

677 "While Shepherds Watched"

1982. Christmas. Carols. Multicoloured.

1202	12½p. Type **677**	25	20
1203	15½p. "The Holly and the Ivy"	50	20
1204	19½p. "I saw Three Ships"	65	75
1205	26p. "We Three Kings"	75	90
1206	29p. "Good King Wenceslas"	1·00	1·00

682 Atlantic Salmon

1983. British River Fish. Multicoloured.

1207	15½p. Type **682**	30	25
1208	19½p. Northern pike	60	60
1209	26p. Brown trout	75	85
1210	29p. Eurasian perch	1·00	1·10

686 Tropical Island

1983. Commonwealth Day. Geographical Regions. Multicoloured.

1211	15½p. Type **686**	40	25
1212	19½p. Desert	75	75
1213	26p. Temperate farmland	75	75
1214	29p. Mountain range	1·00	1·00

690 Humber Bridge

1983. Europa. Engineering Achievements. Multicoloured.

1215	16p. Type **690**	50	25
1216	20½p. Thames Flood Barrier	1·00	1·00
1217	28p. "*Iolair*" (oilfield emergency support vessel)	1·00	1·00

693 Musketeer and Pikeman, The Royal Scots (1633)

1983. British Army Uniforms. Multicoloured.

1218	16p. Type **693**	50	10
1219	20½p. Fusilier and Ensign, The Royal Welch Fusiliers (mid-18th century)	50	60
1220	26p. Riflemen, 95th Rifles (The Royal Green Jackets) (1805)	75	90
1221	28p. Sergeant (khaki service uniform) and Guardsman (full dress), The Irish Guards (1900)	75	90
1222	31p. Paratroopers, The Parachute Regiment (1983)	75	85

698 20th-century Garden, Sissinghurst

1983. British Gardens. Multicoloured.

1223	16p. Type **698**	50	10
1224	20½p. 19th-century garden, Biddulph Grange	50	55
1225	28p. 18th-century garden, Blenheim	75	1·00
1226	31p. 17th-century garden, Pitmedden	1·00	1·00

702 Merry-go-round

1983. British Fairs. Multicoloured.

1227	16p. Type **702**	35	25
1228	20½p. Big wheel, helter-skelter and performing animals	75	75
1229	28p. Side shows	75	1·00
1230	31p. Early produce fair	1·00	1·00

706 "Christmas Post" (pillar-box)

1983. Christmas. Multicoloured.

1231	12½p. Type **706**	25	25
1232	16p. "The Three Kings" (chimney pots)	50	25
1233	20½p. "World at Peace" (dove and blackbird)	75	1·00
1234	28p. "Light of Christmas" (street lamp)	75	1·00
1235	31p. "Christmas Dove" (hedge sculpture)	1·25	1·25

711 Arms of College of Arms

1984. 500th Anniv of College of Arms. Mult.

1236	16p. Type **711**	50	15
1237	20½p. Arms of King Richard III (founder)	50	65
1238	28p. Arms of Earl Marshal of England	1·00	1·10
1239	31p. Arms of City of London	1·25	1·25

715 Highland Cow

1984. Cattle. Multicoloured.

1240	16p. Type **715**	35	15
1241	20½p. Chillingham wild bull	60	60
1242	26p. Hereford bull	80	80
1243	28p. Welsh black bull	90	90
1244	31p. Irish moiled cow	1·00	1·20

720 Garden Festival Hall, Liverpool

1984. Urban Renewal. Multicoloured.

1245	16p. Type **720**	30	10
1246	20½p. Milburngate Centre, Durham	50	60
1247	28p. Bush House, Bristol	1·25	1·25
1248	31p. Commercial Street development, Perth	1·25	1·25

725 Abduction of Europa

1984. 25th Anniv of C.E.P.T. (Europa) (Nos. 1249, 1251), and Second Election to European Parliament (others).

1249	-	16p. grey, blue and gold	50	25
1250	**725**	16p. grey, black, and gold	50	25
1251	-	20½p. red, purple and gold	70	40
1252	**725**	20½p. red, pur, blk gold	70	40

DESIGN: Nos. 1249 and 1251, Bridge (C.E.P.T. 25th anniv logo).

726 Lancaster House

1984. London Economic Summit Conference.

1253	**726**	31p. multicoloured	1·25	1·25

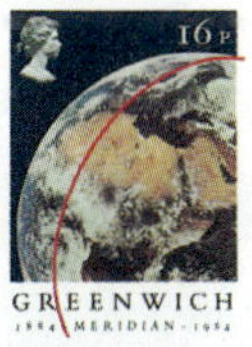

727 View of Earth from "Apollo 11"

1984. Centenary of Greenwich Meridian. Mult.

1254	16p. Type **727**	50	25
1255	20½p. Navigational chart of the English Channel	75	80
1256	28p. Greenwich Observatory	1·00	1·00
1257	31p. Sir George Airey's Transit Telescope	1·00	1·10

731 Bath Mail Coach leaving London, 1784

1984. Bicentenary of First Mail Coach Run, Bath and Bristol to London. Multicoloured.

1258	16p. Type **731**	40	35
1259	16p. Attack on Exeter Mail, 1816	40	35
1260	16p. Norwich Mail in thunderstorm, 1827	40	35
1261	16p. Holyhead and Liverpool Mails leaving London, 1828	40	35
1262	16p. Edinburgh Mail snowbound, 1831	40	35

736 Nigerian Clinic

1984. 50th Anniv of British Council. Mult.

1263	17p. Type **736**	50	25
1264	22p. Violinist and Acropolis, Athens	85	1·00
1265	31p. Building project, Sri Lanka	85	1·00
1266	34p. British Council library, Middle East	1·00	1·00

740 The Holy Family

1984. Christmas. Multicoloured.

1267	13p. Type **740**	25	25
1268	17p. Arrival in Bethlehem	50	50
1269	22p. Shepherd and Lamb	75	75
1270	31p. Virgin and Child	1·00	1·00
1271	34p. Offering of Frankincense	1·00	1·00

745 "Flying Scotsman"

1985. Famous Trains. Multicoloured.

1272	17p. Type **745**	75	25
1273	22p. "Golden Arrow"	75	1·00
1274	29p. "Cheltenham Flyer"	1·00	1·25
1275	31p. "Royal Scot"	1·25	1·50
1276	34p. "Cornish Riviera"	2·50	2·50

750 "*Bombus terrestris*" (bee)

1985. Insects. Multicoloured.

1277	17p. Type **750**	40	10
1278	22p. "*Coccinella septempunctata*" (ladybird)	60	55
1279	29p. "*Decticus verrucivorus*" (bush-cricket)	85	90
1280	31p. "*Lucanus cervus*" (stag beetle)	1·00	1·00
1281	34p. "*Anax imperator*" (dragonfly)	1·00	90

755 "Water Music" (George Frideric Handel)

1985. Europa. European Music Year. British Composers. Multicoloured.

1282	17p. Type **755**	55	10
1283	22p. "The Planets" Suite (Gustav Holst)	75	90
1284	31p. "The First Cuckoo" (Frederick Delius)	1·50	1·25
1285	34p. "Sea Pictures" (Edward Elgar)	1·50	1·25

759 R.N.L.I. Lifeboat and Signal Flags

1985. Safety at Sea. Multicoloured.

1286	17p. Type **759**	40	25
1287	22p. Beachy Head Lighthouse and chart	60	75
1288	31p. "Marecs A" communications satellite and dish aerials	1·00	1·00
1289	34p. Buoys	1·50	1·25

763 Datapost Motorcyclist, City of London

1985. 350 Years of Royal Mail Public Postal Service. Multicoloured.

1290	17p. Type **763**	50	10
1291	22p. Rural postbus	75	70
1292	31p. Parcel delivery in winter	1·00	1·00
1293	34p. Town letter delivery	1·50	1·50

767 King Arthur and Merlin

1985. Arthurian Legends. Multicoloured.

1294	17p. Type **767**	50	25
1295	22p. Lady of the Lake	75	75
1296	31p. Queen Guinevere and Sir Lancelot	1·25	1·25
1297	34p. Sir Galahad	1·25	1·25

771 Peter Sellers (from photo by Bill Brandt)

1985. British Film Year. Multicoloured.

1298	17p. Type **771**	45	25
1299	22p. David Niven (from photo by Cornell Lucas)	60	75
1300	29p. Charlie Chaplin (from photo by Lord Snowdon)	1·00	1·25
1301	31p. Vivien Leigh (from photo by Angus McBean)	1·10	1·50
1302	34p. Alfred Hitchcock (from photo by Howard Coster)	1·40	1·50

776 Principal Boy

1985. Christmas. Pantomime Characters. Mult.

1303	12p. Type **776**	50	15
1304	17p. Genie	50	25
1305	22p. Dame	75	1·10
1306	31p. Good fairy	1·25	1·40
1307	34p. Pantomime cat	1·25	1·40

781 Light Bulb and North Sea Oil Drilling Rig (Energy)

1986. Industry Year. Multicoloured.

1308	17p. Type **781**	75	25
1309	22p. Thermometer and pharmaceutical laboratory (Health)	50	75
1310	31p. Garden hoe and steel-works (Steel)	1·25	1·40
1311	34p. Loaf of bread and corn-field (Agriculture)	1·25	1·40

785 Dr. Edmond Halley as Comet

1986. Appearance of Halley's Comet. Multicoloured.

1312	17p. Type **785**	50	25
1313	22p. "*Giotto*" spacecraft approaching comet	75	75
1314	31p. "Twice in a lifetime"	1·25	1·25
1315	34p. Comet orbiting sun and planets	1·25	1·40

789 Queen Elizabeth II in 1928, 1942 and 1952

1986. 60th Birthday of Queen Elizabeth II. Multicoloured.

1316	17p. Type **789**	60	25
1317	17p. Queen Elizabeth II in 1958, 1973 and 1982	60	25
1318	34p. Type **789**	70	50
1319	34p. As No. 1317	70	50

791 Barn Owl

1986. Europa. Nature Conservation. Endangered Species. Multicoloured.

1320	17p. Type **791**	40	10
1321	22p. Pine marten	80	1·00
1322	31p. Wild cat	1·50	1·25
1323	34p. Natterjack toad	1·65	1·40

795 Peasants working in Fields

1986. 900th Anniv of Domesday Book. Mult.

1324	17p. Type **795**	40	10
1325	22p. Freemen working at town trades	85	85
1326	31p. Knight and retainers	1·25	1·40
1327	34p. Lord at banquet	1·25	1·40

799 Athletics

1986. 13th Commonwealth Games. Edinburgh, and World Hockey Cup for Men, London. Multicoloured.

1328	17p. Type **799**	40	25
1329	22p. Rowing	55	75
1330	29p. Weightlifting	75	1·00
1331	31p. Rifle shooting	1·50	1·75
1332	34p. Hockey	1·75	1·75

804 Prince Andrew and Miss Sarah Ferguson (from photo by Gene Nocon)

1986. Royal Wedding.

1333	**804**	12p. multicoloured	50	30
1334	-	17p. multicoloured	1·00	1·25

DESIGN: 17p. As Type **804** but with naval motif at foot.

806 Stylized Cross on Ballot Paper

1986. 32nd Commonwealth Parliamentary Association Conference.

1335	**806**	34p. multicoloured	1·25	1·25

807 Lord Dowding and Hawker Hurricane Mk I

1986. History of the Royal Air Force. Multicoloured.

1336	17p. Type **807**	50	10
1337	22p. Lord Tedder and Hawker Typhoon IB	75	95
1338	29p. Lord Trenchard and de Havilland DH9A	1·25	1·25
1339	31p. Sir Arthur Harris and Avro Type 683 Lancaster	1·75	1·60
1340	34p. Lord Portal and de Havilland DH98 Mosquito	1·75	1·90

Nos. 1336/40 were issued to celebrate 50th anniv of the first R.A.F. Commands.

812 The Glastonbury Thorn

1986. Christmas. Folk Customs. Multicoloured.

1341	12p. Type **812**	50	50
1342	13p. Type **812**	25	15
1343	18p. The Tanad Valley Plygain	50	15
1344	22p. The Hebrides Tribute	1·00	1·00
1345	31p. The Dewsbury Church Knell	1·25	1·00
1346	34p. The Hereford Boy Bishop	1·25	1·10

817 North American Blanket Flower

1987. Flower Photographs by Alfred Lammer. Multicoloured.

1347	18p. Type **817**	40	10
1348	22p. Globe thistle	70	85
1349	31p. "Echeveria"	1·10	1·25
1350	34p. Autumn crocus	1·10	1·25

821 "*Principia Mathematica*"

1987. 300th Anniv of "Principia Mathematica" by Sir Isaac Newton. Multicoloured.

1351	18p. Type **821**	50	15
1352	22p. "*Motion of Bodies in Ellipses*"	75	75
1353	31p. "*Optick Treatise*"	1·25	1·50
1354	34p. "*The System of the World*"	1·25	1·25

825 Willis Faber Dumas Building, Ipswich

1987. Europa. British Architects in Europe.

1355	18p. Type **825**	50	15
1356	22p. Pompidou Centre, Paris	75	75
1357	31p. Staatsgalerie, Stuttgart	1·25	1·25
1358	34p. European Investment Bank, Luxembourg	1·75	1·25

829 Brigade Members with Ashford Litter, 1887

1987. Centenary of St. John Ambulance Brigade. Multicoloured.

1359	18p. Type **829**	40	25
1360	22p. Bandaging blitz victim, 1940	60	75
1361	31p. Volunteer with fainting girl, 1965	1·25	1·25
1362	34p. Transport of transplant organ by Air Wing, 1987	1·25	1·25

833 Arms of the Lord Lyon, King of Arms

1987. 300th Anniv of Revival of Order of the Thistle. Multicoloured.

1363	18p. Type **833**	50	10
1364	22p. Scottish heraldic banner of Prince Charles	75	90
1365	31p. Arms of Royal Scottish Academy of Painting, Sculpture and Architecture	1·40	1·40
1366	34p. Arms of Royal Society of Edinburgh	1·50	1·40

837 Crystal Palace, "Monarch of the Glen" (Landseer) and Grace Darling

1987. 150th Anniv of Queen Victoria's Accession. Multicoloured.

1367	18p. Type **837**	50	10
1368	22p. "*Great Eastern*", "*Beeton's Book of Household Management*" and Prince Albert	80	75
1369	31p. Albert Memorial, ballot box and Disraeli	1·25	1·50
1370	34p. Diamond Jubilee emblem, newspaper placard for Relief of Mafeking and morse key	1·35	1·60

841 Pot by Bernard Leach

1987. Studio Pottery. Multicoloured.

1371	18p. Type **841**	50	25
1372	26p. Pot by Elizabeth Fritsch	70	75
1373	31p. Pot by Lucie Rie	1·25	1·25
1374	34p. Pot by Hans Coper	1·40	1·50

845 Decorating the Christmas Tree

1987. Christmas. Multicoloured.

1375	13p. Type **845**	30	10
1376	18p. Waiting for Father Christmas	40	20
1377	26p. Sleeping child and Father Christmas in sleigh	80	1·00
1378	31p. Child reading	1·10	1·25
1379	34p. Child playing recorder and snowman	1·25	1·50

850 Short-spined Seascorpion ("Bull-rout") (Jonathan Couch)

1988. Bicentenary of Linnean Society. Archive Illustrations. Multicoloured.

1380	18p. Type **850**	55	10
1381	26p. Yellow Waterlily (Major Joshua Swatkin)	85	1·00
1382	31p. Tundra swan ("Bewick's Swan") (Edward Lear)	1·10	1·25
1383	34p. "*Morchella esculenta*" (James Sowerby)	1·25	1·40

854 Revd. William Morgan (Bible translator, 1588)

1988. 400th Anniversary of Welsh Bible. Mult.

1384	18p. Type **854**	40	10
1385	26p. William Salesbury (New Testament translator, 1567)	70	95
1386	31p. Bishop Richard Davies (New Testament translator, 1567)	1·25	1·25
1387	34p. Bishop Richard Parry (editor of Revised Welsh Bible, 1620)	1·40	1·25

858 Gymnastics (Centenary of British Amateur Gymnastics Association)

1988. Sports Organizations. Multicoloured.

1388	18p. Type **858**	40	15
1389	26p. Downhill skiing (Ski Club of Great Britain)	70	80
1390	31p. Tennis (centenary of Lawn Tennis Association)	1·10	1·25
1391	34p. Football (centenary of Football League)	1·25	1·25

862 "*Mallard*" and Mailbags on Pick-up Arms

1988. Europa. Transport and Mail Services in 1930s. Multicoloured.

1392	18p. Type **862**	50	15
1393	26p. Loading transatlantic mail on liner "*Queen Elizabeth*"	1·00	1·00
1394	31p. Glasgow tram No. 1173 and pillar box	1·25	1·25
1395	34p. Imperial Airways Handley Page H.P.45 G-AAXD "*Horatius*" and airmail van	1·60	1·50

866 Early Settler and Sailing Clipper

1988. Bicentenary of Australian Settlement. Mult.

1396	18p. Type **866**	30	25
1397	18p. Queen Elizabeth II with British and Australian Parliament Buildings	30	25
1398	34p. W. G. Grace (cricketer) and tennis racquet	60	50
1399	34p. Shakespeare, John Lennon (entertainer) and Sydney Opera House	60	50

Stamps in similar designs were also issued by Australia.

870 Spanish Galeasse off The Lizard

1988. 400th Anniv of Spanish Armada. Mult.

1400	18p. Type **870**	30	25
1401	18p. English Fleet leaving Plymouth	30	25
1402	18p. Engagement off Isle of Wight	30	25
1403	18p. Attack of English fire-ships, Calais	30	25
1404	18p. Armada in storm, North Sea	30	25

Nos. 1400/4 were printed together, *se-tenant*, forming a composite design.

875 "The Owl and the Pussy-cat"

1988. Death Centenary of Edward Lear (artist and author).

1405	**875**	19p. black, cream and red	65	20
1406	-	27p. black, cream yellow	1·00	1·00
1407	-	32p. black, cream green	1·25	1·40
1408	-	35p. black, cream and blue	1·40	1·40
MS1409		122×90 mm. Nos. 1405/8 (sold at £1.35)	7·00	8·50

DESIGNS: 27p. "Edward Lear as a Bird" (self-portrait); 32p. "Cat" (from alphabet book); 35p. "There was a Young Lady whose Bonnet ..." (limerick).

The premium on No. **MS**1409 was used to support the "Stamp World London 90" International Stamp Exhibition.

879 Carrickfergus Castle

1988

1410	**879**	£1 green	4·25	60
1411	-	£1.50 red	4·50	1·25
1412	-	£2 blue	8·00	1·50
1413	-	£5 brown	21·00	5·50

DESIGNS: £1.50, Caernarfon Castle; £2, Edinburgh Castle; £5, Windsor Castle.

For similar designs, but with silhouette of Queen's head, see Nos. 1611/14.

883 Journey to Bethlehem

1988. Christmas. Christmas Cards. Multicoloured.

1414	14p. Type **883**	45	25
1415	19p. Shepherds and Star	50	25
1416	27p. Three Wise Men	90	1·00
1417	32p. Nativity	1·10	1·25
1418	35p. The Annunciation	1·40	1·25

888 Atlantic Puffin

1989. Centenary of Royal Society for the Protection of Birds. Multicoloured.

1419	19p. Type **888**	25	20
1420	27p. Pied avocet ("Avocet")	1·25	1·25
1421	32p. Oystercatcher	1·25	1·25
1422	35p. Northern gannet ("Gannet")	1·25	1·25

892 Rose

1989. Greetings Stamps. Multicoloured.

1423	19p. Type **892**	60	50
1424	19p. Cupid	60	50
1425	19p. Yachts	60	50
1426	19p. Fruit	60	50
1427	19p. Teddy bear	60	50

897 Fruit and Vegetables

1989. Food and Farming Year. Multicoloured.

1428	19p. Type **897**	45	15
1429	27p. Meat products	90	85
1430	32p. Dairy produce	1·25	1·40
1431	35p. Cereal products	1·40	1·50

901 Mortar Board

1989. Anniversaries. Multicoloured.

1432	19p. Type **901** (150th anniv of Public Education in England)	50	25
1433	19p. Cross on Ballot paper (3rd Direct Elections to European Parliament)	50	25
1434	35p. Posthorn (26th Postal, Telegraph and Telephone International Congress, Brighton)	75	50
1435	35p. Globe (Inter-Parliamentary Union Centenary Conference, London)	75	50

905 Toy Train and Aeroplanes

1989. Europa. Games and Toys. Multicoloured.

1436	19p. Type **905**	65	25
1437	27p. Building bricks	95	1·00
1438	32p. Dice and board games	1·40	1·25
1439	35p. Toy robot, boat and doll's house	1·50	1·25

909 Ironbridge, Shropshire

1989. Industrial Archaeology. Multicoloured.

1440	19p. Type **909**	60	15
1441	27p. Tin Mine, St. Agnes Head, Cornwall	1·00	1·10
1442	32p. Cotton Mills, New Lanark, Strathclyde	1·10	1·25
1443	35p. Pontcysyllte Aqueduct, Clwyd	1·25	1·50
MS1444	122×90 mm. 19p., 27p., 32p. and 35p. each multicoloured (horiz) (sold at £1.40)	6·00	6·50

The premium on **MS**1444 was used to support "Stamp World London 90" International Stamp Exhibition.

913

1989

1447	**913**	(1st) brownish black	1·75	1·00
1668	**913**	(1st) gold	1·00	1·00
1669	**913**	(E) deep blue	1·25	1·25
1670	**913**	(2nd) bright blue	90	90
1671	**913**	(1st) bright orange-red	1·00	1·00

The above were sold at the current rate for the day.

No. 1669 was valid for the basic European airmail rate.

The 2nd blue and 1st red exist with ordinary or self-adhesive gum.

915 Snowflake (×10)

1989. 150th Anniv of Royal Microscopical Society. Multicoloured.

1453	19p. Type **915**	45	25
1454	27p. "*Calliphora erythrocephala*" (fly) (×5)	95	1·00
1455	32p. Blood cells (×500)	1·10	1·25
1456	35p. Microchip (×600)	1·25	1·25

919 Royal Mail Coach

1989. Lord Mayor's Show, London. Multicoloured.

1457	20p. Type **919**	40	30
1458	20p. Escort of Blues and Royals	40	30
1459	20p. Lord Mayor's Coach	40	30
1460	20p. Coach team passing St. Paul's	40	30
1461	20p. Blues and Royals drum horse	40	30

This issue commemorates the 800th anniv of the installation of the first Lord Mayor of London.

924 14th-century Peasants from Stained-glass Window

1989. Christmas. 800th Anniv of Ely Cathedral.

1462	**924**	15p. gold, silver and blue	40	15
1463	-	15p.+1p. gold, silver and blue	50	40
1464	-	20p.+1p. gold, silver and red	65	80
1465	-	34p.+1p. gold, silver and green	1·25	1·75
1466	-	37p.+1p. gold, silver and green	1·40	1·90

DESIGNS: 15p.+1p. Arches and roundels, West Front; 20p.+1p. Octagon Tower; 34p.+1p. Arcade from West Transept; 37p.+1p. Triple arch from West Front.

929 Queen Victoria and Queen Elizabeth II

1990. 150th Anniv of the Penny Black.

1467	**929** 15p. blue	80	80
1469	**929** 20p. black and cream	1·00	1·00
1471	**929** 29p. mauve	1·75	1·75
1473	**929** 34p. grey	2·00	2·00
1474	**929** 37p. red	2·25	2·25

For this design with "1st" face value see No. 2133.

930 Kitten

1990. 150th Anniv of Royal Society for Prevention of Cruelty to Animals. Multicoloured.

1479	20p. Type **930**	75	50
1480	29p. Rabbit	1·25	1·25
1481	34p. Duckling	1·25	1·50
1482	37p. Puppy	1·50	1·50

934 Teddy Bear

1990. Greetings Stamps. "Smiles". Multicoloured (except No. 1492).

1483	20p. Type **934**	70	60
1484	20p. Dennis the Menace	70	60
1485	20p. Punch	70	60
1486	20p. Cheshire Cat	70	60
1487	20p. The Man in the Moon	70	60
1488	20p. The Laughing Policeman	70	60
1489	20p. Clown	70	60
1490	20p. Mona Lisa	70	60
1491	20p. Queen of Hearts	70	60
1492	20p. Stan Laurel (comedian) (gold and black)	70	60

See also Nos. 1550/9.

944 Alexandra Palace ("Stamp World London 90" Exhibition)

1990. Europa (Nos. 1493 and 1495) and "Glasgow 1990 European City of Culture" (Nos. 1494 and 1496). Multicoloured.

1493	20p. Type **944**	50	25
1494	20p. Glasgow School of Art	50	25
1495	29p. British Philatelic Bureau, Edinburgh	1·25	1·75
1496	37p. Templeton Carpet Factory, Glasgow	1·50	1·75

948 Export Achievement Award

1990. 25th Anniv of Queen's Awards for Export and Technology. Multicoloured.

1497	20p. Type **948**	40	30
1498	20p. Technological Achievement Award	40	30
1499	37p. Type **948**	50	50
1500	37p. As No. 1498	50	50

1990. "Stamp World London 90" International Stamp Exhibition, London. Sheet 122×90 mm, containing No. 1469.

MS1501	**929** 20p. black and cream (sold at £1)	5·50	5·50

The premium on No. **MS**1501 was used to support the "Stamp World London 90" International Stamp Exhibition.

950 Cycad and Sir Joseph Banks Building

1990. 150th Anniv of Kew Gardens. Mult.

1502	20p. Type **950**	55	15
1503	29p. Stone pine and Princess of Wales Conservatory	75	1·00
1504	34p. Willow tree and Palm House	1·25	1·60
1505	37p. Cedar tree and Pagoda	1·50	1·50

954 Thomas Hardy and Clyffe Clump, Dorset

1990. 150th Anniv of Thomas Hardy (author).

1506	**954** 20p. multicoloured	80	75

955 Queen Elizabeth the Queen Mother

1990. 90th Birthday of Queen Elizabeth the Queen Mother. Multicoloured.

1507	20p. Type **955**	95	25
1508	29p. Queen Elizabeth	1·40	1·50
1509	34p. Elizabeth, Duchess of York	2·00	2·50
1510	37p. Lady Elizabeth Bowes-Lyon	2·25	2·50

959 Victoria Cross

1990. Gallantry Awards. Multicoloured.

1517	20p. Type **959**	80	75
1518	20p. George Cross	80	75
1519	20p. Distinguished Service Cross and Distinguished Service Medal (horiz)	80	75
1520	20p. Military Cross and Military Medal (horiz)	80	75
1521	20p. Distinguished Flying Cross and Distinguished Flying Medal (horiz)	80	75

964 Armagh Observatory, Jodrell Bank Radio Telescope and La Palma Telescope

1990. Astronomy. Multicoloured.

1522	22p. Type **964**	65	15
1523	26p. Newton's moon and tides diagram with early telescopes	1·00	1·10
1524	31p. Greenwich Old Observatory and early astronomical equipment	1·25	1·40
1525	37p. Stonehenge, gyroscope and navigating by stars	1·50	1·40

Nos. 1522/5 commemorate the Centenary of the British Astronomical Association and the Bicentenary of the Armagh Observatory.

968 Building a Snowman

1990. Christmas. Multicoloured.

1526	17p. Type **968**	50	15
1527	22p. Fetching the Christmas tree	70	20
1528	26p. Carol singing	70	1·10
1529	31p. Tobogganing	1·25	1·50
1530	37p. Ice-skating	1·25	1·50

973 "King Charles Spaniel"

1991. Dogs. Paintings by George Stubbs. Mult.

1531	22p. Type **973**	50	15
1532	26p. "A Pointer"	75	1·25
1533	31p. "Two Hounds in a Landscape"	1·00	1·25
1534	33p. "A Rough Dog"	1·25	1·25
1535	37p. "Fino and Tiny"	1·25	1·25

978 Song Thrush's Nest

1991. Greetings Stamps. "Good Luck". Mult.

1536	(1st) Type **978**	70	60
1537	(1st) Shooting star and rainbow	70	60
1538	(1st) Black-billed magpies and charm bracelet	70	60
1539	(1st) Black cat	70	60
1540	(1st) River kingfisher with key	70	60
1541	(1st) Mallard and frog	70	60
1542	(1st) Four-leaf clover in boot and match box	70	60
1543	(1st) Pot of gold at end of rainbow	70	60
1544	(1st) Heart-shaped butterflies	70	60
1545	(1st) Wishing well and sixpence	70	60

The background of the stamps forms a composite design.

Nos. 1536/45 were sold at the current rate.

988 Michael Faraday. (inventor of electric motor) (birth bicentenary)

1991. Scientific Achievements. Multicoloured.

1546	22p. Type **988**	60	50
1547	22p. Charles Babbage (computer science pioneer) (birth bicentenary)	60	50
1548	31p. Radar sweep of East Anglia (50th anniv of operational radar network)	1·20	1·50
1549	37p. Gloster Whittle E28/39 airplane over East Anglia (50th anniv of first flight of Sir Frank Whittle's jet engine)	1·35	1·75

992 Teddy Bear

1991. Greetings Stamps. "Smiles". As Nos. 1483/92, but inscr "1st" as in T 992. Multicoloured (except No. 1559).

1550	(1st) Type **992**	70	60
1551	(1st) Dennis the Menace	70	60
1552	(1st) Punch	70	60
1553	(1st) Cheshire Cat	70	60
1554	(1st) The Man in the Moon	70	60
1555	(1st) The Laughing Policeman	70	60
1556	(1st) Clown	70	60
1557	(1st) Mona Lisa	70	60
1558	(1st) Queen of Hearts	70	60
1559	(1st) Stan Laurel (comedian) (gold and black)	70	60

Nos. 1550/9 were sold at the current rate.

993/4 Man looking at Space

1991. Europa. Europe in Space. Multicoloured.

1560	22p. Type **993**	40	30
1561	22p. Type **994**	40	30
1562	37p. Space looking at Man (Queen's head on left)	50	40
1563	37p. Similar to No. 1562 (Queen's head on right)	50	40

Stamps of the same value were printed together in horizontal pairs, each pair forming a composite design.

997 Fencing

1991. World Student Games, Sheffield (Nos. 1564/6) and World Cup Rugby Championship (No. 1567).

1564	22p. Type **997**	60	20
1565	26p. Hurdling	1·00	1·00
1566	31p. Diving	1·25	1·25
1567	37p. Rugby	1·50	1·50

1001 "Silver Jubilee"

1991. 9th World Congress of Roses, Belfast. Multicoloured.

1568	22p. Type **1001**	50	20
1569	26p. "Mme Alfred Carrière"	75	1·25
1570	31p. "*Rosa moyesii*"	1·00	1·25
1571	33p. "Harvest Fayre"	1·25	1·50
1572	37p. "Mutabilis"	1·50	1·50

1006 Iguanodon

1991. 150th Anniv of Dinosaurs' Identification by Owen. Multicoloured.

1573	22p. Type **1006**	60	20
1574	26p. Stegosaurus	1·10	1·25
1575	31p. Tyrannosaurus	1·25	1·25
1576	33p. Protoceratops	1·50	1·50
1577	37p. Triceratops	1·60	1·50

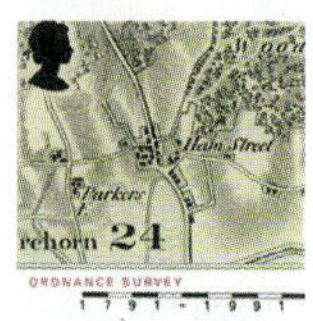

1011 Map of 1816

1991. Bicentenary of Ordnance Survey. Maps of Hamstreet, Kent.

1578	**1011** 24p. black, mauve and cream	60	20
1579	- 28p. multicoloured	1·00	95
1580	- 33p. multicoloured	1·25	1·40
1581	- 39p. multicoloured	1·50	1·40

DESIGNS: 28p. Map of 1906; 33p. Map of 1959; 39p. Map of 1991.

1015 Adoration of the Magi

1991. Christmas. Illuminated Letters from "Acts of Mary and Jesus" Manuscript in Bodleian Library, Oxford. Multicoloured.

1582	18p. Type **1015**	75	10
1583	24p. Mary and Baby Jesus in the Stable	90	10
1584	28p. The Holy Family and Angel	95	1·25
1585	33p. The Annunciation	1·10	1·50
1586	39p. The Flight into Egypt	1·25	1·75

1020 Fallow Deer in Scottish Forest

1992. The Four Seasons. Wintertime. Multicoloured.

1587	18p. Type **1020**	55	25
1588	24p. Hare on North Yorkshire moors	75	25
1589	28p. Fox in the Fens	1·00	1·25
1590	33p. Redwing and Home Counties village	1·25	1·50
1591	39p. Welsh mountain sheep in Snowdonia	1·40	1·75

1025 Flower Spray

1992. Greetings Stamps. "Memories". Mult.

1592	(1st) Type **1025**	70	60
1593	(1st) Double locket	70	60
1594	(1st) Key	70	60
1595	(1st) Model car and cigarette cards	70	60
1596	(1st) Compass and map	70	60
1597	(1st) Pocket watch	70	60
1598	(1st) 1854 1d. Red stamp and pen	70	60
1599	(1st) Pearl necklace	70	60
1600	(1st) Marbles	70	60
1601	(1st) Bucket, spade and starfish	70	60

Nos. 1592/1601 were issued together, *se-tenant*, the backgrounds forming a composite design.

1035 Queen Elizabeth in Coronation Robes and Parliamentary Emblem

1992. 40th Anniv of Accession. Multicoloured.

1602	24p. Type **1035**	50	50
1603	24p. Queen Elizabeth in Garter Robes and Archiepiscopal Arms	50	50
1604	24p. Queen Elizabeth with baby Prince Andrew and Royal Arms	50	50
1605	24p. Queen Elizabeth at Trooping the Colour	50	50
1606	24p. Queen Elizabeth and Commonwealth emblem	50	50

1040 Tennyson in 1888 and "The Beguiling of Merlin" (Sir Edward Burne-Jones)

1992. Death Centenary of Alfred, Lord Tennyson (poet). Multicoloured.

1607	24p. Type **1040**	60	20
1608	28p. Tennyson in 1856 and "April Love" (Arthur Hughes)	85	85
1609	33p. Tennyson in 1864 and "I am Sick of the Shadows" (John Waterhouse)	1·40	1·60
1610	39p. Tennyson as a young man and "Mariana" (Dante Gabriel Rossetti)	1·50	1·60

1044 Carrickfergus Castle

1992. Designs as Nos. 1410/13, but showing Queen's head in silhouette as T 1044.

1611	**1044**	£1 green and gold	5·50	1·00
1612	-	£1.50 purple and gold	6·00	1·20
1613	-	£2 blue and gold	8·00	1·20
1613a	**1044**	£3 violet and gold	19·00	3·00
1614	-	£5 brown and gold	18·00	3·00

The Queen's head on these stamps is printed in optically variable ink which changes colour from gold to green when viewed from different angles.

1045 British Olympic Association Logo (Olympic Games, Barcelona)

1992. Europa. International Events. Mult.

1615	24p. Type **1045**	50	40
1616	24p. British Paralympic Association symbol (Paralympics '92, Barcelona)	50	40
1617	24p. "*Santa Maria*" (500th anniv of discovery of America by Columbus)	1·00	75
1618	39p. "*Kaisei*" (Japanese cadet brigantine) (Grand Regatta Columbus, 1992)	1·40	1·50
1619	39p. British Pavilion, "EXPO '92", Seville	1·40	1·50

1050 Pikeman

1992. 350th Anniv of the Civil War. Multicoloured.

1620	24p. Type **1050**	60	20
1621	28p. Drummer	85	85
1622	33p. Musketeer	1·40	1·50
1623	39p. Standard Bearer	1·50	1·75

1054 *"The Yeomen of the Guard"*

1992. 150th Birth Anniv of Sir Arthur Sullivan (composer). Gilbert and Sullivan Operas. Multicoloured.

1624	18p. Type **1054**	50	20
1625	24p. *"The Gondoliers"*	80	20
1626	28p. *"The Mikado"*	95	1·00
1627	33p. *"The Pirates of Penzance"*	1·50	1·60
1628	39p. *"Iolanthe"*	1·60	1·60

1059 "Acid Rain Kills"

1992. Protection of the Environment. Children's Paintings. Multicoloured.

1629	24p. Type **1059**	70	25
1630	28p. "Ozone Layer"	1·10	1·25
1631	33p. "Greenhouse Effect"	1·25	1·50
1632	39p. "Bird of Hope"	1·40	1·50

1063 European Star

1992. Single European Market.

1633	**1063**	24p. multicoloured	1·00	1·00

1064 "Angel Gabriel", St. James's, Pangbourne

1992. Christmas. Stained Glass Windows. Multicoloured.

1634	18p. Type **1064**	50	15
1635	24p. "Madonna and Child", St. Mary's, Bibury	75	15
1636	28p. "King with Gold", Our Lady and St. Peter, Leatherhead	1·00	1·10
1637	33p. "Shepherds", All Saints, Porthcawl	1·25	1·50
1638	39p. "Kings with Frankincense and Myrrh", Our Lady and St. Peter, Leatherhead	1·25	1·50

1069 Mute Swan Cob and St. Catherine's Chapel, Abbotsbury

1993. 600th Anniv of Abbotsbury Swannery. Multicoloured.

1639	18p. Type **1069**	1·25	25
1640	24p. Cygnet and decoy	1·10	25
1641	28p. Swans and cygnet	1·40	2·25
1642	33p. Eggs in nest and Tithe Barn, Abbotsbury	1·75	2·50
1643	39p. Young swan and the Fleet	1·90	2·50

1074 Long John Silver and Parrot (*"Treasure Island"*)

1993. Greetings Stamps. "Gift Giving". Gold, cream and black (No. 1645) or multicoloured (others).

1644	(1st) Type **1074**	60	50
1645	(1st) Tweedledum and Tweedledee (*"Alice Through the Looking Glass"*)	60	50
1646	(1st) William (*"William"* books)	60	50
1647	(1st) Mole and Toad (*"The Wind in the Willows"*)	60	50
1648	(1st) Teacher and Wilfrid (*"The Bash Street Kids"*)	60	50
1649	(1st) Peter Rabbit and Mrs. Rabbit (*"The Tale of Peter Rabbit"*)	60	50
1650	(1st) Snowman (*"The Snowman"*) and Father Christmas (*"Father Christmas"*)	60	50
1651	(1st) The Big Friendly Giant and Sophie (*"The BFG"*)	60	50
1652	(1st) Bill Badger and Rupert Bear	60	50
1653	(1st) Aladdin and the Genie	60	50

1084 Decorated Enamel Dial

1993. 300th Birth Anniv of John Harrison (inventor of the marine chronometer). Details of "H4" Clock. Multicoloured.

1654	24p. Type **1084**	60	25
1655	28p. Escapement, remontoire and fusee	1·00	1·25
1656	33p. Balance, spring and temperature compensator	1·40	1·25
1657	39p. Back of movement	1·50	1·50

1088 "Britannia"

1993

1658	**1088**	£10 multicoloured	40·00	12·00

1089 *"Dendrobium hellwigianum"*

1993. 14th World Orchid Conference, Glasgow. Multicoloured.

1659	18p. Type **1089**	45	25
1660	24p. *"Paphiopedilum Maudiae"* "Magnificum"	75	25
1661	28p. *"Cymbidium lowianum"*	1·00	1·25
1662	33p. *"Vanda Rothschildiana"*	1·25	1·50
1663	39p. *"Dendrobium vexillarius var albiviride"*	1·60	1·50

1094 "Family Group" (bronze sculpture) (Henry Moore)

1993. Europa. Contemporary Art. Multicoloured.

1767	24p. Type **1094**	60	20
1768	28p. "Kew Gardens" (lithograph) (Edward Bawden)	90	1·00
1769	33p. "St. Francis and the Birds" (Stanley Spencer)	1·25	1·40
1770	39p. "Still Life: Odyssey I" (Ben Nicholson)	1·75	1·75

1098 Emperor Claudius (from gold coin)

1993. Roman Britain. Multicoloured.

1771	24p. Type **1098**	60	20
1772	28p. Emperor Hadrian (bronze head)	90	1·00
1773	33p. Goddess Roma (from gemstone)	1·30	1·50
1774	39p. Christ (Hinton St. Mary mosaic)	1·50	1·60

1102 *"Midland Maid"* and other Narrow Boats, Grand Junction Canal

1993. Inland Waterways. Multicoloured.

1775	24p. Type **1102**	50	20
1776	28p. *"Yorkshire Lass"* and other Humber keels, Stainforth and Keadby Canal	1·00	1·00
1777	33p. *"Valley Princess"* and other horse-drawn barges, Brecknock and Abergavenny Canal	1·25	1·25
1778	39p. Steam barges, including *"Pride of Scotland"*, and fishing boats, Crinan Canal	1·50	1·40

Nos. 1775/8 commemorate the bicentenary of the Acts of Parliament authorizing the canals depicted.

1106 Horse Chestnut

1993. The Four Seasons. Autumn. Fruits and Leaves. Multicoloured.

1779	18p. Type **1106**	50	20
1780	24p. Blackberry	75	20
1781	28p. Hazel	1·10	1·25
1782	33p. Rowan	1·40	1·50
1783	39p. Pear	1·50	1·50

1111 *"The Reigate Squire"*

1993. Sherlock Holmes. Centenary of the Publication of "The Final Problem". Multicoloured.

1784	24p. Type **1111**	50	40
1785	24p. *"The Hound of the Baskervilles"*	50	40
1786	24p. *"The Six Napoleons"*	50	40
1787	24p. *"The Greek Interpreter"*	50	40
1788	24p. *"The Final Problem"*	50	40

1116

1993. Self-adhesive.

1789	**1116** (1st) red	1·25	1·40
1976	**1116** (2nd) blue	2·75	2·50

Nos. 1976/7 were sold at the current rates.

1117 Bob Cratchit and Tiny Tim

1993. Christmas. 150th Anniv of Publication of "A Christmas Carol" by Charles Dickens. Multicoloured.

1790	19p. Type **1117**	60	15
1791	25p. Mr. and Mrs. Fezziwig	90	15
1792	30p. Scrooge	1·25	1·50
1793	35p. The prize turkey	1·40	1·60
1794	41p. Mr. Scrooge's nephew	1·40	1·60

1122 Class 5 No. 44957 and Class B1 No. 61342 on West Highland Line

1994. The Age of Steam. Railway Photographs by Colin Gifford.

1795	**1122** 19p. green, grey black	55	25
1796	- 25p. lilac, grey and black	90	95
1797	- 30p. brown, grey and black	1·40	1·50
1798	- 35p. purple, grey & black	1·75	1·80
1799	- 41p. blue, grey and black	1·80	1·90

DESIGNS: 25p. Class A1 No. 60149 "Amadis" at Kings Cross; 30p. Class 4 No. 43000 on turntable at Blyth North; 35p. Class No. 42455 near Wigan Central; 41p. Class "Castle" No. 7002 "Devizes Castle" on bridge crossing Worcester and Birmingham Canal.

1127 Dan Dare and the Mekon

1994. Greetings Stamps. "Messages". Mult.

1800	(1st) Type **1127**	60	50
1801	(1st) The Three Bears	60	50
1802	(1st) Rupert Bear	60	50
1803	(1st) Alice ("Alice in Wonderland")	60	50
1804	(1st) Noggin and The Ice Dragon	60	50
1805	(1st) Peter Rabbit posting a letter	60	50
1806	(1st) Red Riding Hood and wolf	60	50
1807	(1st) Orlando the Marmalade Cat	60	50
1808	(1st) Biggles	60	50
1809	(1st) Paddington Bear on station	60	50

1137 Castell Y Waun (Chirk Castle), Clwyd, Wales

1994. 25th Anniv of Investiture of the Prince of Wales. Paintings by Prince Charles. Multicoloured.

1810	19p. Type **1137**	55	20
1811	25p. Ben Arkle, Sutherland, Scotland	1·00	20
1812	30p. Mourne Mountains, County Down, Northern Ireland	1·10	1·50
1813	35p. Dersingham, Norfolk, England	1·40	1·75
1814	41p. Dolwyddelan, Gwynedd, Wales	1·50	1·75

1142 Bather at Blackpool

1994. Centenary of Picture Postcards. Mult.

1815	19p. Type **1142**	60	20
1816	25p. "Where's my Little Lad?"	90	20
1817	30p. "Wish You were Here!"	1·10	1·50
1818	35p. Punch and Judy show	1·40	1·75
1819	41p. "The Tower Crane" machine	1·50	1·75

1147 British Lion and French Cockerel over Tunnel

1994. Opening of Channel Tunnel. Multicoloured.

1820	25p. Type **1147**	50	40
1821	25p. Symbolic hands over train	50	40
1822	41p. Type **1147**	60	50
1823	41p. As No. 1821	60	50

1149 Groundcrew replacing Smoke Canisters on Douglas Boston of 88 Sqn

1994. 50th Anniv of D-Day. Multicoloured.

1824	25p. Type **1149**	50	40
1825	25p. H.M.S. "Warspite" (battleship) shelling enemy positions	50	40
1826	25p. Commandos landing on Gold Beach	50	40
1827	25p. Infantry regrouping on Sword Beach	50	40
1828	25p. Tank and infantry advancing, Ouistreham	50	40

1154 The Old Course, St. Andrews

1994. Scottish Golf Courses. Multicoloured.

1829	19p. Type **1154**	50	20
1830	25p. The 18th Hole, Muirfield	75	20
1831	30p. The 15th Hole ("Luckyslap"), Carnoustie	1·10	1·40
1832	35p. The 8th Hole ("The Postage Stamp"), Royal Troon	1·25	1·40
1833	41p. The 9th Hole, Turnberry	1·40	1·40

Nos. 1829/33 commemorate the 250th anniversary of golf's first set of rules produced by the Honourable Company of Edinburgh Golfers.

1159 Royal Welsh Show, Llanelwedd

1994. The Four Seasons. Summertime. Multicoloured.

1834	19p. Type **1159**	50	20
1835	25p. All England Tennis Championships, Wimbledon	75	20
1836	30p. Cowes Week	1·10	1·25
1837	35p. Test Match, Lord's	1·25	1·60
1838	41p. Braemar Gathering	1·40	1·60

1164 Ultrasonic Imaging

1994. Europa. Medical Discoveries. Multicoloured.

1839	25p. Type **1164**	75	25
1840	30p. Scanning electron microscopy	1·00	1·25
1841	35p. Magnetic resonance imaging	1·50	1·75
1842	41p. Computed tomography	1·75	1·75

1168 Mary and Joseph

1994. Christmas. Children's Nativity Plays. Multicoloured.

1843	19p. Type **1168**	50	15
1844	25p. Three Wise Men	75	15
1845	30p. Mary with doll	1·00	1·50
1846	35p. Shepherds	1·25	1·50
1847	41p. Angels	1·50	1·75

1173 Sophie (black cat)

1995. Cats. Multicoloured.

1848	19p. Type **1173**	75	20
1849	25p. Puskas (Siamese) and Tiger (tabby)	75	25
1850	30p. Chloe (ginger cat)	1·00	1·50
1851	35p. Kikko (tortoiseshell) and Rosie (Abyssinian)	1·25	1·50
1852	41p. Fred (black and white cat)	1·50	1·50

1178 Dandelions

1995. The Four Seasons. Springtime. Plant Sculptures by Andy Goldsworthy. Multicoloured.

1853	19p. Type **1178**	75	15
1854	25p. Sweet chestnut leaves	75	15
1855	30p. Garlic leaves	1·00	1·50
1856	35p. Hazel leaves	1·25	1·50
1857	41p. Spring grass	1·50	1·75

1183 "La Danse a la Campagne" (Renoir)

1995. Greetings Stamps. "Greetings in Art".

1858	**1183** (1st) multicoloured	60	50
1859	- (1st) multicoloured	60	50
1860	- (1st) multicoloured	60	50
1861	- (1st) multicoloured	60	50
1862	- (1st) multicoloured	60	50
1863	- (1st) multicoloured	60	50
1864	- (1st) brown and silver	60	50
1865	- (1st) multicoloured	60	50
1866	- (1st) multicoloured	60	50
1867	- (1st) black, yellow and silver	60	50

DESIGNS: No. 1859, "Troilus and Criseyde" (Peter Brookes); 1860, "The Kiss" (Rodin); 1861, "Girls on the Town" (Beryl Cook); 1862, "Jazz" (Andrew Mockett); 1863, "Girls performing a Kathak Dance" (Aurangzeb period); 1864, "Alice Keppel with her Daughter" (Alice Hughes); 1865, "Children Playing" (L. S. Lowry); 1866, "Circus Clowns" (Emily Firmin and Justin Mitchell); 1867, Decoration from "All the Love Poems of Shakespeare" (Eric Gill).

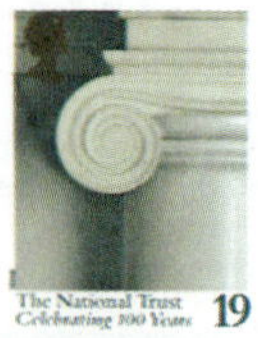

1193 Fireplace Decoration, Attingham Park, Shropshire

1995. Centenary of The National Trust. Multicoloured.

1868	19p. Type **1193**	60	20
1869	25p. Oak seedling	80	20
1870	30p. Carved table leg, Attingham Park	1·00	1·50
1871	35p. St. David's Head, Dyfed, Wales	1·25	1·50
1872	41p. Elizabethan window, Little Moreton Hall, Cheshire	1·40	1·75

1198 British Troops and French Civilians celebrating

1995. Europa. Peace and Freedom.

1873	**1198** 19p. silver, brown and black	70	40
1874	- 19p. multicoloured	70	40
1875	- 25p. silver, blue and black	1·00	1·00
1876	- 25p. multicoloured	1·00	1·00
1877	- 30p. multicoloured	1·25	2·25

DESIGNS: No. 1874, Symbolic hands and Red Cross; 1875, St. Paul's Cathedral and searchlights; 1876, Symbolic hand releasing peace dove; 1877, Symbolic hands.

Nos. 1873 and 1875 commemorate the 50th anniversary of the end of the Second World War, No. 1874 the 125th anniversary of the British Red Cross Society and Nos. 1876/7 the 50th anniversary of the United Nations.

Nos. 1876/7 include the "EUROPA" emblem.

1203 "The Time Machine"

1995. Science Fiction. Novels by H. G. Wells. Multicoloured.

1878	25p. Type **1203**	75	25
1879	30p. "The First Men in the Moon"	1·25	1·50
1880	35p. "The War of the Worlds"	1·25	1·60
1881	41p. "The Shape of Things to Come"	1·50	1·60

Nos. 1878/81 commemorate the centenary of publication of Wells's "The Time Machine".

1207 The Swan, 1595

1995. Reconstruction of Shakespeare's Globe Theatre. Multicoloured.

1882	25p. Type **1207**	50	40
1883	25p. The Rose, 1592	50	40
1884	25p. The Globe, 1599	50	40
1885	25p. The Hope, 1613	50	40
1886	25p. The Globe, 1614	50	40

Nos. 1882/6 were printed together, se-tenant, forming a composite design.

1212 Sir Rowland Hill and Uniform Penny Postage Petition

1995. Pioneers of Communications.

1887	**1212**	19p. silver, red and black	75	30
1888	-	25p. silver, brown and black	1·00	50
1889	-	41p. silver, green and black	1·50	1·75
1890	-	60p. silver, blue and black	1·75	2·25

DESIGNS: 25p. Hill and Penny Black; 41p. Guglielmo Marconi and early wireless; 60p. Marconi and sinking of "Titanic" (liner).

Nos. 1887/8 mark the birth bicentenary of Sir Rowland Hill and Nos. 1889/90 the centenary of the first radio transmissions.

1216 Harold Wagstaff

1995. Centenary of Rugby League. Multicoloured.

1891	19p. Type **1216**	75	25
1892	25p. Gus Risman	75	30
1893	30p. Jim Sullivan	1·00	1·50
1894	35p. Billy Batten	1·00	1·60
1895	41p. Brian Bevan	1·50	1·60

1221 European Robin in Mouth of Pillar Box

1995. Christmas. Christmas Robins. Multicoloured.

1896	19p. Type **1221**	60	20
1897	25p. European robin on railings and holly	85	30
1898	30p. European robin on snow-covered milk bottles	1·25	1·50
1899	41p. European robin on road sign	1·60	1·75
1900	60p. European robin on door knob and Christmas wreath	1·75	1·90

1226 Opening Lines of "To a Mouse" and Fieldmouse

1996. Death Bicent of Robert Burns (Scottish poet).

1901	**1226**	19p. cream, brown and black	75	25
1902	-	25p. multicoloured	1·00	30
1903	-	41p. multicoloured	1·50	2·00
1904	-	60p. multicoloured	1·75	2·50

DESIGNS: 25p. "O my Luve's like a red, red rose" and wild rose; 41p. "Scots, wha hae wi Wallace bled" and Sir William Wallace; 60p. "Auld Lang Syne" and highland dancers.

1230 "MORE! LOVE" (Mel Calman)

1996. Greetings Stamps. Cartoons.

1905	**1230**	(1st) black and mauve	50	40
1906	-	(1st) black and green	50	40
1907	-	(1st) black and blue	50	40
1908	-	(1st) black and violet	50	40
1909	-	(1st) black and red	50	40
1910	-	(1st) black and blue	50	40
1911	-	(1st) black and red	50	40
1912	-	(1st) black and violet	50	40
1913	-	(1st) black and green	50	40
1914	-	(1st) black and mauve	50	40

DESIGNS: No. 1906, "Sincerely" (Charles Barsotti); 1907, "Do you have something for the HUMAN CONDITION?" (Mel Calman); 1908, "MENTAL FLOSS" (Leo Cullum); 1909, "4.55 P.M." (Charles Barsotti); 1910, "Dear lottery prize winner" (Larry); 1911, "I'm writing to you because ..." (Mel Calman); 1912, "FETCH THIS, FETCH THAT" (Charles Barsotti); 1913, "My day starts before I'm ready for it" (Mel Calman); 1914, "THE CHEQUE IN THE POST" (Jack Ziegler).

Nos. 1905/14 were sold at the current rate.

1240 "Muscovy Duck"

1996. 50th Anniv of the Wildfowl and Wetlands Trust. Bird paintings by C. F. Tunnicliffe. Multicoloured.

1915	19p. Type **1240**	70	25
1916	25p. "Lapwing"	90	30
1917	30p. "White-fronted Goose"	1·00	1·25
1918	35p. "Bittern"	1·10	1·50
1919	41p. "Whooper Swan"	1·50	1·60

1245 The Odeon, Harrogate

1996. Centenary of Cinema.

1920	**1245**	19p. multicoloured	50	25
1921	-	25p. multicoloured	70	30
1922	-	30p. multicoloured	1·00	1·75
1923	-	35p. black, red and silver	1·25	2·00
1924	-	41p. multicoloured	1·50	2·25

DESIGNS: 25p. Laurence Olivier and Vivien Leigh in "Lady Hamilton" (film); 30p. Old cinema ticket; 35p. Pathe News still; 41p. Cinema sign, The Odeon, Manchester.

1250 Dixie Dean

1996. European Football Championship. Multicoloured.

1925	19p. Type **1250**	50	20
1926	25p. Bobby Moore	75	20
1927	35p. Duncan Edwards	1·25	1·75
1928	41p. Billy Wright	1·50	1·75
1929	60p. Danny Blanchflower	1·75	2·00

1255 Athlete on Starting Blocks

1996. Olympic and Paralympic Games, Atlanta. Multicoloured.

1930	26p. Type **1255**	50	40
1931	26p. Throwing the javelin	50	40
1932	26p. Basketball	50	40
1933	26p. Swimming	50	40
1934	26p. Athlete celebrating and Olympic Rings	50	40

1260 Prof. Dorothy Hodgkin (scientist)

1996. Europa. Famous Women.

1935	**1260**	20p. green, grey and black	60	25
1936	-	26p. mauve, grey & black	75	25
1937	-	31p. bronze, grey and black	1·10	1·10
1938	-	37p. silver, grey and black	1·25	1·40
1939	-	43p. gold, grey and black	1·50	1·50

DESIGNS: 26p. Dame Margot Fonteyn (ballerina); 31p. Dame Elisabeth Frink (sculptress); 37p. Dame Daphne du Maurier (novelist); 43p. Dame Marea Hartman (sports administrator).

Nos. 1936/7 include the "EUROPA" emblem.

1265 "Muffin the Mule"

1996. 50th Anniv of Children's Television. Multicoloured.

1940	20p. Type **1265**	55	20
1941	26p. "Sooty"	80	20
1942	31p. "Stingray"	1·00	1·50
1943	37p. "The Clangers"	1·40	1·75
1944	43p. "Dangermouse"	1·60	2·00

1270 Triumph TR3

1996. Classic Sports Cars. Multicoloured.

1945	20p. Type **1270**	55	20
1946	26p. MG TD	1·10	20
1947	37p. Austin-Healey 100	1·40	1·90
1948	43p. Jaguar XK120	1·60	1·90
1949	63p. Morgan Plus 4	1·75	2·00

1275 The Three Kings

1996. Christmas. Multicoloured.

1950	(2nd.) Type **1275**	75	20
1951	(1st) The Annunciation	1·00	35
1952	31p. The Journey to Bethlehem	1·25	1·75
1953	43p. The Nativity	1·25	1·75
1954	63p. The Shepherds	1·50	2·00

1280 "Gentiana acaulis" (Georg Ehret)

1997. Greeting Stamps. 19th-century Flower Paintings. Multicoloured.

1955	(1st) Type **1280**	50	40
1956	(1st) "Magnolia grandiflora" (Ehret)	50	40
1957	(1st) "Camellia japonica" (Alfred Chandler)	50	40
1958	(1st) "Tulipa" (Ehret)	50	40
1959	(1st) "Fuchsia" "Princess of Wales" (Augusta Withers)	50	40
1960	(1st) "Tulipa gesneriana" (Ehret)	50	40
1961	(1st) "Guzmania splendens" (Charlotte Sowerby)	50	40
1962	(1st) "Iris latifolia" (Ehret)	50	40
1963	(1st) "Hippeastrum rutilum" (Pierre-Joseph Redoute)	50	40
1964	(1st) "Passiflora coerulea" (Ehret)	50	40

1290 "King Henry VIII"

1997. 450th Death Anniv of King Henry VIII. Multicoloured.

1965	26p. Type **1290**	50	40
1966	26p. "Catherine of Aragon"	50	40
1967	26p. "Anne Boleyn"	50	40
1968	26p. "Jane Seymour"	50	40
1969	26p. "Anne of Cleves"	50	40
1970	26p. "Catherine Howard"	50	40
1971	26p. "Catherine Parr"	50	40

1297 St. Columba in Boat

1997. Religious Anniversaries. Multicoloured.

1972	26p. Type **1297**	75	35
1973	37p. St. Columba on Iona	1·10	1·50
1974	43p. St. Augustine with King Ethelbert	1·50	1·50
1975	63p. St. Augustine with Model of Cathedral	2·00	2·10

Nos. 1972/3 commemorate the 1400th death anniversary of St. Columba and Nos. 1974/5 the 1400th anniversary of the arrival of St. Augustine of Canterbury in Kent.

1303 "Dracula"

1997. Europa. Tales and Legends. Horror Stories. Multicoloured.

1980	26p. Type **1303**	1·00	40
1981	31p. "Frankenstein"	1·10	1·50
1982	37p. "Dr. Jekyll and Mr. Hyde"	1·30	1·75
1983	43p. "The Hound of the Baskervilles"	2·00	1·95

Nos. 1980/3 commemorate the birth bicentenary of Mary Shelley (creator of Frankenstein) with the 26p. and 31p. values incorporating the "EUROPA" emblem.

1307 Reginald Mitchell and Supermarine Spitfire Mk IIA

1997. British Aircraft Designers. Multicoloured.

1984	20p. Type **1307**	75	40
1985	26p. Roy Chadwick and Avro Type 683 Lancaster Mk I	1·10	1·25
1986	37p. Ronald Bishop and de Havilland DH.98 Mosquito *B Mk XVI*	1·40	1·25
1987	43p. George Carter and Gloster Meteor T.Mk7	1·50	1·60
1988	63p. Sir Sidney Camm and Hawker Hunter FGA Mk 9	2·00	2·00

1312 Carriage Horse and Coachman

1997. "All the Queen's Horses". 50th Anniv of the British Horse Society. Multicoloured.

1989	20p. Type **1312**	80	45
1990	26p. Lifeguards horse and trooper	1·10	1·50
1991	43p. Blues and Royals drum horse and drummer	1·50	1·50
1992	63p. Duke of Edinburgh's horse and groom	2·00	2·00

1316 Haroldswick, Shetland

1997. Sub-Post Offices. Multicoloured.

1997	20p. Type **1316**	75	50
1998	26p. Painswick, Gloucestershire	1·00	1·00
1999	43p. Beddgelert, Gwynedd	1·50	1·50
2000	63p. Ballyroney, County Down	2·25	2·25

Nos. 1997/2000 were issued on the occasion of the Centenary of The National Federation of Sub-Postmasters.

1320 "Noddy"

1997. Birth Centenary of Enid Blyton (children's author). Multicoloured.

2001	20p. Type **1320**	50	45
2002	26p. "Famous Five"	1·00	1·25
2003	37p. "Secret Seven"	1·25	1·25

2004 43p. "Faraway Tree" 1·50 2·00
2005 63p. "Malory Towers" 1·75 2·00

1325 Children and Father Christmas pulling Cracker

1997. Christmas. 150th Anniv of the Christmas Cracker. Multicoloured.

2006 (2nd.) Type **1325** 75 20
2007 (1st) Father Christmas with traditional cracker 90 30
2008 31p. Father Christmas riding cracker 1·00 1·50
2009 43p. Father Christmas on snowball 1·25 1·75
2010 63p. Father Christmas and chimney 1·60 2·00

1330 Wedding Photograph, 1947

1997. Royal Golden Wedding.

2011 **1330** 20p. gold, brown and black 85 45
2012 - 26p. multicoloured 1·10 70
2013 **1330** 43p. gold, green and black 1·90 2·25
2014 - 63p. multicoloured 2·50 3·00

DESIGNS: 26p. and 63p. Queen Elizabeth II and Prince Philip, 1997.

1332 Common Dormouse

1998. Endangered Species. Multicoloured.

2015 20p. Type **1332** 60 40
2016 26p. Lady's slipper orchid 75 40
2017 31p. Song thrush 1·00 2·00
2018 37p. Shining ram's-horn snail 1·25 1·25
2019 43p. Mole cricket 1·40 1·75
2020 63p. Devil's bolete 1·90 2·25

1338 Diana, Princess of Wales (photo by Lord Snowdon)

1998. Diana, Princess of Wales Commemoration. Multicoloured.

2021 26p. Type **1338** 50 40
2022 26p. At British Lung Foundation Function, April 1997 (photo by John Stillwell) 50 40
2023 26p. Wearing tiara, 1991 (photo by Lord Snowdon) 50 40
2024 26p. On visit to Birmingham, October 1995 (photo by Tim Graham) (checked suit) 50 40
2025 26p. In evening dress, 1987 (photo by Terence Donovan) 50 40

1343 Lion of England and Griffin of Edward III

1998. 650th Anniv of the Order of the Garter. The Queen's Beasts. Multicoloured.

2026 26p. Type **1343** 90 90
2027 26p. Falcon of Plantagenet and Bull of Clarence 90 90
2028 26p. Lion of Mortimer and Yale of Beaufort 90 90
2029 26p. Greyhound of Richmond and Dragon of Wales 90 90
2030 26p. Unicorn of Scotland and Horse of Hanover 90 90

1348

1998. As Type 157 (Wilding definitive of 1952–54) but with face values in decimal currency as Type 1348.

2031 **1348** 20p. green 70 75
2032 **1348** 26p. brown 90 95
2033 **1348** 37p. purple 2·75 2·75

See also Nos. 2295/8.

1349 St. John's Point Lighthouse, County Down

1998. 300th Anniv of the 1st Lighthouse and Final Year of Manned Lighthouses. Multicoloured.

2034 20p. Type **1349** 50 40
2035 26p. Smalls Lighthouse, Pembrokeshire 75 50
2036 37p. Needles Rock Lighthouse, Isle of Wight, c. 1900 1·10 1·50
2037 43p. Bell Rock Lighthouse, Arbroath, mid-19th century 1·50 1·75
2038 63p. Eddystone Lighthouse, Plymouth, 1698 2·10 2·50

1354 Tommy Cooper

1998. Comedians. Multicoloured.

2041 20p. Type **1354** 50 50
2042 26p. Eric Morecambe 75 85
2043 37p. Joyce Grenfell 1·25 1·25
2044 43p. Les Dawson 1·50 1·50
2045 63p. Peter Cook 1·75 2·10

1359 Hands forming Heart

1998. 50th Anniv of the National Health Service. Multicoloured.

2046 20p. Type **1359** 50 50
2047 26p. Adult and child holding hands 90 90
2048 43p. Hands forming cradle 1·50 1·50
2049 63p. Hand taking pulse 2·10 2·10

1363 "The Hobbit" (J. R. R. Tolkien)

1998. Famous Children's Fantasy Novels. Multicoloured.

2050 20p. Type **1363** 50 45
2051 26p. "The Lion, The Witch and the Wardrobe" (C. S. Lewis) 75 55
2052 37p. "The Phoenix and the Carpet" (E. Nesbit) 1·25 1·50
2053 43p. "The Borrowers" (Mary Norton) 1·50 1·50
2054 63p. "Through the Looking Glass" (Lewis Carroll) 2·10 2·00

Nos. 2050/4 commemorate the birth centenary of C. S. Lewis and the death centenary of Lewis Carroll.

1368 Woman in Yellow Feathered Costume

1998. Europa. Festivals. Notting Hill Carnival. Multicoloured.

2055 20p. Type **1368** 75 45
2056 26p. Woman in blue costume and headdress 95 55
2057 43p. Group of children in white and gold robes 1·50 2·00
2058 63p. Child in "Tree" costume 2·00 2·75

The 20p. and 26p. incorporate the "EUROPA" emblem.

1372 Sir Malcolm Campbell's "Bluebird", 1925

1998. British Land Speed Record Holders. Multicoloured.

2059 20p. Type **1372** 50 25
2060 26p. Sir Henry Segrave's "Sunbeam", 1926 75 30
2061 30p. John G. Parry Thomas's "Babs", 1926 1·25 1·50
2062 43p. John R. Cobb's "Railton Mobil Special", 1947 1·50 1·60
2063 63p. Donald Campbell's "Bluebird CN7", 1964 2·00 2·40

Nos. 2059/63 commemorate the 50th death anniversary of Sir Malcolm Campbell.

1377 Angel with Hands raised in Blessing

1998. Christmas. Angels. Multicoloured.

2064 20p. Type **1377** 50 50
2065 26p. Angel praying 75 60
2066 30p. Angel plaing flute 1·25 1·50
2067 43p. Angel playing lute 1·50 1·60
2068 63p. Angel praying (different) 2·00 2·25

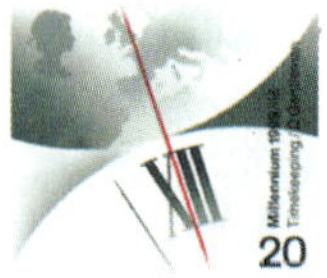

1382 Greenwich Meridian and Clock (John Harrison's chronometer)

1999. Millennium Series. The Inventors' Tale. Multicoloured.

2069 20p. Type **1382** 75 70
2070 26p. Industrial worker and blast furnace (James Watt's discovery of steam power) 95 1·00
2071 43p. Early photos of leaves (Henry Fox-Talbot's photographic experiments) 1·50 1·60
2072 63p. Computer inside human head (Alan Turing's work on computers) 2·25 2·40

1386 Airliner hugging Globe (International air travel)

1999. Millennium Series. The Travellers' Tale.

2073 **1386** 20p. multicoloured 75 70
2074 - 26p. multicoloured 95 1·00
2075 - 43p. black, stone and bronze 1·50 1·60
2076 - 63p. multicoloured 2·25 2·40

DESIGNS: 26p. Women on bicycle (development of the bicycle); 43p. Victorian railway station (growth of public transport); 63p. Captain Cook and Maori (Captain James Cook's voyages).

1390

1999. (a) Self-adhesive.

2077 **1390** (1st) grey (face value) (Queen's head in colourless relief) 3·00 2·50

(b) Ordinary gum.

2078 (1st) black 3·00 2·50

1391 Vaccinating Child (pattern in cow markings) (Jenner's development of smallpox vaccine)

1999. Millennium Series. The Patients' Tale. Multicoloured.

2080 20p. Type **1391** 75 70
2081 26p. Patient on trolley (nursing care) 95 1·00
2082 43p. Penicillin mould (Fleming's discovery of penicillin) 1·50 1·60
2083 63p. Sculpture of test-tube baby (development of in-vitro fertilization) 2·25 2·40

1395 Dove and Norman Settler (medieval migration to Scotland)

1999. Millennium Series. The Settlers' Tale. Multicoloured.

2084 20p. Type **1395** 75 70
2085 26p. Pilgrim Fathers and Red Indian (17th-century migration to America) 95 1·00
2086 43p. Sailing ship and aspects of settlement (19th-century migration to Australia) 2·00 1·75
2087 63p. Hummingbird and superimposed stylized face (20th-century migration to Great Britain) 3·00 3·00

1399 Woven Threads (woollen industry)

1999. Millennium Series. The Workers' Tale. Multicoloured.

2088 19p. Type **1399** 75 70
2089 26p. Salts Mill, Saltaire (cotton industry) 95 1·00
2090 44p. Hull on slipway (shipbuilding) 1·75 1·60
2091 64p. Lloyd's Building (City of London finance centre) 2·25 2·40

1403 Freddie Mercury (lead singer of pop group Queen) ("Popular Music")

1999. Millennium Series. The Entertainers' Tale. Multicoloured.

2092 19p. Type **1403** 75 70
2093 26p. Bobby Moore with World Cup, 1966 ("Sport") 95 1·00
2094 44p. Dalek from "Dr. Who" (science-fiction series) ("Television") 1·50 1·60
2095 64p. Charlie Chaplin (film star) ("Cinema") 2·25 2·40

1407 Prince Edward and Miss Sophie Rhys-Jones (from photo by John Swannell)

1999. Royal Wedding. Multicoloured.

2096	26p. Type **1407**	85	85
2097	64p. Couple in profile	2·50	2·50

1409 Suffragette behind Prison Window (Equal Rights for Women)

1999. Millennium Series. The Citizens' Tale. Multicoloured.

2098	19p. Type **1409**	75	70
2099	26p. Water tap (Right to Health)	95	1·00
2100	44p. Generations of school children (Right to Education)	1·75	1·60
2101	64p. "MAGNA CARTA" (Human Rights)	2·50	2·40

1413 Molecular Structures (DNA Decoding)

1999. Millennium Series. The Scientists' Tale. Multicoloured.

2102	19p. Type **1413**	75	70
2103	26p. Large ground finch and fossilized skeleton (Darwin's Theory of Evolution)	1·50	1·00
2104	44p. Rotation of polarized light by magnetism (Faraday's work on electricity)	1·50	1·60
2105	64p. Saturn (development of astronomical telescopes)	2·25	2·40

1999. Solar Eclipse. Sheet 89×101 mm.

MS2106	No. 2105×4 (sold at £2.56)	22·00	22·00

1417 Upland Landscape (Strip Farming)

1999. Millennium Series. The Farmers' Tale. Multicoloured.

2107	19p. Type **1417**	75	70
2108	26p. Horse-drawn plough (Mechanical Farming)	95	1·00
2109	44p. Man peeling potato (food imports)	2·00	1·60
2110	64p. Aerial view of combine harvester (Satellite Agriculture)	2·50	2·40

1421 Robert the Bruce (Battle of Bannockburn, 1314)

1999. The Millennium Series. The Soldiers' Tale.

2111	**1421**	19p. black, stone and silver	75	70
2112	-	26p. multicoloured	95	1·00
2113	-	44p. grey, black and silver	2·00	1·60
2114	-	64p. multicoloured	2·50	2·40

DESIGNS: 26p. Cavalier and horse (English Civil War); 44p. War Graves Cemetery, The Somme (World Wars); 64p. Soldiers with boy (Peace-keeping).

1425 "Hark the herald angels sing" and Hymnbook (John Wesley)

1999. Millennium Series. The Christians' Tale. Multicoloured.

2115	19p. Type **1425**	75	70
2116	26p. King James I and Bible (Authorised version of Bible)	95	1·00
2117	44p. St. Andrews Cathedral, Fife ("Pilgrimage")	1·50	1·60
2118	64p. Nativity ("First Christmas")	2·25	2·40

1429 "World of the Stage" (Allen Jones)

1999. The Millennium Series. The Artists' Tale. Multicoloured.

2119	19p. Type **1429**	75	70
2120	26p. "World of Music" (Bridget Riley)	95	1·00
2121	44p. "World of Literature" (Lisa Milroy)	1·50	1·60
2122	64p. "New Worlds" (Sir Howard Hodgkin)	2·25	2·40

1433 Clock Face and Map of North America

1434 Clock Face and Map of Asia

1435 Clock Face and Map of Middle East

1436 Clock Face and Map of Europe

1999. Millennium Series. "Millennium Timekeeper". Sheet 120×89 mm. Multicoloured.

MS2123	64p. Type **1433**; 64p. Type **1434**; 64p. Type **1435**; 64p. Type **1436**	26·00	26·00

No. **MS**2123 also exists overprinted **EARLS COURT, LONDON 22–28 MAY 2000 THE STAMP SHOW 2000** from Exhibition Premium Passes, costing £10, available from 1 March 2000.

1437 Queen Elizabeth II

2000. New Millennium.

2124	**1437**	(1st) brown	1·00	1·00

1438 Barn Owl (World Owl Trust, Muncaster)

2000. Millennium Projects (1st series). "Above and Bend".

2125	19p. Type **1438**	1·25	70
2126	26p. Night sky (National Space Science Centre, Leicester)	95	1·00
2126a	(1st) As No. 2126	5·25	4·50
2127	44p. River Goyt and textile mills (Torrs Walkway, New Mills)	1·50	1·75
2128	64p. Northern gannets (Seabird Centre, North Berwick)	2·50	2·50

1442 Millennium Beacon (Beacons across The Land)

2000. Millennium Projects (2nd series). "Fire and Light". Multicoloured.

2129	19p. Type **1442**	75	70
2130	26p. Garratt steam locomotive No. 143 pulling train (Rheilffordd Eryri, Welsh Highland Railway)	1·25	1·00
2131	44p. Lightning (Dynamic Earth Centre, Edinburgh)	1·50	1·50
2132	64p. Multicoloured lights (Lighting Croydon's Skyline)	2·25	2·50

2000. As T 929 but with "1st" face value.

2133	(1st) black and cream	1·50	1·25

1447 Beach Pebbles (Turning the Tide, Durham Coast)

2000. Millennium Projects (3rd series). "Water and Coast".

2134	19p. Type **1447**	75	70
2135	26p. Frog's legs and water lilies (National Pondlife Centre, Merseyside)	1·25	1·00
2136	44p. Cliff Boardwalk (Parc Arfordirol, Llanelli Coast)	1·50	1·50
2137	64p. Reflections in water (Portsmouth Harbour Development)	2·25	2·50

1451 Reed Beds, River Braid (ECOS, Ballymena)

2000. Millennium Projects (4th series). "Life and Earth".

2138	(2nd.) Type **1451**	75	70
2139	(1st) South American leaf-cutter ants ("Web of Life" Exhibition, London Zoo)	1·25	1·00
2140	44p. Solar sensors (Earth Centre, Doncaster)	1·50	1·50
2141	64p. Hydroponic leaves (Project SUZY, Teesside)	2·25	1·50

1455 Pottery Glaze (Ceramica Museum, Stoke-on-Trent)

2000. Millennium Projects (5th series). "Art and Craft".

2142	(2nd.) Type **1455**	75	70
2143	(1st) Bankside Galleries (Tate Modern, London)	1·25	1·00
2144	45p. Road marking (Cycle Network Artworks)	1·50	1·50
2145	65p. People of Salford (Lowry Centre, Salford)	2·25	2·50

2000. "Stamp Show 2000" International Stamp Exhibition, London. Jeffrey Matthews Colour Palette. Sheet 124×70 mm, containing stamps as T 367.

MS2146	4p. blue; 5p. brown; 6p. green; 10p. orange; 31p. mauve; 39p. mauve; 64p. green; £1 violet	30·00	30·00

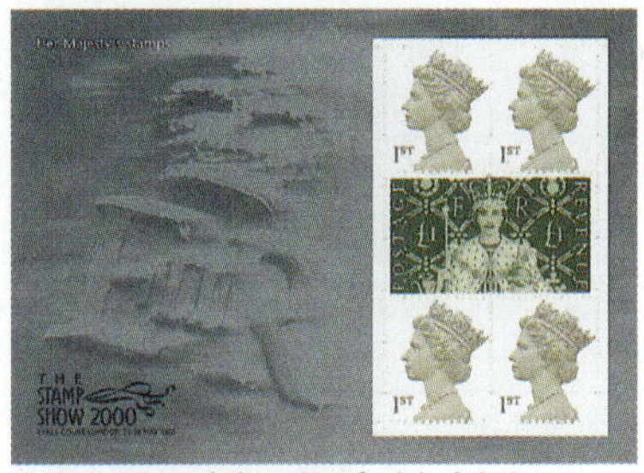

1459a (image scaled to 40% of original size)

2000. "Stamp Show 2000" International Stamp Exhibition, London. "Her Majesty's Stamps". Sheet 121×89 mm.

MS2147	**1459a** (1st) brown (Type **1437**) ×4; £1 green (as Type **163**)	21·00	21·00

The £1 value is an adaptation of the 1953 Coronation 1s.3d. stamp originally designed by Edmund Dulac.

1460 Children playing (Millennium Greens Project)

2000. Millennium Projects (6th series). "People and Places". Multicoloured.

2148	(2nd.) Type **1460**	75	70
2149	(1st) Millennium Bridge, Gateshead	1·25	1·00
2150	45p. Daisies (Mile End Park, London)	1·50	1·50
2151	65p. African Hut and Thatched Cottage ("On the Meridian Line" Project)	2·25	2·50

1464 Raising the Stone (Strangford Stone, Killyleagh)

2000. Millennium Projects (7th series). "Stone and Soil".

2152	**1464**	(2nd.) blk, grey & silver	75	70
2153	-	(1st) multicoloured	1·25	1·00
2154	-	45p. multicoloured	1·50	1·75
2155	-	65p. multicoloured	2·50	2·50

DESIGNS: No. 2153, Horse's Hooves (Trans Pennine Trail, Derbyshire); 2154 Cyclist (Kingdom of Fife Cycle Ways, Scotland); 2155, Bluebell Wood (Groundwork's "Changing Places" Project).

1468 Tree Roots ("Yews for the Millennium" Project)

2000. Millennium Projects (8th series). "Tree and Leaf". Multicoloured.

2156	(2nd.) Type **1468**	75	70
2157	(1st) Sunflower ("Eden" Project, St. Austell)	1·25	1·00
2158	45p. Sycamore seeds (Millennium Seed Bank, Wakehurst Place, Surrey)	1·50	1·60
2159	65p. Forest, Doire Dach ("Forest for Scotland")	2·50	2·50

1472 Queen Elizabeth the Queen Mother

1472a Royal Family on Queen Mother's 99th Birthday (image scaled to 40% of original size)

2000. Queen Elizabeth the Queen Mother's 100th Birthday. Multicoloured.

2160	27p. Type **1472**	2·50	2·75
MS2161	121×89 mm. **1427a** multicoloured	11·00	11·00

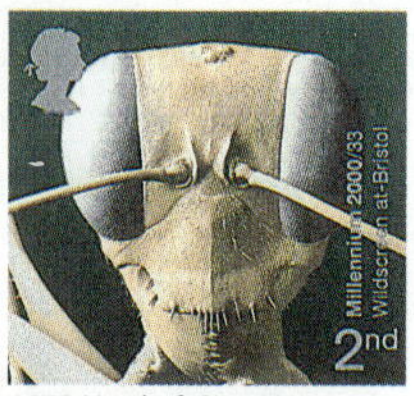

1473 Head of *Gigantiops destructor* (Ant) (Wildscreen at Bristol)

2000. Millennium Projects (9th series). "Mind and Matter". Multicoloured.

2162	(2nd.) Type **1473**	75	70
2163	(1st) Gathering water lilies on Broads (Norfolk and Norwich Project)	1·25	1·00
2164	45p. X-ray of hand holding computer mouse (Millennium Point, Birmingham)	1·50	1·75
2165	65p. Tartan wool holder (Scottish Cultural Resources Access Network)	2·25	2·50

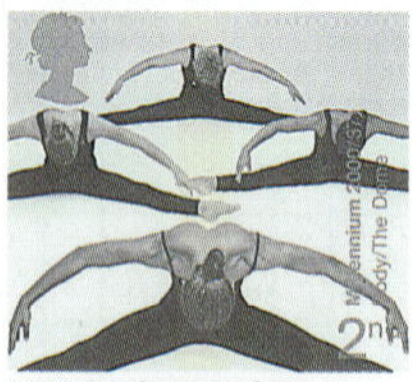

1477 Acrobatic Performers (Millennium Dome)

2000. Millennium Projects (10th series). "Body and Bone".

2166	**1477**	(2nd.) black, blue & silver	75	70
2167	-	(1st) multicoloured	1·25	1·00
2168	-	45p. multicoloured	1·50	1·50
2169	-	65p. multicoloured	2·25	2·50

DESIGNS: No. 2167, Football players (Hampden Park, Glasgow); 2168, Bather (Bath Spa Project); 2169, Hen's egg under magnification (Centre for Life, Newcastle).

1481 Virgin and Child Stained Glass Window, St. Edmundsbury Cathedral (Suffolk Cathedral Millennium Project)

2000. Millennium Projects (11th series). "Spirit and Faith". Multicoloured.

2170	(2nd.) Type **1481**	75	70
2171	(1st) Floodlit church of St. Peter and St. Paul, Overstowey (Church Floodlighting Trust)	1·25	1·00
2172	45p. 12th-cent Latin Gradual (St. Patrick Centre, Downpatrick)	1·50	1·50
2173	65p. Chapter House ceiling, York Minster (York Millennium Mystery Plays)	2·25	2·50

1485 Church Bells (Ringing in the Millennium)

2000. Millennium Projects (12th series). "Sound and Vision". Multicoloured.

2174	(2nd.) Type **1485**	75	70
2175	(1st) Eye (Year of the Artist)	1·25	1·00
2176	45p. Top of harp (Canolfan Mileniwm, Cardiff)	1·50	1·50
2177	65p. Silhouetted figure within latticework (TS2K Creative Enterprise Centres, London)	2·25	2·50

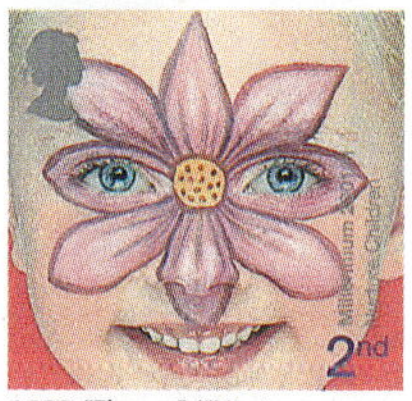

1489 "Flower" ("Nurture Children")

2001. New Millennium. Rights of the Child, Face Paintings. Multicoloured.

2178	(2nd.) Type **1489**	75	75
2179	(1st) "Tiger" ("Listen to Children")	1·00	1·10
2180	45p. "Owl" ("Teach Children")	1·60	1·75
2181	65p. "Butterfly" ("Ensure Children's Freedom")	2·40	2·50

1493 "Love"

2001. "Occasions" Greetings Stamps. Multicoloured.

2182	(1st) Type **1493**	1·30	1·30
2183	(1st) "THANKS"	1·30	1·30
2184	(1st) "abc" "New Baby"	1·30	1·30
2185	(1st) "WELCOME"	1·30	1·30
2186	(1st) "Cheers"	1·30	1·30

The silver-grey backgrounds are printed in Iriodin ink which gives a shiny effect.

1498 Dog and Owner on Bench

2001. Cats and Dogs. Self-adhesive.

2187	**1498**	(1st) black, grey & silver	60	50
2188	-	(1st) black, grey & silver	60	50
2189	-	(1st) black, grey & silver	60	50
2190	-	(1st) black, grey & silver	60	50
2191	-	(1st) black, grey & silver	60	50
2192	-	(1st) black, grey & silver	60	50
2193	-	(1st) black, grey & silver	60	50
2194	-	(1st) black, grey & silver	60	50
2195	-	(1st) black, grey & silver	60	50
2196	-	(1st) black, grey & silver	60	50

DESIGNS: No. 2188 Dog in bath; 2189, Boxer at dog show; 2190, Cat in handbag; 3192, Dog in car; 2193, Cat at window; 2194, Dog behind fence; 2195, Cat watching bird; 2196, Cat in washbasin.

1508 "RAIN"

2001. The Weather. Multicoloured.

2197	19p. Type **1508**	70	75
2198	27p. "FAIR"	85	1·00
2199	45p. "STORMY"	1·50	1·50
2200	65p. "VERY DRY"	2·40	2·50
MS2201	105×105 mm. Nos. 2197/2200	18·00	18·00

The violet on the 27p. and miniature sheet is printed in thermochromic ink, which changes from violet to blue when exposed to heat.

1512 *Vanguard* Class Submarine, 1992

2001. Centenary of Royal Navy Submarine Service. Multicoloured. (a) Ordinary gum.

2202	(2nd) Type **1512**	70	75
2203	(1st) *Swiftsure* Class Submarine, 1973	85	90
2204	45p. *Unity* Class Submarine, 1939	1·75	1·60
2205	65p. "Holland" Type Submarine, 1901	2·40	2·50
MS2206	92×97 mm. (a) (1st) White Ensign; (b) (1st) Union Jack; (c) (1st) Jolly Roger flown by H.M.S. *Proteus* (submarine); (d) (1st) Flag of Chief of Defence Staff	9·00	9·00

(b) Self-adhesive.

2207	(1st) *Swiftsure* Class Submarine, 1973	45·00	40·00
2208	(1st) White Ensign	15·00	15·00
2209	(1st) Jolly Roger Flown by H.M.S. *Proteus* (submarine)	15·00	15·00

1520 Leyland X2 Open-top, London General B Type, Leyland Titan TD1 and AEC Regent 1

1521 AEC Regent 1, Daimler COG5, Utility Guy Arab Mk II and AEC Regent III RT Type

1522 AEC Regent III RT Type, Bristol KSW5G Open-top, AEC Routemaster and Bristol Lodekka FSF6G

1523 Bristol Lodekka FSF6G, Leyland Titan PD3/4, Leyland Atlantean PDR1/1 and Daimler Fleetline CRG6LX-33

1524 Daimler Fleetline CRG6LX-33, MCW Metrobus DR102/43, Leyland Olympian ONLXB/1R and Dennis Trident

2001. 150th Anniv of First Double-decker Bus.

2210	**1520**	(1st) multicoloured	60	50
2211	**1521**	(1st) multicoloured	60	50
2212	**1522**	(1st) multicoloured	60	50
2213	**1523**	(1st) multicoloured	60	50
2214	**1524**	(1st) multicoloured	60	50
MS2215		120×105 mm. Nos. 2210/14	10·50	10·50

In No. **MS**2215 the illustrations of the AEC Regent III RT Type and the Daimler Fleetline CRG6LX-33 appear twice.

1525 Toque Hat by Pip Hackett

2001. Fashion Hats. Multicoloured.

2216	(1st) Type **1525**	85	90
2217	(E) Butterfly hat by Dai Rees	1·10	1·25
2218	45p. Top hat by Stephen Jones	1·60	1·60
2219	65p. Spiral hat by Philip Treacy	2·50	2·50

1529 Common Frog

2001. Europa. Pond Life. Multicoloured.

2220	(1st) Type **1529**	1·00	1·00
2221	(E) Great diving beetle	1·25	1·25
2222	45p. Three-spined stickleback	1·50	1·50
2223	65p. Southern hawker dragonfly	2·00	2·25

The 1st and E values incorporate the "EUROPA" emblem.

1533 Policeman

2001. Punch and Judy Show Puppets. Multicoloured. (a) Ordinary Gum.

2224	(1st) Type **1533**	60	50
2225	(1st) Clown	60	50
2226	(1st) Mr. Punch	60	50
2227	(1st) Judy	60	50
2228	(1st) Beadle	60	50
2229	(1st) Crocodile	60	50

(b) Self-adhesive.

2230	(1st) Mr. Punch	17·00	17·00
2231	(1st) Judy	17·00	17·00

1539 Carbon 60 Molecule (Chemistry)

2001. Centenary of Nobel Prizes.

2232	**1539**	(2nd) black, silver and grey	75	65
2233	-	(1st) multicoloured	1·50	90
2234	-	(E) black, silver and green	1·50	1·25

2235	- 40p. multicoloured	2·00	1·25
2236	- 45p. multicoloured	3·00	1·75
2237	- 65p. black and silver	4·00	2·50

DESIGNS: No. 2233, Globe (Economic Sciences); 2234, Embossed Dove (Peace); 2235, Crosses (Physiology or Medicine); 2236, Poem "The Addressing of Cats" by T. S. Eliot in Open Book (Literature); 2237, Hologram of Boron Molecule (Physics).

The grey on No. 2232 is printed in thermochromic ink which temporarily changes to pale grey when exposed to heat.

The centre of No. 2235 is coated with a eucalyptus scent.

1545 Robins with Snowman

2001. Christmas. Robins. Self-adhesive. Multicoloured.

2238	(2nd) Type **1545**	75	70
2239	(1st) Robins on bird table	1·00	1·00
2240	(E) Robins skating on bird bath	1·50	1·50
2241	45p. Robins with Christmas pudding	2·00	2·00
2242	65p. Robins in paper chain nest	3·00	3·00

1550 "How the Whale got his Throat"

2002. Centenary of Publication of Rudyard Kipling's Just So Stories. Multicoloured. Self-adhesive.

2243	(1st) Type **1550**	50	45
2244	(1st) "How the Camel got his Hump"	50	45
2245	(1st) "How the Rhinoceros got his Skin"	50	45
2246	(1st) "How the Leopard got his Spots"	50	45
2247	(1st) "The Elephant's Child"	50	45
2248	(1st) "The Sing-Song of Old Man Kangaroo"	50	45
2249	(1st) "The Beginning of the Armadillos"	50	45
2250	(1st) "The Crab that played with the Sea"	50	45
2251	(1st) "The Cat that walked by Himself"	50	45
2252	(1st) "The Butterfly that stamped"	50	45

1560 Queen Elizabeth II, 1952 (Dorothy Wilding)

2002. Golden Jubilee. Studio portraits of Queen Elizabeth II by photographers named. Multicoloured.

2253	(2nd) Type **1560**	75	55
2254	(1st) Queen Elizabeth II, 1968 (Cecil Beaton)	1·00	80
2255	(E) Queen Elizabeth II, 1978 (Lord Snowdon)	1·50	1·50
2256	45p. Queen Elizabeth II, 1984 (Yousef Karsh)	1·75	2·00
2257	65p. Queen Elizabeth II, 1996 (Tim Graham)	2·75	3·00

1566

2002. As T 154/5 (Wilding definitive of 1952–54), but with service indicator as T 1566.

2258	**1566** (2nd) red	1·20	1·00
2259	- (1st) green	1·25	1·25

1567 Rabbits ("a new baby")

2002. "Occasions". Greetings Stamps. Mult.

2260	(1st) Type **1567**	1·10	1·10
2261	(1st) "LOVE"	1·10	1·10
2262	(1st) Aircraft sky-writing "hello"	1·10	1·10
2263	(1st) Bear pulling potted topiary tree (Moving Home)	1·10	1·10
2264	(1st) Flowers ("best wishes")	1·10	1·10

No. 2262 also comes self-adhesive.

1572 Studland Bay, Dorset

2002. British Coastlines. Multicoloured.

2265	27p. Type **1572**	60	50
2266	27p. Luskentyre, South Harris	60	50
2267	27p. Cliffs, Dover, Kent	60	50
2268	27p. Padstow Harbour, Cornwall	60	50
2269	27p. Broadstairs, Kent	60	50
2270	27p. St. Abbs Head, Scottish Borders	60	50
2271	27p. Dunster Beach, Somerset	60	50
2272	27p. Newquay Beach, Cornwall	60	50
2273	27p. Portrush, County Antrim	60	50
2274	27p. Sand-spit, Conwy	60	50

1582 Slack Wire Act

2002. Circus. Multicoloured.

2275	(2nd) Type **1582**	50	60
2276	(1st) Lion tamer	75	85
2277	(E) Trick tri-cyclists	1·00	1·25
2278	45p. Krazy kar	1·75	1·50
2279	65p. Equestrienne	2·75	2·25

1587 Queen Elizabeth the Queen Mother

2002. Queen Elizabeth the Queen Mother Commemoration. As Nos. 1507/10 with changed face values and showing both the Queen's head and frame in black.

2280	**1587** (1st) multicoloured	1·00	85
2281	**1587** (E) black and blue	1·25	1·10
2282	**1587** 45p. multicoloured	1·50	1·50
2283	**1587** 65p. black, stone and brown	2·00	2·25

1588 Airbus A340-600 (2002)

2002. 50th Anniv of Passenger Jet Aviation. Airliners. Multicoloured.

2284	(2nd) Type **1588**	75	55
2285	(1st) Concorde (1976)	1·25	1·00
2286	(E) Trident (1964)	1·50	1·50
2287	45p. Vickers VC-10 (1964)	2·00	2·00
2288	65p. de Havilland DH.106 Comet (1952)	3·00	3·00
MS2289	120×105 mm. Nos. 2284/8	12·00	11·00

No. 2285 also comes self-adhesive.

1593 Crowned Lion with Shield of St. George

1594 Top Left Quarter of English Flag, and Football

1595 Top Right Quarter of English Flag, and Football

1596 Bottom Left Quarter of English Flag, and Football

1597 Bottom Right Quarter of English Flag, and Football

2002. World Cup Football Championship, Japan and Korea (2002).

2291	**1593** (1st) blue, red and silver	2·50	2·50
MS2292	145×74 mm. No. 2291; **1594** (1st) multicoloured; **1595** (1st) multicoloured; **1596** (1st) multicoloured; **1597** (1st) multicoloured	7·50	6·50

(b) Self-adhesive.

2293	**1594** (1st) multicoloured	6·00	6·00
2294	**1595** (1st) multicoloured	6·00	6·00

2002. Self-adhesive.

2295	**914** (1st) gold	1·00	1·00
2296	**1093a** (E) blue	2·00	2·00
2297	**367a** 42p. grey	3·00	3·00
2298	**367a** 68p. brown	4·00	4·00

No. 2295 was initially sold for 27p.

1598 Swimming

2002. 17th Commonwealth Games, Manchester. Multicoloured.

2299	(2nd) Type **1598**	75	55
2300	(1st) Running	1·00	80
2301	(E) Cycling	1·25	1·25
2302	47p. Long jumping	1·50	1·50
2303	68p. Wheelchair racing	2·00	2·25

1603 Tinkerbell

2002. 150th Anniv of Great Ormond Street Children's Hospital. Peter Pan by Sir James Barrie. Multicoloured.

2304	(2nd) Type **1063**	75	55
2305	(1st) Wendy, John and Michael Darling in front of Big Ben	1·00	80
2306	(E) Crocodile and alarm clock	1·25	1·25
2307	47p. Captain Hook	1·50	1·50
2308	68p. Peter Pan	2·00	2·25

1608 Millennium Bridge, 2001

2002. Bridges of London. Multicoloured.

2309	(2nd) Type **1608**	75	55
2310	(1st) Tower Bridge, 1894	1·00	80
2311	(E) Westminster Bridge, 1864	2·00	1·50
2312	47p. "Blackfriars Bridge, c 1800" (William Marlow)	2·50	2·00
2313	68p. "London Bridge, c 1670" (Wenceslaus Hollar)	3·50	3·00

No. 2310 also comes self-adhesive.

1613 Galaxies and Nebula (image scaled to 40% of original size)

2002. Astronomy. Sheet 120×89 mm. Multicoloured.

MS2315	**1613** (1st) Planetary nebula in Aquila; (1st) Seyfert 2 galaxy in Pegasus; (1st) Planetary nebula in Norma; (1st) Seyfert 2 galaxy in Circinus	5·25	5·25

1614 Green Pillar Box, 1857

2002. 150th Anniv of the First Pillar Box.

2316	(2nd) Type **1614**	75	55
2317	(1st) Horizontal Aperture Box, 1874	1·00	80
2318	(E) Air Mail Box, 1934	1·75	1·75
2319	47p. Double Aperture Box, 1939	2·00	2·50
2320	68p. Modern Style Box, 1980	2·50	3·00

1619 Blue Spruce Star

2002. Christmas. Self-adhesive.

2321	(2nd) Type **1619**	75	55
2322	(1st) Holly	1·00	80
2323	(E) Ivy	1·50	1·50
2324	47p. Mistletoe	2·00	1·75
2325	68p. Pine cone	3·00	2·75

2002. 50th Anniv of Wilding Definitives (1st issue). Sheet 124×70 mm, containing designs as T 154/5 and 157/60 (1952–54 issue), but with values in decimal currency as T 1348 or with service indicator as T 1566, printed on cream.

MS2326	1p. red; 2p. blue; 5p. brown; (2nd) red; (1st) green; 33p. brown; 37p. mauve; 47p. brown; 50p. green	10·00	10·00

See also No. **MS**2367.

1624 Barn Owl landing

1625 Barn Owl with folded Wings and Legs down

1626 Barn Owl with extended Wings and Legs down

1627 Barn Owl in Flight with Wings lowered

1628 Barn Owl in Flight with Wings raised

1629 Kestrel with Wings folded

1630 Kestrel with Wings fully extended upwards

1631 Kestrel with Wings horizontal

1632 Kestrel with Wings partly extended downwards

1633 Kestrel with Wings fully extended downwards

2003. Birds of Prey.

2327	**1624**	(1st) multicoloured	70	80
2328	**1625**	(1st) multicoloured	70	80
2329	**1626**	(1st) multicoloured	70	80
2330	**1627**	(1st) multicoloured	70	80
2331	**1628**	(1st) multicoloured	70	80
2332	**1629**	(1st) multicoloured	70	80
2333	**1630**	(1st) multicoloured	70	80
2334	**1631**	(1st) multicoloured	70	80
2335	**1632**	(1st) multicoloured	70	80
2336	**1633**	(1st) multicoloured	70	80

1634 "Gold star, See me, Playtime"

2003. "Occasions" Greetings Stamps.

2337	**1634**	(1st) yellow and blue	60	50
2338	-	(1st) red and blue	60	50
2339	-	(1st) purple and green	60	50
2340	-	(1st) green and red	60	50
2341	-	(1st) blue and yellow	60	50
2342	-	(1st) blue and purple	60	50

DESIGNS: No. 2338, "I U, XXXX, S.W.A.L.K."; 2239, "Angel, Poppet, Little terror"; 2340, "Yes, No, Maybe"; 2341, "Oops!, Sorry, Will try harder"; 2342, "I did it!, You did it!, We did it!".

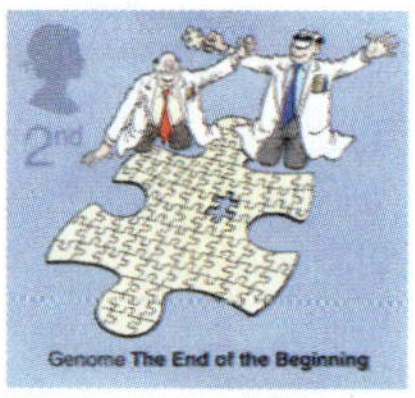

1640 Completing the Genome Jigsaw

2003. 50th Anniv of Discovery of DNA. Multicoloured.

2343	(2nd) Type **1640**	1·00	55
2344	(1st) Ape with Moustache and Scientist	1·00	80
2345	(E) DNA Snakes and Ladders	1·25	1·25
2346	47p. "Animal Scientists"	1·50	1·50
2347	68p. Genome Crystal Ball	2·00	2·25

1645 Strawberry

2003. Fruit and Vegetables. Self-adhesive.

2348	(1st) Type **1645**	70	50
2349	(1st) Potato	70	50
2350	(1st) Apple	70	50
2351	(1st) Red pepper	70	50
2352	(1st) Pear	70	50
2353	(1st) Orange	70	50
2354	(1st) Tomato	70	50
2355	(1st) Lemon	70	50
2356	(1st) Cabbage	70	50
2357	(1st) Aubergine	70	50

Nos. 2348/57 are accompanied by a similar-sized pane of self-adhesive labels showing ears, eyes, mouths, hats etc which are intended for the adornment of fruit and vegetables depicted.

1655

2003. Overseas Stamps. Self-adhesive.

2357a	-	(Worldwide postcard) black, red and blue	85	85
2358	**1655**	(Europe) blue and red	1·10	1·10
2358a	**1655**	(Europe) deep blue, new blue and rosine	1·10	1·10
2359	**1655**	(Worldwide) red and blue	2·10	2·10
2359a	**1655**	(Worldwide) deep mauve, new blue and rosine	2·10	2·10

Nos. 2358/9 were intended to pay postage on mail up to 40 grams to either Europe (52p.) or foreign destinations outside Europe (£1.12). No. 2357a was intended to pay postcard rate to foreign destination (43p.).

1656 Amy Johnson (pilot) and de Havilland DH.60G Gipsy Moth *Jason*

2003. Extreme Endeavours. (British Explorers).

2360	(2nd) Type **1656**	50	50
2361	(1st) Members of 1953 Everest team	75	75
2362	(E) Freya Stark (traveller and writer) and desert	1·50	1·50
2363	42p. Ernest Shackleton (Antarctic explorer) and wreck of *Endurance*	1·75	1·75
2364	47p. Francis Chichester (yachtsman) and *Gipsy Moth IV*	2·00	2·00
2365	68p. Robert Falcon Scott (Antarctic explorer) and Norwegian Expedition at the Pole	2·50	2·50

No. 2361 also comes self-adhesive.

2003. 50th Anniv of Wilding Definitives (2nd issue). Sheet 124×70 mm, containing designs as Nos. 519, 575, 617b and 585 (1952–54 issue), but with values in decimal currency as T 1348 or with service indicator as T 1566, printed on cream.

MS2367 4p. lilac; 8p. blue; (1st) purple; 20p. green; 28p. green; 34p. purple; (1st) chestnut; 42p. blue; 68p. blue	10·50	11·25

1662 Guardsmen in Coronation Procession

2003. 50th Anniv of Coronation.

2368	**1662**	(1st) multicoloured	45	50
2369	-	(1st) black and gold	45	50
2370	-	(1st) multicoloured	45	50
2371	-	(1st) black and gold	45	50
2372	-	(1st) multicoloured	45	50
2373	-	(1st) black and gold	45	50
2374	-	(1st) multicoloured	45	50
2375	-	(1st) black and gold	45	50
2376	-	(1st) multicoloured	45	50
2377	-	(1st) black and gold	45	50

DESIGNS: No. 2369, East End children reading Coronation party poster; 2370, Queen Elizabeth II in Coronation Chair with Bishops of Durham and Bath & Wells; 2371, Children in Plymouth working on Royal Montage; 2372, Queen Elizabeth II in Coronation Robes (photograph by Cecil Beaton); 2373, Childrens Race at East End Street Party; 2374, Coronation Coach passing through Marble Arch; 2375, Children in Fancy Dress; 2376, Coronation Coach outside Buckingham Palace; 2377, Children eating at London street party.

No. 2372 does not show a silhouette of the Queens head in gold as do the other nine designs.

2003. 50th Anniv of Coronation. Designs as Nos. 585, 534 (Wilding definitive of 1952) and 163 (Coronation commemorative of 1953), but with values in decimal currency as T 1348.

2378	47p. brown	5·00	2·50
2379	68p. blue	5·00	2·50
2380	£1 green	50·00	45·00

1672 Prince William in September 2001 (Brendan Beirne)

2003. 21st Birthday of Prince William of Wales.

2381	**1672**	28p. multicoloured	1·00	50
2382	-	(E) mauve, black and green	2·25	1·50
2383	-	47p. multicoloured	2·75	2·00
2384	-	68p. deep green, black and green	4·00	2·50

DESIGNS: No. 2382, Prince William in September 2000 (Tim Graham); 2383, Prince William in September 2001 (Camera Press); 2384, Prince William in September 2001 (Tim Graham).

1676 Loch Assynt, Sutherland

2003. A British Journey: Scotland. Multicoloured.

2385	(2nd) Type **1676**	50	35
2386	(1st) Ben More, Isle of Mull	75	50
2387	(E) Rothiemurchus, Cairngorms	1·25	1·25
2388	42p. Dalveen Pass, Lowther Hills	1·25	1·50
2389	47p. Glenfinnan Viaduct, Lochaber	1·50	2·00
2390	68p. Papa Little, Shetland Islands	2·00	2·50

No. 2386 also comes self-adhesive.

1682 "The Station" (Andrew Davidson)

2003. British Pub Signs. Multicoloured.

2392	(1st) Type **1682**	75	50
2393	(E) "Black Swan" (Stanley Chew)	2·00	2·00
2394	42p. "The Cross Keys" (George Mackenney)	1·50	1·50
2395	47p. "The Mayflower" (Ralph Ellis)	1·75	2·00
2396	68p. "The Barley Sheaf" (Joy Cooper)	2·00	2·25

1687 Meccano Constructor Biplane, c. 1931

2003. Classic Transport Toys. Multicoloured.

2397	(1st) Type **1687**	75	50
2398	(E) Wells-Brimtoy Clockwork Double-decker Omnibus, c. 1938	1·25	1·25
2399	42p. Hornby M1 Clockwork Locomotive and Tender, c. 1948	1·50	1·50
2400	47p. Dinky Toys Ford Zephyr, c. 1956	1·75	1·75
2401	68p. Mettoy Friction Drive Space Ship Eagle, c. 1960	2·50	2·50
MS2402	115×105 mm. Nos. 2397/401	8·00	8·25

No. 2397 also comes self-adhesive.

1692 Coffin of Denytenamun, Egyptian, c. 900BC

2003. 250th Anniv of the British Museum. Multicoloured.

2404	(2nd) Type **1692**	50	35
2405	(1st) Alexander the Great, Greek, c. 200BC	75	50
2406	(E) Sutton Hoo Helmet, Anglo-Saxon, c. AD600	1·25	1·25
2407	42p. Sculpture of Parvati, South Indian, c. AD1550	1·50	1·50
2408	47p. Mask of Xiuhtecuhtli, Mixtec-Aztec, c. AD1500	2·00	2·00
2409	68p. Hoa Hakananai'a, Easter Island, c. AD1000	2·75	2·75

1698 Ice Spiral

2003. Christmas. Ice Sculptures by Andy Goldsworthy. Multicoloured.

2410	(2nd) Type **1698**	75	35
2411	(1st) Icicle Star	1·25	50
2412	(E) Wall of Ice Blocks	1·50	1·50
2413	53p. Ice Ball	2·00	2·00
2414	68p. Ice Hole	2·50	2·50
2415	£1.12 Snow Pyramids	3·00	3·00

1704 (image scaled to 42% of original size)

2003. England's Victory in Rugby World Cup Championship, Australia. Sheet 115×85 mm. Multicoloured.

MS2416	**1704** (1st) England flags and fans; (1st) England team standing in circle before match; 68p. World Cup trophy; 68p. Victorious England players after match	14·00	14·00

1705 Dolgoch, Rheilffordd Talyllyn Railway, Gwynedd

2004. Classic Locomotives. Multicoloured.

2417	20p. Type **1705**	65	65
2418	28p. CR Class 439, Bo'ness and Kinneil Railway, West Lothian	90	90
2419	(E) GCR Class 8K, Leicestershire	1·20	1·20
2420	42p. GWR Manor Class *Bradley Manor*, Severn Valley Railway, Worcestershire	1·50	1·50
2421	47p. SR West Country class *Blackmoor Vale*, Bluebell Railway, East Sussex	2·00	2·00
2422	68p. (1710 BR Standard class, Keighley & Worth Valley Railway, Yorkshire)	3·00	3·50
MS2423	190×67 mm. Nos. 2417/22	35·00	35·00

1711 Postman

2004. Occasions.

2424	**1711**	(1st) mauve and black	50	50
2425	-	(1st) magenta and black	50	50
2426	-	(1st) lemon and black	50	50
2427	-	(1st) green and black	50	50
2428	-	(1st) blue and black	50	50

DESIGNS: No. 2425, Face; 2426, Duck; 2427, Baby; 2428, Aircraft.

1716 Map showing Middle Earth

2004. 50th Anniv of Publication of The Fellowship of the Ring and The Two Towers by J. R. R. Tolkien. Multicoloured.

2429	(1st) Type **1716**	50	50
2430	(1st) Forest of Lothlorien in Spring	50	50
2431	(1st) Dust-jacket for *The Fellowship of the Ring*	50	50
2432	(1st) Rivendell	50	50
2433	(1st) The Hall at Bag End	50	50
2434	(1st) Orthanc	50	50
2435	(1st) Doors of Durin	50	50
2436	(1st) Barad-dur	50	50
2437	(1st) Minas Tirth	50	50
2438	(1st) Fangorn Forest	50	50

1726 Ely Island, Lower Lough Erne

2004. A British Journey: Northern Ireland. Multicoloured.

2439	(2nd) Type **1726**	65	65
2440	(1st) Giant's Causeway, Antrim Coast	90	90
2441	(E) Slemish, Antrim Mountains	1·20	1·20
2442	42p. Banns Road, Mourne Mountains	1·30	1·30
2443	47p. Glenelly Valley, Sperrins	1·50	1·50
2444	68p. Islandmore, Strangford Lough	2·20	2·20

No. 2440 also comes self-adhesive.

1732 "Lace 1 (trial proof) 1968" (Sir Terry Frost)

2004. Centenary of the Entente Cordiale. Contemporary Paintings.

2446	**1732**	28p. grey, black and red	1·00	85
2447	-	57p. multicoloured	2·25	2·00

DESIGN: No. 1733, "Coccinelle" (Sonia Delaunay) Stamps in similar designs were issued by France.

1734 "RMS Queen Mary 2, 2004" (Edward D. Walker)

2004. Ocean Liners. Multicoloured.

2448	(1st) Type **1734**	90	90
2449	(E) "SS Canberra 1961" (David Cobb)	1·30	1·30
2450	42p. "RMS Queen Mary 1936" (Charles Pears)	1·30	1·30
2451	47p. "RMS Mauretania, 1907" (Thomas Henry)	1·50	1·50
2452	57p. "SS City of New York, 1888" (Raphael Monleaon y Torres)	1·80	1·80
2453	68p. "PS Great Western, 1838" (Joseph Walter)	2·20	2·20
MS2454	114×104 mm. Nos. 2448/53	18·00	18·00

No. 2448 also comes self-adhesive.

Nos. 2448/55 commemorate the introduction to service of the *Queen Mary 2*.

1740 Dianthus Allwoodii Group

2004. Bicentenary of the Royal Horticultural Society (1st issue). Multicoloured.

2456	(2nd) Type **1740**	70	70
2457	(1st) Dahlia "Garden Princess"	90	90
2458	(E) Clematis "Arabella"	1·30	1·30
2459	42p. Miltonia "French Lake"	2·00	2·00
2460	47p. Lilium "Lemon Pixie"	2·50	2·50
2461	68p. Delphinium "Clifford Sky"	3·50	3·50
MS2462	115×105 mm. Nos. 2456/61	14·00	14·00

1280 "Gentiana acaulis" (Georg Ehret)

2004. Bicentenary of the Royal Horticultural Society (2nd issue). Designs as Nos. 1955, 1958 and 1962 (1997 Greeting Stamps 19th-century Flower Paintings). Multicoloured.

2463	(1st) Type **1280**	8·00	8·00
2464	(1st) "Tulipa" (Ehret)	4·00	4·00
2465	(1st) "Iris latifolia" (Ehret)	8·00	8·00

1746 Barmouth Bridge

2004. A British Journey: Wales. Multicoloured. (a) Ordinary gum.

2466	(2nd) Type **1746**	70	70
2467	(1st) Hyddgen, Plynlimon	90	90
2468	40p. Brecon Beacons	1·75	1·50
2469	43p. Pen-pych, Rhondda Valley	2·00	2·00
2470	47p. Rhewl, Dee Valley	2·50	3·00
2471	68p. Marloes Sands	3·50	4·00

(b) Self-adhesive.

2472	(1st) Hyddgen, Plynlimon	8·00	8·00

The (1st) and 40p. values include the "EUROPA" emblem.

1752 Sir Rowland Hill Award

2004. 250th Anniv of the Royal Society of Arts.

2473	**1752**	(1st) multicoloured	95	95
2474	-	40p. multicoloured	1·30	1·30
2475	-	43p. multicoloured	1·40	1·40
2476	-	47p. multicoloured	1·50	1·50
2477	-	57p. silver, vermilion and black	2·20	2·20
2478	-	68p. silver, vermilion and black	3·00	3·00

DESIGNS: No. 2474, William Shipley (Founder of Royal Society of Arts); 2475, "RSA" as Typewriter Keys and Shorthand; 2476 Chimney Sweep; 2477, "Gill Typeface"; 2478, "Zero Waste".

1758 Pine Martin

2004. Woodland Animals. Multicoloured.

2479	(1st) Type **1758**	60	50
2480	(1st) Roe deer	60	50
2481	(1st) Badger	60	50
2482	(1st) Yellow-necked mouse	60	50
2483	(1st) Wild cat	60	50
2484	(1st) Red squirrel	60	50
2485	(1st) Stoat	60	50
2486	(1st) Natterer's bat	60	50
2487	(1st) Mole	60	50
2488	(1st) Fox	60	50

1768 Pte. McNamara, 5th Dragoon Guards, Heavy Brigade Charge, Battle of Balaklava

2004. 150th Anniv of the Crimean War. Multicoloured.

2489	(2nd) Type **1768**	70	70
2490	(1st) Piper Muir, 42nd Regt of Foot, Amphibious Assault on Kerch	90	90
2491	40p. Sgt. Maj. Edwards, Scots Fusilier Guards, Gallant Action, Battle of Inkerman	2·00	2·00
2492	57p. Sgt. Powell, 1st Regt of Foot Guards, Battles of Alma and Inkerman	2·50	2·50
2493	68p. Sgt. Maj. Poole, Royal Sappers and Miners, Defensive Line, Battle of Inkerman	2·75	3·00
2494	£1.12 Sgt. Glasgow, Royal Artillery, Gun Battery besieged Sevastopol	4·50	5·00

Nos. 2489/94 show "Crimean Heroes" photographs taken in 1856.

1774 Father Christmas on Snowy Roof

2004. Christmas. Multicoloured. (a) Self-adhesive.

2495	(2nd) Type **1774**	70	70
2496	(1st) Celebrating the sunrise	90	90
2497	40p. On roof in gale	1·30	1·30
2498	57p. With umbrella in rain	1·80	1·80
2499	68p. On edge of roof with torch	2·20	2·20
2500	£1.12 Sheltering behind chimney	3·75	3·75

(b) Ordinary gum.

MS2501	115×105 mm. As Nos. 2495/500	12·00	12·00

1780 British Saddleback Pigs

2005. Farm Animals. Multicoloured.

2502	(1st) Type **1780**	50	60
2503	(1st) Khaki Campbell ducks	50	60
2504	(1st) Suffolk horses	50	60
2505	(1st) Dairy Shorthorn cattle	50	60
2506	(1st) Border collie dog	50	60
2507	(1st) Light Sussex chicks	50	60
2508	(1st) Suffolk sheep	50	60
2509	(1st) Bagot goat	50	60
2510	(1st) Norfolk black turkeys	50	60
2511	(1st) Embden geese	50	60

1790 Old Harry Rocks, Studland Bay

2005. A British Journey: South West England. Multicoloured.

2512	(2nd) Type **1790**	50	50
2513	(1st) Wheal Coates, St. Agnes	50	75
2514	40p. Start Point, Start Bay	1·50	1·75
2515	43p. Horton Down, Wiltshire	1·75	2·00
2516	57p. Chiselcombe, Exmoor	2·50	2·50
2517	68p. St. James's Stone, Lundy	3·50	3·00

1796 "Mr Rochester"

2005. 150th Death Anniv of Charlotte Brontë. Illustrations of scenes from "Jane Eyre" by Paula Rego.

2518	**1796**	(2nd) multicoloured	30	35
2519	-	(1st) multicoloured	50	45
2520	-	40p. multicoloured	1·50	1·50
2521	-	57p. silver, grey and black	3·00	2·50
2522	-	68p. multicoloured	3·75	3·00
2523	-	£1.12 silver, grey and black	4·50	3·50
MS2524		114×105 mm. Nos. 2518/23	10·00	10·00

DESIGNS: No. 1797, "Come to Me"; 1798, "In the Comfort of her Bonnet"; 1799, "La Ligne des Rats"; 1800, "Refectory"; 1801, "Inspection".

1802 Spinning Coin

2005. Centenary of the Magic Circle. Multicoloured.

2525	(1st) Type **1802**	65	45
2526	40p. Rabbit out of Hat Trick	1·00	65
2527	47p. Knotted Scarf Trick	2·50	2·75
2528	68p. Card Trick	3·00	3·00
2529	£1.12 Pyramid under Fez Trick	3·50	3·50

2005. 50th Anniv of First Castles Definitives. Sheet 127×73 mm, containing horiz designs as Nos. 595a/597a and 762 (Castles definitive of 1955–58) but with values in decimal currency.

MS2530	50p. black; 50p. black; £1 vermilion; **168** £1 blue	10·00	10·00

1807 (image scaled to 58% of original size)

2005. Royal Wedding. Sheet 85×115 mm. Multicoloured.

MS2531	**1807** 30p.×2 Prince Charles and Mrs Camilla Parker Bowles laughing; 68p.×2 Prince Charles and Mrs Camilla Parker Bowles smiling into camera	8·00	10·00

1808 Hadrian's Wall, England

2005. World Heritage Sites. Multicoloured.

2532	(2nd) Type **1808**	30	35
2533	(2nd) silver, Uluru-Kata Tjuta National Park, Australia	30	35
2534	(1st) Stonehenge, England	45	45
2535	(1st) Wet Tropics of Queensland, Australia	45	45
2536	47p. Blenheim Palace, England	60	60
2537	47p. Greater Blue Mountains Area, Australia	60	60
2538	68p. Heart of Neolithic Orkney, Scotland	90	90
2539	68p. Purnululu National Park, Australia	90	90

Stamps in these designs were issued by Australia.

1816 Ensign of the Scots Guards, 2002

2005. Trooping the Colour. Multicoloured.

2540	(2nd) Type **1816**	70	80
2541	(1st) Queen taking the salute as Colonel-in-Chief of the Grenadier Guards, 1983	75	90
2542	42p. Trumpeter of the Household Cavalry, 2004	1·00	1·20
2543	60p. Welsh Guardsman, 1990s	2·00	2·00
2544	68p. Queen riding side-saddle, 1972	2·50	2·50
2545	£1.12 Queen and Duke of Edinburgh in carriage, 2004	3·50	3·50
MS2546	115×105 mm. Nos. 2540/5	11·00	11·00

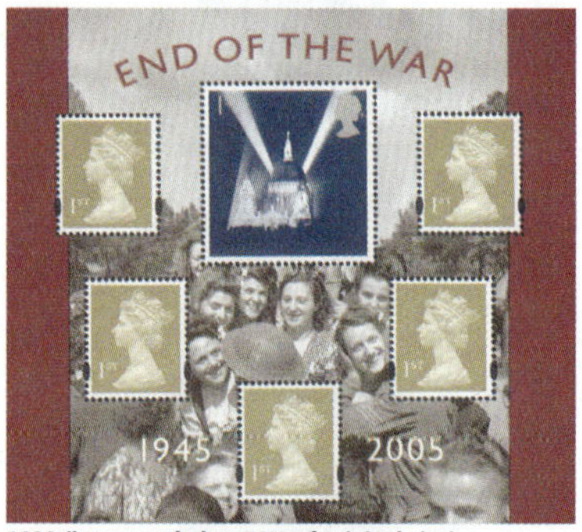

1822 (image scaled to 56% of original size)

2005. 60th Anniv of End of the Second World War. Sheet 115×105 mm containing design as No. 1875 (1995 Peace and Freedom) but with service indicator and No. 1663b×5.

MS2547	**1822** (1st) gold ×5; (1st) silver, blue and black	6·00	6·00

1823 Norton F.1, Road Version of Race Winner (1991)

2005. Motorcycles. Multicoloured.

2548	(1st) Type **1823**	75	80
2549	40p. BSA Rocket 3, Early Three Cylinder "Superbike" (1969)	90	1·00
2550	42p. Vincent Black Shadow, Fastest Standard Motorcycle (1949)	1·25	1·00
2551	47p. Triumph Speed Twin, Two Cylinder Innovation (1938)	1·75	2·00
2552	60p. Brough Superior, Bespoke Luxury Motorcycle (1930)	2·50	2·50
2553	68p. Royal Enfield, Small Engined Motor Bicycle (1914)1	3·00	3·00

1829 (image scaled to 42% of original size)

2005. London's Successful Bid for Olympic Games, 2012. Sheet 115×105 mm containing designs as Nos. 1930/4, but with service indicator. Multicoloured.

MS2554	**1829** (1st) Athlete celebrating×2; (1st) Throwing the javelin; (1st) Swimming; (1st) Athlete on starting blocks; (1st) Basketball	6·00	6·00

Stamps from **MS**2554 are all inscribed "London 2012–Host City" and have imprint date "2005". The design as No. 1934 omits the Olympic rings.

1830 African Woman eating Rice

2005. Europa. Gastronomy. Changing Tastes in Britain. Multicoloured.

2555	(2nd) Type **1830**	60	70
2556	(1st) Indian Woman drinking tea	90	1·00
2557	42p. Boy eating sushi	1·30	1·40
2558	47p. Woman eating pasta	1·50	1·60
2559	60p. Woman eating chips	2·00	1·90
2560	68p. Teenage boy eating apple	2·50	2·20

1836 *Inspector Morse*

2005. 50th Anniv of Independent Television. Classic ITV Programmes. Multicoloured.

2561	(2nd) Type **1836**	60	70
2562	(1st) *Emmerdale*	90	1·00
2563	42p. *Rising Damp*	1·30	1·40
2564	47p. *The Avengers*	1·40	1·50
2565	60p. *The South Bank Show*	2·00	1·90
2566	68p. *Who Wants to be a Millionaire*	2·20	2·20

1842 *Guzmania splendens* (Charlotte Sowerby)

2005. Similar Designs as Nos. 1550, 1896, 1961, MS2206 and 2261/2, but smaller, 20×23 mm and inscribed "1st" as T 1842. Self-adhesive.

2567	(1st) multicoloured	2·00	2·00
2568	(1st) multicoloured	2·00	2·00
2569	(1st) multicoloured	2·00	2·00
2570	(1st) multicoloured	2·00	2·00
2571	(1st) multicoloured	2·00	2·00
2572	(1st) multicoloured	2·00	2·00

1843 Cricket Scenes (image scaled to 42% of original size)

2005. England's Ashes Victory. Sheet 115×90 mm. Multicoloured.

MS2573	**1843** (1st) England team with Ashes trophy; (1st) Kevin Pieterson, Michael Vaughan and Andrew Flintoff on opening day of First Test, Lords; 68p. Michael Vaughan, Third Test, Old Trafford; 68p. Second Test cricket, Edgbaston	7·50	7·50

1844 *Entrepreante* with dismasted *British Belle Isle*

2005. Bicentenary of the Battle of Trafalgar (1st issue). Scenes from "Panorama of the Battle of Trafalgar" by William Heath. Multicoloured.

2574	(1st) Type **1844**	45	45
2575	(1st) Nelson wounded on Deck of HMS *Victory*	45	45
2576	42p. British Cutter *Entrepreante* attempting to rescue Crew of burning French *Achille*	65	65
2577	42p. Cutter and HMS *Pickle* (schooner)	65	65
2578	68p. British Fleet attacking in Two Columns	90	90
2579	68p. Franco/Spanish Fleet putting to Sea from Cadiz	90	90
MS2580	190×68 mm. Nos. 2574/9	10·00	11·00

Nos. 2574/5, 2576/7 and 2578/9 were each printed together, se-tenant, each pair forming a composite design.

2005. Bicentenary of the Battle of Trafalgar (2nd issue). As No. 2208. (2001 White Ensign from Submarine Centenary).

2581	**1516**	(1st) multicoloured	6·75	6·75

1850 Black Madonna and Child from Haiti

2005. Christmas. Madonna and Child Paintings. Multicoloured. (a) Self-adhesive.

2582	(2nd) Type **1850**	60	70
2583	(1st) "Madonna and Child" (Marianne Stokes)	90	1·00
2584	42p. "The Virgin Mary with the Infant Christ"	1·30	1·40
2585	60p. Choctaw Virgin Mother and Child (Fr. John Giuliani)	1·80	1·90
2586	68p. "Madonna and the Infant Jesus" (from India)	2·00	2·20
2587	£1.12 "Come let us adore Him" (Dianne Tchumut)	3·50	3·60

(b) Ordinary gum.

MS2588	115×102 mm. As Nos. 2582/7	10·50	11·00

1856 *The Tale of Mr. Jeremy Fisher* (Beatrix Potter)

2006. Animal Tales. Multicoloured.

2589	(2nd) Type **1856**	40	35
2590	(2nd) *Kipper* (Mick Inkpen)	40	35
2591	(1st) *The Enormous Crocodile* (Roald Dahl)	50	50
2592	(1st) *More About Paddington* (Michael Bond)	50	50
2593	42p. *Comic Adventures of Boots* (Satoshi Kitamura)	65	70
2594	42p. *Alice's Adventures in Wonderland* (Lewis Carroll)	65	70
2595	68p. *The Very Hungry Caterpillar* (Eric Carle)	1·00	1·10
2596	68p. *Maisy's* ABC (Lucy Cousins)	1·00	1·10

1864 Carding Mill Valley, Shropshire

2006. A British Journey: England. Multicoloured.

2597	(1st) Type **1864**	50	50
2598	(1st) Beachy Head, Sussex	50	50
2599	(1st) St. Paul's Cathedral, London	50	50
2600	(1st) Brancaster, Norfolk	50	50
2601	(1st) Derwent Edge, Peak District	50	50
2602	(1st) Robin Hood's Bay, Yorkshire	50	50
2603	(1st) Buttermere, Lake District	50	50
2604	(1st) Chipping Campden, Cotswolds	50	50
2605	(1st) 1872 St. Boniface Down, Isle of Wight	50	50
2606	(1st) Chamberlain Square, Birmingham	50	50

1874 Royal Albert Bridge

2006. Birth Bicentenary of Isambard Kingdom Brunel (engineer) (1st issue).

2607	(1st) Type **1874**	50	50
2608	40p. Box Tunnel	75	75
2609	42p. Paddington Station	1·00	1·00
2610	47p. *Great Eastern* (paddle steamer)	1·50	1·00
2611	60p. Clifton Suspension Bridge design	2·00	1·75
2612	68p. Maidenhead Bridge	2·50	2·25
MS2613	190×65 mm. Nos. 2607/12	8·50	8·50

2006. Birth Bicentenary of Isambard Kingdom Brunel (engineer) (2nd issue). Design as No. 2453 ("PS Great Western" from 2004 Ocean Liners).

2614	**1739**	68p. multicoloured	10·00	10·50

1880 Sabre-tooth Cat

2006. Ice Age Animals.

2615	**1880**	(1st) black and silver	50	50
2616	-	42p. black and silver	75	80
2617	-	47p. black and silver	2·00	2·00
2618	-	68p. black and silver	2·25	2·25
2619	-	£1.12 black and silver	3·25	3·25

DESIGN: 42p.Giant deer; 47p. Woolly rhino; 68p Woolly mammoth; £1.12, Cave bear.

1885 On *Britannia*, 1972

2006. 80th Birthday of Queen Elizabeth II.

2620	**1885**	(2nd) black, green and grey	40	40
2621	-	(2nd) black, green and grey	40	40
2622	-	(1st) black, green and grey	50	45
2623	-	(1st) black, green and grey	50	50
2624	-	44p. black, green and grey	65	65
2625	-	44p. black, green and grey	65	65
2626	-	72p. black, green and grey	1·10	1·10
2627	-	72p. black, green and grey	1·10	1·10

DESIGNS: No. 2621, At Royal Windsor Horse Show, 1985; 2622, At Heathrow Airport, 2001; 2623, As Young Princess Elizabeth with Duchess of York, 1931; 2624, At State Banquet, Ottawa, 1951; 2625, Queen in 1960; 2626, As Princess Elizabeth, 1940;2627. With Duke of Edinburgh, 1951.

1893 England (1966)

2006. World Cup Football Championship, Germany. World Cup Winners. Multicoloured.

2628	(1st) Type **1893**	50	50
2629	42p. Italy (1934, 1938, 1982)	65	70
2630	44p. Argentina (1978, 1986)	1·25	1·25
2631	50p. Germany (1954, 1974, 1990)	2·00	2·00
2632	64p. France (1998)	3·00	3·00
2633	72p. Brazil (1958, 1962, 1970, 1994, 2002)	3·50	3·50

1899 30 St. Mary Axe, London

2006. Modern Architecture. Multicoloured.

2634	(1st) Type **1899**	45	50
2635	42p. Maggie's Centre, Dundee	65	70
2636	44p. Selfridges, Birmingham	1·25	1·25
2637	50p. Downland Gridshell, Chichester	2·00	2·00
2638	64p. An Turas, Isle of Tiree	3·00	3·00
2639	72p. The Deep, Hull	3·50	3·50

1905 "Sir Winston Churchill" (Walter Sickert)

2006. 150th Anniv of National Portrait Gallery, London. Multicoloured.

2640	(1st) Type **1905**	50	50
2641	(1st) "Sir Joshua Reynolds" (self-portrait)	50	50
2642	(1st) "T. S. Eliot" (Patrick Heron)	50	50
2643	(1st) "Emmeline Pankhurst" (Georgina Agnes Brackenbury)	50	50
2644	(1st) "Virginia Woolf" (photo by George Charles Beresford)	50	50
2645	(1st) Bust of Sir Walter Scott (Sir Francis Leggatt Chantry)	50	50
2646	(1st) "Mary Seacole" (Albert Charles Challen)	50	50
2647	(1st) "William Shakespeare" (attrib to John Taylor)	50	50
2648	(1st) "Dame Cicely Saunders" (Catherine Goodman)	50	50
2649	(1st) "Charles Darwin" (John Collier)	50	50

1915

1916

2006. "Pricing in Proportion". (a) Ordinary gum. (i) As T 1915.

2650	(2nd) blue	65	40
2651	(1st) gold	75	50

(ii) As T 1916.

2652	(2nd Large) blue	1·00	60
2653	(1st Large) gold	1·50	70

(b) Self-adhesive. (i) As T 1915.

2654	(2nd) blue	65	40
2655	(1st) gold (2 bands)	75	50

(iii) Self-adhesive. As T 1916.

2656	(2nd Large) blue	1·00	60
2657	(1st Large) gold	1·40	70

1917 (image scaled to 57% of original size)

2006. 70th Anniv of the Year of Three Kings. Sheet 127×72 mm containing No. Y1728. Multicoloured.

MS2658	**1917** £3 mauve	10·00	10·00

1918 Corporal Agansing Rai

2006. 150th Anniv of the Victoria Cross (1st issue). Multicoloured.

2659	(1st) Type **1918**	50	50
2660	(1st) Boy Seaman Jack Cornwell	50	50
2661	64p. Midshipman Charles Lucas	1·25	1·25
2662	64p. Captain Noel Chavasse	1·25	1·25
2663	72p. Captain Albert Ball	2·00	2·25
2664	72p. Captain Charles Upham	2·00	2·25
MS2665	190×67 mm. Nos. 2659/64 and 2666	13·00	13·00

2006. 150th Anniv of the Victoria Cross (2nd issue). Design as No. 1517 (1990 Gallantry Awards).

2666	**959**	20p. multicoloured	6·50	7·00

1924 Sitar Player and Dancer

2006. Europa. Integration. Sounds of Britain.

2667	(1st) Type **1924**	45	50
2668	42p. Reggae bass guitarist and African drummer	1·00	1·00
2669	50p. Fiddler and harpist	1·25	1·25
2670	72p. Sax Player and Blues guitarist	1·75	1·75
2671	£1.19 Maraca player and Salsa dancers	2·50	3·00

The 1st class and 50p. values include the "EUROPA" emblem.

1929 "New Baby" (Alison Carmichael)

2006. "Smiler"s. (2nd series). Occasions. Self-adhesive.

2672	**1929**	(1st) yellow	1·40	1·20
2673	-	(1st) multicoloured	1·40	1·20
2674	-	(1st) vermilion, rosine and yellow	1·40	1·20
2675	-	(1st) multicoloured	1·40	1·20
2676	-	(1st) multicoloured	1·40	1·20
2677	-	(1st) multicoloured	1·40	1·20

DESIGNS: No. 2673, Best Wishes" (Alan Kitching); 2674, "THANK YOU" (Alan Kitching); 2675, Balloons (Ivan Chermayeff); 2676, Firework (Kam Tang); 2677, Champagne, Flowers and Butterflies (Olaf Hajek).

1935 Snowman

2006. Christmas. Multicoloured. (a) Self-adhesive.

2678	(2nd) Type **1935**	35	40
2679	(1st) Father Christmas	50	50
2680	(2nd Large) Snowman	65	65
2681	(1st Large) Father Christmas	75	75
2682	72p. Reindeer	3·25	3·25
2683	£1.19 Christmas Tree	4·50	4·50

(b) Ordinary gum.

MS2684	115×102 mm. As Nos. 2678/83	9·00	9·00

1941 (image scaled to 39% of original size)

2006. "Lest We Forget" (1st issue). 90th Anniv of the Battle of the Somme. Sheet 124×71 mm containing new stamp and designs as Nos. EN15, W107, S118 and NI101.

MS2685	**1941** (1st) Poppies on barbed wire stems; 72p.×4 As Nos. EN15, W107, S118 and NI101	9·00	9·00

1942 "with the beatles"

Beatles Memorabilia (image scaled to 63% of original size)

2007. The Beatles. Album Covers. (a) Self-adhesive.

2686	(1st) Type **1942**	75	70
2687	(1st) "Sgt Pepper's Lonely Hearts Club Band"	75	70
2688	64p. "Help!"	1·50	1·50
2689	64p. "Abbey Road"	1·50	1·50
2690	72p. "Revolver"	1·60	1·60
2691	72p. "Let It Be"	1·60	1·60

Nos. 2686/91 commemorate the 50th anniversary of the first meeting of Paul McCartney and John Lennon.

(b) Ordinary gum.

MS2692	115×89 mm. **1948** (1st) Guitar; (1st) Yellow Submarine lunch-box and key-rings; (1st) Record "Love Me Do"; (1st) Beatles badges	5·00	5·00

2007. "Smilers" (3rd series). As No. 2569. Self-adhesive.

2693	(1st) multicoloured	10·00	10·00

1949 Moon Jellyfish

2007. Sea Life. Multicoloured.

2699	(1st) Type **1949**	75	80
2700	(1st) Beadlet anemone	75	80
2701	(1st) Common starfish	75	80
2702	(1st) Bass	75	80
2703	(1st) Thornback ray	75	80
2704	(1st) Lesser octopus	75	80
2705	(1st) Common mussels	75	80
2706	(1st) Grey seal	75	80
2707	(1st) Shore crab	75	80
2708	(1st) Common sun star	75	80

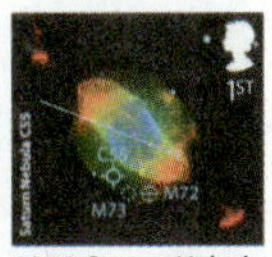

1959 Saturn Nebula C55

2007. 50th Anniv of "The Sky at Night" (TV programme). Nebulae. Multicoloured. Self-adhesive.

2709	(1st) Type **1959**	75	75
2710	(1st) Eskimo Nebula C39	75	75
2711	50p. Cat's Eye Nebula C6	1·20	1·20
2712	50p. Helix Nebula C63	1·20	1·20
2713	72p. Flaming Star Nebula C31	1·70	1·70
2714	72p. The Spindle C53	1·70	1·70

1965 Iron Bridge (Thomas Telford)

2007. World of Invention (1st series). Multicoloured. Self-adhesive.

2715	(1st) Type **1965**	75	50
2716	(1st) Steam locomotive and railway tracks	75	50
2717	64p. Map of British Isles and Australia (telephone)	1·25	1·25
2718	64p. Camera and television (John Logie Baird)	1·25	1·25

No.	Description		
2719	72p. Globe as web (email and internet)	2·00	2·25
2720	72p. Couple with suitcases on Moon (space travel)	2·00	2·25

2007. World of Invention (2nd series). Multicoloured.

No.	Description		
2721	(1st) Type **1965**	75	50
2722	(1st) Steam locomotive and railway tracks	75	50
2723	64p. Map of British Isles and Australia (telephone)	2·50	2·50
2724	64p. Camera and television (John Logie Baird)	2·50	2·50
2725	72p. Globe as web (email and internet)	4·50	4·50
2726	72p. Couple with suitcases on Moon (space travel)	4·50	4·50
MS2727	115×104 mm. Nos. 2721/6	10·00	10·50

1971 William Wilberforce and Anti-slavery Poster

2007. Bicentenary of the Abolition of the Slave Trade. Multicoloured.

No.	Description		
2728	(1st) Type **1971**	75	75
2729	(1st) Olaudah Equiano and map of slave trade routes	75	75
2730	50p. Granville Sharp and slave ship	1·20	1·20
2731	50p. Thomas Clarkson and diagram of slave ship	1·20	1·20
2732	72p. Hannah More and title page of "The Sorrows of Yamba"	1·70	1·70
2733	72p. Ignatius Sancho and trade/business card	1·70	1·70

1977 Ice Cream Cone

2007. "Beside the Seaside". Multicoloured.

No.	Description		
2734	(1st) Type **1977**	75	75
2735	46p. Sandcastle	1·00	1·00
2736	48p. Carousel horse	1·50	1·50
2737	54p. Beach huts	2·00	2·00
2738	69p. Deckchairs	2·50	2·50
2739	78p. Beach donkeys	2·75	2·75

1983 (image scaled to 43% of original size)

2007. New Wembley Stadium, London. Sheet 112×113 mm containing design as Type 1593 but with "WORLD CUP 2002" inscription omitted, and Nos. EN6 and EN15, each×2.

No.	Description		
MS2740	**1983** (1st) As Type **1593**; (2nd) No. EN6×2; 78p. No. EN15×2	7·00	7·00

The design as Type **1593** omits the "WORLD CUP 2002" inscription at the left of the stamp.

1984 Arnold Machin

1985 1967 4d. Machin

1986 (image scaled to 38% of original size)

2007. 40th Anniv of the First Machin Definitives. Sheet 127×73 mm containing new stamps and Nos. Y1725 and Y1725b.

No.	Description		
2741	**1984** (1st) multicoloured	2·00	2·00
2742	**1985** (1st) multicoloured	2·00	2·00
MS2743	**1986** Nos. 2741/2, Y1725 and Y1725b	8·00	8·00

1987 Stirling Moss in Vanwall 2.5L, 1957

2007. Grand Prix. Racing Cars. Multicoloured.

No.	Description		
2744	(1st) Type **1987**	75	75
2745	(1st) Graham Hill in BRM P57, 1962	75	75
2746	54p. Jim Clark in Lotus 26 Climax, 1963	2·00	2·00
2747	54p. Jackie Stewart in Tyrrell 006/2, 1973	2·00	2·00
2748	78p. James Hunt in McLaren M23, 1976	2·50	2·50
2749	78p. Nigel Mansell in Williams FW11, 1986	2·50	2·50

Nos. 2744/9 commemorate the 50th anniv of Stirling Moss victory in the British Grand Prix and the centenary of the opening of the Brooklands race track.

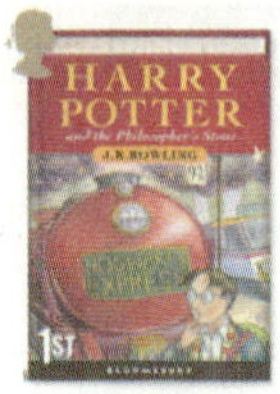

1993 *Harry Potter and the Philosopher's Stone*

2000 Crests of Hogwarts School and its Four Houses (image scaled to 39% of original size)

2007. Publication of Final Book in the Harry Potter Series. (a) Book Covers. Multicoloured.

No.	Description		
2750	(1st) Type **1993**	75	75
2751	(1st) *Harry Potter and the Chamber of Secrets*	75	75
2752	(1st) *Harry Potter and the Prisoner of Azkaban*	75	75
2753	(1st) *Harry Potter and the Goblet of Fire*	75	75
2754	(1st) *Harry Potter and the Order of the Phoenix*	75	75
2755	(1st) *Harry Potter and the Half-Blood Prince*	75	75
2756	(1st) *Harry Potter and the Deathly Hallows*	75	75

(b) Crests of Hogwarts School and its Four Houses. Multicoloured.

No.	Description		
MS2757	123×70 mm. **2000** (1st) Gryffindor; (1st) Hufflepuff; (1st) Hogwarts; (1st) Ravenclaw; (1st) Slytherin	6·00	6·00

2001 Scout and Camp Fire

2007. Europa. Centenary of Scouting and 21st World Scout Jamboree, Chelmsford, Essex. Multicoloured.

No.	Description		
2758	(1st) Type **2001**	75	75
2759	46p. Scouts rock climbing	1·00	1·00
2760	48p. Scout planting tree	1·50	1·50
2761	54p. Adult volunteer teaching scout archery	2·00	2·00
2762	69p. Scouts learning gliding	2·50	2·50
2763	78p. Scouts from many nations	2·75	2·75

The 1st class and 48p. values include the 'EUROPA' emblem.

2007 White-tailed Eagle

2007. Action for Species

No.	Description		
2764	(1st) Type **2007**	75	75
2765	(1st) Bearded tit	75	75
2766	(1st) Red kite	75	75
2767	(1st) Cirl Bunting	75	75
2768	(1st) Marsh harrier	75	75
2769	(1st) Avocet	75	75
2770	(1st) Bittern	75	75
2771	(1st) Dartford warbler	75	75
2772	(1st) Corncrake	75	75
2773	(1st) Peregrine falcon	75	75

See also Nos. 2831/40.

2017 NCO, Royal Military Police, 1999

2007. Military Uniforms (1st series). British Army Uniforms.

No.	Description		
2774	(1st) Type **2017**	80	80
2775	(1st) Tank Commander, 5th Royal Tank Regiment, 1944	80	80
2776	(1st) Observer, Royal Field Artillery, 1917	80	80
2777	78p. Rifleman, 95th Rifles, 1813	1·70	1·70
2778	78p. Grenadier, Royal Regiment of Foot of Ireland, 1704	1·70	1·70
2779	78p. Trooper, Earl of Oxford's Horse, 1661	1·70	1·70

2023 Leaving St. Paul's Cathedral after Thanksgiving Service, 2006

2029 Photographs of the Royal Family (image scaled to 40% of original size)

2007. Diamond Wedding of Queen Elizabeth II and Duke of Edinburgh. (a) Ordinary gum.

No.	Description		
2780	**2023** (1st) brown and black	75	75
2781	- (1st) brown and black	75	75
2782	- 54p. brown and black	1·20	1·20
2783	- 54p. brown and black	1·20	1·20
2784	- 78p. brown and black	1·90	1·90
2785	- 78p. brown and black	1·90	1·90

DESIGNS: No. 2781 Inspecting King's Troop Royal Horse Artillery, Regents Park, 1997; No. 2782 At Garter Ceremony, Windsor, 1980; No. 2783 At Royal Ascot, 1969; No. 2784 At Premiere of *The Guns of Navarone*, 1961; No. 2785 At Clydebank.

(b) Self-adhesive.

No.	Description		
MS2786	115×89 mm. (1st) Royal family, Balmoral, 1972; (1st) Queen and Prince Philip, Buckingham Palace, 2007; 69p. Royal family, Windsor Castle, 1965; 78p. Princess Elizabeth, Prince Philip, Prince Charles and Princess Anne, Clarence House, 1951	6·00	6·00

2030 *Madonna and Child*

2007. Christmas (1st issue). Paintings of the Madonna and Child. Self-adhesive.

No.	Description		
2787	(2nd) Type **2030**	65	50
2788	(1st) *The Madonna of Humility* (Lippo di Dalmasio), c 1390–1400	75	75

2032 Angel playing Trumpet ('PEACE') (William Dyce), c 1827

2007. Christmas (2nd issue). Angels. (a) Self-adhesive.

No.	Description		
2789	(2nd) Type **2032**	65	55
2790	(1st) Angel playing Lute ('GOODWILL')	75	75
2791	(2nd Large) Angel playing Trumpet ('PEACE')	90	90
2792	(1st Large) Angel playing Lute ('GOODWILL')	2·00	2·00
2793	78p. Angel playing Flute ('JOY')	3·00	3·00
2794	£1.24 Angel playing Tambourine ('GLORY')	4·50	4·50

(b) Ordinary gum.

No.	Description		
MS2795	115×102 mm. As Nos. 2789/94	10·00	10·00

2038 (image scaled to 39% of original size)

2007. Lest We Forget

No.	Description		
MS2796	(1st) Soldiers in poppy flower; 78p.×4 As Nos. EN16, NI106, S119 and W108	10·00	10·00

2039 *Casino Royale*

2008. Birth Centenary of Ian Fleming (author of James Bond books). Book Covers. Multicoloured.

No.	Description		
2797	(1st) Type **2039**	75	75
2798	(1st) *Dr. No*	75	75
2799	54p. *Goldfinger*	2·00	1·20
2800	54p. *Diamonds are Forever*	2·00	1·20
2801	78p. *For Your Eyes Only*	3·00	3·00
2802	78p. *From Russia with Love*	3·00	3·00
MS2803	189×68 mm. Nos. 2797/802	10·00	10·00

2008. As Nos. MS2206.

No.	Description		
2805	(1st) multicoloured	85	85

2045 Assistance Dog carrying Letter (Labrador 'Rowan') (image scaled to 39% of original size)

2008. Working Dogs. Multicoloured.

No.	Description		
2806	(1st) Type **2045**	80	80

2807	46p. Mountain rescue dog (Cross-bred 'Merrick')	1·00	1·00
2808	48p. Police dog (German Shepherd 'Max')	1·50	1·50
2809	54p. Customs dog (Springer Spaniel 'Max')	2·00	2·00
2810	69p. Sheepdog (Border Collie 'Bob')	2·50	2·50
2811	78p. Guide dog (Labrador 'Warwick')	2·75	2·75

The 1st value includes the 'EUROPA' emblem.

2051 Henry IV (1399–1413)

2057 The Age of Lancaster and York (image scaled to 39% of original size)

2008. Kings and Queens (1st issue). Houses of Lancaster and York. Multicoloured.

2812	(1st) Type **2051**	80	80
2813	(1st) Henry V (1413–1422)	80	80
2814	54p. Henry VI (1422–1461 & 1470–1)	2·00	2·00
2815	54p. Edward IV (1461–1470 & 1471–1473)	2·00	2·00
2816	69p. Edward V (1483)	2·75	2·75
2817	69p. Edward V (1483)	2·75	2·75
MS2818	123×70 mm. **2057** (1st) Owain Glyn Dwr ('Parliament'), 1404; (1st) Henry V's triumph at Battle of Agincourt, 1415; 78p. Yorkist victory at Battle of Tewkesbury, 1471; 78p. William Caxton, first English printer, 1477	6·50	6·50

2008. 'Smilers' (4th series). As Nos. 2567/8, 2570 and 2675/7. Self-adhesive.

2819	(1st) multicoloured	75	75
2820	(1st) multicoloured	75	75
2821	(1st) multicoloured	75	75
2822	(1st) multicoloured	75	75
2823	(1st) multicoloured	75	75
2824	(1st) multicoloured	75	75

2058 Lifeboat, Barra

2008. Rescue at Sea. Multicoloured.

2825	(1st) Type **2058**	75	75
2826	46p. Lifeboat approaching Dinghy, Appledore	1·00	1·00
2827	48p. Helicopter Winchman, Portland	1·50	1·50
2828	54p. Inshore lifeboat, St Ives	2·00	2·00
2829	69p. Westland Seaking Rescue Helicopter, Lee-on-Solent	2·50	2·50
2830	78p. Launch of Lifeboat, Dinbych-y-Pysgod, Tenby	2·75	2·75

2064 *Lysandra bellargus* (Adonis blue)

2008. Action for Species

2831	(1st) Type **2064**	80	80
2832	(1st) *Coenagrion mercuriale* (southern damselfly)	80	80
2833	(1st) *Formica rufibarbis* (red-barbed ant)	80	80
2834	(1st) *Pareulype berberata* (barberry carpet moth)	80	80
2835	(1st) *Lucanus cervus* (stag beetle)	80	80
2836	(1st) *Cryptocephalus coryli* (hazel pot beetle)	80	80
2837	(1st) *Gryllus campestris* (field cricket)	80	80
2838	(1st) *Hesperia comma* (silver-spotted skipper)	80	80
2839	(1st) *Pseudepipona herrichii* (Purbeck mason wasp)	80	80
2840	(1st) *Gnorimus nobilis* (noble chafer)	80	80

2074 Lichfield Cathedral

2080 St. Paul's Cathedral (Illustration reduced. Actual size 115×89 mm) (image scaled to 42% of original size)

2008. Cathedrals. Multicoloured.

2841	(1st) Type **2074**	85	85
2842	48p. Belfast Cathedral	1·10	1·10
2843	50p. Gloucester Cathedral	1·50	1·50
2844	56p. St. David's Cathedral	2·50	2·50
2845	72p. Westminster Cathedral	3·00	3·00
2846	81p. St. Magnus Cathedral, Kirkwall, Orkney	3·50	3·50
MS2847	115×89 mm. (1st) mult; (1st) mult; 81p. mult; 81p. mult	6·00	6·00

No. **MS**2847 commemorates the 300th anniversary of St. Paul's Cathedral.

2008. Beside the Seaside

2848	**1977**	(1st) multicoloured	80	80

2081 *Carry on Sergeant*

2008. Posters for Carry On and Hammer Horror Films. Multicoloured.

2849	(1st) Type **2081**	85	85
2850	48p. *Dracula*	1·10	1·10
2851	50p. *Carry on Cleo*	1·50	1·50
2852	56p. *The Curse of Frankenstein*	2·50	2·50
2853	72p. *Carry on Screaming*	3·00	3·00
2854	81p. *The Mummy*	3·50	3·50

Nos. 2849/54 commemorate the 50th anniversary of *Dracula* and the first *Carry On* film (*Carry on Sergeant*).

2087 Red Arrows, Dartmouth Regatta Airshow, 2006

2008. Air Displays. Multicoloured.

2855	(1st) Type **2087**	85	85
2856	48p. RAF Falcons Parachute Team, Biggin Hill, 2006	1·10	1·10
2857	50p. Spectator watching Red Arrows, Farnborough, 2006	1·50	1·50
2858	56p. Prototype Avro Vulcan Bombers and Avro 707s, Farnborough, 1953	2·50	2·50
2859	72p. Parachutist Robert Wyndham on Wing of Avro 504, 1933	3·00	3·00
2860	81p. Air Race rounding the Beacon, Hendon, c. 1912	3·50	3·50

2093 Landmarks of Beijing and London (image scaled to 42% of original size)

2008. Handover of Olympic Flag from Beijing to London. Sheet 115×76 mm.

MS2861	(1st) National Stadium, Beijing; (1st) London Eye; (1st) Tower of London; (1st) Corner Tower of the Forbidden City, Beijing	4·00	4·00

The Olympic rings overprinted on **MS**2861 are in silk-screen varnish.

2094 Drum Major, RAF Central Band, 2007

2008. Military Uniforms (2nd series). RAF Uniforms.

2862	(1st) Type 2094	80	80
2863	(1st) Helicopter Rescue Winchman, 1984	80	80
2864	(1st) Hawker Hunter Pilot, 1951	80	80
2865	81p. Lancaster Air Gunner, 1944	1·70	1·70
2866	81p. WAAF Plotter, 1940	1·70	1·70
2867	81p. Pilot, 1918	1·70	1·70

2008. Pilot to Plane

2868	**1307**	20p. multicoloured	3·75	4·00
2869	**2087**	(1st) multicoloured	3·75	4·00

2100 Millicent Garrett Fawcett (suffragist)

2008. Women of Distinction. Multicoloured.

2870	(1st) Type **2100**	85	85
2871	48p. Elizabeth Garrett Anderson (physician – women's health)	1·10	1·10
2872	50p. Marie Stopes (family planning pioneer)	1·50	1·50
2873	56p. Eleanor Rathbone (family allowance campaigner)	2·50	2·50
2874	72p. Claudia Jones (civil rights activist)	3·00	3·00
2875	81p. Barbara Castle (politician – Equal Pay Act)	3·50	3·50

2106 Ugly Sisters from *Cinderella*

2008. Christmas. Multicoloured. (a) Self-adhesive.

2876	(2nd) Type **2106**	55	55
2877	(1st) Genie from *Aladdin*	85	85
2878	(2nd Large) Ugly Sisters from *Cinderella*	90	90
2879	(1st Large) Genie from *Aladdin*	1·10	1·10
2880	50p. Captain Hook from *Peter Pan*	1·30	1·30
2881	81p. Wicked Queen from *Snow White*	2·00	2·00

(b) Ordinary gum.

MS2882	114×102 mm. As Nos. 2876/81	8·00	8·00

2112 Poppies on Barbed Wire Stem

2115 (image scaled to 39% of original size)

2008. Lest We Forget

2883	**2112**	(1st) Type	75	75
2884	**2112**	(1st) Soldiers in poppy flower	75	75
2885	**2112**	(1st) Poppy flower	75	75
MS2886		124×70 mm. **2115** No. 2885 and as Nos. EN18, NI107, S120 and W109	10·00	10·00

2116 Supermarine Spitfire (R. J. Mitchell)

2009. British Design Classics (1st series). Multicoloured.

2887	(1st) Type **2116**	90	90
2888	(1st) Mini skirt (Mary Quant)	90	90
2889	(1st) Mini (Sir Alec Issigonis)	90	90
2890	(1st) Anglepoise lamp (George Carwardine)	90	90
2891	(1st) Concorde (Aerospatiale-BAC)	90	90
2892	(1st) K2 Telephone Kiosk (Sir Giles Gilbert Scott)	90	90
2893	(1st) Polypropylene chair (Robin Day)	90	90
2894	(1st) Penguin Books (Edward Young)	90	90
2895	(1st) London underground map (Harry Beck)	90	90
2896	(1st) Routemaster bus (design team led by AAM Durrant)	90	90

See also Nos. 2897 and 2911/12.

2009. British Design Classics (2nd series). Design as No. 2285 (Concorde from 2002 Passenger Jet Aviation).

2897	**1589**	(1st) multicoloured	3·00	3·00

2126 Charles Darwin

2132 Fauna and Map of the Galapagos Islands (image scaled to 42% of original size)

2009. Birth Bicentenary of Charles Darwin (naturalist and evolutionary theorist) (1st issue). Multicoloured. (a) Self-adhesive.

2898	(1st) Type **2126**	85	85
2899	48p. Marine Iguana	1·10	1·10
2900	50p. Finches	1·50	1·50
2901	56p. Atoll	2·00	2·00
2902	72p. Bee Orchid	2·50	2·50

2903	81p. Orang-utan	3·00	3·00

(b) Ordinary gum.

MS2904	115×89 mm. (1st) Flightless cormorant; (1st) Giant tortoise and cactus finch; 81p. Marine iguana; 81p. Floreana mockingbird	6·50	6·50

See also Nos. 2905/10.

2009. Birth Bicentenary of Charles Darwin (naturalist) (2nd issue). Multicoloured.

2905		(1st) Type **2126**	85	85
2906		48p. As No. 2899	1·10	1·10
2907		50p. As No. 2900	2·00	2·00
2908	**2129**	56p. As No. 2901	2·50	2·50
2909	**2129**	72p. As No. 2902	3·00	3·00
2910	**2129**	81p. As No. 2903	3·50	3·50

2009. Self-adhesive. Designs as T 367, T 913/14, or T 1916.

U2911	(2nd) bright blue	60	60
U2912	(1st) gold	80	80
U2913	(2nd Large) bright blue	90	90
U2914	50p. grey	1·10	1·10
U2915	(1st Large) gold	1·10	1·10
U2916	£1 magenta	2·25	2·25
U2916a	(Recorded Signed for 1st) bright orange-red and lemon	2·25	2·25
U2916b	(Recorded Signed for 1st Large) bright orange-red and lemon	2·75	2·75
U2917	£1.50 brown-red	3·25	3·25
U2918	£2 deep blue-green	4·25	4·25
U2919	£3 deep mauve	6·25	6·25
U2920	£5 azure	10·50	10·50

Nos. U2913 and U2933 were inscr '2nd Large' and initially sold for 42p.

Nos. U2914 and U2934 were inscr '1st Large' and initially sold for 52p.

2009. British Design Classics (3rd series). Designs as Nos. 2892 and 2896. Multicoloured. Self-adhesive.

2911	(1st) K2 Telephone Kiosk (Sir Giles Gilbert Scott)	85	85
2912	(1st) Routemaster Bus (design team led by AAM Durrant)	85	85
2913	(1st) Mini (Sir Alex Issigonis)	85	85
2914	(1st) Concorde (Aerospatiale-BAC)	85	85
2915	(1st) Mini skirt (Mary Quant)	85	85

2133 Matthew Boulton and Factory (Manufacturing)

2009. Pioneers of the Industrial Revolution. Multicoloured.

2916	(1st) Type **2133**	85	85
2917	(1st) James Watt and Boulton & Watt Condensing Engine (steam engineering)	85	85
2918	50p. Richard Arkwright and Spinning Machine (textiles)	1·00	1·00
2919	50p. Josiah Wedgwood and Black Basalt Teapot and Vase (ceramics)	1·00	1·00
2920	56p. George Stephenson and *Locomotion* (railways)	1·25	1·25
2921	56p. Henry Maudslay and Table Engine (machine making)	1·25	1·25
2922	72p. James Brindley and Bridgewater Canal Aqueduct	1·75	1·75
2923	72p. John McAdam (road building)	1·75	1·75

2141 Henry VII (1485–1509)

2147 The Age of the Tudors (image scaled to 39% of original size)

2009. Kings and Queens (2nd issue). The House of Tudor. Multicoloured.

2924	(1st) Type **2141**	85	85
2925	(1st) Henry VIII (1509–47)	85	85
2926	62p. Edward VI (1547–53)	1·40	1·40
2927	62p. Lady Jane Grey (1553)	1·40	1·40
2928	81p. Mary I (1553–8)	1·75	1·75
2929	81p. Elizabeth I (1558–1603)	1·75	1·75
MS2930	123×70 mm. **2147** (1st) *Mary Rose* (galleon), 1510; (1st) Field of Cloth of Gold Royal Conference, 1520; 90p. Royal Exchange (centre of commerce), 1565; 90p. Francis Drake (circumnavigation), 1580	5·75	5·75

2148 *Allium sphaerocephalon* (round-headed leek)

2158 Royal Botanic Gardens, Kew (image scaled to 42% of original size)

2009. 'Action for Species' (3rd series). Plants. Multicolored.

2931	(1st) Type **2148**	85	85
2932	(1st) *Luronium natans* (floating water-plantain)	85	85
2933	(1st) *Cypripedium calceolus* (lady's slipper orchid)	85	85
2934	(1st) *Polygala amarella* (dwarf milkwort)	85	85
2935	(1st) *Saxifraga hirculus* (marsh saxifrage)	85	85
2936	(1st) *Stachys germanica* (downy woundwort)	85	85
2937	(1st) *Euphorbia serrulata* (upright spurge)	85	85
2938	(1st) *Pyrus cordata* (Plymouth pear)	85	85
2939	(1st) *Polygonum maritimum* (Sea knotgrass)	85	85
2940	(1st) *Dianthus armeria* (Deptford pink)	85	85

(b) 250th Anniv of Royal Botanic Gardens, Kew. Multicoloured.

MS2941	115×89 mm. **2158** (1st) Palm House, Kew Gardens; (1st) Millennium Seed Bank, Wakehurst Place; 90p. Pagoda, Kew Gardens; 90p. Sackler Crossing, Kew Gardens	5·75	5·75

2009. 50th Anniv of NAFAS (National Association of Flower Arrangement Societies). Designs as Nos. 1958 and 1962 (1997 Greeting Stamps 19th-century Flower Paintings). Self-adhesive.

2942	(1st) multicoloured	85	85
2943	(1st) multicoloured	85	85

2159 Dragon

2009. Mythical Creatures. Multicoloured.

2944	(1st) Type **2159**	85	85
2945	(1st) Unicorn	85	85
2946	62p. Giant	1·40	1·40
2947	62p. Pixie	1·40	1·40
2948	90p. Mermaid	2·00	2·00
2949	90p. Fairy	2·00	2·00

2165 George V Type B Wall Letter Box, 1933–6

2169 Post Boxes (Illustration reduced. Actual size 145×74 mm) (image scaled to 33% of original size)

2009. Post Boxes (1st series). Multicoloured.

2950	(1st) Type **2165**	85	85
2951	56p. Edward VII Ludlow Letter Box, 1901–10	1·25	1·20
2952	81p. Victorian Lamp Letter Box, 1896	1·75	1·75
2953	90p. Elizabeth II Type A Wall Letter Box, 1962–3	2·00	2·00
MS2954	As Type **2169**Nos. 2950/3	5·75	5·75

2009. 'Treasures of the Archive' (1st series). As Type 929 (1990 150th anniv of the Penny Black).

2955	**929**	20p. brownish-black and grey-brown	45	45
2956	**929**	(1st) brownish-black and grey-brown	90	90

2009. 'Treasures of the Archive' (2nd series). As Type 919 (1989 Lord Mayor's Show). Multicoloured.

2957	**919**	20p. multicoloured	45	45

2170 Firefighting

2009. Fire and Rescue Service. Multicoloured.

2958	(1st) Type **2170**	85	85
2959	54p. Chemical fire	1·10	1·10
2960	56p. Emergency rescue	1·25	1·25
2961	62p. Flood rescue	1·40	1·40
2962	81p. Search and Rescue	1·75	1·75
2963	90p. Fire safety	2·00	2·00

2176 Flight Deck Officer, 2009

2009. Military Uniforms (3rd series). Royal Navy Uniforms. Multicoloured.

2964	(1st) Type **2176**	85	85
2965	(1st) Captain, 1941	85	85
2966	(1st) Second Officer WRNS, 1918	85	85
2967	90p. Able Seaman, 1880	2·00	2·00
2968	90p. Royal Marine, 1805	2·00	2·00
2969	90p. Admiral, 1795	2·00	2·00

2009. Royal Navy Uniforms. As No. 2209 (Jolly Roger flag from 2001 Submarine Centenary).

2970	(1st) multicoloured	90	90

2182 Fred Perry 1909–95 (lawn tennis champion)

2009. Eminent Britons. Multicoloured.

2971	(1st) Type **2182**	85	85
2972	(1st) Henry Purcell 1659–95 (composer and musician)	85	85
2973	(1st) Sir Matt Busby 1909–94 (footballer and football manager)	85	85
2974	(1st) William Gladstone 1809–98 (statesman and Prime Minister)	85	85
2975	(1st) Mary Wollstonecraft 1759–97 (pioneering feminist)	85	85
2976	(1st) Sir Arthur Conan Doyle 1859–1930 (writer and creator of Sherlock Holmes)	85	85
2977	(1st) Donald Campbell 1921–67 (water speed record broken 1959)	85	85
2978	(1st) Judy Fryd 1909–2000 (campaigner and founder of MENCAP)	85	85
2979	(1st) Samuel Johnson 1709–84 (lexicographer, critic and poet)	85	85
2980	(1st) Sir Martin Ryle 1918–84 (radio survey of the Universe 1959)	85	85

2192 Canoe Slalom

2009. Olympic and Paralympic Games, London (2012) (1st issue). Multicoloured.

2981	(1st) Type **2192**	85	85
2982	(1st) Paralympic Games Archery	85	85
2983	(1st) Athletics: Track	85	85
2984	(1st) Diving	85	85
2985	(1st) Paralympic Games Boccia	85	85
2986	(1st) Judo	85	85
2987	(1st) Paralympic Games Dressage	85	85
2988	(1st) Badminton	85	85
2989	(1st) Weightlifting	85	85
2990	(1st) Basketball	85	85

2202 Angel playing Lute (William Morris), Church of St. James, Staveley, Kendal, Cumbria

2009. Christmas. Stained Glass Windows. Multicoloured.

(a) Self-adhesive.

2991	(2nd) Type **2202**	60	60
2992	(1st) Madonna and Child (Henry Holiday), Church of Ormesby St. Michael, Great Yarmouth, Norfolk	85	85
2993	(2nd Large) Angel playing Lute (William Morris), Church of St. James, Staveley, Kendal, Cumbria	95	95
2994	(1st Large) Madonna and Child (Henry Holiday), Church of Ormesby St. Michael, Ormesby, Great Yarmouth, Norfolk	1·25	1·25
2995	56p. Joseph (Henry Holiday), Parish Church of St. Michael, Minehead, Somerse	1·25	1·25
2996	90p. Wise Man (Sir Edward Burne-Jones), Church of St. Mary the Virgin, Rye, East Sussex	2·00	2·00
2997	£1.35 Shepherd (Henry Holiday), St. Mary's Church, Upavon, Wiltshire	2·75	2·75

(b) Ordinary gum.

MS2998	115×102 mm. As Nos. 2991/7	9·50	9·50

2209 *The Division Bell* (Pink Floyd)

2010. Classic Album Covers (1st issue). Multicoloured. Self-adhesive.

2999	(1st) Type **2209**	90	90
3000	(1st) *A Rush of Blood to the Head* (Coldplay)	90	90

3001	(1st) *Parklife* (Blur)	90	90
3002	(1st) *Power Corruption and Lies* (New Order)	90	90
3003	(1st) *Let It Bleed* (Rolling Stones)	90	90
3004	(1st) *London Calling* (The Clash)	90	90
3005	(1st) *Tubular Bells* (Mike Oldfield)	90	90
3006	(1st) *IV* (Led Zeppelin)	90	90
3007	(1st) *Screamadelica* (Primal Scream)	90	90
3008	(1st) *The Rise and Fall of Ziggy Stardust and the Spiders from Mars* (David Bowie)	90	90

The right-hand edges of Nos. 2999/3008 are all cut around to show the vinyl disc protruding from the open edge of the album cover.

2010. Classic Album Covers (2nd issue). Multicoloured.

3009	(1st) As No. 3003	90	90
3010	(1st) As No. 3006	90	90
3011	(1st) As No. 3008	90	90
3012	(1st) As No. 3002	90	90
3013	(1st) As No. 3007	90	90
3014	(1st) As No. 2999	90	90
3015	(1st) As No. 3005	90	90
3016	(1st) As No. 3004		
3017	(1st) As No. 3001	90	90
3018	(1st) As No 3000	90	90
MS3019	223×189 mm. Nos. 3009/18	8·50	8·50

The right-hand edges of Nos. 3009/18 and the miniature sheet **MS**3019 are all cut around in an imperforate section to show the vinyl disc protruding from the open edge of the album cover.

2010. Olympic and Paralympic Games, London (2012) (2nd issue). As Nos. 2982 and 2986. Multicoloured. Self-adhesive.

3020	(1st) As No. 2986	90	90
3021	(1st) As No. 2982	90	90
3022	(1st) As No. 2983	90	90
3023	(1st) As No. 2990	90	90

2219 (Illustration reduced. Actual size 124×71 mm) (image scaled to 39% of original size)

2010. Business and Consumer Smilers. Sheet 124×71 mm. Multicoloured.

MS3024	(1st) Propellor driven airplane (Andrew Davidson); (1st) Vintage sports roadster (Andrew Davidson); (1st) Recreation of crown seal (Neil Oliver); (1st) Birthday cake (Annabel Wright); (1st) Steam locomotive (Andrew Davidson); (1st) Ocean liner (Andrew Davidson); (1st) As Type **2112**; (1st) Birthday present (Annabel Wright); (Europe up to 20 grams) Bird carrying envelope (Lucy Davey); (Worldwide up to 20 grams) 'Hello' in plane vapour trail (Lucy Davey)	10·00	10·00

2220 Girlguiding UK (Illustration reduced. Actual size 190×67 mm) (image scaled to 25% of original size)

2010. Centenary of Girlguiding. Sheet 190×67 mm. Multicoloured.

MS3025	(1st) Rainbows; 56p. Brownies; 81p. Guides; 90p. Senior Section members	6·00	6·00

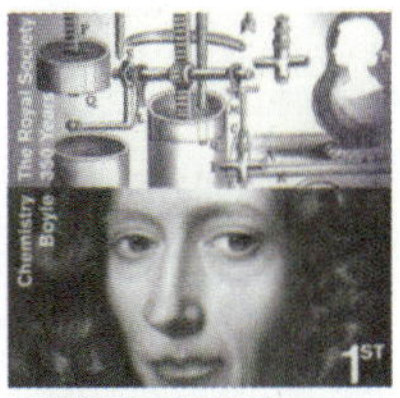

2221 Sir Robert Boyle (chemistry)

2010. 350th Anniv of the Royal Society.

3026	(1st) Type **2221**	90	90
3027	(1st) Sir Isaac Newton (optics)	90	90
3028	(1st) Benjamin Franklin (electricity)	90	90
3029	(1st) Edward Jenner (pioneer of smallpox vaccination)	90	90
3030	(1st) Charles Babbage (computing)	90	90
3031	(1st) Alfred Russel Wallace (theory of evolution)	90	90
3032	(1st) Joseph Lister (antiseptic surgery)	90	90
3033	(1st) Ernest Rutherford (atomic structure)	90	90
3034	(1st) Dorothy Hodgkin (crystallography)	90	90
3035	(1st) Sir Nicholas Shackleton (earth sciences)	90	90

2231 'Pixie' (mastiff cross)

2010. 150th Anniv of Battersea Dogs and Cats Home.

3036	(1st) Type **2231**	90	90
3037	(1st) 'Button'	90	90
3038	(1st) 'Herbie' (mongrel)	90	90
3039	(1st) 'Mr. Tumnus'	90	90
3040	(1st) 'Tafka' (border collie)	90	90
3041	(1st) 'Boris' (bulldog cross)	90	90
3042	(1st) 'Casey' (lurcher)	90	90
3043	(1st) 'Tigger'	90	90
3044	(1st) 'Leonard' (Jack Russell cross)	90	90
3045	(1st) 'Tia' (terrier cross)	90	90

2241 James I (1406–37)

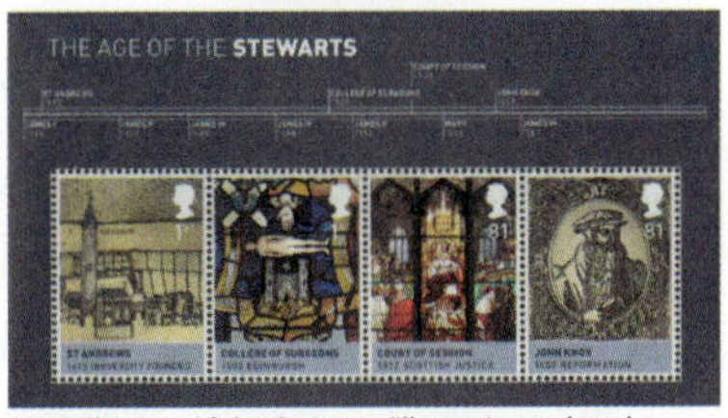

2248 The Age of the Stewarts (Illustration reduced. Actual size 123×70 mm) (image scaled to 39% of original size)

2010. Kings and Queens (3rd series). House of Stewart.

3046	(1st) Type **2241**	90	90
3047	(1st) James II (1437–60)	90	90
3048	(1st) James III (1460–88)	90	90
3049	62p. James IV (1488–1513)	1·40	1·40
3050	62p. James V (1513–42)	1·40	1·40
3051	81p. Mary (1542–67)	1·75	1·75
3052	81p. James VI (1567–1625)	1·75	1·75
MS3053	123×70 mm. **2248** (1st) Foundation of the University of St. Andrews, 1413; (1st) Foundation of the College of Surgeons, Edinburgh, 1505; 81p. Foundation of Court of Session, 1532; 81p. John Knox (Reformation, 1559)	5·25	5·25

2249 Humpback Whale (*Megaptera novaeangliae*)

2010. 'Action for Species' (4th series). Mammals. Multicoloured.

3054	(1st) Type **2249**	90	90
3055	(1st) Wildcat (*Felis silvestris*)	90	90
3056	(1st) Brown Long-eared Bat (*Plecotus auritus*)	90	90
3057	(1st) Polecat (*Mustela putorius*)	90	90
3058	(1st) Sperm Whale (*Physeter macrocephalus*)	90	90
3059	(1st) Water Vole (*Arvicola terrestris*)	90	90
3060	(1st) Greater Horseshoe Bat (*Rhinolophus ferrumequinum*)	90	90
3061	(1st) Otter (*Lutra lutra*)	90	90
3062	(1st) Dormouse (*Muscardinus avellanarius*)	90	90
3063	(1st) Hedgehog (*Erinaceus europaeus*)	90	90

2260 King George V and Queen Elizabeth II (1st); Two portraits of King George V (£1) (image scaled to 34% of original size)

2010. London 2010 Festival of Stamps and Centenary of Accession of King George V. Sheet 141×74 mm.

MS3065	(1st) rosine; £1 blackish brown, grey-brown and silver	3·25	3·25

No. 3064, T **2259** are left for 1st class King George V and Queen Elizabeth II sheet stamp, issued 6 May 2010, not yet received.

A miniature sheet as No. **MS**3065 but inscr 'BUSINESS DESIGN CENTRE, LONDON 8–15 MAY 2010' along the top right margin was only available at London 2010 Festival of Stamps.

2261 King George V and Queen Elizabeth II

2267 (Illustration reduced. Actual size 115×90 mm) (image scaled to 43% of original size)

2010. London 2010 Festival of Stamps.

3066	**2261**	(1st) rosine	90	90
3067	–	(1st) multicoloured	90	90
3068	–	(1st) multicoloured	90	90
3069	–	£1 blackish brown, grey-brown and silver	2·00	2·00
3070	–	£1 multicoloured	2·00	2·00
3071	–	£1 multicoloured	2·00	2·00
MS3072		Nos. 3067/8 and 3070/1	5·75	5·75

DESIGNS: No. 3067, 1924 British Empire Exhibition 1½d. brown stamp; 3068, 1924 British Empire Exhibition 1d. scarlet stamp; 3069, Two Portraits of King George V; 3070, 1913 £1 Green 'Sea Horses' design stamp; 3071, 1913 10s. Blue 'Sea Horses' design stamp.

Nos. 3066 and 3069 also come from miniature sheet **MS**3065.

Nos. 3067/8 and 3070/1 also come from **MS**3072.

2269 Winston Churchill

2010. 'Britain Alone' (1st issue).

3074	**2269**	(1st) pale stone, pale bistre and black	90	90
3075	–	(1st) pale stone, pale bistre and black	90	90
3076	–	60p. pale stone, pale bistre and black	1·25	1·25
3077	–	60p. pale stone, pale bistre and black	1·25	1·25
3078	–	67p. pale stone, pale bistre and black	1·40	1·40
3079	–	67p. pale stone, pale bistre and black	1·40	1·40
3080	–	97p. pale stone, pale bistre and black	2·00	2·00
3081	–	97p. pale stone, pale bistre and black	2·00	2·00

No. **MS**3073, T **2268** are left for London 2010 Exhibition souvenir sheet, issued 8 May 2010, not yet received.

DESIGNS: Nos. 3075, Land Girl; 3076, Home Guard; 3077, Evacuees; 3078, Air Raid Wardens; 3079, Woman working in Factory; 3080, Royal Broadcast by Princess Elizabeth and Princess Margaret; 3081, Fire Service.

2277 Evacuation of British Soldiers from Dunkirk

2281 Evacuation of British Troops from Dunkirk, 1940 (Illustration reduced. Actual size 115×89 mm) (image scaled to 42% of original size)

2010. 'Britain Alone' (2nd issue).

3082	**2277**	(1st) pale stone, pale bistre and black	90	90
3083	–	60p. pale stone, pale bistre and black	1·25	1·25
3084	–	88p. pale stone, pale bistre and black	1·75	1·75
3085	–	97p. pale stone, pale bistre and black	2·00	2·00
MS3086		Nos. 3082/5	6·50	6·50

DESIGNS: 3083, Vessels from Upper Thames Patrol in 'Operation Little Ships'; 3084, Rescued soldiers on board Royal Navy destroyer, Dover; 3085, Steamship and other boat loaded with troops.

REGIONAL ISSUES I. CHANNEL ISLANDS

Islands in the English Channel off N.W. coast of France. Occupied by German forces from June 1940 to May 1945, when separate issueds for both islands were made.

C1 Gathering Vraic (seaweed)

1948. 3rd Anniversary of Liberation.

C1	**C1**	1d. red	25	30
C2	-	2½d. blue	25	30

DESIGN: 2½d. Islanders gathering vraic.

II. GUERNSEY

2

3

1958

6	**2**	2½d. red	35	40
7p	**3**	3d. lilac	15	20
9	**3**	4d. blue	10	20
10	**3**	4d. sepia	10	15
11	**3**	4d. red	20	25
12	**3**	5d. blue	20	30

For War Occupation issues and issues of independent postal administration from 1967 see **GUERNSEY**.

III. ISLE OF MAN

1

2

1958

1	**1**	2½d. red	50	1·20
2	**2**	3d. lilac	50	20
3p	**2**	4d. blue	20	30
5	**2**	4d. sepia	25	30
6	**2**	4d. red	45	75
7	**2**	5d. blue	45	75

3

1971. Decimal Currency.

8	3	2½p. red	20	15
9	3	3p. blue	20	15
10	3	5p. violet	80	80
11	3	7½p. brown	90	90

For issues of independent postal administration from 1973 see **ISLE OF MAN**.

IV. JERSEY

8

9

1958

9	8	2½d. red	30	45
10p	9	3d. lilac	15	15
11p	9	4d. blue	15	25
12	9	4d. sepia	15	25
13	9	4d. red	15	25
14	9	5d. blue	15	50

For War Occupation issues and issues of independent postal administration from 1969 see **JERSEY**.

V. ENGLAND

EN1 Three Lions

2001

EN1	EN 1	(2nd) green and silver	1·00	1·00
EN2	-	(1st) brown and silver	1·00	1·00
EN3	-	(E) green and silver	1·75	1·75
EN4	-	65p. lilac and silver	3·00	3·00
EN5	-	68p. lilac and silver	3·00	3·00

DESIGNS: No. EN2, Crowned Lion with Shield of St. George; EN3, Oak Tree; EN4/5, Tudor Rose.

Nos EN1/3 were initially sold at 19p., 27p. and 36p., the latter representing the basic European airmail rate.

2003. As Nos. EN1/3 and EN5 but with white borders.

EN6	EN1	(2nd) green and silver	75	60
EN7	-	(1st) brown and silver	80	75
EN8	-	(E) green and silver	2·00	2·00
EN9	-	40p. green and silver	1·50	1·50
EN10	-	42p. green and silver	1·25	1·25
EN11	-	44p. green and silver	1·50	1·50
EN12	-	48p. green and silver	1·25	1·25
EN13	-	50p. green	90	85
EN13a	-	56p. green and silver	1·25	1·25
EN13b	-	60p. olive-green and silver	1·75	1·75
EN14	-	68p. lilac and silver	2·50	2·50
EN15	-	72p. lilac and silver	2·50	2·50
EN16	-	78p. lilac and silver	2·50	2·50
EN17	-	81p. lilac and silver	2·00	2·00
EN17a	-	90p. lilac and silver	2·00	2·00
EN17b	-	97p. deep reddish lilac and silver	2·50	2·50

EN 5 (image scaled to 39% of original size)

2007. Celebrating England. Sheet 123×70 mm.
MSEN19 (1st) No. EN7; (1st) St. George's flag; 78p. St. George; 78p. Houses of Parliament, London 9·00 9·00

VI. NORTHERN IRELAND

N1

N2

N3

1958

NI1	N1	3d. lilac	15	10
NI2	N1	4d. blue	15	15
NI3	N 2	6d. purple	30	30
NI4	N 2	9d. green	30	70
NI5	N 3	1s.3d. green	30	70
NI6	N 3	1s.6d. blue	30	70
NI8	N1	4d. sepia	15	15
NI9	N1	4d. red	20	20
NI10	N1	5d. blue	20	20

N4

1971

NI12	N4	2½p. mauve	70	60
NI14	N4	3p. blue	20	15
NI15	N4	3½p. grey	20	25
NI17	N4	4½p. blue	30	25
NI18	N4	5p. violet	1·00	1·00
NI19	N4	5½p. violet	20	20
NI21	N4	6½p. blue	20	20
NI22	N4	7p. brown	35	25
NI23	N4	7½p. brown	1·75	1·75
NI24	N4	8p. red	35	35
NI25	N4	8½p. green	35	40
NI26	N4	9p. violet	40	40
NI27	N4	10p. brown	40	50
NI29	N4	10½p. blue	40	50
NI30	N4	11p. red	50	50
NI31	N4	12p. green	50	50
NI32	N4	13½p. brown	60	70
NI33	N4	15p. blue	60	70
NI34	N4	11½p. drab	85	85
NI36	N4	12½p. green	60	60
NI37	N4	13p. brown	80	50
NI38	N4	14p. blue	75	75
NI41	N4	15½p. violet	80	80
NI42	N4	16p. brown	1·00	1·00
NI43	N4	17p. blue	90	95
NI45	N4	18p. violet	1·00	1·00
NI46	N4	18p. grey	1·00	90
NI47	N4	18p. green	1·00	95
NI49	N4	19p. red	1·00	1·00
NI50	N4	19½p. grey	1·50	1·75
NI51	N4	20p. black	1·00	80
NI52	N4	20½p. blue	4·50	4·25
NI53	N4	22p. blue	1·10	1·10
NI54	N4	22p. green	1·10	1·10
NI55	N4	22p. red	1·25	90
NI56	N4	23p. green	1·25	1·10
NI57	N4	24p. red	1·25	1·25
NI58	N4	24p. brown	1·10	90
NI60	N4	26p. red	1·25	1·25
NI61	N4	26p. drab	1·75	1·75
NI62	N4	28p. blue	1·50	1·50
NI63	N4	28p. grey	1·50	1·50
NI64	N4	31p. purple	1·75	2·00
NI65	N4	32p. blue	1·75	1·75
NI66	N4	34p. grey	1·75	1·75
NI67	N4	37p. red	2·00	2·50
NI68	N4	39p. mauve	2·00	2·25
NI69	N4	19p. bistre	90	80
NI72	N4	25p. red	75	75
NI74	N4	30p. grey	1·25	1·25
NI76	N4	41p. brown	1·50	1·75
NI79	N4	20p. green	90	80
NI81	N4	26p. brown	1·25	1·00
NI82	N4	37p. mauve	2·25	2·25
NI83	N4	38p. blue	8·00	8·00
NI84	N4	40p. blue	2·50	2·50
NI85	N4	63p. green	5·00	5·00
NI86	N4	64p. green	9·00	9·00
NI87	N4	65p. blue	2·75	3·00

2000. As Type N 4 but with "1st" face value.

NI88	(1st) bright red	3·00	3·00

N 6 Basalt Columns, Giant's Causeway

2001

NI89	N 6	(2nd) multicoloured	75	75
NI90	-	(1st) black, blue & yellow	1·20	1·20
NI91	-	(E) black, blue & orange	1·50	1·50
NI92	-	65p. black, mauve & yell	3·00	3·00
NI93	-	68p. black, mauve and yellow	3·25	3·25

DESIGNS: NI90, Aerial view of patchwork fields; NI91, Linen pattern; NI92/3, Vase pattern from Belleck.

Nos. NI89, NI90 and NI91 were initially sold at 19p., 27p. and 36p., the latter representing the basic European airmail rate.

2003. As Nos. NI89/91 and NI93 but with white borders.

NI94	N6	(2nd) multicoloured	1·00	1·00
NI95	-	(1st) black, blue and yellow	1·00	1·00
NI96	-	(E) black and blue	2·50	2·50
NI97	-	40p. black and blue	1·75	1·75
NI98	-	42p. black, blue and orange	1·75	1·75
NI99	-	44p. black, blue and yellow	1·00	1·00
NI101	-	72p. multicoloured	2·50	2·50
NI104	-	48p. grey and black	1·20	1·20
NI105a	-	56p. grey and black	1·25	1·25
NI105b	-	60p. olive-grey and black	1·50	1·50
NI106	-	78p. magenta, yellow and black	2·00	2·00
NI107	-	81p. magenta, yellow and black	2·00	2·00
NI107a	-	90p. magenta, yellow and black	2·00	2·00
NI107b	-	97p. bright magenta, greenish yellow and black	2·40	2·40

N 10 (image scaled to 39% of original size)

2007. Celebrating Northern Ireland. Sheet 123×70 mm.
MS110 (1st) Carrickfergus Castle; (1st) Giant's Causeway; 78p. St. Patrick; 78p. Queen's Bridge and 'Angel of Thanksgiving' sculpture, Belfast 6·00 6·00

REGIONAL ISSUES

N 11 (image scaled to 39% of original size)

2008. 50th Anniv of the Country Definitives. Sheet 124×70 mm, containing designs as Nos. NI1, NI3, NI5, S1, S3, S5, W1, W3 and W5 (regional definitives of 1958) but inscribed 1st and printed on pale cream.
MSNI111 As No. W1; As No. S1; As No. W5; As No. S5; As No. NI1; As No. W3; As No. S3; As No. NI3; As No. NI5 8·25 8·25

See also Nos. NI112/14.

2008. 50th Anniv of the Country Definitives (2nd issue). As Nos. NI1, NI3 and NI5 (definitives of 1958) but inscribed 1st.

NI112	N 1	(1st) lilac	1·25	1·25
NI113	N 3	(1st) green	1·25	1·25
NI114	N 2	(1st) claret	1·25	1·25

VII. SCOTLAND

S1

S2

S3

1958

S3	S 2	6d. purple	20	15
S4	S 2	9d. green	35	40
S5	S 3	1s.3d. green	40	40
S6	S 3	1s.6d. blue	45	50
S7	S1	3d. lilac	10	15
S8	S1	4d. blue	10	15
S9	S1	4d. sepia	10	10
S10	S1	4d. red	10	10
S11	S1	5d. blue	20	10

S4

1971. Decimal Currency.

S14	S4	2½p. mauve	25	20
S16	S4	3p. blue	15	15
S17	S4	3½p. grey	20	25
S19	S4	4½p. blue	30	25
S20	S4	5p. violet	1·00	1·25
S21	S4	5½p. violet	20	20
S23	S4	6½p. blue	20	20
S24	S4	7p. brown	30	30
S25	S4	7½p. brown	1·25	1·25
S26	S4	8p. red	45	40
S27	S4	8½p. green	40	40
S28	S4	9p. violet	40	40
S30	S4	10p. brown	40	50
S31	S4	10½p. blue	45	50
S32	S4	11p. red	50	50
S33	S4	12p. green	50	50
S34	S4	13½p. brown	70	80
S35	S4	15p. blue	60	70
S36	S4	11½p. drab	80	80
S38	S4	12½p. green	60	70
S39	S4	13p. brown	85	75
S41	S4	15½p. violet	80	80
S42	S4	16p. drab	80	85
S44	S4	18p. violet	80	80
S45	S4	19½p. grey	1·75	1·75
S46	S4	20½p. blue	3·50	3·50
S47	S4	22p. blue	1·00	1·00
S49	S4	26p. red	1·25	1·25
S54	S4	14p. blue	60	70
S58	S4	17p. blue	1·00	1·10
S59	S4	18p. grey	1·10	85
S60	S4	18p. green	1·25	90
S62	S4	19p. red	70	70
S64	S4	20p. black	95	95
S65	S4	22p. green	1·25	1·50
S66	S4	22p. red	1·25	90
S67	S4	23p. green	1·25	1·10
S69	S4	24p. red	1·25	1·25
S70	S4	24p. brown	1·40	1·25
S73	S4	26p. drab	1·25	1·25
S74	S4	28p. blue	1·25	1·25
S75	S4	28p. grey	1·25	1·50
S76	S4	31p. purple	2·25	2·25
S77	S4	32p. blue	1·75	2·00
S78	S4	34p. grey	1·75	1·75
S79	S4	37p. red	2·00	2·25
S80	S4	39p. mauve	2·00	2·25
S81	S4	19p. bistre	80	70
S84	S4	25p. red	1·10	1·00
S86	S4	30p. grey	1·25	1·25
S88	S4	41p. brown	1·75	2·00
S90	S4	20p. green	1·00	90
S91	S4	26p. brown	1·20	1·20
S92	S4	37p. mauve	1·50	1·50
S93	S4	63p. green	4·00	4·00

S5 Scottish Flag

1999

S94	S 5	(2nd) blue, deep blue and silver	75	75
S95	-	(1st) multicoloured	1·00	1·00
S96	-	(E) lilac, deep lilac and silver	2·00	2·00
S97	-	64p. multicoloured	9·00	9·00
S98	-	65p. multicoloured	3·00	3·25
S99	-	68p. multicoloured	3·25	3·25

DESIGNS: No. S95, Scottish Lion; S96, Thistle; S97/9, Tartan.

Nos. S94, S95 and S96 were initially sold at 19p., 26p. and 30p., the latter representing the basic European airmail rate.

2000. As Type S 4 but with "1st" face value.

S108	(1st) bright red	3·00	3·25

2003. As Nos. S94/6 and S99 but with white borders.

S109	S5	(2nd) blue, deep blue and silver	60	60
S110	-	(1st) multicoloured	85	85
S111	-	(E) lilac, deep lilac and silver	2·50	2·50
S112	-	40p. lilac, deep lilac and silver	1·75	1·75
S113	-	42p. lilac, deep lilac and silver	1·75	1·75
S114	-	44p. lilac, deep lilac and silver	1·50	1·50
S115	-	48p. lilac, deep lilac and silver	90	90
S116	-	50p. lilac, deep lilac and silver	80	75
S116a	-	50p. lilac, deep lilac and silver	1·25	1·25
S116b	-	60p. olive-grey and black	1·75	1·75
S117	-	68p. multicoloured	2·00	2·00

S118	-	72p. multicoloured	1·75	1·75
S119	-	78p. multicoloured	1·50	1·50
S120	-	81p. multicoloured	1·40	1·30
S120a	-	90p. multicoloured	2·00	2·00
S120b	-	97p. multicoloured	1·90	1·90

2004. Scottish Parliament. Sheet 123×70 mm containing Nos. S109, S110×2 and S112×2.

MSS32 (2nd) deep blue; blue and silver; (1st)×2 yellow; deep red, red and silver; 40p.×2 lilac, deep lilac and silver	6·00	6·00

S 10 (image scaled to 39% of original size)

2006. Celebrating Scotland. Sheet 124×71 mm.

MSS133 (1st) As No. S110; (1st) Scottish Flag; 72p. St. Andrew; 72p. Edinburgh Castle	6·00	3·00

2008. 50th Anniv of the Country Definitives. As Nos. S1, S3 and S5 (definitives of 1958) but inscribed 1st.

S134	S 1	(1st) lilac	1·25	1·25
S135	S 3	(1st) green	1·25	1·25
S136	S 2	(1st) claret	1·25	1·25

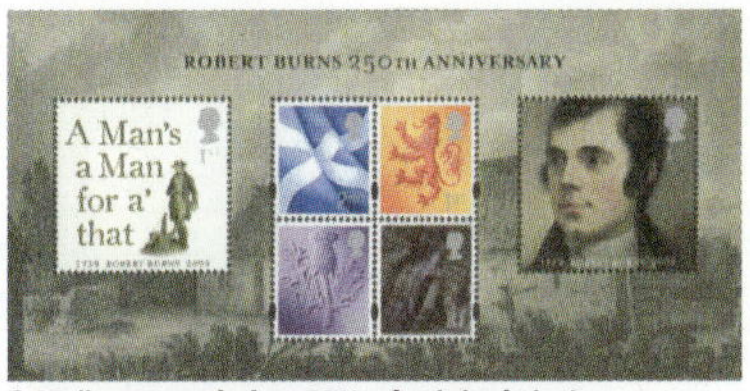

S 11 (image scaled to 33% of original size)

2009. 250th Birth Anniv of Robert Burns (Scottish poet). Sheet 145×74 mm.

MSS137 (2nd) No. S109; (1st) 'A Man's a Man for a' that' and Burns ploughing (detail) (James Sargent Storer) (34×34 mm); (1st) No. S110; (1st) Portrait of Burns (Alexander Nasmyth) (34×34 mm); 50p. No. S116; 81p. S120	8·00	8·00

VIII. WALES

W1

W2

W3

1958

W1	W1	3d. lilac	15	15
W3	W 2	6d. purple	35	30
W4	W 2	9d. green	40	35
W5	W 3	1s.3d. green	40	40
W6	W 3	1s.6d. blue	40	40
W8	W1	4d. blue	10	15
W9	W1	4d. sepia	15	15
W10	W1	4d. red	15	15
W11	W1	5d. blue	15	15

W4

1971. Decimal Currency.

W13	W4	2½p. mauve	20	20
W14	W4	3p. blue	25	20
W16	W4	3½p. grey	20	30
W18	W4	4½p. blue	30	30
W19	W4	5p. violet	1·25	1·25
W20	W4	5½p. violet	25	30
W22	W4	6½p. blue	20	20
W23	W4	7p. brown	25	25
W24	W4	7½p. brown	1·75	1·75
W25	W4	8p. red	30	35
W26	W4	8½p. green	30	35
W27	W4	9p. violet	40	40
W29	W4	10p. brown	40	40
W30	W4	10½p. blue	45	45
W31	W4	11p. red	45	45
W32	W4	12p. green	50	50
W33	W4	13½p. brown	60	70
W34	W4	15p. blue	60	70
W35	W4	11½p. drab	90	80
W37	W4	12½p. green	70	70
W38	W4	13p. brown	60	60
W40	W4	14p. blue	75	75
W42	W4	15½p. violet	75	75
W43	W4	16p. drab	1·75	1·75
W44	W4	17p. blue	70	80
W46	W4	18p. violet	1·00	95
W47	W4	18p. grey	95	90
W48	W4	18p. green	75	75
W50	W4	19p. red	1·00	80
W51	W4	19½p. grey	1·75	2·00
W52	W4	20p. black	90	90
W53	W4	20½p. blue	3·75	3·75
W54	W4	22p. blue	1·10	1·10
W55	W4	22p. green	95	1·10
W56	W4	22p. red	1·00	1·10
W57	W4	23p. green	1·00	1·10
W58	W4	24p. red	1·25	1·25
W59	W4	24p. brown	75	75
W61	W4	26p. red	1·10	1·10
W62	W4	26p. drab	1·75	1·75
W63	W4	28p. blue	1·50	1·50
W64	W4	28p. grey	1·50	1·50
W65	W4	31p. purple	1·75	1·75
W66	W4	32p. blue	1·75	1·75
W67	W4	34p. grey	1·75	1·75
W68	W4	37p. red	2·25	2·25
W69	W4	39p. mauve	2·25	2·25
W70	W4	19p. bistre	80	70
W72	W4	20p. green	1·75	2·00
W73	W4	25p. red	1·25	1·00
W74	W4	26p. brown	2·00	2·25
W75	W4	30p. grey	1·25	1·25
W76	W4	37p. mauve	2·75	3·00
W77	W4	41p. brown	2·00	2·00
W78	W4	63p. green	4·50	4·75

W5 Without "p"

1997

W79	W5	20p. green	80	80
W80	W5	26p. brown	1·00	1·00
W81	W5	37p. mauve	2·75	2·75
W82	W5	63p. green	5·00	5·00

W6 Leek

1999

W83	W6	(2nd) brown, orange and black	60	50
W84	-	(1st) multicoloured	1·00	1·00
W85	-	(E) multicoloured	1·75	1·75
W86	-	64p. multicoloured	9·00	9·00
W87	-	65p. multicoloured	3·25	3·25
W88	-	68p. multicoloured	3·25	3·25

DESIGNS: No. W84, Welsh Dragon; W85, Daffodil; W86/8, Prince of Wales Feathers.

Nos. W83, W84 and W85 were initially sold at 19p., 26p. and 30p., the latter representing the basic European airmail rate.

2000. As Type W 5 but with "1af/st" face value.

W97	(1st) bright red	3·00	2·75

2003. As Nos. W83, W84/5 and W88, but with white borders.

W98	W6	(2nd) orange, brown and black	80	75
W99	-	(1st) multicoloured	80	75
W100	-	(E) blue, deep blue and black	2·50	2·50
W101	-	40p. blue, deep blue and black	1·50	1·50
W102	-	42p. blue, deep blue and black	1·50	1·50
W103	-	44p. blue, deep blue and black	1·50	1·50
W104	-	48p. blue, deep blue and black	90	90
W105	-	50p. blue, deep blue and black	1·00	1·00
W105a	-	56p. blue, deep blue and black	1·25	1·25
W105b	-	60p. greenish blue, deep greenish blue and grey-black	1·75	1·75
W106	-	68p. multicoloured	2·00	2·00
W107	-	72p. multicoloured	2·00	2·00
W108	-	78p. multicoloured	1·40	1·30
W109	-	81p. multicoloured	1·75	1·75
W109a	-	90p. multicoloured	4·25	4·25
W109b	-	97p. multicoloured	2·40	2·40

2006. Opening of New Welsh Assembly Building, Cardiff. Sheet 123×70 mm.

MSW121 Nos. W98, W99×2 and W106×2	5·00	5·00

2008. 50th Anniv of the Country Definitives. As Nos. W1, W3 and W5 (definitives of 1958) but inscribed 1st.

W122	W 1	(1st) lilac	1·25	1·25
W123	W 3	(1st) green	1·25	1·25
W124	W 2	(1st) claret	1·25	1·25

W 11 (image scaled to 39% of original size)

2009. Celebrating Wales. Sheet 123×70 mm.

MSW125 (1st) Red dragon; (1st) No. W120; 81p. St. David; 81p. National Assembly for Wales, Cardiff	6·00	6·00

OFFICIAL STAMP
for Government Departments)

ADMIRALTY

Overprinted ADMIRALTY OFFICIAL

1903. Stamps of King Edward VII.

O101	83	½d. turquoise	27·00	13·00
O102	-	1d. red	16·00	6·50
O103	-	1½d. purple and green	£300	£140
O104	-	2d. green and red	£325	£150
O105	83	2½d. blue	£450	£140
O106	-	3d. purple on yellow	£400	£150

ARMY Overprinted ARMY OFFICIAL

1896. Stamps of Queen Victoria.

O41	71	½d. red	5·00	2·50
O42	71	½d. green	5·00	10·00
O43	57	1d. lilac	5·00	4·00
O44	74	2½d. purple on blue	35·00	25·00
O45	79	6d. purple on red	80·00	45·00

1902. Stamps of King Edward VII.

O48	83	½d. turquoise	5·50	2·25
O49	83	1d. red	5·50	2·25
O50	83	6d. purple	£160	75·00

BOARD OF EDUCATION

Overprinted BOARD OF EDUCATION

1902. Stamps of Queen Victoria.

O81	78	5d. purple on blue	£3500	£850
O82	82	1s. green and red	£8750	£4500

1902. Stamps of King Edward VII.

O83	83	½d. turquoise	£160	38·00
O84	83	1d. red	£160	38·00
O85	83	2½d. blue	£4250	£350
O86	-	5d. purple and blue	£25000	£8500
O87	-	1s. green and red	£130000	

GOVERNMENT PARCELS

Overprinted GOVT. PARCELS

1883. Stamps of Queen Victoria.

O61	62	1½d. purple	£325	70·00
O62	-	6d. green (No. 194)	£2500	£1000
O63	-	9d. green (No. 195)	£2000	£800
O64	25	1s. brown (No. 163)	£1300	£225

1887. Stamps of Queen Victoria.

O65	72	1½d. purple and green	£110	15·00
O66	79	6d. purple on red	£200	50·00
O67	80	9d. purple and blue	£300	75·00
O68	82	1s. green	£550	£225
O69	57	1d. lilac	75·00	18·00
O70	73	2d. green and red	£175	30·00
O71	77	4½d. green and red	£275	£200
O72	82	1s. green and red	£500	£200

1902. Stamps of King Edward VII.

O74	83	1d. red	32·00	13·00
O75	-	2d. green and red	£150	38·00
O76	83	6d. purple	£250	38·00
O77	-	9d. purple and blue	£600	£160
O78	-	1s. green and red	£1300	£275

INLAND REVENUE

Overprinted I.R. OFFICIAL

1882. Stamps of Queen Victoria.

O1	52	½d. green	£110	40·00
O3	57	1d. lilac	6·00	4·00
O4	34	6d. grey (No. 161)	£450	£110
O5	52	½d. blue	70·00	24·00
O6	-	2½d. purple (No. 190)	£400	£150
O7	-	1s. green (No. 196)	£5000	£1500
O9	-	5s. red (No. 181)	£7000	£1900
O10	-	10s. blue (No. 183)	£9000	£2800
O11	61	£1 brown	£60000	£22000

1888

O13	71	½d. red	10·00	4·00
O14	74	2½d. purple on blue	£120	15·00
O15	89	1s. green	£750	£250
O16	61	£1 green	£10000	£2250
O17	71	½d. green	15·00	10·00
O18	79	6d. purple on red	£325	90·00
O19	89	1s. green and red	£3500	£1250

1902. Stamps of King Edward VII.

O20	83	½d. turquoise	24·00	3·25
O21	83	1d. red	17·00	2·25
O22	83	2½d. blue	£900	£250
O23	83	6d. purple	£375000	£170000
O24	-	1s. green and red	£3500	£700
O25	-	5s. red	£25000	£8000
O26	-	10s. blue	£95000	£40000
O27	-	£1 green	£60000	£24000

OFFICE OF WORKS

Overprinted O.W. OFFICIAL

1896. Stamps of Queen Victoria.

O31	71	½d. red	£250	£110
O32	71	½d. green	£350	£160
O33	57	1d. lilac	£400	£110
O34	78	5d. purple and blue	£2800	£1000
O35	81	10d. purple and red	£4800	£1500

1902. Stamps of King Edward VII.

O36	83	½d. turquoise	£550	£160
O37	-	1d. red	£550	£160
O38	-	2d. green and red	£1900	£400
O39	83	2½d. blue	£3250	£600
O40	-	10d. purple and red	£32000	£6000

ROYAL HOUSEHOLD

Overprinted R.H. OFFICIAL

1902. Stamps of King Edward VII.

O91	83	½d. turquoise	£375	£200
O92	83	1d. red	£325	£175

POSTAGE DUE STAMPS

D1

1914

D1	D1	½d. green	50	50
D2	D1	1d. red	50	50
D3	D1	1½d. brown	48·00	48·00
D15	D1	4d. green	15·00	15·00
D17	D1	1s. blue	8·50	8·50
D56	D1	½d. orange	15	1·25
D57	D1	1d. blue	15	50
D58	D1	1½d. green	2·50	2·50
D60	D1	3d. violet	30	30
D61	D1	4d. blue	30	30
D62	D1	5d. brown	45	60
D63	D1	6d. purple	50	30
D64	D1	1s. brown	90	30
D65	D1	2s.6d. purple on yellow	3·00	50
D66	D1	5s. red on yellow	8·25	1·00
D67	D1	10s. blue on yellow	11·50	5·75
D68	D1	£1 black on yellow	45·00	8·25
D69	D1	2d. black	75	1·00
D76	D1	8d. red	50	1·00

On the 2s.6d. to £1 the inscription reads "TO PAY".

D4

1970. Decimal Currency.

D77	-	½p. blue	15	2·50
D78	-	1p. purple	15	15
D79	-	2p. green	20	15
D80	-	3p. blue	20	15
D81	-	4p. brown	25	15
D82	-	5p. violet	25	15
D83	-	7p. brown	35	1·00
D84	D4	10p. red	30	30
D85	D4	11p. green	50	1·00
D86	D4	20p. brown	60	25
D87	D4	50p. blue	2·00	1·25
D88	D4	£1 black	4·00	1·00
D89	D4	£5 yellow and black	36·00	1·50

DESIGN: ½p. to 7p. similar to Type D 4, but with "TO PAY" reading vertically upwards at the left.

D5

1982

D90	**D5**	1p. red	10	30
D91	**D5**	2p. blue	30	30
D92	**D5**	3p. mauve	15	30
D93	**D5**	4p. blue	15	25
D94	**D5**	5p. brown	20	25
D95	-	10p. brown	30	40
D96	-	20p. green	50	60
D97	-	25p. blue	80	90
D98	-	50p. black	1·75	1·75
D99	-	£1 red	3·25	1·25
D100	-	£2 blue	7·00	4·25
D101	-	£5 orange	14·00	2·25

DESIGNS: 10p. to £5, as Type D **5** but with "TO PAY" horizontal.

D7

1994

D102	**D7**	1p. red, yellow and black	10	75
D103	**D7**	2p. mauve, purple blk	10	75
D104	**D7**	5p. yellow, brown blk	15	50
D105	**D7**	10p. yellow, green blk	30	75
D106	**D7**	20p. green, violet blk	75	1·50
D107	**D7**	25p. mauve, red black	1·50	2·00
D108	**D7**	£1 violet, mauve black	7·00	10·00
D109	**D7**	£1.20 blue, green blk	8·00	12·00
D110	**D7**	£5 dp green, green blk	30·00	20·00

Pt. 6

GREAT COMORO

A French island north west of Madagascar. From 1914 to 1950 the stamps of Madagascar were used. In 1950 it became part of the Comoro Islands.

100 centimes = 1 franc.

1897. "Tablet" key-type inscr "GRANDE COMORE" in red or blue.

1	**D**	1c. black on blue	1·10	1·50
2	**D**	2c. brown on buff	1·00	1·60
3	**D**	4c. brown on grey	2·20	2·20
4	**D**	5c. green on light green	2·75	1·10
5	**D**	10c. black on lilac	7·00	5·50
6	**D**	15c. blue	22·00	18·00
7	**D**	20c. red on green	15·00	21·00
8	**D**	25c. black on pink	11·00	11·50
9	**D**	30c. brown on drab	17·00	29·00
10	**D**	40c. red on yellow	22·00	28·00
11	**D**	50c. red on pink	28·00	41·00
12	**D**	75c. brown on blue	42·00	65·00
13	**D**	1f. green	26·00	55·00
14	**D**	10c. red	17·00	26·00
15	**D**	15c. grey	12·00	32·00
16	**D**	25c. blue	15·00	31·00
17	**D**	35c. black on yellow	25·00	23·00
18	**D**	45c. black on green	75·00	95·00
19	**D**	50c. brown on blue	55·00	65·00

1912. Surch.

20A	05 on 2c. brown on buff	1·10	45
21A	05 on 4c. brown on grey	1·40	75
22A	05 on 15c. blue	1·50	90
23A	05 on 20c. red on green	65	4·50
24A	05 on 25c. black on pink	75	75
25A	05 on 30c. brown on drab	1·30	1·50
26A	10 on 40c. red on yellow	1·50	2·30
27A	10 on 45c. black on green	1·20	1·80
28A	10 on 50c. red on pink	75	90
29A	10 on 75c. brown on orange	2·20	6·50

Pt. 3

GREECE

A country in the S.E. of Europe, under Turkish rule till 1830, when it became a kingdom. A republic was established from 1924 to 1935 when the monarchy was restored. The country was under German occupation from April 1941 to October 1944. The monarchy was once again abolished during 1973 and a republic set up.

1861. 100 lepta = 1 drachma.
2002. 100 cents = 1 euro.

1 Hermes

1861. Imperf or perf.

17	1	2l. buff	12·50	35·00
19b	1	10l. orange on blue	£550	80·00
20	1	20l. blue	£275	16·00
22	1	80l. red	90·00	50·00
28	1	40l. mauve on blue	£250	26·00
37	1	40l. orange on green	£600	80·00
43d	1	40l. bistre on blue	33·00	47·00
43f	1	40l. green on blue	70·00	65·00
50	1	40l. buff	22·00	65·00
52	1	60l. green on green	27·00	80·00
53	1	30l. brown	55·00	8·25
54	1	60l. green	£450	47·00
55	1	5l. green	16·00	2·10
56	1	10l. orange	16·00	2·10
59	1	20l. red	2·20	2·10
60	1	30l. blue	£150	7·25
61	1	40l. mauve	43·00	7·25
62	1	1l. brown	11·00	5·25

2

1886. Imperf.

73	2	1l. brown	3·00	2·10
76	2	10l. orange	15·00	2·10
79	2	40l. purple	90·00	21·00
80	2	50l. green	11·00	4·75
81	2	1d. grey	£110	3·75
86	2	2l. buff	1·10	1·30
87b	2	5l. green	2·40	1·60
89c	2	20l. red	33·00	1·00
90d	2	25l. blue	65·00	1·00
91	2	25l. purple	11·00	2·10
93	2	40l. blue	7·50	2·10

1886. Perf.

83	50l. green	16·00	5·75
84	1d. grey	£160	6·25
96	2l. buff	1·10	8·25
100	1l. brown	2·20	1·00
102	5l. green	8·75	1·00
103b	10l. orange	38·00	2·10
104a	20l. red	43·00	1·60
105d	25l. blue	£100	8·25
106a	25l. purple	11·00	2·10
107	40l. purple	£120	31·00
108	40l. blue	13·00	3·25

3 Wrestlers

4 Discus thrower

5 Vase depicting Pallas Athene

6 Quadriga of Chariot driving

1896. 1st International Olympic Games. Perf.

110	3	1l. yellow	2·20	1·80
111	3	2l. red	2·75	2·10
112	4	5l. mauve	11·00	3·25
113	4	10l. grey	11·00	4·50
114	5	20l. brown	24·00	4·75
115	6	25l. red	30·00	6·00
116	5	40l. violet	13·00	7·25
117	6	60l. black	41·00	21·00
118	-	1d. blue	£100	20·00
119	-	2d. olive	£300	80·00
120	-	5d. green	£550	£450
121	-	10d. brown	£600	£500

DESIGNS—As Type **6**—HORIZ: 1d. Acropolis and Stadium; 10d. Acropolis with Parthenon. VERT: 2d. "Hermes" (after statue by Praxiteles); 5d. "Victory" (after statue by Paeonius).

1900. Surch. Imperf.

122	2	20l. on 25l. blue	3·25	1·00
123	2	1d. on 40l. purple	16·00	6·25
124	2	2d. on 40l. purple	£475	
130	1	30l. on 40l. purple	6·50	6·25
131	1	40l. on 2l. buff	8·75	8·25
132	1	50l. on 40l. buff	6·50	6·25
133	1	3d. on 10l. orange	55·00	50·00
134	1	5d. on 40l. purple on blue	£140	£160

1900. Surch. Perf.

125	2	20l. on 25l. blue	3·25	1·00
126	2	1d. on 40l. purple	22·00	10·50
127a	2	2d. on 40l. purple	11·00	12·50
135	1	30l. on 40l. purple	11·00	10·50
136	1	40l. on 2l. buff	16·00	16·00
137	1	50l. on 40l. buff	11·00	10·50
138	1	3d. on 10l. orange	60·00	60·00
139	1	5d. on 40l. purple on blue	£160	£170

1900. Surch AM and value.

140	2	25l. on 40l. purple (No. 79)	5·50	10·50
141	2	50l. on 25l. blue (No. 90d)	27·00	26·00
142	2	25l. on 40l. purple (No. 107)	11·00	16·00
143	2	50l. on 25l. blue (No. 105)	55·00	65·00
144	1	1d. on 40l. brown on blue (No. 43d)	£110	£160
145	1	2d. on 5l. green (No. 55)	16·00	26·00
146	1	1d. on 40l. brown on blue (Perf)	£150	£170
147	1	2d. on 5l. green (No. 102)	22·00	37·00

1900. Olympic Games stamps surch AM and value.

148	-	5l. on 1d. blue	22·00	31·00
149	5	25l. on 40l. violet	£110	85·00
150	-	50l. on 2d. olive	£100	75·00
151	-	1d. on 5d. green	£350	£225
152	-	2d. on 10d. brown	75·00	£120

15

16 Hermes after the "Mercury" of Giovanni da Bologna

17

1901

160	15	30l. purple	13·00	1·60
163	17	1d. black	40·00	2·10
164	17	2d. bronze	11·00	8·25
165	17	3d. silver	15·00	10·50
166	17	5d. gold	17·00	10·50
167A	15	1l. brown	65	20
168A	15	2l. grey	75	20
169A	15	3l. orange	85	30
170A	16	5l. green	75	30
171A	16	10l. red	1·10	30
172A	15	20l. mauve	1·10	30
173A	16	25l. blue	2·00	30
175B	15	40l. brown	1·60	30
176A	15	50l. lake	20·00	1·00

19 Head of Hermes

1902

178	19	5l. orange	2·30	1·00
179	19	25l. green	35·00	2·40
180	19	50l. blue	35·00	2·40
181	19	1d. red	35·00	10·00
182	19	2d. brown	65·00	44·00

20 Athlete throwing Discus

21 Jumper

23 Atlas offering the Apples of Hesperides to Hercules

1906. Olympic Games. Dated "1906".

183	20	1l. brown	55	30
184	20	2l. black	60	30
185	21	3l. orange	70	30
186	21	5l. green	1·20	50
187	-	10l. red	3·25	50
188	23	20l. red	5·50	50
189	-	25l. blue	5·75	65
190	-	30l. purple	6·50	3·25
191	-	40l. brown	6·50	3·25
192	23	50l. purple	15·00	3·25
193	-	1d. black	75·00	19·00
194	-	2d. red	£130	41·00
195	-	3d. yellow	£150	£140
196	-	5d. blue	£200	£150

DESIGNS—As Type **20**: 10l. Victory; 20l. Wrestlers; 40l. "Daemon" or God of the Games. As Type **23**: 25l. Hercules and Antaeus; 1d., 2d., 3d. Race, Ancient Greeks; 5d. Olympic Offerings.

29 Head of Hermes

30 Iris

31 Hermes

32 Hermes and Arcas

1911. Roul.

209		3d. red (20¼×25¼ mm)	33·00	1·30
210		5d. blue (20¼×25¼ mm)	35·00	5·75
211b		10d. blue (20¼×25¼ mm)	80·00	50·00
212	-	25d. blue	65·00	27·00
213	29	1l. green	20	20
214	30	2l. red	20	20
215	29	3l. red	20	20
216	31	5l. green	20	20
217	29	10l. red	20	20
218	30	15l. blue	55	30
219	30	20l. lilac	65	20
220	30	25l. blue	6·50	65
221	31	30l. red	85	30
222	30	40l. blue	2·75	65
223	31	50l. purple	5·50	20
224	31	80l. purple	7·50	1·40
225	32	1d. blue	8·75	50
226	32	2d. red	8·75	65
227	32	3d. red (20×26½ mm)	14·00	65
228		5d. blue (20×26½ mm)	17·00	75
229		10b. blue (20×26½ mm)	17·00	1·00
230	-	25d. slate	17·00	2·30

The 25d. is as Type **29** but larger (24×31 mm).

ΕΛΛΗΝΙΚΗ
ΔΙΟΙΚΗΣΙΣ

(34) "Greek Administration"

1912. Optd with T 34.

231A	15	20l. mauve	65	65
232B	29	1l. green	55	50
233A	30	2l. red	65	65
234A	29	3l. red	65	65
236A	29	10l. red	1·60	1·60
237A	30	20l. lilac	2·75	2·10
238A	30	25l. blue	2·75	2·50
239A	31	30l. red	3·25	2·50
240B	30	40l. blue	2·75	4·25
241B	31	50l. purple	3·25	3·25
242A	32	1d. blue	14·00	2·50
243A	32	2d. red	60·00	31·00
244B	32	3d. red	33·00	31·00
245A	32	5d. blue	27·00	31·00
246B	32	10d. blue	49·00	70·00
249B	31	5l. green	55	50
251B	-	25d. blue (No. 212)	2·20	2·10

35 Vision of Constantine over Athens and Salamis

36 Victorious Eagle over Mt. Olympus

1913. Occupation of Macedonia, Epirus and the Aegean Islands. Rouletted.

252A	35	1l. brown	55	50
253A	36	2l. red	55	50
254A	36	3l. orange	55	50
255A	35	5l. green	1·30	75
256A	35	10l. red	9·75	50
257A	35	20l. violet	27·00	5·25
258A	36	25l. blue	3·25	1·00
259A	35	30l. green	85·00	3·25
260A	36	40l. blue	15·00	5·25
261A	35	50l. blue	5·50	3·25
262A	36	1d. purple	27·00	5·25
263A	35	2d. brown	60·00	8·25
264A	36	3d. blue	£250	42·00
265A	35	5d. grey	£250	48·00
266A	36	10d. red	£275	£375
267A	35	25d. black	£275	£375

37 Hoisting the Greek Flag at Suda Bay, 1 May 1913

1913. Union of Crete with Greece.

268	37	25l. black and blue	12·00	5·25

(38)

1916. Stamps of 1911 optd with T 38.

269	29	1l. green	35	20
270	30	2l. red	35	30
271	29	3l. red	55	50
272	31	5l. green	80	40
273	29	10l. red	1·60	30
274	30	20l. lilac	2·10	30
275	30	25l. blue	1·60	30
277	30	40l. blue	19·00	6·00
278	31	50l. purple	65·00	3·00
280	31	30l. red	2·40	1·20
281	32	1d. blue	60·00	5·75
282	32	2d. red	34·00	5·00
283	32	3d. red	20·00	3·75
284	32	5d. blue	80·00	12·50
285	32	10d. blue	31·00	21·00

39 Iris

1917. Perf or imperf.

286A	39	1l. green	35	30
287A	39	5l. green	35	30
288A	39	10l. red	75	30
289A	39	25l. blue	75	30
290A	39	50l. purple	6·50	2·30
291A	39	1d. blue	4·25	1·00
292A	39	2d. red	5·50	1·70
293A	39	3d. red	22·00	4·25
294A	39	5d. blue	8·75	5·25

295A	39	10d. blue	75·00	21·00
296A	39	25d. grey	£130	£150

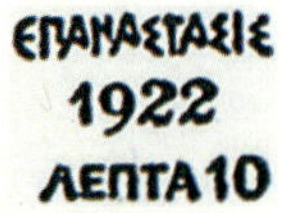

(46) "Revolution, 1922"

1923. Revolution of 1922. Stamps of 1913, surch as T 46.

340	36	5l. on 3l. orange	70	70
341	35	10l. on 20l. violet	3·00	2·50
342	36	10l. on 25l. blue	1·60	1·60
343	35	10l. on 30l. green	1·90	1·60
344	36	10l. on 40l. blue	2·75	2·40
345	35	50l. on 50l. blue	90	90
346	35	2d. on 2d. brown	£120	£110
347	36	3d. on 3d. blue	8·75	8·25
348	35	5d. on 5d. grey	8·75	8·25
349	36	10d. on 1d. purple	20·00	19·00
350	36	10d. on 10d. red	£1900	

1923. Stamps of 1916 surch as T 46.

351	39	5l. on 10l. red	65	65
352	39	50l. on 50l. purple	70	70
353	39	1d. on 1d. blue	70	70
354	39	2d. on 2d. red	80	80
355	39	3d. on 3d. red	3·75	3·75
356	39	5d. on 5d. blue	5·00	3·75
357	39	25d. on 25d. blue	55·00	55·00

1923. Cretan stamps of 1900 surch as T 46.

358	1	5l. on 1l. brown	75·00	
359	3	10l. on 10l. red	65	65
361	3	10l. on 25l. blue	70	70
362	1	50l. on 50l. lilac	80	1·30
363	1	50l. on 50l. blue	16·00	18·00
364	4	50l. on 1d. violet	7·50	8·25
365	-	50l. on 5d. (No. 19)	70·00	

1923. Cretan stamps of 1905 surch as T 46.

366		10l. on 20l. (No. 24)	£250	£225
367		10l. on 25l. (No. 25)	70	70
368		50l. on 50l. (No. 26)	70	70
369	16	50l. on 1d. (No. 27)	6·00	7·75
370	-	3d. on 3d. (No. 28)	28·00	26·00
371	-	5d. on 5d. (No. 29)	19·00	21·00

1923. Cretan stamps of 1907/8 surch as T 46.

372	21	10l. on 10l. red	70	70
373	19	10l. on 25l. black and blue	2·75	2·50
374	19	50l. on 1d. (No. 31)	8·25	7·75

No. 372 is as Crete No. 36 but without "HELLAS" optd. No. 377 is the optd stamp.

1923. Optd stamps of Crete surch as T 46.

375	1	5l. on 1l. brown (No. 32)	70	70
376	-	5l. on 5l. green (No. 34)	70	70
377	21	10l. on 10l. red (No. 36)	70	70
378	-	10l. on 20l. (No. 37)	70	70
379	-	10l. on 25l. (No. 30)	70	70
381	-	50l. on 50l. (No. 39)	1·10	1·00
382	16	50l. on 1d. (No. 40)	9·25	10·50
384	-	3d. on 3d. (No. 42)	28·00	34·00
385	-	5d. on 5d. (No. 43)	£550	£425

1923. Postage Due stamps of Crete of 1900 surch as T 38.

386	D 8	5l. on 5l. red	70	70
387	D 8	5l. on 10l. red	70	70
388	D 8	10l. on 20l. red	24·00	18·00
389	D 8	10l. on 40l. red	75	1·00
390	D 8	50l. on 50l. red	75	1·00
391	D 8	50l. on 1d. red	1·00	1·60
392	D 8	50l. on 1d. on 1d. red	19·00	21·00
393	D 8	2d. on 2d. red	1·60	2·50

1923. Postage Due stamps of Crete of 1908 with opt, surch as T 46.

397	5l. on 5l. red	65	65
398	5l. on 10l. red	65	65
399	10l. on 20l. red	75	75
400	50l. on 50l. red	90	90
401	50l. on 1d. red	8·25	9·00
402	2d. on 2d. red	15·00	16·00

47 Lord Byron

1924. Byron Centenary.

403	47	80l. blue	1·00	30
404	-	2d. black and violet	3·50	95

DESIGN—HORIZ: (45×30 mm): 2d. Byron at Missolonghi.

49 Grave of Marco Botzaris

1926. Centenary of Fall of Missolonghi. Roul.

405	49	25l. mauve	2·20	65

50 Savoia Marchetti S-55C Flying Boat over Fortress

1926. Air. Each showing Savoia Marchetti S-55C flying boat. Multicoloured.

406	2d. Type **50**	5·50	3·75
407	3d. Acropolis	43·00	13·00
408	5d. Map of Greece and Mediterranean	6·00	2·10
409	10d. Colonnade	43·00	16·00

51 Corinth Canal

52 Dodecanese Costume

53 Temple of Theseus, Athens

54 Acropolis

1927

410	51	5l. green	20	10
411	52	10l. red	55	10
412	-	20l. violet	75	10
413	-	25l. green	75	10
414	-	40l. green	1·10	10
415	51	50l. violet	3·25	10
416	51	80l. black and blue	2·20	30
417	53	1d. brown and blue	3·25	20
418b	-	2d. black and green	4·25	20
419d	-	3d. black and violet	11·00	35
419e	-	4d. brown	49·00	1·00
420	-	5d. black and orange	43·00	1·30
421	-	10d. black and red	£150	6·50
422	-	15d. black and green	£225	12·50
423a	54	25d. black and green	£150	16·00

DESIGNS—As Type **52**: 20l. Macedonian costume; 25l. Monastery of Simon Peter, Athos; 40l. White Tower, Salonika. As Type **53**: 2d. Acropolis; 3d. Cruiser "Averoff"; 4d. Mistra Cathedral. As Type **54**: 5, 15d. The Academy of Sciences, Athens; 10d. Temple of Theseus.

55 General Favier and Acropolis

1927. Centenary of Liberation of Athens.

424	55	1d. red	80	35
425	55	3d. blue	9·75	70
426	55	6d. green	44·00	14·00

56 Navarino Bay and Pylos

58 Sir Edward Codrington

1927. Centenary of Battle of Navarino.

427	56	1d.50 green	5·25	45
428	-	4d. blue	24·00	1·70
429	58	5d. black and brown (A)	13·50	4·75
430	-	5d. black and brown (B)	95·00	13·00
431	-	5d. black and blue	85·00	11·00
432	-	5d. black and red	49·00	10·00

DESIGNS: 4d. Battle of Navarino; 5d. (No. 429) "Sir Codrington" (A); 5d. (No. 430) "Sir Edward Codrington" (B); 5d. (No. 431) De Rigny; 5d. (No. 432) Van der Heyden.

59 Righas Ferreo

1930. Centenary of Independence.

433	59	10l. brown	20	10
434	-	20l. black	20	15
435	-	40l. green	25	20
436	-	50l. red	35	30
437	-	50l. blue	35	30
438	-	1d. red	50	30
439	-	1d. orange	50	30
440	-	1d.50 blue	90	20
441	-	1d.50 red	85	25
442	-	2d. orange	1·00	30
443	-	3d. brown	1·90	65
444	-	4d. blue	7·00	70
445	-	5d. purple	3·50	1·40
446	-	10d. black	21·00	7·00
447	-	15d. green	35·00	11·00
448	-	20d. blue	70·00	14·00
449	-	25d. black	65·00	22·00
450	-	50d. brown	£120	60·00

DESIGNS as Type **59**: 20l. Patriarch Gregory V; 40l. A. Ypsilanti; 50l. (No. 436) L. Bouboulina; 50l. (437), Ath. Diakos; 1d. (438), Th. Colocotroni; 1d. (439), C. Kanaris; 1d.50, (440), Karaiskakes; 1d.50 (441), M. Botzaris; 2d. A. Miaoulis; 3d. L. Kondouriotis; 5d. Capo d'Istria; 10d. P. Mavromichalis; 15d. Solomos; 20d. Corais. (27½×40 mm): 4d. Map of Greece. (27×44 mm): 50d. Sortie from Missolonghi. (43×28½ mm): 25d. Declaration of Independence.

64 Monastery of Arkadi, Crete, and Abbott Gabriel

1930

451	64	8d. violet	70·00	1·30

1932. Stamps of 1927 surch.

452	-	1d.50l. on 5d. black and blue (No. 431)	5·50	20
453	-	1d.50l. on 5d. black and red (No. 432)	5·50	20
454	55	2d. on 3d. blue	6·00	35
455	58	2d. on 5d. black and brown (No. 429)	9·25	20
456	-	2d. on 5d. black and brown (No. 430)	23·00	20
457	55	4d. on 6d. green	6·00	1·00

66 Airship LZ-127 "Graf Zeppelin" and Acropolis

1933. Air.

458	66	30d. red	55·00	24·00
459	66	100d. blue	£160	50·00
460	66	120d. brown	£160	50·00

67 Swinging the Propeller

68 "Flight"

1933. Air. Aeroespresso Company issue.

461	67	50l. orange and green	70	50
462	-	1d. orange and blue	1·10	65
463	-	3d. brown and purple	1·70	1·00
464	68	5d. blue and orange	23·00	8·25
465	-	10d. black and red	2·40	2·50
466	-	20d. green and black	42·00	12·50
467	-	50d. blue and brown	£140	80·00

DESIGNS—HORIZ: 1d. Temple of Neptune, Corinth; 3d. Marina Fiat MF.5 flying boat over Hermoupolis; 10d. Map of Italy-Greece-Rhodes-Turkey air routes. VERT: 20d. Hermes and Marina Fiat MF.5 flying boat; 50d. Woman and Marina Fiat MF.5 flying boat.

71 Greece

1933. Air. Government issue.

468	71	50l. green	1·10	65
469	71	1d. red	2·40	75
470	-	2d. violet	3·00	1·40
471	-	5d. blue	21·00	6·25
472	-	10d. red	27·00	10·50
473	71	25d. blue	90·00	26·00
474	-	50d. brown	£130	65·00

DESIGNS—VERT: 2, 10d. Ikarian Islands. HORIZ: 5, 50d. Junkers G.24 airplane and Acropolis.

74 Admiral Kondouriotis and Cruiser "Averoff"

75 "Greece"

1933

475	74	50d. blue and black	£160	4·25
476	75	75d. purple and black	£350	£190
477	-	100d. green and brown	£1600	38·00

DESIGN—VERT: 100d. Statue (Youth of Marathon).

78 Athens Stadium, Entrance

1934

479	78	8d. blue	£225	2·10

79 Sun Chariot

1935. Air. Mythological designs.

484	-	10d. brown	9·75	4·25
485	-	25d. red	11·00	10·50
486	-	30d. green	2·40	3·25
487	-	50d. mauve	11·00	16·00
488	-	100d. brown	3·25	9·50
488a	79	1d. red	55	30
488b	-	2d. blue	55	30
488c	-	5d. mauve	55	40
488d	-	7d. blue	55	40
488e	-	10d. orange	7·50	7·25

DESIGNS—HORIZ: 2d. Iris; 30d. Triptolemus; 100d. Phrixus and Helle. VERT: 5d. Daedalus and Icarus; 7d. Minerva; 10d. Hermes; 25d. Zeus and Ganymede; 50d. Bellerophon on Pegasus.

(81)

(82)

1935. Restoration of Greek Monarchy. Surch with T 81 (489/91) or 82 (492/3).

489	D20	50l. on 40l. blue	55	30
490	D20	3d. on 3d. red	2·20	1·30
492	-	5d. on 100d. green and brown (No. 477)	4·25	1·60
493	75	15d. on 75d. pur & blk	22·00	6·75

83 King Constantine

1936. Re-interment of King Constantine and Queen Sophia.

494	**83**	3d. brown and black	1·10	30
495	**83**	8d. blue and black	2·75	1·80

85 Pallas Athene (Minerva)

1937. Cent of Athens University.

496	**85**	3d. brown	1·10	50

86 Bull-leaping

89 King George II

89a Statue of King Constantine

1937

497	**86**	5l. blue and brown	10	10
498	-	10l. brown and blue	10	10
499	-	20l. green and black	10	10
500	-	40l. black and green	10	10
501	-	50l. black and brown	10	10
502	-	80l. brown and violet	10	10
503	**89**	1d. green	35	10
504	-	2d. blue	20	20
505	**89**	3d. brown	55	20
506	-	5d. red	20	20
507	-	6d. olive	35	25
508	-	7d. brown	1·80	1·60
509	**89**	8d. blue	1·80	50
510	-	10d. brown	35	25
511	-	15d. green	45	30
512	-	25d. blue	35	30
513	**89**	100d. red	31·00	14·00
515	**89a**	1d.50 green	75	30
516	**89a**	30d. red	5·25	4·25

DESIGNS—(Size as Type **89a**). VERT: 10l. Court Lady of Tiryns; 20l. Zeus and Thunderbolt; 80l. Venus of Milo; 25d. "Glory" of Psara. HORIZ: 40l. Amphictyonic Coin; 50l. Chairing Diagoras of Rhodes; 2d. Battle of Salamis; 5d. Panathenaic chariot; 6d. Alexander the Great at Battle of Issus; 7d. St. Paul on Mt. Areopagus; 10d. Temple of St. Demetrius, Salonica; 15d. Leo III (the Isaurian) destroying Saracens.

93 Prince Paul and Princess Frederika Louise

1938. Royal Wedding.

517	**93**	1d. green	25	25
518	**93**	3d. brown	70	25
519	**93**	8d. blue	2·00	1·40

94 Arms of Greece, Rumania, Turkey and Yugoslavia

1938. Balkan Entente.

520	**94**	6d. blue	16·00	2·40

1938. Air. Postage Due stamp optd with Junkers G.24 airplane. Perf or rouletted.

521	**D 20**	50l. brown	20	30

96 Arms of Ionian Islands

97 Corfu Bay and Citadel

1939. 75th Anniv of Cession of Ionian Islands.

523	**96**	1d. blue	1·90	50
524	**97**	4d. green	7·50	2·50
525	-	20d. orange	45·00	24·00
526	-	20d. blue	45·00	24·00
527	-	20d. red	45·00	24·00

DESIGN—HORIZ: 20d. As Type **1** of Ionian Is. but with portraits of George I of Greece and Queen Victoria.

99 Javelin Thrower

1939. 10th Pan-Balkan Games, Athens.

528		50l. green	45	35
529	**99**	3d. red	1·50	40
530	-	6d. brown on orange	8·75	3·25
531	-	8d. blue on grey	9·00	4·25

DESIGNS: 50l. Runner; 6d. Discus-thrower; 8d. Jumper.

100 Arms of Greece, Rumania, Turkey and Yugoslavia

1940. Balkan Entente.

532	**100**	6d. blue	27·00	2·10
533	**100**	8d. slate	24·00	2·40

101 Greek Youth Badge

1940. 4th Anniv of Greek Youth Organization. (a) Postage.

534	**101**	3d. blue, red and silver	2·20	1·00
535	-	5d. black and blue	13·50	5·50
536	-	10d. black and orange	16·00	11·50
537	-	15d. black and green	£120	70·00
538	-	20d. black and red	90·00	41·00
539	-	25d. black and blue	90·00	50·00
540	-	30d. black and purple	90·00	50·00
541	-	50d. black and red	£150	60·00
542	-	75d. gold, brown and blue	£150	60·00
543	**101**	100d. blue, red and silver	£200	95·00

DESIGNS—VERT: 5d. Boy member; 10d. Girl member; 15d. Javelin thrower; 20d. Youths in column formation; 25d. Standard bearer and buglers; 30d. Three youths in uniform; 50d. Youths on parade; 75d. Coat of arms.

103 Meteora Monasteries

(b) Air.

544	**103**	2d. black and orange	3·25	80
545	-	4d. black and green	19·00	3·50
546	-	6d. black and red	24·00	6·25
547	-	8d. black and blue	50·00	10·50
548	-	16d. black and violet	80·00	24·00
549	-	32d. black and orange	£140	60·00
550	-	45d. black and green	£160	65·00
551	-	55d. black and red	£160	65·00
552	-	65d. black and blue	£160	65·00
553	-	100d. black and violet	£190	75·00

DESIGNS (views and aircraft): 4d. Simon Peter Monastery, Mt. Athos; 6, 16d. Isle of Santorin; 8d. Church at Pantanassa; 32d. Ponticonissi, Corfu; 45d. Acropolis; 55d. Erechtheum; 65d. Temple of Nike; 100d. Temple of Zeus.

1941. Postage Due stamps optd with Junkers G.24 airplane, No. 556 also surch. Perf (558/60), perf or rouletted (556/7).

556	**D 20**	1d. on 2d. red	25	30
557	**D 20**	5d. blue	20	30
558	**D 20**	10d. green	20	30
559	**D 20**	25d. red	1·40	3·00
560	**D 20**	50d. orange	1·50	3·25

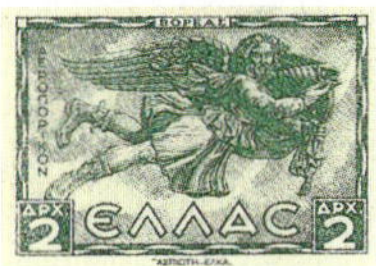

105 "Boreas" (North Wind)

1942. Air. Winds. (Symbolic designs).

561	**105**	2d. emerald and green	25	50
562	-	5d. orange and red	35	50
563	-	10d. red and brown	45	50
564	-	20d. ultramarine and blue	90	1·00
565	-	25d. orange & light orange	55	1·00
566	-	50d. black and grey	2·30	2·10
567	-	10d. red and orange	20	30
568	-	25d. green and grey	20	30
569	-	50d. violet and blue	20	30
570	**105**	100d. black and grey	35	30
571	-	200d. red and pink	35	30
572	-	400d. green and blue	35	30

DESIGNS: 5d. "Notos" (South); 10d. "Apiliotis" (East); 20d. "Lips" (South-west); 25d. "Zephyr" (West); 50d. "Kekias" (North-east); 200d. "Evros" (South-east); 400d. "Skiron" (North-west).

106 Windmills on Mykonos Is.

1942

573	**106**	2d. brown	10	20
574	-	5d. green	10	20
575	-	10d. blue	10	20
576	-	15d. purple	10	20
577	-	25d. orange	10	20
578	-	50d. blue	10	20
579	-	75d. red	10	20
580	-	100d. black	10	20
581	-	200d. blue	10	20
582	-	500d. brown	10	20
583	-	1000d. brown	20	20
584	-	2000d. blue	20	20
585	-	5000d. red	20	20
586	-	15,000d. purple	20	20
587	-	25,000d. green	20	20
588	-	500,000d. blue	40	50
589	**106**	2,000,000d. green	55	1·30
590	-	5,000,000d. red	55	1·30

DESIGNS: 5d., 5,000,000d. Burzi Fortress, Nauplion; 10d., 500,000d. Katokhi on Aspropotamos River; 15d. Heraklion, Crete; 25d. Houses on Hydra Is; 50d., Meteora Monastery; 75d. Edessa; 100d., 200d. Monastery on Mt. Athos; 500d., 5000d. Konitza Bridge; 1000d., 15,000d. Ekatontapiliani Church; 2000d., 25,000d. Kerkyra (Corfu) Is.

110 Child

1943. Children's Welfare Fund.

592	**110**	25d.+25d. green	40	35
593	-	100d.+50d. purple	40	35
594	-	200d.+100d. brown	45	40

DESIGN: 100d. Mother and child; 200d. Madonna and child.

(112)

1944. Children's Convalescent Camp Fund. Surch as T 112.(a) Postage.

595	**106**	50,000d.+450,000d. on 2d. brown	1·00	1·00
596	-	50,000d.+450,000d. on 5d. green (No. 574)	1·00	1·00
597	-	50,000d.+450,000d. on 10d. blue (No. 575)	1·00	1·00
598	-	50,000d.+450,000d. on 15d. purple (No. 576)	1·00	1·00
599	-	50,000d.+450,000d. on 25d. orange (No. 577)	1·00	1·00

(b) Air.

600		50,000d.+450,000d. on 10d. red (No. 567)	1·00	1·00
601		50,000d.+450,000d. on 25d. green (No. 568)	1·00	1·00
602		50,000d.+450,000d. on 50d. blue (No. 569)	1·00	1·00
603	**106**	50,000d.+450,000d. on 100d. black	1·00	1·00
604	-	50,000d.+450,000d. on 200d. claret (No. 571)	1·00	1·00

ΔΡΑΧΜΑΙ ΝΕΑΙ

(113) (Trans "New drachmas")

1944. Optd as T 113.

605		50l. black and brown (No. 501)	30	30
606		2d. blue (No. 504)	30	30
607		5d. red (No. 506)	30	30
608		6d. olive (No. 507)	30	30

92 "Glory" of Psara

1945

609	**92**	1d. purple	40	20
610	**92**	3d. red	40	20
611	**92**	5d. blue	40	20
612	**92**	10d. brown	45	20
613	**92**	20d. violet	80	20
614	**92**	50d. green	1·70	50
615	**92**	100d. blue	17·00	10·50
616	**92**	200d. green	12·00	2·50

For 25d. in Type **92** but larger, see No. 512.

114 "OXI" = No

1945. Resistance to Italian Ultimatum.

617	**114**	20d. orange	40	25
618	**114**	40d. blue	45	30

115 President Roosevelt

1945. Roosevelt Mourning Issue. Black borders.

619	115	30d. purple	50	20
620	115	60d. grey	50	20
621	115	200d. violet	50	20

(116)

1946. Surch as T 116.

622	-	10d. on 10d. (No. 567)	35	20
623	-	10d. on 2000d. (No. 584)	35	20
624	-	20d. on 50d. (No. 569)	35	20
625	-	20d. on 500d. (No. 582)	35	20
626	-	20d. on 1000d. (No. 583)	35	20
627	-	30d. on 5d. (No. 574)	35	20
628	-	50d. on 50d. (No. 578)	35	20
629	-	50d. on 25,000d. (No. 587)	55	20
630	-	100d. on 10d. (No. 575)	1·90	20
631	106	100d. on 2,000,000d.	1·20	20
632	-	130d. on 20l. (No. 499)	1·10	30
633	-	250d. on 20l. (No. 499)	1·10	30
634	-	300d. on 80l. (No. 502)	1·10	40
635	-	450d. on 75d. (No. 579)	2·30	45
636	-	500d. on 5,000,000d. (No. 590)	4·25	75
637	-	1000d. on 500,000d. (No. 588)	18·00	1·60
638	-	2000d. on 5,000d. (No. 585)	60·00	6·50
639	-	5000d. on 15,000d. (No. 586)	£250	43·00

117 E. Venizelos

1946. 10th Anniv of Death of Venizelos (statesman).

640	117	130d. green	55	30
641	117	300d. brown	55	30

1946. Restoration of Monarchy. Surch with value in circle and date 1-9-1946.

642	89	50d. on 1d. green	80	20
643	89	250d. on 3d. brown	1·60	25
644	89	600d. on 8d. blue	14·00	1·60
645	89	3000d. on 100d. red	30·00	1·30

119 Women carrying Munitions, Pindos Mountains

1946. Victory. War Scenes.

646	-	50d. green	45	20
647	-	100d. blue	65	20
648	119	250d. green	90	20
649	-	500d. brown	1·40	30
650	-	600d. brown	1·60	80
651	-	1000d. violet	7·50	40
652	-	2000d. blue	41·00	3·00
653	-	5000d. red	50·00	1·90
682	-	1000d. green	7·75	65

DESIGNS—HORIZ: 50d. Convoy; 500d. Infantry column; 1000d. (No. 651) Supermarine Spitfire Mk IIB and pilot; 1000d. (No. 682) Battle of Crete; 2000d. Torpedo boat "Hyacinth" towing submarine "Perla". VERT: 100d. Torpedoing of Cruiser "Helle"; 600d. Badge, Alpine troops and map of Italy; 5000d. War Memorial at El Alamein.

121 Panayiotis Tsaldaris

1946. 10th Death Anniv of P. Tsaldaris (statesman).

654	121	250d. brown and pink	6·50	1·00
655	121	600d. blue	6·50	1·60

1947. King George II Mourning issue. Surch with value in circle in corner and black border.

656	89	50d. on 1d. green	1·40	25
657	89	250d. on 3d. brown	2·40	25
658	89	600d. on 8d. blue	7·00	95

124 Castelrosso Fortress

126 Apollo (T **1** of Dodecanese Is.)

1947. Restoration of Dodecanese Is. to Greece.

659	124	20d. blue	45	10
660	-	30d. pink and black	45	10
661	-	50d. blue	45	10
662	-	100d. green and olive	45	10
663	-	200d. orange	1·60	10
664	-	250d. grey	1·40	10
665	-	300d. orange	1·80	10
666	-	400d. blue	2·40	10
667	126	450d. blue	3·00	10
668	-	450d. blue	2·40	10
669	126	500d. red	2·20	10
670	-	600d. purple	3·00	25
671	-	700d. mauve	4·00	20
672	-	700d. green	33·00	20
673	-	800d. green and violet	5·25	20
674	-	1000d. olive	3·25	30
675	126	1300d. red	27·00	20
676	124	1500d. brown	£140	40
677	-	1600d. blue	9·75	20
678	-	2000d. red and brown	75·00	30
679	-	2600d. green	16·00	1·20
680	-	5000d. violet	75·00	75
681	-	10,000d. blue	£130	85

DESIGNS—HORIZ: 100, 400d. St. John's Convent, Patmos. VERT: 30, 1600, 2000d. Dodecanese vase; 50, 300d. Woman in national costume; 200, 250d. E. Xanthos; 450 (No. 668), 800d. Casos Is. and 19th-century frigate; 600, 700 (2), 5000d. Statue of Hippocrates; 1000, 2600, 10,000d. Colossus of Rhodes.

129 Column of Women and Children

1949. Abduction of Greek Children to neighbouring Countries.

683	129	450d. violet	9·25	1·00
684	-	1000d. brown	17·00	65
685	-	1800d. red	12·00	65

DESIGNS—VERT: 1000d. Captive children and map of Greece; 1800d. Hand menacing woman and child.

130 Maps and Flags

1950. Battle of Crete.

686	130	1000d. blue	21·00	50

131 "Youth of Marathon"

1950. 75th Anniv of U.P.U. Inscr "1874–1949" in white figures at top.

687	131	1000d. green on buff	3·25	50

133 St. Paul

134 St. Paul

1951. 19th Cent of St. Paul's Travels in Greece.

688	-	700d. purple	4·00	50
689	133	1600d. blue	22·00	3·00
690	134	2600d. brown	30·00	3·75
691	-	10,000d. brown	£250	95·00

DESIGNS—As Type **134**: 700d. Sword and altar (horiz); 10,000d. St. Paul preaching to Athenians (vert).

135 "Industry"

1951. Reconstruction Issue.

692	135	700d. orange	4·25	30
693	-	800d. green	8·50	35
694	-	1300d. blue	13·00	35
695	-	1600d. olive	38·00	40
696	-	2600d. violet	£110	2·10
697	-	5000d. purple	£120	45

DESIGNS—VERT: 800d. Fish and trident; 1300d. Workmen and column; 1600d. Ceres and tractors; 2600d. Women and loom; 5000d. Map and stars ("Electrification").

136 Blessing before Battle

1952. Air. Anti-Communist Campaign.

698	136	1,000d. blue	1·40	30
699	-	1,700d. turquoise	9·25	1·00
700	-	2,700d. brown	20·00	3·50
701	-	7,000d. green	60·00	14·50

DESIGNS—VERT: 1,700d. "Victory" over mountains; 2,700d. Infantry attack; 7,000d. "Victory" and soldiers.

137 King Paul

138 "Spirit of Greece"

1952. 50th Birthday of King Paul.

702	137	200d. green	1·90	30
703	137	1,000d. red	6·50	35
704	138	1,400d. blue	26·00	1·40
705	137	10,000d. purple	75·00	12·50

139 "Oranges"

1953. National Products.

706	139	500d. orange and red	1·90	20
707	-	700d. yellow and brown	2·40	20
708	-	1,000d. green and blue	5·00	20
709	-	1,300d. buff and purple	9·25	30
710	-	2,000d. green and brown	27·00	40
711	-	2,600d. bistre and violet	35·00	1·20
712	-	5,000d. green and brown	49·00	65

DESIGNS—VERT: 700d. "Tobacco" (tobacco plant); 1,300d. "Wine" (wineglass and vase); 2,000d. "Figs" (basket of figs); 2,600d. "Dried Fruit" (grapes and currant bread); 5,000d. "Grapes" (male figure holding grapes). HORIZ: 1,000d. "Olive Oil" (Pallas Athene and olive branch).

140 Bust of Pericles

141 Alexander the Great

1954. Ancient Greek Art. Sculptures, etc.

713	140	100d. brown	55	15
714	-	200d. black	55	15
715	-	300d. violet	1·10	15
716	-	500d. green	1·60	15
717	-	600d. red	1·90	15
718	141	1,000d. black and blue	2·75	15
719	-	1,200d. olive	3·00	15
720	-	2,000d. brown	12·00	20
721	-	2,400d. blue	12·00	35
722	-	2,500d. green	18·00	30
723	-	4,000d. red	38·00	40
724	-	20,000d. purple	£275	1·30

DESIGNS—As Type **140**: VERT: 200d. Mycenaean ox-head vase; 1,200d. Head of charioteer of Delphi; 2,000d. Vase of Dipylon; 2,500d. Man carrying calf; 20,000d. Two pitcher bearers. HORIZ: 2,400d. Hunting wild boar. As Type **141**: VERT: 300d. Bust of Homer; 500d. Zeus of Istiaca; 600d. Youth's head; 4,000d. Dish depicting voyage of Dionysus.

See also Nos. 733a/41.

143 Athlete Bearing Torch

1954. Air. 5th Anniv of N.A.T.O. Inscr "NATO".

725	143	1,200d. orange	5·00	35
726	-	2,400d. green	55·00	3·00
727	-	4,000d. blue	90·00	4·00

DESIGNS—VERT: 2,400d. Amphictyonic coin; 4,000d. Pallas Athene.

144 Extracts from "Hansard" (Parliamentary Debates)

1954. "Enosis" (Union of Cyprus with Greece).

728	144	1.20d. black and yellow	4·25	40
729	144	2d. black and salmon	23·00	4·25
730	144	2d. black and blue	23·00	4·25
731	144	2.40d. black and lavender	23·00	3·00
732	144	2.50d. black and pink	23·00	3·00
733	144	4d. black and lemon	70·00	4·75

On No. 728 the text is in Greek, on Nos. 730/1 in French and on the remainder in English.

1955. As Nos. 713/24 but new colours and values.

733a	140	10l. green	40	15
734	-	20l. myrtle (No. 714)	55	15

734a	-	20l. purple (No. 714)	45	15
735	140	30l. brown	80	20
736	-	50l. lake (No. 716)	1·40	20
736a	-	50l. green (No. 716)	80	10
736b	-	70l. orange (No. 719)	55	10
737	-	1d. green (No. 717)	2·40	15
737a	-	1d. brown (No. 717)	3·00	10
737b	-	1d.50 blue (No. 724)	27·00	20
738	141	2d. black and brown	14·00	15
738a	141	2d.50 black and mauve	24·00	20
739	-	3d. orange (No. 721)	11·00	20
739a	-	3d. blue (No. 722)	3·50	35
740	-	3d.50 red (No. 715)	22·00	65
741	-	4d. blue (No. 723)	95·00	40

145 Samian Coin Depicting Pythagoras

1955. Pythagorean Congress.

742	145	2d. green	5·25	40
743	-	3d.50 black	15·00	3·00
744	145	5d. purple	70·00	2·10
745	-	6d. blue	55·00	39·00

DESIGNS—VERT: 3d.50, Representation of Pythagoras theorem. HORIZ: 6d. Map of Samos.

146 Rotary Emblem and Globe

1956. 50th Anniv of Rotary International.

746	146	2d. blue	21·00	70

147 King George I

1956. Royal Family.

747	-	10l. violet	20	10
748	-	20l. purple	20	10
749	147	30l. brown	20	10
750	-	50l. brown	55	10
751	-	70l. blue	85	20
752	-	1d. blue	1·10	20
753	-	1d.50 grey	4·50	20
754	-	2d. black	5·50	20
755	-	3d. brown	4·25	10
756	-	3d.50 brown	16·00	30
757	-	4d. green	16·00	30
758	-	5d. red	11·00	30
759	-	7d.50 blue	11·00	2·00
760	-	10d. blue	65·00	80

PORTRAITS—HORIZ: 10l. King Alexander; 5d. King Paul and Queen Frederika; 10d. King and Queen and Crown Prince Constantine. VERT: 20l. Crown Prince Constantine; 50l. Queen Olga; 70l. King Otto; 1d. Queen Amalia; 1d.50, King Constantine; 2d. King Paul; 3d. King George II; 3d.50, Queen Sophia; 4d. Queen Frederika; 7d.50, King Paul.

See also Nos. 764/77.

148 Dionysios Solomos

1957. Death Centenary of D. Solomos (national poet).

761		2d. yellow and brown	6·50	40
762	148	3d.50 grey and brown	6·50	2·50
763	-	5d. bistre and green	11·50	10·50

DESIGNS—HORIZ: 2d. Solomos and K. Mantzaros (composer); 5d. Zante landscape and Solomos.

1957. As Nos. 747/60. Colours changed.

764		10l. red	20	15
765		20l. orange	20	15
766	147	30l. black	20	15
767	-	50l. green	40	15
768	-	70l. purple	85	35
769	-	1d. red	1·50	15
770	-	1d.50 green	2·75	15
771	-	2d. red	5·75	15
772	-	3d. blue	6·75	20
773	-	3d.50 purple	13·50	20
774	-	4d. brown	16·00	20
775	-	5d. blue	14·50	20
776	-	7d.50 yellow	3·25	1·50
777	-	10d. green	85·00	80

149 "Argo" (5th Century B.C.)

1958. Greek Merchant Marine Commemoration. Ship designs.

778		50l. multicoloured	40	10
779		1d. ochre, black and blue	45	20
780		1d.50 red, black and blue	1·90	1·20
781		2d. multicoloured	55	30
782		3d.50 black, red and blue	2·75	1·50
783	149	5d. multicoloured	14·00	11·50

SHIPS: 50l. "Michael Carras" (tanker); 1d. "Queen Frederika" (liner); 1d.50, Full-rigged sailing ship, 1821; 2d. Byzantine galley; 3d.50, 6th-century B.C. galley.

150 The Piraeus (Port of Athens)

1958. Air. Greek Ports.

784	150	10d. multicoloured	22·00	20
785	-	15d. multicoloured	2·40	30
786	-	20d. multicoloured	22·00	20
787	-	25d. multicoloured	3·00	65
788	-	30d. multicoloured	1·90	70
789	-	50d. blue, black and brown	7·50	70
790	-	100d. blue, black & brown	60·00	2·75

PORTS: 15d. Salonika; 20d. Patras; 25d. Hermoupolis (Syra); 30d. Volos (Thessaly); 50d. Kavalla; 100d. Heraklion (Crete).

151 "Narcissus" and Flower

1958. International Congress for Protection of Nature, Athens. Mythological and Floral designs. Multicoloured.

791	20l. Type **151**	20	15
792	30l. "Daphne and Apollo"	20	15
793	50l. "Venus and Adonis" (Venus and hibiscus)	25	15
794	70l. "Pan and the Nymph" (Pan and pine cones)	35	20
795	1d. Crocus (21½×26 mm)	35	25
796	2d. Iris (22×32 mm)	75	50
797	3d.50 Tulip (22×32 mm)	70	45
798	5d. Cyclamen (22×32 mm)	6·50	6·75

152 Jupiter's Head and Eagle (Olympia 4th-century B.C. coin)

1959. Ancient Greek Coins. Designs as T 152 showing both sides of each coin. Inscriptions in black.

799	152	10l. green and brown	40	10
800	-	20l. grey and blue	40	10
801	-	50l. grey and purple	45	10
802	-	70l. grey and blue	55	20
803	-	1d. drab and red	2·00	10
804	-	1d.50 grey and ochre	2·50	10
805	-	2d.50 drab and mauve	3·50	10
806	-	4d.50 grey and green	8·50	50
807	-	6d. blue and olive	31·00	20
808	-	8d.50 drab and red	8·25	1·80

COINS—HORIZ: 20l. Athene's head and owl (Athens 5th cent. B.C.); 50l. Nymph Arethusa and chariot (Syracuse 5th cent. B.C.); 70l. Hercules and Jupiter (Alexander the Great 4th cent. B.C.); 1d.50, Griffin and squares (Abdera, Thrace 5th cent. B.C.); 2d.50, Apollo and lyre (Chalcidice, Macedonia 4th cent. B.C.). VERT: 1d. Helios and rose (Rhodes 4th cent. B.C.); 4d.50, Apollo and labyrinth (Crete 3rd cent. B.C.); 6d. Venus and Apollo (Paphos, Cyprus 4th cent. B.C.); 8d.50, Ram's heads and incised squares (Delphi 5th cent. B.C.).

See also Nos. 909/17.

153 Amphitheatre, Delphi

1959. Ancient Greek Theatre.

809		20l. multicoloured	40	15
810		50l. brown and olive	40	20
811		1d. multicoloured	45	25
812		2d.50 brown and blue	85	40
813	153	3d.50 multicoloured	17·00	16·00
814	-	4d.50 brown and black	2·00	90
815	-	6d. brown, grey and black	2·40	1·20

DESIGNS—VERT: 20l. Ancient theatre audience (after a Pharsala Thessaly vase of 580 B.C.); 50l. Clay mask of 3rd century B.C.; 1d. Flute, drum and lyre; 2d.50, Actor (3rd century statuette); 6d. Performance of a satirical play (after a mixing-bowl of 410 B.C.). HORIZ: 4d.50, Performance of Euripides' "Andromeda" (after a vase of 4th century B.C.).

154 "Victory" and Greek Soldiers through the Ages

1959. 10th Anniv of Greek Anti-Communist Victory.

816	154	2d.50 blue, black & brn	6·50	45

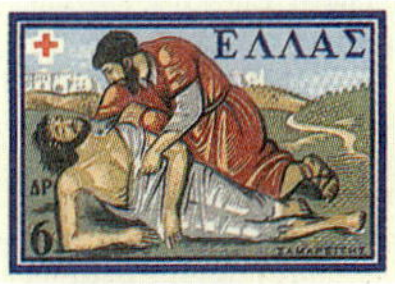

155 "The Good Samaritan"

1959. Red Cross Commem. Cross in red.

817	-	20l. multicoloured	20	20
818	-	50l. grey, red and blue	35	20
819	-	70l. black, brown, bis & bl	50	40
820	-	2d.50 blk, brn, grey & red	85	60
821	-	3d. multicoloured	10·50	10·00
822	-	4d.50 orange and red	2·00	1·30
823	155	6d. multicoloured	2·20	1·00

DESIGNS—HORIZ: 20l. Hippocrates Tree, Cos. VERT: 50l. Bust of Aesculapius; 70l. St. Basil (after mosaic in Hosios Loukas Monastery, Boeotia); 2d.50, Achilles and Patroclus (from vase of 6th cent B.C.); 3d. (32×47½ mm) Red Cross, globe, infirm people and nurses; 4d.50, J. H. Dunant.

156 Imre Nagy (formerly Prime Minister of Hungary)

1959. 3rd Anniv of Hungarian Revolt.

824	156	4d.50 sepia, brown & red	2·00	2·00
825	156	6d. black, blue & ultram	2·00	2·00

157 Kostes Palamas

1960. Birth Cent of Palamas (poet).

826	157	2d.50 multicoloured	8·25	50

158 Brig in Storm

1960. World Refugee Year. Multicoloured.

827	2d.50 Type **158**	70	20
828	4d.50 Brig in calm waters	2·00	95

159 Scout emulating St. George

1960. 50th Anniv of Greek Boy Scout Movement. Multicoloured.

829	20l. Type **159**	25	20
830	30l. Ephebi Oath and Scout Promise	25	20
831	40l. Fire rescue work (horiz)	25	20
832	50l. Planting tree (horiz)	25	20
833	70l. Map reading (horiz)	35	20
834	1d. Scouts on beach (horiz)	75	30
835	2d.50 Crown Prince Constantine in uniform	2·20	85
836	6d. Greek Scout Flag and Medal (horiz)	3·25	2·40

160 Sprinting

1960. Olympic Games.

837	-	20l. brown, black and blue	25	20
838	-	50l. brown and black	35	25
839	-	70l. brown, black & green	35	25
840	-	80l. multicoloured	35	25
841	-	1d. multicoloured	50	35
842	-	1d.50 brown, blk & orge	55	40
843	-	2d.50 brown, black & bl	1·40	65
844	160	4d.50 multicoloured	1·60	1·00
845	-	5d. multicoloured	3·50	1·40
846	-	6d. brown, black & violet	3·50	1·40
847	-	12d.50 multicoloured	21·00	17·00

DESIGNS—VERT: 20l. "Armistice" (official holding plaque); 70l. Athlete taking oath; 2d.50, Discus-throwing; 5d. Javelin-throwing. HORIZ: 50l. Olympic flame; 80l. Cutting branches from crown-bearing olive tree; 1d. Entrance of chief judges; 1d.50 Long jumping; 6d. Crowning the victor; 12d.50, Quadriga or chariot-driving (entrance of the victor).

1960. 1st Anniv of European Postal and Telecommunications Conf. As T 371a of Italy.

848	4d.50 blue	11·00	2·50

162 Crown Prince Constantine and "Nirefs"

1961. Victory of Crown Prince Constantine in Dragon-class Yacht Race, Olympic Games.

849	162	2d.50 multicoloured	1·20	50

163 Kastoria

1961. Tourist Publicity Issue.

850	**163**	10l. blue	15	10
851	-	20l. plum	15	10
852	-	50l. blue	15	10
853	-	70l. purple	20	10
854	-	80l. blue	60	20
855	-	1d. brown	80	10
856	-	1d.50 green	1·40	10
857	-	2d.50 red	3·75	10
858	-	3d.50 violet	1·90	50
859	-	4d. green	13·50	10
860	-	4d.50 blue	1·60	15
861	-	5d. lake	13·50	15
862	-	6d. myrtle	3·25	15
863	-	7d.50 black	80	20
864	-	8d. blue	7·00	20
865	-	8d.50 orange	8·25	50
866	-	12d.50 sepia	2·75	95

DESIGNS—HORIZ: 20l. The Meteora (Monasteries); 50l. Hydra; 70l. Acropolis, Athens; 80l. Mykonos. 1d. Salonika; 1d.50, Olympia; 2d.50, Knossos; 3d.50, Rhodes; 4d. Epidavros; 4d.50, Sounion; 5d. Temple of Zeus, Athens; 7d.50, Yannina; 12d.50, Delos, VERT: 6d. Delphi; 8d. Mount Athos; 8d.50, Santorini (Thira).

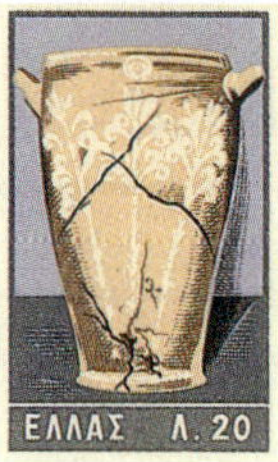

164 Lilies Vase of Knossos

1961. Minoan Art.

867	**164**	20l. multicoloured	50	15
868	-	50l. multicoloured	50	15
869	-	1d. multicoloured	70	20
870	-	1d.50 multicoloured	1·60	20
871	-	2d.50 multicoloured	8·25	20
872	-	4d.50 multicoloured	3·25	2·30
873	-	6d. multicoloured	15·00	1·60
874	-	10d. multicoloured	15·00	9·50

DESIGNS—VERT: 1d.50, Knossos rhyton-bearer; 4d.50, Part of Hagia trias sarcophagus. HORIZ: 50l. Partridges and fig-pecker (Knossos frieze); 1d. Kamares fruit dish; 2d.50, Ladies of Knossos Palace (painting); 6d. Knossos dancer (painting); 10d. Kamares prochus and pithos with spout.

165 Reactor Building

1961. Inauguration of "Democritus" Nuclear Research Centre, Aghia Paraskevi.

875	**165**	2d.50 purple and mauve	80	35
876	-	4d.50 blue and grey	1·60	95

DESIGN: 4d.50, Democritus and atomic symbol.

166 Doves

1961. Europa.

877	**166**	2d.50 red and pink	40	35
878	**166**	4d.50 ultramarine & blue	1·00	70

167 Emperor Nicephorus Phocas

1961. Millenary of Liberation of Crete from the Saracens.

879	**167**	2d.50 multicoloured	1·10	60

168 "Hermes" 1l. Stamp of 1861

1961. Centenary of First Greek Postage Stamps. "Hermes" stamps of 1861. Multicoloured.

880	20l. Type **168**	25	15
881	50l. "2l."	25	15
882	1d.50 "5l."	35	20
883	2d.50 "10l."	35	20
884	4d.50 "20l."	75	30
885	6d. "40l."	1·20	65
886	10d. "80l."	3·00	2·10

169 Ptolemais Steam Plant

1962. Electrification Project. Multicoloured.

887	20l. Tauropos dam (vert)	20	20
888	50l. Ladhon River hydro-electric plant (vert)	25	20
889	1d. Type **169**	35	20
890	1d.50 Louros River dam	40	20
891	2d.50 Aliverion steam plant	1·30	20
892	4d.50 Salonika hydro-electric sub-station	1·50	1·10
893	6d. Agra River power station	4·50	3·50

170 Zappion Building

1962. N.A.T.O. Ministers' Conference, Athens.

894	**170**	2d.50 multicoloured	40	20
895	-	3d. sepia, brown and buff	40	20
896	-	4d.50 black and blue	60	40
897	-	6d. black and red	60	40

DESIGNS—VERT: 3d. Ancient Greek warrior with shield; 4d.50, Soldier kneeling (after Marathon tomb); 6d. (21×37 mm), Soldier (statue in Temple of Aphea, Aegina).

171 Europa "Tree"

1962. Europa.

898	**171**	2d.50 red and black	1·10	35
899	**171**	4d.50 blue and black	3·00	1·20

172 "Protection"

1962. Greek Farmers' Social Insurance Scheme.

900	**172**	1d.50 black, brown & red	50	20
901	**172**	2d.50 black, brown & grn	70	20

173 Demeter, Goddess of Corn

1963. Freedom from Hunger. Multicoloured.

902	2d.50 Type **173**	50	20
903	4d.50 Wheat ears and globe	1·10	60

174 Kings of the Greek Dynasty

1963. Cent of Greek Royal Dynasty.

904	**174**	50l. red	25	10
905	**174**	1d.50 green	75	15
906	**174**	2d.50 brown	1·50	15
907	**174**	4d.50 blue	3·00	80
908	**174**	6d. violet	4·00	40

1963. Ancient Greek Coins. As Nos. 799/808 but colours changed and some designs rearranged. Inscr in black; coins in black and drab or grey; background colours given.

909	50l. blue (As No. 801)	20	15
910	80l. purple (As 802)	25	20
911	1d. green (As 803)	40	15
912	1d.50 red (As 804)	1·50	15
913	3d. olive (As 799)	1·00	15
914	3d.50 red (As 800)	1·00	35
915	4d.50 brown (As 806)	1·00	20
916	6d. turquoise (As 807)	1·00	20
917	8d.50 blue (As 808)	2·20	90

175 "Athens at Dawn" (after watercolour by Lord Baden-Powell)

1963. 11th World Scout Jamboree, Marathon.

918	**175**	1d. multicoloured	35	20
919	-	1d.50 orange, black & bl	35	20
920	-	2d.50 multicoloured	1·50	20
921	-	3d. black, brown & green	90	65
922	-	4d.50 multicoloured	1·70	85

DESIGNS—HORIZ: 3d. A. Lefkadites (founder of Greek Scout Movement) and Lord Baden-Powell. VERT: 1d.50, Jamboree Badge; 2d.50, Crown Prince Constantine, Chief Scout of Greece; 4d.50, Scout bugling with Atlantic trumpet triton shell.

176 Delphi

1963. Red Cross Centenary. Multicoloured.

923	1d. Type **176**	65	35
924	2d. Centenary emblem	25	15
925	2d.50 Queen Olga	35	20
926	4d.50 Henri Dunant	1·20	85

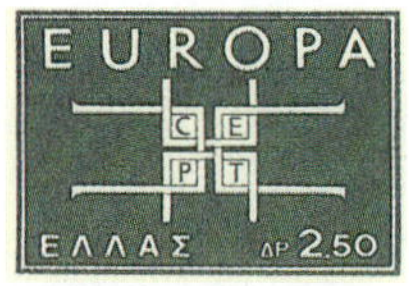

177 "Co-operation"

1963. Europa.

927	**177**	2d.50 green	4·25	50
928	**177**	4d.50 purple	8·25	3·25

178 Great Lavra Church

1963. Millenary of Mt. Athos Monastic Community. Multicoloured.

929	30l. Vatopediou Monastery (horiz)	40	10
930	80l. Dionysion Monastery (horiz)	40	10
931	1d. Protaton Church, Karyae	45	10
932	2d. Stavronikita Monastery (horiz)	1·60	10
933	2d.50 Cover of Nicephorus Phocas Gospel, Great Lavra Church (horiz)	3·50	10
934	3d.50 St. Athanasius the Anthonite (fresco) (horiz)	1·60	95
935	4d.50 11th-century papyrus, Iviron Monastery (horiz)	1·40	45
936	6d. Type **178**	1·60	40

179 King Paul

1964. Death of Paul I.

937	**179**	30l. brown	20	10
938	**179**	50l. violet	25	10
939	**179**	1d. green	1·10	10
940	**179**	1d.50 orange	50	10
941	**179**	2d. blue	85	10
942	**179**	2d.50 sepia	85	10
943	**179**	3d.50 purple	1·40	20
944	**179**	4d. blue	2·20	20
945	**179**	4d.50 blue	2·40	95
946	**179**	6d. red	3·75	20

180 Gold Coin

1964. Byzantine Art Exn, Athens. Mult.

947	1d. Type **180**	20	10
948	1d.50 "Two Saints"	20	15
949	2d. "Archangel Michael"	20	15
950	2d.50 "Young Lady"	40	15
951	4d.50 "Angel"	1·50	90

DESIGN origins: 1d. reign of Emperor Basil II (976–1025); 1d.50, from Harbaville's 10th cent ivory triptych (Louvre); 2d. 14th cent Constantinople icon (Byzantine Museum, Athens); 2d.50, from 14th cent fresco "The Birth of the Holy Virgin" by Panselinos (Protaton Church, Mt. Athos); 4d.50, from 11th cent mosaic (Daphne Church, Athens).

181 Trident of Paxi

1964. Centenary of Union of Ionian Islands with Greece. Inscr "1864–1964".

952	**181**	20l. grey, slate and green	20	10
953	-	30l. multicoloured	20	10
954	-	1d. lt brn, brn & red-brn	20	10
955	-	2d. multicoloured	20	10
956	-	2d.50 pale green, deep green and green	50	10
957	-	4d.50 multicoloured	1·30	90

958	-	6d. multicoloured	1·20	40

DESIGNS: 30l. Venus of Cythera; 1d. Ulysses of Ithaca; 2d. St. George of Levkas; 2d.50, Zakynthos of Zante; 4d.50, Cephalus of Cephalonia; 6d. War galley emblem of Corfu.

182 Greek Child

1964. 50th Anniv of National Institution of Social Welfare (P.I.K.P.A.).

959	**182**	2d.50 multicoloured	1·10	40

183 Europa "Flower"

1964. Europa.

960	**183**	2d.50 red and green	3·25	80
961	**183**	4d.50 brown and drab	5·50	1·30

184 King Constantine II and Queen Anne-Marie

1964. Royal Wedding.

962	**184**	1d.50 green	35	15
963	**184**	2d.50 red	25	15
964	**184**	4d.50 blue	70	35

185 Peleus and Atlanta (amphora)

1964. Olympic Games, Tokyo. Multicoloured.

965	10l. Type **185**	15	10
966	1d. Running (bowl) (horiz)	20	10
967	2d. Jumping (pot) (horiz)	20	10
968	2d.50 Throwing the discus	40	10
969	4d.50 Chariot-racing (sculpture) (horiz)	1·00	60
970	6d. Boxing (vase) (horiz)	45	25
971	10d. Apollo (part of frieze, Zeus Temple, Olympia)	1·00	50

186 "Christ stripping off His garments"

1965. 350th Death Anniv of El Greco. Mult.

972	50l. Type **186**	25	20
973	1d. "Angels' Concert"	25	20
974	1d.50 El Greco's signature (horiz)	25	20
975	2d.50 Self-portrait	25	20
976	4d.50 "Storm-lashed Toledo"	60	45

187 Aesculapius Theatre, Epidavros

1965. Greek Artistic Festivals. Mult.

977	1d.50 Type **187**	40	30
978	4d.50 Herod Atticus Theatre, Athens	70	35

188 ITU Emblem and Symbols

1965. Centenary of I.T.U.

979	**188**	2d.50 red, blue and grey	65	20

189 "New Member making Affirmation" (after Tsokos)

1965. 150th Anniv of "Philiki Hetaeria" ("Friends' Society"). Multicoloured.

980	1d.50 Type **189**	20	10
981	4d.50 Society flag	60	30

190 AHEPA Emblem

1965. American Hellenic Educational Progressive Assn (AHEPA) Congress, Athens.

982	**190**	6d. black, olive and blue	65	35

191 Venizelos as Revolutionary

1965. Birth Cent of E. Venizelos (statesman).

983	**191**	1d.50 green	35	20
984	-	2d. blue	55	45
985	-	2d.50 brown	25	20

DESIGNS: 2d. Venizelos signing Treaty of Sevres (1920); 2d.50, Venizelos.

192 Games' Flag

1965. Balkan Games, Athens. Multicoloured.

986	1d. Type **192**	20	20
987	2d. Victor's medal (vert)	20	20
988	6d. Karaiskakis Stadium, Athens	45	30

193 Symbols of the Planets

1965. Int Astronautic Conference Athens. Mult.

989	50l. Type **193**	20	20
990	2d.50 Astronaut in space	20	20
991	6d. Rocket and space-ship	45	30

194 Europa "Sprig"

1965. Europa.

992	**194**	2d.50 blue, black and grey	1·90	35
993	**194**	4d.50 green, black & olive	2·20	70

195 Hipparchus (astronomer) and Astrolabe

1965. Opening of Evghenides Planetarium, Athens.

994	**195**	2d.50 black, red and green	65	20

196 Carpenter Ants

1965. 50th Anniv of P.O. Savings Bank. Multicoloured.

995	10l. Type **196**	20	20
996	2d.50 Savings Bank and book	50	20

197 St. Andrew's Church, Patras

1965. Restoration of St. Andrew's Head to Greece. Multicoloured.

997	1d. Type **197**	20	20
998	5d. St. Andrew, after 11th-cent mosaic, Hosios Loukas Monastry, Boeotia	40	20

198 T. Brysakes

1966. Modern Greek Painters. Multicoloured.

999	80l. Type **198**	20	15
1000	1d. N. Lytras	20	15
1001	2d.50 C. Volonakes	20	15
1002	4d. N. Gyses	35	20
1003	5d. G. Jacobides	35	20

199 Greek 25d. Banknote of 1867

1966. 125th Anniv of Greek National Bank.

1004	-	1d.50 green	25	10
1005	-	2d.50 brown	25	10
1006	-	4d. blue	35	15
1007	**199**	6d. black	55	30

DESIGNS—VERT: (23×33½ mm): 1d.50, J.-G. Eynard; 2d.50, G. Stavros (founders). HORIZ: (As Type **199**): 4d. National Bank Headquarters, Athens.

200 Geannares (revolutionary leader)

1966. Centenary of Cretan Revolt. Mult.

1008	2d. Type **200**	25	15
1009	2d.50 Explosion of gunpowder machine, Arkadi Monastery (horiz)	25	15
1010	4d.50 Map of Crete (horiz)	40	30

201 "Movement of Water" (Decade of World Hydrology)

1966. U.N.O. Events.

1011	**201**	1d. blue, brown and black	25	15
1012	-	3d. multicoloured	25	15
1013	-	3d. black, blue and red	40	30

DESIGNS—VERT: 3d. U.N.E.S.C.O. emblem (20th anniv); 5d. W.H.O. Building (inauguration of H.Q., Geneva).

202 Tragedian's Mask of 4th Century, B.C.

1966. 2,500th Anniv of Greek Theatre.

1014	**202**	1d. multicoloured	20	15
1015	-	1d.50 black, red & brn	20	15
1016	-	2d.50 black, grn & lt grn	20	15
1017	-	4d.50 multicoloured	50	30

DESIGNS—HORIZ: 1d.50, Dionysus in a Thespian ship-chariot (vase painting, 500–480 B.C.); 2d.50, Theatre of Dionysus, Athens. VERT: 4d.50, Dionysus dancing (after vase painting by Kleophredes, c. 500 B.C.).

203 Boeing 707 Jetliner crossing Atlantic Ocean

1966. Inauguration of Greek Airways Transatlantic Flights.

1018	**203**	6d. indigo, blue & lt blue	60	35

204 Tending Plants

1966. Greek Tobacco. Multicoloured.

1019	1d. Type **204**	25	15
1020	5d. Sorting leaf	70	40

205 Europa "Ship"

1966. Europa.

1021	**205**	1d.50 black, olive & grn	1·10	35

1022	**205**	4d.50 deep brown, brown and light brown	3·00	65

206 Horseman (embroidery)

1966. Greek "Popular" Art. Multicoloured.

1023	10l. Knitting-needle boxes (vert)	20	10
1024	30l. Type **206**	20	10
1025	50l. Cretan lyre (vert)	20	10
1026	1d. "Massa" (Musical instrument) (vert)	20	10
1027	1d.50 "Cross and Angels" (bas-relief after Melios) (vert)	20	10
1028	2d. "Sts. Constantine and Helen" (icon) (vert)	1·20	10
1029	2d.50 Carved altar-screen, St. Nicholas' Church, Galaxidion (vert)	25	10
1030	3d. 19th-century ship of Skyros (embroidery)	25	10
1031	4d. "Psiki" (wedding procession) (embroidery)	1·10	10
1032	4d.50 Distaff (vert)	50	25
1033	5d. Earrings and necklace (vert)	90	10
1034	20d. Detail of handwoven cloth	2·75	60

207 Princess Alexia

1966. Princess Alexia's First Birthday.

1035	**207**	2d. green	30	15
1036	-	2d.50 brown	35	15
1037	-	3d.50 blue	65	30

PORTRAITS: 2d.50, Royal Family; 3d.50, Queen Anne-Marie with Princess Alexia.

208 "Woodcutter" (after D. Filippotes)

1967. Greek Sculpture. Multicoloured.

1038	20l. "Night" (I. Cossos) (vert)	15	10
1039	50l. "Penelope" (L. Drossos) (vert)	15	10
1040	80l. "Shepherd" (G. Phitalis) (vert)	15	10
1041	2d. "Woman's Torso" (K. Demetriades) (vert)	35	10
1042	2d.50 "Kolokotronis" (L. Sochos) (vert)	25	10
1043	3d. "Girl Sleeping" (I. Halepas)	90	35
1044	10d. Type **208**	60	30

209 Olympic Rings ("Olympic Day")

1967. Sports Events. Multicoloured.

1045	1d. Type **209**	25	10
1046	1d.50 Marathon Cup, first Olympics (1896)	25	10
1047	2d.50 Hurdling	35	15
1048	5d. "The Discus-thrower" after C. Demetriades	65	45
1049	6d. Ancient Olympic stadium	1·00	30

The 2d.50, commemorates the European Athletics Cup, 1967. 5d. (vert), The European Highest Award Championships, 1968. 6d. The Inaug of "International Academy" buildings, Olympia.

210 Cogwheels

1967. Europa.

1050	**210**	2d.50 multicoloured	1·40	30
1051	**210**	4d.50 multicoloured	3·50	1·00

211 "Lonchi" (destroyer) and Sailor

1967. Nautical Week. Multicoloured.

1052	20l. Type **211**	25	15
1053	1d. "Eugene Eugenides" (cadet ship) (vert)	25	15
1054	2d.50 Merchant Marine Academy, Aspropyrgos, Attica	25	15
1055	3d. "Averoff" (cruiser) and Naval School, Poros	80	50
1056	6d. "Australis" (liner) and figurehead	60	35

212 The Plaka, Athens

1967. International Tourist Year. Multicoloured.

1057	2d.50 Island of Skopelos (horiz)	20	10
1058	4d.50 Apollo's Temple, Bassai, Peleponnese (horiz)	1·00	30
1059	6d. Type **212**	80	20

213 Soldier and Phoenix

1967. National Revolution of April 21st (1967).

1060	**213**	2d.50 multicoloured	15	10
1061	**213**	3d. multicoloured	20	15
1062	**213**	4d.50 multicoloured	65	45

214 Industrial Skyline

1967. 1st Convention of U.N. Industrial Development Organisation, Athens.

1063	**214**	4d.50 ultramarine, black and blue	65	40

215 "Seaside Scene" (A. Pelaletos)

1967. Children's Drawings. Multicoloured.

1064	20l. Type **215**	20	10
1065	1d.50 "Steamer and Island" (L. Tsirikas)	20	10
1066	3d.50 "Country Cottage" (K. Ambeliotis)	60	50
1067	6d. "The Church on the Hill" (N. Frangos)	50	20

216 Throwing the Javelin

1968. Sports Events, 1968. Multicoloured.

1068	50l. Type **216**	25	10
1069	1d. Long jumping	25	10
1070	1d.50 "Apollo's Head", Temple of Zeus (vert)	25	10
1071	2d.50 Olympic scene on Attic vase (vert)	40	10
1072	4d. Olympic rings (Olympic Day)	50	30
1073	4d.50 "Throwing the Discus", sculpture by Demetriades (European Athletic Championships, 1969) (vert)	1·20	60
1074	6d. Long-distance running (vert)	60	20

The 50l., 1d. and 6d. represent the Balkan Games, and the 1d.50 and 2d.50, the Olympic Academy Meeting.

217 F.I.A. and E.L.P.A. Emblems

1968. General Assembly of International Automobile Federation (F.I.A.), Athens.

1075	**217**	5d. blue and brown	1·10	40

218 Europa "Key"

1968. Europa.

1076	**218**	2d.50 multicoloured	1·90	40
1077	**218**	4d.50 multicoloured	3·00	1·20

219 "Athene defeats Alkyoneus" (from frieze, Altar of Zeus, Pergamos)

1968. "Hellenic Fight for Civilization" Exhibition, Athens. Multicoloured.

1078	10l. Type **219**	20	10
1079	20l. Athene attired for battle (bronze from Piraeus) (vert) (24×37 mm)	20	10
1080	50l. Alexander the Great (from sarcophagus of Alexander of Sidon) (vert) (24×37 mm)	25	10
1081	1d.50 Emperors Constantine and Justinian making offerings to the Holy Mother (Byzantine mosaic)	30	20
1082	2d.50 Emperor Constantine Paleologos (lithograph by D. Tsokos) (vert) (24×37 mm)	30	15
1083	3d. "Greece in Missolonghi" (painting by Delacroix) (vert) (28×40 mm)	30	20
1084	4d.50 "Evzone" (Greek soldier, painting by G. B. Scott) (vert) (28×40 mm)	55	40
1085	6d. "Victory of Samothrace" (statue) (vert) (28×40 mm)	60	45

220 "The Unknown Priest and Teacher" (Rhodes monument)

1968. 20th Anniv of Dodecanese Union with Greece. Multicoloured.

1086	2d. Type **220**	50	10
1087	5d. Greek flag on map (vert)	1·50	75

221 Congress Emblem

1968. 19th Biennial Congress of Greek Orthodox Archdiocese of North and South America.

1088	**221**	6d. multicoloured	1·00	40

222 GAPA Emblem

1968. Regional Congress of Greek-American Progressive Association (GAPA).

1089	**222**	6d. multicoloured	1·00	40

223 "Hand of Aesculapius" (fragment of bas-relief from Asclepios' Temple, Athens)

1968. 5th European Cardiological Congress. Athens.

1090	**223**	4d.50 black, yell & lake	1·90	1·00

224 Panathenaic Stadium

1968. Olympic Games, Mexico. Multicoloured.

1091	2d.50 Type **224**	50	20
1092	5d. Ancient Olympia	90	25
1093	10d. One of Pindar's odes	2·10	90

The 10d. is 28×40 mm.

225 P.Z.L.P 24 ramming Savoia Marchetti S.M.79–11 Sparviero Bomber

1968. Royal Hellenic Air Force. Mult.

1094	2d.50 Type **225**	35	10
1095	3d.50 Mediterranean Flight in Breguet 19 bomber, 1928	50	20
1096	8d. Farman H.F.III biplane and Lockheed F-104G Super Starfighter (vert)	1·10	70

226 Goddess "Hygeia"

1968. 20th Anniv of World Health Organization.

1097	**226**	5d. multicoloured	1·20	40

227 St. Zeno, the Letter-carrier

1969. Greek Post Office Festival.

1098	**227**	2d.50 multicoloured	80	40

228 "Workers' Festival Parade" (detail from Minoan vase)

1969. 50th Anniv of I.L.O. Multicoloured.

1099	1d.50 "Hephaestus and Cyclops" (detail from ancient bas-relief)	40	10
1100	10d. Type **228**	1·30	75

229 Yacht Harbour, Vouliagmeni

1969. Tourism. Multicoloured.

1101	1d. Type **229**	35	10
1102	5d. "Chorus of Elders" (Ancient drama) (vert)	1·30	80
1103	6d. View of Astypalia	45	20

230 Ancient Coin of Kamarina

1969. 20th Anniv of N.A.T.O. Multicoloured.

1104	2d.50 Type **230**	45	20
1105	4d.50 "Going into Battle" (from Corinthian vase) (horiz)	1·20	90

231 Colonnade

1969. Europa.

1106	**231**	2d.50 multicoloured	4·25	30
1107	**231**	4d.50 multicoloured	7·50	1·60

232 Gold Medal

1969. 9th European Athletic Championships, Athens. Multicoloured.

1108	20l. Type **232**	20	15
1109	3d. Pole-vaulting, and ancient pentathlon contest	35	20
1110	5d. Relay-racing, and Olympic race c. 525 B.C. (horiz)	45	20
1111	8d. Throwing the discus, modern and c. 480 B.C.	2·10	95

233 "19th-century Brig and Steamship" (I. Poulakas)

1969. Navy Week and Merchant Marine Year. Multicoloured.

1112	80l. Type **233**	20	10
1113	2d. "Olympic Garland" (tanker) (horiz)	20	10
1114	2d.50 "Themistodes and Karteria, War of Independence, 1821" (anon) (41×29 mm)	35	10
1115	4d.50 "Velos" (modern destroyer) (horiz)	1·30	45
1116	6d. "The Battle of Salamis" (K. Volonakis) (41×29 mm)	1·80	85

234 Raising the Flag on Mt. Grammos

1969. 20th Anniv of Communists' Defeat on Mounts Grammos and Vitsi.

1117	**234**	2d.50 multicoloured	1·10	40

235 Athena Promachos

1969. 25th Anniv of Liberation. Multicoloured.

1118	4d. Type **235**	35	10
1119	5d. "Resistance" (21×37 mm)	1·80	80
1120	6d. Map of Eastern Mediterranean theatre	50	10

236 Demetrius Karatasios (statue by G. Demetriades)

1969. Heroes of Macedonia's Fight for Freedom. Multicoloured.

1121	1d.50 Type **236**	20	10
1122	2d.50 Emmanuel Pappas (statue by N. Perantinos)	20	10
1123	3d.50 Pavlos Melas (from painting by P. Mathiopoulos)	25	25
1124	4d.50 Capetan Kotas	1·00	75

237 Dolphin Mosaic, Delos (110 B.C.)

1970. Greek Mosaics. Multicoloured.

1125	20l. "Angel of the Annunciation", Daphne (11th-century) (vert) (23×34 mm)	20	10
1126	1d. Type **237**	20	10
1127	1d.50 "The Holy Ghost", Hosios Loukas Monastery (11th-century) (vert) (23×34 mm)	25	20
1128	2d. "Hunter", Pella (4th-century B.C.) (vert) (23×34 mm)	55	10
1129	5d. "Bird", St. George's Church, Salonika (5th-century) (vert) (23×34 mm)	65	20
1130	6d. "Christ", Nea Moni Church, Khios (5th-century)	1·40	1·00

238 Overwhelming the Cretan Bull (sculpture)

1970. "The Labours of Hercules".

1131	**238**	20l. multicoloured	20	10
1132	-	30l. multicoloured	20	10
1133	-	1d. black, blue and slate	45	10
1134	-	1d.50 brn, grn & ochre	45	10
1135	-	2d. multicoloured	2·75	10
1136	-	2d.50 brown, red & buff	40	10
1137	-	3d. multicoloured	2·75	10
1138	-	4d.50 multicoloured	40	20
1139	-	5d. multicoloured	55	15
1140	-	6d. multicoloured	55	15
1141	-	20d. multicoloured	2·30	70

DESIGNS—HORIZ: 30l. Hercules and Cerberus (from decorated pitcher); 1d.50, The Lernean Hydra (from stamnos); 2d. Hercules and Geryon (from amphora); 4d.50, Combat with the River-god Achelous (from pitcher); 5d. Overwhelming the Nemean Lion (from amphora); 6d. The Stymphalian Birds (from vase); 20d. Wrestling with Antaeus (from bowl). VERT: 1d. Golden Apples of the Hesperides (sculpture); 2d.50, The Erymanthine Boar (from amphora); 3d. The Centaur Nessus (from vase).

239 "Flaming Sun"

1970. Europa.

1142	**239**	2d.50 yellow and red	3·25	65
1143	-	3d. blue and light blue	3·25	70
1144	**239**	4d.50 yellow and blue	10·50	2·40

DESIGN—VERT: 3d. "Owl" and CEPT emblem.

240 Satellite and Dish Aerial

1970. Satellite Earth Telecommunications Station, Thermopylae.

1145	**240**	2d.50 multicoloured	55	25
1146	**240**	4d.50 multicoloured	1·50	1·00

241 Saints Cyril and Methodius with Emperor Michael III, (from 12th-cent wall-painting)

1970. Saints Cyril and Methodius Commemoration. Multicoloured.

1147	50l. Saints Demetrius, Cyril and Methodius (mosaic) (21×37 mm)	20	15
1148	2d. St. Cyril (Russian miniature) (25×32 mm)	85	65
1149	5d. Type **241**	55	20
1150	10d. St. Methodius (Russian miniature) (25×32 mm)	90	65

Nos. 1148 and 1150 were issued together, se-tenant, forming a composite design.

242 Cephalonian Fir

1970. Nature Conservation Year. Mult.

1151	80l. Type **242**	45	40
1152	2d.50 "Jankaea heldreichii" (plant) (23×34 mm)	1·70	30
1153	6d. Rock Partridge (horiz)	2·75	50
1154	8d. Wild goat	3·75	3·00

243 "Cultural Links"

1970. American–Hellenic Education Progressive Association Congress, Athens.

1155	**243**	6d. multicoloured	1·50	40

244 New U.P.U. Headquarters Building, Berne (Opening)

1970. Anniversaries. Multicoloured.

1156	50l. Type **244**	15	10
1157	2d.50 Emblem (Int Education Year) (vert) (28½×41 mm)	55	10
1158	3d.50 Mahatma Gandhi (birth cent) (vert)	25	20
1159	4d. "25" (25th Anniv of United Nations) (vert)	1·10	10
1160	4d.50 Beethoven (birth bicent) (vert) (28½×41 mm)	2·30	1·40

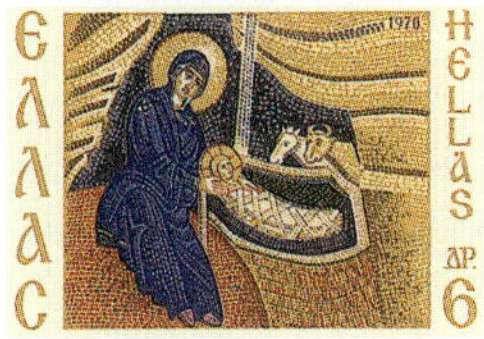

245 "The Nativity"

1970. Christmas. Scenes from "The Mosaic of the Nativity", Hosios Loukas Monastery. Mult.

1161	2d. "The Shepherds" (vert)	30	20
1162	4d.50 "The Magi" (vert)	55	35
1163	6d. Type **245**	1·30	90

246 "Death of Bishop of Salona in Battle, Alamana" (lithograph)

1971. 150th Anniv of War of Independence (1st issue). The Church. Multicoloured.

1164	50l. Warriors taking the oath (medal) (vert)	20	20
1165	2d. Patriarch Gregory V (statue by Phitalis) (vert)	25	20
1166	4d. Type **246**	35	20
1167	10d. "Bishop Germanos blessing the Standard" (Vryzakis)	1·60	1·10

See also Nos. 1168/73, 1178/80, 1181/6 and 1187/89.

1971. 150th Anniv of War of Independence (2nd issue). The War at Sea. As T 246. Multicoloured.

1168	20l. "Leonidas" (warship) (37×24 mm)	25	20
1169	1d. "Pericles" (warship) (37×24 mm)	35	20
1170	1d.50 "Terpsichore" (warship) (from painting by Roux) (37×24 mm)	35	20
1171	2d.50 "Karteria" (warship) (from painting by Hastings) (37×24 mm)	35	20
1172	3d. "Battle of Samos" (contemporary painting) (40×28 mm)	95	40
1173	6d. "Turkish Frigate ablaze, Battle of Yeronda" (Michalis) (40×28 mm)	2·00	95

247 Spyridon Louis winning Marathon, Athens, 1896

1971. 75th Anniv of Olympic Games Revival. Multicoloured.

No.	Type	Description	Unused	Used
1174		3d. Type **247**	80	20
1175		8d. P. de Coubertin and Memorial, Olympia (vert)	2·20	1·10

248 Europa Chain

1971. Europa.

No.	Type	Description	Unused	Used
1176	**248**	2d.50 yellow, grn & blk	3·25	40
1177	**248**	5d. yellow, orange & blk	9·75	1·90

1971. 150th Anniv of War of Independence (3rd issue). "Teaching the People". As T 246. Multicoloured.

No.	Type	Description	Unused	Used
1178		50l. Eugenius Voulgaris (vert)	25	10
1179		2d.50 Dr. Adamantios Korais (vert)	25	20
1180		15d. "The Secret School" (N. Ghyzis) (horiz)	1·90	1·20

SIZES: 50l., 2d.50, 23×34 mm. 15d. as Type **246**.

1971. 150th Anniv of War of Independence (4th issue). The War on Land. As T 246. Mult.

No.	Type	Description	Unused	Used
1181		50l. "Battle of Corinth" (Krazeisen) (vert)	35	20
1182		1d. "Sacrifice of Kapsalia" (Vryzakis) (vert)	35	20
1183		2d. "Suliot Women in Battle" (Deneuville) (horiz)	35	20
1184		5d. "Battle of Athens" (Zographos) (vert)	40	20
1185		6d.50 "Battle of Maniaki" (lithograph) (horiz)	60	20
1186		9d. "Death of Markos Botsaris at Karpenisi" (Vryzakis) (horiz)	1·40	95

SIZES: 50l., 1d., 5d.25×40 mm. 2d.40×25 mm. 6d.50, 9d. as Type **246**.

249 Kaltetsi Monastery and Seal of Peloponnesian Senate

1971. 150th Anniv of War of Independence (5th issue). Government.

No.	Type	Description	Unused	Used
1187	**249**	2d. black, green & brown	40	20
1188	-	2d.50 black, lt blue & bl	40	20
1189	-	20d. black, yellow & brn	2·50	1·70

DESIGNS: 2d.50, National Assembly Memorial, Epidavros, and Seal of Provincial Administration; 20d. Signature and seal of John Capodistria, first President of Greece.

250 Hosios Loukas Monastery, Boeotia

1972. Greek Monasteries and Churches. Mult.

No.	Type	Description	Unused	Used
1190		50l. Type **250**	15	10
1191		1d. Daphni Church, Attica	15	10
1192		2d. St. John the Divine, Patmos	20	10
1193		2d.50 Panaghia Koumbelidiki Church, Kastoria	20	10
1194		4d.50 Panaghia ton Chalkeon, Saloniki	30	20
1195		6d.50 Panaghia Paregoritissa Church, Arta	30	20
1196		8d.50 St. Paul's Monastery, Mount Athos	1·80	1·50

251 Cretan Costume

1972. Greek Costumes (1st series). Mult.

No.	Type	Description	Unused	Used
1197		50l. Type **251**	15	10
1198		1d. Pindus bride	15	10
1199		2d. Warrior-chief Missolonghi	15	10
1200		2d.50 Sarakatsana woman, Attica	15	10
1201		3d. Nisiros woman	20	10
1202		4d.50 Megara woman	25	10
1203		6d.50 Trikeri (rural)	35	10
1204		10d. Pylaia woman, Macedonia	4·00	1·40

See also Nos. 1232/48 and 1282/96.

252 Flag and Map

1972. 5th Anniv of 1967 Revolution. Mult.

No.	Type	Description	Unused	Used
1205		2d.50 Commemorative medal (horiz)	20	10
1206		4d.50 Type **252**	45	25
1207		5d. Facets of modern development	60	40

253 "Communications"

1972. Europa.

No.	Type	Description	Unused	Used
1208	**253**	3d. multicoloured	1·40	35
1209	**253**	4d.50 multicoloured	3·50	1·50

254 Acropolis, Athens

1972. 20th Anniv of Acropolis Motor Rally. Multicoloured.

No.	Type	Description	Unused	Used
1210		4d.50 Type **254**	90	65
1211		5d. Emblem and map	90	65

255 "Gaia delivering Erecthonius to Athene"

1972. Greek Mythology. Museum Pieces (1st series).

No.	Type	Description	Unused	Used
1212	**255**	1d.50 black and green	25	10
1213	-	2d. black and blue	25	20
1214	-	2d.50 black and brown	25	20
1215	-	5d. black and brown	90	50

DESIGNS: 2d. "Uranus" (altar piece); 2d.50, "The Gods repulsing the Giants"; 5d. "Zeus".

See also Nos. 1252/5 and 1271/4.

256 "Young Athlete" (statue)

1972. Olympic Games, Munich. Ancient Olympics. Multicoloured.

No.	Type	Description	Unused	Used
1216		50l. Type **256**	25	15
1217		1d.50 "Wrestlers" (bas-relief) (horiz)	25	15
1218		3d.50 "Female athlete" (statuette)	55	15
1219		4d.50 "Ballgame" (bas-relief) (horiz)	75	20
1220		10d. "Runners" (amphora) (horiz)	2·10	90

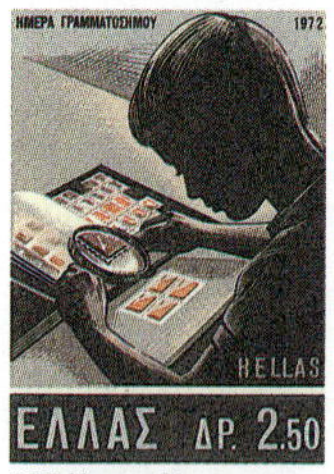

257 Young Stamp Collector

1972. Stamp Day.

No.	Type	Description	Unused	Used
1221	**257**	2d.50 multicoloured	20	20

258 "The Birth of Christ"

1972. Christmas. Multicoloured.

No.	Type	Description	Unused	Used
1222		2d.50 "Pilgrimage of the Magi"	25	20
1223		4d.50 Type **258**	25	20

Nos. 1222/3 were issued together, se-tenant, forming a composite design.

259 University Buildings

1973. Cent of Nat Polytechnic University, Athens.

No.	Type	Description	Unused	Used
1224	**259**	2d.50 multicoloured	40	20

260 "Spring" (wall fresco)

1973. Archaeological Discoveries, Island of Thera. Multicoloured.

No.	Type	Description	Unused	Used
1225		10l. Type **260**	20	15
1226		20l. "Barley" jug	20	15
1227		30l. "Blue Apes" fresco (horiz)	20	15
1228		1d.50 "Bird" (jug)	20	15
1229		2d.50 "Swallows" (detail, "Spring" fresco) (horiz)	20	20
1230		5d. "Wild Goats" fresco (horiz)	20	20
1231		6d.50 "Wrestlers" (detail, fresco) (horiz)	1·10	95

1973. Greek Regional Costumes (2nd series). As Type 251. Multicoloured.

No.	Type	Description	Unused	Used
1232		10l. Peloponnese	10	10
1233		20l. Central Greece	10	10
1234		30l. Locris (Livanates)	10	10
1235		50l. Skyros (male)	10	10
1236		1d. Spetsai	10	10
1237		1d.50 Almyros	10	10
1238		2d.50 Macedonia (Roumlouki)	10	10
1239		3d.50 Salamis	20	10
1240		4d.50 Epirus (Souli)	20	10
1241		5d. Lefkas (Santa Maura)	35	10
1242		6d.50 Skyros (female)	45	10
1243		8d.50 Corinth	60	20
1244		10d. Corfu (Garitsa)	60	10
1245		15d. Epirus	70	10
1246		20d. Thessaly (Karagouniko)	1·90	10
1247		30p. Macedonia (Episkopi)	2·40	10
1248		50d. Thrace (Makra Gefyra)	5·75	3·75

261 Europa "Posthorn"

1973. Europa.

No.	Type	Description	Unused	Used
1249	**261**	2d.50 blue and light blue	70	20
1250	**261**	3d. red, orange and lake	1·20	25
1251	**261**	4d.50 brown, bronze and green	3·00	95

262 "Olympus" (from photograph by Boissonnas)

1973. Greek Mythology (2nd series).

No.	Type	Description	Unused	Used
1252	**262**	1d. black and grey	35	25
1253	-	2d. multicoloured	35	25
1254	-	2d.50 black, grey & brn	35	25
1255	-	4d.50 multicoloured	65	45

DESIGNS: 2d. "Zeus in combat with Typhoeus" (amphora); 2d.50, "Zeus at Battle of Giants" (altar relief); 4d.50, The "Punishment of Atlas and Prometheus" (vase).

263 Dr. G. Papanicolaou

1973. Honouring Dr. George Papanicolaou (cancer specialist).

No.	Type	Description	Unused	Used
1256	**263**	2d.50 multicoloured	15	10
1257	**263**	6d.50 multicoloured	45	35

264 "Our Lady of the Annunciation"

1973. 150th Anniv of Discovery of Miraculous Icon of our Lady of the Annunciation, Tinos.

No.	Type	Description	Unused	Used
1258	**264**	2d.50 multicoloured	40	30

265 "Triptolemus in a Chariot" (vase)

1973. European Transport Ministers Conference, Athens.

No.	Type	Description	Unused	Used
1259	**265**	4d.50 multicoloured	45	35

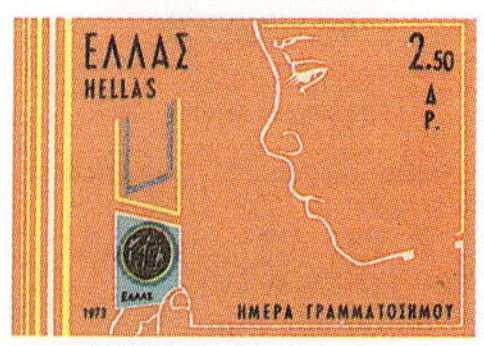

266 Child examining Stamp

1973. Stamp Day.

No.	Type	Description	Unused	Used
1260	**266**	2d.50 multicoloured	25	20

267 G. Averof

1973. National Benefactors (1st series).

1261	**267**	1d.50 brown	15	10
1262	-	2d. red	15	10
1263	-	2d.50 green	15	10
1264	-	4d. lilac	25	15
1265	-	6d.50 black	55	35

DESIGNS: 2d. A. Arsakis; 2d.50, C. Zappas; 4d. A. Syngros; 6d.50, I. Varvakis.

See also Nos. 1315/18.

268 "Lord Byron in Suliot costume" (by Thomas Phillips)

1974. 150th Death Anniv of Lord Byron. Multicoloured.

1266	2d.50 Type **268**	20	15
1267	4d.50 "Byron taking the Oath at Grave of Markos Botsaris" (lithograph)	25	20

269 "Harpist of Keros"

1974. Europa. Ancient Greek Sculptures. Multicoloured.

1268	3d. Type **269**	65	15
1269	4d.50 "Athenian Maiden"	1·00	25
1270	6d.50 "Charioteer of Delphi" (bronze)	3·00	90

270 "Theocracy of Zeus" (vase)

1974. Greek Mythology (3rd series).

1271	**270**	1d.50 black and orange	15	10
1272	-	2d. brown, red & orange	15	10
1273	-	2d.50 black, brn & orge	15	10
1274	-	10d. brown, red & orange	45	30

DESIGNS—HORIZ: 2d. "Athena's Birth" (vase); 2d.50, "Artemis, Apollo and Lito" (vase). VERT: 10d. "Hermes" (vase).

271 U.P.U. Emblem within Mycenaean Vase Design

1974. Centenary of U.P.U. Multicoloured.

1275	2d. Type **271**	15	10
1276	4d.50 Hermes (horiz)	15	10
1277	6d.50 Woman reading letter	45	35

272 Crete 1d. Stamp of 1905

1974. Stamp Day.

1278	**272**	2d.50 black, red & violet	20	20

273 Joseph

1974. Christmas. Multicoloured.

1279	2d. Type **273**	20	15
1280	4d.50 Virgin and Child on donkey	20	15
1281	8d.50 Jacob	20	15

Nos. 1279/81 were issued together, se-tenant, forming a composite design.

1974. Greek Costumes (3rd series). As T 251. Multicoloured.

1282	20l. Megara	10	10
1283	30l. Salamis	10	10
1284	50l. Edipsos	10	10
1285	1d. Kymi	10	10
1286	1d.50 Sterea Hellas	10	10
1287	2d. Desfina	10	10
1288	3d. Epirus	10	10
1289	3d.50 Naousa	10	10
1290	4d. Hasia	10	10
1291	4d.50 Thasos	10	10
1292	5d. Skopelos	10	10
1293	6d.50 Epirus	10	10
1294	10d. Pelion	35	10
1295	25d. Kerkyra	90	10
1296	30d. Boeotia (Tanagra)	2·30	1·80

274 Secret Assembly, Vostitsa

1975. 150th Death Anniv of Girgorios Dikeos Papaflessas (Soldier).

1297	**274**	4d. black, brown & stone	10	10
1298	-	7d. multicoloured	15	10
1299	-	11d. multicoloured	45	35

DESIGNS—VERT: 7d. Papaflessas in uniform. HORIZ: 11d. Aghioi Apostoli (chapel), Kalamala.

275 Roses in Vase

1975. Europa. Multicoloured.

1300	4d. Type **275**	70	20
1301	7d. Erotokritos and Aretussa	1·40	45
1302	11d. Girl and sheep	4·00	1·20

276 Mansion, Kastoria

1975. National Architecture.

1303	**276**	10l. black and blue	15	15
1304	-	40l. black and red	20	15
1305	-	4d. black and brown	20	15
1306	-	6d. black and blue	20	15
1307	-	11d. black and orange	40	30

DESIGNS: 40l. House, Arnea, Halkidiki; 4d. House, Veria; 6d. Mansion, Siatista; 11d. Mansion, Amelakia, Thessaly.

277 Neolithic Goddess

1975. International Women's Year.

1308	**277**	1d.50 brown, deep mauve and mauve	15	10
1309	-	8d.50 black, red and ochre	15	10
1310	-	11d. black, dp blue & bl	45	35

DESIGNS: 8d.50, Confrontation between Antigone and Creon; 11d. Women "Looking to the Future".

278 Alexandros Papanastasiou (founder) and University Buildings

1975. 50th Anniv of Thessaloniki University.

1311	**278**	1d.50 sepia and brown	15	10
1312	-	4d. multicoloured	15	10
1313	-	11d. multicoloured	45	35

DESIGNS: 4d. Original University building; 11d. Plan of University city.

279 Greek 100d. Stamp of 1933

1975. Stamp Day.

1314	**279**	11d. brown, cream & grn	45	35

280 Evangelos Zappas and Zappeion Building

1975. National Benefactors (2nd series).

1315	**280**	1d. black, grey and green	15	10
1316	-	4d. black, grey and brown	15	10
1317	-	6d. black, brown & orge	20	10
1318	-	11d. black, grey and red	45	35

DESIGNS: 4d. Georgios Rizaris and Rizarios Ecclesiastical School; 6d. Michael Tositsas and Metsovion Technical University; 11d. Nicolaos Zosimas and Zosimea Academy.

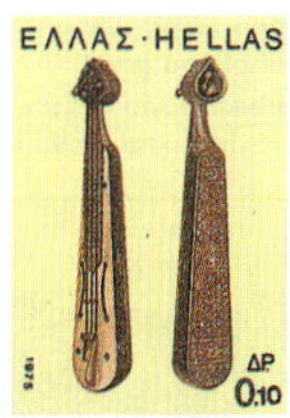

281 Pontos Lyre

1975. Musical Instruments. Multicoloured.

1319	10l. Type **281**	10	10
1320	20l. Musicians (Byzantine mural)	10	10
1321	1d. Cretan lyre	10	10
1322	1d.50 Tambourine	10	10
1323	4d. Cithern-player (from amphora) (horiz)	10	10
1324	6d. Bagpipes	10	10
1325	7d. Lute	10	10
1326	10d. Barrel-organ	10	10
1327	11d. Pipes and zournades	35	10
1328	20d. "Praise God" (Byzantine mural) (horiz)	50	10
1329	25d. Drums	55	10
1330	30d. Kanonaki (horiz)	1·80	1·00

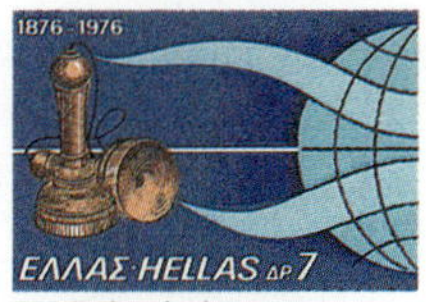

282 Early telephone

1976. Telephone Centenary. Multicoloured.

1331	7d. Type **282**	30	20
1332	11d. Modern telephone and globe	30	20

Nos. 1331/2 were issued together, se-tenant, forming a composite design.

283 Battle of Missolonghi

1976. 150th Anniv of Fall of Missolonghi.

1333	**283**	4d. multicoloured	25	20

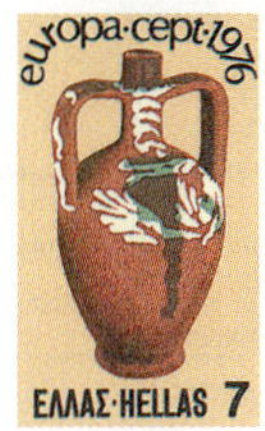

284 Florina Jug

1976. Europa. Multicoloured.

1334	7d. Type **284**	55	25
1335	8d.50 Plate with birds design (25×30 mm)	55	25
1336	11d. Egina pitcher	2·40	85

285 Lion attacking Bull

1976. Ancient Sealing-stones. Multicoloured.

1337	2d. Type **285**	15	10
1338	4d.50 Water birds	15	10
1339	7d. Wounded bull	15	10
1340	8d.50 Head of Silenus (27×40 mm)	20	15
1341	11d. Cow feeding calf (40×27 mm)	40	25

286 Long-jumping

1976. Olympic Games, Montreal. Mult.

1342	50l. Type **286**	15	10
1343	2d. Handball	15	10
1344	3d.50 Wrestling	15	10
1345	4d. Swimming	20	10
1346	11d. Athens and Montreal stadiums (52×37 mm)	25	20
1347	25d. The Olympic flame	1·50	1·10

287 Lemnos

1976. Tourist Publicity. Multicoloured.

1348	30d. Type **287**	45	10
1349	50d. Lesbos (horiz)	1·00	10
1350	75d. Chios (horiz)	1·30	15
1351	100d. Samos (horiz)	2·40	1·50

288 "The Magi speaking to the Jews"

1976. Christmas. Illustrations from manuscripts at Esfigmenou Monastery. Multicoloured.

1352		4d. Type **288**	20	15
1353		7d. "The Adoration of the Magi"	35	25

289 Lascaris Book of Grammar, 1476

1976. 500th Anniv of Printing of First Greek Book.

1354	**289**	4d. multicoloured	25	20

290 Heinrich Schliemann

1976. Centenary of Schliemann's Excavation of the Royal Graves, Mycenae. Multicoloured.

1355		2d. Type **290**	20	10
1356		4d. Gold bracelet (horiz)	20	10
1357		5d. Silver and gold brooch	20	15
1358		7d. Gold diadem (horiz)	35	15
1359		11d. Gold mask	80	50

291 "Patients visiting Aesculapius" (relief)

1977. International Rheumatism Year.

1360	**291**	50l. black, stone and red	15	10
1361	-	1d. black, orange and red	15	10
1362	-	1d.50 black, stone and red	15	10
1363	-	2d. black, orange and red	15	10
1364	-	20d. black, stone and red	40	25

DESIGNS—(22×27 mm): 1d. Ancient clinic; 1d.50, "Asculapius curing a young man" (relief); 2d. Hercules and nurse. (23×34 mm): 20d. "Cured patient offering model of leg" (relief).

292 Fortresses of Mani

1977. Europa. Multicoloured.

1365		5d. Type **292**	90	15
1366		7d. Santorin (vert)	1·00	20
1367		15d. Lassithi Plain, Crete	3·50	60

293 Emblem and Transport

1977. 45th European Conference of Ministers of Transport.

1368	**293**	7d. multicoloured	25	20

294 Alexandria Lighthouse (Roman coin)

1977. "The Civilizing Influence of Alexander the Great". Multicoloured.

1369		50l. Type **294**	20	10
1370		1d. "Placing the Works of Homer in Achilles' tomb" (fresco, Raphael)	20	10
1371		1d.50 Descending to sea bed in special ship (Flemish miniature)	20	10
1372		3d. In search of the water of life (Hindu plate)	25	10
1373		7d. Alexander the Great on horseback (Coptic carpet)	25	10
1374		11d. Listening to oracle (Byzantine manuscript)	40	10
1375		30d. Death of Alexander the Great (Persian miniature)	85	45

295 Wreath in Front of University

1977. Restoration of Democracy.

1376	**295**	4d. blue, green and black	15	10
1377	-	7d. multicoloured	20	10
1378	-	20d. multicoloured	55	35

DESIGNS—HORIZ: (26×22 mm) 7d. Demonstrators at University. VERT: (22×26 mm) 20d. Hand with olive branch, University and flags.

296 Archbishop Makarios

1977. Archbishop Makarios Commemoration.

1379	**296**	4d. black and grey	20	15
1380	-	7d. black, brown & stone	25	25

DESIGN: 7d. Makarios and map of Cyprus.

297 Melas Building, Athens (former post office)

1977. 19th-century Hellenic Architecture.

1381	**297**	50l. black, stone and red	15	10
1382	-	1d. black, stone & green	15	10
1383	-	1d.50 black, stone & bl	15	10
1384	-	2d. black, stone & green	20	10
1385	-	5d. black, stone & yellow	20	10
1386	-	50d. black, stone & orge	75	50

DESIGNS: 1d. Institution for the Blind, Thessalonika; 1d.50, Town Hall of Hermoupolis, Syros; 2d. Branch Office of National Bank, Piraeus; 5d. Ilissia (Palace of Duchess of Plakentia), Athens; 50d. Municipal Theatre, Patras.

298 The Battle of Navarino

1977. 150th Anniv of Battle of Navarino.

1387	**298**	4d. yellow, black & brn	20	15
1388	-	7d. multicoloured	25	20

DESIGN: 7d. Admirals Van der Heyden, Sir Edward Codrington and Comte de Rigny.

299 Parthenon and Industrial Complex

1977. Environmental Protection. Mult.

1389		3d. Type **299**	20	10
1390		4d. Birds and fish (horiz)	20	10
1391		7d. Living and dead trees (horiz)	20	10
1392		30d. Head of Erechtheum caryatid and chimneys	65	50

300 Map of Greece and Ships

1977. "Greeks Abroad". Multicoloured.

1393		4d. Type **300**	15	10
1394		5d. Globe and Greek flag	15	10
1395		7d. Globe and swallows	15	10
1396		11d. Envelope with flags	20	15
1397		13d. Map of the World	50	35

301 "The Port of Kalamata" (C. Parthenis)

1977. Greek Paintings. Multicoloured.

1398		1d.50 Type **301**	20	10
1399		2d.50 "Arsanas" (S. Papaloucas) (vert)	20	10
1400		4d. "Santorin" (C. Maleas)	20	10
1401		7d. "The Engagement" (N. Gyzis)	20	10
1402		11d. "The Straw Hat" (N. Lytras) (vert)	20	10
1403		15d. "Spring" (G. Iacovidis)	40	30

302 "Ebenus cretica"

1978. Greek Flora. Multicoloured.

1404		1d.50 Type **302**	15	10
1405		2d.50 "Fritillaria rhodokanakis"	15	10
1406		3d. "Campanula oreadum"	15	10
1407		4d. "Lilium heldreichii"	15	10
1408		7d. "Viola delphinantha"	20	15
1409		25d. "Paeonia rhodia"	60	45

303 Horse Postman and Pre-stamp Cancel

1978. 150th Anniv of Postal Service. Mult.

1410		4d. Type **303**	15	10
1411		5d. "Maximilianos" (passenger steamer) and Greek "Hermes" stamp	15	10
1412		7d. Steam mail train and 1896 Olympic Games stamp	20	10
1413		30d. Postmen on motor cycles and 1972 "Stamp Day" commemorative	60	45
MS1414		101×92 mm. Nos. 1410/13 (sold at 60d.)	1·40	1·20

304 Lighting the Olympic Flame

1978. 80th International Olympic Committee Session, Athens. Multicoloured.

1415		7d. Type **304**	80	35
1416		13d. Start of 100 m race	1·40	85

305 St. Sophia, Salonika

1978. Europa. Multicoloured.

1417		4d. Type **305**	1·10	30
1418		7d. Lysicrates' Monument, Athens	2·20	75

306 Bust of Aristotle

1978. 2300th Death Anniv of Aristotle. Multicoloured.

1419		2d. Type **306**	20	15
1420		4d. "The School of Athens" (detail Raphael)	20	15
1421		7d. Map of Chalkidiki and statue plinth	35	20
1422		20d. "Aristotle the Wise" (Byzantine fresco) (21×37 mm)	55	35

307 Rotary Emblem (50th anniv)

1978. Anniversaries and Events. Mult.

1423		1d. Type **307**	25	20
1424		1d.50 Surgery (11th Greek Surgery Congress) (vert)	25	20
1425		2d.50 Ugo Foscolo (poet, birth bicentenary)	25	20
1426		5d. Bronze head (25th anniv of European Convention on Human Rights)	25	20
1427		7d. Hand with reins (Conference of Ministers of Culture of Council of Europe countries) (vert)	25	20
1428		13d. *Wright Flyer I* with Daedalus and Icarus (75th anniv of first powered flight) (vert)	55	40

308 The Poor Woman with Five Children

1978. "The Twelve Months" (Greek fairy tale). Multicoloured.

1429		2d. Type **308**	15	10

1430	3d. The poor woman and the twelve months	15	10
1431	4d. The poor woman and the gold coins	20	15
1432	20d. The poor woman with her children and the rich woman with the snakes	40	30

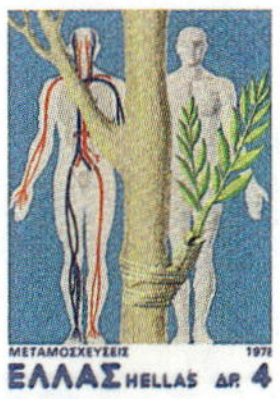

309 Grafted Plant and Circulation Diagram

1978. Transplants. Multicoloured.

1433	4d. Type **309**	20	10
1434	10d. "Miracle of Sts. Cosmas and Damian" (Alonso de Sedano)	35	20

310 "Virgin and Child"

1978. Christmas. Icons from Stavronikita Monastery, Mount Athos. Multicoloured.

1435	4d. Type **310**	20	10
1436	7d. "The Baptism of Christ"	25	20

311 First Academy, Nauplion, and Cadet

1978. 150th Anniv of Military Academy. Multicoloured.

1437	1d.50 Type **311**	15	10
1438	2d. Academy coat of arms (vert)	15	10
1439	10d. Modern Academy, Athens, and cadet	40	30

312 "Antipliarchos Laskos" (destroyer)

1978. Greek Naval Ships. Multicoloured.

1440	50l. Type **312**	15	10
1441	1d. "Andromeda" (motor torpedo-boat)	15	10
1442	2d.50 "Papanicolis" (submarine)	15	10
1443	4d. "Psara" (cruiser)	15	10
1444	5d. "Madonna of Hydra" (armed sailing caique)	20	10
1445	7d. Byzantine dromon	20	15
1446	50d. Athenian trireme	75	45

313 Map of Greece

1978. The Greek State.

1447	**313**	7d. multicoloured	15	10
1448	**313**	11d. multicoloured	20	10
1449	**313**	13d. multicoloured	40	30

314 Kitsos Tsavellas

1979. "The Struggle of the Souliots".

1450	**314**	1d.50 lt brn, blk & brn	15	10
1451	-	3d. multicoloured	15	10
1452	-	10d. multicoloured	20	15
1453	-	20d. ochre, black and brown	35	25

DESIGNS—HORIZ: 3d. Souli Castle; 10d. Fighting Souliots. VERT: 20d. The dance of Zalongo.

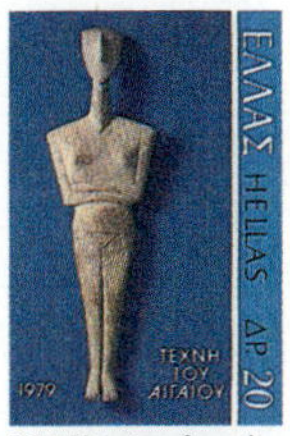

315 Figurine found at Amorgos

1979. Art of the Aegean.

1454	**315**	20d. multicoloured	45	35

316 Cretan Postmen

1979. Europa. Multicoloured.

1455	4d. Type **316**	80	15
1456	7d. Mounted postman	80	25

Nos. 1454/5 were issued in se-tenant pairs, forming a composite design.

317 Nicolas Skoufas

1979. Anniversaries and Events. Mult.

1457	1d.50 Type **317** (founder of Friendly Society, birth bicentenary)	25	20
1458	2d. Steam and diesel locomotives (75th anniv of railway) (horiz)	25	20
1459	3d. Basketball (European Basketball Championship)	25	20
1460	4d. Fossil moonfish "Mene psarianos" (7th International Congress of Mediterranaen Neogene) (horiz)	25	20
1461	10d. Greek church (Balkan Tourist Year)	25	20
1462	20d. Victory of Paeonius and flags (50th anniv of Balkan Sports)	40	35

318 Flags of Member States forming Ear of Wheat

1979. Signing of Treaty, Accession of Greece to European Community. Multicoloured.

1463	7d. Type **318**	20	15
1464	30d. European Parliament (horiz)	50	35

319 "Girl with Dove" (classic statue)

1979. International Year of the Child. Multicoloured.

1465	5d. Type **319**	15	10
1466	8d. Girl with doves	20	15
1467	20d. "Mother and Children" (detail, Iacovides)	35	25

320 Head of Philip of Macedonia

1979. Archaeological Discoveries from Vergina. Multicoloured.

1468	6d. Type **320**	15	10
1469	8d. Gold Wreath	15	10
1470	10d. Copper vessel	20	10
1471	14d. Golden casket (horiz)	25	10
1472	18d. Silver ewer	25	10
1473	20d. Gold quiver	25	15
1474	30d. Iron cuirass	75	50

321 Purple Heron

1979. Endangered Birds. Multicoloured.

1475	6d. Type **321**	15	15
1476	8d. Audouin's gull	15	15
1477	10d. Eleonora's falcon (horiz)	15	15
1478	14d. River kingfisher (horiz)	15	15
1479	20d. Eastern white pelican	35	15
1480	25d. White-tailed sea eagle	1·20	80

322 Agricultural Bank of Greece (50th anniv)

1979. Anniversaries and Events.

1481	**322**	3d. black, yellow & olive	20	20
1482	-	4d. multicoloured	20	20
1483	-	6d. multicoloured	25	20
1484	-	8d. multicoloured	25	20
1485	-	10d. multicoloured	25	20
1486	-	12d. multicoloured	25	20
1487	-	14d. multicoloured	25	20
1488	-	18d. multicoloured	40	25
1489	-	25d. multicoloured	75	50

DESIGNS—HORIZ: 10d. Ionic capital and map of Balkans ("Balkanfila '79" Stamp Exhibition); 25d. Parliamentary Meeting (104th anniv of Greek Parliament). VERT: 4d. Cosmas the Aetolian (monk and martyr) (death bicent.); 6d. Basil the Great (1600th death anniv); 8d. Magnifying glass and map of Balkan countries ("Balkanfila '79" Stamp Exhibition); 12d. Aristolelis Valaoritis (poet) (death centenary); 14d. Golfer (World Golfing Championship); 18d. Bust of Hippocrates (International Hippocratic Foundation, Kos).

323 Parnassos

1979. Landscapes. Multicoloured.

1490	50l. Type **323**	20	10
1491	1d. Tempi (horiz)	20	10
1492	2d. Milos	20	10
1493	4d. Vikos Gorge	20	10
1494	5d. Misolonghi (horiz)	20	10
1495	6d. Louros Aqueduct	20	10
1496	7d. Samothraki	20	10
1497	8d. Sithonia, Chalkidike (horiz)	20	10
1498	10d. Samaria Gorge	20	10
1499	12d. Sifnos	20	10
1500	14d. Kymi (horiz)	25	10
1501	18d. Ios	45	10
1502	20d. Thasos	50	10
1503	30d. Paros (horiz)	85	10
1504	50d. Cephalonia	1·60	70

324 Gate of Galerius

1980. 1st Hellenic Nephrology Congress, Thessalonika.

1505	**324**	8d. blue, black and red	30	20

325 Aegosthena Castle

1980. Castles, Caves and Bridges. Mult.

1506	4d. Type **325**	15	10
1507	6d. Byzantine castle, Thessalonika (horiz)	15	10
1508	8d. Perama cave, Ioannina	15	10
1509	10d. Dyros cave, Mani	15	10
1510	14d. Arta bridge (horiz)	25	15
1511	20d. Kalogiros bridge, Epirus (horiz)	40	20

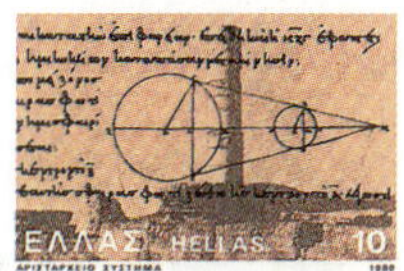

326 Aristarchus' Theorem and Temple of Hera

1980. 2300th Birth Anniv of Aristarchus of Samos (astronomer).

1512	**326**	10d. pink, black & brown	20	15
1513	-	20d. multicoloured	50	30

DESIGN: 20d. Heliocentric system.

327 George Seferis (writer)

1980. Europa.

1514	**327**	8d. brown, blue & black	1·10	15
1515	-	14d. brn, blk and cream	1·60	50

DESIGN: 14d. Maria Callas (opera singer).

328 Open Book

1980. Energy Conservation. Multicoloured.

1516	8d. Type **328**	20	10
1517	20d. Lightbulb and candle (vert)	50	35

329 Fire-fighting

1980. Anniversaries and Events. Mult.

1518	4d. Type **329** (50th anniv of fire brigade)	25	20
1519	6d. St. Demetrius (mosaic) (1700th birth anniv) (vert)	25	20

1520	8d. Revolutionaries (Theriso revolution, 75th anniv)	25	20
1521	10d. Ancient vase and olive branch (World Olive Oil Year) (vert)	25	20
1522	14d. International press emblem (15th International Journalists Federation Congress) (vert)	25	20
1523	20d. Constantinos Ikonomos (cleric and scholar), (birth bicent.) (vert)	40	30

330 Olympia and Coin of Elia

1980. Olympic Games, Moscow. Designs showing Greek stadia. Multicoloured.

1524	8d. Type **330**	20	10
1525	14d. Delphi and Delphic coin	55	40
1526	18d. Epidaurus and coin of Olympia	20	15
1527	20d. Rhodes and coin of Kos	35	15
1528	50d. Panathenaic stadium and First Olympic Games medal	1·20	65

331 Asbestos

1980. Minerals. Multicoloured.

1529	6d. Type **331**	15	10
1530	8d. Gypsum (vert)	15	10
1531	10d. Copper	15	10
1532	14d. Barite (vert)	50	30
1533	18d. Chromite	15	10
1534	20d. Mixed sulphides (vert)	35	15
1535	30d. Bauxite (vert)	60	40

332 Dassault Mirage III Jet Fighter

1980. Anniversaries and Events. Mult.

1536	6d. Breakdown truck (20th anniv of Automobile and Touring Club of Greece road assistance service) (horiz)	25	20
1537	8d. Type **332** (50th anniv of Air Force)	25	20
1538	12d. Piper PA-18 Super Cub light airplane outside hangar (50th anniv of Thessalonika Flying Club) (horiz)	25	20
1539	20d. Harbour scene (50th anniv of Piraeus Port Organization)	40	30
1540	25d. Association for Macedonian Studies Headquarters (40th anniv)	55	35

333 Left Detail of Poulakis' Painting

1980. Christmas. Details from "He is Happy Thanks to You" by T. Poulakis (in St. John's Monastery, Pataros). Multicoloured.

1541	6d. Type **333**	20	20
1542	14d. Virgin and Child (centre)	25	20
1543	20d. Right detail	30	25

Nos. 1541/3 were issued together, se-tenant, forming a composite design.

334 Fresh and Canned Vegetables

1981. Exports. Multicoloured.

1544	9d. Type **334**	15	10
1545	17d. Fruit	20	15
1546	20d. Cotton	25	20
1547	25d. Marble	50	30

335 "Kira Maria" (Alexandrian folk dance)

1981. Europa. Multicoloured.

1548	12d. Type **335**	80	10
1549	17d. "Sousta" (Cretan dance)	1·50	40

336 Olympic Stadium, Kalogreza

1981. European Athletic Championships, Athens (1982) (1st issue).

1550	336	12d. blue, black & lt blue	30	10
1551	-	17d. multicoloured	55	30

DESIGN: 17d. Athletes converging on Greece.

See also Nos. 1586/8.

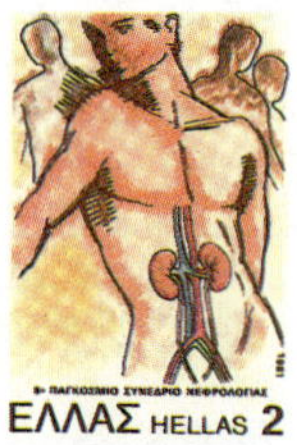

337 Human Figure showing Kidneys

1981. Anniversaries and Events.

1552	337	2d. multicoloured	25	20
1553	-	3d. multicoloured	25	20
1554	-	6d. multicoloured	25	20
1555	-	9d. yellow, black & brn	25	20
1556	-	12d. multicoloured	25	20
1557	-	21d. multicoloured	40	30
1558	-	40d. red, blue & dp blue	65	50

DESIGNS AND EVENTS—VERT: 2d. Type **337** (8th World Nephrology Conference, Athens); 3d. Parachutist, glider, Potez 25 biplane and boy with model glider (50th anniv of Greek National Air Club); 6d. Meteora Monasteries, Thessaly, and Konitsa Bridge, Epirus (International Historical Symposium, Volos, and centenary of incorporation of Thessaly and Epirus into Greece); 12d. Oil rig (first Greek oil production); 40d. Heart (15th World Cardiovascular Surgery Conference Athens). HORIZ: 9d. Bowl with "eye" decoration (50th anniv of Greek Ophthalmological Society); 21d. Globes, plant and coin (Foundation in Athens of World Association for International Relations).

338 Variable Scallops

1981. Shells, Fishes and Butterflies. Mult.

1559	4d. Type **338**	20	10
1560	5d. Painted comber (fish)	20	10
1561	12d. Mediterranean parrotfishes	20	10
1562	15d. Dentex (fish)	20	10
1563	17d. Apollo (butterfly)	60	50
1564	50d. Pale clouded yellow (butterfly)	1·40	95

339 Aegean Island Bell Tower

1981. Bell Towers and Altar Screens. Mult.

1565	4d. Type **339**	20	10
1566	6d. Altar gate, St. Paraskevi Church, Metsovo	20	10
1567	9d. Altar gate, Pelion (horiz)	20	10
1568	12d. Bell tower, Saints Constantine and Helen Church, Halkiades, Epirus	20	10
1569	17d. Altar screen, St. Nicholas Church, Velvendos (horiz)	20	15
1570	30d. Icon of St. Jacob and stand, Alexandroupolis Church Museum	45	20
1571	40d. Upper section of altar gate, St. Nicholas Church, Makrinitsa	85	70

340 Town Scene

1981. Anniversaries and Events. Mult.

1572	3d. Type **340** (Council of Europe Urban Renaissance campaign)	25	20
1573	9d. St. Simeon, Archbishop of Thessalonika (Canonization by Greek Orthodox Church) (vert)	25	20
1574	12d. Child Jesus (detail from Byzantine icon) (Breast feeding campaign) (vert)	40	30
1575	17d. Gina Bachauer (pianist, 5th death anniv) (vert)	45	30
1576	21d. Constantine Broumidis (artist, 175th birth anniv) (vert)	45	30
1577	50d. "Phoenix" banknotes 1831 (first banknotes, 150th anniv)	85	70

341 Old Parliament Building (museum)

1982. Anniversaries and Events. Mult.

1578	2d. Type **341** (centenary of Historical and Ethnological Society)	25	20
1579	9d. Angelos Sikelianos (poet, 31st death anniv) (vert)	25	20
1580	15d. Harilaos Tricoupis (politician, 150th birth anniv) (vert)	25	20
1581	21d. Mermaid (History of Aegean Islands Exhibition) (vert)	40	30
1582	30d. Airbus Industrie A300 jetliner and emblem (25th anniv of Olympic Airways)	55	40
1583	50d. Skull of Petralona man and Petralona cave (3rd European Congress of Anthropology, Petralona) (vert)	80	60

342 "Flight from Missolonghi"

1982. Europa. Multicoloured.

1584	21d. Bust of Miltiades and shield (Battle of Marathon)	3·50	35
1585	30d. Type **342**	5·75	95

343 Pole-vaulter and Wreath

1982. European Athletic Championships (2nd issue). Multicoloured.

1586	21d. Type **343**	25	15
1587	25d. Women runners (vert)	40	15
1588	40d. Athletes at start of race, shot putter, high jumper and hurdler	85	65

344 Lectionary Heading

1982. Byzantine Book Illustrations. Mult.

1589	4d. Type **344**	20	10
1590	6d. Initial letter E (vert)	20	10
1591	12d. Initial letter T (vert)	25	10
1592	15d. Canon-table of Gospel readings (vert)	25	15
1593	80d. Heading from zoology book	1·30	80

345 "Karaiskakis' Camp in Piraeus" (detail, von Krazeisen)

1982. Birth Bicentenary of Georges Karaiskakis (revolutionary leader).

1594	345	12d. green, black & blue	35	15
1595	-	50d. multicoloured	95	70

DESIGN: 50d. Karaiskakis meditating.

346 Cypriot "Disappearances" Demonstration

1982. Amnesty International Year of the "Disappearances". Multicoloured.

1596	15d. Type **346**	25	20
1597	75d. Victims, barbed wire and candle	1·40	1·00

347 "Demonstration in Athens, 25 March 1942–44" (P. Zachariou.)

1982. National Resistance, 1941–44. Mult.

1598	1d. Type **347**	20	10
1599	2d. "Kalavryta's Sacrifice" (S. Vasillou)	20	10
1600	5d. "Resistance in Thrace" (A. Tassos) (vert)	20	10
1601	9d. "The Onset of the Struggle in Crete" (P. Gravalos) (vert)	35	10
1602	12d. Resistance Fighters (vert)	25	10
1603	21d. "Gorgopotamos" (A. Tassos) (vert)	55	30
1604	30d. "Kaisariani, Athens" (G. Sikeliotis)	55	30
1605	50d. "The Struggle in Northern Greece" (V. Katraki)	1·50	95
MS1606	Two sheets (a) 90×81 mm. Nos. 1598/9 and 1604/5; (b) 81×90 mm. Nos. 1600/3	6·00	3·75

348 Mary and Jesus

1982. Christmas. Early Christian Bas-reliefs. Multicoloured.

1607	9d. Type **348**	20	15
1608	21d. Jesus in manger	50	35

349 Figurehead from Tsamados's "Ares" (brig)

1983. 25th Anniv of International Maritime Organization. Ships' Figureheads. Mult.

1609	11d. Type **349**	20	10
1610	15d. Miaoulis's "Ares" (full-rigged ship) (vert)	20	10
1611	18d. Topsail schooner from Sphakia (vert)	40	15
1612	25d. Bouboulina's "Spetses" (full-rigged ship) (vert)	55	30
1613	40d. Babas's "Epameinondas" (brig) (vert)	80	40
1614	50d. "Carteria" (steamer)	1·50	1·00

350 Letter and Map of Greece showing Postcode Districts

1983. Inauguration of Postcode. Multicoloured.

1615	15d. Type **350**	20	15
1616	25d. Hermes' head within posthorn	65	35

351 Archimedes

1983. Europa. Multicoloured.

1617	25d. Acropolis, Athens (49×34 mm)	2·75	50
1618	80d. Type **351**	6·00	1·60

352 Rowing

1983. Sports. Multicoloured.

1619	15d. Type **352**	20	10
1620	18d. Water skiing (vert)	35	10
1621	27d. Windsurfing (vert)	90	65
1622	50d. Ski lift (vert)	70	40
1623	80d. Skiing	2·10	1·30

353 Marinos Antypas (farmers' leader)

1983. Personalities. Multicoloured.

1624	**353**	6d. multicoloured	20	10
1625	-	9d. multicoloured	20	10
1626	-	15d. multicoloured	20	10
1627	-	20d. multicoloured	35	10
1628	-	27d. multicoloured	45	15
1629	-	32d. multicoloured	65	35
1630	-	40d. yellow, brown & blk	85	35
1631	-	50d. multicoloured	1·10	85

DESIGNS: 9d. Nicholas Plastiras (soldier and statesman); 15d. George Papandreou (statesman); 20d. Constantin Cavafy (poet); 27d. Nikos Kazantzakis (writer); 32d. Manolis Calomiris (composer); 40d. George Papanicolaou (medical researcher); 50d. Despina Achladioti, "Matron of Rho" (patriot).

354 Democritus

1983. 1st Int Democritus Congress, Xanthe.

1632	**354**	50d. multicoloured	90	50

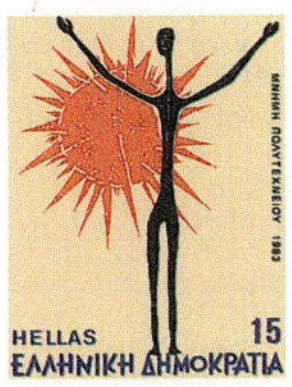

355 Poster by V. Katraki

1983. 10th Anniv of Polytechnic School Uprising. Multicoloured.

1633	15d. Type **355**	20	10
1634	30d. Students leaving Polytechnic	55	35

356 The Deification of Homer

1983. Homeric Odes. Multicoloured.

1635	**356**	2d. sepia and brown	20	10
1636	-	3d. brown, lt orge & orge	20	10
1637	-	4d. yellow, brn & dp brn	20	10
1638	-	5d. multicoloured	20	10
1639	-	6d. orange and brown	20	10
1640	-	10d. lt orge, brn & orge	20	10
1641	-	14d. orge, lt orge & brn	20	10
1642	-	15d. lt orge, orge & brn	25	10
1643	-	20d. bistre, black & brn	25	10
1644	-	27d. brown, pale orange and orange	40	15
1645	-	30d. brown, pale orange and orange	50	10
1646	-	32d. orge, brn & lt orge	60	15
1647	-	50d. brn, lt orge & orge	85	10
1648	-	75d. brown, orange & red	1·20	10
1649	-	100d. sepia, green & brn	2·75	95

DESIGN—HORIZ: 3d. Abduction of Helen by Paris (pot); 4d. Wooden horse; 5d. Achilles throwing dice with Ajax (jar); 14d. Battle between Ajax and Hector (dish); 15d. Priam requesting body of Hector (pot); 27d. Ulysses escaping from Polyphemus's cave; 32d. Ulysses and Sirens; 50d. Ulysses slaying suitors; 75d. Heroes of Iliad (cup). VERT: 6d. Achilles; 10d. Hector receiving arms from his parents (vase); 20d. Binding of Polyphemus; 30d. Ulysses meeting Nausica; 100d. Homer (bust).

357 Horse's Head, Chariot of Seline

1984. Parthenon Marbles. Multicoloured.

1650	14d. Type **357**	75	15
1651	15d. Dionysus	45	15
1652	20d. Hestia, Dione and Aphrodite	65	35
1653	27d. Ilissus	90	35
1654	32d. Lapith and Centaur	1·90	1·00
MS1655	105×81 mm. 15d. Horseman (left); 21d. Horeman (right); 27d. Heroes (left); 32d. Heroes (right)	8·75	7·25

358 Bridge

1984. Europa. 25th Anniv of C.E.P.T.

1656	**358**	15d. multicoloured	80	25
1657	**358**	27d. multicoloured	2·20	1·30

359 Ancient Stadium, Olympia

1984. Olympic Games, Los Angeles. Multicoloured.

1658	14d. Type **359**	25	20
1659	15d. Athletes preparing for training	35	10
1660	20d. Flute player, discus thrower and long jumper	55	25
1661	32d. Athletes training	1·00	60
1662	80d. K. Vikelas and Panathenaic Stadium	3·00	1·50

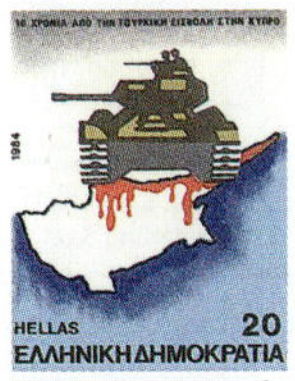

360 Tank on Map of Cyprus

1984. 10th Anniv of Turkish Invasion of Cyprus. Multicoloured.

1663	20d. Type **360**	35	20
1664	32d. Hand grasping barbed wire and map of Cyprus	80	65

361 Pelion Steam Train

1984. Railway Centenary. Multicoloured.

1665	15d. Type **361**	85	30
1666	20d. Steam goods train on Papadia Bridge (vert)	2·20	1·00
1667	30d. Piraeus-Peloponnese steam train	1·00	60
1668	50d. Cogwheel railway, Kalavryta (vert)	2·50	1·10

362 Athens 5th Cent B.C. Silver Coin on Plan of City

1984. 150th Anniv of Athens as Capital. Multicoloured.

1669	15d. Type **362**	50	20
1670	100d. Symbols of ancient Athens and skyline of modern Athens	1·80	1·10

363 "10" enclosing Arms

1984. 10th Anniv of Revolution.

1671	**363**	95d. multicoloured	1·70	60

364 "Annunciation"

1984. Christmas. Multicoloured.

1672	14d. Type **364**	70	40
1673	20d. "Nativity"	80	50
1674	25d. "Presentation in the Temple"	80	50
1675	32d. "Baptism of Christ"	1·10	80

Nos. 1672/5 show scenes from Hagion Panton icon by Athanasios Tountas.

365 Running

1985. 16th European Indoor Athletics Championships, New Phaleron. Multicoloured.

1676	12d. Type **365**	20	20
1677	15d. Putting the shot	25	15
1678	20d. Sports stadium (37×24 mm)	50	25
1679	25d. Hurdling	70	20
1680	80d. High jumping	1·40	85

366 Catacomb Niche

1985. Catacombs of Melos. Multicoloured.

1681	15d. Type **366**	25	15
1682	20d. Martyrs' altars and niches central passageway	40	20
1683	100d. Niches	1·60	1·20

367 Apollo and Marsyas

1985. Europa. Multicoloured.

1684	27d. Type **367**	80	70
1685	80d. Dimitris Mitropoulos and Nikos Skalkotas (composers)	1·90	90

368 Coin (315 B.C.) and "Salonika" (relief)

1985. 2300th Anniv of Salonika. Mult.

1686	1d. Type **368**	20	15
1687	5d. Saints Demetrius and Methodius (mosaics) (49×34 mm)	50	20
1688	15d. Galerius's Arch (detail) (Roman period)	40	15
1689	20d. Salonika's eastern walls (Byzantine period)	50	15
1690	32d. Upper City, Salonika	50	15
1691	50d. Greek army liberating Salonika, 1912	85	15
1692	80d. Soldier's legs and Salonika (German occupation 1941–44)	1·80	35
1693	95d. Contemporary views of Salonika (60th anniv of Aristotelian University and International Trade Fair) (49×34 mm)	3·00	1·60

369 Urn on Map of Cyprus

1985. 25th Anniv of Republic of Cyprus.

1694	**369**	32d. multicoloured	70	45

370 "Democracy crowning the City" (relief)

1985. Athens, "Cultural Capital of Europe".

1695	**370**	15d. multicoloured	25	10
1696	-	20d. black, grey and blue	35	20
1697	-	32d. multicoloured	75	25
1698	-	80d. multicoloured	2·20	1·30

DESIGNS—HORIZ: 20d. Tritons and dolphins (mosaic floor, Roman baths, Hieratis); 80d. Capodistrian University, Athens. VERT: 32d. Angel (fresco, Pentelis Cave).

371 Children of different Races

1985. International Youth Year (1st issue) (15, 25d.) and 40th Anniv of United Nations Organization (27, 100d.). Multicoloured.

1699	15d. Type **371**	20	10
1700	25d. Doves and youths	40	20
1701	27d. Interior of U.N. General Assembly	75	20
1702	100d. U.N. Building, New York, and U.N. emblem	1·60	1·20

See also No. **MS**1703.

372 Girl with Flower Crown

1985. International Youth Year (2nd issue). "Piraeus '85" Stamp Exhibition. Sheet 87×62 mm.

MS1703 **372**	100d. multicoloured	2·50	2·50

373 Folk Dance

1985. Pontic Culture. Multicoloured.

1704	12d. Type **373**	25	20
1705	15d. Monastery of Our Lady of Soumela	25	20
1706	27d. Women's costumes (vert)	65	25
1707	32d. Trapezus High School	70	25
1708	80d. Sinope Castle	1·30	95

374 Hestia

1986. Gods of Olympus.

1709	**374**	5d. orange, black & brn	10	15
1710	-	18d. orange, black & brn	20	15
1711	-	27d. orange, black & bl	35	15
1712	-	32d. orange, black & red	45	25
1713	-	35d. orange, black & brn	45	25
1714	-	40d. orange, black & red	60	20
1715	-	50d. orange, black & grey	75	25
1716	-	110d. orange, blk & brn	95	25
1717	-	150d. orange, blk & grey	1·40	25
1718	-	200d. orange, black & bl	1·60	35
1719	-	300d. orange, black & bl	2·20	90
1720	-	500d. orange, black & bl	5·50	2·50

DESIGNS: 18d. Hermes; 27d. Aphrodite; 32d. Ares; 35d. Athene; 40d. Hephaestus; 50d. Artemis; 110d. Apollo; 150d. Demeter; 200d. Poseidon; 300d. Hera; 500d. Zeus.

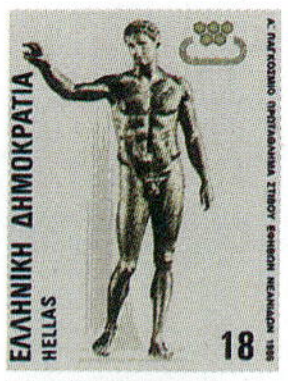

375 "Ephebos of Antikythera"

1986. Sports Events and Anniversaries.

1721	**375**	18d. green, black & grey	50	20
1722	-	27d. yellow, black & red	1·20	55
1723	-	32d. multicoloured	1·70	80
1724	-	35d. green, black & bis	2·40	1·00
1725	-	40d. multicoloured	1·70	95
1726	-	50d. multicoloured	1·70	50
1727	-	110d. multicoloured	6·50	2·10

DESIGNS—VERT: 18d. Type **375** (1st World Junior Athletics Championships); 32d. Footballers (Pan-European Junior Football Finals); 35d. "Wrestlers" (sculpture) (Pan-European Freestyle and Greco-Roman Wrestling Championships); 50d. Cyclists (6th International Round Europe Cycling Meet.). HORIZ: 27d. "Diadoumenos" (sculpture by Polycleitus) (1st World Junior Athletics Championships); 40d. Volleyball players (Men's World Volleyball Championships); 110d. "Victory" (unadopted design by Nikephoros Lytras for first Olympic Games commemoratives, 1896) (90th anniv of modern Olympic Games).

376 Fastening Seat Belt

1986. European Road Safety Year. Mult.

1728	18d. Type **376**	40	10
1729	27d. Motorcyclist in traffic	1·00	70
1730	110d. Child strapped in back seat of car and speed limit signs	2·75	1·60

377 Intelpost

1986. New Postal Services. Multicoloured.

1731	18d. Type **377**	45	20
1732	110d. "Express Mail" banner around globe	1·80	1·60

378 Sapling between Hands and burning Forest

1986. Europa.

1733	**378**	35d. green, black & orge	4·50	2·40
1734	-	110d. blue, black & grn	4·50	2·50

DESIGN: 110d. Dalmatian pelicans on Prespa Lake.

379 Victims' Memorial and Workers

1986. Centenary of Chicago May Day Strike.

1735	**379**	40d. multicoloured	90	50

380 Swearing-in of Venizelos Government

1986. 50th Death Anniv of Eleftherios Venizelos (politician) (18d.) and 6th International Crete Conference, Hania (110d.). Multicoloured.

1736	18d. Type **380**	45	25
1737	110d. Hania harbour	1·80	1·30

381 Dove and Sun

1986. International Peace Year. Multicoloured.

1738	18d. Type **381**	35	25
1739	35d. Dove holding olive branch with flags as leaves	65	50
1740	110d. Dove with olive branch flying out of globe (horiz)	1·70	1·30

382 "Madonna and Child"

1986. Christmas. Designs showing icons. Multicoloured.

1741	22d. Type **382**	25	10
1742	46d. "Adoration of the Magi" (24×32 mm)	90	65
1743	130d. "Christ enthroned with St. John the Evangelist"	2·00	1·00

383 "The Fox and the Grapes"

1987. Aesop's Fables. Multicoloured.

1744A	2d. Type **383**	35	15
1745A	5d. "The North Wind and the Sun"	35	15
1746A	10d. "The Stag at the Spring and the Lion"	55	15
1747A	22d. "Zeus and the Snake"	1·10	15
1748A	32d. "The Crow and the Fox"	1·50	30
1749A	40d. "The Woodcutter and Hermes"	2·40	85
1750A	46d. "The Ass in a Lion's Skin and the Fox"	3·25	85
1751A	130d. "The Hare and the Tortoise"	6·75	1·30

384 "Composition" (Archilleas Apergis)

1987. Europa. Sculptures. Multicoloured.

1752b	40d. Type **384**	4·50	2·10
1753a	130d. "Delphic Light" (Gerassimos Sklavos)	4·50	2·10

385 Player shooting Goal and Indoor Court

1987. 25th European Men's Basketball Championships, Athens. Multicoloured.

1754	22d. Type **385**	80	50
1755	25d. Emblem and spectators (32×24 mm)	45	20
1756	130d. Players	2·30	1·50
MS1757	113×63 mm. 40d. Players; 60d. Players around goal; 100d. Player shooting goal (each 28×40 mm)	8·25	7·25

386 Banner and Students

1987. 150th Annivs. of Athens University (3, 23d.) and National Metsovio Polytechnic Institute (others). Multicoloured.

1758	3d. Type **386**	25	15
1759	23d. Medal and owl	40	15
1760	40d. Building facade, measuring instruments and computer terminal (vert)	70	50
1761	60d. Students outside building (vert)	1·30	1·00

387 Ionic and Corinthian Capitals, Temple of Apollo, Phigaleia-Bassae

1987. Classical Architecture Capitals. Mult.

1762	2d. Type **387**	15	10
1763	26d. Doric capital, Parthenon	50	25
1764	40d. Ionic capital, The Erechtheum	70	40
1765	60d. Corinthian capital, The Tholos, Epidaurus	2·00	1·30

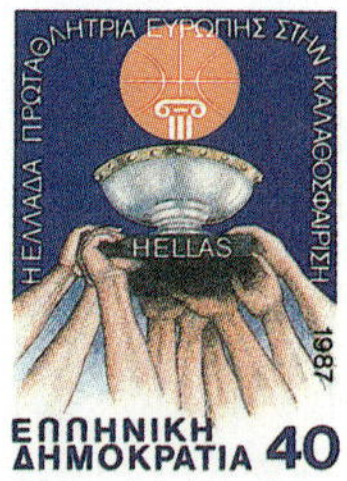

388 Hands holding Cup Aloft

1987. Greek Victory in European Basketball Championship.

1766	**388**	40d. multicoloured	1·10	95

389 Diploma Engraving (Yiannis Kephalinos)

1987. 150th Anniv of Fine Arts High School (1767) and 60th Anniv of Panteios Political Science High School (1768). Multicoloured.

1767	26d. Type **389**	45	15
1768	60d. School campus (horiz)	1·20	95

390 Angel and Christmas Tree (left half)

1987. Christmas.

1769	26d. Type **390**	65	45
1770	26d. Angel and Christmas tree (right half)	65	45

Nos. 1769/70 were printed together, se-tenant, forming a composite design.

391 Eleni Papadaki in "Hecuba" (Euripides) and Philippi Amphitheatre

1987. Greek Theatre. Multicoloured.

1771 2d. Type **391** 20 10
1772 4d. Christopher Nezer in "The Wasps" (Aristophanes) and Dodona amphitheatre 20 10
1773 7d. Emilios Veakis in "Oedipus Rex" (Sophocles) and Delphi amphitheatre 20 10
1774 26d. Marika Kotopouli in "The Shepherdess's Love" (Dimitris Koromilas) 60 40
1775 40d. Katina Paxinou in "Abraham's Sacrifice" (Vitzentzos Cornaros) 1·00 40
1776 50d. Kyveli in "Countess Valeraina's Secret" (Gregory Xenopoulos) 1·10 65
1777 60d. Karolos Koun and stage set 2·00 70
1778 100d. Dimitris Rontiris teaching National Theatre dancers an ancient dance 3·25 50

392 "Codonellina sp." (polyzoan)

1988. Marine Life. Multicoloured.

1779A 30d. Type **392** 1·30 40
1780A 40d. "Diaperoecia major" (polyzoan (clump-forming animals)) 1·30 40
1781A 50d. "Artemia" (marine animal) 1·50 40
1782A 60d. "Posidonia oceanica" (plant) and Marmora sea-bream 3·75 1·50
1783A 100d. "Padina pavonica" (plant) 7·00 2·30

393 Ancient Olympia

1988. Olympic Games, Seoul. Multicoloured.

1784A 4d. Type **393** 60 20
1785A 20d. Ancient athletes in Gymnasium 1·20 20
1786A 30d. Modern Olympics centenary emblem 3·00 95
1787A 60d. Ancient athletes training 5·25 3·25
1788A 170d. Runner with Olympic flame 9·75 2·50

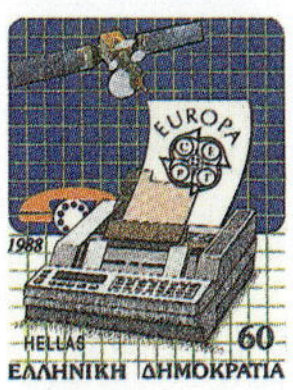

394 Satellite and Fax Machine

1988. Europa. Transport and Communications. Multicoloured.

1789B 60d. Type **394** 6·00 1·90
1790B 150d. Modern express and commuter trains 12·00 2·30

395 Katarraktis Falls

1988. European Campaign for Rural Areas. Waterfalls. Multicoloured.

1791A 10d. Type **395** 2·75 40
1792A 60d. Edessa waterfalls 7·00 3·25
1793A 100d. River Edessaios cascades 8·75 2·50

396 Emblems

1988. 20th European Postal Workers Trade Unions Congress.

1794A **396** 60d. multicoloured 9·75 3·00

397 Mytilene Harbour, Lebos (painting by Theophilos)

1988. Prefecture Capitals (1st series). Mult.

1795B 2d. Type **397** 15 10
1796B 3d. Alexandroupolis lighthouse, Evros (vert) 15 10
1797B 4d. St. Nicholas's bell-tower, Kozani (vert) 20 10
1798B 5d. Workmen's centre, Hermoupolis, Cyclades (vert) 20 10
1799B 7d. Sparta Town Hall, Lakonia 20 10
1800B 8d. Pegasus, Leukas 30 10
1801B 10d. Castle of the Knights, Rhodes, Dodecanese (vert) 30 10
1802B 20d. Acropolis, Athens (vert) 35 15
1803B 25d. Aqueduct, Kavala 40 15
1804B 30d. Castle and statue of Athanasios Diakos, Lamia, Phthiotis (vert) 50 15
1805B 50d. Preveza Cathedral bell-tower and clock (vert) 1·20 20
1806B 60d. Esplanade, Corfu 1·60 45
1807B 70d. Aghios Nicholaos, Lassithi 3·00 25
1808B 100d. Six Springheads, Poligiros, Khalkidiki 5·50 30
1809B 200d. Church of Paul the Apostle, Corinth, Corinthia 6·50 65

See also Nos. 1848/62, 1911/22 and 1955/64.

398 Eleftherios Venizelos, Map and Flag

1988. 75th Annivs. of Union of Crete and Greece (30d.) and Liberation of Epirus and Macedonia (70d.). Multicoloured.

1810A 30d. Type **398** 1·10 35
1811A 70d. Flags, map and "Liberty" 2·20 1·20

399 "Adoration of the Magi" (El Greco)

1988. Christmas. Multicoloured.

1812 30d. Type **399** 1·40 50
1813 70d. "The Annunciation" (Kostas Parthenis) (horiz) 1·90 1·20

400 Map of E.E.C. and Castle of Knights, Rhodes

1988. European Economic Community. Meeting of Heads of State, Rhodes. Multicoloured.

1814A 60d. Type **400** 2·75 1·60
1815A 100d. Members' flags and coin 3·25 1·00

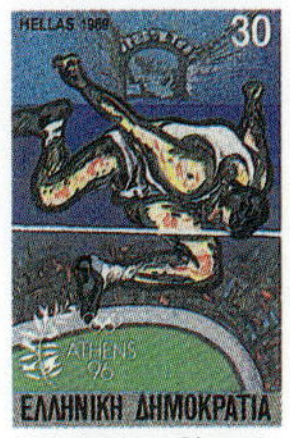

401 Ancient Olympia and High Jumper

1989. Centenary (1996) of Modern Olympic Games (1st issue). Multicoloured.

1816A 30d. Type **401** 70 35
1817A 60d. Wrestlers and Delphi 1·70 1·20
1818A 70d. Acropolis, Athens, and swimmers 2·20 1·50
1819A 170d. Stadium and Golden Olympics emblem 4·25 2·10

See also Nos. 1863/7, **MS**1995 and 1998/2001.

402 Flags

1989. International Anniversaries. Mult.

1820A 30d. Type **402** (5th anniv of Six-nation Initiative for Peace and Disarmament) 1·10 50
1821A 50d. Flag and "Liberty" (bicentenary of French Revolution) 1·40 80
1822A 60d. Flag and ballot box (third direct European Parliament elections) 3·00 1·60
1823A 70d. Coins (cent of Interparliamentary Union) 3·75 1·60
1824A 200d. Flag (40th anniv of Council of Europe) 7·25 1·80

403 Whistling Bird

1989. Europa. Children's Toys. Multicoloured.

1825B 60d. Type **403** 5·00 2·50
1826B 170d. Butterfly 5·00 2·50

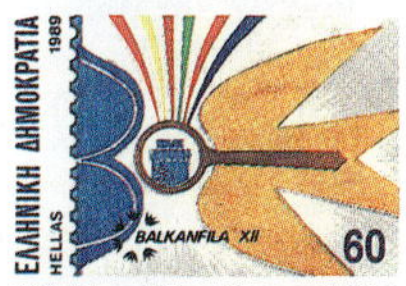

404 Magnifying Glass and Bird

1989. "Balkanfila XII" International Stamp Exhibition, Salonica. Multicoloured.

1827 60d. Type **404** 1·00 45
1828 70d. Eye looking through magnifying glass 1·10 75
MS1829 86×61 mm. 200d. Stamp collectors (42×30 mm) 4·25 4·25

405 Dog Roses

1989. Wild Flowers. Multicoloured.

1830 8d. Type **405** 25 15
1831 10d. Common myrtle 25 15
1832 20d. Common poppies 45 20
1833 30d. Anemones 60 25
1834 60d. Dandelions and chicory 90 40
1835 70d. Mallow 1·40 40
1836 200d. Thistles 3·25 1·70

406 Brown Bear

1990. Endangered Animals. Multicoloured.

1837 40d. Type **406** 80 20
1838 70d. Loggerhead turtle 80 50
1839 90d. Mediterranean monk seal 1·60 60
1840 100d. Lynx 3·00 1·30

407 Gregoris Lambrakis

1990. Politicians' Death Anniversaries. Mult.

1841 40d. Type **407** (27th anniv) 70 50
1842 40d. Pavlos Bakoyiannis (first anniv) 70 50

408 Clasped Hands, Roses and Flag

1990. National Reconciliation. Multicoloured.

1843 40d. Type **408** 55 15
1844 70d. Dove with banner 1·00 50
1845 100d. Map and hands holding roses 1·50 1·30

409 Old Central Post Office Interior

1990. Europa. Post Offices Buildings. Mult.

1846 70d. Type **409** 4·00 1·60
1847 210d. Exterior of modern post office 4·00 1·60

410 "Animal Fair" (D. Gioldassi) (Karditsa)

1990. Prefecture Capitals (2nd series). Mult.

1848B 2d. Type **410** 20 10
1849B 5d. Fort, Trikala (horiz) 20 10
1850B 8d. Street, Veroia (Imathia) 20 10
1851B 10d. Monument to Fallen Heroes, Missolonghi (Aetolia) (horiz) 25 10
1852B 15d. Harbour, Chios (horiz) 25 10
1853B 20d. Street, Tripolis (Arcadia) (horiz) 35 10
1854B 25d. "City and Town Hall" (woodcut, A. Tassos) (Volos, Magnesia) (horiz) 60 30
1855B 40d. Town Hall, Kalamata (Messenia) (horiz) 60 30
1856B 50d. Market, Pyrgos (Elia) (horiz) 75 30
1857B 70d. Lake and island, Yannina (horiz) 85 50
1858B 80d. Harhour sculpture, Rethymnon 1·50 35
1859B 90d. Argostolion (Cephalonia) (horiz) 1·50 50
1860B 100d. Citadel and islet, Nauplion (Argolis) (horiz) 1·60 35
1861B 200d. Lighthouse, Patras (Akhaia) 3·50 45
1862B 250d. Street, Florina (horiz) 5·75 45

411 Yachting

1990. Centenary (1996) of Modern Olympic Games (2nd issue). Multicoloured.

1863	20d. Type **411**	60	20
1864	50d. Wrestling	85	35
1865	80d. Running	1·20	90
1866	100d. Handball	1·70	80
1867	250d. Football	5·00	1·50

412 Schliemann and Lion Gate, Mycenae

1990. Death Cent of Heinrich Schliemann (archaeologist).

1868	**412**	80d. multicoloured	8·50	4·25

413 "Woman knitting" (lithograph, Vasso Katraki)

1990. 50th Anniv of Greek–Italian War. Mult.

1869	50d. Type **413**	80	40
1870	80d. "Virgin Mary protecting Army" (lithograph, George Gounaropoulou)	1·10	80
1871	100d. "Women's War Work" (lithograph, Kosta Grammatopoulou)	1·30	95

414 Hermes

1990. Stamp Day. Sheet 87×62 mm.

MS1872	**414**	300d. multicoloured	15·00	15·00

415 Calliope, Euterpe and Erato

1991. The Nine Muses. Multicoloured.

1873	50d. Type **415**	85	40
1874	80d. Terpsichore, Polyhymnia and Melpomene	1·60	90
1875	250d. Thalia, Clio and Urania	4·25	1·20

416 Battle Scene (Ioannis Anousakis)

1991. 50th Anniv of Battle for Crete. Mult.

1876	60d. Type **416**	2·20	75
1877	300d. Map and flags of allied nations (32×24 mm)	5·00	2·10

417 Icarus pushing Satellite

1991. Europa. Europe in Space. Mult.

1878	80d. Type **417**	4·00	2·40
1879	300d. Chariot of the Sun	5·25	3·50

418 Swimming

1991. 11th Mediterranean Games, Athens. Multicoloured.

1880	10d. Type **418**	35	20
1881	60d. Basketball	80	35
1882	90d. Gymnastics	1·50	35
1883	130d. Weightlifting	2·10	65
1884	300d. Throwing the hammer	4·75	2·50

419 Pillar of Democracy

1991. 2500th Anniv of Birth of Democracy.

1885	**419**	100d. black, stone & blue	1·70	90

420 Europa and Zeus as Bull (from Attic vase)

1991. Greek Presidency of European Postal and Telecommunications Conference. Sheet 81×62 mm.

MS1886	300d. multicoloured	19·00	19·00

421 Pres Konstantinos Karamanlis signing Treaty of Athens

1991. 10th Anniv of Greek Admission to European Community. Multicoloured.

1887	50d. Type **421**	80	35
1888	80d. Map of Europe and Pres. Karamanlis	1·40	65

422 Emblem and Speed Skaters

1991. Winter Olympic Games, Albertville. Multicoloured.

1889	80d. Type **422**	1·90	1·00
1890	300d. Slalom skier	3·75	1·60

423 Throwing the Javelin

1992. Olympic Games, Barcelona. Mult.

1891	10d. Type **423**	40	20
1892	60d. Show jumping	1·40	45
1893	90d. Runner (37×24 mm)	2·10	95
1894	120d. Gymnastics	3·50	75
1895	340d. Runners' heads forming Olympic rings (37×24 mm)	6·50	1·90

424 Couple beneath Umbrella

1992. Health. Multicoloured.

1896	60d. Type **424** (anti-AIDS campaign)	65	25
1897	80d. Doctor examining child (1st European Gastroenterology Week)	1·20	40
1898	90d. Crab killing flower on healthy plant (anti-cancer campaign)	1·40	50
1899	120d. Hephaestus's forge (from 6th-century B.C. urn) (European Year of Social Security, Hygiene and Health in the Workplace)	1·60	1·00
1900	280d. Alexandros Onassis Cardiosurgical Centre	5·50	2·10

425 "Santa Maria", Map and Columbus

1992. Europa. 500th Anniv of Discovery of America by Columbus. Multicoloured.

1901	90d. Type **425**	4·00	2·10
1902	340d. Chios in late 15th century	5·25	3·25

426 Proetus, Bellerophon and Pegasus

1992. European Transport Ministers' Conference, Athens. Sheet 85×59 mm.

MS1903	**426**	300d. multicoloured	11·00	11·00

427 Head of Hercules with Lion Skin (relief)

1992. Macedonia. Multicoloured.

1904	10d. Type **427**	35	10
1905	20d. Map of Macedonia and bust of Aristotle (horiz)	45	10
1906	60d. Alexander the Great at Battle of Issus (mural) (horiz)	1·00	15
1907	80d. Tomb of Philip II at Vergina, and Manolis Andronikos (archaeologist)	1·50	50
1908	90d. Deer hunt (mosaic, Pella)	2·20	50
1909	120d. Macedonian coin	3·00	1·00
1910	340d. 4th-century Church, Philippi, and Apostle Paul	8·75	3·25

428 Piraeus

1992. Prefecture Capitals (3rd series). Mult.

1911B	10d. Type **428**	15	10
1912B	20d. Amphissa (Phocis)	20	10
1913B	30d. The Heraion, Samos	25	10
1914B	40d. Canea	40	10
1915B	50d. Zakynthos	55	20
1916B	60d. Karpenisi (Evrytania)	65	20
1917B	70d. Cave, Kilkis (vert)	80	20
1918B	80d. Door of Town Hall Xanthi (vert)	1·60	20
1919B	90d. Macedonian Struggle Museum, Thessaloniki	1·90	30
1920B	120d. Tsanakleous School, Komotini (Rhodope)	2·75	50
1921B	340d. Spring, Drama	6·00	1·30
1922B	400d. Pinios Bridge, Larissa	7·75	2·10

429 Column, Map, Flags and European Community Emblem

1992. Single European Market.

1923	**429**	90d. multicoloured	1·20	1·00

430 Headstone (4th century B.C.)

1993. 2400th Anniv of Rhodes. Multicoloured.

1924	60d. Type **430**	1·10	40
1925	90d. "Aphrodite bathing" (statue)	1·90	90
1926	120d. "St. Irene" (from St. Catherine's church)	1·40	80
1927	250d. St. Paul's Gate, Naillac Mole	5·50	2·10

431 Georgakis Olympios at Sekkou Monastery, 1821

1993. Historical Events. Multicoloured.

1928	10d. Type **431** (War of Independence)	45	10
1929	30d. Theodore Kolokotronis (War of Independence)	60	20
1930	60d. Pavlos Melas (military hero)	1·00	35
1931	90d. "Glory crowns the Casualties" (Balkan Wars, 1912–13)	2·30	90
1932	120d. Soldiers of Sacred Company, El Alamein, 1942 (horiz)	3·75	1·00
1933	150d. Sacred Company on Aegean Islands, 1943–45 (horiz)	4·25	1·40
1934	200d. Victims' Monument, Kalavryta (destruction of village, 1943)	8·25	2·40

432 "The Benefits of Transportation" (Konstantinos Parthenis) (left half)

1993. Europa. Contemporary Art. Mult.

1935	90d. Type **432**	3·50	2·10
1936	350d. "The Benefits of Transportation" (right half)	5·25	3·75

Nos. 1935/6 were issued together, se-tenant, forming a composite design.

433 Athens Concert Hall

1993. Modern Athens. Multicoloured.

1937	30d. Type **433**	1·10	20
1938	60d. Iliou Melathron (former house of Heinrich Schliemann (archaeologist), now Numismatic Museum)	1·60	30
1939	90d. National Library	1·90	50
1940	200d. Athens Eye Hospital	5·25	1·80

434 Presidency Emblem and Map

1993. Greek Presidency (1994) of European Union (1st issue). Sheet 84×60 mm.

MS1941	**434** 400d. multicoloured	7·50	7·50

See also Nos. 1953/4.

435 "Hermes leading Selene's Chariot" (Boeotian vase)

1994. 2nd Pan-European Transport Conf.

1942	**435**	200d. multicoloured	3·50	1·60

436 "Last Supper" (icon by Michael Damaskinou, St. Catherine's Church, Heraklion, Crete)

1994. Easter. Multicoloured.

1943	30d. Type **436**	55	10
1944	60d. "Crucifixion" (detail of wall painting, Great Meteoron)	80	20
1945	90d. "Burial of Christ" (icon, Church of the Presentation of the Lord, Patmos) (horiz)	1·10	40
1946	150d. "Resurrection" (detail, illuminated manuscript from Mt. Athos) (horiz)	2·75	1·00

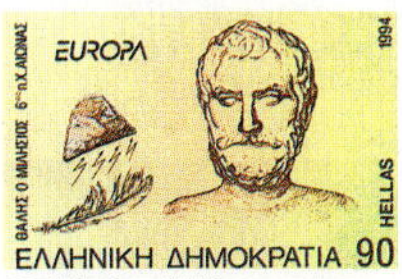

437 Thales of Miletus (philosopher)

1994. Europa. Discoveries. Multicoloured.

1947	90d. Type **437**	3·25	2·10
1948	350d. Konstantinos Karatheodoris (mathematician) and equations	5·50	3·25

438 Demetrios Vikelas (first president, after G. Roilos)

1994. Sports Events and Anniversary. Mult.

1949	60d. Type **438** (centenary of International Olympic Committee)	1·00	25
1950	90d. Modern footballer and ancient relief (World Cup Football Championship, U.S.A.) (horiz)	1·10	70
1951	120d. Ball, net and laurel (World Volleyball Championship, Piraeus and Salonika)	3·25	70
MS1952	68×70 mm. 400d. Modern footballers, Statue of Liberty and ancient relief (World Cup) (41×51 mm)	8·25	8·25

439 "Greece" driving E.U. Chariot

1994. Greek Presidency of European Union. Multicoloured.

1953	90d. Type **439**	1·40	85
1954	120d. Doric columns and E.U. flag	2·20	95

440 Parigoritissas Byzantine Church, Arta

1994. Prefecture Capitals (4th series). Mult.

1955B	10d. Tsalopoulou mansion house, Katerini (Pieria) (vert)	15	10
1956B	20d. Type **440**	15	10
1957B	30d. Bridge and tower, Levadia (Boeotia) (vert)	35	10
1958B	40d. Koumbelidikis church Kastoria	45	10
1959B	50d. Outdoor theatre, Grevena	60	20
1960B	60d. Waterfall, Edessa (Pella)	70	20
1961B	80d. Red House, Chalkida (Euboea)	1·10	25
1962B	90d. Government House, Serres	1·80	35
1963B	120d. Town Hall, Heraklion	1·80	65
1964B	150d. Church of our Lady of the Annunciation, Igoumenitsa (Thesprotia) (vert)	2·75	65

441 "Declaration of Constitution" (detail, Carl Haupt)

1994. 150th Anniv of Constitution. Mult.

1965	60d. Type **441**	55	20
1966	150d. Ioannis Makrygiannis, Andreas Metaxas and Dimitrios Kallergis (from "Neos Aristophanes" (magazine))	1·40	50
1967	200d. "The Night of 3rd September 1843" (anon) (horiz)	3·75	1·00
1968	340d. Article 107 of 1844 Constitution and Parliament Seal (horiz)	6·50	2·10

442 Mercouri and Demonstrators (fighter for Democracy)

1995. Melina Mercouri (actress and Minister of Culture) Commemoration. Multicoloured.

1969	60d. Type **442**	80	20
1970	90d. Mercouri and Acropolis (politician)	90	50
1971	100d. Mercouri in three roles (actress)	2·75	95
1972	340d. Mercouri with flowers (vert)	7·50	2·10

443 Prisoners behind Barbed Wire

1995. Europa. Peace and Freedom. Mult.

1973	90d. Type **443**	3·00	2·50
1974	340d. Doves flying from crushed barbed wire	5·25	2·50

Nos. 1973/4 were issued together, se-tenant, forming a composite design.

444 Emblem

1995. Anniversaries and Events. Mult.

1975	10d. Type **444** (5th World Junior Basketball Championship)	55	10
1976	70d. Agriculture University, Athens (75th anniv) (horiz)	1·10	15
1977	90d. Delphi (50th anniv of U.N.O.)	1·40	30
1978	100d. Greek flag and returning soldier (50th anniv of end of Second World War)	1·60	50
1979	120d. "Peace" (statue by Kifissodotos) (50th anniv of U.N.O.)	1·60	70
1980	150d. Dolphins (European Nature Conservation Year) (horiz)	2·75	90
1981	200d. Old telephone and modern key-pad (cent of telephone in Greece)	4·25	1·00
1982	300d. Owl sitting on ball (29th European Basketball Championship)	8·75	1·90

445 "The First Vision of the Apocalypse" (icon, Thomas Bathas)

1995. 1900th Anniv of the Apocalypse of St. John. Multicoloured.

1983	80d. Type **445**	1·90	40
1984	110d. St. John dictating to Prochoros in front of the Cave of the Apocalypse (miniature from the Four Gospels, Codex 81 of library of Patmos Monastery)	1·90	85
1985	300d. Trumpet of the First Angel (gilded Gospel cover) (horiz)	5·00	2·10

446 Goddess Athene with Argonauts

1995. Jason and the Argonauts. Mult.

1986	80d. Type **446**	80	35
1987	120d. Phineas (blind seer), god Hermes and the Voreadae pursuing Harpies	1·60	50
1988	150d. Medea, Nike and Jason taming bull	1·60	70
1989	200d. Jason and Medea killing snake and taking the Golden Fleece	3·00	1·00
1990	300d. Jason presenting Golden Fleece to Pelias	6·00	1·70

447 Psyttaleia

1995. Lighthouses. Multicoloured.

1991	80d. Type **447**	1·10	50
1992	120d. Sapienza	1·60	75
1993	150d. Kastri, Othonoi	3·25	2·40
1994	500d. Zourva, Hydra	6·50	3·25

448 1l. Stamp

1996. Centenary of Modern Olympic Games (3rd issue). Reproduction of Olympic Games issue of 1896. Three sheets each 88×88 mm, containing designs as T 448. Inscriptions in brown, backgrounds flesh; colour of reproductions listed below.

MS1995	3 sheets (a) 80d. ochre (Type **448**); 120d. pink (2l.); 150d. brown (5l.); 650d. olive (10d.). (b) 80d. red (25l.); 120d. black (60l.); 150d. blue (1d.); 650d. reddish brown (10d.). (c) 80d. brown (20l.); 120d. lilac (40l.); 150l. brown (2d.); 650d. green (5d.) Set of 3 sheets	45·00	45·00

449 Sappho (poet)

1996. Europa. Famous women.

1996	**449**	120d. multicoloured	4·25	3·25
1997	-	430d. brown, black & bl	7·50	5·25

DESIGN: 430d. Amalia Fleming.

450 Running

1996. Centenary of Modern Olympic Games (3rd issue). Mult.

1998	10d. Type **450**	2·20	35
1999	80d. Throwing the discus	1·60	70
2000	120d. Weightlifting	2·75	1·00
2001	200d. Wrestling (horiz)	5·50	2·40

451 Hippocrates

1996. 1st Int Medical Olympiad, Athens.

2002	**451**	80d. brown, pink & black	2·75	1·30
2003	-	120d. brown, green & blk	3·25	1·80

DESIGN: 120d. Galen.

452 Mytilene

1996. Castles (1st series). Multicoloured.

2004B	10d. Type **452**	20	10
2005B	20d. Lindos	25	10
2006B	30d. Rethymnon	35	15
2007B	70d. Assos Cephalonia	60	20
2008B	80d. Castle of the Serbs	1·10	50
2009B	120d. Monemvasia	1·90	65
2010B	200d. Didimotihon	3·50	1·00
2011B	430d. Vonitsas	7·50	1·50
2012B	1000d. Nikopolis	15·00	5·75

See also Nos. 2069/78.

453 Puppets

1996. Shadow Puppets. Multicoloured.

2013	80d. Type **453**	1·60	70
2014	100d. Men courting woman	1·10	80
2015	120d. Soldiers	2·40	1·00
2016	200d. Men fighting dragon	4·25	1·60

454 Inscription on Wine Jug (720 B.C.)

1996. The Greek Language. Multicoloured.

2017	80d. Type **454**	80	65
2018	120d. Homer's "Iliad" (papyrus scroll, 436–45)	1·60	75
2019	150d. Psalm (6th century)	2·20	1·00
2020	350d. Dionysios Solomos (writer) and verse of poem (1824)	9·00	3·25

455 Papandreou, Cap, Degree and Books

1997. Andreas Papandreou (Prime Minister, 1981–89 and 1993–96) Commemoration. Multicoloured.

2021	80d. Type **455** (Doctorate in Economics, Harvard University, 1943)	1·10	50
2022	120d. Return from exile, 1974, and smoking pipe	1·60	75
2023	150d. Parliament building and Papandreou	2·75	95
2024	500d. State flag, dove and Papandreou wearing glasses	7·00	3·50

456 St Dimitrios (patron saint) (fresco, Aghios Nikolaos Orphanos Church)

1997. Thessaloniki, Cultural Capital of Europe. Multicoloured.

2025	80d. Type **456**	80	35
2026	100d. Hippocratic Hospital (horiz)	1·90	65
2027	120d. Marble statue pedestal (2nd century) and circular relief of woman's head	1·90	80
2028	150d. Mosaic (detail) in cupola of Rotunda	2·75	85
2029	300d. 14th-century chalice (horiz)	7·00	2·40

457 Trikomo

1997. Macedonian Bridges. Multicoloured.

2030	80d. Type **457**	1·10	40
2031	120d. Portitsa	1·40	65
2032	150d. Ziakas	2·75	95
2033	350d. Kastro	5·50	2·50

458 Prometheus the Fire-stealer

1997. Europa. Tales and Legends. Mult.

2034	120d. Type **458**	3·25	2·40
2035	430d. Knights (Digenes Akritas)	5·00	2·50

459 Running

1997. 6th World Athletics Championships, Athens. Multicoloured.

2036	20d. Type **459**	45	25
2037	100d. "Nike" (statue)	1·20	60
2038	140d. High jumping	2·20	85
2039	170d. Hurdling	2·75	1·50
2040	500d. Stadium, Athens	8·25	3·00

460 Alexandros Panagoulis (resistance leader)

1997. Anniversaries. Multicoloured.

2041	20d. Type **460** (20th death anniv (1996))	60	50
2042	30d. Grigorios Xenopoulos (writer, 130th birth anniv)	60	50
2043	40d. Odysseas Elytis (poet, first death anniv) (horiz)	60	50
2044	50d. Panayiotis Kanellopoulos (Prime Minister, 1945 and 1967, tenth death anniv (1996))	1·20	50
2045	100d. Harilaos Trikoupis (Prime Minister 1881–85, death centenary (1996)) (horiz)	2·50	95
2046	170d. Maria Callas (opera singer, 20th death anniv) (horiz)	4·00	1·50
2047	200d. Rigas Velestinlis-Feraios (revolutionary writer, death bicent (1998))	5·00	1·90

461 Vassilis Avlonitis

1997. Greek Actors. Multicoloured.

2048	20d. Type **461**	60	45
2049	30d. Vassilis Argyropoulos	60	45
2050	50d. Georgia Vassileiadou	60	45
2051	70d. Lambros Constantaras	60	45
2052	100d. Vassilis Logothetidis	1·70	1·40
2053	140d. Dionysis Papagiannopoulos	2·10	1·70
2054	170d. Nikos Stavrides	2·30	1·90
2055	200d. Mimis Fotopoulos	7·50	6·00

462 "Greece", Greek Flag and Colossus of Rhodes

1998. 50th Anniv of Incorporation of Dodecanese Islands into Greece. Multicoloured.

2056	100d. German commander signing surrender to British and Greek military authorities at Simi, 1945	1·70	1·40
2057	140d. Type **462**	2·10	1·70
2058	170d. Greek and British military representatives at transfer ceremony, Rhodes, 1947	2·30	1·90
2059	500d. Raising Greek flag, Kasos, 1947	7·00	5·50

463 Aghia Sofia Hospital, Athens

1998. Anniversaries and Events. Mult.

2060	20d. Type **463** (cent of Aghia Sofia Children's Hospital)	10	10
2061	100d. St. Xenophon's Monastery (millenary) (vert)	1·20	95
2062	140d. Woman in traditional costume (4th International Thracian Congress, Nea Orestiada) (vert)	1·70	1·40
2063	150d. Parthenon and congress emblem (International Cardiography Research Congress, Rhodes)	1·70	1·40
2064	170d. Sculpture of man and young boy (Cardiography Congress) (vert)	2·30	1·90
2065	500d. Emblem (50th anniv of Council of Europe) (vert)	8·25	6·50

464 Ancient Theatre, Epidavros

1998. Europa. National Festivals. Mult.

2066	140d. Type **464**	1·70	1·40
2067	500d. Festival in Herod Atticus Theatre, Athens	8·25	6·50

465 Players

1998. World Basketball Championship, Athens. Sheet 70×68 mm. containing T 465.

MS2068	300d. multicoloured	4·00	3·25

466 Ierapetra, Crete

1998. Castles (2nd series). Multicoloured.

2069	30d. Type **466**	10	10
2070	50d. Corfu	35	30
2071	70d. Limnos	45	35
2072	100d. Argolis	60	45
2073	150d. Iraklion, Crete	1·00	85
2074	170d. Naupaktos (vert)	1·20	95
2075	200d. Ioannina (vert)	1·30	1·00
2076	400d. Platamona	2·50	2·00
2077	550d. Karitainas (vert)	3·75	3·00
2078	600d. Fragkokastello, Crete	4·00	3·25

467 "Church of St. George of the Greeks" (18th-century copperplate)

1998. 500th Anniv of Greek Orthodox Community in Venice. Multicoloured.

2079	30d. Type **467**	25	20
2080	40d. "Christ Pantocrator" (icon) (vert)	60	45
2081	140d. Illuminated script of hymn "Epi Soi hairei" by Georgios Klontzas (vert)	1·70	1·40
2082	230d. "St. George of the Greeks" (illuminated manuscript, 1640)	3·00	2·30

468 Homer (poet)

1998. Ancient Greek Writers.

2083	**468**	20d. brown and gold	25	20
2084	-	100d. brown and gold	1·70	1·40
2085	-	140d. red and gold	2·30	1·90
2086	-	200d. black and gold	3·50	2·75
2087	-	250d. brown and gold	4·00	3·25

DESIGNS: No. 2084, Sophocles (poet); 2085, Thucydides (historian); 2086, Plato (philosopher); 2087, Demosthenes (orator).

469 Ancient Trireme and Circulation of Mediterranean Sea Currents

1999. International Year of the Ocean. Multicoloured.

2088	40d. Type **469**	25	20
2089	100d. Galleon (detail of icon "Thou art Great, O Lord" by I. Kornaros)	1·20	95
2090	200d. "Aigaio" (oceanographic vessel), astrolabe and seismic sounding of seabed	2·30	1·90
2091	500d. Apollo on ship (3rd-century B.C. silver tetradrachmon coin of Antigonus Dosonos)	4·75	3·75

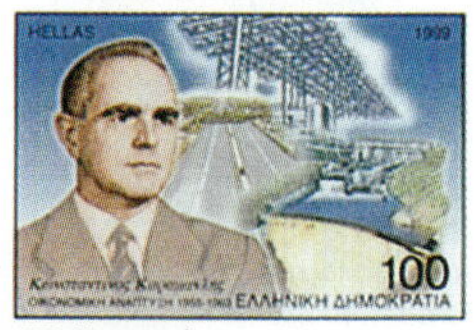

470 Karamanlis

1999. 1st Death Anniv of Konstantinos Karamanlis (Prime Minister 1955–63 and 1974; President 1980–85 and 1990–95). Multicoloured.

2092	100d. Type **470**	95	75
2093	170d. Karamanlis and jubilant crowd, 1974	1·40	1·10
2094	200d. Karamanlis and Council of Europe emblem, 1979	1·70	1·40
2095	500d. Karamanlis and Greek flag (vert)	4·00	3·25

471 Mt. Olympus and Flowers

1999. Europa. Parks and Gardens. Multicoloured.

2096	170d. Type **471**	1·40	1·10
2097	550d. Mt. Olympus and flowers (different)	5·00	4·00

Nos. 2096/7 were issued together, se-tenant, forming a composite design.

472 Ancient Greek and Japanese Noh Theatre Masks

1999. Centenary of Diplomatic Relations between Greece and Japan.

2098	**472**	120d. multicoloured	1·20	95

473 Temple of Hylates Apollo, Kourion

1999. Cyprus–Greece Joint Issue. 4000 Years of Greek Culture. Multicoloured.

2099	120d. Type **473**	95	75
2100	120d. Mycenaean pot depicting warriors (Athens)	95	75
2101	120d. Mycenaean crater depicting horse (Nicosia)	95	75
2102	120d. Temple of Apollo, Delphi	95	75

474 Trains

1999. 5th Anniv of Community Support Programme. Multicoloured.

2103	20d. Type **474** (modernization of railways)	25	20
2104	120d. Bridge over River Antirrio	95	75
2105	140d. Compact disk, delivery lorries and conveyor belt (modernization of Post Office)	1·20	95
2106	250d. Athens underground train	1·70	1·40
2107	500d. Control tower, Eleftherios Venizelos airport, Athens and Boeing 747	4·00	3·25

475 Agusta-Bell 201A Helicopter and Commandos in Inflatable Boat

1999. Armed Forces. Multicoloured.

2108	20d. Type **475**	25	20
2109	30d. Missile corvette	30	25
2110	40d. Lockheed Martin F-16 Fighting Falcons	35	30
2111	50d. Canadier CL-215 aircraft dispersing water on forest fire	45	35
2112	70d. Destroyer	60	45
2113	120d. Forces distributing aid in Bosnia	1·20	95
2114	170d. Dassault Mirage 2000 jet fighter above Aegean	1·70	1·40
2115	250d. Helicopters, tanks and soldiers on joint exercise	2·30	1·90
2116	600d. Submarine "Okeanos"	4·75	3·75

476 Birth of Christ

2000. Birth Bimillenary of Jesus Christ. Icons. Mult.

2117	20d. Type **476**	25	20
2118	50d. Discussion between men of different denominations	60	45
2119	120d. Angels praising God	95	75
2120	170d. Epiphany (horiz)	1·70	1·40
2121	200d. Communion (35×35 mm)	2·10	1·70
2122	500d. Heavenly beings above priests and worshippers (27×57 mm)	4·00	3·25

477 "Building Europe"

2000. Europa.

2123	**477**	170d. multicoloured	3·50	2·75

478 *Ilissos* (steamship)

2000. Ships. Multicoloured.

2124	10d. Type **478**	35	30
2125	120d. *Adrias* (destroyer)	80	65
2126	170d. *Ia II* (steamship)	1·70	1·40
2127	400d. *Vas Olga* (destroyer)	4·75	3·75

479 Rainbow over Village (Spyros Dalakos)

2000. "Stampin' the Future". Winning Entries in Children's International Painting Competition. Mult.

2128	130d. Type **479**	80	65
2129	180d. Robots (Moshovaki-Chaiger Ornella)	1·20	95
2130	200d. Cars and house (Zisis Zariotis)	2·10	1·70
2131	620d. Children astride rocket (Athina Limioudi)	5·25	4·25

480 Torch and Flag

2000. Olympic Games, Sydney. Multicoloured.

2132	200d. Type **480**	1·70	1·40
2133	650d. Torch, flag and Sydney Opera House	5·25	4·25

481 Emblem and Olympic Rings

2000. Olympic Games, Athens (2004) (1st issue).

2134	**481**	10d. multicoloured	25	20
2135	**481**	50d. multicoloured	60	45
2136	**481**	130d. multicoloured	80	65
2137	**481**	180d. multicoloured	1·70	1·40
2138	**481**	200d. multicoloured	2·30	1·90
2139	**481**	650d. multicoloured	4·75	3·75

See also Nos. **MS**2169, 2191/**MS**2196, 2207/10, **MS**2211, 2216/21, **MS**2222, 2234/8, **MS**2239, 2246/51, 2252/**MS**2258, 2259/63, 2264/**MS**2270, **MS**2271, **MS**2272, 2275/**MS**2279, **MS**2285 and 2286/**MS**2288.

482 Create 1901 1d. Stamp

2000. Centenary of First Create Stamp. Sheet 104×73 mm containing T 482 and similar vert designs. Multicoloured.

MS2140 200d. Type **482**; 650d. Create 1901 6d. stamp	17·00	16·00

483 Orpheus Christ (sculpture)

2000. Birth Bimillenary of Jesus Christ. Mult.

2141	20d. Type **483**	10	10
2142	30d. The Good Shepherd (sculpture)	25	20
2143	40d. Christ Pantocrator (mosaic, Holy Monastery of Sina)	35	30
2144	100d. Anapeson in the Protato of Mount Athos (fresco, Manuel Panselinos) (horiz)	60	45
2145	130d. Christ (icon)	80	65
2146	150d. Christ (icon)	95	75
2147	180d. Christ Pantocrator (Encaustic icon)	1·20	95
2148	1000d. Christ Pantocrator (Byzantine coin) (horiz)	8·75	7·00

484 Mother and Child holding Money Box

2001. Anniversaries and Events. Multicoloured.

2149	20d. Type **484** (centenary of Post Office Savings Bank)	25	20
2150	130d. Euro currency and emblem (centenary of Post Office Savings Bank) (horiz)	1·20	95
2151	140d. Refugees (50th anniv of United Nations High Commissioner for Refugees) (horiz)	1·50	1·20
2152	180d. Emblem and crowd (75th anniv of Thessalonika International Trade Fair)	1·70	1·40
2153	200d. University facade (75th anniv of Aristotle University, Thessalonika) (horiz)	2·00	1·60
2154	500d. Academy building (75th anniv of Academy of Athens) (horiz)	4·00	3·25
2155	700d. Ioannis Zigdis (politician, third death anniv)	7·00	5·50

485 Dried Earth

2001. Europa. Water Resources. Multicoloured.

2156	180d. Type **485**	2·30	1·90
2157	650d. Pool of water and droplet	5·75	4·75

486 Little Egret

2001. Flora and Fauna. Multicoloured.

2158	20d. Type **486**	10	10
2159	50d. White storks	35	30
2160	100d. Bearded vulture	70	55
2161	140d. Orchid (vert)	95	75
2162	150d. Dalmatian pelican (vert)	1·00	85
2163	200d. Lily, Plastina Lake, Karditsa	1·40	1·10
2164	700d. Egyptian vulture	4·75	3·75
2165	850d. Black vulture	11·50	9·25

487 Emblem

2001. New Name of Hellenic Post.

2166	**487**	140d. blue and yellow	95	75
2167	**487**	200d. blue	1·40	1·10

488 "The Annuciation" (13th century muniture Athens)

2001. 1700th Anniv of Christianity in Armenia.

MS2168 850d. multicoloured	8·75	7·00

489 Figures of Swimmers from Amphora

2001. Olympic Games, Athens (2004). Sheet 80×70 mm.

MS2169 1200d. multicoloured	11·50	9·25

490 Kamakaki, Salamina

2002. Traditional Dances. Multicoloured.

2170	2c. Type **490**	10	10
2171	3c. Prikia (bride's dowry)	10	10
2172	5c. Zagorissios, Epirus (vert)	10	10
2173	10c. Balos, Aegean Islands	25	20
2174	15c. Synkathistos, Thrace	35	30
2175	20c. Tsakonikos, Peloponnese (vert)	45	35
2176	30c. Pyrrichios (Sera) (Pontian Greek)	70	55
2177	35c. Fourles, Kythnos (vert)	80	65
2178	40c. Apokriatos, Skyros	95	75
2179	45c. Kotsari (Pontian Greek)	1·00	85
2180	50c. Pentozalis, Crete (vert)	1·20	95
2181	55c. Karagouna, Thessaly	1·30	1·00
2182	60c. Hassapiko, Smyrneikos	1·40	1·10
2183	65c. Zalistos, Naoussa	1·50	1·20
2184	85c. Pogonissios, Epirus	2·00	1·60
2185	€1 Kalamtianos, Peloponnese	2·30	1·90
2186	€2 Maleviziotis, Crete	4·75	3·75
2187	€2.15 Tsamikos, Roumeli	5·00	4·00
2188	€2.60 Zeibekikos (vert)	6·00	4·75
2189	€3 Nyfiatikos, Corfou	7·00	5·50
2190	€4 Paschaliatikos	9·25	7·50

491 Runners (vase painting)

2002. Olympics Games, Athens (2004) (3rd issue). Multicoloured.

2191	41c. Type **491**	1·20	95
2192	59c. Charioteer (8th-century bronze statuette) (vert)	1·70	1·40
2193	80c. Javelin thrower (vase painting)	2·00	1·60
2194	€2.05 Doryphoros ("Spear Bearer") (statue, Polycleitos) (vert)	4·75	3·75
2195	€2.35 Weightlifter (vase painting)	5·75	4·75
MS2196	121×80 mm. €5 "Crypt of the ancient Olympic stadium, Olympia" (49×29 mm)	13·00	12·00

492 Performing Elephant

2002. Europa. Circus. Multicoloured.
2197 60c. Type **492** 2·30 1·90
2198 €2.60 Equestrian acrobat 8·25 6·50

493 Navy Scout

2002. Scouts. Multicoloured.
2199 45c. Type **493** 1·00 85
2200 60c. Scout and World Conference emblem 1·40 1·10
2201 70c. Air scout and Cub scouts planting tree 1·60 1·30
2202 €2.15 Scouts, mountains and map 5·25 4·25

494 Fragment of 5th-century B.C. Tablet, Acropolis, Athens

2002. The Greek Language. Multicoloured.
2203 45c. Type **494** 1·00 85
2204 60c. 13th-century B.C. Linear B script tablet, Glay 1·40 1·10
2205 90c. Manuscript and General Makrygiannis (writer) 2·10 1·70
2206 €2.15 Manuscript and page from 11th-century Byzantine manuscript, Mount Athos 5·00 4·00

495 Man wearing Olive Wreath holding Two Ears of Corn

2002. Olympics Games, Athens (2004) (4th issue). Multicoloured.
2207 45c. Type **495** 1·00 85
2208 60c. Man wearing wreath and chewing ear of corn 1·40 1·10
2209 €2.15 Man beside column wearing wreath and chewing ear of corn 5·00 4·00
2210 €2.60 Man beside tilted column holding wreath 6·00 4·75

496 Facade

2002. Olympics Games, Athens (2004) (5th issue). Early Stadia. Sheet 120×75 mm.
MS2211 **496** €6 multicoloured 14·00 11·00

497 Chrysostomos Papadopoulos (1923–38)

2002. Archbishops of Athens. Multicoloured.
2212 10c. Type **497** 25 20
2213 45c. Chrysanthos Philippides (1938–41) 1·20 95
2214 €2.15 Damaskinos Papandreou (1941–49) 5·75 4·75
2215 €2.60 Seraphem Tikas (1974–98) 9·25 7·50

498 Discus

2003. Olympic Games, Athens (2004) (6th issue). Multicoloured.
2216 2c. Type **498** 10 10
2217 5c. Shot put 10 10
2218 47c. Javelin 1·20 95
2219 65c. High jump 1·50 1·20
2220 €2.17 Hurdles 5·00 4·00
2221 €2.85 Dumbbells 6·75 5·25

499 Athena (Girl Mascot)

2003. Olympic Games, Athens (2004) (7th issue). Sheet 128×82 mm containing T 499 and similar horiz design. Multicoloured.
MS2222 €2.50 Type **499**; €2.85 Phevos (boy mascot) 14·00 13·00

500 Globe

2003. Greetings Stamps. Sheet 123×124 containing T 500 and similar square designs. Multicoloured.
MS2223 47c. (a) Type **500** (corporate); 47c. (b) 2004 Olympics emblem (sponsor); 47c. (c) Man wearing wreath (Greece); 47c. (d) Roses (wedding); 47c. (e) Grid and skyline (corporate); 47c. (f) Stylized train (children); 47c. (g) Couple (social occasion); 65c. (h) Statue head (Greece); 65c. (i) Acropolis (Greece) 16·00 15·00

501 Swallow and European Stars

2003. Greek Presidency of the European Union. Multicoloured.
2224 47c. Type **501** 1·20 95
2225 65c. White Tower, Thessaloniki formed from letters 1·70 1·40
2226 €2.17 Swallows (fresco, Thera) 5·25 4·25
2227 €2.85 Stars and flags of member countries as jigsaw puzzle 7·00 5·50

502 Stylized Figure

2003. Europa. Poster Art. Multicoloured.
2228 65c. Type **502** 1·70 1·40
2229 €2.85 House with flag pole and veranda 7·00 5·50

503 Apple floating in Space and Trees

2003. Environmental Protection. Multicoloured.
2230 15c. Type **503** 35 30
2231 47c. Apple floating in water 1·20 95
2232 65c. Wreath above waves 1·60 1·30
2233 €2.85 Planet above apple tree 6·75 5·50

504 High Jump

2003. Olympic Games, Athens (2004) (8th issue). Multicoloured.
2234 5c. Type **504** 10 10
2235 47c. Wrestlers 1·20 95
2236 65c. Runners 1·50 1·20
2237 80c. Cyclists (vert) 1·90 1·50
2238 €4 Windsurfer (vert) 9·25 7·50

505 Athena (Girl Mascot)

2003. Olympic Games, Athens (2004) (9th issue). Sheet 128×80 mm containing T 505 and similar horiz design. Multicoloured.
MS2239 €2.50 Type **505**; €2.85 Phevos (boy mascot) 14·00 13·00

506 Stair Maker

2003. Traditional Trades and Crafts. Multicoloured.
2240 3c. Type **506** 10 10
2241 10c. Shoemaker 25 20
2242 50c. Smith 1·20 1·10
2243 €1 Type setter 2·50 2·20
2244 €1.40 Sponge diver 3·50 3·25
2245 €4 Hand weaver 10·00 9·00
MS2245a 115×149 mm. Nos. 2240/5 16·00 16·00

507 Weightlifting

2003. Olympic Games 2004, Athens (10th issue). Athletes. Multicoloured.
2246 20c. Type **507** 55 50
2247 30c. Throwing javelin 80 75
2248 40c. Charioteers 1·10 1·00
2249 47c. Soldier carrying spear and shield 1·30 1·20
2250 €2 Running 5·25 5·00
2251 €2.85 Throwing discus 7·50 7·00

508 Volos

2004. Olympic Games 2004, Athens (11th issue). Cities. Multicoloured.
2252 1c. Type **508** 10 10
2253 2c. Patra 10 10
2254 5c. Herakleio, Crete 10 10
2255 47c. Athens 1·20 1·20
2256 €1.40 Thessalonika 3·50 3·25
2257 €4 Athens 10·00 9·25
MS2258 120×135 mm. Nos. 2252/7 12·50 12·00

509 Spiros Louis

2004. Olympic Games 2004, Athens (12th issue). Greek Olympic Champions. Multicoloured.
2259 3c. Type **509** (marathon, 1896) 10 10
2260 10c. Aristides Konstantinides (cycling, 1896) 25 25
2261 €2 Ioannis Fokianos (modern Olympic pioneer) 5·00 4·75
2262 €2.17 Ioannis Mitropoulos (gymnast, 1896) 5·50 5·00
2263 €3.60 Konstantinos Tsiklitiras (long jump, 1912) 9·25 8·50

510 Swimming

2004. Olympic Games 2004, Athens (13th issue). Sport Disciplines. Multicoloured.
2264 5c. Type **510** 10 10
2265 10c. Hands applying rosin 25 25
2266 20c. Canoeing 45 40
2267 47c. Relay race 1·10 1·00
2268 €2 Gymnastics floor exercise (vert) 5·00 4·75
2269 €5 Gymnastics ring exercise (vert) 12·50 12·00
MS2270 162×140 mm. Nos. 2264/9 17·00 17·00

511 Woman holding Torch

2004. Olympic Games 2004, Athens (14th issue). Greetings Stamps. Sheet 90×75 mm containing T 511 and similar square design.
MS2271 47c. multicoloured 6·75 6·75

512 Dove and Olympic Rings

2004. Olympic Games 2004, Athens (15th issue). Sheet 128×81 mm containing T 512 and similar horiz design. Multicoloured.
MS2272 47c. Type **512**; €2.50 Dove and children 6·75 6·75

513 Yacht

2004. Europa. Holidays. Multicoloured.
2273 65c. Type **513** 1·40 1·30
2274 €2.85 Hot air balloon 6·00 5·50

514 Obverse and Reverse of 3 Drachma Coin (480—450 BC)

2004. Olympic Games, Athens 2004 (16th issue). Ancient Coins. Multicoloured.

2275	47c. Type **514**	1·20	1·10
2276	65c. Philip of Macedonia gold stater	1·60	1·50
2277	€2 Obverse and reverse of 2 drachma coin (460 BC)	4·75	4·50
2278	€2.17 Obverse and reverse of 4 drachma coin	5·25	5·00
MS2279	140×120 mm. Nos. 2275/8	12·00	11·00

515 Championship Trophy

2004. Greece—European Football Champions, 2004. Multicoloured.

2280	47c. Type **515**	1·20	1·10
2281	65c. Team members	1·60	1·50
2282	€1 Team members with raised arms	2·40	2·20
2283	€2.88 Outstretched hands and trophy	7·00	6·50
MS2284	160×135 mm. Nos. 2280/3	11·00	11·00

516 Sea

2004. Olympic Games, Athens 2004 (17th issue). Modern Art. Three sheets containing T 516 and similar multicoloured designs.

MS2285	(a) 120×80 mm. 50c. Type **516**; €2.50 Rainbow. (b) 120×80 mm. €1 Multicoloured paint brush and glass; €2 Roller making Greek flag. (c) 135×163 mm. As Nos. **MS**2285a/b	27·00	27·00

517 Temple of Heaven, Beijing

2004. Olympic Games, Athens 2004 (18th issue). Athens 2004—Beijing 2008. Multicoloured.

2286	50c. Type **517**	1·20	1·10
2287	65c. Parthenon, Athens	1·60	1·50
MS2288	90×120 mm. Nos. 2286/7	11·00	11·00

518 Athena and Phevos holding Athens 2004 Emblem

2004. Olymphilex 2004, International Olympic Stamp and Memorabilia Exhibition. Sheet 81×70 mm.

MS2289	€6 multicoloured	13·50	13·50

519 Thomas Bimis and Nikos Siranidis

2004. Greek Olympic Medal Winners. Multicoloured.

2290	65c. Type **519** (gold) (synchronised diving)	1·50	1·40
2292	65c. Ilias Iliadis (gold) (judo)	1·50	1·40
2293	65c. Emilia Tsoulfa and Sofia Bekatorou (gold) (women's sailing)	1·50	1·40
2294	65c. Pyrros Dimas (bronze) (weight lifting)	1·50	1·40
2295	65c. Dimosthenis Tabacos (gold) (gymnastics)	1·50	1·40
2296	65c. Anastasia Kelesidou (silver) (discus)	1·50	1·40
2297	65c. Vasilis Polymeros and Nikos Skiathitis (bronze) (rowing)	1·50	1·40
2298	65c. Athanasia Tzoumeleka (gold) (20km.walk)	1·50	1·40
2299	65c. Chrysopigi Devezi (silver) (triple jump)	1·50	1·40
2300	65c. Fani Chalkia (gold) (400m. hurdles)	1·50	1·40
2301	65c. Nikos Kaklamanakis (silver) (sailing)	1·50	1·40
2302	65c. Artiom Kiourgian (bronze) (Greco-roman wrestling)	1·50	1·40
2303	65c. Women's water polo team (silver)	1·50	1·40
2304	65c. Mirela Maniani (bronze) (women's javelin)	1·50	1·40
2305	65c. Elisavet Mystakidou (silver) (women's Taekwondo)	1·50	1·40
2306	65c. Alexandros Nikolaidis (silver) (men's Taekwondo)	1·50	1·40

No. 2291 was later withdrawn from circulation when the athlete, Leonidas Sampanis, was stripped of his medal after failing a drug test.

520 Horse Riders

2004. Paralympics. Multicoloured.

2307	20c. Type **520**	50	50
2308	49c. Disabled runner	1·30	1·20
2309	€2 Wheelchair basket ball players	5·00	4·75
2310	€2.24 Wheelchair archer	6·00	5·50

521 Santorini

2004. Tourism. Greek Islands. Multicoloured.

2311	2c. Type **521**	15	10
2312	3c. Karpathos	15	10
2313	5c. Crete – Vai	15	10
2314	10c. Mykonos	25	25
2315	49c. Chania	1·30	1·20
2316	50c. Kastelorizo	1·30	1·20
2317	€1 Astypalaia	2·50	2·40
2318	€2 Serifos	5·00	4·75
2319	€2.24 Milos	5·75	5·50
2320	€4 Skiathos	10·00	9·50

522 Necklace (730 BC)

2005. Jewellery. Multicoloured.

2321	1c. Type **522**	15	10
2322	15c. Snake-shaped bracelet (2nd—3rd century BC) (vert)	40	35
2323	30c. Necklace with bulls head pendant (5th century)	75	70
2324	49c. Central part of crown (2nd century)	1·30	1·20
2325	€4 Earring (8th century BC) (vert)	10·00	9·50

523 Formula Diagram and "E=mc²" (75th anniv of State Laboratory)

2005. Anniversaries and Events. Multicoloured.

2326	1c. Type **523**	15	10
2327	4c. Sugar cubes and stop sign (41st European Association for Diabetes Meeting) (horiz)	15	10
2328	5c. Electrocardiogram chart and heart (54th European Society for Cardiovascular Surgery Congress) (horiz)	15	10
2329	40c. I. Kondilakis (first president) (90th anniv of ESIA (journalists' union of Athens)	1·00	95
2330	49c. Emblem (2005—Year of Economic Competitiveness)	1·30	1·20
2331	€1.40 Woman examining breast (25th anniv of Senologic Hellenic Society)	3·50	3·25
2332	€3.50 Angel (painting, Alekos Kontopoylos) (birth centenary) (horiz)	9·25	8·75

524 *Gladiolus illyricus*

2005. Flowers. Multicoloured.

2333	20c. Type **524**	50	50
2334	40c. *Crocus sieberi*	1·00	95
2335	49c. *Narcissus tazetta*	1·30	1·20
2336	€1.40 *Rhododendron luteum*	3·50	3·25
2337	€3 *Tulipa boetica*	7·75	7·25

525 *Agiorgitiko Peloponnese*

2005. Wine. Grape varieties. Multicoloured.

2338	20c. Type **525**	50	50
2339	49c. White grapes on cloth (*Assyrtiko Santorini*)	1·30	1·20
2340	65c. Black grapes and coin (*Xinomavro Macedonia*)	1·70	1·60
2341	€2.24 White grapes and barrel (*Robola Kefalonia*)	5·75	5·50
2342	€2.40 Black grapes (*Moschofilero Peloponnese*)	6·25	5·75

526 Dakos

2005. Europa. Gastronomy. Multicoloured.

2343	65c. Type **526**	1·70	1·60
2344	€2.35 Rusk, tomato, herbs, oil and feta cheese	6·00	5·75

Nos. 2343/4 were issued together, se-tenant, forming a composite design.

527 Blackboard

2005. Greetings Stamps. Multicoloured.

2345	49c. Type **527**	1·30	1·20
2346	49c. Envelopes	1·30	1·20
2347	49c. Girl reading	1·30	1·20
2348	49c. Globe and stamp	1·30	1·20
2349	49c. Grid	1·30	1·20
2350	49c. Flowers	1·30	1·20
2351	49c. Figures	1·30	1·20
2352	65c. Church	1·70	1·60

528 Rocket and Mountaineers (Fokion Dimitriadis)

2005. Caricatures. Multicoloured.

2353	15c. Type **528**	40	35
2354	20c. Woman and man (Archelaus)	60	55
2355	30c. Stick figure (Themos Annios)	75	70
2356	50c. Man tying woman's shoe (Dimitris Galanis)	1·30	1·20
2357	65c. Chef icing globe with atomic rocket (Kostas Mitropoulis)	1·70	1·60
2358	€4 Stylized couple (vase painting) (Asteas)	10·00	9·50

529 Two Players, Referee and Ball

2005. Greece—European Basketball Champions, 2005 (Eurobasket 2005, Belgrade). Multicoloured.

2359	30c. Type **529**	75	70
2360	50c. Trophy	1·30	1·20
2361	65c. Team members	1·70	1·60
2362	€3.55 Holding trophy aloft	9·00	8·50
MS2363	165×138 mm. Nos. 2359/62	11·50	11·50

530 Mini Cooper

2005. Cars. Multicoloured.

2364	1c. Type **530**	15	10
2365	30c. Fiat 500	75	70
2366	50c. Citroen 2CV	1·30	1·20
2367	€2.25 Volkswagen Beetle	5·75	5·50
2368	€2.85 Ford Model T	7·50	7·00

531 Ethnikos Sports Club Emblem

2005. Sports Clubs. Multicoloured.

2369	30c. Type **531**	75	70
2370	50c. Panionios Football Club	1·30	1·20
2371	50c. Iraklis Football Club	1·30	1·20
2372	50c. Panathinakos Football Club	1·30	1·20
2373	65c. PAOK Football Club	1·70	1·60
2374	65c. Panellinios Sports Club	1·70	1·60
2375	€4 Omilos Ereton Athletics Club	10·00	9·50

532 Virgin and Child ("Hodeghetria")

2005. Christmas. Icons. Multicoloured.

2376	1c. Type **532**	25	25
2377	20c. "Kardiotissa"	50	50
2378	70c. "Glykophiloussa"	1·80	1·70
2379	€3.20 Virgin, Child and symbols of the Passion	8·25	7·75

533 Building Facade

2006. 50th Anniv of Europa Stamps. Sheet 105×81 mm containing T 533 and similar horiz design.

MS2380	€1.50 Type **533**; €2.50 As No. 1617	13·00	12·00

534 "Ancient Drama" (Dionisis Fotopoulos)

2006. Patras—European Capital of Culture—2006. Multicoloured.

2381	1c. Type **534**	15	10
2382	15c. "Travelling" (Dimitris Milionis)	25	25
2383	20c. "Child and Art" (Rania Kapeliari)	50	50
2384	50c. "Carnival" (Charis Pressas)	1·30	1·20
2385	65c. Patras—2006 emblem (vert)	1·70	1·60
2386	€2.25 "Poetry and Music" (Kelly Mendrinou)	5·50	5·25
2387	€2.30 Icon (vert)	5·75	5·50

535 Kouros of Anavissos (National Archaeological Museum)

2006. Museum Exhibits. Multicoloured.

2388	5c. Type **535**	15	10
2389	20c. Marble seated figure (Museum of Cycladic Art, Athens)	50	50
2390	50c. Spiral (29×30 mm)	1·30	1·20
2391	65c. Parthenon pediment (Acropolis Museum) (horiz)	1·70	1·60
2392	€1.40 Antinopolis (painting) (Benaki Museum, Athens)	3·50	3·25
2393	€2.25 *Concert of the Angels* (Domenicos Theotokopoulos) (National Art Gallery) (horiz)	5·75	5·50

536 As Type **21**

2006. Centenary of Intercalated Olympic Games, Athens. T 536 and similar horiz designs showing 1906 stamps "Second Olympic Games Issue, Athens". Multicoloured.

MS2394	Two sheets, each 105×81 mm. (a) 20c. Type **536**; 30c. As Type **25**; 50c. As Type **22**; €2. As Type **26**; (b) 50c. As Type **23**; 65c. As Type **27**; 85c. As Type **28**; €1. As Type **24**	13·50	13·50

537 Moon and Multicoloured Twisted Strands

2006. Europa. Integration. Multicoloured.

2395	65c. Type **537**	1·50	1·40
2396	€3 Green twisted strands and sun	7·00	6·50

538 Book and Archive Building (90th anniv of state archives)

2006. Anniversaries and Events. Multicoloured.

2397	15c. Type **538**	40	35
2398	20c. European stars (25th anniv of membership of EU)	50	50
2399	50c. Circle of squares (Eurovision Song Contest, Athens)	1·30	1·20
2400	65c. Olive tree (2006—Year of Olive Oil and Olives)	1·70	1·60
2401	€1.40 Tinia (god)	3·50	3·25
2402	€3 Council chamber (Greece's participation in UN Security Council 2005—2006)	7·00	6·50

539 Lesvos

2006. Tourism. Greek Islands. Multicoloured.

2403	1c. Type **539**	15	10
2404	3c. Hydra	15	10
2405	10c. Sifnos	15	10
2406	20c. Lefkada	20	20
2407	40c. Samothrace	1·00	95
2408	50c. Syros	1·30	1·20
2409	65c. Rhodes (30×30 mm)	1·70	1·60
2410	85c. Cephalonia	2·20	2·00
2411	€2.25 Corfu	5·00	4·75
2412	€5 Naxos	11·50	11·00

540 "Olympias" (trireme)

2006. Ancient Technology. Multicoloured.

2413	3c. Type **540**	15	10
2414	5c. 1st-century odometer (Heron of Alexandria)	15	10
2415	50c. 3rd-century piston water pump (Ktesibius) (vert)	1·30	1·20
2416	65c. The Antikythera mechanism, 80 B.C. (vert)	1·70	1·60
2417	€3.80 1st-century automatic temple gates (Heron of Alexandria) (vert)	9·50	9·00

541 Team members (left)

2006. Greece—World Basketball Championship Silver Medallists. Sheet 105×81 mm containing T 541 and similar horiz designs. Multicoloured.

MS2418	50c. Medal; €2 Type **541**; €3 Team members (right)	12·50	12·50

The stamps and margins of **MS**2417 form a composite design.

542 Apollon Kalamarias

2007. Sports Clubs. Multicoloured.

2419	2c. Type **542**	15	10
2420	3c. Atromitos Athinon	15	10
2421	52c. Aris Thessalonikis	1·30	1·20
2422	€2.27 Ethnikos Peiraio	5·75	5·50
2423	€3.20 Apollon Smirnis	8·25	7·75

543 Bleuette (doll, 1905)

2007. Children's Toys. Multicoloured.

2424	5c. Type **543**	10	10
2425	15c. Wooden aircraft (1940—5)	35	35
2426	30c. Paper Mache head dolls (1925—30)	70	65
2427	40c. Wheeled horses and cat (1920—90)	95	90
2428	52c. Clockwork cat, wheeled duck and dominoes (1930—60)	1·30	1·20
2429	72c. Parachutist (c 1950) (vert)	1·80	1·70
2430	€2.27 Airplane carousel (c. 1950) (vert)	6·75	6·25
2431	€4 Puppet show of the Resistance (1941—5) (vert)	9·50	9·00

544 Faces

2007. Greetings Stamps. Multicoloured.

2432	52c. Type **544**	1·30	1·20
2433	52c. Crescents	1·30	1·20
2434	52c. Artemis	1·30	1·20
2435	52c. Earth from space	1·30	1·20
2436	52c. Globe	1·30	1·20
2437	65c. Parthenon	1·60	1·50
2438	65c. Kore Phrasikleia	1·60	1·50
MS2439	118×122 mm. Nos. 2432/8	12·00	11·00

545 Costis Palamas (poet and critic) (engraving by Giannis Gourzis)

2007. Anniversaries and Events. Multicoloured.

2440	2c. Type **545**	10	10
2441	10c. Poseidon and head with gold mask (Year of Greece in China) (horiz)	20	20
2442	20c. Emblem (1st Symposium of Seven Wise Men in Cardiovascular Surgery, Athens and Delphi)	45	40
2443	52c. Figures with arms raised (2nd UNI Postal Global Union World Conference, Athens) (horiz)	1·20	1·20
2444	65c. Rainbow and stars (50th anniv of Treaty of Rome)	1·50	1·40
2445	85c. Georgios Kotzias (30th death anniv)	1·90	1·80
2446	€1 Rigas Velestinlis (revolutionary) (engraving by Giannis Gourzis) (250th birth anniv)	2·20	2·10
2447	€2.27 Light bulb as air balloon (2007–year of innovation)	5·00	4·75
2448	€3 Blind justice (125th anniv of Legal Council of State) (horiz)	6·75	6·25

546 Scorpio

2007. Western Zodiac. Multicoloured.

2449	2c. Type **546**	10	10
2450	3c. Cancer	10	10
2451	5c. Capricorn	10	10
2452	10c. Taurus	20	20
2453	20c. Sagittarius (*vert*)	45	40
2454	40c. Leo (*vert*)	90	85
2455	52c. Virgo (*vert*)	1·20	1·20
2456	65c. Aries	1·50	1·40
2457	85c. Aquarius	1·90	1·80
2458	€1 Libra	2·20	2·10
2459	€2.27 Pisces	5·00	4·75
2460	€2.80 Gemini	6·25	5·75

547 Emblem and Part of Dove

2007. Europa. Centenary of Scouting. Multicoloured.

2461	65c. Type **547**	1·50	1·40
2462	€3.15 Part of Dove and scouts	7·00	6·50

Nos. 2461/2 were issued together, se-tenant, forming a composite design.

548 Asclepius (statue) (Ampuria Museum, Spain)

2007. Asclepius (demigod of medicine). Sheet 120×76 mm containing T 548 and similar vert design. Multicoloured.

MS2463	€2.50×2, Type **548**; Asclepius (head) (National Archaeological Museum)	11·00	11·00

549 Basilica of San Clemente, Rome

2007. Anniversaries and Events. Multicoloured.

2464	2c. Type **549** (150th anniv of excavation and discovery of St Cyril's grave)	10	10
2465	3c. Emblem (50th anniv of University of Macedonia)	10	10
2466	€4 Konstantinos Tsatsos (politician and writer) (president 1975–1980) (50th death anniv) (vert)	10·50	9·75

550 Ergotelis Sports Club

2007. Sports Clubs. Multicoloured.

2467	2c. Type **550**	10	10
2468	4c. OFI Football Club	10	10
2469	54c. Olympiacos Club of Fans of Piraeus (umbrella organization)	1·30	1·20
2470	€2.29 Doxa Dramas Sports Club	5·75	5·25
2471	€5 Mytilini Nautical Club	12·00	11·00

551 *Aphrodite* (Greek)

2007. Statues. Multicoloured.

2472	54c. Type **551**	1·40	1·30
2473	€2.40 *Anahit* (Armenian)	6·00	5·50

Stamps of the same design were issued by Armenia.

552 Chios

2008. Islands. Multicoloured.

2474	2c. Type **552**	10	10
2475	5c. Amorgos	10	10
2476	10c. Nissiros	25	20
2477	20c. Paxi	50	45
2478	40c. Leros	95	90
2479	54c. Kalymnos	1·30	1·20
2480	67c. Kos	1·70	1·60
2481	€1 Simi	2·40	2·20
2482	€2.29 Zakynthos	5·50	5·25
2483	€4 Inousses	9·50	9·00

553 Discus Thrower

2008. Olympic Games, Beijing. Multicoloured.

2494	3c. Type **553**	15	15
2495	35c. Lighting Olympic flame	95	90
2496	67c. Cyclist (horiz)	1·90	1·80
2497	67c. Torch relay	1·90	1·80

554 Heart

2008. Personal Stamps. Multicoloured.

2498	54c. Type **554**	1·60	1·50
2499	54c. Kites	1·60	1·50
2500	54c. Digital symbols	1·60	1·50
2501	54c. Letter	1·60	1·50
2502	67c. Flag	2·00	1·90
2503	67c. Pillar and capitol	2·00	1·90
MS2504	120×122 mm. Nos. 2498/503	9·50	9·00

555 Ink bottle, Pen and Letters

2008. Europa. The Letter. Multicoloured.

2505	67c. Type **555**	1·90	1·80
2506	€3.17 Letter, script and pen	8·25	7·75

Nos. 2505/6 were issued together,se-tenant, forming a composite design.

556 Emblem

2008. Anniversaries. Multicoloured.

2507	3c. Type **556** (180th anniv of Hellenic Post)	15	15
2508	5c. Symbols of Greece (180th anniv of Hellenic Post)	15	15
2509	10c. Ioannis Kapodistrias (180th anniv of his election as first head of state of newly-liberated Greece)	25	25
2510	57c. Dimitris Rodopoulos (M. Karagatsis) (writer) (birth centenary)	1·60	1·50
2511	70c. Fish (International Year of Planet Earth)	2·00	1·90
2512	€1.85 50	5·50	5·00
2513	€3 Emblem (centenary of National Council of Women)	8·25	7·75

557 Feta Cheese

2008. Traditional Products. Multicoloured.

2514	3c. Type **557**	15	15
2515	5c. Mastic gum from Chios	15	15
2516	20c. Olive oil (horiz)	55	50
2517	57c. Ouzo spirit	1·60	1·50
2518	€1 Pistachio nuts from Aigina	3·00	2·75
2519	€4 Honey	11·00	10·00

558 Diagoras Rhodos Sports Club

2008. Sports Clubs. Multicoloured.

2520	40c. Type **558**	1·40	1·30
2521	57c. AEK Football Club	1·90	1·80
2522	70c. Asteras Tripolis Football Club	2·30	2·20
2523	€2 Panserraikos Football Club	6·25	6·00
2524	€3 Keriraikos Sports Club	8·75	8·25

559 Alexander the Great and the Mermaid

2008. Fairy Tales. Multicoloured.

2525	10c. Type **559**	25	20
2526	57c. Little Red Riding Hood	1·60	1·50
2527	€1 The Fairies	3·00	2·75
2528	€1.85 The Girl and the Matches	5·50	5·00
2529	€3 Arion and the Lyre	8·75	8·50

560 Manos Katrakis

2009. Actors. Multicoloured.

2530	1c. Type **560**	10	10
2531	20c. Dinos Iliopoulos	55	50
2532	35c. Elli Lambeti	95	90
2533	40c. Alekos Alexandrakis	95	90
2534	50c. Aliki Vougiouklaki	1·20	1·10
2535	57c. Jenny Karezi	1·60	1·50
2536	€1 Dimitris Horn	3·00	3·75
2537	€2.42 Nikos Kourkoulos	5·75	5·25
2538	€3.50 Thanos Kotsopoulos	9·75	9·25
MS2539	153×148 mm. Nos. 2530/8	24·00	23·00

561 Sivitanidios School

2009. Anniversaries and Events. Multicoloured.

2540	5c. Type **561** (80th anniv)	15	10
2541	10c. Emblem (70th anniv of University of Piraeus) (vert)	25	15
2542	20c. Exhibits (180th anniv of National Archaeological Museum)	30	20
2543	50c. Dove carrying envelope (Greek presidency of UPU Postal Operations Council)	1·30	1·10
2544	57c. Braille (birth bicentenary of Louis Braille (inventor of Braille writing for the blind))	1·70	1·50
2545	70c. €	2·50	2·30
2546	€2.42 Lord Byron (engraving) (Philhellenism and International Solidarity Day) (vert)	5·75	5·25
2547	€3 Buildings (National Real Estate Registry)	9·00	8·50
MS2548	80×121 mm. €1×2, Polar ice; Water (Preserve Polar Regions and Glaciers) (30×30 mm (circular))	6·00	6·00

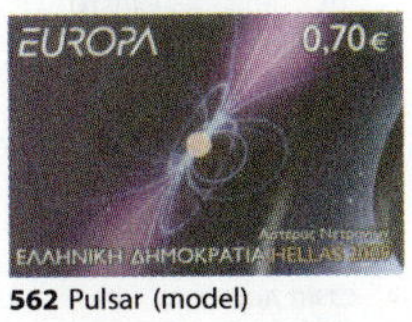

562 Pulsar (model)

2009. Europa. Astronomy. Multicoloured.

2549	70c. Type **562**	2·00	1·70
2550	€3.20 *Aristarchos* telescope	9·00	8·50
2551	70c. As Type **562**	2·00	1·70
2552	€3.20 As No. 2550	9·00	8·50

Nos. 2549/50 were printed, se-tenant, each pair forming a composite design.

563 Acropolis

2009. Greek Monuments of World Cultural Heritage. Multicoloured.

2553	57c. Type **563**	1·60	1·30
2554	57c. Meteora	1·60	1·30
2555	70c. Delphi	1·90	1·70
2556	70c. Mycenae	1·90	1·70
2557	€2 Mystras	5·25	4·75
2558	€3 Delos	8·75	8·25
MS2559	146×136 mm. Nos. 2553/8	21·00	21·00

564 Lighthouse, Didmi Islet, Gaidouronisi

2009. Lighthouses. Multicoloured.

2560	1c. Type **564**	25	15
2561	57c. Tourlitis, Andros	1·60	1·40
2562	70c. Chania	2·30	2·00
2563	€1 Korakas, Paros (horiz)	3·25	3·00
2564	€4.20 Strongyli, Kastellorizo (horiz)	11·50	11·00
MS2565	150×133 mm. Nos. 2560/4	21·00	21·00

565 Minotaur

2009. Myths and Legends. Multicoloured.

2566	1c. Type **565**	25	20
2567	5c. Triton	40	30
2568	57c. Sirens	1·60	1·40
2569	70c. Dioskouroi	2·30	2·10
2570	€5 Pegasus	15·00	14·50

566 Adult and Child's Hands

2009. Rights of the Child. Multicoloured.

2571	20c. Type **566**	55	45
2572	58c. Small girl leaning against wall (horiz)	1·90	1·70
2573	72c. Adults and chilldren's hands linked in circle (horiz)	2·30	2·10
2574	€1 Silhouette of child at window	3·25	3·00
2575	€4 Child's profile against dark background	11·00	10·50

567 2009 European Basketball Championship Gold Medal (men's under-20 team)

2009. Basketball. Three sheets, each 105×81 mm containing T 567 and similar horiz designs showing medals won by Greek athletes in 2009. Multicoloured.

MS2576	Type **567**	6·00	6·00
MS2577	World Championship silver medal (men's under-19 team)	6·00	6·00
MS2578	European Championship bronze medal (men's team)	6·00	6·00

568 *Stuffed Head* (Giannis Gaitis)

2010. Modern Greek Art. Multicoloured.

2579	1c. Type **568**	20	10
2580	5c. *Orpheus, Hermes and Eurydice* (Nikos Engonopoulos)	30	20
2581	50c. *Erotic* (Yannis Moralis)	1·50	1·20
2582	58c. *Sailor at Table* (Yannis Tsarouchis)	1·90	1·60
2583	€2.43 *Wattle Fences* (Nikos Hadjikyriakos-Ghika)	6·00	5·50
2584	€3 *The Drawing* (Diamantis Diamantopoulos)	9·25	8·75
MS2585	148×135 mm. Nos. 2579/84	19·00	10·00

CHARITY TAX STAMPS

C38 Dying Soldier, Widow and Child

1914. Roul.

C269	**C38**	2l. red	65	40
C270	**C38**	5l. blue	75	50

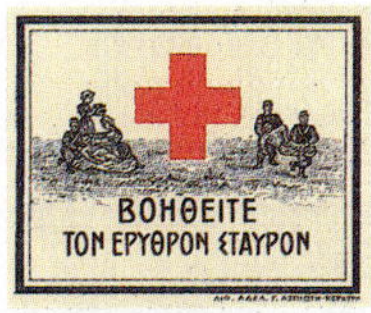

C39 Red Cross, Nurses, Wounded and Bearers

1915. Red Cross. Roul.

C271	**C39**	(5l.) red and blue	21·00	2·40

C40 Greek Women's Patriotic League Badge

1915. Greek Women's Patriotic League.

C272	**C40**	(5l.) red and blue	1·40	1·30

K. Π.
λεπτοῦ
1
(C 42)

1917. Surch as Type C 42.

C297	**15**	1 on 1l. brown	1·10	4·25
C299	**15**	5 on 1l. brown	2·20	2·10
C300	**15**	5 on 20l. mauve	35	2·50
C301	**15**	10 on 30l. purple	65	2·10
C302	**15**	30 on 30l. purple	1·10	2·30
C303	**15**	1 on 3l. orange	35	65
C304	**15**	5 on 40l. brown	60	1·60
C305	**15**	5 on 50l. lake	55	1·60
C306	**17**	5 on 1d. black	1·10	4·25
C307	**36**	5 on 25l. blue	20	50
C308	**36**	5 on 40l. blue	20	30
C309	**35**	5 on 50l. blue	22·00	31·00

K. Π.
λεπτοῦ
1
(C 44)

1917. Fiscal stamps surch as Type C 44. Roul.

C310	**C43**	1l. on 10l. blue	1·10	2·10
C311	**C43**	1l. on 80l. blue	1·10	2·10

C312	C43	5l. on 60l. blue	8·75	10·50
C313	C43	5l. on 80l. blue	4·25	3·25
C315	C43	10l. on 90l. blue	22·00	50·00
C316	C43	20l. on 20l. blue	£8000	£7000
C317	C43	20l. on 30l. blue	11·00	12·50
C318	C43	20l. on 40l. blue	27·00	31·00
C319	C43	20l. on 50l. blue	13·00	16·00
C320	C43	20l. on 60l. blue	£550	
C321	C43	20l. on 80l. blue	£130	
C322	C43	20l. on 90l. blue	7·50	12·50
C326	C43	10l. on 70l. blue	11·00	26·00
C328	C43	1l. on 50l. purple	1·10	2·10
C329	C43	5l. on 10l. blue	1·10	2·10
C330	C43	5l. on 10l. purple	1·10	2·10
C331	C43	10l. on 50l. purple	12·00	19·00
C333	C43	20l. on 2d. blue	15·00	26·00

Κ.Π.
10 ΛΕΠΤΑ 10

(C 46)

1917. Fiscal stamps surch as Type C 46. Roul.

C334	1l. on 10l. blue	1·60	1·60
C335	5l. on 50l. blue	70·00	£120
C338	10l. on 50l. blue	15·00	12·50
C339	20l. on 50l. blue	35·00	29·00
C340	30l. on 50l. blue	26·00	21·00
C341	5l. on 10l. purple & red	13·00	18·00

C48 Wounded Soldier

1918. Red Cross. Roul.

C342	C48	5l. red, blue and yellow	11·00	1·60

1918. Optd P.I.P. in Greek.

C343	5l. red, blue and yellow	16·00	1·60

C49

1922. Greek Women's Patriotic League. Surch as in Type C 49.

C344	C49	5l. on 10l. red and blue	£375	16·00
C345	C49	5l. on 20l. red and blue	£120	80·00
C346	C49	5l. on 50l. red and blue	£375	£275
C347	C49	5l. on 1d. red and blue	11·00	75·00

Nos. C344/7 were not issued without surcharge.

1924. Red Cross. As Type C 48 but wounded soldier and family.

C406	10l. red, blue and yellow	80	50

C77 St. Demetrius

1934. Salonika Int Exn Fund.

C478	C77	20l. brown	65	20

C78 Allegory of Health

1934. Postal Staff Anti-tuberculosis Fund.

C480	C78	10l. orange and green	25	20
C481	C78	20l. orange and blue	55	30
C482	C78	50l. orange and green	4·50	3·75

1935. As Type C 78 but with country inscription at top.

C494	10l. orange and green	65	50
C495	20l. orange and blue	1·10	80
C496	50l. orange and green	2·75	2·50
C497	50l. orange and brown	75	45

ΠΡΟΝΟΙΑ

(C 85)

1937. Nos. D273 and 415 optd with Type C 85.

C498	D20	10l. red	1·90	30
C500	51	50l. violet	1·10	30

Λ.50
ΠΡΟΝΟΙΑ

(C 95)

1938. Surch with Type C 95.

C521	D20	50l. on 5l. green	7·50	1·00
C522	D20	50l. on 20l. slate	7·50	1·00
C523	52	50l. on 20l. violet	1·10	85

C96 Queens Olga and Sophia

1939

C524	C96	10l. red	20	10
C525	C96	50l. green	35	15
C526	C96	1d. blue	55	30

ΠΡΟΣΤΑΣΙΑ ΦΥΜΑΤΙΚΩΝ ΤΤΤ

(C 104)

1940. Postal staff Anti-tuberculosis Fund. Optd with Type C 104.

C554	50l. green	45	30

Κ.Π.
λεπτῶν
50

(C 105)

1941. Social Funds. No. 410 surch with Type C 105.

C561	51	50l. on 5l. green	45	35

1941. Postal Staff Anti-tuberculosis Fund. Surch 50 and bars.

C562	C78	50l. on 10l.	2·10	9·50
C563	-	50l. on 10l. (No. C494)	40	20

ΔΡ. 1

(C 107)

1942. Sample Fair, Salonika. No. C478 surch with Type C 107.

C573	C77	1d. on 20l. brown	45	10

ΦΥΜ· Τ.Τ.Τ.
10 ΔΡ.

(C 109)

1942. Postal Staff Anti-tuberculosis Fund. Nos. 410 and 413 surch with Type C 109.

C591	51	10d. on 5l. green	35	25
C592	51	10l. on 25l. green	35	25

ΦΥΜ· Τ.Τ.Τ.

(C 111)

1944. Postal Staff Anti-tuberculosis Fund. No. 580 optd with Type C 111.

C599	100d. black	25	25

ΦΥΜ· Τ.Τ.Τ.
ΔΡ. 5000

(C 112)

1944. Postal Staff Anti-tuberculosis Fund. No. 579 surch with Type C 112.

C600	5000d. on 75d. red	25	40

ΥΠΕΡ ΤΩΝ
ΦΥΜΑΤΙΚΩΝ Τ.Τ.Τ.
ΔΡΧ.
25.000

(C 113)

1944. Postal Staff Anti-tuberculosis Fund. Surch as Type C 113.

C605	106	25,000d. on 2d.	60	70
C619	-	1d. on 40l. (No. 500)	25	15
C620	-	2d. on 40l. (No. 500)	25	15

ΠΡΟΝΟΙΑ
ΠΡΟΣΩΠΙΚΟΥ Τ.Τ.Τ.
ΔΡΑΧΜΑΙ 50

(C 117)

1946. Postal Staff Anti-tuberculosis Fund. Surch as Type C 117.

C640	C117	20d. on 5l.	1·60	65
C641	C117	20d. on 40l. (No. 500)	65	20

1946. Red Cross. Surch as Type C 117.

C642	C96	50d. on 50l. (No. C525)	70	30

1946. Social Funds. Surch as Type C 117.

C643	50d. on 1d. (No. C526)	55	30

ΔΡ. — 50

(C 123)

1947. Postal Staff Anti-tuberculosis Fund. Additionally surch with T C 123.

C659	50d. on 50l. (C525)	70·00	
C660	50l. on 50d. (C554)	4·50	50

1948. Church Restoration Fund.

C682	C127	50d. brown	35	25

1950. Postal Staff Anti-tuberculosis Fund. Surch with Type C 117.

C686	50d. on 10l. (No. 498)	2·50	50

ΠΡΟΝΟΙΑ
ΤΑΧ. ΥΠΑΛΛΗΛΩΝ
ΔΡΑΧΜΑΙ 50

(C 136)

1951. Postal Staff Welfare Fund. Surch with Type C 136.

C698	86	50d. on 5l. blue & brown	3·00	40

1951. Postal Staff Anti-tuberculosis Fund. Surch with Cross of Lorraine and 50.

C699	89	50d. on 3d. brown	1·60	20

ΠΡΟΣΘΕΤΟΝ
ΔΡ. 100

(C 139)

1952. State Welfare Fund. No. 509 surch with Type C 139.

C706	100d. on 8d. blue	1·80	20

C140 Argostoli, Cephalonia

1953. Ionian Is. Earthquake Fund.

C713	-	300d. slate	3·25	15
C714	C 140	500d. brown & yellow	3·50	90

DESIGN: 300d. Church of Faneromeni, Zante.

C148 Zeus (Macedonian Coin of Philip II)

1956. Macedonian Cultural Fund.

C761	C148	50l. red	1·90	60
C762	-	1d. blue (Aristotle)	6·25	1·50

POSTAGE DUE STAMPS

D2

1875

D73A	D2	1l. green and black	1·90	2·10
D74A	D2	2l. green and black	2·40	2·10
D75A	D2	5l. green and black	2·40	2·10
D78A	D2	40l. green and black	18·00	18·00
D80A	D2	70l. green and black	18·00	18·00
D81A	D2	80l. green and black	22·00	21·00
D82A	D2	90l. green and black	18·00	18·00
D83A	D2	1d. green and black	18·00	18·00
D84A	D2	2d. green and black	27·00	26·00
D88	D2	10l. green and black	1·30	1·30
D89	D2	20l. green and black	2·75	2·50
D91	D2	60l. green and black	9·75	9·50
D95	D2	100l. green and black	16·00	12·50
D96	D2	200l. green and black	£250	£225

D20

1902

D183	D20	1l. brown	55	35
D184	D20	2l. grey	55	35
D185	D20	3l. orange	55	35
D186	D20	5l. green	55	35
D188	D20	20l. mauve	55	35
D190	D20	30l. purple	65	35
D191	D20	40l. brown	80	50
D193	D20	1d. black	1·60	85
D194	D20	2d. bronze	2·40	3·25
D195	D20	3d. silver	3·75	7·25
D196	D20	5d. gold	6·00	22·00
D273	D20	10l. red	35	30
D275	D20	25l. blue	35	30
D451	D20	50l. brown	45	40

1912. Optd with T 34.

D252A	D 20	1l. brown	65	65
D253A	D 20	2l. grey	65	65
D254A	D 20	3l. orange	35	30
D255A	D 20	5l. green	35	30
D256A	D 20	10l. red	1·40	1·40
D257D	D 20	20l. mauve	85	85
D258A	D 20	30l. purple	4·25	4·25
D259D	D 20	40l. brown	85	85
D260D	D 20	50l. brown	85	85
D261D	D 20	1d. black	11·00	10·50
D262D	D 20	2d. bronze	14·00	13·50
D263D	D 20	3d. silver	24·00	23·00
D264D	D 20	5d. gold	38·00	37·00

1913. Perf or roul.

D269	D20	1l. green	10	10
D270	D20	2l. red	10	10
D271	D20	3l. red	10	10
D274	D20	20l. slate	35	30
D276	D20	30l. red	35	30
D277	D20	40l. blue	35	30
D279	D20	80l. purple	55	50
D282	D20	3d. red	12·00	8·25
D452	D20	1d. blue	45	40
D453	D20	2d. red	45	40
D455	D20	5d. blue	45	40
D456	D20	10d. green	45	1·00
D457	D20	15d. brown	45	1·60
D458	D20	25d. red	1·10	2·50
D480	D20	50d. orange	85	5·25
D481	D20	100d. green	85	5·25
D595	D20	10d. orange	35	3·00

D596	**D20**	25d. blue	35	3·00
D597	**D20**	100d. brown	35	3·00
D598	**D20**	200d. violet	35	3·00

1942. Surch 50.

D564	50l. on 30l. red	6·50	13·00

GREEK WAR ISSUES, 1912-1913

For provisional issues used in territories occupied by Greece during the Balkan War, see Stanley Gibbons Part 3 (Balkans) Catalogue

Pt. 3

GREEK OCCUPATION OF ALBANIA

100 lepta = 1 drachma.

Stamps of Greece optd with T 1.

ΕΛΛΗΝΙΚΗ
ΔΙΟΙΚΗΣΙΣ
(1)

1940. Stamps of 1937.

1	**86**	5l. blue and brown	15	30
2	-	10l. brown & blue (No. 498)	15	30
3	-	20l. green & blk (No. 499)	20	50
4	-	40l. black & grn (No. 500)	20	50
5	-	50l. black & brn (No. 501)	20	50
6	-	80l. brown & vio (No. 502)	20	50
7	**89**	1d. green	30	1·30
8	-	2d. blue (No. 504)	35	1·30
9	**89**	3d. brown	45	1·30
10	-	5d. red (No. 506)	65	2·00
11	-	6d. olive (No. 507)	1·00	2·40
12	-	7d. brown (No. 508)	1·00	2·40
13	**89**	8d. blue	1·00	2·40
14	-	10d. brown (No. 510)	1·60	3·00
15	-	15d. green (No. 511)	1·60	5·00
16	-	25d. blue (No. 512)	4·00	9·00
17	**89a**	30d. red	7·50	19·00

1940. Charity Tax Stamps of 1939.

18	**C 96**	10l. red on rose	15	40
19	**C 96**	50l. green on green	25	85
20	**C 96**	1d. blue on blue	65	1·90

1940. Nos. 534/53 (Youth Organization).

26	**101**	3d. blue, red & sil (postage)	55	1·00
27	-	5d. black and blue	2·75	2·10
28	-	10d. black and orange	3·75	5·25
29	-	15d. black and green	13·00	18·00
30	-	20d. black and red	11·00	18·00
31	-	25d. black and blue	11·00	18·00
32	-	30d. black and violet	11·00	18·00
33	-	50d. black and red	11·00	18·00
34	-	75d. gold, blue and brown	14·00	18·00
35	**101**	100d. blue, red and silver	15·00	24·00
36	**103**	2d. black and orange (air)	55	1·00
37	-	4d. black and green	2·75	4·25
38	-	6d. black and red	3·75	5·25
39	-	8d. black and blue	5·50	8·25
40	-	16d. black and violet	11·00	16·00
41	-	32d. black and orange	12·00	19·00
42	-	45d. black and green	12·00	19·00
43	-	55d. black and red	12·00	19·00
44	-	65d. black and blue	12·00	19·00
45	-	100d. black and violet	22·00	16·00

POSTAGE DUE STAMPS

1940. Postage Due stamps of 1913.

D21	**D20**	2d. red	35	95
D22	**D20**	5d. blue	80	1·90
D23	**D20**	10d. green	50	1·60
D24	**D20**	15d. brown	80	1·90

1940. Postage Due stamp surch also.

D25	50l. on 25d. red	35	95

Pt. 11

GREENLAND

A Danish possession N. E. of Canada. On 5 June 1963, Greenland became an integral part of the Danish Kingdom.

100 ore = 1 krone.

1 Christian X

2 Polar Bear

1938

1	**1**	1ore green	20	25
2	**1**	5ore red	1·80	1·10
3	**1**	7ore green	3·25	3·00
4	**1**	10ore violet	95	55
5	**1**	15ore red	95	55
5a	**1**	20ore red	1·80	1·10
6	**2**	30ore blue	7·25	5·75
6a	**2**	40ore blue	41·00	6·75
7	**2**	1k. brown	8·25	6·75

3 Harp Seal

4 King Christian X

5 Eskimo Kayak

1945

8	**3**	1ore violet and black	28·00	25·00
9	**3**	5ore buff and violet	28·00	25·00
10	**3**	7ore black and green	28·00	25·00
11	**4**	10ore olive and purple	28·00	25·00
12	**4**	15ore blue and red	28·00	25·00
13	-	30ore brown and blue	28·00	25·00
14	-	1k. grey and brown	28·00	25·00
15	**5**	2k. green and brown	28·00	25·00
16	-	5k. brown and purple	28·00	25·00

DESIGNS—HORIZ: As Type **5**: 30ore Dog team; 1k. Polar bear; 5k. Eider.

1945. Liberation of Denmark. Nos. 8/16 optd DANMARK BEFRIET 5 MAJ 1945.

17	**3**	1ore violet and black	75·00	50·00
18	**3**	5ore buff and violet	75·00	50·00
19	**3**	7ore black and green	75·00	50·00
20	**4**	10ore olive and purple	80·00	75·00
21	**4**	15ore blue and red	80·00	75·00
22	-	30ore brown and blue	80·00	75·00
23	-	1k. grey and brown	80·00	75·00
24	**5**	2k. green and brown	80·00	75·00
25	-	5k. brown and purple	80·00	75·00

7 King Frederik IX

8 Polar Ship "Gustav Holm"

1950

26	**7**	1ore green	25	15
27	**7**	5ore red	35	25
28	**7**	10ore green	40	25
29a	**7**	15ore violet	50	40
30	**7**	25ore red	2·30	90
31	**7**	30ore blue	28·00	1·70
32	**7**	30ore red	60	30
33	**8**	50ore blue	60·00	11·50
34	**8**	1k. brown	14·50	2·30
35	**8**	2k. red	7·25	2·30
36	**8**	5k. grey	3·25	1·30

1956. Nos. 6a and 7 surch 60 ore.

37	**2**	60ore on 40ore blue	7·25	1·30
38	**2**	60ore on 1k. brown	75·00	6·75

10 "The Boy and the Fox"

1957. Greenland Legends.

39	**10**	50ore red	1·70	80
40	-	60ore blue	2·75	90
41	-	80ore brown	1·80	1·00
42	-	90ore blue	2·75	2·75

DESIGNS: 60ore "Mother of the Sea"; 80ore "The Girl and the Eagle"; 90ore "Great Northern Diver and Raven".

1958. Royal Tuberculosis Relief Fund. No. 33 surch with Cross of Lorraine and 30+10.

43	**8**	30ore+10ore on 50ore blue	3·50	1·10

12 Hans Egede (after J. Horner)

1958. Death Bicent of Hans Egede (missionary).

44	**12**	30ore red	8·75	1·10

1959. Greenland Fund. Surch Gronlandsfonden 30+10 and bars.

45	**7**	30ore+10ore on 25ore red	4·00	3·75

The note below No. 413 of Denmark also applies here.

14 Knud Rasmussen (founder of Thule)

1960. 50th Anniv of Thule Settlement.

46	**14**	30ore red	1·50	85

15 Drum Dance

1961

47	**15**	35ore green	95	60

16 Northern Lights

17 Frederik IX

18 Polar Bear

1963

48	**16**	1ore green	20	15
49	**16**	5ore red	25	20
50	**16**	10ore green	40	30
51	**16**	12ore green	35	35
52	**16**	15ore purple	80	70
53	**17**	20ore blue	3·50	2·75
54	**17**	25ore brown	40	30
54a	**17**	30ore green	35	30
55	**17**	35ore red	35	30
56	**17**	40ore grey	40	30
57	**17**	50ore blue	7·50	6·00
57a	**17**	50ore red	45	30
57b	**17**	60ore red	55	30
58	**17**	80ore orange	85	75
59	**18**	1k. brown	65	25
60	**18**	2k. red	3·00	55
61	**18**	5k. blue	2·30	95
62	**18**	10k. green	3·25	70

18a Prof. Niels Bohr

1963. 50th Anniv of Bohr's Atomic Theory.

63	**18a**	35ore red	30	30
64	**18a**	60ore blue	3·75	3·75

19 S. Kleinschmidt

1964. 150th Birth Anniv of S. Kleinschmidt (philologist).

65	**19**	35ore brown	65	60

20a Princess Margrethe and Prince Henri de Monpezat

1967. Royal Wedding.

66	**20a**	50ore red	3·50	3·00

21a "The Children in the Round Tower" (legend)

1968. Child Welfare.

67	**21a**	60ore+10ore red	80	75

22 King Frederik IX and Map of Greenland

1969. King Frederik's 70th Birthday.

68	**22**	60ore red	1·20	1·00

24 Musk Ox

1969

69	-	1k. blue	55	45
70	-	2k. green	75	50
71	-	5k. blue	1·80	75
72	-	10k. brown	3·00	1·50
73	**24**	25k. olive	7·25	2·40

DESIGN—HORIZ: 1k. Bowhead whale and coastline; 2k. Narwhal; 5k. Polar bear; 10k. Walruses.

25 Celebrations at Jakobshavn

1970. 25th Anniv of Denmark's Liberation.

74	**25**	60ore red	1·80	1·70

26 Egede and Gertrud Rask aboard the "Haabet"

1971. 250th Anniv of Hans Egede's Arrival in Greenland.

75	**26**	60ore red	1·30	1·10
76	-	60ore+10ore red	1·80	1·60

DESIGN: No. 76, Hans Egede and Gertrud Rask meeting Greenlanders.

The premium on No. 76 was for the Greenland Church Building Fund.

27 Mail Kayaks

1971. Greenland Mail Transport.

77	**27**	50ore green	30	30
78	-	70ore red	35	30
79	-	80ore black	40	40
80	-	90ore blue	30	30
81	-	1k. red	55	50
82	-	1k.30 blue	55	50
83	-	1k.50 green	85	55
84	-	2k. blue	70	50

DESIGNS: 70 ore Umiak (women's boat); 80 ore Consolidated PBY-5A Catalina amphibian; 90 ore Mail dog-sledge; 1k. "Kununhuak" (coaster) and "Dlik" (tug); 1k.30 "Sokongen" (schooner); 1k.50 "Karen" (sailing longboat); 2k. Sikorsky S-61N helicopter DY-HAF.

28 King Frederik IX and Royal Yacht "Dannebrog"

1972. King Frederik IX's and Queen Ingrid's Fund.

85	**28**	60ore+10ore red	80	75

29 Queen Margrethe

1973

86	**29**	10ore green	25	20
87	**29**	60ore brown	40	35
88	**29**	90ore brown	50	45
88a	**29**	100ore red	40	25
89	**29**	120ore blue	65	60
89a	**29**	130ore blue	55	50

For values inscribed "KALAALLIT NUNAAT" at top, see Nos. 99/104.

30 Heimaey Eruption

1973. Aid for Victims of Heimaey (Iceland) Eruption.

90	**30**	70ore+20ore blue and red	1·20	1·20

31 "Carl Egede" (trawler) and Kayaks

1974. Bicentenary of Royal Greenland Trade Department.

91	**31**	1k. brown	60	50
92	-	2k. brown	65	50

DESIGN—VERT: 2k. Trade Department Headquarters, Trangraven, Copenhagen.

32 Gyr Falcon and Radio Aerial

1975. 50th Anniv of Greenland's Telecommunications Service.

93	**32**	90ore red	45	45

33 Sirius Sledge Patrol

1975. 25th Anniv of Sirius Sledge Patrol.

94	**33**	1k.20 brown	45	45

34 Arm-wrestling (after H. Egede)

1976. Greenland Sports Publicity.

95	**34**	100ore+20ore brown and green on stone	60	55

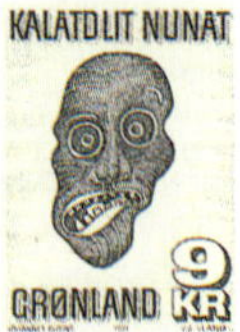

35 Inuit Carved Mask

1977. Eskimo Mask.

96	**35**	9k. grey	2·75	2·30

36 Bronlund and Disko Bay, Jakobshavn

1977. Birth Cent of Jorgen Bronlund (explorer).

97	**36**	1k. brown	35	30

37 Cape York Meteorite and "Ulo" (woman's knife)

1978. Centenary of Commission for Scientific Researches in Greenland.

98	**37**	1k.20 brown	45	35

38 Queen Margrethe

1978

99	**38**	5ore red	25	15
100	**38**	80ore brown	30	25
101	**38**	120ore brown	45	40
102	**38**	130ore red	45	30
103	**38**	160ore blue	65	55
104	**38**	180ore green	60	50

39 Sun rising over Mountains

1978. 25th Anniv of Constitution.

105	**39**	1k.50 blue	45	45

40 Foundation Ceremony

1978. 250th Anniv of Godthab.

106	**40**	2k.50 brown	80	65

41 Tupilak (imaginary animal)

1978. Folk Art.

107	**41**	6k. red	1·80	1·70
108	-	7k. green	1·90	1·70
109	-	8k. blue	2·00	2·00

DESIGNS: 7k. Soapstone figure (Simon Kristoffersen; 8k. "Eskimo Family" (driftwood sculpture by Johannas Kreutzamann).

42 Helmsman

1979. Internal Autonomy.

110	**42**	1k.10 brown	45	40

43 Rasmussen with Eskimos

1979. Birth Centenary of Knud Rasmussen (polar explorer).

111	**43**	1k.30+20ore red	55	50

45 Eskimo Child

1979. International Year of the Child.

112	**45**	2k. green	65	50

47 Queen Margrethe and Map of Greenland

1980

113	**47**	50ore violet	30	25
114	**47**	80ore brown	45	35
115	**47**	1k.30 red	45	45
116	**47**	1k.50 blue	60	55
117	**47**	1k.60 blue	65	55
118	**47**	1k.80 red	80	75
119	**47**	2k.30 green	75	65
120	**47**	2k.50 red	80	60
121	**47**	2k.80 brown	1·30	75
122	**47**	3k. red	1·70	85
122a	**47**	3k.20 red	1·60	80
123	**47**	3k.80 black	1·40	1·30
124	**47**	4k.10 blue	1·90	1·70
124a	**47**	4k.40 blue	2·00	2·00

48 Eskimos and Rasmus Berthelsen in Library

1980. 150th Anniv of Greenland Public Libraries.

125	**48**	2k. brown on yellow	60	60

49 "Reindeer Sledge and the Larva" (drawing, Jens Kreutzmann)

1980. Greenland Art.

126	**49**	1k.60 red	50	50
127	-	2k.70 violet	85	70
128	-	3k. black	85	80

DESIGNS: 2k.70 "Harpooning Walrus" (printing by Jakob Danielsen); 3k. "Foot Race between Quloqutsuk and Aqigssia (woodcut by Aron from Kangeq).

50 Mikkelsen and Eskimo

1980. Birth Centenary of Ejnar Mikkelsen (Inspector of East Greenland).

129	**50**	4k. green	1·30	1·10

52 Atlantic Cod

1981

130	**52**	25k. brown and blue	7·00	4·25

53 Stone Tent Ring, Wolf and King Eiders

1981. Peary Land Expeditions.

131	**53**	1k.60+20ore brown	65	65

54 Reindeer and Hunter (Saqqaq culture, 2000 B.C.)

1981. Greenland Prehistory.

132	**54**	3k.50 blue	1·00	95
133	-	5k. brown	1·40	1·30

DESIGN: 5k. Hunters dragging walrus (Tunit-Dorset culture, 50 B.C.).

55 Shrimps

1982

134	**55**	10k. blue and red	2·75	1·70

57 Eric the Red discovering Greenland, 982

1982. Millenary of Greenland (1st issue).

135	**57**	2k.+40ore brown	1·10	1·00

See also Nos. 136/7, 140/2, 145/7 and 152/3.

58 Eskimos hunting Bowhead Whale (1000–1100)

1982. Millenary of Greenland (2nd issue).

136	**58**	2k. red	60	55
137	-	2k.70 blue	80	75

DESIGN: 2k.70, Bishop Joen Smyrill's staff and house at Gardar (1100–1200).

59 Atlantic Salmon

1983

138	**59**	50k. black and blue	14·00	7·75

60 Blind Person, Armband, Cassette and White Stick

1983. Welfare of the Blind.

139	**60**	2k.50+40ore red	1·20	1·20

61 Eskimos and Northerners bartering (1200–1300)

1983. Millenary of Greenland (3rd issue).

140	**61**	2k.50 brown	70	65
141	-	3k.50 brown	1·00	90
142	-	4k.50 blue	1·40	1·30

DESIGNS: 3k.50, Mummy of Eskimo boy (1300–1400); 4k.50, Hans Pothorst's expedition to America (1400–1500).

62 Herrnhut Bandsmen

1983. 250th Anniv of Herrnhut Moravian Brethren Settlement.

143	**62**	2k.50 brown	85	80

63 "Polar Bear killing Seal Hunter"

1984. 50th Death Anniv of Karale Andreassen (writer and artist).

144	**63**	3k.70 black	1·30	1·10

64 Bowhead Whales and Glass Beads (trading goods) (1500–1600)

1984. Millenary of Greenland (4th issue).

145	**64**	2k.70 brown	1·40	1·20
146	-	3k.70 blue	1·40	1·30
147	-	5k.50 brown	1·50	1·40

DESIGNS: 3k.70 Greenlanders in European dress and apostle spoons (1600–1700); 5k.50, Hans Egede's mission station, Godthab, and key (1700–1800).

65 Prince Henrik of Denmark

1984. Prince Henrik's 50th Birthday.

148	**65**	2k.70 brown	1·60	1·60

66 Danish Grenadier, 1734

1984. 250th Anniv of Christianshab.

149	**66**	3k.70 brown	1·40	1·20

67 Lund

1984. 36th Death Anniv of Henrik Lund (composer).

150	**67**	5k. green	2·50	2·00

68 Spotted Wolffish

1984

151	**68**	10k. black and blue	4·25	3·25

69 "Hvalfisken" (brig) (1800–1900)

1985. Millenary of Greenland (5th issue).

152	**69**	2k.80 purple	1·40	1·20
153	-	6k. black	1·90	1·70

DESIGN: 6k. Communications satellite and globe (1900–2000).

70 Queen Ingrid and "Chrysanthemum frutescens" "Sofiero"

1985. 50th Anniv of Queen Ingrid's Arrival in Denmark.

154	**70**	2k.80 multicoloured	95	80

71 Nesting Birds and I.Y.Y. Emblem

1985. International Youth Year.

155	**71**	3k.80 multicoloured	1·10	1·10

72 "Hare Hunt"

1985. 130th Birth Anniv of Gerhard Kleist (artist).

156	**72**	9k. green	3·00	2·40

73 Greenland Halibut

1985

157	**73**	10k. brown and blue	3·25	2·75

74 Post Office Flags

1986. Postal Independence.

158	**74**	2k.80 red	80	75

75 Towing Man on Bladder (traditional sport)

1986. Greenland Athletic Federation.

159	**75**	2k.80+50ore mult	1·40	1·30

76 Needle Case and Combs

1986. Local Craft Artefacts.

160	**76**	2k.80 brown and red	1·20	1·20
161	-	3k. violet and red	90	85
162	-	3k.80 black and blue	1·10	1·10
163	-	3k.80 purple and blue	1·60	1·50
164	-	5k. brown and green	1·60	1·50
165	-	6k.50 brown and green	2·10	2·10
166	-	10k. brown and purple	3·25	2·75

DESIGNS: 3k. Tubs; 3k.80, (No. 162) Ulos (knives for working sealskins); 3k.80, (No. 163) Eye masks; 5k. Harpoon heads; 6k.50, Lard lamps; 10k. Masks.

77 "Daily Life in Thule" (collage by Aninaaq)

1986. Art from Thule.

167	**77**	2k.80 brown	90	90

78 Capelin

1986

168	**78**	10k. brown and green	3·50	3·50

79 Fulmar and Iceberg

1987. "Hafnia 87" International Stamp Exhibition, Copenhagen (1st issue). Sheet 95×70 mm containing T 79 and similar vert designs showing coastal view of Greenland from sketch by Jens Lorentzen. Multicoloured.

MS169 2k.80 Type **79**; 3k.80 Uummannaq Mountain and ice floes; 6k.50 Fulmars swimming and steamer in bay (sold at 19k.50)		7·25	7·25

See also No. **MS**193.

80 "Ammassalik Fjord" (Peter Rosing)

1987. Greenland Art.

170	**80**	2k.80 brown	1·00	80

81 Father and Son on Ice-floe

1987. Fishing, Sealing and Whaling Industries Year.

171	**81**	3k.80 multicoloured	1·20	1·20

83 Rock Ptarmigans

1987. Birds. Multicoloured.

172	3k. Gyr falcons	1·50	1·20
173	3k.20 Long-tailed ducks	1·20	95
174	4k. Snow geese	1·40	1·10
175	4k.10 Common ravens	2·00	2·00
176	4k.40 Snow buntings	2·00	1·90
177	5k. Type **83**	2·00	1·70
178	5k.50 White-tailed sea eagles	2·75	2·50
179	5k.50 Black guillemots	2·10	1·80
180	6k.50 Brunnich's guillemots	2·75	2·20
181	7k. Great northern divers	3·00	2·75
182	7k.50 Long-tailed skuas	2·75	2·75
183	10k. Snowy owl	4·00	3·00

84 Uummannaq Mountain

1987. "Hafnia 87" International Stamp Exhibition, Copenhagen (2nd issue). Sheet 94×68 mm.

MS193 **84** 2k.80 blue and red (sold at 4k.)		2·50	2·75

85 Telefax, Sledge and de Havilland / Canada DHC-7 Dash Seven

1988. 50 Years of Greenland Postal Administration.

194	**85**	3k.+50ore multicoloured	2·30	2·20

87 National Flag

1989. 10th Anniv of Internal Autonomy. Mult.

195	3k.20 Type **87**	1·20	1·00
196	4k.40 National arms	2·30	2·20

88 Cotton Grass

1989. Flowers. Multicoloured.

197	4k. Bellflower (vert)	50	1·00
198	4k. Hairy lousewort (vert)	1·70	1·20
199	5k. Type **88**	1·60	1·40
200	5k.50 Labrador tea	1·70	1·70
201	6k.50 Arctic white heather	2·50	2·20
202	7k.25 Purple saxifrage	3·00	2·75
203	10k. Arctic poppy (vert)	3·50	2·75

89 Queen Margrethe

1990

210	**89**	25ore green	25	15
213	**89**	1k. brown	40	35
218	**89**	4k. red	1·40	1·20
219	**89**	4k.25 red	2·10	2·00
221	**89**	6k.50 blue	2·50	2·20
222	**89**	7k. violet	2·75	2·50

90 Chained Sledge Dog and nesting Eiders

1990. Greenland Environmental Foundation.

225	**90**	400ore+50ore mult	3·75	3·75

91 Frederik Lynge

1990. Augo and Frederik Lynge (Greenland Members of Danish Folketing).

226	**91**	10k. red and blue	3·75	3·25
227	-	25k. purple and blue	8·00	6·00

DESIGN: 25k. Augo Lynge.

92 Ringed Seal ("Phoca hispida")

1991. Marine Mammals. Multicoloured.

228		4k. Type **92**	1·30	1·20
229		4k. Harp seals ("Pagophilus groenlandicus")	1·30	1·20
230		7k.25 Hooded seals ("Cystophora cristata")	2·50	2·50
231		7k.25 Walrus ("Odobenus rosmarus")	2·50	2·50
232		8k.50 Bearded seal ("Erignatus barbatus")	3·00	3·00
233		8k.50 Common seal ("Phoca vitulina")	3·00	3·00
MS234		142×86 mm. Nos. 228/33	17·00	16·00

93 Dogs and Fisherman

1991. 250th Anniv of Ilulissat (Jakobshavn).

235	**93**	4k. multicoloured	1·60	1·50

94 Iceberg and Summer Flowers

1991. Nordic Countries' Postal Co-operation. Tourism. Multicoloured.

236		4k. Type **94**	1·50	1·50
237		8k.50 Ski party and dog sled in winter	3·25	3·25

95 Birds

1991. 75th Anniv of Blue Cross (health education organization).

238	**95**	4k.+50ore multicoloured	7·50	7·25

96 Jonathan Petersen (composer, 110th anniv)

1991. Birth Anniversaries.

239	**96**	10k. black and blue	3·25	2·40
240	-	50k. brown and blue	12·50	12·00

DESIGN: 50k. Hans Lynge (writer and artist, 85th anniv).

97 Arms and Paamiut

1992. Bicentenary of Paamiut (Fredrikshaab).

241	**97**	7k.25 brown and blue	3·00	2·50

98 Royal Couple in 1992 and in Official Wedding Photograph

1992. Silver Wedding of Queen Margrethe and Prince Henrik.

242	**98**	4k. multicoloured	2·00	2·00

99 Moller and Drawing of Godthab Church

1992. 150th Birth Anniv of Lars Moller (editor and printer).

243	**99**	100k. red and blue	23·00	22·00

100 Rainbow and Landscape

1992. Neriuffik Cancer Research Organization.

244	**100**	4k.+50ore multicoloured	3·75	3·50

101 Mother and Child with Father Christmas

1992. Christmas.

245	**101**	4k. multicoloured	2·00	2·00

102 Flame and Laurel Wreath framed by Dance Drum

1993. Int Year of Indigenous Peoples.

246	**102**	4k. multicoloured	1·80	1·60

103 Flat Crab

1993. Crabs.

247	**103**	4k. red, yellow and green	1·20	1·10
248	-	7k.25 brown and blue	3·75	3·50
249	-	8k.50 multicoloured	3·75	7·75

DESIGNS: 7k.25, Sand crab; 8k.50, Stone crabs.

104 Ummannaq Church

1993. Nordic Countries' Postal Co-operation. Churches. Multicoloured.

250		4k. Type **104**	1·50	1·50
251		8k.50 Hvalso church ruins	3·25	3·00

105 Children in Tent

1993. Anniversaries.

252	**105**	4k.+50ore multicoloured	2·75	2·75
253	-	4k.+50ore red and violet	2·75	2·75
MS254		140×80 mm. Nos. 252/3 each ×2	16·00	18·00

DESIGNS: No. 252 Type **105** (50th anniv of scouts in Greenland); 253, Birds, crosses and landscape (70th anniv of Red Cross in Greenland).

106 Corpuscles and "AIDS"

1993. Anti-AIDS Campaign.

255	**106**	4k. multicoloured	1·50	1·50

107 Wolf

1993. Animals. Multicoloured.

256		4k. Polar bear	1·60	1·30
257		5k. Type **107**	2·00	2·00
258		5k.50 Ermine	2·00	2·00
259		7k.25 Arctic lemmings	3·25	3·00
260		7k.25 Wolverine	3·00	2·75
261		7k.50 Musk ox	3·25	2·75
262		8k.50 Arctic fox	3·25	3·25
263		9k. Mountain hare	3·75	3·50
264		10k. Reindeer	3·75	3·75

108 Dog Sled

1993. Christmas.

265	**108**	4k. multicoloured	2·00	2·00

109 Skiers

1994. Winter Olympic Games, Lillehammer, Norway.

266	**109**	4k.+50ore multicoloured	2·75	2·75
MS267		140×80 mm. No. 266 ×4	16·00	13·00

110 Transmission Line

1994. Inauguration of Buksefjorden Hydroelectric Power Station.

268	**110**	4k. multicoloured	1·40	1·30

111 First Church

1994. Centenary of Ammassalik.

269	**111**	7k.25 blue, brown & grn	2·50	2·50

112 "Danmark" (sail/steam barque)

1994. Europa. Discoveries. "Danmark" Expedition to North-east Coast, 1906–08. Multicoloured.

270		4k. Type **112**	1·40	1·30
271		7k.25 "Danmark" and dogs following ELG Mobil car	2·75	2·75

113 "Ceres" (William Moen)

1994. Figureheads from Greenlandic Ships (1st series). Multicoloured.

272		4k. Type **113**	1·50	1·50
273		8k.50 "Nordlyset" (Johan Heldt)	3·00	3·00

See also Nos. 287/8 and 306/7.

114 Christmas Visiting

1994. Christmas. Multicoloured.

274		4k. Type **114**	1·50	1·50
275		5k. Santa Claus outside igloo	2·30	2·20

115 "Listera cordata"

1995. Arctic Orchids (1st series). Multicoloured.

276		4k. Type **115**	1·40	1·30
277		7k.25 "Leucorchis albida"	2·50	2·50

See also Nos. 293/5.

116 Teacher and Student

1995. 150th Anniv of Nuuk Training College.

278	**116**	4k. multicoloured	1·50	1·50

116a U.N. Emblem and "50"

1995. 50th Anniv of United Nations.

279	**116a**	blue, green and red	2·50	2·75

117 Iceberg and Meadow

1995. Nordic Countries' Postal Co-operation. Tourism.

280 4k. Type **117** 1·80 1·80
281 8k.50 Mountains and valleys 3·75 3·75

118 Airmail Envelope

1995. Europa. Peace and Freedom. Multicoloured.

282 4k. Type **118** 1·80 1·80
283 8k.50 Doves and seascape 3·25 3·50

119 King Christian X

1995. 50th Anniv of Liberation. Three sheets each 140×80 mm, containing reproductions of 1945 "American Series", surcharged in red. Multicoloured.

MS284 (a) 5k. on 10ore Type **119**; 5k. on 15ore Type **119**; (b) 1k. on 1ore Seal; 5k. on 5ore Seal; 7k. on 7ore Seal; (c) 4k. on 30ore Dog team; 4k. on 1k. Polar bear; 4k. on 2k. Eskimo kayak; 4k. on 5k. Eider Set of 3 sheets 21·00 21·00

120 Children with Flag

1995. 10th Anniv of National Flag.

285 **120** 4k.+50ore multicoloured 3·25 3·00
MS286 80×140 mm. No. 285 ×4 14·00 13·50

The premium was for the benefit of the Greenland Flag Society.

1995. Figureheads from Greenlandic Ships (2nd series). As T 113. Multicoloured.

287 4k. "Hvalfisken" (H. J. Moen) (vert) 1·40 1·30
288 8k.50 "Tjalfe" 3·00 3·00

121 Boy running with Lamps

1995. Christmas. Multicoloured.

289 4k. Type **121** 1·20 1·20
290 5k. Boy running with lamp and moon 1·80 1·70

1995. Nos. 210 and 213 surch.

291 **89** 4k.25 on 25ore green 2·40 1·80
292 **89** 4k.50 on 1k. brown 3·00 2·10

1996. Arctic Orchids (2nd series). As T 115. Multicoloured.

293 4k.25 Early coral-root 1·40 1·30
294 4k.50 Round-leaved orchid 1·50 1·50
295 7k.50 Northern green orchid 2·50 2·50

124 Killer Whale

1996. Whales (1st series). Each black, red and blue.

296 25ore Type **124** 45 40
297 50ore Humpback whale 45 45
298 1k. Beluga 60 55
299 4k.50 Sperm whale 1·40 1·30
300 6k.50 Bowhead whale 2·20 2·20
301 9k.50 Minke whale 3·25 3·25
MS302 140×80 mm. Nos. 296/301 10·00 9·50

See also Nos. 318/22.

125 Arnarulunnguaq (Eskimo traveller)

1996. Europa. Famous Women.

303 **125** 4k.50 blue 1·60 1·40

126 Man in Wheelchair at Sea Shore

1996. Greenland Society of Handicapped and Disabled.

304 **126** 4k.25+50ore mult 1·80 1·80
MS305 140×81 mm. No. 304×4 8·00 8·75

1996. Figureheads from Greenlandic Ships (3rd series). As T 113. Multicoloured.

306 15k. "Blaa Hejren" 4·00 4·00
307 20k. "Gertrud Rask" (horiz) 5·25 5·75

127 Child and Angels

1996. Christmas. Multicoloured.

308 4k.25 Type **127** 1·70 1·60
309 4k.50 Star and children 1·70 1·60

128 Arctic Fritillary

1997. Butterflies. Multicoloured.

310 2k. Type **128** 90 85
311 3k. Northern clouded yellow 1·30 1·30
312 4k.75 Arctic blue 1·70 1·40
313 8k. Small copper 2·75 2·75

129 Queen Margrethe in Greenlandic Costume

1997. Silver Jubilee of Queen Margrethe.

314 **129** 4k.50 multicoloured 1·50 1·40

130 Globe and Musicians

1997. Opening of Katuaq Cultural Centre, Nuuk.

315 **130** 4k.50+50ore mult 2·00 2·00
MS316 140×82 mm. No. 315 ×4 9·25 9·00

131 Bear of the Sea inhaling Umiak (boat)

1997. Europa. Tales and Legends.

317 **131** 4k.75 blue 1·90 1·70

1997. Whales (2nd series). As T 124. Mult.

318 5k. Blue whale 1·40 1·40
319 5k.75 Fin whale 2·30 2·20
320 6k. Sei whale 2·30 2·20
321 8k. Narwhal 2·75 2·75
MS322 140×81 mm. Nos. 318/21 9·25 9·00

132 Dancing Children and Church

1997. Bicentenary of Nanortalik.

323 **132** 4k.50 multicoloured 1·80 1·70

133 "Drum Dancer"

1997. Greenland Art (1st series). 20th Death Anniv of Aage Gitz-Johansen. Multicoloured.

324 10k. Type **133** 3·00 3·00
325 16k. "Ammassalik Woman" 4·25 4·25

See also Nos. 342/3 and 353/4.

134 Boy with Huskies

1997. Christmas. Multicoloured.

326 4k.50 Type **134** 2·10 2·00
327 4k.75 Family on sledge and father disentangling traces 2·10 2·00

135 Common Porpoise

1998. International Year of the Ocean. Cetaceans. Multicoloured.

328 2k. Type **135** 75 65
329 3k. White-beaked dolphin 1·10 1·10
330 4k.50 Long-finned pilot whale ("Globicephala melaena") 1·70 1·60
331 4k.50 Northern bottle-nosed whale ("Hyperoodon ampullatus") 1·70 1·60
332 4k.75 Atlantic white-sided dolphin ("Lagenorhynchus acutus") 1·80 1·70
333 4k.75 Black right whale ("Eubalaena glacialis") 1·80 1·70
MS334 141×81 mm. Nos. 328/33 8·25 8·00

136 Augo and Frederik Lynge (first Greenland members of Danish Parliament)

1998. New Order, 1950 (redefinition of Greenland's status).

335 **136** 4k.50 blue, lilac and red 1·40 1·30

137 Kathrine Chemnitz

1998. 20th Death Anniv of Kathrine Chemnitz (founder) and 50th Anniv of Women's Society of Greenland.

336 **137** 4k.50+50ore mult 2·40 2·30
MS337 80×140 mm. No. 336 ×4 7·25 7·00

138 "Children's Faces" (Class 4B, Atuarfik Ukaliusaq School)

1998. Europa. National Festivals. Children's Day. Multicoloured.

338 4k.75 Type **138** 1·50 1·50
339 10k. "Children playing" (Class 5A, Edvard Kruse-p Atuarfia School) 3·00 2·75

139 "Gertrud Rask" (sailing coaster)

1998. Nordic Countries' Postal Co-operation. Sailing Ships. Multicoloured.

340 4k.50 Type **139** 1·90 1·80
341 4k.75 "Hans Egede" (sailing coaster) 1·90 1·80

140 "Breastfeeding Older Brother"

1998. Greenland Art (2nd series). 10th Death Anniv of Hans Lynge (artist). Multicoloured.

342 11k. Type **140** 3·25 3·00
343 25k. "Refuelling" 6·25 6·00

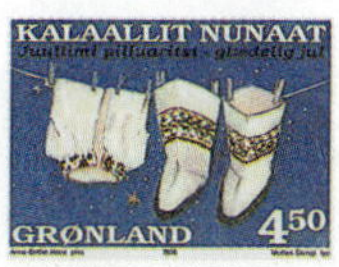

141 Jacket and Slippers on Line

1998. Christmas. Multicoloured.

344 4k.50 Type **141** 1·30 1·30
345 4k.75 Hat and slippers on line 1·60 1·60

142 Owl with Chicks

1999. Endangered Species. The Snowy Owl Multicoloured.

346		1k. Type **142**	60	55
347		4k.75 Owl in flight	1·40	1·30
348		5k.50 Male and female owls	1·70	1·60
349		5k.75 Owl on rock	1·90	1·80

143 Ammassalik Pincushion

1999. Greenland National Museum and Archives.

350	**143**	4k.50+50ore black, blue and red	1·40	1·40
MS351		80×141 mm. No. 350 ×4	8·25	8·00

144 Polar Bear

1999. Europa. Parks and Gardens.

352	**144**	6k. multicoloured	2·00	1·90

145 "The Man from Aluk"

1999. Greenland Art (3rd series). Paintings by Peter Rosing. Multicoloured.

353		7k. Type **145**	1·80	1·70
354		20k. "Homecoming"	5·25	5·00

146 Viking Longship

1999. Greenland Vikings (1st series).

355	**146**	4k.50 green and blue	1·40	1·30
356	-	4k.75 green and blue	1·40	1·40
357	-	5k.75 brown and blue	1·80	1·80
358	-	8k. brown and blue	2·30	2·20
MS359		140×80 mm. Nos. 355/8	6·75	6·50

DESIGNS: 4k.75, Man collecting driftwood; 5k.75, Arrow-head and coins; 8k. Tjodhilde's Church, Brottal.

See also Nos. 363/7 and 390/4.

147 Writing Letter

1999. Christmas. Multicoloured.

360		4k.50 Type **147**	1·40	1·30
361		4k.75 Candles and clasped hands	1·50	1·50

148 Ice Cap

1999. New Millennium.

362	**148**	5k.75 multicoloured	2·10	2·00

2000. Greenland Vikings (2nd series). As T 146.

363		25ore brown and blue	55	45
364		3k. brown and blue	85	80
365		5k.50 blue	1·60	1·50
366		21k. blue	5·50	5·50
MS367		140×81 mm. Nos. 363/6	8·00	7·50

DESIGNS: 25ore Walruses; 3k. Story teller and model of great northern diver; 5k.50, Dog chasing reindeer; 21k. Viking with gyr falcon, polar bear, walrus tusks and straps and bag of ship's tar (trading goods).

149 Huskies pulling Sledge

2000. 50th Anniv of "Sirius" (naval sledge patrol).

368	**149**	10k. multicoloured	2·50	2·50

150 Queen Margrethe II (from photograph by Rigmor Mydtskov)

2000

372	**150**	25ore blue and black	25	15
373	**150**	50ore blue and brown	35	30
374	**150**	4k.50 blue and red	1·20	1·10
375	**150**	4k.75 blue & ultramarine	1·30	1·30
378	**150**	8k. blue and bistre	2·10	2·00
379	**150**	10k. blue and green	2·50	2·40
380	**150**	12k. blue and purple	3·00	2·75

151 "Building Europe"

2000. Europa.

381	**151**	4k.75 multicoloured	2·30	2·20

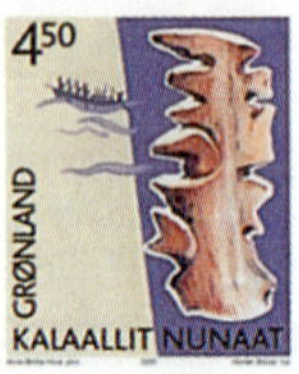

152 Wooden Map

2000. Cultural Heritage (1st series). Multicoloured.

382		4k.50 Type **152**	1·20	1·20
383		4k.75 Sealskin	1·40	1·40

See also Nos. 395/6, 408/9 and 428/9.

153 Drum Dance

2000. "Hafnia 01" International Stamp Exhibition, Copenhagen.

384	**153**	4k.50+1k. multicoloured	1·60	1·60
MS385		80×141 mm. No. 384 ×4	6·50	6·25

154 Candles and Stars

2000. Christmas. Multicoloured.

386		4k.50 Type **154**	1·50	1·40
387		4k.75 Winter landscape and star	1·60	1·50

155 Gymnast and Map

2001. Arctic Winter Games, Nunavut.

388	**155**	4k. 50+50 multicoloured	1·80	1·50
MS389		81×140 mm. No. 388 ×4	6·50	6·25

2001. Greenland Vikings (3rd series). As T 146.

390		1k. red and blue	55	55
391		4k.50 ultramarine and blue	1·20	1·10
392		5k. ultramarine and blue	1·20	1·20
393		10k. red and blue	2·40	2·30
MS394		141×81 mm. Nos. 390/3	5·25	5·00

DESIGNS: 1k. Fisherman and seals; 4k.50, Mouse sitting on food; 5k. Man with packhorses; 10k. Stone wall and common raven.

2001. Cultural Heritage (2nd series). As T 152. Multicoloured.

395		4k.50 Preserving trout	1·20	1·20
396		4k.75 Fishing spear	1·40	1·40

156 Krill

2001. Europa. Water Resources.

397	**156**	15k. multicoloured	4·25	4·00

157 Rock Ptarmigan and Berries

2001. Christmas. Multicoloured.

398		4k.50 Type **157**	1·20	1·10
399		4k.75 Doves flying	1·40	1·40

158 Northern Lights

2001. Essays by Harry Nielsen for First Greenland Stamps. Each black and brown.

400		5k.75 Type **158**	1·80	1·70
401		8k. Seal	2·50	2·40
402		21k. Polar bear	5·75	5·75
MS403		142×80 mm. Nos. 400/2	10·00	9·75

159 Detail of "Stone and Man"

2002. Nordic Countries' Postal Co-operation. Modern Art. Multicoloured.

404		1k. Type **159** (sculpture project, Aka Hoegh and others)	35	30
405		31k. Snow Sculpture (Nuuk Snow Festival, 2001)	8·25	8·00

160 Banner, Igloo Builders and Polar Bears

2002. "Children are People Too" (child welfare project).

406	**160**	4k.50+50ore multicoloured	1·40	1·30
MS407		81×140 mm. No. 406×4	7·50	7·25

2002. Cultural Heritage (3rd series). As T 152. Multicoloured.

408		4k.50 Drum, Thule	1·10	1·10
409		4k.75 Inuit carved mask	1·40	1·40

161 *Nordlyset* (sailing barque)

2002. Ships (1st series). Multicoloured.

410		2k. Type **161**	65	60
411		4k. *Hvidbjornen* (steam/sailing barque)	1·50	1·10
412		6k. *Staerkodder* (sloop)	1·80	1·70
413		16k. *Haabet* (crayer)	4·25	4·25

See also Nos. 438/41, 462/5 and 477/80.

162 Clown, Child and Snow Scene

2002. Europa. Circus.

414	**162**	11k. multicoloured	3·25	3·25

163 Man carrying Gifts and Children on Sledge

2002. Christmas. (a) Ordinary gum.

415		4k.50 Type **163**	1·20	1·20
416		4k.75 Mother with child and carol singers	1·40	1·40

(b) Self-adhesive gum.

417		4k.50 No. 414	1·20	1·20
418		4k.75 No. 416	1·40	1·40

Nos. 417/18 form a composite design.

164 Cliffs and Greenland Shark (*Somniosus microcephalus*)

2002. Centenary of International Council for the Exploration of the Sea. Multicoloured.

419		7k. Type **164**	1·80	1·70
420		19k. Deepwater redfish (*Sebates mentella*)	5·25	5·00
MS421		185×60 mm. Nos. 419/20	7·25	7·00

Stamps of a similar design were issued by Denmark and Faroe Islands.

165 Puppies

2003. Sled Dogs. Each black.

422		4k.50 Type **165**	1·10	1·10
423		4k.75 Adult	1·30	1·20
424		6k. Adult wearing harness	1·60	1·60

166 Tents and mountains

2003. Centenary of the Danish Literary Expedition to Greenland.

425	**166**	15k. agate, green and blue	3·50	3·50
426	-	21k. blue (28×22 mm)	5·00	4·75
MS427 166×61 mm Nos. 424/5 plus label			9·25	9·00

DESIGN: 21k. Knud Ramussen Stamps of a similar design were issued by Denmark.

2003. Cultural Heritage (4th series). As T 152. Multicoloured.

428	25ore Comb, East Greenland	15	15
429	1k. Water bucket, East Greenland	25	25

167 Silamiut Theatre Poster

2003. Europa. Poster Art.

430	**167**	5k.50 multicoloured	1·30	1·20

168 Narwhals and Cliffs

2003. 50th Anniv of Qaanaaq (settlement).

431	**168**	15k. multicoloured	3·50	3·50

169 Children around Christmas Tree

2003. Christmas. (a) Ordinary gum.

432	5k. Type **169**	1·20	1·20
433	5k.50 Family entering church	1·30	1·20

Nos. 434/5 were issued togethert, se-tenant, forming a composite design.

(b) Self-adhesive gum.

434	5k. Type **169**	1·20	1·20
435	5k.50 No. 433	1·30	1·20

170 Santa Claus inside Bauble

2003. Santa Claus of Greenland.

436	**170**	5k.+50ore multicoloured	1·30	1·20
MS437 81×140 mm. No. 436×4			5·75	5·75

2003. Ships (2nd series). As T 161. Multicoloured.

438	6k.75 *Emma* (galleass)	1·60	1·50
439	7k.75 *Gamle Fox* (screw-propelled schooner)	1·90	1·80
440	8k.75 *Godthaab* (screw-propelled barquentine)	2·00	2·00
441	26k. *Sonja* (whaling steamer)	6·00	5·75

171 Moon Man

2004. Nordic Mythology. Multicoloured.

442	5k.50 Type **171**	1·50	1·40
443	6k.50 Northern lights	2·00	2·00
MS444 106×70 mm. Nos. 442/3		3·50	3·25

Stamps of a similar theme were issued by Aland Island, Denmark, Faeroe Islands, Finland, Iceland, Norway and Sweden.

172 Route Map

2004. 50th Anniv of First Scheduled Flight from Denmark to Greenland.

445	**172**	8k.75 multicoloured	2·60	2·50

173 National Arms

2004. 25th Anniv of Home Rule.

446	**173**	11k. multicoloured	1·00	90

174 Rowing Boat attempting Landing on Island

2004. 150th Birth Anniv of Otto Sverdrup (polar explorer).

447	**174**	17k.50 purple and buff	5·25	5·00
MS448 165×60 mm. No. 447 plus 2 labels			5·25	5·00

No. **MS**448 was issued with two stamp-sized labels showing designs of Canada and Norway stamps. Stamps of similar designs were issued by Norway and Canada.

175 Children

2004. 80th Anniv of Society of Greenlandic Children.

449	**175**	5k.+50ore. Multicoloured	1·60	1·50
MS450 140×80 mm. No. 449×4			6·50	6·25

176 Prince Frederik and Mary Donaldson

2004. Marriage of Crown Prince Frederik and Mary Elizabeth Donaldson. Multicoloured.

451	5k. Type **176**	1·70	1·50
452	5k.50 As No. 451 but with design reversed	1·80	1·60
MS453 130×65 mm. Nos. 451/2		3·25	3·00

Stamps of similar design were issued by Denmark and Faroe Islands.

177 *Angelica archangelica*

2004. Edible Plants (1st series). Multicoloured.

454	5k. Type **177**	1·80	1·60
455	5k.50 *Thymus praecox*	1·90	1·80
456	17k. *Empetrum hermaphroditum*	5·50	5·25

See also Nos. 484/6.

178 Family and Decorated Tree

2004. Christmas. (a) Ordinary gum.

457	5k. Type **178**	2·00	1·90
458	5k.50 Family entering church	2·30	2·20

(b) Self-adhesive gum.

459	5k. Type **178**	2·00	1·90
460	5k.50 No. 458	2·30	2·20

179 Girls wearing Traditional Dress

2004. Europa. Holidays.

461	**179**	6k.50 multicoloured	2·75	2·50

2004. Ships (3rd series). As T 161. Multicoloured.

462	6k.50 *Constance* (brig)	2·75	2·50
463	8k.75 *Disko* (passenger ship)	3·50	3·25
464	14k. *Julius Thomsen* (polar ship)	6·00	5·75
465	21k.75 *Misigssut* (tuberculosis hospital ship)	9·00	8·75

180 *Leccinum*

2005. Fungi. Multicoloured. (a) Ordinary or self-adhesive gum.

466	5k.25 Type **180**	2·30	2·20
467	6k. *Russula subrubens*	2·75	2·50
468	7k. *Amanita groenlandica*	3·00	2·75

181 Child's Face

2005. 60th Anniv of Save the Children Fund (charitable organization).

472	**181**	5k.25+50ore multicoloured	2·20	2·10
MS473 140×80 mm. No. 472×4 multicoloured			9·00	8·75

182 Ilulissat Fiord

2005. World Heritage Site. Ilulissat Fiord.

474	**182**	6k. multicoloured	2·50	2·40

183 Mountains and Church Steeple

2005. Centenary of Church Law.

475	**183**	9k.25 multicoloured	3·75	3·50

184 Musk Ox Meat

2005. Europa. Gastronomy.

476	**184**	11k.75 multicoloured	4·75	4·50

2005. Ships (4th series). As T 161. Multicoloured.

477	5k.25 *Dannebrog* (royal yacht)	2·30	2·20
478	6k. *Kista Artica* (polar ship)	2·75	2·50
479	18k.50 *Sarpik Ittuk* (passenger ship)	6·50	6·25
480	23k. *Triton* (naval rescue and helicopter carrier)	10·75	10·50

185 Maps

2005. Completion of Geological Mapping of Greenland.

481	**185**	7k.25 multicoloured	3·00	2·75

186 Limestone Columns

2005. Ikka Fjord Conservation Area.

482	**186**	9k.25 multicoloured	3·50	3·25

187 *Limnognathia Maersk*

2005. Discovery of Limnognathia Maerski (micrognathozoa).

483	**187**	10k. multicoloured	3·75	3·50

2005. Edible Plants (2nd series). As T 177. Multicoloured.

484	75e. *Ligusticum scoticum*	50	40
485	6k.50 *Rhodiola rosea*	3·00	2·75
486	8k.25 *Oxyrias digna*	3·50	3·25

188 Boy and Decoration

2005. Christmas. (a) Ordinary gum.

487	5k.25 Type **188**	2·20	2·10
488	6k. Girl	2·75	2·50

(b) Self-adhesive gum.

489	5k.25 Type **188**	2·20	2·10
490	6k. As. No. 488	2·75	2·50

189 Robert Peary

2005. Robert E. Peary (arctic explorer) Commemoration.

491	**189**	27k.50 multicoloured	10·00	9·75
MS492 167×60 mm **189** 27k.50 multicoloured			10·00	9·75

190 10ore Parcel Post Stamp

2005. Centenary of Parcel Post (1st issue).
493 **190** 50k. blue 19·00 19·00
See also No. 495 and **MS**531.

191 Church

2006. 250th Anniv of Sisimiut.
493a **191** 9k.75 multicoloured 4·00 3·75

192 Doves

2006. 50th Anniv of Norden (postal organization).
494 **192** 19k.50 multicoloured 7·75 7·50

193 5ore Parcel Post Stamp

2006. Centenary of Parcel Post (2nd issue).
495 **193** 25k. brown 10·00 9·75

194 2004 6k.50 Stamp (Type 179)

2006. 50th Anniv of Europa Stamps.
496 **194** 26k.50 multicoloured 10·50 10·00

195 Crown Prince Frederick and Crown Princess Mary

2006. Children in Greenland.
497 **195** 5k.50+50 multicoloured 2·50 2·40
The premium was for children's charities.

196 Mother of the Sea

2006. Nordic Mythology. Multicoloured.
498 7k.50 Type **196** 3·25 3·00
499 13k.50 Mistress of the Wind 5·00 4·75
MS500 105×70 mm. Nos. 498/9 8·25 8·00
Stamps of a similar theme were issued by Aland Islands, Denmark, Faröe Islands, Finland, Iceland, Norway and Sweden.

2006. Fungi. As T 180. Multicoloured. (a) Ordinary Gum.
501 5k.50 *Rozites caperatus* 2·50 2·40
502 7k. *Lactarius dryadophilus* 3·00 2·75
503 10k. *Calvatia cretacea* 4·50 4·25

(b) Self-adhesive.
504 5k.50 As No. 501 2·50 2·40
505 7k. As No. 502 3·00 2·75

197 Ram

2006. Centenary of Sheep Farming in Greenland.
506 **197** 7k.50 multicoloured 3·25 3·00

198 Alfred Wegener

2006. Alfred Wegener (arctic explorer) Commemoration.
507 **198** 20k.75 blue and brown 8·25 8·00
MS508 166×60 mm. **198** 20k.75 blue and brown 8·25 8·00

199 *Vaedderen* (research ship)

2006. Galathea 3—Danish Research Expedition.
509 **199** 9k.75 multicoloured 4·00 3·75

200 Fossilized Tree, Kap Kobenhavn Formation, North East Greenland

2006. Scientific Sites in Greenland.
510 50ore. Type **200** 50 45
511 8k. Rock excavation, Isua (world's oldest mountain) 3·75 3·50
512 15k.50 Qeqertarsuaq Arctic Research Station (centenary) 6·00 5·50

201 Angel and Score

2006. Christmas. Multicoloured. Ordinary or self-adhesive gum.
513 5k.50 Type **201** 2·50 2·40
514 7k. Candle and score 3·00 2·75

202 Water and Power Lines

2007. 10th Anniv of West Nordic Council. Hydropower.
517 **202** 5k. multicoloured 2·10 2·00

203 Children holding Heart-shaped Balloons

2007. Amnesty Kalaallit Nunat (United Nations Children's Convention in Greenland).
518 **203** 5k.75 +50ore multicoloured 2·50 2·40

204 Scouts building Cairn

2007. Europa. Scouting. Multicoloured. Ordinary or self-adhesive gum.
519 5k.75 Type **204** 2·75 2·50
520 7k.50 Building fire and tent 3·25 3·00

205 Ice Core Drilling

2007. International Polar Year. Multicoloured.
523 7k.50 Type **205** 3·00 2·75
524 8k. Three generations (urbanization of Greenland) 3·25 3·00
MS525 105×70 mm. Nos. 523/4 6·25 6·00

206 Crown Prince Frederik, Crown Princess Mary and Prince Christian

2007
526 **206** 14k.25 multicoloured 5·75 5·50

207 *Sled Dogs* (Jens Rosing) (image scaled to 75% of original size)

2007. Greenlandic Artists (1st series). Mult.
527 3k. Type **207** 1·40 1·30
528 8k.50 *Bear and people* (Anne-Birthe Hove) (50×43 mm) 3·75 3·50
529 10k.50 *Face* (Linda Riber Sørensen) (50×43 mm) 4·50 4·25
See also Nos. 542/44.

208 20ore Parcel Post Stamp

2007. Centenary of Parcel Post (3rd issue).
530 **208** 100k. red 32·00 31·00
MS531 200×110 mm. 25k. As No. 495; 50k. As No. 492; 100k. As No. 530 55·00 50·00

209 Tubbiap Queqertaa (Tobias Island) (new island)

2007. Science. Multicoloured.
532 75ore Type **209** 50 40
533 2k. Soapstone lamp 2·00 1·90
534 10k.25 *Cyanobacteria* (green algae (earliest form of life)) (identified by Minik Rosing) 3·75 3·50

210 Landscape

2007. SEPAC (small European mail services).
535 **210** 6k.50 multicoloured 3·00 2·75

211 *Pourquoi-Pas?*

2007. Birth Centenary of Paul-Emile Victor. Jean-Baptiste Charcot (arctic explorer) Commemoration. Multicoloured.
536 **211** 5k.75 multicoloured 2·75 2·50
537 - 7k.50 blue and brown (29×35 mm) 3·25 3·50
MS537a 165×60 mm. As Nos. 536/7 6·00 5·75
DESIGNS: 5k.75 Type **211**; 7k.50 Paul-Emile Victor. No. **MS**537a also contains a stamp size label showing Jean-Baptiste Charcot. Stamps of a similar design were issued by France.

212 Angel and Snowflakes

2007. Christmas. Multicoloured. Ordinary or self-adhesive gum.
538 5k.75 Type **212** 2·75 2·50
539 7k.50 Stars and snowflakes 3·25 3·00

213 Landscape and Figure (Ina Rosing)

2008. Greenlandic Artists (2nd series). Multicoloured.
542 5k.50 Type **213** 2·50 2·30
543 14k.25 Polar bear (Buuti Pedersen) 5·25 5·00
544 30k.50 Abstract (Aka Hoegh) 12·50 12·00

214 Face and Envelope

2008. Europa. Letter Writing. Multicoloured. Ordinary or self-adhesive gum.
545 5k.75 Type **214** 2·75 2·50
546 7k.50 Female face and envelope 3·25 3·00

215 The Rocks

2008. Nordic Mythology. Multicoloured.
549 7k. Type **215** 3·00 3·75
550 8k. The Bear of the Lake 3·75 3·50
MS551 105×70 mm. Nos. 549/50 6·75 6·50
Stamps of a similar theme were issued by Aland Islands, Denmark, Faröe Islands, Finland, Iceland, Norway and Sweden.

216 *Halkieria evangelista*

2008. Fossils. Multicoloured.
552 1k. Type **216** 2·00 1·80
553 20k.50 *Ichthyostega stensioei* 9·50 9·00
554 25k. *Eudimorphodon* 11·50 11·00

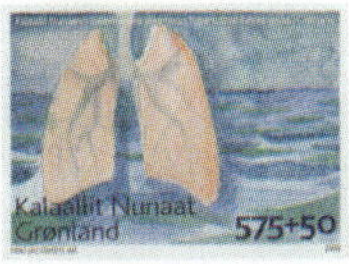

217 Lungs

2008. National Campaign against Tuberculosis.
555 **217** 5k.75+50ore multicoloured 12·00 12·00

218 Prince Joachim and Marie Cavallier

2008. Marriage of Prince Joachim and Marie Cavallier.
556 **218** 10k.25 multicoloured 4·50 4·25

219 Reindeer

2008. Christmas. Multicoloured. (a) Ordinary gum.
557 5k.75 Type **219** 1·50 1·40
558 7k.50 Decorated tree and village 2·00 1·80

(b) Self-adhesive.
559 5k.75 As Type **219** 1·50 1·40
560 7k.50 As No. 558 2·00 1·80

220 Scientists and Equipment

2008. Science. Anniversaries. Multicoloured.
561 6k.50 Type **220** (50th anniv of International Geophysical Year) 3·75 3·50
562 10k.50 French Research Station, Scoresbysund (75th anniv) 7·50 7·25
563 28k. Danish Arctic Station, Nuuk (125th anniv) 10·75 10·50
MS564 166×60 mm. Nos. 561/3 24·00 24·00

221 *Sofia* (expedition ship), 1883

2008. Alfred Erik Nordenskiold's Expeditions to Greenland, 1870–1883. Multicoloured.
565 8k.50 Type **221** 5·50 5·25
566 16k.25 A. E. Nordenskiold (28×33 mm) 6·50 6·25
MS567 166×60 mm. Nos. 565/6 13·00 13·00
Stamps of a similar design were issued by Finland.

222 *Schizoneura carcinoides*

2009. Fossils. Multicoloured.
568 2k. Type **222** 2·25 2·00
569 11k.50 *Scaphites rosenkrantzi* 6·75 6·50
570 22k. *Mallotus villosus* 11·00 10·50
Stamps of a similar design were issued by Finland.

223 Ice Crystal of Humans and Animals

2009. Preserve Polar Regions and Glaciers.
571 **223** 5k. multicoloured 3·00 2·75

224 Ursa Major and Aurora Borealis

2009. Europa. Astronomy. Multicoloured. Ordinary gum.
572 6k.25 Type **224** 3·75 3·50
573 8k. Ursa Major showing bear outline 4·50 4·25

(b) Self-adhesive.
574 6k.25 As Type **224** 3·75 3·50
575 8k. As No. 573 4·50 4·25

225 Enclosed Heart

2009. Neriuffit Kattuffiat (Greenlandic Cancer Society).
576 **225** 6.25k+50ore scarlet-vermilion and black 4·00 4·00
No. 576 the premium was for the benefit of cancer support.

226 Prince Henri

2009. 75th Birth Anniv of Prince Henri.
577 **226** 8k. multicoloured 4·50 4·25

227 Polar Bears (Ivalo Abelsen)

2009. Greenlandic Artists. Multicoloured.
578 6k. Type **227** 3·50 3·25
579 18k. *Window to the World* (fish) (Camilla Nielsen) 9·75 9·25
580 33k. *Gletscher* (Naja Abelsen) 19·00 18·00

228 Mountains and Colours

2009. Self-Governance.
581 **228** 6k.25 multicoloured 4·50 4·25

229 Matthew Henson and Polar Map

2009. Centenary of Matthew Henson's (first Afro-American to the North Pole) Participation in Polar Expedition.
582 **229** 9k. multicoloured 5·50 5·25

230 Scenes from *First Steps* (comic created by Nuka Godtfredsen)

2009. Greenlandic Comics.
583 **230** 15k.50 multicoloured 8·50 8·25
MS584 130×80 mm. As Type **230** 8·50 8·25

231 Flowers, Lake and Mountain

2009. SEPAC (small European mail services).
585 **231** 7k. multicoloured 3·00 2·75

232 Cryolite

2009. Science. Multicoloured.
586 1k. Type **232** 2·20 2·00
587 15k.50 *Himantolophus groenlandicus* 12·00 11·00
588 23k.50 Greenlandic gold 19·00 17·00
MS589 165×60 mm. Nos. 586/8 33·00 33·00

233 Family

2009. Christmas. Multicoloured. (a) Ordinary gum.
590 6k.25 Type **233** 3·75 3·50
591 8k. Baby and star 4·50 4·25

(b) Self-adhesive.
592 6k.25 As Type **233** 3·75 3·50
593 8k. As No. 591 4·50 4·25

234 Family

2009. Centenary of The North Star Mission Station, Thule.
594 **234** 15k.25 black and indigo 8·50 8·25

235 Otto Nordenskjold

2009. Otto Nordenskjold's Expeditions of 1900 and 1909.
595 **235** 30k. deep olive-brown and black 12·00 12·00
MS596 166×60 mm. As Type **235** 12·00 12·00

236 Polar Bear (Maria Paninguak Kjaerulff)

2010. Modern Art. Multicoloured.
597 6k.50 Type **236** 3·75 3·50
598 7k.50 Sun (Miki Jacobsen) (vert) 4·50 4·25
599 50k. Razorbills (Bolatta Sili-Hoegh) 30·00 30·00

237 Figure

2010. 25th Anniv of Silamiut Theatre Group.
600 **237** 7k.+50ore multicoloured 2·00 1·80
The premium was for the benefit of the theatre group.

238 Boy reading

2010. Europa. Children's Books. Multicoloured. (a) Ordinary gum.
601 8k.50 Type **238** 4·50 4·25
602 9k.50 Children reading 5·50 5·25

(b) Self-adhesive.
603 8k.50 As Type **238** 4·50 4·25
604 9k.50 As No. 602 5·50 5·25

239 Aircraft Tailfin and Helicopter

2010. 50th Anniv of Air Greenland Airline.
605 **239** 16k.50 multicoloured 9·50 9·25

240 Women

2010. Centenary of Women's Day.

606	**240**	12k.50 multicoloured	7·50	6·75

241 Waves

2010. Life at the Coast. Paintings by Aka Hoegh. Multicoloured.

607	7k. Type **241**	4·25	3·75
608	8k.50 Port	4·75	4·25
MS609	111×70 mm. Nos. 607/8	17·00	17·00

Stamps of a similar theme were issued by Denmark, Aland Islands, Faröe Islands, Finland, Iceland, Norway and Sweden.

242 Queen Margrethe

2010. 70th Birth Anniv of Queen Margrethe.

610	**242**	35k. multicoloured	24·00	22·00

243 Flag and Ice Floes

2010. 25th Anniv of Erfalasorput, National Flag.

611	**243**	7k. multicoloured	4·00	3·75

244 Scenes from *Boas & Co* (comic created by Robert Holmene)

2010. Greenlandic Comics.

612	**244** 23k.50 multicoloured	19·00	17·00
MS613	140×80 mm. As Type **244**	19·00	17·00

PARCEL POST STAMPS

P1 Arms of Greenland

1905

P4A	**P1**	1ore green	41·00	45·00
P5A	**P1**	2ore yellow	£225	85·00
P6A	**P1**	5ore brown	95·00	95·00
P7A	**P1**	10ore blue	35·00	48·00
P8A	**P1**	15ore violet	£140	£160
P9A	**P1**	20ore red	6·50	9·00
P12A	**P1**	3k. brown	80·00	£140
P13	**P1**	70ore violet	24·00	95·00
P14	**P1**	1k. yellow	24·00	70·00

Prices for used stamps are for rubber stamp cancellations applied in Copenhagen, the various Greenland cancellations being worth much more. Stamps with numeral cancellations have been used as saving stamps.

Pt. 1

GRENADA

One of the Windward Is., Br. W. Indies. Ministerial Government was introduced on 1 January 1960. Achieved Associated Statehood on 3 March 1967 and Independence on 7 February 1974.

1861. 12 pence = 1 shilling; 20 shillings = 1 pound.
1949. 100 cents = 1 West Indian dollar.

1

1861

6	1	6d. red	£600	13·00
14	1	1d. green	85·00	8·00

5

1875. Surch POSTAGE and value in words.

13	5	1s. mauve	£700	12·00
21	5	½d. mauve	14·00	5·50
22	5	2½d. lake	65·00	7·50
23	5	4d. blue	£120	8·00

1883. Revenue stamp surch crown and value (in green) optd POSTAGE.

27	1d. orange	£400	60·00

1883. Revenue stamp as last but optd POSTAGE diagonally on each half.

29	Half of 1d. orange	£275	£110

13

1883

30	13	½d. green	1·50	1·00
31	13	1d. red	80·00	3·25
32	13	2½d. blue	7·00	1·00
33	13	4d. grey	8·00	2·00
34	13	6d. mauve	3·25	4·25
35	13	8d. brown	10·00	13·00
36	13	1s. violet	£140	55·00

1886. Revenue stamps as No. 27 but surch POSTAGE. and value in words or figures.

37	5	1d. on 1½d. orange	55·00	40·00
38	5	1d. on 1s. orange	48·00	38·00
39	5	1d. on 4d. orange	£170	90·00
41	5	4d. on 2s. orange	45·00	20·00
43	5	½d. on 2s. orange	15·00	26·00

1887. As T 13, but inscr "GRENADA POSTAGE & REVENUE" at top.

40	13	1d. red	3·50	1·75

1890. Revenue stamp as No. 27 but surch POSTAGE AND REVENUE 1d.

45	5	1d. on 2s. orange	65·00	65·00

1891. Surch POSTAGE AND REVENUE 1d.

46	13	1d. on 8d. brown	11·00	16·00

1891. Surch 2½d.

47	2½d. on 8d. brown	14·00	11·00

21

1895

48	21	½d. mauve and green	3·00	1·75
49	21	1d. mauve and red	4·50	75
50	21	2d. mauve and brown	40·00	32·00
51	21	2½d. mauve and blue	8·50	1·50
52	21	3d. mauve and orange	6·50	16·00
53	21	6d. mauve and green	18·00	50·00
54	21	8d. mauve and black	12·00	45·00
55	21	1s. green and orange	21·00	55·00

23 Flagship of Columbus (Columbus named Grenada "La Concepcion")

1898. 400th Anniv of Discovery of Grenada by Columbus.

56	23	2½d. blue	18·00	6·00

1902. As T 21, but portrait of King Edward VII.

57	½d. purple and green	3·25	1·25
58	1d. purple and red	5·00	30
59	2d. purple and brown	3·25	10·00
60	2½d. purple and blue	4·00	2·75
61	3d. purple and orange	4·00	9·00
62	6d. purple and green	3·00	17·00
63	1s. green and orange	7·50	30·00
64	2s. green and blue	29·00	60·00
65	5s. green and red	45·00	75·00
66	10s. green and purple	£130	£250

26 Badge of the Colony

1906

77	26	½d. green	4·50	30
78	26	1d. red	7·00	10
79	26	2d. orange	3·00	3·00
80	26	2½d. blue	6·00	1·50
83	26	10s. green and red on green	£120	£250
84	26	3d. purple on yellow	4·75	1·75
85	26	6d. purple	20·00	16·00
86	26	1s. black on green	7·00	4·50
87	26	2s. blue and purple on blue	24·00	12·00
88	26	5s. green and red on yellow	60·00	75·00

28

1913

94	28	2½d. blue	1·75	1·75
96	28	3d. purple on yellow	65	85
97	28	6d. purple	1·50	9·00
98a	28	1s. black on green	1·25	7·50
99	28	2s. purple and blue on blue	6·50	12·00
101	28	10s. green and red on green	55·00	95·00
112	28	½d. green	1·25	30
113	28	1d. red	80	75
114	28	1d. brown	1·50	30
115	28	1½d. red	1·50	1·50
116	28	2d. orange	1·25	30
117	28	2d. grey	2·50	2·75
118	28	2½d. grey	1·00	9·00
121	28	3d. blue	1·25	11·00
123	28	4d. black and red on yellow	1·00	3·75
124	28	5d. purple and green	1·50	4·25
126	28	6d. black and red	2·25	2·50
127	28	9d. purple and black	2·25	9·50
129	28	1s. brown	3·00	10·00
131	28	2s.6d. black & red on blue	7·00	23·00
132	28	3s. green and violet	9·00	27·00
133	28	5s. green and red on yellow	12·00	35·00

1916. Optd WAR TAX.

111	1d. red	30	20

31 Grand Anse Beach

32 Badge of the Colony

1934

135	31	½d. green	15	1·25
136a	32	1d. black and brown	60	35
137a	-	1½d. black and red	1·25	40
138	32	2d. black and orange	1·00	75
139	-	2½d. blue	50	50
140	32	3d. black and olive	1·00	2·75
141	32	6d. black and purple	2·00	1·75
142	32	1s. black and brown	2·25	4·00
143	32	2s.6d. black and blue	8·00	28·00
144	32	5s. black and violet	45·00	50·00

DESIGNS—VERT: 1½d. Grand Etang; 2½d. St. George's.

1935. Silver Jubilee. As T 10a of Gambia.

145	½d. black and green	1·00	1·25
146	1d. blue and grey	1·25	1·75
147	1½d. blue and red	1·25	3·75
148	1s. grey and purple	13·00	32·00

1937. Coronation. As T 10b of Gambia.

149	1d. violet	40	1·75
150	1½d. red	40	50
151	2½d. blue	80	1·25

35 King George VI

1937

152b	35	¼d. brown	30	2·00

40 Badge of the Colony

1938. As 1934, but with portrait of King George VI.

153a	31	½d. green	60	1·25
154a	32	1d. black and brown	50	50
155	-	1½d. black and red	50	1·25
156	32	2d. black and orange	30	50
157	-	2½d. blue	30	30
158ab	32	3d. black and olive	30	80
159	32	6d. black and purple	3·00	40
160	32	1s. black and brown	4·00	40
161	32	2s. black and blue	30·00	1·75
162	32	5s. black and violet	4·50	4·50
163e	40	10s. blue and red	38·00	11·00

1946. Victory. As T 11a of Gambia.

164	1½d. red	10	50
165	3½d. blue	10	1·00

1948. Silver Wedding. As T 11b/c of Gambia.

166	1½d. red	15	10
167	10s. grey	20·00	20·00

1949. U.P.U. As T 11d/g of Gambia.

168	5c. blue	15	10
169	6c. olive	1·50	2·50
170	12c. mauve	15	30
171	24c. brown	15	40

41 King George VI

42 Badge of the Colony

1951

172	41	½c. black and brown	15	1·60
173	41	1c. black and green	15	25
174	41	2c. black and brown	15	50
175	41	3c. black and red	15	10
176	41	4c. black and orange	35	40
177	41	5c. black and violet	20	10
178	41	6c. black and olive	30	60
179	41	7c. black and blue	1·75	10
180	41	12c. black and purple	2·25	30
181	42	25c. black and brown	2·25	80
182	42	50c. black and blue	6·50	40
183	42	$1.50 black and orange	7·50	7·00
184	42	$2.50 slate and red	9·50	5·50

No. 184 is larger, 24½x30½ mm.

43a Arms of University

43b Princess Alice

1951. Inauguration of B.W.I. University College.

185	43a	3c. black and red	45	1·25
186	43b	6c. black and olive	45	50

1951. New Constitution. Nos. 175/7 and 180 optd NEW CONSTITUTION 1951.

187	41	3c. black and red	25	60
188	41	4c. black and orange	25	60
189	41	5c. black and violet	30	80
190	41	12c. black and purple	30	1·00

1953. Coronation. As T 11h of Gambia.

191	3c. black and red	20	10

1953. As T 41, but with portrait of Queen Elizabeth II, and T 42, but Royal Cypher changed.

192		½c. black and brown	10	10
193		1c. black and green	10	10
195		3c. black and red	10	10
196		4c. black and orange	10	10
197		5c. black and violet	10	10
198		6c. black and olive	2·00	1·25
199		7c. black and blue	2·50	10
201	42	25c. black and brown	1·25	20
202	42	50c. black and blue	5·50	1·00
203	42	$1.50 black and orange	11·00	14·00
204	42	$2.50 slate and red	27·00	10·00
214	41	2c. black and brown	60	10
219	41	12c. black and purple	40	50

No. 204 is larger, 24½x30½ mm.

47a Federation Map

1958. British Caribbean Federation.

205	47a	3c. green	35	10
206	47a	6c. blue	45	60
207	47a	12c. red	55	10

48 Queen Victoria, Queen Elizabeth II, Mail Van and Post Office, St. George's

1961. Grenada Stamp Centenary.

208	48	3c. red and black	25	10
209	-	8c. blue and orange	55	25
210	-	25c. lake and blue	55	25

DESIGNS (incorporating Queen Victoria and Queen Elizabeth II): 8c. Flagship of Columbus; 25c. "Solent I" (paddle-steamer) and Douglas DC-3 aircraft.

1963. Freedom from Hunger. As T 21a of Gambia.

211	8c. green	30	15

1963. Centenary of Red Cross. As T 21b of Gambia.

212	3c. red and black	20	15
213	25c. red and blue	40	15

1965. Centenary of I.T.U. As T 45 of Gibraltar.

221	2c. orange and olive	10	10
222	50c. yellow and red	25	20

1965. I.C.Y. As T 46 of Gibraltar.

223	1c. purple and turquoise	10	15
224	25c. green and lavender	20	15

1966. Churchill Commem. As T 47 of Gibraltar.

225	1c. blue	10	15
226	3c. green	10	15
227	25c. brown	15	10
228	35c. violet	25	15

49 Queen Elizabeth II and Duke of Edinburgh

1966. Royal Visit.

229	**49**	3c. black and blue	25	15
230	**49**	35c. black and mauve	1·00	15

52 Hillsborough, Carriacou

1966. Multicoloured.

231	1c. Type **52**	20	1·25
232	2c. Bougainvillea	20	10
233	3c. Flamboyant plant	1·00	1·00
234	5c. Levera Beach	1·25	10
235	6c. Carenage, St. George's	1·00	10
236	8c. Annandale Falls	1·00	10
237	10c. Cocoa pods	50	10
238	12c. Inner Harbour	30	1·25
239	15c. Nutmeg	30	1·25
240	25c. St. George's	30	10
241	35c. Grand Anse beach	30	10
242	50c. Bananas	1·25	2·00
243	$1 Badge of the Colony (vert) (25×39 mm)	7·00	3·75
244	$2 Queen Elizabeth II (vert) (25×39 mm)	5·00	10·00
245	$3 Map of Grenada (vert) (25×39 mm)	4·50	16·00

1966. World Cup Football Championship. As T 48 of Gibraltar.

246	5c. multicoloured	10	10
247	50c. multicoloured	40	90

1966. Inauguration of W.H.O. Headquarters, Geneva. As T 54 of Gibraltar.

248	8c. black, green and blue	20	10
249	25c. black, purple and ochre	45	20

1966. 20th Anniv of UNESCO. As T 56a/c of Gibraltar.

250	2c. multicoloured	10	10
251	15c. yellow, violet and orange	15	10
252	50c. black, purple and orange	30	90

1967. Statehood. Nos. 232/3, 236 and 240 optd ASSOCIATED STATEHOOD 1967.

253	2c. multicoloured	10	15
254	3c. multicoloured	10	10
255	8c. multicoloured	15	10
256	25c. multicoloured	15	15

1967. World Fair, Montreal. Nos. 232, 237, 239 and 243/4 surch or optd expo67 MONTREAL CANADA and emblem.

257	1c. on 15c. multicoloured	10	20
258	2c. multicoloured	10	20
259	3c. on 10c. multicoloured	10	20
260	$1 multicoloured	30	25
261	$2 multicoloured	45	30

1967. Nos. 231/45 optd ASSOCIATED STATEHOOD.

262	**52**	1c. multicoloured	10	10
263	-	2c. multicoloured	10	10
264	-	3c. multicoloured	10	10
265	-	5c. multicoloured	10	10
266	-	6c. multicoloured	10	10
267	-	8c. multicoloured	10	10
268	-	10c. multicoloured	10	10
269	-	12c. multicoloured	10	10
270	-	15c. multicoloured	15	10
271	-	25c. multicoloured	20	10
272	-	35c. multicoloured	55	10
273	-	50c. multicoloured	1·00	20
274	-	$1 multicoloured	1·50	60
275	-	$2 multicoloured	1·25	3·75
276	-	$3 multicoloured	2·50	5·50

70 Kennedy and Local Flower

1968. 50th Birth Anniv of Pres. Kennedy. Multicoloured.

277	1c. Type **70**	10	25
278	15c. Type **70**	10	10
279	25c. Kennedy and strelitzia	10	10
280	35c. Kennedy and roses	10	10
281	50c. As 25c.	15	20
282	$1 As 35c.	25	60

73 Scout Bugler

1968. World Scout Jamboree, Idaho. Mult.

283	1c. Type **73**	10	10
284	2c. Scouts camping	10	10
285	3c. Lord Baden-Powell	10	10
286	35c. Type **73**	25	10
287	50c. As 2c.	35	20
288	$1 As 3c.	50	55

76 "Near Antibes"

1968. Paintings by Sir Winston Churchill. Multicoloured.

289	10c. Type **76**	10	10
290	12c. "The Mediterranean"	15	10
291	15c. "St. Jean, Cap Ferratt"	15	10
292	25c. Type **76**	20	10
293	35c. As No. 291	25	10
294	50c. Sir Winston painting	35	25

1968. No. 275 surch $5.

295	$5 on $2 multicoloured	1·25	2·25

1968. "Children Need Milk". Surch CHILDREN NEED MILK and value. (a) Nos. 244/5.

296	2c.+3c. on $2 multicoloured	10	10
297	3c.+3c. on $3 multicoloured	10	10

(b) Nos. 243/4.

298	1c.+3c. on $1 multicoloured	10	40
299	2c.+3c. on $2 multicoloured	17·00	55·00

83 Edith McGuire (U.S.A.)

1968. Olympic Games, Mexico.

300	**83**	1c. brown, black and blue	20	75
301	-	2c. multicoloured	20	75
302	-	3c. scarlet, brown and green	20	75
303	**83**	10c. multicoloured	30	80
304	-	50c. multicoloured	55	80
305	-	60c. red, brown and orange	60	80

DESIGNS: 2c., 50c. Arthur Wint (Jamaica); 3c., 60c. Ferreira da Silva (Brazil).

86 Hibiscus

1968. Multicoloured.

306	1c. Type **86**	10	10
307	2c. Strelitzia	10	10
308	3c. Bougainvillea	10	10
309	5c. Rock hind (horiz)	10	10
310	6c. Sailfish	10	10
311	8c. Red snapper (horiz)	10	60
312	10c. Marine toad (horiz)	10	10
313	12c. Turtle	15	10
314	15c. Tree boa (horiz)	1·00	60
314a	15c. Thunbergia	2·25	2·50
315	25c. Greater Trinidadian murine opossum	30	10
316	35c. Nine-banded armadillo (horiz)	35	10
317	50c. Mona monkey	45	25
317a	75c. Yacht in St. George's Harbour (horiz)	14·00	8·50
318	$1 Bananaquit	3·00	1·50
319	$2 Brown pelican	8·00	14·00
320	$3 Magnificent frigate bird	4·50	8·00
321	$5 Bare-eyed thrush	11·00	26·00

Nos. 318/21 are larger, 25½×48 mm.

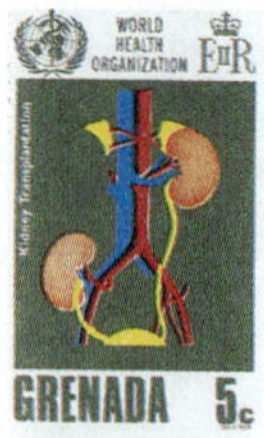

102 Kidney Transplant

1968. 20th Anniv of W.H.O. Multicoloured.

322	5c. Type **102**	20	10
323	25c. Heart transplant	30	10
324	35c. Lung transplant	30	10
325	50c. Eye transplant	40	50

106 "The Adoration of the Kings" (Veronese)

1968. Christmas.

326	**106**	5c. multicoloured	10	10
327	-	15c. multicoloured	10	10
328	-	35c. multicoloured	10	10
329	-	$1 multicoloured	30	40

DESIGNS: 15c. "Madonna and Child with Saints John and Catherine" (Titian); 35c. "The Adoration of the Kings" (Botticelli); $1 "A Warrior Adoring" (Catena).

1969. Caribbean Free Trade Area Exhibition. Nos. 300/5 surch VISIT CARIFTA EXPO '69 April 5-30 and value.

330	**83**	5c. on 1c.	15	30
331	-	8c. on 2c.	15	30
332	-	25c. on 3c.	15	30
333	**83**	35c. on 10c.	15	30
334	-	$1 on 50c.	20	40
335	-	$2 on 60c.	35	60

111 Dame Hylda Bynoe (Governor) and Island Scene

1969. Carifta Expo '69. Multicoloured.

336	5c. Type **111**	10	10
337	15c. Premier E. M. Gairy and island scene	10	10
338	50c. Type **111**	10	30
339	60c. Emblems of 1958 and 1967 World's Fairs	10	65

114 Dame Hylda Bynoe

1969. Human Rights Year. Multicoloured.

340	5c. Type **114**	10	10
341	25c. Dr. Martin Luther King	15	10
342	35c. As 5c.	15	10
343	$1 "Balshazzar's Feast" (Rembrandt) (horiz)	30	45

117 Batsman and Wicket-keeper

1969. Cricket.

344	**117**	3c. yellow, brown and blue	35	1·00
345	-	10c. multicoloured	35	40
346	-	25c. brown, ochre & green	55	85
347	-	35c. multicoloured	75	90

DESIGNS: 10c. Batsman playing defensive stroke; 25c. Batsman sweeping ball; 35c. Batsman playing on-drive.

129 Astronaut handling Moon Rock

1969. First Man on the Moon. Multicoloured.

348	½c. As Type **129** but larger (56×35 mm)	10	20
349	1c. Moon rocket and moon	10	20
350	2c. Module landing	10	20
351	3c. Declaration left on the moon	10	20
352	8c. Module leaving rocket	15	10
353	25c. Rocket lifting-off (vert)	35	10
354	35c. Spacecraft in orbit (vert)	35	10
355	50c. Capsule with parachutes (vert)	45	30
356	$1 Type **129**	60	1·25
MS357	115×90 mm. Nos. 351 and 356. Imperf	1·00	2·75

130 Gandhi

1969. Birth Cent of Mahatma Gandhi. Mult.

358	6c. Type **130**	45	30
359	15c. Gandhi standing	60	10
360	25c. Gandhi walking	70	10
361	$1 Head of Gandhi	1·00	65
MS362	155×122 mm. Nos. 358/61. Imperf	2·25	3·50

1969. Christmas. Nos. 326/9 optd 1969 and surch (No. 363).

363	-	2c. on 15c. multicoloured	10	2·00
364	**106**	5c. multicoloured	10	15
365	-	35c. multicoloured	20	10
366	-	$1 multicoloured	80	2·25

135 "Blackbeard" (Edward Teach)

1970. Pirates.

367	**135**	15c. black	35	10
368	-	25c. green	50	10
369	-	50c. lilac	90	20
370	-	$1 carmine	1·50	75

DESIGNS: 25c. Anne Bonney; 50c. Jean Lafitte; $1 Mary Read.

1970. No. 348 surch 5c.

371	5c. on ½c. multicoloured	10	10

141/2 "The Last Supper" (detail, Del Sarto) (image scaled to 75% of original size)

1970. Easter. Paintings.

372	**141**	5c. multicoloured	10	40
373	**142**	5c. multicoloured	10	40
374	-	15c. multicoloured	15	40
375	-	15c. multicoloured	15	40
376	-	25c. multicoloured	15	40
377	-	25c. multicoloured	15	40
378	-	60c. multicoloured	20	60
379	-	60c. multicoloured	20	60
MS380		120×140 mm. Nos. 376/9	75	1·75

DESIGNS: 15c. "Christ crowned with Thorns" (detail, Van Dyck); 25c. "The Passion of Christ" (detail, Memling); 60c. "Christ in the Tomb" (detail, Rubens).

Each value was issued in sheets containing the two stamps se-tenant. Each design is spread over two stamps as in Types **141/2**.

149 Girl with Kittens in Pram

1970. Birth Bicentenary of Wordsworth. "Children and Pets". Multicoloured.

381	5c. Type **149**	15	15
382	15c. Girl with puppy and kitten	25	15
383	30c. Boy with fishing-rod and cat	30	40
384	60c. Boys and girls with cats and dogs	40	2·00
MS385	Two sheets, each 114×126 mm. Nos. 381, 383 and Nos. 382, 384. Imperf	1·00	2·00

153 Parliament of India

1970. 7th Regional Conference of Commonwealth Parliamentary Association. Parliament Buildings. Multicoloured.

386	5c. Type **153**	10	10
387	25c. Great Britain	10	10
388	50c. Canada	20	15
389	60c. Grenada	20	15
MS390	126×90 mm. Nos. 386/9	50	90

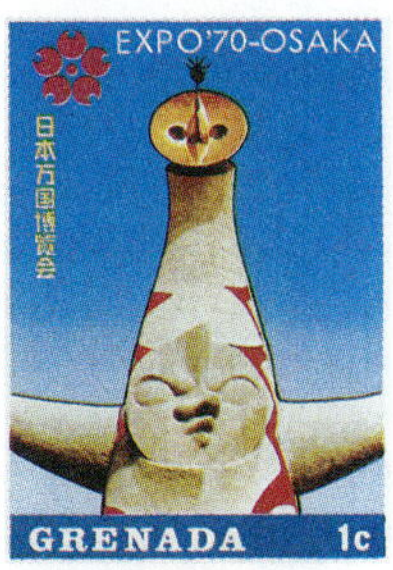

157 Tower of the Sun

1970. World Fair, Osaka. Multicoloured.

391	1c. Type **157**	10	65
392	2c. Livelihood and Industry Pavilion (horiz)	10	65
393	3c. Flower painting, 1634	10	65
394	10c. "Adam and Eve" (Tintoretto) (horiz)	15	10
395	25c. Organization For Economic Co-operation and Development (O.E.C.D.) Pavilion (horiz)	35	10
396	50c. San Francisco Pavilion	40	1·60
MS397	121×91 mm. $1 Japanese Pavilion (56×34 mm)	55	1·50

164 Roosevelt and "Raising U.S. Flag on Iwo Jima"

1970. 25th Anniv of Ending of World War II. Multicoloured.

398	½c. Type **164**	10	1·75
399	5c. Zhukov and "Fall of Berlin"	70	65
400	15c. Churchill and "Evacuation at Dunkirk"	2·00	75
401	25c. De Gaulle and "Liberation of Paris"	1·50	60
402	50c. Eisenhower and "D-Day Landing"	1·75	2·00
403	60c. Montgomery and "Battle of Alamein"	2·25	4·25
MS404	163×113 mm. Nos. 398, 400, 402/3	2·75	7·00

1970. "Philympia 1970" Stamp Exhibition, London. Nos. 353/6 optd PHILYMPIA LONDON 1970.

405	-	25c. multicoloured	10	10
406	-	35c. multicoloured	10	10
407	-	50c. multicoloured	15	15
408	**129**	$1 multicoloured	20	30

170 U.P.U. Headquarters Building and Transport

1970. New U.P.U. Headquarters Building. Multicoloured.

409	15c. Type **170**	1·50	40
410	25c. As Type **170**, but modern transport	1·50	40
411	50c. Sir Rowland Hill and U.P.U. Building (vert)	35	60
412	$1 Abraham Lincoln and U.P.U. Building (vert)	45	3·00
MS413	79×85 mm. Nos. 411/12	1·00	3·50

171 "The Madonna of the Goldfinch" (Tiepolo)

1970. Christmas. Multicoloured.

414	½c. Type **171**	10	35
415	½c. "The Virgin and Child with St. Peter and St. Paul" (Bouts)	10	35
416	½c. "The Virgin and Child" (Bellini)	10	35
417	2c. "The Madonna of the Basket" (Correggio)	10	35
418	3c. Type **171**	10	35
419	35c. As No. 415	35	10
420	50c. As 2c.	45	40
421	$1 As No. 416	65	1·60
MS422	102×87 mm. Nos. 420/1	1·00	3·00

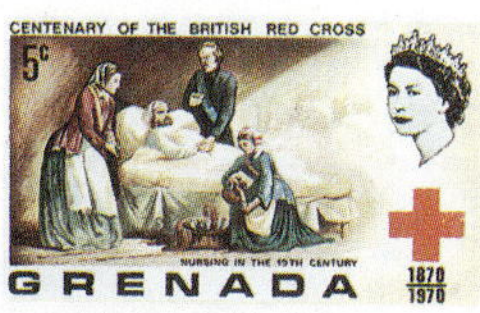

172 19th-Century Nursing

1970. Cent of British Red Cross. Multicoloured.

423	5c. Type **172**	20	10
424	15c. Military ambulance, 1918	25	10
425	25c. First-aid post, 1941	35	10
426	60c. Red Cross transport, 1970	90	1·50
MS427	113×82 mm. Nos. 423/6	2·00	1·60

173 John Dewey and Art Lesson

1971. Int Education Year. Multicoloured.

428	5c. Type **173**	10	10
429	10c. Jean-Jacques Rousseau and "Alphabetization"	15	10
430	50c. Maimonides and laboratory	75	25
431	$1 Bertrand Russell and mathematics class	95	40
MS432	90×98 mm. Nos. 430/1	1·00	2·00

174 Jennifer Hosten and Outline of Grenada

1971. Winner of "Miss World" Competition (1970).

433	**174**	5c. multicoloured	10	10
434	**174**	10c. multicoloured	10	10
435	**174**	15c. multicoloured	15	10
436	**174**	25c. multicoloured	15	10
437	**174**	35c. multicoloured	15	10
438	**174**	50c. multicoloured	35	55
MS439		92×89 mm. **174** 50c. multicoloured. Printed on silk. Imperf	75	1·75

175 French and Canadian Scouts

1971. 13th World Scout Jamboree, Asagiri, Japan. Multicoloured.

440	5c. Type **175**	15	10
441	35c. German and American scouts	30	25
442	50c. Australian and Japanese scouts	30	50
443	75c. Grenada and British scouts	35	1·00
MS444	101×114 mm. Nos. 442/3	1·25	2·50

176 "Napoleon reviewing the Guard" (E. Detaille)

1971. 150th Death Anniv of Napoleon Bonaparte. Paintings. Multicoloured.

445	5c. Type **176**	15	15
446	15c. "Napoleon before Madrid" (Vernet)	20	15
447	35c. "Napoleon crossing Mt. St. Bernard" (David)	25	15
448	$2 "Napoleon in his Study" (David)	50	1·50
MS449	101×76 mm. No. 447. Imperf	1·25	1·60

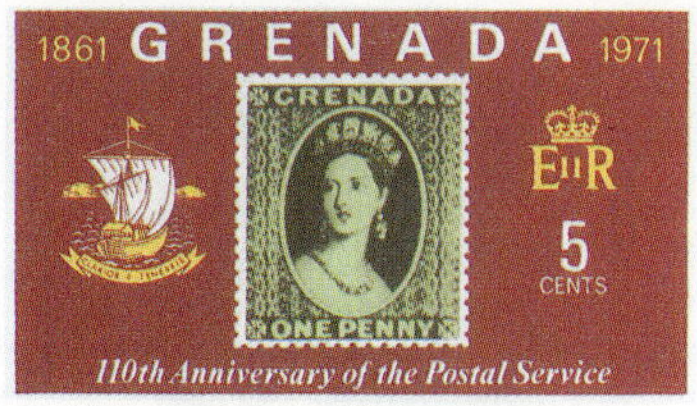

177 1d. Stamp of 1861 and Badge of Grenada

1971. 110th Anniv of the Postal Service. Mult.

450	5c. Type **177**	25	30
451	15c. 6d. stamp of 1861 and Queen Elizabeth II	30	15
452	35c. 1d. and 6d. stamps of 1861 and badge of Grenada	50	20
453	50c. Scroll and 1d. stamp of 1861	60	2·25
MS454	96×114 mm. Nos. 452/3	1·00	1·00

178 Apollo Splashdown

1971. Apollo Moon Exploration Series. Mult.

455	1c. Type **178**	10	50
456	2c. Recovery of "Apollo 13"	10	50
457	3c. Separation of Lunar Module from "Apollo 14"	10	50
458	10c. Shepard and Mitchell taking samples of moon rock	25	10
459	25c. Moon Buggy	75	20
460	$1 "Apollo 15" blast-off (vert)	2·00	3·75
MS461	77×108 mm. 50c. as $1	1·40	1·50

179 67th Regt. of Foot, 1787

1971. Military Uniforms. Multicoloured.

462	½c. Type **179**	10	30
463	1c. 45th Regt. of Foot, 1792	10	30
464	2c. 29th Regt. of Foot, 1794	10	30
465	10c. 9th Regt. of Foot, 1801	45	10
466	25c. 2nd Regt. of Foot, 1815	85	20
467	$1 70th Regt. of Foot, 1764	2·50	2·25
MS468	108×99 mm. Nos. 466/7	2·25	2·75

180 "The Adoration of the Kings" (Memling)

1972. Christmas (1971). Multicoloured.

469	15c. Type **180**	15	10
470	25c. "Madonna and Child" (Michelangelo)	20	10
471	35c. "Madonna and Child" (Murillo)	25	10
472	50c. "The Virgin with the Apple" (Memling)	30	2·00
MS473	105×80 mm. $1 "The Adoration of the Kings" (Mostaert)	75	1·25

1972. Winter Olympic Games, Sapporo, Japan. Nos. 462/4 surch WINTER OLYMPICS FEB.3-13,1972 SAPPORO,JAPAN, Olympic rings and premium. Nos. 476/7 additionally optd AIR MAIL.

474	$2 on 2c. mult (postage)	50	90
MS475	108×99 mm. Nos. 466/7	1·00	1·25
476	35c. on ½c. multicoloured (air)	15	25
477	50c. on 1c. multicoloured	15	35

174 Jennifer Hosten and Outline of Grenada

1972. General Election. Nos. 307/8, 310 and 315 optd VOTE FEB. 28 1972.

478	2c. multicoloured	20	65
479	3c. multicoloured	20	65
480	6c. multicoloured	20	65
481	25c. multicoloured	50	30

183 King Arthur

1972. UNICEF. Multicoloured.

482	½c. Type **183**	10	20
483	1c. Robin Hood	10	20
484	2c. Robinson Crusoe (vert)	10	20
485	25c. Type **183**	10	10
486	50c. As 1c.	25	40
487	75c. As 2c.	30	1·10
488	$1 Mary and her little lamb (vert)	45	1·25
MS489	65×98 mm. No. 488	55	80

1972. "Interpex" Stamp Exbn, New York. Nos. 433/8 optd INTERPEX 1972.

490	5c. multicoloured	10	10
491	10c. multicoloured	10	10
492	15c. multicoloured	10	10
493	25c. multicoloured	10	10
494	35c. multicoloured	15	15
495	50c. multicoloured	25	30
MS496	92×89 mm. **174** 50c. multicoloured. Printed on silk. Imperf	6·00	11·00

1972. Nos. 306/8 and 433 surch 12c.

497	-	12c. on 1c. multicoloured	40	70
498	-	12c. on 2c. multicoloured	40	70
499	-	12c. on 3c. multicoloured	40	70
500	**174**	12c. on 5c. multicoloured	40	70

1972. Air. Optd AIR MAIL or surch in addition.

501	-	5c. mult (No. 309)	10	20
502	-	8c. mult (No. 311)	15	10
503	-	10c. mult (No. 312)	15	10
504	-	15c. mult (No. 314a)	30	10
505	-	25c. mult (No. 315)	35	20
506	-	30c. on 1c. mult (No. 306)	40	25
507	-	35c. mult (No. 316)	40	25
508	-	40c. on 2c. mult (No. 307)	50	25
509	-	45c. on 3c. mult (No. 308)	55	35
510	-	50c. mult (No. 317)	55	35
511	-	60c. on 5c. mult (No. 309)	60	40
512	-	70c. on 6c. mult (No. 310)	70	75
513	-	$1 multicoloured (No. 318)	7·00	1·00
514	-	$1.35 on 8c. mult (No. 311)	3·50	2·25
515	-	$2 multicoloured (No. 319)	9·50	10·00
516	-	$3 multicoloured (No. 320)	10·00	11·00
517	-	$5 multicoloured (No. 321)	12·00	18·00
518	**175**	5c. multicoloured	1·10	20
519	-	35c. mult (No. 441)	2·50	30
520	-	50c. mult (No. 442)	2·50	45
521	-	75c. mult (No. 443)	3·50	1·50

187 Yachting

1972. Olympic Games, Munich. Multicoloured.

522	½c. Type **187** (postage)	10	10
523	1c. Show-jumping	10	10
524	2c. Running (vert)	10	10
525	35c. As 2c.	30	10
526	50c. As 1c.	40	40
527	25c. Boxing (air)	25	10
528	$1 As 25c.	65	85
MS529	82×85 mm. 60c. as 25c. and 70c. as 1c.	1·00	1·40

1972. Royal Silver Wedding. As T 98 of Gibraltar, but with Badge of Grenada and Nutmegs in background.

530	8c. brown	10	10
531	$1 blue	45	55

189 Boy Scout Saluting

1972. 65th Anniv of Boy Scouts. Multicoloured.

532	½c. Type **189** (postage)	10	10
533	1c. Scouts knotting ropes	10	10
534	2c. Scouts shaking hands	10	10
535	3c. Lord Baden-Powell	10	10
536	75c. As 2c.	70	2·75
537	$1 As 3c.	75	2·75
538	25c. Type **189** (air)	40	20
539	35c. As 1c.	50	20
MS540	87×88 mm. 60c. as 3c. and 70c. as 2c.	1·50	1·50

190 Madonna and Child

1972. Christmas. Multicoloured.

541	1c. Type **190**	10	25
542	3c. The Three Kings	10	25
543	5c. The Nativity	10	10
544	25c. Type **190**	15	10
545	35c. As 3c.	15	10
546	$1 As 5c.	40	1·00
MS547	102×76 mm. 60c. Type **190** and 70c. as 3c.	60	80

191 Greater Flamingos

1973. National Zoo. Multicoloured.

548	25c. Type **191**	70	35
549	35c. Brazilian tapir	40	35
550	60c. Blue and yellow macaws	1·25	2·00
551	70c. Ocelot	70	2·25

192 Class II Racing Yacht

1973. Yachting. Multicoloured.

552	25c. Type **192**	25	10
553	35c. Harbour, St. George's	30	10
554	60c. Yacht "Bloodhound"	45	65
555	70c. St. George's	50	75

193 Helios (Greek god) and Earth orbiting the Sun

1973. Centenary of I.M.O./W.M.O. Greek Gods. Multicoloured.

556	½c. Type **193**	10	10
557	1c. Poseidon and "Normad" storm detector	10	10
558	2c. Zeus and radarscope	10	10
559	3c. Iris and weather ballon	10	10
560	35c. Hermes and "ATS-3" satellite	20	10
561	50c. Zephyrus and diagram of pressure zones	25	30
562	75c. Demeter and space photo	25	60
563	$1 Selene and rainfall diagram	25	1·00
MS564	123×92 mm. $2 Computer weather map (42×31 mm.)	1·00	1·25

194 Racing Class Yachts

1973. Carriacou Regatta. Multicoloured.

565	½c. Type **194**	10	10
566	1c. Cruising Class yacht	10	10
567	2c. Open-decked sloops	10	10
568	35c. "Mermaid" (sloop)	30	10
569	50c. St. George's Harbour	35	25
570	75c. Map of Carriacou	40	55
571	$1 Boat-building	55	70
MS572	109×88 mm. $2 End of race	1·00	1·75

195 Ignatius Semmelweis (obstetrician)

1973. 25th Anniv of W.H.O. Multicoloured.

573	½c. Type **195**	10	35
574	1c. Louis Pasteur	10	35
575	2c. Edward Jenner	10	35
576	3c. Sigmund Freud	10	35
577	25c. Emil von Behring (bacteriologist)	65	10
578	35c. Carl Jung	75	20
579	50c. Charles Calmette (bacteriologist)	1·10	1·00
580	$1 William Harvey	1·40	2·50
MS581	105×80 mm. $2 Marie Curie	1·25	1·60

196 Princess Anne and Capt. Mark Phillips

1973. Royal Wedding.

582	**196**	25c. multicoloured	10	10
583	**196**	$2 multicoloured	30	45
MS584		79×100 mm. 75c. and $1 as Nos. 582/3	40	30

197 "Virgin and Child" (Maratti)

1973. Christmas. Multicoloured.

585	½c. Type **197**	10	10
586	1c. "Madonna and Child" (Crivelli)	10	10
587	2c. "Virgin and Child with two Angels" (Verrocchio)	10	10
588	3c. "Adoration of the Shepherds" (Roberti)	10	10
589	25c. "The Holy Family with the Infant Baptist" (Baroccio)	15	10
590	35c. "The Holy Family" (Bronzino)	15	10
591	75c. "Mystic Nativity" (Botticelli)	20	20
592	$1 "Adoration of the Kings" (Geertgen)	25	30
MS593	89×89 mm. $2 "Adoration of the Kings" (Mostaert) (30×45 mm)	1·00	1·10

1974. Independence. Nos. 306/9, 311/13, 315/16 and 317a/21 optd INDEPENDENCE 7TH FEB. 1974.

594	**86**	1c. multicoloured	10	50
595	-	2c. multicoloured	10	50
596	-	3c. multicoloured	10	50
597	-	5c. multicoloured	10	10
598	-	8c. multicoloured	15	10
599	-	10c. multicoloured	20	15
600	-	12c. multicoloured	20	15
601	-	25c. multicoloured	45	25
602	-	35c. multicoloured	75	25
603	-	75c. multicoloured	2·00	1·50
604	-	$1 multicoloured	3·75	1·75
605	-	$2 multicoloured	6·00	6·50
606	-	$3 multicoloured	8·00	8·50
607	-	$5 multicoloured	12·00	17·00

199 Creative Arts Theatre, Jamaica Campus

1974. 25th Anniv of University of West Indies. Multicoloured.

608	10c. Type **199**	10	10
609	25c. Marryshow House	10	10
610	50c. Chapel, Jamaica Campus (vert)	20	10
611	$1 University arms (vert)	30	30
MS612	69×86 mm. $2 as No. 611	50	1·00

200 Nutmeg Pods and Scarlet Mace

1974. Independence. Multicoloured.

613	3c. Type **200**	10	10
614	8c. Map of Grenada	30	10
615	25c. Prime Minister Eric Gairy	15	10
616	35c. Grand Anse Beach and flag	80	10
617	$1 Coat of arms	35	40
MS618	91×125 mm. $2 as $1	55	1·00

201 Footballers (West Germany v. Chile)

1974. World Cup Football Championship, West Germany. Multicoloured.

619	½c. Type **201**	10	10
620	1c. East Germany v. Australia	10	10
621	2c. Yugoslavia v. Brazil	10	10
622	10c. Scotland v. Zaire	10	10
623	25c. Netherlands v. Uruguay	15	10
624	50c. Sweden v. Bulgaria	20	10
625	75c. Italy v. Haiti	35	15
626	$1 Poland v. Argentina	50	25
MS627	114×76 mm. $2 Country flags	1·00	1·75

202 Early U.S. Mail-trains and Concorde

1974. Centenary of U.P.U. Multicoloured.

628	½c. Type **202**	30	10
629	1c. "Caesar" (snow) (1839) and Westland Wessex HU Mk 5 helicopter	30	10
630	2c. Airmail transport	30	10
631	8c. Pigeon post (1480) and telephone dial	30	10
632	15c. 18th-century bellman and tracking antenna	30	10
633	25c. Messenger (1450) and satellite	35	10
634	35c. French pillar-box (1850) and mail-boat	50	10
635	$1 18th-century German post-man and British Advanced Passenger Train	1·50	85
MS636	105×66 mm. $2 St. Gotthard mail-coach (1735)	1·00	1·75

203 Sir Winston Churchill

1974. Birth Centenary of Sir Winston Churchill.

637	**203**	35c. multicoloured	15	10
638	**203**	$2 multicoloured	45	1·00
MS639		126×96 mm. 75c. as 35c. and $1 as $2	75	75

204 "Madonna and Child of the Eucharist" (Botticelli)

1974. Christmas. "Madonna and Child" paintings by named artists. Multicoloured.

640	½c. Type **204**	10	10
641	1c. Niccolo di Pietro	10	10
642	2c. Van der Weyden	10	10
643	3c. Bastiani	10	10
644	10c. Giovanni	10	10
645	25c. Van der Weyden	20	10
646	50c. Botticelli	25	20
647	$1 Mantegna	35	50
MS648	117×96 mm. $2 as 1c.	60	1·00

205 Yachts, Point Saline

1975. Multicoloured.

649	½c. Type **205**	10	85
650	1c. Yacht Club race	10	10
651	2c. Carenage taxi	10	10
652	3c. Large working boats	10	10
653a	5c. Deep-water dock	10	15
654	6c. Cocoa beans in drying trays	10	10
655	8c. Nutmegs	1·25	10
656	10c. Rum distillery, River Antoine Estate, c. 1785	10	10
657	12c. Cocoa tree	30	10
658	15c. Fishermen at Fontenoy	10	10
659	20c. Parliament Building	15	15
660	25c. Fort George cannons	20	15
661	35c. Pearls Airport	20	15
662	50c. General Post Office	15	30
663	75c. Carib's Leap, Sauteurs Bay	45	50
664	$1 Carenage, St. George's	50	70
665	$2 St. George's Harbour by night	50	1·50
666	$3 Grand Anse Beach	55	2·00
667	$5 Canoe Bay and Black Bay	65	3·00
668	$10 Sugar-loaf Island	1·25	6·50

Nos. 663/8 are size 45×28 mm.

206 Sailfish

1975. Big Game Fishing. Multicoloured.

669	½c. Type **206**	10	10
670	1c. Blue marlin	10	10
671	2c. White marlin	10	10
672	10c. Yellow-finned tuna	10	10
673	25c. Wahoo	25	10
674	50c. Dolphin (fish)	40	15
675	70c. Giant grouper	60	20
676	$1 Great barracuda	80	35
MS677	107×80 mm. $2 Short-finned mako	1·25	1·25

207 Granadilla Barbadine

1975. Flowers. Multicoloured.

678	½c. Type **207**	10	10
679	1c. Bleeding Heart (Easter Lily)	10	10
680	2c. Poinsettia	10	10
681	3c. Cocoa flower	10	10
682	10c. Gladioli	10	10
683	25c. Redhead/Yellowhead	20	10
684	50c. Plumbago	30	15
685	$1 Orange flower	50	25
MS686	102×82 mm. $2 Barbados gooseberry	1·10	1·25

208 Dove, Grenada Flag and U.N. Emblem

1975. Grenada's Admission to the U.N. (1974). Multicoloured.

687	½c. Type **208**	10	10
688	1c. Grenada and U.N. flags	10	10
689	2c. Grenada coat of arms	10	10
690	35c. U.N. emblem over map of Grenada	15	10
691	50c. U.N. buildings and flags	20	15
692	$2 U.N. emblem and scroll	45	45
MS693	122×91 mm. 75c. Type **208** and $1 as 2c.	65	90

CANCELLED REMAINDERS*. Some of the following issues have been remaindered, cancelled to order, at a fraction of their face value. For all practical purposes these are indistinguishable from genuine postally used copies. Our used quotations, which are indicated by an asterisk, are the same for cancelled-to-order or postally used copies.

209 Paul Revere's Midnight Ride

1975. Bicentenary of American Revolution (1st issue). Multicoloured.

694	½c. Type **209** (postage)	10	10
695	1c. Crispus Attucks	10	10
696	2c. Patrick Henry	10	10
697	3c. Franklin visits Washington	10	10
698	5c. Rebel troops	10	10
699	10c. John Paul Jones	10	10
700	40c. "John Hancock" (Copley) (vert) (air)	25	10
701	50c. "Benjamin Franklin" (Roslin) (vert)	40	15
702	75c. "John Adams" (Copley) (vert)	55	15
703	$1 "Lafayette" (Casanova) (vert)	60	20
MS704	Two sheets, each 131×102 mm: $2 Grenada arms and U.S. seal; $2 Grenada and U.S. flags	1·00	60

Stamps from No. **MS**704 are horiz and larger: 47½×35 mm.

See also Nos. 785/92.

210 "Blood of the Redeemer" (G. Bellini)

1975. Easter. Multicoloured.

705	½c. Type **210**	10	10
706	1c. "Pieta" (Bellini)	10	10
707	2c. "The Entombment" (Van der Weyden)	10	10
708	3c. "Pieta" (Bellini)	10	10
709	35c. "Pieta" (Bellini)	20	10
710	75c. "The Dead Christ" (Bellini)	25	10
711	$1 "The Dead Christ supported by Angels" (Procaccini)	30	10
MS712	117×100 mm. $2 "Pieta" (Botticelli)	75	30

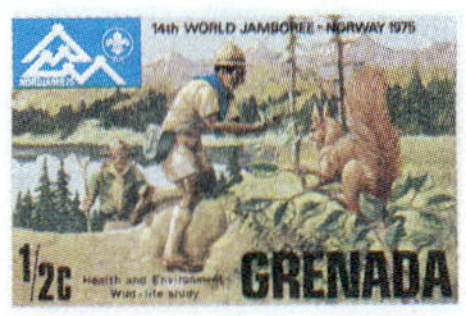

211 Wildlife Study

1975. 14th World Scout Jamboree, Norway. Multicoloured.

713	½c. Type **211**	10	10
714	1c. Sailing	10	10
715	2c. Map-reading	10	10
716	35c. First-aid	30	10
717	40c. Physical training	30	10
718	75c. Mountaineering	40	10
719	$2 Sing-song	70	20
MS720	106×80 mm. $1 Boat-building	1·00	30

212 Leafy Jewel Box

1975. Sea Shells. Multicoloured.

721	½c. Type **212**	10	10
722	1c. Emerald nerite	10	10
723	2c. Yellow American cockle	10	10
724	25c. Common purple janthina	85	10
725	50c. Atlantic turkey wing	1·75	15
726	75c. West Indian fighting conch	2·25	20
727	$1 Noble wentletrap	2·25	20
MS728	102×76 mm. $2 Music volute	2·00	80

213 "Lycorea ceres"

1975. Butterflies. Multicoloured.

729	½c. Type **213**	10	10
730	1c. "Adelpha cytherea"	10	10
731	2c. "Atlides polybe"	10	10
732	35c. "Anteos maerula"	80	10
733	45c. "Parides neophilus"	85	10
734	75c. "Nymula orestes"	1·25	15
735	$2 "Euptychia cephus"	1·75	20
MS736	108×83 mm. $1 "Papilio asty-alus" (sub-species "lycophron")	1·25	40

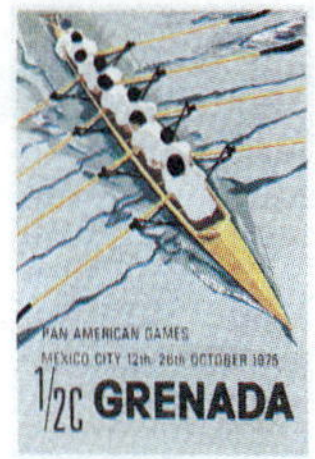

214 Rowing

1975. Pan-American Games, Mexico City. Mult.

737	½c. Type **214**	10	10
738	1c. Swimming	10	10
739	2c. Show-jumping	10	10
740	35c. Gymnastics	15	10
741	45c. Football	15	10
742	75c. Boxing	25	15
743	$2 Cycling	65	20
MS744	106×81 mm. $1 Yachting	1·00	40

215 "The Boy David" (Michelangelo)

1975. 500th Birth Anniv of Michelangelo. Multicoloured.

745	½c. Type **215**	10	10
746	1c. "Young Man" (detail)	10	10
747	2c. "Moses"	10	10
748	40c. "Prophet Zachariah"	30	10
749	50c. "St. John the Baptist"	30	15
750	75c. "Judith and Holofernes"	40	20
751	$2 "Doni Madonna" (detail from "Holy Family")	70	25
MS752	104×89 mm. $1 "Madonna" (head from Pieta)	1·00	30

216 "Madonna and Child" (Filippino Lippi)

1975. Christmas. "Virgin and Child" paintings by artists named. Multicoloured.

753	½c. Type **216**	10	10
754	1c. Mantegna	10	10
755	2c. Luis de Morales	10	10
756	35c. G. M. Morandi	15	10
757	50c. Antonello da Messina	15	10
758	75c. Durer	20	10
759	$1 Velasquez	25	10
MS760	125×95 mm. $2 Bellini	1·00	30

217 Bananaquit

1976. Flora and Fauna. Multicoloured.

761	½c. Type **217**	10	10
762	1c. Brazilian agouti	10	10
763	2c. Hawksbill turtle (horiz)	10	10
764	5c. Dwarf poinciana	10	10
765	35c. Black-finned tuna ("Albacore") (horiz)	90	10
766	40c. Cardinal's guard	95	10
767	$2 Nine-banded armadillo (horiz)	2·50	30
MS768	82×89 mm. $1 Belted kingfisher	7·50	90

218 Carnival Time

1976. Tourism. Multicoloured.

769	½c. Type **218**	10	10
770	1c. Scuba diving	10	10
771	2c. Liner "Southward" at St. George's	10	10
772	35c. Game fishing	65	10
773	50c. St. George's Golf Course	2·25	20
774	75c. Tennis	2·50	25
775	$1 Ancient rock carvings at Mount Rich	2·75	25
MS776	100×73 mm. $2 Small boat sailing	1·75	60

219 "Pieta" (Master of Okolicsno)

1976. Easter. Paintings by artists named. Multicoloured.

777	½c. Type **219**	10	10
778	1c. Correggio	10	10
779	2c. Van der Weyden	10	10
780	3c. Durer	10	10
781	35c. Master of the Holy Spirit	15	10
782	75c. Raphael	30	15
783	$1 Raphael	35	20
MS784	108×86 mm. $2 Crespi	1·00	60

220 Sharpshooters

1976. Bicentenary of American Revolution (2nd issue). Multicoloured.

785	½c. Type **220**	10	10
786	1c. Defending the Liberty Pole	10	10
787	2c. Loading muskets	10	10
788	35c. The Fight for Liberty	30	10
789	50c. Peace Treaty, 1783	35	10
790	$1 Drummers	50	20
791	$3 Gunboat	90	30
MS792	93×79 mm. 75c. as 35c. and $2 as 50c.	75	60

221 Nature Study

1976. 50th Anniv of Girl Guides in Grenada. Multicoloured.

793	½c. Type **221**	10	10
794	1c. Campfire cooking	10	10
795	2c. First aid	10	10
796	50c. Camping	50	10
797	75c. Home economics	65	15
798	$2 First aid	90	25
MS799	111×85 mm. $1 Painting	1·00	70

222 Volleyball

1976. Olympic Games, Montreal. Multicoloured.

800	½c. Type **222**	10	10
801	1c. Cycling	10	10
802	2c. Rowing	10	10
803	35c. Judo	30	10
804	45c. Hockey	60	10
805	75c. Gymnastics	60	20
806	$1 High jump	60	20
MS807	106×81 mm. $3 Equestrian event	1·00	80

223 "Cha-U-Kao at the Moulin Rouge"

1976. 75th Death Anniv of Toulouse-Lautrec. Multicoloured.

808	½c. Type **223**	10	10
809	1c. "Quadrille of the Moulin Rouge"	10	10
810	2c. "Profile of a Woman"	10	10
811	3c. "Salon in the Rue des Moulins"	10	10
812	40c. "The Laundryman"	55	10
813	50c. "Marcelle Lender dancing the Bolero"	65	10
814	$2 "Signor Boileau at the Cafe"	1·75	25
MS815	152×125 mm. $1 "Woman with Boa"	2·25	70

223a Map of the Caribbean

1976. West Indian Victory in World Cricket Cup.

816	35c. Type **223a**	1·00	35
817	$1 The Prudential Cup	1·50	5·00

224 Piper Apache 235

1976. Airplanes. Multicoloured.

818	½c. Type **224**	10	10
819	1c. Beech 50 Twin Bonanza	10	10
820	2c. De Havilland Twin Otter 100	10	10
821	40c. Britten Norman Islander	60	10
822	50c. De Havilland Heron 2	65	10
823	$2 Hawker Siddeley H.S.748	2·00	50
MS824	75×83 mm. $3 B.A.C. One Eleven 500	1·50	80

225 Satellite Assembly

1976. Viking and Helios Space Missions. Multicoloured.

825	½c. Type **225**	10	10
826	1c. Helios satellite	10	10
827	2c. Helios encapsulation	10	10
828	15c. Systems test	10	10
829	45c. Viking lander (horiz)	20	10
830	75c. Lander on Mars	30	15
831	$2 Viking encapsulation	60	25
MS832	110×85 mm. $3 Orbiter and lander	1·00	75

226 S.S. "Geestland"

1976. Ships. Multicoloured.

833	½c. Type **226**	10	10
834	1c. M.V. "Federal Palm"	10	10
835	2c. H.M.S "Blake"	10	10
836	25c. M.V. "Vistafjord"	45	10
837	75c. S.S. "Canberra"	80	15
838	$1 S.S. "Regina"	90	20
839	$5 S.S. "Arandora Star"	1·75	40
MS840	91×78 mm. $2 "Santa Maria"	1·60	4·00

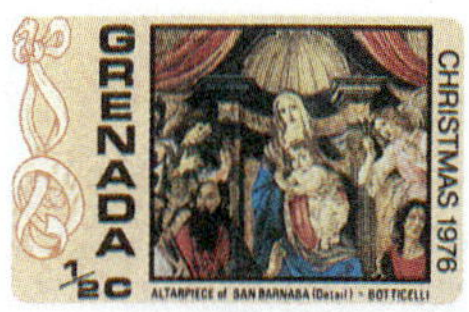

227 "San Barnaba Altarpiece" (Botticelli)

1976. Christmas. Multicoloured.

841	½c. Type **227**	10	10
842	1c. "Annunciation" (Botticelli)	10	10
843	2c. "Madonna of Chancellor Rolin" (Jan van Eyck)	10	10
844	35c. "Annunciation" (Fra Filippo Lippi)	15	10
845	50c. "Madonna of the Magnificat" (Botticelli)	20	10
846	75c. "Madonna of the Pomegranate" (Botticelli)	30	15
847	$3 "Madonna with St. Cosmas and other Saints" (Botticelli)	70	25
MS848	71×57 mm. $2 "Gypsy Madonna" (Titian)	1·00	60

228 Alexander Graham Bell and Telephones

1976. Centenary of First Telephone. Multicoloured.

849	½c. Type **228**	10	10
850	1c. Telephone users within globe	10	10
851	2c. Telephone satellite	10	10
852	18c. Telephone viewer and console	20	10
853	40c. Satellite and tracking stations	25	10
854	$1 Satellite transmitting to ships	35	15
855	$2 Dish aerial and modern telephone	55	25
MS856	107×80 mm. $5 Globe encircled by flags	1·25	75

229 Coronation Scene

1977. Silver Jubilee. Multicoloured.(a) Perf.

857	½c. Type **229**	10	10
858	1c. Sceptre and orb	10	10
859	35c. The Queen on horseback	10	10
860	$2 Spoon and ampulla	25	15
861	$2.50 The Queen and Prince Philip	25	15
MS862	103×79 mm. $5 Royal Visit to Grenada	75	60

(b) Roul. Self-adhesive.

863	35c. As $2.50	15	25
864	50c. As $2	25	1·00
865	$1 As 1c.	50	1·40
866	$3 As 35c.	1·25	2·75

230 Water Skiing

1977. Easter Water Parade. Multicoloured.

867	½c. Type **230**	10	10
868	1c. Speedboat race	10	10
869	2c. Row boat race	10	10
870	22c. Swimming	20	10
871	35c. Work boat race	30	10
872	75c. Water polo	50	15
873	$2 Game fishing	1·00	25
MS874	115×85 mm. $3 Yacht race	1·25	75

231 Meeting Place, Grand Anse Beach

1977. 7th Meeting of Organization of American States.

875	**231**	35c. multicoloured	10	10
876	**231**	$1 multicoloured	25	60
877	**231**	$2 multicoloured	40	1·75

232 Rafting

1977. Caribbean Scout Jamboree, Jamaica. Multicoloured.

878	½c. Type **232**	10	10
879	1c. Tug-of-war	10	10
880	2c. Sea Scouts regatta	10	10
881	18c. Camp fire	20	10
882	40c. Field kitchen	25	10
883	$1 Scouts and sea scouts	55	15
884	$2 Hiking and map reading	75	25
MS885	107×85 mm. $3 Semaphore	2·00	80

233 Angel and Shepherd

1977. Christmas. Ceiling Panels from Church of St. Martin, Zillis. Multicoloured.

886	½c. Type **233**	10	10
887	1c. St. Joseph	10	10
888	2c. Virgin and Child fleeing to Egypt	10	10
889	22c. Angel	10	10
890	35c. Magus on horseback	10	10
891	75c. Three horses	15	15
892	$2 Virgin and Child	40	25

MS893 85×112 mm. $3 Magus offering gift 1·00 70

1977. Royal Visit. Nos. 857/61 optd Royal Visit W.I. 1977.
894 ½c. Type **229** 10 10
895 1c. Sceptre and Orb 10 10
896 35c. Queen on horseback 10 10
897 $2 Spoon and ampulla 30 40
898 $2.50 The Queen and Prince Philip 35 45
MS899 103×79 mm. $5 Royal visit to Grenada 70 80

235 Christjaan Eijkman (Medicine)

1978. Nobel Prize Winners. Multicoloured.
900 ½c. Type **235** 10 10
901 1c. Sir Winston Churchill (Literature) 30 10
902 2c. Woodrow Wilson (Peace) 10 10
903 35c. Frederic Passy (Peace) 15 10
904 $1 Albert Einstein (Physics) 1·00 20
905 $3 Carl Bosch (Chemistry) 1·75 35
MS906 114×99 mm. $2 Alfred Nobel 70 60

236 Count von Zeppelin and First Zeppelin Airship LZ-1

1978. 75th Anniv of First Zeppelin Flight and 50th Anniv of Lindbergh's Transatlantic Flight. Multicoloured.
907 ½c. Type **236** 10 10
908 1c. Lindbergh with "Spirit of St. Louis" 10 10
909 2c. Airship "Deutschland" 10 10
910 22c. Lindbergh's arrival in France 30 10
911 75c. Lindbergh and "Spirit of St. Louis" in flight 60 10
912 $1 "Graf Zeppelin" over Alps 65 15
913 $3 "Graf Zeppelin" over White House 1·40 25
MS914 103×85 mm. Lindbergh in cockpit; $2 Count von Zeppelin and airship LZ-5 1·00 60

237 Rocket Launching

1978. Space Shuttle. Multicoloured.
915 ½c. Type **237** 10 10
916 1c. Booster jettison 10 10
917 2c. External tank jettison 10 10
918 18c. Space Shuttle in orbit 30 10
919 75c. Satellite placement 65 10
920 $2 Landing approach 1·40 20
MS921 103×85 mm. $3 Shuttle after landing 1·40 60

238 Black-headed Gull

1978. Wild Birds of Grenada. Multicoloured.
922 ½c. Type **238** 10 10
923 1c. Wilson's storm petrel ("Wilsons Petrel") 10 10
924 2c. Killdeer plover ("Killdeer") 10 10
925 50c. White-necked jacobin 1·25 10
926 75c. Blue-faced booby 1·50 15
927 $1 Broad-winged hawk 2·00 20
928 $2 Red-necked pigeon 2·50 30
MS929 103×94 mm. $3 Scarlet ibis 6·00 1·00

239 "The Landing of Marie de Medici at Marseilles"

1978. 400th Birth Anniv of Peter Paul Rubens. Multicoloured.
930 5c. Type **239** 10 10
931 15c. "Rubens and Isabella Brandt" 10 10
932 18c. "Marchesa Brigida Spindola-Doria" 10 10
933 25c. "Ludovicus Nonninus" 10 10
934 45c. "Helene Fourment and her Children" 15 10
935 75c. "Clara Serena Rubens" 25 10
936 $3 "Le Chapeau de Paille" 60 20
MS937 65×100 mm. $5 "Self Portrait" 1·00 60

240 Ludwig van Beethoven

1978. 150th Death Anniv of Beethoven. Mult.
938 5c. Type **240** 10 10
939 15c. Woman violinist (horiz) 15 10
940 18c. Musical instruments (horiz) 20 10
941 22c. Piano (horiz) 20 10
942 50c. Violins 40 10
943 75c. Piano and sonata score 50 15
944 $3 Beethoven's portrait and home (horiz) 1·25 25
MS945 83×62 mm. $2 Beethoven and score 1·10 60

241 King Edward's Chair

1978. 25th Anniv of Coronation. Mult. (a) Perf.
946 35c. Type **241** 10 10
947 $2 Queen with regalia 30 35
948 $2.50 St. Edward's Crown 30 40
MS949 102×76 mm. $5 Queen and Prince Philip 80 80

(b) Roul×imperf. Self-adhesive.
950 25c. Queen Elizabeth II taking salute, Trooping the Colour 15 15
951 35c. Queen at Maundy Thursday ceremony 15 25
952 $5 Queen and Prince Philip at Opening of Parliament 1·50 2·50

243 Goalkeeper reaching for Ball

1978. World Cup Football Championship, Argentina.
953 **243** 40c. multicoloured 10 10
954 - 60c. multicoloured 15 20
955 - 90c. multicoloured 25 30
956 - $2 multicoloured 60 60
MS957 130×97 mm. $2.70, multicoloured 1·10 1·10
DESIGNS: 60c. to $2.70, Designs similar to Type **243** with goalkeeper reaching for ball.

244 Aerial Phenomena, Germany, 1561 and U.S.A., 1952

1978. U.F.O. Research. Multicoloured.
958 5c. Type **244** 15 10
959 35c. Various aerial phenomena, 1950 35 25
960 $3 U.F.O.s, 1965 2·00 1·75
MS961 112×89 mm. $2 Sir Eric Gairy and U.F.O. research laboratory 1·25 1·25

245 Wright Flyer III, 1902

1978. 75th Anniv of Powered Flight. Mult.
962 5c. Type **245** 10 10
963 15c. Wright Flyer I, 1903 10 10
964 18c. Wright Type A 10 10
965 22c. Wright Flyer I from above 15 10
966 50c. Orville Wright and Wright Type A 20 20
967 75c. Wright Type A, Pau, France, 1908 25 25
968 $3 Wilbur Wright and Wright glider No. IV 80 70
MS969 114×85 mm. $2 Wright glider No. III 1·00 75

246 Cook and Hawaiian Feast

1978. 250th Birth Anniv of Captain James Cook and Bicentenary of Discovery of Hawaii. Multicoloured.
970 18c. Type **246** 60 20
971 35c. Cook and Hawaiian dance 75 25
972 75c. Cook and Honolulu harbour 1·25 1·00
973 $3 Cook's statue and H.M.S. "Resolution" 1·75 5·50
MS974 116×88 mm. $4 Cook and death scene 3·00 1·50

247 "Paumgartner Altarpiece" (detail)

1978. Christmas. Paintings by Durer. Multicoloured.
975 40c. Type **247** 20 15
976 60c. "The Adoration of the Magi" 25 20
977 90c. "Virgin and Child" 30 20
978 $2 "Virgin and Child with St. Anne" (detail) 55 55
MS979 113×83 mm. $4 "Madonna and Child" 1·10 1·50

248 National Convention and Cultural Centre (interior)

1979. 5th Anniv of Independence.
980 5c. Type **248** 10 10
981 18c. National Convention and Cultural Centre (exterior) 10 10
982 22c. Easter Water Parade, 1978 10 10
983 35c. Sir Eric M. Gairy (Prime Minister) 10 10
984 $3 The Cross, Fort Frederick 45 60

249 "Acalypha hispida"

1979. Flowers. Multicoloured.
985 18c. Type **249** 10 10
986 50c. "Hibiscus rosa sinensis" 20 15
987 $1 "Thunbergia grandiflora" 30 25
988 $3 "Nerium oleander" 80 1·10
MS989 115×90 mm. $2 "Lagerstroemia speciosa" 75 1·00

250 Birds in Flight

1979. 30th Anniv of Declaration of Human Rights. Multicoloured.
990 15c. Type **250** 10 10
991 $2 Bird in Flight 55 65

251 Children playing Cricket

1979. Int Year of the Child (1st issue). Mult.
992 18c. Type **251** 1·50 1·00
993 22c. Children playing baseball 40 30
994 $5 Children playing in a tree 3·25 7·00
MS995 114×92 mm. $4 Children with model spaceship 1·25 2·25
See also Nos. 1006/7 and 1025/34.

252 "Around the World in 80 Days"

1979. 150th Birth Anniv of Jules Verne. Mult.
996 18c. Type **252** 35 20
997 35c. "20,000 Leagues under the Sea" 50 20

998 75c. "From the Earth to the Moon" 60 50
999 $3 "Master of the World" 1·40 2·00
MS1000 110×85 mm. $4 "Clipper of the Clouds" 1·25 1·25

253 Mail Runner, Africa (early 19th-century)

1979. Death Cent of Sir Rowland Hill. Mult.
1001 20c. Type **253** 10 10
1002 40c. Pony Express, America (mid 19th-century) 10 10
1003 $1 Pigeon post 15 25
1004 $3 Mail coach, Europe (18–19th century) 40 80
MS1005 127×100 mm. $5 Sir Rowland Hill and 1891 1d. on 8d.×4 75 1·10

254 "The Pistol of Peace" (vaccination gun), Map of Grenada and Children

1979. International Year of the Child (2nd issue). "Grenada—First Nation 100% Immunized".
1006 **254** 5c. multicoloured 25 75
1007 **254** $1 multicoloured 75 2·50

255 Reef Shark

1979. Marine Wildlife. Multicoloured.
1008 40c. Type **255** 40 30
1009 45c. Spotted eagle ray 40 30
1010 50c. Many-toothed conger 45 40
1011 60c. Golden olive (shell) 70 85
1012 70c. West Indian murex (shell) 85 1·00
1013 75c. Giant tun (shell) 90 1·10
1014 90c. Brown booby 2·25 2·25
1015 $1 Magnificent frigate bird 2·25 2·25
MS1016 109×78 mm. $2.50, Sooty tern 2·50 2·00

256 The Flight into Egypt

1979. Christmas. Tapestries. Multicoloured.
1017 6c. Type **256** 10 10
1018 25c. The Flight into Egypt (detail) 10 10
1019 30c. Angel (vert) 10 10
1020 40c. (Doge Marino Grimani) (detail) (vert) 10 10
1021 90c. The Annunciation to the Shepherds (vert) 15 15
1022 $1 The Flight into Egypt (Rome) (vert) 15 15
1023 $2 The Virgin in Glory (vert) 25 40
MS1024 111×148 mm. $4 Doge Marino Grimani (vert) 70 1·00

257 Mickey Mouse playing Baseball

1979. International Year of the Child (3rd issue). Disney cartoon characters. Multicoloured.
1025 ½c. Type **257** 10 10
1026 1c. Donald Duck high- jumping 10 10
1027 2c. Goofy playing basketbal 10 10
1028 3c. Goofy hurdling 10 10
1029 4c. Donald Duck playing golf 10 10
1030 5c. Mickey Mouse playing cricket 10 10
1031 10c. Mickey Mouse playing football 10 10
1032 $2 Mickey Mouse playing tennis 1·75 3·50
1033 $2.50 Minnie Mouse riding horse 1·75 3·50
MS1034 125×100 mm. $3 Goofy in riding gear 1·50 1·50

258 Paul Harris (founder)

1980. 75th Anniv of Rotary International. Mult.
1035 6c. Type **258** 10 10
1036 30c. "Health" 10 15
1037 90c. "Hunger" 15 30
1038 $2 "Humanity" 40 80
MS1039 104×89 mm. $4 Rotary International emblem 1·00 1·60

1980. 1st Anniv of Revolution (1st issue). Nos. 651/2, 654/7, 659/60 and 662/8 optd PEOPLE'S REVOLUTION 13 MARCH 1979.
1040 2c. Carenage taxi 10 40
1041 3c. Large working boats 10 40
1042 6c. Cocoa beans in drying trays 10 10
1043 8c. Nutmegs 10 10
1044 10c. Rum distillery, River Antoine Estate, c. 1785 10 10
1045 12c. Cocoa tree 10 10
1046 20c. Parliament Building 10 15
1047 25c. Fort George cannons 30 30
1048 50c. General Post Office 30 30
1049 75c. Carib's Leap, Sauteurs Bay 50 40
1050 $1 Carenage, St. George's 60 60
1051 $2 St. George's Harbour by night 1·25 2·00
1052 $3 Grand Anse Beach 1·50 3·25
1053 $5 Canoe Bay and Black Bay 2·00 5·50
1054 $10 Sugar-loaf Island 3·25 8·00
See also Nos. 1069/72.

260 Boxing

1980. Olympic Games, Moscow. Multicoloured.
1055 25c. Type **260** 10 10
1056 40c. Cycling 15 15
1057 90c. Show-jumping 20 30
1058 $2 Running 40 1·00
MS1059 128×95 mm. $4 Sailing 1·00 1·40

261 Tropical Kingbird

1980. Wild Birds. Multicoloured.
1060 20c. Type **261** 85 20
1061 40c. Rufous-breasted hermit 1·25 25
1062 $1 Troupial 1·75 1·75
1063 $2 Ruddy quail dove 2·25 4·00
MS1064 85×114 mm. $3 Prarie warbler 3·75 1·75

1980. "London 1980" International Stamp Exhibition. Nos. 1001/4 optd LONDON 1980.
1065 20c. Type **253** 15 15
1066 40c. Pony Express, America 20 15
1067 $1 Pigeon post 30 30
1068 $3 Mail coach, Europe 85 90

263 Free Hot Lunch at Schools

1980. 1st Anniv of Revolution (2nd issue). Multicoloured.
1069 10c. Type **263** 10 10
1070 40c. "From tree to can" (agro-industry) 15 15
1071 $1 National Health care 30 30
1072 $2 New housing projects 50 70
MS1073 110×85 mm. $5 Prime Minister Maurice Bishop (vert) 75 85

264 Jamb Statues, West Portal, Chartres Cathedral

1980. Famous Works of Art. Multicoloured.
1074 8c. Type **264** 10 10
1075 10c. "Les Demoiselles d' Avignon" (painting, Picasso) 10 10
1076 40c. Winged Victory of Samothrace (statue) 15 15
1077 50c. "The Night Watch" (painting, Rembrandt) 15 15
1078 $1 "Portrait of Edward VI as a Child" (painting, Holbein the Younger) 25 25
1079 $3 Portrait head of Queen Nefertiti (carving) 70 70
MS1080 101×101 mm. $4 "Weier Haws" (detail of painting by Durer) (vert) 75 75

265 Carib Canoes

1980. Shipping. Multicoloured.
1081A ½c. Type **265** 10 40
1082A 1c. Boat building 10 40
1083A 2c. Small working boat 15 40
1084A 4c. Columbus's "Santa Maria" 40 40
1085A 5c. West Indiaman barque, c. 1840 40 30
1086A 6c. "Orinoco" (paddle-steamer), c. 1851 40 40
1087A 10c. Working schooner 50 10
1088A 12c. Trimaran at Grand Anse anchorage 1·00 55
1089A 15c. Spice Island cruising yacht "Petite Amie" 50 10
1090A 20c. Fishing pirogue 1·00 20
1091A 25c. Harbour police launch 2·00 30
1092A 30c. Grand Anse speedboat 1·50 30
1093A 40c. "Seimstrand" (freighter) 2·00 35
1094B 50c. "Ariadne" (cadet schooner) 50 50
1095A 90c. "Geestide" (freighter) 1·75 50
1096A $1 "Cunard Countess" (liner) 3·00 80
1097A $3 Rum-runner 2·50 4·25
1098A $5 "Statendam" (liner) off St. George's 3·50 7·50
1099B $10 Coastguard patrol boat 3·25 8·50
Nos. 1081/99 come with and without date imprint.

1980. Christmas. Scenes from Walt Disney's "Snow White and the Seven Dwarfs". As T 257. Multicoloured.
1100 ½c. Snow White at well 10 10
1101 1c. The Wicked Queen 10 10
1102 2c. Snow White singing to animals 10 10
1103 3c. Snow White doing housework for Dwarfs 10 10
1104 4c. The Seven Dwarfs 10 10
1105 5c. Snow White with Dwarfs 10 10
1106 10c. Witch offering Snow White apple 10 10
1107 $2.50 Snow White with Prince and Dwarfs 3·25 1·75
1108 $3 Snow White and Prince 3·75 2·00
MS1109 127×102 mm. $4 Snow White sleeping (vert) 4·25 1·50

1981. 50th Anniv of Walt Disney's Pluto (cartoon character). As T 257. Multicoloured.
1110 $2 Pluto with birthday cake 1·00 1·00
MS1111 127×102 mm. $4 Pluto in scene from film "Pueblo Pluto" 1·25 1·00

266 Revolution and Grenada Flags

1981. Festival of the Revolution. Multicoloured.
1112 5c. Type **266** 30 10
1113 10c. Teacher, pupil, book and pencil ("education") 10 10
1114 15c. Food processing plant ("industry") 10 10
1115 25c. Selection of fruits and farm scene ("agriculture") 15 10
1116 40c. Crawfish and boat ("fishing") 25 15
1117 90c. "Cunard Countess" arriving at St. George's Harbour ("shipping") 75 30
1118 $1 Straw-work ("native handicrafts") 60 40
1119 $3 Map of Caribbean with expanded view of Grenada 2·00 1·75

1981. Easter. Walt Disney cartoon characters. As T 257. Multicoloured.
1120 35c. Mickey Mouse and Goofy 30 15
1121 40c. Donald Duck, Chip and Daisy Duck 30 15
1122 $2 Minnie Mouse 75 1·00
1123 $2.50 Pluto and Mickey Mouse 75 1·10
MS1124 127×101 mm. $4 Goofy 1·75 1·50

267 "Woman-Flower"

1981. Birth Centenary of Picasso. Multicoloured.
1125 25c. Type **267** 15 10
1126 30c. "Portrait of Madame" 15 10
1127 90c. "Cavalier with Pipe" 25 30
1128 $4 "Large Heads" 70 1·00
MS1129 128×103 mm. $5 "Woman on the Banks of the Seine" (after Courbet). Imperf 2·50 1·40

268 Prince Charles playing Polo

1981. Royal Wedding (1st issue). Multicoloured.
1130 50c. As 30c. 10 10
1131 $2 As 40c. 35 50
1132 $4 Type **268** 50 75

MS1133	98×94 mm. $5 Glass Coach	75	75
1134	30c. Prince Charles and Lady Diana Spencer	20	20
1135	40c. Holyrood House	30	30

269 Lady Diana Spencer

1981. Royal Wedding (2nd issue). Multicoloured. Self-adhesive.

1136	$1 Type **269**	30	65
1137	$2 Prince Charles	30	65
1138	$5 Prince Charles and Lady Diana Spencer	1·00	1·75

270 "The Bath" (Mary Cassatt)

1981. "Decade for Women". Paintings. Mult.

1139	15c. Type **270**	10	10
1140	40c. "Mademoiselle Charlotte du Val d'Ognes" (Constance Marie Charpentier)	20	10
1141	60c. "Self-portrait" (Mary Beale)	30	20
1142	$3 "Woman in White Stockings" (Suzanne Valadon)	1·25	1·00
MS1143	101×77 mm. $5 "The Artist hesitating between the Arts of Music and Painting" (Angelica Kauffman) (horiz)	1·75	2·00

1981. Christmas. As T 257 showing scenes from Walt Disney's cartoon film "Cinderella".

1144	½c. multicoloured	10	10
1145	1c. multicoloured	10	10
1146	2c. multicoloured	10	10
1147	3c. multicoloured	10	10
1148	4c. multicoloured	10	10
1149	5c. multicoloured	10	10
1150	10c. multicoloured	15	10
1151	$2.50 multicoloured	3·50	2·50
1152	$3 multicoloured	3·50	2·75
MS1153	127×103 mm. $5 multicoloured	5·50	3·25

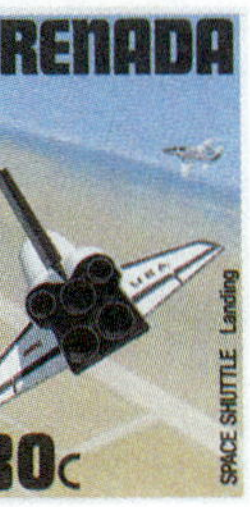

271 Landing

1981. Space Shuttle Project. Multicoloured.

1154	30c. Type **271**	20	15
1155	60c. Working in space	40	30
1156	70c. Lift off	45	35
1157	$3 Separation	1·10	1·25
MS1158	117×89 mm. $5 In orbit	1·75	1·25

272 West German Footballer and Flag

1981. World Cup Football Championship, Spain (1982). Multicoloured.

1159	25c.+10c. Type **272**	75	30
1160	40c.+20c. Argentinian footballer and flag	90	40
1161	50c.+25c. Brazilian footballer and flag	1·00	50
1162	$1+50c. English footballer and flag	1·50	95
MS1163	141×128 mm. $5+50c. Spanish orange mascot and Jules Rimet Trophy (vert)	3·50	2·00

273 General Post Office, St. George's

1981. Cent of U.P.U. Membership. Mult.

1164	25c. Type **273**	20	15
1165	30c. 1861 1d. stamp	30	20
1166	90c. New U.P.U. Headquarters Building 25c. commemorative	70	50
1167	$4 1961 Stamp Centenary 25c. commemorative	1·25	2·25
MS1168	137×87 mm. $5 1974 Centenary of U.P.U. ½c. commemorative	3·25	3·75

274 Artist without Hands

1982. International Year for the Disabled (1981). Multicoloured.

1169	30c. Type **274**	20	10
1170	40c. Computer operator without hands	20	10
1171	70c. Blind schoolteacher teaching braille	50	15
1172	$3 Midget playing drums	1·10	80
MS1173	101×72 mm. $4 Auto mechanic confined to wheelchair	3·00	3·25

275 Tending Vegetable Patch

1982. 75th Anniv of Boy Scout Movement and 125th Birth Anniv of Lord Baden-Powell. Multicoloured.

1174	70c. Type **275**	50	45
1175	90c. Map-reading	55	55
1176	$1 Bee-keeping	65	65
1177	$4 Hospital reading	2·25	2·75
MS1178	100×71 mm. $5 Presentation of trophies	1·25	1·00

276 "Dryas julia"

1982. Butterflies. Multicoloured.

1179	10c. Type **276**	75	30
1180	60c. "Phoebis agarithe"	2·00	1·50
1181	$1 "Anartia amathea"	2·50	2·00
1182	$3 "Battus polydamas"	3·75	7·00
MS1183	111×85 mm. $5 "Junonia evarete"	6·00	2·25

277 "Saying Grace"

1982. Norman Rockwell (painter) Commemoration. Multicoloured.

1184	15c. Type **277**	40	10
1185	30c. "Nothing Up His Sleeve" (inscr "Card Tricks")	65	15
1186	60c. "Pharmacist"	85	25
1187	70c. "Hobo" (inscr "Pals")	90	35

278 Kensington Palace

1982. 21st Birthday of Princess of Wales. Multicoloured.

1188	50c. Type **278**	90	1·00
1189	60c. Type **278**	1·50	50
1190	$1 Prince and Princess of Wales	1·50	1·75
1191	$2 As $1	2·75	1·50
1192	$3 Princess of Wales	2·75	2·75
1193	$4 As $3	3·00	2·50
MS1194	103×75 mm. $5 Princess Diana (different)	3·00	1·50

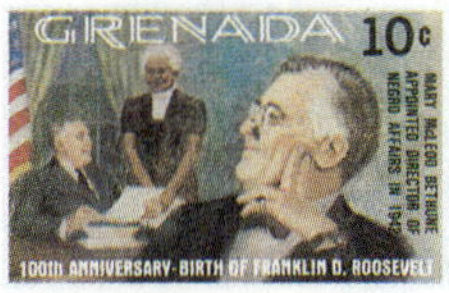

279 Mary McLeod Bethune appointed Director of Negro Affairs, 1942

1982. Birth Centenary of Franklin D. Roosevelt. Multicoloured.

1195	10c. Type **279**	10	10
1196	60c. Huddie Ledbetter "Lead-belly" in concert (Works Progress administration)	30	20
1197	$1.10 Signing bill No. 8802, 1941 (Fair Employment committee)	40	25
1198	$3 Farm Security administration	55	60
MS1199	100×70 mm. $5 William Hastie, first Negro Judicial appointee	1·25	1·25

1982. Birth of Prince William of Wales. Nos. 1188/93 optd ROYAL BABY 21.6.82.

1200	50c. Type **278**	60	1·00
1201	60c. Type **278**	35	35
1202	$1 Prince and Princess of Wales	1·00	1·25
1203	$2 As $1	1·00	1·00
1204	$3 Princess of Wales	1·90	2·25
1205	$4 As $3	1·90	1·90
MS1206	103×75 mm. $5 Princess Diana (different)	2·00	1·25

280 Apostle and Tormentor

1982. Easter. Details from Painting "The Way to Calvary" by Raphael. Multicoloured.

1207	40c. Type **280**	25	10
1208	70c. Captain of the guards (vert)	30	15
1209	$1.10 Christ and apostle (vert)	35	25
1210	$4 Mourners (vert)	70	1·25
MS1211	102×126 mm. $5 Christ falls beneath the cross (vert)	1·50	1·50

281 "Orient Express"

1982. Famous Trains of the World. Mult.

1212	30c. Type **281**	50	35
1213	60c. "Trans-Siberian Express"	60	70
1214	70c. "Fleche d'Or"	70	80
1215	90c. "Flying Scotsman"	85	1·00
1216	$1 German Federal Railways steam locomotive	1·00	1·25
1217	$3 German National Railways Class 05 steam locomotive	2·25	4·00
MS1218	109×81 mm. $5 "20th Century Limited"	2·00	2·00

282 Footballers

1982. World Cup Football Championship Winners.

1219	**282**	60c. multicoloured	35	35
1220	**282**	$4 multicoloured	2·00	2·00
MS1221		93×119 mm. $5 multicoloured	2·50	2·25

1982. Christmas. Scenes from Walt Disney's cartoon film "Robin Hood". As T 257, but horiz.

1222	½c. multicoloured	10	10
1223	1c. multicoloured	10	10
1224	2c. multicoloured	10	10
1225	3c. multicoloured	10	10
1226	4c. multicoloured	10	10
1227	5c. multicoloured	10	10
1228	10c. multicoloured	10	10
1229	$2.50 multicoloured	3·00	3·50
1230	$3 multicoloured	3·00	3·50
MS1231	121×96 mm. $5 multicoloured	6·50	4·00

283 Killer Whale

1983. Save the Whales. Multicoloured.

1232	15c. Type **283**	1·00	30
1233	40c. Sperm whale	2·25	90
1234	70c. Blue whale	2·75	2·75
1235	$3 Common dolphin	3·50	6·50
MS1236	84×74 mm. $5 Humpback whales	6·50	4·00

284 "Construction of Ark"

1983. 500th Birth Anniv of Raphael. Mult.

1237	25c. Type **284**	20	10
1238	30c. "Jacob's Vision"	20	10
1239	90c. "Joseph interprets the Dreams of his Brothers"	30	30
1240	$4 "Joseph interprets Pharaoh's dreams"	1·10	1·40
MS1241	128×100 mm. $5 "Creation of the Animals"	1·25	1·75

285 Dentistry at Health Centre

1983. Commonwealth Day. Multicoloured.

1242	10c. Type **285**	10	10
1243	70c. Airport runway construction	35	35
1244	$1.10 Tourism	40	55
1245	$3 Boat-building	80	1·40

286 Maritime Communications via Satellite

1983. World Communications Year. Multicoloured.

1246	30c. Type **286**	15	15
1247	40c. Rural telephone installation	20	15
1248	$2.50 Satellite weather map	60	1·00
1249	$4 Airport control room	60	1·10
MS1250	111×85 mm. $5 Communications satellite	1·25	1·25

287 Franklin Sport Sedan, 1928

1983. 75th Anniv of Model "T" Ford Car. Multicoloured.

1251	6c. Type **287**	15	20
1252	10c. Delage "D8", 1933	20	10
1253	40c. Alvis, 1938	35	25
1254	60c. Invicta "S-type" tourer, 1931	45	45
1255	70c. Alfa-Romeo "1750 Gran Sport", 1930	55	55
1256	90c. Isotta Fraschini, 1930	60	75
1257	$1 Bugatti "Royale Type 41"	70	75
1258	$2 BMW "328", 1938	1·40	1·75
1259	$3 Marmon "V16", 1931	1·60	2·50
1260	$4 Lincoln "K8" saloon, 1932	1·90	3·00
MS1261	114×90 mm. $5 Cougar "TR 7", 1972	1·50	2·00

288 Airship N.1 "Norge"

1983. Bicentenary of Manned Flight. Multicoloured.

1262	30c. Type **288**	60	30
1263	60c. Gloster VI seaplane	1·00	1·00
1264	$1.10 Curtiss NC-4 flying boat	3·50	4·50
1265	$4 Dornier Do 18 flying boat "Aeolus"	1·60	1·75
MS1266	114×85 mm. $5 Modern hot-air balloon (vert)	1·50	1·50

289 Morty

1983. Christmas. Multicoloured.

1267	½c. Type **289**	10	10
1268	1c. Ludwig von Drake	10	10
1269	2c. Gyro Gearloose	10	10
1270	3c. Pluto and Figaro	10	10
1271	4c. Morty and Ferdie	10	10
1272	5c. Mickey Mouse and Goofy	10	10
1273	10c. Chip n'Dale	10	10
1274	$2.50 Mickey and Minnie Mouse	2·25	3·50
1275	$3 Donald and Grandma Duck	2·25	3·50
MS1276	127×102 mm. $5 Goofy with Christmas tree	4·50	4·50

Nos. 1267/75 show Disney cartoon characters in scenes from "It's beginning to look a lot like Christmas" (song).

290 Daisy Duck on Pommel Horse

1984. Olympic Games. Los Angeles. Multicoloured. A. Inscr "1984 LOS ANGELES".

1277A	½c. Type **290**	10	10
1278A	1c. Mickey Mouse boxing	10	10
1279A	2c. Daisy Duck in archery event	10	10
1280A	3c. Clarabelle Cow on uneven bars	10	10
1281A	4c. Mickey and Minnie Mouse in hurdles race	10	10
1282A	5c. Donald Duck with Chip'n'Dale weightlifting	10	10
1283A	$1 Little Hiawatha in single kayak	2·50	2·25
1284A	$2 The Tortoise and the Hare in marathon	3·00	3·75
1285A	$3 Mickey Mouse polevaulting	3·50	4·00
MS1286A	127×101 mm. $5 Donald Duck in medley relay (vert)	5·50	3·50

B. Inscr "1984 OLYMPICS LOS ANGELES" and Olympic Emblem.

1227B	½c. Type **290**	10	10
1278B	1c. Mickey Mouse boxing	10	10
1279B	2c. Daisy Duck in archery event	10	10
1280B	3c. Clarabelle Cow on uneven bars	10	10
1281B	4c. Mickey and Minnie Mouse in hurdles race	10	10
1282B	5c. Donald Duck with Chip'n'Dale weightlifting	10	10
1283B	$1 Little Hiawatha in single kayak	2·50	2·25
1284B	$2 The Tortoise and the Hare in marathon	3·00	3·75
1285B	$3 Mickey Mouse polevaulting	3·50	4·00
MS1286B	127×100 mm. $5 Donald Duck in medley relay (vert)	6·50	5·50

291 William I

1984. English Monarchs. Multicoloured.

1287	$4 Type **291**	1·75	2·50
1288	$4 William II	1·75	2·50
1289	$4 Henry I	1·75	2·50
1290	$4 Stephen	1·75	2·50
1291	$4 Henry II	1·75	2·50
1292	$4 Richard I	1·75	2·50
1293	$4 John	1·75	2·50
1294	$4 "Henry III"	1·75	2·50
1295	$4 Edward I	1·75	2·50
1296	$4 Edward II	1·75	2·50
1297	$4 Edward III	1·75	2·50
1298	$4 Richard II	1·75	2·50
1299	$4 Henry IV	1·75	2·50
1300	$4 Henry V	1·75	2·50
1301	$4 Henry VI	1·75	2·50
1302	$4 Edward IV	1·75	2·50
1303	$4 Edward V	1·75	2·50
1304	$4 Richard III	1·75	2·50
1305	$4 Henry VII	1·75	2·50
1306	$4 Henry VIII	1·75	2·50
1307	$4 Edward VI	1·75	2·50
1308	$4 Jane Grey	1·75	2·50
1309	$4 Mary I	1·75	2·50
1310	$4 Elizabeth I	1·75	2·50
1311	$4 James I	1·75	2·50
1312	$4 Charles I	1·75	2·50
1313	$4 Charles II	1·75	2·50
1314	$4 James II	1·75	2·50
1315	$4 William III	1·75	2·50
1316	$4 Mary II	1·75	2·50
1317	$4 Anne	1·75	2·50
1318	$4 George I	1·75	2·50
1319	$4 George II	1·75	2·50
1320	$4 George III	1·75	2·50
1321	$4 George IV	1·75	2·50
1322	$4 William IV	1·75	2·50
1323	$4 Victoria	1·75	2·50
1324	$4 Edward VII	1·75	2·50
1325	$4 George V	1·75	2·50
1326	$4 Edward VIII	1·75	2·50
1327	$4 George VI	1·75	2·50
1328	$4 Elizabeth II	1·75	2·50

Although inscribed "Henry III" the portrait on No. 1294 is actually of Edward II.

292 Lantana

1984. Flowers. Multicoloured.

1329	25c. Type **292**	20	15
1330	30c. Plumbago	25	15
1331	90c. Spider lily	60	35
1332	$4 Giant alocasia	1·50	2·75
MS1333	108×90 mm. $5 Orange trumpet vine	1·00	1·50

293 Blue Parrotfish

1984. Coral Reef Fishes. Multicoloured.

1334	10c. Type **293**	1·40	45
1335	30c. Flame-backed angelfish	2·75	1·10
1336	70c. Painted wrasse	4·00	3·25
1337	90c. Rosy razorfish	4·75	3·50
MS1338	81×85 mm. $5 Spanish hogfish	6·50	4·75

1984. Universal Postal Union Congress, Hamburg. Nos. 1331/2 optd 19TH U.P.U CONGRESS HAMBURG.

1339	90c. Spider lily	60	65
1340	$4 Giant alocasia	2·00	2·50
MS1341	108×90 mm. $5 Orange trumpet vine	1·50	2·50

295 Freighter

1984. Ships. Multicoloured.

1342	40c. Type **295**	1·25	55
1343	70c. "Queen Elizabeth 2"	1·50	1·50
1344	90c. Sailing boats	1·60	2·00
1345	$4 "Amerikanis"	3·50	8·00
MS1346	107×80 mm. $5 Spanish galleon	5·00	7·00

296 "The Night" (detail) (Correggio)

1984. 450th Death Anniv of Correggio (painter). Multicoloured.

1347	10c. Type **296**	45	15
1348	30c. "The Virgin adoring the Child"	80	50
1349	40c. "The Mystical Marriage of St. Catherine with St. Sebastian"	2·00	1·75
1350	$4 "The Madonna and the Fruit Basket"	4·50	5·50
MS1351	54×73 mm. $5 "The Madonna at the Spring"	4·25	3·00

297 "L'Absinthe" (Degas)

1984. 150th Birth Anniv of Edgar Degas (painter). Multicoloured.

1352	25c. Type **297**	80	30
1353	70c. "Pouting" (horiz)	1·50	1·25
1354	$1.10 "The Millinery Shop"	2·00	2·00
1355	$3 "The Bellelli Family" (horiz)	3·75	4·25
MS1356	84×54 mm. $5 "The Cotton Market"	4·25	3·00

298 Train on Puffing Billy Line, Victoria

1984. "Ausipex" International Stamp Exhibition, Melbourne. Multicoloured.

1357	$1.10 Type **298**	2·25	1·75
1358	$4 Yacht "Australia II" (winner of America's Cup)	4·75	5·25
MS1359	107×76 mm. $5 Melbourne tram	4·25	4·00

299 George Stephenson's "Locomotion" (1825)

1984. Railway Locomotives. Multicoloured.

1360	30c. Type **299**	80	35
1361	40c. Braithwaite and Ericsson's "Novelty" (1829)	95	40
1362	60c. William Norris's "Washington Farmer" (1836)	1·00	75
1363	70c. French Crampton type (1859)	1·00	1·00
1364	90c. Dutch State Railways (1873)	1·10	1·50
1365	$1.10 "Champion", U.S.A. (1882)	1·25	2·00
1366	$2 Webb Compound type (1893)	1·75	3·25
1367	$4 Berlin "No. 74" (1900)	2·75	5·50
MS1368	Two sheets, each 100×70 mm. (a) $5 Crampton "Phoenix" (1863); (b) $5 Mikado type, Japan (1897) Set of 2 sheets	6·00	6·50

1984. Opening of Point Saline International Airport (1st issue). Nos. 1247 and 1249 optd OPENING OF POINT SALINE INT'L AIRPORT.

1369	40c. Rural telephone installation	30	30
1370	$3 Airport control room	2·00	2·00
MS1371	111×85 mm. $5 Communications satellite	3·50	3·25

See also Nos. 1399/6.

301 Donald Duck as Father Christmas looking into Mirror

1984. Christmas. Walt Disney cartoon characters. Multicoloured.

1372	45c. Type **301**	1·25	40
1373	60c. Donald Duck filling stocking with presents	1·50	55
1374	90c. As Father Christmas pulling a sleigh	2·00	1·10
1375	$2 As Father Christmas decorating Christmas tree	3·50	3·50
1376	$4 Donald Duck and nephews singing carols	5·00	5·50
MS1377	127×102 mm. $5 Father Christmas in sleigh	7·00	8·00

1985. Birth Bicentenary of John J. Audubon (ornithologist) (1st issue). As T 418 of Ghana. Multicoloured.

1378	50c. Clapper rail (vert)	2·00	75
1379	70c. Hooded warbler (vert)	2·25	1·50
1380	90c. Common flicker (vert)	2·75	1·75
1381	$4 Bohemian waxwing (vert)	5·50	8·00
MS1382	82×112 mm. $5 Merlin ("Pigeon Hawk")	9·00	4·50

See also Nos. 1480/4.

302 Honda "XL500R"

1985. Centenary of the Motor Cycle. Multicoloured.

1383	25c. Type **302**	1·00	50
1384	50c. Suzuki "GS1100ES"	1·50	1·00
1385	90c. Kawasaki "KZ700"	2·00	2·25
1386	$4 BMW "K100"	6·00	6·50
MS1387	109×81 mm. $5 Yamaha "500CC V Four"	7·50	5·00

303 "Explorer"

1985. 75th Anniv of Girl Guide Movement. Designs showing work for Guide badges. Multicoloured.

1388	25c. Type **303**	55	30
1389	60c. "Cook"	90	65
1390	90c. "Musician"	1·50	1·10
1391	$3 "Home nurse"	3·00	4·50
MS1392	97×70 mm. $5 Flags of Girl Guides and Grenada	2·50	2·50

304 Hawker Siddeley H.S.748 on Inaugural Flight from Barbados

1985. Opening of Point Saline International Airport (1984) (2nd issue). Multicoloured.

1393	70c. Type **304**	2·50	1·00
1394	$1 Lockheed TriStar 500 on inaugural flight from New York	3·25	1·50
1395	$4 Lockheed TriStar 500 on inaugural flight to Miami	6·50	8·00
MS1396	101×72 mm. $5 Point Saline Airport terminal and Hawker Siddeley H.S.748 on tarmac	5·50	3·75

305 Douglas DC-8-61

1985. 40th Anniv of International Civil Aviation Organization. Multicoloured.

1397	10c. Type **305**	40	20
1398	50c. Lockheed Starliner (inscr "Super Constellation")	1·00	75
1399	60c. Vickers 952 Cargoliner	1·25	85
1400	$4 De Havilland Twin Otter 200/300	4·50	6·00
MS1401	102×64 mm. $5 Hawker Siddeley H.S.748 turboprop	3·00	3·00

306 Model Boat Racing

1985. Water Sports. Multicoloured.

1402	10c. Type **306**	25	10
1403	50c. Scuba diving, Carriacou	55	35
1404	$1.10 Windsurfers on Grand Anse Beach	85	1·25
1405	$4 Windsurfing	2·00	6·00
MS1406	107×77 mm. $5 Beach scene	2·25	2·75

307 Bird of Paradise (flower)

1985. Native Flowers. Multicoloured.

1407	½c. Type **307**	50	60
1408	1c. Passion flower	50	60
1409	2c. Oleander	50	60
1410a	4c. Bromeliad	80	60
1411a	5c. Anthurium	80	40
1412a	6c. Bougainvillea	80	50
1413a	10c. Hibiscus	80	30
1414a	15c. Ginger	1·25	30
1415a	25c. Poinsettia	1·25	30
1417a	40c. Angel's trumpet	1·00	50
1420a	70c. Chenille plant	1·50	1·50
1420b	75c. Cordia	1·50	2·00
1422a	$1.10 Ixora	2·50	2·75
1423a	$3 Shrimp plant	3·00	6·50
1424a	$5 Plumbago	2·50	7·00
1425a	$10 "Lantana camara"	4·00	10·00
1425b	$20 Peregrina	8·50	16·00
1425d	30c. Mexican creeper	30	60
1425e	50c. Amaryllis	40	75
1425f	60c. Prickly pear	50	1·25
1425g	$1 Periwinkle	50	1·25

308 The Queen Mother at Royal Opera House, London

1985. Life and Times of Queen Elizabeth the Queen Mother. Multicoloured.

1426	$1 Type **308**	40	60
1427	$1.50 The Queen Mother playing snooker at London Press Club (horiz)	55	85
1428	$2.50 At Epsom Races, 1960	95	1·50
MS1429	56×85 mm. $5 With Prince of Wales on 80th Birthday	1·75	3·00

Stamps as Nos. 1426/8 but with face values of 90c., $1 and $3 exist from additional sheetlets with changed background colours.

309 Youth Gardening (Horticulture)

1985. International Youth Year. Multicoloured.

1430	25c. Type **309**	25	20
1431	50c. Young people on beach (Leisure)	35	40
1432	$1.10 Girls in classroom (Education)	60	1·10
1433	$3 Nurse and young patient (Health Care)	1·50	2·50
MS1434	111×80 mm. $5 Children of different races	1·50	3·00

309a Crumhorn

1985. 300th Birth Anniv of Johann Sebastian Bach (composer).

1435	**309a**	25c. multicoloured	80	20
1436	-	70c. multicoloured	1·50	85
1437	-	$1 multicoloured	2·00	1·25
1438	-	$3 multicoloured	3·00	5·00
MS1439		104×74 mm. $5 black, grey and cinnamon	3·50	3·75

DESIGNS: 70c. Oboe d'amore; $1 Violin; $3 Harpsichord; $5 Johann Sebastian Bach.

310 Cub Scouts Camping

1985. 4th Caribbean Cuboree. Multicoloured.

1440	10c. Type **310**	30	15
1441	50c. Cub scouts swimming ("Physical Fitness")	65	40
1442	$1 Stamp collecting	1·50	80
1443	$4 Birdwatching	3·50	3·00
MS1444	103×75 mm. $5 Cub scouts saluting leader (vert)	3·25	3·75

310a Flags of Great Britain and Grenada

1985. Royal Visit. Multicoloured.

1445	50c. Type **310a**	1·50	60
1446	$1 Queen Elizabeth II (vert)	1·00	1·25
1447	$4 Royal Yacht "Britannia"	3·00	5·50
MS1448	111×85 mm. $5 Map of Grenada	1·75	3·25

1985. 150th Birth Anniv of Mark Twain (author). As T 145a of Gambia. Design showing Walt Disney cartoon characters in scenes from "The Prince and the Pauper". Multicoloured.

1449	25c. Mortie as Tom meeting the Prince (Ferdie)	60	20
1450	50c. Tom and the Prince exchanging clothes	80	50
1451	$1.10 The Prince with John Cantry	1·75	1·75
1452	$1.50 The Prince knights Mike Hendon (Goofy)	2·25	2·75
1453	$2 Tom and the Whipping Boy	2·50	3·00
MS1454	124×100 mm. $5 The Prince, Tom and Mike Hendon	6·00	6·00

1985. Birth Bicentenaries of Grimm Brothers (folklorists). As T 145b of Gambia, showing Walt Disney cartoon characters in scenes from "The Fisherman and his Wife". Multicoloured.

1455	30c. The Fisherman (Goofy) catching enchanted fish	85	30
1456	60c. The Fisherman scolded by his Wife (Clarabelle)	1·25	80
1457	70c. The Fisherman's Wife with dream cottage	1·40	95
1458	$1 The Fisherman's Wife as King	2·25	1·50
1459	$3 The Fisherman and Wife in their original shack	3·75	4·50
MS1460	126×100 mm. $5 The Fisherman in boat	6·00	6·00

311 Red-spotted Hawkfish

1985. Marine Life. Multicoloured.

1461	25c. Type **311**	1·50	55
1462	50c. Spot-finned butterflyfish	2·25	1·10
1463	$1.10 Fire coral and orange sponges	3·75	3·25
1464	$3 Pillar coral	6·00	7·50
MS1465	127×100 mm. $5 Bigeye	3·75	4·50

311a Mary McLeod Bethune (educationist) and 1975 International Women's Year 10c.

1985. 40th Anniv of U.N.O. Designs showing United Nations (New York) stamps. Mult.

1466	50c. Type **311a**	30	30
1467	$2 Maimonides (physician) and 1966 W.H.O. 5c.	2·50	3·50
1468	$2.50 Alexander Graham Bell (telephone inventor) and 1956 I.T.U. 3c.	2·00	4·00
MS1469	110×85 mm. $5 Dag Hammarskjold (Secretary-General) (vert)	1·25	2·00

312 "Adoration of the Shepherds" (Mantegna)

1985. Christmas. Religious Paintings. Multicoloured.

1470	25c. Type **312**	20	15
1471	60c. "Journey of the Magi" (Sassetta)	30	40
1472	90c. "Madonna and Child enthroned with Saints" (Raphael)	35	70
1473	$4 "Nativity" (Monaco)	1·00	4·25
MS1474	107×81 mm. $5 "Madonna and Child enthroned with Saints" (Gaddi)	1·50	2·50

312a Columbus Monument, 1893

1986. Centenary of Statue of Liberty (1st issue). Multicoloured.

1475	5c. Type **312a**	15	20
1476	25c. Columbus Monument, 1986	30	20
1477	40c. Mounted police, Central Park, 1895 (horiz)	1·75	1·10
1478	$4 Mounted police, 1986 (horiz)	5·00	8·00
MS1479	104×76 mm. $5 Statue of Liberty (vert)	2·75	2·75

See also Nos. 1644/52.

312b Snowy Egret

1986. Birth Bicentenary of John J. Audubon (ornithologist) (2nd issue). Multicoloured.

1480	50c. Type **312b**	2·00	80
1481	90c. Greater flamingo	2·75	2·00
1482	$1.10 Canada goose	2·75	2·50
1483	$3 Smew	4·50	6·00
MS1484	103×72 mm. $5 Brent goose (horiz)	13·00	13·00

1986. Visit of President Reagan. Nos. 1418 and 1424 optd VISIT OF PRES REAGAN 20 FEB. 1986.

1485	50c. Amaryllis	50	50
1486	$5 Plumbago	3·00	5·00

314 Methodist Church, St. George's

1986. Bicentenary of Methodist Church in Grenada. Multicoloured.

1487	60c. Type **314**	70	1·00
MS1488	102×73 mm. $5 St. Georges	1·00	3·00

315 Player with Ball

1986. World Cup Football Championship, Mexico. Multicoloured.

1489	50c. Type **315**	80	55
1490	70c. Player heading ball	1·00	1·00
1491	90c. Player controlling ball	1·50	1·50
1492	$4 Player controlling ball with right foot	5·50	7·00
MS1493	103×71 mm. $5 Player tackling	4·25	5·00

1986. Appearance of Halley's Comet (1st issue). As T 151a of Gambia. Multicoloured.

1494	5c. Clyde Tombaugh (astronomer) and Dudley Observatory, New York	40	40
1495	20c. N.A.S.A. – U.S.A.F. "X-24B" Space Shuttle prototype, 1973	50	30
1496	40c. German comet medal, 1618	70	45
1497	$4 Destruction of Sodom and Gomorrah, 1949 B.C.	3·50	4·50
MS1498	102×70 mm. $5 Halley's Comet over Grenada	6·50	7·00

See also Nos. 1533/7 and 1980/4.

1986. 60th Birthday of Queen Elizabeth II. As T 151b of Gambia.

1499	2c. black and yellow	10	15

1500 $1.50 multicoloured 80 80
1501 $4 multicoloured 1·60 2·50
MS1502 120×85 mm. $5 black and brown 1·75 3·25

DESIGNS: 2c. Princess Elizabeth in 1951; $1.50, Queen presenting trophy at polo match, Windsor, 1965; $4 at Epsom, Derby Day, 1977; $5 King George VI and family, 1939.

315a Goofy as Pitcher

1986. "Ameripex" International Stamp Exhibition, Chicago. Designs showing Walt Disney cartoon characters playing baseball. Multicoloured.

1503 1c. Type **315a** 10 10
1504 2c. Goofy as catcher 10 10
1505 3c. Mickey Mouse striking ball and Donald Duck as catcher 10 10
1506 4c. Huey forcing out Dewey 10 10
1507 5c. Chip n'Dale chasing flyball 10 10
1508 6c. Mickey Mouse, Donald Duck and Clarabelle in argument 10 10
1509 $2 Minnie Mouse and Donald Duck reading baseball rules 1·75 2·75
1510 $3 Ludwig von Drake as umpire with Goofy and Pete colliding 2·25 3·25
MS1511 Two sheets, each 126×101 mm. (a) $5 Donald Duck striking ball. (b) $5 Minnie and Mickey Mouse running between bases Set of 2 sheets 11·00 13·00

1986. Royal Wedding. As T 153b of Gambia. Multicoloured.

1512 2c. Prince Andrew and Miss Sarah Ferguson 10 30
1513 $1.10 Prince Andrew 70 80
1514 $4 Prince Andrew with H.M.S. "Brazen's" Westland Lynx helicopter 3·50 3·50
MS1515 88×88 mm. $5 Prince Andrew and Miss Sarah Ferguson (different) 4·50 5·00

316 Brown-lined Latirus

1986. Sea Shells. Multicoloured.

1516 25c. Type **316** 45 25
1517 60c. Lamellose wentletrap 75 90
1518 70c. Turkey wing 85 1·00
1519 $4 Rooster tail conch 2·00 5·00
MS1520 110×75 mm. $5 Angular triton 2·75 6·00

317 "Lepiota roseolamellata"

1986. Mushrooms. Multicoloured.

1521 10c. Type **317** 60 40
1522 60c. "Lentinus bertieri" 1·75 1·75
1523 $1 "Lentinus retinervis" 2·50 2·50
1524 $4 "Eccilia cystiophorus" 5·75 7·50
MS1525 127×100 mm. $5 "Cystolepiota eriophora" 10·00 13·00

1986. World Cup Football Championship Winners, Mexico. Nos. 1489/92 optd WINNERS Argentina 3 W. Germany 2.

1526 50c. Type **315** 85 85
1527 70c. Player heading ball 1·00 1·00
1528 90c. Player controlling ball 1·40 1·60
1529 $4 Player controlling ball with right foot 4·50 5·00
MS1530 101×71 mm. $5 Player tackling 3·50 4·50

318 Dove on Rifles and Mahatma Gandhi (Disarmament Week)

1986. International Events. Multicoloured.

1531 60c. Type **318** 50 50
1532 $4 Hands passing olive branch and Martin Luther King (International Peace Year) (horiz) 1·50 3·00

1986. Appearance of Halley's Comet (2nd issue). Nos. 1494/7 optd with T 447a of Ghana.

1533 5c. Clyde Tombaugh (astronomer) and Dudley Observatory, New York 60 60
1534 20c. N.A.S.A. – U.S.A.F. "X-24B" Space Shuttle prototype, 1973 85 60
1535 40c. German comet medal, 1618 1·25 70
1536 $4 Destruction of Sodom and Gomorrah, 1949 B.C. 5·00 7·00
MS1537 102×70 mm. $5 Halley's Comet over Grenada 3·50 4·25

318a Mickey Mouse asleep in Armchair

1986. Christmas. Multicoloured.

1538 30c. Type **318a** 45 25
1539 45c. Young Mickey Mouse with Father Christmas 55 30
1540 60c. Donald Duck with toy telephone (horiz) 70 50
1541 70c. Pluto with pushcart (horiz) 80 70
1542 $1.10 Daisy Duck with doll (horiz) 1·25 1·25
1543 $2 Goofy as Father Christmas 2·00 2·25
1544 $2.50 Goofy singing carols at piano 2·25 3·00
1545 $3 Mickey Mouse, Donald Duck and nephew riding toy train (horiz) 2·50 3·50
MS1546 Two sheets, each 127×101 mm. (a) $5 Donald Duck, Goofy and Mickey Mouse delivering presents (vert). (b) $5 Father Christmas playing toy piano Set of 2 sheets 9·00 12·00

319 Cockerel and Hen

1986. Fauna and Flora. Multicoloured.

1547 10c. Type **319** 20 10
1548 30c. Fish-eating bat 35 20
1549 60c. Goat 55 45
1550 70c. Cow 60 50
1551 $1 Anthurium 1·50 1·25
1552 $1.10 Royal poinciana 1·50 1·25
1553 $2 Frangipani 2·50 3·25
1554 $4 Orchid 8·50 9·50
MS1555 Two sheets, each 104×73 mm. (a) $5 Grenada landscape. (b) $5 Horse Set of 2 sheets 12·00 13·00

320 Maserati "Biturbo" (1984)

1986. Centenary of Motoring. Multicoloured.

1556 10c. Type **320** 25 25
1557 30c. AC "Cobra" (1960) 40 40
1558 60c. Corvette (1963) 60 60
1559 70c. Dusenberg "SJ7" (1932) 70 70
1560 90c. Porsche (1957) 85 1·00
1561 $1 Stoewer (1930) 1·00 1·25
1562 $2 Volkswagen "Beetle" (1957) 1·60 2·00
1563 $3 Mercedes "600 Limo" (1963) 1·90 2·50
MS1564 Two sheets, each 106×77 mm. (a) $5 Stutz (1914). (b) $5 Packard (1941) Set of 2 sheets 5·50 7·00

321 Pole Vaulting

1986. Olympic Games, Seoul, South Korea (1988). Multicoloured.

1565 10c.+5c. Type **321** 10 30
1566 50c.+20c. Gymnastics 35 60
1567 70c.+30c. Putting the shot 50 85
1568 $2+$1 High jumping 1·00 2·25
MS1569 80×100 mm. $3+$1 Swimming 1·50 3·25

The premiums on Nos. 1565/9 were to support the participation of the Grenada team.

321a Painting by Chagall

1986. Birth Centenary of Marc Chagall (artist). Designs showing various paintings.

$1.40 x 40 multicoloured
1570-1609 Set of 40 24·00 26·00
MS1610 Ten sheets, each 110×95 mm. $5×10 multicoloured (each 104×89 mm). Imperf Set of 10 sheets 24·00 26·00

321b "Columbia", 1958

1987. America's Cup Yachting Championship. Multicoloured.

1611 10c. Type **321b** 25 20
1612 60c. "Resolute", 1920 55 60
1613 $1.10 "Endeavor", 1934 85 1·25
1614 $4 "Rainbow", 1934 1·75 3·50
MS1615 113×84 mm. $5 "Weatherly", 1962 2·25 4·00

322 Virgin Mary and Outline Map of Grenada

1987. 500th Anniv (1992) of Discovery of America by Christopher Columbus (1st issue). Multicoloured.

1616 10c. Type **322** 30 20
1617 30c. "Santa Maria", "Pinta" and "Nina" (horiz) 80 35
1618 50c. Columbus and outline map of Grenada 90 45
1619 60c. Christopher Columbus 90 55
1620 90c. King Ferdinand and Queen Isabella of Spain (horiz) 90 80
1621 $1.10 Map of Antilles by Columbus 1·25 1·00
1622 $2 Caribs with sailing raft (horiz) 1·40 2·50
1623 $3 Columbus in the New World, 1493 (contemporary drawing) 1·60 2·50
MS1624 Two sheets, each 104×72 mm. (a) $5 Route map and Colombus' signature. (b) $5 Columbus carrying Christ Child Set of 2 sheets 5·00 7·50

See also Nos. 2051/5, 2091/9, 2222/30, 2389/95 and 2423/4.

322a Cornu's First Helicopter, 1907

1987. Milestones of Transportation. Multicoloured.

1625 10c. Type **322a** 1·25 65
1626 15c. "Monitor" and "Merrimack" (first battle between ironclad warships), 1862 1·25 65
1627 30c. LZ1 (first Zeppelin), 1900 1·40 80
1628 50c. "Sirius" (first transatlantic paddle-steamer crossing), 1838 1·50 85
1629 60c. Steam locomotive on Trans-Siberian Railway (longest line) 1·75 1·00
1630 70c. U.S.S "Enterprise" (largest aircraft carrier), 1960 1·75 1·25
1631 90c. Blanchard and Jeffries' balloon (first balloon across English Channel), 1785 1·75 1·40
1632 $1.50 U.S.S. "Holland I" (first steam-powered submarine), 1900 2·50 2·50
1633 $2 "Oceanic I" (first luxury liner), 1871 3·00 3·00
1634 $3 Lamborghini "Countach" (fastest commercial car), 1984 3·25 3·50

323 Black Grouper

1987. "Capex '87" International Stamp Exhibition, Toronto. Game Fishes. Multicoloured.

1635 10c. Type **323** 45 15
1636 30c. Blue marlin (horiz) 60 15
1637 60c. White marlin 80 55
1638 70c. Bigeye threshershark (horiz) 90 70
1639 $1 Bonefish (horiz) 1·25 1·00
1640 $1.10 Wahoo (horiz) 1·40 1·25
1641 $2 Sailfish (horiz) 2·00 2·50
1642 $4 Albacore (horiz) 3·00 3·75
MS1643 Two sheets, each 100×70 mm. (a) $5 Yellow-finned tuna. (b) $5 Great barracuda (horiz) Set of 2 sheets 8·00 11·00

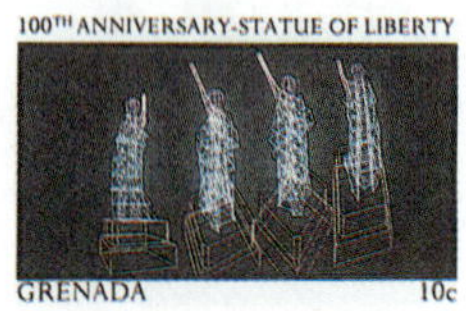

323a Computer Projections on Statue and Base

1987. Centenary of Statue of Liberty (2nd issue). Multicoloured.

1644 10c. Type **323a** 15 15
1645 25c. Statue and fireworks 20 15
1646 50c. Statue and fireworks (different) 35 35
1647 60c. Statue and boats (vert) 45 45
1648 70c. Computer projection of top of Statue 50 50
1649 $1 Rear view of Statue and fireworks (vert) 80 80
1650 $1.10 Aerial view of Statue (vert) 95 1·25
1651 $2 Statue and flotilla (vert) 2·00 2·25
1652 $4 "Queen Elizabeth 2" in New York Harbour (vert) 3·50 4·00

324 Alice and the Rabbit Hole

1987. 50th Anniv of First Full-Length Disney Cartoon Film. Nos. 1653/1706 show scenes from various films and No. MS1707 depict scenes from "Alice in Wonderland", "Cinderella", "Peter Pan", "Pinocchio", "Sleeping Beauty" and "Snow White and the Seven Dwarfs".

	1653-1706 Set of 54	18·00	19·00
1653-1706	30c. x 43 multicoloured		
MS1707	Six sheets, each 127×102 mm. $5×6 multicoloured Set of 6 sheets	30·00	30·00

325 Isaac Newton holding Apple (Law of Gravity)

1987. Great Scientific Discoveries. Multicoloured.

1708	50c. Type **325**	85	85
1709	$1.10 John Jacob Berzelius and symbols of chemical elements	1·75	1·75
1710	$2 Robert Boyle (law of Pressure and Volume)	2·50	3·25
1711	$3 James Watt and drawing of steam engine	5·50	5·00
MS1712	105×75 mm. $5 "Voyager" (experimental aircraft) and Wright glider No. IV	3·00	4·00

No. 1711 is inscribed "RUDOLF DIESEL" and No. **MS**1712 "Flyer I", both in error.

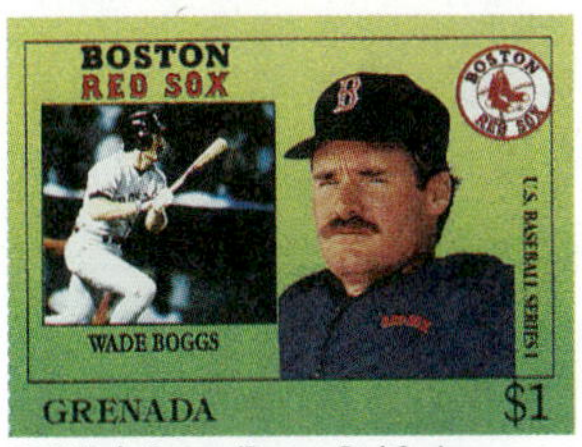

326 Wade Boggs (Boston Red Sox)

1987. All-star Baseball Game, Oakland, California. Sheet 114×82 mm, containing T 326 and similar horiz design. Multicoloured.

MS1713	$1 Type **326**; $1 Eric Davis (Cincinnati Reds)	1·00	1·75

1987. 60th Anniv of International Social Security Association. Nos. 1413, 1418 and 1423 optd INTERNATIONAL SOCIAL SECURITY ASSOCIATION and emblem.

1714	10c. Hibiscus	10	15
1715	50c. Amaryllis	25	35
1716	$3 Shrimp plant	1·40	2·25

327a Independence Hall, Philadelphia

1987. Bicentenary of U.S. Constitution. Mult.

1717	15c. Type **327a**	10	10
1718	50c. Benjamin Franklin (Pennsylvania delegate) (horiz)	25	35
1719	60c. State Seal, Massachusetts (horiz)	25	35
1720	$4 Robert Morris (Pennsylvania delegate)	1·75	2·75
MS1721	105×75 mm. $5 James Madison (Virginia delegate)	1·50	3·50

328 Goofy in "The Shadow"

1987. "Hafnia '87" International Stamp Exhibition. Walt Disney cartoon characters in scenes from Hans Christian Andersen's fairy tales. Multicoloured.

1722	25c. Type **328**	50	30
1723	30c. Mother Stork and brood in "The Storks"	50	30
1724	50c. King Richard, Robin Hood and Little John (from Robin Hood) in "The Emperor's New Clothes"	75	55
1725	60c. Goofy and Pluto in "The Tinderbox"	75	55
1726	70c. Daisy and Donald Duck in "The Shepherdess and the Chimney Sweep"	80	70
1727	$1.50 Mickey and Minnie Mouse in "The Little Mermaid"	1·60	1·75
1728	$3 Clarabelle and Goofy in "The Princess and the Pea"	2·50	3·50
1729	$4 Minnie Mouse and Pegleg Pete in "The Marsh King's Daughter"	2·50	3·50
MS1730	Two sheets, each 127×102 mm. (a) $5 Goofy in "The Flying Trunk". (b) $5 Goofy as "The Sandman" Set of 2 sheets	12·00	14·00

329 "The Annunciation" (Fra Angelico)

1987. Christmas. Religious Paintings. Multicoloured.

1731	15c. Type **329**	55	10
1732	30c. "The Annunciation" (attr. Hubert van Eyck)	90	30
1733	60c. "The Adoration of the Magi" (Januarius Zick)	1·75	1·40
1734	$4 "The Flight into Egypt" (Gerard David)	5·50	7·00
MS1735	99×75 mm. $5 "The Circumcision" (Giovanni Bellini studio)	7·00	8·00

330 T. Albert Marryshow

1988. Birth Centenary of T. Albert Marryshow (nationalist).

1736	330	25c. brown, lt brn & red	30	30

330a Wedding Photograph, 1947

1988. Royal Ruby Wedding. Multicoloured.

1737	**330a**	15c. brown, black & bl	45	10
1738	-	50c. multicoloured	80	50
1739	-	$1 brown and black	1·40	2·00
1740	-	$4 multicoloured	3·25	4·00
MS1741		76×100 mm. $5 multicoloured	2·25	3·25

DESIGNS: 50c. Queen Elizabeth II with Prince Charles and Princess Anne, c. 1955; $1 Queen with Princess Anne, c. 1957; $4 Queen Elizabeth (from photo by Tim Graham), 1980; $5 Princess Elizabeth in wedding dress, 1947.

331 Goofy and Daisy Duck lighting Olympic Torch, Olympia

1988. Olympic Games, Seoul. Designs showing Walt Disney cartoon characters. Multicoloured.

1742	1c. Type **331**	10	10
1743	2c. Donald and Daisy Duck carrying Olympic torch	10	10
1744	3c. Donald Duck, Goofy and Mickey Mouse carrying flags of U.S., Korea and Spain	10	10
1745	4c. Donald Duck releasing doves	10	10
1746	5c. Mickey Mouse flying with rocket belt	10	10
1747	10c. Morty and Ferdie carrying banner with Olympic motto	10	10
1748	$6 Donald Duck, Minnie Mouse and Hodori the Tiger (mascot of Seoul Games)	6·00	5·50
1749	$7 Pluto. Hodori and old post office, Seoul	6·00	5·50
MS1750	Two sheets, each 127×101 mm. (a) $5 Mickey Mouse taking athlete's oath. (b) $5 Donald and Daisy Duck as athletes at Closing Ceremony Set of 2 sheets	8·50	10·00

1988. Stamp Exhibitions. Nos. 1631/4 optd.

1751	90c. Blanchard and Jeffries' balloon, 1785 (optd **OLYMPHILEX '88**, Seoul)	1·25	90
1752	$1.50 U.S.S "Holland I", 1900 (optd **INDEPENDENCE 40**, Israel)	1·75	1·50
1753	$2 "Oceanic I", 1871 (optd **FINLANDIA 88**, Helsinki)	2·25	2·25
1754	$3 Lamborghini "Countach", 1984 (optd **PRAGA 88**, Prague)	2·75	2·75

332 Scout fishing from Boat

1988. World Scout Jamboree, Australia. Mult.

1755	20c. Type **332**	40	15
1756	70c. Scouts hiking through forest (horiz)	1·00	1·00
1757	90c. Practising first aid (horiz)	1·40	1·40
1758	$3 Shooting rapids in inflatable canoe	3·00	3·75
MS1759	114×80 mm. $5 Scout with koala	2·10	3·00

333 "Santa Maria de Guia" (Columbus), 1498 and Map of Rotary District

1988. Rotary District 405 Conference, St. George's. Multicoloured.

1760	$2 Type **333**	80	1·00
MS1761	133×90 mm. $10 Rotary emblem (horiz)	4·25	6·00

334 Roseate Tern

1988. Birds. Multicoloured.

1762	10c. Type **334**	80	30
1763	25c. Laughing gull	1·00	30
1764	50c. Osprey	1·60	70
1765	60c. Rose-breasted grosbeak	1·60	70
1766	90c. American purple gallinule ("Purple Gallinule")	1·60	90
1767	$1.10 White-tailed tropic bird	1·60	1·00
1768	$3 Blue-faced booby	2·25	2·75
1769	$4 Common shoveler	2·25	3·00
MS1770	Two sheets, each 100×71 mm. (a) $5 Belted kingfisher. (b) $5 Grenada flycatcher ("Rusty-tailed Flycatcher") Set of 2 sheets	7·00	9·00

335 Vauxhall Type "OE 30/98", 1925

1988. Cars. Multicoloured.

1771	$2 Type **335**	1·25	1·25
1772	$2 Wills "Sainte Claire", 1926	1·25	1·25
1773	$2 Bucciali, 1928	1·25	1·25
1774	$2 Irving Napier "Golden Arrow", 1929	1·25	1·25
1775	$2 Studebaker "President", 1930	1·25	1·25
1776	$2 Thomas "Flyer", 1907	1·25	1·25
1777	$2 Isotta-Franschini "Tipo J", 1908	1·25	1·25
1778	$2 Fiat 10/14HP, 1910	1·25	1·25
1779	$2 Mercer "Type 35 Raceabout", 1911	1·25	1·25
1780	$2 Marmon "Model 34 Cloverleaf", 1917	1·25	1·25
1781	$2 Tatra "Type 77", 1934	1·25	1·25
1782	$2 Rolls-Royce "Phantom III", 1938	1·25	1·25
1783	$2 Studebaker "Champion Starlight", 1947	1·25	1·25
1784	$2 Porsche "Gmund", 1948	1·25	1·25
1785	$2 Tucker, 1948	1·25	1·25
1786	$2 Peerless "V-16", 1931	1·25	1·25
1787	$2 Minerva "AL", 1931	1·25	1·25
1788	$2 Reo "Royale", 1953	1·25	1·25
1789	$2 Pierce Arrow "Silver Arrow", 1933	1·25	1·25
1790	$2 Hupmobile "Aerodynamic", 1934	1·25	1·25
1791	$2 Peugeot "404", 1965	1·25	1·25
1792	$2 Ford "Capri", 1969	1·25	1·25
1793	$2 Ferrari "312T", 1975	1·25	1·25
1794	$2 Lotus "T-79", 1978	1·25	1·25
1795	$2 Williams-Cosworth "FW07", 1979	1·25	1·25
1796	$2 H.R.G. "1500 Sports", 1948	1·25	1·25
1797	$2 Crosley "Hotshot", 1949	1·25	1·25
1798	$2 Volvo "PV444", 1955	1·25	1·25
1799	$2 Maserati "Tipo 61", 1960	1·25	1·25
1800	$2 Saab "96", 1963	1·25	1·25

1988. 500th Birth Anniv of Titian (artist). As T 166a of Gambia. Multicoloured.

1801	10c. "Lavinia Vecellio"	10	10
1802	20c. "Portrait of a Man"	10	10
1803	25c. "Andrea de Franceschi"	10	15
1804	90c. "Head of a Soldier"	40	45
1805	$1 "Man with a Flute"	45	50
1806	$2 "Lucrezia and Tarquinius"	80	1·00
1807	$3 "Duke of Mantua with Dog"	1·25	1·60
1808	$4 "La Bella di Tiziano"	1·60	2·00
MS1809	Two sheets, each 110×95 mm. (a) $5 "Allegory of Alfonso D'Avalos (detail). (b) $5 "Fall of Man" (detail) (horiz) Set of 2 sheets	4·25	5·50

336 "Graf Zeppelin" over Chicago World's Fair, 1933

1988. Airships. Multicoloured.

1810	10c. Type **336**	50	20
1811	15c. LZ-1 over Lake Constance, 1901 (horiz)	60	25
1812	25c. "Washington" (balloon) and "George Washington Curtis" (balloon barge), 1862	70	30
1813	45c. "Hindenburg" and Maybach "Zeppelin" car (horiz)	80	40
1814	50c. Goodyear Aerospace airship in Statue of Liberty Centenary Race, 1986	80	40
1815	60c. "Hindenburg" over Statue of Liberty, 1937 (horiz)	90	50
1816	90c. Heinkel biplane docking experiment with "Hindenburg", 1936 (horiz)	1·40	80
1817	$2 "Hindenburg" over Olympic Stadium, Berlin, 1936	2·00	2·00
1818	$3 "Hindenburg" over Christ of the Andes Monument, 1937	2·50	2·50
1819	$4 "Hindenburg" and "Bremen" (liner), 1936 (horiz)	2·75	2·75
MS1820	Two sheets. (a) 75×95 mm. $5 LZ-127 "Graf Zeppelin", 1930 (horiz). (b) 95×75 mm. $5 LZ-129 "Hindenburg", 1935 (horiz) Set of 2 sheets	4·75	5·50

337 Tasmanian Wolf, Mickey Mouse and Pluto

1988. "Sydpex '88". National Stamp Exhibition, Sydney and 60th Birthday of Mickey Mouse. Multicoloured.

1821	1c. Type **337**	10	10
1822	2c. Mickey Mouse feeding wallabies	10	10
1823	3c. Mickey Mouse and Goofy with kangaroo	10	10
1824	4c. Mickey and Minnie Mouse riding emus	10	10
1825	5c. Mickey and Minnie Mouse with wombat	10	10
1826	10c. Mickey Mouse and Donald Duck watching platypus	10	10
1827	$5 Mickey Mouse and Goofy photographing blue-winged kookaburra	5·50	5·50
1828	$6 Mickey Mouse and Koala on map of Australia	5·50	5·50
MS1829	Two sheets, each 127×102 mm. (a) $5 Mickey Mouse with birthday cake. (b) $5 Mickey and Minnie Mouse with rainbow lories Set of 2 sheets	12·00	13·00

338 Pineapple

1988. 10th Anniv of International Fund for Agricultural Development. Multicoloured.

1830	25c. Type **338**	35	15
1831	75c. Bananas	70	60
1832	$3 Mace and nutmeg (horiz)	2·50	2·75

339 Lignum Vitae

1988. Flowering Trees and Shrubs. Mult.

1833	15c. Type **339**	15	15
1834	25c. Saman	20	15
1835	35c. Red frangipani	25	20
1836	45c. Flowering maple	30	25
1837	60c. Yellow poui	40	40
1838	$1 Wild chestnut	60	70
1839	$3 Mountain immortelle	1·50	2·25
1840	$4 Queen of flowers	1·75	2·50
MS1841	Two sheets, each 117×88 mm. (a) $5 Flamboyant. (b) $5 Orchid tree Set of 2 sheets	4·25	5·50

340 Mickey Mantle (New York Yankees)

1988. Major League Baseball Players (1st series). Designs showing portraits or league emblems.

340a Donald Duck's Nephew on Mantelpiece

1988. Christmas. "Mickey's Christmas Eve". Designs showing Walt Disney cartoon characters. Multicoloured.

1923	$1 Type **340a**	65	65
1924	$1 Goofy with string of popcorn	65	65
1925	$1 Chip'n'Dale decorating Christmas tree	65	65
1926	$1 Father Christmas in sleigh	65	65
1927	$1 Donald's nephew with stocking	65	65
1928	$1 Donald's nephew unpacking decorations	65	65
1929	$1 Donald Duck with present	65	65
1930	$1 Mickey Mouse with present	65	65
MS1931	Two sheets, each 127×102 mm. (a) $5 Ferdie leaving drink for Father Christmas. (b) $5 Mordie and Ferdie asleep Set of 2 sheets	7·00	8·50

341 Tina Turner

1988. Entertainers. Multicoloured.

1932	10c. Type **341**	30	20
1933	25c. Lionel Ritchie	30	20
1934	45c. Whitney Houston	45	30
1935	60c. Joan Armatrading	60	45
1936	75c. Madonna	90	60
1937	$1 Elton John	1·00	80
1938	$3 Bruce Springsteen	2·00	2·75
1939	$4 Bob Marley	4·00	4·50
MS1940	115×155 mm. 55c.×2 Yoko Minamino; $1×2 Yoko Minamino (different)	1·90	2·75

No. 1935 is incorrectly inscribed "JOAN AMMERTRADING".

342 Atlantic Railway No. 2, 1889, Canada

1989. North American Railway Locomotives. Mult.

1941	$2 Type **342**	1·25	1·25
1942	$2 Virginia & Truckee Railroad "J. W Bowker" type, 1875, U.S.A.	1·25	1·25
1943	$2 Philadelphia & Reading Railway "Ariel", 1872, U.S.A.	1·25	1·25
1944	$2 Chicago & Rock Island Railroad "America" type, 1867, U.S.A.	1·25	1·25
1945	$2 Lehigh Valley Railroad Consolidation No. 63, 1866, U.S.A.	1·25	1·25
1946	$2 Great Western Railway "Scotia", 1860, Canada	1·25	1·25
1947	$2 Grand Trunk Railway Class "Birkenhead", 1854, Canada	1·25	1·25
1948	$2 Camden & Amboy Railroad "Monster", 1837, U.S.A.	1·25	1·25
1949	$2 Baltimore & Ohio Railroad Class "Grasshopper", 1834, U.S.A.	1·25	1·25
1950	$2 Peter Cooper's "Tom Thumb", 1829, Baltimore & Ohio Railroad, U.S.A.	1·25	1·25
1951	$2 United Railways of Yucatan "Yucatan", 1925, Mexico	1·25	1·25
1952	$2 Canadian National Railways Class T2, 1924	1·25	1·25
1953	$2 St. Louis–San Francisco Railroad Class "Light Mikado", 1919, U.S.A.	1·25	1·25
1954	$2 Atlantic Coast Line Railroad Class "Light Pacific", 1919, U.S.A.	1·25	1·25
1955	$2 Edaville Railroad No. 7, 1913, U.S.A.	1·25	1·25
1956	$2 Denver & Rio Grande Western Railroad Class K 27, 1903, U.S.A.	1·25	1·25
1957	$2 Pennsylvania Railroad Class E-2 No. 7002, 1902, U.S.A.	1·25	1·25
1958	$2 Pennsylvania Railroad Class H6, 1899, U.S.A.	1·25	1·25
1959	$2 John Jarvis's "De Witt Clinton", 1831, Mohawk Hudson Railroad, U.S.A.	1·25	1·25
1960	$2 St. Clair Tunnel Company No. 598, 1891, Canada	1·25	1·25
1961	$2 Chesapeake & Ohio Railroad Class M-l steam turbine electric locomotive No. 500, 1947, U.S.A.	1·25	1·25
1962	$2 Rutland Railroad steam locomotive No. 93, 1946, U.S.A.	1·25	1·25
1963	$2 Pennsylvania Railroad Class T1, 1942, U.S.A.	1·25	1·25
1964	$2 Chesapeake & Ohio Railroad Class H-8, 1942, U.S.A.	1·25	1·25
1965	$2 Atchison, Topeka & Santa Fe Railway Model FT diesel, 1941, U.S.A.	1·25	1·25
1966	$2 Gulf, Mobile & Ohio Railroad Models S-l and S-2 diesels, 1940, U.S.A.	1·25	1·25
1967	$2 New York, New Haven & Hartford Railroad Class 15, 1937, U.S.A.	1·25	1·25
1968	$2 Seaboard Air Line Railroad Class R, 1936, U.S.A.	1·25	1·25
1969	$2 Newfoundland Railway Class R-2, 1930	1·25	1·25
1970	$2 Canadian National Railway diesel No. 9000, 1928	1·25	1·25

343 Women's Long Jump (Jackie Joyner-Kersee, U.S.A.)

1989. Olympic Gold Medal Winners, Seoul (1988). Multicoloured.

1971	10c. Type **343**	30	20
1972	25c. Women's Singles Tennis (Steffi Graf, West Germany)	75	35
1973	45c. Men's 1500 m (Peter Rono, Kenya)	80	40
1974	75c. Men's 1000 m single kayak (Greg Barton, U.S.A.)	90	60
1975	$1 Women's team foil (Italy)	1·10	75
1976	$2 Women's 100 m freestyle swimming (Kristin Otto, East Germany)	2·25	2·25
1977	$3 Men's still rings gymnastics (Holger Behrendt, East Germany)	2·50	2·75
1978	$4 Synchronized swimming pair (Japan)	2·75	3·00
MS1979	Two sheets, each 76×100 mm. (a) $6 Olympic flame. (b) $6 Runner with Olympic torch Set of 2 sheets	8·50	9·50

344 Nebulae

1989. Appearance of Halley's Comet (1986) (3rd issue).

1980	**344**	25c.+5c. multicoloured	70	80
1981	-	75c.+5c. black & green	1·10	1·40
1982	-	90c.+5c. multicoloured	1·25	1·60
1983	-	$2+5c. multicoloured	1·75	2·50
MS1984		111×78 mm. $5+5c. multicoloured. Imperf	4·00	5·00

DESIGNS: 75c.+5c. Marine astronomical experiments; 90c.+5c. Moon's surface; $2+5c. Edmond Halley, Sir Isaac Newton and his book "Principia". (102×69 mm)—$5+5c. 17th-century warships and astrological signs.

1989. Japanese Art. Paintings by Hiroshige. As T 177a of Gambia. Multicoloured.

1985	10c. "Shinagawa on Edo Bay"	30	20
1986	25c. "Pine Trees on the Road to Totsuka"	40	30
1987	60c. "Kanagawa on Edo Bay"	60	50
1988	75c. "Crossing Banyu River to Hiratsuka"	65	55
1989	$1 "Windy Shore at Odawara"	80	70
1990	$2 "Snow-Covered Post Station of Mishima"	1·40	1·75
1991	$3 "Full Moon at Fuchu"	1·60	2·00
1992	$4 "Crossing the Stream at Okitsu"	2·25	2·50
MS1993	Two sheets, each 102×76 mm. (a) $5 "Mountain Pass at Nissaka". (b) $5 "Mt Uzu at Okabe" Set of 2 sheets	4·25	5·50

345 Great Blue Heron

1989. Birds. Multicoloured.

1994	5c. Type **345**	40	50
1995	10c. Green-backed heron ("Green Heron")	50	40
1996	15c. Ruddy turnstone	60	40
1997	25c. Blue-winged teal	65	20
1998	35c. Little ringed plover ("Ringnecked Plover") (vert)	70	20
1999	45c. Green-throated carib ("Emerald-throated Hummingbird") (vert)	85	30
2000	50c. Rufous-breasted hermit ("Hairy Hermit") (vert)	90	45
2001	60c. Lesser Antillean bullfinch (vert)	1·00	50
2002	75c. Brown pelican (vert)	1·25	65
2003	$1 Black-crowned night heron (vert)	1·50	90
2004	$3 American kestrel ("Sparrow Hawk") (vert)	2·75	3·00
2005	$5 Barn swallow (vert)	3·50	4·00
2006	$10 Red-billed tropic bird (vert)	6·00	8·50
2007	$20 Barn owl (vert)	12·00	15·00

345a Scotland Player

1989. World Cup Football Championship, Italy (1990) (1st issue). Multicoloured.

2008	10c. Type **345a**	40	20

2009	25c. England and Brazil players	50	30
2010	60c. Paolo Rossi (Italy)	75	55
2011	75c. Jairzinho (Brazil)	90	70
2012	$1 Sweden striker	1·10	90
2013	$2 Pele (Brazil)	2·25	2·00
2014	$3 Mario Kempes (Argentina)	3·00	2·75
2015	$4 Pat Jennings (Northern Ireland)	3·25	3·00
MS2016	Two sheets. (a) 70×93 mm. $6 Players jumping for ball. (b) 82×71 mm. $6 Goalkeeper Set of 2 sheets	8·50	11·00

See also Nos. 2174/8 and **MS**2179.

346 Xebec and Sugar Cane

1989. "Philexfrance '89" International Stamp Exhibition, Paris. Designs showing French sailing vessels and plantation crops. Mult.

2017	25c. Type **346**	1·25	30
2018	75c. Lugger and cotton	1·75	85
2019	$1 Full-rigged ship and cocoa	2·00	1·10
2020	$4 Ketch and coffee	3·75	5·50
MS2021	114×70 mm. $6 "View of Fort and Town of St. George, 1779" (105×63 mm). Imperf	6·00	8·00

347 Alan Shepard and "Freedom 7" Spacecraft, 1961 (first American in Space)

1989. 20th Anniv of First Manned Landing on Moon. Multicoloured.

2022	15c. Type **347**	70	40
2023	35c. "Friendship 7" spacecraft, 1962 (first manned earth orbit)	90	55
2024	45c. "Apollo 8" orbiting Moon, 1968 (first manned lunar orbit)	1·00	65
2025	70c. "Apollo 15" lunar rover, 1972	1·50	85
2026	$1 "Apollo 11" emblem and lunar module "Eagle" on Moon, 1969	1·75	1·10
2027	$2 "Gemini 8" and "Agena" rocket, 1966 (first space docking)	3·00	3·25
2028	$3 Edward White in space, 1965 (first U.S. space walk)	3·00	3·25
2029	$4 "Apollo 7" emblem	3·75	3·50
MS2030	Two sheets, each 101×71 mm. (a) $5 Moon and track of "Apollo 11", 1969. (b) $5 Armstrong and Aldrin raising U.S. flag on Moon, 1969 Set of 2 sheets	12·00	10·00

348 "Hygrocybe occidentalis"

1989. Fungi. Multicoloured.

2031	15c. Type **348**	50	40
2032	40c. "Marasmius haematocephalus"	65	55
2033	50c. "Hygrocybe hypohaemacta"	75	65
2034	70c. "Lepiota pseudoignicolor"	1·00	90
2035	90c. "Cookeina tricholoma"	1·25	1·25
2036	$1.10 "Leucopaxillus gracillimus"	1·50	1·50
2037	$2.25 "Hygrocybe nigrescens"	2·75	3·00
2038	$4 "Clathrus crispus"	3·75	4·00
MS2039	Two sheets, each 57×70 mm. (a) $6 "Mycena holoporphyra". (b) $6 "Xeromphalina tenuipes" Set of 2 sheets	12·00	13·00

349 Y.W.C.A. Logo and Grenada Scenery

1989. Centenary of Young Women's Christian Association. Multicoloured.

2040	50c. Type **349**	45	45
2041	75c. Y.W.C.A. logo and town (horiz)	80	80

350 "Historis odius"

1989. Butterflies. Multicoloured.

2042	6c. Type **350**	30	30
2043	30c. "Marpesia petreus"	55	55
2044	40c. "Danaus gilippus"	60	60
2045	60c. "Dione juno"	80	80
2046	$1.10 "Agraulis vanillae"	1·25	1·25
2047	$1.25 "Danaus plexippus"	1·50	1·50
2048	$4 "Papilio androgeus"	3·25	3·25
2049	$5 "Dryas julia"	3·25	3·25
MS2050	Two sheets, each 87×115 mm. (a) $6 "Anartia jatrophae". (b) $6 "Strymon simaethis" Set of 2 sheets	9·50	11·00

351 Amerindian Hieroglyph

1989. 500th Anniv (1992) of Discovery of America by Columbus (2nd issue). Designs showing different hieroglyphs.

2051	**351**	45c. brown, black & blue	1·00	50
2052	-	60c. brown, black & grn	1·10	60
2053	-	$1 brown, black and violet	1·75	1·00
2054	-	$4 dp brown, black & brn	4·25	4·75
MS2055		74×86 mm. $6 brown, black and red	4·00	5·50

352 Amos leaving Home

1989. "World Stamp Expo '89" International Stamp Exhibition, Washington. Designs showing Walt Disney cartoon characters in scenes from "Ben and Me". Multicoloured.

2056	1c. Type **352**	10	10
2057	2c. Meeting of Benjamin Franklin and Amos	10	10
2058	3c. The Franklin stove	10	10
2059	4c. Ben and Amos with bi-focals	10	10
2060	5c. Amos on page of "Pennsylvania Gazette"	10	10
2061	6c. Ben working printing press	10	10
2062	10c. Conducting experiment with electricity	10	10
2063	$5 Ben disembarking in England	5·00	5·50
2064	$6 Ben with Document of Agreement	5·50	6·00
MS2065	Two sheets, each 127×101 mm. (a) $6 Benjamin Franklin teaching (vert). (b) $6 Signatories of Declaration of Independence Set of 2 sheets	8·00	10·00

352a "Christ in the House of Mary and Martha"

1990. Christmas. Paintings by Rubens. Multicoloured.

2066	20c. Type **352a**	50	25
2067	35c. "The Circumcision"	65	40
2068	60c. "Trinity adored by Duke of Mantua and Family"	1·00	65
2069	$2 "Holy Family with St. Francis"	2·75	2·75
2070	$3 "The Ildefonso Altarpiece"	3·25	3·50
2071	$4 "Madonna and Child with Garland and Putti"	3·75	4·00
MS2072	Two sheets, each 70×95 mm. (a) $5 "Adoration of the Magi". (b) $5 "Virgin and Child adored by Angels" Set of 2 sheets	7·50	9·00

353 Alexander Graham Bell and Early Telephone System (150th anniv of invention)

1990. Anniversaries. Multicoloured.

2073	10c. Type **353**	30	20
2074	25c. George Washington and Capitol (bicentenary of presidential inauguration)	30	20
2075	35c. Shakespeare and birthplace, Stratford (425th birth anniv)	1·50	30
2076	75c. Nehru and Gandhi (birth cent of Nehru)	4·00	1·50
2077	$1 Dr. Hugo Eckener, Ferdinand von Zeppelin and airship "Graf Zeppelin" (80th anniv of first passenger Zeppelin)	2·00	1·25
2078	$2 Charlie Chaplin (birth cent)	5·50	3·00
2079	$3 Container ship in Hamburg Harbour (800th anniv)	2·75	3·50
2080	$4 Friedrich Ebert (first President) and Heidelberg gate (70th anniv of German Republic)	2·75	3·50
MS2081	Two sheets, each 100×72 mm. (a) $6 13th-century ships in Hamburg Harbour (vert) (800th anniv). (b) $6 Concorde (20th anniv of first test flight) Set of 2 sheets	8·50	10·00

No. 2080 is inscribed "40th Anniversary of German Republic" in error.

354 "Odontoglossum triumphans"

1990. "EXPO '90" International Garden and Greenery Exhibition, Osaka. Caribbean Orchids. Multicoloured.

2082	1c. Type **354**	10	30
2083	25c. "Oncidium splendidum"	40	20
2084	60c. "Laelia anceps"	80	60
2085	75c. "Cattleya trianaei"	90	75
2086	$1 "Odontoglossum rossii"	1·25	1·00
2087	$2 "Brassia gireoudiana"	2·00	1·75
2088	$3 "Cattleya dowiana"	2·50	2·50
2089	$4 "Sobralia macrantha"	2·75	2·75
MS2090	Two sheets, each 97×68 mm. (a) $6 "Oncidium lanceanum". (b) $6 "Laelia rubescens" Set of 2 sheets	8·50	9·50

354a "Marpesia petreus"

1990. 500th Anniv (1992) of Discovery of America by Columbus (3rd issue). New World Natural History—Butterflies. Multicoloured.

2091	15c. Type **354a**	75	20
2092	25c. "Junonia evarete"	90	25
2093	75c. "Siproeta stelenes"	1·60	70
2094	90c. "Historis odius"	1·75	85
2095	$1 "Mestra cana"	1·75	90
2096	$2 "Biblis hyperia"	2·75	2·75
2097	$3 "Dryas julia"	3·25	3·75
2098	$4 "Anartia amathea"	3·25	4·00
MS2099	Two sheets, each 101×69 mm. (a) $6 "Pseudolycaena marsyas". (b) $6 "Phoebis philea" Set of 2 sheets	13·00	14·00

354b Caribbean Monk Seal

1990. Local Fauna. Multicoloured.

2100	10c. Type **354b**	50	30
2101	15c. Little brown bat	60	30
2102	45c. Brown rat	70	50
2103	60c. Common rabbit	80	60
2104	$1 Water opossum	1·25	95
2105	$2 White-nosed ichneumon	1·75	1·75
2106	$3 Little big-eared bat (vert)	2·25	2·50
2107	$4 Mouse opossum	2·25	2·50
MS2108	Two sheets, each 107×80 mm. (a) $6 Common rabbit (different). (b) $6 Water opossum (different) Set of 2 sheets	8·50	10·00

354c British Tanks during Operation Battleaxe, 1941

1990. 50th Anniv of Second World War. Mult.

2109	25c. Type **354c**	40	30
2110	35c. Allied tank in southern France, 1944	50	40
2111	45c. U.S. forces landing on Guadalcanal, 1942	60	45
2112	50c. U.S. attack in New Guinea, 1943	60	50
2113	60c. Hoisting U.S. flag on Leyte, Phillippines, 1944	80	60
2114	75c. U.S. tanks entering Cologne, 1945	85	75
2115	$1 Anzio offensive, 1944	1·10	95
2116	$2 Battle of the Bismarck Sea, 1943	2·00	1·75
2117	$3 U.S.S. "Langley" and U.S.S. "Ticonderoga" (aircraft carriers), 1944	2·75	2·75
2118	$4 Focke Wulf Fw 190A fighter attacking Salerno landing, 1943	3·00	3·25
MS2119	111×83 mm. $6 German "U-30" submarine, 1939	3·50	4·00

1990. "Stamp World London '90" International Stamp Exhibition (1st issue). As T 193 of Gambia, but horiz showing Walt Disney cartoon characters and British trains.

2120	5c. Mickey Mouse driving S.R. "King Arthur" class locomotive, 1925	40	20
2121	10c. Mickey and Minnie Mouse with "Puffing Billy", 1813	40	20
2122	20c. Mickey Mouse with Pluto pulling Durham colliery wagon, 1765	65	20
2123	45c. Mickey Mouse timing L.N.E.R. locomotive No. 2509 "Silver Link", 1935	90	25
2124	$1 Mickey Mouse and Donald Duck with locomotive No. 60149 "Amadis", 1948	2·00	1·00
2125	$2 Goofy and Mickey Mouse with Liverpool & Manchester Railway locomotive, 1830	2·75	2·75
2126	$4 Goofy and Donald Duck with Great Northern locomotive No. 1, 1870	3·50	4·25

2127	$5 Mickey Mouse and Gyro the Mechanic with Advanced Passenger Train, 1972	3·50	4·25
MS2128	Two sheets, each 127×101 mm. (a) $6 Minnie Mouse, Donald and Daisy Duck in Trevithick's Catch-Me-Who-Can, 1808 (horiz). (b) $6 Donald Duck and Locomotion, 1825 Set of 2 sheets	13·00	14·00

No. 2126 is inscribed "Flying Scotsman" in error.
See also No. **MS**2146.

355 U.S. Paratroop Drop over Grenada

1990. 50th Anniv of United States Airborne Forces.

2129	75c. Type **355**	1·60	1·25
MS2130	Two sheets, each 115×87 mm. (a) $2.50, Paratrooper landing. (b) $6 Paratroop uniforms of 1940 and 1990 Set of 2 sheets	5·50	6·50

1990. 90th Birthday of Queen Elizabeth the Queen Mother. As T 194 of Gambia showing photographs from the 1960s. Multicoloured.

2131	$2 Queen Mother in coat and hat	1·75	1·75
2132	$2 Queen Mother in evening dress	1·75	1·75
2133	$2 Queen Mother in Garter robes	1·75	1·75
MS2134	90×75 mm. $6 Queen Mother (as No. 2131)	3·50	4·00

1990. Olympic Games, Barcelona (1992) (1st issue). As T 195a of Gambia. Multicoloured.

2135	10c. Men's steeplechase	30	20
2136	15c. Dressage	45	30
2137	45c. Men's 200 m. butterfly swimming	50	45
2138	50c. Men's hockey	1·75	60
2139	65c. Women's beam gymnastics	60	60
2140	75c. "Flying Dutchman" class sailing	1·00	80
2141	$2 Freestyle wrestling	1·75	1·75
2142	$3 Men's springboard diving	2·25	2·75
2143	$4 Women's 1000 m. sprint cycling	4·25	4·25
2144	$5 Men's basketball	5·00	5·00
MS2145	Two sheets, each 101×70 mm. (a) $8 Equestrian three-day event. (b) $8 Men's 10000 metres Set of 2 sheets	9·50	11·00

See also Nos. 2414/22.

356 Map of North America and Logo

1990. "Stamp World London 90" International Stamp Exhibition (2nd issue). Sheet 97×75 mm.

MS2146	**356** $6 mauve	4·25	5·50

357 Yellow Goatfish

1990. Coral Reef Fishes. Multicoloured.

2147	10c. Type **357**	30	30
2148	25c. Black margate	45	35
2149	65c. Blue-headed wrasse	85	75
2150	75c. Puddingwife	95	85
2151	$1 Four-eyed butterflyfish	1·10	95
2152	$2 Honey damselfish	2·00	2·00
2153	$3 Queen angelfish	2·50	2·50
2154	$5 Cherub angelfish	3·00	3·50
MS2155	Two sheets, each 103×72 mm. (a) $6 Smooth trunkfish. (b) $6 Sergeant major Set of 2 sheets	8·00	9·00

358 Tropical Mockingbird

1990. Birds. Multicoloured.

2156	15c. Type **358**	30	30
2157	25c. Grey kingbird	35	35
2158	65c. Bare-eyed thrush	75	75
2159	75c. Antillean crested hummingbird	85	85
2160	$1 House wren	1·00	1·00
2161	$2 Purple martin	1·75	1·75
2162	$4 Lesser Antillian tanager ("Hooded Tanager")	2·50	2·50
2163	$5 Scaly-breasted ground dove	3·00	3·00
MS2164	Two sheets, each 101×72 mm. (a) $6 Fork-tailed flycatcher. (b) $6 Smooth-billed ani Set of 2 sheets	13·00	14·00

359 Coral Crab

1990. Crustaceans. Multicoloured.

2165	5c. Type **359**	20	30
2166	10c. Smoothtail spiny lobster	20	30
2167	15c. Flamestreaked box crab	20	30
2168	25c. Spotted swimming crab	30	25
2169	75c. Sally lightfoot rock crab	70	60
2170	$1 Spotted spiny lobster	90	80
2171	$3 Longarm spiny lobster	2·00	2·50
2172	$20 Caribbean spiny lobster	13·00	18·00
MS2173	Two sheets, 106×75 mm. (a) $6 Copper lobster. (b) $6 Spanish lobster Set of 2 sheets	8·00	9·00

360 Cameroon Player

1990. World Cup Football Championship, Italy (2nd issue). Multicoloured.

2174	10c. Type **360**	20	15
2175	25c. Michel (Spain)	25	15
2176	$1 Brehme (West Germany)	85	85
2177	$5 Nevin (Scotland)	3·00	4·00
MS2178	Two sheets, each 95×90 mm. (a) $6 Giannini (Italy). (b) $6 Perdomo (Uruguay) Set of 2 sheets	9·50	11·00

1990. World Cup Football Championship, Italy (1990) (3rd issue). No. MS2016a optd 1990 W GERMANY 1 ARGENTINA 0.

MS2179	70×93 mm. $6 Players jumping for ball	7·50	8·50

1990. Christmas. Paintings by Raphael. As T 195b of Gambia. Multicoloured.

2180	10c. "The Ansidei Madonna"	20	10
2181	15c. "The Sistine Madonna"	20	10
2182	$1 "The Madonna of the Baldacchino"	1·50	70
2183	$2 "The Large Holy Family" (detail)	2·50	2·75
2184	$5 "Madonna in the Meadow"	4·00	6·00
MS2185	Two sheets, each 71×101 mm. (a) $6 "Madonna of the Diadem" (detail). (b) $6 "The Madonna of the Veil" (detail) Set of 2 sheets	13·00	14·00

1991. 350th Death Anniv of Rubens. As T 195c of Gambia. Multicoloured.

2186	5c. "The Brazen Serpent" (detail)	30	10
2187	10c. "The Garden of Love"	30	10
2188	25c. "Head of Cyrus" (detail)	50	20
2189	75c. "Tournament in Front of a Castle"	1·25	60
2190	$1 "The Brazen Serpent" (different detail)	1·40	75
2191	$2 "Judgement of Paris" (detail)	2·00	2·00
2192	$4 "The Brazen Serpent"	3·00	4·00
2193	$5 "The Karmesse" (detail)	3·25	4·00
MS2194	Two sheets, each 101×70 mm. (a) $6 "Anger of Neptune" (detail). (b) $6 "The Prodigal son" (detail) Set of 2 sheets	13·00	14·00

362 "The Sorcerer's Apprentice"

1991. 50th Anniv of "Fantasia" (cartoon film). Multicoloured.

2195	5c. Type **362**	65	20
2196	10c. Dancing mushrooms ("The Nutcracker Suite")	65	20
2197	20c. Pterodactyls ("The Rite of Spring")	1·00	20
2198	45c. Centaurs ("The Pastoral Symphony")	1·75	40
2199	$1 Bacchus and Jacchus ("The Pastoral Symphony")	2·75	1·25
2200	$2 Dancing ostrich ("Dance of the Hours")	3·75	3·25
2201	$4 Elephant ballet ("Dance of the Hours")	4·75	5·50
2202	$5 Diana ("The Pastoral Symphony")	4·75	5·50
MS2203	Two sheets, each 122×102 mm. (a) $6 Mickey Mouse as the Sorcerer's Apprentice. (b) $6 Mickey Mouse with Leopold Stokowski (conductor) Set of 2 sheets	14·00	15·00
MS2204	176×213 mm. $12 Mickey Mouse as the Sorcerer's Apprentice (vert)	14·00	15·00

363 "Adelpha iphicla"

1991. Butterflies. Multicoloured.

2205	5c. Type **363**	60	60
2206	10c. "Nymphalidae claudina"	60	50
2207	15c. "Brassolidae polyxena"	70	30
2208	20c. "Zebra Longwing"	80	30
2209	25c. "Marpesia corinna"	80	25
2210	30c. "Morpho hecuba"	80	30
2211	45c. "Morpho rhetenor"	1·10	45
2212	50c. "Dismorphia spio"	1·25	55
2213	60c. "Prepona omphale"	1·25	65
2214	70c. "Morpho anaxibia"	1·50	75
2215	75c. "Marpesia iole"	1·50	80
2216	$1 "Amarynthis meneria"	1·75	1·00
2217	$2 "Morpho cisseis"	2·50	2·50
2218	$3 "Danaidae plexippus"	3·00	3·50
2219	$4 "Morpho achilleana"	3·50	4·50
2220	$5 "Calliona argenissa"	4·50	4·75
MS2221	Four sheets, each 118×80 mm. (a) $6 "Anteos clorinde". (b) $6 "Haetera piera". (c) $6 "Papilio cresphontes". (d) $6 "Prepona pheridamas" Set of 4 sheets	17·00	19·00

363a Vitus Bering in Bering Sea, 1728–9

1991. 500th Anniv (1992) of Discovery of America by Columbus. History of Exploration. Mult.

2222	5c. Type **363a**	70	60
2223	10c. De Bougainville off Pacific island, 1766–69	70	50
2224	25c. Polynesian canoe	45	30
2225	50c. De Mendana off Solomon Islands, 1567–69	1·40	60
2226	$1 Darwin's H.M.S. "Beagle", 1831–35	2·50	1·25
2227	$2 Cook's H.M.S. "Endeavour", 1768–71	4·00	3·25
2228	$4 William Schouten in LeMaire Strait, 1615–17	4·00	4·50
2229	$5 Tasman off New Zealand, 1642–44	4·00	4·50
MS2230	Two sheets, each 116×77 mm. (a) $6 "Santa Maria" sinking. (b) $6 Bow of "Santa Maria" (vert) Set of 2 sheets	8·50	9·50

1991. "Phila Nippon '91" International Stamp Exhibition, Tokyo. Horiz designs as T 198c of Gambia showing Walt Disney cartoon characters at Japanese festivals. Multicoloured.

2231	5c. Minnie Mouse and Daisy Duck at Dolls festival	40	20
2232	10c. Morty and Ferdie with Boys' Day display	40	20
2233	20c. Mickey and Minnie Mouse at Star festival	70	20
2234	45c. Minnie and Daisy folk-dancing	1·25	35
2235	$1 Huey, Dewey and Louie wearing Eboshi headdresses	2·00	85
2236	$2 Mickey and Goofy pulling decorated car at Gion festival	3·50	3·50
2237	$4 Minnie and Daisy preparing rice broth, Seven Plants festival	4·25	4·75
2238	$5 Huey and Dewey with straw boat at Lanterns festival	4·25	4·75
MS2239	Three sheets, each 127×101 mm. (a) $6 Minnie Mouse in kimono. (b) $6 Mickey taking photo (horiz). (c) $6 Goofy behind fair stall (horiz) Set of 3 sheets	14·00	15·00

1991. Death Centenary (1990) of Vincent van Gogh (artist). As T 200b of Gambia. Multicoloured.

2240	20c. "Blossoming Almond Branch in Glass" (vert)	50	25
2241	25c. "La Mousme sitting" (vert)	50	25
2242	30c. "Still Life with Red Cabbages and Onions"	55	30
2243	40c. "Japonaiserie: Flowering Plum Tree" (vert)	70	40
2244	45c. "Japonaiserie: Bridge in the Rain" (vert)	70	40
2245	60c. "Still Life with Basket of Apples"	1·00	60
2246	75c. "Italian Woman" (vert)	1·10	70
2247	$1 "The Painter on his Way to Work" (vert)	1·60	1·00
2248	$2 "Portrait of Pere Tanguy" (vert)	2·50	2·25
2249	$3 "Still Life with Plaster Statuette, a Rose and Two Novels" (vert)	3·25	3·25
2250	$4 "Still Life: Bottle, Lemons and Oranges"	3·50	3·75
2251	$5 "Orchard with Blossoming Apricot Trees"	3·50	3·75
MS2252	Five sheets. (a) 76×102 mm. $6 "Roubine du Roi Canal with Washerwoman" (73×99 mm). (b) 102×76 mm. $6 "Farmhouse in a Wheatfield" (99×73 mm). (c) 102×76 mm. $6 "The Gleize Bridge over the Vigueirat Canal" (99×73 mm). (d) 102×76 mm. $6 "Rocks with Oak Tree" (99×73 mm). (e) 76×102 mm. $6 "Japonaiserie: Oiran" (73×99 mm). Imperf. Set of 5 sheets	22·00	24·00

364 "Psilocybe cubensis"

1991. Fungi. Multicoloured.

2253	15c. Type **364**	70	30
2254	25c. "Leptonia caeruleocapitata"	80	30
2255	65c. "Cystolepiota eriophora"	1·40	85
2256	75c. "Chlorophyllum molybdites"	1·40	1·00
2257	$1 "Xerocomus hypoxanthus"	1·60	1·25
2258	$2 "Volvariella cubensis"	2·50	2·75
2259	$4 "Xerocomus coccolobae"	3·25	4·00
2260	$5 "Pluteus chrysophlebius"	3·25	4·00
MS2261	Two sheets, each 100×70 mm. (a) $6 "Psathyrella tuberculata". (b) $6 "Hygrocybe miniata" Set of 2 sheets	14·00	14·00

365 Johannes Kepler (astronomer)

1991. Exploration of Mars. Designs showing astronomers, spacecraft and Martian landscapes. Multicoloured.

	2262-2297 Set of 36	48·00	48·00
2262-2297	75c.×9, $1.25×9, $2×9, $7×9	48·00	
MS2298	Three sheets, each 112×92 mm. (a) $6 Projected spacecraft. (b) $6 Mars and part of spacecraft. (c) $6 Phobos satellite over Mars Set of 3 sheets	11·00	12·00

1991. 65th Birthday of Queen Elizabeth II. As T 198a of Gambia. Multicoloured.

2299	15c. Royal Family on balcony after Trooping the Colour, 1985	60	15
2300	40c. Queen and Prince Philip at Peterborough, 1988	75	35

2301 $2 Queen and Queen Mother at Windsor, 1986 2·50 1·75
2302 $4 Queen and Prince Philip on visit to United Arab Emirates 3·50 3·50
MS2303 68×90 mm. $5 Separate photographs of the Queen and Prince Philip 4·00 4·50

1991. 10th Wedding Anniv of the Prince and Princess of Wales. As T 198b of Gambia. Multicoloured.
2304 10c. Prince and Princess in July 1985 60 10
2305 50c. Separate photographs of Prince, Princess and sons 1·25 45
2306 $1 Prince Henry at Trooping the Colour and Prince William in Majorca 1·50 1·00
2307 $5 Separate photographs of Prince Charles and Princess Diana 4·25 4·50
MS2308 68×90 mm. $5 Prince, Princess and sons on holiday in Majorca 6·50 5·50

366 Anglican High School Pupils

1991. 75th Anniv of Anglican High School (10, 25c.) and 40th Anniv of University of the West Indies (45, 50c.). Multicoloured.
2309 10c. Type **366** 35 20
2310 25c. Artist's impression of new Anglican High School 60 20
2311 45c. Marryshow House, Grenada 85 55
2312 50c. University Administrative Building, Barbados 90 1·00

367 George Stephenson's First Locomotive, 1814 (Great Britain)

1991. Great Railways of the World. Mult.
2313 75c. Type **367** 75 75
2314 75c. George Stephenson 75 75
2315 75c. Killingworth locomotive, 1816 (Great Britain) 75 75
2316 75c. George Stephenson's "Locomotion", 1825 (Great Britain) 75 75
2317 75c. "Locomotion" in Darlington, 1825 (Great Britain) 75 75
2318 75c. Opening of Stockton & Darlington Railway, 1825 75 75
2319 75c. Timothy Hackworth's "Royal George", 1827 (Great Britain) 75 75
2320 75c. Northumbrian T831 (Great Britain) 75 75
2321 75c. "Planet", 1830 (Great Britain) 75 75
2322 $1 "Old Ironsides", 1832 (U.S.A.) 90 90
2323 $1 "Wilberforce", 1832 (Great Britain) 90 90
2324 $1 "Adler", 1835 (Germany) 90 90
2325 $1 "North Star", 1837 (Great Britain) 90 90
2326 $1 London & Birmingham Railway No. 1, 1838 (Great Britain) 90 90
2327 $1 Stephenson's "Austria", 1838 (Austria) 90 90
2328 $1 Baltimore & Ohio Railroad No. 378 "Muddigger", 1840 (U.S.A.) 90 90
2329 $1 Baltimore & Ohio Railroad Norris, 1840 (U.S.A.) 90 90
2330 $1 "Centaur", 1840 (Great Britain) 90 90
2331 $2 "Lion", 1841 (Great Britain) 1·50 1·50
2332 $2 "Beuth", 1843 (Germany) 1·50 1·50
2333 $2 "Derwent", 1845 (Great Britain) 1·50 1·50
2334 $2 "Bets", 1846 (Hungary) 1·50 1·50
2335 $2 Opening of Budapest to Vac railway, 1846 (Hungary) 1·50 1·50
2336 $2 Carriages, Stockton & Darlington Railway, 1846 (Great Britain) 1·50 1·50
2337 $2 "Long Boiler" type, 1847 (France) 1·50 1·50
2338 $2 Baldwin locomotive, 1850 (U.S.A.) 1·50 1·50
2339 $2 Steam locomotive, 1850 (Germany) 1·50 1·50
MS2340 Two sheets, each 116×86 mm. (a) $6 Part of Stephenson's "Locomotion", 1825 (Great Britain). (b) $6 Train on Liverpool & Manchester Railway, 1833 (Great Britain) Set of 2 sheets 14·00 15·00

368 Barbu

1991. Marine Life of the Sandflats. Mult.
2341 50c. Type **368** 80 80
2342 50c. Beau Gregory 80 80
2343 50c. Porcupinefish 80 80
2344 50c. Queen or pink conch and conchfish 80 80
2345 50c. Hermit crab 80 80
2346 50c. Bluestripe lizardfish 80 80
2347 50c. Spot-finned mojarra 80 80
2348 50c. Southern stingray 80 80
2349 50c. Long-spined sea urchin and slippery dick 80 80
2350 50c. Peacock flounder 80 80
2351 50c. West Indian sea star 80 80
2352 50c. Spotted goatfish 80 80
2353 50c. Netted olive and West Indian sea egg 80 80
2354 50c. Pearly razorfish 80 80
2355 50c. Spotted jawfish and yellow-headed jawfish 80 80
MS2356 105×76 mm. $6 Short-nosed batfish 16·00 14·00

Nos. 2341/55 were printed together, se-tenant, forming a composite design.

1991. Christmas. Religious Paintings by Albrecht Durer. As T 200c of Gambia. Mult.
2357 10c. "Adoration of the Magi" (detail) 60 10
2358 35c. "Madonna with the Siskin" (detail) 90 25
2359 50c. "Feast of the Rose Garlands" (detail) 1·25 45
2360 75c. "Virgin with the Pear" (detail) 1·75 80
2361 $1 "Virgin in Half-length" (detail) 2·25 1·00
2362 $2 "Madonna and Child" (detail) 3·25 3·25
2363 $4 "Virgin and Child with St. Anne" (detail) 3·75 5·00
2364 $5 "Virgin and Child" (detail) 3·75 5·00
MS2365 Two sheets, each 102×127 mm. (a) $6 "Virgin with a Multitude of Animals" (detail). (b) $6 "The Nativity" (detail).Set of 2 sheets 13·00 14·00

369 Goofy windsurfing

1992. Thrill Sports. Walt Disney cartoon characters. Multicoloured.
2366 5c. Type **369** 40 30
2367 10c. Mickey Mouse skateboarding 50 30
2368 20c. Daisy Duck gliding 80 30
2369 45c. Mickey's nephews stunt kite flying 1·25 30
2370 $1 Donald Duck mountain biking 2·00 1·10
2371 $2 Donald and Chipmunk parachuting 2·75 2·75
2372 $4 Mickey go-karting 4·00 4·75
2373 $5 Minnie water skiing 4·00 4·75
MS2374 Four sheets, each 128×102 mm. (a) $6 Mickey bungee jumping (vert). (b) $6 Mickey and Minnie river rafting. (c) $6 Donald's nephews playing roller hockey. (d) $6 Mickey hang-gliding Set of 4 sheets 16·00 17·00

1992. 40th Anniv of Queen Elizabeth II's Accession. As T 202a of Gambia. Mult.
2375 10c. Waterfall 65 20
2376 50c. Street in St. George's 75 40
2377 $1 Colonial-style houses, St. George's 1·40 80
2378 $5 St. George's from the sea 4·25 4·50
MS2379 Two sheets, each 75×96 mm. (a) $6 Village on hillside. (b) $6 Yacht at anchor off village Set of 2 sheets 11·00 11·00

1992. "Granada '92" International Stamp Exhibition, Spain. Spanish Paintings. As T 481a of Ghana. Multicoloured.
2380 10c. "The Corpus Christi Procession in Seville" (Manuel Cabral y Aguado) (horiz) 40 20
2381 35c. "The Mancorbo Channel" (Carlos de Haes) 55 20
2382 50c. "Amalia de Llano y Dotres, Countess of Vilches" (Federico de Madrazo y Kuntz) 75 40
2383 75c. "Conchita Serrano y Dominguez, Countess of Santovenia" (Eduardo Rosales Gallina) 1·00 70
2384 $1 "Queen Maria Isabel de Braganza" (Bernardo Lopez Piquer) 1·40 85
2385 $2 "The Presentation of Don John of Austria to Charles V" (detail) (Gallina) 2·25 2·25
2386 $4 "The Presentation of Don John of Austria to Charles V" (different detail) (Gallina) 3·50 4·25
2387 $5 "The Testament of Isabella the Catholic" (Gallina) (horiz) 3·50 4·25
MS2388 Two sheets, each 120×95 mm. (a) $6 "The Horse Corral in the Old Madrid Bullring" (Manuel Castellano) (111×85 mm). (b) $6 "Meeting of Poets in Antonio Mariá Esquivel's Studio" (Antonia Mariá Esquivel y Suárez de Urbina) (111×85 mm). Imperf Set of 2 sheets 8·00 9·00

370 Green-winged Macaw

1992. 500th Anniv of Discovery of America by Columbus (5th issue). World Columbian Stamp "Expo '92", Chicago. Multicoloured.
2389 10c. Type **370** 85 40
2390 25c. "Santa Maria" 90 40
2391 35c. Christopher Columbus 95 40
2392 50c. 15th-century sandglass 95 55
2393 75c. Queen Isabella 1·00 80
2394 $4 Cantino map of 1502 (detail) 5·00 7·00
MS2395 Two sheets, each 80×108 mm. (a) $6 Map of Genoa (detail). (b) $6 Detail of 15th-century map by Thomas Bly Set of 2 sheets 9·00 10·00

370a Ruby-throated Hummingbird

1992. "Genova '92" International Thematic Stamp Exhibition. Hummingbirds. Multicoloured.
2396 10c. Type **370a** 70 25
2397 25c. Vervain hummingbird 90 25
2398 35c. Blue-headed hummingbird 95 25
2399 50c. Cuban emerald 1·25 60
2400 75c. Antillean mango 1·60 75
2401 $2 Purple-throated carib 2·50 2·50
2402 $4 Puerto Rican emerald 3·50 4·25
2403 $5 Green-throated carib 3·50 4·25
MS2404 Two sheets, each 109×80 mm. (a) $6 Young Antillean Crested Hummingbird. (b) $6 Rufous-breasted Hermit Set of 2 sheets 14·00 14·00

371 Gracie Fields

1992. 50th Anniv of United Service Organization (forces' entertainment programme). Multicoloured.
2405 15c. Type **371** 30 20
2406 25c. Jack Benny 30 20
2407 35c. Jinx Falkenburg 30 25
2408 50c. Francis Langford 45 40
2409 75c. Joe E. Brown 80 70
2410 $1 Phil Silvers 1·25 80
2411 $2 Danny Kaye 2·25 2·25
2412 $5 Frank Sinatra 6·50 6·50
MS2413 Two sheets, each 107×80 mm. (a) $6 Bob Hope. (b) $6 Anna May Wong Set of 2 sheets 8·00 9·00

372 Badminton

1992. Olympic Games, Barcelona (2nd issue). Multicoloured.
2414 10c. Type **372** 50 30
2415 25c. Women's long jump 50 20
2416 35c. Women's 100 m 50 30
2417 50c. 1000 m cycling sprint 1·00 50
2418 75c. Decathlon (horiz) 1·00 80
2419 $2 Judo (horiz) 2·00 2·25
2420 $4 Women's gymnastics—asymmetrical bars 3·25 3·75
2421 $5 Men's javelin 3·25 3·75
MS2422 Two sheets, each 100×70 mm. (a) $6 Men's gymnastics – vault. (b) $6 Men's gymnastics – floor exercise Set of 2 sheets 8·00 9·00

372a Columbus meeting Amerindians

1992. 500th Anniv of Discovery of America by Columbus (6th issue). Organization of East Caribbean States. Multicoloured.
2423 $1 Type **372a** 70 70
2424 $2 Ships approaching island 1·40 1·60

372b "The Blue Comet" Locomotive, Boucher (1933)

1992. Toy Trains from American Manufacturers. Multicoloured.
2425 10c. Type **372b** 50 20
2426 35c. No. 2220 switching locomotive, Voltamp (1906) 60 25
2427 40c. No. 221 tunnel locomotive, Knapp (1905) 60 30
2428 75c. "Grand Canyon" locomotive, American Flyer (1931) 90 55
2429 $1 "Streamliner" tin locomotive, Hafner (1930s) 1·25 80
2430 $2 No. 237 switching locomotive, Elektoy (1911) 2·25 2·25
2431 $4 Parlor car, Ives (1928) 3·75 4·25
2432 $5 "Improved President's Special" locomotive, American Flyer (1927) 3·75 4·25
MS2433 Two sheets, each 133×103 mm. (a) $6 No. 1122 locomotive, Ives (1921) (38½×50 mm). (b) $6 No. 3239 locomotive, Ives (1912) (50×38½ mm) Set of 2 sheets 9·00 10·00

1992. Postage Stamp Mega Event, New York. Sheet 100×70 mm, containing multicoloured design as T 207a of Gambia.
MS2434 $6 Guggenheim Museum 3·75 4·50

373 "Matador" (yacht), Newport News Regatta

1992. World Regattas. Multicoloured.
2435 15c. Type **373** 20 20
2436 25c. "Awesome", Antigua 25 25
2437 35c. "Mistress Quickly", Bermuda 30 30
2438 50c. "Emeraude", St. Tropez 50 50
2439 $1 "Diva G", German Admirals Cup 80 80

2440 $2 "Lady Be", French Admirals Cup 1·50 1·75
2441 $4 "Midnight Sun", Admirals Cup 2·75 3·50
2442 $5 "CARAT", Sardinia Cup 2·75 3·50
MS2443 Two sheets, each 113×85 mm. (a) $6 Yachts, Grenada Regatta (horiz). (b) $6 Fastnet Race, 1979 (horiz) Set of 2 sheets 9·00 11·00

1992. Christmas. Religious Paintings. As T 207b of Gambia. Multicoloured.
2444 10c. "Adoration of the Magi" (detail) (Fra Filippo Lippi) 45 15
2445 15c. "Madonna adoring Child in a Wood" (Lippi) 55 20
2446 25c. "Adoration of the Magi" (detail) (Botticelli) 70 20
2447 35c. "The Epiphany—Adoration of the Magi" (detail) (Hieronymus Bosch) 75 20
2448 50c. "Adoration of the Magi" (detail) (Giovanni de Paolo) 1·00 45
2449 75c. "Adoration of the Magi" (Gentile da Fabriano) 1·50 60
2450 90c. "Adoration of the Magi" (detail) (Juan Batista Maino) 1·75 70
2451 $1 "Adoration of the Child" (Master of Liesborn) 1·75 90
2452 $2 "Adoration of the Kings" (Master of Liesborn) 2·75 2·75
2453 $3 "Adoration of the Three Wise Men" (Pedro Berruguete) 3·00 3·50
2454 $4 "Adoration of the Child" (Lippi) 3·75 4·50
2455 $5 "Adoration of the Child" (Correggio) 4·75 4·50
MS2456 Three sheets, each 72×97 mm. (a) $6 "Adoration of the Magi" (detail) (Andrea Mantegna). (b) $6 "Adoration of the Magi" (detail) (Hans Memling). (c) $6 "Adoration of the Shepherds" (La Tour) Set of 3 sheets 16·00 17·00
No. 2447 is inscribed "Hieronymous" in error.

374 Cher

1992. Gold Record Award Winners. Mult.
2457 90c. Type **374** 1·25 1·25
2458 90c. Michael Jackson 1·25 1·25
2459 90c. Elvis Presley 1·25 1·25
2460 90c. Dolly Parton 1·25 1·25
2461 90c. Johnny Mathis 1·25 1·25
2462 90c. Madonna 1·25 1·25
2463 90c. Nat King Cole 1·25 1·25
2464 90c. Janis Joplin 1·25 1·25
MS2465 Two sheets, each 100×70 mm. (a) $3 Chuck Berry; $3 James Brown. (b) $3 Frank Sinatra; $3 Perry Como Set of 2 sheets 12·00 12·00
Nos. 2457/64 were printed together, se-tenant, with a composite background design.

375 Grenada Dove

1992. Anniversaries and Events. Mult.
2466 10c. Type **375** 1·00 65
2467 25c. Airship LZ-1 on maiden flight, 1900 (horiz) 1·00 30
2468 50c. ENDOSAT (robot plane) project (horiz) 1·25 55
2469 75c. Konrad Adenauer (German statesman) and industrial skyline (horiz) 1·25 70
2470 $1.50 Golden lion tamarin (horiz) 2·75 2·00
2471 $2 Mountain gorilla (horiz) 3·50 2·75
2472 $2 Outline of man and heart (horiz) 3·25 2·75
2473 $3 Wolfgang Amadeus Mozart 4·50 4·50
2474 $4 "Voyager 2" and Neptune (horiz) 4·50 4·50
2475 $4 Adenauer with flag and map of West Germany (horiz) 4·50 4·50
2476 $5 Count von Zeppelin and "Graf Zeppelin" (horiz) 4·50 4·75
2477 $6 Admiral Richard Byrd (polar explorer) (horiz) 4·50 4·75
MS2478 Five sheets. (a) 110×80 mm. $6 Count von Zeppelin (horiz). (b) 110×80 mm. $6 Space shuttle recovering "Intelsat 6" satellite. (c) 110×80 mm. $6 Konrad Adenauer (horiz). (d) 95×70 mm. $6 Spotted Little Owl (horiz). (e) 100×70 mm. $6 Papageno costume from "The Magic Flute" Set of 5 sheets 25·00 26·00
ANNIVERSARIES AND EVENTS: No. 2466, National bird; 2467, 2476, **MS**2478a, 75th death anniv of Count Ferdinand von Zeppelin; 2468, 2475, **MS**2478b, International Space Year; 2469, 2475, **MS**2478c, 25th death anniv of Konrad Adenauer; 2470/1, **MS**2478d, Earth Summit '92, Rio; 2472, United Nations World Health Organization Projects; 2473, **MS**2478e, Death bicentenary of Mozart; 2477, 75th anniv of International Association of Lions Clubs.

376 Care Bear on Beach

1992. Ecology.
2479 75c. Type **376** 1·00 60
MS2480 71×101 mm. $2 Care Bear and butterfly (vert) 2·50 2·50

377 Samoyed and St. Basil's Cathedral, Moscow

1993. Dogs of the World. Multicoloured.
2481 10c. Type **377** 70 40
2482 15c. Chow and Ling Yin Monastery, China 85 40
2483 25c. Boxer and Tower of London 90 30
2484 90c. Basenji and Yamma Mosque, Niger 1·60 75
2485 $1 Golden labrador and Parliament Building, Ottawa 1·60 80
2486 $3 St. Bernard and Parsenn, Switzerland 2·75 3·00
2487 $4 Rhodesian ridgeback and Melrose House, South Africa 3·00 3·50
2488 $5 Afghan hound and Mazar-i-Sharif, Afghanistan 3·00 3·50
MS2489 Two sheets, each 100×70 mm. (a) $6 Australian cattle dog. (b) $6 Alaskan malamute Set of 2 sheets 10·00 10·00
No. **MS**2489a is inscribed "Austrailian" in error.

1993. Bicentenary of the Louvre, Paris. Paintings by Jean-Antoine Watteau. As T 209b of Gambia. Multicoloured.
2490 $1 "The Faux-pas" 95 95
2491 $1 "Portrait of a Gentleman" 95 95
2492 $1 "Young Lady with Archlute" 95 95
2493 $1 "Young Man Dancing" 95 95
2494 $1 "Autumn, Pamona and a Cherub" 95 95
2495 $1 "Judgement of Paris" 95 95
2496 $1 "Pierrot" (detail) 95 95
2497 $1 "Pierrot" (different detail) 95 95
MS2498 100×70 mm. $6 "The Embarkation for Cythére" (85×52 mm). 4·75 5·50

378 Baha'i Shrine, Haifa

1993. Centenary of Baha'i Faith.
2499 **378** 75c. multicoloured 1·75 1·00

379 "Citheronia magnifica"

1993. Moths. Multicoloured.
2500 10c. Type **379** 25 25
2501 35c. "Automeris metali" 40 25
2502 45c. "Thysania zenobia" 50 30
2503 75c. "Agrius cingulatus" 70 55
2504 $1 "Composia fidelissima" 80 65
2505 $2 "Synchlora xysteraria" 1·50 1·75
2506 $4 "Eumorpha labruscae" 2·50 2·75
2507 $5 "Ascalapha odorata" 2·50 2·75
MS2508 Two sheets, each 100×70 mm. (a) $6 "Epimecis detexta" (vert). (b) $6 "Xylophanes titana" (vert) Set of 2 sheets 7·50 8·50

380 Heliconia

1993. Flowers. Multicoloured.
2509 10c. Type **380** 30 25
2510 35c. Pansy 50 25
2511 45c. Water lily 60 30
2512 75c. Bougainvillea 80 55
2513 $1 Calla lily 90 65
2514 $2 California poppy 1·75 1·75
2515 $4 Red ginger 2·75 3·25
2516 $5 Anthurium 2·75 3·25
MS2517 Two sheets, each 70×100 mm. (a) $6 Christmas rose (horiz). (b) $6 Moth orchid (horiz) Set of 2 sheets 7·50 8·50

1993. 40th Anniv of Coronation. As T 215a of Gambia.
2518 35c. multicoloured 70 75
2519 70c. multicoloured 80 85
2520 $1 brown and black 85 90
2521 $5 multicoloured 2·25 2·50
MS2522 70×100 mm. $6 multicoloured 6·00 6·50
DESIGNS: 35c. Queen Elizabeth II at Coronation (photograph by Cecil Beaton); 70c. Sceptres; $1 Queen Elizabeth receiving sceptre from Archbishop of Canterbury; $5 Queen and Prince Philip with their children, 1960s. (28½×42½ mm)—$6 "Queen Elizabeth II, 1965" (detail) (Peter Greenham).

381 "Woman with Loaves" (Picasso)

1993. Anniversaries and Events. Each brown, deep brown and black (Nos. 2527, 2535, MS2536d) or multicoloured (others).
2523 25c. Type **381** 40 20
2524 35c. 16th-century telescope 45 20
2525 35c. Public Library building 45 20
2526 35c. Gaetan Boucher (speed skating, 1984) 45 20
2527 50c. Willy Brandt with Senator Edward Kennedy (horiz) 55 30
2528 75c. Carnival float (horiz) 70 40
2529 90c. "Weeping Woman" (Picasso) 85 45
2530 $1 "Marii Prohaska" (Tyrus Czyzewski) 1·00 50
2531 $3 "Marysia et Burek a Geylan" (S. Wirkiewicz) 2·50 2·50
2532 $4 "Woman seated in Airchair" (Picasso) 3·00 3·00
2533 $4 Astronaut on Moon 3·00 3·00
2534 $5 Norbert Schramm (figure skating, 1984) 3·00 3·00
2535 $5 Willy Brandt and Kurt Waldheim (horiz) 3·00 3·00
MS2536 Five sheets. (a) 76×107 mm. $5 Copernicus. (b) 75×105 mm. $6 "Three Women at the Spring" (detail) (Picasso). (c) 76×105 mm. $6 Women's Super G skiing medal winners, 1988 (horiz). (d) 105×75 mm. $6 Newspaper headline, 1974. (e) 105×76 mm. $6 "Parting" (detail) (Witold Wojtkiewicz) Set of 5 sheets 18·00 19·00
ANNIVERSARIES AND EVENTS: Nos. 2523, 2529, 2532, **MS**2536b, 20th death anniv of Picasso (artist); 2524, 2533, **MS**2536a, 450th death anniv of Copernicus (astronomer); 2525, Centenary (1992) of Grenada Public Library; 2526, 2534, **MS**2536c, Winter Olympic Games '94, Lillehammer; 2527, 2535, **MS**2536d, 80th birth anniv (1992) of Willy Brandt (German politician); 2528, Grenada Carnival; 2530/1, **MS**2536e, "Polska '93" International Stamp Exhibition, Poznan.

382 Yellow-green Vireo ("Red-eyed Vireo")

1993. Songbirds. Multicoloured.
2537 15c. Type **382** 60 60
2538 25c. Fork-tailed flycatcher ("Scissor-tailed Flycatcher") 65 65
2539 35c. Palm chat 75 75
2540 35c. Chaffinch 75 75
2541 45c. Yellow wagtail 80 80
2542 45c. Painted bunting 80 80
2543 50c. Short-tailed pygmy tyrant ("Short-tailed Pygmy Flycatcher") 80 80
2544 65c. Orange-breasted bunting ("Rainbow Bunting") 90 90
2545 75c. Red crossbill 90 90
2546 75c. Kauai akialoa 90 90
2547 $1 Yellow-throated longclaw ("Yellow-throated Wagtail") 1·00 1·00
2548 $4 Barn swallow 2·50 2·50
MS2549 Two sheets, each 105×86 mm. (a) $6 Song thrush. (b) $6 White-crested laughing thrush Set of 2 sheets 7·00 8·00
Nos. 2537/48 were printed together, se-tenant, with the backgrounds forming a composite design.

383 Atlantic Grey Cowrie and Atlantic Yellow Cowrie

1993. Seashells. Multicoloured.
2550 15c. Type **383** 55 55
2551 15c. Candy-stick tellin and sunrise tellin 55 55
2552 25c. Caribbean vase 60 60
2553 35c. Lightning venus and royal comb venus 70 70
2554 35c. Crown cone 70 70
2555 45c. Reticulated cowrie-helmet 80 80
2556 50c. Barbados mitre and variegated turret shell 80 80
2557 50c. Common egg cockle and Atlantic strawberry cockle 80 80
2558 75c. Measled cowrie 90 90
2559 75c. Rooster-tail conch 90 90
2560 $1 Lion's-paw scallop and Antillean scallop 1·00 1·00
2561 $4 Dog-head triton 2·25 2·25
MS2562 Two sheets, each 76×106 mm. (a) $6 Dyson's keyhole limpet. (b) $6 Virgin nerite and Emerald nerite Set of 2 sheets 11·00 11·00
Nos. 2550/61 were printed together, se-tenant, with the backgrounds forming a composite design.

1993. Asian International Stamp Exhibitions. As T 219a of Gambia. Mult. (a) "Indopex '93", Surabaya, Indonesia.
2563 35c. Megalithic carving, Sumba Island 35 25
2564 45c. Entrance to Gao Gajah, Bali 45 30
2565 $1.50 Statue of kris holder 1·00 1·00
2566 $1.50 Hanuman protecting Sita 1·00 1·00
2567 $1.50 Sendi of Visu mounted on Garuda 1·00 1·00
2568 $1.50 Wahana (votif figure) 1·00 1·00
2569 $1.50 Hanuman (different) 1·00 1·00
2570 $1.50 Singa (symbolic lion) 1·00 1·00
2571 $2 Loving-mother Bridge, Taroko Gorge National Park 1·40 1·50
2572 $4 Head of Kala over temple gateway, Northern Bali 2·50 2·75
MS2573 104×134 mm. $6 Slow loris 3·75 4·25

(b) "Taipei '93", Taiwan.
2574 35c. Fire-breathing dragon, New Year's Fair, Chongqing 35 25
2575 45c. Stone elephant, Ming Tomb, Nanjing 45 30
2576 $1.50 "Ornamental Cock" (Han Meilin) 1·00 1·00
2577 $1.50 "He's even afraid of Cows" (Meilin) 1·00 1·00
2578 $1.50 "On a Moonlit Night" (Meilin) 1·00 1·00
2579 $1.50 "Eyes that see in the Dark" (Meilin) 1·00 1·00
2580 $1.50 "He's well behaved" (Meilin) 1·00 1·00
2581 $1.50 "He doesn't Bite" (Meilin) 1·00 1·00
2582 $2 Marble peifang, Ming 13 Tombs, Beijing 1·40 1·50
2583 $4 Stone pillar, Nanjing 2·50 3·00

MS2584	104×134 mm. $6 Orang-utan, Mt. Lesuser National Park	3·75	4·25

(c) "Bangkok 1993", Thailand.

2585	35c. Nora Nair, Prasad Phra Thepidon, Wat Phra Kaew	35	25
2586	45c. Stucco deities at Library of Wat Phra Singh	45	30
2587	$1.50 Wooden carved horses	1·00	1·00
2588	$1.50 Wheel of the law	1·00	1·00
2589	$1.50 Lanna bronze elephant	1·00	1·00
2590	$1.50 Kendi in the form of elephant	1·00	1·00
2591	$1.50 Bronze duck	1·00	1·00
2592	$1.50 Horseman	1·00	1·00
2593	$2 Naga snake, Chiang Mai's Temple	1·40	1·50
2594	$4 Stucco figures, Wat Chang Lom	2·50	2·75
MS2595	134×104 mm. $6 Elephant calf (horiz)	3·75	4·25

No. 2590 is incorrectly inscribed "Kendi in the form of an Elphant".

1993. World Cup Football Championship, U.S.A. (1994) (1st issue). As T 221a of Gambia. Mult.

2596	10c. Nikolai Larionov (Russia)	35	30
2597	25c. Andrea Carnevale (Italy)	60	25
2598	35c. Enzo Schifo (Belgium) and Soon-Ho Choi (South Korea)	70	25
2599	45c. Gary Lineker (England)	1·00	30
2600	$1 Diego Maradona (Argentina)	1·50	80
2601	$2 Lothar Mattaeus (Germany)	1·75	2·00
2602	$4 Jan Karas (Poland) and Julio Cesar Silva (Brazil)	2·50	3·25
2603	$5 Claudio Caniggia (Argentina)	2·50	3·25
MS2604	Two sheets, each 75×104 mm. (a) $6 Wlodzimierz (Poland). (b) $6 José Basualdo (Argentina) Set of 2 sheets	7·00	8·00

See also Nos. 2743/9.

384 James K. Spensley

1993. Centenary of Italian Football. Past and present Genoa players. Each blue, red and black.

2605	$3 Type **384**	2·50	2·50
2606	$3 Renzo de Vecchi	2·50	2·50
2607	$3 Giovanni de Pra'	2·50	2·50
2608	$3 Luigi Burlando	2·50	2·50
2609	$3 Felice Levratto	2·50	2·50
2610	$3 Guglielmo Stabile	2·50	2·50
2611	$3 Vittorio Sardelli	2·50	2·50
2612	$3 Juan Carlos Verdeal	2·50	2·50
2613	$3 Fosco Becattini	2·50	2·50
2614	$3 Julio Cesar Abadie	2·50	2·50
2615	$3 Luigi Meroni	2·50	2·50
2616	$3 Roberto Pruzzo	2·50	2·50
MS2617	Two sheets. (a) 100×75 mm. $15 Genoa Football Club badge (29×45 mm). (b) 129×106 mm. $15 Genoa team of 1991–92 (48×35 mm) Set of 2 sheets	22·00	22·00

385 "The Band Concert", 1935

1993. 65th Anniv of Mickey Mouse. Scenes from Walt Disney cartoon films. Multicoloured.

2618	25c. Type **385**	1·00	20
2619	35c. "Mickey's Circus", 1936	1·25	20
2620	50c. "Magician Mickey", 1937	1·50	35
2621	75c. "Moose Hunters", 1937	1·75	60
2622	$1 "Mickey's Amateurs", 1937	2·00	80
2623	$2 "Tugboat Mickey", 1940	2·75	2·50
2624	$4 "Orphan's Benefit", 1941	3·75	4·50
2625	$5 "Mickey's Christmas Carol", 1983	3·75	4·50
MS2626	Two sheets, each 127×102 mm. (a) $6 "Mickey's Birthday Party", 1942. (b) $6 "Mickey's Trailer", 1938 (vert) Set of 2 sheets	11·00	11·00

No. 2624 is inscribed "Oprhan's Benefit" in error.

1993. Christmas. Religious Paintings. As T 221b of Gambia. Black, yellow and red (Nos. 2627/8, 2632 and 2634, MS2635a) or multicoloured (others).

2627	10c. "The Nativity" (Durer)	25	15
2628	25c. "The Annunciation" (Durer)	35	15
2629	35c. "The Litta Madonna" (Da Vinci)	40	20
2630	60c. "The Virgin and Child with St. John the Baptist and St. Anne" (Da Vinci)	50	40
2631	90c. "The Madonna with the Carnation" (Da Vinci)	65	65
2632	$1 "Adoration of the Magi" (Durer)	75	75
2633	$4 "The Benois Madonna" (Da Vinci)	2·50	3·25
2634	$5 "The Virgin Mary in the Sun" (Durer)	2·50	3·25
MS2635	Two sheets, each 102×128 mm. (a) $6 "The Holy Family with Three Hares" (detail) (Dürer). (b) $6 "Adoration of the Magi" (detail) (Da Vinci) Set of 2 sheets	8·00	9·00

Nos. 2629/31, 2633 and **MS**2635b are inscribed "LEONARDO DI VINCI" in error.

386 Blanchard's Balloon over Walnut St. Prison

1993. Aviation Anniversaries. Multicoloured.

2636	35c. Airship "Graf Zeppelin" over Vienna at night	35	20
2637	45c. Type **386**	20	25
2638	50c. Lysander	50	35
2639	75c. "Graf Zeppelin" over Pyramids	75	55
2640	$2 Blanchard waving hat from balloon (vert)	90	95
2641	$3 Hawker Typhoon	2·00	2·50
2642	$5 "Graf Zeppelin" over Rio de Janeiro	3·25	3·75
MS2643	Three sheets, each 106×77 mm. (a) $6 "Graf Zeppelin". (b) Blanchard's balloon (vert). (c) $6 Hawker Hurricane Set of 3 sheets	10·50	11·00

ANNIVERSARIES: Nos. 2636, 2639, 2642, **MS**2643a, 125th birth anniv of Hugo Eckener (airship commander); 2637, 2640, **MS**2643b, Bicentenary of first airmail flight; 2638, 2641, **MS**2643c, 75th anniv of Royal Air Force.

387 Mercedes Benz "370 S" Cabriolet, 1932

1993. Centenaries of Henry Ford's First Petrol Engine (Nos. 2645/6, MS2648b) and Karl Benz's First Four-wheeled Car (others). Multicoloured.

2644	35c. Type **387**	55	20
2645	45c. Ford "Mustang", 1966	65	30
2646	$3 Ford "Model A" Phaeton, 1930	3·25	3·75
2647	$4 Mercedes Benz "300 Sl" Gullwing	3·50	4·00
MS2648	Two sheets, each 76×106 mm. (a) $6 Mercedes Benz "290", 1934. (b) $6 Ford "Model A", 1903 Set of 2 sheets	8·00	9·00

1993. Famous Paintings by Rembrandt and Matisse. As T 221c of Gambia. Multicoloured.

2649	15c. "Self-portrait", 1900 (Matisse)	40	20
2650	35c. "Self-portrait", 1629 (Rembrandt)	45	20
2651	45c. "Self-portrait", 1918 (Matisse)	50	25
2652	50c. "Self-portrait", 1640 (Rembrandt)	60	35
2653	75c. "Self-portrait", 1652 (Rembrandt)	75	55
2654	$2 "Self-portrait", 1906 (Matisse)	1·60	1·75
2655	$4 "Self-portrait", 1900 (different) (Matisse)	2·75	4·00
2656	$5 "Self-portrait", 1625–31 (Rembrandt)	3·00	4·00
MS2657	Two sheets. (a) 100×125 mm. $6 "The Painter in his Studio" (detail) (Matisse). P 13½×14. (b) 125×100 mm. $6 "The Sampling Officials of the Drapers' Guild" (detail) (Rembrandt) (horiz).Set of 2 sheets	7·00	8·00

388 Fishermen with Blue Marlin

1994. 25th Anniv of Spice Island Billfish Tournament. Multicoloured.

2658	15c. Type **388**	50	30
2659	25c. Sailfish with angler	55	30
2660	35c. Yellow-finned tuna with angler	65	30
2661	50c. White marlin with angler	75	60
2662	75c. Catching a sailfish	85	1·00

389 National Flag and Ketch in Bay

1994. 25th Anniv of Independence.

2663	35c. Type **389**	75	40
MS2664	76×106 mm. $6 Map of Grenada	5·50	6·00

1994. "Hong Kong '94" International Stamp Exhibition (1st issue). As T 222a of Gambia. Multicoloured.

2665	40c. Hong Kong 1971 Scouting 50c. stamp and "Hong Kong Post Office, 1846" (left detail) (M. Bruce)	50	65
2666	40c. Grenada 1988 Rotary $2 and "Hong Kong Post Office, 1846" (right detail) (M. Bruce)	50	65

Nos. 2665/6 were printed together, se-tenant, with the centre part of each pair forming the complete painting.

See also Nos. 2667/72.

1994. "Hong Kong '94" International Stamp Exhibition (2nd issue). Qing Dynasty Porcelain. As T 222b of Gambia. Multicoloured.

2667	45c. Vase with dragon decoration	65	65
2668	45c. Hat stand with brown base	65	65
2669	45c. Gourd-shaped vase	65	65
2670	45c. Rotating vase with openwork	65	65
2671	45c. Candlestick with dogs	65	65
2672	45c. Hat stand with orange base	65	65

390 "Hygrocybe acutoconica"

1994. Fungi. Multicoloured.

2673	35c. Type **390**	50	30
2674	45c. "Leucopaxillus gracillimus"	55	30
2675	50c. "Leptonia caeruleocapitata"	55	30
2676	75c. "Leucocoprinus birnbaumii"	70	50
2677	$1 "Marasmius atrorubens"	85	75
2678	$2 "Boletellus cubensis"	1·40	1·50
2679	$4 "Chlorophyllum molybdites"	2·25	2·75
2680	$5 "Psilocybe cubensis"	2·25	2·75
MS2681	Two sheets, each 100×70 mm. (a) $6 "Mycena pura". (b) $6 "Pyrrhoglossum lilaceipes" Set of 2 sheets	9·00	9·00

391 Quetzalcoatlus

1994. Prehistoric Animals. Multicoloured.

2682	75c. Type **391**	70	65
2683	75c. Pteranodon ingens	70	65
2684	75c. Tropeognathus	70	65
2685	75c. Phobetor	70	65
2686	75c. Alamosaurus	70	65
2687	75c. Triceratops	70	65
2688	75c. Tyrannosaurus rex	70	65
2689	75c. Head of Tyrannosaurus rex	70	65
2690	75c. Lambeosaurus	70	65
2691	75c. Spinosaurus	70	65
2692	75c. Parasaurolophus	70	65
2693	75c. Hadrosaurus	70	65
2694	75c. Germanodactylus	70	65
2695	75c. Dimorphodon	70	65
2696	75c. Ramphorynchus	70	65
2697	75c. Apatosaurus	70	65
2698	75c. Pterodactylus	70	65
2699	75c. Stegosaurus	70	65
2700	75c. Brathiosaurus	70	65
2701	75c. Allosaurus	70	65
2702	75c. Plesiosaurus	70	65
2703	75c. Ceratosaurus	70	65
2704	75c. Compsognathus	70	65
2705	75c. Elaphosaurus	70	65
MS2706	Two sheets. (a) 100×70 mm. $6 Pteranodon ingens (different). (b) 70×100 mm. $6 Head of Plateosaurus (vert) Set of 2 sheets	9·00	9·00

Nos. 2682/93 and 2694/2705 respectively were printed together, se-tenant, forming composite designs.

1994. 25th Anniv of First Manned Moon Landing. Space Shuttle "Challenger". As T 227a of Gambia. Multicoloured.

2707	$2 Space shuttle "Challenger"	1·25	1·40
2708	$2 Judith Resnick (astronaut)	1·25	1·40
2709	$2 Aircraft in memorial fly past	1·25	1·40
2710	$2 Dick Scobee (astronaut)	1·25	1·40
2711	$2 Mission logo	1·25	1·40
2712	$2 Michael Smith (astronaut)	1·25	1·40
MS2713	107×76 mm. $6 "Challenger" crew	3·75	4·50

1994. Centenary of International Olympic Committee. Gold Medal Winners. As T 227b of Gambia. Multicoloured.

2714	50c. Heike Drechsler (Germany) (long jump), 1992	50	30
2715	$1.50 Nadia Comaneci (Rumania) (gymnastics), 1976 and 1980	1·60	1·75
MS2716	107×76 mm. $6 Dan Jansen (U.S.A.) (1000 metre speed skating), 1994	3·75	4·25

391a Grenadian Family

1994. International Year of the Family.

2717	**391a** $1 multicoloured	1·00	1·00

1994. 50th Anniv of D-Day. As T 227c of Gambia. Multicoloured.

2718	40c. Sherman amphibious tank leaving landing craft	85	30
2719	$2 Tank on Churchill "Ark" bridging vehicle	2·50	2·00
2720	$3 Churchill "Bobbin" tank laying roadway	2·75	2·50
MS2721	107×76 mm. $6 Churchill AVRE with fascine	3·50	4·00

1994. "Philakorea '94" International Stamp Exhibition, Seoul. As T 227d of Gambia. Multicoloured.

2722	40c. Wonson Park (horiz)	30	25
2723	$1 Pusan (horiz)	55	60
2724	$1 "Lady in a Hooded Cloak" (left detail) (Sin Yunbok)	55	60
2725	$1 "Lady in a Hooded Cloak" (right detail)	55	60
2726	$1 "Kiaseng House" (left detail) (Sin Yunbok)	55	60
2727	$1 "Kiaseng House" (right detail)	55	60
2728	$1 "Amorous Youth on a Picnic" (left detail) (Sin Yunbok)	55	60
2729	$1 "Amorous Youth on a Picnic" (right detail)	55	60
2730	$1 "Chasing a Cat" (left detail) (Sin Yunbok)	55	60
2731	$1 "Chasing a Cat" (right detail)	55	60
2732	$4 Korean orchestra, National Theatre, Seoul (horiz)	2·00	2·50
MS2733	70×102 mm. $6 "Roof Tiling" (detail) (Kim Hongdo)	3·25	3·50

Nos. 2724/31 were printed together, se-tenant, forming composite designs of each painting.

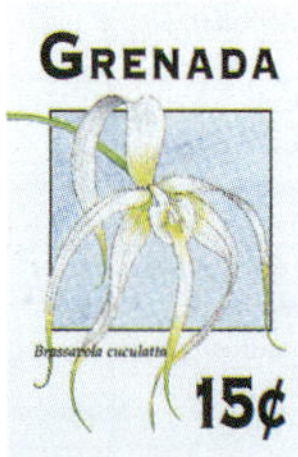

392 "Brassavola cuculatta"

1994. Orchids. Multicoloured.

2734	15c. Type **392**	30	20
2735	25c. "Comparettia falcata"	40	20
2736	45c. "Epidendrum ciliare"	50	30
2737	75c. "Epidendrum cochleatum"	70	50
2738	$1 "Ionopsis utricularioides"	80	70
2739	$2 "Onicidium ceboletta"	1·25	1·40
2740	$4 "Onicidium luridium"	2·25	2·50
2741	$5 "Rodriquezia secunda"	2·25	2·50

MS2742 Two sheets, each 100×70 mm. (a) $6 "Ionopsis utricularioides" (different). (b) $6 "Onicidium luridium" (different) Set of 2 sheets 8·00 8·50

No. **MS**2742b is inscribed "Onicium luridum" in error.

393 Tony Meola (U.S.A.)

1994. World Cup Football Championship, U.S.A. (2nd issue). Multicoloured.

2743	75c. Type **393**	80	80
2744	75c. Steve Mark (Grenada)	80	80
2745	75c. Gianluigi Lentini (Italy)	80	80
2746	75c. Belloumi (Algeria)	80	80
2747	75c. Nunoz (Spain)	80	80
2748	75c. Lothar Matthaus (Germany)	80	80

MS2749 Two sheets. (a) 99×70 mm. $6 World Cup Championship poster, 1930. (b) 70×114 mm. $6 Steve Mark (Grenada) (different) Set of 2 sheets 7·50 8·00

393a Sir Shridath Ramphal

1994. 1st Recipients of Order of the Caribbean Community. Multicoloured.

2750	15c. Type **393a**	10	10
2751	65c. William Demas	40	40
2752	$2 Derek Walcott	1·75	1·75

394 Yellow-tailed Snapper

1994. Fishes. Multicoloured.

2753	15c. Type **394**	40	20
2754	20c. Blue tang	40	20
2755	25c. Porkfish (vert)	40	20
2756	75c. Four-eyed butterflyfish	75	50
2757	$1 Reid's seahorse (vert)	85	70
2758	$2 Spotted moray (vert)	1·50	1·60
2759	$4 Royal gramma ("Fairy basslet")	2·50	2·75
2760	$5 Queen triggerfish (vert)	2·50	2·75

MS2761 Two sheets, each 106×76 mm. (a) $6 Queen angelfish. (b) $6 Long-spined squirrelfish Set of 2 sheets 7·50 8·00

395 Mickey Mouse bathing Pluto

1994. Chinese New Year ("Year of the Dog"). Walt Disney cartoon characters. Multicoloured.

2762	2c. Type **395**	15	10
2763	3c. Dog taking mouthwash	15	10
2764	4c. Dog with curlers in tail	15	10
2765	5c. Brushing dog's eyelashes	15	10
2766	10c. Giving dog manicure	25	10
2767	15c. Mickey spraying Pluto with flea powder	40	15
2768	20c. Dogs on display	40	20
2769	$4 Judge checking Pluto's teeth	4·50	4·75
2770	$5 Pluto wearing "1st Prize" rosette	4·50	4·75

MS2771 Three sheets, each 127×102 mm. (a) $6 King Charles Spaniel rubbing against judge's leg. (b) $6 Pluto holding rosette. (c) $6 Pluto with No. 13 on coat Set of 3 sheets 11·00 12·00

396 "Anartia amathea"

1994. Butterflies. Multicoloured.

2772A	10c. Type **396**	30	20
2773A	15c. "Marpesia petreus"	30	20
2774B	25c. "Hylephila phylaeus"	40	20
2775B	35c. "Junonia evarete"	45	25
2776A	45c. "Pseudolycaena marsyas"	50	30
2777A	50c. "Heliconius charitonius"	50	30
2778A	75c. "Hypolimnas misippus"	70	45
2778cB	90c. "Purgus oilcus"	45	50
2779A	$1 "Cepheuptychia cephus"	75	55
2779cB	$1.50 "Allosmaitia piplea"	80	85
2780A	$2 "Historis odius"	1·75	1·10
2781A	$3 "Phoebis philea"	2·50	2·75
2782A	$4 "Urbanus proteus"	3·25	3·75
2783A	$5 "Battus polydamas"	3·50	4·00
2784A	$10 "Philaethria dido"	6·00	7·50
2785A	$20 "Hamadryas arethusa"	10·00	13·00

1994. Christmas. Religious Paintings by Francisco de Zurbaran. As T 231a of Gambia. Multicoloured.

2786	10c. "The Virgin and Child with St. John" (1658)	20	15
2787	15c. "The Circumcision"	30	20
2788	25c. "Adoration of St. Joseph"	30	20
2789	35c. "Adoration of the Magi"	30	20
2790	75c. "The Portiuncula"	60	45
2791	$1 "The Virgin and Child with St. John" (1662)	75	60
2792	$2 "The Virgin and Child with St. John" (1658/64)	1·25	1·75
2793	$4 "The Flight into Egypt"	2·25	3·25

MS2794 Two sheets. (a) 74×86 mm. $6 "Our Lady of Ransom and Two Mercedarians" (detail). (b) 114×100 mm. $6 "Adoration of the Shepherds" (detail) (horiz) Set of 2 sheets 7·50 8·00

397 Grenada Dove on Nest

1995. Birds. Multicoloured.

2795	25c. Type **397**	1·10	50
2796	35c. Pair of Grenada doves at nest	1·10	50
2797	45c. Cuban tody (vert)	1·25	50
2798	75c. Grenada dove on branch (vert)	1·50	1·50
2799	75c. Painted bunting	1·50	1·50
2800	$1 Grenada dove in flight (vert)	1·60	1·60
2801	$1 Red-legged honeycreeper	1·60	1·60
2802	$5 Green jay	3·50	4·25

MS2803 Two sheets, each 101×71 mm. (a) $6 Chaffinch. (b) $6 Chestnut-sided shrike vireo Set of 2 sheets 7·50 8·00

Nos. 2795/6, 2798 and 2800 also show the W.W.F. Panda emblem.

397a Junior Murray (West Indies)

1995. Centenary of First English Cricket Tour to the West Indies. Multicoloured.

2804	25c. Type **397a**	40	30
2805	35c. Richie Richardson (West Indies)	45	30
2806	$2 Alec Stewart (England) and Wisden Trophy (horiz)	1·60	1·75

MS2807 75×95 mm. $3 West Indian team, 1994 2·25 2·25

398 Hooded Merganser

1995. Water Birds of the World. Multicoloured.

2808	25c. Type **398**	30	30
2809	35c. Green-winged teal	35	30
2810	75c. King eider	70	75
2811	75c. Common shoveler	70	75
2812	75c. Long-tailed duck	70	75
2813	75c. Chiloe wigeon	70	75
2814	75c. Red-breasted merganser	70	75
2815	75c. Falcated teal	70	75
2816	75c. Vericolor teal	70	75
2817	75c. Smew	70	75
2818	75c. Red-crested pochard	70	75
2819	75c. Pintail	70	75
2820	75c. Barrow's goldeneye	70	75
2821	75c. Stellar's eider	70	75
2822	$1 Harlequin duck	75	75
2823	$3 European wigeon	1·75	2·00

MS2824 Two sheets, each 74×104 mm. (a) $5 Common shelduck ("European Wigeon"). (b) $6 Egyptian goose Set of 2 sheets 6·50 7·50

Nos. 2810/21 were printed together, se-tenant, forming a composite design.

No. 2811 is inscribed "Shobeler" in error.

399 Pig Priest, China

1995. Chinese New Year ("Year of the Pig"). Ornaments. Multicoloured.

2825	50c. Type **399**	45	55
2826	75c. Porcelain pig, Scotland	55	65
2827	$1 Seated porcelain pig, Italy	60	75

MS2828 107×77 mm. $2 Jade pig, China 1·25 1·40

400 Yellow-tailed Damselfish

1995. Marine Life. Multicoloured.

2829	$1 Type **400**	75	75
2830	$1 Blue-headed wrasse	75	75
2831	$1 Balloonfish	75	75
2832	$1 Shy hamlet	75	75
2833	$1 Orange tube coral	75	75
2834	$1 Rock beauty	75	75
2835	$1 Creole wrasse	75	75
2836	$1 Queen angelfish	75	75
2837	$1 Trumpetfish	75	75
2838	$1 Barred hamlet	75	75
2839	$1 Tube sponge	75	75
2840	$1 Porcupine fish	75	75
2841	$1 Firecoral	75	75
2842	$1 Royal gramma ("Fairy basslet")	75	75
2843	$1 Sea anemone	75	75

MS2844 Two sheets, each 106×76 mm. (a) $5 Seahorse. (b) $6 Elkhorn coral Set of 2 sheets 4·75 5·00

Nos. 2829/34 and 2835/43 respectively were printed together, se-tenant, forming composite designs.

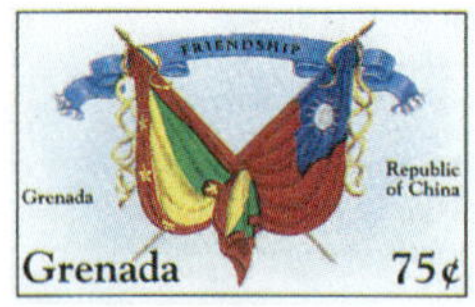

401 National Flags

1995. Grenada–Taiwan (Republic of China) Friendship. Multicoloured.

2845	75c. Type **401**	1·25	75
2846	$1 Prime Minister Brathwaite and President Lee Teng-hui	1·25	80

MS2847 76×106 mm. Nos. 2845/6 2·50 1·75

402 Cocker Spaniel

1995. Domestic Animals. Multicoloured.

2848	10c. Type **402**	50	30
2849	15c. Pinto (horse)	60	30
2850	25c. Rottweiler	70	20
2851	35c. German shepherd	75	20
2852	45c. Persian (cat)	80	25
2853	50c. Snowshoe (cat)	80	30
2854	75c. Percheron (horse)	1·25	60
2855	$1 Scottish fold (cat)	1·25	70
2856	$2 Arabian (horse)	2·00	2·00
2857	$3 Andalusian (horse)	2·25	2·50
2858	$4 C.P. Shorthair (cat)	2·50	3·00
2859	$5 Chihuahua	3·00	3·25

MS2860 Three sheets, each 100×71 mm. (a) $5 Manx (cat). (b) $5 Donkey. (c) $6 Shar Pei Set of 3 sheets 8·00 9·00

1995. Centenary (1992) of Sierra Club (environmental protection society). Endangered Species. As T 224a of Gambia. Multicoloured.

2861	$1 Head of margay at night	80	80
2862	$1 Margay sitting	80	80
2863	$1 Head of margay in daylight	80	80
2864	$1 Head of Andean condor	80	80
2865	$1 Andean condor facing right	80	80
2866	$1 Andean condor facing left	80	80
2867	$1 White-faced saki on branch	80	80
2868	$1 White-faced saki showing mane	80	80
2869	$1 Patagonia landscape	80	80
2870	$1 Lesser rheas feeding (horiz)	80	80
2871	$1 Pair of lesser rheas (horiz)	80	80
2872	$1 Lesser rhea (horiz)	80	80
2873	$1 Sunset over snow-covered mountains, Patagonia (horiz)	80	80
2874	$1 Volcanic eruption, Patagonia (horiz)	80	80
2875	$1 White-faced Saki (horiz)	80	80
2876	$1 Common caracara on branch (horiz)	80	80
2877	$1 Pair of common caracaras at nest (horiz)	80	80
2878	$1 Common caracara facing left (horiz)	80	80

403 Grenadian Scout

1995. 18th World Scout Jamboree, Netherlands. Multicoloured.

2879	75c. Type **403**	45	50
2880	$1 Scout abseiling	55	60
2881	$2 Scout saluting and national flag	85	1·00

MS2882 107×77 mm. $6 Scout in canoe 3·00 3·50

1995. 50th Anniv of End of Second World War in Europe. Fighter Aircraft. As T 237a of Gambia. Multicoloured.

2883	$2 Lavochkin La-7 (fighter)	1·75	1·50
2884	$2 Hawker Hurricane	1·75	1·50

2885	$2 North American P-51D Mustang	1·75	1·50
2886	$2 Messerschmitt Bf 109	1·75	1·50
2887	$2 Bristol Type 152 Beaufighter	1·75	1·50
2888	$2 Messerschmitt Me 262	1·75	1·50
2889	$2 Republic P-47 Thunderbolt	1·75	1·50
2890	$2 Hawker Tempest	1·75	1·50
MS2891	106×76 mm. $6 Nose of Republic P-47 Thunderbolt	3·50	4·00

404 "Swords into Ploughshares"

1995. 50th Anniv of United Nations. Multicoloured.

2892	75c. Type **404**	40	50
2893	$1 Globe and dove	50	60
2894	$2 U.N. Building, New York	85	1·10
MS2895	101×71 mm. $6 Anniversary logo (horiz)	2·50	3·00

405 Woman with Baskets

1995. 50th Anniv of F.A.O. Multicoloured.

2896	75c. Type **405**	40	50
2897	$1 Boy with basket on head	50	60
2898	$2 Men harvesting bananas	85	90
MS2899	72×102 mm. $6 F.A.O. logo	2·50	3·00

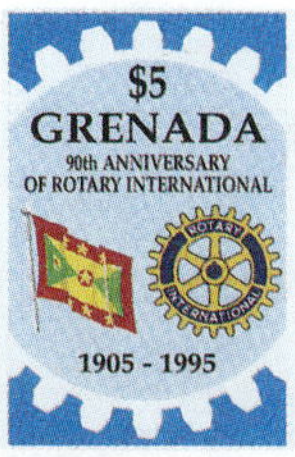

406 National Flag and Rotary Logo

1995. 90th Anniv of Rotary International. Multicoloured.

2900	$5 Type **406**	2·10	2·40
MS2901	76×106 mm. $6 Paul Harris (founder) and logo	2·75	3·25

1995. 95th Birthday of Queen Elizabeth the Queen Mother. As T 239a of Gambia.

2902	$1.50 brown, lt brown & blk	1·75	1·60
2903	$1.50 multicoloured	1·75	1·60
2904	$1.50 multicoloured	1·75	1·60
2905	$1.50 multicoloured	1·75	1·60
MS2906	127×102 mm. $6 multicoloured	6·50	6·50

DESIGNS: No. 2902, Queen Elizabeth the Queen Mother (pastel drawing); 2903, Holding rose; 2904, At desk (oil painting); 2905, In blue hat and white coat; **MS**2906, Wearing floral hat.

1995. 50th Anniv of End of Second World War in the Pacific. As T 239b of Gambia. Multicoloured.

2907	$2 Dogfight over the Marianas	1·75	1·50
2908	$2 U.S. dive-bomber and burning aircraft carrier, Battle of Midway	1·75	1·50
2909	$2 U.S. aircraft attacking Japanese transport, Battle of the Bismarck Sea	1·75	1·50
2910	$2 "Mushashi" (Japanese battleship) on fire in Leyte Gulf	1·75	1·50
2911	$2 U.S. aircraft taking off from Henderson Field	1·75	1·50
2912	$2 Battleships at Guadalcanal	1·75	1·50
MS2913	108×77 mm. $6 U.S. bomber	3·50	4·00

407 Tian Bingyi (China) (badminton)

1995. Olympic Games, Atlanta (1996) (1st issue). Multicoloured.

2914	75c. Type **407**	80	80
2915	75c. Waldemar Leigien (Poland) and Frank Wieneke (West Germany) (judo)	80	80
2916	75c. Nelli Kim (U.S.S.R.) (gymnastics)	80	80
2917	75c. Alessandro Andri (Italy) (shot put)	80	80
2918	$2 Jackie Joyner (U.S.A.) (heptathlon)	1·75	1·75
2919	$2 Mitsuo Tsukahara (Japan) (gymnastics)	1·75	1·75
2920	$2 Flo Hyman (U.S.A.) and Zhang Rung Fang (China) (volleyball)	1·75	1·75
2921	$2 Steffi Graf (West Germany) (tennis)	1·75	1·75
MS2922	Two sheets, each 72×102 mm. (a) $6 Wilma Rudolph (U.S.A.) (athletics). (b) $6 Soling class yacht Set of 2 sheets	7·00	8·00

No. **MS**2922b is inscribed "Sailing" in error.
See also Nos. 3102/24.

408 Junior Murray (West Indies)

1995. Anniversaries and Events. Multicoloured.

2923	25c. Type **408** (centenary of first English cricket tour to the West Indies)	1·50	60
2924	75c. Nutmeg (opening of Grenada Spice Factory)	90	75
2925	$1 Sendall Tunnel (centenary (1994))	1·10	1·25
2926	$1 Caribbean Development Bank building (25th anniv)	1·10	1·25

409 Ajamu

1995. Local Entertainers. Multicoloured.

2927	35c. Type **409**	50	50
2928	35c. Mighty Sparrow	50	50
2929	50c. Mighty Sparrow in evening dress	60	60
2930	75c. Ajamu (different)	75	75

410 Elvis Presley and Signature

1995. Entertainment Legends. Multicoloured.

2931	75c. Type **410**	65	65
2932	75c. Marilyn Monroe	65	65

411 Elvis Presley

1995. 60th Birth Anniv of Elvis Presley (singer). Multicoloured.

2933	$1 Type **411**	70	70
2934	$1 With beard	70	70
2935	$1 With long hair and microphone	70	70
2936	$1 Wearing white shirt	70	70
2937	$1 Wearing pink shirt and purple jacket	70	70
2938	$1 With short hair and microphone	70	70
2939	$1 Wearing magenta shirt	70	70
2940	$1 Wearing orange shirt	70	70
2941	$1 Wearing purple shirt	70	70

412 Film Reel and Oscar Statuette

1995. Centenary of Cinema. Multicoloured.

2942	$1 Type **412**	90	85
2943	$1 "HOLLYWOOD" sign	90	85
2944	$1 Charlie Chaplin	90	85
2945	$1 Shirley Temple	90	85
2946	$1 Spencer Tracy and Katherine Hepburn	90	85
2947	$1 Marilyn Monroe	90	85
2948	$1 John Wayne	90	85
2949	$1 Marlon Brando	90	85
2950	$1 Tom Cruise	90	85
MS2951	107×77 mm. $5 Orson Welles (horiz)	5·50	5·50

Nos. 2942/50 were printed together, se-tenant, forming a composite design.

413 "B1 Level Vista Dome" Electric Locomotive, Japan

1995. Trains of the World (1st series). Multicoloured.

2952	$1 Type **413**	1·00	90
2953	$1 Rolios Rail Class 25NC steam locomotive, South Africa	1·00	90
2954	$1 Class 460 electric locomotive, Switzerland	1·00	90
2955	$1 Central Railway diesel locomotive No. 605, Peru	1·00	90
2956	$1 X2000 tilt body train, Sweden	1·00	90
2957	$1 Via Rail Toronto to Vancouver observation car, Canada	1·00	90
2958	$1 Intercity 125 diesel locomotive, Great Britain	1·00	90
2959	$1 "The Flying Scotsman" steam locomotive, Great Britain	1·00	90
2960	$1 "Indian Pacific" diesel locomotive, Australia	1·00	90
2961	$1 ETR 450 electric train, Italy	1·00	90
2962	$1 Isparta to Bozanonu Line steam locomotive, Turkey	1·00	90
2963	$1 TGV train, France	1·00	90
2964	$1 ICE train, Germany	1·00	90
2965	$1 Nishi Line electric locomotive, Japan	1·00	90
2966	$1 "Hikari" train, Japan	1·00	90
2967	$1 Central Pacific Jupiter steam locomotive, U.S.A.	1·00	90
2968	$1 Amtrak Type 900 electric locomotive, U.S.A.	1·00	90
2969	$1 "Sir Nigel Gresley" steam locomotive, Great Britain	1·00	90
MS2970	Two sheets, each 106×76 mm. (a) $5 Diesel hydraulic train, Korea. (b) $6 Peking–Ulan Bator express, Mongolia Set of 2 sheets	7·00	8·00

See also Nos. 3167/83.

414 Teresa Teng

1995. Teresa Teng (Chinese actress) Commem. Different portraits. Multicoloured unless otherwise indicated.

2971	35c. Type **414**	60	60
2972	35c. As a child (brown, ochre and yellow)	60	60
2973	35c. Wearing feather boa (black, grey and yellow)	60	60
2974	35c. With motor scooter	60	60
2975	35c. Holding microphone	60	60
2976	35c. In white sweater	60	60
2977	35c. Playing flute	60	60
2978	35c. With hand to hair (black, grey and yellow)	60	60
2979	35c. Wearing gold decorated dress	60	60
2980	35c. With fan	60	60
2981	35c. As South-sea islander	60	60
2982	35c. With hands clasped	60	60
2983	35c. In kimono	60	60
2984	35c. Holding bow tie	60	60
2985	35c. Wearing black blouse	60	60
2986	35c. Resting on chair arm	60	60
2987	75c. In army uniform	70	65
2988	75c. In navy uniform	70	65
2989	75c. In air force uniform	70	65
2990	75c. Singing with hand out stretched (black, grey and yellow)	70	65
2991	75c. Singing with flowers in hair	70	65
2992	75c. Singing in blue floral dress	70	65
2993	75c. With pink scarf	70	65
2994	75c. In fringed dress	70	65
2995	75c. In pale green sweater	70	65
2996	75c. With hands to face	70	65

Nos. 2987/96 are larger, 34×46 mm.

415 Mickey Mouse fighting Big Pete

1995. Mickey's Pirate Adventure. Walt Disney cartoon characters. Multicoloured.

2997	15c. Type **415**	40	45
2998	25c. Mickey with treasure chest	45	20
2999	35c. Minnie Mouse trying on plunder	50	20
3000	75c. Goofy with telescope and Mickey swimming with barrel	75	40
3001	$3 Big Pete	2·25	2·25
3002	$5 Mickey with monkey, seagull and handkerchief	2·75	3·25
MS3003	Two sheets, each 108×103 mm. (a) $6 Sea rat pirate. (b) $6 Minnie being thrown overboard by pirates Set of 2 sheets	8·00	8·50

416 Albert Michelson (1907 Physics)

1995. Centenary of Nobel Trust Fund. Multicoloured.

3004	$1 Type **416**	95	85
3005	$1 Ralph Bunche (1950 Peace)	95	85

3006 $1 Edwin Neher (1991 Medicine) 95 85
3007 $1 Klaus Vonklitzing (1985 Physics) 95 85
3008 $1 Johann Deisenhofer (1988 Chemistry) 95 85
3009 $1 Max Delbruck (1969 Medicine) 95 85
3010 $1 J. Georg Bednorz (1987 Physics) 95 85
3011 $1 Feodor Lynen (1964 Medicine) 95 85
3012 $1 Walther Bothe (1954 Physics) 95 85
3013 $1 James Franck (1925 Physics) 95 85
3014 $1 Gustav Hertz (1925 Physics) 95 85
3015 $1 Friedrich Bergius (1931 Chemistry) 95 85
3016 $1 Otto Loewi (1936 Medicine) 95 85
3017 $1 Fritz Lipmann (1953 Medicine) 95 85
3018 $1 Otto Meyerhof (1922 Medicine) 95 85
3019 $1 Paul Heyse (1910 Literature) 95 85
3020 $1 Jane Addams (1931 Peace) 95 85
3021 $1 Carl Braun (1909 Physics) 95 85
3022 $1 Hans Dehmelt (1989 Physics) 95 85
3023 $1 Heinrich Boll (1972 Literature) 95 85
3024 $1 Georges Kohler (1984 Medicine) 95 85
3025 $1 Wolfgang Pauli (1945 Physics) 95 85
3026 $1 Sir Bernard Katz (1970 Medicine) 95 85
3027 $1 Ernest Ruska (1986 Physics) 95 85
3028 $1 William Golding (1983 Literature) 95 85
3029 $1 Hartmut Michel (1988 Chemistry) 95 85
3030 $1 Hans Bethe (1967 Physics) 95 85
MS3031 Three sheets, each 105×76 mm. (a) $6 Theodore Roosevelt (1906 Peace). (b) $6 Woodrow Wilson (1919 Peace). (c) $6 Sir Winston Churchill (1953 Literature) Set of 3 sheets 11·00 12·00

Nos. 3004/12, 3013/21 and 3022/30 respectively were printed together, se-tenant, forming composite designs.
No. 3015 is inscribed "Friedrich" in error.

1995. Christmas. Religious Paintings. As T 245a of Gambia. Multicoloured.
3032 15c. "The Madonna" (Bartolommeo Montagna) 20 10
3033 25c. "Sacred Conversation Piece" (Bonifacio dei Pitati) 20 10
3034 35c. "Nativity" (Van Loo) 25 10
3035 75c. "Madonna of the Fountain" (Van Eyck) 45 40
3036 $2 "The Apparition of the Virgin to St. Philip Neri" (Giovanni Tiepolo) 1·25 1·50
3037 $5 "The Holy Family" (Ribera) 2·50 3·50
MS3038 Two sheets. (a) 127×101 mm. $6 "Madonna and Child" (detail) (Van Dyck). (b) 101×127 mm. $6 "The Vision of St. Anthony" (detail) (Van Dyck) Set of 2 sheets 7·50 8·50

417 Pres. Ronald Reagan at Fort George

1995. 12th Anniv of Liberation of Grenada (1st issue). Multicoloured.
3039 75c. Type **417** 85 85
3040 75c. Pres. Reagan with U.S. and Grenadian flags 85 85
3041 75c. St. George's 85 85
MS3042 Two sheets, each 70×100 mm. (a) $5 Pres. Reagan and beach. (b) $6 Pres. Reagan and waterfall Set of 2 sheets 7·00 7·50

Nos. 3039/41 were printed together, se-tenant, forming a composite design.
See also Nos. 3043/51.

418 Pres. Ronald Reagan

1995. 12th Anniv of Liberation of Grenada (2nd issue). Designs showing Pres. Ronald Reagan. Multicoloured.
3043 $1 With wife 95 85
3044 $1 Type **418** 95 85
3045 $1 With microphones 95 85
3046 $1 Wearing stetson 95 85
3047 $1 In front of U.S. flag 95 85
3048 $1 In front of Brandenburg Gate, Berlin 95 85
3049 $1 Saluting by helicopter 95 85
3050 $1 On horseback 95 85
3051 $1 Addressing troops 95 85

419 Pope John Paul II and Statue of Liberty

1995. Papal Visit to New York. Multicoloured.
3052 $1 Type **419** 95 85
3053 $1 Pope John Paul II and cathedral 95 85
MS3054 105×76 mm. $6 Pope John Paul II 3·50 4·00

420 Rat asleep

1996. Chinese New Year ("Year of the Rat").
3055 **420** 75c. buff, green and brown 70 70
3056 - 75c. orange, red and violet 70 70
3057 - 75c. buff, red and green 70 70
MS3058 95×58 mm. Nos. 3055/7 1·75 2·00
MS3059 76×106 mm. $1 multicoloured 1·00 1·25

DESIGNS—VERT: No. 3056, Rat eating; 3057, Rat asleep (T **420** reversed). HORIZ: No. **MS**3059, Two rats.

421 "Young Woman" (Durer)

1996. Famous Drawings and Paintings by Durer and Rubens. Multicoloured.
3060 15c. Type **421** 40 20
3061 25c. "Four Horsemen of the Apocalypse" (Durer) 45 20
3062 35c. "Assumption and Coronation of the Virgin" (Durer) 50 20
3063 75c. "Mulay Ahmed" (Rubens) 80 50
3064 $1 "Anthony van Dyck aged 15" (Rubens) 90 60
3065 $2 "Head of a Young Monk" (Rubens) 1·75 1·75
3066 $3 "A Scholar inspired by Nature" (Rubens) 2·00 2·25
3067 $5 "Hanns Durer" (Durer) 3·00 3·50
MS3068 Two sheets, each 102×127 mm. (a) $5 "Martyrdom of St. Ursula" (detail) (Rubens). (b) $6 "The Death of the Virgin" (detail) (Durer) Set of 2 sheets 10·00 10·00

422 Goofy Tap-dancing

1996. Famous Dances. Walt Disney cartoon characters Dancing. Multicoloured.
3069 35c. Type **422** 70 20
3070 45c. Donald Duck doing Mexican hat dance (horiz) 80 25
3071 75c. Daisy Duck as hula dancer 1·25 55
3072 90c. Mickey and Minnie Mouse doing the tango (horiz) 1·25 70
3073 $1 Donald and Daisy doing the jitterbug 1·40 85
3074 $2 Mickey and Minnie performing Ukrainian folk dance (horiz) 2·25 2·50
3075 $3 Goofy and Pluto as ballet dancers (horiz) 2·50 2·75
3076 $4 Mickey and Minnie line-dancing 2·50 2·75
MS3077 Two sheets, each 133×109 mm. (a) $5 Minnie doing the can-can (horiz). (b) $6 Scrooge McDuck doing the Scottish sword dance Set of 2 sheets 6·50 7·50

1996. 70th Birthday of Queen Elizabeth II. As T 255a of Gambia showing different photographs. Multicoloured.
3078 35c. As Type **255a** of Gambia 60 25
3079 75c. Wearing white hat 1·00 55
3080 $4 With bouquet 3·00 3·50
MS3081 103×125 mm. $6 Queen and Prince Philip 5·00 5·50

423 Ferrari "125 F1"

1996. Ferrari Racing Cars. Multicoloured.
3082 $1.50 Type **423** 1·50 1·50
3083 $1.50 "Tipo 625" 1·50 1·50
3084 $1.50 "P4" 1·50 1·50
3085 $1.50 "312P" 1·50 1·50
3086 $1.50 "312" Formula 1 1·50 1·50
3087 $1.50 "312B" 1·50 1·50
MS3088 100×71 mm. $6 "F333 SP" (84×28 mm) 4·00 4·00

1996. 50th Anniv of UNICEF. As T 258a of Gambia. Multicoloured.
3089 35c. Child writing in book (horiz) 20 25
3090 $2 Child planting seedling (horiz) 1·00 1·25
3091 $3 Children and UNICEF emblem (horiz) 1·50 2·00
MS3092 75×106 mm. $5 Young boy 2·50 3·00

424 Lions' Gate, Jerusalem

1996. 3000th Anniv of Jerusalem. Multicoloured.
3093 75c. Type **424** 60 45
3094 $2 New Gate 1·40 1·40
3095 $3 Dung Gate 1·75 2·00
MS3096 114×74 mm. $5 The Old City (horiz) 3·25 3·25

1996. Centenary of Radio. Entertainers. As T 259a of Gambia. Multicoloured.
3097 35c. Jack Benny 35 25
3098 75c. Gertrude Berg 55 45
3099 $1 Eddie Cantor 65 60
3100 $2 Groucho Marx 1·25 1·50
MS3101 70×100 mm. $6 George Burns and Gracie Allen (horiz) 3·75 3·75

425 Olympic Stadium, Athens, 1896

1996. Olympic Games, Atlanta (2nd issue). Previous Medal Winners. Multicoloured.
3102 35c. Gold medal of 1896 (vert) 50 25
3103 75c. Type **425** 75 45
3104 $1 Boughera el Quafi (France) (Gold, 1928) 80 80
3105 $1 Gustav Jansson (Sweden) (Bronze, 1952) 80 80
3106 $1 Spiridon Louis (Greece) (Gold, 1896) 80 80
3107 $1 Basil Heatley (Great Britain) (Silver, 1964) 80 80
3108 $1 Emil Zatopek (Czechoslovakia) (Gold, 1952) 80 80
3109 $1 Frank Shorter (U.S.A.) (Gold, 1972) 80 80
3110 $1 Alain Minoun O'Kacha (France) (Gold, 1956) 80 80
3111 $1 Kokichi Tsu Uraya (Japan) (Bronze, 1964) 80 80
3112 $1 Delfo Cabrera (Argentina) (Gold, 1948) 80 80
3113 $1 Harald Sakata (U.S.A.) (Silver—light heavyweight, 1948) 80 80
3114 $1 Tom Kono (U.S.A.) (Gold—middleweight, 1952 and 1956) 80 80
3115 $1 Naim Suleymanoglu (Turkey) (Gold—featherweight, 1988) 80 80
3116 $1 Lee Hyung Kun (South Korea) (Gold—light heavyweight, 1988) 80 80
3117 $1 Vassily Alexeyev (U.S.S.R.) (Gold—super heavyweight, 1972 and 1976) 80 80
3118 $1 Chen Weiqiang (China) (Gold—featherweight, 1984) 80 80
3119 $1 Ye Huanming (China) (Gold—featherweight, 1988) 80 80
3120 $1 Manfred Nerlinger (Germany) (Silver—super heavyweight, 1988) 80 80
3121 $1 Joseph Depietro (U.S.A.) (Gold—bantamweight, 1948) 80 80
3122 $2 Ancient Greek runners 1·75 1·90
3123 $3 Spiridon Louis (Greece) (Gold—marathon, 1896) 2·25 2·50
MS3124 Two sheets, each 75×105 mm. (a) $5 Manfred Nerlinger (Germany) (Silver - super heavyweight weightlifting, 1988) (vert). (b) $6 Thomas Hicks (U.S.A.) (Gold - marathon, 1904) (vert) Set of 2 sheets 7·50 8·50

Nos. 3104/12 (marathon runners) and 3113/21 (weightlifters) respectively were printed together, se-tenant, with the backgrounds forming composite designs.

426 Mercedes-Benz, 1929

1996. Classic Cars. Multicoloured.
3125 35c. Type **426** 35 25
3126 50c. Bugatti Type 35, 1927 45 30
3127 75c. J. Dusenberg, 1935 65 45
3128 $1 Mercer, 1914 70 70
3129 $1 Type 57C Atalante, 1939 70 70
3130 $1 Cannstatt-Daimler, 1900 70 70
3131 $1 Delage, 1925 70 70
3132 $1 Coventry Daimler, 1899 70 70
3133 $1 Vauxhall, 1900 70 70
3134 $1 T-15 Hispano-Suza, 1912 70 70
3135 $2 Alfa Romeo, 1929 1·50 1·60
3136 $3 Rolls Royce, 1910 1·90 2·25
MS3137 Two sheets, each 66×96 mm. (a) $6 L-Head Mercer, 1915 (56×42 mm). (b) $6 Mercedes, 1937 (56×42 mm) Set of 2 sheets 8·00 9·00

427 "Gorch Fock" (cadet barque), Germany, 1916

1996. Ships. Multicoloured.
3138 $1 Type **427** 80 80
3139 $1 "Henry B. Hyde", U.S.A., 1886 80 80

No.	Description		
3140	$1 "Resolution" (galleon), Great Britain, 1652	80	80
3141	$1 U.S.S. "Constitution" (frigate), U.S.A., 1797	80	80
3142	$1 "Nippon Maru" (cadet ship), Japan, 1930	80	80
3143	$1 "Preussen" (full-rigged sailing ship), Germany, 1902	80	80
3144	$1 "Taeping" (clipper), Great Britain, 1852	80	80
3145	$1 "Chariot of Fame" (clipper), U.S.A., 1853	80	80
3146	$1 "Star of India" (clipper), U.S.A., 1861	80	80
3147	$1 H.M.S. "Bounty"	80	80
3148	$1 "Bismark" (German battleship)	80	80
3149	$1 "Chuii Apoo" and two junks	80	80
3150	$1 "Lubeck" (German frigate)	80	80
3151	$1 Dutch galleon	80	80
3152	$1 "Augsburg" (German frigate)	80	80
3153	$1 "Henri Grace a Dieu" (British galleon)	80	80
3154	$1 H.M.S. "Prince of Wales" (battleship)	80	80
3155	$1 "Santa Anna" (Spanish carrack)	80	80
MS3156	Two sheets, each 104×74 mm. (a) $5 H.M.S. "Victory" (ship of the line), Great Britain, 1805. (b) $6 "Cutty Sark" (clipper), Great Britain, 1869 Set of 2 sheets	5·50	6·00

No. 3151 is inscribed "BARBARY CORSAIR" and No. 3153 is stated to be French, both in error.

428 Jacqueline Kennedy

1996. Jacqueline Kennedy Onassis Commemoration. Multicoloured.

No.	Description		
3157	$1 Type **428**	80	80
3158	$1 Wearing mauve blouse	80	80
3159	$1 In evening dress (inscr at right)	80	80
3160	$1 In evening dress (inscr at left)	80	80
3161	$1 Wearing pink dress	80	80
3162	$1 Wearing blue dress with collar embroidered	80	80
3163	$1 Wearing white jacket and brooch	80	80
3164	$1 In yellow jacket and green shirt	80	80
3165	$1 Wearing black jacket	80	80
MS3166	76×106 mm. $6 Jacqueline Kennedy Onassis (different)	3·50	4·25

429 Class C51 Locomotive of Imperial Train, Japan

1996. Trains of the World (2nd series). Multicoloured.

No.	Description		
3167	35c. Type **429**	60	25
3168	75c. "Rheingold" express, Germany	80	45
3169	$1 Atlantic Coast Line locomotive No. 153, 1894, U.S.A.	80	80
3170	$1 Smith Compound No. 1619, Great Britain	80	80
3171	$1 Trans-Siberian Soviet Railways	80	80
3172	$1 Palatinate Railway Krauss locomotive, 1898, Germany	80	80
3173	$1 Paris, Lyons and Mediterranean line, France	80	80
3174	$1 Diesel-electric 0341 locomotive, Italy	80	80
3175	$1 Class C62 locomotive, Japan	80	80
3176	$1 Shantung Railways locomotive, China	80	80
3177	$1 Class C57 locomotive, Japan	80	80
3178	$1 Diesel express train, Japan	80	80
3179	$1 Shanghai–Nanking Railway locomotive, China	80	80
3180	$1 Class D51 locomotive, Japan	80	80
3181	$2 "Pioneer", 1851, U.S.A.	1·60	1·75
3182	$3 "France", France	2·00	2·50
MS3183	Two sheets, each 105×73 mm. (a) $5 Baden State Railways locomotive, Germany. (b) $6 Class C11 locomotive, Japan Set of 2 sheets	8·00	9·00

430 Winter Jasmine

1996. Flowers. Multicoloured.

No.	Description		
3184	$1 Type **430**	80	80
3185	$1 Chrysanthemum	80	80
3186	$1 Lilac	80	80
3187	$1 Japanese iris	80	80
3188	$1 Hibiscus	80	80
3189	$1 Sacred lotus	80	80
3190	$1 Apple blossom	80	80
3191	$1 Gladiolus	80	80
3192	$1 Japanese quince	80	80
3193	$1 Canterbury bell (vert)	80	80
3194	$1 Rose (vert)	80	80
3195	$1 Nasturtium (vert)	80	80
3196	$1 Daffodil (vert)	80	80
3197	$1 Tulip (vert)	80	80
3198	$1 Snapdragon (vert)	80	80
3199	$1 Zinnia (vert)	80	80
3200	$1 Sweetpea (vert)	80	80
3201	$1 Pansy (vert)	80	80
MS3202	Two sheets. (a) 104×74 mm. $5 Aster. (b) 74×104 mm. $6 Peony (vert) Set of 2 sheets	8·00	9·00

Nos. 3184/92 and 3193/3201 respectively were printed together, se-tenant, with the backgrounds forming a composite design.

431 Zeppelin L-31 (Germany)

1996. Airships. Multicoloured.

No.	Description		
3203	30c. Type **431**	50	50
3204	30c. Zeppelin L-35 (Germany)	50	50
3205	50c. Zeppelin L-30 (Germany)	65	50
3206	75c. Zeppelin L-2 10 (Germany)	90	55
3207	$1.50 Zeppelin L-21 (Germany)	1·40	1·60
3208	$1.50 Zodiac Type 13 Spiess (France)	1·40	1·60
3209	$1.50 N1 "Norge" (Roald Amundsen)	1·40	1·60
3210	$1.50 LZ-127 "Graf Zeppelin" (Germany)	1·40	1·60
3211	$1.50 LZ-129 "Hindenburg" (Germany)	1·40	1·60
3212	$1.50 Zeppelin NT (Germany)	1·40	1·60
3213	$3 Zeppelin L-3 (Germany)	2·25	2·50
3214	$3 Beardmore No. 24 (Great Britain)	2·25	2·50
MS3215	Two sheets, each 104×74 mm. (a) $6 Zeppelin ZT (Germany). (b) $6 Zeppelin L-13 (Germany) Set of 2 sheets	9·00	9·00

432 Horned Guan

1996. West Indian Birds. Multicoloured.

No.	Description		
3216	$1.50 Type **432**	1·60	1·60
3217	$1.50 St. Lucia amazon ("St. Lucia Parrot")	1·60	1·60
3218	$1.50 Highland guan ("Black Penelopina")	1·60	1·60
3219	$1.50 Grenada dove	1·60	1·60
3220	$1.50 St. Vincent amazon ("St. Vincent Parrot")	1·60	1·60
3221	$1.50 White-breasted trembler	1·60	1·60
MS3222	Two sheets, each 100×70 mm. (a) $5 Semper's warbler. (b) $6 Yellow warbler ("Barbados Yellow Warbler") Set of 2 sheets	8·75	8·75

The inscriptions on Nos. **MS**3222a and **MS**3222b are transposed in error.

Nos. 3216/21 were printed together, se-tenant, with the backgrounds forming a composite design.

433 Blue Whale

1996. Whales and Turtles. Multicoloured.

No.	Description		
3223	$1.50 Type **433**	1·60	1·60
3224	$1.50 Humpback whale	1·60	1·60
3225	$1.50 Right whale	1·60	1·60
3226	$1.50 Hawksbill turtle	1·60	1·60
3227	$1.50 Leatherback turtle	1·60	1·60
3228	$1.50 Green turtle	1·60	1·60

434 Killer Whale

1996. Marine Life. Multicoloured.

No.	Description		
3229	$1 Type **434**	80	80
3230	$1 Dolphin	80	80
3231	$1 Two dolphins	80	80
3232	$1 Sea lion and regal angelfish	80	80
3233	$1 Dolphins and hawksbill turtle	80	80
3234	$1 Three hawksbill turtles	80	80
3235	$1 Regal angelfish and pennant coralfish	80	80
3236	$1 Pennant coralfish	80	80
3237	$1 Sea lion and squirrelfish	80	80
3238	$1 Brown pelican	80	80
3239	$1 Killer whale (different)	80	80
3240	$1 Whale	80	80
3241	$1 Dolphins and sea lion	80	80
3242	$1 Shortfin pilot whale, blue-ringed octopus and sea lion	80	80
3243	$1 Hammerhead sharks and sea lion	80	80
3244	$1 Blue-striped grunts	80	80
3245	$1 Stingray and Van Gogh fusilier	80	80
3246	$1 Van Gogh fusilier, ribbon moray and percoid fish	80	80
MS3247	Two sheets, each 106×76 mm. (a) $6 Pair of sea lions (horiz). (b) $6 Pair of dolphins (horiz) Set of 2 sheets	8·00	9·00

Nos. 3229/37 and 3238/46 respectively were printed together, se-tenant, with the backgrounds forming a composite design.

1996. Christmas. Religious Paintings. As T 245a of Gambia. Multicoloured.

No.	Description		
3248	25c. "The Visitation" (Tintoretto)	40	20
3249	35c. "Virgin with the Child" (Palma Vecchio)	50	25
3250	50c. "The Adoration of the Magi" (Botticelli)	60	30
3251	75c. "The Annunciation" (Titian)	80	45
3252	$1 "The Flight into Egypt" (Tintoretto)	1·00	65
3253	$3 "The Holy Family with the Infant Saint John" (Andrea del Sarto)	2·25	3·00
MS3254	Two sheets, each 106×76 mm. (a) $6 "Adoration of the Magi" (Paolo Schiavo). (b) $6 "Madonna and Child with Saints" (Vincenzo Ponna) Set of 2 sheets	8·00	8·50

No. 3250 is inscr "Botticeli" in error.

1996. 20th Anniv of Rocky (film). Sheet 143×182 mm, containing vert design as T 266 of Gambia. Multicoloured.

No.	Description		
MS3255	$2×3, Sylvester Stallone in "Rocky V"	4·00	4·50

435 Ox (image scaled to 75% of original size)

1997. Chinese New Year ("Year of the Ox"). Sheet 150×75 mm, containing T 435 and similar triangular designs. Multicoloured. Self-adhesive on silver foil.

No.	Description		
MS3256	$2 Type **435** ("GRENADA" in black); $2 Ox ("GRENADA" in pink); $2 Ox ("GRENADA" in blue)	4·00	4·50

436 Mickey at Tram Stop

1997. "HONG KONG '97" International Stamp Exhibition. Mickey in Hong Kong. Disney cartoon characters. Multicoloured.

No.	Description		
3257	35c. Type **436**	80	90
3258	50c. Mickey and Donald fishing at Victoria Harbour	80	90
3259	75c. Donald and Mickey parachuting	1·00	1·10
3260	90c. Mickey and Minnie visiting Bank of China	1·00	1·10
3261	$1 Mickey with pet parrot	1·25	1·40
3262	$1 Mickey drinking Kung-fu Tea	1·25	1·40
3263	$1 Mickey, Minnie and Goofy shopping at Chinese Wet Market	1·25	1·40
3264	$1 Mickey, Minnie and Goofy with grasshoppers	1·25	1·40
3265	$1 Mickey and Goofy with lanterns	1·25	1·40
3266	$1 Mickey and Minnie practising Tai-chi	1·25	1·40
3267	$2 Goofy delivering bottled gas	1·40	1·60
3268	$3 Mickey, Minnie and Donald at "Jumbo" floating restaurant	1·60	1·75
MS3269	Four sheets, each 132×108 mm. (a) $3 Mickey and skyscrapers (vert). (b) $4 Mickey and Minnie dancing (vert). (c) $5 Mickey pulling rickshaw (vert). (d) $6 Mickey with noodles (vert) Set of 4 sheets	15·00	16·00

1997. 50th Anniv of UNESCO. As T 273a of Gambia. Multicoloured.

No.	Description		
3270	35c. Temple, Kyoto, Japan	50	25
3271	75c. Timbered houses, Quedlinburg, Germany	70	45
3272	90c. View from walls, Dubrovnik, Croatia	80	55
3273	$1 Ruins at Delphi, Greece	80	80
3274	$1 Bryggen Wharf, Bergen, Norway (vert)	80	80
3275	$1 Old city, Berne, Switzerland (vert)	80	80
3276	$1 Warsaw, Poland (vert)	80	80
3277	$1 Fortress walls, Luxembourg (vert)	80	80
3278	$1 Interior of Drottningholm Palace, Sweden (vert)	80	80
3279	$1 Petajavesi Church, Finland (vert)	80	80
3280	$1 Vilnius, Lithuania (vert)	80	80
3281	$1 Jelling Church, Denmark (vert)	80	80
3282	$1 Entrance to caves, Desert of Taklamakan, China (vert)	80	80
3283	$1 House, Desert of Taklamakan, China (vert)	80	80
3284	$1 Monument, Desert of Taklamakan, China (vert)	80	80
3285	$1 Palace of Cielos Purpuras, Wudang, China (vert)	80	80
3286	$1 House, Wudang, China (vert)	80	80
3287	$1 Stone Guardian, The Great Wall, China (vert)	80	80
3288	$1 Ming Dynasty statue, Wudang, China (vert)	80	80
3289	$1 The Great Wall, China (vert)	80	80
3290	$1.50 Segovia Cathedral, Spain	1·10	1·25
3291	$1.50 Wurtzburg, Germany	1·10	1·25
3292	$1.50 Plitvice Lakes, Croatia	1·10	1·25
3293	$1.50 Batalha Monastery, Portugal	1·10	1·25
3294	$1.50 River Seine, Paris, France	1·10	1·25
3295	$2 Tomar, Portugal	1·40	1·60
3296	$3 Palace of Chaillot, Paris, France	1·90	2·25
MS3297	Three sheets, each 127×102 mm. (a) $6 Popocatepetl Monastery, Mexico. (b) $6 Woodland path, Shirakami-Sanchi, Japan. (c) $6 Interior of the Hieronymites' Monastery, Portugal Set of 3 sheets	12·00	14·00

437 Devon Rex

1997. Cats and Dogs. Multicoloured.

3298	35c. Type **437**	50	25
3299	75c. King Charles spaniel	70	45
3300	90c. Japanese bobtail	80	50
3301	$1 Afghan hound	80	80
3302	$1 Turkish van	80	80
3303	$1 Ragdoll	80	80
3304	$1 Siberian	80	80
3305	$1 Egyptian mau	80	80
3306	$1 American shorthair	80	80
3307	$1 Benegal	80	80
3308	$1 Asian longhair	80	80
3309	$1 Somali	80	80
3310	$1 Turkish angora	80	80
3311	$1 Lhasa apso	80	80
3312	$1 Rough collie	80	80
3313	$1 Norwich terrier	80	80
3314	$1 American cocker spaniel	80	80
3315	$1 Chinese crested dog	80	80
3316	$1 Old English sheepdog	80	80
3317	$1 Standard poodle	80	80
3318	$1 German shepherd	80	80
3319	$1 German shorthair pointer	80	80
3320	$2 Cornish rex	1·60	1·75
3321	$3 Pekingese	2·00	2·50
MS3322	Two sheets, each 106×76 mm. (a) $6 Singapura. (b) $6 Bernese mountain dog Set of 2 sheets	8·50	9·00

438 Dunkleosteus

1997. Dinosaurs. Multicoloured.

3323	35c. Type **438**	70	30
3324	75c. Tyrannosaurus rex	1·25	55
3325	$1.50 Sordes	1·40	1·60
3326	$1.50 Dimorphodon	1·40	1·60
3327	$1.50 Diplodocus	1·40	1·60
3328	$1.50 Allosaurus	1·40	1·60
3329	$1.50 Pentaceratops	1·40	1·60
3330	$1.50 Protoceratops	1·40	1·60
3331	$2 Askeptosaurus (vert)	1·40	1·60
3332	$3 Triceratops (vert)	2·00	2·50
MS3333	Two sheets, each 103×74 mm. (a) $6 Tristychius (vert). (b) $6 Maiasaura (vert) Set of 2 sheets	9·00	9·50

Nos. 3325/30 were printed together, se-tenant, with the backgrounds forming a composite design.

439 Porcelain Crab

1997. Marine Life. Multicoloured.

3334	45c. Type **439**	55	30
3335	75c. Humpback whale	1·25	60
3336	90c. Hermit crab	80	50
3337	$1 Great white shark	1·40	1·60
3338	$1.50 Octopus (vert)	1·40	1·60
3339	$1.50 Lei triggerfish (vert)	1·40	1·60
3340	$1.50 Lionfish (vert)	1·40	1·60
3341	$1.50 Harlequin wrasse (vert)	1·40	1·60
3342	$1.50 Clown fish (vert)	1·40	1·60
3343	$1.50 Moray eel (vert)	1·40	1·60
3344	$3 Green sea turtle	2·25	2·50
3345	$4 Whale shark	2·50	2·75
MS3346	Two sheets, each 106×76 mm. (a) $6 Pacific barracudas. (b) $6 Scalloped hammerhead shark Set of 2 sheets	8·50	9·00

Nos. 3338/43 were printed together, se-tenant, with the backgrounds forming a composite design.

1997. 300th Anniv of Mother Goose Nursery Rhymes. Sheet 72×102 mm, containing multicoloured design as T 276a of Gambia.

MS3347	$5 Boy holding umbrella ("Rain") (vert)	3·50	4·00

1997. 10th Anniv of Chernobyl Nuclear Disaster. As T 276a of Gambia. Multicoloured.

3348	$2 As Type **276b** of Gambia	1·40	1·60
3349	$2 As No. 3348, but inscribed "CHABAD'S CHILDREN OF CHERNOBYL" at foot	1·40	1·60

1997. 50th Death Anniv of Paul Harris (founder of Rotary International). As T 276c of Gambia. Multicoloured.

3350	$3 Paul Harris and vocational training programme, Philippines	1·75	2·00
MS3351	78×107 mm. $6 Hands holding globe and doves	3·25	3·75

1997. Golden Wedding of Queen Elizabeth and Prince Philip. As T 276d of Gambia. Multicoloured.

3352	$1 Queen Elizabeth and Prince Philip waving	85	85
3353	$1 Royal coat of arms	85	85
3354	$1 Queen Elizabeth with Prince Philip in naval uniform	85	85
3355	$1 Queen Elizabeth and Prince Philip at Buckingham Palace	85	85
3356	$1 Windsor Castle	85	85
3357	$1 Prince Philip	85	85
MS3358	100×70 mm. $6 Queen Elizabeth with Prince Philip in naval uniform (different)	4·75	5·50

1997. "Pacific '97" International Stamp Exhibition, San Francisco (1st issue). Death Centenary of Heinrich von Stephan (founder of the U.P.U.). As T 276e of Gambia.

3359	$2 green and black	1·25	1·40
3360	$2 brown	1·25	1·40
3361	$2 blue	1·25	1·40
MS3362	82×119 mm. $6 violet and black	3·50	4·25

DESIGNS: No. 3359, Postman on motorcycle; 3360, Von Stephan and Mercury; 3361, Postman on skis, Rocky Mountains, 1900s; **MS**3362, Von Stephan and Chinese letter carrier.

See also Nos. 3392/3409.

1997. Birth Bicentenary of Hiroshige (Japanese painter). As T 541a of Ghana. Multicoloured.

3363	$1.50 "Nihon Embankment, Yoshiwara"	1·25	1·25
3364	$1.50 "Asakusa Ricefields and Torinomachi Festival"	1·25	1·25
3365	$1.50 "Senju Great Bridge"	1·25	1·25
3366	$1.50 "Dawn inside the Yoshiwara"	1·25	1·25
3367	$1.50 "Tile Kilns and Hasiba Ferry, Sumida River"	1·25	1·25
3368	$1.50 "View from Massaki of Suijin Shrine, Uchigawa Inlet and Sekiya"	1·25	1·25
MS3369	Two sheets, each 102×127 mm. (a) $6 "Kinryuzan Temple, Asakusa". (b) $6 "Night view of Saruwaka-machi" Set of 2 sheets	8·50	9·00

1997. 175th Anniv of Brothers Grimm's Third Collection of Fairy Tales. Snow White. As T 277a of Gambia. Multicoloured.

3370	$2 Queen looking in mirror	1·75	1·75
3371	$2 Snow White and the Seven Dwarfs	1·75	1·75
3372	$2 Snow White and Prince	1·75	1·75
MS3373	124×96 mm. $6 Witch with apple	4·00	4·50

440 One-man Luge

1997. Winter Olympic Games, Nagano, Japan. Multicoloured.

3374	45c. Type **440**	50	30
3375	75c. Men's speed skating	75	45
3376	$1 One-man luge (different)	85	85
3377	$1 Ski jumping (blue ski suit)	85	85
3378	$1 Downhill skiing	85	85
3379	$1 Speed skating	85	85
3380	$1 Two-man bobsleigh	85	85
3381	$1 Women's figure skating	85	85
3382	$1 Alpine combined	85	85
3383	$1 Ice hockey	85	85
3384	$1 Ski jumping (yellow ski suit)	85	85
3385	$2 Men's figure skating	1·60	1·75
3386	$3 Slalom	2·00	2·50
MS3387	Two sheets, each 96×69 mm. (a) $6 Four-man bobsleigh. (b) $6 Downhill skiing (vert) Set of 2 sheets	8·50	9·00

441 Bank of China

1997. Return of Hong Kong to China. Multicoloured.

3388	90c. Type **441**	65	50
3389	$1 Skyscrapers	75	55
3390	$1.75 "Hong Kong '97" on modern buildings (63×32 mm)	1·40	1·60
3391	$2 Deng Xiaoping and Hong Kong (63×32 mm)	1·60	1·75

442 Minnie Mouse dancing the Hula

1997. "Pacific '97" International Stamp Exhibition, San Francisco (2nd issue). Centenary of the Cinema. Minnie Mouse in "Hawaiian Holiday". Multicoloured.

3392	50c. Type **442** (Frame 1)	70	70
3393	50c. Frame 2	70	70
3394	50c. Frame 3	70	70
3395	50c. Frame 4	70	70
3396	50c. Frame 5	70	70
3397	50c. Frame 6	70	70
3398	50c. Frame 7	70	70
3399	50c. Frame 8	70	70
3400	50c. Frame 9	70	70
3401	50c. Frame 10	70	70
3402	50c. Frame 11	70	70
3403	50c. Frame 12	70	70
3404	50c. Frame 13	70	70
3405	50c. Frame 14	70	70
3406	50c. Frame 15	70	70
3407	50c. Frame 16	70	70
3408	50c. Frame 17	70	70
MS3409	110×130 mm. $6 Frame 18	7·00	7·50

443 Hercules lifting Rock

1997. "Hercules" (cartoon film) (1st series). Multicoloured.

3410	$1 Type **443**	1·10	1·10
3411	$1 Pegasus	1·10	1·10
3412	$1 Megara	1·10	1·10
3413	$1 Philoktetes	1·10	1·10
3414	$1 Nessus	1·10	1·10
3415	$1 Hydra	1·10	1·10
3416	$1 Pain and Panic	1·10	1·10
3417	$1 Hades	1·10	1·10
MS3418	Two sheets. (a) 131×104 mm. $6 Hercules as a boy. (b) 104×131 mm. $6 The Muses Set of 2 sheets	10·00	11·00

See also Nos. 3561/85.

1997. World Cup Football Championship, France (1998). As T 283a of Gambia. Multicoloured (except Nos. 3422/3 and 3428).

3419	15c. West German and Italian Players, 1982 (vert)	35	20
3420	75c. Italian player holding World Cup, 1982 (vert)	70	45
3421	90c. West German and Italian players wearing "20" shirts, 1982 (vert)	75	50
3422	$1 Uruguay team, 1950 (brown)	75	75
3423	$1 Brazilian team, 1958 (brown)	75	75
3424	$1 West German team, 1974	75	75
3425	$1 Argentine team, 1986	75	75
3426	$1 Italian team, 1982	75	75
3427	$1 West German team, 1990	75	75
3428	$1 Italian team, 1934 (brown)	75	75
3429	$1 Brazilian team, 1970	75	75
3430	$1 Seaman, England	75	75
3431	$1 Klinsmann, Germany	75	75
3432	$1 Berger, Czech Republic	75	75
3433	$1 McCoist, Scotland	75	75
3434	$1 Gascoigne, England	75	75
3435	$1 Djorkaeff, France	75	75
3436	$1 Sammer, Germany	75	75
3437	$1 Futre, Portugal	75	75
3438	$2 Italian player beating goal keeper, 1982 (vert)	1·40	1·60
3439	$3 Goal-mouth melee, 1982 (vert)	1·90	2·25
3440	$4 Two West German players tackling Italian player (vert)	2·50	2·75
MS3441	Two sheets. (a) 102×127 mm. $6 Beckenbaur holding World Cup, Germany (vert). (b) 127×102 mm. $6 Moore, England Set of 2 sheets	9·00	10·00

444 Peacock

1997. Butterflies and Moths. Multicoloured.

3442	45c. Type **444**	50	30
3443	75c. Orange flambeau	75	45
3444	90c. Eastern tailed blue	75	50
3445	$1 Brimstone	75	75
3446	$1 Mocker swallowtail	75	75
3447	$1 American painted lady	75	75
3448	$1 Tiger swallowtail	75	75
3449	$1 Long wing	75	75
3450	$1 Sunset moth	75	75
3451	$1 Australian Blue Mountain swallowtail	75	75
3452	$1 Bird wing	75	75
3453	$2 Black and red	1·40	1·60
3454	$3 Large white	1·90	2·25
3455	$4 Oriental swallowtail	2·50	2·75
MS3456	Two sheets, each 76×106 mm. (a) $5 Monarch. (b) $5 Blue morpho Set of 2 sheets	9·00	10·00

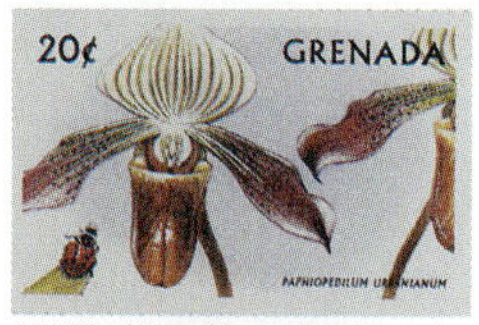

445 "Paphiopedilum urbanianum"

1997. Orchids of the World. Multicoloured.

3457	20c. Type **445**	45	20
3458	35c. "Trichoceros parviflorus"	60	25
3459	45c. "Euanthe sanderiana" (vert)	65	30
3460	75c. "Oncidium macranthum" (vert)	75	45
3461	90c. "Psychopsis kramerianum" (vert)	80	55
3462	$1 "Oncidium hastatum" (vert)	85	60
3463	$2 "Broughtonia sanguinea" (vert)	1·40	1·50
3464	$2 "Anguloa virginalis" (vert)	1·40	1·50
3465	$2 "Dendrobium bigibbum" (vert)	1·40	1·50
3466	$2 "Lucasiana" (vert)	1·40	1·50
3467	$2 "Cymbidium" (vert)	1·40	1·50
3468	$2 "Cymbidium" and vase (vert)	1·40	1·50
3469	$2 "Odontoglossum crispum" (vert)	1·40	1·50
3470	$2 "Cattleya brabantiae" (vert)	1·40	1·50
3471	$2 "Cattleya bicolor" (vert)	1·40	1·50
3472	$2 "Trichopilia suavia" (vert)	1·40	1·50
3473	$2 "Encyclia mariae" (vert)	1·40	1·50
3474	$2 "Angraecum leonis" (vert)	1·40	1·50
3475	$3 "Masdevallia saltatix" (vert)	1·90	2·75
3476	$4 "Cattleya luteola"	2·50	2·75
MS3477	Two sheets. (a) 76×106 mm. $6 "Laelia milleri". (b) 106×76 mm. $6 "Oncidium onustum" Set of 2 sheets	9·00	10·00

Nos. 3463/8 and 3469/74 respectively were printed together, se-tenant, with the backgrounds forming composite designs.

446 "Boletus erythropus"

1997. Fungi of the World. Multicoloured.

3478	35c. Type **446**	60	25
3479	75c. "Armillariella mellea"	70	45
3480	90c. "Amanita flavorubens"	80	50
3481	$1 Indigo milky	85	55
3482	$1.50 "Agaricus solidipes"	1·25	1·40
3483	$1.50 Salmon waxy cap	1·25	1·40
3484	$1.50 Fused maramius	1·25	1·40
3485	$1.50 Shellfish-scented russula	1·25	1·40
3486	$1.50 Red-capped scaber stalk	1·25	1·40
3487	$1.50 "Calocybe gambosum"	1·25	1·40
3488	$1.50 "Boletus parasiticus"	1·25	1·40
3489	$1.50 "Frostis bolete"	1·25	1·40
3490	$1.50 "Amanita myscara flavilolvata"	1·25	1·40
3491	$1.50 "Volvariella volvacea"	1·25	1·40
3492	$1.50 Stuntz's blue legs	1·25	1·40
3493	$1.50 Orange-latex milky	1·25	1·40
3494	$2 "Tylopilus balloui"	1·40	1·90
3495	$4 "Boletus parasiticus"	2·50	2·75

MS3496	Two sheets, each 97×67 mm. (a) $6 "Agaricus argenteus". (b) $6 "Omphalotus illudens" Set of 2 sheets	8·50	9·50

447 Princess Diana with Landmine Victims

1997. Diana, Princess of Wales Commemoration. Multicoloured.

3497	$1.50 Type **447**	1·25	1·25
3498	$1.50 With sick child	1·25	1·25
3499	$1.50 With young boy on crutches	1·25	1·25
3500	$1.50 With leper	1·25	1·25
3501	$1.50 Holding baby	1·25	1·25
3502	$1.50 Walking through minefield	1·25	1·25
MS3503	76×106 mm. $5 With Mother Teresa	3·75	3·75

448 "Angel" (Matthias Grunewald)

1997. Christmas. Religious Paintings. Multicoloured.

3504	35c. Type **448**	45	25
3505	50c. "St. Demetrius" (icon)	60	30
3506	75c. Three-panelled reliquary	75	45
3507	$1 "Angel of the Annunciation" (Jan van Eyck)	85	55
3508	$3 "The Annunciation" (Simone Martini)	2·25	2·50
3509	$4 "St. Michael" (icon)	2·50	3·00
MS3510	Two sheets. (a) 104×114 mm. $6 "The Coronation of the Virgin" (Fra Angelico). (b) 114×104 mm. $6 "The Annunciation" (Titian) (horiz) Set of 2 sheets	9·00	10·00

1998. Chinese New Year ("Year of the Tiger"). Sheet 150×75 mm, containing triangular designs as T 435 showing tigers. Multicoloured. Self-adhesive on silver foil.

MS3511	$1.50, "GRENADA" in pink; $1.50, "GRENADA" in gold; $1.50, "GRENADA" in bronze	3·75	4·00

No. **MS**3511 also exists on gold foil.

449 Black-tailed Damselfish

1998. Fishes. Multicoloured.

3512	65c. Type **449**	55	40
3513	90c. Yellow sweetlips	75	50
3514	$1 Common squirrelfish	80	55
3515	$1.50 Blue tang	1·10	1·25
3516	$1.50 Porkfish	1·10	1·25
3517	$1.50 Banded butterflyfish	1·10	1·25
3518	$1.50 Thread-finned butterflyfish	1·10	1·25
3519	$1.50 Hooded butterflyfish ("Red-headed")	1·10	1·25
3520	$1.50 Emperor angelfish	1·10	1·25
3521	$1.50 Duboulay's angelfish ("Scribbled Anglefish")	1·10	1·25
3522	$1.50 Lemon-peel angelfish	1·10	1·25
3523	$1.50 Bandit angelfish	1·10	1·25
3524	$1.50 Bicoloured angelfish ("Biclor Cherub")	1·10	1·25
3525	$1.50 Palette surgeonfish ("Regal Tang")	1·10	1·25
3526	$1.50 Yellow tang	1·10	1·25
3527	$2 Powder-blue surgeonfish	1·40	1·60
MS3528	Two sheets, each 110×80 mm. (a) $6 Two-banded anemonefish. (b) $6 Forceps butterflyfish ("Long-nosed Butterflyfish")	9·00	10·00

Nos. 3515/20 and 3521/6 respectively were printed together, se-tenant, with the backgrounds forming composite designs.

450 "Sophronitis grandiflora"

1998. Flowers of the World. Multicoloured.

3529	$1.50 Type **450**	1·10	1·10
3530	$1.50 "Phalaenopsis amboinensis"	1·10	1·10
3531	$1.50 "Zygopetalum intermedium"	1·10	1·10
3532	$1.50 "Paphiopedilum purpuratum"	1·10	1·10
3533	$1.50 "Miltonia regnellii"	1·10	1·10
3534	$1.50 "Dendrobium parishii"	1·10	1·10
3535	$1.50 "Arachnis clarkei"	1·10	1·10
3536	$1.50 "Cymbidium eburneum"	1·10	1·10
3537	$1.50 "Dendrobium chrysotoxum"	1·10	1·10
3538	$1.50 "Paphiopedilum insigne"	1·10	1·10
3539	$1.50 "Paphiopedilum venustum"	1·10	1·10
3540	$1.50 "Renanthera imschootiana"	1·10	1·10
MS3541	Two sheets, each 104×72 mm. (a) $6 "Pleione maculata". (b) $6 "Lycaste aromatica" Set of 2 sheets	8·00	9·00

451 Dhow

1998. Famous Ships. Multicoloured.

3542	$1 Type **451**	80	80
3543	$1 Galleon	80	80
3544	$1 Felucca	80	80
3545	$1 Schooner	80	80
3546	$1 Aircraft carrier	80	80
3547	$1 Knau	80	80
3548	$1 Destroyer	80	80
3549	$1 Viking longship	80	80
3550	$1 "Queen Elizabeth 2" (liner)	80	80
3551	$1 Brig	80	80
3552	$1 Clipper	80	80
3553	$1 Caique	80	80
3554	$1 Mississippi riverboat	80	80
3555	$1 Luxury liner	80	80
3556	$1 "Mayflower" (Pilgrim Fathers)	80	80
3557	$1 Frigate	80	80
3558	$1 Janggolan	80	80
3559	$1 Junk	80	80
MS3560	Two sheets, each 100×75 mm. (a) $6 Nuclear submarine (58×43 mm). (b) $6 "Lusitania" (liner) (86×29 mm) Set of 2 sheets	8·00	9·00

Nos. 3542/50 and 3551/9 respectively were printed together, se-tenant, forming composite background designs.

1998. "Hercules" (cartoon film) (2nd series). As T 443 showing Disney cartoon characters. Multicoloured.

3561-3584	Set of 24	18·00	20·00
3561-3568	10c.×8 Hercules and giant statue; Hercules, Pegasus and Philoktetes; Hercules and Philoktetes with shield and arrows; Hercules swinging from blades; Nessus carrying off Megara; Hercules fighting Nessus; Hercules fighting giant lion; Hercules and Pegasus leaving prints on pavement		
3569-3576	$1×8 Baby Hercules with Zeus and Alcmene; Baby Hercules with Hermes; Hades in the Underworld; Baby Hercules and young Pegasus; Baby Hercules with Pain and Panic; Baby Hercules with mortal parents; Hercules towing hay waggon; Hercules receiving gold medallion		
3577-3584	$1×8 Hercules and Megara; Megara and Hades; Hercules training with Philoktetes; Hercules confronting Hades; Giant destroying city; Zeus; Hercules saving Megara by lifting pillar; Hercules diving into sea		
MS3585	Six sheets, each 127×102 mm. (a) $6 Hades. (b) $6 Baby Pegasus. (c) $6 Hercules with sword. (d) $6 Hades on fire. (e) $6 Zeus and Hercules (horiz). (f) $6 Hercules and Megara riding Pegasus (horiz) Set of 6 sheets	27·00	30·00

452 Arctic Skua

1998. Seabirds. Multicoloured.

3586	90c. Type **452**	1·00	60
3587	$1 Fulmar ("Northern Fulmar") (horiz)	1·00	1·00
3588	$1 Black-legged kittiwake (horiz)	1·00	1·00
3589	$1 Pintado petrel ("Cape Petrel") (horiz)	1·00	1·00
3590	$1 Mediterranean gull (horiz)	1·00	1·00
3591	$1 Brandt's cormorant (horiz)	1·00	1·00
3592	$1 Greater shearwater (horiz)	1·00	1·00
3593	$1 Black-footed albatross (horiz)	1·00	1·00
3594	$1 Red-necked phalarope (horiz)	1·00	1·00
3595	$1 Black skimmer (horiz)	1·00	1·00
3596	$1.10 Humboldt penguin	1·10	1·10
3597	$2 Herring gull	1·75	1·75
3598	$3 Red knot	2·25	2·50
MS3599	Two sheets, each 100×70 mm. (a) $5 Black-browed albatross. (b) $5 King penguin Set of 2 sheets	7·50	8·00

Nos. 3587/95 were printed together, se-tenant, with the backgrounds forming a composite design.

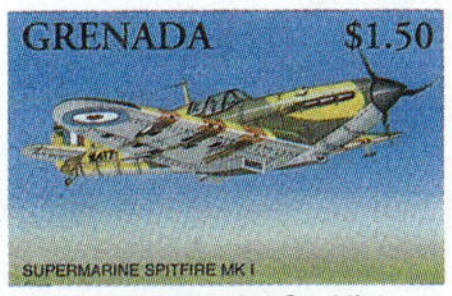

453 Supermarine Spitfire Mk I

1998. History of the Supermarine Spitfire (aircraft). Designs showing different versions. Multicoloured.

3600	$1.50 Type **453**	1·10	1·10
3601	$1.50 Mark VIII	1·10	1·10
3602	$1.50 Mark III	1·10	1·10
3603	$1.50 Mark XVI	1·10	1·10
3604	$1.50 Mark V	1·10	1·10
3605	$1.50 Mark XIX	1·10	1·10
3606	$1.50 Mark IX	1·10	1·10
3607	$1.50 Mark XIV	1·10	1·10
3608	$1.50 Mark XII	1·10	1·10
3609	$1.50 Mark XI	1·10	1·10
3610	$1.50 H.F. Mark VIII	1·10	1·10
3611	$1.50 Mark VB	1·10	1·10
MS3612	Two sheets, each 80×106 mm. (a) $6 Mark IA. (b) $6 Mark IX (different) (both 56×41 mm) Set of 2 sheets	8·50	9·50

454 Walrus

1998. International Year of the Ocean. Multicoloured.

3613	75c. Type **454**	65	65
3614	75c. Jackass penguins ("African Black-footed Penguin")	65	65
3615	75c. Jackass penguin ("African Black-footed Penguin")	65	65
3616	75c. California sealion	65	65
3617	75c. Green turtle	65	65
3618	75c. Redfin anthias	65	65
3619	75c. Sperm whale	65	65
3620	75c. French angelfish and Australian sealion	65	65
3621	75c. Jellyfish	65	65
3622	75c. Sawfish	65	65
3623	75c. Cuckoo wrasse	65	65
3624	75c. Garibaldi	65	65
3625	75c. Spinecheek anemonefish	65	65
3626	75c. Leafy seadragon	65	65
3627	75c. Blue-spotted goatfish	65	65
3628	75c. Two-spot gobies	65	65
MS3629	Two sheets, each 98×68 mm. (a) $5 Atlantic spotted dolphins. (b) $6 Octopus Set of 2 sheets	7·50	8·50

Nos. 3613/28 were printed together, se-tenant, with the backgrounds forming a composite design.

454a Flags of Grenada and CARICOM

1998. 25th Anniv of Caribbean Community.

3630	**454a**	$1 multicoloured	1·00	1·00

454b Stylized Americas

1998. 50th Anniv of Organization of American States.

3631	**454b**	$1 multicoloured	1·00	1·00

1998. 25th Death Anniv of Pablo Picasso (painter). As T 291a of Gambia. Multicoloured.

3632	45c. "The Bathers" (vert)	45	25
3633	$2 "Luncheon on the Grass"	1·50	1·50
3634	$3 "The Swimmer"	2·00	2·25
MS3635	102×127 mm. $5 "Tomato Plant" (vert)	3·50	3·60

1998. Birth Centenary of Enzo Ferrari (car manufacturer). As T 564a of Ghana. Multicoloured.

3636	$2 250 GT Berlinetta Lusso	1·50	1·50
3637	$2 250 GTO	1·00	1·10
3638	$2 250 GT Boano/Ellena cabriolet	1·50	1·50
MS3639	104×70 mm. $5 246 GTS Dino (91×34 mm)	4·00	4·50

454c Scout Saluting

1998. 19th World Scout Jamboree, Chile. Multicoloured.

3640	$2 Type **454c**	1·50	1·25
3641	$3 International scout flag	2·50	2·50
3642	$4 Applying first aid	2·50	2·75
MS3643	106×76 mm. $6 International scout flag	5·00	5·50

454d Mahatma Gandhi

1998. 50th Death Anniv of Mahatma Gandhi.

3644	**454d**	$1 black, grey and mauve	1·25	1·00
MS3645		70×100 mm. $6 multicoloured	6·00	6·00

DESIGN: $6, Gandhi and spinning wheel.

1998. 80th Anniv of Royal Air Force. As T 292a of Gambia. Multicoloured.

3646	$2 Supermarine Spitfire Mk IIa	1·50	1·50
3647	$2 Supermarine Spitfire Mk IXb from above	1·50	1·50
3648	$2 Supermarine Spitfire Mk IXb from side	1·50	1·50
3649	$2 Hawker Hurricane Mk IIC of Battle of Britain Memorial Flight	1·50	1·50
3650	$2 EF-2000 Eurofighter above clouds	1·50	1·50
3651	$2 Nimrod MR2P (maritime reconnaissance)	1·50	1·50
3652	$2 EF-2000 Eurofighter at low level	1·50	1·50
3653	$2 C-47 Dakota (transport)	1·50	1·50

MS3654	Four sheets, each 93×70 mm. (a) $6 Bristol F2B fighter and head of falcon. (b) $6 Bristol F2B fighter and northern goshawk (bird). (c) $6 Jet Provost (trainer) and EF-2000 Eurofighter. (d) $6 VC10 (transport) and EF-2000 Eurofighter Set of 4 sheets	16·00	17·00

455 "Knights in Combat"

1998. Birth Bicentenary of Eugene Delacroix (painter). Multicoloured.

3655	$1 Type **455**	80	80
3656	$1 "Murder of Bishop of Liege"	80	80
3657	$1 "Still Life"	80	80
3658	$1 "Battle of Nancy"	80	80
3659	$1 "Shipwreck of Don Juan"	80	80
3660	$1 "The Death of Ophelia"	80	80
3661	$1 "Attila the Hun"	80	80
3662	$1 "Arab Entertainers"	80	80
MS3663	100×92 mm. $5 "The Capture of Constantinople"	4·00	4·50

1998. 1st Death Anniv of Diana, Princess of Wales. As T 293a of Gambia. Multicoloured.

3664	$1 Diana, Princess of Wales	1·00	1·00

456 Arthur Ashe

1998. Famous Tennis Players. Multicoloured.

3665	45c. Type **456**	50	25
3666	75c. Martina Hingis	60	40
3667	90c. Chris Evert	70	50
3668	$1 Steffi Graf	80	70
3669	$1.50 A. Sanchez Vicario	1·00	1·25
3670	$2 Monica Seles	1·40	1·60
3671	$3 Martina Navratilova	1·75	2·25
MS3672	81×108 mm. $6 Martina Hingis (different)	5·50	6·00

457 Dove of Peace with Stars and Streamers

1998. Grenada's Participation in U.N. Peacekeeping Operations, Beirut, 1982–4.

3673	**457**	$1 multicoloured	1·00	1·00

458 "The Angel's parting from Tobias" (Jean Bilevelt)

1998. Christmas. Religious Paintings. Multicoloured.

3674	35c. Type **458**	30	20
3675	45c. "Allegory of Faith" (Moretto Da Brescia)	40	25
3676	90c. "Crucifixion" (Ugolino Di Tedice)	70	55
3677	$1 "The Triumphal Entry into Jerusalem" (Master of the Thuison Altarpiece)	80	80

459 Antillean Euphonia ("Blue-hooded Euphonia")

1998. Christmas. Birds. Multicoloured.

3678	45c. Type **459**	50	25
3679	75c. Red-billed whistling duck ("Black-bellied Whistling Duck")	70	40
3680	90c. Caribbean martin ("Purple Martin")	75	50
3681	$1 Imperial amazon ("Imperial Parrot")	85	70
3682	$2 Adelaide's warbler	1·50	1·60
3683	$3 Greater flamingo ("Roseate Flamingo")	1·75	2·25
MS3684	Two sheets, each 97×84 mm. (a) $5 Green-throated carib. (b) $6 Purple-throated carib and Canada 1898 Imperial Penny Postage 2c. stamp (37×60 mm) Set of 2 sheets	8·00	8·50

1999. Chinese New Year ("Year of the Rabbit"). Sheet 150×75 mm, containing triangular designs as T 435 showing rabbits. Multicoloured. Self-adhesive on silver foil.

MS3685	$1 "GRENADA" in green; $1 "GRENADA" in orange; $1 "GRENADA" in pink	2·40	2·75

1999. Millennium Series. Famous People of the Twentieth Century. Great Thinkers of the Past and Present. Designs as T 289a of Gambia. Mult.

3686	$1 Martin Luther King Jr (civil rights leader)	1·00	1·00
3687	$1 Socrates (Greek philosopher) (56×41 mm)	1·00	1·00
3688	$1 Sir Thomas More (English scholar) (56×41 mm)	1·00	1·00
3689	$1 Chaim Weizmann (first President of Israel)	1·00	1·00
3690	$1 Alexander Solzhenitsyn (Russian writer)	1·00	1·00
3691	$1 Galileo Galilei (Italian astronomer) (56×41 mm)	1·00	1·00
3692	$1 Michael Servetus (Spanish theologian) (56×41 mm)	1·00	1·00
3693	$1 Salman Rushdie (British novelist)	1·00	1·00
MS3694	106×76 mm. $6 Mother Teresa (founder of Missionaries of Charity)	6·00	6·00

No. 3692 is inscribed "MICHAEL SERVENTUS" in error.

460 Robert H. Goddard (rocket scientist)

1999. Space Exploration. Multicoloured.

3695	$1.50 Type **460**	1·10	1·10
3696	$1.50 Wernher von Braun (rocket scientist)	1·10	1·10
3697	$1.50 Yuri A. Gagarin (first cosmonaut to orbit Earth, 1961)	1·10	1·10
3698	$1.50 "Freedom 7" (first American manned Space flight, 1961)	1·10	1·10
3699	$1.50 Aleksei Leonov (first Russian to walk in Space, 1965)	1·10	1·10
3700	$1.50 Neil Armstrong and Edwin Aldrin (first astronauts on Moon, 1969)	1·10	1·10
3701	$1.50 "Mariner 9" (first space-craft to orbit Mars, 1971)	1·10	1·10
3702	$1.50 "Voyager 1" (Jupiter probe, 1979)	1·10	1·10
3703	$1.50 Bruce McCandless (first astronaut to work in Space unattached, 1984)	1·10	1·10
3704	$1.50 "Giotto" probe (study of Halley's Comet, 1986)	1·10	1·10
3705	$1.50 Space Shuttle "Atlantis" (launch of "Galileo" probe, 1989)	1·10	1·10
3706	$1.50 "Magellan" (Venus probe, 1990)	1·10	1·10
MS3707	Two sheets, each 60×76 mm. (a) $6 John Glenn (first American to orbit Earth, 1962). (b) $6 Neil Armstrong (first astronaut to walk on Moon, 1969) Set of 2 sheets	8·50	9·00

Nos. 3695/3700 and 3701/6 were respectively printed together, se-tenant, with the backgrounds forming composite designs.

461 Goofy as Best Man

1999. 70th Birthday of Mickey Mouse. Mickey's Dream Wedding. Walt Disney cartoon characters. Multicoloured.

3708	$1 Type **461**	80	80
3709	$1 Mickey as groom	80	80
3710	$1 Minnie as bride	80	80
3711	$1 Daisy Duck as bridesmaid	80	80
3712	$1 Donald Duck	80	80
3713	$1 Pluto in love	80	80
3714	$1 Huey, Duey and Louie	80	80
3715	$1 Lady (Pekingese)	80	80
MS3716	Two sheets. (a) 102×127 mm. $6 Mickey's nephew eating cake. (b) 127×102 mm. $6 Mickey and Minnie in carriage (horiz) Set of 2 sheets	10·00	11·00

Nos. 3708/15 were printed together, se-tenant, with the backgrounds forming a composite design.

462 Grand Trunk Western, U.S.A.

1999. Trains of the World. Multicoloured.

3717	25c. Type **462**	50	25
3718	35c. Louisville & Nashville, U.S.A.	55	25
3719	45c. Gulf, Mobile and Ohio, U.S.A.	60	25
3720	75c. Missouri Pacific, U.S.A.	80	35
3721	90c. "RTG" National Railway, France	80	45
3722	$1 Florida East Coast, U.S.A.	90	45
3723	$1.50 Rio Grande, U.S.A.	1·10	1·10
3724	$1.50 Erie Lackawanna, U.S.A.	1·10	1·10
3725	$1.50 New York Central, U.S.A.	1·10	1·10
3726	$1.50 Pennsylvania, U.S.A.	1·10	1·10
3727	$1.50 Milwaukee Road, U.S.A.	1·10	1·10
3728	$1.50 Illinois Central, U.S.A.	1·10	1·10
3729	$1.50 Burlington Route, U.S.A.	1·10	1·10
3730	$1.50 "Texas Special", Missouri, Kansas and Texas, U.S.A.	1·10	1·10
3731	$1.50 City of Los Angeles, U.S.A.	1·10	1·10
3732	$1.50 Northwestern, U.S.A.	1·10	1·10
3733	$1.50 Canadian National	1·10	1·10
3734	$1.50 Rock Island, U.S.A.	1·10	1·10
3735	$1.50 TGV, French National Railways	1·10	1·10
3736	$1.50 HST, British Railways	1·10	1·10
3737	$1.50 TEE, Trans Europe Express	1·10	1·10
3738	$1.50 Ancona Express, Italy	1·10	1·10
3739	$1.50 XPT, Australia	1·10	1·10
3740	$1.50 APT-P, British Railways	1·10	1·10
3741	$1.50 Western Pacific, U.S.A.	1·10	1·10
3742	$1.50 Union Pacific, U.S.A.	1·10	1·10
3743	$1.50 Chesapeake and Ohio, U.S.A.	1·10	1·10
3744	$1.50 Southern Pacific, U.S.A.	1·10	1·10
3745	$1.50 Baltimore and Ohio, U.S.A.	1·10	1·10
3746	$1.50 Wabash, U.S.A.	1·10	1·10
3747	$3 Kansas City Southern, U.S.A.	1·75	2·00
3748	$4 New Haven, U.S.A.	2·00	2·25
MS3749	Four sheets, each 98×68 mm. (a) $6 Eld 4, Netherlands. (b) $6 "Hikari" express train, Japan. (c) $6 Santa Fe, U.S.A. (d) $6 Inter City express, Germany Set of 4 sheets	16·00	7·00

Nos. 3723/8, 3729/34, 3735/40 and 3741/6 respectively were printed together, se-tenant, with the backgrounds forming composite designs.

463 "Papilio blumei" (butterfly)

1999. "Australia '99" World Stamp Exhibition, Melbourne. Wildlife. Multicoloured.

3750	75c. Type **463**	70	70
3751	75c. Great egret ("Egret")	70	70
3752	75c. Kumarahou (flower)	70	70
3753	75c. Javan rhinoceros	70	70
3754	75c. Grey-backed white-eye ("Silver-eye") (bird)	70	70
3755	75c. Kiore (rodent)	70	70
3756	75c. "Cyclorana novaehollandiae" (frog)	70	70
3757	75c. Caterpillar	70	70
3758	75c. Pacific black duck ("Grey Duck")	70	70
3759	75c. Honey blue-eye (fish)	70	70
3760	75c. Krefft's turtle	70	70
3761	75c. Archer fish	70	70
3762	75c. Binturong (vert)	70	70
3763	75c. Two Indian elephants (vert)	70	70
3764	75c. Indian elephant (vert)	70	70
3765	75c. Chestnut-capped laughing thrush ("Garkulax mitratus") (vert)	70	70
3766	75c. "Vanda hookeriana" (orchid) (vert)	70	70
3767	75c. Grey heron ("Heron") (vert)	70	70
3768	75c. Fur seal (vert)	70	70
3769	75c. Black-faced cormorant ("Shag") (bird) (vert)	70	70
3770	75c. Round batfish (vert)	70	70
3771	75c. Loggerhead turtle (vert)	70	70
3772	75c. Three harlequin sweetlips (vert)	70	70
3773	75c. Two harlequin sweetlips (vert)	70	70
3774	$1 Orang-utan	80	80
3775	$2 Douroucouli (monkey)	1·50	1·50
3776	$3 Black caiman (alligator)	1·75	1·90
3777	$4 Panther ("Black Leopard") (vert)	2·00	2·25
MS3778	Two sheets. (a) 110×85 mm. $6 Impala. (b) 85×110 mm. $6 Ring-tailed lemur Set of 2 sheets	9·00	9·00

Nos. 3750/61 and 3762/73 respectively were printed together, se-tenant, with the backgrounds forming composite designs.

Nos. 3753 and 3775 were inscribed "JAUAN RHINOCEROS" and "DOUROCOULI" in error.

1999. "iBRA '99" International Stamp Exhibition, Nuremberg. Horiz designs as T 298a of Gambia. Multicoloured.

3779	75c. Railway locomotive, 1893, and Prussia 1860 ½sgr. stamp	75	45
3780	90c. "Humboldt" (sailing ship) and Mecklenburg-Schwerin 1856 4×½s.	1·00	55
3781	$1 Railway locomotive, 1893, and Saxony 1850 3pf.	1·10	75
3782	$2 "Humboldt" (sailing ship) and Mecklenburg-Strelitz 1864 ½sgr.	1·75	2·00
MS3783	121×104 mm. $6 Saxony 1850 3pf. with Leipzig postmark	5·50	6·00

1999. 150th Death Anniv of Katsushika Hokusai (Japanese artist). As T 298b of Gambia. Multicoloured.

3784	$1.50 "The Actor Ichikawa Danjuro Danjuro as Tomoe Gozen"	1·10	1·10
3785	$1.50 "Washing Clothes" (drawing)	1·10	1·10
3786	$1.50 "The Prostitute of Eguchi"	1·10	1·10
3787	$1.50 "Sudden Shower from a Fine Sky"	1·10	1·10
3788	$1.50 "Hanging Clothes out to dry" (drawing)	1·10	1·10
3789	$1.50 "Shimada"	1·10	1·10
3790	$1.50 "Head of Old Man"	1·10	1·10
3791	$1.50 "Piebald Horse" (drawing)	1·10	1·10
3792	$1.50 "Girl making Cord for binding Hats"	1·10	1·10
3793	$1.50 "Li Po admiring Waterfall of Lo-shan"	1·10	1·10
3794	$1.50 "Bay Horse" (drawing)	1·10	1·10
3795	$1.50 "Potted Dwarf Pine with Basin"	1·10	1·10
MS3796	Two sheets, each 72×102 mm. (a) $6 "The Guardian God Fudo Myoo and his Attendants". (b) $6 "Women on the Beach at Enoshima" Set of 2 sheets	8·00	9·00

No. 3788 is inscribed "DRAWINFS" in error.

1999. 10th Anniv of United Nations Rights of the Child Convention. As T 298c of Gambia. Multicoloured.

3797	$3 Eskimo girl and Russian boy	1·75	2·00
3798	$3 American girl	1·75	2·00
3799	$3 African boy and Indian girl	1·75	2·00
MS3800	110×85 mm. $6 Young boy	4·50	5·00

Nos. 3797/9 were printed together, se-tenant, forming a composite design.

1999. "PhilexFrance '99" International Stamp Exhibition, Paris. Railway Locomotives. Two sheets containing horiz designs as T 299d of Gambia. Multicoloured.

MS3801	(a) 106×76 mm. $6 Paris, Lyons and Mediterranean Railway Compound Pacific. (b) 106×81 mm. $6 French heavy freight locomotive Set of 2 sheets	8·50	9·00

1999. 250th Birth Anniv of Johann von Goethe (German poet and dramatist). Multicoloured designs as T 298d of Gambia.

3802	$3 mauve, purple and black	1·75	1·90

3803	$3 blue, lilac and black	1·75	1·90
3804	$3 violet, deep violet and black	1·75	1·90
MS3805	76×106 mm. $6 orange, brown and black	5·50	6·00

DESIGNS—HORIZ: No. 3802, Faust contemplating Moon; 3803, Goethe and Friedrich von Schiller (dramatist); 3804, Faust talking with Wagner. VERT: No. **MS**3805, Margaret (from "Faust").

1999. 30th Anniv of First Manned Landing on Moon. Horiz designs as T 298e of Gambia. Multicoloured.

3806	$1.50 The Moon	1·10	1·10
3807	$1.50 Edward White on first space walk	1·10	1·10
3808	$1.50 Edwin "Buzz" Aldrin	1·10	1·10
3809	$1.50 The Earth	1·10	1·10
3810	$1.50 Michael Collins	1·10	1·10
3811	$1.50 Neil Armstrong	1·10	1·10
3812	$1.50 Footprint on the Moon	1·10	1·10
3813	$1.50 V2 rocket	1·10	1·10
3814	$1.50 Command module "Columbia"	1·10	1·10
3815	$1.50 Lunar Rover	1·10	1·10
3816	$1.50 Lunar module "Eagle"	1·10	1·10
3817	$1.50 Command module re-entering Earth's atmosphere	1·10	1·10
MS3818	Two sheets. (a) 110×85 mm. $6 Neil Armstrong with American flag. (b) 85×111 mm. $6 Launch of "Apollo 11" (vert) Set of 2 sheets	9·00	9·00

464 Astronaut with Letter

1999. 125th Anniv of Universal Postal Union. Space Mail. Multicoloured.

3819	$2 Type **464**	1·60	1·10
3820	$2 Supply spaceship "Progress"	1·60	1·60
3821	$2 Postmark of space station "MIR"	1·60	1·60
3822	$2 Buran shuttle and "MIR"	1·60	1·60
MS3823	104×75 mm. $6 Space station "MIR"	6·00	6·50

465 "Carry On Doctor"

1999. 50th Anniv of the Variety Club of Great Britain. Scenes from "Carry On" Films. Multicoloured.

3824	$1 "Carry On Dick"	90	90
3825	$1 Type **465**	90	90
3826	$1 "Carry On England"	90	90
3827	$1 "Carry On Matron"	90	90
3828	$1 "Carry On Round The Bend"	90	90
3829	$1 "Carry On Up The Jungle"	90	90
3830	$1 "Carry On Loving"	90	90
3831	$1 "Carry On Up The Khyber"	90	90
MS3832	110×86 mm. $6 Actors from "Carry On" films	5·50	6·00

1999. Royal Wedding. As T 298 of Gambia. Multicoloured.

3833	$3 Prince Edward	2·40	2·50
3834	$3 Sophie and Prince Edward	2·40	2·50
3835	$3 Sophie Rhys-Jones	2·40	2·50
MS3836	78×108 mm. $6 Prince Edward and Sophie Rhys-Jones	6·00	6·50

466 "U.S.S. Enterprise NCC-1701" (from original series)

1999. Spacecraft of "Star Trek". Multicoloured.

3837	$1.50 Type **466**	1·10	1·10
3838	$1.50 Klingon battle cruiser (blue and orange planets in background) (Voyager series)	1·10	1·10
3839	$1.50 "U.S.S. Enterprise" 1701 (green planet in background) (Next Generation series)	1·10	1·10
3840	$1.50 Warbird "Voyager" (below blue planet)	1·10	1·10
3841	$1.50 U.S.S. "Romulan" (in front of orange planet) (original series)	1·10	1·10
3842	$1.50 "U.S.S. Enterprise" 1701 (pink planet in background) (original series)	1·10	1·10
3843	$1.50 "Borg Cube" (Next Generation series)	1·10	1·10
3844	$1.50 "U.S.S. Enterprise NCC" 1701 (in front of multicoloured flames)	1·10	1·10
3845	$1.50 Klingon "Bird of Prey" (original series)	1·10	1·10

1999. "Queen Elizabeth the Queen Mother's Century". As T 304a of Gambia.

3846	$2 black and gold	1·75	1·75
3847	$2 multicoloured	1·75	1·75
3848	$2 black and gold	1·75	1·75
3849	$2 multicoloured	1·75	1·75
MS3850	154×157 mm. $6 multicoloured	5·50	6·50

DESIGNS: No. 3846, Queen Mother with Prince Charles, 1948; 3847, Queen Mother in pink outfit, 1970; 3848, Queen Mother in Australia, 1958; 3849, Queen Mother waving. (37×50 mm)—**MS**3850, Queen Mother in Coronation robes, 1953.

No. **MS**3850 also shows the Royal Arms embossed in gold, and inscr "Good Health and Happiness to Her Majesty The Queen Mother on her 101st Birthday".

467 George Gershwin

1999. American Entertainers. Multicoloured.

3851	$1 Type **467**	80	80
3852	$1 Florence Mills	80	80
3853	$1 Sam Beckett	80	80
3854	$1 Bessie Smith	80	80
3855	$1 Billie Holiday	80	80
3856	$1 Bert Williams	80	80
3857	$1 Cole Porter	80	80
3858	$1 Sofie Tucker	80	80
3859	$1 Lon Chaney	80	80
3860	$1 Buster Keaton	80	80
3861	$1 Norma Shearer	80	80
3862	$1 James Cagney	80	80
3863	$1 Hedda Hopper	80	80
3864	$1 Jean Harlow	80	80
3865	$1 Marlene Dietrich	80	80
3866	$1 Ramon Novarro	80	80
MS3867	Two sheets, each 76×86 mm. (a) $6 Clark Gable. (b) $6 Louis Armstrong Set of 2 sheets	8·50	9·00

Nos. 3885/8 and 3859/66 respectively were printed together, se-tenant, with the backgrounds forming composite designs.

468 Ouranosaurus

1999. Prehistoric Animals. Multicoloured.

3868	35c. Type **468**	50	30
3869	45c. Struthiomimus (vert)	55	30
3870	75c. Parasaurolophus (vert)	75	50
3871	$1 Archaeopteryx	90	90
3872	$1 Brachiosaurus	90	90
3873	$1 Dilophosaurus	90	90
3874	$1 Dimetrodon	90	90
3875	$1 Psittacosaurus	90	90
3876	$1 Acrocanthosaurus	90	90
3877	$1 Stenonychosaurus	90	90
3878	$1 Dryosaurus	90	90
3879	$1 Campsognathus	90	90
3880	$1 Agathaumus	90	90
3881	$1 Camarosaurus	90	90
3882	$1 Quetzalcoatlus	90	90
3883	$1 Alioramus	90	90
3884	$1 Camptosaurus	90	90
3885	$1 Albertosaurus	90	90
3886	$1 Anatosaurus	90	90
3887	$1 Spinosaurus	90	90
3888	$1 Centrosaurus	90	90
3889	$2 Triceratops	1·60	1·60
3890	$3 Stegoceras	2·00	2·25
3891	$4 Stegosaurus	2·25	2·50
MS3892	Two sheets, each 85×110 mm. (a) $6 Velociraptor (vert). (b) $6 Tyrannosaurus (vert) Set of 2 sheets	8·50	9·00

Nos. 3871/9 and 3880/8 were printed together, se-tenant, with the backgrounds forming a composite design.
No. 3871 is inscribed "ARCHEOPTERYX" in error.

469 Christmas Rose

1999. Christmas. Multicoloured.

3893	20c. Type **469**	30	15
3894	75c. Tulip	60	40
3895	90c. Pear	70	50
3896	$1 Hibiscus	80	60
3897	$4 Lily	2·75	3·50
MS3898	106×91 mm. $6 "The Nativity" (Botticelli) (horiz)	5·50	6·00

1999. Faces of the Millennium: Diana, Princess of Wales. Vert designs as T 307 of Gambia showing collage of miniature flower photographs. Multicoloured.

3899	$1 Top of head (face value at left)	90	90
3900	$1 Top of head (face value at right)	90	90
3901	$1 Ear (face value at left)	90	90
3902	$1 Eye and temple (face value at right)	90	90
3903	$1 Cheek (face value at left)	90	90
3904	$1 Cheek (face value at right)	90	90
3905	$1 Blue background (face value at left)	90	90
3906	$1 Chin (face value at right)	90	90

Nos. 3899/906 were printed together, se-tenant, and when viewed as a whole, form a portrait of Diana, Princess of Wales.

470 Green Dragon

2000. Chinese New Year ("Year of the Dragon"). Multicoloured.

3907	$2 Type **470**	1·40	1·50
3908	$2 Dragon ("GRENADA" in red)	1·40	1·50
3909	$2 Dragon ("GRENADA" in violet)	1·40	1·50

471 Roseate Spoonbill

2000. Birds of Grenada. Multicoloured.

3910	75c. Type **471**	70	45
3911	90c. Scarlet ibis	80	55
3912	$1 Adelaide's warbler	90	90
3913	$1 Hispaniolan trogon	90	90
3914	$1 Sun conure ("Sun Parakeet")	90	90
3915	$1 Black-necked stilt	90	90
3916	$1 Sora crake ("Sora")	90	90
3917	$1 Fulvous whistling duck ("Fulvous Tree Duck")	90	90
3918	$1 Blue-headed parrot	90	90
3919	$1 Tropical mockingbird	90	90
3920	$1 Antillean euphonia ("Blue-hooded Euphonia")	90	90
3921	$1 Troupial	90	90
3922	$1 Brown-throated conure ("Caribbean Parakeet")	90	90
3923	$1 Forest thrush	90	90
3924	$1 Lesser Antillean tanager ("Hooded Tanager")	90	90
3925	$1 Stripe-headed tanager	90	90
3926	$1 Ringed kingfisher	90	90
3927	$1 Zenaida dove	90	90
3928	$1.50 Sparkling violetear	1·25	1·40
3929	$2 Northern jacana	1·60	1·75
MS3930	Two sheets, each 70×97 mm. (a) $6 Cedar waxwing (37×50 mm). (b) $6 Antillean siskin (50×37 mm) Set of 2 sheets	11·00	12·00

Nos. 3912/19 and 3920/7 were each printed together, se-tenant, with the backgrounds forming composite designs.
No. 3912 is inscribed "Ade; aode's Warbler" and No. 3919 "Tropical Mockinbird", both in error.

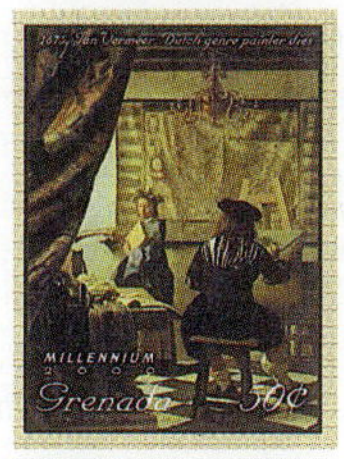

471a Jan Vermeer (Dutch painter) (died 1675)

2000. New Millennium. People and Events of Seventeenth Century (1650–1700). Multicoloured.

3931	50c. Type **471a**	45	45
3932	50c. Antoni van Leeuwenhoek (discovered micro-organisms, 1674)	45	45
3933	50c. Salem Witch Trials, Massachusetts, 1692	45	45
3934	50c. Sir Isaac Newton and reflecting telescope, 1668	45	45
3935	50c. Voltaire (French writer and historian) (born 1694)	45	45
3936	50c. Ivan V and Peter I (joint rulers of Russia, 1682)	45	45
3937	50c. Shun Zhi, first Chinese Emperor of Qing Dynasty (died 1662)	45	45
3938	50c. Christian Huggens and Saturn, 1655	45	45
3939	50c. Microscopic mite (Robert Hooke's experiments in cytology, 1665)	45	45
3940	50c. "Verdant Peaks" (Wang Shih-rnin), 1672	45	45
3941	50c. Rene Descartes (French philosopher) (died 1650)	45	45
3942	50c. Completion of Canal du Midi, 1681	45	45
3943	50c. William of Orange and Bill of Rights, 1688	45	45
3944	50c. William III on horseback (end of King William's War), 1697)	45	45
3945	50c. Cassini (French astronomer) and images of Mars, 1666	45	45
3946	50c. Sir Isaac Newton and apples (law of gravity, 1666) (59×39 mm)	45	45
3947	50c. Jupiter's Moons (Olaus Roemer) (Danish astronomer) (discovered finite speed of light, 1676)	45	45

No. 3936 is dated "1694" in error.

2000. 400th Birth Anniv of Sir Anthony Van Dyck (Flemish painter). As T 312a of Gambia. Mult.

3948	$1 "King Charles I on Horseback"	80	80
3949	$1 "St. Martin dividing his Cloak"	80	80
3950	$1 "Gio. Paolo Babli on Horseback"	80	80
3951	$1 "Marchese Anton Giulio Brignole-Sale on Horseback"	80	80
3952	$1 "Study of a Horse"	80	80
3953	$1 "Oriental on Horseback"	80	80
3954	$1 "Young Woman resting Head on Hand"	80	80
3955	$1 "Self-portrait", 1613–14	80	80
3956	$1 "Woman looking Upwards"	80	80
3957	$1 "Head of an Old Man", c. 1621	80	80
3958	$1 "Head of a Boy"	80	80
3959	$1 "Head of an Old Man", 1616–18	80	80
3960	$1.50 "Portrait of a Man"	1·10	1·10
3961	$1.50 "Portrait of a Man aged Seventy"	1·10	1·10
3962	$1.50 "Portrait of a Woman"	1·10	1·10
3963	$1.50 "Elderly Man"	1·10	1·10
3964	$1.50 "Portrait of a Young Man"	1·10	1·10
3965	$1.50 "Man with a Glove"	1·10	1·10
3966	$1.50 "St. John the Baptist"	1·10	1·10
3967	$1.50 "St. Anthony of Padua and the Ass of Rimini"	1·10	1·10
3968	$1.50 "The Stoning of St. Stephen"	1·10	1·10
3969	$1.50 "The Martyrdom of St. Sebastian"	1·10	1·10
3970	$1.50 "St. Sebastian bound for Martyrdom"	1·10	1·10
3971	$1.50 "St. Jerome"	1·10	1·10
3972	$1.50 "Portrait of Anthony Van Dyck", 1614–15	1·10	1·10
3973	$1.50 "Self-portrait" (after Rubens)	1·10	1·10
3974	$1.50 "Isabella Brant"	1·10	1·10
3975	$1.50 "The Penitent Apostle Peter"	1·10	1·10
3976	$1.50 "Head of a Robber" (used by Rubens in his "Coup de Lance")	1·10	1·10
3977	$1.50 "Heads of the Apostles" (detail from Ruben's "Feast at the House of Simon the Pharisee")	1·10	1·10

MS3978 Six sheets. (a) 103×127 mm. $5 "Prince Thomas-Francis of Savoy on Horseback". (b) 102×127 mm. $5 "Emperor Theodossius refused Entry in Milan Cathedral" (horiz). (c) 102×127 mm. $5 "King Charles I on Horseback". (d) 127×102 mm, $6 "St. Jerome in the Wilderness". (e) 102×127 mm. $6 "St. Martin" (horiz). (f) 127×102 mm. $6 Detail of "Portrait of a Man and His Wife" (horiz) Set of 6 sheets 22·00 24·00

No. **MS**3978b is inscribed "Emperor Theoddosius" in error.

472 *Clitcybe geotropa*

2000. Fungi. Multicoloured.

No.	Description	Unused	Used
3979	35c. Type **472**	50	20
3980	45c. *Psalliota augusta*	55	25
3981	$1 *Amanita rubescens*	90	55
3982	$1.50 *Pholiota spectabilis*	1·10	1·25
3983	$1.50 *Mycena polygramma*	1·10	1·25
3984	$1.50 *Collybia iocephala*	1·10	1·25
3985	$1.50 *Corinus comatus*	1·10	1·25
3986	$1.50 *Amanita muscaria sp.*	1·10	1·25
3987	$1.50 *Boletus aereus*	1·10	1·25
3988	$1.50 *Ungulina marginata*	1·10	1·25
3989	$1.50 *Pleurotus ostreatus*	1·10	1·25
3990	$1.50 *Flammula penetrans*	1·10	1·25
3991	$1.50 *Morchella crassipes*	1·10	1·25
3992	$1.50 *Lepiota procera*	1·10	1·25
3993	$1.50 *Tricholoma aurantium*	1·10	1·25
3994	$4 *Boletus satanas*	3·00	3·25
MS3995	Two sheets. (a) 82×112 mm. $6 *Daedala quercina*. (b) 112×82 mm. $6 *Lepiota acutesquamosa* Set of 2 sheets	10·00	11·00

Nos. 3982/7 and 3988/93 were each printed together, se-tenant, with the backgrounds forming composite designs.

No. 3986 is inscribed "Aminita muscaria" in error.

2000. 18th Birthday of Prince William. As T 312b of Gambia. Multicoloured.

No.	Description	Unused	Used
3996	$1.50 Prince William wearing blue and white tie	1·25	1·25
3997	$1.50 With Prince of Wales	1·25	1·25
3998	$1.50 Prince William waving	1·25	1·25
3999	$1.50 In skiing gear	1·25	1·25
MS4000	100×80 mm. $6 Prince William (37×50 mm)	5·00	5·50

2000. "EXPO 2000" World Stamp Exhibition, Anaheim, U.S.A. Spacecraft. As T 582a of Ghana. Multicoloured.

No.	Description	Unused	Used
4001	$1.50 "Lunik 4"	1·10	1·10
4002	$1.50 "Clemintine"	1·10	1·10
4003	$1.50 "Luna 12"	1·10	1·10
4004	$1.50 "Luna 16"	1·10	1·10
4005	$1.50 Lunar Module *Eagle* from "Apollo 11"	1·10	1·10
4006	$1.50 "Ranger 7"	1·10	1·10
MS4007	117×84 mm. $6 "Apollo 13"	6·00	6·00

Nos. 4001/6 were printed together, se-tenant, with the backgrounds forming a composite design.

2000. 25th Anniv of "Apollo–Soyuz" Joint Project. As T 582b of Ghana. Multicoloured.

No.	Description	Unused	Used
4008	$3 Russian "A-2" rocket	2·00	2·25
4009	$3 "Soyuz 19"	2·00	2·25
4010	$3 "Apollo 18" command module docked with "Soyuz 19"	2·00	2·25
MS4011	88×70 mm. $6 Valeri Kubasov ("Soyuz" engineer) and Thomas Stafford ("Apollo" commander) (horiz)	4·75	5·00

2000. 50th Anniv of Berlin Film Festival. As T 582c of Ghana. Multicoloured.

No.	Description	Unused	Used
4012	$1.50 *Alphaville*, 1965	1·10	1·10
4013	$1.50 Rod Steiger, 1964	1·10	1·10
4014	$1.50 *Os Fuzis*, 1964	1·10	1·10
4015	$1.50 Jean-Pierre Leaud, 1966	1·10	1·10
4016	$1.50 *Cul-de-sac*, 1966	1·10	1·10
4017	$1.50 *Ikiru*, 1961	1·10	1·10
MS4018	97×103 mm. $6 *His Yen*, 1993	4·75	5·00

No. 4012 is inscribed "ALPHAVILE" and No. 4016 "CULDELSAC", both in error.

2000. 175th Anniv of Stockton and Darlington Line (first public railway). As T 582d of Ghana. Multicoloured.

No.	Description	Unused	Used
4019	$3 As Type **582d** of Ghana	2·50	2·50
4020	$3 Robert Stephenson's John Bull locomotive, 1831	2·50	2·50

2000. 250th Death Anniv of Johann Sebastian Bach (German composer). Sheet 77×89 mm, containing vert portrait (24×40 mm) as T 312c of Gambia.

No.	Description	Unused	Used
MS4021	$6 multicoloured	5·50	6·00

2000. Election of Albert Einstein (mathematical physicist) as Time Magazine "Man of the Century". Sheet 117×91 mm, containing vert portrait as T 312d of Gambia.

No.	Description	Unused	Used
MS4022	$6 multicoloured	5·00	5·50

2000. Centenary of First Zeppelin Flight. As T 582e of Ghana, each incorporating a different portrait of Count Ferdinand von Zeppelin. Multicoloured.

No.	Description	Unused	Used
4023	$3 LZ-130 *Graf Zeppelin II*	2·00	2·25
4024	$3 LZ-2, 1906	2·00	2·25
4025	$3 LZ-127 *Graf Zeppelin*, 1928	2·00	2·25
MS4026	119×76 mm. $6 LZ-129 *Hindenburg*, 1936 (50×37 mm)	5·00	5·50

2000. Olympic Games, Sydney. As T 582f of Ghana. Multicoloured.

No.	Description	Unused	Used
4027	$2 Archibald Hahn (athletics), St. Louis (1904)	1·50	1·60
4028	$2 Showjumping	1·50	1·60
4029	$2 Sports Palace, Rome (1960) and Italian flag	1·50	1·60
4030	$2 Ancient Greek chariot racing	1·50	1·60

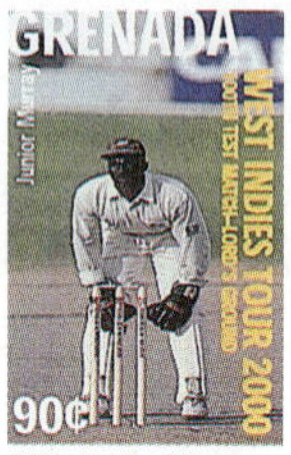

472a Junior Murray

2000. West Indies Cricket Tour and 100th Test Match at Lord's. Multicoloured.

No.	Description	Unused	Used
4031	90c. Type **472a**	1·00	55
4032	$5 Rawl Lewis	4·00	4·25
MS4033	120×105 mm. $6 Lord's Cricket Ground (horiz)	5·50	5·50

473 *Brassolaelio cattleya*

2000. Orchids. Multicoloured.

No.	Description	Unused	Used
4034	75c. Type **473**	75	45
4035	90c. *Maxilbera*	85	50
4036	$1 *Isochilius*	90	55
4037	$1.50 *Lycaste*	1·25	1·25
4038	$1.50 *Cochleanthes*	1·25	1·25
4039	$1.50 *Brassocattleya*	1·25	1·25
4040	$1.50 *Brassolaelio cattleya*	1·25	1·25
4041	$1.50 *Iwanagaara*	1·25	1·25
4042	$1.50 *Sophrocattleya*	1·25	1·25
4043	$1.50 *Laeliocattleya*	1·25	1·25
4044	$1.50 *Saphrocattleya*	1·25	1·25
4045	$1.50 *Epidendrum*	1·25	1·25
4046	$1.50 *Cattleya*	1·25	1·25
4047	$1.50 *Ionopsis*	1·25	1·25
4048	$1.50 *Brassoepidendrum*	1·25	1·25
4049	$2 *Oncidium*	1·25	1·25
MS4050	Two sheets, each 73×103 mm. (a) $6 *Brassocattleya*. (b) $6 *Vanilla* Set of 2 sheets	11·00	12·00

474 Sir Donald Bradman playing a Stroke

2000. Famous Cricketers. Six sheets, each 290×165 mm, containing T 474 and similar vert designs. Multicoloured.

MS4051 (a) $1×8, Type **474** and similar shots in sequence. (b) $1×8, Sequence of Shane Warne bowling. (c) $2×4, Sir Garfield Sobers bowling (two different) or batting (two different). (d) $2×4, Different shots of Sir Jack Hobbs batting. (e) $2×4, Different shots of Sir Viv Richards batting. (f) $2×5, Bradman, Sobers, Hobbs, Warne and Richards Set of 6 sheets 35·00 35·00

475 Maine Coon

2000. Cats and Dogs. Multicoloured.

No.	Description	Unused	Used
4052	75c. Type **475**	75	45
4053	90c. Selkirk rex cat	85	50
4054	$1.50 Spotted tabby British shorthair (horiz)	1·25	1·25
4055	$1.50 Burmilla (horiz)	1·25	1·25
4056	$1.50 British blue shorthair (horiz)	1·25	1·25
4057	$1.50 Siamese (horiz)	1·25	1·25
4058	$1.50 Japanese bobtail (horiz)	1·25	1·25
4059	$1.50 Oriental shorthair (horiz)	1·25	1·25
4060	$1.50 Labrador retriever (horiz)	1·25	1·25
4061	$1.50 Standard poodle (horiz)	1·25	1·25
4062	$1.50 Boxer (horiz)	1·25	1·25
4063	$1.50 Rough-coated jack russell terrier (horiz)	1·25	1·25
4064	$1.50 Tibetan terrier (horiz)	1·25	1·25
4065	$1.50 Welsh corgi (horiz)	1·25	1·25
4066	$2 Shetland sheepdog	1·60	1·75
4067	$3 Central Asian sheepdog	2·00	2·25
MS4068	Two sheets, each 106×76 mm. (a) $6 Scottish fold cat. (b) $6 Irish red and white setter (horiz) Set of 2 sheets	11·00	12·00

Nos. 4054/9 (cats) and 4060/5 (dogs) were each printed together, se-tenant, with the backgrounds forming composite designs.

476 *Marpesia eleuchea bahamaensis*

2000. Butterflies. Multicoloured.

No.	Description	Unused	Used
4069	45c. Type **476**	55	25
4070	75c. *Pterourus palamedes*	75	45
4071	90c. *Dryas julia framptonii*	85	55
4072	$1 *Hypna clytemnestra iphegenia*	90	60
4073	$1.50 *Danaus plexippus*	1·25	1·25
4074	$1.50 *Anartia amathea*	1·25	1·25
4075	$1.50 *Colobura dirce*	1·25	1·25
4076	$1.50 *Parides gundiachianus*	1·25	1·25
4077	$1.50 *Spiroeta stelenes*	1·25	1·25
4078	$1.50 *Hammadryas feronia*	1·25	1·25
4079	$1.50 *Merchantis isthmia*	1·25	1·25
4080	$1.50 *Colias eurytheme*	1·25	1·25
4081	$1.50 *Papilio troilus*	1·25	1·25
4082	$1.50 *Junonia coenia*	1·25	1·25
4083	$1.50 *Doxocopa laure*	1·25	1·25
4084	$1.50 *Pierella hyalinus*	1·25	1·25
MS4085	Two sheets, each 95×68 mm. (a) $6 *Danaus gilippus*. (b) $6 *Agraulis vanilae insularis* Set of 2 sheets	11·00	12·00

Nos. 4073/8 and 4079/84 were each printed together, se-tenant, with the backgrounds forming composite designs.

477 Grenada National Cricket Stadium

2000. New National Cricket Stadium. Multicoloured.

No.	Description	Unused	Used
4086	$2 Type **477**	1·60	1·60
MS4087	102×79 mm. $1 West Indies and New Zealand Test teams; $1 Cricket match in progress	1·60	1·75

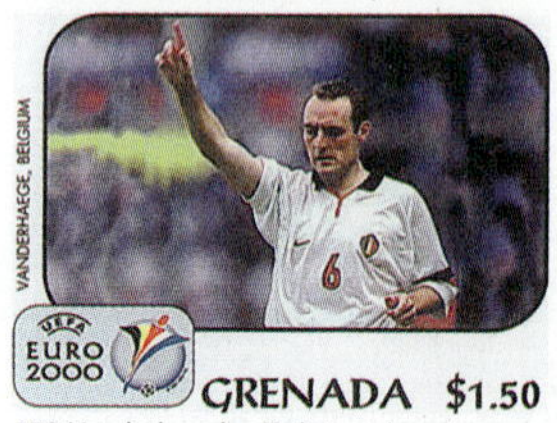

478 Vanderhaeghe (Belgian player)

2000. "Euro 2000" Football Championship. Multicoloured.

No.	Description	Unused	Used
4088	$1.50 Type **478**	1·10	1·10
4089	$1.50 Belgian team	1·10	1·10
4090	$1.50 Ronny Gaspercic (Belgian player)	1·10	1·10
4091	$1.50 Lorenzo Staelens (Belgian player)	1·10	1·10
4092	$1.50 Koning Boudewijn Stadium	1·10	1·10
4093	$1.50 Strupar and Mpenza (Belgian player and coach)	1·10	1·10
4094	$1.50 Sergi Barjuan (Spanish player)	1·10	1·10
4095	$1.50 Spanish team	1·10	1·10
4096	$1.50 Luis Enrique (Spanish player)	1·10	1·10
4097	$1.50 Hierro (Spanish player)	1·10	1·10
4098	$1.50 De Kuip Stadium, Rotterdam	1·10	1·10
4099	$1.50 Raul Gonzales (Spanish player)	1·10	1·10
4100	$1.50 Dejan Savicevic (Yugoslav player)	1·10	1·10
4101	$1.50 Yugoslav team	1·10	1·10
4102	$1.50 Predrag Migatovic (Yugoslav player)	1·10	1·10
4103	$1.50 Savo Milosevic (Yugoslav player)	1·10	1·10
4104	$1.50 Jan Breydel Stadium, Bruges	1·10	1·10
4105	$1.50 Darko Kovacevic (Yugoslav player)	1·10	1·10
MS4106	Three sheets, each 145×95 mm. (a) $6 Robert Waseige (Belgian trainer) (vert). (b) $6 José Antonio Camacho (Spanish trainer) (vert). (c) $6 Vujadin Boskov (Yugoslav trainer) (vert) Set of 3 sheets	13·00	14·00

479 Porkfish

2000. Tropical Fish. Multicoloured.

No.	Description	Unused	Used
4107	45c. Type **479**	45	25
4108	75c. Short bigeye	70	40
4109	90c. Red snapper	80	50
4110	$1 Creole wrasse	80	80
4111	$1 Hawksbill turtle	80	80
4112	$1 Foureye butterflyfish	80	80
4113	$1 Porcupinefish	80	80
4114	$1 Yellowtail damselfish	80	80
4115	$1 Adult French angelfish	80	80
4116	$1 Yellow goatfish	80	80
4117	$1 Blue-striped grunt	80	80
4118	$1 Spanish grunt	80	80
4119	$1 Queen triggerfish	80	80
4120	$1 Juvenile French angelfish	80	80
4121	$1 Beaugregory	80	80
4122	$1 Queen angelfish	80	80
4123	$1 Sergeant major	80	80
4124	$1 Bank butterflyfish	80	80
4125	$1 Spanish hogfish	80	80
4126	$1 Porkfish (different)	80	80
4127	$1 Banded butterflyfish	80	80
4128	$1 Longsnout seahorse	80	80
4129	$2 Indigo hamlet	1·60	1·75
4130	$3 Blue tang	2·00	2·25
MS4131	Two sheets, each 102×73 mm. (a) $6 Blue tang (different). (b) $6 Queen angelfish (different) Set of 2 sheets	10·00	11·00

Nos. 4111/19 and 4120/8 were each printed together, se-tenant, with the backgrounds forming composite designs.

No. 4126 is inscribed "Poskfish" in error.

2000. Monarchs of the Millenium. As T 314a of Gambia.

No.	Description	Unused	Used
4132	$1.50 multicoloured	1·25	1·25
4133	$1.50 multicoloured	1·25	1·25
4134	$1.50 lilac, stone and brown	1·25	1·25
4135	$1.50 lilac, stone and brown	1·25	1·25
MS4136	116×136 mm. $6 multicoloured	5·00	5·50

DESIGNS: No. 4132, King George III of Great Britain; 4133, King George IV of Great Britain; 4134, Duchess Charlotte of Luxembourg; 4135, Duke Jean of Luxembourg; **MS**4136 King Charles VIII of France.

2000. Popes of the Millennium. As T 314b of Gambia. Multicoloured (except MS4143).

No.	Description	Unused	Used
4137	$1.50 Stephen VIII	1·25	1·25
4138	$1.50 Theodore	1·25	1·25
4139	$1.50 Theodore II	1·25	1·25
4140	$1.50 Valentine	1·25	1·25
4141	$1.50 Vitalian	1·25	1·25
4142	$1.50 Zacharias	1·25	1·25
MS4143	116×136 mm. $6 Sylvester II (grey, black and stone)	5·00	5·50

480 500 Mondial Sports Car, 1953

2000. Ferrari Cars. Multicoloured.

4144 20c. Type **480** 30 25
4145 45c. 166 Inter saloon, 1948 45 25
4146 75c. 340 MM sports car, 1953 75 35
4147 90c. 500 Superfast saloon, 1964 85 45
4148 $1 166 MM sports car, 1948 90 55
4149 $1.50 250 S saloon, 1952 1·25 1·25
4150 $2 250 California convertible, 1957 1·60 1·75
4151 $3 365 California convertible, 1966 2·00 2·25

481 Marmon Model 34, 1921

2000. Classic Cars. Multicoloured.

4152 45c. Type **481** 45 25
4153 75c. Buick D44, 1917 75 40
4154 90c. Hudson Runabout Landau, 1918 80 50
4155 $1 Chevrolet Royal Mail, 1915 90 55
4156 $1.50 Rolls Royce, 1929 1·10 1·10
4157 $1.50 Graham Convertible, 1932 1·10 1·10
4158 $1.50 Mercedes-Benz 540K, 1937 1·10 1·10
4159 $1.50 Jaguar Mk V, 1948 1·10 1·10
4160 $1.50 Lagonda Drophead Coupe, 1939 1·10 1·10
4161 $1.50 Alfa Romeo Gran Sport, 1930 1·10 1·10
4162 $1.50 Cadillac V63, 1925 1·10 1·10
4163 $1.50 Plymouth, 1939 1·10 1·10
4164 $1.50 Franklin Club Sedan, 1934 1·10 1·10
4165 $1.50 Fiat Ardita, 1933 1·10 1·10
4166 $1.50 Essex Speedabout, 1929 1·10 1·10
4167 $1.50 Stutz Bearcat, 1932 1·10 1·10
4168 $2 Kissel Speedster, 1925 1·60 1·75
4169 $3 Ford Model T, 1915 2·00 2·25

MS4170 Two sheets, each 94×67 mm. (a) $6 Dodge Tourer, 1915. (b) $6 Chrysler, 1924 Set of 2 sheets 10·00 11·00

482 Borsig Standard Locomotive, 1863

2000. German Railway Locomotives. Mult.

4171 $1.50 Type **482** 1·25 1·25
4172 $1.50 German Federal Railway Austerity Class 52, 1940s 1·25 1·25
4173 $1.50 Stephenson locomotive *Adler* without tender, 1835 1·25 1·25
4174 $1.50 Crampton locomotive *Bardenia*, 1863 1·25 1·25
4175 $1.50 Drache, 1848 1·25 1·25
4176 $1.50 Stephenson locomotive *Adler* with tender, 1835 1·25 1·25
4177 $1.50 German Federal Railway Class 10, 1956 1·25 1·25
4178 $1.50 German Federal Railway Class E10 electric locomotive, 1957 1·25 1·25
4179 $1.50 German Federal Railway Class 23, 1953 1·25 1·25
4180 $1.50 German Federal Railway tank locomotive, 1950s 1·25 1·25
4181 $1.50 East German State Railway rebuilt Class 01 Pacific, 1950s 1·25 1·25
4182 $1.50 East German State Railway diesel railcar on Berlin–Schonefeld service, 1950s 1·25 1·25

MS4183 Two sheets, each 80×72 mm. (a) $6 Borsig locomotive of Berlin and Anhalt Railway, 1841. (b) $6 German Federal Railway V.200 diesel-hydraulic locomotive, 1952 Set of 2 sheets 10·00 11·00

483 Thai State Railway Diesel-electric Locomotive

2000. Modern Railway Locomotives of the World. Multicoloured.

4184 $1.50 Type **483** 1·25 1·25
4185 $1.50 Danish diesel-electric express locomotive 1·25 1·25
4186 $1.50 French-built Turbo train 1·25 1·25
4187 $1.50 Spanish Railways diesel unit 1·25 1·25
4188 $1.50 Spanish Railways diesel locomotive for "Virgen del Rosario" 1·25 1·25
4189 $1.50 Malayan Railways Class 22 diesel-electric locomotive 1·25 1·25
4190 $1.50 British Railways Class 87 electric locomotive 1·25 1·25
4191 $1.50 Iraqi Railway diesel-electric locomotive 1·25 1·25
4192 $1.50 Austrian Railways electric locomotive 1·25 1·25
4193 $1.50 South Australia Railways diesel locomotive 1·25 1·25
4194 $1.50 Black Mesa and Lake Powell Railroad electric locomotive 1·25 1·25
4195 $1.50 Yugoslav Railways diesel-electric unit 1·25 1·25

MS4196 Four sheets, each 96×66 mm. (a) $6 Netherlands Railway Inter-city electric train. (b) $6 Swiss Railways Suburban electric unit. (c) $6 T.E.E. diesel locomotive for "Parsifal". (d) $6 New Zealand Railways "Silver Fern" diesel railcar unit Set of 4 sheets 19·00 20·00

484 Girl at Skylight

2000. Nursery Rhymes. Multicoloured.

4197 $1.50 Type **484** 1·10 1·10
4198 $1.50 Woman and rainbow 1·10 1·10
4199 $1.50 Cow and rainbow 1·10 1·10
4200 $1.50 Boy in nightshirt 1·10 1·10
4201 $1.50 Old Woman with baby 1·10 1·10
4202 $1.50 Boy on show 1·10 1·10
4203 $1.50 Bird in tree and crook 1·10 1·10
4204 $1.50 Little Bo-Peep 1·10 1·10
4205 $1.50 Sheep 1·10 1·10
4206 $1.50 Goose and fence 1·10 1·10
4207 $1.50 Goose and Little Bo-Peep 1·10 1·10
4208 $1.50 Dog 1·10 1·10
4209 $1.50 Sheep and cottage 1·10 1·10
4210 $1.50 Sun and lane 1·10 1·10
4211 $1.50 Cow and haystack 1·10 1·10
4212 $1.50 Two geese 1·10 1·10
4213 $1.50 Dog and Boy Blue's leg 1·10 1·10
4214 $1.50 Little Boy Blue asleep 1·10 1·10
4215 $1.50 Dove and tower 1·10 1·10
4216 $1.50 Cow jumping over moon 1·10 1·10
4217 $1.50 Spoon 1·10 1·10
4218 $1.50 Dog laughing 1·10 1·10
4219 $1.50 Cat playing fiddle 1·10 1·10
4220 $1.50 Dish 1·10 1·10

MS4221 Four sheets, each 106×77 mm. (a) $6 Old Woman and shoe (horiz). (b) $6 Little Bo-Peep (horiz). (c) $6 Little Boy Blue asleep (horiz). (d) $6 Cow jumping over moon (horiz) Set of 4 sheets 18·00 19·00

Nos. 4197/202 (Old Woman that lived in a Shoe), 4203/8 (Little Bo-Peep), 4209/14 (Little Boy Blue) and 4215/20 (The Cat and the Fiddle) were each printed together, se-tenant, with the backgrounds forming composite designs.

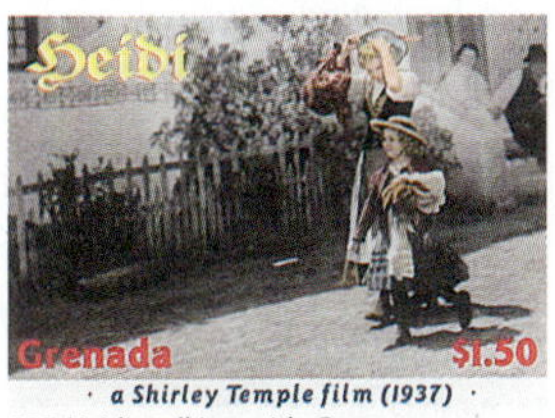

485 Heidi walking with Governess

2000. Shirley Temple in Heidi. Showing scenes from the film. Multicoloured.

4222 $1.50 Type **485** 1·10 1·10
4223 $1.50 Heidi with grandfather 1·10 1·10
4224 $1.50 Heidi with Peter the Goat Boy 1·10 1·10
4225 $1.50 Heidi with doves 1·10 1·10
4226 $1.50 Heidi with grandfather tying knot 1·10 1·10
4227 $1.50 Heidi and governess sitting on bench 1·10 1·10
4228 $1.50 Heidi in bed 1·10 1·10
4229 $1.50 Heidi with Klara Sesemann 1·10 1·10
4230 $1.50 Heidi with Andrews the butler 1·10 1·10
4231 $1.50 Heidi unwrapping Christmas presents with the Sesemanns 1·10 1·10

MS4232 105×75 mm. $6 Heidi sitting on log 4·75 5·00

486 Betty Boop sitting in Sports Car, Hollywood

2000. Betty Boop (cartoon character). Twelve sheets containing vert designs as T **486** showing geographical locations. Multicoloured.

MS4233 (a) 110×90 mm. $6 Type **486**. (b) 110×90 mm. $6 Riding horse, Argentina. (c) 110×90 mm. $6 Sitting on camel, Turkey. (d) 110×90 mm. $6 As flamenco dancer, Spain. (e) 110×90 mm. $6 Drinking champagne, France. (f) 110×90 mm. $6 Fishing, South Pacific. (g) 110×90 mm. $6 As belly dancer, Eygpt. (h) 90×110 mm. $6 With guardsman outside Buckingham Palace, London. (i) 90×110 mm. $6 In floral hat, Switzerland. (j) 90×110 mm. $6 In kimono, Japan. (k) 90×110 mm. $6 As Statue of Liberty, New York. (l) 90×110 mm. $6 Wearing lei, Hawaii Set of 12 sheets 45·00 50·00

2000. Scenes from The Three Stooges (American T.V. comedy series). As T 310 of Gambia. Multicoloured.

4234 $1 Moe pointing bottle at Curly Joe 80 80
4235 $1 Eating straw with horse 80 80
4236 $1 Larry holding flowers 80 80
4237 $1 Reading letter 80 80
4238 $1 Looking in saucepan 80 80
4239 $1 Holding wads of notes 80 80
4240 $1 Moe in breastplate (guard behind in purple and green) 80 80
4241 $1 Indoors with horse 80 80
4242 $1 Larry in breastplate (guard behind in lilac and yellow) 80 80
4243 $1 Western bar brawl 80 80
4244 $1 As "DELIGATES" 80 80
4245 $1 In Victorian dress (two as women) 80 80
4246 $1 Moe pointing gun 80 80
4247 $1 Holding certificate 80 80
4248 $1 Moe using secateurs near Curly's nose 80 80
4249 $1 Larry (picture at right) 80 80
4250 $1 Moe in front of picture 80 80
4251 $1 Curly 80 80

MS4252 Twelve sheets. (a) 108×87 mm. $5 Curly in green shirt holding Moe's arm (vert). (b) 108×87 mm. $5 In evening dress with girl. (c) 108×87 mm. $5 Moe with Larry holding woman's hand (vert). (d) 91×137 mm. $5 With secretary from *He Cooked His Goose* (vert). (e) 108×87 mm. $5 As No. 4243. (f) 108×89 mm. $5 Having heads banged together by cowboy. (g) 97×118 mm. $5 Putting Larry in a jet engine (vert). (h) 98×125 mm. $5 Curly Joe with cigar (vert). (i) 107×88 mm. $5 Listening to jet engine. (j) 107×88 mm. $5 Swinging propeller. (k) 130×100 mm. $6 Larry and Moe in breastplates. (l) 130×100 mm. $6 Curly with hand in mangle Set of 12 sheets 40·00 45·00

487 Kane jumping over Opponent

2000. World Wrestling Federation. Kane. Multicoloured.

4253 $1 Type **487** 80 80
4254 $1 Kneeling by injured opponent 80 80
4255 $1 Jumping 80 80
4256 $1 Kane (red background) 80 80
4257 $1 Kane (blue and yellow background) 80 80
4258 $1 Holding lifting opponent in black tunic 80 80
4259 $1 With arms folded 80 80
4260 $1 Lifting opponent in black and white trousers 80 80
4261 $1 Lifting opponent No. 59 80 80

MS4262 Two sheets, each 77×118 mm. (a) $5 With black glove on right hand. (b) $5 Lifting opponent Set of 2 sheets 7·50 8·50

2000. "Espana 2000" International Stamp Exhibition, Madrid. Paintings from the Prado Museum. As T 326a of Gambia. Multicoloured.

4263 $1.50 King Ferdinand and priest from "The Virgin of the Catholic Monarchs" (anon) 1·10 1·10
4264 $1.50 Virgin and Child from "The Virgin of the Catholic Monarchs" 1·10 1·10
4265 $1.50 Queen Isabella and priest from "The Virgin of the Catholic Monarchs" 1·10 1·10
4266 $1.50 "The Flagellation" (Alejo Fernandez) 1·10 1·10
4267 $1.50 "The Virgin and Souls in Purgatory" (Pedro Machuca) 1·10 1·10
4268 $1.50 "The Holy Trinity" (El Greco) 1·10 1·10
4269 $1.50 "The Saviour's Blessing" (Francisco de Zurbaran) 1·10 1·10
4270 $1.50 "St. John the Baptist" (Francesco Solimena) 1·10 1·10
4271 $1.50 "Noli Me Tangere" (Correggio) 1·10 1·10
4272 $1.50 "St. Casilda" (Francisco de Zurbaran) 1·10 1·10
4273 $1.50 "Nicolas Omazur" (Murillo) 1·10 1·10
4274 $1.50 "Juan Martinez Montanes" (Velazquez) 1·10 1·10
4275 $1.50 "Playing at Giants" (Goya) 1·10 1·10
4276 $1.50 "The Holy Family with Oak Tree" (Raphael and Giulio Romano) 1·10 1·10
4277 $1.50 "Don Gaspar Melchor de Jovellanos" (Goya) 1·10 1·10
4278 $1.50 Courtier from "Joseph in Pharaoh's Palace" (Jacopo Amiconi) 1·10 1·10
4279 $1.50 Pharaoh and Joseph from "Joseph in Pharaoh's Palace" 1·10 1·10
4280 $1.50 Servant with hat from "Joseph in Pharaoh's Palace" 1·10 1·10

MS4281 Three sheets. (a) 90×110 mm. $6 "The Virgin of the Catholic Monarchs" (anon). (b) 90×110 mm. $6 "St. Anne, the Virgin, St. Elizabeth, St. John and the Christ Child" (Fernando Yanez de la Almedina). (c) 110×90 mm. $6 "Joseph in Pharoah's Palace" (Jacopo Amiconi) (horiz) Set of 3 sheets 13·00 14·00

488 American Purple Gallinule

2000. Birds of the Caribbean. Multicoloured.

4282 25c. Type **488** 30 15
4283 40c. Limpkin 40 20
4284 50c. Black-necked stilt 45 25
4285 60c. Painted bunting 50 30
4286 75c. Yellow-breasted flycatcher warbler ("Yellow-breasted Warbler") 60 35
4287 $1 Blackburnian warbler 75 45
4288 $1.25 Blue grosbeak 90 70
4289 $1.50 Black and white warbler 1·10 80
4290 $1.60 Himalayan whistling thrush ("Blue Whistling Thrush") 1·25 1·25
4291 $3 Common yellowthroat 2·00 2·25

4292	$4 Indigo bunting	2·50	2·75
4293	$5 Catbird	3·00	3·25
4294	$10 Bananaquit	6·00	6·50
4295	$20 Blue-grey gnatcatcher	11·00	12·00

489 Messerschmitt Bf 109E under Attack

2000. 60th Anniv of Battle of Britain. Multicoloured.

4296	$1.50 Type **489**	1·40	1·40
4297	$1.50 Supermarine Spitfire Mk XI	1·40	1·40
4298	$1.50 V1 flying bomb	1·40	1·40
4299	$1.50 U-Boat under attack	1·40	1·40
4300	$1.50 Anti-aircraft gun	1·40	1·40
4301	$1.50 Bedford army ambulance	1·40	1·40
4302	$1.50 Messerschmitt Bf 109E	1·40	1·40
4303	$1.50 German pilot parachuting	1·40	1·40
4304	$1.50 Hawker Hurricane MkI	1·40	1·40
4305	$1.50 British airfield under attack	1·40	1·40
4306	$1.50 Heinkel He 111H on fire	1·40	1·40
4307	$1.50 R.A.F. emblem on Supermarine Spitfire Mk XI	1·40	1·40
MS4308	Two sheets, each 99×71 mm. (a) $6 Supermarine Spitfire Mk IX. (b) $6 Hawker Hurricane Mk 1s on tarmac Set of 2 sheets	13·00	14·00

No. 4304 is inscribed "Hanker Hurricane HK1" and No. **MS**4308 "HK1", both in error.

2000. Queen Elizabeth the Queen Mother's 100th Birthday. As T 318 of Gambia. Multicoloured.

4309	$1.50 Queen Mother in grey hat	1·25	1·25

2000. Faces of the Millennium: Queen Elizabeth the Queen Mother's 100th Birthday. As T 307a of Gambia showing collage of miniature flower photographs. Multicoloured.

4310	$1 Top of head (face value at left)	90	90
4311	$1 Top of head (face value at right)	90	90
4312	$1 Eye and temple (face value at left)	90	90
4313	$1 Temple (face value at right)	90	90
4314	$1 Cheek (face value at left)	90	90
4315	$1 Cheek (face value at right)	90	90
4316	$1 Chin (face value at left)	90	90
4317	$1 Neck (face value at right)	90	90

Nos. 4310/17 were printed together, se-tenant, in sheetlets of 8 with the stamps arranged in two vertical columns separated by a gutter also containing miniature photographs. When viewed as a whole the sheetlet forms a portrait of the Queen Mother.

490 *Brassavola nodosa*

2000. Caribbean Flowers. Multicoloured.

4318	25c. Type **490**	30	20
4319	35c. *Laelia anceps* (horiz)	35	20
4320	75c. *Plumeria rubra* (horiz)	65	35
4321	$1 *Bougainvillea glabra* (horiz)	80	60
4322	$1 *Allamanda catharticia*	80	60
4323	$1.50 *Cassia alata*	1·10	1·10
4324	$1.50 *Anthurium andreanum*	1·10	1·10
4325	$1.50 *Ipomea crassicaulis*	1·10	1·10
4326	$1.50 *Laelia anceps*	1·10	1·10
4327	$1.50 *Galeandra baueri*	1·10	1·10
4328	$1.50 *Hibiscus rosa-sinensis*	1·10	1·10
4329	$1.50 *Alpinia purpurata*	1·10	1·10
4330	$1.50 *Strelitzia reginae*	1·10	1·10
4331	$1.50 *Psychlis atropurpurea*	1·10	1·10
4332	$1.50 *Cattleya velutina*	1·10	1·10
4333	$1.50 *Caularthron bicornutum*	1·10	1·10
4334	$1.50 *Cattleya warneri*	1·10	1·10
4335	$1.50 *Mandevilla splendens*	1·10	1·10
4336	$1.50 *Tithonia rotundifolia*	1·10	1·10
4337	$1.50 *Lagerstromia speciosa*	1·10	1·10
4338	$1.50 *Columnea argentea*	1·10	1·10
4339	$1.50 *Brunfelsia calycina*	1·10	1·10
4340	$1.50 *Portlandia albiflora*	1·10	1·10
4341	$1.50 *Pachira insignis*	1·10	1·10
4342	$1.50 *Jatropha integerrima*	1·10	1·10
4343	£1.50 *Jacaranda filicifolia*	1·10	1·10
4344	$1.50 *Cordia sebestena*	1·10	1·10
4345	$1.50 *Allamanda cathartica*	1·10	1·10
4346	$1.50 *Samanea saman*	1·10	1·10
4347	$2 *Lisianthius nigrescens* (horiz)	1·60	1·75
4348	$2 *Aspasia epidendroides*	1·60	1·75
4349	$3 *Oncidium splendidum*	2·00	2·25
MS4350	Four sheets. (a) 68×97 mm. $6 *Anthurium scherzerianum* (horiz). (b) 68×97 mm. $6 *Ipomea learii* (horiz). (c) 94×61 mm. $6 *Fuchsia* (horiz). (d) 94×61 mm. $6 *Heliconia psittaconia* Set of 4 sheets	18·00	19·00

Nos. 4323/8, 4329/34, 4335/40 and 4341/6 were each printed together, se-tenant, each forming a composite floral design.

No. 4320 is inscribed "Plumieria", 4341 "Pachira insigis", 4343 "Jacarancla filicifolia" and 4345 "Corclia filicifolia", all in error.

491 Angel in Red

2000. Christmas. Holy Year. Multicoloured.

4351	15c. Type **491**	20	10
4352	25c. Angel praying	25	15
4353	50c. Type **491**	45	25
4354	$2 As 25c	1·60	1·75
4355	$2 Type **491**	1·60	1·75
4356	$5 As 25c	3·50	4·00
MS4357	110×120 mm. $6 Holy Child (horiz)	4·50	5·50

2001. Chinese New Year. ("Year of the Snake"). As T 470. Multicoloured.

4358	$2 Blue and yellow snake	1·60	1·75
4359	$2 Green snake (inverted triangle)	1·60	1·75
4360	$2 Red snake	1·60	1·75

491a Lucy and Desi with Friends

2001. Scenes from I Love Lucy (American T.V. comedy series). Eight sheets, each containing multicoloured design as T 491a.

MS4361	(a) 80×112 mm. $6 Type **491a**. (b) 80×110 mm. $6 Lucy and Desi dancing. (c) 88×127 mm. $6 Lucy in checked jacket. (d) 92×124 mm. $6 Lucy in checked jacket dancing with Desi. (e) 98×120 mm. $6 Desi laughing with William Frawley. (f) 118×92 mm. $6 Lucy leaning on mantelpiece. (g) 118×100 mm. $6 Lucy sitting at desk. (h) 92×124 mm. $6 William Frawley and Desi at desk (horiz) Set of 8 sheets	32·00	35·00

2001. Bicentenary of Rijksmuseum, Amsterdam. Dutch Paintings. As T 330a of Gambia. Multicoloured.

4362	$1.50 "Syndics of Amsterdam Goldsmiths' Guild" (Thomas de Keyser)	1·10	1·10
4363	$1.50 "Gentleman" (De Keyser)	1·10	1·10
4364	$1.50 "Eva Wtewael" (Joachim Wtewael)	1·10	1·10
4365	$1.50 "Ferry Boat" (Esaias van de Velde)	1·10	1·10
4366	$1.50 "Tares among the Wheat" (Abraham Bloemaert)	1·10	1·10
4367	$1.50 "Princess Henrietta Marie Stuart" (Bartholomeus van der Heist)	1·10	1·10
4368	$1.50 "William I, Prince of Orange" (Adriaen Key)	1·10	1·10
4369	$1.50 "Schimmelpenninck Family" (Pierre-Paul Prud'hon)	1·10	1·10
4370	$1.50 "Johan Rudolf Thorbecke" (Jan Neuman)	1·10	1·10
4371	$1.50 "St. Sebastian" (Wtewael)	1·10	1·10
4372	$1.50 "St. Sebastian" (Hendrick ter Brugghen)	1·10	1·10
4373	$1.50 "Man with a Ring" (Werner van der Valckert)	1·10	1·10
4374	$1.50 "Abraham Casteleyn and his Wife, Margarieta van Bancken" (Jan de Bray)	1·10	1·10
4375	$1.50 Piper and singer from "Concert" (Ter Brugghen)	1·10	1·10
4376	$1.50 "Procuress" (Dirck van Baburen)	1·10	1·10
4377	$1.50 "Woman seated at Virginal" (Vermeer)	1·10	1·10
4378	$1.50 "Elegant Couples courting" (Willem Buytewech)	1·10	1·10
4379	$1.50 "Young Flute player" (Judith Leyster)	1·10	1·10
4380	$1.50 "Merry Fiddler" (Gerard van Honthorst)	1·10	1·10
4381	$1.50 "Merry Drinker" (Frans Hals)	1·10	1·10
4382	$1.50 "Granida and Daifilo" (Van Honthorst)	1·10	1·10
4383	$1.50 "Vertumnus and Pomona" (Paulus Moreelse)	1·10	1·10
4384	$1.50 Piper from "Concert" (Ter Brugghen)	1·10	1·10
4385	$1.50 "Young Student at his Desk" (Pieter Codde)	1·10	1·10
MS4386	Four sheets. (a) 119×88 mm. $6 "Winter Landscape with Skaters" (Hendrick Avercamp) (horiz). (b) 119×88 mm. $6 "Denial of St. Peter" (Rembrandt) (horiz). (c) 98×118 mm. $6 "Portuguese Synagogue, Amsterdam" (Emanuel de Witte). (d) 98×118 mm. $6 "The Raampoortje" (Wouter van Troostwijk) (horiz) Set of 4 sheets	18·00	19·00

No. 4381 is inscribed "Frans Hal" in error.

2001. Characters from "Pokemon" (children's cartoon series). As T 332a of Gambia. Multicoloured.

4387	$1.50 "Rattata No. 19"	1·10	1·10
4388	$1.50 "Sandshrew No. 27"	1·10	1·10
4389	$1.50 "Wartortle No. 08"	1·10	1·10
4390	$1.50 "Primeape No. 57"	1·10	1·10
4391	$1.50 "Golduck No. 55"	1·10	1·10
4392	$1.50 "Persian No. 53"	1·10	1·10
MS4393	74×115 mm. $6 "Jolteon No. 135"	4·50	5·00

492 African Pygmy Goose

2001. "Hong Kong 2001" International Stamp Exhibition. Ducks of the World. Multicoloured.

4394	$1.25 Type **492**	1·00	1·00
4395	$1.25 Versicolor teal ("Silver Teal")	1·00	1·00
4396	$1.25 Marbled teal	1·00	1·00
4397	$1.25 Garganey	1·00	1·00
4398	$1.25 Wandering whistling duck	1·00	1·00
4399	$1.25 Northern shoveler	1·00	1·00
4400	$1.25 Flying steamer duck ("Flightless Steamer Duck")	1·00	1·00
4401	$1.25 Radjah shelduck	1·00	1·00
4402	$1.25 Cape teal	1·00	1·00
4403	$1.25 Hartlaub's duck	1·00	1·00
4404	$1.25 Ruddy shelduck	1·00	1·00
4405	$1.25 Bahama pintail ("White-cheeked Pintail")	1·00	1·00
4406	$1.25 Fulvous whistling duck (vert)	1·00	1·00
4407	$1.25 African black duck (vert)	1·00	1·00
4408	$1.25 Madagascar pochard ("Madagascan White-eye") (vert)	1·00	1·00
4409	$1.25 African pygmy goose ("Pygmy Goose") (vert)	1·00	1·00
4410	$1.25 Wood duck (female) (vert)	1·00	1·00
4411	$1.25 Wood duck (male) (vert)	1·00	1·00
MS4412	Three sheets, each 100×70 mm. (a) $6 Flying steamer duck. (b) $6 Flightless steamer duck. (c) $6 Australian shelduck (vert) Set of 3 sheets	14·00	15·00

493 "Daily Life in Edo" (Miyagawa Choshum)

2001. "Philanippon '01" International Stamp Exhibition, Tokyo. Japanese Paintings. Multicoloured.

4413	75c. Type **493**	60	35
4414	90c. "Twelve Famous Places in Japan" (Kano Isen'in Naganobu)	70	40
4415	$1 "After the Rain" (Kawai Gyokudo)	75	55
4416	$1.25 "Ryogoku Bridge" (Kano Kyuei)	90	65
4417	$2 "Courtesan of Fukagawa" (Katsukawa Shun'ei)	1·60	1·75
4418	$2 "Yugao Chapter" (85×28 mm)	1·60	1·75
4419	$2 "Suetsumuhana Chapter" (85×28 mm)	1·60	1·75
4420	$2 "Wakamurasaki Chapter" (85×28 mm)	1·60	1·75
4421	$2 "Momiji-no-ga Chapter" (85×28 mm)	1·60	1·75
4422	$2 Praying in the woods (vert)	1·60	1·75
4423	$2 Lady with servants (vert)	1·60	1·75
4424	$2 Fire by river (vert)	1·60	1·75
4425	$2 Pagoda by river (vert)	1·60	1·75
4426	$3 "Bear Killing" (unsigned)	1·60	1·75
MS4427	Two sheets. (a) 93×81 mm. $6 "Pomegranates and a Small Bird" (Onishi Keisai). (b) 97×76 mm. $6 from "Bodhisattva: Never Despise" (Enryaku-ji) (vert). Nos. 4418/21 depict "Tale of Genji" Set of 2 sheets	9·50	10·50

Nos. 4418/21 depict "Tale of Genji" (Kano Ryusetsu Hidenobu), and Nos. 4422/5 illustrates "The Lotus Sutra—Tactfulness" (Hompo-ji).

2001. Death Centenary of Queen Victoria. As T 590a of Ghana. Multicoloured.

4428	$3 Princess Victoria as a young girl	2·00	2·25
4429	$3 Young Queen Victoria wearing crown	2·00	2·25
4430	$3 In old age	2·00	2·25
MS4431	77×107 mm. $6 Queen Victoria on throne	5·00	5·50

2001. 25th Death Anniv of Mao Tse-tung (Chinese leader). As T 590b of Ghana. Multicoloured.

4432	$2 Mao Tse-tung in 1936	1·60	1·75
4433	$2 In 1919	1·60	1·75
4434	$2 In 1945	1·60	1·75
MS4435	133×126 mm. $3 Mao Tse-tung encouraging troops in 1938	2·00	2·25

2001. 75th Death Anniv of Claude-Oscar Monet (French painter). As T 590c of Ghana. Multicoloured.

4436	$2 "Boats in Winter Quarters, Etretat"	1·60	1·75
4437	$2 "Regatta at Sainte Adresse"	1·60	1·75
4438	$2 "Bridge at Bougival"	1·60	1·75
4439	$2 "Beach at Sainte Adresse"	1·60	1·75
MS4440	136×111 mm. $6 "Monet's Garden at Vetheuil" (vert)	5·00	5·50

2001. 75th Birthday of Queen Elizabeth II. As T 590d of Ghana. Multicoloured.

4441	$2 Queen in straw boater	1·90	1·90
4442	$2 Queen in red hat	1·90	1·90
4443	$2 Wearing multicoloured pastel hat	1·90	1·90
4444	$2 Wearing mauve turban-style hat	1·90	1·90
MS4445	76×100 mm. $6 Queen wearing mauve hat and coat (37×50 mm)	5·50	6·00

2001. Death Centenary of Giuseppe Verdi (Italian composer). As T 590e of Ghana. Multicoloured.

4446	$2 Character from Ernani (opera)	2·00	1·90
4447	$2 Score from Ernani	2·00	1·90
4448	$2 Verdi as a young man	2·00	1·90
4449	$2 La Scala Opera House, Milan	2·00	1·90
MS4450	76×106 mm. $6 Verdi in old age	6·00	6·50

2001. Death Centenary of Henri de Toulouse-Lautrec (French painter). As T 590f of Ghana. Multicoloured.

4451	$2 "Alone"	1·60	1·75
4452	$2 "Two Half-naked Women"	1·60	1·75
4453	$2 "The Toilette"	1·60	1·75
4454	$2 "Justine Dieuhl"	1·60	1·75
MS4455	66×84 mm. $6 "Mademoiselle Dihau at the Piano"	4·75	5·00

494 Woman on Beach

2001. United Nations Women's Human Rights Campaign. Multicoloured.

4456	90c. Type **494**	70	60
4457	$1 "Caribbean Woman II"	80	80

495 Marlene Dietrich smoking

2001. Birth Centenary of Marlene Dietrich (actress and singer).

4458	**495**	$2 multicoloured	1·60	1·75
4459	-	$2 black, purple and red	1·60	1·75
4460	-	$2 black, purple and red	1·60	1·75
4461	-	$2 black, purple and red	1·60	1·75

DESIGNS No. 4459, Marlene Dietrich on stage with microphone; 4460, Wearing feather boa; 4461, Sitting in armchair.

496 Phoenician Merchant Ship

2001. "Belgica 2001" International Stamp Exhibition, Brussels. Sailing Ships. Mult.

4462	45c. Type **496**	40	25
4463	75c. Portuguese caravel	60	40
4464	90c. Marblehead schooner	75	50
4465	$1 Mala pansi	80	80
4466	$1 English cog	80	80
4467	$1 Roman merchantman	80	80
4468	$1 Greek war galley	80	80
4469	$1 Greek merchantman	80	80
4470	$1 Oseberg Viking longship	80	80
4471	$1 Egyptian sailing craft	80	80
4472	$1 Egyptian galley	80	80
4473	$1 16th-century galleass	80	80
4474	$1 Norman ship	80	80
4475	$1 English carrack	80	80
4476	$1 Mediterranean carrack	80	80
4477	$1 Spanish galleon	80	80
4478	$1 Elizabethan Grumster	80	80
4479	$1 British East Indiaman	80	80
4480	$1 Clipper	80	80
4481	$1 British ship of the line	80	80
4482	$1 British gun boat	80	80
4483	$1 English hoy	80	80
4484	$1 Gloucester fishing schooner	80	80
4485	$1 Sloop-rigged yacht	80	80
4486	$1 Chinese junk	80	80
4487	$1 Sambuk	80	80
4488	$1 Baltimore clipper schooner	80	80
4489	$1 Schooner-rigged yacht	80	80
4490	$1 American clipper	80	80
4491	$1 American frigate	80	80
4492	$1 Sail/steam mail packet	80	80
4493	$1.50 American corvette	1·10	1·10
4494	$2 Racing schooner	1·60	1·75
MS4495	Two sheets, each 60×44 mm. (a) $6 *Suhaili* (yacht), 1968. (b) $6 *Gulf Streamer* (trimaran) and Polynesian outrigger Set of 2 sheets	10·00	11·00

No. 4481 is inscribed "BRITISH GUN SHIP", 4482 "BRITISH FLAGSHIP" and 4484 "GLOUSTER", all in error.

497 Montauk Point Lighthouse, New York

2001. Lighthouses. Multicoloured.

4496	25c. Type **497**	70	30
4497	50c. Alcatraz lighthouse, San Francisco	1·00	55
4498	$1 Barnegat lighthouse, New Jersey	1·40	1·00
4499	$1.50 Point Amour lighthouse, Canada	1·50	1·50
4500	$1.50 Inubo-Saki lighthouse, Japan	1·50	1·50
4501	$1.50 Belle-Ile lighthouse, France	1·50	1·50
4502	$1.50 Faerder lighthouse, Norway	1·50	1·50
4503	$1.50 Cape Agulhas lighthouse, South Africa	1·50	1·50
4504	$1.50 Minicoy lighthouse, India	1·50	1·50
4505	$1.50 Admiralty lighthouse, Washington	1·50	1·50
4506	$1.50 Hooper's Strait lighthouse, Maryland	1·50	1·50
4507	$1.50 Hunting Island lighthouse, South Carolina	1·50	1·50
4508	$1.50 Key West Lighthouse Museum, Florida	1·50	1·50
4509	$1.50 Old Point Loma lighthouse, California	1·50	1·50
4510	$1.50 Old Makinac Point lighthouse, Michigan	1·50	1·50
4511	$1.50 Keri lighthouse, Estonia	1·50	1·50
4512	$1.50 Anholt lighthouse, Denmark	1·50	1·50
4513	$1.50 Porer lighthouse, Croatia	1·50	1·50
4514	$1.50 Laotieshan lighthouse, China	1·50	1·50
4515	$1.50 Sapienza Methoni lighthouse, Greece	1·50	1·50
4516	$1.50 Arkona lighthouse, Germany	1·50	1·50
4517	$2 St. Augustine lighthouse, Florida	1·50	1·50
MS4518	Four sheets, each 70×98 mm. (a) $6 Kvitsoy lighthouse, Norway. (b) $6 Mahota Pagoda lighthouse, China. (c) $6 Boston lighthouse, Massachusetts. (d) $6 Pellworm lighthouse, Germany.	24·00	24·00

Nos. 4503 and 4515 are inscribed "Africca" or "Sapientza", both in error.

497a Anatoly Karpov

2001. First e-World Chess Championship. Sheet 88×103 mm.

MS4518a	**497a** $20 multicoloured	20·00	20·00

498 Commerson's Dolphin

2001. Whales and Dolphins. Multicoloured.

4519	25c. Type **498**	40	15
4520	50c. Pacific white-sided dolphin	55	25
4521	$1.50 Risso's dolphin	1·25	1·25
4522	$1.50 Fraser's dolphin	1·25	1·25
4523	$1.50 Dall's porpoise	1·25	1·25
4524	$1.50 Right whale	1·25	1·25
4525	$1.50 Grey whale	1·25	1·25
4526	$1.50 Minke whale	1·25	1·25
4527	$1.50 Common dolphin	1·25	1·25
4528	$1.50 Antillean beaked whale	1·25	1·25
4529	$1.50 Killer whale's tail and divers	1·25	1·25
4530	$1.50 Bryde's whale	1·25	1·25
4531	$1.50 Cuvier's beaked whale	1·25	1·25
4532	$1.50 Sei whale	1·25	1·25
4533	$1.50 Harbour porpoise	1·25	1·25
4534	$1.50 Beluga	1·25	1·25
4535	$1.50 White-beaked dolphin	1·25	1·25
4536	$1.50 Narwhal	1·25	1·25
4537	$1.50 Bowhead whale	1·25	1·25
4538	$1.50 Fin whale	1·25	1·25
4539	$2 Northern bottlenosed whale	1·60	1·75
4540	$3 Baird's beaked whale	2·00	2·25
MS4541	Four sheets, each 75×52 mm. (a) $6 Humpback whale and calf. (b) $6 Sperm whale calf. (c) $6 Blue whale with calf. (d) $6 Southern right whale	19·00	20·00

Nos. 4521/6, 4527/32 and 4533/8 were printed together, se-tenant, with the backgrounds forming composite designs.

499 World Cup Publicity Poster, Brazil, 1950

2001. World Cup Football Championship, Japan and Korea (2002). Multicoloured.

4542	$1.50 Type **499**	1·10	1·10
4543	$1.50 West German players, Switzerland, 1954	1·10	1·10
4544	$1.50 Just Fontaine (France), Sweden, 1958	1·10	1·10
4545	$1.50 Garrincha (Brazil), Chile, 1962	1·10	1·10
4546	$1.50 Bobby Moore (England), England, 1966	1·10	1·10
4547	$1.50 Pele (Brazil), Mexico, 1970	1·10	1·10
4548	$1.50 Osvaldo Ardiles (Argentina), Argentina, 1978	1·10	1·10
4549	$1.50 Lakhdar Belloumi (Algeria), Spain, 1982	1·10	1·10
4550	$1.50 Diego Maradona (Argentina), Mexico, 1986	1·10	1·10
4551	$1.50 Lothar Matthaus and Rudi Voller (West Germany), Italy, 1990	1·10	1·10
4552	$1.50 Seo Jung Won (South Korea), U.S.A., 1994	1·10	1·10
4553	$1.50 Ronaldo (Brazil), France, 1998	1·10	1·10
MS4554	Two sheets, each 88×75 mm. (a) $6 Detail of Jules Rimet Trophy, Uruguay, 1930. (b) $6 Detail of World Cup Trophy, Japan–Korea, 2002	10·00	11·00

500 Arsenal Football Stadium, Highbury

2001. British Football Clubs (1st series). Multicoloured.

4555	$1.50 Type **500**	1·10	1·10
4556	$1.50 Players celebrating European Cup Winners' Cup success, 1994	1·10	1·10
4557	$1.50 Players celebrating Premiership success, 1998	1·10	1·10
4558	$1.50 Entrance to Highbury	1·10	1·10
4559	$1.50 Dressing room	1·10	1·10
4560	$1.50 Arsenal defenders with trophies and shield, 1998	1·10	1·10
4561	$1.50 Aston Villa emblem at Villa Park	1·10	1·10
4562	$1.50 Villa Park stands at night	1·10	1·10
4563	$1.50 Stands and boxes	1·10	1·10
4564	$1.50 Trinity Road Stand, Villa Park	1·10	1·10
4565	$1.50 Holte End Stand, Villa Park	1·10	1·10
4566	$1.50 Aston Villa supporters	1·10	1·10
4567	$1.50 Reebok Stadium, Bolton (empty)	1·10	1·10
4568	$1.50 Players celebrating Division 1 play-off success, 2001	1·10	1·10
4569	$1.50 Fan holding banner	1·10	1·10
4570	$1.50 Fans celebrating promotion	1·10	1·10
4571	$1.50 Team with Division 1 Cup, 2001	1·10	1·10
4572	$1.50 Reebok Stadium during match	1·10	1·10
4573	$1.50 Everton squad, 2001–02	1·10	1·10
4574	$1.50 Manager Duncan Ferguson, 2000	1·10	1·10
4575	$1.50 Statue of Dixie Dean (former player)	1·10	1·10
4576	$1.50 Everton supporters watching match	1·10	1·10
4577	$1.50 Goodison Park Stadium	1·10	1·10
4578	$1.50 Everton squad, League champions, 1969–70	1·10	1·10
4579	$1.50 Ipswich Town players and Division 1 Cup, 2000	1·10	1·10
4580	$1.50 Ipswich Town squad, 2001–02	1·10	1·10
4581	$1.50 Manager George Burley shaking hands with David Sheepshanks (chairman)	1·10	1·10
4582	$1.50 Pablo Counago running	1·10	1·10
4583	$1.50 Matt Holland (captain), 2001	1·10	1·10
4584	$1.50 George Burley with Manager of the Year Award, 2001	1·10	1·10
4585	$1.50 Anfield Stadium, Liverpool	1·10	1·10
4586	$1.50 Players celebrating Worthington Cup victory, 2000–01	1·10	1·10
4587	$1.50 Players celebrating F.A. Cup victory, 2000–01	1·10	1·10
4588	$1.50 Supporters watching match	1·10	1·10
4589	$1.50 Victorious U.E.F.A. Cup Team, 2000–01	1·10	1·10
4590	$1.50 Players, manager and fans, Treble victory parade, 2001	1·10	1·10
4591	$1.50 Billy Meredith, Denis Law and Bobby Charlton (former players)	1·10	1·10
4592	$1.50 Treble Trophies, 1998–9	1·10	1·10
4593	$1.50 Different views of Old Trafford before 1950s	1·10	1·10
4594	$1.50 Different views of Old Trafford since 1974	1·10	1·10
4595	$1.50 Players celebrating third successive Premiership title, 2000–01	1·10	1·10
4596	$1.50 George Best, Bryan Robson and David Beckham (players)	1·10	1·10
4597	$1.50 Exterior of Ibrox Stadium, Glasgow	1·10	1·10
4598	$1.50 Rangers' European Cup winning team, 1972	1·10	1·10
4599	$1.50 Scottish F.A. and Premier League trophies, 2000	1·10	1·10
4600	$1.50 Ibrox Stadium from the air	1·10	1·10
4601	$1.50 Match in progress at Ibrox Stadium	1·10	1·10
4602	$1.50 Scottish flag and emblem celebrating ninth consecutive league victory, 1997	1·10	1·10

501 Father Christmas and House

2001. Christmas. Father Christmas. Multicoloured.

4603	15c. Type **501**	20	10
4604	50c. Father Christmas with snowman and fir trees	45	25
4605	$1 Father Christmas ice-skating	80	45
4606	$4 Father Christmas with children	3·00	3·50
MS4607	107×76 mm. $6 Father Christmas eating mince pie	4·50	5·50

502 Princess Diana wearing Blue Dress and Tiara

2001. 40th Birth Anniv of Diana, Princess of Wales. Multicoloured.

4608	$1.50 Type **502**	1·25	1·25
4609	$1.50 Wearing white evening dress	1·25	1·25
4610	$1.50 In red dress and tiara	1·25	1·25
MS4611	80×102 mm. $6 Wearing pearl choker	4·50	5·50

503 John F. Kennedy

2001. Presidents John F. Kennedy and Ronald Reagan Commemoration. Multicoloured.

4612	$1.50 Type **503**	1·10	1·10
4613	$1.50 John Kennedy and Empire State Building	1·10	1·10
4614	$1.50 John Kennedy with aircraft	1·10	1·10
4615	$1.50 Ronald Reagan in *Hellcats of the Navy* (film)	1·10	1·10
4616	$1.50 Wearing dark suit and red tie	1·10	1·10
4617	$1.50 Ronald Reagan with American flag	1·10	1·10
MS4618	Two sheets. (a) 67×83 mm. $6 John F. Kennedy. (b) 78×105 mm. $6 Ronald Reagan on telephone	10·00	11·00

2001. Centenary of Nobel Prizes. Prize Winners of 1901 (Nos. 4619/22 and 4629/30) and 1921 (others). As T 595 of Ghana. Multicoloured.

4619	75c. Emil von Behring (Medicine)	70	35
4620	90c. Wilhelm Rontgen (Physics)	75	40
4621	$1 Jacobus van't Hoff (Chemistry)	80	45
4622	$1.50 Frederic Passy (Peace)	1·10	1·10
4623	$1.50 Albert Einstein as a young man (horiz)	1·10	1·10

4624	$1.50 Smoking a pipe (horiz)	1·10	1·10
4625	$1.50 Wearing grey (horiz)	1·10	1·10
4626	$1.50 In pink jumper (horiz)	1·10	1·10
4627	$1.50 Wearing black jacket (horiz)	1·10	1·10
4628	$1.50 In blue jumper (horiz)	1·10	1·10
4629	$2 Jean-Henri Dunant (Peace)	1·60	1·75
4630	$3 Rene Sully-Prudhomme (Literature)	2·00	2·25
MS4631	65×87 mm. $6 Albert Einstein wearing Panama hat	4·50	5·00

504 Brown Horse with Pale Mane

2001. Chinese New Year ("Year of the Horse"). Tang Dynasty Ceramic Horses. Multicoloured.

4632	$1.50 Type **504**	1·10	1·25
4633	$1.50 Purple dappled horse	1·10	1·25
4634	$1.50 Blue horse	1·10	1·25
4635	$1.50 Brown horse with short mane	1·10	1·25
MS4636	100×70 mm. $4 Brown horse with flowers on bridle	3·00	3·25

505 Ruby

2001. Precious Stones and Minerals. Multicoloured.

4637	$1.50 Type **505**	1·60	1·60
4638	$1.50 Sardonyx	1·60	1·60
4639	$1.50 Sapphire	1·60	1·60
4640	$1.50 Opal	1·60	1·60
4641	$1.50 Topaz	1·60	1·60
4642	$1.50 Turquoise	1·60	1·60
4643	$1.50 Garnet	1·60	1·60
4644	$1.50 Amethyst	1·60	1·60
4645	$1.50 Aquamarine	1·60	1·60
4646	$1.50 Diamond	1·60	1·60
4647	$1.50 Emerald	1·60	1·60
4648	$1.50 Pearl	1·60	1·60
4649	$1.50 Ruby (horiz)	1·60	1·60
4650	$1.50 Diamond (horiz)	1·60	1·60
4651	$1.50 Sapphire (horiz)	1·60	1·60
4652	$1.50 Opal (horiz)	1·60	1·60
4653	$1.50 Turquoise (horiz)	1·60	1·60
4654	$1.50 Jade (horiz)	1·60	1·60
MS4655	Three sheets. (a) 82×76 mm. $6 Uraninite (horiz). (b) 92×56 mm. $6 Calcite (horiz). (c) $6 68×78 mm. $6 Quartz	18·00	19·00

Nos. 4637/42 (polished gem stones), 4643/8 (polished gem stones) and 4649/54 (raw stones).

506 U.S. Flag as Statue of Liberty with Grenada Flag

2002. "United We Stand". Support for Victims of 11 September 2001 Terrorist Attacks.

4656	**506**	$2 multicoloured	1·60	1·75

507 Queen Elizabeth with Prince Philip

2002. Golden Jubilee. Multicoloured.

4657	$2 Type **507**	2·00	2·00
4658	$2 Queen Elizabeth in open carriage	2·00	2·00
4659	$2 Queen Elizabeth in evening dress	2·00	2·00
4660	$2 Queen Elizabeth on bridge	2·00	2·00
MS4661	76×109 mm. $6 Queen Elizabeth in Grenadier uniform	5·50	6·00

508 Dale Earnhardt and Car, 1980, within "1"

2002. Dale Earnhardt (stock car driver) Commemoration. Designs each within figures commemorating his seven Winston Cup victories. Multicoloured.

4662	$2 Type **508**	1·60	1·60
4663	$2 With Winston Cup and car, 1986	1·60	1·60
4664	$2 With Winston Cup, 1987	1·60	1·60
4665	$2 With Winston Cup, 1990	1·60	1·60
4666	$2 With Winston Cup, 1991	1·60	1·60
4667	$2 With Winston Cup, 1993	1·60	1·60
4668	$2 With Winston Cup, 1994	1·60	1·60

509 Cannon on C.S.S. *Teaser* (gunboat)

2002. Naval Campaigns of the American Civil War.

4669	**509**	$1 deep brown, brown and black	1·00	1·00
4670	-	$1 deep brown, brown and black	1·00	1·00
4671	-	$1 deep brown, brown and black	1·00	1·00
4672	-	$1 deep brown, brown and black	1·00	1·00
4673	-	$1 deep brown, brown and black	1·00	1·00
4674	-	$1 deep brown, brown and black	1·00	1·00
4675	-	$1.25 brown, ochre and black	1·10	1·10
4676	-	$1.25 brown, ochre and black	1·10	1·10
4677	-	$1.25 brown, ochre and black	1·10	1·10
4678	-	$1.25 brown, ochre and black	1·10	1·10
4679	-	$1.25 brown, ochre and black	1·10	1·10
4680	-	$1.25 brown, ochre and black	1·10	1·10
4681	-	$1.50 deep brown, brown and black	1·40	1·40
4682	-	$1.50 deep brown, brown and black	1·40	1·40
4683	-	$1.50 deep brown, brown and black	1·40	1·40
4684	-	$1.50 deep brown, brown and black	1·40	1·40
4685	-	$1.50 deep brown, brown and black	1·40	1·40
4686	-	$1.50 deep brown, brown and black	1·40	1·40
4687	-	$1.50 brown, yellow and black	1·40	1·40
4688	-	$1.50 brown, yellow and black	1·40	1·40
4689	-	$1.50 brown, yellow and black	1·40	1·40
4690	-	$1.50 brown, yellow and black	1·40	1·40
4691	-	$1.50 brown, yellow and black	1·40	1·40
4692	-	$1.50 brown, yellow and black	1·40	1·40
MS4693		Four sheets, each 72×94 mm. (a) $6 blue, violet and black. (b) $6 violet, blue and black. (c) $6 deep blue, blue and black. (d) $6 deep blue, blue and black	23·00	24·00

DESIGNS: No. 4669, Type **509**; 4670, U.S. gunboats on James River, 1862; 4671, U.S.S. *Tyler* (river gunboat); 4672, U.S.S. *Maratanza* (steam gunboat); 4673, U.S.S. *Metacomet* (steam gunboat); 4674, U.S.S. *Rattler* (river gunboat); 4675, C.S.S. *Tennessee* (ironclad); 4676, U.S.S. *Hartford* (Federal flagship) engaging the *Tennessee*; 4677, U.S.S. *Chickasaw* (river monitor); 4678, U.S.S. *Ossipee* (steam sloop); 4679, Battle of Mobile Bay; 4680, U.S.S. *Chickasaw* in action at Mobile Bay; 4681, C.S.S. *Alabama* (commerce raider); 4682, U.S.S. *Kearsarge* engaging the *Alabama*; 4683, U.S.S. *Hatteras* (paddle gunboat); 4684, C.S.S. *Alabama* attacking merchant ships; 4685, C.S.S. *Sumte* (cruiser); 4686, U.S.S. *Kearsarge* (steam sloop); 4687, C.S.S. *H.L. Hunley* (submarine); 4688, U.S.S. *Cumberland* (frigate); 4689, C.S.S. *Old Dominion* (blockade runner); 4890, U.S.S. *Housatonic* (steam sloop); 4691, U.S.S. *Hartford*; 4692, U.S.S. *Essex* (river gunboat); **MS**4693a U.S.S. *Monitor* (monitor); **MS**4693b Captain Semmes of C.S.S. *Alabama*; **MS**4693c C.S.S. *Tennessee*; **MS**4693d C.S.S. *Florida* (steam corvette).

510 Mickey Mouse

2002. Birth Centenary (2001) of Walt Disney. Mickey Mouse. Multicoloured.

4694	$1 Type **510**	80	80
4695	$1 In "The Nifty Nineties", 1941	80	80
4696	$1 In "Magician Mickey", 1937	80	80
4697	$1 In "Steamboat Willie", 1928	80	80
4698	$1 In "Fantasia", 1940	80	80
4699	$1 In "Mickey Mouse Club", 1955	80	80
4700	$1 In "Cactus Kid", 1930	80	80
4701	$1 In "The Prince and the Pauper", 1990	80	80
4702	$1 In "Brave Little Tailor", 1938	80	80
4703	$1 In "Canine Caddy", 1941	80	80

511 Chiune Sugihara

2002. Chiune Sugihara (Japanese Consul-general in Lithuania who rescued Jews, 1939–40) Commemoration.

4704	**511**	$2 multicoloured	1·60	1·75

512 Mawensi Peak, Kilimanjaro, Kenya

2002. International Year of Mountains. Multi.

4705	$2 Type **512**	1·60	1·75
4706	$2 Mt. Stanley, Uganda	1·60	1·75
4707	$2 Mt. Taweche, Nepal	1·60	1·75
4708	$2 Mt. San Exupery, Argentina	1·60	1·75
MS4709	100×70 mm. $6 Mt. Aso, Japan	4·75	5·00

No. 4708 is inscribed "Exuprey" in error.

513 Church and Bunting

2002. Year of Eco Tourism. Multicoloured.

4710	$1 Type **513**	1·00	1·00
4711	$1 Little ringed plover	1·00	1·00
4712	$1 Relaxing on the patio	1·00	1·00
4713	$1 Scuba diver and grouper	1·00	1·00
4714	$1 Two red snappers	1·00	1·00
4715	$1 Four yachts	1·00	1·00
MS4716	75×75 mm. $6 Purple martin over Grenada	6·00	6·50

514 Downhill Skiing

2002. Winter Olympic Games, Salt Lake City. Multicoloured.

4717	$2 Type **514**	1·60	1·75
4718	$2 Slalom skiing	1·60	1·75
MS4719	82×102 mm. Nos. 4717/18	3·00	3·50

515 Scout in Canoe

2002. 20th World Scout Jamboree, Thailand. Multicoloured.

4720	$2 Type **515**	1·60	1·75
4721	$2 Paddling canoe	1·60	1·75
4722	$2 Scout blowing bugle	1·60	75
4723	$2 Scout saluting	1·60	1·75
MS4724	100×74 mm. $6 Thai scout saluting	4·75	5·00

Nos. 4720/3 were printed together, se-tenant, with the backgrounds forming a composite design.

516 Heidi Klum (model)

2002. APS Stampshow 2002, Atlantic City, U.S.A. Designs showing Heidi Klum. Multicoloured.

4725	$1.50 Type **516**	1·10	1·10
4726	$1.50 Wearing chain earrings	1·10	1·10
4727	$1.50 Close-up of face	1·10	1·10

517 Army Bear

2002. Centenary of the Teddy Bear (1st issue). Multicoloured.

4728	$2 Type **517**	1·60	1·60
4729	$2 Navy bear	1·60	1·60
4730	$2 Air Force bear	1·60	1·60
4731	$2 Marines bear	1·60	1·60
4732	$2 Basketball bear (38×50 mm)	1·60	1·60
4733	$2 Judo bear (38×50 mm)	1·60	1·60
4734	$2 Golf bear (38×50 mm)	1·60	1·60
4735	$2 Baseball bear (38×50 mm)	1·60	1·60
4736	$5 Bear with red hat and pink bow	3·25	3·50
4737	$5 Bear with clogs	3·25	3·50
4738	$5 Bear with black hat and scarf	3·25	3·50
4739	$5 Bear with cheeses	3·25	3·50

Nos. 4728/31 (armed forces bears), 4732/5 (sports bears) and 4736/9 (Dutch bears).

See also Nos. 4851/**MS**4852.

518 "Mareep No. 179"

2002. Pokémon (children's cartoon series). Multicoloured.

4740	$1.50 Type **518**	1·10	1·10
4741	$1.50 "Sunkern No. 191"	1·10	1·10
4742	$1.50 "Teddiursa No. 216"	1·10	1·10
4743	$1.50 "Swinub No. 220"	1·10	1·10
4744	$1.50 "Murkrow No. 198"	1·10	1·10
4745	$1.50 "Snubbull No. 209"	1·10	1·10
MS4746	66×91 mm. $6 "Togepi No. 175"	4·50	5·00

518a Elvis Presley wearing Stetson

2002. 25th Death Anniv of Elvis Presley.

4747	**518a**	$1 multicoloured	1·50	1·25

518b Axel, Zeeland

2002. "Amphilex '02" International Stamp Exhibition, Amsterdam (1st issue). Dutch Women's Traditional Costumes. Sheet, 120×140 mm, containing vert designs, each 37×51 mm. Multicoloured.

MS4748 $3 Type **518b**; $3 Eerde, Noord-Brabant; $3 Volendam, Noord-Holland 5·50 6·00

518c Jacobus van't Hoff (Chemistry, 1901)

2002. "Amphilex '02" International Stamp Exhibition, Amsterdam (2nd issue). (a) Dutch Nobel Prize Winners. Sheet 150×100 mm.

MS4749 $1.50 Type **518c** (black and green); $1.50 Peace Prize medal (black and blue); $1.50 Pieter Zeeman (Physics, 1902) (black and mauve); $1.50 Johannes van der Waals (Physics, 1910) (black and cinnamon); $1.50 Tobias Asser (Peace, 1911) (black and lilac); $1.50 Heike Kamerlingh Onnes (Physics, 1913) (black and green) 5·50 6·00

(b) Dutch Lighthouses. Sheet 128×148 mm. Multicoloured.

MS4750 $1.50 Schiermonnikoog; $1.50 Texel; $1.50 Egmond; $1.50 Scheveningen; $1.50 Schouwen; $1.50 Hellevoetsluis 6·50 6·50

519 Molly Middleton and Father

2002. Shirley Temple in Our Little Girl. Showing scenes from film. Multicoloured.

4751	$1.50 Type **519**	1·10	1·10
4752	$1.50 Family picnic	1·10	1·10
4753	$1.50 Molly with Sniff (dog), talking to park keeper	1·10	1·10
4754	$1.50 Molly with parents and another man	1·10	1·10
4755	$1.50 Molly and Sniff on see-saw	1·10	1·10
4756	$1.50 Molly with Sniff in pink bonnet	1·10	1·10
4757	$2 Molly with mother (vert)	1·60	1·60
4758	$2 Molly watching clown (vert)	1·60	1·60
4759	$2 Molly at prayer (vert)	1·60	1·60
4760	$2 Leaning on father's knee (vert)	1·60	1·60
MS4761	105×76 mm. $6 Molly wearing pink dress	4·50	5·00

520 World Trade Center

2002. 1st Anniv of 11 September 2001 Attacks. Sheet 140×98 mm.

MS4762 **520** $6 multicoloured 4·50 5·00

521 Popeye at Santa Croce Basilica, Florence

2002. "Popeye" (cartoon character). Multicoloured.

4763	$1.50 Type **521**	1·10	1·10
4764	$1.50 With Brutus at Eiffel Tower, Paris	1·10	1·10
4765	$1.50 On steps of Parthenon, Athens	1·10	1·10
4766	$1.50 With Olive Oyl near Rialto Bridge, Venice	1·10	1·10
4767	$1.50 Near Big Ben, London	1·10	1·10
4768	$1.50 In front of traditional wooden building, Norway	1·10	1·10
4769	$2 Sweet Pea on footballer's back (29×44 mm)	1·60	1·60
4770	$2 Jeep (dog) tugging footballer's shorts (29×44 mm)	1·60	1·60
4771	$2 Popeye in football kit (29×44 mm)	1·60	1·60
4772	$2 Brutus being kicked by Popeye (29×44 mm)	1·60	1·60
MS4773	Three sheets. (a) $6 Brutus heading ball (44×29 mm). (b) $6 Popeye celebrating with footballers (44×29 mm). (c) $6 Popeye and Leaning Tower of Pisa (50×78 mm)	13·00	14·00

Nos. 4769/72 were issued together, se-tenant, with the backgrounds forming a composite design.

522 Common Morpho

2002. Flora and Fauna. Multicoloured.

4774	$1.50 Type **522**	1·10	1·10
4775	$1.50 Blue night butterfly	1·10	1·10
4776	$1.50 Small flambeau	1·10	1·10
4777	$1.50 Grecian shoemaker	1·10	1·10
4778	$1.50 Orange-barred sulphur	1·10	1·10
4779	$1.50 Cramer's mesene	1·10	1·10
4780	$1.50 Honey bee	1·10	1·10
4781	$1.50 Dragonfly	1·10	1·10
4782	$1.50 Milkweed bug	1·10	1·10
4783	$1.50 Bumble bee	1·10	1·10
4784	$1.50 Migratory grasshopper	1·10	1·10
4785	$1.50 Monarch caterpillar	1·10	1·10
4786	$1.50 *Boletus crocipodius*	1·10	1·10
4787	$1.50 *Boletus edulis*	1·10	1·10
4788	$1.50 *Flammulina velutipes*	1·10	1·10
4789	$1.50 *Amanita phalloides*	1·10	1·10
4790	$1.50 *Tricholoma aurantium*	1·10	1·10
4791	$1.50 *Amanita muscaria*	1·10	1·10
4792	$1.50 Blue whale and calf	1·10	1·10
4793	$1.50 Pygmy sperm whale	1·10	1·10
4794	$1.50 Humpback whale	1·10	1·10
4795	$1.50 Killer whale	1·10	1·10
4796	$1.50 Bowhead whale	1·10	1·10
4797	$1.50 Grey whale	1·10	1·10
MS4798	Four sheets, each 105×76 mm. (a) $6 Figure of eight butterfly. (b) $6 Hercules beetle. (c) $6 Sharp-scaled parasol (fungus). (d) $6 Blue whale	19·00	20·00

Nos. 4780/5 (butterflies), 4775/80 (insects), 4781/6 (fungi) and 4787/92 (whales) were each printed together, se-tenant, with the backgrounds forming composite designs.

Nos. 4792/7 and 4791 are inscribed "Flammula" or "Aminita", both in error.

523 Norman Wisdom

2002. Sir Norman Wisdom (comedian and actor).

4799	**523**	$1.50 multicoloured	1·50	1·50

523a Madonna and Child, Four Angels and St. Francis (Cimabue)

2002. Christmas. Religious Paintings. Multicoloured.

4800	15c. Type **523a**	20	10
4801	25c. "Madonna and Child and Two Angels" (Cimabue) (vert)	25	15
4802	50c. "Madonna Enthroned" (detail) (Cimabue) (vert)	45	25
4803	$1 "Madonna Enthroned" (Cimabue) (vert)	80	45
4804	$4 "Madonna and Child, Four Angels and St. Francis" (Cimabue) (vert)	3·00	3·50
MS4805	72×98 mm. $6 "Nativity" (Perugino) (vert)	4·75	5·50

524 Astrolabe

2002. 550th Birth Anniv of Amerigo Vespucci (explorer). Sheets containing T 524 and similar multicoloured designs.

MS4806 Two sheets. (a) 98×147 mm. $3 Type **524**; $3 Amerigo Vespucci; $3 Caravel (b) 138×90 mm. $3 Map of South America and caravel (horiz); $3 Compass and caravels (horiz); $3 Map of Africa and Europe (horiz) Set of 2 sheets 9·50 10·50

MS4807 Two sheets. (a) 78×85 mm. $6 Compass rose (28×42 mm). (b) 85×78 mm. $6 Globe and scroll (28×42 mm) Set of 2 sheets 8·00 9·00

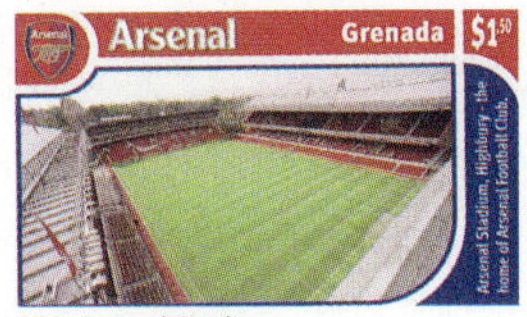

525 Arsenal Stadium

2002. Arsenal Football Club -- FA Community Shield Winners. Sheet 125×125 mm containing T 525 and similar horiz designs. Multicoloured.

MS4808 $1.50 Type **525**; $1.50 Footballers celebrating after winning goal; $1.50 Winning team with FA Shield; $1.50 Arsenal 2002/3 squad with trophies; $1.50 Gilberto with FA Shield; $1.50 Arsenal FC, Stadium and new crest 5·50 6·00

2002. British Football Clubs. Eight sheets, each 125×125 mm, containing horiz designs as T 525. Multicoloured.

MS4809 Arsenal 2001/2 $1.50 Team with FA Cup, Millennium Stadium, Cardiff; $1.50 Winning team with Championship banners; $1.50 Premiership Trophy winning team; $1.50 Winning team with Premiership trophy on rostrum; $1.50 Players celebrating FA Cup winning goal; $1.50 Arsene Wenger (Manager) and Tony Adams (captain) with trophies 5·50 6·00

MS4810 Celtic $1.50 Celtic Park Stadium; $1.50 Martin O'Neill with SPL Trophy; $1.50 Henrik Larsson; $1.50 Celtic squad of 2002/3; $1.50 Celtic scoring goal; $1.50 Celtic Park 5·50 6·00

MS4811 Chelsea $1.50 Crowd watching floodlit match; $1.50 Cup Winners' Cup winning team with trophy, 1988; $1.50 Chelsea supporters at match; $1.50 "The Shed End" at Stamford Bridge ground; $1.50 Stamford Bridge stadium; $1.50 Winning team with FA Cup, 2000 5·50 6·00

MS4812 Liverpool $1.50 Anfield's Centenary stand seen from main stand; $1.50 First team squad, 2002/3; $1.50 Gerard Houllier and Phil Thompson; $1.50 Milan Baros; $1.50 Vladimir Smicer and Danny Murphy; $1.50 The Kop seen from Anfield Road end 5·50 6·00

MS4813 Manchester City $1.50 Maine Road stadium (from above); $1.50 Fans with Division One Champions flags; $1.50 Kevin Keegan (manager) with Division 1 trophy; $1.50 Winning Division 1 with trophy; $1.50 Winning team with medals; $1.50 Maine Road stadium (from stands) 5·50 6·00

MS4814 Manchester United $1.50 David Beckham; $1.50 First team squad, 2002/3; $1.50 Old Trafford stadium (aerial view); $1.50 Players after Ole Gunnar Solskjaer's 100th goal; $1.50 Manchester United fans; $1.50 North stand, Old Trafford 5·50 6·00

MS4815 Norwich City $1.50 Players at The Nest (NCFC ground 1908–35); $1.50 Norwich City players,1971/2; $1.50 With Milk Cup trophy, 1985; $1.50 Carrow Road stadium; $1.50 Winning UEFA Cup,1993; $1.50, Match of 1958/9 5·50 6·00

MS4816 Tottenham Hotspur $1.50 Fans watching match; $1.50 Spurs v. Fulham match, 2001; $1.50 Spurs v. Liverpool match, 2002; $1.50 Winning UEFA Cup team, 1972; $1.50 Players celebrating win against Chelsea, 2002; $1.50 Club Shield and White Hart Lane stadium 5·50 6·00

526 Johan Mjallby (Sweden)

2002. World Cup Football Championship, Japan and Korea. Miniature sheets containing T 526 and similar vert designs. Multicoloured.

MS4817 165×82 mm. $1.50 Type **526**; $1.50 Magnus Hedman (Sweden); $1.50 Fredrik Ljungberg (Sweden); $1.50 Khalilou Fadiga (Senegal); $1.50 El Hadji Diouf (Senegal); $1.50 Papa Bouba Diop (Senegal) 5·50 6·00

MS4818 165×82 mm. $1.50 Roberto Carlos (Brazil); $1.50 Juninho Paulista (Brazil); $1.50 Ronaldinho (Brazil); $1.50 Johan Walem (Belgium); $1.50 Marc Wilmots (Belgium); $1.50 Bart Goor (Belgium) 5·50 6·00

MS4819 Four sheets, each 82×82 mm. (a) $3 Henrik Larsson (Sweden); $3 Niclas Alexandersson (Sweden). (b) $3 Khalilou Fadiga (Senegal); $3 Bruno Metsou (coach, Senegal). (c) $3 Luiz Felipe Scolari (coach, Brazil); $3 Ronaldo (Brazil). (d) $3 Wesley Sonck (Belgium); $3 Robert Waseige (coach, Belgium) Set of 4 sheets 14·00 15·00

527 Foundation Logo and US Flag

2002. National Law Enforcement and Firefighters Children's Foundation. Sheet 75×115 mm.

MS4820 **527** $6 multicoloured 6·50 7·00

528 Princess Diana wearing Bow Tie

2002. 5th Death Anniv of Diana, Princess of Wales. Two sheets containing T 528 and similar vert designs. Multicoloured.

MS4821 137×120 mm. $2 Type **528**; $2 Wearing blue dress; $2 Wearing red and white jacket and hat; $2 Wearing pink dress 5·50 6·00

MS4822 70×100 mm. $6 Wearing headset 4·75 5·50

529 Pres Reagan on the DMZ in Korea, 1983

2002. Presidents Ronald Reagan and John F. Kennedy. Four sheets containing T 529 and similar multicoloured designs.

MS4823 175×117 mm. $1.50 Type **529**; $1.50 Pres Reagan with Prime Minister Margaret Thatcher; $1.50 Speaking at the Berlin Wall, 1987; $1.50 Signing INF Treaty with Soviet Secretary General Gorbachev; $1.50 With Egyptian President Sadat, 1981; $1.50 At home with horse Set of 4 sheets 6·00 6·50

MS4824 175×117 mm. $1.50 Pres Kennedy meeting with Cabinet; $1.50 Signing a bill into law; $1.50 Meeting Civil Rights leaders; $1.50 With astronaut John Glenn; $1.50 On the campaign trail; $1.50 With Jacqueline Kennedy arriving in Dallas, 1963 6·00 6·50

MS4825 Two sheets, each 82×115 mm. (a) $6 Pres. Reagan making speech. (b) Pres. Kennedy making speech (vert) Set of 2 sheets 8·50 9·50

530 Magnifying Glass and Globe

2002. 50th Anniv of International Federation of Stamp Dealers' Associations. P 14.

4826 **530** $2 multicoloured 1·60 1·75

531 Ram

2003. Chinese New Year ("Year of the Ram").

MS4827 130×123 mm. **531** $1.25×4, multicoloured 3·25 3·50

532 Toy Airplane

2003. Learning Resources (1st series). M Gears Childrens' Construction Sets. Sheet 222×152 mm containing T 532 and similar horiz designs showing toys. Multicoloured.

MS4828 $2 Type **532**; $2 Dune buggy; $2 Robot; $2 Racing car 5·50 6·00

See also **MS**4853.

533 David Brown

2003. Columbia Space Shuttle Commemoration. Sheet 184×145 mm, containing T 533 and similar vert designs showing crew members. Multicoloured.

MS4829 $1 Type **533**; $1 Commander Rick Husband; $1 Laurel Clark; $1 Kalpana Chawla; $1 Payload Commander Michael Anderson; $1 Pilot William McCool; $1 Ilan Ramon 5·50 5·50

534 Grenada Dove and "CC" Emblem

2003. 30th Anniv of CARICOM.

4830 **534** $1 multicoloured 1·00 1·00

535 "A Harlot in Repose"

2003. Japanese Art. Paintings of Women by Taiso Yoshitoshi. Multicoloured.

4831 75c. Type **535** 60 35

4832 $1 "A 'Shakuni' or Geisha, who serves Wine or Sake" 75 50

4833 $1.25 "A 'Joro', or Low Ranking Prostitute, having a Snack" 90 65

4834 $3 "A Geisha known as a 'Geiko' or Entertainer relaxing" 2·00 2·25

MS4835 175×135 mm. $2 "Enjoying a Cool Evening Breeze in a Pleasure Boat"; $2 "A Fukagawa Waitress carrying a Wooden Table laden with Food"; $2 "A Spoiled Unmarried Woman pretending to be displeased with an Admirer"; $2 "A Coy Young Girl biting her Sleeve pretending to be Embarrassed" 5·50 6·50

MS4836 66×132 mm. $6 "A Geisha about to Board a Party-Boat" (detail) 4·50 5·50

536 "St. Catherine Altarpiece" (detail of St. Dorothy, St. Agnes and St. Cunigonde)

2003. 450th Death Anniv of Lucas Cranach the Elder (artist). Multicoloured.

4837 50c. Type **536** 45 25

4838 75c. "The St. Catherine Altarpiece" (detail of St. Margaret) (vert) 60 35

4839 $1.25 "The St. Catherine Altarpiece" (detail of St. Barbara) (vert) 90 65

4840 $3 "The St. Catherine Altarpiece" (detail of young girl) (vert) 2·00 2·25

MS4841 158×191 mm. $2 "Lot and his Daughters" (detail); $2 "David and Bathsheba" (detail); $2 "The Agony in the Garden" (detail); $2 "The Adoration of the Magi" 5·50 6·50

MS4842 120×100 mm. $6 "Samson and Delilah" (detail) (vert) 4·50 5·50

537 "Jardin Aux Tournesols"

2003. 85th Death Anniv of Gustav Klimt (artist). Multicoloured.

4843 15c. Type **537** 20 15

4844 25c. "L'allee Aux Poulets" 25 15

4845 75c. "Allee Dans Le Parc Du Schloss Kammer" 60 35

4846 $1 "Portrait de Johanna Staude" 75 45

4847 $1.25 "Portrait de Friederike Maria Beer" 90 65

4848 $3 "Portrait de Mada Primavesi" 2·00 2·25

MS4849 180×105 mm. $2 "La Jeune Fille"; $2 "Les Amies"; $2 "Le Berceau"; $2 "La Vie et la Mort" 5·50 6·50

MS4850 81×102 mm. $6 "Portrait de Margaret Stonborough-Wittgenstein". Imperf 4·50 5·50

538 Embroidery Teddy Bear

2003. Centenary of the Teddy Bear (2nd issue). Embroidered Fabric Teddy Bears. Self-adhesive. Imperf.

4851 **538** $15 ochre, silver and rose-red 8·50 9·50

MS4852 126×157 mm. No. 4851×4 32·00 35·00

539 Children reading Books

2003. Learning Resources (2nd series). Reading Rods. Sheet 222×156 mm containing T 539 and similar horiz designs. Multicoloured.

MS4853 $2 Type **539**; $2 Girl playing with reading rods; $2 Children writing; $2 Teacher and children with book 5·50 6·50

540 Silvere Maes (1939)

2003. Centenary of Tour de France Cycle Race. Designs showing past winners. Multicoloured.

MS4854 160×100 mm. $2 Type **540**; $2 Jean Lazarides (1946); $2 Jean Robic (1947); $2 Gino Bartali (1948) 6·50 7·00

MS4855 160×100 mm. $2 Fausto Coppi (1949); $2 Ferdinand Kubler (1950); $2 Hugo Koblet (1951); $2 Fausto Coppi (1952) 6·50 7·00

MS4856 160×100 mm. $2 Roger Walkowiak (1956); $2 Jacques Anquetil (1957); $2 Charly Gaul (1958); $2 Federico Bahamontes (1959) 6·50 7·00

MS4857 Three sheets, each 100×70 mm. (a) $6 Fausto Coppi (1949). (b) $6 Ferdinand Kubler (1950). (c) $6 Jacques Anquetil (1964) Set of 3 sheets 17·00 18·00

541 Louis Bleriot and *Bleriot* XI (first powered flight across English Channel, 1909)

2003. Centenary of Powered Flight. Multicoloured.

MS4858 128×150 mm. $2 Type **541**; $2 Johnnie Johnson (World War II Ace pilot) and aircraft; $2 Wright Brothers and *Flyer I* (first powered flight, 1903); $2 Jacqueline Cochran and aircraft (first woman to break sound barrier) 6·50 7·00

MS4859 119×119 mm. $2 Alcock and Brown and Vickers FB-27 *Vimy* (first non-stop transatlantic flight, 1919); $2 Amelia Earhart and aircraft; $2 Chuck Yeager and Bell XS-1 rocket airplane (first manned supersonic flight, 1947); $2 Charles Lindbergh and Ryan NYP Special *Spirit of St. Louis* (first solo non-stop transatlantic flight, 1927) 6·50 7·00

542 Queen Elizabeth II flanked by Bishops

2003. 50th Anniv of Coronation. Multicoloured.

4860 $2 Type **542** 1·60 1·60

4861 $2 Holy Communion 1·60 1·60

4863 $2 Enthronement of Queen 1·60 1·60

4864 $2 Queen and Duke of Edinburgh 1·60 1·60

4865 $2 Queen leaving Westminster Abbey in Coronation Coach 1·60 1·60
4866 $2 Queen and family on Palace balcony 1·60 1·60
4867 $2 Westminster Abbey 1·60 1·60
MS4868 106×76 mm. $6 Queen in Coronation Coach 5·00 5·50

No. 4867 is inscr "Floodlit Mall" in error.

543 Levera Pond

2003. International Year of Freshwater. Mult.
MS4869 150×88 mm. $2 Type **543**; $2 Concord Falls; $2 Lake Antoine 4·25 4·50
MS4870 100×70 mm. $6 Lake Grand Etang 4·25 4·50

544 Clive Andrews

2003. Centenary of Circus Clowns. Multicoloured.
MS4871 119×194 mm. $2 Type **544**; $2 Bell Bozo; $2 Bumpsy; $2 Anne Fratellini 5·50 6·50
MS4872 146×218 mm. $2 Stag (acrobat); $2 Olga and Regina Kolpensky with white poodles; $2 Brad Byers; $2 Tiger 5·50 6·50

No. **MS**4871 shows clowns and is cut in the shape of a clown. No. **MS**4872 shows other circus performers and is cut in the shape of a circus elephant.

545 Aerial View of Campus

2003. St. George's University School of Medicine. Multicoloured.
4873 75c. Type **545** 65 45
4874 $1 University buildings 80 80

546 General Sir Mike Jackson and Tank

2003. Operation "Iraqi Freedom". Showing commanders of British armed forces in Iraq (MS4875) or British aircraft, tanks and ships (MS4876). Multicoloured.
MS4875 186×130 mm. $1 Type **546**; $1 Air Vice-Marshal Glenn Torpy and RAF Jaguar fighter; $1 Air Marshal Brian Burridge and RAF Harrier GR7 fighter; $1 Major General Tony Milton and warship; $1 Major General Peter Wall and soldiers; $1 Major General Barney White-Spunner ; $1 Admiral Sir Alan West and aircraft carrier; $1 Air Chief Marshal Peter Squire and surveillance aircraft 6·50 7·00
MS4876 186×130 mm. $1 Royal Marine Gazelle helicopter; $1 Royal Marine hovercraft; $1 RAF Jaguar fighter; $1 HMS *Liverpool*; $1 RAF Harrier GR7; $1 Challenger 2 tank; $1 RAF Chinook helicopter; $1 RAF Tornado F3 6·50 7·00

547 Prince William with Bouquet

2003. 21st Birthday of Prince William of Wales. Multicoloured.
MS4877 79×145 mm. $3 Type **547**; $3 Wearing blue T-shirt; $3 In close-up, looking down 7·50 8·00
MS4878 105×76 mm. $6 Prince William (horiz) 6·00 6·50

548 Yellow Allamanda

2003. Birds, Fish and Flowers of the Caribbean. Multicoloured.
4879 25c. Type **548** 30 15
4880 50c. Queen of the Night (flower) 50 15
4881 75c. Anthurium 70 35
4882 $1 Smallmouthed grunt (fish) 90 90
4883 $1 Spotfinned butterflyfish 90 90
4884 $1 Gold coney (fish) 90 90
4885 $1.25 Osprey 1·40 1·40
4886 $1.25 Red-eyed vireo (bird) 1·40 1·40
4887 $1.25 Northern oriole 1·40 1·40
4888 $3 Oleander 2·25 2·50
4889 $3 Night sergeant (fish) 2·25 2·50
4890 $3 Bahama pintail (duck) 2·25 2·50
MS4891 105×85 mm. $2 Blue passion flower; $2 Chinese hibiscus; $2 Poinsettia; $2 Bird of Paradise (flower) 6·50 7·00
MS4892 105×85 mm. $2 Spot-finned hogfish ("Cuban Hogfish"); $2 Blueheaded wrasse; $2 Black-capped basslet ("Black Cap Gramma"); $2 Cherub angelfish ("Cherubfish") 6·50 7·00
MS4893 105×85 mm. $2 Slaty-capped shrike vireo; $2 Common flicker ("Northern Flicker"); $2 Blackburnian warbler; $2 Common tody flycatcher 7·00 7·50
MS4894 Three sheets, each 96×66 mm. (a) $6 Shrimp plant. (b) $6 Banded butterflyfish. (c) $6 Blue grosbeak (vert) Set of 3 sheets 17·00 18·00

549 Spinosaurus

2003. Prehistoric Animals. Multicoloured.
MS4895 178×117 mm. $2 Type **549**; $2 Herrerasaurus; $2 Protarchaeopteryx; $2 Sinosauropteryx 6·00 6·50
MS4896 178×117 mm. $2 Allosaurus; $2 Crylophosaurus; $2 Eoraptor; $2 Caudipteryx 6·00 6·50
MS4897 Two sheets, each 98×68 mm. (a) $6 Triceratops (vert). (b) $6 Archaeopteryx (vert) Set of 2 sheets 11·00 12·00

550 "Madonna and Child" (detail) (Giotto) from Church of Ognissanti

2003. Christmas. Multicoloured.
4898 35c. Type **550** 30 20
4899 75c. "The Ognissanti Madonna" (detail) (Giotto) 65 35
4900 $1 "Madonna of the Angels" (detail) (Giotto) 80 45
4901 $4 "Madonna and Child" (Giotto) from Florentine Church of San Giorgio alla Costa 3·00 3·50
MS4902 74×95 mm. $6 "Holy Family with John the Baptist and St. Elizabeth" (Nicolas Poussin) (horiz) 4·50 5·50

551 "At the Palmist's" (Jean-Baptiste Le Prince)

2003. 300th Anniv of St. Petersburg. "Treasures of the Hermitage". Multicoloured.
4903 45c. Type **551** 45 25
4904 $1 "A Visit to Grandmother" (Louis Le Nain) (horiz) 75 45
4905 $1.50 "Musicale" (Dirck Hals) (horiz) 1·10 75
4906 $3 "A Young Woman in the Morning" (Frans van Mieris the Elder) 2·00 2·25
MS4907 118×181 mm. $2 "Louis, Grand Dauphin de France" (Louis Tocqué); $2 "Count P. A. Stroganov as a Child" (Jean-Baptiste Greuze); $2 "A Boy with a Book" (Jean- Baptiste Perroneau); $2 "A Girl with a Doll" (Jean-Baptiste Greuze) 5·50 6·50
MS4908 (a) 78×65 mm. $6 "The Lute Player" (Caravaggio). Imperf. (b) 67×77 mm. $6 "The Spoiled Child" (Jean-Baptiste Greuze). Imperf 10·00 11·00

552 "The Spring Tonic"

2003. 25th Death Anniv of Norman Rockwell. Multicoloured.
MS4909 149×179 mm. $2 Type **552**; $2 "The Facts of Life"; $2 "The Proper Gratuity"; $2 "The Runaway" 5·50 6·50
MS4910 91×99 mm. $6 "Boy with Carriage" (detail) (horiz) 4·50 5·50

553 "Claude Drawing"

2003. 30th Death Anniv of Pablo Picasso (artist). Multicoloured.
MS4911 132×168 mm. $2 Type **553**; $2 "Claude and Paloma at Play" (detail); $2 "Paloma at Three Years Old"; $2 "Paloma with an Orange" 5·50 6·50
MS4912 72×99 mm. $6 "Paloma in Blue". Imperf 4·50 5·50

554 Brown and White Monkey

2004. Chinese New Year ("Year of the Monkey"). Multicoloured.
MS4913 116×141 mm. $1.50 Type **554**; $1.50 Proboscis monkey; $1.50 Light brown monkey; $1.50 Grey monkey 4·00 4·50

555 *Lissy* (sail training ship) on River Weser

2004. Opening of Weser Tunnel, Germany. Sheet 113×82 mm.
MS4914 **555** $6 multicoloured 4·00 4·50

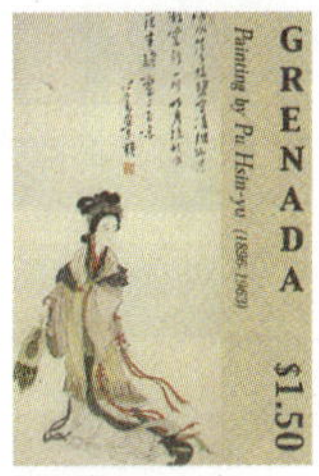

556 Chinese Lady

2004. Hong Kong 2004 International Stamp Exhibition. Paintings by Pu Hsin-yu. Multicoloured.
MS4915 156×112 mm. $1.50 Type **556**; $1.50 Two monkeys in tree; $1.50 Mountain landscape with temple and waterfall; $1.50 Bird in tree with red flower; $1.50 Man sat by gnarled tree; $1.50 Man in red 5·50 6·50
MS4916 107×105 mm. $3 Branch; $3 Bearded man 4·00 4·50

557 Muffy

2004. Arthur the Aardvark and Friends. Multicoloured.
MS4917 165×134 mm. $1.50 Type **557**; $1.50 Francine; $1.50 Brain with potted plants; $1.50 D.W. as astronaut in space; $1.50 Sue Ellen with insects in jam jars; $1.50 Arthur with model of solar system 5·50 6·50
MS4918 150×184 mm. $2 Arthur as Robin Hood; $2 Arthur as Rumpelstiltskin; $2 Arthur with sword; $2 Arthur as King Arthur 5·50 6·50
MS4919 150×184 mm. $1.50 Arthur holding bunch of flowers; $1.50 D.W. holding valentines card; $1.50 Binky holding box of chocolates; $1.50 Muffy holding out box of chocolates; $1.50 D.W. as Cupid; $1.50 Francine and hearts 5·50 6·50
MS4920 150×183 mm. $2 Arthur as Robinson Crusoe; $2 Arthur and map of Treasure Island; $2 Arthur as Tom Sawyer; $2 Arthur swinging on rope 5·50 6·50

558 Concorde, French Flag and Concorde at Take-off

2004. Last Flight of Concorde (2003). Multicoloured.

MS4921	88×129 mm. $3 Type **558**; $3 Concorde, French flag and spectators at perimeter fence; $3 Concorde, French flag and control panel (first flight, Toulouse, Fran, 1969)	8·50	8·50
MS4922	88×129 mm. $3 Concorde, Union Jack, Singapore flag and roof of building; $3 Concorde, Union Jack, Singapore flag and skyscraper; $3 Concorde, Union Jack, Singapore flag and street (London to Singapore flights, 1977)	8·50	8·50
MS4923	88×129 mm. $3 Concorde and dome of US Capitol; $3 Concorde, Capitol building and top of statue; $3 Concorde, Capitol and plinth of statue (last flight, Paris to Washington, 2003)	8·50	8·50

559 Lord Killanin (President of Olympic Committee, 1972—80)

2004. Olympic Games, Athens, Greece. Multicoloured.

4924	75c. Type **559**	60	35
4925	$1 Athletes running 10,000 metre race (horiz)	75	45
4926	$1.25 Commemorative plaque (detail)	90	65
4927	$3 "The Wreath of Olive" (Greek art)	2·00	2·25

560 American Horse

2004. American Indians. Multicoloured.

4928–4939	75c.×12 Type **560**; Blue Bird; Crow King; Crow Man; Gall; Good Horse; Goose; John Grass; Rain-in-the-Face; Red Cloud; Sitting Bull; Wild Horse	7·25	7·50
4940–4945	$1.25×6 "Return of the Blackfoot War Party" (F. Remington); "Ridden Down" (F. Remington); "Smoke Signal" (F. Remington); "Buffalo Hunt" (C.Rssell); "Scouts" (C. Russell); "Piegans" (C. Russell)	6·00	6·25

561 Marilyn Monroe

2004. Marilyn Monroe Commemoration. Mult.

4948	50c. Type **561**	65	55
MS4949	127×116 mm. $2 Wearing one-shoulder red top; $2 Wearing strapless orange top; $2 Wearing white top; $2 Wearing off-shoulder pink top	5·50	6·50

562 Deng Xiaoping

2004. Deng Xiaoping (Chinese politician) Commemoration. Sheet 99×68 mm.

MS4950	$6 multicoloured	4·50	5·50

563 Pres. George W. Bush

2004. Military Operations in Iraq. Sheet 127×118 mm containing T 563 and similar horiz designs. Multicoloured.

MS4951	$2 Type **563**; $2 Paul Bremer; $2 Col. James Hickey; $2 Soldier and Iraqi civilians	6·50	7·00

564 Jan Svehlik (Czech Republic footballer)

2004. European Football Championships 2004, Portugal. T 564 and similar multicoloured designs.

MS4952	147×84 mm. $2 Type **564**; $2 Franz Beckenbauer (German footballer); $2 Karol Dobias (Czech Republic footballer); $2 Crvena Zvezda football ground	5·50	6·50
MS4953	98×84 mm. $6 Czech Republic football team, 1976 (50×37 mm)	4·50	5·50

565 Pope John Paul II

2004. 25th Anniv of the Pontificate of Pope John Paul II. Sheet 163×154 mm containing T 565 and similar horiz designs. Multicoloured.

MS4954	$2 Type **565**; $2 With Mikhail Gorbachev; $2 With arms stretched overhead; $2 Meeting with Polish deportees; $2 With Patriarchate of the Russian Orthodox Church	7·50	8·00

2004. 60th Anniv of D-Day Landings. As T 404 of Dominica. Multicoloured.

4955	45c. Don Sheppard, Royal Engineers	70	40
4956	$1 Air Chief Marshall Sir Arthur Tedder	1·25	75
4957	$1.50 Douglas Kay, 13th/18th Royal Hussars	1·60	1·25
4958	$3 Gen. Sir Bernard Montgomery	2·75	3·00
MS4959	176×107 mm. $2 Germans detect Allied invasion; $2 Germans prepare to engage Allied invasion fleet; $2 British Paratrooper at Merville Battery; $2 Paratroopers and captured Merville Battery	7·50	8·00
MS4960	176×107 mm. $2 HMS *Belfast* fires on German shore batteries; $2 Allies pound German coastal defences; $2 Air strikes over Utah Beach. $2 Allied troops in landing craft approaching Omaha Beach	7·50	8·00
MS4961	Two sheets, each 100×70 mm. (a) $6 PLUTO (Pipe Line Under The Ocean). (b) $6 Fake Landing Craft	13·00	14·00

566 GN Stirling Single

2004. Bicentenary of Steam Locomotives. Mult.

4962–4970	$1×9 Type **566**; Beyer Peacock Mogul; Prussian GB; George Stephenson (engineer); James Nasmyth; James Nasmyth's steam hammer; Raven Z Class; Sir Vincent Raven; Bronze statue of Thomas Cook	8·50	9·00
4971–4979	$1×9 SR Schools class; Indian Railways SGS class; Borsig tram, Paraguay; Richard Trevithick; Herbert Garratt; Isambard Kingdom Brunel; Replica of Trevithick's Coalbrookdale engine; Rhodesian 20th class Garratt; Brunel's Royal Saltash Bridge	8·50	9·00
4980–4988	$1×9 SR Lord Nelson; South African 16CR class Pacific; Florisdorf Fireless, Austria; GWR 57XX class; GWR Castle class; GWR Saint class; GWR Star Class; GWR 28XX class; GWR 51XX class (all horiz)	8·50	9·00
MS4989	Three sheets, each 96×66 mm. (a) $6 California Zephyr (horiz). (b) $6 Steam locomotive, Cumbres and Toltec Railway (horiz). (c) $6 Indian Pacific locomotive (horiz)	16·00	17·00

567 Elvis Presley

2004. 50th Anniv of Elvis Presley's First Record. Multicoloured.

4990–4995	$1.50×6 Type **567**; Playing guitar with overhead microphone (grey background); Playing guitar with overhead microphone (stone background); Playing guitar and singing; Portrait photograph; Playing guitar with overhead microphone (grey background)	7·00	7·50

568 Princess Juliana in 1947 and Palace at Soestdijk

2004. Queen Juliana of the Netherlands Commemoration.

4996	**568**	$2 multicoloured	1·60	1·60

569 Meriwether Lewis

2004. Bicentenary of Lewis and Clark's Expedition to the American West and Pacific North West. T 569 and similar vert designs. Multicoloured.

MS4997	154×180 mm. $3 Type **569**; $3 Sacagawea; $3 William Clark	6·00	6·50

2004. United Nations International Year of Peace. As T 409 of Dominica. Multicoloured.

MS4998	137×77 mm. $3 Jody Williams (Nobel Peace Prize winner, 1997); $3 International Campaign to Ban Landmines; $3 Princess Diana	6·00	6·50

570 Delta II Rocket at blast off

2004. The Mars Exploration Rover Mission. Mult.

MS4999	170×127 mm. $1.50×6 Type **570**; Entering Mars atmosphere; Parachute descent; Landing on the surface; Rover leaving lander; Rover on Mars surface	7·00	7·50

571 *Queen Mary 2* and Queen Elizabeth II (image scaled to 48% of original size)

2004. Ocean Liners. Multicoloured.

MS5000	125×208 mm. $2 Type **571**; $2 *Queen Elizabeth II* and couple at dining table; $2 *Queen Mary* and passengers embarking; $2 *Queen Elizabeth* and couple on deck	7·00	7·50
MS5001	125×203 mm. $2 *Titanic*; $2 *Normandie*; $2 *Mauritania*; $2 *Lusitania*	7·00	7·50
MS5002	115×85 mm. $6 *Queen Mary 2*	6·00	6·50

2004. Centenary of FIFA (Federation Internationale de Football Association). As T 413 of Dominica. Multicoloured.

MS5003	192×96 mm. $2 Gabriel Batistuta, Argentina; $2 Cafu, Brazil; $2 Michel Platini; $2 Gianluca Vialli, Italy	5·50	6·50
MS5004	118×87 mm. $6 Oliver Kahn, Germany	4·75	5·50

572 Pau Gasol, Memphis Grizzlies

2004. US National Basketball Association Players (1st series). Multicoloured.

5005	75c. Type **572**	90	75
5006	75c. Allen Iverson, Philadelphia 76ers	90	75
5007	75c. Stephon Marbury	90	75

See also Nos. 5028/30.

573 President Reagan with Mother Teresa, 1985

2004. Ronald Reagan (US President 1981–9) Commemoration. Multicoloured.

MS5008	170×117 mm. $2 Type **573**; $2 With Gen. Colin Powell, 1988; $2 With Queen Elizabeth II, 1981; $2 With Canadian Prime Minister Brian Mulroney	5·50	6·50

574 Babe Ruth

2004. Centenary of Baseball World Series. T 574 and similar vert designs showing George Herman "Babe" Ruth. Multicoloured.

MS5009	125×115 mm. $2 Type **574**; $2 Looking sideways to left; $2 Standing by helicopter; $2 Wearing stripes	5·50	6·50
MS5010	112×113 mm. $2 Wearing blue cap, facing right; $2 Wearing blue cap, facing left; $2 Wearing stripes and cap; $2 Looking sideways to left, wearing blue cap	5·50	6·50

575 "Merry Christmas" (1920)

2004. Christmas. 25th Death Anniv of Norman Rockwell (artist). Multicoloured.

5011	35c. Type **575**	35	20
5012	75c. "Yuletide Merriment" (1931)	60	35
5013	$1 "Dressing Up" (1916)	75	45
5014	$4 "Christmas" (1927)	3·00	3·50
MS5015	70×100 mm. $6 "The London Coach" (1925) (cover for Saturday Evening Post)	4·75	5·50

576 "Chrysanthemums, Cocks and Hens"

2005. Chinese New Year ("Year of the Rooster"). Paintings by Qi Baishi. Multicoloured.

MS5016	140×108 mm. $1×4 Type 576×4	3·00	3·25
MS5017	70×100 mm. $4 "Taro Leaves and Double Hens"	3·00	3·25

577 Turkey Vulture

2005. Birds of Prey. Multicoloured.

MS5018	160×140 mm. $1.50 Type **577**; $1.50 American bald eagle; $1.50 Peregrine Falcon; $1.50 Prairie Falcon; $1.50 Northern goshawk; $1.50 Cooper's hawk	7·50	8·00
MS5019	82×102 mm. $6 Californian condor (horiz)	6·50	7·00

578 Cheetah

2005. Wild Cats. Multicoloured.

MS5020	115×177 mm. $1.50 Type **578**; $1.50 Lion; $1.50 White tiger; $1.50 Leopard; $1.50 Bobcat; $1.50 Bengal tiger	7·50	8·00
MS5021	97×72 mm. $6 Jaguar	5·50	6·00

579 *Heraclides machaonides*

2005. Butterflies. Multicoloured.

MS5022	177×133 mm. $1.50 Type **579**; $1.50 *Limenitis archippus*; $1.50 *Cithaerias merolina*; $1.50 *Troides hypolitus*; $1.50 *Ornithoptera goliath procus*; $1.50 *Ornithoptera priamus alberio*	7·00	7·50
MS5023	107×89 mm. $6 *Papilio demoleus malayanus*	6·00	6·50

580 Majungatholus

2005. Dinosaurs. Multicoloured.

MS2026	225×110 mm. $2 Pteranodon; $2 Dimorphodon; $2 Pterodactylus; $2 Ramphorhyncus	6·00	6·50
MS2027	Three sheets, each 95×95 mm. (a) $6 Spinosaurus. (b) $6 Pliosaur. (c) $6 Tapejara Imperator	13·00	14·00
MS5024	155×115 mm. $2 Type **580**; $2 Diplodocus; $2 Willo; $2 Velociraptor	6·00	6·50
MS5025	225×110 mm. $2 Archelon; $2 Ammonite; $2 Plesiosaur; $2 Xiphactinus	6·00	6·50

2005. US National Basketball Association Players (2nd series). As T 572. Multicoloured.

5028	75c. Zydrunas Ilgauskas	90	75
5029	75c. Dwyane Wade	90	75
5030	$3 Tracy McGrady	2·75	3·00

581 "Deities overseeing the Transplanting of Rice" (Japanese, artist unknown)

2005. International Year of Rice (2004). Multicoloured.

MS5031	137×92 mm. $3 Type **581**; $3 "The Taoist God overseeing the Rice Planting by the San Chay People of Vietnam" (artist unknown); $3 "Scene of Women transplanting Rice in Late Spring Rain" (Hiroshige)	6·00	6·50

582 Cathedral of Immaculate Conception

2005. Hurricane Ivan—the Aftermath. Sheet 130×90 mm containing T 582 and similar horiz designs showing hurricane damage. Multicoloured.

MS5032	$2 Type **582**; $2 Anglican Church; $2 York House (House of Parliament); $2 Springs Sub-office	5·50	6·50

583 Elvis Presley (1955)

2005. 70th Birth Anniv of Elvis Presley. Multicoloured.

5033-5038	$1.50×6 Type **583**; On outdoor stage, Tupelo (1957); In room, playing guitar (1959); Performing in Memphis Charities Benefit Show (1961); On stage in "68 Special" Show (1968); With guitar on Fall Tour (1970)	7·00	7·50
5039-5044	$1.50×6 *In Jailhouse Rock*, holding door (1957); Playing guitar in *Girl Happy* (1964); On saddle in *Tickle Me* (1965); Playing piano in *Speedway* (1968); Playing guitar in *The Trouble with Girls* (1969); On studio stage in *That's the Way It Is* (1970)	7·00	7·50

584 *Tenement Gentleman, 1947*

2005. Ozu Yasujiro (film director) Commemoration. Sheet 145×175 mm containing T 584 and similar vert designs. Multicoloured.

MS5045	$2 Type **584**; $2 *Tokyo Story*, 1953; $2 *A Hen in the Wind*, 1948; $2 *Floating Weeds, 1959*	5·50	6·50

585 King William I (1815—40)

2005. Silver Jubilee of Queen Beatrix of the Netherlands. T 585 and similar vert designs showing Dutch royalty. Multicoloured.

MS5046	170×235 mm. $2×8 Type **585**; William II (1840—9); William III (1849—90); Wilhelmina (1890—1948); Juliana (1948—80); Queen Beatrix; Crown Prince Willem-Alexander; Princess Catharina-Amalia	11·00	12·00

The stamps within the two horizontal rows of four making up **MS**5046 have composite background designs.

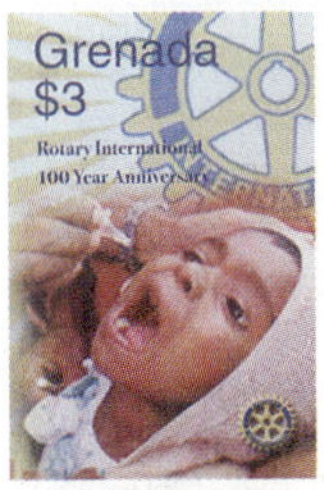

586 Giving Vaccine to Boy

2005. Centenary of Rotary International. Multicoloured.

MS5047	135×105 mm. $3 Type **586**; $3 David Edwards (Governor of District 7030) and his wife Donna; $3 Paul Harris (founder)	6·00	6·50
MS5048	97×67 mm. $6 Richard King (President 2001—2) and two girls	4·50	5·00

The first two designs in **MS**5047 have a composite background design showing the Rotary emblem.

587 "21 Curves" Supply Line from Rangoon to China

2005. 60th Anniv of the End of World War II. "The Route to Victory". Multicoloured.

5049	$2 Type **587**	1·60	1·60
5050	$2 British troops in jungle, Burma	1·60	1·60
5051	$2 Troops at Magwe airstrip	1·60	1·60
5052	$2 Allied troops escorting prisoners	1·60	1·60
5053	$2 Allied troops parachuting behind enemy lines	1·60	1·60
5054	$2 Allied troops firing	1·60	1·60
5055	$2 German troops moving through buildings	1·60	1·60
5056	$2 Aerial view of bridge still under German control	1·60	1·60
MS5057	Two sheets, each 106×97 mm. (a) $6 Troops discussing next move. (b) $6 Allied troops in ruined buildings	8·00	8·50

Nos. 5049/52 depict the Burma Campaign, December 1941 to August 1945, and Nos. 5053/6 Operation Market Garden, Dutch/German border, 17 September 1944.

588 Troops wading Ashore from Landing Craft, D-Day

2005. 60th Anniv of Victory in Europe Day. Multicoloured.

5058	$2 Type **588**	1·75	1·75
5059	$2 Allied soldiers	1·75	1·75
5060	$2 Surrendering German troops	1·75	1·75
5061	$2 Crowd waving US flags on VE Day	1·75	1·75
MS5062	96×66 mm. $6 Fall of Berlin to armies of Soviet Union	6·00	6·50

589 Airstrikes over Pacific Islands

2005. 60th Anniv of Victory in Japan Day. Multicoloured.

5063	$2 Type **589**	1·75	1·75
5064	$2 Allied forces storming beach	1·75	1·75
5065	$2 Gen. McArthur going ashore, Philippines	1·75	1·75
5066	$2 Surrender of Japanese armies	1·75	1·75
MS5067	95×65 mm. $6 Victory celebrations	6·00	6·50

590 Rainbow over Victoria Falls, Africa

2005. EXPO 2005 World Exposition, Aichi, Japan. Multicoloured.

5068	$1.50 Type **590**	1·40	1·40
5069	$1.50 Bald eagle	1·40	1·40
5070	$1.50 Caribbean coral reef	1·40	1·40
5071	$1.50 Mother with new baby	1·40	1·40
5072	$1.50 Neil Armstrong, first man on Moon	1·40	1·40
5073	$1.50 Bee pollinating flower	1·40	1·40

591 Albert Einstein and Galaxy

2005. 50th Death Anniv of Albert Einstein (physicist). Multicoloured.

MS5074	154×90 mm. $2 Type **591**; $2 Einstein and "$E=mc^2$"; $2 Einstein (facing sideways); $2 Einstein as young man	5·50	6·50
MS5075	100×70 mm. $6 Einstein smoking and "$E=mc^2$"	4·75	5·50

592 "Tell's Memorial" Statue (Richard Kissling), Altdorf, Switzerland

2005. Death Bicentenary of Friedrich von Schiller (poet and dramatist). Multicoloured.

5076 $3 Type **592** 2·00 2·25
5077 $3 Scene from modern *William Tell* DVD film 2·00 2·25
5078 $3 William Tell play by Natural Theatre Company of UK, 1997–8 2·00 2·25
MS5079 96×67 mm. $6 Scene from William Tell (horiz) 4·75 5·50

593 Admiral Lord Nelson

2005. Bicentenary of the Battle of Trafalgar. Multicoloured.

5080 $2 Type **593** 2·00 2·00
5081 $2 Napoleon Bonaparte 2·00 2·00
5082 $2 HMS *Victory* 2·00 2·00
5083 $2 "The Nelson Touch" 2·00 2·00
MS5084 100×78 mm. $6 "After the Battle of the Nile" (illustration by Thomas Rowlandson) (horiz) 7·00 7·50

594 "How 'bout a Trade, Dad? My Broccoli, for your Chocolate Cake"

2005. Dennis the Menace (American cartoon character created by Hank Ketcham). Mult.

5085 $2 Type **594** 1·60 1·60
5086 $2 "It's not a Good Idea to Scratch your Nose while you're Finger-Painting, Joey" 1·60 1·60
5087 $2 "I'll bet you were the Top of your Class at Grandpa School" 1·60 1·60
5088 $2 "Boy, I'm Glad I don't have to Clean his Sandbox" 1·60 1·60
5089 $2 "Grandpa got a New Knee Last Year, but it Still Sits like the Old One" 1·60 1·60
5090 $2 "Joey an' Me don't have any Money, but Here's a Brick for the New Church Building" 1·60 1·60
5091 $2 "Good News, Mrs. Wilson! Our Club elected you Vice President in Charge of Cookies!" 1·60 1·60
5092 $2 "I Think the Boy's a 'Born' Realtor. He's been Instrumental in the Sale of Half the Houses in This Neighborhood" 1·60 1·60

595 Private Johnson Beharry VC

2005. Award of Victoria Cross to Private Johnson Beharry. Sheet 70×87 mm.

MS5093 **595** $5 multicoloured 5·00 5·50

596 Jules Verne

2005. Death Centenary of Jules Verne (writer). Multicoloured.

MS5094 110×120 mm. $3 Type **596**; $3 Oval portrait; $3 Jules Verne holding cigar 7·00 7·50
MS5095 100×100 mm. $6 Rocket approaching Moon (*From the Earth to the Moon*) 5·50 6·00

597 Hans Christian Andersen

2005. Birth Bicentenary of Hans Christian Andersen (writer). Multicoloured.

MS5096 150×90 mm. $3 Type **597**; $3 Andersen (looking left); $3 Seated 6·00 6·50
MS5097 70×100 mm. $6 Tombstone 4·50 5·00

598 Purple-throated Carib

2005

5098 **598** 10c. multicoloured 10 10

599 Tel Aviv

2005. TAIPEI 2005 International Stamp Exhibition. Multicoloured.

MS5111 85×115 mm. $2 Type **599**; $2 Empire State Building, New York; $2 Taipei; $2 Eiffel Tower, Paris 5·50 6·50

600 Pope John Paul II with Lech Walesa (Polish trade unionist)

2005. Pope John Paul II Commemoration.

5112 **600** $4 multicoloured 4·00 4·25

601 Prince Charles and Mrs. Camilla Parker-Bowles

2005. Royal Wedding. Designs showing Prince Charles and Mrs. Camilla Parker-Bowles. Multicoloured.

5113 $2 Type **601** 1·90 1·90
5114 $2 Holding book (vert) 1·90 1·90
5115 $2 Holding posy (vert) 1·90 1·90

602 "The Nativity" (detail) (Correggio)

2005. Christmas. Multicoloured.

5116 25c. Type **602** 20 10
5117 75c. "Virgin and Child" (detail) (Lorenzo Lotto) 60 50
5118 $1 "The Holy Family" (detail) (Lorenzo Lotto) 75 55
5119 $5 "Madonna and Child with the Saints" (detail) (Lorenzo Lotto) 4·50 5·00
MS5120 70×100 mm. $6 "Allegory of Music" (Filippo Lippi) 4·75 5·50

603 Stadium

2005. Centenary of Chelsea Football Club. Multicoloured.

5121 $1.50 Type **603** 75 55
5122 $1.50 "1905 2005" and emblem 1·10 1·25
5123 $1.50 Petr Cech, Hernan Crespo and John Terry 1·10 1·25
5124 $1.50 Chelsea team with Premier League trophy 1·10 1·25
5125 $1.50 Fans with "Chelsea FC" banner 1·10 1·25
5126 $1.50 Team with "Champions 2004–2005" banner 1·10 1·25
5127 $1.50 Chelsea players 1·10 1·25
5128 $1.50 Jose Mourinho (manager) 1·10 1·25
5129 $1.50 Emblem and stadium 1·10 1·25
5130 $1.50 Team with FA Charity Shield 1·10 1·25

604 Victory Parade

2005. Liverpool FC Champions of Europe. Multicoloured.

5131 $1.50 Type **604** 1·10 1·25
5132 $1.50 Steven Gerrard and Rafael Benitez (manager) with UEFA Champions League Cup 1·10 1·25
5133 $1.50 Entrance to Liverpool FC ground 1·10 1·25
5134 $1.50 Aerial view of Anfield stadium 1·10 1·25
5135 $1.50 Club banner 1·10 1·25
5136 $1.50 Triumphant team waving to crowd 1·10 1·25
5137 $1.50 Fans with flags 1·10 1·25
5138 $1.50 Match in progress at Anfield stadium 1·10 1·25
5139 $1.50 Victorious team on pitch at end of match 1·10 1·25
5140 $1.50 Victory parade with "Liverpool" banners 1·10 1·25

605 "The Two Hounds" (Hui-Tsung)

2005. Chinese New Year ("Year of the Dog").

5141 **605** $1 multicoloured 1·10 1·25
MS5142 100×70 mm. **605** $4 multicoloured (50×37 mm) 3·00 3·25

606 Pope Benedict XVI

2006. Election of Pope Benedict XVI.

5143 **606** $2 multicoloured 2·00 2·00

2006. 80th Birthday of Queen Elizabeth II. As T 432 of Dominica. Multicoloured.

5144 $3 Queen Elizabeth II (looking left) 2·75 2·75
5145 $3 Princess Elizabeth as teenager 2·75 2·75
5146 $3 Painting of Queen Elizabeth II 2·75 2·75
5147 $3 Queen Elizabeth II (full face) 2·75 2·75
MS5148 120×120 mm. $6 Wearing pearls and dark blue dress 5·50 6·00

607 USA Team

2006. World Cup Football Championship, Germany (1st issue). Designs showing national teams. Multicoloured.

5149-5180 $1.50×32 Type **607**; Brazil; Iran; Netherlands; Czech Republic; Ghana; Serbia & Montenegro; Sweden; Spain; Australia; Ivory Coast; Portugal; Angola; South Korea; Mexico; Poland; Costa Rica; Switzerland; France; England; Croatia; Italy; Ecuador; Japan; Argentina; Trinidad & Tobago; Paraguay; Saudi Arabia; Germany; Ukraine; Tunisia; Togo 27·00 29·00

2006. 80th Birth Anniv of Marilyn Monroe (actress). As T 452 of Gambia. Multicoloured.

5181 $3 Marilyn Monroe 2·00 2·25

2006. Winter Olympic Games, Turin. As T 431 of Dominica but vert. Multicoloured.

5182 75c. Poster for Winter Olympic Games, Lake Placid, 1980 60 50
5183 75c. Poster for Olympic Games, Turin, 2006 60 50
5184 90c. Italy 2006 Winter Olympic €1 Olympic flame stamp (horiz) 75 65
5185 90c. Switzerland 1948 Winter Olympics 30c.+10c. ski-runner stamp 75 65
5186 $2 Poster for Winter Olympic Games, St. Moritz, 1948 1·60 1·75
5187 $3 Switzerland 1948 Winter Olympics 20c.+10c. ice hockey stamp 2·00 2·25

2006. Washington 2006 International Stamp Exhibition. As T 453 of Gambia. Multicoloured.

5188 $3 Rosa Parks 2·00 2·25

608 Stylized Brazil Player (2002) and Trophy

2006. World Cup Football Championship, Germany (2nd issue). Each showing cartoon player in colours of winning team and World Cup trophy. Multicoloured.

5189	75c. Type **608**	60	50
5190	90c. Germany (1990)	75	65
5191	$3 France (1998)	2·00	2·25

609 World Cup Trophy

2006. World Cup Football Championship, Germany (3rd issue). Self-adhesive. Imperf.

5192	**609**	$6 multicoloured	4·00	4·25

2006. 400th Birth Anniv of Rembrandt Harmenszoon van Rijn (artist). As T 458 of Gambia showing paintings. Multicoloured.

5193	50c. "The Little Jewish Bride" (detail)	45	40
5194	$1 "Young Man in Velvet Cap" (detail)	80	80
5195	$1.50 "Old Woman Sleeping" (detail)	1·10	1·10
5196	$3 "Woman Reading" (detail)	2·00	2·25
5197	$3 "Young Woman with Flowers in her Hair" (detail)	2·00	2·25
5198	$3 "Portrait of a Seated Woman" (detail)	2·00	2·25
5199	$3 "Alijdt Adriaensor" (detail)	2·00	2·25
5200	$3 "Amalia van Solms" (detail)	2·00	2·25
5201	$6 "Portrait of a Seated Man" (detail) (69×99 mm)	3·75	4·00
MS5202	70×100 mm. $6 "Portrait of a Scholar" (detail). Imperf	3·75	4·00

610 *Graf Zeppelin* D-LZ-127

2006. 50th Death Anniv of Ludwig Durr (Zeppelin engineer). Multicoloured.

5203	$4 Type **610**	2·75	3·00
5204	$4 *Graf Zeppelin* LT	2·75	3·00
5205	$4 *Graf Zeppelin* L26	2·75	3·00

611 Scene from "The Magic Flute"

2006. 250th Birth Anniv of Wolfgang Amadeus Mozart (composer). Sheet 100×70 mm.

MS5206	**611** $6 multicoloured	3·75	4·00

612 "Girls! Girls! Girls!"

2006. 50th Anniv of Elvis Presley's Film Debut. Sheet 190×127 mm containing T 612 and similar vert designs showing film posters. Multicoloured.

5207	$3 Type **612**	2·50	2·50
5208	$3 "Jailhouse Rock"	2·50	2·50
5209	$3 "Paradise–Hawaiian Style"	2·50	2·50
5210	$3 "It Happened at the World's Fair"	2·50	2·50

613 Halley's Comet

2006. Space Anniversaries. Multicoloured. (a) 20th Anniv of Giotto Comet Probe.

MS5211	150×100 mm. $2×6 Type **613**; Ariane V14 rocket; Halley's Comet (going into distance); Halley's Comet (blue and black background); Giotto Probe Launcher; Halley's Comet and Milky Way	8·50	9·50

The two central stamps in No. **MS**5211 form a composite design showing Ariane V14 rocket on Giotto Probe Launcher.

(b) 50th Anniv of "Sputnik 1".

MS5212	150×100 mm. $2×4 Sergei Korolev; "Sputnik 1" orbiting Earth; Inside "Sputnik 1"; "Sputnik 1" capsule	6·00	6·50

(c) 30th Anniv (2005) of "Apollo"/"Soyuz" Test Project.

MS5213	150×100 mm. $2×4 "Apollo" rocket; Apollo CM with adapter; "Soyuz" spacecraft at Baykonur Cosmodrome; "Soyuz" (all vert)	6·00	6·50
MS5214	Three sheets, each 100×70 mm. (a) $6 Impactor and flyby spacecraft (Comet Tempel I Deep Impact Mission, 2005). (b) $6 Stardust encounters Comet Wild 2, 2004. (c) $6 Space Shuttle "Discovery", 2005	11·00	13·00

614 *Santa Maria* sinking, December 25 1492

2006. 500th Death Anniv of Christopher Columbus. Multicoloured.

5215	$1.50 Type **614**	1·25	1·00
5216	$2 *Santa Maria* replica (vert)	1·75	1·75
5217	$3 Christopher Columbus ashore in New World (vert)	2·25	2·25
5218	$4 Columbus and sailing ship (vert)	2·50	2·50
MS5219	100×70 mm. $6 Columbus's fleet setting sail again, 1493 (horiz)	3·75	4·00

615 *Nymphalis antiopa* (Mourning Cloak)

2006. Butterflies. Multicoloured.

5220	10c. Type **615**	15	15
5221	25c. *Libytheana bachmanii* (snout butterfly)	30	15
5222	$1 *Tithorea pinthias*	90	75
5223	$2 Hypolimnas misippus (Diadem)	1·50	1·50
5224	$4 *Megisto rubricata* (red satyr)	2·75	3·00
5225	$5 *Taygetis chrysogone*	3·00	3·25
5226	$10 *Pierella hortona*	5·50	6·50
5227	$20 *Morpho aega*	9·50	11·00

615a Princess Maxima

2006. Princess Maxima of the Netherlands. Sheet 150×190 mm containing T 615a and similar vert designs. Multicoloured.

5236	$1.50 Type **615a**	1·10	1·10
5237	$1.50 Princess Maxima (half-length portrait)	1·10	1·10

616 Shepherd

2006. Christmas. Showing details from painting "The Adoration of the Shepherds" by Rubens. Multicoloured.

5238	25c. Type **616**	25	15
5239	50c. Virgin Mary	40	30
5240	75c. Shepherd (wearing cloak)	60	45
5241	$1 Baby Jesus	80	65
5242	$2 As Type **616**	1·50	1·60
5243	$2 As No. 5229	1·50	1·60
5244	$2 As No. 5230	1·50	1·60
5245	$2 As No. 5231	1·50	1·60

617 Betty Boop

2006. Betty Boop. Multicoloured.

MS5246	180×128 mm. $1.50×6 Type **617**; Standing, leaning forward, with hands on knees; Seated, with right leg outstretched; Standing with hands clasped; Standing with arms outstretched; Standing with arms and left leg raised	6·50	7·00
MS5247	132×108 mm. $2×4 Standing with hands clasped; Standing with arms outstretched; Standing with arms and left leg raised; With microphone	6·00	6·50
MS5248	100×72 mm. $3×2 Looking over shoulder (head); Seated (body) (both horiz)	4·00	4·25
MS5249	76×106 mm. $3×2 Seated in chair, holding mirror; Wearing Hawaiian style grass skirt, lei and decorated straw hat	4·00	4·25

The two rows of stamps within **MS**5246 each have "BETTY BOOP" printed across them, forming a composite design.

618 Three Players

2007. Arsenal Football Club's New Emirates Stadium, Islington, London. Multicoloured.

MS5250	210×166 mm. $1×5 Type **618**; Match in Emirates Stadium; Terraces of stadium; Entrance to stadium; Four players. $2×5 Arsenal team; Outside of stadium; Arsenal fans; Match in stadium; Stadium at sunset	2·25	2·25

619 Soviet Premier Krushchev at Simferopol Space Control Centre

2007. 90th Birth Anniv of John F. Kennedy (US President 1960–3). Multicoloured.

5251	$2 Type **619**	1·50	1·50
5252	$2 Pres. Kennedy meeting Premier Krushchev	1·50	1·50
5253	$2 Pres. Kennedy pressures Premier Krushchev	1·50	50
5254	$2 Premier Krushchev and Pres. Kennedy in US Ambassador's residence, Vienna, 3 June 1961	1·50	1·50
5255	$2 Premier Krushchev and Cuban President Fidel Castro	1·50	1·50
5256	$2 Pres. Kennedy on television, 22 October 1962	1·50	1·50
5257	$2 Completed SA-2 missile site	1·50	1·50
5258	$2 Pres. Kennedy and Premier Krushchev shaking hands in Vienna	1·50	1·50

620 French Test Pilot Andre Turcat

2007. Concorde. Multicoloured.

5259	$2 Type **620**	1·50	1·50
5260	$2 British test pilot Brian Trubshaw	1·50	1·50

621 Hand giving Salute

2007. Centenary of Scouting. Multicoloured. Background colours given (Nos. 5261/4).

5261	**621**	$3 blue	2·25	2·25
5262	**621**	$3 orange	2·25	2·25
5263	**621**	$3 magenta	2·25	2·25
5264	**621**	$3 green	2·25	2·25
MS5265		110×81 mm. $6 Hand giving salute and "21ST WORLD SCOUT JAMBOREE"	4·25	4·25

622 "The Pig carries the Fortune to the Door" (paper cutting)

2007. Chinese New Year ("Year of the Pig").

MS5266	112×85 mm. [$1] Type **622** (black inscr); $1 As Type **622** (white inscr); $2 As Type **622** (white inscr); $2 As Type **622** (yellow inscr)	4·25	4·25

The colours refer to the "TRADITIONAL CHINESE NEW YEAR PAPER CUTTING" inscription at the top of the stamps.

623 Pope Benedict XVI

2007. 80th Birthday of Pope Benedict XVI.

5267	**623**	$1 multicoloured	80	65

2007. World Cup Cricket, West Indies. As T 448 of Dominica. Multicoloured.

5268	$1 Outline map and flag of Grenada	80	65
5269	$2 Rawl Lewis	1·50	1·50
5270	$3 Queen's Park Stadium (horiz)	2·25	2·25
MS5271	117×90 mm. $6 World Cup Cricket emblem	4·25	4·25

624 Diana, Princess of Wales

2007. 10th Death Anniv of Diana, Princess of Wales. Multicoloured.

5272	$2 Type **624**	1·50	1·50
5273	$2 Wearing turquoise and white jacket and hat	1·50	1·50
5274	$2 Wearing white sleeveless evening dress	1·50	1·50
5275	$2 Wearing green and white jacket and hat	1·50	1·50
MS5276	Two sheets, each 100×70 mm. (a) $6 Wearing green and white dress and white headscarf. (b) $6 Wearing red dress with halter neck (*horiz*)	8·50	8·50

625 Princess Elizabeth and Prince Philip, c. 1947

2007. Diamond Wedding of Queen Elizabeth II and Duke of Edinburgh. Multicoloured.

5277	$2 Type **625**	1·50	1·50
5278	$2 Queen Elizabeth II, c. 2007	1·50	1·50
MS5279	70×100 mm. $6 Queen Elizabeth and Prince Philip, c. 2007	4·25	4·25

626 Emperor Penguin

2007. International Polar Year. Penguins. Multicoloured.

MS5280	150×115 mm. $2×6 Type **626**; Three penguins on the ice; Adult penguin (with head bent); Chick on snow with adult; Chick with wings outstretched; Chick standing on adult's feet	8·50	8·50
MS5281	70×100 mm. $6 Penguin skiing (horiz)	4·25	4·25

The stamps and margins of No. **MS**5280 form a composite design showing Emperor penguins in Antarctica.

2007. Halley's Comet, 1986. As T 473 of Gambia. Frame colours given for Nos. 5282/5. Multicoloured.

5282	$2 orange	1·50	1·50
5283	$2 blue	1·50	1·50
5284	$2 violet	1·50	1·50
5285	$2 red	1·50	1·50
MS5286	100×70 mm. $6 Emblem, Halley's Comet and 'RETURNS 2062'	4·25	4·25

627 George Washington, 1789–97

2007. Presidents of the United States of America. Multicoloured.

MS5287	Three sheets, each 168×115 mm. (a) 1c. Type **627**; 2c. John Adams, 1797–1801; 3c. Thomas Jefferson, 1801–9; 4c. James Madison, 1809–17; 5c. James Monroe, 1817–25; 6c. John Adams, 1825–9; 7c. Andrew Jackson, 1829–37; 8c. Martin Van Buren, 1837–41; 9c. William H. Harrison, 1841; 10c. John Tyler, 1841–5; 11c. James K. Polk, 1845–9; 12c. Zachary Taylor, 1849–50; 13c. Millard Fillmore, 1850–3; 14c. Franklin Pierce, 1853–7; $4 US Arms and flag. (b) 15c. James Buchanan, 1857–61; 16c. Abraham Lincoln, 1861–5; 17c. Andrew Johnson, 1865–9; 18c. Ulysses S. Grant, 1869–77; 19c. Rutherford Hayes, 1877–81; 20c. James Garfield, 1881; 21c. Chester Arthur, 1881–5; 22c. Grover Cleveland, 1885–9; 23c. Benjamin Harrison, 1889–93; 24c. Grover Cleveland, 1893–7; 25c. William McKinley, 1897–1901; 26c. Theodore Roosevelt, 1901–9; 27c. William Taft, 1909–13; 28c. Woodrow Wilson, 1913–21; $2 Capitol, Washington. (c) 29c. Warren G. Harding, 1921–3; 30c. Calvin Coolidge, 1923–9; 31c. Herbert Hoover, 1929–33; 32c. Franklin D. Roosevelt, 1933–45; 33c. Harry S. Truman, 1945–53; 34c. Dwight D. Eisenhower, 1953–61; 35c. John F. Kennedy, 1961–3; 36c. Lyndon B. Johnson, 1963–9; 37c. Richard Nixon, 1969–74; 38c. Gerald R. Ford, 1974–7; 39c. Jimmy Carter, 1977–81; 40c. Ronald Reagan, 1981–9; 41c. George H. W. Bush, 1989–93; 42c. William Clinton, 1993–2001; 43c. George W. Bush, 2001–	12·00	12·00

628 Clymene Dolphin

2007. Endangered Species. Clymene Dolphin (Stenella clymene). Multicoloured.

5288	$1.20 Type **628**	90	75
5289	$1.20 Two dolphins	90	75
5290	$1.20 Dolphin leaping out of water	90	75
5291	$1.20 Two dolphins swimming side by side	90	75
MS5292	115×168 mm. Nos. 5288/91, each ×2	7·25	7·25

2007. Holocaust Remembrance. As T 479 of Gambia. Multicoloured.

5293-5300	$1.40×8 Erasmo Lara-Pena, Dominican Republic; Diego Cordovez, Ecuador; Carmen M. Gallardo Hernandez, El Salvador; Lino Sima Ekua Avomo, Equatorial Guinea; Tina Intelmann, Estonia; Dawit Yohannes, Ethiopia; Isikia Rabiei Savua, Fiji; Lars Wide, Chef de Cabinet, 60th UN GA	8·00	8·00
5301-5308	$1.40×8 Angus Friday, Grenada; Alfredo Lopes Cabral, Guinea-Bissau; Samuel Rudolph Insanally, Guyana; Leo Merares, Haiti; Ivan Romero-Martinez, Honduras; Gabor Brodi, Hungary; Hjalmar W. Hannesson, Iceland; Dan Gillerman, Israel	8·00	8·00
5309-5316	$1.40×8 Colin Beck, Solomon Islands; Dumisani S. Kumalo, South Africa; Juan Antonio Yanez-Barnuevo, Spain; Anders Liden, Sweden; Peter Maurer, Switzerland; K. Laxanachantorn Laohaphan, Thailand; Jose Luis Guterres, Timor-Leste; Fekitamoeloa 'Utoikamanu, Tonga	8·00	8·00
5317-5324	$1.40×8 Srgian Kerim, President, 62nd UN GA; Andrei Dapkiunas, Belarus; Jean-Marie Ehouzou, Benin; Milos Prica, Bosnia & Herzegovina; Samuel O. Outlule, Botswana; Francis K. Butagira, Uganda; Valeriy P. Kuchinsky, Ukraine; Jean Ping, President 59th UN Gen Assem	8·00	8·00

629 Corporal Bryan Budd

2007. 150th Anniv of the First Presentation of the Victoria Cross. Designs showing recipients. Multicoloured.

5325	$1.50 Type **629**	1·10	95
5326	$1.50 Brigadier General James Forbes-Robinson	1·10	95
5327	$1.50 Private Johnson Beharry	1·10	95
5328	$1.50 Sergeant William J. Gordon	1·10	95
5329	$1.50 Private Henry Tandey	1·10	95
5330	$1.50 Private Jorgen Christian Jensen	1·10	95
MS5331	100×70 mm. $6 Seaman Jack Mantel	4·25	4·25

630 Hostage Rescue Helicopter S-65/RH 53D

2007. Centenary of First Helicopter Flight. Multicoloured.

5332	$2 Type **630**	1·50	1·50
5333	$2 Autogyro ('do-it-yourself flying')	1·50	1·50
5334	$2 Multi-role military helicopter BK 117	1·50	1·50
5335	$2 Anti-ship missile helicopter AS-61	1·50	1·50
MS5336	100×70 mm. $6 AH 64 Apache tank destroyer helicopter	4·25	4·25

631 *Susan Bristol* (Bernard Vidal)

2007. Sheet 105×122 mm.

MS5337	$6 multicoloured	4·25	4·25

632 St. George's University

2007. 30th Anniv of St. George's University, Grenada. Sheet 100×70 mm.

MS5338	multicoloured	4·25	4·25

633 Christ Child in Crib

2007. Christmas. Multicoloured.

5339	25c. Type **633**	20	15
5340	50c. Choir of angels	40	35
5341	75c. Praying angels	60	45
5342	$1 Flying cherub	80	65

Nos. 5339/42 all show details from painting *Nativity with the Annunciation to theShepherds* by follower of Jan Joest.

634 Rat

2007. Chinese New Year ('Year of the Rat').

5343	**634**	$2 multicoloured	1·20	1·20

635 Shane Warne bowling, First Test, Bangalore, India, October 2004

2007. 'Shane Warne Collection'. Six sheets each 180×236 mm containing multicoloured designs as T 635.

MS5344	(a) $2×8 'The Power' Shane Warne bowling; (b) $2×6 'The Mastery' Shane Warne celebrates Australia's 1999 World Cup victory; (c) $2×8 'The Artistry' Paintings of Shane Warne bowling by Phillip Howe; (d) $2×6 'The Legendary' Final Test Match, Trent Bridge, London, 2005 Ashes Series; (e) $2×8 'The Revolutionary' Match scenes; (f) $2×8 'The King of Spin' Shane Warne bowling frame by frame	54·00	54·00

2007. Breast Cancer Research. Sheet 100×70 mm containing design as T 481 of Gambia. Multicoloured.

MS5345	Roman Goddess Diana reaching for arrow	4·25	4·25

Similar designs were issued by the USA (in 1998), Belize (2006) and Gambia (2007).

636 Elvis Presley

2008. Elvis Presley Commemoration. Multicoloured.

5346	$1.50 Type **636**	1·10	95
5347	$1.50 Wearing white jumpsuit	1·10	95
5348	$1.50 Wearing green	1·10	95
5349	$1.50 In profile, wearing leather jacket, playing guitar	1·10	95
5350	$1.50 Singing, with guitar and microphone	1·10	95
5351	$1.50 Playing guitar and singing	1·10	95

637 Muhammad Ali

2008. Muhammad Ali (world heavyweight boxing champion, 1964, 1974–8). Multicoloured.

5352	$2 Type **637**	1·50	1·50
5353	$2 Speaking	1·50	1·50
5354	$2 Hitting punch ball in gym	1·50	1·50
5355	$2 Boxing	1·50	1·50
5356	$2 Facing right, towel over back of head (vert)	1·50	1·50
5357	$2 Facing left, towel over back of head (vert)	1·50	1·50
5358	$2 With fist raised (vert)	1·50	1·50
5359	$2 With towel over shoulder (vert)	1·50	1·50
MS5360	Two sheets, each 100×70 mm. (a) $6 Muhammad Ali and audience (vert). (b) $6 Wearing boxing gloves and helmet (vert)	8·50	8·50

2008. 50th Death Anniv of Qi Baishi (2007). As T 475 of Gambia. Multicoloured.

5361	$1 *Magnolias and Bees*	80	65
5362	$1 *Mother Hen, Chicks and Banana Leaves*	80	65
5363	$1 *Fish, Crabs and Watergrass*	80	65
5364	$1 *Cross Returning to Wintry Trees*	80	65
MS5365	60×125 mm. $4 *Morning Glories*	3·00	3·00

638 Greece 1896 40l. Stamp for First International Olympic Games

2008. Olympic Games, Beijing. Multicoloured.

5366	$3 Type **638**	2·25	2·25
5367	$3 Poster for Olympic Games, Athens, 1896	2·25	2·25
5368	$3 Germany 1936 Summer Olympics 25pf.+15pf. double scullers stamp	2·25	2·25
5369	$3 Poster for Olympic Games, Berlin, 1936	2·25	2·25

639 Oolong Tea (*Camellia sinensis* (L.) Kuntze)

2008. Taipei 2008 International Stamp Exhibition. Flora of Taiwan. Multicoloured.

5370	$1 Type **639**	85	65
5371	$1 Pink lotus (*Nelumbo nucifera*)	85	65
5372	$1 Japanese maple (*Acer palmatum*)	85	65
5373	$1 Bitter melon (*Momordica charantia*)	85	65
5374	$1 Rice field (*Oryza sativa*)	85	65
5375	$1 Lychee (*Litchi chinensis* Sonn.)	85	65
MS5376	Shitou Forest, Taiwan (37×50 mm)	3·50	3·50

640 Aerial View of City of David and Walls of Old City of Jerusalem (image scaled to 48% of original size)

2008. Israel 2008 World Stamp Championship, Tel-Aviv. Sheet 100×110 mm. Imperf.

MS5377	multicoloured	4·25	4·25

641 Trevor Ariza

2008. Los Angeles Lakers—NBA Western Conference Champions. Multicoloured.

5378	$1 Type **641**	85	65
5379	$1 Jordan Farmar	85	65
5380	$1 Derek Fisher	85	65
5381	$1 Pau Gasol	85	65
5382	$1 Kobe Bryant		
5383	$1 Lamar Odom	85	65
5384	$1 Vladimir Radmanovic	85	65
5385	$1 Sasha Vujacic	85	65
5386	$1 Luke Walton	85	65

642 Tortoiseshell

2008. Cats of the World. Multicoloured.

5387	$1.40 Type **642**	1·00	85
5388	$1.40 Korat	1·00	85
5389	$1.40 Turkish van	1·00	85
5390	$1.40 Manx	1·00	85
MS5391	100×70 mm. $6 British blue shorthair	4·25	4·25

643 Pope Benedict XVI

2008. 1st Visit of Pope Benedict XVI to the United States. Sheet 176×127 mm containing T 643 and similar vert designs.

MS5392	multicoloured	6·00	6·00

The four stamps within **MS**5392 are as Type **643** but all have slightly different backgrounds of the church ceiling showing through the stamp borders.

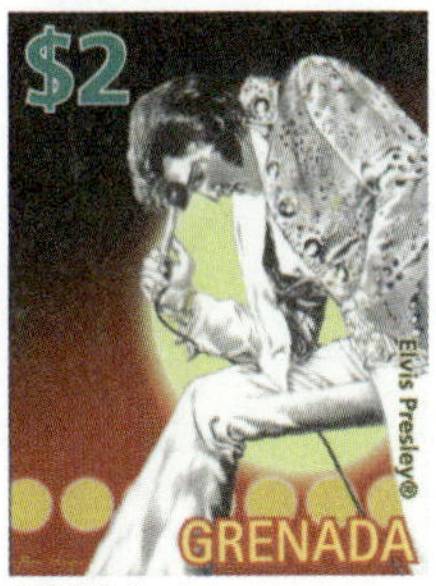

644 Elvis Presley

2008. Elvis Presley Commemoration. Multicoloured.

5393	$2 Type **644**	1·50	1·50
5394	$2 Wearing red shirt and dark grey tie	1·50	1·50
5395	$2 With guitar held over shoulder	1·50	1·50
5396	$2 In close-up	1·50	1·50

647 Karol Wojtyla as a Boy

2008. Pope John Paul II Commemoration. Sheet 133×167 containing T 647 and similar vert designs. Multicoloured.

MS5399	Type **647**; As Cardinal (wearing red skullcap); Wearing biretta (black and blue photo); At his Coronation; With hands raised, giving blessing; Wearing white skullcap	9·00	9·00

648 *Panaeolus papilionaceus*

2009. Mushrooms of the World. Multicoloured.

5400	25c. Type **648**	20	15
5401	50c. *Panaeolus cyanescens*	40	30
5402	75c. *Panaeolus sphinctrinus*	60	50
5403	90c. *Panaeolus fimicola*	80	60
5404	$1 *Copelandia cyanescens*	85	65
5405	$4 *Psilocybe cubensis*	3·00	3·00
MS5406	140×100 mm. $2.50×4 *Panaleus subbalteatus*; *Alboleptonia earlei*; *Porphyrellus portoricensis*; *Psilocybe caerulescens*	7·00	7·00

649 Pres. Barack Obama

2009. Inauguration of President Barack Obama. Sheet 133×94 mm. Multicoloured.

MS5407	Type **649**×4 multicoloured	7·50	7·50

650 International Space Station

2009. 50 Years of Space Exploration. T 650 and similar multicoloured designs. Multicoloured.

MS5408	150×100 mm. $2×6 Type **650**; NASA's new concept for a lunar truck; The Milky Way over Ontario; M16 and the Eagle Nebula; Expedition 16; Dextre robot at work on the Space Station	9·00	9·00
MS5409	150×100 mm. $2×6 304 angstrom wavelength of extreme UV light; Buzz Aldrin on the Moon; Overhead crane lifting Space Shuttle *Atlantis* inside Kennedy's Vehicle Assembly Building; Inside Victoria Crater for extended exploration; Saturn's rings (Cassini Mission); Installation of main engines in *Atlantis*, Kennedy Space Centre	9·00	9·00
MS5410	130×100 mm. $2.50×4 Kennedy Space Centre reveals space shuttle *Atlantis*; ISS from *Discovery*; Saturn Aurora; Kibo Japanese Pressurized Module and Kibo Japanese logistics module (all vert)	7·00	7·00
MS5411	130×100 mm. $2.50×4 Canadarm 2 or space station robotic arm; Shuttle Atlantis-Hubble Space Telescope service mission; Cat's Eye Nebula; NASA's Orion crew capsule (all vert)	7·00	7·00

651 White Crowned Pigeon (*Patagioenas*)

2009. Birds of the Caribbean. Multicoloured.

5412	$1 Type **651**	85	65
5413	$2 Blue winged warbler (*Vermivora pinus*)	1·50	1·50
5414	$4 Bananaquit (*Coereba flaveola*)	3·00	3·00
5415	$5 Monk parakeet (*Myiopsitta monachus*)	3·50	3·50
MS5416	109×100 mm. $3×3 Yellow crowned amazon (*Amazona ochrocephala*); Yellow bellied sap sucker (*Sphyrapicus varius*); Jamaican mango (*Anthracothorax mango*)	6·75	6·75
MS5417	171×121 mm. $3×3 Ringed kingfisher (*Megaceryle torquata*); Tree swallow (*Tachycineta bicolor*); Black and white warbler (*Mniotilta varia.tif*)	6·75	6·75

The stamps and margins of No. **MS**5417 form a composite design showing birds on branches.

652 Ox

2009. Chinese New Year. Year of the Ox. Sheet 190×90 mm.

MS5418	$2.50 Type **652**×4 multicoloured	1·75	1·75

653 Marilyn Monroe

2009. Marilyn Monroe Commemoration. Sheet 100×140 mm. Multicoloured.

MS5419	Type **653**; Looking over shoulder (facing left); Facing right; Looking over shoulder (facing camera)	7·00	7·00

654 Anthony C. George flag designer) and Grenada National Flag

2009. 35th Anniv of Independence. Multicoloured.

5420	**654**	10c. multicoloured	15	15
5421	**654**	25c. multicoloured	30	15
5422	**654**	50c. multicoloured	60	25
5423	**654**	75c. multicoloured	60	50
MS5424		100×70 mm. $6 Anthony C. George and Grenada flag flying from flagstaff (30×40 mm)	4·25	4·25

655 Peony Design on Vase

2009. China 2009 World Stamp Exhibition, Luoyang (1st issue). Peonies. Multicoloured.

5425	75c. Type **655**	60	50
MS5426	70×100 mm. $5 Pink peony (43×43 mm)	3·50	3·50

656 Pole Vault

2009. China 2009 World Stamp Exhibition (2nd issue). Sports of the Summer Games. Sheet 90×130 mm containing T 656 and similar horiz designs. Multicoloured.

MS5427	Type **656**; Hurdles; Relay; High jump	4·50	4·50

657 Orion Upper Stages and Werner von Braun

2009. 40th Anniv of the First Moon Landing. Sheet 150×100 mm containing T 657 and similar horiz designs. Multicoloured.

MS5428 Type **657**; Apollo 11 crew; Lunar orbiter; Ranger 7; Pres. John F. Kennedy, lunar module and Moon; Orion LM on Moon	9·00	9·00

658 Haydn's Birthplace, Rohrau, Austria

2009. Birth Bicentenary of Franz Joseph Haydn (composer). Sheet 164×94 mm containing T 658 and similar vert designs. Multicoloured.

MS5429 Type **658**; Johann Peter Salomon (impresario to Haydn); Austro-Hungarian Haydn Orchestra; Wolfgang Amadeus Mozart; Haydn Haus (home 1766–78), Eisenstadt, Austria; Young Ludwig van Beethoven (Haydn's student)	10·50	10·50

659 Elvis Presley

2009. 40th Anniv of Song Suspicious Minds by Elvis Presley. Sheet 160×130 mm containing T 659 and similar vert designs. Multicoloured.

MS5430 Type **659**; Full length, facing left; Full length, facing right with hand raised; Half length with guitar, facing right	7·00	7·00

661 Pope Benedict XVI and Bethlehem

MS5433 $1.50 Type **661**; $2 As Type **661**; $2.50 As Type **661**; $3 As Type **661**	7·00	7·00

662 Charles Darwin and Finch

MS5434 $2.50 x 4 Type **662;** Charles Darwin and fox; Charles Darwin and dissected tortoise; Charles Darwin and tortoise	7·00	7·00
MS5435 $3.50x3 Type **663**; Pre. Lincoln with Maj. John A. McClernand; Pres. Lincoln with Gen George B. McClellan	6·00	6·00

664 J-5 Airplane

2009. Centenary of Chinese Aviation and Aeropex 2009, Beijing. Showing aircrafts. Multicoloured.

MS5436 145×95 mm. $2×4 Type **664**; J-6; J-7G; J-7	1·50	1·50
MS5437 120×79 mm. $6 JF-17 (50×38 mm)	4·50	4·50

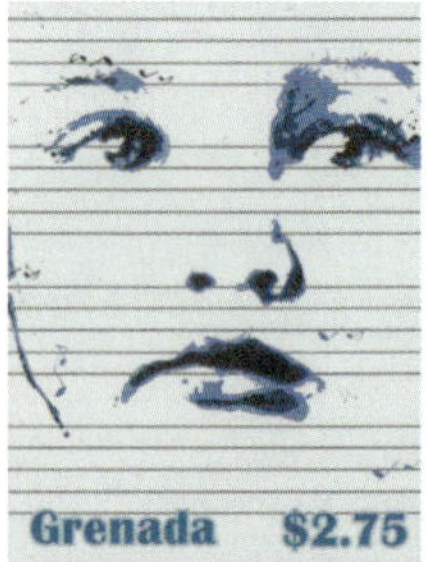

665 Elvis Presley as Young Boy

2010. 75th Birth Anniv of Elvis Presley. Illustrations by Joe Petruccio. Sheet 180×120 mm containing T 665 and similar vert designs. Multicoloured.

MS5438 Type **665**; Singing, with mouth wide open; Singing, looking down; Smiling	7·50	7·50

666 Fish wearing Santa Hats

2010. Christmas. Multicoloured.

5439	$1 Type **666**	80	80
5440	$2 Christmas tree branches decorated with lights and nuts and fruit	1·40	1·40
5441	$4 Christmas bells in window	2·50	2·50
5442	$5 Outline map of Grenada, baubles and stars	3·25	3·25

667 *Brassia caudata*

2010. Orchids of the Caribbean. Multicoloured.

5443	$1.20 Type **667**	1·75	1·75
5444	$1.80 *Epidendrum imatophyllum*	2·25	2·25
5445	$3 *Ionopsis utriculoides*	4·50	4·50
5446	$5 *Habenaria bractescens*	5·75	5·75
MS5447	130×100 mm. $2.75×4 *Vanilla pompona; Caularthron bicornutum; Epidendrum nocturnum; Aspasia variegata*	7·50	7·50
MS5448	100×70 mm. $3×2 *Epidendrum hartii; Brassavola cucullata*	5·50	5·50

OFFICIAL STAMPS

1982. Optd P.R.G. (a) Nos. 1085/97 and 1099.

O1	5c. West Indiaman barque, c. 1840	30	40
O2	6c. R.M.S.P. "Orinoco", c. 1851	30	40
O3	10c. Working schooner	30	30
O4	12c. Trimaran at Grand Anse anchorage	30	30
O5	15c. Spice Island cruising yacht "Petite Amie"	30	30
O6	20c. Fishing pirogue	35	30
O7	25c. Harbour police launch	40	30
O8	30c. Grand Anse speedboat	40	30
O9	40c. M.V. "Seimstrand"	50	30
O10	50c. Three-masted schooner "Ariadne"	60	40
O11	90c. M.V. "Geestide"	90	1·00
O12	$1 M.V "Cunard Countess"	90	1·00
O13	$3 Rum-runner	2·25	4·25
O14	$10 Coast-guard patrol boat	6·00	12·00

(b) Nos. 1130/2 and 1134/5.

O15	30c. Prince Charles and Lady Diana Spencer	1·50	2·25
O16	40c. Holyrood House	2·25	2·75
O17	50c. Prince Charles and Lady Diana Spencer	1·25	2·00
O18	$2 Holyrood House	2·25	3·50
O19	$4 Type **268**	5·00	8·00

POSTAGE DUE STAMPS

D1

1892

D8	**D1**	1d. black	3·50	7·50
D9	**D1**	2d. black	11·00	1·75
D10	**D1**	3d. black	13·00	6·00

1892. Inscr SURCHARGE POSTAGE and value.

D4	**13**	1d. on 6d. mauve	£110	1·25
D5	**13**	1d. on 8d. brown	£1600	3·25
D6	**13**	2d. on 6d. mauve	£180	2·50
D7	**13**	2d. on 8d. brown	£2500	10·00

1921. As Type D 1 but inscr "POSTAGE DUE" instead of "SURCHARGE POSTAGE".

D11	**D1**	1d. black	1·50	1·00
D12	**D1**	1½d. black	9·00	23·00
D13	**D1**	2d. black	2·00	1·75
D14	**D1**	3d. black	2·00	4·50

1952. As last, but currency changed.

D15	3c. black	30	8·50
D16	4c. black	30	16·00
D17	6c. black	45	12·00
D18	8c. black	75	13·00

Pt. 1

GRENADINES OF GRENADA (CARRIACOU AND PETITE MARTINIQUE)

The southern part of the group, attached to Grenada. Main islands Petit Martinique and Carriacou. From 1999 stamps were inscribed "Grenada Carriacou and Petite Martinique".

100 cents = 1 dollar.

1973. Royal Wedding. Nos. 582/3 of Grenada optd GRENADINES.

1	**196** 25c. multicoloured	15	10
2	**196** $2 multicoloured	45	50

1974. Stamps of Grenada optd GRENADINES.

4	1c. multicoloured (No. 306)	10	10
5	2c. multicoloured (No. 307)	10	10
6	3c. multicoloured (No. 308)	10	10
7	5c. multicoloured (No. 309)	15	10
8	8c. multicoloured (No. 311)	15	10
9	10c. multicoloured (No. 312)	15	10
10	12c. multicoloured (No. 313)	20	10
11	25c. multicoloured (No. 315)	45	10
12	$1 multicoloured (No. 318)	2·50	60
13	$2 multicoloured (No. 319)	3·00	1·50
14	$3 multicoloured (No. 320)	3·00	1·75
15	$5 multicoloured (No. 321)	3·75	2·25

1974. World Cup Football Championship. As Nos. 619/27 of Grenada, but inscr "GRENADA GRENADINES".

16	½c. multicoloured	10	10
17	1c. multicoloured	10	10
18	2c. multicoloured	10	10
19	10c. multicoloured	20	10
20	25c. multicoloured	25	10
21	50c. multicoloured	30	15
22	75c. multicoloured	30	20
23	$1 multicoloured	35	25
MS24	114×76 mm. $2 multicoloured	75	80

1974. Cent of U.P.U. As Nos. 628 etc of Grenada, but inscr "GRENADA GRENADINES".

25	8c. multicoloured	10	10
26	25c. multicoloured	15	10
27	35c. multicoloured	15	10
28	$1 multicoloured	70	40
MS29	172×109 mm. $1 as 15c. and $2 as $1	1·00	1·00

1974. Birth Cent of Sir Winston Churchill. As Nos. 637/9 of Grenada, but inscr "GRENADA GRENADINES".

30	35c. multicoloured	15	10
31	$2 multicoloured	40	45
MS32	129×96 mm. 75c. as 35c. and $1 as $2	35	80

1974. Christmas. As Nos. 640/8 of Grenada, but inscr "GRENADA GRENADINES" and background colours changed.

33	**204** ½c. multicoloured	10	10
34	- 1c. multicoloured	10	10
35	- 2c. multicoloured	10	10
36	- 3c. multicoloured	10	10
37	- 10c. multicoloured	10	10
38	- 25c. multicoloured	10	10
39	- 50c. multicoloured	15	15
40	- $1 multicoloured	30	25
MS41	117×96 mm. $2 as 1c.	45	60

1975. Big Game Fishing. As Nos. 669 etc of Grenada, but inscr "GRENADA GRENADINES" and background colours changed.

42	½c. multicoloured	10	10
43	1c. multicoloured	10	10
44	2c. multicoloured	10	10
45	10c. multicoloured	15	10
46	25c. multicoloured	20	10
47	50c. multicoloured	20	15
48	70c. multicoloured	25	20
49	$1 multicoloured	35	35
MS50	107×80 mm. $2 multicoloured	60	90

1975. Flowers. As Nos. 678 etc of Grenada, but inscr "GRENADINES".

51	½c. multicoloured	10	10
52	1c. multicoloured	10	10
53	2c. multicoloured	10	10
54	3c. multicoloured	10	10
55	10c. multicoloured	10	10
56	25c. multicoloured	10	10
57	50c. multicoloured	20	15
58	$1 multicoloured	30	20
MS59	102×82 mm. $2 multicoloured	60	70

CANCELLED REMAINDERS*. Some of the following issues have been remaindered, cancelled-to-order, at a fraction of their face value. For all practical purposes these are indistinguishable from genuine postally used copies. Our used quotations, which are indicated by an asterisk, are the same for cancelled-to-order or postally used copies.

3 "Christ Crowned with Thorns" (Titian)

1975. Easter. Paintings showing Crucifixion and Deposition by artists listed. Multicoloured.

60	½c. Type **3**	10	10
61	1c. Giotto	10	10
62	2c. Tintoretto	10	10
63	3c. Cranach	10	10
64	35c. Caravaggio	15	10
65	75c. Tiepolo	20	10
66	$2 Velasquez	40	15
MS67	105×90 mm. $1 Titian	60	30

4 "Dawn" (detail from Medici Tomb)

1975. 500th Anniv of Michelangelo. Multicoloured.

68	½c. Type **4**	10	10
69	1c. "Delphic Sibyl"	10	10
70	2c. "Giuliano de Medici"	10	10
71	40c. "The Creation" (detail)	15	10
72	50c. "Lorenzo de Medici"	15	10
73	75c. "Persian Sibyl"	20	10
74	$2 "Head of Christ"	30	15
MS75	118×96 mm. $1 "The Prophet Jeremiah"	75	50

1975. Butterflies. As T 213 of Grenada, but inscr "GRENADINES". Multicoloured.

76	½c. "Morpho peleides"	10	10
77	1c. "Danaus eresimus" ("Danaus gilippus")	10	10
78	2c. "Dismorphia amphione"	10	10
79	35c. "Hamadryas feronia"	35	10
80	45c. "Philaethria dido"	45	10
81	75c. "Phoebis argante"	70	15
82	$2 "Prepona laertes"	1·40	30
MS83	104×77 mm. $1 "Siproeta stelenes"	3·00	3·25

5 Progress "Standard" Badge

1975. 14th World Scout Jamboree, Norway. Multicoloured.

84	½c. Type **5**	10	10
85	1c. Boatman's badge	10	10
86	2c. Coxswain's badge	10	10
87	35c. Interpreter's badge	15	10
88	45c. Ambulance badge	20	10
89	75c. Chief Scout's award	25	10
90	$2 Queen's Scout award	35	15
MS91	106×80 mm. $1 Venture award	55	30

6 The Surrender of Lord Cornwallis

1975. Bicentenary of American Revolution (1976) (1st issue). Multicoloured.

92	½c. Type **6**	10	10
93	1c. Minute-men	10	10
94	2c. Paul Revere's ride	10	10
95	3c. Battle of Bunker Hill	10	10
96	5c. Fifer and drummers	10	10
97	45c. Backwoodsman	15	10
98	75c. Boston Tea Party	20	10
99	$2 Naval engagement	35	10
100	$2 George Washington	35	35
101	$2 White House and flags	35	35
MS102	Two sheets 113×128 mm containing No. 100, and 128×113 mm containing No. 101. Imperf	1·10	1·40

Nos. 100/1 are larger, 35×60 mm.
See also Nos. 176/**MS**183.

7 Fencing

1975. Pan-American Games, Mexico City. Multicoloured.

103	½c. Type **7**	10	10
104	1c. Hurdling	10	10
105	2c. Pole-vaulting	10	10
106	35c. Weightlifting	15	10
107	45c. Throwing the javelin	15	10
108	75c. Throwing the discus	15	10
109	$2 Diving	35	15
MS110	78×104 mm. $1 Sprinter	40	20

1975. Nos. 649/68 of Grenada additionally inscr "GRENADINES".

111	½c. Yachts, Point Saline	10	30
112	1c. Yacht Club race, St. George's	10	15
113	2c. Carenage taxi	10	15
114	3c. Large working boats	10	15
115	5c. Deep-water dock, St. George's	10	15
116	6c. Cocoa beans in drying trays	10	15
117	8c. Nutmegs	10	15
118	10c. Rum distillery, River Antoine Estate, c. 1785	10	15
119	12c. Cocoa tree	10	15
120	15c. Fishermen at Fontenoy	10	15
121	20c. Parliament Building	10	40
122	25c. Fort George cannons	10	15
123	35c. Pearls Airport	50	15
124	50c. General Post Office	20	75
125	75c. Carib's Leap, Sauteurs Bay	40	60
126	$1 Carenage, St. George's	60	85
127	$2 St. George's Harbour by night	90	2·00
128	$3 Grand Anse beach	1·10	2·50
129	$5 Canoe Bay and Black Bay	1·50	5·50
130	$10 Sugar-loaf Island	2·25	5·50

8 Virgin and Child" (Durer)

1975. Christmas. "Virgin and Child" paintings by Artists named.

131	½c. Type **8**	10	10
132	1c. Durer	10	10
133	2c. Correggio	10	10
134	40c. Botticelli	15	10
135	50c. Niccolo da Cremona	15	10
136	75c. Correggio	15	10
137	$2 Correggio	30	15
MS138	114×120 mm. $1 Bellini	60	50

9 Bleeding Tooth

1976. Shells. Multicoloured.

139	½c. Type **9**	10	10
140	1c. Toothed donax	10	10
141	2c. Hawk-wing conch	10	10
142	3c. Atlantic distorsio	10	10
143	25c. Scotch bonnet	40	10
144	50c. King helmet	50	10
145	75c. Queen or pink conch	75	15
MS146	79×105 mm. $2 Atlantic trumpet triton	1·00	70

10 Cocoa Thrush

1976. Flora and Fauna. Multicoloured.

147	½c. "Lignum vitae"	10	10
148	1c. Type **10**	10	10
149	2c. "Eurypelma sp." (spider)	10	10
150	35c. Lesser Antillean Tanager ("Hooded Tanager")	1·25	10
151	50c. "Nyctaginaceae"	1·00	15
152	75c. Grenada dove	2·50	25
153	$1 Marine toad	2·50	25
MS154	108×84 mm. $2 Blue-hooded euphonia	4·00	1·00

11 Hooked Sailfish

1976. Tourism. Multicoloured.

155	½c. Type **11**	10	10
156	1c. Careened schooner, Carriacou	10	10
157	2c. Carriacou Annual Regatta	10	10
158	18c. Boat building on Carriacou	20	10
159	22c. Workboat race, Carriacou Regatta	20	10
160	75c. Cruising off Petit Martinique	30	20
161	$1 Water skiing	40	20
MS162	105×87 mm. $2 Yacht racing at Carriacou	70	75

12 Making a Camp Fire

1976. 50th Anniv of Girl Guides in Grenada. Multicoloured.

163	½c. Type **12**	10	10
164	1c. First aid	10	10
165	2c. Nature study	10	10
166	50c. Cookery	50	15
167	$1 Sketching	75	25
MS168	85×110 mm. $2 Guide playing guitar	1·00	75

13 "Christ Mocked" (Bosch)

1976. Easter. Multicoloured.

169	½c. Type **13**	10	10
170	1c. "Christ Crucified" (Antonello da Messina)	10	10
171	2c. "Adoration of the Trinity" (Durer)	10	10
172	3c. "Lamentation of Christ" (Durer)	10	10
173	35c. "The Entombment" (Van der Weyden)	15	10
174	$3 "The Entombment" (Raphael)	60	30
MS175	57×72 mm. $2 "Blood of the Redeemer" (G. Bellini)	65	70

14 "South Carolina" (frigate)

1976. Bicentenary of American Revolution (2nd issue). Multicoloured.

176	½c. Type **14**	10	10
177	1c. "Lee" (schooner)	10	10

178	2c. H.M.S. "Roebuck" (frigate)	10	10
179	35c. "Andrew Doria" (brig)	40	10
180	50c. "Providence" (sloop)	50	15
181	$1 "Alfred" (frigate)	75	20
182	$2 "Confederacy" (frigate)	1·25	30
MS183	72×85 mm. $3 "Revenge" (cutter)	1·00	1·00

15 Piper Apache

1976. Aircraft. Multicoloured.

184	½c. Type **15**	10	10
185	1c. Beech 50 Twin Bonanza	10	10
186	2c. De Havilland Twin Otter	10	10
187	40c. Britten Norman Islander	30	10
188	50c. De Havilland Heron 2	40	10
189	$2 Hawker Siddeley H.S.748	1·25	25
MS190	71×85 mm. $3 B.A.C. One-Eleven 500	1·00	1·00

16 Cycling

1976. Olympic Games, Montreal. Multicoloured.

191	½c. Type **16**	10	10
192	1c. Pommel horse	10	10
193	2c. Hurdling	10	10
194	35c. Shot putting	10	10
195	45c. Diving	15	10
196	75c. Sprinting	15	10
197	$2 Rowing	35	25
MS198	101×76 mm. $3 Sailing	80	75

17 "Virgin and Child" (Cima)

1976. Christmas. Multicoloured.

199	½c. Type **17**	10	10
200	1c. "The Nativity" (Romanino)	10	10
201	2c. "The Nativity" (Romanino) (different)	10	10
202	35c. "Adoration of the Kings" (Bruegel)	15	10
203	50c. "Madonna and Child" (Girolamo)	20	10
204	75c. "Adoration of the Magi" (Giorgione) (horiz)	20	15
205	$2 "Adoration of the Kings" (School of Fra Angelico) (horiz)	40	25
MS206	120×100 mm. $3 "The Holy Family" (Garofalo)	60	2·25

18 Alexander Graham Bell and First Telephone

1977. Centenary of First Telephone Transmission. Designs showing Alexander Graham Bell and telephone. Multicoloured.

207	½c. Type **18**	10	10
208	1c. 1895 telephone	10	10
209	2c. 1900 telephone	10	10
210	35c. 1915 telephone	15	10
211	75c. 1920 telephone	20	10
212	$1 1929 telephone	25	15
213	$2 1963 telephone	35	25
MS214	107×78 mm. $3 Telephone, 1976	1·10	75

19 Coronation Coach

1977. Silver Jubilee. Multicoloured. (a) Perf.

215	35c. Type **19**	10	10
216	$2 Queen entering Abbey	20	10
217	$4 Queen crowned	35	25
MS218	100×70 mm. $5 The Mall on Coronation Night	60	1·25

(b) Imperf×roul. Self-adhesive.

219	35c. Royal visit	15	20
220	50c. Crown of St. Edward	30	80
221	$2 The Queen and Prince Charles	50	1·60
222	$5 Royal Standard	60	1·75

Nos. 219/22 come from booklets.

21 "Disrobing of Christ" (Fra Angelico)

1977. Easter. Paintings by artists named. Mult.

223	½c. Type **21**	10	10
224	1c. Fra Angelico	10	10
225	2c. El Greco	10	10
226	18c. El Greco	10	10
227	35c. Fra Angelico	15	10
228	50c. Giottino	15	10
229	$2 Antonello da Messina	35	25
MS230	121×94 mm. $3 Fra Angelico	65	65

22 "The Virgin adoring the Child" (Correggio)

1977. Christmas. Multicoloured.

231	½c. Type **22**	10	10
232	1c. "Virgin and Child" (Giorgione)	10	10
233	2c. "Virgin and Child" (Morales)	10	10
234	18c. "Madonna della Tenda" (Raphael)	10	10
235	35c. "Rest on the Flight into Egypt" (Van Dyck)	15	10
236	50c. "Madonna and Child" (Lippi)	15	10
237	$2 "Virgin and Child" (Lippi) (different)	35	25
MS238	114×99 mm. $3 "Virgin and Child with Angels and Saints" (Ghirlandaio)	65	65

1977. Royal Visit. Nos. 215/17 optd ROYAL VISIT W.I. 1977.

239	35c. Type **19**	10	10
240	$2 Queen entering Abbey	25	20
241	$4 Queen crowned	40	30
MS242	100×70 mm. $5 The Mall on Coronation Night	70	90

24 Life-saving

1977. Caribbean Scout Jamboree, Jamaica. Multicoloured.

243	½c. Type **24**	10	10
244	1c. Overnight hike	10	10
245	2c. Cubs tying knots	10	10
246	22c. Erecting a tent	15	10
247	35c. Gang show limbo dance	25	10
248	75c. Campfire cooking	40	15
249	$3 Sea Scouts in "Mirror" dinghies	80	30
MS250	109×85 mm. $2 Pioneering project—Spring bridge	1·10	90

25 Blast-off

1977. Space Shuttle. Multicoloured.

251	½c. Type **25**	10	10
252	1c. Booster jettison	10	10
253	2c. External tank jettison	10	10
254	22c. Working in orbit	15	10
255	50c. Shuttle re-entry	25	10
256	$3 Shuttle landing	85	30
MS257	85×103 mm. $2 Shuttle being towed	60	70

26 Alfred Nobel and Physiology/Medicine Medal

1978. Nobel Prize Awards. Multicoloured.

258	½c. Type **26**	10	10
259	1c. Physics and Chemistry medal	10	10
260	2c. Peace medal (reverse)	10	10
261	22c. Nobel Institute, Oslo	25	10
262	75c. Peace Prize committee	50	15
263	$3 Literature medal	1·50	30
MS264	127×103 mm. $2 Peace medal and Nobel's will	50	60

27 German Zeppelin Stamp, 1930

1978. 75th Anniv of First Zeppelin Flight and 50th Anniv of Lindbergh's Transatlantic Flight. Multicoloured.

265	5c. Type **27**	20	10
266	15c. French Concorde stamp, 1970	60	10
267	25c. Liechtenstein Zeppelin stamp, 1931	20	10
268	35c. Panama Lindbergh stamp, 1928	20	10
269	50c. Russia Airship stamp, 1931	25	10
270	$3 Spanish Lindbergh stamp, 1930	75	30
MS271	140×79 mm. 75c. U.S.A. Lindbergh stamp, 1927; $2 German LZ-129 *Hindenburg* stamp, 1936	1·10	90

28 Coronation Ring

1978. 25th Anniv of Coronation. Multicoloured. (a) Horiz designs. Perf.

272	50c. Type **28**	10	10
273	$2 The Orb	25	30
274	$2.50 Imperial State Crown	30	35
MS275	97×67 mm. $5 Queen Elizabeth II	60	60

(b) Vert designs. Roul×imperf. Self-adhesive.

276	18c. Drummer, Royal Regiment of Fusiliers	15	35
277	50c. Drummer, Royal Anglian Regiment	15	45
278	$5 Drum Major, Queen's Regiment	1·00	3·00

30 "Le Chapeau de Paille"

1978. 400th Birth Anniv of Rubens. Mult.

279	5c. Type **30**	10	10
280	15c. "Archilles slaying Hector"	15	10
281	18c. "Helene Fourment and her Children"	15	10
282	22c. "Rubens and Isabella Brandt"	15	10
283	35c. "The Ildefonso Altarpiece"	20	10
284	$3 "Heads of Negroes" (detail)	75	1·00
MS285	85×127 mm. $2 "Self-portrait"	70	1·00

31 Wright Flyer I

1978. 75th Anniv of Powered Flight.

286	**31**	5c. black, blue and brown	10	10
287	-	15c. black, brown and red	10	10
288	-	18c. black, brown and red	10	10
289	-	25c. black, yellow and green	10	10
290	-	35c. black, pink and purple	15	10
291	-	75c. black, lilac and yellow	25	25
292	-	$3 black, violet and mauve	75	75
MS293		126×83 mm. $2 black, blue and green	75	1·00

DESIGNS—HORIZ: 25c. Wright Flyer III, 1905; 35c. Wright glider No. 1; 75c. Wright Flyer I (different); $2 Various Wright aircraft; $3 Wright Type A. VERT: 15c. Orville Wright; 18c. Wilbur Wright.

32 Audubon's Shearwater

1978. Birds. Multicoloured.

294	5c. Type **32**	50	15
295	10c. Semi-palmated plover ("Northern Ring-necked Plover")	70	15
296	18c. Purple-throated carib ("Garnet-throated Humming-bird") (horiz)	80	15
297	22c. Red-billed whistling duck ("Black-bellied Tree Duck") (horiz)	80	20
298	40c. Caribbean martin (horiz)	1·25	35
299	$1 White-tailed tropic bird ("Yellow-tailed Tropicbird")	1·75	50
300	$2 Long-billed curlew	2·25	75
MS301	78×78 mm. $5 Snowy egret	5·00	2·75

33 Players with Ball

1978. World Cup Football Championship, Argentina. Multicoloured.

302	15c. Type **33**	10	10
303	35c. Running with ball	20	10
304	50c. Player with ball	25	20
305	$3 Heading	80	80

MS306	114×85 mm. $2 Player with ball (different)	80	1·25

34 Captain Cook and Kalaniopu (King of Hawaii), 1778

1978. 250th Birth Anniv of Captain James Cook. Multicoloured.

307	18c. Type **34**	45	10
308	22c. Cook and native of Hawaii	60	15
309	50c. Cook and death scene, 1779	1·00	30
310	$3 Cook and offering ceremony	2·25	1·75
MS311	117×113 mm. $4 H.M.S. "Resolution" (vert)	1·50	1·00

35 "Virgin at Prayer"

1978. Christmas. Paintings by Durer. Multicoloured.

312	40c. Type **35**	15	10
313	60c. "The Dresden Altarpiece"	20	15
314	90c. "Madonna and Child with St. Anne"	25	15
315	$2 "Madonna and Child with Pear"	50	50
MS316	114×84 mm. $4 "Salvator Mundi"	1·00	1·40

36 "Strelitzia reginae"

1979. Flowers. Multicoloured.

317	22c. Type **36**	15	10
318	40c. "Euphorbia pulcherrima"	25	15
319	$1 "Heliconia humilis"	45	30
320	$3 "Thunbergia alata"	80	80
MS321	114×90 mm. $2 "Bougainvillaea glabra"	75	1·00

37 Children with Pig

1979. International Year of the Child. Multicoloured.

322	18c. Type **37**	10	10
323	50c. Children with donkey	20	25
324	$1 Children with goats	25	30
325	$3 Children fishing	65	80
MS326	104×86 mm. $4 Child with coconuts	1·00	1·90

38 "20,000 Leagues under the Sea"

1979. 150th Birth Anniv of Jules Verne (author). Multicoloured.

327	18c. Type **38**	50	10
328	38c. "From the Earth to the Moon"	55	20
329	75c. "From the Earth to the Moon" (different)	65	35
330	$3 "Five Weeks in a Balloon"	1·25	1·00
MS331	111×86 mm. $4 "Around the World in 80 Days"	1·00	1·60

39 Sir Rowland Hill and Mail Van

1979. Death Centenary of Sir Rowland Hill. Multicoloured.

332	15c. Type **39**	10	10
333	$1 "Britanis" (cargo liner)	20	20
334	$2 Diesel mail train	30	30
335	$3 Concorde	90	70
MS336	85×67 mm. $4 Sir Rowland Hill	75	1·00

40 "Virgin and Child Enthroned" (11th-century Byzantine)

1979. Christmas. Sculptures. Multicoloured.

337	6c. Type **40**	10	10
338	25c. "Presentation in the Temple" (Andre Beauneveu)	10	10
339	30c. "Flight to Egypt" (Utrecht, c. 1510)	10	10
340	40c. "Madonna and Child" (Jacopo della Quercia)	10	10
341	90c. "Madonna della Mela" (Luca della Robbia)	15	15
342	$1 "Madonna and Child" (Antonio Rossellino)	20	20
343	$2 "Madonna and Child" (Antwerp, 1700)	35	35
MS344	125×95 mm. $4 "Virgin", Krumau	65	1·10

41 Great Hammerhead

1979. Marine Wildlife. Multicoloured.

345	40c. Type **41**	40	30
346	45c. Spot-finned butterflyfish	45	30
347	50c. Permit (fish)	45	40
348	60c. Threaded turban (shell)	65	55
349	70c. Milk conch	75	75
350	75c. Great blue heron	1·25	90
351	90c. Colourful Atlantic moon (shell)	95	1·00
352	$1 Red-footed booby	1·75	1·75
MS353	99×86 mm. $2.50 Collared plover	2·00	1·10

42 Doctor Goofy

1979. International Year of the Child. Walt Disney cartoon characters. Multicoloured.

354	½c. Type **42**	10	10
355	1c. Admiral Mickey Mouse	10	10
356	2c. Fireman Goofy	10	10
357	3c. Nurse Minnie Mouse	10	10
358	4c. Drum Major Mickey Mouse	10	10
359	5c. Policeman Donald Duck	10	10
360	10c. Pilot Donald Duck	10	10
361	$2 Postman Goofy (horiz)	2·25	2·25
362	$2.50 Train driver Donald Duck (horiz)	2·25	2·25
MS363	128×102 mm. $3 Mickey Mouse as fireman	1·75	2·00

1980. 1st Anniv of Revolution. Nos. 116 and 119/30 optd PEOPLE'S REVOLUTION 13 MARCH 1979.

364	6c. Cocoa beans in drying trays	10	10
365	12c. Cocoa tree	10	10
366	15c. Fishermen at Fontenoy	10	10
367	20c. Parliament Building, St. George's	10	10
368	25c. Fort George cannons	15	10
369	35c. Pearls Airport	20	10
370	50c. General Post Office	35	15
371	75c. Carib's Leap, Sauteurs Bay	40	20
372	$1 Carenage, St. George's	55	30
373	$2 St. George's Harbour by night	85	70
374	$3 Grand Anse Beach	1·60	1·60
375	$5 Canoe Bay and Black Bay	2·25	2·50
376	$10 Sugar-loaf Island	3·75	4·25

43 Classroom

1980. 75th Anniv of Rotary International. Multicoloured.

377	6c. Type **43**	10	10
378	30c. Different races encircling Rotary emblem	20	10
379	60c. Rotary executive presenting doctor with cheque	35	20
380	$3 Nurses with young patients	1·25	75
MS381	85×72 mm. $4 Paul P. Harris (founder)	1·00	1·60

44 Yellow-bellied Seedeater

1980. Wild Birds. Multicoloured.

382	25c. Type **44**	50	15
383	40c. Blue-hooded euphonia	55	20
384	90c. Yellow warbler	1·25	65
385	$2 Tropical mockingbird	1·75	1·25
MS386	83×110 mm. $3 Barn Owl	4·00	1·50

45 Running

1980. Olympic Games, Moscow. Multicoloured.

387	30c. Type **45**	20	15
388	40c. Football	15	20
389	90c. Boxing	35	35
390	$2 Wrestling	70	75
MS391	104×75 mm. $4 Athletes in silhouette	75	1·10

1980. "London 1980" International Stamp Exhibition. Nos. 332/5 optd LONDON 1980.

392	15c. Mail van	25	15
393	$1 "Britanis" (cargo liner)	85	35
394	$2 Diesel mail train	1·75	1·00
395	$3 Concorde	2·75	2·00

47 Long-jawed Squirrelfish

1980. Fishes. Multicoloured.

396A	½c. Type **47**	10	10
397A	1c. Blue chromis	10	10
398A	2c. Four-eyed butterflyfish	10	10
399A	4c. Sergeant major	10	10
400A	5c. Yellow-tailed snapper	10	10
401A	6c. Mutton snapper	10	10
402A	10c. Cocoa damselfish	10	10
403A	12c. Royal gramma	10	10
404A	15c. Cherub angelfish	15	10
405A	20c. Black-barred soldierfish	15	10
406A	25c. Mottled grouper	15	15
407A	30c. Caribbean long-nosed butterflyfish	15	20
408A	40c. Puddingwife	20	25
409A	50c. Midnight parrotfish	25	35
410A	90c. Red-spotted hawkfish	40	55
411A	$1 Hogfish	45	60
412A	$3 Beau Gregory	1·25	1·50
413A	$5 Rock beauty	1·50	1·75
414A	$10 Barred hamlet	2·25	2·75

1980. Christmas. Scenes from Walt Disney's "Bambi". As T 42. Multicoloured.

415	½c. Bambi with mother	10	10
416	1c. Bambi with quails	10	10
417	2c. Bambi meets Thumper the rabbit	10	10
418	3c. Bambi meets Flower the skunk	10	10
419	4c. Bambi and Faline	10	10
420	5c. Bambi with his father	10	10
421	10c. Bambi on ice	10	10
422	$2.50 Faline with foals	1·75	1·25
423	$3 Bambi and Faline	1·75	1·25
MS424	127×102 mm. $4 Bambi as Prince of the Forest (vert)	2·00	2·00

48 "The Unicorn in Captivity" (15th century unknown artist)

1981. Art Masterpieces. Multicoloured.

425	6c. Type **48**	10	10
426	10c. "The Fighting 'Temeraire' " (Turner) (horiz)	10	10
427	25c. "Sunday Afternoon on the Ile de la Grande Jatte" (Seurat) (horiz)	15	15
428	90c. "Max Schmitt in a Single Scull" (Eakins) (horiz)	45	45
429	$2 "The Burial of the Count of Orgaz" (El Greco)	85	85
430	$3 "Portrait of George Washington" (Stuart)	1·10	1·10
MS431	66×101 mm. $5 "Kaiser Karl de Grosse" (detail Durer)	1·75	2·00

1981. 50th Anniv of Walt Disney's Pluto (cartoon character). As T 42.

432	$2 Mickey Mouse serving birthday cake to Pluto	1·00	80
MS433	127×101 mm. $4 Pluto in scene from film "Pluto's Dream House"	1·50	1·50

1981. Easter. Walt Disney cartoon characters. As T 42. Multicoloured.

434	35c. Chip	20	20
435	40c. Dewey	20	20
436	$2 Huey	60	60
437	$2.50 Mickey Mouse	75	75
MS438	126×102 mm. $4 Jimmy Cricket	1·50	1·50

49 "Bust of a Woman"

1981. Birth Centenary of Picasso. Mult.

439	6c. Type **49**	10	10
440	40c. Woman (study for "Les Demoiselles d'Avignon")	20	15
441	90c. "Nude with raised Arms (The Dancer of Avignon)"	30	20
442	$4 "The Dryad"	75	75
MS443	103×128 mm. $5 "Les Demoiselles d'Avignon". Imperf	1·40	1·25

50 Balmoral Castle

1981. Royal Wedding (1st issue). Multicoloured.

444	40c. As 30c.	15	15
445	$2 Type **50**	50	50
446	$4 Prince Charles as parachutist	90	90
MS447	97×84 mm. $5 Royal Coach	70	70
448	30c. Prince Charles and Lady Diana Spencer	35	20
449	40c. Type **50**	45	35

51 Lady Diana Spencer

1981. Royal Wedding (2nd issue). Multicoloured. Self-adhesive.

450	$1 Type **51**	20	35
451	$2 Prince Charles	25	50
452	$5 Prince Charles and Lady Diana Spencer (horiz)	1·25	2·00

52 Amy Johnson (1st solo flight, Britain to Australia by Woman, May 1930)

1981. "Decade for Women". Famous Female Aviators. Multicoloured.

453	30c. Type **52**	45	15
454	70c. Mme. La Baronne de Laroche (1st qualified woman pilot, March 1910)	70	30
455	$1.10 Ruth Nichols (solo Atlantic flight attempt, June 1931)	80	40
456	$3 Amelia Earhart (1st North Atlantic solo flight by woman, May 1932)	1·75	1·10
MS457	90×85 mm. $5 Valentina Nikolayeva-Tereshkova (1st woman in space, June 1963)	1·25	1·40

1981. Christmas. Designs as T 42 showing scenes from Walt Disney's cartoon film "Lady and the Tramp".

458	½c. multicoloured	10	10
459	1c. multicoloured	10	10
460	2c. multicoloured	10	10
461	3c. multicoloured	10	10
462	4c. multicoloured	10	10
463	5c. multicoloured	10	10
464	10c. multicoloured	10	10
465	$2.50 multicoloured	3·25	1·50
466	$3 multicoloured	3·25	1·50
MS467	128×103 mm. $5 multicoloured	5·00	3·00

53 Boeing 747 SCA Carrier

1981. Space Shuttle Project. Multicoloured.

468	10c. Type **53**	30	10
469	40c. Re-entry	65	15
470	$1.10 External tank separation	1·25	45
471	$3 Touchdown	1·75	1·00
MS472	117×98 mm. $5 Launch	2·50	1·60

54 Footballer

1981. World Cup Football Championship, Spain (1982).

473	**54**	20c. multicoloured	15	10
474	-	40c. multicoloured	20	15
475	-	$1 multicoloured	35	30
476	-	$2 multicoloured	65	55
MS477		106×128 mm. $4 multicoloured	1·40	1·60

DESIGNS: 40c. to $4 various designs showing footballers.

55 Mail Van and Stagecoach

1982. Cent of U.P.U. Membership. Multicoloured.

478	30c. Type **55**	30	15
479	40c. U.P.U. emblem	30	15
480	$2.50 "Queen Elizabeth 2" (liner) and sailing ship	1·50	70
481	$4 Concorde and De Havilland D.H.9 biplane	2·25	1·25
MS482	117×78 mm. $5 British Advanced Passenger Train and steam mail trains	3·00	2·25

56 National Sports Meeting

1982. 75th Anniv of Boy Scout Movement and 125th Birth Anniv of Lord Baden-Powell. Multicoloured.

483	6c. Type **56**	15	10
484	90c. Sea scouts sailing	50	30
485	$1.10 Handicraft	65	60
486	$3 Animal tending	1·40	1·40
MS487	100×71 mm. $5 Music around campfire	1·40	1·75

57 "Anartia jatrophae"

1982. Butterflies. Multicoloured.

488	30c. Type **57**	75	30
489	40c. "Chioides vintra"	80	35
490	$1.10 "Cynthia cardui"	1·75	75
491	$3 "Historis odius"	2·75	1·60
MS492	103×77 mm. $5 "Dione juno"	3·25	2·50

58 Prince and Princess of Wales

1982. 21st Birthday of Princess of Wales. Multicoloured.

493	50c. Blenheim Palace	1·25	1·75
494	60c. As 50c.	75	75
495	$1 Type **58**	1·75	2·25
496	$2 Type **58**	1·75	2·00
497	$3 Princess of Wales	2·50	2·75
498	$4 As $3	2·50	2·75
MS499	103×75 mm. $5 Princess Diana (different)	5·50	2·50

59 "New Deal"—Soil Conservation

1982. Birth Centenary of Franklin D. Roosevelt. Multicoloured.

500	30c. Type **59**	25	10
501	40c. Roosevelt and George Washington Carver (scientist)	25	10
502	70c. Civilian conservation corps (reafforestation)	30	20
503	$3 Roosevelt with Pres. Barclay of Liberia, Casablanca Conference, 1943	70	80
MS504	100×72 mm. $5 Roosevelt delivering address at Howard University	1·75	1·75

1982. Birth of Prince William of Wales. Nos. 493/8 optd ROYAL BABY 21.6.82.

505	50c. Blenheim Palace	50	75
506	60c. As 50c.	55	60
507	$1 Type **58**	70	1·00
508	$2 Type **58**	1·00	1·25
509	$3 Princess of Wales	1·25	1·75
510	$4 As $3	1·50	1·75
MS511	103×75 mm. $5 Princess Diana (different)	2·10	2·25

60 "Presentation of Christ in the Temple"

1982. Easter. Easter Paintings by Rembrandt. Multicoloured.

512	30c. Type **60**	25	15
513	60c. "Descent from the Cross"	30	10
514	$2 "Raising of the Cross"	45	60
515	$4 "Resurrection of Christ"	80	1·25
MS516	101×126 mm. $5 "The Risen Christ"	2·40	2·00

61 "Santa Fe", U.S.A.

1982. Famous Trains of the World. Mult.

517	10c. Type **61**	50	15
518	40c. "Mistral", France	70	20
519	70c. "Rheingold", Germany	80	45
520	$1 "ET 403", France	1·00	50
521	$1.10 Steam locomotive "Mallard", Great Britain	1·25	60
522	$2 Tokaido Shinkansen "Hikari", Japan	1·40	90
MS523	121×95 mm. $5 "Settebello", Italy	1·50	2·00

62 Footballers

1982. World Cup Football Championship Winners.

524	**62**	60c. multicoloured	75	35
525	**62**	$4 multicoloured	2·00	1·25
MS526		92×134 mm. $5 multicoloured	1·50	1·50

1982. Christmas. Scenes from Walt Disney's cartoon film "The Rescuers". As T 42, but horiz.

527	½c. multicoloured	10	10
528	1c. multicoloured	10	10
529	2c. multicoloured	10	10
530	3c. multicoloured	10	10
531	4c. multicoloured	10	10
532	5c. multicoloured	10	10
533	10c. multicoloured	10	10
534	$2.50 multicoloured	3·25	1·75
535	$3 multicoloured	3·25	1·75
MS536	120×96 mm. $5 multicoloured	5·00	2·75

63 Short-finned Pilot Whale

1982. Save the Whale. Multicoloured.

537	10c. Type **63**	85	55
538	60c. Dall's porpoise	2·00	1·75
539	$1.10 Humpback whale	3·50	2·75
540	$3 Bowhead whale	6·00	7·00
MS541	113×84 mm. $5 Spotted dolphin	4·50	4·00

64 "David and Goliath"

1983. 500th Anniv of Raphael. Multicoloured.

542	25c. Type **64**	15	15
543	30c. "David sees Bathsheba"	15	15
544	90c. "Triumph of David"	30	35
545	$4 "Anointing of Solomon"	70	90
MS546	126×101 mm. $5 "Anointing of David"	80	1·10

65 Voice and Visual Communication

1983. World Communications Year. Mult.

547	30c. Type **65**	10	10
548	60c. Ambulance	25	20
549	$1.10 Westland Whirlwind helicopters	45	45
550	$3 Satellite	1·00	1·00
MS551	127×85 mm. $5 Diver and bottle-nosed dolphin	2·50	2·00

66 Chrysler "Imperial Roadster", 1931

1983. 75th Anniv of Model "T" Ford Car. Multicoloured.

552	10c. Type **66**	15	15
553	30c. Doble steam car, 1925	25	25
554	40c. Ford "Mustang", 1965	25	30
555	60c. Packard tourer, 1930	35	40
556	70c. Mercer "Raceabout", 1913	35	40
557	90c. Corvette "Stingray", 1963	35	40
558	$1.10 Auburn "851 Supercharger Speedster", 1935	40	45
559	$2.50 Pierce-Arrow "Silver Arrow", 1933	65	95
560	$3 Duesenberg dual cowl phaeton, 1929	75	1·25
561	$4 Mercedes-Benz "SSK", 1928	75	1·50
MS562	119×90 mm. $5 McFarlan "Knickerbocker" cabriolet, 1923	1·50	2·50

67 Short Solent 2 Flying Boat

1983. Bicentenary of Manned Flight. Mult.

563	40c. Type **67**	85	20
564	70c. Curtiss R3C-2 seaplane	1·00	35
565	90c. Hawker Nimrod biplane	1·25	40
566	$4 Montgolfier balloon	3·25	2·75
MS567	112×85 mm. $5 LZ-11 "Viktoria Luise" (airship)	1·75	2·00

68 Goofy

1983. Christmas. Disney cartoon characters in scenes from "Jingle Bells" (Christmas carol). Multicoloured.

568	½c. Type **68**	10	10
569	1c. Clarabelle Cow	10	10
570	2c. Donald Duck	10	10
571	3c. Pluto	10	10
572	4c. Morty and Ferdie	10	10

573	5c. Huey, Dewey and Louie	10	10
574	10c. Daisy and Chip n'Dale	10	10
575	$2.50 Big Bad Wolf	4·75	5·00
576	$5 Mickey Mouse	5·00	5·50
MS577	102×124 mm. $5 Donald Duck in sleigh	8·00	8·50

69 Weightlifting

1984. Olympic Games, Los Angeles. Mult.

578	30c. Type **69**	20	15
579	60c. Gymnastics	45	35
580	70c. Archery	50	40
581	$4 Sailing	1·90	1·90
MS582	70×102 mm. $5 Basketball	2·25	2·25

70 Frangipani

1984. Flowers. Multicoloured.

583	15c. Type **70**	15	10
584	40c. Dwarf poinciana	30	25
585	70c. Walking iris	55	45
586	$4 Lady's slipper	1·75	2·50
MS587	66×57 mm. $5 Brazilian glory vine	1·50	2·50

71 Goofy

1984. Easter. Multicoloured.

588	½c. Type **71**	10	10
589	1c. Chip and Dale	10	10
590	2c. Daisy Duck and Huey	10	10
591	3c. Daisy Duck	10	10
592	4c. Donald Duck	10	10
593	5c. Merlin and Madam Mim	10	10
594	10c. Flower	10	10
595	$2 Minnie and Mickey Mouse	1·25	2·00
596	$4 Minnie Mouse	1·75	2·75
MS597	126×100 mm. $5 Minnie Mouse (different)	3·00	3·75

72 Bobolink

1984. Songbirds. Multicoloured.

598	40c. Type **72**	1·75	1·50
599	50c. Eastern kingbird	2·00	1·60
600	60c. Barn swallow	2·25	2·00
601	70c. Yellow warbler	2·25	2·00
602	$1 Rose-breasted grosbeak	2·50	2·50
603	$1.10 Common yellowthroat ("Yellowthroat")	2·75	2·75
604	$2 Catbird	3·50	4·50
MS605	71×65 mm. $5 Fork-tailed flycatcher	6·50	5·00

1984. Universal Postal Union Congress, Hamburg. Nos. 585/6 optd 19th U.P.U. CONGRESS HAMBURG.

606	70c. Walking iris	1·00	1·00
607	$4 Lady's slipper	4·50	5·00
MS608	66×57 mm. $5 Brazilian glory vine	2·25	3·00

74 "Geeststar" (freighter)

1984. Ships. Multicoloured.

609	30c. Type **74**	75	75
610	60c. "Daphne" (liner)	1·00	1·25
611	$1.10 "Southwind" (schooner)	1·25	2·00
612	$4 "Oceanic" (liner)	2·00	5·50
MS613	108×80 mm. $5 Pirate ship	3·00	4·00

1984. 450th Death Anniv of Correggio (painter). As T 296 of Grenada. Multicoloured.

614	10c. "The Hunt—Blowing the Horn"	10	10
615	30c. "St. John the Evangelist" (horiz)	15	15
616	90c. "The Hunt—The Deer's Head"	50	50
617	$4 "The Virgin crowned by Christ" (horiz)	2·00	2·00
MS618	73×63 mm. $5 "Martyrdom of the Four Saints"	2·40	3·00

1984. 150th Birth Anniv of Edgar Degas (painter). As T 297 of Grenada. Multicoloured.

619	25c. "The Song of the Dog"	40	15
620	70c. "Cafe-concert"	70	50
621	$1.10 "The Orchestra of the Opera"	1·50	1·25
622	$3 "The Dance Lesson"	2·75	2·75
MS623	53×73 mm. $5 "Madame Camus at the Piano"	2·40	3·00

1984. "Ausipex" International Stamp Exhibition, Melbourne. As T 298 of Grenada. Multicoloured.

624	$1.10 Queen Victoria Gardens, Melbourne	50	50
625	$4 Ayers Rock	2·00	2·00
MS626	107×76 mm. $5 River Yarra, Melbourne	2·00	3·00

75 Col. Steven's Model (1825)

1984. Railway Locomotives. Multicoloured.

627	20c. Type **75**	55	25
628	50c. "Royal George" (1827)	70	50
629	60c. "Stourbridge Lion" (1829)	75	65
630	70c. "Liverpool" (1830)	80	85
631	90c. "South Carolina" (1832)	90	1·25
632	$1.10 "Monster" (1836)	90	1·50
633	$2 "Lafayette" (1837)	1·10	2·25
634	$4 "Lion" (1838)	1·40	3·75
MS635	Two sheets, each 100×70 mm. (a) $5 Sequin's locomotive (1829). (b) $5 "Adler" (1835). Set of 2 sheets	6·00	8·00

1984. Opening of Point Saline International Airport. Nos. 547, 549 and MS551 optd OPENING OF POINT SALINE INT'L AIRPORT.

636	30c. Type **65**	30	25
637	$1.10 Westland Whirlwind helicopters	95	75
MS638	127×85 mm. Diver and bottle-nosed dolphin	4·25	3·50

1984. Christmas. Walt Disney cartoon characters. As T 301 of Grenada. Multicoloured.

639	45c. Donald Duck and nephews knitting Christmas stockings	70	40
640	60c. Donald Duck and nephews sitting on sofa	80	65
641	90c. Donald Duck getting out of bed	1·25	1·00
642	$2 Donald Duck putting presents in wardrobe	2·00	2·50
643	$4 Nephews singing carols outside Donald Duck's window	3·25	4·25
MS644	126×102 mm. $5 Donald Duck filming nephews	4·25	4·00

1985. Birth Bicentenary of John J. Audubon (ornithologist). As T 418 of Ghana. Mult.

645	50c. Blue-winged teal	2·00	60
646	90c. White ibis	2·50	1·25
647	$1.10 Swallow-tailed kite	3·50	2·00
648	$3 Moorhen	4·50	4·75
MS649	82×111 mm. $5 Mangrove cuckoo (vert)	3·25	3·75

See also Nos. 736/40.

76 Kawasaki "750" (1972)

1985. Centenary of the Motor Cycle. Mult.

650	30c. Type **76**	65	45
651	60c. Honda "Goldwing GL1000" (1974) (horiz)	90	1·00
652	70c. Kawasaki "Z650" (1976) (horiz)	1·00	1·10
653	$4 Honda "CBX" (1977)	4·00	6·50
MS654	113×76 mm. $5 BMW "R100RS" (1978)	3·50	4·25

77 Nursing Cadets folding Bandages (Health)

1985. International Youth Year. Mult.

655	50c. Type **77**	70	45
656	70c. Scuba diver and turtle (Environment)	1·00	80
657	$1.10 Yachting (Leisure)	1·60	1·50
658	$3 Boys playing chess (Education)	6·50	7·00
MS659	98×70 mm. $5 Hands touching globe	2·75	3·00

1985. 40th Anniv of International Civil Aviation Organization. As T 305 of Grenada. Multicoloured.

660	5c. Lockheed Lodestar	40	20
661	70c. Hawker Siddeley H.S.748	1·75	55
662	$1.10 Boeing 727-200	2·25	90
663	$4 Boeing 707	3·50	2·50
MS664	87×68 mm. $4 Pilatus Britten Norman Islander	3·50	3·00

78 Lady Baden-Powell (founder) and Grenadian Guide Leaders

1985. 75th Anniv of Girl Guide Movement. Multicoloured.

665	30c. Type **78**	50	20
666	50c. Guide leader and guides on botany field trip	1·00	30
667	70c. Guide leader and guides camping (vert)	1·10	45
668	$4 Guides sailing (vert)	4·00	2·25
MS669	100×73 mm. $5 Lord and Lady Baden-Powell (vert)	3·75	4·25

79 "Chiomara asychis"

1985. Butterflies. Multicoloured.

670	½c. Type **79**	10	20
671	1c. "Anartia amathea"	10	20
672	2c. "Pseudolycaena marsyas"	10	20
673	4c. "Urbanus proteus"	10	20
674	5c. "Polygonus manueli"	15	20
675a	6c. "Battus polydamas"	20	15
676	10c. "Eurema daira"	30	15
677	12c. "Phoebis agarithe"	45	20
678	15c. "Aphrissa statira"	45	20
679	20c. "Strymon simaethis"	60	20
680	25c. "Mestra cana"	60	25
681	30c. "Agraulis vanillae"	60	30
682	40c. "Junonia evarete"	75	45
683	60c. "Dryas julia"	1·00	65
684	70c. "Philaethria dido"	1·10	75
685	$1.10 "Hamadryas feronia"	1·75	1·25
686	$2.50 "Strymon rufofusca"	3·25	3·00
687	$5 "Appias drusilla"	5·00	4·75
688	$10 "Polites dictynna"	8·00	9·00
688b	$20 "Euptychia cephus"	12·00	16·00

80 The Queen Mother before Prince William's Christening

1985. Life and Times of Queen Elizabeth the Queen Mother. Multicoloured.

689	$1 Type **80**	45	60
690	$1.50 In winner's enclosure at Ascot (horiz)	60	75
691	$2.50 With Prince Charles at Garter ceremony, Windsor Castle	85	1·10
MS692	56×85 mm. $5 At opening of Royal York Hospice, London	1·75	3·00

Stamps as Nos. 689/91 but with face values of 70c., $1.10 and $3 exist from additional sheetlets with changed background colours.

81 Scuba Diving

1985. Water Sports. Multicoloured.

693	15c. Type **81**	30	10
694	70c. Boys playing in waterfall	60	45
695	90c. Water skiing	70	55
696	$4 Swimming	1·50	2·25
MS697	103×78 mm. $5 Scuba diver	2·75	3·25

82 Queen or Pink Conch

1985. Marine Life. Multicoloured.

698	60c. Type **82**	75	40
699	90c. Porcupinefish and fire coral	90	60
700	$1.10 Ghost crab	1·25	1·00
701	$4 West Indies spiny lobster	2·75	4·00
MS702	299×70 mm. $5 Long-spined urchin	5·00	4·00

1985. 300th Birth Anniv of Johann Sebastian Bach (composer). As T 309a of Grenada. Multicoloured.

703	15c. Natural trumpet	50	10
704	60c. Bass viol	85	40
705	$1.10 Flute	1·50	70
706	$3 Double flageolet	2·25	1·75
MS707	110×75 mm. $5 Johann Sebastian Bach	3·25	3·50

1985. Royal Visit. As T 310a of Grenada. Mult.

708	10c. Arms of Great Britain and Grenada	20	20
709	$1 Queen Elizabeth II (vert)	1·00	1·75
710	$4 Royal Yacht "Britannia"	3·00	4·75
MS711	111×83 mm. $5 Map of Grenada Grenadines	3·00	3·75

1985. 40th Anniv of United Nations Organization. Designs as T 311a of Grenada showing United Nations (New York) stamps. Multicoloured.

712	$1 Neil Armstrong (first man on Moon) and 1982 Peaceful Uses of Outer Space 20c.	1·10	1·10
713	$2 Gandhi and 1971 Racial Equality Year 13c.	4·75	5·00
714	$2.50 Maimonides (physician) and 1956 World Health Organization 3c.	6·00	6·50
MS715	110×85 mm. $5 U.N. Under-Secretary	2·50	3·00

1985. 150th Birth Anniv of Mark Twain (author). As T 145a of Gambia showing Walt Disney cartoon characters illustrating scenes from "Letters from Hawaii". Multicoloured.

716	25c. Minnie Mouse dancing the hula	60	30
717	50c. Donald Duck surfing	90	65
718	$1.50 Donald Duck roasting marshmallow in volcano	2·25	2·25
719	$3 Mickey Mouse and Chip n'Dale canoeing	3·75	4·00

MS720 127×120 mm. $5 Mickey Mouse with cat 4·75 3·75

1985. Birth Bicentenaries of Grimm Brothers (folklorists). As T 145b of Gambia, but vert, showing Walt Disney cartoon characters in scenes from "The Elves and the Shoemaker". Multicoloured.

721 30c. Mickey Mouse as the unsuccessful Shoemaker 70 40
722 60c. Two elves making shoes 1·10 85
723 70c. The Shoemaker discovering the new shoes 1·40 1·00
724 $4 The Shoemaker's wife (Minnie Mouse) making clothes for the elves 4·25 5·00
MS725 126×101 mm. $5 The Shoemaker and his wife waving 5·50 5·00

83 "Madonna and Child" (Titian)

1985. Christmas. Religious Paintings. Mult.

726 50c. Type **83** 45 35
727 70c. "Madonna and Child with St. Mary and John the Baptist" (Bugiardini) 55 50
728 $1.10 "Adoration of the Magi" (Di Fredi) 80 1·40
729 $3 "Madonna and Child with Young St. John the Baptist" (Bartolomeo) 1·25 3·75
MS730 112×81 mm. $5 "The Annunciation" (Botticelli) 2·75 6·00

1986. Centenary of Statue of Liberty (1st issue). As T 312a of Grenada. Multicoloured.

731 5c. Croton Reservoir, New York (1875) 10 10
732 10c. New York Public Library (1986) 10 10
733 70c. Old Boathouse, Central Park (1894) 25 40
734 $4 Boating in Central Park (1986) 1·40 2·25
MS735 103×76 mm. $5 Statue of Liberty (vert) 3·75 4·25

See also Nos. 892/903.

1986. Birth Bicentenary of John J. Audubon (ornithologist) (2nd issue). As T 312b of Grenada. Multicoloured.

736 50c. Louisiana heron 1·50 1·00
737 70c. Black-crowned night heron 2·00 1·50
738 90c. American bittern 2·25 2·00
739 $4 Glossy ibis 3·75 6·50
MS740 103×74 mm. $5 King eider 6·50 8·50

1986. Visit of President Reagan of U.S.A. Nos. 684 and 687, optd VISIT OF PRES. REAGAN 20 FEBRUARY 1986.

741 70c. "Philaethria dido" 1·50 1·25
742 $5 "Appias drusilla" 6·50 8·00

85 Two Footballers

1986. World Cup Football Championship, Mexico. Designs showing footballers.

743 **85** 10c. multicoloured 60 40
744 - 70c. multicoloured 1·75 1·25
745 - $1 multicoloured 2·00 1·75
746 - $4 multicoloured 5·00 6·50
MS747 86×104 mm. $5 multicoloured 5·50 5·50

1986. Appearance of Halley's Comet (1st issue). As T 151a of Gambia. Multicoloured.

748 5c. Nicholas Copernicus (astronomer) and Earl of Rosse's six foot reflector telescope 40 40
749 20c. "Sputnik I" (first satellite) orbiting Earth, 1957 60 40
750 40c. Tycho Brahe's notes and sketch of 1577 Comet 80 60
751 $4 Edmond Halley and 1682 Comet 3·75 4·50
MS752 101×70 mm. $5 Halley's Comet 3·00 3·50

See also Nos. 790/4.
The captions of Nos. 750/1 are transposed.

1986. 60th Birthday of Queen Elizabeth II. As T 151b of Gambia.

753 2c. black and yellow 10 15
754 $1.50 multicoloured 80 1·00
755 $4 multicoloured 2·00 2·75
MS756 120×85 mm. $5 black and brown 2·00 3·50

DESIGNS: 2c. Princesses Elizabeth and Margaret, Windsor Park, 1933; $1.50, Queen Elizabeth; $4 In Sydney, Australia, 1970; $5 The Royal Family, Coronation Day, 1937.

1986. "Ameripex '86" International Stamp Exhibition, Chicago. As T 315a of Grenada. Multicoloured.

757 30c. Donald Duck riding mule in Grand Canyon 60 45
758 60c. Daisy Duck, Timothy Mouse and Dumbo on Golden Gate Bridge, San Francisco 85 1·00
759 $1 Mickey Mouse and Goofy in fire engine and Chicago Watertower 1·50 1·75
760 $3 Mickey Mouse as airmail pilot and White House 3·00 4·00
MS761 126×101 mm. $5 Donald Duck and Mickey Mouse watching Halley's Comet over Statue of Liberty 3·75 7·50

1986. Royal Wedding. As T 153b of Gambia. Multicoloured.

762 60c. Prince Andrew and Miss Sarah Ferguson 55 45
763 70c. Prince Andrew in car 65 55
764 $4 Prince Andrew with Westland Lynx naval helicopter 4·00 3·50
MS765 88×88 mm. $5 Prince Andrew and Miss Sarah Ferguson (different) 4·00 5·50

86 "Hygrocybe firma"

1986. Mushrooms of the Lesser Antilles. Mult.

766 15c. Type **86** 80 40
767 50c. "Xerocomus coccolobae" 1·75 1·25
768 $2 "Volvariella cubensis" 3·50 4·00
769 $3 "Lactarius putidus" 4·50 5·00
MS770 76×80 mm. $5 "Leptonia caeruleopitata" 9·00 12·00

87 Giant Atlantic or Dolobrate Pyram

1986. Sea Shells. Multicoloured.

771 15c. Type **87** 90 50
772 50c. Beau's murex 2·00 1·25
773 $1.10 West Indian fighting conch 2·25 2·75
774 $4 Alphabet conch 3·75 7·00
MS775 109×75 mm. $5 Brown-lined paper bubble 6·50 8·50

1986. World Cup Football Championship Winners, Mexico. Nos. 743/6 optd WINNERS Argentina 3 W. Germany 2.

776 **85** 10c. multicoloured 65 40
777 - 70c. multicoloured 1·40 1·10
778 - $1 multicoloured 1·75 1·40
779 - $4 multicoloured 4·00 5·50
MS780 86×104 mm. $5 multicoloured 8·00 10·00

88 Common Opossum

1986. Wildlife. Multicoloured.

781 10c. Type **88** 20 20
782 30c. Giant toad 40 40
783 60c. Land tortoise 80 80
784 70c. Murine opossum (vert) 85 85
785 90c. Burmese mongoose (vert) 90 1·00
786 $1.10 Nine-banded armadillo 1·00 1·25
787 $2 Agouti 1·75 2·25
788 $3 Humpback whale 4·00 4·25
MS789 Two sheets, each 103×72 mm. (a) $5 Mona monkey (vert). (b) $5 Iguana. Set of 2 sheets 11·00 14·00

1986. Appearance of Halley's Comet (2nd issue). Nos. 748/51 optd with T 447a of Ghana.

790 5c. Nicholas Copernicus (astronomer) and Earl of Rosse's six foot reflector telescope 60 60
791 20c. "Sputnik I" orbiting Earth, 1957 80 50
792 40c. Tycho Brahe's notes and sketch of 1577 Comet 1·00 60
793 $4 Edmond Halley and 1682 Comet 5·00 6·00
MS794 102×70 mm. $5 Halley's Comet 4·00 5·50

1986. Christmas. As T 318a of Grenada showing Walt Disney cartoon characters. Multicoloured.

795 25c. Chip n'Dale with hummingbird 50 15
796 30c. Robin delivering card to Mickey Mouse (vert) 50 20
797 50c. Piglet, Pooh and Jose Carioca on beach 65 30
798 60c. Grandma Duck feeding birds (vert) 75 40
799 70c. Cinderella and birds with mistletoe (vert) 80 50
800 $1.50 Huey, Dewey and Louie windsurfing 1·50 2·25
801 $3 Mickey Mouse and Morty on beach with turtle 1·75 3·00
802 $4 Kittens playing on piano (vert) 2·25 4·00
MS803 Two sheets, each 127×102 mm. (a) $5 Mickey Mouse and Willie the Whale. (b) $5 Bambi, Thumper and Blossom in snow (vert). Set of 2 sheets 8·00 11·50

89 Cycling

1986. Olympic Games, Seoul, South Korea (1988). Multicoloured.

804 10c.+5c. Type **89** 75 40
805 50c+20c. Sailing 75 90
806 70c.+30c. Gymnastics 75 1·10
807 $2+$1 Horse trials 2·00 3·00
MS808 80×100 mm. $3+$1 Marathon 2·50 4·50

90 Aston-Martin "Volante" (1984)

1986. Centenary of Motoring. Multicoloured.

809 10c. Type **90** 25 25
810 30c. Jaguar "MK V" (1948) 45 45
811 60c. Nash "Ambassador" (1956) 60 65
812 70c. Toyota "Supra" (1984) 60 70
813 90c. Ferrari "Testarosa" (1985) 70 90
814 $1 BMW "501B" (1955) 70 95
815 $2 Mercedes-Benz "280 SL" (1968) 1·00 2·00
816 $3 Austro-Daimler "ADR8" (1932) 1·25 2·50
MS817 Two sheets, each 116×85 mm. (a) $5 Morgan "+8" (1977). (b) $5 Checker taxi. Set of 2 sheets 5·50 11·00

1986. Birth Centenary of Marc Chagall (artist). As T 321a of Grenada, showing various paintings.

818-857 $1.10×40 multicoloured
MS858 Two sheets, each 110×95 mm. $5×10 multicoloured (each 104×89 mm). Imperf. Set of 10 sheets 28·00 28·00

1987. America's Cup Yachting Championship. As T 321b of Grenada. Multicoloured.

859 25c. "Defender", 1895 60 40
860 45c. "Galatea", 1886 80 60
861 70c. "Azzurra", 1981 1·00 1·00
862 $4 "Australia II", 1983 2·00 3·50
MS863 113×83 mm. $5 "Columbia" defeating "Shamrock", 1899 (horiz) 5·00 7·00

1987. 500th Anniv (1992) of Discovery of America by Christopher Columbus (1st issue). As T 322 of Grenada. Multicoloured.

864 15c. Christopher Columbus 35 25
865 30c. Queen Isabella of Castile 40 30
866 50c. "Santa Maria" 60 50
867 60c. Claiming the New World for Spain 60 60
868 90c. Early Spanish map of Lesser Antilles 80 75
869 $1 King Ferdinand of Aragon 80 80
870 $2 Fort La Navidad (drawing by Columbus) 1·50 2·00
871 $3 Galley and Caribs, Hispaniola (drawing by Columbus) 2·00 2·50
MS872 Two sheets, each 104×72 mm. (a) $5 Caribs pearl fishing. (b) $5 "Santa Maria" at anchor. Set of 2 sheets 8·00 11·00

See also Nos. 1191/5, 1224/32, 1366/74, 1494/1500 and 1519/20.

1987. Milestones of Transportation. As T 322a of Grenada. Multicoloured.

873 10c. Saunders Roe "SRN1" (first hovercraft), 1959 65 30
874 15c. Bugatti "Royale" (largest car), 1931 70 35
875 30c. Aleksei Leonov and "Voskhod II" (first spacewalk), 1965 90 55
876 50c. C.S.S "Hunley" (first submarine to sink enemy ship), 1864 1·25 75
877 60c. Rolls Royce "Flying Bedstead" (first VTOL aircraft), 1954 1·50 85
878 70c. "Jenny Lind" (first mass produced locomotive class), 1847 1·60 1·25
879 90c. Duryea "Buggvaut" (first U.S petrol-driven car), 1893 1·75 1·25
880 $1.50 Steam locomotive, Metropolitan Railway, London (first underground line), 1863 2·50 2·75
881 $2 S.S. "Great Britain" (first transatlantic crossing by screw-steamship), 1843 3·00 3·25
882 $3 "Budweiser Rocket" (fastest car), 1979 3·25 3·75

1987. "Capex '87" International Stamp Exhibition, Toronto. Game Fishes. As T 323 of Grenada but horiz. Multicoloured.

883 6c. Yellow chub 15 15
884 30c. King mackerel 40 30
885 50c. Short-finned mako 55 55
886 60c. Dolphin (fish) 60 60
887 90c. Skipjack tuna ("Bonito") 75 75
888 $1.10 Cobia 1·00 1·25
889 $3 Tarpon 2·25 2·75
890 $4 Swordfish 2·50 3·25
MS891 Two sheets, each 100×70 mm. (a) $5 Spotted jewfish. (b) $5 Amberjack. Set of 2 sheets 8·00 11·00

1987. Centenary of Statue of Liberty (1986) (2nd issue). As T 323a of Grenada. Multicoloured.

892 10c. Cleaning face of statue 20 20
893 15c. Commemorative lapel badges 30 30
894 25c. Band playing and statue 40 40
895 30c. Band on parade and statue 45 45
896 45c. Face of statue 50 50
897 50c. Cleaning head of statue (horiz) 55 55
898 60c. Models of statue (horiz) 65 65
899 70c. Small boat flotilla (horiz) 75 85
900 $1 Unveiling ceremony 85 90
901 $1.10 Statue and Manhattan skyline 90 1·00
902 $2 Parade of warships 1·75 2·00
903 $3 Making commemorative flags 1·90 2·25

1987. Great Scientific Discoveries. As T 325 of Grenada. Multicoloured.

904 60c. Newton medal 1·00 80
905 $1 Louis Daguerre (inventor of daguerreotype) 1·25 1·00
906 $2 Antoine Lavoisier and apparatus 2·25 3·00
907 $3 Rudolf Diesel and first oil engine 7·00 5·50
MS908 105×75 mm. $5 Halley's Comet 6·00 7·50

No. 907 is inscribed "JAMES WATT" in error.

1987. Bicentenary of U.S. Constitution. As T 327a of Grenada. Multicoloured.

909 10c. Washington addressing delegates, Constitutional Convention 25 20
910 50c. Flag and State Seal, Georgia 85 75
911 60c. Capitol, Washington (vert) 85 80
912 $4 Thomas Jefferson (statesman) (vert) 3·25 6·00
MS913 105×75 mm. $5 Alexander Hamilton (New York delegate) (vert) 2·25 4·00

1987. "Hafnia '87" International Stamp Exhibition, Copenhagen. Designs as T 328 of Grenada, but horiz, illustrating Hans Christian Andersen's fairy tales. Multicoloured.

914 25c. Donald and Daisy Duck in "The Swineherd" 50 30
915 30c. Mickey Mouse, Donald and Daisy Duck in "What the Good Man Does is Always Right" 55 35

916 50c. Mickey and Minnie Mouse in "Little Tuk" 75 75
917 60c. Minnie Mouse and Ferdie in "The World's Fairest Rose" 75 75
918 70c. Mickey Mouse in "The Garden of Paradise" 80 80
919 $1.50 Goofy and Mickey Mouse in "The Naughty Boy" 2·00 2·25
920 $3 Goofy in "What the Moon Saw" 2·75 3·00
921 $4 Alice as "Thumbelina" 3·25 3·50
MS922 Two sheets, each 127×101 mm. (a) $5 Daisy Duck in "Hans Clodhopper". (b) $5 Aunt Matilda and Mickey Mouse in "Elder-Tree Mother". Set of 2 sheets 11·00 12·00

91 "The Virgin and Child with Saints Martin and Agnes"

1987. Christmas. Religious Paintings by El Greco. Multicoloured.
923 10c. Type **91** 40 15
924 50c. "St. Agnes" (detail from "The Virgin and Child with Saints Martin and Agnes") 1·25 75
925 60c. "The Annunciation" 1·25 75
926 $4 "The Holy Family with St. Anne" 4·75 7·25
MS927 75×101 mm. $5 "The Adoration of the Shepherds" 7·50 8·50

1988. Royal Ruby Wedding. As T 330a of Grenada. Multicoloured.
928 20c. brown, black and green 50 15
929 30c. brown and black 50 20
930 $2 multicoloured 2·25 2·50
931 $3 multicoloured 2·50 3·25
MS932 76×100 mm. $5 multicoloured 4·50 5·00
DESIGNS: 20c. Queen Elizabeth II with Princess Anne, c. 1957; 30c. Wedding photograph, 1947; $2 Queen with Prince Charles and Princess Anne, c. 1955; $3 Queen Elizabeth (from photo by Tim Graham), 1980; $5 Princess Elizabeth in wedding dress, 1947.

1988. Olympic Games, Seoul. As T 331 of Grenada showing Walt Disney cartoon characters as Olympic competitors. Multicoloured.
933 1c. Minnie Mouse as rhythmic gymnast (horiz) 10 10
934 2c. Pete and Goofy as pankration wrestlers (horiz) 10 10
935 3c. Huey and Dewey as synchronized swimmers (horiz) 10 10
936 4c. Huey, Dewey and Louie in hoplite race (horiz) 10 10
937 5c. Clarabelle and Daisy Duck playing baseball (horiz) 10 10
938 10c. Goofy and Donald Duck in horse race (horiz) 10 10
939 $6 Donald Duck and Uncle Scrooge McDuck windsurfing (horiz) 4·50 5·50
940 $7 Mickey Mouse in chariot race (horiz) 4·75 5·50
MS941 Two sheets, each 127×101 mm. (a) $5 Mickey Mouse throwing discus in pentathalon. (b) $5 Donald Duck playing tennis. Set of 2 sheets 7·50 9·00

92 Scout signalling with Semaphore Flags

1988. World Scout Jamboree, Australia. Mult.
942 50c. Type **92** 50 35
943 70c. Canoeing 60 50
944 $1 Cooking over campfire (horiz) 70 65
945 $3 Scouts around campfire (horiz) 2·00 3·00
MS946 110×77 mm. $5 Erecting tent (horiz) 4·00 4·50

1988. Birds. As T 334 of Grenada. Mult.
947 20c. Yellow-crowned night heron 30 25
948 25c. Brown pelican 30 25
949 45c. Audubon's shearwater 40 35
950 60c. Red-footed booby 50 45
951 70c. Bridled tern 55 50
952 90c. Red-billed tropic bird 70 70
953 $3 Blue-winged teal 1·75 2·25
954 $4 Sora crake ("Sora") 2·00 2·75
MS955 Two sheets, each 105×75 mm. (a) $5 Purple-throated carib. (b) $5 Little blue heron. Set of 2 sheets 6·00 6·50

1988. 500th Birth Anniv of Titian (artist). As T 166a of Gambia. Multicoloured.
956 15c. "Man with Blue Eyes" 15 15
957 30c. "The Three Ages of Man" (detail) 20 20
958 60c. "Don Diego Mendoza" 35 35
959 75c. "Emperor Charles V seated" 50 50
960 $1 "A Young Man in a Fur" 60 60
961 $2 "Tobias and the Angel" 1·10 1·40
962 $3 "Pietro Bembo" 1·60 1·90
963 $4 "Pier Luigi Farnese" 1·75 2·25
MS964 110×95 mm. (a) $5 "Sacred and Profane Love" (detail). (b) $5 "Venus and Adonis" (detail). Set of 2 sheets 7·00 8·00

1988. Airships. As T 336 of Grenada. Multicoloured.
965 10c. "Hindenburg" over Sugarloaf Mountain, Rio de Janeiro, 1937 (horiz) 70 20
966 20c. "Hindenburg" over New York, 1937 (horiz) 85 30
967 30c. U.S. Navy "K" Class airships on Atlantic escort duty, 1944 (horiz) 95 35
968 40c. "Hindenburg" approaching Lakehurst, 1937 1·00 45
969 60c. "Graf Zeppelin" and "Hindenburg" over Germany, 1936 1·25 60
970 70c. "Hindenburg" and "Los Angeles" moored at Lakehurst, 1936 (horiz) 1·25 70
971 $1 "Graf Zeppelin II" over Dover, 1939 1·25 85
972 $2 "Ersatz Deutschland" on scheduled passenger flight, 1912 (horiz) 1·60 1·60
973 $3 "Graf Zeppelin" over Dome of the Rock, Jerusalem, 1931 (horiz) 2·50 2·25
974 $4 "Hindenburg" over Olympic stadium, Berlin, 1936 (horiz) 2·50 2·25
MS975 Two sheets (a) 76×95 mm. $5 LZ-127 "Graf Zeppelin", 1933. (b) 95×76 mm. $5 LZ-127 "Graf Zeppelin", 1931 (horiz). Set of 2 sheets 8·00 10·00

93 Bambi and his mother

1988. Disney Animal Cartoon Films.
976–1029 30c.×54 multicoloured.
MS1030 Six sheets, each 127×102 mm. $5×6 multicoloured. Set of 6 sheets 28·00 30·00
DESIGNS: Scenes from "Bambi", "Dumbo" $5 (vert), "Lady and the Tramp" $5 (vert), "The Aristocats", "The Fox and the Hound" and "101 Dalmatians".

1988. "Sydpex '88" National Stamp Exhibition, Sydney and 60th Birthday of Mickey Mouse. As T 337 of Grenada. Multicoloured.
1031 1c. Mickey Mouse conducting at Sydney Opera House 10 10
1032 2c. Mickey Mouse and Donald Duck at Ayers Rock 10 10
1033 3c. Goofy and Mickey Mouse on sheep station 10 10
1034 4c. Goofy and Mickey Mouse at Lone Pine Koala Sanctuary 10 10
1035 5c. Mickey Mouse, Donald Duck and Goofy playing Australian football 10 10
1036 10c. Mickey Mouse and Goofy camel racing 10 10
1037 $5 Donald Duck and his nephews bowling 4·50 5·00
1038 $6 Mickey Mouse with America's Cup trophy and "Australia II" (yacht) 5·50 6·00
MS1039 Two sheets, each 127×102 mm. (a) $5 Goofy diving on Great Barrier Reef. (b) $5 Donald Duck, Mickey and Minnie Mouse at beach barbecue. Set of 2 sheets 7·50 9·50

1988. Flowering Trees and Shrubs. As T 339 of Grenada. Multicoloured.
1040 10c. Potato tree (vert) 15 15
1041 20c. Wild cotton 15 15
1042 30c. Shower of gold (vert) 20 20
1043 60c. Napoleon's button (vert) 35 30
1044 90c. Geiger tree 60 70
1045 $1 Fern tree 70 80
1046 $2 French cashew 1·25 2·00
1047 $4 Amherstia (vert) 2·00 3·00
MS1048 Two sheets, each 117×88 mm. (a) $5 African tulip tree (vert). (b) $5 Swamp immortelle. Set of 2 sheets 4·25 5·50

1988. Cars. As T 335 of Grenada. Mult.
1049 $2 Doble "Series E", 1925 1·40 1·25
1050 $2 Alvis "12/50", 1926 1·40 1·25
1051 $2 Sunbeam 3-litre, 1927 1·40 1·25
1052 $2 Franklin "Airman", 1928 1·40 1·25
1053 $2 Delage "D8S", 1929 1·40 1·25
1054 $2 Mors, 1897 1·40 1·25
1055 $2 Peerless "Green Dragon", 1904 1·40 1·25
1056 $2 Pope-Hartford, 1909 1·40 1·25
1057 $2 Daniels "Submarine Speedstar", 1920 1·40 1·25
1058 $2 McFarlan 9.3 litre, 1922 1·40 1·25
1059 $2 Frazer Nash "Lemans" replica, 1949 1·40 1·25
1060 $2 Pegaso "Z102", 1953 1·40 1·25
1061 $2 Siata "Spyder V-8", 1953 1·40 1·25
1062 $2 Kurtis-Offenhauser, 1953 1·40 1·25
1063 $2 Kaiser-Darrin, 1954 1·40 1·25
1064 $2 Tracta, 1930 1·40 1·25
1065 $2 Maybach "Zeppelin", 1932 1·40 1·25
1066 $2 Railton "Light Sports", 1934 1·40 1·25
1067 $2 Hotchkiss, 1936 1·40 1·25
1068 $2 Mercedes-Benz "W163", 1939 1·40 1·25
1069 $2 Aston-Martin "Vantage V8", 1982 1·40 1·25
1070 $2 Porsche "956", 1982 1·40 1·25
1071 $2 Lotus "Esprit Turbo", 1983 1·40 1·25
1072 $2 McLaren "MP4/2", 1984 1·40 1·25
1073 $2 Mercedes-Benz "190E 2.3-16", 1985 1·40 1·25
1074 $2 Ferrari "250 GT Lusso", 1963 1·40 1·25
1075 $2 Porsche "904", 1964 1·40 1·25
1076 $2 Volvo "P1800", 1967 1·40 1·25
1077 $2 McLaren-Chevrolet "M8D", 1970 1·40 1·25
1078 $2 Jaguar "XJ6", 1981 1·40 1·25

1988. "Mickey's Christmas Parade". As T 340a of Grenada showing Walt Disney cartoon characters. Multicoloured.
1079 $1 Dumbo 65 65
1080 $1 Goofy as Father Christmas 65 65
1081 $1 Minnie Mouse waving from window 65 65
1082 $1 Clarabelle, Mordie and Ferdie watching parade 65 65
1083 $1 Donald Duck's nephews 65 65
1084 $1 Donald Duck as drummer 65 65
1085 $1 Toy soldiers 65 65
1086 $1 Mickey Mouse on wooden horse 65 65
MS1087 Two sheets, each 127×102 mm. (a) $7 Peter Pan and Captain Hook on float (horiz). (b) $7 Mickey Mouse as Father Christmas and Donald Duck in carnival train (horiz). Set of 2 sheets 10·00 11·00

94 Middleweight Boxing (Gold, Henry Maske, East Germany)

1989. Olympic Medal Winners, Seoul (1988). Multicoloured.
1088 15c. Type **94** 40 20
1089 50c. Freestyle wrestling (130 kg) (Bronze, Andreas Schroeder, East Germany) 60 40
1090 60c. Women's team gymnastics (Bronze, East Germany) 70 50
1091 75c. Platform diving (Gold, Greg Louganis, U.S.A.) 60 80
1092 $1 Freestyle wrestling (52 kg) (Gold, Mitsuru Sato, Japan) 90 80
1093 $2 Men's freestyle 4×200 m relay swimming (Bronze, West Germany) 1·40 1·40
1094 $3 Men's 5000 m (Silver, Dieter Baumann, West Germany) 1·60 2·00
1095 $4 Women's heptathlon (Gold, Jackie Joyner-Kersee, U.S.A.) 2·00 2·50
MS1096 Two sheets, each 70×100 mm. (a) $6 Weightlifting (67.5 kg) (Gold, Joachim Kunz, East Germany). (b) $6 Team Three-Day Event (Gold, West Germany). Set of 2 sheets 6·50 8·50

1989. Japanese Art. Paintings by Hiroshige. As T 177a of Gambia. Multicoloured.
1097 15c. "Crossing the Oi at Shimada by Ferry" 25 25
1098 20c. "Daimyo and Entourage at Arai" 30 30
1099 45c. "Cargo Portage through Goyu" 50 50
1100 75c. "Snowfall at Fujigawa" 75 75
1101 $1 "Horses for the Emperor at Chirifu" 85 85
1102 $2 "Rainfall at Tsuchiyama" 1·60 1·60
1103 $3 "An Inn at Ishibe" 2·25 2·25
1104 $4 "On the Shore of Lake Biwa at Otsu" 2·75 2·75
MS1105 Two sheets, each 102×78 mm. (a) $5 "Fishing Village of Yokkaichi on the Mie". (b) $5 "Pilgrimage to Atsuta Shrine at Miya". Set of 2 sheets 4·75 7·00

1989. World Cup Football Championship, Italy (1990) (1st issue). As T 345a of Grenada. Mult.
1106 15c. World Cup trophy 50 20
1107 20c. Flags of Argentina (winners 1986) and International Federation of Football Associations (FIFA) (horiz) 1·25 20
1108 45c. Franz Beckenbauer (West Germany) with World Cup, 1974 1·00 35
1109 75c. Flags of Italy (winners 1982) and FIFA (horiz) 1·75 55
1110 $1 Pele (Brazil) with Jules Rimet trophy 1·75 85
1111 $2 Flags of West Germany (winners 1974) and FIFA (horiz) 2·25 2·00
1112 $3 Flags of Brazil (winners 1970) and FIFA (horiz) 2·25 2·75
1113 $4 Jules Rimet trophy and Brazil players 2·25 2·75
MS1114 (a) 100×81 mm. $6 Goalkeeper (horiz). (b) 66×95 mm. $6 Péle with Jules Rimet trophy. Set of 2 sheets 8·50 9·00
See also Nos. 1285/9.

1989. North American Railway Locomotives. As T 342 of Grenada. Multicoloured.
1115 $2 Morris & Essex Railroad "Dover", 1841, U.S.A. 1·50 1·50
1116 $2 Baltimore & Ohio Railroad No. 57 "Memnon", 1848, U.S.A. 1·50 1·50
1117 $2 Camden & Amboy Railroad "John Stevens", 1849, U.S.A. 1·50 1·50
1118 $2 Lawrence Machine Shop "Lawrence", 1853, U.S.A. 1·50 1·50
1119 $2 South Carolina Railroad "James S. Corry", 1859, U.S.A. 1·50 1·50
1120 $2 Mine Hill & Schuylkill Haven Railroad flexible beam No. 3, 1860, U.S.A. 1·50 1·50
1121 $2 Delaware, Lackawanna & Western Railroad "Montrose", 1861, U.S.A. 1·50 1·50
1122 $2 Central Pacific Railroad No. 68 "Pequop", 1868, U.S.A. 1·50 1·50
1123 $2 Boston & Providence Railroad "Daniel Nason", 1863, U.S.A. 1·50 1·50
1124 $2 Morris & Essex Railroad "Joe Scranton", 1870, U.S.A. 1·50 1·50
1125 $2 Central Railroad of New Jersey No. 124, 1871, U.S.A. 1·50 1·50
1126 $2 Baldwin tramway steam locomotive, 1876, U.S.A. 1·50 1·50
1127 $2 Lackawanna & Bloomsburg Railroad "Luzerne", 1878, U.S.A. 1·50 1·50
1128 $2 Central Mexican Railroad No. 150, 1892 1·50 1·50
1129 $2 Denver South Park & Pacific Railroad No. 15, Breckenridge, 1879, U.S.A. 1·50 1·50
1130 $2 Miles Planting & Manufacturing Company plantation locomotive "Daisy", 1894, U.S.A. 1·50 1·50
1131 $2 Central of Georgia Railroad Baldwin 854 No. 1136, 1895, U.S.A. 1·50 1·50
1132 $2 Savannah, Florida & Western Railroad No. 111, 1900, U.S.A. 1·50 1·50
1133 $2 Douglas, Gilmore & Company contractors locomotive No. 3, 1902, U.S.A. 1·50 1·50
1134 $2 Lehigh Valley Coal Company compressed air locomotive No. 900, 1903, U.S.A. 1·50 1·50
1135 $2 Louisiana & Texas Railroad McKeen motor locomotive, 1908, U.S.A. 1·50 1·50
1136 $2 Clear Lake Lumber Company Type B Climax locomotive No. 6, 1910, U.S.A. 1·50 1·50
1137 $2 Blue Jay Lumber Company Heisler locomotive No. 10, 1912, U.S.A. 1·50 1·50
1138 $2 Stewartstown Railroad petrol locomotive No. 6, 1920s, U.S.A. 1·50 1·50
1139 $2 Bangor & Aroostock Railroad Class G No. 186, 1921, U.S.A. 1·50 1·50
1140 $2 Hammond Lumber Company Mallet locomotive, No. 6, 1923, U.S.A. 1·50 1·50
1141 $2 Central Railway of New Jersey diesel locomotive No. 1000, 1925, U.S.A. 1·50 1·50
1142 $2 Atchison Topeka & Santa Fe Railroad "Super Chief" diesel express, 1935, U.S.A. 1·50 1·50
1143 $2 Norfolk & Western Railroad Class Y-6, 1948, U.S.A. 1·50 1·50

1144 $2 Boston & Maine Railroad Budd diesel railcar, 1949, U.S.A. 1·50 1·50

94a Mickey Mouse and Donald Duck at Ecole Militaire Inflating Balloon

1989. "Philexfrance '89" International Stamp Exn, Paris. Designs showing Walt Disney cartoon characters in Paris. Multicoloured.

1145 1c. Type **94a** 10 10
1146 2c. Mickey and Minnie Mouse on river boat passing Conciergerie 10 10
1147 3c. Mickey Mouse at Hotel de Ville (vert) 10 10
1148 4c. Mickey Mouse at Genie of the Bastille monument (vert) 10 10
1149 5c. Mickey and Minnie Mouse arriving at Opera House 10 10
1150 10c. Mickey and Minnie Mouse on tandem in Luxembourg Gardens 10 10
1151 $5 Mickey Mouse in aeroplane over L'Arch de La Defense (vert) 5·50 6·50
1152 $6 Mickey Mouse at Place Vendome (vert) 5·50 6·50
MS1153 Two sheets, each 127×102 mm. (a) $6 Mickey and Minnie Mouse on scooter in Place de la Concorde. (b) $6 Donald Duck, Mickey and Minnie Mouse in balloon over Versailles. Set of 2 sheets 11·00 13·00

95 Launch of "Apollo 11"

1989. 20th Anniv of First Manned Landing on Moon. Multicoloured.

1154 25c. Type **95** 30 30
1155 50c. Splashdown (horiz) 50 50
1156 60c. Modules in space 60 60
1157 75c. Aldrin setting up experiment (horiz) 70 70
1158 $1 "Apollo 11" leaving Earth orbit (horiz) 80 80
1159 $2 Moving "Apollo 11" to launch site 1·60 1·90
1160 $3 Lunar module "Eagle" leaving Moon (horiz) 2·00 2·50
1161 $4 "Eagle" landing on Moon 2·25 2·75
MS1162 (a) 71×100 mm. $5 Armstrong stepping onto Moon. (b) 101×72 mm. $5 Armstrong's footprint on Moon. Set of 2 sheets 6·50 8·00

1989. Fungi. As T 348 of Grenada. Mult.

1163 6c. "Agaricus purpurellus" (incorrectly inscr "Collybia aurea") 35 25
1164 10c. "Podaxis pistillaris" 35 25
1165 20c. "Hygrocybe firma" 55 45
1166 30c. "Agaricus rufoaurantiacus" 65 55
1167 75c. "Leptonia howellii" 1·40 1·40
1168 $2 "Marasmiellus purpureus" 2·50 2·75
1169 $3 "Marasmius trinitatis" 3·00 3·25
1170 $4 "Collybia aurea" (incorrectly inscr "Hygrocybe martinicensis") 3·25 3·50
MS1171 Two sheets, each 56×71 mm. (a) $6 "Lentinus crinitus" (incorrectly inscr "Agaricus purpurellus"). (b) $6 "Hygrocybe martinicensis" (incorrectly inscr "Lentinus crinitus"). Set of 2 sheets 12·00 13·00

1989. Butterflies. As T 350 of Grenada. Mult.

1172 25c. "Battus polydamas" (inscr "Papilio androgeus") 40 40
1173 35c. "Phoebis sennae" 45 45
1174 45c. "Hamadryas feronia" 55 55
1175 50c. "Cynthia cardui" 55 55
1176 75c. "Ascia monuste" 80 80
1177 90c. "Eurema lisa" 90 90
1178 $2 "Aphrissa statira" 2·00 2·00
1179 $3 "Hypolimnas misippus" 2·50 2·50
MS1180 Two sheets, each 87×115 mm. (a) $6 "Anartia amathea". (b) $6 "Pseudolycaena marsyas". Set of 2 sheets 9·00 11·00

96 Ethel Barrymore

1989. 425th Birth Anniv of Shakespeare. Shakespearean Actors. Multicoloured.

1181 15c. Type **96** 35 25
1182 $1.10 Richard Burton 1·50 1·25
1183 $2 John Barrymore 2·25 2·25
1184 $3 Paul Robeson 2·50 2·75
MS1185 103×77 mm. $6 Bando Tamasaburo and Nakamura Kanzaburo 4·50 5·50

97 Buddy Holly

1989. Musicians. Multicoloured.

1186 10c. Type **97** 35 25
1187 25c. Jimmy Hendrix 55 40
1188 75c. Mighty Sparrow 70 70
1189 $4 Katsutoji Kineya 3·00 4·00
MS1190 103×77 mm. $6 Kurt Weill 4·25 4·75

97a Arawaks canoeing

1989. 500th Anniv (1992) of Discovery of America by Columbus (2nd issue). Pre-Columbian Arawak Society. As T 247 of Antigua. Multicoloured.

1191 15c. Type **97a** 25 25
1192 75c. Family and campfire 75 75
1193 90c. Using stone tools 95 95
1194 $3 Eating and drinking 2·50 3·00
MS1195 84×87 mm. $6 Making fire 3·50 4·25

1989. "World Stamp Expo '89" International Stamp Exhibition, Washington. Designs showing Walt Disney cartoon characters illustrating proverbs from "Poor Richard's Almanack". As T 352 of Grenada. Multicoloured.

1196 1c. Uncle Scrooge McDuck with gold coins in sinking boat 10 10
1197 2c. Robin Hood shooting apple off Friar Tuck 10 10
1198 3c. Winnie the Pooh with honey 10 10
1199 4c. Goofy, Minnie Mouse and Donald Duck exercising 10 10
1200 5c. Pinnochio holding Jimminy Cricket 10 10
1201 6c. Huey and Dewey putting up wallpaper 10 10
1202 8c. Mickey Mouse asleep in storm 15 10
1203 10c. Mickey Mouse as Benjamin Franklin selling "Pennsylvania Gazette" 15 10
1204 $5 Mickey Mouse with chicken, recipe book and egg 4·00 5·00
1205 $6 Mickey Mouse missing carriage 4·50 5·00
MS1206 Two sheets, each 127×102 mm. (a) $6 Mickey Mouse bowing. (b) $6 Mickey Mouse delivering basket of food (vert). Set of 2 sheets 10·50 11·00

1990. Christmas. Paintings by Rubens. As T 352a of Grenada. Multicoloured.

1207 10c. "The Annunciation" 35 15
1208 15c. "The Flight of the Holy Family into Egypt" 40 15
1209 25c. "The Presentation in the Temple" 55 15
1210 45c. "The Holy Family under the Apple Tree" 70 25
1211 $2 "Madonna and Child with Saints" 2·00 2·50
1212 $4 "The Virgin and Child enthroned with Saints" 3·00 4·00
1213 $5 "The Holy Family" 3·00 4·00
MS1214 Two sheets, each 70×95 mm. (a) $5 "The Adoration of the Magi" (sketch). (b) $5 "The Adoration of the Magi". Set of 2 sheets 12·00 14·00

1990. "EXPO '90" International Garden and Greenery Exhibition, Osaka. Caribbean Orchids. As T 354 of Grenada. Multicoloured.

1215 15c. "Brassocattleya" Thalie 30 30
1216 20c. "Odontocidium" Tigersun 35 35
1217 50c. "Odontioda" Hambuhren 55 55
1218 75c. "Paphiopedium" Delrosi 75 75
1219 $1 "Vuylstekeara" Yokara 95 95
1220 $2 "Paphiopedilum" Geelong 1·75 2·00
1221 $3 "Wilsonara" Tigerwood 2·00 2·25
1222 $4 "Cymbidium" Ormoulu 2·50 2·75
MS1223 Two sheets, each 98×68 mm. (a) $6 "Odontonia" Sappho. (b) $6 "Cymbidium" Vieux Rose. Set of 2 sheets 11·00 11·50

1990. 500th Anniv (1992) of Discovery of America by Columbus (3rd issue). New World Natural History—Insects. As T 354a of Grenada. Mult.

1224 35c. "Dynastes hercules" (beetle) 35 35
1225 40c. "Chalcolepidius porcatus" (beetle) 35 35
1226 50c. "Acrocinus longimanus" (beetle) 40 40
1227 60c. "Battus polydamas" (butterfly) 1·00 75
1228 $1 "Orthemis ferruginea" (skimmer) 1·25 95
1229 $2 "Psiloptera variolosa" (beetle) 1·75 1·75
1230 $3 "Hypolimnas misippus" (butterfly) 3·00 3·00
1231 $4 Scarab beetle 3·00 3·00
MS1232 Two sheets, each 102×70 mm. (a) $6 "Calpodes ethlius" (butterfly). (b) "Danaus plexippus" (butterfly). Set of 2 sheets 8·50 9·50

1990. Wildlife. As T 254 of Antigua. Mult.

1233 5c. West Indies giant rice rat 20 20
1234 25c. Agouti 35 35
1235 30c. Humpback whale 70 65
1236 40c. Pilot whale 70 65
1237 $1 Spotted dolphin 95 95
1238 $2 Egyptian mongoose 1·75 2·00
1239 $3 Brazilian tree porcupine 2·25 2·75
1240 $4 American manatee 2·50 3·00
MS1241 Two sheets, each 107×80 mm. (a) $6 Caribbean monk seal. (b) $6 Egyptian mongoose (different). Set of 2 sheets 8·00 9·00

1990. 50th Anniv of Second World War. As T 354b of Grenada. Multicoloured.

1242 6c. British tanks in France, 1939 30 30
1243 10c. Operation "Crusader", North Africa, 1941 30 30
1244 20c. Retreat of the Afrika Corps, 1942 40 40
1245 45c. American landing on Aleutian Islands, 1943 50 50
1246 50c. U.S marines landing on Tarawa, 1943 55 55
1247 60c. U.S army entering Rome, 1944 60 60
1248 75c. U.S tanks crossing River Seine, 1944 70 70
1249 $1 Battle of the Bulge, 1944 95 95
1250 $5 American infantry in Italy, 1945 3·00 3·50
1251 $6 B-29 "Enola Gay" dropping atomic bomb on Hiroshima, 1945 3·50 3·50
MS1252 112×84 mm. $6 St. Paul's Cathedral in London Blitz, 1940 4·00 5·00

1990. "Stamp World London '90" International Stamp Exhibition. As T 193 of Gambia showing Walt Disney cartoon characters at Shakespeare sites. Multicoloured.

1253 15c. Daisy Duck at Ann Hathaway's Cottage (horiz) 50 20
1254 30c. Minnie and Bill Mouse at Shakespeare's birthplace, Stratford 65 35
1255 50c. Minnie Mouse in front of Mary Arden's house, Wilmcote 85 70
1256 60c. Mickey Mouse leaning on hedge in New Place gardens, Stratford (horiz) 1·00 90
1257 $1 Mickey Mouse walking in New Place gardens, Stratford (horiz) 1·40 1·25
1258 $2 Mickey Mouse carrying books in Scholars Lane, Stratford 2·50 2·50
1259 $4 Mickey Mouse and Royal Shakespeare Theatre, Stratford 3·50 4·00
1260 $5 Ludwig von Drake teaching Mickey Mouse at the Stratford Grammar School (horiz) 3·50 4·00
MS1261 Two sheets, each 126×101 mm. (a) $6 Mickey Mouse as Shakespeare. (b) $6 Mickey and Minnie Mouse in rowing boat on River Avon, Stratford (horiz). Set of 2 sheets 11·00 12·00

1990. 90th Birthday of Queen Elizabeth the Queen Mother. As T 194 of Gambia, showing photographs 1970–79.

1262 $2 Queen Mother wearing pink hat and coat 1·10 1·40
1263 $2 Prince Charles and Queen Mother at Garter ceremony 1·10 1·40
1264 $2 Queen Mother in blue floral outfit 1·10 1·40
MS1265 90×75 mm. $6 Queen Mother in Garter robes 4·25 5·00

1990. Stamp World London 90 International Stamp Exhibition (2nd issue). Sheet 97×75 mm containing horiz designs as T 356 of Grenada.

MS1266 $6 green 5·50 6·50

DESIGN: $6 Map of South America and Logo.

1990. Birds. As T 358 of Grenada, but vert. Multicoloured.

1267 25c. Yellow-bellied seedeater 30 30
1268 45c. Carib grackle 50 50
1269 50c. Black-whiskered vireo 55 55
1270 75c. Bananaquit 70 70
1271 $1 White-collared swift 95 95
1272 $2 Yellow-bellied elaenia 1·50 1·50
1273 $3 Blue-hooded euphonia 2·00 2·00
1274 $5 Eared dove 3·25 3·25
MS1275 Two sheets, each 101×72 mm. (a) $6 Mangrove cuckoo. (b) $6 Scaly-breasted thrasher. Set of 2 sheets 8·50 10·00

1990. Crustaceans. As T 359 of Grenada. Mult.

1276 10c. Slipper lobster 20 20
1277 25c. Green reef crab 30 30
1278 65c. Caribbean lobsterette 60 60
1279 75c. Blind deep sea lobster 70 70
1280 $1 Flattened crab 95 95
1281 $2 Ridged slipper lobster 1·75 2·00
1282 $3 Land crab 2·25 2·75
1283 $4 Mountain crab 2·50 2·75
MS1284 Two sheets, each 108×76 mm. (a) $6 Caribbean king crab. (b) $6 Purse crab. Set of 2 sheets 8·00 10·00

98 Lineker, England

1990. World Cup Football Championship, Italy (2nd issue). Multicoloured.

1285 15c. Type **98** 25 25
1286 45c. Burruchaga, Argentina 45 45
1287 $2 Hysen, Sweden 1·75 2·25
1288 $4 Sang Ho, South Korea 2·75 3·75
MS1289 Two sheets, each 76×90 mm. (a) $6 Ramos, U.S.A. (b) $6 Stojkovic, Yugoslavia. Set of 2 sheets 8·50 9·50

1990. Olympic Games, Barcelona (1992). As T 195a of Gambia. Multicoloured.

1290 10c. Boxing 10 10
1291 25c. Olympic flame 20 20
1292 50c. Football 40 40
1293 75c. Discus throwing 60 60
1294 $1 Pole vaulting 85 85
1295 $2 Show jumping 1·75 2·00
1296 $4 Women's basketball 3·50 3·75
1297 $5 Men's gymnastics 3·00 3·75
MS1298 Two sheets. (a) 101×70 mm. $6 Sailboards. (b) 70×101 mm. $6 Decathlon. Set of 2 sheets 8·50 9·50

1991. 350th Death Anniv of Rubens. As T 195c of Gambia. Multicoloured.

1299 5c. "Adam and Eve" (Eve detail) (vert) 30 20
1300 15c. "Esther before Ahasuerus" (detail) 50 20
1301 25c. "Adam and Eve" (Adam detail) (vert) 60 25
1302 50c. "Expulsion from Eden" 90 60
1303 $1 "Cain slaying Abel" (detail) (vert) 1·60 1·10
1304 $2 "Lot's Flight" 2·25 2·25
1305 $4 "Samson and Delilah" (detail) 3·50 4·00
1306 $5 "Abraham and Melchizedek" 3·75 4·00
MS1307 Two sheets, each 101×71 mm. (a) $6 "The Meeting of David and Abigail" (detail). (b) $6 "Daniel in the Lions' Den" (detail). Set of 2 sheets 10·00 12·00

1991. Coral Reef Fishes. As T 357 of Grenada. Multicoloured.
1308 15c. Barred hamlet 50 25
1309 35c. Long-spined squirrelfish 80 50
1310 45c. Red-spotted hawkfish 85 60
1311 75c. Bigeye 1·25 1·00
1312 $1 Balloonfish ("Spiny puffer") 1·50 1·25
1313 $2 Small-mouth grunt 2·25 2·50
1314 $3 Harlequin bass 2·75 3·25
1315 $4 Creole fish 3·00 3·50
MS1316 Two sheets, each 103×72 mm. (a) $6 Copper sweeper. (b) $6 Royal gramma ("Fairy Basslet"). Set of 2 sheets 8·50 10·00

99 Angel with Star and Lantern

1991. Christmas (1990). Hummel Figurines. Multicoloured.
1317 10c. Type **99** 40 10
1318 15c. Christ Child and Angel playing mandolin 50 15
1319 25c. Shepherd 60 25
1320 50c. Angel with trumpet and lantern 1·10 50
1321 $1 Nativity scene 1·75 95
1322 $2 Christ Child and Angel holding candle 2·75 2·50
1323 $4 Angel with baskets 3·75 4·25
1324 $5 Angels singing 4·00 4·25
MS1325 Two sheets, each 99×122 mm. (a) 5c. As No. 1318; 40c. As No. 1320; 60c. As No. 1321; $3 As No. 1324. (b) 20c. As Type **99**; 30c. As No. 1319; 75c. As No. 1322; $6 As No. 1323. Set of 2 sheets 10·00 11·00

100 "Brassia maculata"

1991. Orchids. Multicoloured.
1326 5c. Type **100** 30 30
1327 10c. "Oncidium lanceanum" 30 30
1328 15c. "Broughtonia sanguinea" 35 20
1329 25c. "Diacrium bicornutum" 40 20
1330 35c. "Cattleya labiata" 40 20
1331 45c. "Epidendrum fragrans" 50 25
1332 50c. "Oncidium papilio" 55 30
1333 75c. "Neocogniauxia monophylla" 70 50
1334 $1 "Epidendrum polybulbon" 80 70
1335 $2 "Spiranthes speciosa" 1·40 1·40
1336 $4 "Epidendrum ciliare" 2·25 2·75
1337 $5 "Phais tankervilliae" 2·50 3·00
1338 $10 "Brassia caudata" 4·50 5·50
1339 $20 "Brassavola cordata" 9·25 11·00

1991. Butterflies. As T 363 of Grenada. Mult.
1340 5c. Crimson-patched longwing 40 30
1341 10c. "Morpho helena" 40 30
1342 15c. "Morpho sulkowskyi" 55 35
1343 20c. "Dynastor napoleon" 60 40
1344 25c. "Pieridae callinira" 60 45
1345 30c. "Anartia amathea" 65 50
1346 35c. "Heliconiidae dido" 65 50
1347 45c. "Papilionidae columbus" 75 65
1348 50c. "Nymphalidae praeneste" 85 70
1349 60c. "Panacea prola" 1·00 80
1350 75c. "Dryas julia" 1·00 90
1351 $1 "Papilionidae orthosilaus" 1·25 1·10
1352 $2 "Pyrrhopyge cometes" 1·75 2·00
1353 $3 "Papilionidae paeon" 2·00 2·50
1354 $4 "Morpho cypris" 2·50 3·00
1355 $5 Choringa 3·00 3·25
MS1356 Four sheets, each 118×80 mm. (a) $6 "Danaus plexippus". (b) $6 "Caligo idomenides". (c) $6 "Nymphalidae amydon". (d) $6 "Papilio childrenae". Set of 4 sheets 15·00 15·00

101 Donald and Daisy Duck with Solar-powered Car

1991. Ecology Conservation. Walt Disney cartoon characters. Multicoloured.
1357 10c. Type **101** 60 20
1358 15c. Goofy saving water 70 20
1359 25c. Donald and Daisy on nature hike 90 35
1360 45c. Donald Duck returning chick to nest 1·25 55
1361 $1 Donald Duck and balloons 2·00 1·25
1362 $2 Minnie Mouse and Daisy Duck on hot day 3·00 2·25
1363 $4 Mickey's nephews cleaning beach 3·75 4·25
1364 $5 Donald Duck on pedal generator 3·75 4·25
MS1365 Three sheets, each 127×102 mm. (a) $6 Hiawatha and felled forest. (b) $6 Donald Duck recycling (vert). (c) $6 Mickey Mouse with Arbor Day notice. Set of 3 sheets 14·00 15·00

1991. 500th Anniv (1992) of Discovery of America by Columbus (4th issue). History of Exploration. As T 363a of Grenada. Multicoloured.
1366 15c. Magellan's "Vitoria" rounding Cape Horn, 1519–21 1·00 50
1367 20c. Drake's Golden Hind, 1577–80 1·40 50
1368 50c. Cook's H.M.S "Resolution", 1768–71 2·00 90
1369 60c. Douglas World Cruiser seaplane, 1924 2·00 80
1370 $1 "Sputnik I" satellite, 1957 2·00 1·00
1371 $2 Gagarin's space flight, 1961 2·25 2·25
1372 $4 Glenn's space flight, 1962 2·50 3·50
1373 $5 Space shuttle, 1981 3·00 3·50
MS1374 Two sheets. (a) 105×78 mm. $6 Bow of "Pinta" (vert). (b) 78×105 mm. $6 Fleet of Columbus. Set of 2 sheets 8·00 10·00

1991. "Phila Nippon '91" International Stamp Exhibition, Tokyo. As T 198c of Gambia but horiz showing Walt Disney cartoon characters in Japanese scenes. Multicoloured.
1375 15c. Minnie Mouse with silkworms 65 20
1376 30c. Mickey, Minnie, Morty and Ferdie at Torii Gate 85 35
1377 50c. Donald Duck and Mickey Mouse trying origami 1·25 60
1378 60c. Mickey and Minnie diving for pearls 1·40 70
1379 $1 Minnie Mouse in kimono 2·00 1·10
1380 $2 Mickey making masks 2·75 2·50
1381 $4 Donald and Mickey making paper 3·50 3·75
1382 $5 Minnie and Pluto making pottery 3·75 4·00
MS1383 Four sheets, each 122×102 mm. (a) $6 Mickey flower-arranging. (b) $6 Mickey carving a netsuke. (c) $6 Mickey at tea ceremony. (d) $6 Mickey making printing plate. Set of 4 sheets 16·00 16·00

1991. Fungi. As T 364 of Grenada. Multicoloured.
1384 5c. "Pyrrhoglossum pyrrhum" 35 25
1385 45c. "Agaricus purpurellus" 85 50
1386 50c. "Amanita craseoderma" 85 55
1387 90c. "Hygrocybe acutoconica" 1·50 1·25
1388 $1 "Limacella guttata" 1·50 1·25
1389 $2 "Lactarius hygrophoroides" 2·00 2·00
1390 $4 "Boletellus cubensis" 3·25 3·50
1391 $5 "Psilocybe caerulescens" 3·25 3·50
MS1392 Two sheets, each 100×70 mm. (a) $6 "Marasmius haematocephalus". (b) $6 "Lepiota spiculata". Set of 2 sheets 12·00 13·00

1991. 65th Birthday of Queen Elizabeth II. As T 198a of Gambia. Multicoloured.
1393 20c. Queen, Prince Philip, Prince Charles and Prince William at Trooping the Colour, 1990 30 20
1394 25c. Queen and Prince Charles at polo match, 1985 30 20
1395 $2 Queen and Prince Philip at Maundy service, 1989 2·00 2·50
1396 $4 Queen with Queen Mother on her 87th birthday, 1987 3·25 3·75
MS1397 68×90 mm. $5 The Queen at Caen Hill, 1990, and Prince Philip at R.A.F. Benson, 1989 3·75 4·50

1991. 10th Wedding Anniv of Prince and Princess of Wales. As T 198b of Gambia. Multicoloured.
1398 5c. Prince and Princess of Wales kissing, 1987 65 25
1399 60c. Portraits of Prince, Princess and sons 1·50 70
1400 $1 Prince Harry in 1988 and Prince William in 1987 1·50 1·10
1401 $5 Princess Diana in 1990 and Prince Charles in 1988 5·50 4·75
MS1402 68×90 mm. $5 Princess with Prince Harry in Majorca, and Prince and Princess with Prince Harry at polo match 5·50 5·00

1991. Death Centenary (1990) of Vincent van Gogh (artist). As T 200b of Gambia. Multicoloured.
1403 5c. "Two Thistles" 50 30
1404 10c. "Baby Marcelle Roulin" 55 30
1405 15c. "Still Life: Basket with Six Oranges" (horiz) 75 20
1406 25c. "Orchard in Blossom" 90 20
1407 45c. "Armand Roulin" 1·25 35
1408 50c. "Wood Gatherers in Snow" (detail) (horiz) 1·25 50
1409 60c. "Almond Tree in Blossom" 1·50 50
1410 $1 "An Old Man" 2·00 1·25
1411 $2 "The Seine Bridge at Asnieres" (horiz) 2·75 2·50
1412 $3 "Vase with Lilacs, Daises and Anemones" 3·00 3·00
1413 $4 "Self Portrait" 3·25 3·50
1414 $5 "Patience Escalier" 3·25 3·50
MS1415 Three sheets. (a) 127×102 mm. $6 "Quay with Men unloading Sand Barges" (horiz). (b) 127×102 mm. $6 "Sunset: Wheat Fields near Arles" (horiz). (c) 102×127 mm. "Les Alyscamps". Imperf. Set of 3 sheets 12·00 13·00

102 Sargassum Triggerfish

1991. Reef Fishes. Multicoloured.
1416 50c. Type **102** 90 90
1417 50c. Tobaccofish 90 90
1418 50c. Caribbean long-nosed butterflyfish 90 90
1419 50c. Cherub angelfish 90 90
1420 50c. Black jack 90 90
1421 50c. Masked goby and black jack 90 90
1422 50c. Spot-finned hogfish 90 90
1423 50c. Royal gramma ("Fairy basslet") 90 90
1424 50c. Orange-backed bass 90 90
1425 50c. Candy basslet 90 90
1426 50c. Black-capped basslet 90 90
1427 50c. Long-jawed squirrelfish 90 90
1428 50c. Jackknife-fish 90 90
1429 50c. Bigeye 90 90
1430 50c. Short bigeye 90 90
MS1431 106×66 mm. $6 Caribbean flashlight fish 9·00 11·00
Nos. 1416/30 were printed together, se-tenant, forming a composite design.

1991. Christmas. Religious Paintings by Martin Schongauer. As T 200c of Gambia.
1432 10c. black and brown 60 15
1433 35c. multicoloured 1·00 30
1434 50c. multicoloured 1·40 50
1435 75c. multicoloured 1·75 80
1436 $1 multicoloured 2·00 1·25
1437 $2 multicoloured 3·25 3·00
1438 $4 black and brown 4·00 4·25
1439 $5 black, grey and red 4·00 4·50
MS1440 Two sheets, each 102×127 mm. (a) $6 multicoloured. (b) $6 multicoloured. Set of 2 sheets 9·50 11·00
DESIGNS: 10c. "Angel of the Annunciation"; 35c. "Madonna of the Rose Hedge" (detail); 50c. "Madonna of the Rose Hedge" (different detail); 75c. "Nativity" (detail); $1 "Adoration of the Shepherds" (detail); $2 "The Nativity"; $4 "Nativity" (different); $5 "Symbol of St. Matthew"; $6 (No. **MS**1440a) "Adoration of the Shepherds" (different detail); $6 (No. **MS**1440b) "Nativity".

1992. Great Railways of the World. As T 367 of Grenada. Multicoloured.
1441 75c. Medoc locomotive No. J-S 58, 1857 (Switzerland) 1·10 1·10
1442 75c. Stirling single locomotive No. 1, 1870 (Great Britain) 1·10 1·10
1443 75c. Paris–Lyon–Mediterranee locomotive No. 90, 1877 (France) 1·10 1·10
1444 75c. Standard type, 1880 (U.S.A.) 1·10 1·10
1445 75c. Class 650 "Vittorio Emanuel II", 1884 (Italy) 1·10 1·10
1446 75c. Johnson single, 1887 (Great Britain) 1·10 1·10
1447 75c. Locomotive No. 999, 1893 (U.S.A.) 1·10 1·10
1448 75c. Class Q1, 1896 (Great Britain) 1·10 1·10
1449 75c. "Claud Hamilton", 1900 (Great Britain) 1·10 1·10
1450 $1 Class P8, 1906 (Germany) 1·10 1·10
1451 $1 Class P, 1910 (Denmark) 1·10 1·10
1452 $1 Southern Railway Ps4, 1926 (U.S.A.) 1·10 1·10
1453 $1 "Kestrel", 1932 (Ireland) 1·10 1·10
1454 $1 Southern Pacific Class GS2, 1937 (U.S.A.) 1·10 1·10
1455 $1 Class 12, 1938 (Belgium) 1·10 1·10
1456 $1 Norfolk and Western Railroad Class J No. 600, 1941 (U.S.A.) 1·10 1·10
1457 $1 Alco PA series diesel, 1946 (U.S.A.) 1·10 1·10
1458 $1 Class 4E electric, 1954 (South Africa) 1·10 1·10
1459 $2 Trans Europe Express train, 1957 1·50 1·50
1460 $2 New Haven Railroad Type FL9 diesel, 1960 (U.S.A.) 1·50 1·50
1461 $2 "Hikari" train, 1964 (Japan) 1·50 1·50
1462 $2 Class 103.1 electric, 1970 (Germany) 1·50 1·50
1463 $2 RTG diesel, 1972 (France) 1·50 1·50
1464 $2 ETR 401 Pendolino train, 1976 (Italy) 1·50 1·50
1465 $2 Advanced Passenger Train Class 370, 1981 (Great Britain) 1·50 1·50
1466 $2 Via Rail LRC diesel, 1982 (Canada) 1·50 1·50
1467 $2 MAV BZMOT 601, 1983 (Hungary) 1·50 1·50
MS1468 Two sheets, each 120×80 mm. (a) $6 Werner von Siemens's electric locomotive, 1879 (Germany). (b) ETR 401 Pendolino train, 1976 (Italy). Set of 2 sheets 11·00 11·00

1992. 40th Anniv of Queen Elizabeth II's Accession. As T 202a of Gambia. Multicoloured.
1469 60c. Swimming jetty on beach 1·10 40
1470 75c. View of Grenadines 1·25 45
1471 $2 Surf on beach 2·50 1·75
1472 $4 Secluded bay 3·75 3·25
MS1473 Two sheets, each 74×92 mm. (a) $6 Plantation house. (b) $6 St. George's. Set of 2 sheets 9·00 9·50

1992. Olympic Games, Barcelona. As T 372 of Grenada. Multicoloured.
1474 10c. Women's backstroke swimming 60 30
1475 15c. Women's handball 65 30
1476 25c. Men's 4×100 m relay 75 30
1477 35c. Men's hammer throw 80 35
1478 50c. Men's 110 m hurdles 90 60
1479 75c. Men's pole vault 1·25 80
1480 $1 Men's volleyball 1·40 1·00
1481 $2 Men's weightlifting 2·50 2·75
1482 $5 Men's gymnastics 3·25 4·00
1483 $6 Football 3·75 4·25
MS1484 Two sheets, each 100×70 mm. (a) $15 Finn class single-handed dinghy sailing. (b) $15 Baseball. Set of 2 sheets 16·00 17·00

1992. Granada '92 Int Stamp Exn, Spain. Spanish Paintings. As T 481a of Ghana. Mult.
1485 10c. "The Surrender of Seville" (Zurbaran) 30 20
1486 35c. "The Liberation of St. Peter by an Angel" (Antonio de Pereda) 50 35
1487 50c. "Joseph explains the Dreams of the Pharaoh" (Antonio del Castillo Saavedra) (horiz) 75 60
1488 75c. "The Flower Vase" (Juan de Arellano) 1·00 70
1489 $1 "The Duke of Pastrana" (Juan Carreno de Miranda) 1·25 90
1490 $2 "The Annunciation" (detail) (Francisco Rizi) 2·00 2·00
1491 $4 "The Annunciation" (different detail) (Rizi) 3·00 3·50
1492 $5 "Old Women Seated" (attr Antonio Puga) 3·00 3·50
MS1493 Two sheets. (a) 95×120 mm. $6 "The Triumph of Saint Hermenegildo" (Francisco de Herrera the younger) (86×111 mm). (b) 120×95 mm. $6 "Relief of Genoa" (De Pereda) (110×84 mm). Imperf. Set of 2 sheets 7·00 8·00

103 Don Isaac Abarbanel, Minister of Finance

1992. 500th Anniv of Discovery of America by Columbus (5th issue). World Columbian Stamp Expo '92, Chicago. Multicoloured.
1494 10c. Type **103** 15 15
1495 25c. Columbus on voyage 25 25

1496 35c. Look-out sighting land 30 30
1497 50c. King Ferdinand and Queen Isabella of Spain 50 50
1498 60c. Columbus showing map to Queen Isabella 55 55
1499 $5 "Santa Maria" and bird 4·00 5·50
MS1500 Two sheets, each 100×71 mm. (a) $6 Christopher Columbus. (b) $6 Columbus with hand to face. Set of 2 sheets 7·00 8·00

1992. "Genova '92" International Thematic Stamp Exhibition. Hummingbirds. As T 370a of Grenada. Multicoloured.
1501 5c. Male blue-headed hummingbird 25 30
1502 10c. Female rufous-breasted hermit 25 25
1503 20c. Female blue-headed hummingbird 30 25
1504 45c. Male green-throated carib 45 30
1505 90c. Male Antillean crested hummingbird 60 70
1506 $2 Male purple-throated carib 1·40 1·60
1507 $4 Female purple-throated carib 2·40 2·75
1508 $5 Female Antillean crested hummingbird 2·50 2·75
MS1509 Two sheets, each 104×75 mm. (a) $6 Male Rufous-breasted Hermit. (b) $6 Female Green-throated Carib. Set of 2 sheets 9·50 11·00

1992. 50th Anniv of United Service Organization (forces' entertainment programme). As T 371 of Grenada. Multicoloured.
1510 10c. James Cagney 60 25
1511 15c. Anne Sheridan 60 25
1512 35c. Jerry Colonna 60 25
1513 50c. Spike Jones 70 40
1514 75c. Edgar Bergen 90 55
1515 $1 The Andrews Sisters 1·40 80
1516 $2 Dinah Shore 2·00 2·00
1517 $5 Bing Crosby 4·50 4·50
MS1518 Two sheets, each 107×80 mm. (a) $6 Fred Astaire. (b) $6 Marlene Dietrich. Set of 2 sheets 7·00 7·50

No. 1515 is incorrectly inscribed "THE ANDREW SISTERS".

1992. 500th Anniv of Discovery of America by Columbus (6th issue). Organization of East Caribbean States. As Nos. 2423/4 of Grenada.
1519 $1 Columbus meeting Amerindians 65 65
1520 $2 Ships approaching island 1·25 1·50

1992. Toy Trains from American Manufacturers. As T 372b of Grenada. Multicoloured.
1521 15c. No. 2220 switcher locomotive, Voltamp (1910) 25 15
1522 25c. Clockwork locomotive of Bridge Port Line, American Miniature Railroad (1907) 35 20
1523 50c. First electric toy locomotive, Ives (1910) 60 40
1524 75c. "J.C. Penney Special" locomotive, American Flyer (1920s) 80 60
1525 $1 Clockwork cast-metal locomotive, Hafner (1916) 95 80
1526 $2 Pull toy copper-plated locomotive, probably Hubley (1900) 1·75 2·00
1527 $4 "Mayflower" locomotive, American Flyer (1928) 3·00 3·50
1528 $5 "Olympian" locomotive, Ives (1929) 3·00 3·50
MS1529 Two sheets. (a) 128×93 mm. $6 Clockwork locomotive, Ives (1910) (50×38½ mm). (b) 142×95 mm. $6 "Statesman" locomotive, American Flyer (50×38½ mm). P 13. Set of 2 sheets 7·50 8·50

1992. Postage Stamp Mega Event, New York. Sheet 100×70 mm containing multicoloured design as T 207a of Gambia.
MS1530 $6 Brooklyn Bridge 3·50 4·25

1992. Christmas. Religious Paintings. "The Annunciation" by various artists. As T 207b of Gambia. Multicoloured.
1531 5c. Robert Campin 15 10
1532 15c. Melchior Broederlam 25 10
1533 25c. Fra Filippo Lippi (two-panel diptych) 30 15
1534 35c. Simone Martini 40 20
1535 50c. Lippi (detail from left panel) 55 45
1536 75c. Lippi (detail from right panel) 70 60
1537 90c. Albert Bouts 80 80
1538 $1 D. di Michelino 90 90
1539 $2 Rogier van der Weyden 1·75 2·00
1540 $3 Sandro Botticelli (detail of angel) 2·25 2·75
1541 $4 Botticelli (detail of Virgin Mary) 2·75 3·50
1542 $5 Bernardo Daddi (horiz) 2·75 3·50
MS1543 Three sheets, each 72×97 mm. (a) $6 Van der Weyden (different). (b) $6 Botticelli (as $3). (c) $6 Hubert van Eyck. Set of 3 sheets 10·50 12·00

1992. Gold Record Award Winners. As T 374 of Grenada. Multicoloured.
1544 90c. Leonard Bernstein 1·50 1·25
1545 90c. Ray Charles 1·50 1·25
1546 90c. Bob Dylan 1·50 1·25
1547 90c. Barbra Streisand 1·50 1·25
1548 90c. Frank Sinatra 1·50 1·25
1549 90c. Harry Belafonte 1·50 1·25
1550 90c. Aretha Franklin 1·50 1·25
1551 90c. Garth Brooks 1·50 1·25
MS1552 Two sheets, each 100×70 mm. (a) $3 Charlie Parker; $3 Miles Davis. (b) $3 Johnny Cash; $3 Willie Nelson. Set of 2 sheets 7·00 8·00

Nos. 1544/51 were printed together, se-tenant, with a composite background design.

1992. 60th Anniv of Goofy (Disney cartoon character). Scenes from various cartoon films. As T 207c of Gambia. Multicoloured.
1553 5c. "Father's Day Off", 1953 30 20
1554 10c. "Cold War", 1951 35 20
1555 15c. "Home Made Home", 1951 40 20
1556 25c. "Get Rich Quick", 1951 50 25
1557 50c. "Man's Best Friend", 1952 70 40
1558 75c. "Aquamania", 1961 1·00 55
1559 90c. "Tomorrow We Diet", 1951 1·10 65
1560 $1 "Teachers Are People", 1952 1·25 75
1561 $2 "The Goofy Success Story", 1955 2·00 1·75
1562 $3 "Double Dribble", 1946 2·50 3·00
1563 $4 "Hello Aloha", 1952 2·75 3·25
1564 $5 "Father's Lion", 1952 3·00 3·50
MS1565 Three sheets, each 128×102 mm. (a) $6 "Motor Mania", 1956. (b) $6 "Hold that Pose", 1950 (vert). (c) $6 "Father's Weekend", 1953 (vert). Set of 3 sheets 12·00 13·00

1992. Anniversaries and Events. As T 375 of Grenada. Multicoloured, except No. 1571.
1566 25c. Zeppelin "Viktoria Luise" over Kiel Harbour (horiz) 75 30
1567 50c. Space shuttle "Columbia" landing (horiz) 85 35
1568 75c. German Federal Republic flag and arms (horiz) 85 50
1569 $1.50 Giant anteater (horiz) 1·00 1·00
1570 $2 Scarlet macaw 2·50 2·00
1571 $2 W.H.O. emblem (black and blue) (horiz) 1·50 1·50
1572 $3 Wolfgang Amadeus Mozart 4·00 3·00
1573 $4 The Berlin Airlift (horiz) 3·25 3·50
1574 $4 Repairing "Intelsat VI" satellite in space (horiz) 3·25 3·50
1575 $5 Zeppelin "Hindenburg" on fire (horiz) 3·25 3·50
1576 $5 Admiral Richard Byrd's Ford Trimotor aircraft (horiz) 3·25 3·50
MS1577 Five sheets. (a) 110×80 mm. $6 Zeppelin LZ-4, 1913 (51½×39½ mm). (b) 110×80 mm. $6 First flight of space shuttle "Endeavour" (51½×39½ mm). (c) 110×80 mm. $6 Map of West Germany (39½×51½ mm). (d) 110×80 mm. $6 Jaguar (51½×39½ mm). (e) 98×67 mm. $6 Figaro costume from "The Marriage of Figaro". Set of 5 sheets 18·00 20·00

ANNIVERSARIES AND EVENTS: Nos. 1566, 1575, **MS**1577a, 75th death anniv of Count Ferdinand von Zeppelin; 1567, 1574, **MS**1577b, International Space Year; 1568, 1573, **MS**1577c, 25th death anniv of Konrad Adenauer (German statesman); 1569/70, **MS**1577d, Earth Summit '92, Rio; 1571, United Nations World Health Organization Projects; 1572, **MS**1577e, Death bicentenary of Mozart; 1576, 75th anniv of International Association of Lions Clubs.

104 "Atalanta" and "Mischief" (yachts), 1881

1992. History of The Americas Cup Challenge Trophy. Multicoloured.
1578 15c. Type **104** 60 20
1579 25c. "Valkyrie III" and "Defender", 1895 75 30
1580 35c. "Shamrock IV" and "Resolute", 1920 90 45
1581 75c. "Endeavour II" and "Ranger", 1937 1·40 70
1582 $1 "Sceptre" and "Columbia", 1958 1·60 85
1583 $2 "Australia II" and "Liberty", 1983 2·25 2·25
1584 $4 "Stars & Stripes" and "Kookaburra III", 1987 3·25 4·00
1585 $5 "New Zealand" and "Stars & Stripes", 1988 3·25 4·00
MS1586 Two sheets, each 114×85 mm. (a) $6 "America" (schooner), 1851 (57×43 mm). (b) $6 Americas Cup emblems (57×43 mm). Set of 2 sheets 10·00 11·00

1993. Dogs of the World. As T 377 of Grenada, but vert. Multicoloured.
1587 35c. Irish setter and Glendalough, Ireland 50 25
1588 50c. Boston terrier and Boston State House, U.S.A. 70 50
1589 75c. Beagle and Temple to Athena, Greece 1·00 60
1590 $1 Weimaraner and Nesselwang, Germany 1·25 85
1591 $3 Norwegian elkhound and Urnes Stave Church, Norway 2·50 3·00
1592 $4 Mastiff and Sphinx, Egypt 2·75 3·00
1593 $5 Akita and Torii Temple, Kyoto, Japan 2·75 3·00
1594 $5 Saluki and Rub'al Khali, Saudi Arabia 2·75 3·00
MS1595 Two sheets, each 99×71 mm. (a) $6 Bull dog, Great Britain. (b) $6 Shar Pei, China. Set of 2 sheets 7·50 8·50

1993. Bicentenary of the Louvre, Paris. As T 209b of Gambia. Multicoloured (except No. 1599).
1596 $1 "Madonna and Child with the young John the Baptist" (Botticelli) 1·00 1·00
1597 $1 "The Buffet" (Chardin) 1·00 1·00
1598 $1 "Return from Market" (Chardin) 1·00 1·00
1599 $1 "Erasmus" (Durer) (black and grey) 1·00 1·00
1600 $1 "Self-portrait with Eryngium" (Durer) 1·00 1·00
1601 $1 "Jeanne of Aragon" (Raphael) 1·00 1·00
1602 $1 "La Belle Jardiniere" (detail) (Raphael) 1·00 1·00
1603 $1 "La Belle Jardiniere" (different detail) (Raphael) 1·00 1·00
MS1604 70×100 mm. $6 "King Charles I Hunting" (Van Dyck) (52×85 mm) 3·75 4·50

105 "Battus polydamus"

1993. Butterflies. Multicoloured.
1605 15c. Type **105** 40 20
1606 35c. "Astraptes talus" 55 20
1607 45c. "Pseudolycaena marsyas" 55 25
1608 75c. "Siproeta stelenes" 70 50
1609 $1 "Phoebis sennae" 80 60
1610 $2 "Dione juno" 1·40 1·40
1611 $4 "Chlorostrymon simaethis" 2·25 2·75
1612 $5 "Urbanus proteus" 2·50 2·75
MS1613 Two sheets, each 100×70 mm. (a) $6 "Historis odius" ("Orion"). (b) $6 "Heliconius charithonia" ("Zebra"). Set of 2 sheets 7·00 8·00

1993. Flowers. As T 380 of Grenada. Mult.
1614 35c. Hibiscus 50 20
1615 35c. Columbine 50 20
1616 45c. Red ginger 50 25
1617 75c. Bougainvillea 70 50
1618 $1 Crown imperial 80 60
1619 $2 Fairy orchid 1·40 1·40
1620 $4 Heliconia 2·25 2·75
1621 $5 Tulip 2·50 2·75

1993. 40th Anniv of Coronation. As T 215a of Gambia.
1623 35c. multicoloured 30 55
1624 50c. multicoloured 40 60
1625 $2 green and black 1·10 1·40
1626 $4 multicoloured 1·90 2·00
MS1627 70×100 mm. $6 multicoloured 6·00 6·50

DESIGNS—(38×27 mm): 35c. Queen Elizabeth II at Coronation (photograph by Cecil Beaton); 50c. Ampulla and spoon; $2 Queen Elizabeth II leaving for Coronation; $4 Prince Harry's christening. (28½×42½ mm)—$6 "Queen Elizabeth II, 1954" (detail) (Pietro Annigoni).

1993. Anniversaries and Events. As T 381 of Grenada. Multicoloured.
1628 15c. "Painter and Model" (Picasso) (horiz) 55 30
1629 35c. Keith Tkachuk and Dmitri Mironov (ice hockey, 1992) (horiz) 1·00 40
1630 50c. Early telescope 85 50
1631 75c. "Gra w Gudziki" (Ludomir Slerdinski) (horiz) 90 90
1632 75c. Willy Brandt and Lyndon Johnson, 1961 (horiz) 90 90
1633 $1 "Artist and his Model" (Picasso) (horiz) 1·00 1·00
1634 $2 "Pocalunek Mongolskiego Ksiecia" (S. Wirkiewicz) (horiz) 1·40 1·60
1635 $4 "The Drawing Lesson" (Picasso) (horiz) 2·25 2·75
1636 $4 Radio telescope 2·25 2·75
1637 $5 Alberto Tomba (Giant Slalom, 1984) (horiz) 2·25 2·75
1638 $5 Willy Brandt and Eleanor Hulles, 1957 (horiz) 2·25 2·75
MS1639 Five sheets. (a) 105×75 mm. $5 Copernicus. (b) 105×75 mm. $6 Picasso (horiz). (c) 75×105 mm. $6 Emil Zogragski (70 metre ski jump, 1984). (d) 75×105 mm. $6 "Allegory" (detail) (Jan Wydra). (e) 105×75 mm. $6 Willy and Rut Brandt (grey and black) (horiz) Set of 5 sheets 17·00 19·00

ANNIVERSARIES AND EVENTS: Nos. 1628, 1633, 1635, **MS**1639b, 20th death anniv of Picasso (artist); 1629, 1637, **MS**1639c, Winter Olympic Games '94, Lillehammer; 1630, 1636, **MS**1639a, 450th death anniv of Copernicus (astronomer); 1631, 1634, **MS**1639d, Polska '93 International Stamp Exhibition, Poznan; 1632, 1638, **MS**1639e, 80th birth anniv of Willy Brandt (German politician).

1993. Songbirds. As T 382 of Grenada. Multicoloured.
1640 15c. Painted bunting 80 80
1641 15c. White-throated sparrow 80 80
1642 25c. Common grackle 90 90
1643 25c. Royal flycatcher 90 90
1644 35c. Swallow tanager 95 95
1645 35c. Vermilion flycatcher 95 95
1646 45c. Black-headed bunting 1·00 1·00
1647 50c. Rose-breasted grosbeak 1·00 1·00
1648 75c. Corn bunting 1·25 1·25
1649 75c. Rose-breasted thrush tanager 1·25 1·25
1650 $1 Buff-throated saltator 1·40 1·40
1651 $4 Plush-capped finch 2·75 2·75
MS1652 Two sheets, each 115×86 mm. (a) $6 Pine grosbeak. (b) $6 Bohemian waxwing. Set of 2 sheets 12·00 12·00

Nos. 1640/51 were printed together, se-tenant, with the backgrounds forming a composite design.

Nos. 1645/6 show the scientific inscriptions transposed between the designs.

1993. Shells. As T 383 of Grenada. Mult.
1653 15c. Hawk-wing conch 35 35
1654 15c. Music volute 35 35
1655 25c. Globe vase and deltoid rock shell 40 40
1656 35c. Spiny Caribbean vase 40 40
1657 35c. American common sundial and common purple janthina 40 40
1658 45c. Toothed donax and gaudy asaphis 40 40
1659 45c. Mouse cone 40 40
1660 50c. Gold-mouthed triton 50 50
1661 75c. Tulip mussel and trigonal tivela 60 60
1662 75c. Common dove shell and chestnut latirus 60 60
1663 $1 Wide-mouthed purpura 70 70
1664 $4 American thorny oyster and Atlantic wing oyster 2·25 2·25
MS1665 Two sheets, each 70×106 mm. (a) $6 Atlantic turkey wing. (b) $6 Zebra or zigzag periwinkle. Set of 2 sheets 10·00 10·00

Nos. 1653/64 were printed together, se-tenant, with the backgrounds forming a composite design.

1993. Asian International Stamp Exhibitions. As T 219a of Gambia. Multicoloured. (a) "Indopex '93", Surabaya, Indonesia.
1666 35c. National Museum, Central Jakarta (horiz) 40 20
1667 45c. Sacred wheel and deer (horiz) 45 25
1668 $1 Ramayana relief, Panataran Temple (horiz) 70 60
1669 $1.50 "Bullock Carts" (Batara Lubis) (horiz) 1·25 1·25
1670 $1.50 "Surat Irsa II" (A. D. Pirous) (horiz) 1·25 1·25
1671 $1.50 "Self-portrait with Goat" (Kartika) (horiz) 1·25 1·25
1672 $1.50 "The Cow-est Cow" (Ivan Sagito) (horiz) 1·25 1·25
1673 $1.50 "Rain Storm" (Sudjana Kerton) (horiz) 1·25 1·25
1674 $1.50 "Story of Pucuk Flower" (Effendi) (horiz) 1·25 1·25
1675 $5 Candi Tikus, Trawulan, East Java (horiz) 2·50 3·00
MS1676 134×105 mm. $6 Banteng cattle (horiz) 3·50 4·00

(b) "Taipei '93", Taiwan.
1677 35c. Macau Palace Casino, Hong Kong (horiz) 40 20
1678 45c. Stone lion, Ming Tomb, Nanjing (horiz) 45 25
1679 $1 Stone camels, Ming Tomb, Nanjing (horiz) 70 60
1680 $1.50 Nesting quail incense burner (horiz) 1·25 1·25
1681 $1.50 Standing quail incense burner (horiz) 1·25 1·25
1682 $1.50 Seated qilin incense burner (horiz) 1·25 1·25

1683 $1.50 Pottery horse, Han period (horiz) 1·25 1·25
1684 $1.50 Seated caparisoned elephant (horiz) 1·25 1·25
1685 $1.50 Cow in imitation of Delft faience (horiz) 1·25 1·25
1686 $5 Stone lion and elephant, Ming Tomb, Nanjing (horiz) 2·50 3·00
MS1687 134×105 mm. $6 Sumatran tiger, Mt. Leuser National Park 3·50 4·00

(c) "Bangkok 1993", Thailand.
1688 35c. Three Naga snakes, Chiang Mai's Temple (horiz) 40 20
1689 45c. Sri Mariamman Temple, Singapore (horiz) 45 25
1690 $1 Topiary, Hua Hin Resort (horiz) 70 60
1691 $1.50 "Buddha's Victory over Mara" (horiz) 1·25 1·25
1692 $1.50 "Mythological Elephant" (horiz) 1·25 1·25
1693 $1.50 "Battle with Mara" (Thon Buri) (horiz) 1·25 1·25
1694 $1.50 "Untitled" (Panya Wijinthanasarn) (horiz) 1·25 1·25
1695 $1.50 "Temple Mural" (horiz) 1·25 1·25
1696 $1.50 "Elephants in Pahcekha Buddha's Heaven" (horiz) 1·25 1·25
1697 $5 Pak Tai Temple, Cheung Chau Island (horiz) 2·50 3·00
MS1698 134×105 mm. $6 Monkey from Chiang Kong 3·50 4·00

1993. World Cup Football Championship, U.S.A. (1994) (1st issue). As T 221a of Gambia. Mult.
1699 15c. McCall (Scotland) and Verri (Brazil) (horiz) 70 20
1700 25c. Verri (Brazil) and Maradona (Argentina) (horiz) 75 20
1701 35c. Schillaci (Italy) and Saldana (Uruguay) (horiz) 80 25
1702 45c. Gullit (Holland) and Wright (England) (horiz) 90 35
1703 $1 Verri (Brazil) and Maradona (Argentina) (different) (horiz) 1·25 80
1704 $2 Zubizarreta and Fernandez (Spain) with Albert (Belgium) (horiz) 1·75 1·75
1705 $4 Hagi (Rumania) and McGrath (Ireland) (horiz) 2·50 3·25
1706 $5 Gorriz (Spain) and Scifo (Belgium) (horiz) 2·50 3·25
MS1707 Two sheets, each 104×75 mm. (a) $6 Foxboro Stadium, Massachusetts (horiz). (b) $6 Rudi Voeller (Germany). Set of 2 sheets 8·00 9·00

See also Nos. 1810/16.

1993. 65th Anniv of Mickey Mouse. Scenes from Walt Disney cartoon films. As T 385 of Grenada.
1708 15c. "Mickey's Rival", 1936 65 25
1709 35c. "The Worm Turns", 1937 80 25
1710 50c. "The Pointer", 1939 95 55
1711 75c. "Society Dog Show", 1939 1·50 90
1712 $1 "A Gentleman's Gentleman", 1941 1·60 1·00
1713 $2 "The Little Whirlwind", 1941 2·25 2·50
1714 $4 "Mickey Down Under", 1948 3·00 3·50
1715 $5 "R'coon Dawg", 1951 3·00 3·50
MS1716 Two sheets, each 127×102 mm. (a) $6 "Lonesome Ghosts", 1937. (b) $6 "Mickey's Garden", 1935 (vert). Set of 2 sheets 8·00 8·50

1993. Christmas. Religious Paintings. As T 211b of Gambia. Black, yellow and red (Nos. 1717, 1721/3 and MS1725a) or multicoloured (others).
1717 10c. "Adoration of the Shepherds" (detail) (Durer) 30 20
1718 25c. "Adoration of the Magi" (detail) (Raphael) 40 20
1719 35c. "Presentation at the Temple" (detail) (Raphael) 45 20
1720 50c. "Adoration of the Magi" (different detail) (Raphael) 55 35
1721 75c. "Adoration of the Shepherds" (different detail) (Durer) 90 60
1722 $1 "Adoration of the Shepherds" (different detail) (Durer) 1·00 85
1723 $4 "Adoration of the Shepherds" (different detail) (Durer) 2·50 3·25
1724 $5 "Presentation at the Temple" (different detail) (Raphael) 2·50 3·25
MS1725 Two sheets. (a) 102×128 mm. $6 "Adoration of the Shepherds" (different detail) (Dürer) (horiz). (b) 128×102 mm. $6 "Annunciation" (detail) (Raphael). Set of 2 sheets 7·00 8·00

1993. Aviation Anniversaries. As T 386 of Grenada. Multicoloured.
1726 15c. Avro Lancaster 30 25
1727 35c. Blanchard's balloon crossing the River Delaware 15 25
1728 50c. Airship "Graf Zeppelin" over Rio de Janeiro 50 35
1729 75c. Hugo Eckener 65 50
1730 $3 Pres. Washington handing passport to Blanchard 1·40 1·75
1731 $5 Short Sunderland flying boat 2·50 3·00
1732 $5 Eckener in "Graf Zeppelin" 2·50 3·00
MS1733 Three sheets. (a) 76×107 mm. $6 Supermarine Spitfire. (b) 107×76 mm. $6 Blanchard's balloon (vert). (c) 107×76 mm. $6 Eckener with Pres. Hoover. Set of 3 sheets 11·50 12·50

ANNIVERSARIES: Nos. 1726, 1731, **MS**1733a, 75th anniv of Royal Air Force; 1727, 1730, **MS**1733b. Bicentenary of first airmail flight; 1728/9, 1732, **MS**1733c, 125th birth anniv of Hugo Eckener (airship commander).

1993. Centenaries of Henry Ford's First Petrol Engine (Nos. 1735/6) and Karl Benz's First Four-wheeled Car (others). As T 387 of Grenada. Multicoloured.
1734 25c. Mercedes Benz "300 SLR", 1955 85 25
1735 45c. Ford "Thunderbird", 1957 1·00 25
1736 $4 Ford "150-A" station wagon, 1929 3·50 3·75
1737 $5 Mercedes Benz "540 K" 3·50 3·75
MS1738 Two sheets, 76×107 mm. (a) $6 Mercedes Benz "SSK", 1929. (b) $6 Ford "Model T", 1924. Set of 2 sheets 8·00 9·00

1993. Famous Paintings by Rembrandt and Matisse. As T 221c of Gambia. Multicoloured.
1739 15c. "Hendrickje Stoffels as Flora" (Rembrandt) 40 25
1740 35c. "Lady and Gentleman in Black" (Rembrandt) 50 25
1741 50c. "Aristotle with the Bust of Homer" (Rembrandt) 60 40
1742 75c. "Interior: Flowers and Parakeets" (Matisse) 85 60
1743 $1 "Goldfish" (Matisse) 1·00 85
1744 $2 "The Girl with Green Eyes" (Matisse) 1·75 2·25
1745 $3 "Still Life with a Plaster Figure" (Matisse) 2·00 2·75
1746 $5 "Christ and the Woman of Samaria" (Rembrandt) 2·50 3·25
MS1747 Two sheets. (a) 100×125 mm. $6 "Anna accused of stealing the Kid" (detail) (Rembrandt). (b) 125×100 mm. $6 "Tea in the Garden" (detail) (Matisse) (horiz). Set of 2 sheets 8·00 9·00

1994. "Hong Kong '94" International Stamp Exhibition (1st issue). As T 222a of Gambia. Multicoloured.
1748 40c. Hong Kong 1984 $5 aviation stamp and airliner at Kai Tak Airport 80 85
1749 40c. Grenada Grenadines 1988 20c. airships stamp and junk in Kowloon Bay 80 85

Nos. 1748/9 were printed together, se-tenant, forming a composite design.

See also Nos. 1750/5.

1994. "Hong Kong '94" International Stamp Exhibition (2nd issue). Jade Sculptures. As T 222b of Gambia, but horiz. Multicoloured.
1750 45c. White jade brush washer 65 65
1751 45c. Archaic jade brush washer 65 65
1752 45c. Dark green jade brush washer 65 65
1753 45c. Green jade almsbowl 65 65
1754 45c. Archaic jade dog 65 65
1755 45c. Yellow jade brush washer 65 65

1994. Fungi. As T 390 of Grenada, but with white backgrounds. Multicoloured.
1756 35c. "Hygrocybe hypohaemacta" 45 30
1757 45c. "Cantharellus cinnabarinus" 55 35
1758 50c. "Marasmius haematocephalus" 60 40
1759 75c. "Mycena pura" 80 60
1760 $1 "Gymnopilus russipes" 90 80
1761 $2 "Calocybe cyanocephala" 1·40 1·50
1762 $4 "Pluteus chrysophlebius" 2·50 3·00
1763 $5 "Chlorophyllum molybdites" 2·50 3·00
MS1764 Two sheets, each 100×70 mm. (a) $6 "Xeromphalina tenuipes". (b) "Collybia fibrosipes". Set of 2 sheets 7·50 8·00

No. 1757 is inscribed "Cantherellus cinnabarinus" and No. 1762 "Pleuteus chrysophlebius", both in error.

1994. Prehistoric Animals. As T 391 of Grenada. Multicoloured.
1765 15c. Spinosaurus 30 25
1766 35c. Apatosaurus (Brontosaurus) 45 30
1767 45c. Tyrannosaurus rex 50 35
1768 55c. Triceratops 50 40
1769 $1 Pachycephalosaurus 85 75
1770 $2 Pteranodon 1·40 1·75
1771 $4 Parasaurolophus 2·50 3·00
1772 $5 Brachiosaurus 2·50 3·00
MS1773 Two sheets, each 100×70 mm. (a) $6 Head of Brachiosaurus (vert). (b) $6 Spinosaurus and Tyrannosaurus rex fighting (vert). Set of 2 sheets 7·50 8·00

1994. 25th Anniv of First Manned Moon Landing. Space Shuttle "Challenger". As T 227a of Gambia. Multicoloured.
1774 $1.10 "Challenger" crew in training 1·00 1·25
1775 $1.10 Christa McAuliffe (astronaut) 1·00 1·25
1776 $1.10 "Challenger" on launch pad 1·00 1·25
1777 $1.10 Gregory Jarvis (astronaut) 1·00 1·25
1778 $1.10 Ellison Onizuka (astronaut) 1·00 1·25
1779 $1.10 Ronald McNair (astronaut) 1·00 1·25
MS1780 107×76 mm. $6 Judith Resnick (astronaut) (vert) 4·00 4·50

1994. Centenary of International Olympic Committee. Gold Medal Winners. As T 227b of Gambia. Multicoloured.
1781 50c. Silke Renk (Germany) (javelin), 1992 35 35
1782 $1.50 Mark Spitz (U.S.A.) (swimming), 1972 90 1·40
MS1783 106×77 mm. $6 Japanese team (Nordic skiing), 1994 3·25 3·75

1994. International Year of the Family. As T 391a of Grenada. Multicoloured.
1784 $1 Grenadines family 60 60

1994. 50th Anniv of D-Day. As T 227c of Gambia. Multicoloured.
1785 40c. Churchill bridge-laying tank 35 30
1786 $2 Sherman "Firefly" tank leaving landing craft 1·00 1·25
1787 $3 Churchill "Crocodile" flame-thrower 1·60 1·50
MS1788 107×76 mm. $6 Sherman "Crab" flail tank 3·25 3·75

1994. "Philakorea '94" International Stamp Exhibition, Seoul (1st issue). As T 227d of Gambia. Multicoloured.
1789 40c. Onung Tomb (horiz) 30 30
1790 $1 Stone pagoda, Mt. Namsam (horiz) 55 65
1791 $1 "Admiring Spring in the Country" (left detail) (Sin Yunbok) 55 65
1792 $1 "Admiring Spring in the Country" (right detail) 55 65
1793 $1 "Woman on Dano Day" (left detail) (Sin Yunbok) 55 65
1794 $1 "Woman on Dano Day" (right detail) 55 65
1795 $1 "Enjoying Lotuses while Listening to Music" (left detail) (Sin Yunbok) 55 65
1796 $1 "Enjoying Lotuses while Listening to Music" (right detail) 55 65
1797 $1 "Women by a Crystal Stream" (left detail) (Sin Yunbok) 55 65
1798 $1 "Women by a Crystal Stream" (right detail) 55 65
1799 $4 Pusan (horiz) 2·25 2·75
MS1800 70×102 mm. $6 "Blacksmith Shop" (detail) (Kim Duksin) 3·25 3·75

The two details of each painting on Nos. 1791/8 were printed together, se-tenant, each pair forming a composite design.

See also Nos. 1817/31.

1994. Orchids. As T 392 of Grenada. Multicoloured.
1801 15c. "Cattleya aurantiaca" 35 25
1802 25c. "Blettia patula" 40 25
1803 45c. "Sobralia macrantha" 50 30
1804 75c. "Encyclia belizensis" 70 55
1805 $1 "Sophrolaeliocattleya" 85 75
1806 $2 "Encyclia fragrans" 1·40 1·75
1807 $4 "Schombocattleya" 2·50 3·00
1808 $5 "Brassolaeliocattleya" 2·50 3·00
MS1809 Two sheets, each 100×70 mm. (a) $6 "Ornithidium coccineum" (horiz). (b) $6 "Brassavola nodosa" (horiz). Set of 2 sheets 8·50 9·00

1994. World Cup Football Championship, U.S.A. (2nd issue). As T 393 of Grenada. Multicoloured.
1810 75c. Steve Mark (Grenada) 70 70
1811 75c. Jurgen Kohler (Germany) 70 70
1812 75c. Almir (Brazil) 70 70
1813 75c. Michael Windiscmann (U.S.A.) 70 70
1814 75c. Guiseppe Giannini (Italy) 70 70
1815 75c. Rashidi Yekini (Nigeria) 70 70
MS1816 Two sheets, each 90×70 mm. (a) $6 Kemari (ancient Japanese game). (b) Hand holding trophy. Set of 2 sheets 7·50 8·50

106 Mickey Mouse and Unjin Miruk Window from Kwanch Ok Temple

1994. "Philakorea '94" International Stamp Exhibition, Seoul (2nd issue). Walt Disney cartoon characters. Multicoloured.
1817 3c. Type **106** 30 40
1818 4c. Goofy imitating statue of Admiral Yi, Chonju 30 40
1819 5c. Cousin Gus and Donald Duck eating dinner 30 40
1820 10c. Mickey playing flute 45 35
1821 15c. Goofy with Tolharubang (statue) 60 20
1822 15c. Type **106** 60 20
1823 20c. Mickey and Minnie at Hyang-Wonjong 60 20
1824 35c. As 4c. 75 25
1825 50c. As 5c. 90 35
1826 75c. As 10c. 1·10 60
1827 $1 As 15c. 1·40 90
1828 $2 As 20c. 2·25 2·50
1829 $4 Mickey as Somori-Kut shaman 3·00 3·50
1830 $5 Minnie holding ceremonial fan 3·00 3·50
MS1831 Two sheets, each 130×103 mm. (a) $6 Minnie beating Buk drum (vert). (b) $6 Mickey in swimming pool at Pugok Hawaii (vert). Set of 2 sheets 8·00 9·00

1994. 1st Recipients of Order of the Caribbean Community. As Nos. 2750/2 of Grenada. Multicoloured.
1832 25c. Sir Shridath Ramphal 10 10
1833 50c. William Demas 25 30
1834 $2 Derek Walcott 2·75 2·50

1994. Fishes. As T 394 of Grenada. Multicoloured.
1835 75c. Porkfish 85 80
1836 75c. Blue chromis 85 80
1837 75c. Caribbean reef shark (facing left) 85 80
1838 75c. Long-spined squirrelfish 85 80
1839 75c. Four-eyed butterflyfish 85 80
1840 75c. Blue head 85 80
1841 75c. Royal gramma 85 80
1842 75c. Sharp-nosed puffer 85 80
1843 75c. Reid's seahorse 85 80
1844 75c. Black-barred soldierfish 85 80
1845 75c. Red-lipped blenny 85 80
1846 75c. Painted wrasse 85 80
1847 75c. Yellow-tailed snapper 85 80
1848 75c. Caribbean reef shark (facing right) 85 80
1849 75c. Great barracuda 85 80
1850 75c. Red-tailed parrotfish 85 80
1851 75c. Blue tang 85 80
1852 75c. Queen angelfish 85 80
1853 75c. Red hind 85 80
1854 75c. Rock beauty 85 80
1855 75c. Queen parrotfish 85 80
1856 75c. Spanish hogfish 85 80
1857 75c. Spotted moray 85 80
1858 75c. Queen triggerfish 85 80
MS1859 Two sheets, each 102×72 mm. (a) $6 Head of queen angelfish. (b) $6 Head of painted wrasse. Set of 2 sheets 8·00 9·00

Nos. 1835/46 and 1847/58 respectively were printed together, se-tenant, forming composite designs.

1994. Christmas. Religious Paintings by Bartolome Murillo. As T 231a of Gambia. Multicoloured.
1860 15c. "The Annunciation" 30 20
1861 35c. "The Adoration of the Shepherds" 40 20
1862 50c. "Virgin and Child with St. Rose" 50 30
1863 50c. "Flight into Egypt" 50 30
1864 75c. "Virgin and Child" 70 45
1865 $1 "Virgin of the Rosary" 85 70
1866 $4 "The Holy Family" 2·50 3·25
MS1867 Two sheets. (a) 85×95 mm. $6 "Adoration of the Shepherds" (different) (detail). (b) 95×125 mm. $6 "The Holy Family with a Little Bird" (detail). Set of 2 sheets 7·50 8·00

1995. Birds. As T 397 of Grenada. Multicoloured.
1868 25c. Scaly-breasted ground dove ("Ground Dove") (vert) 1·25 40
1869 50c. White-winged dove 1·75 60
1870 $2 Inca dove (vert) 3·00 2·50
1871 $4 Mourning dove 4·00 5·50

1995. Centenary of First English Cricket Tour to the West Indies. As T 397a of Grenada. Multicoloured.
1872 50c. Mike Atherton (England) and Wisden Trophy 1·10 65
1873 75c. Curtly Ambrose (West Indies) (vert) 1·40 1·10
1874 $1 Brian Lara (West Indies) (vert) 1·50 1·50
MS1875 75×95 mm. $3 West Indian team, 1994 3·00 3·00

107 Aspects of London, National Flag and Map

1995. Capitals of the World. Aspects of various cities, national flags and maps. Multicoloured.

1876 $1 Type **107** 65 70
1877 $1 Cairo 65 70
1878 $1 Vienna 65 70
1879 $1 Paris 65 70
1880 $1 Rome 65 70
1881 $1 Budapest 65 70
1882 $1 Moscow 65 70
1883 $1 Peking ("Beijing") 65 70
1884 $1 Tokyo 65 70
1885 $1 Washington 65 70

108 Pig

1995. Chinese New Year ("Year of the Pig"). Multicoloured designs showing "GRENADA GRENADINES" in colours indicated.

1886 75c. Type **108** (violet) 50 60
1887 75c. Pig (carmine) 50 60
1888 75c. Pig (brown) 50 60
1889 75c. Pig (vermilion) 50 60
MS1890 Two sheets. (a) 106×77 mm. $2 Two pigs (horiz). (b) 67×83 mm. Nos. 1886/9. Set of 2 sheets 3·25 3·50

109 Bull Shark and Diver

1995. Marine Life of the Caribbean. Multicoloured.

1891 $1 Type **109** 75 75
1892 $1 Great white shark 75 75
1893 $1 Octopus and shoal of fish 75 75
1894 $1 Great barracuda 75 75
1895 $1 Green moray 75 75
1896 $1 Spotted eagle ray 75 75
1897 $1 Sea snake 75 75
1898 $1 Stingray 75 75
1899 $1 Grouper 75 75
1900 $1 Dolphins 75 75
1901 $1 Lionfish 75 75
1902 $1 Sea turtle and rock beauty (fish) 75 75
1903 $1 Blue-cheeked butterflyfish and nurse shark 75 75
1904 $1 Queen angelfish 75 75
1905 $1 Grouper and coney 75 75
1906 $1 Rainbow eel and spotted moray 75 75
1907 $1 Sun flower-star and coral crab 75 75
1908 $1 Octopus on sea bed 75 75
MS1909 Two sheets each 107×77 mm. (a) $5 French angelfish. (b) $6 Smooth hammerhead. Set of 2 sheets 6·50 7·00

110 Suffolk Punch

1995. Domestic Animals. Multicoloured.

1910 15c. Type **110** 60 40
1911 25c. Shetland pony 60 40
1912 75c. Blue persian (cat) 60 65
1913 75c. Sorrel abyssinian (cat) 60 65
1914 75c. White angora (cat) 60 65
1915 75c. Brown Burmese (cat) 60 65
1916 75c. Red tabby exotic shorthair (cat) 60 65
1917 75c. Seal-point birman (cat) 60 65
1918 75c. Korat (cat) 60 65
1919 75c. Norwegian forest cat 60 65
1920 75c. Lilac-point Balinese (cat) 60 65
1921 75c. British shorthair (cat) 60 65
1922 75c. Red self longhair (cat) 60 65
1923 75c. Calico Manx (cat) 60 65
1924 75c. Shetland sheepdog 60 65
1925 75c. Bull terrier 60 65
1926 75c. Afghan hound 60 65
1927 75c. Scottish terrier 60 65
1928 75c. Labrador retriever 60 65
1929 75c. English springer spaniel 60 65
1930 75c. Samoyed (dog) 60 65
1931 75c. Irish setter 60 65
1932 75c. Border collie 60 65
1933 75c. Pekingese 60 65
1934 75c. Dachshund 60 65
1935 75c. Weimaraner (dog) 60 65
1936 $1 Arab 85 85
1937 $3 Shire horse 1·75 2·00
MS1938 Two sheets, each 105×75 mm. (a) $6 Seal-point colourpoint (cat). (b) $6 English setter. Set of 2 sheets 7·00 7·50

1995. Centenary (1992) of Sierra Club (environmental protection society). Endangered Species. As T 224a of Gambia. Multicoloured.

1939 $1 Spotted owl ("Northern Spotted Owl") 90 80
1940 $1 Brown pelican on perch 90 80
1941 $1 Head of brown pelican 90 80
1942 $1 Head of jaguarundi 90 80
1943 $1 Jaguarundi looking over shoulder 90 80
1944 $1 Maned wolf in undergrowth 90 80
1945 $1 American wood stork ("Wood Stork") standing on two legs 90 80
1946 $1 American wood stork standing on one leg 90 80
1947 $1 Close-up of maned wolf 90 80
1948 $1 Brown pelican (horiz) 90 80
1949 $1 Close-up of spotted owl ("Northern Spotted Owl") (horiz) 90 80
1950 $1 Spotted owl ("Northern Spotted Owl") chick (horiz) 90 80
1951 $1 Jaguarundi (horiz) 90 80
1952 $1 Central American spider monkey sitting with young (horiz) 90 80
1953 $1 Central American spider monkey carrying young (horiz) 90 80
1954 $1 Central American spider monkey swinging from branch (horiz) 90 80
1955 $1 American wood stork ("Wood Stork") (horiz) 90 80
1956 $1 Pair of maned wolfs (horiz) 90 80

1995. 18th World Scout Jamboree, Netherlands. As T 403 of Grenada. Multicoloured.

1957 75c. Grenadian scout on beach 60 70
1958 $1 Scout with staff on hill 80 90
1959 $2 Scout saluting and national flag 1·10 1·50
MS1960 107×77 mm. $6 Scout snorkelling 3·50 4·00

1995. 50th Anniv of End of Second World War in Europe. Bombers. As T 237a of Gambia. Mult.

1961 $2 Avro Type **683** Lancaster 1·50 1·50
1962 $2 Junkers Ju 88 1·50 1·50
1963 $2 North American B-25 Mitchell 1·50 1·50
1964 $2 Boeing B-17 Flying Fortress 1·50 1·50
1965 $2 Petlyakov Pe-2 1·50 1·50
1966 $2 Martin B-26 Marauder 1·50 1·50
1967 $2 Heinkel He 111H 1·50 1·50
1968 $2 Consolidated B-24 Liberator 1·50 1·50
MS1969 105×75 mm. $6 Pres. Truman and newspaper headline (57×43 mm) 3·00 3·50

1995. 50th Anniv of United Nations. As T 404 of Grenada. Multicoloured.

1970 75c. U.N. Headquarters, New York, and flag 60 90
1971 $1 Trygve Lie (first Secretary-General) 80 1·10
1972 $2 U.N. soldier 1·10 1·40
MS1973 101×76 mm. $6 Peace dove over emblem 2·50 3·00

Nos. 1970/2 were printed together, se-tenant, forming a composite design.

1995. 50th Anniv of F.A.O. As T 405 of Grenada. Multicoloured.

1974 75c. Man hoeing 60 90
1975 $1 Woman hoeing 80 1·10
1976 $2 Man and woman hoeing 1·10 1·40
MS1977 106×76 mm. $6 Child eating with chopsticks 2·50 3·00

Nos. 1974/6 were printed together, se-tenant, forming a composite design.

1995. 90th Anniv of Rotary International. As T 406 of Grenada. Multicoloured.

1978 $5 Paul Harris (founder) and logo (horiz) 2·50 3·00
MS1979 106×76 mm. $6 Rotary Club and International logos (horiz) 2·75 3·25

1995. 95th Birthday of Queen Elizabeth the Queen Mother. As T 239a of Gambia.

1980 $1.50 brown, light brown and black 1·40 1·40
1981 $1.50 multicoloured 1·40 1·40
1982 $1.50 multicoloured 1·40 1·40
1983 $1.50 multicoloured 1·40 1·40
MS1984 102×127 mm. $6 multicoloured 6·00 5·50

DESIGNS: No. 1980, Queen Elizabeth the Queen Mother (pastel drawing); 1981, At Remembrance Day service; 1982, At desk (oil painting); 1983, Wearing green hat; **MS**1984, Unveiling memorial to Blitz victims.

1995. 50th Anniv of End of Second World War in the Pacific. As T 239b of Gambia. Multicoloured.

1985 $2 Mitsubishi G4M1 "Betty" (bomber) 1·40 1·50
1986 $2 Japanese submarine "I 14" with seaplane on catapault 1·40 1·50
1987 $2 Mitsubishi GM31 "Nell" (bomber) 1·40 1·50
1988 $2 "Akizuki" (Japanese destroyer) 1·40 1·50
1989 $2 "Kirishima" (Japanese battleship) 1·40 1·50
1990 $2 "Asigari" (Japanese cruiser) 1·40 1·50
MS1991 108×76 mm. $6 Japanese Aichi D3A1 "Val" dive bomber 3·50 3·75

1995. Olympic Games, Atlanta (1996). As T 407 of Grenada. Multicoloured.

1992 15c. Rosemary Ackerman (East Germany) (high jump) (horiz) 50 60
1993 15c. Li Ning (China) (gymnastics) (horiz) 50 60
1994 15c. Denise Parker (U.S.A.) (archery) (horiz) 50 60
1995 $3 Terry Carlisle (U.S.A.) (skeet shooting) (horiz) 2·00 2·50
1996 $3 Kathleen Nord (East Germany) (swimming) (horiz) 2·00 2·50
1997 $3 Brigit Schmidt (East Germany) (canoeing) (horiz) 2·00 2·50
MS1998 Two sheets, each 102×72 mm. (a) $6 Dan Gable (U.S.A.) and Kikuo Wada (Japan) (wrestling). (b) $6 George Foreman (U.S.A.) (boxing). Set of 2 sheets 7·00 8·00

111 Brown Pelican

1995. Birds of the Caribbean. Multicoloured.

1999 10c. Type **111** 40 40
2000 15c. Black-necked stilt ("Common Stilt") 50 40
2001 25c. Cuban trogon ("Cuban Trogan") 55 30
2002 35c. Greater flamingo ("Flamingo") 60 30
2003 75c. Imperial amazon ("Parrot") 80 45
2004 $1 Pintail ("Pintail Duck") 90 1·00
2005 $1 Great blue heron 1·90 1·90
2006 $1 Jamaican tody 90 1·00
2007 $1 Laughing gull 90 1·00
2008 $1 Purple-throated carib 90 1·00
2009 $1 Red-legged thrush 90 1·00
2010 $1 Ruddy duck 90 1·00
2011 $1 Common shoveler ("Shoveler Duck") 90 1·00
2012 $1 Great red-bellied woodpecker ("West Indian Red-bellied Woodpecker") 90 1·00
2013 $2 Ringed kingfisher 1·40 1·75
2014 $3 Strip-headed tanager 1·75 2·25
MS2015 Two sheets, each 104×73 mm. (a) $5 Village weaver. (b) $5 Blue-hooded euphonia. Set of 2 sheets 7·00 7·50

No. 2001 is inscr "Cuban Trogan", No. 2008 "Purple-throated Carb" and No. 2013 "Ringed King Fisher", all in error.

No. **MS**2015, carry the "Singapore '95" exhibition logo.

1995. Mickey's Pirate Adventure. Walt Disney cartoon characters. As T 415 of Grenada. Multicoloured.

2016 10c. Goofy and Donald Duck with treasure chests (horiz) 35 25
2017 35c. Mickey and Minnie Mouse at ship's wheel (horiz) 55 25
2018 75c. Mickey, Donald and Goofy opening chest (horiz) 90 55
2019 $1 Big Pete and rats confronting Mickey (horiz) 1·00 75
2020 $2 Mickey, Goofy and Donald in boat (horiz) 1·75 2·00
2021 $5 Goofy fighting rat pirate with mop (horiz) 3·25 4·25
MS2022 Two sheets, each 108×130 mm. (a) $6 Goofy and cannon-balls. (b) $6 Monkey pinching Mickey's nose. Set of 2 sheets 8·00 8·50

1995. Centenary of Nobel Trust Fund. As T 416 of Gambia. Multicoloured.

2023-2051 75c.×2, $1×27
MS2052 Three sheets, each 105×76 mm. (a) $6 Sir Winston Churchill (1953 Literature). (b) $6 Willy Brandt (1971 Peace). (c) $6 Albert Schweitzer (1952 Peace). Set of 3 sheets 15·00 14·00

DESIGNS: 75c. W. Arthur Lewis (1979 Economics); Derek Walcott (1992 Literature); $1 Jules Border (1919 Medicine); Rene Cassin (1968 Peace); Verner von Heidenstam (1916 Literature); Jose Echegaray (1904 Literature); Otto Wallach (1910 Chemistry); Corneille Heymans (1938 Medicine); Ivar Giaever (1973 Physics); Sir William Cremer (1903 Peace); John Strutt (1904 Physics); James Franck (1925 Physics); Tobias Asser (1911 Peace); Carl Spitteler (1919 Literature); Christiaan Eijkman (1929 Medicine); Ragnar Granit (1967 Medicine); Frederic Passy (1901 Peace); Louis Neel (1970 Physics); Sir William Ramsay (1904 Chemistry); Philip Noel-Baker (1959 Peace); Heike Onnes (1913 Physics); Fridtjof Nansen (1922 Peace); Sir Ronald Ross (1902 Medicine); Paul Muller (1948 Medicine); Allvar Gullstrand (1911 Medicine); Gerhart Hauptmann (1912 Literature); Hans Spemann (1935 Medicine); Cecil Powell (1950 Physics); Walther Bothe (1954 Physics).

Nos. 2025/33, 2034/42 and 2043/51 respectively were printed together, se-tenant, forming composite designs.

No. 2027 (Von Heidenstam) is inscribed "1906" and No. 2044 "Fridtjof Nanser", both in error.

112 Nita Naldi and Rudolph Valentino

1995. Centenary of Cinema. Multicoloured.

2053 $1 Type **112** 75 75
2054 $1 Ramon Novaro and Alice Terry 75 75
2055 $1 Frederic March and Joan Crawford 75 75
2056 $1 Clark Gable and Vivien Leigh 75 75
2057 $1 Barbara Stanwyck and Burt Lancaster 75 75
2058 $1 Warren Beatty and Natalie Wood 75 75
2059 $1 Spencer Tracy and Katharine Hepburn 75 75
2060 $1 Humphrey Bogart and Lauren Bacall 75 75
2061 $1 Omar Sharif and Julie Christie 75 75
2062 $1 Marion Davies 75 75
2063 $1 Marlene Dietrich 75 75
2064 $1 Lillian Gish 75 75
2065 $1 Bette Davis 75 75
2066 $1 Elizabeth Taylor 75 75
2067 $1 Veronica Lake 75 75
2068 $1 Ava Gardner 75 75
2069 $1 Grace Kelly 75 75
2070 $1 Kim Novak 75 75
MS2071 Two sheets. (a) 72×102 mm. $6 Sophia Loren. (b) 102×72 mm. $6 Greta Garbo and John Gilbert (horiz). Set of 2 sheets 7·00 8·00

Nos. 2053/61 and 2062/70 respectively were printed together, se-tenant, forming composite designs.

1995. Racing Cars. As T 423 of Grenada. Multicoloured.

2072 10c. Williams-Renault Formula 1, 1990s 30 20
2073 25c. Porsche "956", Le Mans, 1980s 45 20
2074 35c. Lotus "John Player Special", 1970s 50 20
2075 75c. Ford "GT-40", 1960s 75 45
2076 $2 Mercedes-Benz "W196", 1950s 1·50 2·00
2077 $3 Mercedes "SSK", 1920s 2·00 2·50
MS2078 103×73 mm. $6 Jackie Stewart in Tyrell-Ford, 1971 (vert) 3·75 4·00

113 Man on Donkey

1995. Local Transport. Multicoloured.

2079 35c. Type **113** 50 25
2080 75c. Local bus 1·00 85

1995. Evolution of Sailing Ships. As T 427 of Grenada. Multicoloured.
2081 $1 "Preussen" (full-rigged ship) 90 1·00
2082 $1 Japanese junk 90 1·00
2083 $1 Caribbean pirate ship 90 1·00
2084 $1 "Mayflower" (Pilgrim Fathers) 90 1·00
2085 $1 Chinese junk 90 1·00
2086 $1 "Santa Maria" (Columbus) 90 1·00
MS2087 103×73 mm. $5 Spanish galleon (56×41 mm) 3·25 3·50

1995. Christmas. Religious Paintings. As T 245a of Gambia. Multicoloured.
2088 10c. "Immaculate Conception" (Piero di Cosimo) 30 20
2089 15c. "St. Michael dedicating Arms to the Madonna" (Le Nain) 35 20
2090 35c. "Annunciation" (Lorenzo di Credi) 55 20
2091 50c. "The Holy Family" (Jacob Jordaens) 70 30
2092 $3 "Madonna and Child" (Lippi) 2·25 3·00
2093 $5 "Madonna and Child with Ten Saints" (Fiorentino) 3·25 4·00
MS2094 102×127 mm. (a) $6 "Adoration of the Shepherds" (detail) (Van Oost). (b) $6 "Holy Family" (detail) (Del Start). Set of 2 sheets 7·50 8·00

114 Symbolic Rat and Candle

1996. Chinese New Year ("Year of the Rat"). Multicoloured, background colours given.
2095 **114** 75c. blue 55 60
2096 **114** 75c. lilac 55 60
2097 **114** 75c. brown 55 60
2098 **114** 75c. green 55 60
MS2099 69×84 mm. Nos. 2095/8 2·00 2·20
MS2100 76×106 mm. $2 Two rats (horiz) 1·40 1·50
The four designs show different Chinese characters.

1996. Works of Art by Durer and Rubens. As T 421 of Grenada. Multicoloured.
2101 15c. "The Centaur Family" (Durer) 30 20
2102 35c. "Oriental Ruler Seated" (Durer) 40 20
2103 50c. "The Entombment" (Durer) 55 30
2104 75c. "Man in Armour" (Rubens) 70 50
2105 $1 "Peace embracing Plenty" (Rubens) 85 75
2106 $2 "Departure of Lot" (Rubens) 1·50 1·75
2107 $3 "The Four Evangelists" (Rubens) 1·75 2·25
2108 $5 "Knight, Death and Devil" (Durer) 3·00 3·75
MS2109 Two sheets, each 101×127 mm. (a) $5 "The Fathers of the Church" (detail) (Rubens). (b) $6 "St. Jerome" (detail) (Durer). Set of 2 sheets 6·50 7·50

115 Mickey and Minnie at New Year's Day "Hopping John" Tradition

1996. Traditional Holidays. Walt Disney cartoon characters. Multicoloured.
2110 25c. Type **115** 50 15
2111 50c. Disney characters dancing around maypole 70 30
2112 75c. Mickey, Minnie and Pluto watching Independence Day fireworks 95 40
2113 90c. Gyro Gearloose and Donald's nephews in Halloween costumes 1·00 55
2114 $3 Donald Duck as Puritan and nephews as Indians on Thanksgiving Day 2·75 3·25
2115 $4 Huey and Dewey with Hanukkah dreidle 2·75 3·50
MS2116 Two sheets, each 124×98 mm. (a) $6 Mickey, Minnie and Donald taking part in Caribbean carnival. (b) $6 Traditional pot of gold in St. Patrick's Day parade (vert). Set of 2 sheets 9·50 10·00

116 Gateway in Imperial Palace, Peking (image scaled to 67% of original size)

1996. "CHINA '96" 9th Asian International Stamp Exhibition, Peking. Multicoloured.
2117 $1 Type 116 65 70
2118 $1 Eastern end of Great Wall at Shanhaiguan 65 70
2119 $1 Great Wall fortress, Shanhaiguan 65 70
2120 $1 Gate of Heavenly Peace, Peking 65 70
2121 $1 Sun Yat-sen's Mausoleum, Nanjing 65 70
2122 $1 Summer Palace, Peking 65 70
2123 $1 Temple of Heaven, Peking 65 70
2124 $1 Hall of Supreme Harmony, Forbidden City, Peking 65 70
MS2125 Three sheets. (a) 150×100 mm. $2 Traditional Chinese painting (39×50 mm). (b) 90×68 mm. $6 Great Wall of China from the air (39×50 mm). (c) 90×68 mm. $6 Marble Boat, Summer Palace, Peking (50×39 mm). Set of 3 sheets 7·00 7·50

1996. 70th Birthday of Queen Elizabeth II. As T 255a of Gambia. Multicoloured.
2126 35c. As Type **255a** of Gambia 40 25
2127 $2 Queen wearing tiara and green dress 1·25 1·40
2128 $4 Windsor Castle 2·50 2·75
MS2129 103×125 mm. $6 Queen Elizabeth at Windsor 3·75 4·00

1996. Flowers. As T 430 of Grenada. Multicoloured.
2130 35c. "Camellia" "Apple Blossom" 40 25
2131 75c. "Odontoglossum" 60 60
2132 75c. "Cattleya" 60 60
2133 75c. "Paphiopedilum" "Venus's Slipper" 60 60
2134 75c. "Laeliocattleya" "Marysville" 60 60
2135 75c. Fuchsia "Citation" 60 60
2136 75c. Fuchsia "Amy Lye" 60 60
2137 75c. "Clysonimus" (butterfly) and temple 60 60
2138 75c. Foxglove ("Digitalis purpurea") 60 60
2139 75c. Martagon lily ("Lilium martagon") 60 60
2140 75c. "Tulipa" "Couleur Cardinal" 60 60
2141 75c. Snowdrop ("Galanthus nivalis") 60 60
2142 75c. "Rosa" "Superstar" 60 60
2143 75c. Crocus "Dutch Yellow Mammoth" 60 60
2144 75c. Japanese lily ("Lilium speciosum") 60 60
2145 75c. "Lilium" "Joan Evans" 60 60
2146 75c. "Rosa" "Rosemary Harkness" 60 60
2147 90c. "Camellia japonica" "Extravaganza" 60 60
2148 $1 Chrysanthemum "Primrose Dorothy Else" 60 60
2149 $2 Dahlia "Brandaris" 1·25 1·40
MS2150 Two sheets, each 68×98 mm. (a) $5 Narcissus "Rembrandt". (b) $6 Gladiolus "Flowersong". Set of 2 sheets 6·50 7·50
Nos. 2135/46 were printed together, se-tenant, with the backgrounds forming a composite design.
No. 2135 is inscribed "Fuschcia", No. 2133 "Mammouth" and **MS**2150b "Gladiollus", all in error.

1996. 50th Anniv of UNICEF. As T 258a of Gambia. Multicoloured.
2151 75c. Child's face (horiz) 55 45
2152 $2 Child with spoon (horiz) 1·10 1·40
2153 $3 Girl sewing (horiz) 1·60 1·90
MS2154 105×75 mm. $6 Mother carrying child 3·00 3·50

1996. 3000th Anniv of Jerusalem. Multicoloured designs as T 424 of Grenada, but horiz.
MS2155 137×47 mm. $1 Pool of Bethesda and "Papaver rhoeas"; $2 Damascus Gate and "Chrysanthemum coronarium"; $3 Church of All Nations and "Myrtus communis". 4·00 3·75
MS2156 82×62 mm. $6 Church of the Holy Sepulchre 4·00 3·75

1996. Centenary of Radio. Entertainers. As T 259a of Gambia. Multicoloured.
2157 35c. Ed Wynn 35 25
2158 75c. Red Skelton 55 45
2159 $1 Joe Penner 65 55
2160 $3 Jerry Colonna 1·75 2·00
MS2161 70×99 mm. $6 Bob Elliot and Ray Goulding (horiz) 3·25 3·75

1996. Olympic Games, Atlanta. Previous Medal Winners. As T 425 of Grenada. Multicoloured.
2162 35c. Los Angeles Memorial Coliseum 35 25
2163 75c. Connie Carpenter-Phinney (U.S.A.) (Cycling) 75 55
2164 $1 Josef Neckermann (Germany) (vert) 70 70
2165 $1 Harry Boldt (Germany) (vert) 70 70
2166 $1 Elena Petouchkova (Russia) (vert) 70 70
2167 $1 Alwin Schockemoehle (Germany) (vert) 70 70
2168 $1 Hans Winkler (Germany) (vert) 70 70
2169 $1 Joe Fargis (U.S.A.) (vert) 70 70
2170 $1 David Broome (Great Britain) (vert) 70 70
2171 $1 Reiner Klimke (Germany) (vert) 70 70
2172 $1 Richard Meade (Great Britain) (vert) 70 70
2173 $1 Julianne McNamara (U.S.A.) (vert) 70 70
2174 $1 Takuti Hayata (Japan) (vert) 70 70
2175 $1 Nikolai Adriana (Russia) (vert) 70 70
2176 $1 Mitch Gaylord (U.S.A.) (vert) 70 70
2177 $1 Ludmilla Tourischeva (Russia) (vert) 70 70
2178 $1 Karin Janz (Germany) (vert) 70 70
2179 $1 Peter Kormann (U.S.A.) (vert) 70 70
2180 $1 Sawoo Kato (Japan) (vert) 70 70
2181 $1 Nadia Comaneci (Rumania) (vert) 70 70
2182 $2 Mohamed Bouchighe (Algeria) (Boxing) (vert) 1·25 1·40
2183 $3 Jackie Joyner Kersee (U.S.A.) (Javelin) 1·75 1·90
MS2184 Two sheets, each 103×74 mm. (a) $5 Child waving flag (vert). (b) $6 William Steinkraus (U.S.A.) (Show jumping). Set of 2 sheets 6·50 7·00
Nos. 2164/72 (equestrians) and 2173/81 (gymnasts) respectively were printed together, se-tenant, with the backgrounds forming composite designs.

1996. Classic Cars. As T 426 of Grenada. Multicoloured.
2185 35c. Chevrolet Belair convertible 40 25
2186 50c. V.I.P. car 55 30
2187 75c. Rolls-Royce Torpedo 65 45
2188 $1 Nissan "Cepric" type 70 70
2189 $1 Delaunay-Belleville HB6 70 70
2190 $1 Bugatti Type-15 70 70
2191 $1 Mazda Type 800 70 70
2192 $1 Mercedes 24/100/140 Sport 70 70
2193 $1 MG K3 Rover 70 70
2194 $1 Plymouth Fury 70 70
2195 $2 Mercedes-Benz 500K 1·25 1·40
2196 $3 Bugatti Type-13 1·75 1·90
MS2197 Two sheets, each 106×76 mm. (a) $5 Bugatti "Roadster" Type-55. (b) $6 Lincoln Type-L. Set of 2 sheets 6·50 7·00

1996. Ships. As T 427 of Grenada. Multicoloured.
2198 35c. Grenada schooner 60 25
2199 75c. Grenada schooner (different) 85 45
2200 $1 Athenian triremes, 1000 B.C. 95 95
2201 $1 Egyptian Nile galley, 30 B.C. 95 95
2202 $1 Bangladesh dinghi, 310 B.C. 95 95
2203 $1 Warship of Queen Hatshepsut, 476 B.C. 95 95
2204 $1 Chinese Junk, 200 B.C. 95 95
2205 $1 Polynesian ocean-going canoe, 600 B.C 95 95
2206 $1 "Europa" (liner), 1957 95 95
2207 $1 "Lusitania" (liner), 1906 95 95
2208 $1 "Queen Mary" (liner), 1936 95 95
2209 $1 "Bianca C" (liner) 95 95
2210 $1 "France" (liner), 1952 95 95
2211 $1 "Orion" (liner), 1915 95 95
MS2212 Two sheets, each 104×74 mm. (a) $5 "Queen Elizabeth 2" (liner), 1969 (56×42 mm). (b) $6 Viking longship, 610 (42×56 mm). Set of 2 sheets 6·50 7·00

117 Felix Mendelssohn

1996. Composers. Multicoloured.
2213 $1 Type **117** 90 70
2214 $1 Franz Schubert 90 70
2215 $1 Franz Joseph Haydn 90 70
2216 $1 Robert Schumann 90 70
2217 $1 Ludwig van Beethoven 90 70
2218 $1 Gioacchino Rossini 90 70
2219 $1 George Frederick Handel 90 70
2220 $1 Pyotr Tchaikovsky 90 70
2221 $1 Frederic Chopin 90 70
2222 $1 Bela Bartok 90 70
2223 $1 Giacomo Puccini 90 70
2224 $1 George Gershwin 90 70
2225 $1 Leonard Bernstein 90 70
2226 $1 Kurt Weill 90 70
2227 $1 John Cage 90 70
2228 $1 Aaron Copland 90 70
2229 $1 Sergei Prokofiev 90 70
2230 $1 Igor Stravinsky 90 70
MS2231 Two sheets, each 74×104 mm. (a) $5 Richard Strauss. (b) $6 Wolfgang Amadeus Mozart. Set of 2 sheets 8·50 7·50
Nos. 2213/21 and 2222/30 respectively were printed together, se-tenant, with the backgrounds forming composite designs.

1996. Railway Steam Locomotives. As T 429 of Grenada. Multicoloured.
2232 $1.50 Class 38 No. 382, Germany 1·10 1·10
2233 $1.50 "Duchess of Hamilton", Great Britain 1·10 1·10
2234 $1.50 Class W.P., India 1·10 1·10
2235 $1.50 Class 141R "Americaine", France 1·10 1·10
2236 $1.50 Class A4 "Mallard", Great Britain 1·10 1·10
2237 $1.50 Class 18 No. 201, Germany 1·10 1·10
2238 $1.50 Class A2 "Blue Peter", Great Britain 1·10 1·10
2239 $1.50 Class P36, Russia 1·10 1·10
2240 $1.50 Class QJ, China 1·10 1·10
2241 $1.50 Class 12, Belgium 1·10 1·10
2242 $1.50 Class "Challenger", U.S.A. 1·10 1·10
2243 $1.50 Class 25, South Africa 1·10 1·10
MS2244 Two sheets, each 100×70 mm. (a) $5 Class "King", Great Britain. (b) $6 Class "Royal Scot", Great Britain. Set of 2 sheets 7·00 7·50

1996. Christmas. Religious Paintings. As T 245a of Gambia. Showing different details from "Suffer Little Children to Come Unto Me" by Van Dyck.
2245 15c. multicoloured 40 20
2246 25c. multicoloured 40 20
2247 $1 multicoloured 1·00 65
2248 $1.50 multicoloured 1·25 1·25
2249 $2 multicoloured 1·60 1·60
2250 $4 multicoloured 2·50 3·25
MS2251 Two sheets, each 106×76 mm. (a) $6 "Suffer Little Children to Come Unto Me" (detail) (Van Dyck) (horiz). (b) $6 "Adoration of the Magi" (Rembrandt) (horiz). Set of 2 sheets 7·50 8·50

118 Man Ho Temple, 1841

1997. "HONG KONG '97" International Stamp Exhibition. Hong Kong Past and Present. T 118 and similar horiz designs. Multicoloured.
MS2252 Five sheets, each 120×96 mm. (a) $3 Type **118**; $3 Man Ho Temple, 1983. (b) $3 St. John's Cathedral, Victoria 1886; $3 St. John's Cathedral, Victoria 1983. (c) $3 Victoria Harbour, 1858; $3 Victoria Harbour, 1983. (d) $3 Waterfront skyscraper; $3 Aerial view of central Victoria. (e) $3 Signing of Treaty of Nanking, 1852. $3 Margaret Thatcher signing The Joint Declaration, 1984. Set of 5 sheets 22·00 20·00

1997. 50th Anniv of UNESCO. As T 273a of Gambia. Multicoloured.
2253 15c. Temple, Kyoto, Japan 40 20
2254 25c. Roman ruins, Trier, Germany 40 20
2255 $1 Gateway, Mount Taishan, China 80 80
2256 $1 Temple guardian, Kyoto, Japan (vert) 80 80
2257 $1 Temple deity, Kyoto, Japan (vert) 80 80
2258 $1 Temple lamp, Kyoto, Japan (vert) 80 80
2259 $1 Ayutthaya, Thailand (vert) 80 80
2260 $1 Statue, Borobudur Temple, Indonesia (vert) 80 80
2261 $1 Monuments at Pattadakal, India (vert) 80 80
2262 $1 Sleeping buddha, Polonnaruwa, Sri Lanka (vert) 80 80
2263 $1 Sagarmatha National Park, Nepal (vert) 80 80
2264 $1 Congonhas Sanctuary, Brazil (vert) 1·10 1·10
2265 $1 Cartagena, Colombia (vert) 1·10 1·10

2266 $1 Pueblo, Guatemala (vert) 1·10 1·10
2267 $1 Maya statue, Honduras (vert) 1·10 1·10
2268 $1 Popocatepetl Monastery, Mexico (vert) 1·10 1·10
2269 $1 Galapagos Islands, Ecuador (vert) 1·10 1·10
2270 $1 Waterfall, Costa Rica (vert) 1·10 1·10
2271 $1 Glaciares National Park, Argentina (vert) 1·10 1·10
2272 $1.50 Notre Dame Cathedral, Paris, France 1·10 1·10
2273 $1.50 Timbered house, Maulbronn, Germany 1·10 1·10
2274 $1.50 Gateway, Himeji-jo, Japan 1·10 1·10
2275 $1.50 Lion statues, Delphi, Greece 1·10 1·10
2276 $1.50 Palace of Fontainebleau, France 1·10 1·10
2277 $1.50 Scandola Nature Reserve, France 1·10 1·10
2278 $2 Citadel, Dubrovnik, Croatia 1·50 1·60
2279 $4 Angra do Heroismo, Portugal 2·50 3·00
MS2280 Three sheets, each 127×102 mm. (a) $6 Mont St. Michel, France. (b) $6 Ruins of Teotihuacau, Mexico. (c) $6 Temple, Chengde, China. Set of 3 sheets 10·00 11·00

119 Springer Spaniel

1997. Cats and Dogs. Multicoloured.
2281 35c. Type **119** 50 25
2282 45c. Abyssinian blue 50 30
2283 50c. Burmese cream (vert) 50 30
2284 75c. Doberman pinscher 75 50
2285 90c. Persian tortoiseshell and white 75 50
2286 $1 Italian spinone (vert) 85 55
2287 $1.50 Siamese chocolate point 1·10 1·10
2288 $1.50 Oriental shorthair white 1·10 1·10
2289 $1.50 Burmese sable 1·10 1·10
2290 $1.50 Abyssinian tabby 1·10 1·10
2291 $1.50 Persian shaded silver 1·10 1·10
2292 $1.50 Tonkinese natural mink 1·10 1·10
2293 $1.50 Leonberger 1·10 1·10
2294 $1.50 Newfoundland 1·10 1·10
2295 $1.50 Boxer 1·10 1·10
2296 $1.50 St. Bernard 1·10 1·10
2297 $1.50 Silky terrier 1·10 1·10
2298 $1.50 Miniature schnauzer 1·10 1·10
2299 $2 Cocker spaniel (vert) 1·50 1·60
2300 $3 Oriental shorthair agouti (vert) 2·00 2·25
MS2301 Two sheets. (a) 75×105 mm. $6 Sphynx (vert). (b) 105×75 mm. $6 Golden retriever puppy. Set of 2 sheets 7·50 8·00

Nos. 2287/92 (cats) and Nos. 2293/8 (dogs) respectively were printed together, se-tenant, with the backgrounds forming composite designs.

1997. Dinosaurs. As T 438 of Grenada. Mult.
2302 45c. Stegosaurus 60 30
2303 90c. Diplodocus 80 50
2304 $1 Pteranodon (vert) 80 55
2305 $1.50 Rhamphorhynchus and head of Brachiosaurus 1·10 1·10
2306 $1.50 Archaeopteryx 1·10 1·10
2307 $1.50 Anurognathus and body of Brachiosaurus 1·10 1·10
2308 $1.50 Head of Albertosaurus 1·10 1·10
2309 $1.50 Herrerasaurus and legs of Brachiosaurus 1·10 1·10
2310 $1.50 Platyhystrix and body of Albertosaurus 1·10 1·10
2311 $2 Deinonychus and Ankylasaurus (vert) 1·50 1·60
MS2312 Two sheets, each 103×74 mm. (a) $6 Allosaurus (vert). (b) $6 Hydacrosaurus. Set of 2 sheets 8·00 8·50

Nos. 2305/10 were printed together, se-tenant, with the backgrounds forming a composite design.

1997. 300th Anniv of Mother Goose Nursery Rhymes. Sheet 72×102 mm containing vert design as T 276a of Gambia. Multicoloured.
MS2313 $6 Girl and sheep ("Baa, Baa, Black Sheep") 3·50 4·00

1997. 50th Death Anniv of Paul Harris (founder of Rotary International). As T 276b of Gambia. Multicoloured.
2314 $3 Paul Harris and village women with water pump, Burkina Faso 1·50 1·60
MS2315 78×108 mm. $6 Early Rotary parade float 3·00 3·50

1997. Golden Wedding of Queen Elizabeth and Prince Philip. As T 276c of Gambia. Multicoloured (except Nos. 2318/19).
2316 $1 Engagement photograph, 1947 1·00 90
2317 $1 Royal coat of arms 1·00 90
2318 $1 Queen Elizabeth and Duke of Edinburgh, 1953 (brown) 1·00 90
2319 $1 Formal portrait of Queen Elizabeth with Prince Philip in uniform (brown) 1·00 90
2320 $1 Sandringham House 1·00 90
2321 $1 Queen Elizabeth and Prince Philip in carriage 1·00 90
MS2322 100×70 mm. $6 Wedding photograph, 1947 5·50 5·00

1997. "Pacific '97" International Stamp Exhibition, San Francisco. Death Centenary of Heinrich von Stephan (founder of the U.P.U.). As T 276d of Gambia.
2323 $1.50 green 1·10 1·10
2324 $1.50 brown 1·10 1·10
2325 $1.50 violet 1·10 1·10
MS2326 82×118 mm. $6 blue and black 3·25 3·75

DESIGNS: No. 2323, Pony Express, 1860; 2324, Von Stephan and Mercury; 2325, American steam locomotive; **MS**2326 Von Stephan and camel courier, Baghdad.

1997. Birth Bicentenary of Hiroshige (Japanese painter). "100 Famous Views of Edo". As T 541a of Ghana but horiz. Multicoloured.
2327 $1.50 "Koume Embankment" 1·00 1·00
2328 $1.50 "Azuma Shrine and the Entwined Camphor" 1·00 1·00
2329 $1.50 "Yanagishima" 1·00 1·00
2330 $1.50 "Inside Akiba Shrine, Ukeji" 1·00 1·00
2331 $1.50 "Distant View of Kinryuzan Temple and Azuma Bridge" 1·00 1·00
2332 $1.50 "Night View of Matsuchiyama and the San'ya Canal" 1·00 1·00
MS2333 Two sheets, each 102×127 mm. (a) $6 "Five Pines, Onagi Canal". (b) $6 "Spiral Hall, Five Hundred Rakan Temple". Set of 2 sheets 7·00 7·50

1997. 175th Anniv of Brothers Grimm's Third Collection of Fairy Tales. "The Fox and the Geese". As T 277a of Gambia. Multicoloured.
2334 $2 Fox and geese 1·60 1·60
2335 $2 Fox with knife and fork and geese 1·60 1·60
2336 $2 Fox asleep and singing geese 1·60 1·60
MS2337 124×96 mm. $6 Fox (horiz) 3·75 4·00

1997. Winter Olympic Games, Nagano, Japan. As T 440 of Grenada. Multicoloured.
2338 90c. Slalom 65 50
2339 $1 Downhill skiing 70 70
2340 $1 Freestyle ski-jumping (blue and green ski suit) 70 70
2341 $1 Curling 70 70
2342 $1 Ski-jumping (pink ski suit) 70 70
2343 $1 Four-man bobsleigh 70 70
2344 $1 Nordic combined 70 70
2345 $1 Speed skating 70 70
2346 $1 Ice hockey 70 70
2347 $1 Cross-country skiing 70 70
2348 $2 One-man luge 1·25 1·40
2349 $3 Men's figure-skating 1·75 1·90
2350 $5 Speed skating (different) 2·75 3·00
MS2351 Two sheets, each 97×67 mm. (a) $6 Figure skating. (b) $6 One-man luge (vert). Set of 2 sheets 6·00 6·50

120 Hong Kong

1997. Return of Hong Kong to China. Multicoloured.
2352 **120** $1 multicoloured 70 60
2353 - $1.25 multicoloured 80 85
2354 - $1.50 mult (63×32 mm) 95 1·00
2355 - $2 mult (63×32 mm) 1·25 1·40

DESIGNS: $1.25 to $2 Modern Hong Kong shown through inscriptions.

1997. Marine Life. As T 439 of Grenada. Mult.
2356 10c. Wimplefish 10 10
2357 15c. Clown triggerfish 10 10
2358 25c. Ringed emperor angelfish 15 20
2359 35c. Hooded butterflyfish 20 25
2360 45c. Semicircle angelfish 25 30
2361 75c. Scribbled angelfish 40 45
2362 90c. Threadfin butterflyfish 45 50
2363 $1 Clown surgeonfish 60 65
2364 $2 Bottle-nosed dolphin 1·00 1·10
2365 $5 Triggerfish 2·50 2·75
2366 $10 Lionfish 5·00 5·50
2367 $20 Jackknifefish 10·00 10·50

121 Winnie the Pooh as Monday's Child

1997. "Monday's Child" (poem). Disney cartoon characters from Winnie the Pooh illustrating various verses. Multicoloured.
2368 $1 Type **121** 1·25 1·25
2369 $1 Kanga as Tuesday's child 1·25 1·25
2370 $1 Eeyore as Wednesday's child 1·25 1·25
2371 $1 Tigger as Thursday's child 1·25 1·25
2372 $1 Piglet as Friday's child 1·25 1·25
2373 $1 Rabbit as Saturday's child 1·25 1·25
MS2374 128×107 mm. $6 Christopher Robin as Sunday's child 5·50 5·50

122 Snow White kissing Grumpy

1997. Disney Sweethearts. Disney cartoon characters kissing. Multicoloured.
2375 $1 Type **122** 1·10 1·10
2376 $1 Figaro the Cat and Cleo the Fish 1·10 1·10
2377 $1 Peter Pan and Wendy 1·10 1·10
2378 $1 Cinderella and the Prince 1·10 1·10
2379 $1 Ariel and Eric 1·10 1·10
2380 $1 Beauty and the Prince 1·10 1·10
2381 $1 Aladdin and Jasmine 1·10 1·10
2382 $1 Pocahontas and Captain John Smith 1·10 1·10
2383 $1 Phoebus and Esmeralda 1·10 1·10
MS2384 127×102 mm. $6 Georges Hautecourt kissing cats tail (vert) 6·00 6·00

1997. World Cup Football Championship, France (1998). As T 283a of Gambia.
2385 10c. blue 25 25
2386 20c. multicoloured 30 30
2387 45c. brown 40 30
2388 $1 black 70 70
2389 $1 brown 70 70
2390 $1 black 70 70
2391 $1 brown 70 70
2392 $1 multicoloured 70 70
2393 $1 multicoloured 70 70
2394 $1 black 70 70
2395 $1 brown 70 70
2396 $1 multicoloured 70 70
2397 $1 black 70 70
2398 $1 black 70 70
2399 $1 black 70 70
2400 $1 black 70 70
2401 $1 black 70 70
2402 $1 black 70 70
2403 $1 black 70 70
2404 $1 black 70 70
2405 $1.50 multicoloured 95 1·00
2406 $5 black 2·75 3·00
MS2407 Two sheets. (a) 127×102 mm. $6 black. (b) 102×127 mm. $6 black. Set of 2 sheets 8·50 9·00

DESIGNS—HORIZ: No. 2385, Italian team, 1934; 2386, Angolan team; 2387, Brazilian team, 1958; 2388, Uruguay team, 1950; 2389, Winning England team, 1966; 2390, West German team, 1954; 2391, Uruguayan officials with Jules Rimet trophy, 1930; 2392, West German players celebrating, 1990; 2393, Maradona (Argentine player), 1986; 2394, Brazilian players, 1994; 2395, Argentine players, 1978; 2396, West German player holding World Cup, 1974; 2405, West German team, 1974; 2406, Italian team, 1938; **MS**2407b, Paulao, Angola. VERT: No. 2397, Ademir, Brazil; 2398, Kocsis, Hungary; 2399, Leonidas, Brazil; 2400, Nejedly, Czechoslavakia; 2401, Schiavio, Italy; 2402, Stabile, Uruguay; 2403, Pele, Brazil; 2404, Fritzwalter, West Germany; **MS**2407a, Shearer, England.

1997. Butterflies. As T 444 of Grenada. Mult.
2408 75c. "Polyura dehaani" 65 45
2409 90c. "Polyura dolon" 70 50
2410 $1 "Charaxes candiope" 70 55
2411 $1.50 "Pantaporia punctata" 95 95
2412 $1.50 "Euthalia confucius" 95 95
2413 $1.50 "Euthalia kardama" 95 95
2414 $1.50 "Limenitis albomaculata" 95 95
2415 $1.50 "Hestina assimilis" 95 95
2416 $1.50 "Kallima inachus" 95 95
2417 $1.50 "Euthalia teutoides" 95 95
2418 $1.50 "Euphaedra francina" 95 95
2419 $1.50 "Euphaedra eleus" 95 95
2420 $1.50 "Euphaedra harpalyce" 95 95
2421 $1.50 "Euphaedra cyparissa" 95 95
2422 $1.50 "Euphaedra gausape" 95 95
2423 $1.50 "Euphaedra imperialis" 95 95
2424 $2 "Charaxes etesippe" 1·25 1·40
2425 $3 "Charaxes castor" 1·75 1·90
MS2426 Two sheets, each 106×76 mm. (a) $5 "Charaxes nobilis" (vert). (b) $6 "Charaxes numenes" (vert). Set of 2 sheets 6·50 7·00

Nos. 2412/17 and 2418/23 respectively were printed together, se-tenant, with the backgrounds forming composite designs.

123 James Dean

1997. James Dean (actor) Commemoration. Different portaits. Multicoloured.
2427 $1 Type **123** 70 70
2428 $1 Wearing purple jumper 70 70
2429 $1 Wearing stetson and smoking 70 70
2430 $1 Wearing dinner jacket and tie 70 70
2431 $1 Full-face portrait 70 70
2432 $1 Grimacing 70 70
2433 $1 Wearing stetson 70 70
2434 $1 Leaning on arms 70 70
2435 $1 Smoking 70 70

124 "Symphyglossum sanguineum"

1997. Orchids of the World. Multicoloured.
2436 35c. Type **124** 40 25
2437 45c. "Doritaenopsis" "Mythic Beauty" 50 30
2438 75c. "Odontoglossum cervantesii" 65 45
2439 90c. "Cattleya" "Pumpernickel" 70 50
2440 $1 "Vanda" "Patricia Low" 70 55
2441–2449 $1×9 ("Lycaste" "Aquila"; "Brassolaeliocattleya" "Dorothy Bertsch"; "Phalaenopsis" "Zuma Urchin"; "Promenaea xanthina"; "Amesiella philippinensis"; "Brassocattleya" "Angel Lace"; "Brassoepidendrum" "Peggy Ann"; "Miltonia seine"; "Sophralaeliocattleya" "Precious Stones") 5·50
2450–2458 $1×9 ("Cymbidium" "Showgirl"; "Disa blackii"; "Phalaenopsis aphrodite"; "Iwanagaara" "Apple Blossom"; "Masdevallia" "Copper Angel"; "Paphiopedilum micranthum"; "Paphiopedilum" "Clare de Lune"; "Cattleya forbesii"; "Dendrobium" "Dawn Maree") 5·50
2459 $1.50 "Odontonia" "Debutante" 1·00 1·00
2460–2465 $1.50×6 ("Miltoniopsis" "Jean Sabourin"; "Cymbidium" "Red Beauty"; "Brassocattleya" "Green Dragon"; "Phalaenopsis" hybrid; "Laeliocattleya" "Mary Ellen Carter"; "Disa" hybrid) 5·50
2466–2471 $1.50×6 ("Lycaste macrobulbon"; "Cochleanthes discolor"; "Cymbidium" "Nang Carpenter"; "Paphiopedilum" "Claire de Lune"; "Masdevallia caudata"; "Cymbidium" "Showgirl") 5·50
2472 $2 "Laeliocattleya" "Mini Purple" 1·25 1·40
2473 $3 "Phragmipedium dominianum" 1·75 1·90

MS2474 Two sheets, each 76×106 mm. (a) $5 "Phalenopsis" "Medford Star". (b) $6 "Brassolaelio-cattleya" "Dorothy Bertsch". Set of 2 sheets 7·00 7·50

Nos. 2460/5 and 2466/71 respectively were printed together, se-tenant, with the backgrounds forming composite designs.

125 "Clitocybe metachroa"

1997. Fungi. Multicoloured.

2475	75c. Type **125**	65	45
2476	90c. "Clavulinopsis helvola"	70	50
2477	$1 "Lycoperdon pyriforme"	70	55
2478	$1.50 "Auricularia auricula-judae"	95	95
2479	$1.50 "Entoloma incanum"	95	95
2480	$1.50 "Coprinus atramentarius"	95	95
2481	$1.50 "Mycena polygramma"	95	95
2482	$1.50 "Lepista nuda"	95	95
2483	$1.50 "Pleurotis cornucopiae"	95	95
2484	$1.50 "Laccaria amethystina"	95	95
2485	$2 "Clathrus archeri"	1·25	1·40
2486	$3 "Lactarius trivialis"	1·75	1·90
MS2487	Two sheets, each 106×76 mm. (a) $6 "Morchella esculenta". (b) $6 "Amanita muscaria". Set of 2 sheets	7·50	8·00

126 Ludwig van Beethoven

1997. Classical Composers. Multicoloured.

2488	$1 Type **126**	85	80
2489	$1 Pyotr Tchaikovsky	85	80
2490	$1 Johann Christian Bach	85	80
2491	$1 Frederic Chopin	85	80
2492	$1 Igor Stravinsky	85	80
2493	$1 Franz Joseph Haydn	85	80
2494	$1 Gustav Mahler	85	80
2495	$1 Gioacchino Antonio Rossini	85	80
MS2496	Two sheets, each 106×76 mm. (a) $6 Wolfgang Amadeus Mozart. (b) $6 Franz Schubert. Set of 2 sheets	9·50	9·50

127 Diana, Princess of Wales and Buckingham Palace

1997. Diana, Princess of Wales Commemoration. Multicoloured.

2497	$1.50 Type **127**	1·10	1·10
2498	$1.50 Princess Diana and lake at Althorp	1·10	1·10
2499	$1.50 Princess Diana and Westminster Abbey	1·10	1·10
2500	$1.50 Princess Diana and gates to Althorp	1·10	1·10
2501	$1.50 Princess Diana in pink hat and gates to Kensington Palace	1·10	1·10
2502	$1.50 Princess Diana and Althorp House	1·10	1·10
MS2503	115×80 mm. $6 Holding bouquet (60×40 mm)	3·75	4·00

1997. Christmas. Religious Paintings. As T 448 of Grenada. Multicoloured.

2504	20c. "Choir of Angels (Simon Marmion)	30	15
2505	75c. "The Annunciation" (Giotto)	65	45
2506	90c. "Festival of the Rose Garlands" (Albrecht Durer)	70	50
2507	$1.50 "Madonna with Two Angels" (Hans Memling)	95	1·00
2508	$2 "The Ognissanti Madonna" (Giotto)	1·25	1·40
2509	$3 "Angel with Candlestick" (Michelangelo)	1·75	1·90
MS2510	Two sheets, each 114×104 mm. (a) $6 "The Rising of the Sun" (detail) (horiz) (Francois Boucher). (b) $6 "Cupid" (detail) (horiz) (Jean-Baptiste Huet). Set of 2 sheets	7·50	7·50

No. 2506 is inscribed "DUER" in error.

1998. Fishes. As T 449 of Grenada. Multicoloured.

2511	$1 Queen angelfish	75	75
2512	$1 Clown triggerfish	75	75
2513	$1 Four-spot butterflyfish	75	75
2514	$1 Yellow-tailed damselfish	75	75
2515	$1 Yellow-headed wrasse	75	75
2516	$1 Royal gramma	75	75
2517	$1 Candy basslet	75	75
2518	$1 Smooth trunkfish	75	75
2519	$1 Coral hind	75	75
MS2520	Two sheets. (a) 102×72 mm. $6 Black-finned reef shark. (b) 72×102 mm. $6 Yellow-headed jawfish (vert). Set of 2 sheets	8·50	8·50

Nos. 2511/19 were printed together, se-tenant , with the backgrounds forming a composite design.

128 Tiger (hologram)

1998. Chinese New Year ("Year of the Tiger").

2521	**128** $1.50 black on silver foil	1·25	1·25
MS2522	64×76 mm. **128** $3 black on silver foil (52×65 mm)	2·00	2·00

129 "Alabama" (Confederate warship)

1998. Famous Ships. Multicoloured. (a) Ships of the 1860s.

2523	75c. Type **129**	75	75
2524	75c. "Persia" (paddle-steamer)	75	75
2525	75c. "Ariel" (clipper)	75	75
2526	75c. "Florida" (Confederate warship)	75	75
2527	75c. "Great Eastern" (paddle-steamer)	75	75
2528	75c. "Jacob Bell" on fire	75	75
2529	75c. "Star of India" (clipper)	75	75
2530	75c. "Robert E. Lee" (Mississippi paddle-steamer)	75	75
2531	75c. U.S.S. "Passaic" (monitor)	75	75
2532	75c. "Madagascar" (clipper)	75	75
2533	75c. H.M.S. "Devastation" (battleship)	75	75
2534	75c. "General Grant" (clipper)	75	75

(b) Ships of the American Civil War.

2535	$1 Clark Gable as Rhett Butler in "Gone with the Wind" (vert)	75	75
2536	$1 Crew abandoning blockade runner wrecked on Sullivan's Island (vert)	75	75
2537	$1 Margaret Mitchell (author of "Gone with the Wind") (vert)	75	75
2538	$1 George Alfred Trenholm (ship owner) (vert)	75	75
2539	$1 Dock Street Theatre, Charleston (vert)	75	75
2540	$1 "Howlett" (paddle-steamer) sinking (vert)	75	75
2541	$1 U.S.S. "Tecumseh" on fire (vert)	75	75
2542	$1 City Jail, Charleston (vert)	75	75
MS2543	Two sheets, each 106×76 mm. (a) $6 "Nashville" sinking Union clipper "Harvey Birch" (57×42 mm). (b) $6 "Hatteras" (paddle-steamer) on fire (42×57 mm). Set of 2 sheets	8·00	8·50

130 Concept Strike Fighter

1998. Aircraft Designs of the Future. Multicoloured.

2544	70c. Type **130**	50	40
2545	90c. Concept space shuttle	45	60
2546	$1 Velocity 173 RG Elite	75	75
2547	$1 Davis DA-9	75	75
2548	$1 Concorde	75	75
2549	$1 Voyager	75	75
2550	$1 Factimobile	75	75
2551	$1 RAF 2000	75	75
2552	$1 Boomerang	75	75
2553	$1 N1M Flying Wing	75	75
2554	$2 Concept air and space jet	1·40	1·40
2555	$3 V Jet II	1·75	1·75
MS2556	Two sheets, each 100×70 mm. (a) $6 Concept aeropod. (b) $6 Delmar. Set of 2 sheets	8·00	8·50

131 "Lycaste deppei"

1998. Orchids of the World. Multicoloured.

2557	$1 Type **131**	70	70
2558	$1 "Dendrobium victoriae"	70	70
2559	$1 "Dendrobium nobile"	70	70
2560	$1 "Cymbidium dayanum"	70	70
2561	$1 "Cymbidium" "Starbright"	70	70
2562	$1 "Cymbidium giganteum"	70	70
2563	$1 "Chysis aurea"	70	70
2564	$1 "Broughtonia sanguinea"	70	70
2565	$1 "Cattleya guttata"	70	70
2566	$1 "Calanthe vestita"	70	70
2567	$1 "Cattleya bicolor"	70	70
2568	$1 "Laelia anceps"	70	70
2569	$1 "Epidendrum prismatocarpum"	70	70
2570	$1 "Coelogyne ochracea"	70	70
2571	$1 "Doritaenopsis eclantant"	70	70
2572	$1 "Laelia gouldiana"	70	70
2573	$1 "Encyclia vitellina"	70	70
2574	$1 "Maxillaria praestans"	70	70
2575	$1 "Laelia tenebrosa"	70	70
2576	$1.50 "Phragmipedium besseae"	1·10	1·10
2577	$2 "Pschopsis papilio"	1·40	1·40
2578	$3 "Masdevallia coccinea"	1·75	1·75
MS2579	Two sheets, each 29×43 mm. (a) $6 "Masdevallia ignea". (b) $6 "Encyclia brassavolae". Set of 2 sheets	8·00	8·50

1998. Seabirds. As T 452 of Grenada. Multicoloured.

2580	75c. Bonaparte's gull (horiz)	60	40
2581	90c. Western sandpiper (horiz)	70	50
2582	$1.50 Common tern (horiz)	1·00	1·00
2583	$1.50 Brown pelican (horiz)	1·00	1·00
2584	$1.50 Black-legged kittiwake and white tern (horiz)	1·00	1·00
2585	$1.50 Herring gull (horiz)	1·00	1·00
2586	$1.50 Lesser noddy (horiz)	1·00	1·00
2587	$1.50 Black-legged kittiwake (horiz)	1·00	1·00
2588	$1.50 Whimbrel (horiz)	1·00	1·00
2589	$1.50 Golden white-tailed tropic bird (horiz)	1·00	1·00
2590	$1.50 Arctic tern (horiz)	1·00	1·00
2591	$1.50 Ruddy turnstone (horiz)	1·00	1·00
2592	$1.50 Blue-eyed cormorant ("Imperial Shag") (horiz)	1·00	1·00
2593	$1.50 Magellan gull (horiz)	1·00	1·00
2594	$2 Great black-backed gull (horiz)	1·40	1·40
2595	$3 Dotterell (horiz)	1·75	1·75
MS2596	Two sheets, each 100×70 mm. (a) $5 Broad-billed prion (horiz). (b) $5 Yellow-nosed albatross. Set of 2 sheets	7·50	8·00

1998. International Year of the Ocean. As T 454 of Grenada. Multicoloured.

2597	75c. Great black-backed gull	50	50
2598	75c. Common dolphin	50	50
2599	75c. Seal	50	50
2600	75c. Amazonian catfish	50	50
2601	75c. Shark	50	50
2602	75c. Goldfish	50	50
2603	75c. Cyathopharynx	50	50
2604	75c. Killer whale	50	50
2605	75c. Telmatochromis	50	50
2606	75c. Crab	50	50
2607	75c. Octopus	50	50
2608	75c. Turtle	50	50
2609	90c. Two dolphins	55	55
2610	90c. Seal	55	55
2611	90c. Turtle on rock	55	55
2612	90c. Leopard shark	55	55
2613	90c. Flame angelfish	55	55
2614	90c. Syndontis	55	55
2615	90c. Lamprologus	55	55
2616	90c. "Krptopterus bicirrhus"	55	55
2617	90c. "Pterophyllum scalare"	55	55
2618	90c. Swimming pancake	55	55
2619	90c. Cowfish	55	55
2620	90c. Seahorse	55	55
MS2621	Two sheets, each 98×68 mm. (a) $6 "Tetraodon mbu". (b) $6 Goldfish. Set of 2 sheets	8·00	8·50

Nos. 2597/2608 and 2609/20 respectively were printed together, se-tenant, with the backgrounds forming composite designs.

1998. 50th Anniv of Organization of American States. As T 454a of Grenada.

2622	$1 violet, orange and black	75	75

1998. 25th Death Anniv of Pablo Picasso (painter). As T 291a of Gambia. Multicoloured.

2623	45c. "Bust of a Woman" (vert)	50	30
2624	$2 "Three Musicians"	1·25	1·25
2625	$3 "Studio at La Californie"	1·75	1·75
MS2626	102×127 mm. $5 "Woman with a Blue Hat"	3·00	3·25

1998. Birth Centenary of Enzo Ferrari (car manufacturer). As T 454b of Grenada. Multicoloured.

2627	$2 275 GTB	1·50	1·50
2628	$2 340 MM	1·50	1·50
2629	$2 250 GT SWB Berlinetta "Hot Rod"	1·50	1·50
MS2630	104×72 mm. $5 First Ferrari cabriolet (91×34 mm). P 14×14½	3·50	3·75

1998. 19th World Scout Jamboree, Chile. As T 455 of Grenada. Multicoloured.

2631	90c. Scout greeting	60	40
2632	$1.50 Lord Baden-Powell	90	90
2633	$5 Scout salute	2·50	3·00
MS2634	76×106 mm. $6 Lord Baden-Powell (vert)	3·50	4·00

1998. 50th Death Anniv of Mahatma Gandhi. As T 455a of Grenada.

2635	$1 grey, brown and black	1·00	80
MS2636	100×70 mm. $6 grey, brown and black	4·00	4·00

1998. 80th Anniv of Royal Air Force. As T 292a of Gambia. Multicoloured.

2637	$2 Tornado GR1	1·60	1·60
2638	$2 BAe Hawk T1A	1·60	1·60
2639	$2 Sepecat Jaguar GR1	1·60	1·60
2640	$2 Harrier GR7	1·60	1·60
2641	$2 Chinook helicopter carrying three loads	1·60	1·60
2642	$2 Silhouette of BAe Harrier GR5	1·60	1·60
2643	$2 Panavia Tornado F3 ADV at sunset	1·60	1·60
2644	$2 Chinook HC2 carrying 105 mm light gun	1·60	1·60
MS2645	Four sheets, each 93×70 mm. (a) $6 Bristol F2B fighter and head of golden eagle (bird). (b) $6 Bristol F2B fighter and montagu's harrier in flight. (c) $6 Hawker Hunter and EF-2000 Eurofighter. (d) $6 Tornado and EF-2000 Eurofighter. Set of 4 sheets	15·00	16·00

1998. Birth Bicentenary of Eugene Delacroix (painter). As T 294 of Gambia. Multicoloured.

2646	$1 "The Natchez"	80	80
2647	$1 "Christ and His Disciples Crossing the Sea of Galilee"	80	80
2648	$1 "Sunset"	80	80
2649	$1 "Moroccans outside the Walls of Tangier"	80	80
2650	$1 "The Fireplace"	80	80
2651	$1 "Forest View with an Oak Tree"	80	80
2652	$1 "View of the Harbour at Dieppe"	80	80
2653	$1 "Arab Tax Collectors"	80	80
MS2654	85×105 mm. $5 "Young Orphan"	3·00	3·25

1998. 1st Death Anniv of Diana, Princess of Wales. As T 293a of Gambia.

2655	$1.50 multicoloured	60	65

132 Father Christmas and Hare

1998. Disney's Christmas Trains. Walt Disney cartoon characters in train carriages. Multicoloured.

2656	$1 Type **132**	85	85
2657	$1 Giraffe, elephant and tiger	85	85
2658	$1 Three Pigs and Wolf	85	85
2659	$1 Pied Piper, Jiminy Cricket, penguins and children	85	85
2660	$1 Swans, Little Hiawatha and tortoise	85	85
2661	$1 Mickey Mouse as train driver	85	85
2662	$1 Pluto, Chip and Dale	85	85
2663	$1 Donald and Daisy Duck	85	85
2664	$1 Goofy, Huey, Dewey and Louie	85	85
2665	$1 Minnie Mouse and presents	85	85
2666	$1 Piglet as train driver	85	85
2667	$1 Winnie the Pooh and honey	85	85

2668 $1 Rabbit and Owl 85 85
2669 $1 Kanga, Roo and Christopher Robin 85 85
2670 $1 Eeyore and Tigger 85 85
MS2671 Three sheets, each 133×109 mm. (a) $6 Father Christmas and toy train. (b) $6 Mickey Mouse as train driver. (c) $6 Rabbit, Winnie the Pooh, Piglet and Eeyore. Set of 3 sheets 12·00 13·00

1999. Chinese New Year ("Year of the Rabbit"). Sheet 150×76 mm, containing triangular designs as T 435 of Grenada each showing rabbits. Multicoloured. Self-adhesive on gold foil.
MS2672 $1.50, "GRENADA GRENADINES" in green; $1.50 "GRENADA GRENADINES" in orange; $1.50 "GRENADA GRENADINES" in red 2·25 2·50

133 Troodon

1999. "Australia '99" World Stamp Exhibition, Melbourne. Prehistoric Animals. Multicoloured.
2673 $1 Type **133** 75 75
2674 $1 Camptosaurus 75 75
2675 $1 Parasaurolophus 75 75
2676 $1 Dryosaurus 75 75
2677 $1 Gallimimus 75 75
2678 $1 Camarasaurus 75 75
2679 $1.50 Duckbill (horiz) 1·00 1·00
2680 $1.50 Lambeosaurus (horiz) 1·00 1·00
2681 $1.50 Igaunodon (horiz) 1·00 1·00
2682 $1.50 Euoplocephalus (horiz) 1·00 1·00
2683 $1.50 Triceratops (horiz) 1·00 1·00
2684 $1.50 Brachiosaurus (horiz) 1·00 1·00
2685 $1.50 Ponoptosaurus (horiz) 1·00 1·00
2686 $1.50 Stegosaurus (horiz) 1·00 1·00
MS2687 Three sheets. (a) 106×76 mm. $6 Edmontosaurus (horiz). (b) 76×106 mm. $6 "Tyrannosaurus Rex". (c) 76×106 mm. $6 Halticosaurus. Set of 3 sheets 11·00 12·00

134 Great Indian Peninsula Passenger and Mail Locomotive

1999. Steam Trains of the World. Multicoloured.
2688 15c. Type **134** 50 25
2689 75c. Midland Great Western passenger locomotive (Ireland) 60 45
2690 90c. Canada Pacific express locomotive 70 55
2691 $1.50 East Indian Railway express locomotive 1·00 1·00
2692 $2 Victorian Railways suburban tank locomotive (Australia) 1·25 1·25
2693 $2 Eastern Railways compound locomotive (France) 1·25 1·25
2694 $2 Govt Railways Class WF tank locomotive (New Zealand) 1·25 1·25
2695 $2 Burma Railways oil-burning tank locomotive, 1899 1·25 1·25
2696 $2 Federated Malay States Railway Class G steam locomotive, 1899 1·25 1·25
2697 $2 Belfast and Northern Counties Railway narrow-gauge tank locomotive 1·25 1·25
2698 $2 Shunting tank locomotive (Russia) 1·25 1·25
2699 $2 G.N.R. Ivatt large-boilered "Atlantic" type 1·25 1·25
2700 $2 Palatine Railway "Atlantic" type express locomotive (Germany) 1·25 1·25
2701 $2 Belgian State Railways "Dunalastair" type locomotive 1·25 1·25
2702 $2 Swedish State Railways Class Cc locomotive 1·25 1·25
2703 $2 Antofagasta and Bolivian Railway tank locomotive (Chile) 1·25 1·25
2704 $2 Bolivian State Fairlie type locomotive 1·25 1·25
2705 $2 Belgian State Railways express locomotive 1·25 1·25
2706 $2 London and South Western Railway Drummond's mixed traffic locomotive 1·25 1·25
2707 $2 Belfast and Northern Counties Railways Compound locomotive 1·25 1·25
2708 $2 Dutch State Railway express passenger locomotive 1·25 1·25
2709 $2 Gothard Railway heavy freight locomotive (Switzerland) 1·25 1·25
2710 $2 Waterford, Limerick and Western railway goods locomotive (Ireland) 1·25 1·25
2711 $2 Atchison, Topeka and Santa Fe railway tandem compound express locomotive (U.S.A.) 1·25 1·25
2712 $2 Midland Railway Class "Prince of Wales" locomotive (Great Britain) 1·25 1·25
2713 $3 Glasgow and South Western Railway Stirling type locomotive 1·60 1·75
MS2714 Two sheets, each 100×70 mm. (a) $6 Paris, Lyons and Mediterranean compound locomotive (France). (b) $6 Italian Southern Railway compound locomotive. Set of 2 sheets 7·50 7·50

No. 2701 is inscribed "Dunalastiar" in error.

135 Porkfish

1999. Fauna and Flora. Multicoloured.
2715 75c. Type **135** 60 40
2716 90c. Leatherback turtle 70 55
2717 $1 Red-billed tropic bird ("White-tailed Tropicbird") (vert) 70 70
2718 $1 Laughing gull (vert) 70 70
2719 $1 Palm tree (vert) 70 70
2720 $1 Humpback whale (vert) 70 70
2721 $1 Painted bunting (vert) 70 70
2722 $1 Common grackle (vert) 70 70
2723 $1 Green anole (lizard) (vert) 70 70
2724 $1 "Morpho peleides" (butterfly) (vert) 70 70
2725 $1 "Prepona meander" (butterfly) (vert) 70 70
2726 $1 Common dolphin (vert) 70 70
2727 $1 "Catonephele numilia" (butterfly) (vert) 70 70
2728 $1 Sooty tern (vert) 70 70
2729 $1 Vermilion flycatcher (vert) 70 70
2730 $1 Blue grosbeak (vert) 70 70
2731 $1 Great egret (vert) 70 70
2732 $1 "Actinate pellenea" (butterfly) (vert) 70 70
2733 $1 "Anteos clorinde" (butterfly) (vert) 70 70
2734 $1 Common iguana (vert) 70 70
2735 $1.50 Ruby-throated hummingbird 70 70
2736 $2 "Theope eudocia" (butterfly) 1·40 1·40
MS2737 Two sheets, each 85×110 mm. (a) $6 Bananaquit. (b) $6 Beaugregory (fish). Set of 2 sheets 7·50 8·00

Nos. 2717/25 and 2726/34 respectively were printed together, se-tenant, with the backgrounds forming composite designs.

No. 2727 is inscribed "numili" in error.

136 John H. Glenn (astronaut), 1998

1999. John Glenn's (first American to orbit Earth) Return to Space. Multicoloured, except Nos. 2716, 2718 and 2720/1.
2738 $1 Type **136** 70 70
2739 $1 Glenn and Pres. John F. Kennedy (brown and red) 70 70
2740 $1 Inside "Discovery", 1998 70 70
2741 $1 Climbing from "Friendship 7" capsule, 1962 (brown and red) 70 70
2742 $1 Medical checkup 70 70
2743 $1 Climbing into space capsule, 1962 (brown and red) 70 70
2744 $1 As Democratic Senator for Ohio, 1974 (vert) (brown and red) 70 70
2745 $1 In space suit, 1962 (vert) 70 70
2746 $1 Smiling during suit up test, 1998 (vert) 70 70
2747 $1 Preparing for "Discovery" flight (vert) 70 70
2748 $1 At press conference (with microphone) (vert) 70 70
2749 $1 Smiling at camera (wearing glasses) (vert) 70 70
2750 $1 Participating in medical research (vert) 70 70
2751 $1 Posing in space suit, 1998 (vert) 70 70

No. 2744 was inscribed "Junior Senator form Ohio (1974)" in error.

1999. "iBRA '99" International Stamp Exhibition, Nuremberg. As T 298a of Gambia. Multicoloured.
2752 35c. "Luckenbach" (full-rigged ship) and Thurn and Taxis Northern District 1852 ¼sgr. stamp 45 40
2753 45c. Leipzig–Dresden Railway carriage and Schleswig-Holstein 1850 1s. 45 40
2754 $1.50 Leipzig–Dresden Railway carriage and Oldenburg 1852⅓sgr. 1·50 1·25
2755 $3 "Luckenbach" (full-rigged ship) and North German Confederation 1868 ¼g. 2·25 2·25
MS2756 154×86 mm. $6 Thurn and Taxis Northern District 1865 ¼sgr. rouletted pair used on cover 3·50 3·75

1999. 150th Death Anniv of Katsushika Hokusai (Japanese artist). As T 298b of Gambia. Multicoloured.
2757 $1.50 "Fuchu" 90 90
2758 $1.50 "Doll Fair at Fikkendana" 90 90
2759 $1.50 "Sumo Wrestlers" (in arm hold) 90 90
2760 $1.50 "Sumo Wrestlers" (in head lock) 90 90
2761 $1.50 "Sojo Henjo" 90 90
2762 $1.50 "Twin Gardens Gateway of Asakusa Kannon Temple" 90 90
2763 $1.50 "A Breeze on a Fine Day" 90 90
2764 $1.50 "Ejiri" 90 90
2765 $1.50 "Horse Drawings" (galloping) 90 90
2766 $1.50 "Horse Drawings" (stationary) 90 90
2767 $1.50 "View along Bank of Sumida River" 90 90
2768 $1.50 "Thunderstorm Below the Mountain" 90 90
MS2769 Two sheets, each 102×72 mm. (a) $6 "Stretching Cloth" (vert). (b) $6 "Kobo Daishi exorcising Demon that causes Sickness" (vert). Set of 2 sheets 7·00 8·00

No. 2762 is inscribed "TWIN GARDAINS GATEWAY" in error.

1999. 10th Anniv of United Nations Rights of the Child Convention. As T 298c of Gambia. Multicoloured.
2770 $3 African boy 1·60 1·75
2771 $3 Liv Ullman (UNICEF's first female ambassador) 1·60 1·75
2772 $3 African woman in head scarf 1·60 1·75
MS2773 110×84 mm. $6 Maurice Pate (Founding Director of UNICEF) 2·75 3·25

Nos. 2770/2 were printed together, se-tenant, forming a composite design.

1999. "PhilexFrance '99" International Stamp Exhibition, Paris. Railway Locomotives. Two sheets containing horiz designs as T 299d of Gambia. Multicoloured.
MS2774 (a) 106×81 mm. $6 Paris, Orleans and Mediterranean Railway Cha Pelon type steam locomotive. (b) 106×76 mm. $6 French National Railways Class 7000 high speed electric locomotive. Set of 2 sheets 7·50 8·00

1999. 250th Birth Anniv of Johann von Goethe (German writer). As T 298d of Gambia.
2775 $3 multicoloured 1·60 1·75
2776 $3 blue and black 1·60 1·75
2777 $3 blue, violet and black 1·60 1·75
MS2778 71×106 mm. $6 brown, chestnut and black 2·75 3·25

DESIGNS—HORIZ: No. 2775, Peasants dancing under linden-tree; 2776, Goethe and Schiller; 2777, Faust dreams of soaring above the mortal. VERT: **MS**2778, Johann von Goethe.

1999. Royal Wedding. As T 298 of Gambia. Multicoloured.
2779 $3 Sophie Rhys-Jones 1·75 1·90
2780 $3 Sophie and Prince Edward 1·75 1·90
2781 $3 Prince Edward 1·75 1·90
MS2782 78×108 mm. $6 Sophie and Prince Edward on wedding day 4·75 5·00

1999. "Queen Elizabeth the Queen Mother's Century". As T 304a of Gambia.
2783 $2 black and gold 1·40 1·40
2784 $2 multicoloured 1·40 1·40
2785 $2 black and gold 1·40 1·40
2786 $2 multicoloured 1·40 1·40
MS2787 153×157 mm. $6 multicoloured 3·50 3·50

DESIGNS: No. 2783, Lady Elizabeth Bowes-Lyon as a child; 2784, Queen Mother in Rhodesia, 1957; 2785, Queen Mother with Princesses Elizabeth and Anne, 1950; 2786, Queen Mother, 1988. (37×50 mm)—**MS**2787, Queen Mother reviewing Black Watch, Berlin.

138 George Raft

1999. Early Cinema Actors.
2788 **138** $1 multicoloured 70 70
2789 - $1 grey and black 70 70
2790 - $1 grey and black 70 70
2791 - $1 multicoloured 70 70
2792 - $1 multicoloured 70 70
2793 - $1 black and grey 70 70
2794 - $1 black, blue and grey 70 70
2795 - $1 multicoloured 70 70
2796 - $2 multicoloured 1·10 1·10
2797 - $2 black and grey 1·10 1·10
2798 - $2 multicoloured 1·10 1·10
2799 - $2 black and grey 1·10 1·10
MS2800 $6 multicoloured 3·50 3·50

DESIGNS: No. 2791, Fatty Arbuckle; 2792, Buster Keaton; 2795, Harold Lloyd; 2796, James Cagney; 2798, Edward G. Robinson; **MS**2800, Charlie Chaplin. (53×39 mm): No. 2789, George Raft in "Scarface"; 2790, Fatty Arbuckle with nurse; 2793, Buster Keaton on locomotive cow-catcher; 2794, Harold Lloyd hanging on clockface; 2797, James Cagney in "The Public Enemy"; 2799, Edward G. Robinson in "Little Caesar".

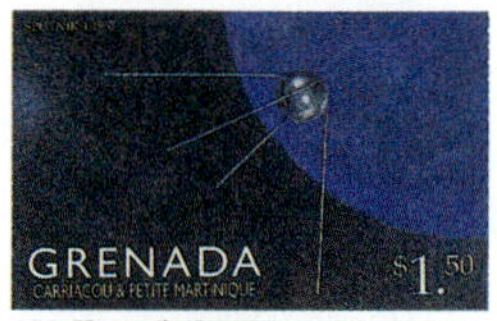

139 "Sputnik I", 1957

1999. Space Exploration. Multicoloured.
2801 $1.50 Type **139** 1·00 1·00
2802 $1.50 "Explorer I", 1958 1·00 1·00
2803 $1.50 "Telstar I" satellite, 1962 1·00 1·00
2804 $1.50 "Maristat I", 1976 1·00 1·00
2805 $1.50 Long Duration Exposure facility, 1984 1·00 1·00
2806 $1.50 Hubble Space Telescope, 1990 1·00 1·00
2807 $1.50 X-15 rocket plane, 1960 (vert) 1·00 1·00
2808 $1.50 "Freedom 7" rocket, 1961 (vert) 1·00 1·00
2809 $1.50 "Friendship 7", 1962 (vert) 1·00 1·00
2810 $1.50 "Gemini 4" rocket and Edward H. White, 1965 (vert) 1·00 1·00
2811 $1.50 Saturn V rocket and Edwin E. Aldrin stepping onto Moon, 1969 (vert) 1·00 1·00
2812 $1.50 Lunar Rover, "Apollo 15" mission, 1971 (vert) 1·00 1·00
MS2813 Two sheets, each 110×85 mm. (a) $6 "Mars Pathfinder", 1997 (55×42 mm); (b) $6 Space shuttle "Columbia", 1981 (55×42 mm). Set of 2 sheets 11·00 11·00

Nos. 2801/6 and 2807/12 were each printed together, se-tenant, with the backgrounds forming composite designs.

140 Kirk Douglas

1999. Kirk Douglas (American actor). Multicoloured.
2814 $1.50 Type **140** 90 90
2815 $1.50 As a boxer in "Champion" 90 90
2816 $1.50 As Van Gogh in "Lust for Life" 90 90
2817 $1.50 With white hair and wearing black shirt 90 90
2818 $1.50 In French uniform for "Paths of Glory" 90 90
2819 $1.50 As a cowboy in "The Bad and the Beautiful" 90 90
MS2820 93×106 mm. $6 As Spartacus 3·00 3·25

141 Elvis Presley

1999. Elvis Presley Commemoration. Each grey, silver and black.

2821	$1.50 Type **141**	1·00	1·00
2822	$1.50 Resting chin on hand	1·00	1·00
2823	$1.50 Wearing roll-neck sweater	1·00	1·00
2824	$1.50 Leaning against brick wall	1·00	1·00
2825	$1.50 Singing into microphone	1·00	1·00
2826	$1.50 Singing with eyes closed	1·00	1·00

141a Howard Thurston (magician)

1999. Famous Magicians. Multicoloured.

2826a	$1.50 Type **141a**	90	90
2826b	$1.50 Harry Houdini	90	90
2826c	$1.50 Harry Kellar	90	90

142 Poinsettia and Candle

1999. Christmas. Foliage and Candles. Mult.

2827	15c. Type **142**	15	10
2828	35c. Holly	25	25
2829	75c. Fir tree	60	35
2830	$1.50 Ivy	90	85
2831	$3 Geranium	1·60	2·00
MS2832	83×108 mm. $6 "The Adoration of the Magi" (horiz)	3·25	3·50

No. 2829 is inscribed "FUR TREE" in error.

2000. New Millennium. People and Events of Fourteenth Century (1300–30). As T 471a of Grenada. Multicoloured.

2833	50c. Robert the Bruce, King of Scotland, 1306	40	40
2834	50c. Fresco by Giotto, 1306	40	40
2835	50c. Mansa Musa, ruler of Mali, 1307	40	40
2836	50c. Dante and *The Divine Comedy*, 1321	40	40
2837	50c. Noh Theatre masks, Japan, 1325	40	40
2838	50c. Staircase, Tenochtitlan (Aztec capital, founded 1325)	40	40
2839	50c. Ibn Batuta on camel (start of journey, 1325)	40	40
2840	50c. Great Munich Fire, 1327	40	40
2841	50c. Grand Duke Ivan I (transfer of capital to Moscow, 1328)	40	40
2842	50c. Archers and castle (beginning of Hundred Years War, 1337)	40	40
2843	50c. Cannon at siege of Calais, 1346 (first recorded use of cannon)	40	40
2844	50c. "Death" (Black Death in Europe, 1348)	40	40
2845	50c. Boccaccio composing *The Decameron*, 1348	40	40
2846	50c. Early Italian spectacles, 1350	40	40
2847	50c. Knight (introduction of plate armour, 1350)	40	40
2848	50c. Junks (completion of Grand Canal of China, 1326) (59×39 mm)	40	40
2849	50c. Maori canoe (Maori migration to New Zealand, 1350)	40	40

143 Dragon

2000. Chinese New Year ("Year of the Dragon"). Sheet 79×60 mm.

MS2850	**143** $4 multicoloured	2·25	2·40

144 Barn Swallow

2000. Birds. Multicoloured.

2851	75c. Type **144**	60	45
2852	90c. Caribbean coot	70	70
2853	$1 Turquoise parrot	70	70
2854	$1 Scarlet-chested parrot	70	70
2855	$1 Red-capped parrot	70	70
2856	$1 Eastern rosella	70	70
2857	$1 Budgerigar	70	70
2858	$1 Superb parrot ("Orange-Flanked Parakeet")	70	70
2859	$1 Mallee ringneck parrot	70	70
2860	$1 Red-rumped parrot	70	70
2861	$1 Yellow-fronted parakeet	70	70
2862	$1 Rainbow lory ("Red-collared Lorikeet")	70	70
2863	$1 Lesser sulphur-crested cockatoo ("Citron-crested Cockatoo")	70	70
2864	$1 Papuan lory ("Stella's Lorikeet")	70	70
2865	$1 Major Mitchell's cockatoo ("Leadbeator's Cockatoo")	70	70
2866	$1 Golden conure	70	70
2867	$1 Red-spotted lorikeet	70	70
2868	$1 Red-shouldered macaw ("Nobel macaw")	70	70
2869	$1 Goffin's cockatoo	70	70
2870	$1 Sun conure	70	70
2871	$1.50 Puerto Rican emerald	1·00	1·00
2872	$1.50 Green mango	1·00	1·00
2873	$1.50 Red-legged thrush	1·00	1·00
2874	$1.50 Green-cheeked amazon ("Red-crowned Parrot")	1·00	1·00
2875	$1.50 Hispaniolan amazon ("Hispaniolan Parrot")	1·00	1·00
2876	$1.50 Yellow-headed parrot ("Yellow-crowned Parrot")	1·00	1·00
2877	$1.50 Yellow-shouldered blackbird	1·00	1·00
2878	$1.50 Troupial	1·00	1·00
2879	$1.50 Green-throated carib	1·00	1·00
2880	$1.50 Nanday conure ("Black-hooded Parakeet")	1·00	1·00
2881	$1.50 Scarlet tanager	1·00	1·00
2882	$1.50 Golden bishop ("Yellow-crowned Bishop")	1·00	1·00
2883	$2 Moorhen ("Common Moorhen")	1·40	1·50
2884	$3 Orange-winged amazon ("Orange-winged Parrot")	1·75	1·90
MS2885	Four sheets. (a) 74×98 mm. $6 Crimson rosella ("Pennant's Parakeet"). (b) 74×98 mm. $6 Scarlet macaw (vert). (c) 75×107 mm. $6 Puerto Rican lizard cuckoo. (d) 75×107 mm. $6 Pin-tailed whydah (vert). Set of 4 sheets	14·00	15·00

Nos. 2853/61, 2862/70, 2871/6 and 2877/82 were each printed together, se-tenant, with the backgrounds forming composite designs.

No. 2859 is inscribed "Rigneck", No. 2863 "Cocatoo", No. 2865 "Cockatto" and No. 2869 "GoffinsCocatto", all in error.

145 *Cantharellus cinnabarinus*

2000. Fungi. Multicoloured.

2886	$2 Type **145**	1·25	1·25
2887	$2 *Hygrocybe conica*	1·25	1·25
2888	$2 *Cortinarius violaceus*	1·25	1·25
2889	$2 *Leccinum versipelle*	1·25	1·25
2890	$2 *Russula xerampelina*	1·25	1·25
2891	$2 *Entoloma nitidum*	1·25	1·25
2892	$2 *Lentinus tigrinus*	1·25	1·25
2893	$2 *Mycena flavoalba*	1·25	1·25
2894	$2 *Boletus legaliae* (horiz)	1·25	1·25
2895	$2 *Russula emetica* (horiz)	1·25	1·25
2896	$2 *Cortinarius alboviolaceus* (horiz)	1·25	1·25
2897	$2 *Volvariella bombycina* (horiz)	1·25	1·25
MS2898	Two sheets, each 103×81 mm. (a) $6 *Gomphus floccosus* (horiz). (b) $6 *Collybia dryophila* (horiz). Set of 2 sheets	14·00	15·00

No. 2886 is inscribed "Canharellus", No. 2889 "Lecinum", and No. **MS**2898 (a) "Comphus", all in error.

146 Ferdinand Magellan (Spanish navigator)

2000. New Millennium. Sea Exploration. Mult.

2899	50c. Type **146**	40	40
2900	50c. Ship in storm	40	40
2901	50c. Queen Elizabeth I's hand on globe	40	40
2902	50c. Two wandering albatrosses ("Albatrosses")	40	40
2903	50c. Emperor penguins	40	40
2904	50c. Tahitian woman	40	40
2905	50c. Breadfruit	40	40
2906	50c. Moai (carved statue) on Easter Island	40	40
2907	50c. Maori carving	40	40
2908	50c. Lobster	40	40
2909	50c. Orchid	40	40
2910	50c. Walrus	40	40
2911	50c. Kangaroo	40	40
2912	50c. H.M.S. *Beagle* (Charles Darwin) careened	40	40
2913	50c. Magnificent frigate bird ("Frigatebird")	40	40
2914	50c. Ship and boats in the Strait of Magellan (59×39 mm)	40	40
2915	50c. Captain James Cook (English navigator)	40	40

146a Salvador Allende elected President of Chile, 1970

2000. New Millennium. People and Events of Twentieth Century (1970–79). Multicoloured.

2916	20c. Type **146a**	35	35
2917	20c. Cartoon characters around globe (introduction of Earth Day holiday, 1970)	35	35
2918	20c. Computerized Axial Tomography (CAT) scanner, 1971	35	35
2919	20c. Pres. Richard Nixon in China (re-opening of U.S. relations with People's Republic, 1972)	35	35
2920	20c. Terrorist and flag (murder of Israeli athletes at Munich Olympics 1972)	35	35
2921	20c. Petrol ration sign (OPEC oil price rises, 1973)	35	35
2922	20c. Sydney Opera House, 1973	35	35
2923	20c. Pres. Richard Nixon leaving helicoptor (resignation 1974)	35	35
2924	20c. Stylized black hole (new theory, 1974)	35	35
2925	20c. U.S. Bicentennial celebrations, 1976	35	35
2926	20c. Louise Brown, first test tube baby, born (born 1978)	35	35
2927	20c. Pope John Paul II visiting Poland, 1978	35	35
2928	20c. Ayatollah Khomeini (Iran's Islamic Revolution, 1978)	35	35
2929	20c. Concorde (first flight, 1979)	35	35
2930	20c. Charles de Gaulle (died 1970) and Eiffel Tower	35	35
2931	20c. Pres. Sadat, Prime Minister Begin and Pres. Carter (Camp David Talks 1978/9) (59×39 mm)	35	35
2932	20c. Mother Teresa (Nobel Peace Prize, 1979)	35	35

No. 2932 is inscribed "Noble Peace Prize" in error.

147 Elongate Mbuna ("Slender Mbuna")

2000. Tropical Fish. Multicoloured.

2933	35c. Type **147**	30	25
2934	45c. *Pygoplites diacanthus*	30	60
2935	75c. *Pomacanthus semicirclatus*	60	60
2936	75c. Siamese fighting fish	60	60
2937	90c. *Zanclus canescens*	70	60
2938	$1 *Xiphophorus maculatus*	70	70
2939	$1 Dwarf pencilfish	70	70
2940	$1 Bumblebee goby	70	70
2941	$1 Black-headed blenny	70	70
2942	$1 Velvet boarfish	70	70
2943	$1 Red-tailed surgeonfish ("Achilles Tang")	70	70
2944	$1 Swordtail	70	70
2945	$1 Moorish idol	70	70
2946	$1 Banded pipefish	70	70
2947	$1 Striped catfish	70	70
2948	$1 Emperor angelfish	70	70
2949	$1 Magenta dottyback ("Strawberryfish")	70	70
2950	$1 Jackknife-fish	70	70
2951	$1 Flame angelfish	70	70
2952	$1 Yellow-tailed ("Clarke's") anemonefish	70	70
2953	$1 Flash-back dottyback	70	70
2954	$1 Coral trout	70	70
2955	$1 Foxface	70	70
2956	$1.65 *Bodianus rufus*	1·10	1·10
2957	$1.65 *Coris aygula*	1·10	1·10
2958	$1.65 *Centropyge bicolor*	1·10	1·10
2959	$1.65 *Balistoides conspicillum*	1·10	1·10
2960	$1.65 *Poecilia reticulata*	1·10	1·10
2961	$1.65 *Heniochus acuminatus*	1·10	1·10
2962	$1.65 *Plectorhinchus chaetodonoides*	1·10	1·10
2963	$1.65 *Bodianus pulchellus*	1·10	1·10
2964	$1.65 *Acanthurus leucosternon*	1·10	1·10
2965	$1.65 *Chromileptis altivelis*	1·10	1·10
2966	$1.65 *Pterophyllum scalare*	1·10	1·10
2967	$1.65 *Premnas biaculeatus*	1·10	1·10
2968	$2 Pennant coralfish ("Wimplefish")	1·40	1·60
2969	$2 *Gramma loreto*	1·40	1·60
2970	$3 *Zebrasoma xanthurum*	1·60	1·75
MS2971	Four sheets. (a) 97×68 mm. $6 Harlequin Tuskfish. (b) 97×68 mm. $6 Purple Queen. (c) 93×65 mm. $6 *Equetus punctatus*. (d) 93×65 mm. $6 *Pomacanthus imperator* (vert). Set of 4 sheets	14·00	15·00

Nos. 2940/7, 2948/55, 2956/61 and 2962/7 were each printed together, se-tenant, with the backgrounds forming composite designs.

No. 2942 is inscribed "CCAPROS APER", No. 2949 "PSEUDOCHROMIS ORPHYREUS", No. 2954 "CEPHALOPHELIS MINIATUS", No. 2962 "PLECTORHYNCHUS CHAETODONOIDS" and No. 2963 "BODIANUS PUCHELLUS", all in error.

2000. 400th Birth Anniv of Sir Anthony Van Dyck (Flemish painter). As T 312a of Gambia. Mult.

2972	$1.50 "Portrait of an Elderly Woman"	90	90
2973	$1.50 "Head of a Young Woman"	90	90
2974	$1.50 "Portrait of a Man"	90	90
2975	$1.50 "Jan van den Wouwer"	90	90
2976	$1.50 "Portrait of a Young Man"	90	90
2977	$1.50 "Everhard Jabach"	90	90
2978	$1.50 "Man in Armour"	90	90
2979	$1.50 "Portrait of a Young General"	90	90
2980	$1.50 "Emanuele Filiberto, Prince of Savoy"	90	90
2981	$1.50 "Donna Polixena Spinola Guzman de Leganes"	90	90
2982	$1.50 "Luigia Cattaneo Gentile"	90	90
2983	$1.50 "Giovanni Battista Cattaneo"	90	90
2984	$1.50 "Marchesa Paolina Adorno Brignole-Sale" (1623–25)	90	90
2985	$1.50 "Marchesa Geronima Spinola"	90	90
2986	$1.50 "Marchesa Paolina Adorna Brignole-Sale" (1627)	90	90
2987	$1.50 "Marcello Durazzo"	90	90
2988	$1.50 "Marchesa Grimaldi Cattaneo with a Black Page"	90	90
2989	$1.50 "Young Man of the House of Spinola"	90	90
2990	$1.50 "Cardinal Bentivoglio"	90	90
2991	$1.50 "Cardinal Infante Ferdinand"	90	90

2992 $1.50 "Cesare Alessandro Scaglia, Abbe of Staffarda and Mandanici" 90 90
2993 $1.50 "A Roman Clergyman" 90 90
2994 $1.50 "Jean-Charles della Faille" 90 90
2995 $1.50 "Cardinal Domenico Rivarola" 90 90
MS2996 Six sheets. (a) 100×123 mm. $5 "Hendrick van der Bergh". (b) 100×123 mm. $5 "Jaques le Roy". (c) 100×123 mm. $6 "Justus van Meerstraeten". (d) 100×123 mm. $6 "Frederik Hendrik, Prince of Orange". (e) 100×123 mm. $6 "Maria Louisa de Tassis" (horiz). (f) 123×100 mm. $6 "Abbot Scaglia adoring the Virgin and Child" (horiz). Set of 6 sheets 19·00 21·00

Nos. 2972/3 are inscribed "Women", No. 2983 "Cattanaeo" and No. 2992 "Stafford", all in error.

2000. 18th Birthday of Prince William. As T 312b of Gambia. Multicoloured.
2997 $1.50 Prince William with birthday gift 1·25 1·25
2998 $1.50 In Eton uniform 1·25 1·25
2999 $1.50 Wearing checked shirt 1·25 1·25
3000 $1.50 Wearing grey suit 1·25 1·25
MS3001 100×80 mm. $6 Wearing blue jumper (37×50 mm) 4·50 4·50

2000. "EXPO 2000" World Stamp Exhibition, Anaheim, U.S.A. Spacecraft. As T 582a of Ghana. Multicoloured.
3002 $1.50 "Foton" and comet 1·00 1·00
3003 $1.50 "Sub-Satellite" and rock particle 1·00 1·00
3004 $1.50 Satellite near Eros 1·00 1·00
3005 $1.50 "Explorer 16" 1·00 1·00
3006 $1.50 Space Shuttle *Challenger* 1·00 1·00
3007 $1.50 Giotto facing right and Halley's Comet 1·00 1·00
3008 $1.50 Circular satellite with aerial (inscr "Foton") 1·00 1·00
3009 $1.50 Giotto facing left (inscr "Sub-Satellite") 1·00 1·00
3010 $1.50 Satellite with solar panels extended (inscr "Near Eros") 1·00 1·00
3011 $1.50 Satellite over planet surface (inscr "Explorer XVI") 1·00 1·00
3012 $1.50 Satellite with folded solar panels (inscr "Astro Challenger") 1·00 1·00
3013 $1.50 Circular satellite with cones on base (inscr "Giotto Halley's Comet") 1·00 1·00
MS3014 Two sheets. (a) 76×106 mm. $6 "Pegasus" over Saturn. (b) 106×76 mm. $6 "Lunar Prospector". Set of 2 sheets 7·50 8·00

Nos. 3002/7 and 3008/13 were each printed together, se-tenant, with the backgrounds forming composite designs.

Inscriptions on Nos. 3008/13 repeat those of Nos. 3002/7 in error.

2000. 25th Anniv of "Apollo–Soyuz" Joint Project. As T 582b of Ghana. Multicoloured.
3015 $3 Thomas P. Stafford (Commander of "Apollo 18") 1·75 1·90
3016 $3 Joint Mission Badge 1·75 1·90
3017 $3 Donald D. Slayton ("Apollo 18") 1·75 1·90
MS3018 70×88 mm. $6 Alexei Leonov (Commander of "Soyuz 19") 3·00 3·25

2000. 50th Anniv of Berlin Film Festival. As T 582c of Ghana. Multicoloured.
3019 $1.50 James Stewart in *Mr. Hobbs takes a Vacation*, 1962 1·00 1·00
3020 $1.50 Sachiko Hidari in *Kanojo To Kare*, 1964 1·00 1·00
3021 $1.50 Juliette Mayniel in *Kirmes*, 1960 1·00 1·00
3022 $1.50 *Le Bonheur*, 1965 1·00 1·00
3023 $1.50 *La Notte*, 1961 1·00 1·00
3024 $1.50 Lee Marvin in *Cat Ballou*, 1965 1·00 1·00
MS3025 97×103 mm. $6 *The Thin Red Line*, 1999 3·50 3·75

2000. 175th Anniv of Stockton and Darlington Line (first public railway). As T 582d of Ghana. Multicoloured.
3026 $3 As Type **582d** of Ghana 2·25 2·25
3027 $3 George Stephenson's *Rocket* 2·25 2·25

2000. 250th Death Anniv of Johann Sebastian Bach (German composer). Sheet, 75×88 mm, containing vert design as T 312c of Gambia. Multicoloured.
MS3028 $6 Statue of Johann Sebastian Bach 4·50 4·75

2000. Election of Albert Einstein (mathematical physicist) as Time Magazine "Man of the Century". Sheet, 117×90 mm, containing vert design as T 312d of Gambia. Multicoloured.
MS3029 $6 Albert Einstein 3·50 3·75

2000. Centenary of First Zeppelin Flight. As T 582e of Ghana, each incorporating a portrait of Count Ferdinand von Zeppelin. Multicoloured.
3030 $3 LZ-3, 1906 2·00 2·00
3031 $3 LZ-56, 1915 2·00 2·00
3032 $3 LZ-88, 1917 2·20 2·00
MS3033 118×75 mm. $6 LZ-1, 1900 (50×37 mm) 4·25 4·50

2000. Olympic Games, Sydney. As T 582f of Ghana. Multicoloured.
3034 $2 Frantz Reichel (rugby), Paris (1900) 1·60 1·60
3035 $2 Modern discus-thrower 1·60 1·60
3036 $2 Seoul Sports Complex (1988) and South Korean flag 1·60 1·60
3037 $2 Ancient Greek wrestlers 1·60 1·60

148 *Euplagia quadripunctaria*

2000. Butterflies and Moths. Multicoloured.
3038 $1.50 Type **148** 1·00 1·00
3039 $1.50 *Oenosandra boisduvalii* 1·00 1·00
3040 $1.50 *Thinopteryx erocopterata* 1·00 1·00
3041 $1.50 *Euschemon rafflesia* 1·00 1·00
3042 $1.50 *Milionia isodoxa* 1·00 1·00
3043 $1.50 *Oysphania euprina* 1·00 1·00
3044 $1.50 *Thaloina clara* 1·00 1·00
3045 $1.50 *Zerynthnia rumina* 1·00 1·00
3046 $1.50 *Attacus atlas* 1·00 1·00
3047 $1.50 *Lasiocampa quercus* 1·00 1·00
3048 $1.50 *Pararge schakra* 1·00 1·00
3049 $1.50 *Arhopala amantes* 1·00 1·00
3050 $1.50 *Heliconius charithonia* 1·00 1·00
3051 $1.50 *Dismorphia amphione* 1·00 1·00
3052 $1.50 *Theela coronata* 1·00 1·00
3053 $1.50 *Cithaerias esmeralda* 1·00 1·00
3054 $1.50 *Zerene eurydice* 1·00 1·00
3055 $1.50 *Theela eudoela* 1·00 1·00
3056 $1.50 *Catonephele numilia* 1·00 1·00
3057 $1.50 *Diaethria clymena* 1·00 1·00
3058 $1.50 *Mesene phareus* 1·00 1·00
3059 $1.50 *Estigmene aerea* 1·00 1·00
3060 $1.50 *Marpesia petreus* 1·00 1·00
3061 $1.50 *Cepheuptychia cephus* 1·00 1·00
MS3062 Six sheets. (a) 70×95 mm. $6 *Tajuria cippus*. (b) 78×97 mm. $6 *Ecpantheria serifonia*. (c) 75×105 mm. $6 *Ornithoptera alexandrae*. (d) 127×100 mm. $6 *Hyalophora cecropia* (vert). (e) 100×73 mm. $2 *Cyrestis thyodamos*; $2 *Papilionidae*; $2 *Apatura iris*; $2 *Crypsiphona ocyltaria*. (f) 100×73 mm. $2 *Hemaris thysbe*; $2 *Helicopis cupido*; $2 *Aretia eaja*; $2 *Erateina staudingeri*. Set of 6 sheets 23·00 25·00

Nos. 3038/43, 3044/9, 3050/5 and 3056/61 were each printed together, se-tenant, with the backgrounds forming composite designs.

No. 3038 is inscribed "quadripunctama", No. 3041 "Eusehemon zafflesia", No. 3045 "Zerynthia", No. 3048 "Parage", No. 3050 "charitonius", No. 3056 "numili", **MS**3062 (d) "Hyalophor", all in error.

150 Golsdorf Compound Tank Locomotive, Vienna Metropolitan Railway

2000. Railways of the World. Multicoloured.
3066 90c. Type **150** 75 50
3067 $1 Vauxhall, Dublin and Kingstown Railway 75 55
3068 $1.50 Electric railcar, South Jersey Transit 90 90
3069 $1.50 "Metroliner", Amtrak 90 90
3070 $1.50 Maglev train, H.S.S.T. 90 90
3071 $1.50 Model E60C electric locomotive, Amtrak 90 90
3072 $1.50 "Parsifal" diesel express, T.E.E. 90 90
3073 $1.50 Class G.G.I. electric locomotive, Pennsylvania 90 90
3074 $1.50 Electric locomotive, Norwegian State Railways 90 90
3075 $1.50 Diesel-electric locomotive, Jamaica Railway 90 90
3076 $1.50 Diesel-electric locomotive, China 90 90
3077 $1.50 Electric locomotive, Portuguese Railways 90 90
3078 $1.50 "Re-6/6" electric locomotive, Swiss Federal Railways 90 90
3079 $1.50 Dual-purpose electric locomotive, Turkish State Railways 90 90
3080 $1.50 Passenger steam locomotive, Perak Govt Railway 90 90
3081 $1.50 Tank locomotive, Rhondda & Swansea Railway 90 90
3082 $1.50 Aspinal tank locomotive, Lancashire & Yorkshire Railway 90 90
3083 $1.50 Tank locomotive, North-western Railway, India 90 90
3084 $1.50 Imperial Mail locomotive, Shanghai–Nanking Railway 90 90
3085 $1.50 Passenger tank locomotive, Danish State Railway 90 90
3086 $1.50 Braithwait steam locomotive, Eastern Counties Railway 90 90
3087 $1.50 *Philadelphia*, Austria 90 90
3088 $1.50 Stephenson locomotive of 1836 90 90
3089 $1.50 *Aigle* locomotive, Western Railway, France 90 90
3090 $1.50 Borsig Standard steam locomotive, Germany 90 90
3091 $1.50 *Ajax*, Great Western Railway 90 90
3092 $2 Metro-Cammell diesel-electric locomotive, Nigerian Railways 1·25 1·25
3093 $3 T.G.V. 001 high-speed turbo train, French National Railways 1·60 1·75
MS3094 Four sheets, each 81×57 mm. (a) $6 *The Experiment*, U.S.A. (b) $6 Freight steam locomotive, South African Railway. (c) $6 Diesel-electric locomotive, South African Railway. (d) $6 "Prospector" diesel railcar, Western Australia. Set of 4 sheets 14·00 15·00

151 Irish Setter

2000. Cats and Dogs. Multicoloured.
3095 45c. Type **151** 45 30
3096 75c. Blue point snowshoe 60 45
3097 90c. Dalmatian 70 55
3098 $1.50 California spangled cat 90 90
3099 $1.50 Russian blue 90 90
3100 $1.50 Seal point Siamese 90 90
3101 $1.50 Black Devon rex 90 90
3102 $1.50 Silver tabby British shorthair 90 90
3103 $1.50 Tricolour Japanese bobtail 90 90
3104 $1.50 Great Dane 90 90
3105 $1.50 Newfoundland 90 90
3106 $1.50 Rottweiler 90 90
3107 $1.50 Bulldog 90 90
3108 $1.50 Japanese spitz 90 90
3109 $1.50 Bull terrier 90 90
3110 $1.50 British white shorthair 90 90
3111 $1.50 Blue-cream American shorthair 90 90
3112 $1.50 Bombay 90 90
3113 $1.50 Red Burmese 90 90
3114 $1.50 Sorrel Abyssinian 90 90
3115 $1.50 Ocicat 90 90
3116 $1.50 Alaskan malamute 90 90
3117 $1.50 Golden retriever 90 90
3118 $1.50 Afghan hound 90 90
3119 $1.50 Long-haired dachshund 90 90
3120 $1.50 Irish terrier 90 90
3121 $1.50 Miniature poodle 90 90
3122 $2 German shepherd 1·25 1·25
3123 $3 Black and white maine coon 1·60 1·75
3124 $4 Brown tabby British shorthair 1·90 2·00
MS3125 Four sheets. (a) 106×76 mm. $5 Silver Classic Tabby Persian (horiz). (b) 76×106 mm. $5 Red-white Bicolor British Shorthair. (c) 106×76 mm. $6 Basset Hound (horiz). (d) 76×106 mm. $6 Labrador Retriever. Set of 4 sheets 13·00 14·00

Nos. 3098/103 (cats), 3104/9 (dogs), 3110/15 (cats) and 3116/21 (dogs) were each printed together, se-tenant, with the backgrounds forming composite designs.

No. 3108 is inscribed "Sptz" and No. 3121 "Minature", both in error.

2000. "Euro 2000" Football Championship. As T 479 of Grenada. Multicoloured.
3126 $1.50 Tofting (Danish player) 90 90
3127 $1.50 Danish team 90 90
3128 $1.50 Michael Laudrup (Danish player) 90 90
3129 $1.50 Jorgensen (Danish player) 90 90
3130 $1.50 Philips Stadium, Eindhoven 90 90
3131 $1.50 Moller (Danish player) 90 90
3132 $1.50 Thuram (French player) 90 90
3133 $1.50 French team 90 90
3134 $1.50 Barthez (French player) 90 90
3135 $1.50 Zidane (French player) 90 90
3136 $1.50 Jan Breydel Stadium, Bruges 90 90
3137 $1.50 Michel Platini (French player) 90 90
3138 $1.50 Giovanni van Bronckhorst (Dutch player) 90 90
3139 $1.50 Dutch team 90 90
3140 $1.50 Patrick Kluivert (Dutch player) 90 90
3141 $1.50 Johan Cruyff (Dutch player) 90 90
3142 $1.50 Amsterdam Arena Stadium 90 90
3143 $1.50 Zenden (Dutch player) 90 90
MS3144 Three sheets, each 145×96 mm. (a) $6 Bo Johansson (Danish trainer) (vert). (b) $6 Roger Lemerre (French trainer) (vert). (c) $6 Frank Rijkaard (Dutch trainer) (vert). Set of 3 sheets 10·00 10·50

152 St. Lucia Amazon

2000. "The Stamp Show 2000" International Stamp Exhibition, London. South American Fauna. Multicoloured.
3145 75c. Type **152** 60 45
3146 90c. Three-toed sloth 60 45
3147 $1 Hispaniolan solenodon 70 55
3148 $1.50 Red vakari 1·00 1·00
3149 $1.50 St. Andrews virea ("San Andreas Vireo") 1·00 1·00
3150 $1.50 Golden lion tamarin 1·00 1·00
3151 $1.50 American crocodile 1·00 1·00
3152 $1.50 Spectacled caimen 1·00 1·00
3153 $1.50 Rhinoceros iguana 1·00 1·00
3154 $1.50 Jaguarundis 1·00 1·00
3155 $1.50 Andean condor 1·00 1·00
3156 $1.50 Lesser rhea ("Darwin's Rhea") 1·00 1·00
3157 $1.50 Central American tapir 1·00 1·00
3158 $1.50 Jaguar 1·00 1·00
3159 $1.50 Jamaican hutia 1·00 1·00
3160 $2 Thick-billed parrot 1·40 1·50
MS3161 Two sheets, each 106×71 mm. (a) $6 Kemp Ridley Sea Turtle. (b) $6 Pronghorn. Set of 2 sheets 7·50 8·00

Nos. 3148/53 and 3154/9 were each printed together, se-tenant, with the backgrounds forming composite designs.

2000. Monarchs of the Millennium. As T 314a of Gambia. Multicoloured (except Nos. 3162 and 3166).
3162 $1.50 King Louis XVI of France (lilac, green and brown) 1·00 1·00
3163 $1.50 King Louis XVIII of France 1·00 1·00
3164 $1.50 Kublai Khan's Empress, China 1·00 1·00
3165 $1.50 Queen Mary I of England 1·00 1·00
3166 $1.50 Mohammed Ali, Shah of Iran (black, green and brown) 1·00 1·00
3167 $1.50 Emperor Qianlong of China 1·00 1·00
MS3168 116×136 mm. $6 Grand Duke Vladimir I of Kiev 3·25 3·50

2000. Popes of the Millennium. As T 314b of Gambia. Multicoloured (except No. MS3173).
3169 $1.50 Adrian VI 1·40 1·40
3170 $1.50 Paul II 1·40 1·40
3171 $1.50 Callistus III 1·40 1·40
3172 $1.50 Eugene IV 1·40 1·40
MS3173 116×136 mm. $6 Gregory XI (grey, black and green) 3·50 3·50

153 "Wind"

2000. "The Storm Riders" (Chinese comic series by Ma Wing Sing). Multicoloured.
3174 $4 Type **153** 1·90 2·00
3175 $4 "Cloud" with sword 1·90 2·00
3176 $4 "Cloud" with dragon 1·90 2·00
3177 $4 "Wind" with waves 1·90 2·00

154 David Copperfield (portrait at left with levitating legs at right)

2000. David Copperfield (conjurer). Multicoloured.

3178	$1.50 Type **154**	90	90
3179	$1.50 Portrait at right with levitating body at left	90	90
3180	$1.50 Portrait at right with levitating legs at left	90	90
3181	$1.50 Portrait at left with levitating body at right	90	90

2000. "Espana 2000" International Stamp Exhibition, Madrid. Paintings from the Prado. As T 326a of Gambia. Multicoloured.

3182	$1.50 "St. John the Baptist and the Franciscan Maestro, Henricus Werl" (Robert Campin)	90	90
3183	$1.50 "Justice and Peace" (Corrado Giaquinto)	90	90
3184	$1.50 "St. Barbara" (Robert Campin)	90	90
3185	$1.50 "John Fane, 10th Earl of Westmoreland" (Thomas Lawrence)	90	90
3186	$1.50 "The Marchioness of Manzanedo" (Jean-Louis-Ernest Meissonier)	90	90
3187	$1.50 "Mr. Storer" (Martin Archer Shee)	90	90
3188	$1.50 "Isabella Carla Eugenia" (Alonso Sanchez Coello)	90	90
3189	$1.50 "Nobleman with his Hand on his Chest" (El Greco)	90	90
3190	$1.50 "King Philip III" (Juan Pantoja de la Cruz)	90	90
3191	$1.50 Madonna and Child from "The Holy Family with Sts. Ildefonsus and John the Evangelist, and the Master Alonso de Villegas" (Blas del Prado)	90	90
3192	$1.50 "The Last Supper" (Bartolme Carducci)	90	90
3193	$1.50 St. John from "The Holy Family with Sts. Ildefonsus and John the Evangelist, and the Master Alonso de Villegas"	90	90
3194	$1.50 "St. Dominic of Silos" (Bartolome Bermejo)	90	90
3195	$1.50 "Head of a Prophet" (Jaume Huguet)	90	90
3196	$1.50 "Christ giving His Blessing" (Fernando Gallego)	90	90
3197	$1.50 "The Mystic Marriage of St. Catherine" (Alonso Sanchez Coello)	90	90
3198	$1.50 "St. Catherine of Alexandria" (Fernando Yanez de la Almedina)	90	90
3199	$1.50 "Virgin and Child" (Luis de Morales)	90	90
MS3200	Three sheets, each 110×90 mm. (a) $6 As No. 3192 (horiz). (b) $6 "The Coronation of the Virgin" (El Greco) (horiz). (c) $6 As No. 3191. Set of 3 sheets	9·50	10·00

155 Barbara Taylor Bradford

2000. Great Writers of the 20th Century: Barbara Taylor Bradford. Sheet 126×87 mm.

MS3201	**155** $6 multicoloured	3·00	3·50

2000. 60th Anniv of Battle of Britain. As T 327 of Gambia. Multicolourred.

3202	$1 R.A.F. Pilots running to their planes	1·00	90
3203	$1 Barrage balloons	1·00	90
3204	$1 Supermarine Spitfire B aircraft (fighter)	1·00	90
3205	$1 Princess Elizabeth broadcasting, 1940	1·00	90
3206	$1 Fire Watcher and auxilary fireman	1·00	90
3207	$1 Painting white bands round posts	1·00	90
3208	$1 Bombed building	1·00	90
3209	$1 Air Raid Wardens and auxilary policewoman	1·00	90
3210	$1 Women fire-fighters	1·00	90
3211	$1 Family leaving bombed home	1·00	90
3212	$1 Searchlight	1·00	90
3213	$1 Winston Churchill inspecting bomb damage in Coventry	1·00	90
3214	$1 Rescue team evacuating casualty	1·00	90
3215	$1 Re-united family	1·00	90
3216	$1 After air raid on Buckingham Gate	1·00	90
3217	$1 Aftermath of air raid on Coventry	1·00	90
MS3218	Two sheets, each 106×76 mm. (a) $6 Hawker Hurricane (fighter). (b) $6 British family outside air raid shelter (vert). Set of 2 sheets	9·00	9·00

No. 3215 is inscribed "RESCUSE" in error.

156 Queen Elizabeth, the Queen Mother

2000. 100th Birthday of Queen Elizabeth, the Queen Mother.

3219	**156**	$1.50 multicoloured	1·50	1·50

2000. Faces of the Millennium: Queen Elizabeth the Queen Mother. As T 307a of Gambia showing collage of miniature flower photographs. Multicoloured.

3220	$1 Top of head (face value at left)	1·00	1·00
3221	$1 Top of head (face value at right)	1·00	1·00
3222	$1 Eye and temple (face value at left)	1·00	1·00
3223	$1 Temple (face value at right)	1·00	1·00
3224	$1 Cheek (face value at left)	1·00	1·00
3225	$1 Cheek (face value at right)	1·00	1·00
3226	$1 Chin (face value at left)	1·00	1·00
3227	$1 Neck (face value at right)	1·00	1·00

Nos. 3220/7 were printed together, se-tenant, in sheetlets of 8 with the stamps arranged in two vertical columns separated by a gutter also containing miniature photographs. When viewed as a whole the sheetlet forms a portrait of the Queen Mother.

2000. Faces of the Millennium: Pope John Paul II. As T 307a of Gambia showing collage of miniature religious photographs. Multicoloured.

3228	$1 Top of head (face value at left)	1·00	1·00
3229	$1 Top of head (face value at right)	1·00	1·00
3230	$1 Ear (face value at left)	1·00	1·00
3231	$1 Temple and eye (face value at right)	1·00	1·00
3232	$1 Neck and collar (face value at left)	1·00	1·00
3233	$1 Cheek and fingertips (face value at right)	1·00	1·00
3234	$1 Shoulder (face value at left)	1·00	1·00
3235	$1 Hands (face value at right)	1·00	1·00

Nos. 3228/35 were printed together, se-tenant, in sheetlets of 8 with the stamps arranged in two vertical columns separated by a gutter also containing miniature photographs. When viewed as a whole the sheetlet forms a portrait of Pope John Paul II.

157 Rat Snake

2001. Chinese New Year. "Year of the Snake". Multicoloured.

3236	90c. Type **157**	60	70
3237	90c. Mangrove snake	60	70
3238	90c. Boomslang	60	70
3239	90c. Emerald tree boa	60	70
3240	90c. African egg-eating snake	60	70
3241	90c. Chinese green tree viper	60	70
MS3242	74×88 mm. $4 King Cobra	2·25	2·50

2001. Bicentenary of Rijksmuseum, Amsterdam. Dutch Paintings. As T 330a of Gambia. Multicoloured.

3243	$1.50 Harpist from "A Music Party" (Rembrandt)	85	90
3244	$1.50 Woman singing from "A Music Party"	85	90
3245	$1.50 Boy and girl from "Rutger Jan Schimmelpenninck with his Wife and Children" (Pierre-Paul Prud'hon)	85	90
3246	$1.50 Girl from "Rutger Jan Schimmelpenninck with his Wife and Children"	85	90
3247	$1.50 "The Syndics" (Thomas de Keyser)	85	90
3248	$1.50 "Marriage Portrait of Isaac Massa and Beatrix van der Laen" (Frans Hals)	85	90
3249	$1.50 Bride from "Marriage Portrait of Isaac Massa and Beatrix van der Laen"	85	90
3250	$1.50 "Winter Landscape with Ice Skaters" (Hendrick Avercamp)	85	90
3251	$1.50 Woman and clerk from "The Spendthrift" (Cornelis Troost)	85	90
3252	$1.50 Beggars from "The Spendthrift"	85	90
3253	$1.50 Two men and a Woman from "The Art Gallery of Jan Gildemeester Jansz" (Adriaan de Lelie)	85	90
3254	$1.50 Man examining painting from "The Art Gallery of Jan Gildemeester Jansz"	85	90
3255	$1.50 Couple with musicians from "Garden Party" (Dirck Hals)	85	90
3256	$1.50 "Still Life with Gilt Goblet" (Willem Claesz Heda)	85	90
3257	$1.50 Two men arguing from "Orestes and Pylades disputing at the Altar" (Pieter Lastman)	85	90
3258	$1.50 Women at altar from "Orestes and Pylades disputing at the Altar"	85	90
3259	$1.50 "Self-portrait in a Yellow Robe" (Jan Lievens)	85	90
3260	$1.50 Couples with monkey from "Garden Party"	85	90
3261	$1.50 Goatherd and goats from "Dune Landscape" (Jan van Goyen)	85	90
3262	$1.50 "The Raampoortje" (Wouter Johannes van Troostwijk)	85	90
3263	$1.50 Houses from "The Ferryboat" (Esaias van de Velde)	85	90
3264	$1.50 "The Departure of a Dignitary from Middleburg" (Adriaen van de Venne)	85	90
3265	$1.50 Cart on ferry from "The Ferryboat"	85	90
3266	$1.50 Group of peasants by fence from "Dune Landscape"	85	90
MS3267	Four sheets. (a) 87×118 mm. $6 "Anna accused by Tobit of Stealing a Kid" (Rembrandt). (b) 118×87 mm. $6 "Cleopatra's Banquet" (Gerard Lairesse) (horiz). (c) 118×87 mm. $6 "View of Tivoli" (Isaac de Moucheron) (horiz). (d) 87×118 mm. $6 "A Music Party" (Rembrandt). Set of 4 sheets	14·00	15·00

No. 3248 is inscribed "Marraige" and "dr" in error.

158 Greater Flamingo

2001. Tropical Fauna. Multicoloured.

3268	75c. Type **158**	75	50
3269	90c. Cuban crocodile (horiz)	75	50
3270	$1 Jaguarundi	75	55
3271	$1.50 Red-breasted toucan	1·25	1·25
3272	$1.50 Mexican black howler monkey	1·25	1·25
3273	$1.50 Fieck's pygmy boa	1·25	1·25
3274	$1.50 Red-eyed tree frog	1·25	1·25
3275	$1.50 Caimen	1·25	1·25
3276	$1.50 Jaguar	1·25	1·25
3277	$1.50 Cuban pygmy owl	1·25	1·25
3278	$1.50 Woody spider monkey	1·25	1·25
3279	$1.50 Bee hummingbirds	1·25	1·25
3280	$1.50 Dragonfly, leaf frog and poison dart frog	1·25	1·25
3281	$1.50 Red brocket deer	1·25	1·25
3282	$1.50 Cuban stream anole	1·25	1·25
3283	$2 Wedge-capped capuchin monkey (horiz)	1·50	1·50
MS3284	Two sheets. (a) 72×104 mm. $6 Ocelot. (b) 72×98 mm. $6 Western knight anole. Set of 2 sheets	7·50	8·00

Nos. 3271/6 and 3277/82 were each printed together, se-tenant, with the backgrounds forming composite designs.

No. 3271 is inscribed "Red-Breated" in error.

2001. Characters from "Pokemon" (children's cartoon series). As T 332a of Gambia. Multicoloured.

3285	$1.50 "Bellsprout No. 69"	85	90
3286	$1.50 "Vulpix No. 37"	85	90
3287	$1.50 "Dewgong No. 87"	85	90
3288	$1.50 "Oddish No. 43"	85	90
3289	$1.50 "Dratini No. 147"	85	90
3290	$1.50 "Jigglypuff No. 39"	85	90
MS3291	74×114 mm. $6 "Pikachu No. 25"	3·00	3·25

159 *Scarus vetula*

2001. Endangered Species. Fish. Multicoloured.

3292	75c. Type **159**	75	75
3293	75c. *Scarus taeniopterus*	75	75
3294	75c. *Sparisoma viride*	75	75
3295	75c. *Sparisoma rubripinne*	75	75

160 Falkland Islands Flightless Streamer Duck ("Falklands Streamer Duck")

2001. Caribbean Ducks and Waterfowl. Mult.

3296	$1.50 Type **160**	1·25	1·25
3297	$1.50 Black-crowned night heron	1·25	1·25
3298	$1.50 Muscovy duck	1·25	1·25
3299	$1.50 Ruddy duck	1·25	1·25
3300	$1.50 Northern screamer ("Black necked Screamer")	1·25	1·25
3301	$1.50 White-faced whistling duck	1·25	1·25
MS3302	60×93 mm. $6 Great egret (vert)	4·00	4·25

Nos. 3296/301 were printed together, se-tenant, with the backgrounds forming a composite design.

161 Virgie Cary (Shirley Temple) sitting on Chair

2001. Shirley Temple in The Littlest Rebel. Showing scenes from the film. Multicoloured.

3303	$2 Type **161**	1·10	1·25
3304	$2 Virgie with her mother (Karen Morley)	1·10	1·25
3305	$2 Virgie with her father, Captain Cary (John Boles)	1·10	1·25
3306	$2 Virgie comforting her mother	1·10	1·25
3307	$2 Virgie with Uncle Billy (Bill Robinson) and Col. Morrison (Jack Holt)	1·10	1·25
3308	$2 Virgie hugging her father	1·10	1·25
3309	$2 Virgie being admonished by Col. Morrison (horiz)	1·10	1·25
3310	$2 Virgie disguised as a negro slave (horiz)	1·10	1·25
3311	$2 Virgie escaping with her father in buggy (horiz)	1·10	1·25
3312	$2 Virgie with Abraham Lincoln (Frank McGlynn Sr.) (horiz)	1·10	1·25
MS3313	105×75 mm. $6 Virgie tap dancing with Uncle Billy	3·00	3·50

2001. Betty Boop (cartoon character). As T 486 of Grenada showing Betty in various geographical locations. Multicoloured.

3314	$1 Flamenco dancing, Spain	65	70
3315	$1 In national dress, Turkey	65	70
3316	$1 Wearing lei, Hawaii	65	70
3317	$1 As belly-dancer, Egypt	65	70

3318 $1 With flower in hair, South Pacific 65 70
3319 $1 Riding horse, Argentina 65 70
3320 $1 Drinking champagne, France 65 70
3321 $1 Sitting in sports car, Hollywood 65 70
3322 $1 As Statue of Liberty, New York 65 70
MS3323 Two sheets, each 90×110 mm. (a) $6 On a gondola, Venice. (b) $6 By river, India. Set of 2 sheets 7·50 8·00

162 Clark Gable smoking Cigar

2001. Birth Centenary of Clark Gable (American film star). Multicoloured.
3324 $1.50 Type **162** 85 90
3325 $1.50 In *Gone With the Wind* 85 90
3326 $1.50 Sitting in director's chair 85 90
3327 $1.50 Signing autograph 85 90
3328 $1.50 Wearing checked tie 85 90
3329 $1.50 In pin-stripe suit with legs crossed 85 90
3330 $1.50 Seated in car 85 90
3331 $1.50 In grey suit 85 90
3332 $1.50 In casual dress 85 90
3333 $1.50 Arm resting on knee 85 90
3334 $1.50 On telephone 85 90
3335 $1.50 In evening dress 85 90
MS3336 Two sheets. (a) 114×88 mm. $6 Wearing U.S. Air Force uniform. (b) 98×110 mm. $6 As Rhett Butler in *Gone With the Wind*. Set of 2 sheets 8·50 9·00

2001. "Philanippon '01" International Stamp Exhibition, Tokyo. Japanese Paintings. As T 493 of Grenada. Multicoloured.
3337 75c. "Daily Life in Edo" (Miyagawa Choshun) 50 45
3338 90c. "Twelve Famous Places in Japan" (Kani Isen'in Naganobu) 60 50
3339 $1 "Along the Sumida River" (Kano Kyuei) 70 75
3340 $1.25 "Cranes" (Kano Eisen'in Michinobu) 80 70
3341 $2 "Courtesan of Yoshiwara" (Katsukawa Shun'ei) 1·25 1·40
3342 $2 "Kiritsubo Chapter" (86×28 mm) 1·25 1·40
3343 $2 "Akahsi Chapter" (86×28 mm) 1·25 1·40
3344 $2 "Hatsune Chapter" (86×28 mm) 1·25 1·40
3345 $2 "E-Awase Chapter" (86×28 mm) 1·25 1·40
3346 $2 Buddha on golden elephant (vert) 1·25 1·40
3347 $2 Buddha on white elephant (vert) 1·25 1·40
3348 $2 Buddha on elephant and temple (vert) 1·25 1·40
3349 $2 Buddha on elephant with crowd (vert) 1·25 1·40
3350 $3 "Bear killing" (unsigned) 1·60 1·75
MS3351 Two sheets. (a) 86×74 mm. $6 "Sage pointing to the Moon" (Katagiri Ranseki). (b) 97×77 mm. $6 Frontispiece from "Devadatta" (Itsukushima-Jinja) (vert). Set of 2 sheets 7·50 8·00

Nos. 3342/5 depicts "Tale of Genji" (Kano Ryusetsu Hidenobu), and 3346/9 illustrates "The Lotus Sutra".

2001. Death Centenary of Queen Victoria. As 590a of Ghana. Multicoloured.
3352 $3 Queen Victoria at her Coronation 1·75 1·90
3353 $3 Princess Victoria as a young girl, standing 1·75 1·90
3354 $3 In old age 1·75 1·90
MS3355 107×77 mm. $6 Queen Victoria within royal arms 3·25 3·50

2001. 25th Death Anniv of Mao Tse-tung (Chinese leader). As T 590b of Ghana. Multicoloured.
3356 $1.50 Young Mao Tse-tung on steps (horiz) 85 90
3357 $1.50 Mao talking with country people on the Long March (horiz) 85 90
3358 $1.50 Visiting a rural market place (horiz) 85 90
3359 $1.50 Explaining doctrines to soldiers (horiz) 85 90
MS3360 93×134 mm. $3 Mao Tse-tung in 1939 proclaiming the People's Republic of China 1·60 1·90

2001. 75th Death Anniv of Claude-Oscar Monet (French painter). As T 590c of Ghana. Mult.
3361 $1 "The Magpie" 80 80
3362 $1 "La Pointe de la Heve at Low Tide" 80 80
3363 $1 "Regatta at Argenteuil" 80 80
3364 $1 "La Grenouillere (the Frog Pond)" 80 80
MS3365 138×110 mm. $6 "J. F. Jacquemart with Parasol" (vert) 3·50 3·75

2001. 75th Birthday of Queen Elizabeth II. As T 590d of Ghana. Multicoloured.
3366 $1.25 Princess Elizabeth wearing pearl necklace 1·00 1·00
3367 $1.25 Queen in blue coat with brooch 1·00 1·00
3368 $1.25 Wearing tiara 1·00 1·00
3369 $1.25 Queen Elizabeth in pink 1·00 1·00
3370 $1.25 Queen in Order of the Bath robes 1·00 1·00
3371 $1.25 Wearing blue hat and coat 1·00 1·00
3372 $2 Young Queen in red hat with feathers 1·60 1·60
3373 $2 Queen Elizabeth in evening dress with orders 1·60 1·60
3374 $2 Young Queen wearing tiara 1·60 1·60
MS3375 119×147 mm. $5 Queen Elizabeth at Coronation (38×51 mm) 3·50 3·75

2001. Death Centenary of Giuseppe Verdi (Italian composer). As T 590e of Ghana. Showing various portraits of the composer.
3376 25c. multicoloured 75 75
3377 75c. multicoloured 1·25 1·25
3378 $2 multicoloured 1·75 1·75
3379 $3 multicoloured 2·00 2·00
MS3380 78×112 mm. $6 multicoloured 5·00 5·00

Nos. 3376/9 were printed together, se-tenant, with the backgrounds forming a composite design.

2001. Death Centenary of Henri de Toulouse-Lautrec (French painter). As T 590f of Ghana. Multicoloured.
3381 $1 "Helene V" (horiz) 80 80
3382 $1 "Clownesse" (horiz) 80 80
3383 $1 "Madame Berthe Bady" (horiz) 80 80
3384 $1 "Woman with the Black Boa" (horiz) 80 80
MS3385 55×85 mm. $6 "Loie Fuller at the Folies Bergere" 3·50 3·75

2001. Birth Centenary of Marlene Dietrich (German actress). As T 495 of Grenada. Multicoloured.
3386 $2 Singing on stage 1·25 1·25
3387 $2 With feather boa 1·25 1·25
3388 $2 In floral dress 1·25 1·25
3389 $2 Wearing hat, coat and gloves 1·25 1·25

163 *Creole* (racing schooner), 1927

2001. Ships. Multicoloured.
3390 90c. Type **163** 80 45
3391 $1 *Britannia* (steamer), 1887 80 55
3392 $1.25 *Santa Maria* and Christopher Columbus, 1492 1·00 1·00
3393 $1.25 *Sao Gabriel* and Vasco da Gama, 1498 1·00 1·00
3394 $1.25 *Vitoria* and Ferdinand Magellan, 1519 1·00 1·00
3395 $1.25 *Golden Hind* and Sir Francis Drake, 1577 1·00 1·00
3396 $1.25 H.M.S. *Endeavour* and Captain James Cook, 1768 1·00 1·00
3397 $1.25 H.M.S. *Erebus* and John Franklin 1·00 1·00
3398 $1.25 *William Fawcett* (paddle steamer), 1829 1·00 1·00
3399 $1.25 *Sirius* (paddle steamer), 1838 1·00 1·00
3400 $1.25 *Great Britain* (steam/sail vessel), 1843 1·00 1·00
3401 $1.25 *Oriental* (American clipper), 1849 1·00 1·00
3402 $1.25 *Lightning* (clipper), 1854 1·00 1·00
3403 $1.25 *Great Eastern* (paddle steamer), 1858 1·00 1·00
3404 $1.25 *Mayflower* (Pilgrim Fathers), 1620 (vert) 1·00 1·00
3405 $1.25 *Sv. Petr* (Bering), 1728 (vert) 1·00 1·00
3406 $1.25 H.M.S. *Beagle* (Darwin), 1825 (vert) 1·00 1·00
3407 $1.25 H.M.S. *Challenger* (survey ship), (vert) 1·00 1·00
3408 $1.25 *Vega* (Nordenskjold), 1872 (vert) 1·00 1·00
3409 $1.25 *Fram* (Amundsen and Nansen), 1892 (vert) 1·00 1·00
3410 $2 *Ariel* (clipper), 1865 1·75 1·75
3411 $3 *Sindia* (barque), 1887 2·00 2·00
MS3412 Two sheets, each 60×45 mm. (a) $6 *Cutty Sark* (clipper), 1869. (b) $6 *Challenger* (American clipper), 1851. Set of 2 sheets 10·00 10·00

No. 3405 is inscribed "GABRIEL" in error. The same stamp shows two different incorrect spellings of Bering.
No. 3407 is inscribed "1852" in error.

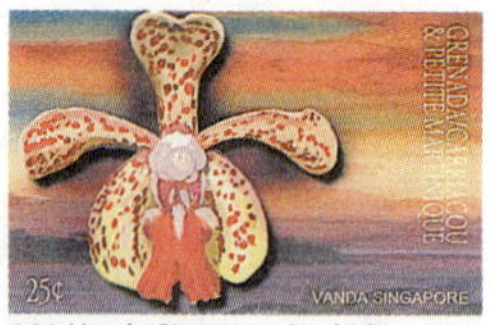
164 *Vanda Singapore* (orchid)

2001. Orchids. Multicoloured.
3413 25c. Type **164** 45 20
3414 50c. *Vanda Joan Warne* 65 30
3415 75c. *Vanda lamellata* 80 45
3416 $1.50 *Papilionanthe teres* 1·25 1·25
3417 $1.50 *Vanda flabellata* 1·25 1·25
3418 $1.50 *Vanda tessellata* (name bottom left) 1·25 1·25
3419 $1.50 *Vanda pumila* 1·25 1·25
3420 $1.50 *Rhynchostylis gigantea* 1·25 1·25
3421 $1.50 *Vandopsis gigantea* 1·25 1·25
3422 $1.50 *Vanda tessellata* (name centre left) 1·25 1·25
3423 $1.50 *Vanda helvola* 1·25 1·25
3424 $1.50 *Vanda brunnea* 1·25 1·25
3425 $1.50 *Vanda stageana* 1·25 1·25
3426 $1.50 *Vanda limbata* 1·25 1·25
3427 $1.50 *Vandopsis tricolor* 1·25 1·25
3428 $2 *Vanda merrillii* 1·75 1·75
MS3429 Two sheets, each 68×97 mm. (a) $6 *Vanda insignis*. (b) $6 *Vandopsis lissochiloides*. Set of 2 sheets 9·00 9·50

No. 3425 is inscribed "STANGEANA" in error.

165 Richard Petty (stock car driver)

2001. Richard Petty (stock car driver). Two sheets each containing vert designs as T 165. Multicoloured.
MS3430 (a) 92×130 mm. $6 Type **165**. (b) 92×135 mm. $6 Richard Petty being interviewed. Set of 2 sheets 7·50 8·00

166 Dale Earnhardt in Yellow Overalls, 1980

2001. Dale Earnhardt (stock car driver) Commemoration. Multicoloured.
3431 $2 Type **166** 1·10 1·25
3432 $2 With Winston Cup, 1986 1·10 1·25
3433 $2 With Winston Cup, 1987 1·10 1·25
3434 $2 With Winston Cup, 1990 1·10 1·25
3435 $2 With Winston Cup, 1991 1·10 1·25
3436 $2 With Winston Cup, 1993 1·10 1·25
3437 $2 With Winston Cup, 1994 1·10 1·25
3438 $4 Dale Earnhardt's Chevrolet cars (76×52 mm) 1·10 1·25

167 Ferrari F1 86, 1986

2001. Ferrari Formula 1 Racing Cars. Multicoloured.
3439 $1.50 Type **167** 1·00 1·00
3440 $1.50 Ferrari F1 89, 1989 1·00 1·00
3441 $1.50 Ferrari F92A, 1992 1·00 1·00
3442 $1.50 Ferrari F1 93, 1993 1·00 1·00
3443 $1.50 Ferrari 412T1, 1994 1·00 1·00
3444 $1.50 Ferrari F310, 1996 1·00 1·00

168 World Cup Publicity Poster, Brazil, 1950

2001. World Cup Football Championship, Japan and Korea (2002). Designs showing publicity posters and badges from previous World Cups. Multicoloured.
3445 $1.50 Type **168** 1·00 1·00
3446 $1.50 Switzerland, 1954 1·00 1·00
3447 $1.50 Sweden, 1958 1·00 1·00
3448 $1.50 Chile, 1962 1·00 1·00
3449 $1.50 England, 1966 1·00 1·00
3450 $1.50 Mexico, 1970 1·00 1·00
3451 $1.50 Argentina, 1978 1·00 1·00
3452 $1.50 Spain, 1982 1·00 1·00
3453 $1.50 Mexico, 1986 1·00 1·00
3454 $1.50 Italy, 1990 1·00 1·00
3455 $1.50 U.S.A., 1994 1·00 1·00
3456 $1.50 France, 1998 1·00 1·00
MS3457 Two sheets, 88×75 mm. (a) $6 Uruguay, 1930. (b) $6 Detail of World Cup trophy, Japan-Korea, 2002. Set of 2 sheets 8·50 9·00

169 "Coronation of the Virgin" (Filipo Lippi)

2001. Christmas. Italian Renaissance Religious Paintings. Multicoloured.
3458 25c. Type **169** 30 15
3459 75c. "Virgin and Child" (Andrea Mantegna) 70 35
3460 $1.50 "Madonna and Child" (Tommaso Masaccio) 1·25 1·25
3461 $3 "Madonna and Child" (Raffaelo Sanzio) 2·00 2·50
MS3462 96×136 mm. $6 "Virgin and Child enthroned with Angels" (Mantegna) 3·75 4·00

170 "Battle of Solebay, 1672"

2001. Royal Navy Commemoration. Marine Paintings. Multicoloured.
3463 75c. "H.M.S. Renown (battle cruiser), Portsmouth Harbour, 1922" (vert) 70 45
3464 90c. "Battle of the Saintes, 1782" (vert) 85 50
3465 $1.50 Type **170** 1·25 1·25
3466 $1.50 "Royal Prince, 1679" 1·25 1·25
3467 $1.50 "Battle of Texel, 1673" 1·25 1·25
3468 $1.50 "Battle of Scheveningen, 1653" 1·25 1·25
3469 $1.50 "Battle against Barbary Pirates, 1600s" 1·25 1·25
3470 $1.50 "Capture of Royal Charles, 1667" 1·25 1·25
3471 $1.50 "The Glorious First of June, 1794" 1·25 1·25
3472 $1.50 "The Moonlight Battle, 1780" 1·25 1·25
3473 $1.50 "Great Ships of the Jacobean Navy, 1623" 1·25 1·25
3474 $1.50 "Battle of the Gulf of Genoa, 1795" 1·25 1·25
3475 $1.50 "Battle of the Nile, 1798" 1·25 1·25
3476 $1.50 "Battle of St. Lucia, 1778" 1·25 1·25
3477 $2 "Battle of Trafalgar, 1805" (vert) 1·50 1·60
3478 $3 "Henry VIII embarking at Dover, 1520" (vert) 2·00 2·25

MS3479 Two sheets, each 135×67 mm. (a) $6 "H.M.S. *Repulse* (battle cruiser), 1924". (b) $6 "Battle of Navarino, 1827". Set of 2 sheets 9·50 10·00

The date on No. 3466 is incorrect. The *Royal Prince* was sunk by the Dutch in 1666.

171 Lady Elizabeth Bowes-Lyon as a Young Child

2001. 101st Birthday of Queen Elizabeth, the Queen Mother.

3480	**171**	$2 black and yellow	1·60	1·60
3481	-	$2 multicoloured	1·60	1·60
3482	-	$2 black and yellow	1·60	1·60
3483	-	$2 multicoloured	1·60	1·60

MS3484 151×155 mm. $6 multicoloured 4·00 4·00

DESIGNS: No. 3481, Queen Mother in Rhodesia, 1957; 3482, Queen Elizabeth with Princess Elizabeth and Princess Anne, 1950; 3483, Queen Mother in blue hat, 1988. (37×50 mm); No. **MS**3484, Queen Mother inspecting Black Watch.

172 John F. Kennedy on *P.T. 109*

2001. John F. Kennedy (American President) Commemoration. Multicoloured.

3485	$1.50 Type **172**	90	90
3486	$1.50 John Kennedy in chair	90	90
3487	$1.50 Facing left	90	90
3488	$1.50 Facing forward, smiling	90	90
3489	$1.50 Wearing spotted tie	90	90
3490	$1.50 Wearing striped tie	90	90

MS3491 120×82 mm. $6 John Kennedy with Nikita Khrushchev (First Secretary of U.S.S.R.) (horiz) 3·25 3·50

173 Jacqueline Kennedy Onassis

2001. Jacqueline Kennedy Onassis (widow of American president) Commemoration. Multicoloured.

3492	$1.50 Type **173**	90	90
3493	$1.50 Wearing red coat	90	90
3494	$1.50 In green dress	90	90
3495	$1.50 Wearing evening cloak	90	90
3496	$1.50 In matching pink hat and coat	90	90
3497	$1.50 Jacqueline Kennedy Onassis and hot air balloon	90	90

MS3498 Two sheets. (a) 68×83 mm. $6 Portrait with face value at top right. (b) 83×68 mm. $6 Portrait with face value at top left 7·50 8·00

174 General George Patton and Tank

2001. American Military Leaders. Multicoloured.

3499	75c. Type **174**	55	55
3500	75c. General Joseph Stilwell with President and Mrs. Chiang Kai-shek	55	55
3501	75c. Admiral Thomas Kinkaid and marine landing	55	55
3502	75c. General Jonathan Wainwright and Filipino troops	55	55
3503	75c. Lt.-General James Doolittle and aircraft carrier	55	55
3504	75c. General Matthew Ridgway and cheering crowd	55	55
3505	75c. General Maxwell Taylor and B-17s	55	55
3506	75c. Admiral Richmond Turner and island landing	55	55
3507	75c. General Curtis LeMay and heavy bombers	55	55
3508	75c. General Hoyt Vandenberg and fighter aircraft	55	55
3509	75c. General Carl Spaatz and explosion of atomic bomb	55	55
3510	75c. Admiral Raymond Spruance and burning Japanese battleship	55	55
3511	75c. General Omar Bradley and D-Day landings	55	55
3512	75c. General George Marshall and Marine Corps memorial	55	55
3513	75c. General Douglas MacArthur and return to the Philippines	55	55
3514	75c. Admiral William Halsey and carrier landing	55	55
3515	75c. General Dwight Eisenhower and reviewing troops	55	55
3516	75c. Admiral Chester Nimitz and beach landing	55	55
3517	75c. Admiral William Leahy and aircraft carriers	55	55
3518	75c. General Henry Arnold and heavy bomber	55	55
3519	75c. Admiral Ernest King and battleships	55	55
3520	75c. General George Washington and seated with his wife	55	55
3521	75c. General John Pershing and parade	55	55

MS3522 Two sheets, each 150×139 mm. (a) $6 General Dwight Eisenhower (38×49 mm). (b) $6 General Douglas MacArthur (38×49 mm) 7·50 8·00

175 Princess Diana in Evening Dress

2001. 40th Birth Anniv of Diana, Princess of Wales. Multicoloured.

3523	$1.50 Type **175**	1·25	1·25
3524	$1.50 Wearing ski suit	1·25	1·25
3525	$1.50 In pale blue hat	1·25	1·25

176 *Nudaurelia cytheria* (moth)

2001. Moths. Multicoloured.

3526	75c. Type **176**	65	45
3527	90c. *Janomima westwoodi*	80	50
3528	$1.50 *Actias selene*	1·25	1·25
3529	$1.50 *Amphicallia bellatrix*	1·25	1·25
3530	$1.50 *Citheronia regalis*	1·25	1·25
3531	$1.50 *Arctica caja*	1·25	1·25
3532	$1.50 *Leto venus*	1·25	1·25
3533	$1.50 *Alcides zodiaca*	1·25	1·25
3534	$1.50 *Graellsia isabellae*	1·25	1·25
3535	$1.50 *Dysphania cuprina*	1·25	1·25
3536	$1.50 *Automeris io*	1·25	1·25
3537	$1.50 *Agarista agricola*	1·25	1·25
3538	$1.50 *Callioratis millari*	1·25	1·25
3539	$1.50 *Othreis fullonia*	1·25	1·25
3540	$2 *Lasiocampa quercus*	1·50	1·60
3541	$3 *Chrysiridia riphearia*	2·00	2·25

MS3542 Two sheets, each 77×106 mm. (a) $6 *Divana diva* (vert). (b) $6 *Argema mimosae* (vert) 8·50 9·00

No. 3539 is inscribed "Otthreis" in error.

177 Queen Elizabeth in Spotted Dress

2002. Golden Jubilee. Multicoloured.

3543	$2 Type **177**	1·60	1·60
3544	$2 Queen Elizabeth wearing pink hat	1·60	1·60
3545	$2 Queen Elizabeth in evening dress	1·60	1·60
3546	$2 Queen Elizabeth wearing sunglasses	1·60	1·60

MS3547 76×109 mm. $6 Princess Elizabeth with family 4·00 4·25

178 Horse on Background of Chinese Characters

2002. Chinese New Year ("Year of the Horse"). Showing different horses.

3548	**178**	75c. multicoloured	65	40
3549	-	$1.25 multicoloured	90	95
3550	-	$2 multicoloured	1·40	1·60

MS3551 **178** 70×102 mm. $6 black, light orange and orange 3·25 3·75

179 US Flag on Twin Towers

2002. "United We Stand". Support for Victims of 11 September 2001 Attacks.

3552	**179**	80c. multicoloured	60	60

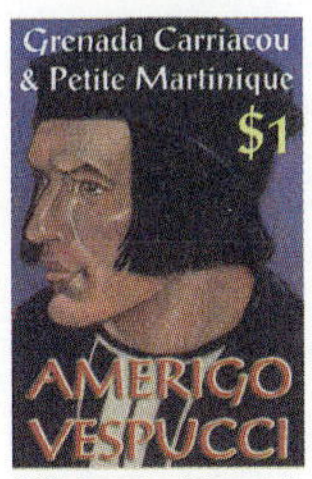

180 Amerigo Vespucci

2002. 550th Birth Anniv of Amerigo Vespucci (explorer).

3553	**180**	$1 multicoloured	80	60
3554	-	$2 multicoloured	1·40	1·50
3555	-	$3 multicoloured	1·90	2·00

MS3556 75×58 mm. $6 multicoloured 3·75 4·00

DESIGNS: $2 to $6 Various portraits.

181 F1 86, 1986

2002. Ferrari Racing Cars. Sheet 147×165 mm containing T 181 and similar horiz designs. Multicoloured.

MS3557 $1.50 Type **181**; $1.50 F1 89, 1989; $1.50 F 92 A, 1992; $1.50 F1 93, 1993; $1.50 412 T1, 1994; $1.50 F310, 1996 4·50 4·75

2002. International Year of Mountains. Two sheets containing horiz designs as T 512 of Grenada. Multicoloured.

MS3558 143×93 mm. $2 Kilimanjaro, Tanzania; $2 Mount Kenya; $2 Mount Kea, Hawaii; $2 Mount Fuji, Japan 4·75 5·50

MS3559 115×65 mm. $6 Ko'olau Mountains, Hawaii 3·25 3·50

182 Waterfall

2002. International Year of Ecotourism. Two sheets containing T 182 and similar horiz designs. Multicoloured.

MS3560 137×105 mm. $1.50 Type **182**; $1.50 Ringed kingfisher; $1.50 Butterfly; $1.50 Rock beauty (fish); $1.50 Cactus; $1.50 Orchid 3·50 3·50

MS3561 80×98 mm. $6 Blue-hooded euphonias 4·75 4·75

183 Olympic Rings and Skier (airborne)

2002. Winter Olympic Games, Salt Lake City. Multicoloured.

3562	$3 Type **183**	1·75	1·90
3563	$3 Olympic rings and skier (different)	1·75	1·90

MS3564 82×113 mm. Nos. 3562/3 3·50 3·75

2002. World Scout Jamboree, Thailand. Two sheets each containing multicoloured designs as T 515 of Grenada.

MS3565 107×90 mm. $2 Scout badge and campfire; $2 Scout hiking; $2 Boy scout feeding calf; $2 Girl saluting 4·50 4·75

MS3566 98×70 mm. $2 Scout at seashore (vert) 1·25 1·40

2002. Chiune Sugihara (Japanese Consul-general in Lithuania who rescued Jews, 1939–40) Commemoration. Two sheets each 60×90 mm containing vert designs as T 511 of Grenada.

MS3567 (a) $6 Sugihara and map showing route from Lithuania to Japan. (b) $6 Sugihara and wife Set of 2 sheets 7·50 8·00

184 *Bombus auricomus* (bumble bee)

2002. Flora and Fauna. Miniature sheets containing T 184 and similar multicoloured designs.

MS3568 135×170 mm. $1 Type **184**; $1 *Anax junius* (dragonfly); $1 *Dynastes tityus* (Hercules beetle); $1 *Coccinella novemrotata* (ladybug); $1 *Callicore maimuna* (figure-of-eight butterfly); $1 *Tenodera aridifolia sinensis* (praying mantis) 3·25 3·50

MS3569 135×170 mm. $1 Sperm whale; $1 Bottlenose whale; $1 Sei Whale; $1 Killer whale; $1 Humpback whale ("Humback Whale"); $1 Pygmy sperm whale 3·25 3·50

MS3570 135×170 mm. $2 *Anartia jatrophae*; $2 *Phoebis philea*; $2 *Cepheuptychia cephus*; $2 *Prepona meander*; $2 *Mesene phareus*; $2 *Morpho peleides* 6·50 7·00

MS3571 135×170 mm. $2 *Coprinus comatus*; $2 *Leucocoprinus rachodes*; $2 *Collybia iocephala*; $2 *Lepiota acutesquamosa*; $2 *Morchella crassipes*; $2 *Mycena galericulata* 6·50 7·00

MS3572 Four sheets, each 100×70 mm. (a) $6 *Anax junius* (dragonfly) (horiz). (b) $6 Blue whale (horiz). (c) $6 *Cepheuptychia cephus* (butterfly) (horiz). (d) $6 *Amanita phalloides* (mushroom) (horiz) Set of 4 sheets 13·00 14·00

No. **MS**3568 shows insects, **MS**3569 shows whales, **MS**3570 shows butterflies and **MS**3571 fungi.

2002. 25th Death Anniv of Elvis Presley. As T 518a of Grenada. Multicoloured (No. 3573) or black and brown (No. MS3574).

3573	$1 Elvis Presley with guitar	1·00	1·00

MS3574 150×215 mm. $1×9 containing nine different portraits of Elvis Presley 7·50 7·50

2002. "Amphilex '02" International Stamp Exhibition, Amsterdam. As T 518b of Grenada. (a) Dutch Nobel Prize Winners. Sheet 150×100 mm.

MS3575 $1.50 Paul J. Crutzen (Chemistry, 1995) (black and green); $1.50 Nobel medal (black and brown); $1.50 Martinus Veltman (Physics, 1999) (black and mauve); $1.50 Hendrik Lorentz (Physics, 1902) (black and blue); $1.50 Christiaan Eijkman (Medicine, 1929) (black and green); $1.50 Gerard 't Hooft (Physics, 1999) (black and brown) 5·50 5·50

(b) Dutch Lighthouses. Sheet 128×148 mm. Multicoloured.

MS3576 $1.50 Ameland; $1.50 Vlieland; $1.50 Julianadorp; $1.50 Noordwijk; $1.50 Hoek van Holland; $1.50 Goeree 6·50 6·50

(c) Dutch Women's Traditional Costumes. Sheet 120×140 mm containing multicoloured designs, each 36×50 mm.

MS3577 $3 Marken, Noord-Holland; $3 Staphorst, Overijsel; $3 Walchheren, Zeeland 5·50 5·50

185 Teddy Bear holding "HAPPY BIRTHDAY" in Heart

2002. Centenary of the Teddy Bear (1st issue). T 185 and similar vert designs. Multicoloured.

MS3578 140×142 mm. 50c. Type **185**; $1 With waistcoat, briefcase and bowler hat; $2 Wearing raincoat, sunglasses and hat; $5 Wearing boxer shorts with heart pattern 5·00 5·00

MS3579 85×115 mm. 15c. Teddy Bear wearing Guardsmans plumed helmet; $2 Panda teddy bear wearing black hat; $3 Wearing beret and ruff; $4 White teddy bear wearing grey top hat 5·50 5·50

No. **MS**3578 is heart-shaped.

See also Nos. 3611/12.

2002. World Cup Football Championship, Japan and Korea. Miniature sheets containing vert designs as T 524 of Grenada. Multicoloured.

MS3580 165×82 mm. $1.50 Oliver Neuville (Germany) and Eddie Pope (USA); $1.50 Claudio Reyna (USA) and Miroslav Klose (Germany); $1.50 Christian Ziege (Germany) and Frankie Hejduk (USA); $1.50 Nadal (Spain) and Jung Hwan Ahn (South Korea); $1.50 Luis Enrique (Spain) and Chong Gug Song (South Korea); $1.50 Park Ji Sung (South Korea) and Mendieta Gaizka (Spain) 5·50 5·50

MS3581 165×82 mm. $1.50 Danny Mills (England) and Ronaldo (Brazil); $1.50 Roque Junior (Brazil) and Emil Heskey (England); $1.50 Sol Campbell (England) and Rivaldo (Brazil); $1.50 Lamine Diatta (Senegal) and Hakan Sukur (Turkey); $1.50 Umit Davala (Turkey) and Khalilou Fadiga (Senegal); $1.50 El Hadji Diouf (Senegal) and Tugay Kerimoglu (Turkey) 5·50 5·50

MS3582 Four sheets, each 82×82 mm. (a) $3 Oliver Kahn (Germany); $3 Brad Friedel (Germany). (b) $3 Chun Soo Lee (South Korea); $3 Juan Carlos Valeron (Spain). (c) $3 David Beckham (England) and Roberto Carlos (Brazil); $3 Ronaldinho (Brazil) and Nicky Butt (England). (d) $3 Alpay Ozalan (Turkey); $3 Khalilou Fadiga (Senegal) Set of 4 sheets 13·00 13·00

2002. Christmas. Religious Paintings. As T 523a of Grenada. Multicoloured.

3583 15c. "The Redeemer and the Four Apostles" (Carpaccio) 25 10

3584 25c. "The Miracle of the Relic of the Cross" (Carpaccio) (vert) 30 15

3585 50c. "The Presentation in the Temple" (Carpaccio) 40 25

3586 $2 "The Visitation" (Carpaccio) 1·60 1·75

3587 $3 "The Birth of the Virgin" (Carpaccio) 1·90 2·25

MS3588 62×90 mm. $6 "Madonna and Child and Two Angels" (detail) (Cimabue) (vert) 3·25 3·50

186 "Year of Ram" (Ren Yi)

2003. Chinese New Year ("Year of the Ram").

MS3589 179×108 mm. $1.25×4 multicoloured 3·00 3·25

2003. Columbia Space Shuttle Commemoration. Sheet 183×146 mm, containing vert designs as T 533 of Grenada showing crew members. Multicoloured.

MS3590 $1 David Brown; $1 Commander Rick Husband; $1 Laurel Clark; $1 Kalpana Chawla; $1 Michael Anderson; $1 William McCool; $1 Ilan Ramon 4·50 4·75

2003. Japanese Art. Paintings by Toyohara Kunichika showing Famous Actors. As T 535 of Grenada. Multicoloured.

3591 50c. "Ichikawa Danjuro IX as the Beggar Akushichibyoe Kagekiyo" 35 25

3592 75c. "Ichikawa Danjuro IX as the Female Demon Ewanari" 55 40

3593 $1.25 "Sawamura Tossho II as Sutewakamaru" 80 80

3594 $3 "Bando Hikosaburo V as Nikki Damjo" 1·60 1·75

MS3595 175×137 mm. $2 "Nakamura Shikan IV as Keyamura Rokusuke"; $2 "Bando Hikosaburo V as Ichimisai no Musume Osono"; $2 "Ichikawa Sadanji I as Wada no Shimobe Busuke"; $2 "Ichikawa Sadanji I as Kiyomizu no Yoshitaka" 4·50 4·75

MS3596 122×82 mm. $6 "Onoe Kikugoro V as Torii Tsuneemon returning to Mikawa" (horiz) 3·25 3·50

2003. 450th Death Anniv of Lucas Cranach the Elder (artist). As T 536 of Grenada. Multicoloured.

3597 25c. "The St. Mary Altarpiece" (detail) (vert) 25 15

3598 $1 "The St. Mary Altarpiece" (different detail) (vert) 70 55

3599 $1.25 "Altar Piece of the Princes" (detail) (vert) 80 80

3600 $3 Frederick the Wise with St. Bartholomew (detail of altarpiece) (vert) 1·60 1·75

MS3601 150×160 mm. $2 "Judith at the Table of Holofernes" (detail); $2 "St. Catherine Altarpiece" (detail); $2 "Judith killing Holofernes" (detail); $2 "The Martyrdom of St. Catherine" (detail) 4·50 4·75

MS3602 102×123 mm. $6 "Cardinal Albrecht of Brandenbourg as St. Jerome in the Wilderness" (vert) 3·25 3·50

2003. 85th Death Anniv of Gustav Klimt (artist). As T 537 of Grenada. Multicoloured.

3603 15c. "Le Chapeau de Plumes Noires" 20 15

3604 25c. "Le Schloss Kammer am Attersee" 25 15

3605 50c. "Malcesine sur le Lac de Garde" 35 25

3606 75c. "Ferme en Haute-Autriche" 55 40

3607 $1.25 "Portrait d'une Dame" 80 75

3608 $4 "La Frise Beethoven" (detail) 1·90 2·00

MS3609 126×178 mm. $2 "Portrait de la Baronne Elisabeth Bachofen-Echt"; $2 "Portrait d'une Dame"; $2 "Portrait d'Emilie Floge"; $2 "Portrait d'Adele Bloch-Bauer" 4·50 4·75

MS3610 103×81 mm. $6 "Le Baiser" (detail). Imperf 3·25 3·50

2003. Centenary of the Teddy Bear (2nd issue). Embroidered Fabric Teddy Bears. As T 538 of Grenada. Self-adhesive. Imperf.

3611 $15 ochre, silver and red 8·00 8·50

MS3612 126×157 mm. No. 3611×4 28·00 29·00

2003. Centenary of Tour de France Cycle Race. As T 540 of Grenada showing past winners. Multicoloured.

MS3613 160×100 mm. $2 Ferdinand Kubler (1950); $2 Hugo Koblet (1951); $2 Fausto Coppi (1952); $2 Louison Bobet (1953) 5·50 5·50

MS3614 160×100 mm. $2 Louison Bobet (1954); $2 Louison Bobet (1955); $2 Roger Walkowiak (1956); $2 Jacques Anquetil (1957) 5·50 5·50

MS3615 160×100 mm. $2 Gastone Nencini (1960); $2 Jacques Anquetil (1961); $2 Jacques Anquetil (1962); $2 Jacques Anquetil (1963) 5·50 5·50

MS3616 Three sheets, each 100×70 mm. (a) $6 Louison Bobet (1953–1955). (b) $6 Jacques Anquetil (1957). (c) $6 Eddy Merckx (1969) Set of 3 sheets 10·00 10·00

187 John Kennedy, Choate Graduate, 1935

2003. 40th Death Anniv of President John F. Kennedy.

MS3617 144×131 mm. $2 Type **187** (agate, black and); $2 John Kennedy, 1946 (multicoloured); $2 With Jacqueline Kennedy on tennis court (multicoloured); $2 With young John F. Kennedy Jnr (multicoloured) 4·50 4·75

MS3618 144×131 mm. $2 With Jacqueline Kennedy (black, brown and grey); $2 Announcing Cuban blockade, 1962 (agate and mauve); $2 Sitting in chair, White House, 1962 (brown and black); $2 Jackie Kennedy with children at funeral, 1963 (black, mauve and purple) 4·50 4·75

188 Charles Lindbergh

2003. 75th Anniv of First Solo Trans-atlantic Flight. Multicoloured (No. MS3620).

MS3619 129×144 mm. $2 Type **188** (blue, grey and red); $2 Lindbergh and Ryan NYP Special *Spirit of St. Louis* (purple, blue and red); $2 Lindbergh and *Spirit of St. Louis* (black and red); $2 Lindbergh (purple, blue and red) 5·00 5·00

MS3620 129×144 mm. $2 Lindbergh (looking forward); $2 Lindbergh (looking left); $2 Lindbergh on arrival in Paris, 1927; $2 Lindbergh and *Spirit of St. Louis* 5·00 5·00

189 La Sagesse

2003. International Year of Freshwater. Multicoloured.

MS3621 150×88 mm. $2 Type **189**; $2 Annadale Falls; $2 Grand Etang 3·25 3·50

MS3622 100×70 mm. $6 St. George 3·25 3·50

2003. Centenary of Circus Clowns. As T 544 of Grenada. Multicoloured.

MS3623 119×194 mm. $2 Anton Pilossian; $2 Victor Vashnikov; $2 Dan Rice; $2 Tom Comet 3·25 3·25

MS3624 146×218 mm. $2 Boxer dog; $2 Macaw; $2 Monigue; $2 Vassily Trofimov 3·25 3·25

No. **MS**3623 shows clowns and is cut in the shape of a clown. No. **MS**3624 shows others circus performers and circus animals and is cut in the shape of an elephant.

190 Wright Flyer

2003. Centenary of Powered Flight. Multicoloured.

MS3625 176×97 mm. $2 Type 190; $2 NC-4; $2 Douglas World Cruiser; $2 Fokker Eindecker 3·25 3·25

MS3626 176×97 mm. $2 Hansa Brandenburg D.1; $2 B.E.2e; $2 Handley Page 0/400; $2 Avro 504 3·25 3·25

MS3627 176×97 mm. $2 Hawker Hart; $2 Martin B-10; $2 Armstrong Whitworth Siskin IIIA; $2 Loening OL-8 3·25 3·25

MS3628 (a) 67×97 mm. $6 Wright Glider No. III. (b) 106×76 mm. $6 Wright *Flyer II*. (c) 106×76 mm. $6 Gloster Gamecock 7·00 7·00

191 Princess Elizabeth as Young Woman

2003. 50th Anniv of Coronation. Multicoloured.

MS3629 160×86 mm. $3 Type **191**; $3 Queen wearing azure blue; $3 Riding side saddle at Trooping the Colour 3·50 3·50

MS3630 76×106 mm. $6 Queen wearing tiara 3·00 3·00

2003. 21st Birthday of Prince William. As T 547 of Grenada. Multicoloured.

MS3631 160×86 mm. $3 Prince William (half-length photo); $3 Prince William (in close-up); $3 Prince William (looking left) 4·00 4·00

MS3632 106×76 mm. $6 Wearing hat and ski goggles 3·00 3·00

192 Rose-breasted Grosbeak

2003. Birds, Tropical Fish and Flowers of the World. Multicoloured.

3633 25c. Type **192** 30 20

3634 25c. Three-spotted dascyllus ("Domino Damselfish") 30 20

3635 50c. Northern oriole ("Bullock's Oriole") 45 35

3636 50c. Catbird ("Gray Catbird") 45 35

3637 75c. Porcupinefish 60 60

3638 75c. Wild rhododendron (vert) 60 60

3639 $1 Blue grosbeak 90 90

3640 $1 Peony (vert) 90 90

3641 $1.25 Black-tailed damselfish 1·00 1·00

3642 $1.25 Camellia (vert) 1·00 1·00

3643 $2 Reticulate damselfish ("Clown Fish") 1·60 1·60

3644 $2 Laurel (vert) 1·60 1·60

MS3645 110×138 mm. $2 Lazuli bunting; $2 Indigo bunting; $2 Broad-tailed Hummingbird; $2 Scarlet tanager (all vert) 5·00 5·00

MS3646 129×109 mm. $2 Halfmoon triggerfish; $2 Blackeye thicklip ("Half and Half Wrasser"); $2 Pennant coralfish ("Long-fin Banner Fish"); $2 Hump-headed bannerfish ("Butterfly Fish") 4·50 4·50

MS3647 110×130 mm. $2 Apple blossom; $2 Mock orange; $2 Wild rose; $2 Hibiscus (all vert) 4·50 4·50

MS3648 98×68 mm. (a) $6 Barn swallow. (b) $6 Blue-girdled angelfish. (c) $6 Violets (vert) 10·00 10·00

No. **MS**3647 is inscribed "ASDA Postage Stamp Mega-Event" on the sheet margin.

193 "Madonna and Child" (detail), Carnesecchii Tabernacle (Domenico Veneziano)

2003. Christmas. Multicoloured.

3649 35c. Type **193** 25 20

3650 75c. "Madonna and Child" (detail), Magnoli Altarpiece (Domenico Veneziano) 60 45

3651 90c. "Crevole Madonna" (detail) (Duccio di Buoninsegna) 70 55

3652 $3 "Madonna and Child" (detail) (Domenico Veneziano) 1·90 2·25

MS3653 71×96 mm. $6 "Madonna and the Child by the Fireplace" (detail) (Robert Campin) 3·50 3·75

2003. 300th Anniv of St. Petersburg. "Treasures of the Hermitage". As T 551 of Grenada. Multicoloured.

3654 75c. "Abraham and Isaac" (Rembrandt) 55 40
3655 $1 "David and Jonathan" (Rembrandt) 75 60
3656 $1.25 "Saint Onuphrus" (Juisepe de Ribera) 85 80
3657 $2 "Pope Paul III" (Titian) 1·75 1·75
MS3658 115×145 mm. $2 "Rest on the Flight into Egypt" (Murillo); $2 "Esther before Ahasuerus" (Nicolas Poussin); $2 "Abraham's Servant and Rebecca" (Jacob Hogers); $2 "The Prophet Elisha and Naaman" (Lambert Jacobsz) (all horiz) 4·50 4·75
MS3659 (a) 66×78 mm. $6 "The Building of Noah's Ark" (Guido Reni). Imperf. (b) 78×66 mm. $6 "Hagar flees Abram's House" (Rubens). Imperf 6·00 6·50

2003. 25th Death Anniv of Norman Rockwell (artist). As T 552 of Grenada. Multicoloured.

MS3660 150×181 mm. $2 "The Trumpeter"; $2 "Waiting for the Vet"; $2 "The Diving Board"; $2 "The Discovery" 3·50 3·75
MS3661 $6 "Day in a Boy's Life" (detail) (horiz) 3·50 3·75

2003. 30th Death Anniv of Pablo Picasso (artist). As T 553 of Grenada. Multicoloured.

MS3662 128×168 mm. $2 "Jacqueline Sitting"; $2 "Jacqueline with Flower"; $2 "Seated Nude"; $2 "Woman in Armchair" 3·75 4·00
MS3663 74×98 mm. $6 "Head of a Woman". Imperf 3·25 3·50

2004. Chinese New Year ("Year of the Monkey"). As T 554 of Grenada. Multicoloured.

MS3664 118×144 mm. $1.50 Cotton-top tamarin; $1.50 Chimpanzee; $1.50 Baboon; $1.50 Bald uakari 3·25 3·50

194 "The Mind Landscape of Xie Youyu" (Zhao Mengfu)

2004. Hong Kong 2004 International Stamp Exhibition. Paintings by Zhao Mengfu (1254—1322). Multicoloured.

MS3665 120×119 mm. $2 Type **194**; $2 Mountains and trees; $2 "Twin Pines"; $2 Mountain range and plains 4·00 4·25
MS3666 87×81 mm. $6 "Autumn" 3·25 3·50

2004. Arthur the Aardvark and Friends. As T 557 of Grenada. Multicoloured.

MS3667 150×183 mm. $1.50 Brain as molecule; $1.50 Binky as pirate; $1.50 Francine as vampire; $1.50 Prunella as fairy; $1.50 Arthur as skeleton; $1.50 Muffy as witch 4·00 4·25
MS3668 150×184 mm. $2 Francine as clown; $2 Buster as Frankenstein's monster; $2 Muffy and spider; $2 Sue Ellen as cat 3·75 4·00
MS3669 150×183 mm. $2 Francine and butterfly; $2 Binky and world map; $2 Brain and maths equation; $2 Arthur and model of planet 3·75 4·00

2004. Marilyn Monroe Commemoration. As T 560 of Grenada.

3670 50c. multicoloured 50 50
MS3671 multicoloured 127×112 mm. $2 black, grey and red; $2 black, grey and red; $2 black, grey and red; $2 black, grey and red 4·25 4·50

DESIGNS: 50c. Wearing halter-neck dress and drop earrings; $2 Wearing white top and short hair; $2 Wearing beret; $2 Wearing white backless dress; $2 With long dark hair and black dress.

195 Deng Xiaoping

2004. Deng Xiaoping (Chinese politician) Commemoration. Sheet 98×68 mm.

MS3672 **195** $6 black, grey and red 3·25 3·50

2004. 25th Anniv of the Pontificate of Pope John Paul II. Sheet 163×153 mm containing horiz designs as T 564 of Grenada. Multicoloured.

MS3673 $2 Pope with Lech Walesa; $2 Pope with Chief Rabbi of Israel, Yisrael Meir Lau; $2 Pope with children; Pope using laptop; $2 Pope wearing mitre and gesturing 6·50 6·50

2004. Olympic Games, Athens, Greece. As T 559 of Grenada. Multicoloured.

3674 25c. Long jump 25 15
3675 50c. Avery Brundage 40 25
3676 $1 Commemorative medal 65 65
3677 $4 Greek vase showing "The Paidotribe" ("Paidotribai") 2·25 2·50

2004. 60th Anniv of D-Day Landings. As T 404 of Dominica. Multicoloured.

3678 25c. Admiral Sir Bertram Ramsay 40 25
3679 50c. Lt Gen. Miles Dempsey 70 50
3680 75c. Bob Shrimpton "Ping", Higher Submarine Detector, HMS *Belfast* 90 65
3681 $4 Denis Edwards, 6th Airborne Division 2·50 2·75
MS3682 177×107 mm. $2 US troops landing and map of Omaha Beach; $2 Troops moving inland from Omaha Beach; $2 Soldier with rifle and map of Sword Beach; $2 Meeting of German generals and Allied troops leaving landing craft 6·00 6·50
MS3683 177×107 mm. $2 Winston Churchill; $2 Churchill (wearing hat); $2 British link up with Airborne Troops; $2 British troops and map showing Horsa Bridge on Orne River 7·50 7·00
MS3684 100×70 mm. (a) $6 Gunner in British bomber 7·50 8·00
MS3684a 100×70 mm. (b) $6 Assault landing craft coming ashore 3·75 4·00

2004. Bicentenary of Steam Locomotives. Multicoloured As T 566 of Grenada but horiz.

3685-3693 $1×9 Britannia class; Indian Railways XD class; China Railways KD6 class (USATC S160); SE+CR 01 class; Battle of Britain light Pacific; SR King Arthur class; SR Marsh 13 class; SR N class; SR School class 7·00 7·50
3694-3702 $1×9 LNER V2 class; Sudan Railways locomotive; China Railways DF4 Co Co; LMS 2F with Black 5; LMS Lickey Banker; LMS *Princess Royal Pacific*; LMS Reboilered Claughton class; LMS Stanier 8F; Midland Railway compound 7·00 7·50
3703-3711 $1×9 SR Merchant Navy Pacific; Gazira Cotton Railway, Sudan; Spanish Railways; LNER 04-1 class; LNER A1 Pacific;LNER A3 class; LNER A4 class Pacific; LNER B1 class; LNER Ivatt Large Atlantic A4 Pacific 7·00 7·50
MS3712 Three sheets, each 97×66 mm. (a) $6 London to Holyhead train. (b) $6 Dublin to Tralee train crossing viaduct. (c) $6 Modern Aberdeen to Penzance train crossing bridge 11·00 12·00

2004. Queen Juliana of the Netherlands Commemoration. As T 568 of Grenada. Mult.

3713 $2 Wedding portrait of Princess Juliana, 1937 1·40 1·40

196 Start of Donkey Race

2004. 40th Carriacou Regatta Festival. Mult.

3714 75c. Type **196** 60 60
3715 90c. Start of model boat race 70 75
3716 $1 Dinghy race (vert) 70 75

2004. Centenary of FIFA (Federation Internationale de Football Association). As T 413 of Dominica. Multicoloured.

MS3717 192×96 mm. $2 David Beckham (England); $2 Marcel Desailly (France); $2 Guido Buchwald (Germany) $2 Alfonso (Spain) 4·50 4·75
MS3718 $6 Bobby Charlton (England) 3·75 4·00

197 Elvis Presley

2004. 50th Anniv of Elvis Presley's First Record. Two sheets, each 187×136 mm, containing T 197 and similar vert designs. Multicoloured.

MS3719 $2 Type **197**; $2 Wearing spotted shirt, singing with guitar; $2 Wearing shirt, guitar slung over one shoulder; $2 Wearing grey jacket 3·75 4·00
MS3720 $2 Wearing mauve shirt; $2 Wearing spotted shirt, strumming guitar; $2 Wearing jacket and tie, guitar slung over one shoulder; $2 Wearing blue patterned shirt 4·50 4·75

198 *Titanic*

2004. Ocean Liners. Multicoloured.

3721 25c. Type **198** 30 20
3722 75c. *Michaelangelo* 70 55
3723 $1 *America* 85 70
3724 $1.25 *Vaterland* 1·00 1·00
3725 $2 *Deutschland* 1·50 1·60
3726 $3 *Mauritania* 2·00 2·25
MS3727 75×70 mm. $6 *Ile de France* 3·75 4·00

2004. Ronald Reagan (US President 1981–9) Commemoration. As T 573 of Grenada. Mult.

MS3728 179×107 mm. $2 With Press Secretary James Brady; $2 With German Chancellor Helmut Kohl; $2 Pres. Reagan at desk and with family; $2 With Princess Diana, 1983 4·50 4·75

2004. Centenary of Baseball World Series. As T 574 of Grenada showing George Herman "Babe" Ruth. Multicoloured.

MS3273 1 120×114 mm. $2 Holding bat; $2 Full-face portrait; $2 Facing right; $2 Holding baseball 4·00 4·50
3729 50c. George Herman "Babe" Ruth (white background) 35 35
3730 50c. As No. 2929 (blue background) 35 35

2004. Christmas. 25th Death Anniv of Norman Rockwell (artist). As T 575 of Grenada. Mult.

3732 35c. "Follow Me in Merry Measure" (1928) 30 25
3733 75c. "The Merrie Old Coach Driver" (1929) 55 45
3734 90c. "Joy to the World" (1930) 70 60
3735 $3 "Santa Reading His Mail" (1935) 1·90 2·25
MS3736 62×80 mm. $6 "Wartime Santa" (1942). Imperf 3·25 3·50

199 "Double Chickens and Peony"

2005. Chinese New Year ("Year of the Rooster"). Paintings by Ren Yi. Multicoloured.

MS3737 135×115 mm. 75c.×4 Type **199** 1·75 2·00
MS3738 100×70 mm. $3 "A Rooster" (59×39 mm) 1·75 2·00

200 Scarlet-bodied Wasp Moth

2005. Moths. Multicoloured.

3739 75c. Type **200** 60 60
3740 90c. Bella moth 70 70
3741 $1 Sphinx moth 70 70
3742 $3 Faithful beauty moth 1·90 2·25
MS3743 93×73 mm. $6 Spotted oleander moth (inscr "Spotted Oleander Caterpillar" in error) 3·50 3·75

201 *Heliamphora tatei*

2005. Carnivorous Plants of the Caribbean. Multicoloured.

MS3744 150×100 mm. $2 Type **201**; $2 *Sarracenia flava and Genlisea pygmaea*; $2 *Nepenthes bicalcarata*; $2 *Utricularia intermedia* 4·50 4·75
MS3745 93×73 mm. $6 *Dionaea muscipula* 3·50 3·75

202 Poison Dart Frog

2005. Reptiles of the Caribbean. Multicoloured.

MS3746 150×100 mm. $2 Type **202**; $2 Western Antillean anoles; $2 Black iguana; $2 American crocodile 4·50 4·75
MS3747 93×73 mm. $6 Anolis lizard 3·50 3·75

203 Rice Plants

2005. International Year of Rice (2004). Multicoloured.

MS3748 202×140 mm. $1.50 Type **203**; $1.50 Rice plants and perched bird; $1.50 Rice plants and bird (flying downwards); $1.50 Clump of rice; $1.50 Rice plants with bird (flying upwards); $1.50 Two clumps of rice 5·00 6·00
MS3749 100×70 mm. $6 Rice farming in Bali, Indonesia, 1930s (artist anon) (horiz) 3·25 3·50

The stamps in **MS**3748 form a composite design showing a screen painting by Maruyama Oshen of rice plants heavy with grain in autumn.

204 *Swiftsure*

2005. US National Basketball Association Players. As T 572 of Grenada. Multicoloured.

3750	75c. Tracy McGrady, Houston Rockets	50	55
3751	75c. Shaquille O'Neal, Miami Heat	50	55
3752	75c. Steve Nash, Phoenix Suns	50	55
3753	75c. Chris Webber, Sacramento Kings	50	55
3754	75c. Allan Houston, New York Knicks	50	55
3755	75c. Steve Francis, Orlando Magic	50	55

2005. Bicentenary of the Battle of Trafalgar. Multicoloured.

3756	75c. Type **204**	85	60
3757	$1 British fleet sailing into Cape Trafalgar towards French and Spanish fleet (horiz)	1·00	85
3758	$2 Captain Alexander Ball	1·75	1·75
3759	$3 Vice Admiral Francois Paul Brueys d'Aigalliers	2·50	2·50
MS3760	96×66 mm. $6 Admiral Aristide Aubert du Petit-Thouars	3·75	4·00

2005. 70th Birth Anniv of Elvis Presley. As T 583 of Grenada. Multicoloured.

3761–3766	$1.50×6 With guitar, 1955; Performing on Milton Berle Show, 1956; $1.50 Seated in studio, 1958; $1.50 Portrait photograph, 1962; Performing for the "68 Special", 1968; On tour, 1972	5·50	6·00
3767–3772	$1.50×6 "In GI Blues", 1958; "Blue Hawaii", 1961; "It Happened at the World's Fair", 1963; "Harum Scarum", 1965; "Sitting on car, Spinout", 1966; "Change of Habit", 1969	5·50	6·00

2005. Ozu Yasujiro (film director) Commemoration. AS T 584 of Grenada. Multicoloured.

MS3773	145×175 mm. $2 A "Mother Should be Loved", 1934; $2 "An Inn in Tokyo", 1935; $2 "Dragnet Gir", 1933; $2 "There was a Father", 1942	4·50	5·00

2005. Prehistoric Animals. A T 580 of Grenada. Multicoloured.

MS3774	Three sheets, each 133×100 mm. (a) Animals: $2 Psittacosaurus; $2 Deinonychus; $2 Suchomimus; $2 Smilodon. (b) Fish: $2 Eurypholis; $2 Ichthyosaurus; $2 Plesiosaur; $2 Varnerxiphactinus. (c) Birds: $2 Pterosaurus; $2 Archaeopteryx; Pterosaurian; $2 Microraptor	12·00	14·00
MS3775	Three sheets, each 98×69 mm. (a) $6 Tenotosaurus. (b) $6 Uintatherium. (c) $6 Mammoth (vert)	11·00	13·00

2005. 60th Anniv of the End of World War II. "The Route to Victory". As T 587 of Grenada. Multicoloured.

3776	$2 Field Marshal Montgomery directing troops forward	1·40	1·40
3777	$2 Field Marshal Rommel	1·40	1·40
3778	$2 Troops moving forward into battle	1·40	1·40
3779	$2 German prisoners after Battle of El Alamein	1·40	1·40
3780	$2 Russian troops at the gates of Berlin	1·40	1·40
3781	$2 Two surrendering German soldiers	1·40	1·40
3782	$2 Berlin in ruins	1·40	1·40
3783	$2 Soldier carrying child	1·40	1·40
MS3784	Two sheets, each 107×97 mm. (a) $6 Troops attacking, North African desert. (b) $6 "Give me five years and you will not recognise Germany again" (Hitler quotation) and ruins of Berlin	7·00	7·50

205 "E=mc²" and Sunlight on Planet Mars

2005. 50th Death Anniv of Albert Einstein (physicist). Multicoloured.

MS3785	175×80 mm. $3 Type **205**; $3 Albert Einstein; $3 David Ben-Gurion (first Prime Minister of Israel)	6·50	6·50

The two right-hand designs in **MS**2785 form a composite design showing Einstein with David Ben-Gurion.

2005. 60th Anniv of Victory in Japan Day. As T 589 of Grenada. Multicoloured.

3786	$2 P-38 J Lightning	1·40	1·40
3787	$2 P-51D Mustang	1·40	1·40
3788	$2 F4 fighter plane	1·40	1·40
3789	$2 Douglas C-47 Skytrain	1·40	1·40
3790	$2 Officer reading VJ Day message to troops	1·40	1·40
3791	$2 Chaplain's prayer	1·40	1·40
3792	$2 "PEACE" placard	1·40	1·40
3793	$2 USS Missouri, Tokyo Bay, 2 September 1945	1·40	1·40

206 Moses Maimonides

2005. 800th Death Anniv of Moses Maimonides (Rabbi Moses Ben Maimon) (Jewish scholar)).

3794	**206** $2 multicoloured	1·50	1·50

207 Pope John Paul II

2005. Pope John Paul II Commemoration.

3795	**207** $3 multicoloured	2·00	2·00

2005. Christmas. As T 602 of Grenada. Mult.

3796	35c. "Madonna and Child" (detail) (Andrea del Sarto)	25	20
3797	75c. "Madonna Pesaro" (detail) (Tiziano Vecellio)	60	45
3798	90c. "Madonna and Child" (detail) (Tiziano Vecellio)	70	60
3799	$3 "Madonna and Child" (detail) (Rubens)	1·75	2·00
MS3800	100×70 mm. $6 "Madonna and Child" (Dominico Veneziano)	3·50	4·00

208 Dog

2005. Chinese New Year ("Year of the Dog"). Painting of Dog by Chang Dai-Chien.

3801	**208** $1 multicoloured	1·00	1·00

209 Pope Benedict XVI

2006. Election of Pope Benedict XVI.

3802	**209** $2 multicoloured	1·40	1·40

2006. 80th Birthday of Queen Elizabeth II. As T 432 of Dominica. Multicoloured.

3803	$3 Wearing white hat and jacket, 1960s	1·90	1·90
3804	$3 Wearing tiara	1·90	1·90
3805	$3 With baby Princess Anne	1·90	1·90
3806	$3 Wearing pearls and dark blue dress	1·90	1·90
MS3807	120×120 mm. $6 Wearing uniform	3·50	3·75

2006. 80th Birth Anniv of Marilyn Monroe (actress). As T 452 of Gambia. Multicoloured.

3808	$3 Marilyn Monroe	1·75	1·90

2006. 400th Birth Anniv of Rembrandt Harmenszoon van Rijn (artist). As T 458 of Gambia showing paintings. Multicoloured.

3809	75c. "The Strolling Musicians" (detail)	50	35
3810	90c. "The Great Jewish Bride" (detail)	60	45
3811	$1 "Old Haaringh" (detail)	65	50
3812	$3 "Lady and Gentleman in Black" (detail of man)	1·75	1·90
3813	$3 "Lady and Gentleman in Black" (detail of woman)	1·75	1·90
3814	$3 "The Shipbuilder and his Wife" (detail of shipbuilder)	1·75	1·90
3815	$3 "The Shipbuilder and his Wife" (detail of wife)	1·75	1·90
3816	$4 "Beggars receiving Alms at the Door of a House" (detail)	1·90	2·00
3817	$6 "Young Woman in a Pearl-trimmed Beret" (detail) (69×99 mm)	3·25	3·50
3818	$6 "Portrait of a Boy" (detail) (69×99 mm)	3·25	3·50

2006. 250th Birth Anniv of Wolfgang Amadeus Mozart (composer). Sheet 100×70 mm containing vert design as T 435 of Dominica. Multicoloured.

MS3819	$6 "Don Giovanni" (opera)	4·00	4·00

210 Space Shuttle *Columbia* at Pad 39-A

2006. Space Anniversaries. Multicoloured. (a) 25th Anniv of First Flight of Space Shuttle Columbia.

3820	$2 Type **210**	1·40	1·40
3821	$2 Astronauts John Young and Robert Crippen	1·40	1·40
3822	$2 *Columbia* first flight take-off	1·40	1·40
3823	$2 *Columbia* in space	1·40	1·40
3824	$2 *Columbia* crew in cabin	1·40	1·40
3825	$2 *Columbia* landing	1·40	1·40

2005. (b) Launch of Space Shuttle Discovery.

3826	$3 Mission STS-114 on pad	1·90	1·90
3827	**3826** $3 Mission STS-114 crew	1·90	1·90
3828	**3826** $3 Building of first ISS elements	1·90	1·90
3829	**3826** $3 STS-114 in space walk	1·90	1·90

(c) 30th Anniv (2005) of "Apollo"—"Soyuz" Test Project.

3830	$3 Liftoff of "Soyuz 19" from Baikonur Cosmodrome, Kazakhstan	1·90	1·90
3831	$3 ASTP crew	1·90	1·90
3832	$3 Soviet and American crew in the cabin	1·90	1·90
3833	$3 Spacecraft "Soyuz" 19	1·90	1·90
MS3834	Three sheets, each 100×70 mm. (a) $6 "Luna 9" flight apparatus (first lunar soft landing, 1966). (b) $6 "Venus Express" (first European mission to Venus). (c) $6 Mars Reconnaissance "Orbiter" Set of 3 sheets	11·00	13·00

The stamp within No. **MS**3834(c) is incorrectly inscribed "Reconaissance".

2006. 500th Death Anniv of Christopher Columbus. As T 614 of Grenada. Multicoloured.

3835	75c. *Pinta* (vert)	50	35
3836	$1.50 Columbus's fleet setting sail	90	70
3837	$2 *Santa Maria* and map showing voyage	1·40	1·50
3838	$3 Columbus discovers San Salvador, 1492	1·75	2·00
MS3839	100×70 mm. $6 Christopher Columbus	3·50	3·75

2006. Christmas. Vert designs as T 616 of Grenada showing details from painting "Saint Willibrod in Adoration before Mary Mother of God" by Rubens. Multicoloured.

3840	25c. Joseph	25	20
3841	50c. Cherubs	35	30
3842	75c. Madonna and Christ Child	50	35
3843	$1 Saint Willibrod	65	50
3844	$2 As No. 3840	1·40	1·40
3845	$2 As No. 3841	1·40	1·40
3846	$2 As No. 3842	1·40	1·40
3847	$2 As No. 3843	1·40	1·40

211 *LZ-127* Zeppelin

2007. 50th Death Anniv (2006) of Ludwig Durr (Zeppelin designer). Multicoloured.

3848	$3 Type **211**	2·25	2·25
3849	$3 *Hindenburg's* dining room	2·25	2·25
3850	$3 Marine Airship L53	2·25	2·25

212 John Kennedy running for Congress

2007. 90th Birth Anniv of John F. Kennedy (US President 1960–3). Multicoloured.

3851	$2 Type **212**	1·50	1·50
3852	$2 Campaign for Congress	1·50	1·50
3853	$2 Campaigning in New Hampshire	1·50	1·50
3854	$2 John Kennedy as President	1·50	1·50
3855	$2.50 Naru Island	2·00	2·00
3856	$2.50 Lieut. John Kennedy on Solomon Islands (in forest, wearing cap)	2·00	2·00
3857	$2.50 Lieut. Kennedy on Solomon Islands (standing on boardwalk)	2·00	2·00
3858	$2.50 SOS coconut carved by John Kennedy	2·00	2·00

Nos. 3851/4 ('Elected to the House of Representatives 1946–52') and 3855/8 ('John F. Kennedy Joins the Navy 1941–44').

213 '100' containing Emblem

2007. Centenary of Scouting. Multicoloured.

3859	$2 Type **213**	1·50	1·50
MS3860	111×80 mm. $6 As Type **213**	4·25	4·25

The stamp within **MS**3860 differs from Type **213** in having different colours and no frame around '100' emblem.

214 Elvis Presley

2007. 30th Death Anniv of Elvis Presley. Mult.

3861	$3 Type **214**	2·25	2·25
3862	$3 Elvis Presley playing guitar (guitarist in background)	2·25	2·25
3863	$3 Seated, with hands resting on guitar	2·25	2·25
3864	$3 Singing into microphone, hands raised	2·25	2·25

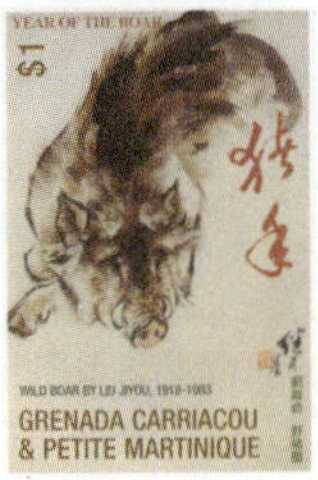

215 *Wild Boar* (Liu Jiyou)

2007. Chinese New Year ('Year of the Boar').

MS3865 85×112 mm. $1×2 Type **215**; $2×2 Type **215**		4·25	4·25

216 Pied-billed Grebe

2007. Birds of the Caribbean. Multicoloured.

3866	75c. Type **216**	55	40
3867	$1 Black-crowned night-heron	80	65
3868	$1 Turkey vulture	80	65
3869	$2 Hooded warbler (horiz)	1·50	1·50
3870	$2 Northern flicker (horiz)	1·50	1·50
3871	$2 Mockingbird (horiz)	1·50	1·50
3872	$2 Blue tit (horiz)	1·50	1·50
3873	$2 Caspian tern (horiz)	1·50	1·10
3874	$2 Scarlet tanager (horiz)	1·50	1·50
3875	$2 Common nighthawk (horiz)	1·50	1·50
3876	$2 Osprey (horiz)	1·50	1·50
3877	$4 Green honeycreeper	4·00	4·00
MS3878 Three sheets, each 71×100 mm. (a) $5 White-winged parakeet. (b) $5 Blackpoll warbler (horiz). (c) $5 Yellow-green vireo (horiz)		11·00	11·00

217 *Goodyera tesselata*

2007. Orchids of the World. Multicoloure.

3879	75c. Type **217**	55	40
3880	$1.50 *Oncidium floridanum*	1·10	95
3881	$2 *Hexalectris spicata*	1·50	1·50
3882	$2 *Platanthera grandiflora*	1·50	1·50
3883	$2 *Platanthera peramoena*	1·50	1·50
3884	$2 *Cyrtopodium punctatum*	1·50	1·50
3885	$2 *Spiranthes odorata*	1·50	1·50
3886	$2 *Platanthera blephariglottis*	1·50	1·50
3887	$2 *Epipactis helleborine*	1·50	50
3888	$2 *Cypripedium alaskanum*	1·50	1·50
3889	$2 *Zeuxine strateumatica*	1·50	1·50
3890	$3 *Pogonia ophioglossoides*	2·25	2·25
MS3891 Three sheets, each 70×100 mm. (a) $6 *Macradenia lutescens* (horiz). (b) $6 *Bletilla striata* (horiz). (c) $6 *Platanthera chapmanii*		13·00	13·00

218 *Morchella semilibera*

2007. Fungi of the World. Multicoloured.

3892	75c. Type **218**	55	40
3893	$1 *Ganoderma resinaceum*	80	65
3894	$1 *Helvella crispa*	80	65
3895	$2 *Aleuria aurantia*	1·50	1·50
3896	$2 *Boletus*sp.	1·50	1·50
3897	$2 *Boletellus russellii*	1·50	1·50
3898	$2 *Otidea onotica*	1·50	1·50
3899	$2 *Russula sardonia*	1·50	1·50
3900	$2 *Amanita cruzii*	1·50	1·50
3901	$2 *Macrocybe titans*	1·50	1·50
3902	$2 *Amanita microspora*	1·50	1·50
3903	$4 *Ganoderma*sp.	4·00	4·00
MS3904 Three sheets, each 103×73 mm. (a) $5 *Cantharellus cibarius*. (b) $5 *Amanitapolypyramis*. (c) $5 *Boletellus ananas*		11·00	11·00

219 Wicked Stepmother Queen holding Magic Mirror

2007. Betty Boop in Snow White (cartoon film, 1933). Multicoloured.

MS3905 Two sheets, each 195×175 mm. (a) $1×3 Type **219**; Wicked Stepmother Queen shouting; Bimbo and Koko in knight costumes falling down hole; $2×3 Betty Boop at palace door; Magic mirror pointing at Betty Boop; Betty Boop rolled into snowball (b) $2×4 Queen finding hole; Koko, Bimbo and Queen turned into Hag; Koko as ghost; Betty Boop asleep and Koko and Bimbo turned into ice figures		13·00	13·00
MS3906 106×76 mm. $6 Betty Boop fleeing (vert)		4·25	4·25

220 Royal Penguins

2007. International Polar Year. Penguins. Mult.

MS3907 150×115 mm. $2×6 Type **220** (country inscr at right); Penguins preening, with heads bent (country inscr at top); Head of penguin (foreground) and penguin (country inscr at right); Penguin (in foreground) and penguin showing feet (country inscr at bottom); Penguins preening, with heads bent (country inscr at bottom); Penguin (in foreground) and back of penguin (country inscr at left)		9·00	9·00
MS3908 100×70 mm. $6 African penguin swimming		4·25	4·25

The stamps and margins of No. **MS**3907 forms a composite design showing a colony of royal penguins.

221 Queen Elizabeth II and Prince Philip

2007. Diamond Wedding of Queen Elizabeth II and Prince Philip. Multicoloured.

3909	$1.50 Type **221**	1·10	95
3910	$1.50 Queen Elizabeth II	1·10	95

222 Pope Benedict XVI

2007. 80th Birthday of Pope Benedict XVI.

3911	**222** $1 multicoloured	80	65

223 Helicopter D-HBKS

2007. Centenary of the Helicopter. Multicoloured.

3912	$1.50 Type **223**	1·10	95
3913	$1.50 UH-1 Iroquois troop carrier	1·10	95
3914	$1.50 S-65/RH-53D 'Hostage rescue helicopter'	1·10	95
3915	$1.50 UH-1B/C Iroquois helicopter	1·10	95
3916	$1.50 Autogyro	1·10	95
3917	$1.50 BO 105 rescue helicopter	1·10	95
MS3918 100×70 mm. $6 AH-64 Apache armoured gunship		4·25	4·25

224 *The Virgin and Child with Saints Jerome*

2007. Christmas. Multicoloured.

3919	25c. Type **224**	20	25
3920	50c. *The Virgin and Child between Saints Thomas and Jerome* (Guido Reni)	80	35
3921	75c. *The Virgin and Child* (Giovanni Batista Salvi)	60	45
3922	$1 *The Madonna of Decemviri* (Pietro Perugino)	80	65

225 Rat

2007. Chinese New Year ('Year of the Rat').

3923	**225** $1 multicoloured	80	65

226 Princess Diana *and Bartholomew* (Alessandro Bonvicino)

2007. 10th Death Anniv of Princess Diana. Multicoloured.

3924	$1.50 Type **226**	1·10	95
3925	$1.50 Wearing dark coat and plumed hat	1·10	95
3926	$1.50 Wearing emerald green	1·10	95
3927	$1.50 As Type **226** in close-up	1·10	95
3928	$1.50 As No. 3925 in close-up	1·10	95
3929	$1.50 As No. 3926 in close-up	35	35
MS3930 70×100 mm. $6 Princess Diana and Prince Charles with baby Prince William at his Christening (horiz)		4·25	4·25

2008. Elvis Presley Commemoration. As T 635 of Grenada. Multicoloured.

3931	$1.50 Silhouette (back view)	1·10	95
3932	$1.50 Wearing green shirt	1·10	95
3933	$1.50 Silhouette (side view)	1·10	95
3934	$1.50 Playing guitar (seen from back, looking over shoulder)	1·10	95
3935	$1.50 Silhouette (front view)	1·10	95
3936	$1.50 Wearing orange jacket	1·10	95

227 Aerial View of City of David and Walls of Old City, Jerusalem (Illustration reduced. Actual size 150×125 mm) (image scaled to 32% of original size)

2008. Israel 2008 World Stamp Championship, Tel-Aviv. Sheet 150×125 mm. Imperf.

MS3937 multicoloured		4·25	4·25

228 Elvis Presley

2008. Elvis Presley Commemoration. Multicoloured.

3954	$1.50 Type **228**	1·10	95
3955	$1.50 Wearing blue shirt and jeans, striped background	1·10	95
3956	$1.50 Wearing white (seen full length)	1·10	95
3957	$1.50 Wearing blue shirt and jeans (green and black background)		
3958	$1.50 Wearing white (seen three quarter length)	1·10	95
3959	$1.50 Wearing red shirt (green, blue and black background)	1·10	95

229 Bauble in Surf on Beach

2008. Christmas. Multicoloured.

3960	25c. Type **229**	20	25
3961	50c. 'MERRY CHRISTMAS' and shapes of wrapped parcels in lights	40	35
3962	75c. 'Merry Christmas' written in beach sand and palm fronds	60	45
3963	$1 Christmas lights including outlines of seashells and star (vert)	1·00	85

230 *Mariner 9* and the Valles Marineris on Mars

2008. 50 Years of Space Exploration and Satellites. Multicoloured.

3964	$2 Type **230**	1·50	1·50
3965	$2 *Mariner 9* and technicians	1·50	1·50
3966	$2 *Mariner 9* and the Olympus Mons on Mars	1·50	1·50
3967	$2 Valles Marineris on Mars	1·50	1·50
3968	$2 Atlas-Centaur rocket launches *Mariner 9*	1·50	1·50
3969	$2 *Mariner 9* and Mars moon Phobos	1·50	1·50

3970	$2 Venus and Mercury (horiz)	1·50	1·50
3971	$2 Jupiter	1·50	1·50
3972	$2 Earth and Mars	1·50	1·50
3973	$2 Saturn	1·50	1·50
3974	$2 Neptune	1·50	1·50
3975	$2 Uranus	1·50	1·50
3976	$2.50 *Mariner 10* and Venus	2·00	2·00
3977	$2.50 Atlas-Centaur rocket and *Mariner 10*	2·00	2·00
3978	$2.50 *Mariner 10* and technicians	2·00	2·00
3979	$2.50 *Mariner 10* and Mercury	2·00	2·00
3980	$2.50 Pillars of Creation in the Eagle Nebula	2·00	2·00
3981	$2.50 Orion Nebula	2·00	2·00
3982	$2.50 Crab Nebula		
3983	$2.50 Horsehead Nebula	2·00	2·00

231 True Tulip Shell (*Fasciolaria tulipa*)

2009. Seashells of the World. Multicoloured.

3984	25c. Type **231**	20	25
3985	50c. Twisted plait olive (*Olivancillaria contortuplicata*)	40	35
3986	75c. The Junonia (*Scaphella junonia*)	60	45
3987	$1 Royal comb venus (*Pitar dione*)	85	60
MS3988	141×101 mm. $2×6 Lion's paw (*Lyropecten nodosus*); Banded tulip (*Fasciolaria lilium*); Flame auger (*Terebra taurinus*); Miniature melo (*Micromelo undata*); West Indian worm shell (*Vermiculariaspirata*); Mouse cowrie (*Cypraea mus*) (wrongly spelt 'cowry') (all vert)	9·00	9·00

The stamps and margins of No. **MS**3988 form a composite design showing a beach.

232 Blue Chromis (*Chromis cyaneus*)

2009. Tropical Fish. Multicoloured.

3989	$1 Type **232**	80	65
3990	$2 Clown wrasse (*Coris gaimard*)	1·50	1·50
3991	$4 Orange spotted filefish (*Oxymonacanthus longirostris*)	3·00	3·00
3992	$5 Palometa (*Trachinotus goodei*)	3·75	3·75
MS3993	140×100 mm. $2×6 Tiger grouper (*Mycteroperca tigris*); Bluehead wrasse (*Thalassoma bifasciatum*); Squirrel fish (*Sargocentron speniferun*); Queen parrotfish (*Scarus vetula*); Yellowtail snapper (*Ocyurus chrysurus*); Barred hamlet (*Hypoplectrus puella*)	9·00	9·00

The stamps and margins of No. **MS**3993 form a composite background design.

233 Pres. Barack Obama

2009. Inauguration of President Barack Obama. Multicoloured.

MS3994	130×100 mm. $2.75×4 Type **233**; Facing camera; Speaking, hand raised; Facing left	7·00	7·00
MS3995	100×70 mm. $10 Barack Obama and Capitol, Washington (37×50 mm)	9·50	9·50

The stamps and margins of Nos. **MS**3994/5 form a composite designs showing the US flag.

234 Ox Symbols on Prayer Wheels

2009. Chinese New Year. Year of the Ox. Sheet 190×78 mm. Multicoloured.

MS3996	$2.50 Type **234**×4 multicoloured	8·00	8·00

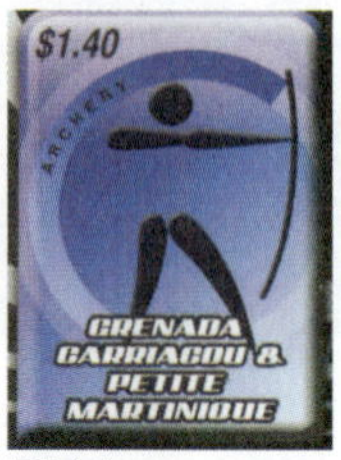

235 Archery

2009. China 2009 World Stamp Exhibition, Luoyang (1st issue). Sports of the Summer Games. Sheet 138×95 mm containing T 235 and similar vert designs. Multicoloured.

MS3997	Type **235**; Cycling; Wrestling; Boxing	4·00	4·00

236 Qianglong Emperor

2009. China 2009 World Stamp Exhibition (2nd issue). Qianglong Emperor (1736–96). Sheet 150×120 mm containing T 236 and similar vert designs. Multicoloured.

MS3998	Type **236**; Emperor and his court sitting by table; Sitting at writing desk; Qianglong Emperor (three quarter length portrait)	4·00	4·00

237 Elvis Presley

2009. Elvis Presley Commemoration. Sheet 153×124 mm containing T 237 and similar horiz designs. Multicoloured.

MS3999	Type **237**; In close up (blue inscriptions); Half length, holding microphone (magenta inscriptions); In close-up, singing (turquoise inscriptions)	8·00	8·00

238 Caribbean Spiny Lobsters

2009. Endangered Species. Caribbean Spiny Lobster (Panulirus argus). Multicoloured.

4000	$3 Type **238**	2·00	2·00
4001	$3 Three lobsters	2·00	2·00
4002	$3 Spiny lobster (side view)	2·00	2·00
4003	$3 Spiny lobster (front view)	2·00	2·00
MS4004	112×165 mm. Nos. 4000/3, each ×2	16·00	16·00
MS4005	112×94 mm. Nos. 4000/3	16·00	16·00

239 *Psilocybe mexicana*

2009. Fungi of the Caribbean. Multicoloured.

4006	25c. Type **239**	20	25
4007	$1 *Crinipellis piceae*	1·00	1·00
4008	$2 *Psilocybe subcubensis*	1·50	1·50
4009	$5 *Psilocybe cubensis*	3·75	3·75
MS4010	190×90 mm. $2.50×4 *Panaeolus fimicola; Psilocybe yungensis; Panaeolus subbalteatus; Russula cremeolilacina*	8·00	8·00
MS4011	124×95 mm. $3 *Psilocybe guilartensis*; $3 *Psilocybe aztecorum* (both 29×40 mm)	4·50	4·50

240 Abraham Lincoln as Young Man

2009. Birth Bicentenary of Abraham Lincoln (US President 1861–5). Sheet 175×136 mm containing T 240 and similar vert designs showing portraits. Multicoloured.

MS4012	Type **240**; Older, no beard; With beard; With beard, head and shoulders portrait	8·00	8·00

241 Pope Benedict XVI

2009. Visit of Pope Benedict XVI to Israel. Sheet 100×150 mm containing T 241 and similar horiz designs. Multicoloured. Litho.

MS4013	Type **241**; Pope Benedict XVI and Israel's President Shimon Peres at the President's residence; Pope visiting the Temple Mount, Jerusalem; Pope visiting Heichal Shlomo, Jerusalem	8·00	8·00

242 Don

2009. 25th Anniv of Teenage Mutant Ninja Turtles. Sheet 132×132 mm. containing T 242 and similar vert designs. Multicoloured.

MS4014	Type **242**; Leo; Rafe; Mike	8·00	8·00

243 Voyager 1, Saturn and Titan

2009. 40th Anniv of First Manned Moon Landing and International Year of Astronomy. T 243 and similar vert designs. Multicoloured.

MS4015	150×100 mm. $2×6 Type **243**×2; Apollo 11 Lunar Module×2; Voyager 1, Jupiter and its moons Europa, Io, Callisto and Ganymede×2	9·00	9·00
MS4016	100×70 mm. $6 Apollo 11 Lunar Module	4·50	4·50

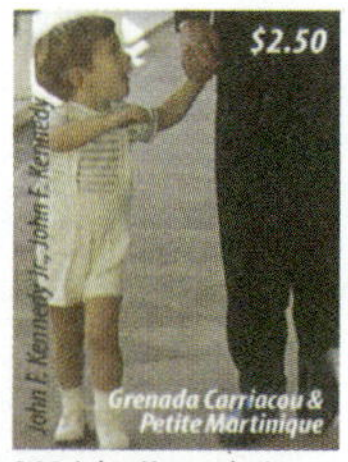

244 John Kennedy Jnr with Pres. Kennedy

2009. Tenth Death Anniv of John Kennedy Jnr. Sheet 130×100 mm containing T 244 and similar vert designs. Multicoloured.

MS4017	Type **244**; John Kennedy Jnr and his mother Jackie Onassis; John Kennedy Jnr; Pres. and Mrs. Kennedy with young John and Caroline	8·00	8·00

245 Elvis Presley

2010. 75th Birth Anniv of Elvis Presley. Sheet 190×127 mm containing T 245 and similar vert designs. Multicoloured.

MS4018	Type **245**; On stage, facing left, audience in background; In close-up, singing, facing left; Half kneeling, holding microphone	9·50	9·50

246 Elvis Presley as Tulsa McClean

2010. Elvis Presley in GI Blues. Multicoloured.

MS4019	90×125 mm. $6 Type **246**	4·25	4·25
MS4020	125×90 mm. $6 Poster for *GI Blues*	4·25	4·25
MS4021	125×90 mm. $6 Elvis Presley as Tulsa McClean (yellow background)	4·25	4·25
MS4022	90×125 mm. $6 As Tulsa McClean (seated on ground)	4·25	4·25

247 *Dendrophylax lindenii*

2010. Orchids of the Caribbean. Multicoloured.

4023	$1.20 Type **247**	95	95
4024	$1.80 *Scaphyglottis imbricata*	1·25	1·25
4025	$3 *Encyclia ceratistes*	2·25	2·25
4026	$5 *Scaphyglottis stellata*	4·25	4·25
MS4027	140×100 mm. $2.50×4 *Oncidium excavatum; Brassavola nodosa; Cattleya gaskelliana; Phalaenopsis cultivars*	8·00	8·00
MS4028	100×70 mm. $3×2 *Lepanthopsis floripecten*; Equitant *Oncidium*	4·25	4·25

248 Pres. Barack Obama

2010. Pres. Barack Obama's Nobel Peace Prize (2009). Sheet 126×178 mm containing T 248 and similar vert designs. Multicoloured.

MS4029	Type **248**; Smiling, facing towards left; Facing camera; Speaking	8·00	8·00

OFFICIAL STAMPS

1982. Optd P.R.G. (a) Nos. 400/12 and 414.

O1	5c. Yellow-tailed snapper	10	20
O2	6c. Mutton snapper	10	20
O3	10c. Cocoa damselfish	10	20
O4	12c. Royal gramma	10	20
O5	15c. Cherub angelfish	10	20
O6	20c. Black-barred soldierfish	10	20
O7	25c. Mottled grouper	10	20
O8	30c. Long-snouted butterflyfish	15	20
O9	40c. Puddingwife	15	25
O10	50c. Midnight parrotfish	20	30
O11	90c. Redspotted hawkfish	40	55
O12	$1 Hogfish	40	60
O13	$3 Beau Gregory	1·25	2·50
O14	$10 Barred hamlet	4·25	6·50

(b) Nos. 444/6 and 448/9.

O15	30c. Prince Charles and Lady Diana Spencer	2·00	2·00
O16	40c. Prince Charles and Lady Diana Spencer	1·60	1·60
O17	40c. Type **50**	2·00	2·75
O18	$2 Type **50**	2·50	3·50
O19	$4 Prince Charles as parachutist	6·50	8·50

(c) Nos. 473/6.

O20	**54**	20c. multicoloured	10	20
O21	-	40c. multicoloured	15	25
O22	-	$1 multicoloured	35	70
O23	-	$2 multicoloured	70	1·60

Pt. 1

GRENADINES OF ST VINCENT

Part of a group of Islands south of St. Vincent that include Bequia, Mustique, Canouan and Union.

100 cents = 1 dollar.

1973. Royal Wedding. As T 101a of Gibraltar. Multicoloured. Background colours given.

1	25c. green	10	10
2	$1 brown	15	15

1974. Nos. 286/300 of St. Vincent optd GRENADINES OF.

3	1c. Green-backed heron ("Green Heron")	10	10
4	2c. Lesser Antillean bullfinches ("Bullfinch")	15	15
6	4c. Rufous-throated solitaire ("Soufriere Bird") (vert)	10	10
7	5c. Red-necked pigeon ("Ramier") (vert)	10	10
8	6c. Bananaquits	10	10
9	8c. Purple-throated carib ("Humming Bird")	10	10
10	10c. Mangrove cuckoo (vert)	10	10
11	12c. Common black hawk ("Black Hawk") (vert)	20	15
12	20c. Bare-eyed thrush	20	20
13	25c. Lesser Antillean tanager ("Prince")	20	20
14	50c. Blue hooded euphonia	30	40
15	$1 Barn owl (vert)	60	75
16	$2.50 Yellow-bellied elaenia ("Crested Elaenia") (vert)	60	1·00
17	$5 Ruddy quail dove	80	1·75
25	3c. St. Vincent amazon ("St. Vincent Parrot")	25	30

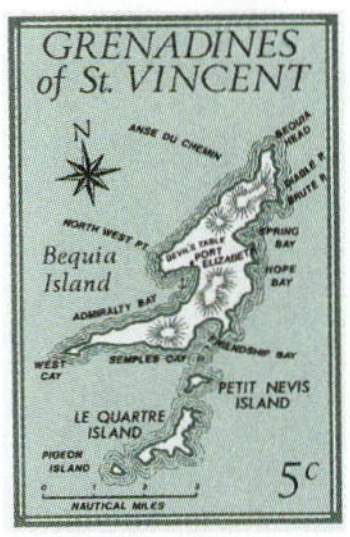

2 Map of Bequia

1974. Maps (1st series).

18	**2**	5c. black, green & deep green	10	10
19	-	15c. multicoloured	10	10
20	-	20c. multicoloured	10	10
21	-	30c. black, pink and red	10	10
22	-	40c. black, violet and purple	10	10
23	-	$1 black, ultramarine and blue	20	20

MAPS: 15c. Prune Island; 20c. Mayreau Island and Tobago Cays; 30c. Mustique Island; 40c. Union Island; $1 Canouan Island.

See also Nos. 85/8.

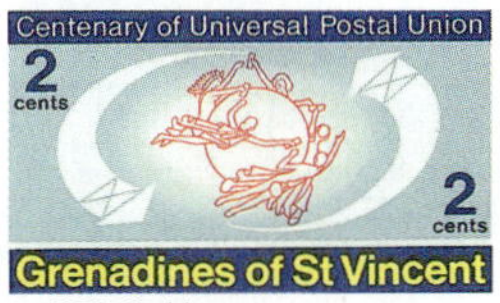

3a U.P.U. Emblem

1974. Centenary of U.P.U. Multicoloured.

26	2c. Type **3a**	10	10
27	15c. Globe within posthorn	10	10
28	40c. Map of St. Vincent and hand-cancelling	10	10
29	$1 Map of the World	25	15

4 Boat-building

1974. Bequia Island (1st series). Multicoloured.

31	30c. Careening at Port Elizabeth	10	15
32	35c. Admiralty Bay	10	15
33	$1 Fishing-boat race	15	25
34	5c. Type **4**	10	15

See also Nos. 185/88.

5 Music Volute

1974. Shells and Molluscs. Multicoloured.

35A	1c. American thorny oyster	10	10
36A	2c. Zigzag scallop	10	10
37A	3c. Reticulated cowrie-helmet	10	10
38A	4c. Type **5**	10	10
39A	5c. Amber pen shell	10	10
40A	6c. Angular triton	10	10
41A	8c. Flame helmet	10	10
42A	10c. Caribbean olive	10	10
43A	12c. American or common sundial	10	10
44A	15c. Glory of the Atlantic cone	25	20
45B	20c. Flame auger	30	20
46A	25c. King venus	50	20
47A	35c. Long-spined star shell	35	25
48A	45c. Speckled tellin	35	30
49A	50c. Rooster-tail conch	40	25
50B	$1 Green star shell	60	60
51A	$2.50 Antillean or incomparable cone	60	75
52A	$5 Rough file clam	75	80
52cA	$10 Measled cowrie	3·50	1·00

Nos. 38/42, 45, 47 and 49/50 come with and without an imprint below the design.

1974. Birth Centenary of Sir Winston Churchill. As Nos. 403/6 of St. Vincent, but inscr "GRENADINES OF ST. VINCENT" and values (Nos. 53/5) and colours changed.

53	**75**	5c. multicoloured	10	15
54	-	40c. multicoloured	10	15
55	-	50c. multicoloured	10	15
56	-	$1 multicoloured	20	50

6 Cotton House, Mustique

1975. Mustique Island. Multicoloured.

57	5c. Type **6**	10	10
58	35c. "Blue Waters", Endeavour Bay	10	10
59	45c. Endeavour Bay	10	10
60	$1 "Les Jolies Eaux", Gelliceaux Bay	25	20

7 "Danaus plexippus"

1975. Butterflies. Multicoloured.

61	3c. Type **7**	20	10
62	5c. "Agraulis vanillae"	20	10
63	35c. "Battus polydamas"	35	10
64	45c. "Evenus dindymus" and "Junonia evarete"	35	10
65	$1 "Anartia jatrophae"	60	45

8 Resort Pavilion

1975. Petit St. Vincent. Multicoloured.

66	5c. Type **8**	10	20
67	35c. The Harbour	10	20
68	45c. The Jetty	15	20
69	$1 Sailing in coral lagoon	50	1·10

9 Ecumenical Church, Mustique

1975. Christmas. Multicoloured.

70	5c. Type **9**	10	10
71	25c. Catholic Church, Union Island	10	10
72	50c. Catholic Church, Bequia	10	10
73	$1 Anglican Church, Bequia	25	15

10 Sunset Scene

1976. Union Island (1st series). Multicoloured.

74	5c. Type **10**	10	25
75	35c. Customs and Post Office, Clifton	10	20
76	45c. Anglican Church, Ashton	10	20
77	$1 Mail schooner, Clifton Harbour	25	80

See also Nos. 242/5.

11 Staghorn Coral

1976. Corals. Multicoloured.

78	5c. Type **11**	10	10
79	35c. Elkhorn coral	20	10
80	45c. Pillar coral	20	10
81	$1 Brain coral	40	20

12 25c. Bicentennial Coin

1976. Bicentenary of American Revolution.

82	**12**	25c. silver, black and blue	10	10
83	-	50c. silver, black and red	20	10
84	-	$1 silver, black and mauve	25	20

DESIGNS: 50c. Half-dollar coin; $1 One dollar coin.

1976. Maps (2nd series). As T 2.

85	5c. black, deep green and green	15	15
86	10c. black, green and blue	15	10
87	35c. black, brown and red	30	20
88	45c. black, red and orange	30	25

Nos. 85/8 exist in 7 different designs to each value as follows: A, Bequia, B, Canouan, C, Mayreau, D, Mustique, E, Petit St. Vincent, F, Prune, G, Union. To indicate any particular design use the appropriate catalogue No. together with the suffix for the island concerned.

13 Station Hill School and Post Office

1977. Mayreau Island. Multicoloured.

89	5c. Type **13**	10	10
90	35c. Church at Old Wall	10	10
91	45c. La Sourciere Anchorage	20	10
92	$1 Saline Bay	35	15

14 Coronation Crown Coin

1977. Silver Jubilee. Multicoloured.

93	25c. Type **14**	15	10
94	50c. Silver Wedding crown	20	10
95	$1 Silver Jubilee crown	20	15

15 Fiddler Crab

1977. Crustaceans. Multicoloured.

96	5c. Type **15**	15	15
97	35c. Ghost crab	25	15
98	50c. Blue crab	30	20
99	$1.25 Spiny lobster	60	90

16 Snorkel Diving

1977. Prune Island. Multicoloured.

100	5c. Type **16**	15	10
101	35c. Palm Island Resort	20	15
102	45c. Casuarina Beach	20	15
103	$1 Palm Island Beach Club	60	1·10

17 Mustique Island

1977. Royal Visit. Surch as in T 17.

104	**17**	40c. turquoise and green	20	10
105	**17**	$2 ochre and brown	45	25

18 The Clinic, Charlestown

1977. Canouan Island (1st series). Mult.

106	5c. Type **18**	10	15
107	35c. Town jetty, Charlestown	20	15
108	45c. Mail schooner arriving at Charlestown	20	15
109	$1 Grand Bay	40	1·00

See also Nos. 307/10.

19 Tropical Mockingbird

1978. Birds and their Eggs. Multicoloured.

110	1c. Type **19**	10	60
111	2c. Mangrove cuckoo	15	60
112	3c. Osprey	20	60
113	4c. Smooth-billed ani	20	60
114	5c. House wren	20	40
115	6c. Bananaquit	20	40
116	8c. Carib grackle	20	45
117	10c. Yellow-bellied elaenia	20	45
118	12c. Collared plover	30	1·25
119	15c. Cattle egret	30	45
120	20c. Red-footed booby	30	45
121	25c. Red-billed tropic bird	30	45
122	40c. Royal tern	45	1·00
123	50c. Grenada flycatcher ("Rusty-tailed Flycatcher")	45	1·00
124	80c. American purple gallinule ("Purple Gallinule")	70	1·00
125	$1 Broad-winged hawk	75	1·00
126	$2 Scaly-breasted ground dove ("Common Ground Dove")	75	1·60
127	$3 Laughing gull	1·00	1·75
128	$5 Common noddy ("Brown Noddy")	1·00	1·75
129	$10 Grey kingbird	1·25	2·25

19a Worcester Cathedral

1978. 25th Anniv of Coronation. British Cathedrals. Multicoloured.

130	5c. Type **19a**	10	10
131	40c. Coventry Cathedral	10	10
132	$1 Winchester Cathedral	15	20
133	$3 Chester Cathedral	25	45
MS134	130×102 mm. Nos. 130/3	45	80

20 Green Turtle

1978. Turtles. Multicoloured.

135	5c. Type **20**	10	10
136	40c. Hawksbill turtle	15	10
137	50c. Leatherback turtle	15	10
138	$1.25 Loggerhead turtle	40	40

21 Three Kings following Star

1978. Christmas. Scenes and Verses from the Carol "We Three Kings". Multicoloured.

139	5c. Type **21**	10	10
140	10c. King presenting gold	10	10
141	25c. King presenting frankincense	10	10
142	50c. King presenting myrrh	10	10
143	$2 Kings paying homage to infant Jesus	30	20
MS144	154×175 mm. Nos. 139/43	70	1·25

22 Sailing Yachts

1979. National Regatta.

145	**22** 5c. multicoloured	10	10
146	- 40c. multicoloured	20	10
147	- 50c. multicoloured	25	10
148	- $2 multicoloured	75	60

DESIGNS: 40c. to $2, Various sailing yachts.

22a Green Iguana

1979. Wildlife. Multicoloured.

149	20c. Type **22a**	10	25
150	40c. Common opossum ("Manicou")	15	25
151	$2 Red-legged tortoise	60	1·10

22b Sir Rowland Hill

1979. Death Centenary of Sir Rowland Hill. Multicoloured.

152	80c. Type **22b**	15	15
153	$1 Great Britain 1d. and 4d. stamps of 1858 with "A10" (Kingstown, St. Vincent) postmark	15	25
154	$2 St. Vincent ½d and 1d. stamps of 1894 with Bequia postmark	25	40
MS155	165×115 mm. Nos. 124/6 and 152/4	1·40	2·50

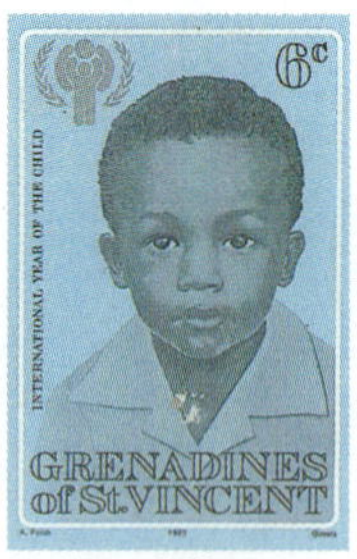

22c Young Child

1979. International Year of the Child. Designs showing portraits of young children.

156	**22c** 6c. black, silver and blue	10	10
157	- 40c. black, silver & salmon	10	10
158	- $1 black, silver and buff	20	10
159	- $3 black, silver and lilac	45	30

22d National Flag and "Ixora salicifolia" (flower)

1979. Independence. Multicoloured.

160	5c. Type **22d**	10	10
161	40c. House of Assembly and "Ixora odorata" (flower)	10	10
162	$1 Prime Minister R. Milton Cato and "Ixora javanica" (flower)	20	20

23 False Killer Whale

1980. Whales and Dolphins. Multicoloured.

163	10c. Type **23**	45	30
164	50c. Spinner dolphin	45	35
165	90c. Bottle-nosed dolphin	50	80
166	$2 Short-finned pilot whale ("Blackfish")	1·25	2·25

23a Queen Elizabeth II

1980. "London 1980" International Stamp Exhibition. Multicoloured.

167	40c. Type **23a**	10	15
168	50c. St. Vincent 2c. stamp of 1965	15	15
169	$3 First Grenadines stamps	40	1·25
MS170	165×115 mm. Nos. 122/3, 127 and 167/9	2·00	2·50

23b Running

1980. Sport. Multicoloured.

171	25c. Type **23b**	10	10
172	50c. Sailing	10	10
173	$1 Long-jumping	20	20
174	$2 Swimming	30	30

1980. Hurricane Relief. Nos. 171/4 optd HURRICANE RELIEF 50c.

175	**22** 25c.+50c. multicoloured	10	30
176	- 50c.+50c. multicoloured	15	40
177	- $1+50c. multicoloured	20	50
178	- $2+50c. multicoloured	30	70

24 Scene and Verse from the Carol "De Borning Day"

1980. Christmas. Multicoloured.

179	5c. Type **24**	10	10
180	50c. "Mary and de Baby lonely"	10	10
181	60c. "Mary and de Baby weary"	10	10
182	$1 "Mary and de Baby rest easy"	15	15
183	$2 "Star above shine in de sky"	25	25
MS184	159×178 mm. Nos. 179/83	50	1·40

25 Post Office, Port Elizabeth

1981. Bequia Island (2nd series). Mult.

185	50c. Type **25**	15	20
186	60c. Moonhole	15	20
187	$1.50 Fishing boats, Admiralty Bay	30	55
188	$2 "The Friendship Rose" (yacht) at jetty	50	70

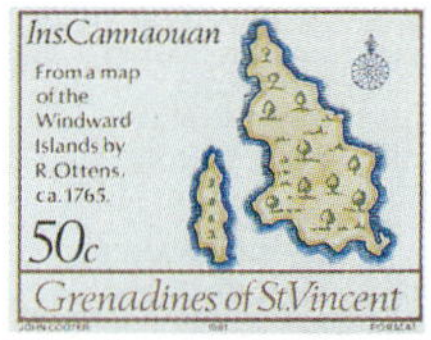

26 Ins. Cannaouan (from map of Windward Islands by R. Ottens, c. 1765)

1981. Details from Early Maps. Multicoloured.

189	50c. Type **26**	30	30
190	50c. Cannouan Is. (from chart by J. Parsons, 1861)	30	30
191	60c. Ins. Moustiques (from map of Windward Islands by R. Ottens, c. 1765)	30	35
192	60c. Mustique Is. (from chart by J. Parsons, 1861)	30	35
193	$2 Ins. Bequia (from map of Windward Islands by R. Ottens, c.1765)	50	75
194	$2 Bequia Is. (from map surveyed in 1763 by T. Jefferys)	50	75

26a "Mary"

1981. Royal Wedding. Royal Yachts. Multicoloured.

195	50c. Type **26a**	10	15
196	50c. Prince Charles and Lady Diana Spencer	35	40
197	$3 "Alexandra"	20	30
198	$3 As No. 196	60	90
199	$3.50 "Britannia"	25	35
200	$3.50 As No. 196	65	90
MS201	120×109 mm. $5 As No. 196	75	75

27 Bar Jack

1981. Game Fish. Multicoloured.

204	10c. Type **27**	15	10
205	50c. Tarpon	30	10
206	60c. Cobia	35	10
207	$2 Blue marlin	1·00	70

28 H.M.S. "Experiment" (frigate)

1982. Ships. Multicoloured.

208	1c. Type **28**	10	20
209	3c. "Lady Nelson" (cargo liner)	15	20
210	5c. "Daisy" (brig)	20	20
211	6c. Carib canoe	10	20
212	10c. "Hairoun Star" (freighter)	20	10
213	15c. "Jupiter" (liner)	40	10
214	20c. "Christina" (steam yacht)	40	10
215	25c. "Orinoco" (mail paddle-steamer)	40	15
216	30c. H.M.S. "Lively" (frigate)	40	15
217	50c. "Alabama" (Confederate warship)	50	30
218	60c. "Denmark" (freighter)	60	30
219	75c. "Santa Maria"	1·00	50
220	$1 "Baffin" (research vessel)	80	55
221	$2 "Queen Elizabeth 2" (liner)	1·00	1·00
222	$3 R.Y. "Britannia"	1·00	1·50
223	$5 "Geeststar" (freighter)	1·00	1·75
224	$10 "Grenadines Star" (ferry)	1·25	4·00

29 Prickly Pear Fruit

1982. Prickly Pear Cactus. Multicoloured.

225	10c. Type **29**	15	15
226	50c. Prickly pear flower buds	35	35
227	$1 Flower of prickly pear cactus	60	60
228	$2 Prickly pear cactus	1·25	1·25

30 Anne Neville, Princess of Wales, 1470

1982. 21st Birthday of Princess of Wales. Multicoloured.

229	50c. Type **30**	10	15
230	60c. Coat of arms of Anne Neville	10	15
231	$6 Diana, Princess of Wales	60	80

31 Old and New Uniforms

1982. 75th Anniv of Boy Scout Movement. Multicoloured.

232	$1.50 Type **31**	50	75
233	$2.50 Lord Baden-Powell	60	1·00

1982. Birth of Prince William of Wales. Nos. 224/6 optd ROYAL BABY and Island name.

234	50c. Type **30**	10	15
235	60c. Coat of arms of Anne Neville	10	15
236	$6 Diana, Princess of Wales	60	80

Nos. 229/32 exist optd with 5 different island names as follows: A, Bequia, B, Canouan, C, Mayreau, D, Mustique, E, Union Island. To indicate any particular overprint use the appropriate catalogue No. together with the suffix for the island concerned.

33 Silhouette Figures of Mary and Joseph

1982. Christmas. Silhouette of figures. Multicoloured.

237	10c. Type **33**	10	10
238	$1.50 Animals in stable	45	45
239	$2.50 Mary and Joseph with baby Jesus	60	60
MS240	168×99 mm. Nos. 237/9	1·00	2·00

1983. No. 123 surch 45c.

241	45c. on 50c. Grenada flycatcher	55	30

35 Power Station, Clifton

1983. Union Island (2nd issue). Multicoloured.

242	50c. Type **35**	25	15
243	60c. Sunrise, Clifton harbour	25	15
244	$1.50 Junior Secondary School, Ashton	60	40
245	$2 Frigate Rock and Conch Shell Beach	85	55

36 British Man-of-war

1983. Bicentenary of Treaty of Versailles. Mult.

246	45c. Type **36**	35	15
247	60c. American man-of-war	35	15
248	$1.50 Soldiers carrying U.S flags	75	45
249	$2 British troops in battle	80	55

37 Montgolfier Balloon, 1783

1983. Bicentenary of Manned Flight. Mult.

250	45c. Type **37**	15	15
251	60c. Ayres Turbo Thrush Commander (horiz)	15	15
252	$1.50 Lebaudy-Juillot airship No. 1 "La Jaune" (horiz)	40	45
253	$2 Space shuttle "Columbia" (horiz)	40	55
MS254	110×145 mm. Nos. 250/3	1·00	1·50

38 Coat of Arms of Henry VIII

1983. Leaders of the World. British Monarchs. Multicoloured.

255	60c. Type **38**	10	25
256	60c. Henry VIII	10	25
257	60c. Coat of Arms of James I	10	25
258	60c. James I	10	25
259	75c. Henry VIII at Hampton Court	10	25
260	75c. Hampton Court	10	25
261	75c. James I at Edinburgh Castle	10	25
262	75c. Edinburgh Castle	10	25
263	$2.50 The "Mary Rose"	25	35
264	$2.50 Henry VIII and Portsmouth harbour	25	35
265	$2.50 Gunpowder Plot	25	35
266	$2.50 James I and Gunpowder Plot	25	35

39 Quarter Dollar and Half Dollar, 1797

1983. Old Coinage. Multicoloured.

267	20c. Type **39**	10	10
268	45c. Nine Bitts, 1811–14	15	15
269	75c. Twelve Bitts and Six Bitts, 1811–14	25	25
270	$3 Sixty-six Shillings, 1798	80	80

40 Class D13

1984. Leaders of the World. Railway Locomotives (1st series). The first design in each pair shows technical drawings and the second the locomotive at work.

271	5c. multicoloured	10	10
272	5c. multicoloured	10	10
273	10c. multicoloured	10	10
274	10c. multicoloured	10	10
275	15c. multicoloured	10	15
276	15c. multicoloured	10	15
277	35c. multicoloured	10	20
278	35c. multicoloured	10	20
279	45c. multicoloured	10	20
280	45c. multicoloured	10	20
281	60c. multicoloured	15	20
282	60c. multicoloured	15	20
283	$1 multicoloured	15	25
284	$1 multicoloured	15	25
285	$2.50 multicoloured	25	35
286	$2.50 multicoloured	25	35

DESIGNS: Nos. 271/2, Class D13, U.S.A., 1892 (Type **40**); 273/4, High Speed Train 125, Great Britain (1980); 275/6, Class T9, Great Britain (1899); 277/8, "Claud Hamilton", Great Britain (1900); 279/80, Class J, U.S.A. (1941); 281/2, Class D16, U.S.A. (1895); 283/4, "Lode Star", Great Britain (1907); 285/6, "Blue Peter", Great Britain (1948).

See also Nos. 321/26, 351/8, 390/7, 412/9, 443/58, 504/19 and 520/35.

41 Spotted Eagle Ray

1984. Reef Fishes. Multicoloured.

287	45c. Type **41**	25	20
288	60c. Queen triggerfish	25	35
289	$1.50 White spotted filefish	40	1·25
290	$2 Schoolmaster	40	1·50

42 R. A. Woolmer

1984. Leaders of the World. Cricketers (1st series). The first design in each pair shows a portrait and the second the cricketer in action.

291	1c. multicoloured	10	10
292	1c. multicoloured	10	10
293	3c. multicoloured	10	10
294	3c. multicoloured	10	10
295	5c. multicoloured	10	10
296	5c. multicoloured	10	10
297	30c. multicoloured	30	30
298	30c. multicoloured	30	30
299	60c. multicoloured	40	40
300	60c. multicoloured	40	40
301	$1 multicoloured	40	40
302	$1 multicoloured	40	40
303	$2 multicoloured	45	70
304	$2 multicoloured	45	70
305	$3 multicoloured	55	80
306	$3 multicoloured	55	80

DESIGNS: Nos. 291/2, R. A. Woolmer (Type **42**); K. S. Ranjitsinhji; 295/6, W. R. Hammond; 297/8, D. L. Underwood; 299/300, W. G. Grace; 301/2, E. A. E. Baptiste; 303/4, A. P. E. Knott; 305/6, L. E. G. Ames.

See also Nos. 331/8 and 364/9.

43 Junior Secondary School

1984. Canouan Island (2nd series). Multicoloured.

307	35c. Type **43**	20	20
308	45c. Police Station	50	25
309	$1 Post Office	50	55
310	$3 Anglican Church	1·00	1·75

1984. Leaders of the World. Railway Locomotives (2nd issue). As T 40. The first design in each pair shows technical drawings and the second the locomotive at work.

311	1c. multicoloured	10	10
312	1c. multicoloured	10	10
313	5c. multicoloured	10	10
314	5c. multicoloured	10	10
315	20c. multicoloured	15	15
316	20c. multicoloured	15	15
317	35c. multicoloured	15	15
318	35c. multicoloured	15	15
319	60c. multicoloured	25	25
320	60c. multicoloured	25	25
321	$1 multicoloured	25	30
322	$1 multicoloured	25	30
323	$1.50 multicoloured	30	40
324	$1.50 multicoloured	30	40
325	$3 multicoloured	35	55
326	$3 multicoloured	35	55

DESIGNS: Nos. 311/12, Class C62, Japan (1948); 313/14, Class V, Great Britain (1903); 315/16, Richard Trevithick's "Catch-Me-Who-Can", Great Britain (1808); 317/18, Class E10, Japan (1948); 319/20, "J. B. Earle", Great Britain (1904); 321/2, No. 762 "Lyn", Great Britain (1898); 323/4, "Talyllyn", Great Britain (1865); 325/6, "Cardean", Great Britain (1906).

44 Lady of the Night

1984. Night-blooming Flowers. Mult.

327	35c. Type **44**	30	30
328	45c. Four o'clock	35	35
329	75c. Mother-in-law's tongue	45	60
330	$3 Queen of the night	1·10	2·75

1984. Leaders of the World. Cricketers (2nd series). As T 42. The first in each pair listed shows a head portrait and the second the cricketer in action.

331	5c. multicoloured	10	10
332	5c. multicoloured	10	10
333	30c. multicoloured	25	20
334	30c. multicoloured	25	20
335	$1 multicoloured	35	40
336	$1 multicoloured	35	40
337	$2.50 multicoloured	45	80
338	$2.50 multicoloured	45	80

DESIGNS: Nos. 331/2, S. F. Barnes; 333/4, R. Peel; 335/6, H. Larwood; 337/8, Sir John Hobbs.

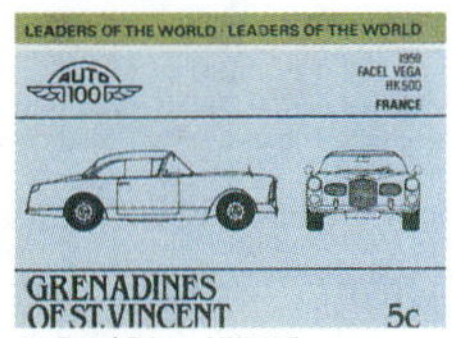

45 Facel "Vega HK500"

1984. Leaders of the World. Automobiles (1st series). The first design in each pair shows technical drawings and the second paintings.

339	5c. black, blue and green	10	10
340	5c. multicoloured	10	10
341	25c. black, lilac and pink	10	10
342	25c. multicoloured	10	10
343	50c. black, blue and orange	15	15
344	50c. multicoloured	15	15
345	$3 black, stone and brown	30	45
346	$3 multicoloured	30	45

DESIGNS: Nos. 339/40, Facel "Vega HK500" (Type **45**); 341/2, BMW "328"; 343/4, Frazer-Nash "TT Replica 1.5L"; 345/6, Buick "Roadmaster Riviera".

See also Nos. 378/85 and 431/42.

46 Three Wise Men and Star

1984. Christmas. Multicoloured.

347	20c. Type **46**	10	10
348	45c. Journeying to Bethlehem	15	25
349	$3 Presenting gifts	70	1·40
MS350	177×107 mm. Nos. 347/9	1·00	2·00

1985. Leaders of the World. Railway Locomotives (3rd series). As T 40. The first in each pair shows technical drawings and the second the locomotive at work.

351	1c. multicoloured	10	10
352	1c. multicoloured	10	10

353	15c. multicoloured	10	10
354	15c. multicoloured	10	10
355	75c. multicoloured	20	25
356	75c. multicoloured	20	25
357	$3 multicoloured	50	70
358	$3 multicoloured	50	70
MS359	142×122 mm. Nos. 355/8	1·75	6·50

DESIGNS: Nos. 351/2, P.L.M. "Grosse C", France (1898); 353/4, Class C12, Japan (1932); 355/6, Class D50, Japan (1923); 357/8, "Fire Fly", Great Britain (1840).

47 Caribbean King Crab

1985. Shell Fish. Multicoloured.

360	25c. Type **47**	20	15
361	60c. Queen or pink conch	30	35
362	$1 White sea urchin	35	60
363	$3 West Indian top shell or wilk	75	2·00

1985. Leaders of the World. Cricketers (3rd series). As T 42 (55, 60c.) the first in each pair showing a head portrait and the second the cricketer in action, or horiz designs showing teams ($2).

364	55c. multicoloured	25	35
365	55c. multicoloured	25	35
366	60c. multicoloured	25	40
367	60c. multicoloured	25	40
368	$2 multicoloured	40	85
369	$2 multicoloured	40	85

DESIGNS—VERT (As T **42**): Nos. 364/5 M. D. Moxon; 366/7, L. Potter. HORIZ (59×42 mm): No. 368, Kent team; 369, Yorkshire team.

48 "Cypripedium calceolus"

1985. Leaders of the World. Flowers. Multicoloured.

370	5c. Type **48**	10	10
371	5c. "Gentiana asclepiadea"	10	10
372	55c. "Clianthus formosus"	15	20
373	55c. "Clemisia coriacea"	15	20
374	60c. "Erythronium americanum"	15	20
375	60c. "Laelia anceps"	15	20
376	$2 "Leucadendron discolor"	35	50
377	$2 "Meconopsis horridula"	35	50

1985. Leaders of the World. Automobiles (2nd series). As T 45. The first in each pair shows technical drawings and the second paintings.

378	5c. black, yellow and blue	10	10
379	5c. multicoloured	10	10
380	60c. black, yellow and orange	15	15
381	60c. multicoloured	15	15
382	$1 black, green and blue	15	20
383	$1 multicoloured	15	20
384	$1.50 black, blue and green	15	25
385	$1.50 multicoloured	15	25

DESIGNS: Nos. 378/9, Winton (1903); 380/1, Invicta 4½ litre (1932); 382/3, Daimler "SP250 Dart" (1959); 384/5, Brabham "Repco BT19" (1966).

49 Windsurfing

1985. Tourism. Watersports. Multicoloured.

386	35c. Type **49**	15	15
387	45c. Water-skiing	15	15
388	75c. Scuba-diving	15	25
389	$3 Deep-sea game fishing	30	1·40

1985. Leaders of the World. Railway Locomotives (4th series). As T 40. The first design in each pair shows technical drawings and the second the locomotive at work.

390	10c. multicoloured	10	10
391	10c. multicoloured	10	10
392	40c. multicoloured	20	20
393	40c. multicoloured	20	20
394	50c. multicoloured	20	20
395	50c. multicoloured	20	20
396	$2.50 multicoloured	70	80
397	$2.50 multicoloured	70	80

DESIGNS: Nos. 390/1, Class 581 electric train, Japan (1968); 392/3, 231-132BT, Algeria (1936); 394/5, "Slieve Gullion", Ireland (1913); 396/7, Class "Beattie" well tank, Great Britain (1874).

50 Passion Fruits and Blossom

1985. Fruits and Blossoms. Multicoloured.

398	30c. Type **50**	15	20
399	75c. Guava	25	40
400	$1 Sapodilla	35	55
401	$2 Mango	50	1·10
MS402	145×120 mm. Nos. 398/401	2·00	2·25

51 Queen Elizabeth, the Queen Mother

1985. Leaders of the World. Life and Times of Queen Elizabeth, the Queen Mother. Various vertical portraits.

403	51	40c. multicoloured	10	20
404	-	40c. multicoloured	10	20
405	-	75c. multicoloured	15	20
406	-	75c. multicoloured	15	20
407	-	$1.10 multicoloured	15	20
408	-	$1.10 multicoloured	15	20
409	-	$1.75 multicoloured	15	30
410	-	$1.75 multicoloured	15	30
MS411		85×114 mm. $2 multicoloured; $2 multicoloured	50	1·50

Each value, issued in pairs, shows a floral pattern across the bottom of the portraits which stops short of the left-hand edge on the first stamp and of the right-hand edge on the second.

1985. Leaders of the World. Railway Locomotives (5th series). As T 40. The first design in each pair shows technical drawings and the second the locomotive at work.

412	35c. multicoloured	15	20
413	35c. multicoloured	15	20
414	70c. multicoloured	20	30
415	70c. multicoloured	20	30
416	$1.20 multicoloured	30	40
417	$1.20 multicoloured	30	40
418	$2 multicoloured	40	65
419	$2 multicoloured	40	65

DESIGNS: Nos. 412/13, "Coronation", Great Britain (1937); 414/15, Class E18, Germany (1935); 416/17, Hayes type, U.S.A. (1854); 418/19, Class 2120, Japan (1890).

1985. Royal Visit. Nos. 199/200, 222, 287, 398 and 407/8 optd CARIBBEAN ROYAL VISIT 1985 or surch also.

420	**50**	30c. multicoloured	80	1·50
421	**41**	45c. multicoloured	1·00	1·75
422	-	$1.10 multicoloured (No. 407)	1·75	4·00
423	-	$1.10 multicoloured (No. 408)	1·75	4·00
424	-	$1.50 on $3.50 mult (No. 199)	2·00	2·25
425	-	$1.50 on $3.50 mult (No. 200)	20·00	23·00
426	-	$3 multicoloured (No. 222)	2·75	3·75

52 Donkey Man

1985. Traditional Dances. Multicoloured.

427	45c. Type **52**	10	30
428	75c. Cake dance (vert)	15	40
429	$1 Bois-Bois man (vert)	15	55
430	$2 Maypole dance	25	1·10

1986. Leaders of the World. Automobiles (3rd series). As T 45. The first in each pair shows technical drawings and the second paintings.

431	15c. black, lilac and mauve	10	10
432	15c. multicoloured	10	10
433	45c. black, yellow and brown	10	20
434	45c. multicoloured	10	20
435	60c. black, green and blue	10	25
436	60c. multicoloured	10	25
437	$1 black, brown and green	15	25
438	$1 multicoloured	15	25
439	$1.75 black, yellow and orange	15	35
440	$1.75 multicoloured	15	35
441	$3 multicoloured	25	45
442	$3 multicoloured	25	45

DESIGNS: Nos. 431/2, Mercedes-Benz 4.5 litre (1914); 433/4, Rolls Royce "Silver Wraith" (1954); 435/6, Lamborghini "Countach" (1974); 437/8, Marmon "V-16" (1932); 439/40, Lotus-Ford "49 B" (1968); 441/2, Delage 1.5 litre (1927).

1986. Leaders of the World. Railway Locomotives (6th series). As T 40. The first in each pair shows technical drawings and the second the locomotive at work.

443	15c. multicoloured	15	10
444	15c. multicoloured	15	10
445	45c. multicoloured	20	20
446	45c. multicoloured	20	20
447	60c. multicoloured	20	30
448	60c. multicoloured	20	30
449	75c. multicoloured	20	35
450	75c. multicoloured	20	35
451	$1 multicoloured	25	40
452	$1 multicoloured	25	40
453	$1.50 multicoloured	25	50
454	$1.50 multicoloured	25	50
455	$2 multicoloured	30	65
456	$2 multicoloured	30	65
457	$3 multicoloured	30	80
458	$3 multicoloured	30	80

DESIGNS: Nos. 443/4, Class T15, Germany (1897); 445/6, Class 13, Great Britain (1900); 447/8, "Halesworth", Great Britain (1879); 449/50, Class "Problem", Great Britain (1859); 451/2, Class "Western" diesel, Great Britain (1961); 453/4, Drummond's "Bug", Great Britain (1899); 455/6, Class "Clan", Great Britain (1951); 457/8, Class 1800, Japan (1884).

52a Queen Elizabeth II

1986. 60th Birthday of Queen Elizabeth II. Mult.

459	5c. Type **52a**	15	15
460	$1 At Princess Anne's christening, 1950	30	40
461	$4 Princess Elizabeth	60	1·25
462	$6 In Canberra, 1982 (vert)	75	1·50
MS463	85×115 mm. $8 Queen Elizabeth II (different)	1·50	4·50

53 Handmade Dolls

1986. Handicrafts. Multicoloured.

464	10c. Type **53**	10	10
465	60c. Basketwork	20	35
466	$1 Scrimshaw work	30	50
467	$3 Model sailing dinghy	80	2·25

54 Uruguayan Team

1986. World Cup Football Championship, Mexico. Multicoloured.

468	1c. Type **54**	10	10
469	10c. Polish team	10	10
470	45c. Bulgarian player (28×42 mm)	25	30
471	75c. Iraqi player (28×42 mm)	35	40
472	$1.50 South Korean player (28×42 mm)	60	90
473	$2 Northern Irish player (28×42 mm)	70	1·10
474	$4 Portuguese team	1·00	1·50
475	$5 Canadian team	1·00	1·50
MS476	Two sheets, 85×114 mm. (a) $1 As No. 474. (b) $3 Type **54**. Set of 2 sheets	1·50	2·75

55 "Marasmius pallescens"

1986. Fungi. Multicoloured.

477	45c. Type **55**	2·25	75
478	60c. "Leucocoprinus fragilissimus"	2·50	1·10
479	75c. "Hygrocybe occidentalis"	2·75	1·60
480	$3 "Xerocomus hypoxanthus"	8·00	7·00

55a Miss Sarah Ferguson and Princess Diana applauding

1986. Royal Wedding (1st issue). Multicoloured.

481	60c. Type **55a**	20	30
482	60c. Prince Andrew at shooting match	20	30
483	$2 Prince Andrew and Miss Sarah Ferguson (horiz)	60	90
484	$2 Prince Charles with Prince Andrew, Princess Anne and Princess Margaret on balcony (horiz)	60	90
MS485	115×85 mm. $8 Duke and Duchess of York in carriage after wedding (horiz)	2·75	4·50

1986. Royal Wedding (2nd issue). Nos. 481/4 optd Congratulations to T.R.H. The Duke & Duchess of York.

486	60c. Miss Sarah Ferguson and Princess Diana applauding	30	65
487	60c. Prince Andrew at shooting match	30	65
488	$2 Prince Andrew and Miss Sarah Ferguson (horiz)	1·00	1·25
489	$2 Prince Charles, Prince Andrew, Princess Anne and Princess Margaret on balcony (horiz)	1·00	1·25

56 "Brachymesia furcata"

1986. Dragonflies. Multicoloured.

490	45c. Type **56**	25	20
491	60c. "Lepthemis vesiculosa"	30	40
492	75c. "Perithemis domitta"	30	45
493	$2.50 "Tramea abdominalis (vert)	45	1·40

1986. Centenary of Statue of Liberty. Vert views of Statue as T 323a of Grenada in seperate miniature sheets. Multicoloured.

MS494	Nine sheets, each 85×115 mm. $1.50; $1.75; $2; $2.50; $3; $3.50; $5; $6; $8. Set of 9 sheets	3·00	12·00

57 American Kestrel ("Sparrow Hawk")

1986. Birds of Prey. Multicoloured.

495	10c. Type **57**	75	45

496	45c. Common black hawk ("Black Hawk")	1·90	50
497	60c. Peregrine falcon ("Duck Hawk")	2·25	1·25
498	$4 Osprey ("Fish Hawk")	5·00	6·50

58 Santa playing Steel Band Drums

1986. Christmas. Multicoloured.

499	45c. Type **58**	30	30
500	60c. Santa windsurfing	35	35
501	$1.25 Santa skiing	60	85
502	$2 Santa limbo dancing	1·10	1·60
MS503	166×128 mm. Nos. 499/502	7·00	8·00

1987. Railway Locomotives (7th series). As T 40. The first in each pair shows technical drawings and the second the locomotive at work.

504	10c. multicoloured	15	10
505	10c. multicoloured	15	10
506	40c. multicoloured	25	25
507	40c. multicoloured	25	25
508	50c. multicoloured	30	30
509	50c. multicoloured	30	30
510	60c. multicoloured	30	30
511	60c. multicoloured	30	30
512	75c. multicoloured	30	40
513	75c. multicoloured	30	40
514	$1 multicoloured	30	50
515	$1 multicoloured	30	50
516	$1.25 multicoloured	30	60
517	$1.25 multicoloured	30	60
518	$1.50 multicoloured	40	75
519	$1.50 multicoloured	40	75

DESIGNS: Nos. 504/5, Class 1001, No. 1275, Great Britain (1874); 506/7, Class 4P Garratt, Great Britain (1927); 508/9, "Papyrus", Great Britain (1929); 510/11, Class VI, Great Britain (1930); 512/13, Class 40 diesel, No. D200, Great Britain (1958); 514/15, Class 42 "Warship" diesel, Great Britain (1958); 516/17, Class P-69, U.S.A. (1902); 518/19, Class 60-3 Shay, No. 15, U.S.A. (1913).

1987. Railway Locomotives (8th series). As T 40. The first in each pair shows technical drawings and the second the locomotive at work.

520	10c. multicoloured	15	15
521	10c. multicoloured	15	15
522	40c. multicoloured	25	30
523	40c. multicoloured	25	30
524	50c. multicoloured	30	35
525	50c. multicoloured	30	35
526	60c. multicoloured	30	40
527	60c. multicoloured	30	40
528	75c. multicoloured	30	45
529	75c. multicoloured	30	45
530	$1 multicoloured	30	45
531	$1 multicoloured	30	45
532	$1.50 multicoloured	40	55
533	$1.50 multicoloured	40	55
534	$2 multicoloured	45	70
535	$2 multicoloured	45	70

DESIGNS: Nos. 520/1, Class 142, East Germany (1977); 522/3, Class 120, West Germany (1979); 524/5, Class X, Australia (1954); 526/7, Class 59, Great Britain (1986); 528/9, New York Elevated Railroad "Spuyten Duyvel", U.S.A. (1875); 530/1, Camden & Amboy Railroad "Stevens" and rebuilt "John Bull", U.S.A. (1832); 532/3, Class Hl-d, No. 2850, Canada (1938); 534/5, "Pioneer Zephyr" 3-car diesel set, U.S.A. (1934).

59 Queen Elizabeth with Prince Andrew

1987. Royal Ruby Wedding and 150th Anniv of Queen Victoria's Accession.

536	**59**	15c. multicoloured	20	15
537	-	45c. brown, black and yellow	25	20
538	-	$1.50 multicoloured	30	55
539	-	$3 multicoloured	45	1·00
540	-	$4 multicoloured	50	1·25
MS541		85×115 mm. $6 multicoloured	2·00	3·25

DESIGNS: 45c. Queen Victoria and Prince Albert, c. 1855; $1.50, Queen and Prince Philip after Trooping the Colour, 1977; $3 Queen and Duke of Edinburgh, 1953; $4 Queen in her study, c. 1980; Princess Elizabeth, 1947.

60 Banded Coral Shrimp

1987. Marine Life. Multicoloured.

542	45c. Type **60**	55	35
543	50c. Arrow crab and flamingo tongue	60	50
544	65c. Cardinal fish	70	90
545	$5 Moray eel	2·00	4·00
MS546	85×115 mm. $5 Porcupinefish ("Puffer Fish")	2·50	5·00

61 "Australia IV"

1988. Ocean Racing Yachts. Multicoloured.

547	50c. Type **61**	30	35
548	65c. "Crusader II"	35	50
549	75c. "New Zealand II"	40	60
550	$2 "Italia"	60	1·25
551	$4 "White Crusader"	70	2·00
552	$5 "Stars and Stripes"	70	2·25
MS553	100×140 mm. $1 "Champosa V"	1·25	2·00

62 Seine-fishing Boats racing

1988. Bequia Regatta. Multicoloured.

554	5c. Type **62**	10	15
555	50c. "Friendship Rose" (cruising yacht)	15	30
556	75c. Fishing boats racing	20	45
557	$3.50 Yachts racing	75	2·25
MS558	115×85 mm. $8 Port Elizabeth, Bequia (60×40 mm)	3·25	6·00

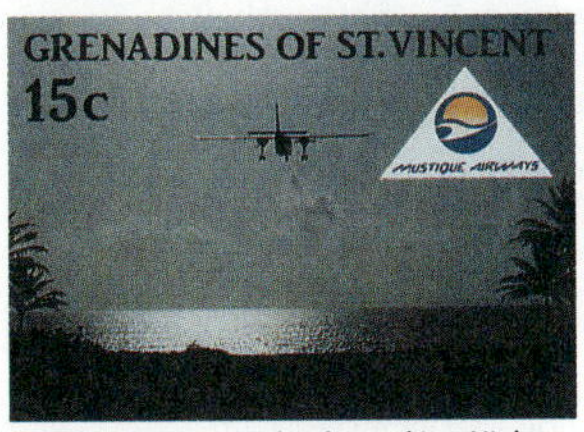

63 Britten Norman Islander making Night Approach

1988. Mustique Airways. Multicoloured.

559	15c. Type **63**	10	15
560	65c. Beech Baron aircraft in flight	15	35
561	75c. Britten Norman Islander over forest	15	35
562	$5 Beech Baron on airstrip	1·00	2·25
MS563	115×85 mm. $10 Baleine Falls (36×56 mm)	2·50	5·50

64 "Sv. Pyotr" in Arctic (Bering)

1988. Explorers. Multicoloured.

564	15c. Type **64**	35	20
565	75c. Bering's ships in pack ice	40	30
566	$1 Livingstone's steam launch "Ma-Robert" on Zambesi	40	40
567	$2 Meeting of Livingstone and H. M. Stanley at Ujiji	50	75
568	$3 Speke and Burton at Tabori	50	1·00
569	$3.50 Speke and Burton in canoe on Lake Victoria	50	1·25
570	$4 Sighting the New World, 1492	60	1·40
571	$4.50 Columbus trading with Indians	60	1·50
MS572	Two sheets, each 115×85 mm. (a) $5 Sextant and coastal scene. (b) $5 "Santa Maria" at anchor. Set of 2 sheets	2·50	5·50

65 Asif Iqbal Razvi

1988. Cricketers of 1988 International Season. Multicoloured.

573	20c. Type **65**	40	30
574	45c. R. J. Hadlee	60	50
575	75c. M. D. Crowe	80	80
576	$1.25 C. H. Lloyd	90	1·25
577	$1.50 A. R. Boarder	1·00	1·50
578	$2 M. D. Marshall	1·25	2·00
579	$2.50 G. A. Hick	1·25	2·25
580	$3.50 C. G. Greenidge (horiz)	1·25	2·75
MS581	115×85 mm. $3 As $2	3·75	7·00

66 Pam Shriver

1988. International Tennis Players. Mult.

582	15c. Type **66**	20	20
583	50c. Kevin Curran (vert)	20	30
584	75c. Wendy Turnbull (vert)	25	35
585	$1 Evonne Cawley (vert)	35	50
586	$1.50 Ilie Nastase	40	65
587	$2 Billie Jean King (vert)	45	75
588	$3 Bjorn Borg (vert)	55	1·25
589	$3.50 Virginia Wade with Wimbledon trophy (vert)	60	1·50
MS590	115×85 mm. $2.25, Stefan Edberg with Wimbledon cup; $2.25, Steffi Graf with Wimbledon trophy	1·50	3·50

No. 584 is inscribed "WENDY TURNBALL" in error.

67 Mickey and Minnie Mouse visiting Fatehpur Sikri

1989. "India-89" International Stamp Exhibition. Designs showing Walt Disney cartoon characters in India. Multicoloured.

591	1c. Type **67**	10	10
592	2c. Mickey and Minnie Mouse aboard "Palace on Wheels" train	10	10
593	3c. Mickey and Minnie Mouse passing Old Fort, Delhi	10	10
594	5c. Mickey and Minnie Mouse on camel, Pinjore Gardens, Haryana	10	10
595	10c. Mickey and Minnie Mouse at Taj Mahal, Agra	15	10
596	25c. Mickey and Minnie Mouse in Chandni Chowk, Old Delhi	20	10
597	$4 Goofy on elephant with Mickey and Minnie Mouse at Agra Fort, Jaipur	3·25	3·50
598	$5 Goofy, Mickey and Minnie Mouse at Gandhi Memorial Cape Comorin	3·00	3·50
MS599	Two sheets, each 127×102 mm. (a) $6 Mickey and Minnie Mouse in vegetable cart, Jaipur. (b) $6 Mickey and Minnie Mouse leaving carriage, Qutab Minar, New Delhi (vert). Set of 2 sheets	8·50	10·00

1989. Japanese Art. As T 177a of Gambia but horiz. Multicoloured.

600	5c. "The View at Yotsuya" (Hokusai)	20	20
601	30c. "Landscape at Ochanomizu" (Hokuju)	50	50
602	45c. "Itabashi" (Eisen)	60	60
603	65c. "Early Summer Rain" (Kunisada)	75	75
604	75c. "High Noon at Kasumigaseki" (Kuniyoshi)	80	80
605	$1 "The Yoshiwara Embankment by Moonlight" (Kuniyoshi)	1·00	1·00
606	$4 "The Bridge of Boats at Sano" (Hokusai)	2·75	3·00
607	$5 "Lingering Snow on Mount Hira" (Kunitora)	2·75	3·00
MS608	Two sheets, each 103×76 mm. (a) $6 "Colossus of Rhodes" (Kunitora). (b) $6 "Shinobazu Pond" (Kokan). Set of 2 sheets	7·00	8·00

68 Player with Ball and Mt. Vesuvius

1989. World Cup Football Championship, Italy (1st issue). Designs showing players and Italian landmarks. Multicoloured.

609	$1.50 Type **68**	1·40	1·40
610	$1.50 Fallen player, opponent kicking ball and Coliseum	1·40	1·40
611	$1.50 Player blocking ball and Venice	1·40	1·40
612	$1.50 Player tackling and Forum, Rome	1·40	1·40
613	$1.50 Two players competing for ball and Leaning Tower, Pisa	1·40	1·40
614	$1.50 Goalkeeper and Florence	1·40	1·40
615	$1.50 Two players competing for ball and St. Peter's, Vatican	1·40	1·40
616	$1.50 Player kicking ball and Pantheon	1·40	1·40

Nos 609/16 were printed together, se-tenant, forming a composite foreground design.

See also Nos. 680/3.

1989. 500th Anniv (1992) of Discovery of America by Columbus (1st issue). Pre-Columbian Arawak Society. As T 97a of Grenadines of Grenada. Multicoloured.

617	25c. Arawak smoking tobacco	45	30
618	75c. Arawak rolling cigar	75	65
619	$1 Applying body paint	90	80
620	$1.50 Making fire	1·25	1·50
621	$1.50 Cassava production	1·25	1·50
622	$1.50 Woman baking bread	1·25	1·50
623	$1.50 Using stone implement	1·25	1·50
624	$4 Arawak priest	2·50	3·00
MS625	Two sheets, each 70×84 mm. (a) $6 Arawak chief. (b) $6 Men returning from fishing expedition. Set of 2 sheets	11·00	12·00

Nos. 620/3 were printed together, se-tenant, forming a composite design.

See also Nos. 818/23 and 864/5.

70 Command Module "Columbia"

1989. 20th Anniv of First Manned Landing on Moon. Multicoloured.

626	5c. Type **70**	40	40
627	40c. Astronaut Neil Armstrong saluting U.S. flag	1·25	85
628	55c. "Columbia" above lunar surface	1·50	1·00
629	65c. Lunar module "Eagle" leaving moon	1·50	1·25
630	70c. "Eagle" on Moon	1·50	1·25
631	$1 "Columbia" re-entering Earth's atmosphere	1·60	1·60
632	$3 "Apollo 11" emblem	3·00	3·25
633	$5 Armstrong and Aldrin on Moon	3·25	3·75
MS634	Two sheets, each 110×82 mm. (a) $6 Launch of "Apollo 11" (vert). (b) $6 "Apollo 11" splashdown. Set of 2 sheets	11·00	12·00

71 "Marpesia petreus"

1989. Butterflies. Multicoloured.

635	5c. Type **71**	50	50
636	30c. "Papilio androgeus"	1·25	60
637	45c. "Strymon maesites"	1·50	65
638	65c. "Junonia coenia"	1·75	1·40
639	75c. "Eurema gratiosa"	2·00	1·50
640	$1 "Hypolimnas misippus"	2·00	1·75
641	$4 "Urbanus proteus"	4·25	4·50
642	$5 "Junonia evarete"	4·25	4·50
MS643	Two sheets. (a) 76×104 mm. $6 "Phoebis agarithe". (b) 104×76 mm. $6 "Dryas julia". Set of 2 sheets	15·00	13·00

72 "Solanum urens"

1989. Flowers from St. Vincent Botanical Gardens. Multicoloured.

644	80c. Type **72**	1·50	1·50
645	$1.25 "Passiflora andersonii"	2·00	2·00
646	$1.65 "Miconia andersonii"	2·25	2·25
647	$1.85 "Pitcairnia sulphurea"	2·50	2·50

1989. Christmas. As T 183 of Gambia. Mult.

648	5c. Goofy and Mickey Mouse in Rolls Royce "Silver Ghost", 1907	20	15
649	10c. Daisy Duck driving first Stanley Steamer, 1897	20	15
650	15c. Horace Horsecollar and Clarabelle Cow in Darracq "Genevieve", 1904	25	20
651	45c. Donald Duck driving Detroit electric coupe, 1914	50	40
652	55c. Mickey and Minnie Mouse in first Ford, 1896	55	40
653	$2 Mickey Mouse driving Reo "Runabout", 1904	2·00	2·00
654	$3 Goofy driving Winton mail truck, 1899	2·75	2·75
655	$5 Mickey and Minnie Mouse in Duryea car, 1893	3·50	4·00
MS656	Two sheets, each 127×102 mm. (a) $6 Mickey and Minnie Mouse in Pope-Hartford, 1912. (b) $6 Mickey and Minnie Mouse in Buick "Model 10", 1908. Set of 2 sheets	10·00	12·00

1990. 50th Anniv of Second World War. As T 354c of Grenada. Multicoloured.

657	10c. Destroyer in action, First Battle of Narvik, 1940	35	25
658	15c. Allied tank at Anzio, 1944	45	35
659	20c. U.S. carrier under attack, Battle of Midway, 1942	50	40
660	45c. North American B-25 Mitchell bombers over Gustav Line, 1944	80	70
661	55c. Map showing Allied zones of Berlin, 1945	85	75
662	65c. German U-boat pursuing convoy, Battle of the Atlantic, 1943	90	80
663	90c. Allied tank, North Africa, 1943	1·25	1·00
664	$3 U.S. forces landing on Guam, 1944	2·75	2·75
665	$5 Crossing the Rhine, 1945	3·75	3·75
666	$6 Japanese battleships under attack, Lete Gulf, 1944	4·25	4·25
MS667	100×70 mm. $6 Avro Type **683** Lancaster Mk III on "Dambusters" raid, 1943	5·00	6·00

1990. "Stamp World London 90" International Stamp Exhibition (1st issue). Mickey's Shakespeare Company. As T 193 of Gambia showing Walt Disney cartoon characters. Multicoloured.

668	20c. Goofy as Mark Anthony ("Julius Caesar")	40	20
669	30c. Clarabelle Cow as the Nurse ("Romeo and Juliet")	45	25
670	45c. Pete as Falstaff ("Henry IV")	60	40
671	50c. Minnie Mouse as Portia ("The Merchant of Venice")	65	40
672	$1 Donald Duck as Hamlet ("Hamlet")	1·25	85
673	$2 Daisy Duck as Ophelia ("Hamlet")	2·00	2·00
674	$4 Donald and Daisy Duck as Benedick and Beatrice ("Much Ado About Nothing")	3·50	3·50
675	$5 Minnie Mouse and Donald Duck as Katherine and Petruchio ("The Taming of the Shrew")	3·50	3·50
MS676	Two sheets, each 127×101 mm. (a) $6 Clarabelle as Titania ("A Midsummer Night's Dream") (vert). (b) $6 Mickey Mouse as Romeo ("Romeo and Juliet") (vert). Set of 2 sheets	11·00	12·00

74 Exhibition Emblem

1990. "Stamp World London 90" International Stamp Exhibition (2nd issue). 150th Anniv of the Penny Black.

677	74	$1 black, pink and mauve	1·50	1·25
678	-	$5 black, lilac and blue	3·75	4·25
MS679		130×100 mm. $6 black and pale blue	5·00	6·00

DESIGNS: $5 Negative image of Penny Black; $6 Penny Black.

74a McCleish, Scotland

1990. World Cup Football Championship, Italy (2nd issue). Multicoloured.

680	25c. Type **74a**	80	40
681	50c. Rasul, Egypt	1·10	80
682	$2 Lindenberger, Austria	2·75	2·75
683	$4 Murray, U.S.A.	3·75	4·25
MS684	Two sheets, each 102×77 mm. (a) $6 Robson, England. (b) $6 Gullit, Netherlands. Set of 2 sheets	16·00	12·00

74b "Paphiopedilum"

1990. "EXPO 90" International Garden and Greenery Exposition, Osaka. Orchids. Mult.

685	5c. Type **74b**	80	50
686	25c. "Dendrobium phalaenopsis" and "Cymbidium hybrid"	1·75	90
687	30c. "Miltonia candida hybrid"	1·75	90
688	50c. "Epidendrum ibaguense" and "Cymbidium" Elliot Rogers	2·25	1·25
689	$1 "Rossioglossum grande"	2·75	1·75
690	$2 "Phalaenopsis" Elisa Chang Lou and "Masdevallia coccinea"	3·25	2·50
691	$4 "Cypripedium acaule" and "Cypripedium calceolus"	3·75	4·00
692	$5 "Orchis spectabilis"	3·75	4·00
MS693	Two sheets, each 108×78 mm. (a) $6 "Dendrobium anosmum". (b) $6 "Epidendrum ibaguense" and "Phalaenopsis". Set of 2 sheets	13·00	13·00

75 Scaly-breasted Ground Dove ("Common Ground Dove")

1990. Birds of the Caribbean. Multicoloured.

694	5c. Type **75**	20	20
695	25c. Purple martin	40	40
696	45c. Painted bunting	70	70
697	55c. Blue-hooded euphonia	80	80
698	75c. Blue-grey tanager	1·00	1·00
699	$1 Red-eyed vireo	1·25	1·25
700	$2 Palm chat	2·00	2·00
701	$3 Northern jacana ("North American Jacana")	2·50	2·50
702	$4 Green-throated carib	2·75	2·75
703	$5 St. Vincent amazon ("St. Vincent Parrot")	3·00	3·00
MS704	Two sheets, each 117×87 mm. (a) $3 Magnificent frigate bird; $3 Bananaquit. (b) $6 Red-legged honeycreeper. Set of 2 sheets	9·50	10·00

1991. 90th Birthday of Queen Elizabeth the Queen Mother. As T 194 of Gambia.

705	$2 multicoloured	1·90	1·25
706	$2 multicoloured	1·90	1·25
707	$2 multicoloured	1·90	1·25
708	$2 multicoloured	1·90	1·25
709	$2 multicoloured	1·90	1·25
710	$2 multicoloured	1·90	1·25
711	$2 multicoloured	1·90	1·25
712	$2 multicoloured	1·90	1·25
713	$2 multicoloured	1·90	1·25
714	$2 multicoloured	1·90	1·25
715	$2 multicoloured	1·90	1·25
716	$2 multicoloured	1·90	1·25
717	$2 multicoloured	1·90	1·25
718	$2 multicoloured	1·90	1·25
719	$2 multicoloured	1·90	1·25
720	$2 multicoloured	1·90	1·25
721	$2 multicoloured	1·90	1·25
722	$2 multicoloured	1·90	1·25
723	$2 multicoloured	1·90	1·25
724	$2 multicoloured	1·90	1·25
725	$2 multicoloured	1·90	1·25
726	$2 multicoloured	1·90	1·25
727	$2 multicoloured	1·90	1·25
728	$2 multicoloured	1·90	1·25
729	$2 multicoloured	1·90	1·25
730	$2 multicoloured	1·90	1·25
731	$2 multicoloured	1·90	1·25
MS732	Nine sheets containing details of designs indicated. (a) 120×115 mm. $5 As No. 705. (b) 115×120 mm. $5 As No. 710. (c) 115×120 mm. $5 As No. 712. (d) 115×120 mm. $5 As No. 715. (e) 120×115 mm. $5 As No. 719. (f) 120×115 mm. $5 As No. 720. (g) 120×115 mm. $5 As No. 724. (h) 120×115 mm. $5 As No. 726. (i) 120×115 mm. $5 As No. 730. Set of 9 sheets	30·00	27·00

DESIGNS: No. 705, Lady Elizabeth Bowes-Lyon with sister; 706, Young Lady Elizabeth in long dress; 707, Young Lady Elizabeth wearing a hat; 708, Lady Elizabeth leaning on wall; 709, Lady Elizabeth on pony; 710, Studio portrait; 711, Lady Elizabeth in evening dress; 712, Duchess of York in fur-lined cloak; 713, Duchess of York holding rose; 714, Coronation, 1937; 715, King and Queen with Princess Elizabeth at Royal Lodge, Windsor; 716, Queen Elizabeth in blue hat; 717, King George VI and Queen Elizabeth; 718, Queen Elizabeth with Princess Elizabeth; 719, Queen Elizabeth watching sporting fixture; 720, Queen Elizabeth in white evening dress; 721, Princess Anne's christening, 1950; 722, Queen Mother with yellow bouquet; 723, Queen Mother and policewoman; 724, Queen Mother at ceremonial function; 725, Queen Mother in pink coat; 726, Queen Mother in academic robes; 727, Queen Mother in carriage with Princess Margaret; 728, Queen Mother in blue coat and hat; 729, Queen Mother with bouquet; 730, Queen Mother outside Clarence House on her birthday; 731, Queen Mother in turquoise coat and hat.

1991. Death Centenary (1990) of Vincent van Gogh (artist). As T 200b of Gambia. Mult.

733	5c. "View of Arles with Irises"	40	30
734	10c. "Saintes-Maries" (vert)	40	30
735	15c. "Old Woman of Arles" (vert)	50	30
736	20c. "Orchard in Blossom, bordered by Cypresses"	55	30
737	25c. "Three White Cottages in Saintes-Maries"	55	30
738	35c. "Boats at Saintes-Maries"	70	40
739	40c. "Interior of a Restaurant in Arles"	75	45
740	45c. "Peasant Women" (vert)	80	50
741	55c. "Self-portrait" (vert)	90	60
742	60c. "Pork Butcher's Shop from a Window" (vert)	1·00	70
743	75c. "The Night Cafe in Arles"	1·10	80
744	$1 "2nd Lieut. Millet of the Zouaves"	1·40	95
745	$2 "The Cafe Terrace, Place du Forum, Arles at Night" (vert)	2·25	2·25
746	$3 "The Zouave" (vert)	2·75	3·00
747	$4 "The Two Lovers" (detail) (vert)	3·50	3·75
748	$5 "Still Life"	3·75	4·00
MS749	Four sheets, each 112×76 mm. (a) $5 "Street in Saintes-Maries" (horiz). (b) $5 "Lane near Arles" (horiz). (c) $6 "Harvest at La Crau, with Montmajour in the Background" (horiz). (d) $6 "The Sower". Imperf. Set of 4 sheets	21·00	19·00

1991. 65th Birthday of Queen Elizabeth II. As T 198a of Gambia. Multicoloured.

750	15c. Inspecting the Yeomen of the Guard	30	20
751	40c. Queen Elizabeth II with the Queen Mother at the Derby, 1988	55	30
752	$2 The Queen and Prince Philip leaving Euston, 1986	2·00	2·00
753	$4 The Queen at the Commonwealth Institute, 1987	2·75	3·00
MS754	68×90 mm. $5 Queen Elizabeth and Prince Philip with Prince Andrew in naval uniform	4·75	4·75

1991. 10th Wedding Anniv of Prince and Princess of Wales. As T 198b of Gambia. Multicoloured.

755	10c. Prince and Princess at polo match, 1987	1·00	30
756	50c. Separate family portraits	1·75	55
757	$1 Prince William and Prince Henry at Kensington Palace, 1991	1·75	1·00
758	$5 Portraits of Prince Charles and Princess Diana	4·75	4·00
MS759	68×90 mm. $5 Separate portraits of Prince and Princess and sons	8·00	5·00

76 Class 150 Steam Locomotive and Map

1991. "Phila Nippon '91" International Stamp Exhibition, Toyko. Japanese Railway Locomotives. Each in black, red and green.

760	10c. Type **76**	80	50
761	25c. Class 7100 locomotive, "Benkei", 1880	1·10	80
762	35c. Class 8620 steam locomotive, 1914	1·40	90
763	50c. Class C53 steamlined steam locomotive, 1928	1·90	1·25
764	$1 Class DD51 diesel-hydraulic locomotive, 1962	2·50	1·90
765	$2 Class KTR001 electric railcar Tango Explorer (inscr "RF 22327")	3·00	3·00
766	$4 Class EF55 electric locomotive, 1936	3·50	4·25
767	$5 Class EF58 electric locomotive, 1946	3·50	4·25
MS768	Four sheets, each 114×73 mm showing frontal views. (a) $6 Class 9600 steam locomotive (1913) (vert). (b) $6 Class C57 steam locomotive (1937) (vert). (c) $6 Class C62 steam locomotive (1948) (vert). (d) $6 Class 4100 tank locomotive (1912) (vert). Set of 4 sheets	19·00	19·00

77 President Gorbachev and Brandenburg Gate

1991. Anniversaries and Events. Multicoloured.

769	45c. Type **77**	40	40
770	60c. General de Gaulle in Djibouti, 1959	1·25	55
771	65c. "DIE MAUER MUSS WEG!" slogan	65	65
772	80c. East German border guard escaping to West	80	80
773	$1 "Abduction from the Seraglio"	4·25	1·75
774	$1.50 Lilienthal and glider	2·00	1·75
775	$1.75 Trans-Siberian identity plate	3·50	2·75
776	$1.75 Trans-Siberian steam locomotive (vert)	3·50	2·75
777	$2 Czechoslovakia 1918 20h. stamp and scout delivering mail	3·00	3·00
778	$2 Zurich couple maypole dancing	3·00	3·00
779	$2 Man and woman in Vaud traditional costumes	3·00	3·00
780	$2 Georg Laves (architect) and Hoftheater	3·00	3·00
781	$3 Dresden, 1749	7·00	5·00
782	$4 Scouts and cog train on Snowdon (vert)	4·50	5·00
MS783	Eleven sheets. (a) 100×71 mm. $5 Arms of Berlin. (b) 100×71 mm. $5 Berlin police badge. (c) 77×112 mm. $5 De Gaulle in civilian dress. (d) 69×101 mm. $5 General Charles de Gaulle (vert). (e) 75×101 mm. $5 Portrait of Mozart (vert). (f) 75×101 mm. $5 Bust of Mozart (vert). (g) 115×85 mm. $5 Trans-Siberian Class P36 No. 0250 steam locomotive leaving Moscow at night (43×56 mm). (h) 118×89 mm. $5 Jamboree emblem (buff background) (vert). (i) 118×89 mm. $5 Jamboree emblem (bluish violet background) (vert). (j) 101×72 mm. $5 Arms of Appenzell and Thurgau. (k) 101×72 mm. $5 Old Hanover Set of 11 sheets	38·00	38·00

Anniversaries and Events:—Nos. 769, 771/2, **MS**783a/b, Bicentenary of Brandenburg Gate; 770, **MS**783c/d, Birth centenary of Charles de Gaulle (French statesman); 773, 781, **MS**783e/f, Death bicentenary of Mozart; 774, Centenary of Otto Lilienthal's gliding experiments; 775/6, **MS**783g, Centenary of Trans-Siberian Railway; 777, 782, **MS**783h/i. 50th death anniv of Lord Baden-Powell and World Scout Jamboree, Korea; 778/9, **MS**783j, 700th anniv of Swiss Confederation; 780, **MS**783k, 750th anniv of Hanover.

78 Japanese Aircraft and Submarines leaving Truk

1991. 50th Anniv of Japanese Attack on Pearl Harbor. Multicoloured.

784	$1 Type **78**	2·00	1·60
785	$1 "Akagi" (Japanese aircraft carrier)	2·00	1·60
786	$1 Nakajima B5N2 "Kate" bombers	2·00	1·60
787	$1 Nakajima B5N2 "Kate" bombers attacking Battleship Row	2·00	1·60
788	$1 Burning aircraft, Ford Island airfield	2·00	1·60
789	$1 Doris Miller winning Navy Cross	2·00	1·60
790	$1 U.S.S. "West Virginia" and "Tennessee" (battleships) ablaze	2·00	1·60
791	$1 U.S.S. "Arizona" (battleship) sinking	2·00	1·60
792	$1 U.S.S. "New Orleans" (cruiser)	2·00	1·60
793	$1 President Roosevelt declaring war	2·00	1·60

78a Pluto pulling Mickey Mouse in Sledge, 1974

1991. Christmas. Walt Disney Company Christmas Cards. Multicoloured.

794	10c. Type **78a**	60	30
795	55c. Mickey, Pluto and Donald Duck watching toy band, 1961	1·25	70
796	65c. "The Same Old Wish", 1942	1·40	85
797	75c. Mickey, Peter Pan, Donald and Nephews with Merlin the magician, 1963	1·50	95
798	$1.50 Mickey and Donald with leprechauns, 1958	2·50	2·50
799	$2 Mickey and friends with book "Old Yeller", 1957	2·75	2·75
800	$4 Mickey controlling Pinocchio, 1953	4·00	4·25
801	$5 Cinderella and Prince dancing, 1987	4·00	4·25
MS802	Two sheets, each 128×102 mm. (a) $6 Santa Claus and American bomber, 1942. (b) $6 Snow White, 1957. Set of 2 sheets	13·00	14·00

1992. 40th Anniv of Queen Elizabeth II's Accession. As T 202a of Gambia. Multicoloured.

803	15c. View across bay	75	20
804	45c. Schooner at anchor, Mayreau	1·25	25
805	$2 Hotel on hillside	1·75	1·75
806	$4 Tourist craft at anchor	3·75	3·75
MS807	Two sheets, each 74×97 mm. (a) $6 Beach and palms. (b) $6 Aerial view of hotel by beach. Set of 2 sheets	9·50	10·00

78b Big Pete as Hernando Cortes in Mexico

1992. International Stamp Exhibitions. Walt Disney cartoon characters. Multicoloured. (a) "Grenada '92", Spain. Spanish Explorers.

808	15c. Type **78b**	30	15
809	40c. Mickey Mouse as Hernando de Soto at Mississippi River	50	30
810	$2 Goofy as Vasco Nunez de Balboa sights Pacific	1·75	1·75
811	$4 Donald Duck as Francisco Coronado on Rio Grande	2·75	3·00
MS812	127×102 mm. $6 Mickey as Ponce de Leon	4·25	4·75

(b) "World Columbian Stamp Expo '92", Chicago. Local Personalities.

813	10c. Mickey Mouse and Pluto outside Walt Disney's birthplace	35	20
814	50c. Donald Duck and nephews in George Pullman's railway sleeping car	1·50	55
815	$1 Daisy Duck as Jane Addams (social reformer) and Hull House	1·60	85
816	$5 Mickey as Carl Sandburg (novelist, poet and historian)	3·75	4·00
MS817	127×102 mm. $6 Daisy as Mrs O'Leary with her cow (source of Chicago fire of 1871)	4·25	4·75

79 King Ferdinand and Queen Isabella of Spain

1992. 500th Anniv of Discovery of America by Columbus (2nd issue). Multicoloured.

818	10c. Type **79**	25	25
819	45c. "Santa Maria" and "Nina" in Acul Bay, Haiti	50	50
820	55c. "Santa Maria" (vert)	55	55
821	$2 Ships of Columbus (vert)	1·40	1·40
822	$4 Wreck of "Santa Maria"	2·50	2·50
823	$5 "Pinta" and "Nina"	2·75	2·75
MS824	Two sheets, each 114×85 mm. (a) $6 Columbus landing on San Salvador. (b) $6 "Santa Maria" in storm. Set of 2 sheets	7·00	8·00

79a "Paulogramma sp."

1992. "Genova '92" International Thematic Stamp Exhibition (1st issue). Butterflies. Multicoloured.

825	15c. Type **79a**	75	65
826	20c. "Heliconius cydno"	80	70
827	30c. "Eutresis hypereia"	85	75
828	45c. "Eurytides columbus" (vert)	1·40	1·25
829	55c. "Papilio ascolius"	1·40	1·00
830	75c. "Anaea pasibula"	1·40	1·25
831	80c. "Heliconius doris"	1·40	1·25
832	$1 "Perisama pitheas"	1·40	1·25
833	$2 "Batesia hypochlora"	2·00	2·00
834	$3 "Heliconius erato"	2·50	2·50
835	$4 "Elzunia cassandrina"	2·75	2·75
836	$5 "Sais ivcidice"	2·75	2·75
MS837	Three sheets, each 109×79 mm. (a) $6 "Oleria tigilla" (horiz). (b) $6 "Dismorphia orise" (horiz). (c) $6 "Podotricha telesiphe" (horiz). Set of 3 sheets	11·00	12·00

See also Nos. 851/62.

79b "Entoloma bakeri"

1992. Fungi. Multicoloured.

838	10c. Type **79b**	60	50
839	15c. "Hydropus paraensis"	65	55
840	20c. "Leucopaxillus gracillimus"	70	60
841	45c. "Hygrotrama dennisianum"	90	80
842	50c. "Leucoagaricus hortensis"	90	80
843	65c. "Pyrrhoglossum pyrrhum"	1·25	1·00
844	75c. "Amanita craeoderma"	1·25	1·00
845	$1 "Lentinus bertieri"	1·50	1·25
846	$2 "Dennisiomyces griseus"	2·00	2·00
847	$3 "Xerulina asprata"	2·50	2·50
848	$4 "Hygrocybe acutoconica"	3·00	3·00
849	$5 "Lepiota spiculata"	3·00	3·00
MS850	Three sheets, each 101×68 mm. (a) $6 "Pluteus crysophlebius". (b) $6 "Amanita lilloi". (c) $6 "Lepiota volvatua". Set of 3 sheets	12·00	13·00

1992. "Genova '92" International Thematic Stamp Exhibition (2nd issue). Hummingbirds. As T 370a of Grenada. Multicoloured.

851	5c. Antillean crested hummingbird (female) (horiz)	40	30
852	10c. Blue-tailed emerald (female)	40	30
853	35c. Antillean mango (male) (horiz)	55	45
854	45c. Antillean mango (female) (horiz)	55	45
855	55c. Green-throated carib (horiz)	65	55
856	65c. Green violetear (male)	80	70
857	75c. Blue-tailed emerald (male) (horiz)	90	80
858	$1 Purple-throated carib	1·25	1·00
859	$2 Copper-rumped hummingbird (horiz)	2·25	2·00
860	$3 Rufous-breasted hermit	3·25	2·75
861	$4 Antillean crested hummingbird (male)	4·00	3·50
862	$5 Green-breasted mango (male)	4·25	3·75
MS863	Three sheets, each 105×74 mm. (a) $6 Blue-tailed emerald. (b) $6 Antillean mango. (c) $6 Antillean crested hummingbird. Set of 3 sheets	13·00	14·00

1992. 500th Anniv of Discovery of America by Columbus (3rd issue). Organization of East Caribbean States. As T 372a of Grenada. Multicoloured.

864	$1 Columbus meeting Amerindians	75	75
865	$2 Ships approaching island	2·75	2·50

1992. Olympic Games, Albertville and Barcelona. As T 372 of Grenada. Multicoloured.

866	10c. Men's volleyball	70	40
867	15c. Men's gymnastics (horiz)	85	50
868	25c. Men's cross-country skiing	1·00	60
869	30c. Men's 110 m hurdles (horiz)	1·00	60
870	45c. Men's 120 m ski-jumping (horiz)	1·10	70
871	55c. Women's 4×100 m relay	1·25	80
872	75c. Men's triple jump	1·60	1·00
873	80c. Men's mogul skiing	1·60	1·00
874	$1 Men's 110 m butterfly swimming (horiz)	1·60	1·25
875	$2 "Tornado" Class yachting (horiz)	2·25	1·75
876	$3 Men's decathlon (horiz)	2·50	2·75
877	$5 Show jumping (horiz)	3·75	3·75
MS878	Three sheets, each 101×70 mm. (a) $6 Ice hockey (horiz). (b) $6 Men's single luge (horiz). (c) $6 Football. Set of 3 sheets	14·00	14·00

1992. Christmas. Religious Paintings. As T 207b of Gambia. Multicoloured.

879	10c. "Our Lady with St. Roch and St. Anthony of Padua" (Giorgione)	60	30
880	40c. "Anthony of Padua" (Master of the Embroidered Leaf)	80	55
881	45c. "Madonna and Child" (detail) (Orazio Gentileschi)	90	60
882	50c. "Madonna and Child with St. Anne" (detail) (Da Vinci)	95	65
883	55c. "The Holy Family" (Crespi)	1·00	70
884	65c. "Madonna and Child" (Del Sarto)	1·10	80
885	75c. "Madonna and Child with Sts. Lawrence and Julian" (Gentile da Fabriano)	1·25	90
886	$1 "Virgin and Child" (detail) (School of Parma)	1·50	1·10
887	$2 "Madonna with the Iris" (detail) (style of Durer)	2·50	2·25
888	$3 "Virgin and Child with St. Jerome and St. Dominic" (Lippi)	3·00	3·00
889	$4 "Rapolano Madonna" (Ambrogio Lorenzetti)	3·50	3·75
890	$5 "The Virgin and Child with Angels in a Garden with a Rose Hedge" (Stefano da Verona)	3·50	3·75
MS891	Three sheets, each 73×98 mm. (a) $6 "Madonna and Child with Grapes" (detail) (Cranach the Elder). (b) $6 "Virgin and Child with St. John the Baptist" (detail) (Botticelli). (c) $6 "Madonna and Child with St. Anne" (different detail) (Da Vinci). Set of 3 sheets	15·00	15·00

80 "Nina" in Baracoa Harbour

1992. Anniversaries and Events. Multicoloured.

892	10c. Type **80**	1·75	75
893	75c. Airship LZ-3	2·50	1·75
894	75c. Blind man with guide dog	3·00	1·75
895	75c. Training guide dog	3·00	1·75
896	$1 Ships of Columbus	2·75	1·75
897	$1 Adenauer, state arms and German flag	3·00	1·75
898	$1 "America III" and "Il Moro" (yachts) with trophy	1·50	1·50
899	$1 Hands breaking bread and emblem (vert)	1·50	1·50
900	$2 "Voyager 2" and planet	3·25	2·50
901	$3 Adenauer and children watching Berlin Airlift	2·75	3·50
902	$4 Airship LZ-37 in flames	3·25	4·00
903	$4 Adenauer and ruins in Cologne	3·00	4·00
904	$4 Mozart with his wife Constanze (vert)	7·00	5·00
905	$5 Adenauer and modern office blocks	3·00	5·00
MS906	Seven sheets. (a) 100×70 mm. $6 Columbus sighting land. (b) 100×70 mm. $6 Count von Zeppelin facing left. (c) 110×70 mm. $6 Count von Zeppelin facing right. (d) 100×70 mm. $6 Konrad Adenauer (vert). (e) 100×70 mm. $6 Konrad Adenauer. (f) 100×70 mm. $6 "Mars Observer" spacecraft. (g) 100×70 mm. $6 Costume for "Don Giovanni" by Cassandre. Set of 7 sheets	35·00	38·00

ANNIVERSARIES AND EVENTS: Nos. 892, 896, **MS**906a, 500th anniv of discovery of America by Columbus; Nos. 893, 902, **MS**906b/c, 75th death anniv of Count Ferdinand von Zeppelin (airship pioneer); Nos. 894/5, 75th anniv of International Association of Lions Clubs; Nos. 897, 901, 903, 905, **MS**906d/e, 25th death anniv of Konrad Adenauer (German statesman); No. 898, Americas Cup yachting championship; No. 899, International Conference on Nutrition, Rome; No. 900, **MS**906f, International Space Year; No. 904, **MS**906g, Death bicentenary of Mozart.

81 Olivia and Flaversham

1992. Walt Disney Cartoon Films.

907-950	60c.×44 multicoloured		
MS951	Ten sheets, each 127×103 mm. $6×10 multicoloured. Set of 10 sheets	35·00	38·00

Nos. 907/50 were printed as five se-tenant sheetlets, each of nine different designs except that for "Darkwing Duck" which contains eight vertical designs (Nos. 943/50). The other four sheetlets depict scenes from "The Great Mouse Detective", "Oliver and Company", "The Legend of Sleepy Hollow" and "Ducktales the Movie".

No. **MS**951 contains two sheets for each film. On one sheet in the pairs for "The Legend of Sleepy Hollow", "Ducktales the Movie" and "Darkwing Duck" the stamp design is vertical.

1992. 15th Death Anniv of Elvis Presley (singer). As T 260 of Dominica. Mult.

952	$1 Elvis Presley	2·75	2·25
953	$1 Elvis with guitar	2·75	2·25
954	$1 Elvis with microphone	2·75	2·25

82 Prince Mickey searching for Bride

1992. "Tales of Uncle Scrooge" (fairy stories). Walt Disney cartoon characters.

955-1008	60c.×54 multicoloured		
MS1009	Twelve sheets, each 128×102 mm or 102×128 mm. $6×12 multicoloured. Set of 12 sheets	45·00	48·00

Nos. 955/1008 (issued as six sheetlets each of nine different designs) depict scenes from "The Princess and the Pea", "Little Red Riding Hood", "Goldilocks and the Three Bears", "The Pied Piper of Hamelin", "Hop O'-My-Thumb" and "Puss in Boots".

No. **MS**1009 contains two sheets for each story, all being horizontal with the exception of the second sheet for "Puss in Boots". Of the stamp designs in these miniature sheets the two for "Little Red Riding Hood" and one of each for "Goldilocks and the Three Bears", "The Pied Piper of Hamelin" and "Puss in Boots" are vertical.

83 Oleander

1994. Medicinal Plants. Multicoloured.

1010	5c. Type **83**	55	50
1011	10c. Beach morning glory	60	30
1012	30c. Calabash	85	30
1013	45c. Portia tree	95	30
1014	55c. Cashew	1·00	40
1015	75c. Prickly pear	1·40	70
1016	$1 Shell ginger	1·60	80
1017	$1.50 Avocado pear	2·25	2·00
1018	$2 Mango	2·50	2·50
1019	$3 Blood flower	3·00	3·25
1020	$4 Sugar apple	3·25	4·00
1021	$5 Barbados lily	3·25	4·00

OFFICIAL STAMPS

1982. Nos. 195/200 optd OFFICIAL.

O1	50c. "Mary"	10	15
O2	50c. Prince Charles and Lady Diana Spencer	30	35
O3	$3 "Alexandra"	20	20
O4	$3 Prince Charles and Lady Diana Spencer	65	70
O5	$3.50 "Britannia"	20	20
O6	$3.50 Prince Charles and Lady Diana Spencer	65	70

APPENDIX

The following stamps have either been issued in excess of postal needs, or have been made available to the public in reasonable quantities at face value.

BEQUIA

The following stamps have either been issued in excess of postal needs, or have not been made available to the public in reasonable quantities at face value.

1984

Leaders of the World. Railway Locomotives (1st series). Two designs for each value, the first showing technical drawings and the second the locomotive at work. 1, 5, 10, 25, 35, 45c., $1.50, $2, each×2.
Grenadines of St. Vincent 1982 Ships definitives (Nos. 208/24) optd **BEQUIA**. 1, 3, 5, 6, 10, 15, 20, 25, 30, 50, 60, 75c., $1, $2, $3, $5, $10.
Leaders of the World. Automobiles (1st series). Two designs for each value, the first showing technical drawings and the second the car in action. 5, 40c., $1, $1.50, each×2.
Leaders of the World. Olympic Games, Los Angeles. 1, 10, 60c., $3, each×2.
Leaders of the World. Railway Locomotives (2nd series). Two designs for each value, the first showing technical drawings and the second the locomotive at work. 1, 5, 10, 35, 75c., $1, $2.50, $3, each×2.
Leaders of the World. Automobiles (2nd series). Two designs for each value, the first showing technical drawings and the second the car in action. 5, 10, 20, 25, 75c., $1, $2.50, $3, each×2.

1985

Leaders of the World. Railway Locomotives (3rd series). Two designs for each value, the first showing technical drawings and the second the locomotive at work. 25, 55, 60c., $2, each×2.
Leaders of the World. Dogs. 25, 35, 55c., $2, each×2.
Leaders of the World. Warships of the Second World War. Two designs for each value, the first showing technical drawings and the second the ship at sea. 15, 50c., $1, $1.50, each×2.
Leaders of the World. Flowers. 10, 20, 70c., $2.50, each×2.
Leaders of the World. Automobiles (3rd series). Two designs for each value, the first showing technical drawings and the second the car in action. 5, 25, 50c., $1, $1.25, $2, each×2.
Leaders of the World. Railway Locomotives (4th series). Two designs for each value, the first showing technical drawings and the second the locomotive at work. 25, 55, 60, 75c., $1, $2.50, each×2.
Leaders of the World. Life and Times of Queen Elizabeth the Queen Mother. Two designs for each value showing different portraits. 20, 65c., $1.35, $1.80, each×2.
Leaders of the World. Automobiles (4th series). Two designs for each value, the first showing technical drawings and the second the car in action. 20, 45c., $1.50, $2, each×2.

1986

Leaders of the World. Automobiles (5th series). Two designs for each value, the first showing technical drawings and the second the car in action. 25, 50, 65, 75c., $1, $3, each×2.
60th Birthday of Queen Elizabeth II. 5, 75c., $2, $8.
World Cup Football Championship, Mexico. 1, 2, 5, 10, 45, 60, 75c., $1.50, $1.50, $2, $3.50, $6.
Royal Wedding (1st issue). 60c., $2, each×2.
Railway Engineers and Locomotives. $1, $2.50, $3, $4.
Royal Wedding (2nd issue). Previous issue optd "**Congratulations T.R.H. The Duke & Duchess of York**". 60c., $2, each×2.
Automobiles (6th series). Two designs for each value, the first showing technical drawings and the second the car in action. 20, 60, 75, 90c., $1, $3, each×2.

1987

Automobiles (7th series). Two designs for each value, the first showing technical drawings and the second the car in action. 5, 20, 35, 60, 75, 80c., $1.25, $1.75, each×2.
Royal Ruby Wedding. 15, 75c., $1, $2.50, $5.
Railway Locomotives (5th series). Two designs for each value, the first showing technical drawings and the second the locomotive at work. 15, 25, 40, 50, 60, 75c., $1, $2, each×2.

1988

Explorers. 15, 50c., $1.75, $2, $2.50, $3, $3.50, $4.
International Lawn Tennis Players. 15, 45, 80c., $1.25, $1.75, $2, $2.50, $3.

1989

"Philexfrance '89" International Stamp Exhibition, Paris. Walt Disney Cartoon Characters. 1, 2, 3, 4, 5, 10c., $5, $6.

1991

Centenary of Otto Lilienthal's Gliding Experiments. $5.
50th Anniv of Japanese Attack on Pearl Harbor. 50c., $1.
Death Anniv of Mozart. 10, 75c., $4.
50th Death Anniv of Lord Baden-Powell and World Jamboree, Korea. 50c., $1, $2, $3.

1997

Diana, Princess of Wales Commemoration. $1.

2000

Faces of the Millennium: Queen Elizabeth the Queen Mother. Collage of miniature flower photographs. $1×8.

2001

Endangered Species. Turtles. $1.40×4.

2002

Ferrari Racing Cars. $1.10×8.
Chinese New Year ("Year of the Horse"). $1.40×4.
Golden Jubilee. 80c.×4.
25th Death Anniv of Elvis Presley (1st issue). $1 (in sheetlet of 9).
Shirley Temple in Captain January. $1.40×6, $2×4.
Queen Elizabeth the Queen Mother Commemoration. $2×2.
"United We Stand". Support for Victims of 11 September 2001 Terrorist Attacks. $2 (in sheetlet of 4).

2003

Centenary of the Teddy Bear. $2×8.
Chinese New Year ("Year of the Ram"). $1×6.
5th Death Anniv of Diana, Princess of Wales. $2×8.
50th Anniv of General Motors Chevrolet Corvette. $2×4.
40th Death Anniv of President John F. Kennedy. $2×4.
25th Death Anniv of Elvis Presley (2nd issue). 90c.×2 (in sheetlet of 9).
Birds of the Caribbean. 90c., $1, $1.40, $2.

2004

Chinese New Year ("Year of the Monkey"). $1.40×4
Centenary of World Series Baseball. Babe Ruth. 70c.×12
Marilyn Monroe. 70c.×12
Ancient Greece. 30c., 70c.,. £1, $1.40, $2, $3
Ronald Reagan. $1.40×6 Christmas. 55c., 90c., $1, $4
30th Death Anniv of Pablo Picasso. $2×4
Bicentenary of Steam Locomotives. $2×16
Bicentenary of Steam Locomotives. $1×27

2005

Prehistoric Animals. $2×12
Pope John Paul II Commemoration. 70c, $4
Marine Life. $2×4
Moths. 90c, $1, $1.40, $2
Flowers. $2×4
Liberation of Paris. $2×4
Sinking of the Bismarck. $2×4
60th Anniv of the End of World War II. "The Route to Victory". $2×8
70th Birth Anniv of Elvis Presley. $2×5

2006

80th Birthday of Queen Elizabeth II. $2×4
80th Birth Anniv of Marilyn Monroe. $2×4
50th Death Anniv of Ludwig Durr (Zeppelin engineer). $3×3
50th Anniv of "Loving You" (Elvis Presley). $2.50×4
500th Death Anniv of Christopher Columbus. 20c., 90c., $1.10, $2Luna 9 $2×6 Mars Reconnaissance Orbiter $3×4

2007

Centenary of World Scouting $3
Diamond Wedding of Queen Elizabeth II and Duke of Edinburgh $1.40×6
Tenth Death Anniv of Diana, Princess of Wales. $1.40×6
Final Flight of Concorde, 2003. $1.40×4
Centenary of the First New York City Taxis. $1.40×6
50th Anniv of Elvis Presley's Purchase of Gracelands. $2×4
90th Birth Anniv of John F. Kennedy (US President 1960–3). $2×8
Halley's Comet, 1986. $2×4
80th Birthday of Pope Benedict XVI. $1
Holocaust Remembrance. $1.40×8

CANOUAN

1997

Diana, Princess of Wales Commemoration. $1.

2000

100th Birthday of Queen Elizabeth the Queen Mother. $1.40 (in sheetlet of 6).

2003

40th Death Anniv of President John F. Kennedy. $2×4.
"United We Stand". Support for Victims of 11 September 2001 Terrorist Attacks. $2 (in sheetlet of 4).
25th Death Anniv of Elvis Presley. 90c. (in sheetlet of 9).
Butterflies of the Caribbean. 90c., $1, $1.40, $2.

2007

Centenary of World Scouting. 75c.×20
Centenary of First New York City Taxis. $1.40×6
90th Birth Anniv of John F. Kennedy (US President 1960–3). $2×4Holocaust Remembrance $1.40×8.
30th Death Anniv of Elvis Presley $1.50×6.
10th Death Anniv of Princess Diana. $2×4.
80th Birthday of Pope Benedict XVI. Photomosaic. $2.25×4.

MUSTIQUE

1997

Diana, Princess of Wales Commemoration. $1.

2000

Faces of the Millennium: Queen Elizabeth the Queen Mother. Collage of miniature flower photographs. $1×8.

2003

21st Birthday of Prince William of Wales. $3×3.
50th Anniv of Coronation. $3×3.
Centenary of Circus Clowns. $2×4.
50th Anniv of General Motors Chevrolet Corvette. $2×4.
Centenary of General Motors Cadillac. $2×4.
40th Death Anniv of President John F. Kennedy. $2×4.
"United We Stand". Support for Victims of 11 September 2001 Terrorist Attacks. $2 (in sheetlet of 4).
25th Death Anniv of Elvis Presley. 90c. (in sheetlet of 9).
Birds of the Caribbean. $1, $1.10, $1.40, $2

2005

Pope John Paul II Commemoration. $2

2007

Centenary of World Scouting. $1.50×6
Holocaust Remembrance. $1.40×8.

MYREAU

2006

90th Birth Anniv of John F. Kennedy. $2×8

2007

Diamond Wedding of Queen Elizabeth II and Duke of Edinburgh. $1.40×6
Tenth Death Anniv of Diana, Princess of Wales. $1.40×6
80th Birthday of Pope Benedict XVI. $1.50

PALM ISLAND

2003

Centenary of the Circus Clown. $2×4.
"United We Stand". Support for Victims of 11 September 2001 Terrorist Attacks. $2 (in sheetlet of 4).
25th Death Anniv of Elvis Presley. 90c. (in sheetlet of 9).
Marine Life of the Caribbean. 50c., 60c., 70c., 90c

2004

Butterflies. $2×4

TOBAGO CAYS

2003

21st Birthday of Prince William of Wales. $3×3.
50th Anniv of Coronation. $3×3.
50th Anniv of General Motors Chevrolet Corvette. $2×4.
Centenary of General Motors Cadillac. $2×4.
40th Death Anniv of President John F. Kennedy. $2×4.
"United We Stand". Support for Victims of 11 September 2001 Terrorist Attacks. $2 (in sheetlet of 4).

UNION ISLAND

1984

Leaders of the World. British Monarchs. Two designs for each value forming a composite picture. 1, 5, 10, 20, 60c., $3, each×2.
Leaders of the World. Railway Locomotives (1st series). Two designs for each value, the first showing technical drawings and the second the locomotive at work. 5, 60c., $1, $2.
Grenadines of St. Vincent 1982 Ships definitives (Nos. 208/24) optd **UNION ISLAND**. 1, 3, 5, 6, 10, 15, 20, 25, 30, 50, 60, 75c., $1, $2, $3, $5, $10.
Leaders of the World. Cricketers. Two designs for each value, the first showing a portrait and the second the cricketer in action. 1, 10, 15, 55, 60, 75c., $1.50, $3, each×2.
Leaders of the World. Railway Locomotives (2nd series). Two designs for each value, the first showing technical drawings and the second the locomotive at work. 5, 10, 20, 25, 75c., $1, $2.50, $3, each×2.
Centenary of the First Helicopter Flight. 10, 25, 90c., $2×4, $5.
Elvis Presley through the Decades. $3×4.

1985

Leaders of the World. Automobiles (1st series). Two designs for each value, the first showing technical drawings and the second the car in action. 1, 50, 75c., $2.50, each×2.
Leaders of the World. Birth Bicentenary of John J. Audubon (ornithologist). Birds. 15, 50c., $1, $1.50, each×2.
Leaders of the World. Railway Locomotives (3rd series). Two designs for each value, the first showing technical drawings and the second the locomotive at work. 5, 50, 60c., $2, each×2.
Leaders of the World. Butterflies. 15, 25, 75c., $2, each×2.
Leaders of the World. Automobiles (2nd series). Two designs for each value, the first showing technical drawings and the second the car in action. 5, 60c., $1, $1.50, each×2.
Leaders of the World. Automobiles (3rd series). Two designs for each value, the first showing technical drawings and the second the car in action. 10, 55, 60, 75, 90c., $1, $1.50, $2, each×2.
Leaders of the World. Life and Times of Queen Elizabeth the Queen Mother. Two designs for each value showing different portraits. 55, 70c., $1.05, $1.70, each×2.

1986

Leaders of the World. Railway Locomotives (4th series). Two designs for each value, the first showing technical drawings and the second the locomotive at work. 15, 30, 45, 60, 75c., $1.50, $2.50, $3, each×2.
60th Birthday of Queen Elizabeth II. 10, 60c., $2, $8.
World Cup Football Championship, Mexico. 1, 10, 30, 75c., $1, $2.50, $3, $6.
Royal Wedding (1st issue). 60c., $2, each×2.
Automobiles (4th series). Two designs for each value, the first showing technical drawings and the second the car in action. 10, 60, 75c., $1, $1.50, $3, each×2.
Royal Wedding (2nd issue). Previous issue optd as Bequia. 60c., $2, each×2.
Railway Locomotives (5th series). Two designs for each value, the first showing technical drawings and the second the locomotive at work. 15, 45, 60, 75c., $1, $1.50, $2, $3, each×2.

1987

Railway Locomotives (6th series). Two designs for each value, the first showing technical drawings and the second the locomotive at work. 15, 25, 40, 50, 60, 75c., $1, $2, each×2.
Royal Ruby Wedding. 15, 45c., $1.50, $3, $4.
Railway Locomotives (7th series). Two designs for each value, the first showing technical drawings and the second the locomotive at work. 15, 20, 30, 45, 50, 75c., $1, $1.50, each×2.

1989

"Philexfrance 89" International Stamp Exhibition, Paris. Walt Disney Cartoon Characters. 1, 2, 3, 4, 5, 10c., $5, $6.

1997

Diana, Princess of Wales Commemoration. $1.

2000

Faces of the Millennium: Queen Elizabeth the Queen Mother. Collage of miniature flower photographs. $1x8.

2002

Chinese New Year ("Year of the Horse"). $1.40×4.
Endangered Species. Shortfin Mako Shark. $1×4.
"United We Stand". Support for Victims of 11 September 2001 Terrorist Attacks. $2 (in sheetlet of 4).
Queen Elizabeth the Queen Mother Commemoration. $2×3.
Ferrari Cars. $1.10×8.
WWF. Shorefin Mako Shark. $1×16

2003

Centenary of the Teddy Bear. $2×8.
Chinese New Year ("Year of the Ram"). $1×6.
25th Death Anniv of Diana, Princess of Wales. $1.40×6, $2×4.
40th Death Anniv of President John F. Kennedy. $2×4.
25th Death Anniv of Elvis Presley. 90c.×9.
Fish. 90c., $1, $1.40, $2

2004

Chinese New Year ("Year of the Monkey"). "Monkey and Cat" painting by Yi Yuan-Chi. $1.40 (in sheetlet of 4).
Ronald Reagan. $1.40×6
Marilyn Monroe. 75c.×20
Babe Ruth. 75c.×10

2005

25th Anniv of the Pontificate of Pope John Paul II. $2×4
Commemoration of Pope John Paul II. $3×6
Bicentenary of Steam Trains. $1×18
National Basketball Association. 90c.×6
Pope John Paul II Commemoration. 70c.
70th Birth Anniv of Elvis Presley. $2×2

2006

80th Birthday of Queen Elizabeth II. $2×3

2006

500th Death Anniv of Christopher Columbus. 10c., 90c., $2, $3
Venus Express. $2×4
First Flight of Space Shuttle Columbia, 1981. $3×6
400th Birth Anniv of Rembrandt. 50c., 75c., $1, $2×9

2007

90th Birth Anniv of John F. Kennedy. $2×8
Centenary of World Scouting. $4
Diamond Wedding of Queen Elizabeth II and Duke of Edinburgh. $1.40×6
Tenth Death Anniv of Diana, Princess of Wales. $1.40×6; $2×4
80th Birthday of Pope Benedict XVI. $1.50

YOUNG ISLAND

2007

90th Birth Anniv of John F. Kennedy. $2×8

Pt. 1

GRIQUALAND WEST

A British colony, later annexed to the Cape of Good Hope and now part of South Africa, whose stamps it uses.

12 pence = 1 shilling; 20 shillings = 1 pound.

1874. Stamp of Cape of Good Hope ("Hope" seated) with pen-and-ink surch.

1	4	1d. on 4d. blue	£1600	£2500

1877. Stamps of Cape of Good Hope ("Hope" seated) optd G. W.

2	6	1d. red	£600	90·00
3	6	4d. blue	£400	80·00

1877. Stamps of Cape of Good Hope ("Hope" seated) optd G.W.

6a	4	4d. blue	£350	50·00
14	6	½d. grey	19·00	19·00
16	6	1d. red	20·00	15·00
26	6	4d. blue	45·00	7·00
27	4	6d. violet	£180	11·00
28	4	1s. green	£160	7·50
29	6	5s. orange	£550	18·00

Pt. 6

GUADELOUPE

An overseas department of France, formerly a Fr. colony in the W. Indies, consisting of a group of islands between Antigua and Dominica. Now uses the stamps of France.

100 centimes = 1 franc.

1894. French Colonies, "Peace and Commerce" type, surch G. P. E. and new value in frame.

6	H	20 on 30c. brown	50·00	60·00
7	H	25 on 35c. black on orange	48·00	55·00

1889. French Colonies, "Commerce" type, surch GUADELOUPE and value in figures and words in plain frame.

8	J	3c. on 20c. red on green	1·00	4·00
9	J	15c. on 20c. red on green	9·25	6·50
10	J	25c. on 20c. red on green	9·25	6·50

1889. French Colonies, "Commerce" type, surch GUADELOUPE and value in figures and words in ornamental frame.

11		5c. on 1c. black on blue	4·25	4·50
12		10c. on 40c. red on yellow	13·00	21·00
13		15c. on 20c. red on green	14·00	11·00
14		25c. on 30c. brown on drab	20·00	23·00

1890. French Colonies, "Commerce" type, surch 5 C. GPE.

15		5c. on 10c. black on lilac	6·50	5·50
16		5c. on 1f. olive on green	5·50	4·50

1891. French Colonies, "Ceres" and "Commerce" types, optd GUADELOUPE.

19	F	30c. brown	£275	£300
20	F	80c. red	£850	£900
21	J	1c. black on blue	45	35
22	J	2c. brown on buff	1·40	90
23	J	4c. brown on grey	6·00	7·75
24	J	5c. green on light green	4·50	3·75
25	J	10c. black on lilac	25·00	12·00
26	J	15c. blue on light blue	23·00	2·30
27	J	20c. red on green	55·00	50·00
28	J	25c. black on pink	46·00	3·75
29	J	30c. brown on drab	50·00	55·00
30	J	35c. black on orange	£100	85·00
31	J	40c. red on yellow	75·00	65·00
32	J	75c. red on pink	£140	£140
33	J	1f. green	£120	£110

1892. "Tablet" key-type inscr "GUADELOUPE ET DEPENDANCES" in red (1, 5, 15, 25, 50 (No. 52), 75c., 1f.) or blue (others).

34	D	1c. black on blue	85	1·00
35	D	2c. brown on buff	2·50	1·60
37	D	4c. brown on grey	2·00	3·75
38	D	5c. green on light green	3·75	1·20
39	D	10c. black on lilac	16·00	5·50
40	D	15c. blue	25·00	45
41	D	20c. red on green	3·75	12·00
42	D	25c. black on pink	3·75	75
43	D	30c. brown on drab	34·00	46·00
44	D	40c. red on yellow	32·00	23·00
45	D	50c. red on pink	28·00	22·00
46	D	75c. brown on yellow	32·00	60·00
47	D	1f. green	28·00	60·00
49	D	10c. red	6·00	1·40
50	D	15c. grey	10·50	45
51	D	25c. blue	95·00	£110
52	D	50c. brown on blue	16·00	60·00

1903. "Tablet" key-type surch G & D (5, 15c., 1f.) or G et D (10, 40c.) and new value.

53b		5 on 30c. brown on buff	4·00	9·25
54		10 on 40c. red on yellow	6·50	24·00
55		15 on 50c. red	14·00	19·00
56		40 on 1f. green	9·25	22·00
57		1f. on 75c. brown on yellow	65·00	75·00

49 Mt. Houllemont, Basse-Terre

50 La Soufriere

51 Pointe-a-Pitre, Grande Terre

1904. Nos. 56/7 further optd 1903 in frame.

59c		40 on 1f. green	60·00	70·00
60c		1f. on 75c. brown on yellow	95·00	95·00

1905

61	49	1c. black on blue	45	20
62	49	2c. brown on yellow	30	10
63	49	4c. brown on grey	50	65
64	49	5c. green	2·75	45
65	49	10c. red	4·00	45
66	49	15c. lilac	1·20	35
67	50	20c. red on green	55	35
68	50	25c. blue	2·00	35
69	50	30c. black	4·50	3·25
70	50	35c. black on yellow	1·80	90
71	50	40c. red on yellow	2·00	1·50
72	50	45c. brown on lilac	3·00	2·75
73	50	50c. green on yellow	7·75	4·00
74	50	75c. red on blue	1·70	2·50
75	51	1f. black on green	1·80	2·50
76	51	2f. red on orange	1·70	4·75
77	51	5f. blue on orange	9·25	25·00
83	49	5c. blue	40	45
84	49	10c. green	2·50	2·30
85	49	10c. red on blue	75	70
86	50	20c. green	65	2·50
87	50	25c. green	1·10	20
88	50	30c. red	1·10	2·50
89	50	30c. olive on lilac	2·00	90
90	50	45c. red	1·10	2·75
91	50	50c. blue	65	1·40
92	50	50c. mauve	80	55
93	50	65c. blue	3·00	6·50
94	51	1f. blue	1·60	2·20

1912. Nos. 37 and 43/4 surch in figures.

78A	D	05 on 4c. brown on grey	1·20	3·25
79A	D	05 on 30c. brown on drab	1·70	4·25
80A	D	10 on 40c. red on yellow	2·10	4·25

1915. Surch 5c and red cross.

81	49	10c.+5c. red	3·75	4·50
82	49	15c.+5c. lilac	1·80	11·50

1924. Surch in figures and bars.

95	51	25c. on 5f. blue on orange	45	7·75
96	51	65 on 1f. green	1·40	4·00
97	51	85 on 1f. green	2·00	8·25
98	50	90c. on 75c. red	1·50	3·50
99	51	1f.05 on 2f. red	45	6·00
100	51	1f.25 on 1f. blue	65	3·25
101	51	1f.50 on 1f. blue	1·50	1·80
102	51	3f. on 5f. brown	1·80	3·25
103	51	10f. on 5f. red on yellow	6·00	30·00
104	51	20f. on 5f. mauve on red	12·00	32·00

53 Sugar Refinery

54 Saints Harbour

55 Pointe-a-Pitre Harbour

1928

105	53	1c. mauve and yellow	35	3·75
106	53	2c. red and black	20	90
107	53	3c. mauve and yellow	30	5·75
108	53	4c. brown and green	20	2·50
109	53	5c. green and red	25	1·00
110	53	10c. blue and brown	10	10
111	53	15c. black and red	20	35
112	53	20c. brown and mauve	30	75
113	54	25c. olive and blue	60	30
114	54	30c. green and deep green	10	10
115	54	35c. green	1·00	3·75
116	54	40c. mauve and yellow	40	20
117	54	45c. grey and purple	70	3·00
118	54	45c. deep green and green	1·20	8·50
119	54	50c. red and green	35	20
120	54	55c. red and blue	1·70	6·00
121	54	60c. red and blue	50	6·25
122	54	65c. red and black	70	70
123	54	70c. red and black	45	5·50
124	54	75c. green and red	80	1·10
125	54	80c. brown and red	90	2·00
126	54	90c. red	2·00	2·75
127	54	90c. blue and red	90	7·75
128	55	1f. blue and red	4·50	1·40
129	55	1f. orange and red	3·75	6·50
130	55	1f. brown and blue	55	4·25
131	55	1f.05 red and blue	3·00	8·50
132	55	1f.10 green and orange	5·00	11·00
133	55	1f.25 brown and blue	2·00	5·00
134	55	1f.25 orange and red	2·50	8·25
135	55	1f.40 mauve and blue	2·00	8·00
136	55	1f.50 light blue and blue	35	20
137	55	1f.60 orange and mauve	2·50	8·00
138	55	1f.75 brown and mauve	5·75	1·80
139	55	1f.75 blue	14·00	18·00
140	55	2f. brown and green	80	65
141	55	2f.25 blue	85	7·75
142	55	2f.50 green and orange	1·20	8·25
143	55	3f. black and brown	55	2·00
144	55	5f. red and blue	90	75
145	55	10f. brown and mauve	1·10	2·75
146	55	20f. red and green	65	7·50

1931. "Colonial Exhibition" key-types inscr "GUADELOUPE".

147	E	40c. black and green	5·25	6·25
148	F	50c. black and mauve	2·50	4·00
149	G	90c. black and red	8·50	19·00
150	H	1f.50 black and blue	7·00	12·50

57 Richelieu founding W. India Co., 1635

58 Victor Hughes and Corsairs, 1793

1935. West Indies Tercentenary.

151	57	40c. brown	17·00	23·00
152	57	50c. red	14·00	12·00
153	57	1f.50 blue	14·00	16·00
154	58	1f.75 mauve	14·00	12·00
155	58	5f. brown	14·00	12·00
156	58	10f. green	17·00	12·00

58a Sailing Ships

1937. International Exhibition, Paris.

157	-	20c. violet	1·90	8·25
158	58a	30c. green	90	4·00
159	-	40c. red	1·00	8·00
160	-	50c. brown	1·20	3·25
161	-	90c. red	1·10	5·25
162	-	1f.50 blue	1·40	3·50

MS162a 120×100 mm. 3f. blue (as T **58a**). Imperf — 17·00 42·00

DESIGNS—VERT: 20c. Allegory of Commerce; 50c. Allegory of Agriculture. HORIZ: 40c. Berber Negress and Annamite; 90c. France with torch of Civilization; 1f.50, Diane de Poitiers.

58b Pierre and Marie Curie

1938. International Anti-cancer Fund.

163	58b	1f.75+50c. blue	5·50	34·00

58c

1939. New York World's Fair.

164	58c	1f.25 red	2·30	4·00
165	58c	2f.25 blue	2·30	3·00

58d Storming the Bastille

1939. 150th Anniv of French Revolution.

166	58d	45c.+25c. green and black	8·25	20·00
167	58d	70c.+30c. brown & black	8·25	20·00
168	58d	90c.+35c. orange & black	9·25	20·00
169	58d	1f.25+1f. red and black	9·25	20·00
170	58d	2f.25+2f. blue and black	9·75	20·00

1944. Surch Un franc (No. 177) or in figures (others). (a) On Nos. 164/5.

178		40c. on 1f.25 red	3·25	7·00
179		40c. on 2f.25 blue	4·25	8·25

(b) On Issue of 1928.

172	54	40c. on 35c. green	1·10	6·00
173	54	50c. on 25c. olive and blue	65	75
174	54	50c. on 65c. red and black	1·10	3·25
175	54	1f. on 90c. red	2·50	9·25
176	54	1f. on 90c. blue and red	1·40	5·00
177	54	1f. on 65c. red and black	75	6·00

(c) On No. 99.

171	51	4f. on 1f.05 on 2f. red	5·00	9·25

58e

1944. Mutual Aid and Red Cross Funds.

180	58e	5f.+20f. blue	45	8·50

58f Felix Eboue

1945

181	58f	2f. black	20	45
182	58f	25f. green	65	7·75

63

1945

183	**63**	10c. blue and orange	65	5·00
184	**63**	30c. green and orange	65	3·50
185	**63**	40c. blue and red	75	5·25
186	**63**	50c. orange and green	35	1·00
187	**63**	60c. grey and blue	45	6·25
188	**63**	70c. grey and green	1·00	7·00
189	**63**	80c. green and yellow	75	6·75
190	**63**	1f. purple and green	55	1·30
191	**63**	1f.20 mauve and green	1·00	4·25
192	**63**	1f.50 brown and red	80	1·40
193	**63**	2f. red and blue	90	1·20
194	**63**	2f.40 red and green	1·60	6·25
195	**63**	3f. brown and blue	1·10	50
196	**63**	4f. blue and orange	1·10	1·70
197	**63**	4f.50 orange and green	75	1·70
198	**63**	5f. violet and green	90	2·00
199	**63**	10f. green and mauve	65	45
200	**63**	15f. grey and orange	90	1·00
201	**63**	20f. grey and orange	1·10	75

63a Fairey FC-1

1945. Air.

202	**63a**	50f. green	1·30	4·00
203	**63a**	100f. red	1·50	2·50

63b "Victory"

1946. Air. Victory.

204	**63b**	8f. brown	65	3·00

63c Chad

1946. Air. From Chad to the Rhine.

205	**63c**	5f. olive	1·00	5·50
206	-	10f. blue	1·00	6·00
207	-	15f. purple	1·00	3·25
208	-	20f. red	1·70	7·75
209	-	25f. black	1·00	3·25
210	-	50f. brown	1·20	2·75

DESIGNS: 10f. Koufra; 15f. Mareth; 20f. Normandy; 25f. Paris; 50f. Strasbourg.

64 Woman and Port Basse-Terre

65 Cutting Sugar Cane

66 Guadeloupe Woman

67 Sud Ouest Bretagne over Guadeloupe Woman and Fishing Boats

1947

211	**64**	10c. lake (postage)	10	3·50
212	**64**	30c. brown	10	6·25
213	**64**	50c. green	35	5·75
214	**65**	60c. brown	45	6·50
215	**65**	1f. red	30	5·75
216	**65**	1f.50 blue	90	6·25
217	-	2f. green	1·30	6·75
218	-	2f.50 red	1·70	7·75
219	-	3f. blue	1·70	6·00
220	-	4f. violet	2·20	6·75
221	-	5f. green	2·00	8·25
222	-	6f. red	2·50	2·00
223	-	10f. blue	2·75	5·75
224	-	15f. purple	2·75	4·75
225	-	20f. red	3·25	4·25
226	**66**	25f. green	4·25	8·25
227	**66**	40f. orange	4·00	11·00
228	-	50f. purple (air)	8·25	20·00
229	-	100f. blue	9·25	22·00
230	**67**	200f. red	14·00	30·00

DESIGNS—As Type **66**: 2f. to 3f. Women carrying pineapples; 4f. to 6f. Woman in kerchief facing left; 10f. to 20f. Picking coffee. As Type **67**: 50f. Latecoere 631 flying boat over village; 100f. Short Hythe flying boat landing in bay.

POSTAEG DUE STAMPS

D1

1876

D1	**D1**	15c. black on blue	60·00	50·00
D2	**D1**	25c. black on white	£850	£650
D3	**D1**	30c. black on white	£110	80·00
D4	**D1**	40c. black on blue	†	£37000
D5	**D1**	40c. black on white	£1100	£850

D3

1884. Imperf.

D8	**D3**	5c. black on white	10·00	18·00
D9	**D3**	10c. black on blue	75·00	65·00
D10	**D3**	15c. black on lilac	£120	75·00
D11	**D3**	20c. black on red	£130	£130
D12	**D3**	30c. black on yellow	£130	£130
D13	**D3**	35c. black on grey	60·00	50·00
D14	**D3**	50c. black on green	22·00	18·00

1903. Postage Due stamps of French Colonies surch G & D 30 in frame.

D59	**U**	30 on 60c. brown on buff	£275	£300
D61	**U**	30 on 1f. red on yellow	£275	£325

D48 Gustavia Bay, Island of St. Bartholomew

1905

D63	**D48**	5c. blue	20	35
D64	**D48**	10c. brown	35	35
D65	**D48**	15c. green	40	6·75
D66	**D48**	20c. brown on yellow	45	1·20
D67	**D48**	30c. red	55	4·75
D68	**D48**	50c. black	85	7·00
D69	**D48**	60c. orange	75	7·75
D70	**D48**	1f. lilac	1·80	8·50

1926. Surch in figures and words and a percevoir.

D105	2f. on 1f. grey	75	7·50
D106	3f. on 1f. blue	1·80	10·50

D56 Allee Dumanoir, Capesterre

1928

D147	**D56**	2c. mauve and brown	10	3·25
D148	**D56**	4c. brown and blue	10	3·00
D149	**D56**	5c. brown and green	10	2·00
D150	**D56**	10c. yellow and mauve	20	2·00
D151	**D56**	15c. olive and red	20	3·25
D152	**D56**	20c. olive and orange	30	3·25
D153	**D56**	25c. green and red	55	4·00
D154	**D56**	30c. yellow and blue	45	3·00
D155	**D56**	50c. red and brown	50	6·25
D156	**D56**	60c. black and blue	60	6·75
D157	**D56**	1f. red and green	90	4·00
D158	**D56**	2f. red and brown	65	7·75
D159	**D56**	3f. blue and mauve	1·30	7·50

D68 Palms and Houses

1947

D231	**D68**	10c. black	10	5·00
D232	**D68**	30c. green	10	4·75
D233	**D68**	50c. blue	35	4·75
D234	**D68**	1f. green	50	7·25
D235	**D68**	2f. blue	55	6·75
D236	**D68**	3f. brown	1·10	8·25
D237	**D68**	4f. purple	1·00	8·75
D238	**D68**	5f. violet	1·00	9·50
D239	**D68**	10f. red	1·30	10·00
D240	**D68**	20f. purple	2·00	11·00

Pt. 22

GUAM

An island in the Pacific Ocean belonging to the United States. Now uses U.S. stamps.

100 cents = 1 dollar.

1899. Stamps of United States optd GUAM.

1	1c. green (No. 283)	23·00	28·00
2	2c. red (No. 270)	19·00	28·00
4	3c. violet (No. 271)	£140	£190
5	4c. brown (No. 285)	£150	£190
6	5c. blue (No. 286)	34·00	50·00
7	6c. purple (No. 287a)	£140	£225
8	8c. brown (No. 275)	£140	£225
9	10c. brown (No. 289)	50·00	65·00
11	15c. green (No. 290)	£170	£190
12	50c. orange (No. 278)	£400	£450
13	$1 black (No. 279)	£400	£450

SPECIAL DELIVERY STAMP

1899. Special Delivery stamp of United States optd GUAM.

E15	**E46**	10c. blue (No. E283)	£170	£225

Pt. 15

GUANACASTE

A province of Costa Rica whose stamps it now uses.

100 centavos = 1 peso.

Stamps of Costa Rica optd.

1885. Stamps of 1883 optd Guanacaste or GUANACASTE.

G1	**8**	1c. green	2·00	2·00
G3	**8**	5c. violet	8·00	3·00
G4	**8**	10c. orange	8·00	8·00
G5	**8**	40c. blue	15·00	15·00
G36	**8**	2c. red	1·60	2·00

1887. Stamps of 1887 optd Guanacaste.

G37	**14**	5c. violet	11·00	2·20
G39	**14**	10c. orange	2·30	2·50

1887. Fiscal stamps optd Guanacaste or GUANACASTE.

G41	2c. blue	25·00	25·00
G44	1c. red	£150	£150

1889. Stamps of 1889 optd GUANACASTE.

G56	**17**	20c. green	70	75
G57	**17**	50c. red	1·30	1·10
G59	**17**	1p. blue	2·75	2·75
G60	**17**	2p. violet	4·50	4·50
G61	**17**	5p. olive	27·00	25·00
G62	**17**	1c. brown	75	75
G63	**17**	2c. blue	75	75
G64	**17**	5c. orange	75	75
G65	**17**	10c. lake	75	75

Pt. 15

GUATEMALA

A republic of Central America; independent since 1847.

1871. 100 centavos = 8 reales = 1 peso.
1927. 100 centavos de quetzal = 1 quetzal.

1 Arms

1871

1	1	1c. bistre	2·00	35·00
2	1	5c. brown	6·00	15·00
3	1	10c. blue	7·75	17·00
4	1	20c. red	6·00	16·00

2

1873

5	2	4r. mauve	£475	£120
6	2	1p. yellow	£250	£150

3 Liberty

1875. Various frames.

7	3	¼r. black	30·00	15·00
8	3	½r. green	30·00	9·50
9	3	1r. blue	30·00	9·50
10	3	2r. red	30·00	9·50

4 Native Indian

1878

11	4	½r. green	2·00	4·75
12	4	2r. red	3·00	9·00
13	4	4r. mauve	3·00	10·00
14	4	1p. yellow	3·50	25·00

5 Resplendent Quetzal

1879

15	5	¼r. green and brown	11·00	14·00
16	5	1r. green and black	16·00	20·00

For similar stamps, but inscr differently, see Nos. 21/25.

1881. Surch.

17		1c. on ¼r. green and brown	18·00	23·00
18	4	5c. on ½r. green	13·00	20·00
19	5	10c. on 1r. green and black	27·00	35·00
20	4	20c. on 2r. red	70·00	£100

1881. As T 5 inscr "UNION POSTAL UNIVERSAL—GUATEMALA". Centres in green.

21	5	1c. black	4·25	3·00
22	5	2c. brown	4·25	3·00
23	5	5c. red	9·00	3·75
24	5	10c. lilac	4·25	3·00
25	5	20c. yellow	4·25	3·50

7 President J. Rufino Barrios

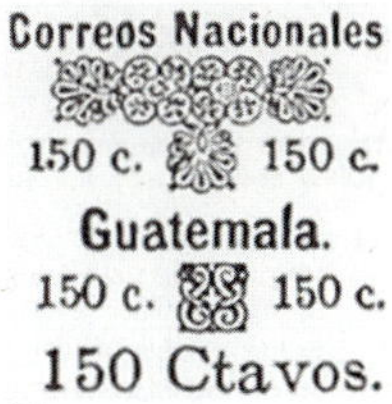

(8)

1886. Railway stamp variously surch as T 8.

26	7	25c. on 1p. red	1·10	1·10
27	7	50c. on 1p. red	1·10	1·10
28	7	75c. on 1p. red	1·10	1·10
29	7	100c. on 1p. red	2·10	3·50
30	7	150c. on 1p. red	2·10	3·50

9 Arms of Guatemala

1886

37	9	50c. olive	16·00	4·75
38	9	75c. red	16·00	4·50
39	9	100c. brown	16·00	9·00
40	9	150c. blue	22·00	13·00
41	9	200c. yellow	24·00	13·00
43a	9	1c. blue	1·70	50
44	9	2c. brown	3·50	50
46	9	5c. violet	4·00	50
47	9	6c. mauve	4·00	50
48	9	10c. red	4·00	50
49	9	20c. green	7·50	1·50
50	9	25c. orange	12·00	2·00

See also Nos. 101/9.

1886. Surch PROVISIONAL. 1886. 1 UN CENTAVO.

42h	1c. on 2c. brown	3·50	2·00

1894. Surch 1894, bar and value.

51	2c. on 100c. brown	6·50	5·50
53	10c. on 75c. red	8·50	7·00
54	10c. on 200c. yellow	9·75	5·50
55	1c. on 2c. brown	1·50	1·00
57	6c. on 150c. blue	12·00	6·50

1895. Surch 1895 1 CENTAVO and bar.

59	1c. on 5c. violet	60	50

16 Steamship, arms, portrait of Pres. J. M. Reyna Barrios and locomotive in centre. Arms of El Salvador, Honduras, Nicaragua and Costa Rica in corners

1897. Central American Exhibition.

62	16	1c. black on grey	85	80
63	16	2c. black on green	85	80
64	16	6c. black on orange	85	80
65	16	10c. black on blue	85	80
66	16	12c. black on red	85	80
67	16	18c. black on white	14·50	14·00
68	16	20c. black on red	1·60	1·50
69	16	25c. black on brown	1·60	1·50
70	16	50c. black on brown	1·60	1·50
71	16	75c. black on blue	80·00	75·00
72	16	100c. black on green	1·60	1·50
73	16	150c. black on pink	£160	£200
74	16	200c. black on mauve	1·60	1·50
75	16	500c. black on green	1·60	1·50

1897. Surch UN CENTAVO 1898.

76	1c. on 12c. black on red	1·20	1·20

1898. Surch 1898, bar and value.

77	9	1c. on 5c. violet	1·40	1·40
78	9	1c. on 25c. orange	3·50	3·50
79	9	1c. on 50c. olive	3·00	3·00
80	9	1c. on 75c. red	3·00	3·00
81	9	6c. on 5c. violet	5·50	2·30
82	9	6c. on 10c. red	12·00	12·00
83	9	6c. on 20c. green	6·00	5·00
84	9	6c. on 100c. brown	6·00	5·00
85	9	6c. on 150c. blue	6·00	5·00
86	9	6c. on 200c. yellow	6·00	5·00
87	9	10c. on 20c. green	6·00	5·00

20

1898. Fiscal stamps as T 20 optd CORREOS NACIONALES or surch 2 CENTAVOS also.

88	20	1c. blue	2·20	2·10
89	20	2c. on 1c. blue	3·50	3·50

22

1898. Fiscal stamps dated "1898" as T 22 surch CORREOS NACIONALES and value.

90	22	1c. on 10c. blue	1·20	1·20
91	22	2c. on 1c. red	5·50	3·00
92	22	2c. on 5c. violet	1·90	1·50
93	22	2c. on 10c. blue	10·50	10·50
94	22	2c. on 25c. red	11·50	11·50
95	22	2c. on 50c. blue	14·50	14·00
96	22	6c. on 1p. violet	6·00	6·50
97	22	6c. on 5p. blue	13·50	11·50
98	22	6c. on 10p. green	13·50	11·50

1899. Surch Un 1 Centavo 1899.

99	9	1c. on 5c. violet	60	35

1900. Surch 1900 1 CENTAVO.

100	1c. on 10c. red	85	80

1900

101	1c. green	95	35
102	2c. red	95	35
103	5c. blue	3·50	1·80
104	6c. green	1·20	50
105	10c. brown	12·00	1·50
106	20c. mauve	11·00	10·50
107	20c. brown	14·50	14·00
108	25c. yellow	11·00	10·50
109	25c. green	14·50	14·00

1901. Surch 1901 and value.

110	1c. on 20c. green	85	80
111	1c. on 25c. orange	95	95
112	2c. on 20c. green	2·40	2·30

1902. Fiscal stamp surch CORREOS NACIONALES 1902 and value in figures and words.

113	20	1c. on 1c. blue	1·80	1·80
114	20	2c. on 1c. blue	1·80	1·80

1902. Fiscal stamp, dated "1898", surch CORREOS 1902 Seis 6 Cts.

115	22	6c. on 25c. red	3·50	3·50

30 Arms

31 J. Rufino Barrios Statue

35 Statesmen discussing Independence (after painting by E. Bravo)

47 President Manuel Estrada Cabrera

1902. Inscr "U.P.U. 1902".

116	30	1c. purple and green	50	45
117	31	2c. black and red	50	45
118a	-	5c. black and blue	50	45
119	-	6c. green and yellow	50	45
120	-	10c. blue and orange	60	60
121	35	12½c. black and blue	60	60
122	-	20c. black and red	95	60
123a	-	50c. blue and brown	70	60
124	-	75c. black and lilac	85	60
125	-	1p. black and brown	1·30	60
126	-	2p. black and orange	1·60	1·30
141	-	25c. black and blue	85	35
142	47	5p. black and red	95	95

DESIGNS—HORIZ: 5c. La Reforma Palace; 6c. Temple of Minerva; 10c. Lake Amatitlan; 20c. Cathedral; 25c. G.P.O.; 50c. Columbus Theatre; 75c. Artillery Barracks; 1p. Columbus Monument; 2p. Indian Institute.

1903. Surch 1903 25 CENTAVOS.

127	9	25c. on 1c. green	1·90	80
128	9	25c. on 2c. red	2·40	80
129	9	25c. on 6c. green	3·75	2·50
130	9	25c. on 10c. brown	12·00	10·50
131	9	25c. on 75c. red	14·50	14·00
132	9	25c. on 150c. blue	14·50	14·00
133	9	25c. on 200c. yellow	16·00	15·00

1908. Surch 1908 and value in figures and words.

134	-	1c. on 10c. blue and orange (No. 120)	50	35
135	35	2c. on 12½c. black and blue	50	50
136	-	6c. on 20c. black and red (No. 122)	70	35

1909. Surch 1909 and value in figures and words.

137	2c. on 75c. blk & lil (No. 124)	85	80
138	6c. on 50c. bl & brn (No. 123)	50	45
139	12½c. on 2p. black and orange (No. 126)	50	45

45 M. Garcia Granados

1910. Granados Centenary.

140	45	6c. black and bistre	85	60

1911. Surch 1911 Un Centavo.

143	1c. on 6c. black and bistre	36·00	14·00

1911. Surch Correos de Guatemala 1911 and value.

144	2c. on 5c. (No. 118a)	2·40	1·20
145	6c. on 10c. (No. 120)	1·90	1·90

1912. Surch 1912 and value.

146	1c. on 20c. (No. 122)	50	45
147	2c. on 50c. (No. 123a)	50	50
148	5c. on 75c. (No. 124)	1·20	1·20

1913. Surch 1913 and value.

149	1c. on 50c. (No. 123a)	35	35
150	6c. on 1p. (No. 125)	50	45
151	12½c. on 2p. (No. 126)	50	45

1916. Surch with value only.

152	30	6c. on 1c. purple and green	35	35
153	30	12½c. on 1c. purple & green	35	35
154	31	25c. on 2c. black and red	35	35
156	30	2c. on 1c. purple and green	35	35

59 Pres. Manuel Estrada Cabrera

1917. Re-election of President Cabrera.

155	59	25c. brown and blue	35	35

60

1918

157	60	1p.50 blue	1·00	35

61 Arms

64 Technical School

1919. Buildings and Obligatory Tax G.P.O. Rebuilding Fund (No. 158).

158	61	12½c. red (obligatory tax)	50	25
159	-	30c. black and red (postage)	3·25	1·20
160	-	60c. black and olive	1·20	70

161	**64**	90c. black and brown	1·20	1·20
162	-	3p. black and green	2·75	70
169	-	1p.50 orange and blue	1·30	35
170	-	5p. green and sepia	4·00	1·90
171	-	15p. red and black	34·00	19·00

DESIGNS—Dated 1918: 30c. Radio station; 60c. Maternity hospital; 3p. Arms. Dated 1921: 1p.50, Monolith at Quirigua; 5p. Garcia Granados Monument; 15p. La Penitenciaria railway bridge, Guatemala City.

1920. Nos. 159/60 surch 1920 2 centavos.

163		2c. on 30c. black and red	35	35
164		2c. on 60c. black and olive	35	35

1920. No. 126 surch 25 Centavos and bars.

165		25c. on 2p. black and orange	50	35

68

1920. Telegraph stamp as T 68 optd CORREOS.

166	**68**	25c. green	35	25

1921. Surch 1921 and value in words.

167		12½c. on 20c. black and red (No. 122)	35	25
168		50c. on 75c. black and lilac (No. 124)	60	35

1921. Optd 1921 CORREOS.

173	**63**	25c. green	35	35

1921. Surch 1921 CORREOS DOCE Y MEDIO.

172	**68**	12½c. on 25c. green	35	35

1922. Surch 1922 and value in words.

174	-	12½c. on 20c. (No. 122)	35	35
175	-	12½c. on 60c. (No. 160)	70	70
176	**64**	12½c. on 90c. (No. 161)	85	80
179	-	12½c. on 3p. (No. 162)	35	35
180	-	12½c. on 5p. (No. 170)	70	70
181	-	12½c. on 15p. (No. 171)	70	70
184	-	25c. on 15p. (No. 171)	2·00	2·00
185	-	25c. on 30c. (No. 159)	1·40	1·40
186	-	25c. on 60c. (No. 160)	1·40	1·40
187	-	25c. on 75c. (No. 124)	45	45
188	**64**	25c. on 90c. (No. 161)	1·40	1·40
189	-	25c. on 1p. (No. 125)	35	35
190	-	25c. on 1p.50 (No. 169)	35	35
191	-	25c. on 2p. (No. 126)	55	55
192	-	25c. on 3p. (No. 162)	45	45
193	-	25c. on 5p. (No. 170)	1·10	1·10

80 Independence Centenary Palace

82 Columbus Theatre

1922

195	**80**	12½c. green	50	25
196	**81**	25c. brown	50	25

82 Columbus Theatre

83 Resplendent Quetzal

1923

197	**82**	50c. red	70	35
198	**83**	1p. green	3·50	35
199	**84**	5p. orange	1·80	70

1924. Surch 1924 and value.

200	-	1p. on 1p.50 (No. 169)	50	35
201	**84**	1p.25 on 5p. orange	70	70

87 Pres. J. R. Barrios

88 Dr. L. Montufar

1924

202	-	6c. olive (as No. 119)	25	25
203	**81**	25c. brown	25	25
204	-	50c. red (as No. 123a)	25	25
205	-	1p. brown (as No. 125)	25	25
206	**87**	1p.25 blue	60	25
207	-	2p. orange (as No. 126)	50	35
208	**88**	2p.50 purple	1·40	40
209	-	3p. green (as No. 162)	3·50	70
210	-	15p. black (as No. 171)	7·25	4·25

These all have imprint "PERKINS BACON & CO. LD. LONDRES" at foot.

1925. No. 201 further surch with two bars.

211	**84**	1p. on 5p. orange	70	70

89 Aurora Park

90 General Post Office

91 National Observatory

1926. Dated "1926".

212	-	6c. bistre (as No. 119)	20	20
213	**89**	12½c. green	20	20
214	**81**	25c. brown	20	20
215	**90**	50c. red	25	25
216	-	1p. brown (as No. 125)	25	25
217	**87**	1p.50 blue	25	25
218	**91**	2p. orange	1·80	1·40
219	**88**	2p.50 purple	2·20	1·80
220	-	3p. green (as No. 162)	60	35
221	-	5p. lilac (as No. 170)	1·40	60
222	-	15p. black (as No. 171)	9·00	4·00

These all have imprint "WATERLOW & SONS LIMITED, LONDRES" at foot.

92 Proposed new G.P.O.

1927. Obligatory Tax. G.P.O. Rebuilding Fund.

223	**92**	1c. olive	50	35

1928. Surch 1928 and value.

224	**91**	½c. de q. on 2p. orange	85	70
225	-	½c. de q. on 5p. lilac (No. 221)	50	35
226	**88**	1c. de q. on 2p.50 purple (No. 219)	50	35

95 Pres. J. R. Barrios

96 Dr. L. Montufar

97 Garcia Granados

98 General Orellana

99 City Arms, Guatemala

1929

227	**91**	½c. green	90	25
228	**81**	1c. sepia	35	25
229	**95**	2c. blue	35	25
230	**96**	3c. lilac	25	25
231	**97**	4c. yellow	35	25
232	**98**	5c. red	70	25
233	-	10c. brown (as No. 119)	60	25
234	-	15c. blue (as No. 125)	85	25
235	**31**	25c. brown	1·40	35
236	**89**	30c. green	1·30	60
237	-	50c. red (as No. 120)	3·00	1·20
238	**99**	1q. black	4·50	70

These all have imprint "T. DE LA RUE & CO. LD. LONDRES" at foot.

1929. Air. Nos. 210 and 222 surch SERVICIO POSTAL AEREO ANO DE 1928 and new value.

239		3c. on 15p. black (222)	1·70	2·00
240		5c. on 15p. black (222)	85	70
240a		5c. on 15p. black (210)	5·00	3·25
241		15c. on 15p. black (222)	2·40	70
242		20c. on 15p. black (222)	3·50	3·25

1929. Air. Surch SERVICIO POSTAL AEREO ANO DE 1929 Q0.03.

243	**88**	3c. on 2p.50 purple (No. 208)	1·40	1·40

1929. Opening of Guatemala–El Salvador Railway. No. 220 surch FERROCARRIL ORIENTAL 1929 and new value.

244		3c. on 3p. green	1·80	2·30
245		5c. on 3p. green	1·80	2·30

1930. Opening of Los Altos Railway. No. 222 surch FERROCARRIL DE LOS ALTOS Inaugurado en 1929 and value in words.

246		1c. on 15p. black	1·90	2·10
247		2c. on 15p. black	1·90	2·10
248		3c. on 15p. black	1·90	2·10
249		5c. on 15p. black	1·90	2·10
250		15c. on 15p. black	1·90	2·10

104 Bridge and Permanent Way

1930. Opening of Los Altos Railway.

251	-	2c. black and purple	2·10	2·10
252	**104**	3c. black and red	4·00	4·00
253	-	5c. blue and orange	4·00	4·00

DESIGNS: 2c. Quetzaltenango Dam; 5c. Quetzaltenango railway station.

105 Fokker Super Trimotor over Mt. Agua

1930. Air.

254	**105**	6c. red	95	60

1930. Air. Surch SERVICIO AEREO INTERIOR 1930 and value in words.

255		1c. on 3p. green (No. 220)	60	60
256		2c. on 3p. green	1·80	2·30
257		3c. on 3p. green	1·80	2·30
258		4c. on 3p. green	1·80	2·30
259		10c. on 15p. black (No. 222)	7·75	7·50

1931. Air. Optd EXTERIOR - 1931.

260		6c. red	2·10	2·00

1931. Air. Optd AEREO EXTERIOR 1931.

261	**97**	4c. yellow	60	45

1931. Air. Optd AEREO INTERNACIONAL 1931.

262	-	15c. blue (No. 234)	2·20	25
263	**89**	30c. green (No. 236)	3·50	1·20

1931. Air. Optd Primer Vuelo Posta BARRIOS-MIAMI 1931.

264	**95**	2c. blue	3·50	4·25
265	**96**	3c. lilac	3·50	4·25
266	-	15c. blue (No. 234)	3·50	4·25

1932. Air. Surch SERVICIO AEREO INTERIOR 1932 and value.

267	**87**	2c. on 1p.50 blue (217)	1·20	80
268	-	3c. on 3p. green (220)	1·20	35
270	-	10c. on 15p. black (222)	12·00	9·50
271	-	15c. on 15p. black (222)	14·50	13·00

114 Monolith of Quirigua

1932

272	**114**	3c. red	3·00	60

See also Nos. 416a/b.

1933. Air. Optd AEREO INTERIOR 1933.

273	**97**	4c. yellow	35	35

116 Flag of the Race, Columbus and Tecum Uman

1933. 441st Anniv of Departure of Columbus from Palos.

274	**116**	½c. green	1·10	75
275	**116**	1c. brown	1·80	1·50
276	**116**	2c. blue	1·80	1·50
277	**116**	3c. mauve	1·40	1·20
278	**116**	5c. red	1·80	1·50

1934. Air. (a) Optd AERO EXTERIOR 1934.

280	**98**	5c. red	2·40	35
281	-	15c. blue (No. 234)	2·40	35

(b) Optd AEREO INTERIOR 1934.

279	**95**	2c. blue	85	25

117 Barrios' Birthplace

118 Barrios and "Agamemnon" (freighter)

1935. Birth Centenary of J. R. Barrios.

282	**117**	½c. pink & green (postage)	75	70
283	-	1c. blue and orange	75	70
284	-	2c. black and orange	75	70
285	-	3c. blue and red	75	70
286	-	4c. red and blue	6·75	6·75
287	-	5c. brown and green	5·00	5·00
288	-	10c. red and green	7·25	7·00
289	-	15c. brown and green	7·25	7·00
290	-	25c. black and red	7·25	7·00
291	**118**	10c. blue and brown (air)	2·50	2·50
292	-	15c. brown and grey	2·50	2·50
293	-	30c. violet and red	2·50	1·80

DESIGNS—POSTAGE—HORIZ: 1c. San Lorenzo; 2c. Barrios and Official Decree; 3c. Arms and locomotive; 5c. Telegraph office and Barrios; 10c. Polytechnic School; 15c. Police H.Q.; 25c. Pres. Ubico, arms and Barrios. VERT: 4c. G.P.O. AIR—HORIZ: Barrios and (15c.) tomb, (30c.) statue.

120 Lake Atitlan

121 Resplendent Quetzal

122 Arms and Map of Guatemala

1935

293a		½c. blue and green	35	35
294	**120**	1c. red and brown	35	35
295	**121**	3c. green and orange	1·10	35
296	**121**	3c. green and red	1·10	35
297	-	4c. red and blue	50	35
297a	**122**	5c. brown and blue	1·20	35

DESIGNS—As Type **120**: ½c. Govt. Printing Works; 4c. National Assembly.

123 Lake Amatitlan

1935. Air. (a) Inscr "INTERIOR" (37×17 mm).

298	**123**	2c. brown	35	35
299	-	3c. blue	35	35
300	-	4c. black	35	35
300a	-	4c. blue	35	35
301	-	6c. green	35	35

301a	-	6c. violet	6·00	35
302	-	10c. red	70	35
303	-	15c. orange	95	60
303a	-	15c. green	95	95
304	-	30c. olive	9·00	9·50
304a	-	30c. brown	1·10	70
305	-	50c. purple	27·00	21·00
305a	-	50c. blue	6·00	4·25
306	-	1q. orange	27·00	29·00
306a	-	1q. red	6·75	4·25

DESIGNS: 3c. Puerto Barrios; 4c. San Felipe; 6c., 1q. Different view of Lake Amatitlan; 10c. Livingston; 15c. San Jose; 30c. Atitlan; 50c. La Aurora Airport.

(b) Inscr "EXTERIOR" (34×15 mm) (except Nos. 319/20 which are 46×20 mm).

307	1c. brown	35	35
308	2c. red	35	35
309	3c. mauve	70	35
309a	4c. yellow	2·75	2·10
309b	4c. red	1·40	1·10
310	5c. blue	35	35
310a	5c. orange	35	35
311	10c. brown	70	60
311a	10c. green	70	45
312	15c. red	35	35
312a	15c. orange	35	35
313	20c. blue	4·25	4·25
313a	20c. red	70	35
314	25c. black	5·00	5·00
314a	25c. green	70	35
315	30c. green	2·30	2·20
315a	30c. red	1·60	35
316	50c. red	11·00	11·50
316a	50c. violet	10·50	11·00
317	1q. blue	38·00	38·00
318	1q. green	11·00	10·50
319	2q.50 olive and red	7·25	5·50
320	5q. blue and orange	11·00	7·00

DESIGNS: 1c. Guatemala City; 2c., 15c. (No. 312) Views of Central Park; 3c. Cerrito del Carmen; 4c. Estuary of R. Dulce; 5c. Plaza J. R. Barrios; 10c. National Liberators' Monument; 15c. (No. 312a) R. Dulce; 20c. Quezaltenango; 25c. Antigua; 30c. Puerto Barrios; 50c. San Jose; 1q. Aurora Airport; 2q.50, Islet; 5q. Rocks on Atlantic Coast.

1936. Obligatory Tax. 65th Anniv of Liberal Revolution. Optd 1871 30 DE JUNIO 1936.

321	**92**	1c. green	85	80

1936. Obligatory Tax. 115th Anniv of Independence. Optd 1821 15 de SEPTIEMBRE 1936.

322	1c. green	70	60

1936. Obligatory Tax. National Fair. Optd FERIA NACIONAL 1936.

323	1c. olive	85	70

1937. Philatelic Exhibition Fund. Optd EXPOSICION FILATELICA 1937 or surch +1 also.

324		1c. olive	85	80
325	**120**	1c.+1c. red and brown	1·20	1·50
326	**121**	3c.+1c. green and orange	1·20	1·50
327	**121**	3c.+1c. green and red	1·20	1·50
328	**122**	5c.+1c. brown and blue	1·20	1·50
329	-	4c.+1c. (No. 300a)	1·30	1·60
330	-	6c.+1c. (No. 301a)	1·30	1·60
331	-	10c.+1c. (No. 311a)	1·30	1·60
332	-	15c.+1c. (No. 312a)	1·30	1·60

128 Resplendent Quetzal

129 General Ubico on horseback

1937. Second Term of Pres. Ubico. (a) Postage.

333	**128**	½c. red and blue	95	70
334	-	1c. brown and grey	70	45
335	-	2c. red and violet	85	45
336	-	3c. blue and purple	70	35
337	-	4c. olive and yellow	3·00	3·00
338	-	5c. purple and red	3·00	2·50
339	-	10c. black and purple	4·25	5·00
340	-	15c. red and blue	3·50	5·00
341	-	25c. violet and orange	4·50	5·25
342	-	50c. orange and green	6·75	8·25
343	**129**	1q. purple and brown	35·00	35·00
344	-	1q.50 brown and olive	35·00	35·00

DESIGNS: As Type **128**—VERT: 1c. Tower of the Reformer; 5c. National Congress entrance; 10c. Customs House. HORIZ: 2c. Union Park, Quezaltenango; 3c. G.P.O; 4c. Government Building, Retalhuleu; 15c. Aurora Airport; 25c. National Fair; 50c. Presidential Guards' Barracks. As Type **129**: 1q.50, Gen. Ubico.

130 Quezaltenango

(b) Air. As T 130, inscr "INTERIOR" and optd with aeroplane.

345	**130**	2c. black and red	35	35
346	-	3c. black and blue	1·40	1·80
347	-	4c. black and yellow	35	35
348	-	6c. black and green	60	35
349	-	10c. black and purple	3·00	3·25
350	-	15c. black and orange	2·20	1·40
351	-	30c. black and olive	5·50	4·25
352	-	50c. black and blue	7·25	6·50
353	-	75c. black and violet	14·50	15·00
354	-	1q. black and red	16·00	16·00

DESIGNS: 3c. Lake Atitlan; 4c. Progressive colony on Lake Amatitlan; 6c. Carmen Hill; 10c. Relief map; 15c. National University; 30c. Plaza Espana; 50c. Aurora Police Station; 75c. Aurora Amphitheatre; 1q. Aurora Airport.

(c) Air. As T 130 inscr "EXTERIOR" and optd with aeroplane.

355	1c. blue and orange	35	35
356	2c. violet and red	35	35
357	3c. brown and purple	70	70
358	5c. red and green	6·00	4·25
359	10c. green and red	1·80	1·40
360	15c. olive and pink	70	35
361	20c. black and blue	4·25	2·50
362	25c. red and grey	3·50	3·50
363	30c. violet and green	1·80	1·80
364	50c. blue and purple	14·00	14·00
365	1q. purple and olive	14·50	14·50
366	1q.50 brown and red	18·00	18·00

DESIGNS: 1c. Seventh Avenue; 2c. Liberators' Monument; 3c. National Printing Offices; 5c. National Museum; 10c. Central Park; 15c. Escuintla Park; 20c. Mobile Police; 25c. Slaughter-house, Escuintla; 30c. Campo de Marte Stadium; 50c. Plaza Barrios; 1q. Polytechnic; 1q.50, Aurora Airport.

132a George Washington

1938. 150th Anniv of U.S. Constitution. Optd 1787-1789 CL ANIVERSARIO DE LA CONSTITUCION EE. UU. 1937-1939.

367	**92**	1c. olive (postage)	30	25

MS367b 105×114 mm comprising 4c. brown and red (i); 4c. blue and red (ii); 15c. brown and blue (i); 15c. olive and blue (ii) (air) 8·75 8·50

DESIGNS: 4c. (i) President Roosevelt; 4c. (ii) Map of the Americas; 15c. (i), T **132a**; 15c. (ii) Pan-American Building, Washington.

1938. Obligatory Tax. No. 223 optd 1938.

368a	1c. olive	50	35

134

1938. 1st Central American Philatelic Exhibition. (a) Air. As T 134 inscr "PRIMERA EXPOSICION FILATELICA CENTRO AMERICANA".

369	**134**	1c. brown and orange	35	35
370	-	2c. brown and red	35	35
371	-	3c. brown, buff and green	60	60
372	-	4c. brown and purple	85	80
373	-	5c. brown and grey	70	80
374	-	10c. brown and blue	1·40	2·00

DESIGNS: 2c. to 10c. Various portraits as Type **134**.

(b) Postage. No. 223 optd Primera Exposicion Filatelica Centroamericana 1938.

375	**92**	1c. olive	60	45

136 Flag of Guatemala

(c) T 136 and similar horiz designs. Flags in national colours, frame colours given.

MS375a 145×96 mm. comprising 1c. orange (T **136**); 2c. carmine (El Salvador); 3c. green (Honduras); 4c. purple (Nicaragua); 5c. green (Costa Rica); 10c. bistre (Panama) 3·50 3·50

137 La Merced Church

1939. Optd with flying quetzal. (a) Inland Air Mail. As T 137 inscr "CORREO AEREO INTERIOR".

376	**137**	1c. brown and olive	35	35
377	-	2c. green and red	35	35
378	-	3c. olive and blue	35	35
379	-	4c. green and pink	35	35
380	-	5c. blue and purple	50	35
381	-	6c. grey and orange	60	35
382	-	10c. grey and brown	70	35
383	-	15c. black and purple	1·30	35
384	-	30c. red and blue	1·90	35
385	-	50c. violet and orange	2·75	60
386	-	1q. blue and green	3·75	1·90

DESIGNS: 2c. Christ's Church Ruins, Antigua; 3c. Aurora Airport; 4c. Campo de Marte Stadium; 5c. Cavalry Barracks; 6c. Palace of Justice; 10c. Customs House, San Jose; 15c. Post Office, Retalhuleu; 30c. Municipal Theatre, Quezaltenango; 50c. Customs House, Retalhuleu; 1q. Departmental Palace, Retalhuleu.

(b) Foreign Air Mail. As T 137 inscr "AEREO EXTERIOR" (10c. and 25c.) or "AEREO INTERNACIONAL".

387	1c. brown and sepia	35	35
388	2c. black and green	50	35
389	3c. green and blue	35	35
390	4c. green and brown	35	35
391	5c. red and green	60	35
392	10c. slate and red	3·25	35
393	15c. red and blue	2·75	35
394	20c. yellow and green	95	35
395	25c. olive and purple	95	35
396	30c. grey and red	1·40	35
397	50c. orange and red	2·30	35
398	1q. green and orange	4·50	45

DESIGNS: 1c. Mayan Altar, Aurora Park; 2c. Ministry of Health; 3c. Lake Amatitlan; 4c. Lake Atitlan; 5c. Bridge over Tamazulapa; 10c. National Liberators' Monument; 15c. Palace of the Captains General; 20c. Carmen Hill; 25c. Barrios Square; 30c. Mayan Altar, Archaeological Museum; 50c. Carlos III Fountain; 1q. Antigua.

1939. Obligatory Tax. No. 223 optd 1939.

399	**92**	1c. olive	60	35

140 National Flower (White Nun)

142 Arms and Map of Guatemala

1939

400	-	½c. brown and green	1·00	35
401	**140**	2c. black and blue	5·50	45
402	-	3c. green and brown	4·75	80
403	-	3c. green and red	4·75	80
404	**142**	5c. red and blue	6·75	2·50

DESIGNS: ½c. Mayan calendar; 3c. Resplendent quetzal.

1939. No. 229 surch UN CENTAVO.

405	**95**	1c. on 2c. blue	35	35

1940. Obligatory Tax. No. 223 optd 1940.

406	**92**	1c. olive	60	35

1940. 50th Anniv of Pan-American Union. (a) Optd Conmemorativo Union Panamericana 1890-1940.

407	1c. olive	60	35

(b) Air. Optd UNION PANAMERICANA 1890-1940 CORREO AEREO.

408	15c. blue (No. 234)	85	35

1940. Surch with new values.

409	**31**	1c. on 25c. brown	35	35
410	-	5c. on 50c. red (No. 237)	35	35

1941. Obligatory Tax. Optd 1941.

411	**92**	1c. olive	85	35

1941. Obligatory Tax. Surch CONSTRUCCION (twice) and UN CENTAVO.

412	**95**	1c. on 2c. blue	50	35

1941. Air. 2nd Pan-American Health Day. Optd DICIEMBRE 2 1941 SEGUNDO DIA PAN-AMERICANO DE LA SALUD.

414	2c. black and green (No. 388)	60	35

1941. Surch ½ MEDIO CENTAVO ½.

415	**31**	½c. on 25c. brown	50	45

1942. Obligatory Tax. Surch CONSTRUCCION 1942 UN CENTAVO.

416	**95**	1c. on 2c. blue	85	35

1942. As T 114, but tablet dated "1942".

416a	3c. green	1·40	35
416b	3c. blue	1·40	35

153 Archway between wings of new G.P.O.

1942. Obligatory Tax.

417a	**153**	1c. brown	60	35

154 Guastatoya Vase

1942

418	**154**	½c. brown	50	25
419	-	1c. red	50	25

DESIGN—HORIZ: 1c. Old people's home.

156 Ruins of Zakuleu

157 National Printing Works

158 National Police H.Q.

159 San Carlos Borromeo University, Antigua

1943

420	**156**	½c. brown (postage)	35	25
421	**157**	2c. red	35	25
422	**158**	10c. mauve (air)	70	25
423	**159**	15c. brown	85	25

160 Don Pedro de Alvarado

1943. Air. 400th Anniv of Founding of Antigua.

424	**160**	15c. blue	24·00	16·00

161 Archway between wings of new G.P.O.

1943. Obligatory Tax.

425	**161**	1c. orange	60	35

162 Rafael Maria Landivar

1943. 150th Death Anniv of R. M. Landivar (poet).

426	**162**	5c. blue	50	35

163 National Palace

1944. Inauguration of National Palace.

427	**163**	3c. green (postage)	50	25
444	**163**	5c. red (air)	85	35
445	**163**	10c. lilac	35	35
446	**163**	15c. blue	85	35

1945. Optd 25 de junio de 1944 PALACIO NACIONAL and bar.

428	3c. blue	70	35

1945. Air. Optd PALACIO NACIONAL and bar.

429	5c. red	60	35

165 Archway between wings of new G.P.O.

1945. Obligatory Tax.

430	**165**	1c. orange	60	35
479	**165**	1c. blue	60	35

166 Allegory of the Revolution

1945. Revolution of 20 October 1944.

431	**166**	3c. blue (postage)	50	35
432	**166**	5c. red (air)	95	35
433	**166**	6c. green	95	35
434	**166**	10c. violet	95	35
435	**166**	15c. blue	95	35

1945. Air. Book Fair. No. 389 surch 1945 FERIA DEL LIBRO 2½ CENTAVOS.

436	2½c. on 3c. green and blue	3·00	2·30

168 Jose Milla y Vidaurre (author)

169 Archbishop Pavo Enriquez de Rivera

1945

437	**168**	1c. green (postage)	50	25
438	**169**	2c. violet	50	35
439	**169**	5c. red (air)	60	35
440	**168**	7½c. purple	2·40	1·80
441	**168**	7½c. blue	1·20	60
678	**169**	5c. olive	50	25
679	**169**	5c. blue	50	25
680	**169**	5c. green	50	25
681	**169**	5c. orange	50	25
682	**169**	5c. violet	50	25
683	**169**	5c. grey	50	25

For stamps as Type **169** but dated "1660 1951" see Nos. 523/27.

170 Torch

1945. 1st Anniv of Revolution of 20 October 1944.

442	**170**	3c. blue (postage)	35	25
443	**170**	5c. mauve (air)	95	35

MS443a 90×71 mm. No. 443 (×2). Imperf 3·00 1·90

See also Nos. 458/61.

171 Jose Batres y Montufar (military leader and writer)

1945

447	**171**	½c. brown (postage)	35	25
448	**171**	3c. blue	35	25
449	**171**	3c. green	35	35
450	-	10c. green (air)	70	35

DESIGN—HORIZ: 10c. Montufar.

174 Rowland Hill

1946. Centenary of First Postage Stamps.

451		1c. olive & violet (postage)	50	35
452	**174**	5c. brown and grey (air)	50	35
453	-	15c. blue, green and red	85	45

DESIGNS: 1c. U.P.U. Monument, Berne; 15c. Hemispheres and quetzal.

175 Signing the Declaration of Independence

1946. Air. 125th Anniv of Independence.

454	**175**	5c. red	25	25
455	**175**	6c. brown	35	25
456	**175**	10c. violet	50	35
457	**175**	20c. blue	60	35

1947. Air. 2nd Anniv of Revolution of 20 October 1944. As T 170 but inscr "1944 1946" instead of "1944 1945" and "II" for "I".

458	1c. green	60	35
459	2c. red	60	35
460	3c. violet	60	35
461	5c. blue	60	35

176 Franklin D. Roosevelt

1947. Air.

462	**176**	5c. red	35	35
463	**176**	6c. blue	35	35
464	**176**	10c. blue	50	35
465	**176**	30c. black	2·20	1·40
466	**176**	50c. violet	3·50	3·50
467	**176**	1q. green	6·00	5·75

177 "Labour"

1948. Labour Day and 1st Anniv of Adoption of Labour Code.

468	**177**	1c. green	60	35
469	**177**	2c. purple	60	35
470	**177**	3c. blue	60	35
471	**177**	5c. red	60	35

1948. Optd 1948.

472	**142**	5c. red and blue	60	45

1948. Air. Optd 1948 AEREO.

473	5c. red and blue	60	45

180 Football Match

1948. Air. 4th Central American and Caribbean Football Championship Games.

474	**180**	3c. black and red	1·20	45
475	**180**	5c. black and green	1·40	70
476	**180**	10c. black and mauve	1·60	1·40
477	**180**	30c. black and blue	3·25	5·25
478	**180**	50c. black and yellow	7·25	7·00

181 Fray Bartolome de Las Casas and Indian

1949. Fray Bartolome de Las Casas ("Apostle of the Indians").

480	**181**	½c. red	35	25
481	**181**	1c. brown	35	25
484	**181**	4c. blue	35	25
661	**181**	½c. blue	35	25
662	**181**	1c. violet	35	25
663	**181**	2c. green	60	25
664	**181**	3c. red	50	25
665a	**181**	4c. brown	35	25

182 Seal of University of Guatemala

1949. Air. Latin-American Universities' Congress.

485	**182**	3c. blue and red	85	70
486	**182**	10c. blue and green	1·70	1·20
487	**182**	50c. blue and yellow	5·00	5·25

183 Gathering Coffee

1950. Tourist Propaganda. (a) Postage.

488	**183**	½c. olive, blue and pink	35	25
489	-	½c. blue and brown	85	35
490	-	1c. olive, brown and yellow	35	25
491	-	1c. green and orange	85	35
492	-	2c. blue, green and red	35	25
493	-	2c. brown and red	85	35
494	-	3c. brown, blue and violet	35	25
495	-	6c. violet, orange & green	50	25

DESIGNS—As Type **183**: ½c. (No. 489), 3c. Cutting sugar canes; 1c. (No. 490), 2c. (No. 493), Agricultural colony; 1c. (No. 491), 2c. (No. 492), Banana trees; 6c. International Bridge.

184 Tecum Uman Monument

(b) Air. Multicoloured centres.

496		3c. red	60	35
497	**184**	5c. lake	60	35
498	-	8c. black	70	35
499	-	13c. brown	1·10	35
500	-	35c. violet	3·50	4·50

DESIGNS—As Type **184**—HORIZ: 3c. Lake Atitlan; 8c. San Cristobal Church; 35c. Momostenango Cliffs. VERT: 13c. Weaver.

185 Footballers

1950. Air. 6th Central American and Caribbean Games. Inscr "VI JUEGOS DEPORTIVOS 1950".

501	**185**	1c. black and violet	95	35
502	-	3c. black and red	1·10	35
503	-	4c. black and brown	1·40	45
504	-	8c. black and purple	1·70	60
505	-	35c. black and blue	3·75	5·00
506	-	65c. green	7·75	8·25

DESIGNS—HORIZ: 4c. Pole vaulting; 35c. Diving; 65c. Stadium. VERT: 3c. Runners; 8c. Tennis.

186 Ministry of Health Badge

1950. Social Assistance and Public Health Fund.

507	**186**	1c. blue and red (postage)	35	35
508	-	3c. red and green (Nurse)	50	35
509	-	5c. brown and blue (Map)	70	35

MS510 130×80 mm. Nos. 507/9. Imperf or perf 4·25 4·00

187 Nursing School

511		5c. red, green & violet (air)	35	35
512	**187**	10c. green and brown	95	60
513	-	50c. purple, green and red	3·25	4·00
514	-	1q. olive, green and yellow	4·50	4·50

MS515 150×100 mm. Nos. 511/14. Imperf or perf 12·00 11·50

DESIGNS—As Type **187**: 5c. Nurse; 50c., 1q. Zacapa and Roosevelt Hospitals.

1951. No. E479 without surcharge for use as ordinary postage.

517	**E181**	4c. black and green	70	35

1951. 75th Anniv (in 1949) of UPU. Sheet containing stamps similar to Type 5. Imperf.

MS518 111×69 mm. 1c. carmine (As T **195**); 10c. blue (as T **5**) 3·75 3·75

188 School

1951. Aerial views of schools as T 188.

519	188	½c. brown and violet	60	45
520	-	1c. green and lake	60	45
521	188	2c. brown and blue	60	60
522	-	4c. purple and black	60	60

1952. As No. 438 but dated "1660 1951" below portrait.

523	169	½c. violet	35	35
524	169	1c. red	35	35
525	169	2c. green	35	35
526	169	4c. orange	70	35
527	169	4c. blue	50	25

189 Ceremonial Axehead

1953. Air.

528	189	3c. drab and blue	35	35
529	189	5c. brown and slate	50	35
530	189	10c. slate and violet	70	35

190 Flag and Constitution

1953. Air. Presidential Succession, 1951.

531	190	1c. multicoloured	35	25
532	190	2c. multicoloured	35	25
533	190	4c. multicoloured	50	25

191 R. Alvarez Ovalle (music), J. J. Palma (words)

1953. National Anthem.

534	191	½c. grey and violet	50	35
535	191	1c. brown and grey	50	35
536	191	2c. olive and brown	50	35
537	191	3c. olive and blue	50	35

192 "Work and Play" 193 Horse Racing

1953. Air. National Fair. Inscr "FERIA NACIONAL".

538	-	1c. red and blue	35	35
539	-	4c. green and orange	1·90	45
540	192	5c. brown and green	1·20	60
541	193	15c. lilac and brown	1·80	1·50
542	-	20c. blue and red	1·60	1·40
543	-	30c. blue and sepia	1·80	2·00
544	-	50c. black and violet	2·10	2·00
545	-	65c. green and blue	3·75	4·00
546	-	1q. green and red	31·00	19·00

DESIGNS—VERT: 1c. National dance; 4c. National flower (white nun); 30c. Picture and corn cob; 1q. Resplendent quetzal. HORIZ: 20c. Ruins of Zakuleu; 50c. Champion bull; 65c. Cycle-racing.

194 Indian Warrior

1954. Air. National Revolutionary Army Commemoration.

547	194	1c. red	50	35
548	194	2c. blue	50	35
549	194	4c. green	50	35
550	194	5c. turquoise	85	35
551	194	6c. orange	85	35
552	194	10c. violet	1·70	45
553	194	20c. sepia	5·00	5·00

1954. As T 5 but inscr "UNION POSTAL UNIVERSAL GUATEMALA" around oval.

554	1c. blue	1·60	35
555	2c. violet	85	35
556	2c. brown	85	35
557	3c. red	1·10	35
558	3c. blue	1·10	35
559	4c. orange	1·80	35
560	4c. violet	1·60	35
561	5c. brown	2·40	35
562	5c. red	2·40	35
563	5c. green	1·80	35
564	5c. grey	3·25	35
565	6c. green	2·40	80
1222	1c. green	35	30
1222a	2c. blue	35	30
1225	3c. brown	25	20
1226	3c. green	25	20
1227	3c. orange	25	20
1228	4c. brown	35	30
1228a	5c. mauve	35	30
1229	6c. blue	45	30

196 Flags of Guatemala and ODECA

1954. Air. 3rd Anniv of Organization of Central American States.

566	196	1c. multicoloured	70	60
567	196	2c. multicoloured	70	60
568	196	4c. multicoloured	70	60

197 Goalkeeper

1955. Golden Jubilee of Football in Guatemala. Inscr "1902–1952".

569	-	4c. violet (Camposeco)	1·60	35
570	-	4c. red (Camposeco)	1·60	35
571	-	4c. green (Camposeco)	1·60	35
572	-	10c. green (Matheu)	4·75	1·20
573	197	15c. blue	4·75	3·00

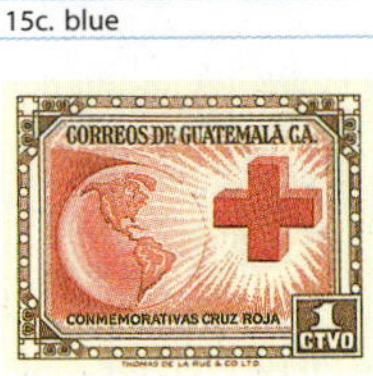

198 Red Cross and Globe

1956. Red Cross. Inscr "CONMEMORATIVAS CRUZ ROJA".

574	198	1c. red & brown (postage)	50	35
575	-	3c. red and green	50	35
576	-	4c. red and black	50	35
577	-	5c.+15c. red and blue	1·60	2·10
578	-	15c.+50c. red and lilac	3·50	4·00
579	198	25c.+50c. red and blue	3·50	4·00
580	-	35c.+1q. grn & red (air)	8·50	8·75
581	-	50c.+1q. red and blue	8·50	8·75
582	-	1q.+1q. red and green	8·50	8·75

DESIGNS: 3c., 15c. Telephone and red cross; 4c., 5c. Nurse, patient and red cross; 35c. Red Cross ambulance; 50c. Nurse and hospital; 1q. Red Cross nurse.

199 Road Map of Guatemala 200 Maya Warrior

1956. Revolution of 1954–55. Inscr "LIBERACION 1954-55".

583		½c. violet (postage)	35	35
584	199	1c. green	35	35
585	-	3c. sepia	35	35
586	200	2c. multicoloured (air)	35	35
587	-	4c. black and red	35	35
588	-	5c. brown and blue	35	35
589	-	6c. blue and sepia	50	35
590	-	20c. brown, blue and violet	2·50	2·20
591	-	30c. olive and blue	3·00	2·75
592	-	65c. green and brown	4·50	3·75
593	-	1q. multicoloured	5·75	5·50
594	-	5q. brown, blue and green	23·00	22·00

DESIGNS: ½c. Liberation dagger symbol; 3c. Oil production; 4c. Family; 5c. Sword smashing Communist emblems; 6c. Hands holding map and cogwheel; 20c. Martyrs' Monument; 30c. Champerico Port; 65c. Telecommunications symbols; 1q. Flags of ODECA countries;-5q. Pres. Armas.

201 Rotary Emblem and Road Map

1956. Air. 50th Anniv of Rotary International.

595	201	4c. bistre and blue	35	35
596	201	6c. bistre and green	35	25
597	201	35c. bistre and violet	3·00	2·20

1957. Air. Red Cross Fund. Nos. 577/9 optd AEREO-1957 and ornaments.

598	-	5c.+15c. red and blue	11·50	11·50
599	-	15c.+50c. red and lilac	11·50	11·50
600	198	25c.+50c. red and blue	11·50	11·50

203 Esquipulas Cathedral and "Black Christ"

1957. Esquipulas Highway Fund. Inscr "PRO-CARRETERA ESQUIPULAS JUNIO 1957".

601	203	1½c.+½c. violet and brown (postage)	85	35
602	-	10c.+1q. brown and green (air)	11·00	11·00
603	-	15c.+1q. green and sepia	11·00	11·00
604	-	20c.+1q. slate and brown	11·00	11·00
605	-	25c.+1q. red and lilac	11·00	11·00

DESIGNS—HORIZ: 10c. Esquipulas Cathedral. VERT: 15c. Cathedral and "Black Christ"; 20c. Map of Guatemala and "Black Christ"; 25c. Bishop of Esquipulas.

204 Red Cross, Map and Resplendent Quetzal

1958. Air. Red Cross.

606	204	1c. multicoloured	70	35
607	-	2c. red, brown and blue	50	25
608	-	3c. brown, red and blue	50	25
609	-	4c. red, green and brown	50	25

DESIGNS—VERT: 2c. J. R. Angulo, Mother and Child. HORIZ: 3c. P. de Bethancourt and Invalid; 4c. R. Ayau and Red Cross.

1959. Birth Centenary of R. A. Ovalle (composer of National Anthem). Optd 1858 1958 CENTENARIO.

610	191	½c. grey and violet	60	60

1959. Air. Pres. Castillo Armas Commem. As No. 594 but inscr "LIBERACION 3 DE JULIO DE 1954", etc. Centre in blue and yellow. Frame colours given.

615	1c. black	50	35
616	2c. red	50	35
617	4c. brown	50	35
618	6c. green	50	35
619	10c. violet	60	45
620	20c. green	1·60	1·20
621	35c. grey	2·75	2·10

1959. Air. United Nations. Optd HOMENAJE A LAS NACIONES UNIDAS.

622	168	7½c. blue	1·80	1·90

207 Caravel of 1532 and freighter "Quetzaltenango"

1959. Air. Central American Merchant Marine Commemoration.

623	207	6c. blue and red	1·60	45

1959. Air. Guatemala's Claim to Belize (British Honduras). As No. 509 optd BELICE ES NUESTRO and AEREO.

624	5c. brown and blue	85	35

1959. Air. Centenary of First Export of Coffee. No. 589 optd 1859 CENTENARIO PRIMERA EXPORTACION DE CAFE 1959.

625	6c. blue and sepia	95	35

210 Pres. and Senora Morales

1959. Air. Visit of President of Honduras.

626	210	6c. brown	60	45

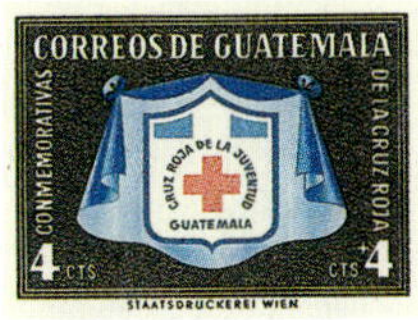

211 Red Cross Shield

1960. Red Cross Commemoration. Cross in red.

627	211	1c.+1c. blue and brown (postage)	35	60
628	-	3c.+3c. blue and lilac	35	60
629	211	4c.+4c. blue and black	35	60
630	-	5c.+5c. blue, pink and red (air)	3·75	4·00
631	-	6c.+6c. green and red	3·75	4·00
632	-	10c.+10c. pink, blue and deep blue	3·75	4·00
633	-	15c.+15c. red, blue and brown	3·75	4·00
634	-	20c.+20c. green, pink and purple	3·75	4·00
635	-	25c.+25c. pink, blue and grey	3·75	4·00
636	-	30c.+30c. multicoloured	3·75	4·00

DESIGNS—3c., 5c. Wounded soldier at Solferino; 6c., 20c. Houses and debris afloat on flood waters; 10c., 25c. Earth, Moon and planets; 15c., 30c. Red Cross H.Q., Guatemala City.

1960. Air. World Refugee Year. Nos. 606/9 optd ANO MUNDIAL DE REFUGIADOS or surch also.

637	1c. multicoloured	3·25	2·50
638	2c. red, brown and blue	1·40	1·40
639	3c. brown, red and blue	1·40	1·40
640	4c. red, green and brown	1·40	1·40
641	6c. on 1c. multicoloured	7·75	3·75
642	7c. on 2c. red, brown and blue	3·50	3·00
643	10c. on 3c. brown, red & blue	5·50	5·75
644	20c. on 4c. red, green & brown	6·75	6·50

1960. Air. Founding of City of Melchor de Mencos. No. 589 optd Fundacion de la cuidad Melchor de Mencos 30-IV-1960.

645		6c. blue and sepia	1·90	2·10

213 Abraham Lincoln

1960. Air. 150th Birth Anniv of Abraham Lincoln.

646	**213**	5c. blue	35	35
647	**213**	30c. violet	1·70	2·10
648	**213**	50c. slate	8·50	10·00

214 UNESCO Headquarters, Paris

1960. Air. Inauguration of UNESCO. Headquarters Building, Paris (1958).

649	**214**	5c. violet and mauve	35	35
650	**214**	6c. sepia and blue	35	35
651	**214**	8c. red and green	60	35
652	**214**	20c. blue and brown	2·20	2·10

1961. Air. Red Cross. Nos. 606/9 optd MAYO DE 1960.

653		1c. multicoloured	60	45
654		2c. red, brown and blue	25	45
655		3c. brown, red and blue	60	45
656		4c. red, green and brown	60	45

216 Romulus, Remus and Wolf

1961. Plaza Italia Inauguration.

657	**216**	3c. blue	95	35

217 Independence Ceremony

1962. Air. 140th Anniv of Independence.

658	**217**	4c. sepia	35	25
659	**217**	5c. blue	50	25
660	**217**	15c. violet	1·90	95

1962. Air. Malaria Eradication. Optd 1962 EL MUNDO UNIDO CONTRA LA MALARIA.

666	**214**	6c. sepia and blue	1·30	2·10

219 Dr. Jose Luna

1962. Air. Guatemalan Doctors.

667	**219**	1c. violet and olive	1·20	35
668	-	4c. green and yellow	1·20	35
669	-	5c. brown and blue	1·20	35
670	-	6c. black and salmon	1·20	35
671	-	10c. brown and green	1·80	35
672	-	20c. blue and mauve	2·10	1·20

DOCTORS: 4c. R. Robles; 5c. N. Esparragoza; 6c. J. Ortega; 10c. D. Gonzalez; 20c. J. Flores.

1962. Air. Pres. Ydigoras's Tour of Central America. No. 589 optd PRESIDENTE YDIGORAS FUENTES RECORRE POR TIERRA CENTRO AMERICA 14 A 20 DIC. 1962.

673		6c. blue and sepia	1·70	1·20

1963. Air. New ODECA Charter Commemoration. Optd CONMEMORACION FIRMA NUEVA CARTA ODECA.—1962.

674	**214**	6c. sepia and blue	60	35
675	**214**	8c. red and green	70	35

222 Girl with Basket of Fruit on head

1963. Air. National Fair, 1960.

676	**222**	1c. multicoloured	35	25

1963. Air. Presidential Meeting. No. 589 with 11-line opt starting REUNION PRESIDENTES: KENNEDY.

677		6c. blue and sepia	8·50	4·25

224 Arms

1963

684	**224**	10c. red	60	35
685	**224**	10c. black	60	35
686	**224**	10c. brown	60	35
687	**224**	20c. violet	95	45
688	**224**	20c. blue	95	45

225 Harvester (after "The Reaper", Mathieson)

1963. Air. Freedom from Hunger.

689	**225**	5c. turquoise	50	35
690	**225**	10c. blue	95	45

226 Ceiba (national tree)

1963. Air.

691	**226**	4c. green and sepia	60	35

227 Pedro Bethancourt tending sick man

1964. Campaign for Canonization of Pedro Bethancourt.

692	**227**	2½c. brown (postage)	35	25
693	**227**	2½c. blue (air)	25	25
694	**227**	3c. orange	25	25
695	**227**	4c. violet	35	25
696	**227**	5c. green	50	25

228 Patzun Palace

1964. Air. Guatemalan Palaces.

697	**228**	1c. brown and red	60	35
698	-	3c. green and mauve	60	35
699	-	4c. lake and blue	60	35
700	-	5c. blue and brown	70	35
701	-	6c. blue and green	70	35

PALACES: 3c. Coban; 4c. Retalhuleu; 5c. San Marcos; 6c. Los Capitanes Generales.

229 Municipal Building

1964. Air. New Buildings. (a) As T 229.

702	**229**	3c. brown and blue	50	35
703	-	4c. blue and brown	60	45

DESIGN: 4c. Social Security Building.

(b) Designs as Nos. 702/3 but different style frame and inscr, and new designs.

704		3c. green (As No. 703)	85	35
705		4c. slate	85	35
706	**229**	7c. blue	95	35
707	-	7c. bistre	85	35

DESIGNS: 4c. University Rectory; 7c. (No. 707), Engineering Faculty.

1964. Air. Olympic Games, Tokyo. Optd with Olympic rings and OLIMPIADAS TOKIO-1964.

708	**204**	1c.	1·40	1·60
709	-	2c. (No. 607)	1·40	1·60
710	-	3c. (No. 608)	1·40	1·60
711	-	4c. (No. 609)	1·40	1·60

1964. Air. New York World's Fair. Optd FERIA MUNDIAL DE NEW YORK.

712	**204**	1c.	1·20	1·30
713	-	2c. (No. 607)	1·20	1·30
714	-	3c. (No. 608)	1·20	1·30
715	-	4c. (No. 609)	1·20	1·30

1964. Air. Surch HABILITADA 1964 and value.

716	**204**	7c. on 1c.	50	35
717	-	9c. on 2c. (No. 607)	60	60
718	-	13c. on 3c. (No. 608)	85	70
719	-	21c. on 4c. (No. 609)	1·60	1·30

1964. Air. 8th Cycle Race. Optd VIII VUELTA CICLISTICA.

720	**204**	1c.	1·80	1·60
721	-	2c. (No. 607)	1·80	1·60
722	-	3c. (No. 608)	1·80	1·60
723	-	4c. (No. 609)	3·25	2·50

234 Pres. Kennedy

1964. Air. Pres. Kennedy Commemoration.

724	**234**	1c. violet	1·40	85
725	**234**	2c. green	1·40	85
726	**234**	3c. brown	1·40	85
727	**234**	7c. blue	1·40	85
728	**234**	50c. green	10·50	9·00

1964. Air. 15th UPU Congress, Vienna. Sheet containing two stamps similar to T 224.

MS729 86×60 mm. 10c. blue; 20c. carmine		11·50	12·00

235 Centenary Emblem

1964. Air. Red Cross Centenary. Emblem in silver and red.

730	**235**	7c. blue	85	45
731	**235**	9c. orange	85	55
732	**235**	13c. violet	1·30	95
733	**235**	21c. green	1·30	1·60
734	**235**	35c. brown	2·20	2·30
735	**235**	1q. bistre	6·25	3·75

1964. 15th Anniv (1963) of International Society of Guatemala Collectors. No. 559 optd HOMENAJE A LA "I.S.G.C." 1948–1963.

736		4c. orange	70	35

237 Bishop F. Marroquin

1985. Air. 400th Death Anniv of Bishop Marroquin.

737	**237**	4c. brown and purple	35	25
738	**237**	7c. sepia and grey	60	25
739	**237**	9c. black and blue	70	35

1965. Air. Optd AYUDENOS MAYO 1965. Emblem in silver and red.

740	**235**	7c. blue	60	50
741	**235**	9c. orange	70	60
742	**235**	13c. violet	75	65
743	**235**	21c. green	1·10	95
744	**235**	35c. brown	1·30	1·50

239 Scout Badge

1966. Air. 5th Regional Scout Training Conference, Guatemala City. Multicoloured.

745	5c. Type **239**	70	65
746	9c. Scouts by campfire	90	85
747	10c. Scout carrying torch and flag	1·10	1·00
748	15c. Scout saluting	1·40	1·30
749	20c. Lord Baden-Powell	2·00	1·90

240 Flags

1966. Air. "Centro America". 145th Anniv of Central American Independence.

750	**240**	6c. multicoloured	50	20

241 Nefertari's Temple, Abu Simbel

1966. Air. Nubian Monuments Preservation.

751	**241**	21c. violet and bistre	1·10	55

242 Arms

1966. Air.

752 **242** 5c. orange 40 20
753 **242** 5c. green 40 20
754 **242** 5c. grey 40 25
755 **242** 5c. violet 40 25
756 **242** 5c. blue 40 25
757 **242** 5c. deep blue 40 20
758 **242** 5c. violet 40 20
759 **242** 5c. green 40 20
760 **242** 5c. lake 70 25
761 **242** 5c. green on yellow 75 25

243 Mgr. M. Rossell y Arellano

1966. Air. Monseigneur Rossell Commem.

765 **243** 1c. violet 30 20
766 **243** 2c. green 40 20
767 **243** 3c. sepia 40 20
768 **243** 7c. blue 60 50
769 **243** 50c. slate 2·50 2·40

244 Mario M. Montenegro (revolutionary)

1966. Air. Montenegro Commemoration.

770 **244** 2c. red 30 15
771 **244** 3c. orange 40 20
772 **244** 4c. red 50 20
773 **244** 5c. grey 70 20
774 **244** 5c. blue 70 20
775 **244** 5c. green 70 20
776 **244** 5c. black 70 20

245 Morning Glory

1967. Air. Flowers. Multicoloured.

777 4c. Type **245** 60 30
778 8c. "Bird of Paradise" (horiz) 60 30
779 10c. "White Nun" orchid (national flower) (horiz) 85 45
780 20c. "Nymphs of Amatitlan" 1·90 1·30

246 Institute Emblem

1967. Air. 8th General Assembly of Pan-American Geographical and Historical Institute (1965).

781 **246** 4c. purple, black & brown 35 20
782 **246** 5c. blue, black and bistre 70 20
783 **246** 7c. blue, black and yellow 1·10 30

247 Map of Guatemala and British Honduras

1967. Guatemala's Claim to British Honduras.

784 **247** 4c. blue, red and green 50 30
785 **247** 5c. blue, red and yellow 50 30
786 **247** 6c. blue, grey and orange 50 30

1967. Air. Guatemalan Victory in "Norceca" Football Games. No. 704 optd GUATEMALA CAMPEON III Norceca Foot-Ball and football motif.

787 3c. green 2·00 1·40

1967. Air. American Heads of State Meeting, Punta del Este. No. 705 optd REUNION JEFES DE ESTADO AMERICANO, PUNTA DEL ESTE etc.

788 4c. slate 1·40 1·40

250 "Peace and Progress"

1967. Air. International Co-operation.

789 **250** 7c. multicoloured 70 30
790 **250** 21c. multicoloured 1·10 65

251 Yurrita Church

1967. Air. Religion in Guatemala.

791 **251** 1c. brown, green and blue 50 30
792 - 2c. brown, pur & salmon 60 30
793 - 3c. indigo, red and blue 60 30
794 - 4c. green, purple & salmon 60 30
795 - 5c. brown, purple & green 60 30
796 - 7c. black, blue and mauve 70 30
797 - 10c. blue, violet and yellow 1·20 35

DESIGNS—HORIZ: 2c. Santo Domingo Church; 3c. San Francisco Church; 7c. Mercy Church, Antigua; 10c. Metropolitan Cathedral. VERT: 4c. Antonio Jose de Irisarri; 5c. Church of the Recollection.

252 Lincoln

1967. Air. Death Centenary (1965) of Abraham Lincoln.

798 **252** 7c. red and blue 60 30
799 **252** 9c. black and green 70 30
800 **252** 11c. black and brown 65 35
801 **252** 15c. red and blue 80 50
802 **252** 30c. green and purple 1·80 1·90

1967. Air. 8th Central American Scout Camporee. Nos. 745/9 optd VIII Camporee Scout Centroamericano Diciembre 1-8/1967.

803 5c. Type **239** 50 50
804 9c. Scouts by campfire 80 75
805 10c. Scout carrying torch and flag 1·10 1·00
806 15c. Scout saluting 1·10 1·00
807 20c. Lord Baden-Powell 1·30 1·20

1967. Air. Award of Nobel Prize for Literature to Miguel Angel Asturias (1st issue). Nos. 694/5 optd "Premio Nobel de Literatura - 10 diciembre 1967 - Miguel Angel Asturias".

808 **227** 3c. orange 70 65
809 - 4c. violet 70 65

See also No. 838.

255 UNESCO Emblem and Children

1967. Air. 20th Anniv (1966) of UNESCO.

810 **255** 4c. green 30 15
811 **255** 5c. blue 40 20
812 **255** 7c. grey 50 30
813 **255** 21c. purple 1·20 1·10

256 Institute Emblem

1967. Air. 25th Anniv of Inter-American Institute of Agricultural Sciences.

814 **256** 9c. black and green 1·00 95
815 **256** 25c. red and brown 1·90 1·90
816 **256** 1q. ultramarine and blue 5·00 4·75

1968. Air. 3rd Meeting of Central American Presidents. Optd III REUNION DE PRESIDENTES Nov. 15-18, 1967.

817 **204** 1c. (No. 606) 1·20 80
819 - 2c. (No. 607) 1·00 1·00
821 - 3c. (No. 608) 1·00 1·00
823 **235** 7c. (No. 730) 1·00 1·00
824 **235** 9c. (No. 731) 1·40 1·40
825 **235** 13c. (No. 732) 2·00 1·40
826 **235** 21c. (No. 733) 2·75 1·40
827 **235** 35c. (No. 734) 2·30 2·40

258 "Madonna of the Choir"

1968. Air. 400th Anniv of "Madonna of the Choir".

828a **258** 4c. blue 60 30
829 **258** 7c. slate 60 30
830 **258** 9c. green 70 30
830a **258** 9c. lilac 75 25
831 **258** 10c. red 1·00 30
832 **258** 10c. grey 65 30
832a **258** 10c. blue 50 15
833 **258** 1q. purple 5·00 4·25
834 **258** 1q. yellow 5·00 4·25

1968. Air. 11th Cycle Race. Nos. 784/6 optd AEREO XI VUELTA CICLISTICA 1967.

835 **247** 4c. blue, red and green 1·10 1·00
836 **247** 5c. blue, red and yellow 1·10 1·00
837 **247** 6c. blue, grey and orange 85 85

260 Miguel Angel Asturias

1968. Air. Award of Nobel Prize for Literature to Miguel Angel Asturias.

838 **260** 20c. blue 1·40 50

1968. Air. Campaign for Conservation of the Forests. No. 789 optd AYUDA A CONSERVAR LOS BOSQUES.–1968.

839 **250** 7c. multicoloured 50 30

1968. Air. Human Rights Year. No. 626 optd 1968.–ANO INTERNACIONAL DERECHOS HUMANOS.–ONU.

840 **210** 6c. brown 70 35

1968. Air. Nahakin Scientific Expedition. No. 589 optd Expedicion Cientifica etc.

841 6c. blue and sepia 40 35

264 "Visit Guatemala"

1968. Air. Tourism.

842 **264** 10c. red and green 70 30
843 **264** 20c. red and black 1·10 75
844 **264** 50c. blue and red 1·90 1·80

265 Mayan Ball Game Ring and Resplendent Quetzal

1968. Olympic Games, Mexico. Quetzal in green and red.

845 **265** 1c. black 50 20
846 **265** 5c. yellow 70 30
847 **265** 8c. orange 80 30
848 **265** 15c. blue 1·40 30
849 **265** 30c. violet 2·50 1·30
850 **265** 1c. slate 40 30
851 **265** 5c. pink 70 30
852 **265** 5c. brown 70 30
853 **265** 5c. blue 70 70

1968. Air. 20th Anniv of Federation of Central American Universities. No. 705 optd CONFEDERACION DE UNIVERSIDADES CENTROAMERICANAS 1948 1968.

854 4c. slate 40 35

267 Presidents Gustavo Diaz Ordaz and Julio Cesar Mendez Montenegro

1968. Air. Exchange Visits of Mexican and Guatemalan Presidents.

855 **267** 5c. multicoloured 30 30
856 **267** 10c. blue and ochre 50 30
857 **267** 25c. blue and ochre 1·20 1·00

268 I.T.U. Emblem and Symbols

1968. Air. Centenary (1965) of I.T.U.

858 **268** 7c. blue 30 20
859 **268** 15c. black and green 60 20
859a **268** 15c. brown and orange 70 30
860 **268** 21c. purple 85 55
861 **268** 35c. red and green 1·20 55
862 **268** 75c. green and red 3·00 2·75
863 **268** 3q. brown and red 11·50 9·50

269 Young Girl and Poinsettia

1969. Help for Abandoned Children.

864	**269**	2½c. ochre, red and green	40	20
865	**269**	2½c. orange, red and green	60	65
866	**269**	5c. black, red and green	60	20
867	**269**	21c. violet, red and green	1·30	1·00

1969. Air. Nos. 845/9 optd AEREO and motifs. Quetzal in green and red.

868	**265**	1c. black	1·00	50
869	**265**	5c. yellow	1·30	65
870	**265**	8c. orange	1·20	1·00
871	**265**	15c. blue	1·40	1·20
872	**265**	30c. violet	2·00	1·60

271 Dante

1969. Air. 700th Birth Anniv (1965) of Dante.

873	**271**	7c. blue and plum	50	30
874	**271**	10c. blue	60	30
875	**271**	20c. green	85	30
876	**271**	21c. slate and brown	1·40	95
877	**271**	35c. violet and green	3·50	2·10

272 Map of Central and South America

1969. Air. 20th Anniv of Latin-American Universities Union.

878	**272**	2c. mauve and black	30	20
879	-	9c. black and grey	70	30
MS880 118×75 mm. As Nos. 878/9, but colours changed; 2c. blue and black; 9c. black and red. Imperf			1·60	1·40

DESIGN: 26×27 mm 9c. University seal.

273 "Apollo 11" and Moon Landing

1969. Air. 1st Man on the Moon.

881	**273**	50c. black and purple	3·50	3·25
882	**273**	1q. black and blue	5·75	5·75
MS883 111×81 mm. **273** 1q. blue and green. Imperf			8·25	8·00

1970. 50th Anniv of Int Labour Organization. Nos. 847/8 optd Cincuentenario O.I.T. and ornaments.

884	**265**	8c. orange, green and red	60	20
886	**265**	15c. blue, green and red	85	30

275 Lake Atitlan

1970. Air. Conservation of Atitlan Grebes. Multicoloured.

888	4c. Type **275**	1·20	30
889	9c. Family of Atitlan Grebes	1·70	35
890	20c. Young grebe in nest (vert)	3·00	1·00

276 Dr. V. M. Calderon

1970. Air. 1st Death Anniv of Dr. Victor M. Calderon (medical scientist).

892	**276**	1c. black and blue	20	20
893	**276**	2c. black and green	30	20
894	**276**	9c. black and yellow	70	20

277 Hand holding Bible

1970. Air. 400th Anniv of Spanish Bible.

895	**277**	5c. multicoloured	40	30

1971. Air. Surch VALE Q0.50.

896	**268**	50c. on 3q. brown and red	2·50	2·40

279 Arms and Newspaper

1971. Air. Stamp Centenary (1st issue) and Centenary of Newspaper "Gaceta de Guatemala".

897	**279**	2c. blue and red	15	15
899	**279**	25c. blue and red	80	50
899b	**279**	5c. brown and red	30	30
899c	**279**	50c. mauve and brown	1·70	65

See also Nos. 988/9d.

280 Maya Indians and C.A.R.E. Package

1971. 25th Anniv of C.A.R.E. (Co-operative for American Relief Everywhere). Mult.

900	1c. Type **280** (black inscr) (postage)	30	30
901	1c. Type **280** (brown inscr)	30	30
902	1c. Type **280** (violet inscr)	30	30
903	2c. Maya porter and C.A.R.E. parcel (air)	35	25
904	5c. Two Maya warriors and parcel	50	40
905	10c. C.A.R.E. parcel within Maya border	65	45
MS906 141×96 mm. Nos. 900 and 904. Imperf		3·00	3·00
MS907 141×96 mm. Nos. 903 and 905. Imperf		1·40	1·40

SIZES: 2c. (36×30 mm); 50c. (46×27 mm); 10c. (28×31 mm).

281 Decree of 1870

1971. Air. Stamp Centenary. Sheet 140×110 mm containing T 281 and four designs similar to T 1.

MS908 1c. yellow; 4c, black (T **281**); 5c. brown; 10c. blue; 20c. red	2·50	2·40

282 J. Rufino Barrios, M. Garcia Granados and Emblems

1971. Air. Centenary of Liberal Reforms.

909	**282**	2c. multicoloured	1·00	20
910	**282**	10c. multicoloured	1·90	35
911	**282**	50c. multicoloured	8·25	4·00
912	**282**	1q. multicoloured	14·50	8·00

283 J. A. Chavarry Arrue (stamp engraver) and Leon Bilak (philatelist)

1971. Air. "Homage to Philately".

913	**283**	1c. black and green	30	20
914	**283**	2c. black and brown	40	30
915	**283**	5c. black and orange	60	35

1971. Air. "INTERFER 71" Int Fair, Guatemala. Optd FERIA INTERNACIONAL "INTERFER–71" 30 Oct. al 21 Nov.

916	**207**	6c. blue and red	40	20

285 Flag and Map

1971. Air. 150th Anniv of Central American Independence.

917	**285**	1c. blue, black and lilac	25	20
918	**285**	3c. blue, brown and pink	25	20
919	**285**	5c. blue, brown & orange	30	25
920	**285**	9c. blue, black and green	35	25

286 Maya Statue and UNICEF Emblem

1971. Air. 25th Anniv of UNICEF.

921	**286**	1c. green	30	20
921a	**286**	2c. purple	30	25
922	**286**	50c. purple	2·30	2·30
923	**286**	1q. blue	3·75	3·75

287 Boeing "Peashooter" and North American P-51 Mustang

1972. Air. 50th Anniv of Guatemala Air Force.

924	**287**	5c. blue and brown	70	25
925	-	10c. blue	1·30	30

DESIGN—56×32 mm: 10c. Bleriot XI airplane.

1972. Olympic Games, Munich. Sheet No. MS518 cut down to size 61×47 mm and optd JUEGOS OLIMPICOS MUNICH 1972.

MS926 1c. carmine (As T **5**); 10c. blue (as T **244**)	1·90	1·90

289 Ruins of Capuchin Monastery

1972. Air. Tourism. Ruins of Antigua.

927	**289**	1c. blue and light blue	30	10
928	**A**	1c. blue and light blue	30	10
929	**B**	1c. blue and light blue	30	10
930	**C**	1c. blue and light blue	30	10
931	**D**	1c. blue and light blue	30	10
932	**E**	1c. blue and light blue	30	10
933	**289**	2c. black and brown	30	25
934	**A**	2c. black and brown	30	25
935	**B**	2c. black and brown	30	25
936	**C**	2c. black and brown	30	25
937	**D**	2c. black and brown	30	25
938	**E**	2c. black and brown	30	25
939	**289**	2½c. black, mauve & silver	60	25
940	**A**	2½c. black, mauve & silver	60	25
941	**B**	2½c. black, mauve & silver	60	25
942	**C**	2½c. black, mauve & silver	60	25
943	**D**	2½c. black, mauve & silver	60	25
944	**E**	2½c. black, mauve & silver	60	25
945	**289**	5c. black, blue and orange	95	35
946	**A**	5c. black, blue and orange	95	35
947	**B**	5c. black, blue and orange	95	35
948	**C**	5c. black, blue and orange	95	35
949	**D**	5c. black, blue and orange	95	35
950	**E**	5c. black, blue and orange	95	35
951	**289**	20c. black and yellow	85	55
952	**A**	20c. black and yellow	85	55
953	**B**	20c. black and yellow	85	55
954	**C**	20c. black and yellow	85	55
955	**D**	20c. black and yellow	85	55
956	**E**	20c. black and yellow	85	55
957	**289**	1q. lt blue, red and blue	5·75	3·00
958	**A**	1q. lt blue, red and blue	5·75	3·00
959	**B**	1q. lt blue, red and blue	5·75	3·00
960	**C**	1q. lt blue, red and blue	5·75	3·00
961	**D**	1q. lt blue, red and blue	5·75	3·00
962	**E**	1q. lt blue, red and blue	5·75	3·00

DESIGNS: A, "La Recoleccion" archways; B, Cathedral ruins; C, Santa Clara courtyard; D, San Francisco gateway; E, Fountain, Central Park.

See also Nos. 1230/41.

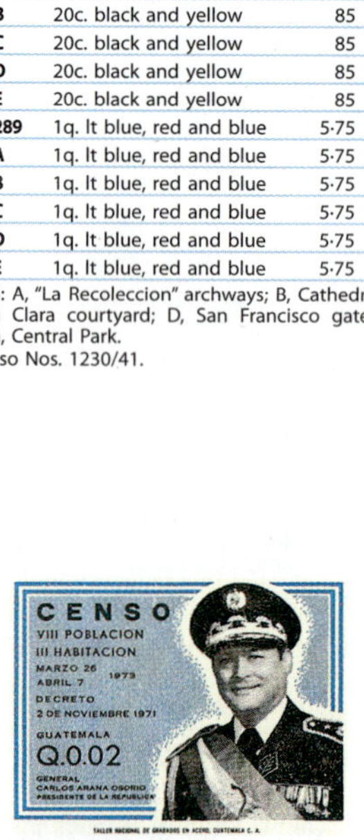

290 Pres. Carlos Arana Osorio

1973. National Census.

963	**290**	2c. black and blue	20	10
964	-	3c. brown, pink & orange	30	10
965	**290**	5c. purple, mauve & black	40	10
966	-	8c. green, black & emerald	70	20

DESIGNS—VERT: 3c. Pres. Osorio seated; 8c. Pres. Osorio standing.

291 Francisco Ximenez

1973. International Book Year (1972).

No.	Type	Description		
967	**291**	2c. black and green	30	20
968	**291**	3c. brown and orange	30	20
969	**291**	6c. black and blue	35	25
969a	**291**	3c. black and yellow	30	20

292 Simon Bolivar and Map

1973. Air. Simon Bolivar, "The Liberator".

No.	Type	Description		
970	**292**	3c. black and red	30	20
971	**292**	3c. blue and orange	30	20
972	**292**	5c. black and yellow	35	30
973	**292**	5c. black and green	35	30

293 Eleanor Roosevelt

1973. Air. 90th Birth Anniv (1974) of Eleanor Roosevelt (sociologist).

No.	Type	Description		
974	**293**	7c. blue	30	20

294 Star Emblem

1973. Air. Centenary of Polytechnic School.

No.	Type	Description		
975	**294**	5c. yellow, brown & blue	40	30

See also Nos. 1000/1.

1973. Air. Nos. 927/32 optd "II Feria Internacional" INTERFER/73 31 Octubre-Noviembre 18 1973 GUATEMALA.

No.	Type	Description		
976	**289**	1c. blue and light blue	50	35
977	**A**	1c. blue and light blue	50	35
978	**B**	1c. blue and light blue	50	35
979	**C**	1c. blue and light blue	50	35
980	**D**	1c. blue and light blue	50	35
981	**E**	1c. blue and light blue	50	35

296 1c. Stamp of 1871

1973. Air. Stamp Centenary (1971). (2nd issue).

No.	Type	Description		
988	**296**	1c. brown	30	20
988a	**296**	6c. orange	30	30
988b	**296**	6c. green	30	30
988c	**296**	6c. blue	30	30
988d	**296**	6c. grey	30	30
989	**296**	1q. red	3·75	3·00

297 School Building

1973. Air. Centenary of Instituto Varones, Chiquimula.

No.	Type	Description		
990	**297**	3c. multicoloured	30	25
991	**297**	5c. red and black	30	25

268 I.T.U. Emblem and Symbols

1974. No. 863 surch Desvalorizadas a Q0.50 and leaves.

No.	Type	Description		
992	**268**	50c. on 3q. brown and red	2·50	2·40

1974. Air. Centenary of Universal Postal Union. Nos. 927/32 optd UPU HOMENAJE CENTENARIO 1874 1974 and U.P.U. emblem.

No.	Type	Description		
993	**289**	1c. blue and light blue	50	35
994	**A**	1c. blue and light blue	50	35
995	**B**	1c. blue and light blue	50	35
996	**C**	1c. blue and light blue	50	35
997	**D**	1c. blue and light blue	50	35
998	**E**	1c. blue and light blue	50	35
MS999 141×96 mm			11·50	11·00

300 Barrios and Granados

1974. Air. Centenary (1973) of Polytechnic School (2nd issue).

No.	Type	Description		
1000	**300**	6c. red, grey and blue	30	30
1001	-	25c. multicoloured	60	35

DESIGN—VERT: 25c. School building.

1974. Air. Protection of the Resplendent Quetzal (Guatemala's national bird). No. 800 surch with bars, VALE 10c. Proteccion del Ave Nacional el Quetzal and bird.

No.	Type	Description		
1002	**252**	10c. on 11c. black & brn	85	50

302 Costume of San Martin Sacatepequez

1974. Air. Guatemalan Costumes. Mult.

No.	Type	Description		
1003		2c. Solola costume	30	30
1004		2½c. Type **302**	30	25
1005		9c. Coban costume	40	30
1006		20c. Chichicastenango costume	70	30

303 Mayan Girl and Resplendent Quetzals

1975. Air. International Women's Year.

No.	Type	Description		
1007	**303**	8c. multicoloured	85	30
1008	**303**	20c. multicoloured	1·60	50

304 Rotary Emblem

1975. Air. 50th Anniv of Guatemala City Rotary Club.

No.	Type	Description		
1009	**304**	10c. multicoloured	30	10
1010	**304**	15c. multicoloured	55	20

305 I.W.Y. Emblem and Orchid

1975. Air. International Women's Year (2nd series).

No.	Type	Description		
1011	**305**	1c. multicoloured	35	30
1012	**305**	8c. multicoloured	50	30
1013	**305**	26c. multicoloured	1·10	40

306 Ruined Village

1976. Air. Earthquake of 4 February 1976. Multicoloured.

No.	Type	Description		
1014		1c. Type **306**	20	20
1015		3c. Food queue	20	20
1016		5c. Jaguar Temple, Tikal	20	20
1017		10c. Broken bridge	35	20
1018		15c. Open-air casualty station	55	20
1019		20c. Harvesting sugarcane	55	25
1020		25c. Ruined house	95	30
1021		30c. Reconstruction, Tecpan	1·10	35
1022		50c. Ruined church, Cerrodel Carmen	1·50	50
1023		75c. Clearing debris	2·40	90
1024		1q. Military aid	3·75	1·20
1025		2q. Lake Atitlan	7·00	2·75
MS1026 Three sheets each 112×83 mm. 50c. Map and bell; 1q. Encampment and helicopter; 2q. No. 1025 Set of three sheets			21·00	19·00

Text in panels expresses gratitude for foreign aid.

307 Eagle and Resplendent Quetzal Emblems

1976. Air. Bicentenary of American Revolution. Multicoloured.

No.	Type	Description		
1029		1c. Type **307**	30	20
1030		2c. Boston Tea Party	20	20
1031		3c. Thomas Jefferson (after G. Stuart) (vert)	20	20
1032		4c. Eagle and resplendent quetzal emblems (vert)	30	20
1033		5c. "Death of Gen. Warren at Bunker Hill" (detail, Trumbull)	20	20
1034		10c. "Washington reviewing his Ragged Army" (detail, Trego)	30	20
1035		15c. "Washington rallying the Troops at Monmouth" (detail, Leutze)	30	20
1036		20c. Eagle and resplendent quetzal emblems (diff)	55	25
1037		25c. "Meeting of Generals at Yorktown after the Surrender" (detail, Peale)	70	25
1038		30c. "Washington crossing the Delaware" (detail, Leutze)	95	25
1039		35c. Eagle and resplendent quetzal emblems (diff)	1·00	50
1040		40c. "Declaration of Independence" (detail, Trumbull)	1·00	55
1041		45c. "Patrick Henry before Virginia House of Burgesses" (detail, Rothermel) (vert)	1·20	65
1042		50c. "Congress voting Independence" (detail, Savage)	1·60	50
1043		1q. George Washington (after G. Stuart) (vert)	2·75	2·20
1044		2q. Abraham Lincoln (after D. D. Eisenhower) (vert)	4·75	4·25
1045		3q. Benjamin Franklin (after C. W. Peale) (vert)	6·75	5·75
1046		5q. John F. Kennedy (35×55 mm)	11·50	3·75
MS1047 Four sheets (a) 141×103 mm. No. 1043; (b) 147×108 mm. No. 1044; (c) 140×101 mm. No. 1045; (d) 143×105 mm. No. 1046. Imperf Set of four sheets			39·00	34·00

308 Quetzal Coin

1976. Air. 50th Anniv of Quetzal Currency.

No.	Type	Description		
1051	**308**	8c. black, orange and blue	30	20
1052	**308**	20c. black, mauve & blue	85	25

309 "The Engineers" (sculpture)

1976. Air. Centenary of Engineering School, Guatemala City.

No.	Type	Description		
1053	**309**	9c. blue	35	20
1054	**309**	10c. green	35	20

310 Sculpture of Christ (Pedro de Mendoza)

1977. Holy Week. Multicoloured.

No.	Type	Description		
1055		6c. Type **310** (postage)	50	25
1056		8c. Sculpture of Christ (Lanuza Brothers)	50	25
1057		3c. Statue of Christ (air)	50	25
1058		4c. Statue of Christ (vert)	50	25
1059		7c. Statue of Christ (vert)	50	25
1060		9c. Statue of Christ (vert)	55	25
1061		20c. Statue of Christ and Virgin (vert)	1·10	60
1062		26c. Statue of Christ	1·50	75
MS1063 100×70 mm. 30c. Christ bearing the Cross (horiz)			2·40	2·20

311 Deed to Site of Guatemala City

1977. Air. Bicentenary of Nueva Guatemala de la Asuncion (Guatemala City). Multicoloured.

No.	Type	Description		
1064		6c. Type **311**	50	25
1065		7c. City Hall and Bank of Guatemala (horiz)	50	25
1066		8c. Site of first legislative assembly (horiz)	50	25
1067		9c. Archbishop's arms (horiz)	65	25
1068		22c. Arms of Guatemala City	1·00	25
MS1069 Two sheets each 110×80 mm. (a) No. 1067; (b) No. 1068. Imperf Set of two sheets			2·40	2·10

312 Arms of Quetzaltenango

1977. Air. 150th Anniv of Founding of Quetzaltenango.

No.	Type	Description		
1071	**312**	7c. black and silver	30	15
1072	-	30c. orange and blue	1·00	35

DESIGN: 30c. City Hall and torch.

313 "Interfer 77" Emblem

1977. 4th International Fair, Guatemala City.

1073	**313**	7c. multicoloured	30	25

314 Mayan Bas-relief

1977. Air. 14th Congress of Latin Notaries.

1074	**314**	10c. black and red	35	20

315 "The Holy Family"

1977. Air. Christmas. Multicoloured.

1075	1c. Type **315**	30	25
1076	2c. Boy and girl with animals, and Jesus in crib	30	25
1077	4c. Boy and girl with Mary and Jesus	30	25

316 Man from Almolongo

1978. Air. Guatemalan Costumes. Mult.

1078	1c. Type **316**	15	15
1079	2c. Woman from Nebaj	15	15
1080	5c. Couple from San Juan Cotzal	20	15
1081	6c. Couple from Todos Santos	35	15
1082	20c. Couple from Regidores	1·30	25
1083	30c. Woman from San Cristobal	1·30	35
MS1084	70×90 mm. No. 1082	1·50	1·30

317 Virgin of Sorrows, Antigua

1978. Air. Holy Week. Multicoloured.

1085	2c. Type **317**	50	25
1086	4c. Virgin of Mercy, Antigua	50	25
1087	5c. Virgin of Anguish, Yurrita	50	25
1088	6c. Virgin of the Rosary, Santo Domingo	50	25
1089	8c. Virgin of Sorrows, Santo Domingo	50	25
1090	9c. Virgin of the Rosary, Quetzaltenango	50	25
1091	10c. Virgin of the Immaculate Conception, Church of St. Francis	50	25
1092	20c. Virgin of the Immaculate Conception, Cathedral Church	1·20	25
MS1093	71×101 mm. 30c. Pieta, Cavalry Church, Antigua. Imperf	3·50	3·00

318 Footballer

1978. Air. World Cup Football Championship, Argentina.

1094	**318**	10c. multicoloured	35	15

319 Gymnastics

1978. Air. 13th Central American and Caribbean Games, Medellin, Colombia.

1095	**319**	6c. mauve, blue and black	30	25
1096	-	6c. brt blue, blue & black	30	25
1097	-	6c. blue, brt blue & black	30	25
1098	-	6c. blue, mauve and black	30	25
1099	-	8c. mauve, blue and black	30	25

DESIGNS: No. 1096, Volleyball; 1097, Target Shooting; 1098, Weightlifing; 1099, Running.

320 "Cattleya pachecoi"

1978. Air. Orchids. Multicoloured.

1100	1c. Type **320**	30	25
1101	1c. "Sobralia xantholeuca"	35	25
1102	1c. "Cypripedium irapeanum"	35	25
1103	1c. "Oncidium splendidum"	35	25
1104	3c. "Cattleya bowringiana"	40	25
1105	3c. "Encyclia cordigera"	40	25
1106	3c. "Epidendrum imatophyllum"	40	25
1107	3c. "Barkeria skinneri"	40	25
1108	8c. "Spiranthes speciosa"	75	60
1109	20c. "Lycaste skinneri"	2·75	2·40

321 University Seal

1978. Air. 300th Anniv of San Carlos University of Guatemala. Multicoloured.

1110	6c. Type **321**	20	15
1111	7c. Students from different faculties (26×46 mm)	30	15
1112	12c. 17th-century student	35	20
1113	14c. Student and molecular model	55	20

322 Brown and White Children

1978. Air. Guatemalan Children's Year (1977). Multicoloured.

1114	6c. Type **322**	20	15
1115	7c. Child skipping	30	15
1116	12c. "Helping Hand"	35	20
1117	14c. Hands protecting Indian girl	55	20

323 Planting Seedling

1979. Air. Forestry. Multicoloured.

1118	6c. Type **323**	35	25
1119	8c. Burnt forest	35	25
1120	9c. Woodland scene	35	25
1121	10c. Sawmill	35	25
1122	26c. Forest conservation	65	25
MS1123	140×100 mm. Nos. 1118/22 with label showing FAO emblem	2·30	2·10

324 Ocellated Turkey

1979. Air. Wildlife Conservation. Mult.

1124	1c. Type **324**	75	25
1125	3c. White-tailed deer (horiz)	50	25
1126	5c. King vulture	2·40	25
1127	7c. Great horned owl	5·25	1·00
1128	9c. Ocelot	1·10	25
MS1129	98×69 mm. 30c. Resplendent quetzal (35×45 mm)	12·00	11·00

325 Clay Jar

1979. Air. Archaeological Treasures from Tikal. Multicoloured.

1130	2c. Type **325**	50	25
1131	3c. Ceramic head of Mayan woman	65	40
1132	4c. Earring	95	60
1133	5c. Vase	1·10	65
1134	6c. Ceramic figure	1·50	85
1135	7c. Carved bone	1·60	1·00
1136	8c. Striped vase	1·90	1·10
1137	10c. Tripod vase with lid	2·40	1·40

326 Presidential Guard Headquarters

1979. 30th Anniv of Presidential Guard. Multicoloured.

1138	10c. Type **326** (postage)	30	25
1139	8c. Presidential Guard insignia (air)	30	25

327 National Coat of Arms

1979. Air. Municipal Arms. Multicoloured.

1140	8c. Type **327**	55	25
1141	8c. Alta Verapaz	55	25
1142	8c. Baja Verapaz	55	25
1143	8c. Chimal Tenango	55	25
1144	8c. Chiquimula	55	25
1145	8c. Escuintla	55	25
1146	8c. Flores (Peten)	55	25
1147	8c. Guatemala	55	25
1148	8c. Huehuetenango	55	25
1149	8c. Izabal	55	25
1150	8c. Jalapa	55	25
1151	8c. Jutiapa	55	25
1152	8c. Mazatenango	55	25
1153	8c. El Progreso	55	25
1154	8c. Quezaltenango	55	25
1155	8c. Quiche	55	25
1156	8c. Retalhuleu	55	25
1157	8c. Sacatepequez	55	25
1158	8c. San Marcos	55	25
1159	8c. Santa Rosa	55	25
1160	8c. Solola	55	25
1161	8c. Totonicapan	55	25
1162	8c. Zacapa	55	25
MS1163	100×72 mm. 50c. First and present national arms. Imperf	4·25	3·75

328 Rotary Emblem and Girl with Flowers

1980. 75th Anniv of Rotary International. Multicoloured.

1164	4c. Type **328**	95	25
1165	6c. Diamond, emblem and resplendent quetzal	95	25
1166	10c. Paul P. Harris (founder), emblem and resplendent quetzal	1·10	65

329 The Creation of the World

1981. Air. "Popol Vuh". Designs showing medallic illustrations of Guatemalan history and legends from the Sacred Book of the Ancient Quiches of Guatemala. (a) The Creation.

1167	**329**	1c. black and mauve	10	10
1168	-	2c. black and green	10	10
1169	-	4c. black and blue	35	20
1170	-	8c. black and yellow	70	40
1171	-	10c. black and pink	80	50
1172	-	22c. black and brown	1·90	1·10

(b) The Adventures of Hun Ahpu and Xbalanque.

1173	1c. black and mauve	10	10
1174	4c. black and violet	35	20
1175	6c. black and brown	45	30
1176	8c. black and green	70	40
1177	10c. black and yellow	80	50
1178	26c. black and green	2·10	1·20

(c) The Founding of the Quiche Race.

1179	2c. black and mauve	10	10
1180	4c. black and blue	35	20
1181	6c. black and pink	45	30
1182	8c. black and yellow	70	40
1183	10c. black and green	80	50
1184	30c. black and green	2·50	1·60

(d) The Territorial Expansion of the Quiches.

1185	3c. black and blue	25	10
1186	4c. black and violet	35	20
1187	6c. black and pink	45	30
1188	8c. black and grey	70	40
1189	10c. black and green	80	50
1190	50c. black and mauve	4·25	2·50

DESIGNS: No. 1168, Populating the earth; 1169, Birth of the stick-men; 1170, Destruction of the stick-men; 1171, Creation of the men of corn; 1172, "Thanks to the creator"; 1173, Origin of the twin semi-gods; 1174, Punishment of the Princess Xquic; 1175, Odyssey of Hun Ahpu and Xbalanque; 1176, The test in Xibalba; 1177, Multiplication of the prodigies; 1178, The deification of Hun Ahpu and Xbalanque; 1179, Balam Quitze, father of CavIquib; 1180, Caha Paluma, wife of Balam Quitze; 1181, Balam Acab, father of Nihaibab; 1182, Chomiia, wife of Balam Acab; 1183, Mahucutah, father of Ahau Quiche; 1184, Tzununiha, wife of Mahucutah; 1185, Cotuha, Quiche monarch; 1186, The invincible Cotuha and Iztayul; 1187, Cucumatz, the prodigious king; 1188, Warrior with captive; 1189, "None can conquer or kill the king"; 1190, "This was the greatness of the Quiches".

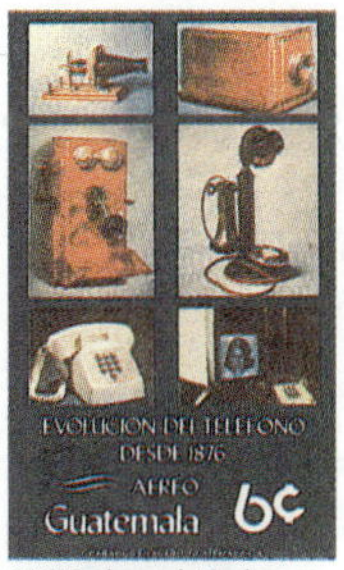

330 Early and Modern Telephones (cent)

1981. Air. Anniversaries.

1191	-	3c. red and black	35	30
1192	-	5c. blue and black	45	30
1193	**330**	6c. multicoloured	60	30
1194	-	7c. multicoloured	70	40
1195	-	12c. multicoloured	1·20	60
1196	-	25c. multicoloured	2·30	1·30

DESIGNS—26×46 mm: 3c. Thomas Edison (centenary of gramophone). 29×39 mm: 7c. Charles Lindbergh (50th anniv of solo Atlantic flight); 12c. Jose Cecilio del Valle (patriot, birth bicentenary), 25c. Jesues Castillo (composer, birth centenary). 46×26 mm: 5c. Spool of film (50th anniv of sound film).

331 Roderico Toledo and German Chupina (first and present Police Chiefs)

1981. Air. Centenary of National Police. Multicoloured.

1197	2c. Type **331**	60	30
1198	4c. Police Headquarters	60	30

332 Mayan Sun Calendar

1981. Air. 7th Latin American Aviculture Congress.

1199	**332**	1c. green, yellow & black	35	30

333 Bernardo O'Higgins (Chile)

1982. Air. Liberators of the Americas.

1200	**333**	2c. multicoloured	35	30
1201	-	3c. multicoloured	35	30
1202	-	4c. multicoloured	35	30
1203	-	10c. grey and black	35	30

DESIGNS—(31×45 mm): 4c. Jose de San Martin (Argentine); 10c. Miguel Garcia Granados (Guatemala). (26×35 mm): 3c. Jose Artigas (Uruguay).

334 General Barrios and Bank

1982. Air. Centenary of Banco de Occidente.

1204	**334**	1c. multicoloured	35	30
1205	-	2c. black, red and blue	35	30
1206	-	3c. multicoloured	35	30
1207	-	4c. multicoloured	35	30

DESIGNS—HORIZ: 2c. Bank building. VERT: 3c. Centenary emblem; 4c. Centenary medals.

335 Old and New Bank Buildings, Guatemala City

1982. Air. 50th Anniv of National Mortgage Bank.

1208	**335**	1c. multicoloured	35	30
1209	-	2c. black, yellow & green	35	30
1210	-	5c. multicoloured	35	30
1211	-	10c. black, yellow & grn	35	30

DESIGNS—HORIZ: 2c. Bank emblem; 10c. Bank and Anniversary emblems. VERT: 5c. Bronze anniversary medallion.

336 Brother Pedro

1983. Air. Blessed Brother Pedro. Mult.

1212	1c. Type **336**	25	20
1213	20c. Apparition of Virgin Mary	95	50

337 I.T.U. and W.H.O. Emblems with Ribbons forming Caduceus

1983. Air. World Communications and Health Day.

1214	**337**	10c. yellow, red and black	45	30

338 Hands holding Bible

1983. Air. Centenary (1982) of Evangelical Church in Guatemala. Multicoloured.

1215	3c. Type **338**	60	30
1216	5c. Central Evangelical Church	60	30

339 Train crossing Las Vacas Bridge

1983. Air. Centenary (1980) of Guatemalan Railways. Multicoloured.

1217	10c. Type **339**	1·10	85
1218	25c. General Barrios and trains at station	3·00	1·80
1219	30c. Train crossing Lake Amatitlan Dam	3·50	2·20

340 F.A.O. Emblem and Starving Children

1983. Air. World Food Day (1981). Mult.

1220	8c. Maize and Globe	35	10
1221	1q. Type **340**	3·25	1·80

1984. Air. As Nos. 927/32 and 945/50 but colours changed. Values inscribed in black.

1230	**289**	1c. black and green	25	20
1231	**A**	1c. black and green	25	20
1232	**B**	1c. black and green	25	20
1233	**C**	1c. black and green	25	20
1234	**D**	1c. black and green	25	20
1235	**E**	1c. black and green	25	20
1236	**289**	5c. black and orange	35	20
1237	**A**	5c. black and orange	35	20
1238	**B**	5c. black and orange	35	20
1239	**C**	5c. black and orange	35	20
1240	**D**	5c. black and orange	35	20
1241	**E**	5c. black and orange	35	20

341 Pope John Paul II

1984. Air. Papal Visit. Multicoloured.

1242	4c. Type **341**	35	30
1243	8c. Woman kneeling before Pope	35	30

342 Rafael Landivar

1984. Air. 250th Birth Anniv of Rafael Landivar (poet). Multicoloured.

1244	2c. Type **342**	35	30
1245	4c. Landivar's tomb, Antigua Guatemala (horiz)	35	30

343 Casariego y Acevedo

1984. Air. 1st Death Anniv of Cardinal Mario Casariego y Acevedo, Archbishop of Guatemala.

1246	**343**	10c. multicoloured	60	30

344 Bank's Emblem

1984. Air. 20th Anniv of Central American Bank for Economic Integration.

1247	**344**	30c. multicoloured	1·60	85

345 Planting Coffee, 1870

1984. Air. Coffee.

1248	**345**	1c. black and brown	25	20
1249	-	2c. black and flesh	25	20
1250	-	3c. black and stone	25	20
1251	-	4c. black and buff	25	20
1252	-	5c. multicoloured	45	30
1253	-	10c. multicoloured	95	50
1254	-	12c. multicoloured	1·20	60
1255	-	25c. multicoloured	2·30	1·30
1256	-	25c. black and brown	£130	10
1257	-	30c. multicoloured	£160	10

DESIGNS: As T **345**: 2c. Harvesting coffee, 1870; 3c. Drying coffee beans, 1870; 4c. Exporting coffee, 1870; 5c. Grafting seedlings; 10c. Instant coffee; 12c. Harvesting and processing coffee; 25c. (1255) Exporting coffee (different). (81×108 mm): 25c. (1256) Women picking coffee. (100×81 mm): 30c. Globe and coffee beans.

346 "Beaver" Cub and Tikal Pyramid

1985. Air. 75th Anniv of Boy Scout Movement. Multicoloured.

1258	5c. Type **346**	35	20
1259	6c. "Wolf" cub and Captains Palace, Old Guatemala	50	25
1260	8c. Scout, xylophone player and countryside	55	35
1261	10c. Rover scout and dancers	70	40
1262	20c. Lord Baden-Powell (founder) and Carlos Cipriani (founder of Guatemalan scouts)	1·50	90

347 Family

1985. Air. Inter-American Family Year.

1263	**347**	10c. multicoloured	55	35

348 Emblem

1985. Air. 25th Anniv of Central American Air Navigation Services Association.

1264	**348**	10c. multicoloured	50	25

349 Morse Key, Samuel Morse, J. Rufino Barrios and Telegraph Aerial

1985. Air. National Telegraph Service.

1265	**349**	4c. black and brown	30	25

350 Olympic Rings and Maya Pelota Player

1986. Air. 90th Anniv of First Modern Olympic Games and Foundation of International Olympic Committee. Multicoloured.

1266 8c. Type **350** 35 25
1267 10c. Rings and Baron Pierre de Coubertin 50 25

351 Rescue Team with Person in Cradle

1986. Air. Volunteer Firemen (1st series).

1268 **351** 6c. multicoloured 75 25

See also Nos. 1271/2.

352 Temple of Minerva, Quetzaltenango

1986. Air. Centenary (1984) of Independence Fair, Quetzaltenango. Multicoloured.

1269 8c. Type **352** 30 20
1270 10c. City arms in courtyard of Quetzaltenango Municipal Palace 35 25

353 Fire behind Fireman carrying Child

1986. Air. Volunteer Firemen (2nd series). Multicoloured.

1271 8c. Type **353** 75 25
1272 10c. Searching rubble after explosion (33×24 mm) 75 30

354 Arms

1986. Air. 25th Anniv (1976) of Association of Telegraphists and Radio-Telegraph Operators.

1273 **354** 6c. multicoloured 30 20

355 Architect with Plans looking at Building

1987. Air. 25th Anniv of San Carlos University Architecture Faculty.

1274 **355** 10c. multicoloured 35 20

356 Emblem and Boeing 727

1987. Air. 40th Anniv of I.C.A.O. Mult.

1275 8c. Type **356** 30 20
1276 10c. Boeing 727 airplane on runway (vert) 35 20

357 Aerial View of Site

1987. Air. Chixoy Hydro-electric Plant.

1277 **357** 2c. multicoloured 30 25

358 Dr. Cayetano Francos y Monroy, Archbishop of Guatemala (founder)

1987. Air. Bicentenary (1981) of St. Joseph Children's College. Multicoloured.

1278 8c. Type **358** 30 20
1279 10c. College emblem 35 25

359 Column beside Man studying Book

1987. Air. Regional Book Promotion Centre for Latin America and Caribbean.

1280 **359** 12c. multicoloured 50 25

360 Girls in Traditional Costumes

1987. Coban Folklore Festival. Mult.

1281 50c. Girl weaving 3·25 1·00
1282 1q. Type **360** 6·75 2·10

361 Cesar Branas

1987. Air. Writers (1st series).

1283 **361** 6c. orange and black 30 20
1284 - 8c. red and black 30 20
1285 - 9c. purple and black 30 20

DESIGNS: 8c. Rafael Arevalo Martinez; 9c. Jose Milla y Vidaurre.

See also Nos. 1297/8 and 1307/11.

362 Footballer

1987. Air. Pan-American Games National Football Selection.

1286 **362** 10c. blue and black 35 20

363 Miguel Angel Asturias Cultural Centre

1987

1287 **363** 1c. blue 30 20
1287a **363** 2c. brown 30 20
1288 **363** 3c. blue 30 20
1289 **363** 4c. mauve 30 20
1290 **363** 5c. orange 30 20
1291 **363** 6c. green 30 20
1292 **363** 7c. red 30 20
1293 **363** 8c. mauve 30 20
1294 **363** 9c. black 30 20
1295 **363** 10c. green 35 25

1988. Air. Writers (2nd series). As T 361.

1297 4c. red and black 30 20
1298 5c. brown and black 30 20

DESIGNS: 4c. Enrique A. Hidalgo; 5c. Enrique Gomez Carrillo.

364 Stylized Dove

1988. Air. "Esquipulas II—A Firm Step towards Peace".

1299 **364** 10c. green 50 25
1300 - 40c. red 1·90 1·10
1301 - 60c. blue 2·75 1·60

DESIGNS—HORIZ: 40c. Three stylized doves. VERT: 60c. Stylized dove.

365 Festival Performers

1988. National Folklore Festival, Coban. Sheet 81×100 mm. Imperf.

MS1302 **365** 2q. multicoloured 12·00 11·00

366 St. John and Boys

1989. Death Centenary of St. John Bosco (founder of Salesian Brothers).

1303 **366** 40c. black and gold 1·10 60

367 Birds

1989. Air. Bicentenary of French Revolution.

1304 **367** 1q. red, blue and black 6·00 2·10

368 Madrid Codex (detail)

1990. Air. America. Pre-Columbian Culture. Multicoloured.

1305 10c. Type **368** 2·10 1·20
1306 20c. Tikal Pyramid 4·25 2·50

1990. Air. Writers (3rd series). As T 361.

1307 1c. mauve and black 30 20
1308 2c. orange and black 30 20
1309 3c. blue and black 30 20
1310 7c. black and green 30 20
1311 10c. black and yellow 30 20

DESIGNS: 1c. Flavio Herrera; 2c. Rosendo Santa Cruz; 3c. Werner Ovalle Lopez; 7c. Clemente Marroquin Rojas; 10c. Miguel Angel Asturias.

369 Games Emblem

1990. 6th Central American and Caribbean University Games. Multicoloured.

1312 15c. Type **369** 35 25
1313 20c. Mascot holding flame (vert) 55 25
1314 25c. Mascot playing volleyball 75 25
1315 30c. Mascot playing football 85 25
1316 45c. Mascot performing judo movement 1·30 35
1317 1q. Mascot playing baseball 3·00 80
1318 2q. Mascot playing basketball 5·50 1·60
1319 3q. Mascot hurdling 9·00 2·75

370 Family, Cereal and Emblem

1990. Air. 40th Anniv of Central America and Panama Nutrition Institute.

1320 **370** 20c. multicoloured 65 25

371 Palais de l'Athenee, Geneva (venue of founding meeting)

1990. Air. 125th Anniv (1988) of International Red Cross.

1321 **371** 50c. multicoloured 1·50 40

372 Arms

1991. Air. Centenary of National Defence Staff.

1322 **372** 20c. multicoloured 55 20

373 Atitlan Lake

1991. America. Natural World. Multicoloured.

1323 10c. Pacaya Volcano in eruption 30 25
1324 60c. Type **373** 2·10 40

374 Martin and Vicente Pinzon

1992. Air. America. 500th Anniv of Discovery of America by Columbus. Each black and green.

1325	40c. Type **374**	1·10	50
1326	60c. Christopher Columbus and "Santa Maria" (vert)	1·70	75

375 Crops

1992. Air. 50th Anniv of International Institute for Agricultural Co-operation.

1327	**375**	10c. multicoloured	65	25

376 Emblem

1992. International Anti-AIDS Campaign.

1328	**376**	1q. multicoloured	3·00	85

377 "Encyclia cochleata"

1994. Air. Orchids (1st series). Multicoloured.

1329	50c. Type **377**	1·40	85
1330	1q. "Encyclia vitellina"	2·75	85
1331	2q. "Odontoglossum uroskinneri"	5·25	1·60

See also Nos. 1355/6.

378 Family around Tree

1994. 50th Anniv of 20 October Revolution. Multicoloured.

1332	40c. Type **378**	35	25
1333	60c. Dove on hand (horiz)	55	35
1334	1q. Man holding book and rifle	95	60
1335	2q. Representations of social developments since 1944	1·90	1·20
1336	3q. Three youths supporting torch ("Revolution, Liberty, Justice and Peace")	3·00	1·60

379 City Buildings

1995. Air. Tourism. Multicoloured.

1337	20c. White water rafting	50	25
1338	40c. Windsurfing	50	25
1339	60c. Pleasure boat on Lake Atitlan	65	35
1340	80c. Tourist launch "Crucero"	75	40
1341	1q. Erupting volcano	75	35
1342	2q. Type **379**	1·50	65
1343	3q. Parrots on perch (vert)	2·10	90
1344	4q. Mayan ruins (vert)	3·00	1·30
1345	5q. Ceremony (vert)	3·75	1·80

380 Greeting Crowd

1996. Air. Papal Visit. Pope John Paul II. Multicoloured.

1350	10c. Type **380**	20	15
1351	1q. Holding child	55	50
1352	1q.75 Holding crucifix and wearing mitre	1·00	90
1353	1q.90 Wearing cross and red cloak	1·10	1·00
1354	2q.90 Wearing red hat	1·80	1·60

1996. Air. Orchids (2nd series). As T 377. Mult.

1355	20c. "Phragmipedium caudatum"	75	65
1356	1q.50 "Odontoglossum laeve"	5·75	5·00

381 Carlos Merida

1996. Air. Personalities.

1357	**381**	40c. lt blue, blue & black	30	25
1358	-	50c. brown, blue & black	30	25
1359	-	60c. brown, blue & black	35	35

DESIGNS: 50c. Jose Eulalio Samayoa; 60c. Manuel Montufar y Coronado.

382 University Hall

1997. Buildings. Multicoloured.

1360	50c. Type **382**	35	35
1361	1q. Brewery	75	70

383 Breastfeeding

1997. Air. Breastfeeding Campaign.

1362	**383**	1q. multicoloured	75	65

384 Parent and Child (Marion Contreras Castanaza)

1997. 50th Anniv (1996) of UNICEF "Children and Peace". Multicoloured.

1363	10c. Type **384**	30	20
1364	20c. Child riding birds (Marvin Sac Coyoy) (horiz)	30	20

385 Child writing (Education)

1997. Air. Public Finance Projects. Mult.

1365	20c. Type **385**	20	20
1366	60c. Child receiving medication (health)	35	25
1367	80c. Road (infrastructure)	55	40
1368	1q. Family (security)	75	50

386 Jorge Rybar (pioneer) and Machinery

1998. Air. 50th Anniv of Guatemala Plastics Industry.

1369	**386**	10c. multicoloured	30	25

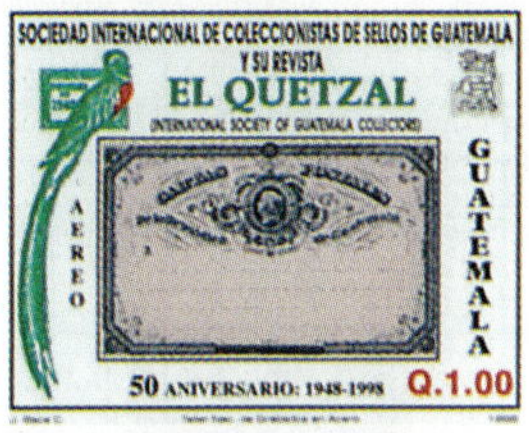

387 1875 Postcard and Emblem

1999. Air. 50th Anniv (1998) of El Quetzal (International Society of Guatemala Stamp Collectors).

1370	**387**	1q. multicoloured	75	65

388 Francisco Marroquin (first bishop of Guatemala)

2001. Birth Anniversaries (1999). Multicoloured.

1371	3q. Type **388** (500th anniv)	3·00	2·75
1372	4q. Jacinto Rodriguez Diaz (aviation pioneer) (centenary)	4·00	3·50
1373	8q.75, Miguel Angel Asturias (Nobel Prize winner for Literature) (centenary)	8·75	7·75
1374	10q. Cesar Branas (writer and historian) (centenary)	10·00	8·75

389 Church Architecture, Antigua and Hermano Pedro

2002. Air. 3rd Visit of Pope John Paul II (50c., 2, 5, 8q.75). 12th Anniv Canonisation of Hermano Pedro (monk and humanitarian) (20, 25c., 1q.). Multicoloured.

1375	20c. Type **389**	25	20
1376	25c. Hermano Pedro holding bell rope	25	20
1377	50c. Hermano Pedro and Pope John Paul II (horiz)	45	40
1378	1q. Nativity, his alms bell and Hermano Pedro (head)	95	85
1379	2q. Pope John Paul II and Archbishop Rudolfo Toruno (horiz)	2·00	1·80
1380	5q. Fountain, part of door lintel and Pope John Paul II (horiz)	5·00	4·50
1381	8q. 75 Pope John Paul II, clock tower and Government Palace (horiz)	8·75	7·75
MS1382	153×128 mm. As Nos. 1375/81	18·00	16·00

390 Guatemalan Flag, Globe, Envelopes, Quetzal Bird and Flags

2002. Air. 125th Anniv of Universal Postal Union (1999). Multicoloured.

1383	20c. Type **390**	25	20
1384	2q. UPU emblem	1·50	1·30
1385	3q. Globe with map of Americas encircled by bird	2·20	2·00
1386	5q. Globe with hands holding envelopes and flags	3·75	3·25

391 Mt. Everest

2002. Air. 1st Anniv of Jaime Vinals' Ascent of Everest.

1387	**391**	3q. multicoloured	2·10	1·40

392 Children

2002. Air. Centenary of Pan-American Health Organization.

1388	**392**	4q. multicoloured	2·50	1·90

393 Dance of the Conquest Mask, Totonicapan

2003. Masks. Masks. Multicoloured.

1389	20c. Type **393**	25	20
1390	2q. Dance of Moors and Christians, Sacatepequez	1·40	1·20
1391	3q. Deer dance, Alta Verapaz	2·10	1·90
1392	4q. Jaguar mask, Deer dance, Totonicapan	2·75	2·50
MS1393	100×71 mm. 5q. Paabanc	3·50	3·00

394 Field Worker and Josemaria Escriva de Balaguer

2003. Birth Centenary of Josemaria Escriva de Balaguer (2002) (founder of Opus Dei (religious organization)). Multicoloured.

1394	20c. Type **394**	25	20
1395	50c. Josemaria Escriva and fisherman	45	40
1396	3q. Facing left	2·30	2·10
1397	10q. Church and Josemaria Escriva	7·50	6·75

395 Man carrying Bananas

2003. 50th Anniv of Regional Organization for Farming Health (OIRSA). Multicoloured.

1398	20c. Type **395**	20	20
1399	1q. Hands holding corn	85	75
1400	2q. Cow's face	1·80	1·60
1401	4q. Field of crop	3·25	2·75
1402	5q. Meats	4·50	4·00
1403	10q. Eye and maize	9·00	7·75
MS1404	101×62 mm. 3q. Fruit	1·20	1·00

396 Pier, Punta de Manabique, Izabel Department

2004. Tourism. Izabel Department (1405/7). Multicoloured.

1405	20c. Type **396**	20	20
1406	50c. Las Siete Altares, Izabel Department	40	35
1407	1q. Las Escobas waterfalls, Izabel Department	85	75
1408	1q.50 Barrios y Pichilingo harbour (America. Cultural Heritage)	1·40	1·20
1409	2q. Mayan acropolis, Quirigua	1·80	1·60
1410	3q. Livingston beach, Rio Dulce	2·75	2·40
1411	4q. San Felipe castle	3·50	3·25
1412	5q. Sunset, El Estor	4·50	4·00
1413	8q.75 Agua Caliente waterfalls	7·75	7·00
1414	10q. Rio Polochi river	9·00	7·75
MS1415	102×63 mm. 4q. Carving, Mayan acropolis, Quirigua (America. Cultural Heritage)	1·50	1·30

398 *Sarcoramphus papa* (inscr "Sarcoranphus")

2005. Flora and Fauna. America 2003 Endangered Species. Multicoloured.

1427	50c. Type **398**	40	35
1428	3q. *Heliconia collinsiana* (vert)	2·75	2·40
1429	5q. *Felis concolor*	4·50	4·00
1430	12q. *Heliconius petiveranus*	8·75	7·70
MS1431	100×64 mm. 12q. *Tapirus vairdii*	10·50	9·25

399 Flags, Water-pipe and Girl

2005. 70th Anniv of Guatemala—Japan Diplomatic Relations. Multicoloured.

1432	1q. Type **399**	85	75
1433	1q. Flags, hospital and girl	85	75
MS1434	114×51 mm. 14q. Mount Fuji	10·50	9·25

400 Incense Burner

2005. Pottery. Multicoloured.

1435	1q. Type **400**	85	75
1436	2q. Jars with owl faces	1·40	1·20
1437	6q.50 Plate and bowl	4·25	2·10
1438	8q. Lantern	5·50	5·00
MS1439	64×51 mm. 12q. Jars	10·50	9·25

401 Clasped Hands

2005. Centenary of Rotary International. Multicoloured.

1440	2q. Type **401**	1·40	1·20
1441	6q.50 Child's face and water droplets	4·25	2·10
MS1442	51×64 mm. 8q. Emblem	5·50	5·00

402 Hand reaching

2006. America. Struggle against Poverty. Multicoloured.

1443	50c. Type **402**	40	35
1444	50c. Child's face	40	35
1445	5q. Clasped hands	4·50	4·00
1446	5q. Child's face (different)	4·50	4·00

Nos. 1443/4 and 1445/6, respectively, were issued together, se-tenant, forming a composite design.

403 Jose Pardo

2006. Birth Centenary (2005) of Jose Joaquin Pardo Gallardo (historian).

1447	**403**	3q. multicoloured	2·10	1·90

404 Santa Cruz Hermitage

2006. Churches. Multicoloured.

1448	50c. Type **404**	45	40
1449	1q. San Jacinto Church	85	75
1450	2q. San Andreas Xecul Church (vert)	1·40	1·20
1451	3q. El Calvario Church (vert)	2·10	1·90
1452	4q. San Cristobel (vert)	2·75	2·50
1453	5q. La Antigua Cathedral	4·50	4·00
1454	8q. San Pedro Church and Hospital	5·50	5·00
1455	10q. San Pedro Las Huertas Church	7·50	6·75
MS1456	57×70 mm. 14q. Metropolitan Cathedral, Guatemala City	10·50	9·25

405 Nativity (clay)

2006. Christmas. Multicoloured.

1457	20c. Type **405**	25	20
1458	6q.50 Nativity (decorated pottery)	5·00	4·75

406 Coffee Grower (Acatenango)

2006. Coffee. Multicoloured.

1459	50c. Type **406**	45	40
1460	1q. Antigua	85	75
1461	2q. Atitlan	1·40	1·20
1462	6q.50 Coban	5·00	4·75
1463	8q. Fraijanes	5·50	5·00
1464	10q. Huehue	7·50	6·75
MS1465	102×64 mm. 5q. Oriente; 20q. San Marcos	21·00	19·00

407 Baile de la Conquista

2006. Centenary of Guatemala—Brazil Diplomatic Relations. Multicoloured.

1466	4q. Type **407**	2·75	2·50
1467	4q. Maracatua	2·75	2·50

408 Oil Derricks and Petrol Pump

2006. America. Energy Conservation. Multicoloured.

1468	3q. Type **408**	2·10	1·90
1469	10q. Switch and solar panels	7·50	6·75

2007. Nos. 1293, 1338/40, 1357, 1359 and 1366 surch.

1470	50c. on 40c. light blue, blue and black (No. 1357) (air)	45	40
1471	50c. on 40c. multicoloured (No. 1338)	45	40
1472	1q. on 60c. multicoloured (No. 1339)	85	75
1473	2q. on 80c. multicoloured (No. 1367)	1·40	1·20
1474	3q. on 60c. grey-brown, blue and black (No. 1359)	2·10	1·90
1475	8q. on 80c. multicoloured (No. 1340)	5·50	5·00
1476	10q. on 60c. multicoloured (No. 1366)	7·50	6·75
1477	5q. on 9c. black (No. 1293) (postage)	4·50	4·00

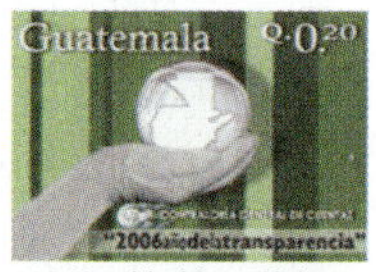

410 Hand holding Globe

2007. 2006—Year of Honesty and Transparency. Multicoloured.

1478	20c. Type **408**	25	20
1479	6q.50 Magnifying glass and finger print (44×25 mm)	5·00	4·75

411 1c. Stamp of 1881 (as No. 21)

2007. 75th Anniv of Guatemala Philatelic Association. Multicoloured.

1480	1q. Type **411**	85	75
1481	3q. 2c. Stamp of 1881 (as No. 22)	2·10	1·90
1482	6q.50 5c. Stamp of 1881 (as No. 23)	5·00	4·75
1483	8q. 10c. Stamp of 1881 (as No. 24)	5·50	5·00
MS1484	108×64 mm. 25q. 20c. Stamp of 1881 (as No. 25)	21·00	19·00

412 Early Buildings, Guatemala

2007. Centenary of Uruguay–Guatemala Diplomatic Relations. Multicoloured.

1485	4q. Type **412**	2·75	2·50
1486	4q. Colonia del Sacramento	2·75	2·50

Stamps of a similar design were issued by Uruguay.

413 Stylized Children

2007. America. Education for All. Designs showing stylized children. Multicoloured.

1487	4q. Type **413**	2·75	2·50
1488	4q. Drawing	2·75	2·50
1489	4q. In house	2·75	2·50
1490	4q. Reading and drawing	2·75	2·50

Nos. 1487/90 were issued together, se-tenant, forming a composite design.

414 Holy Family

2007. Christmas. Multicoloured.

1491	20c. Type **414**	25	20
1492	6q.50 Three Kings (40×35 mm)	5·00	4·75

415 Emblem

2007. Centenary of World Scouting.

1493	**415**	20c. multicoloured	25	20

416 Institute Building

2008. Municipal Development Institute.

1494	**416**	3q. multicoloured	2·10	1·90

417 Gerardi Conedera

2008. 10th Death Anniv of Juan Jose Gerardi Conedera (bishop and human rights activist).

1495	**417**	8q. multicoloured	5·50	5·00

418 San Rafael de Matamoros

2008. Forts. Multicoloured.

1496	1q. Type **418**	85	75
1497	1q. San Josede Buena Vista	85	75

Nos. 1496/7 were issued together, se-tenant, forming a composite design.

419 Mayan Ball Player

2008. Olympic Games, Beijing.

1498	**419**	6q.50 multicoloured	5·00	4·75

420 *Trogon violaceus braccatus* (violaceous trogon)

2008. Birds. Multicoloured.

1499	50c. Type **420**	40	45
1500	1q. *Amazilia beryllina viola* (berylline hummingbird)	85	75
1501	2q. *Turdus rufitorques* (rufous-collared thrush)	1·40	1·20
1502	4q. *Glaucidium brasilianum ridgwayi* (ferruginous pygmy owl)	2·75	2·50
MS1503	108×63 mm. 20q. *Brotogeris jugularis* (inscr 'julularis') (orange-chinned parakeet)	15·00	13·50

421 Embroidered Christmas Rose

2008. Christmas. Multicoloured.

1504	20c. Type **421**	25	20
1505	8q. Embroidered Christmas tree	5·50	5·00

422 Virgen Inmaculaada Concepcion (Mary of Immaculate Conception), St. Francis Temple

2008. 500th Anniv of Franciscan Order.

1506	**422**	3q. multicoloured	2·10	1·90

423 Building Facade

2009. 250th Anniv of Basilica del Senor de Esqipulas.

1507	**423**	50c. multicoloured	40	45

424 Boats

2009. 50th Anniv of National Marine Defence.

1508	**424**	1q. multicoloured	85	75

425 Masquerade Ball, Comalapa

2009. America (2008). Festivals. Multicoloured.

1509	50c. Type **425**	40	45
1510	2q. Feast of All Saints, Santiago Sacatepequez	1·40	1·20
1511	3q. Marimba dance festival	2·10	1·90
1512	5q. Son dance festival	3·25	2·75
MS1513	82×89 mm. 8q. The brethren and captains festival	5·50	5·50

426 Man, San Juan Atitan

2009. Traditional Costumes. Multicoloured.

1514	50c. Type **426**	40	45
1515	1q. Woman, San Juan Sacatepequez	85	75
1516	2q. Woman, Tamahu	1·40	1·20
1517	3q. Woman, San Rafael Petzal	2·10	1·90
1518	4q. Man, Totonicapan	2·75	2·50
1519	5q. Woman, Palzicia	3·25	2·75
1520	8q. Woman, San Pedro San Marcos	5·50	5·00
MS1521	51×64 mm. 10q. Couple, San Juan Cotzal	11·00	11·00

EXPRESS LETTER STAMPS

1940. No. 231 optd EXPRESO.

E411	**97**	4c. yellow	2·30	45

E181 Motorcyclist

1948. Surch.

E479	**E181**	10c. on 4c. blk & grn	5·00	1·30

OFFICIAL STAMPS

O41

1902

O127	**O41**	1c. green	8·50	5·50
O128	**O41**	2c. red	8·50	5·50
O129	**O41**	5c. blue	8·50	4·25
O130	**O41**	10c. purple	11·50	4·25
O131	**O41**	25c. orange	11·50	4·25

O100

1929

O239	**O100**	1c. blue	50	45
O240	**O100**	2c. sepia	50	45
O241	**O100**	3c. green	50	45
O242	**O100**	4c. purple	60	45
O243	**O100**	5c. lake	60	60
O244	**O100**	10c. brown	95	95
O245	**O100**	25c. blue	2·20	1·60

134

1939. Air. Nos. 369/74 optd OFICIAL OFICIAL.

O400	**134**	1c. brown and orange	1·70	1·60
O401	-	2c. brown and red	1·70	1·60
O402	-	3c. brown, buff & green	1·70	1·60
O403	-	4c. brown and purple	1·70	1·60
O404	-	5c. brown and grey	1·70	1·60
O405	-	10c. brown and blue	1·70	1·60

1939. Air. No. MS375a optd OFFICIAL OFFICIAL on each stamp in sheet.

MSO405	As No. **MS**375a	2·50	2·10

Pt. 1

GUERNSEY

An island in the English Channel off N.W. coast of France. Occupied by German Forces from June 1940 to May 1945. "Regional" issues were introduced from 1958 (see after GREAT BRITAIN). The island's postal service was organised as a separate postal administration in 1969.

(a) War Occupation Issues

1

1941

1f	**1**	½d. green	4·00	3·00
2b	**1**	1d. red	3·50	2·00
3a	**1**	2½d. blue	10·00	7·00

(b) Independent Postal Administration

4 Castle Cornet and Edward the Confessor

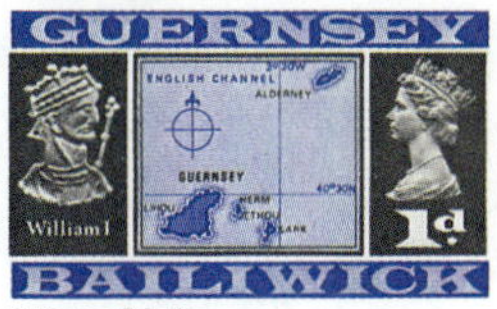

5 View of Sark

1969

13	**4**	½d. mauve and black	10	10
14	-	1d. blue and black*	10	10
14b	-	1d. blue and black*	30	30
15	-	1½d. brown and black	10	10
16	-	2d. multicoloured	10	10
17	-	3d. multicoloured	15	15
18	-	4d. multicoloured	20	25
19	-	5d. multicoloured	20	20
20	-	6d. multicoloured	20	30
21	-	9d. multicoloured	30	30
22	-	1s. multicoloured	30	30
23	-	1s.6d. green and black*	25	30
23b	-	1s.6d. green and black*	2·00	1·70
24	-	1s.9d. multicoloured	80	80
25	-	2s.6d. violet and black	3·50	3·00
26	**5**	5s. multicoloured	2·50	2·50
27	-	10s. multicoloured	16·00	18·00
28a	-	£1 multicoloured	2·20	2·20

DESIGNS—As Type **4**: 1d. Map and William I; 1½d. Martello tower and Henry II; 2d. Arms of Sark and King John; 3d. Arms of Alderney and Edward III; 4d. Guernsey lily and Henry V; 5d. Arms of Guernsey and Elizabeth I; 6d. Arms of Alderney and Charles II; 9d. Arms of Sark and George III; 1s. Arms of Guernsey and Queen Victoria; 1s.6d., As 1d.; 1s.9d. Guernsey lily and Elizabeth I; 2s.6d. Martello tower and King John. As Type **5**: 10s. View of Alderney; 20s. View of Guernsey.

*On Nos. 14 and 23 the degree of latitude is inscr (incorrectly) as 40° 30'N. On Nos. 14b and 23b it has been corrected to 49° 30'.

19 Isaac Brock as Colonel

1969. Birth Bicent of Sir Isaac Brock. Mult.

29	4d. Type **19**	20	20
30	5d. Sir Isaac Brock as Major-General	20	20
31	1s.9d. Isaac Brock as Ensign	90	75
32	2s.6d. Arms and flags (horiz)	90	75

23 H.M.S. "L103" (landing craft) entering St. Peter's Harbour and Hawker Hurricans Mk II

1970. 25th Anniv of Liberation.

33	**23**	4d. blue	20	20
34	-	5d. brown, lake and grey	40	20
35	-	1s.6d. brown and buff	1·20	90

DESIGNS—HORIZ: 5d. H.M.S. "Bulldog" and H.M.S. "Beagle" (destroyers) entering St. Peter Port. VERT: 1s.6d. Brigadier Snow reading Proclamation.

26 Guernsey "Toms"

1970. Agriculture and Horticulture. Mult.

36	4d. Type **26**	55	20
37	5d. Guernsey cow	70	20
38	9d. Guernsey bull	2·50	1·30
39	1s.6d. Freesias	2·75	2·40

32 St. Peter's Church, Sark

1970. Christmas. Churches (1st series). Mult.

40	4d. St. Anne's Church, Alderney (horiz)	20	10
41	5d. St. Peter's Church (horiz)	20	10
42	9d. Type **32**	1·20	1·00
43	1s.6d. St. Tugual Chapel, Herm	1·50	1·20

See also Nos. 63/6.

34 Martello Tower and King John

1971. Decimal Currency. Nos. 13, etc, but with new colours and decimal values as T 34.

44	½p. mauve and black (as No. 13)	10	15
45	1p. blue and black (as No. 14b)	10	10
46	1½p. brown & black (as No. 15)	15	15
47	2p. multicoloured (as No. 18)	15	15
48	2½p. multicoloured (as No. 19)	15	10
49	3p. multicoloured (as No. 17)	20	20
50	3½p. multicoloured (as No. 24)	20	20
51	4p. multicoloured (as No. 16)	20	20
52	5p. green and black (as No. 14b)	20	20
53	6p. multicoloured (as No. 20)	20	20
54	7½p. multicoloured (as No. 22)	30	35
55	9p. multicoloured (as No. 21)	65	65
56a	10p. violet & black (as No. 25)	1·20	1·20
57	20p. multicoloured (as No. 26)	70	70
58	50p. multicoloured (as No. 27)	1·20	1·20

35 Hong Kong 2c. of 1862

1971. Thomas De La Rue Commemoration.

59	**35**	2p. purple	35	15
60	-	2½p. red	35	15
61	-	4p. green	1·10	1·00
62	-	7½p. blue	1·40	1·20

DESIGNS (Each showing portraits of Queen Elizabeth and Thomas De La Rue): 2½p. Great Britain 4d. of 1855–7; 4p. Italy 5c. of 1862; 7½p. Confederate States 5c. of 1862.

1971. Christmas. Churches (2nd series). As T 32. Multicoloured.

63	2p. Ebenezer Church, St. Peter Port (horiz)	10	10
64	2½p. Church of St. Pierre du Bois (horiz)	10	10
65	5p. St. Joseph's Church, St. Peter Port	1·00	1·00
66	7½p. Church of St. Philippe de Torteval	1·00	1·00

43 "Earl of Chesterfield" (1794)

1972. Mail Packet Boats (1st series). Mult.

67	2p. Type **43**	15	10
68	2½p. "Dasher" (1827)	15	10
69	7½p. "Ibex" (1891)	40	35
70	9p. "Alberta" (1900)	60	50

See also Nos. 80/3.

1972. World Conference of Guernsey Breeders, Guernsey. As No. 38 but size 48×29 mm, and additional inscription with face value changed.

71	5p. multicoloured	30	30

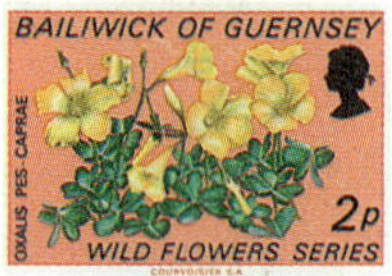

48 Bermuda Buttercup

1972. Wild Flowers. Multicoloured.

72	2p. Type **48**	10	10
73	2½p. Heath spotted orchid (vert)	10	10
74	7½p. Kaffir fig	50	50
75	9p. Scarlet pimpernel (vert)	60	60

52 Angels adoring Christ

1972. Royal Silver Wedding and Christmas. Stained-glass Windows from Guernsey Churches. Multicoloured.

76	2p. Type **52**	10	10
77	2½p. The Epiphany	15	10
78	7½p. The Virgin Mary	30	25
79	9p. Christ	35	35

See also Nos. 89/92.

1973. Mail Packet Boats (2nd series). As T 43. Multicoloured.

80	2½p. "St. Julien" (1925)	10	10
81	3p. "Isle of Guernsey" (1930)	20	20
82	7½p. "St. Patrick" (1947)	40	40
83	9p. "Sarnia" (1961)	45	45

60 Supermarine Sea Eagle Amphibian G-EBGS

1973. 50th Anniv of Air Service. Mult.

84	2½p. Type **60**	10	10
85	3p. Westland Wessex trimotor G-ADEW	10	10
86	5p. de Havilland DH.89 Dragon Rapide G-AGSH *James Hardie*	25	25
87	7½p. Douglas DC-3	35	30
88	9p. Vickers Viscount 800 "Anne Marie"	45	40

65 "The Good Shepherd"

1973. Christmas. Stained-glass Windows from Guernsey Churches. Multicoloured.

89	2½p. Type **65**	10	10
90	3p. Christ at the well of Samaria	10	10
91	7½p. St. Dominic	30	30
92	20p. Mary and the Child Jesus	40	40

69 Princess Anne and Capt. Mark Phillips

1973. Royal Wedding.

93	**69** 25p. multicoloured	45	45

70 "John Lockett", 1875

1974. 150th Anniv of Royal National Lifeboat Institution. Multicoloured.

94	2½p. Type **70**	10	10
95	3p. "Arthur Lionel", 1912	10	10
96	8p. "Euphrosyne Kendal", 1954	30	20
97	10p. "Arun", 1972	35	25

74 Private, East Regt, 1815

89 Driver, Field Battery, Royal Guernsey Artillery, 1848

1974. Guernsey Militia. Multicoloured. (a) As T 74.

98	½p. Type **74**	10	10
99	1p. Officer, 2nd North Regt, 1825	10	10
100	1½p. Gunner, Guernsey Artillery, 1787	10	10
101	2p. Gunner, Guernsey Artillery, 1815	10	10
102	2½p. Corporal, Royal Guernsey Artillery, 1868	10	10
103	3p. Field Officer, Royal Guernsey Artillery, 1895	10	10
104	3½p. Sergeant, 3rd Regt, 1867	10	10
105	4p. Officer, East Regt, 1822	10	10
105a	5p. Field Officer, Royal Guernsey Artillery, (1895)	15	15
106	5½p. Colour-Sergeant of Grenadiers, East Regt, 1833	10	10
107	6p. Officer, North Regt, 1832	10	10
107a	7p. Officer, East Regt, 1822	25	25
108	8p. Field Officer, Rifle Company, 1868	15	10
109	9p. Private, 4th West Regt, 1785	15	10
110	10p. Field Officer, 4th West Regt, 1824	15	10

(b) As T 46.

111	20p. Type **89**	75	40
112	50p. Officer, Field Battery, Royal Guernsey Artillery, 1868	2·00	1·00
113	£1 Cavalry Trooper, Light Dragoons, 1814 (horiz)	2·50	1·75

92 Badge of Guernsey and U.P.U. Emblem

1974. Centenary of U.P.U. Multicoloured.

114	2½p. Type **92**	10	10
115	3p. Map of Guernsey	10	10
116	8p. U.P.U. Building, Berne, and Guernsey flag	20	20
117	10p. "Salle des Etats"	20	20

96 "Cradle Rock"

1974. Renoir Paintings. Multicoloured.

118	3p. Type **96**	10	10
119	5½p. "Le Baie de Moulin Huet"	10	10
120	8p. "Au Bord de la Mer" (vert)	25	25
121	10p. Self-portrait (vert)	25	25

100 Guernsey Spleenwort

1975. Guernsey Ferns. Multicoloured.

122	3½p. Type **100**	10	10
123	4p. Sand quilwort	10	10
124	8p. Guernsey quilwort	25	25
125	10p. Least adder's tongue	25	25

104 Victor Hugo House

1975. Victor Hugo's Exile in Guernsey. Mult.

126	3½p. Type **104**	10	10
127	4p. Candie Gardens (vert)	10	10
128	8p. United Europe Oak, Hauteville (vert)	25	25
129	10p. Tapestry Room, Hauteville	25	25
MS130	114×143 mm. Nos. 126/9	65	90

108 Globe and Seal of Bailiwick

1975. Christmas. Multicoloured.

131	4p. Type **108**	10	10
132	6p. Guernsey flag	10	10
133	10p. Guernsey flag and Alderney shield (horiz)	25	25
134	12p. Guernsey flag and Sark shield (horiz)	25	25

112 Les Hanois

1976. Bailiwick Lighthouses. Multicoloured.

135	4p. Type **112**	10	10
136	6p. Les Casquets	10	10
137	11p. Quesnard	20	20
138	13p. Point Robert	25	25

116 Milk Can

1976. Europa.

139	**116** 10p. brown and green	20	20
140	- 25p. grey and blue	40	35

DESIGN: 25p. Christening cup.

118 Pine Forest, Guernsey

1976. Bailiwick Views. Multicoloured.

141	5p. Type **118**	10	10
142	7p. Herm and Jethou	10	10
143	11p. Grand Greve Bay, Sark (vert)	25	25
144	13p. Trois Vaux Bay, Alderney (vert)	25	25

122 Royal Court House, Guernsey

1976. Christmas. Buildings. Multicoloured.

145	5p. Type **55**	10	10
146	7p. Elizabeth College, Guernsey	10	10
147	11p. La Seigneurie, Sark	25	25
148	13p. Island Hall, Alderney	25	25

126 Queen Elizabeth II

1977. Silver Jubilee. Multicoloured.

149	7p. Type **126**	20	15
150	35p. Queen Elizabeth (half-length portrait)	55	40

128 Woodland, Talbot's Valley

1977. Europa. Multicoloured.

151	7p. Type **128**	15	15
152	25p. Pastureland, Talbot's Valley	45	45

130 Statue-menhir, Castel

1977. Prehistoric Monuments. Multicoloured.

153	5p. Type **130**	10	10

154		7p. Megalithic tomb, St. Saviour (horiz)	10	10
155		11p. Cist, Tourgis (horiz)	25	25
156		13p. Statue-menhir, St. Martin	25	25

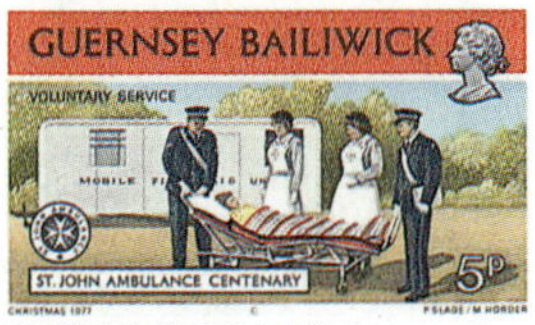

134 Mobile First Aid Unit

1977. Christmas and St. John Ambulance Centenary. Multicoloured.

157		5p. Type **134**	10	10
158		7p. Mobile radar unit	10	10
159		11p. Marine ambulance "Flying Christine II" (vert)	25	25
160		13p. Cliff rescue (vert)	25	25

138 View from Clifton, c. 1830

1978. Old Guernsey Prints (1st series).

161	**138**	5p. black and green	10	10
162	-	7p. black and stone	10	10
163	-	11p. black and pink	25	25
164	-	13p. black and blue	25	25

DESIGNS: 7p. Market Square, St. Peter Port, c. 1838; 11p. Petit-Bo Bay, c. 1839; 13p. The Quay, St. Peter Port, c. 1830.

See also Nos. 249/52.

142 "Prosperity" Memorial

1978. Europa. Multicoloured.

165		5p. Type **142**	10	10
166		7p. Victoria Monument (vert)	25	25

144 Queen Elizabeth II

1978. 25th Anniversary of Coronation.

167	**144**	20p. black, grey and blue	45	45

1978. Royal Visit. As T 62, but inscr "VISIT OF H.M THE QUEEN AND H.R.H THE DUKE OF EDINBURGH JUNE 28–29, 1978 TO THE BAILIWICK OF GUERNSEY".

168		7p. black, grey and green	20	20

146 Northern Gannet

1978. Birds. Multicoloured.

169		5p. Type **146**	10	10
170		7p. Firecrest	20	15
171		11p. Dartford warbler	30	20
172		13p. Spotted redshank	40	30

150 Solanum

1978. Christmas. Multicoloured.

173		5p. Type **150**	10	10
174		7p. Christmas rose	10	10
175		11p. Holly (vert)	20	20
176		13p. Mistletoe (vert)	25	25

154 One Double Coin, 1830

1979. Coins.

177	**154**	½p. multicoloured	10	10
178	-	1p. multicoloured	10	10
179	-	2p. multicoloured	10	10
180	-	4p. multicoloured	10	10
181	-	5p. black, silver and brown	10	10
182	-	6p. black, silver and red	15	10
183	-	7p. black, silver and green	15	15
184	-	8p. black, silver and brown	15	15
185	-	9p. multicoloured	15	15
186	-	10p. multicoloured (green background)	30	25
187	-	10p. multicoloured (orange background)	20	15
188	-	11p. multicoloured	20	15
189	-	11½p. multicoloured	20	15
190	-	12p. multicoloured	20	15
191	-	13p. multicoloured	25	20
192	-	14p. black, silver and blue	25	20
193	-	15p. black, silver and brown	25	25
194	-	20p. black, silver and brown	30	30
195	-	50p. black, silver and red	85	60
196	-	£1 black, silver and green	1·70	1·10
197	-	£2 black, silver and blue	3·75	2·00
198	-	£5 multicoloured	8·00	8·00

DESIGNS—VERT (As Type **65**): 1p. Two doubles, 1899; 2p. Four doubles, 1902; 4p. Eight doubles, 1959; 5p. Three pence, 1956; 6p. Five new pence, 1968; 7p. Fifty new pence, 1969; 8p. Ten new pence, 1970; 9p. Half new penny, 1971; 10p. (both) One new penny, 1971; 11p. Two new pence, 1971; 11½p. Half penny, 1979; 12p. One penny, 1977; 13p. Two pence, 1977; 14p. Five pence, 1977; 15p. Ten pence, 1977; 20p. Twenty-five pence, 1972. (26×45 mm): 50p. William I commemorative 10s., 1966; £5 Seal of the Bailiwick. HORIZ (45×26 mm): £1 Silver Jubilee crown, 1977; £2 Royal Silver Wedding crown, 1972.

175 Pillar-box and Postmark, 1853, and Mail Van and Postmark, 1979

1979. Europa. Communications. Multicoloured.

201		6p. Type **175**	10	10
202		8p. Telephone, 1897 and telex machine, 1979	20	20

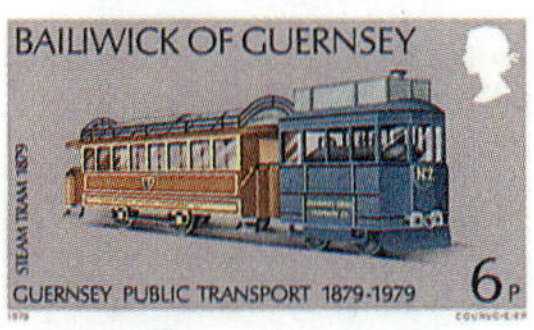

177 Steam Tram, 1879

1979. History of Public Transport. Multicoloured.

203		6p. Type **177**	10	10
204		8p. Electric tram, 1896	15	10
205		11p. Motor bus, 1911	20	15
206		13p. Motor bus, 1979	20	25

181 Bureau and Postal Headquarters

1979. 10th Anniv of Guernsey Postal Administration. Multicoloured.

207		6p. Type **181**	10	10
208		8p. "Mails and telegrams"	15	10
209		13p. "Parcels"	20	15
210		15p. "Philately"	25	25
MS211		120×80 mm. Nos. 207/10	80	80

185 Major-General Le Marchant

1980. Europa. Personalities. Multicoloured.

212		10p. Type **185**	15	15
213		13½p. Admiral Lord de Saumarez	30	25

187 Policewoman with Lost Child

1980. 60th Anniv of Guernsey Police Force. Mult.

214		7p. Type **187**	15	15
215		15p. Motorcycle escort	25	25
216		17½p. Dog-handler	30	25

190 Golden Guernsey Goat

1980. Golden Guernsey Goats. Multicoloured.

217		7p. Type **190**	10	10
218		10p. Head of goat	20	15
219		15p. Goat	25	20
220		17½p. Goat and kids	40	35

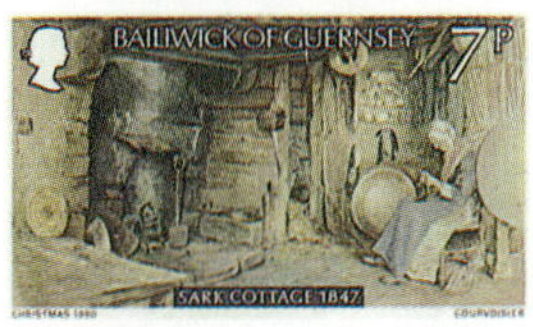

194 "Sark Cottage"

1980. Christmas. Peter Le Lievre Paintings. Multicoloured.

221		7p. Type **194**	15	10
222		10p. "Moulin Huet"	20	15
223		13½p. "Boats at Sea"	25	20
224		15p. "Cow Lane" (vert)	25	25
225		17½p. "Peter Le Lievre" (vert)	40	35

199 "Polyommatus icarus"

1981. Butterflies. Multicoloured.

226		8p. Type **199**	15	15
227		12p. "Vanessa atalanta"	20	20
228		22p. "Aglais urticae"	35	35
229		25p. "Lasiommata megera"	40	40

203 Sailors paying respect to "Le Petit Bonhomme Andriou" (rock resembling head of a man)

1981. Europa. Folklore.

230	**203**	12p. gold, brown & lt brn	25	15
231	-	18p. gold, blue and light blue	30	35

DESIGN: 18p. Fairies and Guernsey lily.

205 Prince Charles

1981. Royal Wedding. Multicoloured.

232		8p. Type **205**	15	10
233		8p. Prince Charles and Lady Diana Spencer	15	10
234		8p. Lady Diana	15	10
235		12p. Type **205**	25	25
236		12p. As No. 233	25	25
237		12p. As No. 234	25	25
238		25p. Royal Family (49×32 mm)	65	60
MS239		104×127 mm. Nos. 232/8	2·50	2·50

209 Sark Launch

1981. Inter-island Transport. Multicoloured.

240		8p. Type **209**	15	15
241		12p. Britten-Norman BN-2A MKIII "short nose" Trislander aircraft	25	20
242		18p. Hydrofoil	30	35
243		22p. Herm catamaran	45	65
244		25p. "Sea Trent" (coaster)	55	75

214 Rifle Shooting

1981. Int Year for Disabled Persons. Mult.

245		8p. Type **214**	15	10
246		12p. Riding	25	20
247		22p. Swimming	45	35
248		25p. Circuit construction	55	55

1982. Old Guernsey Prints (2nd series). Prints from Sketches by T. Compton. As T 138.

249		8p. black and blue	15	15
250		12p. black and green	25	20
251		22p. black and brown	40	40
252		25p. black and lilac	50	50

DESIGNS: 8p Jethou; 12p. Fermain Bay; 22p. The Terres; 25p. St. Peter Port.

222 Sir Edgar MacCulloch (founder-president) and Guille-Alles Library, St. Peter Port

1982. Cent of La Societe Guernesiaise. Mult.

253		8p. Type **222**	15	15
254		13p. French invasion fleet crossing English Channel, 1066 ("history")	30	15
255		20p. H.M.S "Crescent", 1793 ("history")	40	25
256		24p. Dragonfly ("entomology")	50	40

No.	Description	Mint	Used
257	26p. Common snipe caught for ringing ("ornithology")	60	50
258	29p. Samian bowl, 160–200 A.D. ("archaeology").	65	55

The 13p. and 20p. designs also include the Europa C.E.P.T. emblem.

228 "Sea Scouts"

1982. 75th Anniv of Boy Scout Movement. Mult.

No.	Description	Mint	Used
259	8p. Type **228**	15	25
260	13p. "Scouts"	30	25
261	26p. "Cub Scouts"	55	50
262	29p. "Air Scouts"	65	1·10

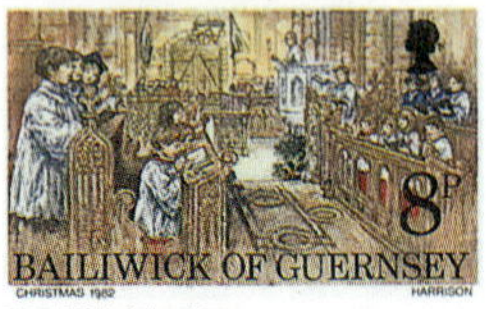

232 Midnight Mass

1982. Christmas. Multicoloured.

No.	Description	Mint	Used
263	8p. Type **232**	15	15
264	13p. Exchanging gifts	25	15
265	24p. Christmas meal	50	45
266	26p. Exchanging cards	55	50
267	29p. Queen's Christmas message	65	55

237 Flute Player and Boats

1982. Centenary of Boys' Brigade. Multicoloured.

No.	Description	Mint	Used
268	8p. Type **237**	15	10
269	13p. Cymbal player and tug o' war	25	20
270	24p. Trumpet player and bible class	40	40
271	26p. Drummer and cadets marching	55	50
272	29p. Boys' Brigade band	65	55

242 Building Albert Pier Extension, 1850s

1983. Europa. Development of St. Peter Port Harbour. Multicoloured.

No.	Description	Mint	Used
273	13p. Type **242**	20	15
274	13p. St. Peter Port harbour, 1983	20	15
275	20p. St. Peter Port, 1680	30	30
276	20p. Artist's impression of future development scheme	30	30

246 "View at Guernsey" (Renoir)

1983. Cent of Renoir's Visit to Guernsey. Mult.

No.	Description	Mint	Used
277	9p. Type **246**	20	15
278	13p. "Children on the Seashore" (25×39 mm)	25	25
279	26p. "Marine, Guernesey"	55	50
280	28p. "La Bale du Moulin Huet a travers les Arbres"	85	80
281	31p. "Brouillard a Guernesey"	1·00	90

251 Launching "Star of the West", 1869, and Capt. J. Lenfestey

1983. Guernsey Shipping (1st series). Mult.

No.	Description	Mint	Used
282	9p. Type **251**	20	20
283	13p. Leaving St. Peter Port	25	15
284	26p. Off Rio Grande Bar	50	50
285	28p. Off St. Lucia	85	75
286	31p. Map of 1879–80 voyage	95	80

See also Nos. 415/19.

256 Dame of Sark as Young Woman

1984. Birth Centenary of Sibyl Hathaway, Dame of Sark. Multicoloured.

No.	Description	Mint	Used
287	9p. Type **256**	20	20
288	13p. German occupation, 1940–45	30	15
289	26p. Royal visit, 1957	70	55
290	28p. Chief Pleas	75	70
291	31p. The "Dame of Sark" rose	80	75

261 C.E.P.T. 25th Anniversary Logo

1984. Europa.

No.	Description	Mint	Used
292	**261** 13p. light blue, blue & black	25	15
293	**261** 20½p. green, dp green & blk	55	50

262 The Royal Court and St. George's Flag

1984. Links with the Commonwealth. Mult.

No.	Description	Mint	Used
294	9p. Type **262**	20	15
295	31p. Castle Cornet and Union flag	85	85

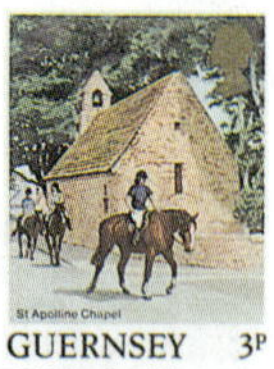

266 St. Apolline Chapel

1984. Views. Multicoloured.

No.	Description	Mint	Used
296	1p. Little Chapel	10	10
297	2p. Fort Grey (horiz)	10	10
298	3p. Type **266**	10	10
299	4p. Petit Port (horiz)	10	10
300	5p. Little Russel (horiz)	15	10
301	6p. The Harbour, Herm (horiz)	15	15
302	7p. Saints (horiz)	15	15
303	8p. St. Saviour	20	15
304	9p. New Jetty (inscr "Cambridge Berth") (horiz)	20	10
305	10p. Belvoir, Herm (horiz)	25	15
306	11p. La Seigneurie, Sark (horiz)	25	15
306b	12p. Petit Bot	35	15
307	13p. St. Saviours reservoir (horiz)	25	25
308	14p. St. Peter Port	25	20
309	15p. Havelet	30	30
309c	16p. Hostel of St. John (horiz)	30	20
309d	18p. Le Variouf	30	20
310	20p. La Coupee, Sark (horiz)	45	25
310b	21p. King's Mills (horiz)	45	30
310c	26p. Town Church	70	50
311	30p. Grandes Rocques (horiz)	65	60
312	40p. Torteval Church	70	70
313	50p. Bordeaux (horiz)	80	75
314	£1 Albecq (horiz)	1·90	1·50
315	£2 L' Ancresse (horiz)	3·75	3·50

See also Nos. 398/9a.

289 "A Partridge in a Pear Tree"

1984. Christmas. "The Twelve Days of Christmas". Multicoloured.

No.	Description	Mint	Used
316	5p. Type **289**	15	15
317	5p. "Two turtle doves"	15	15
318	5p. "Three French hens"	15	15
319	5p. "Four colly birds"	15	15
320	5p. "Five gold rings"	15	15
321	5p. "Six geese a-laying"	15	15
322	5p. "Seven swans a-swimming"	15	15
323	5p. "Eight maids a-milking"	15	15
324	5p. "Nine drummers drumming"	15	15
325	5p. "Ten pipers piping"	15	15
326	5p. "Eleven ladies dancing"	15	15
327	5p. "Twelve lords a-leaping"	15	15

301 Sir John Doyle and Coat of Arms

1984. 150th Death Anniv of Lt.-General Sir John Doyle. Multicoloured.

No.	Description	Mint	Used
328	13p. Type **301**	30	25
329	29p. Battle of Germantown, 1777 (horiz)	65	60
330	31p. Reclamation of Braye du Valle, 1806 (horiz)	75	70
331	34p. Mail for Alderney, 1812 (horiz)	90	85

305 Cuckoo Wrasse

1985. Fishes. Multicoloured.

No.	Description	Mint	Used
332	9p. Type **305**	30	25
333	13p. Red gurnard	40	25
334	29p. Red mullet	90	90
335	31p. Mackerel	90	90
336	34p. Oceanic sunfish	90	90

310 Dove

1985. 40th Anniv of Peace in Europe.

No.	Description	Mint	Used
337	**310** 22p. multicoloured	60	60

311 I.Y.Y. Emblem and Young People of Different Races

1985. International Youth Year. Multicoloured.

No.	Description	Mint	Used
338	9p. Type **311**	25	15
339	31p. Girl Guides cooking over campfire	75	70

313 Stave of Music enclosing Flags

1985. Europa. European Music Year. Multicoloured.

No.	Description	Mint	Used
340	14p. Type **313**	30	25
341	22p. Stave of music and musical instruments	60	55

315 Guide Leader, Girl Guide and Brownie

1985. 75th Anniv of Girl Guide Movement.

No.	Description	Mint	Used
342	**315** 34p. multicoloured	1·00	90

316 Santa Claus

1985. Christmas. Gift-bearers. Multicoloured.

No.	Description	Mint	Used
343	5p. Type **316**	25	15
344	5p. Lussibruden (Sweden)	25	15
345	5p. King Balthazar	25	15
346	5p. Saint Nicholas (Netherlands)	25	15
347	5p. La Befana (Italy)	25	15
348	5p. Julenisse (Denmark)	25	15
349	5p. Christkind (Germany)	25	15
350	5p. King Wenceslas (Czechoslovakia)	25	15
351	5p. Shepherd of Les Baux (France)	25	15
352	5p. King Caspar	25	15
353	5p. Baboushka (Russia)	25	15
354	5p. King Melchior	25	15

328 "Vraicing"

1985. Paintings by Paul Jacob Naftel. Multicoloured.

No.	Description	Mint	Used
355	9p. Type **328**	20	20
356	14p. "Castle Cornet"	25	25
357	22p. "Rocquaine Bay"	65	65
358	31p. "Little Russel"	1·00	1·00
359	34p. "Seaweedgatherers"	1·20	1·20

333 Squadron off Nargue Island, 1809

1986. 150th Death Anniv of Admiral Lord De Saumarez. Multicoloured.

No.	Description	Mint	Used
360	9p. Type **333**	30	25
361	14p. Battle of the Nile, 1798	40	30
362	29p. Battle of St. Vincent, 1797	75	70
363	31p. H.M.S "Crescent" off Cherbourg, 1793	1·10	95
364	34p. Battle of the Saints, 1782	1·20	1·00

338 Profile of Queen Elizabeth II (after R. Maklouf)

1986. 60th Birthday of Queen Elizabeth II.

365	**338**	60p. multicoloured	1·20	1·20

339 Northern Gannet and Nylon Net ("Operation Gannet")

1986. Europa. Nature and Environmental Protection. Multicoloured.

366	10p. Type **339**	30	30
367	14p. Whitsun orchid	40	40
368	22p. Guernsey elm	70	70

342 Prince Andrew and Miss Sarah Ferguson

1986. Royal Wedding. Multicoloured.

369	14p. Type **342**	60	50
370	34p. Prince Andrew and Miss Sarah Ferguson (different) (47×30 mm)	1·00	90

344 Bowls

1986. Sport in Guernsey. Multicoloured.

371	10p. Type **344**	25	20
372	14p. Cricket	35	20
373	22p. Squash	50	45
374	29p. Hockey	90	80
375	31p. Swimming (horiz)	90	80
376	34p. Shooting (horiz)	1·00	90

350 Guernsey Museum and Art Gallery, Candie Gardens

1986. Cent of Guernsey Museums. Mult.

377	14p. Type **350**	30	15
378	29p. Fort Grey Maritime Museum	85	80
379	31p. Castle Cornet	85	80
380	34p. National Trust of Guernsey Folk Museum	1·00	90

354 "While Shepherds Watched their Flocks by Night"

1986. Christmas. Carols. Multicoloured.

381	6p. Type **354**	20	10
382	6p. "In The Bleak Midwinter"	20	10
383	6p. "O Little Town of Bethlehem"	20	10
384	6p. "The Holly and the Ivy"	20	10
385	6p. "O Little Christmas Tree"	20	10
386	6p. "Away in a Manger"	20	10
387	6p. "Good King Wenceslas"	20	10
388	6p. "We Three Kings of Orient Are"	20	10
389	6p. "Hark the Herald Angels Sing"	20	10
390	6p. "I Saw Three Ships"	20	10
391	6p. "Little Donkey"	20	10
392	6p. "Jingle Bells"	20	10

366 Duke of Richmond and Portion of Map

1987. Bicentenary of Duke of Richmond's Survey of Guernsey. Sheet 134×103 mm containing T 106 and similar horiz designs showing sections of map. Multicoloured.

MS393	14p. Type **366**; 29p. North-east; 31p. South-west; 34p. South-east	2·50	2·75

The stamps within No. **MS**393 show a composite design of the Duke of Richmond's map of Guernsey.

367 Post Office Headquarters

1987. Europa. Modern Architecture. Mult.

394	15p. Type **371**	25	20
395	15p. Architect's elevation of Post Office Headquarters	25	20
396	22p. Guernsey Grammar School	30	35
397	22p. Architect's elevation of Grammar School	30	35

1987. Designs as Nos. 306, 306b, 309 and 309c but smaller.

398	11p. La Seigneurie, Sark (22x18 mm)	50	50
398a	12p. Petit Bot (18x22 mm)	40	40
399	15p. Havelet (18x22 mm)	60	60
399a	16p. Hostel of St. John (22x18 mm)	50	50

371 Sir Edmund Andros and La Plaiderie, Guernsey

1987. 350th Birth Anniv of Sir Edmund Andros (colonial administrator). Multicoloured.

400	15p. Type **371**	30	15
401	29p. Governor's Palace, Virginia	80	60
402	31p. Governor Andros in Boston	85	75
403	34p. Map of New Amsterdam (New York), 1661	1·10	1·00

375 The Jester's Warning to Young William

1987. 900th Death Anniv of William the Conqueror. Multicoloured.

404	11p. Type **375**	20	15
405	15p. Hastings battlefield	30	25
406	15p. Norman soldier with pennant	30	25
407	22p. William the Conqueror	60	60
408	22p. Queen Matilda and Abbaye aux Dames, Caen	60	60
409	34p. William's coronation regalia and Halley's Comet	1·00	1·10

381 John Wesley preaching on the Quay, Alderney

1987. Bicentenary of John Wesley's Visit to Guernsey. Multicoloured.

410	7p. Type **381**	20	15
411	15p. Wesley preaching at Mon Plaisir, St. Peter Port	25	25
412	29p. Preaching at Assembly Rooms	80	75
413	31p. Wesley and La Ville Baudu (early Methodist meeting place)	90	85
414	34p. Wesley and first Methodist Chapel, St. Peter Port	90	85

386 "Golden Spur" off St. Sampson Harbour

1988. Guernsey Shipping (2nd series). "Golden Spur". Multicoloured.

415	11p. Type **386**	25	25
416	15p. "Golden Spur" entering Hong Kong harbour	35	35
417	29p. Anchored off Macao	1·00	1·00
418	31p. In China Tea Race	1·00	1·00
419	34p. "Golden Spur" and map showing voyage of 1872–74	1·20	1·20

391 Rowing Boat and Bedford "Rascal" Mail Van

1988. Europa. Transport and Communications. Multicoloured.

420	16p. Type **391**	35	35
421	16p. Rowing boat and Vickers Viscount 800 mail plane	35	35
422	22p. Postman on bicycle and horse-drawn carriages, Sark	70	70
423	22p. Postmen on bicycles and carriage	70	70

Nos. 420/1 and 422/3 were each printed together, se-tenant, the two stamps of each value forming a composite design.

395 Frederick Corbin Lukis and Lukis House, St. Peter Port

1988. Birth Bicentenary of Frederick Corbin Lukis (archaeologist). Multicoloured.

424	12p. Type **395**	25	25
425	16p. Natural history books and reconstructed pot	30	25
426	29p. Lukis directing excavation of Le Creux es Faies and prehistoric beaker	90	85
427	31p. Lukis House Observatory and garden	90	85
428	34p. Prehistoric artifacts	90	90

400 "Cougar", "Rocky" and "Annabella" (powerboats) and Westland Wessex HU Mk5 Rescue Helicopter off Jethou

1988. World Offshore Powerboat Championships. Multicoloured.

429	16p. Type **400**	35	25
430	30p. "Paul Pilot" (powerboat) in Gouliot Passage	85	85
431	32p. Start of race at St. Peter Port (vert)	1·00	90
432	35p. Admiralty chart showing course (vert)	1·10	1·00

404 Joshua Gosselin and Herbarium

1988. Bicentenary of Joshua Gosselin's "Flora Sarniensis". Multicoloured.

433	12p. Type **404**	25	25
434	16p. Hares-tail grass	40	35
435	16p. Dried hares-tail grass	40	35
436	23p. Variegated catchfly	55	50
437	23p. Dried variegated catchfly	55	50
438	35p. Rock sea lavender	1·00	1·00

410 Coutances Cathedral, France

1988. Christmas. Ecclesiastical Links. Mult.

439	8p. Type **410**	20	10
440	8p. Interior of Notre Dame du Rosaire Church, Guernsey	20	10
441	8p. Stained glass, St. Sampson's Church, Guernsey	20	10
442	8p. Dol-de-Bretagne Cathedral, France	20	10
443	8p. Bishop's throne, Town Church, Guernsey	20	10
444	8p. Winchester Cathedral	20	10
445	8p. St. John's Cathedral, Portsmouth	20	10
446	8p. High altar, St. Joseph's Church, Guernsey	20	10
447	8p. Mont Saint-Michel, France	20	10
448	8p. Chancel, Vale Church, Guernsey	20	10
449	8p. Lychgate, Forest Church, Guernsey	20	10
450	8p. Marmoutier Abbey, France	20	10

422 Le Cat (Tip Cat)

1989. Europa. Children's Toys and Games. Multicoloured.

451	12p. Type **422**	25	20
452	16p. Girl with Cobo Alice doll	40	40
453	23p. Le Colimachaon (hopscotch)	80	85

425 Outline Map of Guernsey

1989. Coil Stamp. No value expressed.

454	425 (-) blue	60	60
455	425 (-) green	65	70

No. 454 is inscribed "MINIMUM BAILIWICK POSTAGE PAID" and No. 455 "MINIMUM FIRST CLASS POSTAGE TO UK PAID". They were initally sold at 14p. and 18p. but this was changed in line with postage rate rises.

426 Guernsey Airways de Havilland DH.86 Dragon Express and Mail Van

1989. 50th Anniv of Guernsey Airport (Nos. 456, 458 and 460) and 201 Squadron's Affiliation with Guernsey (Nos. 457, 459 and 461). Mult.

456	12p. Type **426**	35	30
457	12p. Supermarine Southampton II flying boat at mooring	35	30
458	18p. B.E.A. de Havilland DH.89 Dragon Rapide G-AGSH	50	50
459	18p. Short S.25 Sunderland Mk V flying boat taking off	50	50
460	35p. Air U.K. British Aerospace BAe 146	1·00	90
461	35p. Avro Shackleton M.R.3	1·00	1·00

432 "Queen Elizabeth II" (June Mendoza)

1989. Royal Visit.

462	432 30p. multicoloured	75	80

433 "Ibex" at G.W.R. Terminal, St. Peter Port

1989. Centenary of Great Western Railway Steamer Service to Channel Islands. Multicoloured.

463	12p. Type **433**	20	20
464	18p. "Great Western" (paddle-steamer) in Little Russel	45	45
465	29p. "St. Julien" passing Casquets Light	70	75
466	34p. "Roebuck" off Portland	1·00	95
467	37p. "Antelope" and boat train on Weymouth Quay	1·20	1·10
MS468	115×117 mm. Nos. 463/7	3·00	3·25

438 Two-toed Sloth

1989. 10th Anniv of Guernsey Zoological Trust. Animals of the Rainforest. Multicoloured.

469	18p. Type **438**	70	70
470	29p. Capuchin monkey	70	70
471	32p. White-lipped tamarin	70	70
472	34p. Common squirrel-monkey	70	70
473	37p. Common gibbon	70	70

443 Star

1989. Christmas. Christmas Tree Decorations. Multicoloured.

474	10p. Type **443**	25	15
475	10p. Fairy	25	15
476	10p. Candles	25	15
477	10p. Bird	25	15
478	10p. Present	25	15
479	10p. Carol-singer	25	15
480	10p. Christmas cracker	25	15
481	10p. Bauble	25	15
482	10p. Christmas stocking	25	15
483	10p. Bell	25	15
484	10p. Fawn	25	15
485	10p. Church	25	15

455 Sark Post Office, c. 1890

1990. Europa. Post Office Buildings.

486	455 20p. deep brown, sepia and light brown	45	45
487	- 20p. multicoloured	45	45
488	- 24p. deep brown, sepia and light brown	60	65
489	- 24p. multicoloured	60	65

DESIGNS: No. 487, Sark Post Office, 1990; 488, Arcade Post Office counter, St. Peter Port, c. 1840; 489, Arcade Post Office counter, St. Peter Port, 1990.

459 Penny Black and Mail Steamer off St. Peter Port, 1840

1990. 150th Anniv of the Penny Black. Mult.

490	14p. Type **459**	35	35
491	20p. Penny Red, 1841 and pillar box of 1853	45	45
492	32p. Bisected 2d., 1940 and German Army band	80	80
493	34p. Regional 3d., 1958 and Guernsey emblems	1·00	1·00
494	37p. Independent postal administration 1½d., 1969 and queue outside Main Post Office	1·00	1·00
MS495	151×116 mm. Nos. 490/4	3·25	3·50

No. **MS**495 also commemorates "Stamp World London '90" International Stamp Exhibition.

464 Lt. Philip Saumarez writing Log Book

1990. 250th Anniv of Anson's Circumnavigation. Multicoloured.

496	14p. Type **464**	30	30
497	20p. Anson's squadron leaving Portsmouth, 1740	40	40
498	29p. Ships at St. Catherine's Island, Brazil	80	80
499	34p. H.M.S. "Tryal" (sloop) dismasted, Cape Horn, 1741	1·00	90
500	37p. Crew of H.M.S. "Centurion" on Juan Fernandez	1·10	95

469 Grey Seal and Pup

1990. Marine Life. Multicoloured.

501	20p. Type **469**	45	45
502	26p. Bottle-nosed dolphin	95	95
503	31p. Basking shark	1·00	1·00
504	37p. Common porpoise	1·20	1·20

473 Blue Tit and Great Tit

1990. Christmas. Winter Birds. Multicoloured.

505	10p. Type **473**	35	15
506	10p. Snow bunting	35	15
507	10p. Common kestrel ("Kestrel")	35	15
508	10p. Common starling ("Starling")	35	15
509	10p. Western greenfinch ("Greenfinch")	35	15
510	10p. European robin ("Robin")	35	15
511	10p. Winter wren	35	15
512	10p. Barn owl	35	15
513	10p. Mistle thrush	35	15
514	10p. Grey heron ("Heron")	35	15
515	10p. Chaffinch	35	15
516	10p. River kingfisher ("Kingfisher")	35	15

485 Air Raid and 1941 1/2d. Stamp

1991. 50th Anniv of First Guernsey Stamps. Multicoloured.

517	37p. Type **485**	1·00	1·10
518	53p. 1941 1d. stamp	1·30	1·50
519	57p. 1944 2½d. stamp	1·30	1·50

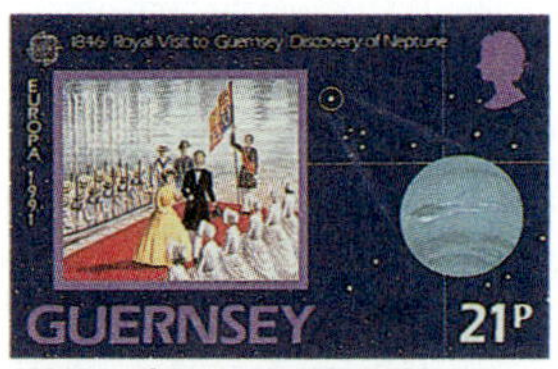

488 Visit of Queen Victoria to Guernsey, and Discovery of Neptune, 1846

1991. Europa. Europe in Space. Multicoloured.

520	21p. Type **488**	55	50
521	21p. Visit of Queen Elizabeth II and Prince Philip to Sark, and "Sputnik" (first artificial satellite), 1957	55	50
522	26p. Maiden voyage of "Sarnia" (ferry) and "Vostok I" (first manned space flight), 1961	65	60
523	26p. Cancelling Guernsey stamps, and first manned landing on Moon, 1969	65	60

492 Children in Guernsey Sailing Trust "GP14" Dinghy

1991. Centenary of Guernsey Yacht Club. Mult.

524	15p. Type **492**	45	15
525	21p. Guernsey Regatta	70	25
526	26p. Lombard Channel Islands' Challenge race	80	80
527	31p. Rolex Swan Regatta	90	1·10
528	37p. Old Gaffers' Association gaff-rigged yacht	1·00	1·40
MS529	163×75 mm. As Nos. 524/8, but "GUERNSEY" and face values in yellow	3·50	4·00

497 Pair of Oystercatchers

1991. Nature Conservation. L'Eree Shingle Bank Reserve. Multicoloured.

530	15p. Type **497**	35	20
531	15p. Three ruddy turnstones	35	20
532	15p. Dunlins and ruddy turnstones	35	20
533	15p. Curlew and ruddy turnstones	35	20
534	15p. Ringed plover with chicks	35	20
535	21p. Gull, sea campion and sea radish	35	20
536	21p. Yellow horned poppy	35	20
537	21p. Pair of common stone-chats, hare's foot clover and fennel	35	20
538	21p. Hares's foot clover, fennel and slender oat	35	20
539	21p. Sea kale on shore	35	20

Nos. 530/4 and 535/9 were each printed together, se-tenant, with the backgrounds forming composite designs.

507 "Rudolph the Red-nosed Reindeer" (Melanie Sharpe)

1991. Christmas. Children's Paintings. Mult.

540	12p. Type **507**	30	15
541	12p. "Christmas Pudding" (James Quinn)	30	15
542	12p. "Snowman" (Lisa Guille)	30	15
543	12p. "Snowman in Top Hat" (Jessica Ede-Golightly)	30	15
544	12p. "Robins and Christmas Tree" (Sharon Le Page)	30	15
545	12p. "Shepherds and Angels" (Anna Coquelin)	30	15
546	12p. "Nativity" (Claudine Lihou)	30	15
547	12p. "Three Wise Men" (Jonathan Le Noury)	30	15
548	12p. "Star of Bethlehem and Angels" (Marcia Mahy)	30	15
549	12p. "Christmas Tree" (Laurel Garfield)	30	15
550	12p. "Santa Claus" (Rebecca Driscoll)	30	15
551	12p. "Snowman and Star" (Ian Lowe)	30	15

519 Queen Elizabeth II in 1952

1992. 40th Anniv of Accession. Multicoloured.

552	23p. Type **519**	50	50
553	28p. Queen Elizabeth in 1977	65	65
554	33p. Queen Elizabeth in 1986	90	90
555	39p. Queen Elizabeth in 1991	1·10	1·10

523 Christopher Columbus

1992. 500th Anniv of Discovery of America by Columbus. Multicoloured.

556	23p. Type **523**	65	60
557	23p. Examples of Columbus's signature	65	60
558	28p. "Santa Maria"	1·20	1·20
559	28p. Map of first voyage	1·20	1·20
MS560	157×77 mm. Nos. 556/9	4·50	5·00

527 Guernsey Calves

1992. 150th Anniv of Royal Guernsey Agricultural and Horticultural Society. Sheet, 93×71 mm.

MS561	**527** 75p. multicoloured	2·10	2·00

528 Stock

1992. Horticultural Exports. Multicoloured.

562	1p. "Stephanotis floribunda"	10	10
563	2p. Potted hydrangea	10	10
564	3p. Type **528**	10	10
565	4p. Anemones	15	15
566	5p. Gladiolus	15	15
567	6p. "Asparagus plumosus" and "Gypsophila paniculata"	15	15
568	7p. Guernsey lily	20	20
569	8p. Enchantment lily	20	20
570	9p. Clematis "Freckles"	20	25
571	10p. Alstroemeria	25	25
572	16p. Standard carnation (horiz)	50	35
572b	18p. Standard rose	55	45
573	20p. Spray rose	60	50
574	23p. Mixed freesia (horiz)	60	55
575	24p. Standard rose (horiz)	70	60
576	25p. Iris "Ideal" (horiz)	70	60
576b	26p. Freesia "Pink Glow"	70	60
577	28p. Lisianthus (horiz)	80	65
578	30p. Spray chrysanthemum (horiz)	80	70
579	40p. Spray carnation	1·00	75
580	50p. Single freesia (horiz)	1·20	90
581	£1 Floral arrangement (35×26½ mm)	2·00	1·50
582	£2 Chelsea Flower Show exhibit (35×26½ mm)	4·00	3·00
582a	£3 "Floral Fantasia" (exhibit) (35×28 mm)	6·00	5·00

552 Building the Ship

1992. "Operation Asterix" (excavation of Roman ship). Multicoloured.

583	16p. Type **552**	45	35
584	23p. Loading the cargo	60	45
585	28p. Ship at sea	80	70
586	33p. Ship under attack	95	90
587	39p. Crew swimming ashore	1·10	1·00

557 Tram No. 10 decorated for Battle of Flowers

1992. Guernsey Trams. Multicoloured.

588	16p. Type **557**	45	30
589	23p. Tram No 10 passing Hougue a la Perre	60	35
590	28p. Tram No. 1 at St. Sampsons	75	80
591	33p. First steam tram at St. Peter Port, 1879	90	1·00
592	39p. Last electric tram, 1934	1·10	1·10

562 Man in Party Hat

1992. Christmas. Seasonal Fayre. Multicoloured.

593	13p. Type **562**	30	15
594	13p. Girl and Christmas tree	30	15
595	13p. Woman and balloons	30	15
596	13p. Mince pies and champagne	30	15
597	13p. Roast turkey	30	15
598	13p. Christmas pudding	30	15
599	13p. Christmas cake	30	15
600	13p. Fancy cakes	30	15
601	13p. Cheese	30	15
602	13p. Nuts	30	15
603	13p. Ham	30	15
604	13p. Chocolate log	30	15

Nos. 593/604 were printed together, se-tenant, forming a composite design.

574 Rupert Bear, Bingo and Dog

1993. Rupert Bear and Friends (cartoon characters created by Mary and Herbert Tourtel).

605	**574** 24p. multicoloured	50	75
MS606	116×97 mm. 16p. Airplane and castle; 16p. Professor's servant and Autumn Elf; 16p. Algy Pug; 16p. Baby Badger on sledge; 24p. Bill Badger, Willie Mouse, Reggie Rabbit and Podgy playing in snow; 24p. Type **574**; 24p. The Balloonist avoiding Gregory on toboggan; 24p. Tiger Lily and Edward Trunk	4·50	4·00

The 24p. values in No. **MS**606 are as Type **574**; the 16p. designs are smaller, each 25½×26 mm.

575 Tapestry by Kelly Fletcher

1993. Europa. Contemporary Art. Multicoloured.

607	24p. Type **575**	70	70
608	24p. "Le Marchi a Paissaon" (etching and aquatint, Sally Reed) (48×33½ mm)	70	70
609	28p. "Red Abstract" (painting, Molly Harris)	80	80
610	28p. "Dress Shop, King's Road" (painting, Damon Bell) (48×33½ mm)	80	80

579 Arrest of Guernsey Parliamentarians, Fermain Bay

1993. 350th Anniv of Siege of Castle Cornet. Multicoloured.

611	16p. Type **579**	35	35
612	24p. Parliamentary ships attacking Castle Cornet	60	60
613	28p. Parliamentary captives escaping	75	75
614	33p. Castle cannon firing at St. Peter Port	85	85
615	39p. Surrender of Castle Cornet, 19 December 1651	90	90
MS616	203×75 mm. Nos. 611/15	3·25	4·00

584 Playing Cards

1993. Birth Bicentenary of Thomas de la Rue (printer).

617	**584** 16p. multicoloured	40	45
618	- 24p. multicoloured	65	65
619	- 28p. multicoloured	80	80
620	- 33p. red	95	95
621	- 39p. green	1·10	1·10

DESIGNS: 24p. Fountain pens; 28p. Envelope-folding machine; 33p. Great Britain 1855 4d. stamp; 39p. Thomas de la Rue and Mauritius £1 banknote.

589 "The Twelve Pearls"

1993. Christmas. Stained Glass Windows by Mary-Eily de Putron from the Chapel of Christ the Healer. Multicoloured.

622	13p. Type **589**	30	15
623	13p. "Healing rays"	30	15
624	13p. "Hand of God over the Holy City"	30	15
625	13p. "Wing and Seabirds" (facing left)	30	15
626	13p. "Christ the Healer"	30	15
627	13p. "Wing and Seabirds" (facing right)	30	15
628	13p. "The Young Jesus in the Temple"	30	15
629	13p. "The Raising of Jairus' Daughter"	30	15
630	13p. "Suffer little Children to come unto Me"	30	15
631	13p. "Pilgrim's Progress"	30	15
632	13p. "The Light of the World"	30	15
633	13p. "Raphael, Archangel of Healing, with Tobias"	30	15

601 Les Fouaillages (ancient burial ground)

1994. Europa. Archaeological Discoveries. Multicoloured.

634	24p. Type **601**	55	55
635	24p. Mounted Celtic warrior	55	55
636	30p. Jars, arrow heads and stone axe from Les Fouaillages	80	75
637	30p. Sword, spear head and torque from King's Road burial	80	75

605 Supermarine Spitfires Mk V over Normandy Beaches

1994. 50th Anniv of D-Day. Sheet 93×71 mm.

MS638	**605** £2 multicoloured	4·00	4·25

606 Peugeot "Type 3", 1894

1994. Cent of First Car in Guernsey. Mult.

639	16p. Type **606**	40	40
640	24p. Mercedes "Simplex", 1903	60	45
641	35p. Humber tourer, 1906	90	1·00
642	41p. Bentley sports tourer, 1936	1·00	1·00
643	60p. MG TC Midget, 1948	1·50	1·40

1994. "Philakorea '94" International Stamp Exhibition, Seoul. Sheet 110×90 mm containing No. 581.

MS644	£1 multicoloured	3·25	3·00

611 "Trident" (Herm ferry)

1994. 25th Anniv of Guernsey Postal Administration. Multicoloured.

645	16p. Type **611**	35	30
646	24p. Handley Page HPR.7 Herald of Channel Express	55	50
647	35p. Britten Norman BN-2A MkIII Trislander of Aurigny Air Services	85	75
648	41p. "Bon Marin de Serk" (Sark ferry)	1·00	85
649	60p. Map of Bailiwick	1·40	1·20
MS650	150×100 mm. Nos. 645/9	4·00	4·25

616 Dolls' House

1994. Christmas. Bygone Toys. Multicoloured.

651	13p. Type **616**	40	15
652	13p. Doll	40	15
653	13p. Teddy in bassinette	40	15
654	13p. Sweets in pillar box and playing cards	40	15
655	13p. Spinning top	40	15
656	13p. Building blocks	40	15
657	24p. Rocking horse	75	30
658	24p. Teddy bear	75	30
659	24p. Tricycle	75	30
660	24p. Wooden duck	75	30
661	24p. Hornby toy locomotive	75	30
662	24p. Ludo game	75	30

Nos. 651/6 and 657/62 respectively were printed together, se-tenant, forming composite designs.

628 Seafood "Face"

1995. Greetings Stamps. "The Welcoming Face of Guernsey". Multicoloured.

663	24p. Type **628**	60	55
664	24p. Buckets and spade "face"	60	55
665	24p. Flowers "face"	60	55
666	24p. Fruit and vegetables "face"	60	55
667	24p. Sea shells and seaweed "face"	60	55
668	24p. Anchor and life belts "face"	60	55
669	24p. Glasses, cork and cutlery "face"	60	55
670	24p. Butterflies and caterpillars "face"	60	55
MS671	137×109 mm. Nos. 663/70	4·25	4·25

636 Winston Churchill and Wireless

1995. 50th Anniv of Liberation. Multicoloured.

672	16p. Type **636**	45	30
673	24p. Union Jack and Royal Navy ships off St. Peter Port	60	50
674	35p. Royal Arms and military band	90	90
675	41p. "Vega" (Red Cross supply ship)	90	90
676	60p. Rejoicing crowd	1·50	1·20
MS677	189×75 mm. Nos. 672/6	4·50	4·75

641 Silhouette of Doves on Ground (image scaled to 64% of original size)

1995. Europa. Peace and Freedom. Multicoloured.

678	25p. Type **641**	55	65
679	30p. Silhouette of doves in flight	75	85

The designs of Nos. 678/9 each provide a stereogram or hidden three-dimensional image of a single dove.

643 Prince Charles, Castle Cornet and Bailiwick Arms

1995. Royal Visit.

680	**643**	£1.50 multicoloured	3·00	3·25

1995. "Singapore '95" International Stamp Exhibition. Sheet 110×90 mm. containing No. 581.

MS681	£1 multicoloured	3·00	2·75

644 Part of United Nations Emblem (face value at top left)

1995. 50th Anniv of United Nations. Designs showing different segments of the United Nations Emblem. Each blue and gold.

682	50p. Type **644**	1·10	1·10
683	50p. Face value at top right	1·10	1·10
684	50p. Face value at bottom left	1·10	1·10
685	50p. Face value at bottom right	1·10	1·10

648 "Christmas Trees for Sale in Bern" (Cornelia Huisboum-Weibel)

1995. Christmas. 50th Anniv of UNICEF Multicoloured.

686	13p. Type **648** (face value at left)	40	15
687	13p. "Christmas Trees for Sale in Bern" (face value at right)	40	15
688	13p.+1p. "Evening Snowfall" (Katerina Mertikas) (face value at left)	40	20
689	13p.+1p. "Evening Snowfall" (face value at right)	40	20
690	24p. "It came upon a Midnight Clear" (Georgia Guback) (face value at left)	70	30
691	24p. "It came upon a Midnight Clear" (Georgia Guback) (face value at right)	70	30
692	24p.+2p. "Children of the World" (face value at left)	70	30
693	24p.+2p. "Children of the World" (face value at right)	70	30

Nos. 686/7, 688/9, 690/1 and 692/3 were printed together, se-tenant, each pair forming a composite design.

656 Princess Anne (President, Save the Children Fund) and Children

1996. Europa. Famous Women. Multicoloured.

694	25p. Type **656**	55	50
695	30p. Queen Elizabeth II and people of the Commonwealth	70	75

658 England v. U.S.S.R., 1968 (value at right)

1996. European Football Championship, England. Multicoloured.

696	16p. Type **658**	55	20
697	16p. England v. U.S.S.R., 1968 (value at left)	55	20
698	24p. Italy v. Belgium, 1972 (value at right)	75	25
699	24p. Italy v. Belgium, 1972 (value at left)	75	25
700	35p. Ireland v. Netherlands, 1988 (value at right)	80	40
701	35p. Ireland v. Netherlands, 1988 (value at left)	80	40
702	41p. Denmark v. Germany, 1992 final (value at right)	95	45
703	41p. Denmark v. Germany, 1992 final (value at left)	95	45

666 Maj-Gen. Brock meeting Tecumseh (Indian chief)

1996. "CAPEX '96" International Stamp Exhibition, Toronto. Sheet 110×90 mm. containing T 666 and similar horiz design.

MS704	24p. Type **666**; £1 Major-General Sir Isaac Brock on horseback, 1812	3·00	2·75

667 Ancient Greek Runner

1996. Centenary of Modern Olympic Games. Ancient Greek Athletes. Each black, yellow and orange.

705	16p. Type **677**	50	40
706	24p. Throwing the javelin	95	90
707	41p. Throwing the discus	1·10	1·20
708	55p. Wrestling (53×31 mm)	1·40	1·50
709	60p. Jumping	1·60	1·70
MS710	192×75 mm. Nos. 705/9	4·50	4·75

No. 708 also includes the "OLYMPHILEX '96" International Stamp Exhibition, Atlanta, logo.

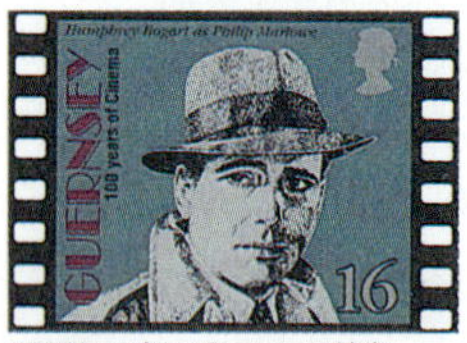

672 Humphrey Bogart as Philip Marlowe

1996. Centenary of Cinema. Screen Detectives. Multicoloured.

711	16p. Type **672**	40	40
712	24p. Peter Sellers as Inspector Clouseau	60	60
713	35p. Basil Rathbone as Sherlock Holmes	85	85
714	41p. Margaret Rutherford as Miss Marple	90	90
715	60p. Warner Oland as Charlie Chan	1·40	1·40

677 The Annunciation

1996. Christmas. Multicoloured.

716	13p. Type **677**	30	15
717	13p. Journey to Bethlehem	30	15
718	13p. Arrival at the inn	30	15
719	13p. Angel and shepherds	30	15
720	13p. Mary, Joseph and Jesus in stable	30	15
721	13p. Shepherds worshipping Jesus	30	15
722	13p. Three Kings following star	30	15
723	13p. Three Kings with gifts	30	15
724	13p. The Presentation in the Temple	30	15
725	13p. Mary and Jesus	30	15
726	13p. Joseph warned by angel	30	15
727	13p. The Flight into Egypt	30	15
728	24p. Mary cradling Jesus (horiz)	30	15
729	25p. The Nativity (horiz)	30	15

691 Holly Blue

1997. Endangered Species. Butterflies and Moths. Multicoloured.

730	18p. Type **691**	55	50
731	25p. Hummingbird hawk- moth	65	60
732	26p. Emperor moth	85	85
733	37p. Brimstone	1·10	1·10
MS734	92×68 mm. £1 Painted Lady	3·00	2·50

No. **MS**734 includes the "HONG KONG '97" International Stamp Exhibition logo on the sheet margin.

696 Gilliatt fighting Octopus

1997. Europa. Tales and Legends. Scenes from "Les Travailleurs de la Mer" by Victor Hugo. Multicoloured.

735	26p. Type **696**	55	60
736	31p. Gilliatt grieving on rock	75	65

698 Shell Beach, Herm

1997. Guernsey Scenes (1st series). Multicoloured. Self-adhesive.

737	18p. Type **698**	60	30
738	25p. La Seigneurie, Sark (vert)	70	60
739	26p. Castle Cornet, Guernsey	80	75

701 19th-century Shipyard, St. Peter Port

1997. "Pacific '97" World Philatelic Exhibition, San Francisco. Sheet 110×90 mm. containing T 701 and similar horiz design.

MS740	30p. green and gold; £1 multicoloured ("Costa Rica Packet" (barque))	4·00	4·00

See also Nos. 770/3.

702 Transistor Radio, Microphone and Radio Logos

1997. Methods of Communication. Multicoloured.

741	18p. Type **702**	40	40
742	25p. Television, video camera and satellite dish	60	60
743	26p. Fax machine, telephones and mobile phone	60	60
744	37p. Printing press, newspaper and type	90	85
745	43p. Stamp, coding machine and postbox	1·20	1·20
746	63p. CD, computer and disk	1·50	1·70

708 Teddy Bear making Cake

1997. Christmas. Teddy Bears. Multicoloured.

747	15p. Type **708**	45	45
748	25p. Teddy bears decorating Christmas tree	70	70
749	26p. Two teddy bears in armchair	70	70
750	37p. Teddy bear as Father Christmas	1·00	1·00
751	43p. Teddy bears unwrapping presents	1·10	1·10
752	63p. Teddy bears eating Christmas dinner	1·60	1·60
MS753	123×107 mm. Nos. 747/52	6·00	6·00

714 Visiting Guernsey, 1957

1997. Golden Wedding of Queen Elizabeth and Prince Philip. Multicoloured.

754	18p. Type **714**	40	40
755	25p. Coronation Day, 1953	60	60
756	26p. Royal Family, 1957	60	60
757	37p. On royal yacht, 1972	90	90
758	43p. Queen Elizabeth and Prince Philip at Trooping the Colour, 1987	1·00	1·00
759	63p. Queen Elizabeth and Prince Philip, 1997	1·40	1·40

No. 755 is inscribed "1947" in error.

720 Tapestry of 11th-century Guernsey (St. Martin)

1998. The Millennium Tapestries Project. Each showing a different century contributed by individual parishes. Multicoloured.

760	25p. Type **720**	60	30
761	25p. 12th-century (St. Saviour)	60	30
762	25p. 13th-century (Vale)	60	30
763	25p. 14th-century (St. Sampson)	60	30
764	25p. 15th-century (Torteval)	60	30
765	25p. 16th-century (Castel)	60	30
766	25p. 17th-century (St. Andrew)	60	30
767	25p. 18th-century (Forest)	60	30
768	25p. 19th-century (St. Pierre du Bois)	60	30
769	25p. 20th-century (St. Peter Port)	60	30

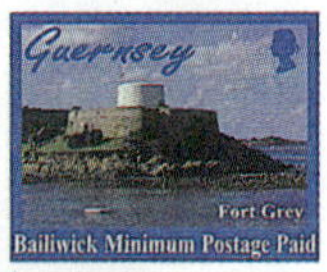

730 Fort Grey

1998. Guernsey Scenes (2nd series). Multicoloured. Self-adhesive.

770	(20p.) Type **730**	45	55
771	(20p.) Grand Havre	45	55
772	(25p.) Little Chapel	50	65
773	(25p.) Guernsey cow	55	65

Nos. 770/1 are inscribed "Bailiwick Minimum Postage Paid" and were intially sold at 20p. Nos. 772/3 are inscribed "UK Minimum Postage Paid" and were initially sold at 25p.

734 Fairey IIIC, Balloon, Sopwith Camel and Avro 504

1998. 80th Anniv of the Royal Air Force. Multicoloured.

774	20p. Type **734**	50	50
775	25p. Fairey Swordfish, de Havilland DH.82 Tiger Moth, Supermarine Walrus and Gloster Gladiator	60	60
776	30p. Hawker Hurricane, Supermarine Spitfire, Vickers Type **271** Wellington, Short S.25 Sunderland (flying boat), Westland Lysander and Bristol Type **142** Blenheim	70	70

777	37p. de Havilland DH.98 Mosquito, Avro Type **683** Lancaster, british Taylorcraf-tAuster III, Gloster Meteor and Airspeed Horsa glider	90	85
778	43p. English Electric Canberra, Hawker Sea Fury, Bristol Sycamore, Hawker Hunter, Handley Page HP.80 Victor and English Electric BAe Lightning	1·00	1·20
779	63p. Pavania Tornado GRI, BAe Hawk, BAe Sea Harrier, Westland Lynx (helicopter) and Hawker Siddeley (BAe) Nimrod	1·40	1·50

740 Jules Rimet (first President of F.I.F.A)

1998. 150th Anniv of the Cambridge Rules for Football. Sheet 110×90 mm containing T 173 and similar horiz design.

MS780	30p. Type **740**; £1.75, Bobby Moore and Queen Elizabeth II, 1966	4·00	4·00

741 Girls in Traditional Costume watching Sheep Display, West Show

1998. Europa. Festivals. Multicoloured.

781	20p. Type **741**	45	45
782	25p. Marching band and "Battle of Flowers" exhibit, North Show	55	55
783	30p. Prince Charles, monument and tank, Liberation Day	65	65
784	37p. Goat, dahlias and show-jumping, South Show	85	85

The 25p. and 30p. incorporate the "EUROPA" emblem.

745 Outward Motorboat

763 Royal Yacht "Britannia"

1998. Maritime Heritage. Multicoloured.

785	1p. Type **745**	10	10
786	2p. St. John Ambulance inshore rescue dinghy	10	10
787	3p. Pilot boat, St. Peter Port	10	10
788	4p. "Flying Christine III" (St. John Ambulance launch)	10	10
789	5p. Crab fishing boat	10	10
790	6p. Herm Island ferry	10	10
791	7p. "Sarnia" (St. Peter Port Harbour Authority launch)	15	20
792	8p. "Leopardess" (States' fisheries protection launch)	15	20
793	9p. Trawler	20	25
794	10p. Powerboat (27×27 mm)	20	25
795	20p. Dart 18 racing catamaran (27×27 mm)	40	45
796	30p. 30ft Bermuda-rigged sloop (27×27 mm)	60	65
797	40p. Motor cruiser (27×27 mm)	80	85
798	50p. Ocean-going sailing yacht (27×27 mm)	1·00	1·10
799	75p. Motor yacht "Beaucette Marina" (27×27 mm)	1·50	1·30
800	£1 "Queen Elizabeth 2" (liner) (35×26 mm)	2·00	1·80
801	£3 "Oriana" (liner) (35×26 mm)	6·00	5·50
802	£4 "Queen Mary 2" (liner)	9·00	9·00
803	£5 Type **763**	13·00	10·00

769 Modern Tree, Teletubby and Playstation

1998. 150th Anniv of the Introduction of the Christmas Tree. Multicoloured.

810	17p. Type **769**	40	40
811	25p. 1960s tinsel tree, toy bus and doll	60	60
812	30p. 1930s gold foil tree, panda and toy tank	70	70
813	37p. 1920s tree, model of "Bluebird" and doll	90	90
814	43p. 1900s tree, teddy bear and toy train	90	90
815	63p. 1850s tree, wooden doll and spinning top	1·50	1·50
MS816	160×94 mm. Nos. 810/15	6·00	6·00

775 Elizabeth Bowes Lyon, 1907

1999. Life and Times of Queen Elizabeth the Queen Mother. Multicoloured.

817	25p. Type **775**	70	30
818	25p. On wedding day, 1923	70	30
819	25p. Holding Princess Elizabeth, 1926	70	30
820	25p. At Coronation, 1937	70	30
821	25p. Visiting bombed areas of London, 1940 (wearing green hat)	70	30
822	25p. Fishing near Auckland, New Zealand, 1966	70	30
823	25p. At Guernsey function, 1963 (wearing tiara)	70	30
824	25p. Receiving flowers on her birthday, 1992	70	30
825	25p. Presenting trophy, Sandown Park races, 1989	70	30
826	25p. Opening Royal Norfolk Regimental Museum, Norwich, 1990 (wearing blue hat)	70	30

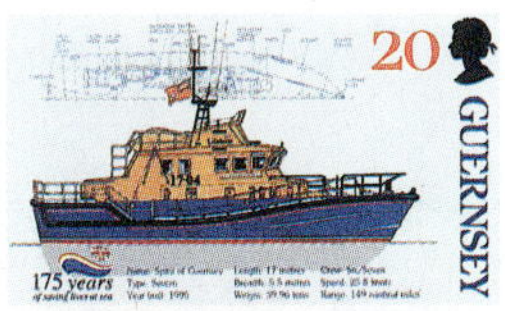

785 "Spirit of Guernsey", 1995

1999. 175th Anniv of Royal National Lifeboat Institution. Multicoloured.

827	20p. Type **785**	50	50
828	25p. "Sir William Arnold", 1973	60	60
829	30p. "Euphrosyne Kendal", 1954	70	70
830	38p. "Queen Victoria", 1929	90	90
831	44p. "Arthur Lionel", 1912	1·10	1·10
832	64p. "Vincent Kirk Ella", 1888	1·50	1·50

791 Burnet Rose and Local Carriage Label

1999. Europa. Parks and Gardens. Herm Island. Designs each showing a different local carriage label. Multicoloured.

833	20p. Type **791**	50	45
834	25p. Atlantic puffin	60	75
835	30p. Small heath butterfly	70	80
836	38p. Shells on Shell Beach	90	1·20

795 Prince Edward and Miss Sophie Rhys-Jones

1999. Royal Wedding. Sheet 93×70 mm.

MS837	**795** £1 Multicoloured	2·50	3·00

796 Major-General Le Marchant (founder) and Cadet at Sword Drill

1999. Bicentenary of The Royal Military Academy, Sandhurst. Multicoloured.

838	20p. Type **796**	50	45
839	25p. The Duke of York (official sponsor) and Cadet on Horseback	60	55
840	30p. Field-Marshal Earl Haig and cadets on parade	75	70
841	38p. Field-Marshal Viscount Montgomery and bridging exercise	90	95
842	44p. David Niven (actor) and rifle practice	1·10	1·20
843	64p. Sir Winston Churchill and tank	1·50	1·75

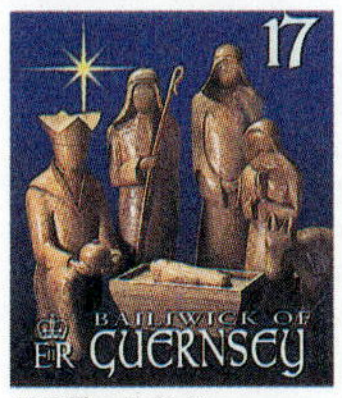

802 The Nativity

1999. Christmas. Wood Carvings by Denis Brehaut from Notre Dame Church. Multicoloured.

844	17p. Type **802**	45	40
845	25p. Virgin Mary and Child	60	55
846	30p. Holy Family	75	70
847	38p. Cattle around manger	90	85
848	44p. Adoration of the Shepherds	1·10	1·20
849	64p. Adoration of the Magi	1·50	1·70
MS850	159×86 mm. Nos. 844/9	5·50	5·50

808 "Space Bus" (Fallon Ephgrave)

2000. New Millennium. "Stampin' the Future" (children's stamp design competition). Multicoloured.

851	20p. Type **808**	60	45
852	25p. "Children holding hands" (Abigail Downing)	60	55
853	30p. "No Captivity" (Laura Martin)	70	65
854	38p. "Post Office of the Future" (Sarah Haddow)	90	80
855	44p. "Solar-powered car" (Sophie Medland)	1·20	1·50
856	64p. "Woman flying" (Danielle McIver)	1·50	1·75

814 Bristol Type 142 Blenheim

2000. 60th Anniv of Battle of Britain. R.A.F. Aircraft. Multicoloured.

857	21p. Type **814**	50	50
858	26p. Hawker Hurricane	60	55
859	36p. Boulton Paul P.28 Defiant II	95	85
860	40p. Gloster Gladiator	1·00	95
861	45p. Bristol Type 156 Beaufighter IF	1·10	1·20
862	65p. Supermarine Spitfire IIC	1·50	1·50

820 Guernsey Flag on Kite and "2000"

2000. Europa. Multicoloured.

863	21p. Type **820**	50	45
864	26p. Stylized sails bearing national flowers	60	55
865	36p. "Building Europe"	1·00	1·00
866	65p. Rainbow and three doves	1·60	1·75

824 *Iris stylosa*

2000. "A Botanist's Sketchbook". Restoration of Candie Gardens, St. Peter Port. Multicoloured.

867	26p. Type **824**	45	30
868	26p. *Watsonia*	45	30
869	26p. *Richardia maculata*	45	30
870	26p. *Narcissus bulbocodium*	45	30
871	26p. *Triteleia laxa*	45	30
872	26p. *Tigridia pavonia*	45	30
873	26p. *Agapanthus umbellatus*	45	30
874	26p. *Sparaxis*	45	30
875	26p. *Pancratium maritimum*	45	30
876	26p. *Nerine sarniensis*	45	30

834 Town Church, St. Peter Port

2000. Christmas. Guernsey Churches. Multicoloured.

877	18p. Type **834**	40	40
878	26p. Children leaving St. Sampson's Church	60	55
879	36p. Flying kite by Vale Church	90	85
880	40p. Carol singing outside St. Pierre du Bois Church	95	1·00
881	45p. Building snowman near St. Martin's Church	1·10	1·40
882	65p. Street scene including St. John's Church, St. Peter Port	1·50	1·75
MS883	160×86 mm. Nos. 877/82	6·00	6·00

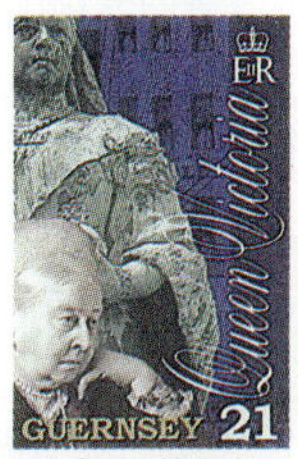

840 Queen Victoria and Diamond Jubilee Statue

2001. Death Centenary of Queen Victoria. Each incorporating a different portrait of Queen Victoria. Multicoloured.

884	21p. Type **840**	50	50
885	26p. Letter of thanks to Guernsey, 1846	60	55
886	36p. Statues of Queen Victoria and Prince Albert	90	85
887	40p. Stone commemorating 1846 visit	95	95
888	45p. Statue of Prince Albert	1·10	1·10
889	65p. Victoria Tower, 1848	1·50	1·50
MS890	165×80 mm. Nos. 884/9	6·00	7·00

No. **MS**890 includes the logo of the "Hong Kong 2001" Stamp Exhibition on the sheet margin.

846 River kingfisher ("Kingfisher")

2001. Europa. Water Birds. Multicoloured.

891	21p. Type **846**	60	40
892	26p. Garganey	90	75
893	36p. Little egret	1·20	1·50
894	65p. Little ringed plover	1·70	1·90

850 Cavalier King Charles Spaniel

2001. Centenary of Guernsey Dog Club. Mult.

895	22p. Type **850**	55	50
896	27p. Miniature schnauzer	65	60
897	36p. German shepherd dog	90	85
898	40p. Cocker spaniel	95	95
899	45p. West highland white terrier	1·10	1·10
900	65p. Dachshund	1·50	1·50

856 La Corbiere Sunset

2001. Island Scenes. Multicoloured. Self-adhesive.

901	(22p.) Type **856**	45	50
902	(22p.) Rue des Hougues	45	50
903	(22p.) St. Saviour's Reservoir	45	50
904	(22p.) Shell Beach, Herm	45	50
905	(22p.) Telegraph Bay, Alderney	45	50
906	(27p.) Alderney Railway	55	60
907	(27p.) Vazon Bay	55	60
908	(27p.) La Coupee, Sark	55	60
909	(27p.) Les Hanois Lighthouse	55	60
910	(27p.) Albecq Beach	55	60

Nos. 901/5 were intended for postage within the Bailiwick and are inscribed "GY". They were each initially sold at 22p. Nos. 906/10 were intended for postage to Great Britain and are inscribed "UK". They were each initially sold at 27p.

866 Droplet of Water on Leaf ("Vision")

2001. Incorporation of Guernsey Post Ltd. Multicoloured.

(a) Square designs as T 193.

921	22p. Type **866**	45	50
922	27p. Hummingbird ("Understanding")	55	60
923	36p. Butterfly's wing ("Individuality")	70	75
924	40p. Sea shell ("Strength")	80	85
925	45p. Honeycomb ("Community")	90	95
926	65p. Dandelion ("Maturity")	1·20	1·40

(b) Design as No. 28a (1969 £1), but redrawn.

927	£1 View of Guernsey from the sea	5·00	5·50

No. 927 differs from the original 1969 stamp by showing the Queen's portrait without a tiara and by showing "GUERNSEY BALIWICK" in white instead of grey.

872 "Tree of Joy", St. Peter Port

2001. Christmas. Festive Lights. Multicoloured.

928	19p. Type **872**	40	45
929	27p. Cross, Les Cotils Christian Centre	55	60
930	36p. Les Ruettes Cottage, St. Saviour's	75	80
931	40p. Farmhouse, Le Preel, Castel	1·00	1·10
932	45p. Sark Post Office	1·10	1·20
933	65p. High Street, St. Peter Port	1·50	1·60
MS934	150×100 mm. Nos. 928/33	6·00	6·50

878 Victor Hugo and St. Peter Port

2002. Birth Bicentenary of Victor Hugo (French author). Les Miserables (novel). Multicoloured.

935	22p. Type **878**	45	50
936	27p. Cosette	55	60
937	36p. Valjean	75	80
938	40p. Inspector Javert	90	95
939	45p. Cosette and Marius	1·10	1·10
940	65p. Novel and score for *Les Miserables* (musical by Alain Boublil and Claude-Michel Schonberg)	1·50	1·60
MS941	150×100 mm. Nos. 935/40	5·50	6·00

The 27p. value reproduces the main image from promotional material for Cameron Mackintosh's musical production.

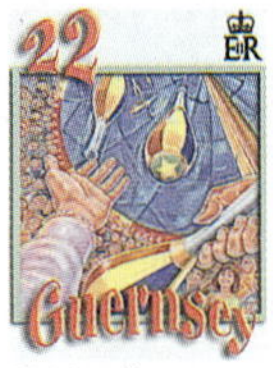

884 Juggling

2002. Europa. The Circus. Multicoloured.

942	22p. Type **884**	45	50
943	27p. Clowns	55	60
944	36p. Trapeze artists	70	75
945	40p. Knife thrower	80	90
946	45p. Acrobat	90	95
947	65p. High-wire cyclist	1·20	1·40

890 Queen Elizabeth and Crowd

2002. Golden Jubilee. Multicoloured.

948	22p. Type **890**	45	50
949	27p. Queen Elizabeth at St. Peter Port	55	60
950	36p. Queen Elizabeth and Prince Philip at St. Anne's School, Alderney	70	75
951	40p. Queen Elizabeth and La Seigneurie, Sark	80	85
952	45p. At Millennium Stone, L'Ancresse	90	95
953	65p. In evening dress and floodlit Castle Cornet	1·20	1·40

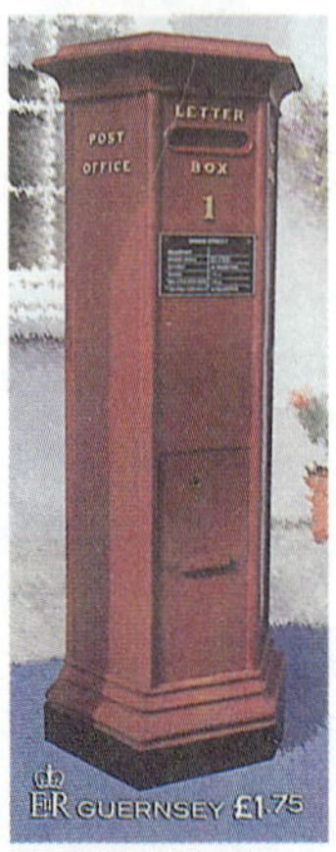

896 Original Pillar Box, Union Street

2002. 150th Anniv of First Pillar Box. Sheet, 55×90 mm.

MS954	**896** £1.75 multicoloured	4·00	4·50

897 Family and Ferry, La Maseline

2002. Holidays on Sark. Multicoloured.

955	27p. Type **897**	45	30
956	27p. Passenger tractors	45	30
957	27p. Campsite	45	30
958	27p. Cyclists at La Coupee	45	30
959	27p. Swimming in Venus Pool	45	30
960	27p. La Seigneurie gardens	45	30
961	27p. Posting cards	45	30
962	27p. Carriage ride	45	30
963	27p. Tea at a café	45	30
964	27p. On the beach at Creux Harbour	45	30

907 Elizabeth College and Cadet Corps Parade, 1934

2002. 60th Anniv of Herbert Le Patourel's Victoria Cross. Multicoloured.

965	22p. Type **907**	45	50
966	27p. Captain Le Patourel in action, Tunisia 1942, and V.C	55	60
967	36p. Captain Le Patourel and nurse, 1943	70	75
968	40p. Award ceremony, Cairo, 1943	80	85
969	45p. Major Le Patourel welcomed home to Guernsey, 1948	90	95
970	65p. Hebert Le Patourel carrying the King's Colour, 1968	1·20	1·40

913 Queen Elizabeth the Queen Mother and Bouquet (1/2-size illustration)

2002. Queen Elizabeth the Queen Mother Commemoration. Sheet 140×98 mm.

MS971	**913** £2 multicoloured	4·50	4·25

914 Mary and Jesus

2002. Christmas. Multicoloured.

972	22p. Type **914**	45	50
973	27p. Mary, Joseph and Jesus in the stable	55	60
974	36p. Angel appearing to shepherds	70	75
975	40p. Shepherds with Mary and Jesus	80	85
976	45p. Three Wise Men	1·00	95
977	65p. Stable with star overhead	1·50	1·40
MS978	131×101 mm. Nos. 972/7	5·00	5·00

920 Avro Type 683 Lancaster Bomber and Crew

2003. Memories of the Second World War. 60th Anniv of Operation Tunnel (£1.50) and Dambusters Raid (others) (1st issue). Multicoloured.

979	22p. Type **920**	45	50
980	27p. Flight of Lancaster bombers crossing English coast	55	60
981	36p. Lancaster bombers in enemy searchlights	70	75
982	40p. Dropping bouncing bombs	80	85
983	£1.50 H.M.S. *Charybdis* (cruiser) and H.M.S. *Limbourne* (destroyer) (40×30 mm)	3·00	3·25

See also Nos. 1027/31 and 1060/4.

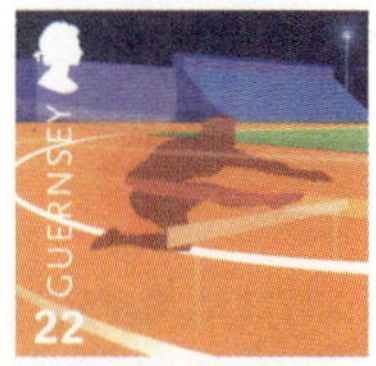

925 Hurdling

2003. Island Games, Guernsey. Multicoloured.

984	22p. Type **925**	45	50
985	27p. Cycling	55	60
986	36p. Gymnastics	75	80
987	40p. Sailing	80	85
988	45p. Golf	90	95
989	65p. Running	1·20	1·40
MS990	140×75 mm. Nos. 984/9	5·00	5·00

931 St. Peter Port Harbour ("Naturally Guernsey", 2003)

2003. Europa. Poster Art. Multicoloured.

991	22p. Type **931**	45	50
992	27p. Motor-cruiser off Guernsey ("The islands of Guernsey", 1995)	55	60
993	36p. "Children on the Seashore" (Renoir) ("Holiday Guernsey", 1988)	75	80
994	40p. St. Peter Port Harbour ("Bailiwick of Guernsey", 1978)	80	85
995	45p. St. Peter Port and cliffs ("Guernsey - The Charming Channel Island", 1968)	90	95
996	65p. Secluded bay ("Guernsey", 1956)	1·20	1·40

937 H.M.S. *Guernsey*

2003. Decommissioning of H.M.S. Guernsey (fishery protection patrol vessel). Sheet 117×84 mm.

MS997	**206** £1.50 multicoloured	4·50	4·00

938 Princess Diana and Baby Prince William

2003. 21st Birthday of Prince William of Wales. Multicoloured.

998	27p. Type **938**	55	30
999	27p. Prince William, aged 3, with Prince Charles and Prince Harry at Kensington Palace	55	30

1000	27p. Aged 4, in Parachute Regiment uniform	55	30
1001	27p. Aged 7, with Prince Harry on his first day at Wetherby School	55	30
1002	27p. Aged 8, with Prince Charles at Guards Polo	55	30
1003	27p. Aged 9, on ski slopes with Princess Diana	55	30
1004	27p. On first day at Eton, 1995	55	30
1005	27p. With Prince Charles and Prince Harry at Balmoral, 1997	55	30
1006	27p. Wearing hard hat during Community project in Chile, 2000	55	30
1007	27p. Playing polo, 2002	55	30

948 Letters of Alphabet

2003

1008	**948**	£5 orange, blue and silver	10·00	10·50

The alphabet letters are printed in thermochromic ink which fades from pale orange to white when exposed to heat.

949 Sleeping Boy and Christmas Tree

2003. Christmas. Scenes from Poem "Twas the Night before Christmas" by Clement Clarke Moore. Multicoloured.

1009	10p. Type **949**	20	25
1010	27p. Boy opening shutter to see Santa's sleigh	55	60
1011	36p. Santa on roof with reindeer	70	75
1012	40p. Santa with presents	80	85
1013	45p. Santa leaving presents under Christmas tree	1·20	1·30
1014	65p. Santa in sleigh	1·50	1·70
MS1015	130×104 mm. Nos. 1009/14	4·75	4·75

955 Golden Snub-nosed Monkey

2004. Endangered Species (1st series). Golden Snub-nosed Monkey. Sheet 120×85 mm.

MS1016	£2 multicoloured	6·50	6·50

See also Nos. **MS**1085, **MS**1096, **MS**1173 and **MS**1266.

956 Clematis "Rosemoor"

2004. Raymond Evison's Guernsey Clematis. Multicoloured. Self-adhesive.

1017	(22p.) Type **956**	75	75
1018	(22p.) "Arctic Queen"	75	75
1019	(22p.) "Harlow Carr"	75	75
1020	(22p.) "Guernsey Cream"	75	75
1021	(22p.) "Josephine"	75	75
1022	(27p.) "Blue Moon"	85	85
1023	(27p.) "Wisley"	85	85
1024	(27p.) "Liberation"	85	85
1025	(27p.) "Royal Velvet"	85	85
1026	(27p.) "Hyde Hall"	85	85

Nos. 1017/21 were intended for postage within the Bailiwick and are inscribed "GY". They were each initially sold at 22p. Nos. 1022/6 were intended for postage to Great Britain and are inscribed "UK". They were each initially sold at 27p.

2004. Memories of the Second World War (2nd issue). 60th Anniv of D-Day Landings. As T 920. Multicoloured.

1027	26p. Supermarine Spitfire	85	85
1028	32p. Landing craft and ship	1·00	1·00
1029	36p. Troops going ashore at Gold Beach	1·20	1·20
1030	40p. Troops in water	1·30	1·30
1031	£1.50 *Vega* (Red Cross supply ship) (40×29 mm)	5·00	5·00

971 Sandcastle, Rider, Bucket and Spade, Deckchair and Canoeist

2004. Europa. Holidays. Multicoloured.

1032	26p. Type **971**	85	85
1033	32p. Pathway sign, walking trails, bench and Guernsey landscapes	1·10	1·10
1034	36p. Lighthouse and yachts in marina, St. Peter Port	1·20	1·20
1035	40p. Glasses of red wine and meals on table	1·30	1·30
1036	45p. Statue-menhir at Castel and Loop Holed Tower, Le Gran'mere statue-menhir, Little Chapel and Victor Hugo statue	1·50	1·50
1037	65p. Guernsey Lily, wildflowers and robin	2·10	2·10

977 Three Crowns (Loyalty)

2004. 800th Anniv of Allegiance to England. Multicoloured.

1038	26p. Type **977**	85	85
1039	32p. Three ships (Trade)	1·10	1·10
1040	36p. Knotted rope (Unity)	1·20	1·20
1041	40p. Three castle turrets (Protection)	1·30	1·30
1042	45p. Three scrolls (Justice)	1·50	1·50
1043	65p. Three leaping fish (Industry)	2·10	2·10
MS1044	140×80 mm. Nos. 1038/43	8·00	8·00

983 Discus Thrower

2004. Olympic Games, Athens, Greece. Multicoloured.

1045	32p. Type **983**	1·00	1·00
1046	36p. Javelin thrower	1·20	1·20
1047	45p. Runners	1·50	1·50
1048	65p. Wrestlers	2·10	2·10
MS1049	152×98 mm. £1 Olympic sports (40×29 mm)	3·50	3·50

988 "Little Donkey"

2004. Christmas. Multicoloured.

1050	20p. Type **988**	65	25
1051	20p. "While Shepherds Watched"	65	25
1052	20p. "Away in a Manger"	65	25
1053	20p. "Unto Us a Child is Born"	65	25
1054	20p. "We Three Kings"	65	25
1055	32p. Angels wings (33×26 mm)	1·10	1·10
1056	36p. Bauble (33×26 mm)	1·20	1·20
1057	40p. Holly (33×26 mm)	1·30	1·30
1058	45p. Detail of snowman (33×26 mm)	1·50	1·50
1059	65p. Star on top of tree (33×26 mm)	2·20	2·20

Nos. 1050/4 were printed together, se-tenant, with the backgrounds forming a composite design.

2005. Memories of the Second World War (3rd issue). 60th Anniv of Liberation. As T 920. Multicoloured.

1060	26p. British soldiers in Landrover and welcoming crowd	50	55
1061	32p. Guernsey woman waving and Liberty sign and flags on building	65	70
1062	36p. Parents and children reunited	70	75
1063	40p. Return of local men from Hampshire Regiment	80	85
1064	£1.50 Winston Churchill (40×29 mm)	3·00	3·25

1003 Iris "Dorothea" and "Royal"

2005. Birth Centenary of William J. Caparne (artist and iris breeder). Watercolour paintings of flowers. Multicoloured.

1065	26p. Type **1003**	50	55
1066	32p. Nerine Fothergilli "Major"	65	70
1067	36p. Iris "Garnet"	70	95
1068	40p. Narcissus "Sir Watkin"	85	1·00
1069	45p. Narcissus "Rip van Winkle"	1·00	1·10
1070	65p. Narcissus "Sulphur Phoenix"	1·50	1·50
MS1071	140×85 mm. Nos. 1065/70	5·00	5·50

1009 Spider Crab

2005. Europa. Gastronomy. Seafood and coastal scenes. Multicoloured.

1072	26p. Type **1007**	50	55
1073	32p. Seared red mullet and crab cake	65	70
1074	36p. Lobster salad	70	75
1075	40p. Brill on spinach with local moules	80	85
1076	45p. Prawn salad	90	95
1077	65p. Salmon wrapped in spinach with local moules	1·30	1·40

1015 King George VI

2005. 60th Anniv of Liberation of Guernsey. Multicoloured.

1078	£1 Type **1015**	1·80	1·30
1079	£1 Queen Elizabeth II	1·80	1·30

1017 Fishing Boat

2005. "Sea Guernsey 2005". Multicoloured.

1080	26p. Type **1017**	50	55
1081	32p. Yacht off Herm Harbour	65	70
1082	36p. Windsurfer	70	75
1083	40p. Sea angler on rocks at Albecq	80	85
1084	65p. Horse and rider on beach, Vazon Bay	1·50	1·40

1022 Basking Shark (image scaled to 40% of original size)

2005. Endangered Species (2nd issue). Basking Shark. Sheet 185×65 mm.

MS1085	**1022**	£2 multicoloured	5·00	5·00

1023 Christ holding Guernsey Flag, St. Pierre du Bois

2005. Christmas. Stained-glass Windows from Guernsey and Alderney Parish Churches. Multicoloured.

1086	20p. Type **1023**	40	45
1087	20p. Madonna and Child, St. Saviour	40	45
1088	20p. John baptising Christ, St. Martin	40	45
1089	20p. Christ, the Light of the World, Torteval	40	45
1090	20p. Madonna and Child, St. Sampson	40	45
1091	32p. Madonna and Child, Vale	65	70
1092	36p. Three Kings, Castel	70	75
1093	40p. St. Nicholas, Alderney	80	85
1094	45p. Madonna and Child, St. Andrew	90	95
1095	65p. St. Marguerite, Forest	1·30	1·40

1033 Atlantic Leatherback Turtle

2006. Endangered Species of the Florida Everglades. Sheet 110×90 mm containing T 1033 and similar horiz design. Multicoloured.

MS1096	£1 Type **1033**; £1.50 American wood ibis	6·00	6·00

1034 Iraq Conflict, 2004

2006. 150th Anniv of the Victoria Cross. Multicoloured.

1097	29p. Type **1034**	60	65
1098	34p. Falklands war, 1982	70	75
1099	38p. Battle of El Alamein, 1942	75	80
1100	42p. Gallipoli campaign, 1915	85	90
1101	47p. Battle of Rorke's Drift, 1879	95	1·00
1102	68p. Charge of the Light Brigade, 1854	1·40	1·50

1040 Pilbeam MP58, British Speed Hill Climb Championship, 1995

2006. Andy Priaulx's Motor Racing Victories. Multicoloured.

1103	29p. Type **1040**	60	65
1104	34p. Renault Spider Cup, 1999	70	75
1105	42p. British Formula 3, 2001	85	90
1106	45p. FIA European Touring Car Championship, 2004	90	95
1107	47p. Nurburgring, Germany, 2005	1·20	1·20
1108	68p. FIA World Touring Car Championship, 2005	1·70	1·70
MS1109	160×100 mm. Nos. 1103/8	6·00	6·00

1046 Brunel and Mailbags at Paddington Station

2006. Birth Bicentenary of Isambard Kingdom Brunel (engineer). Multicoloured.

1110	29p. Type **1046**	60	65
1111	34p. Duke class locomotive No. 3258 *King Arthur* at Paddington Station	70	75
1112	42p. *King Arthur* on Wharncliffe Viaduct	85	90
1113	45p. Loading mail from train onto *Ibex* at Weymouth harbour	90	95
1114	47p. Weymouth & Channel Island steam packet *Ibex*	1·20	1·20
1115	68p. Unloading mail from *Ibex* at St. Peter Port harbour	1·70	1·70

1052 Student working as Waiter in Paris

2006. Europa. Integration. Showing student's gap year travels. Multicoloured.

1116	29p. Type **1052**	60	65
1117	34p. Sphinx, Egypt	70	75
1118	42p. Great Wall of China	85	90
1119	45p. Student and aborigines at Ayers Rock, Australia	1·00	95
1120	47p. Head of Statue of Liberty, New York	1·20	1·00
1121	68p. Students at Taj Mahal, India	1·50	1·50

1058 Queen Elizabeth II

2006. 80th Birthday of Queen Elizabeth II.

1122	**1058**	£10 multicoloured	22·00	22·00

1059 Grey Seal

2006. Designation of L'Eree Wetland as Ramsar Site. Multicoloured.

1123	29p. Type **1059**	60	65
1124	34p. Ormer	70	75
1125	42p. Common blenny	85	90
1126	45p. Le Creux es Faies (Neolithic grave)	1·00	95
1127	47p. Yellow horned poppy	1·20	1·00
1128	68p. Oystercatcher	1·50	1·50
MS1129	140×95 mm. Nos. 1123/8	6·50	5·75

1065 A Partridge in a Pear Tree

2006. Christmas. "The Twelve Days of Christmas" (carol). Multicoloured.

1130	22p. Type **1065**	45	50
1131	22p. Two turtle doves	45	50
1132	22p. Three French hens	45	50
1133	22p. Four calling birds	45	50
1134	22p. Five gold rings	45	50
1135	22p. Six geese a-laying	45	50
1136	29p. Seven swans a-swimming	60	65
1137	34p. Eight maids a-milking	70	75
1138	42p. Nine ladies dancing	85	90
1139	45p. Ten lords a-leaping	90	95
1140	47p. Eleven pipers piping	95	1·00
1141	68p. Twelve drummers drumming	1·40	1·50

1077 Departure of Troops on *Queen Elizabeth 2*, Southampton

2007. 25th Anniv of the Battle for the Falklands. Multicoloured.

1142	32p. Type **1077**	75	75
1143	37p. Troops landing at San Carlos Bay	90	90
1144	45p. BAe Sea Harriers flying over SS *Canberra*	1·10	1·10
1145	48p. Lt. Col. H. Jones firing machine gun	1·10	1·10
1146	50p. Westland Sea King helicopter and *Invincible*	1·20	1·50
1147	71p. Troops marching with Union Jack towards Port Stanley	1·70	2·00
MS1148	150×100 mm. Nos. 1142/7	6·75	7·00

1083 Rocks at Albecq

2007. 125th Anniv of La Societe Guernesiaise. Multicoloured. Self-adhesive.

1149	(32p.) Type **1083**	80	80
1150	(32p.) Ivy bee	80	80
1151	(32p.) Vale Church	80	80
1152	(32p.) Common frog	80	80
1153	(32p.) Parasol mushroom	80	80
1154	(37p.) Southern marsh orchid	80	80
1155	(37p.) Shore crab	80	80
1156	(37p.) Alderney blonde hedgehog	80	80
1157	(37p.) Barn owl	80	80
1158	(37p.) Le Trepied dolmen	80	80

Nos. 1149/53 were intended for postage within the Bailiwick, are inscribed "GY" and sold for 32p. each.

Nos. 1154/8 were intended for postage to Great Britain, are inscribed "UK" and sold for 37p. each.

1093 Scouts Camping, 1907

2007. Europa. Centenary of Scouting. Multicoloured.

1159	32p. Type **1093**	75	75
1160	37p. Scout sailing, 1924	90	90
1161	45p. Two scouts fishing from rocks, 1947	1·10	1·10
1162	48p. Scouts making and flying model aircraft, 1968	1·10	1·10
1163	50p. Scouts on caving expedition, 1990	1·50	1·20
1164	71p. Scouts rollerblading, Cambridge Park, St. Peter Port, 2007	2·00	1·70

1099 Mike Hawthorn, 1958

2007. British Formula One World Champions. Multicoloured.

1165	32p. Type **1099**	75	75
1166	32p. Jackie Stewart, 1971	75	75
1167	37p. Graham Hill, 1962	85	85
1168	37p. James Hunt, 1976	85	85
1169	45p. Jim Clark, 1963	1·20	1·10
1170	48p. Nigel Mansell, 1992	1·50	1·10
1171	50p. John Surtees, 1964	1·70	1·20
1172	71p. Damon Hill, 1996	2·50	1·70

1107 Mountain Gorilla (image scaled to 53% of original size)

2007. Endangered Species (4th series). Mountain Gorilla (Gorilla beringeiberingei). Sheet 118×84 mm.

MS1173	£2.50 multicoloured	7·00	7·00

1108 Engagement, c. 1947

2007. Diamond Wedding of Queen Elizabeth II and Duke of Edinburgh. Multicoloured.

1174	32p. Type **1108**	75	75
1175	37p. With baby Princess Anne	90	90
1176	45p. Off-duty, wearing casual clothes	1·10	1·10
1177	48p. On tour	1·10	1·10
1178	50p. With Princes William and Harry	1·20	1·50
1179	71p. In recent years	1·70	1·90

1114 St. Peter Port Harbour

2007. Sea Guernsey. Multicoloured.

1180	32p. Type **1114**	75	75
1181	37p. Fort Grey, Rocquaine Bay	90	90
1182	45p. Point Robert Lighthouse, Sark	1·10	1·10
1183	48p. Islands at dusk (Brecqhou seen from Sark)	1·10	1·10
1184	50p. Vazon Bay	1·50	1·50
1185	71p. Fontenelle Bay	2·00	1·90

The 45p. value includes the 'sepac' emblem.

1120 Crystal Angel

2007. Christmas. 'Deck the Halls'. Showing decorations. Multicoloured.

1186	27p. Type **1120**	60	60
1187	27p. Crystal decoration	60	60
1188	27p. Pine cone	60	60
1189	27p. White bauble with leaf design	60	60
1190	27p. Snowflake	60	60
1191	27p. Decoration with star	60	60
1192	32p. Gold bauble	75	75
1193	37p. Candles	90	90
1194	45p. Gold bell	1·10	1·10
1195	48p. Wrapped present with ribbons	1·10	1·10
1196	50p. Spiky star	1·20	1·20
1197	71p. Tree fairy	1·70	1·70

1132 World Touring Car Championship, 2005

2008. Andy Priaulx Triple World Touring Car Champion 2005–2007. Sheet 140×95 mm containing T 1132 and similar horiz designs. Multicoloured.

MS1198	£1 Type **1132**; £1 World Touring Car Championship, 2006; World Touring Car Championship, 2007 (60×48 mm)	7·00	7·50

1133 Beadlet Anemones

2008. Designation of Gouliot Headland and Caves, Sark as RAMSAR Site. Multicoloured.

1199	34p. Type **1133**	80	80
1200	40p. Sand crocus	95	95
1201	48p. Fulmar	1·10	1·10
1202	51p. Sheep's-bit (flower)	1·20	1·20
1203	53p. Thick-lipped grey mullet	1·30	1·30
1204	74p. Light bulb sea-squirt	1·70	1·70
MS1205	140×95 mm. Nos. 1199/204	7·00	7·00

1139 Red Campion

2008. Wild Flowers (1st series). Multicoloured.

1211	10p. Type **1139**	25	25
1212	20p. Great bindweed	45	45
1213	30p. Spear thistle	70	70
1214	40p. Greater bird's-foot trefoil	95	95
1215	50p. Sheep's-bit	1·20	1·20
1216	£1 Marguerite (vert)	2·30	2·30
1217	£2 Sea campion (vert)	4·75	4·75

See also Nos. 1273/83.

1153 'A la perchoine' ('Till the next time')

2008. Europa. The Letter. Designs showing quotations in Guernsiais (Guernsey French) and their English translations. Multicoloured.

1220	34p. Type **1153**	80	80
1221	40p. Banjour	95	95
1222	48p. Oh! Te v	1·10	1·10
1223	51p. Mais oy-ous!	1·20	1·20
1224	53p. Cor chapin!	1·30	1·30
1225	74p. L	1·70	1·70

1159 *Mr. Happy*

2008. Mr. Men and Little Miss Series of Children's Books by Roger Hargreaves. Multicoloured.

1226	34p. Type **1159**	80	80
1227	40p. *Mr. Bump*	95	95
1228	48p. *Little Miss Naughty*	1·10	1·10
1229	51p. *Mr. Greedy*	1·20	1·20
1230	53p. *Mr. Strong*	1·30	1·30
1231	74p. *Mr. Tickle*	1·70	1·70

1165 Pleimont Point

2008. Abstract Guernsey

1232	(34p.) Type **1165**	80	80

1233	(34p.) Saint's Harbour	80	80
1234	(34p.) Rocks at Albecq	80	80
1235	(34p.) Groynes at Vazon Bay	80	80
1236	(34p.) La Bette Bay	80	80
1237	(40p.) Bordeaux Harbour	95	95
1238	(40p.) St. Saviour's Reservoir	95	95
1239	(40p.) Vazon Bay	95	95
1240	(40p.) St. Peter Port Lighthouse	95	95
1241	(40p.) Petit Port	95	95

Nos. 1232/6 were intended for postage within the Bailiwick and are inscribed 'GY'. They were each initially sold at 34p. Nos. 1237/41 were intended for postage to Great Britain and are inscribed 'UK'. They were each initially sold at 40p.

1175 Ford Model T Touring Car, 1913

2008. Centenary of the Ford Model T. Multicoloured.

1242	34p. Type **1175**	80	80
1243	40p. Delivery van, 1912	95	95
1244	48p. Pick-up, 1925	1·10	1·10
1245	51p. Couplet, 1917	1·20	1·20
1246	53p. First World War army ambulance	1·30	1·30
1247	74p. Roadster, 1912	1·70	1·70

1181 Early Drawing of St. Paul's Cathedral

2008. Guernsey Granite at St. Paul's Cathedral, London. Multicoloured.

1248	34p. Type **1181**	80	80
1249	40p. Cathedral and River Thames, 1860s	95	95
1250	48p. Cathedral during World War II Blitz	1·10	1·10
1251	51p. Cathedral illuminated at night	1·20	1·20
1252	53p. Close-up of St. Paul's Cathedral	1·30	1·30
1253	74p. Cathedral seen from Millennium Bridge	1·70	1·70

Nos. 1248/53 have powdered Guernsey granite applied to the value tablets.

1187 Spruce

2008. Christmas. Festive Foliage. Multicoloured.

1254	29p. Type **1187**	70	70
1255	29p. Christmas cactus	70	70
1256	29p. Ivy	70	70
1257	29p. Cyclamen	70	70
1258	29p. Mistletoe	70	70
1259	29p. Butchers Broom	70	70
1260	34p. Holly	80	80
1261	40p. Poinsettia	95	95
1262	48p. Bracken	1·10	1·10
1263	51p. Hawthorn	1·20	1·20
1264	53p. Clematis 'Peppermint'	1·20	1·20
1265	74p. Pyracantha	1·70	1·70

1199 Amur Leopard (image scaled to 41% of original size)

2009. Endangered Species (5th series). Amur Leopard (Panthera pardus orientalis). Sheet 116x84 mm.

MS1266	multicoloured	8·50	8·50

1200 Land Iguana

2009. 'Darwin's Discoveries'. Multicolored.

1267	36p. Type **1200**	85	85
1268	43p. Wallaby	1·00	1·00
1269	51p. Giant tortoise	1·25	1·25
1270	54p. Marine iguana	1·25	1·25
1271	56p. Guanaco	1·25	1·25
1272	77p. Komodo dragon	1·75	1·75
MS1273	144x80 mm. Nos. 1267/72	7·50	7·50

Nos. 1267/72 commemorate the birth bicentenary of Charles Darwin.

1206 Stinking Onion

2009. Wild Flowers (2nd series). Multicoloured.

1274	1p. Type **1206**	10	10
1275	2p. Common mallow	10	10
1276	3p. Primrose	10	10
1277	4p. Loose-flowered prchid	10	10
1278	5p. Common centaury	10	10
1279	6p. Yellow horned poppy	15	15
1280	7p. Sea kale	20	20
1281	8p. Bluebell	25	25
1282	9p. Sea bindweed	25	25
1283	£3 Common poppy	8·50	8·50

1216 Quasar (digital enhancement)

2009. Europa. Astronomy. 400th Anniv of the Telescope. Multicoloured.

1284	36p. Type **1216**	85	85
1285	43p. Asteroid	1·00	1·00
1286	51p. Satellite View of Sunrays falling on the Earth's Surface	1·25	1·25
1287	54p. Jupiter, Sun in Background (digital composite)	1·25	1·25
1288	56p. The Moon touches the Sun before a Total Eclipse	1·40	1·40
1289	77p. Solar Eruption from the Sun (satellite image)	1·75	1·75

1222 Henry VIII as Young Man

2009. 500th Anniv of the Coronation of King Henry VIII. Multicoloured.

1289	36p. Type **1222**	85	85
1290	43p. Coronation of Henry VIII and Katherine of Aragon, 1509	1·00	1·00
1291	51p. Meeting of Henry VIII and Francis I, Field of the Cloth of Gold, 1520	1·25	1·25
1292	54p. Thomas Wolsey presenting Hampton Court Palace to Henry VIII	1·25	1·25
1293	56p. Henry VIII dancing with Anne Boleyn	1·40	1·40
1294	77p. Henry VIII watching his Navy as *Mary Rose* sinks, 1545	1·75	1·75

1228 'The Psychedelic 60's'

2009. 40th Anniv of Postal Independence. Multicoloured.

1295	36p. Type **1228**	85	85
1296	43p. 'God Save the 70s'	1·00	1·00
1297	51p. 'The POPular 80s'	1·25	1·25
1298	54p. 'The Urban 90s'	1·25	1·25
1299	56p. 'The Seductive 00s'	1·40	1·40
1300	77p. 'Looking to the Future'	1·75	1·75

1234 Jerbourg Point

2009. Sea Guernsey (2nd series). Multicoloured.

1302	36p. Type **1234**	85	85
1303	43p. Vazon Bay	1·00	1·00
1304	51p. Saints Bay Moorings	1·25	1·25
1305	54p. Le Jaonnet Bay	1·25	1·25
1306	56p. Rocquaine Bay	1·40	1·40
1307	77p. Bordeaux Harbour	1·75	1·75

The 51p. value includes the 'sepac' emblem.

1240 Castel Church

2009. Christmas. Churches. Multicoloured.

1308	31p. Type **1240**	75	75
1309	31p. Torteval Church	75	75
1310	31p. St. Martin's Church	75	75
1311	31p. St. John's Church	75	75
1312	31p. St. Sampson's Church	75	75
1313	31p. St. Peter Port Church	75	75
1314	36p. St. Mathew's Church	85	85
1315	43p. St. Saviour's Church	1·00	1·00
1316	51p. Forest Church	1·25	1·25
1317	54p. St. Andrew's Church	1·25	1·25
1318	56p. Vale Churchmulticoloured	1·40	1·40
1319	77p. St. Peter's Church	1·75	1·75

1252 Asian Elephant (image scaled to 41% of original size)

2010. Endangered Species (6th series). Asian Elephant (Elephas maximus). Sheet 118x84 mm.

MS1320	multicoloured	7·25	7·25

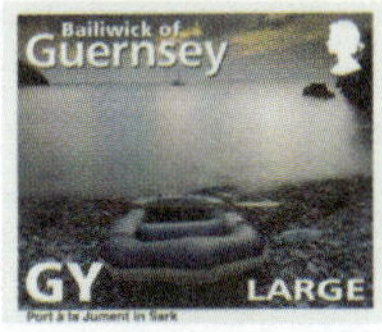

1253 Port a la Jument, Sark

2010. Abstract Guernsey (2nd series). Multicoloured. (a) Ordinary gum.

1321	(48p.) Type **1253**	1·10	1·10
1322	(48p.) The Dog and Lion Rocks-multicoloured	1·10	1·10
1323	(50p.) Fort Grey	1·25	1·25
1324	(58p.) Sunset on West Coast of Guernsey	1·40	
1325	(58p) Slipway at Havelet Bay at Sunrise	1·40	1·40
1326	(80p) Castle Cornet	1·90	1·90

(b) Self-adhesive.

1327	(48p.) As Type No. **1253**	1·10	1·10
1328	(48p.) As No. 1322	1·10	1·25
1329	(50p.) As No. 1323	1·25	1·25
1330	(58p.) As No. 1324	1·40	1·40
1331	(58p.) As No. 1325	1·40	1·40
1332	(80p.) As No. 1326	1·90	1·90

Nos. 1321/2 and 1327/8 were intended for postage within the Bailiwick and are inscribed 'GY LARGE'. They were each initially sold at 48p.

Nos. 1324/5 and 1330/1 were intended for postage to Great Britain and are inscribed 'UK LARGE'. They were each initially sold at 58p.

Nos. 1323 and 1329 for postage to Europe are inscribed 'EUR' and were initially sold at 50p. each.

Nos. 1326 and 1332 for postage to rest of world are inscribed 'ROW' and were initially sold at 80p. each.

1259 Penny the Postie and Pirate Captain Titch in Boat made from Wooden Chest

2010. Europa. Children's Books. The Adventures of Penny the Postie by Keith Robinson. Multicoloured.

1333	45p. Type **1259**	1·00	1·00
1334	50p. Captain Titch spies enemy Captain Bullybones	1·25	1·25
1335	£2 Captain Titch reclaiming his Stolen Ship	4·50	4·50
MS1336	149x96 mm. Nos. 1333/5	6·75	6·75

1262 Guide kayaking ('Outdoor Activities')

2010. Centenary of Girl Guiding. Embroidered Badges. Multicoloured.

1337	36p. Type **1262**	80	80
1338	45p. Spitfire crossing Searchlights ('Help during WW1&2')	1·00	1·00
1339	48p. Crystal Palace Maze (renovated to celebrate Centenary)	1·10	1·10
1340	50p. Agnes Baden-Powell (founder) wearing First Guide Uniform	1·25	1·25
1341	58p. Mount Everest (Guide trek to base camp, 2009)	1·40	1·40
1342	80p. Queen's Guide Award	1·75	1·75

POSTAGE DUE STAMPS

D1 Castle Cornet

1969. Face values in black.

D1	**D1**	1d. plum	2·00	1·20
D2	**D1**	2d. green	2·00	1·20
D3	**D1**	3d. red	3·00	4·00
D4	**D1**	4d. blue	4·00	5·00
D5	**D1**	5d. ochre	6·00	4·00
D6	**D1**	6d. turquoise	6·00	4·50
D7	**D1**	1s. brown	10·00	8·00

1971. Decimal Currency. Face values in black.

D8	½p. plum	10	10
D9	1p. green	10	10
D10	2p. red	10	10
D11	3p. blue	10	10
D12	4p. ochre	10	10
D13	5p. blue	10	10
D14	6p. violet	10	10
D15	8p. orange	20	40
D16	10p. brown	20	20
D17	15p. grey	30	50

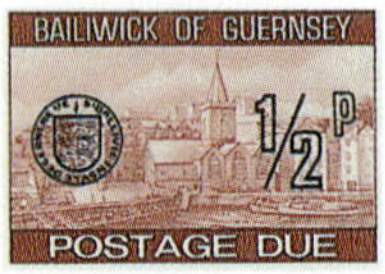

D3 St. Peter Pan

1977. Face values in black.

D18	**D3**	½p. brown	10	10
D19	**D2**	1p. purple	10	10
D20	**D2**	2p. orange	10	10
D21	**D2**	3p. red	10	10
D22	**D2**	4p. blue	10	10
D23	**D2**	5p. green	10	10
D24	**D2**	6p. green	10	10
D25	**D2**	8p. brown	10	10
D26	**D2**	10p. blue	10	10
D27	**D2**	14p. green	20	20
D28	**D2**	15p. violet	20	20
D29	**D2**	16p. red	30	30

D4 Milking Cow

1982. Guernsey Scenes, c. 1990.

D30	**D4**	1p. blue and green	10	10
D31	-	2p. brown, lt brown & blue	10	10
D32	-	3p. green and lilac	10	10
D33	-	4p. green and orange	10	10
D34	-	5p. blue and green	10	10
D35	-	16p. blue and light blue	30	35
D36	-	18p. blue and green	35	40
D37	-	20p. green and blue	40	45
D38	-	25p. blue and pink	50	55
D39	-	30p. green and yellow	60	65
D40	-	50p. brown and blue	1·00	1·10
D41	-	£1 lt brown and brown	2·00	2·10

DESIGNS: 2p. Vale Mill; 3p. Sark cottage; 4p. Quay-side, St. Peter Port; 5p. Well, Water Lane, Moulin Huet; 16p. Seaweed gathering; 18p. Upper Walk, White Rock; 20p. Cobo Bay; 25p. Saint's Bay; 30p. La Coupee, Sark; 50p. Old Harbour, St. Peter Port; £1 Greenhouses, Doyle Road, St. Peter Port.

ALDERNEY

The following issues are provided by the Guernsey Post Office for use on Alderney. They are also valid for postal purposes throughout the rest of the Bailiwick of Guernsey.

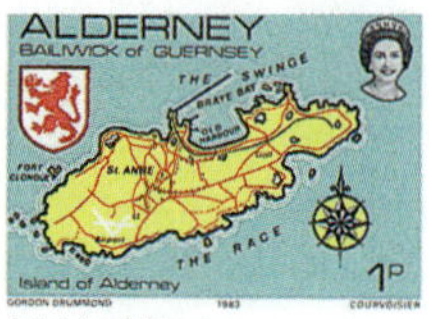

A 1 Island Map

1983. Island Scenes. Multicoloured.

A1	1p. Type A **1**	10	10
A2	4p. Hanging Rock	10	10
A3	9p. States' Building, St. Anne	15	15
A4	10p. St. Anne's Church	20	15
A5	11p. Yachts in Braye Bay	20	20
A6	12p. Victoria St., St. Anne	25	20
A7	13p. Map of Channel	25	20
A8	14p. Fort Clonque	30	20
A9	15p. Corblets Bay and Fort	35	20
A10	16p. Old Tower, St. Anne	35	25
A11	17p. Golf course and Essex Castle	40	30
A12	18p. Old Harbour	40	30
A12a	20p. Quesnard Lighthouse	1·00	90
A12b	21p. Braye Harbour	1·00	90
A12c	23p. The Island Hall	95	85
A12d	24p. "J.T. Daly" (steam locomotive)	1·70	1·70
A12e	28p. "Louis Marchesi of the Round Table" (lifeboat)	2·20	2·20

Nos. A12a/e are larger, 38×27 mm.

A 13 Oystercatcher

1984. Birds. Multicoloured.

A13	9p. Type A **13**	1·10	60
A14	13p. Ruddy turnstone ("Turnstone")	1·10	75
A15	26p. Ringed plover	2·50	2·75
A16	28p. Dunlin	2·50	2·75
A17	31p. Curlew	2·50	1·70

A 18 Westland Wessex HU.4 Mk5 Helicopter XV732 of The Queen's Flight

1985. 50th Anniv of Alderney Airport. Mult.

A18	9p. Type A **18**	1·40	70
A19	13p. Britten Norman BN-2AMkIII "long nose" Trislander	1·70	1·00
A20	29p. de Havilland Heron 1B G-AOXL	3·00	2·75
A21	31p. de Havilland Dragon Rapide DH.89A "Sir Henry Lawrence"	3·50	3·50
A22	34p. Saro A21 G-AHLL Wind-hover amphibian flying boat G-ABJP "City of Portsmouth"	3·50	3·50

A 23 Royal Engineers, 1890

1985. Regiments of the Alderney Garrison. Multicoloured.

A23	9p. Type A **23**	25	20
A24	14p. Duke of Albany's Own Highlanders, 1856	80	40
A25	29p. Royal Artillery, 1855	80	70
A26	31p. South Hampshire Regiment, 1810	1·10	1·10
A27	34p. Royal Irish Regiment, 1782	1·40	1·50

A 28 Fort Grosnez

1986. Alderney Forts. Multicoloured.

A28	10p. Type A **28**	80	20
A29	14p. Fort Tourgis	90	80
A30	31p. Fort Clonque	2·50	3·00
A31	34p. Fort Albert	2·50	3·00

A 32 "Liverpool" (full-rigged ship), 1902

1987. Alderney Shipwrecks. Multicoloured.

A32	11p. Type A **32**	1·60	50
A33	15p. "Petit Raymond" (schooner), 1906	1·70	60
A34	29p. "Maina" (yacht), 1910	3·00	3·50
A35	31p. "Burton" (steamer), 1911	3·75	3·50
A36	34p. "Point Law" (oil tanker), 1975	4·00	4·25

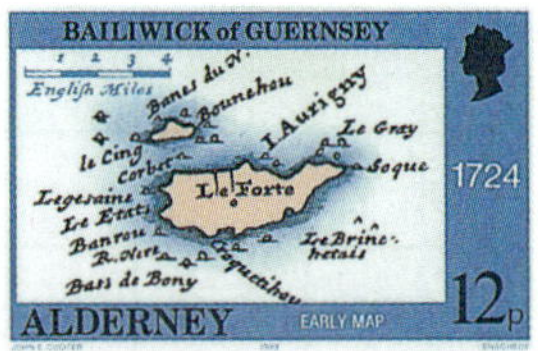

A 37 Moll's Map of 1724

1989. 250th Anniv of Bastide's Survey of Alderney.

A37	**A37**	12p. multicoloured	25	25
A38	-	18p. black, blue & brown	45	30
A39	-	27p. black, blue and green	95	1·10
A40	-	32p. black, blue and red	1·10	1·10
A41	-	35p. multicoloured	1·50	1·40

DESIGNS: 18p. Bastide's survey of 1739; 27p. Goodwin's map of 1831; 32p. General Staff map of 1943; 35p. Ordnance Survey map, 1988.

A 42 H.M.S. "Alderney" (bomb ketch), 1738

1990. Royal Navy Ships named after Alderney.

A42	**A42**	14p. black and bistre	25	20
A43	-	20p. black and brown	45	35
A44	-	29p. black and brown	1·00	1·00
A45	-	34p. black and blue	1·10	1·50
A46	-	37p. black and blue	1·40	1·50

DESIGNS: 20p. H.M.S. "Alderney" (sixth-rate), 1742; 29p. H.M.S. "Alderney" (sloop), 1755; 34p. H.M.S. "Alderney" (submarine), 1945; 37p. H.M.S. "Alderney" (patrol vessel), 1979.

A 47 Wreck of H.M.S. "Victory", 1744

1991. Automation of The Casquets Lighthouse. Multicoloured.

A47	21p. Type A **47**	80	50
A48	26p. Lighthouse keeper's daughter rowing back to the Casquets	1·90	1·70
A49	31p. MBB-Bolkow Bo105D helicopter G-BATC leaving pad on St. Thomas Tower	2·00	2·20
A50	37p. Northern wheater and yellow wagtail over lighthouse	2·75	3·25
A51	50p. Trinity House vessel "Patricia" and arms	3·75	3·50

A 52 Two French Warships on Fire

1992. 300th Anniv of the Battle of La Hogue. Multicoloured.

A52	23p. Type A **52**	1·10	1·00
A53	28p. Crews leaving burning ships	2·40	2·50
A54	33p. French warship sinking	2·75	3·00
A55	50p. "The Battle of La Hogue" (47×32 mm)	3·00	3·50

Nos. A52/4 show details of the painting on the 50p. value.

A 56 Spiny Lobster

1993. Endangered Species. Marine Life. Mult.

A56	24p. Type A **56**	60	30
A57	28p. Plumose anemone	60	35
A58	33p. Starfish	70	40
A59	39p. Sea urchin	90	60

Nos. A56/9 were printed together, se-tenant, the backgrounds forming a composite design.

A 60 Blue-tailed Damselfly, Dark Hair Water Crowfoot and Branched Bur-reed

1994. Flora and Fauna. Multicoloured.

A60	1p. Type A **60**	10	10
A61	2p. White-toothed shrew and flax-leaved St. John's wort	10	10
A62	3p. Fulmar and kaffir fig	10	10
A63	4p. Clouded yellow (butterfly) and red clover	10	10
A64	5p. Bumble bee, prostrate broom and giant broom-rape	10	10
A65	6p. Dartford warbler and lesser dodder	15	20
A66	7p. Peacock (butterfly) and stemless thistle	15	20
A67	8p. Mole and bluebell	15	20
A68	9p. Great green grasshopper and common gorse	20	25
A69	10p. Six-spot burnet (moth) and viper's bugloss	20	25
A70	16p. Common blue (butterfly) and pyramidal orchid	55	40
A70b	18p. Small tortoiseshell (butterfly) and buddleia	35	40
A71	20p. Common rabbit and creeping buttercup	40	45
A72	24p. Greater black-backed gull and sand crocus	50	55
A72b	25p. Rock pipit and sea stock	50	55
A72c	26p. Sand digger wasp and sea bindweed (horiz)	50	55
A73	30p. Atlantic puffin and English stonecrop	60	65
A74	40p. Emperor (moth) and bramble	80	85
A75	50p. Pale-spined hedgehog and pink oxalis	1·50	1·20
A76	£1 Common tern and Bermuda grass (horiz)	2·50	2·20
A77	£2 Northern gannet and "Fucus vesiculosus" (seaweed) (horiz)	5·00	4·50

A 78 Royal Aircraft Factory SE5A

1995. Birth Cent of Tommy Rose (aviator). Mult.

A78	35p. Type A **78**	95	95
A79	35p. Miles M.19 Master II and other Miles aircraft	95	95
A80	35p. Miles M.57 Aerovan and Miles Monitor M.33	95	95
A81	41p. Miles M.38 Falcon Six winning King's Cup air race, 1935	1·10	1·10
A82	41p. Miles M.2 Hawk Speed Six winning Manx Air Derby, 1947	1·10	1·10
A83	41p. Miles M.3B Falcon Six breaking U.K.–Cape record, 1936	1·10	1·10

A 84 Returning Islanders

1995. 50th Anniv of Return of Islanders to Alderney. Sheet 93×70 mm.

MSA84	A **84** £1.65, multicoloured	5·00	5·00

A 85 Signallers training on Alderney

1996. 25th Anniv of Adoption of 30th Signal Regiment by Alderney. Multicoloured.

A85	24p. Type A **85**	45	35
A86	41p. Communications station, Falkland Islands	75	55
A87	60p. Dish aerial and Land Rover, Gulf War	1·10	80
A88	75p. Service with United Nations	1·10	1·10

Nos. A85/8 were printed together, se-tenant, forming a composite design.

A 89 Cat with Butterfly

1996. Cats. Multicoloured.

A89	16p. Type A **89**	45	35
A90	24p. Blue and white on table	65	40
A91	25p. Tabby kitten grooming blue and white persian kitten	65	65
A92	35p. Red persian under table	1·20	1·20
A93	41p. White cat with tortoise-shell and white in toy cart	1·50	1·70
A94	60p. Siamese playing with wool	2·00	2·00
MSA95	144×97 mm. Nos. A89/94	6·50	6·50

A 95 Harold Larwood

1997. 150th Anniv of Cricket on Alderney. Multicoloured.

A96	18p. Type A **95**	50	30
A97	25p. John Arlott	65	35
A98	37p. Pelham J. Warner	1·00	1·20
A99	43p. W. G. Grace	1·20	1·50
A100	63p. John Wisden	1·60	1·70
MSA101	190×75 mm. Nos. A96/100 and label	9·00	9·00

A 100 Railway under Construction

1997. Garrison Island (1st series). 150th Anniv of Harbour. Multicoloured.

A102	18p. Type A **100**	45	20
A103	18p. "Ariadne" (paddle steamer) at anchor	45	20
A104	25p. Quarrying stone	65	30
A105	25p. Quarry railway	65	30
A106	26p. Queen Victoria and Prince Albert on Alderney	70	30
A107	26p. Royal Yacht "Victoria and Albert" and guard of honour	70	30
A108	31p. Railway workers greet Queen Victoria	80	35
A109	31p. Royal party in railway wagons	80	35

See also Nos. A116/23, A132/9, A154/61 and A176/83.

A 108 Modern Superlite Helmet and Wreck of "Point Law" (oil tanker)

1998. 21st Anniv of Alderney Diving Club. Multicoloured.

A110	20p. Type A **108**	60	40
A111	30p. Cousteau-Gagnan demand valve and wreck of "Stella" (steamer)	85	85
A112	37p. Heinke closed helmet and "Liverpool" (full-rigged ship)	1·20	1·20
A113	43p. Siebe closed helmet	1·70	1·70
A114	63p. Deane open helmet	2·20	2·30
MSA115	190×75 mm. Nos. A110/14 and label	8·00	8·00

1998. Garrison Island (2nd series). As Type A 100. Multicoloured.

A116	20p. Alderney Post Office	50	25
A117	20p. Traders in Victoria Street	50	25
A118	25p. Court House	60	30
A119	25p. Police Station and fire engine	60	30
A120	30p. St. Anne's Church	70	35
A121	30p. Wedding party at Albert Gate	70	35
A122	37p. "Courier" (ferry) at Braye Bay	85	40
A123	37p. Fishermen at quay	85	40

A 121 Stained Glass Window commemorating Mary Rogers (Chief Stewardess)

1999. Centenary of the Wreck of "Stella" (mail steamer). Sheet 110×90 mm containing Type A 121 and similar horiz design.

MSA124	25p. Type A **121**; £1.75, "Stella" leaving Southampton	6·00	6·00

A 122 Solar Eclipse at 10.15 am

1999. Total Eclipse of the Sun (11 August). Designs showing stages of the eclipse. Multicoloured.

A125	20p. Type A **122**	50	50
A126	25p. At 10.51 am	60	60
A127	30p. At 11.14 am	70	70
A128	38p. At 11.16 am	1·00	1·00
A129	44p. At 11.17 am	1·50	1·50
A130	64p. At 11.36 am	1·70	1·90
MSA131	191×80 mm. Nos. A125/30 and label	6·50	6·50

No. **MS**A131 also includes the "PHILEX FRANCE '99", Paris, and the "iBRA '99", Nuremberg, emblems on the sheet margin.

1999. Garrison Island (3rd series). Forts. As Type A 100. Multicoloured.

A132	20p. Field gun and crew, Fort Grosnez, c. 1855	45	25
A133	20p. Parade of 9th Bn, Royal Garrison Artillery	45	25
A134	25p. The Arsenal, Fort Albert, c. 1862	55	30
A135	25p. Royal Engineers loading wagons	55	30
A136	30p. 2nd Bn, Royal Scots on parade	65	35
A137	30p. Garrison at work, Fort Tourgis, c. 1865	65	35
A138	38p. Gun emplacement, Fort Houmet Herbe, c. 1870	80	40
A139	38p. Royal Alderney Artillery Militia loading cannon	80	40

Nos. A132/3, A134/5, A136/7 and A138/9 respectively were printed together, se-tenant, forming composite designs.

A 136 Peregrine Falcon attacking Ruddy Turnstone

2000. Endangered Species. Peregrine Falcon. Multicoloured.

A140	21p. Type A **136**	50	45
A141	26p. Two falcons and prey	55	55
A142	34p. Falcon guarding eggs	95	95
A143	38p. Falcon feeding young	1·00	1·00
A144	44p. Falcon and prey	1·50	1·50
A145	64p. Two young falcons	2·00	2·00

A 142 Wombles around Map of Alderney

2000. "A Wombling Holiday" (characters from children's television programme). Multicoloured.

A146	21p. Type A **142**	45	45
A147	26p. Alderney and Shansi on beach	55	55
A148	36p. Wellington by lighthouse	95	95
A149	40p. Madame Cholet and Bungo having picnic	1·10	1·10
A150	45p. Tomsk playing golf	1·50	1·50
A151	65p. Orinoco at airport	2·00	2·00
MSA152	160×86 mm. Nos. A146/51	6·50	6·50

A 148 Queen Elizabeth the Queen Mother on Alderney, 1984

2000. Queen Elizabeth the Queen Mother's 100th Birthday. Sheet 93×70 mm.

MSA153	A **148** £1.50 multicoloured	4·00	4·50

2000. Garrison Island (4th series). Events. As Type A 100. Multicoloured.

A154	21p. Regimental boxing tournament	45	25
A155	21p. Sports Day, Alderney Gala Week, 1924	45	25
A156	26p. Regimental orchestra playing at Ball	55	30
A157	26p. Garrison Ball in Fort Albert Mess, 1873	55	30
A158	36p. Royal Engineers' colour party, 1859	75	40
A159	36p. Royal Artillery on parade, Queen's 40th Birthday, 1859	75	40
A160	40p. Royal Artillery guard of honour	90	45
A161	40p. Arrival of Maj.-Gen. Marcus Slade, 1863	90	45

Nos. A154/5, A156/7, A158/9 and A160/1 were each printed together, se-tenant, forming a composite design.

A 157 Queen Elizabeth II

2001. 75th Birthday of Queen Elizabeth II. Sheet 70×70 mm.

MSA162	A **157** £1.75 multicoloured	4·50	4·50

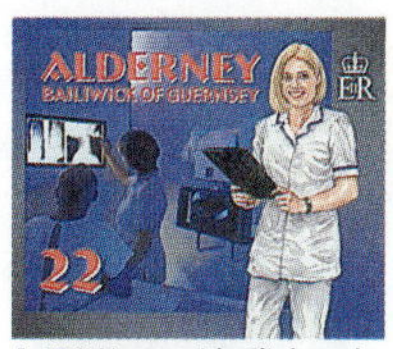

A 158 Nurse with Clipboard and Patient in X-Ray

2001. Community Services (1st series). Healthcare. Multicoloured.

A163	22p. Type A **158**	45	50
A164	27p. Nurse with tray and Mignot Memorial Hospital	55	60
A165	36p. Doctor and Princess Anne visiting hospital, 1972	70	75
A166	40p. Nurse from 1960s and maternity unit	80	85
A167	45p. Nurse from 1957 and Queen Elizabeth II laying hospital foundation stone	90	95
A168	65p. Nurse of 1926 with baby and opening of original hospital	1·20	1·40

See also Nos. A197/202, A217/22 and A242/7.

A 164 "Feathery" Golf Ball, 1901

2001. 30th Anniv of Alderney Golf Club. Multicoloured.

A169	22p. Type A **164**	45	50
A170	27p. Golfing fashions of the 1920s	55	60
A171	36p. Alderney Golf Course in 1970s	80	75
A172	40p. Modern putter	1·10	1·10
A173	45p. Modern golf gloves and shoes	1·50	1·50
A174	65p. Modern "lofted wood"	1·70	1·70
MSA175	190×75 mm. Nos. A169/74	6·50	6·50

No. **MS**A175 includes the "Philanippon '01" logo on the sheet margin.

A 170 Construction of New Breakwater, 1853

2001. Garrison Island (5th series). The Royal Navy. Multicoloured.

A176	22p. Type A **170**	45	25
A177	22p. Official party inspecting harbour, 1853	45	25
A178	27p. H.M.S. *Emerald*, (steam frigate), 1860	55	30
A179	27p. Disembarking troops from H.M.S. *Emerald*, 1860	55	30
A180	36p. Moored torpedo boats, 1890	70	40
A181	36p. Quick-firing gun on railway wagon, 1890	70	40
A182	40p. H.M.S. *Majestic* (battleship) at anchor, 1901	80	45
A183	40p. Torpedo boats outside harbour, 1901	80	45

Nos. A176/7, A178/9, A180/1 and A182/3 were each printed together, se-tenant, each pair forming a composite design.

A 178 Queen Elizabeth and Prince Philip arriving at London Airport, Feb 1952

2002. Golden Jubilee. Sheet 159×98 mm.

MSA184	A **178** £2 purple and gold	4·00	4·25

A 179 Northern Hobby

2002. Migrating Birds (1st series). Raptors. Multicoloured.

A185	22p. Type A **179**	45	50
A186	27p. Black kite	55	60
A187	36p. Merlin	85	85
A188	40p. Honey buzzard	1·00	1·00
A189	45p. Osprey	1·20	1·20
A190	65p. Marsh harrier	1·70	1·70
MSA191	170×80 mm. Nos. A185/90	6·50	6·50

See also Nos. A210/**MS**A216, A235/**MS**A41 and A259/**MS**265.

A 185 Coal Fire Beacon, 1725

2002. 50th Anniv of Electrification of Les Casquets Lighthouse. Multicoloured.

No.	Description	Mint	Used
A192	22p. Type A **185**	50	50
A193	27p. Oil lantern, 1779	60	60
A194	36p. Argand lamp, 1790	75	75
A195	45p. Revolving light, 1818	1·10	1·10
A196	65p. Electric light, 1952	1·50	1·50

No. A196 is inscribed "Elctrification" in error.

2002. Community Services (2nd series). Emergency Medical Aid. As Type A 158. Multicoloured.

No.	Description	Mint	Used
A197	22p. Ambulance technician, and ambulance station	45	50
A198	27p. Ambulance technician using radio, and ambulance	55	60
A199	36p. Doctor, and loading patient onto aircraft	95	95
A200	40p. Pilot, and Britten-Norman BN-2A MkIII Trislander over Alderney	1·10	1·10
A201	45p. Emergency operator, and patient on stretcher	1·70	1·70
A202	65p. Lifeboatman, and *Roy Barker One* (lifeboat)	2·00	2·00

A 196 St. Edward's Crown (image scaled to 38% of original size)

2003. 50th Anniv of Coronation. Sheet 128×90 mm.

No.	Description	Mint	Used
MSA203	A **196** £2 multicoloured	4·50	4·25

A 197 Wright Brothers' *Flyer I*, 1903

2003. Centenary of Powered Flight. Multicoloured.

No.	Description	Mint	Used
A204	22p. Type A **197**	50	50
A205	27p. Alcock and Brown's Vickers FB-27 Vimy, 1919	75	75
A206	36p. Douglas DC-3, 1936	85	85
A207	40p. de Havilland DH106 Comet 4, 1946	1·00	1·00
A208	45p. British Aerospace/Aerospatiale Concorde, 1969	1·20	1·20
A209	65p. Airbus Industrie Airbus A380	1·50	1·50

2003. Migrating Birds (2nd series). Seabirds. Type A 179. Multicoloured.

No.	Description	Mint	Used
A210	22p. Arctic tern	45	50
A211	27p. Great skua	55	60
A212	36p. Sandwich tern	75	75
A213	40p. Sooty shearwater	1·00	1·00
A214	45p. Arctic skua	1·50	1·50
A215	65p. Manx shearwater	2·00	2·00
MSA216	80×170 mm. Nos. A210/15	6·00	6·00

2003. Community Services (3rd series). Alderney Police. As Type A 158. Multicoloured.

No.	Description	Mint	Used
A217	22p. Policeman with clipboard and constables on beat	50	50
A218	27p. Policeman and Land Rover	60	60
A219	36p. Forensic team	80	80
A220	40p. Police constable and policeman with child cyclist	1·00	1·00
A221	45p. Policeman directing traffic and police at scene of accident	1·50	1·50
A222	65p. Policewoman and policeman with customs officer	2·00	2·00

A 215 *Hypholoma fasciculare*

2004. Fungi. Multicoloured.

No.	Description	Mint	Used
A223	22p. Type A **215**	70	70
A224	27p. *Aleuria aurantia*	85	85
A225	36p. *Coprinus micaceus*	1·20	1·20
A226	40p. *Langermannia gigantean*	1·30	1·30
A227	45p. *Macrolepiota procera*	1·40	1·40
A228	65p. *Xylaria hypoxylon*	2·10	2·10

A 221 Boys playing Football, Tourgis Close

2004. Centenary of FIFA (Federation Internationale de Football Association). Multicoloured.

No.	Description	Mint	Used
A229	26p. Type A **221**	85	85
A230	32p. Three children playing football, Braye Beach	1·10	1·10
A231	36p. Two boys playing football in playground	1·20	1·20
A232	40p. Teenagers playing football, Arch Bay	1·30	1·30
A233	45p. Football match	1·50	1·50
A234	65p. Father and two children playing football, Arch Bay	2·10	2·10

2004. Migrating Birds (3rd series). Passerines. As Type A 179. Multicoloured.

No.	Description	Mint	Used
A235	26p. Northern wheatear	85	85
A236	32p. Common redstart	1·10	1·10
A237	36p. Yellow wagtail	1·20	1·20
A238	40p. Hoopoe	1·30	1·30
A239	45p. Ring ousel ("Ouzel")	1·50	1·50
A240	65p. Sand martin	2·10	2·10
MSA241	170×80 mm. Nos. A235/40	8·00	8·00

2004. Community Services (4th series). Fire Service. As Type A 158. Multicoloured.

No.	Description	Mint	Used
A242	26p. Fire engine	85	85
A243	32p. Fireman up ladder and fire engine at Fort Tourgis	1·10	1·10
A244	36p. Airport service fire truck	1·20	1·20
A245	40p. Alderney Fire Station	1·30	1·30
A246	45p. Airport training ground	1·50	1·50
A247	65p. Road accident training exercise	2·10	2·10

A 239 Mermaid at her Undersea Home

2005. Birth Bicentenary of Hans Christian Andersen. Scenes from The Little Mermaid. Multicoloured.

No.	Description	Mint	Used
A248	26p. Type A **239**	50	55
A249	32p. Mermaid rescuing drowning Prince	65	70
A250	36p. Mermaid with Sea Witch bargaining her voice for a human life	1·00	1·00
A251	40p. Mermaids waving to Prince and his lover on seashore	2·00	2·00
A252	65p. Mermaid carried away by angels	3·00	3·00

A 244 Admiral Horatio Nelson

2005. Bicentenary of Battle of Trafalgar. Mult.

No.	Description	Mint	Used
A253	26p. Type A **244**	50	55
A254	32p. HMS *Victory*	65	70
A255	36p. Marine firing musket	70	75
A256	40p. Wounded Nelson with Captain Hardy	80	85
A257	45p. HMS *Victory* in battle with *Redoutable*	1·50	1·70
A258	65p. Admiral James Lord de Saumarez	2·00	2·50

2005. Migrating Birds (4th series). Waders. As Type A 179. Multicoloured.

No.	Description	Mint	Used
A259	26p. Little stint	50	55
A260	32p. Common greenshank	65	70
A261	36p. Golden plover	70	75
A262	40p. Bar-tailed godwit	1·00	85
A263	45p. Green sandpiper	2·00	2·00
A264	65p. Sanderling	3·00	3·00
MS265	170×80 mm. Nos. A259/64	8·00	8·00

A 256 Alderney Arms and Sunset (image scaled to 46% of original size)

2005. 60th Anniv of Return of War Evacuees. Sheet 140×80 mm.

No.	Description	Mint	Used
MSA266	A **256** £2 multicoloured	6·00	7·50

A 257 Young King Arthur

2006. "The Once and Future King". Multicoloured.

No.	Description	Mint	Used
A267	29p. Type A **39**	60	65
A268	34p. Merlyn	70	75
A269	38p. Morgause	1·00	1·00
A270	42p. Queen Guenever	1·50	1·50
A271	47p. Lancelot	1·90	1·90
A272	68p. Mordred	2·20	2·20
MSA273	120×90 mm. Nos. A267/72	8·50	8·50

Nos. A267/**MS**A273 commemorate the birth centenary of Terence Hanbury White, author of "The Once and Future King".

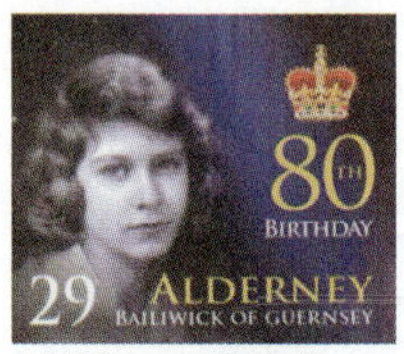

A 263 Princess Elizabeth

2006. 80th Birthday of Queen Elizabeth II. Multicoloured.

No.	Description	Mint	Used
A274	29p. Type A **263**	30	30
A275	29p. Princess Elizabeth (facing right)	30	30
A276	34p. Queen Elizabeth II, c. 1955	50	50
A277	34p. Wearing brown coat and hat	50	50
A278	42p. Wearing tiara	85	90
A279	42p. Wearing red jacket and red and white hat	85	90
A280	45p. Wearing pale pink hat	90	95
A281	45p. Wearing mauve dress and hat	90	95

A 271 Fulmar

2006. Resident Birds (1st series). Seabirds. Multicoloured.

No.	Description	Mint	Used
A282	29p. Type A **271**	65	65
A283	34p. Gannet	75	75
A284	42p. Lesser black-backed gull	1·00	1·00
A285	45p. Storm petrel	1·50	1·50
A286	47p. Kittiwake	2·00	2·00
A287	68p. Puffin	3·00	3·00

See also Nos. A316/21, A336/41, A363/368.

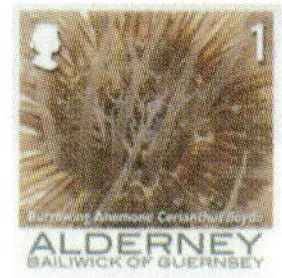

A 277 *Ceriantius lloydii* (burrowing anemone)

2006. Corals and Anemones. Multicoloured.

No.	Description	Mint	Used
A288	1p. Type A **277**	10	10
A289	2p. *Parazoanthus axinellae* (colonial anemone)	10	10
A290	3p. *Corynactis viridis* (jewel anemone colony)	10	10
A291	4p. *Sagartia elegans* (anemone)	10	15
A292	5p. *Alcyonium glomeratum* (red fingers)	10	15
A293	6p. *Metridium senile* (plumose anemone)	10	15
A294	7p. *Eunicella verrucosa* (fan coral)	15	20
A295	8p. *Corynactis viridis* (close-up of jewel anemone)	15	20
A296	9p. *Actinothoe sphyrodeta* (anemone)	20	25
A297	10p. *Anemonia viridis* (snake-locks anemone)	20	25
A298	20p. *Caryophyllia smithii* (Devonshire cup coral)	45	45
A301	40p. *Actinothoe sphyrodeta* (fried egg anemone)	95	95
A304	50p. *Calliactis parasitica* (parasitic anemone)	1·20	1·20
A306	£1 *Actinia equina* (beadlet anemone) (23×29 mm)	2·00	2·10
A307	£2 *Leptopsammia pruvoti* (sunset cup coral) (23×29 mm)	4·00	4·25
A308	£4 *Actinia fragacea* (strawberry anemone)	9·50	9·50

A 298 Cushion Starfish

2007. Designation of Alderney West Coast and the Burhou Islands as Ramsar Site. Multicoloured.

No.	Description	Mint	Used
A309	32p. Type A **298**	75	75
A310	37p. Gannet colony at Les Etacs	90	90
A311	45p. Spiny squat lobster	1·10	1·10
A312	48p. Grey seal	1·10	1·10
A313	50p. Golden samphire near Fort Clonque	1·20	1·20
A314	71p. Little egret and oystercatchers	1·70	1·70
MSA315	140×95 mm. Nos. A309/14	6·75	6·75

2007. Resident Birds (2nd series). Passerines. As Type A 271. Multicoloured.

No.	Description	Mint	Used
A316	32p. Blackbird	75	75
A317	37p. Dartford warbler	90	90
A318	45p. Blue tit	1·10	1·10
A319	48p. Wren	1·25	1·25
A320	50p. House sparrow	1·25	1·25
A321	71p. Jackdaw	1·75	1·75

A 310 'How the Camel got his Hump' A 45 *Vanessa cardui* (painted lady)

2007. Rudyard Kipling's Just So Stories. Multicoloured.

No.	Description	Mint	Used
A322	32p. Type A **310**	75	75
A323	37p. How the Whale got his Throat	90	90
A324	45p. The Elephant	1·10	1·10
A325	48p. How the Leopard got his Spots	1·25	1·25
A326	50p. The Cat that walked by Himself	1·25	1·25
A327	71p. How the Rhinoceros got his Skin	1·75	1·75
MSA328	140×95 mm. Nos. A322/7	7·00	6·75

A 316 *Vanessa cardui* (painted lady)

2008. Butterflies. Multicoloured.

A329	34p. Type A **316**	80	80
A331	48p. *Callophrys rubi* (green hairstreak)	1·10	1·10
A332	51p. *Pararge aegeria* (speckled wood)	1·20	1·20
A333	53p. *Polyommatus icarus* (common blue)	1·30	1·30
A334	74p. *Melitaea cinxia* (Glanville fritillary)	1·70	1·70
A330	40p. *Hipparchia semele* (grayling)	95	95
MSA335	140×100 mm. Nos. A329/34	7·00	7·00

2008. Resident Birds (3rd series). Raptors. As Type A 271. Multicoloured.

A336	34p. Common buzzard	80	80
A337	40p. Peregrine falcon	95	95
A338	48p. Kestrel	1·10	1·10
A339	51p. Barn owl	1·20	1·20
A340	53p. Long-eared owl	1·30	1·30
A341	74p. Sparrowhawk	1·70	1·70

A 328 Old Harbour

2008. 25th Anniv of Alderney Stamps. Multicoloured.

A342	34p. Type A **328**	80	80
A343	40p. The Breakwater	95	95
A344	48p. Fort Clonque Causeway	1·10	1·10
A345	51p. Golf Course	1·20	1·20
A346	53p. Hanging Rock	1·30	1·30
A347	74p. Fort Clonque	1·70	1·70

A 334 Lion Rampant from Alderney Flag

2008

A348	**A 334** £5 multicoloured	12·00	12·00

A 335 Britten-Norman Islander

2008. 40th Anniv of Aurigny Air Services. Multicoloured.

A349	34p. Type A **335**	80	80
A350	40p. Britten-Norman Trislander	95	95
A351	48p. DHC-6 Twin Otter	1·10	1·10
A352	51p. Short 360	1·20	1·20
A353	53p. Saab 340	1·30	1·30
A354	74p. ATR 72	1·70	1·70
MSA355	140×95 mm. Nos. A349/54	7·00	7·00

A 341 Tawny Mining Bee (*Andrena fulva*)

2009. Alderney Bees. Multicoloured.

A356	36p. Type A **341**	90	90
A357	43p. Early bumble bee (*Bombus pratorum*)	1·00	1·00
A358	51p. Bug mining bee (*Colletes daviesanus*)	1·25	1·25
A359	54p. Cuckoo bee (*Nomada goodeniana*)	1·25	1·25
A360	56p. Solitary bee (*Halictus scabiosae*)	1·40	1·40
A361	77p. Honey bee (*Apis mellifera*)	1·75	1·75
MSA362	140×100 mm. Nos. A356/61	8·00	8·00

A 347 Turnstone

2009. Resident Birds (4th series). Waders. Multicoloured.

A363	36p. Type A**347**	85	75
A364	43p. Curlew	1·10	1·10
A365	51p. Oystercatcher	1·25	1·25
A366	54p. Snipe	1·25	1·25
A367	56p. Dunlind	1·40	1·40
A368	77p. Ringed Plover	1·60	1·60

A 353 Felixstowe F2A Flying Boat with 'Dazzle' Paint over Castle Cornet, 1918

2009. Centenary of Naval Aviation. Multicoloured.

A369	36p. Type A**354**	85	85
A370	43p. Fairey Swordfish NE874 attacking U-boat	1·00	1·25
A371	51p. Blackburn Skuas dive bombing *Scharnhorst*	1·25	1·25
A372	54p. Hawker Sea Fury FB11 (VR930) over Alderney	1·25	1·25
A373	56p. Hawker Seahawk and Sea Furym	1·40	1·40
A374	77p. Agusta Westland HM101 Merlin Helicopter landing on HMS *Daring*	1·75	1·75

A 359 Alice West reporting Theft of Bull to Sherlock Holmes

2009. 150th Birth Anniv of Sir Arthur Conan Doyle. Scenes from new story Sherlock Holmes and the Curious Case of theAlderney Bull. Multicoloured.

A375	36p. Type A**359**	85	85
A376	43p. Holmes studying Coded Message and Arrest of Herdsman	1·00	1·00
A377	51p. Holmes studying Message on Harbour Wall	1·25	1·25
A378	54p. Sherlock Holmes and Farmer West	1·25	1·25
A379	56p. Holmes and Watson observing Half-Built Lighthouse	1·40	1·40
A380	77p. Arrest of Thief	1·75	1·75

A 365 Common Darter (*Sympetrum striolatum*)

Dragonflies. Multicoloured.

A381	36p. Type A**365**	85	85
A382	45p. Emperor dragonfly (*Anax imperator*)	1·10	1·10
A383	56p. Blue-tailed damselfly (*Ischnura elegans*)	1·40	1·40
A384	66p. Brown hawker (*Aeshna grandis*)	1·50	1·50
A385	75p. Black-tailed skimmer (*Orthetrum cancellatum*)	1·75	1·75
A386	83p. Red veined darter (*Sympetrum fonscolumbii*)	2·00	2·00
MS387	140×100 mm. Nos. A381/6	8·50	8·50

A 371 Pilot Keith Gilman

A 377 Sir Douglas Bader (birth centenary) (Actual size 110×70 mm)

2010. 70th Anniv of the Battle of Britain. Multicoloured.

A388	36p. Type **A 372**	80	80
A389	45p. Hurricanes	1·00	1·00
A390	48p. Pilots scramble	1·10	1·10
A391	50p. Spitfire sortie	1·25	1·25
A392	58p. Air Raid Warden	1·40	1·40
A393	80p. Evacuees	1·75	1·75
MS394	110×70 mm. A **377** £2 multicoloured	4·50	2·00

Pt. 13

GUINEA

The former French Colony on the W. coast of Africa which became fully independent in 1958.

1959. 100 centimes = 1 franc.
1973. 100 caury = 1 syli.
1986. 100 centimes = 1 franc.

1959. Stamps of Fr. West Africa optd REPUBLIQUE DE GUINEE or surch also.

No.	Type	Description	Unused	Used
188	-	10f. mult (No. 118)	3·25	3·75
189	20	45f. on 20f. pur, grn & ol	3·75	3·75

10 Pres. Sekou Toure

1959. Proclamation of Independence.

No.	Type	Description	Unused	Used
190	10	5f. red	35	10
191	10	10f. blue	55	30
192	10	20f. orange	90	60
193	10	65f. green	2·75	1·60
194	10	100f. violet	4·00	2·50

12 Tamara Lighthouse and Fishing Boats

13 Flying Doves

1959

No.	Type	Description	Unused	Used
201	12	1f. red (postage)	20	10
202	12	2f. green	20	10
203	12	3f. brown	20	10
204	-	5f. blue	40	10
205	-	10f. purple	40	20
206	-	15f. brown	1·20	40
207	-	20f. purple	1·20	35
208	-	25f. brown	2·20	60
209	13	40f. blue (air)	45	35
210	13	50f. green	65	55
211	13	100f. lake	1·30	90
212	13	200f. red	2·75	1·60
213	13	500f. red	7·75	4·50

DESIGNS—VERT: 5f. Palms and dhow; 20f. Pres. Sekou Toure. HORIZ: 10f. Pirogue being launched; 15f. African Elephant (front view); 25f. African Elephant (side view).

14 Mangoes

1959. Fruits in natural colours. Frame colours given.

No.	Type	Description	Unused	Used
214	-	10f. red (Bananas)	25	25
215	-	15f. green (Grapefruit)	40	25
216	-	20f. brown (Lemons)	60	30
217	14	25f. blue	80	45
218	-	50f. violet (Pineapple)	1·50	60

15 Lockheed Super Constellation Airliner

1959. Air.

No.	Type	Description	Unused	Used
219	15	100f. blue, brown & mauve	2·40	1·30
220	15	200f. mauve, brown & grn	5·75	1·90
221	-	500f. multicoloured	8·25	4·00

DESIGN: 500f. Lockheed Super Constellation airliner on ground.

16 "Raising the Flag"

1959. 1st Anniv of Independence.

No.	Type	Description	Unused	Used
222	16	50f. multicoloured	1·20	60
223	16	100f. multicoloured	2·00	1·00

18 Africans acclaiming U.N. Headquarters Building

1959. U.N.O.

No.	Type	Description	Unused	Used
230	18	1f. blue & orange (postage)	15	10
231	18	2f. purple and green	15	10
232	18	3f. brown and red	30	15
233	18	5f. brown and turquoise	30	20
234	18	50f. green, blue & brn (air)	90	70
235	18	100f. green, red and blue	1·60	1·20

Nos. 234/5 are larger (45×26 mm).

19 Eye-testing

1960. National Health. Inscr "POUR NOTRE SANTE NATIONALE".

No.	Type	Description	Unused	Used
236	19	20f.+10f. red and blue	95	90
237	-	30f.+20f. violet & orange	1·00	95
238	-	40f.+20f. blue and red	1·60	1·30
239	-	50f.+50f. brown and green	2·50	2·10
240	-	100f.+100f. green & pur	4·00	3·25

DESIGNS—HORIZ: 30f. Laboratory assistant; 40f. Spraying trees. VERT: (28½×40 mm): 50f. Research with microscope; 100f. Operating theatre.

20 "Uprooted Tree"

1960. World Refugee Year.

No.	Type	Description	Unused	Used
241	20	25f. multicoloured	70	40
242	20	50f. multicoloured	1·10	75

21 U.P.U. Monument, Berne

1960. 1st Anniv of Admission to U.P.U. Background differs for each value.

No.	Type	Description	Unused	Used
243	21	10f. black and brown	25	10
244	21	15f. lilac and mauve	45	25
245	21	20f. indigo and blue	55	25
246	-	25f. myrtle and green	75	30
247	-	50f. sepia and orange	1·10	55

DESIGN: 25f., 50f. As Type **10** but vert.

1960. Olympic Games. Optd Jeux Olympiques Rome 1960 and Olympic rings.

No.	Type	Description	Unused	Used
248	16	50f. multicoloured (postage)	8·00	7·75
249	16	100f. multicoloured	12·00	11·50
250	15	100f. blue, grn & mve(air)	10·50	7·75
251	15	200f. mauve, brown & grn	18·00	11·00
252	-	500f. multi (No. 221)	47·00	37·00

23 Flag and Map

1960. 2nd Anniv of Independence.

No.	Type	Description	Unused	Used
253	23	25f. multicoloured	50	45
254	23	30f. multicoloured	70	65

1960. 15th Anniv of U.N.O. Optd XVEME ANNIVERSAIRE DES NATIONS UNIES. (a) Nos. 214/18. Fruits in natural colours.

No.	Type	Description	Unused	Used
255	-	10f. red	30	25
256	-	15f. green	45	25
257	-	20f. brown	55	40
258	14	25f. blue	55	40
259	-	50f. violet	1·10	80

(b) Nos. 230/35.

No.	Type	Description	Unused	Used
260	18	1f. blue & orange (postage)	10	10
261	18	2f. purple and green	10	10
262	18	3f. brown and red	10	10
263	18	5f. brown and turquoise	10	10
264	18	50f. green, blue & brn (air)	95	70
265	18	100f. green, red and blue	1·60	1·10

1961. Surch 1961 and value.

No.	Type	Description	Unused	Used
266	20	25f.+10f. multicoloured	7·25	7·25
267	20	50f.+20f. multicoloured	7·25	7·25

27 Bohar Reedbuck

1961. Centres in brown, green and blue. Inscriptions and value tablets in colours given.

No.	Type	Description	Unused	Used
268	27	5f. turquoise	15	10
269	27	10f. green	15	10
270	27	25f. violet	45	30
271	27	40f. orange	80	40
272	27	50f. red	1·60	60
273	27	75f. blue	2·50	1·00

28 Guinea Flag and Exhibition Hall, Conakry

1961. First Three-Year Plan. Flag in red, yellow and green.

No.	Type	Description	Unused	Used
274	28	5f. blue and red	15	15
275	28	10f. brown and red	20	20
276	28	25f. green and red	45	40

29 Helmeted Guineafowl

1961. Guineafowl in purple and blue.

No.	Type	Description	Unused	Used
277	29	5f. mauve and blue	15	15
278	29	10f. red and blue	45	15
279	29	25f. red and blue	55	25
280	29	40f. brown and blue	95	40
281	29	50f. bistre and blue	1·30	55
282	29	75f. olive and blue	2·40	95

1961. Protection of Animals. Surch POUR LA PROTECTION DE NOS ANIMAUX +5 FRS.

No.	Type	Description	Unused	Used
283	27	5f.+5f. turquoise	70	15
284	27	10f.+5f. green	70	25
285	27	25f.+5f. violet	1·90	35
286	27	40f.+5f. orange	2·40	65
287	27	50f.+5f. red	3·50	80
288	27	75f.+5f. blue	5·50	1·30

31 Patrice Lumumba

1962. 1st Death Anniv of Lumumba (Congo leader).

No.	Type	Description	Unused	Used
289	31	10f. multicoloured	40	25
290	31	25f. multicoloured	60	45
291	31	50f. multicoloured	85	50

1962. Malaria Eradication (1st issue). Nos. 236/40 optd with Malaria Eradication emblem and ERADICATION DE LA MALARIA.

No.	Type	Description	Unused	Used
292	19	20f.+10f. red and blue	55	55
293	-	30f.+20f. violet and orange	65	65
294	-	40f.+20f. blue and red	1·20	1·10
295	-	50f.+50f. brown & green	1·70	1·60
296	-	100f.+100f. green & pur	3·75	3·50

33 King Mohammed V and Map

1962. 1st Anniv of Casablanca Conference.

No.	Type	Description	Unused	Used
297	33	25f. multicoloured	95	40
298	33	75f. multicoloured	2·75	75

34 Mosquito and Emblem

1962. Air. Malaria Eradication (2nd issue).

No.	Type	Description	Unused	Used
299	34	25f. black and orange	75	30
300	34	50f. black and red	95	50
301	34	100f. black and green	1·80	80
MS302		103×77 mm. 100f. sepia and green	11·50	11·00

34a Posthorn on North Africa

1962. African Postal Union Commemoration.

No.	Type	Description	Unused	Used
303	34a	25f. green, brown & orge	75	20
304	34a	100f. orange and brown	2·30	70

1962. Guinea-fowl stamps surch POUR LA PROTECTION DE NOS OISEAUX +5 FRS.

No.	Type	Description	Unused	Used
305	29	5f.+5f.	45	25
306	29	10f.+5f.	45	30
307	29	25f.+5f.	95	45
308	29	40f.+5f.	1·30	70
309	29	50f.+5f.	2·20	90
310	29	75f.+5f.	4·25	1·70

36 Bote-player

1962. Native Musicians.

No.	Type	Description	Unused	Used
311	36	30c. red, grn & bl (postage)	15	10
312	A	50c. green, brown & salmon	15	10
313	B	1f. purple and green	15	10
314	C	1f.50 turquoise, red & yell	15	10
315	D	2f. green, red and mauve	15	10
316	C	3f. violet, green & turquoise	30	10
317	B	10f. blue, brown and orange	40	25
318	D	20f. red, sepia and olive	45	60
319	36	25f. violet, sepia and olive	60	45

320	A	40f. mauve, green and blue	30	30
321	36	50f. blue, red and rose	45	50
322	A	75f. blue, brown and ochre	3·50	1·00
323	D	100f. blue, red & pink (air)	1·70	70
324	D	200f. red and blue	3·00	1·20
325	E	500f. blue, violet and brown	8·25	3·25

DESIGNS—(Musicians playing). HORIZ: A, Bolon; C, Koni; D, Kora; E, Balafon. VERT: B, Flute.

37 Hippopotamus

1962. Wild Game.

326	37	10f. sepia, green and orange	35	10
327	-	25f. brown, sepia and green	55	25
328	-	30f. sepia, yellow and olive	90	45
329	37	50f. sepia, green and blue	1·20	65
330	-	75f. brown, purple and lilac	1·80	85
331	-	100f. sepia, yellow & turq	2·50	1·00

DESIGNS: 25f., 75f. Lion; 30f., 100f. Leopard.

38 Boy at Blackboard

1962. Campaign Against Illiteracy.

332	38	5f. sepia, yellow and red	10	10
333	-	10f. sepia, orange and purple	10	10
334	38	15f. sepia, green and red	35	20
335	-	20f. sepia, turquoise & pur	45	30

DESIGN: 10f., 20f. Teacher at blackboard.

39 Alfa Yaya

1962. African Heroes and Martyrs.

336	39	25f. sepia, turquoise & gold	40	10
337	-	30f. sepia, ochre and gold	55	25
338	-	50f. sepia, purple and gold	85	25
339	-	75f. sepia, green and gold	1·50	55
340	-	100f. sepia, red and gold	2·10	80

PORTRAITS: 30f. King Behanzin; 50f. King Ba Bemba of Sikasso; 75f. Almamy Samory; 100f. Chief Tierno Aliou of the Goumba.

1962. Algerian Refugees Fund. Surch Aide aux Refugies Algeriens and premium.

341	33	25f.+15f. multicoloured	95	95
342	33	75f.+25f. multicoloured	1·80	1·80

1962. Air. "The Conquest of Space". Optd with capsule and La Conquete De L'Espace.

343	13	40f. blue	75	30
344	13	50f. green	1·00	40
345	13	100f. lake	1·60	75
348	13	200f. red	3·25	1·40

43 Crowned Crane

1962. Birds. Multicoloured.

349	30c. Type **43** (postage)	10	10
350	50c. Grey parrot (horiz)	10	10
351	1f. Abyssinian ground hornbill (horiz)	30	10
352	1f.50 White spoonbill (horiz)	30	10
353	2f. Bateleur (horiz)	30	10
354	3f. Type **43**	30	10
355	10f. As 50c. (horiz)	60	30
356	20f. As 1f. (horiz)	95	30
357	25f. As 1f.50 (horiz)	1·20	25
358	40f. As 2f. (horiz)	1·50	45
359	50f. Type **43**	2·20	65
360	75f. As 50c. (horiz)	3·00	80
361	100f. As 1f. (horiz) (air)	2·75	80
362	200f. As 1f.50 (horiz)	5·00	1·50
363	500f. As 2f. (horiz)	10·50	3·50

44 Handball

1963. Sports.

364	44	30c. purple, red and green (postage)	10	10
365	A	50c. violet, lilac and blue	10	10
366	B	1f. sepia, orange and green	10	10
367	C	1f.50 blue, orange & purple	10	10
368	D	2f. blue, turquoise & purple	10	10
369	44	3f. purple, olive and blue	10	10
370	A	4f. violet, mauve and blue	10	10
371	B	5f. sepia, green and purple	20	10
372	C	10f. blue and bright purple	30	10
373	D	20f. blue, orange and red	45	25
374	44	25f. purple, green and black	55	25
375	A	30f. violet, black and blue	55	40
376	B	100f. sepia, lake & grn (air)	1·90	70
377	C	200f. blue, brown & purple	4·00	1·40
378	D	500f. blue, brown & purple	8·75	3·50

DESIGNS: A, Boxing; B, Running; C, Cycling; D, Canoeing.

45 Campaign Emblem

1963. Freedom from Hunger.

379	45	5f. yellow and red	10	10
380	45	10f. yellow and green	15	10
381	45	15f. yellow and brown	30	15
382	45	25f. yellow and olive	45	25

46 "Amauris niavius"

1963. Butterflies. Multicoloured.

383	10c. Type **46** (postage)	10	10
384	30c. "Papilio demodocus"	10	10
385	40c. As 30c.	10	10
386	50c. "Graphum policenes"	10	10
387	1f. "Papilio nireus"	30	10
388	1f.50 Type **46**	30	10
389	2f. "Papilio menestheus"	30	10
390	3f. As 30c.	30	10
391	10f. As 50c.	50	10
392	20f. As 1f.	90	10
393	25f. Type **46**	1·50	25
394	40f. As 2f.	2·00	45
395	50f. As 30c.	2·50	60
396	75f. As 1f.	4·50	95
397	100f. Type **46** (air)	2·50	50
398	200f. As 50c.	4·50	1·10
399	500f. As 2f.	10·00	3·75

47 "African Unity"

1963. Conf of African Heads of State, Addis Ababa.

400	47	5f. sepia, blk & turq on grn	10	10
401	47	10f. sepia, black and yellow on yellow	15	10
402	47	15f. sepia, black & ol on ol	30	10
403	47	25f. sepia, black and brown on cinnamon	45	25

48 Capsule encircling Globe

1963. Centenary of Red Cross.

404	48	5f. red and green (postage)	10	10
405	48	10f. red and blue	35	10
406	48	15f. red and yellow	50	25
407	48	25f. red and black (air)	85	40

MS408 102×76 mm. 100f. carmine and green 4·25 4·25

1963. Air. 1st Pan-American Conakry–New York Direct Air Service. Optd PREMIER SERVICE DIRECT CONAKRY–NEW YORK PAN AMERICAN 30 JUILLET 1963.

409	15	10f. blue, green and mauve	2·75	1·10
410	15	200f. mauve, brown & green	4·75	2·20

1963. Olympic Games Preparatory Commission, Conakry. Nos. 364/6 surch COMMISSION PREPARATOIRE AUX JEUX OLYMPIQUES A CONAKRY, rings and new value.

411	40f. on 30c. purple, red and green	1·50	1·10
412	50f. on 50c. violet, lilac and blue	2·20	1·70
413	75f. on 1f. sepia, orange & grn	3·75	2·75

51 Jewel Cichlid

1964. Guinea Fishes. Multicoloured.

414	30c. Type **51** (postage)	10	10
415	40c. Golden pheasant panchax	10	10
416	50c. Blue gularis	10	10
417	1f. Banded jewelfish and jewel cichlid	10	10
418	1f.50 Yellow gularis	30	10
419	2f. Six-banded lyretail	30	25
420	5f. Type **51**	50	25
421	30f. As 40c.	85	40
422	40f. As 50c.	1·50	70
423	75f. As 1f.	3·25	95
424	100f. As 1f.50 (air)	2·10	80
425	300f. As 2f.	6·75	2·20

52 President Kennedy

1964. Pres. Kennedy Memorial Issue. Flag in red and blue.

426	52	5f. violet & black (postage)	10	10
427	52	25f. violet and green	45	25
428	52	50f. violet and brown	85	40
429	52	100f. black and violet (air)	1·90	1·20

53 Pipeline under Construction

1964. Inaug of Piped Water Supply, Conakry.

430	53	5f. red	10	10
431	-	10f. violet	15	10
432	-	20f. brown	35	15
433	-	30f. blue	55	25
434	-	50f. green	1·00	50

DESIGNS—HORIZ: 10f. Reservoir; 20f. Joining pipes; 30f. Transporting pipes; 50f. Laying pipes.

54 Ice hockey

1964. Winter Olympic Games, Innsbruck. Rings, frame and tablet in gold.

435	54	10f. olive & green (postage)	30	10
436	-	25f. slate and violet	70	25
437	-	50f. black and blue	1·30	60
438	-	100f. black & brn (air)	2·20	95

DESIGNS: 25f. Ski-jumping; 50f. Skiing; 100f. Figure-skating.

1964. Air. Olympic Games, Tokyo (1st issue). Nos. 376/8 optd JEUX OLYMPIQUES TOKYO 1964 and Olympic rings.

439	100f. sepia, lake and green	1·90	1·30
440	200f. blue, brown and purple	3·50	2·40
441	500f. blue, brown and purple	8·25	5·25

56 Eleanor Roosevelt with Children

1964. 15th Anniv of Declaration of Human Rights.

442	56	5f. green (postage)	10	10
443	56	10f. orange	10	10
444	56	15f. blue	30	10
445	56	25f. red	45	25
446	56	50f. violet (air)	1·10	50

57 Striped Hyena

1964. Animals.

447	**57**	5f. sepia and yellow	30	10
448	**57**	30f. sepia and blue	55	25
449	-	40f. black and mauve	80	25
450	-	75f. sepia and green	1·60	60
451	-	100f. sepia and ochre	2·20	80
452	-	300f. deep violet and orange	5·75	2·50

ANIMALS: 40f., 300f. African buffalo; 75f., 100f. African elephant.

58 Guinea Pavilion

1964. New York World's Fair.

453	**58**	30f. green and lilac	45	15
454	**58**	40f. green and purple	55	25
455	**58**	50f. green and brown	75	30
456	**58**	75f. blue and red	1·10	50
MS457		Two sheets each 100×76 mm. 59 (a) 100f. orange and blue; (b) 200f. green and carmine Set of 2 sheets	5·75	5·75

See also Nos. 484/**MS**488.

60 Nefertari, Isis and Hathor

1964. Nubian Monuments Preservation. Mult.

458	10f. Type **60** (postage)	30	10
459	25f. Pharaoh in battle	35	10
460	50f. The Nile—partly submerged sphinxes	65	35
461	100f. Rameses II, entrance hall of Great Temple, Abu Simbel	1·50	60
462	200f. Lower part of Colossi, Abu Simbel	2·75	1·10
463	300f. Nefertari (air)	4·75	1·90

61 Athlete with Torch

1965. Olympic Games, Tokyo (2nd issue). Multicoloured.

464	5f. Weightlifter and children (postage)	25	15
465	10f. Type **61**	45	10
466	25f. Pole vaulting	45	25
467	40f. Running	60	40
468	50f. Judo	85	45
469	75f. Japanese hostess	1·50	75
470	100f. Air hostess and Convair Coronado airliner (horiz) (air)	1·90	75
MS471	Two sheets. (a) 85×120 mm. 200f. Sun setting over Mt. Fuji; (b) 120×85 mm. 300f. Snow-clad Mt. Fuji set of 2 sheets	13·00	13·00

62 Doudou (Boke) Mask

1965. Native Masks and Dancers. Mult.

472	20c. Type **62** (postage)	10	10
473	40c. Niamou (Nzerekore) mask	10	10
474	60c. "Yoki" (Boke) statuette	10	10
475	80c. Guekedou dancer	10	10
476	1f. Niamou (Nzerekore) mask	15	10
477	2f. Macenta dancer	15	10
478	15f. Niamou (Nzerekore) mask	30	25
479	20f. Tom-tom beater (forest region)	50	25
480	60f. Macenta "Bird-man" dancer	1·50	45
481	80f. Bassari (Koundara) dancer	1·70	75
482	100f. Karana sword dancer	2·20	90
483	300f. Niamou (Nzerekore) mask (air)	6·50	2·20

1965. New York World's Fair. As Nos. 453/6 but additionally inscr "1965".

484	30f. orange and green	40	15
485	40f. green and red	55	25
486	50f. violet and blue	75	40
487	75f. violet and brown	1·00	55
MS488	Two sheets each 100×70 mm. 59 (a) 100f. green and sepia; (b) 200f. magenta and green Set of 2 sheets	6·50	6·50

63 Metal-work

1965. Native Handicrafts. Multicoloured.

489	15f. Type **63** (postage)	30	10
490	20f. Pottery	30	25
491	60f. Dyeing	85	40
492	80f. Basket-making	1·00	50
493	100f. Ebony-work (air)	1·80	80
494	300f. Ivory-work	5·00	1·80

64 I.T.U. Emblem and Symbols

1965. I.T.U. Centenary.

495	**64**	25f. multicoloured (postage)	45	25
496	**64**	50f. multicoloured	75	40
497	**64**	100f. multicoloured (air)	1·90	70
498	**64**	200f. multicoloured	3·00	1·30

65 Major Grissom

66 Grissom and Young in "Gemini 2" Spaceship

1965. American and Russian Achievements in Space. Two sheets each 145×215 mm containing fifteen stamps as T 65/6. Multicoloured.

MS499	America in Space. 5f. Type **65**; 10f. Lt. Com. John W. Young; 15f. Moon from 258 miles; 25f. Moon from 115 miles; 30f. Moon from 58 miles; 100f. Type **66**	11·00	11·00
MS500	Russia in Space. 5f. Col. Pavel Belyayev; 10f. Lt. Col. Alexei Leonov; 15f. Vostoks 3 and 4 in space; 25f. Sputnik over earth; 30f. Vostoks 5 and 6 over earth; 100f. Leonov floating in space	11·00	11·00

67 U.N. Headquarters and I.C.Y. Emblem

1965. I.C.Y.

501	**67**	25f. red and green (postage)	30	15
502	**67**	45f. red and violet	45	25
503	**67**	75f. red and brown	95	50
504	**67**	100f. orange and blue (air)	1·50	70

68 Polytechnic Institute, Conakry

1965. 7th Anniv of Independence. Mult.

505	25f. Type **68** (postage)	30	10
506	30f. Camayenne Hotel	45	30
507	40f. Gbessia Airport	75	45
508	75f. "28 Septembre" Stadium	1·00	65
509	200f. Polytechnic Institute, North facade (air)	2·20	1·30
510	500f. Ditto, West facade	6·50	3·25

Nos. 509/10 are larger, 53×23 mm.

69 Moon, Globe and Satellite

1965. "To the Moon". Multicoloured.

511	5f. Type **69** (postage)	15	10
512	10f. Trajectory of "Ranger 7"	50	10
513	25f. "Relay" satellite	60	30
514	45f. "Vostok 1, 2" and Globe	95	35
515	100f. "Ranger 7" approaching Moon (vert) (25×36 mm) (air)	1·30	45
516	200f. Launching of "Ranger 7" (vert) (25×36 mm)	2·75	90

Nos. 512/14 are larger, 36×25½ mm.

1965. Gemini 5 and Pictures of Mars Commemoration. Sheet MS499 variously optd. The 5, 10 and 100f. are optd in English or French and the 15, 25 and 30f. are optd in French, English and French respectively.

MS517	145×215 mm	10·00	10·00
MS518	155×215 mm. Sheet **MS**499 optd as last but the 15, 25 and 30f. are optd in English, French and English respectively	10·00	10·00

70 Sabre Dance, Karana

1966. Guinean Dances. Multicoloured.

519	10c. Type **70** (postage)	10	10
520	30c. Young girls' dance, Lower Guinea	10	10
521	50c. Tiekere musicians, "Eyora" (bamboo) dance, Bandjinguene (horiz) (36×29 mm)	10	10
522	5f. Doundouba dance, Kouroussa	30	10
523	40f. Bird-man's dance, Macenta	1·50	50
524	100f. Kouyate Kandia, national singer (horiz) (36×29 mm) (air)	1·80	75

See also Nos. 561/6.

1966. Stamp Cent Exn, Cairo. Nos. 460 and 463 optd CENTENAIRE DU TIMBRE CAIRE 1966.

525	50f. multicoloured (postage)	95	80
526	300f. multicoloured (air)	3·75	1·80

1966. Pan Arab Games, Cairo (1965). Nos. 464/5, 467/9 optd JEUX PANARABES CAIRE 1965 and pyramid motif.

527	-	5f. multicoloured (postage)	45	25
528	**61**	10f. multicoloured	45	25
529	-	40f. multicoloured	90	45
530	-	50f. multicoloured	1·00	70
531	-	75f. multicoloured	1·80	1·10
532	-	100f. multicoloured (air)	1·80	75
MS533		Two sheets as No. **MS**471 optd 200f. and 300f. Price for 2 sheets	15·00	15·00

73 Vonkou Rocks, Telimele

1966. Landscapes (1st series). Multicoloured.

534	20f. Type **73** (postage)	15	10
535	25f. Artificial lake, Coyah	30	10
536	40f. Waterfalls, Kate	35	15
537	50f. Bridge, Forecariah	55	25
538	75f. Liana bridge	95	45
539	100f. Lighthouse and bay, Boulbinet (air)	85	1·20

See also Nos. 603/608.

74 UNESCO Emblem

1966. 20th Anniv of UNESCO (a) Postage.

540	**74**	25f. multicoloured	70	25

(b) Air. Nos. 509/10 optd vingt ans 1946 1966 and UNESCO Emblem.

541	200f. multicoloured	2·40	1·50
542	500f. multicoloured	5·75	3·00

76

1966. Guinean Flora and Female Headdresses. Similar designs.

543	**76**	10c. multicoloured (postage)	10	10
544	-	20c. multicoloured	10	10
545	-	30c. multicoloured	10	10
546	-	40c. multicoloured	10	10
547	-	3f. multicoloured	10	10
548	-	4f. multicoloured	10	10
549	-	10f. multicoloured	30	10
550	-	25f. multicoloured	75	15
551	-	30f. multicoloured	95	25
552	-	50f. multicoloured	1·40	35
553	**76**	80f. multicoloured	1·80	60
554	-	200f. multicoloured (air)	4·00	1·30
555	-	300f. multicoloured	5·75	2·20

Nos. 551/555 are 29×42 mm.

1966. Landing of "Luna 9" on Moon. Sheet No. MS500 LUNA 9 FEBRUARY 3 1966. (a) Inscr English on each stamp.

MS556	145×215 mm. As No **MS**500	9·00	9·00

(b) Inscr French on each stamp.

MS557	145×215 mm. As No **MS**500	9·00	9·00

78 Decade and UNESCO Symbols

1966. Int Hydrological Decade.

No.	Type	Description	Mint	Used
558	**78**	5f. red and blue	10	10
559	**78**	25f. red and green	35	10
560	**78**	100f. red and purple	1·20	70

1966. Guinean National Ballet. Designs show various dances as T 70.

No.	Description	Mint	Used
561	60c. multicoloured	10	10
562	1f. multicoloured	10	10
563	1f.50 multicoloured	30	10
564	25f. multicoloured	50	25
565	50f. multicoloured	1·00	50
566	75f. multicoloured	1·70	75

SIZES—VERT: (26×36 mm): 60c., 1f., 1f.50, 50f. HORIZ: (36×29 mm): 25f., 75f.

79 "Village"

1966. 20th Anniv of UNICEF Multicoloured designs showing children's drawings.

No.	Description	Mint	Used
567	2f. "Elephant"	10	10
568	3f. "Doll"	10	10
569	10f. "Girl"	10	10
570	20f. Type **79**	30	10
571	25f. "Footballer"	55	25
572	40f. "Still Life"	70	25
573	50f. "Bird in Tree"	85	25

80 Dispensing Medicine

1967. Inauguration of W.H.O. Headquarters, Geneva. Multicoloured.

No.	Description	Mint	Used
574	30f. Type **80**	30	10
575	50f. Doctor examining child	45	25
576	75f. Nurse weighing baby	65	40
577	80f. W.H.O. Building and flag	95	55

81 Niamou Mask

1967. Guinean Masks. Multicoloured.

No.	Description	Mint	Used
578	10c. Banda-di (Kanfarade Boke region)	10	10
579	30c. Niamou (N'zerekore region) (different)	10	10
580	50c. Type **81**	10	10
581	60c. Yinadjinkele (Kankan region)	10	10
582	1f. As 10c.	10	10
583	1f.50 As 30c.	10	10
584	5f. Type **81**	25	10
585	25f. As 60c.	30	10
586	30f. As 10c.	45	30
587	50f. As 30c.	85	25
588	75f. As Type **81**	1·40	50
589	100f. As 60c.	2·10	85

82 Research Institute

1967. Pastoria Research Institute. Mult.

No.	Description	Mint	Used
590	20c. Type **82** (postage)	10	10
591	30c. "Python regius" (snake)	10	10
592	50c. Extracting snake's venom	10	10
593	1f. "Python sebae"	10	10
594	2f. Attendants handling viper	10	10
595	5f. Gabon viper	15	10
596	20f. "Dendroaspis viridis"	45	10
597	30f. As 5f.	95	20
598	50f. As 1f.	1·80	25
599	75f. As 50c.	2·50	60
600	200f. As 20c. (air)	2·75	1·10
601	300f. As 2f.	5·75	1·80
MS602	105×125 mm. Nos. 596, 599/600	7·00	6·25

Nos. 596/601 are 56×26 mm.

1967. Landscapes (2nd series). As T 73. Mult.

No.	Description	Mint	Used
603	5f. Loos Islands (postage)	10	10
604	30f. Tinkisso waterfalls	30	10
605	70f. The "Elephant's Trunk", Kakoulima	65	20
606	80f. Seashore, Ratoma	95	35
607	100f. House of explorer Olivier de Sanderval (air)	1·30	55
608	200f. Aerial view of Conakry	2·00	95

83 People's Palace, Conakry

1967. 20th Anniv of Guinean Democratic Party and Inaug of People's Palace. Multicoloured.

No.	Description	Mint	Used
609	5f. Type **83** (postage)	10	10
610	30f. African elephant's head	60	30
611	55f. Type **83**	60	35
612	200f. As 30f. (air)	1·90	1·00

1967. 50th Anniv of Lions Int Landscape series optd AMITE DES PEUPLES GRACE AU TOURISME 1917 – 1967 and Lions Emblem.

No.	Description	Mint	Used
613	5f. (No. 603) (postage)	35	10
614	30f. (No. 604)	45	35
615	40f. (No. 536)	60	30
616	50f. (No. 537)	95	50
617	70f. (No. 605)	1·30	55
618	75f. (No. 538)	2·10	60
619	80f. (No. 606)	2·50	80
620	100f. (No. 539) (air)	2·00	80
621	100f. (No. 607)	2·00	80
622	200f. (No. 608)	4·00	1·60

85 Section of Mural

1967. Air. "World of Tomorrow". Jose Vanetti's Mural, Conference Building, U.N. Headquarters.

No.	Type	Description	Mint	Used
623	-	30f. multicoloured	30	15
624	-	50f. multicoloured	55	25
625	**85**	100f. multicoloured	1·30	55
626	-	200f. multicoloured	2·75	90
MS627		126×85 mm. 50f.×2 100f. Inscr in English or French	5·75	5·75

DESIGNS: Various sections of mural. The 30, 50, 100f. are horiz designs. **MS**627 contains two different 50f. vert designs and 100f. similar to T **85**.

86 W.H.O. Building, Brazzaville

1967. Inaug of W.H.O. Building, Brazzaville.

No.	Type	Description	Mint	Used
628	**86**	30f. olive, ochre and blue	45	10
629	**86**	75f. red, ochre and blue	90	45

87 Human Rights Emblem

1968. Human Rights Year.

No.	Type	Description	Mint	Used
630	**87**	30f. red, green and ochre	50	15
631	**87**	40f. red, blue and violet	70	25

88 Coyah, Oubreka Region

1968. Regional Costumes and Habitations. Multicoloured.

No.	Description	Mint	Used
632	20c. Type **88** (postage)	10	10
633	30c. Kankan Region	10	10
634	40c. Kankan, Upper Guinea	10	10
635	50c. Forest region	10	10
636	60c. Foulamory, Gaoual Region	10	10
637	5f. Cognagui, Koundara Region	10	10
638	15f. As 50c.	25	10
639	20f. As 20c.	40	10
640	30f. As 30c.	55	25
641	40f. Fouta-Djallon, Middle Guinea	95	35
642	100f. Labe, Middle Guinea	2·10	55
643	300f. Bassari, Koundara Region (air)	4·50	1·60

The 60c. to 300f. are larger (60×39 mm).

89 "The Village Story-teller"

1968. Paintings of African Legends (1st series). Multicoloured.

No.	Description	Mint	Used
644	25f. Type **89** (postage)	20	10
645	30f. "The Moon and the Stars"	20	10
646	75f. "Leuk the Hare sells his Sister" (vert)	85	45
647	80f. "The Hunter and the Female Antelope"	95	55
648	100f. "Old Faya's Inheritance" (vert) (air)	1·40	75
649	200f. "Soumangourou Kante killed by Djegue"	2·75	90
MS650	106×141 mm. Nos. 646/9. Imperf	11·50	11·50

1968. Paintings of African Legends (2nd series). As T 89. Multicoloured.

No.	Description	Mint	Used
651	15f. "Little Demons of Mount Nimba" (postage)	10	10
652	30f. "Lan, the Baby Buffalo" (vert)	30	25
653	40f. "The Nianablas and the Crocodiles"	45	25
654	50f. "Leuk the Hare and the Drum" (vert)	65	25
655	70f. "Malissadio—the Young Girl and the Hippopotamus" (air)	95	25
656	300f. "Little Goune, Son of the Lion" (vert)	4·75	1·60
MS657	106×141 mm. Nos. 653/6. Imperf	7·00	7·00

90 Olive Baboon

1968. African Fauna. Multicoloured.

No.	Description	Mint	Used
658	5f. Type **90** (postage)	30	10
659	10f. Leopards	30	10
660	15f. Hippopotami	45	15
661	20f. Crocodile	75	25
662	30f. Warthog	95	25
663	50f. Kob	1·30	45
664	75f. African buffalo	2·00	60
665	100f. Lions (air)	2·30	50
666	200f. African elephant	4·75	1·30
MS667	Three sheets each 120×100 mm. Nos. 658/60; 661/3 and 664/6 each with se-tenant stamp-size label	17·00	12·00

Nos. 665/6 are 50×35 mm.

91 Robert F. Kennedy

1968. "Martyrs of Liberty". Multicoloured.

No.	Description	Mint	Used
668	30f. Type **91** (postage)	45	10
669	75f. Martin Luther King	1·00	40
670	100f. John F. Kennedy	1·60	70
671	50f. Type **91** (air)	90	35
672	100f. Martin Luther King	1·90	70
673	200f. John F. Kennedy	4·00	1·60

92 Running

1969. Olympic Games, Mexico (1968). Multicoloured.

No.	Description	Mint	Used
674	5f. Type **92** (postage)	10	10
675	10f. Boxing	30	10
676	15f. Throwing the javelin	30	10
677	25f. Football	45	10
678	30f. Steeplechase	55	10
679	50f. Throwing the hammer	70	25
680	75f. Cycling	1·10	40
681	100f. Gymnastics (air)	1·20	45
682	200f. Exercising on rings	2·40	90
683	300f. Pole-vaulting	4·50	1·20

The 25, 100, 200 and 300f. are larger, 57×30 mm.

Each design also shows one of three different sculptured figures.

1969. Moon Flight of "Apollo 8". Nos. 514/16 optd APOLLO 8 DEC. 1968 and earth and moon motifs or surch also.

No.	Description	Mint	Used
684	30f. on 45f. mult (postage)	1·30	1·20
685	45f. multicoloured	1·30	1·20
686	25f. on 200f. mult (air)	55	45
687	100f. multicoloured	1·70	90
688	200f. multicoloured	3·50	1·40

95 "Tarzan"

1969. "Tarzan" (famous Guinea Chimpanzee). Multicoloured.

No.	Description	Mint	Used
689	25f. Type **95**	40	15
690	30f. "Tarzan" in front of Pastoria Institute	50	25
691	75f. "Tarzan" and family	1·00	45
692	100f. "Tarzan" squatting on branch	1·90	65

96 Pioneers lighting Fire

1969. Guinean Pioneer Youth Organization. Multicoloured.

693	5f. Type **96**	10	10
694	25f. Pioneer and village	30	10
695	30f. Pioneers squad	45	10
696	40f. Playing basketball	50	25
697	45f. Two pioneers	70	25
698	50f. Pioneers emblem	90	40
MS699	120×135 mm. Nos. 693/8	3·75	3·00

97 "Apollo" Launch

1969. 1st Man on the Moon. Multicoloured.

700	25f. Type **97**	30	10
701	30f. View of Earth	30	10
702	50f. Modules descent to the Moon	45	10
703	60f. Astronauts on Moon	55	25
704	75f. Landing module on Moon	75	30
705	100f. Take-off from Moon	1·30	65
706	200f. "Splashdown"	2·75	1·20

No. 705 is 35×71 mm.
The above stamps were issued with English and French inscriptions.

98 Pylon and Heavy Industry

1969. 50th Anniv of I.L.O. Multicoloured.

707	25f. Type **98**	30	10
708	30f. Broadcasting studio	30	10
709	75f. Harvesting	75	25
710	200f. Making pottery	2·30	85

99 Child suffering from Smallpox

1970. Campaign Against Measles and Smallpox. Multicoloured.

711	25f. Type **99**	30	10
712	30f. Mother and child with measles	30	10
713	40f. Inoculating girl	40	25
714	50f. Inoculating boy	60	25
715	60f. Inoculating family	95	35
716	200f. Dr. Edward Jenner	2·75	1·20

100 O.E.R.S. Countries on Map of Africa

1970. Meeting of Senegal River Riparian States Organization (Organisation des Etats Riverains du Fleuve Senegal).

717	**100**	30f. multicoloured	25	25
718	**100**	200f. multicoloured	2·00	1·20

NOTE: The Riparian States are Guinea, Mali, Mauritania and Senegal.

101 Dish Aerial and Open book

1970. World Telecommunications Day.

719	**101**	5f. black and blue	30	10
720	**101**	10f. black and red	30	25
721	**101**	50f. black and yellow	55	25
722	**101**	200f. black and lilac	2·30	1·20

102 Lenin

1970. Birth Centenary of Lenin. Multicoloured.

723	5f. Type **102**	10	10
724	20f. "Lenin in the Smolny" (Serov)	35	10
725	30f. "Lenin addressing Workers" (Serov)	45	25
726	40f. "Lenin speaking to Service-men" (Vasiliev)	55	30
727	100f. "Lenin with Crowd" (Vasilev)	1·70	65
728	200f. Type **102**	3·25	1·50

103 Congo Tetra

1971. Fishes. Multicoloured.

729	5f. Type **103**	10	10
730	10f. Red-spotted gularis	30	10
731	15f. Red-chinned panchax	35	10
732	20f. Six-barred distichodus	40	10
733	25f. Jewel cichlid	50	20
734	30f. Rainbow krib	65	30
735	40f. Two-striped lyretail	90	35
736	45f. Banded jewelfish	1·10	40
737	50f. Red-tailed notho	1·40	50
738	75f. Freshwater butterflyfish	2·20	85
739	100f. Golden trevally	3·00	1·00
740	200f. African mouth-brooder	6·50	2·10

104 Violet-crested Turaco

1971. Wild Birds. Multicoloured.

741	5f. Type **104** (postage)	15	15
742	20f. Golden oriole	45	15
743	30f. Blue headed coucal	75	20
744	40f. Great grey shrike	1·00	40
745	75f. Vulturine guineafowl	2·50	90
746	100f. Southern ground hornbill	3·25	1·20
747	50f. Type **104** (air)	1·50	55
748	100f. As 20f.	3·00	1·10
749	200f. As 75f.	6·50	1·60

105 UNICEF Emblem on Map of Africa

1971. 25th Anniv of UNICEF.

750	**105**	25f. multicoloured	10	10
751	**105**	30f. multicoloured	30	10
752	**105**	50f. multicoloured	55	25
753	**105**	60f. multicoloured	75	25
754	**105**	100f. multicoloured	1·20	60

106 John and Robert Kennedy and Martin Luther King

1972. Air. Martyrs for Peace. Embossed on silver or gold foil.

755	**106**	300f. silver		
756	**106**	1500f. gold, cream and green		

107 Jules Verne and Moon Rocket

1972. Air. Moon Exploration. Embossed on silver or gold foil.

757	**107**	300f. silver		
758	**107**	1200f. gold		

108 Pres. Richard Nixon

1972. Air. Pres. Nixon's Visit to Peking. Embossed on gold or silver foil.

759	**108**	90f. silver
760	-	90f. silver
761	-	90f. silver
762	-	90f. silver
763	**108**	290f. gold
764	-	290f. gold
765	-	290f. gold
766	-	290f. gold
767	-	1200f. gold and red

DESIGNS—VERT: Nos. 760, 764, Chinese table-tennis player; 761, 765, American table-tennis player; 762, 766, Mao Tse-tung. HORIZ: (45×35 mm): No. 767, Pres. Nixon and Mao Tse-tung.

109 "Flying Flatfish"

1972. Imaginary Space Creatures. Mult.

768	5f. Type **109**	10	10
769	20f. "Radioactive crab"	30	10
770	30f. "Space octopus"	45	10
771	40f. "Rocket-powered serpent"	60	20
772	100f. "Winged eel"	1·30	60
773	200f. "Flying dragon"	2·75	1·10

110 African Child

1972. Racial Equality Year. Multicoloured.

774	15f. Type **110** (postage)	10	10
775	20f. Asiatic child	30	10
776	30f. Indian youth	30	10
777	50f. European girl	75	25
778	100f. Heads of four races	1·20	50
779	100f. As No. 778 (air)	1·50	65

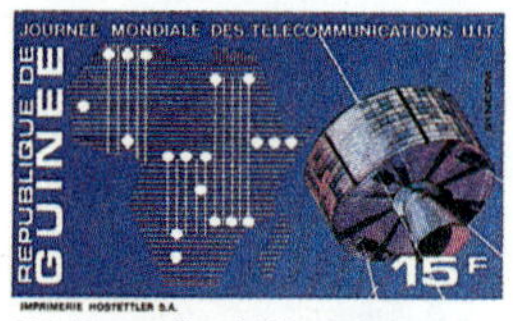

111 "Syncom" and African Map

1972. World Telecommunications Day. Mult.

780	15f. Type **111** (postage)	10	10
781	30f. "Relay"	45	10
782	75f. "Early Bird"	95	25
783	80f. "Telstar"	1·00	40
784	100f. As 30f. (air)	1·50	50
785	200f. As 75f.	3·00	1·00

112 APU Emblem and Dove with Letter

1972. 10th Anniv of African Postal Union.

786	**112**	15f. mult (postage)	10	10
787	**112**	30f. multicoloured	30	25
788	**112**	75f. multicoloured	80	30
789	**112**	80f. multicoloured	95	50
790	-	100f. multicoloured (air)	1·20	50
791	-	200f. multicoloured	2·20	95

DESIGNS: 100f. to 200f. APU emblem and airmail envelope.

113 Child reading Book

1972. International Book Year. Multicoloured.

792	5f. Type **113**	10	10
793	15f. Book with sails	10	10
794	40f. Girl with book and plant	45	10
795	50f. "Key of Knowledge" and open book	75	25

796	75f. "Man" reading book and globe	95	55
797	200f. Open book and laurel sprigs	2·30	95

114 Throwing the Javelin

1972. Olympic Games, Munich. Mult.

798	5f. Type **114** (postage)	10	10
799	10f. Pole-vaulting	10	10
800	25f. Hurdling	45	10
801	30f. Throwing the hammer	55	10
802	40f. Boxing	75	25
803	50f. Gymnastics (horse)	95	45
804	75f. Running	1·50	55
805	100f. Gymnastics (rings) (air)	2·20	65
806	200f. Cycling	3·75	1·40
MS807	111×75 mm. 300f. Football	6·75	5·75

1972. U.N. Environmental Conservation Conf, Stockholm. Nos. 750/4 optd UNE SEULE TERRE and emblem.

808	**105**	25f. multicoloured	45	10
809	**105**	30f. multicoloured	60	30
810	**105**	50f. multicoloured	1·10	40
811	**105**	60f. multicoloured	1·60	50
812	**105**	100f. multicoloured	2·10	95

116 Dimitrov addressing "Reichstag Fire" Court

1972. 90th Birth Anniv of George Dimitrov (Bulgarian statesman).

813	**116**	5f. blue, gold and green	10	10
814	-	25f. blue, gold and green	30	10
815	-	40f. blue, gold and green	55	25
816	-	100f. blue, gold and green	1·30	45

DESIGNS: 25f. In Moabit Prison, Berlin, 1933; 40f. Writing memoirs; 100f. G. Dimitrov.

117 Emperor Haile Selassie

1972. Emperor Haile Selassie of Ethiopia's 80th Birthday. Multicoloured.

817	40f. Type **117**	60	35
818	200f. Emperor Haile Selassie in military uniform	3·00	1·40

118 "Syntomeida epilais"

1973. Guinean Insects. Multicoloured.

819	5f. Type **118**	25	10
820	15f. "Hippodamia californica"	40	10
821	30f. "Tettigonia viridissima"	1·20	30
822	40f. "Apis mellifica"	1·50	45
823	50f. "Photinus pyralis"	2·00	45
824	200f. "Ancyluris formosissima"	6·25	1·70

119 Dr. Kwame Nkrumah

1973. 10th Anniv of Organization of African Unity.

825	**119**	1s.50 black, gold & green	30	10
826	-	2s.50 black, gold & green	45	25
827	-	5s. black, gold and green	75	25
828	-	10s. violet and gold	1·50	50

DESIGNS: Nos. 826/8, different portraits of Dr. Kwame Nkrumah similar to Type **119**.

120 Institute of Applied Biology, Kindia

1973. 25th Anniv of W.H.O. Multicoloured.

829	1s. Type **120**	10	10
830	2s.50 Preparing vaccine from an egg	40	25
831	3s. Filling ampoules with vaccine	45	25
832	4s. Sterilization of vaccine	55	25
833	5s. Packing vaccines	95	40
834	10s. Preparation of vaccine base	1·50	55
835	20s. Inoculating patient	3·50	1·10

Nos. 833/35 are 48×31 mm.

121 Volcanic Landscape

1973. 500th Birth Anniv of Copernicus. Mult.

836	50c. Type **121**	10	10
837	2s. Sun over desert	30	10
838	4s. Earth and Moon	45	10
839	5s. Lunar landscape	95	25
840	10s. Jupiter	1·60	55
841	20s. Saturn	3·00	85
MS842	133×133 mm. 20s.×4 Copernicus (44×44 mm)	20·00	16·00

122 Loading Bauxite at Quayside

1974. Air. Bauxite Industry, Bok. Mult.

843	4s. Type **122**	60	10
844	6s. Bauxite train	1·60	50
845	10s. Bauxite mining	2·50	50

123 "Clappertonia ficifolia"

1974. Flowers of Guinea. Multicoloured.

846	50c. Type **123** (postage)	10	10
847	1s. "Rothmannia longiflora"	10	10
848	2s. "Oncoba spinosa"	30	10
849	3s. "Venidium fastuosum"	45	10
850	4s. "Bombax costatum"	55	25
851	5s. "Clerodendrum splendens"	1·20	25
852	7s.50 "Combretuni grandiflorum"	1·50	40
853	10s. "Mussaendra erythrophylla"	1·80	55
854	12s. "Argemone mexicana"	2·30	80
855	20s. "Thunbergia alata" (air)	4·00	1·30
856	25s. "Diascia barberae"	4·50	1·60
857	50s. "Kigelia africana"	10·00	2·20

SIZES—VERT: Nos. 847/9, As Type **123**; 850/3, 36×47 mm. DIAMOND: Nos. 854/7, 61×61 mm.

No. 855 is wrongly inscr "Thunbegia alata".

124 Drummers and Pigeon

1974. Centenary of U.P.U. Multicoloured.

858	5s. Type **124**	40	25
859	6s. Runner and pigeon	95	35
860	7s.50 Monorail train, lorry and pigeon	1·20	50
861	10s. Boeing 707, "United States" (liner) and pigeon	1·50	70
MS862	Two sheets (a) 71×60 mm. 10s. Balloon, canoe and pigeon; (b) 113×95 mm. 20s.×4 Space satellites	17·00	17·00

125 Pioneers testing Rope-bridge

1974. National Pioneers (Scouting) Movement. Multicoloured.

863	50c. Type **125**	10	10
864	2s. "On safari"	30	10
865	4s. Using field-telephone	45	20
866	5s. Cooking on camp-fire	75	30
867	7s.50 Saluting	1·00	35
868	10s. Playing basketball	1·80	75
MS869	78×60 mm. Nos. 867/8	3·75	4·00

126 Limes

1974. Fruits. Sheet 128×113 mm containing T 126 and similar vert designs. Multicoloured.

MS870	(a) 4s. Type **126**; (b) 4s. Oranges; (c) 5s. Bananas; (d) 5s. Mangoes; (e) 12s. Pineapple	6·50	6·50

127 Chimpanzee

1975. Wild Animals. Multicoloured.

871	1s. Type **127**	30	10
872	2s. Impala	45	25
873	3s. Warthog	55	25
874	4s. Waterbuck	65	30
875	5s. Leopard	95	40
876	6s. Greater kudu	1·10	45
877	6s.50 Common zebra	1·20	55
878	7s.50 African buffalo	1·70	70
879	8s. Hippopotamus	2·40	90
880	10s. Lion	2·75	1·10
881	12s. Black rhinoceros	3·25	1·10
882	15s. African elephant	4·50	1·60
MS883	Three sheets each 96×96 mm. (a) Nos. 871/4; (b) Nos. 875/8; (c) Nos. 879/82 (air). Perf or imperf	37·00	18·00

128 Lion and Lioness beside Pipeline

1975. 10th Anniv of African Development Bank.

884	5s. Type **128**	95	25
885	7s. African elephants beside pipeline	1·20	25
886	10s. Lions beside pipeline (horiz)	1·70	45
887	20s. African elephant and calf beside pipeline (horiz)	3·50	85

129 Women playing Saxophones

1976. Int Women's Year (1975). Mult.

888	5s. Type **129**	55	25
889	7s. Women playing guitars	95	30
890	9s. Woman railway shunter	1·50	40
891	15s. Woman doctor	2·20	75
892	20s. Genetics emblems	2·75	1·10
MS893	Two sheets. (a) 70×82 mm. No. 891; (b) 90×125 mm. No. 892×4	16·00	10·50

130 Gymnastics

1976. Olympic Games, Montreal. Mult.

894	3s. Type **130**	45	10
895	4s. Long jump	55	25
896	5s. Throwing the hammer	55	25
897	6s. Throwing the discus	75	25
898	6s.50 Hurdling	80	25
899	7s. Throwing the javelin	95	40
900	8s. Running	1·00	40
901	8s.50 Cycling	1·50	40
902	10s. High-jumping	1·60	55
903	15s. Putting the shot	2·40	85
904	20s. Pole vaulting	3·25	1·10
905	25s. Football	4·00	1·30
MS906	Two sheets. (a) 82×62 mm. 25s. Swimming; (b) 82×112 mm. No. 905×4	22·00	16·00

131 Bell and Early Telephone

1976. Telephone Centenary. Multicoloured.

907	5s. Type **131**	75	15
908	7s. Bell and wall telephone	1·00	25
909	12s. Bell and satellite "Syncom"	1·70	55
910	15s. Bell and satellite "Telstar"	2·50	80
MS911	Two sheets. (a) 70×58 mm. 15s. Bell and telephonist; (b) 110×93 mm. Nos. 907/10	10·00	5·25

132 "Collybia fusipes"

1977. Mushrooms. Multicoloured.

912	5s. Type **132** (postage)	1·70	35
913	7s. "Lycoperdon perlatum"	2·50	40
914	9s. "Boletus edulis"	3·25	65
915	9s.50 "Lactarius deliciosus"	3·50	80
916	11s.50 "Agaricus campestris"	5·00	1·40
917	10s. "Morchella esculenta" (air)	3·50	90
918	12s. "Lepiota procera"	4·75	1·20
919	15s. "Cantharellus cibarius"	6·75	1·70
MS920	115×86 mm. Nos. 912 and 914	7·25	3·75

133 Duplex Murex

1977. Sea Shells. Multicoloured.

921	1s. Type **133**	20	10
922	2s. Wavy-leaved turrid	45	20
923	4s. Queen marginella	1·00	40
924	5s. "Tympanotonos radula"	1·30	45
925	7s. Striped marginella	1·80	50
926	8s. Doris harp	2·10	60
927	10s. Obtuse demoulia	2·75	80
928	20s. Pitted frog shell	5·00	90
929	25s. Adanson's marginella	6·25	1·50

Nos. 927/9 are 50×34 mm.

134 President Sekou Toure

1977. 30th Anniv of Guinean Democratic Party (PDG). Multicoloured.

930	5s. Type **134**	75	25
931	10s. Labourers and oxen	1·20	55
932	20s. Soldier driving tractor	3·00	90
933	25s. Pres. Toure addressing U.N. General Assembly	3·50	1·60
934	30s. Pres. Toure (vert)	4·50	1·80
935	40s. As 30s.	5·50	2·20
MS936	Two sheets. (a) 121×97 mm. Nos. 930/933; (b) 96×76 mm. Nos. 934/935	23·00	21·00

135 "Varanus niloticus"

1977. Reptiles. Multicoloured.

937	3s. Type **135** (postage)	45	15
938	4s. "Hyperolius quinquevittatus"	55	20
939	5s. "Uromastix"	70	25
940	6s. "Scincus scincus"	1·10	45
941	6s.50 "Agama agama"	1·40	50
942	7s. "Naja melanoleuca"	1·90	60
943	8s.50 "Python regius"	2·30	80
944	20s. "Bufo mauritanicus"	5·75	1·10
945	10s. "Chamaeleo diepis" (air)	3·25	60
946	15s. "Crocodylus niloticus"	4·75	80
947	25s. "Testudo elegans"	6·75	1·30

136 Eland (male)

1977. Endangered Animals. Multicoloured.

948	1s. Type **136** (postage)	30	10
949	1s. Eland (female)	30	10
950	1s. Eland (young)	30	10
951	2s. Chimpanzee (young)	45	10
952	2s. Chimpanzee	45	10
953	2s. Chimpanzee sitting	45	10
954	2s.50 African elephant	70	25
955	2s.50 African elephant	70	25
956	2s.50 African elephant	70	25
957	3s. Lion	95	25
958	3s. Lioness	95	25
959	3s. Lion Cub	95	25
960	4s. Indian palm squirrel	1·30	25
961	4s. Indian palm squirrel	1·30	25
962	4s. Indian palm squirrel	1·30	25
963	5s. Hippopotamus	1·80	30
964	5s. Hippopotamus	1·80	30
965	5s. Hippopotamus	1·90	30
966	5s. Type **136** (air)	1·30	30
967	5s. As No. 949	1·30	30
968	5s. As No. 950	1·30	30
969	8s. As No. 954	1·90	35
970	8s. As No. 955	1·90	35
971	8s. As No. 956	2·00	35
972	9s. As No. 963	2·20	50
973	9s. As No. 964	2·20	50
974	9s. As No. 965	2·20	50
975	10s. As No. 951	2·50	55
976	10s. As No. 952	2·50	55
977	10s. As No. 953	2·50	55
978	12s. As No. 960	2·75	70
979	12s. As No. 961	2·75	70
980	12s. As No. 962	2·75	70
981	13s. As No. 957	3·25	90
982	13s. As No. 958	3·25	95
983	13s. As No. 959	3·25	95

Issued se-tenant in strips of three within the sheet, each strip showing different views of the same animal.

137 Lenin taking Parade in Red Square, Moscow

1976. 60th Anniv of Russian Revolution. Multicoloured.

984	2s.50 Lenin's first speech in Moscow (postage)	45	10
985	5s. Lenin addressing revolutionary crowd	95	25
986	7s.50 Lenin with militiamen	1·50	30
987	8s. Type **137**	1·80	35
988	10s. Russian ballet (air)	3·00	60
989	30s. Pushkin Monument	6·75	1·30

138 Pres. Giscard d'Estaing at Microphones

1979. Visit of President Giscard d'Estaing of France.

990	138	3s. brown and light brown (postage)	50	15
991	-	5s. brown, green and deep green	1·00	20
992	-	6s.50 brown, mauve and deep mauve	1·50	25
993	-	7s. brown, light blue and blue	1·80	30
994	-	8s.50 brown, rose & red	2·50	55
995	-	10s. brown, light violet and violet	3·00	90
996	-	20s. brown, green and deep green	5·75	1·20
997	-	25s. multicoloured (air)	7·25	1·70

DESIGNS—HORIZ: 5s. President Giscard d'Estaing and Sekou Toure in conference; 6s.50, Presidents signing agreement; 7s. Presidents at official meeting; 8s.50, Presidents with their wives; 10s. Presidents in conference; 20s. Toasting the agreement. VERT: 25s. President Giscard d'Estaing.

139 "20,000 Leagues Under the Sea"

1979. 150th Birth Anniv (1978) of Jules Verne. Multicoloured.

998	1s. Type **139** (postage)	10	10
999	3s. "The Children of Captain Grant"	45	10
1000	5s. "The Mysterious Island"	95	30
1001	7s. "A Captain of Fifteen Years"	1·50	55
1002	10s. "The Amazing Adventure of Barsac"	2·00	80
1003	20s. "Five Weeks in a Balloon" (air)	3·00	55
1004	25s. "Robur the Conqueror"	4·50	80

140 William Henson's "Aerial Steam Carriage", 1842

1979. Aviation History. Multicoloured.

1005	3s. Type **140**	45	10
1006	5s. Wright Type A (inscr "Flyer I"), 1903	75	25
1007	6s.50 Caudron C-460, 1934	95	25
1008	7s. Charles Lindbergh's "Spirit of St. Louis", 1927	1·30	25
1009	8s.50 Bristol Beaufighter, 1940	1·70	40
1010	10s. Bleriot XI, 1909	2·10	40
1011	20s. Boeing 727-100, 1963	3·75	80
1012	20s. Concorde	3·75	80

141 Hafla Football Team

1979. Hafla Football Club's Victories. Mult.

1013	1s. Type **141**	10	10
1014	2s. Team members with cup (vert)	30	10
1015	5s. President Toure presenting medals	75	10
1016	7s. President Toure presenting cup (vert)	1·20	40
1017	8s. Ahmed Sekou Toure Cup (vert)	1·60	40
1018	10s. Team captains shaking hands (vert)	1·70	65
1019	20s. The winning goal	3·50	1·20

142 Children dancing round Tree

1980. International Year of the Child. Mult.

1020	2s. Type **142**	30	10
1021	4s. "Heureuse Enfance"	55	10
1022	5s. Steam train (horiz)	95	30
1023	7s. Village (horiz)	1·10	25
1024	10s. Boy climbing tree (horiz)	1·70	40
1025	25s. Children of different races (horiz)	4·25	1·00

143 Buckler Dory

1980. Fishes. Multicoloured.

1026	1s. Robust butterflyfish (horiz)	10	10
1027	2s. Blue-pointed porgy (horiz)	30	10
1028	3s. Type **143**	55	10
1029	4s. African hind (horiz)	75	25
1030	5s. Spotted seahorse	95	30
1031	6s. Marine hatchetfish (horiz)	1·20	25
1032	7s. Half-banded snake-eel (horiz)	1·50	25
1033	8s. Flying gurnard	1·70	25
1034	9s. West African squirrel-fish (horiz)	2·00	25
1035	10s. Guinean fingerfish	2·50	25
1036	12s. African sergeant major (horiz)	3·50	60
1037	15s. West African trigger-fish (horiz)	5·00	85

144 Rocket on Launch Pad

1980. 10th Anniv of 1st Moon Landing. Mult.

1038	1s. Type **144**	10	10
1039	2s. Earth from the Moon	30	10
1040	4s. Armstrong descending from lunar module	45	10
1041	5s. Armstrong on the Moon	75	25
1042	7s. Astronaut collecting samples	95	25
1043	8s. Parachute descent	1·50	40
1044	12s. Winching capsule aboard recovery vessel	2·40	60
1045	20s. Astronauts	4·50	85

145 Dome of the Rock

1981. Palestinian Solidarity.

1046	145	8s. multicoloured	1·40	55
1047	145	11s. multicoloured	2·50	95

146 Map of Member States and Agricultural Produce

1982. 5th Anniv of Economic Community of West African States. Multicoloured.

1048	6s. Type **146**	1·20	40
1049	7s. Transport	1·50	55
1050	9s. Heavy industry	2·00	75

147 Ataturk as Soldier

1982. Birth Centenary of Kemal Ataturk (Turkish statesman). Multicoloured.

1051	7s. Type **147** (postage)	1·20	40
1052	10s. Ataturk as statesman	1·70	55
1053	25s. Equestrian statue (horiz)	5·00	1·20
1054	25s. As No. 1053 (air)	5·50	1·00

148 Football

1982. Olympic Games, Moscow. Multicoloured.

1055	1s. Type **148** (postage)	10	10
1056	2s. Basketball	30	10
1057	3s. Diving	45	10
1058	4s. Gymnastics	55	10
1059	5s. Boxing	95	25
1060	6s. High jumping	1·20	25
1061	7s. Running	1·30	40
1062	8s. Long jumping	2·00	60
1063	9s. Fencing (air)	1·70	25
1064	10s. Football (vert)	1·80	45
1065	11s. Basketball (vert)	2·00	60
1066	20s. Diving (vert)	4·25	75
1067	25s. Boxing (vert)	5·00	90

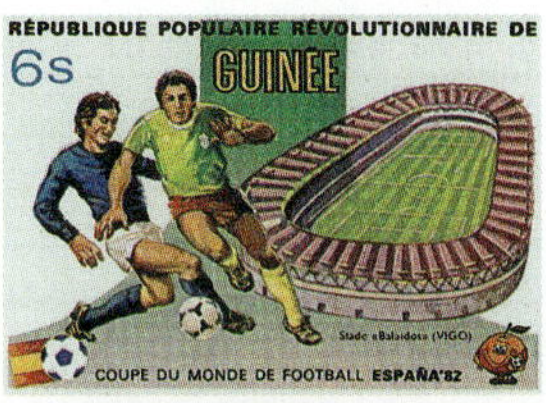

149 Balaidos Stadium, Vigo

1982. World Cup Football Championship, Spain. Football Stadia. Mult.

1068	6s. Type **149** (postage)	95	10
1069	8s. El Molinon, Gijon	1·50	25
1070	9s. San Mames, Bilbao	2·00	50
1071	10s. Sanchez Pizjuan, Seville	2·20	65
1072	10s. Luis Casanova, Valencia (air)	2·75	80
1073	20s. Nou Camp, Barcelona	4·50	1·10
1074	25s. Santiago Bernabeu, Madrid	6·50	1·50

150 Wrestling

1983. Olympic Games, Los Angeles. Multicoloured.

1075	5s. Type **150** (postage)	1·10	30
1076	7s. Weightlifting	1·40	50
1077	10s. Gymnastics	2·10	75
1078	15s. Discus	3·00	1·10
1079	20s. Kayak (air)	4·00	1·10
1080	25s. Equestrian	5·25	1·40
MS1081	89×89 mm. 30s. Running	4·50	1·60

See also Nos. 843/9.

151 Marquis d'Arlandes, Pilatre de Rozier and Montgolfier Balloon, 1783

1983. Bicentenary of Manned Flight. Mult.

1082	5s. Type **151** (postage)	75	25
1083	7s. Jean-Francois Pilatre de Rozier and Montgolfier balloon "Marie Antoinette", 1784	1·00	40
1084	10s. Henri Dupuy de Lome and airship, 1872 (horiz)	1·50	55
1085	15s. Major A. Parseval and "Airship No. 1", 1906 (horiz)	2·30	90
1086	20s. Count Zeppelin and airship "Bodensee", 1919 (horiz) (air)	2·75	90
1087	25s. Balloon "Double Eagle II" and crew, 1978	3·50	1·30
MS1088	81×81 mm. 30s. Nadar and "Le Geant", 1863, and Santos Dumont and his dirigible, 1919 (horiz 50×41 mm)	4·50	1·60

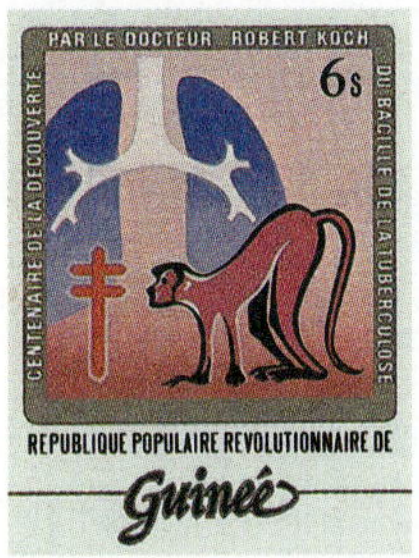

152 Lungs and Monkey

1983. Centenary of Discovery of Tubercle Bacillus. Multicoloured.

1089	6s. Type **152**	1·40	35
1090	10s. Cow	2·30	50
1091	11s. Robert Koch and microscope	2·40	65
1092	12s. Koch using microscope	2·50	80
1093	15s. Laboratory	3·50	1·00
1094	20s. Scientist with test tube and monkey	4·75	1·30
1095	25s. Doctor examining young boy	6·00	1·60

153 Disabled and Emblem

1983. International Year of Disabled Persons.

1096	**153**	10s. multicoloured	2·75	1·30
1097	**153**	20s. multicoloured	5·75	2·00

154 Mosque, Conakry

1983. 25th Anniv of Independence.

1098	**154**	1s. multicoloured (postage)	15	10
1099	**154**	2s. multicoloured	45	25
1100	**154**	5s. multicoloured	1·10	45
1101	**154**	10s. multicoloured	2·00	65
MS1102		86×109 mm. **154** 25s. multicoloured (air)	4·00	1·70

155 Citizens with Scrolls

1983. 10th Anniv of Mano River Union. Multicoloured.

1103	2s. Type **155** (postage)	35	10
1104	7s. Union emblem	95	40
1105	8s. Map and presidents of Guinea, Sierra Leone and Liberia	1·00	50
1106	10s. Signing the Declaration of Union	1·50	60
MS1107	83×72 mm. 20s. As No. 1106 (air)	3·00	1·70

156 Biathlon

1983. Winter Olympic Games, Sarajevo. Mult.

1108	5s. Type **156** (postage)	75	25
1109	7s. Luge	95	40
1110	10s. Slalom	1·50	55
1111	15s. Speed skating	2·20	80
1112	20s. Ski jump (air)	2·50	75
1113	25s. Ice dancing	3·25	1·20
MS1114	90×90 mm. 30s. Ice Hockey	4·50	1·60

157 Raphael and "Virgin with the Blue Diadem"

1984. Anniversaries (1983). Multicoloured.

1115	5s. Type **157**	75	25
1116	7s. Rubens and "Holy Family"	95	40
1117	10s. Rembrandt and "Portrait of Saskia"	1·80	55
1118	15s. Goethe and scene from "The Young Werther"	2·00	80
1119	20s. Lord Baden-Powell and scout camp	2·75	75
1120	25s. P. P. Harris and speaker at Rotary meeting	3·00	1·20
MS1121	69×90 mm. 30s. John Kennedy and first moon landing	5·00	1·50

158 Abraham Lincoln

1984. Personalities. Multicoloured.

1122	5s. Type **158** (postage)	55	15
1123	7s. Jean-Henri Dunant (founder of Red Cross)	95	35
1124	10s. Gottlieb Daimler (automobile designer)	1·50	45
1125	15s. Louis Bleriot (pilot)	2·30	65
1126	20s. Paul P. Harris (founder of Rotary Club) (air)	2·75	80
1127	25s. Auguste Piccard (ocean explorer)	3·25	1·20
MS1128	100×70 mm. 30s. Anatoli Karpov (world chess champion)	5·25	1·60

159 "The Mystic Marriage of Sts. Catherine and Sebastian" (detail, Correggio)

1984. Paintings. Multicoloured.

1129	5s. Type **159** (postage)	60	15
1130	7s. "The Holy Family" (A. Durer)	1·00	35
1131	10s. "The Veiled Lady" (Raphael)	1·70	45
1132	15s. "Portrait of a Young Man" (A. Durer)	2·50	65
1133	20s. "Portrait of Soutine" (A. Modigliani) (air)	3·00	1·00
1134	25s. "The Esterhazy Madonna" (Raphael)	3·75	1·30
MS1135	77×100 mm. 30s. "Madonna dell Impannata" (Raphael)	5·50	1·60

160 Congo River Steamer and Canoe

1984. Transport. Multicoloured.

1136	5s. Type **160** (postage)	95	30
1137	7s. Airship "Graf Zeppelin"	1·10	40
1138	10s. Daimler car, 1886	2·30	60
1139	15s. Beyer-Garratt steam locomotive	2·50	85
1140	20s. Latecoere seaplane "Comte de la Vaulx" (air)	2·75	90
1141	25s. Savoia Marchetti S-73 airplane	3·25	1·30
MS1142	101×95 mm. 30s. "B" locomotive (46×37 mm)	5·50	1·80

161 W. Hoppe and D. Schauerhammer (bobsleigh)

1984. Winter Olympic Gold Medal Winners. Multicoloured.

1143	5s. Type **161** (postage)	55	25
1144	7s. T. L. Wassberg (cross- country skiing)	85	25
1145	10s. G. Boucher (speed skating)	1·40	55
1146	15s. K. Witt (ladies figure skating)	2·00	75
1147	20s. W. D. Johnson (downhill skiing) (air)	2·75	1·00
1148	25s. U.S.S.R. (ice hockey)	3·25	1·20
MS1149	97×82 mm. 30s. J. Weissflog (ski jumping)	5·00	1·60

162 T. Ruiz and C. Costie (Synchronized Swimming Duet)

1985. Olympic Games Gold Medal Winners. Multicoloured.

1150	5s. Type **162** (postage)	55	25
1151	7s. R. Klimke, H. Krug and U. Sauer, West Germany (team dressage)	85	25
1152	10s. McKee and Buchan, U.S.A. (sailing, "Flying Dutchman" class)	1·40	55
1153	15s. Mark Todd (equestrian three-day event)	2·00	75
1154	20s. Daley Thompson (decathlon) (air)	2·75	1·00

1155	25s. M. Smith, C. Homfeld, L. Burr and J. Fargis, U.S.A. (equestrian team jumping)	3·25	1·20
MS1156	78×78 mm. 30s. Carl Lewis (100, 200 metres, 4×100 metres relay and long jump)	5·75	1·60

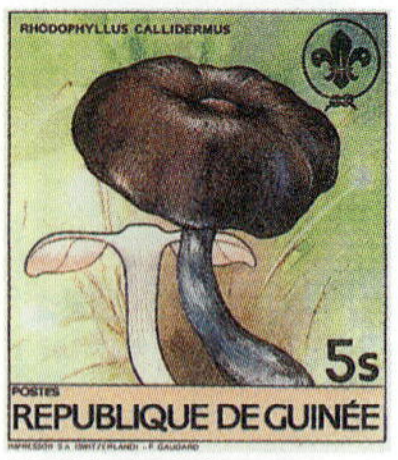

163 "Rhodophyllus callidermus"

1985. Fungi. Multicoloured.

1157	5s. Type **163** (postage)	1·00	35
1158	7s. "Agaricus niger"	1·60	50
1159	10s. "Thermitomyces globulus"	2·20	80
1160	15s. "Amanita robusta"	3·00	1·10
1161	20s. "Lepiota subradicans" (air)	3·75	1·40
1162	25s. "Cantharellus rhodophylus"	4·75	1·90
MS1163	69×93 mm. 30s. "Phlebopus silvaticus"	5·25	1·90

164 Hermann Oberth and 2-Stage Conical Motor Rocket

1985. Space Achievements. Multicoloured.

1164	7s. Type **164** (postage)	75	25
1165	10s. "Lunik 1"	1·50	50
1166	15s. "Lunik 2" on Moon, 1959	2·00	65
1167	20s. "Lunik 3" photographing hidden face of Moon	2·75	85
1168	30s. Armstrong, Aldrin and Collins (first manned landing on Moon) (air)	4·25	1·10
1169	35s. Sally Ride (first American woman in space)	5·00	1·40
MS1170	76×94 mm. 50s. Recovering "Palapa V2" satellite	6·75	2·20

165 Maimonides in Jewish Quarter (850th birth anniv)

1985. Anniversaries and Events. Multicoloured.

1171	7s. Type **165** (postage)	85	25
1172	10s. Christopher Columbus departing from Palos, 1492	1·50	45
1173	15s. Frederic Bartholdi and Statue of Liberty (centenary)	2·00	60
1174	20s. Queen Mother with Duke of York and Princess Elizabeth (85th birthday)	2·75	85
1175	30s. Ulf Merbold and space shuttle "Columbia" (air)	4·00	1·00
1176	35s. Prince Charles and Lady Diana Spencer (Royal Wedding)	4·50	1·20
MS1177	95×80 mm. 50s. Prince and Princess of Wales with their children	5·75	2·30

166 Black-billed Cuckoo

1995. Birth Bicentenary of John J. Audubon (ornithologist). Multicoloured.

1178	7s. Type **166** (postage)	1·00	35
1179	10s. Carolina parakeet	1·60	50
1180	15s. American darter (vert)	2·10	75
1181	20s. Red-shouldered hawk	3·00	1·00
1182	30s. Eastern screech owl (air)	4·00	1·20
1183	35s. Brown thrasher (vert)	5·00	1·60
MS1184	64×83 mm. 50s. Mourning dove (wrongly inscr "Zenaidura")	7·50	2·30

167 Blue-point Siamese

1985. Cats and Dogs. Multicoloured.

1185	7s. Type **167** (postage)	95	30
1186	10s. Cocker spaniel	1·50	50
1187	15s. Poodles	2·30	70
1188	20s. Persian blue cat	3·00	85
1189	25s. European tortoiseshell cat	4·00	1·00
1190	30s. German shepherd dog (air)	4·25	1·20
1191	35s. Abyssinian cats	4·75	1·50
1192	40s. Boxer dog	5·50	1·80
MS1193	100×60 mm. 50s. Pyrenean mountain dog and Chartreux cat (49×28 mm)	7·25	2·20

168 Bebeto and Footballers

1985. World Cup Football Championship, Mexico (1986) (1st issue). Multicoloured.

1194	7s. Type **168** (postage)	85	30
1195	10s. Rinat Dassaev	1·50	50
1196	15s. Phil Neal	2·10	75
1197	20s. Jean Tigana	3·00	95
1198	30s. Fernando Chalana (air)	3·75	1·30
1199	35s. Michel Platini	4·75	1·60
MS1200	90×90 mm. 50s. Karl Heinz Rummenigge (49×29 mm)	6·75	2·10

See also Nos. 1268/**MS**1272.

1985. Air. Nos. 1126 and 1119/20 optd.

1201	20s. **80e ANNIVERSAIRE 1905 1985** (1126)	2·50	1·10
1202	20s. **Rassemblement Jamb-ville-1985** (1119)	2·50	1·10
1203	25s. **80e ANNIVERSAIRE 1905 1985** (1120)	3·50	1·50

1985. Nos. 1157/62 surch.

1205	1s. on 5s. Type **163** (postage)	35	10
1206	2s. on 7s. "Agaricus niger"	75	25
1207	8s. on 10s. "Thermitomyces globulus"	2·10	50
1208	30s. on 15s. "Amanita robusta"	6·00	1·20
1209	35s. on 20s. "Lepiota subradicans" (air)	7·00	1·80
1210	40s. on 25s. "Cantharellus rhodophyllus"	8·25	2·50
MS1211	69×93 mm. 50s. on 30s. "Phlebopus silvaticus"	8·75	2·75

171 Class 8 F Locomotive

1985. Trains (1st series). Multicoloured.

1212	7s. Type **171** (postage)	1·10	40
1213	15s. Class III electric locomotive, Germany	2·30	80
1214	25s. Pacific steam locomotive No. 270	3·50	1·20
1215	35s. German electric commuter train Series 420 (air)	5·00	1·80
MS1216	99×88 mm. 50s. "ICE", German high speed train	7·25	2·50

Nos. 1213 and 1215/**MS**1216 commemorate 150th anniv of German railways.

See also Nos. 1252/5.

172 Columbus and "Pinta"

1985. 480th Death Anniv of Christopher Columbus (explorer) (1st issue). Multicoloured.

1217	10s. Type **172** (postage)	1·50	50
1218	20s. "Santa Maria"	3·00	1·00
1219	30s. "Nina" (air)	4·00	1·30
1220	40s. "Santa Maria" and crow's nest	5·75	1·80
MS1221	99×88 mm. 50s. Columbus and "Nina"	7·25	2·40

See also Nos. 1257/**MS**1261.

173 Chopin, aged Eight, playing Piano

1986. International Youth Year. Multicoloured.

1222	10s. Type **173** (postage)	1·50	45
1223	20s. Sandro Botticelli and "Birth of Venus"	3·00	95
1224	35s. Gioachino Antonio Rossini, aged 15, conducting orchestra	4·50	1·50
1225	25s. Pablo Picasso and "Paul as Harlequin" (air)	3·75	1·30
MS1226	100×75 mm. 50s. Michelangelo and Doni Tondo (horiz)	7·25	2·40

174 Bayeux Tapestry

1986. Appearance of Halley's Comet. Multicoloured.

1227	5f. Type **174** (postage)	10	10
1228	30f. Comet as seen by the Arabs	30	10
1229	40f. Comet as seen by Montezuma II	45	25
1230	50f. Edmond Halley and trajectory diagram	55	25
1231	300f. Halley and Sir Isaac Newton (air)	2·75	85
1232	500f. Comet, Earth, sun, "Giotto", Soviet and N.A.S.A. space probes	4·50	1·50
MS1233	95×65 mm. 600f. Medal (wrongly inscr Sir Edmund), comet and "Giotto" space probe	6·25	2·10

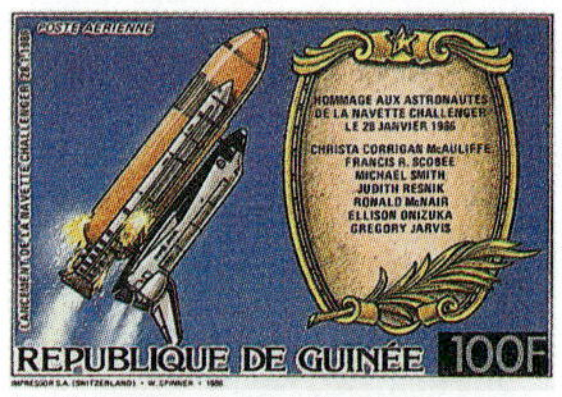

175 "Challenger" Space Shuttle Memorial Roll

1986. Air. "Challenger" Astronauts Commem. Multicoloured.

1234	100f. Type **175**	1·00	50
1235	170f. Shuttle diagram and Christa McAuliffe holding model	1·70	75
MS1236	65×95 mm. 600f. Shuttle lifting off	6·25	2·10

1986. Various stamps surch. (a) Nos. 1212/15 (Trains).

1237	2f. on 7s. multicoloured	25	10
1238	25f. on 15s. multicoloured	45	20
1239	50f. on 25s. multicoloured	80	30
1240	90f. on 35s. multicoloured	1·40	55
MS1241	99×88 mm. 500f. on 50s. multicoloured	5·25	2·40

(b) Nos. 1217/20 (Columbus).

1242	5f. on 10s. multicoloured	20	20
1243	35f. on 20s. multicoloured	65	45
1244	70f. on 30s. multicoloured	95	30
1245	200f. on 40s. multicoloured	2·40	85
MS1246	99×88 mm. 500f. on 50s. multicoloured	6·00	2·40

(c) Nos. 1222/5 (International Youth Year).

1247	5f. on 10s. mult (postage)	30	10
1248	35f. on 20s. multicoloured	50	25
1249	90f. on 35s. multicoloured	1·30	45
1250	50f. on 25s. mult (air)	60	25
MS1251	100×75 mm. 500f. on 50s. multicoloured	6·00	2·75

177 Dietrich Autorail Diesel Railcar

1986. Trains (2nd series). Multicoloured.

1252	20f. Type **177** (postage)	30	10
1253	100f. Class T.13 steam locomotive No. 7906, Prussia	1·00	25
1254	300f. German steam locomotive No. 01220	2·75	90
1255	400f. Autorail ABH-3 type 5020 diesel train (air)	4·00	1·30
MS1256	87×67 mm. 600f. Renault Autorail ABH 3 and "Adler"	6·25	1·80

Nos. 1253/4 and **MS**1256 were inscr for the 150th Anniv of German railways.

178 Building Fort Navidad and Map of First Voyage, 1492–93

1986. 480th Death Anniv of Christopher Columbus (explorer) (2nd issue). Multicoloured.

1257	40f. Type **178** (postage)	45	15
1258	70f. Disembarking at Hispaniola and map of second voyage, 1493–96	75	35
1259	200f. Columbus on deck with natives and map of third voyage, 1498–1500	2·00	65
1260	500f. Columbus and crew with natives and map of fourth voyage, 1502–04 (air)	5·50	1·60
MS1261	87×67 mm. 600f. Columbus before King Ferdinand of Spain	6·25	1·80

179 Prince and Princess of Wales and Prince William

1986. Celebrities. Multicoloured.

1262	30f. Type **179** (postage)	35	10
1263	40f. Alain Prost (1985 Formula I world champion)	75	10
1264	100f. Duke and Duchess of York	1·10	40
1265	300f. Elvis Presley (entertainer)	3·50	1·00
1266	500f. Michael Jackson (entertainer) (air)	5·75	1·80
MS1267	109×79 mm. 600f. Marcel Dassault (aircraft engineer) and airplane (47×35 mm)	7·50	2·75

180 Pfaff, Trophy and Satellite

1986. World Cup Football Championship, Mexico (2nd issue). Multicoloured.

1268	100f. Type **180** (postage)	95	25
1269	300f. Michel Platini	2·75	80
1270	400f. Matthaus	3·50	1·20
1271	500f. Diego Maradona (air)	4·50	1·30
MS1272	103×88 mm. 600f. Maradona holding trophy (50×41 mm)	6·25	1·80

181 Judo

1987. Olympic Games, Seoul (1988). Mult.

1273	20f. Type **181** (postage)	30	10
1274	30f. High jumping	30	10
1275	40f. Handball	45	25
1276	100f. Gymnastics	95	30
1277	300f. Javelin throwing (air)	2·75	80
1278	500f. Showjumping	4·75	1·40
MS1279	71×99 mm. 600f. Satellite, stadium and Pierre de Coubertin (founder of modern Olympic Games)	6·25	1·80

182 Rifle shooting

1987. Winter Olympic Games, Calgary (1988) (1st issue). Multicoloured.

1280	50f. on 40f. Type **182** (postage)	45	10
1281	100f. Cross-country skiing	95	25
1282	400f. Ski jumping (air)	4·00	95
1283	500f. Two-man bobsleigh	4·50	1·20
MS1284	116×81 mm. 600f. Women's figure skating and satellite	6·25	1·80

183 Skiing

1987. Winter Olympic Games, Calgary (1988) (2nd issue). Multicoloured.

1285	25f. Type **183** (postage)	30	10
1286	50f. Ice hockey	45	25
1287	100f. Men's figure skating	95	30
1288	150f. Slalom	1·40	40
1289	300f. Speed skating (air)	2·50	75
1290	500f. Four-man bobsleigh	4·50	1·40
MS1291	79×68 mm. 600f. Ski-jumping	6·25	1·80

184 S. K. Doe, Gen. Lansana Conte, Gen. J. Momoh and National Flags

1987. 10th Anniv of River Mano Reconciliation.

1292	**184**	40f. multicoloured	40	15
1293	**184**	50f. multicoloured	50	20
1294	**184**	75f. multicoloured	75	30
1295	**184**	100f. multicoloured	1·00	40
1296	**184**	150f. multicoloured	1·50	55

185 Dimetrodon

1987. Prehistoric Animals. Multicoloured.

1297	50f. Type **185** (postage)	80	20
1298	100f. Iguanodon	1·70	50
1299	200f. Tylosaurus	3·25	85
1300	300f. Cave bear	4·50	1·30
1301	400f. Sabre-tooth tiger (air)	5·00	1·00
1302	500f. Stegosaurus	6·00	1·20
MS1303	124×78 mm. 600f. Triceratops	7·25	2·10

186 Statue and Portrait of Marquis de Lafayette (revolutionary)

1987. Celebrities. Multicoloured.

1304	50f. Type **186** (230th birth anniv) (postage)	45	10
1305	100f. Ettore Bugatti (motor manufacturer) (40th death anniv) and "White Elephant"	95	50
1306	200f. Gary Kasparov (world chess champion) and game diagram of Kasparov v. Karpov, 1986	2·00	60
1307	300f. Flag and George Washington (first U.S. President) (bicentenary of American constitution)	2·75	90
1308	400f. Boris Becker (tennis player) (air)	3·50	95
1309	500f. Winston Churchill (statesman)	4·50	1·20

187 Towers, Chicago, Capitol, Washington and Statue of Liberty, New York (image scaled to 55% of original size)

1987. Air. International Cardiology congress, Chicago, Washington. and New York. Sheet 136×92 mm.

MS1310	**187** 1500f. multicoloured	14·00	3·75

188 Tennis Player and Emblem

1987. Olympic Games, Seoul (1988). Tennis.

1311	**188**	50f. mult (postage)	45	10
1312	-	100f. multicoloured	95	30
1313	-	150f. multicoloured	1·40	45
1314	-	200f. multicoloured	1·80	55
1315	-	300f. multicoloured (air)	2·75	85
1316	-	500f. multicoloured	4·75	1·30
MS1317		95×70 mm. 600f. multicoloured (35×41 mm)	6·25	1·80

DESIGNS: 100f. to 600f. Various tennis players.

189 Discus thrower and Courtyard of Hospital of the Holy Cross and St. Paul

1987. Olympic Games, Barcelona (1992). Multicoloured.

1318	50f. Type **189** (postage)	45	10
1319	100f. Statue of Pablo Casals (cellist) and pole vaulter	95	30
1320	150f. Long jumper and Labyrinth of Horta	1·40	45
1321	170f. Lizard in Guell Park and javelin thrower	1·80	55
1322	400f. Gymnast and Church of Mercy (air)	3·75	1·00
1323	500f. Tennis player and Picasso Museum	4·75	1·50
MS1324	105×82 mm. 600f. Runner and Miro tapestry (41×50 mm)	6·25	1·80

190 African Wild Dogs

1987. Endangered Wildlife. Multicoloured.

1325	50f. Type **190** (postage)	1·20	30
1326	70f. African wild dog	1·40	45
1327	100f. African wild dogs stalking prey	1·80	60
1328	170f. African wild dog chasing prey	2·40	90
1329	400f. South African crowned cranes (air)	4·50	1·10
1330	500f. Giant eland	5·50	1·40
MS1331	83×72 mm. 600f. Savanna monkeys (41×35 mm)	7·25	2·10

191 "Galaxy"–"Grasp"

1988. Space Exploration. Multicoloured.

1332	50f. Type **191** (postage)	45	10
1333	150f. "Energia"–"Mir" link-up	1·50	25
1334	200f. NASA space station	2·00	40
1335	300f. "Ariane-5" rocket depositing satellite payload	3·00	75
1336	400f. Mars "Rover" space vehicle (air)	3·75	95
1337	450f. Venus "Vega" space probe	4·25	1·20
MS1338	108×81 mm. 500f. Mars "Phobos" space probe (41×35 mm)	5·00	1·80

192 Red-headed Bluebill

1988. Scouts, Birds and Butterflies. Designs showing scouts studying featured animals. Multicoloured.

1339	50f. Type **192** (postage)	50	10
1340	100f. "Medon nymphalidae" (butterfly)	1·00	35
1341	150f. Red bishop	1·50	50
1342	300f. Beautiful sunbird	3·00	80
1343	400f. "Sophia nymphalidae" (butterfly) (air)	4·25	1·10
1344	450f. "Rumia nymphalidae" (butterfly)	4·75	1·40
MS1345	116×88 mm. 750f. "Opus nymphalidae" (butterfly) and rose-ringed parakeet	7·25	2·30

193 Queen Elizabeth II and Prince Philip

1988. Celebrities. Multicoloured.

1346	200f. Type **193** (40th wedding anniv (1987)) (postage)	1·80	45
1347	250f. Fritz von Opel (car designer) and "Rak 2 Opel", 1928	2·30	55
1348	300f. Wolfgang Amadeus Mozart (composer)	3·75	80
1349	400f. Steffi Graf (tennis player)	3·75	90
1350	450f. Edwin "Buzz" Aldrin (astronaut) (air)	4·00	1·00
1351	500f. Paul Harris (founder of Rotary International)	4·75	1·20
MS1352	101×77 mm. 750f. Thomas Jefferson (US President) (41×35 mm)	6·75	2·00

194 Vreni Schneider (Women's Slalom and Giant Slalom)

1988. Calgary Winter Olympic Games Gold Medal Winners. Multicoloured.

1353	50f. Type **194** (postage)	45	10
1354	150f. Matti Nykaenen (Ski jumping)	1·40	45
1355	250f. Marina Kiehl (Women's downhill)	2·30	60
1356	400f. Frank Piccard (Men's super giant slalom)	3·50	90
1357	100f. Frank-Peter Roetsch (Biathlon) (air)	95	40
1358	450f. Katarina Witt (Women's figure skating)	4·00	1·20
MS1359	90×66 mm. 750f. Pirmin Zurbriggen (Men's downhill)	7·25	2·00

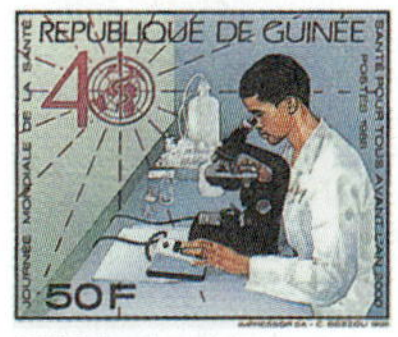

195 Scientist using Microscope

1988. World Health Day. Multicoloured.

1360	50f. Type **195**	45	10
1361	150f. Nurse vaccinating boy	1·50	40
1362	500f. Dental check	4·50	1·30

196 Baron Pierre de Coubertin (founder of modern Olympics)

1988. International Olympic Committee.

1363	**196**	50f. multicoloured	45	10
1364	**196**	100f. multicoloured	95	25
1365	**196**	150f. multicoloured	1·50	45
1366	**196**	500f. multicoloured	4·50	1·40

197 Hands exchanging Letter

1988. 25th Anniv of Pan-African Postal Union.

1367	**197**	50f. multicoloured	45	10
1368	**197**	75f. multicoloured	75	25
1369	**197**	100f. multicoloured	95	30
1370	**197**	150f. multicoloured	1·40	45

198 Earth Communications Station

1988. Inauguration of MT 20 International Transmission Centre.

1371	**198**	50f. multicoloured	45	10

1372	**198**	100f. multicoloured	95	30
1373	**198**	150f. multicoloured	1·30	50

199 "Helix Nebular"

1989. Appearance of Halley's Comet. Nebulae. Multicoloured.

1374	100f.+25f. Type **199** (postage)	1·00	25
1375	150f.+25f. Orion	1·50	40
1376	200f.+25f. "The Eagle"	2·00	60
1377	250f.+25f. "Triffid"	2·30	80
1378	300f.+25f. Eta-Carinae (air)	2·75	80
1379	500f.+25f. NGC 2264	5·25	1·20
MS1380	124×99 mm. 750f.+50f. "Horse's Head" and Edmond Halley (astronomer)	7·50	2·00

200 Diving

1989. Olympic Games, Barcelona (1992) (1st issue). Multicoloured.

1381	50f. Type **200** (postage)	55	10
1382	100f. Running (vert)	1·10	25
1383	150f. Shooting	1·70	40
1384	250f. Tennis (vert)	2·75	60
1385	400f. Football (air)	4·50	1·10
1386	500f. Equestrian (dressage) (vert)	5·50	1·30
MS1387	84×99 mm. 750f. Yachting (vert)	7·25	2·00

201 Oath of the Tennis Court and Jean Sylvain Bailly (President of National Assembly)

1989. "Philexfrance 89" Stamp Exhibition and Bicentenary of French Revolution. Mult.

1388	250f. Type **201** (postage)	2·40	65
1389	300f. King addressing the Three Estates and Comte de Mirabeau	3·00	1·00
1390	400f. 18th July 1790 celebrations and Marquis de La Fayette	4·00	1·30
1391	450f. The King's arrest at Varennes and Jerome Petion (first President of the Convention) (air)	4·75	1·40
MS1392	140×103 mm. 750f. Storming of the Bastille and Camille Desmoulins	7·50	2·30

202 Girl carrying Plants

1989. 10th Anniv (1987) of International Fund for Agricultural Development. Campaign for Self-sufficiency. Multicoloured.

1393	25f. Type **202**	30	10
1394	50f. Men irrigating crops	45	10
1395	75f. Family with cattle	75	25
1396	100f. Fishermen	95	25
1397	150f. Harvesting crops	1·50	40
1398	300f. Pumping water	3·00	80

203 Buildings, Vehicles and Envelopes on Map

1989. 15th Anniv of Mano River Union. Mult.

1399		150f. Type **203**	1·80	55
1400		300f. Map and Presidents of member countries	2·75	80

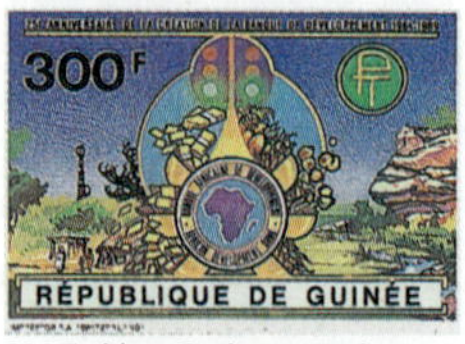

204 Emblem, Banknotes and Produce

1989. 25th Anniv of African Development Bank.

1401	**204**	300f. multicoloured	3·00	1·40

205 Skiing and Super-Tignes

1990. Winter Olympic Games, Albertville (1992). Multicoloured.

1402	150f. Type **205** (postage)	95	30
1403	250f. Cross-country skiing and Le Lavachet	2·30	60
1404	400f. Bobsleighing and Val-Claret	3·75	85
1405	500f. Speed skating and Meribel (air)	4·75	1·40
MS1406	97×71 mm. 750f. Skiing and Albertville	7·00	1·80

206 Presidents Bush and Gorbachev (1989 Summit, Malta)

1990. Multicoloured.

1407	200f. Type **206** (postage)	1·80	45
1408	250f. De Gaulle's appeal to resist, June 1940	3·00	80
1409	300f. Pope Jean-Paul II, President Gorbachev and dove (1989 meeting)	3·00	75
1410	400f. Concorde and TGV Atlantique express train, France	4·25	85
1411	450f. Robin Yount (cent of Baseball) (air)	4·50	1·00
1412	500f. "Galileo" space probe	5·00	1·40
MS1413	83×100 mm. 750f. Crew of "Apollo 11", 1969 (vert)	7·50	2·00

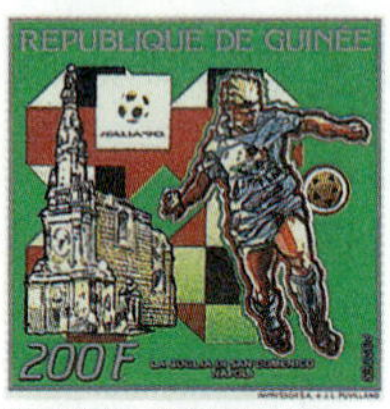

207 St. Dominic's, Naples

1990. World Cup Football Championship, Italy. Multicoloured.

1414	200f. Type **207** (postage)	1·80	40
1415	250f. Piazza San Carlo, Turin	2·20	60
1416	300f. San Cataldo church	2·75	75
1417	450f. St. Francis's Church, Udine (air)	4·50	1·20
MS1418	87×72 mm. 750f. Trophy and statue of Dante, Florence	6·50	1·40

1991. "Telecom 91" International Telecommunications Exhibition. Multicoloured.

1419	150f. Type **208**	1·50	75
1420	300f. Emblem (horiz)	2·75	1·40

209 Health Centre

1991. Medecins sans Frontieres.

1421	**209**	300f. multicoloured	3·00	1·40

210 "Madonna della Tenda"

1991. Christmas (1990). Paintings by Raphael. Multicoloured.

1422	50f. Type **210** (postage)	45	10
1423	100f. Small Cowper Madonna	95	25
1424	150f. Tempi Madonna	1·50	40
1425	250f. Niccolini Madonna	2·50	55
1426	300f. Orleans Madonna (air)	2·75	75
1427	500f. Solly Madonna	4·50	1·20
MS1428	81×105 mm. 750f. "Madonna of the Fisherman"	7·25	1·70

211 Rudi Voller

1991. West Germany, 1990 World Cup Football Champion. West German Players and Goals Scored. Multicoloured.

1429	200f. Type **211** (postage)	2·00	45
1430	250f. Uwe Bein	2·30	60
1431	300f. Pierre Littbarski	2·75	80
1432	400f. Jurgen Klinsmann	4·00	90
1433	450f. Lothar Matthaus (air)	3·25	75
1434	500f. Andreas Brehme	4·50	1·20
MS1435	116×89 mm. 750f. Andreas Brehme	7·00	1·60

212 Fairey Swordfish sinking "Bismarck" (German battleship) and Admirals Raeder and Tovey

1991. Battles of Second World War. Mult.

1436	100f. Type **212** (postage)	1·20	25
1437	150f. Aichi D3A "Val" bombers sinking U.S.S. "Yorktown" (aircraft carrier) and Admirals Yamamoto and Nimitz (Battle of Midway)	1·50	45
1438	200f. American torpedo boat and Admirals Kondo and Halsey (Guadalcanal)	1·80	55
1439	250f. "Crusader III" tanks, Hawker Hurricane Mk II aircraft, Rommel and Montgomery (El Alamein)	2·50	80
1440	300f. "Tiger II" tanks and Generals Guderian and Patton (Ardennes) (air)	3·00	75
1441	450f. Grumman TBF Avenger aircraft sinking "Yamato" (Japanese battleship) and Admiral Kogo and General MacArthur	4·50	1·20
MS1442	120×86 mm. 750f. Boeing "B 17 G Flying Fortress" and Eisenhower	7·00	1·40

1991. Various stamps surch.

1443	100f. on 170f. mult (No. 1321) (postage)	95	45
1444	100f. on 170f. mult (No. 1328)	95	45
1445	100f. on 250f. mult (No. 1388)	95	45
1446	100f. on 400f. mult (No. 1270)	95	45
1447	100f. on 400f. mult (No. 1349)	95	45
1448	100f. on 400f. mult (No. 1356)	95	45
1449	100f. on 400f. mult (No. 1404)	95	45
1450	100f. on 400f. mult (No. 1410)	95	45
1451	100f. on 500f. mult (No. 1362)	95	45
1452	100f. on 500f. mult (No. 1366)	95	45
1453	100f. on 400f. mult (No. 1301) (air)	1·00	45
1454	100f. on 400f. mult (No. 1308)	1·00	45
1455	100f. on 400f. mult (No. 1322)	1·00	45
1456	100f. on 400f. mult (No. 1329)	1·00	45
1457	100f. on 400f. mult (No. 1343)	1·00	45
1458	100f. on 400f. mult (No. 1385)	1·00	45
1459	300f. on 450f. mult (No. 1350)	2·75	90
1460	300f. on 450f. mult (No. 1411)	2·75	90

214 Nat King Cole Trio

1991. Music and Films. Multicoloured.

1461	100f. Type **214** (postage)	1·20	25
1462	150f. Yul Brynner and scene from "The Magnificent Seven"	1·40	40
1463	250f. Judy Garland and scene from "The Wizard of Oz"	2·50	55
1464	300f. Steve McQueen and scene from "Papillon"	2·75	80
1465	500f. Gary Cooper and scene from "Sergeant York" (air)	4·50	80
1466	600f. Bing Crosby and scene from "High Society"	5·50	1·30
MS1467	84×106 mm. 750f. John Wayne and scene from "Conquest of the West"	7·50	1·70

215 Dancer

1991. African Tourism Year. Multicoloured.

1468	100f. Type **215**	1·10	60
1469	150f. Baskets (horiz)	1·70	90
1470	250f. Drum (horiz)	3·00	1·60
1471	300f. Flautist	3·25	2·10

216 Doves, Map and Pope John Paul II

1991. Papal Visit. Litho.

1472	**216**	150f. multicoloured	2·75	1·50

217 "ERS-1" Observation Satellite and Earth

1991. Anniversaries and Events. Mult.

1473	100f. Type **217** (postage)	95	30
1474	150f. "Sunflowers" (Vincent van Gogh, 1888)	1·40	25
1475	200f. Napoleon I (170th death anniv)	2·00	40

1476	250f. Henri Dunant (founder of Red Cross) and Red Cross volunteers	2·30	45
1477	300f. Bicentenary of Brandenburg Gate and second anniversary of fall of Berlin Wall	2·75	60
1478	400f. Pope John Paul II's tour of Africa, 1989	3·75	70
1479	450f. Garry Kasparov and Anatoli Karpov (World Chess Championship, 1990) (air)	4·25	4·50
1480	500f. Boy feeding dove and Rotary International and Lions International emblems	5·25	1·30

218 Care-a-Lot and Care Bears around Globe

1991. Ecology. Care Bear cartoon characters. Multicoloured.

1481	50f. Type **218** (postage)	50	25
1482	100f. Care Bears around sink ("Save Water!")	1·00	45
1483	200f. Care Bears in tree ("Recycle!")	1·90	80
1484	300f. Traffic jam and Care Bear ("Control Noise")	3·00	1·40
1485	400f. Elephant and Care Bear ("Protect Our Wild Life") (horiz)	4·00	2·10
MS1486	Two sheets. (a) 64×95 mm. 500f. Care Bears' emblem and waterfall (39×27 mm) (postage); (b) 95×65 mm. 600f. Scout, tent and Baden-Powell (17th World Scout Jamboree, Korea) (39×26 mm) (air)	4·50	3·00

219 Player, Trophy and Little Five Points

1992. World Cup Football Championship, U.S.A. (1994) (1st issue). Multicoloured.

1487	100f. Type **219** (postage)	95	50
1488	300f. Germany player and Fulton Stadium, Atlanta	3·00	60
1489	400f. Player and Inman Park	3·75	90
1490	500f. Player and Museum of Fine Art (air)	4·50	1·30
MS1491	110×80 mm. 1000f. USA player, "Intelstat VI" satellite and Capitol	6·50	2·10

See also Nos. 1565/**MS**1569.

220 Emblem

1992. 75th Anniv of Lions International.

1492	**220**	150f. multicoloured	1·40	75
1493	**220**	400f. multicoloured	3·75	2·10

221 Emblem

1992. International Nutrition Conference, Rome.

1494	**221**	150f. mult (postage)	2·10	45
1495	**221**	400f. multicoloured	3·00	45
1496	**221**	500f. multicoloured (air)	3·75	60

222 Scene from "The Devil and Catherine" and Antonin Dvorak (composer)

1992. Anniversaries and Events. Multicoloured.

1497	200f. Type **222** (150th birth (1991)) (postage)	2·10	45
1498	300f. Antonio Vivaldi (composer) (250th death (1991)) and as choirmaster to the Hospital of the Pieta, Venice	3·00	45
1499	350f. Meeting of airship "Graf Zeppelin" and Santos-Dumont's flying boat and Count Ferdinand von Zeppelin (airship pioneer)	3·75	60
1500	400f. Projected locomotive emerging from Channel Tunnel (construction)	4·00	80
1501	450f. Konrad Adenauer (German statesman) and Brandenburg Gate, Berlin (bicentenary of Gate) (air)	4·75	90
1502	500f. Emperor Hirohito of Japan (third death anniv)	5·25	1·40
MS1503	77×115 mm. 750f. Cross-channel locomotive (59×41 mm)	7·50	1·80

223 Charlie Chaplin (actor) and Scene from "Modern Times"

1992. Anniversaries and Events. Multicoloured.

1504	50f. Type **223** (15th death anniv) (postage)	50	30
1505	100f. Pavilion and Christopher Columbus ("Expo '92" World's Fair, Seville)	1·00	30
1506	150f. St. Peter's Square, Rome	1·50	45
1507	200f. Marlene Dietrich (actress, death) in scene from "Shanghai Express"	2·10	60
1508	250f. Michael Schumacher and Formula 1 racing car	2·40	60
1509	300f. Rocket launch and John Glenn (30th anniv of Glenn's three-orbit flight in "Mercury" space capsule)	2·75	75
1510	400f. Bill Koch (skipper) and "America 3" (yacht) (winner of Americas Cup) (air)	3·75	1·00
1511	450f. Victory of Washington Redskins in 26th American Superbowl baseball championships	4·50	1·00
1512	500f. Recovery of "Intelsat VI" satellite by "Endeavour" space shuttle	5·00	1·20
MS1513	750f. Brandenburg Gate and Willy Brandt (politician and Mayor of Berlin, 1957–66, death (49×35 mm)	6·75	1·70

1993. 50th Death Anniv (1991) of Robert Baden-Powell (founder of Scouting Movement). Nos. 1339/MS1345 optd 50eme ANNIVERSAIRE DE LA MORT DE BADEN POWEL.

1515	**192**	50f. mult (postage)	95	25
1516	-	100f. multicoloured	95	25
1517	-	150f. multicoloured	1·40	55
1518	-	300f. multicoloured	2·75	75
1519	-	400f. multicoloured (air)	3·75	25
1520	-	450f. multicoloured	4·25	25
MS1521		116×87 mm. 750f. multicoloured	1·40	1·40

1993. Bicentenary of Year One of First Republic of France. Nos. 1388/MS1392 optd BICENTENAIRE DE L'AN I DE LA REPUBLIQUE FRANCAISE.

1522	**201**	250f. mult (postage)	2·75	25
1523	-	300f. multicoloured	3·75	25
1524	-	400f. multicoloured	4·75	45
1525	-	450f. multicoloured (air)	5·75	45
MS1526		140×102 mm. 750f. multicoloured	8·50	8·50

1993. Winter Olympic Games, Albertville, Gold Medal Winners. Nos. 1402/MS1406 variously optd.

1527	150f. **SLALOM GEANT Alberto Tomba, Italie** (postage)	1·90	30
1528	250f. **SKI NORDIQUE Vegard Ulvang, Norvege**	2·75	40
1529	400f. **BOB A DEUX G. Weder/D. Acklin, Suisse**	3·75	40
1530	500f. **PATINAGE DE VITESSE Olaf Zinke 1000m., Allemagne** (air)	4·75	40
MS1531	97×71 mm. 750f. As No. 1527	2·75	2·75

1993. World Cup Football Championship, Italy, Results. Nos. 1414/MS1418 optd 1. ALLEMAGNE 2. ARGENTINE 3. ITALIE.

1532	**207**	200f. mult (postage)	1·90	45
1533	-	250f. multicoloured	2·75	60
1534	-	300f. multicoloured	3·25	60
1535	-	450f. multicoloured (air)	4·25	60
MS1536		87×72 mm. 750f. multicoloured	4·75	4·75

1993. Air. Bobby Fischer–Boris Spassky Chess Match (1537) and 75th Anniv of Lions International (1538). Nos. 1479/80 optd.

1537	450f. **RENCONTRE FISCHER - SPASSKY 3 SEPT au 5 NOV 1992 AU MONTENEGRO**	3·75	55
1538	500f. **75eme ANNIVERSAIRE LIONS**	4·75	65

230 West Germany Footballer and Little White House

1993. Olympic Games, Atlanta (1996) (1st issue). Multicoloured.

1539	150f. Type **230** (postage)	1·60	45
1540	250f. Cyclist and Georgia World Congress Center	2·50	75
1541	400f. Basketball player and underground station	4·00	90
1542	500f. Baseball player and steam train, New Georgia Railroad (air)	4·75	1·10
MS1543	123×90 mm. 1000f. Table tennis player and Atlanta at night	9·00	9·00

See also Nos. 1623/**MS**1628.

231 Ice Hockey and "Whale Hunt" (sculpture)

1993. Winter Olympic Games, Lillehammer, Norway (1994). Multicoloured.

1544	150f. Type **231** (postage)	1·40	40
1545	250f. Two-man bobsleigh and Edvard Grieg's house	2·30	75
1546	400f. Biathlon and Fredrikstad Park (air)	3·50	90
1547	450f. Ski jumping and Eidsvoll Manor	4·25	1·20
MS1548	100×72 mm. 1000f. Skiing and Lillehammer	8·75	8·75

232 "Luna 3" and Dark Side of Moon

1993. 25th Anniv (1994) of First Manned Moon Landing. Multicoloured.

1549	150f. Type **232**	1·40	30
1550	150f. "Ranger 7"	1·40	30
1551	150f. "Luna 9"	1·40	30
1552	150f. "Surveyor 1" (first lunar probe)	1·40	30
1553	150f. Lunar "Orbiter 1" and moon	1·40	30
1554	150f. Launch of "Saturn 5" (rocket) carrying "Apollo 11"	1·40	30
1555	150f. "Apollo 11" command module in lunar orbit	1·40	30
1556	150f. Astronaut climbing from "Apollo 11"	1·40	30
1557	150f. "Apollo 12" astronaut recovering "Surveyor 1" camera	1·40	30
1558	150f. Explosion of "Apollo 13"	1·40	30
1559	150f. "Luna 16" probe (first collection of lunar samples by automatic probe)	1·40	30
1560	150f. Lunokhod of "Luna 17" (first lunar vehicle)	1·40	30
1561	150f. Alan Shepard playing golf on moon	1·40	30
1562	150f. First lunar jeep from "Apollo 15" mission	1·40	30
1563	150f. First lunar telescope from "Apollo 16" mission	1·40	30
1564	150f. Astronaut from "Apollo 17" (last "Apollo" mission)	1·40	30

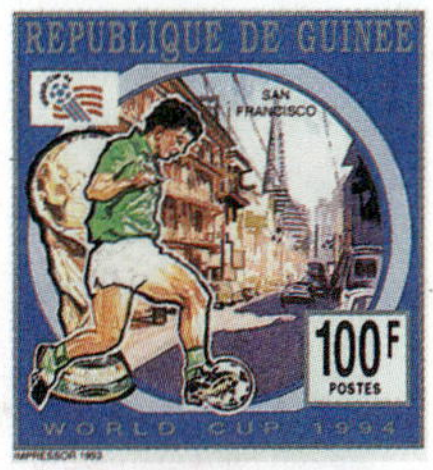

233 San Francisco

1993. World Cup Football Championship, U.S.A. (1994) (2nd issue). Multicoloured.

1565	100f. Type **233** (postage)	1·40	30
1566	300f. Washington D.C.	2·75	55
1567	400f. Renaissance Center, Detroit	3·75	80
1568	500f. Dallas (air)	4·50	1·10
MS1569	106×84 mm. 1000f. New York	9·00	9·00

234 Euparkeria

1993. Prehistoric Animals. Multicoloured.

1570	50f. Type **234**	45	25
1571	50f. Plateosaurus	45	25
1572	50f. Anchisaurus	45	25
1573	50f. Ornithosuchus	45	25
1574	100f. Megalosaurus	95	30
1575	100f. Scelidosaurus	95	30
1576	100f. Camptosaurus	95	30
1577	100f. Ceratosaurus	95	30
1578	250f. Ouranosaurus	2·30	25
1579	250f. Dicraeosaurus	2·30	25
1580	250f. Tarbosaurus	2·30	25
1581	250f. Gorgosaurus	2·30	25
1582	250f. Polacanthus	2·30	25
1583	250f. Deinonychus	2·30	25
1584	250f. Corythosaurus	2·30	25
1585	250f. Spinosaurus	2·30	25
MS1586	170×120 mm. 1000f. "Tyrannosaurus rex" (50×60 mm)	10·00	10·00

235 Prince Johann I of Liechtenstein

1994. Multicoloured. (a) Battle of Austerlitz, 1805.
1587 150f. Type **235** 1·50 75
1588 150f. Marshal Joachim Murat 1·50 75
1589 600f. Napoleon (59×47 mm) 5·50 1·20
Nos. 1587/9 were issued together, se-tenant, forming a composite design of a battle scene.

(b) Battle of the Moskva, 1912.
1590 150f. Marshal Michel Ney 1·60 80
1591 150f. Prince Pyotr Ivanovich Bagration 1·60 80
1592 600f. Napoleon on horseback (59×47 mm) 6·00 1·30
Nos. 1590/2 were issued together, se-tenant, forming a composite design of a battle scene.

(c) Normandy Landings, 1944.
1593 150f. Field-Marshal Erwin Rommel (wrongly inscr "Romel") 1·50 75
1594 150f. Gen. George Patton 1·50 75
1595 600f. Gen. Dwight David Eisenhower (59×47 mm) 5·50 1·20
Nos. 1593/5 were issued together, se-tenant, forming a composite design of a battle scene.

(d) Battle of the Ardennes, 1944.
1596 150f. Lt.-Gen. William H. Simpson 1·50 75
1597 150f. Gen. Heinz Guderian 1·50 75
1598 600f. Tank battle scene (59×47 mm) 5·50 1·20
Nos. 1596/8 were issued together, se-tenant, forming a composite design of a battle scene.

236 Johann Kepler and "Pluto" Space Probe

1994. Astronomers. Multicoloured.
1599 300f. Type **236** 2·75 75
1600 300f. Sir Isaac Newton and "Voyager" space probe 2·75 75
1601 500f. Nicolas Copernicus and "Galileo" space probe (59×47 mm) 4·25 1·20
Nos. 1599/1601 were issued together, se-tenant, forming a composite design.

1994. Winter Olympic Games, Lillehammer. Gold Medal Winners. Nos. 1544/MS1545 variously optd.
1602 150f. **MEDAILLE D'OR SUEDE** (postage) 1·50 75
1603 250f. **G. WEDER D. ACKLIN SUISSE** 2·50 90
1604 400f. **F.B. LUNDBERG NORVEGE** (air) 3·50 1·40
1605 450f. **J. WEISSFLOG ALLEMAGNE** 4·00 1·40
MS1606 100×72 mm. 1000f. T. Moe USA 8·75 8·75

1994. World Cup Football Championship, U.S.A., Winners. Nos. 1565/MS1569 optd 1. BRESIL 2. ITALIE 3. SUEDE.
1607 **233** 100f. mult (postage) 1·30 45
1608 - 300f. multicoloured 2·75 70
1609 - 400f. multicoloured 3·50 80
1610 - 500f. multicoloured (air) 4·50 1·10
MS1611 106×84 mm. 1000f. multicoloured 8·75 8·50

239 Banea Dam

1995. Garafiri Water Management. Mult.
1612 100f. Type **239** 45 25
1613 150f. Donkea 75 40
1614 200f. Tinkisso overflow (vert) 95 45
1615 250f. Waterfalls 1·20 75
1616 500f. Water works, Kinkon 2·50 1·20

240 Red and White Persian

1995. Cats. Multicoloured.
1617 150f. Type **240** (inscr "Tortoiseshell") 75 35
1618 250f. Tabby and white 1·30 65
1619 500f. Black smoke persian ("Smoke long-haired") 2·50 90
1620 500f. Red tabby 2·50 90
1621 500f. Tortoiseshell and white persian ("longhair") 2·50 90
MS1622 48×78 mm. 1000f. Chinchilla (38×30 mm) 5·75 3·75

241 Throwing the Javelin

1995. Olympic Games, Atlanta (1996) (2nd issue). Multicoloured.
1623 150f. Type **241** 40 25
1624 250f. Boxing 75 45
1625 500f. Football 1·30 85
1626 500f. Basketball 1·30 85
1627 500f. Weightlifting 1·30 85
MS1628 48×82 mm. 1000f. Archery (31×39 mm) 4·25 2·75

242 Eurasian Goldfinch

1995. Birds. Multicoloured.
1629 150f. Type **242** 40 25
1630 250f. Nightingale ("Luscinia megarhynchos") 75 45
1631 500f. Island canary ("Serinus canaria") 1·30 85
1632 500f. Chaffinch ("Fringilla coelebs") 1·30 85
1633 500f. Western greenfinch ("Carduelis chloris") 1·30 85
MS1634 60×75 mm. 1000f. European robin (31×37 mm) 5·75 3·75

243 Mona Monkey

1995. Mammals. Multicoloured.
1635 150f. Type **243** 40 25
1636 250f. Savanna monkey 75 45
1637 500f. Demidoff's galago ("Galagoides demidovi") 1·30 85
1638 500f. Hare ("Lepus crawshayi") (horiz) 1·30 85
1639 500f. Giant ground pangolin ("Manis gigantea") (horiz) 1·30 85
MS1640 49×74 mm. 1000f. African clawless otter (31×39 mm) 5·75 3·75

244 Pup-150 (Great Britain)

1995. Aircraft. Multicoloured.
1641 100f. Type **244** 45 20
1642 150f. Gardan GY-80 "Horizon" (France) 75 25
1643 250f. Piper J-3 Cub (U.S.A.) 1·30 45
1644 500f. Piper PA-28 Cherokee Arrow (U.S.A.) 2·50 90
1645 500f. Pilatus PC-6 Porter (Switzerland) 2·50 90
1646 500f. Valmet L-90TP Redigo (Finland) 2·50 90
MS1647 79×49 mm. 1000f. Stol DO-27 (Germany) (39×30 mm) 5·00 2·30

245 Yoked Oxen

1995. 50th Anniv of F.A.O. Multicoloured.
1648 200f. Type **245** 95 45
1649 750f. Nutrition lesson 4·00 1·40

246 Jacobean Lily

1995. Flowers. Multicoloured.
1650 100f. Type **246** 45 10
1651 150f. "Rudbeckia purpurea" 75 25
1652 250f. Himalayan blue poppy 1·30 45
1653 500f. Iris "Starshine" 2·50 90
1654 500f. Rose "Gail Borden" 2·50 90
1655 500f. Sweet pea ("Lathyrus odoratus") 2·50 90
MS1656 55×70 mm. 100f. Orchid (28×36 mm) 5·00 2·30

247 Players

1995. World Cup Football Championship, France (1998) (1st issue). Multicoloured.
1657 150f. Type **247** 40 25
1658 250f. Player challenging player No. 2 75 45
1659 500f. Players in blue and white shirt and red shirt in tackle 1·30 85
1660 500f. Players Nos. 3 and 10 running after ball 1·30 85
1661 500f. Player No. 2 high-kicking ball 1·30 85
MS1662 90×51 mm. 1000f. Two players opposing player No. 19 (31×39 mm) 5·75 3·75
See also Nos. 1719/**MS**1725.

248 Arab Horse

1995. Arab Horses. Multicoloured.
1663 100f. Type **248** 40 25
1664 150f. Dark brown horse with white star 65 40
1665 250f. Chestnut 1·00 80
1666 500f. Grey 1·70 85
1667 500f. Bay 1·70 85
1668 500f. Bay with harness and rein (horiz) 1·70 1·10
MS1669 69×91 mm. 1000g. Grey (different) (31×39 mm) 5·75 3·75

249 "Leccinum nigrescens"

1995. Fungi. Multicoloured.
1670 150f. Type **249** 40 25
1671 250f. "Boletus rhodoxanthus" 75 45
1672 500f. "Cantharellus lutescens" 1·30 85
1673 500f. Brown roll-rim ("Paxillus involutus") 1·30 85
1674 500f. "Xerocomus rubellus" 1·30 85
MS1675 66×83 mm. 1000f. "Gymnopilus junonius" (31×38 mm) 5·75 3·75

250 Enterprise, 1832

1995. Veteran Omnibuses. Multicoloured.
1676 250f. Type **250** 55 35
1677 300f. Daimler, 1898 75 50
1678 400f. V.H. Bussing, 1904 1·30 80
1679 450f. M.A.N. autobus, 1906 1·30 80
1680 500f. M.A.N. autocar, 1934 1·30 85

251 Locomotive "Tom Thumb", 1829, U.S.A.

1996. Rail Transport. Multicoloured.
1681 200f. Type **251** 95 30
1682 250f. Locomotive "Genf", 1858, Switzerland (68×27 mm) 1·20 45
1683 300f. Canterbury Frozen Meat Company Dubs locomotive, 1873, New Zealand 1·50 70
1684 400f. Bagnall fireless steam accumulator locomotive No. 2, Great Britain 1·70 70
1685 450f. Werner von Siemen's first electric locomotive, 1879, and passenger carriage (68×27 mm) 2·00 80
1686 500f. North London Tramways Company tram, 1885–89, Great Britain 2·50 90
MS1687 80×90 mm. 1000f. Steam locomotive "General", 1862 (39×31 mm) 5·00 2·30

252 Rock Formation

1996. Multicoloured.
1688 200f. Type **252** 95 45
1689 750f. Child 4·00 1·40
1690 1000f. Women carrying faggots 5·00 1·90

253 Red Siskin

1996. Birds. Multicoloured.

1691	200f. Type **253**	95	30
1692	250f. Red-cheeked cordon-bleu	1·20	45
1693	300f. Chestnut-breasted minnikin	1·50	70
1694	400f. Paradise sparrow	1·70	70
1695	450f. Gouldian finch	2·00	80
1696	500f. Red bishop	2·50	90
MS1697	100×70 mm. 1000f. Spotted-sided finch (31×39 mm)	5·00	2·30

254 Bull Terrier

1996. Dogs. Multicoloured.

1698	200f. Type **254**	95	30
1699	250f. Elkhound	1·20	45
1700	300f. Akita	1·50	70
1701	400f. Collie	1·70	70
1702	450f. Rottweiler	2·00	80
1703	500f. Boxer	2·50	90
MS1704	69×89 mm. 1000f. German short-haired setter (31×39 mm)	5·00	2·30

255 Tortoiseshell and White Shorthair

1996. Cats. Multicoloured.

1705	200f. Type **255**	95	30
1706	250f. Bicolour shorthair	1·20	45
1707	300f. Tortoiseshell and white Japanese bobtail	1·50	70
1708	400f. Chocolate point Himalayan	1·70	70
1709	450f. Red longhair	2·00	80
1710	500f. Blue Persian	2·50	90
MS1711	109×88 mm. 1000f. Tortoise-shell and white longhair (31×39 mm)	5·00	2·30

256 Chestnut

1996. Fungi. Multicoloured.

1712	200f. Type **256**	95	30
1713	250f. Granular	1·20	45
1714	300f. Destroying angel	1·50	70
1715	400f. Milky blue	1·70	70
1716	450f. Violet cortinarius	2·00	80
1717	500f. Rough-stemmed	2·50	90
MS1718	90×70 mm. 1000f. Hygrophoris (31×39 mm)	5·00	2·30

257 Players

1997. World Cup Football Championship, France (1998) (2nd issue). Multicoloured.

1719	200f. Type **257**	95	30
1720	250f. Player No. 5	1·20	45
1721	300f. Three players	1·50	70
1722	400f. Player dribbling ball past opposition (horiz)	1·70	70
1723	450f. Player No. 12 with opposing player on ground (horiz)	2·00	80
1724	500f. Ball passing lunging goalkeeper (horiz)	2·50	90
MS1725	92×70 mm. 1000f. Goalkeeper looking at ball in net (31×39 mm)	5·00	2·30

258 "Paphiopedilum millmoore"

1997. Orchids. Multicoloured.

1726	200f. Type **258**	95	30
1727	250f. "Paphiopedilum ernest read"	1·20	45
1728	300f. "Paphiopedilum harrisianum"	1·50	70
1729	400f. "Paphiopedilum gaudianum"	1·70	70
1730	450f. "Paphiopedilum papa rohl"	2·00	80
1731	500f. "Paphiopedilum sea cliff"	2·50	90
MS1732	69×89 mm. 1000f. "Paphiopedilum gowerianum" (31×39 mm)	5·00	2·30

259 Giraffe

1997. Mammals. Multicoloured.

1733	200f. Type **259**	95	30
1734	250f. White rhinoceros (vert)	1·20	45
1735	300f. Warthog	1·50	70
1736	400f. Cheetah	1·70	70
1737	450f. African elephant (vert)	2·00	80
1738	500f. Pygmy hippopotamus	2·50	90
MS1739	90×70 mm. 1000f. Okapi (38×30 mm)	5·00	2·30

260 H.M.S. "Captain" (turret ship, Great Britain, 1870)

1997. 19th-Century Warships. Multicoloured.

1740	200f. Type **260**	95	30
1741	250f. "Kaiser Wilhelm" (ironclad, Germany, 1869)	1·20	45
1742	300f. H.M.S. "Temeraire" (turret ship, Great Britain, 1871)	1·50	70
1743	400f. "Mouillage" (turret ship, Italy, 1866)	1·70	70
1744	450f. H.M.S. "Inflexible" (battle-ship, Great Britain, 1881)	2·00	80
1745	500f. "Magenta" (ironclad, France, 1862)	2·50	90
MS1746	107×90 mm. 1000f. "Redoutable" (iron-clad warships, France, 1878) (31×39 mm)	5·00	2·30

261 "Siganus trispilos"

1997. Fishes. Multicoloured.

1747	200f. Type **261**	95	30
1748	250f. Dusky parrotfish	1·20	45
1749	300f. Harlequin tuskfish	1·50	70
1750	400f. Masked unicornfish	1·70	70
1751	450f. "Hypoplectrus gemma"	2·00	80
1752	500f. Red-tailed surgeon-fish	2·50	90
MS1753	90×70 mm. 1000f. Yellow tang (39×31 mm)	5·00	2·30

262 Officer, Von Witerfeldt's Regiment

1997. Prussian Infantry Uniforms. Mult.

1754	200f. Type **262**	95	40
1755	250f. Non-commissioned officer, Von Kanitz's Regiment	1·20	55
1756	300f. Private, Prince Franz von Anhalt-Dessau's Regiment	1·50	70
1757	400f. Private, Von Kalnein's Regiment	1·70	85
1758	450f. Grenadier, Duke Ferdinand of Brunswick's Regiment	2·00	1·00
1759	500f. Grenadier musician, Rekow's Guards Battalion	2·50	1·10
MS1760	91×111 mm. 1000f. Pioneer (31×39 mm)	5·75	2·75

263 Baldwin Steam Locomotive

1997. Steam Locomotives. Multicoloured.

1761	200f. Type **263**	95	40
1762	250f. Steam locomotive No. 1	1·20	55
1763	300f. Vulcan steam locomotive	1·50	70
1764	400f. Commonwealth Edison Company Baldwin steam locomotive No. 2	1·70	85
1765	450f. TCID Railroad steam locomotive No. 108	2·00	1·00
1766	500f. Pittsburgh-Hanover Coal Company steam locomotive No. 3	2·50	1·10
MS1767	110×91 mm. 1000f. Baldwin steam locomotive (39×31 mm)	6·75	3·25

264 14th-century Thai Knight, Rook and King

1997. Chess Pieces. Multicoloured.

1768	200f. Type **264**	75	45
1769	250f. Chinese pawn, king and knight, 1930	95	55
1770	300f. Portuguese ivory "seahorse" pawn, queen and king, 1920	1·20	65
1771	400f. German pewter "military" knight, king and pawn	1·40	90
1772	450f. Russian amber queen, king, bishop and knight from reign of Catherine II	1·60	1·00
1773	500f. Max Ernst's designs for queen, king, bishop and knight	2·00	1·10
MS1774	106×90 mm. 1000f. 18th-century French knight (27×36 mm)	5·75	3·75

265 Siberian Husky

1997. Dogs. Multicoloured.

1775	200f. Type **265**	55	45
1776	250f. Teckel	75	55
1777	300f. Boston terrier	95	65
1778	400f. Basset hound	1·20	90
1779	450f. Dalmatian	1·40	1·00
1780	500f. Rottweiler	1·50	1·20
MS1781	110×80 mm. 1000f. Golden retriever	5·75	3·75

POSTAGE DUE STAMPS

D11

1959

D195	**D11**	1f. green	15	15
D196	**D11**	2f. red	15	15
D197	**D11**	3f. brown	15	15
D198	**D11**	5f. blue	45	25
D199	**D11**	10f. orange	10	90
D200	**D11**	20f. mauve	2·20	1·60

D17

1959

D224	**D17**	1f. red	30	15
D225	**D17**	2f. orange	30	15
D226	**D17**	3f. lake	45	25
D227	**D17**	5f. green	95	60
D228	**D17**	10f. sepia	2·00	90
D229	**D17**	20f. blue	4·00	2·10

APPENDIX

The following stamps have either been issued in excess of postal needs or have not been available to the public in reasonable quantities at face value. Such stamps may be given full listing if there is evidence of regular postal use.

1982

World Cup Winners. Nos. 1068/74 optd.

1983

Olympic Games, Los Angeles. 100s.
Bicentenary of Manned Flight. 100s.
Winter Olympic Games, Sarajevo. 100s.

1984

Winter Olympic Gold Medal Winners. 100s.

1985

Space Achievements. 200s.
Anniversaries and Events. 85th Birthday of Queen Elizabeth the Queen Mother. 100s.

1986

Appearance of Halley's Comet. 1500f.

1987

Winter Olympic Games, Seoul. 1500f.

1989

Embossed on gold foil.Scout and Butterfly. Air 1500f.
Bicentenary of French Revolution. Air 1500f.

1990

Embossed on gold foil. World Cup Football Championship, Italy. Air 1500f.
Winter Olympic Games, Albertville (1992). Air 1500f.
De Gaulle and Free French Forces. Air 1500f.

1992

Embossed on gold foil.Olympic Games, Barcelona. Air 1500f.
World Cup Football Championship, U.S.A. (1994) (1st issue). Air 1500f. (vert design).
Elvis Presley. Air 1500f.
Pope John Paul II's African Tour. Air 1500f.

1993

Embossed on gold foil.Bicentenary of Year One of First Republic of France. Air. Optd on 1989 French Revolution issue. 1500f.
Olympic Games, Atlanta. Air 1500f.
Winter Olympic Games, Lillehammer, Norway. Air 1500f.
World Cup Football Championship, U.S.A. (1994) (2nd issue). Air 1500f. (square design).

1995

Embossed on gold foil.Normandy Landing, 1944. Air. Optd on 1990 De Gaulle Appendix. 1500f.

Pt. 13

GUINEA-BISSAU

Following an armed rebellion against Colonial rule, the independence of former Portuguese Guinea was recognised on 10 September 1974.

1974. 100 centavos = 1 escudo.
1976. 100 centavos = 1 peso.

77 Amilcar Cabral, Map and Flag

1974. 1st Anniv of Proclamation of Republic. Country name inscr in white.

426	**77**	1p. multicoloured	50	40
427	**77**	2.5p. multicoloured	75	65
428	**77**	5p. multicoloured	15·00	8·50
429	**77**	10p. multicoloured	2·50	2·00

1975. No. 425 of Portuguese Guinea optd REP. DA BISSAU.

430	2e. multicoloured	60	60

79 Amilcar Cabral, Map and Flag

1975. 2nd Anniv of Proclamation of Republic (1st issue). Country name inscr in black.

431	**79**	1p. multicoloured	45	30
432	**79**	2.5p. multicoloured	60	45
433	**79**	5p. multicoloured	2·50	1·40
434	**79**	10p. multicoloured	2·50	2·25

See also Nos. 439/440.

80 Amilcar Cabral, Arms and Flag

1975. 51st Birth Anniv of Amilcar Cabral (founder of P.A.I.G.C.).

435	**80**	1e. multicoloured	20	10
436	**80**	10e. multicoloured	80	40

81 Family, Arms and Flag

1975. 19th Anniv of P.A.I.G.C. (Partido Africano da Independencia da Guine e do Cabo Verde).

437	**81**	2e. multicoloured	50	20
438	**81**	10e. multicoloured	2·00	75

82 Pres. Luis Cabral, Arms and Flag

1975. 2nd Anniv of Proclamation of Republic (2nd issue).

439	**82**	3e. multicoloured	40	20
440	**82**	5e. multicoloured	85	30

83 General Henry Knox (after Stuart) and Cannons of Ticonderoga (after Lovell)

1976. Bicentenary of American Independence (1st issue). Multicoloured.

441	5e. Type **83** (postage)	25	15
442	10e. General Putnam and Battle of Bunker Hill	55	30
443	15e. Washington and Crossing of the Delaware	80	35
444	20e. General Kosciuszko and Battle of Saratoga	1·25	50
445	30e. General von Steuben and Valley Forge (air)	1·75	90
446	40e. Lafayette and Monmouth Court House	2·00	1·00
MS447	122×83 mm. 50p. "The Declaration of Independence" (Trumbell)	2·10	2·10

See also Nos. 503/6.

84 Masked Dancer

1976. Dancers. Multicoloured.

448	2p. Type **84** (postage)	30	10
449	3p. Dancer and drummer	35	15
450	5p. Dancers on stilts	60	20
451	10p. Dancers with spears and bows (air)	65	40
452	15p. Masked dancer	1·00	50
453	20p. "Devil" dancer	1·50	65
MS454	78×104 mm. 50p. As No. 453	3·50	3·50

1976. Cent of Universal Postal Union (1st issue). Nos. 1448/MS1454 optd CENTENARIO DA U.P.U. 1874. MEMBRO DA U.P.U. 1974 and emblem.

455	**84**	2p. multicoloured (post)	10	10
456	-	3p. multicoloured	20	10
457	-	5p. multicoloured	25	15
458	-	10p. multicoloured (air)	50	25
459	-	15p. multicoloured	65	40
460	-	20p. multicoloured	90	50
MS461		78×104 mm. 50p. multicoloured	2·00	2·00

See also Nos. 518/**MS**524.

1976. Nos. 435/40 surch in new currency.

462	1p. on 1e. multicoloured	10	10
463	2p. on 2e. multicoloured	10	10
464	3p. on 3e. multicoloured	15	10
465	5p. on 5e. multicoloured	25	15
466	10p. on 10e. multicoloured	50	30
467	10p. on 10e. multicoloured	50	30

87 Amilcar Cabral and Funeral

1976. 3rd Anniv of Amilcar Cabral's Assassination.

468	**87**	3p. multicoloured	15	10
469	**87**	5p. multicoloured	20	15
470	**87**	6p. multicoloured	25	20
471	**87**	10p. multicoloured	40	25

88 Party Emblem

1976. 20th Anniv of P.A.I.G.C.

472	**88**	3p. multicoloured	15	15
473	**88**	15p. multicoloured	65	50
474	**88**	50p. multicoloured	1·60	1·25

89 Launch of "Soyuz" Spacecraft

1976. Air. "Apollo–Soyuz" Space Link. Mult.

475	5p. Type **89**	25	15
476	10p. Launch of "Apollo" spacecraft	45	30
477	15p. Leonov, Stafford and meeting in Space	80	45
478	20p. Eclipse of the Sun	1·25	55
479	30p. Infra-red photograph of Earth	1·75	85
480	40p. Return of Spacecraft to Earth	2·25	95
MS481	117×80 mm. 50p. Spacecraft docking (59×39 mm)	2·00	2·00

90 Bell Telephone of 1876 and Laying First Atlantic Cable

1976. Telephone Centenary. Multicoloured.

482	2p. Type **90** (postage)	15	10
483	3p. French telephone of 1890 and first telephone box, 1893	20	10
484	5p. German automatic telephone of 1908 and automatic telephone, 1898	25	15
485	10p. English telephone of 1910 and trans-horizon link, 1963 (air)	55	25
486	15p. French telephone of 1924 and communications satellite	85	45
487	20p. Modern telephone and "Molnya" satellite	1·25	50
MS488	126×83 mm. 50p. Visionphone and people of different races (68×42 mm)	2·00	2·00

91 Women's Figure Skating

1976. Winter Olympic Games, Innsbruck. Mult.

489	1p. Type **91** (postage)	15	10
490	3p. Ice-hockey	30	10
491	5p. Bobsleighing	30	15
492	10p. Pairs figure-skating (air)	55	30
493	20p. Cross-country skiing	1·25	45
494	30p. Speed skating	1·75	85
MS495	116×78 mm. 50p. Slalom skiing	2·25	2·25

92 Footballers and Montreal Skyline

1976. Olympic Games, Montreal. Mult.

496	1p. Type **92**	10	10
497	3p. Pole vaulting	15	10
498	5p. Hurdling	25	15
499	10p. Discus throwing	45	25
500	20p. Running	90	50
501	30p. Wrestling	1·40	75
MS502	120×90 mm. 50p. Cycling (47×38 mm)	2·25	2·25

93 "Viking" orbiting Mars

1976. Bicentenary of American Revolution (2nd issue). Multicoloured. (a) Postage. Horiz designs as T 83.

503	3p.50 Crispus Attuck and Boston Massacre	30	10
504	5p. Martin Luther King and Capitol	40	20

(b) Air. Success of "Viking" Mission. Vert.

505	25p. Type **93**	1·25	65
506	35p. Lander scooping samples from surface of Mars	1·75	90

94 Amilcar Cabral

1977. 4th Death Anniv of Amilcar Cabral. Multicoloured.

507	50c. Type **94** (postage)	15	10
508	3p.50 Luis Cabral addressing U.N. Assembly	35	10
509	15p. Type **94** (air)	55	30
510	30p. As No. 508	1·25	50

95 Henri Dunant (Peace, 1901)

1977. 75th Anniv of 1st Nobel Prizes. Mult.

511	3p.50 Type **95** (postage)	30	10
512	5p. Albert Einstein (Physics, 1921)	35	20
513	6p. Irene and Jean-Frederic Joliot-Curie (Chemistry, 1935)	75	20
514	30p. Alexander Fleming (Medicine, 1945)	1·75	90
515	35p. Ernest Hemingway (Literature, 1954) (air)	2·00	90
516	40p. J. Tinbergen (Economic Sciences, 1969)	2·25	1·00
MS517	101×80 mm. 50p. Nobel Prize medal (56×38 mm)	2·25	2·25

96 Postal Runner and "Telstar" Satellite

1977. Centenary (1974) of Universal Postal Union (2nd issue). Multicoloured.

518	3p.50 Type **96** (postage)	25	15
519	5p. A.E.G. J-II biplane, and satellites circling globe	35	15
520	6p. Mail van and satellite control room	55	15
521	30p. Stage-coach and astronaut cancelling letters on Moon	1·75	50
522	35p. French locomotive (1844) and "Intelsat 4" satellite (air)	6·50	2·75
523	40p. Aircraft and "Apollo"–"Soyuz" link	2·50	90
MS524	115×87 mm. 50p. Chappe's optical telegraph and dish aerial	2·25	2·25

97 Coronation Coach

1977. Silver Jubliee of Queen Elizabeth II. Multicoloured.

525	3p.50 Type **97** (postage)	20	10
526	5p. Coronation ceremony	25	15
527	10p. Yeoman of the Guard and Crown Jewels	45	25
528	20p. Trumpeter sounding fanfare	90	45
529	25p. Royal Horse Guard (air)	1·25	50
530	30p. Royal Family on balcony	1·50	70
MS531	85×102 mm. 50p. Queen Elizabeth, Westminster Abbey and Coronation Chair (39×35 mm)	2·25	2·25

98 Congress Emblem

1977. 3rd P.A.I.G.C. Congress, Bissau.

532	**98**	3p.50 multicoloured	25	15

99 "Massacre of the Innocents" (detail)

1977. 400th Birth Anniv of Peter Paul Rubens (artist). Multicoloured.

533	3p.50 Type **99** (postage)	20	10
534	5p. "Rape of the Daughters of Leukippos"	25	15
535	6p. "Lamentation of Christ" (horiz)	35	15
536	30p. "Francisco IV Gonzaga, Prince of Mantua"	1·60	50
537	35p. "The Four Continents" (detail) (horiz) (air)	1·75	50
538	40p. "Marquise Brigida Spinola Doria"	2·25	60
MS539	89×78 mm. 50p. "Wounding of Christ with a Spear"	2·25	2·25

100 Santos-Dumont's Airship "Ballon No. 6"

1978. Airships. Multicoloured.

540	3p.50 Type **100** (postage)	25	15
541	5p. Beardmore airship R-34 crossing Atlantic	35	15
542	10p. "Norge" over North Pole	55	20
543	20p. "Graf Zeppelin" over Abu Simbel	1·40	50
544	25p. "Hindenburg" over New York (air)	1·75	70
545	30p. "Graf Zeppelin", Concorde airliner and space shuttle	2·25	75
MS546	110×78 mm. 50p. Count Ferdinand von Zeppelin (56×38 mm)	2·75	2·75

101 Footballers, Cup and Poster (Uruguay, 1930)

1978. World Cup Football Championship, Argentina. Multicoloured.

547	3p.50 Type **101** (postage)	20	10
548	5p. "Coupe du Monde, 1938"	25	15
549	10p. Brazil, 1950	55	25
550	20p. Chile, 1962	1·10	45
551	25p. Mexico, 1970 (air)	1·40	50
552	30p. "FIFA World Cup 1974" (Germany)	1·60	65
MS553	102×77 mm. 50p. Argentina 78 emblem	2·25	2·25

DESIGNS: Showing match scenes and posters from previous championships.

102 Black Antelope

1978. Endangered Animals. Multicoloured.

554	3p.50 Type **102** (postage)	30	10
555	5p. Fennec	75	30
556	6p. Secretary bird	1·00	50
557	30p. Hippopotamuses	2·00	65
558	35p. Cheetahs (air)	2·25	65
559	40p. Gorillas	2·50	75
MS560	94×75 mm. 50p. "Cercopithecus erythotis"	2·25	2·25

103 Microwave-antenna

1978. Telecommunications Day.

561	**103**	3p.50 multicoloured	20	15
562	**103**	10p. multicoloured	55	30

104 Child

1978. Children's Day.

563	**104**	50c. blue and green	10	10
564	-	3p. bright red and red	15	10
565	-	5p. light brown and brown	25	15
566	-	30p. brown and red	1·40	1·00

DESIGNS: 3p. Amilcar Cabral and child; 5p. Children; 30p. Two children playing.

105 Reading the Proclamation

1978. 25th Anniv of Coronation of Queen Elizabeth II. Multicoloured.

567	3p. Type **105** (postage)	20	10
568	5p. Queen and Prince Philip in Coronation Coach	25	15
569	10p. Queen and Prince Philip	45	25
570	20p. Mounted drummer	90	45
571	25p. Imperial State Crown and St. Edward's Crown (air)	1·25	50
572	30p. Queen holding orb and sceptre	1·25	65
573	100p. Queen, stained glass window and Imperial State Crown (55×38 mm)	4·50	1·50
MS574	Two sheets (a) 84×105 mm. 50p. Queen on throne with Archbishops (49×40 mm); (b) 87×119 mm. 100p. Coronation Coach (55×38 mm)	7·00	

106 Wright Brothers and Wright Flyer I

1978. History of Aviation. Multicoloured.

575	3p.50 Type **106** (postage)	20	10
576	10p. Alberto Santos-Dumont	45	20
577	15p. Louis Blériot	75	35
578	20p. Charles Lindbergh (air)	90	40
579	25p. Moon landing	1·25	50
580	30p. Space shuttle	1·50	65
MS581	120×83 mm. 50p. Concorde	3·00	3·00

1978. World Cup Football Championship Results. Nos. 547/52 optd 10 ARGENTINA 20 HOLANDA 30 BRAZIL.

582	3p.50 multicoloured (postage)	20	10
583	5p. multicoloured	25	15
584	10p. multicoloured	45	25
585	20p. multicoloured	1·10	55
586	25p. multicoloured (air)	1·25	55
587	30p. multicoloured	1·50	70
MS588	102×77 mm. 50p. multicoloured	2·25	2·25

108 "Virgin and Child", 1497

1978. 450th Death Anniv of Albrecht Durer (artist). Multicoloured.

589	3p.50 Type **108** (postage)	20	10
590	5p. "Virgin and Child", 1507	25	15
591	6p. "Virgin and Child", 1512	30	15
592	30p. "Virgin", 1518	1·40	70
593	35p. "Virgin and Child with St. Anne", 1519 (air)	1·75	50
594	40p. "Virgin of the Pear", 1526	2·00	75
MS595	95×85 mm. 50p."Adoration of the Magi" (49×55 mm)	2·25	1·25

109 Rowland Hill and Wurttemberg 70k. Stamp, 1873

1978. Death Centenary of Rowland Hill.

596	3p.50 Type **109** (postage)	15	10
597	5p. Belgian 10c. stamp, 1849	25	15
598	6p. Monaco 5f. stamp, 1885	30	20
599	30p. Spanish 10r. stamp, 1851	1·50	70
600	35p. Swiss 5r. stamp, 1851 (air)	1·75	50
601	40p. Naples ½t. stamp, 1860	2·00	75
MS602	99×78 mm. 50p. Portuguese Guinea stamp, 1885 (49×41 mm)	2·25	2·25

DESIGNS: 5p. to 40p. show Rowland Hill and stamp.

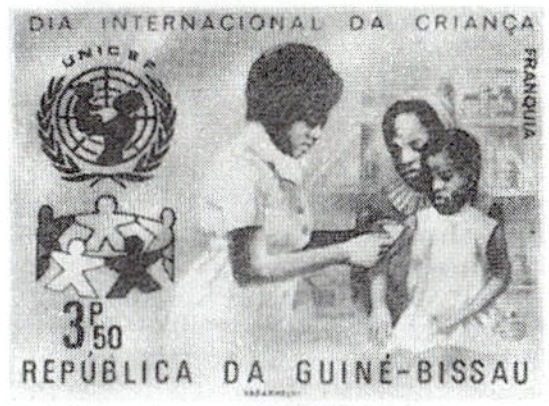

110 Nurse immunising Child

1979. International Year of the Child (1st issue). Multicoloured.

603	3p.50 Type **110** (postage)	20	10
604	10p. Children drinking	55	25
605	15p. Children with book	1·00	35
606	20p. Space shuttle (air)	1·00	40
607	25p. "Skylab" space station	1·40	50
608	30p. Children playing chess	2·00	75
MS609	117×81 mm. 50p. Children watching space ship orbiting planet	2·25	2·25

See also Nos. 616/**MS**619.

111 Family

1979. National Census.

610	**111**	50c. brown, blue and pink	10	10
611	**111**	2p. brown, blue & lt blue	15	10
612	**111**	4p. brown, blue and yellow	25	15

112 Wave Pattern and Human Figures

1979. World Telecommunications Day. Mult.

613	50c. Type **112**	10	10
614	4p. Wave pattern and human figures (different)	20	15

113 Monument

1979. 20th Anniv of Pindjiuouiti Massacre.

615	**113**	4p.50 multicoloured	30	15

114 Classroom Scene

1980. International Year of the Child (2nd issue). Multicoloured.

616	6p. Type **114** (postage)	30	25
617	10p. Jules Verne and child reading novel (vert)	45	30
618	25p. Locomotive "Northumbrian" (1831), Japanese "Hikari" express train and child with toy steam locomotive (vert)	9·00	1·25
619	35p. Man and child with bows and arrows (vert)	1·60	75
MS620	102×77 mm. 50p. Children with microscope (air)	2·25	2·25

115 Amilcar Cabral, Workers and Children reading Books

1980. Literacy Campaign. Multicoloured.

621	3p.50 Type **115** (postage)	20	10
622	5p. Luis Cabral displaying school textbooks	30	15
623	15p. Type **115** (air)	80	50
624	25p. As No. 622	1·40	75

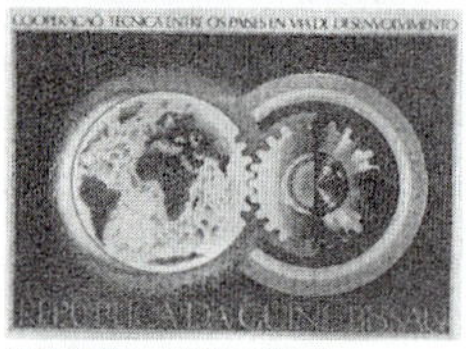

116 Globe and Cogwheel

1980. Technical Co-operation among Developing Countries.

625	**116**	3p.50 multicoloured	20	10
626	**116**	6p. multicoloured	30	20
627	**116**	10p. multicoloured	45	30

117 Wood Carvings

1980. Handicrafts. Multicoloured.

628	3p. Type **117**	20	10
629	6p. Weaving (horiz)	30	20
630	20p. Bust and statuette (horiz)	1·00	50

118 Ernst Udet

1980. History of Aviation. Air Aces of 1st World War. Multicoloured.

631	3p.50 Type **118** (postage)	25	15
632	5p. Charles Nungesser	35	25
633	6p. Manfred von Richthofen	55	25
634	30p. Francesco Baracca	1·75	70
635	35p. Willy Coppens de Houthulst (air)	2·10	75
636	40p. Charles Guynemer	2·50	90
MS637	117×80 mm. 50p. Commandant de Rose (37×55 mm)	2·25	2·25

119 Speed Skating

1980. Winter Olympic Games, Lake Placid. Multicoloured.

638	3p. Type **119** (postage)	20	10
639	5p. Downhill	30	20
640	6p. Luge	40	25
641	30p. Cross country skiing	1·75	70
642	35p. Downhill skiing (air)	2·00	75
643	40p. Figure skating	2·40	90
MS644	99×79 mm. 50p. Ice hockey (46×37 mm)	2·25	2·25

120 Putting the Shot

1980. Olympic Games, Moscow. Multicoloured.

645	3p.50 Type **120** (postage)	20	15
646	5p. Gymnastics (ring exercise)	25	20
647	6p. Long jump	35	25
648	30p. Fencing	1·50	70
649	35p. Gymnastics (backward somersault) (air)	1·75	75
650	40p. Running	2·00	90
MS651	84×69 mm. 50p. Olympic emblems and runner (41×50 mm)	2·25	2·25

121 Congress Meeting

1980. 16th Anniv of Cassaca Congress.

652	**121**	3p.50 multicoloured	15	10
653	**121**	6p.50 multicoloured	30	20
654	**121**	10p. multicoloured	40	30

122 Satellites

1981. Space Achievements. Multicoloured.

655	3p.50 Type **122** (postage)	20	10
656	5p. Satellite	25	15
657	6p. Rocket	30	15
658	30p. Space Shuttle "Columbia"	1·75	95
659	35p. "Viking I" (air)	1·75	75
660	40p. U.S.–Soviet space link	2·00	90
MS661	131×80 mm. 50p. "Apollo 11" crew and badge (horiz 59×41 mm)	2·25	2·25

123 Platini (France) and Football Scene

1981. World Cup Football Championship, Spain. Multicoloured.

662	3p.50 Type **123** (postage)	30	10
663	5p. Bettega (Italy)	35	15
664	6p. Rensenbrink (Netherlands)	40	15
665	30p. Rivelino (Brazil)	1·90	80
666	35p. Rummenigge (West Germany) (air)	1·90	80
667	40p. Kempes (Argentina)	2·00	90
MS668	116×82 mm. 50p. Juanito (Spain)	2·25	2·25

124 Lady Diana Spencer with Horse

1981. Wedding of Prince of Wales. Multicoloured.

669	3p.50 Type **124** (postage)	20	15
670	5p. Investiture of Prince of Wales	25	15
671	6p. Lady Diana Spencer with Children	30	15
672	30p. St. Paul's Cathedral	1·25	95
673	35p. Althorp House (air)	1·40	1·00
674	40p. Arms of Prince of Wales	1·50	1·25
MS675	85×103 mm. 50p. Lady Diana Spencer and Prince of Wales	2·00	2·00

125 Eric the Red and Viking Ship

1981. Navigators. Multicoloured.

676	3p.50 Type **125** (postage)	25	15
677	5p. Vasco da Gama and "Sao Gabriel"	30	15
678	6p. Magellan and "Vitoria"	35	20
679	30p. Cartier and "Emerillon"	2·00	1·00
680	35p. Drake and "Golden Hind" (air)	2·50	1·25
681	40p. Cook and H.M.S. "Endeavour"	2·75	1·60
MS682	97×94 mm. 50p. Columbus and "Santa Maria"	3·00	3·00

126 "Girl with Bare Feet"

1981. Birth Centenary of Pablo Picasso. Multicoloured.

683	3p.50 Type **126** (postage)	20	15
684	5p. "Acrobat on Ball"	25	15
685	6p. "Pierrot"	30	15
686	30p. "Girl in front of a Mirror"	1·50	95
687	35p. "The First Steps" (air)	2·00	1·00
688	40p. "Woman in Turkish Dress"	2·25	1·25
MS689	93×111 mm. 50p. "Portrait of Sylvette" (41×50 mm)	2·50	2·50

127 "Retable of St. Zeno" (Mantegna)

1981. Christmas. Multicoloured.

690	3p.50 Type **127** (postage)	20	15
691	5p. "Virgin with Child" (Bellini)	25	15
692	6p. "Virgin and Child with Cherubs" (Mantegna)	30	15
693	25p. "Madonna Campori" (Correggio)	1·50	1·00
694	30p. "Virgin and Child" (Memling) (air)	2·00	1·10
695	35p. "Virgin and Child" (Bellini)	2·25	1·25
MS696	68×117 mm. 50p. "Cortone Triptych" (Fra Angelico) (35×59 mm)	3·00	3·00

128 Archery

1982. 75th Anniv of Boy Scout Movement. Multicoloured.

697	3p.50 Type **128** (postage)	15	10
698	5p. First aid	20	15
699	6p. Bugler	25	15
700	30p. Cub scouts	1·60	80
701	35p. Girl scout in canoe (air)	2·25	90
702	40p. Scouts with model aircraft	2·40	1·25
MS703	100×80 mm. 50p. Scouts playing chess (horiz 47×38 mm)	2·60	2·60

129 Keegan

1982. World Cup Football Championship, Spain. Multicoloured.

704	3p.50 Type **129** (postage)	20	10
705	5p. Rossi	20	15
706	6p. Zico	25	15
707	30p. Arconada	1·60	80
708	35p. Kempes (air)	2·25	1·00
709	40p. Kaltz	2·50	1·10
MS710	100×72 mm. 50p. Player, World Cup and stadium	2·75	2·75

130 Lady Diana Spencer

1982. 21st Birthday of Princess of Wales. Multicoloured.

711	3p.50 Type **130** (postage)	15	10
712	5p. Playing croquet	25	15
713	6p. Lady Diana with pony	30	15
714	30p. Fishing	1·75	80
715	35p. Engagement picture (air)	1·90	90
716	40p. Honeymoon picture	2·00	1·10
MS717	100×80 mm. 50p. Princess of Wales with Prince William (vert)	2·25	2·25

1982. Birth of Prince William of Wales. Nos. 711/MS717 optd 21 DE JULHO 1982. GUILHERMO ARTHUR FILIPE LUIS PRINCIPE DE GALES.

718	3p.50 multicoloured (postage)	20	10

719	5p. multicoloured	25	15
720	6p. multicoloured	30	15
721	30p. multicoloured	1·60	95
722	35p. multicoloured (air)	1·90	1·10
723	40p. multicoloured	2·00	1·25
MS724	100×80 mm. 50p. multicoloured	2·25	2·25

132 National Colours

1982. Visit of President Eanes of Portugal. Multicoloured.

725	4p.50 Type **132**	10	10
726	20p. Doves on national colours	20	10

133 Montgolfier Balloon

1983. Bicentenary of Manned Flight. Mult.

727	50c. Type **133**	10	10
728	2p.50 Charles's hydrogen balloon	15	10
729	3p.50 Charles Green's balloon "Royal Vauxhall"	20	10
730	5p. Gaston Tissandier's balloon "Zenith"	30	10
731	10p. Salomon Andree's balloon "Ornen" over Arctic	60	20
732	20p. Stratosphere balloon "Explorer II"	1·25	40
733	30p. Modern hot-air balloons	2·00	60
MS734	75×87 mm. 50p. Gas balloon (47×47 mm)	3·00	3·00

134 Hamadryas Baboon

1983. African Primates. Multicoloured.

735	1p. Type **134**	10	10
736	1p.50 Gorilla	20	10
737	3p.50 Gelada	30	10
738	5p. Mandrill	40	15
739	8p. Chimpanzee	80	20
740	20p. Eastern black-and-white colobus	1·50	50
741	30p. Diana monkey	2·40	85

135 USA Space Rocket

1983. "Tembal 83" International Thematic Stamp Exhibition, Basle. Sheet 91×57 mm.

MS742	**135** 50p. multicoloured	3·25	3·25

136 Satellite

1983. Cosmonautics Day. Multicoloured.

743	1p. Type **136**	10	10
744	1p.50 Satellite (different)	15	10
745	3p.50 Rocket carrying space shuttle	20	10
746	5p. Satellite (different)	30	15
747	8p. Satellite (different)	60	20
748	20p. Satellite (different)	1·25	45
749	30p. "Soyuz" docking with "Salyut"	2·00	70
MS750	95×54 mm. 50p. "Soyuz"–"Salyut" complex (28×36 mm)	3·25	3·25

137 Woodcut from Caxton's "Game and Playe of Chesse", Arabian Pawn and Rook

1983. Chess. Multicoloured.

751	1p. Type **137**	15	10
752	1p.50 12th-century European king and knight	15	10
753	3p.50 Mid 18th-century German rook, queen and king	25	10
754	5p. Late 12th/early 13th-century Danish bishop and knight	40	10
755	10p. 18th-century French king and queen	80	25
756	20p. 18th-century Venetian king, knight and queen	1·75	55
757	40p. 19th-century faience knight, queen and rook	3·00	1·10
MS758	83×70 mm. 50p. brown and black (15th-century engraving of chess players) (31×36 mm)	3·50	3·50

138 "Vision of Ezekiel"

1983. 500th Birth Anniv of Raphael (artist). Multicoloured.

759	1p. Type **138**	10	10
760	1p.50 "Tempi Madonna"	10	10
761	3p.50 "Della Tenda Madonna"	20	10
762	5p. "Orleans Madonna"	25	10
763	8p. "La Belle Jardiniere"	45	20
764	15p. "Small Cowper Madonna"	90	35
765	30p. "St. George and the Dragon"	2·00	60
MS766	74×58 mm. 50p. "Solby Madonna" (31×39 mm)	3·25	3·25

139 Swimming

1983. Olympic Games, Los Angeles (1932 and 1984) (1st issue). Multicoloured.

767	1p. Type **139**	10	10
768	1p.50 Hurdling	15	10
769	3p.50 Fencing	20	10
770	5p. Weightlifting	30	10
771	10p. Marathon	60	15
772	20p. Show jumping	1·10	35
773	40p. Cycling	2·40	65
MS774	86×81 mm. 50p. Stadium	2·60	2·60

See also Nos. 843/**MS**850.

140 Portuguese Caravel

1983. Brasiliana 83 International Stamp Exhibition, Rio de Janeiro. Sheet 90×89 mm.

MS775	**140** 50p. multicoloured	2·60	2·60

141 Rowland Hill and Penny Black

1983. World Communications Year. Mult.

776	50c. Type **141**	10	10
777	2p.50 Samuel Morse and morse machine	15	10
778	3p.50 Heinrich Rudolf Hertz and electromagnetic wave diagrams	20	10
779	5p. Lord Kelvin and "Agamemnon" (cable ship)	50	10
780	10p. Alexander Graham Bell and telephones	60	15
781	20p. Guglielmo Marconi and wireless apparatus	1·40	40
782	30p. Vladimir Kosma Zworykin and television	1·60	55
MS783	98×64 mm. 50p. Satellites	3·00	3·00

142 JAAC Emblem

1983. First JAAC Congress. Multicoloured.

784	4p. Crowd and emblem	25	15
785	5p. Type **142**	30	15

143 Speed Skating

1983. Winter Olympic Games, Sarajevo (1st issue). Multicoloured.

786	1p. Type **143**	10	10
787	1p.50 Ski jumping	15	10
788	3p. Cross-country skiing	20	10
789	5p. Bobsleigh	25	10
790	10p. Ice hockey	70	25
791	15p. Ice skating	1·10	30
792	20p. Luge	1·25	35
MS793	94×54 mm. 50p.Skiing	3·25	3·25

See also Nos. 816/**MS**823.

144 Hoeing Vegetable Patch

1983. World Food Day.

794	**144**	1p.50 multicoloured	10	10
795	**144**	2p. multicoloured	15	10
796	**144**	4p. multicoloured	30	15
MS797		60×61 mm. 10p. Man hoeing plantation	75	25

145 U.D.E.M.U. Emblem

1983. Democratic Union of Women. Multicoloured.

798	4p.50 Type **145**	30	15
799	7p.50 Flag and woman	50	20
800	9p. Woman sewing	70	30
801	12p. Women working on plantation	1·00	45

146 "Canna coccinea"

1983. Flowers. Multicoloured.

802	1p. Type **146**	15	10
803	1p.50 "Bougainvillea litoralis"	20	10
804	3p.50 "Euphorbia milii"	25	10
805	5p. "Delonix regia"	30	10
806	8p. "Bauhinia variegata"	50	15
807	10p. "Spathodea campanulata"	70	20
808	30p. "Hibiscus rosa-sinensis"	2·00	60

147 Guinean Fingerfish

1983. Fishes. Multicoloured.

809	1p. Type **147**	20	15
810	1p.50 Clown loach	25	15
811	3p.50 Spotted climbing-perch	35	20
812	5p. Berthold's panchax	50	20
813	8p. Red-barred lyretail	75	30
814	10p. Two-striped lyretail	1·10	40
815	30p. Lyre-tailed panchax	3·50	1·40

148 Ski Jumping

1984. Winter Olympic Games, Sarajevo (2nd issue). Multicoloured.

816	50c. Type **148**	10	10
817	2p.50 Speed skating	15	10
818	3p.50 Ice hockey	30	10
819	5p. Cross-country skiing	35	10
820	6p. Downhill skiing	60	15
821	20p. Ice skating	1·25	40
822	30p. Two-man bobsleigh	2·00	60
MS823	71×92 mm. 50p. Skiing	3·00	3·00

149 Duesenberg, 1928

1984. 150th Birth Anniv of Gottlieb Daimler (automobile designer). Multicoloured.

No.	Description	Unused	Used
824	5p. Type **149**	15	10
825	8p. MG "Midget", 1932	25	10
826	15p. Mercedes, 1928	50	20
827	20p. Bentley, 1928	60	30
828	24p. Alfa Romeo, 1929	85	30
829	30p. Datsun, 1932	1·25	35
830	35p. Lincoln, 1932	1·75	40
MS831	78×112 mm. 100p. Gottlieb Daimler and car (49×42 mm)	3·50	3·50

150 Sud Aviation Caravelle

1984. 40th Anniv of I.C.A.O. Multicoloured.

No.	Description	Unused	Used
832	8p. Type **150**	25	10
833	22p. Douglas DC-6B	80	30
834	80p. Ilyushin Il-76	2·25	90

151 "Dona Tadea Arias de Enriquez" (Goya)

1984. "Espana 84" International Stamp Exhibition, Madrid. Multicoloured.

No.	Description	Unused	Used
835	3p. "Virgin and Child" (Morales)	15	10
836	6p. Type **151**	20	10
837	10p. "Saint Cassilda" (Zurbaran)	30	10
838	12p. "Saints Andrew and Francis" (El Greco)	35	15
839	15p. "Infanta Isabel Clara Eugenia" (Coello)	55	15
840	35p. "Queen Maria of Austria" (Velazquez)	1·40	45
841	40p. "The Trinity" (El Greco)	1·75	55
MS842	76×81 mm. 100p. "The Clothed Maja" (Goya) (49×28 mm)	3·25	3·25

152 Football

1984. Olympic Games, Los Angeles (2nd issue). Multicoloured.

No.	Description	Unused	Used
843	6p. Type **152**	15	10
844	8p. Show jumping	25	10
845	15p. Sailing	50	15
846	20p. Hockey	70	20
847	22p. Handball	75	20
848	30p. Canoeing	1·10	35
849	40p. Boxing	1·75	60
MS850	79×92 mm. 100p. Windsurfing	3·75	3·75

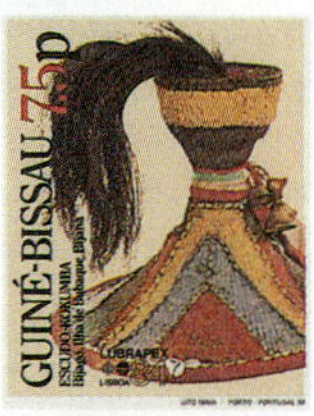

153 Fabric Headdress

1984. "Lubrapex 84" Portuguese-Brazilian Stamp Exhibition, Lisbon. Multicoloured.

No.	Description	Unused	Used
851	7p.50 Type **153**	25	15
852	7p.50 Headdress	25	15
853	7p.50 Carved bird headdress	25	15
854	7p.50 Wooden mask	25	15
855	7p.50 Carving of horse	25	15
856	7p.50 Statuette	25	15

154 Tiger

1984. Wild Cats. Multicoloured.

No.	Description	Unused	Used
857	3p. Type **154**	15	10
858	6p. Lions	25	10
859	10p. Clouded leopard	35	15
860	12p. Cheetahs	45	20
861	15p. Lynx	60	25
862	35p. Leopard	1·40	55
863	40p. Snow leopard	1·75	65

155 Pearl Throne, Cameroun

1984. World Heritage. Multicoloured.

No.	Description	Unused	Used
864	3p. Type **155**	10	10
865	6p. Antelope (carving), West Sudan	20	10
866	10p. Setial, East Africa	30	15
867	12p. Mask, West African coast	40	20
868	15p. Leopard (statuette), Guinea coast	60	25
869	35p. Carved statuette of woman, Zaire	1·25	50
870	40p. Funeral figures, South-east Africa and Madagascar	1·25	55

156 Amilcar Cabral making Speech

1984. 60th Birth Anniv of Amilcar Cabral. Multicoloured.

No.	Description	Unused	Used
871	5p. Type **156**	15	10
872	12p. Amilcar Cabral in combat dress	35	15
873	20p. Amilcar Cabral memorial	60	25
874	50p. Amilcar Cabral mausoleum	1·50	60

157 Mechanic working on Engine

1984. 11th Anniv of Independence. Mult.

No.	Description	Unused	Used
875	3p. Type **157**	10	10
876	6p. Children in school	20	10
877	10p. Laying bricks	30	10
878	12p. Doctor tending child (vert)	35	20
879	15p. Sewing (vert)	40	20
880	35p. Telephonist and switchboard	1·25	50
881	40p. P.A.I.G.C. headquarters	1·25	55

158 Grey Whales

1984. Whales. Multicoloured.

No.	Description	Unused	Used
882	5p. Type **158**	25	10
883	8p. Blue whales	30	15
884	15p. Bottle-nosed dolphins	60	25
885	20p. Sperm whale	70	25
886	24p. Killer whale	85	35
887	30p. Bowhead whale	1·50	40
888	35p. Sei whale	1·75	45

159 "Hypolimnas dexithea"

1984. Butterflies and Moths. Multicoloured.

No.	Description	Unused	Used
889	3p. Type **159**	15	15
890	6p. "Papilio arcturus"	20	15
891	10p. "Morpho menelaus terrestris"	35	15
892	12p. "Apaturina erminea"	45	20
893	15p. "Prepona praeneste"	70	25
894	35p. "Ornithoptera paradisea"	1·60	55
895	40p. "Morpho hecuba obidona"	1·60	60

160 Carl Lewis (400 m relay)

1984. Olympic Gold Medallists, Los Angeles. Multicoloured.

No.	Description	Unused	Used
896	6p. Type **160**	15	10
897	8p. Koji Gushiken (men's gymnastics)	15	10
898	15p. Dr. Reiner Klimke (individual dressage)	45	20
899	20p. Tracie Ruiz (synchronized swimming)	55	20
900	22p. May Lou Retton (women's gymnastics)	65	25
901	30p. Michael Gross (100 m free-style and 100 m butterfly)	90	35
902	40p. Edwin Moses (400 m hurdles)	1·25	50
MS903	54×62 mm. 100p. Daley Thompson (decathlon) (30×38 mm)	2·75	2·75

161 White Mountain Central Railway locomotive, 1926, U.S.A.

1984. Locomotives. Multicoloured.

No.	Description	Unused	Used
904	5p. Type **161**	20	15
905	8p. Talyllyn Mountain Railway locomotive No. 86, 1886, Great Britain	25	15
906	15p. Wuppetal Overhead Railway, 1901, Germany	50	20
907	20p. Peruvian mountain rack railway locomotive	60	25
908	24p. Steam locomotive, Achensee rack railway, Austria	80	30
909	30p. Vitznau–Rigi rack railway locomotive, Switzerland	1·10	40
910	35p. Vitznau–Rigi rack railway locomotive No. 7, Switzerland	1·60	60
MS911	91×66 mm. 100p. As No. 906 (36×27 mm)	3·50	3·50

162 Harley Davidson Motor Cycle

1985. Centenary of Motor Cycle. Mult.

No.	Description	Unused	Used
912	5p. Type **162**	20	15
913	8p. Kawasaki	25	15
914	15p. Honda	45	20
915	20p. Yamaha	70	30
916	25p. Suzuki	1·00	35
917	30p. BMW	1·40	45
918	35p. Moto Guzzi	1·50	50
MS919	90×72 mm. 100p. Daimler single track motor cycle, 1885 (27×36 mm)	3·75	3·75

163 Brown Pelican

1985. Air. Birth Bicentenary of John J. Audubon (ornithologist). Multicoloured.

No.	Description	Unused	Used
920	5p. Type **163**	45	20
921	10p. American white pelican	75	30
922	20p. Great blue heron	1·40	45
923	40p. Greater flamingo	3·00	1·00

164 "Clitocybe gibba"

1985. Fungi. Multicoloured.

No.	Description	Unused	Used
924	7p. Type **164**	35	15
925	9p. "Morchella elata"	50	20
926	12p. "Lepista nuda"	75	25
927	20p. "Lactarius deliciosus"	90	30
928	30p. "Russula virescens"	1·25	35
929	35p. "Chroogomphus rutilus"	1·75	50

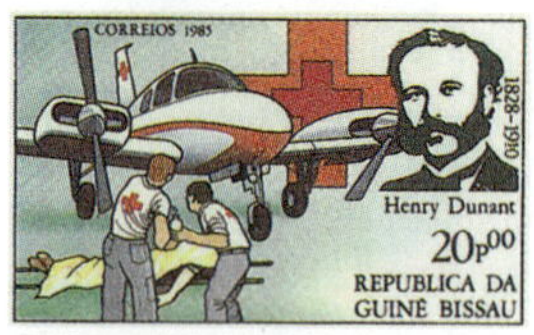

165 Dunant, Piper Twin Commanche and Volunteers attending Patient

1985. 75th Death Anniv of Henri Dunant (Red Cross founder). Multicoloured.

No.	Description	Unused	Used
930	20p. Type **165**	40	15
931	25p. Doctor and volunteer putting patient in ambulance	50	15
932	40p. Helicopter team attending wounded soldier	75	35
933	80p. Volunteers in boat rescuing man from water	1·40	55

166 Long-haired White Cat

1985. Cats. Multicoloured.

No.	Description	Unused	Used
934	7p. Type **166**	20	15

935	10p. Siamese cat	25	15
936	12p. Grey cat	30	15
937	15p. Tortoiseshell cat	40	15
938	20p. Ginger cat	55	20
939	40p. Tabby cat	1·00	35
940	45p. Short-haired white cat	1·40	35
MS941	80×70 mm. 100p. Tabby kittens (39×31 mm)	2·75	2·75

167 Vincenzo Bellini, 1820 Harp and 16th-century Descant Viol

1985. International Music Year. Composers. Multicoloured.

942	4p. Type **167** (150th death anniv of Bellini)	15	15
943	5p. Robert Schumann (175th birth anniv) and pyramid piano, 1829	15	15
944	7p. Frederic Chopin (175th birth anniv) and piano, 1817	15	15
945	12p. Luigi Cherubini (225th birth anniv), 1720 baryton and 18th-century quinton	20	15
946	20p. Giovanni Battista Pergolesi (275th birth anniv) and harpsichord, 1734	45	15
947	30p. Georg Friedrich Handel (300th birth anniv), 1825 valve trumpet and 18th-century timpani	65	20
948	50p. Heinrich Schutz (400th birth anniv), 17th-century bass viol and 1680 oboe	1·00	45
MS949	77×90 mm. 100p. Johann Sebastian Bach (300th birth anniv) and organ from Thomas Church, Leipzig (28×49 mm3	75	3·75

168 "Santa Maria"

1985. Sailing Ships. Multicoloured.

950	8p. Type **168**	30	15
951	15p. 16th-century Dutch carrack	40	15
952	20p. "Mayflower"	50	15
953	30p. "St. Louis" (French galleon)	75	20
954	35p. "Royal Sovereign" (galleon), 1660	85	20
955	45p. "Soleil Royal" (17th- century French warship)	1·25	35
956	80p. 18th-century British naval brig	1·90	60

169 U.N. Emblem, Rainbow and Peace Doves

1985. 40th Anniv of U.N.O.

957	**169**	10p. multicoloured	25	15
958	-	20p. blue and brown	50	35

DESIGN: 20p. U.N. emblem in "40".

170 "Madonna of the Rose Garden" (detail)

1985. "Italia '85" International Stamp Exhibition, Rome. Paintings by Botticelli. Multicoloured.

959	7p. Type **170**	15	10
960	10p. "Venus and Mars" (detail)	15	10
961	12p. "St. Augustine in his Study" (detail)	20	15
962	15p. "Spring" (detail)	25	15
963	20p. "Virgin and Child" (detail)	35	15
964	40p. "Virgin and Child with St. John" (detail)	1·00	30
965	45p. "Birth of Venus" (detail)	1·10	35
MS966	73×107 mm. 100p. "Virgin and Child with Two Angels" (detail) (31×39 mm)	2·50	2·50

171 Youths dancing

1985. International Youth Year. Mult.

967	7p. Type **171**	10	10
968	13p. Windsurfing	20	15
969	15p. Roller skating	20	15
970	25p. Hang-gliding	35	15
971	40p. Surfing	55	25
972	50p. Skateboarding	75	40
973	80p. Free-falling from airplane	1·50	60
MS974	75×75 mm. 100p. Judo (39×31 mm)	3·25	3·25

172 Alfa Touring Car

1986. Anniversaries and Events. Mult.

975	15p. Tail of comet	1·25	50
976	15p. Head of comet	1·25	50
977	15p. Type **172**	1·25	50
978	15p. Frankfurt am Main railway station, 1914	2·25	75
979	15p. Top of trophy	2·50	1·00
980	15p. Base of trophy	2·50	1·00
981	15p. Olympic rings	3·00	1·00
982	15p. View of Barcelona	3·00	1·00
983	15p. Part of space station	1·25	50
984	15p. Deflectors	1·25	50
985	15p. Space station and Shuttle	1·25	50
986	15p. Part of space station and Earth	1·25	50
987	15p. Boris Becker's head and arm	1·50	75
988	15p. Becker's body	1·50	75
989	15p. Lendl's head and arms	1·50	75
990	15p. Lendl's body and legs	1·50	75
MS991	103×67 mm. 100p. Comet and "Giotto" space probe	8·00	8·00

ANNIVERSARIES: Nos. 975/6, Appearance of Halley's Comet; 977, Centenary of motor car; 978, 150th anniv of German railways; 979/80, World Cup Football Championship, Mexico; 981, Olympic Games, Seoul (1988); 982, "500th anniv of discovery of America by Columbus" Exhibition and Olympic Games, Barcelona (1992); 983/6, 25 years of manned space flights; 987/8, Wimbledon Men's Singles champion, 1986; 989/90, Ivan Lendl, winner of U.S. Masters Tournament, 1986.

Nos. 975/90 were printed together in se-tenant sheetlets of 16 stamps, stamps for the same event forming a composite design.

173 "Santa Maria"

1987. 500th Anniv (1992) of Discovery of America by Columbus. Multicoloured.

992	50p. Type **173**	2·25	80
993	50p. View of Seville	2·25	80
994	50p. Pedro Alvares Cabral disembarking at Bahia	2·00	60
995	50p. View of Seville (different)	2·25	80
MS996	103×67 mm. 150p. 15th-century galleon in Lisbon harbour	5·75	5·75

1987. Nos. 352/5, 359 and 362/3 of Portuguese Guinea surch DA BISSAU and new value.

997	100p. on 20c. Type **51**	35	15
998	200p. on 35c. African rock python	70	25
999	300p. on 70c. Boomslang	1·10	35
1000	400p. on 80c. West African mamba	1·25	40
1001	500p. on 3e.50 Brown house snake	1·50	50
1002	1000p. on 15e. Striped beauty snake	3·00	1·00
1003	2000p. on 20e. African egg-eating snake (horiz)	6·00	3·00

1987. No. 430 surch 2500,00.

1004	**76**	2500p. on 2e. mult	7·00	3·25

176 Ice Dancing

1988. Winter Olympic Games, Calgary. Mult.

1005	5p. Type **176**	10	10
1006	10p. Luge	10	10
1007	50p. Skiing	30	15
1008	200p. Downhill skiing	75	30
1009	300p. Ski-bobbing	1·25	40
1010	500p. Ski jumping (vert)	2·00	55
1011	800p. Speed skating (vert)	3·00	1·10
MS1012	90×47 mm. 900p. Two-man luge (39×31 mm)	3·25	3·25

177 Yachting

1988. Olympic Games, Seoul. Multicoloured.

1013	5p. Type **177**	10	10
1014	10p. Equestrian events (horiz)	10	10
1015	50p. High jumping (horiz)	15	10
1016	200p. Rifle shooting (horiz)	70	30
1017	300p. Triple jumping	1·10	40
1018	500p. Tennis	2·00	50
1019	800p. Archery	2·75	1·00
MS1020	70×45 mm. 900p. Football (39×31 mm)	3·00	3·00

178 Football

1988. "Essen 88" Stamp Fair and European Football Championship, Germany.

1021	**178**	5p. multicoloured	10	10
1022	-	10p. multicoloured	10	10
1023	-	50p. multicoloured	15	10
1024	-	200p. multicoloured	70	30
1025	-	300p. multicoloured	1·10	40
1026	-	500p. multicoloured	2·00	50
1027	-	800p. multicoloured	2·75	1·10
MS1028		60×75 mm. 900p. multicoloured	3·00	3·00

DESIGNS: 10 to 900p. Various footballing scenes.

179 Lioness

1988. Animals. Multicoloured.

1029	5p. Type **179**	10	10
1030	10p. Ferruginous pygmy owl	10	10
1031	50p. Hoopoe (horiz)	25	10
1032	200p. Common zebra (horiz)	30	10
1033	300p. African elephant	50	20
1034	500p. Vulturine guineafowl	3·00	1·25
1035	800p. Black rhinoceros	1·25	50

180 Machel

1988. 2nd Death Anniv of Pres. Samora Machel of Mozambique. Multicoloured.

1036	10p. Type **180**	10	10
1037	50p. With arm raised	10	10
1038	200p. With soldier	30	10
1039	300p. Wearing suit	50	20

181 Henry Dunant (founder)

1988. 125th Anniv of Int Red Cross. Mult.

1040	10p. Type **181**	10	10
1041	50p. Dr. T. Maunoir	10	10
1042	200p. Dr. Louis Appia	30	10
1043	800p. Gustave Moynier	1·25	50

182 Basset Hound

1988. Dogs. Multicoloured.

1044	5p. Type **182**	10	10
1045	10p. Grand bleu de Gascogne	10	10
1046	50p. Italian spinone	10	10
1047	200p. Yorkshire terrier	30	10
1048	300p. Munsterlander	50	20
1049	500p. Pointer	80	30
1050	800p. German shorthaired pointer	1·25	50
MS1051	81×50 mm. 900p. German shepherd (40×32 mm)	1·40	1·40

183 Egyptian Ship, 3300 B.C.

1988. Sailing Ships. Multicoloured.

1052	5p. Type **183**	10	10
1053	10p. Ship of Sahu Re, 2500 B.C. (wrongly inscr "2700 B.C.")	10	10
1054	50p. Ship of Hatshepshut, 1500 B.C	10	10
1055	200p. Ship of Rameses III, 1200 B.C	35	10
1056	300p. Greek trireme, 480 B.C	60	25
1057	500p. Etruscan bireme, 600 B.C	1·00	40
1058	800p. 12th-century Venetian galley	1·50	65

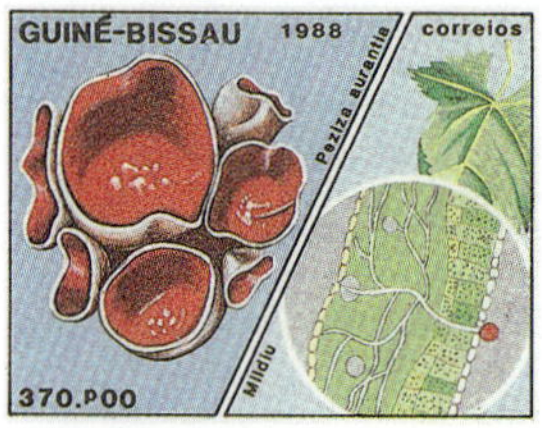

184 "Peziza aurantia"

1988. Fungi. Multicoloured.

1059	370p. Type **184**	75	30
1060	470p. Morel	1·00	35
1061	600p. Caesar's mushroom	1·25	45
1062	780p. Fly agaric	1·60	55
1063	800p. Deadly amanite	1·60	55
1064	900p. Cultivated mushroom	1·90	70
1065	945p. Pixie stool	2·10	75

185 Francois-Andre Philidor and Rook

1988. "Finlandia 88" International Stamp Exhibition, Helsinki. Chess. Multicoloured.

1066	5p. Type **185**	10	10
1067	10p. Howard Staunton and chessmen	10	10
1068	50p. Adolf Anderssen and queen	10	10
1069	200p. Paul Morphy and pawn	30	10
1070	300p. Wilhelm Steinitz and knight	50	20
1071	500p. Emanuel Lasker and bishop	80	30
1072	800p. Jose Capablanca and king	1·25	50
MS1073	93×62 mm. 900p. Ruy Lopez (37×32 mm)	1·40	1·40

186 Trumpeter, Flag Bearer and Drummer

1988. Abel Djassi Pioneers Organisation. Multicoloured.

1074	10p. Type **186**	10	10
1075	50p. Girls saluting	10	10
1076	200p. Drawing on floor (horiz)	30	10
1077	300p. Playing ball (horiz)	50	20

187 Monument

1988. 400th Anniv of Cacheu. Multicoloured.

1078	10p. Type **187**	10	10
1079	50p. Fort (horiz)	10	10
1080	200p. Early building (horiz)	35	10
1081	300p. Church (horiz)	50	20

188 Woman with Long Hair

1989. Traditional Hairstyles.

1082	188	50p. multicoloured	10	10
1083	-	100p. multicoloured	15	10
1084	-	200p. multicoloured	30	10
1085	-	350p. multicoloured	60	25
1086	-	500p. multicoloured	80	30
1087	-	800p. multicoloured	1·25	50
1088	-	1000p. multicoloured	1·60	65

DESIGNS: 100p. to 1000p. Different hairstyles.

189 Bombalon

1989. Traditional Musical Instruments. Mult.

1089	50p. Type **189**	10	10
1090	100p. Flute	15	10
1091	200p. Tambor	35	15
1092	350p. Dondon	65	25
1093	500p. Balafon	90	35
1094	800p. Kora	1·50	60
1095	1000p. Nhanhero	1·75	70

190 Seychelles Blue Pigeon

1989. Birds. Multicoloured.

1096	50p. Type **190**	15	15
1097	100p. Laughing dove	20	15
1098	200p. Namaqua dove	50	30
1099	350p. Purple-breasted ground dove	80	50
1100	500p. African collared dove	1·25	70
1101	800p. Pheasant pigeon	2·10	1·25
1102	1000p. Emerald dove	2·75	1·40
MS1103	71×80 mm. 1500f. Reinwardt's long-tailed pigeon (32×40 mm)	3·75	3·75

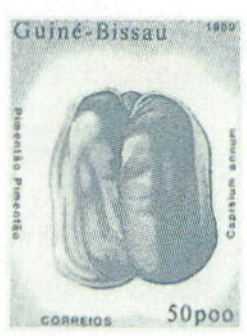

191 Pimento

1989. Plants.

1104	191	50p. blue	10	10
1105	-	100p. violet	15	10
1106	-	200p. green	35	15
1107	-	350p. red	65	25
1108	-	500p. brown	90	35
1109	-	800p. brown	1·50	60
1110	-	1000p. green	1·75	70

DESIGNS: 100p. Solanum; 200p. "Curcumis peco"; 350p. Tomato; 500p. "Solanum itiopium"; 800p. "Hibiscus esculentus"; 1000p. Baguiche.

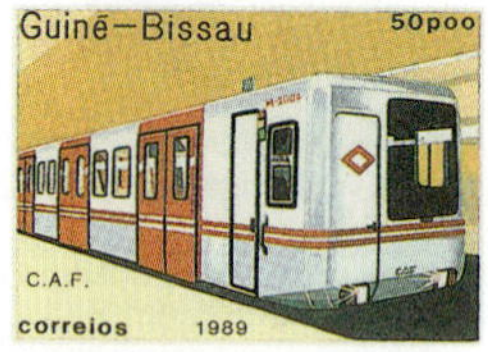

192 Madrid Rapid Transit Train No. M-2004, Spain

1989. Trains. Multicoloured.

1111	50p. Type **192**	15	10
1112	100p. Class TEM-2 diesel locomotive, Russia	20	10
1113	200p. Diesel locomotive, Brazil	50	15
1114	350p. Diesel railcar, Spain	95	25
1115	500p. Type 55E electric locomotive, Czechoslovakia	1·40	35
1116	800p. Class Tu-7E diesel shunting locomotive, Russia	2·25	60
1117	1000p. Electric multiple unit, Spain (68×27 mm)	2·60	70
MS1118	89×59 mm. 1500p. Class 593 diesel multiple unit train, Spain (31×39 mm)	3·75	3·75

193 Hurdling

1989. Olympic Games, Barcelona (1992) (1st issue). Multicoloured.

1119	50p. Type **193**	10	10
1120	100p. Boxing	20	10
1121	200p. High jumping	35	15
1122	350p. Sprinters in starting blocks	60	25
1123	500p. Runner leaving starting block	90	35
1124	800p. Gymnastics	1·50	60
1125	1000p. Pole vaulting	1·75	70
MS1126	82×61 mm. 1500p. Football (31×39 mm)	2·60	2·60

See also Nos. 1245/8.

194 "Limelight"

1989. Lilies. Multicoloured.

1127	50p. Type **194**	10	10
1128	100p. "Lilium candidum"	20	10
1129	200p. "Lilium pardalinum"	35	15
1130	350p. "Lilium auratum"	65	25
1131	500p. "Lilium canadense"	90	35
1132	800p. "Enchantment"	1·50	60
1133	1000p. "Black Dragon"	1·75	70
MS1134	43×70 mm. 1500p. "Lilium pyrenaicum" (31×39 mm)	2·60	2·60

195 "La Marseillaise" (relief by Rude from Arc de Triomphe)

1989. "Philex France 89" International Stamp Exhibition, Paris. Multicoloured.

1135	50p. Type **195**	10	10
1136	100p. Champ de Mars	20	10
1137	200p. Storming of the Bastille	35	15
1138	350p. Fete (27×44 mm)	65	25
1139	500p. Dancing round Tree of Liberty	90	35
1140	800p. Rouget de Lisle singing "The Marseillaise"	1·50	60
1141	1000p. Storming of the Bastille (different)	1·75	70
MS1142	99×74 mm. 1500p. Motto of the Republic	2·60	2·60

196 Teotihuacan Pot

1989. "Brasiliana 89" International Stamp Exhibition, Rio de Janeiro. Multicoloured.

1143	50p. Type **196**	10	10
1144	100p. Mochica jar	20	10
1145	200p. Jaina statuette	35	15
1146	350p. Nayarit anthrozoomorphic jug	65	25
1147	500p. Inca vase	90	35
1148	800p. Hopewell statuette of mother and child	1·50	60
1149	1000p. Taina mask	1·75	70
MS1150	56×70 mm. 1500p. Ecuador statuette (31×39 mm)	2·75	2·75

197 Players Tackling

1989. World Cup Football Championship, Italy (1990). Multicoloured.

1151	50p. Type **197**	10	10
1152	100p. Players and ball	20	10
1153	200p. Players and ball (different)	35	15
1154	350p. "Scissors" kick	65	25
1155	500p. Goalkeeper	90	35
1156	800p. Foul	1·50	60
1157	1000p. Player scoring goal	1·75	70
MS1158	55×96 mm. 1500p. Legs and ball (37×29 mm)	2·75	2·75

198 Trachodon

1989. Prehistoric Animals. Multicoloured.

1159	50p. Type **198**	10	10
1160	100p. Edaphosaurus (68×22 mm)	20	10
1161	200p. Mesosaurus	35	15
1162	350p. "Elephas primigenius"	65	25
1163	500p. Tyrannosaurus (horiz)	90	35
1164	800p. Stegosaurus (horiz)	1·50	60
1165	1000p. "Cervus megaceros"	1·75	70

No. 1162 is inscribed "Elephius primigenius" in error.

199 Speed Skating

1989. Winter Olympic Games, Albertville (1992). Multicoloured.

1166	50p. Type **199**	10	10
1167	100p. Figure skating	20	10
1168	200p. Ski jumping	35	15
1169	350p. Skiing	65	25

1170	500p. Skiing (different)	90	35
1171	800p. Bobsleighing	1·50	60
1172	1000p. Ice hockey	1·75	70
MS1173	102×61 mm. 1500p. Ice hockey (different) (31×39 mm)	2·75	2·75

200 African Buffalo

1989. Animals.

1174	**200**	50p. brown and red	10	10
1175	-	100p. ultramarine & blue	20	10
1176	-	200p. green & light green	35	15
1177	-	350p. purple and lilac	65	25
1178	-	500p. chestnut and brown	90	35
1179	-	800p. violet & deep violet	1·50	60
1180	-	1000p. deep red and red	1·75	70
1181	-	1500p. red and yellow	2·75	1·10

DESIGNS: 100p. Steppe zebra; 200p. Black rhinoceros; 350p. Okapi; 500p. Rhesus macacque; 800p. Hippopotamus; 1000p. Cheetah; 1500p. Lion.

201 "Adoration of Baby Jesus" (Fra Filippo Lippi)

1989. Christmas. Multicoloured.

1182	50p. Type **201**	10	10
1183	100p. "Adoration of the Kings" (Pieter Brueghel)	20	10
1184	200p. "Adoration of the Kings" (Jan Mostaert)	35	15
1185	350p. "Nativity" (Albert Durer)	65	25
1186	500p. "Adoration of the Kings" (Peter Paul Rubens)	90	35
1187	800p. "Adoration of the Kings" (Roger van der Weyden)	1·50	60
1188	1000p. "Adoration of the Kings" (Francesco Francia) (horiz)	1·75	70

202 Pope John-Paul II and Map

1990. Papal Visit. Multicoloured.

1189	500p. Type **202**	80	20
1190	1000p. Pope and couple	1·60	40
MS1191	109×137 mm. 1500p. Cathedral (vert)	2·75	2·75

203 Dove flying over Exhibition

1990. Belgica 90 International Stamp Exhibition, Brussels. Sheet 111×122 mm.

MS1192	**203** 3000p. multicoloured	4·25	4·25

204 Cockerel and Hen

1990. "Lubrapex 90" Brazilian–Portuguese Stamp Exhibition, Brasilia. Coop Fowls. Multicoloured.

1193	500p. Type **204**	85	35
1194	800p. Common turkey	1·25	50
1195	1000p. Duck and ducklings	1·60	65
MS1196	112×141 mm. 1500p. Red junglefowl, common turkey, ducks and ducklings	2·25	2·25

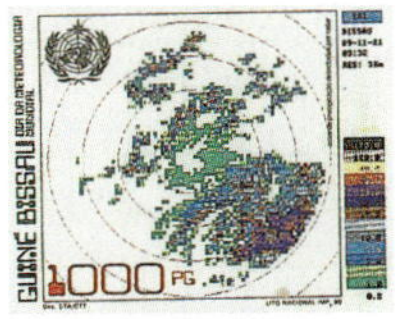

205 Radar Rainfall Map

1990. World Meteorology Day. Multicoloured.

1197	1000p. Type **205**	1·60	65
1198	3000p. Campbell-Stokes heliograph	5·00	2·00

206 Crying Man and Baby in Womb

1990. 40th Anniv of U.N. Development Programme.

1199	**206**	1000p. multicoloured	1·60	65

207 Cotton Plant

1991. Traditional Cotton Weaving. Mult.

1200	400p. Type **207**	60	25
1201	500p. Weaver	75	30
1202	600p. Traditional cloth pattern	95	40
MS1203	156×228 mm. 150p. Type **207**; 150p. Woman preparing cotton; 150p. Girl spinning cotton; 150p. Picking cotton; 150p. "Earius insulana" (cotton pest) and larvae; 150p. Dyeing cloth; 150p. As No. 1201; 150p. As No. 1202; 150p. Pattern with lozenges and stripes; 150p. Striped pattern	5·00	5·00

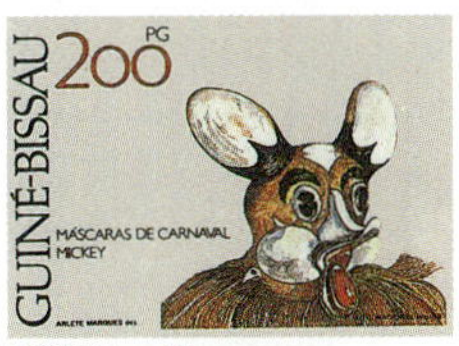

208 Mickey Mouse

1991. Carnival Masks. Multicoloured.

1204	200p. Type **208**	30	10
1205	300p. Hippopotamus	45	20
1206	600p. Buffalo	75	30
1207	1200p. Buffalo (different)	95	40

209 Royal Threadfin

1991. Fishes. Multicoloured.

1208	300p. Type **209**	45	20
1209	400p. Guinean fingerfish	95	55
1210	500p. Goree spadefish	1·60	85
1211	600p. Long-finned pompano	2·00	90

210 Fire Engine with Water Cannons

1991. Fire and First Aid Service. Mult.

1212	200p. Type **210**	30	10
1213	500p. Fire engine with ladders	75	30
1214	800p. Emergency vehicle with ladders	1·25	50
1215	1500p. Ambulance	2·25	90

211 Lizard Buzzard

1991. Birds. Multicoloured.

1216	100p. Type **211**	25	15
1217	250p. Crowned crane	75	15
1218	350p. Abyssinian ground hornbill	1·10	35
1219	500p. Saddle-bill stork	1·50	40
MS1220	111×139 mm. 1500p. Lizard buzzard (different) (40×49)	4·25	4·25

212 "Best Wishes"

1991. Greetings Stamps. Multicoloured.

1221	250p. Type **212**	40	10
1222	400p. Couple embracing ("With love")	65	25
1223	800p. Horn-blower and map of Africa ("Congratulations")	1·25	50
1224	1000p. Doves ("Season's greetings")	1·50	60

213 Fula

1992. Traditional Costume. Multicoloured.

1225	400p. Type **213**	10	10
1226	600p. Balanta	15	10
1227	1000p. Fula (different)	25	10
1228	1500p. Manjaco	40	15

214 "Landolfia owariensis"

1992. Fruits. Multicoloured.

1229	500p. Type **214**	15	10
1230	1500p. "Dialium guineensis"	40	15
1231	2000p. "Adansonia digitata"	50	20
1232	3000p. "Parkia biglobosa"	75	30

215 Cigarette and Fruit "Hearts"

1992. World Health Day. "Health in Rhythm with the Heart". Multicoloured.

1233	1500p. Type **215**	40	15
1234	4000p. "Heart" running over food	1·00	40

216 "Cassia alata"

1992. "Lubrapex 92" Brazilian–Portuguese Stamp Exhibition, Lisbon. Plants. Multicoloured.

1235	100p. Type **216**	10	10
1236	400p. "Perlebia purpurea"	10	10
1237	1000p. "Caesalpinia pulcherrima"	25	15
1238	1500p. "Adenanthera pavonina"	40	15
MS1239	110×140 mm. 3000p. "Caesalpina pulcherrima"	80	80

Nos. 1235/8 were issued together, se-tenant, forming a composite design.

217 Canoe

1992. Canoes. Multicoloured.

1240	750p. Type **217**	35	10
1241	800p. Pirogue	35	10
1242	1000p. Pirogue (different)	45	10
1243	1300p. Skiff	60	20
MS1244	70×96 mm. 1500p. Malachite kingfisher	85	85

The canoe appears in the margin of No. **MS**1244.

218 Volleyball

1992. Olympic Games, Barcelona (2nd issue). Multicoloured.

1245	600p. Basketball	15	10
1246	1000p. Type **218**	25	10
1247	1500p. Handball	40	15
1248	2000p. Football	50	20

219 "Afzelia africana"

1992. Forest Preservation. Multicoloured.

1249	1000p. Type **219**	25	10
1250	1500p. African mahogany	40	15
1251	2000p. Iroko	50	20
1252	3000p. Ambila	75	30

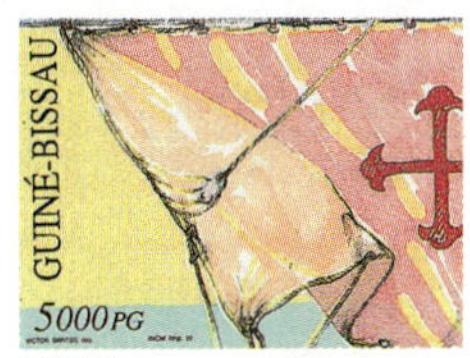

220 Sail

1992. 500th Anniv of Discovery of America by Columbus. Sheet 71×96 mm.

MS1253	**220** 5000p. multicoloured	1·25	1·25

221 Colobus

1992. The Red Colobus. Multicoloured.

1254	2000p. Type **221**	50	20
1255	2000p. Colobus sitting in tree fork	50	20
1256	2000p. Mother and young	50	20
1257	2000p. Two colobus on tree branch	50	20

222 Puff Adder

1993. Reptiles. Multicoloured.

1258	1500p. Type **222**	40	15
1259	3000p. African dwarf crocodile	80	30
1260	4000p. Nile monitor	1·10	45
1261	5000p. Rainbow lizard	1·40	55
MS1262	130×106 mm. Nos. 1258/61	4·00	4·00

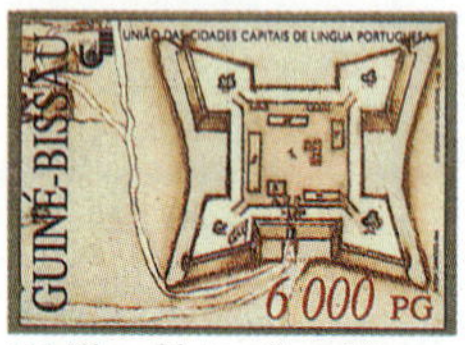

223 "Plan of S. Jose Bissau" (Jose Luis Braun)

1993. Union of Portuguese speaking capital Cities. Sheet 71×97 mm.

MS1263	**223** 6000p. multicoloured	1·60	1·60

224 Waterside Village

1993. Tourism. Multicoloured.

1264	1000p. Type **224**	25	10
1265	2000p. Masked villagers on shore and crops	55	20
1266	4000p. Villages on offshore islands	1·10	45
1267	5000p. Crops on island	1·40	55

Nos. 1264/7 were issued together, se-tenant, forming a composite design.

225 Bracelet

1994. Jewellery. Multicoloured.

1268	1500p. Type **225**	40	15
1269	3000p. Tribal mask pendant	80	30
1270	4000p. Circles pendant	1·10	45
1271	5000p. Filigree pendant	1·40	55
MS1272	76×76 mm. 18000p. Detail of tribal mask pendant	1·90	1·90

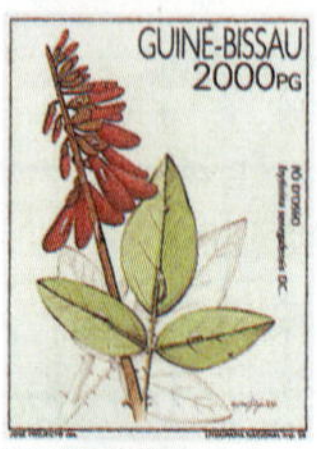

226 "Erythrina senegalensis"

1994. Medicinal Plants. Multicoloured.

1273	2000p. Type **226**	20	10
1274	3000p. "Cassia occidentalis"	30	10
1275	4000p. "Gardenia ternifolia"	45	20
1276	6000p. "Cochlospermum tinctorium"	65	25

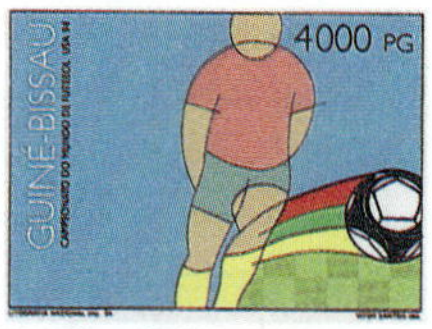

227 Player kicking Ball

1994. World Cup Football Championship, U.S.A. Multicoloured.

1277	4000p. Type **227**	40	15
1278	5000p. Goalkeeper making save	55	20
1279	5500p. Heading the ball	60	25
1280	6500p. Dribbling the ball	70	30

228 Common Egg-eater (Dasypeltis scabra)

1994. "Philakorea 1994" International and "Singpex '94" Stamp Exhibitions. Snakes. Multicoloured.

1281	5000p. Type **228**	45	20
1282	5000p. Green snake ("Philothamnus sp.")	45	20
1283	5000p. Black-lipped cobra ("Naja melanoleuca")	45	20
1284	5000p. African python ("Python sebae")	45	20
MS1285	145×105 mm. 15000p. Superb sunbird and tree snake (60×49 mm)	1·40	1·40

229 Collecting Fruits

1995. Palm Oil. Multicoloured.

1286	3000p. Type **229**	20	10
1287	6500p. Crushing fruit	45	20
1288	7500p. Palm oil production	55	20
1289	8000p. Animals and pot of palm oil	80	35

230 Women fishing

1995. 50th Anniv of United Nations Food and Agriculture Organization. Multicoloured.

1290	3000p. Type **230**	20	10
1291	6500p. Farmer on tractor	45	10
1292	7500p. Basket of fruit	55	15
1293	8000p. Women and children queuing	60	15
MS1294	140×110 mm. Nos. 1292/3	1·10	1·10

231 Hands and Emblem

1995. 50th Anniv of United Nations. Multicoloured.

1295	4000p. Type **231**	30	10
1296	5500p. United Nations emblem	40	10
1297	7500p. Guinea-Bissau flag and emblem	55	15
1298	8000p. Hands holding dove and emblem	60	15
MS1299	95×90 mm. 15000p. Emblem	2·00	1·00

Pt. 1

GUYANA

Formerly British Guiana. Attained independence on 26 May 1966, and changed its name to Guyana.

100 cents = 1 dollar

CANCELLED REMAINDERS* In 1969 remainders of some issues were put on the market cancelled-to-order in such a way as to be indistinguishable form genuine postally used copies for all practical purposes. Our used quotations which are indicated by an asterisk are the same for cancelled-to-order or postally used copies.

1966. Nos. 331 etc. of British Guiana optd GUYANA INDEPENDENCE 1966.

388	-	5c. red and black	40	10
391	-	12c. black and brown	10	10
393	-	36c. red and black	30	30
395	-	72c. red and green	50	65
396	-	$1 multicoloured	4·50	35
397	-	$2 mauve	1·50	1·50
398	-	$5 blue and black	1·00	3·25
399	**55**	1c. black	10	10
400	-	4c. violet	10	10
401	-	8c. blue	10	10
405	-	48c. blue and red	30	30
421	-	2c. green	10	10
422	-	3c. green and brown	30	10
424	-	6c. green	10	10
435	-	24c. black and orange	5·00	10

74 Flag and Map

1966. Independence. Multicoloured.

408	5c. Type **74**	30	10
409	15c. Type **74**	40	10
410	25c. Arms of Guyana	40	10
411	$1 Arms of Guyana	1·10	1·25

76 Bank Building

1966. Opening of Bank of Guyana.

412	**76**	5c. multicoloured	10	10
413	**76**	25c. multicoloured	10	10

77 British Guiana One Cent Stamp of 1856

1967. World's Rarest Stamp Commemoration.

414	**77**	5c. multicoloured*	10	10
415	**77**	25c. multicoloured*	10	10

78 Chateau Margot

1967. 1st Anniv of Independence. Multicoloured.

416	6c. Type **78***	10	10
417	15c. Independence Arch*	10	10
418	25c. Fort Island (horiz)*	10	10
419	$1 National Assembly (horiz)	20	15

83 "Millie" (Blue and Yellow Macaw)

1967. Christmas.

441	**83**	5c. yellow, blue, black grn*	10	10
442	**83**	25c. yellow, blue, blk vio*	15	10
443	**83**	5c. yellow, blue, black red*	10	10
444	**83**	25c. yellow, blue, blk grn*	15	10

84 Wicket-keeping

1968. M.C.C.'s West Indies Tour. Multicoloured.

445	5c. Type **84***	10	10
446	6c. Batting*	10	10
447	25c. Bowling*	30	10

87 Pike Cichlid

1968. Multicoloured.

448	1c. Type **87**	10	10
449	2c. Red paranha ("Pirai")	10	10
450	3c. Peacock cichlid ("Lukunani")	10	10
451	5c. Armoured catfish ("Hassar")	10	10
455	20c. Hoatzin (vert)	60	10
459	60c. White-lipped peccary	1·00	10
460	$1 Paca ("Labba")	80	10
461	$2 Nine-banded armadillo	1·25	2·00
462	$5 Ocelot	1·00	3·00
489	6c. Black acara ("Patua")	10	1·00
490	10c. Spix's guan (vert)	30	60
491	15c. Harpy eagle (vert)	30	10
493	25c. Guianan cock of the rock (vert)	30	10
494	40c. Great kiskadee (vert)	60	1·00
495	50c. Brazilian agouti ("Accouri")	35	15

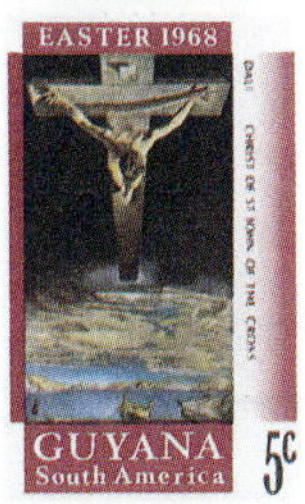

102 "Christ of St. John of the Cross" (Salvador Dali)

1968. Easter.

463	**102**	5c. multicoloured*	10	10
464	**102**	25c. multicoloured*	20	10

103 "Efficiency Year"

1968. "Savings Bonds and Efficiency". Multicoloured.

465	6c. Type **103***	10	10
466	25c. Type **103***	10	10
467	30c. "Savings Bonds"*	10	10
468	40c. "Savings Bonds"*	10	10

105 Open Book, Star and Crescent

1968. 1400th Anniv of Holy Quran.

469	**105**	6c. black, gold and flesh*	10	10
470	**105**	25c. black, gold and lilac*	10	10
471	**105**	30c. black, gold and green*	10	10
472	**105**	40c. black, gold and blue*	10	10

107 Broadcasting Greetings

1968. Christmas.

473	**107**	6c. brown, black and green	10	10
474	**107**	25c. brown, violet green	10	10
475	-	30c. green and turquoise*	10	10
476	-	40c. red and turquoise*	10	10

DESIGNS: 30c. and 40c. Map showing radio link, Guyana–Trinidad.

109 Festival Ceremony

1969. Hindu Festival of Phagwah. Multicoloured.

477	6c. Type **109**	10	10
478	25c. Ladies spraying scent	10	10
479	30c. Type **109**	10	10
480	40c. As No. 478	10	10

111 "Sacrament of the Last Supper" (Dali)

1969. Easter.

481	**111**	6c. multicoloured	10	10
482	**111**	25c. multicoloured	10	10
483	**111**	30c. multicoloured	10	10
484	**111**	40c. multicoloured	10	10

112 Map showing "CARIFTA" Countries

1969. 1st Anniv of "CARIFTA".

500	**112**	6c. red, blue and turquoise	15	15
501	-	25c. lemon, brown and red	15	15

DESIGN—HORIZ: 25c. "Strength in Unity".

114 Building "Independence" (first aluminium ship)

1969. 50th Anniv of I.L.O.

502	**114**	30c. blue, black and silver	40	25
503	-	40c. multicoloured	50	25

DESIGN—HORIZ: 40c. Bauxite processing plant.

116 Scouts raising Flag

1969. 3rd Caribbean Scout Jamboree and Diamond Jubilee of Scouting in Guyana. Multicoloured.

504	6c. Type **116**	10	10
505	8c. Camp-fire cooking	10	10
506	25c. Type **116**	10	10
507	30c. As 8c.	10	10
508	50c. Type **116**	15	15

118 Gandhi and Spinning-wheel

1969. Birth Centenary of Mahatma Gandhi.

509	**118**	6c. black, brown and olive	65	65
510	**118**	15c. black, brown and lilac	65	65

119 "Mother Sally" Dance Troupe

1969. Christmas. Unissued stamps optd as in T 119. Multicoloured.

511	5c. Type **119**	10	10
512	6c. City Hall, Georgetown	10	10
513	25c. Type **119**	10	10
514	60c. As 6c.	20	25

121 Forbes Burnham and Map

1970. Republic Day.

515	**121**	5c. sepia, ochre and blue	10	10
516	-	6c. multicoloured	10	10
517	-	15c. multicoloured	15	10
518	-	25c. multicoloured	20	15

DESIGNS—VERT: 6c. Rural self-help. HORIZ: 15c. University of Guyana; 25c. Guyana House.

125 "The Descent from the Cross"

1970. Easter. Paintings by Rubens. Multicoloured.

No.	Description	Mint	Used
519	5c. Type **125**	10	10
520	6c. "Christ on the Cross"	10	10
521	15c. Type **125**	20	15
522	25c. As 6c.	20	15

127 "Peace" and U.N. Emblem

1970. 25th Anniv of United Nations. Mult.

No.	Description	Mint	Used
523	5c. Type **127**	10	10
524	6c. U.N. emblem, gold-panning and drilling	10	10
525	15c. Type **127**	10	10
526	25c. As 6c.	15	15

128 "Mother and Child" (Philip Moore)

1970. Christmas.

No.	Type	Description	Mint	Used
527	**128**	5c. multicoloured	10	10
528	**128**	6c. multicoloured	10	10
529	**128**	15c. multicoloured	15	15
530	**128**	25c. multicoloured	15	15

129 National Co-operative Bank

1971. Republic Day.

No.	Type	Description	Mint	Used
531	**129**	6c. multicoloured	10	10
532	**129**	15c. multicoloured	15	15
533	**129**	25c. multicoloured	15	15

130 Racial Equality Symbol

1971. Racial Equality Year.

No.	Type	Description	Mint	Used
534	**130**	5c. multicoloured	10	10
535	**130**	6c. multicoloured	10	10
536	**130**	15c. multicoloured	15	15
537	**130**	25c. multicoloured	15	15

131 Young Volunteer felling Tree (from painting by J. Criswick)

1971. 1st Anniv of Self-help Road Project.

No.	Type	Description	Mint	Used
538	**131**	5c. multicoloured	10	10
539	**131**	20c. multicoloured	20	10
540	**131**	25c. multicoloured	20	10
541	**131**	50c. multicoloured	30	1·75

132 Yellow Allamanda

1971. Flowering Plants. Multicoloured.

No.	Description	Mint	Used
542	1c. Pitcher Plant of Mt. Roraima	10	10
543	2c. Type **132**	10	10
544	3c. Hanging heliconia	10	10
545	5c. Annatto tree	10	10
546	6c. Cannon-ball tree	10	10
547	10c. Cattleya	3·25	10
548a	15c. Christmas orchid	65	10
549	20c. "Paphinia cristata"	3·00	20
550	25c. Marabunta	5·50	7·50
550ab	25c. Marabunta	45	10
551	40c. Tiger beard	3·50	10
552	50c. "Guzmania lingulata"	40	85
553	60c. Soldier's cap	30	65
554	$1 "Chelonanthus uliginoides"	30	55
555	$2 "Norantea guianensis"	35	55
556	$5 "Odontadenia grandiflora"	55	55

No. 550 shows the flowers facing upwards and has the value in the centre. No. 550ab has the flowers facing downwards with the value to the right.

133 Child praying at Bedside

1971. Christmas. Multicoloured.

No.	Description	Mint	Used
557	5c. Type **133**	10	10
558	20c. Type **133**	10	10
559	25c. Carnival masquerader (vert)	10	10
560	50c. As 25c.	20	60

134 Obverse and Reverse of Guyana $1 Coin

1972. Republic Day.

No.	Type	Description	Mint	Used
561	**134**	5c. silver, black and red	10	10
562	-	20c. silver, black and red	15	10
563	**134**	25c. silver, black and blue	15	15
564	-	50c. silver, black and green	25	45

DESIGN: 20c., 50c. Reverse and obverse of Guyana $1 coin.

135 Hands and Irrigation Canal

1972. Youman Nabi (Mohammed's Birthday).

No.	Type	Description	Mint	Used
565	**135**	5c. multicoloured	10	10
566	**135**	25c. multicoloured	10	10
567	**135**	30c. multicoloured	10	10
568	**135**	60c. multicoloured	20	20

136 Map and Emblem

1972. Conference of Foreign Ministers of Non-aligned Countries.

No.	Type	Description	Mint	Used
569	**136**	8c. multicoloured	10	10
570	**136**	25c. multicoloured	10	10
571	**136**	40c. multicoloured	15	15
572	**136**	50c. multicoloured	20	20

137 Hand reaching for Sun

1972. 1st Caribbean Festival of Arts.

No.	Type	Description	Mint	Used
573	**137**	8c. multicoloured	10	10
574	**137**	25c. multicoloured	10	10
575	**137**	40c. multicoloured	15	20
576	**137**	50c. multicoloured	20	25

138 Joseph, Mary and the Infant Jesus

1972. Christmas.

No.	Type	Description	Mint	Used
577	**138**	8c. multicoloured	10	10
578	**138**	25c. multicoloured	10	10
579	**138**	40c. multicoloured	15	25
580	**138**	50c. multicoloured	15	25

139 Umana Yana (Meeting-house)

1973. Republic Day. Multicoloured.

No.	Description	Mint	Used
581	8c. Type **139**	10	10
582	25c. Bethel Chapel	10	10
583	40c. As 25c.	20	20
584	50c. Type **139**	25	20

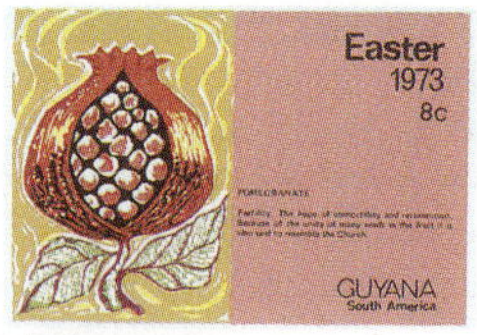

140 Pomegranate

1973. Easter. Multicoloured.

No.	Description	Mint	Used
585	8c. Type **140**	10	10
586	25c. Cross and map (34×17 mm)	10	10
587	40c. As 25c.	10	10
588	50c. Type **140**	15	15

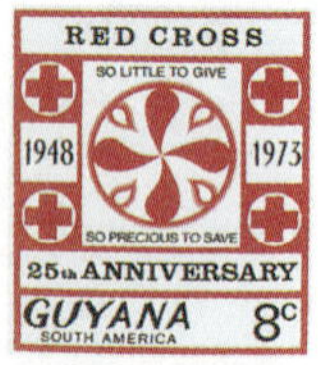

141 Stylised Blood Cell

1973. 25th Anniv of Guyana Red Cross.

No.	Type	Description	Mint	Used
589	**141**	8c. red and black	10	10
590	**141**	25c. red and purple	25	15
591	**141**	40c. red and blue	35	50
592	**141**	50c. red and green	50	1·00

142 Steel-Band Players

1973. Christmas. Multicoloured.

No.	Description	Mint	Used
593	8c. Type **142**	10	10
594	25c. Type **142**	20	10
595	40c. "Virgin and Child" stained-glass window (34×47 mm)	40	75
596	50c. As 40c.	40	75

143 Symbol of Progress

1974. Republic Day. Multicoloured.

No.	Description	Mint	Used
597	8c. Type **143**	10	10
598	25c. Wai-Wai Indian	10	10
599	40c. Type **143**	15	30
600	50c. As 25c.	15	40

1974. No. 546 surch 8c.

No.	Description	Mint	Used
601	8c. on 6c. multicoloured	10	10

145 Kite with Crucifixion Motif

1974. Easter.

No.	Type	Description	Mint	Used
602	**145**	8c. multicoloured	10	10
603	-	25c. black and green	10	10
604	-	40c. black and mauve	10	15
605	**145**	50c. multicoloured	15	25

DESIGN: Nos. 603/4, "Crucifixion" in pre-Columbian style.

146 British Guiana 24c. Stamp of 1874

1974. Centenary of Universal Postal Union.

606	**146**	8c. multicoloured	25	10
607	-	25c. lt green, green black	35	10
608	**146**	40c. multicoloured	35	20
609	-	50c. green, brown black	45	45

DESIGN—VERT (42×25 mm): 25, 50c. U.P.U. emblem and Guyana postman.

147 Guides with Banner

1974. Golden Jubilee of Girl Guides. Mult.

610	8c. Type **147**	20	10
611	25c. Guides in camp	30	15
612	40c. As 25c.	45	40
613	50c. Type **147**	45	45

148 Buck Toyeau

1974. Christmas. Multicoloured.

615	8c. Type **148**	10	10
616	35c. Five-fingers and awaras	10	10
617	50c. Pawpaw and tangerine	15	10
618	$1 Pineapple and sapodilla	30	60
MS619	127×94 mm. Nos. 615/18	70	2·50

1975. No. 544 surch 8c.

620	8c. on 3c. multicoloured	10	10

149 Golden Arrow of Courage

1975. Republic Day. Guyana Orders and Decorations. Multicoloured.

621	10c. Type **149**	10	10
622	35c. Cacique's Crown of Honour	10	15
623	50c. Cacique's Crown of Valour	15	20
624	$1 Order of Excellence	35	60

150 Old Sluice Gate

1975. Silver Jubilee of International Commission on Irrigation and Drainage. Multicoloured.

625	10c. Type **150**	10	10
626	35c. Modern sluice gate (horiz)	10	15
627	50c. Type **150**	15	30
628	$1 As 35c.	35	60
MS629	162×121 mm. Nos. 625/8	75	2·75

151 I.W.Y. Emblem and Rock Drawing

1975. International Women's Year. Designs showing different rock drawings.

630	**151**	10c. green and yellow	10	10
631	-	35c. violet and blue	15	10
632	-	50c. blue and orange	20	15
633	-	$1 brown and blue	30	45
MS634		178×89 mm. Nos. 630/3	75	3·00

152 Freedom Monument

1975. Namibia Day. Multicoloured.

635	10c. Type **152**	10	10
636	35c. Unveiling of Monument	15	10
637	50c. Type **152**	25	10
638	$1 As 35c.	35	35

153 G.N.S. Emblem

1975. 1st Anniv of National Service.

639	**153**	10c. yellow, green & violet	10	10
640	-	35c. orange, green & violet	10	10
641	-	50c. blue, green and brown	15	15
642	-	$1 mauve, green & lt green	40	40
MS643		196×133 mm. Nos. 639/42	75	2·00

Nos. 640/2 are as Type **153** but have different symbols within the circle.

154 Court Building, 1875, and Forester's Badge

1975. Centenary of Guyanese Ancient Order of Foresters. Multicoloured.

644	10c. Type **154**	10	10
645	35c. Rock drawing of hunter and quarry	10	10
646	50c. Crossed axes and bugle-horn	15	10
647	$1 Bow and arrow	40	40
MS648	129×97 mm. Nos. 644/7	75	2·25

1976. No. 553 surch 35c.

649	35c. on 60c. Soldier's cap	20	15

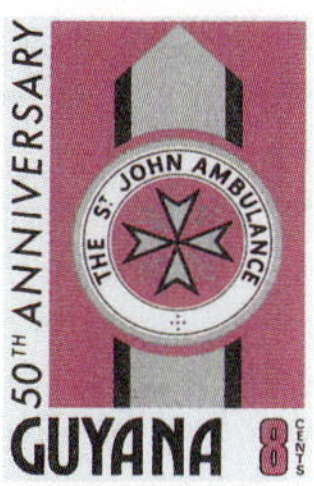

156 Shoulder Flash

1976. 50th Anniv of St. John Ambulance in Guyana.

650	**156**	8c. silver, black and mauve	10	10
651	-	15c. silver, black & orange	10	10
652	-	35c. silver, black and green	20	20
653	-	40c. silver, black and blue	25	25

Nos. 651/3 are as Type **156** but show different shoulder flashes.

157 Triumphal Arch

1976. 10th Anniv of Independence. Multicoloured.

654	8c. Type **157**	10	10
655	15c. Stylised Victoria Regia lily	10	10
656	35c. "Onward to Socialism"	15	15
657	40c. Worker pointing the way	15	15
MS658	120×100 mm. Nos. 654/7	50	1·50

1976. West Indies Victory in World Cricket Cup. As T 223a of Grenada.

659	15c. Map of the Caribbean	90	1·50
660	15c. Prudential Cup	90	1·50

158 Flame in Archway

1976. Deepavali Festival. Multicoloured.

661	8c. Type **158**	10	10
662	15c. Flame in hand	10	10
663	35c. Flame in bowl	15	20
664	40c. Goddess Latchmi	15	25
MS665	94×109 mm. Nos. 661/4	50	1·50

159 Festival Emblem and "Musical Instrument"

1977. Second World Black and African Festival of Arts and Culture, Nigeria.

666	**159**	10c. red, black and gold	10	10
667	**159**	25c. violet, black and gold	15	10
668	**159**	50c. blue, black and gold	20	25
669	**159**	$1 green, black and gold	35	75
MS670		90×157 mm. Nos. 666/9	75	3·00

160 1c. and 5c. Coins

1977. New Coinage.

671	**160**	8c. multicoloured	20	10
672	-	15c. brown, grey and black	25	10
673	-	35c. green, grey and black	45	30
674	-	40c. red, grey and black	50	35
675	-	$1 multicoloured	80	1·25
676	-	$2 multicoloured	1·25	2·75

DESIGNS: 15c.10 and 25c. coins; 35c., 50c. and $1 coins; 40c. $5 and $10 coins; $1 $50 and $100 coins; $2 Reverse of $1 coin.

161 Hand Pump, c. 1850

1977. National Fire Prevention Week. Mult.

677	8c. Type **161**	1·10	10
678	15c. Steam engine, c. 1860	1·50	10
679	35c. Fire engine, c. 1930	1·75	60
680	40c. Fire engine, 1977	1·75	85

162 Cuffy Monument

1977. Cuffy Monument (commemorating 1763 Slave Revolt). Multicoloured.

681	8c. Type **162**	10	10
682	15c. Cuffy Monument (different view)	10	10
683	35c. Type **162**	15	20
684	40c. As 15c.	15	30

163 American Manatee

1978. Wildlife Conservation. Multicoloured.

685	8c. Type **163**	65	10
686	15c. Giant sea turtle	85	20
687	35c. Harpy eagle (vert)	4·00	1·50
688	40c. Iguana (vert)	3·50	1·50

164 L.F.S. Burnham (Prime Minister) and Parliament Buildings, Georgetown

1978. 25th Anniv of Prime Minister's Entry into Parliament.

689	**164**	8c. black, violet and grey	10	10
690	-	15c. black, blue and grey	10	10
691	-	35c. black, red and grey	15	20
692	-	40c. black, orange and grey	15	20
MS693		176×118 mm. Nos. 689/92	55	1·00

DESIGNS: 15c. Burnham, graduate and children ("Free Education"); 35c. Burnham and industrial works (Nationalization of Bauxite Industry); 40c. Burnham and village scene ("The Co-operative Village").

165 Dr. George Giglioli (scientist and physician)

1978. Nat Science Research Council. Mult.

694	10c. Type **165**	15	10
695	30c. Institute of Applied Science and Technology	20	15
696	50c. Emblem of National Science Research Council	25	25
697	60c. Emblem of Commonwealth Science Council (commemorating the 10th meeting) (horiz)	25	25

166 "Prepona pheridamas"

1978. Butterflies. Multicoloured.

698	5c. Type **166**	1·50	10
699	10c. "Archonias bellona"	1·50	10
700	15c. "Eryphanis polyxena"	1·50	10
701	20c. "Helicopis cupido"	1·50	10
702	25c. "Nessaea batesii"	1·50	10
702a	30c. "Nymphidium mantus"	1·25	2·50
703	35c. "Anaea galanthis"	1·50	10
704	40c. "Morpho rhetenor" (male)	1·50	10
705	50c. "Hamadryas amphinome"	1·50	20
705a	60c. "Papilio androgeus"	1·25	1·00
706	$1 "Agrias claudina" (vert) (25x39 mm)	3·75	20
707	$2 "Morpho rhetenor" (female) (vert) (25x39 mm)	5·50	35
708	$5 "Morpho deidamia" (vert) (25x39 mm)	6·50	90
708a	$10 "Elbella patrobas" (vert) (25x39 mm)	4·50	4·25

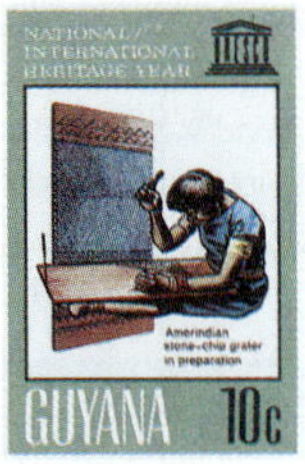

168 Amerindian Stone-chip Grater in Preparation

1978. National/International Heritage Year. Multicoloured.

709	10c. Type **168**	10	10
710	30c. Cassiri and decorated Amerindian jars	15	10
711	50c. Fort, Kyk-over-al	20	15
712	60c. Fort Island	20	20

169 Dish Aerial by Night

1979. Satellite Earth Station. Multicoloured.

713	10c. Type **169**	10	10
714	30c. Dish aerial by day	20	15
715	50c. Satellite with solar veins	30	15
716	$3 Cylinder satellite	1·00	90

170 Sir Rowland Hill and British Guiana 1850 12c. "Cottonreel" Stamp

1979. Death Cent of Sir Rowland Hill. Mult.

717	10c. Type **170**	15	10
718	30c. British Guiana 1856 1c. black on magenta stamp (vert)	20	15
719	50c. British Guiana 1898 1c. Mount Roraima stamp	30	15
720	$3 Printing press used for early British Guiana stamps (vert)	45	80

171 "Me and my Sister"

1979. International Year of the Child. Children's Paintings. Multicoloured.

721	10c. Type **171**	10	10
722	30c. "Fun with the Fowls" (horiz)	15	15
723	50c. "Two Boys catching Ducks" (horiz)	15	20
724	$3 "Mango Season" (horiz)	45	1·25

172 "An 8 Hour Day"

1979. 60th Anniv of Guyana Labour Union. Multicoloured.

725	10c. Type **172**	10	10
726	30c. "Abolition of Night Baking" (horiz)	10	10
727	50c. "Introduction of the Workmen's Compensation Ordinance"	15	15
728	$3 H. N. Critchlow (founder)	55	90

173 Guyana Flag

1980. 10th Anniv of Republic.

729	**173**	10c. multicoloured	10	10
730	-	35c. black and orange	30	10
731	-	60c. multicoloured	50	20
732	-	$3 multicoloured	80	90

DESIGNS: 35c. Demerara River Bridge; 60c. Kaieteur Falls; $3 "Makanaima, the Great Ancestral Spirit of the Amerindians".

174 Common Snook

1980. "London 1980" International Stamp Exhibition. Fishes. Multicoloured.

733	35c. Type **174**	20	20
734	35c. Trahira ("Haimara")	20	20
735	35c. Electric eel	20	20
736	35c. Golden rivulus	20	20
737	35c. Golden pencilfish	20	20
738	35c. Four-eyed fish	20	20
739	35c. Red piranha ("Pirai")	20	20
740	35c. Smoking hassar	20	20
741	35c. Manta	20	20
742	35c. Festival cichlid ("Flying patwa")	20	20
743	35c. Arapaima	20	20
744	35c. Peacock cichlid ("Lukanani")	20	20

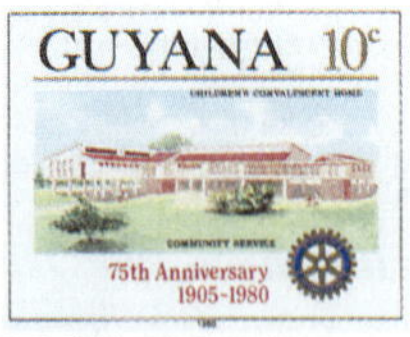

175 Children's Convalescent Home (Community Service)

1980. 75th Anniv of Rotary International. Multicoloured.

745	10c. Type **175**	10	10
746	30c. Georgetown Rotary Club and Rotary International emblems	10	10
747	50c. District 404 emblem (vert)	20	20
748	$3 Rotary anniversary emblem (vert)	80	80

176 "C" encircling Globe, Caduceus Emblem and Sea

1980. 25th Anniv of Commonwealth Caribbean Medical Research Council. Multicoloured.

749	10c. Type **176**	10	10
750	60c. Researcher with microscope, Caduceus emblem, stethoscope and beach scene	40	20
751	$3 Caduceus emblem, "C" encircling researcher and island silhouettes	1·10	1·00

177 "Virola surinamensis"

1980. Christmas. Trees and Foliage. Multicoloured.

752	10c. Type **177**	10	10
753	30c. "Hymenaea courbaril"	20	10
754	50c. "Mora excelsa"	30	15
755	$3 "Peltogyne venosa"	80	1·10

178 Brazilian Tree Porcupine

1981. Wildlife. Multicoloured.

756	30c. Type **178**	25	40
757	30c. Red howler	25	40
758	30c. Common squirrel-monkey	25	40
759	30c. Two-toed sloth	25	40
760	30c. Brazilian tapir	25	40
761	30c. Collared peccary	25	40
762a	30c. Six-banded armadillo	25	40
763	30c. Tamandua	25	40
764	30c. Giant anteater	25	40
765	30c. Murine opossum	25	40
766	30c. Brown four-eyed opossum	25	40
767	30c. Brazilian agouti	25	40

1981. Liberation of Southern Africa Conference. No. 635 surch 1981 CONFERENCE $1.05.

768	$1.05 on 10c. Type **152**	40	30

1981. Royal Wedding (1st issue). Nos. 554 and 556 surch ROYAL WEDDING 1981 and value.

769c	$3.60 on $5 "Odontadenia grandiflora"	60	65
770	$7.20 in $1 "Chelonanthus uliginoides"	60	60

See also Nos. 841/3 and 930/6.

181 Map of Guyana

1981. Fiscal stamps surch for postal use.

771	**181**	10c. on 3c. black, blue and red	30	10
772	**181**	30c. on 2c. black, blue and grey	45	15
773	**181**	50c. on 2c. black, blue and grey	40	15
774	**181**	60c. on 2c. black, blue and grey	45	15
775	**181**	75c. on 3c. black, blue and red	45	20
940	**181**	15c. on 2c. black, blue and grey	50	15
941	**181**	20c. on 2c. black, blue and grey	4·75	30
945	**181**	45c. on 2c. black, blue and grey	1·75	45
948	**181**	75c. on 2c. black, blue and grey	6·00	25
949	**181**	80c. on 2c. black, blue and grey	8·00	20
950	**181**	85c. on 2c. black, blue and grey	75	25
951	**181**	100c. on 3c. black, blue and red	1·00	35
952	**181**	110c. on 3c. black, blue and red	80	30
953	**181**	120c. on 3c. black, blue and red	8·00	35
954	**181**	125c. on 3c. black, blue and red	2·25	35
955	**181**	130c. on 3c. black, blue and red	1·00	35
956	**181**	150c. on 3c. black, blue and red	8·50	40
957	**181**	160c. on 3c. black, blue and red	2·00	40
958	**181**	170c. on 3c. black, blue and red	1·40	45
959	**181**	175c. on 3c. black, blue and red	6·00	45
960	**181**	180c. on 3c. black, blue and red	2·00	60
961	**181**	200c. on 3c. black, blue and red	2·25	45
962	**181**	210c. on 3c. black, blue and red	7·00	50
963	**181**	220c. on 3c. black, blue and red	8·50	50
964	**181**	235c. on 3c. black, blue and red	8·00	50
965	**181**	240c. on 3c. black, blue and red	9·00	50
966	**181**	250c. on 3c. black, blue and red	2·25	50
967	**181**	300c. on 3c. black, blue and red	12·00	55
968	**181**	330c. on 3c. black, blue and red	2·75	65
969	**181**	375c. on 3c. black, blue and red	8·00	75
970	**181**	400c. on 3c. black, blue and red	10·00	75
971	**181**	440c. on 3c. black, blue and red	4·00	75
972	**181**	500c. on 3c. black, blue and red	3·50	1·10
973	**181**	550c. on 3c. black, blue and red	4·00	1·25
974	**181**	625c. on 3c. black, blue and red	2·75	1·75
975	**181**	1500c. on 2c. black, blue and grey	11·00	3·00
976	**181**	2000c. on 2c. black, blue and grey	11·00	3·75
989	**181**	40c. on 2c. black, blue and grey	1·00	15
1029	**181**	25c. on 2c. black, blue and grey	50	10

1981. No. 544 surch 7.20.

775c	720c. on 3c. multicoloured	80·00	15·00

1981. Various stamps optd 1981.

776	**105**	25c. black, gold and lilac	10	10
777	**105**	30c. black, gold and green	15	10
778	-	35c. mult (No. 645)	15	10
791	-	15c. mult (No. 491)	16·00	10
792	-	40c. mult (No. 457)	10·00	40
810	-	15c. mult (No. 659)	7·00	20
811	-	15c. mult (No. 660)	8·00	35
811c	-	40c. mult (No. F5)		£200
812	-	50c. mult (No. 623)	60	20
813	**150**	50c. multicoloured	1·00	20
814	-	50c. blue and orange (No. 632)	23·00	2·25
815	-	50c. mult (No. 646)	2·75	20
816	**159**	50c. blue, black and gold	13·00	2·00
817	-	50c. mult (No. F6)	4·00	20
818	-	60c. mult (No. 731)	60	20
819	-	60c. mult (No. 750)	60	20
820	-	$1 mult (No. 624)	6·00	55
821	**159**	$1 green, black and gold	5·00	30
823	-	$3 mult (No. 732)	2·00	65
824	-	$5 mult (No. 556)	3·25	1·25
864	-	15c. mult (No. 548a)	4·00	10
865	-	$1 mult (No. 554)	40	20
866	-	$2 mult (No. 555)	90	35

1981. Nos. 545 and 556 surch.

780	75c. on 5c. Annatto tree	50	50
781	210c. on $5 "Odontadenia grandiflora"	80	1·00
781b	220c. on 5c. Annatto tree	95·00	8·50

1981. Nos. D8/11 surch ESSEQUIBO IS OURS.

782A	**D2**	10c. on 2c. black	15	10
783A	**D2**	15c. on 12c. red	15	15
784A	**D2**	20c. on 1c. green	15	20
785B	**D2**	45c. on 2c. black	30	15
786A	**D2**	55c. on 4c. blue	20	20
787B	**D2**	60c. on 4c. blue	30	10
788A	**D2**	65c. on 2c. black	30	15
789B	**D2**	70c. on 4c. blue	30	30
790A	**D2**	80c. on 4c. blue	30	20

1981. Nos. 545, 554, 556, 716, 843, F7 and F9 surch.

794	50c. on 5c. Annatto tree (postage)	30	20
795	120c. on $1 "Chelonanthus uliginoides"	75	40
796	140c. on $1 "Chelonanthus uliginoides"	70	40
797	150c. on $2 "Norantea guianensis" (F9)	75	40
798	360c. on $2 "Norantea guianensis" (F9)	3·00	60
799	720c. on 60c. Soldier's Cap (F7)	3·00	1·00
800	220c. on $3 Cylinder satellite	1·75	45
801	250c. on $5 "Odontadenia grandiflora"	1·25	45
802	280c. on $5 "Odontadenia grandiflora"	1·50	50
803	375c. on $5 "Odontadenia grandiflora"	1·75	55

804 $1.10 on $2 "Norantea guianensis" (843) (air) 1·00 1·00
No. 804 has the Royal Wedding opt cancelled by three bars.

1981. No. 448 surch.
805 **87** 15c. on 1c. mult (postage) 70 20
806 **87** 100c. on 1c. mult (air) 70 40
807 **87** 110c. on 1c. multicoloured 70 40

1981. No. 700 optd ESSEQUIBO IS OURS.
808 15c. "Eryphanis polyxena" 7·50 25

1981. Various stamps surch.
825 **116** 55c. on 6c. multicoloured 3·00 80
826 **111** 70c. on 6c. multicoloured 1·00 20
827 **111** 100c. on 6c. mult 1·25 20
828 - 100c. on 8c. multicoloured (No. 505) 3·00 20
829 **152** 100c. on $1.05 on 10c. mult (No. 768) 32·00 4·00
830 **116** 110c. on 6c. mult 2·00 30
831 **149** 110c. on 10c. mult 2·50 30
832 **151** 110c. on 10c. green and yellow 6·00 45
834 - 125c. on $2 multicoloured (No. 555) 13·00 80
835 **116** 180c. on 6c. mult 2·25 45
836 **116** 400c. on 6c. mult 3·50 80
837a **116** 440c. on 6c. mult 1·00 55
838 - 550c. on $10 multicoloured (No. O21) 9·00 1·00
839 - 625c. on 40c. mult (No. F5) 14·00 1·75
840 - 240c. on $3 multicoloured (No. 728) 8·00 75

1981. Royal Wedding (2nd issue). Nos. 544 and 555/6 surch Royal Wedding 1981 (No. 843 Air Mail also) and value.
841 60c. on 3c. Hanging heliconia (postage) 30 35
842 75c. on $5 "Odontadenia grandiflora" 30 35
843 $1.10 on $2 "Norantea guianensis" (air) 30 35

1981. World Cup Football Championship, Spain (1982) (1st issue). No. 781a optd Espana 82.
844 220c. on 5c. Annatto tree 2·25 40
See also Nos. 937/9 and 1218.

1981. 150th Birth Anniv of Heinrich von Stephan (founder of U.P.U.) No. 720 surch 1831-1981 Von Stephan 330.
845 330c. on $3 Printing press used for early British Guiana stamps 1·10 55

1981. No. 489 surch with large figure over smaller figure.
847 12c. on 12c. on 6c. Black acara ("Patua") 20 25
848 15c. on 10c. on 6c. Black acara ("Patua") 15 10
849 15c. on 30c. on 6c. Black acara ("Patua") 15 15
850 15c. on 50c. on 6c. Black acara ("Patua") 15 10
851 15c. on 60c. on 6c. Black acara ("Patua") 15 10
Nos. 847/51 are further surcharges on previously unissued stamps.

214 Coromantyn Free Negro Armed Ranger, c. 1772, and Cuffy Monument

1981. 16th Anniv of Guyana Defence Force. Multicoloured.
853 15c. on 10c. Type **214** 20 10
854 50c. Private, 27th Foot Regiment, c. 1825 30 30
855 $1 on 30c. Private, Col. Fourgeoud's Marines, c. 1775 30 45
856 $1.10 on $3 W.O. and N.C.O., Guyana Defence Force, 1966 35 70
The 15c., $1 and $1.10 values are surcharged on previously unissued stamps.

215 Louis Braille

1981. International Year for Disabled Persons. Famous Disabled People. Multicoloured.
857 15c. on 10c. Type **215** 20 10
858 50c. Helen Keller and Rajkumari Singh 30 40
859 $1 on 60c. Beethoven and Sonny Thomas 40 50
860 $1.10 on $3 Renoir 25 55
The 15c., $1 and $1.10 values are surcharged on previously unissued stamps.

1981. No. 489 surch (Nos. 862/3 optd AIR also).
861 12c. on 6c. Black acara ("Patua") (postage) 15 10
862b 50c. on 6c. Black acara ("Patua") (air) 20 15
863 $1 on 6c. Black acara ("Patua") 50 30

1981. Nos. 601, 620, 644, O13, 717, 720, 728, 749, 751 and 755 surch (Nos. 868/9 twice).
867 110c. on 10c. Type **154** 3·00 30
868 110c. on 110c. on 8c. on 3c. Hanging heliconia 3·00 40
869 110c. on 110c. on 8c. on 6c. Cannon-ball tree 3·00 40
869b 110c. on 10c. on 25c. Marabunta 2·25 40
870 110c. on 10c. Type **170** 2·00 30
871 110c. on 10c. Type **176** 8·00 50
872 110c. on $3 Printing press used for early British Guiana stamps 1·75 30
873 110c. on $3 H. N. Critchlow 6·50 45
874 110c. on $3 Caduceus emblem, "C" encircling researcher and island silhouettes 1·50 30
875 110c. on $3 "Peltogyne venosa" 4·00 50

1981. No. 698 surch Nov 81 50c.
876 50c. on 5c. Type **166** 8·50 20

222 Yellow Allamanda ("Allamanda cathartica")

1981. Flowers.
877 **222** 15c. on 2c. lilac, blue and green 15 15
878 - 15c. on 8c. lilac, blue and mauve 15 15
DESIGN: 15c. on 8c. Mazaruni pride ("Sipanea prolensis").
Nos. 877/8 are surcharged on previously unissued stamps.

1981. Air. Human Rights Day. No. 748 surch Human Rights Day 1981 110 AIR.
879 110c. on $3 Rotary anniversary emblem 1·00 60

1981. 35th Anniv of UNICEF No. 724 surch UNICEF 1946 - 1981 125.
880 125c. on $2 "Mango Season" 1·25 40

1981. "Cancun 81" International Conference. No. 698 surch Cancun 81 50c.
880c 50c. on 5c. Type **166** 4·00 55

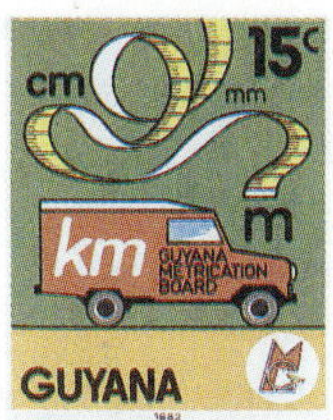

225 Tape Measure and Guyana Metrication Board Van

1982. Metrication. Multicoloured.
881 15c. Type **225** 45 45
882 15c. "Metric man" 45 45
883 15c. "Postal service goes metric" 45 45
884 15c. Weighing child on metric scales 45 45
885 15c. Canje Bridge 45 45
886 15c. Tap filling litre bucket 45 45

1982. Various stamps optd 1982.
887 - 20c. multicoloured (No. 549) 1·00 20
888 **105** 25c. black, gold and lilac 60 15
889 - 25c. mult (No. 550ab) 1·25 20
See also Nos. 914/17, 919/21, 923/4, 977, 992/8, 1001, 1004, 1006/8, 1015, 1017, 1059, 1117 and OP3/4.

1982. No. 506 optd POSTAGE and Nos. 546 and 601 surch.
890 20c. on 6c. Cannon-ball tree 20 10
892 25c. Type **116** 1·00 10
893 125c. on 8c. on 6c. Cannon-ball tree 20 20

230 Guyana Soldier and Flag

1982. Savings Campaign.
894 **230** $1 multicoloured 30 20
No. 894 is a fiscal stamp optd for postal use. See also Nos. 913 and 990.

1982. 125th Birth Anniv of Lord Baden-Powell and 75th Anniv of Boy Scout Movement. Nos. 543, 545 and 601 surch as given in brackets.
895 15c. on 2c. Type **132 (BADEN POWELL 1857–1982)** 30 45
896 15c. on 2c. Type **132 (Scout Movement 1907–1982)** 30 40
897 15c. on 2c. Type **132 (1907–1982)** 2·00 2·25
898 15c. on 2c. Type **132 (1857–1982)** 2·00 2·25
899 15c. on 2c. Type **132 (1982)** 10 10
900 110c. on 5c. Annatto tree **(BADEN POWELL 1857–1982)** 60 20
901 110c. on 5c. Annatto tree **(Scout Movement 1907–1982)** 60 20
902 110c. on 5c. Annatto tree **(1907–1982)** 2·50 2·75
903 110c. on 5c. Annatto tree **(1857–1982)** 2·50 2·75
904 110c. on 5c. Annatto tree **(1982)** 60 20
905 125c. on 8c. on 6c. Cannon-ball tree **(BADEN POWELL 1857–1982)** 60 20
906 125c. on 8c. on 6c. Cannon-ball tree **(Scout Movement 1907–1982)** 60 20
907 125c. on 8c. on 6c. Cannon-ball tree **(1907–1982)** 2·50 2·75
908 125c. on 8c. on 6c. Cannon-ball tree **(1857–1982)** 2·50 2·75
909 125c. on 8c. on 6c. Cannon-ball tree **(1982)** 60 20

1982. 250th Birth Anniv of George Washington. Nos. 718 and 720 surch Geo Washington 1732 . . . 1982 and value and No. 708 optd GEORGE WASHINGTON 1732–1982.
910 100c. on $3 Printing press used for early British Guiana stamps 45 30
911 400c. on 30c. British Guiana 1856 1c. black on purple 1·60 1·25
912 $5 "Morpho deidamia" 10·00 5·50

1982. Savings Campaign. As T 230. Mult.
913 110c. on $5 Guyana male and female soldiers with flag 50 20
No. 913 is a fiscal stamp surch for postal use. See also No. 990.

1982. Easter. Optd 1982 or surch also.
914 **111** 25c. multicoloured 20 15
915 **111** 30c. multicoloured 20 15
916 **111** 45c. on 6c. multicoloured 20 25
917 **111** 75c. on 40c. multicoloured 35 25

1982. No. 703 surch 20.
918 20c. on 35c. "Anaea galanthis" 6·00 10

1982. No. F5 optd 1982 180.
919 180c. on 40c. Tiger beard 3·50 40

1982. Nos. 555/6 optd 1982.
920 $2 "Norantea guianensis" 80 30
921 $5 "Odontadenia grandiflora" 1·00 70

1982. No. 542 surch 220.
922 220c. on 1c. Pitcher Plant of Mt. Roraima 1·00 40

1982. Nos. 472 and 684 optd 1982.
923 **105** 40c. black, gold and blue 35 15
924 - 40c. multicoloured 50 25

1982. Nos. 469, 751 and 842/3 surch.
925 **105** 80c. on 6c. black, gold and flesh 30 20
926 **105** 85c. on 6c. black, gold and flesh 50 20
927 - 160c. on $1.10 on $2 mult (No. 843) 40 30
928 - 210c. on $3 mult (No. 751) 8·00 40
929 - 235c. on 75c. on 85 mult (No. 842) 1·75 60

1982. Royal Wedding (3rd issue). Nos. 841/3 surch.
930 85c. on 60c. on 3c. Hanging heliconia 4·25 50
931 130c. on 60c. on 3c. Hanging heliconia 2·75 45
932 160c. on. $1.10 on $2 "Norantea guianensis" 3·25 1·00
933 170c. on $1.10 on $2 "Norantea guianensis" 6·50 4·50
934 210c. on 75c. on $5 "Odontadenia grandiflora" 2·50 40
935 235c. on 75c. on $5 "Odontadenia grandiflora" 3·75 1·40
936 330c. on $1.10 on $2 "Norantea guianensis" 1·75 40

1982. World Cup Football Championship, Spain (2nd issue). Nos. 544, 546 and 554 optd ESPANA 1982 or surch also.
937 $1 "Chelonanthus uliginoides" 1·00 40
938 110c. on 3c. Hanging heliconia 1·00 25
939 250c. on 6c. Cannon-ball tree 1·40 60
See also No. 1218.

1982. No. 548a optd 1982.
977 15c. Christmas orchid 9·00 10

1982. No. O26 optd POSTAGE.
978 110c. on 6c. Type **116** 2·75 35

1982. Air. 21st Birthday of Princess of Wales. Nos. 542, 545 and 555 surch AIR Princess of Wales 1961–1982.
979 110c. on 5c. Annatto tree 1·75 30
980 220c. on 1c. Pitcher Plant of Mt. Roraima 2·00 80
981 330c. on $2 "Norantea guianensis" 2·00 1·25

1982. Birth of Prince William of Wales. Surch H.R.H Prince William 21st June 1982. (a) On stamps of British Guiana with additional opt GUYANA.
982 50c. on 2c. green (No. 332) 1·25 30
983 $1.10 on 3c. green and brown (No. 333) 2·00 50

(b) On stamps of Guyana previously optd GUYANA INDEPENDENCE 1966.
984 50c. on 2c. green (No. 421) 17·00 3·50
985 $1.10 on 3c. green and brown (No. 422) 28·00 3·50
986 $1.25 on 6c. green (No. 424) 60 60
987 $2.20 on 24c. black and orange (No. 435) 1·50 1·50

1982. Savings Campaign. As No. 913 but showing inverted comma before "OURS" in opt.
990 110c. on $5 Guyana male and female soldiers with flag 5·50 75

1982. Italy's Victory in World Cup Football Championship. No. F7 surch ESPANA 1982 ITALY $2.35.
991 $2.35 on 180c. on 60c. Soldier's cap 3·75 55

1982. Wildlife Protection. Nos. 687 and 733/8 optd 1982.
992 35c. Harpy eagle 2·00 40
993 35c. Type **174** 2·00 40
994 35c. Trahira ("Haimara") 2·00 40
995 35c. Electric eel 2·00 40
996 35c. Golden rivulus 2·00 40
997 35c. Golden pencilfish 2·00 40
998 35c. Four-eyed fish 2·00 40

1982. Central America and Caribbean Games, Havana. Nos. 542/3 surch C.A. & CARIB GAMES 1982.
999 50c. on 2c. Type **132** 1·00 25
1000 60c. on 1c. Pitcher plant of Mt. Roraima 1·25 15

1982. No. 730 optd 1982.
1001 35c. black and orange 50 20

1982. Nos. 841 and 979 further surch.
1002 130c. on 60c. on 3c. Hanging heliconia 40 30
1003 170c. on 110c. on 5c. Annatto tree 70 45

1982. No. 841 surch 1982 440.
1004 440c. on 60c. on 3c. Hanging heliconia 75 45

1982. Commonwealth Games, Brisbane, Australia. No. 546 surch Commonwealth GAMES AUSTRALIA 1982 1.25.
1005 $1.25 on 6c. Cannon-ball tree 1·00 30

1982. Nos. 552, 641 and 719 optd 1982.
1006 50c. multicoloured (No. 552) 1·50 25
1007 50c. blue, green and brown (No. 641) 1·00 25
1008 50c. multicoloured (No. 719) 60 25

1982. Various Official stamps additionally optd POSTAGE.
1009 15c. Christmas Orchid (No. O 23) 14·00 30
1010 50c. "Guzmania lingulata" (No. O14) 90 15
1011 100c. on $3 Cylinder satellite (No. O19) 1·00 35

1982. International Food Day. No. 617 optd INT. FOOD DAY 1982.
1012 50c. Pawpaw and tangerine 7·50 65

1982. International Year of the Elderly. No. 747 optd INT. YEAR OF THE ELDERLY.
1013 50c. District 404 emblem 7·00 50

1982. Centenary of Robert Koch's Discovery of Tubercle Bacillus. No. 750 optd Dr. R. KOCH CENTENARY TBC BACILLUS DISCOVERY.
1014 60c. Researcher with microscope, Caduceus emblem, stethoscope and beach scene 2·00 30

1982. International Decade for Women. No. 633 optd 1982.
1015 $1 brown and blue 2·00 60

1982. Birth Centenary of F. D. Roosevelt (American statesman). No. 706 optd F. D. ROOSEVELT 1882-1982.
1016 $1 "Agrias claudina" 6·00 50

1982. 1st Anniv of G.A.C. Inaugural Flight Georgetown to Boa Vista, Brazil. No. 842 optd 1982 GAC Inaug. Flight Georgetown–Boa Vista, Brasil 200.
1017 200c. on 75c. on $5 "Odontadenia grandiflora" 5·00 1·40

1982. CARICOM Heads of Government Conference, Kingston, Jamaica. Nos. 881/6 surch 50 CARICOM Heads of Gov't Conference July 1982.
1018 50c. on 15c. Type **225** 1·50 50
1019 50c. on 15c. "Metric man" 1·50 50
1020 50c. on 15c. "Postal service goes metric" 1·50 50
1021 50c. on 15c. Weighing child on metric scales 1·50 50
1022 50c. on 15c. Canje Bridge 1·50 50
1023 50c. on 15c. Tap filling litre bucket 1·50 50

1982. Christmas. Nos. 895/9 optd CHRISTMAS 1982.
1024 15c. on 2c. Type **132** (surch **BADEN POWELL 1857–1982**) 25 15
1025 15c. on 2c. Type **132** (surch **Scout Movement 1907–1982**) 25 15
1026 15c. on 2c. Type **132** (surch **1907–1982**) 85 75
1027 15c. on 2c. Type **132** (surch **1857–1982**) 85 75
1028 15c. on 2c. Type **132** (surch **1982**) 11·00 12·00

1982. Nos. 543 and 546 surch in figures (no "c" after face value).
1034 15c. on 2c. Type **132** 15 10
1035 20c. on 6c. Cannon-ball tree 15 10
See also No. 1086.

1982. No. 489 surch.
1032 50c. on 6c. Black acara ("Patua") 20 15
1033 100c. on 6c. Black acara ("Patua") 40 30

1983. Optd 1983.
1036 - 15c. mult (No. 655) 3·50 1·50
1037 - 15c. brown, grey and black (No. 672) 3·75 10
1038 - 15c. mult (No. 682) 40 10
1039 **214** 15c. on 10c. mult 35 10
1040 **215** 15c. on 10c. mult 15 10
1041 - 50c. mult (No. 646) 4·00 25
1042 - 50c. mult (No. 696) 4·00 25
1043 - 50c. mult (No. 719) 1·50 25
See also Nos. 1060/1, 1069/70, 1072/9c, 1096, 1101 and 1110/16.

1983. No. O17 optd POSTAGE.
1044 15c. Harpy Eagle 13·00 10

1983. National Heritage. Nos. 710/12 and 778 surch.
1045 90c. on 30c. Cassiri and decorated Amerindian jars 85 50
1046 90c. on 35c. Rock drawing of hunter and quarry 35 20
1047 90c. on 50c. Fort Kyk-over-al 85 50
1048 90c. on 60c. Fort Island 1·25 20

258 Guyana Flag (inscr. "60TH BIRTHDAY ANNIVERSARY")

1983. 60th Birthday of President Burnham and 30 Years in Parliament. Multicoloured.
1049 25c. Type **258** 15 20
1050 25c. As T **258** but position of flag reversed and inscr "30th ANNIVERSARY IN PARLIAMENT" 15 20
1051 $1.30 Youth display (41×25 mm) 40 65
1052 $6 Presidential standard (43½×25 mm) 70 2·75

1983. Surch in words.
1053 **170** 50c. on 10c. mult (No. 717) 2·75 30
1054 - 50c. on 400c. on 30c. mult (No. 911) 3·25 30
1055 **152** $1 on 10c. mult (No. 635) 7·50 45
1056 **152** $1 on $1.05 on 10c. mult (No. 768) 6·50 45
1056a - $1 on $1.10 on $2 mult (No. 843) 1·00 2·50
1057 - $1 on 220c. on 5c. mult (No. 844) 7·50 75
1058 - $1 on 330c. on $2 mult (as No. 981) 5·00 45
1059 - $1 on $12 on $1.10 on $2 multicoloured (No. P3) 1·75 2·00
See also Nos. 1080/4.

1983. No. 859 optd 1983.
1060 $1 on 60c. Beethoven and Sonny Thomas 6·00 45

1983. Conference of Foreign Ministers of Non-aligned Countries, New Delhi. No. 569 surch FIFTY CENTS and No. 570 optd 1983.
1061 **136** 25c. multicoloured 75 25
1062 **136** 50c. on 8c. multicoloured 1·00 25

1983. No. 771 further surch 20.
1064 **181** 20c. on 10c. on 3c. black, blue and red 55 10

1983. Commonwealth Day. Nos. 424 and 435 surch Commonwealth Day 14 March 1983, emblem and value.
1065 **60** 25c. on 6c. green 1·00 20
1066 **60** $1.20 on 6c. green 50 50
1067 **63** $1.30 on 24c. black and orange 3·50 55
1068 **63** $2.40 on 24c. black and orange 4·00 1·50

1983. Easter. Nos. 482/3 optd 1983.
1069 **111** 25c. multicoloured 15 10
1070 **111** 30c. multicoloured 30 15

262

1983. 25th Anniv of International Maritime Organization. British Guiana fiscal stamp optd.
1071 **262** $4.80 blue and green 2·00 4·00

1983. Optd 1983.
1072 **152** 50c. mult (No. 637) 1·50 25
1073 **159** 50c. blue, black and yellow (No. 668) 1·50 25
1073a - 50c. mult (No. 723) 27·00 2·00
1074 - 50c. mult (No. 854) 60 25
1075 - 50c. mult (No. 858) 7·50 25
1076 - $1 mult (No. 628) 3·00 45
1077 - $1 mult (No. 638) 4·00 45
1078 - $1 mult (No. 675) 4·00 45
1079 - $1 on 30c. mult (No. 855) 1·25 45
1079a - $3 mult (No. 720) 27·00 1·75
1079b - $3 mult (No. 724) 42·00 3·00
1079c - $3 mult (No. 748) £100 9·50

1983. Surch FIFTY CENTS.
1080 **148** 50c. on 8c. mult (No. 615) 1·75 25
1081 **162** 50c. on 8c. mult (No. 681) 6·00 25
1082 **171** 50c. on 10c. mult (No. 721) 3·00 25
1083 - 50c. on 10c. on 25c. mult (No. O13) 8·00 25
1084 - 50c. on 330c. on $3 mult (No. 845) 4·00 25

1983. Surch in figures with c after new face value.
1087 **111** 50c. on 6c. multicoloured (No. 481) 40 30
1098 **105** 15c. on 6c. black, gold and pink (No. 469) 10 10
1099 - 50c. on 6c. multicoloured (No. 489) 30 30
1100 - 20c. on 6c. multicoloured (No. 546) 15 10

1983. No. 489 surch $1.
1088 $1 on 6c. Black acara ("Patua") 1·75 30

1983. No. 639 surch 110.
1089 **153** 110c. on 10c. yellow, green and violet 1·75 50

1983. Nos. 551 and 556 surch.
1090 250c. on 40c. Tiger beard 7·50 55
1091 400c. on $5 "Odontadenia grandiflora" 5·50 70

1983. World Telecommunications and Health Day. Nos. 842 and 980 further surch.
1092 25c. on 220c. on 1c. Pitcher plant of Mt. Roraima (surch **ITU 1983 25**) 40 40
1093 25c. on 220c. on 1c. Pitcher plant of Mt. Roraima (surch **WHO 1983 25**) 40 40
1094 25c. on 220c. on 1c. Pitcher plant of Mt. Roraima (surch **17 MAY '83 ITU/WHO 25**) 40 40
1095 $4.50 on 75c. on $5 "Odontadenia grandiflora" (surch **ITU/ WHO 17 MAY 1983**) 13·00 1·50
1095a 235c. on 75c. on $5 (No. 929) 1·00 1·00

1983. 30th Anniv of President's Entry into Parliament. Nos. 690 and 692 surch in words, No. 1096 additionally optd 1983.
1096 $1 on 15c. black, blue and grey 6·00 50
1097 $1 on 40c. black, orange and grey 10·00 50

1983. No. 611 optd 1983.
1101 25c. Guides in camp 48·00 4·00

1983. 15th World Scout Jamboree, Alberta. Nos. 835/6 and O25 optd CANADA 1983, Nos. 1103 and 1105 additionally surch.
1103 - $1.30 on 100c. on 8c. multicoloured 1·50 1·00
1104 **116** 180c. on 6c. mult 1·50 1·50
1105 **116** $3.90 on 400c. on 6c. multicoloured 2·25 3·50

1983. Nos. 659/60 surch.
1106 60c. on 15c. Map of the Caribbean 13·00 55
1107 $1.50 on 15c. Prudential Cup 15·00 1·75

1983. As Nos. 1049/50, but without commemorative inscr above flag.
1108 25c. As Type **258** 15 15
1109 25c. As No. 1050 15 15

1983. Optd 1983.
1110 **105** 30c. black, gold and green (No. 471) 75 20
1111 - 30c. multicoloured (No. 695) 9·50 30
1112 - 30c. multicoloured (No. 718) 4·50 20
1113 - 30c. multicoloured (No. 722) 8·00 20
1114 - 30c. multicoloured (No. 746) 14·00 20
1115 - 60c. multicoloured (No. 697) 16·00 20
1116 - 60c. multicoloured (No. 731) 5·50 20

1983. No. 553 optd 1982.
1117 60c. Soldier's cap 4·00 35

1983. Surch.
1118 **157** 120c. on 8c. mult (No. 654) 2·25 40
1119 - 120c. on 10c. red, black and gold (No. 666) 2·25 40
1120 - 120c. on 35c. mult (No. 622) 2·25 40
1121 - 120c. on 35c. orange, green and violet (No. 640) 2·25 40

1983. Nos. 716 and 729 surch.
1122 120c. on 10c. Type **173** 2·00 40
1123 120c. on 375c. on $3 Cylinder satellite 1·75 40
No. 1123 also carries an otherwise unissued surcharge in red reading **INTERNATIONAL SCIENCE YEAR 1982 375**. As issued much of this is obliterated by two heavy bars.

1983. British Guiana No. D1a and Guyana No. D8 surch 120 GUYANA.
1124 **D 1** 120c. on 1c. green 1·50 45
1125 **D 2** 120c. on 1c. olive 1·50 45

1983. CARICOM Day. No. 823 additionally surch CARICOM DAY 1983 60.
1126 60c. on $3 "Makanaima the Great Ancestral Spirit of the Amerindians" 1·00 35

271 "Kurupukari"

1983. Riverboats.
1127 **271** 30c. black and red 15 20
1128 - 60c. black and violet 15 35
1129 - 120c. black and yellow 20 60
1130 - 130c. black 20 65
1131 - 150c. black and green 20 80
DESIGNS: 60c. "Makouria"; 120c. "Powis"; 130c. "Pomeroon"; 150c. "Lukanani".

1983. Unissued Royal Wedding surch similar to No. 843 additionally surch.
1132 $2.30 on $1.10 on $2 "Norantea guianensis" 60 40
1133 $3.20 on $1.10 on $2 "Norantea guianensis" 60 40

1983. Bicentenary of Manned Flight and 20th Anniv of Guyana Airways. Nos. 701/2a optd as indicated in brackets.
1134 20c. multicoloured (**BW**) 80 35
1135 20c. multicoloured (**LM**) 80 35
1136 20c. multicoloured (**GY 1963 1983**) 80 35
1137 20c. multicoloured (**JW**) 80 35
1138 20c. multicoloured (**CU**) 80 35
1139 20c. multicoloured (**Mont Golfier 1783-1983**) 80 35
1140 25c. multicoloured (**BGI**) 1·75 60
1141 25c. multicoloured (**GEO**) 35 10
1142 25c. multicoloured (**MIA**) 1·75 60
1143 25c. multicoloured (**BVB**) 1·75 60
1144 25c. multicoloured (**PBM**) 1·75 60
1145 25c. multicoloured (**Mont Golfier 1783-1983**) 40 15
1146 25c. multicoloured (**POS**) 1·75 60
1147 25c. multicoloured (**JFK**) 1·75 60
1148 30c. multicoloured (**AHL**) 80 30
1149 30c. multicoloured (**BCG**) 80 30
1150 30c. multicoloured (**BMJ**) 80 30
1151 30c. multicoloured (**EKE**) 80 30
1152 30c. multicoloured (**GEO**) 80 30
1153 30c. multicoloured (**GFO**) 80 30
1154 30c. multicoloured (**IBM**) 80 30
1155 30c. multicoloured (**Mont Golfier 1783-1983**) 35 15
1156 30c. multicoloured (**KAI**) 80 30
1157 30c. multicoloured (**KAR**) 80 30
1158 30c. multicoloured (**KPG**) 80 30
1159 30c. multicoloured (**KRG**) 80 30
1160 30c. multicoloured (**KTO**) 80 30
1161 30c. multicoloured (**LTM**) 80 30
1162 30c. multicoloured (**MHA**) 80 30
1163 30c. multicoloured (**MWJ**) 80 30
1164 30c. multicoloured (**MYM**) 80 30
1165 30c. multicoloured (**NAI**) 80 30
1166 30c. multicoloured (**ORJ**) 80 30
1167 30c. multicoloured (**USI**) 80 30
1168 30c. multicoloured (**VEG**) 80 30

1983. No. 649 further surch 240.
1169 240c. on 35c. on 60c. Soldier's cap 2·75 1·25

1983. F.A.O. Fisheries Project. Nos. 448 and 450 surch FAO 1983 and value.
1170 30c. on 1c. Type **87** 1·00 15
1171 $2.60 on 3c. Peacock cichlid ("Lukunani") 3·50 3·25

277 G.B. 1857 1d. with Georgetown "AO3" Postmark

1983. 125th Anniv of Use of Great Britain Stamps in Guyana. (a) Inscriptions in black.
1172 **277** 25c. brown and black 15 10
1173 - 30c. red and black 15 15
1174 - 60c. violet and black 25 30
1175 - 120c. green and black 50 55

(b) Inscriptions in blue.
1176 **277** 25c. brown and black 15 10
1177 - 25c. red and black 15 10
1178 - 25c. violet and black 15 10
1179 - 25c. green and black 15 10
1180 **277** 30c. brown and black 15 15
1181 - 30c. red and black 15 15
1182 - 30c. violet and black 15 15
1183 - 30c. green and black 15 15
1184 **277** 45c. brown and black 20 25
1185 - 45c. red and black 20 25
1186 - 45c. violet and black 20 25
1187 - 45c. green and black 20 25
1188 **277** 120c. brown and black 20 55
1189 - 130c. red and black 20 60
1190 - 150c. violet and black 20 70
1191 - 200c. green and black 20 95
DESIGNS: Nos. 1173, 1177, 1181, 1185, 1189, G.B. 1857 4d. red; Nos. 1174, 1178, 1182, 1186, 1190, G.B. 1856 6d. lilac; Nos. 1175, 1179, 1183, 1187, 1191, G.B. 1856 1s. green.
Each design incorporates the "AO3" postmark except Nos. 1189/91 which show mythical post-marks of the Crowned-circle type inscribed "DEMERARA", "BERBICE" or "ESSEQUIBO".

1983. International Communications Year. No. 716 surch INT. COMMUNICATIONS YEAR 50.
1192 50c. on 375c. on $3 Cylinder satellite 4·50 30

No. 1192 also carries an otherwise unissued "375" surcharge. As issued much of this surcharge is obliterated by two groups of six horizontal lines.

1983. St. John Ambulance Commemoration. Nos. 650 and 653 surch.
1193 **156** 75c. on 8c. silver, black and mauve 4·50 50
1194 - $1.20 on 40c. silver, black and blue 6·50 75

1983. International Food Day. No. 616 surch $1.20 Int. Food Day 1983.
1195 $1.20 on 35c. Five-fingers and awaras 1·00 50

1983. 65th Anniv of I.L.O. and 25th Death Anniv of H. N. Critchlow (founder of Guyana Labour Union). No. 840 further optd 1918-1983 I.L.O.
1196 240c. on $3 H. N. Critchlow 1·50 1·50

1983. Deepavali Festival. Nos. 661 and 663/4 surch.
1197 25c. on 8c. Type **158** 20 10
1198 $1.50 on 35c. Flame in bowl 1·25 60
1199 $1.50 on 40c. Goddess Latchmi 80 60

1983. No. 732 optd 1982 and No. 798 further optd 1983.
1200 $3 "Makanaima the Great Ancestral Spirit of the Amerindians" 1·00 70
1201 360c. on $2 "Norantea guianensis" 1·10 80

1983. Wildlife Protection. Nos. 686 and 688 surch and No. 852 optd 1983.
1202 30c. Six-banded armadillo 75 15
1203 60c. on 15c. Giant sea turtle 1·25 30
1204 $1.20 on 40c. Iguana 1·75 50

1983. Human Rights Day. No. 1079c optd Human Rights Day.
1205 $3 Rotary anniversary emblem 2·00 1·25

1983. Olympic Games, Los Angeles (1984) (1st issue). Nos. 733/44 surch LOS ANGELES 1984 125, Nos. 1206/17 further surch 55.
1206 55c. on 125c. on 35c. Type **174** 25 25
1207 55c. on 125c. on 35c. Trahira ("Haimara") 25 25
1208 55c. on 125c. on 35c. Electric eel 25 25
1209 55c. on 125c. on 35c. Golden rivulus 25 25
1210 55c. on 125c. on 35c. Golden pencilfish 25 25
1211 55c. on 125c. on 35c. Four-eyed fish 25 25
1212 55c. on 125c. on 35c. Red piranha ("Pirai") 25 25
1213 55c. on 125c. on 35c. Smoking hassar 25 25
1214 55c. on 125c. on 35c. Manta 25 25
1215 55c. on 125c. on 35c. Festive cichlid ("Flying patwa") 25 25
1216 55c. on 125c. on 35c. Arapaima 25 25
1217 55c. on 125c. on 35c. Peacock cichlid ("Lukanani") 25 25
1217a 125c. on 35c. Type **174** 7·50
1217b 125c. on 35c. Trahira ("Haimara") 7·50
1217c 125c. on 35c. Electric eel 7·50
1217d 125c. on 35c. Golden rivulus 7·50
1217e 125c. on 35c. Golden pencilfish 7·50
1217f 125c. on 35c. Four-eyed fish 7·50
1217g 125c. on 35c. Red piranha ("Pirai") 7·50
1217h 125c. on 35c. Smoking hassar 7·50
1217i 125c. on 35c. Manta 7·50
1217j 125c. on 35c. Festive cichlid ("Flying patwa") 7·50
1217k 125c. on 35c. Arapaima 7·50
1217l 125c. on 35c. Peacock cichlid ("Lukanani") 7·50

See also Nos. 1308/17 and 1420.

1983. No. F7 with unissued ESPANA 1982 surch further optd 1983.
1218 180c. on 60c. Soldier's cap 3·25 65

1983. Commonwealth Heads of Government Meeting, New Delhi. No. 542 surch COMMONWEALTH HEADS OF GOV'T MEETING–INDIA 1983 150.
1219 150c. on 1c. Pitcher plant of Mt. Roraima 4·75 80

1983. Christmas. No. 861 further surch CHRISTMAS 1983 20c.
1220 20c. on 12c. on 6c. Black acara ("Patua") 2·25 10

1984. Nos. 838 and F9 optd POSTAGE.
1221 $2 "Norantea guianensis" 3·50 70
1221b 550c. on $10 "Elbella patrobas" 19·00 8·50

1984. Flowers. Unissued stamps as T 222 surch.
1222 17c. on 2c. lilac, blue and green 4·25 2·25
1223 17c. on 8c. lilac, blue and mauve 4·25 2·25

1984. Republic Day. No. 703 and 705a variously optd or surch.
1224 25c. on 35c. mult (surch **ALL OUR HERITAGE 25**) 50 20
1225 25c. on 35c. mult (surch **1984 25**) 75 30
1226 25c. on 35c. mult (surch **REPUBLIC DAY 25**) 75 30
1227 25c. on 35c. mult (surch **25**) 75 30
1228 25c. on 35c. mult (surch **BERBICE 25**) 4·25 4·25
1229 25c. on 35c. mult (surch **DEMERARA 25**) 4·25 4·25
1230 25c. on 35c. mult (surch **ESSEQUIBO 25**) 4·25 4·25
1232 60c. mult (optd **ALL OUR HERITAGE**) 2·25 75
1233 60c. mult (optd **REPUBLIC DAY**) 2·25 75
1234 60c. mult (optd **1984**) 2·25 75

1984. Guyana Olympic Committee Appeal. Nos. 841/3 surch OLYMPIC GAMES 84 25c POSTAGE (+2.25 SURTAX) and rings, the whole surch inverted.
1235 25c.+$2.25 on 60c. on 3c. Hanging heliconia 2·25 6·00
1236 25c.+$2.25 on 75c. on $5 "Odontadenia grandiflora" 2·25 6·00
1237 25c.+$2.25 on $1.10 on $2 "Norantea guianensis" 2·25 6·00

1984. Nature Protection. Various stamps optd Protecting our Heritage, some additionally surch.
1238 20c. on 15c. mult (No. 491) 16·00 25
1239 20c. on 15c. mult (No. 791) 16·00 25
1240a 20c. on 15c. mult (No. 1044) 26·00 1·25
1241 25c. mult (No. 550ab) 24·00 25
1242 30c. on 15c. mult (No. 548a) 22·00 30
1243 40c. multicoloured (No. 457) 18·00 30
1244 50c. multicoloured (No. 552) 3·50 30
1245 50c. multicoloured (No. F6) 3·50 30
1246 60c. multicoloured (No. 459) 10·00 30
1247 90c. on 40c. mult (No. 551) 18·00 65
1248 180c. on 40c. mult (No. 919) 18·00 1·00
1249 $2 multicoloured (No. 461) 55·00 1·75
1250 225c. on 10c. mult (No. 490) 24·00 1·25
1251 260c. on $1 mult (No. 460) 12·00 1·00
1252 320c. on 40c. mult (No. 551) 13·00 2·25
1253 350c. on 40c. mult (No. 551) 22·00 3·00
1254 380c. on 50c. mult (No. 495) 12·00 2·75
1255 450c. on $5 mult (No. 462) 8·00 2·75

1984. Easter. Nos. 483 and 916/17 optd 1984 and No. 481 surch 130.
1256 **111** 30c. multicoloured 20 20
1257 **111** 45c. on 6c. multicoloured 25 25
1258 **111** 75c. on 40c. multicoloured 35 35
1259 **111** 130c. on 6c. multicoloured 65 60

1984. Nos. 937/9 and 991 surch.
1260 75c. on $1 "Chelonanthus uliginoides" 9·50 35
1261 75c. on 110c. on 3c. Hanging heliconia 9·50 35
1262 225c. on 250c. on 6c. Cannon-ball tree 3·00 1·25
1263 230c. on $2.35 on 180c. on 60c. Soldier's cap 3·00 1·00

1984. Nos. 899/901, 904/6 and 909 surch.
1264 20c. on 15c. on 2c. Type **132** (No. 899) 1·50 30
1265 75c. on 110c. on 5c. Annatto tree (No. 904) 9·00 70
1266 90c. on 110c. on 5c. Annatto tree (No. 900) 5·50 85
1267 90c. on 110c. on 5c. Annatto tree (No. 901) 7·00 85
1268 120c. on 125c. on 8c. on 6c. Cannon-ball tree (No. 905) 7·00 1·00
1269 120c. on 125c. on 8c. on 6c. Cannon-ball tree (No. 906) 7·00 1·00
1270 120c. on 125c. on 8c. on 6c. Cannon-ball tree (No. 909) 2·75 1·00

1984. World Telecommunications and Health Day. Nos. 802 and 980 surch.
1271 25c. on 220c. on 1c. Pitcher plant of Mt. Roraima (surch **ITU DAY 1984 25**) 60 60
1272 25c. on 220c. on 1c. Pitcher plant of Mt. Roraima (surch **WHO DAY 1984 25**) 60 60
1273 25c. on 220c. on 1c. Pitcher plant of Mt. Roraima (surch **ITU/WHO DAY 1984 25**) 60 60
1274 $4.50 on 280c. on $5 "Odontadenia grandiflora" (surch **ITU/WHO DAY 1984 $4.50**) 2·75 2·75

1984. No. 1005 surch 120.
1275 120c. on $1.25 on 6c. Cannon-ball tree 7·00 55

1984. World Forestry Conference. No. 755 optd 1984 and Nos. 752/4 and 875 surch.
1276 55c. on 30c. "Hymenaea courbaril" 2·75 30
1277 75c. on 110c. on $3 "Peltogyne venosa" 40 35
1278 160c. on 50c. "Mora excelsa" 75 70
1279 260c. on 10c. Type **177** 1·25 1·25
1280 $3 "Peltogyne venosa" 1·40 1·40

1984. No. 625 surch.
1281 55c. on 110c. on 10c. Type **150** 1·00 30
1282 90c. on 110c. on 10c. Type **150** 1·25 45

Nos. 1281/2 also carry an otherwise unissued 110c. surch.

1984. U.P.U. Congress, Hamburg. Nos. 1188/91 optd UPU Congress 1984 Hamburg.
1283 120c. brown and black 50 60
1284 130c. red and black 55 70
1285 150c. violet and black 60 75
1286 200c. green and black 80 90

1984. Nos. 982/3 and 986/7 surch.
1287 45c. on 50c. on 2c. green 60 25
1288 60c. on $1.10 on 3c. olive and brown 3·00 40
1289 120c. on $1.25 on 6c. green 75 65
1290 200c. on $2.20 on 24c. black and orange 8·00 3·25

1984. Nos. 979/80 and 1003 surch and No. 981 optd 1984.
1291 75c. on 110c. on 5c. Annatto tree 1·50 35
1292 120c. on 170c. on 110c. on 5c. Annatto tree 1·75 55
1293 200c. on 220c. on 1c. Pitcher plant of Mt. Roraima 30·00 2·25
1294 330c. on $2 "Norantea guianensis" 2·25 2·50

1984. CARICOM Day. No. 1200 additionally surch CARICOM DAY 1984 60.
1295 60c. on $3 "Makanaima the Great Ancestral Spirit of the Amerindians" 60 30

1984. No. 544 surch 150.
1296 150c. on 3c. Hanging heliconia 1·25 65

1984. CARICOM Heads of Government Conference. No. 544 surch 60 CARICOM HEADS OF GOV'T CONFERENCE JULY 1984.
1297 60c. on 3c. Hanging heliconia 60 30

301 Children and Thatched School

1984. Cent of Guyana Teachers' Association. Mult.
1298 25c. Type **301** 10 15
1299 25c. Torch and graduates 10 15
1300 25c. Torch and target emblem 10 15
1301 25c. Teachers of 1884 and 1984 in front of school 10 15

1984. 60th Anniv of International Chess Federation. No. 1048 optd or surch also.
1302 25c. on 90c. on 60c. Fort Island (surch **INT. CHESS FED. 1924–1984 25**) 2·50 50
1303 25c. on 90c. on 60c. Fort Island (surch **1984 25**) 3·50 90
1304 75c. on 90c. on 60c. Fort Island (surch **INT. CHESS FED. 1924–1984 75**) 2·50 75
1305 75c. on 90c. on 60c. Fort Island (surch **1984 75**) 3·50 1·25
1306 90c. on 60c. Fort Island (optd **INT. CHESS FED. 1924–1984**) 2·50 80
1307 90c. on 60c. Fort Island (optd **1984**) 3·50 1·50

1984. Olympic Games, Los Angeles (2nd issue). No. 1051 surch.
1308 25c. on $1.30 mult (surch **TRACK AND FIELD 25**) 35 40
1309 25c. on $1.30 mult (surch **BOXING 25**) 40 45
1310 25c. on $1.30 mult (surch **OLYMPIC GAMES 1984 LOS ANGELES 25**) 40 45
1311 25c. on $1.30 mult (surch **CYCLING 25**) 3·25 50
1312 25c. on $1.30 mult (surch **OLYMPIC GAMES 1984 25**) 4·50 1·25
1313 $1.20 on $1.30 mult (surch **TRACK AND FIELD $1.20**) 1·25 1·40
1314 $1.20 on $1.30 mult (surch **BOXING $1.20**) 1·25 1·40
1315 $1.20 on $1.30 mult (surch **OLYMPIC GAMES 1984 LOS ANGELES $1.20**) 1·25 1·40
1316 $1.20 on $1.30 mult (surch **CYCLING $1.20**) 4·75 2·00
1317 $1.20 on $1.30 mult (surch **OLYMPIC GAMES 1984 $1.20**) 4·75 4·50

1984. 60th Anniv of Girl Guide Movement in Guyana. Nos. 900/9 surch 25 GIRL GUIDES 1924-1984.
1318 25c. on 110c. on 5c. Annatto tree (No. 900) 25 20
1319 25c. on 110c. on 5c. Annatto tree (No. 901) 25 20
1320 25c. on 110c. on 5c. Annatto tree (No. 902) 80 60
1321 25c. on 110c. on 5c. Annatto tree (No. 903) 80 60
1322 25c. on 110c. on 5c. Annatto tree (No. 904) 10·00 11·00
1323 25c. on 125c. on 8c. on 6c. Cannon-ball tree (No. 905) 25 20
1324 25c. on 125c. on 8c. on 6c. Cannon-ball tree (No. 906) 25 20
1325 25c. on 125c. on 8c. on 6c. Cannon-ball tree (No. 907) 80 60
1326 25c. on 125c. on 8c. on 6c. Cannon-ball tree (No. 908) 80 60
1327 25c. on 125c. on 8c. on 6c. Cannon-ball tree (No. 909) 10·00 11·00

1984. Various stamps surch.
1328 20c. on 15c. on 2c. Type **132** (No. 1034) 30 10
1331 60c. on 110c. on 8c. on 3c. Hanging heliconia (As No. 868 but with only one **110**) 35·00 5·00
1332 120c. on 125c. on 8c. on 6c. Cannon-ball tree (No. 893) 7·00 50
1333 120c. on 125c. on $2 "Norantea guianensis" (No. 834) 70·00 7·50
1334 120c. on 125c. on $2 "Norantea guianensis" (No. O20) 5·50 50
1335 120c. on 140c. on $1 "Chelonanthus uliginoides" (No. 796) 5·50 50
1336 200c. on 220c. on 1c. Pitcher plant of Mt. Roraima (No. 922) 23·00 75
1337 320c. on $1.10 on $2 "Norantea guianensis" (No. 804) 1·50 75
1338 350c. on 375c. on $5 "Odontadenia grandiflora" (No. 803) 5·50 1·00
1339 390c. on 400c. on $5 "Odontadenia grandiflora" (No. 1091) 6·00 1·25
1340 450c. on $5 "Odontadenia grandiflora" (No. O16) 9·00 3·00
1341 25c. on 10c. Cattleya (No. 547) 55·00 2·25
1342 25c. on 15c. Christmas orchid (No. 864) 28·00 50
1342a 25c. on 60c. Soldier's cap (No. 649) 95·00 4·75
1343 25c. on 15c. Christmas orchid (No. 548a) £120 5·50
1346 25c. on 15c. Christmas orchid (No. 977) 17·00 20
1347 25c. on 15c. Christmas orchid (No. 1009) 17·00 20
1348 25c. on 15c. Christmas orchid (No. O23) 17·00 20
1349 130c. on 110c. on $2 "Norantea guianensis" (No. 804) 90·00 5·00
1350 130c. on 110c. on $2 "Norantea guianensis" (No. O22) 1·25 1·25
1351a 600c. on $7.20 on $1 "Chelonanthus uliginoides" (No. 770) 50 60

1984. Various stamps optd 1984.
1352 20c. "Paphinia cristata" (No. 549) 28·00 40
1354 50c. on 8c. Type **136** (No. 1062) 10·00 25
1355 60c. on 1c. Pitcher plant of Mt. Roraima (No. 1000) 2·25 25
1356 $2 "Norantea guianensis" (No. O33) 1·25 60
1358 25c. Marabunta (No. 550) 85·00 4·50
1359 25c. Marabunta (No. F4) 6·50 50
1359a 25c. Marabunta (No. F4a) 2·00 30
1360 $3.60 on $5 "Odontadenia grandiflora" (No. 769) 85 1·10

1984. No. 899 optd with fleur-de-lis.
1358a 25c. Marabunta 85·00 4·50

1984. 40th Anniv of I.C.A.O. Nos. 981, 1017 and 1148/68 optd ICAO or as indicated.
1361 30c. multicoloured (No. 1148) 1·40 1·00
1362 30c. multicoloured (No. 1149) 1·40 1·00
1363 30c. multicoloured (No. 1150) 1·40 1·00
1364 30c. multicoloured (No. 1151) 1·40 1·00
1365 30c. multicoloured (No. 1152) 1·40 1·00
1366 30c. multicoloured (No. 1153) 1·40 1·00
1367 30c. multicoloured (No. 1154) (optd **IMB/ICAO**) 1·40 1·00
1368 30c. multicoloured (No. 1155) (optd **KCV/ICAO**) 1·40 1·00
1369 30c. multicoloured (No. 1156) (optd **KAI/ICAO**) 1·40 1·00
1370 30c. multicoloured (No. 1157) 1·40 1·00
1371 30c. multicoloured (No. 1158) 1·40 1·00
1372 30c. multicoloured (No. 1155) (optd **1984**) 1·40 1·00
1373 30c. multicoloured (No. 1155) (optd **KPM/ICA**) 1·40 1·00
1374 30c. multicoloured (No. 1159) 1·40 1·00
1375 30c. multicoloured (No. 1160) 1·40 1·00
1376 30c. multicoloured (No. 1161) 1·40 1·00
1377 30c. multicoloured (No. 1155) (optd **PMT/ICAO**) 1·40 1·00

1378 30c. multicoloured (No. 1162) 1·40 1·00
1379 30c. multicoloured (No. 1163) 1·40 1·00
1380 30c. multicoloured (No. 1164) 1·40 1·00
1381 30c. multicoloured (No. 1165) 1·40 1·00
1382 30c. multicoloured (No. 1166) 1·40 1·00
1383 30c. multicoloured (No. 1167) 1·40 1·00
1384 30c. multicoloured (No. 1168) 1·40 1·00
1385 200c. on 330c. on $2 multicoloured (No. 981) 75 85
1386 200c. on 75c. on $5 multicoloured (No. 1017) 3·00 2·00

No. 1385 also carries an otherwise unissued surch **G.A.C. Inaug. Flight Georgetown–Toronto 200**.

1984. Wildlife Protection. Nos. 756/67 optd 1984.
1387 30c. Type **178** 30 25
1388 30c. Red howler 30 25
1389 30c. Common squirrel-monkey 30 25
1390 30c. Two-toed sloth 30 25
1391 30c. Brazilian tapir 30 25
1392 30c. Collared peccary 30 25
1393 30c. Six-banded armadillo 30 25
1394 30c. Tamandua ("Ant Eater") 30 25
1395 30c. Giant anteater 30 25
1396 30c. Murine opossum 30 25
1397 30c. Brown four-eyed opossum 30 25
1398 30c. Brazilian agouti 30 25

1984. Nos. D10/11 surch 120 GUYANA.
1399 **D 2** 120c. on 4c. blue 1·50 45
1402 **D 2** 120c. on 12c. red 1·50 45

1984. 175th Birth Anniv of Louis Braille (inventor of alphabet for the blind). No. 1040 surch $1.50.
1403 $1.50 on 15c. on 10c. Type **215** 6·50 55

1984. International Food Day. No. 1012 surch 1.
1404 150c. on 50c. Pawpaw and tangerine 2·50 55

The surcharge places a "1" alongside the original face value and obliterates the "1982" date on the previous overprint.

1984. Birth Centenary of H. N. Critchlow (founder of Guyana Labour Union). No. 873 surch 240 and No. 1196, both optd 1984.
1405 240c. on 110c. on $3 H. N. Critchlow (No. 873) 1·00 65
1406 240c. on $3 H. N. Critchlow (No. 1196) 7·50 1·25

1984. Nos. 910/12 and 1184/7 surch.
1407 **277** 25c. on 45c. brown and black 15 25
1408 - 25c. on 45c. red and black (No. 1185) 15 25
1409 - 25c. on 45c. violet and black (No. 1186) 15 25
1410 - 25c. on 45c. green and black (No. 1187) 15 25
1411 - 120c. on 100c. on $3 mult (No. 910) 9·50 75
1412 - 120c. on 400c. on 30c. mult (No. 911) 1·00 75
1413 - 320c. on $5 multicoloured (No. 912) 17·00 2·50

1984. Deepavali Festival. Nos. 544/5 surch MAHA SABHA 1934-1984 and new value.
1414 25c. on 5c. Annatto tree 50 10
1415 $1.50 on 3c. Hanging heliconia 2·75 1·00

1984. A.S.D.A. Philatelic Exhibition, New York. Nos. 1188/91 optd Philatelic Exhibition New York 1984.
1416 **277** 120c. brown and black 40 45
1417 - 130c. red and black 45 50
1418 - 150c. violet and black 50 55
1419 - 200c. green and black 70 75

1984. Olympic Games, Los Angeles (3nd issue). Design as No. 1051, but with Olympic rings and inscr "OLYMPIC GAMES 1984 LOS ANGELES".
1420 $1.20 Youth display (41×25 mm) 1·50 70

1984. Nos. 847, 861, 1099 and 1088 surch.
1421 20c. on 12c. on 12c. on 6c. multicoloured (No. 847) 60 10
1422 20c. on 12c. on 6c. mult (No. 861) 85·00 6·00
1423 25c. on 50c. on 6c. mult (No. 1099) 30 10
1424 60c. on $1 on 6c. mult (No. 1088) 45 25

318 Pair of Swallow-tailed Kites on Tree

1984. Christmas. Swallow-tailed Kites. Mult.
1425 60c. Type **318** 3·00 1·75
1426 60c. Swallow-tailed kite on branch 3·00 1·75
1427 60c. Kite in flight with wings raised 3·00 1·75
1428 60c. Kite in flight with wings lowered 3·00 1·75
1429 60c. Kite gliding 3·00 1·75

Nos. 1425/9 were printed together, se-tenant, with the backgrounds forming a composite design. Each stamp is inscribed "CHRISTMAS 1982".

319 St. George's Cathedral, Georgetown

1985. Georgetown Buildings. Each black and stone.
1430 25c. Type **319** 10 10
1431 60c. Demerara Mutual Life Assurance Building 15 25
1432 120c. As No. 1431 30 45
1433 120c. Town Hall 30 45
1434 120c. Victoria Law Courts 30 45
1435 200c. As No. 1433 30 75
1436 300c. As No. 1434 30 1·10

Nos. 1432/4 were printed together, se-tenant, forming a composite design.

1985. International Youth Year. No. 1420 optd International Youth Year 1985.
1437 $1.20 Youth display 2·50 45

Examples of No. 1420 used for this overprint all show the second line of the original inscription as "LOS ANGLELLES".

1985. Republic Day. Nos. 1049/50 and 1052 optd or surch Republic Day 1970-1985.
1438 25c. Type **238** 40 40
1439 25c. Flag (inscr "30th ANNIVERSARY IN PARLIAMENT") 40 40
1440 120c. on $6 Presidential standard 1·00 1·00
1441 130c. on $6 Presidential standard 1·10 1·10

322 Young Ocelot on Branch

1985. Wildlife Protection. Multicoloured.
1442A 25c. Type **322** (green background) 1·75 10
1443A 60c. Young ocelot (different) (brown background) 30 25
1444B 120c. As No. 1443 15 20
1445B 120c. Type **322** 15 20
1446B 120c. Young ocelot (different) (brown background) 15 20
1447A 130c. As No. 1446 45 60
1448A 320c. Scarlet macaw (28×46 mm) 3·25 2·00
1449A 330c. Young ocelot reaching for branch (28×46 mm) 90 2·00

1985. Revenue stamp as T 181, and Nos. 912, 940, 1016 and No. O24 surch.
1450 30c. on 50c. mult (No. O24) 50 10
1451 55c. on 2c. black, blue and grey 65 20
1452 55c. on 15c. on 2c. black, blue and grey (940) 65 20
1453 90c. on $1 mult (No. 1016) 7·00 50
1454 225c. on $5 mult (No. 912) 17·00 2·00
1455 230c. on $5 mult (No. 912) 17·00 2·25
1456 260c. on $5 mult (No. 912) 17·00 2·50

1985. International Youth Year Save the Children Fund Campaign. Nos. 880, 1073a, 1079b and 1082 optd International Youth Year 1985 or surch also.
1457 50c. "Two Boys catching Ducks" (No. 1073a) 2·25 20
1458 50c. on 10c. Type **171** (No. 1082) 7·00 20
1459 120c. on 125c. on $3 "Mango Season" (No. 880) 2·25 45
1460 $3 "Mango Season" (No. 1079b) 2·25 1·50

1985. 125th Anniv of British Guiana Post Office (1st issue). No. 699 surch 25 and names of post offices and postal agencies open in 1860.
1461 25c. on 10c. mult (**Airy Hall**) 1·25 1·25
1462 25c. on 10c. multicoloured (**Belfield Arab Coast**) 1·25 1·25
1463 25c. on 10c. multicoloured (**Belfield E. C. Dem.**) 1·25 1·25
1464 25c. on 10c. mult (**Belladrum**) 1·25 1·25
1465 25c. on 10c. multicoloured (**Beterver-wagting**) 1·25 1·25
1466 25c. on 10c. multicoloured (**Blairmont Ferry**) 1·25 1·25
1467 25c. on 10c. mult (**Boeraserie**) 1·25 1·25
1468 25c. on 10c. mult (**Brahm**) 1·25 1·25
1469 25c. on 10c. mult (**Bushlot**) 1·25 1·25
1470 25c. on 10c. mult (**De Kinderen**) 1·25 1·25
1471 25c. on 10c. multicoloured (**Fort Wellington**) 1·25 1·25
1472 25c. on 10c. mult (**Georgetown**) 1·25 1·25
1473 25c. on 10c. mult (**Hague**) 1·25 1·25
1474 25c. on 10c. mult (**Leguan**) 1·25 1·25
1475 25c. on 10c. mult (**Mahaica**) 1·25 1·25
1476 25c. on 10c. mult (**Mahaicony**) 1·25 1·25
1477 25c. on 10c. multicoloured (**New Amsterdam**) 1·25 1·25
1478 25c. on 10c. mult (**Plaisance**) 1·25 1·25
1479 25c. on 10c. multicoloured (**No. 6 Police Station**) 1·25 1·25
1480 25c. on 10c. mult (**Queenstown**) 1·25 1·25
1481 25c. on 10c. multicoloured (**Vergenoegen**) 1·25 1·25
1482 25c. on 10c. mult (**Vigilance**) 1·25 1·25
1483 25c. on 10c. multicoloured (**Vreed-en-Hoop**) 1·25 1·25
1484 25c. on 10c. mult (**Wakenaam**) 1·25 1·25
1485 25c. on 10c. multicoloured (**Windsor Castle**) 1·25 1·25

See also Nos. 1694/1717, 2140/64 and 2278/2301.

1985. I.T.U./W.H.O. Day. Nos. 1148/68 optd 1985 or with single capital letter.
1486 30c. multicoloured (1148) 1·25 1·25
1487 30c. multicoloured (1149) 1·25 1·25
1488 30c. multicoloured (1150) 1·25 1·25
1489 30c. multicoloured (1151) 1·25 1·25
1490 30c. multicoloured (1152) 1·25 1·25
1491 30c. multicoloured (1153) 1·25 1·25
1492 30c. multicoloured (1154) (**I**) 1·25 1·25
1493 30c. multicoloured (1155) (**T**) 1·25 1·25
1494 30c. multicoloured (1156) (**U**) 1·25 1·25
1495 30c. multicoloured (1157) 1·25 1·25
1496 30c. multicoloured (1158) 1·25 1·25
1497 30c. multicoloured (1155) (**W**) 1·25 1·25
1498 30c. multicoloured (1155) (**H**) 1·25 1·25
1499 30c. multicoloured (1155) (**O**) 1·25 1·25
1500 30c. multicoloured (1159) 1·25 1·25
1501 30c. multicoloured (1160) 1·25 1·25
1502 30c. multicoloured (1161) (**D**) 1·25 1·25
1503 30c. multicoloured (1155) (**A**) 1·25 1·25
1504 30c. multicoloured (1162) (**Y**) 1·25 1·25
1505 30c. multicoloured (1163) 1·25 1·25
1506 30c. multicoloured (1164) 1·25 1·25
1507 30c. multicoloured (1165) 1·25 1·25
1508 30c. multicoloured (1166) 1·25 1·25
1509 30c. multicoloured (1167) 1·25 1·25
1510 30c. multicoloured (1168) 1·25 1·25

1985. No. 861 surch 20.
1511 20c. on 12c. on 6c. Patua 5·50 10

1985. 10th Anniv of Caribbean Agricultural Research Development Institute. No. 544 surch 60 CARDI 1975-1985.
1512 60c. on 3c. Hanging heliconia 5·50 35

1985. No. 839 surch 600.
1513 600c. on 625c. on 40c. Tiger beard 48·00 4·50

1985. 80th Anniv of Rotary International. Nos. 707 and 879 surch ROTARY INTERNATIONAL 1905-1985.
1514 120c. on 110c. on $3 Rotary anniversary emblem 27·00 1·75
1515 300c. on $2 "Morpho rhetenor" 17·00 5·50

1985. CARICOM Day. No. 1200 surch CARICOM DAY 1985 60.
1516 60c. on $3 "Makanaima the Great Ancestral Spirit of the Amerindians" 3·00 40

1985. 135th Anniv of First British Guiana Stamps. No. 870 surch 135th Anniversary Cotton Reel 1850-1985 120.
1517 120c. on 110c. on 10c. Type **170** 1·50 70

Series 1

"REICHENBACHIA" ISSUES. Due to the proliferation of these designs the catalogue uses the book plate numbers as description for each design. The following index gives the species on each plate.

Plate No. 1 (Series 1) "Odontoglossum crispum"
Plate No. 2 (Series 1) "Cattleya percivaliana"
Plate No. 3 (Series 1) "Cypripedium sanderianum"
Plate No. 4 (Series 1) "Odontoglossum rossi"
Plate No. 5 (Series 1) "Cattleya dowiana aurea"
Plate No. 6 (Series 1) "Coelogyne cristata maxima"
Plate No. 7 (Series 1) "Odontoglossum insleayi splendens"
Plate No. 8 (Series 1) "Laelia euspatha"
Plate No. 9 (Series 1) "Dendrobium wardianum"
Plate No. 10 (Series 1) "Laelia autumnalis xanthotropis"
Plate No. 11 (Series 1) "Phalaenopsis grandiflora aurea"
Plate No. 12 (Series 1) "Cattleya lawrenceana"
Plate No. 13 (Series 1) "Masdevallia shuttleworthii" and "M. xanthocorys"
Plate No. 14 (Series 1) "Aeranthus sesquipedalis"
Plate No. 15 (Series 1) "Cattleya mendelii Duke of Marlborough"
Plate No. 16 (Series 1) "Zygopetalum intermedium"
Plate No. 17 (Series 1) "Phaius humblotii"
Plate No. 18 (Series 1) "Chysis bractescens"
Plate No. 19 (Series 1) "Masdevallia backhousiana"
Plate No. 20 (Series 1) "Cattleya citrina"
Plate No. 21 (Series 1) "Oncidium jonesianum" and "Oncidium jonesianum phaeanthum"
Plate No. 22 (Series 1) "Saccolabium giganteum"
Plate No. 23 (Series 1) "Cypripedium io"
Plate No. 24 (Series 1) "Odontoglossum blandum"
Plate No. 25 (Series 1) "Maxillaria sanderiana"
Plate No. 26 (Series 1) "Odontoglossum Edward II"
Plate No. 27 (Series 1) "Vanda teres"
Plate No. 28 (Series 1) "Odontoglossum hallii xanthoglossum"
Plate No. 29 (Series 1) "Odontoglossum crispum hrubyanum"
Plate No. 30 (Series 1) "Oncidium concolor"
Plate No. 31 (Series 1) "Trichopilia suavis alba"
Plate No. 32 (Series 1) "Cattleya superba splendens"
Plate No. 33 (Series 1) "Odontoglossum luteo-purpureum"
Plate No. 34 (Series 1) "Cypripedium niveum"
Plate No. 35 (Series 1) "Stanhopea shuttleworthii"
Plate No. 36 (Series 1) "Laelia anceps percivaliana"
Plate No. 37 (Series 1) "Odontoglossum hebraicum"
Plate No. 38 (Series 1) "Cypripedium oenanthum superbum"
Plate No. 39 (Series 1) "Dendrobium superbiens"
Plate No. 40 (Series 1) "Laelia harpophylla"
Plate No. 41 (Series 1) "Lycaste skinneri" and "alba"
Plate No. 42 (Series 1) "Phalaenopsis stuartiana"
Plate No. 43 (Series 1) "Cattleya trianaei ernesti"
Plate No. 44 (Series 1) "Sobralia xantholeuca"
Plate No. 45 (Series 1) "Odontoglossum crispum kinlesideanum"
Plate No. 46 (Series 1) "Cattleya trianaei schroederiana"
Plate No. 47 (Series 1) "Epidendrum vitellinum"
Plate No. 48 (Series 1) "Laelia anceps stella" and "barkeriana"
Plate No. 49 (Series 1) "Odontoglossum harryanum"
Plate No. 50 (Series 1) "Dendrobium leechianum"
Plate No. 51 (Series 1) "Phalaenopsis speciosa"
Plate No. 52 (Series 1) "Laelia elegans schilleriana"
Plate No. 53 (Series 1) "Zygopetalum wendlandi"
Plate No. 54 (Series 1) "Cypripedium selligerum majus"
Plate No. 55 (Series 1) "Angraecum articulatum"
Plate No. 56 (Series 1) "Laelia anceps sanderiana"
Plate No. 57 (Series 1) "Vanda coerulea"
Plate No. 58 (Series 1) "Dendrobium nobile sanderianum"
Plate No. 59 (Series 1) "Laelia gouldiana"
Plate No. 60 (Series 1) "Odontoglossum grande"
Plate No. 61 (Series 1) "Cypripedium rothschildianum"
Plate No. 62 (Series 1) "Vanda sanderiana"
Plate No. 63 (Series 1) "Dendrobium aureum"
Plate No. 64 (Series 1) "Oncidium macranthum"
Plate No. 65 (Series 1) "Cypripedium tautzianum"
Plate No. 66 (Series 1) "Cymbidium mastersi"
Plate No. 67 (Series 1) "Angraecum caudatum"
Plate No. 68 (Series 1) "Laelia albida"
Plate No. 69 (Series 1) "Odontoglossum roezlii"
Plate No. 70 (Series 1) "Oncidium ampliatum majus"
Plate No. 71 (Series 1) "Renanthera lowii"
Plate No. 72 (Series 1) "Cattleya warscewiczii"
Plate No. 73 (Series 1) "Oncidium lanceanum"
Plate No. 74 (Series 1) "Vanda hookeriana"
Plate No. 75 (Series 1) "Cattleya labiata gaskelliana"
Plate No. 76 (Series 1) "Epidendrum prismatocarpum"
Plate No. 77 (Series 1) "Cattleya guttata leopoldi"
Plate No. 78 (Series 1) "Oncidium splendidum"
Plate No. 79 (Series 1) "Odontoglossum hebraicum aspersum"
Plate No. 80 (Series 1) "Cattleya dowiana var chrysotoxa"
Plate No. 81 (Series 1) "Cattleya trianae alba"
Plate No. 82 (Series 1) "Odontoglossum humeanum"
Plate No. 83 (Series 1) "Cypripedium argus"
Plate No. 84 (Series 1) "Odontoglossum luteo-purpureum prionopetalum"
Plate No. 85 (Series 1) "Cattleya rochellensis"
Plate No. 86 (Series 1) "Odontoglossum triumphans"
Plate No. 87 (Series 1) "Phalaenopsis casta"
Plate No. 88 (Series 1) "Oncidium tigrinum"
Plate No. 89 (Series 1) "Cypripedium lemoinierianum"
Plate No. 90 (Series 1) "Catasetum bungerothii"
Plate No. 91 (Series 1) "Cattleya ballantiniana"
Plate No. 92 (Series 1) "Dendrobium brymerianum"
Plate No. 93 (Series 1) "Cattleya eldorado crocata"
Plate No. 94 (Series 1) "Odontoglossum sanderianum"
Plate No. 95 (Series 1) "Cattleya labiata warneri"
Plate No. 96 (Series 1) "Odontoglossum schroderianum"

Series 2

Plate No. 1 (Series 2) "Cypripedium morganiae burfordiense"
Plate No. 2 (Series 2) "Cattleya bowringiana"
Plate No. 3 (Series 2) "Dendrobium formosum"
Plate No. 4 (Series 2) "Phaius tuberculosus"
Plate No. 5 (Series 2) "Odontoglossum crispum mundyanum"
Plate No. 6 (Series 2) "Laelia praestans"
Plate No. 7 (Series 2) "Dendrobium phalaenopsis var statterianum"
Plate No. 8 (Series 2) "Cypripedium boxalli atratum"
Plate No. 9 (Series 2) "Odontoglossum wattianum"
Plate No. 10 (Series 2) "Cypripedium lathamianum inversum"
Plate No. 11 (Series 2) "Paphinia rugosa" and "Zygopetalum xanthinum"
Plate No. 12 (Series 2) "Dendrobium melanodiscus"
Plate No. 13 (Series 2) "Laelia anceps schroderiana"
Plate No. 14 (Series 2) "Phaius hybridus cooksonii"
Plate No. 15 (Series 2) "Disa grandiflora"
Plate No. 16 (Series 2) "Selenipedium hybridum grande"
Plate No. 17 (Series 2) "Cattleya schroederae alba"
Plate No. 18 (Series 2) "Lycaste skinnerii armeniaca"
Plate No. 19 (Series 2) "Odontoglossum excellens"
Plate No. 20 (Series 2) "Laelio-cattleya elegans var blenheimensis"
Plate No. 21 (Series 2) "Odontoglossum coradinei"
Plate No. 22 (Series 2) "Odontoglossum wilckeanum var rothschildianum"
Plate No. 23 (Series 2) "Cypripedium lawrenceanum hyeanum"
Plate No. 24 (Series 2) "Cattleya intermedia punctatissima"
Plate No. 25 (Series 2) "Laelia purpurata"
Plate No. 26 (Series 2) "Masdevallia harryana splendens"
Plate No. 27 (Series 2) "Selenipedium hybridum nitidissimum"
Plate No. 28 (Series 2) "Cattleya mendelii var measuresiana"
Plate No. 29 (Series 20 "Odontoglossum vexillarium" ("miltonia vexillaria")
Plate No. 30 (Series 2) "Saccolabium coeleste"
Plate No. 31 (Series 2) "Cypripedium hybridum youngianum"
Plate No. 32 (Series 2) "Miltonia (hybrida) bleuana"

Plate No. 33 (Series 2) "Laelia grandis"
Plate No. 34 (Series 2) "Cattleya labiata var lueddemanniana"
Plate No. 35 (Series 2) "Odontoglossum coronarium"
Plate No. 36 (Series 2) "Cattleya granulosa var schofieldiana"
Plate No. 37 (Series 2) "Odontoglossum (hybridum) leroyanum"
Plate No. 38 (Series 2) "Cypripedium (hybridum) laucheanum" and "eyermanianum"
Plate No. 39 (Series 2) "Cychnoches chlorochilon"
Plate No. 40 (Series 2) "Cattleya O'Brieniana"
Plate No. 41 (Series 2) "Odontoglossum ramosissimum"
Plate No. 42 (Series 2) "Dendrobium phalaenopsis var"
Plate No. 43 (Series 2) "Cypripedium (hybridum) pollettianum" and "maynardii"
Plate No. 44 (Series 2) "Odontoglossum naevium"
Plate No. 45 (Series 2) "Cypripedium (hybridum) castleanum"
Plate No. 47 (Series 2) "Cattleya amethystoglossa"
Plate No. 48 (Series 2) "Cattleya (hybrida) arnoldiana"
Plate No. 49 (Series 2) "Cattleya labiata"
Plate No. 50 (Series 2) "Dendrobium (hybridum) venus" and "cassiope"
Plate No. 51 (Series 2) "Selenipedium (hybridum) weidlichianum"
Plate No. 52 (Series 2) "Cattleya mossiae var reineckiana"
Plate No. 53 (Series 2) "Cymbidium lowianum"
Plate No. 54 (Series 2) "Oncidium loxense"
Plate No. 56 (Series 2) "Coelogyne sanderae"
Plate No. 58 (Series 2) "Coelogyne pandurata"
Plate No. 59 (Series 2) "Schomburgkia sanderiana"
Plate No. 60 (Series 2) "Oncidium superbiens"
Plate No. 61 (Series 2) "Dendrobium johnsoniae"
Plate No. 62 (Series 2) "Laelia hybrida behrensiana"
Plate No. 63 (Series 2) Hybrid "Calanthes Victoria Regina", "Bella" and "Burfordiense"
Plate No. 64 (Series 2) "Cattleya mendelii Quorndon House var"
Plate No. 65 (Series 2) "Arachnanthe clarkei"
Plate No. 66 (Series 2) "Zygopetalum burtii"
Plate No. 67 (Series 2) "Cattleya (hybrida) parthenia"
Plate No. 68 (Series 2) "Phalaenopsis sanderiana" and "intermedia portei"
Plate No. 69 (Series 2) "Phaius blumei var assamicus"
Plate No. 70 (Series 2) "Angraecum humblotii"
Plate No. 71 (Series 2) "Odontoglossum pescatorei"
Plate No. 72 (Series 2) "Cattleya rex"
Plate No. 73 (Series 2) "Zygopetalum crinitum"
Plate No. 74 (Series 2) "Cattleya lueddemanniana alba"
Plate No. 75 (Series 2) "Cymbidium (hybridum) winnianum"
Plate No. 76 (Series 2) Hybrid "Masdevallias courtauldiana", "geleniana" and "measuresiana"
Plate No. 77 (Series 2) "Cypripedium (hybridum) calypso"
Plate No. 78 (Series 2) "Masdevallia chimaera var mooreana"
Plate No. 79 (Series 2) "Miltonia phalaenopsis"
Plate No. 80 (Series 2) "Lissochilus giganteus"
Plate No. 82 (Series 2) "Thunia brymeriana"
Plate No. 83 (Series 2) "Miltonia moreliana"
Plate No. 84 (Series 2) "Oncidium kramerianum"
Plate No. 85 (Series 2) "Cattleya Victoria Regina"
Plate No. 86 (Series 2) "Zygopetalum klabochorum"
Plate No. 87 (Series 2) "Laelia autumnalis alba"
Plate No. 88 (Series 2) "Spathoglottis kimballiana"
Plate No. 89 (Series 2) "Laelio-cattleya" ("The Hon. Mrs. Astor")
Plate No. 90 (Series 2) "Phaius hybridus amabilis" and "marthiae"
Plate No. 91 (Series 2) "Zygopetalum rostratum"
Plate No. 92 (Series 2) "Coelogyne swaniana"
Plate No. 93 (Series 2) "Laelio-cattleya (hybrida) phoebe"
Plate No. 94 (Series 2) "Epidendrum atro-purpureum var randianum"
Plate No. 95 (Series 2) "Dendrobium imperatrix"
Plate No. 96 (Series 2) "Vanda parishii var marriottiana"

331 "Cattleya lawrenceana" (Plate No. 12 (Series 1))

1985. Centenary of Publication of Sanders' "Reichenbachia" (1st issue). Orchids. Mult.

1518	25c. Type **331**	50	30
1519	60c. Plate No. 2 (Series 1)	60	35
1520	60c. Plate No. 7 (Series 1)	60	35
1521	60c. Plate No. 10 (Series 1)	60	35
1522	60c. Plate No. 19 (Series 1)	60	35
1523	60c. Plate No. 31 (Series 1)	60	35
1524	120c. Plate No. 27 (Series 1)	75	55
1525	130c. Plate No. 3 (Series 1)	75	55
1528	130c. Plate No. 18 (Series 1)	4·50	55
1531	130c. Plate No. 29 (Series 1)	3·25	55
1532	130c. Plate No. 30 (Series 1)	3·25	55
1533	200c. Plate No. 4 (Series 1)	3·25	85
1759	130c. Plate No. 6 (Series 1)	75	20
1760	130c. Plate No. 13 (Series 1)	75	20
1761	130c. Plate No. 20 (Series 1)	75	20
1762	130c. Plate No. 25 (Series 1)	75	20

See also Nos. 1551/66, 1571/1806, 1597, 1620/1863, 1663/73, 1679/83, 1731/8, 1747/54, 1809/19, 1822, 1868/9, 1872/81, 1884/7, 1907, 1912/15, 1916/24, 1925/9, 2066/73, 2171/8, 2180/2, 2190/3, 2216/18, 2219/20, 2225/7, 2235/42, **MS**2275, 2314/18, 2322/5, 2328, **MS**2332, 2314/18, 2322/5, 2329, 2468/71, 2498/2511 and 2605/8.

332 Arms of Guyana

1985

1535b **332** 25c. multicoloured 15 20

For Type **332** within frame, see No. 2183.

1985. 85th Birthday of Queen Elizabeth the Queen Mother (1st issue). Nos. 1528 and 1531/2 optd QUEEN MOTHER 1900-1985.

1536	130c. Plate No. 18 (Series 1)	80	80
1537	130c. Plate No. 29 (Series 1)	80	80
1538	130c. Plate No. 30 (Series 1)	80	80

MS1539 100×126 mm. 200c.×4 Plate 4 (Series 1) 7·50 5·50

The four stamps in No. **MS**1539 are overprinted **LADY BOWES-LYON 1900-1923, DUCHESS OF YORK 1923-1937, QUEEN ELIZABETH 1937-1952** or **QUEEN MOTHER 1952-1985**.

See also No. **MS**1570.

1985. International Youth Year. Nos. 900/4 surch 25 International Youth Year 1985.

1540	25c. on 110c. on 5c. multicoloured (900)	25	25
1541	25c. on 110c. on 5c. multicoloured (901)	25	25
1542	25c. on 110c. on 5c. multicoloured (902)	1·00	1·00
1543	25c. on 110c. on 5c. multicoloured (903)	1·00	1·00
1544	25c. on 100c. on 5c. multicoloured (904)	12·00	12·00

1985. 75th Anniv of Girl Guide Movement. No. 612 surch 225 1910-1985.

1545 225c. on 350c. on 225c. on 40c. Guides in camp 48·00 5·50

No. 1545 also carries two otherwise unissued surcharges at top right.

1985. Birth Bicentenary of John J. Audubon (ornithologist). No. 992 surch J. J. Audubon 1785-1985 240.

1546 240c. on 35c. Harpy eagle 48·00 7·00

337 Leaders of the 1763 Rebellion

1985. 150th Anniv (1984) of Abolition of Slavery (1st issue).

1547	**337**	25c. black and grey	25	10
1548	-	60c. black and mauve	20	25
1549	-	130c. black and blue	25	50
1550	-	150c. black and lilac	60	55

DESIGNS: 60c. Damon and Parliament Buildings, Georgetown; 130c. Quamina and Demerara, 1823; 150c. "Den Arendt" (slave ship), 1627.

For these designs in changed colours see Nos. 2552/5.

1985. Centenary of Publication of Sanders' "Reichenbachia" (2nd issue). As T 331 showing orchids. Multicoloured.

1551	25c. Plate No. 52 (Series 1)	2·50	25
1556	60c. Plate No. 44 (Series 1)	70	35
1557	60c. Plate No. 47 (Series 1)	70	35
1558	120c. Plate No. 36 (Series 1)	2·75	55
1559	130c. Plate No. 16 (Series 1)	2·75	55
1560	130c. Plate No. 38 (Series 1)	2·75	55
1561	150c. Plate No. 32 (Series 1)	2·75	55
1562	150c. Plate No. 34 (Series 1)	2·75	55
1563	150c. Plate No. 35 (Series 1)	2·75	55
1564	150c. Plate No. 41 (Series 1)	2·75	55
1565	150c. Plate No. 48 (Series 1)	2·75	55
1566	150c. Plate No. 62 (Series 1)	2·75	55
1763	55c. Plate No. 9 (Series 1)	55	10
1764	55c. Plate No. 22 (Series 1)	55	10
1765	55c. Plate No. 49 (Series 1)	55	10
1766	55c. Plate No. 64 (Series 1)	55	10

1985. Signing of Guyana–Libya Friendship Treaty. No. 621 surch Guyana/Libya Friendship 1985 150.

1567 **149** 150c. on 10c. mult 9·00 2·75

1985. Namibia Day. No. 636 surch 150.

1568 150c. on 35c. Unveiling of monument 2·75 55

1985. World Cup Football Championship, Mexico (1986) (1st issue). No. F2 surch Mexico 1986 275.

1569 275c. on 3c. Hanging heliconia 22·00 5·00

See also No. 1727.

1985. 85th Birthday of Queen Elizabeth the Queen Mother (2nd issue). Sheet 120×129 mm containing No. 1529×4 optd as No. MS1539, each stamp surch 200.

MS1570 200c. on 130c.×4 Plate No. 20 (Series 1) 20·00 7·50

1985. Centenary of Publication of Sanders' "Reichenbachia" (3rd issue). As T 331 showing orchids. Multicoloured.

1571	25c. Plate No. 8 (Series 1)	2·25	20
1572	25c. Plate No. 23 (Series 1)	2·25	20
1573	25c. Plate No. 51 (Series 1)	2·25	20
1574	25c. Plate No. 61 (Series 1)	2·25	20
1575	25c. Plate No. 63 (Series 1)	2·25	20
1576	25c. Plate No. 70 (Series 1)	2·25	20
1577	25c. Plate No. 72 (Series 1)	2·25	20
1578	120c. Plate No. 1 (Series 1) (horiz)	2·25	55
1579	120c. Plate No. 11 (Series 1) (horiz)	2·25	55
1580	120c. Plate No. 28 (Series 1) (horiz)	2·25	55
1584	200c. Plate No. 14 (Series 1)	2·50	80
1585	200c. Plate No. 21 (Series 1) (horiz)	2·50	80
1767	150c. Plate No. 40 (Series 1) (horiz)	50	20
1768	150c. Plate No. 42 (Series 1) (horiz)	50	20
1769	150c. Plate No. 45 (Series 1) (horiz)	50	20
1770	200c. Plate No. 43 (Series 1) (horiz)	55	30

1985. 30th Anniv of Commonwealth Caribbean Medical Research Council. Nos. 819, 871, 874, 928 and 1014 optd 1955–1985 or surch also.

1587	-	60c. mult (No. 819)	20	25
1588	-	60c. mult (No. 1014)	20	25
1589	**176**	120c. on 110c. on 10c. multicoloured (No. 871)	40	45
1590	-	120c. on 110c. on $3 mult (No. 874)	40	45
1592	-	120c. on 210c. on $3 mult (No. 928)	40	45

1985. 20th Anniv of Guyana Defence Force. No. 856 surch 1965-1985.

1593	25c. on $1.10 on $3 W.O. and N.C.O; Guyana Defence Force, 1966	1·00	10
1594	225c. on $1.10 on $3 W.O. and N.C.O; Guyana Defence Force, 1966	2·50	1·75

1985. Fire Prevention. Nos. 678 and 680 optd 1985 and surch.

1595	25c. on 40c. Fire engine, 1977	18·00	60
1596	320c. on 15c. Steam engine, circa 1860	28·00	9·00

1985. Centenary of Publication of Sanders' "Reichenbachia" (4th issue). As T 331. Mult.

1597 60c. Plate No. 55 (Series 1) 1·75 30

1985. Columbus Day. Unissued value as T 331 surch 350 CRISTOBAL COLON 1492-1992. Mult.

1598 350c. on 120c. Plate No. 65 (Series 1) 12·00 6·00

1985. 20th Death Anniv of Sir Winston Churchill. No. 707 optd SIR WINSTON CHURCHILL 1965-1985.

1599 $2 "Morpho rhetenor" (female) 24·00 7·50

1985. 35th Anniv of International Commission of Irrigation and Drainage. No. 625 with unissued surcharge further surch 1950-1985.

1600	**150**	25c. on 110c. on 10c. multicoloured	30	10
1601	**150**	200c. on 110c. on 10c. multicoloured	1·25	85

1985. 40th Anniv of U.N.O. Nos. 714/16, 800 and O19 optd United Nations 1945-1985.

1602	30c. multicoloured (No. 714)	1·75	10
1603	50c. multicoloured (No. 715)	1·75	20
1604	100c. on $3 mult (No. O19)	1·50	40
1605	225c. on 220c. on $3 mult (No. 800)	25·00	2·75
1606	$3 multicoloured (No. 716)	3·50	4·00

1985. Nos. 551/3, O14/15, O18, O21, OP1/2 and F7 optd POSTAGE.

1607	30c. on $2 "Norantea guianensis" (No. O18)	40	10
1608	40c. Tiger beard (No. 551)	50·00	1·00
1609	50c. "Guzmania lingulata" (No. 552)	40	20
1610	50c. "Guzmania lingulata" (No. O14)	40	20
1611	60c. Soldier's cap (No. 553)	4·25	25
1612	60c. Soldier's cap (No. O15)	3·50	25
1613	60c. Soldier's cap (No. F7)	1·75	25
1614	$10 "Elbella patrobas" (No. O21)	32·00	8·50
1615	$15 on $1 "Chelonanthus uliginoides" (No. OP1)	8·00	10·00
1616	$20 on $1 "Chelonanthus uliginoides" (No. OP2)	9·00	11·00

1985. Deepavali Festival. Nos. 542/3 surch Deepavali 1985.

1617	25c. on 2c. Type **132**	2·00	25
1618	150c. on 1c. Pitcher plant of Mt. Roraima	4·50	1·75

1985. Christmas. Sheet 120×129 mm containing No. 1764×4 optd Christmas 1985.

MS1619 55c.×4 Plate No. 22 (Series 1), each with a different overprint (Type **350**, **Happy New Year, Merry Christmas** or **Happy Holidays**) 7·00 4·00

1985. Centenary of Publication of Sanders' "Reichenbachia" (5th issue). As T 331 showing orchids. Multicoloured.

1620	25c. Plate No. 59 (Series 1)	1·25	20
1622	60c. Plate No. 57 (Series 1) (horiz)	1·50	35
1623	60c. Plate No. 73 (Series 1) (horiz)	1·50	35
1624	60c. Plate No. 75 (Series 1) (horiz)	1·50	35
1627	120c. Plate No. 37 (Series 1)	2·25	55
1628	120c. Plate No. 46 (Series 1)	2·25	55
1629	120c. Plate No. 56 (Series 1)	2·25	55
1630	120c. Plate No. 58 (Series 1)	2·25	55
1631	120c. Plate No. 67 (Series 1)	2·25	55
1632	130c. Plate No. 66 (Series 1)	2·25	65
1633	150c. Plate No. 26 (Series 1)	2·50	75
1634	200c. Plate No. 33 (Series 1) (horiz)	2·75	85
1771	30c. Plate No. 53 (Series 1)	30	10
1772	75c. Plate No. 55 (Series 1)	35	15
1773	100c. Plate No. 65 (Series 1)	35	15
1774	225c. Plate No. 24 (Series 1)	50	35

The 30, 75, 100 and 225c. values have "GUYANA" in blue.

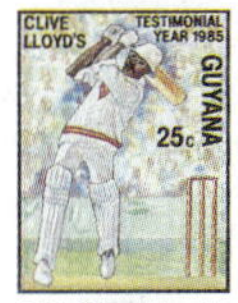

351 Clive Lloyd (cricketer)

1985. Clive Lloyd's Testimonial Year. Multicoloured.

1636	25c. Type **351**	50	80
1637	25c. Clive Lloyd, bat and wicket	50	80
1638	25c. Cricket equipment	50	80
1639	60c. As No. 1638 (25×33 mm)	50	40
1640	$1.30 As No. 1637 (25×33 mm)	50	85
1641	$2.25 Type **351** (25×33 mm)	60	1·50
1642	$3.50 Clive Lloyd with the Prudential Cup (36×56 mm)	60	2·00

1985. Wildlife Protection. Nos. 756/67 optd 1985.

1643	30c. Type **178**	75	75
1644	30c. Red howler	75	75
1645	30c. Common squirrel-monkey	75	75
1646	30c. Two-toed sloth	75	75
1647	30c. Brazilian tapir	75	75
1648	30c. Collared peccary	75	75
1649	30c. Six-banded armadillo	75	75
1650	30c. Tamandua	75	75
1651	30c. Giant anteater	75	75
1652	30c. Murine opossum	75	75
1653	30c. Brown four-eyed opossum	75	75
1654	30c. Brazilian agouti	75	75

1985. No. 847 surch 20.

1655 20c. on 12c. on 12c. on 6c. Black acara ("Patua") 7·00 20

1986. Centenary of the Appearance of "Reichenbachia" Volume 1. Nos. 1768 and 1770 optd REICHENBACHIA 1886-1986.

1657	150c. Plate No. 42 (Series 1)	6·00	90
1658	200c. Plate No. 43 (Series 1)	6·00	1·10

1986. Republic Day. Nos. 1108/9 and 1052 optd Republic Day 1986 or surch also.

1659	25c. As Type **258**	10	20
1660	25c. As No. 1050	10	20
1661	120c. on $6 Presidential standard	40	50
1662	225c. on $6 Presidential standard	70	1·00

1986. Centenary of Publication of Sanders' "Reichenbachia" (6th issue). As T 331. Mult.

1663	40c. Plate No. 77 (Series 1)	75	20
1664	45c. Plate No. 54 (Series 1)	75	25
1665	50c. Plate No. 92 (Series 1)	75	25
1666	60c. Plate No. 95 (Series 1)	80	30
1667	75c. Plate No. 5 (Series 1)	85	35
1668	90c. Plate No. 84 (Series 1)	95	40
1669	150c. Plate No. 78 (Series 1)	1·25	60
1670	200c. Plate No. 79 (Series 1)	1·60	80
1671	300c. Plate No. 83 (Series 1)	2·25	1·40
1672	320c. Plate No. 50 (Series 1)	2·25	1·60
1673	360c. Plate No. 85 (Series 1)	2·50	1·75

1986. Easter. No. 481 optd 1986 and surch also.

1674	**111**	25c. on 6c. multicoloured	25	10
1675	**111**	50c. on 6c. multicoloured	40	20
1676	**111**	100c. on 6c. mult	60	40
1677	**111**	200c. on 6c. mult	1·00	70

1986. 60th Anniv of St. John's Ambulance in Guyana. No. 652 surch 1926 1986 150.
1678 150c. on 35c. silver, black and green 3·00 55

1986. Centenary of Publication of Sanders' "Reichenbachia" (7th issue). As T 331. Mult.
1679 25c. Plate No. 71 (Series 1) (horiz) 1·50 20
1680 120c. Plate No. 69 (Series 1) (horiz) 2·25 55
1681 150c. Plate No. 87 (Series 1) (horiz) 2·50 65
1682 225c. Plate No. 60 (Series 1) 2·50 1·25
1683 350c. Plate No. 94 (Series 1) (horiz) 2·75 2·00

1986. 60th Birthday of Queen Elizabeth II. No. 1759/60 optd 1926 1986 QUEEN ELIZABETH.
1684 130c. Plate No. 13 (Series 1) 7·00 2·50
MS1685 100×126 mm. 130c. on 130c., 200c. on 130c., 260c. on 130c., 330c. on 130c., Plate No. 6 (Series 1) 8·50 8·50
The original face values on No. **MS**1685 are obliterated by a floral pattern.

1986. Wildlife Protection. Nos. 685, 739/44 and 993/8 surch Protect the and value.
1686 60c. on 35c. Type **174** 35 40
1687 60c. on 35c. Trahira ("Haimara") 35 40
1688 60c. on 35c. Electric eel 35 40
1689 60c. on 35c. Golden rivulus 35 40
1690 60c. on 35c. Golden pencilfish 35 40
1691 60c. on 35c. Four-eyed fish 35 40
1691a 60c. on 35c. Red piranha ("Pirai") 10·00 3·00
1691b 60c. on 35c. Smoking hassar 10·00 3·00
1691c 60c. on 35c. Manta 10·00 3·00
1691d 60c. on 35c. Festive cichlid ("Flying patwa") 10·00 3·00
1691e 60c. on 35c. Arapaima 10·00 3·00
1691f 60c. on 35c. Peacock cichlid ("Lukanani") 10·00 3·00
1692 $6 on 8c. Type **163** 3·00 3·25

1986. No. 799 surch 600.
1693 600c. on 720c. on 60c. Soldier's cap 23·00 2·75

1986. 125th Anniv of British Guiana Post Office (2nd issue). No. 702a surch 25 and names of postal agencies opened between 1860 and 1880.
1694 25c. on 30c. mult (surch **Abary**) 1·25 1·00
1695 25c. on 30c. multicoloured (surch **Anna Regina**) 1·25 1·00
1696 25c. on 30c. multicoloured (surch **Aurora**) 1·25 1·00
1697 25c. on 30c. multicoloured (surch **Bartica Grove**) 1·25 1·00
1698 25c. on 30c. multicoloured (surch **Bel Air**) 1·25 1·00
1699 25c. on 30c. multicoloured (surch **Belle Plaine**) 1·25 1·00
1700 25c. on 30c. multicoloured (surch **Clonbrook**) 1·25 1·00
1701 25c. on 30c. multicoloured (surch **T.P.O. Dem. Railway**) 1·25 1·00
1702 25c. on 30c. multicoloured (surch **Enmore**) 1·25 1·00
1703 25c. on 30c. multicoloured (surch **Fredericksburg**) 1·25 1·00
1704 25c. on 30c. multicoloured (surch **Good Success**) 1·25 1·00
1705 25c. on 30c. mult (surch **1986**) 1·25 1·00
1706 25c. on 30c. multicoloured (surch **Mariabba**) 1·25 1·00
1707 25c. on 30c. multicoloured (surch **Massaruni**) 1·25 1·00
1708 25c. on 30c. mult (surch **Nigg**) 1·25 1·00
1709 25c. on 30c. multicoloured (surch **No. 50**) 1·25 1·00
1710 25c. on 30c. multicoloured (surch **No. 63 Benab**) 1·25 1·00
1711 25c. on 30c. multicoloured (surch **Philadelphia**) 1·25 1·00
1712 25c. on 30c. multicoloured (surch **Sisters**) 1·25 1·00
1713 25c. on 30c. multicoloured (surch **Skeldon**) 1·25 1·00
1714 25c. on 30c. multicoloured (surch **Suddie**) 1·25 1·00
1715 25c. on 30c. multicoloured (surch **Taymouth Manor**) 1·25 1·00
1716 25c. on 30c. mult (surch **Wales**) 1·25 1·00
1717 25c. on 30c. mult (surch **Whim**) 1·25 1·00

1986. 20th Anniv of Independence. (a) No. 332 of British Guiana surch GUYANA INDEPENDENCE 1966-1986, Nos. 424 and 435 of Guyana surch 1986 and No. 656 surch 25.
1718 25c. on 2c. green (No. 332) 15 10
1719 25c. on 35c. mult (No. 656) 15 10
1720 60c. on 2c. green (No. 332) 25 10
1721 120c. on 6c. green (No. 424) 40 35
1722 130c. on 24c. black and orange (No. 435) 11·00 1·75

(b) Nos. 1188/91 surch INDEPENDENCE 1966-1986.
1723 **277** 25c. on 120c. brown, black and blue (No. 1188) 25 40
1724 - 25c. on 130c. red, black and blue (No. 1189) 25 40
1725 - 25c. on 150c. violet and blue (No. 1190) 25 40
1726 - 225c. on 200c. green, black and blue (No. 1191) 65 75

1986. World Cup Football Championship, Mexico (2nd issue). No. 544 surch MEXICO 1986 225.
1727 225c. on 3c. Hanging heliconia 23·00 5·00

1986. CARICOM Day. No. 705a optd CARICOM DAY 1986.
1728 60c. "Papilio androgeus" 11·00 60

1986. CARICOM Heads of Government Conference, Georgetown. Nos. 544 and 601 surch CARICOM HEADS OF GOV'T CONFERENCE JULY 1986 and value.
1729 25c. on 8c. on 6c. Cannon-ball tree 2·75 30
1730 60c. on 3c. Hanging heliconia 3·50 70

1986. Centenary of Publication of Sanders' "Reichenbachia" (8th issue). As T 331. Mult.
1731 30c. Plate No. 86 (Series 1) 1·50 15
1732 55c. Plate No. 17 (Series 1) 50 20
1733 60c. Plate No. 93 (Series 1) 50 20
1734 100c. Plate No. 68 (Series 1) 2·50 20
1735 130c. Plate No. 91 (Series 1) 2·75 30
1736 250c. Plate No. 74 (Series 1) 75 1·00
1737 260c. Plate No. 39 (Series 1) 75 1·00
1738 375c. Plate No. 90 (Series 1) 4·25 1·50

1986. International Peace Year. Nos. 542 and 546 surch INT. YEAR OF PEACE and value.
1739 25c. on 1c. Pitcher plant of Mt. Roraima 80 40
1740 60c. on 6c. Cannon-ball tree 1·75 1·75
1741 120c. on 6c. Cannon-ball tree 1·75 1·75
1742 130c. on 6c. Cannon-ball tree 1·75 1·75
1743 150c. on 6c. Cannon-ball tree 1·75 1·75

363 Halley's Comet and British Guiana 1907 2c. Stamp

1986. Appearance of Halley's Comet.
1744 **363** 320c. red, black and lilac 40 1·00
1745 - 320c. multicoloured 40 1·00
MS1746 76×50 mm. Nos. 1744/5. Imperf 1·50 2·00
DESIGN: No. 1745, Guyana 1985 320c. scarlet macaw stamp.

1986. Centenary of Publication of Sanders' "Reichenbachia" (9th issue). As T 331. Mult.
1747 40c. Plate No. 96 (Series 1) 2·25 15
1748 45c. Plate No. 81 (Series 1) 30 15
1749 90c. Plate No. 89 (Series 1) 50 20
1750 100c. Plate No. 88 (Series 1) 3·75 20
1751 150c. Plate No. 76 (Series 1) 3·75 35
1752 180c. Plate No. 15 (Series 1) 50 40
1753 320c. Plate No. 82 (Series 1) 60 90
1754 330c. Plate No. 80 (Series 1) 3·75 1·25

1986. No. 489 surch 20.
1755 20c. on 6c. Patua 10·00 25

1986. 50th Anniv of Guyana United Sadr Islamic Association. Nos. 469/70 optd GUSIA 1936-1986, No. 1757 surch also.
1756 **105** 25c. black, gold and lilac 6·00 50
1757 **105** $1.50 on 6c. black, gold and flesh 11·00 4·50

1986. Regional Pharmacy Conference. No. 545 surch REGIONAL PHARMACY CONFERENCE 1986 130.
1758 130c. on 5c. Annatto tree 11·00 1·75

1986. Centenary of Publication of Sanders' "Reichenbachia" (10th issue). As T 331. Mult.
1809 30c. Plate No. 30 (Series 2) 1·25 15
1810 45c. Plate No. 21 (Series 2) (horiz) 50 15
1811 75c. Plate No. 8 (Series 2) 50 15
1812 80c. Plate No. 42 (Series 2) (horiz) 50 15
1813 90c. Plate No. 4 (Series 2) 55 25
1814 130c. Plate No. 38 (Series 2) 3·00 35
1815 160c. Plate No. 5 (Series 2) (horiz) 3·00 40
1816 200c. Plate No. 9 (Series 2) 75 50
1817 320c. Plate No. 12 (Series 2) 1·75 90
1818 350c. Plate No. 29 (Series 2) (horiz) 2·00 90
1819 360c. Plate No. 34 (Series 2) 5·50 90

1986. 20th Anniv of Independence (2nd issue). As T 332 but additionally inscr "1966–1986" at foot.
1820 25c. multicoloured 20 25

1986. Centenary of Publication of Sanders' "Reichenbachia" (11th issue). Design as No. 1735, but with different face value. Mult.
1822 40c. Plate No. 91 (Series 1) 1·00 15

1986. Nos. 1361/84 surch 120.
1823 120c. on 30c. mult (No. 1361) 2·00 1·50
1824 120c. on 30c. mult (No. 1362) 2·00 1·50
1825 120c. on 30c. mult (No. 1363) 2·00 1·50
1826 120c. on 30c. mult (No. 1364) 2·00 1·50
1827 120c. on 30c. mult (No. 1365) 2·00 1·50
1828 120c. on 30c. mult (No. 1366) 2·00 1·50
1829 120c. on 30c. mult (No. 1367) 2·00 1·50
1830 120c. on 30c. mult (No. 1368) 2·00 1·50
1831 120c. on 30c. mult (No. 1369) 2·00 1·50
1832 120c. on 30c. mult (No. 1370) 2·00 1·50
1833 120c. on 30c. mult (No. 1371) 2·00 1·50
1834 120c. on 30c. mult (No. 1372) 2·00 1·50
1835 120c. on 30c. mult (No. 1373) 2·00 1·50
1836 120c. on 30c. mult (No. 1374) 2·00 1·50
1837 120c. on 30c. mult (No. 1375) 2·00 1·50
1838 120c. on 30c. mult (No. 1376) 2·00 1·50
1839 120c. on 30c. mult (No. 1377) 2·00 1·50
1840 120c. on 30c. mult (No. 1378) 2·00 1·50
1841 120c. on 30c. mult (No. 1379) 2·00 1·50
1842 120c. on 30c. mult (No. 1380) 2·00 1·50
1843 120c. on 30c. mult (No. 1381) 2·00 1·50
1844 120c. on 30c. mult (No. 1382) 2·00 1·50
1845 120c. on 30c. mult (No. 1383) 2·00 1·50
1846 120c. on 30c. mult (No. 1384) 2·00 1·50

1986. 12th World Orchid Conference, Tokyo (1st issue). Unissued design as No. 1731, but with different face value, surch 12th World Orchid Conference TOKYO JAPAN MARCH 1987 650.
1847 650c. on 40c. Plate No. 86 (Series 1) 19·00 6·50
No. 1847 is inscribed "ONTOGLOSSUM TRIUMPHANS" in error.
See also No. 2138.

1986. Columbus Day. Unissued design as No. 1774, but with different face value, surch 1492-1992 CHRISTOPHER COLUMBUS 320.
1864 320c. on 150c. Plate No. 24 (Series 1) 7·00 3·00

1986. International Food Day. Nos. 1170/1 further surch 1986 and value.
1866 50c. on 30c. on 1c. Type **87** 5·50 60
1867 225c. on $2.60 on 3c. Peacock cichlid ("Lukanani") 17·00 4·75

1986. Centenary of Publication of Sanders' "Reichenbachia" (12th issue). As T 331, one as No. 1731 with different face value. Mult.
1868 40c. Plate No. 86 (Series 1) 75 15
1869 90c. Plate No. 10 (Series 2) 1·00 30

1986. Air. 40th Annivs of UNICEF and UNESCO No. 706 surch.
1870 120c. on $1 "Agrias claudina" (surch **UNICEF 1946-1986 AIR 120**) 13·00 11·00
1871 120c. on $1 "Agrias claudina" (surch **UNESCO 1946-1986 AIR 120**) 13·00 11·00

1986. Centenary of Publication of Sanders' "Reichenbachia" (13th issue). As T 331. Mult.
1872 45c. Plate No. 17 (Series 2) 40 15
1873 50c. Plate No. 33 (Series 2) 40 15
1874 60c. Plate No. 27 (Series 2) 60 15
1875 75c. Plate No. 56 (Series 2) 70 25
1876 85c. Plate No. 45 (Series 2) 12·00 75
1877 90c. Plate No. 13 (Series 2) 1·00 30
1878 200c. Plate No. 44 (Series 2) 1·50 55
1879 300c. Plate No. 50 (Series 2) 2·00 75
1880 320c. Plate No. 10 (Series 2) 2·00 90
1881 390c. Plate No. 6 (Series 2) 2·00 1·50

1986. Deepavali Festival. Nos. 543 and 601 surch Deepavali 1986 and value.
1882 25c. on 2c. Type **132** 3·00 50
1883 200c. on 8c. on 6c. Cannon-ball tree 11·00 4·00

1986. Centenary of Publication of Sanders' "Reichenbachia" (14th issue). As T 331, two as Nos. 1732 and 1734 with different face values. Multicoloured.
1884 40c. Plate No. 68 (Series 1) 2·00 25
1885 80c. Plate No. 17 (Series 1) 6·50 90
1886 200c. Plate No. 2 (Series 2) 1·60 1·00
1887 225c. Plate No. 24 (Series 2) 1·60 1·25

1986. Christmas. No. 489 surch CHRISTMAS 1986 20.
1888 20c. on 6c. Black acara ("Patua") 5·00 20
MS1889 215×75 mm. 120c. on 60c.×5 Nos. 1425/9 7·00 7·00

1986. Wildlife Protection. Nos. 756/67 optd 1986.
1894 30c. Type **178** 2·00 1·75
1895 30c. Red howler 2·00 1·75
1896 30c. Common squirrel-monkey 2·00 1·75
1897 30c. Two-toed sloth 2·00 1·75
1898 30c. Brazilian tapir 2·00 1·75
1899 30c. Collared peccary 2·00 1·75
1900 30c. Six-banded armadillo 2·00 1·75
1901 30c. Tamandua 2·00 1·75
1902 30c. Giant anteater 2·00 1·75
1903 30c. Murine opossum 2·00 1·75
1904 30c. Brown four-eyed opossum 2·00 1·75
1905 30c. Brazilian agouti 2·00 1·75

1986. No. 1642 surch $15.
1906 $15 on $3.50 Clive Lloyd with Prudential Cup 48·00 22·00

1986. Centenary of Publication of Sanders' "Reichenbachia" (15th issue). Design as No. 1877, but with different face value. Mult.
1907 50c. Plate No. 13 (Series 2) 1·00 25

375 Memorial

1986. President Burnham Commemoration. Multicoloured.
1908 25c. Type **375** 10 10
1909 120c. Map of Guyana and flags 30 20
1910 130c. Parliament Buildings and mace 20 20
1911 $6 L. F. Burnham and Georgetown mayoral chain (vert) 60 1·75

1986. Centenary of Publication of Sanders' "Reichenbachia" (16th issue). As Nos. 1765/6, 1874 and 1887 but with different face values. Multicoloured.
1912 50c. Plate No. 49 (Series 1) 75 20
1913 50c. Plate No. 64 (Series 1) 75 20
1914 85c. Plate No. 24 (Series 2) 75 40
1915 90c. Plate No. 27 (Series 2) 9·00 1·50

1986. Centenary of Publication of Sanders' "Reichenbachia" (17th issue). As T 331. Mult.
1916 25c. Plate No. 20 (Series 2) 20 20
1917 40c. Plate No. 7 (Series 2) 45 15
1918 85c. Plate No. 15 (Series 2) 6·50 50
1919 90c. Plate No. 3 (Series 2) 60 20
1920 120c. Plate No. 14 (Series 2) 60 30
1921 130c. Plate No. 32 (Series 2) 60 30
1922 150c. Plate No. 22 (Series 2) 70 45
1923 320c. Plate No. 18 (Series 2) 90 75
1924 330c. Plate No. 28 (Series 2) 90 90

1987. Centenary of Publication of Sanders' "Reichenbachia" (18th issue). As Nos. 1772, 1876, 1886, 1918 and 1923 but with different face values. Multicoloured.
1925 35c. Plate No. 45 (Series 2) 40 15
1926 50c. Plate No. 15 (Series 2) 40 20
1927 50c. Plate No. 55 (Series 1) 40 20
1928 85c. Plate No. 18 (Series 2) 8·00 60
1929 90c. Plate No. 2 (Series 2) 50 30

1987. 10th Anniv of Guyana Post Office Corporation (1st issue). Unissued designs as Nos. 1771 and 1774, but with different face values, surch or optd G P O C 1977 1987.
1930 $2.25 Plate No. 53 (Series 1) 4·50 75
1931 $10 on 150c. Plate No. 24 (Series 1) 11·00 12·00
See also Nos. 2074/80.

1987. Various "Reichenbachia" issues surch.
1932 200c. on 40c. Plate No. 90 (Series 1) 80 50
1933 200c. on 25c. Plate No. 8 (Series 1) (No. 1571) 80 50
1934 200c. on 25c. Plate No. 51 (Series 1) (No. 1573) 80 50
1937 200c. on 40c. Plate No. 68 (Series 1) (No. 1884) 80 50
1939 200c. on 50c. Plate No. 92 (Series 1) (No. 1665) 80 50
1940 200c. on 50c. Plate No. 22 (Series 1) 80 50
1941 200c. on 55c. Plate No. 22 (Series 1) (No. 1764) 80 50
1942 200c. on 60c. Plate No. 5 (Series 1) 80 50
1943 200c. on 75c. Plate No. 5 (Series 1) (No. 1667) 80 50
1944 200c. on 75c. Plate No. 60 (Series 1) 80 50
1945 200c. on 75c. Plate No. 92 (Series 1) 80 50
1946 200c. on 85c. Plate No. 18 (Series 2) (No. 1928) 80 50
1947 200c. on 375c. Plate No. 90 (Series 1) (No. 1738) 80 50
1949 200c. on 25c. Plate No. 52 (Series 1) (No. 1551) 80 50
1951 200c. on 25c. Plate No. 72 (Series 1) (No. 1577) 80 50
1952 200c. on 25c. Plate No. 71 (Series 1) (No. 1679) 80 50
1953 200c. on 30c. Plate No. 86 (Series 1) (No. 1731) 80 50

1954 200c. on 30c. Plate No. 53 (Series 1) (No. 1771) 80 50
1955 200c. on 40c. Plate No. 77 (Series 1) (No. 1663) 80 50
1956 200c. on 40c. Plate No. 86 (Series 1) (No. 1868) 80 50
1957 200c. on 45c. Plate No. 81 (Series 1) (No. 1748) 80 50
1958 200c. on 45c. Plate No. 77 (Series 1) 80 50
1959 200c. on 45c. Plate No. 78 (Series 1) 80 50
1960 200c. on 45c. Plate No. 85 (Series 1) 80 50
1961 200c. on 50c. Plate No. 24 (Series 1) 80 50
1962 200c. on 50c. Plate No. 53 (Series 1) 80 50
1963 200c. on 50c. Plate No. 65 (Series 1) 80 50
1964 200c. on 55c. Plate No. 49 (Series 1) (No. 1765) 80 50
1965 200c. on 55c. Plate No. 17 (Series 1) (No. 1732) 80 50
1967 200c. on 60c. Plate No. 7 (Series 1) (No. 1520) 80 50
1968 200c. on 60c. Plate No. 10 (Series 1) (No. 1521) 80 50
1969 200c. on 60c. Plate No. 19 (Series 1) (No. 1522) 80 50
1970 200c. on 60c. Plate No. 31 (Series 1) (No. 1523) 80 50
1971 200c. on 60c. Plate No. 44 (Series 1) (No. 1556) 80 50
1972 200c. on 60c. Plate No. 47 (Series 1) (No. 1557) 80 50
1973 200c. on 60c. Plate No. 57 (Series 1) (No. 1622) 80 50
1974 200c. on 60c. Plate No. 73 (Series 1) (No. 1623) 80 50
1975 200c. on 60c. Plate No. 75 (Series 1) (No. 1624) 80 50
1976 200c. on 60c. Plate No. 71 (Series 1) 80 50
1977 200c. on 60c. Plate No. 87 (Series 1) 2·25 1·25
1978 225c. on 90c. Plate No. 89 (Series 1) (No. 1749) 80 55
1980 120c. on 55c. Plate No. 9 (Series 1) (No. 1763) 50 40
1981 120c. on 55c. Plate No. 64 (Series 1) (No. 1766) 50 30
1987 225c. on 40c. Plate No. 91 (Series 1) (No. 1822) 70 60
1988 225c. on 40c. Plate No. 90 (Series 1) 14·00 3·50
1988a 225c. on 50c. Plate No. 92 (Series 1) (No. 1665) 14·00 3·50
1989 225c. on 50c. Plate No. 22 (Series 1) 70 60
1990 225c. on 60c. Plate No. 55 (Series 1) (No. 1597) 14·00 3·50
1990a 225c. on 60c. Plate No. 95 (Series 1) (No. 1666) 14·00 3·50
1991 225c. on 60c. Plate No. 93 (Series 1) (No. 1733) 70 60
1992 225c. on 80c. Plate No. 93 (Series 1) 70 60
1993 225c. on 150c. Plate No. 42 (Series 1) (No. 1657) 70 60
1994 120c. on 50c. Plate No. 49 (Series 1) (No. 1912) 60 40
1995 120c. on 50c. Plate No. 64 (Series 1) (No. 1913) 60 40
2003 120c. on 55c. Plate No. 49 (Series 1) (No. 1765) 60 40
2006 120c. on 55c. Plate No. 22 (Series 1) (No. 1764) 60 40
2009 120c. on 55c. Plate No. 15 (Series 1) 60 40
2010 120c. on 55c. Plate No. 81 (Series 1) 60 40
2011 120c. on 55c. Plate No. 82 (Series 1) 60 40
2012 120c. on 55c. Plate No. 89 (Series 1) 60 40
2019 120c. on 50c. Plate No. 24 (Series 1) 60 40
2020 120c. on 50c. Plate No. 53 (Series 1) 60 40
2021 120c. on 50c. Plate No. 65 (Series 1) 60 40
2027 120c. on 60c. Plate No. 10 (Series 1) (No. 1521) 60 40
2028 120c. on 60c. Plate No. 19 (Series 1) (No. 1522) 60 40
2029 120c. on 60c. Plate No. 31 (Series 1) (No. 1523) 60 40
2030 120c. on 60c. Plate No. 5 (Series 1) 60 40
2034 120c. on 60c. Plate No. 71 (Series 1) 60 40
2036 120c. on 60c. Plate No. 87 (Series 1) 60 40
2038 120c. on 75c. Plate No. 60 (Series 1) 60 40
2039 120c. on 75c. Plate No. 83 (Series 1) 60 40
2040 120c. on 75c. Plate No. 92 (Series 1) 60 40
2041 120c. on 75c. Plate No. 95 (Series 1) 60 40
2044 200c. on 45c. Plate No. 84 (Series 1) 60 40
2046 200c. on 50c. Plate No. 55 (Series 1) (No. 1927) 1·00 50
2050 200c. on 55c. Plate No. 15 (Series 1) 3·50 60
2051 200c. on 55c. Plate No. 81 (Series 1) 3·50 60
2052 200c. on 55c. Plate No. 82 (Series 1) 10·00 1·25
2053 200c. on 55c. Plate No. 89 (Series 1) 3·50 60
2055 225c. on 40c. Plate No. 86 (Series 1) (No. 1868) 2·50 70
2056 225c. on 40c. Plate No. 68 (Series 1) (No. 1884) 90 60
2058 225c. on 65c. Plate No. 76 (Series 1) 90 60
2059 225c. on 65c. Plate No. 80 (Series 1) 90 60
2060 225c. on 65c. Plate No. 88 (Series 1) 90 60
2061 225c. on 65c. Plate No. 96 (Series 1) 90 60
2062 600c. on 80c. Plate No. 17 (Series 1) (No. 1885) 1·50 1·75
2063 600c. on 80c. Plate No. 39 (Series 1) 1·50 1·75
2064 600c. on 80c. Plate No. 74 (Series 1) 1·50 1·75
2065 600c. on 80c. Plate No. 93 (Series 1) 1·50 1·75
2375 120c. on 40c. Plate No. 91 (Series 1) (No. 1822) 60 40
2380 120c. on 40c. Plate No. 90 (Series 1) 60 40
2387 120c. on 50c. Plate No. 9 (Series 1) 60 40
2388 120c. on 50c. Plate No. 22 (Series 1) 60 40
2389 120c. on 50c. Plate No. 3 (Series 2) 60 40
2390 120c. on 50c. Plate No. 6 (Series 2) 60 40
2391 120c. on 50c. Plate No. 20 (Series 2) 60 40
2392 120c. on 50c. Plate No. 32 (Series 2) 60 40
2394 120c. on 60c. Plate No. 2 (Series 1) (No. 1519) 60 30
2403 120c. on 60c. Plate No. 50 (Series 1) 60 40
2404 120c. on 60c. Plate No. 54 (Series 1) 60 40
2405 120c. on 60c. Plate No. 69 (Series 1) 60 40
2406 120c. on 60c. Plate No. 79 (Series 1) 60 40
2407 120c. on 60c. Plate No. 94 (Series 1) 60 40

1987. Nos. 1518 and 1572 surch TWO DOLLARS.
1935 $2 on 25c. Plate No. 12 (Series 1) (No. 1518) 2·00 60
1936 $2 on 25c. Plate No. 23 (Series 1) (No. 1572) 2·00 90

1987. Various "Reichenbachia" issues surch 1987.
1983 $10 on 25c. Plate No. 53 (Series 1) 3·00 3·50
1984 $12 on 80c. Plate No. 74 (Series 1) 3·25 3·75
1985 $15 on 80c. Plate No. 39 (Series 1) 3·50 4·00
1986 $25 on 25c. Plate No. 53 (Series 1) 6·00 7·00

1987. Centenary of Publication of Sanders' "Reichenbachia" (19th issue). Multicoloured.
2066 180c. Plate 41 (Series 2) 75 40
2067 230c. Plate 25 (Series 2) 80 50
2068 300c. Plate 85 (Series 2) 8·50 1·50
2069 330c. Plate 82 (Series 2) 9·00 1·75
2070 425c. Plate 87 (Series 2) 9·00 1·75
2071 440c. Plate 88 (Series 2) 9·00 1·75
2072 590c. Plate 52 (Series 2) 1·50 1·75
2073 650c. Plate 65 (Series 2) 1·75 2·00

1987. 10th Anniv of Guyana Post Office Corporation (2nd issue). Nos. 543, 545, 548a and 601 surch Post Office Corp. 1977-1987.
2074 25c. on 2c. Type **132** 15 10
2075 25c. on 5c. Annatto tree 15 10
2076 25c. on 8c. on 6c. Cannon-ball tree 15 10
2077 25c. on 15c. Christmas orchid 5·50 30
2078 60c. on 15c. Christmas orchid 11·00 30
2079 $1.20 on 2c. Type **132** 75 75
2080 $1.30 on 15c. Christmas orchid 12·00 3·00

1987. No. 1535b surch 1987 200.
2081 **332** 200c. on 25c. mult 6·00 2·00

1987. Various "Reichenbachia" issues optd 1987.
2084 130c. Plate No. 3 (Series 1) (No. 1525) 60 40
2087 130c. Plate No. 18 (Series 1) (No. 1536) 60 40
2088 130c. Plate No. 29 (Series 1) (No. 1537) 60 40
2089 130c. Plate No. 30 (Series 1) (No. 1538) 60 40
2090 130c. Plate No. 16 (Series 1) (No. 1559) 60 40
2091 130c. Plate No. 66 (Series 1) (No. 1632) 60 40
2092 130c. Plate No. 13 (Series 1) (No. 1684) 60 40
2093 130c. Plate No. 6 (Series 1) (No. 1759) 60 40
2094 130c. Plate No. 20 (Series 1) (No. 1761) 60 40
2095 200c. Plate No. 4 (Series 1) (No. 1533) 70 50
2096 200c. Plate No. 14 (Series 1) (No. 1584) 70 50
2097 200c. Plate No. 21 (Series 1) (No. 1585) 70 50
2098 200c. Plate No. 33 (Series 1) (No. 1634) 70 50
2099 200c. Plate No. 43 (Series 1) (No. 1658) 70 50
2100 200c. Plate No. 79 (Series 1) (No. 1670) 70 50
2101 200c. Plate No. 9 (Series 2) (No. 1816) 70 50
2102 200c. Plate No. 2 (Series 2) (No. 1886) 70 50
2103 250c. Plate No. 74 (Series 1) (No. 1736) 80 60
2104 260c. Plate No. 39 (Series 1) (No. 1737) 80 60
2109 130c. Plate No. 91 (Series 1) (No. 1735) 60 40
2111 130c. Plate No. 25 (Series 1) (No. 1762) 60 40
2112 120c. Plate No. 1 (Series 1) (No. 1578) 3·50 75
2113 120c. Plate No. 11 (Series 1) (No. 1579) 2·75 70
2114 120c. Plate No. 28 (Series 1) (No. 1580) 3·25 75
2115 120c. Plate No. 37 (Series 1) (No. 1627) 1·75 70
2116 120c. Plate No. 46 (Series 1) (No. 1628) 8·50 90
2117 120c. Plate No. 56 (Series 1) (No. 1629) 2·75 70
2118 120c. Plate No. 58 (Series 1) (No. 1630) 2·75 70
2123 150c. Plate No. 40 (Series 1) (No. 1767) 2·50 80
2124 150c. Plate No. 45 (Series 1) (No. 1769) 1·75 70
2125 150c. Plate No. 42 (Series 1) (No. 1657) 6·50 1·00
2132 120c. Plate No. 67 (Series 1) (No. 1631) 60 40
2137 150c. Plate No. 26 (Series 1) (No. 1633) 60 50

1987. 12th World Orchid Conference, Tokyo (2nd issue). Nos. 1763 surch 12th World Orchid Conference 650.
2138 650c. on 55c. Plate No. 9 (Series 1) 11·00 6·00

1987. 125th Anniv of British Guiana Post Office (3rd issue). No. 699 surch 25 and names of postal agencies opened by 1885.
2140 25c. on 10c. multicoloured (surch **AGRICOLA**) 1·50 1·10
2141 25c. on 10c. multicoloured (surch **BAGOTVILLE**) 1·50 1·10
2142 25c. on 10c. multicoloured (surch **BOURDA**) 1·50 1·10
2143 25c. on 10c. multicoloured (surch **BUXTON**) 1·50 1·10
2144 25c. on 10c. multicoloured (surch **CABACABURI**) 1·50 1·10
2145 25c. on 10c. mult (surch **CARMICHAEL STREET**) 1·50 1·10
2146 25c. on 10c. mult (surch **COTTON TREE**) 1·50 1·10
2147 25c. on 10c. multicoloured (surch **DUNOON**) 1·50 1·10
2148 25c. on 10c. multicoloured (surch **FELLOWSHIP**) 1·50 1·10
2149 25c. on 10c. multicoloured (surch **GROVE**) 1·50 1·10
2150 25c. on 10c. multicoloured (surch **HACKNEY**) 1·50 1·10
2151 25c. on 10c. multicoloured (surch **LEONORA**) 1·50 1·10
2152 25c. on 10c. mult (surch **1987**) 1·50 1·10
2153 25c. on 10c. multicoloured (surch **MALLALI**) 1·50 1·10
2154 25c. on 10c. multicoloured (surch **PROVIDENCE**) 1·50 1·10
2155 25c. on 10c. multicoloured (surch **RELIANCE**) 1·50 1·10
2156 25c. on 10c. multicoloured (surch **SPARTA**) 1·50 1·10
2157 25c. on 10c. multicoloured (surch **STEWARTVILLE**) 1·50 1·10
2158 25c. on 10c. multicoloured (surch **TARLOGY**) 1·50 1·10
2159 25c. on 10c. mult (surch **T.P.O. BERBICE RIV.**) 1·50 1·10
2160 25c. on 10c. multicoloured (surch **T.P.O. DEM. RIV.**) 1·50 1·10
2161 25c. on 10c. multicoloured (surch **T.P.O. ESSEO. RIV.**) 1·50 1·10
2162 25c. on 10c. mult (surch **T.P.O. MASSARUNI RIV.**) 1·50 1·10
2163 25c. on 10c. multicoloured (surch **TUSCHEN** (**De VRIENDEN**)) 1·50 1·10
2164 25c. on 10c. multicoloured (surch **ZORG**) 1·50 1·10

1987. 50th Anniv of First Georgetown to Port-of-Spain Flight by P.A.A. No. 708a optd 28 MARCH 1927 PAA GEO-POS.
2165 $10 "Elbella patrobas" 26·00 13·00

1987. No. 704 surch 25.
2166 25c. on 40c. "Morpho rhetenor" (male) 15·00 30

1987. Easter. Nos. 481/2 and 484 optd 1987 or surch also.
2167 **111** 25c. multicoloured 50 10
2168 **111** 120c. on 6c. mult 75 20
2169 **111** 320c. on 6c. mult 1·25 90
2170 **111** 500c. on 40c. mult 1·75 2·25

1987. Centenary of Publication of Sanders' "Reichenbachia" (20th issue). As T 331. Mult.
2171 240c. Plate No. 47 (Series 2) 80 45
2172 260c. Plate No. 39 (Series 2) 90 55
2173 275c. Plate No. 58 (Series 2) (horiz) 90 55
2174 390c. Plate No. 37 (Series 2) (horiz) 1·10 70
2175 450c. Plate No. 19 (Series 2) (horiz) 1·50 90
2176 460c. Plate No. 54 (Series 2) (horiz) 1·50 90
2177 500c. Plate No. 51 (Series 2) 1·75 1·10
2178 560c. Plate No. 1 (Series 2) 2·00 1·50

1987. No. 706 optd 1987.
2179 **167** $1 multicoloured 16·00 90

1987. Centenary of Publication of Sanders' "Reichenbachia" (21st issue). As T 331. Mult.
2180 500c. Plate No. 86 (Series 2) 1·50 1·10
2181 520c. Plate No. 89 (Series 2) 1·50 1·25
2182 $20 Plate No. 83 (Series 2) 4·50 7·00

1987. As T 332 but within frame.
2183 25c. multicoloured 30 30
2184 25c. multicoloured 30 30

No. 2183 has a bird with a short tail (as in Type **332**) in the lower part of the arms; No. 2184 has a bird with crest and long tail.

1987. "Capex '87" International Stamp Exhibition, Toronto. Nos. 1744/5 optd CAPEX '87.
2185 **363** 320c. red, black and lilac 3·00 3·25
2186 - 320c. multicoloured 3·00 3·25

1987. Commonwealth Heads of Government Meeting, Vancouver. Nos. 1066/8 further optd 1987.
2187 $1.20 on 6c. green 75 20
2188 $1.30 on 24c. black orange 11·00 75
2189 $2.40 on 24c. black orange 14·00 4·50

1987. Centenary of Publication of Sanders' "Reichenbachia" (22nd issue). As T 331. Mult.
2190 400c. Plate No. 80 (Series 2) 1·25 80
2191 480c. Plate No. 77 (Series 2) 1·50 1·00
2192 600c. Plate No. 94 (Series 2) 1·50 1·50
2193 $25 Plate No. 72 (Series 2) 4·50 8·00

396 Steam Locomotive No. 4 "Alexandra"

1987. Guyana Railways.
2194 **396** $1.20 green 25 30
2195 - $1.20 green 25 30
2196 - $1.20 green 25 30
2197 - $1.20 green 25 30
2198 **396** $1.20 purple 25 30
2199 - $1.20 purple 25 30
2200 - $1.20 purple 25 30
2201 - $1.20 purple 25 30
2202 **396** $3.20 blue 60 90
2203 - $3.20 blue 60 90
2204 - $3.20 blue 60 90
2205 - $3.20 blue 60 90
2206 - $3.20 blue 60 90
2207 - $3.30 black 60 90
2208 **396** $3.30 black 60 90
2209 - $3.30 black 60 90
2210 - $3.30 black 60 90
2211 - $3.30 black 60 90
2212 - $10 multicoloured 60 1·50
2213 - $12 multicoloured 60 1·75

DESIGNS—As T **396**: Nos. 2195, 2199, 2203, 2207, Front view of diesel locomotive; Nos. 2196, 2200, 2204, 2210, Steam locomotive with searchlight; Nos. 2197, 2201, 2205, 2209, Side view of diesel locomotive No. 21. (82×55 mm): No. 2206, Molasses warehouses and early locomotive; No. 2211, Diesel locomotive and passenger train. (88×39 mm): No. 2212, Cattle train and Parika–Rosignol Railway route map; No. 2213, Molasses train and Parika–Rosignol Railway route map.

1987. 50th Anniv of First Flights from Georgetown to Massaruni and Mabaruma. No. 706 optd.

2214 $1 multicoloured (optd **FAIREY NICHOLL 8 AUG 1927 GEO-MAZ**) 13·00 10·00
2215 $1 multicoloured (optd **FAIREY NICHOLL 15 AUG 1927 GEO-MAB**) 13·00 10·00

1987. Centenary of Publication of Sanders' "Reichenbachia" (23rd issue). As T 331. Mult.

2216 200c. Plate No. 43 (Series 2) 7·50 1·75
2217 200c. Plate No. 48 (Series 2) 7·50 1·75
2218 200c. Plate No. 92 (Series 2) 7·50 1·75

1987. Centenary of Publication of Sanders' "Reichenbachia" (24th issue). No. 2219 surch 600. Multicoloured.

2219 600c. on 900c. Plate No. 74 (Series 2) 6·00 7·00
2220 900c. Plate No. 74 (Series 2) 6·00 7·00

1987. Columbus Day.

2221 225c. on 350c. on 120c. Plate No. 65 (Series 1) (No. 1598 further surch **225**) 1·75 80
2222 950c. on 900c. Plate No. 74 (Series 2) (No. 2220 surch **950 CRISTOVAO COLOMBO 1492 – 1992**) 3·00 3·50
2223 950c. on 900c. Plate No. 74 (Series 2) (No. 2220 surch **950 CHRISTOPHE COLOMB 1492 – 1992**) 3·00 3·50
MS2224 76×50 mm. $20 on 320c.×2 Nos. 1744/5 7·00 9·00

1987. Centenary of Publication of Sanders' "Reichenbachia" (25th issue). As T 331. Mult.

2225 325c. Plate No. 68 (Series 2) (horiz) 1·50 1·10
2226 420c. Plate No. 95 (Series 2) (horiz) 1·75 1·75
2227 575c. Plate No. 60 (Series 2) 15·00 6·50

1987. Deepavali Festival. Nos. 544/5 surch DEEPAVALI 1987 and new value.

2228 25c. on 3c. Hanging heliconia 2·50 25
2229 $3 on 5c. Annatto tree 8·50 4·50

1987. Christmas. No. 489 surch CHRISTMAS 1987 20, and previously unissued miniature sheet containing Nos. 1425/9 and No. MS1619 surch.

2230 20c. on 6c. Black acara ("Patua") 4·50 20
MS2231 215×75 mm. 120c. on 60c.×5 Nos. 1425/9 8·00 4·00
MS2232 120×129 mm. 225c. on 55c.×4 Plate No. 22 (Series 1), each with a different overprint (**Christmas 1985 ,Happy New Year, Merry Christmas** or **Happy Holidays**) 1·60 1·75

1987. Royal Ruby Wedding. Nos. 1684/5 optd 1987 (130c.) or surch 120.

2233 130c. Plate No. 13 (Series 1) 5·50 1·75
MS2234 600c. on 130c. on 130c., 600c. on 200c. on 130c., 600c. on 260c. on 130c., 600c. on 330c. on 130c., Plate No. 6 (Series 1) 9·00 10·00

1987. Centenary of Publication of Sanders' "Reichenbachia" (26th issue). As T 331. Mult.

2235 255c. Plate No. 61 (Series 2) 4·75 1·25
2236 290c. Plate No. 53 (Series 2) 4·75 1·50
2237 375c. Plate No. 96 (Series 2) 2·00 1·60
2238 680c. Plate No. 64 (Series 2) 13·00 3·75
2239 720c. Plate No. 49 (Series 2) 14·00 6·00
2240 750c. Plate No. 66 (Series 2) 3·00 5·00
2241 800c. Plate No. 79 (Series 2) 3·00 5·50
2242 850c. Plate No. 76 (Series 2) 3·00 5·50

1987. Air. No. 1620 surch AIR 75.

2243 75c. on 25c. Plate No. 59 (Series 1) 12·00 1·40

1987. Wildlife Protection. Nos. 756/67 optd 1987, Nos. 1432/4 surch Protect our Heritage '87 320 and Nos. 1631/3, 1752/3 and 1847 optd PROTECT OUR HERITAGE '87.

2244 30c. Type **178** 40 25
2245 30c. Red howler 40 25
2246 30c. Common squirrel-monkey 40 25
2247 30c. Two-toed sloth 40 25
2248 30c. Brazilian tapir 40 25
2249 30c. Collared peccary 40 25
2250 30c. Six-banded armadillo 40 25
2251 30c. Tamandua 40 25
2252 30c. Giant anteater 40 25
2253 30c. Murine opossum 40 25
2254 30c. Brown four-eyed opossum 40 25
2255 30c. Brazilian agouti 40 25
2256 120c. Plate No. 67 (Series 1) 1·00 30
2257 130c. Plate No. 66 (Series 1) 1·00 30
2258 150c. Plate No. 26 (Series 1) 1·10 35
2259 180c. Plate No. 15 (Series 1) 1·25 40
2260 320c. Plate No. 82 (Series 1) 1·40 60
2261 320c. on 120c. Demerara Mutual Life Assurance Building 1·40 1·75
2262 320c. on 120c. Town Hall 1·40 1·75
2263 320c. on 120c. Victoria Law Courts 1·40 1·75
2264 650c. on 40c. Plate No. 86 (Series 1) 2·75 3·50

1987. Air. Various "Reichenbachia" issues optd AIR.

2265 60c. Plate No. 55 (Series 1) (No. 1597) 8·50 10·00
2463 75c. Plate No. 55 (Series 1) (No. 1772) 1·50 1·00
2464 75c. Plate No. 5 (Series 1) (No. 1667) 1·50 1·00
2466 75c. Plate No. 83 (Series 1) 1·50 1·00
2467 75c. Plate No. 95 (Series 1) 1·50 1·00

1988. World Scout Jamboree, Australia. No. 837a optd AUSTRALIA 1987 JAMBOREE 1988 and Nos. 830, 837a and 1104 surch $10 AUSTRALIA 1987 JAMBOREE 1988.

2266 **116** 440c. on 6c. mult (No. 837a) 7·50 60
2267 **116** $10 on 110c. on 6c. mult (No. 830) 75 90
2268 **116** $10 on 180c. on 6c. mult (No. 1104) 75 90
2269a **116** $10 on 440c. on 6c. mult (No. 837a) 75 90

1988. 10th Anniv of International Fund for Agricultural Development. Nos. 448 and 450 surch IFAD For a World Without Hunger.

2270 25c. on 1c. Type **87** 2·50 25
2271 $5 on 3c. Lukunani 9·50 7·00

1988. Republic Day. Nos. 545, 548a and 555 surch Republic Day 1988.

2272 25c. on 5c. Annatto tree 10 10
2273 120c. on 15c. Christmas orchid 12·00 70
2274 $10 on $2 "Norantea guianensis" 2·75 3·50

1988. Centenary of Publication of Sanders' "Reichenbachia" (27th issue). Four sheets, each 102×127 mm, containing vert designs as T 331. Multicoloured.

MS2275 (a) 320c. Plate No. 46 (Series 2); 330c. Plate No. 55 (Series 2); 350c. Plate No. 57 (Series 2); 500c. Plate No. 81 (Series 2). (b) 320c. Plate No. 55 (Series 2); 330c. Plate No. 46 (Series 2); 350c. Plate No. 81 (Series 2); 500c. Plate No. 57 (Series 2). (c) 320c. Plate No. 57 (Series 2); 330c. Plate No. 81 (Series 2); 350c. Plate No. 46 (Series 2); 500c. Plate No. 55 (Series 2). (d) 320c. Plate No. 81 (Series 2); 330c. Plate No. 57 (Series 2); 350c. Plate No. 55 (Series 2); 500c. Plate No. 46 (Series 2). Set of 4 sheets 17·00 13·00

1988. Centenary of Publication of Sanders' "Reichenbachia" (28th series). As T 331. Multicoloured.

2276 $10 Plate No. 40 (Series 2) 1·50 2·25
2277 $12 Plate No. 91 (Series 2) 1·50 2·25

1988. 125th Anniv of British Guiana Post Office (4th issue). No. 702a surch 25 and names of postal agencies opened between 1886 and 1900.

2278 25c. on 30c. multicoloured (surch **Albouystown**) 1·25 1·00
2279 25c. on 30c. multicoloured (surch **Anns Grove**) 1·25 1·00
2280 25c. on 30c. multicoloured (surch **Amacura**) 1·25 1·00
2281 25c. on 30c. multicoloured (surch **Arakaka**) 1·25 1·00
2282 25c. on 30c. multicoloured (surch **Baramanni**) 1·25 1·00
2283 25c. on 30c. multicoloured (surch **Cuyuni**) 1·25 1·00
2284 25c. on 30c. multicoloured (surch **Hope Placer**) 1·25 1·00
2285 25c. on 30c. multicoloured (surch **H M P S**) 1·25 1·00
2286 25c. on 30c. mult (surch **Kitty**) 1·25 1·00
2287 25c. on 30c. multicoloured (surch **M'M'Zorg**) 1·25 1·00
2288 25c. on 30c. multicoloured (surch **Maccaseema**) 1·25 1·00
2289 25c. on 30c. mult (surch **1988**) 1·25 1·00
2290 25c. on 30c. multicoloured (surch **Morawhanna**) 1·25 1·00
2291 25c. on 30c. multicoloured (surch **Naamryck**) 1·25 1·00
2292 25c. on 30c. mult (surch **Purini**) 1·25 1·00
2293 25c. on 30c. multicoloured (surch **Potaro Landing**) 1·25 1·00
2294 25c. on 30c. multicoloured (surch **Rockstone**) 1·25 1·00
2295 25c. on 30c. multicoloured (surch **Rosignol**) 1·25 1·00
2296 25c. on 30c. multicoloured (surch **Stanleytown**) 1·25 1·00
2297 25c. on 30c. multicoloured (surch **Santa Rosa**) 1·25 1·00
2298 25c. on 30c. multicoloured (surch **Tumatumari**) 1·25 1·00
2299 25c. on 30c. multicoloured (surch **Weldaad**) 1·25 1·00
2300 25c. on 30c. multicoloured (surch **Wismar**) 1·25 1·00
2301 25c. on 30c. mult (surch **TPO Berbice Railway**) 1·25 1·00

1988. Olympic Games, Seoul (1st issue). Nos. 1206/17 further surch 120 Olympic Games 1988.

2302 120c. on 55c. on 125c. on 35c. Type **174** 1·50 1·50
2303 120c. on 35c. on 125c. on 35c. Trahira ("Haimara") 1·50 1·50
2304 120c. on 55c. on 125c. on 35c. Electric eel 1·50 1·50
2305 120c. on 55c. on 125c. on 35c. Golden rivulus 1·50 1·50
2306 120c. on 55c. on 125c. on 35c. Golden pencilfish 1·50 1·50
2307 120c. on 55c. on 125c. on 35c. Four-eyed fish 1·50 1·50
2308 120c. on 55c. on 125c. on 35c. Red piranha ("Pirai") 1·50 1·50
2309 120c. on 55c. on 125c. on 35c. Smoking hassar 1·50 1·50
2310 120c. on 55c. on 125c. on 35c. Manta 1·50 1·50
2311 120c. on 55c. on 125c. on 35c. Festive cichlid ("Flying patwa") 1·50 1·50
2312 120c. on 55c. on 125c. on 35c. Arapaima 1·50 1·50
2313 120c. on 55c. on 125c. on 35c. Peacock cichlid ("Lukanani") 1·50 1·50

See also Nos. 2476/95.

116 Scouts raising Flag

1988. Centenary of Publication of Sanders' "Reichenbachia" (29th issue). As T 331. Mult.

2314 320c. Plate No. 62 (Series 2) 3·00 50
2315 475c. Plate No. 73 (Series 2) 4·00 1·75
2316 525c. Plate No. 36 (Series 2) 4·50 2·00
2317 530c. Plate No. 69 (Series 2) 1·00 2·00
2318 $15 Plate No. 67 (Series 2) 2·50 4·50

1988. CARICOM Day. Nos. 545/6 and 555 surch Caricom Day 1988 and new value.

2319 25c. on 5c. Annatto tree 25 10
2320 $1.20 on 6c. Cannon-ball tree 75 10
2321 $10 on $2 "Norantea guianensis" 4·50 5·50

1988. Centenary of Publication of Sanders' "Reichenbachia" (30th issue). As T 331. Mult.

2322 700c. Plate No. 62 (Series 2) 1·00 1·75
2323 775c. Plate No. 59 (Series 2) 1·25 2·00
2324 875c. Plate No. 31 (Series 2) 13·00 4·50
2325 950c. Plate No. 78 (Series 2) 1·75 4·50

1988. 40th Anniv of World Health Day. No. 705a optd.

2326 60c. "Papilio androgeus" (optd **WHO 1948-1988**) 18·00 19·00
2327 60c. "Papilio androgeus" (optd **1988**) 35 10

1988. Centenary of Publication of Sanders' "Reichenbachia" (31st issue). As T 331. Mult.

2328 350c. Plate No. 74 (Series 2) 3·50 1·75

1988. Centenary of Publication of Sanders' "Reichenbachia" (32nd issue). As T 331, but additionally inscr "1985–1988". Multicoloured.

2329 130c. Plate No. 73 (Series 2) 3·00 35
2330 200c. Plate No. 96 (Series 2) 50 45
2331 260c. Plate No. 16 (Series 2) 6·50 2·50
MS2332 Four sheets, each 102×127 mm. (a) 120c. Plate No. 81 (Series 2); 120c. Plate No. 57 (Series 2); 120c. Plate No. 55 (Series 2); 120c. Plate No. 46 (Series 2). (b) 150c. Plate No. 57 (Series 2); 150c. Plate No. 81 (Series 2); 150c. Plate No. 46 (Series 2); 150c. Plate No. 55 (Series 2). (c) 225c. Plate No. 46 (Series 2); 225c. Plate No. 55 (Series 2); 225c. Plate No. 57 (Series 2); 225c. Plate No. 81 (Series 2). (d) 305c. Plate No. 55 (Series 2); 305c. Plate No. 46 (Series 2); 305c. Plate No. 81 (Series 2); 305c. Plate No. 57 (Series 2). Set of 4 sheets 7·50 5·00

1988. Conservation of Resources. (a) Nos. 1444/6 optd.

2333 120c. Young Ocelot (No. 1444) (optd **CONSERVE TREES**) 1·00 80
2334 120c. Young Ocelot (No. 1444) (optd **CONSERVE ELECTRICITY**) 1·00 80
2335 120c. Young Ocelot (No. 1444) (optd **CONSERVE WATER**) 1·00 80
2336 120c. Type **322** (optd **CONSERVE ELECTRICITY**) 1·00 80
2337 120c. Type **322** (optd **CONSERVE WATER**) 1·00 80
2338 120c. Type **322** (optd **CONSERVE TREES**) 1·00 80
2339 120c. Young Ocelot (No. 1446) (optd **CONSERVE WATER**) 1·00 80
2340 120c. Young Ocelot (No. 1446) (optd **CONSERVE TREES**) 1·00 80
2341 120c. Young Ocelot (No. 1446) (optd **CONSERVE ELECTRICITY**) 1·00 80

(b) Nos. 1634, 1670, 1683 and 1774 optd CONSERVE WATER.

2342 200c. Plate No. 33 (Series 1) 1·00 1·00
2343 200c. Plate No. 79 (Series 1) 1·00 1·00
2344 225c. Plate No. 24 (Series 1) 1·00 1·00
2345 350c. Plate No. 94 (Series 1) 1·00 1·00

1988. Road Safety Campaign. Nos. 2194/2201 optd.

2346 **396** $1.20 green (optd **BEWARE OF ANIMALS**) 1·10 1·10
2347 - $1.20 green (No. 2195) (optd **BEWARE OF CHILDREN**) 1·10 1·10
2348 - $1.20 green (No. 2196) (optd **DRIVE SAFELY**) 1·10 1·10
2349 - $1.20 green (No. 2197) (optd **DO NOT DRINK AND DRIVE**) 1·10 1·10
2350 **396** $1.20 purple (optd **BEWARE OF ANIMALS**) 1·10 1·10
2351 - $1.20 purple (No. 2199) (optd **BEWARE OF CHILDREN**) 1·10 1·10
2352 - $1.20 purple (No. 2200) (optd **DRIVE SAFELY**) 1·10 1·10
2353 - $1.20 purple (No. 2201) (optd **DO NOT DRINK AND DRIVE**) 1·10 1·10

1988. No. 706 optd 1988 or surch 120.

2354 $1 "Agrias claudina" 9·00 1·25
2355 120c. on $1 "Agrias claudina" 9·00 1·25

1988. Various "Reichenbachia" issues surch.

2356 120c. on 25c. Plate No. 61 (Series 1) (No. 1574) 1·00 70
2357 120c. on 25c. Plate No. 63 (Series 1) (No. 1575) 1·00 70
2358 120c. on 25c. Plate No. 70 (Series 1) (No. 1576) 1·00 70
2359 120c. on 25c. Plate No. 59 (Series 1) (No. 1620) 1·00 70
2360 120c. on 25c. Plate No. 71 (Series 1) (No. 1679) 1·00 70
2361 120c. on 30c. Plate No. 53 (Series 1) (No. 1771) 1·00 70
2362 120c. on 30c. Plate No. 86 (Series 1) (No. 1731) 1·00 70
2363 120c. on 30c. Plate No. 30 (Series 2) (No. 1809) 1·00 70
2365 120c. on 30c. Plate No. 7 (Series 2) 1·00 70
2366 120c. on 30c. Plate No. 14 (Series 2) 1·00 70
2368 120c. on 30c. Plate No. 22 (Series 2) 1·00 70
2369 120c. on 30c. Plate No. 28 (Series 2) 1·00 70
2371 120c. on 35c. Plate No. 45 (Series 2) (No. 1925) 1·00 70
2372 120c. on 40c. Plate No. 77 (Series 1) (No. 1663) 1·00 70
2374 120c. on 40c. Plate No. 96 (Series 1) (No. 1747) 1·00 70
2377 120c. on 40c. Plate No. 86 (Series 1) (No. 1868) 1·00 70
2378 120c. on 40c. Plate No. 68 (Series 1) (No. 1884) 1·00 70
2381 120c. on 45c. Plate No. 54 (Series 1) (No. 1664) 1·00 70
2382 120c. on 45c. Plate No. 81 (Series 1) (No. 1748) 1·00 70
2383 120c. on 45c. Plate No. 21 (Series 2) (No. 1810) 1·00 70
2384 120c. on 50c. Plate No. 92 (Series 1) (No. 1665) 1·00 70
2385 120c. on 50c. Plate No. 13 (Series 2) (No. 1907) 1·00 70
2386 120c. on 50c. Plate No. 15 (Series 2) (No. 1926) 1·00 70
2393 120c. on 55c. Plate No. 17 (Series 1) (No. 1732) 1·00 70
2395 120c. on 60c. Plate No. 57 (Series 1) (No. 1622) 1·00 70
2397 120c. on 60c. Plate No. 73 (Series 1) (No. 1623) 1·00 70
2398 120c. on 60c. Plate No. 75 (Series 1) (No. 1624) 1·00 70
2400 120c. on 60c. Plate No. 95 (Series 1) (No. 1666) 1·00 70
2401 120c. on 60c. Plate No. 93 (Series 1) (No. 1733) 1·00 70
2402 120c. on 60c. Plate No. 27 (Series 2) (No. 1874) 1·00 70
2408 120c. on 70c. Plate No. 8 (Series 2) 1·00 70
2409 120c. on 70c. Plate No. 9 (Series 2) 1·00 70
2411 120c. on 70c. Plate No. 12 (Series 2) 1·00 70
2413 120c. on 70c. Plate No. 17 (Series 2) 1·00 70
2414 120c. on 80c. Plate No. 39 (Series 1) 1·00 70
2415 120c. on 80c. Plate No. 74 (Series 1) 1·00 70

2416 120c. on 80c. Plate No. 93 (Series 1) 1·00 70
2417 120c. on 85c. Plate No. 45 (Series 2) (No. 1876) 1·00 70
2418 120c. on 85c. Plate No. 24 (Series 2) (No. 1914) 1·00 70
2419 120c. on 85c. Plate No. 15 (Series 2) (No. 1918) 1·00 70
2420 120c. on 85c. Plate No. 18 (Series 2) (No. 1928) 1·00 70
2421 120c. on 90c. Plate No. 84 (Series 1) (No. 1668) 1·00 70
2422 120c. on 90c. Plate No. 89 (Series 1) (No. 1749) 1·00 70
2423 120c. on 90c. Plate No. 10 (Series 2) (No. 1869) 1·00 70
2424 120c. on 90c. Plate No. 13 (Series 2) (No. 1877) 1·00 70
2425 120c. on 90c. Plate No. 27 (Series 2) (No. 1915) 1·00 70
2426 120c. on 90c. Plate No. 2 (Series 2) (No. 1929) 1·00 70
2427 200c. on 80c. Plate No. 42 (Series 2) (No. 1812) 1·00 70
2428 200c. on 90c. Plate No. 4 (Series 2) (No. 1813) 1·00 70
2429 120c. on 25c. Plate No. 72 (Series 1) (No. 1577) 1·00 70
2430 240c. on 140c. Plate No. 30 (Series 2) 1·00 70
2431 240c. on 140c. Plate No. 34 (Series 2) 1·00 70
2432 240c. on 425c. Plate No. 87 (Series 2) (No. 2070) 1·00 70
2433 260c. on 375c. Plate No. 90 (Series 1) (No. 1378) 1·00 70

1988. Conservation of Resources. Various "Reichenbachia" issues optd CONSERVE OUR RESOURCES.
2434 100c. Plate No. 65 (Series 1) (No. 1773) 1·00 70
2435 100c. Plate No. 68 (Series 1) (No. 1734) 1·00 70
2436 100c. Plate No. 88 (Series 1) (No. 1750) 1·00 70
2438 120c. Plate No. 27 (Series 1) (No. 1524) 1·00 70
2439 120c. Plate No. 36 (Series 1) (No. 1558) 1·00 70
2440 120c. Plate No. 37 (Series 1) (No. 1627) 1·00 70
2441 120c. Plate No. 56 (Series 1) (No. 1629) 1·00 70
2442 120c. Plate No. 58 (Series 1) (No. 1630) 1·00 70
2443 120c. Plate No. 67 (Series 1) (No. 1631) 1·00 70
2444 120c. Plate No. 69 (Series 1) (No. 1680) 1·00 70
2445 130c. Plate No. 38 (Series 1) (No. 1560) 1·00 70
2446 130c. Plate No. 66 (Series 1) (No. 1632) 1·00 70
2447 130c. Plate No. 91 (Series 1) (No. 1735) 1·00 70
2448 130c. Plate No. 13 (Series 1) (No. 1760) 1·00 70
2449 130c. Plate No. 20 (Series 1) (No. 1761) 1·00 70
2450 150c. Plate No. 26 (Series 1) (No. 1633) 1·00 70
2451 150c. Plate No. 78 (Series 1) (No. 1669) 1·00 70
2452 150c. Plate No. 87 (Series 1) (No. 1681) 1·00 70
2453 150c. Plate No. 76 (Series 1) (No. 1751) 1·00 70
2454 250c. Plate No. 74 (Series 1) (No. 1736) 1·00 70

1988. 125th Anniv of International Red Cross. Nos. 2202/5 and 2207/10 optd with cross.
2455 **396** $3.20 blue 1·50 1·50
2456 - $3.20 blue (No. 2203) 1·50 1·50
2457 - $3.20 blue (No. 2204) 1·50 1·50
2458 - $3.20 blue (No. 2205) 1·50 1·50
2459 - $3.30 black (No. 2207) 1·50 1·50
2460 **396** $3.30 black 1·50 1·50
2461 - $3.30 black (No. 2209) 1·50 1·50
2462 - $3.30 black (No. 2210) 1·50 1·50

1988. Centenary of Publication of Sanders' "Reichenbachia" (33rd issue). As T 331. Mult.
2468 270c. Plate No. 90 (Series 2) 8·50 70
2469 360c. Plate No. 84 (Series 2) 75 1·00
2470 550c. Plate No. 70 (Series 2) (horiz) 2·00 2·50
2471 670c. Plate No. 71 (Series 2) (horiz) 2·25 3·00

1988. 60th Anniv of Cricket in Guyana. Nos. 1584, 1670, 1681 and 1815 optd 1928 – 1988 CRICKET JUBILEE or surch also.
2472 200c. Plate No. 14 (Series 1) 20·00 25·00
2473 200c. Plate No. 79 (Series 1) 1·00 40
2474 800c. on 150c. Plate No. 87 (Series 1) 8·50 13·00
2475 800c. on 160c. Plate No. 5 (Series 2) 3·25 3·25

1988. Olympic Games, Seoul. (a) Nos. 1628, 1634, 1671, 1681, 1683, 1814, 1818/19, 1880 and 2069 optd OLYMPIC GAMES 1988 or surch also.
2476 120c. Plate No. 46 (Series 1) 50 50
2477 130c. Plate No. 38 (Series 2) 50 50
2478 150c. Plate No. 87 (Series 1) 50 50
2479 200c. Plate No. 33 (Series 1) 50 50
2480 300c. Plate No. 83 (Series 1) 70 70
2481 300c. on 360c. Plate No. 34 (Series 2) 70 70
2482 320c. Plate No. 10 (Series 2) 70 70
2483 330c. Plate No. 82 (Series 2) 70 70
2484 350c. Plate No. 94 (Series 1) 70 70
2485 350c. Plate No. 29 (Series 2) 70 70

(b) Design as No. 1420 but incorrectly inscr "LOS ANGELLES" optd or surch OLYMPICS 1988 (A) or KOREA 1988 (B).
2486 $1.20 multicoloured (A) 50 50
2487 $1.20 multicoloured (B) 50 50
2488 130c. on $1.20 mult (A) 50 50
2489 130c. on $1.20 mult (B) 50 50
2490 150c. on $1.20 mult (A) 50 50
2491 150c. on $1.20 mult (B) 50 50
2492 200c. on $1.20 mult (A) 60 60
2493 200c. on $1.20 mult (B) 60 60
2494 350c. on $1.20 mult (A) 70 70
2495 350c. on $1.20 mult (B) 70 70

1988. Columbus Day. Nos. 1672/3 optd or surch V CENTENARY OF THE LANDING OF CHRISTOPHER COLUMBUS IN THE AMERICAS.
2496 320c. Plate No. 50 (Series 1) 2·75 60
2497 $15 on 360c. Plate No. 85 (Series 1) 4·75 6·50

1988. Centenary of Publication of Sanders' "Reichenbachia" (34th issue). As T 331. Mult.
2498 100c. Plate No. 44 (Series 2) 60 55
2499 130c. Plate No. 42 (Series 2) (horiz) 60 55
2500 140c. Plate No. 4 (Series 2) 75 65
2501 160c. Plate No. 50 (Series 2) 75 65
2502 175c. Plate No. 51 (Series 2) 90 75
2503 200c. Plate No. 11 (Series 2) 6·00 1·50
2504 200c. Plate No. 23 (Series 2) 6·00 1·50
2505 200c. Plate No. 26 (Series 2) 6·00 1·50
2506 200c. Plate No. 75 (Series 2) 6·00 1·50
2507 200c. Plate No. 93 (Series 2) 6·00 1·50
2508 250c. Plate No. 79 (Series 2) 1·00 1·00
2509 280c. Plate No. 62 (Series 2) 1·25 1·50
2510 285c. Plate No. 63 (Series 2) 8·50 2·50
2511 380c. Plate No. 35 (Series 2) 9·00 3·00

1988. Christmas (1st issue). Various "Reichenbachia" issues optd or surch. (a) Optd or surch SEASON'S GREETINGS.
2512 150c. Plate No. 32 (Series 1) (No. 1561) 70 70
2513 150c. Plate No. 62 (Series 1) (No. 1566) 70 70
2514 225c. Plate No. 60 (Series 1) (No. 1682) 70 70
2515 260c. Plate No. 39 (Series 1) (No. 1737) 70 70
2516 320c. Plate No. 82 (Series 1) (No. 1753) 70 70
2517 330c. Plate No. 80 (Series 1) (No. 1754) 70 70
2518 360c. Plate No. 85 (Series 1) (No. 1673) 70 70
2519 120c. on 100c. Plate No. 6 (Series 1) 70 70
2520 120c. on 100c. Plate No. 13 (Series 1) 70 70
2521 120c. on 100c. Plate No. 20 (Series 1) 70 70
2522 120c. on 100c. Plate No. 25 (Series 1) 70 70
2523 120c. on 100c. Plate No. 40 (Series 1) (horiz) 70 70
2524 120c. on 100c. Plate No. 42 (Series 1) (horiz) 70 70
2525 120c. on 100c. Plate No. 43 (Series 1) (horiz) 70 70
2526 120c. on 100c. Plate No. 45 (Series 1) (horiz) 70 70
2532 240c. on 180c. Plate No. 15 (Series 1) (No. 1752) 80 80

(b) Optd SEASON'S GREETINGS 1988.
2527 225c. Plate No. 24 (Series 1) (No. 1774) 1·25 1·25
2528 225c. Plate No. 60 (Series 1) (No. 1682) 1·25 1·25
2530 225c. on 350c. on 120c. Plate No. 65 (Series 1) (No. 2221) 1·25 1·25
MS2531 120×129 mm. 225c. on 55c.×4 Plate No. 22 (Series 1) each with a different overprint (**Christmas 1987**, **Happy New Year**, **Merry Christmas** or **Happy Holidays**) (No. **MS**2232) 3·75 3·75

1988. Christmas (2nd issue). Nos. 489, 1188/91 and 1449 surch or optd CHRISTMAS 1988.
2533 - 20c. on 6c. mult (No. 489) 35 10
2534 **277** 120c. brown, black bl 1·00 1·50
2535 - 120c. on 130c. red, black and blue (No. 1189) 1·00 1·50
2536 - 120c. on 150c. violet, black and blue (No. 1190) 1·00 1·50
2537 - 120c. on 200c. green, black and blue (No. 1191) 1·00 1·50
2538 - 500c. on 330c. mult (No. 1449) 2·25 3·00

1988. AIDS Information Campaign. Nos. 707/8a optd or surch with various slogans.
2539 120c. on $5 "Morpho deidamia" (A) 3·00 3·00
2540 120c. on $5 "Morpho deidamia" (B) 3·00 3·00
2541 120c. on $5 "Morpho deidamia" (C) 3·00 3·00
2542 120c. on $5 "Morpho deidamia" (D) 3·00 3·00
2543 120c. on $5 "Morpho deidamia" (E) 3·00 3·00
2544 120c. on $10 "Elbella patrobas" (A) 3·00 3·00
2545 120c. on $10 "Elbella patrobas" (B) 3·00 3·00
2546 120c. on $10 "Elbella patrobas" (C) 3·00 3·00
2547 120c. on $10 "Elbella patrobas" (D) 3·00 3·00
2548 120c. on $10 "Elbella patrobas" (E) 3·00 3·00
2549 $2 "Morpho rhetenor" (female) (E) 9·50 2·75
2550 $5 "Morpho deidamia" (E) 11·00 7·00
2551 $10 "Elbella patrobas" (E) 13·00 11·00
OVERPRINTS: (A) **Be compassionate towards AIDS victims.**; (B) **Get information on AIDS. it may save your life.**; (C) **Get the facts. Education helps to prevent AIDS.**; (D) **Say no to Drugs and limit the spread of AIDS.**; (E) **Protect yourself from AIDS. Better safe than sorry.**

1988. 150th Anniv of Abolition of Slavery (1984) (2nd issue). Designs as Nos. 1547/50, but colours changed.
2552 **337** 25c. black and brown 20 10
2553 - 60c. black and lilac 25 15
2554 - 130c. black and green 30 70
2555 - 150c. black and blue 35 90

1989. Olympic Medal Winners, Seoul. Nos. 1672, 1923 and 2178 surch SALUTING WINNERS OLYMPIC GAMES 1988.
2556 550c. on 560c. Plate No. 1 (Series 2) 1·50 1·25
2557 900c. on 320c. Plate No. 18 (Series 2) 2·00 2·50
2558 1050c. on 320c. Plate No. 50 (Series 1) 2·50 3·25

1989. Republic Day. Nos. 2194/2201 and 2212 optd REPUBLIC DAY 1989.
2559 **396** $1.20 green 70 90
2560 - $1.20 green (No. 2195) 70 90
2561 - $1.20 green (No. 2196) 70 90
2562 - $1.20 green (No. 2197) 70 90
2563 **396** $1.20 purple 70 90
2564 - $1.20 purple (No. 2199) 70 90
2565 - $1.20 purple (No. 2200) 70 90
2566 - $1.20 purple (No. 2201) 70 90
2567 - $10 multicoloured 4·00 5·00

1989. Nos. 2202/5 and 2207/10 surch $5.00.
2568 **396** $5 on $3.20 blue 2·75 3·25
2569 - $5 on $3.20 blue (No. 2203) 2·75 3·25
2570 - $5 on $3.20 blue (No. 2204) 2·75 3·25
2571 - $5 on $3.20 blue (No. 2205) 2·75 3·25
2572 - $5 on $3.30 black (No. 2207) 2·75 3·25
2573 **396** $5 on $3.30 black 2·75 3·25
2574 - $5 on $3.30 black (No. 2209) 2·75 3·25
2575 - $5 on $3.30 black (No. 2210) 2·75 3·25

1989. Various "Reichenbachia" issues surch.
2576 120c. on 140c. Plate No. 25 (Series 2) 2·50 2·50
2577 120c. on 140c. Plate No. 52 (Series 2) 2·50 2·50
2578 120c. on 140c. Plate No. 65 (Series 2) 2·50 2·50
2579 120c. on 175c. Plate No. 54 (Series 2) 2·50 2·50
2580 120c. on 140c. Plate No. 38 (Series 2) 2·50 2·50
2581 120c. on 140c. Plate No. 41 (Series 2) 2·50 2·50
2582 170c. on 175c. Plate No. 58 (Series 2) 2·75 2·75
2583 250c. on 280c. Plate No. 66 (Series 2) 3·00 3·00
2584 250c. on 280c. Plate No. 67 (Series 2) 3·00 3·00
2585 300c. on 290c. Plate No. 53 (Series 2) (No. 2236) 3·00 3·00

1989. Nos. 1744/5 and 2185/6 surch TEN DOLLARS $10.00 (Nos. 2586, 2588) or TEN DOLLARS (Nos. 2587, 2589).
2586 **363** $10 on 320c. red, black and lilac (No. 1744) 4·50 5·00
2587 - $10 on 320c. mult (No. 1745) 4·50 5·00
2588 **363** $10 on 320c. red, black and lilac (No. 2185) 4·50 5·00
2589 - $10 on 320c. mult (No. 2186) 4·50 5·00

1989. Nos. O54/7, O59/63 and O65/9 optd POSTAGE or surch also.
2591 125c. on 130c. Plate No. 92 (Series 2) 2·25 2·25
2592 125c. on 140c. Plate No. 36 (Series 2) 2·25 2·25
2593 150c. Plate No. 43 (Series 2) 2·25 2·25
2594 150c. on 175c. Plate No. 31 (Series 2) 2·25 2·25
2595 250c. Plate No. 59 (Series 2) 2·50 2·50
2596 250c. on 225c. Plate No. 26 (Series 2) 2·50 2·50
2597 250c. on 230c. Plate No. 68 (Series 2) 2·50 2·50
2598 250c. on 275c. Plate No. 69 (Series 2) 2·50 2·50
2599 300c. on 275c. Plate No. 90 (Series 2) 2·50 2·50
2600 350c. Plate No. 95 (Series 2) 2·50 2·50
2601 350c. on 330c. Plate No. 23 (Series 2) 2·50 2·50
2602 600c. Plate No. 70 (Series 2) 2·75 3·00
2603 $12 Plate No. 71 (Series 2) 3·25 5·00
2604 $15 Plate No. 84 (Series 2) 3·50 5·50

1989. Centenary of Publication of Sanders' "Reichenbachia" (35th issue). As T 331. Mult.
2605 200c. Plate No. 49 (Series 2) 3·50 3·50
2606 200c. Plate No. 53 (Series 2) 3·50 3·50
2607 200c. Plate No. 60 (Series 2) 3·50 3·50
2608 200c. Plate No. 64 (Series 2) 3·50 3·50

1989. No. 1442 surch 250.
2609 **322** 250c. on 25c. mult 9·00 1·25

1989. 40th Anniv of Guyana Red Cross. No. 1872 surch RED CROSS 1948 1988 and new value.
2610 375c. on 45c. Plate No. 17 (Series 2) 3·50 3·50
2611 425c. on 45c. Plate No. 17 (Series 2) 3·50 3·50

1989. World Health Day. Nos. 1875 and 2239 surch with new value and inscr as indicated.
2612 250c. on 75c. Plate No. 56 (Series 2) surch **HEALTH FOR ALL** 2·50 2·50
2613 250c. on 75c. Plate No. 56 (Series 2) surch **ALL FOR HEALTH** 2·50 2·50
2614 675c. on 720c. Plate No. 49 (Series 2) surch **ALL FOR HEALTH** 3·25 4·00
2615 675c. on 720c. Plate No. 49 (Series 2) surch **HEALTH FOR ALL** 3·25 4·00

1989. Scouting Anniversaries. Nos. 1873, 1879, 2322, 2509 and unissued value as No. 1873 optd or surch also.
2616 250c. on 50c. Plate No. 33 (Series 2) (surch **BOY SCOUTS 1909 1989**) 1·25 1·25
2617 250c. on 50c. Plate No. 33 (Series 2) (surch **GIRL GUIDES 1924 1989**) 1·25 1·25
2618 250c. on 100c. Plate No. 33 (Series 2) (surch **BOY SCOUTS 1909 1989**) 1·25 1·25
2619 250c. on 100c. Plate No. 33 (Series 2) (surch **GIRL GUIDES 1924 1989**) 1·25 1·25
2620 300c. Plate No. 50 (Series 2) (optd **BOY SCOUTS 1909 1989**) 1·25 1·25
2621 300c. Plate No. 50 (Series 2) (optd **GIRL GUIDES 1924 1989**) 1·25 1·25
2622 $25 on 280c. Plate No. 62 (Series 2) (surch **LADY BADEN POWELL 1889 – 1989**) 5·50 7·00
2623 $25 on 700c. Plate No. 62 (Series 2) (surch **LADY BADEN POWELL 1889 – 1989**) 5·50 7·00
The events commemorated are the 80th anniv of Boy Scout Movement in Guyana, 65th anniv of Girl Guide Movement in Guyana and birth centenary of Lady Baden-Powell.

1989. 150 Years of Photography. No. 1881 surch PHOTOGRAPHY 1839 – 1989 and new value.
2624 550c. on 390c. Plate No. 6 (Series 2) 3·75 4·00
2625 650c. on 390c. Plate No. 6 (Series 2) 3·75 4·00

1989. 70th Anniv of International Labour Organization. No. 1875 surch I.L.O. 1919-1989 300.
2627 300c. on 75c. Plate No. 56 (Series 2) 7·50 2·75

1989. Various stamps surch.
2628 80c. on 6c. Patua (No. 489) 40 20
2629 $1 on 2c. Type **132** 40 20

2630	$2.05 on 3c. Hanging heliconia (No. 544)	40	25
2633	$5 on 6c. Type **111**	40	30
2634	$6.40 on 10c. "Archonias bellona" (No. 699)	7·00	75
2635	$8.90 on 60c. "Papilio androgeus" (No. 705a)	9·00	1·50
2637a	$7.65 on 35c. "Anaea galanthus" (No. 703)	7·00	1·50
2638	$7.65 on 40c. "Morpho retenor" (male) (No. 704)	8·00	1·50
2641	$2.55 on 5c. Annatto tree (No. 545)	40	25
2642	$3.25 on 6c. Cannon-ball tree (No. 546)	40	25
2643	$50 on $2 "Morpho rhetenor" (female) (No. 707)	18·00	9·00
2644	$100 on $2 "Morpho rhetenor" (female) (No. 707)	26·00	19·00
2646	640c. on 675c. on 720c. Plate No. 49 (Series 2) (No. 2614)	1·75	2·00
2647	640c. on 675c. on 720c. Plate No. 49 (Series 2) (No. 2615)	1·75	2·00
2648	$6.40 on $3.30 black (No. 2207)	9·00	7·50
2649	$6.40 on $3.30 black (No. 2208)	9·00	7·50
2650	$6.40 on $3.30 black (No. 2209)	9·00	7·50
2651	$6.40 on $3.30 black (No. 2210)	9·00	7·50
2652	$7.65 on $3.20 blue (No. 2202)	9·00	7·50
2653	$7.65 on $3.20 blue (No. 2203)	9·00	7·50
2654	$7.65 on $3.20 blue (No. 2204)	9·00	7·50
2655	$7.65 on $3.20 blue (No. 2205)	9·00	7·50

1989. CARICOM Day. No. 1878 surch CARICOM DAY 125.

2656	125c. on 200c. Plate No. 44 (Series 2)	4·50	1·00

454 "Stalachtis calliope"

1989. Butterflies (1st series). Multicoloured.

2657	80c. Type **454**	60	10
2658	$2.25 "Morpho rhetenor"	70	15
2659	$5 "Agrias claudia"	80	15
2660	$6.40 "Marpesia marcella"	85	20
2661	$7.65 "Papilio zagreus"	90	30
2662	$8.90 "Chorinea faunus"	1·00	30
2663	$25 "Euptychia cephus"	2·75	2·75
2664	$100 "Nessaea regina"	7·00	9·00

See also Nos. 2789/2861 and **EMS**18/19.

455 Kathryn Sullivan (first U.S. woman to walk in space)

1989. 25 Years of Women in Space. Mult.

2665	$6.40 Type **455**	70	20
2666	$12.80 Svetlana Savitskaya (first Soviet woman to walk in space)	1·10	45
2667	$15.30 Judy Resnik and Christa McAuliffe and "Challenger" logo	1·10	45
2668	$100 Sally Ride (first U.S. woman astronaut)	8·00	9·00

1989. Centenary of Ahmadiyya (Moslem organization). Nos. 543/5 surch AHMADIYYA CENTENARY 1899-1989.

2669	80c. on 2c. Type **132**	4·75	60
2670	$6.40 on 3c. Hanging heliconia	14·00	5·50
2671	$8.90 on 5c. Annatto tree	16·00	8·00

457 Head of Harpy Eagle

1990. Endangered Species. Harpy Eagle. Multicoloured.

2672	$2.25 Type **457**	75	25
2673	$5 Harpy eagle with monkey prey	1·00	30
2674	$8.90 Eagle on branch (facing right)	1·50	50
2675	$30 Eagle on branch (facing left)	3·25	3·50

458 Channel-billed Toucan

1990. Birds of Guyana. Multicoloured.

2676	$15 Type **458**	1·50	70
2677	$25 Blue and yellow macaw	1·75	50
2678	$50 Wattled jacana (horiz)	3·25	2·50
2679	$60 Hoatzin	3·50	2·75
MS2680	Two sheets, each 110×80 mm. (a) $100 Great kiskadee. (b) $100 Amazon kingfisher Set of 2 sheets	9·00	5·75

1990. 85th Anniv of Rotary International. Optd Rotary International 1905-1990 and emblem. (a) On Nos. 2657/64.

2681	80c. Type **454**	1·50	30
2682	$2.25 "Morpho rhetenor"	1·75	50
2683	$5 "Agrias claudia"	2·25	50
2684	$6.40 "Marpesia marcella"	2·25	55
2685	$7.65 "Papilio zagreus"	2·25	55
2686	$8.90 "Chorinea faunus"	2·50	65
2687	$25 "Euptychia cephus"	5·00	5·50
2688	$100 "Nessaea regina"	12·00	14·00

(b) On Nos. 2665/8.

2689	$6.40 Type **455**	1·25	40
2690	$12.80 Svetlana Savitskaya (first Soviet woman to walk in space)	1·75	1·00
2691	$15.30 Judy Resnik and Christa McAuliffe with "Challenger" logo	1·75	1·10
2692	$100 Sally Ride (first U.S. woman astronaut)	9·00	11·00

460 Indian Post Runner, 1837

1990. 150th Anniv of the Penny Black and 500th Anniv of Thurn and Taxis Postal Service. Multicoloured.

	2693-2746 Set of 54	32·00	35·00
2693-2746	$15.30×27, $17.80×9, $20×18		
MS2747	Three sheets, each 116×86 mm. (a) $150 Post boy. (b) $150 Thurn and Taxis (Northern District) 3sgr. of 1852. (c) $150 Thurn and Taxis (Southern District) 6k. of 1852 Set of 3 sheets	13·00	14·00

Nos. 2693/2746 depict various forms of mail transport.

1990. 9th Conference of Rotary District 405, Georgetown. Nos. 1759, 1762/3 and 1765/6 surch ROTARY DISTRICT 405 9th CONFERENCE MAY 1990 GEORGETOWN and new value.

2748	80c. on 55c. Plate No. 9 (Series 1)	2·00	1·00
2749	80c. on 55c. Plate No. 49 (Series 1)	2·00	1·00
2750	80c. on 55c. Plate No. 64 (Series 1)	2·00	1·00
2751	$6.40 on 130c. Plate No. 6 (Series 1)	7·50	6·00
2752	$6.40 on 130c. Plate No. 25 (Series 1)	7·50	6·00
2753	$7.65 on 130c. Plate No. 25 (Series 1)	7·50	6·00

1990. 90th Birthday of Queen Elizabeth the Queen Mother. Nos. 2657/64 surch 90th Birthday H.M. The Queen Mother.

2754	80c. Type **454**	1·75	50
2755	$2.25 "Morpho rhetenor"	2·00	60
2756	$5 "Agrias claudia"	2·50	70
2757	$6.40 "Marpesia marcella"	2·75	75
2758	$7.65 "Papilio zagreus"	3·00	80
2759	$8.90 "Chorinea faunus"	3·00	1·00
2760	$25 "Euptychia cephus"	7·50	6·50
2761	$100 "Nessaea regina"	17·00	22·00

See also Nos. **EMS**31/3.

463 Collared Trogon

1990. Birds. Multicoloured.

2762	80c. Marbled wood quail ("Guiana Partridge") (horiz)	30	10
2763	$2.55 Type **463**	40	15
2764	$3.25 Chestnut-tipped toucanet ("Derby Aracari")	40	15
2765	$5 Black-necked aracari	50	20
2766	$5.10 Green aracari	50	30
2767	$5.80 Ivory-billed aracari	50	30
2768	$6.40 Guiana toucanet	50	30
2769	$6.50 Channel-billed toucan ("Sulphur-breasted Toucan")	50	30
2770	$7.55 Red-billed toucan	65	30
2771	$7.65 Toco toucan	65	30
2772	$8.25 Tawny-tufted toucanet ("Natterers Toucanet")	65	30
2773	$8.90 Eared trogon ("Welcome Trogon")	65	30
2774	$9.75 Elegant trogon ("Doubtful Trogon")	65	30
2775	$11.40 Collared trogon ("Banded Aracari")	75	40
2776	$12.65 Golden-headed quetzal ("Golden-headed Train Bearer")	75	40
2777	$12.80 Rufous-breasted hermit	75	40
2778	$13.90 Band tail barbthroat	75	40
2779	$15.30 White-tipped sickle-bill	80	50
2780	$17.80 Black jacobin	90	60
2781	$19.20 Fiery topaz	90	60
2782	$22.95 Tufted coquette	1·00	70
2783	$26.70 Ecuadorian pied-tail	1·00	70
2784	$30 Resplendent quetzal ("Quetzal")	1·00	70
2785	$50 Green-crowned brilliant	1·75	1·25
2786	$100 Emerald-chinned hummingbird	2·75	2·75
2787	$190 Lazuline sabre-wing	4·50	5·00
2788	$225 Beryline hummingbird	4·50	5·50

464 "Melinaea idae"

1990. Butterflies (2nd series). Multicoloured.

	2789-2860 Set of 72	30·00	35·00
2789-2860	80c., $2.55, $5, $6.40, $7.65, $8.90, $10×64, $50 and $100		
MS2861	Four sheets, each 102×71 mm. (a) $150 "Heliconius aoede". (b) $150 "Phyciodes clio" (horiz). (c) $190 "Thecla hemon". (d) $190 "Nymphidium caricae" Set of 4 sheets	20·00	24·00

DESIGNS—VERT: $2.55, "Rhetus dysonii"; $5 "Actinote anteas"; $6.40, "Heliconius tales"; $7.65, "Thecla telemus"; $8.90, "Theope eudocia"; $10 (2795), "Heleconius vetustus"; 2796, "Mesosemia eumene"; 2797, "Parides phosphorus"; 2798, "Polystichtis emylius"; 2799, "Xanthocleis aedesia"; 2800, "Doxocopa agathina"; 2801, "Adelpha plesaure"; 2802, "Heliconius wallacei"; 2803, "Notheme eumeus"; 2804, "Melinaea mediatrix"; 2805, "Theritas coronata"; 2806, "Dismorphia orise"; 2807, "Phyciodes ianthe"; 2808, "Morpho aega"; 2809, "Zaretis isidora"; 2810, "Pierella lena"; 2811, "Heliconius silvana"; 2812, "Eunica alcmena"; 2813, "Mechanitis polymnia"; 2814, "Mesosemia ephyne"; 2815, "Thecla erema"; 2816, "Callizona acesta"; 2817, "Stalachtis phaedusa"; 2818, "Battus belus"; 2819, "Nymula phliasus"; 2820, "Parides childrenae"; 2821, "Stalachtis euterpe"; 2822, "Dysmathia portia"; 2823, "Tithorea hermias"; 2824, "Prepona pheridamas"; 2825, "Dismorphia fortunata"; 2826, "Hamadryas amphinome"; $50 "Heliconius vicini"; $100 "Amarynthis meneria". HORIZ: $10 (2827), "Thecla falerina"; 2828, "Pheles heliconides"; 2829, "Echenias leucocyana"; 2830, "Heliconius xanthocles"; 2831, "Mesopthalma idotea"; 2832, "Parides aeneas"; 2833, "Heliconius numata"; 2834, "Thecla critola"; 2835, "Themone pais"; 2836, "Nymula agle"; 2837, "Adelpha cocala"; 2838, "Anaea eribotes"; 2839, "Prepona demophon"; 2840, "Selenophanes cassiope"; 2841, "Consul hippona"; 2842, "Antirrhaea avernus"; 2843, "Thecla telemus"; 2844, "Thyridia confusa"; 2845, "Heliconius burneyi"; 2846, "Parides lysander"; 2847, "Eunica orphise"; 2848, "Adelpha melona"; 2849, "Morpho menelaus"; 2850, "Nymula phylleus"; 2851, "Stalachtis phlegia"; 2852, "Theope barea"; 2853, "Morpho perseus"; 2854, "Lycorea ceres"; 2855, "Archonias bellona"; 2856; "Caeronis chorinaeus"; 2857, "Vila azeca"; 2858, "Nessaea batesii".

Nos. 2795/2810, 2811/26, 2827/42 and 2843/58 respectively were printed together, se-tenant, forming composite designs.

465 "Vanillia inodora"

1990. Flowers. Multicoloured.

	2862-2965 Set of 104	30·00	30·00
2862-2965	$7.65, $8.90, $10×32, $12.80×65, $15.30, $17.80, $20, $25 and $100		
MS2966	Five sheets. (a) 65×95 mm. $150 "Delonix regia" (horiz). (b) 86×65 mm. $150 "Hexisea bidentata" (horiz). (c) 70×105 mm. $150 "Galeandra devonianal" (horiz). (d) 68×110 mm. $150 "Lecythis ollaria". (e) 74×104 mm. $190 "Ionopsis utricularioides" Set of 5 sheets	18·00	20·00

DESIGNS—VERT: $8.90, "Epidendrum ibaguense"; $10 (2864), "Dichea muricata"; 2865, "Octomeria erosilabia"; 2866, "Spiranthes orchioides"; 2867, "Brassavola nodosa"; 2868, "Epidendrum rigidum"; 2869, "Brassia caudata"; 2870, "Pleurothallis diffusa"; 2871, "Aspasia variegata"; 2872, "Stenia pallida"; 2873, "Cyrtopodium punctatum"; 2874, "Cattleya deckeri"; 2875, "Cryptarrhena lunata"; 2876, "Cattleya violacea"; 2877, "Caularthron bicornutum"; 2878, "Oncidium carthagenense"; 2879, "Galeandra devoniana"; 2880, "Bifrenaria aurantiaca"; 2881, "Epidendrum ciliare"; 2882, "Dichaea picta"; 2883, "Scaphyglottis violacea"; 2884, "Cattleya percivaliana"; 2885, Map and national flag; 2886, "Epidendrum difforme"; 2887, "Eulophia maculata"; 2888, "Spiranthes tenuis"; 2889, "Peristoria guttata"; 2890, "Pleurothallis pruinosa"; 2891, "Cleistes rosea"; 2892, "Maxillaria variabilis"; 2893, "Brassavola cucullata"; 2894,"Epidendrum moyobambae"; 2895, "Oncidium orthostate"; $12.80, "Maxillaria parkeri"; $12.80 (2897), "Brassavola martiana"; 2898, "Paphinia cristata"; 2899, "Aganisia pulchella"; 2900, "Oncidium lanceanum"; 2901, "Lockhartia imbricata"; 2902, "Caularthron bilamellatum"; 2903, "Oncidium nanum"; 2904, "Pleurothallis ovalifolia"; 2905, "Galeandra dives"; 2906, "Cycnoches loddigesii"; 2907, "Ada aurantiaca"; 2908, "Catasetum barbatum"; 2909, "Palmorchis pubescens"; 2910, "Epidendrum anceps"; 2911, "Huntleya meleagris"; 2912, "Sobralia sessilis"; $15.30, "Epidendrum nocturnum"; $17.80, "Catasetum discolor"; $20 "Scuticaria hadwenii"; $25 "Epidendrum fragrans"; $100 "Epistephium parviflorum". HORIZ: $12.80 (2913), "Cochlospermum vitifolium"; 2914, "Eugenia malaccensis"; 2915, "Plumiera rubra"; 2916, "Erythrina glauca"; 2917, "Spathodea campanulata"; 2918, "Jacaranda filicifolia"; 2919, "Samanea saman"; 2920, "Cassia fistula"; 2921, "Abutilon integerrimum"; 2922, "Lagerstroemia speciosa"; 2923, "Tabebuia serratifolia"; 2924, "Guaiacum officinale"; 2925, "Solanum macranthum"; 2926, "Peltophorum roxburghii"; 2927, "Bauhinia variegata"; 2928, "Plumiera alba"; 2929, "Maxillaria camaridii"; 2930, "Vanilla pompona"; 2931, "Stanhopea grandiflora"; 2932, "Oncidium pusillum"; 2933, "Polycycnis vittata"; 2934, "Cattleya lawrenceana"; 2935, "Menadenium labiosum"; 2936, "Rodriguezia secunda"; 2937, "Mormodes buccinator"; 2938, "Otostylis brachystalix"; 2939, "Maxillaria discolor"; 2940, "Liparis elata"; 2941, "Gongora maculata"; 2942, "Koellensteinia graminea"; 2943, "Rudolfiella aurantiaca"; 2944, "Scuticaria steelei"; 2945, "Gloriosa rothschildiana"; 2946, "Pseudocalymma alliaceum"; 2947, "Callichlamys latifolia"; 2948, "Distictis riversii"; 2949, "Maurandya barclaiana"; 2950, "Beaumontia fragrans"; 2951, "Phaseolus caracalla"; 2952, "Mandevilla splendens"; 2953, "Solandra longiflora"; 2954, "Passiflora coccinea"; 2955, "Allamanda cathartica"; 2956, "Bauhinia galpini"; 2957, "Verbena maritima"; 2958, "Mandevilla sauveolens"; 2959, "Phryganocydia corymbosa"; 2960, "Jasminum sambac".

Nos. 2864/79, 2880/95, 2897/2912, 2913/28, 2929/44 and 2945/60 respectively were printed together, se-tenant, forming composite designs.

466 Ivory-billed Woodpecker

1990. Fauna. Multicoloured.
2967-3046 Set of 80 32·00 32·00
2967-2986 $12.80×20 (vert designs showing endangered birds)
2987-3006 $12.80×20 (vert designs showing tropical birds)
3007-3036 $12.80×20 (vert designs showing prehistoric animals)
3027-3046 $12.80×20 (horiz designs showing endangered wildlife)

DESIGNS—VERT: No. 2968, Cauca guan; 2969, Sun conure; 2970, Resplendent quetzal ("Quetzal"); 2971, Long-wattled umbrellabird; 2972, Banded cotinga; 2973, Blue-throated conure ("Blue-chested Parakeet"); 2974, West Mexican chachalaca ("Rufous-bellied Chachalaca"); 2975, Yellow-faced amazon; 2976, Toucan barbet; 2977, Red siskin; 2978, Guianan cock-of-the-rock ("Cock-of-the-Rock"); 2979, Hyacinth macaw; 2980, Yellow cardinal; 2981, Bare-necked umbrellabird; 2982, Saffron toucanet; 2983, Red-billed curassow; 2984, Spectacled parrotlet; 2985, Lovely cotinga; 2986, Black-bellied gnateater ("Black-breasted Gnateater"); 2987, Swallow-tailed kite; 2988, Hoatzin; 2989, Ruby-topaz hummingbird; 2990, American black vulture; 2991, Rufous-tailed jacamar; 2992, Scarlet macaw; 2993, Rose-breasted thrush tanager; 2994, Toco toucan; 2995, Bearded bellbird; 2996, Blue-crowned motmot; 2997, Green oropendola; 2998, Pompadour cotinga; 2999, Vermilion flycatcher; 3000, Blue and yellow macaw; 3001, White-barred piculet; 3002, Great razor-billed curassow; 3003, Ruddy quail dove; 3004, Paradise tanager; 3005, American darter ("Anhinga"); 3006, Greater flamingo; 3007, Palaelodus; 3008, Archaeotrogon; 3009, Teratornis mirabilis ("Vulture"); 3010, Bradypus tridactylus; 3011, Natalus stramineus bat; 3012, Cebidae; 3013, Cuvieronius; 3014, Phororhacos; 3015, Smilodectes; 3016, Megatherium; 3017, Titanotylopus; 3018, Teleoceras; 3019, Macrauchenia; 3020, Mylodon; 3021, Smilodon; 3022, Glyptodon; 3023, Protohydrocherus; 3024, Archaeohyrax; 3025, Pyrotherium; 3026, Platypittamys. HORIZ: $12.80 (3027), Harpy eagle and hyacinth macaw; 3028, Andean condor; 3029, Amazonian umbrellabird; 3030, Spider monkeys; 3031, Hyacinth macaws; 3032, Red siskin; 3033, Toucan barbet; 3034, Three-toed sloth; 3035, Guanacos; 3036, Spectacled bear; 3037, White-lipped peccary; 3038, Maned wolf; 3039, Jaguar; 3040, Spectacled cayman; 3041, Giant armadillo; 3042, Giant anteater; 3043, South American river otter; 3044, Yapok; 3045, Central American river turtle; 3046, Cauca guan.

Nos. 2967/86, 2987/3006, 3007/26 and 3027/46 respectively were printed together, se-tenant, forming composite designs.

No. 2982 is inscribed "Toucanette" and No. 2995 "Bellbird", both in error.

See also **E**MS34/5.

467 National Flag

1991. 25th Anniv of Independence. Sheet 100×70 mm. Litho. Imperf.
MS3047 **467** $225 multicoloured 5·50 6·00

468 Ramon Folist (Cuba) (fencing, 1990)

1991. Winter Olympic Games, Albertville (1st issue), and Olympic Games, Barcelona. Previous Gold Medal Winners. Multicoloured.
3048-3119 Set of 72 32·00 35·00
3048-3119 $15.30×9, $17.80×9, $20×18, $25×18 and $30×18
MS3120 Three sheets, each 98×70 mm. (a) $150 Johannes Kolehmainen (Finland) (10,000 metres, 1912) (vert). (b) $150 Paavo Nurmi (Finland) (5000 metres, 1924) (vert). (c) $190 Nedo Nadi (Italy) (fencing, 1920) (vert) Set of 3 sheets 11·00 12·00

DESIGNS: $15.30 (3049), Lucien Gaudin (France) (fencing, 1924); 3050, Ole Lilloe-Olsen (Norway) (shooting, 1924); 3051, Morris Fisher (U.S.A.) (rifle shooting, 1924); 3052, Ray Ewry (U.S.A.) (long jump, 1900); 3053, Hubert van Innes (Belgium) (archery, 1900); 3054, Alvin Kraenzlein (U.S.A.) (hurdles, 1900); 3055, Johnny Weissmuller (U.S.A.) (swimming, 1924); 3056, Hans Winkler (West Germany) (show jumping, 1956); $17.80 (3057), Viktor Chukarin (Russia) (gymnastics, 1952); 3058, Agnes Keleti (Hungary) (gymnastics, 1952); 3059, Barbel Wochel (East Germany) (200 metres, 1980); 3060, Eric Heiden (U.S.A.) (speed skating, 1980); 3061, Alvodar Gerevich (Hungary) (fencing, 1932); 3062, Giuseppe Delfino (Italy) (fencing, 1952); 3063, Alexander Tikhonov (Russia) (skiing, 1980); 3064, Pahud de Mortanges (Netherlands) (equestrian, 1932); 3065, Patricia McCormick (U.S.A.) (diving, 1952); $20 (3066), Olga Korbut (Russia) (gymnastics, 1972); 3067, Lyudmila Turischeva (Russia) (gymnastics, 1972); 3068, Lasse Viren (Finland) (10,000 metres, 1972); 3069, George Miez (Switzerland) (gymnastics, 1936); 3070, Roland Matthes (East Germany) (swimming, 1972); 3071, Pal Kovaks (Hungary) (fencing, 1936); 3072, Jesse Owens (U.S.A.) (200 metres, 1936); 3073, Mark Spitz (U.S.A.) (swimming, 1972); 3074, Eduardo Mangiarotti (Italy) (fencing, 1936); 3075, Nelli Kim (Russia) (gymnastics, 1976); 3076, Viktor Krovopuskov (Russia) (fencing, 1976); 3077, Viktor Sidiak (Russia) (fencing, 1976); 3078, Nikolai Andrianov (Russia) (gymnastics, 1976); 3079, Nadia Comaneci (Rumania) (gymnastics, 1976); 3080, Mitsuo Tsukahara (Japan) (gymnastics, 1976); 3081, Yelena Novikova-Belova (Russia) (fencing, 1976); 3082, John Naber (U.S.A.) (swimming, 1976); 3083, Kornella Ender (Rumania) (swimming, 1976); $25 (3084), Lydia Skoblikova (Russia) (speed skating, 1964); 3085, Ivar Ballangrud (Norway) (speed skating, 1936); 3086, Clas Thunberg (Finland) (speed skating, 1928); 3087, Anton Heida (U.S.A.) (gymnastics, 1904); 3088, Akinori Nakayama (Japan) (gymnastics, 1968); 3089, Sixten Jernberg (Sweden) (skiing, 1964); 3090, Yevgeniy Grischin (Russia) (speed skating, 1956); 3091, Paul Radmilovic (East Germany) (waterpolo, 1920); 3092, Charles Daniels (U.S.A.) (swimming, 1904); 3093, Sawao Kato (Japan) (gymnastics, 1968); 3094, Rudolf Karpati (Hungary) (fencing, 1948); 3095, Jeno Fuchs (Hungary) (fencing, 1908); 3096, Emil Zatopek (Czechoslovakia) (10,000 metres, 1948); 3097, Fanny Blankers-Koen (Netherlands) (hurdles, 1948); 3098, Melvin Sheppard (U.S.A.) (4 x 400 metres relay, 1908); 3099, Gert Fredriksson (Sweden) (kayak, 1948); 3100, Paul Elvstrom (Denmark) (sailing, 1948); 3101, Harrison Dillard (U.S.A.) (100 metres, 1948); $30 (3102), Al Oerter (U.S.A.) (discus, 1956); 3103, Polina Atsakhova (Russia) (gymnastics, 1956); 3104, Takashi Ono (Japan) (gymnastics, 1956); 3105, Valentin Muratov (Russia) (gymnastics, 1956); 3106, Henri St. Cyr (Sweden) (equestrian, 1956); 3107, Iain Murray Rose (Australia) (swimming, 1956); 3108, Larisa Latynina (Russia) (gymnastics, 1956); 3109, Carlo Pavesi (Italy) (fencing, 1956); 3110, Dawn Fraser (Australia) (swimming, 1956); 3111, Betty Cuthbert (Australia) (400 metres, 1964); 3112, Vera Caslavska (Czechoslovakia) (gymnastics, 1964); 3113, Galin Kulakova (Russia) (skiing, 1972); 3114, Yukio Endo (Japan) (gymnastics, 1972); 3115, Vladimir Morozov (Russia) (kayak, 1972); 3116, Boris Shaklin (Russia) (gymnastics, 1964); 3117, Don Schollander (U.S.A.) (swimming, 1964); 3118, Gyozo Kulscar (Hungary) (fencing, 1964); 3119, Christian D'Oriloa (France) (fencing, 1956).

Nos. 3048/56, 3057/65, 3066/74, 3075/83, 3084/92, 3093/3101, 3102/10 and 3111/19 respectively were printed together, se-tenant, forming composite designs.

Sheetlets containing Nos. 3057/65, 3084/92 and 3111/19 were subsequently re-issued with Nos. 3063, 3086 and 3113 overprinted "ALBERTVILLE '92".

See also Nos. 3186/94 and 3246/54.

1991. 85th Anniv of Rotary International (1990). (a) Nos. 2789/94 and 2859/60 optd or surch Paul Percy Harris Founder 1868-1947 and emblem (A) or with Rotary emblem and 1905-1990 (B).
3121 80c. Type **464** (B) 10 10
3122 $2.55 "Rhetus dysonii" (A) 10 10
3123 $5 "Actinote anteas" (A) 10 10
3124 $6.40 "Heliconius tales" (A) 15 15
3125 $7.65 "Thecla telemus" (A) 15 15
3126 $100 on $8.90 "Theope eudocia" (A) 1·75 1·90
3127 $190 on $50 "Heliconius vicini" (B) 2·75 3·00
3128 $225 on $100 "Amarynthis meneria" (B) 3·00 3·50

(b) Nos. 2795/2810 optd or surch as Nos. 3121/8 or with emblems and inscriptions of other international organizations.
3129 $10 "Heliconius vetustus" (B) 20 20
3130 $10 "Mesosemia eumene" (optd Boy Scout emblem and **1907–1992**) 20 20
3131 $10 "Parides phosphorus" (optd Lions Club emblem and **1917–1992**) 20 20
3132 $10 "Polystichtis emylius" (A) 20 20
3133 $10 "Xanthocleis aedesia" (optd **125 Years Red Cross** and cross) 20 20
3134 $10 "Doxocopa agathina" (optd with part Rotary emblem) 20 20
3135 $10 "Adelpha plesaure" (optd with part Rotary emblem) 20 20
3136 $10 "Heliconius wallacei" (optd **125 Years Red Cross** and cross) 20 20
3137 $10 "Notheme eumeus" (optd Lions Club emblem and **1917–1992**) 20 20
3138 $10 "Melinaea mediatrix" (optd with part Rotary emblem) 20 20
3139 $10 "Theritas coronata" (optd with part Rotary emblem) 20 20
3140 $10 "Dismorphia orise" (optd Boy Scout emblem and **1907–1992**) 20 20
3141 $50 on $10 "Phyciodes ianthe" (A) 80 80
3142 $75 on $10 "Morpho aega" (surch Boy Scout emblem and **1907–1992**) 1·60 1·60
3143 $100 on $10 "Zaretis isidora" (surch Lions Club emblem and **1917–1992**) 1·75 1·90
3144 $190 on $10 "Pierella lena" (B) 2·75 3·25
MS3145 Two sheets, each 102×71 mm. (a) $400 on $150 "Heliconius aoede". (b) $500 on $150 "Phyciodes clio" Set of 2 sheets 10·00 10·50

Nos. **MS**3145a/b only show the new face values on the stamps and have international organization emblems overprinted on the sheet margins.

1991. 65th Birthday of Queen Elizabeth II and 70th Birthday of Prince Philip. As T 198a of Gambia. Multicoloured.
3146 $12.80 Queen and Prince Philip in evening dress 25 20
3147 $15.30 Queen Elizabeth II 25 20
3148 $100 Queen and Prince Philip 1·25 1·40
3149 $130 Prince Philip 1·50 1·60
3150 $150 Prince Philip in R.A.F. uniform 1·75 1·90
3151 $200 The Queen with Queen Elizabeth the Queen Mother 2·50 2·75
MS3152 68×90 mm. $225 Queen Elizabeth II 3·25 3·50

1991. 10th Wedding Anniv of Prince and Princess of Wales. As T 198b of Gambia. Multicoloured.
3153 $8.90 Prince and Princess of Wales 30 20
3154 $50 Separate portraits of Princess and sons 1·00 80
3155 $75 Prince Charles with Prince William 1·25 1·50
3156 $190 Princess Diana with Prince Henry 2·75 3·50
MS3157 68×90 mm. $225 Separate portraits of Prince Charles, Prince William and Princess Diana with Prince Henry 3·75 3·75

1991. 75th Anniv of Lions International (1992). (a) Nos. 2789/94 and 2859/60 optd or surch Melvin Jones Founder 1880-1961 (A) or with Lions Club emblem and Lions International 1917–1992 (B).
3158 80c. Type **464** (B) 15 10
3159 $2.55 "Rhetus dysonii" (B) 20 15
3160 $5 "Actinote anteas" (A) 30 20
3161 $6.40 "Heliconius tales" (A) 30 25
3162 $7.65 "Thecla telemus" (A) 40 25
3163 $100 on $8.90 "Theope eudocia" (A) 1·50 1·50
3164 $190 on $50 "Heliconius vicini" (B) 2·50 2·75
3165 $225 on $100 "Amarynthis meneria" (B) 2·50 2·75

(b) Nos. 2843/58 optd or surch as Nos. 3158/65 or with emblems and inscriptions of other international organizations.
3166 $10 "Thecla telemus" (optd Lions Club emblem and **1917–1992**) 15 15
3167 $10 "Thyridia confusa" (optd Rotary emblem and **1905–1990**) 15 15
3168 $10 "Heliconius burneyi" (optd Boy Scout emblem and **1907–1992**) 15 15
3169 $10 "Parides lysander" (A) 15 15
3170 $10 "Eunica orphise" (optd **125 Years Red Cross** and cross) 15 15
3171 $10 "Adelpha melona" (optd with part Lions Club emblem) 15 15
3172 $10 "Morpho menelaus" (optd with part Lions Club emblem) 15 15
3173 $10 "Nymula phylleus" (optd **125 Years Red Cross** and cross) 15 15
3174 $10 "Stalachtis phlegia" (optd Rotary emblem and **1905–1990**) 15 15
3175 $10 "Theope barea" (optd with part Lions Club emblem) 15 15
3176 $10 "Morpho perseus" (optd with part Lions Club emblem) 15 15
3177 $10 "Lycorea ceres" (optd Boy Scout emblem and **1907–1992**) 15 15
3178 $50 on $10 "Archonias bellona" (A) 70 70
3179 $75 on $10 "Caerois chorinaeus" (surch Boy Scout emblem and **1907–1992**) 1·25 1·40
3180 $100 on $10 "Vila azeca" (surch Rotary emblem and **1905–1990**) 1·50 1·60
3181 $190 on $10 "Nessaea batesii" (surch Lions Club emblem and **1917–1992**) 2·50 3·00
MS3182 Two sheets, each 102×71 mm. (a) $400 on $190 "Nymphidium caricae". (b) $500 on $190 "Thecla hemon" Set of 2 sheets 10·00 11·00

Nos. **MS**3182a/b only show new face values on the stamps and have international organization emblems overprinted on the sheet margins.

1991. "Phila Nippon '91" International Stamp Exhibition, Tokyo. Sheetlets containing Nos. 2880/95 and 2897/2912, now sold as miniature sheets, and **MS**2966d with some stamps surch $50 and inscriptions and exhibition logo on the sheet margins, all in red.
MS3183 135×203 mm. $10×12; $25 on $10; $50 on $10; $75 on $10; $130 on $10 11·00 12·00
MS3184 135×203 mm. $12.80×12; $25 on $12.80; $50 on $12.80; $75 on $12.80; $100 on $12.80 11·00 12·00
MS3185 68×110 mm. $250 on $150 "Lecythis ollaria" 3·75 4·00

1991. Winter Olympic Games, Albertville (1992) (2nd issue). Nos. 2738/46 optd or surch ALBERTVILLE 92 or XVIth Olympic Winter Games in Albertville (No. 3190).
3186-3194 Set of 9 22·00 23·00
3186-3194 $20 x 6, $70 on $20, $100 on $20, $190 on $20

1991. John F. Kennedy and Sir Winston Churchill Commemorations. Nos. MS2966c and MS2966e surch $600 in black or red.
MS3195 70×105 mm. $600 on $150 "Galeandra devoniana" (horiz)
MS3196 74×104 mm. $600 on $190 "Ionopsis utricularioides"

No. **MS**3195 is additionally overprinted with "IN MEMORIAM John F. Kennedy 1917–1963", "First Man on Moon July 20, 1969" and "Apollo 11" emblem, and No. **MS**3196 "IN MEMORIAM Sir Winston S. Churchill 1874–1965" and "50th Anniversary World War II" on sheet margins.

474 "Akagi" (Japanese aircraft carrier)

1991. 50th Anniv of Japanese Attack on Pearl Harbor. Each blue, red and black.
3197 $50 Type **474** 85 85
3198 $50 Beached Japanese midget submarine 85 85
3199 $50 Mitsubishi A6M Zero-Sen fighter 85 85
3200 $50 U.S.S. "Arizona" (battleship) under attack 85 85
3201 $50 Aichi D3A1 "Val" dive bomber 85 85
3202 $50 U.S.S. "California" (battleship) sinking 85 85
3203 $50 Curtiss P-40 fighters taking off 85 85
3204 $50 U.S.S. "Cassin" and U.S.S. "Downes" damaged in dry dock 85 85
3205 $50 Boeing B-17 Flying Fortress crash landing at Bellows Field 85 85
3206 $50 U.S.S. "Nevada" (battleship) on fire 85 85

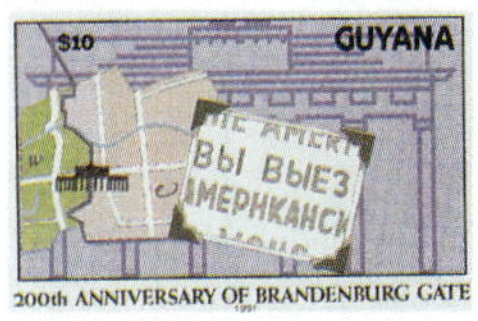

475 Brandenburg Gate and Location Plan

1991. Anniversaries and Events. Multicoloured.
3207 $10 Type **475** 20 20
3208 $25 President Bush, President Lech Walesa of Poland and Brandenburg Gate 50 50
3209 $25 Scout handshake 50 50
3210 $30 Scouts hiking at Philmont Scout Ranch 60 60
3211 $40 Jamboree and Scout Movement emblems 70 70
3212 $60 General de Gaulle at Venice, 1944 90 90
3213 $75 De Gaulle with Khrushchev, 1960 1·25 1·25
3214 $75 Mozart and Castle of Laxenburg 2·00 1·50
3215 $75 Caroline Herschel (astronomer) and Old Town Hall, Hanover 1·25 1·25
3216 $75 Map of Switzerland and woman in Valais costume 1·75 1·25
3217 $80 De Gaulle at Algiers, 1958 1·40 1·40
3218 $80 Mozart and death of Leopold II 2·00 1·50
3219 $80 Otto Lilienthal and "Flugzeug Nr. 3" 1·60 1·40
3220 $100 Chancellor Kohl, Foreign Minister Genscher and Brandenburg Gate 1·50 1·50
3221 $100 Lord Baden-Powell (vert) 1·75 1·75
3222 $100 De Gaulle with Pope Paul VI, 1967 2·50 1·75

3223 $100 Mozart and birthplace, Salzburg 2·50 1·75
3224 $100 Class P36 steam locomotive 2·50 1·75
MS3225 Six sheets. (a) 67×99 mm. $150 General De Gaulle (vert). (b) 75×104 mm. $190 General De Gaulle (different) (vert). (c) 101×71 mm. $190 Ceremonial helmet and statues from Brandenburg Gate. (d) 114×83 mm. $190 Rocket-flown commemorative cover, 1960. (e) 73×104 mm. $190 Mozart cameo (vert). (f) 103×74 mm. $190 Arms of Berne and Solothurn Set of 6 sheets 17·00 19·00

ANNIVERSARIES and EVENTS—Nos. 3207/8, 3220, **MS**3225c, Bicentenary of Brandenburg Gate, Berlin; 3209/11, 3221, **MS**3225d, 17th World Scout Jamboree, Korea; 3212/13, 3217, 3222, **MS**3225a/b, Birth centenary (1990) of Charles de Gaulle (French statesman); 3214, 3218, 3223, **MS**3225e, Death bicentenary of Mozart; 3215, 750th anniv of Hanover; 3216, **MS**3225f, 700th anniv of Swiss Confederation; 3219, Centenary of Otto Lilienthal's first gliding experiments; 3224, Centenary of Trans-Siberian Railway.

No. 3222 is inscribed "Pope John VI" in error.

476 Disney Characters Carol Singing, 1989

1991. Christmas. Walt Disney Christmas Cards. Multicoloured.
3226 80c. Type **476** 10 10
3227 $2.55 Disney characters and carol singers in tram, 1962 15 15
3228 $5 Donald Duck and Pluto with parcel, 1971 20 20
3229 $6.40 "SEASON'S GREETINGS" and Mickey Mouse with candle, 1948 30 20
3230 $7.65 Mickey Mouse as Father Christmas, 1947 30 20
3231 $8.90 Shadow of Pinocchio with candle, 1939 30 20
3232 $50 Three Little Pigs dancing on wolf rug, 1933 1·25 1·25
3233 $50 Conductor and Donald Duck, 1940 (vert) 1·25 1·25
3234 $50 Elephant and ostrich carol singing, 1940 (vert) 1·25 1·25
3235 $50 Hippo, centaurs, Pinocchio and Goofy, 1940 (vert) 1·25 1·25
3236 $50 Snow White, Dopey, Mickey and Minnie, 1940 (vert) 1·25 1·25
3237 $50 Dino, Pluto and Walt Disney, 1940 (vert) 1·25 1·25
3238 $50 Mickey Mouse in sleigh, 1974 (vert) 1·25 1·25
3239 $50 Three Little Pigs, Winnie the Pooh, Bambi and Thumper, 1974 (vert) 1·25 1·25
3240 $50 Baloo, King Louis, Lady and the Tramp, 1974 (vert) 1·25 1·25
3241 $50 Alice, Robin Hood, the Cheshire Cat and Goofy, 1974 (vert) 1·25 1·25
3242 $50 Dumbo, Pinocchio, Peter Pan, Tinkerbelle, Seven Dwarfs and Donald Duck, 1974 (vert) 1·25 1·25
3243 $50 Pluto pulling sleigh, 1974 (vert) 1·25 1·25
3244 $200 Mickey and mice carol singing, 1949 4·00 5·00
MS3245 Eight sheets. (a) 127×101 mm. $260 Mickey, Minnie, Clarabelle and Pluto in mail coach, 1932 (vert). (b) 127×101 mm. $260 Mickey's House, 1935 (vert). (c) 101×127 mm. $260 Jose Carioca, Rooster and Donald Duck on flying carpet, 1944 (vert). (d) 101×127 mm. $260 Casey at the Bat and dancers, 1945. (e) 127×101 mm. $260 Mickey, Donald and Goofy on musical score, 1946. (f) 127×101 mm. $260 Picture of Winnie the Pooh, 1969. (g) 127×101 mm. $260 Father Christmas in chimney, 1969 (vert). (h) 101×127 mm. $260 Letters of film titles forming Mickey Mouse, 1978 (vert) Set of 8 sheets 30·00 30·00

477 Gus Gander playing Ice Hockey

1991. Winter Olympic Games, Albertville (1992) (3rd issue). Walt Disney Cartoon Characters. Multicoloured.
3246 $6.40 Type **477** 35 15
3247 $7.65 Mickey and Minnie Mouse in bobsleigh 40 15
3248 $8.90 Donald's Nephews on luge and skis 45 15
3249 $12.80 Goofy freestyle skiing 60 20
3250 $50 Goofy ski jumping 1·75 1·25
3251 $100 Donald and Daisy Duck speed skating 2·50 2·00
3252 $130 Pluto cross-country skiing 2·75 2·75
3253 $190 Mickey and Minnie Mouse ice dancing 3·50 4·50
MS3254 Two sheets, each 125×100 mm. (a) $225 Donald's nephew curling. (b) $225 Donald Duck slalom skiing Set of 2 sheets 8·00 8·50

478 Columbus landing on Trinidad

1992. 500th Anniv of Discovery of America by Columbus. Multicoloured.
3255 $6.40 Type **478** 55 40
3256 $7.65 Columbus the map-maker 65 45
3257 $8.90 Fleet blown off course 65 45
3258 $12.80 Map of third voyage and Columbus in chains 65 55
3259 $15.30 Sighting land 65 55
3260 $50 "Nina" and "Pinta" 1·75 1·00
3261 $75 "Santa Maria" 2·00 1·25
3262 $100 Columbus trading with Amerindians 2·25 1·75
3263 $125 Crew and sea monster 2·75 2·75
3264 $130 Columbus landing on San Salvador and map of first voyage 2·75 2·75
3265 $140 Priest and Amerindians 2·75 2·75
3266 $150 Columbus before King Ferdinand and Queen Isabella of Spain 2·75 2·75
MS3267 Three sheets, each 126×91 mm. (a) $280 "Nina" (vert). (b) $280 Columbus (vert). (c) $280 Early map of Caribbean Set of 3 sheets 14·00 16·00

479 Tom Mix in "The Great K & A Train Robbery", 1926

1992. Classic Movie Posters. Multicoloured.
3268 $8.90 Type **479** 50 40
3269 $12.80 Richard Dix and Irene Dunne in "Cimarron", 1931 60 50
3270 $15.30 Fatty Arbuckle in "Buzzin' Around", 1934 60 50
3271 $25 Tom Tyler in "The Adventures of Captain Marvel", 1941 80 70
3272 $30 Boris Karloff in "The Mummy", 1932 1·25 85
3273 $50 Rudolph Valentino in "A Sainted Devil", 1924 1·40 1·10
3274 $75 Seven posters for "A Tale of Two Cities", 1935 1·75 1·40
3275 $100 Chester Conklin in "A Tugboat Romeo", 1916 2·50 1·90
3276 $130 Douglas Fairbanks in "The Thief of Bagdad", 1924 2·75 2·25
3277 $150 Laurel and Hardy in "Bacon Grabbers", 1929 3·25 3·00
3278 $190 Marx Brothers in "A Night at the Opera", 1935 4·00 4·25
3279 $200 Orson Welles in "Citizen Kane", 1941 4·00 4·25
MS3280 Four sheets. (a) 70×99 mm. $225 Babe Ruth in "Babe Comes Home", 1927. (b) 70×99 mm. $225 Mae West in "She Done Him Wrong", 1933. (c) 70×99 mm. $225 Charlie Chaplin in "The Circus", 1928. (d) 99×70 mm. $225 Poster for never-made film "Zeppelin", 1933. Imperf Set of 4 sheets 15·00 17·00

1992. Easter. Paintings by Durer. As T 204a of Gambia. Multicoloured.
3281 $6.40 "The Martyrdom of Ten Thousand" (detail) 25 10
3282 $7.65 "Adoration of the Trinity" (detail of Virgin Mary) 25 10
3283 $12.80 "The Martyrdom of Ten Thousand" (execution detail) 40 20
3284 $15.30 "Adoration of the Trinity" (different detail) 45 25
3285 $50 "The Martyrdom of Ten Thousand" (detail of bishop) 1·00 75
3286 $100 "Adoration of the Trinity" (different detail) 1·50 1·50
3287 $130 "The Martyrdom of Ten Thousand" (different detail) 1·75 2·00
3288 $190 "Adoration of the Trinity" (different detail) 3·25 4·00
MS3289 Two sheets, each 71×101 mm. (a) $225 "The Martyrdom of Ten Thousand". (b) $225 "Adoration of the Trinity" (detail of Christ on cross) Set of 2 sheets 8·00 8·50

1992. Baha'i Holy Year. Surch BAHA'I HOLY YEAR 1992 and value.
3290 $6.40 on 60c. Plate No. 10 (Series 1) (No. 1521)
3291 $7.65 on 60c. Plate No. 31 (Series 1) (No. 1523)
3292 $8.90 on 60c. Plate No. 19 (Series 1) (No. 1522)
3293 $50 on 60c. Plate No. 2 (Series 1) (No. 1519)

481 Queen Elizabeth II and Duke of Edinburgh

1992. 40th Anniv of Queen Elizabeth II's Accession. Multicoloured.
3294 $8.90 Type **481** 65 25
3295 $12.80 Queen at Trooping the Colour 75 30
3296 $100 Queen at Coronation 3·50 2·50
3297 $130 Queen in Garter robes 4·00 3·25
MS3298 Two sheets, each 119×79 mm. (a) $225 Queen in Coronation robes. (b) $225 Queen in blue dress Set of 2 sheets 9·00 9·50

482 Holy Cross Church, Annai Rupununi

1992. 150th Anniv of Diocese of Guyana. Multicoloured.
3299 $6.40 Type **482** 15 10
3300 $50 St. Peter's Church 80 65
3301 $100 Interior of St. George's Cathedral (vert) 1·50 1·60
3302 $190 Map of Guyana (vert) 2·75 3·75
MS3303 104×70 mm. $225 Religious symbols 3·75 4·50

483 Burmese

1992. Cats. Multicoloured.
3304 $5 Type **483** 20 10
3305 $6.40 Turkish van 20 10
3306 $12.80 American shorthair 30 20
3307 $15.30 Sphynx 30 20
3308 $50 Egyptian mau 1·00 1·00
3309 $50 Russian blue 1·00 1·00
3310 $50 Havana brown 1·00 1·00
3311 $50 Himalayan 1·00 1·00
3312 $50 Manx 1·00 1·00
3313 $50 Cornish rex 1·00 1·00
3314 $50 Black Persian 1·00 1·00
3315 $50 Scottish fold 1·00 1·00
3316 $50 Siamese 1·00 1·00
3317 $100 Japanese bobtail 1·50 1·25
3318 $130 Abyssinian 1·75 1·75
3319 $225 Oriental shorthair 2·75 3·25
MS3320 Four sheets, each 99×69 mm. (a) $250 Chartreuse (vert). (b) $250 Turkish angora (vert). (c) $250 Maine coon (vert). (d) $250 Chinchilla (vert) Set of 4 sheets 14·00 15·00

484 Red Howler

1992. Animals of Guyana. Multicoloured.
3321 $8.90 Type **484** 20 10
3322 $12.80 Ring-tailed coati 25 20
3323 $15.30 Jaguar 30 20
3324 $25 Two-toed sloth 50 30
3325 $50 Giant armadillo 1·00 80
3326 $75 Giant anteater 1·50 1·75
3327 $100 Capybara 1·75 1·90
3328 $130 Ocelot 2·00 2·25
MS3329 Two sheets, each 70×100 mm. (a) $225 Woolly opossum (vert). (b) $225 Night monkey (vert) Set of 2 sheets 8·00 9·00

No. **MS**3329a is inscribed "WOLLY OPOSSUM" in error.

485 Oligocene Mammoth

1992. Elephants. Multicoloured.
3330 $50 Type **485** 1·50 1·50
3331 $50 Mid-Miocene stegodon 1·50 1·50
3332 $50 Pliocene mammoth 1·50 1·50
3333 $50 Carthaginian elephant crossing Alps, 219 B.C. 1·50 1·50
3334 $50 Ceremonial elephant of Maharaja of Mysore, India 1·50 1·50
3335 $50 Elephant pulling teak trunks, Burma 1·50 1·50
3336 $50 Tiger-hunting by elephant, India 1·50 1·50
3337 $50 Elephant towing raft on River Kwai, Thailand 1·50 1·50
MS3338 110×80 mm. $225 African elephant 6·00 6·00

486 Palomino

1992. Horses. Multicoloured.
3339 $190 Type **486** 3·00 3·00
3340 $190 Appaloosa 3·00 3·00
3341 $190 Clydesdale 3·00 3·00
3342 $190 Arab 3·00 3·00
3343 $190 Morgan 3·00 3·00
3344 $190 Friesian 3·00 3·00
3345 $190 Pinto 3·00 3·00
3346 $190 Thoroughbred 3·00 3·00
MS3347 109×80 mm. $190 Lipizzaner (47×29 mm) 4·50 4·50

No. 3340 is inscribed "APALOOSA" in error.

1992. International Conference on Nutrition, Rome. Surch INT. CONFERENCE ON NUTRITION 1992 and value.
3348 $6.40 on 150c. Plate No. 45 (Series 1) (No. 1769)
3349 $7.65 on 150c. Plate No. 42 (Series 1) (No. 1768)
3350 $8.90 on 150c. Plate No. 40 (Series 1) (No. 1767)
3351 $10 on 200c. Plate No. 43 (Series 1) (No. 1658)
3352 $50 on 200c. Plate No. 43 (Series 1) (No. 1658)

488 Marklin Swiss "Crocodile" Locomotive, 1933

1992. "Genova '92" International Thematic Stamp Exhibition. Toy Trains from German Manufacturers. Multicoloured.

No.	Description	Unused	Used
3353-3361	$45×9 Made by Marklin: Type **488**; French tramcar, 1902; British "Flatiron" tank engine, 1913; German switching engine, 1970; Third class carriage, 1909; American style locomotive, 1904; Zurich tramcar, 1928; Central London Railway locomotive in Paris-Orleans livery, 1904; British GWR "Great Bear" locomotive, 1909		
3353-3424	3393-3424 Set of 72	45·00	48·00
3362-3370	$45×9 Made by Marklin: LMS "Precursor" tank engine, 1923; American "Congressional Limited" passenger carriage, 1908; Swiss Type "Ae 3/6" locomotive, 1934; German Class 80, 1975; British Southern Railways third class carriage, 1926; LNWR Bowen-Cooke tank engine, 1913; London Underground "Two Penny Tube", 1901; French Paris-Orsay steeplecab, 1920; Passenger locomotive, 1895		
3371-3379	$45×9 Made by Marklin: American style locomotive, 1907; German passenger carriage, 1908; British Great Eastern Railway locomotive, 1908; London Underground steeplecab, 1904; Santa Fe Railroad diesel locomotive, 1962; British GNR locomotive, 1903; Caledonian Railway "Cardean", 1906; British LNWR passenger carriage, 1903; Swiss St. Gotthard Railway locomotive, 1920		
3380-3388	$45×9 Made by Marklin: British LB SCR tank engine No. 22, 1920; Central London Railway steeplecab locomotive, 1904; German "Borsig" streamlined, 1935; French Paris-Lyon-Mediterranee first class carriage, 1929; American style locomotive No. 1021, 1904; French Paris-Orsay long-nose steeplecab, 1920; British LNER "Cock o' the North", 1936; Prussian State Railways Class P8, 1975; German diesel railcar set, 1937		
3389-3397	$45×9 Marklin North British Railway "Atlantic", 1913; Bing British LNWR "Precursor", 1916; Marklin British GWR "King George V", 1937; Marklin "Kaiser Train" passenger carriage, 1901; Bing side tank locomotive No. 88, 1904; Marklin steeplecab, 1912; Marklin "Adler", 1935; Bing British GWR "County of Northampton", 1909; Bing British Midland Railway "Black Prince", 1908		
3398-3406	$45×9 Made by Bing: Midland Railway "Deeley Type" No. 483, 1909; British Midland Railway No. 2631, 1903; German Pacific, 1927; British GWR third class coach, 1926; British LSWR "M7" No. 109, 1909; Side tank engine "Pilot", 1901; British LNWR Webb "Cauliflower", 1912; Side tank locomotive No. 112, 1910; British GNR "Stirling Single", 1904		
3407-3315	$45×9 Carette tin "Penny Bazaar" train, 1904; Winteringham locomotive, 1917; Carette British Northeastern Railway Smith Compound, 1905; Carette S.E. C.R. steam railcar, 1908; Carette British Great Northern Railway Stirling Single No. 776, 1903; Carette British Midland Railways locomotive No. 1132M, 1911; Carette London Metropolitan Railway Co. "Westinghouse" locomotive No. 5, 1908; Carette Clestory carriage, 1907; Carette steam railcar No. 1, 1906		
3416-3324	$45×9 Made by Bing: Engine and tender, 1895; British Midland Railway "Single" No. 650, 1913; No. 524/510 reversible locomotive, 1916; "Kaiser Train" passenger carriage, 1902; British rural station, 1915; British LSWR M7 tank locomotive, 1909; "Windcutter", 1912; British Great Central Railway "Sir Sam Fay", 1914; Scottish Caledonian Railway "Dunalastair" locomotive, 1910		
MS3425	Eight sheets, each 116×83 mm. (a) $350 Bing contractor's locomotive No. 18, 1904 (51×39 mm). (b) $350 Marklin rack railway steeplecab locomotive, 1908 (51×39 mm). (c) $350 Bing British GWR "County of Northampton" locomotive, 1909 (51×39 mm).(d) $350 Marklin French Paris–Lyon–Mediterranean Pacific locomotive, 1912 (51×39 mm). (e) $350 Bing Pabst Blue Ribbon beer refrigerator wagon, 1925 (51×39 mm). (f) $350 Marklin French "Mountain Etat" locomotive, 1933 (51×39 mm). (g) $350 Marklin German National Railroad Class 0-1 Pacific locomotive, 1937 (51×39 mm). (h) $350 Marklin American "Commodore Vanderbilt" locomotive, 1937 (51×39 mm) Set of 8 sheets	30·00	32·00

1992. Postage Stamp Mega Event, New York. Sheet 100×70 mm, containing multicoloured design as T 207a of Gambia, but vert.

No.	Description	Unused	Used
MS3426	$325 Statue of Liberty	6·00	7·50

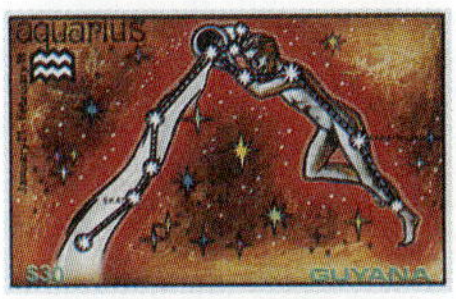

489 Aquarius

1992. Signs of the Zodiac. Multicoloured.

No.	Description	Unused	Used
3427	$30 Type **489**	85	85
3428	$30 Pisces	85	85
3429	$30 Aries	85	85
3430	$30 Taurus	85	85
3431	$30 Gemini	85	85
3432	$30 Cancer	85	85
3433	$30 Leo	85	85
3434	$30 Virgo	85	85
3435	$30 Libra	85	85
3436	$30 Scorpio	85	85
3437	$30 Sagittarius	85	85
3438	$30 Capricorn	85	85

490 City Walls and Two Birds

1992. Bible Stories (1st series). David and Goliath. Multicoloured.

No.	Description	Unused	Used
3439	$25 Type **490**	50	50
3440	$25 City walls and one bird at right	50	50
3441	$25 Sun over city gateway	50	50
3442	$25 City walls and one bird at left	50	50
3443	$25 City walls and no birds	50	50
3444	$25 Philistine army and edge of shield	50	50
3445	$25 Goliath's head and torso	50	50
3446	$25 Goliath's arm and spear	50	50
3447	$25 Philistine army and spearhead	50	50
3448	$25 Philistine infantry	50	50
3449	$25 Philistine cavalry and infantry	50	50
3450	$25 Goliath's shield	50	50
3451	$25 Goliath's waist and thigh	50	50
3452	$25 David with sling	50	50
3453	$25 Israelite soldier with spear	50	50
3454	$25 Two Israelite soldiers with spears and shields	50	50
3455	$25 Goliath's right leg	50	50
3456	$25 Goliath's left leg (face value at foot)	50	50
3457	$25 David's legs and Israelite standard	50	50
3458	$25 Three Israelite soldiers	50	50
3459	$25 Israelite soldier and parts of two shields	50	50
3460	$25 Israelite soldier with sword	50	50
3461	$25 Back of Israelite soldier	50	50
3462	$25 Israelite soldier leaning on rock	50	50
3463	$25 Israelite soldier looking left	50	50

Nos. 3439/63 were printed together, se-tenant, forming a composite design.

See also Nos. 4020/4116.

491 Count Von Zeppelin and Airship over Lake Constance, 1909

1992. Anniversaries and Events. Multicoloured.

No.	Description	Unused	Used
3464	$12.80 Type **491**	50	35
3465	$50 "Voyager I" and Jupiter	1·50	1·00
3466	$50 Adenauer with Pres. Kennedy, 1961	1·00	1·00
3467	$100 Aeromedical airlift	2·00	2·00
3468	$100 Boutu ("Amazon Dolphin")	2·00	2·00
3469	$130 Baby gorilla	2·50	2·50
3470	$130 Mobile eye screening unit and doctor with child	2·50	2·50
3471	$130 "Stars and Stripes" (winning yacht, 1987)	2·50	2·50
3472	$130 Lift-off of "Voyager I", 1977	2·50	2·50
3473	$190 Adenauer with President De Gaulle of France, 1962	3·25	3·25
3474	$225 Von Zeppelin and airship preparing for take-off, 1905	3·50	3·50
MS3475	Four sheets. (a) 76×105 mm. $225 Ferdinand von Zeppelin (vert). (b) 116×80 mm. $225 Earth from Space (vert). (c) 84×111 mm. $225 Konrad Adenauer (vert). (d) 87×111 mm. $225 "Hyperohus marmoratus" (tree frog) (vert) Set of 4 sheets	15·00	16·00

ANNIVERSARIES and EVENTS: Nos. 3464, 3474, **MS**3475a, 75th death anniv of Count Ferdinand von Zeppelin; 3465, 3472, **MS**3475b, International Space Year; 3466, 3473, **MS**3475c, 75th death anniv of Konrad Adenauer (German statesman); 3467, United Nations World Health Organization projects; 3468/9, **MS**3475d, Earth Summit '92, Rio; 3470, 75th anniv of International Association of Lions Clubs; 3471, Americas Cup Yachting Championship.

492 Hyacinth Macaw

1993. South American Parrots. Multicoloured.

No.	Description	Unused	Used
3476	80c. Type **492**	30	15
3477	$6.40 Scarlet macaw (preening)	50	25
3478	$7.65 Buffon's macaw ("Green Macaw") (vert)	50	25
3479	$15.30 Orange-chinned parakeet ("Tovi Parakeet")	70	50
3480	$50 Blue and yellow macaw	1·00	80
3481	$100 Military macaw (vert)	1·50	1·25
3482	$130 Green-winged macaw ("Red and Green Macaw") (vert)	1·75	1·75
3483	$190 Chestnut-fronted macaw ("Severa Macaw")	2·50	3·00
MS3484	Two sheets, each 108×74 mm. (a) $225 Scarlet macaw. (b) $225 Monk parakeet (vert) Set of 2 sheets	7·00	7·50

493 Crimson Topaz

1993. Birds of Guyana. Multicoloured.

No.	Description	Unused	Used
3485	$50 Type **493**	75	75
3486	$50 Bearded bellbird	75	75
3487	$50 Amazonian umbrellabird	75	75
3488	$50 Paradise jacamar	75	75
3489	$50 Paradise tanager	75	75
3490	$50 White-tailed trogon	75	75
3491	$50 Scarlet macaw	75	75
3492	$50 Hawk-headed parrot ("Redfan Parrot")	75	75
3493	$50 Red-billed toucan	75	75
3494	$50 White-faced antcatcher ("White-plumed Antbird")	75	75
3495	$50 Crimson-hooded manakin	75	75
3496	$50 Guianan cock of the rock	75	75
MS3497	70×100 mm. $325 Tufted coquette (horiz)	5·00	5·50

Nos. 3485/96 were printed together, se-tenant, with the backgrounds forming a composite design.

494 Manatee surfacing

1993. Endangered Species. American Manatee ("Caribbean Manatee"). Multicoloured.

No.	Description	Unused	Used
3498	$6.40 Type **494**	60	30
3499	$7.60 Cow and calf feeding	60	30
3500	$8.90 Manatee underwater	60	30
3501	$50 Two manatees	2·25	2·25

495 Tamandua

1993. Animals of Guyana. Multicoloured.

No.	Description	Unused	Used
3502	$50 Type **495**	75	75
3503	$50 Pale-throated sloth ("Three-toed Sloth")	75	75
3504	$50 Red howler	75	75
3505	$50 Four-eyed opossum	75	75
3506	$50 Black spider monkey	75	75
3507	$50 Giant otter	75	75
3508	$50 Red brocket	75	75
3509	$50 Brazilian tree porcupine	75	75
3510	$50 Tayra	75	75
3511	$50 Brazilian tapir	75	75
3512	$50 Ocelot	75	75
3513	$50 Giant armadillo	75	75
MS3514	100×70 mm. $325 Paca	4·50	5·00

Nos. 3502/13 were printed together, se-tenant, the backgrounds forming a composite design.

No. 3505 is inscribed "Four-eyed Opossium" in error.

496 Pteranodon

1993. Prehistoric Animals. Multicoloured.

No.	Description	Unused	Used
	3515-3550 Set of 36	17·00	19·00
3515-3526	$30×12 (Type **496**; Cearadactylus; Eudimorphodon; Pterodactylus; Stauirkosaurus; Euoplocephalus; Tuojiangosaurus; Oviraptor; Protoceratops; Panaoplosaurus; Psittacosaurus; Corythosaurus)		
3527-3538	$30×12 (Sordes; Quetzalcoatlus; Archaeopteryx in flight; Rhamphorynchus; Spinosaurus; Anchisaurus; Stegosaurus; Leaellynosaurus; Minmi; Heterdontosaurus; Esothosaurus; Deninonychus)		
3539-3550	$30×12 (Archaeopteryx on branch; Pteranodon (different); Quetzalcoatlus (three); Protoavis; Dicraeosaurus; Moschops; Lystrosaurus; Dimetrondon; Staurikosaurus; Cacops; Diarthrognathus; Estemmenosuchus)		

Nos. 3515/26, 3527/38 and 3539/50 respectively were printed together, se-tenant, with the backgrounds forming composite designs.

1993. 40th Anniv of Coronation. As T 215a of Gambia. Multicoloured.

No.	Description	Unused	Used
3551	$25 Queen Elizabeth II in Coronation robes (photograph by Cecil Beaton)	85	85
3552	$50 Royal gems	1·25	1·25
3553	$75 Queen Elizabeth and Prince Philip	1·40	1·40
3554	$130 Queen opening Parliament	1·75	2·00
MS3555	69×100 mm. $325 "Queen in Coronation Robes" (Sir James Gunn) (28½×42½ mm)	5·00	5·50

497 Gabriel Marquez (author)

1993. Famous People of the Twentieth Century. Multicoloured. (a) Arts and Literature.

3556 $50 Type **497** 75 75
3557 $50 Pablo Picasso (artist) 75 75
3558 $50 Cecil De Mille (film director) 75 75
3559 $50 Martha Graham (dancer) 75 75
3560 $50 Peace dove (inscr "20th Century Arts and Literature") 75 75
3561 $50 Charlie Chaplin (actor) 75 75
3562 $50 Paul Robeson (actor) 75 75
3563 $50 Rudolph Dunbar (musician) 75 75
3564 $50 Louis Armstrong (musician) 75 75
MS3565 100×70 mm. $250 Elvis Presley (singer) (vert) 3·50 3·50

(b) Science and Medicine.

3566 $50 Louis Leakey (archaeologist and anthropologist) 75 75
3567 $50 Jonas Salk (discoverer of polio vaccine) 75 75
3568 $50 Hideyo Noguchi (bacteriologist) 75 75
3569 $50 Karl Landsteiner (pathologist) 75 75
3570 $50 As No. 3550, but inscr "20th Century Science and Medicine" 75 75
3571 $50 Sigmund Freud (founder of psychoanalysis) 75 75
3572 $50 Louis Pasteur (chemist) 75 75
3573 $50 Madame Curie (physicist) 75 75
3574 $50 Jean Baptiste Perrin (physicist) 75 75
MS3575 100×70 mm. $250 Einstein's Theory of Relativity equation (vert) 3·50 3·50

(c) Sports Personalities.

3576 $50 O. J. Simpson (American football) 75 75
3577 $50 Rohan Kanhai (cricket) 75 75
3578 $50 Gabriela Sabatini (tennis) 75 75
3579 $50 Severiano Ballesteros (golf) 75 75
3580 $50 As No. 3550, but inscr "20th Century Sports" 75 75
3581 $50 Franz Beckenbauer (football) 75 75
3582 $50 Pele (football) 75 75
3583 $50 Wilt Chamberlain (basketball) 75 75
3584 $50 Nadia Comaneci (gymnastics) 75 75
MS3585 100×70 mm. $250 Jackie Robinson (baseball) (vert) 3·50 3·50

(d) Peace and Humanity.

3586 $100 Mahatma Gandhi (India) 1·10 1·10
3587 $100 Dalai Lama (Tibet) 1·10 1·10
3588 $100 Michael Manley (Jamaica) 1·10 1·10
3589 $100 Perez de Cuellar (U.N. Secretary-General) 1·10 1·10
3590 $100 Peace dove and globe 1·10 1·10
3591 $100 Mother Teresa (India) 1·10 1·10
3592 $100 Martin Luther King (U.S.A.) 1·10 1·10
3593 $100 Pres. Nelson Mandela (South Africa) 1·10 1·10
3594 $100 Raoul Wallenberg (Sweden) 1·10 1·10
MS3595 100×70 mm. $250 Nobel Peace Prize scroll (vert) 3·50 3·50

(e) Politics.

3596 $100 Nehru (India) 1·10 1·10
3597 $100 Dr. Eric Williams (Trinidad and Tobago) 1·10 1·10
3598 $100 Pres. John F. Kennedy (U.S.A.) 1·10 1·10
3599 $100 Pres. Hugh Desmond Hoyte (Guyana) 1·10 1·10
3600 $100 Peace dove and map of the Americas 1·10 1·10
3601 $100 Friedrich Ebert (Germany) 1·10 1·10
3602 $100 Pres F. D. Roosevelt (U.S.A.) 1·10 1·10
3603 $100 Mikhail Gorbachev (Russia) 1·10 1·10
3604 $100 Sir Winston Churchill (Great Britain) 1·10 1·10
MS3605 100×70 mm. $250 Flags of United Nations and member countries (vert) 3·50 3·50

(f) Transportation and Technology.

3606 $100 Douglas DC-3 cargo plane 1·25 1·25
3607 $100 Space Shuttle 1·25 1·25
3608 $100 Concorde 1·25 1·25
3609 $100 Count Ferdinand von Zeppelin and "Graf Zeppelin" 1·25 1·25
3610 $100 Peace dove and rocket trails 1·25 1·25
3611 $100 Marconi and aerial tower 1·25 1·25
3612 $100 Adrian Thompson (mountaineer) and Mt. Roraima 1·25 1·25
3613 $100 "Hikari" express train, Japan 1·25 1·25
3614 $100 Johann von Neumann and computer 1·25 1·25
MS3615 100×70 mm. $250 Lunar module "Eagle" on Moon 4·00 4·00

Nos. 3556/64, 3566/74, 3576/84, 3586/94, 3596/3604 and 3606/14 respectively were printed together, se-tenant, with composite background designs on Nos. 3586/94, 3596/3604 and 3606/14.

No. 3562 is inscribed "Paul Roebeson" in error.

498 "Bather, Paris" (Picasso)

1993. Anniversaries and Events. Multicoloured (except No. MS3628c).

3616 $15.30 Type **498** 15 20
3617 $25 Willy Brandt with Prime Minister of Israel Golda Meir, 1969 (horiz) 40 40
3618 $50 "Pantaloons" (left half) (Tadeusz Brzozowski) 50 55
3619 $50 Georg Hackl (men's single luge, 1992) 70 70
3620 $50 Astrolabe 70 70
3621 $75 Miedzyrecz Castle 75 80
3622 $100 "Two Nudes" (Picasso) 1·00 1·10
3623 $130 "Pantaloons" (right half) (Tadeusz Brzozowski) 1·25 1·40
3624 $130 Karen Magnussen (women's figure skating, 1972) 1·50 1·50
3625 $190 "Nude seated on a Rock" (Picasso) 1·90 2·25
3626 $190 Willy Brandt at Georgsmarienhutten Steel Mill, 1969 (horiz) 2·25 2·50
3627 $190 Dish aerial 2·25 2·50
MS3628 Five sheets. (a) 104×75 mm. $300 Copernicus. (b) 75×104 mm. $325 "The Rescue" (detail) (Picasso). (c) 104×75 mm. $325 Willy Brandt giving interview, 1969 (brown and black). (d) 99×70 mm. $325 "Children in the Garden" (Wladyslaw Podkowinski) (horiz). (e) 75×104 mm. $325 German four-man bobsleigh team, 1992 Set of 5 sheets 20·00 22·00

ANNIVERSARIES and EVENTS: Nos. 3616, 3622, 3625, **MS**3628b, 20th death anniv of Picasso (artist); 3617, 3626, **MS**3628c, 80th birth anniv (1992) of Willy Brandt (German politician); 3618, 3621, 3623, **MS**3628d, "Polska '93" International Stamp Exhibition, Poznan; 3619, 3624, **MS**3628e, Winter Olympic Games '94, Lillehammer; 3620, 3627, **MS**3628a, 450th death anniv of Copernicus (astronomer).

Nos. 3618 and 3623 were printed together, se-tenant, forming a composite design showing the complete painting.

499 Audie Murphy (most decorated U.S. serviceman)

1993. 50th Anniv of Second World War (1st issue). Multicoloured.

3629 $6.40 Type **499** 70 20
3630 $7.65 Allied troops in Normandy (8 June 1944) 70 25
3631 $8.90 American howitzer crew, Battle of Montecassino (18 May 1944) 75 30
3632 $12.80 American aircraft attacking "Yamato" (Japanese battleship), Battle of East China Sea (7 April 1945) 80 50
3633 $15.30 St. Basil's Cathedral, Moscow (Foreign Ministers' Conference, 19 October 1943) 80 50
3634 $50 American troops crossing Rhine at Remagen (7 March 1945) 1·50 75
3635 $100 Boeing B-29 Superfortresses raiding Japan from China (15 June 1944) 2·25 1·75
3636 $130 General Patton and map of Sicily (17 August 1943) 2·50 2·25
3637 $190 Destruction of "Tirpitz" (German battleship) (12 November 1944) 3·25 3·25
3638 $200 American forces in Brittany (1 August 1944) 3·25 3·25
3639 $225 American half-track (ceasefire in Italy, 2 May 1945) 3·50 3·75
MS3640 100×69 mm. $325 Meeting of American and Russian troops on the Elbe (25 April 1945) 5·00 6·00

No. 3631 is inscribed "Monte Casino" in error. See also Nos. 3641/60 and 3942/61.

500 R.A.A.F. Bristol Type 156 Beaufighter, Battle of the Bismarck Sea (2-4 March 1943)

1993. 50th Anniv of Second World War (2nd issue). Multicoloured.

3641 $50 Type **500** 80 80
3642 $50 Lockheed P-38 Lightning attacking Admiral Yamamoto's plane, Bougainville (7 April 1943) 80 80
3643 $50 Consolidated B-24 Liberator bombers, Tarawa (17-19 September 1943) 80 80
3644 $50 North American B-25 Mitchell bomber, Rabaul (12 October 1943) 80 80
3645 $50 U.S. Navy aircraft attacking Makin (19 November 1943) 80 80
3646 $50 U.S.A.A.F. bombers on first daylight raid over Germany (27 January 1943) 80 80
3647 $50 R.A.F. De Havilland D.H.98 Mosquito bombers on first daylight raid over Berlin (30 January 1943) 80 80
3648 $50 Allied aircraft over Hamburg (24-30 July 1943) 80 80
3649 $50 Consolidated B-24 Liberators bombing Ploesti oil refineries, Rumania (1 August 1943) 80 80
3650 $50 German nightfighter attacking Allied bombers over Berlin (18 November 1943) 80 80
3651 $50 Japanese aircraft carriers during Operation 1 (7 April 1943) 80 80
3652 $50 Lt. John F. Kennedy's motor torpedo boat U.S.S. "PT109" in Blackett Strait (1 August 1943) 80 80
3653 $50 U.S.S. "Enterprise" (aircraft carrier) 80 80
3654 $50 American battleships bombarding Rabaul (12 October 1943) 80 80
3655 $50 American landing craft at Cape Gloucester (26 December 1943) 80 80
3656 $50 Commissioning of U.S.S. "Bogue" (first anti-submarine escort carrier) (February 1943) 80 80
3657 $50 Grumman FM-2 Wildcat fighters from U.S.S. "Bogue" sinking "U-118" 80 80
3658 $50 U-boat launching torpedo during peak of Battle of the Atlantic (March 1943) 80 80
3659 $50 Surrender of Italian fleet at Malta (10 September 1943) 80 80
3660 $50 H.M.S. "Duke of York" (battleship) sinking "Scharnhorst" (26 December 1943) 80 80

501 Stuart Pearce (England)

1993. World Cup Football Championship, U.S.A. (1994) (1st issue). Multicoloured.

3661 $5 Type **501** 15 10
3662 $6.40 Ronald Koeman (Netherlands) 15 10
3663 $7.65 Gianluca Vialli (Italy) 20 10
3664 $12.80 McStay (Scotland) and Alemao (Brazil) 30 20
3665 $15.30 Ceulemans (Belgium) and Butcher (England) 30 20
3666 $50 Dragan Stojkovic (Yugoslavia) 75 65
3667 $100 Ruud Gullit (Netherlands) 1·25 1·25
3668 $130 Miloslav Kadlec (Czechoslovakia) 1·40 1·50
3669 $150 Ramos (Uruguay) and Berthold (Germany) 1·75 2·00
3670 $190 Baggio (Italy) and Wright (England) 2·25 2·50
3671 $200 Yarentchuck (Russia) and Renquin (Belgium) 2·40 2·75
3672 $225 Timofte (Rumania) and Aleinikov (Russia) 2·50 3·00
MS3673 Two sheets. (a) 101×73 mm. $325 Salvatore Schillaci (Italy) and Jose Pintos (Uruguay) (horiz). (b) 73×101 mm. $325 Rene Higuita (Colombia) Set of 2 sheets 9·00 9·50

See also Nos. 4142/58.

502 Sir Shridath Ramphal

1993. 1st Recipients of Order of the Caribbean Community. Multicoloured.

3674 $7.65 Type **502** 60 50
3675 $7.65 William Demas 60 50
3676 $7.65 Derek Walcott 1·00 65

1993. Christmas. Paintings by Rubens and Durer. As T 211b of Gambia. Each black, yellow and red (Nos. 3678, 3680/1, 3684) or multicoloured (others).

3677 $6.40 "The Holy Family under the Apple Tree" (detail) (Rubens) 15 10
3678 $7.65 "The Virgin in Glory" (detail) (Durer) 15 10
3679 $12.80 "The Holy Family under the Apple Tree" (different detail) (Rubens) 20 15
3680 $15.30 "The Virgin in Glory" (different detail) (Durer) 20 20
3681 $50 "The Virgin in Glory" (different detail) (Durer) 70 55
3682 $130 "The Holy Family under the Apple Tree" (different detail) (Rubens) 1·50 1·60
3683 $190 "The Holy Family under the Apple Tree" (different detail) (Rubens) 2·25 2·50
3684 $250 "The Virgin in Glory" (different detail) (Durer) 2·75 3·25
MS3685 Two sheets. (a) 126×101 mm. $325 "The Holy Family under the Apple Tree" (Rubens). (b) 101×126 mm. $325 "The Virgin in Glory" (woodcut by Durer from "The Life of the Virgin") Set of 2 sheets 7·00 8·50

1993. Bicentenary of the Louvre, Paris. As T 209b of Gambia. Multicoloured.

3686 $50 "Mona Lisa" (Leonardo da Vinci) 60 60
3686-3726 Set of 41 26·00 28·00
3687-3694 $50×8 "Self-portrait with Spectacles" (Chardin); "Infanta Maria Theresa" (Velazquez); "Spring" (Arcimboldo); "The Virgin of Sorrows" (Bouts); "The Student" (Fragonard); "Francois I" (Clouet); "Le Condottiere" (Antonello da Messina); "La Bohemienne" (Hals)
3695-3702 $50×8 "The Village Bride" (left detail) (Greuze); "The Village Bride" (centre detail); "The Village Bride" (right detail); "Self-portrait" (Melendez); "The Knight, the Girl and the Mountain" (Baldung-Grien); "The Young Beggar" (Murillo); "The Pilgrims of Emmaus" (left detail) (Le Nain); "The Pilgrims of Emmaus" (right detail)
3703-3710 $50×8 "Woman with a Flea" (detail) (Crespi); "The Woman with Dropsy" (detail) (Dou); "Portrait of a Couple" (Ittenbach); "Cleopatra" (Moreau); "Riches" (Vouet); "Old Man and Young Boy" (Ghirlandaio); "Louis XIV" (Rigaud); "The Drinker" (Pieter de Hooch)
3711-3718 $50×8 "Woman with a Flea" (Crespi); "Self-portrait at Easel" (Rembrandt); "Algerian Women" (detail) (Delacroix); "Head of a Young Man" (Raphael); "Venus and The Graces" (detail) (Botticelli); "Still Life with Chessboard" (detail) (Lubin Baugin); "Lady Macbeth" (Fussli); "The Smoke-filled Room" (detail) (Chardin)
3719-3726 $50×8 "The Virgin with the Rabbit" (Titian); "The Virgin with the Rabbit" (detail of head) (Titian); "The Beautiful Gardener" (detail) (Raphael); "The Lace-maker" (Vermeer); "Jeanne d'Aragon" (detail) (Raphael); "The Astronomer" (Vermeer); "The Rialto Bridge" (detail) (Canaletto); "Sigismond Malatesta" (Piero della Francesca)

MS3727 Six sheets, each 95×70 mm. (a) $325 "Mona Lisa" and details (Leonardo da Vinci) (84×56 mm). (b) $325 "The Coronation of Napoleon I" (David) (84×56 mm). (c) $325 "Farmyard" (Jan Brueghel the Younger) (84×56 mm). (d) $325 "The Marriage Feast at Cana" (Veronese) (84×56 mm). (e) $325 "The Fortune-teller" (Caravaggio) (84×56 mm). (f) $325 "The Rialto Bridge" (Canaletto) (84×56 mm) Set of 6 sheets 23·00 25·00

503 "Donald's Better Self", 1938

1993. Donald Duck Film Posters. Multicoloured.

3728-3735 $60×8 Type **503**; "Donald's Golf Game", 1938; "Sea Scouts", 1939; "Donald's Penguin", 1939; "A Good Time for a Dime", 1941; "Truant Officer Donald"; "Orphan's Benefit", 1941; "Chef Donald", 1941

3728-3781 Set of 56 45·00 50·00

3736-3743 $60×8 "The Village Smithy"; "Donald's Snow Fight"; "Donald's Garden"; "Donald's Gold Mine"; "The Vanishing Private"; "Sky Trooper"; "Bellboy Donald"; "The New Spirit", all 1942

3744-3751 $60×8 "Saludos Amigos", 1943; "The Eyes Have It", 1945; "Donald's Crime", 1945; "Straight Shooters", 1947; "Donald's Dilemma", 1947; "Bootle Beetle", 1947; "Daddy Duck", 1948; "Soup's On", 1948

3752-3759 $80×8 "Donald's Happy Birthday", 1949; "Sea Salts", 1949; "Honey Harvester", 1949; "All in a Nutshell", 1949; "The Greener Yard", 1949; "Slide, Donald, Slide", 1949; "Lion Around", 1950; "Trailer Horn", 1950

3760-3767 $80×8 "Bee at the Beach", 1950; "Out on a Limb", 1950; "Corn Chips", 1951; "Test Pilot Donald", 1951; "Lucky Number", 1951; "Out of Scale", 1951; "Bee on Guard", 1951; "Let's Stick Together", 1952

3768-3775 $80×8 "Trick or Treat", 1952; "Don's Fountain of Youth", 1953; "Rugged Bear", 1953; "Canvas Back Duck", 1953; "Dragon Around", 1954; "Grin and Bear It", 1954; "The Flying Squirrel", 1954; "Up a Tree", 1955

3776-3781 $80×8 Scenes from "Pirate Gold": In the crow's nest; Aracuan Bird carrying treasure chest; Donald with treasure map; Donald at souvenir stall; Aracuan Bird with Donald; Donald on jetty (all horiz)

MS3782 Five sheets, each 129×103 mm. (a) $500 Book cover of "The Wise Little Hen", 1934 (horiz). (b) $500 Sketch for "Timber", 1941. (c) $500 Fan-card for "The Three Caballeros", 1945 (horiz). (d) $500 Fan-card for "Melody Time", 1948. Imperf. (e) $500 Donald Duck Set of 5 sheets 27·00 29·00

504 Aladdin

1993. "Aladdin" (film). Disney Cartoon Characters. Multicoloured.

3783-3790 $7.65×8 Type **504**; Abu the monkey; Jasmine; Rajah the tiger; Jafar; Iago the parrot; The Sultan; The Genie

3783-3808 Set of 26 15·00 16·00

3791-3799 $50×9 Jafar and magic scarab; Tiger Head entrance, Cave of Wonders; Jafar; Aladdin and Abu at breakfast; Aladdin rescuing Jasmine; Aladdin, Jasmine and Abu; Rajah comforts Jasmine; Jafar disguised as an old man; Aladdin and Abu in treasure chamber (all horiz)

3800-3808 $65×9 Aladdin with lamp and magic carpet; The Genie measuring Aladdin; Abu turned into an elephant; Aladdin in disguise at palace; Aladdin and Jasmine on magic carpet; Aladdin in disguise, Jasmine and Sultan; Aladdin fighting Jafar; Aladdin and Jasmine; The Genie with suitcase and golf clubs (all horiz)

MS3809 Four sheets, each 127×102 mm. (a) $325 Aladdin, The Genie, Abu and magic carpet in Cave of Wonders (horiz). (b) $325 Aladdin in disguise on elephant. (c) $325 Aladdin and Jasmine on magic carpet (horiz). (d) $325 The Genie, The Sultan, Jasmine, Aladdin and Abu (horiz) Set of 4 sheets 18·00 19·00

505 President Dr. Cheddi Jagan

1993. 1st Anniv of Election of President Jagan.

3810 **505** $6.40 multicoloured 40 30

MS3811 97×69 mm. $325 "REBIRTH OF DEMOCRACY" emblem 3·50 4·00

1994. "Hong Kong '94" International Stamp Exhibition (1st issue). As T 222a of Gambia. Multicoloured.

3812 $50 Hong Kong 1984 Royal Hong Kong Jockey Club $1.30 stamp and Happy Valley Racecourse 80 90

3813 $50 Guyana 1992 Movie Posters $190 stamp and Happy Valley Racecourse 80 90

Nos. 3812/13 were printed together, se-tenant, with the centre part of each pair forming a composite design.

1994. "Hong Kong '94" International Stamp Exhibition (2nd issue). Ch'ing Dynasty Snuff Boxes (Nos. 3814/19) or Porcelain (Nos. 3820/5). As T 222b of Gambia. Multicoloured.

3814 $20 Painted enamel in shape of bamboo 35 40

3815 $20 Painted enamel showing woman 35 40

3816 $20 Amber with lions playing ball 35 40

3817 $20 Agate in shape of two gourds 35 40

3818 $20 Glass overlay with dog design 35 40

3819 $20 Glass with foliage design 35 40

3820 $20 Covered jar with dragon design 35 40

3821 $20 Rotating brush-holder 35 40

3822 $20 Covered jar with horses design 35 40

3823 $20 Amphora vase with bats and peaches 35 40

3824 $20 Tea caddy with Fo dogs 35 40

3825 $20 Vase with camellias and peaches design 35 40

1994. Centenary of the Sign for the Mahdi. Nos. 1622/4 and 1634 surch CENTENARY Sign For The MAHDI 1894-1994 and new value.

3826 $6 on 60c. Plate No. 73 (Series 1) (horiz)

3827 $20 on 200c. Plate No. 33 (Series 1) (horiz)

3828 $30 on 60c. Plate No. 57 (Series 1) (horiz)

3829 $35 on 60c. Plate No. 75 (Series 1) (horiz)

The surcharges on Nos. 3826 and 3828 show the third line as "MADHI".

1994. Hummel Figurines. As T 501a of Ghana. Multicoloured.

3830 $20 Girl holding inscribed heart 25 25

3831 $25 Boy with heart under arm 30 30

3832 $35 Baker 40 40

3833 $50 Girl with pot of flowers 60 55

3834 $60 Girl with trumpet, pot plant and bird 70 65

3835 $130 Four girls 1·50 1·50

3836 $190 Boy and two girls with dog 2·25 2·50

3837 $250 Boy with cake and dog 2·75 3·50

MS3838 Two sheets, each 92×124 mm. (a) $6 As No. 3835; $25 No. 3831; $30 As No. 3830; $190 No. 3836. (b) $20 As No. 3832; $35 As No. 3837; $60 No. 3834; $130 As No. 3833 Set of 2 sheets 6·00 6·50

1994. 75th Anniv of I.L.O. Nos. 1760 and 1629/30 surch I L O 75th Anniversary 1919-1994 and new value.

3839 $6 on 130c. Plate No. 13 (Series 1)

3840 $30 on 120c. Plate No. 58 (Series 1)

3841 $35 on 120c. Plate No. 56 (Series 1)

1994. Centenary (1992) of Sierra Club (environmental protection society). Endangered Species. As T 224a of Gambia. Multicoloured.

3842 $70 Red Kangaroo with young 90 90

3843 $70 Head of American alligator 90 90

3844 $70 Head of bald eagle 90 90

3845 $70 Giant panda eating bamboo 90 90

3846 $70 Head of red kangaroo 90 90

3847 $70 Alaskan brown bear sitting 90 90

3848 $70 Bald eagle 90 90

3849 $70 Head of giant panda 90 90

3850 $70 Red kangaroo (horiz) 90 90

3851 $70 Whooping crane facing left (horiz) 90 90

3852 $70 Male whooping crane in courtship display (horiz) 90 90

3853 $70 Whooping crane looking right (horiz) 90 90

3854 $70 Alaskan brown bear and cub (horiz) 90 90

3855 $70 Alaskan brown bear fishing (horiz) 90 90

3856 $70 Bald eagle on branch (horiz) 90 90

3857 $70 Giant panda (horiz) 90 90

3858 $70 American alligator (logo at left) (horiz) 90 90

3859 $70 American alligator (logo at right) (horiz) 90 90

3860 $70 Italian Alps at sunrise (horiz) 90 90

3861 $70 Italian Alps and meadow (horiz) 90 90

3862 $70 Mono Lake at sunset (horiz) 90 90

3863 $70 Rock pinnacles, Mono Lake (horiz) 90 90

3864 $70 Sea lion 90 90

3865 $70 Head of sea lion 90 90

3866 $70 Sea lions on rocks 90 90

3867 $70 Rock pinnacles, Mono Lake 90 90

3868 $70 Sierra Club Centennial emblem (black, brown and green) 90 90

3869 $70 Lake, Italian Alps 90 90

3870 $70 Summit of Matterhorn 90 90

3871 $70 Matterhorn and village 90 90

3872 $70 Clouds over Matterhorn 90 90

1994. Royal Visit. Nos. 3551/4 optd ROYAL VISIT FEB 19-22, 1994.

3873 $25 Queen Elizabeth II in Coronation robes (photograph by Cecil Beaton) 1·50 1·60

3874 $50 Royal gems 2·00 2·25

3875 $75 Queen Elizabeth and Prince Philip 2·25 2·50

3876 $130 Queen opening Parliament 2·50 2·75

MS3877 69×100 mm. $325 "Queen in Coronation Robes" (Sir James Gunn) (28½×42½ mm) 6·50 7·00

509 "Cestrum parqui"

1994. Flowers. Multicoloured.

3878 $6.40 Type **509** 15 10

3879 $7.65 "Brunfelsia calycina" 15 10

3880 $12.80 "Datura rosei" 20 15

3881 $15.30 "Ruellia macrantha" 20 20

3882 $50 "Portlandia albiflora" 50 55

3883 $50 "Clusia grandiflora" 50 55

3884 $50 "Begonia haageana" 50 55

3885 $50 "Fuchsia simplicicaulis" 50 55

3886 $50 "Guaiacum officinale" 50 55

3887 $50 "Pithecoctenium cynanchoides" 50 55

3888 $50 "Sphaeralcea umbellata" 50 55

3889 $50 "Erythrina poeppigiana" 50 55

3890 $50 "Steriphoma paradoxa" 50 55

3891 $50 "Allemanda violacea" 50 55

3892 $50 "Centropogon cornutus" 50 55

3893 $50 "Passiflora quadrangularis" 50 55

3894 $50 "Victoria amazonica" 50 55

3895 $50 "Cobaea scandens" 50 55

3896 $50 "Pyrostegia venusta" 50 55

3897 $50 "Petrea kohautiana" 50 55

3898 $50 "Hippobroma longiflora" 50 55

3899 $50 "Cleome hassleriana" 50 55

3900 $50 "Verbena peruviana" 50 55

3901 $50 "Tropaeolum peregrinum" 50 55

3902 $50 "Plumeria rubra" 50 55

3903 $50 "Selenicereus grandiflorus" 50 55

3904 $50 "Mandevilla splendens" 50 55

3905 $50 "Pereskia aculeata" 50 55

3906 $50 "Ipomoea learii" 50 55

3907 $130 "Pachystachys coccinea" 1·25 1·40

3908 $190 "Beloperone guttata" 1·90 2·25

3909 $250 "Ferdinandusa speciosa" 2·50 3·00

MS3910 Two sheets, each 99×70 mm. (a) $325 "Lophospermum erubescens". (b) $325 "Columnea fendleri" Set of 2 sheets 7·50 8·50

Nos. 3883/94 and 3895/3906 respectively were printed together, se-tenant, forming composite background designs.

1994. 25th Anniv of First Moon Landing (1st issue). As T 227a of Gambia. Multicoloured.

3911 $60 Walter Dornberger and launch of first A-4 rocket 90 90

3912 $60 Rudolph Nebel and "Surveyor 1" 90 90

3913 $60 Robert H. Goddard and "Apollo 7" 90 90

3914 $60 Kurt Debus and view of Earth from Moon ("Apollo 8") 90 90

3915 $60 James T. Webb and "Apollo 9" 90 90

3916 $60 George E. Mueller and "Apollo 10" lunar module 90 90

3917 $60 Wernher von Braun and launch of "Apollo 11" 90 90

3918 $60 Rocco A. Petrone and "Apollo 11" astronaut on Moon 90 90

3919 $60 Eberhard Rees and "Apollo 12" astronaut on Moon 90 90

3920 $60 Charles A. Berry and damaged "Apollo 13" 90 90

3921 $60 Thomas O. Paine and "Apollo 14" before splashdown 90 90

3922 $60 A. F. Staats and "Apollo 15" on Moon 90 90

3923 $60 Robert R. Gilruth and "Apollo 16" astronaut on Moon 90 90

3924 $60 Ernst Stuhlinger and "Apollo 17" crew on Moon 90 90

3925 $60 Christopher C. Kraft and X-30 National Aero-Space Plane 90 90

3926 $60 Rudolf Opitz and Messerschmitt Me 163B Komet (rocket engine), 1943 90 90

3927 $60 Clyde W. Tombaugh and "face" on Mars 90 90

3928 $60 Hermann Oberth and scene from "The Girl in the Moon" 90 90

MS3929 125×112 mm. $325 Frank J. Everest Jr and "Apollo 11" anniversary logo 4·50 5·00

See also Nos. 4169/87.

1994. Centenary of International Olympic Committee. Medal Winners. As T 227b of Gambia. Multicoloured.

3930 $20 Nancy Kerrigan (U.S.A.) (1994 figure skating silver) 30 30

3931 $35 Sawao Kato (Japan) (1976 gymnastics gold) 50 50

3932 $130 Florence Griffith Joyner (U.S.A.) (1988 100 and 200 metres gold) 1·75 2·00

MS3933 110×80 mm. $325 Mark Wasmeier (Germany) (1994 super giant slalom and giant slalom gold) 4·00 4·50

1994. Centenary of First English Cricket Tour to the West Indies (1995). As T 397a of Grenada. Multicoloured.

3934 $20 Clive Lloyd (Guyana and West Indies) (vert) 65 30

3935 $35 Carl Hooper (Guyana and West Indies) and Wisden Trophy 75 50

3936 $60 Graham Hick (England) and Wisden Trophy 1·40 1·50

MS3937 79×100 mm. $200 English team of 1895 (black and brown) 3·25 3·00

1994. 50th Anniv of D-Day. Aircraft. As T 227c of Gambia. Multicoloured.

3938 $6 Supermarine Spitfire Mk XI fighter on photo reconnaissance 40 15

3939 $35 North American B-25 Mitchell bomber 85 50

3940 $190 Republic P-47 Thunderbolt fighters 3·00 3·50

MS3941 109×79 mm. $325 Avro Type **683** Lancaster bomber of 419 Squadron 4·75 5·00

1994. 50th Anniv of Second World War (3rd issue). As T 500. Multicoloured.

3942 $60 Paratroops drop, D-Day 90 80

3943 $60 Glider assault, D-Day 90 80

3944	$60 U.S.S. "Arkansas" (battle-ship) bombarding Omaha Beach, D-Day	90	80
3945	$60 U.S. fighters attacking train	90	80
3946	$60 Allied landing craft approaching beaches	90	80
3947	$60 Troops in beach obstacles	90	80
3948	$60 Commandos leaving landing craft	90	80
3949	$60 U.S. flail tank destroying mines	90	80
3950	$60 U.S. tank breaking through sea wall	90	80
3951	$60 Tanks and infantry advancing	90	80
3952	$60 Landings at Anzio (22 January 1944)	90	80
3953	$60 R.A.F. attacking Amiens Prison (18 February 1944)	90	80
3954	$60 Soviet Army tank in Sevastopol (9 May 1944)	90	80
3955	$60 British bren-gun carriers at the Gustav Line (19 May 1944)	90	80
3956	$60 D-Day landings (6 June 1944)	90	80
3957	$60 "V-1" over London (13 June 1944)	90	80
3958	$60 Allies entering Paris (19 August 1944)	90	80
3959	$60 German "V-2" rocket ready for launch (8 September 1944)	90	80
3960	$60 Sinking of "Tirpitz" (German battleship) (12 November 1944)	90	80
3961	$60 U.S. tanks at Bastogne (29 December 1944)	90	80

1994. "Philakorea '94" International Stamp Exhibition, Seoul (1st issue). As T 227d of Gambia. Multicoloured.

3962	$6 Socialist ideals statue, Pyongyang (vert)	10	10
3963	$25 Statue of Admiral Yi Sun-sin (vert)	30	30
3964	$60 Fruits and mountain peaks	70	75
3965	$60 Manchurian crane, bamboo and peaks	70	75
3966	$60 Rising sun and two cranes on pine	70	75
3967	$60 Five cranes on pine and peak	70	75
3968	$60 Three cranes in flight	70	75
3969	$60 Sea, rocky shore and fungi	70	75
3970	$60 Sea, rocky shore and fruit	70	75
3971	$60 Hind at seashore and fruit	70	75
3972	$60 Stag in pine forest	70	75
3973	$60 Deer and fungi by waterfall	70	75
3974	$60 Tops of pines and mountain peaks	70	75
3975	$60 Manchurian crane in flight	70	75
3976	$60 Three cranes on pine tree	70	75
3977	$60 Crane on pine tree	70	75
3978	$60 Top of fruit tree	70	75
3979	$60 Stag and two hinds on mountainside	70	75
3980	$60 Deer and fungi	70	75
3981	$60 Stag by waterfall and hind drinking	70	75
3982	$60 Pine tree, fruit and fungi	70	75
3983	$60 Fungi on mountainside	70	75
3984	$120 Sokkat'ap Pagoda, Pulguksa	1·40	1·60
3985	$130 Village Guardian (statue), Chejudo Island	1·40	1·60
MS3986	Two sheets. (a) 104×73 mm. $325 Europeans at the Korean Court (early lithograph). (b) 73×104 mm. $325 Pagoda by Ch'urae-am Rock Set of 2 sheets	7·00	8·00

Nos. 3964/73 and 3974/83, all 23×49 mm, were printed together, se-tenant, in sheetlets of 10, each sheetlet forming a composite design showing panels from a screen painting of longevity symbols from the late Chosun dynasty.

See also Nos. 4117/41.

510 Miki Maya

1994. 80th Anniv of Takarazuka Revue of Japan. Multicoloured.

3987	$20 Type **510**	55	60
3988	$20 Fubuki Takane	55	60
3989	$20 Seika Kuze	55	60
3990	$20 Saki Asaji	55	60
3991	$60 Mira Anju (34×47 mm)	75	80
3992	$60 Yuki Amami (34×47 mm)	75	80
3993	$60 Maki Ichiro (34×47 mm)	75	80
3994	$60 Yu Shion (34×47 mm)	75	80

511 "Heliconius melpomene"

1994. Butterflies. Multicoloured.

3995	$6 Type **511**	20	20
3996	$20 "Helicopis cupido"	45	45
3997	$25 "Agrias claudina"	50	50
3998	$30 "Parides coelus"	60	60
3999	$50 "Heliconius hecale"	75	75
4000	$50 "Anaea marthesia"	75	75
4001	$50 "Brassolis astyra"	75	75
4002	$50 "Heliconius melpomene"	75	75
4003	$50 "Haetera piera"	75	75
4004	$50 "Morpho diana"	75	75
4005	$50 "Parides coelus"	75	75
4006	$50 "Catagramma pitheas"	75	75
4007	$50 "Nessaea obrinus"	75	75
4008	$50 "Automeris janus"	75	75
4009	$50 "Papilio torquatus"	75	75
4010	$50 "Eunica sophonisba"	75	75
4011	$50 "Ceratinia nise"	75	75
4012	$50 "Panacea procilla"	75	75
4013	$50 "Pyrrhogyra neaerea"	75	75
4014	$50 "Morpho deidamia"	75	75
4015	$50 "Dismorphia orise"	75	75
4016	$60 "Morpho diana"	85	85
4017	$190 "Dismorphia orise"	2·50	3·00
4018	$250 "Morpho deidamia"	3·00	3·50
MS4019	Four sheets. (a) 104×76 mm. $325 "Anaea eribotes". (b) 104×76 mm. $325 "Eunica sophonisba". (c) 110×80 mm. $325 "Hamadryas velutina" (39×30 mm). (d) 110×80 mm. $325 Agrias claudina (39×30 mm) Set of 4 sheets	14·00	16·00

512 Jacob

1994. Bible Stories (2nd series). Multicoloured. (a) Joseph.

4020-4116 Set of 97 — 28·00 29·00

4020-4043 $20×24 arranged as blocks of 4 depicting Jacob giving Joseph a coat of many colours (Type **512** at top left); Joseph thrown into a pit; Joseph sold as a slave; Joseph accused by Potiphar's wife; Joseph interprets Pharoah's dreams; Joseph reunited with his brothers

(b) The Parting of the Red Sea.

4044-4067 $20×24 Palm trees on shore; Pyramids; Palm trees on shore and black cloud; Three palm trees; Blue and white dove; Red and white bird; Egyptian army engulfed by sea; Yellow and white dove; Red and green fishes; Egyptian chariot with wall of water at left; Chariots between walls of water; Dolphins; Two doves; Israelites and water to left; Israelites and water to right; Turquoise and purple fishes; Israelites with tree at left; Iraelites with goats; Moses; Israelites with tree at right; Israelites with woman on horse; Israelites with old man and woman carrying pack; Israelites with woman carrying young child; Israelites with cart

(c) Ruth.

4068-4091 $20×24 arranged as blocks of 6 depicting Ruth and Naomi; Ruth gleaning in cornfield; Boaz establishing kinsman's rights; Naomi with Ruth, Boaz and Obed

(d) Daniel in the Lions' Den.

4092-4116 $20×25 Palm fronds and hibiscus flower; Magnificent frigate bird and palm fronds; Magnificent frigate birds and tops of stone pillars; Magnificent frigate bird, pillars and sail at bottom right; Hibiscus, sails of ship and top of pillar; Yellow arum lilies and palm trees; Heads of adult and immature magnificent frigate birds and palm trees; Palm trees, butterfly and stone pillars; Two butterflies and stone pillars; Stone pillar and sailing ship; Great egret (standing); Purple irises and palm trees; Daniel; Angel; Donkey foal; Orchids; Lioness and two cubs; Daniel's legs and lions; Lion; Three crowns; Goat and kid; Kid; Cub and head of lion; Lioness; Great egret in flight

Nos. 4020/43, 4044/67, 4068/91 and 4092/4116 respectively were printed together, se-tenant, forming composite designs.

513 Peregrine Falcon

1994. "Philakorea '94" International Stamp Exhibition, Seoul (2nd issue). Birds of the World. Multicoloured.

4117	$35 Type **513**	55	55
4118	$35 Great spotted woodpecker	55	55
4119	$35 White-throated kingfisher	55	55
4120	$35 Andean cock of the rock ("Peruvian Cock of the Rock")	55	55
4121	$35 Yellow-headed amazon	55	55
4122	$35 Victoria crowned pigeon	55	55
4123	$35 Little owl	55	55
4124	$35 Common pheasant ("Ring-necked Pheasant")	55	55
4125	$35 Eurasian goldfinch ("Goldfinch")	55	55
4126	$35 Jay	55	55
4127	$35 Keel-billed toucan ("Sulphur-breasted Toucan")	55	55
4128	$35 Blue and white flycatcher ("Japanese Blue Flycatcher")	55	55
4129	$35 Northern goshawk	55	55
4130	$35 Northern lapwing ("Lapwing")	55	55
4131	$35 Long-wattled umbrellabird ("Ornate Umbrellabird")	55	55
4132	$35 Slaty-headed parakeet	55	55
4133	$35 Regent bowerbird	55	55
4134	$35 Egyptian goose	55	55
4135	$35 White-winged crossbill	55	55
4136	$35 Bohemian waxwing ("Waxwing")	55	55
4137	$35 Ruff	55	55
4138	$35 Hoopoe	55	55
4139	$35 Superb starling	55	55
4140	$35 Great jacamar	55	55
MS4141	Two sheets, each 70×100 mm. (a) $325 American bald eagle. (b) $325 Gould's violetear Set of 2 sheets	11·00	11·00

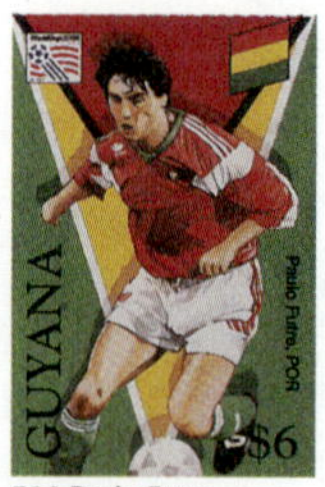

514 Paulo Futre (Portugal)

1994. World Cup Football Championship, U.S.A. (2nd issue). Multicoloured.

4142	$6 Type **514**	15	10
4143	$35 Lyndon Hooper (Canada)	50	40
4144	$60 Enzo Francescoli (Uruguay)	65	65
4145	$60 Paolo Maldini (Italy)	65	65
4146	$60 Guyana player	65	65
4147	$60 Bwalya Kalusha (Zambia)	65	65
4148	$60 Diego Maradona (Argentina)	65	65
4149	$60 Andreas Brehme (Germany)	65	65
4150	$60 Eric Wynalda (U.S.A.) (pursuing ball)	65	65
4151	$60 John Doyle (U.S.A.)	65	65
4152	$60 Eric Wynalda (U.S.A.) (kicking ball)	65	65
4153	$60 Thomas Dooley (U.S.A.)	65	65
4154	$60 Ernie Stewart (U.S.A.)	65	65
4155	$60 Marcelo Balboa (U.S.A.)	65	65
4156	$60 Bora Milutinovic (U.S.A. coach)	65	65
4157	$190 Freddy Rincon (Colombia)	1·90	3·00
MS4158	Two sheets. (a) 105×75 mm. $325 "94" symbol and player. (b) 75×105 mm. $325 Oiler Watson (U.S.A.) Set of 2 sheets	7·50	8·50

Nos. 4145/50 and 4151/6 respectively were printed together, se-tenant, forming composite background designs.

515 Anja Fichtel (individual foil, 1988)

1994. Olympic Games, Atlanta (1996) (1st issue). Previous German Gold Medal Winners. Mult.

4159	$6 Type **515**	15	10
4160	$25 Annegret Richter (100 m, 1976) (vert)	35	30
4161	$30 Heike Henkel (high jump, 1992) (vert)	40	35
4162	$35 Armin Hary (100 m, 1960) (vert)	40	40
4163	$50 Heide Rosendahl (long jump, 1972) (vert)	60	65
4164	$60 Josef Neckermann (dressage, 1968) (vert)	90	75
4165	$130 Heike Drechsler (long jump, 1988) (vert)	1·50	1·75
4166	$190 Ulrike Mayfarth (high jump, 1984) (vert)	2·50	2·75
4167	$250 Michael Gross (200 m freestyle and 100 m butterfly, 1984)	3·00	3·50
MS4168	Three sheets. (a) 105×75 mm. $135 Markus Wasmeier (skiing, 1994) (vert); $190 Katja Seizinger (skiing, 1994) (vert). (b) 105×75 mm. $325 Franziska van Almsick (swimming, 1992) (vert). (c) 75×105 mm. $325 Steffi Graf (tennis, 1988, 1992) (vert) Set of 3 sheets	11·00	11·00

See also Nos. 4492/4508 and 4739/88.

516 Dog Laika and Rocket, 1957

1994. 25th Anniv of First Moon Landing (2nd issue). Multicoloured.

4169	$60 Type **516**	90	80
4170	$60 Yuri Gagarin (first man in space), 1961	90	80
4171	$60 John Glenn (first American to orbit Earth), 1962	90	80
4172	$60 Edward White walking in space, 1965	90	80
4173	$60 Neil Armstrong, walking on Moon and "Apollo 11" logo	90	80
4174	$60 "Luna 16" leaving Moon, 1970	90	80
4175	$60 Lunar Module 1 on Moon, 1970	90	80
4176	$60 Skylab 1, 1973	90	80
4177	$60 Astronauts and Apollo–Soyuz link-up, 1975	90	80
4178	$60 "Mars 3"	90	80
4179	$60 "Mariner 10"	90	80
4180	$60 "Voyager"	90	80
4181	$60 "Pioneer"	90	80
4182	$60 "Giotto"	90	80
4183	$60 "Magellan"	90	80
4184	$60 "Galileo"	90	80
4185	$60 "Ulysses"	90	80
4186	$60 "Cassini"	90	80
MS4187	Two sheets, each 142×104 mm. (a) $325 "Apollo 11" astronauts. (b) $325 "Galileo" Set of 2 sheets	8·50	9·00

Nos. 4178/86 were printed together, se-tenant, with the backgrounds forming a composite design of Space.

517 South Caroline Railroad "Best Friend of Charleston", 1830, U.S.A.

1994. History of Trains. Steam Locomotives. Multicoloured.

4188 $25 Type **517** 40 40
4189 $25 South Eastern Railway No. 285, 1882 40 40
4190 $30 Camden Amboy Railway No. 1 "John Bull", 1831, U.S.A. 45 45
4191 $30 Stephenson "Patentee" type locomotive, 1837 45 45
4192 $30 "Atlantic", 1832 45 45
4193 $30 "Stourbridge Lion", 1829, U.S.A. 45 45
4194 $30 Polonceau locomotive, 1854 45 45
4195 $30 "Thomas Rogers", 1855, U.S.A. 45 45
4196 $30 "Vulcan", 1858 45 45
4197 $30 "Namur", 1846 45 45
4198 $30 John Jarvis's "De Witt Clinton", 1831, U.S.A. 45 45
4199 $30 Seguin locomotive, 1829 45 45
4200 $30 Stephenson's "Planet", 1830 45 45
4201 $30 Norris locomotive, 1840 45 45
4202 $30 "Sampson", 1867, U.S.A. 45 45
4203 $30 "Andrew Jackson", 1832 45 45
4204 $30 "Herald", 1831 45 45
4205 $30 "Cumberland", 1845, U.S.A. 45 45
4206 $30 Pennsylvania Railroad Class K, 1880 45 45
4207 $30 Cooke locomotive No. 11, 1885 45 45
4208 $30 "John B. Turner", 1867, U.S.A. 45 45
4209 $30 Baldwin locomotive, 1871 45 45
4210 $30 Richard Trevithick's locomotive, 1803 45 45
4211 $30 John Stephens's locomotive, 1825 45 45
4212 $30 John Blenkinsop's locomotive, 1814 45 45
4213 $30 "Pennsylvania," 1803 45 45
4214 $300 Mount Washington Cog Railway locomotive No. 6, 1886 3·25 3·50
4215 $300 Stroudley locomotive "Brighton", 1872 3·25 3·50
MS4216 Two sheets, each 100×70 mm. (a) $250 Est Railway locomotive, 1878. (b) $300 "Claud Hamilton", 1900 Set of 2 sheets 7·50 8·00

No. 4198 is inscribed "West Point Foundry 1832 Locomotive" and No. 4202 "Union Iron Works os San Francisco", both error.

1994. Christmas. Religious Paintings. As T 231a of Gambia. Multicoloured.

4217 $6 "Joseph with the Christ Child" (Guido Reni) 15 10
4218 $20 "Adoration of the Christ Child" (Girolamo Romanino) 30 25
4219 $25 "Adoration of the Christ Child with St. Barbara and St. Martin" (Raffaello Botticini) 35 30
4220 $30 "Holy Family" (Pompeo Batoni) 40 35
4221 $35 "Flight into Egypt" (Bartolommeo Carducci) 45 40
4222 $60 "Holy Family and the Baptist" (Andrea del Sarto) 80 70
4223 $120 "Sacred Conversation" (Cesare de Sesto) 2·00 2·25
4224 $190 "Madonna and Child with Saints Joseph and John the Baptist" (Pontormo) 2·75 3·50
MS4225 Two sheets. (a) 112×93 mm. $325 "Presentation of Christ in the Temple" (Fra Bartolommeo). (b) 85×95 mm. $325 "Holy Family and St. Elizabeth and St. John the Baptist" (Francisco Primaticcio) Set of 2 sheets 7·50 8·00

518 Riker and Dr. Crusher

1994. "Star Trek Generations" (film). Designs showing "Enterprise" crew in 19th-century naval uniforms (Nos. 4226/34) or in 23rd-century (Nos. 4235/43). Multicoloured.

4226 $100 Type **518** 1·75 1·50
4227 $100 Geordi, Dr. Crusher with Lt. Worf in chains 1·75 1·50
4228 $100 Captain Picard 1·75 1·50
4229 $100 Data and Geordi 1·75 1·50
4230 $100 "U.S.S. Enterprise" (sailing ship) 1·75 1·50
4231 $100 Captain Picard and Riker on quarterdeck 1·75 1·50
4232 $100 Data 1·75 1·50
4233 $100 Lt. Worf 1·75 1·50
4234 $100 Dr. Crusher 1·75 1·50
4235 $100 Captain Picard 1·75 1·50
4236 $100 Riker 1·75 1·50
4237 $100 Captain Kirk 1·75 1·50
4238 $100 Soron with phaser 1·75 1·50
4239 $100 Captains Kirk and Picard on horseback 1·75 1·50
4240 $100 Klingon women 1·75 1·50
4241 $100 Captains Kirk and Picard 1·75 1·50
4242 $100 Troi 1·75 1·50
4243 $100 Captain Picard and Data 1·75 1·50
4244 $100 "BOLDLY GO" film poster 1·75 1·50
MS4245 86×103 mm. $500 U.S.S. "Enterprise" from film poster (horiz) 6·00 6·50

519 Cross and Map of Guyana

1994. Centenary of Sisters of Mercy in Guyana.

4246 **519** $60 multicoloured 1·00 80

1994. 1st Recipients of Order of the Caribbean Community. As T 393a of Grenada. Mult.

4247 $60 Sir Shridath Ramphal 65 75
4248 $60 William Demas 65 75
4249 $60 Derek Walcott 1·60 75

520 Garfield Sobers congratulating Brian Lara

1995. Brian Lara's Achievements in Cricket. Multicoloured.

4250 $20 Type **520** 35 25
4251 $30 Brian Lara setting world record for highest Test Match score (vert) 45 35
4252 $375 Lara and Chanderpaul 4·25 4·75
MS4253 70×100 mm. $300 Brian Lara (vert) 3·25 3·50

521 Babe Ruth

1995. Birth Centenary of Babe Ruth (baseball player). Each brown and black.

4254 $65 Type **521** 70 80
4255 $65 Preparing to bat (full-length photo) 70 80
4256 $65 Head and shoulders portrait (cap with limp brim) 70 80
4257 $65 In retirement (bare-headed) 70 80
4258 $65 Running (in plain shirt) 70 80
4259 $65 Head and shoulders portrait (cap with emblem and stiff brim) 70 80
4260 $65 Wearing "NEW YORK" shirt 70 80
4261 $65 Preparing to hit (in "NEW YORK" shirt) 70 80
4262 $65 Wearing "YANKEES" shirt 70 80
4263 $65 At base with bat on shoulder (in striped shirt) 70 80
4264 $65 Watching the ball (in striped shirt) 70 80
4265 $65 In cap and coat at Old Timer's Day, Yankee Stadium, 1948 70 80
MS4266 89×118 mm. $500 Babe Ruth (horiz) 5·00 5·25

522 Mickey Mouse as Family Doctor

1995. Disney Characters at Work. Multicoloured.

4267-4317 Set of 51 22·00 24·00

4267-4275 $30×9 Type **522**; Goofy and optometrist; Daisy Duck as nurse; Scrooge McDuck as psychiatrist; Daisy Duck as physiotherapist; Horace Horsecollar and dentist; Goofy and radiologist; Goofy as pharmacist; Big Pete as chiropractor

4276-4284 $30×9 Mickey Mouse as vet; Donald Duck training seals; Ludwig von Duck as animal psychiatrist; Goofy as ornithologist; Daisy Duck grooming Old English sheepdog; Minnie Mouse as herpetologist; Mickey Mouse as pet shop keeper with Pluto; J. Audubon Woodlore as park ranger; Donald Duck as aquarist

4285-4293 $30×9 Mickey Mouse as animator with Pluto; Goofy the tailor with Mickey Mouse; Pete the glassblower with Morty; Minnie Mouse painting Clarabelle; Daisy Duck sculpting Donald; Donald Duck as potter; Chip and Dale the watchmakers; Donald Duck the locksmith; Grandma Duck making quilt

4294-4301 $35×8 Mickey Mouse as policeman; Donald Duck as fireman; Uncle Scrooge as ambulance driver; Grandma Duck as crossing patrol; Daisy Duck as museum attendant and Donald as visitor; Goofy as census taker and family of rabbits; Horace Horsecollar and Big Pete as street maintenance workers; Donald Duck as sanitation worker at recycling bin (all vert)

4302-4309 $35×8 Mickey Mouse with Pluto driving lorry; Mickey Mouse as carpenter sawing; Goofy riding road drill; Minnie Mouse with electric drill; Donald Duck driving forklift; Minnie Mouse and Goofy as construction contractors; Mickey Mouse with Pluto as carpenter making table; Pluto driving bulldozer (all vert)

4310-4317 $35×8 Mickey Mouse as plumber; Mickey Mouse the paperboy; Huey, Dewey and Louie moving furniture; Big Pete as handyman; Donald Duck and nephews house painting; Goofy as washing machine repairman; Minnie Mouse as babysitter; Daisy Duck as carer (all vert)

MS4318 Six sheets. (a) 132×107 mm. $200 Goofy as surgeon. (b) 107×129 mm. $200 Goofy the zookeeper. (c) 132×107 mm. $200 Ferdie riding Pluto for photographer (vert). (d) 107×129 mm. $200 Horace Horsecollar campaigning for mayor. (e) 132×107 mm. $200 Minnie Mouse as carpenter and puppies. (f) 107×129 mm. $200 Minnie Mouse as maid Set of 6 sheets 25·00 25·00

No. 4271 is inscribed "PHYSICAL THEREPIST" in error.

1995. Centenary of Salvation Army. Nos. 1519 and 1521/3 surch SALVATION ARMY 1895 – 1995 and new value.

4319 $6 on 60c. Plate No. 10 (Series 1)
4320 $20 on 60c. Plate No. 19 (Series 1)
4321 $30 on 60c. Plate No. 2 (Series 1)
4322 $35 on 60c. Plate No. 31 (Series 1)

524 Pig

1995. Chinese New Year ("Year of the Pig"). Symbolic pigs. Multicoloured.

4323 $20 Type **524** 60 55
4324 $30 Pig facing left 65 60
4325 $50 Pig facing front (face value bottom right) 80 80
4326 $100 Pig facing front (face value bottom left) 1·25 1·40
MS4327 67×89 mm. $50×4 As Nos. 4323/6 3·25 3·25
MS4328 104×76 mm. $150 Pig's head 2·25 2·50

525 Northern Goshawk ("Goshawk")

1995. Birds. Multicoloured.

4329 $5 Type **525** 15 10
4330 $6 Northern lapwing ("Lapwing") 15 10
4331 $8 Long-wattled umbrellabird ("Ornate Umbrellabird") 20 10
4332 $15 Slaty-headed parakeet 30 15
4333 $19 Regent bowerbird 35 15
4334 $20 Egyptian goose 35 15
4335 $25 White-winged crossbill 40 20
4336 $30 Bohemian waxwing ("Waxwing") 45 25
4337 $35 Ruff 45 25
4338 $60 Hoopoe 80 40
4339 $100 Superb starling 1·00 1·10
4340 $500 Great jacamar 4·50 5·00

526 Norwegian Forest Cat

1995. "Singapore '95" International Stamp Exhibition. Multicoloured.

4341-4376 Set of 35 16·00 18·00

4341-4352 $35×12 Cats (Type **526**; Scottish fold; Red Burmese; British blue-hair; Abyssinian; Siamese; Exotic shorthair; Turkish van cat; Black Persian; Black-tipped burmilla; Singapura; Calico shorthair)

4353-4364 $35×12 Dogs (Gordon setter; Long-haired chihuahua; Dalmatian; Afghan hound; Old English bulldog; Miniature schnauzer; Clumber spaniel; Pekingese; St. Bernard; English cocker spaniel; Alaskan malamute; Rottweiler)

4365-4376 $35×12 Horses (chestnut thoroughbred colt; liver chestnut quarter horse; black Friesian; chestnut Belgian; Appaloosa; Lippizaner; chestnut hunter; British shire; Palomino; pinto ("Seal Brown Point"); Arab; Afghanistan kabardin)

MS4377 Three sheets, each 87×71 mm. (a) $300 Maine coon. (b) $300 Golden retriever. (c) $300 American anglo-arab Set of 3 sheets 9·00 9·50

No. 4355 is inscribed "Dalmation", No. 4367 "Freisian" and No. 4370 "Lipizzanas", all in error.

527 Captain John Smith leaving for New World, 1607

1995. "Pocahontas". Characters and scenes from Disney cartoon film. Multicoloured. (a) Vert designs showing characters.

4378-4412 Set of 35 30·00 32·00

4378-4385 $50×8 Pocahontas and Meeko; John Smith; Chief Powhatan; Kocoum; Ratcliffe; Wiggins; Nakoma; Thomas

(b) Horiz designs showing film scenes.

4386-4394 $8×9 Type **527**; Ratcliffe; Chief Powhatan greeted by his people; Pocahontas standing on cliff; Pocahontas, Nakoma and Meeko in canoe; Powhatan asking Pocahontas to marry Kocoum; Pocahontas receiving her mother's necklace; Pocahontas seeking guidance from Grandmother Willow; Pocahontas watching arrival of "Susan Constant"

4395-4403 $30×9 Ratcliffe claiming land for English Crown; Kekata having vision; Meeting of John Smith and Pocahontas; Namantack watching settlers; Powhatan and wounded Namantack; Pocahontas showing John Smith the colours of the wind; Nakoma finds Pocahontas with John Smith; Pocahontas offering John "Indian gold" (corn); Pocahontas, John Smith and Grandmother Willow

4404-4412 $35×9 Kocoum telling Pocahontas about the war council; Nakoma trying Kocoum to find Pocahontas; John Smith and Kocoum wrestling over knife; Powhatan sentencing John to death; Pocahontas and Grandmother Willow; Pocahontas saving John Smith; Ratcliffe under arrest; Powhatan draping his cloak over wounded John Smith; Pocahontas and John Smith saying goodbye

MS4413 Four sheets. (a) 98×120 mm. $300 Meeko. (b) 132×107 mm. $325 Pocahontas hiding. (c) 132×107 mm. $325 Powhatan and Pocahontas. (d) 132×107 mm. $325 Pocahontas kneeling (vert) Set of 4 sheets 26·00 27·00

1995. 95th Birthday of Queen Elizabeth the Queen Mother. As T 239a of Gambia.

4414 $100 brown, light brown and black 1·50 1·50
4415 $100 multicoloured 1·50 1·50
4416 $100 multicoloured 1·50 1·50
4417 $100 multicoloured 1·50 1·50
MS4418 – 101×126 mm. $325 multicoloured 4·25 4·50

DESIGNS: No. 4414, Queen Elizabeth the Queen Mother (pastel drawing); 4415, Wearing purple hat; 4416, Wearing turquoise hat; 4417, At desk (oil painting); **MS**4418, Wearing blue dress and mink stole.

528 Paul Harris (founder) and Rotary Emblem

1995. 90th Anniv of Rotary International. Multicoloured.

4419 **528** $200 multicoloured 2·00 2·50
MS4420 104×74 mm. $300 Rotary emblems 3·00 3·50

529 Girl carrying Sack on Head

1995. 50th Anniv of F.A.O. Multicoloured.

4421 $35 Type **529** 50 65
4422 $60 Man and woman carrying sacks of food aid 80 95
4423 $200 Woman holding sack 2·00 2·40
MS4424 104×74 mm. $300 Bowl of food and F.A.O. emblem 3·00 3·50

Nos. 4421/3 were printed together, se-tenant, forming a composite design.

530 Scouts around Campfire

1995. 18th World Scout Jamboree, Netherlands. Multicoloured.

4425 $20 Type **530** 35 25
4426 $25 Scout on beach 40 30
4427 $30 Scouts hiking 45 35
4428 $35 Scout snorkelling 50 40
4429 $60 Scout saluting and flag of Guyana 90 65
4430 $200 Scout fishing from boat 2·00 2·50
MS4431 Two sheets, each 100×70 mm. (a) $300 Scout putting up tent. (b) Scout canoeing Set of 2 sheets 6·50 7·00

1995. 50th Anniv of End of World War II in Europe. As T 237a of Gambia. Multicoloured.

4432 $60 American tank during Battle of the Bulge 85 90
4433 $60 Allied tanks crossing Siegfried Line 85 90
4434 $60 Liberated concentration camp prisoners 85 90
4435 $60 Allied plane dropping food to Dutch 85 90
4436 $60 U.S. infantry patrol, North Italy 85 90
4437 $60 "Daily Mail" headline announcing Hitler's death 85 90
4438 $60 Soviet tanks entering Berlin 85 90
4439 $60 Surrender of "U858" in U.S. waters 85 90
MS4440 105×74 mm. $300 Soviet troops raising flag on Brandenburg Gate (56×42 mm) 3·00 3·25

No. 4433 is incorrectly inscribed "SIGFRIED LINE".

1995. 50th Anniv of End of Second World War in the Pacific. As T 239b of Gambia. Multicoloured.

4441 $60 P61 Black Widow 75 75
4442 $60 PT boat 75 75
4443 $60 Martin B-26 Marauder bomber 75 75
4444 $60 U.S.S. "San Juan" (cruiser) 75 75
4445 $60 "Gato" class submarine 75 75
4446 $60 Destroyer 75 75
MS4447 107×77 mm. $300 Cruiser and aircraft carrier 3·00 3·25

531 Thanksgiving (U.S.A.)

1995. Holidays of the World. Multicoloured.

4448 $60 Type **531** 85 90
4449 $60 Christmas (Germany) 85 90
4450 $60 Hanukkah (Israel) 85 90
4451 $60 Easter (Spain) 85 90
4452 $60 Carnivale (Brazil) 85 90
4453 $60 Bastille Day (France) 85 90
4454 $60 Independence Day (India) 85 90
4455 $60 St. Patrick's Day (Ireland) 85 90
MS4456 105×76 mm. $300 Chinese New Year (China) 3·00 3·25

532 Map of the Americas and U.N. Soldier

1995. 50th Anniv of United Nations. Multicoloured.

4457 $35 Type **532** 55 50
4458 $60 Map of Africa and Western Asia 85 75
4459 $200 Map of Eastern Asia and Australasia with refugees 2·50 3·00
MS4460 74×104 mm. $300 Secretary-General Boutros Boutros Ghali 3·00 3·50

Nos. 4457/9 were printed together, se-tenant, forming a composite design.

533 Four-eyed Butterflyfish

1995. Marine Life. Multicoloured.

4461 $30 Type **533** 70 75
4462 $30 Lemon shark 70 75
4463 $35 Blue-headed wrasse 70 75
4464 $35 Green turtle 70 75
4465 $60 Three-spotted damselfish 70 75
4466 $60 Sawfish 70 75
4467 $60 Sei whales 70 75
4468 $60 Great barracuda 70 75
4469 $60 Mutton snapper 70 75
4470 $60 Hawksbill turtle 70 75
4471 $60 Spanish hogfish 70 75
4472 $60 Queen angelfish 70 75
4473 $60 Porkfish 70 75
4474 $60 Trumpetfish 70 75
4475 $60 Lesser electric ray 70 75
4476 $60 Tiger shark 70 75
4477 $60 Needlefish 70 75
4478 $60 Horse-eyed jack 70 75
4479 $60 Princess parrotfish 70 75
4480 $60 Yellow-tailed snapper 70 75
4481 $60 Spotted snake eel 70 75
4482 $60 Buffalo trunkfish 70 75
4483 $60 Cherubfish angelfish 70 75
4484 $60 French angelfish 70 75
4485 $80 Cocoa damselfish (vert) 90 1·00
4486 $80 Sergeant major (vert) 90 1·00
4487 $80 Beaugregory (vert) 90 1·00
4488 $80 Yellow-tailed damselfish (vert) 90 1·00
4489 $200 Fin-spot wrasse 2·25 2·40
4490 $200 Stingray 2·25 2·40
MS4491 Two sheets, each 100×70 mm. (a) $300 Great white shark. (b) $300 Leatherback turtle Set of 2 sheets 11·00 11·00

Nos. 4461, 4463, 4465 and 4489; Nos. 4462, 4464, 4466 and 4490; Nos. 4467/75; Nos. 4476/84 and Nos. 4485/8 respectively were printed together, se-tenant, the backgrounds forming composite designs.

534 Pole Vaulting

1995. Olympic Games, Atlanta (1996) (2nd issue). Multicoloured.

4492 $60 Type **534** 90 85
4493 $60 Long jumping 90 85
4494 $60 Woman with relay baton 90 85
4495 $60 Wrestling 90 85
4496 $60 Discus (side view) 90 85
4497 $60 Basketball 90 85
4498 $60 Boxing 90 85
4499 $60 Weightlifting 90 85
4500 $60 Shot put 90 85
4501 $60 Man in relay race 90 85
4502 $60 Female gymnast on beam 90 85
4503 $60 Cycling 90 85
4504 $60 Synchronized swimming 90 85
4505 $60 Hurdling 90 85
4506 $60 Male gymnast on pommel horse 90 85
4507 $60 Discus (front view) 90 85
MS4508 Two sheets. (a) 105×75 mm. $300 Athletes at start of race. (b) 75×105 mm. $300 Long jumping Set of 2 sheets 6·50 7·00

Nos. 4492/9 and 4500/7 respectively were printed together, se-tenant, the backgrounds forming composite designs.

535 Sand Martin

1995. Wildlife. Multicoloured.

4509 $20 Type **535** 70 70
4510 $35 House martin 70 70
4511 $60 Northern hobby ("Hobby") 75 75
4512 $60 Olive colobus 90 90
4513 $60 Violet-backed starling 90 90
4514 $60 Diana monkey 90 90
4515 $60 African palm civet 90 90
4516 $60 Giraffe and zebras 90 90
4517 $60 African linsang 90 90
4518 $60 Royal antelope 90 90
4519 $60 Duikers 90 90
4520 $60 Palm squirrel 90 90
4521 $200 Long-tailed skua 1·40 1·40
MS4522 Two sheets, each 110×80 mm. (a) $300 Brush pig and giant forest hog. (b) $300 Chimpanzee Set of 2 sheets 6·50 7·00

Nos. 4509/11 and 4521; and 4512/20 respectively were printed together, se-tenant, forming composite background designs.

536 Queenstown Jama Masjid

1995. Centenary of Queenstown Jama Masjid (mosque), Georgetown.

4523 **536** $60 multicoloured 75 60

537 Woman Soldier with Sub-machine Gun

1995. 30th Anniv of Guyana Defence Force. Multicoloured.

4524 $6 Type **537** 15 10
4525 $60 Soldier with rifle 85 70

538 Bank Logo and Headquarters

1995. 25th Anniv of Caribbean Development Bank.

4526 **538** $60 multicoloured 70 60

1995. Christmas. Religious Paintings. As T 245a of Gambia. Multicoloured.

4527 $25 "Angel of the Annunciation" (Carracci) 50 30
4528 $30 "Virgin of the Annunciation" (Carracci) 55 35
4529 $35 "Assumption of the Madonna" (Carracci) 60 40
4530 $60 "Baptism of Christ" (Carracci) 90 70
4531 $100 "Madonna and Child with Saints" (detail) (Carracci) 1·60 1·75
4532 $300 "Birth of the Virgin" (Carracci) 3·75 5·00
MS4533 Two sheets, each 101×127 mm. (a) $325 "Madonna and Child enthroned with Ten Saints" (Rosso Fiorentino). (b) $325 "Mystic Marriage of St. Catherine" (Carracci) Set of 2 sheets 7·00 8·00

539 John Lennon

1995. 15th Death Anniv of John Lennon (musician).
4534 **539** $35 multicoloured 1·00 80

540 Albrecht Kossel (1910 Medicine)

1995. Centenary of Nobel Trust Fund. Multicoloured.
4535-4588 Set of 54 38·00 40·00

4535-4543 $35×9 Type **540**; Arthur H. Compton (1927 Physics); N. M. Butler (1931 Peace); Charles Laveran (1907 Medicine); George R. Minot (1934 Medicine); Henry H. Dale (1936 Medicine); Jacques Monod (1965 Medicine); Alfred Hershey (1969 Medicine); Par Lagerkvist (1951 Literature)

4544-4552 $35×9 Norman F. Ramsey (1989 Physics); Chen Ning Yang (1957 Physics); Earl W. Sutherland Jr. (1971 Medicine); Paul Karrer (1937 Chemistry); Harmut Michel (1988 Chemistry); Richard Kuhn (1938 Chemistry); P. A. M. Dirac (1933 Physics); Victor Grignard (1912 Chemistry); Richard Willstatter (1915 Chemistry)

4553-4561 $35×9 Adolf von Baeyer (1905 Chemistry); Hideki Yukawa (1949 Physics); George W. Beadle (1958 Medicine); Edwin M. McMillan (1951 Chemistry); Samuel C. C. Ting (1976 Physics); Saint-John Perse (1960 Literature); John F. Enders (1954 Medicine); Felix Bloch (1952 Physics); P. B. Medawar (1960 Medicine)

4562-4570 $35×9 Nikolai Basov (1964 Physics); Klas Arnoldson (1908 Peace); Rene Sully-Prudhomme (1901 Literature); Robert W. Wilson (1978 Physics); Hugo Theorell (1955 Medicine); Nelly Sachs (1966 Literature); Hans von Euler-Chelpin (1929 Chemistry); Mairead Corrigan (1976 Peace); Willis E. Lamb Jr. (1955 Physics)

4571-4579 $35×9 Francis Crick (1962 Medicine); Manne Siegbahn (1924 Physics); Eisaku Sato (1974 Peace); Robert Koch (1905 Medicine); Edgar D. Adrian (1932 Medicine); Erwin Neher (1991 Medicine); Henry Taube (1983 Chemistry); Norman Angell (1933 Peace); Robert Robinson (1947 Chemistry)

4580-4588 $35×9 Henri Becquerel (1903 Physics); Igor Tamm (1958 Physics); Georges Kohler (1984 Medicine); Gerhard Domagk (1939 Medicine); Yasunari Kawabata (1968 Literature); Maurice Allais (1988 Economic Sciences); Aristide Briand (1926 Peace); Pavel Cherenkov (1958 Physics); Feodor Lynen (1964 Medicine)

MS4589 Six sheets, each 106×76 mm. (a) $300 Lech Walesa (1983 Peace). (b) $300 Heinrich Böll (1972 Literature). (c) $300 Henry A. Kissinger (1973 Peace). (d) $300 Kenichi Fukui (1981 Chemistry). (e) $300 Yasunari Kawabata (1968 Literature). (f) $300 Le Duc Tho (1973 Peace) Set of 6 sheets 23·00 24·00

Nos. 4535/43, 4544/52, 4553/61, 4562/70, 4571/9 and 4580/8 respectively were printed together, se-tenant, with the backgrounds forming composite designs.

541 David Copperfield

1995. David Copperfield (magician). Multicoloured.
4590 $60 Type **541** 70 75
4591 $60 David Copperfield in cloak and top hat 70 75
4592 $60 With flaming torch 70 75
4593 $60 David Copperfield in close up 70 75
4594 $60 Head of Statue of Liberty 70 75
4595 $60 David Copperfield climbing rope 70 75
4596 $60 With handcuffs 70 75
4597 $60 With woman dancer 70 75
4598 $60 David Copperfield wearing white shirt 70 75
MS4599 76×106 mm. $300 David Copperfield with rose 3·00 3·50

Nos. 4590/8 were printed together, se-tenant, forming a composite background design.

542 Marilyn Monroe

1995. 70th Birth Anniv of Marilyn Monroe (entertainer). Multicoloured.
4600 $60 Type **542** 65 65
4601 $60 Marilyn Monroe with circular earrings 65 65
4602 $60 Marilyn Monroe (red top right corner) 65 65
4603 $60 Marilyn Monroe (signature at bottom right) 65 65
4604 $60 With hair over left eye 65 65
4605 $60 With pink satin at left 65 65
4606 $60 With arm raised 65 65
4607 $60 With pink satin at bottom right 65 65
4608 $60 With square earring 65 65
MS4609 76×105 mm. $300 Marilyn Monroe in pink satin dress (horiz) 3·00 3·25

Nos. 4600/8 were printed together, se-tenant, with the background forming a composite design.

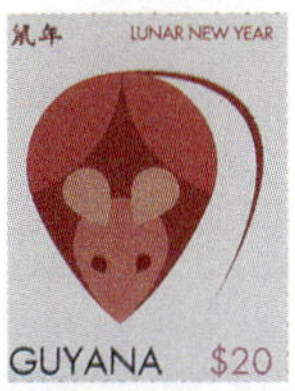

543 Rat

1995. Chinese New Year ("Year of the Rat").
4610 **543** $20 multicoloured 25 20
4611 - $30 multicoloured (face value bottom left) 35 30
4612 - $50 multicoloured (face value top right) 65 50
4613 - $100 multicoloured (face value top left) 1·10 1·25
MS4614 68×92 mm. $50×4 As Nos. 4610/13 2·10 2·00
MS4615 106×76 mm. $150 multicoloured 2·00 2·25

DESIGNS: $30 to $150 Symbolic rats.

544 City Children

1996. 50th Anniv of UNICEF. Sheet 110×87 mm, containing T **544** and similar horiz designs. Multicoloured.
MS4616 $1100 Type **544**; $1100 Youth worker and children (face value at top right); $1100 City children (face value at bottom right; $1100 Youth worker and children (face value at bottom right) 45·00 45·00

1996. Paintings by Rubens. As T 421 of Grenada. Multicoloured.
4617 $6 "The Garden of Love" (detail) 15 10
4618 $10 "Two Sleeping Children" 20 10
4619 $20 "All Saints Day" 35 20
4620 $25 "Sacrifice of Abraham" 35 25
4621 $30 "The Last Supper" 40 30
4622 $35 "The Birth of Henry of Navarre" 45 30
4623 $40 Study of standing female saint 50 35
4624 $50 "The Garden of Love" (different detail) 60 45
4625 $60 "The Garden of Love" (different detail) 70 50
4626 $200 "The Martyrdom of St. Livinus" 2·00 2·25
4627 $200 "St. Francis of Paola" 2·00 2·25
4628 $300 "The Union of Maria de Medici and Henry IV" 3·00 3·75
MS4629 Three sheets. (a) 70×100 mm. $325 "The Three Crosses" (56×84 mm). (b) 100×70 mm. $325 "Decius Mus addressing the Legions" (84×56 mm). (c) 100×70 mm. $325 "Triumph of Henry IV" (84×56 mm). P 14 Set of 3 sheets 11·00 12·00

545 Apatosaurus

1996. Prehistoric Animals. Multicoloured.
4630-4677 Set of 48 21·00 22·00

4630-4641 $35×12 Type **545**; Archaeopteryx; Dimorphodon; Deinonychus; Coelophysis; Tyranosaurus; Triceratops; Anatosaurus; Saltasaurus; Allosaurus; Oviraptor; Stegosaurus

4642-4653 $35×12 Ornithomimus; Pteranodon; Rhamphorynchus; Ornitholestes; Brachiosaurus; Parasaurolophus; Ceratosaurus; Camarasaurus; Euoplocephalus; Scutellosaurus; Compsognathus; Stegoceras

4654-4665 $35×12 Eudimorphodon; Criorhynchus; Elasmosaurus; Ceresiosaurus; Mesosaurus; Grendelius; Nothosaurus; Mixosaurus; Placodus; Coelacanth; Mosasaurus

4666-4677 $35×12 Tarbosaurus; Hadrosaurus; Polacanthus; Psittacosaurus; Ornitholestes; Yangchuanosaurus; Scelidosaurus; Kentrosaurus; Coelophysis; Lesothosaurus; Plateosaurus; Staurikosaurus (all vert)

MS4678 Two sheets, each 101×58 mm. (a) $60 Saurolophus; $60 Muttaburrasaurus; $60 Dicraeosaurus. (b) $60 Heterodontosaurus; $60 Compsognathus; $60 Ornithomimosaure (all vert) Set of 2 sheets 4·50 5·50

MS4679 Five sheets. (a) 106×76 mm. $300 Struthiomimus. (b) 76×106 mm. $300 Tyrannosaurus rex (vert). (c) 76×106 mm. $300 Apatosaurus and Allosaurus. (d) 106×76 mm. $300 Quetzalcoatlus. (e) 106×76 mm. $300 Lagosuchus Set of 5 sheets 19·00 21·00

Nos. 4630/41, 4642/53, 4654/65 and 4666/77 respectively were printed together, se-tenant, with the backgrounds forming composite designs.

1996. "CHINA 96" International Stamp Exhibition, Beijing. T **546** and similar vert designs. Multicoloured.
MS4680 130×95 mm. $60 Summer Palace, Beijing (39×51 mm) 1·25 1·40
MS4681 Two sheets, each 146×116 mm. (a) $60 Type **546**; $60 Panda holding bamboo stem; $60 Eating bamboo stalk; $60 On all fours. (b) $60 Panda lying on tree branch (logo at left); $60 Lying on branch (logo at right; $60 Exploring hollow in tree (logo at left); $60 Sitting on trunk (logo at right) Set of 2 sheets 7·00 7·00

The stamps in No. **MS**4681 form composite designs showing rocks and stream (a) or dead tree (b).

546a Deng Xiaoping writing Inscription

1996. Deng Xiaoping (Chinese leader) Commemoration. Multicoloured.
4681c $30 Type **546a** 35 40
4681d $30 Deng Xiaoping addressing meeting (value in red) 35 40
4681e $30 Signing first day cover for army officer (value in yellow) 35 40
4681f $30 Waving 35 40
4681g $30 As No. 4681d (value in yellow) 35 40
4681h $30 As No. 4681e (value in red) 35 40
MS4681i 73×101 mm. $300 Deng Xiaoping applauding (vert) 3·25 3·50

547 "Morchella esculenta" and "Doryphorella princeps" (leaf beetle)

1996. Fungi of Guyana. Multicoloured.
4682 $20 Type **547** 55 30
4683 $25 Green-spored mushroom 55 30
4684 $30 Common mushroom and leaf beetle 60 40
4685 $35 Pine cone mushroom and "Danaus plexippus" caterpillar 60 40
4686 $60 "Armillaria mellea" 80 80
4687 $60 "Gomphus floccosus" 80 80
4688 $60 "Pholiota astragalina" 80 80
4689 $60 "Helvellaa crispa" 80 80
4690 $60 "Hygrophorus miniatus" 80 80
4691 $60 "Omphalotus olearius" 80 80
4692 $60 "Hygrocybe acutoconica" 80 80
4693 $60 "Mycena viscosa" 80 80
4694 $60 Cockle-shell lentinus 80 80
4695 $60 "Volvariella surrecta" 80 80
4696 $60 "Lepiota josserandii" 80 80
4697 $60 "Boletellus betula" 80 80
4698 $60 "Amanita muscaria" 80 80
4699 $60 "Russula claroflava" and "Semiotus angulatus" (click beetle) 80 80
4700 $60 "Dictyophora duplicata" and "Musca domestica" (house fly) 80 80
4701 $60 "Stropharia" and "Editha magnifica" (butterfly hunter) 80 80
4702 $60 "Leotia viscosa" 80 80
4703 $60 "Calostoma cinnabarina" 80 80
4704 $60 Stalkless paxillus 80 80
4705 $60 "Amanita spissa" 80 80
MS4706 Two sheets, each 114×84 mm. (a) $300 "Mycena leaiana" and Yellow grosbeak (bird). (b) $300 "Tubifera ferryginosa", "Clavulina amethystina" and "Ramaria formosa" (horiz) Set of 2 sheets 8·00 8·50

Nos. 4686 and 4692 are inscribed "Armillauella mellea" and "Hygzocybe acutoconica", both in error.

1996. 70th Birthday of Queen Elizabeth II. As T 255a of Gambia. Multicoloured.
4707 $100 Queen Elizabeth II 1·40 1·50
4708 $100 Queen wearing green and blue jacket and hat 1·40 1·50
4709 $100 Queen at State Opening of Parliament 1·40 1·50
MS4710 103×125 mm. $325 Queen in Garter robes 4·25 4·50

1996. Commonwealth Pharmacy Week. Unissued values in designs of Nos. 1810 and 1873 surch COMMONWEALTH PHARMACY WEEK JUNE 16th 22nd 1996.
4711 $6 on 130c. Plate No. 21 (Series 2)
4712 $60 on 100c. Plate No. 33 (Series 2)

1996. Centenary of Radio. Entertainers. As T 259a of Gambia. Multicoloured.
4713 $20 Frank Sinatra 50 30
4714 $35 Gene Autry 50 30
4715 $60 Groucho Marx 60 50
4716 $200 Red Skelton 2·00 2·25

MS4717	104×74 mm. $300 Burl Ives	3·50	4·00

549 Hulda Gates

1996. 3000th Anniv of Jerusalem. Multicoloured.

4718	$30 Type **549**	80	40
4719	$35 Church of St. Mary Magdalene	80	40
4720	$200 Absalom's Tomb, Kidron Valley	2·50	3·00
MS4721	105×76 mm. $300 Children's Holocaust Memorial, Yad Vashem	4·00	4·25

550 Long-billed Starthroat

1996. Birds of the World. Multicoloured.

4722	$60 Type **550**	70	70
4723	$60 Velvet-purple coronet	70	70
4724	$60 Racquet-tailed coquette	70	70
4725	$60 Violet-tailed sylph	70	70
4726	$60 Broad-tailed hummingbird	70	70
4727	$60 Blue-tufted starthroat	70	70
4728	$60 White-necked jacobin	70	70
4729	$60 Ruby-throated hummingbird	70	70
4730	$60 Blue and yellow macaw	70	70
4731	$60 Andean condor	70	70
4732	$60 Guiana crested eagle ("Crested Eagle")	70	70
4733	$60 White-tailed trogon	70	70
4734	$60 Toco toucan	70	70
4735	$60 Great horned owl	70	70
4736	$60 Andean cock-of-the-rock	70	70
4737	$60 Great curassow	70	70
MS4738	Two sheets, each 101×70 mm. (a) $300 Sparkling violetear ("Gould's Sparkling Violet-ear"). (b) $300 Ornate hawk eagle (horiz) Set of 2 sheets	7·50	8·00

Nos. 4722/9 and 4730/7 respectively were printed together, se-tenant, the backgrounds forming composite designs.

551 Pancratium (ancient Olympic event)

1996. Olympic Games, Atlanta (3rd issue). Multicoloured.

	4739-4787 Set of 49	25·00	27·00
4739	$20 Type **551**	40	30
4740	$30 Olympic Stadium, Melbourne, 1956	40	30
4741-4749	$50×9 Volleyball; Basketball; Tennis; Table tennis; Baseball; Handball; Hockey; Water polo; Football		
4750/8	$50×9 Cycling; Hurdling; High jumping; Diving; Weightlifting; Canoeing; Wrestling; Gymnastics; Running (all vert)		
4759-4767	$50×9 Florence Griffith-Joyner (track and field) (U.S.A.); Ines Geissler (swimming) (Germany); Nadia Comaneci (gymnastics) (Rumania); Tatiana Gutsu (gymnastics) (Unified team); Ogla Korbut (gymnastics) (Russia); Barbara Krause (swimming) (Germany); Olga Bryzgina (track and field) (Russia); Fanny Blankers-Koen (track and field) (Holland); Irena Szewinska (track and field) (Poland) (all vert)		
4768-4776	$50×9 Gerd Wessig (Germany); Jim Thorpe (U.S.A.); Norman Read (New Zealand); Lasse Viren (Finland); Milt Campbell (U.S.A.); Abebe Bikila (Ethiopia); Jesse Owens (U.S.A.); Viktor Saneev (Russia); Waldemer Cierpinski (Germany) (all track and field) (all vert)		
4777-4785	$50×9 Ditmar Schmidt (handball) (Germany); Pam Shriver (tennis doubles) (U.S.A.); Zina Garrison (tennis doubles) (U.S.A); Hyun Jung-Hua (table tennis doubles) (Korea); Steffi Graf (tennis) (Germany); Michael Jordan (basketball) (U.S.A.); Karch Kiraly (volleyball) (U.S.A.); "Magic" Johnson (basketball) (U.S.A.); Ingolf Weigert (handball) (Germany) (all vert)		
4786	$60 Leonid Spirin winning 20 kilometre walk, 1956 (vert)	60	60
4787	$200 Lars Hall, Gold medal winner, Modern Pentathalon, 1952 and 1956 (Sweden) (vert)	1·75	2·00
MS4788	Two sheets. (a) 104×74 mm. $300 Carl Lewis, Gold medal winner, track and field, 1984, 1988 and 1992 (U.S.A.). (b) 74×104 mm. $300 U.S.A. defeating Korea at baseball, 1988 Set of 2 sheets	6·50	7·50

Nos. 4741/9, 4750/8, 4759/67, 4768/76 and 4777/85 (the last three showing Gold medal winners) respectively were printed together, se-tenant, forming composite background designs.

No. **MS**4788a is inscribed "1985" in error.

552 Mickey's Bait Shop

1996. Mickey Mouse and Friends Outdoors. Multicoloured.

4789	$60 Type **552**	1·00	1·00
4790	$60 Mickey and Pluto as lumberjacks	1·00	1·00
4791	$60 Mickey fishing	1·00	1·00
4792	$80 Donald Duck in BMX bike championships (vert)	1·25	1·25
4793	$80 Goofy as ice hockey superstar (vert)	1·25	1·25
4794	$80 Donald Duck at Malibu Surf City (vert)	1·25	1·25
4795	$100 Mickey as naval captain (vert)	1·40	1·40
4796	$100 Captain Mickey's Seamanship School (vert)	1·40	1·40
4797	$100 Mickey as sailor with ship's wheel and full-rigged sailing ship (vert)	1·40	1·40
MS4798	Five sheets. (a) 124×101 mm. $250 Mickey as Pinkerton detective (vert). (b) 104×126 mm. $250 Mickey as U.S. Marshal (vert). (c) 125×104 mm. $250 Mickey as train conductor and Transcontinental Railroad locomotive. (d) 101×124 mm. $300 Donald Duck as mountaineer. (e) 104×124 mm. $325 Mickey as trapper (vert) Set of 5 sheets	21·00	22·00

553 Two Gun Mickey

1996. Disney Antique Toys. Multicoloured.

4799	$6 Type **553**	50	50
4800	$6 Wood-jointed Mickey figure	50	50
4801	$6 Donald jack-in-the-box	50	50
4802	$6 Rocking Minnie	50	50
4803	$6 Fireman Donald Duck	50	50
4804	$6 Long-billed Donald Duck	50	50
4805	$6 Painted-wood Mickey figure	50	50
4806	$6 Wind-up Jiminy Cricket	50	50
MS4807	Two sheets, each 131×105 mm. (a) $300 Mickey doll. (b) $300 Carousel Set of 2 sheets	10·00	10·00

554 Elvis Presley

1996. 60th Birth Anniv (1995) of Elvis Presley. Multicoloured, background colours given.

4808	**554**	$100 red	1·40	1·25
4809	-	$100 mauve	1·40	1·25
4810	-	$100 brown	1·40	1·25
4811	-	$100 blue	1·40	1·25
4812	-	$100 purple	1·40	1·25
4813	-	$100 blue	1·40	1·25

DESIGNS: Nos. 4809/13, Various portraits.

555 Piece of Meteorite showing Fossil

1996. Mars Meteorite. Sheet 104×76 mm.

MS4814	**555** $50 multicoloured	2·00	1·75

556 Birman

1996. Cats of the World. Multicoloured.

4815	$60 Type **556**	70	70
4816	$60 American curl	70	70
4817	$60 Turkish angora	70	70
4818	$60 European shorthair (Italy)	70	70
4819	$60 Persian (Great Britain)	70	70
4820	$60 Scottish fold	70	70
4821	$60 Sphynx (Canada)	70	70
4822	$60 Malayan (Thailand)	70	70
4823	$60 Cornish rex (Great Britain)	70	70
4824	$60 Norwegian forest (vert)	70	70
4825	$60 Russian shorthair (vert)	70	70
4826	$60 European shorthair (Italy) (vert)	70	70
4827	$60 Birman (vert)	70	70
4828	$60 Ragdoll (U.S.A.) (vert)	70	70
4829	$60 Egyptian mau (vert)	70	70
4830	$60 Persian (Great Britain) (vert)	70	70
4831	$60 Turkish angora (vert)	70	70
4832	$60 Siamese (vert)	70	70
MS4833	Two sheets, each 107×72 mm. (a) $300 Himalayan (U.S.A.). (b) $300 Maine coon (U.S.A.) (vert) Set of 2 sheets	7·00	8·00

Nos. 4815/23 and 4824/32 respectively were printed together, se-tenant, with the backgrounds forming composite designs.

557 Hyed Snapper

1996. Marine Life. Multicoloured.

4834	$6 Type **557**	15	15
4835	$6 Angelfish	15	15
4836	$20 Boxfish	30	20
4837	$25 Golden damselfish	30	25
4838	$30 Goblin shark and coelacanth	35	35
4839	$30 "Jason" (American remote-controlled submersible)	35	35
4840	$30 Deep-water invertebrates	35	35
4841	$30 Submarine NR-1	35	35
4842	$30 Giant squid	35	35
4843	$30 Sperm whale	35	35
4844	$30 Volcanic vents and "Alvin" (submersible)	35	35
4845	$30 Air-recycling pressure suits and shipwreck	35	35
4846	$30 "Shinkai" 6500 (submersible)	35	35
4847	$30 Giant tube worms	35	35
4848	$30 Anglerfish	35	35
4849	$30 Six-gill shark	35	35
4850	$30 Autonomous underwater vehicle ABE	35	35
4851	$30 Octopus and viperfish	35	35
4852	$30 Swallower and hatchetfish	35	35
4853	$35 Clown triggerfish	35	30
4854	$60 Red gorgonians	65	65
4855	$60 Soft coral and butterflyfish	65	65
4856	$60 Soft coral and slender snapper	65	65
4857	$60 Common clownfish, anemone and mushroom coral	65	65
4858	$60 Anemone and horse-eyed jack	65	65
4859	$60 Splendid coral trout	65	65
4860	$60 Anemones	65	65
4861	$60 Brain coral	65	65
4862	$60 Cup coral	65	65
4863	$200 Harlequin tuskfish	2·25	2·50
MS4864	Two sheets, each 98×68 mm. (a) $300 Caribbean flower coral. (b) $300 Sea anemone Set of 2 sheets	6·50	7·50

Nos. 4838/52 and 4854/62 respectively were printed together, se-tenant, with the backgrounds forming composite designs.

No. 4853 is inscribed "CLOWN TUGGERFISH" in error.

558 Snow White and Reindeer

1996. Christmas. Disney's "Snow White and the Seven Dwarfs". Multicoloured.

4865	$6 Type **558**	30	10
4866	$20 Doc with presents	80	25
4867	$25 Dopey and Sneezy	80	30
4868	$30 Sleepy, Happy and Bashful	80	35
4869	$35 Dopey and Santa Claus	80	40
4870	$60 Dopey with socks at fireplace	1·50	1·00
4871	$100 Dopey and Grumpy	2·50	2·50
4872	$200 Dopey dressed as Santa Claus	3·75	4·50
MS4873	Two sheets, each 122×102 mm. (a) $300 Snow White, Doc and squirrel. (b) $300 Dopey and Christmas tree Set of 2 sheets	12·00	12·00

559 Hotel Tower

1996. 50th Anniv of Hotel Tower, Georgetown.

4874	**559**	$30 multicoloured	70	40

561 Ox

1997. Chinese New Year. "Year of the Ox".

4882	**561**	$20 multicoloured	35	25
4883	-	$30 multicoloured	50	40
4884	-	$35 multicoloured	55	50
4885	-	$50 multicoloured	75	80
MS4886		101×72 mm. $150 multicoloured	2·00	2·25
MS4887		68×90 mm. $50 As No. 4882 (value bottom right); $50 As No. 4883 (value bottom left); $50 As No. 4884 (value top right); $50 As No. 4885 (value top left)	2·00	2·25

DESIGNS: Nos. 4883/7 depict symbolic oxen.

562 Mickey with Traditional Box of Sweets

1997. Mickey Mouse and Friends celebrate Chinese New Year. Multicoloured.

4888 $6 Type **562** 40 25
4889 $20 Mickey and Minnie at home with friends 50 35
4890 $25 Mickey and Minnie hanging fortune lantern 50 35
4891 $30 Minnie and Daisy with paper silhouette 55 55
4892 $30 Mickey and friends receiving traditional red money 55 55
4893 $30 Mickey in lion dance 55 55
4894 $30 Mickey preparing Chinese calligraphy wall hangings 55 55
4895 $30 Mickey with symbols of surplus 55 55
4896 $30 Donald Duck playing with fireworks 55 55
4897 $30 Donald, Mickey and Minnie on ox 55 55
4898 $35 Donald Duck and friends at New Year flower market 55 55
4899 $60 Mickey and Minnie as "harmonious man and woman" 90 90
MS4900 Two sheets, each 133×109 mm. (a) $150 Mickey Mouse marching (vert). (b) $200 Mickey and ox Set of 2 sheets 6·50 6·50

563 Burgess Meredith as Ernie Pyle in "The Story of G.I. Joe"

1997. Centenary of Cinema. Second World War Films. Multicoloured.

4901 $50 Type **563** 70 70
4902 $50 M. E. Clifton-James as General Montgomery in "I was Monty's Double" 70 70
4903 $50 Audie Murphy as himself in "To Hell and Back" 70 70
4904 $50 Gary Cooper as Dr. Wassell in "The Story of Dr. Wassell" 70 70
4905 $50 James Mason as Erwin Rommel in "The Desert Fox" 70 70
4906 $50 Manart Kippen as Stalin in "Mission to Moscow" 70 70
4907 $50 Robert Taylor as Col. Paul Tibbets in "Above and Beyond" 70 70
4908 $50 James Cagney as Admiral Bill Halsey in "The Gallant Hours" 70 70
4909 $50 John Garfield as Al Schmid in "Pride of the Marines" 70 70
MS4910 105×75 mm. $300 George C. Scott as Gen. George S. Patton in "Patton" (horiz) 5·50 6·00

564 "Washington in Battle"

1997. Bicentenary of George Washington's Retirement from U.S. Presidency. Multicoloured.

4911 $60 Type **564** 60 60
4912 $60 "Washington taking Presidential Oath" 60 60
4913 $60 "Washington seated in Armchair" (engraving after Chappel) 60 60
4914 $60 "Col. Washington of the Virginia Militia" (Charles W. Peale) 60 60
4915 $60 "George Washington" (Rembrandt Peale) 60 60
4916 $60 "Washington addressing Constitutional Convention" (Junius B. Stearns) 60 60
4917 $60 "Washington on his way to Continental Congress" 60 60
4918 $60 "Washington on a White Charger" (John Faed) 60 60
4919 $60 "Washington surveying" (engraving by G. R. Hall) 60 60
4920 $60 "Washington praying at Valley Forge" (bas-relief) 60 60
4921 $60 "Death of Gen. Mercer at Battle of Princeton" (John Trumbull) 60 60
4922 $60 "Washington taking Command at Cambridge" 60 60
4923 $60 "Washington before Battle of Trenton" (John Trumbull) 60 60
4924 $60 "Washington and his Family at Mount Vernon" (Alonzo Chappel) 60 60
4925 $60 "Washington's Inauguration" (Chappel) 60 60
4926 $60 "Washington" (Adolph Ulrich Wertmuller) 60 60
4927 $60 "Washington accepts Commission as Commander-in-Chief" (Currier & Ives lithograph) 60 60
4928 $60 "Washington" (mezzotint by Sartain) 60 60
4929 $60 "Mount Vernon" 60 60
4930 $60 "Washington with Farm Workers" (print by Junius B. Stearns) 60 60
4931 $60 "Wedding of Nellie Custis" (Ogden) 60 60
4932 $60 "Washington crossing the Delaware" (Leutze) 60 60
4933 $60 "Washington and Gen. Braddock" 60 60
4934 $60 "Washington's Birthplace" (Currier & Ives lithograph) 60 60
4935 $300 "George Washington" (Gilbert Stuart) (66×91 mm) 2·50 3·00
4936 $300 "Washington at Yorktown" (James Peale) (66×91 mm) 2·50 3·00

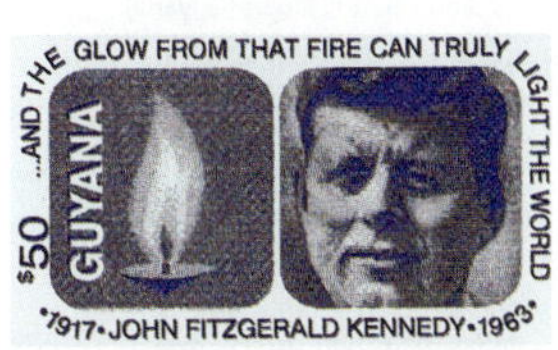

565 Pres. Kennedy and "Eternal Flame"

1997. 80th Birth Anniv of Pres. John F. Kennedy.

4937 **565** $50 violet 1·00 1·00

No. 4937 is in the same design as the U.S.A. Memorial Issue of 1964.

1997. 50th Anniv of UNESCO. Multicoloured. As T 273a of Gambia.

4938 $20 Hall at Horyu-ji, Japan 20 20
4939 $25 Coastline, Scandola Nature Reserve, France 25 25
4940 $30 Great Wall turret, China 30 30
4941 $35 Bedroom in the Residenz, Wurzburg, Germany 35 30
4942 $60 Monastery of Batalha, Portugal 60 60
4943 $60 Cathedral of Aquisgran, Aachen, Germany (vert) 60 60
4944 $60 Trier Cathedral, Germany (vert) 60 60
4945 $60 Column of Augusta Treveror, Trier (vert) 60 60
4946 $60 The Residenz and garden, Wurzburg (vert) 60 60
4947 $60 Interior of church, Wurzburg (vert) 60 60
4948 $60 The Residenz and lake, Wurzburg (vert) 60 60
4949 $60 Riverside houses, Inselstadt, Bamberg, Germany (vert) 60 60
4950 $60 Cathedral interior, Speyer, Germany (vert) 60 60
4951 $60 Monastery of Thessaloniki, Greece (vert) 60 60
4952 $60 Church tower, Monastery of Mystras, Greece (vert) 4·25 4·25
4953 $60 Interior of Church of Santa Sofia, Thessaloniki (vert) 60 60
4954 $60 Monastery and ruins, Mystras (vert) 60 60
4955 $60 Aerial view of Monastery at Mystras (vert) 60 60
4956 $60 City wall, Thessaloniki (vert) 60 60
4957 $60 Wall painting, Mystras Monastery (vert) 60 60
4958 $60 Paintings in Museum of Byzantine Art, Thessaloniki (vert) 60 60
4959 $60 Monastery of Poblet, Catalonia, Spain (vert) 60 60
4960 $60 Salamanca, Spain (vert) 4·25 4·25
4961 $60 Toledo, Spain (vert) 60 60
4962 $60 Florence Cathedral, Italy (vert) 60 60
4963 $60 Leaning Tower of Pisa, Italy (vert) 60 60
4964 $60 Courtyard and tower, Convent of Cristo in Tomas, Portugal (vert) 60 60
4965 $60 Main door, Convent of Cristo in Tomas (vert) 60 60
4966 $60 Cloisters, Convent of Cristo in Tomas (vert) 60 60
4967 $80 Tower, Horyu-ji, Japan 70 70
4968 $80 Temple with verandah, Kyoto, Japan 70 70
4969 $80 Temple and pillar, Kyoto 70 70
4970 $80 Temples and lake, Horyu-Ji 70 70
4971 $80 Three-storey temple, Horyu-Ji 70 70
4972 $80 University of Virginia, U.S.A. 70 70
4973 $80 Yosemite National Park, U.S.A. 70 70
4974 $80 Yellowstone National Park, U.S.A. 70 70
4975 $80 Olympic National Park, U.S.A. 70 70
4976 $80 Everglades, U.S.A. 70 70
4977 $80 Street, Cuzco, Peru 70 70
4978 $80 Potosi, Bolivia 70 70
4979 $80 Fortress of San Lorenzo, Panama 70 70
4980 $80 Sangay National Park, Ecuador 70 70
4981 $80 Los Glaciares National Park, Argentina 70 70
4982 $200 City walls, Dubrovnik, Croatia 1·75 2·00
MS4983 Four sheets, each 126×101 mm. (a) $300 Golden Buddha, Mount Taishan, China. (b) $300 Monastery garden, Batalha, Portugal. (c) $300 Virgin and Child (statue), Bamberg Cathedral, Germany. (d) $300 Monastery, Mount Athos, Greece Set of 4 sheets 11·00 12·00

566 "Morchella hortensis"

1997. Fungi of the World. Multicoloured.

4984 $6 Type **566** 20 15
4985 $20 "Boletus chrysenteron" 25 20
4986 $25 "Hygrophorus agathosmus" 30 25
4987 $30 "Cortinarius violaceus" 35 30
4988 $35 "Acanthocystis geogenius" 40 30
4989 $60 "Mycena polygramma" 65 50
4990 $80 "Coprinus picaceus" 75 75
4991 $80 "Stropharia umbonatescens" 75 75
4992 $80 "Paxillus involutus" 75 75
4993 $80 "Amanita inaurata" 75 75
4994 $80 "Lepiota rhacodes" 75 75
4995 $80 "Russula amoena" 75 75
4996 $80 "Volvaria volvacea" 75 75
4997 $80 "Psalliota augusta" 75 75
4998 $80 "Tricholoma aurantium" 75 75
4999 $80 "Pholiota spectabilis" 75 75
5000 $80 "Cortinarius armillatus" 75 75
5001 $80 "Agrocybe dura" 75 75
5002 $200 "Hebeloma radicosum" 1·75 2·00
5003 $300 "Coprinus comatus" 2·75 3·00
MS5004 Two sheets, each 76×105 mm. (a) $300 "Pholiota mutabilis". (b) $300 "Amanita muscaria" Set of 2 sheets 6·50 7·00

567 Pineapple Lily

1997. Flowers. Multicoloured.

5005 $6 Type **567** 15 15
5006 $6 Blue columbine 15 15
5007 $20 Petunia 20 20
5008 $25 Lily of the Nile 25 25
5009 $30 Bird of paradise 30 30
5010 $35 African daisy 35 30
5011 $60 Cape daisy 60 60
5012 $60 Monarch slipperwort 60 60
5013 $60 Passion flower 60 60
5014 $60 Butterfly iris 60 60
5015 $60 Red-hot poker 60 60
5016 $60 Water lily "Dir G. T. Moore" 60 60
5017 $60 Painted tongue "Superbissima" 60 60
5018 $60 Canariensis orchid 60 60
5019 $60 Annual chrysanthemum 60 60
5020 $80 Tulips 70 70
5021 $80 Liatris 70 70
5022 $80 Roses 70 70
5023 $80 Gerber daisies 70 70
5024 $80 Sunflowers 70 70
5025 $80 Chrysanthemums 70 70
5026 $80 Gazania 70 70
5027 $80 Cape water lily 70 70
5028 $200 Insigne lady's slipper 1·75 2·25
MS5029 105×75 mm. $300 Petunias 3·00 3·50

568 Deng Xiaoping inspecting Rural Sichuan, 1980

1997. Deng Xiaoping (Chinese leader) Commem.

5030 **568** $100 multicoloured 1·00 1·00
MS5031 100×70 mm. $150 Deng Xiaoping on visit to foundry 1·50 1·60

1997. 10th Anniv of Chernobyl Nuclear Disaster. As T 276a of Gambia. Multicoloured.

5032 $200 As Type **276a** of Gambia 1·75 2·00
5033 $200 As Type **276a** of Gambia, but inscribed "CHABAD'S CHILDREN OF CHERNOBYL" at foot 1·75 2·00

1997. 50th Death Anniv of Paul Harris (founder of Rotary International). As T 276b of Gambia. Mult.

5034 $200 Paul Harris and volunteers with children ("Health, hunger and humanity") 1·75 2·00
MS5035 77×107 mm. $300 Group of boys ("Mutual respect among all faiths, races and cultures") 2·50 3·00

1997. Golden Wedding of Queen Elizabeth II and Prince Philip. As T 276c of Gambia. Multicoloured (except Nos. 5038/9).

5036 $60 Queen Elizabeth II wearing tiara 90 90
5037 $60 Royal coat of arms 90 90
5038 $60 Wedding photograph, 1947 (black) 90 90
5039 $60 Engagement photograph (black) 90 90
5040 $60 Broadlands, Romsey (honeymoon residence) 90 90
5041 $60 Duke of Edinburgh 90 90
MS5042 99×70 mm. $300 Queen and Duke of Edinburgh 4·00 4·25

1997. "Pacific '97" International Stamp Exhibition, San Francisco. Death Centenary of Heinrich von Stephan (founder of U.P.U.). As T 276d of Gambia.

5043 $100 sepia 1·00 1·25
5044 $100 brown 1·00 1·25
5045 $100 green 1·00 1·25
MS5046 82×118 mm. $300 black and blue 2·75 3·00

DESIGNS: No. 5043, Roman post cart from frieze; 5044, Von Stephan and Mercury; 5045, Cable car, Boston, 1907; **MS**5046, Von Stephan and ancient Egyptian messenger.

1997. 175th Anniv of Brothers Grimm's Third Collection of Fairy Tales. Hansel and Gretel. As T 277a of Gambia. Multicoloured.

5047 $100 Hansel and Gretel lost in forest 1·40 1·40
5048 $100 Gingerbread house 1·40 1·40
5049 $100 Witch 1·40 1·40
MS5050 124×96 mm. $500 Gretel pushing witch into oven (horiz) 6·00 6·50

1997. 300th Anniv of Mother Goose Nursery Rhymes. Multicoloured design as T 276a of Gambia. Sheet 75×101 mm.

MS5051 $300 "Cock-a-doodle-doo" (vert) 3·75 4·00

1997. Birth Bicentenary of Hiroshige (Japanese painter). "One Hundred Famous Views of Edo". As T 541a of Ghana. Multicoloured.

5052 $80 "Oumayagashi" 1·00 1·00
5053 $80 "Ryogoku Ekoin and Moto-Yanagibashi Bridge" 1·00 1·00
5054 $80 "Pine of Success and Oumayagashi, Asakusa River" 1·00 1·00
5055 $80 "Fireworks at Ryogoku" 1·00 1·00
5056 $80 "Dyers' Quarter, Kanda" 1·00 1·00
5057 $80 "Cotton-goods Lane, Odenma-cho" 1·00 1·00
MS5058 Two sheets, each 102×127 mm. (a) $300 "Suruga-cho". (b) $300 "Yatsukoji, inside Sujikai Gate" Set of 2 sheets 7·00 8·00

569 Tortoise

1997. "Hong Kong '97" International Stamp Exhibition. Return of Hong Kong to China. Mult.

5059	$80 Type **569**	80	80
5060	$80 Dragon	80	80
5061	$80 Unicorn	80	80
5062	$80 Phoenix	80	80
5063	$80 Barn swallow ("Swallow") and willow (vert)	80	80
5064	$80 River kingfisher ("Kingfisher") and chrysanthemum (vert)	80	80
5065	$80 Common crane ("Crane") and pine (vert)	80	80
5066	$80 Common peafowl ("Peacock") and peony (vert)	80	80
5067	$80 "Bird of Paradise" kite with two tail feathers (vert)	80	80
5068	$80 Large "eyed" kite with blue tail ribbons (vert)	80	80
5069	$80 "Phoenix" kite with "flaming" tail (vert)	80	80
5070	$80 "Insect" kite with red tail ribbons (vert)	80	80
5071	$200 Chinese landscape (face value at top left) (50×75 mm)	2·00	2·25
5072	$200 Chinese landscape (face value at bottom right) (50×75 mm)	2·00	2·25
MS5073	159×110 mm. $500 Junk in Hong Kong harbour (50×75 mm)	5·00	5·50

570 Markus Wasmeier (skier)

1997. Winter Olympic Games, Nagano, Japan (1998). Multicoloured.

5074	$30 Type **570**	35	35
5075	$30 Jens Weissflog (ski-jumper)	35	35
5076	$30 Erhard Keller	35	35
5077	$30 Rosi Mittermaier (skier)	35	35
5078	$30 Gunda Niemann (speed skater)	35	35
5079	$30 Peter Angerer (skier)	35	35
5080	$30 Gorg Thoma (ski-jumper)	35	35
5081	$35 Katja Seizinger (skier)	35	35
5082	$60 Gorg Hackl (luge)	70	70
5083	$60 Gunda Niemann (Germany) (3000 and 5000 m speed skating gold medals, 1992)	70	70
5084	$60 Tony Nash and Robin Dixon (Great Britain) (bobsleigh gold medal, 1964)	70	70
5085	$60 Switzerland (4 man bobsleigh gold medal, 1988)	70	70
5086	$60 Piet Kleine (Holland) (speed skating gold medal, 1976)	70	70
5087	$60 Oksana Baiul (Ukraine) (figure skating gold medal, 1994)	70	70
5088	$60 Cathy Turner (U.S.A.) (500 m speed skating gold medal, 1994)	70	70
5089	$60 Brian Boitano (U.S.A.) (figure skating gold medal, 1988)	70	70
5090	$60 Nancy Kerrigan (U.S.A.) (figure skating silver medal, 1994)	70	70
5091	$200 Katarina Witt (skater)	2·00	2·25
MS5092	Three sheets. (a) 106×81 mm. $300 Jean-Claude Killy (France) (slalom skiing gold medal), 1968. (b) 106×81 mm. $300 Chen Lu (China) (figure skating gold medal, 1992). (c) 76×106 mm. $300 Swiss 4-man bobsleigh team Set of 3 sheets	9·50	10·00

No. 5081 is inscribed "KATIA", No. 5087 "BAIUI", No. 5091 "KATHARINA" and No. **MS**5092c "GERMANY", all in error.

571 Chihuahua

1997. Cats and Dogs. Multicoloured.

5093	$20 Type **571**	45	25
5094	$25 Norfolk terrier	45	25
5095	$30 Norwegian forest cat	45	30
5096	$35 Oriental spotted tabby	45	30
5097	$60 Welsh terrier	70	70
5098	$60 Abyssinian (horiz)	70	70
5099	$60 Chocolate colorpoint shorthair (horiz)	70	70
5100	$60 Silver tabby (horiz)	70	70
5101	$60 Persian (horiz)	70	70
5102	$60 Maine coon cat and kitten (horiz)	70	70
5103	$60 Brown-shaded Burmese (horiz)	70	70
5104	$60 Persian kitten (horiz)	70	70
5105	$60 Siamese (horiz)	70	70
5106	$60 British shorthair (horiz)	70	70
5107	$60 Shar-pei	70	70
5108	$60 Chihuahua	70	70
5109	$60 Chow chow	70	70
5110	$60 Sealyham terrier	70	70
5111	$60 Collie	70	70
5112	$60 German shorthair pointer	70	70
5113	$60 Bulldog	70	70
5114	$60 German shepherd dog	70	70
5115	$60 Old English sheepdog	70	70
5116	$200 Asian smoke (cat)	2·00	2·25
MS5117	Two sheets, each 105×76 mm. (a) $300 Manx cat. (b) $300 Tibetan spaniel Set of 2 sheets	8·00	8·00

572 Verdin

1997. Birds of the World. Multicoloured.

5118	$25 Type **572**	50	30
5119	$30 Wood thrush (vert)	50	30
5120	$60 Rufous-sided towhee	75	50
5121	$80 Groove-billed ani	90	90
5122	$80 Green honeycreeper	90	90
5123	$80 Emerald toucanet	90	90
5124	$80 Wire-tailed manakin	90	90
5125	$80 Hoatzin	90	90
5126	$80 Rufescent tiger heron ("Tiger Heron")	90	90
5127	$80 Magenta-throated woodstar	90	90
5128	$80 Anna's hummingbird	90	90
5129	$80 Long-tailed hermit	90	90
5130	$80 White-tipped sicklebill	90	90
5131	$80 Red-footed plumeleteer	90	90
5132	$80 Fiery-throated hummingbird	90	90
5133	$200 Pygmy nuthatch (vert)	2·00	2·25
MS5134	Two sheets, each 70×100 mm. (a) $300 Pinnated bittern. (b) $300 Keel-billed toucan Set of 2 sheets	8·00	8·00

573 Pres. Cheddi Jagan in 1947 and 1997 with National Assembly Building

1997. 50th Anniv of Pres. Cheddi Jagan's Election to Parliament.

5135	**573**	$6 multicoloured	15	15
5136	**573**	$30 multicoloured	50	50

574 Princess Diana

1997. Diana, Princess of Wales Commemoration. Multicoloured.

5137	$80 Type **574**	90	90
5138	$80 Princess Diana in black V-neck dress	90	90
5139	$80 In red dress with diamante pattern on front	90	90
5140	$80 In white evening dress with narrow shoulder straps	90	90
5141	$80 In white evening dress with one shoulder bare	90	90
5142	$80 In lavender dress	90	90
MS5143	Two sheets, each 107×108 mm. (a) $300 In red sleeveless dress (33×51 mm). (b) $300 In white blouse (33×51 mm) Set of 2 sheets	7·00	7·50

575 Presidents Clinton (U.S.A.) and Cheddi Jagan (Guyana)

1997. President Clinton's Caribbean Visit. Mult.

5144	$6 Type **575**	15	10
5145	$30 As Type **575**, but different portrait of Pres. Jagan	45	35
5146	$30 Presidents Clinton and Jagan, flags and sunrise over sea (horiz)	45	35
5147	$100 Presidents Clinton and Jagan, flags and sunrise over beach (horiz)	1·50	1·75

576 President Jiang Zemin, Flags, and New York Skyline by Day

1997. Visit of President Jiang Zemin of China to New York. Two sheets, each 125×84 mm, containing T 576 and similar horiz design. Multicoloured.

MS5148	Two sheets. (a) $200 Type **576**. (b) $300 President Jiang Zemin, flags, and New York at night Set of 2 sheets	5·50	6·00

1997. Christmas. Paintings. As T 284a of Gambia. Multicoloured.

5149	$25 Cupid from "The Triumph of Galatea" (Raphael)	30	10
5150	$30 Different Cupid from "The Triumph of Galatea" (Raphael)	30	10
5151	$35 Cupid from "Primavera" (Botticelli)	35	15
5152	$60 "Angel Musicians" (Agostino di Duccio)	70	30
5153	$100 Cupid from illustration No. 1212, *Life Magazine* 28/1/06	1·40	1·50
5154	$200 Angels from "Madonna and Saints" (Rosso Fiorentino)	2·50	3·25
MS5155	Two sheets. (a) 95×105 mm. $300 "The Gardens of Love" (Rubens). (b) 105×95 mm. $300 "Cherubs" (Philippe de Champaigne) Set of 2 sheets	8·50	9·00

577 Abraham Lincoln

1997. 75th Anniversaries, 1997–2001. Multicoloured.

5156	$60 Type **577** (Dedication of Lincoln Memorial, Washington, 1922)	75	75
5157	$60 Mask of Tutankhamun (discovery of tomb, 1922)	75	75
5158	$60 Alexander Graham Bell and early telephone, 1922 (75th death anniv)	75	75
5159	$60 John L. Baird and first television, 1923	75	75
5160	$60 President Warren G. Harding, 1923 (75th death anniv)	75	75
5161	$60 Presidency of Calvin Coolidge, 1923	75	75
5162	$60 Skier (first Winter Olympics, Chamonix, France, 1924)	75	75
5163	$60 Sun Yat-sen (Chinese leader), 1925 (75th death anniv)	75	75
5164	$60 Charles Darwin (ban on teaching of evolution, Tennessee, U.S.A., 1925)	75	75
5165	$60 Robert Goddard (first liquid fuel rocket, 1926)	75	75
5166	$60 Richard E. Byrd (first flight over North Pole, 1926)	75	75
5167	$60 Liberty Bell (Sesquicentennial Exposition, Philadelphia, 1926)	75	75

578 Fogarty's Department Store, Georgetown

1997. Buildings in Guyana. Multicoloured.

5168	$6 Type **578**	15	15
5169	$30 St. Rose's High School (150th anniv)	50	50

579 Tiger sitting (face value at bottom right)

1998. Chinese New Year ("Year of the Tiger"). Multicoloured.

5170	$50 Type **579**	50	55
5171	$50 Tiger sitting (face value bottom left)	50	55
5172	$50 Tiger standing (face value top right)	50	55
5173	$50 Tiger standing (face value top left)	50	55
MS5174	102×72 mm. $150 Tiger with Chinese characters in background	1·40	1·60

580 Kentrosaurus

1998. Prehistoric Animals. Multicoloured.

5175	$25 Type **580**	40	30
5176	$30 Lesothosaurus	40	30
5177	$35 Stegoceras	40	30
5178	$55 Ceresiosaurus	65	70
5179	$55 Nothosaurus	65	70
5180	$55 Rhomaleosaurus	65	70
5181	$55 Grendelius	65	70
5182	$55 Mixosaurus	65	70
5183	$55 Mesosaurus	65	70
5184	$55 Placodus	65	70
5185	$55 Stethacanthus	65	70
5186	$55 Coelacanth	65	70
5187	$55 Quetzalcoatlus	65	70
5188	$55 Pteranodon	65	70
5189	$55 Peteinosaurus	65	70
5190	$55 Criorhychus	65	70
5191	$55 Pterodaustro	65	70
5192	$55 Eudimorphodon	65	70
5193	$55 Archeopteryx	65	70
5194	$55 Dimorphodon	65	70
5195	$55 Sharovipteryx	65	70
5196	$60 Lagosuchus	65	60
5197	$100 Herrerasaurus	1·00	1·10
5198	$200 Iguanodon	1·90	2·25

MS5199 Two sheets, each 106×76 mm. (a) $300 Yangchuanosaurus (vert). (b) $300 Styracosaurus (vert) Set of 2 sheets 6·00 6·50

Nos. 5178/86 and 5187/95 were each printed together, se-tenant, with the backgrounds forming composite designs.

581 Bryan Berard

1998. Ice Hockey Players. Multicoloured.

5200 $35 Type **581** 35 35
5201 $35 Ray Bourque 35 35
5202 $35 Martin Brodeur 35 35
5203 $35 Pavel Bure 35 35
5204 $35 Chris Chelios 35 35
5205 $35 Sergei Fedorov 35 35
5206 $35 Peter Forsberg 35 35
5207 $35 Wayne Gretzky 35 35
5208 $35 Dominik Hasek 35 35
5209 $35 Brett Hull 35 35
5210 $35 Jarome Iginla 35 35
5211 $35 Jaromir Jagr 35 35
5212 $35 Paul Kariya 35 35
5213 $35 Saku Koivu 35 35
5214 $35 John LeClair 35 35
5215 $35 Brian Leetch 35 35
5216 $35 Eric Lindros 35 35
5217 $35 Patrick Marleau 35 35
5218 $35 Mark Messier 35 35
5219 $35 Mike Modano 35 35
5220 $35 Chris Osgood 35 35
5221 $35 Zigmund Palffy 35 35
5222 $35 Felix Potvin 35 35
5223 $35 Jeremy Roenick 35 35
5224 $35 Patrick Roy 35 35
5225 $35 Joe Sakic 35 35
5226 $35 Sergei Samsonov 35 35
5227 $35 Teemu Selanne 35 35
5228 $35 Brendan Shanahan 35 35
5229 $35 Ryan Smyth 35 35
5230 $35 Jocelyn Thibault 35 35
5231 $35 Joe Thornton 35 35
5232 $35 Keith Tkachuk 35 35
5233 $35 John Vanbiesbrouck 35 35
5234 $35 Steve Yzerman 35 35
5235 $35 Dainius Zubrus 35 35

582 Argentine Team

1998. World Cup Football Championship, France. Showing competing teams and trophy. Multicoloured.

5236 $30 Type **582** 30 30
5237 $30 Austria 30 30
5238 $30 Belgium 30 30
5239 $30 Brazil 30 30
5240 $30 Bulgaria 30 30
5241 $30 Cameroon 30 30
5242 $30 Chile 30 30
5243 $30 Colombia 30 30
5244 $30 Croatia 30 30
5245 $30 Denmark 30 30
5246 $30 England 30 30
5247 $30 France 30 30
5248 $30 Germany 30 30
5249 $30 Holland 30 30
5250 $30 Iran 30 30
5251 $30 Italy 30 30
5252 $30 Jamaica 30 30
5253 $30 Japan 30 30
5254 $30 Mexico 30 30
5255 $30 Morocco 30 30
5256 $30 Nigeria 30 30
5257 $30 Norway 30 30
5258 $30 Paraguay 30 30
5259 $30 Rumania 30 30
5260 $30 Saudi Arabia 30 30
5261 $30 Scotland 30 30
5262 $30 South Africa 30 30
5263 $30 South Korea 30 30
5264 $30 Spain 30 30
5265 $30 Tunisia 30 30
5266 $30 U.S.A. 30 30
5267 $30 Yugoslavia 30 30

MS5268 Two sheets, each 110×85 mm. (a) $300 Okada, Japan (vert). (b) $300 Nakata, Japan (vert) Set of 2 sheets 5·00 5·50

583 Dutch Fluyt

1998. Sailing Ships. Multicoloured.

5269 $80 Type **583** 75 75
5270 $80 *Alastor* (barque) 75 75
5271 $80 *Falcon* (medieval ship) 75 75
5272 $80 *Red Rover* (barque) 75 75
5273 $80 *British Anglesey* (full-rigged ship) 75 75
5274 $80 *Archibald Russell* (barque) 75 75
5275 $80 14th century double-ended Scandinavian ship 75 75
5276 $80 Portuguese caravel 75 75
5277 $80 *Nina* (Columbus) 75 75
5278 $80 *Fannie* (schooner) 75 75
5279 $80 *Vitoria* (Magellan) 75 75
5280 $80 Arab sambook 75 75

MS5281 Two sheets. (a) 76×106 mm. $300 *Half Moon* (Hudson). (b) 106×76 mm. $300 Osberg ship Set of 2 sheets 5·00 5·50

No. 5274 is inscribed "ARCHIBALD RUSSEL" in error.

584 J. Bruce Ismay (Managing Director of White Star Line)

1998. 85th Anniv of Sinking of the Titanic (liner). Multicoloured.

5282 $80 Type **584** 80 80
5283 $80 Jack Phillips (wireless operator) 80 80
5284 $80 Margaret Brown (passenger) 80 80
5285 $80 Capt. Edward J. Smith 80 80
5286 $80 Frederick Fleet (crew member) 80 80
5287 $80 Thomas Andrews (Managing Director of Harland & Wolff) 80 80

MS5288 100×70 mm. $300 *Titanic* sinking 3·00 3·25

1998. 25th Anniv of Caribbean Community. As T 454a of Grenada. Multicoloured.

5289 $20 Flags of Grenada and CARICOM 30 20

585 Queen Elizabeth the Queen Mother

1998. 98th Birthday of Queen Elizabeth the Queen Mother.

5290 **585** $90 multicoloured 90 90

1998. France's Victory in World Cup Football Championship. Nos. 5239, 5244/5, 5247, 5251, 5258, 5260 and 5262 optd FRANCE WINNERS. Multicoloured.

5291 $30 Brazil 30 35
5292 $30 Croatia 30 35
5293 $30 Denmark 30 35
5294 $30 France 30 35
5295 $30 Italy 30 35
5296 $30 Paraguay 30 35
5297 $30 Saudi Arabia 30 35
5298 $30 South Africa 30 35

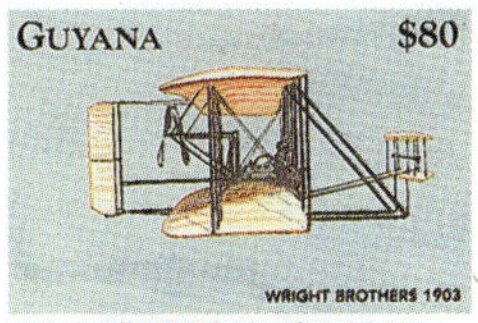

587 Orville Wright in *Flyer I*, 1903

1998. Aircraft. Multicoloured.

5299 $80 Type **587** 75 75
5300 $80 Bleriot, 1911 75 75
5301 $80 Curtiss Jenny, 1919 75 75
5302 $80 Zeppelin LZ-10 *Schwaben*, 1911 75 75
5303 $80 W-8B, 1923 75 75
5304 $80 DH66, 1926 75 75
5305 $80 A7K Corsair II 75 75
5306 $80 A6E Intruder 75 75
5307 $80 U2 spy plane 75 75
5308 $80 Blackhawk helicopter 75 75
5309 $80 F-16 75 75
5310 $80 Phantom II 75 75

MS5311 Two sheets, each 70×100 mm. (a) $300 A-10 Warthog. (b) $300 HH-65A Dolphin helicopter Set of 2 sheets 5·00 5·50

Nos. 5299/304 and 5305/10 were each printed together, se-tenant, with the backgrounds forming composite designs.

588 Panda climbing Tree

1998. Giant Pandas. Multicoloured.

5312 $80 Type **588** 75 75
5313 $80 Panda sitting on tree trunk 75 75
5314 $80 Panda climbing bamboo 75 75
5315 $80 Panda chewing bamboo 75 75
5316 $80 Panda snapping bamboo stalk 75 75
5317 $80 Panda eating foliage 75 75

MS5318 100×70 mm. $300 Panda with leaves 2·75 3·00

Nos. 5312/17 were printed together, se-tenant, with the backgrounds forming a composite design.

589 Mountain Gorilla

1998. Mountain Gorillas. Multicoloured.

5319 $80 Type **589** 75 75
5320 $80 Gorilla climbing tree 75 75
5321 $80 Gorilla eating foliage 75 75
5322 $80 Female gorilla sitting on ground 75 75
5323 $80 Baby gorilla eating twig 75 75
5324 $80 Male gorilla in forest 75 75

MS5325 100×70 mm. $300 Young gorilla eating leaf 2·75 3·00

Nos. 5319/24 were printed together, se-tenant, with the backgrounds forming a composite design.

590 Christian Lautenschlager in Grand Prix Mercedes, 1914

1998. History of Grand Prix Motor Racing. Mult.

5326 $80 Type **590** 70 70
5327 $80 P. Etancelin in Bugatti Type 35B, 1930 70 70
5328 $80 Louis Chiron in Alfa Romeo P3, 1934 70 70
5329 $80 Richard Seaman in Mercedes-Benz W154, 1938 70 70
5330 $80 Tazio Nuvolari in Auto Union D Type, 1938 70 70
5331 $80 Juan Fangio in Alfa Romeo 158, 1951 70 70
5332 $80 Stirling Moss in Mercedes-Benz W196, 1955 70 70
5333 $80 Phil Hill in Ferrari Dino 246, 1960 70 70
5334 $80 Jack Brabham in Brabham-Repco BT19, 1966 70 70
5335 $80 John Miles in Lotus Ford 72, 1970 70 70
5336 $80 Alain Prost in Renault RE40, 1983 70 70
5337 $80 David Coulthard in McLaren Mercedes MP4/13, 1998 70 70

MS5338 Two sheets, each 100×70 mm. (a) $300 Ferenc Szisz in Grand Prix Renault, 1906 (56×42 mm). (b) $300 Stirling Moss in Maserati 250F, 1956 (56×42 mm) Set of 2 sheets 5·00 5·50

591 Comic Book Title (1/2-size illustration) (image scaled to 51% of original size)

1998. 50th Anniv of Disney's Uncle Scrooge Character. Designs showing text and illustrations from comic book Christmas on Bear Mountain (drawn by C. Barks). Mult.

5339 $35 Type **591** 60 60
5340 $35 Uncle Scrooge sitting in armchair 60 60
5341 $35 Uncle Scrooge looking out window 60 60
5342 $35 James the butler holding telephone 60 60
5343 $35 Uncle Scrooge at foot of staircase 60 60
5344 $35 Donald Duck with open fridge 60 60
5345 $35 Uncle Scrooge entering attic 60 60
5346 $35 Uncle Scrooge in limousine 60 60
5347 $35 Huey, Dewey and Louie at window 60 60
5348 $35 Car in snow 60 60
5349 $35 Ducks in bed 60 60
5350 $35 Donald in chair with nephews 60 60
5351 $35 Donald refusing nephews 60 60
5352 $35 Ducks and rabbit 60 60
5353 $35 Ducks with Christmas tree 60 60
5354 $35 Baby bear climbing down Christmas tree 60 60
5355 $35 Ducks in panic 60 60
5356 $35 Baby bear running 60 60
5357 $35 Ducks searching 60 60
5358 $35 Nephews and tree 60 60
5359 $35 Huey, Dewey and Louie tripping on roller skate 60 60
5360 $35 Frightened nephew 60 60
5361 $35 Baby bear on roller skate 60 60
5362 $35 Donald hiding in light fitting 60 60
5363 $35 Baby bear with chocolate 60 60
5364 $35 Louie climbing Christmas tree 60 60
5365 $35 Baby bear evading Louie 60 60
5366 $35 Nephews searching bedroom 60 60
5367 $35 Donald peering down from light fitting 60 60
5368 $35 Mother bear chasing Donald 60 60
5369 $35 Donald jumping through window 60 60
5370 $35 Bears after eating 60 60
5371 $35 Ducks looking through window 60 60
5372 $35 Donald and sleeping mother bear 60 60
5373 $35 Uncle Scrooge outside cabin 60 60
5374 $35 Uncle Scrooge in bear suit behind sofa 60 60
5375 $35 Uncle Scrooge in bear suit surprised 60 60
5376 $35 Uncle Scrooge with James 60 60
5377 $35 Ducks on Christmas Day 60 60
5378 $35 Donald fainting 60 60

MS5379 220×175 mm. $300 Carl Barks (37×50 mm); $300 Uncle Scrooge pursued by bear (50×37 mm) 7·00 7·00

Only issued in stamp booklets in which each pane contains two pairs separated by a horizontal gutter margin showing further parts of the comic strip. Each stamp shows two drawings of which the first in each instance is described for the listing.

1998. 50th Anniv of Organization of American States. As T 454b of Grenada.

5380 $40 yellow, violet and black 40 30

1998. 25th Death Anniv of Pablo Picasso (painter). As T 291a of Gambia. Multicoloured.
5381 $25 "Sleeping Peasants" 25 20
5382 $60 "Large Nude in Red Armchair" (vert) 55 40
5383 $200 "Female Head" (vert) 1·75 1·90
MS5384 102×126 mm. $300 "Man and Woman" (vert) 2·75 3·00

592 James E. West (first Scout executive) and Early Eagle Scouts

1998. 19th World Scout Jamboree, Chile. Mult.
5385 $160 Type **592** 1·40 1·50
5386 $160 Pres. John F. Kennedy greeting Explorers, 1961 1·40 1·50
5387 $160 Walter Schirra (astronaut) receiving Special Merit badge, 1962 1·40 1·50

593 Mahatma Gandhi as Lawyer in South Africa, 1906

1998. 50th Death Anniv of Mahatma Gandhi. Mult.
5388 $100 Type **593** 90 90
5389 $100 Gandhi on Bengal walk, 1946 (56×42 mm) 90 90
5390 $100 Gandhi with Jawaharlal Nehru and Sardar Patel, 1948 (56×42 mm) 90 90
5391 $100 Gandhi during fast, 1947 90 90
MS5392 70×66 mm. $300 Gandhi and Jawaharlal Nehru (horiz) 2·75 3·00

1998. 80th Anniv of Royal Air Force. As T 292a of Gambia. Multicoloured.
5393 $100 Avro Lancaster B2 90 90
5394 $100 PBY-5A Catalina amphibian 90 90
5395 $100 Hawk T1As of Red Arrows 90 90
5396 $100 Avro Lancaster and De Havilland D.H. 98 Mosquito 90 90
5397 $100 BAe Hawk T1A 90 90
5398 $100 C-130 Hercules 90 90
5399 $100 Panavia Tornado GR1 90 90
5400 $100 BAe Hawk 200 in desert camouflage 90 90
5401 $150 BAe Nimrod R1P 1·25 1·25
5402 $150 Panavia Tornado F3 ADV 1·25 1·25
5403 $150 CH-47 Chinook helicopter 1·25 1·25
5404 $150 Panavia Tornado GR1A in front of hangar 1·25 1·25
MS5405 Set of six sheets, each 91×68 mm. (a) $200 Eagle and Bristol F2B fighter. (b) $200 Spitfire and EF2000 Eurofighter. (c) $300 Tiger Moth and EF2000 Eurofighter. (d) $300 Eurofighter. (e) $300 Bristol F2B fighter and two Montagu's harrier (birds). (f) $300 Bristol F2B fighter and Golden eagle Set of 6 sheets 12·00 13·00

1998. 1st Death Anniv of Diana, Princess of Wales. As T 293a of Gambia.
5406 $60 multicoloured 60 60

1998. Birth Bicentenary of Eugene Delacroix (painter). As T 293 of Gambia. Multicoloured.
5407 $60 "Corner of the Studio" (vert) 50 55
5408 $60 "Count Mornay's Apartment" (vert) 50 55
5409 $60 "Hamlet and the Two Gravediggers" (vert) 50 55
5410 $60 "George Sand" (vert) 50 55
5411 $60 "The Fiancee of Abydos" (vert) 50 55
5412 $60 "The Champs-Elysses" (vert) 50 55
5413 $60 "Lioness" (vert) 50 55
5414 $60 "Alfred Bruyas" (vert) 50 55
5415 $60 "The Sultan of Morocco" (vert) 50 55
5416 $60 "Indian with Kukri" (vert) 50 55
5417 $60 "Man in Turkish Dress" (vert) 50 55
5418 $60 "Studies of Jewish Women" (vert) 50 55
5419 $60 "Arab Horseman giving Signal" (vert) 50 55
5420 $60 "Arab Horsemen charging" (vert) 50 55
5421 $60 "A Seated Moor" (vert) 50 55
5422 $60 "Jewish Woman in Traditional Dress" (vert) 50 55
MS5423 Two sheets, each 100×90 mm. (a) $300 "Death of Sardanpole". (b) $300 "Jewish Wedding, Morocco" Set of 2 sheets 5·00 5·50

594 St. Andrew's Kirk, Georgetown

1999. 180th Anniv of St. Andrew's Kirk, Georgetown. Multicoloured.
5424 $6 Type **594** 10 10
5425 $30 Front of church 30 25
5426 $60 Front and side of church 55 50

595 Rabbit

1999. Chinese New Year ("Year of the Rabbit"). Multicoloured.
5427 $50 Type **595** 45 50
5428 $50 Rabbit (face value at bottom left) 45 50
5429 $50 Rabbit (face value at top right) 45 50
5430 $50 Rabbit (face value at top left) 45 50
MS5431 112×70 mm. $150 Rabbit on background of Chinese characters 1·25 1·40

596 Pongo driving Steam Locomotive

1999. Disney Trains. Cartoon characters. Multicoloured.
5432 $100 Type **596** 1·00 1·00
5433 $100 Puppies watching television 1·00 1·00
5434 $100 Perdita, Roger and Anita 1·00 1·00
5435 $100 Nanny with puppies 1·00 1·00
5436 $100 Horace, Jasper and Cruella De Vil 1·00 1·00
5437 $100 Rhino pulling Little John and Friar Tuck 1·00 1·00
5438 $100 Maid Marian, Robin Hood and Lady Kluck 1·00 1·00
5439 $100 Sir Hiss and Prince John 1·00 1·00
5440 $100 Allan-a-Dale on elephant 1·00 1·00
5441 $100 Rabbit family and Toby Turtle 1·00 1·00
5442 $100 Doc driving train 1·00 1·00
5443 $100 Grumpy, Happy, Sleepy and Bashful singing 1·00 1·00
5444 $100 Snow White and Prince with diamonds 1·00 1·00
5445 $100 Old Witch, animals from forest and Sneezy 1·00 1·00
5446 $100 Dopey and racoon on trolley 1·00 1·00
5447 $100 Triton driving locomotive 1·00 1·00
5448 $100 Flounder with pearls 1·00 1·00
5449 $100 Ariel, The Little Mermaid 1·00 1·00
5450 $100 Sebastian and friends in band 1·00 1·00
5451 $100 Ursula 1·00 1·00
MS5452 Five sheets. (a) 127×112 mm. $300 Horace, Jasper and Cruella De Vil (*101 Dalmatians*). (b) 127×112 mm $300 Robin Hood and Little John (*Robin Hood*). (c) 230×180 mm. $200 Doc driving train and $200 Dopey and racoon on trolley (vert) (*Snow White*). (d) 110×27 mm. $300 Ariel kissing statue (*The Little Mermaid*). (e) 127×110 mm. $300 Ariel holding starfish (*The Little Mermaid*) Set of 5 sheets 13·00 13·00

Nos. 5432/6 (characters from *101 Dalmatians*), Nos. 5437/41 (*Robin Hood*), Nos. 5442/6 (*Snow White*) and Nos. 5447/51 (*The Little Mermaid*) were each printed together, se-tenant, forming composite designs.

597 Huey skateboarding

1999. 70th Birthday of Mickey Mouse. Multicoloured.
5453 $80 Type **597** 80 80
5454 $80 Mickey Mouse skateboarding 80 80
5455 $80 Dewey skateboarding (purple cap) 80 80
5456 $80 Louie skateboarding (red cap) 80 80
5457 $80 Goofy skateboarding (lilac boots) 80 80
5458 $80 Donald Duck skateboarding (with cap) 80 80
5459 $80 Minnie Mouse rollerblading 80 80
5460 $80 Goofy rollerblading 80 80
5461 $80 Daisy Duck rollerblading (red boots) 80 80
5462 $80 Baby Duck rollerblading (yellow wheels) 80 80
5463 $80 Donald Duck rollerblading 80 80
5464 $80 Mickey Mouse rollerblading (red helmet) 80 80
5465 $80 Baby Duck rollerblading (mauve wheels) 80 80
5466 $80 Daisy Duck rollerblading (mauve boots) 80 80
5467 $80 Mickey Mouse rollerblading (mauve helmet) 80 80
5468 $80 Goofy skateboarding (red boots) 80 80
5469 $80 Dewey rollerblading 80 80
5470 $80 Donald Duck skateboarding (without cap) 80 80
MS5471 Three sheets. (a) 112×127 mm. $300 Dewey skateboarding. (b) 127×112 mm. $300 Daisy Duck. (c) 127×112 mm. $300 Goofy (horiz) Set of 3 sheets 8·50 8·50

598 *Pelargonium domesticum*

1999. Flowers of the World. Multicoloured.
5472 $60 Type **598** 60 60
5473 $60 *Oncidium macranthum* and butterfly 60 60
5474 $60 *Bepi orchidglades* 60 60
5475 $60 *Helianthus maximiliani* (two flowers) 60 60
5476 $60 *Cattleya walkeriana* 60 60
5477 $60 *Cattleya frasquita* 60 60
5478 $60 *Helianthus maximiliani* (single bloom) 60 60
5479 $60 *Paphiopedilum insigne sanderae* and *lilium longifolium* 60 60
5480 $60 *Lilium longifolium* 60 60
5481 $60 *Dendrobium nobile* 60 60
5482 $60 *Phalaenopsis schilleriana* 60 60
5483 $60 *Cymbidium alexette* 60 60
5484 $60 *Rhododendron nudiflorum* and hummingbird 60 60
5485 $60 *Phragmipedium besseae* and *laelia cinnabarina* 60 60
5486 $60 *Masdevallia veitchiana, laelia cinnabarina* and hummingbird 60 60
5487 $60 *Calochortus nuttallii* 60 60
5488 $60 *Brassolaelio cattleya* "Puregold" 60 60
5489 $60 *Laelia cinnabarina* 60 60
5490 $90 *Leptotes bicolor* and *masdevallia ignea* 60 60
5491 $90 *Sophrolaelio cattleya* and *anguloa clowesii* 60 60
5492 $90 *Laelia pumila* 60 60
5493 $90 *Masdevallia ignea* 60 60
5494 $90 *Dendrobium phalaenopsis* 60 60
5495 $90 *Anguloa clowesii* 60 60
MS5496 Two sheets, each 106×75 mm. (a) $300 *Iris pseudacorus*. (b) $300 *Ascocentrum miniatum* (vert) Set of 2 sheets 5·50 6·00

Nos. 5472/80, 5481/9 and 5490/5 were each printed together, se-tenant, with the backgrounds forming composite designs.

No. **MS**5496b is inscribed "Asocentrum" in error.

599 *Philaethria dido*

1999. Caribbean Butterflies. Multicoloured.
5497 $80 Type **599** 80 80
5498 $80 *Papilio troilus* 80 80
5499 $80 *Eueides isabella* 80 80
5500 $80 *Colobura dirce* 80 80
5501 $80 *Agraulis vanillae* 80 80
5502 $80 *Callicore maimuna* 80 80
5503 $80 *Thecla coronata* 80 80
5504 $80 *Battus polydamus* 80 80
5505 $80 *Morpho peleides* 80 80
5506 $80 *Doxocopa cherubina* 80 80
5507 $80 *Metamorpha stelenes* 80 80
5508 $80 *Catonephele numili* 80 80
MS5509 Two sheets. (a) 76×107 mm. $300 *Papilio cresphontes* (vert). (b) 107×76 mm. $300 *Battus philenor* (vert) Set of 2 sheets 5·50 6·00

Nos. 5504 and 5509b are both inscribed "Baltus" in error.

600 Actor from *The Dream*

1999. Akira Kurosawa (Japanese film director) Commemoration. Multicoloured (except No. 5519).
5510 $80 Type **600** 70 70
5511 $80 Actor from *Red Beard* 70 70
5512 $80 Scene from *Rashomon* 70 70
5513 $80 Scene from *Seven Samurai* 70 70
5514 $80 Actor from *Kagemusha* 70 70
5515 $80 Scene from *Yojimbo* 70 70
5516 $130 Akira Kurosawa wearing blue cap (horiz) 1·10 1·10
5517 $130 Resting head on right hand (horiz) 1·10 1·10
5518 $130 Wearing black jumper (horiz) 1·10 1·10
5519 $130 Looking through camera (horiz) (brown and black) 1·10 1·10
MS5520 98×68 mm. $300 Actor from *Dreams* 2·75 3·00

601 *Boletus aereus*

1999. Fungi. Multicoloured.
5521 $25 *Coprinus atramentarius* (28×33 mm) 30 20
5522 $35 *Hebeloma crustuliniforme* (28×33 mm) 40 25
5523 $60 Type **601** 60 60
5524 $60 *Coprinus comatus* 60 60
5525 $60 *Inocybe godeyi* 60 60
5526 $60 *Morchella crassipes* 60 60
5527 $60 *Lepiota acutesquamosa* 60 60
5528 $60 *Amanita phalloides* 60 60
5529 $60 *Boletus spadiceus* 60 60
5530 $60 *Cortinarius collinitus* 60 60
5531 $60 *Lepiota procera* 60 60
5532 $60 *Russula ochroleuca* 60 60
5533 $60 *Hygrophorus hypotheius* 60 60
5534 $60 *Amanita rubescens* 60 60
5535 $60 *Boletus satanas* 60 60
5536 $60 *Amanita echinocephala* 60 60
5537 $60 *Amanita muscaria* 60 60
5538 $60 *Boletus badius* 60 60
5539 $60 *Hebeloma radicosum* 60 60
5540 $60 *Mycena polygramma* 60 60
5541 $100 *Russula nigricans* (28×33 mm) 90 90
5542 $200 *Tricholoma aurantium* (28×33 mm) 1·60 1·75

MS5543 Two sheets. (a) 70×98 mm. $300 *Pluteus cervinus*. (b) 98×70 mm. $300 *Lepiota acutesquamosa* Set of 2 sheets 5·50 6·00

No. **MS**5543b is inscribed "Acutesquamoso" in error.

602 Shinkansen 100 Series Bullet Train, Japan (1984)

1999. "Australia '99" International Stamp Exhibition, Melbourne. Trains. Multicoloured (except Nos. 5550/5, each brown, yellow and black, and MS5568b/d).

5544 $80 Type **602** 75 75
5545 $80 Ukrainian ZMGR diesel locomotive, Russia (1983) 75 75
5546 $80 Rhatische Bahn electric locomotive No. 706, Germany 75 75
5547 $80 Eurostar T.G.V. train, France (1986) 75 75
5548 $80 Atlantique T.G.V. train, France (1989) 75 75
5549 $80 Class 86-6 diesel locomotive No. 86604, Great Britain 75 75
5550 $80 Joseph Clark steam locomotive, U.S.A. (1868) 75 75
5551 $80 Diamond Stack Bethel steam locomotive, U.S.A. (1863) 75 75
5552 $80 New York Central steam locomotive No. 999, U.S.A. (1890) 75 75
5553 $80 Boston and Maine steam locomotive *Ballardville*, U.S.A. (1876) 75 75
5554 $80 Portland Rochester Railroad steam locomotive, U.S.A. (1863) 75 75
5555 $80 Baltimore and Ohio Railroad steam locomotive, U.S.A. (1881) 75 75
5556 $80 Burlington Northern GP 39-2 diesel locomotive, U.S.A. (1974) 75 75
5557 $80 CSX GP40-2 diesel locomotive, U.S.A. (1967) 75 75
5558 $80 Erie Lackawana Railroad GP 9 diesel locomotive, U.S.A. (1956) 75 75
5559 $80 Amtrak P 42 Genesis No. 82 train, U.S.A. (1993) 75 75
5560 $80 Erie Railroad S-2 diesel locomotive, U.S.A. (1948) 75 75
5561 $80 Pennsylvania Railroad S-1 diesel locomotive, U.S.A. (1947) 75 75
5562 $80 Northern and Western steam locomotive No. 610, U.S.A. (1933) 75 75
5563 $80 Pennsylvania Railroad M1B Mountain steam locomotive, U.S.A. (1930) 75 75
5564 $80 Reading Railroad FP7A diesel locomotive, U.S.A. (1951) 75 75
5565 $80 New York Central steam locomotive No. 765, U.S.A. (1940) 75 75
5566 $80 Union Pacific steam locomotive No. 3985, U.S.A. (1963) 75 75
5567 $80 GP 15-15-1 diesel locomotive, U.S.A. (1956) 75 75

MS5568 Four sheets. (a) 70×98 mm. $300 George Nagelmackers (founder of International Sleeping Car Co.) (vert). (b) 70×98 mm. $300 R. F. Trevithick (engineer, Japanese National Railways) (vert) (violet and black). (c) 70×98 mm. $300 Alfred de Glehn (locomotive designer) (vert) (brown and black). (d) 98×70 mm. $300 George Stephen (president of Canadian Pacific) (vert) (brown and black) Set of 4 sheets 10·00 11·00

1999. Royal Wedding. As T 298 of Gambia. Multicoloured.

5569 $150 Sophie Rhys-Jones in multicoloured dress 1·25 1·25
5570 $150 Prince Edward with Sophie Rhys-Jones inspecting guard of honour 1·25 1·25
5571 $150 Sophie Rhys-Jones wearing grey jacket 1·25 1·25
5572 $150 Prince Edward wearing striped shirt 1·25 1·25
5573 $150 Prince Edward and Sohpie Rhys-Jones at the races 1·25 1·25
5574 $150 Sophie Rhys-Jones holding blue folder 1·25 1·25
5575 $150 Prince Edward wearing blue shirt 1·25 1·25
5576 $150 Sophie Rhys-Jones wearing black outfit 1·25 1·25

MS5577 Two sheets, each 83×66 mm. (a) $300 Prince Edward and Sophie Rhys-Jones in front of blossom (horiz). (b) $300 Prince Edward and Sophie Rhys-Jones in front of building (horiz) Set of 2 sheets 5·00 5·50

1999. John Glenn's Return to Space. As T 136 of Grenadines of Grenada. Multicoloured.

5578 $100 John Glenn (American astronaut) in spacesuit, 1962 90 90
5579 $100 Relaxing after landing, 1962 90 90
5580 $100 As Senator for Ohio, 1974 90 90
5581 $100 In spacesuit and helmet for Space Shuttle flight, 1998 90 90
5582 $100 In spacesuit without helmet, 1998 90 90

No. 5582 is dated "1992" in error.

1999. "iBRA '99" International Stamp Exhibition, Nuremberg. As T 299a of Gambia. Multicoloured.

5583 $60 Class E10 electric locomotive, Germany, 1952 (vert) 60 50
5584 $200 Early steam locomotive, Der Adler, Germany, 1835 1·75 1·90

No. 5584 is inscribed "CLASS 01 STEAM EXPRESS TRAIN, GERMANY, 1926" in error.

1999. 150th Death Anniv of Katsushika Hokusai (Japanese artist). As T 299b of Gambia. Multicoloured.

5585 $80 "Travellers climbing a Mountain Path" 70 75
5586 $80 "Washing Clothes in a River" 70 75
5587 $80 "The Blind" (old man smiling) 70 75
5588 $80 "The Blind" (man with beard) 70 75
5589 $80 "Convolvulus and Tree-frog" 70 75
5590 $80 "Fishermen hauling a Net" 70 75
5591 $80 "Hibiscus and Sparrow" 70 75
5592 $80 "Hydrangea and Swallow" 70 75
5593 $80 "The Blind" (man yawning) 70 75
5594 $80 "The Blind" (old man frowning) 70 75
5595 $80 "Irises" 70 75
5596 $80 "Lilies" 70 75

MS5597 Two sheets, each 101×72 mm. (a) $300 "Flowering Cherries at Mount Yoshino" (vert). (b) $300 "View of Stone Causeway" (vert) Set of 2 sheets 5·00 5·50

1999. 10th Anniv of U.N. Rights of the Child Convention. As T 299c of Gambia. Multicoloured.

5598 $150 Two girls 1·25 1·40
5599 $150 Two boys 1·25 1·40
5600 $150 One boy 1·25 1·40

MS5601 $300 Prince Talal, UNICEF special envoy, 1980 2·75 3·00

Nos. 5598/600 were printed together, se-tenant, with the backgrounds forming a composite design.

1999. "PhilexFrance '99" International Stamp Exhibition, Paris. Railway Locomotives. Two sheets, each 106×82 mm, containing horiz designs as T 299d of Gambia. Multicoloured.

MS5602 (a) $300 Class 7000 high-speed locomotive, 1949–55. (b) $300 Class 241-P steam locomotive, 1947–49 Set of 2 sheets 5·50 6·00

1999. 250th Birth Anniv of Johann von Goethe (German writer). As T 299e of Gambia.

5603 $150 green, black and blue 1·25 1·40
5604 $150 blue, violet and black 1·25 1·40
5605 $150 blue, brown and black 1·25 1·40

MS5606 78×109 mm. $300 brown, chocolate and black 2·75 3·00

DESIGNS—HORIZ: No. 5603, Lynceus singing from the watchtower; 5604, Von Goethe and Von Schiller; 5605, The Fallen Icarus. VERT: **MS**5606, Mephistopheles as a salamander.

603 Kurt Masur (German conductor and musician)

1999. Year of the Older Person. Multicoloured (except No. MS5625).

5607 $50 Type **603** 50 50
5608 $50 Rupert Murdoch (newspaper publisher) 50 50
5609 $50 Margaret Thatcher (former British Prime Minister) 50 50
5610 $50 Pope John Paul II 50 50
5611 $50 Mikhail Gorbachev (Russian leader) 50 50
5612 $50 Ted Turner (American politician) 50 50
5613 $50 Sophia Loren (Italian actress) 50 50
5614 $50 Nelson Mandela (South African leader) 50 50
5615 $50 John Glenn (American astronaut) 50 50
5616 $50 Luciano Pavarotti (Italian opera singer) 50 50
5617 $50 Queen Elizabeth, the Queen Mother 50 50
5618 $50 Jimmy Carter (former American President) 50 50
5619 $100 Ronald Reagan (former American president) in football shirt 80 80
5620 $100 Ronald Reagan wearing black shirt 80 80
5621 $100 Ronald Reagan in military uniform 80 80
5622 $100 Ronald Reagan wearing stetson 80 80
5623 $100 Ronald Reagan feeding chimp with bottle 80 80
5624 $100 Ronald Reagan in evening dress 80 80

MS5625 111×111 mm. $300 Ronald Reagan in star (black) 2·75 3·00

604 Pope John Paul II praying

1999. Pope John Paul II. Multicoloured.

5626 $80 Type **604** 80 80
5627 $80 Pope John Paul II (face value at top right) 80 80
5628 $80 Pope John Paul II smiling (face value at bottom left) 80 80
5629 $80 With crucifix 80 80
5630 $80 Pope John Paul II wearing black cloak 80 80
5631 $80 Pope John Paul II (face value at bottom right) 80 80

1999. 30th Anniv of First Manned Landing on Moon. As T 298c of Gambia but horiz. Multicoloured.

5632 $80 Konstantin Tsiolkovsky and first Russian artificial satellite, 1959 (vert) 70 75
5633 $80 Launch of "Apollo 11" (vert) 70 75
5634 $80 Astronaut descending onto Moon (vert) 70 75
5635 $80 Collecting samples of lunar rock (vert) 70 75
5636 $80 "Apollo 11" lunar module, *Eagle* (vert) 70 75
5637 $80 Splashdown of command module *Columbia* (vert) 70 75
5638 $80 "Apollo 11" after launch 70 75
5639 $80 "Apollo 11" modules after separation from rocket 70 75
5640 $80 Astronaut leaving *Eagle* for moon walk 70 75
5641 $80 Seismic experiments equipment 70 75
5642 $80 *Eagle* leaving Moon 70 75
5643 $80 *Eagle* after splashdown 70 75

MS5644 Two sheets, each 106×83 mm. (a) $300 Astronaut saluting American flag on Moon. (b) $300 Astronaut Michael Collins Set of 2 sheets 5·00 5·50

605 *Breitling Orbiter* 3 (balloon)

1999. 1st Non-stop Round-the-World Balloon Flight by Breitling Orbiter 3. Multicoloured.

5645 $150 Type **605** 1·25 1·40
5646 $150 Flight logo 1·25 1·40
5647 $150 Bertrand Piccard (balloonist) 1·25 1·40
5648 $150 Brian Jones (balloonist) 1·25 1·40

MS5649 100×70 mm. $300 *Breitling Orbiter 3* 2·75 3·00

606 Sidney Sheldon

1999. Great Authors of the 20th Century. Sidney Sheldon.

5650 **606** $80 multicoloured 70 70

607 Scarlet Macaw ("Marron Macaw")

1999. South American Lories and Parrots. Multicoloured.

5651 $60 Type **607** 60 60
5652 $60 Thick-billed parrot 60 60
5653 $60 Golden-crowned conure 60 60
5654 $60 Yellow-collared macaw 60 60
5655 $60 Double yellow-headed amazon 60 60
5656 $60 Mountain parakeet ("Golden-fronted Parakeet") 60 60
5657 $60 Maroon-bellied conure 60 60
5658 $60 Nanday conure 60 60
5659 $60 Hyacinth macaw 4·50 4·50
5660 $60 Blue and yellow macaw ("Blue and Gold Macaw") 60 60
5661 $60 Blue-fronted amazon 60 60
5662 $60 Amazon parrot 60 60
5663 $60 Sun conure 60 60
5664 $60 Orange-chinned parakeet ("Tivi Parakeet") 60 60
5665 $60 Golden conure ("Bavaria's Conure") 60 60
5666 $60 Fairy lorikeet 60 60

MS5667 Two sheets, each 110×85 mm. (a) $300 Jendaya conure (horiz). (b) $300 Grey-cheeked parakeet Set of 2 sheets 5·50 6·00

Nos. 5651/8 and 5659/66 were each printed together, se-tenant, with the backgrounds forming composite designs.

Nos. 5653, 5657 and 5658 are inscribed "CANURE", "BILLED" and "NANDAYA", all in error.

608 Queen Elizabeth the Queen Mother during Second World War

1999. Queen Elizabeth the Queen Mother's 99th Birthday. Multicoloured.

5668 $60 Type **608** 60 60
5669 $60 Wedding of Duke and Duchess of York, 1923 60 60
5670 $60 Lady Elizabeth Bowes-Lyon as a child 60 60
5671 $60 At Coronation, 1937 60 60
5672 $60 Queen Mother, 1971 60 60
5673 $60 Queen Mother wearing red hat, 1991 60 60
5674 $60 Lady Elizabeth Bowes-Lyon, 1914 60 60
5675 $60 Queen Mother, 1988 60 60
5676 $60 At Royal Agricultural Show during 1950s 60 60
5677 $60 Queen Mother, 1960 60 60

MS5678 50×76 mm. $1000 Queen Mother holding bouquet (43×69 mm). Imperf 9·00 9·50

1999. "Queen Elizabeth the Queen Mother's Century". As T 305a of Gambia.

5679 $130 multicoloured 1·25 1·25
5680 $130 black and gold 1·25 1·25
5681 $130 black and gold 1·25 1·25
5682 $130 multicoloured 1·25 1·25

MS5683 154×158 mm. $400 multicoloured 3·75 4·00

DESIGNS: No. 5679, Duchess of York with Princess Elizabeth, 1928; 5680, Lady Elizabeth Bowes-Lyon, 1914; 5681, Queen Elizabeth with Princess Elizabeth, 1940; 5682, Queen Elizabeth the Queen Mother in Venice, 1984. (37×50 mm)—**MS**5683, Queen Mother in Canada, 1988.

609 Mei Lanfang

1999. "China '99" International Stamp Exhibition, Beijing. 40th Death Anniv of Mei Lanfang (Chinese opera singer). Sheet 118×78 mm.

MS5684 $400 multicoloured 3·00 3·25

610 Wang Guangning

1999. Chinese Football League Players. Multicoloured.

5685 $50 Type **610** 45 50
5686 $50 Gao Feng ("H" emblem) 45 50
5687 $50 Jian Hong (goalkeeper) (bull emblem) 45 50
5688 $50 Gao Zhongxun (Yanbian football club) 45 50
5689 $50 Yao Xia (SCQXFC) 45 50
5690 $50 Zhang Yuning ("E" emblem) 45 50
5691 $50 Zhang Weihua (Matsunichi) 45 50
5692 $50 Dragon logo 45 50
5693 $60 Cai Sheng (winged comma logo) 50 55
5694 $60 Li Weifeng ("A" emblem) 50 55
5695 $60 Xie Zhaoyang (Beijing Guoan) 50 55
5696 $60 Li Xiaopeng (LNTS) 50 55
5697 $60 Hao Haidong (Dalian Wanda) 50 55
5698 $60 Zhang Xiaorui (TEDA) 50 55
5699 $60 Qi Hong (Shenhu) 50 55
5700 $60 Dragon logo 50 55

1999. John F. Kennedy Jr. Commemoration. As T 307 of Gambia. Multicoloured.

5701 $80 John Junior as a child with mother 70 75
5702 $80 John Junior under father's desk 70 75
5703 $80 John and Jacqueline Kennedy as a young couple 70 75
5704 $80 Jacqueline Kennedy 70 75
5705 $80 John Junior with sister, Caroline 70 75
5706 $80 President John Kennedy 70 75
5707 $160 John Junior at father's funeral 1·25 1·40
5708 $160 John Junior as an adult with mother, Jacqueline 1·25 1·40
5709 $160 John Junior in front of U.S. flag 1·25 1·40

1999. Birth Centenary of Enzo Ferrari, 1998 (car manufacturer). As T 564a of Ghana. Multicoloured.

5710 $30 312 T2 racing car 30 25
5711 $35 553 F.1 racing car 35 25
5712 $60 D 50 racing car 50 40
5713 $100 212 Export sports car 1·00 1·00
5714 $100 410 Superamerica saloon 1·00 1·00
5715 $100 125 S sports car 1·00 1·00
5716 $200 246 F.1 racing car 1·50 1·60
5717 $300 126/C2 racing car 2·25 2·50
5718 $400 312/B2 racing car 2·75 3·00
MS5719 104×70 mm. $300 512 S sports cars (93×35 mm) 2·50 2·75

611 Inter-American Development Bank Logo

1999. 40th Anniv of Inter-American Development Bank.

5720 **611** $30 multicoloured 30 25

1999. New Millennium (1st issue). People and Events of Eleventh Century (1050–1100). As T 310b of Gambia. Multicoloured.

5721 $35 Indians with pots (Anasazi trading centre, 1050) 35 35
5722 $35 Catalan "Black Virgin" statue (carved, 1050) 35 35
5723 $35 Horse archer (Seljuk conquest of Armenia, 1064) 35 35
5724 $35 Halley's Comet (appearance, 1066) 35 35
5725 $35 Norman cavalry (Battle of Hastings, 1066) 35 35
5726 $35 William I of England (crowned, 1066) 35 35
5727 $35 Samurai warriors (power of Fujiwara clan checked, 1068) 35 35
5728 $35 Henry IV, Holy Roman Emperor (excommunicated, 1076) 35 35
5729 $35 Timbuktu (founded, 1087) 35 35
5730 $35 Students (foundation of Bologna University, 1088) 35 35
5731 $35 Gondola, Venice (introduction, 1094) 35 35
5732 $35 El Cid (Spanish warrior) (capture of Valencia, 1094) 35 35
5733 $35 Mounted knights (First Crusade, 1095) 35 35
5734 $35 Saracen infantry (capture of Jerusalem, 1099) 35 35
5735 $35 Statue of Guanyin (Chinese deity) (carved, 1100) 35 35
5736 $35 Couple and quote from the Rubiayat of Omar Khayyam (written, 1100) (55×36 mm) 35 35
5737 $35 Decorating jar (introduction of Syrian style storage jars, 1100) 35 35

1999. New Millennium (2nd issue). People and Events of Twentieth Century (1910–1919). As T 471a of Grenada. Multicoloured.

5738 $35 Poster for Grafton Gallery's Post Impressionist Exhibition, 1910 35 35
5739 $35 Trial scene and oil rig (Standard Oil case, 1911) 35 35
5740 $35 Harriet Quimby (first American woman pilot, 1911) 35 35
5741 $35 U.S. Senate (declaration of war, 1917) 35 35
5742 $35 Sinking of *Titanic*, 1912 35 35
5743 $35 Emperor Pu Yi (formation of Chinese Republic, 1913) 35 35
5744 $35 Statue over entrance (opening of Grand Central Station, New York, 1913) 35 35
5745 $35 Archduke Francis Ferdinand of Austria and cavalry (assassinated, 1914) 35 35
5746 $35 Map and lock gates (opening of Panama Canal, 1914) 35 35
5747 $35 Lawrence of Arabia (Arab revolt, 1916) 35 35
5748 $35 Burning buildings, Dublin (Easter Rising, 1916) 35 35
5749 $35 Lenin and revolutionaries (Russian Revolution, 1917) 35 35
5750 $35 Tsar Nicholas II and family (murdered, 1917) 35 35
5751 $35 Treaty of Versailles, 1918 35 35
5752 $35 Three patients and poster (influenza epidemic, 1919) 35 35
5753 $35 Leo Tolstoy and Mark Twain (deaths, 1910) (55×36 mm) 35 35
5754 $35 Walter Gropius and Bauhaus (opened 1919) 35 35

Dates on Nos. 5750 and 5751 are transposed. No. 5754 is inscribed "Bahaus" in error.

1999. Faces of the Millennium. Diana, Princess of Wales. As T 307a of Gambia. Multicoloured.

5755 $80 Top of head (face value at left) 70 75
5756 $80 Top of head (face value at right) 70 75
5757 $80 Ear (face value at left) 70 75
5758 $80 Eye and temple (face value at right) 70 75
5759 $80 Cheek (face value at left) 70 75
5760 $80 Cheek (face value at right) 70 75
5761 $80 Blue background (face value at left) 70 75
5762 $80 Chin (face value at right) 70 75

Nos. 5755/62 were printed together, se-tenant, in sheetlets of 8 with the stamps arranged in two vertical columns separated by a gutter also containing miniature flower photographs. When viewed as a whole the sheetlet forms a portrait of Diana, Princess of Wales.

612 Dragon

2000. Chinese New Year ("Year of the Dragon"). Multicoloured.

5763 $100 Type **612** (face value bottom right) 85 90
5764 $100 Dragon (face value bottom left) 85 90
5765 $100 Dragon (face value top right) 85 90
5766 $100 Dragon (face value top left) 85 90
MS5767 102×70 mm. $300 Dragon on background of Chinese characters 2·50 2·75

613 Cugnot's Steam-powered Fardier (1769)

2000. Cars. Multicoloured.

5768 $100 Type **613** 80 80
5769 $100 Marcus's motor carriage (1875) 80 80
5770 $100 Benz Velo (1894) 80 80
5771 $100 Bordino's steam carriage (1854) 80 80
5772 $100 Benz Motorwagen (1886) 80 80
5773 $100 Black Model T Ford (1908) 80 80
5774 $100 Duesenberg Model A phaeton (1926) 80 80
5775 $100 Mercedes-Benz Model K (1927) 80 80
5776 $100 Rolls-Royce Phantom I (1928) 80 80
5777 $100 Auburn 851 Speedster (1935) 80 80
5778 $100 Mercedes-Benz 540K Cabriolet B (1936) 80 80
5779 $100 Volkswagen Beetle (1949) 80 80
5780 $100 Ford Thunderbird (1957) 80 80
5781 $100 Jaguar XK150 (1957) 80 80
5782 $100 Chevrolet Corvette Sting-ray (1968) 80 80
5783 $100 BMW 2002 Turbo (1973) 80 80
5784 $100 Porsche 911 Turbo (1975) 80 80
5785 $100 Volkswagen Beetle (1999) 80 80
5786 $100 Daimler (1886) 80 80
5787 $100 Opel Luzman (1898) 80 80
5788 $100 Benz Landaulet Coupe (1899) 80 80
5789 $100 Peugeot Vis-a-vis (1892) 80 80
5790 $100 Benz Patent Motor Car (1886) 80 80
5791 $100 Benz Velo (1894) 80 80
5792 $100 Ford (1896) 80 80
5793 $100 De Dion-Bouton Populare (1903) 80 80
5794 $100 Adler (1900) 80 80
5795 $100 Vauxhall (1904) 80 80
5796 $100 Rolls Royce Silver Ghost (1908) 80 80
5797 $100 Model T Ford (1908) (different) 80 80
MS5798 Five sheets. (a) 105×80 mm. $400 Mercedes Benz 60/70 (1904) (50×38 mm). (b) 105×80 mm. $400 Mercedes Benz Type 320 Cabriolet (1939) (50×38 mm). (c) 105×80 mm. $400 Mercedes Benz 300 SL Gullwing (1954) (50×38 mm). (d) 81×63 mm. $400 Runabout (1910) (50×38 mm). (e) 81×63 mm. $400 Turner Miesse (1904) (50×38 mm) Set of 5 sheets 14·00 15·00

No. 5791 is inscribed "VELD" in error.

614 Top of Head

2000. Faces of the Millennium. George Washington. Designs showing a collage of miniature bank note photographs. Multicoloured.

5799 $80 Type **614** 70 75
5800 $80 Top of head (face value at right) 70 75
5801 $80 Ear (face value at left) 70 75
5802 $80 Cheek (face value at right) 70 75
5803 $80 Right shoulder (face value at left) 70 75
5804 $80 Left shoulder (face value at right) 70 75
5805 $80 Right upper arm (face value at left) 70 75
5806 $80 Left upper arm (face value at right) 70 75

Nos. 5799/806 were printed together, se-tenant, in sheetlets of 8 with the stamps arranged in two vertical columns separated by a gutter also containing miniature photographs. When viewed as a whole the sheetlet forms a portrait of George Washington.

615 Hogfish (*Lachnolaimus maximus*)

2000. Tropical Marine Life. Multicoloured.

5807 $30 Type **615** 30 25
5808 $35 Flamingo-tongue cowrie (*Cyphoma gibbosum*) 35 25
5809 $60 Permit (*Trachinotus falcatus*) 60 40
5810 $80 Lionfish (*Pterois volitans*) (vert) 70 75
5811 $80 Bottle-nosed dolphin (*Tursiops truncatus*) (vert) 70 75
5812 $80 Jellyfish (*Diplulmaris antarctica*) (vert) 70 75
5813 $80 Grey angelfish (*Pomacanthus arcuatus*) (vert) 70 75
5814 $80 Spotted eagle ray (*Aetobatus narinari*) (vert) 70 75
5815 $80 Grey reef shark (*Carcharhinus amblyrhynchos*) (vert) 70 75
5816 $80 Sea bass (*Sacura margaritacea*) (vert) 70 75
5817 $80 Giant octopus (*Octopus dolfeini*) (vert) 70 75
5818 $80 Great barracuda (*Sphyraena barracuda*) 70 75
5819 $80 Gulper eel (*Saccopharynx sp*) 70 75
5820 $80 Sea slug (*Chromodoris amoena*) 70 75
5821 $80 Blue marlin (*Makaira nigricans*) 70 75
5822 $80 Killer whale (*Orcinus orca*) 70 75
5823 $80 Reid's seahorse (*Hippocampus reidi*) 70 75
5824 $80 Green sea turtle (*Chelonia mydas*) 70 75
5825 $80 Sailfin blenny (*Emblemaria pandionis*) 70 75
5826 $80 Indigo hamlet (*Hypoplectrus indigo*) 70 75
5827 $80 Scallop (*Chlamys hastata*) 70 75
5828 $80 Flag rockfish (*Sebastes rubrivinctus*) 70 75
5829 $80 Lookdown (*Selene vomer*) 70 75
5830 $80 Orange marginella (*Marginella carnea*) 70 75
5831 $80 Harbour seal (*Phocus vitulina*) 70 75
5832 $80 Dolphin fish (*Coryphaena hippurus*) 70 75
5833 $80 Coney (*Epinephelus fulvus*) 70 75
5834 $100 Spot-finned hogfish (*Bodianus pulchellus*) 90 90
5835 $200 Porkfish (*Anisotremus virginicus*) 1·60 1·75
5836 $300 Orange-throated darter (*Etheostoma spectabile*) 2·25 2·50
MS5837 Three sheets. (a) 85×110 mm. $400 Snakestar (*Asteroschema tenue*) (vert). (b) 85×110 mm. $400 Penpoint gunnel (*Apodichthys flavidus*) (vert). (c) 110×85 mm. $400 Spotted cleaner shrimp (*Periclimenes pedersoni* (57×42 mm) Set of 3 sheets 9·00 9·50

Nos. 5810/17, 5818/25 and 5826/33 were each printed together, se-tenant, with the backgrounds forming composite designs.

2000. 18th Birthday of Prince William. As T 312b of Gambia. Multicoloured.

5838 $100 Prince William with Prince Harry 1·00 1·00
5839 $100 As a young boy, holding present 1·00 1·00
5840 $100 Prince William wearing suit and white shirt 1·00 1·00
5841 $100 Wearing suit and blue shirt 1·00 1·00
MS5842 100×80 mm. $400 Dressed for skiing (37×50 mm) 3·75 4·00

2000. "EXPO 2000" World Stamp Exhibition, Anaheim, USA. Space Satellites. As T 582a of Ghana. Multicoloured.

5843 $100 "Apollo 11" 80 85
5844 $100 "Pioneer" and Saturn 80 85
5845 $100 Nasa/Esa "Soho" Satellite 80 85
5846 $100 Nasa "Mars Orbiter" and Mars 80 85
5847 $100 Space Shuttle and International Space Station 80 85
5848 $100 "Giotto" and Halley's Comet 80 85
5849 $100 "Amsat IIIC" (vert) 80 85
5850 $100 "Sret" (vert) 80 85
5851 $100 "Inspector" (vert) 80 85
5852 $100 "Stardust" (vert) 80 85
5853 $100 "Temisat" (vert) 80 85
5854 $100 "Arsene" (vert) 80 85
5855 $100 "Cesar" with Argentine and Spanish flags 80 85
5856 $100 "Sirio 2" with Italian flag 80 85
5857 $100 "Taos S 80" with French flag 80 85
5858 $100 "Viking" with Swedish flag 80 85
5859 $100 "SCD 1" with Brazilian flag 80 85
5860 $100 "Offeq 1" with Israeli flag 80 85
MS5861 Two sheets. (a) 106×76 mm. $400 "Solar Max". (b) 76×106 mm. $400 Clementine French Satellite "Ariane V 124" (vert) 6·00 6·50

No. 5845 is inscribed "Satellit" in error.

2000. 25th Anniv of "Apollo-Soyuz" Joint Project. As T 582a of Ghana. Multicoloured.

5862 $200 Thomas Stafford and Vance Brand ("Apollo 18" astronauts) 1·60 1·75
5863 $200 "Apollo 18" command module 1·60 1·75
5864 $200 Thomas Stafford and Valeri Kubasov (Russian cosmonaut) 1·60 1·75
MS5865 88×71 mm. $400 Donald Slayton and Thomas Stafford ("Apollo 18" astronauts) (horiz) 2·75 3·00

2000. 50th Anniv of Berlin Film Festival. As T 582c of Ghana. Multicoloured.

5866 $100 "Das Boot ist Voll", 1981 80 85
5867 $100 "David", 1979 80 85
5868 $100 "Hong Gaoliang", 1988 80 85
5869 $100 "Die Ehe der Maria Braun", 1979 80 85
5870 $100 "The Whisperers", 1967 80 85
5871 $100 "Le Vieil Homme et L'Enfant", 1967 80 85
MS5872 97×103 mm. $400 "Love Streams", 1984 3·00 3·25

No. 5871 omits "L'ENFANT" from the film title.

2000. 175th Anniv of Stockton and Darlington Line (first public railway). As T 582c of Ghana. Multicoloured.

5873 $200 Timothy Hackworth 2·25 2·25
5874 $200 Hackworth's "Sans Pareil" engine 2·25 2·25
5875 $200 Bramhope Tunnel, Otley 2·25 2·25

Nos. 5874 and 5875 are inscribed "Sansareil" and "Branhope", both in error.

616 Johann Sebastian Bach

2000. 250th Death Anniv of Johann Sebastian Bach (German composer). Sheet 88×76 mm.

MS5876 **616** $400 multicoloured 5·00 5·00

2000. Election of Albert Einstein (mathematical physicist) as Time Magazine "Man of the Century". Sheet 117×91 mm, containing vert design as T 312d of Gambia. Multicoloured.

MS5877 $400 Albert Einstein 3·25 3·50

2000. Centenary of First Zeppelin Flight. As T 582c of Ghana. Multicoloured.

5878 $200 Count von Zeppelin and LZ-1 airship, 1900 1·75 1·90
5879 $200 Von Zeppelin and LZ-2, 1906 1·75 1·90
5880 $200 Von Zeppelin and LZ-9, 1911 1·75 1·90
MS5881 84×114 mm. $400 LZ-127 Zeppelin, 1928 (50×38 mm) 3·50 3·75

2000. Olympic Games, Sydney. As T 582f of Ghana. Multicoloured.

5882 $160 Henry Robert Pearce (single sculls rower), Los Angeles (1932) 1·25 1·40
5883 $160 Volleyball 1·25 1·40
5884 $160 Olympic Park, Canada (1976) and Canadian flag 1·25 1·40
5885 $160 Ancient Greek athletes 1·25 1·40

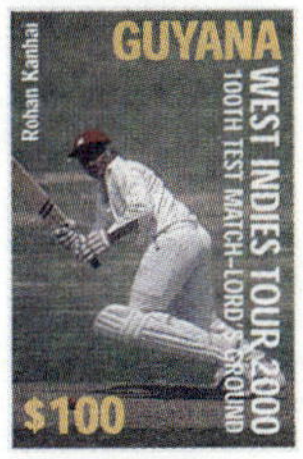

617 Rohan Kanhai

2000. West Indies Cricket Tour and 100th Test Match at Lord's. Multicoloured.

5886 $100 Type **617** 1·50 1·00
5887 $300 Clive Lloyd 3·00 3·00
MS5888 121×104 mm. $400 Lord's Cricket Ground, London (horiz) 4·50 4·75

618 Flags of China and Macau

2000. Return of Macau to Chinese Sovereignty. Sheet 144×119 mm, containing T 618 and similar horiz design. Multicoloured.

MS5889 $150 Type **618**; $150 Downtown Macau 2·50 2·75

2000. Betty Boop (cartoon character). As T 308 of Gambia. Multicoloured.

5890 $80 Betty Boop wearing striped shirt 65 70
5891 $80 With shopping bags 65 70
5892 $80 Kneeling on cushion 65 70
5893 $80 As belly dancer 65 70
5894 $80 Putting on shoe 65 70
5895 $80 Wearing cowboy boots 65 70
5896 $80 Betty Boop dancing 65 70
5897 $80 In flowered trousers 65 70
5898 $80 In black dress 65 70
MS5899 Twenty-two sheets. (a) 137×87 mm. $400 In blue dress and fur stole; (b) 137×87 mm. $400 In polka dot dress; (c) 120×95 mm. $400 Standing in shell; (d) 111×127 mm. $400 In red dress by the sea; (e) 121×95 mm. $400 Wearing brown coat and red scarf; (f) 120×95 mm. $400 With tennis racket; (g) 121×101 mm. $400 Winking; (h) 120×96 mm. $400 Wearing black feather boa and brown hat; (i) 95×133 mm. $400 With sad expression (horiz). (j) 91×143 mm. $400 Wearing ruff; (k) 90×140 mm. $400 Wearing orange t-shirt and baseball hat (horiz). (l) 90×140 mm. $400 Wearing red vest top; (m) 140×90 mm. $400 Wearing pink baseball hat; (n) 90×140 mm. $400 Wearing red dress and orange sash; (o) 89×139 mm. $400 Holding present; (p) 89×139 mm. $400 Wearing party hat (horiz). (q) 89×139 mm. $400 Wearing sailor's hat; (r) 89×139 mm. $400 In red bikini; (s) 89×139 mm. $400 With sunglasses on head; (t) 89×139 mm. $400 In mauve vest top and blue dungarees (horiz). (u) 89×139 mm. $400 In mauve vest top; (v) 89×139 mm. $400 With mauve flower in hair Set of 22 sheets 55·00 60·00

2000. Scenes from I Love Lucy (American T.V. comedy series). As T 309 of Gambia, but vert. Multicoloured.

5900 $60 Lucy reading a thriller 50 55
5901 $60 Lucy and Ricky talking 50 55
5902 $60 Ricky whispering to Lucy 50 55
5903 $60 Lucy looking out of window 50 55
5904 $60 Lucy behind Ethel 50 55
5905 $60 Ricky holding red scarf over Lucy 50 55
5906 $60 Ethel and Lucy with frying pan 50 55
5907 $60 Ricky with frying pan 50 55
5908 $60 Lucy and Ethel sitting on sofa next to coffee table 50 55
MS5909 Ten sheets. (a) 120×95 mm. $400 Lucy in pink dressing gown. (b) 120×95 mm. $400 Lucy with dustbin lid. (c) 100×134 mm. $400 Lucy wearing glasses. (d) 138×100 mm. $400 Lucy wearing blue hat and green coat. (e) 93×137 mm. $400 Lucy dancing the rumba. (f) 137×100 mm. $400 Lucy wearing green hat. (g) 100×134 mm. $400 Lucy with knives. (h) 137×100 mm. $400 Lucy wearing black hat. (i) 93×137 mm. $400 Lucy in checked shirt. (j) 137×100 mm. $400 Lucy wearing leis Set of 10 sheets 27·00 29·00

2000. Scenes from The Three Stooges (American T.V. comedy series). As T 310 of Gambia. Multicoloured.

5910 $80 Larry, Moe and Curly (The Three Stooges) with man in green jacket 65 70
5911 $80 Larry and Moe with skeleton 65 70
5912 $80 Shemp with hair standing on end 65 70
5913 $80 Larry, Moe and Curly with fingers in mouths 65 70
5914 $80 Larry, Moe and Curly reading a book 65 70
5915 $80 Larry, Moe and Curly holding man in bowler hat 65 70
5916 $80 Shemp pointing a gun at Larry and Moe 65 70
5917 $80 Moe and Shemp holding Larry (being kicked in stomach by man in blue) 65 70
5918 $80 Moe and Shemp looking at man in window 65 70
5919 $80 Moe pointing syphon bottle at Larry, with Shemp behind 65 70
5920 $80 Larry, Moe and Shemp as cave men (Moe with rock on head) 65 70
5921 $80 Moe with cow 65 70
5922 $80 Shemp with bucket on head 65 70
5923 $80 Moe, Shemp and Larry as cavemen (three wise monkeys) 65 70
5924 $80 Moe, Shemp and Larry as cavemen (Shemp holding large rock) 65 70
5925 $80 Larry, Moe and Shemp wearing pith helmets 65 70
5926 $80 Moe, Shemp and Larry in front of painting 65 70
5927 $80 Moe, Larry and Shemp with false beards 65 70
MS5928 Four sheets (a) 92×122 mm. $400 Shemp wearing tam-o'-shanter (vert). (b)122×92 mm. $400 Larry with skeleton. (c) 131×103 mm. $400 Larry with lady in blue dress (vert). (d) 131×103 mm. $400 Moe being pulled by collar Set of 4 sheets 11·00 12·00

619 Outline Drawing of Dove on Head

2000. 3rd Annual Caribbean Media Conference, Georgetown.

5929 **619** $100 multicoloured 85 85

2000. "Euro 2000" Football Championship. As T 316 of Gambia. Multicoloured.

5930 $80 Turkish team 70 75
5931 $80 Slovenian team 70 75
5932 $80 Yugoslavian team 70 75
5933 $80 Swedish team 70 75
5934 $80 Belgian team 70 75
5935 $80 Spanish team 70 75
5936 $80 French team 70 75
5937 $80 English team 70 75
5938 $80 Danish team 70 75
5939 $80 German team 70 75
5940 $80 Italian team 70 75
5941 $80 Dutch team 70 75
5942 $80 Portuguese team 70 75
5943 $80 Romanian team 70 75
5944 $80 Czech team 70 75
5945 $80 Norwegian team 70 75
MS5946 Two sheets, each 102×80 mm. (a) $400 Stefan Kuntz, 1966 (vert). (b) $400 Jurgen Klinsmann holding trophy, 1996 (vert) Set of 2 sheets 6·50 7·00

620 Lee Hyo-Ri (Korean singer)

2000. Fine Killing Liberty (FIN.K.L), Korean Girl Group. Multicoloured (except No. 5954).

5947 $80 Type **620** 70 75
5948 $80 Ok Ju-Hyun (head tilted to left) 70 75
5949 $80 Lee Jin (looking sideways) 70 75
5950 $80 Lee Jin (facing forwards) 70 75
5951 $80 FIN.K.L 70 75
5952 $80 Sung Yu-Ri (head tilted to left) 70 75
5953 $80 Lee Hyo-Ri (no hat) 70 75
5954 $80 Sung Yu-Ri (facing forwards) (purple, black and blue) 70 75
5955 $80 Ok Ju-Hyun smiling 70 75

621 *Amanita calyptroderma*

2000. "The Stamp Show 2000" International Stamp Exhibition, London. Fungi. Multicoloured.

5956 $100 Type **621** 85 90
5957 $100 *Polyporus brumalis* 85 90
5958 $100 *Hygrophorus pudorinus* 85 90
5959 $100 *Aeryginosa stropharia geophila* 85 90
5960 $100 *Amanita muscaria* 85 90
5961 $100 *Armillaria mellea* 85 90
5962 $100 *Hygrophoracaea* 85 90
5963 $100 *Russula xerampelina* 85 90
5964 $100 *Hygrophorus coccineus* 85 90
5965 $100 *Psilocybe stuntzii* 85 90
5966 $100 *Rhodotus palmatus* 85 90
5967 $100 *Lactarius indigo* 85 90
5968 $100 *Gomphus floccosus* 85 90
5969 $100 *Amanita caesarea* 85 90
5970 $100 *Leotia viscose* 85 90
5971 $100 *Entoloma salmoneum* 85 90
5972 $100 *Cheimonophyllum candidissimus* 85 90
5973 $100 *Cortinarius multiformis* 85 90
MS5974 Three sheets. (a) 99×69 mm. $400 *Marasmius rotula*. (b) 69×99 mm. $400 *Volvariella pusilla* (vert). (c) 99×69 mm. $400 *Trametes versicolour* Set of 3 sheets 9·00 9·50

Nos. 5956/61, 5962/7 and 5968/73 were each printed together, se-tenant, with the backgrounds forming composite designs.

Nos. 5956/8, 5961/2, 5964/5, 5967, 5969, 5972, **MS**5974a and **MS**5974c are inscribed "calyptzoderma", "crumalis", "pydorinus", "Armillariella", "Hygrophotaceae", "cocineus", "psilcybe stuntaii", "lactaius", "Aminita", "candidissimis", "zotula" and "Tzametes", all in error.

622 *Bougainvillea spectabilis*

2000. Flowers. Multicoloured.

5975 $35 Type **622** 35 25
5976 $60 *Euphorbia milii* 60 40
5977 $100 *Cordia sebestena* (vert) 80 85
5978 $100 *Heliconia wagneriana* (vert) 80 85
5979 $100 *Dendrobium phalaenopsis* (vert) 80 85
5980 $100 *Passiflora caerulea* (vert) 80 85
5981 $100 *Oncidium nubigenum* (vert) 80 85
5982 $100 *Hibiscus rosa-sinensis* (vert) 80 85
5983 $100 *Lantana camara* 80 85
5984 $100 *Jatropha integerrima* 80 85
5985 $100 *Plumeria alba* 80 85
5986 $100 *Strelitzia reginae* 80 85
5987 $100 *Clerodendrum splendens* 80 85
5988 $100 *Thunbergia grandiflora* 80 85
5989 $200 *Catharanthus roseus* 1·50 1·60
5990 $300 *Ipomoea carnea* 2·10 2·25
MS5991 Two sheets (a) 83×103 mm. $400 *Cattleya granulose* (vert). (b) 103×83 mm. $400 *Guzmania lingulata* Set of 2 sheets 6·00 6·50

Nos. 5983/8 were printed together, se-tenant, the backgrounds forming a composite design.

623 *Russelia equisetiformis*

2000. Flowers of Central America. Multicoloured.

5992	$35 Type **623**	35	25
5993	$60 *Sprekelia formosissima*	60	40
5994	$100 *Bignonia capreolata*	80	85
5995	$100 *Calceolaria herbeo-hybrida*	80	85
5996	$100 *Canna generalis*	80	85
5997	$100 *Bauhinia grandiflora*	80	85
5998	$100 *Amaranthus caudatus*	80	85
5999	$100 *Abutilon megapotamicum*	80	85
6000	$100 *Ipomoea tricolor* ("Morning Glory")	80	85
6001	$100 *Lantana camara*	80	85
6002	$100 *Cantua buxifolia*	80	85
6003	$100 *Fuschia*	80	85
6004	$100 *Eichhornia crassipes*	80	85
6005	$100 *Cosmos sulphureus*	80	85
6006	$200 *Passiflora quadrangularis*	1·50	1·60
6007	$300 *Mirabilis jalapa*	2·10	2·25
MS6008	Two sheets, each 100×70 mm. (a) $400 *Oeceoclades maculate*. (b) $400 *Passiflora van-volxemii* ("Tasconia")	6·00	6·50

No. 6004 is inscribed "Eichornia", in error.

2000. Victims of Munich Olympics Massacre (1972) Commemoration. As T 328 of Gambia showing Israeli athletes and officials. Multicoloured.

6009	$40 Yaakov Springer (weightlifting referee)	50	50
6010	$40 Andrei Schpitzer (fencing referee)	50	50
6011	$40 Amitsur Shapira (athletics coach)	50	50
6012	$40 David Berger (weightlifter)	50	50
6013	$40 Ze'ev Friedman (weightlifter)	50	50
6014	$40 Joseph Gottfreund (wrestling referee)	50	50
6015	$40 Moshe Weinberg (wrestling referee)	50	50
6016	$40 Kahat Shor (shooting coach)	50	50
6017	$40 Mark Slavin (wrestler)	50	50
6018	$40 Eliezer Halffin (wrestler)	50	50
6019	$40 Joseph Romano (weightlifter)	50	50
6020	$40 Munich Olympics stadium	50	50
MS6021	127×101 mm. $400 Israeli athlete with Olympic torch (vert)	3·75	4·00

2000. Queen Elizabeth the Queen Mother's 100th Birthday. As T 318 of Gambia. Multicoloured.

6022	$100 Queen Elizabeth the Queen Mother	1·50	1·50

624 Heads of Two Angels

2000. Christmas and Holy Year. Multicoloured.

6023	$60 Type **624**	50	40
6024	$90 Two angels	80	60
6025	$120 Heads of two angels (different)	1·00	75
6026	$180 As $90	1·40	1·60
6027	$180 Type **624**	1·40	1·60
6028	$180 As $120	1·40	1·60
6029	$180 Two angels with drapery	1·40	1·60
6030	$400 As No. 6029	1·40	1·60
MS6031	121×110 mm. $400 Holy Child (horiz)	3·25	3·50

625 Snake

2001. Chinese New Year ("Year of the Snake"). Multicoloured.

6032	$80 Type **625**	70	70
6033	$80 Snake (face value at top right)	70	70
6034	$80 Snake (face value at bottom right)	70	70
6035	$80 Snake (face value at bottom left)	70	70
MS6036	85×65 mm. $250 Snake (vert)	2·00	2·50

626 Prime Minister's Residence, Georgetown

2001. Tourist Attractions. Multicoloured.

6037	$90 Type **626**	1·00	1·00
6038	$90 Kaieteur Falls (vert)	1·00	1·00

2001. Faces of the Millennium. Queen Elizabeth the Queen Mother's 100th Birthday. As T 307a of Gambia showing collage of miniature flower photographs. Multicoloured.

6039	$80 Top left side of head	75	75
6040	$80 Top right side of head	75	75
6041	$80 Eye and temple	75	75
6042	$80 Temple	75	75
6043	$80 Right cheek	75	75
6044	$80 Left cheek	75	75
6045	$80 Chin	75	75
6046	$80 Neck	75	75

Nos. 6039/46 were printed together, se-tenant, in sheetlets of 8 with the stamps arranged in two vertical columns separated by a gutter also containing miniature photographs. When viewed as a whole, the sheetlet forms a portrait of the Queen Mother.

2001. Faces of the Millennium: 80th Birthday of Pope John Paul II. As T 307a of Gambia showing collage of miniature religious photographs. Multicoloured.

6047	$100 Back of head	1·10	1·10
6048	$100 Front of forehead	1·10	1·10
6049	$100 Ear	1·10	1·10
6050	$100 Eye	1·10	1·10
6051	$100 Neck	1·10	1·10
6052	$100 Cheek	1·10	1·10
6053	$100 Shoulder of robe	1·10	1·10
6054	$100 Hands	1·10	1·10

Nos. 6047/54 were printed together, se-tenant, in sheetlets of 8 with the stamps arranged in two vertical columns separated by a gutter also containing miniature photographs. When viewed as a whole, the sheetlet forms a portrait of the Pope.

627 Chow Yun-Fat

2001. Chow Yun-Fat (Hong Kong actor). Multicoloured.

6055	$60 Type **627**	50	55
6056	$60 Wearing maroon coat	50	55
6057	$60 Wearing dark suit and grey shirt	50	55
6058	$60 In cream jacket, black shirt and white T-shirt	50	55
6059	$60 Wearing dark suit, white shirt and grey tie	50	55
6060	$60 In dark overcoat	50	55

2001. Characters from Pokemon (children's cartoon series). As T 332a of Gambia. Multicoloured.

6061	$100 "Staryu No. 120"	85	85
6062	$100 "Seaking No. 119"	85	85
6063	$100 "Tentacool No. 72"	85	85
6064	$100 "Magikarp No. 129"	85	85
6065	$100 "Seadra No. 117"	85	85
6066	$100 "Goldeen No. 118"	85	85
MS6067	74×114 mm. $400 "Horsea No. 116" (vert)	3·00	3·25

628 Boxer Dog

2001. "Hong Kong 2001" Stamp Exhibition. Cats and Dogs. Multicoloured.

6068	$35 Type **628**	35	25
6069	$60 Cinnamon ocicat	55	55
6070	$60 Devon Rex	55	55
6071	$60 Egyptian Mau	55	55
6072	$60 Turkish angora	55	55
6073	$60 Sphynx	55	55
6074	$60 Persian	55	55
6075	$60 American wirehair	55	55
6076	$60 Exotic shorthair	55	55
6077	$60 American curl	55	55
6078	$80 Airedale terrier	70	70
6079	$80 Greyhound	70	70
6080	$80 Afghan hound	70	70
6081	$80 Samoyed	70	70
6082	$80 Field spaniel	70	70
6083	$80 Scottish terrier	70	70
6084	$80 Brittany spaniel (brown and white)	70	70
6085	$80 Boston terrier	70	70
6086	$100 Smooth dachshund	90	90
6087	$300 White Manx	2·50	2·75
MS6088	Two sheets, each 100×80 mm. (a) $400 Birman (cat). (b) $400 Dalmatian Set of 2 sheets	6·50	7·00

Nos. 6070/7 (cats) and 6078/85 (dogs) were each printed together, se-tenant, with the backgrounds forming composite designs. No. 6081 is inscribed "Samoyeo" in error. Nos. 6070/85 and **MS**6088 all show the "Hong Kong 2001" logo on the sheet margins.

629 "Tom"

2001. Cats and Dogs of the Cinema. Multicoloured.

6089	$100 Type **629**	90	90
6090	$100 "Puff" (Siamese)	90	90
6091	$100 "Jag" (silver tabby)	90	90
6092	$100 "Fritz" (Burmese, with paw curled)	90	90
6093	$100 "Smokey" (Burmese)	90	90
6094	$100 "Thor" (white cat)	90	90
6095	$100 "Pup" (small black and tan dog)	90	90
6096	$100 "Yogi" (white dog in snow)	90	90
6097	$100 "Hooch" (mastiff)	90	90
6098	$100 "Huxley Blu" (collie)	90	90
6099	$100 "Snowflake" (small white dog)	90	90
6100	$100 "Red" (Irish setter)	90	90
MS6101	Two sheets, each 67×86 mm. (a) $400 "Spike" (kitten). (b) $400 "Baron of Fillmore" (German shepherd dog) Set of 2 sheets	6·50	7·00

630 Chihuahua

2001. Dogs and Cats in the Caribbean. Multicoloured.

6102	$35 Type **630**	35	25
6103	$60 Persian tabby	60	40
6104	$80 Rottweiler	70	70
6105	$80 German shepherd	70	70
6106	$80 Burmese mountain dog	70	70
6107	$80 Shar Pei	70	70
6108	$80 Dachshund	70	70
6109	$80 Jack Russell	70	70
6110	$80 Boston terrier	70	70
6111	$80 Corgi	70	70
6112	$80 American shorthair	70	70
6113	$80 Somali	70	70
6114	$80 Balinese	70	70
6115	$80 Egyptian Mau	70	70
6116	$80 Scottish fold	70	70
6117	$80 Sphynx	70	70
6118	$80 Korat	70	70
6119	$100 Colourpoint shorthair	90	90
6120	$200 Cocker spaniel	1·60	1·75
MS6121	Two sheets, each 76×86 mm. (a) $400 Beagle. (b) $400 Abyssinian (cat) Set of 2 sheets	6·50	7·00

Nos. 6104/11 (dogs) and 6112/18 (cats) were each printed together, se-tenant, with the backgrounds forming composite designs that extend onto the sheetlet margins.

631 George Washington (image scaled to 71% of original size)

2001. George Washington (American president) Commemoration.

6122	**631**	$300 multicoloured	2·50	2·75

632 Hello Kitty in Alice in Wonderland

2001. Hello Kitty (cartoon character). Twelve sheets, each 100×100 mm, containg vert designs as T 632 of Hello Kitty in European (No. MS6120a/f) or Japanese (No. MS6120g/l) fairy tales. Multicoloured.

MS6123	(a) $400 Type **632**. (b) $400 Cinderella. (c) $400 Heidi. (d) $400 The Wizard of Oz. (e) $400 Peter Pan. (f) $400 Little Red Riding Hood. (g) $400 Three in a Boat. (h) $400 Bamboo Princess. (i) $400 The Fisherman. (j) $400 Up a Tree. (k) $400 On a Bear. (l) $400 In the Snow Set of 12 sheets	32·00	35·00

633 American Securities and Exchange Commission Office (founded 1934)

2001. People and Events of Early 20th Century. Multicoloured.

6124	$60 Type **633**	55	60
6125	$60 Herbert Hoover (American President, elected 1928)	55	60
6126	$60 Al Jolson in *The Jazz Singer* (first talking film, 1927)	55	60
6127	$60 J. Edgar Hoover (Director of F.B.I., appointed 1924)	55	60
6128	$60 Alexander Fleming (discovered penicillin, 1928)	55	60
6129	$60 Radio and microphone (Federal Communications Commission set up, 1927)	55	60
6130	$60 Charles Lindbergh (first solo transatlantic flight, 1927)	55	60

6131	$60 Albert Einstein (awarded Nobel physics prize, 1921)	55	60
6132	$60 Paul von Hindenburg (German leader, died 1934, succeeded by Hitler)	55	60
6133	$60 American flag and certificate (American Social Security Act, 1935)	55	60
6134	$60 Amelia Earhart (first solo flight from Hawaii to California)	55	60
6135	$60 Marcus Garvey (founder of Universal Negro Improvement Association, prison sentence commuted and deported, 1927)	55	60

634 Ronald Reagan

2001. 90th Birthday of Ronald Reagan (American President). Multicoloured (except Nos. 6136/8).

6136	$60 Type **634** (lilac and black)	55	60
6137	$60 With chimp in *Bedtime for Bonzo* (lilac and black)	55	60
6138	$60 Wearing cowboy hat (grey and black)	55	60
6139	$60 In dark suit and black tie	55	60
6140	$60 With Nancy Reagan	55	60
6141	$60 Pointing	55	60
6142	$60 Getting into car and waving	55	60
6143	$60 Signing reduction of nuclear arms treaty with Mikhail Gorbachev, 1987	55	60
6144	$60 Helping demolish Berlin Wall, 1989	55	60
6145	$60 With President Clinton	55	60

635 "Girl at a Hot Spring Resort" (Hashiguchi Goyo)

2001. "Philanippon '01" International Stamp Exhibition, Tokyo. Japanese Paintings. Multicoloured.

6146	$25 Type **635**	20	20
6147	$25 "Hanaogi with Maidservant" (Eishosai Choki)	20	20
6148	$30 "Morokoshi of the Echizenya" (Rekisentei Eiri)	25	25
6149	$30 "Courtesan receiving a Letter of Invitation" (Suzuki Harunobu)	25	25
6150	$35 "Mother and Daughter on an Outing" (Katsushika Hokusai)	30	30
6151	$35 "Two Girls on Way to (or from) the Bathhouse" (S. Harunobu)	30	30
6152	$60 "Matron in Love" (Kitagawa Utamaro)	55	55
6153	$60 "Girl and Frog" (S. Harunobu)	55	55
6154	$80 "Insects, reptiles and amphibians at a Pond" (38×72 mm)	70	70
6155	$80 "Rose Mallow and Fowl" (38×72 mm)	70	70
6156	$80 "Rooster, Sunflower and Morning Glories" (38×72 mm)	70	70
6157	$80 "Group of Roosters" (38×72 mm)	70	70
6158	$80 "Black Rooster and Nandina" (38×72 mm)	70	70
6159	$80 "Birds and Autumn Maples" (38×72 mm)	70	70
6160	$80 "Wagtail and Roses" (38×72 mm)	70	70
6161	$80 "Cockatoos in a Pine" (38×72 mm)	70	70
6162	$100 "Three Beauties of High Fame" (K. Utamaro)	85	85
6163	$100 "The Courtesan Midorigi" (Chokosai Eisho)	85	85
6164	$100 Bridge (38×72 mm)	85	85
6165	$100 Causeway and summer house (38×72 mm)	85	85
6166	$100 Island in lake with single tree (38×72 mm)	85	85
6167	$100 Rocky islet and waterfalls tumbling into lake (38×72 mm)	85	85
6168	$100 Shugakuin Imperial Villa with Japanese letters (38×72 mm)	85	85
6169	$100 Trees with Japanese letters (38×72 mm)	85	85
6170	$120 "Girls After the Bath" (K. Utamaro) (38×72 mm)	85	85
6171	$120 "Summer Evening on Riverbank at Hama-Cho" (Torii Kiyonaga) (38×72 mm)	90	90
6172	$120 "A Beauty in the Wind" (Kaigetsudo Ando) (38×72 mm)	90	90
6173	$120 "Sisters (Shimainozu)" (Tsuji Kako) (38×72 mm)	90	90
6174	$120 "Kasamori Osen" (S. Harunobu) (38×72 mm)	90	90
6175	$160 "Ichikawa Ebizo" behind Screen (30×38 mm)	1·25	1·25
6176	$160 "Ichikawa Ebizo" in red jacket (30×38 mm)	1·25	1·25
6177	$160 "Ichikawa Ebizo" with musicians (30×38 mm)	1·25	1·25
6178	$160 "Ichikawa Ebizo" being dressed as warrior (30×38 mm)	1·25	1·25
6179	$200 "Girl breaking off Branch of Flowering Tree" (S. Harunobu)	1·60	1·75
6180	$200 "Maiko" (Tsuchida Bakusen)	1·60	1·75
MS6181	Five sheets. (a) 120×80 mm. $400 "Wintry Sky" (Higashibara Hosen). (b)120×80 mm. $400 "Woman holding a Flower" (Kajiwara Hisako). (c) 120×80 mm. $400 "Palace of Immortals in an Autumn Valley" (Okochi Yako). (d) 80×120 mm. $400 Fish and Octopus from the "Colourful Realm of living Beings" (I. Jakuchu). (e) 80×120 mm. $400 "Portrait of Takami Senseki" (Watanabe Kazan). All imperf set of 5 sheets	14·00	15·00

Nos. 6154/61 (paintings by Ito Jakuchu), 6164/9 ("Procession to the Shugakuin Imperial Villa" by Kakimoto Sesshin), 6170/4 (Japanese Women) and 6175/8 ("Ichikawa Ebizo" (actor) by Toshusai Sharaku) were each printed together, se-tenant, in sheetlets of 4, 5, 6 or 8 with enlarged inscribed margins.

Nos. 6164/9 and 6175/8 each form a composite design.

636 Queen Victoria, 1850

2001. Death Centenary of Queen Victoria. Multicoloured.

6182	$200 Type **636**	2·00	2·00
6183	$200 Queen Victoria, 1843	2·00	2·00
6184	$200 Queen Victoria wearing crown, 1859	2·00	2·00
6185	$200 Queen Victoria in feathered hat, 1897	2·00	2·00
6186	$200 Princess Victoria, 1829	2·00	2·00
6187	$200 Queen Victoria with hair in bun, 1837	2·00	2·00
6188	$200 In uniform for troop review, 1840	2·00	2·00
6189	$200 Wearing crown and white veil, 1897	2·00	2·00
MS6190	Two sheets, each 88×120 mm. (a) $400 Queen Victoria. (b) $400 Queen Victoria in old age Set of 2 sheets	7·50	8·00

2001. 75th Death Anniv of Claude-Oscar Monet (artist). As T 339 of Gambia. Multicoloured.

6191	$150 "Village Street near Honfleur"	1·25	1·40
6192	$150 "Road to Chailly"	1·25	1·40
6193	$150 "Train in the Countryside"	1·25	1·40
6194	$150 "Quai du Louvre"	1·25	1·40
MS6195	136×111 mm. $400 "Flowering Garden" (vert)	3·50	3·75

2001. 75th Birthday of Queen Elizabeth II. As T 340 of Gambia. Multicoloured.

6196	$150 Queen Elizabeth wearing pink hat	1·75	1·75
6197	$150 Wearing red coat and hat	1·75	1·75
6198	$150 Wearing white turban style hat	1·75	1·75
6199	$150 Wearing tiara	1·75	1·75
MS6200	80×110 mm. $400 Queen Elizabeth wearing yellow dress and pearls (38×50 mm)	4·50	4·75

2001. Death Centenary of Giuseppe Verdi (Italian composer). Vert designs as T 342 of Gambia. Multicoloured.

6201	$160 Verdi (face value at bottom left)	2·25	2·25
6202	$160 Rigoletto and score	2·25	2·25
6203	$160 Ernani and opera score	2·25	2·25
6204	$160 Verdi (face value at bottom right)	2·25	2·25
MS6205	77×117 mm. $400 Verdi	5·00	5·00

Nos. 6201/4 were printed together, se-tenant, with the backgrounds forming a composite design.

2001. Death Centenary of Henri de Toulouse-Lautrec (artist). As T 343 of Gambia. Multicoloured.

6206	$160 "Maurice Joyant in the Baie de Somme" (horiz)	1·25	1·40
6207	$160 "Monsieur Boileau" (horiz)	1·25	1·40
6208	$160 "Monsieur, Madame and the Dog" (horiz)	1·25	1·40
MS6209	66×85 mm. $400 "Monsieur"	3·50	3·75

637 Top Right of Head

2001. Faces of the Millennium. John F. Kennedy. Showing collage of miniature photographs from Kennedy's years as President. Multicoloured.

6210	$80 Type **637**	65	70
6211	$80 Top left of head	65	70
6212	$80 Top of right cheek	65	70
6213	$80 Top of left cheek	65	70
6214	$80 Bottom of right cheek	65	70
6215	$80 Bottom of left cheek	65	70
6216	$80 Bottom right of chin	65	70
6217	$80 Bottom left of chin	65	70

Nos. 6210/17 were printed together, se-tenant, in sheetlets of 8 with the stamps arranged in two vertical columns separated by a gutter also containing miniature photographs. When viewed as a whole, the sheetlet forms a portrait of JFK.

2001. 75th Birthday of Queen Elizabeth II. As T 368 of Dominica.

6218	$80 multicoloured	1·00	1·10

No. 6218 was also issued, in the same format, inscribed "In Celebration of the 50th Anniversary of H.M. Queen Elizabeth II's Accession to the Throne' in the margin.

638 Rainbow Lory ("Rainbow Lorikeet")

2001. Tropical Birds. Multicoloured.

6219	$100 Type **638**	60	65
6220	$100 King bird of paradise	60	65
6221	$100 Canary-winged parakeet ("Yellow-Chevroned Parakeet")	60	65
6222	$100 Masked lovebird	60	65
6223	$100 Scarlet ibis	60	65
6224	$100 Toco toucan	60	65
6225	$100 Hyacinth macaw	60	65
6226	$100 Wire-tailed manakin	60	65
6227	$100 Scarlet macaw	60	65
6228	$100 Sun conure ("Sun Parakeet")	60	65
6229	$100 Roseate spoonbill	60	65
6230	$100 Red-billed toucan	60	65
MS6231	Two sheets, each 85×110 mm. (a) $400 Eclectus parrot (vert). (b) $400 Sulphur-crested cockatoo (vert) Set of 2 sheets	4·75	4·75

Nos. 6219/24 and 6225/30 were each printed together, se-tenant, with the backgrounds forming composite designs.

639 Alamosaurus head

2001. "Vegaspex 2001", Nevada. Prehistoric Creatures. Multicoloured.

6232	$20 Allosaurus (vert)	10	15
6233	$30 Spinosaurus (vert)	20	25
6234	$35 Pteranodon (vert)	20	25
6235	$60 Cetiosaurus (vert)	35	40
6236	$100 Type **639**	60	65
6237	$100 Archaeopteryx	60	65
6238	$100 Pachycephalosaurus head and Alamosaurus body	60	65
6239	$100 Parasaurolophus	60	65
6240	$100 Edmontosaurus head	60	65
6241	$100 Triceratops	60	65
6242	$100 Brachiosaurus head, neck and back	60	65
6243	$100 Dimorphodon	60	65
6244	$100 Coelophysis head and Brachiosaurus body	60	65
6245	$100 Velociraptor	60	65
6246	$100 Antrodemus	60	65
6247	$100 Euparkeria	60	65
6248	$100 Brachiosaurus head and neck	60	65
6249	$100 Pteranodon	60	65
6250	$100 Compsognathus and Brachiosaurus neck	60	65
6251	$100 Corythosaurus	60	65
6252	$100 Allosaurus	60	65
6253	$100 Torosaurus	60	65
6254	$100 Ichthyostega	60	65
6255	$100 Eryops	60	65
6256	$100 Ichthyosaur	60	65
6257	$100 Pliosaur	60	65
6258	$100 Dunklosteus	60	65
6259	$100 Eogyrinus	60	65
6260	$200 Archaeopteryx (vert)	1·20	1·20
6261	$300 Parasaurolophus (vert)	1·80	1·80
MS6262	Four sheets. (a) 88×68 mm. $400 Pteranodon. (b) 88×68 mm. $400 Ichthyosaur. (c) 88×68 mm. $400 Torosaurus. (d) 68×88 mm. $400 Brachiosaurus (vert) Set of 4 sheets	9·50	9·50

Nos. 6236/41, 6242/7, 6248/53 and 6254/9 were each printed together, se-tenant, with the backgrounds forming composite designs.

640 Elephant

2001. Tropical Rainforest. Multicoloured.

6263	$35 Mandrill (vert)	30	25
6264	$80 Type **640**	50	55
6265	$80 Impala	50	55
6266	$80 Leopard head and shoulders	50	55
6267	$80 Grey parrot and leopard body	50	55
6268	$80 Hippopotamus	50	55
6269	$80 Pygmy chimp	50	55
6270	$80 African green python	50	55
6271	$80 Mountain gorilla	50	55
6272	$80 Three-toed sloth	50	55
6273	$80 Lion tamarind	50	55
6274	$80 Ring-tailed lemur	50	55
6275	$80 Sugar glider	50	55
6276	$80 Toco toucan	50	55
6277	$80 Trogon	50	55
6278	$80 Pygmy marmoset	50	55
6279	$80 Poison arrow frog	50	55
6280	$100 Leaf-cutting ants	70	75
MS6281	Two sheets, each 110×85 mm. (a) $400 Tapir (vert). (b) $400 Sable antelope (vert) Set of 2 sheets	4·75	4·75

Nos. 6264/71 and 6272/9 were each printed together, se-tenant, with the backgrounds forming composite designs.

641 Prince Willem-Alexander of Orange and Miss Maxima Zorreguieta

2002. Royal Wedding. Multicoloured.

MS6282	158×240 mm. $120 Type **641**; $120 Prince Willem-Alexander on right and Miss Maxima on left; $120 Prince Willem-Alexander on left and Miss Maxima on right; $120 Hugging from the side; $120 Prince Willem-Alexander; $120 Miss Maxima	4·25	4·25

642 U.S. Flag as Statue of Liberty and Flag of Guyana

2002. "United We Stand". Support for Victims of 11 September 2001 Terrorist Attacks.

MS6283 120×120 mm. **642** $200 ×4 multicoloured 4·75 4·75

643 Queen Elizabeth II

2002. Golden Jubilee (1st issue). Multicoloured.

MS6284 132×100 mm. $150 Type **643**; $150 Queen Elizabeth and Prince Philip; $150 Queen Elizabeth and Prince Philip waving; $150 Queen Elizabeth and horse 4·50 4·50

MS6285 76×109 mm. $400 Queen Elizabeth and Princess Margaret 3·25 3·25

See also Nos. **MS**6370/ and **MS**6371.

644 Harold C. Urey (Chemistry, 1934)

2002. Nobel Prize Winners (1st issue). Multicoloured.

MS6286 Two sheets each 183×129 mm. (a) $100 Type **644**; $100 Willard F. Libby (Chemistry, 1960); $100 Frederick Sanger (Chemistry, 1958 and 1980); $100 Teodor Svedberg (Chemistry, 1926); $100 Cyril N. Hinshelwood (Chemistry, 1956); $100 Nicolay Semenov (Chemistry, 1956). (b) $100 Alexander Todd (Chemistry, 1957); $100 John Steinbeck (Literature, 1962); $100 Edward C. Kendall (Physiology and Medicine, 1950); $100 Frederick G. Banting (Physiology and Medicine, 1923); $100 Charles Nicolle (Physiology and Medicine, 1928); $100 Charles Richet (Physiology and Medicine, 1913) Set of 2 sheets 7·25 7·25

MS6287 Three sheets each 106×75 mm. (a) $400 International Red Cross (Peace, 1917). (b) $400 John J. R. MacLeod (Physiology and Medicine, 1923). (c) $400 Derek H. R. Barton (Chemistry, 1969) Set of 3 sheets 7·25 7·25

2002. Nobel Prize Winners (2nd issue). Albert Einstein Photomosaic. Sheet 160×244 mm containing vert designs as T 637 showing miniature scientific images. Multicoloured.

MS6288 $80 Left of forehead; $80 Right of forehead; $80 Left eye; $80 Right eye; $80 Left cheek; $80 Right cheek; $80 Left of jaw; $80 Right of jaw 4·00 4·00

The stamps of No. **MS**6288 were printed in two vertical columns of 4, separated by a central gutter. When viewed as a whole, the miniature sheet forms a portrait of Albert Einstein.

645 Chinese Character meaning "Horse" (Qin Dynasty)

2002. Chinese New Year ("Year of the Horse"). Multicoloured.

6289	$100 Type **645**	60	65
6290	$100 Yin Dynasty	60	65
6291	$100 Tang Dynasty	60	65
6292	$100 Shang and Zhou Dynasties	60	65

MS6293 125×116 mm. (a) $150 Decorated person riding purple horse; (b) $150 Decorated Person riding orange horse. (37×50 mm) 1·80 1·80

Nos. 6282/5 show Chinese characters for "Horse" from various dynasties and an explanation of the Chinese characters inscribed on the bottom margin.

646 Obdulio Varela (Uruguay) (Brazil, 1950)

2002. World Cup Football Championship, Japan and South Korea. Tournament posters. Multicoloured.

6294	$100 Type **646**	60	65
6295	$100 Jules Rimet (Switzerland, 1954)	60	65
6296	$100 Pele and team mates (Brazil) (Sweden, 1958)	60	65
6297	$100 Zito (Brazil) (Chile, 1962)	60	65
6298	$100 English players (England, 1966)	60	65
6299	$100 Jairzinho (Brazil) (Mexico, 1970)	60	65
6300	$100 Daniel Passarella (Argentina) (Argentina, 1978)	60	65
6301	$100 Paolo Rossi (Italy) (Spain, 1982)	60	65
6302	$100 Diego Maradona (Argentina) (Mexico, 1986)	60	65
6303	$100 Lothar Matthaus and Rudi Voller (West Germany) (Italy, 1990)	60	65
6304	$100 Brazilian players (U.S.A., 1994)	60	65
6305	$100 Zinedine Zidane (France) (France, 1998)	60	65

MS6306 Two sheets, each 88×75 mm. (a) $400 Detail of Jules Rimet Trophy (Uruguay, 1930). (b) $400 Detail of World Cup Trophy (Japan and South Korea, 2002) Set of 2 sheets 4·75 4·75

647 The Devil's Tower, U.S.A

2002. International Year of Mountains (1st issue). Multicoloured.

MS6307 136×95 mm. $200 Type **647**; $200 Schreckhorn, Switzerland; $200 Mt. Rainer (U.S.A); $200 Mt. Everest, Tibet 4·75 4·75

MS6308 84×56 mm. $400 Mt. McKinley 2·40 2·40

2002. International Year of Mountains (2nd issue). As T 647. Multicoloured.

6309	$80 Mt. Kosciuszko, Australia	50	55
6310	$100 Mt. Elbrus, Russia	60	65
6311	$150 Mt. Vinson, Antarctica	90	95

MS6312 73×90 mm. $400 Mt. Everest, Nepal 2·40 2·40

648 Skiing

2002. Winter Olympic Games, Salt Lake City. Multicoloured.

6313	$200 Type **648**	1·20	1·30
6314	$200 Ice Skating	1·20	1·30

MS6315 82×113 mm. Nos. 6313/14 2·50 2·40

649 Owl

2002. United Nations Year of Eco Tourism. Multicoloured.

MS6316 81×137 mm. $100 Type **649**; $100 Waterfall; $100 Baboon; $100 Butterfly; $100 Flower; $100 Ferret 4·50 4·50

MS6317 86×69 mm. $400 Leopard 2·40 2·40

650 Environmental Science Merit Badge

2002. 20th World Scout Jamboree, Thailand. Multicoloured.

MS6318 161×67 mm. $200 Type **650**; $200 World Citizen Merit badge; $200 Life Saving Merit badge 3·50 3·50

MS6319 98×67 mm. $400 Jamboree mascot saluting 2·40 2·40

651 Kaieteur Falls, Guyana

2002. 30th Anniv of Diplomatic Relations with Republic of China. Multicoloured.

6320	$100 Type **651**	60	65
6321	$100 Great Wall of China	60	65

652 Volunteer Cleaning Globe and Emblem

2002. International Year of Volunteers. Multicoloured.

6322	$35 Type **652**	20	25
6323	$60 Two styles of emblem	35	40
6324	$300 Volunteer "embracing the nation"	1·80	1·90

653 Sperm Whale

2002. Whales. Multicoloured.

MS6325 140×67 mm. $100 Type **653**; $100 Pygmy Sperm whale; $100 Blue whale; $100 Bottlenose whale; $100 Killer whale; $100 True's Beaked whale 4·50 4·50

MS6326 75×62 mm. $400 Beluga whale 3·25 3·25

654 *Masdevallia tovarensis*

2002. Orchids. Multicoloured.

MS6327 94×103 mm. $100 Type **654**; $100 *Encyclia vitellina*; $100 *Dendrobium nobile*; $100 *Masdevallia falcate*; $100*Calanthe vestita*; $100 *Brassolaelia cattleya* 4·50 4·50

MS6328 74×62 mm. $400 *Brassavola nodosa* (horiz) 3·25 3·25

2002. Birds. As T 654. Multicoloured.

MS6329 94×103 mm. $100 Flycatcher; $100 Barbary shrike; $100 Red-faced mousebird; $100 Red-footed booby; $100 White-fronted goose; $100 Great crested grebe 4·50 4·50

MS6330 74×62 mm. $400 Whiskered tern 3·25 3·25

2002. Butterflies. As T 654. Multicoloured.

MS6331 94×103 mm. $100 Sweet oil butterfly; $100 Swallowtail; $100 Southern white admiral; $100 Pre-pona pheridamas; $100 Plain tiger; $100 Common eggfly 4·50 4·50

MS6332 62×75 mm. $400 Zebra butterfly 3·25 3·25

2002. Moths. As T 654. Multicoloured.

MS6333 94×103 mm. $100 *Burgena varia*; $100 *Mimas tiliae*; $100 *Hyles euphorbiae*; $100 *Eligma laetipicta*; $100 *Autometris io*; $100 *Hyloicus pinastri* 4·50 4·50

MS6334 75×62 mm. $400 *Callimorpha quadripuntaria* 3·25 3·25

655 Elvis Presley

2002. 25th Death Anniv of Elvis Presley. Multicoloured.

MS6335 Two sheets each 200×170 mm. (a) $60 Type **655**×9. (b) $60 Elvis in army uniform in front of U.S. flag×9 Set of 2 sheets 5·50 5·50

656 Popeye

2002. Popeye (cartoon character). Multicoloured.

MS6336 187×125 mm. $100 Type **656**; $100 Olive Oyl; $100 Wimpy; $100 Eugene the Jeep; $100 Sweet Pea racing for ball; $100 Sweet Pea holding tennis ball 3·50 3·50

MS6337 118×86 mm. $400 Popeye wearing white tennis shirt 2·40 2·40

657 Ronald Reagan

2003. Ronald Reagan (President of U.S.A 1981–1989). T 657 and Multicoloured.

MS6338	167×136 mm. $100 Ronald Reagan and eagle; $100 Type **657**; $100 In front of Mt. Rushmore; $100 Kissing Nancy Reagan; $100 With hand to forehead and White House; $100 On horseback	3·50	3·50
MS6339	106×76 mm. $400 Ronald Reagan and Mikhail Gorbachev shaking hands (horiz)	2·40	2·40

658 Ram

2003. Chinese New Year ("Year of the Ram").

MS6340	**658** 109×86 mm. $100×4 multicoloured	2·40	2·40

659 John F. Kennedy

2003. John F. Kennedy Commemoration. T 659 and similar multicoloured designs.

MS6341	158×128 mm. $100 Addressing the nation; $100 Type **659**; $100 Space scene in background; $100 With miniature model of White House; $100 In front of rocket; $100 Jackie Kennedy at funeral	3·50	3·50
MS6342	106×76 mm. $400 John F. Kennedy and Jackie Kennedy in open top car (horiz)	2·40	2·40

660 Princess Diana

2003. Diana, Princess of Wales Commemoration. Multicoloured.

MS6343	157×127 mm. $100 Type **660**; $100 Wearing tiara; $100 Wearing high collared top; $100 Wearing wedding veil; $100 Looking straight ahead; $100 Looking left	3·50	3·50
MS6344	104×75 mm. $400 Wearing pink and black hat and pearl choker	2·40	2·40

661 "The Actor Nakamura Shikan IV"

2003. Famous Actors in Japanese Art. Paintings by Toyohara Kunichika. Multicoloured.

6345	$60 Type **661**	35	40
6346	$80 "The Actor Ichikawa Danjuro IX as Sukeroku" (1883)	50	55
6347	$100 "The Actor Onoe Tatsunosuke"	60	65
6348	$300 "The Actor Ichikawa Sadanji I as Kyusuke"	1·80	1·90
MS6349	182×143 mm. $150 "The Actor Kawarazak Sansho as Watonai"; $150 "The Actor Ichikawa Danjuro IX as Kamakura Gongoro Kagemasa"; $150 The Actor Ichikawa Sadanji I as Sadajkuro"; $150 "The Actor Ichikawa Danjuro IX as Sukeroku" (1898)	3·50	3·50
MS6350	127×83 mm. $400 "The Actor Ichikawa Danjuro IX as Kato Shukeigashira Kiyomasa" (horiz)	2·40	2·40

662 "Tension Red"

2003. Wassily Kandinsky (artist) Commemoration. Multicoloured.

6351	$25 Type **662**	15	20
6352	$30 "Black Accompaniment"	20	25
6353	$35 "Calm Tension"	20	25
6354	$60 "Hard and Soft"	35	40
6355	$100 "Yellow Point" (horiz)	60	65
6356	$300 "Composition VIII" (horiz)	1·80	1·90
MS6357	130×156 mm. $150 "Red Oval", 1920; $150 On the White II", 1923; $150 "Mutual Agreement", 1942; $150 "Inclination", 1931	3·50	3·50
MS6358	Two sheets each 104×84 mm. (a) $400 "White Center", 1921. (b) $400 "Black Weft", 1922. Imperf	4·75	4·75

663 "Portrait of a Man"

2003. 450th Death Anniv of Lucas Cranach the Elder (artist). Multicoloured.

6359	$35 Type **663**	20	25
6360	$60 "Portrait of a Woman"	35	40
6361	$100 "Duchess Catherine of Mecklenburg" (detail)	60	65
6362	$200 "Portrait of Duke Henry of Saxony" (detail)	1·20	1·20
MS6363	160×117 mm. $150 "The Virgin", c. 1518 (detail); $150 "The Virgin and Child Under the Apple Tree" (detail); $150 "The Virgin"(detail); $150 "The Virgin"	3·50	3·50
MS6364	93×130 mm. $400 "The Virgin and Child Holding a Piece of Bread" (detail)	2·40	2·40

664 Outline of Guyana

2003. 30th Anniv of the Caribbean Community ("CARICOM"). Multicoloured.

6365	$20 Type **664**	10	10
6366	$60 Bank of Guyana (horiz)	35	40
6367	$100 Hands holding torch	60	65
6368	$160 AIDS ribbon and stethoscope	95	1·00

665 Queen Elizabeth II

2003. Golden Jubilee (2nd issue). Multicoloured.

MS6370	166×108 mm. $200 Type **665**; $200 Wearing purple top; $200 Wearing pink top	5·00	5·00
MS6371	76×106 mm. $400 Wearing Imperial State Crown	3·50	3·50

666 Top of Kaieteur Falls

2003. International Year of Freshwater. Multicoloured.

MS6372	143×150 mm. $200 Type **666**; $200 Middle of Kaieteur Falls; $200 Kaieteur Falls and part of Cliffside	4·00	4·00
MS6373	76×106 mm. $400 Amazon River	2·75	2·75

667 Jacques Anquetil (1964)

2003. Centenary of Tour de France Cycle Race. Multicoloured.

MS6374	163×104 mm. $150 Type **667**; $150 Felice Gimondi (1965); $150 Lucien Aimar (1966); $150 Roger Pingeon (1967)	5·00	5·00
MS6375	106×76 mm. $400 Jan Janssen (1968)	3·50	3·50

668 Brown Teddy Bear

2003. Centenary of Teddy Bears. Multicoloured.

MS6376	178×140 mm. $80 Type **668**×9; lilac; green; blue; light green; light blue; stone; mauve; pale green; light mauve	4·50	4·50
MS6377	178×102 mm. $150 Bear dressed in red dress and white apron; $150 Blue bear dressed in yellow bow tie; $150 Bear decorated with fairy lights and star; $150 Bear dressed in blue dress and ribbon	3·50	3·50

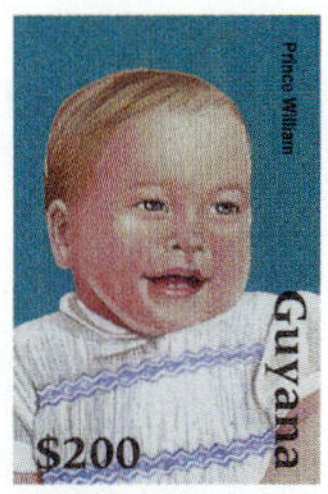

669 Prince William as a Baby

2003. 21st Birthday of Prince William. Multicoloured.

MS6378	166×108 mm. $200 Type **669**; $200 Wearing round neck sweater; $200 Wearing christening robe	3·50	3·50
MS6379	76×106 mm. $400 Wearing blue shirt and tie	2·40	2·40

670 Sixty Special (1948)

2003. Centenary of the Cadillac. Multicoloured.

MS6380	126×176 mm. $150 Type **670**; $150 Fleetwood Sixty Special (1966); $150 Eldorado (1967); Eldorado Convertible (1976)	1·75	1·75
MS6381	90×126 mm. $400 Red vintage Cadillac	2·40	2·40

671 Corvette Stingray (1964)

2003. 50th Anniv of the Corvette. Multicoloured.

MS6382	146×126 mm. $150 Type **671**; $150 Corvette Stingray (1963); $150 Corvette Stingray (1966); $150 Corvette (1969)	3·50	3·50
MS6383	126×90 mm. $400 Corvette (1971)	2·40	2·40

672 AVRO Plane (Sir Alliot Verdon Roe)

2003. Centenary of Powered Flight. Multicoloured.

6384	$100 Type **672**	90	80
6385	$160 First British powered flight	1·40	1·60
MS6386	Two sheets. (a) 186×106 mm. $150 Wright Brothers' plane; $150 SPAD 13; $150 Sopwith F.1; $150 Albatross D.II. (b) 106×186 mm. $150 Nieuport 17; $150 Scout Experimental 5a; $150 De Havilland 4; $150 Wright Brothers plane (black crosses on tail) Set of 2 sheets	6·00	6·00
MS6387	Two sheets each 76×106 mm. (a) $400 Fokker D.VIIs. (b) $400 Wright Brothers plane over water	6·00	6·00

673 Grecian Shoemaker

2003. Butterflies. Multicoloured.

6388	$20 Type **673**	10	15
6389	$55 Clorinde	30	35
6390	$80 Orange-barred sulphur	50	55
6391	$100 The atala	60	65
6392	$160 White peacock	95	1·00
6393	$200 Polydamas swallowtail	1·20	1·30
6394	$300 Giant swallowtail	1·80	1·90
6395	$400 Banded king shoemaker	2·40	2·50
6396	$500 Blue night	3·00	3·25
6397	$1000 Orange theope	6·00	6·25
6398	$2000 Small lace-wing	12·00	12·50
6399	$3000 Common morpho	18·00	19·00

674 *Clitocybe clavipes*

2003. Mushrooms. Multicoloured.

6400	$20 Type **674**	30	20
6401	$20 *Clitocybe gibba*	30	20
6402	$30 *Calocybe carnea*	35	25
6403	$300 *Marasmius*	2·50	3·00
MS6404	133×92 mm. $150 *Amanita spissa*; $150 *Boletus aestivalis*; $150 *Boletus rubellus*; $150 *Clathrus archeri*	4·50	4·50
MS6405	96×66 mm. $400 *Volvariella bombycina*	3·00	3·25

675 Toucan

2003. Endangered Species. Toucan. Multicoloured.

6406 $100 Toucan with chick 90 1·00

6407 $100 Type **675** 90 1·00

6408 $100 Two Toucans on branch 90 1·00

6409 $100 One Toucan on branch 90 1·00

MS6410 204×169 mm. Designs as Nos. 6406/9, each×2 6·50 7·00

676 *Begonia sedeni*

2003. Flowers. Multicoloured.

6411 $20 Type **676** 15 15

6412 $30 Dahlia 25 25

6413 $35 *Eschecholzia californica* 25 30

6414 $300 *Lupinus perennis* 2·25 2·50

MS6415 116×116 mm. $150 *Agapanthus africanus*; $150 *Hyacinth cultivars*; $150 *Protea linearis*; $150 *Hippestrum aulicum* 4·00 4·50

MS6416 66×96 mm. $400 *Crocus sativus* (horiz) 2·75 3·00

677 Regal Tang

2003. Fish. Multicoloured.

6417 $25 Type **677** 20 20

6418 $60 Pajama tang 50 40

6419 $100 Coral beauty 85 80

6420 $200 Emperor angelfish 1·50 1·75

MS6421 145×100 mm. $150 High hat; $150 Regal angelfish; $150 Fire clown; $150 Domino damselfish 4·00 4·50

MS6422 66×96 mm. $400 Tomato clown 2·75 3·00

678 Common Tenrec

2003. Animals. Multicoloured.

6423 $25 Type **678** 20 20

6424 $60 Woolly monkey (vert) 50 40

6425 $100 Gundi 85 80

6426 $200 Hooded seal 1·50 1·75

MS6427 135×127 mm. $150 Prevost's squirrel; $150 Mountain tapir; $150 Sea otter; $150 Indus dolphin 4·00 4·50

MS6428 67×96 mm. $400 Peter's disk-winged bat (vert) 2·75 3·00

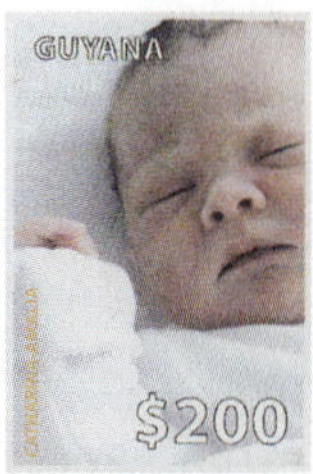

679 Princess Catharina-Amalia

2003. Birth of Princess Catharina-Amalia of the Netherlands. Sheet 185×115 mm containing T 679 and similar vert designs. Multicoloured.

MS6429 $200 Type **679**; $200 Prince Willem-Alexander and Princess Catharina-Amalia; $200 Princess Catharina-Amalia (looking to left) 4·00 4·50

No. **MS**6429 is cut around in the shape of a baby.

680 Handshake

2003. 35th Anniv of Guyana—Brazil Diplomatic Relations.

6430 **680** $20 multicoloured 50 50

681 Dark Brown Monkey

2004. Chinese New Year ("Year of the Monkey"). Sheet 140×117 mm containing T 681 and similar vert designs. Multicoloured.

MS6431 $100 Type **681**; $100 Black and white monkey; $100 Light brown monkey; $100 Red Howler Monkey 2·40 2·50

682 "Concubines of Emperor Chu"

2004. Hong Kong 2004 International Stamp Exhibition. Paintings by Tang Yin. T 682 and similar multicoloured designs.

MS6432 140×140 mm. $150 Type **682**; $150 Woman standing on boardwalk; $150 Woman standing on rocky slope; $150 Mountain landscape 3·50 3·75

MS6433 108×78 mm. $400 "Mountain Scene" (horiz) 2·40 2·50

683 "Doctor and Doll"

2004. 25th Death Anniv of Norman Rockwell (artist).

Multicoloured.

MS6434 142×173 mm. $150 Type **683**; $150 "Babysitter with Screaming Infant"; $150 "Girl with Black Eye"; $150 "Checkup" 3·50 3·75

MS6435 95×103 mm. $400 "Girl running with Wet Canvas (Wet Paint)" (detail) (horiz) 2·40 2·50

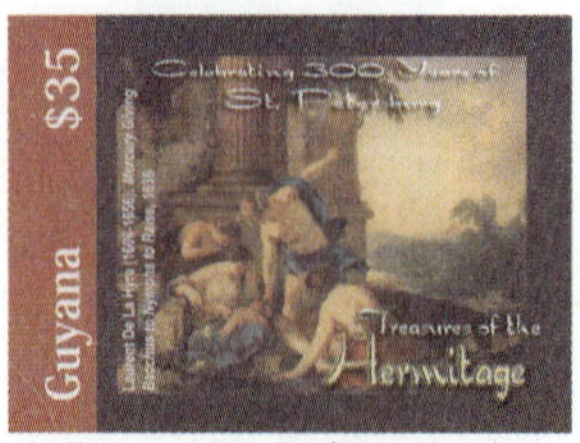

684 "Mercury giving Bacchus to Nymphs to Raise" (Laurent de la Hyre)

2004. 00th Anniv of St. Petersburg. "Treasures of the Hermitage". Multicoloured.

6436 $35 Type **684** 20 25

6437 $60 "Satyr and Bacchante" (Nicolas Poussin) (vert) 35 40

6438 $100 "Parting of Abelard and Eloisa" (Angelica Kauffmann) 60 65

6439 $200 "Pastoral Scene" (Francois Boucher) 1·20 1·30

MS6440 147×126 mm. $150 "The Union of Earth and Water" (Rubens); $150 "Hercules between Love and Wisdom" (Pompeo Girolano Batoni); $150 "Innocence choosing Love over Wealth" (Pierre-Paul Prud'hon); $150 "Mars and Venus" (Joseph-Marie Vien) (all vert) 3·50 3·75

MS6441 Two sheets. (a) 77×55 mm. $400 "Allegory of Virtuous Life" (Hendrik van Balen). (b) 55×77 mm. $400 "Statue of Ceres" (Rubens). Both imperf. Set of 2 sheets 3·00 3·25

685 "Woman in Yellow Hat"

2004. 30th Death Anniv (2003) of Pablo Picasso (artist). Multicoloured.

MS6442 130×167 mm. $150 Type **685**; $150 "Seated Woman"; $150 "Head of a Woman"; $150 "Large Profile" 3·50 3·75

MS6443 72×98 mm. $400 "Seated Woman". Imperf 2·40 2·50

686 "A Woman Bathing"

2004. Paintings by Rembrandt. Multicoloured.

6444 $35 Type **686** 30 25

6445 $60 "Flora" 35 40

6446 $100 "The Poet, Jan Hermansz Krul" 60 65

6447 $200 "Portrait of a Young Man" 1·20 1·30

MS6448 182×183 mm. $150 "The Apostle James"; $150 "The Apostle Bartholomew"; $150 "The Evangelist Matthew inspired by an Angel"; $150 "The Apostle Peter Standing" 3·50 3·75

MS6449 113×146 mm. $400 "Balaam and the Ass" 2·40 2·50

687 Uruguay (1930)

2004. Centenary of FIFA (Federation Internationale de Football Association). World Cup winning teams. Multicoloured.

6450 $80 Type **687** 50 55

6451 $80 Italy (1934) 50 55

6452 $80 Italy (1938) 50 55

6453 $80 Uruguay (1950) 50 55

6454 $80 Germany (1954) 50 55

6455 $80 Brazil (1958) 50 55

6456 $80 Brazil (1962) 50 55

6457 $80 England (1966) 50 55

6458 $80 Brazil (1970) 50 55

688 Poster for Olympic Games, Stockholm, 1912

2004. Olympic Games, Athens. Multicoloured.

6459 $60 Type **688** 45 40

6460 $80 Competitor in high jump, Los Angeles, 1932 (horiz) 65 65

6461 $100 Commemorative medal for Olympic Games, Los Angeles, 1932 80 85

6462 $200 Ancient Greek athletes in 192 metre first foot race (horiz) 1·60 1·75

2004. European Football Championship, Portugal. Commemoration of Match between France and Spain (1984). As T 407 of Dominica. Mult.

MS6463 147×85 mm. $150 Michelle Platini; $150 Luis Arconada; $150 Bruno Bellone; $150 Parc des Princes Stadium, Paris 5·50 6·00

MS6464 96×85 mm. $400 Winning French team, 1984 (50×37 mm) 3·25 3·50

2004. 25th Anniv of Pontificate of Pope John Paul II. Sheet 164×154 mm containing horiz designs as T 408 of Dominica. Multicoloured.

MS6465 $100 Pope John Paul II with Fidel Castro, 1998; $100 With US President Clinton, 1999; $100 Audience with Pope, 2000; $100 Pope in prayer, 2003; $100 In popemobile, 2003 4·50 4·75

689 Deng Xiaoping

2004. Birth Centenary of Deng Xiaoping (Chinese leader). Sheet 95×65 mm.

MS6466 **689** $400 multicoloured 3·25 3·50

2004. Centenary of FIFA (Federation Internationale de Football Association). As T 413 of Dominica. Multicoloured.

MS6467 192×96 mm. $150 Alf Ramsey (England); $150 Pele (Brazil); $150 Lothar Matthaus; $150 Dennis Bergkamp (Holland) 4·75 5·00

MS6468 107×86 mm. $400 Fabien Barthez (France) 3·25 3·50

690 Michael Wittmann, 101st Sturmmorser Kompanie

2004. 60th Anniv of D-Day Landings. Mult.

MS6469 97×137 mm. $150 Type **690**; $150 Lt. Robert Edlin, 2nd Battalion Army Ranger; $150 CSM Stanley Hollis, 6th Green Howards; $150 Kurt Meyer, 12th SS Panzer Division 5·50 6·00

MS6470 156×109 mm. $150 Rear Adm. John Hall; $150 Rear Adm. Carlton Bryant; $150 Gen. Dwight Eisenhower; $150 Gen. H. Arnold 4·50 4·75

MS6471 133×97 mm. $150 Anti-aircraft battery and map of Utah Beach ("Operation Overlord begins"); $150 Troops in landing craft storm Normandy beaches; $150 Troops drop behind enemy lines; $150 Churchill announces landings a success (all horiz) 4·50 4·75

MS6472 137×97 mm. $150 Royal Scots Fusiliers; $150 2nd Company 101st Heavy Tank Battalion; $150 Six-pounder anti-tank gun of the 7th Green Howards; $150 229th Engineer Combat Battalion (all horiz) 4·50 4·75

MS6473 Four sheets. (a) 97×66 mm. $400 Maj. Gen. Maxwell Taylor (horiz). (b) 67×97 mm. $400 T/Sgt. Clifton Barker, 743rd Tank Battalion. (c) 97×66 mm. $400 Tank battle, Cotentin Peninsula, Normandy (horiz). (d) 97×66 mm. $400 Seaforth Highlanders of Canada (horiz) 10·00 11·00

691 *Hercules*, United States

2004. Bicentenary of Steam Locomotives. Multicoloured.

6474–6477 $150×9 Type **691**; *Stirling* 8ft Single Class, Great Britain; Class YP, India; Class 01.10, Germany 4·50 4·75

6478–6481 $150×9 GWR "King" Class, Great Britain; 4500 Class, France; Class F, Sweden; Class 231C, France 4·50 4·75

6482- 6485 $150×9 Train near Santa Fe Depot; LD Porta; D9000 Royal Scots Grey; French TGV train 4·50 4·75

MS6486 Four sheets, each 156×84 mm. (a) $150×4 Western Railway, France, 1856; Dutch State Railway, 1880; Southern Railway, England, 1890; Madras and Southern Mahratta Railway, India, 1891. (b) $150×4 Shantung Railway, China, 1919; Great Indian Peninsula Railway, 1898; Cumberland Valley Railroad, USA, 1851; Central Pacific Railroad, USA, 1863. (c) $150×4 Great Northern Railway, Ireland, 1876; London and Northwestern Railways, 1873; Shanghai—Nanking Railway, China, 1910; London, Brighton and South Coast Railway, 1846. (d) $150×4 Baltimore and Ohio Railroad, USA, 1856; Utica and Schenectady Railroad, USA, 1837; Great Southern Railway, Spain, 1913; Victorian Government Railway, Australia, 1906 14·00 15·00

MS6487 Seven sheets. (a) 97×68 mm. $400 TGV Atlantique train. (b) 97×68 mm. $400 *Northumbrian*, Great Britain (vert). (c) 67×97 mm. $400 No. 999, United States. (d) 97×68 mm. $400 Austrian State Railway, 1868 (e) 97×68 mm. $400 Pennsylvania Railroad, 1848 (f) 97×68 mm. $400 Netherlands State Railway, 1886 (g) 97×68 mm. $400 London, Midland and Scottish Railway, 1923 21·00 22·00

No. **MS**6486a/d consist of four stamps in two horizontal pairs, each pair forming a composite background design showing a railway in a landscape.

692 Mexican Funnel-eared Bat

2005. Fauna and Flora of South America. Multicoloured.

6488 $160 Type **692** 1·50 1·60
6489 $160 Greater bulldog bat 1·50 1·60
6490 $160 Vampire bat 1·50 1·60
6491 $160 Geoffroy's tailess bat 1·50 1·60
6492 $160 Blue passion flower (vert) 1·50 1·60
6493 $160 Scarlet passion flower (vert) 1·50 1·60
6494 $160 Passion vine (vert) 1·50 1·60
6495 $160 Bromeliad flower (vert) 1·50 1·60

MS6496 Two sheets, each 110×97 mm. (a) $160×4 Fish: Velvet cichlid; Freshwater stingray; Splash tetra; Red piranha. (b) $160×4 Reptiles: Red-foot tortoise; Emerald tree boa; Green iguana; Cuvier's dwarf caiman 12·00 13·00

MS6497 Two sheets, each 100×70 mm. (a) $400 Short-tailed fruit bat (vert). (b) $400 Epiphytic blueberry (vert). (c) $400 Tambaqui (vert). (d) $400 Eyelash viper 13·00 14·00

693 Dark Brown Rooster

2005. Chinese New Year ("Year of the Rooster"). Multicoloured.

6498 $50 Type **693** 50 50
6499 $50 White rooster 50 50

694 Moeritherium

2005. Prehistoric Animals. Multicoloured.

MS6500 Three sheets, each 177×96 mm. (a) $150×4 Moeritherium; Deinonychys; Ophthalmosaurus; Grendelius. (b) $150×4 Eustreptospondylus; Rhamphorhynchus; Utahraptor; Entelodonts. (c) $150×4 Spinosaurus; Tarbosaurus; Coelophysis; Sinosauropteryx prima 10·00 11·00

MS6501 (a) 100×70 mm. $400 Ophtalmosaurus baby. (b) 100×70 mm. $400 Iguanodon bernissartensis (vert). (c) 70×100 mm. $400 Velociraptors hatching from eggs (vert) 10·00 11·00

The stamps within Nos. **MS**6500a/c form composite background designs.

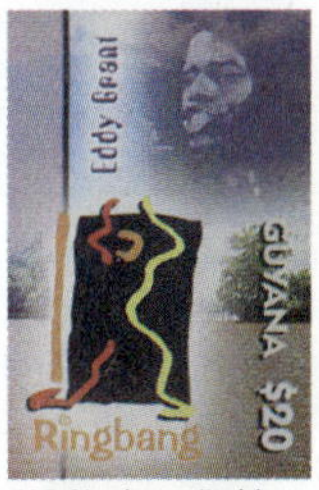

695 Ringbang Emblem, Guyana Landscape and Eddy Grant

2005. Eddy Grant (singer and music producer). Multicoloured.

6502 $20 Type **695** 15 15
6503 $80 Eddy Grant and Ringbang emblem 65 65
6504 $190 Eddy Grant (blue background) (38×49 mm) 1·60 1·75
6505 $190 As No. 6504 (stone background) (38×49 mm) 1·60 1·75
6506 $190 As No. 6504 (lavender background) (38×49 mm) 1·60 1·75
6507 $190 As No. 6504 (lilac background) (38×49 mm) 1·60 1·75

MS6508 100×70 mm. $400 Eddy Grant singing with guitar (38×49 mm) 3·25 3·50

696 Chamberlain on Peace Mission to Nazi Germany, 1938

2005. 60th Anniv of Victory in Europe Day. Multicoloured.

6509 $200 Type **696** 1·75 1·90
6510 $200 RAF Spitfire 1·75 1·90
6511 $200 VE Day poster and cover of *The Illustrated London News* 1·75 1·90

MS6512 100×70 mm. $400 Netherlands 1945 Liberation stamp (vert) 3·25 3·50

697 Japanese Attack on Pearl Harbour, 1945

2005. 60th Anniv of Victory in Japan Day. Multicoloured.

6513 $200 Type **697** 1·75 1·90
6514 $200 Iwo Jima War Memorial, Harlington, Texas 1·75 1·90
6515 $200 "JAPAN SURRENDERS!" newspaper headline 1·75 1·90

MS6516 100×70 mm. $400 US Navy "Seabees" celebrating Japanese surrender 3·25 3·50

2005. Pope John Paul II Commemoration. As T 600 of Grenada. Multicoloured.

6517 $300 Pope John Paul II with US President Ronald Reagan 2·00 2·10

2005. 75th Anniv of First World Cup Football Championship, Uruguay. As T 420 of Dominica showing scenes from World Cup, Switzerland, 1954. Multicoloured.

6518 $150 German Federal Republic team 1·40 1·50
6519 $150 Winning goal in net and Gyula Grosics (Hungarian goalkeeper), Germany v. Hungary final 1·40 1·50
6520 $150 Wankdorf Stadium, Berne 1·40 1·50
6521 $150 Helmut Rahn about to score winning goal for West Germany 1·40 1·50

MS6522 115×90 mm. $400 Victorious German team members 3·25 3·50

698 Friedrich von Schiller

2005. Death Bicentenary of Friedrich von Schiller (poet and dramatist). Multicoloured.

6523 $200 Type **698** 1·75 1·90
6524 $200 Schiller and his house, Gohlis, Saxony 1·75 1·90
6525 $200 Ludwig von Beethoven (composer) 1·75 1·90
6526 $400 Schiller, Beethoven and "Ode to Joy" (written by Schiller, set to music by Beethoven) (60×55 mm) 3·50 3·75

699 Jules Verne

2005. Death Centenary of Jules Verne (writer). Multicoloured.

6527 $150 Type **699** 1·50 1·60
6528 $150 Interior of space capsule in *From the Earth to the Moon* 1·50 1·60
6529 $150 Space capsule in *From the Earth to the Moon* 1·50 1·60
6530 $150 Apollo 11 command module, 1969 1·50 1·60

MS6531 100×70 mm. $400 Neil Armstrong and lunar module on Moon, 1969 (horiz) 3·25 3·50

2005. Bicentenary of the Battle of Trafalgar. As T 423 of Dominica. Multicoloured.

6532 $25 Vice-Admiral Collingwood (vert) 40 30
6533 $35 Admiral Nelson wounded, Battle of Santa Cruz, 1797 (vert) 50 40
6534 $60 Nelson's funeral car arriving at St. Paul's Cathedral, 1806 75 55
6535 $80 Admiral Lord Nelson and Flag Captain Thomas Hardy (vert) 90 65
6536 $100 First shots fired in Battle of Trafalgar 1·25 1·00
6537 $300 British ship hoisting signals to begin pincer movement (vert) 3·25 3·75

MS6538 70×100 mm. $400 Admiral Lord Nelson (vert) 4·50 4·50

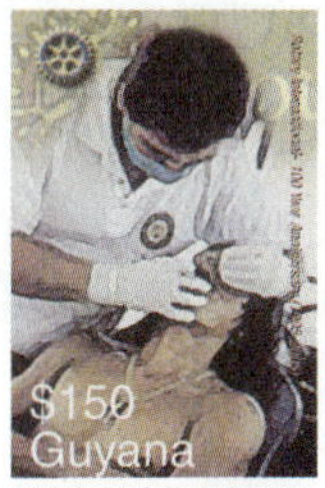

700 Dental Examination

2005. Centenary of Rotary International. Multicoloured.

MS6539 140×109 mm. $150 Type **700**; $150 Carl-Wilhelm Steinhammar (2005 President-elect); $150 First Couple—District of Guyana 4·25 4·50

MS6540 100×70 mm. $400 Homer Wood (founder) 3·25 3·50

The stamps within No. **MS**6540 form a composite background design.

701 *The Travelling Companion*

2005. Birth Bicentenary of Hans Christian Andersen (writer). Multicoloured.

6541 $200 Type **701** 1·75 1·90
6542 $200 *The Shadow* 1·75 1·90
6543 $200 *The Drop of Water* 1·75 1·90

MS6544 100×70 mm. $400 *The Emperor's New Suit* (50×38 mm) 3·25 3·50

702 "Luna 9"

2006. Space Anniversaries. Multicoloured. (a) 40th Anniv of "Luna 9" Moon Landing.

6545 $160 Type **702** 1·50 1·50
6546 $160 "Luna 9" capsule 1·50 1·50
6547 $160 Moon's *Oceanus Procellarum* 1·50 1·50
6548 $160 Sergei Korolev 1·50 1·50
6549 $160 Image of Moon's surface 1·50 1·50
6550 $160 Take-off of Molniya 8K78M rocket 1·50 1·50

(b) Muse Itokawa Comet Encounter.

6551 $200 Take-off of MV-5 rocket (vert) 1·75 1·75
6552 $200 Spacecraft *Hayabusa* (vert) 1·75 1·75
6553 $200 Itokawa composite colour image (vert) 1·75 1·75
6554 $200 Projected return to Earth (vert) 1·75 1·75

(c) 25th Anniv of First Flight of Space Shuttle Columbia.

6555 $200 Launch of space shuttle *Columbia* (vert) 1·75 1·75
6556 $200 Astronaut Robert Crippen (vert) 1·75 1·75
6557 $200 Astronaut John Young (vert) 1·75 1·75
6558 $200 Mission control (vert) 1·75 1·75

(d) Launch of Space Shuttle Discovery.

6559 $200 SS *Discovery* docked at ISS Destiny Laboratory 1·75 1·75
6560 $200 Astronaut Stephen Robinson attached to foot restraint on ISS Canadarm2 1·75 1·75
6561 $200 SS *Discovery* seen from ISS during docking operations 1·75 1·75
6562 $200 SS *Discovery* safe return 1·75 1·75

MS6563 Four sheets each 98×68 mm. (a) $400 Lunar Reconnaissance Orbiter. (b) $400 *Hayabusa* spacecraft over Asteroid Itokawa. (c) $400 Calipso satellite. (d) $400 Venus Express (first European mission to Venus) 11·00 12·00

2006. 80th Birthday of Queen Elizabeth II. As T 432 of Dominica. Multicoloured.

6564 $200 Queen Elizabeth II and Parliament Building, Guyana, 1966 2·00 2·00
6565 $200 Queen Elizabeth wearing black edged fawn jacket and hat, c. 1990 2·00 2·00

MS6566 120×120 mm. $400 Queen Elizabeth, c. 1955 and flags of Guyana and Great Britain 4·00 4·00

703 De Beers Zeppelin NT

2006. Hot Air Balloons and Airships. Multicoloured.

6567 $200 Type **703** 1·75 1·75
6568 $200 Lockhead Martin LTA 2004 1·75 1·75
6569 $200 Stratellite concept airship 1·75 1·75

MS6570 100×70 mm. $400 Skybus airship, Switzerland 3·00 3·25

2006. 400th Birth Anniv of Rembrandt Harmenszoon van Rijn (artist). As T 458 of Gambia. Multicoloured.

6571 $160 Man playing violin 1·50 1·50
6572 $160 Woman wearing shawl 1·50 1·50
6573 $160 Man playing harp 1·50 1·50
6574 $160 Woman with sheet music 1·50 1·50

MS6575 57×84 mm. $400 "Old Man with a Jewelled Cross" (detail). Imperf 3·00 3·25

Nos. 6571/4 all show details from painting "The Music Makers".

704 *Nina*

2006. 500th Death Anniv of Christopher Columbus. Multicoloured.

6576 $300 Type **704** 2·75 2·75
6577 $300 *Pinta* 2·75 2·75
6578 $300 *Santa Maria* 2·75 2·75

705 British Guiana 1856 1c. Black on Magenta Stamp

2006. 150th Anniv of Printing of the World's Rarest Stamp. Sheet 100×68 mm.

MS6579 **705**	$400 multicoloured	3·00	3·25

706 Japanese Kemari Player, 7th-century

2006. World Cup Football Championship, Germany. History of Soccer. Sheet 102×127 mm containing T 706 and similar vert designs. Multicoloured.

MS6580	$80 Type **706**; $100 Kemari game, 7th-century; $160 Chinese Tsu Chu game, 2500BC; $300 1986 50f. Chinese stamp showing tsu chu game, 2500BC	4·75	5·00

707 Betty Boop with Hat and Cane

2006. Betty Boop. Multicoloured.

6581	$100 Type **707**	80	80
6582	$100 Seated on chair, holding mirror	80	80
6583	$100 With bouquet of red roses	80	80
6584	$100 Standing on grating with dress blowing upwards	80	80
6585	$100 With microphone	80	80
6586	$100 Lifting dress to show heart-shaped garter	80	80
MS6587	72×102 mm. $200 Seated, wearing black dress (horiz); $200 In car (horiz)	3·25	3·50

708 Marilyn Monroe

2007. 80th Birth Anniv (2006) of Marilyn Monroe (actress). Multicoloured.

6588	$200 Type **708**	1·60	1·60
6589	$200 Wearing pink dress, standing sideways with head and shoulders turned towards camera	1·60	1·60
6590	$200 Wearing pink dress, standing sideways with head turned towards camera	1·60	1·60
6591	$200 In close-up, speaking	1·60	1·60
MS6592	70×100 mm. $400 In close-up, smiling	2·75	3·00

709 *Bletia florida*

2007. Orchids. Multicoloured.

6593	$25 Type **709**	25	30
6594	$35 *Basiphyllaea corallicola*	30	35
6595	$60 *Calopogon multiflorus*	45	50
6596	$160 *Cypripedium acaule*	1·50	1·50
6597	$160 *Calopogon tuberosus*	1·50	1·50
6598	$160 *Calopogon pallidus*	1·50	1·50
6599	$160 *Bletia patula*	1·50	1·50
6600	$300 *Bletia purpurea*	1·50	1·50
MS6601	66×95 mm. $400 *Cypripedium reginae*	2·75	3·00

710 Summer Tanager

2007. Birds of South America. Multicoloured.

6602	$25 Type **710**	25	30
6603	$35 Gray-cheeked thrush	30	35
6604	$60 Blackpoll warbler	45	50
6605	$160 Golden-tailed warbler (vert)	1·50	1·50
6606	$160 Blue-crowned parakeet (vert)	1·50	1·50
6607	$160 White-winged parakeet (vert)	1·50	1·50
6608	$160 Yellow-green vireo (vert)	1·50	1·50
6609	$300 Thick-billed parrot	2·50	2·50
MS6610	95×66 mm. (a) $400 Bobolink (vert). (b) $400 Pacific golden plover (vert)	5·50	6·00

711 *Morpho vitrea*

2007. Butterflies of South America. Multicoloured.

6611	$25 Type **711**	25	30
6612	$35 *Rothschildia Hesperus*	30	35
6613	$60 *Anaea nessus*	45	50
6614	$300 *Dryas iulia*	2·50	2·50
MS6615	$160×4 *Callithea sapphire*; *Prepona buckleyana*; *Lycorea pasinuntia*; *Danaus eresimus*	6·50	7·00
MS6616	Two sheets, each 100×70 mm. (a) $400 *Eurytides protesilaus*. (b) $400 *Cithaerias aurorina*	5·50	6·00

The stamps and margins of No. **MS**6615 form a composite background design showing a butterfly's wing.

712 Chartreux

2007. Cats. Multicoloured.

6617	$25 Type **712**	25	30
6618	$35 Siamese Seal snowshoe point	30	35
6619	$60 Maine coon	45	50
6620	$300 Turkish angora	2·50	2·50
MS6621	70×101 mm. $400 Blue Burmese (vert)	2·75	3·00

713 Papillon

2007. Dogs. Multicoloured.

6622	$160 Type **713**	1·50	1·50
6623	$160 Dogue de Bordeaux	1·50	1·50
6624	$160 Cavalier King Charles spaniel	1·50	1·50
6625	$160 Neapolitan mastiff	1·50	1·50
MS6626	70×100 mm. $400 Basset hound wearing tweed hat	2·75	3·00

714 Mozart in 1770

2007. 250th Birth Anniv (2006) of Wolfgang Amadeus Mozart (composer). Multicoloured.

6627	$190 Type **714**	1·75	1·75
6628	$190 Mozart in 1762	1·75	1·75
6629	$190 Mozart, c. 1789	1·75	1·75
6630	$190 Portrait by Joseph Grassi	1·75	1·75

715 Lord Robert Baden-Powell (founder), Peace Dove and Globe

2007. Centenary of World Scouting and 21st World Scout Jamboree, England. Multicoloured.

6631	$180 Type **715**	1·60	1·60
6632	$180 Scouts rafting	1·60	1·60
6633	$180 Scouts in tug-of-war	1·60	1·60
MS6634	111×80 mm. $400 Peace dove (vert)	2·75	3·00

716 Pig

2007. Chinese New Year ("Year of the Pig"). Multicoloured.

6635	$55 Type **716**	35	40
6636	$80 Pig (facing right)	50	55
6637	$100 As Type **716**	80	85
6638	$160 As No. 6636	1·40	1·50

717 Oath of Office

2007. 90th Birth Anniv of John F. Kennedy (US President 1960–3). Multicoloured.

MS6639	Two sheets, each 108×130 mm. (a) $80 Type **717**; $100 Inaugural speech; $160 John Kennedy; $190 With Jacqueline Kennedy at Inaugural Ball. (b) $80 The Peace Corps; $100 The Space Program; $160 Civil Rights; $190 John Kennedy, 1941	8·50	8·75

718 Elvis Presley

2007. 30th Death Anniv of Elvis Presley. Multicoloured.

6640	$160 Type **718**	1·40	1·40
6641	$160 Poster in bright scarlet and brown-rose	1·40	1·40
6642	$160 Young Elvis Presley (wearing black shirt)	1·40	1·40
6643	$160 Wearing sunglasses, facing left	1·40	1·40

2007. World Cup Cricket, West Indies. As T 448 of Dominica. Multicoloured.

6644	$100 Outline map and flag of Guyana	1·25	60
6645	$200 Victorious Guyana team, Stanford 20/20 (horiz)	2·00	2·00
MS6646	117×90 mm. $500 World Cup Cricket emblem	3·50	3·75

719 Pope Benedict XVI

2007. 80th Birthday of Pope Benedict XVI.

6647	**719**	$80 multicoloured	75	75

720 Concorde Prototype 002 rolled out, Filton, September 1968

2007. Concorde. Multicoloured.

6648	$100 Type **720**	1·00	1·00
6649	$100 Prototype 002 (seen from above, gangway down), Filton, September 1968	1·00	1·00
6650	$100 Concorde and Red Arrows, 1985	1·00	1·00
6651	$100 Silhouettes of Concorde, Red Arrows and *Queen Elizabeth II*	1·00	1·00

Nos. 6650/1 commemorate Concorde's flight in formation with the Red Arrows and the liner *Queen Elizabeth* in 1985.

721 Hockey

2008. Olympic Games, Beijing. Multicoloured.

6652	$100 Type **721**	80	80
6653	$100 Basketball	80	80
6654	$100 Judo	80	80
6655	$100 Shooting	80	80

722 Emblem and 'Carifesta X'

2008. Carifesta Caribbean Festival of Arts, Guyana. Multicoloured, background colours given.

6656	**722**	$20 red	25	30
6657	**722**	$55 green and yellow	35	40
6658	**722**	$80 green	50	55
6659	**722**	$160 yellow	1·40	1·40

723 St. Stanislaus College, Georgetown

2008. 150th Anniv (2007) of Jesuits in Guyana. Multicoloured.

6660	$80 Type **723**	50	55
6661	$100 Sacred Heart Church, 1861–2004, Georgetown	80	55
6662	$160 Fr. Cuthbert Cary-Elwes, missionary among the Amerindians, 1909–23	1·40	1·40

724 Sir James Douglas

2008. 150th Anniv of Appointment of Sir James Douglas (born in Guyana) as First Governor of British Columbia, Canada. Sheet 70×100 mm.

MS6663 multicoloured 1·40 1·40

725 White Peony

2009. China 2009 World Stamp Exhibition, Luoyang (1st issue). Peonies.

6664 **725** $80 multicoloured 50 55

726 Red Peony

2009. China 2009 World Stamp Exhibition, Luoyang (2nd issue). The Art of Wang Hui (1632–1717). Sheet 150×120 mm containing T 726 and similar horiz designs. Multicoloured.

MS6665 Type **726**; River valley and coast; Clouds and forest; Coastal rocks with pines 5·50 5·50

727 Elvis Presley

2009. Elvis Presley Commemoration. Sheet 128×190 mm containing T 727 and similar vert designs. Multicoloured.

MS6666 Type **727**; Wearing orange jacket; Wearing white jacket; In profile; In close-up, singing into microphone; Wearing black shirt 8·50 8·50

728 Pres. Barack Obama

2009. Inauguration of Pres. Barack Obama. Sheet 107×145 mm containing T 728 and similar vert designs showing Pres. Obama. Multicoloured.

MS6667 Type **728**; In profile; Wearing red tie; Wearing pale grey tie 4·50 4·50

729 50th Anniversary Commemorative Magazine

2009. 50th Anniv of Rotary Club of Georgetown, Guyana. Sheet 140×90 mm containing T 729 and similar horiz designs. Multicoloured.

MS6668 $80 Type **729**; $80 'Christmas Cheers for the Elderly'; $160 Poster showing people in wheelchairs ('Physically challenged sports'); $160 Boy receiving award 4·50 4·50

730 500 F2, 1952

2009. Ferrari Racing Cars. Sheet 120×100 mm containing T 730 and similar horiz designs. Multicoloured.

MS6669 $200×4 Type **730**; 500 F2, 1953; 246 F1, 1958; 312 T2, 1976 6·50 6·50

730a Takutu Bridge

2009. Opening of Takutu Bridge linking Guyana to Brazil. Sheet 100×70 mm.

MS6669a multicoloured 3·50 3·50

731 Guyana Scouts Centenary Parade

2009. Centenary of Scouting in Guyana and 14th Caribbean Scout Jamboree, Georgetown. Multicoloured.

6670 $55 Type **731** 35 40
6671 $55 Archery (vert) 35 40
6672 $80 Helping the homeless 50 55
6673 $80 Erecting shelter at Scout jamboree 50 55
6674 $160 '1909 Scouting Guyana 2009' and national flag 1·40 1·50
6675 $160 '2009 14th Caribbean Scout jamboree Celebrating 100 years of Scouting in Guyana' 1·40 1·50

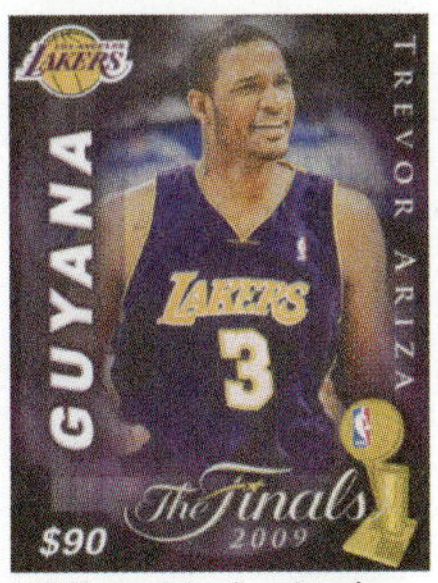

732 Trevor Ariza (Los Angeles Lakers)

2009. NBA Basketball Finals. Multicoloured.

6676 $90 Type **732** 65 70
6677 $90 Shannon Brown 65 70
6678 $90 Jordan Farmar 65 70
6679 $90 Andrew Bynum 65 70
6680 $90 Kobe Bryant 65 70
6681 $90 Derek Fisher 65 70
6682 $90 Pau Gasol 65 70
6683 $90 Lamar Odom 65 70
6684 $90 Luke Walton 65 70
6685 $90 Rafer Alston 65 70
6686 $90 Marcin Gortat 65 70
6687 $90 Rashard Lewis 65 70
6688 $90 Courtney Lee 65 70
6689 $90 Dwight Howard 65 70
6690 $90 Jameer Nelson 65 70
6691 $90 Mickael Pietrus 65 70
6692 $90 J. J. Redick 65 70
6693 $90 Hedo Turkoglu 65 70

Nos. 6676/84 show players from Los Angeles Laker, the 2009 NBA champions.

Nos. 6685/93 show players from Orlando Magic, the 2009 Eastern Conference champions.

733 Michael Jackson

2009. Michael Jackson Commemoration. Two sheets, each 178×127 mm, containing T 733 and similar multicoloured designs.

MS6694 Type **733**; With arm raised and other hand on belt buckle; Seen from side, right arm outstretched; Both hands at waist level 6·00 6·00

MS6695 Wearing red waistcoat; Wearing black hat, black glittery jacket and white T shirt; Wearing black sequinned jacket and white T shirt; Wearing red T shirt with black diagonal band (all horiz) 6·00 6·00

734 Parliament Building, Georgetown

2009. 60th Anniv of the Commonwealth. Sheet 170×114 mm.

MS6696 multicoloured 2·50 2·50

735 National Library, Georgetown

2009. Centenary of National Library, Georgetown. Sheet 120×100 mm containing T 735 and similar horiz designs. Multicoloured.

MS6697 Type **735**; Aerial view; Students in library; Students in library (black and white photo) 4·00 4·00

736 J-8II

2009. Centenary of Chinese Aviation and Aeropex 2009 Exhibition, Beijing. T 736 and similar horiz designs showing fighter jets. Multicoloured.

MS6698 145×95 mm. $150×4 Type **736**; J-11; J-10 (pale blue background); J-10 (blue sky and white clouds background) 5·00 5·00

MS6699 120×80 mm. $400 J-10 (50×37 mm) 3·25 3·25

737 Pope John Paul II and Cardinal Joseph Ratzinger

2009. Pope Benedict XVI and Pope John Paul II. Multicoloured.

MS6700 120×140 mm. $200×4 As Type **737** 3·25 3·25

MS6701 110×100 mm. $400×2 Cardinal Joseph Ratzinger; Pope John Paul II 6·50 6·50

The stamps within **MS**6700 are all as Type **737** with a yellow border at the foot of the stamp which depicts portions of the sheet background illustration of the portico of St. Peter's Basilica.

EXPRESS LETTER STAMPS

1986. Various stamps surch EXPRESS and new values.

E1 $12 on 350c. on 120c. multicoloured (No. 1598) 7·00 7·00
E2 $15 on 40c. multicoloured (No. 1868) 9·00 9·00
E3 $20 on $6.40 multicoloured 7·00 7·00
E4 $25 on 25c. multicoloured (as No. 1771, but value changed) 13·00 13·00

No. E3 was previously a miniature sheet for Halley's Comet containing two 320c. stamps. As surch the original values on both designs have been cancelled and replaced by a single $20 face value.

1987. No. E3 additionally optd with small Maltese cross above surch.

E5 $20 on $6.40 multicoloured 7·00 7·00

1987. Centenary of Publication of Sanders' "Reichenbachia". As T 331 additionally inscr "EXPRESS". Multicoloured.

E6 $15 Plate No. 11 (Series 2) 6·00 6·00
E7 $20 Plate No. 93 (Series 2) 3·50 4·00
E8 $25 Plate No. 63 (Series 2) 5·00 6·50
E9 $45 Plate No. 35 (Series 2) 8·00 10·00

1987. Nos. 1744/5 imperf between surch EXPRESS FORTY DOLLARS and star.

E10 $40 on $6.40 multicoloured 12·00 12·00

1987. No. E2 additionally optd 1987.

E11 $15 on 40c. multicoloured 11·00 7·00

1988. Nos. 2206 and 2211 surch SPECIAL DELIVERY and new value.

E12 $40 on $3.20 blue 10·00 11·00
E13 $45 on $3.30 black 10·00 11·00

1989. Imperf between pairs of Nos. 1744/5 and 2185/6 surch EXPRESS FORTY DOLLARS (without stars).

E14 $40 on $6.40 multicoloured (Nos. 1744/5) 6·00 6·50
E15 $40 on $6.40 multicoloured (Nos. 2185/6) 6·00 6·50

1989. Nos. 2206 and 2211 surch SPECIAL DELIVERY and new value.

E16 $190 on $3.30 black 17·00 19·00
E17 $225 on $3.20 blue 18·00 20·00

1989. Butterflies. Two sheets, each 97×67 mm, containing vert designs as T 454 optd EXPRESS. Multicoloured.

EMS18 $130 "Phareas coeleste" 5·00 5·00
EMS19 $190 "Papilio torquatus" 6·00 6·00

1989. Women in Space. Sheet 92×67 mm, containing vert design as T 455 optd EXPRESS. Multicoloured.

EMS20 $190 Valentina Tereshkova (first woman cosmonaut) 4·25 4·50

1989. "World Stamp Expo '89" International Stamp Exhibition, Washington. Nos. EMS18/19 optd with logo.

EMS21 $130 "Phareas coeleste" 4·00 4·00
EMS22 $190 "Papilio torquatus" 4·50 4·50

Nos. **EMS**21/22 show additional overprints on sheet margins.

1990. 85th Anniv of Rotary International. Nos. EMS18/20 optd ROTARY INTERNATIONAL 1905–1990 and emblem on sheet margins only.

EMS23 $130 "Phareas coeleste" 4·00 4·00
EMS24 $190 "Papilio torquatus" 6·50 6·50
EMS25 $190 Valentina Tereshkova (first woman cosmonaut) 4·25 6·00

1990. "Stamp World London '90" International Stamp Exhibition. Nos. EMS18/20 optd Stamp World London '90 and emblem on sheet margins only.

EMS26 $130 "Phareas coeleste" (R.) 3·75 3·75
EMS27 $190 "Papilio torquatus" 5·50 5·50
EMS28 $190 Valentina Tereshkova (first woman cosmonaut) 4·00 5·50

1990. "Belgica '90" International Stamp Exhibition, Brussels. Nos. EMS18 and EMS20 additionally optd BELGICA PHILATELIC EXPOSITION 1990 and emblem in black on sheet margins only.

EMS29 $130 "Phareas coeleste" 4·00 4·00
EMS30 $190 Valentina Tereshkova (first woman cosmonaut) 4·50 5·00

1990. 90th Birthday of Queen Elizabeth the Queen Mother. Nos. EMS18/20 optd 90TH BIRTHDAY H.M. THE QUEEN MOTHER on sheet margins only.

EMS31 $130 "Phareas coeleste" 3·50 3·50
EMS32 $190 "Papilio torquatus" 4·00 4·00
EMS33 $190 Valentina Tereshkova (first woman cosmonaut) 4·00 4·00

1990. Fauna. Two sheets, each 110×80 mm, containing vert designs as T 466, but larger (40×55 mm) inscr EXPRESS. Multicoloured.

EMS34 $130 Harpy Eagle 4·50 4·50
EMS35 $150 Ocelot 4·50 4·50

OFFICIAL STAMPS

1981. Nos. 556, F4a and F6/7 optd OPS or surch also.

O13 10c. on 25c. Marabunta 3·50 2·25
O14 50c. "Guzmania lingulata" 1·00 30
O15 60c. Soldier's cap 1·00 20
O16 $5 "Odontadenia grandiflora" 1·75 1·75

1981. Nos. 491, 708a, 716, 804, 834 and F9 optd OPS or surch also.

O17 15c. Harpy eagle (postage) 9·50 65
O18 30c. on $2 "Norantea guianensis" (F9) 45 30
O19 100c. on $3 Cylinder satellite 2·00 40
O20 125c. on $2 "Norantea guianensis" 1·00 60
O21 $10 "Elbella patrobas" 11·00 11·00

O22		$1.10 on $2 "Norantea guianensis" (804) (air)	1·00	2·00

1981. Nos. 548a, 719, 828 and 830 optd OPS or surch also.

O23		15c. Christmas orchid	8·50	1·50
O24		50c. British Guiana 1898 1c. stamp	1·25	35
O25		100c. on 8c. Camp-fire cooking	1·25	50
O26		110c. on 6c. Type **116**	2·00	1·25

1982. Various stamps optd OPS.

O27	-	20c. multicoloured (No. 701)	7·00	80
O28	**136**	40c. multicoloured	75	15
O29	-	40c. red, grey and black (No. 674)	1·00	15
O30	-	$2 multicoloured (No. 676)	7·00	75

1982. Nos. 911 and 980 optd or surch OPS.

O31		250c. on 400c. on 30c. multicoloured (postage)	80	60
O32		220c. on 1c. multicoloured (air)	1·00	60

1982. No. F9 optd OPS.

O33		$2 "Norantea guianensis"	8·00	2·00

1982. Air. No. 979 optd OPS.

O34		110c. on 5c. Annatto tree	1·25	40

1984. No. 912 surch OPS.

O35		150c. on $5 multicoloured	6·00	2·75
O36		200c. on $5 multicoloured	6·50	3·00
O37		225c. on $5 multicoloured	6·50	3·25
O38		230c. on $5 multicoloured	6·50	3·25
O39		260c. on $5 multicoloured	6·50	3·50
O40		320c. on $5 multicoloured	8·00	4·00
O41		350c. on $5 multicoloured	8·50	4·50
O42		600c. on $5 multicoloured	10·00	6·50

1984. Nos. O32 and O34 surch and No. 981 optd OPS.

O43		25c. on 110c. on 5c. Annatto tree	1·50	40
O44		30c. on 110c. on 5c. Annatto tree	1·50	45
O45		45c. on 220c. on 1c. Pitcher plant of Mt. Roraima	1·60	55
O46		55c. on 110c. on 5c. Annatto tree	1·75	60
O47		60c. on 220c. on 1c. Pitcher plant of Mt. Roraima	1·75	60
O48		75c. on 220c. on 1c. Pitcher plant of Mt. Roraima	2·00	70
O49		90c. on 220c. on 1c. Pitcher plant of Mt. Roraima	2·00	80
O50		120c. on 220c. on 1c. Pitcher plant of Mt. Roraima	2·25	1·25
O51		130c. on 220c. on 1c. Pitcher plant of Mt. Roraima	2·25	1·25
O52		330c. on $2 "Norantea guianensis"	4·00	4·00

1987. Centenary of Publication of Sanders' "Reichenbachia". As T 331 additionally inscr "OFFICIAL". Multicoloured.

O53		120c. Plate No. 48 (Series 2)	1·75	45
O54		130c. Plate No. 92 (Series 2)	1·75	45
O55		140c. Plate No. 36 (Series 2)	75	35
O56		150c. Plate No. 43 (Series 2)	1·75	50
O57		175c. Plate No. 31 (Series 2)	80	40
O58		200c. Plate No. 61 (Series 2)	1·75	60
O59		225c. Plate No. 26 (Series 2)	1·75	60
O60		230c. Plate No. 68 (Series 2) (horiz)	50	50
O61		250c. Plate No. 59 (Series 2)	50	60
O62		260c. Plate No. 69 (Series 2)	50	60
O63		275c. Plate No. 90 (Series 2)	1·75	75
O64		320c. Plate No. 75 (Series 2)	1·75	80
O65		330c. Plate No. 23 (Series 2)	3·00	1·00
O66		350c. Plate No. 95 (Series 2) (horiz)	50	80
O67		600c. Plate No. 70 (Series 2) (horiz)	75	1·60
O68		$12 Plate No. 71 (Series 2) (horiz)	1·40	2·50
O69		$15 Plate No. 84 (Series 2)	1·50	2·75

OFFICIAL PARCEL POST STAMPS

1981. Nos. P1/2 optd OPS.

OP1		$15 on $1 "Chelonanthus uliginoides"	10·00	2·25
OP2		$20 on $1 "Chelonanthus uliginoides"	10·00	2·75

1983. No. 843 surch OPS Parcel Post $12.00 and additionally optd 1982.

OP3		$12 on $1.10 on $2 "Norantea guianensis"	75·00	17·00

1983. No. OP3 with additional OPS opt.

OP4		$12 on $1.10 on $2 "Norantea guianensis"	22·00	4·00

1983. No. P4 optd OPS.

OP5		$12 on $1.10 on $2 "Norantea guianensis"	7·50	4·00

1981. No. 554 surch PARCEL POST and new value.

P1		$15 on $1 "Chelonanthus uliginoides"	10·00	3·00
P2		$20 on $1 "Chelonanthus uliginoides"	10·00	6·00

1983. No. 843 surch PARCEL POST $12.00.

P3		$12 on $1.10 on $2 "Norantea guianensis"	2·25	2·50

1983. Unissued Royal Wedding surch, similar to No. 843, further surch Parcel Post $12.00.

P4		$12 on $1.10 on $2 "Norantea guianensis"	1·00	1·75

1985. No. 673 surch TWENTY FIVE DOLLARS PARCEL POST 25.00.

P5		$25 on 35c. green, grey and black	27·00	19·00

POSTAGE DUE STAMPS

D2

1987.

D8	**D2**	1c. green	25	3·75
D9	**D2**	2c. black	25	3·75
D10	**D2**	4c. blue	25	3·75
D11	**D2**	12c. red	35	3·75

POSTAL FISCAL STAMPS

1975. Nos. 543/5 and 550ab/6 optd REVENUE ONLY.

F1		2c. Type **132**	50	40
F2		3c. Hanging heliconia	50	50
F3		5c. Annatto tree	75	30
F4		25c. Marabunta	3·25	30
F4a		25c. Marabunta (No. 550)	15·00	13·00
F5		40c. Tiger beard	5·50	30
F6		50c. "Guzmania lingulata"	70	40
F7		60c. Soldier's cap	75	50
F8		$1 "Chelonanthus uliginoides"	75	1·25
F9		$2 "Norantea guianensis"	1·00	2·75
F10		$5 "Odontadenis grandiflora"	1·75	9·00

Although intended for fiscal use Nos. F1/F10 were allowed by the postal authorities as an "act of grace" to do duty as postage stamps until 30 June 1976.

Pt. 1

GWALIOR

A "convention" state of Central India.

12 pies = 1 anna; 16 annas = 1 rupee.

1885. Queen Victoria stamps of India optd GWALIOR at foot and native opt at top.

1	**23**	½a. turquoise	£170	35·00
2	-	1a. purple	£100	35·00
3	-	2a. blue	85·00	18·00
6	-	1a.6p. brown	95·00	
8	-	4a. green (No. 69)	£110	
9	-	6a. brown (No. 80)	£110	
10	-	8a. mauve	85·00	
11	-	1r. grey (No. 101)	85·00	

Stamps of India overprinted **GWALIOR** above native overprint unless otherwise stated.

1885. Queen Victoria.

14		4a. green (No. 69)	35·00	20·00
16c	**23**	½a. turquoise	50	10
17	-	9p. red	35·00	65·00
18	-	1a. purple	2·25	20
20c	-	1a.6p. brown	2·25	1·25
21c	-	2a. blue	3·00	10
23	-	2a.6p. green	11·00	22·00
25c	-	3a. orange	5·00	15
27c	-	4a. green (No. 96)	6·00	1·40
29	-	6a. brown (No. 80)	4·25	9·50
30c	-	8a. mauve	6·50	1·40
32c	-	12a. purple on red	3·25	65
33c	-	1r. grey (No. 101)	4·50	3·50
34	**37**	1r. green and red	8·50	7·50
35	**38**	2r. red and orange	5·50	3·00
36	**38**	3r. brown and green	7·50	3·50
37	**38**	5r. blue and violet	14·00	6·50

1899. Queen Victoria.

38	**40**	3p. red	50	20
39	**40**	3p. grey	7·50	60·00
40	**23**	½a. green	1·40	1·60
41	-	1a. red	1·25	35
42	-	2a. lilac	3·25	5·50
43	-	2½a. blue	2·00	7·50

1903. King Edward VII.

46A	**41**	3p. grey	1·40	20
48A	-	½a. green (No. 122)	20	10
49A	-	1a. red (No. 123)	20	10
50A	-	2a. lilac	2·25	1·00
52B	-	2a.6p. blue	1·25	9·50
53A	-	3a. orange	2·25	35
54A	-	4a. olive	3·50	40
56B	-	6a. bistre	7·50	1·60
57A	-	8a. mauve	6·00	1·60
59B	-	12a. purple on red	3·75	3·25
60A	-	1r. green and red	4·00	1·75
61B	**52**	2r. red and orange	9·00	11·00
62B	**52**	3r. brown and green	30·00	60·00
63B	**52**	5r. blue and violet	19·00	27·00

1907. King Edward VII inscr "INDIA POSTAGE AND REVENUE".

65		½a. green (No. 149)	1·75	20
66		1a. red (No. 150)	1·50	20

1912. King George V.

67	**55**	3p. grey	10	10
68	**58**	½a. green	20	10
69	**57**	1a. red	25	10
70	**59**	2a. purple	1·00	10
71	**62**	3a. orange	70	15
72	**63**	4a. olive	60	60
73a	**64**	6a. bistre	1·40	1·50
74	**65**	8a. mauve	2·50	80
75	**66**	12a. red	1·40	4·00
76	**67**	1r. brown and green	12·00	1·00
77	**67**	2r. red and brown	6·00	4·50
78	**67**	5r. blue and violet	24·00	6·50
80	**57**	1a. brown	1·10	10
81	**58**	1½a. brown (No. 165)	2·75	50
82	**58**	1½a. red	20	20
83	**61**	2½a. blue	2·25	1·75
84	**61**	2½a. orange	35	50
88	**80**	9p. green	3·50	30
90	**82**	1a.3p. mauve	50	15
91	**70**	2a. lilac	75	30
92	**62**	3a. blue	1·00	40
93	**71**	4a. green	1·25	1·00
102	**79**	½a. green	50	20
103	**81**	1a. brown	20	10
104	**59**	2a. red	3·50	3·50

1922. No. 192 (King George V) optd GWALIOR only.

79	**57**	9p. on 1a. red	10	50

1928. King George V. Optd in larger type (19 mm long).

96	**67**	1r. brown and green	4·00	4·50
97w	**67**	2r. red and orange	8·00	4·50
98	**67**	5r. blue and violet	22·00	28·00
99	**67**	10r. green and red	80·00	48·00
100	**67**	15r. blue and olive	£130	75·00
101	**67**	25r. orange and blue	£275	£190

1938. King George VI.

105	**91**	3p. slate	11·00	10
106	**91**	½a. brown	11·00	10
107	**91**	9p. green	55·00	4·50
108	**91**	1a. red	10·00	15
109	**91**	3a. green (No. 253)	35·00	6·00
110	**91**	4a. brown (No. 255)	50·00	4·00
111	**91**	6a. green (No. 256)	4·50	13·00
112	**93**	1r. slate and brown	13·00	1·75
113	**93**	2r. purple and brown	55·00	10·00
114	**93**	5r. green and blue	32·00	45·00
115	**93**	10r. purple and red	32·00	48·00
116	**93**	15r. brown and green	90·00	£190
117	**93**	25r. slate and purple	80·00	£150

1942. King George VI.

118	**100a**	3p. slate	45	10
119	**100a**	½a. mauve	1·00	10
120	**100a**	9p. green	1·00	10
121	**100a**	1a. red	1·00	10
122	**101**	1½a. violet	8·00	1·00
123	**101**	2a. red	2·25	20
124	**101**	3a. violet	16·00	2·25
125	**102**	4a. brown	4·25	20
126	**102**	6a. green	14·00	27·00
127	**102**	8a. violet	4·50	2·75
128	**102**	12a. purple	6·50	24·00

OFFICIAL STAMPS

Stamps of India overprinted with native inscription at top and bottom, unless otherwise stated.

1895. Queen Victoria.

O1	**23**	½a. turquoise	60	10
O3	-	1a. purple	3·00	10
O5	-	2a. blue	2·25	50
O7	-	4a. green (No. 96)	3·25	1·40
O9	-	8a. mauve	5·00	2·75
O10	**37**	1r. green and red	10·00	3·00

1901. Queen Victoria.

O23	**40**	3p. red	1·75	25
O24	**40**	3p. grey	2·50	3·75
O26	**23**	½a. green	75	10
O27	-	1a. red	7·00	10
O28	-	2a. lilac	1·75	1·50

1903. King Edward VII.

O29	**41**	3p. grey	70	10
O32	-	1a. red (No. 123)	1·10	10
O33a	-	2a. lilac	2·25	30
O36	-	8a. mauve	9·50	70
O38	-	1r. green and red	2·75	2·00
O41	-	½a. green (No. 122)	4·50	15
O44	-	4a. olive	3·00	1·00

1907. King Edward VII inscr "POSTAGE & REVENUE".

O48		1a. red (No. 150)	9·50	15
O49		½a. green (No. 149)	1·75	15

1913. King George V.

O51	**55**	3p. grey	40	10
O53a	**57**	1a. red	30	10
O55	**59**	2a. purple	1·75	1·00
O58	**67**	1r. brown and green	35·00	28·00
O62	**56**	½a. green	10	15
O63	**80**	9p. green	10	15
O64	**57**	1a. brown	10	10
O65	**82**	1a.3p. mauve	50	15
O66	**70**	2a. lilac	20	15
O67	**71**	4a. green	75	30
O68	**65**	8a. mauve	60	1·10
O73	**79**	½a. green	15	15
O74	**81**	1a. brown	15	15
O75	**59**	2a. red	20	40
O77	**63**	4a. olive	60	75

1922. No. O97 (King George V Official) optd GWALIOR only.

O59	**57**	9p. on 1a. red	10	30

1927. King George V. Optd in large type (21 mm long).

O69	**67**	1r. brown and green	1·00	1·75
O70	**67**	2r. red and orange	23·00	23·00
O71	**67**	5r. blue and violet	27·00	£200
O72	**67**	10r. green and red	£180	£500

1938. King George VI.

O78	**91**	½a. brown	6·50	30
O79	**91**	1a. red	2·00	20
O91	**93**	1r. slate and brown	12·00	24·00
O92	**93**	2r. purple and brown	18·00	£110
O93	**93**	5r. green and blue	30·00	£650
O94	**93**	10r. purple and red	80·00	£1300

1940. King George VI. Optd at bottom only.

O80	**O20**	3p. slate	50	10
O81	**O20**	½a. brown	6·00	25
O82	**O20**	½a. purple	1·00	10
O83	**O20**	9p. green	70	70
O84	**O20**	1a. red	2·25	10
O85	**O20**	1a.3p. brown	50·00	1·75
O86	**O20**	1a.6p. violet	1·75	30
O87	**O20**	2a. orange	2·00	30
O88	**O20**	4a. brown	2·25	3·25
O89	**O20**	8a. violet	6·00	9·50

1942. No. O65 surch 1A 1A and bar.

O90	**82**	1a. on 1¼a. mauve	25·00	3·00

Pt. 15

HAITI

The W. portion of the island of Hispaniola in the West Indies. A republic, independent from 1804.

100 centimes = 1 gourde or piastre.

1 Liberty

1881. Imperf.

1	1	1c. red	8·25	5·00
2	1	2c. purple	10·00	5·00
3	1	3c. bistre	18·00	7·50
4	1	5c. green	31·00	15·00
5	1	7c. blue	20·00	3·75
6	1	20c. brown	75·00	28·00

1882. Perf.

7	1c. red	5·25	1·90
9	2c. purple	8·50	2·50
12	3c. bistre	10·50	3·00
15	5c. green	7·00	1·30
17	7c. blue	9·50	1·90
20	20c. brown	11·00	2·40

2 Pres. Salomon

1887

24	2	1c. lake	35	30
25	2	2c. mauve	90	65
26	2	3c. blue	65	40
27	2	5c. green	4·25	50

1890. Surch DEUX 2 CENT.

28	2c. on 3c. blue	60	50

4 Tree with Leaves upright

1891. Tree with leaves upright.

29	4	1c. mauve	45	30
30	4	2c. blue	65	30
31	4	3c. lilac	90	40
31a	4	3c. grey	80	50
32	4	5c. orange	3·00	45
33	4	7c. red	6·75	2·50

1892. Surch DEUX 2 CENT.

34	2c. on 3c. lilac	1·20	85
34a	2c. on 3c. grey	1·40	95

5 Tree with Leaves drooping

1893. Tree with leaves drooping.

35a	5	1c. purple	35	15
36	5	2c. blue	45	20
37	5	3c. lilac	65	40
38	5	5c. orange	2·50	45
39	5	7c. red	45	20
40	5	20c. brown	1·60	1·00
41	5	1c. blue	50	65
42	5	2c. red	60	1·10
43	5	3c. brown	50	1·10
44	5	5c. green	60	1·10
45	5	7c. grey	80	1·60
46	5	20c. orange	1·00	2·10

1898. Surch DEUX 2 CENT.

47	2c. on 20c. brown	1·20	80
48	2c. on 20c. orange	80	60

6

1898

49a	6	2c. red	45	20
50a	6	5c. green	45	20

8 Pres. Simon Sam

9

1898

51	8	1c. blue	15	10
52	8	2c. orange	15	15
53	8	3c. green	15	15
54	9	4c. red	15	15
55	8	5c. brown	15	15
56	8	7c. grey	15	15
57	9	8c. red	15	15
58	9	10c. orange	15	15
59	9	15c. olive	55	40
60	8	20c. black	55	40
61	8	50c. lake	65	45
62	8	1g. mauve	2·00	1·50
67	9	1c. green	15	10
68	9	2c. red	15	15
69	9	5c. blue	15	15

1902. Optd MAI Gt Pre 1902 in frame.

70	8	1c. blue	55	40
71	9	1c. green	40	25
72	8	2c. orange	70	65
73	9	2c. red	40	25
74	8	3c. green	40	40
75	9	4c. red	55	50
76	8	5c. brown	1·10	1·00
77	9	5c. blue	40	40
78	8	7c. grey	85	80
79	9	8c. red	85	80
80	9	10c. orange	85	80
81	9	15c. olive	4·00	2·50
82	8	20c. black	4·00	3·00
83	8	50c. lake	9·75	5·50
84	8	1g. mauve	15·00	13·00

12 Arms

13 J.-J. Dessalines

1904. Cent of Independence. Optd 1804 POSTE PAYE 1904 in frame. T 12 and portraits as T 13.

89	12	1c. green	45	40
90	-	2c. black and red	45	40
91	-	5c. black and blue	45	40
92	13	7c. black and red	45	40
93	-	10c. black and yellow	45	40
94	-	20c. black and grey	45	40
95	-	50c. black and olive	45	40

DESIGNS: 2, 5c. Toussaint l'Ouverture; 20, 50c. Petion.

1904. Nos. 89/95 but without opt.

96	1c. green	30	30
97	2c. black and red	30	30
98	5c. black and blue	30	30
99	7c. black and red	30	30
100	10c. black and yellow	30	30
101	20c. black and grey	30	30
102	50c. black and olive	30	30

15 Pres. Nord Alexis

1904. External Mail. Optd 1804 POSTE PAYE 1904 in frame.

103	15	1c. green	55	50
104	15	2c. red	55	50
105	15	5c. blue	55	50
106	15	10c. brown	55	50
107	15	20c. orange	55	50
108	15	50c. plum	55	50

1904. Nos. 103/108, but without opt.

109	1c. green	30	30
110	2c. red	30	30
111	5c. blue	30	30
112	10c. brown	30	30
113	20c. orange	30	30
114	50c. plum	30	30

1906. Optd SERVICE EXTERIEUR PROVISOIRE EN PIASTRES FORTES in oval.

117	8	1c. blue	1·10	75
118	9	1c. green	60	60
119	8	2c. orange	2·00	1·90
120	9	2c. red	1·10	1·00
121	8	3c. green	1·10	1·00
122	9	4c. red	4·75	3·75
123	8	5c. brown	6·00	4·50
124	9	5c. blue	85	50
125	8	7c. grey	4·00	3·75
126	9	8c. red	85	80
127	9	10c. orange	1·60	95
128	9	15c. olive	2·00	1·00
129	8	20c. black	4·75	3·75
130	8	50c. lake	4·75	3·00
131	8	1g. mauve	9·50	6·00

19 Pres. Nord Alexis

20 Arms

1906

132	19	1c. de g. blue	30	20
133	20	2c. de g. orange	40	20
134	20	2c. de g. yellow	60	25
135	19	3c. de g. grey	35	20
136	20	7c. de g. green	1·10	40

21 Iron Market, Port-au-Prince

1906. Currency changed from "gourdes" to "piastres".

137		1c. de p. green	30	25
138	19	2c. de p. red	40	25
139	21	3c. de p. sepia	55	25
140	21	3c. de p. orange	6·25	3·00
141	-	4c. de p. red	55	30
142	19	5c. de p. blue	2·00	25
143	-	7c. de p. grey	1·60	75
144	-	8c. de p. red	1·60	70
145	-	10c. de p. orange	1·10	25
146	-	15c. de p. olive	2·00	80
147	19	20c. de p. blue	2·00	80
148	20	50c. de p. red	3·00	2·10
149	-	1pi. red	6·50	4·00
167	-	4c. de p. olive	11·50	8·25
168	-	7c. de p. red	38·00	28·00
169	-	8c. de p. olive	23·00	17·00
170	-	10c. de p. brown	23·00	17·00
171	-	15c. de p. yellow	11·50	5·50
172	20	50c. de p. yellow	11·50	8·25
173	-	1pi. red	11·50	10·00

DESIGNS—As Type **21**: 4c. Palace of Sans Souci-Milot; 7c. Independence Palace, Gonaives; 8c. Entrance to Catholic College, Port-au-Prince; 10c. Catholic Monastery and Church, Port-au-Prince; 15c. Government Offices, Port-au-Prince; 1pi. President's Palace, Port-au-Prince.

1906. Surch with value in double-lined frame Without opt.

154	15	1c. on 5c. blue	35	30
155	15	1c. on 10c. brown	45	20
156	15	1c. on 20c. orange	35	20
157	15	2c. on 10c. brown	35	20
158	15	2c. on 20c. orange	35	35
159	15	2c. on 50c. plum	45	35

24 Pres. A. T. Simon

1910

160	24	1c. de g. black and red	25	20
161	24	2c. de p. black and red	60	45
162	24	5c. de p. black and blue	11·50	65
163	24	20c. de p. black and green	9·50	6·50

25 Pres. C. Leconte

1912. Various frames.

164	25	1c. de g. lake	35	35
165	25	2c. de g. orange	45	35
166	25	5c. de p. blue	80	35

1914. Optd GL O.Z. 7 FEV. 1914 in frame. A. On 1898 issue.

174	9	8c. red	11·50	8·75

B. On 1904 issue, without opt.

175	15	1c. green (No. 109)	29·00	24·00
176	15	2c. red	29·00	24·00
177	15	5c. blue	60	35
178	15	10c. brown	60	35
179	15	20c. orange	95	45
180	15	50c. plum	2·30	1·10

C. On pictorial stamps of 1906.

181	20	2c. de g. yellow	45	35
182	19	3c. de g. grey	45	35

D. On pictorial stamps of 1906.

183	20	1c. de p. green (No. 137)	45	35
184	19	2c. de p. red (No. 138)	60	35
185	21	3c. de p. sepia (No. 139)	95	55
186	21	3c. de p. orange (No. 140)	45	35
187	-	4c. de p. red (No. 141)	95	45
188	-	7c. de p. grey (No. 143)	2·30	2·20
189	-	8c. de p. red (No. 144)	4·00	3·75
190	-	10c. de p. orange (No. 145)	1·20	55
191	-	15c. de p. olive (No. 146)	3·25	3·00
192	19	20c. de p. blue (No. 147)	3·00	1·10
194	20	50c. de p. red (No. 148)	5·25	5·00
195	-	1pi. red (No. 149)	5·25	5·00
198	-	4c. de p. olive (No. 167)	2·50	1·30
200	-	7c. de p. red (No. 168)	5·75	5·50
201	-	8c. de p. olive (No. 169)	7·50	7·25
202	-	10c. de p. brown (No. 170)	3·00	1·90
203	-	15c. de p. yellow (No. 171)	2·50	1·30
204	20	50c. de p. yellow (No. 172)	8·75	8·25
205	-	1pi. red (No. 173)	9·50	8·75

E. On stamp of 1910.

193	24	20c. de p. black and green	3·50	3·25

F. On stamps of 1912.

196	25	1c. de g. lake	45	35
197	25	2c. de g. orange	60	45
199	25	5c. de p. blue	95	35

1914. Stamps of 1904, without the opt, surch GL O.Z 7 FEV 1914 7 CENT in diamond frame.

213	15	7c. on 20c. orange (No. 113)	45	20
214	15	7c. on 50c. plum (No. 114)	40	20

1914. Pictorial stamps of 1906 (Nos. 148/73), surch GL OZ 1 CENT DE PIASTRE 7 FEV. 1914 in frame.

215	20	1c. de p. on 50c. red	45	35
216	20	1c. de p. on 50c. yellow	60	45
217	-	1c. de p. on 1p. red	60	45
218	-	1c. de p. on 1p. red	60	45

38

1915

219		2c. de g. black and yellow	80
220	38	5c. de g. black and green	1·30
221	-	7c. de g. black and red	80

PORTRAIT: 2, 7c. O. Zamor.

1915. As T 24, inscr "EMISSION 1914".

222	1c. de p. black and green	2·50
223	3c. de p. black and olive	25
224	5c. de p. black and blue	45
225	7c. de p. black and orange	1·20
226	10c. de p. black and brown	35
227	15c. de p. black and olive	45
228	20c. de p. black and brown	45

DESIGNS: 1c., 5c., 10c., 15c. O. Zamor; 3c., 20c. Arms; 7c. T. Auguste.

1915. Surch with figure in frame.

229		1 on 5c. blue (No. 111)	1·40	1·30
230		1 on 7c. grey (No. 143)	45	45
231		1 on 10c. brown (No. 112)	60	55
232		1 on 20c. orange (No. 107)	45	45
233		1 on 20c. orange (No. 113)	80	75
234		1 on 50c. plum (No. 108)	2·10	55
235		1 on 50c. plum (No. 114)	45	45
236		2 on 1pi. red (No. 172)	45	45

1917. Surch GOURDE and value in frame. A. On provisional stamps of 1906.

237	8	1c. on 50c. lake (No. 130)	23·00	17·00
238	8	1c. on 1g. mauve (No. 131)	26·00	20·00

B. On pictorial stamps of 1906.

239	-	1c. on 4c. de p. red (No. 141)	60	55
240	-	1c. on 4c. de p. olive (No. 167)	60	55
241	-	1c. on 7c. de p. red (No. 168)	45	45
242	-	1c. on 10c. de p. orange (No. 145)	60	55
243	-	1c. on 15c. de p. yellow (No. 171)	45	45
244	19	1c. on 20c. de p. blue (No. 147)	60	55
246	24	1c. on 20c. de p. black and green (No. 163)	60	55
247	20	1c. on 50c. de p. red (No. 148)	60	55
249	-	1c. on 50c. de p. yellow (No. 172)	1·50	1·30
250	-	1c. on 1p. red (No. 173)	1·20	1·20
251	21	2c. on 3c. de p. sepia (No. 139)	60	55
252	21	2c. on 3c. de p. orange (No. 140)	60	55
253	-	2c. on 8c. de p. red (No. 144)	60	55
255	-	2c. on 8c. de p. olive (No. 169)	45	45
256	-	2c. de p. on 10c. brown (No. 170)	45	20
257	-	2c. on 15c. de p. olive (No. 146)	60	55
258	-	2c. on 15c. de p. yellow (No. 171)	60	55
259	19	2c. on 20c. de p. blue (No. 147)	60	55
260	-	5c. on 10c. de p. brown (No. 170)	80	75
261	-	5c. on 15c. de p. yellow (No. 171)	4·00	3·75

1919. For inland use. Provisionals of 1914. (a) Surch with new value without frame.

262		1c. on 15c. de p. olive (No. 191)	45	45
263	19	1c. on 20c. de p. blue (No. 192)	45	45
264	24	1c. on 20c. de p. black and green (No. 193)	45	45
265	-	1c. on 1p. red (No. 195)	45	45
267	-	1c. on 1p. red (No. 205)	45	45

(b) Surch with new value in frame.

268		2c. on 4c. de p. red (No. 187)	45	45
269		2c. on 8c. de p. red (No. 189)	60	55
270		2c. on 8c. de p. olive (No. 201)	45	45
271	24	2c. on 20c. de p. black and green	60	55
272	20	2c. on 50c. de p. red (No. 194)	35	20
274	20	2c. on 50c. de p. yellow (No. 204)	45	35
275	-	2c. on 1p. red (No. 195)	2·30	2·00
276	-	2c. on 1p. red (No. 205)	1·80	1·70
277	21	3c. on 3c. de p. sepia (No. 185)	45	45
278	-	3c. on 7c. de p. red (No. 200)	45	35
279	21	5c. on 3c. de p. sepia (No. 185)	45	35
280	21	5c. on 3c. de p. orange (No. 186)	1·70	1·50
281	-	5c. on 4c. de p. red (No. 187)	60	55
282	-	5c. on 4c. de p. olive (No. 198)	35	35
283	-	5c. on 7c. de p. grey (No. 188)	35	35
284	-	5c. on 7c. de p. red (No. 200)	45	45
285	15	5c. on 7c. on 20c. orange (No. 213)	45	45
286	15	5c. on 7c. on 50c. plum (No. 214)	3·25	3·00
287	19	5c. on 10c. de p. orange (No. 190)	45	45
288	-	5c. on 15c. de p. yellow (No. 203)	45	45
289	-	5c. on 10c. de p. orange (No. 190)	45	45

No. 289 has the word "PIASTRE" in the surcharge.

1919. Postage Due stamps surch POSTES and new value in frame.

290	D23	5c. de g. on 10c. de p. purple (No. D211)	35	35
291	D23	5c. de g. on 50c. de p. olive (No. D153)	10·00	7·75
292	D23	5c. de g. on 50c. de p. olive (No. D212)	45	45

48 "Agriculture"

1920

294	48	3c. de g. orange	35	35
295	48	5c. de g. green	35	35
296	-	10c. de g. red	45	35
297	-	15c. de g. violet	45	35
298	-	25c. de g. blue	60	45

DESIGN: 10c., 15c., 25c. "Commerce".

50 Pres. L. J. Borno

51 Christophe's Citadel

54 Coffee

1924

299	50	5c. green	35	20
300	51	10c. red	35	20
301	-	20c. blue	80	35
302	50	50c. black and orange	80	35
303	-	1g. olive	1·50	45
304	54	35c. green	3·50	55

DESIGNS—VERT: 20c. Map of W. Indies. HORIZ: 1g. National Palace.

55 Pres. Borno

1929. Frontier Agreement between Haiti and Dominican Republic.

305	55	10c. red	45	35

56 Fokker Super Trimotor over Port-au-Prince

1929. Air.

306	56	25c. green	45	35
307	56	50c. violet	60	35
308	56	75c. red	1·50	1·10
309	56	1g. blue	1·60	1·40

57 Salomon and S. Vincent

1931. 50th Anniv of U.P.U. Membership.

310	57	5c. green	1·20	45
311	-	10c. red (S. Vincent)	1·20	45

1933. Air. "Columbia" New York–Haiti Flight. Surch COLUMBIA VOL-DIRECT N.-Y.–P.AU-P. BOYD-LYON 60 CTS.

311a		60c. on 20c. blue (No. 301)	60·00	65·00

59 Pres. S. Vincent

60 Prince's Aqueduct

1933. T 59 and designs as T 60.

312	59	3c. orange	25	10
313	59	3c. green	25	10
316	60	5c. green	25	10
317	60	5c. olive	45	20
318	-	10c. red	45	20
320	-	10c. brown	45	15
321	-	25c. blue	80	20
322	-	50c. brown	2·30	50
323	-	1g. green	2·30	50
324	-	2g.50 olive	4·00	80

DESIGNS: 10c. Fort National; 25c. Palace of Sans Souci; 50c. Christophe's Chapel, Milot; 1g. King's Gallery, Citadel; 2g.50, Vallieres Battery.

62 Fokker Super Trimotor over Christophe's Citadel

1933. Air.

325	62	50c. orange	4·75	75
326	62	50c. olive	4·75	75
327	62	50c. red	3·00	1·70
328	62	50c. black	1·80	75
329	62	60c. brown	95	45
330	62	1g. blue	1·50	45

63 Alexandre Dumas and his Father and Son

1935. Visit of French Delegation to West Indies.

331	63	10c. brown & red (postage)	80	35
332	63	25c. brown and blue	1·50	45
333	63	60c. brown and violet (air)	4·00	2·20

64 Arms of Haiti, and George Washington

1938. Air. 150th Anniv of U.S. Constitution.

334	64	60c. blue	60	35

1939. Surch 25c between bars.

335	54	25c. on 35c. green	80	35

66 Pierre de Coubertin

1939. Port-au-Prince Athletic Stadium Fund.

336	66	10c.+10c. red (postage)	25·00	25·00
337	66	60c.+40c. violet (air)	22·00	22·00
338	66	1g.25+60c. black	22·00	22·00

67

1941. 3rd Caribbean Conference.

339	67	10c. red (postage)	95	45
340	67	25c. blue	80	35
341	67	60c. olive (air)	3·00	75
342	67	1g.25 violet	3·00	55

68 Our Lady of Perpetual Succour

1942. Our Lady of Perpetual Succour (National Patroness).

343	68	3c. purple (postage)	35	20
344	68	5c. green	45	20
345	68	10c. red	45	20
346	68	15c. orange	60	45
347	68	20c. brown	60	45
348	68	25c. blue	1·20	45
349	68	50c. red	1·60	65
350	68	2g.50 brown	5·25	1·30
351	68	5g. violet	10·50	4·00

The 5g. is larger (32½×47 mm).

352		10c. olive (air)	35	20
353		25c. blue	45	35
354		50c. green	80	35
355		60c. red	1·20	45
356		1g.25 black	2·30	45

MS357 Three sheets each 140×128 mm. (a) Nos. 352, 354; (b) 353, 355; (c) No. 356 — 14·00 13·00

69 Admiral Killick and Flagship "Crete-a-Pierrot"

1943. 41st Death Anniv of Admiral Killick.

358	69	3c. orange (postage)	35	20
359	69	5c. green	45	35
360	69	10c. red	45	35
361	69	25c. blue	60	35
362	69	50c. olive	1·20	45
363	69	5g. brown	5·25	2·75
364	69	60c. violet (air)	60	35
365	69	1g.25 black	1·80	1·40

1944. Surch (a) Postage.

366	59	0.02 on 3c. green	25	20
367	59	0.05 on 3c. green	35	35
368	68	0.10 on 15c. orange	35	20
369	69	0.10 on 25c. blue	35	20
370	-	0.10 on 1g. olive (No. 303)	45	35
371	-	0.20 on 2g.50 olive (No. 324)	45	35

(b) Air.

372	62	0.10 on 60c. brown	45	35

71

1944. Obligatory Tax. United Nations Relief Fund.

373	71	5c. blue	1·20	55
374	71	5c. black	1·20	55
375	71	5c. olive	1·20	55
376	71	5c. violet	1·20	55
377	71	5c. brown	1·20	55
378	71	5c. green	1·20	55
379	71	5c. red	1·20	55

72 Nurse and Wounded Soldier

1945. Red Cross stamps. Cross in red.

381	**72**	3c. black (postage)	10	10
382	**72**	5c. green	20	10
383	**72**	10c. orange	25	15
384	**72**	20c. brown	25	15
385	**72**	25c. blue	35	20
386	**72**	35c. orange	45	20
387	**72**	50c. red	45	20
388	**72**	1g. olive	80	35
389	**72**	2½g. violet	2·30	45
390	**72**	20c. orange (air)	35	20
391	**72**	25c. blue	35	20
392	**72**	50c. brown	35	20
393	**72**	60c. purple	45	20
394	**72**	1g. yellow	1·20	35
395	**72**	1g.25c. red	1·00	35
396	**72**	1g.35c. green	1·00	55
397	**72**	5g. black	6·50	2·20

73 Franklin D. Roosevelt

1946. Air.

398	**73**	20c. black	35	20
399	**73**	60c. black	45	20

74 Capois-la-Mort

1946

400	**74**	3c. orange (postage)	20	10
401	**74**	5c. green	20	10
402	**74**	10c. red	20	10
403	**74**	20c. black	20	10
404	**74**	25c. blue	25	15
405	**74**	35c. orange	35	20
406	**74**	50c. brown	45	35
407	**74**	1g. olive	45	35
408	**74**	2g.50 grey	1·20	45
409	**74**	20c. red (air)	20	15
410	**74**	25c. green	20	15
411	**74**	50c. orange	25	15
412	**74**	60c. purple	35	15
413	**74**	1g. slate	45	15
414	**74**	1g.25 violet	65	35
415	**74**	1g.35 black	65	45
416	**74**	5g. red	2·00	1·10

75 J.-J. Dessalines

1947. 141st Death Anniv of Emperor Jean-Jacques Dessalines, founder of National Independence.

417	**75**	3c. orange (postage)	10	10
418	**75**	5c. green	10	10
419	**75**	5c. violet	60	15
420	**75**	10c. red	20	10
421	**75**	25c. blue	35	15
422	**75**	20c. brown (air)	35	15

1947. Surch.

423	**74**	10c. on 35c. orge (postage)	35	20
424	**74**	5c. on 1g.35 black (air)	50	35
425	**74**	30c. on 50c. orange	45	35
426	**74**	30c. on 1g.35 black	45	35

77 Sanatorium and Mosquito

1949. Air. Anti-T.B. and Malaria Fund. Cross in red.

427	**77**	20c.+20c. sepia	9·50	5·50
428	**77**	30c.+30c. green	9·50	5·50
429	**77**	45c.+45c. brown	9·50	5·50
430	**77**	80c.+80c. violet	9·50	5·50
431	**77**	1g.25+1g.25 red	9·50	5·50
432	**77**	1g.75+1g.75 blue	9·50	5·50

MS433 Two sheets each 120×80 mm. (a) No. 431; (b) No. 432 — 60·00 — 40·00

78 Washington, Dessalines and Bolivar

1949. Obligatory Tax. Bicent of Port-au-Prince.

434	**78**	5c. red	45	35
435	**78**	5c. brown	45	35
436	**78**	5c. orange	45	35
437	**78**	5c. grey	45	35
438	**78**	5c. violet	45	35
439	**78**	5c. blue	45	35
440	**78**	5c. green	45	35
441	**78**	5c. black	45	35

79 Arms of Port-au-Prince

80 Columbus and "Santa Maria"

1950. Bicentenary of Port-au-Prince Exhibition. (a) Postage. Multicoloured arms.

442	**79**	10c. red	35	20

(b) Air.

443	**80**	30c. blue and grey	80	45
444	-	1g. black (Pres. D. Estime)	80	45

1950. 75th Anniv of U.P.U. Optd U P U 1874 1949 or surch also.

445	**78**	3 on 5c. grey (postage)	20	15
446	**78**	5c. green	35	20
447	**78**	10 on 5c. red	35	20
448	**78**	20 on 5c. blue	45	45
449	**74**	30 on 25c. green (air)	35	20
450	**74**	1g. slate	50	45
451	**74**	1.50 on 1g.35 black	1·50	1·30

83 Cocoa

1951. National Products.

456	**83**	5c. green (postage)	35	20
457	-	30c. orange (Bananas) (air)	1·20	35
458	-	80c. pink and green (Coffee)	3·00	55
459	-	5g. grey (Sisal)	10·00	3·25

84 Isabella the Catholic

1951. Air. 5th Birth Cent of Isabella the Catholic.

460	**84**	15c. brown	25	20
461	**84**	30c. blue	35	35

85 Pres. Magloire and Nursery, La Saline

1953. Projects realized by Pres. Magloire. Designs with medallion of president.

462	**85**	5c. green (postage)	20	10
463	-	10c. red	25	15
464	-	20c. blue (air)	25	20
465	-	30c. brown	35	20
466	-	1.50g. black	75	45
467	-	2.50g. violet	1·40	75

DESIGNS—HORIZ: 10c. Road-making; 20c. Anchorage, Cap-Haitien; 30c. Workers' estate, St. Martin; 1.50g. Old Cathedral restoration; 2.50g. School canteen.

1953. 150th Death Anniv of Toussaint l'Ouverture. No. 405 surch 7 AVRIL 1803 - 1953 50.

469	**74**	50c. on 35c. orange	45	35

1953. Air. 150th Anniv of National Flag. Surch 18 MAI 1803 - 1953 50.

470	50c. on 60c. purple	35	20
471	50c. on 1g.35 black	35	20

87 J.-J. Dessalines and Pres. Magloire

88 Toussaint l'Ouverture

89 Marie-Jeanne and Lamartiniere on La Crete-a-Pierrot

1954. 150th Anniv of Independence. (a) As T 87/8.

472	**87**	3c. black and blue (postage)	10	10
473	**88**	5c. black and green	25	15
474	-	5c. black and green	25	15
475	-	5c. black and green	35	25
476	-	5c. black and green	25	15
477	**87**	10c. black and red	25	15
478	-	15c. black and lilac	35	20
479	**88**	50c. black and green (air)	40	25
480	-	50c. black and green	40	25
481	-	50c. black and red	40	25
482	-	50c. black and brown	40	25
483	-	50c. black and blue	40	25
484	-	1g. black and grey	70	45
485	-	1g.50 black and mauve	1·30	95
486	**87**	7g.50 black and orange	5·00	4·50

PORTRAITS—As Type **88**. Nos. 474, 482, Lamartiniere; Nos. 475, 482, Boisrond-Tonnerre; Nos. 476, 483, 485, A. Petion; No. 478, Capois-La-Mort; No. 480, J. J. Dessalines; No. 481, H. Christophe.

For stamps as No. 480 without dates see Nos. 533/4.

(b) As T 89.

487	**89**	25c. orange (postage)	35	20
488	-	25c. slate	35	20
489	**89**	50c. red (air)	35	20
490	**89**	50c. black	35	30
491	-	50c. pink	35	20
492	-	50c. blue	35	20

DESIGN—HORIZ: Nos. 488, 491, 492, Battle of Vertieres; Nos. 489/92 are larger (31½×26 mm).

90 Mme. Magloire

1954

493	**90**	10c. orange (postage)	25	15
494	**90**	10c. blue	25	15
495	**90**	20c. red (air)	20	15
496	**90**	50c. brown	35	35
497	**90**	1g. green	45	35
498	**90**	1g.50 red	65	45
499	**90**	2g.50 green	1·00	80
500	**90**	5g. blue	2·50	2·00

91 Tomb and Arms of King Henri Christophe

92 Christophe, Citadel and Pres. Magloire

1954. Restoration of Christophe's Citadel. (a) T 91. Flag in black and red.

501	**91**	10c. red (postage)	25	15
502	**91**	50c. orange (air)	35	20
503	**91**	1g. blue	70	45
504	**91**	1g.50 green	1·00	55
505	**91**	2g.50 grey	1·60	80
506	**91**	5g. red	3·00	1·70

(b) T 92.

507	**92**	10c. red (postage)	20	15
508	**92**	50c. black and orange (air)	35	20
509	**92**	1g. black and blue	70	45
510	**92**	1g.50 black and green	1·00	55
511	**92**	2g.50 black and grey	1·60	80
512	**92**	5g. black and red	3·00	1·70

93 Columbus's Drawing of Fort de la Nativite

1954. Air.

513	**93**	50c. red	60	45
514	**93**	50c. slate	60	45

94 Sikorsky S-55 Helicopter over Ruins

1955. Obligatory Tax. Cyclone "Hazel" Relief Fund (1st issue).

515	**94**	10c. blue	25	15
516	**94**	10c. green	25	15
517	**94**	10c. orange	25	15
518	**94**	10c. black	25	15
519	**94**	20c. red	30	15
520	**94**	20c. green	30	15

95 Sikorsky S-55 Helicopter

1955. Obligatory Tax. Cyclone "Hazel" Relief Fund (2nd issue).

521	95	10c. black & grey (postage)	25	15
522	95	20c. deep blue and blue	30	15
523	95	10c. red and brown (air)	25	15
524	95	20c. red and pink	30	15

96 J.-J. Dessalines

1955. Dessalines Commemoration.

525	96	3c. black & brown (postage)	15	10
526	96	5c. black and lilac	15	10
527	96	10c. black and red	20	10
528	96	10c. black and pink	15	10
529	96	25c. black and blue	25	15
530	96	25c. black and light blue	25	15
531	96	20c. black and green (air)	15	10
532	96	20c. black and orange	15	10

1955. Air. As No. 480 but without dates and colours changed.

533	50c. black and blue	35	20
534	50c. black and grey	35	20

97 Pres. Magloire and Monument

1955. 21st Anniv of Haitian Army.

535	97	10c. blue & black (postage)	35	20
536	97	10c. red and black	35	20
537	97	1g.50 green and black (air)	60	20
538	97	1g.50 blue and black	60	20

98 Mallard

99 Douglas DC-4, Liner and Map

1955

539	-	10c. blue (postage)	1·30	25
540	98	25c. green and turquoise	1·80	30
541	99	50c. black and grey (air)	65	20
542	-	50c. red and grey	40	20
543	99	75c. green and turquoise	90	45
544	-	1g. olive and blue	75	25
545	-	2g.50 orange	8·25	1·50
546	98	5g. red and buff	12·50	2·50

DESIGNS—VERT: 10c., 2g.50, Greater flamingo. HORIZ: 50c. (No. 542), 1g. Car on coast road.

100 Immanuel Kant

1956. 10th Anniv of 1st Int Philosophical Congress.

547	100	10c. blue (postage)	25	15
548	100	50c. brown (air)	35	20
549	100	75c. green	45	35
550	100	1g.50 mauve	1·10	45

MS551 155×50 mm. Nos. 548/9 and 1g.25 indigo in same design 7·00 4·50

101 Zim Basin and Waterfall

1957

552	101	10c. orange & bl (postage)	25	10
553	101	50c. green & turq (air)	35	20
554	101	1g.50 green and blue	55	35
555	101	2g.50 blue and light blue	85	55
556	101	5g. violet and blue	2·00	1·40

102 J.-J. Dessalines and Monument

1958. Birth Bicentenary of J. J. Dessalines.

557	102	5c. green & black (postage)	25	10
558	102	10c. red and black	25	10
559	102	25c. blue and black	35	10
560	102	20c. grey and black (air)	25	10
561	102	50c. orange and black	60	35

103 The "Atomium"

1958. Brussels International Exhibition.

562	103	50c. brown (postage)	35	20
563	-	75c. green	35	20
564	103	1g. violet	65	20
565	-	1g.50 orange	65	35
566	103	2g.50 red (air)	1·00	45
567	-	5g. blue	1·20	75

MS568 108×69 mm. Nos. 566/7. Imperf 3·75 3·50

DESIGN—HORIZ: 75c. 1g.50 and 5g. Exhibition view.

104 Sylvio Cator making Long Jump

1958. Sylvio Cator (athlete) Commem.

569	104	5c. green (postage)	15	10
570	104	10c. brown	15	10
571	104	20c. purple and mauve	20	10
572	-	50c. black (air)	25	15
573	-	50c. green	25	15
574	-	1g. brown	45	35
575	-	5g. black and grey	2·00	75

DESIGN—HORIZ: Nos. 572/75, Sylvio Cator making long jump (head-on view).

1958. Red Cross. Nos. 564/66 surch with red cross and +50 CENTIMES.

576	103	1g.+50c. violet (postage)	2·30	2·20
577	-	1g.50+50c. orange	2·30	2·20
578	103	2g.50+50c. red (air)	2·30	2·20

106 Head of U.S. Satellite

1958. I.G.Y. Inscr as in T 106.

579	106	10c. lake & turq (postage)	25	15
580	-	20c. black and orange	1·10	45
581	-	50c. red and green	65	25
582	-	1g. black and blue	75	25
583	106	50c. lake and blue (air)	45	25
584	-	1g.50 brown and red	2·75	65
585	-	2g. red and blue	1·80	35

MS586 82×112 mm. Nos. 583/5. Imperf 7·00 6·50

DESIGNS: 20c., 1g.50, King penguins on icefloe; 50c., 2g. Giant radio telescope; 1g. Ocean-bed exploration.

107 Duvalier

1958. 1st Anniv of Installation of President Francois Duvalier. Commemorative inscr in blue.

587	107	10c. blk & pink (postage)	25	10
588	107	50c. black and green	35	20
589	107	1g. black and red	45	35
590	107	5g. black and salmon	2·10	1·40
591	-	50c. black and red (air)	85	20
592	-	2g.50 black and orange	1·20	55
593	-	5g. black and mauve	1·60	1·10
594	-	7g.50 black and green	2·40	1·80

MS595 132×78 mm. Nos. 590 and 593/4 8·25 7·75

DESIGN: Nos. 591/94 as Type **107** but horiz.

1958. As T 107 but without commem. inscr. (a) Postage. Vert portrait.

596	5c. black and blue	10	10
597	10c. black and pink	10	10
598	20c. black and yellow	15	15
599	50c. black and green	25	15
600	1g. black and red	45	35
601	1g.50 black and pink	60	45
602	2g.50 black and lavender	80	45
603	5g. black and salmon	1·50	1·00

(b) Air. Horiz portrait.

604	50c. black and red	35	20
605	1g. black and violet	45	20
606	1g.50 black and brown	65	35
607	2g. black and pink	85	35
608	2g.50 black and orange	95	45
609	5g. black and mauve	1·80	1·10
610	7g.50 black and green	2·50	1·40

108 Map of Haiti

1958. United Nations.

611	108	10c. red (postage)	20	10
612	108	25c. green	25	15
613	-	50c. red and blue (air)	35	20
614	108	75c. blue	35	20
615	108	1g. brown	45	35

MS616 109×67 mm. Nos. 613 and 615. Imperf 3·00 3·00

DESIGN: 50c. Flags of Haiti and U.N.

1959. 10th Anniv of Declaration of Human Rights. Nos. 611/15 optd 10TH ANNIVERSARY OF THE UNIVERSAL DECLARATION OF HUMAN RIGHTS.

(a) Postage. (i) English.

617		10c. red	25	15
618		25c. green	35	20

(ii) French.

617		10c. red	25	15
618		25c. green	35	20

(iii) Portuguese.

617		10c. red	25	15
618		25c. green	35	20

(iv) Spanish.

617		10c. red	25	15
618		25c. green	35	20

(b) Air. (i) English.

619	-	20c. red and blue	50	50
620	108	75c. blue	70	70
621	108	1g. brown	1·30	1·20

(ii) French.

619	-	20c. red and blue	50	50
620	108	75c. blue	70	70
621	108	1g. brown	1·30	1·20

(iii) Portuguese.

619	-	20c. red and blue	50	50
620	108	75c. blue	70	70
621	108	1g. brown	1·30	1·20

(iv) Spanish.

619	-	20c. red and blue	50	50
620	108	75c. blue	70	70
621	108	1g. brown	1·30	1·20

Overprinted alternately in different languages through the sheet of 25.

110 Pope Pius XII with Children

1959. Pope Pius XII Commemoration. Inscr "PIE XII PAPE DE LA PAIX".

622	110	10c. olive & blue (postage)	15	10
623	-	50c. brown and green	35	20
624	-	2g. sepia and lake	80	45
625	110	50c. violet and green (air)	25	15
626	-	1g.50 brown and olive	55	35
627	-	2g.50 blue and purple	85	35

DESIGNS: 50c. (No. 623), 1g.50, Pope at prayer; 2g., 2g.50, Pope giving blessing.

1959. Red Cross. (a) United Nations stamps surch with red cross and +25 CENTIMES.

628	108	10c.+25c. (postage)	35	20
629	108	25c.+25c.	35	20
630	-	50c.+25c. (air)	35	30
631	108	75c.+25c.	40	40
632	108	1g.+25c.	60	55

(b) Pope Pius XII stamps surch with red cross and +50 CENTIMES.

633	110	10c.+50c. (postage)	65	45
634	-	50c.+50c.	65	50
635	-	2g.+50c.	1·00	80
636	110	50c.+50c. (air)	85	80
637	-	1g.50+50c.	85	80
638	-	2g.50+50c.	1·00	1·00

111 Abraham Lincoln when a young man

1959. 150th Birth Anniv of Abraham Lincoln.

639	111	50c. purple & bl (postage)	35	20
640	-	1g. brown and green (air)	45	35
641	-	2g. myrtle and green	60	45
642	-	2g.50 blue and buff	65	35

MS643 120×105 mm. Nos. 639/42. Imperf 2·40 2·30

PORTRAITS of Lincoln (bearded): 1g. Looking right; 2g., 2g.50, Looking left. The designs include various buildings associated with Lincoln.

1959. World Refugee Year (1st issue). Nos. 639/42 surch Nations Unies ANNEE DES REFUGIES 1959-1960 + 20 Centimes.

644	111	50c.+20c. purple and blue (postage)	70	65
645	-	1g.+20c. brown and green (air)	85	70
646	-	2g.+20c. myrtle and green	90	85
647	-	2g.50+20c. blue & buff	95	90

MS648 120×105 mm. As Nos. 644/7 but each stamp surch 50c. Imperf 23·00 22·00

113 Chicago's First House and Modern Skyline

1959. 3rd Pan-American Games, Chicago.

649	113	25c. sepia & blue (postage)	35	20
650	-	50c. multicoloured	45	35
651	-	75c. sepia and blue	60	45
652	-	50c. brown & turq (air)	60	20
653	113	1g. turquoise and purple	85	35
654	-	1g.50 multicoloured	1·10	45

DESIGNS—HORIZ: 50c., 1g.50, Discus-thrower and Haitian flag. VERT: 50c. (air), 75c. J. B. Paul Dessables (founder of Chicago) and map.

114

1959. Obligatory Tax. Literacy Fund. (a) Postage. (i) Size 40×23 mm.

655	**114**	5c. green	20	15
656	**114**	10c. black	20	15
657	**114**	10c. red	20	15

(ii) Size 29×17 mm.

658	5c. green	20	15
659	5c. red	20	15
660	10c. blue	20	15

(b) Air. Size 29×17 mm.

661	5c. yellow	20	15
662	10c. blue	20	15
663	10c. orange	20	15

1959. Sports Fund. Nos. 649/54 surch POUR LE SPORT + 0.75 CENTIMES.

664	25c.+75c. sepia and blue (postage)	60	55
665	50c.+75c. multicoloured	80	55
666	75c.+75c. sepia and blue	80	55
667	50c.+75c. brown & turq (air)	85	70
668	1g.+75c. turquoise and purple	85	70
669	1g.50+75c. multicoloured	85	70

1960. UNICEF Commem. Nos. 600 and 607/8 surch Hommage a l'UNICEF +G.0,50.

670	1g.+50c. blk & red (postage)	80	80
671	2g.+50c. black and pink (air)	85	85
672	2g.50+50c. black and orange	1·50	1·50

1960. Winter Olympic Games. Nos. 650 and 652/4 optd with Olympic rings and VIIIEME JEUX OLYMPIQUES D'HIVER CALIFORNIE USA 1960.

673	50c. multicoloured (postage)	1·50	1·10
674	50c. brown and turquoise (air)	1·10	1·10
675	1g. turquoise and purple	1·60	1·60
676	1g.50 multicoloured	2·10	2·10

118 "Uprooted Tree"

1960. World Refugee Year (2nd issue).

677	**118**	10c. grn & orge (postage)	15	10
678	**118**	50c. purple and violet	35	20
679	**118**	50c. brown and blue (air)	35	20
680	**118**	1g. red and green	45	35
MS681		134×76 mm. Nos. 677/80. Imperf	5·00	4·75

1960. Surch in figures.

682	**96**	5c. on 3c. black and brown	20	15
683	**96**	10c. on 3c. black and brown	30	15

1960. 28th Anniv of Haitian Red Cross. 1945 Red Cross stamps optd "28eme ANNIVERSAIRE" or surch also.

684	**72**	1g. on 2½g. violet (postage)	80	45
685	**72**	2½g. violet	1·20	90
686	**72**	20c. on 1g.35 green (air)	35	20
687	**72**	50c. on 60c. purple	60	35
688	**72**	50c. on 1g.35 green	35	35
689	**72**	50c. on 2½g. violet	35	35
690	**72**	60c. purple	35	35
691	**72**	1g. on 1g.35 green	55	45
692	**72**	1g.35 green	60	45
693	**72**	2g. on 1g.35 green	1·20	90

No. 689 is also optd **Avion.**

121 "Sugar Queen, 1960" and Beach

1960. Election of Miss Claudinette Fouchard ("Miss Haiti") as World "Sugar Queen, 1960".

694	-	10c. violet & brn (postage)	25	15
695	-	20c. black and brown	35	15
696	**121**	50c. brown and blue	60	20
697	-	1g. brown and green	1·20	35
698	-	50c. brown and mauve (air)	65	20
699	**121**	2g.50 brown and blue	1·60	45

DESIGNS: Sugar Queen and—10c., 1g. Plantation (different views); 20c., 50c. Harvesting.

1960. Education Campaign. Surch ALPHABETISATION and premium.

700	**118**	10c.+20c. green and orange (postage)	30	20
701	**118**	10c.+30c. green & orge	35	20
702	**118**	50c.+20c. purple & vio	35	20
703	**118**	50c.+30c. purple & vio	50	45
704	**118**	50c.+20c. black and blue (air)	35	30
705	**118**	50c.+30c. black and blue	60	50
706	**118**	1g.+20c. red and green	80	65
707	**118**	1g.+30c. red and green	80	65

123 Olympic Torch, Victory Parade at Athens, 1896, and Melbourne Stadium

1960. Olympic Games, Rome.

708	**123**	10c. blk & orge (postage)	10	10
709	-	20c. blue and red	15	10
710	-	50c. green and brown	35	20
711	-	1g. blue and black	45	35
712	-	50c. purple and bistre (air)	35	20
713	-	1g.50 mauve and green	60	20
714	-	2g.50 slate, purple & blk	85	35
MS715		104×57 mm. Nos. 711 and 714. Imperf	3·00	3·00

DESIGNS: 20c. and 1g.50, "The Discus-thrower" and Rome Stadium; 50c. (No. 710), Pierre de Coubertin (founder) and Athletes Parade, Melbourne; 50c. (No. 712), As Type **123** but P. de Coubertin inset; 1g. Athens Stadium, 1896; 2g.50, Victory Parade, Athens, 1896, and Athletes' Parade, Melbourne.

1960. Nos. 710/3 surch +25 CENTIMES.

716	50c.+25c. grn & brn (postage)	35	20
717	1g.+25c. blue and black	45	35
718	50c.+25c. purple & bis (air)	35	20
719	1g.50+25c. mauve and green	55	40

125 Occide Jeanty

1960. Birth Cent of Occide Jeanty (composer).

720	**125**	10c. pur & orge (postage)	25	10
721	-	20c. purple and blue	35	20
722	**125**	50c. sepia and green	45	35
723	**125**	50c. blue and yellow (air)	40	20
724	-	1g.50 slate and mauve	65	20

DESIGN: 20c., 1g.50, Jeanty and Capitol, Port-au-Prince.

126 U.N., New York

1960. 15th Anniv of U.N.O.

731	**126**	1g. black & grn (postage)	45	35
732	**126**	50c. black and red (air)	35	20
733	**126**	1g.50 black and blue	45	35
MS734		106×77 mm. Nos. 731/3. Imperf	2·30	2·20

127 Sud Aviation Caravelle

1960. Air. Aviation Week.

735	**127**	20c. blue and red	15	10
736	-	50c. brown and green	40	20
737	-	50c. blue and green	40	20
738	-	50c. black and green	40	20
739	**127**	1g. green and red	90	20
740	-	1g.50 pink and blue	95	35
MS741		80×125 mm. Nos. 738/40. Imperf	2·30	1·90

DESIGNS: 50c. (3) Boeing 707 airliner and Wright Flyer I; 1g.50, Boeing 707 and 60c. "Columbia" stamp of 1933.

1961. UNICEF Child Welfare Fund. Surch UNICEF +25 centimes.

748	**126**	1g.+25c. black and green (postage)	45	35
749	**126**	50c.+25c. black and red (air)	35	20
750	**126**	1g.50+25c. black & bl	55	40

129 Alexandre Dumas (father and son)

1961. Alexandre Dumas Commemoration.

751	-	5c. brown & blue (postage)	15	10
752	-	10c. black, purple and red	15	10
753	**129**	50c. blue and red	35	20
754	-	50c. black and blue (air)	45	20
755	-	1g. red and black	60	35
756	-	1g.50 black and green	80	45

DESIGNS—HORIZ: 5c. Dumas' House; 50c. (No. 754), A. Dumas and horseman in "Twenty Years After"; 1g. A. Dumas (son) and "The Lady of the Camellias" (Marguerite Gauthier); 1g.50, A. Dumas, and "The Count of Monte Cristo".

130 Pirates

1961. Tourist Publicity.

761		5c. yellow & blue (postage)	15	10
762	**130**	10c. yellow and mauve	15	10
763	-	15c. orange and green	20	10
764	-	20c. orange and brown	25	15
765	-	50c. yellow and blue	35	20
766	-	20c. yellow and blue (air)	25	10
767	-	50c. orange and violet	45	20
768	-	1g. yellow and green	50	35

DESIGNS: Nos. 761, 768, Map of Tortuga; No. 763, Two pirates on beach; Nos. 764, 766, Pirate ships attacking galleon; Nos. 765, 767, Pirate in rigging.

1961. Re-election of Pres. Duvalier. Optd Dr. F. Duvalier President 22 Mai 1961.

769	**102**	5c. green & blk (postage)	10	10
770	**102**	10c. red and black	15	10
771	**102**	25c. blue and black	25	15
772	**74**	2g.50 grey	95	55
773	**102**	20c. grey and black (air)	15	10
774	**102**	50c. orange and black	25	20
775	**99**	75c. green and turquoise	35	35

1961. Air. 18th World Scout Conference, Lisbon. Nos. 735 and 739/40 surch 18e CONFERENCE INTERNATIONALE DU SCOUTISME MONDIAL. LISBONNE SEPTEMBRE 1961 +0,25 and Scout emblem.

776	20c.+25c. blue and red	30	25
777	1g.+25c. green and red	40	30
778	1g.50+25c. pink and blue	50	45
MS779	No. **MS**741 surch. Imperf	22·00	22·00

1961. U.N. and Haitian Malaria Eradication Campaign. Surch OMS SNEM +20 CENTIMES.

780	**126**	1g.+20c. black and green (postage)	70	55
781	**126**	50c.+20c. black and red (air)	1·30	1·20
782	**126**	1g.50+20c. black & bl	1·80	1·70

1961. Duvalier-Ville Reconstruction Fund Nos. 598, 600, 602, 604/5 and 608/10 surch with UNICEF emblem, Duvalier-Ville and premium.

783	20c.+25c. black and yellow (postage)	25	20
784	50c.+25c. black and red (air)	35	35
785	1g.+50c. black and violet	45	45
786	5g.+50c. black and mauve	95	90
787	1g.+50c. black and red	45	45
788	2g.50+50c. black and blue	80	55
789	2g.50+50c. black and orange	55	50
790	7g.50+50c. black and green	1·30	1·10

1962. Colonel Glenn's Space Flight. Nos. 761, 768 optd EXPLORATION SPATIALE JOHN GLENN and outline of capsule or surch also.

795	50c. on 5c. yell & bl (postage)	35	20
796	1g.50 on 5c. yellow and blue	1·20	75
797	1g. yellow and green (air)	45	35
798	2g. on 1g. yellow and green	1·20	90

136 Campaign Emblem

1962. Malaria Eradication.

799	**136**	5c. blue and red (postage)	15	10
800	-	10c. green and brown	15	10
801	**136**	50c. red and blue	35	20
802	-	20c. red and violet (air)	15	10
803	**136**	50c. red and green	35	20
804	-	1g. blue and orange	45	35
MS805		140×70 mm. Nos. 801 and 803/4 in slightly different colours. Imperf	2·30	2·20

DESIGN: 10c., 20c., 1g. As Type **136** but with long side of triangle at top.

See also No. **MS**826.

1962. World Refugee Year (3rd issue). As T 118 but additionally inscr "1962" and colours changed.

806	**118**	10c. orange & bl (postage)	15	15
807	**118**	50c. green and mauve	35	35
808	**118**	50c. brown and blue (air)	30	25
809	**118**	1g. black and buff	35	35
MS810		133×76 mm. Nos. 806/9. Imperf	2·30	2·20

137 Scout Badge

1962. 22nd Anniv of Haitian Boy Scout Movement.

811	**137**	3c. orange, black and violet (postage)	15	15
812	-	5c. brown, olive and black	15	15
813	-	10c. brown, black & green	15	15
814	**137**	25c. black, lake and olive	20	15
815	-	50c. green, violet and red	35	20
816	-	20c. slate, green and purple (air)	20	15
817	**137**	50c. brown, green and red	45	35
818	-	1g.50 turq, sepia & brn	60	35
MS819		102×60 mm. Nos. 817/18. Imperf	1·40	1·30

DESIGNS—VERT: 5c., 20c., 50c. (post) Scout and camp. HORIZ: 10c., 1g.50, Lord and Lady Baden-Powell.

1962. Surch with premium. (a) Nos. 799/804.

820	**136**	5c.+25c. (postage)	25	20
821	-	10c.+25c.	25	20
822	**136**	50c.+25c.	35	20
823	-	20c.+25c. (air)	25	20
824	**136**	50c.+25c.	35	20
825	-	1g.+25c.	45	35
MS826		140×70 mm. As No. **MS**810 but sheet additionally inscribed "Contribution d'Haiti a l'OM" below stamps	1·80	1·70

(b) Nos. 806/9.

827	**118**	10c.+20c. (postage)	25	20
828	**118**	50c.+20c.	35	35
829	**118**	50c.+20c. (air)	35	35
830	**118**	1g.+20c.	45	35

1962. Air. Port-au-Prince Airport Construction Fund. Optd AEROPORT INTERNATIONAL 1962, with No. 832 additionally optd Poste Aerienne.

831	-	20c. No. 816	25	20
832	-	50c. No. 815	35	20
833	**137**	50c. No. 817	35	20
834	-	1g.50 No. 818	50	35

140 Tower, World's Fair

1962. "Century 21" Exn (World's Fair), Seattle.

835	140	10c. purple & bl (postage)	10	10
836	140	20c. blue and red	15	10
837	140	50c. green and yellow	35	20
838	140	1g. red and green	45	35
839	140	50c. black and lilac (air)	35	15
840	140	1g. red and grey	50	35
841	140	1g.50 purple and orange	60	35
MS842		133×82 mm. Nos. 840/1. Imperf	3·00	2·75

141 Town plan and 1904 10c. stamp

1963. Duvalier-ville Commemoration.

843	141	5c. black, yellow and violet (postage)	10	10
844	141	10c. black, yellow and red	15	10
845	141	25c. black, yellow and grey	25	20
846	-	50c. brown & orange (air)	40	20
847	-	1g. brown and blue	65	35
848	-	1g.50 brown and green	80	45

DESIGN: Nos. 846/8 Houses and 1881 2c. stamp.

1963. "Peaceful Uses of Outer Space". Nos. 837/38 and 841/2 optd UTILISATIONS PACIFIQUES DE L'ESPACE and space capsule.

853	140	50c. green and yellow (postage)	60	35
854	140	1g. red and green	1·20	45
855	140	1g. red and grey (air)	1·20	55
856	140	1g.50 purple and orange	1·50	95

1963. Literacy Campaign. Surch ALPHABETISATION + 0,10.

857	141	25c.+10c. (postage)	20	15
858	-	50c.+10c. (No. 846) (air)	35	20
859	-	1g.50+10c. (No. 848)	45	35

143 Harvesting

1963. Freedom from Hunger.

860	143	10c. orange and black (postage)	10	10
861	143	20c. turquoise and black	15	15
862	143	50c. mauve and black (air)	35	20
863	143	1g. green and black	45	35

144 Dag Hammarskjold and U.N. Emblem

1963. Air. Dag Hammarskjold Commemoration. Portrait in blue.

864	144	20c. brown and bistre	15	10
865	144	50c. red and blue	35	20
866	144	1g. blue and mauve	35	20
867	144	1g.50 green and grey	60	45
MS868		110×65 mm. Nos. 865 and 868 (but in brown and light brown). Imperf	1·80	1·70

Nos. 864/67 were printed in sheets of 25 (5×5) with a map of Sweden in the background covering most stamps in the second and third vertical rows.

145 Dessalines Statue

1963. Dessalines Commemoration.

869	145	5c. red & brown (postage)	15	10
870	145	10c. blue, green and ochre	15	10
871	145	50c. green and brown (air)	25	15
872	145	50c. purple, violet and blue	25	15

146 "Alphabetisation"

1963. Obligatory Tax. Education Fund.

873	146	10c. red (postage)	10	10
874	146	10c. blue	10	10
875	146	10c. olive	10	10
876	146	10c. brown (air)	10	10
877	146	10c. violet	10	10
878	146	10c. violet	10	10

See also Nos. 974/78, 1157/63 and 1260/1.

1964. Mothers' Festival. Optd FETE DES MERES 1964 or surch also.

879	145	10c. blue, green and ochre (postage)	15	10
880	145	50c. green and brown (air)	35	20
881	145	50c. purple, violet and blue	35	20
882	145	1g.50 on 80c. pink and green (No. 458)	50	35

1964. Winter Olympic Games, Innsbruck. Surch JEUX OLYMPIQUES D'HIVER INNSBRUCK 1964 0.50+0.10, Olympic rings and Games emblem.

883	137	50c.+10c. on 3c. (postage)	55	35
884	137	50c.+10c. on 5c. (No. 812)	55	35
885	-	50c.+10c. on 10c. (No. 813)	55	35
886	137	50c.+10c. on 25c.	55	35
887	101	50c.+10c. on 2g.50 (air)	80	70

1964. Air. Red Cross Cent (1963). Optd 18631963 and Centenary Emblem, on surch also. Portrait in blue.

888	144	20c. brown and bistre	30	15
889	144	50c. red and blue	35	20
890	144	1g. blue and mauve	50	35
891	144	1g.50 green and grey	60	45
892	144	2g.50+1g.25 on 1g.50 green and grey	1·20	1·00

150 Weightlifting

1964. Olympic Games, Tokyo (1st issue).

893	150	10c. sepia & blue (postage)	15	10
894	150	25c. sepia and salmon	20	15
895	-	50c. sepia and mauve	35	20
896	150	50c. sepia and purple (air)	35	20
897	-	50c. sepia and green	35	20
898	-	75c. sepia and yellow	45	35
899	-	1g.50 sepia and grey	60	45
MS900		75×89 mm. Nos. 896/9 in new colours. Imperf	2·30	2·20

DESIGN: Nos. 895, 896/9, Hurdling.

151 Our Lady of Perpetual Succour and Airport

1964. International Airport.

901	151	10c. blk & ochre (postage)	20	10
902	151	25c. black and turquoise	25	15
903	151	50c. black and green	35	20
904	151	1g. black and red	45	35
905	151	50c. black and orange (air)	35	20
906	151	1g.50 black and mauve	60	35
907	151	2g.50 black and violet	1·20	55

1965. International Airport Opening. Optd 1965.

908		10c. blk & ochre (postage)	15	10
909		25c. black and turquoise	25	20
910		50c. black and green	35	20
911		1g. black and red	45	35
912		50c. black and orange (air)	35	20
913		1g.50 black and mauve	60	35
914		2g.50 black and violet	95	65

1965. Olympic Games. Tokyo (2nd issue). Nos. 893/9 surch +5 c.

915	150	10c.+5c. (postage)	15	10
916	-	25c.+5c.	25	20
917	-	50c.+5c.	45	35
918	150	50c.+5c. (air)	35	20
919	-	50c.+5c.	35	20
920	-	75c.+5c.	45	35
921	-	1g.50+5c.	70	55
MS922		No. MS900 surch 25c.	9·50	8·75

154 Unisphere

1965. New York World's Fair.

923	154	10c. mult (postage)	15	10
924	-	20c. purple and yellow	25	15
925	154	50c. multicoloured	35	20
926	-	50c. blue and yellow (air)	35	20
927	-	1g.50 black and yellow	45	35
928	154	5g. multicoloured	2·10	1·70

DESIGN: 20c., 50c. (No. 926), 1g.50, "Reaching for the Stars" (statue).

1965. Haitian Merchant Marine Commemoration.

929	155	10c. mult (postage)	15	10
930	155	50c. multicoloured	35	20
931	155	50c. multicoloured (air)	35	20
932	155	1g.50 multicoloured	65	45

155 "Likala" (freighter) in Port

1965. Air 20th Anniv of U.N. Optd O.N.U. 1945-1965. Portrait in blue.

933	144	20c. brown and bistre	15	10
934	144	50c. red and blue	35	20
935	144	1g. blue and mauve	45	35
936	144	1g.50 green and grey	60	45

157 I.T.U. Emblem and Symbols

1965. Centenary of I.T.U.

937	157	10c. mult (postage)	15	10
938	157	25c. multicoloured	25	10
939	157	50c. multicoloured	35	15
940	157	50c. multicoloured (air)	35	15
941	157	1g. multicoloured	45	35
942	157	1g.50 multicoloured	75	45
943	157	2g. multicoloured	1·10	55
MS944		116×67 mm. Nos. 940 and 943. Imperf	12·00	10·00

1965. 25th Anniv of U.N.E.S.C.O. Nos. 937/41 optd 20e Anniversaire UNESCO.

945		10c. mult (postage)	25	20
946		25c. multicoloured	30	25
947		50c. multicoloured	50	40
948		50c. multicoloured (air)	1·20	45
949		1g. multicoloured	2·30	75
MS950		116×67 mm. No. MS944 optd	23·00	

158 Cathedral Facade

1965. Bicentenary of Cathedral of Our Lady of the Assumption, Port-au-Prince. Mult.

951		5c. Type **158** (postage)	15	10
952		10c. High Altar (vert)	15	10
953		25c. "Our Lady of the Assumption" (painting) (vert)	25	15
954		50c. Type **158** (air)	35	20
955		1g. High Altar (vert)	60	45
956		7g.50 As 25c. but larger, 38×51 mm	2·30	2·00

159 "Passiflora quadrangularis"

1965. Haitian Flowers. Multicoloured.

957		3c. Type **159** (postage)	15	15
958		5c. "Sambucus canadensis"	15	15
959		10c. "Hibiscus esculentus"	15	15
960		15c. As 5c.	25	15
961		50c. Type **159**	45	35
962		50c. Type **159** (air)	35	20
963		50c. As 5c.	35	20
964		50c. As 10c.	35	20
965		1g.50 As 5c.	60	45
966		1g.50 As 10c.	60	45
967		5g. Type **159**	1·80	1·40

160 Amulet

1966. "Culture". Multicoloured.

968		5c. Type **160** (postage)	15	15
969		10c. Carved stool and Veve decoration (horiz)	15	15
970		50c. Type **160**	35	20
971		50c. Carved stool and Veve decoration (horiz) (air)	35	20
972		1g.50 Type **160**	60	45
973		2g.50 Modern abstract painting (52×37 mm)	1·30	75

1966. Obligatory Tax. Education Fund. As T 146 but larger (17×25½ mm).

974	146	10c. green (postage)	20	15
975	146	10c. violet	20	15
977	146	10c. orange (air)	20	15
978	146	10c. blue	20	15

1966. State Visit of Emperor Haile Selassie of Ethiopia. Nos. 969 and 971/3 optd Hommage Haile Selassie 1er 24-25 Avril 1966.

979	-	10c. mult (postage)	25	20
980	-	50c. multicoloured (air)	35	20
981	160	1g.50 multicoloured	60	45
982	-	2g.50 multicoloured	1·20	90

162 Astronauts and "Gemini" Capsules

1966. Space Rendezvous. Astronauts and capsules in brown.

No.	Type	Description	Unused	Used
983	162	5c. indigo & blue (postage)	15	15
984	162	10c. violet and blue	15	15
985	162	25c. green and blue	25	20
986	162	50c. red and blue	35	20
987	-	50c. indigo and blue (air)	35	20
988	-	1g. green and blue	45	35
989	-	1g.50 red and blue	70	45

DESIGN: Nos. 987/9, Astronauts and "Gemini" capsules (different arrangement).

163 Football and Pres. Duvalier

1966. Caribbean Football Championships. Portrait in black. (i) Inscr "CHAMPIONNAT DE FOOTBALL DES CARAIBES".

No.	Type	Description	Unused	Used
990	163	5c. green & flesh (postage)	15	15
991	-	10c. green and blue	15	15
992	163	15c. green and apple	25	15
993	-	50c. green and lilac	35	20
994	163	50c. purple and sage (air)	35	20
995	-	1g.50 purple and pink	60	45

(ii) As Nos. 990/5 but additionally inscr "COUPE DR. FRANCOIS DUVALIER 22 JUIN".

No.	Type	Description	Unused	Used
996	163	5c. grn & flesh (postage)	15	15
997	-	10c. green and blue	15	10
998	163	15c. green and apple	20	15
999	-	50c. green and lilac	35	20
1000	163	50c. purple and sage (air)	35	35
1001	-	1g.50 purple and pink	60	45

DESIGN: 10c., 50c. (No. 991, 993), 1g.50, Footballer and Pres. Duvalier.

164 Audio-visual Aids

1966. National Education.

No.	Type	Description	Unused	Used
1002		5c. purple, green and pink (postage)	15	15
1003		10c. sepia, lake & brown	15	15
1004	164	25c. violet, blue and green	25	20
1005	-	50c. pur, grn & yell (air)	35	20
1006	-	1g. sepia, brown & orge	45	35
1007	164	1g.50 blue, turq & grn	60	45

DESIGNS—VERT: 5c., 50c. Young Haitians walking towards ABC "sun"; 10c., 1g. Scouting—hat, knot and saluting hand.

165 Dr. Albert Schweitzer and Maps of Alsace and Gabon

1967. Schweitzer Commem. Multicoloured.

No.	Description	Unused	Used
1008	5c. Type **165** (postage)	15	15
1009	10c. Dr. Schweitzer and organ pipes	15	15
1010	20c. Dr. Schweitzer and Hospital Deschapelles, Haiti	35	20
1011	50c. As 20c. (air)	45	35
1012	1g. As 20c.	45	35
1013	1g.50 Type **165**	60	45
1014	2g. As 10c.	80	65

166 J.-J. Dessalines and Melon

1967. Dessalines Commem. With Portrait of Dessalines. Multicoloured.

No.	Description	Unused	Used
1015	5c. Type **166** (postage)	15	15
1016	10c. Chou (cabbage)	15	15
1017	20c. Mandarine (orange)	25	20
1018	50c. Mirliton (gourd)	35	20
1019	50c. Type **166** (air)	35	20
1020	1g. As 20c.	45	35
1021	1g.50 As 20c.	60	45

1967. World Scout Jamboree, Idaho. Nos. 957/8, 960/1, 963 and 965 surch 12e Jamboree Mondial 1967 or with additional premium only.

No.	Description	Unused	Used
1022	10c.+10c. on 5c. (postage)	10	10
1023	15c.+10c.	15	15
1024	50c. on 3c.	25	20
1025	50c.+10c.	25	35
1026	50c.+10c. (air)	45	35
1027	1g.50+50c.	60	45

1967. World Fair, Montreal. Nos. 968/70 and 972 optd EXPO CANADA 1967 and emblem, also surch with new values (1g. and 2g.).

No.	Type	Description	Unused	Used
1028	160	5c. mult (postage)	15	15
1029	-	10c. multicoloured	15	15
1030	160	50c. multicoloured	25	20
1031	160	1g. on 5c. multicoloured	45	35
1032	160	1g.50 multicoloured (air)	60	45
1033	160	2g. on 1g.50 mult	95	65

169 Head of Duvalier and Guineafowl Emblem

1967. 10th Anniv of Duvalierists Revolution.

No.	Type	Description	Unused	Used
1034	169	5c. gold and red (postage)	15	15
1035	169	10c. gold and blue	15	15
1036	169	25c. gold and brown	25	15
1037	169	50c. gold and purple	35	20
1038	169	1g. gold and green (air)	45	35
1039	169	1g.50 gold and violet	60	45
1040	169	2g. gold and red	95	65

170 "Literacy"

1967. National Education. Multicoloured.

No.	Description	Unused	Used
1041	5c. Type **170** (postage)	15	15
1042	10c. "Scouting" (Scout badge) (vert)	15	15
1043	25c. "Visual Aids" (slide projection)	25	15
1044	50c. Type **170** (air)	25	20
1045	1g. As 10c. (vert)	45	35
1046	1g.50 As 25c.	60	45

1968. Olympic Games, Mexico. Nos. 990, 992 and 995 surch MEXICO 1968 with Olympic rings and value or optd only (1g.50).

No.	Type	Description	Unused	Used
1047	163	50c. on 15c. (postage)	35	20
1048	163	1g. on 5c.	45	35
1049	-	1g.50 (air)	60	45
1050	-	2g.50+1g.25 on 1g.50	1·40	1·10

1968. Winter Olympic Games, Grenoble. Nos. 986/9 optd Xeme JEUX OLYMPIQUES D'HIVER-GRENOBLE 1968 and Games emblem.

No.	Type	Description	Unused	Used
1051	162	50c. red & blue (postage)	80	75
1052	-	50c. indigo and blue (air)	60	35
1053	-	1g. green and blue	1·20	55
1054	-	1g.50 red and blue	2·10	1·00

173 Bois Caiman Ceremony

1968. Slaves' Revolt Commem.

No.	Type	Description	Unused	Used
1055	173	5c. mult (postage)	10	10
1056	173	10c. multicoloured	15	10
1057	173	25c. multicoloured	20	15
1058	173	50c. multicoloured	35	20
1059	173	50c. multicoloured (air)	35	20
1060	173	50c. multicoloured	35	20
1061	173	1g. multicoloured	45	35
1062	173	1g. multicoloured	45	35
1063	173	1g.50 multicoloured	70	55
1064	173	2g. multicoloured	80	65
1065	173	5g. multicoloured	1·80	1·30

Nos. 1060 and 1062/4 are in a larger size—49½×36 mm.

174 "The Unknown Slave"

1968. Inaug of Slavery Freedom Monument.

No.	Type	Description	Unused	Used
1066	174	5c. black & blue (postage)	15	15
1067	174	10c. black and brown	15	10
1068	174	20c. black and violet	10	15
1069	174	25c. black and blue	25	20
1070	174	50c. black and green	35	20
1071	174	50c. black and ochre (air)	35	20
1072	174	1g. black and red	45	35
1073	174	1g.50 black and orange	70	45

1968. Air. Nos. 1044/6 surch CULTURE + 0.10.

No.	Type	Description	Unused	Used
1074	170	50c.+10c. mult	35	20
1075	-	1g.+10c. multicoloured	45	35
1076	-	1g.50+10c. mult	60	45

176 Various Arms and Palm

1968. Consecration of Haitian Bishopric.

No.	Type	Description	Unused	Used
1077	176	5c. mult (postage)	15	15
1078	-	10c. multicoloured	15	10
1079	-	25c. multicoloured	20	15
1080	176	50c. multicoloured (air)	35	20
1081	-	1g. multicoloured	45	35
1082	-	1g.50 multicoloured	60	45
1083	-	2g.50 multicoloured	1·20	90

DESIGNS—HORIZ: (50×30 mm): 10c., 1g., 2g.50, Virgin Mary; 25c., 1g.50, Cathedral, Port-au-Prince.

177 Boeing 727-100 over Control Tower

1968. Inauguration of Duvalier Airport, Port-au-Prince. Portrait in black.

No.	Type	Description	Unused	Used
1084	177	5c. brown & bl (postage)	15	15
1085	177	10c. brown and blue	15	10
1086	177	25c. brown and lilac	25	15
1087	-	50c. purple & violet (air)	35	20
1088	-	1g.50 purple and blue	60	45
1089	-	2g.50 purple & turquoise	80	75

DESIGN: 50c., 1g.50, 2g.50, Boeing 727-100 over airport entrance.

178 President Duvalier, Emblems and Map

1968. Air. 4th Anniv of Francois Duvalier's "Life Presidency". Die-stamped in gold.

No.	Type	Description	Unused	Used
1090	178	30g. gold, black and red	35·00	33·00

179 Slave breaking Chains

1968. "Revolt of the Slaves" (1791).

No.	Type	Description	Unused	Used
1091	179	5c. mauve, purple and blue (postage)	15	15
1092	179	10c. mauve, pur & orge	15	10
1093	179	25c. mauve, pur & ochre	25	15
1094	179	50c. mauve, pur & lil (air)	35	20
1095	179	1g. mauve, purple & grn	45	35
1096	179	1g.50 mauve, pur & bl	60	45
1097	179	2g. mauve, purple & turq	70	55

180 "Learning the Alphabet"

1968. "National Education". Multicoloured.

No.	Description	Unused	Used
1098	5c. Type **180** (postage)	15	15
1099	10c. Children watching TV screen ("Education by Audio-visual Methods")	15	10
1100	50c. Hands with ball ("Education Through Sport")	35	20
1101	50c. As No. 1099 (air)	35	20
1102	1g. As No. 1100	45	35
1103	1g.50 As No. 1099	60	45

181 Boesman and Balloon

1968. Air. Boesman's Balloon Flight.

No.	Type	Description	Unused	Used
1104	181	70c. brown and green	60	45
1105	181	1g.75 brown and blue	1·20	90

182 Airmail Cachet of 1925

1968. Air. Galiffet's Balloon Flight of 1784. Each black and purple on mauve.

No.	Description	Unused	Used
1106	70c. Airplane and "AVION" ("2 May 1925")	45	55
1107	70c. Type **182**	45	55
1108	70c. "AVION" and airplane ("28 March 1927")	45	55
1109	70c. "HAITI POSTE AVION" and airplane ("12 July 1927")	45	55
1110	70c. Airplane and "AVION" within ring ("13 Sept 1927")	45	55
1111	70c. "LINDBERGH" and airplane ("6th February 1928")	45	55

Nos. 1106/11 were issued together se-tenant within a small sheet containing two blocks of six (3×2) with an overall background design representing Galiffet's balloon.

183 Churchill as Elder Brother of Trinity House

1968. Churchill Commemoration. Mult.

No.	Description	Unused	Used
1112	3c. Type **183** (postage)	10	10

1113	5c. Churchill painting	10	10
1114	10c. As Knight of the Garter	15	10
1115	15c. 79th birthday portrait and troops	20	15
1116	20c. Churchill and Farman M.F.7 floatplane	20	15
1117	25c. Karsh portrait and taking leave of the Queen	25	20
1118	50c. Giving "V" sign and Houses of Parliament	35	20
1119	50c. As No. 1116 (air)	35	20
1120	75c. As No. 1115	45	35
1121	1g. As No. 1117	60	45
1122	1g.50 As No. 1118	70	55
MS1123	101×75 mm. 3g. Karsh portrait and Arms (horiz)	3·50	3·25

1969. Nos. 1070/2 surch.

1124	**174**	70c. on 50c. (postage)	45	35
1125	**174**	70c. on 50c. (air)	45	35
1126	**174**	1g.75 on 1g.	70	45

185 Blue-hooded Euphonia

1969. Birds. Multicoloured.

1127	5c. Type **185** (postage)	1·60	45
1128	10c. Hispaniolan trogon	1·60	45
1129	20c. Palm chat	1·90	45
1130	25c. Stripe-headed tanager	2·20	55
1131	50c. Type **185**	3·00	55
1132	50c. As 10c. (air)	2·50	75
1133	1g. Black-cowled oriole	3·00	1·30
1134	1g.50 As 25c.	3·75	1·80
1135	2g. Hispaniolan woodpecker	4·25	2·20

186 "Theato, Paris-1900"

1969. Winners of Olympic Marathon showing commemorative inscr and stamp of "host" country. Multicoloured.

1136	5c. "Louis, Athens-1896" (postage)	15	15
1137	10c. Type **186**	25	20
1138	15c. "Hicks, St. Louis-1904"	25	20
1139	20c. "Hayes, London-1908"	45	45
1140	20c. "McArthur, Stock-holm-1912"	45	45
1141	25c. "Kolehmainen, Ant-werp-1920"	70	65
1142	25c. "Steenroos, Paris-1924"	70	65
1143	25c. "El Quafi, Amsterdam-1928"	70	65
1144	30c. "Zabala, Los Angeles-1932" (air)	80	75
1145	50c. "Son, Berlin-1936"	1·20	1·10
1146	60c. "Cabrera, London-1948"	1·60	1·50
1147	75c. "Zatopek, Helsinki-1952"	2·30	2·20
1148	75c. "Mimoun, Melbourn-1956"	2·30	2·20
1149	90c. "Bikila, Rome-1960"	2·50	2·40
1150	1g. "Bikila, Tokyo-1964"	3·25	3·00
1151	1g.25 "Wolde, Mexico-1968"	4·50	4·25
MS1152	Two sheets each 128×71 mm. 1g.50 Design as No. 1144; 2g. Design as No. 1151	28·00	26·00

Nos. 1136, 1139, 1142 and 1149 are larger, size 66×36 mm.

187 Pylons and Electric Light Bulb

1969. Construction of Duvalier Hydro-electric Scheme.

1153	**187**	20c. violet & bl (postage)	15	10
1154	**187**	20c. blue and violet (air)	25	15
1155	**187**	25c. green and red	25	15
1156	**187**	25c. red and green	25	15

189 Practising the Alphabet

1969. Obligatory Tax. Education Fund. As Nos. 974/8.

1157	**146**	10c. brown (postage)	25	20
1158	**146**	10c. blue	25	20
1159	**146**	10c. purple (air)	25	20
1160	**146**	10c. red	25	20
1161	**146**	10c. yellow	25	20
1162	**146**	10c. green	25	20
1163	**146**	10c. maroon	25	20

1969. 50th Anniv of League of Red Cross Societies. Various stamps surch 50 eme. Anniversaire de la Ligue des Societes de la Croix Rouge.

1164	10c.+10c. (No. 1099) (postage)	15	10
1165	50c.+20c. (No. 1100)	45	35
1166	50c.+20c. (No. 1101) (air)	45	35
1167	1g.50+25c. (No. 1103)	80	45

1969. "National Education". Multicoloured.

1168	5c. Type **189** (postage)	15	15
1169	10c. Children at play (vert)	15	10
1170	50c. Audio-visual education (vert)	25	15
1171	50c. As No. 1170 (vert) (air)	25	20
1172	1g. Type **189**	45	35
1173	1g.50 As No. 1169 (vert)	70	45

190 I.L.O. Emblem

1969. 50th Anniv of I.L.O.

1174	**190**	5c. green & blk (postage)	15	15
1175	**190**	10c. brown and black	15	10
1176	**190**	20c. blue and black	20	15
1177	**190**	25c. red and black (air)	25	20
1178	**190**	70c. orange and black	60	35
1179	**190**	1g.75 violet and black	1·20	65

191 "Papilio zonaria"

1969. Haitian Butterflies. Multicoloured.

1180	10c. Type **191** (postage)	1·10	35
1181	20c. "Zerene cesonia"	2·30	50
1182	25c. "Papilio machaonides"	3·50	55
1183	50c. "Danaus eresimus" (air)	4·75	70
1184	1g.50 "Anaea marthesia"	9·75	1·70
1185	2g. "Prepona antimache"	14·00	2·75

192 Dr. Martin Luther King

1970. Dr. Martin Luther King (American Civil Rights leader) Commemoration.

1186	**192**	10c. brown, red and ochre (postage)	15	10
1187	**192**	20c. black, red & bl	15	10
1188	**192**	25c. black, red and pink	20	20
1189	**192**	50c. black, red and green (air)	40	30
1190	**192**	1g. black, red and orange	50	40
1191	**192**	1g.50 black, red and blue	60	50

193 "Laeliopsis dominguensis"

1970. Haitian Orchids. Multicoloured.

1192	10c. Type **193** (postage)	15	10
1193	20c. "Oncidium haitiense"	30	30
1194	25c. "Oncidium calochilum"	40	30
1195	50c. "Tetramicra elegans" (air)	40	30
1196	1g.50 "Epidendrum truncatum"	70	50
1197	2g. "Oncidium desertorum"	1·00	75

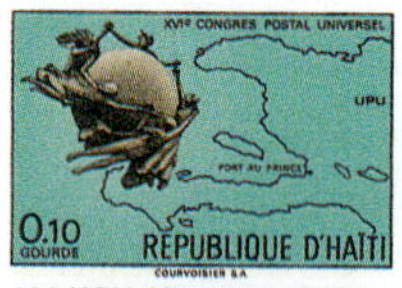

194 U.P.U. Monument Berne, and Map of Haiti

1970. 16th U.P.U. Congress, Tokyo.

1198	**194**	10c. brown, black and green (postage)	15	10
1199	-	25c. yellow, black and red	20	20
1200	-	50c. green, black and blue	30	20
1201	-	50c. brn, blk & vio (air)	30	20
1202	-	1g.50 yellow, blk & red	60	40
1203	**194**	2g. brown, black & green	85	60
MS1204		130×74 mm. Nos. 1201/3. Imperf	2·10	1·90

DESIGNS—VERT: 25c., 1g.50, Stylized "propeller". HORIZ: 50c. (both), Doves and globe.

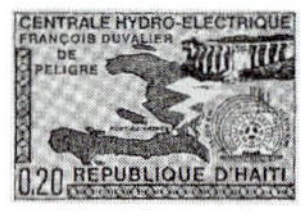

195 Map, Dam and Generator

1970. Construction of Duvalier Central Hydro-electric Power Station. Multicoloured.

1205	20c. Type **195**	20	10
1206	25c. Map, dam and pylon	20	15

1970. 25th Anniv of United Nations. Nos. 1200/203 optd XXVe ANNIVERSAIRE O.N.U. and emblem.

1207	-	50c. green, black and blue (postage)	30	20
1208	-	50c. brown, blk & bl (air)	30	20
1209	-	1g.50 yellow, blk & red	60	40
1210	**194**	2g. brown, black & green	85	60
MS1211		130×73 mm. As Nos. 1208/10. Imperf	2·10	1·90

197 Power Station and Pylon

1970. Obligatory Tax. Duvalier Hydro-electric Project.

1212	**197**	20c. brown & lil (post-age)	20	10
1213	**197**	20c. grey and brown (air)	20	10
1214	**197**	20c. violet and blue	20	10
1214a	**197**	25c. black and olive		

See also No. 1268.

198 Fort Nativity, 1492

1970. Christmas.

1215	**198**	3c. brn & yell (postage)	15	10
1216	**198**	5c. black and green	25	20
1217	-	1g.50 mult (sepia panel) (air)	60	40
1218	-	1g.50 mult (blue panel)	60	40
1219	-	2g. multicoloured	1·00	60

DESIGN—SQUARE (33×33 mm): Nos. 1217/19, "Haitian Nativity" (Toussaint Auguste).

199 "The Oriental" (Rembrandt)

1971. Paintings. Multicoloured.

1220	5c. Type **199** (postage)	15	15
1221	10c. "The Ascension" (C. Bazile)	15	15
1222	20c. "Irises in a vase" (Van Gogh)	20	15
1223	50c. "The Baptism of Christ" (C. Bazile)	30	20
1224	50c. "The Nativity" (R. Benoit) (air)	30	20
1225	1g. "Head of a Negro" (Rubens)	50	40
1226	1g.50 As 10c.	65	50
MS1227	Two sheets each 66×86 mm. (a) 3g. "Young Mother Sewing" (Cassatt); (b) 3g. "The Card-players" (Cezanne) (25×37 mm). Imperf	2·30	2·30

200 Football

1971. World Cup Football Championship, Mexico (1970).

1228	**200**	5c. black and orange	15	10
1229	**200**	50c. black and brown	40	30
1230	-	50c. black, yellow & pink	40	30
1231	-	1g. black, yellow and lilac	60	40
1232	**200**	1g.50 black and drab	70	50
1233	-	5g. black, yellow and grey	2·10	1·40
MS1234		84×66 mm. 70c. black and vio-let (T **200**); 1g. multicoloured (Jules Rimet Cup). Imperf	10·50	7·75

DESIGNS: Nos. 1230/31, 1233, Jules Rimet Cup.

1971. Inauguration of Duvalier Central Power Station. Surch INAUGURATION 22-7-71 and premium.

1235	**195**	20c.+50c. mult	40	30
1236	-	25c.+1g.50 mult (No. 1206)	70	40

202 Balloon and Airmail Stamp of 1929

1971. Air. 40th Anniv of Airmail Service (1969).

1237	**202**	20c. black, red and blue	20	15
1238	**202**	50c. black, red and blue	35	20
1239	-	1g. black and orange	80	40
1240	-	1g.50 black and mauve	1·20	50
MS1241		85×71 mm. 50c. purple and emerald	5·75	3·75

DESIGNS: Nos. 1239/40, Concorde and 1929 air stamp; **MS**1241, 1929 50c. Air stamp.

1971. Obligatory Tax. Education Fund. Nos. 1205/6 surch ALPHABETISATION and value.

1242	**195**	20c.+10c. mult	30	20
1243	-	25c.+10c. mult	30	20

1972. Air. "INTERPEX" International Stamp Exhibition, New York Nos. 1237/40 optd INTERPEX 72 and emblem.

1244	**202**	20c. black, red and blue	20	20
1245	**202**	50c. black, red and blue	30	30
1246	-	1g. black and orange	50	40
1247	-	1g.50 black and mauve	60	50

205 J.-J. Dessalines and Emblem

1972. Jean-Jacques Dessalines ("founder of Haiti") Commemoration (1st issue).

No.	Type	Description	Mint	Used
1248	**205**	5c. black & grn (postage)	15	10
1249	**205**	10c. black and blue	20	20
1250	**205**	25c. black and orange	20	20
1251	**205**	50c. black and green (air)	30	20
1252	**205**	2g.50 black and lilac	1·00	60

See also Nos. 1304/10, 1343/52, 1357/60, 1413/17 and 1451/2.

1972. Air. 5th "Haipex" Congress. Nos. 1237/40 optd HAIPEX 5eme. CONGRES and emblem.

No.	Type	Description	Mint	Used
1253	**202**	20c. black, red and blue	15	10
1254	-	50c. black, red and blue	30	20
1255	-	1g. black and orange	40	30
1256	-	1g.50 black and mauve	60	40

1972. Air. "Belgica 72" Stamp Exhibition, Brussels. Nos. 1238/40 optd BELGICA 72 and emblem.

No.	Description	Mint	Used
1257	50c. black, red and blue	30	20
1258	1g. black and orange	40	30
1259	1g.50 black and mauve	60	40

1972. Obligatory Tax. As Nos. 974/8.

No.	Type	Description	Mint	Used
1260	**146**	5c. red	20	20
1261	**146**	5c. blue	20	20

208 "Sun" and "EXPO" Emblem

1972. "EXPO 70" World Fair, Osaka, Japan (1970).

No.	Type	Description	Mint	Used
1262	**208**	10c. mult (postage)	15	10
1263	-	25c. multicoloured	20	20
1264	-	50c. multicoloured (air)	30	20
1265	-	1g. multicoloured	50	30
1266	-	1g.50 multicoloured	60	40
1267	-	2g.50 multicoloured	85	50

DESIGNS—HORIZ: Nos. 1264/7, Sun Tower and emblem.

1972. Obligatory Tax. Duvalier Hydro-electric Project. As Nos. 1212/14.

No.	Type	Description	Mint	Used
1268	**197**	20c. brown and blue	20	20

209 Basket Vendors

1973. 20th Anniv of Caribbean Travel Assn. Multicoloured.

No.	Description	Mint	Used
1269	50c. Type **209**	30	20
1270	80c. Postal bus service	40	30
1271	1g.50 Type **209**	60	40
1272	2g.50 As 80c.	1·20	70

1973. Air. Education Fund. As Nos. 977/8 but larger size 17×25 mm.

No.	Type	Description	Mint	Used
1273	**146**	10c. brown and blue	30	20
1274	**146**	10c. brown and green	30	20
1275	**146**	10c. brown and orange	30	20

210 Headquarters and Map

1973. Air. 70th Anniv of Pan-American Health Organization. Multicoloured.

No.	Type	Description	Mint	Used
1276	**210**	50c. multicoloured	30	20
1277	**210**	80c. multicoloured	40	30
1278	**210**	1g.50 multicoloured	50	40
1279	**210**	2g. multicoloured	65	50

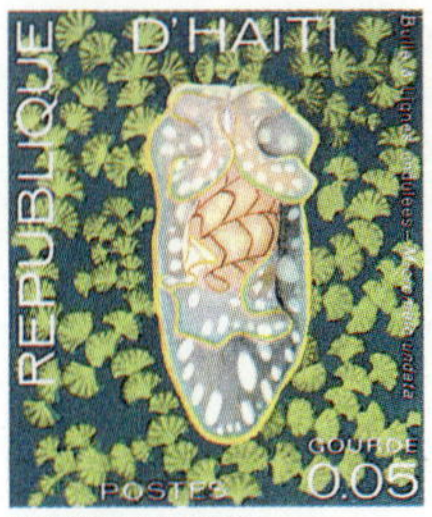

211 Miniature Melo

1973. Marine Life. Multicoloured.

No.	Description	Mint	Used
1280	5c. Type **211** (postage)	15	15
1281	10c. "Nemaster rubiginosa"	20	15
1282	25c. "Cyerce cristallina"	35	20
1283	50c. "Desmophyllum riisei"	60	20
1284	50c. "Platypodia spectabilis" (air)	60	30
1285	85c. "Goniaster tessellatus"	85	30
1286	1g.50 "Stephanocyathus diadema"	1·10	40
1287	2g. "Phyllangia americana"	1·40	50

211a Royal Gramma

1973. Fishes. Multicoloured.

No.	Description	Mint	Used
1288	10c. Type **211a** (postage)	30	20
1289	50c. Blue tang	40	30
1290	50c. Black-capped basslet (air)	40	30
1291	85c. Rock beauty	50	40
1292	1g.50 Peppermint basslet	75	50
1293	5g. Creole wrasse	2·50	1·20

212 Haitian Flag

1973. Air.

No.	Type	Description	Mint	Used
1294	**212**	80c. black and red	40	30
1295	-	80c. black and red	40	30
1296	-	1g.85 black and red	85	60
1297	-	1g.85 black and red	85	60

DESIGNS—As Type **212**: No. 1295, Flag and arms (framed). (47×29 mm): No. 1296, Flag and arms; No. 1297, Flag and Pres. Jean-Claude Duvalier.

213 Football Stadium

1973. World Cup Football Championship. Preliminary Games between Caribbean Countries.

No.	Type	Description	Mint	Used
1298	**213**	10c. green, black and brown (postage)	15	10
1299	-	20c. mauve, black & brn	20	20
1300	**213**	50c. green, blk & red (air)	30	20
1301	**213**	80c. green, black & blue	40	30
1302	-	1g.75 green, black & brn	85	40
1303	-	10g. green, black & brn	3·00	2·10

DESIGNS: 20c., 1g.75, 10g. World Cup stamp of 1971.

214 J.-J. Dessalines

1974. Jean-Jacques Dessalines Commemoration (2nd issue).

No.	Type	Description	Mint	Used
1304	**214**	10c. green & bl (postage)	15	10
1305	**214**	20c. black and red	20	20
1306	**214**	25c. violet and brown	20	20
1307	**214**	50c. blue and brown (air)	30	20
1308	**214**	80c. brown and grey	40	30
1309	**214**	1g. purple and green	50	40
1310	**214**	1g.75 green and mauve	85	50

215 Symbol of Solar System

1974. 500th Birth Anniv (1973) of Nicolas Copernicus (astronomer). Multicoloured.

No.	Description	Mint	Used
1311	10c. Type **215** (postage)	15	10
1312	25c. Copernicus	20	20
1313	50c. Type **215** (air)	30	20
1314	50c. As 25c.	30	20
1315	80c. Type **215**	40	30
1316	1g. As 25c.	50	40
1317	1g.75 Type **215**	85	50
MS1318	96×65 mm. 1g.50 Type **215**; 2g.50 As 25c. Imperf	2·10	1·90

216 Pres. Jean-Claude Duvalier

1974

No.	Type	Description	Mint	Used
1319	**216**	10c. grn & gold (postage)	15	10
1320	**216**	20c. purple and gold	20	20
1321	**216**	50c. blue and gold	30	20
1322	**216**	50c. purple and gold (air)	30	20
1323	**216**	80c. red and gold	40	30
1324	**216**	1g. purple and gold	50	40
1325	**216**	1g.50 blue and gold	85	60
1326	**216**	1g.75 violet and gold	1·00	65
1327	**216**	5g. grey and gold	2·50	1·40

1975. Air. Nos. 1296/7 surch.

No.	Description	Mint	Used
1328	80c. on 1g.85 black and red	50	40
1329	80c. on 1g.85 black and red	50	40

1975. Air. Centenary of U.P.U. Nos. 1296/7 optd 1874 UPU 1974 100 ANS.

No.	Description	Mint	Used
1330	1g.85 black and red	85	60
1331	1g.85 black and red	85	60

219 Haiti 60c. Stamp of 1937

1976. Bicentenary of American Revolution.

No.	Type	Description	Mint	Used
1332	**219**	10c. mult (postage)	20	20
1333	-	50c. multicoloured (air)	30	20
1334	-	80c. multicoloured	50	30
1335	-	1g.50 multicoloured	70	50
1336	-	7g.50 multicoloured	2·50	1·70

DESIGN: 50c. to 7g.50, text with names of Haitians at Siege of Savannah.

1976. Surch.

No.	Type	Description	Mint	Used
1337	**205**	80c. on 25c. black and pink (postage)	50	30
1338	-	80c. on 10c. mult (No. 1288)	50	30
1339	**214**	80c. on 25c. violet & brn	50	30
1340	**215**	80c. on 10c. mult	50	30
1341	-	80c. on 85c. mult (No. 1285) (air)	50	30
1342	-	80c. on 85c. mult (No. 1291)	50	30

1977. Jean-Jacques Dessalines Commem (3rd issue).

No.	Type	Description	Mint	Used
1343	**205**	20c. black and brown (postage)	15	10
1344	**205**	50c. black and mauve	30	20
1345	**205**	75c. black and yellow (air)	30	30
1346	**205**	1g. black and blue	30	30
1347	**205**	1g.25 black and olive	40	30
1348	**205**	1g.50 black and grey	40	30
1349	**205**	1g.75 black and red	50	40
1350	**205**	2g. black and yellow	60	50
1351	**205**	5g. black and blue	1·60	95
1352	**205**	10g. black and brown	3·00	1·90

1977. Air. Lindbergh's Transatlantic Flight Nos. 1313/14 and 1316/17 optd or surch C. LINDBERGH. N.Y.-PARIS 1927-1977.

No.	Description	Mint	Used
1353	1g. Copernicus	40	30
1354	1g.25 on 50c. Type **215**	50	40
1355	1g.25 on 50c. Copernicus	50	40
1356	1g.25 on 1g.75 Type **215**	50	40

1977. Jean-Jacques Dessalines Commem (4th issue).

No.	Description	Mint	Used
1357	10c. black and mauve (postage)	15	10
1358	50c. black and brown	30	20
1359	80c. black and green (air)	40	30
1360	1g. black and brown	50	40

1977. Air. Various stamps surch G. 0.80.

No.	Type	Description	Mint	Used
1361	-	80c. on 1g.50 mult (No. 1266)	50	30
1362	-	80c. on 2g.50 mult (No. 1267)	50	30
1363	-	80c. on 1g.85 black and red (No. 1296)	50	30
1364	**215**	80c. on 1g.75 mult	50	30
1365	**216**	80c. on 1g.75 violet and gold	50	30
1366	-	80c. on 1g.50 mult (No. 1335)	50	30

1978. Surch 1.00.

No.	Type	Description	Mint	Used
1367	**205**	1g. on 20c. black & brn	40	30
1368	**205**	1g. on 1g.75 black and red	40	30
1369	**205**	1g.25 on 75c. black and yellow	40	30
1370	**205**	1g.25 on 1g.50 black and green	40	30

Nos. 1368/70 have the inscription "AVION" obliterated by the surcharge.

224 J.-C. Duvalier Telecommunications Stations

1978. Telephone Centenary (1976). Mult.

No.	Description	Mint	Used
1372	10c. Type **224** (postage)	15	15
1373	20c. Video telephone	20	20
1374	50c. Alexander Graham Bell (vert)	30	20
1375	1g. Satellite over Earth (air)	40	30
1376	1g.25 Type **224**	50	40
1377	2g. Wall telephone, 1890 (vert)	70	50

225 Flag-raising Ceremony

1978. Olympic Games, Montreal (1976). Multicoloured.

No.	Description	Mint	Used
1378	5c. Type **225** (postage)	15	10
1379	25c. Cycling	20	20
1380	50c. High jump	30	20
1381	1g.25 Horse jumping (air)	60	50
1382	2g.50 Basketball	1·20	95
1383	5g. Yachting	2·75	1·20

226 Mother feeding Baby

1979. 50th Anniv of Inter-American Child Institute. Multicoloured.

No.	Description	Mint	Used
1384	25c. Type **226** (postage)	20	20
1385	1g.25 Type **226** (air)	50	30
1386	2g. Nurse vaccinating child	70	50

227 Mother feeding Child

1979. 30th Anniv of Co-operative for American Relief Everywhere (CARE). Multicoloured.

1387	25c. Type **227** (postage)	20	20
1388	50c. Type **227**	30	20
1389	1g. Spinning cotton (air)	60	50
1390	1g.25 As No. 1389	85	60
1391	2g. As No. 1389	1·20	75

228 Human Rights Emblem

1979. 30th Anniv of Declaration of Human Rights.

1392	**228**	25c. mult (postage)	25	20
1393	**228**	1g. multicoloured (air)	60	50
1394	**228**	1g.25 multicoloured	85	60
1395	**228**	2g. multicoloured	1·20	75

229 Anteor Firmin and Book

1979. International Anti-Apartheid Year.

1396	**229**	50c. pink and brown (postage)	35	20
1397	**229**	1g. green and brown (air)	70	50
1398	**229**	1g.25 blue and brown	85	60
1399	**229**	2g. olive and brown	1·30	75

230 Children playing

1979. International Year of the Child.

1400	**230**	10c. mult (postage)	15	10
1401	**230**	25c. multicoloured	20	20
1402	**230**	50c. multicoloured	30	20
1403	**230**	1g. multicoloured (air)	60	50
1404	**230**	1g.25 multicoloured	85	60
1405	**230**	2g.50 multicoloured	2·30	95
1406	**230**	5g. multicoloured	3·00	1·40

1980. Air. Wedding of President Duvalier. Nos. 1322 and 1325/6 optd 27 5 80 JOUR FASTE.

1407	**216**	50c. purple and gold	30	20
1408	**216**	1g.50 blue and gold	85	40
1409	**216**	1g.75 violet and gold	1·00	50

1980. Nos. 1252, 1357 and 1359 surch TIMBRE POSTE with value changed.

1410	**205**	1g. on 2g.50 black & lil	50	40
1411	**205**	1g.25 on 10c. blk & mve	60	50
1412	**205**	1g.25 on 80c. blk & grn	60	50

1980. Jean-Jacques Dessalines Commemoration (5th issue).

1413	25c. black and orange (postage)	25	15
1414	1g. black and grey (air)	50	40
1415	1g.25 black and pink	60	50
1416	2g. black and green	1·00	75
1417	5g. black and blue	2·10	1·40

233 Henri Christophe Citadel

1980. World Tourism Conference, Manila. Multicoloured.

1418	5c. Type **233** (postage)	15	10
1419	25c. Sans-Souci Palace	20	20
1420	50c. Vallieres market	30	20
1421	1g. Type **233** (air)	50	40
1422	1g.25 As No. 1419	60	50
1423	1g.50 Carnival dancers	85	50
1424	2g. Women with flowers	1·00	75
1425	2g.50 As No. 1424	1·20	95

234 Players and Flag of Uruguay (1930)

1980. 50th Anniv of First World Cup Football Championship. Multicoloured.

1426	10c. Type **234** (postage)	15	10
1427	20c. Italy (1934)	15	15
1428	25c. Italy (1938)	20	20
1429	50c. Uruguay (air)	30	20
1430	75c. West Germany (1954)	40	30
1431	1g. Brazil (1958)	60	40
1432	1g.25 Brazil (1962)	70	50
1433	1g.50 England (1966)	95	60
1434	1g.75 Brazil (1970)	1·10	75
1435	2g. West Germany (1974)	1·20	85
1436	5g. Argentina (1978)	3·00	1·90

235 "Woman with Birds and Flowers" (Hector Hyppolite)

1981. Paintings. Multicoloured.

1437	5c. Type **235** (postage)	15	10
1438	10c. "Going to Church" (Gregoire Etienne)	15	15
1439	20c. "Street Market" (Petion Savain)	15	15
1440	25c. "Market Sellers" (Michele Manual)	20	15
1441	50c. Type **235** (air)	30	20
1442	1g.25 As No. 1438	60	50
1443	2g. As No. 1439	1·10	75
1444	5g. As No. 1440	2·10	1·40

1981. Various stamps surch 1.25.

1445	**233**	1g.25 on 5c. mult (postage)	60	50
1446	**235**	1g.25 on 5c. mult	60	50
1447	-	1g.25 on 10c. mult (No. 1438)	60	50
1448	-	1g.25 on 20c. mult (No. 1427)	60	50
1449	-	1g.25 on 1g.50 mult (No. 1423) (air)	60	50
1450	**205**	2g. on 5g. black and blue (No. 1417)	80	60

The surcharge on No. 1446 is inverted.

1982. Jean-Jacques Dessalines ("founder of Haiti") Commemoration (6th issue).

1451	1g.25 black and brown	60	50
1452	2g. black and violet	1·00	75

237 President Duvalier, Dish Aerial and Freighter at Quayside

1982. 10th Anniv of Duvalier Reforms ("Jean-Claudisme").

1453	**237**	25c. green and black	20	20
1454	**237**	50c. green and black	30	20
1455	**237**	1g. purple and black	50	40
1456	**237**	1g.25 blue and black	60	50
1457	**237**	2g. orange and black	1·00	75
1458	**237**	5g. orange and black	2·10	1·40

1982. Nos. 1453 and 1455/7 optd 1957- 1982 25 ANS DE REVOLUTION.

1459	25c. green and black	20	20
1460	1g. purple and black	50	40
1461	1g.25 blue and black	60	50
1462	2g. orange and black	1·00	75

239 Scouts planting Trees

1983. 75th Anniv of Boy Scout Movement. Multicoloured.

1463	5c. Type **239** (postage)	15	10
1464	10c. Lord Baden-Powell (vert)	20	20
1465	25c. Scout teaching villagers to read	20	20
1466	50c. As No. 1464	35	20
1467	75c. As No. 1465 (air)	75	30
1468	1g. Type **239**	90	40
1469	1g.25 As No. 1465	1·30	60
1470	2g. As No. 1464	1·70	75

240 Our Lady of Perpetual Succour

1983. Centenary of Miracle of Our Lady of Perpetual Succour.

1471	**240**	10c. mult (postage)	15	10
1472	**240**	20c. multicoloured	20	15
1473	**240**	25c. multicoloured	20	15
1474	**240**	50c. multicoloured	30	20
1475	**240**	75c. multicoloured (air)	40	30
1476	**240**	1g. multicoloured	50	40
1477	**240**	1g.25 multicoloured	60	50
1478	**240**	1g.50 multicoloured	85	60
1479	**240**	1g.75 multicoloured	95	70
1480	-	2g. multicoloured	1·10	75
1481	-	5g. multicoloured	2·00	1·40

MS1482 Two sheets each containing No. 1481. (a) 90×115 mm; (b) 115×90 mm 4·00 3·50

Nos. 1480/1 differ slightly in design of the frame.

241 Arms of Haiti and U.P.U. Monument, Berne

1983. Centenary (1981) of U.P.U. Membership.

1483	**241**	5c. brown, red and black (postage)	15	15
1484	-	10c. brown, black & blue	25	20
1485	-	25c. green, black and red	25	20
1486	-	50c. green, red and black	25	20
1487	-	75c. lilac, black and blue (air)	45	30
1488	-	1g. blue, red and black	60	40
1489	-	1g.25 blue, black and red	70	50
1490	-	2g. blue, black and red	1·20	75

DESIGNS: 50c., 1g. Type **241**; 10, 75c. L. F. Salomon and J. C. Duvalier; 25c., 1g.25, 2g. First Haitian stamp and U.P.U. Monument, Berne.

242 Argentine and Belgian Footballers

1983. World Cup Football Championship, Spain.

1491	**242**	5c. black & bl (postage)	15	10
1492	-	10c. black and brown	20	20
1493	-	20c. black and green	20	20
1494	-	25c. black and green	20	20
1495	-	50c. black and yellow	30	20
1496	-	1g. multicoloured (air)	50	40
1497	-	1g.25 multicoloured	60	50
1498	-	1g.50 multicoloured	85	60
1499	-	2g. multicoloured	1·00	75
1500	-	2g.50 multicoloured	1·20	95

DESIGNS—VERT: 10c. Northern Ireland and Yugoslavia; 20c. England and France; 25c. Spain and Northern Ireland; 50c. Italian player with Cup. HORIZ: 1g. Brazil and Scotland; 1g.25, Northern Ireland and France; 1g.50, Poland and Cameroun; 2g. Italy and West Germany; 2g.50, Argentine and Brazil.

243 1c. Stamp of 1881

1984. Stamp Centenary (1981).

1501	**243**	5c. mult (postage)	15	10
1502	-	10c. multicoloured	25	20
1503	-	25c. multicoloured	25	20
1504	-	50c. multicoloured	30	20
1505	-	75c. yellow, brown and silver (air)	40	30
1506	-	1g. blue, red and gold	50	40
1507	-	1g.25 multicoloured	60	50
1508	-	2g. gold, brown and green	1·00	75

DESIGNS: 10c. 1881 2c. stamp; 25c., 1881 3c. stamp; 50c. 1881 7c. stamp; 75c., 1g. Pres. Salomon; 1g.25, 2g. Pres. Duvalier.

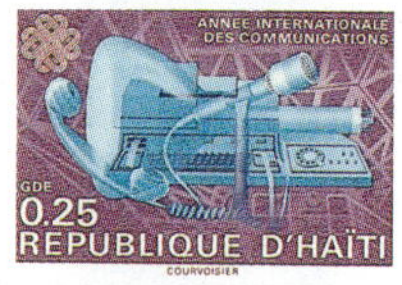

244 Modern Communications Equipment

1984. World Communications Year.

1509	**244**	25c. blue and purple	20	20
1510	**244**	50c. blue and olive	30	20
1511	-	1g. orange, brown & grn	50	40
1512	-	1g.25 orange, brown & bl	60	50
1513	-	2g. blue, orange and black	1·00	75
1514	-	2g.50 blue, bistre & blk	1·20	95

DESIGNS—VERT: 1g., 1g.25, Pres. Petion's drum; 2g., 2g.50, W.C.Y. emblem as satellite over globe.

245 Javelin-thrower, Runner and Polevaulter

1984. Olympic Games, Los Angeles.

1515	**245**	5c. black, green and red	15	10
1516	**245**	10c. black, olive and red	20	20
1517	-	25c. black, green and red	20	20
1518	-	50c. black, ochre and red	30	20
1519	-	1g. black, blue and red	50	40
1520	-	1g.25 black, blue & orge	70	50
1521	-	2g. black, violet and red	1·00	75

MS1522 52×72 mm. 2g.50 black, green and orange 1·70 95

DESIGNS—HORIZ: 25c., 50c. Hurdler. VERT: 1g. to 2g.50, Long jumper.

246 Head of "The Unknown Indian", Toussaint Square, Louverture

1984. 500th Anniv of Arrival of Europeans in America (1st issue).

1523	**246**	5c. mult (postage)	30	20
1524	**246**	10c. multicoloured	30	25
1525	**246**	25c. multicoloured	30	25
1526	**246**	50c. multicoloured	45	30
1527	-	1g. multicoloured (air)	60	40
1528	-	1g.25 multicoloured	90	55
1529	-	2g. multicoloured	2·50	1·30

MS1530 124×79 mm. Nos. 1526 and 1529 7·75 6·75

DESIGN: 1 to 2g. "The Unknown Indian".

See also Nos. 1539/44.

247 Simon Bolivar and Alexandre Petion

1985. Birth Bicentenary of Simon Bolivar. Mult.

1531	5c. Type **247** (postage)	15	15
1532	25c. Bolivar and Alexandre Petion (different)	25	20
1533	50c. Bolivar and flags of members of Grand Colombian Confederation	30	20
1534	1g. Type **247** (air)	50	40
1535	1g.25 As No. 1532	60	50
1536	2g. Type **247**	1·00	75
1537	7g.50 As No. 1532	3·00	1·90
MS1538	90×61 mm. 4g.50 As No. 1533	2·75	1·70

248 Chief Henri

1986. 500th Anniv of Arrival of Europeans in America (2nd issue).

1539	**248**	10c. mult (postage)	45	20
1540	**248**	25c. multicoloured	45	20
1541	**248**	50c. multicoloured	50	20
1542	-	1g. multicoloured (air)	85	40
1543	-	1g.25 multicoloured	1·10	50
1544	-	2g. multicoloured	1·70	75
MS1545		69×89 mm. 3g. mult	7·75	7·00

DESIGN: 1 to 3g. Chief Henri hunting.

1986. Various stamps surch.

1546	**241**	25c. on 5c. brown, red and black (postage)	25	20
1547	**242**	25c. on 5c. black & blue	25	20
1548	**243**	25c. on 5c. multicoloured	25	20
1549	-	25c. on 75c. mult (1430) (air)	25	20
1550	-	25c. on 75c. mult (1467)	25	20
1551	-	25c. on 1g.50 mult (1122)	25	20

250 Planting Saplings

1986. International Youth Year (1985). Mult.

1552	10c. Type **250** (postage)	15	10
1553	25c. I.Y.Y. emblem	20	20
1554	50c. Boy and girl scouts and flag	30	20
1555	1g. Type **250** (air)	50	40
1556	1g.25 As No. 1553	60	50
1557	2g. As No. 1554	1·00	75
MS1558	100×80 mm. 3g. green, red and black	4·75	4·25

251 Dove above Peace Year Emblem on Globe

1987. International Peace Year (1986) and 40th Anniv of United Nations Educational, Scientific and Cultural Organization.

1559	**251**	10c. mult (postage)	20	20
1560	**251**	25c. multicoloured	20	20
1561	**251**	50c. multicoloured	30	20
1562	**251**	1g. multicoloured (air)	50	40
1563	**251**	1g.25 multicoloured	60	50
1564	**251**	2g.50 multicoloured	1·20	95

MS1565	56×66 mm. 2g. mult	1·60	1·50

252 Peralte and Flag

1989. Charlemagne Peralte Commemoration.

1566	**252**	25c. mult (postage)	20	20
1567	**252**	50c. multicoloured	30	20
1568	**252**	1g. multicoloured (air)	50	40
1569	**252**	2g. multicoloured	1·00	75
1570	**252**	3g. multicoloured	1·60	1·20
MS1571		102×85 mm. No. 1569	2·10	1·90

253 Slaves and Tree forming Fist

1991. Bicentenary of Uprising of Slaves. Mult.

1572	25c. Type **253** (postage)	25	20
1573	50c. Type **253**	40	25
1574	1g. Gathering of slaves around fire (air)	75	50
1575	2g. As No. 1574	1·50	95
1576	3g. As No. 1574	2·30	1·40
MS1577	132×85 mm. 50c. No. 1573; 2g. No. 1575	6·50	6·00

254 Amerindian watching Europeans landing

1993. America. 500th Anniv (1992) of Discovery of America by Columbus. Multicoloured.

1578	25c. Type **254** (postage)	20	20
1579	50c. Type **254**	30	20
1580	1g. Columbus's fleet at anchor and rowing boats on shore (vert) (air)	50	40
1581	2g. As No. 1580	1·00	75
1582	3g. As No. 1580	1·60	1·20
MS1583	120×82 mm. Nos. 1580/1	7·25	6·75

255 Map of Haiti and Emblem

1995. 25th General Assembly of Organization of American States. Multicoloured.

1584	50c. Type **255**	30	20
1585	75c. Type **255**	40	30
1586	1g. Map of Americas and emblems (vert)	50	40
1587	2g. As No. 1586	1·00	75
1588	3g. As No. 1586	1·60	1·20
1589	5g. As No. 1586	2·30	1·40
MS1590	72×59 mm. 7g.50 Type **255**	4·25	3·25

256 Dove holding Flags in Beak

1995. 50th Anniv of U.N.O. Multicoloured.

1591	50c. Type **256** (postage)	35	20
1592	75c. Type **256**	45	30
1593	1g. Dove with olive branch flying over flags (air)	60	40
1594	2g. As No. 1593	1·30	75
1595	3g. As No. 1593	2·00	1·10
1596	5g. As No. 1593	3·00	1·90
MS1597	103×84 mm. 5g. Dove carrying olive branch	6·00	4·50

1996. Various stamps surch XXIIIES JEUX OLYMPIQUES LOS ANGELES 1984.

1598	2g. on 1g.25 black, blue and orange (1520) (postage)	50	40
1599	1g. on 1g.25 mult (1556) (air)	1·00	75
1600	3g. on 1g.25 mult (1535)	2·10	1·50
1601	3g. on 1g.25 mult (1477)	3·00	2·30

259 Players

1996. Olympic Games, Atlanta. Multicoloured. (a) Centenary of Volleyball.

1605	50c. Type **259**	30	20
1606	75c. Umpire and players	40	30
1607	1g. Players holding Olympic Flame	50	40
1608	2g. Players jumping for ball	1·00	75

(b) 1984 Medal Winners.

1609	3g. 400 m hurdles (U.S.A.)	60	40
1610	10g. Decathlon (gold, Great Britain)	2·00	1·40
MS1611	110×80 mm. 15g. Volleyball player	5·75	5·25

Nos. 1605/6 were issued together, se-tenant, forming a composite design of a match scene and Nos. 1607/8 a composite design of a map.

260 "Virgin and Child" (Jacopo Bellini)

1996. Christmas. Multicoloured.

1612	2g. Type **260**	40	30
1613	3g. "Adoration of the Shepherds" (Bernardo Strozzi)	60	50
1614	6g. "Virgin and Child" (Giovanni Bellini)	1·30	95
1615	10g. "Virgin and Child" (Francesco Mazzola)	2·30	1·50
1616	25g. "Adoration of the Magi" (Gentile da Fabriano)	5·75	4·00
MS1617	106×76 mm. 25g. "Nativity" (Jan de Beer)	4·25	3·75

261 Children in Street

1997. 50th Anniv (1996) of UNICEF.

1618	**261**	4g. multicoloured	60	40
1619	**261**	5g. multicoloured	70	60
1620	**261**	6g. multicoloured	85	60
1621	**261**	10g. multicoloured	1·40	1·20
1622	**261**	20g. multicoloured	3·00	2·10
MS1622a		100×70 mm. 25g. Crowd	4·25	3·75

262 Sleeping Beauty

1998. 175th Anniv (1997) of 3rd Collection of Fairy Tales by Brothers Grimm. Multicoloured.

1623	2g. Type **262**	1·00	95
1624	3g. Snow White	1·60	1·40
1625	4g. Sleeping Beauty and Prince	2·10	1·90
1626	6g. Man in bed (Water of Life)	3·00	3·00
1627	10g. Cinderella	5·75	5·25
1628	20g. Serving patient with the Water of Life	11·50	10·50
MS1629	195×150 mm. As Nos. 1623/8 but each with decorated frame and size 37×50 mm	12·00	11·00

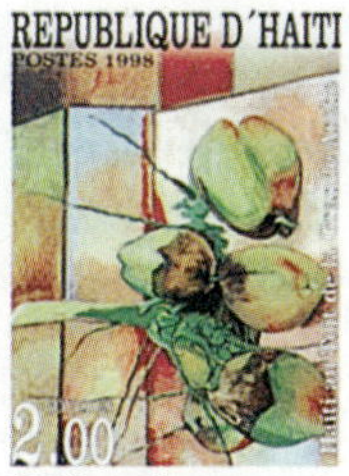

263 Cocoa Beans

1998. Grande Arche Roof Competition, Paris. "Haiti: Women and Creation". Multicoloured.

1630	2g. Type **263**	1·40	1·40
1631	3g. Swords and flags	2·10	1·90
1632	5g. Boy with model churches	3·50	3·50
1633	6g. Woman with artist's palette and brush	4·25	4·00
MS1634	80×110 mm. 15g. La Grande Arche	11·50	10·50

264 Animals, Birds and Coastline

1999. Nature Protection. Sheet 100×85 mm.

MS1635	**264** 20g. multicoloured	3·00	3·00

265 *Hyla vasta*

1999. Endangered Species. Amphibians and Reptiles. Multicoloured.

1636	2g. Type **265**	40	40
1637	2g. *Cyclura ricordii*	40	40
1638	4g. Head of *Hyla vasta*	70	70
1639	4g. Head of *Cyclura ricordiii*	70	70

266 *Priotelus roseigaster*

1999. Birds. Multicoloured.

1640	2g. Type **266**	40	40
1641	4g. *Xenoligea mantana* (inscr "Xenoligeo mantana")	70	70
1642	10g. *Phoenicophilus poliocephalus*	1·60	1·40
1643	20g. *Phoenicopterus rubber*	3·00	3·00
MS1644	120×90 mm. Nos. 1640/3	6·25	5·75

267 Diamond Sutra (868 AD) (first moveable type) (11th-century)

1999. Chinese Inventions. Multicoloured.

1645	2g. Type **267**	30	30
1646	3g. Paper making (2nd-century BC)	50	50
1647	6g. Cannon (gunpowder 9th-century)	1·00	95
1648	10g. Compass (4th-century BC)	1·70	1·50
MS1649	171×121 mm. Nos. 1645/8	3·00	3·00

268 The Nativity

269 Flight into Egypt

1999. Christmas.

1650	**268**	1g. multicoloured	10	10
1651	**268**	3g. multicoloured	40	40
1652	**268**	5g. multicoloured	70	70
1653	**269**	10g. multicoloured	1·60	1·40
1654	**269**	15g. multicoloured	2·30	2·10
1655	**269**	20g. multicoloured	3·00	2·75

270 Pirogue

2000. Tourism. Multicoloured.

1656	2g. Type **270**	40	40
1657	3g. Child	50	50
1658	4g. Bassin Zim waterfall (vert)	70	70
1659	5g. Ardadins Island (vert)	95	85
1660	6g. Gingerbread house	1·30	1·20
1661	10g. National Palace	1·70	1·50
1662	20g. Peligre Lake (vert)	2·10	1·90
MS1663	Two sheets. (a) 130×180 mm. Nos. 1656/72. (b) 78×100 mm. 25g. Sail boat (vert)	8·25	7·75

271 Open Book

2001. Air. Bicentenary of the Constitution.

1664	**271**	1g. multicoloured	20	10
1665	**271**	2g. multicoloured	40	40
1666	**271**	5g. multicoloured	95	85
1667	**271**	10g. multicoloured	1·70	1·50
1668	**271**	25g. multicoloured	2·50	2·40
1669	**271**	50g. multicoloured	3·00	3·00
MS1670		141×100 mm. 25g.×2, Toussaint Louverture; As Type **271**	5·25	4·75

272 Toussaint Louverture

2003. Death Bicentenary of Toussaint Louverture.

1671	**272**	1g. multicoloured	20	10
1672	**272**	2g. multicoloured	40	40
1673	**272**	3g. multicoloured	50	50
1674	**272**	5g. multicoloured	95	85
1675	**272**	6g. multicoloured	1·30	1·20
1676	**272**	10g. multicoloured1	1·70	1·50
MS1677		160×220 mm. **272** 15g. multicoloured. Imperf	2·10	1·90

OFFICIAL STAMPS

1960. Nos. 736/40 optd OFFICIEL.

O742	-	50c. brown and green	†	55
O743	-	50c. blue and green	†	55
O744	-	50c. black and green	†	55
O745	**127**	1g. green and red	†	75
O746	-	1g.50 pink and blue	†	1·20
MSO747		No. **MS**741 optd UNICEF+25 centimes on each stamp	†	3·25

The above were only issued precancelled.

O135 Dessalines' Statue

1962. Air. (a) Size 20½×37½ mm.

O791	**O135**	50c. sepia and blue	45	35
O792	**O135**	1g. red and blue	70	45
O793	**O135**	1g.50 blue and bistre	95	65

(b) Size 30½×40 mm.

O794	5g. green and red	2·50	2·20

PARCEL POST STAMPS

1960. Optd COLIS POSTAUX.

P725	**102**	5c. green & blk (postage)	10	10
P726	**102**	10c. red and black	20	15
P727	**102**	25c. blue and black	30	20
P728	**74**	2g.50 grey	2·40	2·20
P729	**102**	50c. orange & black (air)	45	35
P730	**101**	5g. violet and blue	3·00	2·40

P130 Arms

1961

P757	**P130**	50c. violet and bistre (postage)	45	35
P758	**P130**	1g. blue and red	70	45
P759	**P130**	2g.50 lake & grn (air)	1·80	1·30
P760	**P130**	5g. green and orange	2·30	1·50

POSTAGE DUE STAMPS

D10

1898

D63	**D10**	2c. blue	45	35
D64	**D10**	5c. brown	80	55
D65	**D10**	10c. orange	1·20	80
D66	**D10**	50c. grey	2·00	1·10

1902. Optd MAI Gt Pre 1902 in frame.

D85	2c. blue	1·30	90
D86	5c. brown	1·10	70
D87	10c. orange	1·50	75
D88	50c. grey	8·25	4·00

D23

1906

D150	**D23**	2c. red	90	50
D151	**D23**	5c. blue	2·40	2·30
D152	**D23**	10c. purple	2·40	2·30
D153	**D23**	50c. olive	8·50	5·00

1914. Optd GL O. Z. 7 FEV. 1914 in frame.

D206	**D10**	5c. brown	95	55
D207	**D10**	10c. orange	80	75
D208	**D10**	50c. grey	5·25	3·25

1914. Optd GL O. Z 7 FEV. 1914 in frame.

D209	**D 23**	2c. red	70	45
D210	**D 23**	5c. blue	1·10	65
D211	**D 23**	10c. purple	4·00	3·25
D212	**D 23**	50c. olive	7·00	4·50

D83

1951

D452	**D83**	10c. red	20	15
D453	**D83**	20c. brown	25	20
D454	**D83**	40c. green	35	35
D455	**D83**	50c. yellow	45	45

SPECIAL DELIVERY STAMP

S 86 G.P.O.

1953

E468	**S 86**	25c. red	55	40

APPENDIX

The following stamps have either been issued in excess of postal needs or have not been available to the public in reasonable quantities at face value. Such stamps may later be given full listing if there is evidence of regular postal use.

1968

Medal Winners, Winter Olympic Games, Grenoble. Postage 5, 10, 20, 25, 50c., 1g.50; Air 2g.

1969

Moon Landing of "Apollo 11". Optd on 1969 Birds issue. Nos. 1132/5. Air 50c., 1g.50, 2g.

Space Flights of "Apollo 7" and "Apollo 8". Postage 10, 15, 20, 25c.; Air 70c., 1g., 1g.25, 1g.50.

1970

Moon Mission of "Apollo 12". Postage 5, 10, 15, 20, 25, 30, 40, 50c.; Air 25, 30, 40, 50, 75c., 1g., 1g.25, 1g.50.

1971

Safe Return of "Apollo 13". Optd on 1970 "Apollo 12" issue. Postage 5, 10, 15, 20, 25, 30, 40, 50c.; Air 25, 30, 40, 50, 75c., 1g., 1g.25, 1g.50.

1972

Gold Medal Winners Olympic Games, Munich. Air 50, 75c., 1g.50, 2g.50, 5g.

1973

American and Russian Space Exploration. Postage 5, 10, 20, 25, 50c., 2g.50, 5g.; Air 50, 75c., 1g.50, 2g.50, 5g.

Moon Mission of "Apollo 17". Optd on 1973 Space Exploration issue. 50c., 2g.50, 5g.

Pt. 7

HAMBURG

A port in north-west Germany, formerly a Free City. In 1867 it joined the North German Confederation.

16 schillinge = 1 mark.

1

1859. Imperf.

1	**1**	½s. black	£110	£650
2	**1**	1s. brown	£110	90·00
3	**1**	2s. red	£110	£110
4	**1**	3s. blue	£110	£140
6	**1**	4s. green	£130	£1400
7	**1**	7s. orange	95·00	44·00
10	**1**	9s. yellow	£225	£2250

3

4

1864. Imperf.

11	**3**	1¼s. lilac	£550	£1100
15	**3**	1¼s. grey	£180	£110
17	**3**	1¼s. blue	£550	£1100
18	**4**	2½s. green	£160	£160

1864. Perf.

19	**1**	½s. black	7·00	13·00
20	**1**	1s. brown	14·00	19·00
21	**3**	1¼s. mauve	£110	11·50
25	**1**	2s. red	18·00	22·00
27	**4**	2½s. green	£130	35·00
30	**1**	3s. blue	44·00	90·00
33	**1**	4s. green	£250	44·00
34	**1**	7s. orange	£180	£130
37	**1**	7s. mauve	10·50	18·00
38	**1**	9s. yellow	31·00	£2250

5

1866. Roul.

44	**5**	1¼s. mauve	44·00	40·00
45	**5**	1½s. pink	8·75	£140

1867. Perf.

46	**1**	2½s. green	13·00	90·00

Pt. 7

HANOVER

In north-east Germany. An independent kingdom until 1866, when it was annexed by Prussia.

1850. 12 pfennige = 1 gutegroschen. 24 gutengroschen = 1 thaler.

1858. 10 (new) pfennige = 1 (new) groschen. 30 (new) groschen = 1 thaler.

2

1850. On coloured paper. Imperf.

1	**2**	1ggr. black on blue	£4500	55·00
2	**2**	1ggr. black on green	£110	26·00
3	**2**	1/30th. black on orange	£130	55·00
4	**2**	1/30th. black on red	£130	55·00
5	**2**	1/15th. black on blue	£200	90·00
6	**2**	1/10th. black on orange	£275	65·00

1853. Imperf.

18	**4**	3pf. pink	£150	£180

4

1855. With coloured network. Imperf.

10	**2**	1/10th. black and orange	£475	£300
12	**4**	3pf. pink and black	£450	£400
14	**2**	1ggr. black and green	90·00	10·50
15	**2**	1/30th. black and pink	£180	35·00
16	**2**	1/15th. black and blue	£130	80·00

5 King George V

1859. Imperf.

23	**5**	1gr. pink	8·00	2·75
25a	**5**	2gr. blue	18·00	48·00
28	**5**	3gr. yellow	£180	£110
29	**5**	3gr. brown	31·00	55·00
31	**5**	10gr. green	£275	£950

6

1860. Imperf.

32a	**6**	½gr. black	£190	£225

1863. Imperf.

34	**4**	3pf. green	£450	£1100

1864. Roul.

35a		3pf. green	35·00	65·00
36a	6	½gr. black	£300	£300
37a	5	1gr. pink	10·50	4·00
38	5	2gr. blue	£130	65·00
39a	5	3gr. brown	80·00	80·00

Pt. 16

HATAY

Hatay was returned to Turkey in June 1939.

1939. 100 santims = 40 paras = 1 kurus.

1939. Stamps of Turkey surch HATAY DEVLETI and value.

32	112	10s. on 20pa. orange	80	40
33	112	25s. on 1k. green	80	40
34	112	50s. on 2k. violet	80	40
35	112	75s. on 2½k. green	80	40
36	112	1k. on 4k. grey	40	1·20
37	112	1k. on 5k. red	80	40
38	112	1½k. on 3k. brown	1·20	55
39	112	2½k. on 4k. grey	1·60	80
40	112	5k. on 8k. blue	4·75	2·40
41	112	12½k. on 20k. green	7·00	3·50
42	112	20k. on 25k. blue	8·00	4·00

9 Map of Hatay

10 Flag of Hatay

1939

48	9	10pa. orange and blue	45	15
49	9	30pa. violet and blue	55	25
50	9	1½k. olive and blue	80	40
51	-	2½k. green	85	40
52	-	3k. blue	95	45
53	-	5k. red	1·20	55
54	10	6k. red and blue	1·30	65
55	10	7½k. red and green	1·30	80
56	10	12k. red and violet	2·00	1·20
57	10	12½k. red and blue	2·40	1·20
58	-	17½k. red	4·75	2·40
59	-	25k. olive	6·00	2·75
60	-	50k. blue	13·50	6·25

DESIGNS—HORIZ: 2½, 3, 5k. Lions of Antioch; 17½, 25, 50k. Parliament House, Antioch.

1939. Commemorating Turkish Annexation. Optd T. C. ilhak tarihi 30-6-1939.

65	9	10pa. orange and blue	65	25
66	9	30pa. violet and blue	80	40
67	9	1½k. olive and blue	80	40
68	-	2½k. green (No. 51)	1·20	55
69	-	3k. blue (No. 52)	1·30	65
70	-	5k. red (No. 53)	1·30	65
71	10	6k. red and blue	1·30	65
72	10	7½k. red and green	1·60	80
73	10	12k. red and violet	2·00	95
74	10	12½k. red and blue	2·00	1·00
75	-	17½k. red (No. 58)	4·25	2·00
76	-	25k. olive (No. 59)	8·75	4·25
77	-	50k. blue (No. 60)	17·00	9·50

POSTAGE DUE STAMPS

1939. Postage Due stamps of Turkey optd HATAY DEVLETI or surch also.

D43	D121	1k. on 2k. blue	1·60	80
D44	D121	3k. violet	3·25	1·60
D45	D121	4k. on 5k. green	3·25	1·60
D46	D121	5k. on 12k. red	4·00	2·40
D47	D121	12k. red	47·00	24·00

D11 Castle at Antioch

1939

D61	D11	1k. red	1·60	80
D62	D11	3k. brown	2·00	80
D63	D11	4k. green	2·75	80
D64	D11	5k. grey	4·00	1·20

1939. Nos. D61/4 optd T. C. ilhak tarihi 30-6-1939.

D73	1k. red	2·75	1·20
D74	3k. brown	3·25	1·20
D75	4k. green	4·00	1·60
D76	5k. grey	4·25	1·60

Pt. 22

HAWAII

A group of islands in the central Pacific, an independent kingdom till 1893 when a provisional government was set up. Annexed in 1898 by the United States. Now a State of the U.S.A.

100 cents = 1 dollar.

1

1851. Inscr "Hawaiian Postage". Imperf.

1	1	2c. blue	£750000	£340000
2	1	5c. blue	£70000	£40000
3	1	13c. blue	£35000	£30000

On Nos. 1/2 the value is expressed in words.

1852. Inscr "H.L. & US. Postage". Imperf.

4		13c. blue	£45000	£32000

3 Kamehameha III

1853. Imperf.

18	3	5c. blue	28·00	
19	3	13c. red	£275	

5

1859. Inter-island post.

9	5	1c. blue	£18000	£12000
10	5	2c. blue	£7000	£5500
12	5	1c. black	£1000	£2000
14d	5	2c. black	£1100	£800

6 Kamehameha IV

1862. Imperf.

22	6	2c. red	65·00	

7 Princess Victoria Kamamalu

1864. Perf.

27	7	1c. mauve	12·50	10·00
30	-	6c. green	34·00	12·50
31	-	18c. red	£110	45·00
41	-	2c. red	75·00	25·00
42	-	5c. blue	20·00	4·50

DESIGNS: 2c. Kamehameha IV; 5c., 6c. Portraits of Kamehameha V; 18c. H.E. Mataio Kekuanaoa.

12

1865. Inter-island post.

32	12	1c. blue	£400	
33	12	2c. blue	£400	
34	12	5c. blue on blue	£750	£1300
35	-	5c. blue on blue	£1100	£800

DESIGN: No. 35, As Type **12** but inscr "HAWAIIAN POSTAGE" on left side of frame.

16 Princess Likelike

1875

36		2c. brown	10·00	4·00
37		12c. black	75·00	39·00
38	16	1c. blue	8·00	11·50
39	16	1c. green	3·50	2·75
40b	-	2c. red	5·50	1·40
44	-	10c. black	48·00	27·00
45	-	10c. red	45·00	17·00
46	-	10c. brown	41·00	13·50
47	-	12c. lilac	£100	45·00
48	-	15c. brown	75·00	34·00
49	-	25c. purple	£170	70·00
50	-	50c. red	£225	95·00
51	-	$1 red	£275	£325

DESIGNS: 2c. King Kalakaua; 10c. Same in uniform; 12c. Prince Leleiohoku; 15c. Queen Kapiolani; 25c. Statute of Kamehameha I; 50c. King Lunalilo; $1, Queen Emma Kaleleonalani.

22 Princess (later Queen) Liliuokalani

1890

53	22	2c. violet	5·75	1·70

1893. Stamps of 1864, 1875 and 1889, optd Provisional GOVT. 1893.

54	7	1c. mauve	10·00	14·00
55	16	1c. blue	9·75	14·00
56	16	1c. green	2·00	3·50
57	-	2c. brown	13·50	27·00
58	22	2c. violet	1·70	2·00
60	-	5c. blue	8·50	3·50
61	-	6c. green	20·00	34·00
62	-	10c. black	12·50	20·00
64	-	12c. black	12·50	25·00
65	-	12c. lilac	£190	£275
66	-	25c. purple	36·00	55·00
67	-	2c. red (No. 41)	90·00	£100
68	-	2c. red (No. 40b)	1·70	3·25
70	-	10c. red	20·00	34·00
71	-	10c. brown	10·00	17·00
73	-	15c. brown	27·00	41·00
74	-	18c. red	34·00	48·00
75	-	50c. red	85·00	£130
76	-	$1 red	£150	£225

24 Arms

26 Statue of King Kamehameha I

1894

77	24	1c. orange	2·75	1·70
78	-	2c. brown	3·25	90
79	26	5c. red	5·50	2·00
80	-	10c. green	8·50	6·25
81	-	12c. blue	17·00	25·00
82	-	25c. blue	25·00	20·00
89	24	1c. green	2·00	1·70
90	-	2c. pink	1·90	1·40
91	26	5c. blue	9·00	4·00

DESIGNS—HORIZ: 2c. Honolulu; 12c. "Arawa" (steamer). VERT: 10c. Star and palms; 25c. President S. B. Dole.

OFFICIAL STAMPS

O30 Secretary L. A. Thurston

1896

O83	O30	2c. green	55·00	25·00
O84	O30	5c. brown	55·00	25·00
O85	O30	6c. blue	55·00	25·00
O86	O30	10c. red	55·00	25·00
O87	O30	12c. orange	55·00	25·00
O88	O30	25c. violet	55·00	25·00

Pt. 1

HELIGOLAND

An island off the N. coast of Germany, ceded to that country by Great Britain in 1890.

1867. 16 schillings = 1 mark.
1875. 100 pfennig = 1 mark.

Many of the Heligoland stamps found in old collections and the majority of those offered at a small fraction of catalogue prices today, are reprints which have very little value.

1

1867. Perf (½, 1, 2 and 6 sch. also roul).

3	1	2sch. red and green	13·00	60·00
4	1	6sch. green and red	15·00	£250
5	1	¼sch. green and red	28·00	£1500
6b	1	½sch. green and red	£100	£160
7	1	¾sch. red and green	38·00	£1100
8a	1	1sch. red and green	£130	£190
9	1	1½sch. green and red	75·00	£250

2

3

4

5

1875

10	2	1pf. (¼d.) green and red	15·00	£500
11	2	2pf. (½d.) red and green	15·00	£600
12a	3	3pf. (⅝d.) green, red yellow	£160	£850
13	2	5pf. (¾d.) green and red	18·00	19·00
14a	2	10pf. (1½d.) red and green	15·00	22·00
15b	3	20pf. (2½d.) green, red and yellow	20·00	29·00
16	2	25pf. (3d.) green and red	20·00	28·00
17	2	50pf. (6d.) red and green	22·00	40·00
18	4	1m. (1s.) green, red and black	£150	£200
19	5	5m. (5s.) green, red and black	£190	£950

Pt. 17

HOI-HAO (HOIHOW)

An Indo-Chinese post office in China, closed in 1922.

1901. 100 centimes = 1 franc.
1918. 100 cents = 1 piastre.

HOI HAO
州 瓊

(1)

1902. Stamps of Indo-China "Tablet" key-type, optd with T 1. Chinese characters read "HOI-HAO" and are the same on every value.

1	D	1c. black on blue	2·30	2·75
2	D	2c. brown on yellow	5·00	3·75
3	D	4c. red on grey	3·25	3·25
4	D	5c. green	2·75	4·50
5	D	10c. black on lilac	6·50	7·75
6	D	15c. blue	£1300	£550
7	D	15c. grey	2·50	2·00
8	D	20c. red on green	28·00	30·00
9	D	25c. black on red	9·75	6·00
10	D	30c. brown	54·00	56·00
11	D	40c. red on yellow	44·00	54·00
12	D	50c. red on rose	42·00	60·00
13	D	75c. brown on orange	£200	£180
14	D	1f. olive	£650	£525
15	D	5f. mauve on lilac	£550	£450

1903. Stamps of Indo-China, "Tablet" key-type, surch as T 1. Chinese characters indicate the value and differ for each denomination.

16	1c. black on blue	1·80	2·25
17	2c. brown on yellow	3·00	3·25
18	4c. red on grey	2·75	5·50
19	5c. green	2·50	6·00

20	10c. red	2·50	2·50
21	15c. grey	2·50	5·00
22	20c. red on green	8·25	13·50
23	25c. blue	2·30	4·50
24	25c. black on red	6·00	7·25
25	30c. brown	4·00	7·25
26	40c. red on yellow	58·00	70·00
27	50c. red on rose	22·00	65·00
28	50c. brown on blue	£120	£120
29	75c. brown on orange	54·00	65·00
30	1f. olive	75·00	80·00
31	5f. mauve on lilac	£160	£160

1906. Stamps of Indo-China surch HOI-HAO and with value in Chinese.

32	**8**	1c. olive	3·25	4·75
33	**8**	2c. red on yellow	3·00	4·00
34	**8**	4c. mauve on blue	3·25	4·50
35	**8**	5c. green	6·00	7·75
36	**8**	10c. red	5·50	7·75
37	**8**	15c. brown on blue	6·50	7·75
38	**8**	20c. red on green	7·50	10·00
39	**8**	25c. blue	7·75	11·50
40	**8**	30c. brown on cream	13·00	14·50
41	**8**	35c. black on yellow	14·50	25·00
42	**8**	40c. black on grey	11·00	32·00
43	**8**	50c. brown	22·00	34·00
44	**D**	75c. brown on orange	50·00	60·00
45	**8**	1f. green	50·00	55·00
46	**8**	2f. brown on yellow	55·00	60·00
47	**D**	5f. mauve on lilac	£110	£120
48	**8**	10f. red on green	£130	£130

1908. Native types of Indo-China surch HOIHAO (1 to 50c.) or HOI-HAO (others) and with value in Chinese.

49	**10**	1c. black and olive	75	55
50	**10**	2c. black and brown	85	1·10
51	**10**	4c. black and blue	1·30	1·80
52	**10**	5c. black and green	1·50	2·50
53	**10**	10c. black and red	2·30	3·75
54	**10**	15c. black and violet	5·50	8·75
55	**11**	20c. black and violet	5·50	11·00
56	**11**	25c. black and blue	5·25	11·50
57	**11**	30c. black and brown	5·75	13·00
58	**11**	35c. black and green	7·25	13·00
59	**11**	40c. black and brown	6·00	12·00
60	**11**	50c. black and red	7·75	18·00
61	**12**	75c. black and orange	11·00	20·00
62	**12**	1f. black and red	28·00	40·00
63	**12**	2f. black and green	50·00	60·00
64	**12**	5f. black and blue	80·00	£100
65	**12**	10f. black and violet	£120	£120

1919. Stamps as last surch in addition with value in figures and words.

66	**10**	⅖c. on 1c. black and olive	1·30	4·75
67	**10**	⅘c. on 2c. black and brown	55	3·50
68	**10**	1⅗c. on 4c. black and blue	2·00	5·00
69	**10**	2c. on 5c. black and green	1·50	3·00
70	**10**	4c. on 10c. black and red	3·25	5·50
71	**10**	6c. on 15c. black and violet	2·30	2·50
72	**11**	8c. on 20c. black and violet	4·00	6·75
73	**11**	10c. on 25c. black and blue	9·00	11·00
74	**11**	12c. on 30c. black & brown	2·75	5·50
75	**11**	14c. on 35c. black and green	3·75	5·75
76	**11**	16c. on 40c. black & brown	2·75	6·50
77	**11**	20c. on 50c. black and red	4·75	6·25
78	**12**	30c. on 75c. black & orange	4·25	7·75
79	-	40c. on 1f. black and red	10·50	19·00
80	-	80c. on 2f. black and green	36·00	40·00
81	-	2p. on 5f. black and blue	55·00	90·00
82	-	4p. on 10f. black and violet	£140	£170

Pt. 15

HONDURAS

A republic of C. America, independent since 1838.

1866. 8 reales = 1 peso.
1878. 100 centavos = 1 peso.
1933. 100 centavos = 1 lempira.

1 Seal of Honduras

1866. Imperf.

1	**1**	2r. black on green	65	
2	**1**	2r. black on red	65	

5 Pres. F. Morazan

1878. Perf.

31	**5**	1c. violet	60	60
32	**5**	2c. brown	60	60
33	**5**	½r. black	4·50	60
34	**5**	1r. green	25·00	1·20
35	**5**	2r. blue	3·75	4·75
36	**5**	4r. red	5·00	9·25
37	**5**	1p. orange	6·25	19·00

6

1890

45	**6**	1c. green	35	35
46	**6**	2c. red	35	35
47	**6**	5c. blue	35	35
48	**6**	10c. orange	50	50
49	**6**	20c. bistre	50	50
50	**6**	25c. red	50	50
51	**6**	30c. violet	60	70
52	**6**	40c. blue	60	95
53	**6**	50c. brown	75	95
54	**6**	75c. green	75	2·40
55	**6**	1p. lake	85	3·00

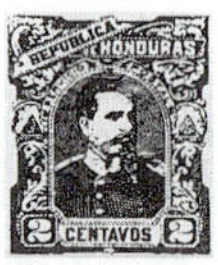

8 President Bogran

1891

56	**8**	1c. blue	35	35
57	**8**	2c. brown	35	35
58	**8**	5c. green	35	35
59	**8**	10c. red	35	35
60	**8**	20c. lake	35	35
61	**8**	25c. red	50	70
62	**8**	30c. grey	50	70
63	**8**	40c. green	50	70
64	**8**	50c. sepia	60	95
65	**8**	75c. violet	60	1·60
66	**8**	1p. brown	60	1·90
67	-	2p. black and brown	1·90	6·00
68	-	5p. black and violet	1·90	7·25
69	-	10p. black and green	1·90	7·25

DESIGN (LARGER): 2, 5, 10p. Pres. Bogran facing left.

10

1892. 400th Anniv of Discovery of America.

70	**10**	1c. grey	75	60
71	**10**	2c. blue	75	60
72	**10**	5c. green	75	60
73	**10**	10c. green	75	60
74	**10**	20c. red	75	60
75	**10**	25c. brown	85	70
76	**10**	30c. blue	85	70
77	**10**	40c. orange	85	1·10
78	**10**	50c. brown	1·10	1·10
79	**10**	75c. lake	1·20	1·60
80	**10**	1p. violet	1·20	1·70

11 Gen. Cabanas

1893

81	**11**	1c. green	35	1·80
82	**11**	2c. red	35	1·80
83	**11**	5c. blue	35	1·80
84	**11**	10c. brown	35	1·80
85	**11**	20c. brown	35	1·80
86	**11**	25c. blue	35	1·80
87	**11**	30c. orange	60	1·80
88	**11**	40c. black	60	1·80
89	**11**	50c. sepia	60	1·80
90	**11**	75c. violet	75	1·80
91	**11**	1p. brown	75	2·20

12

1895

92	**12**	1c. red	35	35
93	**12**	2c. blue	35	35
94	**12**	5c. grey	35	60
95	**12**	10c. lake	50	60
96	**12**	20c. lilac	50	70
97	**12**	30c. lilac	50	1·10
98	**12**	50c. brown	60	1·60
99	**12**	1p. green	75	1·90

13 President Arias

1896

100	**13**	1c. blue	35	50
101	**13**	2c. brown	35	50
102	**13**	5c. purple	35	50
103	**13**	10c. red	50	50
104	**13**	20c. green	1·00	60
105	**13**	30c. blue	85	85
106	**13**	50c. lake	1·20	1·20
107	**13**	1p. sepia	1·70	1·80

14 Steam Train

1898

108	**14**	1c. brown	50	35
109	**14**	2c. red	50	35
110	**14**	5c. blue	50	35
111	**14**	6c. purple	85	60
112	**14**	10c. blue	90	60
113	**14**	20c. bistre	1·90	1·70
114	**14**	50c. orange	4·00	3·75
115	**14**	1p. green	4·75	5·50

16 General Santos Guardiola

1903

118	**16**	1c. green	50	25
119	**16**	2c. red	50	35
120	**16**	5c. blue	50	35
121	**16**	6c. lilac	50	35
122	**16**	10c. brown	50	35
123	**16**	20c. blue	60	50
124	**16**	50c. red	1·60	1·30
125	**16**	1p. orange	1·60	1·30

17 President Medina

1907. Perf or imperf.

127	**17**	1c. green	25	25
128a	**17**	2c. red	35	35
129	**17**	5c. blue	35	35
130	**17**	6c. violet	50	35
131	**17**	10c. sepia	50	50
132	**17**	20c. blue	1·10	95
133	**17**	50c. red	1·40	1·30
134	**17**	1p. orange	1·90	1·80
136	**17**	1c. black	21·00	21·00

1910. Surch in figures.

137	1 on 20c. blue	9·25	7·25
138	5 on 20c. blue	9·25	7·25
139	10 on 20c. blue	9·25	7·25

20

1911

140	**20**	1c. violet	50	25
141	**20**	2c. green	50	25
142	**20**	5c. red	50	25
143	**20**	6c. blue	60	35
144	**20**	10c. blue	75	50
145	**20**	20c. yellow	75	60
146	**20**	50c. brown	2·50	2·20
147	**20**	1p. olive	3·00	2·40

1911. Optd XC Aniversario de la Independencia.

157	2c. green	22·00	22·00

23

1912. Election of President Manuel Bonilla.

158	**23**	1c. red	15·00	14·50

1913. 90th Anniv of Independence. Surch 2 CENTAVOS.

159	**20**	2c. on 1c. violet	1·60	95

1913. Surch in figures and words.

161	2c. on 1c. violet	8·75	7·25
162	2c. on 10c. blue	3·50	3·00
163	2c. on 20c. yellow	8·75	8·50
164	5c. on 1c. violet	2·40	70
165	5c. on 10c. blue	3·75	2·20
166	6c. on 1c. violet	3·75	3·00

26 Gen. T. Sierra

27 Gen. M. Bonilla

1913

167	**26**	1c. brown	25	25
168	**26**	2c. red	35	25
169	**27**	5c. blue	50	25
170	**27**	5c. blue	50	25
171	**27**	6c. violet	60	35
172	**27**	6c. mauve	50	35
173	**26**	10c. blue	1·00	95
174	**26**	10c. brown	1·60	1·60
175	**26**	20c. brown	1·20	1·10
176	**27**	50c. red	2·50	2·40
177	**27**	1p. green	3·00	3·00

1914. Surch.

178	**26**	1c. on 2c. red	1·00	95
179	**26**	5c. on 2c. red	1·60	1·20

180	**27**	5c. on 6c. violet	2·50	2·40
181	**26**	5c. on 10c. brown	3·00	2·20
182	**26**	10c. on 2c. red	2·50	2·40
184	**27**	10c. on 6c. violet	3·00	3·00
185	**27**	10c. on 50c. red	8·00	6·00

32 Railway Bridge over River Ulua at Pimienta

1915. Dated "1915".

186	**32**	1c. brown	25	25
187	**32**	2c. red	25	25
188	-	5c. blue	35	25
189	-	6c. violet	50	25
190	**32**	10c. blue	1·00	25
191	**32**	20c. brown	1·60	1·20
192	-	50c. red	1·90	1·80
193	-	1p. green	3·00	3·00

DESIGN: 5c., 6c., 50c., 1p. Bonilla Theatre.

34 Pres. Francisco Bertrand

1916

194	**34**	1c. orange	2·50	2·40

1918. No. O206 optd CORRIENTE and bar.

195	5c. blue	2·50	1·80

36 Statue of Francisco Morazan

1919. Dated "1919" at top.

196	**36**	1c. brown	25	25
197	**36**	2c. red	35	25
198	**36**	5c. red	35	25
199	**36**	6c. mauve	35	25
200	**36**	10c. blue	35	35
201	**36**	15c. blue	1·00	25
202	**36**	15c. violet	75	25
203	**36**	20c. brown	1·20	35
204	**36**	50c. brown	5·00	3·00
205	**36**	1p. green	9·25	24·00

36a

1920. Assumption of Power by Gen. R. L. Gutierrez.

206	**36a**	2c. red	3·00	3·00
207	**36a**	2c. gold (51×40 mm)	15·00	14·50
208	**36a**	2c. silver (51×40 mm)	15·00	14·50
209	**36a**	2c. red (51×40 mm)	15·00	14·50

1921. As T 36, but dated "1920" at top.

210	**36**	6c. purple	12·50	6·00

1922. Surch VALE SEIS CTS.

211	6c. on 2c. red	60	60

1923. Surch HABILITADO VALE and value in words and figures.

212	$0.10 on 1c. brown	1·90	1·80
213	$0.50 on 2c. red	2·50	2·40
214	1p. on 5c. red	4·25	4·25

39 Dionisio de Herrera

1923

215	**39**	1c. olive	35	25
216	**39**	2c. red	50	25
217	**39**	6c. purple	50	25
218	**39**	10c. blue	50	25
219	**39**	20c. brown	1·00	50
220	**39**	50c. red	2·20	1·30
221	**39**	1p. green	5·00	3·50

40 M. Paz Baraona

1925. Inaug of President Baraona. Imperf or perf.

222A	**40**	1c. blue	2·50	2·40
224B	**40**	1c. red	11·00	11·00
225B	**40**	1c. brown	11·00	11·00

1925. Air. Nos. 186/93 optd AERO CORREO or surch also.

227	5c. blue	£110	£110
229	10c. blue	£225	£225
231	20c. brown	£225	£225
233	50c. red	£550	£350
234	1p. green	£750	£700
235	25c. on 1c. brown	£160	£160
236	25c. on 5c. blue	£275	£275
236c	25c. on 10c. blue	£84000	
237	25c. on 20c. brown	£250	£250

1926. Optd Acuerdo Mayo 3 de 1926 HABILITADO.

238	**36**	6c. mauve	1·60	1·30

1926. Optd HABILITADO 1926.

242	**32**	2c. red	35	35
243	**36**	2c. red	35	35

1926. Optd 1926.

239	-	6c. violet (No. 189)	2·75	2·75
240	**36**	6c. violet	3·00	3·00

1926. Surch Vale 6 Cts. 1926 and bar.

243d	6c. on 10c. blue	60	25

1927. Surch vale 6 cts. 1927 and bar.

244		6c. on 15c. violet	1·00	95
245	**32**	6c. on 20c. brown	1·00	95
246	**36**	6c. on 20c. brown	75	70

47 Copan Ruins

1927. Various designs as T 47.

247	-	1c. blue (Road)	35	25
248	**47**	2c. red	35	25
249	-	5c. purple (Pine tree)	35	25
250	-	5c. blue (Pine tree)	20·00	8·50
251	-	6c. black (Palace)	1·00	70
252	-	6c. blue (Palace)	1·00	60
253	-	10c. blue (P. Leiva)	1·00	25
254	-	15c. blue (Pres. Soto)	1·20	60
255	-	20c. blue (Lempira)	1·60	70
256	-	30c. brown (Map)	2·00	1·20
257	-	50c. green (Pres. Lindo)	3·25	1·90
258	-	1p. red (Columbus)	6·25	3·00

50 President Colindres and Vice-President Chavez

1929. Installation of President Colindres.

259	**50**	1c. lake	3·75	3·50
260	-	2c. green	3·75	3·50

DESIGN—VERT: 2c. Pres. Colindres.

51a L. Garay (Pilot)

1929. Air. Planned Flight from New York to Honduras.

260a	**51a**	50c. carmine	2·75	2·40

1929. Air. No. 260a surch.

260b	50c.+5c. carmine	60	35
260c	50c.+10c. carmine	75	50
260d	50c.+15c. carmine	1·00	60
260e	50c.+20c. carmine	1·40	95

The flight did not take place, however, the stamps were sold at the post office and had validity. The face value was for the pilot and the premium for the Department of Public Health for a tuberculosis hospital.

1929. Air. (a) Surch Servicio aereo Vale, value and 1929.

261	**39**	25c. on 50c. red	6·25	4·75
262	**39**	5c. on 20c. brown	1·90	1·80
263	**39**	10c. on 50c. red	3·00	2·40
264	**39**	15c. on 1p. green	5·00	4·75

(b) Surch Servicio Aereo Internacional 1929 and value.

265	5c. on 10c. blue	75	70
266	20c. on 50c. red	1·50	1·40

1929. Herrera Monument type, dated "1924–1928". Surch Vale 1 cts. XI 1929.

267	1c. on 6c. mauve	1·00	95

1929. Nos. 247/58 optd 1929a1930.

268	-	1c. blue	35	25
269	**47**	2c. red	60	35
270	-	5c. purple	50	35
271	-	5c. blue	1·40	95
272	-	6c. black	3·00	2·75
273	-	6c. blue	50	25
274	-	10c. blue	50	25
275	-	15c. blue	60	35
276	-	20c. blue	60	50
277	-	30c. brown	1·00	70
278	-	50c. green	2·50	1·20
279	-	1p. red	6·25	3·00

1930. Air. No. O264 optd HABILITADO Servicio Aereo Internacional 1930.

281	50c. green and yellow	1·60	1·60

1930. Air. Surch Servicio Aereo Internacional Vale, value and 1930.

282	**39**	5c. on 10c. blue	75	70
284	**39**	5c. on 20c. brown	£160	£160
285	**39**	10c. on 20c. brown	1·00	95
287	-	25c. on 50c. red (No. 192)	1·40	1·30

1930. Air. Surch Vale and value in addition in large letters and figures.

290	**39**	10c. on 5c. on 20c. brown (No. 284)	1·20	1·20
291	**39**	10c. on 10c. on 20c. brown (No. 285)	£120	£120
292	-	50c. on 25c. on 1p. green (No. 193)	5·50	5·50

1930. Air. Surch Servicio aereo Vale, value and Marzo–1930.

293	**39**	5c. on 10c. blue	75	60
294	**39**	15c. on 20c. brown	1·00	70
295	-	20c. on 50c. red (No. 192)	1·50	1·30

1930. Surch Vale, value and 1930.

297	**39**	1c. on 10c. blue	60	50
298	**39**	2c. on 10c. blue	60	50

1930. Nos. O259/60 optd Habilitado para el servicio publico 1930.

299	-	1c. blue	75	70
300	**O50**	2c. red	1·50	1·40

1930. Air. Surch Servicio aereo Vale 5 centavos oro Mayo.

301	**39**	5c. on 20c. brown	1·90	1·80

1930. Air. Nos. O264/5 optd. HABILITADO Servicio Aereo MAYO 1930.

302	20c. blue	1·90	1·80
303	50c. green and yellow	1·90	1·80
304	1p. red	2·50	2·40

1930. Optd Habilitado julio.–1930.

305	**32**	1c. brown	1·20	1·20
306	**36**	1c. brown	21·00	21·00
307	**36**	20c. brown	21·00	21·00
308	**36**	$0.50 on 2c. red (No. 213)	£120	£120
309	**39**	1c. olive	50	35
310	**39**	2c. red	1·20	1·20

66 Title Page, First Issue Government Gazette

1930. Newspaper Centenary.

311	**66**	2c. blue	1·20	1·20
312	**66**	2c. orange	1·20	1·20
313	**66**	2c. red	1·20	1·20

67 National Palace, Tegucigalpa

1930. Air.

314	**67**	5c. yellow	60	35
315	**67**	10c. red	1·10	70
316	**67**	15c. green	1·50	95
317	**67**	20c. violet	1·70	85
318	**67**	1p. brown	6·25	5·50

68 Pres. Baraona

69 Amapala

1931

319	**68**	1c. sepia	70	25
320	-	2c. red	70	25
321	-	5c. violet	85	25
322	-	6c. green	85	25
323	**69**	10c. brown	1·40	35
324	-	15c. blue	1·60	35
325	-	20c. black	3·25	50
326	-	50c. olive	4·25	1·90
327	-	1p. slate	8·75	3·25

DESIGNS—As Type **68**: 2c. Pres. Bonilla; 15c. Copan Ruins; 20c. Columbus. As Type **69**: 5c. Lake Yojoa; 6c. Tegucigalpa Palace; 50c. Discovery of America; 1p. Loarq Bridge at Loarq.

1931. Nos. 319/27 and 314/18 optd T.S.de.C.

328	**68**	1c. sepia (postage)	50	35
329	-	2c. red	75	35
330	-	5c. violet	85	50
331	-	6c. green	85	50
332	**69**	10c. brown	1·20	50
333	-	15c. blue	1·40	70
334	-	20c. black	2·50	70
335	-	50c. olive	7·50	6·00
336	-	1p. slate	9·50	8·50
337	**67**	5c. yellow (air)	3·75	3·50
338	**67**	10c. red	5·50	5·50
339	**67**	15c. green	9·25	9·00
339a	**67**	20c. violet	9·25	9·00
339b	**67**	1p. brown	19·00	18·00

1931. Air. Surch Servicio aereo interior Vale 15 cts Octubre 1931.

340	**39**	15c. on 20c.	5·00	3·50
341	-	15c. on 1p. (No. O265)	7·50	6·00
342	**36**	15c. on 20c. (No. O218)	7·50	6·00
343	-	15c. on 50c. (No. O210)	7·50	6·00
344a	**32**	15c. on 20c. (No. O209)	10·00	9·75
344c	**39**	15c. on 20c. (No. O226)	4·25	4·00
346	**36**	15c. on 50c. (No. O219)	4·75	3·75

Nos. 342/3 come with or without the original OFICIAL overprint obliterated.

1932. Air. Surch S.–Aereo Vl. 15 cts. XI 1931.

347	**39**	15c. on 20c. brown	5·00	4·25
348	**36**	15c. on 50c. (No. O219)	5·00	4·25
349	-	15c. on 50c. (No. O264)	4·75	4·00
350	-	15c. on 1p. (No. O265)	3·75	3·00

1932. Air. Nos. O328/36 optd Servicio Aereo Exterior. Habilitado X. 1931.

350c	**O70**	1c. blue	50	50
350d	**O70**	2c. purple	1·10	1·10
350e	**O70**	5c. olive	1·40	1·30
350f	**O70**	6c. red	1·40	1·30
350g	**O70**	10c. green	1·60	1·60
350h	**O70**	15c. brown	2·75	2·40
350i	**O70**	20c. brown	2·75	2·40
350j	**O70**	50c. violet	2·00	1·90
350k	**O70**	1p. orange	2·75	2·40

1932. Nos. O223/25 surch Aereo interior VALE 15 Cts. 1932.

351	**39**	15c. on 2c. red	1·00	95
352	**39**	15c. on 6c. purple	1·00	95
353	**39**	15c. on 10c. blue	1·00	95

78 Pres. Carias and Vice-Pres. Williams

1933. Inauguration of Pres. Carias.

355	**78**	2c. red	75	60
356	**78**	6c. green	1·00	70

357	78	10c. blue	1·20	85
358	78	15c. orange	1·50	95

79 Flag of the Race

1933. 441st Anniv of Departure of Columbus from Palos.

359	79	2c. blue	90	70
360	79	6c. yellow	1·10	85
361	79	10c. yellow	1·40	1·10
362	79	15c. violet	1·90	1·40
363	79	50c. red	7·50	6·00
364	79	1l. green	12·50	12·00

80 Pres. T. Carias

1935. Inscr as in T 80.

365	-	1c. green	60	25
366	80	2c. red	60	25
367	-	5c. blue	60	35
368	-	6c. brown	60	35

DESIGNS: 1c. Masonic Temple, Tegucigalpa; 5c. National Flag; 6c. Pres. T. E. Palma.

82 Tegucigalpa

1935. Air. Inscr as in T 82.

369		8c. blue	25	25
370	82	10c. grey	35	25
371	-	15c. olive	75	25
372	-	20c. green	1·20	60
373	-	40c. brown	1·40	35
374	-	50c. yellow	12·50	4·75
375	-	1l. green	4·50	3·50

DESIGNS: 8c. G.P.O. and Congress Building; 15c. Map of Honduras; 20c. Presidential Palace and Mayol Railway Bridge; 40c. Different view of Tegucigalpa; 50c. Great horned owl; 1l. National Arms.

84 President Carias and Carias Bridge

1937. Re-election of President Carias.

376	84	6c. red and olive	1·20	60
377	84	21c. green and violet	2·50	1·20
378	84	46c. orange and brown	3·00	2·20
379	84	55c. blue and black	5·00	3·50

85 Book of the Constitution and Flags of U.S. and Honduras

1937. Air. 150th Anniv of U.S. Constitution.

380	85	46c. multicoloured	3·00	1·80

86 Comayagua Cathedral

1937. Air. 400th Anniv of Comayagua.

381	86	2c. red	35	25
382	-	8c. blue	75	35
383	-	15c. black	1·10	70
384	-	50c. brown	6·75	3·00

DESIGNS: 8c. Founding of Comayagua; 15c. Portraits of Caceres and Carias; 50c. Lintel of Royal Palace.

90 Arms of Honduras

91 Copan Ruins

1939. Dated "1939 1942".

385	90	1c. yellow (postage)	25	25
386	-	2c. red	25	25
387	-	3c. red	35	25
388	-	5c. orange	50	35
389	-	8c. blue	60	50

DESIGNS: 2c. Central District Palace; 3c. Map of Honduras; 5c. Choluteca Bridge; 8c. National flag.

390	91	10c. brown (air)	35	10
391	-	15c. blue	50	10
392	-	21c. slate	85	10
393	-	30c. green	1·10	25
394	-	40c. violet	1·90	25
395	-	46c. brown	1·90	1·10
396	-	55c. green	2·40	1·40
397	-	66c. black	3·75	2·10
398	-	1l. olive	4·25	1·30
399	-	2l. red	6·25	4·25

DESIGNS: 15c. Pres. Carias; 21c. Mayan Temple; 30c. J. C. del Valle; 40c. The Presidency; 46c. Statue of Lempira; 55c. Suyapa Church; 66c. J. T. Reyes; 1l. Choluteca Hospital; 2l. R. Rosa.

92 Flags of Honduras, U.S.A., and Francisco Morazan

1940. Air. 50th Anniv of Pan-American Union. Sheet 130×114 mm containing T 92 and similar multicoloured designs with different inset portraits.

MS399a 14c. Type 92; 16c. Washington, J.C. del Valle; 40c. Bolivar		5·50	5·50

1940. Air. Dedication of Columbus Memorial Lighthouse. Official stamps optd Correo Aereo Habilitado para Servicio Publico Pro-Faro-Colon-1940.

400	O92	2c. blue and green	25	25
401	O92	5c. blue and orange	35	35
402	O92	8c. blue and brown	35	35
403	O92	15c. blue and red	75	70
404	O92	46c. blue and olive	1·00	95
405	O92	50c. blue and violet	1·20	1·20
406	O92	1l. blue and brown	5·00	4·75
407	O92	2l. blue and red	11·00	11·00

97 Francisco Morazan

1941. Obligatory Tax. Death Centenary of Gen. Morazan.

408	97	1c. brown	60	25

98 Red Cross

1941. Obligatory Tax. Red Cross.

409	98	1c. blue and red	35	25

1941. Air. Official stamps optd Habilitada para el Servicio Publico 1941.

410	O92	5c. blue and orange	5·00	35
411	O92	8c. blue and brown	7·50	35

1941. Air. Official stamps surch Rehabilitada para el Servicio Publico 1941 Vale and value in words.

412	3c. on 2c. blue and green	60	35
413	8c. on 2c. blue and green	75	60
414	8c. on 15c. blue and red	75	25
415	8c. on 46c. blue & olive	1·20	70
416	8c. on 50c. blue & violet	1·50	70
417	8c. on 1l. blue & brown	2·00	1·40
418	8c. on 2l. blue and red	2·50	2·20

1942. Air. Surch Correo Aereo and value.

419 8c. on 15c. blue (No. 391)	1·20	35
420 16c. on 46c. brown (No. 395)	1·20	35

102 Morazan's Birthplace **103** Tomb

1942. Air. Death Centenary of Gen. Morazan.

421	-	2c. orange	25	10
422	-	5c. blue	25	10
423	102	8c. purple	25	10
424	103	14c. black	50	35
425	-	16c. olive	25	25
426	-	21c. blue	1·60	1·20
427	-	1l. blue	4·25	3·50
428	-	2l. brown	11·00	10·50

DESIGNS—HORIZ: 2c. Commemoration plate; 5c. Battle of La Trinidad; 16c. Morazan's monument (as in Type **36**); 21c. Church where Morazan was baptised; 1l. Arms of C. American Federation. VERT: 2l. Morazan.

105 Coat of Arms **106** Western Hemisphere

1943. Air.

429	105	1c. green	25	25
430	-	2c. blue	25	25
431	-	5c. green	50	25
432	-	6c. green	35	25
433	-	8c. purple	35	25
434	-	10c. brown	50	25
435	-	15c. red	50	25
436	-	16c. red	60	25
437	-	21c. blue	1·00	25
438	-	30c. brown	75	25
439	-	40c. red	75	25
440	-	55c. black	1·50	85
441	-	1l. green	2·50	2·20
442	106	2l. lake	8·00	5·50
443	-	5l. orange	20·00	19·00

DESIGNS—HORIZ: 2c. National flag; 5c. Cattle; 8c. Rosario; 15c. Tobacco plant; 21c. Orchid; 30c. Oranges; 40c. Wheat; 5l. Map of Honduras. VERT: 6c. Banana Tree; 10c. Pine tree; 16c. Sugar cane; 55c. Coconut palms; 1l. Maize.

114 Agricultural College

1944. Air. Inauguration of Pan-American Agricultural College.

444	114	21c. green	60	35

1944. Optd HABILITADO 1944-45.

445	90	1c. yellow	50	50
446	-	2c. red (No. 386)	1·60	95

1945. Air. Surch Correo Aereo HABILITADO Acd. No 798-1945 and value.

447		1c. on 50c. (No. 384)	10	10
448	86	2c. on 2c. red	10	10
449	-	8c. on 15c. (No. 383)	25	25
450	91	10c. on 10c. brown	60	50
451	-	15c. on 15c. (No. 391)	35	25
452	-	30c. on 21c. (No. 392)	7·50	4·75
453	-	40c. on 40c. (No. 394)	3·00	1·70
454	-	1l. on 46c. (No. 395)	3·00	2·40
455	-	2l. on 66c. (No. 397)	7·50	4·75

1945. Air. Allied Victory in Europe. MS399a optd VICTORIA DE LAS NACIONES UNIDAS ALEMANIA SE RINDE INCONDICIONALMENTE 8 DE MAYO DE 1945 ACDO. No. 1231 QUE AUTORIZA LA CONTRAMARCA.

MS455a 103×114 mm	6·25	4·75

117 Flag, mother and child

1945. Obligatory Tax. Red Cross.

456	117	1c. brown and red	35	25
456a	-	1c. red and brown	35	25

DESIGN: No. 456a, Red Cross.

118 Arms of Honduras

1946. Air. Coats of Arms.

457	118	1c. red	25	25
458	-	2c. orange	25	25
459	-	5c. violet	35	25
461	-	15c. purple	1·00	25
462	-	21c. blue	1·20	35
463	-	1l. green	4·25	1·90
464	-	2l. grey	7·50	3·50

ARMS: 2c. Von Gracias and Trujillo; 5c. Comayagua and S. J. de Olancho; 15c. Honduras Province and S. J. de Puerto Caballos; 21c. Comayagua and Tencoa; 1l. Jerez de la Frontera de Choluteca and San Pedro de Zula; 2l. San Miguel de Heredia de Tegucigalpa.

119 Broken Column and F. D. Roosevelt

1946. Air. Allied Victory over Japan and Death of Pres. Roosevelt. (a) Inscr "F.D.R.".

460	119	8c. brown	1·20	60

(b) Inscr "FRANKLIN D. ROOSEVELT".

465 8c. brown	75	35

120 Honduras and Copan Antiquities

1947. Air. 1st International Conference of Caribbean Archaeologists. Various frames.

466	120	16c. green	35	25
467	120	22c. yellow	60	35
468	120	40c. orange	1·20	95
469	120	1l. blue	1·50	1·20
470	120	2l. mauve	6·25	4·75
471	120	5l. brown	15·00	11·00

121 Flag and Arms of Honduras **122** Galvez, Carias and Lozano

123 National Stadium **124** President Galvez

1949. Air. Inauguration of President Juan Manuel Galvez. Inscr "CONMEMORATIVA DE LA SUCESION PRESIDENCIAL", etc.

472	121	1c. blue	10	10
473	124	2c. red	10	10
474	-	5c. blue	10	10
475	-	9c. brown	10	10

476	-	15c. brown	10	10
477	**122**	21c. black	25	25
478	**123**	30c. olive	1·20	60
479	-	40c. grey	25	25
480	-	1l. brown	1·90	1·20
481	-	2l. violet	5·00	3·25
482	-	5l. red	12·50	7·25

DESIGNS—HORIZ: 40c. Toncontin Customs House; 5l. Galvez and Lozano. VERT: 5c., 15c. Lozano (different frames); 9c. Galvez; 1l. Palace of Tegucigalpa; 2l. Carias.

1951. Air. 75th Anniv of U.P.U. Optd U.P.U. 75 Aniversario 1874-1949.

483	**120**	16c. green	1·00	60
484	-	22c. yellow	1·20	95
485	-	40c. orange	1·20	1·20
486	-	1l. blue	3·00	1·80
487	-	2l. mauve	6·25	4·75
488	-	5l. brown	37·00	30·00
MS488a		103×114 mm. Imperf	£375	£350

1951. Air. Founding of Central Bank. Nos. 472/81 optd Conmemorativa Fundacion Banco Central Administracion Galvez–Lozano Julio 1o. de 1950.

489	1c. blue	10	10
490	2c. red	10	10
491	5c. blue	10	10
492	9c. brown	10	10
493	15c. brown	25	10
494	21c. black	35	25
495	30c. olive	75	60
496	40c. grey	1·20	85
497	1l. brown	3·75	1·90
498	2l. violet	9·50	6·25

127 Discovery of America

128 Isabella the Catholic

1952. Air. 500th Anniv of Birth of Isabella the Catholic.

499	**127**	1c. slate and orange	10	10
500	-	2c. brown and blue	10	10
501	-	8c. sepia and green	25	25
502	**128**	16c. black and blue	75	60
503	-	30c. green and violet	1·20	1·20
504	-	1l. black and red	2·50	1·90
505	**127**	2l. violet and brown	5·25	4·25
506	**128**	5l. olive and purple	10·50	9·50

DESIGNS—HORIZ: 2c.1l. King Ferdinand and Queen Isabella receive Columbus; 8c. Surrender of Granada; 30c. Queen Isabella pledging her jewels.

1953. Air. Surch HABILITADO 1953 and value.

507	**122**	5c. on 21c. black	35	10
508	**122**	8c. on 21c. black	75	25
509	**122**	16c. on 21c. black	1·40	50

1953. Air. Nos. O507/509 and O512/14 surch HABILITADO 1953 and value or optd only.

510	**127**	10c. on 1c. olive & purple	25	10
511	**127**	12c. on 1c. olive & purple	25	25
512	-	15c. on 2c. violet & brn	35	25
513	-	20c. on 2c. violet & brn	75	60
514	-	24c. on 2c. violet & brn	75	60
515	-	25c. on 2c. violet & brn	75	60
516	-	30c. on 8c. black and red	75	60
517	-	35c. on 8c. black and red	85	70
518	-	50c. on 8c. black and red	1·20	95
519	-	60c. on 8c. black and red	1·60	1·20
520	-	1l. sepia and green	3·50	2·75
521	**127**	2l. brown and blue	8·25	6·50
522	**128**	5l. slate and orange	20·00	17·00

130 U.N. Emblem

1953. Air. United Nations. Inscr as in T 130.

523	-	1c. blue and black	10	10
524	**130**	2c. blue and black	10	10
525	-	3c. violet and black	25	10
526	-	5c. green and black	25	10
527	-	15c. brown and black	60	35
528	-	30c. brown and black	1·20	70
529	-	1l. red and black	10·00	70
530	-	2l. orange and black	12·50	95
531	-	5l. green and black	25·00	18·00

DESIGNS: 1c. U.N. and Honduras flags; 3c. U.N. Building, New York; 5c. Arms of U.S.A; 15c. Pres. J. M. Galvez; 30c. Indian girl (U.N.I.C.E.F.); 1l. Refugee mother and child (U.N.R.R.A.); 2l. Torch and open book (U.N.E.S.C.O.); 5l. Cornucopia (F.A.O.).

1955. Air. 50th Anniv of Rotary International. Nos. O532/38 optd with rotary emblem, 1905 1955, clasped hands and laurel sprigs or surch also.

532	1c. blue and black	25	25
533	2c. green and black	25	25
534	3c. orange and black	25	25
535	5c. red and black	25	25
536	8c. on 1c. blue and black	25	25
537	10c. on 2c. green and black	25	25
538	12c. on 3c. orange and black	35	25
539	15c. sepia and black	35	35
540	30c. purple and black	1·50	1·20
541	1l. olive and black	27·00	24·00

1956. Air. 10th Anniv of U.N.O. Nos. O523/5 and 527/31 optd ONU X ANIVERSARIO 1945-1955.

542	1c. blue and black	25	25
543	2c. green and black	25	25
544	3c. orange and black	25	25
545	5c. red and black	35	35
546	15c. brown and black	50	35
547	30c. brown and black	75	60
548	1l. red and black	5·50	3·75
549	2l. orange and black	8·00	7·25
550	5l. green and black	21·00	19·00

133 J. Lozano Diaz

134 Southern Highway

1956. Air.

551	-	1c. blue and black	25	25
552	**133**	2c. blue and black	25	25
553	**134**	3c. sepia and black	25	25
554	-	4c. purple and black	25	25
555	-	5c. red and black	25	25
556	-	8c. multicoloured	25	25
557	-	10c. green and black	25	25
558	-	12c. green and black	25	25
559	-	15c. black and red	25	25
560	-	20c. blue and black	25	25
561	**133**	24c. purple and black	35	25
562	-	25c. green and black	35	35
563	-	30c. red and black	50	35
564	-	40c. brown and black	60	35
565	-	50c. turquoise and black	75	50
566	-	60c. orange and black	1·00	70
567	-	1l. purple and black	2·50	1·60
568	-	2l. red and black	5·00	3·50
569	-	5l. lake and black	10·50	7·75

DESIGNS—HORIZ: 1c. Suyapa Basilica; 8c. Landscape and cornucopia; 10c. National Stadium; 12c. United States School; 15c. Projected Central Bank of Honduras; 20c. Legislative Building; 25c. Projected Development Bank; 30c. Toncontin Airport; 40c. J. R. Molina Bridge; 60c. Treasury Building; 1l. Blood Bank. VERT: 4c. Dona de Estrada Palma; 5c. Dona de Morazan; 50c. Peace Memorial; 2l. Electrical Communications Building; 5l. Presidential Palace.

135 Revolutionary Flag

1957. Air. Revolution of October 21, 1956. Frames in black.

570	**135**	1c. blue and yellow	10	10
571	-	2c. purple, green & orange	10	10
572	**135**	5c. blue and pink	25	10
573	-	8c. violet, olive and orange	25	10
574	-	10c. brown and violet	25	25
575	**135**	12c. blue and turquoise	35	25
576	-	15c. brown and green	60	35
577	-	30c. grey and pink	75	60
578	-	1l. brown and blue	3·75	2·10
579	-	2l. grey and green	6·25	3·75

DESIGNS: 2c., 8c. Obelisk and mountains; 10c., 15c., 1l. Indian with bow and arrow; 30c., 2l. Arms of 1821.

NOTE. In July 1958 after stocks of current issues had been looted, eighteen different facsimile signatures validated the remaining stamps for use.

136 Flags of Honduras and the U.S.A. and Book

1958. Air. Bi-national Centre Commem. (Institute of American Culture). Flags in national colours.

580	**136**	1c. blue	25	10
581	**136**	2c. red	25	10
582	**136**	5c. green	25	10
583	**136**	10c. brown	35	25
584	**136**	20c. orange	60	35
585	**136**	30c. red	75	50
586	**136**	50c. grey	1·00	60
587	**136**	1l. yellow	2·00	1·70
588	**136**	2l. olive	3·25	2·75
589	**136**	5l. blue	7·50	6·00

137 Abraham Lincoln

1959. Air. 150th Birth Anniv of Abraham Lincoln. Flags in blue and red.

590	**137**	1c. green	25	25
591	-	2c. blue	25	25
592	-	3c. violet	25	25
593	-	5c. red	25	25
594	-	10c. slate	35	25
595	-	12c. sepia	35	25
596	**137**	15c. orange	50	25
597	-	25c. purple	85	35
598	-	50c. blue	1·10	70
599	-	1l. brown	2·50	1·60
600	-	2l. olive	4·00	2·40
601	-	5l. yellow	8·00	5·50
MS601a		180×140 mm. As Nos. 590, 592, 594, 597, 599 and 601. Imperf	15·00	12·00

DESIGNS—HORIZ: 2c., 25c. Lincoln's birthplace; 3c., 50c. Gettysburg Address; 5c., 1l. Lincoln at conference to free slaves; 10c., 2l. Assassination of Lincoln; 12c., 5l. Lincoln Memorial, Washington.

138 Henri Dunant

1959. Obligatory Tax. Red Cross.

602	**138**	1c. red and blue	35	25
647	**138**	1c. red and green	35	25
648	**138**	1c. red and brown	35	25

Nos. 647/8 have no frame around portrait and values are at left.

139 Constitution of 21 December 1957

1959. Air. 2nd Anniv of New Constitution. Inscr "21 DE DICIEMBRE DE 1957".

603	**139**	1c. red, blue and brown	10	10
604	-	2c. brown	10	10
605	-	3c. blue	10	10
606	-	5c. orange	25	10
607	**139**	10c. red, blue and green	35	25
608	-	12c. red	50	25
609	-	25c. violet	1·20	70
610	-	50c. grey-blue	2·20	95

DESIGNS—HORIZ: 2, 12c. Inaug of Pres. R. V. Morales. VERT: 3, 25c. Pres. R. V. Morales; 5, 50c. Flaming torch.

140 King Alfonso XIII of Spain and Map

1961. Air. Settlement of Boundary Dispute with Nicaragua.

611	**140**	1c. blue	10	10
612	-	2c. pink	10	10
613	-	5c. green	25	25
614	-	10c. brown	25	25
615	-	20c. red	60	60
616	-	50c. brown	1·40	85
617	-	1l. slate	2·20	1·70

DESIGNS: 2c. 1906 award (document); 5c. Arbitration commission, 1907; 10c. International Court of Justice, The Hague; 20c. 1960 award (document); 50c. Pres. Morales Foreign Minister Puerto and map; 1l. Presidents Davila and Morales.

1964. Air. Freedom from Hunger. Flags in National colours. Optd FAO Luncha Contra el Hambre.

621	**136**	1c. blue	25	25
622	**136**	2c. red	25	25
623	**136**	5c. green	35	35
624	**136**	30c. red	1·90	1·80
625	**136**	2l. olive	8·00	7·75

1964. Air. Olympic Games, Tokyo. Optd with Olympic Rings and 1964.

626	-	1c. blue & black (No. 523)	25	25
627	**130**	2c. blue and black	35	35
628	-	3c. violet & blk (No. 525)	60	60
629	-	15c. brn & blk (No. 527)	1·20	1·20

See also No. O646.

144 Ancient Stadium

1964. Air. "Homage to Sport" and Olympic Games, Tokyo.

630	**144**	1c. black and green	10	10
631	-	2c. black and mauve	25	10
632	-	5c. black and yellow	25	10
633	-	8c. black and grey-green	35	25
634	**144**	10c. black and bistre	75	60
635	-	12c. black and yellow	1·00	60
636	-	1l. black and buff	3·00	1·80
637	-	2l. black and olive	6·75	6·00
638	**144**	3l. black and red	8·75	8·50
MS638a		130×110 mm. Nos. 632/3, 635 and 638	60·00	60·00

DESIGNS: 2c., 12c. Boundary stones; 5c., 1l. Mayan ball player; 8c., 2l. Olympic Stadium, Tokyo.

1964. Air. Surch.

618	**137**	6c. on 15c.	35	25
619	-	8c. on 25c. (No. 597)	50	25
620	-	10c. on 50c. (No. 598)	60	35
639	-	4c. on 5c. (No. 593)	25	25
640	-	10c. on 15c. (No. 476)	25	25
641	-	12c. on 16c. (No. 425)	35	25
642	-	12c. on 21c. (No. 426)	35	35
643	**120**	12c. on 22c.	35	35
644	**120**	30c. on 1l.	85	50
645	-	40c. on 1l. (No. 480)	1·20	85
646	**120**	40c. on 2l.	1·20	85

See also Nos. 716/18 and O647/18.

1965. Air. Presidential Investiture of General Lopez. Optd Toma de Posesion General Oswaldo Lopez A. Junio 6, 1965. Flags in blue and red.

649	**137**	1c. green	10	10
650	-	2c. green	10	10
651	-	3c. violet (No. 592)	25	25
652	-	5c. red (No. 593)	25	25
653	**137**	15c. orange	35	25
654	-	25c. purple (No. 597)	60	50
655	-	50c. red	1·20	1·10
656	-	2l. olive (No. 600)	4·50	3·75
657	-	5l. yellow (No. 601)	10·00	9·00

147 Ambulance and Clinic

1965. Air. Order of Malta Campaign Against Leprosy.

658	**147**	1c. blue	60	60
659	-	5c. green	60	60

660	-	12c. black	85	85
661	-	1l. brown	3·25	3·25

DESIGNS: 5c. Hospital; 12c. Patients receiving treatment; 1l. Map of Honduras.

148 Father Subirana

1965. Air. Death Cent of Father Manuel de Jesus Subirana. Centres in black and gold; inscr in black.

662		1c. violet	10	10
663		2c. flesh	10	10
664	**148**	8c. pink	25	25
665	-	10c. purple	25	25
666	-	12c. brown	35	35
667	-	20c. green	75	60
668	-	1l. sage	3·00	2·75
669	-	2l. blue	5·50	4·50

MS670 99×148 mm. Nos. 664, 666 and 668/9 31·00 24·00

DESIGNS: 1c. Abraham, Jicaque Indian; 2c. Allegory of Catechism; 10c. Msgr. Juan de Jesus Zepeda; 12c. Pope Pius IX; 20c. Subirana's Tomb, Yoro; 1l. Hermitage; 2l. Jicaque Indian woman and child.

1965. Air. Churchill Commemoration. Nos. 499/500 and 470 optd IN MEMORIAM Sir Winston Churchill 1874-1965.

671	**127**	1c. black and orange	60	60
672	-	2c. brown and blue	1·20	1·20
673	-	2l. mauve	10·50	10·50

See also No. O674.

1966. Air. Pope Paul's Visit to U.N. Organisation. Nos. 662/68 optd CONMEMORATIVA Visita S. S. Pablo VI a la ONU. 4-X-1965.

675		1c. violet	10	10
676		2c. flesh	10	10
677	**148**	8c. pink	35	25
678	-	10c. purple	60	35
679	-	12c. brown	60	35
680	-	20c. green	85	70
681	-	1l. sage	5·00	4·25

151 2r. Stamp of 1866

1966. Air. Stamp Centenary. Inscriptions in black (1c., 2c.) or in gold (others).

682	**151**	1c. black, green and gold	10	10
683	-	2c. blue, black and orange	10	10
684	-	3c. purple and red	25	10
685	-	4c. indigo and blue	25	10
686	-	5c. purple and mauve	4·50	1·30
687	-	6c. violet and lilac	25	25
688	-	7c. slate and turquoise	25	25
689	-	8c. indigo and blue	25	25
690	-	9c. blue and cobalt	25	25
691	-	10c. black and olive	25	25
692	-	12c. yellow, black & green	25	25
693	-	15c. purple and mauve	35	35
694	-	20c. black and orange	35	35
695	-	30c. blue and yellow	75	60
696	-	40c. multicoloured	1·10	95
697	-	1l. green and emerald	2·75	1·70
698	-	2l. black and grey	5·50	4·00

MS699 139×121 mm. Nos. 682/3, 691/2 and 697/8 6·75 6·75

DESIGNS—VERT: 2c. Honduras; 5c. air stamp of 1925; 3c. T. Estrada Palma, 1st Director of Posts; 8c. Sir Rowland Hill; 10c. Pres. Arellano; 12c. Postal emblem; 15c. H. von Stephan; 30c. Honduras flag; 40c. Honduras arms; 1l. U.P.U. Monument, Berne; 2l. J. M. Medina (statesman). HORIZ: 4c. Post Office, Tegucigalpa; 5c. Steam locomotive No. 59; 6c. 19th-century mule transport; 7c. 19th-century sorting office; 9c. Mail van; 20c. Curtiss C-46 Commando mail plane.

See also No. E700.

1966. Air. World Cup Football Championship, Final Match between England and West Germany. Optd CAMPEONATO DE FOOTBALL Copa Mundial 1966 Inglaterra-Alemania Wembley, Julio 30.

701		2c. vio & brn (No. O508)	25	25
702	**128**	16c. black and blue	60	60
703	**127**	2l. violet and brown	13·50	13·50

1967. Air. 20th Anniv of U.N.O. Nos. 662/4 and 666/9 optd CONMEMORATIVA del XX Aniversario ONU 1966.

704	-	1c. violet	25	25
705	-	2c. flesh	25	25
706	**148**	8c. pink	35	25
707	-	12c. brown	50	25
708	-	20c. green	60	25
709	-	1l. sage	1·90	60
710	-	2l. blue	5·25	5·00

1967. Birth Bicentenary of Simeon Canas y Villacorta (slave liberator). Nos. 551, 553, 559, 552 and 568. Optd Simeon Canas y Villacorta Libertador de los esclavos en Centro America 1767-1967.

711		1c. blue and black	25	25
712		3c. sepia and black	50	35
713		15c. black and red	85	70
714		25c. green and black	1·60	1·20
715		2l. red and black	3·75	3·00

1967. Air. Nos. E570 and 480/1 surch.

716	**E135**	10c. on 20c. grey, black and red	60	25
717	-	10c. on 1l. brown	60	25
718	-	10c. on 2l. violet	60	25

156 J. C. del Valle (Honduras)

1967. Air. Founding of Central-American Journalists' Federation.

719	**156**	11c. black, blue and gold	25	25
720	-	12c. black, yellow and blue	25	25
721	-	14c. black, green and silver	25	25
722	-	20c. black, green & mauve	25	25
723	-	30c. black, yellow and lilac	35	25
724	-	40c. gold, blue and violet	1·50	1·20
725	-	50c. green, red and olive	1·60	1·20

DESIGNS: 12c. Ruben Dario (Nicaragua); 14c. J. B. Montufar (Guatemala); 20c. F. Gavidia (El Salvador); 30c. J. M. Fernandez (Costa Rica); 40c. Federation emblem; 50c. Central American map.

157 Olympic Rings and Flags of Mexico and Honduras

1968. Air. Olympic Games, Mexico. Mult.

726		1c. Type **157**	25	25
727		2c. Type **157**	35	35
728		5c. Italian flag and boxing	60	60
729		10c. French flag and skiing	75	70
730		12c. West German flag and show-jumping	85	85
731		50c. British flag and athletics	5·25	5·00
732		1l. U.S. flag and running	8·00	7·75

MS733 110×70 mm. **157** 20c. multicoloured; 40c. multicoloured 12·50 12·00

158 J. F. Kennedy and Rocket Launch

1968. Air. International Telecommunications Union Centenary. Multicoloured.

734		1c. Type **158**	25	25
735		2c. Dish aerial and telephone	25	25
736		3c. Dish aerial and television	25	25
737		5c. Dish aerial, globe and I.T.U. emblem as satellite	60	60
738		8c. "Early Bird" satellite	85	85
739		10c. Type **158**	1·00	95
740		20c. Type **158**	1·20	1·20

1969. Air. Robert F. Kennedy Commemoration. Nos. 734 and 739/40 optd In-Memoriam Robert F. Kennedy 1925-1968.

741		1c. multicoloured	75	50
742		10c. multicoloured	75	50
743		20c. multicoloured	75	50

1969. Air. Gold Medal Winners, Olympic Games. Nos. 735/8 optd Medallas de Oro Mexico 1968.

744		2c. multicoloured	50	35
745		3c. multicoloured	75	65
746		5c. multicoloured	1·20	1·00
747		8c. multicoloured	1·80	1·60

161 Patient and Nurse

1969. Obligatory Tax. Red Cross.

748	**161**	1c. red and blue	35	25

162 Rocket Launch

1969. Air. First Man on the Moon. Mult.

749		5c. Type **162**	10	10
750		10c. Moon	25	10
751		12c. Lunar landing module leaving space-ship (horiz)	35	10
752		20c. Astronaut on Moon (horiz)	85	35
753		24c. Lunar landing module taking off from Moon	1·10	60
754		30c. Capsule re-entering Earth's atmosphere (horiz)	1·60	85

1970. No. E700 optd with "HABILITADO" for use as ordinary postage stamp.

755		20c. brown, orange and gold	1·20	95

1970. Air. Various stamps surch in figures.

756	**151**	4c.+1c. (No. 682)	35	25
757	-	4c.+3c. (No. 525)	35	25
758	-	5c.+1c. (No. 662)	50	25
759	-	5c.+7c. (No. 688)	35	25
760	-	8c.+2c. (No. 663)	1·00	50
761	-	10c.+2c. (No. 500)	1·20	60
762	**133**	10c.+2c. (No. 552)	1·20	60
763	-	10c.+3c. (No. 525)	1·20	60
764	**134**	10c.+3c. (No. 553)	1·20	60
765	-	10c.+3c. (No. 684)	1·20	60
766	-	10c.+9c. (No. 690)	50	25
767	**156**	10c.+11c. (No. 719)	50	25
768	-	12c.+14c. (No. 721)	60	35
769	**E135**	12c.+20c. (No. E570)	60	35
770	-	12c.+1l. (No. 480)	60	35
771	-	15c.+12c. (No. 783)	1·60	85
772	-	30c.+12c. (No. 783)	2·00	1·20
773	-	40c.+24c. (No. 753)	3·25	2·40
774	-	40c.+50c. (No. 731)	3·25	2·40

1970. Air. Safe Return of "Apollo 13". Nos. 749/54 optd Admiracion al Rescate del Apolo XIII, James A. Lovell, Fred W. Haise Jr., John L. Swigert Jr.

775		5c. multicoloured	10	10
776		10c. multicoloured	25	25
777		12c. multicoloured	35	25
778		20c. multicoloured	60	50
779		24c. multicoloured	75	60
780		30c. multicoloured	1·20	1·10

165 J. A. Sanhueza (firefighter)

1970. Air. Campaign Against Forest Fires. Multicoloured.

781		5c. Type **165**	25	25
782		8c. R. Ordonez Rodriguez (firefighter)	35	25
783		12c. Fire Brigade emblems (horiz)	50	25
784		20c. Flag, map and emblems	75	50
785		1l. Emblems, and flags of Honduras, U.N. and U.S.A.	4·25	2·40

MS786 120×130 mm. Nos. 781/4 (sold at 1l.45). Imperf 4·25 3·50

166 Hotel Honduras Maya

1970. Air. Opening of Hotel Honduras Maya, Tegucigalpa.

787	**166**	12c. black and blue	60	35

1972. Air. 50th Anniv of Honduras Masonic Grand Lodge. Nos. 749 and 751/3. optd Aniversario Gran Logia de Honduras 1922-1972 or surch also.

791		5c. multicoloured	1·20	60
792		12c. multicoloured	1·60	1·10
793		1l. on 20c. multicoloured	4·25	3·25
794		2l. on 24c. multicoloured	8·00	6·25

168 Soldiers' Bay, Guanaja

1972. Air. 150th Anniv of Independence (1970). Multicoloured.

795		4c. Type **168**	25	10
796		5c. Bugler sounding "Last Post" (vert)	25	10
797		6c. Lake Yojoa	25	10
798		7c. "The Banana Carrier" (R. Aguilar) (vert)	25	10
799		8c. Soldiers marching and fly-past	35	10
800		9c. "Brassavola digbyana" (national flower) (vert)	35	10
801		10c. As 9c.	50	25
802		12c. Machine-gunner	50	25
803		15c. Tela beach at sunset	60	25
804		20c. Stretcher-bearers	60	25
805		30c. "San Antonio de Oriente" (A. Velasquez)	85	60
806		40c. Ruins of Copan	1·50	70
807		50c. "Woman from Huacal" (P. Zelaya Sierra)	1·50	70
808		1l. Trujillo Bay	3·50	2·40
809		2l. As 9c.	4·25	3·00

MS810 Four sheets each 122×112 mm. (a) Nos. 795, 799, 802 and 808; (b) Nos. 796/7, 804 and 807; (c) Nos. 798, 803 and 805/6; (d) Nos. 800/1 and 809 Set of four sheets 16·00 16·00

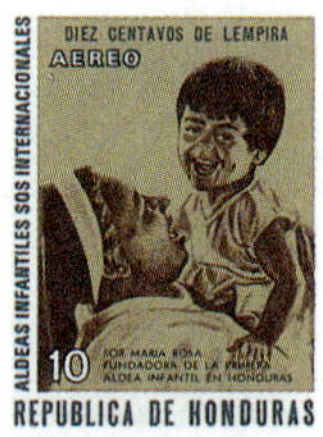

169 Sister Maria Rosa and Child

1972. Air. "S.O.S." Children's Villages in Honduras. Each brown, green and gold.

812		10c. Type **169**	35	25
813		15c. "S.O.S. Villages" emblem (horiz)	60	35
814		30c. Father J. T. Reyes (educationalist)	75	50
815		40c. First Central American "S.O.S." village (horiz)	85	60
816		1l. "Future Citizen" (boy)	2·50	1·90

170 Map of Honduras

1973. Air. 25th Annivs of National Cartographic Service (10c.) and Joint Cartographic Work (12c.).

817	**170**	10c. multicoloured	75	50
818	-	12c. multicoloured	1·00	70

DESIGN: 12c. Similar to Type **170** but with two badges and inscr "25 Anos de Labor Cartografica Conjunta".

171 Illustration from "Habitante de la Osa"

1973. Air. 25th Anniv of U.N.E.S.C.O. and Juan Ramon Molina (poet) Commem. Multicoloured.

819	8c. Type **171**	35	10
820	20c. Juan Ramon Molina	1·00	60
821	1l. Illustration from "Tierras Mares y Cielos"	2·50	1·40
822	2l. U.N.E.S.C.O. emblem	4·25	3·25
MS823	140×128 mm. Nos. 819/22	9·25	8·50

1973. Air. Census and World Population Year. Various stamps optd Censos de Poblacion y Vivienda, marzo 1974. 1974 Ano Mundial de Poblacion.

824	**169**	10c. brown, green and gold	25	25
825	-	15c. brown, green and gold (No. 813)	25	25
826	-	30c. brown, green and gold (No. 814)	60	50
827	-	40c. brown, green and gold (No. 815)	60	50
828	**170**	10c. multicoloured	25	25
829	-	12c. mult (No. 818)	25	25

1974. Air. Various stamps surch.

830		2c. on 1c. blue and black (No. 551)	25	10
831	**137**	2c. on 1c. green	25	10
832	-	3c. on 1c. blue and black (No. 551)	25	10
833	**137**	3c. on 1c. green	25	10
834	-	16c. on 1c. bl & blk (551)	25	10
835	**135**	16c. on 1c. bl, yell & blk	25	10
836	**137**	16c. on 1c. green	25	10
837	-	16c. on 1c. mult (O602)	75	50
838	-	16c. on 1c. violet (662)	25	10
839	**170**	18c. on 10c. mult	35	25
840	-	18c. on 12c. mult (818)	85	25
841	**171**	18c. on 8c. mult	35	25
842	**169**	18c. on 10c. mult	35	25
843	-	50c. on 30c. mult (814)	1·20	35
844	**137**	1l. on 2l. mauve	2·50	1·90
845	-	1l. on 2l. violet (No. 481)	2·50	1·90
846	-	1l. on 50c. blue (610)	2·50	1·90
847	-	1l. on 30c. mult (814)	2·10	1·40

1974. Air. Honduras' Children's Villages. 25th Anniv. Nos. 786/9 optd 1949-1974 SOS Kinderdorfer Internacional Honduras-Austria.

851	**169**	10c. multicoloured	25	10
852	-	15c. multicoloured	50	35
853	-	30c. multicoloured	60	50
854	-	40c. multicoloured	85	70

175 Flags of West Germany and Austria

1975. Air. Centenary (1974) of U.P.U. Mult.

855	1c. Type **175**	25	25
856	2c. Belgium and Denmark	25	25
857	3c. Spain and France	25	25
858	4c. Hungary and Russia	25	25
859	5c. Great Britain and Italy	25	25
860	10c. Norway and Sweden	25	25
861	12c. Honduras	35	35
862	15c. United States and Switzerland	50	50
863	20c. Greece and Portugal	60	60
864	30c. Rumania and Yugoslavia	1·10	1·10
865	1l. Egypt and Netherlands	2·75	2·75
866	2l. Luxembourg and Turkey	5·50	5·50
MS867	150×122 mm. As Nos. 855/66 but different backgrounds	19·00	18·00

176 Jalteva Youth Centre

1976. Air. International Women's Year (1975). Multicoloured.

868	8c. Humuya Youth Centre	25	10
869	16c. Type **176**	35	25
870	18c. Sra Arellano and I.W.Y. emblem	35	25
871	30c. El Carmen Youth Centre, San Pedro Sula	60	35
872	55c. Flag of National Social Welfare Organization (vert)	1·10	85
873	1l. Sports and recreation grounds, La Isla	1·80	1·20
874	2l. Women's Social Centre	4·25	2·50

177 "CARE" Package

1976. Air. 20th Anniv of "CARE" (Co-operative for American Relief Everywhere) in Honduras.

875	**177**	1c. blue and black	10	10
876	-	5c. mauve and black	10	10
877	**177**	16c. red and black	25	25
878	-	18c. green and black	35	25
879	**177**	30c. blue and black	60	50
880	-	50c. green and black	1·00	70
881	**177**	55c. brown and black	1·00	70
882	-	70c. purple and black	1·20	95
883	**177**	1l. blue and black	1·70	1·20
884	-	2l. orange and black	3·75	2·50

DESIGN—HORIZ: 5c., 18c., 50c., 70c., 2l. "CARE" on globe.

Each of the above stamps has a different inscription detailing "CARE's" various fields of activities in Honduras.

178 White-tailed Deer in Burnt Forest

1976. Air. Forest Protection. Multicoloured.

885	10c. Type **178**	25	10
886	16c. COHDEFOR emblem	25	25
887	18c. Forest stream (horiz)	35	25
888	30c. Live and burning trees	75	35
889	50c. Type **178**	1·00	70
890	70c. Protection emblem	1·40	95
891	1l. Forest of young trees (horiz)	1·80	1·40
892	2l. As 30c.	4·25	3·00

COHDEFOR = Corporacion Hondurena de Desarollo Forestal.

179 Boston Tea Party and "Liberty" Flag

1976. Air. Bicentenary of American Revolution. Multicoloured.

894	1c. Type **179**	10	10
895	2c. Hoisting the "Liberty and Union" flag	10	10
896	3c. Battle of Bunker Hill and Pine Tree flag	10	10
897	4c. Loading stores aboard "Washington" and "An Appeal to Heaven" flag	10	10
898	5c. First naval ensign and navy warship	35	35
899	6c. Presidential Palace, Tegucigalpa, and Honduras flag	25	25
900	18c. Capitol, Washington and U.S. flag	75	70
901	55c. Washington at Valley Forge and Grand Union flag	1·00	95
902	2l. Battle scene and Bennington flag	3·50	3·25
903	3l. Betsy Ross flag	5·75	5·75
MS904	Three sheets each 110×85 mm. (a) Nos. 896 and 899/901; (b) Nos. 894, 897 and 902; (c) Nos. 895, 898 and 903. Imperf	19·00	18·00

180 Queen Sophia of Spain

1977. Air. Visit of King and Queen of Spain. Multicoloured.

905	16c. Type **180**	25	25
906	18c. King Juan Carlos	25	25
907	30c. Queen Sophia and King Juan Carlos	60	50
908	2l. Arms of Honduras and Spain (horiz)	2·75	2·40

181 Mayan Stelae

1978. Air. "Honduras 78". Stamp Exhibition. Multicoloured.

909	15c. Type **181**	25	25
910	18c. Giant head	60	25
911	30c. Kneeling figure	85	70
912	55c. Sun God	1·50	1·20
MS913	160×110 mm. 1l.50 Mayan pelota court. Imperf	4·00	3·75

182 Del Valle's Birthplace

1978. Air. Birth Bicentenary of Jose Cecelio del Valle. Multicoloured.

914	8c. Type **182**	10	10
915	14c. La Merced Church, Choluteca	10	10
916	15c. Baptismal font (vert)	25	10
917	20c. Reading Independence Act	25	10
918	25c. Portrait, documents and map of Central America	35	25
919	40c. Portrait (vert)	60	35
920	1l. Monument, Choluteca (vert)	1·60	1·10
921	3l. Bust (vert)	5·50	4·25

183 Rural Heath Centre

1978. Air. 75th Anniv (1977) of Panamerican Health Organization. Multicoloured.

922	5c. Type **183**	10	10
923	6c. Child at water tap	10	10
924	10c. Los Laureles Dam, Tegucigalpa	25	10
925	20c. Rural aqueduct	35	25
926	40c. Teaching hospital, Tegucigalpa	75	50
927	2l. Parents and child	2·75	2·20
928	3l. Vaccination of child	4·00	3·00
929	5l. Panamerican Health Organization Building, Washington	5·75	5·00

184 Luis Landa and "Botanica"

1978. Air. Birth Centenary of Professor Luis Landa (botanist). Multicoloured.

930	14c. Type **184**	10	10
931	16c. Map of Honduras	25	10
932	18c. Medals received by Landa	25	10
933	30c. Birthplace, San Ignacio	35	35
934	2l. "Brassavola" (national flower)	4·00	2·50
935	3l. Women's normal school	5·50	5·00

1978. Air. Argentina's Victory in World Cup Football Championship. Nos. 909/12 optd with Argentina Campeon Holanda sub-Campeon XI Campeonato Mundial de Football and emblem.

936	**181**	15c. multicoloured	25	10
937	-	18c. multicoloured	35	25
938	-	30c. multicoloured	60	35
939	-	55c. multicoloured	1·20	70
MS940		160×110 mm. 1l.50 multicoloured	41·00	

186 Central University

1978. Air. 400th Anniv of Founding of Tegucigalpa.

941	**186**	6c. brown and black	10	10
942	-	6c. multicoloured	10	10
943	-	8c. brown and black	10	10
944	-	8c. multicoloured	10	10
945	-	10c. brown and black	10	10
946	-	10c. multicoloured	10	10
947	-	16c. brown and black	10	10
948	-	16c. multicoloured	10	10
949	-	20c. brown and black	25	10
950	-	20c. multicoloured	25	10
951	-	40c. brown and black	35	35
952	-	40c. multicoloured	35	35
953	-	50c. brown and black	85	60
954	-	50c. multicoloured	85	60
955	-	5l. brown and black	9·75	8·25
956	-	5l. multicoloured	9·75	8·25
MS957		160×110 mm. 1l.50 multicoloured	4·25	4·25

DESIGNS—HORIZ: No. 942, University City; No. 943, Manuel Bonilla Theatre; No. 944, Present Manuel Bonilla Theatre; No. 947, National Palace; No. 948, Presidential House; No. 949, General San Felipe Hospital; No. 950, Teaching Hospital; No. 951, Parish Church and Convent of San Francisco; No. 952, Metropolitan Cathedral; No. 953, Old view of Tegucigalpa; No. 954, Modern view of Tegucigalpa; **MS**957, Aerial view of Tegucigalpa. VERT: No. 945, Court House; No. 946, North Boulevard highway intersection; No. 955, Arms of San Miguel de Tegucigalpa; No. 956, President Marco Aurelio Soto.

187 Footballers jumping for Ball

1978. Air. 7th Youth Football Championship of Central American Football League. Multicoloured.

958	15c. Type **187**	25	10
959	30c. Goalkeeper (horiz)	60	10
960	55c. Tackling	85	35
961	1l. Goalkeeper and players (horiz)	1·80	1·10
962	2l. Players at goalmouth (horiz)	3·00	2·40

188 National Postal Emblem

1979. Air. Centenary of Honduras's U.P.U. Membership (1st issue). Multicoloured.

963	2c. Type **188**	10	10
964	15c. U.P.U. emblem	25	25
965	25c. Roman Rosa (vert)	50	50
966	50c. Marco Aurelio Soto (vert)	1·00	95

See also Nos. 975/6.

189 Rotary Emblem and "50"

1979. Air. 50th Anniv of Tegucigalpa Rotary Club.

967	189	3c. orange, turquoise & bis	10	10
968	189	5c. green, emerald & bistre	10	10
969	189	50c. ochre, mauve & bistre	85	60
970	189	2l. blue, violet and bistre	2·75	2·40

190 Map of Caratasca Lagoon

1979. Air. 50th Anniv of Pan-American Institute of History and Geography. Multicoloured.

971	5c. Type **190**	10	10
972	10c. Aerial view of Fort San Fernando de Omoa	10	10
973	24c. Institute anniversary emblem (vert)	35	25
974	5l. Map of Santanilla Islands	6·25	5·50

191 Model of New General Post Office Building

1980. Air. Centenary (1979) of U.P.U. Membership (2nd issue).

975	191	24c. multicoloured	35	25
976	-	3l. brown, yellow & black	4·00	3·50

DESIGN: 3l. 19th century Post Office.

192 "Landscape" (Roman E. Cooper)

1980. Air. International Year of the Child (1979). Multicoloured.

977	1c. "Workers in a Field (J. E. Mejia) (horiz)	25	25
978	5c. Type **192**	25	25
979	15c. "Sitting boy" (D. M. Zavala)	25	25
980	20c. I.Y.C. emblem	35	35
981	30c. "Beach scene" (M. A. Hernandez) (horiz)	60	60
MS982	105×79 mm. 1l. United Nation's Children's Fund (UNICEF) emblem	2·20	2·20

193 Hill and "Maltese Cross" Cancellations

1980. Air. Death Centenary (1979) of Sir Rowland Hill. Multicoloured.

983	1c. Type **193**	10	10
984	2c. Great Britain "Penny Black"	10	10
985	5c. 1866 Honduras 2r. green	25	25
986	10c. 1866 Honduras 2r. rose	35	35
987	15c. Honduras postal emblem	75	70
988	20c. Flags of Honduras and United Kingdom	85	85
MS989	105×79 mm. 1l. Stamp Centenary stamp, 1966 (46×34 mm)	1·90	1·80

Nos. 987/8 are 46×34 mm.

194 Visitacion Padilla (founder of Honduras section)

1981. Air. 50th Anniv of Inter-American Women's Commission. Multicoloured.

990	2c. Type **194**	25	25
991	10c. Maria Trinidad del Cid (founder of Honduras section)	25	25
992	40c. Intubucana Indian mother and child	60	50
993	1l. Emblem (horiz)	1·40	1·20

195 "O'Higgins during the Liberation of Chile" (Cosmo San Martin)

1981. Air. Bernardo O'Higgins Commemoration. Multicoloured.

994	16c. Type **195**	25	25
995	20c. Don Ambrosio O'Higgins (father) (vert)	25	25
996	30c. "Bernardo O'Higgins" (Jose Gil de Castro) (vert)	35	35
997	1l. "Bernardo O'Higgins laying-down Office" (M. Antonio Caro)	1·50	85

196 National Sports Emblem

1981. Air. World Cup Football Championship Preliminary Round. Multicoloured.

998	20c. Type **196**	75	35
999	50c. Footballer and map of Honduras	1·70	1·30
1000	70c. Flags of Honduras, CONCACAF and FIFA	2·50	1·80
1001	1l. National stadium	3·75	2·10
MS1002	110×80 mm. 1l.50 Type **196**	3·00	2·40

197 Curtiss Condor II Biplane

1983. Air. 50th Anniv of Honduras Air Force. Multicoloured.

1003	3c. Type **197**	10	10
1004	15c. North America Texan	25	10
1005	25c. Chance Vought F4U-5 Corsair	50	35
1006	65c. Douglas C-47 Skytrain	1·00	60
1007	1l. Cessna Dragonfly	1·50	95
1008	2l. Dassault Super Mystere SMB-11	3·00	2·40
MS1009	80×55 mm. 11.55 Air Force Headquarters and Bell "UH-1H" helicopter	3·00	3·00

198 U.P.U. Monument, Berne

1983. Air. Election to U.P.U. Executive Council (1979). Multicoloured.

1010	16c. Type **198**	25	25
1011	18c. 18th U.P.U. Congress emblem	25	25
1012	30c. Honduras's postal emblem	35	35
1013	55c. View of Rio de Janeiro	75	70
1014	2l. "Stamp" showing pigeon on globe (vert)	2·75	2·75
MS1015	80×110 mm. 1l. mult	1·50	1·40

DESIGNS—HORIZ: 18c. 18th UPU Congress emblem; 30c. Honduras's postal emblem; 55c. View of Rio de Janeiro. VERT: 1, 2l. "Stamp showing pigeon on globe.

199 I.Y.D.P. Emblem

1983. Air. International Year of Disabled Persons.

1016	199	25c. multicoloured	60	50

200 National Library, Tegucigalpa

1983. Air. Centenary (1980) of National Library and Archives. Multicoloured.

1017	9c. Type **200**	25	15
1018	1l. Books	1·10	45

1983. Air. Papal Visit. Nos. 951/2 optd CONMEMORATIVA DE LA VISITA DE SS. JUAN PABLO II 8 de marzo de 1983.

1019	40c. brown and black	3·00	2·40
1020	40c. multicoloured	3·00	2·40

202 Agricultural Produce

1983. Air. World Food Day (1981).

1021	202	65c. multicoloured	70	70

203 Hands reaching for Open Book

1983. Air. Literacy Campaign (1980). Mult.

1022	40c. Type **203**	55	45
1023	1l.50 Family with books	2·20	1·70

204 Motorway Bridge over River Comayagua

1983. 20th Anniv of Inter-American Development Bank. Multicoloured.

1024	1l. Type **204**	1·60	85
1025	2l. Luis Borgran Technical Institute	2·75	1·70

205 Arms

1984. Air. 2nd Anniv of Return of Constitutional Government. Multicoloured.

1026	20c. Type **205**	25	15
1027	20c. President Roberto Suazo Cordova	25	15

206 Hand, Dove and Map on Globe

1984. "Internationalization of Peace".

1028	206	78c. black, blue and green	90	70
1029	206	85c. black, orange & grn	1·00	35
1030	206	95c. black, orange & grn	1·10	45
1031	206	1l.50 black, red & green	1·80	60
1032	206	2l. black, lt grn & green	2·00	80
1033	206	5l. black, purple & green	5·50	1·90

207 Front Page of "La Gaceta"

1984. Air. 150th Anniv of "La Gaceta".

1034	207	10c. brown, black & grn	25	15
1035	207	20c. brown, black & sepia	35	25

1986. Various stamps surch.

1036	184	60c. on 14c. mult (postage)	80	45
1037	177	5c. on 1c. blue and black (air)	10	10
1038	-	10c. on 8c. mult (No. 868)	10	10
1039	176	20c. on 16c. mult	25	15
1040	-	50c. on 14c. mult (No. 915)	50	25
1041	-	85c. on 6c. mult (No. 942)	90	50
1042	186	85c. on 6c. brown & blk	90	50
1043	-	95c. on 6c. brown & blk	1·10	70
1044	-	95c. on 6c. mult (No. 942)	1·10	70
1045	177	1l. on 1c. blue and black	1·20	85

1986. Air. "Exfilhon '86" Stamp Exhibition and World Cup Winners. Nos. 951/2 optd.

1046	40c. **"EXFILHON '86"/ ARGENTINA CAMPEON/ MEXICO'86** (951)	45	25
1047	40c. **"EXFILHON '86"/ ALEMANIA FEDERAL Sub Campeon/ MEXICO'86** (952)	45	25
1048	40c. **"EXFILHON '86"/ "FRANCIA TERCER LUGAR"/ MEXICO'86** (952)	45	25
1049	40c. **"EXFILHON '86"/ "BELG-ICA–CUARTO LUGAR"/ MEXICO'86** (951)	45	25

210 Phulapanzak

1986. Air. Tourism. Multicoloured.

1050		20c. Type **210**	25	15
1051		78c. Aerial view of Bahia Island beach and jetty (horiz)	70	35
1052		85c. Yacht off Bahia Islands (horiz)	90	45
1053		95c. Yojoa lake	1·00	45
1054		1l. Woman painting pottery	1·10	50
MS1055		84×58 mm. 1l.50 San Fernando Castle, Omoa (80×55 mm). Imperf	1·80	1·70

211 Pres. Jose Azcona and Flag

1987. Air. 1st Anniv of Democratic Government.

1056	**211**	20c. multicoloured	35	15
1057	**211**	85c. multicoloured	1·40	50

212 Edward Warner Award Medal

1987. 25th Anniv (1985) of Central American Air Navigation Services Association. Mult.

1058		2c. Type **212**	20	15
1059		5c. Flags of member countries (horiz)	20	15
1060		60c. Transmission mast, arrows and airplane (horiz)	70	25
1061		75c. Emblem	90	35
1062		1l. Members' flags and emblem (horiz)	1·30	45
MS1063		100×80 mm. 1l.50 As No. 1062	2·20	2·20

213 "Eupatorium cyrillinelsonii"

1987. Air. Flowering Plants. Multicoloured.

1064		10c. Type **213**	25	15
1065		20c. "Salvia ernestivargasii"	35	25
1066		95c. "Robinsonella erasmi-sosae"	90	50

214 Turquoise-browed Motmot

1987. Air. Birds. Multicoloured.

1067		50c. Type **214**	1·80	35
1068		60c. Keel-billed toucan	2·20	45
1069		85c. Yellow-headed amazon	3·25	60

215 Family and House on Emblem

1987. 30th Anniv of Housing Institute.

1070	**215**	5c. multicoloured	20	15
1071	-	95c. black, brown & blue	90	45

DESIGN: 95c. Emblem.

216 Emblem

1987. Air. 30th Anniv of Honduras National Autonomous University.

1072	**216**	1l. red, black and yellow	1·30	60

217 Emblem

1987. Air. 50th Anniv of Honduras Red Cross.

1073	**217**	20c. red and blue	35	25

218 Emblem of President

1988. Air. 17th Lions International Latin-American and Caribbean Forum, Honduras.

1074	**218**	95c. blue and yellow	1·10	45

219 1913 Headquarters Building, La Ceiba

1988. Air. 75th Anniv of Banco Atlantida.

1075		10c. Type **219**	20	10
1076		85c. Present headquarters building, Tegucigalpa	1·20	60
MS1077		112×81 mm. Nos. 1075/6 (sold at 1l.). No. gum	1·30	1·30

1988. Nos. 941/4 surch.

1078		5c. on 6c. brown and black	20	10
1079		5c. on 6c. multicoloured	20	10
1080		20c. on 8c. brown and black	30	15
1081		20c. on 8c. multicoloured	30	15

221 Postal Messenger

1988. Air. "Exfilhon 88" Stamp Exhibition, Honduras.

1082	**221**	85c. brown	90	50
1083	-	2l. brown and red	2·20	1·40
MS1084		115×83 mm. 3l. orange-brown and ultramarine (Ship carrying mail). Imperf	3·50	3·50

DESIGN: 2l. Handstamp on cover.

222 Athletes

1988. Air. Olympic Games, Seoul.

1085	**222**	85c. black, yellow & mve	1·00	50
1086	-	1l. yellow, black & orge	1·30	70
MS1087		114×83 mm. 4l. Single sculls designs as Nos. 1085/6. Imperf	4·50	4·25

DESIGN: 1l. Ball games equipment.

223 Three-legged Tub

1988. Air. 500th Anniv (1992) of Discovery of America by Christopher Columbus. Mult.

1088		10c. Type **223**	35	15
1089		25c. Bowl (horiz)	80	25
1090		30c. Dish with legs shaped as animal heads (horiz)	1·10	35
1091		50c. Jug	1·80	50
MS1092		114×83 mm. 1l.Square dish. Imperf	3·50	3·50

1989. Air. Various stamps surch.

1093	-	10c. on 16c. brown and black (No. 947)	20	10
1094	-	10c. on 16c. mult (No. 948)	20	10
1095	-	15c. on 6c. mult (No. 923)	20	15
1096	**195**	20c. on 16c. mult	45	15
1097	**176**	50c. on 16c. mult	70	45
1098	-	95c. on 18c. mult (No. 910)	1·30	50
1099	-	1l. on 16c. mult (No. 836)	1·30	1·00

1990. Air. 4th Central American Games. Nos. 887 and 878 surch IV Juegos Olimpicos Centroamericanos and value.

1101		75c. on 18c. multicoloured	1·10	85
1102		85c. on 18c. green and black	1·20	95

1990. Air. Nos. 915 and 870 surch L. 0.20.

1103		20c. on 14c. multicoloured	25	15
1104		20c. on 18c. multicoloured	25	15

1990. Air. 50th Anniv (1989) of I.H.C.I. Nos. 930 and 915 surch "50 Aniversario IHCI" 1939–1989 and new value.

1105	**184**	20c. on 14c. mult	20	10
1106	-	1l. on 14c. multicoloured	65	45

228 Monkey swinging through Trees

1990. Air. The Black-handed Spider Monkey. Multicoloured.

1107		10c. Type **228**	1·70	95
1108		10c. Mother and baby	1·70	95
1109		20c. Monkey swinging through trees (different)	3·00	1·50
1110		20c. Mother and baby (different)	3·00	1·50

1990. Air. World Cup Football Championship, Italy. No. 960 surch ITALIA '90 L.1.00.

1111		1l. on 55c. multicoloured	65	45
MS1112		110×80 mm. 1l.50 multicoloured (optd **CAMPEONATO MUNDIAL/DE FUTBOL/ITALIA '90**) and mascot	90	85

230 Institute Building

1990. Air Centenary of Luis Bogran Technical Institute, Tegucigalpa.

1113	**230**	20c. red, black and green	20	10
1114	-	85c. multicoloured	65	45
MS1115		114×82 mm. **230** 2l. red, black and emerald	1·60	1·60

DESIGN: 85c. Cogwheel, globe and Institute emblem.

231 Emblem

1990. Air. 45th Anniv of F.A.O.

1116	**231**	95c. multicoloured	70	50

232 "Santa Maria", Shoreline, Fish and Fruit

1990. America. The Natural World. Mult.

1117		20c. Type **232**	20	15
1118		1l. Maize, fish, fruit and palm (horiz)	70	50

233 Congress Emblem

1990. Air. 30th Anniv and 17th Congress of Inter-American Construction Industry Federation.

1119	**233**	20c. black and green	20	10
1120	-	1l. black and blue	70	50

DESIGN—HORIZ: 1l. Jose Cecilio del Valle Palace, Tegucigalpa (Ministry of Foreign Relations).

234 Virgin and Child with Apostles

1990. Air. Christmas. Multicoloured.

1121		20c. Type **234**	20	10
1122		95c. Virgin and Child (vert)	70	45
MS1123		101×82 mm. 3l. Poinsetta. Imperf	2·20	2·20

235 St. John Bosco (founder) (after Mario Caffaro Roke)

1990. Air. 80th Anniv of Salesian Brothers in Honduras. Multicoloured.

1124		75c. Type **235**	55	35
1125		1l. Bosco and National Youth Sanctuary, Tegucigalpa	80	50

236 Pres. Callejas

1991. Air. 1st Anniv of Presidency of Rafael Leonardo Callejas. Multicoloured.
1126 30c. Type **236** 20 10
1127 2l. Pres. Callejas wearing sash 1·40 95

237 "Strymon melinus"

1991. Air. Butterflies. Multicoloured.
1128 85c. Type **237** 90 45
1129 90c. "Diorina sp." 1·20 50
1130 1l.50 "Hyalophora cecropia" 1·80 80
MS1131 114×82 mm. 5l. "Papilio polixenes". Imperf 3·50 3·25

238 "Rhyncholaelia glauca"

1991. Air. Orchids. Multicoloured.
1132 30c. Type **238** 20 10
1133 50c. "Oncidium splendidum" (vert) 35 25
1134 95c. "Laelia anceps (vert) 70 50
1135 1l.50 "Cattleya skinneri" 1·40 1·00

239 International Latin Lawyers Union Emblem and Flags

1991. Air. 6th Caribbean and North and Central American Lawyers' Day.
1136 **239** 50c. multicoloured 45 25

241 Emblem, Flags and Carving

1991. Air. 25th Anniv of Italian–Latin American Institute.
1138 **241** 1l. multicoloured 70 45

242 Meeting of Old and New Worlds

1991. Air. "Espamer '91" Spain–Latin America Stamp Exhibition, Buenos Aires.
1139 **242** 2l. multicoloured 2·20 85
MS1140 102×83 mm. **242** 5l. multicoloured. Imperf 3·50 3·50

243 Valle

1991. Air. Birth Centenary of Rafael Heliodoro Valle.
1141 **243** 2l. black and red 1·30 95

244 Show Jumping

1991. Air. 11th Pan-American Games, Havana. Multicoloured.
1142 30c. Type **244** 20 10
1143 85c. Judo 65 45
1144 95c. Swimming 70 45
MS1145 115×83 mm. 5l. Swimmers diving into pool. Imperf 3·50 3·50

245 St Manuel de Colohete's Church, Gracias, Lempira

1991. Air. Churches. Multicoloured.
1146 30c. Type **245** 20 10
1147 95c. Church of Mercy, Gracias, Lempira 70 45
1148 1l. Comayagua Cathedral 70 45

246 Stone Carving and Cobs of Corn

1991. Air. America. Pre-Columbian Civilizations. Multicoloured.
1149 25c. Type **246** 20 10
1150 40c. Stone carving, dried corn and map 40 20
1151 1l.50 Stone carving and map of Honduras 1·10 70

247 Means of Control

1991. Air. 4th International Congress on Pest Control. Multicoloured.
1152 30c. Type **247** 55 15
1153 75c. Hoeing crop (scientific co-operation) 1·30 35
1154 1l. Co-operation of scientists and producers 1·80 50
MS1155 115×83 mm. 5l. Biological control. Imperf 3·50 3·50

248 Poinsettias in Basket

1991. Christmas. Multicoloured.
1156 1l. Type **248** 70 45
1157 2l. Poinsettia in chicken-shaped pot 1·50 95

249 "Taking Possession of the New Continent" (Enrique Escher)

1992. Air. 75th Anniv of Savings Bank of Honduras. Multicoloured.
1158 85c. Type **249** 55 35
1159 1l. "First Celebration of Mass in the Americas" (Maury Flores) 70 45
MS1160 114×83 mm. 5l. As T **249** but larger. Imperf 3·50 3·50

250 Presidents Callejas and Cossiga of Italy

1992. Air. 2nd Year in Office of President Rafael Leonardo Callejas. Multicoloured.
1161 20c. Type **250** 15 10
1162 2l. Callejas with Pope 1·30 85

251 View From Crow's Nest

1992. Air. America 1991. 500th Anniv of Discovery of America. Multicoloured.
1163 90c. Type **251** 70 50
1164 1l. Fleet 80 60
1165 2l. Ship approaching island 1·80 1·30

252 Skiing

1992. Winter Olympic Games, Albertville. Mult.
1166 50c. Type **252** 25 15
1167 3l. Jenny Palacios de Stillo (cross-country skier) 2·00 1·30

253 Athletics

1992. Olympic Games, Barcelona. Mult.
1168 20c. Type **253** 20 10
1169 50c. Tennis 35 15
1170 85c. Football 65 45

254 "Seller" (Manuel Rodriguez)

1992. Mother's Day. Paintings. Multicoloured.
1171 20c. Type **254** 20 10
1172 50c. "Grandmother and Baby" (Manuel Rodriguez) 25 15
1173 5l. "Sellers" (Maury Flores) 3·25 2·20

255 "Chlosyne janais"

1992. Butterflies. Multicoloured.
1174 25c. Type **255** 25 15
1175 85c. "Agrilus vanillae" 80 45
1176 3l. "Morpho granadensis" 2·75 1·30
MS1177 107×76 mm. 5l. "Dryadula phalusa". Imperf 4·25 4·00

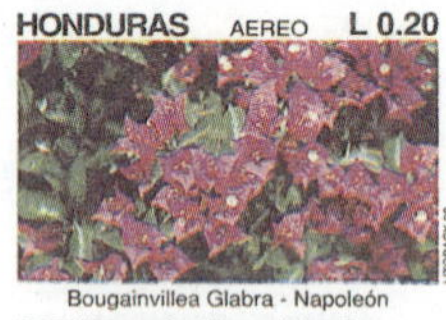

256 "Bougainvillea glabra" "Napoleon"

1992. Air. Flowers. Multicoloured.
1178 20c. Type **256** 25 15
1179 30c. "Canna indica" 25 15
1180 75c. "Epiphyllum sp." 70 50
1181 95c. "Sobralia macrantha" 1·00 70

257 Dam

1992. Air. General Francisco Morazan Hydroelectric Project. Multicoloured.
1182 85c. Type **257** 55 35
1183 4l. Inner view of dam (horiz) 2·75 1·70

258 Crops

1992. Air. 50th Anniv of Inter-American Institute for Agricultural Co-operation.
1184 **258** 95c. multicoloured (white background) 65 50
1185 **258** 95c. multicoloured (black background) 65 50

259 "Huancasco" (Arturo Lopez Rodezno)

1992. Air. Children's Day. Multicoloured.
1186 25c. Type **259** 20 10
1187 95c. "Bougainvillea" (Enrique Escher) 65 35
1188 2l. "Melissa" (Cesar Ordonez) 1·30 85

260 Morazan on Horseback (after Francisco Cisneros)

1992. Air. Birth Bicentenary of General Francisco Morazan. Multicoloured.

1189 5c. Type **260** 20 15
1190 10c. Statue of Morazan, Ampala 20 15
1191 50c. Morazan's watch and sword (horiz) 25 15
1192 95c. Josefa Lastiri de Morazan (wife) 65 45
MS1193 77×107 mm. 5l. "The Glory of Morazan" (after Zuniga Figueroa). Imperf 3·25 2·50

261 Globe as Pot filled with Food

1992. Air. Int Nutrition Conference, Rome.

1194 **261** 1l.05 multicoloured 70 50

262 Cinnamon Hummingbird

1992. Air. "Exfilhon '92" National Stamp Exhibition, Tegucigalpa. Multicoloured.

1195 1l.50 Type **262** 1·80 1·70
1196 2l.45 Scarlet macaw 2·75 2·50
MS1197 76×108 mm. 5l. Resplendent quetzal ("Pharomachrus mocinno"). Imperf 3·50 3·50

263 Bee-keeping

1992. Air. 50th Anniv of Pan-American School of Agriculture. Multicoloured.

1198 20c. Type **263** 10 10
1199 85c. Tending goats 55 35
1200 1l. Ploughing with oxen 65 45
1201 2l. Hoeing (vert) 1·30 85

264 Fruit, Locomotive, Clock and Bridge

1992. Air. Centenary of El Progreso (City).

1202 **264** 1l.55 multicoloured 1·20 70

265 Amerindian Village

1992. Air. America. 500th Anniv of Discovery of America by Columbus. Multicoloured.

1203 35c. Type **265** 20 10
1204 5l. Columbus's landing party meeting Amerindians 2·50 1·80

266 Columbus's Fleet and Landing Craft

1992. Air. 500th Anniv of Discovery of America by Columbus. Details of "The First Mass" by Roque Zelaya. Multicoloured.

1205 95c. Type **266** 55 45
1206 1l. Mass (horiz) 70 50
1207 2l. View of village (horiz) 1·40 1·10

267 Road and Bridge

1992. Air. 1st Central America–Panama Highway Maintenance Congress, San Pedro Sula. Multicoloured.

1208 20c. Type **267** 20 10
1209 85c. Bulldozer 55 35

268 The Greasy Pole

1992. Air. Christmas. Multicoloured.

1210 20c. Type **268** 20 10
1211 85c. Crib, San Antonio de Flores (horiz) 55 35

269 Globes, Children and Emblem

1992. Air. 90th Anniv of Pan-American Health Organization.

1212 **269** 3l.95 multicoloured 2·30 1·90

1992. Air. Nos. 894 and 899/900 surch.

1213 **179** 20c. on 1c. multicoloured 20 15
1214 - 20c. on 6c. multicoloured 25 15
1215 - 85c. on 18c. mult 55 35

271 Pres. Callejas at Ceremony

1993. Air. 3rd Year of Rafael L. Callejas's Presidential Term and International Court of Justice's Decision on Border with El Salvador. Multicoloured.

1216 90c. Type **271** 55 35
1217 1l.05 Map (horiz) 65 45

272 Mother and Child

1993. Air. Mother's Day. Multicoloured.

1218 50c. Type **272** 25 15
1219 95c. Mother and child (different) 55 35

273 American Manatee

1993. Air. Endangered Mammals. Mult.

1220 85c. Type **273** 65 45
1221 2l.45 Puma 1·60 1·30
1222 10l. Jaguar (vert) 5·75 3·75

274 Scarlet Macaws

1993. Air. National Symbols. Multicoloured.

1223 25c. Type **274** 1·30 1·00
1224 95c. White-tailed deer 1·60 1·40

1993. Air. Various stamps surch.

1225 - 20c. on 3c. mult (No. 896) 25 15
1226 **189** 20c. on 3c. orange, blue and bistre 25 15
1227 **197** 20c. on 3c. multicoloured 25 15
1228 - 20c. on 8c. mult (No. 868) 25 15
1229 **182** 20c. on 8c. multicoloured 25 15
1230 **176** 50c. on 16c. mult 25 15
1231 **177** 50c. on 16c. red and black 25 15
1232 - 50c. on 16c. mult (No. 886) 25 15
1233 **180** 50c. on 16c. mult 25 15
1234 - 50c. on 16c. mult (No. 931) 45 15
1235 **195** 50c. on 16c. mult 45 25
1236 - 50c. on 18c. mult (No. 870) 25 15
1237 - 50c. on 18c. mult (No. 910) 25 15
1238 - 50c. on 18c. mauve and black (No. 1011) 25 15
1239 - 85c. on 18c. green and black (No. 878) 45 35
1240 - 85c. on 18c. mult (No. 906) 45 35
1241 - 85c. on 18c. mult (No. 932) 55 35
1242 - 85c. on 18c. mult (No. 937) 45 35
1243 - 85c. on 24c. mult (No. 973) 45 35
1244 **191** 85c. on 24c. mult 45 35

276 30r. "Bull's Eye" Stamp

1993. Air. 150th Anniv of 1st Brazilian Stamps. Multicoloured.

1245 20c. Type **276** 20 10
1246 50c. 60r. "Bull's eye" stamp 25 15
1247 95c. 90r. "Bull's eye" stamp 55 45

277 Atlantida

1993. Air. Departments. Multicoloured.

1248 20c. Type **277** 15 10
1249 20c. Colon 15 10
1250 20c. Cortes 15 10
1251 20c. Choluteca 15 10
1252 20c. El Paraiso 15 10
1253 20c. Francisco Morazan 15 10
1254 50c. Comayagua (vert) 35 25
1255 50c. Copan (vert) 35 25
1256 50c. Intibuca (vert) 35 25
1257 50c. Bahia Islands (vert) 35 25
1258 50c. Lempira (vert) 35 25
1259 50c. Ocotepeque (vert) 35 25
1260 1l.50 La Paz 90 80
1261 1l.50 Olancho 90 80
1262 1l.50 Santa Barbara 90 80
1263 1l.50 Valle 90 80
1264 1l.50 Yoro 90 80
1265 1l.50 Gracias a Dios 90 80

278 Muscovy Duck

1993. Air. America. Endangered Birds. Mult.

1266 20c. Ornate hawk eagle (vert) 25 15
1267 80c. Type **278** 1·10 70
1268 2l. Harpy eagle 2·75 1·70

279 Painting by Julia Padilla

1993. Air. 40th Anniv of United Nations Development Programme.

1269 **279** 95c. multicoloured 55 35

280 Church

1993. Air. Christmas. Paintings by Aida Lara de Pedemonte. Multicoloured.

1270 20c. Type **280** 20 10
1271 85c. Flower vendor 45 35

281 Ramon Rosa

1993. Air. Personalities. Multicoloured.

1272 25c. Type **281** 20 10
1273 65c. Jesus Aguilar Paz 35 25
1274 85c. Augusto Coello 45 35

282 Grey Angelfish

1993. Air. Fishes. Multicoloured.

1275 20c. Type **282** 25 15
1276 85c. Queen angelfish 55 45
1277 3l. Banded butterflyfish 1·90 1·50

283 Norma Callejas planting Tree

1994. Air. 4th Year of Rafael L. Callejas's Presidential Term. Multicoloured.

1278 95c. Type **283** 45 35
1279 1l. Pres. Callejas and Government House (horiz) 45 35

284 Family with Rushes (Aida Lara de Pedemonte)

1994. International Year of the Family.

1280 **284** 1l. multicoloured 45 35

285 Dove and Maps on Globe

1994. Air. International Peace and Development in Central America Conference, Tegucigalpa.

1281 **285** 1l. multicoloured 45 35

286 "Madonna and Child"

1994. Air. Christmas. Paintings by Gelasio Gimenez. Multicoloured.

1282 95c. Type **286** 45 35
1283 1l. "Holy Family" 55 45

287 "Family Scene" (Delmer Mejia)

1995. Air. 50th Anniv of U.N.O. Mult.

1284 1l. "The Sowing: Ecological Family" (Elisa Dulcey) 55 45
1285 2l. Type **287** 90 80
1286 3l. Anniversary emblem 1·30 1·20

288 Pres. Reina

1995. Air. 1st Anniv of Presidency of Carlos Roberto Reina. Multicoloured.

1287 80c. Type **288** 45 35
1288 95c. Pres. Reina with arms raised (horiz) 45 35
1289 1l. Pres. Reina at summit conference (horiz) 55 45

289 Postman loading Mail Van

1995. Air. America. Postal Transport. Paintings by Ramiro Rodriguez Zelaya. Multicoloured.

1290 1l.50 Type **289** 70 60
1291 2l. Postman on motor cycle 90 80

290 "Boletellus russelli"

1995. Air. Fungi. Multicoloured.

1292 1l. "Marasmius cohaerens" (horiz) 45 35
1293 1l. Blue leg ("Lepista nuda") (horiz) 45 35
1294 1l. "Polyporus pargamenus" (horiz) 45 35
1295 1l. "Fomes sp." (horiz) 45 35
1296 1l. "Paneolus sphinctrinus" (horiz) 45 35
1297 1l. "Hygrophorus aurantiaca" (horiz) 45 35
1298 1l.50 The blusher ("Amanita rubescens") 65 50
1299 1l.50 "Boletus frostii" 65 50
1300 1l.50 "Fomes annosus" 65 50
1301 1l.50 "Psathyrella sp." 65 50
1302 1l.50 Type **290** 65 50
1303 1l.50 "Marasmius spegazzinii" 65 50
1304 2l. "Amanita sp." 90 80
1305 2l. Golden tops ("Psilocybe cubensis") 90 80
1306 2l. Royal boletus ("Boletus regius") 90 80
1307 2l. Black trumpet ("Craterellus cornucopioides") 90 80
1308 2l. "Auricularia delicata" 90 80
1309 2l. "Clavariadelphus pistilaris" 90 80
1310 2l.50 "Scleroderma aurantium" (horiz) 1·10 95
1311 2l.50 "Amanita praegraveolens" (horiz) 1·10 95
1312 2l.50 Chanterelle ("Cantharellus cibarius") (horiz) 1·10 95
1313 2l.50 "Geastrum triplex" (horiz) 1·10 95
1314 2l.50 "Russula emetica" (horiz) 1·10 95
1315 2l.50 "Boletus pinicola" (horiz) 1·10 95
1316 3l. "Fomes versicolor" (horiz) 1·30 1·20
1317 3l. "Cantharellus purpurascens" (horiz) 1·30 1·20
1318 3l. "Lyophyllum decastes" (horiz) 1·30 1·20
1319 3l. Oyster fungus ("Pleurotus ostreatus") (horiz) 1·30 1·20
1320 3l. "Boletus ananas" (horiz) 1·30 1·20
1321 3l. Caesar's mushroom ("Amanita caesarea") (horiz) 1·30 1·20

291 "Food for All"

1995. Air. 50th Anniv of F.A.O.

1322 **291** 3l. multicoloured 90 50

292 Family and Farm over Globe

1995. Air. 50th Anniv of CARE (Co-operative for Assistance and Remittances Overseas). Multicoloured.

1323 1l.40 Type **292** 65 50
1324 5l.40 Crop farming 2·20 1·90
1325 5l.40 Keel-billed toucan, orchid, planting tree and animals at waterfall 2·20 1·90

293 Archaeological Site (1/2-size illustration) (image scaled to 66% of original size)

1995. Air. El Puente Archaeological Park. Sheet 83×58 mm. Imperf.

MS1326 **293** 20l. multicoloured 7·25 7·00

294 People around Japanese Character

1995. 20th Anniv of Japanese Overseas Co-operation Voluntary Workers in Honduras. Multicoloured.

1327 1l.40 Type **294** (postage) 65 50
1328 4l.30 Amerindian-style figures on pages of leaflet (horiz) (air) 1·40 1·30
1329 5l.40 Volunteer and people in traditional costumes (horiz) 1·90 1·70

295 Scorpion Mud Turtle

1995. Air. America. Environmental Protection. Multicoloured.

1330 1l.40 Type **295** 55 45
1331 4l.54 "Alpinia purpurata" (flower) (vert) 1·40 1·30
1332 10l. Common caracara ("Caracara") (vert) 3·25 3·00

296 "Agalychnis sp."

1995. Air. Reptiles and Amphibians. Mult.

1333 5l.40 Type **296** 2·20 2·20
1334 5l.40 Iguana 2·20 2·20

297 Bell

1995. Air. Christmas. Multicoloured.

1335 1l.40 Type **297** 55 50
1336 5l.40 Crib figures (horiz) 2·20 2·10
1337 6l.90 Deer (carving) 2·75 2·50

298 "SICA" over Map

1996. Air. 3rd Anniv of Central American Integration System. Multicoloured.

1338 1l.40 Type **298** (signing of Protocol, 1991) 45 45
1339 4l.30 Emblem 1·50 1·50
1340 5l.40 Presidents of Central American countries at 17th Summit 2·00 1·90

299 Allegorical Design

1996. Air. United Nations Decade against Drug Abuse and Drug Trafficking. Multicoloured.

1341 1l.40 Type **299** 45 45
1342 5l.40 Woman's head with butterfly as hat (vert) 1·80 1·70
1343 10l. Guitar and bar of music 2·75 2·50

300 Traditional Headdress

1996. Air. Bicentenary of Arrival of Garifunas Tribe in Honduras. Multicoloured.

1344 1l.40 Type **300** 45 35
1345 5l.40 Tribesmen dancing to music (horiz) 1·80 1·40
1346 10l. Drums (horiz) 2·75 2·20

301 Steam Locomotive "San Jose"

1996. Air. "Exfilhon 96" National Stamp Exn, Tegucigalpa. Railway Locomotives. Mult.

1347 5l.40 Type **301** 1·80 1·70
1348 5l.40 Diesel railcar No. 203 1·80 1·70
MS1349 75×52 mm. 20l.+2l. Locomotive "San Jose". Imperf 7·25 7·00

302 Football

1996. Air. 6th Central American Games, San Pedro Sula (1997). Multicoloured.

1350 4l.30 Type **302** 1·30 85
1351 4l.54 Volleyball and games emblem 1·40 90
1352 5l.40 Games mascot (vert) 1·80 1·10

303 Honduran and International Badges

1996. Air. 75th Anniv of Honduran Scouts' Association. Multicoloured.

1353 2l.15 Type **303** 55 35
1354 5l.40 Anniversary emblem (vert) 1·80 1·00
1355 6l.90 Scout feeding deer (vert) 2·20 1·30

304 Poinsettia and Candles

1996. Air. Christmas. Multicoloured.

1356 1l.40 Type **304** 55 35
1357 3l. Poinsettia 1·30 75

1358	5l.40 As Type **304** but vert	2·75	1·40

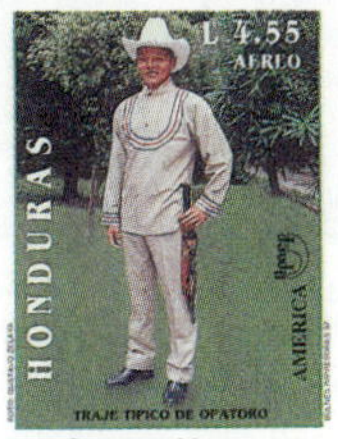
305 Opatoro Man

1997. Air. America (1996). Traditional Costumes. Multicoloured.

1359	4l.55 Type **305**	1·30	75
1360	5l.40 Jocomico woman	1·80	1·00
1361	10l. Intibuca couple	3·25	1·80

306 Children playing in River (Oscar Moncada)

1997. Air. 20th Anniv of Honduran Plan and 60th Anniv of International Plan. Multicoloured.

1362	1l.40 Type **306**	55	30
1363	5l.40 Girl beside river (Nataly Alexandra Reyes) (horiz)	1·80	95
1364	9l.70 Street (Walter Enrique Martinez) (horiz)	3·00	2·40

307 Red-tailed Hawk

1997. Birds. Multicoloured.

1365	1l.40 Type **307** (postage)	55	35
1366	1l.50 Keel-billed toucan	55	35
1367	2l. Red-billed whistling duck	70	50
1368	2l.15 Collared forest falcon	80	60
1369	3l. Common caracara	1·10	85
1370	5l.40 King vulture (air)	2·00	1·70
MS1371	57×84 mm. 20l. As No. 1370 (41×61 mm). Imperf	6·75	6·50

308 Von Stephan

1997. Air. Death Centenary of Dr. Heinrich von Stephan (founder of U.P.U.).

1372	**308** 5l.40 multicoloured	1·40	80

309 Children and Adults in Room (Yorvin Ramon Toro)

1997. Air. World Population Day. Mult.

1373	1l.40 Type **309**	45	25
1374	6l.90 Family group and house (Marvin Lamberth Harry)	1·80	85

310 "Rothschildia forbesi"

1997. Air. Butterflies and Moths. Mult.

1375	1l. Type **310**	25	15
1376	1l.40 "Parides photinus"	35	15
1377	2l.15 Emperor	55	45
1378	3l. Jamaican kite swallowtail	90	70
1379	4l.30 "Parides iphidamas"	1·30	1·00
1380	5l.40 Monarch	1·80	1·30
MS1381	89×64 mm. 20l.+2l. "Hamadryas arinome". Imperf	4·50	3·50

311 St. Theresa

1997. Air. Death Centenary of St. Theresa of Lisieux. Multicoloured.

1382	1l.40 Type **311**	45	30
1383	5l.40 St. Theresa (different)	1·30	70

312 Observatory

1997. Air. 150th Anniv of National University and 40th Anniv of Free University. Multicoloured.

1384	1l.40 Type **312**	35	25
1385	5l.40 Statue of Fr. Jose Trinidad Reyes (founder)	1·30	70
1386	10l. Woman with book guiding boy	2·30	1·30

313 Diana, Princess of Wales

1997. Air. Diana, Princess of Wales Commemoration. Multicoloured.

1387	1l.40 Type **313**	35	25
1388	5l.40 Visiting minefield (horiz)	1·80	85
MS1389	57×83 mm. 20l. Mother Teresa (founder of Missionaries of Charity) and Princess of Wales. Imperf	5·50	3·50

314 Children around Statue (Nelson Leonel Rodriguez)

1997. Air. 37th Anniv of Alcoholics Anonymous (rehabilitation organization).

1390	**314** 5l.40 multicoloured	1·60	85

315 "Christ of Picacho" (statue)

1997. Air. Christmas. Multicoloured.

1391	1l.40 Type **315**	35	25
1392	5l.50 "Virgin of Suyapa"	1·40	1·00

316 Basketball

1997. Air. 6th Central American Games, San Pedro Sula. Multicoloured.

1393	1l.40 Type **316**	45	35
1394	1l.40 Baseball (batting)	45	35
1395	1l.40 Football	45	35
1396	1l.40 Squash	45	35
1397	1l.40 Volleyball	45	35
1398	1l.40 Handball	45	35
1399	1l.40 Bowls	45	35
1400	1l.40 Table tennis	45	35
1401	1l.40 Rings on map of Honduras	45	35
1402	1l.40 Baseball (bowling)	45	35
1403	1l.50 Taekwondo (kicking)	55	45
1404	1l.50 Karate (one hand raised)	55	45
1405	1l.50 Judo (bowing)	55	45
1406	1l.50 Wrestling	55	45
1407	1l.50 Weightlifting	55	45
1408	1l.50 Boxing	55	45
1409	1l.50 Body-building	55	45
1410	1l.50 Fencing	55	45
1411	1l.50 Games emblem	55	45
1412	1l.50 Shooting	55	45
1413	2l.15 Cycling (on bicycle)	70	60
1414	2l.15 Road cycle racing (running beside bicycle)	70	60
1415	2l.15 Swimming	70	60
1416	2l.15 Water polo	70	60
1417	2l.15 Hurdling	70	60
1418	2l.15 Gymnastics (ring exercise)	70	60
1419	2l.15 Horse riding	70	60
1420	2l.15 Tennis	70	60
1421	2l.15 Pedrito Pichete (Games mascot)	70	60
1422	2l.15 Chess	70	60

317 "Cichlasoma dovii"

1997. Air. Fishes. Multicoloured.

1423	1l.40 Type **317**	35	25
1424	2l. "Cichlasoma spilurum" (facing left)	55	45
1425	3l. "Cichlasoma spilurum" (facing right)	70	60
1426	5l.40 "Astyanay fasciatus"	1·30	1·00

318 Queen Triggerfish

1998. Air. 50th Anniv of Bancahsa. Marine Life of Bahia Coral Reef. Multicoloured.

1427	2l.50 Type **318**	90	70
1428	2l.50 White grunt ("Haemulon plumieri")	90	70
1429	2l.50 French angelfish ("Pomacanthus paru")	90	70
1430	2l.50 Wrasse (juvenile) ("Halichoeres garnoti")	90	70
1431	2l.50 Grey angelfish (complete fish) ("Pomacanthus arcuatus")	90	70
1432	2l.50 Queen angelfish ("Holacanthus ciliaris")	90	70
1433	2l.50 Diver and "Pseud opterogorgia" (coral)	90	70
1434	2l.50 Diver's oxygen tank and "Pseud opterogorgia"	90	70
1435	2l.50 Six fingers of pillar coral ("Dendrogyra cylindrus") (inscr in Latin)	90	70
1436	2l.50 Squirrelfish facing right ("Holocentrus adscensionis")	90	70
1437	2l.50 Three fingers of pillar coral ("Dendrogyra cylindrus") (inscr in Latin)	90	70
1438	2l.50 "Stegastes fuscus" (fish)	90	70
1439	2l.50 "Gorgonia mariae" (coral)	90	70
1440	2l.50 Three fingers of pillar coral (inscr in English)	90	70
1441	2l.50 Head of grey angelfish ("Pomacanthus arcuatus")	90	70
1442	2l.50 Squirrelfish facing left ("Holocentrus adscensionis")	90	70
1443	2l.50 "Eusmilia fastigiata" (coral)	90	70
1444	2l.50 Midnight parrotfish ("Scarus coelestinus")	90	70
1445	2l.50 One finger of pillar coral (inscr in English)	90	70
1446	2l.50 Hogfish ("Lachnolaimus maximus")	90	70

Nos. 1427/46 were issued together, se-tenant, forming a composite design.

319 Postman on Motor Cycle

1998. Air. America (1997). Postal Service. Multicoloured.

1447	5l.40 Type **319**	1·30	85
1448	5l.40 Post Office	1·30	85

320 Sculpted Skull from Temple 16

1998. Air. Maya Culture. Multicoloured.

1449	1l. Type **320**	35	25
1450	1l.40 Stone carving	45	35
1451	2l.15 Steles H and F	65	50
1452	5l.40 Carved water vessel	1·30	1·00
MS1453	89×64 mm. 20l. Temple ruins, Copan. Imperf	4·50	2·50

321 Players and Trophy

1998. Air. World Cup Football Championship, France. Multicoloured.

1454	5l.40 Type **321**	1·30	85
1455	10l. Players in tackle and trophy (vert)	2·75	1·70
MS1456	67×95 mm. 10l. Tegucigalpa Stadium, Honduras (63×42 mm); 10l. St. Denis Stadium, France (63×46 mm)	8·00	7·75

322 Green Iguana

1998. Air. Reptiles. Multicoloured.

1457	1l.40 Type **322**	35	25
1458	2l. Eyelash viper	55	45
1459	3l. Green lizards	80	70
1460	5l.40 Coral snake	1·40	1·00
MS1461	89×64 mm. 20l.+2l. Turtle. Imperf	3·50	2·20

323 Robin giving Gift to Girl

1998. Air. Christmas. Multicoloured.

1462	3l. Type **323**	65	45
1463	5l.40 Child Jesus in crib (horiz)	1·20	85
1464	10l. Child leading donkey	2·20	1·70

324 Flores and his Wife greeting Pope

1999. Air. 1st Anniv of Inauguration of President Carlos Roberto Flores.

1465	5l.40 Type **324**	1·30	85
1466	10l. President and Mary Flores (vert)	2·00	1·30

325 Floods, Central Zone

1999. Air. Hurricane Mitch Victims' Fund. Mult.

1467	5l.40 Type **325**	1·10	1·00
1468	5l.40 Man carrying boy on back through flood and black-tailed trogon	1·10	1·00
1469	5l.40 Prince Felipe of Spain and Mary Flores (President's wife)	1·10	1·00
1470	5l.40 Child crying and orchid	1·10	1·00
1471	5l.40 People clearing timber in Comayaguela and orchid	1·10	1·00
1472	5l.40 People wading through flood in North Zone and spectacled owl	1·10	1·00
1473	5l.40 Destruction of La Hoya quarter, Tegucigalpa, and orchid	1·10	1·00
1474	5l.40 Soldier helping woman and child in North Zone and lance-tailed manakin	1·10	1·00
1475	5l.40 Collapsed houses in rural zone and orchids	1·10	1·00
1476	5l.40 Collapsed bridge and damaged motor cars ("Red Vial") and red-capped manakin	1·10	1·00
1477	5l.40 Damaged houses, motor cars and uprooted trees ("Red Vial") and orchids	1·10	1·00
1478	5l.40 Mexican soldiers with dogs and airplane	1·10	1·00
1479	5l.40 Two children swimming in North Zone and sinaloa martin	1·10	1·00
1480	5l.40 Mary and President Flores with Hillary Clinton (wfe of U.S. President)	1·10	1·00
1481	5l.40 Crowd before collapsed building in South Zone and rufous motmot	1·10	1·00
1482	5l.40 President Flores and George Bush (U.S. President, 1988–92)	1·10	1·00
1483	5l.40 Three men digging out rubble and tufted jay	1·10	1·00
1484	5l.40 Helicopter on beach and orchid	1·10	1·00
1485	5l.40 Car submerged under flood water in North Zone and bare-necked umbrel-labird	1·10	1·00
1486	5l.40 Tipper Gore (U.S. Vice-president's wife) and Mary Flores in flooded building	1·10	1·00
1487	5l.40 Flooded banana plantation and orchid	1·10	1·00
1488	5l.40 Tegucigalpa submerged under flood water and red-breasted blackbird and green bird	1·10	1·00
1489	5l.40 Traffic jam behind rocks from landslide ("Red Vial")	1·10	1·00
1490	5l.40 Comayaguela and ridgway's cotinga	1·10	1·00
1491	5l.40 Destruction of Comayaguela street and orchid	1·10	1·00
1492	5l.40 People carrying plank in Eastern Zone and scarlet macaw	1·10	1·00
1493	5l.40 Mexican truck being filled with debris and orchid	1·10	1·00
1494	5l.40 Bulldozer clearing street and white-tipped sicklebill	1·10	1·00
1495	5l.40 President Flores and President Chirac of France	1·10	1·00
1496	5l.40 Comayaguela commercial zone flooded and tooth-billed hummingbird	1·10	1·00
1497	5l.40 People looking at flood water in Tegucigalpa and lineated woodpecker	1·10	1·00
1498	5l.40 Stranded BMW motor car in Comayaguela street and hoffmann's conure	1·10	1·00

326 Pilar Salinas

1999. Air. America (1998). Famous Women. Mult.

1499	2l.60 Type **326**	55	35
1500	7l.30 Clementina Suarerz (poet)	1·60	85
1501	10l.65 Mary Flores (President's wife)	2·30	1·40

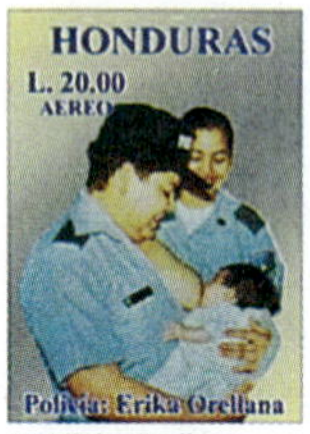

327 Enka Orellana breast-feeding Baby

1999. Air. Mothers' Day. Multicoloured.

1502	20l. Type **327**	4·00	3·00
1503	30l. *Paphiopedilum urbanianum* (horiz)	5·75	4·00
1504	50l. *Miltoniopsis vexillaria* (horiz)	9·75	6·00

1999. No. 748 surch.

1505	2l.60 on 1c. blue and red	70	45
1506	7l.85 on 1c. blue and red	2·00	1·40
1507	10l.65 on 1c. blue and red	2·75	1·90
1508	11l.55 on 1c. blue and red	3·00	2·10
1509	12l.45 on 1c. blue and red	3·25	2·30
1510	13l.85 on 1c. blue and red	3·50	2·50

329 Orange-fronted Conure

1999. Air. 30th Anniv of Sogerin Bank. Birds. Mult.

1511	3l. Type **329**	70	45
1512	3l. White-fronted amazon (*Amazona albifrons*)	70	45
1513	3l. Yellow-naped amazon (*Amazona auropalliata*)	70	45
1514	3l. Red-lored amazon (*Amazona autumnalis*)	70	45
1515	3l. Sun-bittern (*Eurypga helias*)	70	45
1516	3l. Great curassow (*Crax rubra*)	70	45
1517	3l. Orange-chinned parakeet (*Brotogeris jugularis*)	70	45
1518	3l. White-capped parrot (*Pionus senilis*)	70	45
1519	3l. Brown-throated conure (*Aratinga rubritorques*)	70	45
1520	3l. Great tinamou (*Tinamus major*)	70	45
1521	5l. King vulture (*Sarcorhamphus papa*)	1·30	85
1522	5l. White hawk (*Leucopternis albicollis*)	1·30	85
1523	5l. Harpy eagle (*Harpia harpyja*)	1·30	85
1524	5l. Spectacled owl (*Pulsatrix perspicillata*)	1·30	85
1525	5l. Ornate hawk eagle (*Spizaetus ornatus*)	1·30	85
1526	5l. Resplendent quetzal (*Pharomachrus mocinno*)	1·30	85
1527	5l. Emerald toucanet (*Aulacorhynchus prasinus*)	1·30	85
1528	5l. Honduras emerald (*Amazilia luciae*)	1·30	85
1529	5l. Scarlet macaw (*Ara macao*)	1·30	85
1530	5l. Yucatan woodpecker (*Centurus pygmaeus*)	1·30	85
1531	10l. Jabiru (*Jabiru mycteria*) (wrongly inscr "Jaberu")	2·20	1·50
1532	10l. Hook-billed kite (*Chondrohierax uncinatus*)	2·20	1·50
1533	10l. Resplendent quetzal (*Pharomachrus mocinno*) (different)	2·20	1·50
1534	10l. Keel-billed toucan (*Ramphastos sulfuratus*)	2·20	1·50

Nos. 1511/30 were issued together, se-tenant, forming a composite design.

330 Salvador Moncada (scientist) and Pipette

1999. Air. New Millennium. Multicoloured.

1535	2l. Type **330**	45	35
1536	8l.65 Albert Einstein (scientist, formulator of Theory of Relativity, 1905)	1·40	1·00
1537	10l. Wilhelm Rontgen (scientist, discoverer of X-rays, 1895)	1·70	1·40
1538	14l.95 George Stephenson (engineer) (inventor of steam locomotive, 1829) and *Rocket* (horiz)	2·75	2·00

331 Headquarters

1999. Air. 40th Anniv of Inter-American Development Bank.

1539	331	18l.30 multicoloured	3·50	2·20

332 Josemaria Escriva de Balaguer (founder)

1999. Air. 70th Anniv (1998) of Founding of Opus Dei (religious organization).

1540	332	2l.60 multicoloured	70	45
1541	332	16l.40 multicoloured	3·75	2·20

333 Statue and View of Cedros, Francisco Morazan Province

1999. Air. 175th Anniv of National Congress. Mult.

1542	4l.30 Type **333**	90	45
1543	10l. Rafael Pineda Ponce (Congress President) and building	2·10	1·40

334 St. Peter

2000. Holy Year 2000. Multicoloured.

1544	4l. Open gateway into garden	1·00	70
1545	4l.30 Type **334**	1·10	80
1546	4l.30 As Type **334**, but with country name and face value in yellow	1·10	80
1547	6l.90 Jesus (statue) and Jerusalem (horiz)	1·70	1·20
1548	7l.30 Pope John Paul II addressing crowd (horiz)	1·90	1·30
1549	10l. Pope John Paul II	2·75	1·80
1550	14l. Pope John Paul II and Pres. Carlos Roberto Flores	3·00	2·10
1551	14l. As No. 1550 but with country name at right	3·50	2·40

335 Pres. Flores and Reunion Consultative Group, Stockholm, Sweden

2000. 2nd Anniv of Inauguration of President Carlos Roberto Flores. Multicoloured.

1552	10l. Type **335**	2·50	1·80
1553	10l.65 Flores and General Mario Hung Pacheco	2·75	1·90

336 Left Half of Marimba

2000. Air. Musical Instruments. Multicoloured.

1554	1l.40 Type **336**	45	35
1555	1l.40 Right half of Marimba	45	35
1556	1l.40 Ayotl	45	35
1557	2l.60 Maracas	80	65
1558	2l.60 Guiro	80	65
1559	2l.60 Chinchin	80	65
1560	2l.60 Raspador	80	65
1561	2l.60 Quijada de Caballo	80	65
1562	3l. Fish-shaped whistle	90	70
1563	3l. Aztec drum	90	70
1564	3l. Whistle ("Pito Zoomorfo de un tono")	90	70
1565	3l. Whistle ("Pito Zoomorfo de dos tonos")	90	70
1566	3l. Tun	90	70
1567	4l. Tecomate	1·10	85
1568	4l. Deerskin drum	1·10	85
1569	4l. Guacalitos	1·10	85
1570	4l. Women standing to left of marimba	1·10	85
1571	4l. Men standing to right of marimba	1·10	85
1572	10l. Maya drum	3·25	2·50
1573	10l. Teponaxtle	3·25	2·50
MS1574a	Inscribed Pro filatelia in black, 221×139 mm. 10l.+1l. Drummer, Garifuna (horiz); 10l.+1l. Tolteca drum (horiz); 10l.+1l. Flutes (horiz); 10l.+1l. Chirimia (horiz); 10l.+1l. Maya drum (different) (horiz); 10l.+1l. Man blowing conch shell (horiz)	15·00	14·50
MS1574b	As **MS**1574a but inscription Pro filatelia in red	17·00	16·00

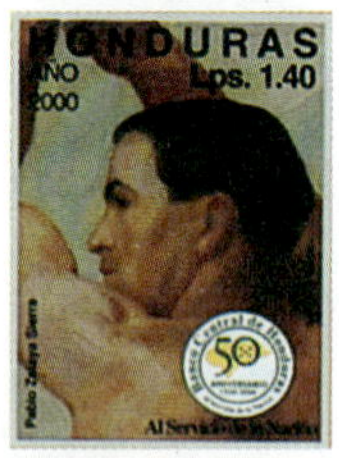

337 Man

2000. 50th Anniv of Central Honduras Bank. Paintings by Pablo Zelaya Sierra. Multicoloured.

1575	1l.40 Type **337**	45	35
1576	1l.40 Dog barking	45	35
1577	1l.40 View of town on hillside	45	35
1578	1l.40 Back of woman's head	45	35
1579	1l.40 Woman holding bowl	45	35
1580	2l. Building surrounded by trees	70	60
1581	2l. Old woman wearing black gown	70	60
1582	2l. Two women talking	70	60
1583	2l. Woman wrapped in white sheet	70	60
1584	2l. View of walled town	70	60
1585	2l.60 Birds and animals	90	70
1586	2l.60 Trees	90	70
1587	2l.60 Nun beside harp	90	70
1588	2l.60 Archers	90	70
1589	2l.60 Moon over sea	90	70
1590	2l.60 Sculpture of woman's head	90	70
1591	2l.60 Gardener in grounds of large house	90	70
1592	2l.60 Sculpture of man's head and open fan	90	70
1593	10l. Lemons on white table cloth	3·50	3·00

1594	10l. Pile of books	3·50	3·00

338 1925 25c. on 10c. Airmail Stamp

2000. Air. 75th Anniv of Honduras Airmail Stamps. Multicoloured.

1595	7l.30 Type **338**	1·80	90
1596	10l. Thomas Canfield Pounds (founder of Central American Airline) (vert)	2·50	1·30
1597	10l.65 General Rafael Lopez Gutierrez (President of Honduras, 1920–24) (vert)	2·75	1·40
MS1598	111×89 mm. 50l.+5l. Biplane and Sumner B. Margan (pilot) (80×59 mm)	18·00	17·00

339 Flower and Rifle

2000. Air. America (1999). A New Millennium without Arms. Multicoloured.

1599	10l. Type **339**	2·75	1·80
1600	10l.65 White dove and soldier	3·25	1·90
1601	14l. Steam train and bomb (horiz)	4·00	2·50

340 Ivan Guerrero and Mario Chirinos (football)

2000. Air. Olympic Games, Sydney. Multicoloured.

1602	2l.60 Type **340**	1·30	1·10
1603	10l.65 Ramon Valle (swimming) (vert)	4·50	3·50
1604	12l.45 Gina Coello (running) (vert)	5·00	4·00
MS1605	122×90 mm. 4l.30 Swimming; 4l.30 Danilo Turcios (football); 10l.65 David Suazo (football); 10l.65 Pedro Ventura (running). Perf or imperf	8·50	8·25

L.48.50 +

(341)

2000. No. MS913 surch with T 341 in black and red.

MS1606	160×110 mm. 48l.50 on 1l.50, Mayan pelota court	13·00	12·50

342 Children and White-crowned Parrot

2000. Air. International Year of Volunteers. Multicoloured.

1607	2l.60 Type **342**	70	45
1608	10l.65 Boy and flower	2·75	1·70

343 Mary and Jesus

2000. Air. Christmas. Multicoloured.

1609	1l.60 Type **343**	70	45
1610	7l.30 Nativity (vert)	2·20	1·30
1611	14l. Pavement art	2·75	1·40

344 Yellow-naped Amazon (*Amazona auroalliata*)

2001. Air. America. AIDS Awareness Campaign. Monogamy. Multicoloured.

1612	2l.60 Type **344**	45	35
1613	4l.30 Common ground dove (*Columbina passerine*) (horiz)	75	60
1614	10l.65 Scarlet macaw (*Ara macao*)	2·30	2·00
1615	20l. Harpy eagle (*Aguila harpia*)	4·50	3·50

2001. Air. Various stamps surch.

1616	2l. on 16c. brown and black (No. 947)	35	25
1617	2l. on 16c. multicoloured (No. 948)	35	25
1618	2l.60 on 3c. orange, blue and brown (No. 967)	45	35
1619	2l.60 on 3c. multicoloured (No. 1003)	45	35
1620	2l.60 on 8c. multicoloured (No. 914)	45	35
1621	2l.60 on 16c. multicoloured (No. 931)	45	35
1622	3l. on 16c. multicoloured (No. 886)	55	45
1623	4l. on 9c. multicoloured (No. 1017)	55	45
1624	4l.30 on 6c. multicoloured (No. 899)	70	50
1625	7l.30 on 6c. brown and black (No. 941)	1·30	60
1626	7l.30 on 6c. multicoloured (No. 942)	1·30	60
1627	10l. on 16c. orange-red and black (No. 877)	1·80	85
1628	10l.65 on 16c. multicoloured (No. 994)	2·00	1·00
1629	14l. on 16c. multicoloured (No. 905)	3·25	1·40

346 Cardinal Rodriguez as a Child with his Father

2001. Air. Cardinal Oscar Andreas Rodriguez. Multicoloured.

1630	2l.60 Type **346**	90	70
1631	2l.60 Seated, wearing white vestments	90	70
1632	2l.60 Seated, at Seminary, 1964	90	70
1633	2l.60 Consecration as Archbishop	90	70
1634	2l.60 At home, 1960	90	70
1635	2l.60 Kneeling before Pope John Paul II and other clergy, Vatican, 2001	90	70
1636	2l.60 Celebrating Mass, 1970	90	70
1637	2l.60 Woman wearing dark glasses, Cardinal Rodriguez and crowd, Vatican	90	70
1638	2l.60 Pope John Paul II and Cardinal Rodriguez wearing sash, 1993	90	70
1639	2l.60 Leaving airplane as Cardinal, 2001	90	70
1640	10l.65 Woman, Cardinal Rodriguez and Pope John Paul II, 1993 (47×40 mm)	3·50	3·00
1641	10l.65 Audience with Pope John Paul II, 2001 (47×40 mm)	3·50	3·00
1642	10l.65 Receiving cardinal ring from Pope John Paul II (47×40 mm)	3·50	3·00
1643	10l.65 Addressing crowd, 2001 (47×40 mm)	3·50	3·00
1644	10l.65 Kneeling before Pope John Paul II, Rome, 1993 (47×40 mm)	3·50	3·00
1645	10l.65 Pope John Paul II and Cardinal Rodriguez, 2000 (47×40 mm)	3·50	3·00
1646	15l. As No. 1645 enlarged to show crowd (164×132 mm)	4·50	3·50

347 Stylized Mother and child

2001. Air. 50th Anniv of United Nations High Commissioner for Refugees. Multicoloured.

1647	2l.60 Type **347**	90	60
1648	10l.65 Refugees (horiz)	3·50	2·30

348 Jug

2001. Air. 50th Anniv of Banco Occidente. Mayan Ceramics. Multicoloured.

1649	2l. Type **348**	70	60
1650	2l. Man-shaped jar	70	60
1651	2l. Seated figure with raised arms	70	60
1652	2l. Three-legged cylindrical vase	70	60
1653	2l. Textured censer with crouching animal on lid	70	60
1654	3l. Seated figure (scribe)	1·10	85
1655	3l. Cylindrical decorated jar	1·10	85
1656	3l. Three conjoined pots	1·10	85
1657	3l. Head	1·10	85
1658	3l. Man-shaped jar, arms forming handles	1·10	85
1659	5l. Decorated pot with handles and legs	1·80	1·40
1660	5l. Curved pot with lip and handles	1·80	1·40
1661	5l. Censer with large animal on lid	1·80	1·40
1662	5l. Seated figure with hands on knees	1·80	1·40
1663	5l. Man-shaped jar showing teeth	1·80	1·40
1664	6l.90 Pot with handles and narrow base	2·30	1·90
1665	6l.90 Seated figure with hands on knees (different)	2·30	1·90
1667	6l.90 Jar in shape of seated figure holding pole	2·30	1·90
1668	6l.90 Tall cylindrical vase	2·30	1·90
1669	6l.90 Textured pot with animal-shaped handles	2·30	1·90

349 Juan Ramon Molina Bridge

2001. Air. Honduras–Japan Diplomatic Relations. Sheet 153×127 mm containing T 349 and similar horiz designs showing views of bridge. Multicoloured.

MS1670	2l.60 Type **349**; 10l.65, Side view; 13l.65 From beneath	11·50	11·00

350 Turquoise-browed Motmot, Lago de Yojoa

2002. Air. America (2001). UNESCO World Heritage Sites. Multicoloured.

1671	10l. Type **350**	3·50	3·00
1672	10l.65 Iguana, Islas del Cisne	3·50	3·00
1673	20l. Chrysina quetzalcoatli, Cataratas de Pulaphanzhak (horiz)	7·25	5·75

351 Centenary Emblem

2002. Air. Centenary of Pan American Health Organization.

1674	**351** 10l. multicoloured	3·50	3·50

352 Statues and Buildings (2/3-size illustration)

2002. Air. Inauguration of Miguel Pastor, Mayor of Tegucigalpa. Multicoloured.

1675	1l.40 Type **352**	55	45
1676	1l.40 Chimpanzee dropping banana skin in rubbish bin	55	45
1677	1l.40 Municipal building	55	45
1678	2l.60 Flags and Mayor Pastor (27×35 mm)	90	70
1679	2l.60 Mayor Pastor sitting under tree (27×35 mm)	90	70
1680	2l.60 With elderly woman (27×35 mm)	90	70
1681	2l.60 With children (27×35 mm)	90	70
1682	2l.60 Mayor Pastor crouching (27×35 mm)	90	70
1683	2l.60 With family (27×35 mm)	90	70
1684	10l. Mayor Pastor and committee members	3·50	3·00
1685	10l. Mayor Pastor and guests on roof top	3·50	3·00
1686	10l.65 Type **352** (114×75 mm)	3·75	3·00

353 Natives and Cross

2002. Air. America. Literacy Campaign. Two sheets, each 114×92 mm containing T 353 and similar horiz designs. Multicoloured.

MS1687	(a) 2l.60 Type **353**; 3l. Santa Barbara fortress, Trujillo; 10l. "400 Years of History" (detail) (Mario Castillo); 10l. Arrival of missionaries (500th anniv of arrival of first Catholics on mainland America); (b) 10l.65 River and forest; 12l.45 Natives landing on beach; 13l.65 Spaniards landing craft; 20l. Spanish ship (500th anniv of discovery of Honduras)	10·00	9·75

354 Building and Emblems

2002. 10th Anniv of Banco del Pais, Tegucigalpa.

1688	**354**	2l. multicoloured	35	30
1689	**354**	2l.60 multicoloured	45	35
1690	**354**	10l. multicoloured	1·60	1·30
1691	**354**	10l.65 multicoloured	1·70	1·40

355 *Vanilla planifolia*

2002. Air. Orchids. Multicoloured.

No.	Description	Mint	Used
1692	1l.40 Type **355**	25	20
1693	2l.60 *Lycaste virginalis* (inscr "virginalis")	45	35
1694	3l. *Coelia bella*	55	45
1695	4l.30 *Chysis laevis*	70	60
1696	8l.65 *Myrmecophilia brysiana*	1·40	1·20
1697	10l. *Rhyncholaelia digbyana* (inscr "Rhyncolaelia")	1·60	1·30
MS1698	96×66 mm. 20l. *Mormodes aromatica*. Imperf	3·50	3·50

356 The Nativity (figurines)

2002. Air. Christmas. Multicoloured.

No.	Description	Mint	Used
1699	2l.60 Type **356**	45	35
1700	10l.65 Nativity (painting)	1·70	1·40
1701	14l. Crowd and outdoor Nativity	2·30	1·90

357 Children

2002. Air. 120th Anniv of PANI (social awareness organization). Multicoloured.

No.	Description	Mint	Used
1702	2l.60 Type **357**	45	35
1703	10l. Elderly men	1·60	1·30
1704	10l.65 Carving, instruments, building and birds (vert)	1·70	1·40

358 *Chrysina spectabilis*

2003. Air. 90th Anniv of Banco Atlantida. Insects. Multicoloured.

No.	Description	Mint	Used
170-1712	2l. 60×4, *Chrysina cusuquensis; Calomacraspis haroldi; Pelidnota strigosa; Odontocheila tawahka*	1·80	1·40
1705-1708	2l.×4, Type **358**; *Chrysina strasseni; Viridimicus omensis; Hoplopyga liturata*	1·40	1·20
1713-1716	3l.×4, *Chrysina cavei; Macropoides crassipes; Pelidnota velutipes; Tragidion cyanovestis*	2·20	1·80
1717-1720	4l.×4, *Chrysina pastori; Platycoelia humeralis; Phanaeus eximius; Acanthoderes cavei*	2·80	2·40
1721-1724	10l. 65×4, *Chrysina quetzalcoatli; Cyclocephala abrelata; Aegithus rufipennis; Callipogen barbatum*	6·75	5·50
MS1725	120×72 mm. 10l.×3, Eggs; Larva; Pupa	4·50	4·25

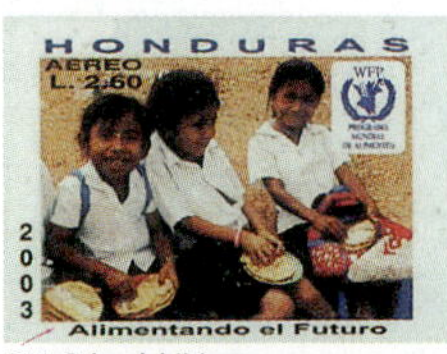

359 Schoolchildren

2003. Air. World Food Programme. Multicoloured.

No.	Description	Mint	Used
1726	2l.60 Type **359**	45	35
1727	6l.90 Girl eating from red bowl	1·20	95
1728	10l.65 Child eating, spoon in right hand	1·70	1·40

360 Pope John Paul II

2003. Air. 25th Anniv of Pontificate of Pope John Paul II. 20th Anniv of visit of Pope John Paul II to Honduras. Sheet 185×82 mm containing T 360 and similar vert designs. Multicoloured.

No.	Description	Mint	Used
MS1729	13l.65 Type **360**; 14l.55 Disembarking from aircraft; 15l.45 Wearing mitre; 16l.65 Holding rosary	9·25	9·00

361 Foodstuffs

2003. Air. 50th Anniv of OIRSA (Organization for Farming Health). Multicoloured.

No.	Description	Mint	Used
1730	2l.60 Type **361**	55	45
1731	10l. Vegetables as eye	2·00	1·60
1732	10l.65 Emblem	2·10	1·70
1733	14l. Basket of vegetables	2·75	2·10
1734	20l. Sweet corn, squash and fish	3·75	3·00

362 Llama Bridge

2003. Air. Bridges. Sheet 169×182 mm containing T 362 and similar horiz designs. Multicoloured.

No.	Description	Mint	Used
MS1735	3l. Type **362**; 3l. Sol Naciente; 4l.30 Rio Hondo; Iztoca; 4l.30 El Chile; 10l. La Democracia; 10l. Guasaule	9·00	8·50

363 Flag and Emblem

2003. Air. Telethon. Multicoloured.

No.	Description	Mint	Used
1736	1l.40 Type **363**	25	20
1737	2l.60 Emblem and outstretched hand	55	45
1738	7l.30 As No. 1737 but design enlarged	1·40	1·20
1739	10l. Map and emblem	1·80	1·40

364 Angel

2003. Air. Christmas. Multicoloured.

No.	Description	Mint	Used
1740	10l.65 Type **364**	1·80	1·40
1741	14l. The Nativity	2·75	2·10

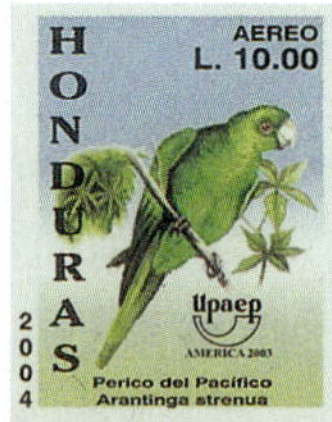

365 *Arantinga strenua*

2003. Air. America. Endangered Species. Birds. Sheet 94×105 mm containing T 365 and similar vert designs. Multicoloured.

No.	Description	Mint	Used
MS1742	10l. Type **365**; 10l.65 *Falco deiroleucus*; 14l. *Spizaetus melanoleucos*; 20l. *Amazona xantholora*	7·25	7·00

370 Journey to Bethlehem

2004. Air. Christmas. Multicoloured.

No.	Description	Mint	Used
1766	2l.60 Type **370**	55	45
1767	7l.85 Santa enclosed in bauble	1·50	1·30
1768	10l.65 Three kings	2·10	1·70
1769	20l. The Nativity	3·75	3·00

Nos. 1743/54 and Type **366** have been left for 'Fauna', issued on 24 May 2004, not yet received.

Nos. 1755/9 and Type **367** have been left for 'Shells', issued on 19 July 2004, not yet received.

Nos. 1760 and Type **368** have been left for 'Surcharges', issued on 13 August 2004, not yet received.

Nos. 1761/5 and Type **369** have been left for 'Football', issued on 13 September 2004, not yet received.

371 Family

2005. Air. Family Unity. Multicoloured.

No.	Description	Mint	Used
1770	10l. Type **371**	2·00	1·60
1771	20l. Virgen de Suyapa (Virgin of Suyapa) (vert)	3·75	3·00

372 Paul Harris (founder) and Early Leaders

2005. Air. Centenary of Rotary International. Multicoloured.

No.	Description	Mint	Used
1772	2l.60 Type **372**	55	40
1773	5l. Rotary emblem (vert)	1·00	85
1774	8l. Community bank and Rotary emblems	1·70	1·40
1775	10l.65 Polio plus emblem	2·10	1·70
1776	14l. Carved monument	2·75	2·10

373 Pope John Paul II

2005. Air. Pope John Paul II Commemoration. Multicoloured.

No.	Description	Mint	Used
1777	10l. Type **373**	2·00	1·60
1778	15l. Facing left	2·75	2·40

No. 1779 is left for stamp not yet received.

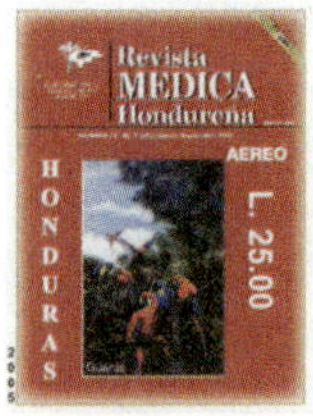

374 Macaws

2005. Air. 75th Anniv of Medical Review. Sheet 92×118 mm T 374 and similar vert designs. Multicoloured.

No.	Description	Mint	Used
MS1784	25l.×4, Type **374**; Macaw and bananas; Cockerel; Turkeys	19·00	19·00

Nos. 1780/3 have been left for single stamps not yet received.

No. 1785 is vacant.

376 *One Hundred Sacks of Rice* (play)

2005. Air. 70th Anniv of Honduras–Japan Diplomatic Relations. Multicoloured.

No.	Description	Mint	Used
1836	8l. Type **376**	1·70	1·40
1837	15l. Emblem	2·75	2·40
1838	30l. National Congress and Princess Sayako of Japan	5·50	4·75
MS1839	106×99 mm. 25l.×4, Japanese ceramics; Cherry blossom and *Rhyncholaelia digbyana*; Mayan ceramic; Mount Fuji and Pico bonito National Park	19·00	19·00

Nos. 1786/835 and Type **375** have been left for 'Surcharges', issued on 3 June 2005, not yet received.

377 Jose Trinidad Cabanas

2005. Air. Birth Bicentenary of Jose Trinidad Cabanas (president 1852–1855). Multicoloured.

No.	Description	Mint	Used
1840	3l. Type **377**	60	45
1841	8l. University City (horiz)	1·70	1·40
1842	15l. As older man	2·75	2·40

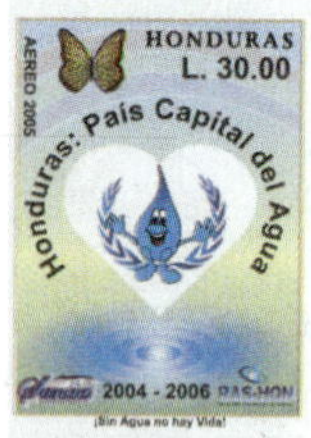

378 Emblem

2005. Air. Water Capital. Multicoloured.

No.	Description	Mint	Used
1843	30l. Type **378**	5·50	4·75
MS1844	99×73 mm. 50l. As Type **378**	9·25	9·25

383 Ruins, Copan

2006. Air. Debt Reduction. Multicoloured.

No.	Description	Mint	Used
1857	14l. Type **383**	2·75	2·10
1858	15l. Flags of supporting countries	2·75	2·40
1859	30l. Ricardo Maduro (pres. 2002–2006) (vert)	5·50	4·75

Nos. 1845/9 and Type **379** have been left for 'Mail Transport', issued on 6 December 2005, not yet received.

No. 1850 and Type **380** have been left for 'Fungi', issued 2005, not yet received.

Nos. 1851/4 and Type **381** have been left for 'Surcharges', issued 2005, not yet received.

Nos. 1855/6 and Type **382** have been left for 'Winter Olympic Games, Turin', issued on 24 January 2006, not yet received.

No. 1860 is vacant.

387 Roberto Micheletti Bain (pres. Congress), Manuel Zelaya (pres. 2006–) and Vilma Cecilia Morales (pres. supreme court)

2007. Air. 25th Anniv of National Constitution. Multicoloured.

1867	5l. Type **387**	1·00	85
1868	10l. First constituent assembly meeting venue	2·00	1·60
1869	15l. Presidential palace (1922–91) (vert)	2·75	2·40
1870	20l. Legislative building	3·75	3·00

Nos. 1861/13 and Type **384** have been left for '70th Anniv of Chamber of Commerce', issued 2006, not yet received.

Nos. 1864/5 and Type **385** have been left for 'Honduras-Brazil Diplomatic Relations', issued 2006, not yet received.

No. 1866 and Type **386** have been left for 'Honduras–Japan Friendship', issued 2006, not yet received.

390 Launch

2007. 50th Anniv of Space Exploration. Sputnik. Sheet 79×100 mm containing T 390 and similar multicoloured designs.

MS1878 25l. Type **390**; 35l. *Sputnik*; 50l. Orbit (60×40 mm) 4·75 3·75

Nos. 1871/6 and Type **388** have been left for '50th Anniv of Central Bank', issued on 13 March 2007, not yet received.

No. 1877 and Type **389** have been left for 'Children's Rights', issued on 18 October 2007, not yet received.

2007. Air. Various stamps surch.

1881	2l. on 8l.65 multicoloured (1696)	40	35
1883	3l. on 1l.40 multicoloured (1692)	60	45
1884	3l. on 1l.40 multicoloured (1736)	60	45
1885	3l. on 2l.60 multicoloured (1737)	60	45
1887	3l. on 7l.30 multicoloured (1738)	60	45
1889	3l. on 18l.30 multicoloured (1539)	60	45
1892	5l. on 2l.60 multicoloured (1693)	1·50	1·30
1893	5l. on 4l.30 multicoloured (1695)	1·50	1·30

Nos. 1879/80; 1882; 1886; 1888; 1890/1 and1894/5 have been left for stamps not yet received.

392 Struggle against Poverty

2008. Air. Exfilhon 2008 Stamp Exhibition. America–2005, 2006, 2007 and 2008. Sheet 108×92 mm containing T 392 and similar horiz designs. Multicoloured.

MS1896 2l. Type **392**; 3l. Alternative energy; 5l. Education for all; 10l. National festivals 4·50 4·50

393 *Medusa de las Islas*

2008. Air. Paintings by Gaye–Darlene Bidart de Satulsky. Sheet 110×155 mm containing T 393 and similar vert designs. Multicoloured.

MS1897 3l. Type **393**; 3l. *Nido de Amor*; 3l. *Guitarrista Isleno*; 5l. *'M' Hombre Cruz*; 5l. *Amor a Martillazos*; 5l. *Sor Maria Rosa*; 5l. *Islena, Luna y Mar*; 5l. *Clementina Suarez*; 5l. *La Naranjera*; 7·75 7·75

394 Olympic Torch

2008. Air. Olympic Games, Beijing. Multicoloured.

1898	3l. Type **394**	60	45
1899	5l. Athletics	1·00	85
1900	5l. Judo	1·00	85
1901	25l. Football	4·75	3·75

395 'El Emprendedor'

2008. Air. Centenary of Honduras–Mexico Diplomatic Relations. Sheet 139×113 mm containing T 395 and similar multicoloured designs, inscriptions given.

MS1902 5l. Type **395**; 10l. 'La Estrellas se aceranal Aguia'; 15l. 'Hermano de Antano' (horiz); 20l. 'Lazos y Vientos de Amistad'; 25l. 'Eclipse Maya' (horiz); 50l. 'Ciclico' (horiz) 19·00 19·00

No. 1903 is vacant.

396 Juan Ramon Molina

2008. Air. Death Centenary of Juan Ramon Molina (writer). Multicoloured.

1904	10l. Type **396**	2·00	1·60
1905	25l. Bust	4·75	3·75

397 School Building

2009. Air. Supporting Education. Escuela Normal 'Espana', Villa Ahumada, Danli. Multicoloured.

1906	2l. Type **397**	45	35
1907	5l. Emblem	1·50	1·30

398 Hopscotch

2009. Air. Amercia. Games. Multicoloured.

1908	3l. Type **398**	60	45
1909	10l. Kite flying	2·00	1·60
1910	20l. Spinning top	3·75	3·00
1911	50l. Children playing games	9·00	7·75

EXPRESS LETTER STAMPS

1953. No. O507 surch ENTREGA INMEDIATA 1953 L 0.20.

E523 **127** 20c. on 1c. olive & pur 3·75 1·80

1956. Air. Optd ENTREGA INMEDIATA as in Type E 135.

E570 **E135** 20c. grey and black 1·40 60

1966. Stamp Cent. Design similar to T 144.

E700 20c. brown, gold & lt brown 85 40

DESIGN—HORIZ: 20c. Motor cyclist.

E135 Lockheed Constellation

1972. As T 168, but inscr "ENTREGA INMEDIATA". Multicoloured.

E811 20c. Chance Vought F4U-5 Corsair fighter aircraft 60 60

1975. No. E811 surch.

E848 60c. on 20c. multicoloured 1·90 1·20

1976. As T 178.

E893 60c. Deer in forest 1·20 85

OFFICIAL STAMPS

Various stamps overprinted OFICIAL.

1890. Stamps of 1890.

O56	**6**	1c. yellow	35	
O57	**6**	2c. yellow	35	
O58	**6**	5c. yellow	35	
O59	**6**	10c. yellow	35	
O60	**6**	20c. yellow	35	
O61	**6**	25c. yellow	35	
O62	**6**	30c. yellow	35	
O63	**6**	40c. yellow	35	
O64	**6**	50c. yellow	35	
O65	**6**	75c. yellow	35	
O66	**6**	1p. yellow	35	

1891. Stamps of 1891.

O70	**8**	1c. yellow	35	
O71	**8**	2c. yellow	35	
O72	**8**	5c. yellow	35	
O73	**8**	10c. yellow	35	
O74	**8**	20c. yellow	35	
O75	**8**	25c. yellow	35	
O76	**8**	30c. yellow	35	
O77	**8**	40c. yellow	35	
O78	**8**	50c. yellow	35	
O79	**8**	75c. yellow	35	
O80	**8**	1p. yellow	35	

1898. Stamps of 1898.

O116	**14**	5c. blue	60	
O117	**14**	10c. blue	1·20	
O118	**14**	20c. bistre	1·90	
O119	**14**	50c. orange	3·75	
O120	**14**	1p. green	5·00	

1911. Stamps of 1911.

O148	**20**	1c. violet	2·20	85
O149	**20**	2c. green	1·40	95
O150	**20**	5c. red	2·20	1·80
O151	**20**	6c. blue	4·00	3·00
O152	**20**	10c. blue	2·20	1·80
O153	**20**	20c. yellow	7·50	7·25
O154	**20**	50c. brown	12·50	10·50
O155	**20**	1p. olive	19·00	14·50

1914. No. O150 and O148 surch.

O186	1c. on 5c. red	2·75	2·20
O187	2c. on 5c. red	3·00	2·20
O188	10c. on 1c. violet	5·50	4·75
O189	10c. on 5c. red	31·00	30·00
O190	20c. on 1c. violet	4·25	3·50

1914. No. O190 and O146 surch OFICIAL and value.

O191	10c. on 20c. on 1c. violet	31·00	30·00
O193	20c. on 50c. brown	7·50	7·25

1915. Stamps of 1913.

O194	**26**	1c. brown	40	40
O195	**26**	2c. red	40	40
O197	**27**	5c. blue	45	45
O198	**27**	6c. violet	1·50	1·40
O199	**26**	10c. brown	1·20	1·20
O200	**26**	20c. brown	3·00	2·75
O202	**27**	50c. red	5·75	5·75

1915. No. 168 surch OFICIAL $0.01.

O203 **26** 1c. on 2c. red 3·00 3·00

1915. Stamps of 1915.

O204	**32**	1c. brown	35	35
O205	**32**	2c. red	50	50
O206	-	5c. blue	50	50
O207	-	6c. violet	60	60
O208	**32**	10c. blue	75	70
O209	**32**	20c. brown	1·00	95
O210	-	50c. red	2·50	2·40
O211	-	1p. green	5·00	4·75

1921. Stamps of 1919.

O212	**36**	1c. brown	3·75	3·50
O213	**36**	2c. red	10·00	9·75
O214	**36**	5c. red	10·00	9·75
O215	**36**	6c. mauve	85	85
O216	**36**	10c. blue	1·00	95
O217	**36**	15c. blue	1·20	1·20
O218	**36**	20c. brown	1·60	1·60
O219	**36**	50c. brown	2·20	2·20
O220	**36**	1p. green	4·25	4·25

1925. Stamps of 1923.

O222	**39**	1c. olive	25	25
O223	**39**	2c. red	35	35
O224	**39**	6c. purple	50	50
O225	**39**	10c. blue	75	70
O226	**39**	20c. brown	1·10	1·10
O227	**39**	50c. red	2·00	1·90
O228	**39**	1p. green	3·00	3·00

O50 J. R. Molina

1929

O259	-	1c. blue	25	10
O260	**O50**	2c. red	25	25
O261	-	5c. violet	50	50
O262	-	10c. green	60	50
O263	-	20c. blue	75	70
O264	-	50c. green and yellow	1·50	1·40
O265	-	1p. brown	3·00	3·00

DESIGNS: J. C. Valle; 5c. Coffee tree; 10c. J. T. Reyes; 20c. Tegucigalpa Cathedral; 50c. Lake Yojoa; 1p. Wireless station.

1930. Air. Nos. O224/8 surch Servicio aereo Vale 5 centavos VI-1930 or optd Servicio aereo Habilitado VI-1930.

O319	**39**	5c. on 6c. purple	1·40	1·30
O320	**39**	6c. purple	£120	£120
O321	**39**	10c. blue	1·60	1·60
O322	**39**	20c. brown	1·60	1·60
O323	**39**	50c. red	2·00	1·90
O324	**39**	1p. green	1·60	1·60

O70 Tegucigalpa

1931

O328	**O70**	1c. blue	35	25
O329	**O70**	2c. purple	50	35
O330	**O70**	5c. olive	60	50
O331	**O70**	6c. red	60	50
O332	**O70**	10c. green	75	50
O333	**O70**	15c. brown	1·00	60
O334	**O70**	20c. brown	1·20	85
O335	**O70**	50c. violet	1·50	1·10
O336	**O70**	1p. orange	2·75	2·75

1933. Air. Various stamps surch Aereo Oficial Vale 1933 and new value.

O354	**66**	20c. on 2c. blue	5·00	4·75
O355	**66**	20c. on 2c. orange	5·00	4·75
O356	**66**	20c. on 2c. red	5·00	4·75
O357	**66**	40c. on 2c. orange	4·50	4·25
O358	**66**	40c. on 2c. red	6·75	6·75
O360	-	40c. on 5c. purple (249)	6·75	6·75
O361	-	40c. on 5c. blue (250)	9·25	9·00
O362	-	40c. on 5c. purple (270)	6·75	6·75
O363	-	40c. on 5c. blue (271)	12·50	12·00
O365	-	70c. on 5c. blue (188)	8·00	7·75
O366	**39**	70c. on 10c. blue	7·50	7·25
O367	**36**	1l. on 20c. brown	2·10	2·10
O368	**39**	1l. on 50c. red	16·00	15·00
O369	**36**	1.20l. on 1p. green	2·50	2·40
O370	-	40c. on 5c. violet (O261)	2·40	2·40
O372	**39**	60c. on 6c. purple (O224)	1·50	1·40
O374	-	70c. on 5c. blue (O206)	8·00	7·75
O375	**32**	70c. on 10c. blue (O208)	12·50	12·00
O377	**36**	70c. on 10c. blue (O216)	5·50	5·50
O378	**39**	70c. on 10c. blue (O225)	7·50	7·25
O380	**36**	70c. on 15c. blue (O217)	£150	£140
O381	**36**	90c. on 10c. blue (O216)	8·00	7·75
O382	**36**	90c. on 15c. blue (O217)	5·75	5·50
O383	**39**	1l. on 2c. red	2·10	2·10
O384	**36**	1l. on 20c. brown (O218)	5·75	5·50
O385	**39**	1l. on 20c. brown (O226)	5·00	4·75
O386	**36**	1l. on 50c. brown (O219)	3·00	3·00
O387	**39**	1l. on 50c. red (O227)	6·75	6·75
O388	-	1.20l. on 1p. grn (O211)	13·50	10·50
O389	**39**	1.20l. on 1p. grn (O288)	2·50	2·40

1935. Stamps of 1931 optd HABILITADO 1935–1938 between thick lines.

O390	**O70**	1c. blue	35	35
O391	**O70**	2c. purple	35	35
O392	**O70**	5c. olive	50	50
O393	**O70**	6c. red	60	60
O394	**O70**	10c. green	60	60
O395	**O70**	15c. brown	75	70
O396	**O70**	20c. brown	1·50	1·40
O397	**O70**	50c. violet	5·50	5·50

O92 Coat of Arms and National Flag

1939. Air.

No.	Type	Description	Mint	Used
O400	**O92**	2c. blue and green	25	25
O401	**O92**	5c. blue and orange	25	25
O402	**O92**	8c. blue and brown	25	25
O403	**O92**	15c. blue and red	35	25
O404	**O92**	46c. blue and olive	60	35
O405	**O92**	50c. blue and violet	75	35
O406	**O92**	1l. blue and brown	2·50	1·80
O407	**O92**	2l. blue and red	5·00	3·25

1952. Air. 500th Birth Anniv of Isabella the Catholic. As Nos. 499/506 but colours changed, optd OFICIAL.

No.	Type	Description	Mint	Used
O507	**127**	1c. olive and purple	10	10
O508	-	2c. violet and brown	25	25
O509	-	8c. black and red	35	35
O510	**128**	16c. green and violet	50	50
O511	-	30c. black and blue	75	70
O512	-	1l. sepia and green	2·00	1·90
O513	**127**	2l. brown and blue	4·00	3·75
O514	**128**	5l. slate and orange	10·50	10·00

1953. Air. United Nations. As Nos. 523/31 but colours changed (except 1c.), optd OFICIAL.

No.	Type	Description	Mint	Used
O532	-	1c. blue and black	25	25
O533	**130**	2c. green and black	25	25
O534	-	3c. orange and black	25	25
O535	-	5c. red and black	25	25
O536	-	15c. sepia and black	35	25
O537	-	30c. purple and black	60	50
O538	-	1l. olive and black	6·25	3·50
O539	-	2l. purple and black	7·50	4·25
O540	-	5l. blue and black	19·00	10·50

1956. Air. As Nos. 551/69 but colours changed, optd OFICIAL.

No.	Description	Mint	Used
O570	1c. lake and black	25	25
O571	2c. red and black	25	25
O572	3c. purple and black	25	25
O573	4c. orange and black	25	25
O574	5c. turquoise and black	25	25
O575	8c. multicoloured	25	25
O576	10c. brown and black	25	25
O577	12c. red and black	25	25
O578	15c. black and red	25	25
O579	20c. olive and black	25	25
O580	24c. blue and black	35	25
O581	25c. purple and black	35	25
O582	30c. green and black	35	25
O583	40c. orange and black	35	35
O584	50c. red and black	60	50
O585	60c. purple and black	60	60
O586	1l. sepia and black	2·50	1·60
O587	2l. blue and black	5·00	3·50
O588	5f. blue and black	10·50	7·75

1957. Air. Revolution of 21 October 1956. Nos. 570/9 optd OFICIAL. Frames in black.

No.	Description	Mint	Used
O589	1c. blue and yellow	10	10
O590	2c. purple, green and orange	10	10
O591	5c. blue and pink	10	10
O592	8c. violet, olive and orange	10	10
O593	10c. brown and violet	25	25
O594	12c. blue and turquoise	25	25
O595	15c. brown and green	35	35
O596	30c. grey and pink	85	85
O597	1l. brown and blue	2·75	2·75
O598	2l. grey and green	6·25	6·00

1959. Air. Abraham Lincoln. 150th Birth Anniv No. 590/601 but colours changed and optd OFICIAL. Flags in blue and red.

No.	Description	Mint	Used
O602	1c. yellow	25	25
O603	2c. olive	25	25
O604	3c. brown	25	25
O605	5c. blue	25	25
O606	10c. purple	25	25
O607	12c. orange	25	25
O608	15c. sepia	25	25
O609	25c. slate	35	25
O610	50c. red	60	35
O611	1l. violet	1·20	95
O612	2l. blue	3·50	1·80
O613	5l. green	7·00	6·25
MSO614 180×140 mm. As Nos. O603, O605, O607/8, O610 and O612. Imperf		4·25	3·50

1964. Air. Pres. Kennedy Memorial Issue. Optd IN MEMORIAM JOHN F. KENNEDY 22 NOVIEMBRE 1963.

No.	Description	Mint	Used
O626	1c. yellow (No. O602)	10	10
O627	2c. olive (No. O603)	25	25
O628	3c. brown (No. O604)	35	25
O629	5c. blue (No. O605)	60	50
O630	15c. sepia (No. O608)	2·50	2·20
O631	50c. red (No. O610)	12·00	10·50
MSO632 On No. **MS**614		75·00	70·00

1964. Air. Nos. O611/14 surch.

No.	Description	Mint	Used
O621	20c. on 25c. slate	75	50
O647	10c. on 50c. red	35	35
O648	12c. on 15c. sepia	50	35
O649	12c. on 25c. slate	50	35

1964. Air. Olympic Games, Tokyo. Optd with Olympic Rings and 1964.

No.	Description	Mint	Used
O632	2l. purple & black (No. O539)	10·00	9·75

1965. Air. Nos. 630/38 optd OFICIAL.

No.	Type	Description	Mint	Used
O650	**144**	1c. black and green	10	10
O651	-	2c. black and mauve	10	10
O652	-	5c. black and blue	25	25
O653	-	8c. black and green	25	25
O654	**144**	10c. black and bistre	50	50
O655	-	12c. black and yellow	60	60
O656	-	1l. black and buff	5·50	5·50
O657	-	2l. black and olive	10·50	10·00
O658	**144**	3l. black and red	14·00	13·50

1965. Air. Churchill Commem. Optd IN MEMORIAM Sir Winston Churchill 1874-1965.

No.	Type	Description	Mint	Used
O674	**128**	16c. green and violet	1·50	1·40

1971. Air. Various official stamps surch in figures.

No.	Type	Description	Mint	Used
O788	**134**	10c. on 3c. (O572)	50	35
O789	-	10c. on 2c. (O603)	50	35
O790	-	10c. on 3c. (O604)	50	35

1974. Air. Nos. O570 and O602 surch.

No.	Description	Mint	Used
O849	2c. on 1c. lake and black	25	10
O850	2c. on 1c. yellow	25	10

Pt. 1, Pt. 17

HONG KONG

Former British colony at the mouth of the Canton R., consisting of the island of Hong Kong and peninsula of Kowloon. Under Japanese Occupation from 25 December 1941, until liberated by British forces on 16 September 1945.

Hong Kong became a Special Administrative Region of the People's Republic of China on 1 July 1997.

Hong Kong.
100 cents = 1 Hong Kong dollar.

Japanese Occupation of Hong Kong.
100 sen = 1 yen.

1

1862

4	1	18c. lilac	£600	60
8a	1	2c. brown	£130	7·00
10	1	6c. lilac	£450	18·00
11b	1	8c. yellow	£475	13·00
12a	1	12c. blue	32·00	8·50
14	1	24c. green	£600	75·00
15a	1	30c. red	£850	15·00
16	1	30c. mauve	£275	£275
17a	1	48c. red	£900	29·00
18	1	96c. olive	£55000	4·50
19	1	96c. grey	£1400	2·25
22	1	16c. yellow	£1900	16·00
34	1	4c. grey	21·00	2·50

1877. Surch in figures and words, thus 5 cents.

20	16c. on 18c. lilac	£2250	2·25
21	28c. on 30c. mauve	£1500	4·25
23	5c. on 8c. yellow	£1000	4·50
24	5c. on 18c. lilac	£950	5·00
25	10c. on 12c. blue	£1000	75·00
26	10c. on 16c. yellow	£4250	£225
27	10c. on 24c. green	£1500	75·00

1880

30	10c. mauve	£700	15·00
31	48c. brown	£1400	£100
33	2c. red	50·00	2·50
35	5c. blue	35·00	85
37a	10c. green	£160	1·50
38	10c. purple on red	35·00	1·50
39a	30c. green	90·00	27·00
56	2c. green	27·00	85
57	4c. red	19·00	85
58	5c. yellow	22·00	6·50
59	10c. blue	50·00	2·25
61	30c. brown	50·00	24·00

1885. Surch in figures and words, thus 20 CENTS.

40	20c. on 30c. red	£180	5·50
41	50c. on 48c. brown	£400	45·00
42	$1 on 96c. olive	£750	85·00
45a	20c. on 30c. green	£110	£150
46	50c. on 48c. purple	£275	£300
47	$1 on 96c. purple on red	£800	£350
53a	$1 on 96c. black	£2750	£3750
54	10c. on 30c. green	£600	£1200

1891. Surch in figures and words, thus 7 cents.

43	7c. on 10c. green	80·00	9·00
44	14c. on 30c. mauve	£180	70·00

13 (20c.)

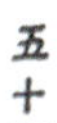

14 (50c.)

15 ($1)

1891. T 1 surch with figures and words and with Chinese surch also.

48a	13	20c. on 30c. green	42·00	9·00
49	14	50c. on 48c. purple	80·00	5·50
50	15	$1 on 96c. purple on red	£450	22·00
52a	15	$1 on 96c. black	£180	27·00
55	-	10c. on 30c. green	60·00	80·00

The Chinese surch on No. 55 is larger than Type **13**.

1891. 50th Anniv of Colony. Optd 1841 Hong Kong JUBILEE 1891.

51	1	2c. red	£475	£130

20

1903

62	20	1c. purple and brown	2·00	50
66	20	8c. grey and violet	11·00	1·25
68	20	12c. green & purple on yell	9·00	4·50
76	20	$10 grey and orange on blue	£1200	£425
77	20	2c. green	16·00	2·25
78a	20	4c. purple on red	16·00	1·00
79a	20	5c. green and orange	19·00	6·00
81	20	10c. purple and blue on blue	26·00	1·25
83a	20	20c. grey and brown	45·00	2·75
84	20	30c. green and black	50·00	27·00
85	20	50c. green and purple	90·00	12·00
86	20	$1 purple and olive	£160	32·00
87a	20	$2 grey and red	£275	£120
88	20	$3 grey and blue	£275	£250
89	20	$5 purple and green	£475	£425
91	20	1c. brown	6·50	1·00
93	20	4c. red	14·00	40
94	20	6c. brown and purple	26·00	7·00
95	20	10c. blue	40·00	40
96	20	20c. purple and green	45·00	42·00
97	20	30c. purple and yellow	55·00	32·00
98	20	50c. black on green	45·00	17·00
99	20	$2 red and black	£350	£350

24

1912

103	24	6c. orange	5·50	2·25
104	24	8c. grey	27·00	8·00
106	24	12c. purple on yellow	9·00	10·00
116	24	$10 purple and black on red	£600	90·00
117	24	1c. brown	1·00	40
118	24	2c. green	3·50	70
118c	24	2c. grey	22·00	8·00
119	24	3c. grey	10·00	1·50
120a	24	4c. red	7·00	30
121	24	5c. violet	18·00	30
123	24	8c. orange	5·50	1·50
124	24	10c. blue	7·00	30
125	24	20c. purple and olive	8·50	30
126	24	25c. purple	7·50	1·50
127	24	30c. purple and orange	11·00	1·50
128	24	50c. black on green	23·00	30
129	24	$1 purple and blue on blue	45·00	50
130	24	$2 red and black	£140	7·50
131	24	$3 green and purple	£190	65·00
132	24	$5 green and red on green	£475	80·00

1935. Silver Jubilee. As T 10a of Gambia.

133	3c. blue and black	4·00	4·00
134	5c. green and blue	8·50	3·50
135	10c. brown and blue	20·00	1·75
136	20c. grey and purple	40·00	10·00

1937. Coronation. As T 10b of Gambia.

137	4c. green	4·50	6·50
138	15c. red	10·00	3·25
139	25c. blue	13·00	4·50

29 King George VI

1938

140	29	1c. brown	1·75	4·00
141	29	2c. grey	2·00	30
142	29	4c. orange	5·00	4·00
143	29	5c. green	1·25	20
144	29	8c. brown	1·75	2·75
145b	29	10c. violet	7·00	1·25
146	29	15c. red	2·00	30
147	29	20c. black	1·25	30
148	29	20c. red	7·50	40
149	29	25c. blue	29·00	3·50
150	29	25c. olive	4·75	2·75
151a	29	30c. olive	25·00	9·50
152	29	30c. blue	7·00	20
153c	29	50c. purple	9·00	20
154	29	80c. red	5·00	1·00
155	29	$1 purple and blue	8·00	3·75
156	29	$1 orange and green	22·00	30
157	29	$2 orange and green	80·00	27·00
158a	29	$2 violet and red	42·00	1·00
159	29	$5 purple and red	65·00	50·00
160	29	$5 green and violet	80·00	14·00
161	29	$10 green and violet	£550	£130
162	29	$10 violet and blue	£140	45·00

30 Street Scene

1941. Centenary of British Occupation. Dated "1841 1941".

163	30	2c. orange and brown	7·00	2·00
164	-	4c. purple and red	8·00	4·50
165	-	5c. black and green	3·25	50
166	-	15c. black and red	8·00	2·50
167	-	25c. brown and blue	17·00	8·00
168	-	$1 blue and orange	50·00	11·00

DESIGNS—HORIZ: 4c. "Empress of Japan" (liner) and junk; 5c. University; 15c. Harbour; $1 "Falcon" (clipper) and Short S.23 Empire "C" Class flying boat. VERT: 25c. Hong Kong Bank.

For Japanese issues see "Japanese Occupation of Hong Kong".

36 King George VI and Pheonix

1946. Victory.

169	36	30c. blue and red	2·75	1·75
170	36	$1 brown and red	3·75	75

1948. Silver Wedding. As T 11b/c of Gambia.

171	10c. violet	3·50	1·50
172	$10 red	£300	£110

1949. U.P.U. As T 11d/g of Gambia.

173	10c. violet	4·50	1·00
174	20c. red	17·00	5·00
175	30c. blue	15·00	5·00
176	80c. mauve	35·00	8·00

1953. Coronation. As T 11h of Gambia.

177	10c. black and purple	3·50	30

1954. As T 29 but portrait of Queen Elizabeth, facing left.

178	5c. orange	1·75	20
179	10c. lilac	2·50	10
180a	15c. green	4·50	1·00
181	20c. brown	6·00	30
182a	25c. red	4·00	3·00
183	30c. grey	5·00	20
184	40c. blue	6·00	40
185	50c. purple	6·50	20
186	65c. grey	19·00	13·00
187	$1 orange and green	7·50	20
188	$1.30 blue and red	23·00	2·50
189	$2 violet and red	12·00	60
190	$5 green and purple	75·00	3·25
191	$10 violet and blue	65·00	10·00

38 University Arms

1961. Golden Jubilee of Hong Kong University.

192	38	$1 multicoloured	4·00	2·00

39 Statue of Queen Victoria

1962. Stamp Centenary.

193	39	10c. black and mauve	45	10
194	39	20c. black and blue	1·50	2·25
195	39	50c. black and bistre	2·75	40

40 Queen Elizabeth II (after Annigoni)

1962

196	40	5c. orange	75	60
198	40	15c. green	3·25	2·75
199	40	20c. brown	2·50	1·25
200	40	25c. red	3·00	4·00
201	40	30c. blue	2·50	10
202	40	40c. turquoise	4·00	70
203	40	50c. red	1·75	30
206	-	$1.30 multicoloured	3·50	20
207	-	$2 multicoloured	5·00	1·00
208	-	$5 multicoloured	14·00	1·50
209	-	$10 multicoloured	28·00	2·75
210	-	$20 multicoloured	£110	25·00
223	40	10c. violet	70	60
230	40	65c. blue	6·50	9·00
231	40	$1 sepia	18·00	1·75

Nos. 206/10 are as T **40** but larger 26×40½ mm.

1963. Freedom from Hunger. As T 20a of Gambia.

211	$1.30 green	26·00	8·00

1963. Cent of Red Cross. As T 20b of Gambia.

212	10c. red and black	1·50	30
213	$1.30 red and blue	9·50	8·00

1965. Centenary of I.T.U. As T 44 of Gibraltar.

214	10c. purple and yellow	1·50	25
215	$1.30 olive and green	9·50	5·50

1965. I.C.Y. As T 45 of Gibraltar.

216	10c. purple and turquoise	1·50	25
217	$1.30 green and lavender	10·00	5·50

1966. Churchill Commem. As T 46 of Gibraltar.

218	10c. blue	2·50	15
219	50c. green	2·75	30
220	$1.30 brown	10·00	3·00
221	$2 violet	20·00	10·00

1966. Inauguration of W.H.O. Headquarters, Geneva. As T 54 of Gibraltar.

237	10c. black, green and blue	1·50	30
238	50c. black, purple and ochre	4·50	1·75

1966. 20th Anniv of U.N.E.S.C.O. As T 56a/c of Gibraltar.

239	10c. multicoloured	2·50	20
240	50c. yellow, violet and olive	5·50	90
241	$2 black, purple and orange	32·00	20·00

49 Rams' Heads on Chinese Lanterns

1967. Chinese New Year ("Year of the Ram").

242	49	10c. red, olive and yellow	2·00	50
243	-	$1.30 green, red and yellow	13·00	9·00

DESIGN: $1.30, Three rams.

50 Cable Route Map

1967. Completion of Malaysia–Hong Kong Link of SEACOM Telephone Cable.

244	50	$1.30 blue and red	6·00	3·50

51 Rhesus Macaques in Tree

1968. Chinese New Year ("Year of the Monkey").

245	51	10c. gold, black and red	2·00	50
246	-	$1.30 gold, black and red	13·00	10·00

DESIGN: $1.30, Family of rhesus macaques.

52 "Iberia" (liner) at Ocean Terminal

1968. Sea Craft.

No.	Type	Description	Unused	Used
247	**52**	10c. multicoloured	1·75	15
248	-	20c. blue, black and brown	2·50	1·50
249	-	40c. orange, black & mauve	8·00	12·00
250	-	50c. red, black and green	5·00	75
251	-	$1 yellow, black and red	9·00	7·00
252	-	$1.30 blue, black and pink	27·00	4·25

DESIGNS: 20c. Pleasure launch; 40c. Car ferry; 50c. Passenger ferry; $1 Sampan; $1.30, Junk.

53 "Bauhinia blakeana"

1968. Multicoloured.

No.	Type	Description	Unused	Used
253		65c. Type **53**	8·00	50
254		$1 Arms of Hong Kong	8·00	40

55 "Aladdin's Lamp" and Human Rights Emblem

1968. Human Rights Year.

No.	Type	Description	Unused	Used
255	**55**	10c. orange, black and green	75	75
256	**55**	50c. yellow, black & purple	1·75	2·25

56 Cockerel

1969. Chinese New Year ("Year of the Cock"). Multicoloured.

No.	Type	Description	Unused	Used
257		10c. Type **56**	2·00	1·00
258		$1.30 Cockerel (vert)	26·00	9·00

58 Arms of Chinese University

1969. Establishment of Chinese University of Hong Kong.

No.	Type	Description	Unused	Used
259	**58**	40c. violet, gold and blue	2·75	3·00

59 Earth Station and Satellite

1969. Opening of Communications Satellite Tracking Station.

No.	Type	Description	Unused	Used
260	**59**	$1 multicoloured	6·00	3·50

60 Chow's Head

1970. Chinese New Year ("Year of the Dog"). Multicoloured.

No.	Type	Description	Unused	Used
261		10c. Type **60**	2·50	1·00
262		$1.30 Chow standing (horiz)	30·00	10·00

62 "Expo '70" Emblem

1970. World Fair, Osaka. Multicoloured.

No.	Type	Description	Unused	Used
263		15c. Type **62**	65	85
264		25c. "Expo '70" emblem and junks (horiz)	1·40	1·50

64 Plaque in Tung Wah Hospital

1970. Centenary of Tung Wah Hospital.

No.	Type	Description	Unused	Used
265	**64**	10c. multicoloured	50	25
266	**64**	50c. multicoloured	1·00	1·50

65 Symbol

1970. Asian Productivity Year.

No.	Type	Description	Unused	Used
267	**65**	10c. multicoloured	1·00	60

66 Pig

1971. Chinese New Year ("Year of the Pig").

No.	Type	Description	Unused	Used
268	**66**	10c. multicoloured	2·50	90
269	**66**	$1.30 multicoloured	20·00	11·00

67 "60" and Scout Badge

1971. Diamond Jubilee of Scouting in Hong Kong.

No.	Type	Description	Unused	Used
270	**67**	10c. black, red and yellow	75	10
271	**67**	50c. black, green and blue	3·00	1·00
272	**67**	$2 black, mauve and violet	16·00	12·00

68 Festival Emblem

1971. Hong Kong Festival.

No.	Type	Description	Unused	Used
273	**68**	10c. orange and purple	1·25	20
274	-	50c. multicoloured	2·25	1·00
275	-	$1 multicoloured	7·00	7·00

DESIGNS—39×23 mm: 50c. Coloured streamers. 23×39 mm: $1 "Orchid".

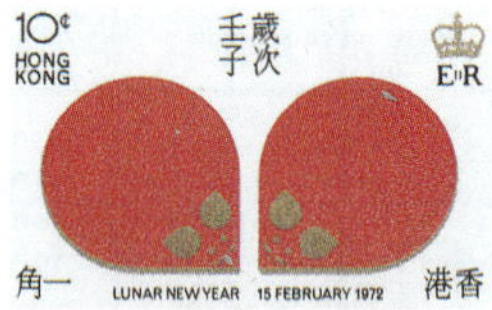

69 Stylized Rats

1972. Chinese New Year. ("Year of the Rat").

No.	Type	Description	Unused	Used
276	**69**	10c. red, black and gold	2·50	50
277	**69**	$1.30 red, black and gold	28·00	11·00

70 Tunnel Entrance

1972. Opening of Cross-Harbour Tunnel.

No.	Type	Description	Unused	Used
278	**70**	$1 multicoloured	4·50	2·25

1972. Royal Silver Wedding. As T 98 of Gibraltar, but with Phoenix and Dragon in background.

No.	Type	Description	Unused	Used
279		10c. multicoloured	30	15
280		50c. multicoloured	1·10	1·40

72 Ox

1973. Chinese New Year ("Year of the Ox").

No.	Type	Description	Unused	Used
281	**72**	10c. orange, brown & black	1·00	50
282	-	$1.30 yellow, orange & black	4·00	6·00

DESIGN—HORIZ: $1.30, Ox.

73 Queen Elizabeth II

1973

No.	Type	Description	Unused	Used
284	**73**	15c. green	7·00	9·00
286	**73**	25c. brown	11·00	8·50
289	**73**	50c. red	1·50	60
290	**73**	65c. brown	16·00	13·00
291	**73**	$1 green	2·25	80
311	**73**	10c. orange	55	30
313	**73**	20c. violet	50	10
315	**73**	30c. blue	70	70
316	**73**	40c. blue	1·25	2·50
318	**73**	60c. lavender	1·75	2·50
320	**73**	70c. yellow	1·75	75
321	**73**	80c. red	2·25	3·25
321c	**73**	90c. brown	4·00	2·25
323	-	$1.30 yellow and violet	2·50	30
324	-	$2 green and brown	3·00	1·25
324c	-	$5 pink and blue	4·75	1·75
324d	-	$10 pink and green	5·00	6·00
324e	-	$20 pink and black	9·00	12·00

Values of $1.30 and above are size 27×32 mm.

1973. Royal Wedding. As T 101a of Gibraltar. Multicoloured. Background colours given.

No.	Type	Description	Unused	Used
297		50c. brown	50	15
298		$2 mauve	1·50	2·00

75 Festival Symbols forming Chinese Character

1973. Hong Kong Festival.

No.	Type	Description	Unused	Used
299	**75**	10c. red and green	40	10
300	-	50c. mauve and orange	1·50	95
301	-	$1 green and mauve	3·50	4·00

DESIGNS—Festival symbols arranged to form a Chinese character: 10c. "Hong"; 50c. "Kong"; $1 "Festival".

76 Tiger

1974. Chinese New Year ("Year of the Tiger").

No.	Type	Description	Unused	Used
302	**76**	10c. multicoloured	2·00	50
303	-	$1.30 multicoloured	6·50	12·00

DESIGN—VERT: $1.30, similar to Type **76**.

77 Chinese Mask

1974. Arts Festival.

No.	Type	Description	Unused	Used
304	**77**	10c. multicoloured	75	10
305	-	$1 multicoloured	3·75	4·25
306	-	$2 multicoloured	6·50	8·50
MS307		159×94 mm. Nos. 304/6	30·00	35·00

DESIGNS: $1, $2, Chinese masks similar to T **77**.

78 Pigeons with Letters

1974. Centenary of U.P.U.

No.	Type	Description	Unused	Used
308	**78**	10c. blue, green and black	40	10
309	-	50c. mauve, orange & black	75	40
310	-	$2 multicoloured	3·25	4·25

DESIGNS: 50c. Globe within letters; $2 Hands holding letters.

79 Stylized Hare

1975. Chinese New Year ("Year of the Hare").

No.	Type	Description	Unused	Used
327	**79**	10c. silver and red	1·00	60
328	-	$1.30 gold and green	5·00	6·50

DESIGN: $1.30, Pair of hares.

80 Queen Elizabeth II, the Duke of Edinburgh and Hong Kong Arms

1975. Royal Visit.

No.	Type	Description	Unused	Used
329	**80**	$1.30 multicoloured	2·00	1·50
330	**80**	$2 multicoloured	3·00	3·75

81 Mid-Autumn Festival

1975. Hong Kong Festivals of 1975. Mult.

No.	Type	Description	Unused	Used
331		50c. Type **81**	2·00	50

332	$1 Dragon-boat Festival	6·50	2·50
333	$2 Tin Hau Festival	25·00	9·50
MS334	102×83 mm. Nos. 331/3	60·00	35·00

82 Melodious Laughing Thrush ("The Hwamei")

1975. Birds. Multicoloured.

335	50c. Type **82**	2·50	50
336	$1.30 Chinese bulbul	7·00	3·50
337	$2 Black-capped kingfisher	13·00	11·00

83 Dragon

1976. Chinese New Year ("Year of the Dragon").

338	**83**	20c. mauve, purple and gold	75	10
339	-	$1.30 green, red and gold	4·00	2·50

DESIGN: $1.30, As Type **83** but dragon reversed.

84 "60" and Girl Guides Badge

1976. Diamond Jubilee of Girl Guides. Multicoloured.

354	20c. Type **84**	50	10
355	$1.30 Badge, stylized diamond and "60"	4·00	4·00

85 "Postal Services" in Chinese Characters

1976. Opening of New G.P.O.

356	**85**	20c. green, grey and black	75	10
357	-	$1.30 orange, grey and black	2·75	1·50
358	-	$2 yellow, grey and black	5·00	4·00

DESIGNS: $1.30, Old G.P.O; $2 New G.P.O.

86 Tree Snake on Branch

1977. Chinese New Year ("Year of the Snake"). Multicoloured.

359	20c. Type **86**	50	15
360	$1.30 Snake facing left	2·50	4·00

87 Presentation of the Orb

1977. Silver Jubilee. Multicoloured.

361	20c. Type **87**	40	10
362	$1.30 The Queen's visit, 1975	1·00	75
363	$2 The Orb (vert)	1·25	1·50

88 Tram Cars

1977. Tourism. Multicoloured.

364	20c. Type **88**	55	10
365	60c. Star ferryboat	1·75	2·00
366	$1.30 The Peak Railway	2·00	2·00
367	$2 Junk and sampan	2·00	3·50

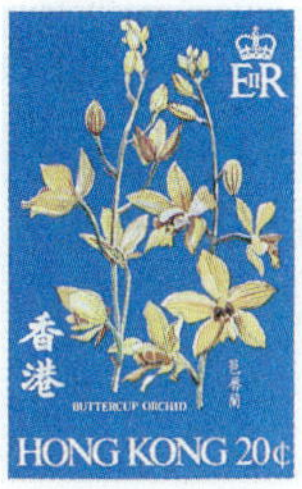

89 Buttercup Orchid

1977. Orchids. Multicoloured.

368	20c. Type **89**	1·25	20
369	$1.30 Lady's slipper orchid	3·00	1·50
370	$2 Susan orchid	5·00	4·50

90 Horse

1978. Chinese New Year ("Year of the Horse").

371	**90**	20c. mauve, olive and bistre	50	10
372	**90**	$1.30 orange, brn & lt brn	2·75	4·50

91 Queen Elizabeth II

1978. 25th Anniv of Coronation.

373	**91**	20c. mauve and blue	40	10
374	**91**	$1.30 blue and mauve	1·00	1·75

92 Girl and Boy holding Hands

1978. Centenary of Po Leung Kuk (children's charity). Multicoloured.

375	20c. Type **92**	25	15
376	$1.30 Ring of children	1·00	2·00

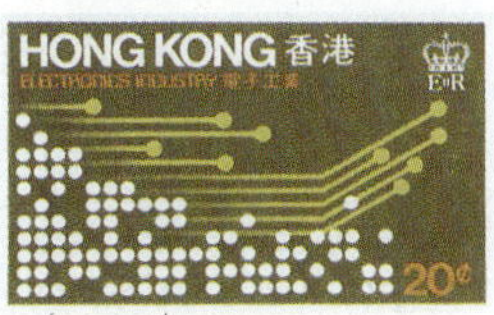

93 Electronics Industry

1979. Hong Kong Industries.

377	**93**	20c. yellow, olive & orange	30	10
378	-	$1.30 multicoloured	80	1·75
379	-	$2 multicoloured	85	2·25

DESIGNS: $1.30, Toy industry; $2 Garment industry.

94 "Precis orithya"

1979. Butterflies. Multicoloured.

380	20c. Type **94**	45	10
381	$1 "Graphium sarpedon"	85	55
382	$1.30 "Heliophorus epicles"	90	1·00
383	$2 "Danaus genutia"	1·25	3·75

95 Diagrammatic View of Railway Station

1979. Mass Transit Railway. Multicoloured.

384	20c. Type **95**	45	10
385	$1.30 Diagrammatic view of car	1·00	55
386	$2 Plan showing route of railway	1·00	2·00

96 Tsui Shing Lau Pagoda

1980. Rural Architecture.

387	**96**	20c. black, mauve & yellow	35	20
388	-	$1.30 multicoloured	60	80
389	-	$2 multicoloured	80	2·00

DESIGNS—HORIZ: $1.30, Village house, Sai O; $2 Ching Chung Koon Temple.

97 Queen Elizabeth the Queen Mother

1980. 80th Birthday of The Queen Mother.

390	**97**	$1.30 multicoloured	1·00	1·25

98 Botanical Gardens

1980. Parks. Multicoloured.

391	20c. Type **98**	20	15
392	$1 Ocean Park	35	35
393	$1.30 Kowloon Park	40	50
394	$2 Country parks	70	2·25

99 Red-spotted Grouper

1981. Fishes. Multicoloured.

395	20c. Type **99**	25	15
396	$1 Golden thread-finned bream	50	45
397	$1.30 Scar-breasted tuskfish	55	60
398	$2 Blue-barred orange parrotfish	70	2·25

100 Wedding Bouquet from Hong Kong

1981. Royal Wedding. Multicoloured.

399	20c. Type **100**	20	10
400	$1.30 Prince Charles in Hong Kong	45	30
401	$5 Prince Charles and Lady Diana Spencer	1·25	2·25

101 Suburban Development

1981. Public Housing.

402	**101**	20c. multicoloured	20	10
403	-	$1 multicoloured	55	40
404	-	$1.30 multicoloured	60	65
405	-	$2 multicoloured	70	1·75
MS406		148×105 mm. Nos. 402/5	3·50	5·50

DESIGNS: $1 to $2, Various suburban developments.

102 "Victoria from the Harbour, c.1855"

1982. Hong Kong Port, Past and Present. Multicoloured.

407	20c. Type **102**	50	15
408	$1 "West Point, Hong Kong, 1847"	1·25	80
409	$1.30 Fleet of junks	1·40	85
410	$2 Liner "Queen Elizabeth 2" at Hong Kong	2·50	3·00

103 Large Indian Civet

1982. Wild Animals.

411	**103**	20c. black, pink and brown	25	15
412	-	$1 multicoloured	45	45
413	-	$1.30 black, green & orange	50	55
414	-	$5 black, brown and yellow	1·25	3·25

DESIGNS: $1 Chinese pangolin; $1.30, Chinese porcupine; $5 Indian muntjac.

104 Queen Elizabeth II

1982

415	**104**	10c. light red, red & yellow	80	60
416	**104**	20c. blue, violet & lavender	1·00	1·00
417	**104**	30c. lt violet, violet & pink	1·50	30
418	**104**	40c. red and blue	1·50	30

No.	Type	Description	Mint	Used
475	104	50c. chestnut, brn & grn	1·00	40
476	104	60c. purple and grey	1·50	1·10
477	104	70c. green, myrtle & yellow	3·50	60
478	104	80c. bistre, brown & green	3·75	3·00
479	104	90c. dp green, grn & turq	4·25	75
480	104	$1 dp orange, orange & red	1·75	40
481	104	$1.30 blue and mauve	2·50	45
482	104	$1.70 dp blue, blue & grn	4·00	1·50
483	104	$2 blue and pink	3·75	1·50
484	-	$5 red, purple and yellow	9·00	3·50
485	-	$10 brown and light brown	9·00	4·50
486	-	$20 red and blue	10·00	7·50
487	-	$50 red and grey	32·00	27·00

Nos. 484/7 are as Type **104** but larger, 26×30 mm.

106 Table Tennis

1982. Sport for the Disabled. Multicoloured.

No.	Description	Mint	Used
431	30c. Type **106**	50	10
432	$1 Racing	75	80
433	$1.30 Basketball	2·75	1·50
434	$5 Archery	3·75	6·50

107 Dancing

1983. Performing Arts.

No.	Type	Description	Mint	Used
435	107	30c. light blue and blue	40	10
436	-	$1.30 red and purple	1·25	1·25
437	-	$5 green and deep green	3·00	5·00

DESIGNS: $1.30, "Theatre"; $5 "Music".

108 Aerial View of Hong Kong

1983. Commonwealth Day. Multicoloured.

No.	Description	Mint	Used
438	30c. Type **108**	70	10
439	$1 "Liverpool Bay" (container ship)	1·50	1·25
440	$1.30 Hong Kong flag	1·50	1·25
441	$5 Queen Elizabeth II and Hong Kong	3·00	6·50

109 Victoria Harbour

1983. Hong Kong by Night. Multicoloured.

No.	Description	Mint	Used
442	30c. Type **109**	1·25	15
443	$1 Space Museum, Tsim Sha Tsui Cultural Centre	3·00	1·50
444	$1.30 Fireworks display	4·00	2·00
445	$5 "Jumbo", floating restaurant	11·00	10·00

110 Old and new Observatory Buildings

1983. Centenary of Hong Kong Observatory.

No.	Type	Description	Mint	Used
446	110	40c. orange, brown & black	75	10
447	-	$1 mauve, dp mauve & blk	1·50	1·25
448	-	$1.30 blue, dp blue & black	1·75	1·40
449	-	$5 yellow, green and black	5·00	9·00

DESIGNS: $1 Wind measuring equipment; $1.30, Thermometer; $5 Ancient and modern seismometers.

111 De Havilland D.H.86 Dragon Express "Dorado" (Hong Kong–Penang Service, 1936)

1984. Aviation in Hong Kong. Multicoloured.

No.	Description	Mint	Used
450	40c. Type **111**	1·00	15
451	$1 Sikorsky S-42B flying boat (San Francisco–Hong Kong Service, 1937)	1·75	1·50
452	$1.30 Cathay-Pacific Boeing 747 jet leaving Kai Tak Airport	2·00	1·50
453	$5 Baldwin brothers' balloon, 1891 (vert)	4·75	11·00

112 Map by Capt. E. Belcher, 1836

1984. Maps of Hong Kong.

No.	Description	Mint	Used
454	40c. Type **112**	1·00	20
455	$1 Bartholomew map of 1929	1·75	1·25
456	$1.30 Early map of Hong Kong waters	2·00	1·75
457	$5 Chinese-style map of 1819	10·00	12·00

113 Cockerel

1984. Chinese Lanterns. Multicoloured.

No.	Description	Mint	Used
458	40c. Type **113**	1·00	15
459	$1 Dog	2·00	1·40
460	$1.30 Butterfly	3·00	1·75
461	$5 Fish	9·50	12·00

114 Jockey on Horse and Nurse with Baby ("Health Care")

1984. Centenary of Royal Hong Kong Jockey Club. Designs showing aspects of Club's charity work. Multicoloured.

No.	Description	Mint	Used
462	40c. Type **114**	1·25	20
463	$1 Disabled man playing hand-ball ("Support for Disabled")	2·00	1·75
464	$1.30 Ballerina ("The Arts")	3·00	2·00
465	$5 Humboldt penguins ("Ocean Park")	9·00	11·00
MS466	178×98 mm. Nos. 462/5	22·00	24·00

115 Hung Sing Temple

1985. Historic Buildings. Multicoloured.

No.	Description	Mint	Used
467	40c. Type **115**	60	20
468	$1 St. John's Cathedral	1·00	1·10
469	$1.30 The Old Supreme Court Building	1·10	1·25
470	$5 Wan Chai Post Office	4·50	9·00

116 Prow of Dragon Boat

1985. 10th International Dragon Boat Festival. Designs showing different parts of dragon boat. Multicoloured.

No.	Description	Mint	Used
488	40c. Type **116**	50	15
489	$1 Drummer and rowers	1·75	1·25
490	$1.30 Rowers	3·00	1·60
491	$5 Stern of boat	9·25	11·00
MS492	190×100 mm. Nos. 488/91	18·00	18·00

117 The Queen Mother with Prince Charles and Prince William, 1984

1985. Life and Times of Queen Elizabeth the Queen Mother. Multicoloured.

No.	Description	Mint	Used
493	40c. At Glamis Castle, aged 7	60	10
494	$1 Type **117**	1·75	1·25
495	$1.30 The Queen Mother, 1970 (from photo by Cecil Beaton)	2·00	1·40
496	$5 With Prince Henry at his christening (from photo by Lord Snowdon)	3·25	5·50

118 Melastoma

1985. Native Flowers. Multicoloured.

No.	Description	Mint	Used
497	40c. Type **118**	1·50	20
498	50c. Chinese lily	1·50	40
499	60c. Grantham's camellia	1·75	1·25
500	$1.30 Narcissus	2·75	1·25
501	$1.70 Bauhinia	3·00	1·50
502	$5 Chinese New Year flower	6·00	12·00

119 Hong Kong Academy for Performing Arts

1985. New Buildings. Multicoloured.

No.	Description	Mint	Used
503	50c. Type **119**	80	15
504	$1.30 Exchange Square (vert)	1·50	1·00
505	$1.70 Hong Kong Bank Headquarters (vert)	1·75	1·10
506	$5 Hong Kong Coliseum	2·75	10·00

120 Halley's Comet in the Solar System

1986. Appearance of Halley's Comet. Mult.

No.	Description	Mint	Used
507	50c. Type **120**	1·25	20
508	$1.30 Edmond Halley and Comet	1·50	1·40
509	$1.70 Comet over Hong Kong	1·75	1·50
510	$5 Comet passing the Earth	7·50	11·00
MS511	135×80 mm. Nos. 507/10	17·00	21·00

120a At Wedding of Miss Celia Bowes-Lyon, 1931

1986. 60th Birthday of Queen Elizabeth II. Multicoloured.

No.	Description	Mint	Used
512	50c. Type **120a**	50	10
513	$1 Queen in Garter procession, Windsor Castle, 1977	85	60
514	$1.30 In Hong Kong, 1975	1·10	70
515	$1.70 At Royal Lodge, Windsor, 1980 (from photo by Norman Parkinson)	1·25	75
516	$5 At Crown Agents Head Office, London, 1983	4·00	6·50

121 Mass Transit Train, Boeing 747 Airliner and Map of World

1986. "Expo '86" World Fair, Vancouver. Multicoloured.

No.	Description	Mint	Used
517	50c. Type **121**	80	30
518	$1.30 Hong Kong Bank Headquarters and map of world	1·50	1·00
519	$1.70 Container ship and map of world	2·25	1·40
520	$5 Dish aerial and map of world	5·00	8·00

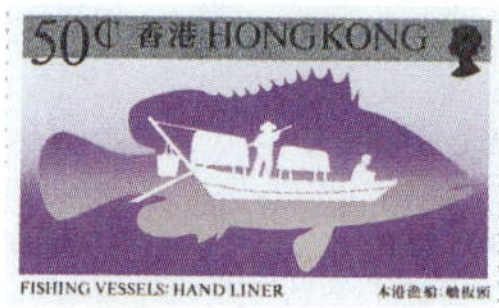

122 Hand-liner Sampan

1986. Fishing Vessels. Designs showing fishing boat and outline of fish. Multicoloured.

No.	Description	Mint	Used
521	50c. Type **122**	80	15
522	$1.30 Stern trawler	1·50	1·10
523	$1.70 Long liner junk	1·75	1·40
524	$5 Junk trawler	5·50	9·50

123 "The Second Puan Khequa" (attr Spoilum)

1986. 19th-century Hong Kong Portraits. Multicoloured.

No.	Description	Mint	Used
525	50c. Type **123**	40	15
526	$1.30 "Chinese Lady" (19th-century copy)	1·25	1·25
527	$1.70 "Lamqua" (self-portrait)	1·40	1·40
528	$5 "Wife of Wo Hing Qua" (attr G. Chinnery)	3·25	6·50

124 Rabbit

1987. Chinese New Year ("Year of the Rabbit"). Designs showing stylized rabbits.

No.	Type	Description	Mint	Used
529	124	50c. multicoloured	75	15
530	-	$1.30 multicoloured	1·40	1·10
531	-	$1.70 multicoloured	1·50	1·10
532	-	$5 multicoloured	6·00	6·50
MS533		133×84 mm. Nos. 529/32	25·00	26·00

Nos. 530/1 have the "0" omitted from their face values.

125 "Village Square, Hong Kong Island, 1838" (Auguste Borget)

1987. 19th-century Hong Kong Scenes. Mult.

534	50c. Type **125**	70	15
535	$1.30 "Boat Dwellers, Kowloon Bay, 1838 (Auguste Borget)	2·00	1·25
536	$1.70 "Flagstaff House, 1846" (Murdoch Bruce)	2·50	1·40
537	$5 "Wellington Street, late 19th-century" (C. Andrasi)	7·50	11·00

126 Queen Elizabeth II and Central Victoria

1987

538B	126	10c. multicoloured	75	65
539A	126	40c. multicoloured	1·50	2·25
547A	126	$1.70 multicoloured	3·00	80
602	126	50c. multicoloured	1·25	1·00
603	126	60c. multicoloured	1·75	30
604	126	70c. multicoloured	2·25	2·00
605	126	80c. multicoloured	2·00	1·75
606	126	90c. multicoloured	1·75	1·25
607	126	$1 multicoloured	2·25	1·00
607a	126	$1.20 multicoloured	3·50	3·75
608	126	$1.30 multicoloured	3·25	1·25
609	126	$1.40 multicoloured	3·25	1·25
610	126	$1.80 multicoloured	1·75	60
611	126	$2 multicoloured	2·50	50
611a	126	$2.30 multicoloured	3·50	3·75
612	-	$5 multicoloured	6·00	1·75
613	-	$10 multicoloured	8·00	6·00
614	-	$20 multicoloured	12·00	11·00
615	-	$50 multicoloured	19·00	22·00

DESIGNS—25×31 mm: Queen Elizabeth II and $5 Kowloon; $10 Victoria Harbour; $20 Legislative Council Building; $50 Government House.

With the exception of Nos. 607a and 611a which are dated, all the above exist with or without a date in the design.

127 Hong Kong Flag

1987

554a	127	10c. multicoloured	1·00	1·00
554b	-	50c. brown, red and black	1·25	1·75
554c	-	80c. mauve, green & blk	1·25	2·75
554d	-	90c. blue, brown & black	1·25	1·75
554e	-	$1.30 green, blue & black	1·75	2·50
554f	-	$2.30 brown, violet & blk	2·00	3·25

DESIGN: 50c. to $2.30, Map of Hong Kong.

128 Alice Ho Miu Ling Nethersole Hospital, 1887

1987. Hong Kong Medical Centenaries. Mult.

555	50c. Type **128**	1·25	20
556	$1.30 Matron and nurses, Nethersole Hospital, 1891	2·50	1·40
557	$1.70 Scanning equipment, Faculty of Medicine	3·00	1·40
558	$5 Nurse and patient, Faculty of Medicine	9·00	9·00

129 Casual Dress with Fringed Hem, 220–589

1987. Historical Chinese Costumes. Multicoloured.

559	50c. Type **129**	55	10
560	$1.30 Two-piece dress and wrap, 581–960	1·40	1·25
561	$1.70 Formal dress, Song Dynasty, 960–1279	1·50	1·50
562	$5 Manchu empress costume, 1644–1911	4·00	7·50

130 Dragon

1988. Chinese New Year ("Year of the Dragon"). Designs showing dragons.

563	130	50c. multicoloured	60	15
564	-	$1.30 multicoloured	1·25	1·00
565	-	$1.70 multicoloured	1·50	1·10
566	-	$5 multicoloured	2·75	5·50
MS567		134×88 mm. Nos. 563/6	9·00	12·00

131 White-throated Kingfisher ("White-breasted Kingfisher")

1988. Hong Kong Birds. Multicoloured.

568	50c. Type **131**	1·00	30
569	$1.30 Fukien niltava	2·00	1·60
570	$1.70 Black kite	2·50	1·75
571	$5 Lesser pied kingfisher	4·00	7·00

132 Chinese Banyan

1988. Trees of Hong Kong. Multicoloured.

572	50c. Type **132**	35	10
573	$1.30 Hong Kong orchid tree	70	65
574	$1.70 Cotton tree	90	85
575	$5 Schima	2·50	5·50
MS576	135×85 mm. Nos. 572/5	10·00	7·50

133 Lower Terminal, Peak Tramway

1988. Centenary of The Peak Tramway. Mult.

577	50c. Type **133**	35	10
578	$1.30 Tram on incline	70	1·00
579	$1.70 Peak Tower Upper Terminal	90	1·25
580	$5 Tram	2·50	5·00
MS581	160×90 mm. Nos. 577/80	8·00	8·00

134 Hong Kong Catholic Cathedral

1988. Centenary of Hong Kong Catholic Cathedral.

582	134	60c. multicoloured	1·25	1·50

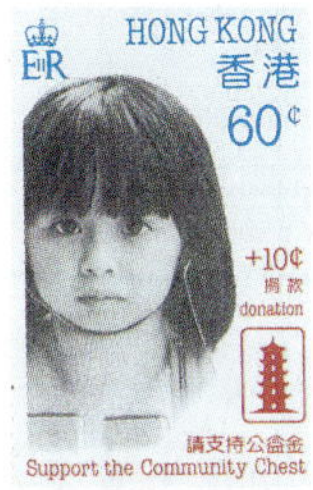

135 Deaf Girl

1988. Community Chest Charity.

583	135	60c.+10c. black, red & bl	60	1·25
584	-	$1.40+20c. black, red and green	75	1·40
585	-	$1.80+30c. black, red and orange	90	1·75
586	-	$5+$1 black, red & brn	2·00	5·00

DESIGNS: $1.40, Elderly woman; $1.80, Blind boy using braille typewriter; $5 Mother and baby.

136 Snake

1989. Chinese New Year ("Year of the Snake"). Multicoloured.

587	60c. Type **136**	45	15
588	$1.40 Snake and fish	1·75	70
589	$1.80 Snake on branch	1·90	85
590	$5 Coiled snake	5·00	7·25
MS591	135×85 mm. Nos. 587/90	12·00	7·50

137 Girl and Doll

1989. Cheung Chau Bun Festival. Multicoloured.

592	60c. Type **137**	55	15
593	$1.40 Girl in festival costume	1·25	80
594	$1.80 Paper effigy of god Taai Si Wong	1·40	90
595	$5 Floral gateway	3·50	6·00

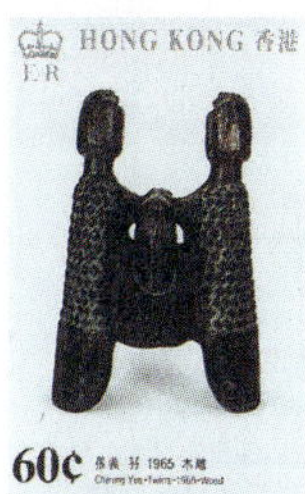

138 "Twins" (wood carving, Cheung Yee)

1989. Modern Art. Multicoloured.

596	60c. Type **138**	50	15
597	$1.40 "Figures" (acrylic on paper, Chan Luis)	1·25	80
598	$1.80 "Lotus" (copper sculpture, Van Lau)	1·40	90
599	$5 "Zen Painting" (ink and colour on paper, Lui Shou-kwan)	3·00	4·75

139 Lunar New Year Festivities

1989. Hong Kong People. Multicoloured.

616	60c. Type **139**	75	10
617	$1.40 Shadow boxing and horse racing	2·00	80
618	$1.80 Foreign-exchange dealer and traditional builder	2·00	90
619	$5 Multi-racial society	4·50	8·00

140 University of Science and Technology

1989. Building for the Future.

620	140	60c. black, yellow & brn	45	15
621	-	70c. blk, pale pink & pink	50	40
622	-	$1.30 black, lt green & grn	1·00	1·00
623	-	$1.40 black, lt blue & blue	1·00	70
624	-	$1.80 black, turquoise & bl	1·25	1·00
625	-	$5 brown, orange and red	6·50	8·50

DESIGNS: 70c. Cultural Centre; $1.30, Eastern Harbour motorway interchange; $1.40, New Bank of China Building; $1.80, Convention and Exhibition Centre; $5 Mass Transit electric train.

141 Prince and Princess of Wales and Hong Kong Skyline

1989. Royal Visit. Multicoloured.

626	60c. Type **141**	1·50	30
627	$1.40 Princess of Wales	2·50	1·10
628	$1.80 Prince of Wales	1·75	1·10
629	$5 Prince and Princess of Wales in evening dress	7·50	9·00
MS630	128×75 mm. No. 629	12·00	9·00

143 Horse

1990. Chinese New Year ("Year of the Horse").

631	143	60c. multicoloured	55	20
632	-	$1.40 multicoloured	1·75	1·25
633	-	$1.80 multicoloured	1·90	1·25
634	-	$5 multicoloured	6·50	8·50
MS635		135×85 mm. Nos. 631/4	13·00	10·00

DESIGNS: $1.40 to $5, Different horse designs.

144 Chinese Lobster Dish

1990. International Cuisine. Designs showing various dishes. Multicoloured.

No.	Description		
636	60c. Type **144**	60	15
637	70c. Indian	60	50
638	$1.30 Chinese vegetables	1·00	1·25
639	$1.40 Thai	1·00	70
640	$1.80 Japanese	1·25	95
641	$5 French	4·25	8·50

145 Air Pollution and Clean Air

1990. U.N. World Environment Day. Mult.

No.	Description		
642	60c. Type **145**	40	15
643	$1.40 Noise pollution and music	85	80
644	$1.80 Polluted and clean water	1·00	80
645	$5 Litter on ground and in bin	2·75	4·00

1990. "New Zealand 1990" International Stamp Exhibition, Auckland. Sheet 130×75 mm, containing design as No. 613.

No.	Description		
MS646	$10 multicoloured	80·00	85·00

146 Street Lamp and Des Voeux Road, 1890

1990. Centenary of Electricity Supply.

No.	Type	Description		
647	**146**	60c. black, bistre & brown	50	15
648	-	$1.40 multicoloured	90	80
649	-	$1.80 black, bistre and blue	1·00	80
650	-	$5 multicoloured	2·25	4·50
MS651		155×85 mm. Nos. 648 and 650	4·50	6·00

DESIGNS: $1.40, Street Lamp and "Jumbo" (floating restaurant), 1940; $1.80, Street lamp and pylon, 1960; $5 Street lamp and Hong Kong from harbour, 1980.

147 Christmas Tree and Skyscrapers

1990. Christmas. Multicoloured.

No.	Description		
652	50c. Type **147**	25	10
653	60c. Dove with holly	25	15
654	$1.40 Firework display	80	40
655	$1.80 Father Christmas hat on skyscraper	1·00	50
656	$2 Children with Father Christmas	1·40	1·40
657	$5 Candy stick with bow and Hong Kong skyline	3·00	6·00

148 Ram

1991. Chinese New Year ("Year of the Ram").

No.	Type	Description		
658	**148**	60c. multicoloured	25	15
659	-	$1.40 multicoloured	65	60
660	-	$1.80 multicoloured	80	75
661	-	$5 multicoloured	2·75	5·50
MS662		135×85 mm. Nos. 658/61	6·50	7·50

DESIGNS: $1.40 to $5, Different ram designs.

149 Letter "A", Clock, Teddy Bear and Building Bricks (Kindergarten)

1991. Education. Multicoloured.

No.	Description		
663	80c. Type **149**	50	20
664	$1.80 Globe, laboratory flask and mathematical symbols (Primary and Secondary)	1·25	80
665	$2.30 Machinery (Vocational)	1·40	1·40
666	$5 Mortar board, computer and books (Tertiary)	3·50	6·50

150 Rickshaw

1991. 100 Years of Public Transport. Mult.

No.	Description		
667	80c. Type **150**	30	15
668	90c. Double-decker bus	70	75
669	$1.70 Harbour ferry	1·10	1·25
670	$1.80 Double-deck tram	1·40	80
671	$2.30 Mass Transit electric train	2·00	2·25
672	$5 Jetfoil	3·50	6·50

151 Victorian Pillar Box and Cover of 1888

1991. 150th Anniv of Hong Kong Post Office. Multicoloured.

No.	Description		
673	80c. Type **151**	50	15
674	$1.70 Edwardian pillar box and cover	1·00	1·00
675	$1.80 King George V pillar box and cover of 1935	1·10	75
676	$2.30 King George VI pillar box and cover of 1938	1·50	2·00
677	$5 Queen Elizabeth II pillar box and cover of 1989	4·00	7·50
MS678	130×75 mm. $10 As No. 677	13·00	16·00

See also Nos. **MS**745 and **MS**899.

152 Bronze Buddha, Lantau Island

1991. Landmarks.

No.	Type	Description		
679	**152**	80c. red and black	50	15
680	-	$1.70 green and black	1·00	1·25
681	-	$1.80 violet and black	1·75	80
682	-	$2.30 blue and black	1·25	2·00
683	-	$5 orange and black	3·50	7·25

DESIGNS: $1.70, Peak Pavilion; $1.80, Clocktower of Kowloon–Canton Railway Station; $2.30, Catholic Cathedral; $5 Wong Tai Sin Temple.

1991. "Phila Nippon '91" International Stamp Exhibition, Tokyo. Sheet 130×75 mm, containing design as No. 613.

No.	Description		
MS684	$10 multicoloured	32·00	30·00

1991. Olympic Games, Barcelona (1992) (1st issue). Sheet 130×75 mm, containing design as No. 613.

No.	Description		
MS685	$10 multicoloured	18·00	18·00

See also Nos. 696/700 and **MS**722.

153 Monkey

1992. Chinese New Year ("Year of the Monkey").

No.	Type	Description		
686	**153**	80c. multicoloured	40	15
687	-	$1.80 multicoloured	80	70
688	-	$2.30 multicoloured	1·25	1·75
689	-	$5 multicoloured	2·75	7·00
MS690		135×85 mm. Nos. 686/9	9·50	11·00

DESIGNS: $1.80 to $5, Different monkey designs.

1992. 40th Anniv of Queen Elizabeth II's Accession. As T 179a of Gibraltar. Multicoloured.

No.	Description		
691	80c. Royal barge in Hong Kong harbour	30	15
692	$1.70 Queen watching dancing display	60	70
693	$1.80 Fireworks display	60	35
694	$2.30 Three portraits of Queen Elizabeth	90	1·00
695	$5 Queen Elizabeth II	1·50	3·25

154 Running

1992. Olympic Games, Barcelona. Multicoloured.

No.	Description		
696	80c. Type **154**	40	20
697	$1.80 Swimming and javelin	90	1·00
698	$2.30 Cycling	2·00	2·00
699	$5 High jump	2·25	5·50
MS700	130×75 mm. As Nos. 696/9*	7·00	8·50

*The stamps from No. **MS**700 show the inscriptions in different colours, instead of the black on Nos. 696/9. The designs of the $1.80 and $5 values from the miniature sheet have also been rearranged so that "HONG KONG" and the Royal Cypher occur at the right of the inscription.

1992. "World Columbian Stamp Expo '92" Exhibition, Chicago. Sheet 130×75 mm, containing design as No. 613, but colours changed.

No.	Description		
MS701	$10 multicoloured	3·50	6·50

155 Queen Elizabeth II

1992

No.	Type	Description		
702	**155**	10c. mauve, blk & cerise	30	50
702b	**155**	20c. black, indigo & bl	1·00	1·75
703	**155**	50c. red, black and yellow	30	30
704	**155**	60c. blue, black and light blue	2·00	1·50
705	**155**	70c. mauve, black and lilac	2·00	75
706	**155**	80c. mauve, black and pink	30	45
707	**155**	90c. green, blk & grey	30	60
708	**155**	$1 brown, black and yellow	35	20
708b	**155**	$1.10 red, black & orge	2·00	1·50
709	**155**	$1.20 violet, blk & lilac	45	25
709c	**155**	$1.40 green, black and yellow	2·25	1·75
709d	**155**	$1.50 brown, black and blue	2·25	2·50
709e	**155**	$1.60 green, black and lilac	2·00	2·25
710	**155**	$1.70 ultram, blk & bl	1·00	1·00
711	**155**	$1.80 mauve, black and grey	1·25	55
711a	**155**	$1.90 green, black and stone	1·00	1·75
712b	**155**	$2.10 red, black & green	2·25	2·50
713	**155**	$2.30 brown, black and pink	2·50	75
713b	**155**	$2.50 green, black and yellow	2·25	2·50
713c	**155**	$2.60 choc, blk & brn	1·50	2·50
713d	**155**	$3.10 brown, black and blue	2·25	1·00
715	-	$10 brown, black and cinnamon	2·50	2·75
716	-	$20 red, black & orange	4·25	4·50
717	-	$50 dp grey, blk & grey	8·50	11·00
757c	**155**	$1.30 blue, black and orange	50	1·00
759	**155**	$2.40 blue, blk & grey	1·10	1·50
759e	**155**	$5 green, black & lt grn	1·50	3·25
764	**155**	$2 blue, black and green	60	80

Nos. 715/17 are as Type **155**, but larger, 26×30 mm.

156 Stamps and Perforation Gauge

1992. Stamp Collecting. Multicoloured.

No.	Description		
718	80c. Type **156**	30	25
719	$1.80 Handstamp of 1841, 1891 Jubilee overprint and tweezers	60	75
720	$2.30 Stamps of 1946 and 1949 under magnifying glass	85	1·25
721	$5 2c. of 1862 and watermark detector	2·00	4·00

1992. Olympic Games, Barcelona (3rd issue). As No. MS700, but additionally inscribed "To Commemorate the Opening of the 1992 Summer Olympic Games 25 July 1992", in English and Chinese, at foot of sheet.

No.	Description		
MS722	130×75 mm. As Nos. 696/9	3·75	6·00

1992. "Kuala Lumpur '92" International Stamp Exhibition. Sheet 130×75 mm, containing design as No. 715, but colours changed.

No.	Description		
MS723	$10 blue, black and light blue	3·50	7·00

157 Principal Male Character

1992. Chinese Opera. Multicoloured.

No.	Description		
724	80c. Type **157**	1·25	25
725	$1.80 Martial character	2·00	1·60
726	$2.30 Principal female character	2·25	2·50
727	$5 Comic character	4·50	10·00

158 Hearts

1992. Greetings Stamps. Multicoloured.

No.	Description		
728	80c. Type **158**	30	20
729	$1.80 Stars	55	60
730	$2.30 Presents	75	1·00
731	$5 Balloons	1·60	3·50

159 Cockerel

1993. Chinese New Year ("Year of the Cock").

No.	Type	Description		
732	**159**	80c. multicoloured	30	20
733	-	$1.80 multicoloured	70	80
734	-	$2.30 multicoloured	95	1·25
735	-	$5 multicoloured	1·75	4·25
MS736		133×84 mm. Nos. 732/5	4·00	6·50

DESIGNS: $1.80 to $5, Different cock designs.

160 Pipa

1993. Chinese String Musical Instruments. Multicoloured.

No.	Description		
737	80c. Type **160**	40	20
738	$1.80 Erhu	70	75
739	$2.30 Ruan	95	1·25

740	$5 Gehu	2·00	3·75

161 Central Waterfront, Hong Kong in 1954

1993. 40th Anniv of Coronation. Multicoloured.

741	80c. Type **161**	40	20
742	$1.80 Hong Kong in 1963	70	75
743	$2.30 Hong Kong in 1975	90	1·25
744	$5 Hong Kong in 1992	2·25	4·00

1993. 150th anniv of Hong Kong Post Office (2nd issue). Sheet 130×75 mm, containing design as No. 715.

MS745	$10 brown, black and cinnamon	3·50	6·00

1993. "Hong Kong '94" International Stamp Exhibition. Sheet 115×78 mm, containing design as No. 715, but colours changed.

MS746	$10 purple, black, yellow and blue	3·50	5·00

162 University of Science and Technology Building and Student

1993. Hong Kong's Contribution to Science and Technology. Multicoloured.

747	80c. Type **162**	25	20
748	$1.80 Science Museum building and energy machine exhibit	40	40
749	$2.30 Governor's Award and circuit board	60	90
750	$5 Dish aerials and world map	1·25	3·50

1993. "Bangkok '93" International Stamp Exhibition. Sheet 131×75 mm, containing design as No. 715, but colours changed.

MS751	$10 emerald, deep green and green	2·75	3·75

163 Red Calico Egg-fish

1993. Goldfish. Multicoloured.

752	$1 Type **163**	50	20
753	$1.90 Red cap oranda	80	50
754	$2.40 Red and white fringetail	1·00	1·25
755	$5 Black and gold dragon-eye	2·25	5·00
MS756	130×75 mm. Nos. 752/5	4·75	8·50

164 Dog

1994. Chinese New Year ("Year of the Dog").

766	164	$1 multicoloured	30	20
767	-	$1.90 multicoloured	50	55
768	-	$2.40 multicoloured	70	1·00
769	-	$5 multicoloured	1·75	4·00
MS770		133×84 mm. Nos. 766/9	5·50	8·00

DESIGNS: $1.90 to $5, Different dog designs.

1994. "Hong Kong '94" International Stamp Exhibition. Sheet 130×75 mm, containing design as No. 759e.

MS771	**155** $5 green, black and light green	2·50	5·00

165 Modern Police Constables on Traffic Duty

1994. 150th Anniv of Royal Hong Kong Police Force. Multicoloured.

772	$1 Type **165**	30	20
773	$1.20 Marine policeman with binoculars	40	50
774	$1.90 Police uniforms of 1950	55	50
775	$2 Tactical firearms unit officer with sub-machine gun	75	1·00
776	$2.40 Early 20th-century police uniforms	90	1·25
777	$5 Sikh and Chinese constables of 1900	2·75	4·25

166 Dragon Boat Festival

1994. Traditional Chinese Festivals. Multicoloured.

778	$1 Type **166**	35	20
779	$1.90 Lunar New Year	60	70
780	$2.40 Seven Sisters Festival	85	1·25
781	$5 Mid-Autumn Festival	1·75	4·25

1994. Conference of Commonwealth Postal Administrations, Hong Kong. Sheet 134×83 mm, containing design as No. 715.

MS782	$10 brown, black and cinnamon	4·00	7·00

167 Swimming

1994. 15th Commonwealth Games, Victoria, Canada. Multicoloured.

783	$1 Type **167**	25	20
784	$1.90 Bowls	40	55
785	$2.40 Gymnastics	50	1·00
786	$5 Weightlifting	90	3·25

168 Dr. James Legge and Students

1994. Dr. James Legge (Chinese scholar) Commemoration.

787	**168** $1 multicoloured	1·00	1·00

169 Alcyonium Coral

1994. Corals. Multicoloured.

788	$1 Type **169**	25	20
789	$1.90 Zoanthus	35	60
790	$2.40 Tubastrea	45	1·00
791	$5 Platygyra	80	3·00
MS792	130×75 mm. Nos. 788/91	4·50	6·50

170 Pig

1995. Chinese New Year ("Year of the Pig").

793	170	$1 multicoloured	30	30
794	-	$1.90 multicoloured	60	80
795	-	$2.40 multicoloured	60	1·10
796	-	$5 multicoloured	1·25	4·00
MS797		130×84 mm. Nos. 793/6	4·25	6·50

DESIGNS: $1.90 to $5, Different pig designs.

171 Hong Kong Rugby Sevens

1995. International Sporting Events in Hong Kong. Multicoloured.

798	$1 Type **171**	45	20
799	$1.90 The China Sea Yacht Race	60	80
800	$2.40 International Dragon Boat Races	85	1·10
801	$5 Hong Kong International Horse Races	1·75	4·25

172 Tsui Shing Lau Pagoda

1995. Hong Kong Traditional Rural Buildings. Multicoloured.

802	$1 Type **172**	30	25
803	$1.90 Sam Tung Uk village	45	65
804	$2.40 Lo Wai village	60	1·10
805	$5 Man Shek Tong house	1·10	3·50

173 Regimental Badge

1995. Disbandment of the Royal Hong Kong Regiment. Multicoloured.

806	$1.20 Type **173**	70	25
807	$2.10 Regimental guidon (horiz)	80	65
808	$2.60 Colour of Hong Kong Volunteer Defence Corps, 1928 (horiz)	80	1·10
809	$5 Cap badge of Royal Hong Kong Defence Force, 1951	1·10	4·00

1995. "Singapore '95" International Stamp Exhibition. Sheet 130×75 mm, containing design as No. 715, but colours changed.

MS810	$10 mauve, green, yellow and lilac	4·00	6·50

1995. 50th Anniv of End of Second World War. Sheet 130×75 mm, containing design as No. 715.

MS811	$10 brown, black and cinnamon	4·50	7·00

174 Bruce Lee

1995. Hong Kong Film Stars. Multicoloured.

812	$1.20 Type **174**	2·00	75
813	$2.10 Leung Sing-por	2·25	1·40
814	$2.60 Yam Kim-fai	3·00	2·25
815	$5 Lin Dai	3·50	5·00

175 Rat

1996. Chinese New Year ("Year of the Rat").

816	175	$1.20 multicoloured	25	30
817	-	$2.10 multicoloured	50	55
818	-	$2.60 multicoloured	50	65
819	-	$5 multicoloured	1·50	1·75
MS820		133×83 mm. Nos. 816/19	3·50	3·50

DESIGNS: $2.10 to $5, Rats (different).

1996. Visit "HONG KONG '97" Stamp Exhibition (1st issue). Sheet 130×80 mm, containing design as No. 715, but colours changed.

MS821	$10 orange, black and green	4·00	6·50

See also Nos. **MS**827, **MS**841 and **MS**872/3.

176 Rhythmic Gymnastics

1996. Olympic Games, Atlanta. Multicoloured with Royal cypher and face values in black and Olympic rings multicoloured.

822	$1.20 Type **176**	20	25
823	$2.10 Diving	35	65
824	$2.60 Athletics	40	75
825	$5 Basketball	1·50	3·25
MS826	130×75 mm. As Nos. 822/5, but Royal Cypher and Olympic Rings in gold and face values in black (medal in bottom sheet margin)	2·50	4·25

See also Nos. 832/5.

1996. Visit "HONG KONG '97" Stamp Exhibition (2nd issue). Sheet 130×80 mm, containing design as No. 715, but colours changed.

MS827	$10 green, deep green and violet	2·50	3·00

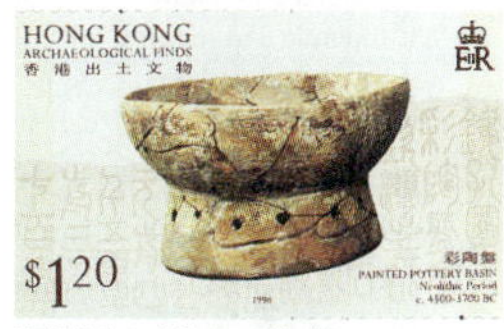

177 Painted Pottery Basin, c. 4500–3700 B.C.

1996. Archaeological Discoveries. Multicoloured.

828	$1.20 Type **177**	45	25
829	$2.10 Stone "yue" (ceremonial axe), c. 2900–2200 B.C.	50	65
830	$2.60 Stone "ge" (halberd), c. 2200–1500 B.C.	55	1·00
831	$5 Pottery tripod, c. 25–220 A.D.	1·00	2·50

1996. Opening of Centennial Olympic Games, Atlanta. Designs as Nos. 822/5, but with Royal Cypher and Olympic Rings in gold and face values in colours quoted.

832	$1.20 Type **176** (mauve)	35	25
833	$2.10 As No. 823 (blue)	40	60
834	$2.60 As No. 824 (green)	45	90
835	$5 As No. 825 (red)	1·00	2·75
MS836	130×75 mm. As No. **MS**826, but with medal in top margin	2·75	4·50

The stamps in Nos. **MS**826 and **MS**836 are similar. The miniature sheets differ in the marginal inscriptions and illustrations. No. **MS**826 is inscribed "1996 OLYMPIC GAMES" and has a Gold Medal in the bottom margin. No. **MS**836 is inscribed "TO COMMEMORATE THE OPENING OF THE CENTENNIAL OLYMPIC GAMES 19 JULY 1996" and has the medal in the top margin.

178 Pat Sin Leng Mountain

1996. Mountains. Multicoloured.

837	$1.30 Type **178**	45	35
838	$2.50 Ma On Shan (40×35 mm)	65	1·00
839	$3.10 Lion Rock (35×40 mm)	85	1·40
840	$5 Lantau Peak (25×46½ mm)	1·10	2·75

1996. Visit "HONG KONG '97" Stamp Exhibition (3rd issue). Sheet 130×80 mm, containing design as No. 715, but colours changed.

MS841	$10 green, black and red	2·50	3·50

1996. Hong Kong Team's Achievements at Atlanta Olympic Games. Sheet 130×75 mm, containing No. 715.

MS842	$10 brown, black and cinnamon	2·75	3·25

179 Main Building, University of Hong Kong, 1912

1996. Urban Heritage. Multicoloured.

843	$1.30 Type **179**	30	70

844	$2.50 Western Market, 1906	50	85
845	$3.10 Old Pathological Institute, 1905	55	1·00
846	$5 Flagstaff House, 1846	70	2·25

1996. Serving the Community. Sheet 130×75 mm, containing design as No. 619, but smaller, 25×35 mm. Multicoloured.

MS847	$5 Multi-racial society	1·00	1·25

180 Part of Hong Kong Skyline

1997

848	180	10c. purple and pink	15	30
849	-	20c. brown and red	30	30
850	-	50c. green and orange	20	40
851	-	$1 blue and yellow	30	20
852	-	$1.20 green and yellow	30	50
853	-	$1.30 violet and green	30	25
854	-	$1.40 purple and green	30	50
855	-	$1.60 purple and green	30	60
856	-	$2 green and blue	40	50
857	-	$2.10 turquoise and blue	40	60
858	-	$2.50 violet and mauve	50	1·00
859	-	$3.10 purple and mauve	60	70
860	-	$5 mauve and orange	1·25	1·00
861	-	$10 multicoloured (28×32 mm)	2·00	2·50
862	-	$20 multicoloured (28×32 mm)	3·50	5·00
863	-	$50 multicoloured (28×32 mm)	8·00	11·00
MS864		273×53 mm. Nos. 848/60	3·50	4·00
MS865		95×72 mm. Nos. 861/3	13·00	13·50

DESIGNS: 20c. to $50, Different sections of Hong Kong skyline.

See also Nos. MS872/3 and MS892.

1997. Visit "HONG KONG '97" Stamp Exhibition (4th issue). Sheet 130×80 mm, containing No. 861, with marginal illustration in violet.

MS872	$10 multicoloured	1·75	3·50

1997. Visit "HONG KONG '97" Stamp Exhibition (5th issue). Sheet 130×80 mm, containing No. 861, with marginal illustration in brown.

MS873	$10 multicoloured	1·75	3·50

181 Ox

1997. Chinese New Year ("Year of the Ox").

874	181	$1.30 multicoloured	25	25
875	181	$2.50 multicoloured	40	55
876	181	$3.10 multicoloured	55	90
877	181	$5 multicoloured	85	2·00
MS878		133×84 mm. Nos. 874/7	1·75	3·00

182 Yellow-breasted Bunting

1997. Migratory Birds. Multicoloured.

884	$1.30 Type **182**	30	35
885	$2.50 Great knot	40	55
886	$3.10 Falcated teal	55	90
887	$5 Black-faced spoonbill	85	2·00

183 Hong Kong Stadium

1997. Modern Landmarks. Multicoloured.

888	$1.30 Type **183**	30	25
889	$2.50 Peak Tower	60	55
890	$3.10 Hong Kong Convention and Exhibition Centre	85	1·10
891	$5 Lantau bridge	1·40	2·50
MS892	130×76 mm. No. 891	1·00	1·75

1997. Paralympic Games, Atlanta (1996). Sheet 130×75 mm, containing No. 861.

MS898	$10 multicoloured	1·50	2·25

1997. History of the Hong Kong Post Office. Sheet 130×75 mm, containing design as No. 677, but redrawn smaller, 22×38 mm.

MS899	$5 multicoloured	1·00	1·75

184 House of Sam Tung Uk

1997. Establishment of Hong Kong as Special Administrative Region of People's Republic of China. Multicoloured.

900	$1.30 Type **184**	45	40
901	$1.60 Hong Kong Bank and vehicles	55	40
902	$2.50 Buildings and Hong Kong Convention and Exhibition Centre	75	50
903	$2.60 Container Terminal	85	50
904	$3.10 Junks and dolphins	1·10	60
905	$5 Bauhinia flower and clouds	1·60	60
MS906	131×75 mm. No. 905	2·50	2·10

185 Graphs and Hong Kong Bank (Finance and Banking)

1997. World Bank Group and International Monetary Fund Annual Meetings. Multicoloured.

907	$1.30 Type **185**	45	40
908	$2.50 Share prices (Investment) and Stock Exchange	75	60
909	$3.10 Map on printed circuit and dish aerial (Trade and Telecommunications)	1·10	1·00
910	$5 Satellite image and road junctions (Infrastructure and Transport)	1·60	1·00

186 Clam

1997. Sea Shells. Multicoloured.

911	$1.30 Type **186**	45	40
912	$2.50 Cowrie	75	60
913	$3.10 Cone	1·10	1·00
914	$5 Murex	1·60	1·00

187 Tiger

1998. Chinese New Year ("Year of the Tiger").

915	187	$1.30 multicoloured	55	30
916	187	$2.50 multicoloured	75	60
917	187	$3.10 multicoloured	1·10	70
918	187	$5 multicoloured	1·40	80
MS919		133×84 mm. Nos. 915/18	6·50	6·25

188 "Star", 1900s

1998. Centenary of Star Ferry. Multicoloured.

920	$1.30 Type **188**	45	40
921	$2.50 "Star", 1910s–20s	75	60
922	$3.10 "Star", 1920s–1950s	1·10	70
923	$5 "Star", 1950s onwards	1·50	80

189 Observation Lounge

1998. Inauguration of Hong Kong International Airport, Chek Lap Kok. Multicoloured.

924	$1.30 Type **189**	40	35
925	$1.60 Couple boarding train	50	45
926	$2.50 Train and suspension bridge	70	55
927	$2.60 Concourse and mail vans at Airmail Centre	80	55
928	$3.10 Aircraft in bays	1·00	55
929	$5 Airplane taking off	1·60	55
MS930	145×79 mm. No. 929	2·50	2·20

190 De Havilland D.H.86 Dragon Express "Dorado" (Hong Kong—Penang Service, 1936)

1998. Closure of Kaj Tak Airport. Sheet 130×75 mm.

MS931	$5 multicoloured	2·50	2·20

Type **190** is a redrawn version of Type **111**.

191 Grasshopper and Cub Scouts and Knot

1998. 85th Anniv of Hong Kong Scout Association. Multicoloured.

932	$1.30 Type **191**	40	35
933	$2.50 Two scouts, knot, watch-tower and tents	70	65
934	$3.10 Two venture scouts, knot, sailing dinghies and helicopter	1·00	65
935	$5 Rover scout and adult leader, knot and buildings	1·50	65

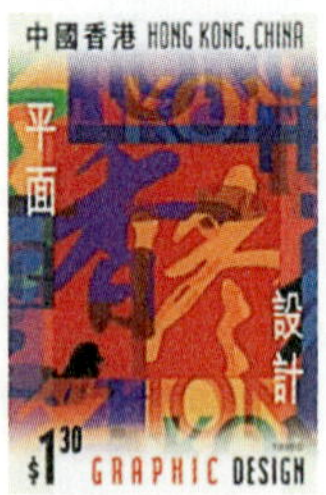

192 Graphic Design

1998. Hong Kong Design. Multicoloured.

936	$1.30 Type **192**	40	35
937	$2.50 Product design	70	65
938	$3.10 Interior design	90	80
939	$5 Fashion design	1·50	90

193 Dragonfly Kite

1998. Kites. Multicoloured.

940	$1.30 Type **193**	40	35
941	$2.50 Dragon kite	70	65
942	$3.10 Butterfly kite	90	80
943	$5 Goldfish kite	1·50	90
MS944	135×85 mm. Nos. 940/3	4·00	3·50

194 Rabbit ("Kung Hei Fat Choi")

1999. Chinese New Year ("Year of the Rabbit"). Multicoloured.

945	$1.30 Type **194**	40	35
946	$2.50 Rabbit and scroll ("Good Health")	70	65
947	$3.10 Rabbit and tangerine ("Good Luck")	1·00	80
948	$5 Rabbit and sweet tray ("May all your wishes come true")	1·50	90

The gold panels of the designs can be scratched off to reveal a greeting in Chinese characters as given in brackets. Prices for Nos. 945/8 are for examples with the gold panels intact.

195 Rabbit

1999. Chinese Lunar Cycle. Sheet 250×48 mm containing similar designs to 1987—98 New Year issues but with inscriptions as in T 195 and some face values altered. Multicoloured.

MS949	$1.30 As Type **175**; $1.30 As Type **181**; $1.30 As Type **187**; $1.30 As Type **195**; $1.30 As Type **170**; $1.30 As Type **130**; $1.30 As No. 768; $1.30 As Type **136**; $1.30 As No. 735; $1.30 As Type **53**; $1.30 As Type **148**; $1.30 As Type **143**	6·75	6·75

196 Calligraphy

1999. International Year of the Elderly. Mult.

950	$1.30 Type **196**	40	35
951	$2.50 Holding bird cage	70	65
952	$3.10 Playing chess	1·00	80
953	$5 Holding walking stick (voluntary services)	1·50	90

1999. Hong Kong Team's Achievements at 13th Asian Games, Bangkok (1998). Sheet 135×85 mm.

MS954	Nos. 856/7	3·50	3·50

197 An An

1999. Presentation of Giant pandas An An and Jia Jia to Hong Kong. Sheet 132×78 mm.

MS955	$10 multicoloured	6·25	6·25

198 Bus

1999. Public Transport. Multicoloured.

956	$1.30 Type **198**	40	35
957	$2.40 Minibus	70	55
958	$2.50 Tram	90	70

959	$2.60 Taxi	1·20	70
960	$3.10 "Airport Express" train	1·40	90

199 Hong Kong Harbour

1999. Hong Kong–Singapore Joint Issue. Mult.

961	$1.20 Type **199**	30	25
962	$1.30 Singapore skyline	40	35
963	$2.50 Giant Buddha, Lantau Island, Hong Kong	70	65
964	$2.60 Merlion statue, Sentosa Island, Singapore	80	65
965	$3.10 Street scene, Hong Kong	1·00	80
966	$5 Bugis Junction, Singapore	1·60	90
MS967	133×76 mm. Nos. 961/6	5·00	5·00

1999. "China 1999" International Stamp Exhibition, Peking. Sheet 130×75 mm.

MS968	No. 861	3·50	3·50

200 Flags of Hong Kong and People's Republic, and Hong Kong

1999. 50th Anniv of People's Republic of China. Multicoloured.

969	$1.30 Type **200**	70	35
970	$2.50 "Bauhinia blakeana" and Hong Kong harbour	90	65
971	$3.10 Chinese dragon dance	1·20	80
972	$5 Firework display over Hong Kong	1·90	1·10

201 Museum of Tea Ware

1999. Hong Kong Landmarks and Tourist Attractions. Multicoloured. (a) Size 24×29 mm (10c. to $5) or 26×31 mm (others).

973	10c. Type **201**	20	20
974	20c. St. John's Cathedral	20	20
975	50c. Legislative Council building	20	20
976	$1 Tai Fu Tai	30	20
977	$1.20 Wong Tai Sin Temple	40	20
978	$1.30 Victoria Harbour	40	20
979	$1.40 Hong Kong Railway Museum	40	20
980	$1.60 Tsim Sha Tsui clocktower	50	25
980a	$1.80 Hong Kong Stadium	60	25
980b	$1.90 Western Market	60	25
981	$2 Happy Valley racecourse	70	25
982	$2.10 Kowloon–Canton Railway	60	35
982a	$2.40 Repulse Bay	90	25
983	$2.50 Chi Lin Nunnery, Kowloon	90	25
983b	$3 The Peak Tower	1·20	25
984	$3.10 Giant Buddha, Po Lin Monastery, Lantau Island	1·20	25
985	$5 Pagoda, Aw Boon Haw Gardens	1·50	45
986	$10 Tsing Ma bridge	2·50	1·30
986a	$13 Hong Kong Cultural Centre	4·50	1·80
987	$20 Hong Kong Convention and Exhibition Centre	5·75	2·75
988	$50 Hong Kong International Airport	14·50	5·25
MS989	210×153 mm. Nos. 973/85	7·25	7·25
MS990	118×89 mm. Nos. 986/8	26·00	26·00

(b) Size 20×24 mm.

991	10c. As Type **201**	60	45
992	50c. As No. 975	80	45
993	$1.30 As No. 978	1·40	45
993a	$1.40 As No. 979	1·40	45
994	$1.60 As No. 980	1·50	45
994a	$1.80 As No. 980a	1·50	55
994b	$2.40 As No. 982a	1·80	65
994c	$3 As No. 984	2·00	70

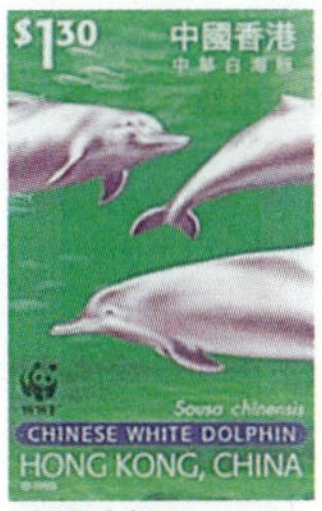

202 Dolphins

1999. Endangered Species. Indo-Pacific Hump- backed Dolphin ("Chinese White Dolphin").

995	**202**	$1.30 multicoloured	40	25
996	-	$2.50 multicoloured	70	55
997	-	$3.10 multicoloured	90	70
998	-	$5 multicoloured	1·50	90
MS999		150×80 mm. Nos. 995/8	5·00	5·25

DESIGNS: $2.50 to $5 Various designs showing dolphins as Type **202**.

203 Dragon Boat Race (fire) and City Skyline (metal)

1999. New Millennium (1st issue). The Five Elements. Sheet 130×75 mm containing T 203 and similar horiz designs. Multicoloured.

MS1000	$5 Type **203**; $5 Tsing Ma bridge (wood) and birds flying over Mai Po Marches (water)	4·00	4·00

204 Victoria Harbour

2000. New Millennium.

1001	**204**	$50 multicoloured	26·00	26·00

No. 1001 is embossed with 22 carat gold.

205 Scales on Globe (Au Chung-yip)

2000. New Millennium. Winning Entries in Children's Millennium Stamp Design Competition. Mult.

1002	$1.30 Type **205**	40	20
1003	$2.50 Globe, space shuttle, houses and children watering (Cheung Hang)	80	45
1004	$3.10 Planets (Valerie Teh)	90	65
1005	$5 Planets, spacecraft and satellite (Tsui Ming-yin)	1·40	90

206 Dragon

2000. Chinese New Year ("Year of the Dragon").

1006	**206**	$1.30 multicoloured	40	30
1007	-	$2.50 multicoloured	80	65
1008	-	$3.10 multicoloured	90	70
1009	-	$5 multicoloured	1·50	90
MS1010		Two sheets, each 135×85 mm. (a) Nos. 1006/9. (b) $5 No. 1009. Imperf Set of 2 sheets	15·00	15·00

DESIGNS: $2.50 to $5 Various dragons.

2000. Establishment of the Certification Authority (1st issue). Sheet 140×90 mm containing design as No. 986.

MS1011	$10 multicoloured	4·00	4·00

2000. Visit "HONG KONG 2001" Stamp Exhibition (1st issue). Sheet 130×74 mm containing design as No. 986, and with marginal illustrations showing bird.

MS1012	$10 multicoloured	5·00	5·00

See also Nos. **MS**1017, **MS**1022, **MS**1027, **MS**1028, **MS**1037 and **MS**1052.

207 Hong Kong Heritage Museum, Sha Tin

2000. Museums and Libraries. Multicoloured.

1013	$1.30 Type **207**	60	35
1014	$2.50 Central Library, Causeway Bay	1·10	70
1015	$3.10 Museum of Coastal Defence, Shau Kei Wan	1·20	80
1016	$5 Museum of History, Tsim Sha Tsui East	1·90	1·30

2000. Visit "HONG KONG 2001" Stamp Exhibition (2nd issue). Sheet 130×75 mm containing design as No. 986, and with marginal illustration showing flowers.

MS1017	$10 multicoloured	4·00	4·00

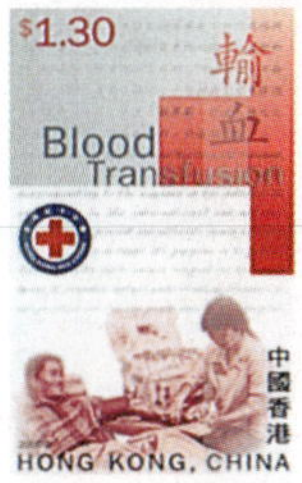

208 Patient and Nurse (Blood Transfusion)

2000. 50th Anniv of Hong Kong Red Cross. Multicoloured.

1018	$1.30 Type **208**	50	35
1019	$2.50 Doctor and child (Special Education and Care for the Disabled)	90	65
1020	$3.10 Man distributing blankets (Disaster relief)	1·00	70
1021	$5 Volunteer and young man (Youth and Voluntary services)	1·60	1·10
MS1022	130×75 mm. Nos. 1018/21	4·00	4·00

209 Lantern Fly

2000. Insects. Multicoloured.

1023	$1.30 Type **209**	60	25
1024	$2.50 Yellow-spotted emerald	1·00	55
1025	$3.10 Hong Kong birdwing (butterfly)	1·10	65
1026	$5 Red-cap tortoise beetle	1·80	1·30
MS1027	130×75 mm. Nos. 1023/6	4·75	4·75

210 Lion Rock

2000. Visit "HONG KONG 2001" Stamp Exhibition (3rd issue). Sheet 130×75 mm.

MS1028	$10 multicoloured	4·00	4·00

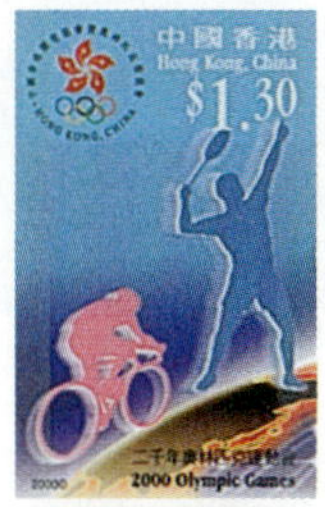

211 Cycling and Tennis

2000. Olympic Games, Sydney. Multicoloured.

1029	$1.30 Type **211**	50	35
1030	$2.50 Table tennis and running	90	70
1031	$3.10 Wrestling and rowing	1·10	80
1032	$5 Diving and wind surfing	1·70	1·10

212 View of Street (Establishment of Chamber, 1900)

2000. Centenary of General Chamber of Commerce. Multicoloured.

1033	$1.30 Type **212**	50	35
1034	$2.50 Old and new headquarters (relocation, 1922)	90	70
1035	$3.10 Victims of Pak Tin village fire receiving aid	1·10	80
1036	$5 Man using abacus and hand using mouse	1·70	1·10

213 Corals

2000. Visit "HONG KONG 2001" Stamp Exhibition (4th issue). 129×75 mm.

MS1037	$10 multicoloured	4·00	4·00

2000. I.T.U. Telecome, Asia 2000. Sheet 130×75 mm containing design as No. 986.

MS1038	$10 multicoloured	4·00	4·00

214 Hong Kong Convention and Exhibition Centre

2000. New Millennium. Sheet 91×151 mm.

MS1039	$20 multicoloured	6·75	6·75

215 Snake

2001. Chinese New Year ("Year of the Snake").

1040	**215**	$1.30 multicoloured	50	35
1041	-	$2.50 multicoloured	90	70
1042	-	$3.10 multicoloured	1·10	80
1043	-	$5 multicoloured	1·70	1·10
MS1044		Two sheets, each 135×85 mm. (a) $5 Nos. 1040/3. (b) $5 No. 1043. Imperf	7·25	7·25

DESIGNS: $2.50 to $5 Showing various snakes.

216 Leaves and Pebbles ("Happy Memories")

2001. Greetings Stamps. Multicoloured.

1045	$1.30 Type **216**	40	25
1046	$1.60 Swans ("Happy Valentine's Day")	50	35
1047	$2.50 Chicks ("Happy Birthday")	1·00	65
1048	$2.60 Cherry blossom ("Happy New Year")	1·00	65
1049	$3.10 Bamboo ("A Successful Year")	1·20	80
1050	$5 Poinsettia ("Merry Christmas")	1·70	1·30

217 Dragon ("Year of the Dragon")

2001. "HONG KONG 2001" Stamp Exhibition. Sheet 135×90 mm.

MS1051	$50 Type **217**; $50 Snake ("Year of the Snake")	41·00	41·00

218 Schima tree

2001. Visit "HONG KONG 201" Stamp Exhibition (5th issue). Sheet 130×75 mm.

MS1052	$5 multicoloured	2·00	2·00

219 Tai Tam Tuk Reservoir

2001. 150th Anniv of Hong Kong's Public Water Supply. Multicoloured.

1053	$1.30 Type **219**	50	35
1054	$2.50 Plover Cove Reservoir	90	70
1055	$3.10 Guangdong to Hong Kong water pipeline	1·10	90
1056	$5 Water monitoring equipment and chemical symbols	1·70	1·40

220 Ng Cho-fan and Pak Yin

2001. Hong Kong Film Stars. Multicoloured.

1057	$1.30 Type **220**	50	35
1058	$2.50 Sun Ma Si-tsang and Tang Bik-wan	90	70
1059	$3.10 Cheung Wood-yau and Wong Man-lei	1·10	90
1060	$5 Mak Bing-wing and Fung Wong-nui	1·70	1·40

2001. 9th National Games, Guangzhou, People's Republic of China. Preliminary Contest for Sanda (discipline in National Game), Hong Kong. Sheet 130×75 mm containing design as No. 985 and with marginal illustrations showing boxing gloves.

MS1061	$5 multicoloured	2·40	2·40

221 Dragon Boat and Sydney Opera House

2001. Dragon Boat Racing. Multicoloured.

1062	$5 Type **221**	1·60	1·10
1063	$5 Dragon boat racing and Hong Kong Convention and Exhibition Centre	1·60	1·10
MS1064	106×70 mm. Nos. 1062/3	3·50	3·50

222 Emblem

2001. Choice of Beijing as 2008 Olympic Host City.

1065	**222**	$1.30 multicoloured	90	45

2001. "PHILA NIPPON 02" International Stamp Exhibition, Tokyo. Sheet 130×75 mm containing design as No. 986.

MS1066	$10 multicoloured	3·50	3·50

223 Pouring Tea (Gongfu tea)

2001. Tea Culture. Multicoloured.

1067	$1.30 Type **223**	45	30
1068	$2.50 Hong Kong style tea	80	55
1069	$3.10 Pouring water (Yum Cha and Dim Sum)	1·10	70
1070	$5 Pouring hot water in to tea pot	1·60	1·10

224 *Centella asiatica*

2001. Medicinal Herbs. Multicoloured.

1071	$1.30 Type **224**	45	30
1072	$2.50 *Lobelia chinensis*	80	55
1073	$3.10 *Gardenia jasminoides*	1·10	70
1074	$5 *Scutellaria indica*	1·60	1·10

225 Child dressed as Bear

2001. Children's Stamps. Self-adhesive gum.

1075	$1.30 Type **225**	45	30
1076	$2.50 Child dressed as duck	80	55
1077	$3.10 Child dressed as pot plant	1·10	70
1078	$5 Child dressed as bee	1·60	1·10
MS1079	130×92 mm. Nos. 1075/8	4·25	4·25

The stamps had portions of the design left white for users to colour as they wished. Such embellishments did not affect the postal validity of the stamps.

226 Horse

2002. Chinese New Year ("Year of the Horse").

1080	**226**	$1.30 multicoloured	45	30
1081	-	$2.50 multicoloured	80	55
1082	-	$3.10 multicoloured	1·10	70
1083	-	$5 multicoloured	1·60	1·10
MS1084		Two sheets, each 135×85 mm. (a) Nos. 1080/3. (b) No. 1083. Imperf	6·00	6·00

DESIGNS: Nos. 1081/3, showing horses.

2002. Serving the Community Festival 2002. Sheet 75×130 mm, containing design as No. 985.

MS1085	$5 multicoloured	2·10	2·10

227 Snake

2002. Chinese New Year ("Year of the Snake"). Sheet 135×90 mm.

MS1086	$50 Type **227**; $50 Horse ("Year of the Horse")	45·00	45·00

No. **MS**1086 has the snake and the horse embossed in gold and silver foil.

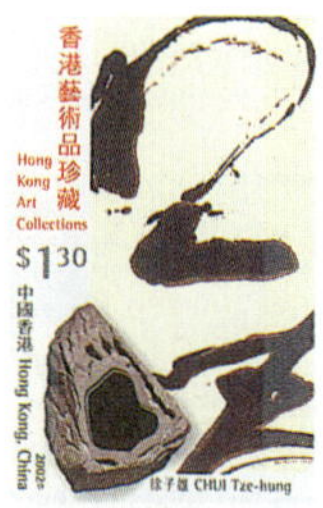

228 "Lines in Motion" (detail, Chui Tze-hung)

2002. Modern Art. Multicoloured.

1087	$1.30 Type **228**	50	35
1088	$2.50 "Volume and Time" (detail, Hon Chi-fun)	80	55
1089	$3.10 "Bright Sun" (sculpture, detail, Aries Lee)	1·00	70
1090	$5 "Midsummer" (detail, Irene Chou)	1·70	1·20

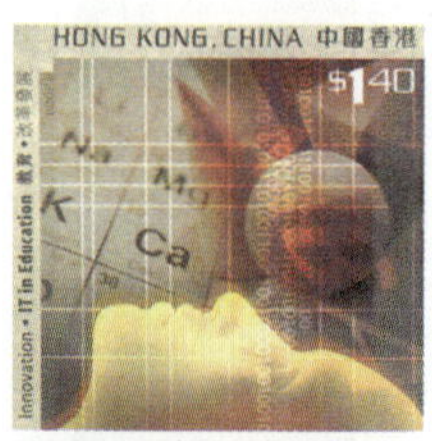

229 Face and Periodic Table (Education)

2002. Information Technology. Multicoloured.

1091	$1.40 Type **229**	50	35
1092	$2.40 Face, world map and internet symbols (communications)	80	55
1093	$3 Face, film and musical notes (entertainment)	1·00	70
1094	$5 Face, buildings and city (commerce)	1·70	1·20

230 Player and Football

2002. World Cup Football Championship. Japan and South Korea. Multicoloured.

1095	$1.40 Type **230**	70	35
1096	$1.40 Players tackling and crowd	70	35

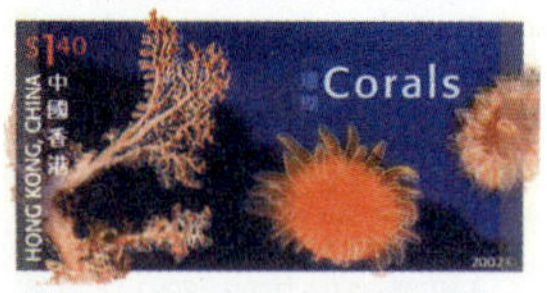

231 North Atlantic Pink Tree Coral, Pacific Orange Cup Coral and North Pacific Horn Coral

2002. Corals. Multicoloured.

1097	$1.40 Type **231**	50	30
1098	$2.40 North Atlantic giant orange tree coral and black coral	80	50
1099	$3 *Dendronepthea gigantea* and *Dendronepthea*	1·00	65
1100	$5 *Tubastrea* and *Echinogorgia* and island	1·60	1·10
MS1101	161×85 mm. Nos. 1097/1100	4·00	4·00

Stamps in similar designs were issued by Canada.

232 Hong Kong Buildings and Train

2002. 5th Anniv of Bejing—Kowloon Through Train Service. Multicoloured.

1102	$1.40 Type **232**	50	30
1103	$2.40 Wuhan—Changjiang Bridge and train	80	50
1104	$3 Pagodas, Shaolin Monastery, Zhengzhou and train	1·00	65
1105	$5 Temple of Heaven, Beijing and front of train	1·60	1·10

Nos. 1102/5 were issued together, forming a composite design of a train.

233 Chinese White Dolphins and Coral

2002. 5th Anniv of Hong Kong's Status as Special Administrative Region of People's Republic of China. Multicoloured.

1106	$1.40 Type **233**	50	30
1107	$2.40 School children and bauhinia flowers	80	50
1108	$3 Birds in flight over Hong Kong airport	1·00	65
1109	$5 Flags of China and Hong Kong, buildings and fireworks	1·60	1·00
MS1110	135×85 mm. Nos. 1106/9	4·00	4·00

2002. "PHILAKOREA 2002" World Stamp Exhibition, Seoul, South Korea. Sheet 131×75 mm, containing design as No. 986.

MS1111	$10 multicoloured	4·00	4·00

2002. "AMPHILEX 2002" World Stamp Exhibition, Amsterdam. Sheet 130×75 mm, containing design as No. 986.

MS1112	$10 multicoloured	4·00	4·00

2002. Hukou Waterfall Shanxi, People's Republic of China. Sheet 140×90 mm, containing design as No. 986.

MS1113	$10 multicoloured	4·00	4·00

234 Ping Chau

2002. Geology of Hong Kong. Multicoloured.

1114	$1.40 Type **234**	50	30
1115	$2.40 Port Island	80	50
1116	$3 Po Pin Chau	1·20	65
1117	$5 Lamma Island	3·00	1·30

MS1118 136×81 mm. Nos. 1114/17 5·50 5·50

235 Radar Signal and Luopan (fengshui compass)

2002. Cultural Diversity. Multicoloured.

1119 10c. Type **235** 20 10
1120 20c. Calculator and abacus 20 10
1121 50c. Incense coils and stained-glass window 20 10
1122 $1 Chair and Luohan (bed) 30 15
1123 $1.40 Dim Sum (dumplings) and loaves of bread 40 15
1124 $1.80 Cutlery and chopsticks 50 20
1125 $1.90 Canned drinks and tea caddies 55 20
1126 $2 European and oriental wedding cakes 60 25
1127 $2.40 Erhu (stringed instrument) and violin 70 30
1128 $2.50 Oriental letterbox and internet symbol 75 30
1129 $3 Yachts and Dragon boat 90 40
1130 $5 Traditional tiled roof and modern office block 1·50 55
1131 $10 Ballet dancers and Chinese opera character 3·00 65
1132 $13 Chess pieces and Xiangqi pieces (Chinese chess) 4·00 95
1133 $20 Christmas lights and mid-autumn festival lantern 6·00 1·30
1134 $50 Sculptures "Oval with points" (Henry Moore) and "Tai Chi series: Single Whip" (Ju Ming) 18·00 4·00
MS1135 Two sheets (a) 210×150 mm. Nos. 1119/30 (b) 122×101 mm. Nos. 1131/4 29·00 25·00

236 Christmas Tree

2002. Christmas. Multicoloured.

1146 $1.40 Type **236** 40 25
1147 $2.40 Bauble 70 45
1148 $3 Snowman 1·00 65
1149 $5 Bell 1·50 95

237 Train and Station (Main Street)

2003. Disneyland Hong Kong. Multicoloured.

1150 $1.40 Type **237** 50 30
1151 $2.40 Castle (Fantasyland) 80 50
1152 $3 Tree house (Adventureland) 90 55
1153 $5 Pylons (Tomorrowland) 1·50 95
MS1154 135×85 mm. Nos. 1150/3 4·00 4·00

Nos. 1150/**MS**1154 each have an embossed figure of Mickey Mouse in the lower left corner.

238 Argali Ram

2003. Chinese New Year ("Year of the Ram"). Multicoloured.

1155 $1.40 Type **238** 50 30
1156 $2.40 Sheep 80 50
1157 $3 Tahr ram 90 55
1158 $5 Gazella ram 1·50 95

MS1159 Two sheets, each 135×85 mm. (a) Nos. 1155/8; (b) $5 No. 1158 Set of 2 sheets 6·75 7·00

(b) Flocked paper. P 13. Litho Cartor.

1160 $10 As No. 1008 ("Year of the Dragon") 3·00 1·90
1161 $10 As No. 1042 ("Year of the Snake") 3·00 1·90
1162 $10 As No. 1081 ("Year of the Horse") 3·00 1·90
1163 $10 As No. 1158 ("Year of the Ram") 3·00 1·90

(c) Size 38×51 mm. Ordinary paper.

MS1164 135×90 mm. $50 As No. 1162 ("Year of the Horse") (37×50 mm); $50 As No. 1157 (37×50 mm) 35·00 35·00

No. **MS**1164 has the horse and ram embossed with gold and silver foil.

239 Letter Writing

2003. Traditional Trades and Crafts. Multicoloured.

1165 $1.40 Type **239** 50 30
1166 $1.80 Bird cage maker (vert) 60 40
1167 $2.40 Qipao tailoring (women's clothes) 70 45
1168 $2.50 Hairdressing (vert) 80 50
1169 $3 Making dough figures (vert) 90 55
1170 $5 Olive seller 1·50 95
MS1171 219×123 mm. Nos. 1165/70 5·00 5·00

240 Hong Kong Skyline

2003. Hong Kong 2004 International Stamp Exhibition (1st issue). Sheet 135×85 mm.

MS1172 **240** $10 multicoloured 4·00 4·00

See also Nos. **MS**1190, **MS**1213 and 1214/1230.

241 The Master-of-Nets Garden, Suzhou

2003. Mainland Landscapes (1st issue). Sheet 140×90 mm.

MS1173 **241** $10 multicoloured 4·00 4·00

See also Nos. **MS**1243, **MS**1324, **MS**1349, **MS**1447 and **MS**1495.

242 Fukien Tea (semi-cascade)

2003. Miniature Landscapes. Multicoloured.

1174 $1.40 Type **242** 50 30
1175 $2.40 Hedge Sageretia (informal upright) 80 50
1176 $3 Fire-thorn (cascade) (vert) 1·00 65
1177 $5 Chinese Hackberry (root on rock) (vert) 1·50 95

243 Ear-spot Angelfish

2003. Aquarium Fish. Multicoloured.

1178 $1.40 Type **243** 40 25
1179 $2.40 Copper-banded butterflyfish 70 45
1180 $3 Dwarf gourami 1·00 65
1181 $5 Red discus 1·40 90

244 Bottles and Man holding Firework ("Celebrations")

2003. Greetings Stamps. With service indicator. Multicoloured.

1182 ($1.40) Type **244** ("Local Mail Postage") 50 30
1183 ($1.40) Man and heart-shaped tree ("Care and Love") 50 30
1184 ($3) No. 1182 ("Air Mail Postage") 1·00 65
1185 ($3) No. 1183 1·00 65

No. 1182/3 were for use on letters up to 30 grams within Hong Kong and 1184/5 were for use on airmail letters up to 20 grams to addresses outside Hong Kong.

245 Pied Avocet

2003. Water Birds. Multicoloured.

1186 $1.40 Type **245** 40 25
1187 $2.40 Horned grebe 60 40
1188 $3 Great crested grebe 90 55
1189 $5 Black-throated diver 1·50 95

Stamps of the same design were issued by Sweden.

246 Sha Tin Park

2003. Hong Kong 2004 International Stamp Exhibition (2nd issue). Sheet 135×85 mm.

MS1190 **246** $10 multicoloured 4·00 4·00

247 Astronaut and Satellite

2003. First Chinese Manned Space Flight. Multicoloured.

1191 $1.40 Type **247** 80 50
1192 $1.40 Shenzhou-5 space craft 80 50

248 Drum

2003. Traditional Instruments. Multicoloured.

1193 $1.40 Type **248** 40 25
1194 $2.40 Clappers 70 45
1195 $3 Cymbals 1·00 65
1196 $5 Gongs 1·40 90
MS1197 130×75 mm. $13 Bell (35×45 mm) 4·00 4·00

249 Potola Palace, Lhasa

2003. UNESCO World Heritage Sites in China. Multicoloured.

1198 $1.40 Type **249** 40 25
1199 $1.80 Imperial Palace, Beijing (47×39 mm) 60 40
1200 $2.40 First Qin Emperor's Mausoleum, Shaanxi Province (47×39 mm) 70 45
1201 $2.50 Mount Huangshan, Anhui Province (39×47 mm) 75 45
1202 $3 Old Town, Lijang (39×47 mm) 90 55
1203 $5 Jiuzhaigou valley, Sichuan Province (77×30 mm) 1·30 80

250 Building Development and People on Walkways

2003. Development of Public Housing. Multicoloured.

1204 $1.40 Type **250** 50 30
1205 $2.40 L-shaped development and women through window 80 50
1206 $3 High-rise development and man reading with children 1·00 65
1207 $5 High-rise development and family walking in park 1·50 95

251 Monkey

2004. New Year. "Year of the Monkey". Multicoloured.

1208 $1.40 Type **251** 40 25
1209 $2.40 Mother and baby 70 45
1210 $3 Walking 80 50
1211 $5 Holding branch 1·30 80
MS1212 Two sheets, each 136×85 mm (a/b). (a) Nos. 1208/11. (b) As No. 1211. Imperf. (c) 135×90 mm $50×2, As No. 1155 (38×52 mm); As No. 1211 (38×52 mm) Set of 2 sheets 21·00 21·00

252 Round Pudding and Greeting

2004. Hong Kong 2004 International Stamp Exhibition (3rd issue). Tourism. Six sheets, each 135×86 mm containing T 252 and similar horiz designs. Multicoloured.

MS1213 (a) $10 Type **252**; (b) $10×2, As No. **MS**1213a: (c) $10 New Year parade; (d) $10 Jade pendant; (e) $10 Fire dragon 18·00 18·00

2004. Hong Kong 2004 International Stamp Exhibition (4th issue). Hong Kong Landmarks and Tourist Attractions. Multicoloured.

1214	$1.40 As Type **201**	30	20
1215	$1.40 As No. 973	30	20
1216	$1.40 As No. 974	30	20
1217	$1.40 As No. 975	30	20
1218	$1.40 As No. 976	30	20
1219	$1.40 As No. 977	30	20
1220	$1.40 As No. 978	30	20
1221	$1.40 As No. 979	30	20
1222	$1.40 As No. 980a	30	20
1223	$1.40 As No. 980b	30	20
1224	$1.40 As No. 981	30	20
1225	$1.40 As No. 982	30	20
1226	$1.40 As No. 982a	30	20
1227	$1.40 As No. 983	30	20
1228	$1.40 As No. 984	30	20
1229	$1.40 As No. 984b	30	20
1230	$1.40 As No. 985	30	20
1231	$1.40 As No. 986	30	20
1232	$1.40 As No. 986a	30	20
1233	$1.40 As No. 987	30	20
1234	$1.40 As No. 988	30	20

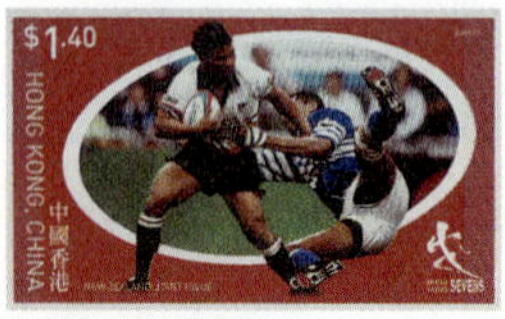

253 Hong Kong Team

2004. Rugby Sevens. Multicoloured.

1235	$1.40 Type **253**	40	25
1236	$2.40 New Zealand team	70	45
1237	$3 Hong Kong Stadium	90	55
1238	$5 Westpac Stadium, Wellington	1·30	80

Stamps of the same design were issued by New Zealand.

254 Scissors, Paper, Stone (Ka-lai Tsoi)

2004. Winning Entries in Children's Stamp Design Competition. Games. Multicoloured.

1239	$1.40 Type **254**	40	25
1240	$2.40 Chinese chess (Belinda Hoi-yan Chan)	70	45
1241	$3 Bubble blowing (April Nga-pui Yuen)	90	55
1242	$5 Hopscotch (Chap-yin Lui)	1·30	80

255 The Chen Clan Academy, Guangzhou

2004. Mainland Landscapes (2nd series). Sheet 140×90 mm.

MS1243	**255** $10 multicoloured	3·25	3·25

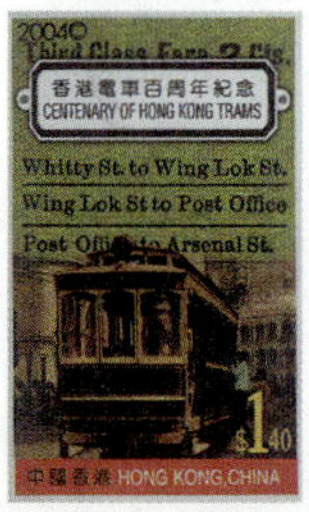

256 First Tram (1904)

2004. Centenary of Hong Kong Tramway.

1244	$1.40 Type **256**	40	25
1245	$2.40 Open-topped tram	60	40
1246	$3 Canvas-topped tram	90	55
1247	$5 Modern tram	1·30	80
MS1248	Two sheets, each 136×85 mm. (a) Nos. 1240/3; (b) $5 Millennium new tram Set of 2 sheets	6·00	6·00

257 Soldiers, Sailors and Airmen

2004. Armed Forces. Multicoloured.

1249	$1.40 Type **257**	40	25
1250	$1.80 Serviceman giving blood	50	30
1251	$2.40 Servicemen and children	60	40
1252	$2.50 Soldiers	70	45
1253	$3 Sailors	90	55
1254	$5 Airmen	1·30	80

258 Preparing to Dive

2004. Olympic Games, Athens. Sports. Multicoloured.

1255	$1.40 Type **258**	40	25
1256	$1.40 Diver twisting forward	40	25
1257	$1.40 Descending with arms extended	40	25
1258	$1.40 Entering water	40	25
1259	$1.40 Volleyball player with bent knees	40	25
1260	$1.40 Jumping to hit ball	40	25
1261	$1.40 Hitting ball	40	25
1262	$1.40 Opponent trying to save	40	25
1263	$1.40 Two cyclists	40	25
1264	$1.40 Cyclist	40	25
1265	$1.40 Cyclists at speed	40	25
1266	$1.40 Victory salute	40	25
1267	$1.40 Badminton player preparing to hit shuttlecock	40	25
1268	$1.40 Player with arm extended	40	25
1269	$1.40 Player leaning backwards	40	25
1270	$1.40 Player leaning to right	40	25
1271	$1.40 Start of relay race	40	25
1272	$1.40 Runners	40	25
1273	$1.40 Baton exchange	40	25
1274	$1.40 Runner with baton raised	40	25
MS1275	130×75 mm. $5×2, Classical Olympic runner; Modern runner	3·00	3·00

259 Flags and Deng Xiaoping

2004. Birth Centenary of Deng Xiaoping (leader of China, 1978–89). Two sheets containing T 259 and similar horiz designs. Multicoloured.

MS1276	(a) 175×130 mm. $1.40 Type **259**; $1.40 Wearing blue suit, each×4 (b) 130×75 mm. $10 As young man	6·75	6·75

260 First Bronze Coin, 1863

2004. Currency. Multicoloured.

1277	$1.40 Type **260**	40	25
1278	$2.40 First silver coin, 1866	60	40
1279	$3 First paper currency, 1935	90	55
1280	$5 Gold coin to commemorate Hong Kong Special Administrative Region, 1997	1·30	80
MS1281	(a) 130×80 mm. Nos. 1277/80 (b) 130×75 mm. $5 Reverse of $10 dollar coin, 1997	5·00	5·00

261 Building and Bridge

2004. Development of Pearl River Delta Region. Multicoloured.

1282	$1.40 Type **261**	40	25
1283	$2.40 Container and crane	60	40
1284	$3 Views of Hong Kong, Guangdong and Macau	90	55
1285	$5 Harbour views and men shaking hands	1·30	80

262 Straw Mushrooms

2004. Fungi. Multicoloured.

1286	$1.40 Type **262**	40	25
1287	$2.40 Red-orange mushroom	60	40
1288	$3 Violet marasmius	90	55
1289	$5 Lingzhi	1·30	80
MS1290	(a) 130×85 mm. Nos. 1286/9. (b) 130×75 mm. $5 Hexagon fungus	5·50	5·50

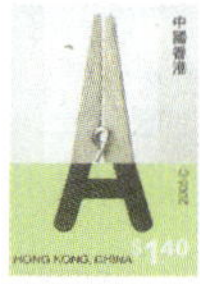

263 Clothes Peg (A)

2005. Greetings Stamps. Alphabet. Sheet 230×162 mm containing T 263 and similar vert designs showing household objects as letters of the alphabet. Multicoloured. Ordinary of self-adhesive gum.

MS1291	$1.40×30, Type **263**×2; Scissors handle (B); Lamp (C); Plastic lid (D); Rack (E) x 2; Gauge (F); Clamp (G); Bamboo (H); Torch (I) x 2; Cleaning mop (J); Stapler (K); Sock (L); Maths equipment (M); Swiss Army knife (N); Elastic band (O) x 2; Sieve (P); Stainless steel ring (Q); Sunglasses (R); Coat hanger (S); Brush (T); Flip flops (U); Drawing compass (V); Corkscrew (W); Tap (X); Meat skewer (Y); Paint roller (Z)	12·00	12·00

The stamps and margin of **MS**1291 form a composite design.

264 Rooster

2005. New Year. "Year of the Rooster". Multicoloured.

1292	$1.40 Type **264**	40	25
1293	$2.40 With black neck feathers	70	45
1294	$3 With leg raised	80	50
1295	$5 Crowing	1·30	80
MS1296	Three sheets. (a) 136×85 mm Nos. 1292/5. (b) 136×85 mm As No. 1295. Imperf. (c) 135×90 mm $50×2, As No. 1209 (38×52 mm); As No. 1292 (38×52 mm)	3·25	3·25

No. **MS**1296c has the ram and monkey embossed with gold and silver foil.

265 "The Ugly Duckling"

2005. Birth Bicentenary of Hans Christian Andersen (writer).

1297	**265**	$1.40 blue	40	25
1298	-	$2.40 green	70	45
1299	-	$3 orange	80	50
1300	-	$5 magenta	1·30	80

DESIGNS: $1.40 Type **265**; $2.40 "The Little Mermaid"; $3 "The Little Match Girl"; $5 "The Emperor's New Clothes".

266 Opera House, Sydney

2005. Pacific Explorer 2005 International Stamp Exhibition, Australia. Sheet 130×75 mm.

MS1301	**266** $10 multicoloured	3·25	3·25

267 Variegated Pearl-scale

2005. Goldfish. Multicoloured.

1302	$1.40 Type **267**	40	25
1303	$2.40 Red and white swallowtail	70	45
1304	$3 Pale bronze egg phoenix 45	80	50
1305	$5 Blue wenyu	1·30	80
MS1306	Two sheets, each 130×75 mm. (a) Nos. 1302/5. (b) $5 Red and white dragon-eye (45×35 mm)	5·00	5·00

268 Zheng He

2005. 600th Anniv of the Voyages of Zheng He (Ma Sanbao). Multicoloured.

1307	$1.40 Type **268**	40	25
1308	$1.40 Giraffe, jars and ship	40	25
1309	$1.40 Ships and compass	40	25
MS1310	139×80 mm. $10 Nine-masted "Treasure ship" (50×30 mm)	3·00	3·00

Stamps of a similar design were issued by China and Macau.

269 Coloured Shapes

2005. Creative Industries. Multicoloured.

1311	$1.40 multicoloured	40	25
1312	$2.40 green and black	70	45
1313	$3 scarlet, black and bronze	80	50
1314	$5 multicoloured	1·30	80

DESIGNS: $1.40 Type **269** (advertising, architecture and design); $2.40 Digital symbols (digital entertainment, publishing and computers); $3 Coloured grids (media); $5 Streamers (arts, antiques, crafts and performing arts).

270 Early Compass

2005. Chinese Inventions. Multicoloured.

1315	$1.40 Type **270**	40	25
1316	$2.40 Printing	70	45
1317	$3 Gunpowder	80	50
1318	$5 Paper making	1·30	80

271 Mickey and Minnie (Main Street, USA)

2005. Disneyland Hong Kong. Grand Opening. Multicoloured.

1319	$1.40 Type **271**	40	25
1320	$2.40 Dumbo (Fantasyland)	70	45
1321	$3 Simba and Nala (Adventureland)	80	50
1322	$5 Pluto (Tomorrowland)	1·30	80
MS1323	Three sheets, each 135×85 mm. (a) Nos. 1319/22. (b) $5 Mickey. (c) $50 As No. **MS**1323b	23·00	23·00

No. **MS**1323c has Mickey embossed with gold foil.

272 Qiantang Bore (image scaled to 64% of original size)

2005. Mainland Scenery (3rd issue). Sheet 141×90 mm.

MS1324	**272** $10 multicoloured	3·25	3·25

273 Boat, Tai O, Hong Kong

2005. Fishing Villages. Multicoloured.

1325	$1.40 Type **273**	40	25
1326	$2.40 Fisherman and boats, Aldeia da Carrasqueira	70	45
1327	$3 Wrapped fish, Tai O	80	50
1328	$5 Moorings and pier, Aldeia da Carrasqueira	1·30	80

Nos. 1325 and 1327, and 1326 and 1328, respectively were issued together, se-tenant, each pair forming a composite design. Stamps of the same design were issued by Portugal.

274 Wong ka Kui

2005. Pop Singers. Multicoloured.

1329	$1.40 Type **274**	40	25
1330	$1.80 Danny Chan	50	30
1331	$2.40 Roman Tam	80	50
1332	$3 Leslie Chung	90	55
1333	$5 Anita Mui	1·30	80

275 Dog

2006. New Year. "Year of the Dog". Multicoloured.

1334	$1.40 Type **275**	40	25
1335	$2.40 Pekinese	70	45
1336	$3 German shepherd	80	50
1337	$5 Beagle	1·30	80
MS1338	Two sheets, each 136×85 mm. (a) Nos. 1334/7. (b) As No. 1337. Imperf	5·25	5·25
MS1339	135×90 mm Size 38×52 mm. $50×2, As No. 1292; As No. 1335	25·00	25·00

No. **MS**1339 has the rooster and dog embossed with gold and silver foil.

276 Lantern enclosing Woman

2006. Chinese Lanterns. Multicoloured.

MS1340	108×131 mm. $1.40×2, Type 276×2; $1.80×2, Lantern enclosing flowers×2; $2.40×2, Lantern enclosing birds×2	4·25	4·25
MS1341	130×75 mm $5 Children holding dragon lantern (38×49 mm)	5·00	5·00

277 Bear wearing Hakka Costume (Yuen-ching Lee)

2006. Dress up Bear. Winning Entries in Children's Design a Stamp Competition. Multicoloured.

1342	$1.40 Type **277**	40	25
1343	$1.80 Wearing wedding costume (Sean Sheung-nam Lam)	60	40
1344	$2.40 Wearing pleated skirt (Chun-hin Chow)	70	45
1345	$2.50 Wearing embroidered apron and shoes (Hong-wan Lau)	75	45
1346	$3 Wearing striped top and hat (Man-lok Chiu)	90	55
1347	$5 Wearing leaf skirt (Michelle Hiu-tung Lau)	1·30	80
MS1348	115×115 mm. Nos. 1342/7	5·00	5·00

278 Mount Taishan

2006. Mainland Scenery (4th issue). Sheet 140×90 mm.

MS1349	$10 multicoloured	2·75	2·75

279 Rainbow

2006. Washington 2006 Philatelic Exhibition. Sheet 130×75 mm.

MS1350	$10 multicoloured	2·75	2·75

280 "Respect makes a Successful Marriage"

2006. Chinese Idioms. Multicoloured.

1351	$1.40 Type **280**	40	25
1352	$2.40 "Reading is always rewarding"	70	45
1353	$3 "Prepare for success"	80	50
1354	$5 "All in the same boat"	1·30	80
MS1355	135×85 mm. Nos. 1351/4	3·25	3·25

281 Central and Western District

2006. Hong Kong Districts. Multicoloured.

1356	$1.40 Type **281**	40	25
1357	$1.40 Eastern	40	25
1358	$1.40 Southern	40	25
1359	$1.40 Wan Chai	40	25
1360	$1.40 Yau Tsim Mong	40	25
1361	$1.40 Wong Tai Sin	40	25
1362	$1.40 Kwun Tong	40	25
1363	$1.40 Sham Shui Po	40	25
1364	$1.40 Kowloon City	40	25
1365	$1.40 Sai Kung	40	25
1366	$1.40 Kwai Tsing	40	25
1367	$1.40 Tai Po	40	25
1368	$1.40 North	40	25
1369	$1.40 Tsuen Wan	40	25
1370	$1.40 Sha Tin	40	25
1371	$1.40 Tuen Mun	40	25
1372	$1.40 Yuen Long	40	25
1373	$1.40 Islands district	40	25

282 Fireworks over Victoria Harbour

2006. Fireworks. Multicoloured.

1374	$5 Type **282**	1·30	80
1375	$5 Fireworks over Giant Ferris Wheel, Vienna, Austria	1·30	80
MS1376	146×85 mm. $50×2, As Type **282**; As No. 1375	20·00	20·00

MS1376 has crystals applied to the surface of the stamps and was sold in a folder. Stamps of a similar design were issued by Austria.

283 Love

2006. International Day of Peace. Multicoloured.

1377	$1.40 Type **283**	40	25
1378	$1.80 Peace	50	30
1379	$2.40 Hope	60	40
1380	$3 Caring	80	50
1381	$5 Harmony	1·30	80
MS1382	150×85 mm. Nos. 1377/81	3·25	3·25

284 Security Bus

2006. Government Transport. Multicoloured.

1383	$1.40 Type **284**	40	25
1384	$1.80 Mobile X-ray unit	50	30
1385	$2.40 Hydraulic lift fire appliance	60	40
1386	$2.50 Super Puma helicopter	65	40
1387	$3 Traffic Control motorcycle	80	50
1388	$5 Immigration Dept launch	1·30	80

285 Sun Yat-Sen

2006. 140th Birth Anniv of Sun Yat-Sen (revolutionary). Multicoloured.

1389	$1.40 Type **285**	40	25
1390	$2.40 Seated wearing suit	70	45
1391	$3 Standing wearing suit	80	50
1392	$5 As older man	1·40	90
MS1393	130×75 mm. $5 Seated wearing traditional dress	1·50	1·50

286 Bottles

2006. Greetings Stamps. Multicoloured.

1394	($1.40) Type **286** (postage)	40	25
1395	($1.40) Hearts	40	25
1396	($3) Glasses (air)	80	50
1397	($3) Flowers	80	50

287 White-bellied Sea Eagle

2006. Birds. Multicoloured. (a) 23×29 mm.

1398	10c. Type **287**	10	10
1399	20c. Collared scops owl	15	10
1400	50c. Scarlet minivet	20	15
1401	$1 Kingfisher	30	20
1402	$1.40 Fork-tailed sunbird	40	25
1403	$1.80 Roseate tern	50	30
1404	$1.90 Black-faced spoonbill	50	30
1405	$2 Little egret	55	35
1406	$2.40 Greater painted snipe	70	45
1407	$2.50 Swallow	75	45
1408	$3 Red-whiskered bulbul	80	50
1409	$5 Long-tailed shrike	1·30	80

(b) Size 28×33 mm.

1410	$10 White wagtail	2·50	1·60
1411	$13 Northern shoveler	3·50	2·20
1412	$20 Magpie	5·00	3·25
1413	$50 Dalmatian pelican	12·00	6·25
MS1414	220×160 mm. Nos. 1398/409	5·75	5·75
MS1415	150×90 mm. Nos. 1410/13	20·00	20·00

288 Pig and Piglet

2007. New Year. "Year of the Pig". Multicoloured.

1425	$1.40 Type **288**	40	25
1426	$2.40 Pot-bellied pig	60	40
1427	$3 Spotted pig	80	50
1428	$5 Piglet	1·20	75
MS1429	Two sheets, each 135×85 mm. (a) Nos. 1425/8; (b) $5 No. 1428	5·00	5·00

2007

1430	$10 As No. 1210 ("Year of the Monkey")	2·40	1·50
1431	$10 As No. 1292 ("Year of the Rooster")	2·40	1·50
1432	$10 As No. 1335 ("Year of the Dog")	2·40	1·50
1433	$10 As No. 1417 ("Year of the Pig")	2·40	1·50
MS1434	136×90 mm. $50 As No. 1337 ("Year of the Dog"); $50 As No. 1425	25·00	25·00

No. **MS**1434 has the beagle and pig embossed with gold and silver foil.

289 Robert Baden-Powell (founder)

2007. Centenary of World Scouting. Multicoloured.

1435	$1.40 Type **289**	40	25
1436	$2.40 Emblem and compass	60	40
1437	$3 Rucksack and reef knot	80	50
1438	$5 Scouts	1·20	75

MS1439	130×75 mm. Nos. 1435/8	3·25	3·25

290 Two Rabbits (Spot the differences)

2007. Children's Stamps. Bunny Fun and Games. Multicoloured.

1440	$1.40 Type **290**	40	25
1441	$1.80 Outline (colour in dotted areas)	50	30
1442	$2.40 Maize (trace your way out)	60	40
1443	$2.50 Rabbit and Easter eggs (hunt for Easter eggs)	65	40
1444	$3 Tree containing rabbits (spot ten rabbits)	80	50
1445	$5 Rabbit in egg (look for a star)	1·20	75
MS1446	140×90 mm. Nos. 1440/5	4·00	4·00

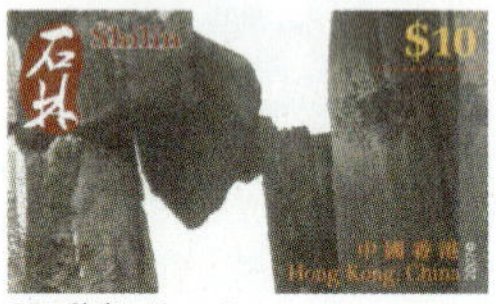

291 Shilin, Kunming

2007. Mainland Scenery (5th issue). Sheet 140×90 mm.

MS1447	$10 multicoloured	2·50	2·50

292 Southern Lion Dance

2007. Lion Dance and Martial Arts. Multicoloured.

1448	$1.40 Type **292**	40	25
1449	$2.40 Nanquan	60	40
1450	$3 Northern lion dance	80	50
1451	$5 Beitui	1·20	75
MS1452	130×90 mm. Nos. 1448/51	3·25	3·25

Nos. 1448/51 each has a small gold symbol signifying the design in lower left ($1.40 and $5) or right ($2.40 and $3) corners.

293 *Faunis eumeus*

2007. Butterflies. Multicoloured.

1453	$1.40 Type **293**	40	25
1454	$1.80 *Prioneris philpnome*	50	30
1455	$2.40 *Polyura nepenthes*	60	40
1456	$3 *Tajura maculata*	80	50
1457	$5 *Acraea issoria*	1·20	75

294 Children

2007. 10th Anniv of Re-unification of Hong Kong. Multicoloured.

1458	$1.40 Type **294**	40	25
1459	$1.40 Forever Blooming Bauhinia	40	25
1460	$1.80 Heritage Museum	50	30
1461	$2.40 Tsing Ma bridge	60	40
1462	$2.50 International Wetland Park	65	40
1463	$3 Two IFC building	80	50
1464	$5 Fireworks over city	1·20	75
MS1465	130×91 mm. Size 30×60 mm. $10×3, Victoria Harbour waterfront	6·50	6·50
MS1465a	110×150 mm. No. 1459 and Nos. 5189/91 of China	9·75	9·75

The stamps and margins of **MS**1465 form a composite view of Victoria Harbour waterfront from the sea.

A stamp of a similar design to No. 1459 was issued by China.

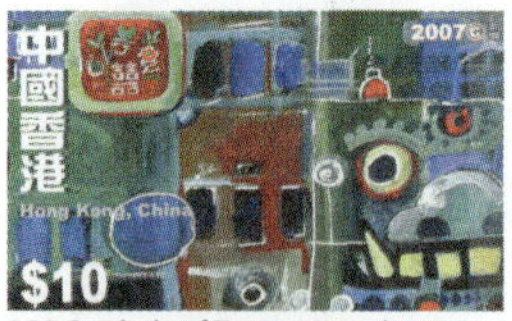

295 Symbols of Transport and Guardian God

2007. Bangkok 2007, International Philatelic Exhibition. Sheet 130×75 mm.

MS1466	$10 multicoloured	2·20	2·20

296 Scales and People of Many Nations (Human Rights)

2007. Civil Responsibility. Multicoloured.

1467	$1.40 Type **296**	45	30
1468	$2.40 Buildings with faces (Rule of Law)	55	35
1469	$3 Clasped hands (Social Participation)	70	45
1470	$5 Rainbow and hands enclosing fruit (Corporate Citizenship)	1·10	65

297 Tin Hau Temple, Causeway Bay

2007. Official Monuments. Multicoloured.

1471	$1.40 Type **297**	45	30
1472	$1.80 Old Post Office, Wan Chai	50	30
1473	$2.40 Former Central Police Station Compound	55	35
1474	$2.50 Former Yamen building, Kowloon Walled City	60	35
1475	$3 Kun Lung Gate Tower, Lung Yeuk Tau	70	45
1476	$5 Tang Lung Chai lighthouse	1·10	65
MS1477	145×78 mm. Nos. 1471/6	3·75	3·75

298 Stocking

2007. Christmas. Multicoloured.

1478	$1.40 Type **298**	50	30
1479	$2.40 Gingerbread man	60	35
1480	$3 Inscribed bell	70	45
1481	$5 Snowman	1·10	65

299 Qing Dynasty Carved Chair

2007. Woodcraft. Multicoloured.

1482	$5 Type **299**	1·00	60
1483	$5 Wooden bowls	1·00	60
MS1484	106×70 mm. Nos. 1482/3	2·20	2·20

Stamps of a similar design were issued by Finland.

300 Firework

2007. Greetings Stamps. With service indicator. Multicoloured. (a) Inscr "Local Mail Postage"

1485	($1.40) Type **300**	50	30
1486	($1.40) Two birds	50	30

(b) AIR. Inscr "Air Mail Postage"

1487	($3) Parcels and balloons	70	45
1488	($3) Slippers	70	45

No. 1485/6 were for use on letters up to 30 grams within Hong Kong and 1487/8 were for use on airmail letters up to 20 grams to addresses outside Hong Kong.

301 Rat

2008. New Year. 'Year of the Rat'. Multicoloured.

1489	$1.40 Type **301**	30	20
1490	$2.40 Rat seated	50	30
1491	$3 Rat facing left	70	45
1492	$5 Rat facing right	1·10	65
MS1493	Two sheets, each 135×85 mm. (a) Nos. 1489/92 (b) $5 As No. 1492	4·00	4·00

(b) Size 38×51 mm.

MS1494	136×90 mm. $50 As No. 1425 ('Year of the Pig'); $50 As No. 1492	20·00	20·00

302 Huanglong

2008. Mainland Scenery (6th issue). Sheet 140×90 mm.

MS1495	$10 multicoloured	2·20	2·20

303 Hibiscus

2008. Flowers. Multicoloured.

1496	$1.40 Type **303**	30	20
1497	$1.80 Cotton tree blooms	45	30
1498	$2.40 Allamanda	55	35
1499	$2.50 Azalea	60	40
1500	$3 Lotus blossom	75	50
1501	$5 Morning glory	1·20	80
MS1502	220×123 mm. Nos. 1496/501	3·75	3·75

304 Bauhinia (Yu-tong Chua)

2008. Paper Folding. Multicoloured.

1503	$1.40 Type **304**	30	20
1504	$1.80 Bear (Shing-him (Bernard) Yeung) (horiz)	45	30
1505	$2.40 New Year decorations (Wing-tung Lau; Ka-wing Cheung)	55	35
1506	$2.50 Rainbow and lotus blossom (Hiu-yu Chau; Hiu-ling Wong) (horiz)	60	40
1507	$3 Koala bears and monkey holding banana (Wing-tung Lo; Ka-wing Cheung)	75	50
1508	$5 Christmas scene and Santa Claus (Po-chu Yeung and Lesley Chu; Hon-keung and Hazel Li Hin) (horiz)	1·20	80
MS1509	218×122 mm. Nos. 1503/8	3·75	3·75

305 Flower Hat Jellyfish

2008. Jellyfish. Multicoloured.

1510	$1.40 Type **305**	30	20
1511	$1.80 Octopus jellyfish (horiz)	45	30
1512	$2.40 Brown sea nettle	55	35
1513	$2.50 Moon jellyfish (horiz)	60	40
1514	$3 Lion's mane jellyfish	75	50
1515	$5 Pacific sea nettle	1·20	80
MS1516	135×85 mm. Nos. 1510/15	3·75	3·75

306 Ying Ying and Le Le

2008. Pandas. Multicoloured.

1517	$1.40 Type **306**	35	25
1518	$2.40 Ying Ying	60	40
1519	$3 Le Le	80	55
1520	$5 Ying Ying and Le Le in tree	1·30	90
MS1521	176×210 mm. Nos. 1517/20, each×2	5·75	5·75

307 Show Jumping

2008. Olympic Games, Beijing. Equestrian Events in Hong Kong. Multicoloured.

1522	$1.40 Type **307**	35	25
1523	$2.40 Dressage	60	45
1524	$3 Eventing	85	65
1525	$5 Stylized winning horse and rider	1·40	1·00
MS1526	135×85 mm. Nos. 1522/5	3·25	3·25

308 Cityscape

2008. Praga 2008 International Stamp Exhibition, Prague, Czech Republic. Sheet 130×75 mm. Multicoloured.

MS1527	multicoloured	2·75	2·75

309 Chwibari (Bongsan Mask Dance)

2008. Masks. Multicoloured.

1528	$5 Type **309**	1·40	1·00
1529	$5 Big Head Buddha (Chinese Lion Dance)	1·40	1·00
MS1530	106×70 mm. $5×2, Nos. 1528/9	3·00	3·00

Stamps of a similar design were issued by Korea.

310 Justice

2008. The Judiciary. Multicoloured.

1531	$1.40 Type **310**	45	30
1532	$2.40 Court building	70	50
1533	$3 Barristers and judges	1·00	70
1534	$5 Gavel	1·60	1·10
MS1535	136×85 mm. Nos. 1531/4	3·75	3·50

311 Ox

2009. New Year. Year of the Ox. Multicoloured.

1536	$1.40 Type 311	45	30
1537	$2.40 Friesian cow	70	50
1538	$3 Yak	1·00	70
1539	$5 Water buffalo	1·60	1·10
MS1540	135×85 mm. Nos. 1536/8	3·75	3·75
MS1541	135×85 mm. $5 No. 1539. Imperf	1·60	1·60

Size 38×51 mm.

MS1542	136×90 mm. $50 As No. 1489 (Year of the Rat); $50 As No. 1536	30·00	30·00

No. **MS**1542 has the rat and ox embossed with gold and silver foil.

312 Mount Tianshan

2009. Mainland Scenery (7th issue). Sheet 140×90 mm. Multicoloured.

MS1543	multicoloured	3·00	3·00

313 Peony and *Bauhinia blakeana* (flowers of Hong Kong and Luoyang)

2009. China 2009 International Stamp Exhibition, Luoyang. Sheet 130×75 mm.

MS1544	multicoloured	14·00	14·00

314 Tangram Pieces as Figure

2009. Hong Kong 2009, 23rd Asian International Stamp Exhibition. Sheet 135×85 mm.

MS1545	multicoloured	14·00	14·00

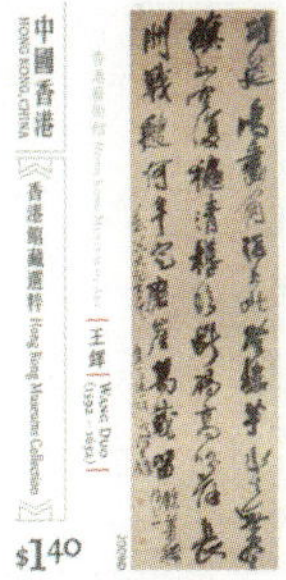

315 Calligraphy (Wang Duo)

2009. Hong Kong Museums Collections. Multicoloured.

1546	$1.40 Type **315**	25	15
1547	$1.80 Mountains (Wang Yuanqi)	35	15
1548	$2.40 Calligraphy (Wang Xizhi)	55	25
1549	$2.50 Moon and bird on blossom branch	55	25
1550	$3 Fan (Ju Lian) (horiz)	1·10	55
1551	$5 Calligrapher and assistants (Gu Huai) (horiz)	1·80	90
MS1552	140×90 mm. Nos. 1546/51	4·50	4·50

316 Flowers

2009. Greetings Stamps. With service indicator. Showing felt applique. Multicoloured. (a) Inscr 'Local Mail Postage'.

1553	($1.40) Type **316**	30	15
1554	($1.40) Lion costume	30	15

(b) Air. Inscr 'Air Mail Postage'.

1555	($3) Conical hats and musical notes	1·10	55
1556	($3) Butterflies	1·10	55

No. 1553/4 were for use on letters up to 30 grams within Hong Kong and 1555/6 were for use on airmail letters up to 20 grams to addresses outside Hong Kong.

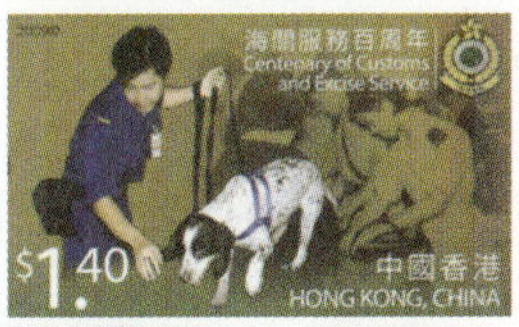

317 Sniffer Dog

2009. Centenary of Customs and Excise Service. Multicoloured.

1557	$1.40 Type **317**	25	10
1558	$2.40 Custom and Excise vehicle	55	25
1559	$3 Coast guard vessel	90	45
1560	$5 Service men	1·30	65
MS1561	135×85 mm. Nos. 1557/60	3·00	3·00

318 Victoria Harbour and Tiananmen Square

2009. 60th Anniv of People's Republic of China. T 318 and similar vert (MS1569) or fan shaped (others) designs. Multicoloured.

1562	$1.40 Type **318**	25	10
1563	$1.80 National flag and 'Forever Blooming Bauhina' (symbol of Hong Kong)	35	15
1564	$2.40 National stadium	55	25
1565	$2.50 CZ-2F rocket	55	25
1566	$3 Temple of Heaven, Beijing	1·10	55
1567	$5 Dragon and Great Wall of China	1·80	90
MS1568	140×90 mm. Nos. 1562/7	4·50	4·50
MS1569	140×90 mm. $5×2, Forbidden City; Hong Kong skyline	3·75	3·75

319 Hong Kong Player

2009. Hong Kong–Brazil Diplomatic Relations. Football. Multicoloured.

1570	$1.40 Type **319**	25	10
1571	$2.40 Hong Kong goalkeeper	55	25
1572	$3 Brazilian player	1·10	1·10
1573	$5 Brazilian player (different)	1·80	90
MS1574	135×85 mm. Nos. 1570/3	3·75	3·75

320 Judo, Football and Kayaking

2009. East Asian Games, Hong Kong. Designs showing athletes, colours of athletes given. Multicoloured.

1575	$1.40 Type **320**	25	10
1576	$1.40 Badminton, athletics, martial arts and rifle shooting (gold)	25	10
1577	$2.40 Cycling, weightlifting and tennis (silver)	55	25
1578	$2.40 Men's volleyball, hockey, women's table tennis and diving (silver)	55	25
1579	$3 Men's table tennis, women's volleyball, dance and snooker (bronze)	1·10	55
1580	$3 Wind surfing, football, basketball and taekwondo (bronze)	1·10	55
MS1581	150×90 mm. Nos. 1575/81	3·50	3·50

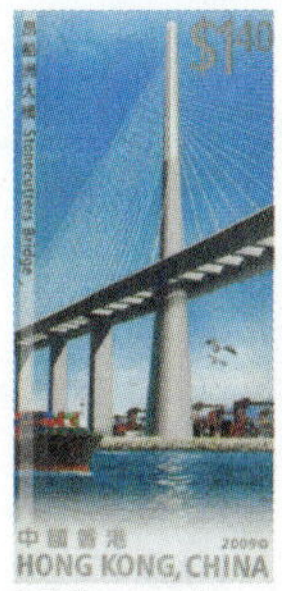

321 Tower and Suspension Cables

2009. Opening of Stonecutters Bridge. Multicoloured.

1582	$1.40 Type **321**	25	10
1583	$2.40 Aerial view of bridge	55	25
1584	$3 Bridge from river	1·10	55
1585	$5 Aerial view of tower and suspension cables	1·80	90
MS1586	150×90 mm. Nos. 1582/5	3·75	3·75

POSTAGE DUE STAMPS

D1 Post-office Scales

1923

D1ab	**D1**	1c. brown	30	1·00
D2a	**D1**	2c. green	11·00	5·00
D3a	**D1**	4c. red	28·00	6·00
D4	**D1**	6c. yellow	30·00	13·00
D5	**D1**	10c. blue	25·00	8·50
D6a	**D1**	2c. grey	1·10	10·00
D7a	**D1**	4c. orange	2·50	10·00
D8	**D1**	6c. red	8·50	5·50
D9	**D1**	8c. brown	4·50	32·00
D15	**D1**	10c. violet	3·50	5·50
D16	**D1**	20c. black	6·00	4·25
D18	**D1**	5c. red (21×18 mm)	2·50	5·50
D22	**D1**	50c. blue	4·50	10·00

1976. As Type D 1 but smaller design 21×17 mm with redrawn value.

D25a	10c. violet	80	2·00
D26a	20c. grey	1·50	2·25
D27a	50c. blue	1·50	2·75
D28a	$1 yellow	1·40	4·00

D2

1987

D31	**D2**	10c. green	10	60
D32	**D2**	20c. brown	10	60
D33	**D2**	50c. violet	10	20
D34	**D2**	$1 orange	15	20
D35	**D2**	$5 blue	80	1·60
D36	**D2**	$10 red	1·60	3·00

D3

2004

D37	**D3**	10c. ultramarine	10	15
D38	**D3**	20c. blue	10	15
D39	**D3**	50c. orange	25	25
D40	**D3**	$1 pink	60	70
D41	**D3**	$5 green	1·40	1·60
D42	**D3**	$10 magenta	3·00	3·25

JAPANESE OCCUPATION OF HONG KONG

(1) (2)

1945. Stamps of Japan surch as T 1 (No. J1) or T 2.

J1	**126**	1.50yen on 1s. brown	35·00	29·00
J2	**84**	3yen on 2s. red	12·00	25·00
J3	**84**	5yen on 5s. red (No. 396)	£900	£150

Pt. 9

HORTA

A district of the Azores for which separate issues were used from 1892 to 1905.

1865. 1000 reis = 1 milreis.

1892. As T 4 of Funchal, but inscr "HORTA".

2	25r. green	8·25	3·75
4	5r. yellow	2·10	1·70
5	10r. mauve	2·10	1·80
6	15r. brown	2·10	2·10
7	20r. lilac	2·50	2·50
8	50r. blue	6·25	3·00
10	80r. green	9·25	8·25
22	75r. red	6·75	4·50
23	100r. brown on yellow	38·00	18·00
24	150r. red on rose	46·00	38·00
25	200r. blue on blue	46·00	38·00
26	300r. blue on brown	46·00	38·00

1897. "King Carlos" key-type inscr "HORTA". Name and value in red (Nos. 46 and 41) or black (others).

28	**S**	2½r. grey	50	30
29	**S**	5r. orange	50	30
30	**S**	10r. green	50	30
31	**S**	15r. brown	7·25	5·50
32	**S**	20r. lilac	1·40	1·20
33	**S**	25r. green	2·40	95
34	**S**	50r. blue	2·75	1·10
35	**S**	75r. red	2·50	1·20
36	**S**	80r. mauve	1·50	95
37	**S**	100r. blue on blue	2·75	95
38	**S**	150r. brown on yellow	1·90	95
39	**S**	200r. purple on pink	5·25	4·50
40	**S**	300r. blue on pink	9·50	6·75
41	**S**	500r. black on blue	12·00	11·50
42	**S**	15r. green	1·40	1·10
43	**S**	25r. red	1·40	75
45	**S**	65r. blue	1·00	75
46	**S**	75r. brown on yellow	11·00	9·75
47	**S**	115r. red on pink	1·90	1·50
48	**S**	130r. brown on yellow	1·90	1·50
49	**S**	180r. black on pink	1·90	1·50

Pt. 2

HUNGARY

A country in central Europe. A Kingdom ruled by the Emperor of Austria until 1918. A Republic was then proclaimed, and later a Soviet style constitution was adopted. In 1919 parts of the country were occupied by France, Serbia and Rumania, including Budapest. Following the withdrawal of the Rumanians a National Republic was instituted, and in 1920 Hungary was declared a Monarchy with Admiral Nicholas Horthy as Regent. In 1946 Hungary became a Republic again.

Hungary.
1858. 100 krajczar = 1 forint.
1900. 100 filler (heller) = 1 korona (krone).
1926. 100 filler = 1 pengo.
1946. 100 filler = 1 forint.

Szeged.
100 filler = 1 korona.

1

1871

8	1	2k. yellow	£100	17·00
9	1	3k. green	£225	65·00
10	1	5k. red	£100	2·30
11	1	10k. blue	£500	37·00
12	1	15k. brown	£600	50·00
13	1	25k. lilac	£325	£130

2

1874

28a	2	20k. grey	10·00	85
29b	2	2k. lilac	1·60	40
30b	2	3k. green	1·60	40
31b	2	5k. red	8·00	40
32b	2	10k. blue	4·75	55

1888. Numerals in black on the krajczar values, in red on the forint values.

38i	3fo. brown and gold	14·00	8·75
39a	1k. black	18·00	2·20
40	2k. mauve and light mauve	£180	49·00
41	3k. green and light green	60·00	17·00
42	5k. red and pink	60·00	2·75
43	8k. orange and yellow	11·00	1·60
44	10k. blue	£425	£375
45	12k. brown and green	15·00	1·60
46	15k. red and blue	11·00	1·60
47	20k. grey	£1100	£750
48	24k. purple and red	38·00	2·20
51	1fo. grey and silver	£225	6·50
62B	30k. olive and brown	9·75	6·50
63	50k. red and orange	14·50	22·00

7 "Turul" (mythical bird of the Magyars)

8 King Francis Joseph wearing Hungarian Crown

1900. Figures of value in black.

67	7	4f. mauve	85	45
69a	7	6f. purple	†	55·00
81	8	3k. blue	£160	8·00
99	7	1f. grey	30	10
100	7	2f. yellow	20	10
102	7	5f. green	20	10
103	7	6f. drab	30	10
105	7	12f. lilac	55	10
111	7	50f. red	95	10
112	7	60f. green	5·50	20
118	7	3f. orange	10	10
120	7	6f. green	10	10
121	7	10f. red	10	10
122	7	12f. lilac on yellow	15	10
123	7	16f. green	15	15
124	7	20f. brown	20	10
125	7	25f. blue	20	10
126	7	30f. brown	20	10
127	7	35f. purple	20	10
128	7	50f. red on blue	20	10
130	7	60f. green on pink	90	10
131	7	70f. brown and green	30	10
132	7	80f. violet	30	10
133	8	1k. red	2·00	10
134	8	2k. blue	4·50	10
135	8	5k. red	4·75	2·00

12

1913. Flood Charity stamps. As T 7/8, but with label as T 12.

136	12	1f.+2f. grey	1·20	1·20
137	12	2f.+2f. yellow	60	60
138	12	3f.+2f. orange	60	60
139	12	5f.+2f. green	60	60
140	12	6f.+2f. drab	1·20	1·20
141	12	10f.+2f. red	60	25
142	12	12f.+2f. lilac on yellow	1·70	1·70
143	12	16f.+2f. green	1·20	1·20
144	12	20f.+2f. brown	3·00	2·30
145	12	25f.+2f. blue	1·20	80
146	12	30f.+2f. brown	1·70	1·20
147	12	35f.+2f. purple	1·70	80
148	12	50f.+2f. lake on blue	6·00	3·00
149	12	60f.+2f. green on red	7·25	1·70
150	8	1k.+2f. red	29·00	14·00
151	8	2k.+2f. blue	65·00	60·00
152	8	5k.+2f. red	29·00	23·00

1914. War Charity. Nos. 136/52 (with labels) surch Hadi segely Ozvegyeknek es arvaknak ket (2) filler.

153	12	1f.+2f. grey	1·20	60
154	12	2f.+2f. yellow	1·20	60
155	12	3f.+2f. orange	1·20	60
156	12	5f.+2f. green	60	25
157	12	6f.+2f. drab	1·20	60
158	12	10f.+2f. red	60	25
159	12	12f.+2f. lilac on yellow	1·40	60
160	12	16f.+2f. green	1·40	60
161	12	20f.+2f. brown	1·70	80
162	12	25f.+2f. blue	1·70	80
163	12	30f.+2f. brown	2·30	80
164	12	35f.+2f. purple	5·75	1·70
165	12	50f.+2f. lake on blue	3·00	1·20
166	12	60f.+2f. green on red	8·75	1·70
167	8	1k.+2f. red (No. 150)	75·00	47·00
168	8	2k.+2f. blue (No. 151)	29·00	41·00
169	8	5k.+2f. red (No. 152)	30·00	35·00

1915. War Charity. Stamps of 1900 (without labels) surch as last round the stamp.

170	7	1f.+2f. grey	10	10
171	7	2f.+2f. yellow	10	10
172	7	3f.+2f. orange	10	10
173	7	5f.+2f. green	10	10
174	7	6f.+2f. drab	10	10
175	7	10f.+2f. red	10	10
176	7	12f.+2f. lilac on yellow	10	10
177	7	16f.+2f. green	60	60
178	7	20f.+2f. brown	60	60
179	7	25f.+2f. blue	25	25
180	7	30f.+2f. brown	25	25
181	7	35f.+2f. purple	35	35
182	7	50f.+2f. lake on blue	60	60
183	7	60f.+2f. green on red	1·20	1·20
185	8	1k.+2f. red (No. 133)	1·90	1·90
186	8	2k.+2f. blue (No. 134)	5·75	5·75
187	8	5k.+2f. red (No. 135)	14·00	14·00

18 Harvesters

1916. As T 18 but with white figures in top corners.

243	18	10f. red	95	35
244	18	15f. purple	95	35

19 Parliament Buildings, Budapest

1916. Inscr "MAGYAR KIR. POSTA".

245		2f. brown	10	10
246		3f. red	10	10
247		4f. slate	10	10
248		5f. green	10	10
249		6f. blue	10	10
250		10f. red	1·20	10
251		15f. violet	10	10
252		20f. brown	10	10
253		25f. blue	10	10
254		35f. brown	10	10
255		40f. olive	10	10
256	19	50f. purple	25	10
257	19	75f. blue	25	10
258	19	80f. green	25	10
259	19	1k. lake	25	10
260	19	2k. brown	25	10
261	19	3k. grey and violet	1·20	25
262	19	5k. brown	1·40	35
263	19	10k. mauve and brown	1·70	1·00

In Type **19** the colours of the centres differ slightly from those of the frames.

For later issues in Types **18** and **19**, see Nos. 372/86 and 404/11.

20 In Trenches

22 "Turul" at bay

1916. War Charity.

264	20	10f.+2f. red	25	25
265	-	15f.+2f. violet	35	35
266	22	40f.+2f. lake	50	50

DESIGN: 15f. Hand to hand combat.

23 Queen Zita

1916. Coronation.

267	23	10f. mauve	85	85
268	-	15f. red (Emperor Charles IV)	85	85

1917. War Charity Exhibition. Nos. 243/4 surch Jozsef foherczeg vezerezredes hadi kiallitasa 1 korona (= "Prince Joseph. Chief Colonel General War Exhibition").

269	18	10f.+1k. red	85	85
270	18	15f.+1k. violet	85	85

1918. Air. Surch REPULO POSTA and value.

271	19	1k.50 on 75f. blue	19·00	24·00
272	19	4k.50 on 2k. brown	18·00	22·00

27 Charles IV

28 Zita

1918

273	27	10f. red	25	25
274	27	15f. violet	25	25
275	27	20f. brown	25	25
276	27	25f. blue	25	25
277	28	40f. olive	25	25
278	28	50f. purple	25	25

1918. Optd KOZTARSASAG. (a) War Charity Stamps (Nos. 264/6).

279	20	10+2f. red	25	25
280	-	15+2f. violet	25	25
281	22	40+2f. red	25	25

(b) Harvesters and Parliament.

282	18	2f. brown	15	15
283	18	3f. red	15	15
284	18	4f. grey	15	15
285	18	5f. green	15	15
286	18	6f. blue	15	15
287	18	10f. red	15	15
288	18	20f. brown	15	15
289	18	40f. green	15	15
290	19	1k. red	15	15
291	19	2k. brown	40	55
292	19	3k. grey and violet	70	90
293	19	5k. brown	2·75	3·50
294	19	10k. mauve and brown	3·00	3·50

(c) Charles and Zita.

295	27	10f. pink	10	15
296	27	15f. purple	10	15
297	27	20f. brown	10	15
298	27	25f. blue	15	15
299	28	40f. green	45	55
300	28	50f. purple	25	25

1919. As T 18/19, but inscr "MAGYAR POSTA".

301	18	2f. brown	10	10
302	18	4f. grey	10	10
303	18	5f. green	10	10
304	18	6f. blue	10	10
305	18	10f. red	20	10
306	18	15f. violet	10	10
307	18	20f. brown	10	10
308	18	20f. green	10	10
309	18	25f. blue	10	10
310	18	40f. green	10	10
311	18	40f. red	10	10
312	18	45f. orange	10	10
313	19	50f. purple	10	10
314	19	60f. blue and brown	10	10
315	19	95f. blue	10	10
316	19	1k. red	10	10
317	19	1k. blue and indigo	10	10
318	19	1k.20 green	10	20
319	19	1k.40 green	10	20
320	19	2k. brown	10	10
321	19	3k. grey and violet	15	20
322	19	5k. brown	10	55
323	19	10k. mauve and brown	85	70

32 Karl Marx

1919

324	32	20f. red and brown	90	90
325	-	45f. green and orange	90	90
326	-	60f. brown and grey	6·75	6·75
327	-	75f. brown and red	6·75	6·75
328	-	80f. brown and olive	6·75	6·75

PORTRAITS: 45f. S. Petofi; 60f. Ignacs Martinovics; 75f. G. Dozsa; 80f. F. Engels.

1919. Nos. 301 etc optd MAGYAR TANACSKOZTARSASAG. (second word hyphenated on 2 to 45f.) (= "Hungarian Soviet Republic").

329	18	2f. brown	30	40
330	18	3f. purple	30	40
331	18	4f. grey	30	40
332	18	5f. green	30	40
333	18	6f. blue	30	40
334	18	10f. red	30	40
335	18	15f. violet	30	40
336	18	20f. brown	30	40
337	18	25f. blue	30	40
338	18	40f. green	30	40
339	18	45f. orange	30	40
340	19	50f. purple	30	40
341	19	95f. blue	30	40
342	19	1k. red	30	40
343	19	1k.20 green	1·20	1·20
344	19	1k.40 green	1·20	1·20
345	19	2k. brown	1·80	1·80
346	19	3k. grey and violet	1·80	1·80
347	19	5k. brown	1·80	1·80
348	19	10k. mauve and brown	2·40	2·40

1919. Entry of National Army into Budapest. Nos. 303 etc optd A nemzeti hadsereg bevonulasa. 1919. XI/16.

348a	18	5f. green	1·00	1·00
348b	18	10f. red	1·00	1·10
348c	18	15f. violet	1·00	1·10
348d	18	20f. brown	1·00	1·10
348e	18	25f. blue	1·00	1·10

(36)

(37)

1920. Nos. 329/48 optd with T 36 (2 to 45f.) or 37 (others).

349		2f. brown	1·50	1·50
350		3f. purple	30	30
351		4f. grey	1·50	1·50
352		5f. green	20	20
353		6f. blue	35	35
354		10f. red	20	20
355		15f. violet	20	20
356		20f. brown	20	20
357		25f. blue	30	30
358		40f. green	1·90	1·90
359		45f. orange	1·90	1·90
360	19	50f. purple	1·90	1·90
361	19	95f. blue	1·90	1·90
362	19	1k. red	1·90	1·90
363	19	1k.20 green	2·30	2·30
364	19	1k.40 green	2·30	2·30
365	19	2k. brown	13·00	13·00
366	19	3k. grey and violet	13·00	13·00

367	19	5k. brown	45	45
368	19	10k. mauve and brown	13·00	13·00

38 Returning P.O.W.

1920. Returned Prisoners-of-War Fund.

369B	38	40f.+1k. lake	1·90	1·90
370A	-	60f.+2k. brown	3·00	3·00
371A	-	1k.+5k. blue	1·60	1·60

DESIGNS—HORIZ: 60f. Prison Camp. VERT: 1k. Family Reunion.

1920. Re-issue of T 18 inscr "MAGYAR KIR. POSTA".

372	18	5f. brown	15	15
373	18	10f. purple	15	15
374	18	40f. red	15	15
375	18	50f. green	15	15
376	18	50f. blue	15	15
377	18	60f. black	15	15
378	18	1k. green	15	15
379	18	1½k. purple	15	15
380	18	2k. blue	20	15
381	18	2½k. green	20	15
382	18	3k. brown	20	15
383	18	4k. red	20	15
384	18	4½k. violet	30	15
385	18	5k. brown	25	15
386	18	6k. blue	25	15
387	18	10k. brown	25	15
388	18	15k. black	35	15
389	18	20k. red	35	15
390	18	25k. orange	35	15
391	18	40k. green	35	15
392	18	50k. blue	35	15
393	18	100k. purple	40	15
394	18	150k. green	60	15
395	18	200k. green	60	15
397	18	350k. violet	1·80	40
442	18	300k. red	40	15
443	18	400k. blue	40	15
444	18	500k. black	40	25
445	18	600k. bistre	40	25
446	18	800k. yellow	50	40

1920. Air. No. 263 surch LEGI POSTA and value.

401	19	3k. on 10k. mauve & brn	3·75	4·50
402	19	8k. on 10k. mauve & brn	3·75	4·50
403	19	12k. on 10k. mauve & brn	3·75	4·50

1920. Re-issue of T 19 inscr "MAGYAR KIR. POSTA".

404	2k.50 blue	25	15
405	3k.50 grey	30	15
406	10k. brown	60	15
407	15k. grey	25	15
408	20k. red	35	20
409	25k. orange	40	15
410	30k. lake	50	15
411	40k. green	50	15
412	50k. blue	65	15
413	100k. brown	65	15
414	400k. green	1·00	40
415	500k. violet	75	20
416	1000k. red	1·80	25
448	2000k. red	1·90	75

42 Madonna and Child

1921

418	42	50k. blue and brown	65	50
419	42	100k. brown and bistre	1·30	75
420	42	200k. ultramarine and blue	1·30	40
421	42	500k. mauve and purple	1·50	40
422	42	1000k. purple and mauve	1·70	40
423	42	2000k. mauve and green	2·75	90
424	42	2500k. brown and bistre	2·40	65
425	42	3000k. mauve and red	3·00	65
426	42	5000k. light green and green	3·25	1·50
427	42	10000k. blue and violet	4·50	1·50

44 Statue of Petofi in National Dress

45 John, the hero, on flying dragon

47 Death of Petofi

1923. Birth Centenary of Petofi (poet).

428	44	10k. (+ 10k.) blue	1·30	1·30
429	45	15k. (+ 15k.) blue	2·50	2·50
430	-	25k. (+ 25k.) brown	1·30	1·30
431	47	40k. (+ 40k.) red	3·75	3·75
432	-	50k. (+ 50k.) purple	3·75	3·75

DESIGNS—VERT (As Type **45**): 25k. Petofi; 50k. Petofi addressing the people.

49 Icarus over Budapest

1924. Air.

433	49	100k. pink and brown	4·00	4·00
434	49	500k. light green and green	4·00	4·00
435	49	1000k. brown and bistre	4·00	4·00
436	49	2000k. blue and deep blue	4·00	4·00
436a	49	5000k. mauve and purple	6·25	6·25
436b	49	10000k. purple and red	6·25	6·25

50

1924. Tuberculosis Relief Fund.

437	50	300k. (+ 300k.) blue	7·50	7·50
438	-	500k. (+ 500k.) brown	7·50	7·50
439	-	1000k. (+ 1000k.) green	7·50	7·50

DESIGNS: 500k. Mother and child; 1000k. Bowman.

53 M. Jokai

1925. Birth Cent of Maurus Jokai (novelist).

449	53	1000k. brown and green	9·50	8·75
450	53	2000k. brown	3·25	1·30
451	53	2500k. brown and blue	9·50	8·75

55

1925. Sports Association Fund.

452	-	100k.(+100k.) brn & grn	6·25	3·75
453	-	200k.(+200k.) grn & brn	6·25	5·00
454	-	300k.(+300k.) blue	15·00	7·00
455	-	400k.(+400k.) green & bl	15·00	8·75
456	-	500k.(+500k.) purple	16·00	9·50
457	-	1000k.(+1000k.) red	19·00	10·00
458	55	2000k.(+2000k.) purple	21·00	10·50
459	-	2500k.(+2500k.) sepia	25·00	11·50

DESIGNS—HORIZ: 100k. Athletes; 500k. Fencing. VERT: 200k. Skiing; 300k. Skating; 400k. Diving; 1000k. Scouts; 2500k. Hurdles.

56 Crown of St. Stephen

57 Matthias Church and Fisher's Bastion

58 Royal Palace, Budapest

59

60 Madonna and Child

1926. T 59 is without boat.

460	56	1f. black	1·00	25
461	56	2f. blue	1·00	25
462	56	3f. orange	1·00	25
463	56	4f. mauve	1·00	25
464	56	6f. green	1·00	25
465	56	8f. mauve	2·00	25
466	57	10f. blue	2·00	25
467	57	16f. violet	2·00	25
468	57	20f. red	2·00	25
469	57	25f. brown	2·00	25
470	59	30f. green	6·25	40
471	58	32f. violet	6·25	25
472	58	40f. blue and deep blue	9·50	25
473	59	46f. blue	8·25	40
474	59	50f. black	8·50	40
475	59	70f. red	9·50	40
476	60	1p. violet	65·00	1·30
477	60	2p. red	65·00	1·90
478	60	5p. blue	65·00	9·50

See also Nos. 502/6.

61 The fabulous "Turul"

62 Mercury astride a "Turul"

1927. Air.

478a	61	4f. orange	65	65
479	61	12f. green	2·00	90
480	61	16f. brown	2·00	90
481	61	20f. red	2·00	90
482	61	32f. purple	6·25	3·25
483	61	40f. blue	5·00	1·90
484	62	50f. red	5·00	1·90
485	62	72f. olive	6·25	2·10
486	62	80f. violet	7·00	2·50
487	62	1p. green	6·25	2·75
488	62	2p. red	12·50	4·50
489	62	5p. blue	44·00	45·00

66 Royal Palace, Budapest

1928. T 66 has the boat in a different place and a redrawn frame.

502	66	30f. green	6·25	15
503	66	32f. purple	8·75	40
504	66	40f. blue	8·75	25
505	66	46f. green	8·75	25
506	66	50f. brown	8·25	25

67 St. Stephen

1928. 890th Death Anniv of St. Stephen of Hungary.

507	67	8f. green	1·90	65
508	67	16f. red	1·90	65
509	67	32f. blue	7·50	4·50

1929. Colours changed.

510	8f. red	1·30	50
511	16f. violet	1·50	65
512	32f. bistre	6·25	3·25

68 Admiral Horthy

1930. 10th Anniv of Regency.

513	68	8f. green	1·90	30
514	68	16f. violet	1·90	40
515	68	20f. red	11·50	1·50
516	68	32f. brown	9·50	4·50
517	68	40f. blue	12·50	1·90

69 St. Emeric

1930. 900th Death Anniv of St. Emeric.

518	69	8f.+2f. green	1·90	1·30
519	-	16f.+4f. purple	2·50	1·30
520	-	20f.+4f. red	6·25	3·75
521	-	32f.+8f. blue	8·75	6·25

DESIGNS—VERT: 16f. St. Stephen and Queen Gisela; 20f. St. Ladislas. HORIZ: 32f. Sts. Gellert and Emeric.

1931. Surch.

525	57	20 on 25f. brown	3·75	1·90
526	56	2 on 3f. orange	3·25	40
527	56	6 on 8f. mauve	3·25	25
528	57	10 on 16f. violet	3·25	25

1931. Air. Optd Zeppelin 1931.

529	62	1p. orange	£130	£130
530	62	2p. purple	£130	£130

73 St. Elizabeth

1932. 700th Death Anniv of St. Elizabeth of Hungary.

531	73	10f. blue	1·30	65
532	73	20f. red	1·30	65
533	-	32f. purple	7·50	3·25
534	-	40f. blue	5·75	1·90

DESIGN—18×28 mm: 32, 40f. St. Elizabeth giving cloak to the poor.

75 Madonna and Child

1932

535	75	1p. green	65·00	2·75
536	75	2p. red	65·00	4·25
537	75	5p. blue	£190	14·00
538	75	10p. brown	£225	90·00

1932. No. 527 further surch 2.

540	56	2 on 6 on 8f. mauve	3·50	95

77

1932. Famous Hungarians.

541	-	1f. grey	90	15
542	-	2f. orange	90	15
543	-	4f. blue	90	15
543a	77	5f. brown	1·30	25
544	-	6f. green	90	15
545	-	10f. green	90	15
546	-	16f. violet	90	25
547	-	20f. red	1·50	25
547a	-	25f. green	2·50	25
548	-	30f. brown	1·50	40
549	-	32f. purple	3·25	40
550	-	40f. blue	4·50	1·50

551	-	50f. green	4·50	1·50
552	-	70f. red	6·25	1·00

DESIGNS: 1f. I. Madach, poet, 1823–64; 2f. J Arany, poet, 1817–82; 4f. I. Semmelweis, physician, 1818–65; 5f. F. Kolcsey, poet, 1790–1838; 6f. L. Eotvos, physicist, 1848–1919; 10f. I. Szechenyi, statesman, 1791–1860; 16f. F. Deak, statesman, 1803–76; 20f. F. Liszt, composer, 1811–86; 25f. M. Vorosmarty, poet, 1800–55; 30f. L. Kossuth, statesman, 1802–94; 32f. I. Tisza, statesman, 1861–1918; 40f. M. Munkacsy, painter, 1844–1900; 50f. S. Korosi Csoma, explorer, 1784–1842; 70f. F. Bolyai, mathematician, 1775–1856.

1933. Surch 10.

553	**59**	10 on 70f. red	6·25	65

79 "Justice for Hungary" over Danube

80 Gift Plane from Mussolini

1933. Air.

554	**79**	10f. green	3·25	65
555	**79**	16f. violet	3·25	65
556	**80**	20f. red	9·50	1·30
557	**80**	40f. blue	9·50	1·30
558	-	48f. black	25·00	3·25
559	-	72f. brown	65·00	3·75
560	-	1p. green	65·00	4·50
561	-	2p. red	95·00	25·00
562	-	5p. grey	£190	£225

DESIGNS—VERT: As Type **80**: 48, 72f. "Spirit of Flight" on wing of Lockheed Model 8A Sirius; 1, 2, 5p. Mercury and propeller.

83 "The Stag of Hungary"

1933. International Scout Jamboree, Godollo.

563	**83**	10f. green	1·90	1·30
564	**83**	16f. red	6·25	3·75
565	**83**	20f. red	4·50	1·90
566	**83**	32f. yellow	14·00	9·50
567	**83**	40f. blue	15·00	6·25

1934. 2nd Hungarian Philatelic Exhibition, Budapest, and Jubilee of First Hungarian Philatelic Society (L.E.H.E.). Sheet 64×76 mm containing No. 547 in changed colour.

MS568 20f. red	£225	£180

84 Ferenc Rakoczi II

1935. Death Bicentenary of Prince Rakoczi.

569	**84**	10f. green	1·90	65
570	**84**	16f. violet	11·50	5·00
571	**84**	20f. red	3·25	1·90
572	**84**	32f. red	15·00	9·50
573	**84**	40f. blue	19·00	11·50

85 Cardinal Peter Pazmany

1935. Tercentenary of Budapest University.

574	**85**	6f. green	3·25	1·50
575	-	10f. green	65	40
576	**85**	16f. violet	4·50	2·50
577	**85**	20f. mauve	65	65
578	-	32f. red	7·50	5·25
579	-	40f. blue	6·25	5·25

DESIGN—HORIZ (35×25 mm): 10f., 32f., 40f. Pazmany signing deed.

87 Fokker F.VIIb/3m

1936. Air.

580	**87**	10f. green	1·30	65
581	**87**	20f. red	1·30	65
582	**87**	36f. brown	1·30	65
583	-	40f. blue	1·30	65
584	-	52f. orange	1·90	65
585	-	60f. violet	24·00	3·25
586	-	80f. green	5·00	65
587	-	1p. green	5·00	90
588	-	2p. lake	6·25	3·25
589	-	5p. blue	25·00	25·00

DESIGNS: 40f. to 80f. Fokker F.VIIb/3m over Parliament Buildings; 1p. to 5p. Fokker F.VIIb/3m (different).

88 Ancient Buda

1936. 250th Anniv of Recapture of Buda from Turks.

590	**88**	10f. green	1·30	40
591	-	16f. mauve	7·50	5·00
592	-	20f. red	1·30	40
593	-	32f. brown	7·50	5·00
594	**88**	40f. blue	7·50	5·00

DESIGNS: 16f. Angel of Peace over Buda; 20f. Arms of Buda; 32f. Colour bearer and bugler.

89 "Commerce", "May Fair, 1937" and R. Danube

1937. Budapest International Fair.

595	**89**	2f. orange	25	10
596	**89**	6f. green	65	15
597	**89**	10f. green	90	25
598	**89**	20f. red	1·90	65
599	**89**	32f. violet	2·50	90
600	**89**	40f. blue	2·75	1·30

90 St. Stephen, the Church Builder

1938. 900th Death Anniv of St. Stephen. (1st issue).

601	-	1f. violet	65	25
602	**90**	2f. sepia	25	25
603	-	4f. blue	1·30	25
604	-	5f. mauve	1·90	25
605	-	6f. green	2·50	25
606	-	10f. red	1·90	25
607	**90**	16f. violet	3·25	90
608	-	20f. red	1·90	25
609	-	25f. green	2·50	1·30
610	-	30f. bistre	3·75	25
611	-	32f. red on yellow	3·75	3·25
612	-	40f. blue	3·75	25
613	-	50f. purple on green	4·50	25
614	-	70f. green on blue	7·00	90
MS614a 146×106 mm. No. 608 for 34th International Eucharistic Congress and Philatelic Exhibition, Budapest			50·00	44·00

DESIGNS: 1f., 10f. Abbot Astrik receiving Crown from Pope; 4f., 20f. St. Stephen enthroned; 5f., 25f. St. Gellert, St. Emeric and St. Stephen; 6f., 30f. St. Stephen offering Crown to Virgin Mary; 32f., 50f. St. Stephen; 40f. Madonna and Child; 70f. Crown of St. Stephen.

See also Nos. 620/**MS**621a.

92 Admiral Horthy

1938

615	**92**	1p. green	4·50	25
616	**92**	2p. sepia	5·00	25
617	**92**	5p. blue	6·25	2·75

93 Eucharistic Symbols

1938. 34th International Eucharistic Congress.

618	-	16f.+16f. blue	8·25	8·25
619	**93**	20f.+20f. red	8·25	8·25
MS619a 130×149 mm 6f.+6f. green; 10f.+10f. red; 16f.+16f. blue; 20f.+20f. red; 32f.+32f. purple; 40f.+40f. blue; 50f.+50f. mauve			75·00	75·00

DESIGNS: 6f. St. Stephen; 10f.St. Emeric; 16f. (619), St Ladislas; 16f. St. Laszio; 20f. Offering crown to Virgin Mary; 32f. St. Elizabeth; 40f. Bishop Maurice and Pecs Cathedral; 50f. St. Margaret.

94 St. Stephen the Victorious

1938. 900th Death Anniv of St. Stephen (2nd issue).

620	**94**	10f.+10f. purple	5·00	5·00
621	-	20f.+20f. red	5·00	5·00
MS621a 153×113 mm. 6f.+6f. green; 10f.+10f. red; 16f.+16f. brown; 20f.+20f. red; 32f.+32f. blue; 40f.+40f. blue; 50f.+50f. purple			65·00	70·00

DESIGNS: St. Stephen the missionary; 16f. On throne; 20f. Offering crown to Virgin Mary; 32f. Receiving bishops and monks; 40f. Queen Gisela, St. Stephen and St. Emeric; 50f. On bier.

95 Debrecen College

1938. 400th Anniv of Debrecen College.

622	**95**	6f. green	65	15
623	-	10f. brown	65	15
624	-	16f. red	65	40
625	-	20f. red	65	25
626	-	32f. green	1·50	1·10
627	-	40f. blue	1·50	90

DESIGNS—HORIZ: 10, 20f. 18th and 19th-cent views of College. VERT: 16f. 18th-century students as firemen; 32f. Prof. Marothi; 40f. Dr. Hatvani.

1938. Acquisition of Czech Territory. As Nos. 608 and 614 optd HAZATERES 1938.

628	20f. red	3·25	2·50
629	70f. brown on blue	3·25	2·50

100 Statue representing Northern Provinces

1939. "Hungary for Hungarians" Patriotic Fund.

630	**100**	6f.+3f. green	1·50	90
631	-	10f.+5f. green	90	65
632	-	20f.+10f. red	90	65
633	-	30f.+15f. green	1·90	1·30
634	-	40f.+20f. blue	2·50	1·30

DESIGNS: 10f. Fort at Munkacs; 20f. Admiral Horthy leading troops into Komarom; 30f. Cathedral of St. Elizabeth of Hungary, Kassa; 40f. Girls offering flowers to soldiers.

101 Crown of St. Stephen

102 Esztergom Basilica

1939

635	**101**	1f. purple	15	15
636	**101**	2f. green	15	15
637	**101**	4f. brown	15	15
638	**101**	5f. violet	15	15
639	**101**	6f. green	15	15
640	**101**	10f. brown	15	15
641	**101**	16f. violet	15	15
642	-	20f. red	15	15
643	-	25f. blue	15	15
645	-	32f. brown	25	15
690	**101**	3f. brown	15	15
693	**101**	8f. green	15	15
695	**101**	12f. red	15	15
697	-	24f. red	15	15
698	-	80f. brown	65	25
699	-	30f. mauve	15	15
700	**102**	40f. green	25	25
701	-	50f. green	25	25
702	-	70f. red	25	25

DESIGNS—As T **101**: 20, 24f. St. Stephen; 25, 80f. Madonna and Child. As T **102**: 30f. Buda Cathedral; 32f. Debrecen Reformed Church; 50f. Budapest Evangelical Church; 70f. Kassa Cathedral.

For further issues in these designs, see Nos. 751/5.

103 Guides' Salute

1939. Girl Guides' Rally, Godollo. Inscr "I. PAX-TING".

649	**103**	2f. orange	75	50
650	-	6f. green	75	50
651	-	10f. brown	1·30	75
652	-	20f. pink	1·90	1·30

DESIGNS: 6f. Lily symbol and Hungarian arms; 10f. Guide and girl in national costume; 20f. Dove of peace.

104 Memorial Tablets

1939. National Protestant Day and Int Protestant Cultural Fund.

653	**104**	6f.+3f. green	1·50	90
654	-	10f.+5f. purple	1·50	90
655	-	20f.+10f. red	2·30	1·90
656	-	32f.+16f. brown	2·50	2·50
657	-	40f.+20f. blue	3·25	3·00
MS657a 77×112 mm. No. 656 32f. brown. Perf or imperf			65·00	65·00

DESIGNS—HORIZ: 10f., 20f. G. Karoli and A. Molnar di Szenci (translators of the Bible and the Psalms). VERT: 32f. Prince Gabriel Bethlen; 40f. Zsuzsanna Lorantffy.

106 Boy Scout with Kite

1940. Admiral Horthy Aviation Fund.

658	**106**	6f.+6f. green	90	90
659	-	10f.+10f. brown	1·50	1·50
660	-	20f.+20f. red	2·10	2·10

DESIGNS: 10f. "Spirit of Flight"; 20f. St. Elizabeth carrying Crown and Cross of St. Stephen.

107 Regent and Szeged Cathedral

1940. 20th Anniv of Regency.

661	107	6f. green	25	25
662	-	10f. brown and olive	40	40
663	-	20f. red	1·30	90

DESIGNS: 10f. Admiral Horthy (dated "1920 1940"); 20f. Kassa Cathedral and Angelic bellringer (dated "1939").

108 Stemming the Flood

1940. Flood Relief Fund.

664	108	10f.+2f. purple	65	40
665	108	20f.+4f. orange	65	40
666	108	20f.+50f. brown	1·90	2·00
MS666a		77×112 mm. T **108**. 20f.+1p. green	8·25	8·25

109 Hunyadi Family Arms

110 Hunyadi Castle

1940. 500th Birth Anniv of King Matthias Hunyadi and Cultural Institutes Fund.

667	109	6f.+3f. green	90	90
668	110	10f.+5f. brown	90	90
669	-	16f.+8f. olive	1·10	1·10
670	-	20f.+10f. red	1·10	1·10
671	-	32f.+16f. grey	1·50	1·50
MS671a		89×113 mm. 20f.+1p. green (as No. 670)	8·25	8·25

DESIGNS—VERT: 16f. Bust of King Matthias (dated "1440–1490"); 32f. Corvin Codex (dated "1473"). HORIZ: 20f. Equestrian Statue of King Matthias.

111 Crown of St. Stephen

1940. Recovery from Rumania of North-Eastern Transylvania.

672	111	10f. green and yellow	65	25

112 Madonna and Martyr

1940. Transylvanian Relief Fund. Various designs dated "1940".

673	-	10f.+50f. green	1·50	1·50
674	112	20f.+50f. red	1·60	1·60
675	-	32f.+50f. brown	2·00	2·00

DESIGNS: 10f. Prince Csaba and soldier; 32f. Mother offering child to Fatherland.

113 Spirit of Music

1940. Artists' Relief Fund. Inscr "MAGYAR MUVESZETERT".

676	113	6f.+6f. green	2·10	1·90
677	-	10f.+10f. brown	2·10	1·90
678	-	16f.+16f. violet	2·10	1·90
679	-	20f.+20f. red	2·10	1·90
MS679a		123×84 mm. 6f.+6f. brown; 10f.+10f. red; 16f.+16f. green; 20f.+20f. lilac	9·50	9·50

DESIGNS—VERT: 10f. Sculpture; 16f. Painting. HORIZ: 20f. Poetry (Pegasus).

114 Pilot

1941. Air. Horthy Aviation Fund. Various allegorical designs inscribed "HORTHY MIKLOS NEMZETI REPULO ALAP".

680	114	6f.+6f. olive	90	90
681	-	10f.+10f. brown	90	90
682	-	20f.+20f. red	90	90
683	-	32f.+32f. blue	2·50	2·50

DESIGNS: 10f. Youth releasing model glider; 20f. Glider; 32f. Madonna.

1941. Acquisition of Yugoslav Territory. Overprinted DELVISSZATER ("The South Comes Home").

684	101	10f. brown	65	15
685	-	20f. red (No. 642)	65	15

116 Admiral Horthy

1941

686A	116	1p. green and yellow	40	25
687B	116	2p. brown and yellow	40	40
688B	116	5p. purple and yellow	1·30	50

118 Szechenyi

119 Giant opening Straits of Kazan

1941. 150th Birth Anniv of Count Szechenyi.

703	118	10f. olive	25	15
704	-	16f. brown	40	25
705	119	20f. red	40	25
706	-	32f. orange	90	50
707	-	40f. blue	1·00	50

DESIGNS: 16f. Count Szechenyi and Academy of Science; 32f. Budapest Chain Bridge; 40f. Mercury, Locomotive and "Szent Istvan" (river steamer).

120 Infantry in Action

1941. Soldiers' Gifts Fund. Inscr "HONVEDEINK KARACSONYARA 1941". (a) 1st issue.

708	120	8f.+12f. green	75	65
709	-	12f.+18f. brown	75	65
710	-	20f.+30f. blue	90	65
711	-	40f.+60f. brown	90	65

DESIGNS: 12f. Artillery; 20f. Tanks; 40f. Cavalryman and cyclist.

(b) 2nd Issue (for Christmas gifts).

712		20f.+40f. red	3·75	3·75

DESIGN: Soldier in helmet; cross and sword.

121 Pilot and Airplane

1942. Air. Horthy Aviation Fund. Inscr "HORTHY MIKLOS NEMZETI REPULO ALAP".

713	121	8f.+8f. green	1·30	1·30
714	-	12f.+12f. blue	1·30	1·30
715	-	20f.+20f. brown	1·30	1·30
716	-	30f.+30f. red	1·30	1·30

DESIGNS—VERT: 30f. Airmen and Turul. HORIZ: 12f. Aircraft and horsemen; 20f. Airplane and archer.

122 Blood Transfusion

1942. Red Cross Fund. Cross in red.

717	122	3f.+18f. green	2·10	2·10
718	-	8f.+32f. brown	2·10	2·10
719	-	12f.+50f. purple	2·10	2·10
720	-	20f.+1p. blue	2·10	2·10

DESIGNS: 8f. First aid; 12f. Wireless and carrier-pigeon service; 20f. Bereaved parents and orphans.

123 Vice-regent Stephen Horthy

1942. Air. Mourning for Stephen Horthy and Horthy Aviation Fund.

721		20f. black	65	65
722	123	30f.+20f. violet	75	75

No. 721 is squarer in shape than No. 722 and is dated "1904–1942".

124 Stephen Horthy's Widow

1942. Red Cross Fund. Cross and Crown in red.

723	124	6f.+1p. blue	4·50	4·50
724	-	8f.+1p. green	4·50	4·50
725	-	20f.+1p. brown	4·50	4·50

DESIGNS—HORIZ: 8f. Nurse and wounded soldier. VERT: 20f. Stephen Horthy's mother.

125 King Ladislas

1942. Cultural Funds.

726	125	6f.+6f. brown	90	90
727	-	8f.+8f. green	90	90
728	-	12f.+12f. brown	90	90
729	-	20f.+20f. green	90	90
730	-	24f.+24f. brown	90	90
731	-	30f.+30f. red	90	90

DESIGNS—Statuettes: 8f. Ladislas on horseback; 20f. Bela IV with architect; 30f. Lajos the Great enthroned. King's heads; 12f. Bela IV; 24f. Lajos the Great.

126 Prince Arpad

127 St. Stephen's Crown

1943

732	126	1f. grey	15	15
733	-	2f. orange	15	15
734	-	3f. blue	15	15
735	-	4f. brown	15	15
736	-	5f. red	15	15
737	-	6f. blue	15	15
738	-	8f. green	15	15
739	-	10f. brown	20	15
740	-	12f. green	20	15
741	-	18f. black	20	15
742	127	20f. brown	20	15
743	-	24f. purple	25	15
744	127	30f. red	25	15
745	-	30f. red	25	15
746	127	50f. blue	25	15
747	127	80f. brown	25	15
748	127	1p. green	25	15
749	127	2p. brown	35	65
750	127	5p. purple	50	1·30

DESIGNS: 2f. King Ladislas; 3f. Miklos Toldi; 4f. Janos Hunyadi; 5f. Pal Kinizsi; 6f. Miklos Zrinyi; 8f. Ferenc Rakoczi II; 10f. Andre Hadik; 12f. Artur Gorgey; 18f. and 24f. Madonna; 30f. (No. 745), St. Margaret.

1943. As T 102 (designs and colours changed).

751	-	30f. red	25	15
752	-	40f. grey	25	15
753	102	50f. blue	25	15
754	-	70f. green	25	15
755	-	80f. brown	25	15

DESIGNS: 30f. Kassa Cathedral; 40f. Debrecen Reformed Church; 70f. Budapest Evangelical Church; 80f. Buda Cathedral.

128 Mounted Archer

1943. Wounded Soldiers' Relief Fund. Inscr as in T 128.

756	128	1f.+1f. grey	15	15
757	-	3f.+1f. lilac	75	1·30
758	-	4f.+1f. brown	25	20
759	-	8f.+2f. green	25	20
760	-	12f.+2f. brown	25	20
761	-	20f.+2f. brown	25	20
762	-	40f.+4f. grey	30	20
763	-	50f.+6f. brown	40	20
764	-	70f.+8f. blue	50	40

DESIGNS—VERT: 3f., 4f. Magyar soldier with battle-axe and buckler; 8f. Warrior with shield and sword; 20f. Musketeer; 50f. Artilleryman; 70f. Magyar Arms. HORIZ: 12f. Lancer; 40f. Hussar.

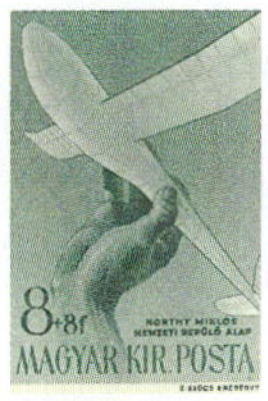

129 Model Glider

1943. Air. Horthy Aviation Fund. Inscr "HORTHY MIKLOS NEMZETI REPULO ALAP".

765	129	8f.+8f. green	1·30	1·10
766	-	12f.+12f. blue	1·30	1·10
767	-	20f.+20f. brown	1·30	1·10
768	-	30f.+30f. red	1·30	1·10

DESIGNS: 12f. Gliders in flight; 20f. White-tailed sea eagle and aircraft; 30f. Cant Z.1007 bis Alcione bomber and gliders.

130 Shepherds and Angels

1943. Christmas.

769	130	4f. green	40	40
770	-	20f. blue	40	40
771	-	30f. red	40	40

DESIGNS: 20f. Nativity; 30f. Adoration of the Wise Men.

131 Nurse and Soldier

1944. Red Cross Fund. Cross and Crown in red.

772	131	20f.+20f. brown	90	75
773	-	30f.+30f. brown	90	75
774	-	50f.+50f. purple	90	75
775	-	70f.+70f. blue	90	75

DESIGNS: 30f. Soldier, nurse, mother and child; 50f. Nurse shielding a lamp over the Fallen; 70f. Soldier with crutches, nurse and sapling.

132 Drummer and Flags

1944. 50th Death Anniv of Kossuth (statesman).

776		4f. brown	40	25

777	**132**	20f. green	40	25
778	-	30f. red	40	25
779	-	50f. blue	40	25

DESIGNS—VERT: 4f. Kossuth and family group; 50f. Portrait. HORIZ: 30f. Kossuth speaking before an assembly.

133 St. Elizabeth

1944. Famous Women.

780	**133**	20f. bistre	40	40
781	-	24f. purple	40	40
782	-	30f. red	40	40
783	-	50f. blue	40	40
784	-	70f. red	40	40
785	-	80f. brown	40	40

PORTRAITS: 24f. St. Margaret; 30f. Elizabeth Szilagyi; 50f. Dorothy Kanizsai; 70f. Zsuzsanna Lorantffy; 80f. Ilona Zrinyi.

1945. Stamps as Nos. 732/48, surch FELSZABADULAS (= Liberation) 1945 apr 4 and value. On yellow or blue surface-tinted paper (same price).

786	10f. on 1f. grey	2·50	2·50
787	20f. on 3f. blue	2·50	2·50
788	30f. on 4f. brown		2·50
789	40f. on 6f. blue	2·50	2·50
790	50f. on 8f. green	2·50	2·50
791	1p. on 10f. brown	2·50	2·50
792	150f. on 12f. green	2·50	2·50
793	2p. on 18f. black	2·50	2·50
794	3p. on 20f. brown	2·50	2·50
795	5p. on 24f. purple	2·50	2·50
796	6p. on 50f. blue	2·50	2·50
797	10p. on 80f. brown	2·50	2·50
798	20p. on 1p. green	2·50	2·50

135 Bajcsy-Zsilinszky

1945. Bajcsy-Zsilinszky (patriot).

799	**135**	1p.+1p. purple	1·30	1·30

1945. Provisionals. 1st issue. Surch 1945 and value. (a) On stamps of 1943, Nos. 732/50, surface-tinted paper.

800	10f. on 4f. brown on blue	15	15
801	10f. on 10f. brown on blue	40	40
802	10f. on 12f. green on yellow	15	15
803	20f. on 1f. grey on yellow	15	15
804	20f. on 18f. black on yellow	15	15
805	28f. on 5f. red on blue	15	15
806	30f. on 30f. red on blue (No. 745)	15	15
807	30f. on 30f. red on blue (No. 744)	15	15
808	40f. on 24f. purple on yellow	15	15
809	42f. on 20f. brown on yellow	15	15
810	50f. on 50f. blue on yellow	15	15
811	60f. on 8f. green on yellow	15	15
812	1p. on 80f. brown on blue	15	15
813	1p. on 1p. green on yellow	15	15
814	150f. on 6f. blue on yellow	1·50	1·50
815	2p. on 2p. brown on blue	15	15
816	3p. on 3f. blue on yellow	40	40
817	5p. on 5p. purple on yellow	25	25
818	10p. on 2f. orange on blue	12·50	12·50

(b) On Famous Women Series of 1944 (Nos. 780/5), surface-tinted paper.

819	20f. on 20f. bistre on blue	15	15
820	30f. on 30f. red on blue	15	15
821	40f. on 24f. purple on yellow	15	15
822	50f. on 50f. blue on yellow	15	15
823	80f. on 80f. brown on yellow	15	15
824	1p. on 70f. red on blue	25	25

1945. Provisionals. 2nd issue. Surch 1945 and value. (a) On stamps of 1943, Nos. 732/48, surface-tinted paper.

825	40f. on 10f. brown on blue	15	15
826	1p. on 20f. brown on yellow	15	15
827	1.60p. on 12f. green on yellow	15	15
828	2p. on 4f. brown on blue	15	15
829	4p. on 30f. red on blue (No. 744)	15	15
830	5p. on 8f. green on yellow	15	15
831	6p. on 50f. blue on yellow	15	15
832	7p. on 1p. green on yellow	15	15
833	9p. on 1f. grey on yellow	15	15
834	10p. on 80f. brown on blue	15	15

(b) On Famous Women Series of 1944. (Nos. 780/3), surface-tinted paper.

835	80f. on 24f. purple on yellow	25	25
836	3p. on 50f. blue on yellow	15	15
837	8p. on 20f. bistre on blue	15	15
838	20p. on 30f. red on blue	15	15

1945. National High School Fund. Nos. 776/9, with coloured surfaces, surch BEKE A NEPFOISKOLAKERT, new value and premium.

839	**132**	3p.+9p. on 20f. green on yellow	65	1·10
840	-	4p.+12p. on 4f. brown on blue	65	1·10
841	-	8p.+24p. on 50f. blue on yellow	65	1·10
842	-	10p.+30p. on 30f. red on blue	65	1·10

138 Mining

1945. Int Trade Union Conference, Paris.

843	**138**	40f. grey	8·75	10·00
844	-	1p.60 brown	8·75	10·00
845	-	2p. green	8·75	10·00
846	-	3p. purple	8·75	10·00
847	-	5p. red	8·75	10·00
848	-	8p. brown	8·75	10·00
849	-	10p. red	8·75	10·00
850	-	20p. blue	8·75	10·00

DESIGNS: Trade Symbols—1p.60, Hammer and anvil (ironworking); 2p. Winged wheel (railway workers); 3p. Trowel and bricks (building); 5p. Plough (agriculture); 8p. Carrier pigeon (communications); 10p. Compasses (engineering); 20p. Winged pen and book (clerks).

139 I. Sallai and S. Furst

1945. National Relief Fund.

851	**139**	2p.+2p. brown	2·50	2·75
852	-	3p.+3p. red	2·50	2·75
853	-	4p.+4p. violet	2·50	2·75
854	-	6p.+6p. green	2·50	2·75
855	-	10p.+10p. red	2·50	2·75
856	-	15p.+15p. olive	2·50	2·75
857	-	20p.+20p. brown	2·50	2·75
858	-	40p.+40p. blue	2·50	2·75

PORTRAITS: 3p. L. Kabok and I. Monus; 4p. F. Rozsa and Z. Schonherz; 6p. A. Koltoi and P. Knurr; 10p. G. Sarkozi and I. Nagy; 15p. V. Tartsay and J. Nagy; 20p. J. Kiss and E. Bajcsy-Zsilinszky; 40p. E. Sagvari and O. Hoffmann.

1945. Provisionals. 3rd issue. Nos. 738, 740/1 and 745 (coloured surfaces) surch 1945 and new value.

859	40p. on 8f. green on yellow	15	15
860	60p. on 18f. black on yellow	15	15
861	100p. on 12f. green on yellow	15	15
862	300p. on 30f. red on blue	25	25

140 Reconstruction

1945

863	**140**	12p. olive	65	65
864	**140**	20p. green	25	40
865	**140**	24p. brown	65	65
866	**140**	30p. black	25	40
867	**140**	40p. green	25	40
868	**140**	60p. red	25	40
869	**140**	100p. orange	25	40
870	**140**	120p. blue	25	40
871	**140**	140p. red	90	1·00
872	**140**	200p. brown	25	40
873	**140**	240p. blue	25	40
874	**140**	300p. red	25	40
875	**140**	500p. green	25	40
876	**140**	1000p. purple	25	40
877	**140**	3000p. red	25	40

Owing to the collapse of the pengo, the following stamps were overprinted to show the postage rate for which they were valid, and they were sold at the appropriate rate for the day. **Any** or **Nyomtatv** = Sample Post or Printed Matter. **Hlp** or **Helyi lev. lap** = Local Postcard. **Hl** or **Helyi level** = Local Letter. **Tlp** or **Tavolsagi lev.-lap** = Inland Postcard. **Tl** or **Tavolsagi level** = Inland Letter. **Ajl** or **Ajanlas** = Registered Letter. **Cs.** or **Csomag** = Parcel.

1946. Optd as above. (a) First Issue.

878	**126**	"Any. 1" on 1f. grey	15	15
879	-	"Hlp. 1" on 8p. on 20f. bistre on blue (No. 837)	15	15
880	-	"Hl. 1" on 50f. blue (No. 783)	15	15
881	-	"Tlp. 1" on 4f. brown (No. 735)	15	15
882	-	"Tl. 1" on 10f. brown (No. 739)	15	15
883	**133**	"Ajl. 1" on 20f. bistre	15	15
883b	**127**	"Cs. 5-1" on 30f. red (No. 744)	31·00	31·00
884	-	"Cs. 5-1" on 70f. red (No. 784)	15	15
885	-	"Cs. 10-1" on 70f. red (No. 784)	15	15
885a	**127**	"Cs. 10-1" on 80f. brown (No. 747)	50·00	50·00

(b) Second Issue.

886	**126**	"Any. 2" on 1f. grey	25	25
887	-	"Hlp. 2" on 8p. on 20f. bistre on blue (No. 837)	25	25
888	-	"Hl. 2" on 40f. on 10f. brown on blue (No. 825)	25	25
889	-	"Tlp. 2" on 4f. brown (No. 735)	25	25
890	-	"Tl. 2" on 10f. on 4f. brown on blue (No. 800)	25	25
891	-	"Ajl. 2" on 12f. green (No. 740)	25	25
892	-	"Cs. 5-2" on 24f. purple (No. 743)	25	25
893	-	"Cs. 10-2" on 80f. brown (No. 785)	25	25

(c) Third Issue.

894	"Nyomtatv. 20gr." on 60f. on 8f. green on yellow (No. 811)	25	25
895	"Helyi lev.-lap" on 2f. bistre on blue (as No. 780)	25	25
896	"Helyi level" on 10f. brown on blue (as No. 739)	25	25
897	"Tavolsagi lev.-lap" on 4f. brown (No. 735)	25	25
898	"Tavolsagi level" on 18f. black (No. 741)	25	25
899	"Ajanlas" on 24f. purple (No. 781)	25	25
900	"Csomag 5 kg" on 2p. on 4f. brown on blue (No. 828)	25	25
901	"Csomag 10kg." on 30f. red on blue (as No. 782)	25	25

ez(er) p. = thousand pengos.
m(illio) p. = million pengos.
m.p. (milpengo) = million pengos.
md.p. (milliard. p) = thousand million pengos.
b.p. (billio. p) = million million pengos.
ez. ap (ezer adopengo) = thousand "tax" pengos.
m. ap. (millio adopengo) = million "tax" pengos.

143

1946. Foundation of Republic.

902	**143**	3ez. p. brown	25	25
903	**143**	15ez. p. blue	25	25

144

1946

904	**144**	4ez. p. brown	25	25
905	**144**	10ez. p. red	25	25
906	**144**	15ez. p. blue	25	25
907	**144**	20ez. p. brown	25	25
908	**144**	30ez. p. purple	25	25
909	**144**	50ez. p. grey	25	25
910	**144**	80ez. p. blue	25	25
911	**144**	100ez. p. red	25	25
912	**144**	160ez. p. green	25	25
913	**144**	200ez. p. green	25	25
914	**144**	500ez. p. red	25	25
915	**144**	640ez. p. olive	25	25
916	**144**	800ez. p. violet	25	25

145

1946. 75th Anniv of First Hungarian Stamps.

917	**145**	500+500ez. p. green	3·25	3·50
918	**145**	1+1m. p. brown	3·25	3·50
919	**145**	1.5+1.5m. p. red	3·25	3·50
920	**145**	2+2m. p. blue	3·25	3·50

146

1946

921	**146**	1m.p. red	40	65
922	**146**	2m.p. blue	40	65
923	**146**	3m.p. brown	40	65
924	**146**	4m.p. grey	40	65
925	**146**	5m.p. violet	40	65
926	**146**	10m.p. green	40	65
927	**146**	20m.p. red	40	65
928	**146**	50m.p. green	40	65

147 Posthorn and Arms

1946

929	**147**	100m.p. red	30	65
930	**147**	200m.p. red	30	65
931	**147**	500m.p. red	30	65
932	**147**	1000m.p. red	30	65
933	**147**	2000m.p. red	30	65
934	**147**	3000m.p. red	30	65
935	**147**	5000m.p. red	30	65
936	**147**	10,000m.p. red	30	65
937	**147**	20,000m.p. red	30	65
938	**147**	30,000m.p. red	30	65
939	**147**	50,000m.p. red	30	65

148 Posthorn

1946

940	**148**	100md.p. green and red	40	65
941	**148**	200md.p. green and red	40	65
942	**148**	500md.p. green and red	40	65

149 Dove and Letter

1946

943	**149**	1b.p. black and red	25	65
944	**149**	2b.p. black and red	25	65
945	**149**	5b.p. black and red	25	65
946	**149**	10b.p. black and red	25	65
947	**149**	20b.p. black and red	25	65
948	**149**	50b.p. black and red	25	65
949	**149**	100b.p. black and red	25	65
950	**149**	200b.p. black and red	25	65
951	**149**	500b.p. black and red	25	65
952	**149**	1000b.p. black and red	25	65
953	**149**	10,000b.p. black and red	1·10	1·30
954	**149**	50,000b.p. black and red	1·10	1·30
955	**149**	100,000b.p. black and red	1·10	1·30
956	**149**	500,000b.p. black and red	1·10	1·30

150 Locomotive "Heves", 1846

1946. Centenary of Hungarian Railways.

957	**150**	10000ap. brown	5·50	5·75
958	-	20000ap. blue	5·50	5·75
959	-	30000ap. green	5·50	5·75
960	-	40000ap. red	5·50	5·75

DESIGNS: 20000ap. Class 424 steam locomotive; 30000ap. Class V44 electric locomotive; 40000ap. "Arpad" diesel railcar, 1935.

151 Posthorn

1946

961	151	5ez. ap. green and black	25	65
962	151	10ez. ap. green and black	25	65
963	151	20ez. ap. green and black	25	65
964	151	50ez. ap. green and black	25	65
965	151	80ez. ap. green and black	25	65
966	151	100ez. ap. green and black	25	65
967	151	200ez. ap. green and black	25	65
968	151	500ez. ap. green and black	25	65
969	151	1m. ap. red and black	65	1·30
970	151	5m. ap. red and black	65	1·30

152 Industry

153 Agriculture

1946. Currency Reform.

971	152	8fi. brown	25	15
972	152	10fi. brown	25	15
973	152	12fi. brown	25	15
974	152	20fi. brown	25	15
975	152	30fi. brown	25	15
976	152	40fi. brown	25	15
977	152	60fi. brown	25	15
978	153	1fo. green	1·00	15
979	153	1fo. 40 green	1·00	15
980	153	2fo. green	1·90	15
981	153	3fo. green	6·25	15
982	153	5fo. green	1·90	15
983	153	10fo. green	3·75	65

154 Ceres

1946. Agricultural Fair.

984	154	30fi.+60fi. green	7·50	8·75
985	154	60fi.+1fo. 20 red	7·50	8·75
986	154	1fo.+2fo. blue	7·50	8·75

155 Liberty Bridge

1947. Air. Views.

987	-	10fi. red	25	15
988	-	20fi. grey	25	15
989	155	50fi. brown	65	15
990	-	70fi. green	80	15
991	-	1fo. blue	2·00	15
992	-	1fo. 40 brown	2·00	25
993	-	3fo. green	2·00	25
994	-	5fo. lilac	8·00	2·10

DESIGNS: 10fi. Loyalty Tower, Sopron; 20fi. Esztergom Cathedral; 70fi. Palace Hotel, Lillafured; 1fo. Vajdahunyad Castle, Budapest; 1fo. 40, Visegrad Fortress; 3fo. "Falcone" (racing yacht) on Lake Balaton; 5fo. Parliament Buildings and Kossuth Bridge.

156 Gyorgy Dozsa

1947. Liberty issue.

995	156	8fi. red	65	15
996	-	10fi. blue	65	15
997	-	12fi. brown	65	15
998	-	20fi. green	95	15
999	-	30fi. brown	95	15
1000	-	40fi. purple	1·20	15
1001	-	60fi. red	1·20	15
1002	-	1fo. blue	1·30	15
1003	-	2fo. violet	2·75	65
1004	-	4fo. green	4·00	95

PORTRAITS: 10fi. A. Budai Nagy; 12fi. T. Esze; 20fi. I. Martinovics; 30fi. J. Batsanyi; 40fi. L. Kossuth; 60fi. M. Tancsics; 1fo. S. Petofi; 2fo. E. Ady; 4fo. A. Jozsef.

157 Doctor examining X-Ray

1947. Welfare Organizations. Inscr "SIESS! ADJ! SEGITS!" (trans. "Come! Give! Help!").

1005		8fi.+50fi. blue	6·00	8·00
1006	157	12fi.+50fi. brown	6·00	8·00
1007	-	20fi.+50fi. green	6·00	8·00
1008	-	60fi.+50fi. red	2·50	1·30

DESIGNS: 8fi. Doctor testing syringe; 20fi. Nurse and child; 60fi. Released prisoner-of-war.

158 Emblem of Peace

1947. Peace Treaty.

1009	158	60fi. red	80	40

159 Liberty Statue

1947. 30th Anniv of Soviet Union and Hungarian–Soviet Cultural Society Fund.

1010	-	40fi.+40fi. brn & grn	6·75	6·75
1011	159	60fi.+60fi. grey and red	3·25	3·25
1012	-	1fo.+1fo. black & blue	6·75	6·75

PORTRAITS: 40fi. Lenin; 1fo. Stalin.

161 Savings Bank

1947. Savings Day. Inscr "TAKAREKOS JELENBOLDOG JOVO".

1013		40fi. red (beehive)	65	25
1014	161	60fi. red	65	25

162 16th-century Mail Coach

1947. Stamp Day.

1015	162	30fi. (+ 50fi.) brown	14·50	14·50

165 Arms of Hungary

1948. Centenary of Insurrection.

1016	-	8fi. red	25	15
1017	-	10fi. blue	25	15
1018	-	12fi. brown	40	15
1019	-	20fi. green	80	15
1020	-	30fi. brown	40	15
1021	-	40fi. purple	40	15
1022	-	60fi. red	1·60	15
1023	165	1fo. blue	1·60	15
1024	165	2fo. brown	3·25	40
1025	165	3fo. green	4·00	80
1026	165	4fo. red	6·75	1·30

DESIGNS—HORIZ: 8fi., 40fi. Hungarian independence flag; 10fi. Printing press; 12fi. Latticed window; 20fi. Shako, trumpet and sword; 30fi., 60fi. Slogan.

167 Johann Gutenberg

1948. Air. Explorers and Inventors.

1027	167	1fi. red	40	40
1028	-	2fi. mauve	40	40
1029	-	4fi. blue	40	40
1030	-	5fi. brown	55	55
1031	-	6fi. green	55	55
1032	-	8fi. purple	55	55
1033	-	10fi. brown	65	65
1034	-	12fi. green	65	65
1035	-	30fi. red	2·30	2·30
1036	-	40fi. violet	2·75	2·75

PORTRAITS: 2fi. Christopher Columbus; 4fi. Robert Fulton; 5fi. George Stephenson; 6fi. David Schwarz and Count Ferdinand von Zeppelin; 8fi. Thomas Edison; 10fi. Louis Bleriot; 12fi. Roald Amundsen; 30fi. Kalman Kando; 40fi. Alexander Popov.

168 Chain Bridge, Budapest

1948. Air. Re-opening of Budapest Chain Bridge. Sheets 74×65 mm.

MS1036a	2fo.+18fo. Red	£160	£160
MS1036b **168**	3fo.+18fo. blue	£160	£160

DESIGN: 20fo. Shows a more distant view of the bridge.

169 Lorand Eotvos

1948. Birth Centenary of L. Eotvos (physicist).

1037	169	60fi. red	2·00	65

170 William Shakespeare

1948. Air. Writers.

1038	170	1fi. blue	40	40
1039	-	2fi. red	40	40
1040	-	4fi. green	40	40
1041	-	5fi. mauve	55	55
1042	-	6fi. blue	55	55
1043	-	8fi. brown	55	55
1044	-	10fi. red	65	65
1045	-	12fi. violet	65	65
1046	-	30fi. brown	2·30	2·30
1047	-	40fi. brown	2·75	2·75

PORTRAITS: 2fi. Voltaire; 4fi. Goethe; 5fi. Byron; 6fi. Victor Hugo; 8fi. Edgar Allan Poe; 10fi. Petofi; 12fi. Mark Twain; 30fi. Tolstoy; 40fi. Gorki.

171 Globe and Pigeon

1948. 5th National Philatelic Exhibition.

1048	171	30fi. blue	8·00	8·00

Sold at 1fo.30 (incl 1fo. entrance fee).

172 Symbolizing Industry, Agriculture and Culture

1948. 17th Trades' Union Congress.

1049	172	30fi. red	1·30	1·30

173 Agricultural Worker

1949. International Women's Day.

1050	173	60fi.+60fi. mauve	2·75	2·75

174 Reproduction of T **32**

1949. 30th Anniv of Bolshevist Regime.

1051	174	40fi. brown and red	65	65
1052	-	60fi. olive and red	65	65

DESIGN: 60fi. Reproduction of No. 325.

175 Pushkin holding Torch and Scroll

1949. 150th Birth Anniv of A. S. Pushkin (poet).

1053	175	1fo.+1fo. red	13·50	13·50
MS1053a		52×62 mm. 1fo.+1fo. Red	20·00	20·00

DESIGN—HORIZ: No. **MS**1053a, Puhkin writing.

176 Symbolising Workers of Five Continents

1949. 2nd World Federation of Trade Unions Congress, Milan. Flag in red.

1054	176	30fi. brown	4·75	4·75
1055	176	40fi. purple	4·75	4·75
1056	176	60fi. red	4·75	4·75
1057	176	1fo. blue	4·75	4·75

177 Sandor Petofi

1949. Death Centenary of Petofi (poet).

1058	177	40fi. purple	95	55
1059	177	60fi. red	65	25
1060	177	1fo. blue	80	40
1096	177	40fi. brown	95	55
1098	177	1fo. green	80	55

178 Heads and Globe

1949. World Youth Festival, Budapest.

1061	**178**	20fi. brown	1·60	1·60
1062	-	30fi. green	2·00	2·00
1063	-	40fi. bistre	2·75	2·75
1064	-	60fi. red	2·75	2·75
1065	-	1fo. blue	3·50	3·50
MS1065a 100×130 mm. Nos. 1061/5, but colours changed			60·00	60·00

DESIGNS: 30fi. Three clenched fists; 40fi. Man breaking chains; 60fi. Young people and banner; 1fo. Workers and tractor.

179 Hungarian Coat-of-Arms

1949. Ratification of Constitution. Arms in blue, brown, red and green.

1066A	**179**	20fi. green	2·00	95
1067B	**179**	60fi. red	1·60	65
1068B	**179**	1fo. blue	1·70	65

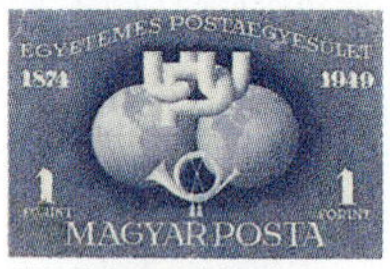

181 Globes and Posthorn

1949. 75th Anniv of U.P.U.

1069	**181**	60fi. red (postage)	95	95
1070	**181**	1fo. blue	95	95
1071	-	2fo. brown (air)	2·00	2·00
MS1072 128×98 mm. 3fo. (×4) brown and red			£750	£750

DESIGN: 2, 3fo. Lisunov Li-2 airplane replaces posthorn.

182 Chain Bridge

1949. Centenary of Budapest Chain Bridge.

1073	**182**	40fi. green (postage)	95	65
1074	**182**	60fi. brown	95	65
1075	**182**	1fo. blue	95	65
1076	**182**	1fo.60 red (air)	2·00	1·30
1077	**182**	2fo. olive	2·00	1·30
MS1077a 136×100 mm. 50 fo. Lilac			£600	£600

DESIGN—VERT: 50fo. Drawing board, plans, etc.

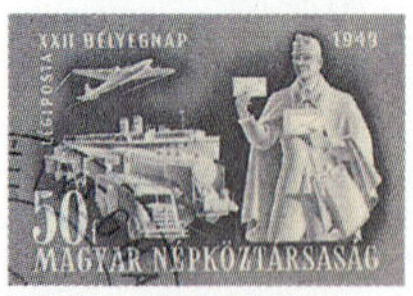

183 Postman and Forms of Transport

1949. Air. Stamp Day.

1078	**183**	50fi. grey	10·00	10·00

184 Joseph Stalin

1949. Stalin's 70th Birthday.

1079	**184**	60fi. red	1·30	55
1080	**184**	1fo. blue	2·00	80
1081	**184**	2fo. brown	2·75	1·60

185 Miners

1950. Five Year Plan.

B1082	**185**	8fi. grey	1·30	15
1083B	-	10fi. purple	65	15
1084B	-	12fi. red	65	15
1085B	-	20fi. green	65	15
1086B	-	30fi. purple	80	15
1087B	-	40fi. brown	1·60	15
1088B	-	60fi. red	1·60	15
1089B	-	1fo. violet and yellow	2·00	15
1090B	-	1fo.70 green and yellow	3·25	15
1091B	-	2fo. red and orange	4·00	45
1092B	-	3fo. blue and buff	4·25	55
1093B	-	4fo. green and orange	4·75	65
1094B	-	5fo. purple and yellow	8·00	1·90
1095B	-	10fo. brown and yellow	10·00	4·75

DESIGNS: 10fi. Iron foundry; 12fi. Power station; 20fi. Textiles; 30fi. Factory workers' entertainment; 40fi. Mechanical farming; 60fi. Village co-operative office; 1fo. Class 303 steam locomotive on bridge; 1fo.70, Family at health resort; 2fo. Soldier and tank; 3fo. Freighter and Lisunov Li-2 airplane; 4fo. Cattle; 5fo. Draughtsman and factory; 10fo. Sportsman, woman and football match.

186 Philatelic Museum

1950. 20th Anniv of P.O. Philatelic Museum.

1099	**186**	60fi. brown and black (postage)	13·50	13·50
1100	-	2fo. red and yellow (air)	16·00	16·00

DESIGN—HORIZ: 2fo. Globe, coach, Douglas DC-4 airliner and stamps.

188 Family Greeting Soviet Troops

1950. 5th Anniv of Liberation.

1101	**188**	40fi. black	2·00	1·30
1102	**188**	60fi. lake	1·30	25
1103	**188**	1fo. blue	1·30	65
1104	**188**	2fo. brown	2·00	95

189 Chess Match

1950. 1st International Candidates Chess Tournament, Budapest. Designs incorporate rook and chessboard.

1105	**189**	60fi. mauve (postage)	3·25	95
1106	-	1fo. blue	6·75	2·00
1107	-	1fo.60 brown (air)	10·00	3·50

DESIGNS: 1fo. Trade Union Building; 1fo.60, Map.

190 Workers and Star

1950. May Day. Inscr as in T 190.

1108	**190**	40fi. brown	3·50	1·30
1109	-	60fi. red	1·60	25
1110	**190**	1fo. blue	3·00	95

DESIGN: 60fi. Two workers.

191 Workers and Flag

1950. World Federation of Trade Unions Congress, Budapest.

1111	-	40fi. green (postage)	3·50	1·30
1112	**191**	60fi. red	1·60	35
1113	-	1fo. brown (air)	3·00	95

DESIGNS: 40fi. Statue, dove and globes; 1fo. Globes, Chain Bridge and Parliament Buildings.

192 Baby and Nursery

1950. Children's Day.

1114	**192**	20fi. brown and grey	2·75	2·30
1115	-	30fi. mauve and brown	1·10	40
1116	-	40fi. green and blue	1·10	40
1117	-	60fi. red and brown	£1600	£1600
1117a	-	60fi. red and brown	1·10	40
1118	-	1fo.70 blue and green	2·30	1·30

DESIGNS: 30fi. Baby boy and holiday scene; 40fi. Schoolgirl and classroom; 60fi. Pioneer boy and camp; 1fo.70, Pioneer boy and girl and model glider class.

No. 1117 is inscr "UTANPOTLASUNK A JOVO HARCAIHOZ" and No. 1117a is inscr "SZABAD HAZABAN BOLDOG IFJUSAG".

193 Workers and Globe

1950. 1st Congress of Young Workers, Budapest.

1119	**193**	20fi. green	1·60	80
1120	-	30fi. orange	40	25
1121	-	40fi. brown	40	25
1122	-	60fi. mauve	1·10	40
1123	-	1fo.70 green	3·00	95

DESIGNS—HORIZ: 30fi. Foundry worker and cauldron. VERT: 40fi. Man, woman and banner; 60fi. Workers, banner and Liberty Statue; 1fo.70, Three workers and banner.

194 Peonies

1950. Flowers.

1124	**194**	30fi. purple and green	1·90	65
1125	-	40fi. green, yellow & mve	1·90	75
1126	-	60fi. brown, yellow & grn	3·25	1·00
1127	-	1fo. violet, red and green	6·25	4·50
1128	-	1fo.70 violet, grn & lilac	6·00	2·75

DESIGNS: 40fi. Pasque flowers; 60fi. Yellow pheasant's-eye; 1fo. Geranium; 1fo.70, Campanulas.

195 Miner

1950. 2nd National Inventions Exhibition.

1129	**195**	40fi. brown	2·50	75
1130	-	60fi. red	2·10	65
1131	-	1fo. blue	3·25	1·40

DESIGNS: 60fi. Turner; 1fo. Building factory.

196 Liberty Statue

1950. Air.

1132	**196**	20fi. red	25	15
1133	-	30fi. violet	25	15
1134	-	70fi. purple	65	15
1135	-	1fo. brown	65	15
1136	-	1fo.60 blue	1·30	15
1137	-	2fo. red	1·50	15
1138	-	3fo. black	1·90	15
1139	-	5fo. blue	3·25	90
1140	-	10fo. brown	9·50	1·50
1140a	-	20fo. green	19·00	8·25

DESIGNS—VERT: 30fi. Crane and buildings; 70fi. Diosgyor steelworks; 1fo. "Stalinyec" tractor; 1fo.60, "Szeged" (freighter); 2fo. Combine harvester; 3fo. Class 303 steam locomotive; 5fo. Matyas Rakosi steel-mill; 10, 20fo. Lisunov Li-2 airplane at Budaors airport.

For No. 1139 but on silver paper see No. 1437.

198 Worker signing Peace Petition

1950. Peace Propaganda.

1141	**198**	40fi. brown and blue	16·00	16·00
1142	-	60fi. green and orange	3·75	3·75
1143	-	1fo. brown and green	16·00	16·00

DESIGNS—VERT: 60fi. Girl holding dove. HORIZ: 1fo. Soldier, mother and children.

199 Swimmers

1950

1144	**199**	10fi. blue and light blue (postage)	15	15
1145	-	20fi. brown and orange	15	15
1146	-	1fo. green and olive	1·30	90
1147	-	1fo.70 red and vermilion	1·90	1·50
1148	-	2fo. violet and brown	3·75	2·10
1149	-	30fi. mauve & violet (air)	65	25
1150	-	40fi. blue and green	1·30	25
1151	-	60fi. orange, brown & grn	1·90	65
1152	-	70fi. brown and grey	2·50	90
1153	-	3fo. chestnut and brown	5·75	2·10

DESIGNS—POSTAGE: 20fi. Vaulting; 1fo. Mountaineering; 1fo.70, Basketball; 2fo. Motor cycling. AIR: 30fi. Volleyball; 40fi. Throwing the javelin; 60fi. Emblem of "Ready for work and action" movement; 70fi. Football; 3fo. Gliding.

200 Jozef Bem and Battle of Piski

1950. Death Centenary of Gen. Bem.

1154	**200**	40fi. brown	1·50	65
1155	**200**	60fi. red	1·50	65
1156	**200**	1fo. blue	3·25	90
MS1156a 98×78 mm. **200** 2fo. (+2fo.) purple. Imperf			65·00	65·00

201 Workers and Soldier

1951. 2nd Hungarian Communist Party Congress.

1157	**201**	10fi. green	65	25
1158	-	30fi. brown	90	65
1159	-	60fi. red	1·30	90

1160	-	1fo. blue	2·10	1·30

DESIGNS—HORIZ: 30fi. Workers, soldier and banner; 60fi. Portrait and four workers with flags. VERT: 1fo. Procession with banner.

202 Flags

1951. Hungarian–Soviet Amity. Inscr "MAGYAR SZOVJET BARATSAG HONAPJA 1951".

1161	**202**	60fi. red	65	25
1162	-	1fo. violet	1·30	65

DESIGN: 1fo. Hungarian and Russian workers.

203 Mare and Foal

1951. Livestock Expansion Plan.

1163	**203**	10fi. brown and ochre (postage)	40	25
1164	-	30fi. brown and red	65	65
1165	-	40fi. brown and green	90	65
1166	-	60fi. brown and orange	1·30	90
1167	**203**	20fi. brown & green (air)	50	40
1168	-	70fi. ochre and brown	1·30	1·00
1169	-	1fo. brown and blue	5·00	2·10
1170	-	1fo.60 chestnut & brown	8·75	3·25

DESIGNS: 30, 70fi. Sow and litter; 40fi., 1fo. Ewe and lamb; 60fi., 1fo.60, Cow and calf.

204 Worker

1951. May Day. Inscr "1951 MAJUS".

1171	**204**	40fi. brown	1·40	1·30
1172	-	60fi. red	1·30	25
1173	-	1fo. blue	1·30	90

DESIGNS—VERT: 60fi. People with banners. HORIZ: 1fo. Labour Day rally.

205 Leo Frankel

206 Street-fighting

1951. 80th Anniv of Paris Commune.

1174	**205**	60fi. brown	1·30	25
1175	**206**	1fo. blue and red	1·90	65

207 Children's Heads

1951. Int Children's Day. Inscr "NEMZETKOZI GYERMEKNAP 1951".

1176	**207**	30fi. brown	65	25
1177	-	40fi. green	90	25
1178	-	50fi. brown	90	65
1179	-	60fi. mauve	1·30	65
1180	-	1fo.70 blue	1·90	1·90

DESIGNS: 40fi. Flying model airplane; 50fi. Diesel train on Budapest Pioneer Railway; 60fi. Chemistry experiment; 1fo.70, Blowing bugle.

208 Ganz Wagon Works

1951. Rebuilding Plan (1st series).

1180a		8fi. green	90	15
1180b		10fi. violet	90	15
1180c		12fi. red	90	15
1181	**208**	20fi. green	90	25
1182	-	30fi. orange	1·10	25
1183	-	40fi. brown	1·10	25
1183a	-	50fi. blue	1·30	25
1184	-	60fi. red	1·50	25
1184a	-	70fi. brown	1·90	25
1184b	-	80fi. purple	1·90	25
1185	-	1fo. blue	2·50	25
1185a	-	1fo.20 red	3·25	25
1185b	-	1fo.70 blue	2·10	25
1185c	-	2fo. green	2·10	25
1186	-	3fo. purple	3·75	25
1186a	-	4fo. olive	4·00	40
1186b	-	5fo. black	6·25	40

BUILDINGS: 8fi. Stalin School; 10fi. Szekesfehervar railway station; 12fi. Ujpest medical dispensary; 30fi. Flats; 40fi. Central Railway Station, Budapest; 50fi. Inota power station; 60fi. Matyas Rakosi Cultural Institute; 70fi. Hajdunanas grain elevator; 80fi. Tiszalok dam; 1fo. Kilian Road School; 1fo.20, Mining Apprentices Institute, Ajkacsingervolgy; 1fo.70, Iron and Steel Apprentices Institute, Csepel; 2fo. Cultural Centre, Hungarian Optical Works; 3fo. Building Workers' Union Headquarters; 4fo. Miners' Union Headquarters; 5fo. Flats.

See also Nos. 1296/1304.

209 Gorky

1951. 15th Death Anniv of Maksim Gorky (Russian writer).

1187	**209**	60fi. red	40	25
1188	**209**	1fo. blue	75	40
1189	**209**	2fo. purple	2·50	1·30

210 Engineers and Tractors

1951. 1st Anniv of Five Year Plan.

1190	**210**	20fi. sepia (postage)	25	25
1191	-	30fi. blue	40	30
1192	-	40fi. red	90	40
1193	-	60fi. brown	1·00	40
1194	-	70fi. brown (air)	1·40	65
1195	-	1fo. green	1·50	90
1196	-	2fo. purple	2·10	1·30

DESIGNS: 30fi. Doctor X-raying patient; 40fi. Workman instructing apprentices; 60fi. Girl driving tractor; 70fi. Electrical engineers constructing pylon; 1fo. Young people and recreation home; 2fo. Lisunov Li-2 airplane over Stalin (later Arpad) Bridge.

211 1871 Stamp without portrait and Hungarian Arms

1951. 80th Anniv of 1st Hungarian Postage Stamp.

1197	**211**	60fi. green	3·75	3·75
1198	**211**	1fo.+1fo. red	19·00	19·00
1199	**211**	2fo.+2fo. blue	21·00	21·00

MS1199a Air. Three sheets each 78×97 mm. Nos. 1197/9 Set of 3 sheets £275 £275

212 Soldiers Parading

1951. Army Day.

1200	**212**	1fo. brown (postage)	2·10	40
1201	-	60fi. blue (air)	1·30	40

DESIGN—VERT: 60fi. Tanks and Liberty Statue.

213 Lily of the Valley

1951. Flowers.

1202		30fi. violet, blue and green	65	25
1203	**213**	40fi. myrtle and green	2·10	1·00
1204	-	60fi. red, pink and green	1·50	65
1205	-	1fo. blue, red and green	2·50	1·30
1206	-	1fo.70 brown, yell & grn	5·75	3·75

FLOWERS: 30fi. Cornflowers; 60fi. Tulips; 1fo. Poppies; 1fo.70, Cowslips.

214 Revolutionaries and Flags

1951. 34th Anniv of Russian Revolution.

1207	**214**	40fi. green	1·50	90
1208	-	60fi. blue	1·30	65
1209	-	1fo. red	1·50	90

DESIGNS: 60fi. Lenin addressing revolutionaries; 1fo. Lenin and Stalin.

215 Parade before Stalin Statue

1951. Stalin's 72nd Birthday.

1210	**215**	60fi. red	2·30	1·00
1211	**215**	1fo. blue	2·30	1·00

216 Bolshoi State Theatre, Moscow

1952. Views of Moscow.

1212	**216**	60fi. lake and green	75	25
1213	-	1fo. brown and red	1·10	50
1214	-	1fo.60 olive and lake	1·90	1·00

DESIGNS: 1fo. Lenin Mausoleum; 1fo.60, Kremlin.

217 Rakosi and Peasants

218 Rakosi

1952. 60th Birth Anniv of Rakosi.

1215	**217**	60fi. purple	1·30	65
1216	**218**	1fo. brown	1·30	65
1217	-	2fo. blue	3·25	1·30

DESIGN: 2fo. Rakosi and foundry workers.

219 L. Kossuth

1952. Heroes of 1848 Revolution.

1218	**219**	20fi. green	25	25
1219	-	30fi. purple (Petofi)	40	25
1220	-	50fi. black (Bem)	75	40
1221	-	60fi. lake (Tancsics)	90	40
1222	-	1fo. blue (Damjanich)	1·00	65
1223	-	1fo.50 brown (Nagy)	1·30	1·30

220 Pied Avocet

1952. Air. Birds.

1224	**220**	20fi. black and green	25	15
1225	-	30fi. black and green	25	15
1226	-	40fi. black, yellow & brn	40	25
1227	-	50fi. black and orange	50	25
1228	-	60fi. black and red	75	40
1229	-	70fi. black, orange & red	90	50
1230	-	80fi. black, yellow & grn	1·30	65
1231	-	1fo. black, red and blue	1·50	75
1232	-	1fo.40 multicoloured	1·90	90
1233	-	1fo.60 black, grn & brn	2·10	1·10
1234	-	2fo.50 black and purple	4·50	1·90

DESIGNS: 30fi. White stork; 40fi. Golden oriole; 50fi. Kentish plover; 60fi. Black-winged stilt; 70fi. Lesser grey strike; 80fi. Great bustard; 1fo. Western red-footed falcon; 1fo.40, European bee eater; 1fo.60, Glossy ibis; 2fo.50, Great egret.

1952. Budapest Philatelic Exn. No. 1050 with bars obliterating inscription and premium.

1235	**173**	60fi. mauve	75·00	75·00

222 Drummer and Flags

1952. May Day. Inscr "1952 MAJUS I".

1236	**222**	40fi. red and green	2·50	1·00
1237	-	60fi. red and brown	1·90	1·00
1238	-	1fo. red and brown	1·90	1·00

DESIGNS: 60fi. Workers; 1fo. Workman and globe.

223 Running

1952. 15th Olympic Games, Helsinki.

1239	**223**	30fi. brown (postage)	1·00	25
1240	-	40fi. green	1·00	25
1241	-	60fi. red	1·50	25
1242	-	1fo. blue	2·50	50
1243	-	1fo.70 orange (air)	3·25	1·90
1244	-	2fo. brown	3·75	2·00

DESIGNS: 40fi. Swimming; 60fi. Fencing; 1fo. Gymnastics; 1fo.70, Throwing the hammer; 2fo. Stadium.

224 Leonardo da Vinci

1952. Air. 500th Birth Anniv of Leonardo da Vinci and 150th Birth Anniv of Victor Hugo.

1245	**224**	1fo.60 blue	1·50	90
1246	-	2fo. purple (Victor Hugo)	2·50	1·50

225 Train and Railwayman

1952. Railway Day. Inscr "1952 VIII 10".

1247	**225**	60fi. brown	1·50	65
1248	-	1fo. green	2·10	65

DESIGN: 1fo. Railway tracks.

226 Mechanical Coal-cutter

1952. Miners' Day. Inscr as in T 226.

1249	**226**	60fi. brown	1·50	40
1250	-	1fo. green	2·10	65

DESIGN: 1fo. Miners operating machinery.

227 L. Kossuth

1952. 150th Birth Anniv of Kossuth (statesman).

1251	**227**	40fi. olive on pink	1·50	40
1252	-	60fi. black on blue	65	40
1253	**227**	1fo. lilac on yellow	1·50	90

DESIGN: 60fi. Statue of Kossuth.

228 Gy Dozsa

1952. Army Day. Inscr as T 228.

1254	20fi. lilac (J. Hunyadi)	40	15
1255	30fi. green (T **228**)	40	15
1256	40fi. blue (M. Zrinyi)	40	15
1257	60fi. purple (I. Zrinyi)	75	65
1258	1fo. turquoise (B. Vak)	1·30	65
1259	1fo.50 brown (A. Stromfeld)	2·50	90

229 Boy, Girl and Stamp Exhibition

1952. Air. Stamp Day. Inscr "XXV. BELYEGNAP 1952".

1260	-	1fo.+1fo. blue	12·50	12·50
1261	**229**	2fo.+2fo. red	12·50	12·50

DESIGN: 1fo. Children examining stamps.

230 Lenin and Revolutionary Council

1952. 35th Anniv of Russian Revolution.

1262	**230**	40fi. olive and purple	2·50	65
1263	-	60fi. olive and black	1·30	25
1264	-	1fo. olive and red	2·50	65

DESIGNS: 60fi. Stalin and Cossacks; 1fo. Marx, Engels, Lenin, Stalin and Spassky Tower.

231 Harvester

1952. 3rd Hungarian Peace Congress. Inscr as in T 231.

1265	**231**	60fi. red on yellow	1·30	25
1266	-	1fo. brown on green	1·30	65

DESIGN—HORIZ: 1fo. Workers' discussion group.

232 Tunnel Construction

1953. Budapest Underground Railway. Inscr "BUDAPESTI FOLDALATTI GYORSVASUT".

1267	**232**	60fi. green	1·90	65
1268	-	1fo. lake	1·90	90

DESIGN—HORIZ: 1fo. Underground map and station.

233 Russian Flag and Tank

1953. 10th Anniv of Battle of Stalingrad.

1269	**233**	40fi. red	1·90	25
1270	-	60fi. brown	1·90	90

DESIGN: 60fi. Soldier, map and flags.

234 Eurasian Red Squirrel

1953. Air. Forest Animals.

1271	**234**	20fi. brown and olive	40	25
1272	-	30fi. sepia and brown	50	40
1273	-	40fi. sepia and green	55	50
1274	-	50fi. sepia and brown	75	65
1275	-	60fi. brown and turquoise	1·00	75
1276	-	70fi. brown and olive	1·10	90
1277	-	80fi. brown and green	1·50	1·30
1278	-	1fo. brown and green	2·00	1·50
1279	-	1fo.50 black and bistre	4·25	2·10
1280	-	2fo. sepia and brown	4·50	2·50

DESIGNS—HORIZ: 30fi. West European hedgehog; 40fi. Brown hare; 60fi. European otter; 70fi. Red fox; 1fo. Roe deer; 1fo.50, Wild boar. VERT: 50fi. Beech marten; 80fi. Fallow deer; 2fo. Red deer.

235 Stalin

1953. Death of Stalin.

1281	**235**	60fi. black	65	40
MS1281a		51×72 mm. 2fo. purple (T **235**)	50·00	50·00

236 Rest Home, Galyateto

1953. Workers' Rest Homes.

1282	**236**	30fi. brown (postage)	25	15
1283	-	40fi. blue	35	15
1284	-	50fi. ochre	40	25
1285	-	60fi. green	50	25
1286	-	70fi. red	65	40
1287	-	1fo. turquoise (air)	90	50
1288	-	1fo.50 purple	1·30	65

DESIGNS: 40fi. Terrace, Mecsek; 50fi. Parad Spa; 60fi. Sports field, Kekes; 70fi. Balaton-fured Spa; 1fo. Children paddling at Balaton; 1fo.50, Lillafured Rest Home.

237 Young People and Banners

1953. May Day.

1289	**237**	60fi. brown & red on yell	1·30	40

238 Karl Marx

1953. 70th Death Anniv of Karl Marx.

1290	**238**	1fo. black on pink	1·30	40

See also No. 2354.

239 Peasants and Flag

1953. 250th Anniv of Rakoczi Rebellion.

1291	**239**	20fi. orange & grn on grn	1·30	90
1292	-	30fi. orange and purple	1·50	1·30
1293	-	40fi. orange & blue on pk	1·90	1·50
1294	-	60fi. orange & grn on yell	3·25	2·50
1295	-	1fo. red & brown on yell	4·50	3·25

DESIGNS: 30fi. Drummer and insurgents; 40fi. Battle scene; 60fi. Cavalryman attacking soldier; 1fo. Ferenc Rakoczi II.

1953. Rebuilding Plan (2nd series). As T 208.

1296	8fi. green	40	15
1297	10fi. lilac	65	15
1298	12fi. red	1·30	15
1299a	20fi. green	2·50	25
1300	30fi. orange	1·30	15
1301	40fi. brown	1·90	15
1302	50fi. blue	1·90	15
1303a	60fi. red	5·00	25
1304	70fi. brown	2·50	25

BUILDINGS: 8fi. Day nursery, Ozd; 10fi. Nursing school, Szombathely; 12fi. Workers houses, Komlo; 20fi. Department store, Ujpest; 30fi. Factory, Maly; 40fi. General Hospital, Fovaros; 50fi. Gymnasium, Sztalinvaros; 60fi. Post Office, Csepel; 70fi. Blast-furnace, Diosgyor.

240 Cycling

1953. Opening of People's Stadium. Budapest. Inscr "1953 NEPSTADION".

1313	**240**	20fi. brown and orange (postage)	15	15
1314	-	30fi. brown and green	15	15
1315	-	40fi. brown and blue	25	15
1316	-	50fi. brown and olive	30	15
1317	-	60fi. brown and yellow	40	15
1318	-	80fi. brown & turq (air)	65	25
1319	-	1fo. brown and purple	90	40
1320	-	2fo. brown and green	2·10	1·30
1321	-	3fo. brown and red	3·25	1·30
1322	-	5fo. turquoise and brown	5·00	3·25

DESIGNS: 30fi. Swimming; 40fi. Gymnastics; 50fi. Throwing the discus; 60fi. Wrestling; 80fi. Water polo; 1fo. Boxing; 2fo. Football; 3fo. Running; 5fo. Stadium.

241 Kazar

1953. Provincial Costumes.

1323	**241**	20fi. green	1·90	65
1324	-	30fi. brown	2·50	65
1325	-	40fi. blue	3·25	65
1326	-	60fi. red	4·50	2·50
1327	-	1fo. turquoise	5·00	2·50
1328	-	1fo.70 green	6·25	3·75
1329	-	2fo. red	10·00	5·00
1330	-	2fo.50 purple	12·50	10·00

PROVINCES: 30fi. Ersekcsanad; 40fi. Kalocsa; 60fi. Sioagard; 1fo. Sarkoz; 1fo.70, Boldog; 2fo. Orhalom; 2fo.50, Hosszuheteny.

242 Postwoman Delivering Letters

1953. Stamp Day.

1331	**242**	1fo.+1fo. turquoise	6·25	6·25
1332	**242**	2fo.+2fo. lilac	6·25	6·25

1953. Air. Hungarian Football Team's Victory at Wembley. No. 1320 optd LONDON-WEMBLEY 1953. XI 25. 6:3.

1333	2fo. brown and green	35·00	31·00

244 Bihari

1953. Air. Hungarian Composers.

1334	**244**	30fi. grey and brown	40	25
1335	-	40fi. orange and brown (Erkel)	50	30
1336	-	60fi. green & brn (Liszt)	65	40
1337	-	70fi. red and brown (Mosonyi)	75	50
1338	-	80fi. blue and brown (Goldmark)	90	65
1339	-	1fo. bistre and brown (Bartok)	1·30	1·00
1340	-	2fo. lilac and brown (Kodaly)	2·10	1·90

245 Lenin

1954. 30th Death Anniv of Lenin.

1341	**245**	40fi. green	1·90	1·30
1342	-	60fi. brown	2·50	65
1343	-	1fo. lake	3·75	1·90

DESIGNS: 60fi. Lenin addressing meeting; 1fo. Profile portrait of Lenin.

246 Turnip Beetle

1954. Air. Insects.

1344	**246**	30fi. brown and orange	55	40
1345	-	40fi. brown and green	65	50
1346	-	50fi. black and red	90	70

1347	-	60fi. brown, yell & lilac	1·00	75
1348	-	80fi. claret, purple & grn	1·40	1·10
1349	-	1fo. black and brown	1·60	1·30
1350	-	1fo.20 brown and green	1·90	1·50
1351	-	1fo.50 dp brown & brn	2·50	1·90
1352	-	2fo. brown and chestnut	3·25	2·50
1353	-	3fo. brown and green	4·75	3·25

INSECTS—HORIZ: 40fi. Crawling cockchafer; 50fi. Long-horn beetle; 60fi. Hornet; 1fo.20, European field cricket; 1fo.50, European rhinoceros beetle; 2fo. Stag beetle. VERT: 80fi. Apple beetle; 1fo. Corn beetle; 3fo. Great silver water beetle.

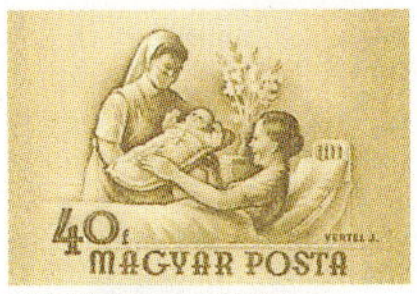

247 Mother and Baby

1954. Child Welfare.

1354		30fi. blue (postage)	40	20
1355	**247**	40fi. bistre	65	25
1356	-	60fi. lilac	90	40
1357	-	1fo. green (air)	1·50	65
1358	-	1fo.50 red	2·10	75
1359	-	2fo. turquoise	3·75	1·90

DESIGNS: 30fi. Woman having blood-test; 60fi. Doctor examining child; 1fo. Children in creche; 1fo.50, Doctor, mother and child; 2fo. Children in nursery school.

248 Worker and Flag

1954. 35th Anniv of Proclamation of Hungarian Soviet Republic.

1360		40fi. blue and red	2·50	2·30
1361	**248**	60fi. brown and red	6·25	3·75
1362	-	1fo. black and red	8·75	5·00

DESIGNS—HORIZ: 40fi. Worker reading book; 1fo. Soldier with rifle.

249 Maypole

1954. May Day. Inscr "1954-MAJUS I".

1363	**249**	40fi. olive	65	15
1364	-	60fi. red	65	25

DESIGN: 60fi. Worker and flag.

250 Agricultural Worker

1954. 3rd Hungarian Communist Party Congress, Budapest.

1365	**250**	60fi. red on yellow	1·00	50

251 Boy building Model Glider

1954. Air.

1366	**251**	40fi. grey and brown	40	20
1367	-	50fi. brown and grey	45	25
1368	-	60fi. grey and brown	50	30
1369	-	80fi. brown and violet	55	40
1370	-	1fo. grey and brown	65	50
1371	-	1fo.20 brown and green	90	65
1372	-	1fo.50 grey and purple	2·50	90
1373	-	2fo. brown and blue	3·25	2·10

DESIGNS—As Type **251**: 60fi. Gliders; 1fo. Parachutists; 1fo.50, Lisunov Li-2 airplane. 43×43 mm; 50fi. Boy flying model airplane; 80fi. Libis KB-6T Matajur aircraft and hangar; 1fo.20, Letov C-4 biplane; 2fo. Mikoyan Gurevich MiG-15 jet fighters.

252 Hungarian National Museum

1954. 5th Anniv of Constitution.

1374	**252**	40fi. blue	2·10	1·30
1375	-	60fi. brown	1·90	75
1376	-	1fo. brown	2·10	1·00

DESIGNS: 60fi. Hungarian Coat of Arms; 1fo. Dome of Parliament Buildings, Budapest.

253 Paprika

1954. Fruits. Multicoloured.

1377	40fi. Type **253**	95	35
1378	50fi. Tomatoes	95	35
1379	60fi. Grapes	95	35
1380	80fi. Apricots	1·10	50
1381	1fo. Apples	1·40	60
1382	1fo.20 Plums	2·10	1·20
1383	1fo.50 Cherries	4·25	2·40
1384	2fo. Peaches	6·00	3·00

254 M. Jokai

1954. 50th Death Anniv of Jokai (novelist).

1385	**254**	60fi. green	1·30	65
1386	**254**	1fo. purple	2·50	1·90

255 C. J. Apacai

1954. Hungarian Scientists.

1387	**255**	8fi. black on yellow	15	15
1388	-	10fi. lake on pink	15	15
1389	-	12fi. black on blue	15	15
1390	-	20fi. brown on yellow	15	15
1391	-	30fi. blue on pink	25	15
1392	-	40fi. green on yellow	30	15
1393	-	50fi. brown on green	40	20
1394	-	60fi. blue on pink	50	25
1395	-	1fo. olive	80	25
1396	-	1fo.70 red on yellow	1·30	40
1397	-	2fo. turquoise	2·20	65

PORTRAITS: 10fi. S. Korosi Csoma; 12fi. A. Jedlik; 20fi. I. Semmelweis; 30fi. J. Irinyi; 40fi. F. Koranyi; 50fi. A. Vambery; 60fi. K. Than; 1fo. O. Herman; 1fo.70, T. Puskas; 2fo. E. Hogyes.

256 Speed Skaters

1955. Air. Winter Sports.

1398		40fi. brown, blue & black	1·00	40
1399		50fi. red, green and brown	1·00	40
1400		60fi. red, blue and brown	1·30	65
1401		80fi. green, brown & blk	1·60	65
1402		1fo. red, blue and brown	2·50	1·30
1403	**256**	1fo.20 red, green & blk	2·50	1·90
1404	-	1fo.50 red, green & brn	3·75	2·30
1405	-	2fo. red, green and brown	4·00	2·50

DESIGNS—VERT: 40fi. Boys on toboggan; 60fi. Ice-yacht; 1fo. Ski jumper; 1fo.50, Skier turning. HORIZ: 50fi. Cross-country skier; 80fi. Ice-hockey players; 2fo. Figure skaters.

257 Blast Furnace

1955. 10th Anniv of Liberation.

1406		40fi. brown and red	80	40
1407	**257**	60fi. red and green	90	50
1408	-	1fo. green and brown	1·60	1·00
1409	-	2fo. brown and green	2·20	1·50

DESIGNS—VERT: 40fi. Reading room; 2fo. Liberty statue. HORIZ: 1fo. Combine harvester.

258 "1st May"

1955. May Day.

1410	**258**	1fo. red	80	40

259 State Printing Works

1955. Cent of Hungarian State Printing Office.

1411	**259**	60fi. brown and green	65	40
MS1411a 97×77 mm. Air. T **259** 5fo. red and green			50·00	50·00

260 Young Workers and Flag

1955. 2nd Congress of Young Workers' Federation.

1412	**260**	1fo. brown	80	40

261 Postilion

1955. Opening of P.O. Museum.

1413	**261**	1fo. purple	80	40

262 Radio Mechanic

1955. Workers.

1414	-	8fi. brown	15	15
1415	-	10fi. turquoise	15	15
1416	-	12fi. orange	15	15
1417	**262**	20fi. olive	15	15
1418	-	30fi. red	15	15
1419	-	40fi. brown	15	15
1420	-	50fi. blue	15	15
1421	-	60fi. red	20	15
1422	-	70fi. olive	20	15
1423	-	80fi. purple	25	15
1424	-	1fo. blue	25	15
1425	-	1fo.20 bistre	60	15
1426	-	1fo.40 green	65	15
1427	-	1fo.70 lilac	85	15
1428	-	2fo. lake	90	15
1429	-	2fo.60 red	1·30	15
1430	-	3fo. green	1·60	15
1431	-	4fo. blue	5·25	15
1432	-	5fo. brown	3·25	15
1433	-	10fo. violet	5·75	15

DESIGNS: 8fi. Market gardener; 10fi. Fisherman; 12fi. Bricklayer; 30fi. Potter; 40fi. Railway guard; 50fi. Shop assistant; 60fi. Post Office worker; 70fi. Herdsman; 80fi. Mill-girl; 1fo. Boat-builder; 1fo.20, Carpenter; 1fo.40, Tram conductor; 1fo.70, Swineherd; 2fo. Welder; 2fo.60, Tractor-driver; 3fo. Horse and groom; 4fo. Bus driver; 5fo. Telegraph lineman; 10fo. Miner.

263 M. Csokonai Vitez

1955. Hungarian Poets.

1434	**263**	60fi. black	1·30	25
1435	-	1fo. blue	1·30	65
1436	-	2fo. red	1·30	90

PORTRAITS: 1fo. M. Vorosmarty; 2fo. A. Jozsef.

1955. Air. Light Metal Industries Int Congress, Budapest. As No. 1139.

1437	5fo. blue on silver	28·00	28·00

264 Bela Bartok

1955. 10th Death Anniv of Bartok (composer).

1438	**264**	60fi. brown (postage)	1·30	25
1439	**264**	1fo. green (air)	3·25	2·75
1440	**264**	1fo. brown	5·75	3·75

265 "Hargita" Diesel Multiple Unit

1955. Transport.

1441	**265**	40fi. brown and green	40	15
1442	-	60fi. bistre and green	50	25
1443	-	80fi. brown and green	65	40
1444	-	1fo. green and brown	90	65
1445	-	1fo.20 black and brown	1·30	90
1446	-	1fo.50 brown and black	1·60	1·00
1447	-	2fo. brown and green	2·20	1·30

DESIGNS: 60fi. Motor coach; 80fi. Motor cyclist; 1fo. Lorry; 1fo.20, Class 303 steam locomotive; 1fo.50, Tipper; 2fo. "Beke" (freighter).

266 Puli Sheepdog

1956. Hungarian Dogs.

1448	**266**	40fi. black, red and yellow	40	15
1449	-	50fi. black, buff and blue	50	20
1450	-	60fi. black, red and green	65	25
1451	-	80fi. black, orge & grey	80	40
1452	-	1fo. black, orange & turq	90	50
1453	-	1fo.20 black, brn & orge	1·30	65
1454	-	1fo.50 black, buff & bl	1·90	90

1455	-	2fo. black, brown & mve	3·25	1·50

DESIGNS—RECTANGULAR (36×26 mm): 50fi. Puli and cattle; 1fo.50, Kuvasz sheepdog and cottage. (27×35 mm): 80fi. Hungarian retriever. (27×38 mm): 1fo. Hungarian retriever carrying mallard. As Type **266**: 60fi. Pumi; 1fo.20, Kuvasz sheepdog; 2fo. Komondor sheepdog.

268 Pioneers' Badge

1956. 10th Anniv of Pioneers Movement.

1456	**268**	1fo. red	65	25
1457	**268**	1fo. grey	65	25

269 Hunyadi on Horseback

1956. 500th Death Anniv of Janos Hunyadi.

1458	**269**	1fo. brown on yellow	90	90

270 Miner

1956. Miners' Day.

1459	**270**	1fo. blue	80	40

271 Horse-jumping

1956. Olympic Games. Inscr "1956". Centres in brown.

1460	-	20fi. blue (Canoeing)	20	20
1461	**271**	30fi. olive	25	20
1462	-	40fi. brown (Fencing)	35	20
1463	-	60fi. turquoise (Hurdling)	40	20
1464	-	1fo. red (Football)	50	25
1465	-	1fo.50 violet (Weightlifting)	80	40
1466	-	2fo. green (Gymnastics)	1·30	75
1467	-	3fo. mauve (Basketball)	2·50	1·30

272 Chopin

1956. Hungarian–Polish Philatelic Exn, Budapest.

1468		1fo. blue (Liszt)	3·25	3·25
1469	**272**	1fo. mauve	3·25	3·25

1957. Hungarian Red Cross Fund. Nos. 1417 etc., surch with shield, cross and premium.

1470	**262**	20fi.+20fi. olive	25	25
1471	-	30fi.+30fi. red	65	40
1472	-	40fi.+40fi. brown	80	65
1473	-	60fi.+60fi. red	90	75
1474	-	1fo.+1fo. blue	1·90	1·60
1475	-	2fo.+2fo. lake	3·25	2·10

274 Dr. L. Zamenhof

1957. Air. 70th Anniv of Esperanto.

1476		60fi. brown	80	40
1477	**274**	1fo. green	1·00	50

DESIGN—HORIZ: 60fi. Esperanto Star.

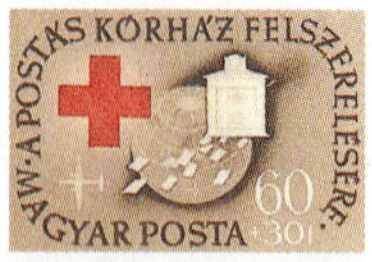

275 Letters, Letter-box and Globe

1957. Air. Hungarian Red Cross Fund. Cross in red.

1478	**275**	60fi.+30fi. brown	50	35
1479	-	1fo.+50fi. lilac	65	40
1480	-	2fo.+1fo. red	1·90	50
1481	-	3fo.+1fo.50 blue	2·50	1·90
1482	-	5fo.+2fo.50 grey	4·50	3·25
1483	-	10fo.+5fo. green	7·75	5·00

DESIGNS: 1fo. Postal coach; 2fo. Top of telegraph pole; 3fo. Radio aerial mast; 5fo. Desk telephone; 10fo. (46×31 mm) Posthorn.

276 Janos Arany

1957. 75th Death Anniv of Janos Arany (poet).

1484	**276**	2fo. blue	1·00	40

277 Arms

1957. Inauguration of National Emblem.

1485	**277**	60fi. red	65	25
1486	**277**	1fo. green	1·30	40

278 Congress Emblem

1957. 4th W.F.T.U. Congress, Leipzig.

1487	**278**	1fo. red	65	40

279 Courier

1957. Air. Stamp Day.

1488	**279**	1fo.(+4fo.) brown and bistre on cream	1·30	1·30
1489	-	1fo.(+4fo.) brown and bistre on cream	1·30	1·30

DESIGN: No. 1489, Tupolev Tu-104A airplane over Budapest.

280 Dove of Peace and Flags

1957. 40th Anniv of Russian Revolution. Flags multicoloured.

1490	**280**	60fi. black and grey	40	15
1491	-	1fo. black and drab	80	40

DESIGN: 1fo. Lenin.

281 Komarom Tumbler Pigeons

1957. Int Pigeon-fanciers' Exn, Budapest.

1492	**281**	30fi. brown, yellow and green (postage)	15	15
1493	-	40fi. black and brown	15	15
1494	-	60fi. grey and blue	40	15
1495	-	1fo. brown and grey	80	15
1496	-	2fo. grey and mauve	1·40	75
1497	-	3fo. grn, grey & red (air)	1·60	90

DESIGNS: 40fi. Two short-beaked Budapest pigeons; 60fi. Giant domestic pigeon; 1fo. Three Szeged pigeons; 2fo. Two Hungarian fantail pigeons; 3fo. Two carrier pigeons.

IMPERFORATE STAMPS. Most modern Hungarian stamps issued up to the end of 1991 also exist imperforate.

282 Television Building

1958. Inaug of Hungarian Television Service.

1498	**282**	2fo. purple	1·90	75
MS1498a		49×70 mm. **282** 2fo. (+23fo.) green	60·00	60·00

283 Mother and Child

1958. Savings Campaign.

1499	**283**	20fi. deep green and green	25	15
1500	-	30fi. purple and green	40	15
1501	-	40fi. brown and bistre	80	15
1502	-	60fi. myrtle and red	90	15
1503	-	1fo. brown and green	1·60	15
1504	-	2fo. green and orange	2·20	1·50

DESIGNS: 30fi. Old man feeding pigeons; 40fi. Schoolboys with savings stamps; 60fi. "The Cricket and the Ant."; 1fo. Bees on honeycomb; 2fo. Hands holding banknotes.

284 Hungarian Pavilion

1958. Air. Brussels International Exhibition. Inscr "BRUXELLES 1958".

1505	**284**	20fi. brown and red	40	15
1506	-	40fi. sepia and blue	40	15
1507	-	60fi. sepia and red	40	15
1508	-	1fo. brown and ochre	65	15
1509	-	1fo.40 multicoloured	90	15
1510	-	2fo. sepia and brown	1·30	15
1511	-	3fo. sepia and green	2·20	90
1512	-	5fo. multicoloured	4·00	1·90
MS1512a		72×98 mm. 10fo. mauve	50·00	50·00

DESIGNS—HORIZ: 40fi. Map of Hungary and exhibits; 60fi. Parliament Buildings, Budapest; 1fo. Chain Bridge, Budapest; 1fo.40, Arms of Belgium and Hungary and Exhibition emblem; 5fo. Exhibition emblem. VERT: 2fo. "Mannekin Pis" statue, Brussels; 3fo. Town Hall, Brussels; 10fo. Girl in national costume as T **241**.

285 Arms of Hungary

1958. 1st Anniv of Amended Constitution. Arms multicoloured.

1513	**285**	60fi. red	25	15
1514	**285**	1fo. green	50	25
1515	**285**	2fo. drab	1·00	50

286 Youth with Book

1958. 5th Youth Festival, Keszthely.

1516	**286**	1fo. brown	1·00	1·00

287 Town Hall, Prague and Posthorn

1958. Organization of Socialist Countries' Postal Administrations Conference, Prague.

1517	**287**	60fi. green (postage)	80	40
1518	-	1fo. lake (air)	80	40

DESIGN: 1fo. Prague Castle, telegraph pole and wires.

288 "Linum dolomiticum"

1958. Flowers.

1519	**288**	20fi. yellow and purple	25	15
1520	-	30fi. brown and blue	40	15
1521	-	40fi. brown, buff & sepia	75	15
1522	-	60fi. mauve and green	90	15
1523	-	1fo. green and red	1·40	40
1524	-	2fo. yellow and green	2·75	50
1525	-	2fo.50 pink and blue	3·25	1·00
1526	-	3fo. pink, lt green & grn	4·00	1·40

FLOWERS—TRIANGULAR: 30fi. "Kitaibelia vitifolia"; 2fo.50, "Dianthus collinus"; 3fo. "Rosa sancti andreae". VERT: (20½×31 mm): 40fi. "Doronicum hungaricum"; 60fi. "Colchicum arenarium"; 1fo. "Helleborus purpuracens"; 2fo. "Hemerocallis lilio-asphodelus".

For miniature sheet containing stamps as T **288**, see No. **MS**1533a.

289 Table-tennis Bat and Ball

1958. European Table-tennis and Swimming Championships, and World Wrestling Championships, Budapest.

1527	**289**	20fi. red on pink	15	15
1528	-	30fi. olive on green	25	15
1529	-	40fi. purple on yellow	40	15
1530	-	60fi. brown on blue	65	25
1531	-	1fo. blue on blue	90	50
1532	-	2fo.50 red on yellow	1·90	1·10
1533	-	3fo. blue on turquoise	3·25	1·60

DESIGNS—VERT: 30fi. Table-tennis player; 40fi. Wrestlers; 1fo. Water-polo player; 2fo.50, High-diver. HORIZ: 60fi. Wrestlers; 3fo. Swimmer.

1958. International Philatelic Federation Congress, Brussels.

MS1533a		111×111 mm. Nos. 1519/20 and 1525/6 in new colours	50·00	50·00

290

1958. Air. (a) Int Correspondence Week.

1534	**290**	60fi. bistre and purple	65	25
1535	-	1fo. bistre and blue	90	65

(b) National Stamp Exhibition, Budapest.

1536		1fo.(+2fo.) bistre and red	1·40	1·40
1537	**290**	1fo.(+2fo.) bistre and green	1·40	1·40

DESIGNS: No. 1535, Posthorn, envelope and transport; No. 1536, Stamp and magnifier.

291 Airliner over Millennium Monument Budapest

1958. Air. 40th Anniv of 1st Hungarian Air Mail Stamp.

1538	**291**	3fo. purple, red and drab	1·30	65
1539	-	5fo. blue, red and drab	2·50	90

DESIGN: 5fo. Airliner over Sopron Tower.

For similar stamps but without commemorative inscription see Nos. 1542/51.

292 Red Flag

1958. 40th Anniv of Hungarian Communist Party and Founding of the "Red Journal".

1540	**292**	1fo. red and brown	65	25
1541	-	2fo. red and blue	90	65

DESIGN: 2fo. Hand holding up the newspaper "Voros Ujsag" (Red Journal).

1958. Air. As T 291 but with "LEGIPOSTA" at top in place of commem inscription. On cream paper.

1542		20fi. green and red	15	15
1543		30fi. violet and red	15	15
1544		70fi. purple and red	25	15
1545		1fo. blue and red	40	15
1546		1fo.60 purple and red	65	25
1547		2fo. green and red	75	25
1548		3fo. brn & red	90	40
1549	**291**	5fo. green and red	1·50	50
1550	-	10fo. blue and red	4·50	1·00
1551	-	20fo. sepia and red	9·50	2·50

DESIGNS: Airliner over: 20fi. Town Hall, Szeged; 30fi. Sarospatak Castle; 70fi. Town Hall, Gyor; 1fo. Opera House, Budapest; 1fo.60, Old City of Veszprem; 2fo. Chain Bridge, Budapest; 3fo. Sopron Tower; 10fo. Danube Embankment, Budapest; 20fo. Budapest Cathedral.

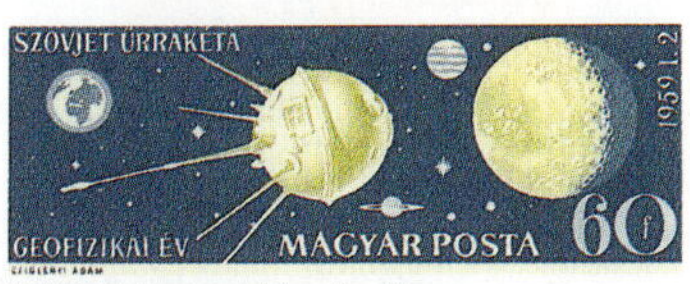
293 Rocket approaching the Moon

1959. I.G.Y. Achievements.

1552		10fi. brown and red	25	15
1553		20fi. black and blue	65	15
1554		30fi. buff and green	90	25
1555		40fi. light blue and blue	1·30	40
1556	**293**	60fi. green and blue	1·40	65
1557	-	1fo. brown and red	1·60	75
1558	-	5fo. brown & deep brown	3·75	1·30

DESIGNS—(31½×21 mm): 10fi. Eotvos torsion balance (gravimetry); 20fi. Ship using echo-sounder (oceanography); 30fi. "Northern Lights" and polar scene. (35½×26½ mm): 40fi. Russian polar camp and Antarctic route map; 1fo. Observatory and the sun; 5fo. Russian "Sputnik" and American "Vanguard" (artificial satellites).

See also No. 1605.

294 Revolutionary

1959. 40th Anniv of Proclamation of Hungarian Soviet Republic.

1559	**294**	20fi. red and purple	15	15
1560	**294**	60fi. red and blue	50	25
1561	**294**	1fo. red and brown	1·10	50

295 Rose

1959. May Day.

1562	**295**	60fi. red, green and lilac	65	25
1563	**295**	1fo. red, green and brown	90	40

296 Nagy Model of Locomotive "Deru", 1847

1959. Transport Museum issue.

1564	**296**	20fi. mult (postage)	15	15
1565	-	30fi. green, black and buff	25	15
1566	-	40fi. multicoloured	40	15
1567	-	60fi. multicoloured	50	15
1568	-	1fo. multicoloured	75	25
1569	-	2fo. multicoloured	1·30	25
1570	-	2fo.50 multicoloured (blue background)	1·50	35
1571	-	3fo. multicoloured (air)	3·75	2·30

DESIGNS—HORIZ: 30fi. Ganz diesel railcar; 60fi. Csonka motor car; 1fo. Ikarusz rear-engine motor coach; 2fo. First Lake Balaton steamer "Kisfaludy"; 2fo.50, Stagecoach; 3fo. Aladar Zselyi's monoplane. VERT: 40fi. Early railway semaphore signal.

See also No. 1572.

1959. Int Philatelic Federation Congress, Hamburg. As No. 1570 but colours changed.

1572	2fo.50 multicoloured (yellow background)	3·25	3·25

297 Posthorn

1959. Organization of Socialist Countries' Postal Administration Conference, Berlin.

1573	**297**	1fo. red	1·30	1·30

298 Great Cormorant

1959. Water Birds. Inscr "1959".

1574	**298**	10fi. black and green	25	15
1575	-	20fi. green and blue	40	15
1576	-	30fi. violet, myrtle & orge	65	25
1577	-	40fi. grey and green	75	65
1578	-	60fi. brown and purple	90	70
1579	-	1fo. black and turquoise	1·10	75
1580	-	2fo. black and red	2·10	90
1581	-	3fo. brown and bistre	3·25	1·90

DESIGNS: 20fi. Little egret; 30fi. Purple heron; 40fi. Great egret; 60fi. White spoonbill; 1fo. Grey heron; 2fo. Squacco heron; 3fo. Glossy ibis.

299 10th-century Man-at-Arms

1959. 24th World Fencing Championships, Budapest. Inscr as in T 299.

1582	**299**	10fi. black and blue	15	15
1583	-	20fi. black and lemon	15	15
1584	-	30fi. black and violet	25	15
1585	-	40fi. black and red	25	15
1586	-	60fi. black and purple	40	15
1587	-	1fo. black and turquoise	75	15
1588	-	1fo.40 black and orange	1·30	25
1589	-	3fo. black and green	2·50	90

DESIGNS (Evolution of Hungarian swordsmanship): 20fi. 15th-century man-at-arms; 30fi. 18th-century soldier; 40fi. 19th-century soldier; 60fi. 19th-century cavalryman. Fencer: at the assault (1fo.); on guard (1fo.40); saluting (3fo.).

300 Bathers at Lake Balaton

1959. Lake Balaton Summer Courses.

1590		30fi. bl on yell (postage)	15	15
1591		40fi. red on green	25	15
1592	**300**	60fi. brown on pink	40	15
1593	-	1fo.20 violet on pink	90	25
1594	-	2fo. red on yellow	1·50	50
1595	-	20fi. green (air)	15	15
1596	-	70fi. blue	40	15
1597	-	1fo. red and blue	65	25
1598	-	1fo.70 brown on yellow	1·30	90

DESIGNS—VERT: 20fi. Tihany (view); 30fi. "Kek Madar" (yacht); 70fi. "Tihany" (waterbus); 1fo. Waterlily and view of Heviz; 1fo.20, Anglers; 1fo.70, "Saturnus" (yacht) and statue of fisherman (Balaton pier); 2fo. Holiday-makers and "Beloiannis" (lake steamer). HORIZ: 40fi. Vintner with grapes.

301

1959. 150th Death Anniv of Haydn (composer).

1599	**301**	40fi. yellow and purple	65	25
1600	-	60fi. buff and slate	1·30	25
1601	-	1fo. orange and violet	1·90	40

MS1601a 94×76 mm. 3fo. purple; 3fo. green (each 27×35 mm) 19·00 19·00

DESIGNS—HORIZ: 60fi. Fertod Chateau. VERT: 1fo. Hayden; 3fo (purple) "J h" and music score; 3fo. Green "F SCH" and prose quotation.

No. **MS**1601a also commemorates Schiller's birth bicentenary.

1959. Birth Bicentenary of Schiller (poet). As T 301 but inscr "F. SCHILLER" etc.

1602	40fi. yellow and olive	65	25
1603	60fi. pink and blue	1·30	25
1604	1fo. yellow and purple	1·90	40

DESIGNS—VERT: 40fi. Stylized initials "F" and "Sch" and Schiller's birthplace; 1fo. Schiller. HORIZ: 60fi. Pegasus.

See also No. **MS**1601a.

1959. Landing of Russian Rocket on the Moon. As T 293 with addition of Russian Flag and "22 h 0234" on Moon in red.

1605	**293**	60fi. green and blue	90	40

302 Shepherd with Letter

1959. Stamp Day and National Stamp Exn.

1606	**302**	2fo. purple	3·25	3·25

303 "Taking Delivery"

1959. International Correspondence Week.

1607	**303**	60fi. multicoloured	90	40

304 Lenin and Szamuely

1959. Russian Stamp Exhibition, Budapest.

1608	**304**	20fi. brown and red	15	15
1609	-	40fi. lake & brown on bl	40	25
1610	-	60fi. buff and blue	65	50
1611	-	1fo. multicoloured	90	75

DESIGNS: 40fi. Pushkin; 60fi. Mayakovsky; 1fo. Arms with hands clasping flag.

305 Swallowtail

1959. Butterflies and Moths. Butterflies in natural colours, background colours given.

1612	**305**	20fi. black and green (postage)	65	25
1613	-	30fi. black and blue	65	25
1614	-	40fi. black and brown	90	40
1615	-	60fi. black and bistre	1·30	65
1616	-	1fo. black and green (air)	1·90	75
1617	-	2fo. black and lilac	4·00	1·50
1618	-	3fo. black and green	6·25	2·50

DESIGNS—HORIZ: 30fi. Hebe tiger moth; 40fi. Adonis blue; 2fo. Death's-head hawk moth. VERT: 60fi. Purple emperor; 1fo. Scarce copper; 3fo. Red emperor.

306

1959. 7th Socialist Workers' Party Congress. Flag in red and green.

1619	**306**	60fi. brown	25	15
1620	-	1fo. red	50	25

DESIGN: 1fo. Flag inscr "MSZMP VII. KONGRESSZUSA".

307 "Fairy Tales"

1959. Fairy Tales (1st series). Centres and inscr in black.

No.	Type	Description	Mint	Used
1621	307	20fi. multicoloured	25	15
1622	-	30fi. pink	40	15
1623	-	40fi. turquoise	65	20
1624	-	60fi. blue	90	25
1625	-	1fo. yellow	1·00	50
1626	-	2fo. green	1·30	65
1627	-	2fo.50 salmon	1·90	70
1628	-	3fo. red	1·90	75

FAIRY TALE SCENES: 30fi. "The Sleeping Beauty"; 40fi. "Mat the Goose"; 60fi. "The Cricket and the Ant"; 1fo. "Mashenka and the Bears"; 2fo. "The Babes in the Wood"; 2fo.50, "The Pied Piper of Hamelin"; 3fo. "Little Red Riding Hood".

See also Nos. 1702/9 and 2133/41.

308 Sumeg Castle

1960. Hungarian Castles. On white paper.

No.	Type	Description	Mint	Used
1629	308	8fi. purple	15	15
1630	-	10fi. brown	15	15
1631	-	12fi. blue	15	15
1632	-	20fi. green	15	15
1633	-	30fi. brown	15	15
1634	-	40fi. turquoise	15	15
1635	-	50fi. brown	15	15
1636	-	60fi. red	40	15
1637	-	70fi. green	40	15
1638	-	80fi. purple	25	15
1639	-	1fo. blue	40	15
1640	-	1fo.20 purple	50	15
1641	-	1fo.40 blue	50	15
1642	-	1fo.70 lilac ("SOMLO")	50	15
1642a	-	1fo.70 lilac ("SOMLYO")	90	25
1643	-	2fo. bistre	90	15
1644	-	2fo.60 blue	1·30	15
1645	-	3fo. brown	1·30	25
1646	-	4fo. violet	1·80	15
1647	-	5fo. green	2·10	50
1648	-	10fo. red	4·50	75

CASTLES—As Type **308**: 10fi. Kisvarda; 12fi. Szigliget; 20fi. Tata; 30fi. Diosgyor; 40fi. Simon Tornya; 50fi. Fuzer; 60fi. Sarospatak; 70fi. Nagyvazsony; 80fi. Egervar. 28½×21½ mm: 1fo. Vitany; 1fo.20, Sirok; 1fo.40, Siklos; 1fo.70, Somlyo; 2fo. Boldogko; 2fo.60, Holloko; 4fo. Eger. 21½×28½ mm: 3fo. Csesznek; 5fo. Koszeg; 10fo. Sarvar.

See also Nos. 1694/700.

309 Halas Lace

1960. Halas Lace (1st series). Designs showing lace as T 309. Inscriptions and values in orange.

No.	Type	Description	Mint	Used
1649	304	20fi. sepia	25	10
1650	-	30fi. violet	35	10
1651	-	40fi. turquoise	50	25
1652	-	60fi. brown	70	35
1653	-	1fo. green	1·30	60
1654	-	1fo.50 green	1·40	70
1655	-	2fo. blue	2·75	1·10
1656	-	3fo. red	4·75	1·40

Nos. 1650/1, 1654/5 are larger 38×44 mm.

See also Nos. 1971/8.

310 Cross-country Skiing

1960. Winter Olympic Games.

No.	Type	Description	Mint	Used
1657	310	30fi. bistre and blue	25	10
1658	-	40fi. bistre and green	25	10
1659	-	60fi. bistre and red	50	10
1660	-	80fi. bistre and violet	60	25
1661	-	1fo. bistre and turquoise	1·20	60
1662	-	1fo.20 bistre and lake	1·20	70
1663	-	2fo.+1fo. mult	3·50	85

DESIGNS: 40fi. Ice hockey; 60fi. Ski jumping; 80fi. Speed skating; 1fo. Skiing; 1fo.20, Figure skating; 2fo. Games emblem.

311 Kato Haman

1960. Celebrities and Anniversaries. Portrait as T 311.

No.	Type	Description	Mint	Used
1664		60fi. purple (T **311**)	35	10
1665		60fi. brown (Clara Zetkin)	35	10
1666		60fi. violet (Garibaldi)	35	10
1667		60fi. green (I. Turr)	35	10
1668		60fi. red (I. Tukory)	35	10
1669		60fi. deep blue and blue (O. Herman)	35	10
1670		60fi. brown (Beethoven)	35	10
1671		60fi. red (F. Mora)	35	10
1672		60fi. black and grey (B. I. Toth)	35	10
1673		60fi. purple and mauve (D. Banki)	35	10
1674		60fi. deep green and green (A. G. Pattantyus)	35	10
1675		60fi. blue and cobalt (I. P. Semmelweis)	35	10
1676		60fi. brown (Joliot-Curie)	35	10
1677		60fi. red (F. Erkel)	35	10
1678		60fi. blue and light blue (J. Bolyai)	35	10
1679		60fi. red (V. I. Lenin)	35	10

COMMEMORATIVE EVENTS: Nos. 1664/5, Int Women's Day: 1666, Centenary of Sicilian Expedition; 1669, 125th Birth Anniv; 1670, Martonvasar Beethoven Concerts: 1671, Szeged Festival: 1672, Miners' Day: 1677, 150th Birth Anniv; 1678, Birth Centenary; 1679, 90th Birth Anniv.

312 Yellow Pheasant's-eye and Quill

1960. Stamp Exhibition Budapest.

No.	Type	Description	Mint	Used
1680	312	2fo.(+4fo.) yellow, green and brown	2·20	2·20

313 Soldier

1960. 15th Anniv of Liberation.

No.	Type	Description	Mint	Used
1681	313	40fi. brown and red	60	35
1682	-	60fi. red, green and brown	1·20	50

DESIGN—HORIZ: 60fi. Student with flag (inscr "1945 FELSZABADULASUNK... 1960").

314 Rowing

1960. Summer Olympic Games. Centres and inscr in black (3fo. multicoloured). Circular frames in bistre. Background colours given.

No.	Type	Description	Mint	Used
1683		10fi. blue (T **314**)	10	10
1684		20fi. brown (Boxing)	10	10
1685		30fi. lilac (Archery)	10	10
1686		40fi. ochre (Discus)	10	10
1687		50fi. red (Ball game)	10	10
1688		60fi. green (Javelin)	25	10
1689		1fo. purple (Horse-riding)	60	10
1690		1fo.40 blue (Wrestling)	70	10
1691		1fo.70 brown (Swordplay)	1·20	25
1692		2fo.+1fo. red (Romulus, Remus and Wolf)	1·30	35
1693		3fo. grey (Olympic Rings and Arms of Hungary)	3·50	1·40
MS1693a		67×95 mm. 10fo. multicoloured	30·00	30·00

1960. International Philatelic Federation Congress, Warsaw. Sheet 161×122 mm containing four of No. 1656, each in different colours, side by side with commemorative labels.

No.	Description	Mint	Used
MS1693b	3fo. (×4)	18·00	18·00

1960. Hungarian Castles. As Nos. 1629, 1632/3, 1636/7 and 1641/2 but printed on coloured paper.

No.	Type	Description	Mint	Used
1694		8fi. purple on blue	10	10
1695		20fi. bronze on green	25	10
1696		30fi. brown on yellow	25	10
1697		60fi. red on pink	35	10
1698		70fi. green on blue	60	10
1699		1fo.40 blue on blue	85	10
1700		1fo.70 lilac on blue ("SOMLO")	1·90	25

315 Girl in Mezokovesd Provincial Costume

1960. Stamp Day.

No.	Type	Description	Mint	Used
1701	315	2fo.(+4fo.) mult	3·00	3·00

316 "The Turnip"

1960. Fairy Tales (2nd series). Multicoloured.

No.	Type	Description	Mint	Used
1702		20fi. Type **316**	10	10
1703		30fi. "Snow White and the Seven Dwarfs"	10	10
1704		40fi. "The Miller, Son and Donkey"	25	10
1705		60fi. "Puss in Boots"	35	20
1706		80fi. "The Fox and the Raven"	60	25
1707		1fo. "The Maple-wood Pipe"	1·20	35
1708		1fo.70 "The Stork and the Fox"	1·40	60
1709		2fo. "Momotaro" (Japanese tale)	3·00	70

317 F. Rozsa

1961. Celebrities and Anniversaries. Portraits as T 317.

No.	Type	Description	Mint	Used
1710		1fo. brown (T **317**)	35	10
1711		1fo. turquoise (G. Kilian)	35	10
1712		1fo. red (J. Rippi-Ronai)	35	10
1713		1fo. olive (S. Latinka)	35	10
1714		1fo. green (M. Zalka)	35	10
1715		1fo. lake (J. Katona)	35	10

COMMEMORATIVE EVENTS: No. 1710, Press Day; No. 1711, Gyorgy Kilian Sports Movement; No. 1712, Birth Cent; No. 1713, 75th Birth Anniv; No. 1714, 65th Birth Anniv.

318 Eastern Grey Kangaroo with Young

1961. Budapest Zoo Animals. Inscr "ZOO 1961".

No.	Type	Description	Mint	Used
1716	318	20fi. black and orange	25	10
1717	-	30fi. sepia and green	35	10
1718	-	40fi. brown and chestnut	50	10
1719	-	60fi. grey and mauve	60	10
1720	-	80fi. yellow and black	70	10
1721	-	1fo. brown and green	1·10	25
1722	-	1fo.40 sepia and turquoise	1·60	25
1723	-	2fo. black and red	1·80	95
1724	-	2fo.60 brown and violet	2·40	1·40
1725	-	3fo. multicoloured	3·75	1·80

DESIGNS—HORIZ: 30fi. American bison; 60fi. Indian elephant and calf; 80fi. Tiger and cubs; 1fo.40, Polar bear; 2fo. Common zebra and foal; 2fo.60, European bison cow with calf. VERT: 40fi. Brown bear; 1fo. Ibex; 3fo. Main entrance, Budapest Zoo.

319 Child chasing Butterfly

1961. Health. Inscr "1961". Cross in red.

No.	Type	Description	Mint	Used
1726	319	30fi. black, purple & brn	10	10
1727	-	40fi. sepia, blue & turq	25	10
1728	-	60fi. yellow, grey & violet	30	10
1729	-	1fo. multicoloured	35	10
1730	-	1fo.70 yellow, blue & grn	95	25
1731	-	4fo. green and grey	2·10	85

DESIGNS—As Type **319**: 40fi. Patient on operating table. LARGER (29½×35 mm): 60fi. Ambulance and stretcher; 1fo. Traffic lights and scooter; 1fo.70, Syringe and jars; 4fo. Emblem of Health Department.

320 Launching of Rocket "Vostok"

1961. World's First Manned Space Flight. Inscr "1961. IV.12".

No.	Type	Description	Mint	Used
1732	320	1fo. brown and blue	1·80	1·20
1733	-	2fo. brown and blue	5·50	4·75

DESIGN: 2fo. Gagarin and "Vostok" in flight.

321 Roses

1961. May Day.

No.	Type	Description	Mint	Used
1734	321	1fo. red and green	60	25
1735	-	2fo. red and green	1·20	60

DESIGN: 2fo. As Type **321** but roses and inscr reversed.

322 "Venus" Rocket

1961. Launching of Soviet "Venus" Rocket. Inscr "VENUSZ RAKETA 1961 11.12".

No.	Type	Description	Mint	Used
1736	322	40fi. black, bistre and blue	70	70
1737	-	60fi. black, bistre and blue	1·20	1·20
1738	-	80fi. black and blue	1·30	1·30
1739	-	2fo. bistre and violet-blue	3·50	3·50

DESIGNS: 60fi. Separation of rocket capsule in flight; 80fi. Capsule and orbit diagram; 2fo. Allegory of flying woman and crescent moon.

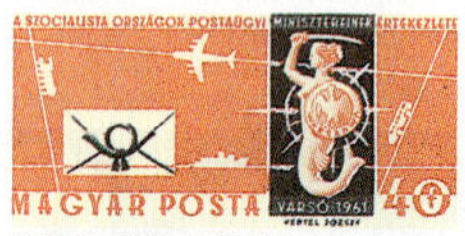

323 Conference Emblem, Letter and Transport

1961. Organization of Socialist Countries' Postal Administrations Conference.

No.	Type	Description	Mint	Used
1740	323	40fi. black and orange	55	10
1741	-	60fi. black and mauve	65	10
1742	-	1fo. black and blue	1·10	75

DESIGNS: 60fi. Television aerial; 1fo. Radar receiving equipment.

324 Hungarian Flag

1961. International Stamp Exhibition, Budapest. (a) 1st issue. Background in silver.

No.	Type	Description	Mint	Used
1743	324	1fo. red, green and black	65	60

1744	-	1fo.70 multicoloured	1·30	1·10
1745	-	2fo.60 multicoloured	1·90	1·20
1746	-	3fo. multicoloured	2·50	1·90

(b) 2nd issue. Background in gold. Inscriptions at left altered on 1fo. and 3fo.

1747	324	1fo. red, green and black	80	75
1748	-	1fo.70 multicoloured	1·30	1·20
1749	-	2fo.60 multicoloured	1·90	1·90
1750	-	3fo. multicoloured	2·30	2·20

DESIGNS: 1fo.70, Late spider orchids; 2fo.60, Small tortoiseshell; 3fo. Eurasian goldfinch.

See also Nos. 1765/8.

325 George Stephenson

1961. Communications Ministers' Conference, Budapest. Inscr "KOZLEKEDESUGYI", etc.

1751	325	60fi. olive	25	10
1752	-	1fo. bistre, black and blue	65	10
1753	-	2fo. brown	1·00	35

DESIGNS: 1fo. Communications emblems; 2fo. J. Landler (Minister of Communications).

326 Football and Club Badge

1961. 50th Anniv of VASAS Sports Club. Badge in gold, red and blue.

1754	326	40fi. orange, black and gold	15	10
1755	-	60fi. green, black and gold	40	10
1756	-	1fo. bistre, black and gold	50	35
1757	-	2fo.+1fo. blue, blk & gold	1·60	1·10

DESIGNS: 60fi. Wrestling; 1fo. Vaulting; 2fo. Sailing.

327 Three Racehorses

1961. Racehorses.

1758	327	30fi. multicoloured	25	10
1759	-	40fi. multicoloured	40	25
1760	-	60fi. multicoloured	65	35
1761	-	1fo. black, green and orange	75	60
1762	-	1fo.70 sepia, black and green	1·50	75
1763	-	2fo. black, blue and brown	1·90	1·40
1764	-	3fo. multicoloured	3·25	1·90

DESIGNS: 40fi. Three hurdlers; 60fi. Trotting race (two horses); 1fo. Trotting race (three horses); 1fo.70, Two racehorses and two foals; 2fo. Hungarian trotter "Baka"; 3fo. 19th century champion mare, "Kincsem".

328 Budapest

1961. Stamp Day and International Stamp Exhibition, Budapest (3rd issue). Designs as T 328.

1765	328	2fo.+1fo. bl, brn & ol	2·30	2·30
1766	-	2fo.+1fo. bl, brn & ol	2·30	2·30
1767	-	2fo.+1fo. bl, brn & ol	2·30	2·30
1768	-	2fo.+1fo. bl, brn & ol	2·30	2·30

Nos. 1765/8 are printed together in sheets of 40 (4×10) with one vertical row of each design. Horizontal strips of four form a composite panorama of Budapest.

329 Music, Keyboard and Silhouette

1961. 150th Birth and 75th Death Anniv of Liszt (composer).

1769	329	60fi. black and gold	60	25
1770	-	1fo. black	80	60
1771	-	2fo. green and blue	1·70	1·20

MS1771a 71×98 mm. 10fo. multicoloured 17·00 17·00

DESIGNS—VERT: 1fo. Statue; 10fo. Head profile over piano keys. HORIZ: 2fo. Music Academy.

330 Lenin

1961. 22nd Soviet Communist Party Congress, Moscow.

1772	330	1fo. brown	60	25

331 Monk's Hood

1961. Medicinal Plants. Multicoloured.

1773		20fi. Type **331**	10	10
1774		30fi. Centaury	10	10
1775		40fi. Blue iris	25	10
1776		60fi. Thorn-apple	35	10
1777		1fo. Purple hollyhock	80	15
1778		1fo.70 Hop	1·20	25
1779		2fo. Poppy	1·70	60
1780		3fo. Mullein	2·30	1·00

332 Nightingale

1961. Birds of Woods and Fields. Multicoloured. Inscr "1961".

1781		30fi. Type **332**	10	10
1782		40fi. Great tit	25	10
1783		60fi. Chaffinch (horiz)	35	10
1784		1fo. Jay	60	15
1785		1fo.20 Golden oriole (horiz)	70	25
1786		1fo.50 Blackbird (horiz)	1·20	35
1787		2fo. Yellowhammer	1·40	40
1788		3fo. Northern lapwing (horiz)	2·30	80

333 M. Karolyi

1962. Celebrities and Anniversaries. Inscr "1962".

1789	333	1fo. sepia	35	10
1790	-	1fo. brown (F. Berkes)	35	10
1791	-	1fo. blue (J. Pech)	35	10
1792	-	1fo. violet (A. Chazar)	35	10
1793	-	1fo. blue (Dr. F. Hutyra)	35	10
1794	-	1fo. red (G. Egressy)	35	10

ANNIVERSARIES: Nos. 1789/90, 5th Co-operative Movement Congress; 1791, 75th anniv of Hydrographic Institute; 1792, 50th anniv of Sports Club for the Deaf; 1793, 175th anniv of Hungarian Veterinary Service; 1794, 125th anniv of National Theatre.

333a Globe and Gagarin, Titov and Glenn (image scaled to 59% of original size)

1962. World Space Flights of Gagarin, Titov and Glenn. Sheet 109×70 mm.

MS1794a **333a** 10fo. multicoloured 17·00 17·00

334 Railway Signals

1962. 14th Int Railwaymen's Esperanto Congress.

1795	334	1fo. green	30	10

335 Green Swordtail

1962. Ornamental Fishes. Inscr "1962". Mult.

1796		20fi. Type **335**	10	10
1797		30fi. Paradise fish	10	10
1798		40fi. Fan-tailed guppy	15	10
1799		60fi. Siamese fighting fish	25	10
1800		80fi. Tiger barb	35	10
1801		1fo. Freshwater angelfish	60	25
1802		1fo.20 Sunfish	70	35
1803		1fo.50 Lyretail panchax	1·00	45
1804		2fo. Neon tetra	1·30	60
1805		3fo. Blue discus	1·70	1·30

336 Flags of Argentina and Bulgaria

1962. World Football Championships, 1962. Inscr "CHILE 1962". Flags in national colours: ball, flagpole, value, etc., in bistre.

1806	-	30fi. mauve	25	10
1807	-	40fi. green	35	15
1808	-	60fi. lilac	60	25
1809	-	1fo. blue	70	35
1810	336	1fo.70 orange	1·40	45
1811	-	2fo. turquoise	1·60	50
1812	-	3fo. red	1·70	60
1813	-	4fo.+1fo. green	3·50	1·20

MS1813a 72×92 mm. 10fo. multicoloured 11·50 11·50

FLAGS: 30fi. Colombia and Uruguay; 40fi. U.S.S.R. and Yugoslavia; 60fi. Switzerland and Chile; 1fo. German Federal Republic and Italy; 2fo. Hungary and Great Britain; 3fo. Brazil and Mexico; 4fo. Spain and Czechoslovakia. The two flags on each stamp represent the football teams playing against each other in the first round. VERT: (28½×39 mm)—10fo. Goal keeper and map.

337 Gutenberg

1962. Centenary of Hungarian Printing Union.

1814	337	1fo. blue	35	10
1815	-	1fo. brown	35	10

PORTRAIT: No. 1815, Miklos Kis (first Hungarian printer).

338 Campaign Emblem

1962. Malaria Eradication.

1816	338	2fo.50 bistre and black	1·70	80

MS1816a 111×76 mm. 2fo.50 (×4) green and black 15·00 15·00

339 "Beating Swords into Ploughshares"

1962. World Peace Congress, Moscow.

1817	339	1fo. brown	35	10

340 Festival Emblem

1962. World Youth Festival, Helsinki.

1818	340	3fo. multicoloured	1·20	45

341 Icarus

1962. Air. Development of Flight.

1819	341	30fi. bistre and blue	10	10
1820	-	40fi. blue and green	25	10
1821	-	60fi. red and blue	35	10
1822	-	80fi. silver, blue & turq	45	10
1823	-	1fo. silver, blue & purple	60	15
1824	-	1fo.40 orange and blue	70	35
1825	-	2fo. brown and turquoise	95	45
1826	-	3fo. blue, silver and violet	1·20	60
1827	-	4fo. silver, black & green	1·70	70

DESIGNS: 40fi. Modern glider and Lilienthal monoplane glider; 60fi. Zlin Trener 6 and Rakos's monoplane; 80fi. Airship "Graf Zeppelin" and Montgolfier balloon; 1fo. Ilyushin Il-18B and Wright Flyer I; 1fo.40, Nord 3202 sports airplane and Peter Nesterov's Nieuport biplane; 2fo. Mil Mi-6 helicopter and Asboth's helicopter; 3fo. Myasichev Mya-4 airliner and Zhukovsky's wind tunnel; 4fo. Space rocket and Tsiolkovsky's rocket.

342 Hybrid Tea

1962. Rose Culture. Roses in natural colours. Background colours given.

1828		20fi. brown	25	10
1829	342	40fi. myrtle	45	10
1830	-	60fi. violet	60	10
1831	-	80fi. red	80	15
1832	-	1fo. myrtle	1·20	45
1833	-	1fo.20 orange	1·40	60
1834	-	2fo. turquoise	3·00	80

ROSES: 20fi. Floribunda; 60fi. to 2fo. Various hybrid teas.

343 Globe, "Vostok 3" and "Vostok 4" (image scaled to 75% of original size)

1962. Air. 1st "Team" Manned Space Flight.

1835	343	1fo. brown and blue	80	60
1836	-	2fo. brown and blue	1·70	1·20

DESIGN: 2fo. Cosmonauts Nikolaev and Popovich.

344 Weightlifting

1962. European Weightlifting Championships, Budapest.

1837	**344**	1fo. brown	80	35

345 Austrian 2kr. stamp of 1850

1962. 35th Stamp Day.

1838	**345**	2fo.+1fo. brown & yell	1·70	1·70
1839	-	2fo.+1fo. brown & pk	1·70	1·70
1840	-	2fo.+1fo. brown & bl	1·70	1·70
1841	-	2fo.+1fo. brown & grn	1·70	1·70

MS1841a 91×110 mm. Nos. 1838/41 in block of four 10·50 10·50

DESIGNS: Hungarian stamps of: No. 1839, 1919 (75fi. Dozsa); No. 1840, 1955 (1fo. 50 Skiing); No. 1841, 1959 (3fo. "Vanessa atalanta").

346 Primitive and Modern Oilwells

1962. 25th Anniv of Hungarian Oil Industry.

1842	**346**	1fo. green	35	10

347 Gagarin

1962. Air. Astronautical Congress, Paris.

1843	**347**	40fi. ochre and purple	25	10
1844	-	60fi. ochre and green	60	15
1845	-	1fo. ochre and turquoise	80	25
1846	-	1fo.40 ochre and brown	1·20	35
1847	-	1fo.70 ochre and blue	1·60	60
1848	-	2fo.60 ochre and violet	1·70	80
1849	-	3fo. ochre and brown	3·00	1·40

ASTRONAUTS: 60fi. Titov; 1fo. Glenn; 1fo.40, Scott Carpenter; 1fo.70, Nikolaev; 2fo.60, Popovich; 3fo. Schirra.

348 Cup and Football

1962. "Budapest Vasas" Football Team's Victory in Central European Cup Competition.

1850	**348**	2fo.+1fo. mult	1·20	95

349 Osprey

1962. Air. Birds of Prey. Multicoloured.

1851	30fi. Eagle owl	25	10
1852	40fi. Type **349**	25	25
1853	60fi. Marsh harrier	60	35
1854	80fi. Booted eagle	80	60
1855	1fo. African fish eagle	1·20	80
1856	2fo. Lammergeier	1·70	95
1857	3fo. Golden eagle	2·30	1·20
1858	4fo. Common kestrel	3·00	1·40

350 Racing Motor Cyclist

1962. Motor Cycle and Car Sports. Mult.

1859	20fi. Type **350**	10	10
1860	30fi. Sidecar racing	15	10
1861	40fi. "Scrambling" (hill climb)	25	10
1862	60fi. Dirt-track racing	35	15
1863	1fo. Wearing "garland"	70	25
1864	1fo.20 Speed trials	80	35
1865	1fo.70 Sidecar trials	1·30	40
1866	2fo. "Go-kart" racing	1·50	45
1867	3fo. Car racing	1·70	1·40

351 Ice Skater

1963. European Figure Skating and Ice Dancing Championships, Budapest.

1868	**351**	20fi. green, brown & lilac	10	10
1869	-	40fi. black, brn & salmon	25	15
1870	-	60fi. multicoloured	60	35
1871	-	1fo. multicoloured	80	45
1872	-	1fo.40 multicoloured	1·20	60
1873	-	2fo. red, brown and green	1·70	80
1874	-	3fo. multicoloured	3·00	1·20

MS1874a 66×94 mm. 10fo. multicoloured 11·50 11·50

DESIGNS—VERT: 40fi., 2fo. Skater leaping; 60fi., 1fo. Pairs dancing; 1fo.40, Skater turning; 10fo. (29×38 mm), Figure skater and flags. HORIZ: 3fo. Pair dancing.

352 J. Batsanyi

1963. Celebrities and Anniversaries.

1875	40fi. lake (Type **352**)	10	10
1876	40fi. green (F. Entz)	10	10
1877	40fi. blue (I. Markovits)	10	10
1878	40fi. olive (L. Weiner)	25	10
1879	60fi. purple (Dr. F. Koranyi)	60	10
1880	60fi. bronze (G. Gardonyi)	25	10
1881	60fi. brown (P. de Coubertin)	60	10
1882	60fi. violet (J. Eotvos)	35	10

ANNIVERSARIES: No. 1875, Revolutionary, birth bicent; No. 1876. Horticulture College founder, Horticulture cent; No. 1877, Inventor, Hungarian Shorthand, cent; No. 1878, Composer, Budapest Music Competitions; No. 1879, Tuberculosis researcher, 50th death anniv; No. 1880, Novelist, birth cent; No. 1881, Olympic Games reviver, birth cent; No. 1882, Author, 150th birth anniv.

353 Bulgarian 21. Rocket Stamp of 1959

1963. Organization of Socialist Countries Postal Administrations Conference, Budapest.

1883	-	20fi. red, yellow and green	10	10
1884	**353**	30fi. red, brown & purple	10	10
1885	-	40fi. purple and blue	10	10
1886	-	50fi. violet and blue	15	10
1887	-	60fi. multicoloured	25	10
1888	-	80fi. turquoise, black & bl	35	10
1889	-	1fo. multicoloured	45	10
1890	-	1fo.20 yellow, violet & bl	50	15
1891	-	1fo.40 blue, red & brown	60	15
1892	-	1fo.70 brn, grn & lt brn	1·00	25
1893	-	2fo. orange, blue & pur	1·20	35
1894	-	2fo.60 violet, red & grn	1·30	1·20

DESIGNS: Various "space" stamps—HORIZ: 20fi. Albania 1l.50 (1962); 40fi. Czechoslovakia 80h. (1962); 50fi. China 8f. (1958); 60fi. N. Korea 10ch. (1961); 80fi. Poland 40g. (1959); 1fo. Hungary 60fi. (1961); 1fo.40, East Germany 25pf. (1961); 1fo.70, Rumania 1l.20 (1957); 2fo.60, N. Vietnam 6x. (1961). VERT: 1fo.20, Mongolia 30m. (1959); 2fo. Russia 6k. (1961).

354 Fair Emblem

1963. International Fair, Budapest.

1895	**354**	1fo. violet	60	10

355 Erkel (composer)

1963. Students' Erkel Memorial Festival, Gyula.

1896	**355**	60fi. brown	60	10

356 Roses

1963. 5th National Rose Show, Budapest.

1897	**356**	2fo. red, green and brown	1·20	10

357 Helicon Monument

1963. 10th Youth Festival, Keszthely.

1898	**357**	40fi. blue	10	10

358 Chain Bridge and "Snow White" (Danube steamer)

1963. Transport and Communications.

1899	**358**	10fi. blue	10	10
1900	-	20fi. green	10	10
1901	-	30fi. blue	10	10
1902	-	40fi. orange	10	10
1902b	-	40fi. grey	35	35
1903	-	50fi. brown	10	10
1904	-	60fi. red	10	10
1905	-	70fi. olive	10	10
1906	-	80fi. brown	10	10
1906a	-	1fo. brown	25	25
1907	-	1fo. purple	25	10
1908	-	1fo.20 brown	2·00	60
1909	-	1fo.20 violet	25	10
1910	-	1fo.40 green	35	10
1911	-	1fo.70 brown	45	10
1912	-	2fo. turquoise	60	10
1913	-	2fo.50 purple	70	25
1914	-	2fo.60 olive	80	25
1915	-	3fo. blue	60	10
1916	-	4fo. blue	80	10
1917	-	5fo. brown	1·20	10
1918	-	6fo. ochre	1·30	10
1919	-	8fo. mauve	2·00	45
1920	-	10fo. green	2·30	1·20

DESIGNS—As Type **358**: HORIZ: 20fi. Tramcar; 30fi. Open-deck bus; 40fi. (No. 1902), Articulated bus; 40fi. (No. 1902b), Budapest 100 Post Office; 50fi. Railway truck with gas cylinders; 60fi. Trolley bus; 70fi. Railway T.P.O. coach; 80fi. Motor cyclist. VERT: 1fo. (No. 1906a), Hotel Budapest. 28½×21 mm: 1fo. (No. 1907) Articulated trolley bus; 1fo.40, Postal coach; 1fo.70, Diesel-electric multiple unit train; 2fo. T.V. broadcast coach; 2fo.50, Tourist coach; 2fo.60, Signalbox and train; 3fo. Parcels conveyor; 5fo. Railway fork-lift truck; 6fo. Telex operator; 8fo. Telephonist and map; 10fo. Postwoman. 21×28½ mm: 1fo.20, (No. 1908), Mail plane and trolley on tarmac; 1fo.20, (No. 1909), Control tower, Miskole; 4fo. Pylon, Pecs.

See also Nos. 2767/70.

359 Holidaymaker and "Beloiannis" (lake steamer)

1963. Cent of Siofok Resort, Lake Balaton.

1921		20fi. black, green and red	60	25
1922	**359**	40fi. multicoloured	60	25
1923	-	60fi. orange, brown & bl	60	35

DESIGNS—TRIANGULAR: 20fi. "Tihany" (water bus); 60fi. Yacht.

359a Spaceship over Globe

1963. Air. Space Flights of "Vostok 5" and "Vostok 6". Sheet 64×94 mm.

MS1923a **359a** 10fo. light blue, blue and gold 14·00 14·00

360 Mail Coach and Arc de Triomphe, Paris

1963. Centenary of Paris Postal Conference.

1924	**360**	1fo. red	60	25

361 Performance in front of Szeged Cathedral

1963. Summer Drama Festival, Szeged.

1925	**361**	40fi. blue	25	25

362 Child with towel

1963. Red Cross Cent. Inscr "1863–1963". Mult.

1926		30fi. Type **362**	10	10
1927		40fi. Girl with medicine bottle and tablets	10	10
1928		60fi. Girls of three races	25	10
1929		1fo. Girl and "heart"	35	15
1930		1fo.40 Boys of three races	60	25
1931		2fo. Child being medically examined	70	35
1932		3fo. Hands tending plants	2·00	70

363 Pylon and Map

1963. Village Electrification.

1933	**363**	1fo. black and grey	60	25

364 Karancssag

1963. Provincial Costumes.

1934	**364**	20fi. lake	25	10
1935	-	30fi. green (Kapuvar)	30	15
1936	-	40fi. brown (Debrecen)	35	25
1937	-	60fi. blue (Hortobagy)	60	30
1938	-	1fo. red (Csokoly)	80	35
1939	-	1fo.70 violet (Dunantul)	95	50
1940	-	2fo. turquoise (Bujak)	1·20	60
1941	-	2fo.50 red (Alfold)	1·40	1·00
1942	-	3fo. blue (Mezokovesd)	3·00	1·20

365 Hyacinth

1963. Stamp Day. Flowers. Multicoloured.

1943		2fo.+1fo. Type **365**	1·30	1·30
1944		2fo.+1fo. Narcissus	1·30	1·30
1945		2fo.+1fo. Chrysanthemum	1·30	1·30
1946		2fo.+1fo. Tiger lily	1·30	1·30
MS1946a		76×91 mm. Nos. 1943/6 but smaller (20×27 mm) in block of four	6·50	6·50

366 Skiing (slalom)

1963. Winter Olympic Games, Innsbruck, 1964. "MAGYAR" and emblems red and black; centres brown: background colours given.

1947	**366**	40fi. green	10	10
1948	-	60fi. violet	10	10
1949	-	70fi. blue	15	10
1950	-	80fi. green	25	10
1951	-	1fo. orange	35	15
1952	-	2fo. blue	80	25
1953	-	2fo.60 purple	2·00	80
1954	-	4fo.+1fo. blue	2·30	95

DESIGNS: 60fi. Skiing (biathlon); 70fi. Ski jumping; 80fi. Rifle-shooting on skis; 1fo. Figure skating (pairs); 2fo. Ice hockey; 2fo.60, Speed skating; 4fo. Bobsleighing.

367 Calendar

1963. New Year Issue. Hungarian Postal and Philatelic Museum Fund. Multicoloured.

1955		20fi. Type **367**	10	10
1956		30fi. Young chimney-sweep with glass of wine	10	10
1957		40fi. Four-leafed clover	10	10
1958		60fi. Piglet in top-hat	10	10
1959		1fo. Young pierrot	35	15
1960		2fo. Chinese lanterns and mask	60	25
1961		2fo.50+1fo.20 Holly, mistletoe, clover and horseshoe	95	35
1962		3fo.+1fo.50 Piglets with balloon	2·00	70

SIZES: As Type **367**—HORIZ: 20fi., 1fo., 3fo. VERT: 40fi. LARGER (28×38 mm.): 30fi., 60fi., 2fo., 2fo.50.

368 Moon Rocket

1964. Space Research. Multicoloured.

1963		30fi. Type **368**	25	10
1964		40fi. Venus rocket	35	10
1965		60fi. "Vostok 1" (horiz)	45	15
1966		1fo. U.S. spaceship	60	20
1967		1fo.70 Soviet team space flights	1·00	25
1968		2fo. "Telstar" (horiz)	1·20	35
1969		2fo.60 Mars rocket	1·30	60
1970		3fo. "Space Research" (rockets and tracking equipment) (horiz)	1·70	70

368a Skier racing

1964. Winter Olympic Games, Innsbruck, 1964. Sheet 65×60 mm.

MS1970a	**368a**	10fo. multicoloured	8·75	8·75

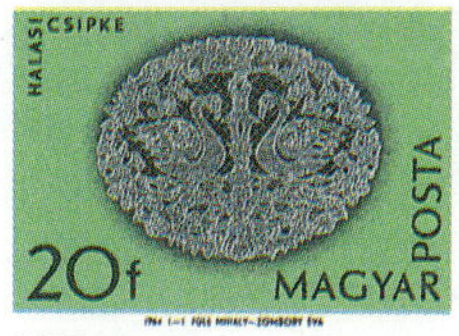

369 Swans

1964. Halas Lace (2nd series). Lace patterns die-stamped in white on black; inscriptions black.

1971	**369**	20fi. green	25	10
1972	-	30fi. yellow	60	10
1973	-	40fi. red	80	15
1974	-	60fi. olive	1·20	20
1975	-	1fo. orange	1·40	25
1976	-	1fo.40 blue	1·70	30
1977	-	2fo. turquoise	2·00	60
1978	-	2fo.60 violet	2·50	80

LACE PATTERNS—VERT: (38½×45 mm.): 30fi. Peacocks; 40fi. Pigeons; 60fi. Peacock; 1fo. Deer; 1fo.40, Fisherman; 2fo. Pigeons. As Type **369**: 2fo.60, Butterfly.

370 Armour and Swords

371 Basketball

372 Dozsa and Kossuth

373 Fair and Emblem

374 "Breasting the Tape"

1964. Anniversaries and Events of 1964. Designs as T 370/4, some showing portraits. (a) As T 370.

1979		60fi. purple (I. Madach)	25	25
1980		60fi. olive (E. Szabo)	35	25
1981		60fi. olive (A. Fay)	35	25
1982		1fo. red (Skittles)	60	25
1983		2fo. brown (T **370**)	60	25

ANNIV OR EVENT: No. 1979, (author, death cent.); No. 1980, (founder of Municipal Libraries, 60th anniv); No. 1981, (death cent.); No. 1982, (1st European Skittles Championships, Budapest); No. 1983, (50th anniv of Hungarian Fencing Assn.).

(b) As T 371.

1984		60fi. turquoise (Stalactites and stalagmites)	25	25
1985		60fi. blue (Bauxite excavator)	35	25
1986		1fo. green (Forest and waterfall)	60	25
1987		2fo. brown (Galileo)	80	25
1988		2fo. lake (Shakespeare)	80	25
1989		2fo. blue (T **371**)	1·70	60
1990		60fi. red (K. Marx)	35	25

ANNIV OR EVENT—VERT: No. 1984, (Aggteleki Cave); No. 1985, (30th anniv or Hungarian Aluminium Production); No. 1986, (National Forestry Federation Congress); No. 1987, (400th birth anniv); No. 1988 (400th birth anniv); No. 1989, (European Women's Basketball Championships). HORIZ: No. 1990, (cent of "First International").

(c) As T 372.

1991		1fo. blue (T **372**)	60	25
1992		3fo.+1fo.50, black, grey and orange (Sports Museum, Budapest)	1·40	35

ANNIV OR EVENT: No. 1991, (60th Anniv of City of Cegled); No. 1992, (Lawn Tennis Historical Exn, Budapest).

(d) T 373.

1993		1fo. green (Budapest Int Fair)	60	25

(e) As T 374.

1994		60fi. slate ("Alba Regia" statue)	35	25
1995		1fo. brown (M. Ybl)	60	25
1996		2fo. brown (T **374**)	80	25
1997		2fo. dull pur (Michelangelo)	80	25

ANNIV OR EVENT: No. 1994, (Szekesfehervar Days); No. 1995, (architect, 150th birth anniv); No. 1996, (50th anniv of Hungarian–Swedish Athletic Meeting); No. 1997, (400th death anniv).

375 Eleanor Roosevelt

1964. Eleanor Roosevelt Commemoration.

1998	**375**	2fo. ochre, deep brown and brown	80	60
MS1998a		112×76 mm. 4×2 fo. (each 39×20 mm) in different colours, showing portrait	5·25	5·25

376 Fencing

1964. Olympic Games, Tokyo. Multicoloured.

1999		30fi. Type **376**	10	10
2000		40fi. Gymnastics	10	10
2001		60fi. Football	10	10
2002		80fi. Horse-jumping	10	10
2003		1fo. Running	25	10
2004		1fo.40 Weightlifting	35	10
2005		1fo.70 Gymnastics (trapeze)	45	10
2006		2fo. Throwing the hammer, and javelin	70	15
2007		2fo. 50 Boxing	1·50	25
2008		3fo.+1fo. Water-polo	1·70	95

377 Peaches ("Magyar Kajszi")

1964. National Peaches and Apricots Exn, Budapest. Designs of peaches or apricots. Multicoloured.

2009		40fi. "J.H. Hale"	10	10
2010		60fi. Type **377**	10	10
2011		1fo. "Mandula Kajszi"	35	10
2012		1fo.50 "Borsi Rozsa"	60	10
2013		1fo.70 "Alexander"	80	15
2014		2fo. "Champion"	1·20	25
2015		2fo.60 "Elberta"	1·40	60
2016		3fo. "Mayflower"	2·50	80

378 Lilac

1964. Stamp Day. Multicoloured.

2017	2fo.+1fo. Type **378**	1·40	1·40
2018	2fo.+1fo. Mallard	1·40	1·40
2019	2fo.+1fo. Gymnast	1·40	1·40
2020	2fo.+1fo. Rocket and globe	1·40	1·40
MS2020a	85×100 mm. Nos. 2017/20 but smaller (20×27½ mm) in block of four	6·50	6·50

378a Mt. Fuji and Stadium

1964. Air. Summer Olympic Games, Tokyo. Sheet 56×83 mm.

MS2020b	**378a** 10fo. multicoloured	10·50	10·50

379 Pedestrian Road Crossing

1964. Road Safety. Multicoloured.

2021	20fi. Type **379**	25	10
2022	60fi. Child with ball running into road	60	10
2023	1fo. Woman and child waiting to cross road	80	60

379a Venus, Rocket and Globe

1964. Three-manned Space Flight. Sheet 87×74 mm.

MS2023a	**379a** 10fo. multicoloured	10·50	10·50

380 Arpad Bridge, Budapest

1964. Opening of Reconstructed Elizabeth Bridge, Budapest.

2024	**380**	20fi. grey, green and blue (postage)	10	10
2025	-	30fi. green, blue & brown	10	10
2026	-	60fi. brown, grn & dp brn	35	10
2027	-	1fo. brown, bl & dp brn	70	10
2028	-	1fo.50 grey, blue & brn	1·20	25
2029	-	2fo. grey, green & brown	1·50	60
2030	-	2fo.50 grey, blue & brn	2·30	1·30

(b) Air.

MS2030a	95×49 mm. 10fo. green	10·50	10·50

BUDAPEST BRIDGES: 30fi. Margaret; 60fi. Chain; 1fo. Elizabeth; 1fo.50, Liberty; 2fo. Petofi; 2fo.50, South; 10fo. Elizabeth (different).

381 Common Pheasant

1964. "Hunting". Multicoloured.

2034	20fi. Type **381**	10	10
2035	30fi. Wild boar	10	10
2036	40fi. Grey partridges	15	10
2037	60fi. Brown hare	25	10
2038	80fi. Fallow deer	35	10
2039	1fo. Mouflon	60	10
2040	1fo.70 Red deer	1·20	15
2041	2fo. Great bustard	1·30	25
2042	2fo.50 Roe deer	1·40	60
2043	3fo. Emblem of Hunters' Federation	2·30	1·20

382 Horse-riding and Medals

1965. Olympic Games, Tokyo—Hungarian Winners' Medals. Medals: Gold and brown (G); Silver and black (S); Bronze and brown (B).

2044	20fi. brown and olive (G)	10	10
2045	30fi. brown and violet (S)	10	10
2046	50fi. brown and olive (G)	10	10
2047	60fi. brown and light blue (G)	15	10
2048	70fi. brown, slate & stone (B)	25	10
2049	80fi. brown and grey (G)	35	15
2050	1fo. brown, violet & mauve (S)	60	25
2051	1fo.20 brown and blue (S)	80	35
2052	1fo.40 brown and grey (S)	1·20	45
2053	1fo.50 brown and bistre (G)	1·40	60
2054	1fo.70 brown and red (S)	1·70	80
2055	3fo. brown and turquoise (G)	2·30	1·40

DESIGNS: 20fi. Type **382**; 30fi. Gymnastics; 50fi. Rifle-shooting; 60fi. Water-polo; 70fi. Putting the shot; 80fi. Football; 1fo. Weightlifting; 1fo.20, Canoeing; 1fo.40, Throwing the hammer; 1fo.50, Wrestling; 1fo.70, Throwing the javelin; 3fo. Fencing.

383 Mil Mi-4 Helicopter and Polar Station

1965. International Quiet Sun Year.

2056	**383**	20fi. orange, black & blue	10	10
2057	-	30fi. green, black & grey	10	10
2058	-	60fi. yellow, black & mve	10	10
2059	-	80fi. yellow, black & grn	25	10
2060	-	1fo.50 multicoloured	45	10
2061	-	1fo.70 black, mauve & bl	60	15
2062	-	2fo. red, black and blue	70	25
2063	-	2fo.50 yellow, blk & brn	1·20	60
2064	-	3fo. black, blue & yellow	1·70	1·20
MS2065		62×85 mm. 10fo. black, orange and blue	5·75	5·75

DESIGNS: 30fi. Rocket and radar aerials; 60fi. Rocket and diagram; 80fi. Radio telescope; 1fo.50, Compass needle on Globe; 1fo.70, Weather balloon; 2fo. Northern Lights and Adelie Penguins; 2fo.50, Space satellite; 3fo. I.Q.S.Y. emblem and world map; 10fo. Sun flares, snow crystals and rain.

384 Asters

1965. 20th Anniv of Liberation. Multicoloured.

2066	20fi. Type **384**	10	10
2067	30fi. Peonies	10	10
2068	50fi. Carnations	15	10
2069	60fi. Roses	25	10
2070	1fo.40 Lilies	60	10
2071	1fo.70 Godetia	70	15
2072	2fo. Gladiolus	75	25
2073	2fo.50 Parrot tulips	80	60
2074	3fo. Mixed bouquet	2·00	1·20

385 Leonov in Space

1965. Air. "Voskhod 2" Space Flight.

2075	**385**	1fo. grey and violet	60	25
2076	-	2fo. brown and purple	1·70	1·40

DESIGN: 2fo. Belyaev and Leonov.

386 "Red Head" (after Leonardo da Vinci)

1965. Int Renaissance Conference, Budapest.

2077	**386**	60fi. brown and ochre	45	10

387 Nikolaev, Tereshkova and View of Budapest

1965. Visit of Astronauts Nikolaev and Tereshkova.

2078	**387**	1fo. brown and blue	60	10

388 I.T.U. Emblem and Symbols

1965. Centenary of I.T.U.

2079	**388**	60fi. blue	35	10

389 Reproduction of Austria Type 109

1965. International Philatelic Exhibition, Vienna ("WIPA 1965"). Sheet 102×75 mm containing two of T 389 and two labels showing commemorative covers.

MS2080	**389** 2fo. (×2) blue and grey	1·00	1·00

390 French 13th-cent Tennis

1965. "History of Tennis".

2081	**390**	30fi.+10fi. lake on buff	10	10
2082	-	40fi.+10fi. blk on lilac	10	10
2083	-	60fi.+10fi. green on bis	25	10
2084	-	70fi.+30fi. pur on turq	35	10
2085	-	80fi.+40fi. blue on lav	60	15
2086	-	1fo.+50fi. green on yell	70	25
2087	-	1fo.50+50fi. brown on green	80	35
2088	-	1fo.70+50fi. blk on bl	1·20	60
2089	-	2fo.+1fo. red on green	1·30	80

DESIGNS: 40fi. Hungarian 16th-cent game; 60fi. French 18th-cent "long court"; 70fi. 16th-cent "tennys courte"; 80fi. 16th-cent court at Fontainebleau; 1fo. 17th-cent game; 1fo.50, W. C. Wingfield and Wimbledon Cup, 1877; 1fo.70, Davis Cup, 1900. 2fo. Bela Kehrling in play.

391 Marx and Lenin

1965. Organization of Socialist Countries' Postal Administrations Congress, Peking.

2090	**391**	60fi. multicoloured	35	10

392 I.C.Y. Emblem and Pulleys

1965. International Co-operation Year.

2091	**392** 2fo. red	60	10
MS2092	75×98 mm T **392** but smaller (21×29 mm) in blokc of four, each in a different colour	5·25	5·25

393 Equestrian Act

1965. "Circus 1965". Multicoloured.

2093	20fi. Type **393**	10	10
2094	30fi. Musical clown	15	10
2095	40fi. Performing elephant	25	10
2096	50fi. Performing seal	35	15
2097	60fi. Lions	60	25
2098	1fo. Wild cat leaping through burning hoops	70	35
2099	1fo.50 Black panthers	1·20	35
2100	2fo.50 Acrobat with hoops	1·40	60
2101	3fo. Performing panther and dogs	2·00	80
2102	4fo. Bear on bicycle	3·00	2·10

394 Rescue Boat

1965. Danube Flood Relief.

2103	**394** 1fo.+50fi. brown & bl	1·70	1·70
MS2104	113×79 mm. 10fo.+5 fo. brown (Another rescue boat as T **394**)	5·75	5·75

395 Dr. I. Semmelweis

1965. Death Cent of Ignac Semmelweis (physician).

2105	**395**	60fi. brown	35	25

396 Running

1965. University Games, Budapest. Multicoloured (except MS2115).

2106	20fi. Type **396**	10	10
2107	30fi. Start of swimming race	10	10
2108	50fi. Diving	10	10
2109	60fi. Gymnastics	20	10
2110	80fi. Tennis	25	10
2111	1fo.70 Fencing	60	15
2112	2fo. Volleyball	70	25
2113	2fo.50 Basketball	1·20	60
2114	4fo. Water-polo	1·70	1·60
MS2115	195×75 mm. Horiz design (38×28 mm) showing stadium. 10fo. chestnut, ochre and grey	8·75	8·75

397 Congress Emblem

1965. 6th W.F.T.U. Congress, Warsaw.

2116	**397**	60fi. blue	35	10

398 "Phyllocactus hybridum"

1965. Succulents and Orchids. Multicoloured.

2117	20fi. Type **398**	10	10
2118	30fi. "Cattleya warszewiczii"	10	10
2119	60fi. "Rebutia calliantha"	20	10
2120	70fi. "Paphiopedilum hybridum"	25	10
2121	80fi. "Opuntia rhodantha"	60	10
2122	1fo. "Laelia elegans"	70	10
2123	1fo.50 "Zygocactus truncatus"	80	15
2124	2fo. "Strelitzia reginae"	1·20	25
2125	2fo.50 "Lithops weberi"	1·40	60
2126	3fo. "Victoria amazonica"	3·00	1·20

399 Reproduction of No. 1127

1965. Stamp Day. Designs show reproductions of Hungarian stamps. Multicoloured.

2127	2fo.+1fo. Type **399**	1·50	1·50
2128	2fo.+1fo. No. 1280	1·50	1·50
2129	2fo.+1fo. No. 1873	1·50	1·50
2130	2fo.+1fo. No. 1733	1·50	1·50
MS2131	100×85 mm. Nos. 2127/30 but smaller	7·50	7·50

400 F.I.R. Emblem

1965. 5th International Federation of Resistance Fighters Congress, Budapest.

2132	**400**	2fo. blue	80	25

401 The Magic Horse

1965. Fairy Tales (3rd series). Scenes from "The Arabian Nights Entertainments". Multicoloured.

2133	20fi. Type **401**	10	10
2134	30fi. Sultan Schahriah and Scheherazade	10	10
2135	50fi. Sinbad's 5th Voyage (ship)	10	10
2136	60fi. Aladdin and Genie of the Lamp	25	10
2137	80fi. Haroun al Rashid	35	10
2138	1fo. The Magic Carpet	80	25
2139	1fo.70 The Fisherman and the Genie	1·20	45
2140	2fo. Ali Baba	1·40	80
2141	3fo. Sinbad's 2nd Voyage (roc—legendary bird)	2·30	1·20

402 "Mariner 4"

1965. Air. Space Research.

2142	**402**	20fi. black, yellow & blue	25	10
2143	-	30fi. violet, yellow & brn	25	10
2144	-	40fi. brown, mauve & bl	45	10
2145	-	60fi. multicoloured	60	25
2146	-	1fo. multicoloured	1·20	35
2147	-	2fo.50 black, grey & pur	1·70	60
2148	-	3fo. black, green & brn	2·30	80
MS2149		105×85 mm. 10fo. multicoloured	7·50	7·50

DESIGNS—VERT: 30fi. "San Marco" (Italian satellite); 40fi. "Molnyija 1" (Polish satellite); 60fi. Moon rocket; 1fo. "Shapir" rocket; 2fo.50, "Szonda 3" satellite; 3fo. "Syncom 3" satellite. HORIZ: 10fo. Satellites orbiting Globe.

403 Scarlet Tiger Moth

1966. Butterflies and Moths. Multicoloured.

2150	20fi. Type **403**	10	10
2151	60fi. Orange tip	25	10
2152	70fi. Meleager's blue	60	10
2153	80fi. Scarce swallowtail	70	10
2154	1fo. Common burnet	80	10
2155	1fo.50 Southern festoon	95	35
2156	2fo. Camberwell beauty	1·20	45
2157	2fo.50 Nettle-tree butterfly	1·40	45
2158	3fo. Clouded yellow	1·90	1·20

404 Bela Kun

1966. Anniversaries of 1966.

2159	60fi. black and red (T **404**)	35	25
2160	60fi. black and blue (T. Esze)	80	25
2161	1fo. violet (Shastri)	60	25
2162	2fo. brown and ochre (I. Szechenyi)	80	25
2163	2fo. sepia and bistre (M. Zrinyi)	80	25
2164	2fo. sepia and green (S. Koranyi)	80	25

EVENTS: No. 2159, 80th Birth anniv (workers' leader); 2160, (after statue by M. Nemeth) 300th Birth anniv (war hero); 2161, Death commem (Indian Prime Minister); 2162, 175th Birth anniv (statesman); 2163, 400th Death anniv (military commander); 2164, Birth cent (scientist).

405 "Luna 9" in Space

1966. Moon Landing of "Luna 9".

2165	**405**	2fo. black, yellow & violet	60	25
2166	-	3fo. black, yellow & blue	1·70	1·20

DESIGN—HORIZ: 3fo. "Luna 9" on Moon.

406 Crocus

1966. Flower Protection. Multicoloured.

2167	20fi. Type **406**	40	10
2168	30fi. European cyclamen	50	25
2169	60fi. Ligularia	80	35
2170	1fo.40 Orange lily	1·20	45
2171	1fo.50 Fritillary	1·40	80
2172	3fo. "Dracocephalum ruyschiana"	2·50	1·20

407 Order of Labour (bronze)

1966. Hungarian Medals and Orders. Mult.

2173	20fi. Type **407**	10	10
2174	30fi. Order of Labour (silver)	10	10
2175	50fi. Banner Order of Republic, 3rd class (21½×28½ mm)	10	10
2176	60fi. Order of Labour (gold)	10	10
2177	70fi. Banner Order of Republic, 2nd class (25×30½ mm)	25	10
2178	1fo. Red Banner Order of Labour	35	15
2179	1fo.20 Banner Order of Republic, 1st class (28½×38 mm)	45	35
2180	2fo. Order of Merit of Republic	95	60
2181	2fo.50 Hero of Socialist Labour	1·40	95

408 Early Transport and Budapest Railway Station, 1846

1966. Re-opening of Transport Museum, Budapest.

2182	**408**	1fo. brown, green & yell	60	25
2183	-	2fo. blue, brown & green	1·20	60

DESIGN: 2fo. Modern transport and South Station, Budapest.

409 Barn Swallows

1966. Protection of Birds. Multicoloured.

2184	20fi. Type **409**	25	10
2185	30fi. Long-tailed tits	35	10
2186	60fi. Red crossbill	60	15
2187	1fo.40 Middle-spotted woodpecker	1·40	35
2188	1fo.50 Hoopoe	1·70	70
2189	3fo. Forest and emblem of National Forestry Association	2·50	1·40

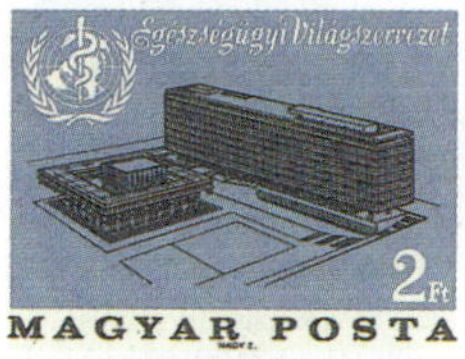

410 W.H.O. Building

1966. Inaug of W.H.O. Headquarters, Geneva.

2190	**410**	2fo. black and blue	80	25

411 Football

1966. World Cup Football Championships (1st issue). Sheet 76×108 mm.

MS2191	**411** 10fo. multicoloured	10·00	10·00

See also Nos. 2194/2202.

412 Nuclear Research Institute

1966. 10th Anniv of United Nuclear Research Institute, Dubna (U.S.S.R.).

2192	**412**	60fi. black and green	80	25

413 Buda Fortress, after Schedel's "Chronicle" (1493)

1966. 20th Anniv of U.N.E.S.C.O. and 72nd Executive Board Session, Budapest.

2193	413	2fo. violet and blue	1·20	35

414 Jules Rimet, Football and Cup

1966. World Cup Football Championship (2nd issue). Multicoloured.

2194	20fi. Type **414**	10	10
2195	30fi. Montevideo, 1930	25	10
2196	60fi. Rome, 1934	35	10
2197	1fo. Paris, 1938	45	10
2198	1fo.40 Rio de Janeiro, 1950	60	15
2199	1fo.70 Berne, 1954	1·00	25
2200	2fo. Stockholm, 1958	1·20	60
2201	2fo.50 Santiago de Chile, 1962	1·70	80
2202	3fo.+1fo. World Cup emblem on Union Jack, and map of England	2·50	2·00

415 Girl Pioneer and Emblem

1966. 20th Anniv of Hungarian Pioneers Movement.

2203	415	60fi. red and violet	80	25

416 Fire Engine

1966. Centenary of Voluntary Fire Brigades.

2204	416	2fo. black and orange	1·20	60

417 Red Fox

1966. Hunting Trophies. Multicoloured.

2205	20fi. Type **417**	10	10
2206	60fi. Wild boar	25	10
2207	70fi. Wild cat	35	10
2208	80fi. Roe deer	35	10
2209	1fo.50 Red deer	60	15
2210	2fo.50 Fallow deer	70	25
2211	3fo. Mouflon	1·70	95

418 Throwing the Discus

1966. 8th European Athletic Championships, Budapest. Multicoloured.

2212	20fi. Type **418**	10	10
2213	30fi. High-jumping	25	10
2214	40fi. Throwing the javelin	35	10
2215	50fi. Throwing the hammer	45	10
2216	60fi. Long-jumping	70	15
2217	1fo. Putting the shot	1·20	35
2218	2fo. Pole-vaulting	2·00	95
2219	3fo. Running	3·00	1·20
MS2220	105×75 mm. 10fo. Hurdling	10·50	10·50

419 Archery

1966. Stamp Day. Multicoloured.

2221	2fo.+50fi. Types **419**	1·50	1·50
2222	2fo.+50fi. Grapes	1·50	1·50
2223	2fo.+50fi. Poppies	1·50	1·50
2224	2fo.+50fi. Space dogs	1·50	1·50
MS2225	98×84 mm. Nos. 2221/4	7·00	7·00

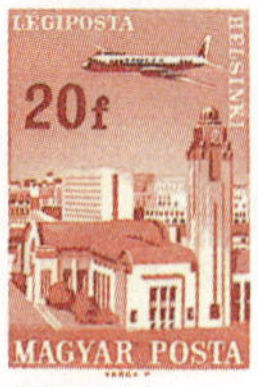

420 Helsinki

1966. Air.

2226	**420**	20fi. red	10	10
2227	-	50fi. brown	10	10
2228	-	1fo. blue	25	10
2229	-	1fo.10 black	30	10
2230	-	1fo.20 orange	35	10
2231	-	1fo.50 green	40	10
2232	-	2fo. blue	50	15
2233	-	2fo.50 red	60	25
2234	-	3fo. green	65	30
2235	-	4fo. brown	3·00	2·10
2236	-	5fo. violet	1·20	35
2237	-	10fo. blue	3·00	60
2238	-	20fo. green	4·75	1·20

DESIGNS—Ilyushin Il-18 over: 50fi. Athens; 1fo. Beirut; 1fo.10, Frankfurt; 1fo.20, Cairo; 1fo.50, Copenhagen; 2fo. London; 2fo.50, Moscow; 3fo. Paris; 4fo. Prague; 5fo. Rome; 10fo. Damascus; 20fo. Budapest.

For 2fo.60 in similar design see No. 2369.

421 "Girl in the Woods" (after Barabas)

1966. Paintings in Hungarian National Gallery (1st series). Multicoloured.

2239	60fi. Type **421**	60	25
2240	1fo. "Mrs. Istvan Bitto" (Barabas)	80	35
2241	1fo.50 "Laszlo Hunyadi Farewell" (Benczur)	1·40	60
2242	1fo.70 "Woman Reading" (Benczur) (horiz)	2·00	70
2243	2fo. "The Faggot-carrier" (Munkacsy)	2·30	80
2244	2fo.50 "The Yawning Apprentice" (Munkacsy)	2·50	85
2245	3fo. "Woman in Lilac" (Szinyei)	3·50	95
MS2246	97×79 mm. 10fo. "Picnic in May" (Szinyei)	16·00	16·00

See also Nos. 2282/8, 2318/**MS**2325, 2357/**MS**2364, 2411/**MS**2418, 2449/**MS**2456 and 2525/**MS**2532.

422 "Vostok 3" and "Vostok 4" (Nikolaev and Popovich)

1966. Twin Space Flights. Multicoloured.

2247	20fi. Type **422**	10	10
2248	60fi. Borman and Lovell, Schirra and Stafford	30	10
2249	80fi. Bykovsky and Tereshkova	35	10
2250	1fo. Stafford and Cernan	60	25
2251	1fo.50 Belyaev and Leonov (Leonov in space)	80	35
2252	2fo. McDivitt and White (White in space)	1·20	45
2253	2fo.50 Komarov, Feoktistov and Yegorov	2·00	70
2254	3fo. Conrad and Gordon	2·50	80

423 Kitaibel and "Kitaibelia vitifolia"

1967. 150th Death Anniv of Pal Kitaibel (botanist). Carpathian Flowers. Multicoloured.

2255	20fi. Type **423**	10	10
2256	60fi. "Dentaria glandulosa"	35	10
2257	1fo. "Edraianthus tenuifolius"	45	10
2258	1fo.50 "Althaea pallida"	80	25
2259	2fo. "Centaurea mollis"	1·00	35
2260	2fo.50 "Sternbergia colchiciflora"	2·00	45
2261	3fo. "Iris hungarica"	2·10	1·30

424 Militiaman

1967. 10th Anniv of Workers' Militia.

2262	**424**	2fo. blue	80	25

425 Faustus Verancsics' Parachute Descent, 1617

1967. Air. "Aerofila 67". Airmail Stamp Exhibition, Budapest. (a) 1st issue.

2263	2fo.+1fo. sepia and yellow	1·50	1·50
2264	2fo.+1fo. sepia and blue	1·50	1·50
2265	2fo.+1fo. sepia and green	1·50	1·50
2266	2fo.+1fo. sepia and pink	1·50	1·50
MS2267	116×90 mm. Nos. 2263/6	7·00	7·00

(b) 2nd issue.

2268	2fo.+1fo. blue and green	1·50	1·50
2269	2fo.+1fo. blue and orange	1·50	1·50
2270	2fo.+1fo. blue and yellow	1·50	1·50
2271	2fo.+1fo. blue and pink	1·50	1·50
MS2272	116×90 mm. Nos. 2268/71	7·00	7·00

DESIGNS: No. 2263, Type **425**; No. 2264, David Schwartz's aluminium airship, 1897; No. 2265, Erno Horvath's monoplane, 1911; No. 2266, PKZ-2 helicopter, 1918; No. 2268, Parachutist; No. 2269, Mil Mi-1 helicopter; No. 2270, Tupolev Tu-154 airliner; No. 2271, "Luna 12".

426 I.T.Y. Emblem and Transport

1967. International Tourist Year.

2273	**426**	1fo. black and blue	60	25

427 "Milton", after Orial Petrics

1967. "Amphilex" Stamp Exhibition, Amsterdam. Sheet 81×91 mm.

MS2274 **427**	10fo. multicoloured	10·50	10·50

428 "Ferenc Deak" (paddle-steamer), Schonbuchel Castle and Austrian Flag (image scaled to 74% of original size)

1967. 25th Session of Danube Commission. Vessels of Mahart Shipping Company.

2275	**428**	30fi. multicoloured	60	25
2276	-	60fi. multicoloured	80	45
2277	-	1fo. multicoloured	1·70	60
2278	-	1fo.50 multicoloured	3·50	1·00
2279	-	1fo.70 multicoloured	5·25	1·20
2280	-	2fo. multicoloured	5·75	2·30
2281	-	2fo.50 multicoloured	8·75	3·00

DESIGNS (Vessels, backgrounds and flags): 60fi. River-bus "Revfulop" Bratislava Castle, Czechoslovakia; 1fo. Diesel passenger boat "Hunyadi", Buda Castle, Hungary; 1fo.50, Diesel tug "Szekszard", Golubac Castle, Yugoslavia; 1fo.70, Tug "Miscolc", Vidin Castle, Bulgaria; 2fo. Motor-freighter "Tihany", Galati shipyard. Rumania; 2fo.50, Hydrofoil "Siraly I", port of Izmail, U.S.S.R.

429 "Szidonia Deak" (A. Gyorgyi)

1967. Paintings in National Gallery, Budapest (2nd series). Multicoloured.

2282	60fi. "Liszt" (M. Munkacsy)	35	25
2283	1fo. "Self-portrait" (S. Lanyi)	60	30
2284	1fo.50 "Portrait of a Lady" (J. Borsos)	80	35
2285	1fo.70 "The Lovers" (after P. Szinyei Merse) (horiz)	1·30	40
2286	2fo. Type **429**	1·40	45
2287	2fo.50 "National Guardsman" (J. Borsos)	1·60	60
2288	3fo. "Louis XV and Madame Dubarry" (G. Benczur)	1·90	70

430 Poodle

1967. Dogs. Multicoloured.

2289	30fi. Type **430**	15	10
2290	60fi. Collie (23½×35 mm)	25	10
2291	1fo. Pointer	45	10
2292	1fo.40 Fox terriers (23½×35 mm)	80	15
2293	2fo. Pumi	1·20	35
2294	3fo. Alsatian (23½×35 mm)	1·40	80
2295	4fo. Puli	2·50	1·40

431 Sterlet

1967. 14th International Anglers' Federation Congress, and World Angling Championships, Dunaujvaros. Multicoloured.

2296	20fi. Type **431**	10	10
2297	60fi. Zander	25	10
2298	1fo. Common carp	35	10
2299	1fo.70 Wels	95	15
2300	2fo. Northern pike	1·20	35
2301	2fo.50 Asp	1·40	70
2302	3fo.+1fo. Anglers' and C.I.P.S. (Federation) emblem	2·50	1·30

432 "Prince Igor" (Borodin)

1967. Popular Operas. Designs showing scenes from various operas. Multicoloured.

2303	20fi. Type **432**	25	10
2304	30fi. "Der Freischutz" (Weber)	25	10
2305	40fi. "The Magic Flute" (Mozart)	60	15
2306	60fi. "Bluebeard's Castle" (Bartok)	80	25
2307	80fi. "Carmen" (Bizet) (vert)	1·20	35
2308	1fo. "Don Carlos" (Verdi) (vert)	1·40	60
2309	1fo.70 "Tannhauser" (Wagner) (vert)	1·70	1·20
2310	3fo. "Laszlo Hunyadi" (Erkel) (vert)	2·30	2·10

433 "Teaching" (14th-cent class)

1967. 600th Anniv of Higher Education in Hungary.

2311	**433**	2fo. green and gold	1·40	25

434 Faculty Building

1967. 300th Anniv of Political Law and Science Faculty, Lorand Eotvos University, Budapest.

2312	**434**	2fo. green	1·40	25

435 "Lenin as Teacher"

1967. 50th Anniv of October Revolution. Multicoloured.

2313	60fi. Type **435**	25	10
2314	1fo. "Lenin"	25	10
2315	3fo. "Lenin aboard the Aurora"	1·20	60

436 "Venus 4"

1967. Landing of "Venus 4" on planet Venus.

2316	**436**	5fo. multicoloured	2·00	1·50

437 19th-centenary Mail Coach

1967. Centenary of Hungarian Postal Administration. Sheet 85×95 mm.

MS2317	**437**	10fo. multicoloured	5·75	5·75

437a "Brother and Sister" (A. Fenyes)

1967. Paintings in National Gallery, Budapest (3rd series). Multicoloured.

2318	60fi. Type **437a**	25	10
2319	1fo. "Boys Wrestling on Beach" (O. Glatz)	60	10
2320	1fo.50 "October" (K. Ferenczy)	75	15
2321	1fo.70 "Women by the River" (I. Szonyi) (horiz)	80	25
2322	2fo. "Godfather's Breakfast" (I. Csok)	85	30
2323	2fo.50 "The Eviction Order" (G. Derkovits)	1·00	60
2324	3fo. "Self-Portrait" (T. Csontvary)	1·20	80
MS2325	78×100 mm. 10fo. "The Apple Pickers" (B. Uitz) (larger 37½×60 mm)	2·25	3·00

"Women by the River" (1fo.70) is in a private collection in Budapest.

See also Nos. 2357/**MS**2364 and 2411/**MS**2418.

438 Rifle-shooting on Skis

1967. Winter Olympic Games, Grenoble. Multicoloured.

2326	30fi. Type **438**	10	10
2327	60fi. Figure skating (pairs)	25	10
2328	1fo. Bobsleighing	35	10
2329	1fo.40 Downhill skiing	60	15
2330	1fo.70 Figure skating	80	25
2331	2fo. Speed skating	95	45
2332	3fo. Ski jumping	1·20	80
2333	4fo.+1fo. Ice stadium, Grenoble	1·70	1·20
MS2334	116×99 mm. 10fo. Ice hockey goal keeper (61×61 mm)	4·75	4·75

439 Kalman Kando, Class V43 Electric Locomotive and Map

1968. Kando Commemoration.

2335	**439**	2fo. blue	80	25

440 Cat

1968. Cats. Multicoloured.

2336	20fi. Type **440**	25	10
2337	60fi. Cream angora	35	25
2338	1fo. Smoky angora	60	30
2339	1fo.20 Domestic kitten	70	35
2340	1fo.50 White angora	1·20	60
2341	2fo. Striped angora	1·40	80
2342	2fo.50 Siamese	2·00	95
2343	5fo. Blue angora	3·50	1·40

441 Zoltan Kodaly (composer)

1968. Kodaly Commemoration.

2344	**441**	5fo. multicoloured	2·00	1·20

442 City Hall, Arms, Grapes and Apricot

1968. 600th Anniv of Kecskemet.

2345	**442**	2fo. brown	80	25

443 White Stork

1968. International Council for Bird Preservation Congress, Budapest. Protected Birds. Mult.

2346	20fi. Type **443**	25	10
2347	50fi. Golden orioles	35	15
2348	60fi. Imperial eagle	45	25
2349	1fo. Western red-footed falcons	60	30
2350	1fo.20 Eurasian scops owl	70	35
2351	1fo.50 Great bustard	80	40
2352	2fo. European bee eaters	2·30	60
2353	2fo.50 Greylag goose	3·00	1·30

444 Karl Marx

1968. 150th Birth Anniv of Karl Marx.

2354	**444**	1fo. purple	60	25

See also No. 1290.

445 Icarus falling in space

1968. In Memoriam. Astronauts White, Gagarin and Komarov. Sheet 95×77 mm.

MS2355	**445**	10fo. multicoloured	5·75	5·75

446 Student

1968. 150th Anniv of Mosonmagyarovar Agricultural College.

2356	**446**	2fo. green	80	25

1968. Paintings in National Gallery, Budapest (4th series). As T 437a. Multicoloured.

2357	40fi. "Girl with a Pitcher" (Goya)	10	10
2358	60fi. "Head of an Apostle" (El Greco)	25	10
2359	1fo. "Boy with Apples" (Nunez) (horiz)	45	25
2360	1fo.50 "The Repentant Magdalen" (El Greco)	95	35
2361	2fo.50 "The Breakfast" (Velasquez) (horiz)	1·40	40
2362	4fo. "St. Elizabeth" (detail from "The Holy Family"; El Greco)	1·60	95
2363	5fo. "The Knife-grinder" (Goya)	1·70	1·20
MS2364	88×95 mm. 10fo. "Portrait of a Girl" (Palma Vecchio)	3·00	3·75

447 Lake Steamer, Flags and Badacsony Hills

1968. Lake Balaton Resorts. Multicoloured.

2365	20fi. Type **447**	25	10
2365a	40fi. Type **447**	25	10
2366	60fi. Tihany peninsula, tower and feather	25	10
2367	1fo. Yachts and buoy, Balatonalmadi	25	10
2368	2fo. Szigliget bay, vineyard, wine and fish	60	25

448 Ilyushin Il-18 over St. Stephen's Cathedral, Vienna

1968. Air. 50th Anniv of Budapest–Vienna Airmail Service.

2369	**448**	2fo.60 violet	1·20	35

449 Class 424 Steam Locomotive No. 176

1968. Centenary of Hungarian State Railways.

2370	**449**	2fo. multicoloured	2·00	60

450 Grazing Stud

1968. Horse-breeding on the Hortobagy "puszta" (Hungarian steppe). Multicoloured.

2371	30fi. Type **450**	15	10
2372	40fi. Horses in storm	15	10
2373	60fi. Grooms horse-racing	25	10
2374	80fi. Horse-drawn sleigh	45	10
2375	1fo. Four-in-hand	60	30
2376	1fo.40 Seven-in-hand	70	35
2377	2fo. Driving five horses	85	40
2378	2fo.50 Groom preparing evening meal	95	60
2379	4fo. Five-in-hand	1·20	95

451 M. Tompa

1968. Death Centenary of Mihaly Tompa (poet).

2380	**451**	60fi. violet	35	10

452 Festival Emblem, Bulgarian and Hungarian Couples in National Costume

1968. 9th World Youth Festival, Sofia.

2381	**452**	60fi. multicoloured	35	10

453 Breasting the Tape

454 Swimming

1968. Air. Olympic Games, Mexico. Mult.

MS2382 81×101 mm **453** 10fo. multi-coloured (postage)		6·50	6·50
2383	20fi. Type **454** (air)	10	10
2384	60fi. Football	10	10
2385	80fi. Wrestling	10	10
2386	1fo. Canoeing	15	10
2387	1fo.40 Gymnastics	35	10
2388	2fo.+1fo. Horse-jumping	1·20	35
2389	3fo. Fencing	1·40	45
2390	4fo. Throwing the Javelin	1·70	65

455 Baja Plate, 1870

1968. Stamp Day. Hungarian Ceramics. Mult.

2391	1fo.+50fi. Type **455**	1·20	1·20
2392	1fo.+50fi. West Hungarian jug, 1618	1·20	1·20
2393	1fo.+50fi. Tiszafured flagon, 1847	1·20	1·20
2394	1fo.+50fi. Mezocsat flask, 1848	1·20	1·20
MS2395 74×96 mm. 2fo.+50fi. North Hungarian jug, 1672; 2fo.+50fi. Mezocsat plate, 1843; 2fo.+50fi. Moragy plate, 1860; 2fo.+50fi. Debrecen pitcher, 1793		5·75	5·75

The designs from the miniature sheet are smaller, measuring 25×35 mm.

456 Society Emblem

1968. "Hungarian Society for Popularization of Scientific Knowledge".

2396	**456**	2fo. black and blue	80	25

457 Rocket Hesperus

1968. Garden Flowers. Multicoloured.

2397	20fi. Type **457**	35	10
2398	60fi. Pansy	45	10
2399	80fi. Zinnias	60	35
2400	1fo. Morning Glory	95	45
2401	1fo.40 Petunia	1·20	60
2402	1fo.50 Purslane	1·40	65
2403	2fo. Michaelmas daisies	1·60	70
2404	2fo.50 Dahlia	1·70	1·20

458 Two Girls waving Flags

1968. Children's Stamp Designs for 50th Anniv of Hungarian Communist Party. Multicoloured.

2405	40fi. Type **458**	35	10
2406	60fi. Children with flags and banner	80	25
2407	1fo. Pioneer bugler in camp	1·40	60

459 "Workers of the World Unite" (Bertalan Por's 1918 poster)

1968. 50th Anniv of Hungarian Communist Party.

2408	**459**	1fo. black, red and gold	35	25
2409	-	2fo. multicoloured	45	35

DESIGN—HORIZ: 2fo. "Martyrs" (statue by Zoltan Kiss).

460 Human Rights Emblem

1968. Human Rights Year.

2410	**460**	1fo. brown	80	25

1968. Paintings in National Gallery, Budapest (5th series). Italian Masters. As T 437a. Mult.

2411	40fi. "Esterhazy Madonna" (Raphael)	10	10
2412	60fi. "The Annunciation" (Strozzi)	10	10
2413	1fo. "Portrait of a Young Man" (Raphael)	25	10
2414	1fo.50 "The Three Graces" (Naldini)	60	10
2415	2fo.50 "Portrait of a Man" (Sebastian del Piombo)	1·00	35
2416	4fo. "The Doge Marcantonio Trevisani" (Titian)	1·70	80
2417	5fo. "Venus, Cupid and Jealousy" (Bronzino)	2·50	1·30
MS2418 116×73 mm. 10fo. "Bathsheba bathing" (Ricci). Imperf		6·50	6·50

461 Endre Ady

1969. 50th Death Anniv of Endre Ady (poet).

2419	**461**	1fo. black, purple & gold	60	25

462 Press Emblem

1969. Centenary of Athenaeum Press.

2420	**462**	2fo. multicoloured	80	25

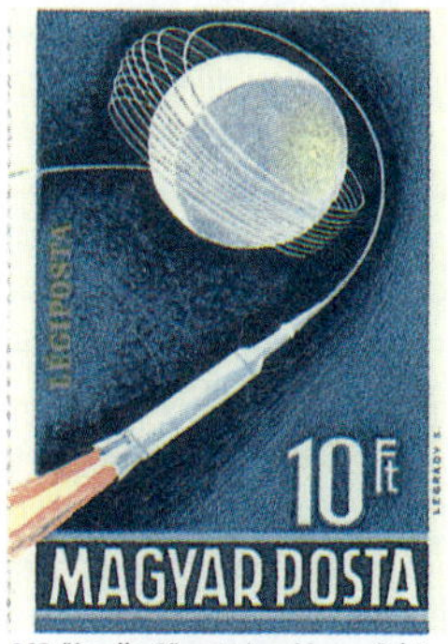

463 "Apollo 8" entering Moon Orbit

1969. Air. Moon Flight of "Apollo 8". Sheet 111×81 mm.

MS2421 **463** 10fo. multicoloured	70	70

464 Throwing the Javelin

1969. Olympic Gold Medal Winners. Mult.

2422	40fi. Type **464**	15	10
2423	60fi. Canoeing	25	10
2424	1fo. Football	30	10
2425	1fo.20 Throwing the Hammer	35	15
2426	2fo. Fencing	50	25
2427	3fo. Wrestling	60	30
2428	4fo. Kayak-canoeing	1·40	35
2429	5fo. Horse-jumping	1·70	95
MS2430 111×84 mm. 10fo. Ancient Greek Athlete and Olympic Flame		7·50	7·50

465 Poster by O. Danko

1969. 50th Anniv of Proclamation of Hungarian Soviet Republic.

2431	**465**	40fi. black, red and gold	10	10
2432	-	60fi. black, red and gold	10	10
2433	-	1fo. black, red and gold	35	15
2434	-	2fo. multicoloured	60	25
2435	-	3fo. multicoloured	1·20	60
MS2436 97×71 mm. 10fo. black, red and grey			4·75	4·75

DESIGNS: 60fi. "Lenin" by unknown artist; 1fo. "Young Man Breaking Chains" (R. Steiner); 2fo. "Worker" (I. Foldes and G. Vegh); 3fo. "Soldier" (unknown artist). HORIZ—(52×40 mm): 10fo. "Workers with Banner" (R. Bereny).

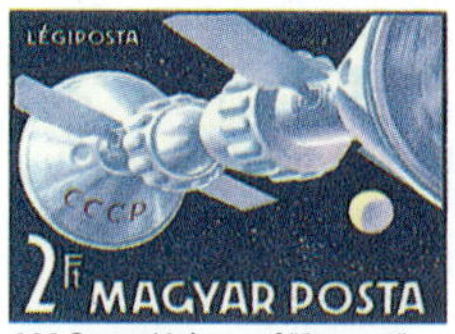

466 Space Link-up of "Soyuz 4" and "Soyuz 5"

1969. Air. Space Flights of "Soyuz 4" and "Soyuz 5". Multicoloured.

2437	2fo. Type **466**	80	80
2438	2fo. Link-up and astronauts "walking" in Space	80	80

467 Jersey Tiger Moth

1969. Butterflies and Moths. Multicoloured.

2439	40fi. Type **467**	25	10
2440	60fi. Eyed hawk moth	25	10
2441	80fi. Painted lady	25	10
2442	1fo. Foxy charaxes	30	10
2443	1fo.20 Lesser fiery copper	40	10
2444	2fo. Large blue	80	25
2445	3fo. Dark crimson underwing	1·60	60
2446	4fo. Peacock	1·70	1·20

468 I.L.O. Emblem

1969. 50th Anniv of Int Labour Organisation.

2447	**468**	1fo. brown and red	60	25

469 Chain Bridge, Budapest

1969. "Budapest 71" Stamp Exhibition.

2448	**469**	5fo.+2fo. multicoloured	2·30	2·30

470 "Black Pigs" (Gauguin)

1969. Paintings in National Gallery, Budapest (6th series). French Masters. Multicoloured.

2449	40fi. Type **470**	15	10
2450	60fi. "The Ladies" (Toulouse-Lautrec) (horiz)	25	10
2451	1fo. "Venus on Clouds" (Vouet)	35	15
2452	2fo. "Lady with Fan" (Manet) (horiz)	80	25
2453	3fo. "Petra Camara" (Chasseriau)	1·70	35
2454	4fo. "The Cowherd" (Troyon) (horiz)	2·30	70
2455	5fo. "The Wrestlers" (Courbet)	2·50	1·20
MS2456 75×97 mm. 10fo. "Pomona" (Fouche)		7·00	7·00

471 Vac

1969. Danube Towns. Multicoloured.

2457	40fi. Type **471**	10	10
2458	1fo. Szentendre	10	10

2459 1fo.20 Visegrad 60 10
2460 3fo. Esztergom 95 25

472 "PAX"

1969. 20th Anniv of Int Peace Movement.
2461 **472** 1fo. gold, dp blue & blue 60 25

473 Astronauts on Moon (image scaled to 64% of original size)

1969. Air. First Man on the Moon (1st issue). Sheet 133×89 mm.
MS2462 **473** 10fo. multicoloured 10·50 10·50
See also Nos. 2487/94.

474 Zelkova Leaf (fossil)

1969. Centenary of Hungarian Geological Institute. Minerals and Fossils. Multicoloured.
2463 40fi. Type **474** 15 10
2464 60fi. Greenockite calcite sphalerite crystals 25 10
2465 1fo. Hungarian herring (fossilized fish) 30 10
2466 1fo.20 Quartz crystals 35 15
2467 2fo. "Reineckia crassicostata" (ammonite) 45 25
2468 3fo. Copper ore 95 35
2469 4fo. "Placochelys placodonta" (fossilized turtle) 1·70 95
2470 5fo. Cuprite crystals 3·00 1·20

475 Okorag Stirrupcup, 1880

1969. Stamp Day. Hungarian Folk Art. Wood-carvings. Multicoloured.
2471 1fo.+50fi. Type **475** 1·40 1·40
2472 1fo.+50fi. Felsotizavidek jar, 1898 1·40 1·40
2473 1fo.+50fi. Somogyharsagy pot, 1935 1·40 1·40
2474 1fo.+50fi. Alfold smoking-pipe, 1740 1·40 1·40
MS2475 75×96 mm. 2fo.+50fi. ×4 (a) Csorna panel, 1879; (b) Okany mug, 1914; (c) Sellye casket, 1899; (d) Lengyeltoti box, 1880 5·75 5·75
The designs in **MS**2475 are smaller, each 31×40 mm.

476 "The Scientist at his Table" (Rembrandt)

1969. Int "History of Art" Congress, Budapest.
2476 **476** 1fo. sepia 60 25

477 Horse-jumping

1969. World Pentathlon Championships, Budapest. Multicoloured.
2477 40fi. Type **477** 30 15
2478 60fi. Fencing 60 35
2479 1fo. Pistol-shooting 95 60
2480 2fo. Swimming 1·00 70
2481 3fo. Running 1·20 95
2482 5fo. All five sports 2·30 1·40

478 Postcard and Letterbox

1969. Centenary of 1st Hungarian Postcard.
2483 **478** 60fi. ochre and red 35 25

479 Mahatma Gandhi

1969. Birth Centenary of Mahatma Gandhi.
2484 **479** 5fo. multicoloured 1·70 1·20

480 Hemispheres

1969. World Trade Unions Federations Congress, Budapest.
2485 **480** 2fo. blue and brown 80 25

481 "Janos Nagy" (self-portrait)

1969. 50th Death Anniv of Janos Nagy (painter).
2486 **481** 5fo. multicoloured 1·70 1·20

482 "Flight to the Moon" (after Jules Verne)

1969. Air. 1st Man on the Moon (2nd issue). Multicoloured.
2487 40fi. Type **482** 10 10
2488 60fi. Tsiolkovsky's "space station" 25 10
2489 1fo. "Luna 1" 35 10
2490 1fo.50 "Ranger 7" 70 15
2491 2fo. "Luna 9" 95 25
2492 2fo.50 "Apollo 8" 1·00 35
2493 3fo. "Soyuz 4" and "5" 1·40 70
2494 4fo. "Apollo 10" 1·70 1·00

483 "St John the Evangelist" (Van Dyck)

1969. Dutch Paintings in Hungarian Museums. Multicoloured.
2495 40fi. Type **483** 10 10
2496 60fi. "Peasants" (P. de Molyn) 10 10
2497 1fo. "Boy lighting Pipe" (H. Terbruggen) 45 15
2498 2fo. "The Musicians" (detail, Jan Steen) 80 25
2499 3fo. "Woman reading Letter" (P. de Hooch) 1·50 35
2500 4fo. "The Fiddler" (Dirk Hals) 1·70 70
2501 5fo. "J. Asselyn" (Frans Hals) 2·30 1·40
MS2502 73×97 mm. 10fo. "Mucius Scaevola before Porsenna" (Rubens and Van Dyck) 5·75 5·75

484 Kiskunfelegyhaza Pigeon

1969. International Pigeon Exn, Budapest.
2503 **484** 1fo. multicoloured 60 25

485 Daimler (1886)

1970. Air. Old Motor Cars. Multicoloured.
2504 40fi. Type **485** 35 10
2505 60fi. Peugeot (1894) 45 15
2506 1fo. Benz (1901) 60 35
2507 1fo.50 Cudell (1902) 70 45
2508 2fo. Rolls-Royce (1908) 1·00 60
2509 2fo.50 Ford "T" (1908) 1·20 80
2510 3fo. Vermorel (1912) 1·70 95
2511 4fo. Csonka (1912) 2·30 1·20

486 View of Budapest

1970. "Budapest 71" Stamp Exhibition and Centenary of Hungarian Stamps (1st series). Multicoloured. Background colours given.
2512 **486** 2fo.+1fo. brown 1·00 1·00
2513 - 2fo.+1fo. lilac 1·00 1·00
2514 - 2fo.+1fo. blue 1·00 1·00
DESIGNS: Nos. 2513/4 show different views of Budapest, in style as Type **486**.
See also Nos. 2572/**MS**2576 and 2604/**MS**2608.

487 "Soyuz 6, 7, 8"

1970. Air. Space Exploration. Multicoloured.
2515 3fo.(×4) Type **487** 1·20 1·20
2516 3fo.(×4) Astronauts on Moon ("Apollo 12") 1·20 1·20
Nos. 2515/6 were only available each in small sheets of four, and are priced thus.

488 Underground Train at Station

1970. Opening of Budapest Underground Railway.
2517 **488** 1fo. blue, turquoise & blk 60 25

489 Budapest Panorama, 1945 (image scaled to 37% of original size)

1970. 25th Anniv of Liberation. Sheet 159×83 mm containing T 489 and similar horiz design. Multicoloured.
MS2518 5fo. ×2 (a) Type **489**; (b) Budapest panorama, 1970 5·75 5·75

490 Cloud Formation, Satellite and Globe

1970. Cent of Hungarian Meteorological Service.
2519 **490** 1fo. multicoloured 60 25

491 Lenin

1970. Birth Centenary of Lenin. Mult.
2520 1fo. Lenin Statue, Budapest 25 10
2521 2fo. Type **491** 60 35

492 Lehar and Music

1970. Birth Cent of Franz Lehar (composer).

2522 **492** 2fo. multicoloured 80 35

493 Fujiyama and Hungarian Pavilion

1970. Air. Expo 70. Multicoloured.

2523 2fo. Type **493** 1·20 1·20
2524 3fo. Tower of the Sun and Peace Bell 1·70 1·70

494 "Samson and Delilah" (M. Rocca)

1970. Paintings in National Gallery, Budapest (7th series). Multicoloured.

2525 40fi. Type **494** 10 10
2526 60fi. "Joseph's Dream" (G. B. Langetti) 25 10
2527 1fo. "Clio" (P. Mignard) 35 15
2528 1fo.50 "Venus and Satyr" (S. Ricci) (horiz.) 45 25
2529 2fo.50 "Andromeda" (F. Furini) 95 35
2530 4fo. "Venus, Adonis and Cupid" (L. Giordano) 1·50 80
2531 5fo. "Allegory" (woman) (C. Giaquinto) 1·70 1·20
MS2532 100×85 mm. 10fo. "Diane and Callisto" (Janssens) (horiz) 7·00 7·00

The design of **MS**2532 is larger, 64×46 mm.

495 "Apollo 13" over Moon

1970. Air. Space Flight of "Apollo 13". Sheet 112×90 mm containing T 495 and three other similar horiz designs. Multicoloured.

MS2533 2fo.50 ×4 (a) Type **495**; (b) In flight; (c) Descent; (d) In sea 5·25 5·25

496 Beethoven (from statue at Martonvasar)

1970. Birth Bicentenary of Beethoven.

2534 **496** 1fo. green, lilac & yellow 1·40 35

497 Foundryman

1970. Bicent of Diosgyor Foundry, Miskolc.

2535 **497** 1fo. multicoloured 60 25

498 St. Stephen

1970. 1,000th Birth Anniv of St. Stephen (King Stephen I of Hungary).

2536 **498** 3fo. multicoloured 1·40 45

499 Rowing Four

1970. 17th European Women's Rowing Championships, Lake Tata.

2537 **499** 1fo. multicoloured 80 25

500 Illuminated Initial

1970. Stamp Day. Paintings and Illuminated Initials from Codices of King Matthias.

2538 1fo.+50fi. Type **500** 1·40 1·40
2539 1fo.+50fi. "N" and flowers 1·40 1·40
2540 1fo.+50fi. "O" and ornamentation 1·40 1·40
2541 1fo.+50fi. "King Matthias" 1·40 1·40
MS2542 66×86 mm. 2fo.+50fi. ×4 (a) "Bishop Ransanus with King Matthias and Queen Beatrix"; (b) "Q" and "Old Humanist"; (c) "C" and "Appianus of Alexandria"; (d) "A" and "King David on Throne" 7·50 7·50

501 "Soyuz 9" on Transporter

1970. Air. "Soyuz 9" Space Mission. Sheet 108×87 mm containing T 501 and three similar horiz designs. Multicoloured.

MS2543 2fo.50 ×4 (a) Type **501**; (b) Launch; (c) In flight; (d) Cosmonauts 5·25 5·25

502 "Bread" (sculpture by I. Szabo) and F.A.O. Emblem

1970. 7th F.A.O. European Regional Conference, Budapest.

2544 **502** 1fo. multicoloured 60 25

503 Boxing

1970. 75th Anniv of Hungarian Olympic Committee. Multicoloured.

2545 40fi. Type **503** 10 10
2546 60fi. Canoeing 10 10
2547 1fo. Fencing 25 15
2548 1fo.50 Water-polo 35 25
2549 2fo. Gymnastics 95 35
2550 2fo.50 Throwing the Hammer 95 45
2551 3fo. Wrestling 1·20 60
2552 5fo. Swimming 1·30 65

504 Family and "Flame of Knowledge"

1970. 5th Education Congress, Budapest.

2553 **504** 1fo. blue, green & orange 60 25

505 Chalice of Benedek Suky, c. 1400

1970. Goldsmiths' Craft. Treasures from Budapest National Museum and Esztergom Treasury. Multicoloured.

2554 40fi. Type **505** 10 10
2555 60fi. Altar-cruet, c. 1500 10 10
2556 1fo. "Nadasdy" goblet, 16th-century 25 10
2557 1fo.50 Coconut goblet with gold case, c. 1600 45 15
2558 2fo. Silver tankard of M. Toldalaghy, c. 1623 60 35
2559 2fo.50 Communion-cup of G.I. Rakoczi, c. 1670 95 45
2560 3fo. Tankard, c. 1690 1·20 60
2561 4fo. "Bell-flower" cup, c. 1710 1·70 1·20

506 "The Virgin and Child" ("Giampietrino", G. Pedrini)

1970. Paintings. Religious Art from Christian Museum, Esztergom. Multicoloured.

2562 40fi. Type **506** 10 10
2563 60fi. "Love" (G. Lazzarini) 10 10
2564 1fo. "Legend of St. Catherine of Alexandria" ("Master of Bat") 25 15
2565 1fo.50 "Adoration of the Shepherds" (F. Fontebasso) (horiz.) 70 25
2566 2fo.50 "Adoration of the Magi" ("Master of Aranyosmarot") 1·40 35
2567 4fo. "Temptation of St. Anthony the Hermit" (J. de Cock) 1·90 70
2568 5fo. "St. Sebastian" (Palmezzano) 2·00 80

MS2569 72×84 mm. 10fo. "The Maid and the Unicorn" (unknown Lombard painter) 7·50 7·50

507 Mauthausen Camp Memorial (A. Makrisz)

1970. 25th Anniv of Liberation of Concentration Camps.

2570 **507** 1fo. brown and blue 60 25

508 "Luna 16" in Flight

1971. Air. "Luna 16" Space Mission. Sheet 108×87 mm containing T 508 and three other similar horiz designs. Multicoloured.

MS2571 2fo.50 ×4 (a) Type **508**; (b) Parachute landing; (c) On Moon's surface; (d) Nosecone 5·25 5·25

509 Budapest, 1470

1971. "Budapest 71" Stamp Exhibition and Centenary of Hungarian Stamps (2nd series). "Budapest Through the Ages".

2572 **509** 2fo.+1fo. black & yell 1·00 1·00
2573 - 2fo.+1fo. black & mve 1·00 1·00
2574 - 2fo.+1fo. black & grn 1·00 1·00
2575 - 2fo.+1fo. black & orge 1·00 1·00
MS2576 110×75 mm. 2fo.+1fo. ×4 (a) black and orange; (b) black and pale green; (c) black and violet; (d) black and mauve 4·75 4·75

DESIGNS: Budapest in: No. 2573, 1600; No. 2574, 1638; No. 2575, 1770. Smaller (40×18 mm)—No. **MS**2575, Budapest in (a) 1777, (b) 1850, (c) 1895, (d) 1970.

510 "Lunokhod 1" on Module

1971. Air. Moon Mission of "Luna 17" and "Lunokhod 2". Sheet 108×87 mm containing T 510 and three other similar horiz designs. Multicoloured.

MS2577 2fo.50 ×4 (a) Type **510**; (b) "Luna 17" leaving Earth; (c) "Luna 17" nearing Moon; (d) "Lunokhod 1" on Moon's surface 5·25 5·25

511 "The Marseillaise" (sculpture by Rude)

1971. Centenary of Paris Commune.

2578 **511** 3fo. brown and green 1·30 60

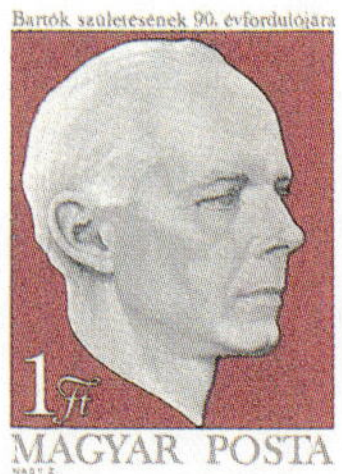

512 Bela Bartok

1971. 90th Birth Anniv of Bela Bartok (composer).
2579 **512** 1fo. black, grey and red 1·40 25

513 Gyor in 1594

1971. 700th Anniv of Gyor.
2580 **513** 2fo. multicoloured 80 35

514 Astronauts on Moon

1971. Air. "Apollo 14" Moon Mission. Sheet 120×70 mm.
MS2581 **514** 10fo. multicoloured 5·75 5·75

1971. Birth Centenary of Andras L. Achim (peasant leader). Portrait in similar style to T 512.
2582 1fo. black, grey and green 60 25

516 Hunting European Bison

1971. World Hunting Exhibition, Budapest. Multicoloured.
2583 40fi. Type **516** (postage) 25 10
2584 60fi. Hunting wild boar 35 25
2585 80fi. Deer-stalking 60 30
2586 1fo. Falconry 95 35
2587 1fo.20 Stag-hunting 1·00 45
2588 2fo. Great bustards with young 1·20 60
2589 3fo. Netting fish 1·70 70
2590 4fo. Angling 2·30 80

MS2591 145×100 mm. 10fo. Herd of roe deer (air) 8·75 8·75
The design of the 10fo. is larger, 72×46 mm.

517 "Portrait of a Man" (Durer)

1971. 500th Birth Anniv of Albrecht Durer (artist). Sheet 80×100 mm.
MS2592 **517** 10fo. multicoloured 4·75 4·75

518 Emblem on Flower

1971. 25th Anniv of Hungarian Young Pioneers.
2593 **518** 1fo. multicoloured 1·20 25

519 F.I.R. Emblem

1971. 20th Anniv of International Federation of Resistance Fighters.
2594 **519** 1fo. multicoloured 1·20 25

520 "Walking in the Garden" (Toyokuni School)

1971. Japanese Colour Prints from Ferenc Hopp Collection, Budapest. Multicoloured.
2595 40fi. Type **520** 10 10
2596 60fi. "Geisha in boat" (Yeishi) 15 10
2597 1fo. "Woman with scroll-painting" (Yeishi) 35 15
2598 1fo.50 "Oirans" (Kiyonaga) 60 25
2599 2fo. "Awabi Fishers" (Utamaro) 95 30
2600 2fo.50 "Scated Oiran" (Harunobu) 1·00 35
2601 3fo. "Peasant Girl carrying Faggots" (Hokusai) 1·20 1·00
2602 4fo. "Women and Girls Walking" (Yeishi) 1·70 1·40

521 Locomotive "Bets" and Route Map (1846)

1971. 125th Anniv of Hungarian Railways.
2603 **521** 1fo. multicoloured 80 25

522 Hungarian Newspaper Stamp of 1871

1971. "Budapest 71" Stamp Exhibition and Centenary of Hungarian Stamps (3rd series). Mult.
2604 2fo.+1fo. Type **522** 1·40 1·40
2605 2fo.+1fo. 45f. "Petofi" stamp of 1919 1·40 1·40
2606 2fo.+1fo. 40k. "Harvesters" stamp of 1920 1·40 1·40
2607 2fo.+1fo. 16f.+16f. "Art" stamp of 1940 1·40 1·40
MS2608 115×99 mm. 2fo.+1fo. ×4 (a) 60f.+60f. "Liberty" stamp of 1947; (b) 2fo. "Costume" stamp of 1953; (c) 2fo. Air stamp of 1958; (d) 1fo. "Space" stamp of 1965 5·75 5·75

523 Griffin with Inking Balls

1971. Cent of State Printing Office, Budapest.
2609 **523** 1fo. multicoloured 80 80

524 O.I.J. Emblem and Page of "Magyar Sajto"

1971. 25th Anniv of Int Organisation of Journalists.
2610 **524** 1fo. gold and blue 60 25

525 Volkov, Dobrovolsky and Patsaev (image scaled to 53% of original size)

1971. Air. "Soyuz 11" Cosmonauts Memorial Issue. Sheet 133×90 mm.
MS2611 **525** 10fo. multicoloured 5·75 5·75

526 J. Winterl (founder) and "Waldsteinia geoides"

1971. Bicentenary of Botanical Gardens, Budapest. Multicoloured.
2612 40fi. Type **526** 10 10
2613 60fi. "Bromeliaceae" 20 10
2614 80fi. "Titanopsis calcarea" 25 15
2615 1fo. "Vinca herbacea" 35 20
2616 1fo.20 "Gymnocalycium mihanovichii" 45 25
2617 2fo. "Nymphaea gigantea" 95 35
2618 3fo. "Iris arenaria" 1·20 60
2619 5fo. "Paeonia banatica" 2·30 1·20

527 Horse-racing

1971. Equestrian Sport. Multicoloured.
2620 40fi. Type **527** 15 10
2621 60fi. Trotting 25 10
2622 80fi. Cross-country riding 35 10
2623 1fo. Show-jumping 45 10
2624 1fo.20 Start of race 60 15
2625 2fo. Polo 95 35
2626 3fo. Steeplechasing 1·40 70
2627 5fo. Dressage 2·30 1·30

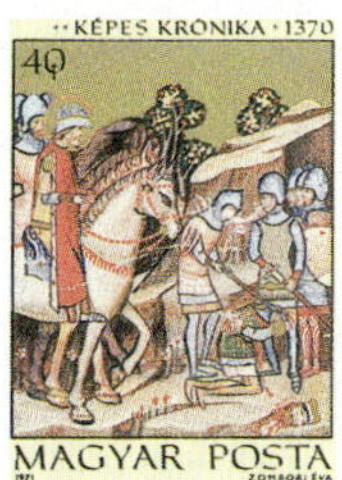

528 "Execution of Koppany"

1971. Miniatures from the "Illuminated Chronicle" of King Lajos I of Hungary. Multicoloured.
2628 40fi. Type **528** 20 10
2629 60fi. "The Pursuit of King Peter" 25 10
2630 1fo. "Bazarad's Victory over King Karoly I" 35 15
2631 1fo.50 "The Strife between King Salamon and Prince Geza" 70 25
2632 2fo.50 "The Founding of Obuda Monastery by King Stephen and Queen Gisela" 1·00 35
2633 4fo. "Reconciliation of King Kalman and his brother, Almos" 1·60 80
2634 5fo. "King Ladislas I supervising the construction of Nagyvarad Church" 1·70 1·20
MS2635 84×87 mm. 10fo. "The Funeral of Prince Emeric and the Binding of Vazul" 5·25 5·25
The design of the 10fo. is larger, 51×60 mm.

529 Racial Equality Year Emblem

1971. Racial Equality Year.
2636 **529** 1fo. multicoloured 60 25

530 Ice Hockey

1971. Winter Olympic Games, Sapporo, Japan (1972). Multicoloured.
2637 40fi. Type **530** 10 10
2638 60fi. Downhill skiing 25 10
2639 80fi. Figure skating (female) 30 10
2640 1fo. Ski jumping 35 10
2641 1fo.20 Cross-country skiing 60 15
2642 2fo. Figure skating (male) 70 25
2643 3fo. Bobsleighing 95 80
2644 4fo. Rifle-shooting (Biathlon) 1·20 1·30
MS2645 133×89 mm. 10fo. Buddha 7·50 7·50
The design of the 10fo. is larger, 89×51 mm.

531 Astronauts aboard Moon Rover (image scaled to 68% of original size)

1972. Air. Moon Flight of "Apollo 15". Sheet 120×76 mm.
MS2646 **531** 10fo. multicoloured 5·75 5·75

532 Class 303, 1950

1972. Railway Steam Locomotives. Mult.
2647 40fi. Type **532** 30 10
2648 60fi. Class P6, 1902, Prussia 35 15
2649 80fi. Class 380, 1894, Italy 60 35
2650 1fo. Class P36, 1950, Russia 55 15
2651 1fo.20 Heisler locomotive, Japan 60 30
2652 2fo. Scottish Caledonian tank locomotive, 1837 1·40 70
2653 4fo. Class 166, 1882, Austria 1·70 1·20
2654 5fo. Locomotive "Continent", 1854 2·30 1·40

533 "J. Pannonius" (A. Mantegna)

1972. 500th Death Anniv of Janus Pannonius (poet).

2655	**533**	1fo. multicoloured	35	25

534 "Mariner 9"

1972. Exploration of Mars. Multicoloured.

2656	2fo. Type **534**	80	80
2657	2fo. "Mars 2 and 3"	80	80

535 Doorway of Csempeszkopacs Church

1972. Protection of Monuments.

2658	**535**	3fo. green	1·40	60

536 Hungarian Greyhound

1972. Dogs. Multicoloured.

2659	40fi. Type **536**	15	10
2660	60fi. Afghan hound (head)	25	10
2661	80fi. Irish wolfhound	30	15
2662	1fo.20 Borzoi (head)	45	25
2663	2fo. Greyhound	95	35
2664	4fo. Whippet (head)	2·10	60
2665	6fo. Afghan hound	2·30	1·40

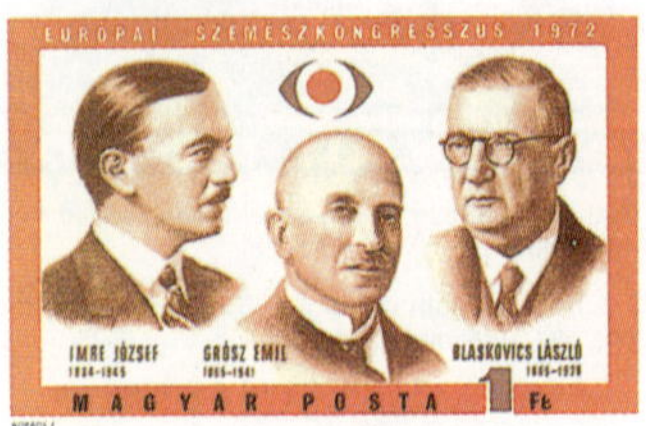

537 J. Imre, E. Grosz and L. Blaskovics

1972. 1st. European Oculists' Congress, Budapest. Famous Oculists.

2666	**537**	1fo. brown and red	1·20	25
2667	-	2fo. brown and blue	1·70	95

DESIGN: 2fo. A. Gullstrand, V. P. Filatov and J. Gonin.

538 Footballers and Flag of Hungary

1972. Air. European Football Championships. Footballers and Flags of participating countries. Multicoloured.

2668	40fi. Type **538**	25	15
2669	60fi. Rumania	30	25
2670	80fi. West Germany	35	30
2671	1fo. England	60	45
2672	1fo.20 Yugoslavia	80	50
2673	2fo. Russia	1·40	60
2674	4fo. Italy	2·10	70
2675	5fo. Belgium	2·30	1·20

539 "V. Miskolcz" postmark, 1818–43

1972. Stamp Day.

2676	**539**	2fo.+1fo. black & blue	1·20	1·20
2677	-	2fo.+1fo. black & yell	1·20	1·20
2678	-	2fo.+1fo. black & grn	1·20	1·20
2679	-	2fo.+1fo. mult	1·20	1·20

MS2680 105×90 mm. 2fo.+1fo. ×4 (a) Wax impression of signet ring, 1953; (b) Letter of Rakoczi era, 1705; (c) Courier letter of 1708; (d) V. Tokai postmark, 1752 — 7·50 — 7·50

DESIGNS: No. 2677, "Szegedin" postmark, 1827–48; 2678, "Esztergom" postmark, 1848–51; 2679, "Budapest 71" stamp cent, cancellation, 1971.

540 Girl reading Book

1972. International Book Year.

2681	**540**	1fo. multicoloured	70	25

541 Roses

1972. National Rose Exhibition.

2682	**541**	1fo. multicoloured	80	25

542 Globe and Olympic Rings

1972. Air. Olympic Games, Munich (1st issue). Sheet 117×68 mm.

MS2683 **542** 10fo. multicoloured — 16·00 — 16·00

See also Nos. 2687/**MS**2695.

543 G. Dimitrov

1972. 90th Birth Anniv of Georgi Dimitrov (Bulgarian leader).

2684	**543**	3fo. multicoloured	80	45

544 "St. Martin and the Beggar"

1972. "Belgica '72" Stamp Exhibition, Brussles. Sheet 69×94 mm.

MS2685 **544** 10fo. multicoloured — 4·75 — 4·75

545 Gy. Dozsa

1972. 500th Birth Anniv of Gyorgy Dozsa (revolutionary).

2686	**545**	1fo. multicoloured	60	25

546 Football

1972. Olympic Games, Munich (2nd issue). Multicoloured.

2687	40fi. Type **546** (postage)	10	10
2688	60fi. Water-polo	10	10
2689	80fi. Javelin-throwing	20	10
2690	1fo. Kayak-canoeing	25	10
2691	1fo.20 Boxing	60	10
2692	2fo. Gymnastics	80	15
2693	3fo.+1fo. Wrestling	1·40	45
2694	5fo. Fencing	2·30	1·20

MS2695 115×90 mm. 10fo. Show-jumping (air) — 7·00 — 7·00

The design on the 10fo. is larger, 43×43 mm.

547 Prince Geza indicating Site of Szekesfehervar

1972. Millenary of Szekesfehervar and 750th Anniv of "Aranybulla" (legislative document). Multicoloured.

2696	40fi. Type **547**	10	10
2697	60fi. King Stephen and shield	10	10
2698	80fi. Soldiers and cavalry	20	10
2699	1fo.20 King Stephen drawing up legislation	45	15
2700	2fo. Mason sculpting column	95	25
2701	4fo. Merchant displaying wares to King Stephen	1·70	45
2702	6fo. Views of Szekesfehervar and Palace	2·30	80

MS2703 136×90 mm. 10fo. King Andrew II at presentation of "Aranybulla" to the court — 5·25 — 5·25

The design on the 10fo. is larger, 95×47 mm.

548 Parliament Building, Budapest

1972. Constitution Day. Multicoloured.

2704	5fo. Type **548**	1·40	25
2705	6fo. Parliament in session	1·70	60

549 Eger and "Bulls Blood"

1972. World Wines Competition, Budapest Multicoloured.

2706	1fo. Type **549**	60	10
2707	2fo. Tokay and "Tokay Aszu"	1·70	60

550 Ear of Wheat and Emblems on Open Book

1972. 175th Anniv of Georgikon Agricultural Academy, Keszthely.

2708	**550**	1fo. multicoloured	35	25

551 "Rothschild" Vase

1972. Herendi Porcelain. Multicoloured.

2709	40fi. Type **551**	20	10
2710	60fi. "Poisson" bonboniere	25	10
2711	80fi. "Victoria" vase	30	10
2712	1fo. "Miramare" dish	35	10
2713	1fo.20 "Godollo" pot	45	15
2714	2fo. "Empire" tea-set	70	25
2715	4fo. "Apponyi" dish	1·40	80
2716	5fo. "Baroque" vase	1·70	80

The 60fi., 1fo.20, and 4fo. are size 34×36 mm.

552 Class M62 Diesel Train and U.I.C. Emblem

1972. 50th Anniv of Int Railway Union.

2717	**552**	1fo. red	80	25

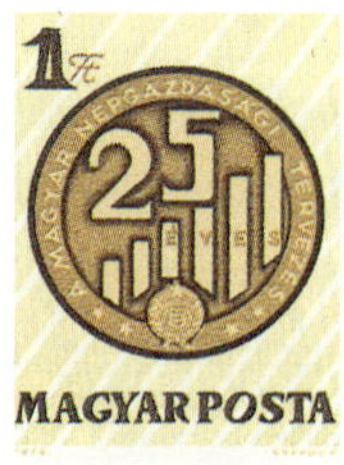

553 Commemorative Emblem

1972. 25th Anniv of National Economy Plan.
2718 **553** 1fo. yellow, sepia & brn 60 25

554 River Steamer and Old Obuda

1972. Centenary of Unification of Buda, Obuda and Pest as Budapest.

2719	**554**	1fo. purple and blue	35	10
2720	-	1fo. blue and purple	35	10
2721	-	2fo. green and brown	60	15
2722	-	2fo. brown and green	60	15
2723	-	3fo. brown and green	70	35
2724	-	3fo. green and brown	70	35

DESIGNS: No. 2720, River hydrofoil and modern Obuda; 2721, Buda, 1872; 2722, Budapest, 1972; 2723, Pest, 1872; 2724, Parliament Buildings, Budapest.

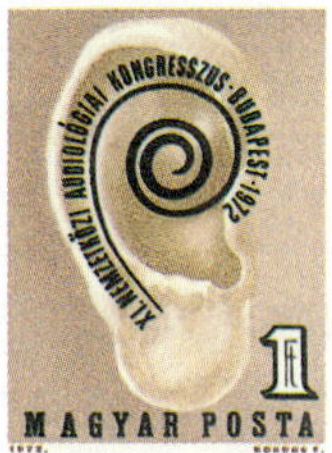

555 Congress Emblem within Ear

1972. Int Audiological Congress, Budapest.
2725 **555** 1fo. multicoloured 60 25

556 "Apollo 16"

1972. Air. Moon Flight of "Apollo 16". Sheet 120×75 mm.
MS2726 **556** 10fo. multicoloured 5·25 5·25

557 Postbox, Bell Telephone and Satellite "Molnya"

1972. Reopening of Postal and Philatelic Museums, Budapest. Multicoloured.

2727		4fo.+2fo. Type **557**	1·70	1·70
2728		4fo.+2fo. Globe, posthorn and stamps	1·70	1·70

558 Miklos Radnoti (poet)

1972. Radnoti Commemoration.
2729 **558** 1fo. multicoloured 35 25

559 F. Martos

1972. 75th Birth Anniv of Flora Martos (patriot).
2730 **559** 1fo. multicoloured 35 25

560 "The Muses" (J. Rippl-Ronai)

1972. Stained Glass Windows. Multicoloured.

2731	40fi. Type **560**	20	10
2732	60fi. "16th-century Scribe" (F. Sebestenyl)	20	15
2733	1fo. "Exodus to Egypt" (K. Lotz and B. Szekely)	35	20
2734	1fo.50 "Prince Arpad's Messenger" (J. Percz)	60	25
2735	2fo.50 "The Nativity" (L. Sztehlo)	95	30
2736	4fo. "Prince Arpad and Leaders" (K. Kernstock)	1·40	60
2737	5fo. "King Matthias reprimands the Rich Aristocrats" (J. Haranghy)	1·70	95

561 "Textiles"

1972. Opening of Textiles Technical Museum, Budapest.
2738 **561** 1fo. multicoloured 80 25

562 Main Square, Szarvas

1972. Views.

2739	**562**	40fi. brown and orange	10	10
2739a	-	40fi. black and green	10	10
2740	-	1fo. blue and light blue	15	10
2741	-	1fo. brown and yellow	15	10
2742	-	3fo. green and blue	60	25
2743	-	4fo. red and orange	60	25
2743a	-	4fo. brown and pink	1·20	35
2744	-	5fo. blue and cobalt	60	10
2745	-	6fo. brown and red	1·70	25
2746	-	7fo. violet and lilac	1·20	35
2747	-	8fo. deep green & green	1·20	10
2748	-	10fo. brown and yellow	1·20	25
2749	-	20fo. multicoloured	4·75	80
2750	-	50fo. multicoloured	9·25	3·00

DESIGNS: 21×18 mm: 40fi. (No. 2739a) Rotunda (public health centre), Vasvar; 1fo. (No. 2740) Salgotarjan; 1fo. (No. 2741) Nyirbator. 28×22 mm: 3fo. Tokay; 4fo. (No. 2743) Esztergom; 4fo. (No. 2743a) Szentendre; 5fo. Szolnok; 6fo. Dunaujvaros; 7fo. Kaposvar; 8fo. Vac; 10fo. Kiskunfelegyhaza; 20fo. Veszprem; 50ra. Pecs.

563 S. Petofi

1972. 150th Birth Anniv of Sandor Petofi (poet and patriot).

2762		1fo. red	25	10
2763	**563**	2fo. lilac	60	15
2764	-	3fo. green	95	45

DESIGNS: 1fo. Petofi making speech in Cafe Pilvax; 3fo. Petofi on horseback during War of Independence, 1848–49.

564 Arms of U.S.S.R.

1972. 50th Anniv of U.S.S.R.
2765 **564** 1fo. multicoloured 35 25

565 Code Map and Crow Symbol

1973. Introduction of Postal Codes.
2766 **565** 1fo. black and red 35 25

1973. As Nos. 1912, 1915/16 and 1918 but smaller.

2767	2fo. blue (22×19 mm)	45	25
2768	3fo. blue (22×19 mm)	60	45
2769	4fo. green (19×22 mm)	95	60
2770	6fo. ochre (22×19 mm)	1·40	1·00

566 Astronaut on Moon

1973. Air. Moon Flight of "Apollo 17". Sheet 69×110 mm.
MS2771 **566** 10fo. multicoloured 7·00 7·00

567 I. Madach

1973. 150th Birth Anniv of Imre Madach (writer).
2772 **567** 1fo. multicoloured 60 25

568 Carnival Mask

1973. Busho-Walking Ceremony, Mohacs. Carnival Masks.

2773	**568**	40fi. multicoloured	15	10
2774	-	60fi. multicoloured	25	10
2775	-	80fi. multicoloured	35	10
2776	-	1fo.20 multicoloured	70	15
2777	-	2fo. multicoloured	95	35
2778	-	4fo. multicoloured	1·20	60
2779	-	6fo. multicoloured	2·30	95

569 Copernicus

1973. 500th Birth Anniv of Copernicus.
2780 **569** 3fo. blue 1·70 80

570 "Venus 8"

1973. Air. Space Flight of "Venus 8". Sheet 110×93 mm.
MS2781 **570** 10fo. multicoloured 5·75 5·75

571 Show-jumping (Pentathlon) and Gold Medal

1973. Hungarian Medal Winners, Olympic Games, Munich. Multicoloured.

2782	40fi. Type **571**	10	10
2783	60fi. Weightlifting (Gold)	25	10
2784	1fo. Canoeing (Silver)	45	10
2785	1fo.20 Swimming (Silver)	60	15
2786	1fo.80 Boxing (Gold)	65	25
2787	4fo. Wrestling (Gold)	1·20	60
2788	6fo. Fencing (Gold)	1·70	95

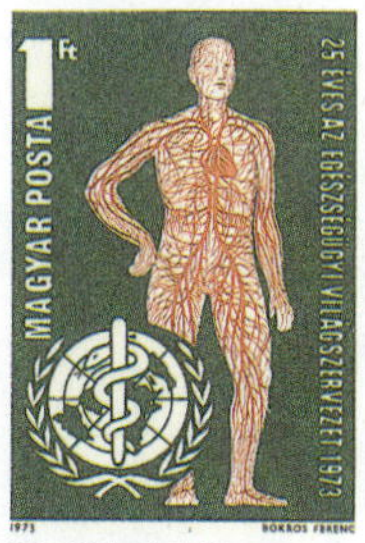

572 Biological Man

1973. 25th Anniv of W.H.O.
2790 **572** 1fo. brown and green 35 25

573 Winter Wrens

1973. Air. Hungarian Birds. Multicoloured.

2791	40fi. Type **573** (postage)	25	10
2792	60fi. Rock thrush	30	10
2793	80fi. European robins	40	10
2794	1fo. Firecrests	60	25
2795	1fo.20 Linnets	85	35
2796	2fo. Blue tits	95	45
2797	4fo. Bluethroat	1·40	50
2798	5fo. Grey wagtails	1·70	60

MS2789 132×88 mm. 10fo. Girl igniting Olympic Flame (air) 4·50 60

The design of the 10fo. is larger, 83×46 mm.

574 Soldier and Weapons

1973. Military Stamp Collectors' Exn, Budapest.
2799 **574** 3fo. multicoloured 80 35

575 "Budapest 61" 1fo. Stamp

1973. "IBRA 73" Stamp Exn, Munich, and "POLSKA '73", Poznan. Repoductions of Hungary Exhibition stamps. Multicoloured.

2800	40fi. Type **575** (postage)	10	10
2801	60fi. "Budapest 61" 1fo.70 stamp	10	10
2802	80fi. "Budapest 61" 2fo.60 stamp	25	10
2803	1fo. "Budapest 61" 3fo. stamp	35	10
2804	1fo.20 "Budapest 71" 2fo. stamp	40	10
2805	2fo. "Budapest 71" 2fo. stamp	60	25
2806	4fo. "Budapest 71" 2fo. stamp	1·20	60
2807	5fo. "Budapest 71" 2fo. stamp	1·30	65

MS2808 130×81 mm. 10fo. Bavaria's first stamp, Town Hall and Olympic complex, Munich (air) 5·25 5·25

The design of the 10fo. is larger, 83×46 mm.

576 Setting Type and Preparing Ink

1973. 500th Anniv of Book-printing in Hungary.

2809	**576**	1fo. black and gold	25	10
2810	-	3fo. black and gold	95	25

DESIGN: 3fo. Printer operating press.

577 "Storm over Hortobagy Puszta"

1973. Paintings by Csontvary Kosztka. Mult.

2811	40fi. Type **577**	10	10
2812	60fi. "Mary's Well, Nazareth"	20	10
2813	1fo. "Carriage drive by Moon-light" (vert)	30	25
2814	1fo.50 "Pilgrimage to the Lebanese Cedars" (vert)	45	10
2815	2fo.50 "The Lone Cedar"	60	25
2816	4fo. "Waterfall at Jajce"	1·30	60
2817	5fo. "Ruins of Greek Theatre at Taormina"	1·40	95

MS2818 114×75 mm. 10fo. "Riding at the Seaside" 4·75 4·75

The design of the 10fo. is larger, 91×43 mm.

578 "Europa" Poster

1973. European Security and Co-operation Conference, Helsinki.
2819 **578** 2fo.50 brown and black 3·75 3·75

579 "Rosa gallica"

1973. Wild Flowers. Multicoloured.

2820	40fi. Type **579**	10	10
2821	60fi. "Cyclamen europaeum"	10	10
2822	80fi. "Pulmonaria mollissima"	25	10
2823	1fo.20 "Bellis perennis"	45	15
2824	2fo. "Adonis vernalis"	80	25
2825	4fo. "Viola cyanea"	1·40	60
2826	6fo. "Papaver rhoeas"	2·10	1·20

580 "Let's be friends...!"

1973. Road Safety.

2827	**580**	40fi. green and red	10	10
2828	-	60fi. violet and orange	15	10
2829	-	1fo. blue and red	35	25

DESIGNS: 60fi. "Not even a glass!" (hand reaching for tumbler); 1fo. "Cyclist – use a lamp" (car running down cyclist).

581 Silver "Eagle" Disc

1973. Jewelled Treasures, National Museum. Multicoloured.

2830	2fo.+50fi. Type **581**	1·40	1·40
2831	2fo.+50fi. Serpent's head ring	1·40	1·40
2832	2fo.+50fi. "Loving couple" buckle	1·40	1·40
2833	2fo.+50fi. Silver "floral" buckle	1·40	1·40

MS2834 75×101 mm. 2fo.+50fi. ×4 (a) Opaline pendant; (b) Jewelled buckle; (c) Floral pin; (d) Rosette pendant 6·50 6·50

The designs in **MS**2834 are each 25×36 mm.

582 "Skylab" photographing Earth

1973. Air. "Skylab" Space-station. Sheet 114×75 mm.
MS2835 **582** 10fo. multicoloured 6·50 6·50

583 "The Three Kings" (Master of the High Altar, Szmrecsany)

1973. Esztergom Millennium. "Old Master" Paintings in the Christian Museum. Mult.

2836	40fi. Type **583**	10	10
2837	60fi. "Angels making Music" (Master "B.E.")	10	10
2838	1fo. "The Adoration of the Magi" (anon.)	35	15
2839	1fo.50 "The Annunciation" (Szmrecsany Master)	50	20
2840	2fo.50 "Angels making Music" (different Master "B.E.")	60	25
2841	4fo. "The Visitation of Mary and Elizabeth" (Szmrecsany Master)	1·00	35
2842	5fo. "The Legend of St. Catharine of Alexandria" (Master Bati)	1·20	95

MS2843 73×101 mm. 10fo. "The Birth of Jesus" (Szmrecsany Master) 5·25 5·25

584 Csokonai's Statue, Debrecen

1973. Birth Bicentenary of M. Csokonai Vitez (poet).
2844 **584** 2fo. multicoloured 80 25

585 J. Marti

1973. 120th Birth Anniv of Jose Marti (Cuban patriot).
2845 **585** 1fo. brown, red and blue 35 25

586 B. Pesti

1973. 30th Death Anniv of Barnabas Pesti (patriot).
2846 **586** 1fo. lt brown, brown & bl 35 25

588 Kayak-canoeing

1973. World Aquatic Sports Championships, Belgrade and Tampere. Multicoloured.

2855	40fi. Type **588**	10	10
2856	60fi. Water polo	10	10
2857	80fi. Men's solo kayak	30	10
2858	1fo.20 Swimming	35	10
2859	2fo. Men's kayak fours	60	15
2860	4fo. Men's solo canoe	1·20	60
2861	6fo. Men's double canoe	1·50	95

589 Map of Europe

1974. European Security and Co-operation Conference, Geneva. Sheet 143×71 mm containing two stamps as T 589 together with a double-size label depicting Geneva.
MS2862 **589** 50fo.×2 gold, blue and green 11·50 11·50

590 Lenin

1974. 50th Death Anniv of Lenin.
2863 **590** 2fo. brown, blue and gold 95 25

591 J. Boczor, I. Bekes and T. Elek

1974. Hungarian Heroes of the French Resistance.
2864 **591** 3fo. multicoloured 1·20 35

592 "Comecon" Building, Moscow, and Flags

1974. 25th Anniv of Council for Mutual Economic Aid.
2865 **592** 1fo. multicoloured 60 25

593 Savings Bank Emblem, Note and Coins

1974. 25th Anniv of National Savings Bank.
2866 **593** 1fo. multicoloured 35 25

594 "Mariner 4" on course for Mars

1974. Mars Research Projects. Multicoloured.

2867	40fi. Type **594** (postage)	10	10
2868	60fi. "Mars 2" approaching Mars	10	10
2869	80fi. "Mariner 4" space probe	35	10
2870	1fo. Mt. Palomar telescope and Mars photo	60	10
2871	1fo.20 "Mars 3" on planet's surface	80	15
2872	5fo. "Mariner 9" approaching Mars and satellites	1·90	60
2873	6fo. G. Schiaparelli and Martian "canals" map (air)	2·00	1·40

MS2874 96×91 mm. 10fo. "Mars 7" in Space 4·75 4·75

595 Pres. Salvador Allende

1974. Pres. Allende of Chile Commemoration.

2875	**595**	1fo. multicoloured	35	25

596 "Mona Lisa" (Leonardo da Vinci)

1974. Exhibition of "Mona Lisa" in Japan.

2876	**596**	4fo. multicoloured	17·00	17·00

597 2k. Stamp of 1874 and Mallow

1974. Centenary of Hungarian "Envelope Design" Stamps. Sheet 103×87 mm containing T 597 and similar horiz design. Multicoloured.

MS2877 2fo.50 ×5 (a) Type **597**; (b) 3k. stamp and aster; (c) 5k. stamp and daisy; (d) 10k. stamp and columbine 4·75 4·75

598 Dove with Letter

1974. Centenary of U.P.U. Multicoloured.

2878	40fi. Type **598**	10	10
2879	60fi. Mail coach	10	10
2880	80fi. Early mail van and postbox	35	10
2881	1fo.20 Balloon post	45	15
2882	2fo. Diesel mail train	95	25
2883	4fo. Post-bus	1·40	60
2884	6fo. Tupolev Tu-154 mail plane	1·90	1·20

MS2885 132×106 mm. 2fo.50 ×4 (a) As 60fi.; (b) As 80fi. but design reversed; (c) As 6fo.; (d) "Apollo 15" 6·50 6·50

The designs in **MS**2885 are smaller, 45×30 mm. and are redrawn so that only part of the U.P.U. Monument falls on each stamp.

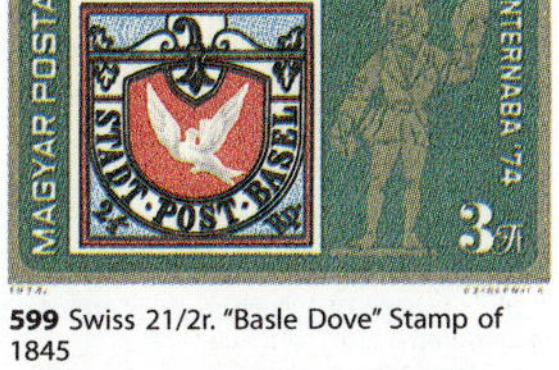

599 Swiss 21/2r. "Basle Dove" Stamp of 1845

1974. "Internaba 1974" Stamp Exn, Basle.

2886	**599**	3fo. multicoloured	2·30	2·30

600 13th-century miniature from King Alfonso X's "Book of Chess, Dice and Tablings" and Pawn

1974. 50th Anniv of International Chess Federation and 21st Chess Olympiad, Nice.

2887	**600**	40fi. black, green and blue	30	10
2888	-	60fi. black, brown & lilac	60	15
2889	-	80fi. black, yellow & grn	95	25
2890	-	1fo.20 black, yellow and lilac	1·20	35
2891	-	2fo. black, stone and blue	1·50	45
2892	-	4fo. black, yellow & pink	1·70	1·00
2893	-	6fo. black, brown & grn	2·00	1·20

DESIGNS: 60fi. 15th-century woodcut from "The Game and Playe of Chesse" by William Caxton and knight; 80fi. 15th-century illustration from Italian chess book and bishop; 1fo.20, "The Chess Players" (17th-century engraving by Jacob van der Heyden) and rook; 2fo. Kempelen's chess playing machine (1769) and king; 4fo. Geza Maroczy (Hungarian master) and queen; 6fo. View of Nice and tournament emblem.

601 Passenger Train, 1874

1974. Centenary of the Budapest Rack Railway. Sheet 132× 96 mm. containing T 601 and similar horiz designs. Multicoloured.

MS2894 2fo.50 Type **601**; 2fo.50 Goods train, 1874; 2fo.50 Passenger train, 1929; 2fo.50 Passenger train, 1973 7·50 7·50

602 Congress Emblem

1974. 4th International Economists' Congress, Budapest.

2895	**602**	2fo. black, blue and silver	1·20	25

603 "Woman Bathing" (K Lotz)

1974. Nudes. Paintings. Multicoloured.

2896	40fi. Type **603**	20	10
2897	60fi. "Awakening" (K. Brocky)	25	10
2898	1fo. "Venus and Cupid" (K. Brocky) (horiz)	60	25
2899	1fo.50 "After Bathing" (K. Lotz)	80	35
2900	2fo.50 "Honi soit qui mal y pense" (reclining nude) (I. Csok) (horiz)	1·20	60
2901	4fo. "After Bathing" (B. Szkely)	1·70	75
2902	5fo. "Devotion" (E. Korb)	1·70	80

MS2903 75×102 mm. 10fo. "Lark" (P.M. Szinyei) (50×71 mm) 7·50 7·50

604 "Mimi" (Czobel)

1974. 91st Birth Anniv of Bela Czobel (painter).

2904	**604**	1fo. multicoloured	1·70	25

605 "Intersputnik" Satellite Tracking Radar

1974. 25th Anniv of Technical and Scientific Co-operation between Hungary and Soviet Union.

2905	**605**	1fo. violet and blue	45	10
2906	-	3fo. mauve and green	1·30	15

DESIGN—HORIZ: 3fo. Power installations.

606 Neruda

1974. Pablo Neruda (Chilean poet) Commem.

2907	**606**	1fo. brown, deep brown and blue	35	25

607 Swedish 3s. Stamp, 1855, and "Swedish Lion"

1974. "Stockholmia 74" International Stamp Exhibition.

2908	**607**	3fo. green, blue and gold	2·00	2·00

608 Tanks and Infantry

1974. Military Day.

2909	**608**	1fo. black, red and gold (postage)	35	10
2910	-	2fo. blk, grn & gold (air)	60	25
2911	-	3fo. black, blue and gold	80	45

DESIGNS—VERT: 2fo. Guided missile and radar. HORIZ: 3fo. Parachutist, helicopter and jet fighter.

609 J. A. Segner and Moon

1974. 270th Birth Anniv of Janos Segner (scientist).

2912	**609**	3fo. multicoloured	1·30	35

610 Hansa Brandenburg C-1 Biplane, 1918

1974. Air. "Aerofila 1974" International Airmail Exhibition, Budapest. Multicoloured.

2913	2fo.+1fo. Type **610**	1·70	1·70
2914	2fo.+1fo. Airship "Graf Zeppelin"	1·70	1·70
2915	2fo.+1fo. Hot air balloon	1·70	1·70
2916	2fo.+1fo. Mil Mi-1 helicopter	1·70	1·70

MS2917 107×92 mm. 2fo.+1fo. Hungarian 1k.50 stamp, 1918; 2fo. + 1fo. Hungarian 500k. stamp, 1924; 2fo.+1fo. Hungarian 3fo. stamp, 1970; 2fo. + 1fo. Hungarian 3fo. stamp, 1970; 2fo.+1fo. Hungarian 10fo. stamp, 1972 7·00 7·00

611 Purple Tiger Moth

1974. Butterflies and Moths. Multicoloured.

2918	40fi. Type **611**	25	10
2919	60fi. Marbled white	45	15
2920	80fi. Apollo	60	25
2921	1fo. Spurge hawk moth	70	35
2922	1fo.20 Clifden's nonpareil	95	60
2923	5fo. Purple emperor	2·20	95
2924	6fo. Purple-edged copper	2·30	1·40

612 Istvan Pataki

1974. Hungarian Antifascist Martyrs. Mult.

2925	1fo. Type **612**	35	10
2926	1fo. Robert Kreutz	35	10

613 Mother and Child

1974. "Mothers".

2927	**613**	1fo. black, yellow & blue	35	10

614 Puppy

1974. Young Animals. (1st series). Mult.

2928	40fi. Type **614**	15	10
2929	60fi. Kittens (horiz)	20	15

2930	80fi. Rabbit	25	20
2931	1fo.20 Foal (horiz)	35	25
2932	2fo. Lamb	80	35
2933	4fo. Calf (horiz)	1·40	60
2934	6fo. Piglet	1·70	1·50

See also Nos. 3014/20.

615 Lambarene Hospital

1975. Birth Centenary of Dr. Albert Schweitzer (Nobel Peace Prize Winner). Multicoloured.

2935	40fi. Type **615**	10	10
2936	60fi. Casualty being treated	20	10
2937	80fi. Casualty being transported by canoe	25	10
2938	1fo.20 Charitable goods arriving by freighter	35	10
2939	2fo. View of Lambarene, doves, globe and Red Cross emblem	80	15
2940	4fo. Schweitzer's Nobel Peace Prize medal and inscription	1·40	35
2941	6fo. Schweitzer and organ-pipes	1·90	80

616 F. Bolyai

1975. Birth Bicentenary of Farkas Bolyai (mathematician).

2942	616	1fo. grey and red	60	25

617 Carrier-pigeon

1975. Air. Pigeon-racing Olympics, Budapest.

2943	617	3fo. multicoloured	1·70	1·70

618 Karolyi

1975. Birth Centenary of Count Mihaly Karolyi (politician).

2944	618	1fo. brown and blue	60	25

619 Woman's Head

1975. International Woman's Year.

2945	619	1fo. black and blue	60	25

620 "Railway Rebuilding" (2/3-size illustration)

1975. 30th Anniv of Liberation. Mult.

2946	40fi. Type **620**	10	10
2947	60fi. Hammer and sickle representing agriculture	25	10
2948	2fo. Blacksmith's hammer representing Communist party action	60	15
2949	4fo. Power hammer as "3" representing the "Three Year Heavy Industry Plan"	1·20	25
2950	5fo. Blocks of Flats representing "developed socialist society"	1·40	70

621 1915 "Arrow"

1975. 75th Anniv of Hungarian Automobile Club. Vintage Motor Cars. Multicoloured.

2951	40fi. Type **621**	25	10
2952	60fi. 1911 "Swift"	30	10
2953	80fi. 1908 Ford "T"	35	25
2954	1fo. 1901 Mercedes	60	35
2955	1fo.20 1912 Panhard Levassor	70	60
2956	5fo. 1906 Csonka	2·00	80
2957	6fo. Hungarian Automobile Club and international motoring organizations' emblems	3·75	1·20

622 "Creation of Adam" (from ceiling of Sistine Chapel) (image scaled to 51% of original size)

1975. 500th Birth Anniv of Michelangelo. Sheet 126×90 mm.

MS2958	**622** 10fo. multicoloured	8·75	8·75

623 Academy Building

1975. 150th Anniv of National Academy of Sciences. Multicoloured.

2959	1fo. Type **623**	60	25
2960	2fo. Dates "1825" and "1975"	1·00	60
2961	3fo. Count Istvan Szechenyi (statesman)	1·20	80

624 Olympic Stadium, Moscow

1975. "Socphilex V" International Stamp Exhibition, Moscow.

2962	624	5fo. multicoloured	3·00	3·00

625 French 1f. Stamp, 1964

1975. "Arphila 75" International Stamp Exhibition, Paris.

2963	625	5fo. multicoloured	2·30	2·30

626 Electric Railway Locomotive and Transformer

1975. 75th Anniv of Hungarian Electro-technical Association.

2964	626	1fo. multicoloured	1·20	25

627 "Sputnik 2"

1975. Air. "Apollo–Soyuz" Space Link. Mult.

2965	40fi. Type **627**	10	10
2966	60fi. "Mercury Atlas 5"	10	10
2967	80fi. "Lunokhod 1" (moon vehicle)	25	10
2968	1fo.20 "Apollo 15" (moon vehicle)	35	15
2969	2fo. Launch of "Soyuz" from Baikonur	70	25
2970	4fo. Launch of "Apollo"	1·70	60
2971	6fo. "Apollo–Soyuz" link-up	2·30	1·20
MS2972	129×100 mm. 10fo. "Apollo" and "Soyuz" in linking manoeuvre (65×42 mm)	5·75	5·75

628 Sword, Epee, Rapier, and Globe

1975. World Fencing Championships, Budapest.

2973	628	1fo. multicoloured	35	25

629 Whale Pavilion

1975. International Exposition, Okinawa (1st issue). Sheet 116×95 mm.

MS2974	**629** 10fo. multicoloured	4·00	4·00

See also Nos. 2986/92.

630 Map of Europe and Cogwheel (image scaled to 53% of original size)

1975. Air. European Security and Co-operation Conference, Helsinki. Sheet 157×82 mm.

MS2975	**630** 10fo. multicoloured	7·00	7·00

631 A. Zimmermann

1975. Birth Centenary of Dr. Agoston Zimmermann (veterinary surgeon).

2976	631	1fo. dp brown, brn & bl	35	25

632 Branches of Tree symbolizing 14 Languages

1975. Int Finno-Ugrian Congress, Budapest.

2977	632	1fo. multicoloured	60	25

633 (image scaled to 51% of original size)

1975. Air. Hungarian Stamps since 1945. Sheet 150×95 mm. Multicoloured.

MS2978	Hungarian 1fo. Stamp, 1964, 2fo. Stamp, 1961 and 2fo.50 Stamp, 1973	6·50	6·50

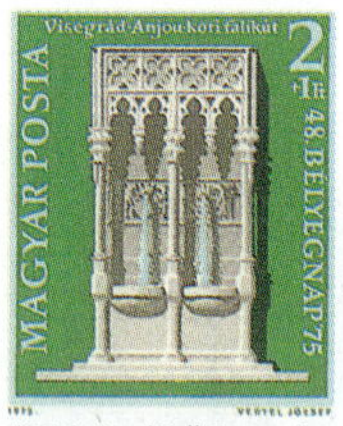

634 Anjou Wall Fountain

1975. Stamp Day. Preservation of Monuments. Monuments in Visegrad Palace. Multicoloured.

2979	2fo.+1fo. Type **634**	2·30	2·30
2980	2fo.+1fo. Anjou well house	2·30	2·30
2981	2fo.+1fo. Hunyadi wall fountain	2·30	2·30
2982	2fo.+1fo. Hercules fountain	2·30	2·30
MS2983	128×100 mm. 2fo.+1fo. Detail of Hunyadi wall fountain (26×37 mm); 2fo.+1fo. Madonna of Visegrad (52×37 mm); 2fo.+1fo. Detail of Hercules fountain (26×37 mm); 2fo.+1fo. View of Visegrad in 1480 (105×37 mm)	7·00	7·00

635 Hungarian Arms and Map

1975. 25th Anniv of Hungarian Council System. Multicoloured.

2984	1fo. Type **635**	35	10
2985	1fo. Voters participating in council election	35	10

636 Ocean Pollution

1975. International Exposition, Okinawa. Environmental Protection (2nd issue). Multicoloured.

2986	40fi. Type **636**	10	10
2987	60fi. Strangled rose (water pollution)	15	10
2988	80fi. Clown anemonefish struggling for uncontaminated water (river pollution)	25	10
2989	1fo. Dead carnation (soil pollution)	35	10
2990	1fo.20 Falling bird (air pollution)	60	15
2991	5fo. Infected lung (smoke pollution)	1·50	45
2992	6fo. Healthy and skeletal hands (life and death)	2·00	1·20

637 Mariska Gardos (writer) (1885–1973)

1975. Birth Annivs of Celebrities. Each black and red.

2993	1fo. Type **637**	35	10
2994	1fo. Imre Tarr (soldier) (1900–1937)	35	10
2995	1fo. Imre Meso (Communist martyr) (1905–1956)	35	10

638 Treble Clef, Organ and Orchestra

1975. Centenary of Ferenc Liszt Music Academy, Budapest.

2996	**638**	1fo. multicoloured	35	25

639 18th-century Icon of Szigetcsep

1975. Hungarian Icons depicting the Virgin and Child. Multicoloured.

2997	40fi. Type **639**	10	10
2998	60fi. 18th-century Icon of Graboc	25	10
2999	1fo. 18th-century Icon of Esztergom	45	10
3000	1fo.50 18th-century Icon of Vatoped	80	15
3001	2fo.50 17th-century Icon of Tottos	1·20	25
3002	4fo. 17th-century Icon of Gyor	1·60	45
3003	5fo. 18th-century Icon of Kazan	1·70	1·50

640 Mother and Child, Flags and Radar Equipment (image scaled to 73% of original size)

1975. 20th Anniv of Warsaw Treaty.

3004	**640**	1fo. multicoloured	35	25

641 Ice Hockey

1975. Winter Olympic Games, Innsbruck. Multicoloured.

3005	40fi. Type **641**	25	10
3006	60fi. Slalom skiing	25	10
3007	80fi. Slalom skiing (different)	30	10
3008	1fo.20 Ski jumping	45	10
3009	2fo. Speed skating	70	25
3010	4fo. Cross-country skiing	1·40	60
3011	6fo. Bobsleighing	1·90	80
MS3012	130×80 mm. 10fo. Pairs figure skating (65×42 mm)	5·75	5·75

642 Banknotes of 1925 and 1975

1976. 50th Anniv of State Banknote Printing Office, Budapest.

3013	**642**	1fo. multicoloured	70	25

1976. Young Animals (2nd series). As T 614. Multicoloured.

3014	40fi. Wild boars (horiz)	10	10
3015	60fi. Eurasian red squirrels	20	10
3016	80fi. Lynx (horiz)	25	10
3017	1fo.20 Wolf cubs	35	10
3018	2fo. Red fox cubs (horiz)	70	15
3019	4fo. Brown bear cubs	1·40	60
3020	6fo. Lion cubs (horiz)	2·10	80

643 Alexander Graham Bell, Telecommunications Satellite and Dish Aerial

1976. Telephone Centenary.

3021	**643**	3fo. multicoloured	1·40	1·40

644 "Horses in Storm" (K. Lotz)

1976. Air. Tourist Publicity. Paintings. Sheet 95×135 mm containing T 644 and similar square design. Multicoloured.

MS3022	5fo. Type **644**; 5fo. "Morning at Tihany" (J. Halapy)	4·75	4·75

645 "Clash between Rakoczi's Kuruts and Hapsburg Soldiers"

1976. 300th Birth Anniv of Prince Ferenc Rakoczi II (soldier). Paintings. Multicoloured.

3023	40fi. Type **645**	10	10
3024	60fi. "Meeting of Rakoczi and Tamas Esze"	25	10
3025	1fo. "The Parliament of Onod" (Mor Than)	60	15
3026	2fo. "Kuruts' Encampment"	1·20	25
3027	3fo. "Ilona Zrinyi" (Rakoczi's mother) (vert)	2·30	35
3028	4fo. "Kuruts Officers" (vert)	3·00	80
3029	5fo. "Prince Rakoczi II" (A. Manyoki) (vert)	4·00	1·40

646 Metric System Act, 1876

1976. Centenary of Introduction of Metric System into Hungary. Multicoloured.

3030	1fo. Type **646**	25	10
3031	2fo. Istvan Krusper (scientist) and vacuum balance	80	35
3032	3fo. Interferometer, space rocket and emblem	1·20	60

647 Knight

1976. Stamp Day. Gothic Statues from Buda Castle.

3033	2fo.50+1fo. Type **647**	1·30	1·30
3034	2fo.50+1fo. Armour bearer	1·30	1·30
3035	2fo.50+1fo. Apostle	1·30	1·30
3036	2fo.50+1fo. Bishop	1·30	1·30
MS3037	107×100 mm. 2fo.50+1fo. Man wearing brimmed hat; 2fo.50+1fo. Woman in wimple; 2fo.50+1fo. Man wearing cloth hat; 2fo.50+1fo. Man in fur cap	4·00	4·00

The designs in **MS** are horiz, 35×28 mm, and show statue heads only.

648 U.S. 6c. Stamp, 1968

1976. "Interphil '76" Int Stamp Exn, Philadelphia.

3038	**648**	5fo. multicoloured	2·50	2·50

649 "Children Playing" (E. Gebora) within "30"

1976. 30th Anniv of Hungarian Pioneers Movement.

3039	**649**	1fo. multicoloured	45	25

650 Truck, Tractor and Safety Headgear with Emblem

1976. Industrial Safety.

3040	**650**	1fo. multicoloured	45	25

651 "Intelstar IV" Telecommunications Satellite

1976. Olympic Games, Montreal. Mult.

3041	40fi. Type **651** (postage)	10	10
3042	60fi. Horse-jumping	15	10
3043	1fo. Swimming	25	10
3044	2fo. Canoeing	35	10
3045	3fo. Fencing	80	15
3046	4fo. Javelin-throwing	1·20	35
3047	5fo. Gymnastics	1·40	60
MS3048	135×85 mm. 20fo. black, grey and red (air)	9·25	9·25

DESIGN: 44×57 mm. 20fo. Olympic Stadium, Montreal.

652 Danish 1851 4 R.B.S. Stamp and "Little Mermaid" Statue

1976. "Hafnia '76" International Stamp Exhibition, Copenhagen.

3049	**652**	3fo. multicoloured	2·00	2·00

653 "Flora" (Titian)

1976. 400th Death Anniv of Titian (painter).

3050	**653**	4fo. multicoloured	1·40	35

654 "Discovery of King Lajos II's Body" (B. Szekely)

1976. 450th Anniv of Battle of Mohacs. Sheet 82×81 mm.

MS3051	**654** 20fo. multicoloured	5·75	5·75

655 Pal Gyulai (1826–1909)

1976. Writers' Anniversaries.

3052	**655**	2fo. black and red	70	25
3053	-	2fo. black, yellow & gold	70	25

DESIGN: No. 3053, Daniel Berzsenyi (1776–1836).

656 "Hussar" (Zs. Kisfaludy-Strobl)

1976. 150th Anniv of Herend China Factory.

3054	**656**	4fo. multicoloured	1·40	25

657 Tuscany 1q. Stamp, 1851 and Arms of Milan

1976. "Italia '76" International Stamp Exhibition, Milan.

3055	**657**	5fo. multicoloured	5·25	5·25

658 Russian Dancer, Flags and Building

1976. 2nd Anniv of House of Soviet Culture and Science, Budapest.

3056	**658**	1fo. multicoloured	35	25

659 Ignac Bogar

1976. Hungarian Labour Movement Celebrities.

3057	**659**	1fo. brown and red	35	10
3058	-	1fo. brown and red	35	10
3059	-	1fo. brown and red	35	10

PORTRAITS: No. 3058, Rudolf Golub; No. 3059, Jozsef Madzsar.

660 Dr. F. Koranyi and Dispensary

1976. 75th Anniv of Koranyi T.B. Dispensary.

3060	**660**	2fo. multicoloured	80	25

661 Launch of "Viking" Mission

1976. Air. Space Probes to Mars and Venus. Multicoloured.

3061	40fi. Type **661**	10	10
3062	60fi. "Viking" in flight	20	10
3063	1fo. "Viking" on Mars	25	10
3064	2fo. Launch of "Venera"	60	15
3065	3fo. "Venera 9" in flight	95	25
3066	4fo. "Venera 10" descending to Venus	1·40	35
3067	5fo. "Venera" on Venus	1·70	1·20
MS3068	97×81 mm. 20fo. "Viking 1" landing on Mars (42×65 mm)	5·25	5·25

662 Locomotive No. 4, 1875

1976. Cent of Gyor-Sopron Railway. Mult.

3069	40fi. Type **662**	20	10
3070	60fi. Locomotive No. 17, 1885	25	10
3071	1fo. Rail-bus. 1925	35	10
3072	2fo. Steam locomotive, 1920	80	15
3073	3fo. Diesel railcar, 1926	1·30	25
3074	4fo. Diesel railcar, 1934	2·00	60
3075	5fo. Diesel railcar, 1971	2·30	1·20

663 Tree Foliage and Map

1976. "Afforestation of 1,000,000th Hectare".

3076	**663**	1fo. multicoloured	70	25

664 Weightlifting and Wrestling (silver medals)

1976. Olympic Games, Montreal. Hungarian Medal-winners. Multicoloured.

3077	40fi. Type **664**	10	10
3078	60fi. Men's solo kayak and Women's pairs kayak (silver medals)	25	10
3079	1fo. Men's gymnastics (horse) (gold medal)	35	15
3080	4fo. Women's rapier (gold medal)	1·50	60
3081	6fo. Men's javelin (gold medal)	3·00	1·50
MS3082	80×95 mm. 20fo. Water-polo (Gold medal)	5·75	5·75

665 White Spoonbill

1977. Birds of Hortabagy National Park. Multicoloured.

3083	40fi. Type **665**	25	10
3084	60fi. White stork	35	15
3085	1fo. Purple heron	60	25
3086	2fo. Great bustard	70	35
3087	3fo. Common crane	1·20	60
3088	4fo. Pied wagtail	2·00	80
3089	5fo. Garganey	3·00	1·20

666 Imre Abonyi (champion driver) and Carriage, 1976

1977. Historic Horse-drawn Vehicles. Mult.

3090	40fi. Type **666**	20	10
3091	60fi. Omnibus, 1870	25	10
3092	1fo. Hackney-carriage, 1890	30	10
3093	2fo. 19th-century mail coach	60	15
3094	3fo. 18th-century covered wagon	1·20	25
3095	4fo. Coach, 1568	1·50	60
3096	5fo. Saint Elizabeth's carriage, 1430	1·90	1·00

667 Common Peafowl

1977. Peafowl and Pheasants. Multicoloured.

3097	40fi. Type **667**	20	10
3098	60fi. Green peafowl	25	10
3099	1fo. Congo peafowl	30	10
3100	3fo. Great Argus pheasant	95	25
3101	4fo. Himalayan monal pheasant	1·70	35
3102	6fo. Burmese peacock- pheasant	2·30	1·40

668 Front Page of "Nepszava" and Printing Works

1977. Centenary of Newspaper "Nepszava".

3103	**668**	1fo. black, red and gold	35	25

669 Flower painting (Mihaly Munkacsy)

1977. Flower Paintings by Hungarian Artists. Multicoloured.

3104	40fi. Type **669**	10	10
3105	60fi. Jakab Bogdany	15	10
3106	1fo. Istvan Csok (horiz)	25	15
3107	2fo. Janos Halapy	60	25
3108	3fo. Jozsef Rippl-Ronai (horiz)	1·20	35
3109	4fo. Janos Tornyai	1·50	60
3110	5fo. Jozsef Koszta	1·90	1·50

670 Isaac Newton and Lens

1977. 250th Death Anniv of Isaac Newton (mathematician).

3111	**670**	3fo. black, brown and red	1·40	1·40

671 Children Running

1977. Youth Sports.

3112	**671**	3fo.+1fo. 50 mult	1·70	1·20

672 "Acrofila 74" 2fo.+1fo. Stamp

1977. Stamp Exhibitions.

3113	**672**	3fo. multicoloured	2·00	2·00

673 Janos Vajda

1977. 150th Birth Anniv of Janos Vajda (poet).

3114	**673**	1fo. stone, black & green	45	25

674 Netherlands 5c. Stamp, 1852

1977. "Amphilex 77" International Stamp Exhibition, Amsterdam.

3115	**674**	3fo. multicoloured	1·90	1·90

675 "Wedding at Nagyrede" Dance

1977. 25th Anniv of State Folk Ensemble.

3116	**675**	3fo. multicoloured	1·70	25

676 "Bathsheba at the Fountain"

1977. 400th Birth Anniv of Peter Paul Rubens. Sheet 70×94 mm.

MS3117	**676**	20fo. multicoloured	14·00	14·00

677 View of Sopron (from medieval engraving), Arms and Fidelity Tower

1977. 700th Anniv of Sopron.

3118	**677**	1fo. multicoloured	3·00	3·00

678 Kincsem (champion racehorse)

1977. 150th Anniv of Horse Racing in Hungary.

3119	**678**	1fo. multicoloured	2·30	2·30

679 East German 10pf. Stamp, 1957

1977. "Sozphilex 77" Stamp Exhibition, East Berlin.

3120	**679**	3fo. multicoloured	2·00	2·00

680 Scythian Iron Bell (6th century B.C.)

1977. Stamp Day and 175th Anniv of Hungarian National Museum. Art Treasures.

3121	**680**	2fo. brown and blue	1·20	1·20
3122	-	2fo. brown and violet	1·20	1·20
3123	-	2fo. brown & deep brown	1·20	1·20
3124	-	2fo. gold and mauve	1·20	1·20
MS3125		73×83 mm. 10fo. multicoloured	7·00	7·00

DESIGNS: No. 3122, Bronze candlestick, 12-13th century; 3123, Copper aquamanile, 13th century; 3124, Cast gold Christ (from crucifix), 11th century. 32×47 mm—10fo. Plate from crown of Constantinus Monomakhosz, 11th century.

681 "Sputnik 1"

1977. Space Research. Multicoloured.

3126		40fi. Type **681** (postage)	10	10
3127		60fi. "Skylab"	15	10
3128		1fo. "Soyuz–Salyut 5" space station	25	10
3129		3fo. "Luna 24"	80	15
3130		4fo. "Mars 3"	2·00	30
3131		6fo. "Viking"	2·30	1·40
MS3132		98×78 mm. 20fo. Viking Lander on Mars (air)	7·50	7·50

682 Map, Dove and "Europa"

1977. Air. European Security Conference, Belgrade. Sheet 125×75 mm.

MS3133	**682**	20fo. multicoloured	7·00	7·00

683 Tupolev Tu-154

1977. Air.

3134	**683**	60fl. black and orange	15	10
3135	-	1fo.20 black and lilac	20	10
3136	-	2fo. black and orange	30	10
3137	-	2fo.40 black & turquoise	35	10
3138	-	4fo. black and blue	60	10
3139	-	5fo. black and mauve	80	15
3140	-	10fo. black and blue	2·00	30
3141	-	20fo. black and green	4·00	80

DESIGNS—As T **683**: 1fo.20, Douglas DC-8-62; 2fo. Ilyushin Il-62M; 2fo.40, Airbus Industrie A300B4; 4fo. Boeing 747; 5fo. Tupolev Tu-144; 10fo. Concorde. 38×28 mm: 20fo. Ilyushin Il-86.

684 Montgolfier Brothers and Balloon

1977. Air. Airships. Multicoloured.

3142		40fi. Type **684**	10	10
3143		60fi. David Schwarz and his aluminium airship	20	10
3144		1fo. Alberto Santos-Dumont and airship "Ballon No. 5" over Paris	30	10
3145		2fo. K. E. Tsiolkovsky and airship "Lebedi" over Kremlin	60	10
3146		3fo. Roald Amundsen and airship "Norge" over North Pole	80	25
3147		4fo. Hugo Eckener and airship "Graf Zeppelin" over Mount Fuji	1·40	30
3148		5fo. Ferdinand Zeppelin and "Graf Zeppelin" over Chicago World Exhibition	2·30	80
MS3149		98×78 mm. 20fo. Airship LZ-127 "Graf Zeppelin" over Budapest (58×36 mm)	7·00	7·00

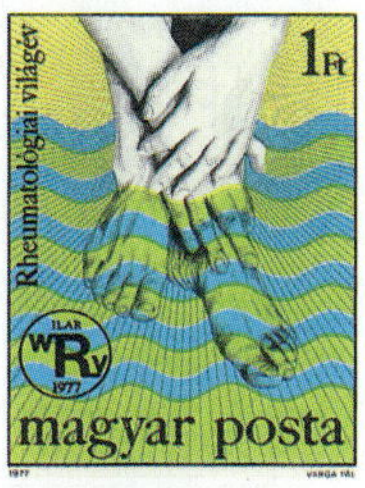

685 Feet Immersed in Water

1977. World Rheumatism Year.

3150	**685**	1fo. multicoloured	70	25

686 Ervin Szabo

1977. Anniversaries.

3151	-	1fo. black and red	35	25
3152	**686**	1fo. grey, black and red	35	25

DESIGNS: No 3151, Jamos Szanto Kovacs (agrarian socialist movement leader, 125th birth anniv); 3152, Type **686** (director of Municipal Libraries, journalist and labour movement leader, birth centenary).

687 Monument to Hungarian Participants, Omsk

1977. 60th Anniv of Russian Revolution.

3153	**687**	1fo. black and red	35	25

688 Endre Ady

1977. Birth Centenary of Endre Ady (poet).

3154	**688**	1fo. blue	60	60

689 Lesser Panda

1977. Bears. Multicoloured.

3155		40fi. Type **689**	15	10
3156		60fi. Giant panda	20	10
3157		1fo. Asiatic black bear	40	15
3158		4fo. Polar bear	1·50	25
3159		6fo. Brown bear	3·50	1·20

690 Austrian Flag and Passenger Ship

1977. 30th Anniv of Re-establishment of Danube Commission. Sheet 130×93 mm containing T 690 and similar horiz designs.

MS3160		2fo.×11 multicoloured	14·00	14·00

DESIGNS—Flags and ships of : Austria, Bulgaria, Czechoslovakia, France, Netherlands, Yugoslavia, Hungary, West Germany, Rumania, Switzerland, Soviet Union.

691 Border-country Lancer, 17th-cent

1978. Hussars. Multicoloured.

3161		40fi. Type **691**	15	10
3162		60fi. Kuruts horseman, 1710	20	10
3163		1fo. Baranya hussar, 1762	30	10
3164		2fo. Palatine Hussars officer, 1809	60	15
3165		4fo. Alexander Hussar, 1848	1·20	45
3166		6fo. Trumpeter, 5th Honved Regiment, 1900	2·50	80

692 Moon Station

1978. Air. Science Fiction in Space Research. Multicoloured.

3167		40fi. Type **692**	10	10
3168		60fi. Moon settlement	15	10
3169		1fo. Phobos	30	10
3170		2fo. Exploring an asteroid	60	10
3171		3fo. Spacecraft in gravitational field of Mars	80	10
3172		4fo. One of Saturn's rings	1·40	25
3173		5fo. "Jupiter 3"	1·70	70

693 School of Arts and Crafts

1978. Bicent of School of Art and Crafts.

3174	**693**	1fo. multicoloured	35	25

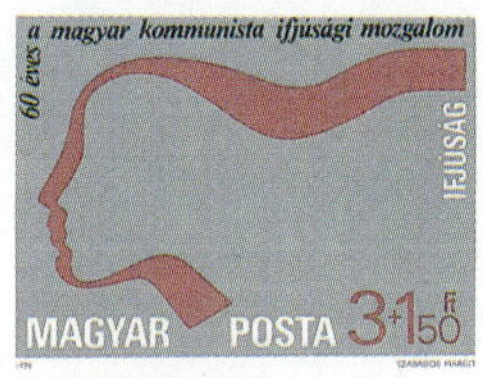

694 Profile Heads

1978. Youth Stamp Exhibition, Hatvan.

3175	**694**	3fo.+1fo.50 silver, red and black	3·50	3·50

695 "Generations" (Gyula Derkovits)

1978. "Socphilex 78" Stamp Exhibition, Szombathely.

3176	**695**	3fo.+1fo.50 mult	1·70	1·70

696 Louis Bleriot

1978. Air. Famous Aviators and their Airplanes. Multicoloured.

3177		40fi. Type **696**	15	10
3178		60fi. John Alcock and Arthur Whitten Brown	20	10
3179		1fo. Albert C. Read	25	10
3180		2fo. Hermann Kohl, Gunther Hunefeld and James Fitzmaurice	70	15
3181		3fo. Amy Johnson and Jim Mollison	1·00	25
3182		4fo. Georgy Endresz and Sandor Magyar	1·50	30
3183		5fo. Wolfgang von Gronau	1·90	1·20
MS3184		96×79 mm. 20fo. Wright Brothers and "Flyer" (74×25 mm)	7·00	7·00

697 Glass Vase and Glass-blowing Tube

1978. Centenary of Ajka Glass Works.

3185	**697**	1fo. multicoloured	35	25

698 West Germany and Poland

1978. World Cup Football Championship, Argentina. Multicoloured.

3186	2fo. Type **698**	80	35
3187	2fo. Hungary and Argentina	80	35
3188	2fo. France and Italy	80	35
3189	2fo. Tunisia and Mexico	80	35
3190	2fo. Sweden and Brazil	80	35
3191	2fo. Spain and Austria	80	35
3192	2fo. Peru and Scotland	80	35
3193	2fo. Iran and Netherlands	80	35
MS3194	98×76 mm. 20fo. World Cup emblem and goal mouth (37×27 mm)	8·25	8·25

699 Canadian 3d. Stamp, 1851

1978. "Capex 78" International Stamp Exhibition, Toronto.

3195	**699**	3fo. multicoloured	1·70	1·70

700 Diesel MK 45 Locomotive

702 Festival Emblem

1978. 30th Anniv of Budapest Pioneer Railway.

3196	**700**	1fo. multicoloured	35	25

701 Leif Eriksson

1978. Explorers. Two sheets each 130×100 mm containing horiz designs as T 701.

MS3197	Two sheets (a) 2fo. ×4 yellow and black (T **701**); orange and black (Christopher Columbus); orange and black (Vasco da Gama); pink and black (Ferdinand Magellan). (b) 2fo. ×4 yellow and black (Sir Francis Drake); apple green and black (Henry Hudson); green and black (James Cook); light blue and black (Robert Peary) 2 sheets	14·00	14·00

702 Festival Emblem

1978. 11th World Youth and Students' Festival, Havana. Multicoloured.

3198	1fo. Type **702**	35	10
3199	1fo. Map of Cuba and emblem	35	10

703 Human Torso and Heart

1978. World Hypertension Year.

3200	**703**	1fo. red, black and blue	35	10

704 Jules Verne and illustration from "A Journey to the Moon"

1978. Air. 150th Birth Anniv of Jules Verne (novelist). Sheet 97×78 mm.

MS3201 **704**	20fo. black and yellow	7·00	7·00

705 Dove and Fist holding Olive Branch

1978. 20th Anniv of Communist Party Review "Peace and Socialism".

3202	**705**	1fo. red and black	35	10

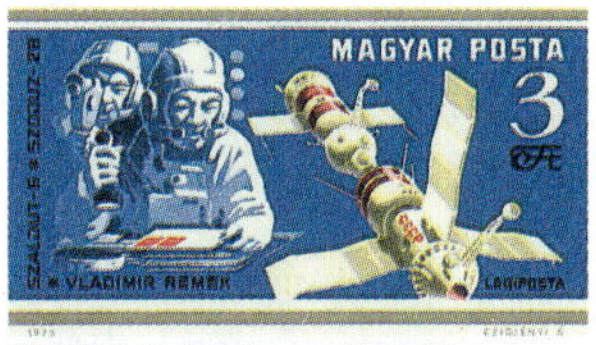

706 Vladimir Remek cancelling Letters, "Salyut 6" and "Soyuz 28"

1978. Air. "Praga 1978" International Stamp Exhibition, Prague.

3203	**706**	3fo. multicoloured	1·70	1·70

707 Toshiba Automatic Letter Sorting Equipment

1978. Automation of Letter Sorting.

3204	**707**	1fo. multicoloured	60	60

708 Putto offering Grapes

1978. Stamp Day. Mosaics. Multicoloured.

3205	2fo. Type **708**	2·50	2·50
3206	2fo. Tiger	2·50	2·50
3207	2fo. Bird	2·50	2·50
3208	2fo. Dolphin	2·50	2·50
MS3209	88×61 mm. 10fo. Hercules aiming arrow at Centaur Nessus fleeing with Nymph Deianeira (51×32 mm)	11·50	11·50

709 Methods of Communication

1978. Organization of Socialist Countries' Postal Administrations Conference, Tbilisi.

3210	**709**	1fo. multicoloured	60	25

710 Imre Thokoly

1978. 300th Anniv of Thokoly's Revolt.

3211	**710**	1fo. black and yellow	60	25

711 Hungarian Regalia

1978. Return of Hungarian Regalia. Sheet 76×96 mm.

MS3212 **711**	20fo. multicoloured	10·50	10·50

712 "The Red Coach" (novel)

1978. Birth Cent of Gyula Krudy (novelist).

3213	**712**	3fo. red and black	1·00	25

713 St. Ladislas (bust, Gyor Cathedral)

1978. 900th Anniv of Accession of St. Ladislas.

3214	**713**	1fo. multicoloured	70	25

714 Buildings and Arms of Koszeg

1978. 650th Anniv of Koszeg.

3215	**714**	1fo. multicoloured	70	25

715 Samu Czaban and Gizella Berzeviczy

1978. Birth Centenaries of Samu Czaban and Gizella Berzeviczy (teachers).

3216	**715**	1fo. multicoloured	70	60

716 Communist Party Emblem

1978. 60th Anniv of Hungarian Communist Party.

3217	**716**	1fo. red, grey and black	25	10

717 "Girl cutting Bread"

1978. Ceramics by Margit Kovacs. Mult.

3218	1fo. Type **717**	45	10
3219	2fo. "Girl with Pitcher"	60	35
3220	3fo. "Boy Potter"	1·20	60

718 "Self-portrait in Fur Coat"

1978. 450th Death Anniv of Albrecht Durer (artist). Multicoloured.

3221	40fi. "Madonna with Child"	10	10
3222	60fi. "Adoration of the Magi" (horiz)	10	10
3223	1fo. Type **718**	25	10
3224	2fo. "St. George"	60	10
3225	3fo. "Nativity" (horiz)	1·20	15
3226	4fo. "St. Eustace"	1·40	25
3227	5fo. "The Four Apostles"	2·00	1·20
MS3228	78×99 mm. 20fo. sepia and stone ("Dancing Peasant Couple") (36×59 mm)	7·00	7·00

719 Human Rights Emblem

1979. 30th Anniv of Declaration of Human Rights.

3229	**719**	1fo. blue and light blue	1·70	1·70

720 Child with Dog

1979. International Year of the Child (1st issue). Multicoloured.

3230	1fo. Type **720**	1·20	1·20
3231	1fo. Family group	1·20	1·20
3232	1fo. Children of different races	7·00	7·00

See also Nos. 3287/93.

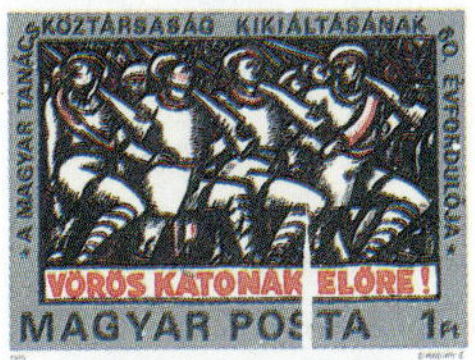

721 "Soldiers of the Re l Army, Forward!" (poster by Be a Uitz)

1979. 60th Anniv of First Hungari n Soviet Republic.

3233	**721**	1fo. black, red and (rey	25	10

722 "Girl Reading" ·erenc Kovacs)

1979. Youth Stamp Exhibition, Be :scsaba.

3234	**722**	3fo.+1fo.50 grey, bl and black	1·20	1·20

723 Chessmen and Cu

1979. 23rd Chess Olympiad, Buer ; Aires (1978).

3235	**723**	3fo. multicoloured	2·00	1·70

724 Alexander Nevski Cat dral, Sofia, and First Bulgarian Stamp

1979. "Philaserdica 79" Internat ıal Stamp Exhibition, Sofia.

3236	**724**	3fo. multicoloured	1·50	1·50

725 Stephenson's "R ', 1829

1979. International Transpor :hibition, Hamburg. Depicting development of t ailway. Mult.

3237	40fi. Type **725**	25	10
3238	60fi. Siemens's electric lo(no-tive, 1879	40	10
3239	1fo. Locomotive "Pioneer' 51 (wrongly dated "1936")	65	20
3240	2fo. Hungarian Class MA\ pulling "Orient Express 83	75	25
3241	3fo. "Trans-Siberian Expre 1898	1·30	50
3242	4fo. Japanese "Hikari" ex train, 1964	1·90	75
3243	5fo. German "Transrapid 05" Maglev train, 1979	2·10	1·50
MS3244	78×95 mm. 20fo. European railway map (51×36 mm)	10·50	10·50

726 Soyuz Gas Pipeline and Compressor Station

1979. 30th Anniv of Council of Mutual Economic Aid. Multicoloured.

3245	1fo. Type **726**	25	10
3246	2fo. Pylon and dam, Lenin hydro-electric power station, Dnepropetrovsk	65	20
3247	3fo. Council building, Moscow	90	25

727 Zsigmond Moricz (after J. Rippl-Ronai)

1979. Birth Centenary of Zsigmond Moricz (writer).

3248	**727**	1fo. multicoloured	25	10

728 City Hall, Helsinki (1952 Games)

1979. Olympic Games, Moscow (1980) (1st issue). Multicoloured.

3249	40fi. Type **728**	15	10
3250	60fi. Colosseum, Rome (1960)	25	10
3251	1fo. Asakusa Temple, Tokyo (1964)	65	20
3252	2fo. Cathedral, Mexico City (1968)	90	25
3253	3fo. Frauenkirche, Munich (1972)	1·30	35
3254	4fo. Modern quarter, Montreal (1976)	1·50	60
3255	5fo. Lomonosov University, Moscow, and Misha the bear (mascot) (1980)	2·10	1·20

See also Nos. 3323/29.

729 "Child with Horse and Greyhounds" (Janos Vaszary)

1979. Animal Paintings. Multicoloured.

3256	40fi. Type **729**	20	10
3257	60fi. "Coach and Five" (Karoly Lotz)	25	10
3258	1fo. "Lads on Horseback" (Celesztin Pallya)	40	25
3259	2fo. "Farewell" (Karoly Lotz)	65	35
3260	3fo. "Horse Market" (Celeztin Pallya)	90	60
3261	4fo. "Wandering" (Bela Ivanyi-Grunwald)	1·30	85
3262	5fo. "Ready for Hunting" (Karoly Sterio)	2·50	1·20

730 Sturgeon, Cousteau's Ship "Calypso" and Black Sea

1979. Sea and River Purity.

3263	**730**	3fo. multicoloured	1·30	25

731 Globe and Five Pentathlon Sports

1979. Pentathlon World Championship, Budapest.

3264	**731**	2fo. multicoloured	1·30	35

732 Stephen I Denarius (reverse)

1979. 9th International Numismatic Congress, Berne. Designs showing old Hungarian coins. Multicoloured.

3265	1fo. Type **732**	20	25
3266	2fo. Bela III copper coin (obverse)	65	60
3267	3fo. Louis the Great groat (reverse)	90	85
3268	4fo. Matthias I gold forint (obverse)	1·30	1·20
3269	5fo. Wladislaw II gulden (reverse)	1·50	1·50

733 Design for Proposed Hungarian Stamp of 1848

1979. Stamp Day. Sheet 70×56 mm.

MS3270	**733**	10fo. multicoloured	7·50	7·50

734 Light Passenger Locomotive

1979. Centenary of Gyor—Sopron—Ebenfurt Railway. Sheet 98×79 mm containing T 734 and similar horiz designs. Multicoloured.

MS3271	5fo. Type **734**; 5fo. Class 424 steam locomotive; 5fo. Class 520 locomotive; 5fo. Diesel locomotive Type M41	7·50	7·50

735 Flags and Globe filled with Coins

1979. World Savings Day.

3272	**735**	1fo. multicoloured	25	10

736 "Vega-Chess" (Victor Vasarely)

1979. Modern Art.

3273	**736**	1fo. multicoloured	50	25

737 European Otter

1979. Protected Animals. Multicoloured.

3274	40fi. Type **737**	25	10
3275	60fi. Wild cat	30	10
3276	1fo. Pine marten	40	10
3277	2fo. Eurasian badger	75	20
3278	4fo. Steppe polecat	1·50	60
3279	6fo. Beech marten	3·75	1·40

738 Ski Jumping

1979. Air. Winter Olympic Games, Lake Placid (1980). Multicoloured.

3280	40fi. Type **738**	30	10
3281	60fi. Figure skating	65	20
3282	1fo. Slalom	70	35
3283	2fo. Ice hockey	1·30	50
3284	4fo. Bobsleigh	1·90	60
3285	6fo. Cross-country skiing	2·50	1·90
MS3286	97×73 mm. 20fo. Ice dancing (square, 49×49 mm)	8·25	8·25

739 "Tom Thumb"

1979. International Year of the Child (2nd issue). Designs depicting children's stories. Mult.

3287	40fi. Type **739**	25	10
3288	60fi. "The Ugly Duckling" (Andersen)	65	10

3289	1fo. "The Fisher and the Goldfish"	75	20
3290	2fo. "Cinderella"	1·30	25
3291	3fo. "Gulliver's Travels" (Swift)	1·40	35
3292	4fo. "The Little Pig and the Wolves"	1·50	60
3293	5fo. "Gallant John"	2·50	1·00
MS3294	78×98 mm. 20fo. "Fairy Ilona"	8·25	8·25

740 Achillea and Bee-eating Beetles

1980. Pollination. Multicoloured.

3295	40fl. Type **740**	20	10
3296	60fl. Gaillardia and bee	25	10
3297	1fo. Rudbeckia and red admiral	40	10
3298	2fo. Dog rose and rose chafer	75	20
3299	4fo. "Petroselinum hortense" and striped bug	1·50	35
3300	6fo. Achillea and longhorn beetle	2·40	1·20

741 Hanging Gardens of Babylon

1980. Seven Wonders of the Ancient World. Mult.

3301	40fi. Type **741**	15	10
3302	60fi. Temple of Artemis, Ephesus	20	10
3303	1fo. Statue of Zeus, Olympia	25	10
3304	2fo. Mausoleum of Halicarnassus	65	20
3305	3fo. Colossus of Rhodes	1·00	25
3306	4fo. Pharos, Alexandria	1·40	35
3307	5fo. Pyramids of Egypt	3·00	1·00

742 Gabor Bethlen (copperplate)

1980. 400th Birth Anniv of Gabor Bethlen (Prince of Transylvania).

3308	**742**	1fo. multicoloured	25	10

743 Tihany Abbey

1980. 925th Anniv of Foundation of Tihany Abbey.

3309	**743**	1fo. multicoloured	25	10

744 Easter Sepulchre

1980. Easter Sepulchre of Garamszentbenedek. Designs showing details of sepulchre. Mult.

3310	1fo. Type **744**	25	25
3311	2fo. Three Marys	65	60
3312	3fo. Apostle Jacob	1·00	1·00
3313	4fo. Apostle Thaddeus	1·30	1·20
3314	5fo. Apostle Andrew	1·60	1·60

745 Bunch of Wild Flowers

1980. 35th Anniv of Liberation.

3315	**745**	1fo. multicoloured	40	25

746 Watch symbolising Environmental Protection

1980. Youth Stamp Exhibition, Dunaujvaros.

3316	**746**	3fo.+1fo.50 mult	1·30	1·30

747 Attila Jozsef

1980. 75th Birth Anniv of Attila Jozsef (poet).

3317	**747**	1fo. green and red	40	25

748 "Madonna and Child" Stamp of 1921 with Inverted Centre

1980. 50th Anniv of Hungarian Stamp Museum.

3318	**748**	1fo. multicoloured	2·30	2·30

749 Great Britain 2d. Blue and Life Guard

1980. "London 1980" International Stamp Exhibition.

3319	**749**	3fo. multicoloured	1·30	1·30

750 Soviet and Hungarian Cosmonauts

1980. Air. Soviet–Hungarian Space Flight.

3320	**750**	5fo. multicoloured	2·50	60

751 Margit Kaffka

1980. Birth Centenary of Margit Kaffka (writer).

3321	**751**	1fo. yellow, black & vio	40	25

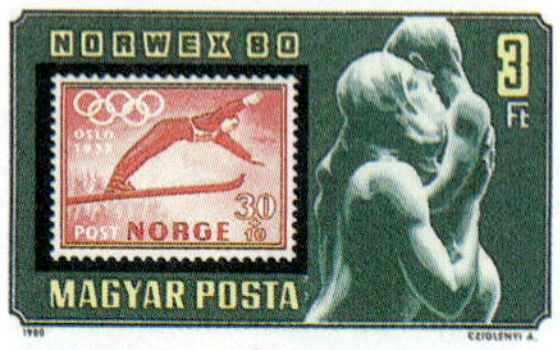

752 Norwegian 1951 Olympic Stamp and Statue "Mother and Child" (Gustav Vigeland)

1980. "Norwex 80" International Stamp Exhibition, Oslo.

3322	**752**	3fo. multicoloured	1·50	1·50

753 Handball

1980. Air. Olympic Games, Moscow (2nd issue). Multicoloured.

3323	40fi. Type **753**	15	10
3324	60fi. Double kayak	20	10
3325	1fo. Running	25	10
3326	2fo. Gymnastics	65	10
3327	3fo. Show-jumping (modern pentathlon)	1·00	20
3328	4fo. Wrestling	1·60	60
3329	5fo. Water polo	1·90	1·50
MS3330	71×87 mm. 20fo. Runners with Olympic flame	8·25	8·25

754 Endre Hogyes (physician) and Congress Emblem

1980. 28th International Congress of Physiological Sciences, Budapest.

3331	**754**	1fo. multicoloured	30	10

755 B. Farkos, V. Kubasov and Space Station

1980. Air. Soviet–Hungarian Space Flight (2nd issue). Sheet 72×93 mm.

MS3332	**755** 20fo. multicoloured	10·50	10·50

756 Zoltan Schonherz

1980. 75th Birth Anniv of Zoltan Schonherz (Workers' Movement member).

3333	**756**	1fo. multicoloured	30	10

757 Decanter

1980. Stamp Day. Glassware. Multicoloured.

3334	1fo. Type **757**	40	25
3335	2fo. Wine glass, Budapest	75	60
3336	3fo. Drinking glass, Zay-Ugrocz	1·30	85
MS3337	68×79 mm. 10fo. Drinking glass, Pecs (25×35 mm)	4·50	4·50

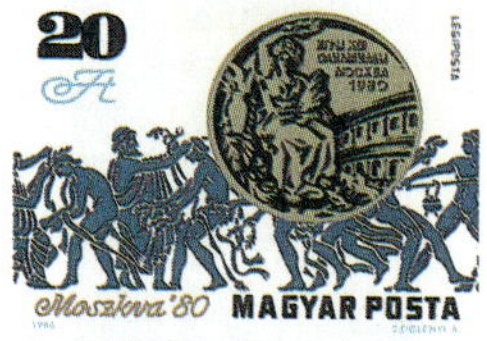

758 Greek Athletes and Olympic Gold Medal

1980. Air. Olympic Champions. Sheet 84×65 mm.

MS3338	**758** 20fo. multicoloured	7·00	7·00

759 Bertalan Por (self-portrait)

1980. Birth Centenary of Bertalan Por (artist).

3339	**759**	1fo. multicoloured	30	20

760 Greylag Goose

1980. Protected Birds. Multicoloured.

3340	40fi. Type **760**	15	10
3341	60fi. Black-crowned night herons	25	10
3342	1fo. Common shovelers	30	20
3343	2fo. White-winged black tern	65	25
3344	4fo. Great crested grebes	1·90	85
3345	6fo. Black-winged stilts	3·25	1·50
MS3346	75×95 mm. 20fo. Great egrets (40×63 mm)	6·25	6·25

761 Peace Dove and Map of Europe

1980. European Security and Co-operation Conference, Madrid. Sheet 99×78 mm.
MS3347 **761** 20fo. multicoloured 3·75 3·75

762 Johannes Kepler

1980. 350th Death Anniv of Johannes Kepler (astronomer).
3348 **762** 1fo. multicoloured 65 25

763 Karoly Kisfaludy

1980. 150th Death Anniv of Karoly Kisfaludy (dramatist and poet).
3349 **763** 1fo. multicoloured 50 20

764 U.N. Building, New York

1980. 25th Anniv of United Nations Membership. Multicoloured.

3350	40fi. Type **764**	15	10
3351	60fi. U.N. building, Geneva	20	10
3352	1fo. International Centre, Vienna	25	10
3353	2fo. U.N. and Hungarian flags	65	20
3354	4fo. U.N. emblem and Hungarian arms	1·30	25
3355	6fo. World map	3·75	2·10

765 Ferenc Erdei

1980. 70th Birth Anniv of Ferenc Erdei (agricultural economist and politician).
3356 **765** 1fo. multicoloured 25 10

766 Bela Szanto

1981. Birth Centenary of Bela Szanto (founder member of Hungarian Communist Party).
3357 **766** 1fo. multicoloured 25 10

767 Lajos Batthyany (after Miklos Barabas)

1981. 175th Birth Anniv of Lajos Batthyany (politician).
3358 **767** 1fo. multicoloured 25 10

768 Cheetah

1981. Air. Birth Centenary of Kalman Kittenberger (explorer and zoologist). Multicoloured.

3359	40fi. Type **768**	20	10
3360	60fi. Lion	20	10
3361	1fo. Leopard	30	20
3362	2fo. Black rhinoceros	65	25
3363	3fo. Greater kudu	1·00	30
3364	4fo. African elephant	1·40	35
3365	5fo. Kittenberger and Hungarian National Museum	3·25	1·90

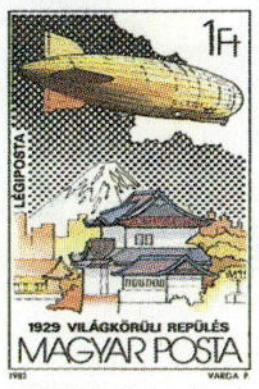

769 "Graf Zeppelin" over Tokyo

1981. Air. "Luraba" International Exhibition of Aero- and Astro-philately, Lucerne. "Graf Zeppelin" Flights. Multicoloured.

3366	1fo. Type **769** (first round-the-world flight, 1929)	25	10
3367	2fo. Franz Josef Land and icebreaker "Malygin" (Polar flight, 1931)	50	20
3368	3fo. Nine-arch Bridge, Hortobagy (Hungary flight, 1931)	75	25
3369	4fo. Hostentor, Lubeck (Baltic flight, 1931)	1·00	30
3370	5fo. Tower Bridge (England flight, 1931)	1·10	35
3371	6fo. Federal Palace, Chicago (World Exhibition flight, 1933)	1·30	50
3372	7fo. Lucerne (1st Swiss flight, 1929)	1·90	1·60

770 Bela Bartok (after Ferenczy Beni)

1981. Birth Centenary of Bela Bartok (composer). Sheet 100×80 mm containing T 770 and similar vert design. Multicoloured.
MS3373 10fo. Type **770**; 10fo. Illustration for "Cantata Profana" 8·25 8·25

771 Flag of House of Arpad (11th century)

1981. Historical Hungarian Flags. Mult.

3374	40fi. Type **771**	20	10
3375	60fi. Hunyadi Family flag (15th century)	40	15
3376	1fo. Flag of Gabor Bethlen (1600)	75	20
3377	2fo. Flag of Ferenc Rakoczi II (1706)	1·10	25
3378	4fo. "Honved" (1848–49)	1·50	35
3379	6fo. Troop Flag (1919)	2·10	1·10

772 Red Deer seen through Binoculars

1981. Cent of Association of Hungarian Huntsmen.
3380 **772** 2fo. multicoloured 65 25

773 First Hungarian Telephone Exchange

1981. Centenary of First Hungarian Telephone Exchange, Budapest.
3381 **773** 2fo. multicoloured 1·30 25

774 Henri Dunant (founder) and Map of Europe

1981. 3rd European Conference of Red Cross and Red Crescent Societies, Budapest. Sheet 98×78 mm.
MS3382 **774** 20fo. multicoloured 6·25 6·25

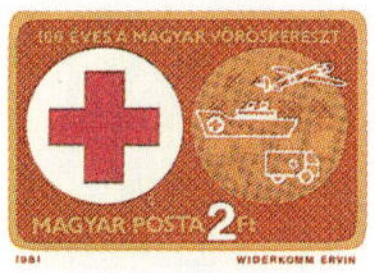

775 Red Cross, Transport and Globe

1981. Cent of Hungarian Red Cross.
3383 **775** 2fo. orange and red 65 25

776 Airship LZ-127 "Graf Zeppelin"

1981. "WIPA 1981" International Stamp Exhibition, Vienna. Sheet 80×60 mm containing T 776 and similar horiz designs depicting "WIPA 1933" souvenir labels.
MS3384 5fo. green and black (Type **776**); 5fo. purple and black (Rocket); 5fo. brown and black (Dispatch rider); 5fo. blue and black (Sailing ship) 8·25 8·25

777 I.Y.D.P. Emblem and Person pushing Wheelchair

1981. International Year of Disabled Persons.
3385 **777** 2fo.+1fo. green & yell 1·90 1·20

778 Young People and Factory

1981. 10th Young Communist League Congress, Budapest.
3386 **778** 4fo.+2fo. mult 2·50 2·50

779 Stephenson and "Locomotion"

1981. Birth Bicentenary of George Stephenson (railway pioneer).
3387 **779** 2fo. yellow, grey & brown 1·30 35

780 Bela Vago

1981. Birth Centenary of Bela Vago (founder member of Hungarian Communist Party).
3388 **780** 2fo. green and brown 90 25

781 Alexander Fleming

1981. Birth Centenary of Alexander Fleming (discoverer of penicillin).
3389 **781** 2fo. multicoloured 90 35

782 Bridal Chest from Szentgal

1981. Stamp Day. Bridal Chests. Mult.

3390	1fo. Type **782**	65	50
3391	2fo. Chest from Hodmezovasarhely	1·30	1·10
MS3392	76×55 mm. 10fo. Chest from Bacs (43×23 mm)	7·00	7·00

783 Calvinist College

1981. 450th Anniv of Calvinist College, Papa.
3393 **783** 2fo. multicoloured 90 25

784 Hands holding F.A.O. Emblem

1981. World Food Day.
3394 **784** 2fo. multicoloured 1·90 25

785 German Costume

1981. National Costumes of Hungarian Ethnic Minorities. Multicoloured.

3395	1fo. Slovakian costume	1·80	1·80
3396	2fo. Type **785**	1·80	1·80
3397	3fo. Croatian costume	1·80	1·80

3398	4fo. Rumanian costume	1·80	1·80

786 "Franz I" (1830) and "Ferene Deak" on 30fi. Stamp

1981. 125th Anniv of Danube Commission. Paddle-steamers and Danube Commission stamps issued in 1967. Multicoloured.

3399	1fo. Type **786**	40	25
3400	1fo. "Arpad" (1834) and "Revfulop" on 60fi. stamp	45	30
3401	2fo. "Szechenyi" (1853) and "Hunyadi" on 1fo. stamp	65	50
3402	2fo. "Grof Szechenyi Istvan" (1896) and "Szekszard" on 1fo.50 stamp	70	50
3403	4fo. "Zsofia" (1914) and "Miscolc" on 1fo.70 stamp	1·10	85
3404	6fo. "Felszabadulas" (1917) and "Tihany" on 2fo. stamp	2·00	1·50
3405	8fo. "Rakoczi" (1964) and "Siraly I" on 2fo.50 stamp	2·75	1·90
MS3406	96×77 mm. 20fo. Hydrofoil "Solyom" and 1fo. stamp (49×39 mm)	7·00	7·00

787 "Mother Breast-feeding" (pottery, Margit Kovacs)

1981. Christmas. Multicoloured.

3407	1fo. Type **787**	65	35
3408	2fo. "Madonna of Csurgo" (bronze Amerigo Tot)	1·30	50

788 "Pen Pals" (Rockwell)

1981. Illustrations by Norman Rockwell and Anna Lesznai. Multicoloured.

3409	1fo. Type **788**	20	20
3410	2fo. "Courting under the Clock at Midnight" (Rockwell)	30	25
3411	2fo. "Maiden Voyage" (Rockwell)	30	25
3412	4fo. "Threading the Needle" (Rockwell)	1·30	1·10
3413	4fo. "At the End of the Village" (detail) (Lesznai)	1·30	1·10
3414	5fo. "Dance" (detail) (Lesznai)	1·90	1·70
3415	6fo. "Sunday" (detail) (Lesznai)	2·10	2·10

789 "La Tolette"

1981. Birth Centenary of Pablo Picasso (artist). Sheet 61×86 mm.

MS3416	**789** 20fo. multicoloured	8·25	8·25

790 Militiaman at Shooting Practice

1982. 25th Anniv of Workers' Militia. Mult.

3417	1fo. Type **790**	25	20
3418	4fo. Three generations of militiamen	1·30	35

791 Congress Emblem and Havana

1982. 10th World Trade Unions Federation Congress, Havana.

3419	**791**	2fo. multicoloured	65	25

792 Gyula Alpari

1982. Birth Centenary of Gyula Alpari (journalist).

3420	**792**	2fo. yellow, purple & brn	65	25

793 Dr. Robert Koch

1982. Cent of Discovery of Tubercle Bacillus.

3421	**793**	2fo. multicoloured	65	25

794 Tennis Racket and Ball

1982. Youth Stamp. European Junior Tennis Cup.

3422	**794**	4fo.+2fo. mult	1·90	1·90

795 Hungary v. Egypt, 1934

1982. World Cup Football Championship, Spain. Multicoloured.

3423	1fo. Type **795**	40	10
3424	1fo. Italy v. Hungary, 1938	40	10
3425	2fo. West Germany v. Hungary, 1954	75	20
3426	2fo. Hungary v. Mexico, 1958	75	20
3427	4fo. Hungary v. England, 1962	1·50	25
3428	6fo. Hungary v. Brazil, 1966	1·90	35
3429	8fo. Argentina v. Hungary, 1978	2·50	1·50
MS3430	100×68 mm. 10fo. Barcelona stadium; 10fo. Madrid stadium	7·50	7·50

796 Table Tennis Player and Map of Europe

1982. European Table Tennis Championship, Budapest.

3431	**796**	2fo. multicoloured	1·00	25

797 "Pascali"

1982. Roses. Multicoloured.

3432	1fo. Type **797**	40	10
3433	1fo. "Michele Meilland"	40	10
3434	2fo. "Diorama"	75	20
3435	2fo. "Wendy Cussons"	75	20
3436	3fo. "Blue Moon"	1·10	25
3437	3fo. "Invitation"	1·10	25
3438	4fo. "Tropicana"	2·10	1·40
MS3439	70×92 mm. 10fo. Bunch of roses (35×57 mm)	6·25	6·25

798 Georgi Dimitrov

1982. Birth Centenary of Georgi Dimitrov (Bulgarian statesman).

3440	**798**	2fo. grey, green & brown	65	60

799 "Columbia" Space Shuttle

1982. Space Research. Multicoloured.

3441	1fo. Type **799**	25	10
3442	1fo. Neil Armstrong (first man on Moon)	25	10
3443	2fo. A. Leonov (first space-walker)	65	20
3444	2fo. Yuri Gagarin (first man in space)	65	20
3445	4fo. Laika (first dog in space)	1·30	25
3446	4fo. "Sputnik I" (first artificial satellite)	1·30	25
3447	6fo. K. E. Tsiolkovsky (Russian scientist)	2·00	1·00

800 Watermark

1982. Bicentenary of Diosgyor Paper-mill.

3448	**800**	2fo. multicoloured	65	25

801 Rubik Cube

1982. World Rubik Cube Championship, Budapest.

3449	**801**	2fo. multicoloured	65	25

802 World Cup 20fi. Stamp, 1966, and Paris Arms

1982. "Philexfrance 82" International Stamp Exhibition, Paris. Sheet 98×72 mm.

MS3450	**802** 20fo.+10fo. mult	6·25	6·25

803 Col. Mihaly Kovats (after S. Finta)

1982. 250th Birth Anniv of George Washington. Sheet 90×72 mm containing T 803 and similar vert design. Multicoloured.

MS3451	5fo. Type **803**; 5fo. Washington on horseback (after F. Kemmelmeyer)	5·00	5·00

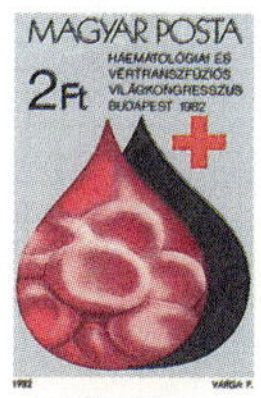

804 Blood Drop

1982. World Haematology Congress, Budapest.

3452	**804**	2fo. multicoloured	65	25

805 Zirc Abbey and Seal of King Bela III

1982. 800th Anniv of Zirc Abbey.

3453	**805**	2fo. multicoloured	65	25

806 Fisherman's Bastion, Budapest

1982. Stamp Day. Multicoloured.

3454	4fo.+2fo. Type **806**	1·90	1·90
3455	4fo.+2fo. Cupola of Parliament, Budapest	1·90	1·90

807 Budapest (image scaled to 59% of original size)

1982. 10th Anniv of European Security and Co-operation Conference, Brussels. Sheet 100×84 mm.
MS3456 **807** 20fo.+10fo. mult 5·75 5·75

808 Kner Emblem

1982. Cent of Kner Printing Office, Gyoma.
3457 **808** 2fo. yellow, black and red 65 25

809 Agricultural Symbols on Map of Hungary

1982. "Agrofila '82" Stamp Exhibition, Godollo.
3458 **809** 5fo. multicoloured 1·90 1·90

810 Horse-drawn Bus and Underground Train

1982. 150th Anniv of Public Transport in Budapest.
3459 **810** 2fo. multicoloured 65 25

811 Budapest Polytechnic University

1982. Bicentenary of University Engineering Education.
3460 **811** 2fo. brown, stone & blue 65 25

812 Gyorgy Boloni

1982. Birth Centenary of Gyorgy Boloni (journalist).
3461 **812** 2fo. yellow, brown and deep brown 65 25

813 Lenin

1982. 65th Anniv of Russian Revolution.
3462 **813** 5fo. multicoloured 1·50 25

814 Vuk and Bird

1982. Vuk the Fox Cub (cartoon character). Multicoloured.

3463	1fo. Type **814**	25	10
3464	1fo. Two dogs	25	10
3465	2fo. Vuk and cock	75	20
3466	2fo. Vuk and owl	75	20
3467	4fo. Vuk and geese	1·50	25
3468	6fo. Vuk and frog	2·50	1·00
3469	8fo. Vuk, old fox and butterflies	3·25	1·70

815 St. Stephen (sculpture, Imre Varga)

1982. Works of Art in Hungarian Chapel, Vatican. Multicoloured.

3470	2fo. Type **815**	75	75
3471	2fo. "Pope Silvester II making donation to St. Stephen" (37×18 mm)	75	75
3472	2fo. "St. John of Capistrano ringing Angelus to commemorate Hungarian victory over Turks" (37×18 mm)	75	75
3473	2fo. "Pope Paul VI showing Cardinal Lekai site of Hungarian Chapel" (37×18 mm)	75	75
3474	2fo. "Pope John Paul II consecrating chapel" (37×18 mm)	75	75
3475	2fo. "Madonna" (sculpture, Imre Varga)	75	75

Nos. 3471/5 were printed together, se-tenant, forming a composite design of a relief by Amerigo Tot.

816 Dog and Cat crossing road

1982. New Year.
3476 **816** 2fo. multicoloured 65 25

817 Zoltan Kodaly

1982. Birth Centenary of Zoltan Kodaly (composer). Sheet 66×95 mm.
MS3477 **817** 20fo. brown and stone 5·75 5·75

818 Goethe (after Heinrich Kolbe)

1982. 150th Death Anniv of Johann Wolfgang Goethe (writer). Sheet 93×74 mm.
MS3478 **818** 20fo. multicoloured 6·25 6·25

819 Raven and Envelope Address Marks

1983. 10th Anniv of Postal Codes.
3479 **819** 2fo. black, grey and red 65 25

820 "Ship of Peace" (Endre Szasz)

1983. Budapest Spring Festival.
3480 **820** 2fo. grey, gold and black 65 25

821 Student at School Door

1983. Youth Stamp Exhibition, Baja.
3481 **821** 4fo.+2fo. mult 1·90 1·90

822 Gyula Juhasz

1983. Birth Cent of Gyula Juhasz (writer).
3482 **822** 2fo. dp brown, brn & blk 65 25

823 Menner's Balloon, 1811

1983. Air. Bicent of Manned Flight. Mult.

3483	1fo. Type **823** (1st manned flight in Hungary)	25	10
3484	1fo. Captive observation balloon at Budapest Exhibition, 1896	25	10
3485	2fo. Pursuit race, 1904	65	10
3486	2fo. Hot-air balloon "Pannonia", 1977	65	10
3487	4fo. Hot-air balloon "Malev", 1981	1·30	20
3488	4fo. Hungarian National Defence Union balloon, 1982	1·30	20
3489	5fo. Non-rigid airship over Mecsek television tower, 1981	1·50	75
MS3490	88×74 mm. 20fo. Hot-air balloons (39×49 mm)	5·75	5·75

824 Szentgotthard Monastery and Seal

1983. 800th Anniv of Szentgotthard.
3491 **824** 2fo. multicoloured 65 25

825 Watermill, Tapolca

1983. "Tembal 83" Thematic Stamps Exhibition, Basel.
3492 **825** 5fo. multicoloured 1·90 1·90

826 Parliament Buildings, Budapest

1983. 5th Inter-Parliamentary Union Conference, Budapest. Sheet 95×77 mm.
MS3493 **826** 20fo. multicoloured 5·75 5·75

827 Jeno Hamburger

1983. Birth Centenary of Jeno Hamburger (doctor and revolutionary).
3494 **827** 2fo. brown, blue and red 65 25

828 "Giovanna d'Aragona"

1983. 500th Birth Anniv of Raphael (artist). Mult.

3495	1fo. Type **828**	20	10
3496	1fo. "Lady with Unicorn"	20	10
3497	2fo. "Madonna of the Chair"	40	10
3498	2fo. "Madonna of the Grand Duke"	40	10
3499	4fo. "La Muta"	1·10	25
3500	6fo. "Lady with a Veil"	1·60	35
3501	8fo. "La Fornaria"	2·10	75
MS3502	66×89 mm. 20fo. "Esterhazy Madonna" (24×37 mm)	7·00	7·00

829 Vagi and Newspapers

1983. Birth Centenary of Istvan Vagi (secretary of Socialist Workers' Party).
3503 **829** 2fo. multicoloured 65 25

830 Bolivar and Map of Americas

1983. Birth Bicent of Simon Bolivar.

3504	**830**	2fo. multicoloured	65	25

831 Globe and Congress Emblem

1983. 68th Universal Esperanto Congress, Budapest.

3505	**831**	2fo. multicoloured	65	25

832 Martin Luther

1983. 500th Anniv of Martin Luther (religious reformer). Sheet 80×65 mm.

MS3506 **832** 20fo. multicoloured	7·00	7·00

833 Lesser Spotted Eagle

1983. Birds of Prey. Multicoloured.

3507	1fo. Type **833**	25	10
3508	1fo. Imperial eagle	25	10
3509	2fo. White-tailed sea eagle	65	10
3510	2fo. Western red-footed falcon	65	10
3511	4fo. Saker falcon	1·30	60
3512	6fo. Rough-legged buzzard	2·30	1·20
3513	8fo. Common buzzard	3·25	2·10

834 Bee collecting Pollen

1983. 29th Apimondia (Bee Keeping) Congress, Budapest.

3514	**834**	1fo. multicoloured	25	10

835 Old National Theatre (after R. Alt)

1983. Stamp Day. Engravings of Budapest Buildings.

3515	**835**	4fo.+2fo. yellow, brown and black	2·10	2·10
3516	-	4fo.+2fo. yellow, brown and black	2·10	2·10

MS3517 80×63 mm. 20fo.+10fo. yellow and brown	7·00	7·00

DESIGNS—As T **835**: No. 3516, Municipal concert hall, Pest (after H. Luders). 27×44 mm—**MS**3517, Holy Trinity Square, Buda (after Rudolf Alt).

836 "Fruit-piece"

1983. Birth Centenary of Bela Czobel (artist).

3518	**836**	2fo. multicoloured	65	25

837 "Molnya" Satellite and Kekes TV Tower

1983. World Communications Year. Mult.

3519	1fo. Type **837**	25	10
3520	1fo. Dish aerials and rockets	25	10
3521	2fo. Manual telephone exchange and modern "TMM-81" telephone	65	10
3522	3fo. Computer terminal	90	25
3523	5fo. Automatic letter-storing equipment	1·50	35
3524	8fo. Teletext and newspaper mastheads	2·50	60
MS3525	70×90 mm. 20fo. "Molnya" satellite (29×44 mm)	7·00	7·00

838 Flags encircling Globe

1983. 34th International Astronautical Federation Congress, Budapest.

3526	**838**	2fo. multicoloured	65	25

839 Kremlin, Moscow

1983. "Sozphilex '83" Stamp Exhibition, Moscow.

3527	**839**	2fo. multicoloured	90	90

840 Congress Palace, Madrid

1983. European Security and Co-operation Conference, Madrid. Sheet 98×78 mm.

MS3528 **840** 20fo. multicoloured	5·00	5·00

841 Babits (after Jozsef Rippl-Ronai)

1983. Birth Cent of Mihaly Babits (writer).

3529	**841**	2fo. multicoloured	65	25

842 "Madonna with Rose"

1983. Christmas. Multicoloured.

3530	1fo. Type **842**	25	10
3531	2fo. Altar painting, Csikmenasag	65	20

843 Zanka

1983. Hungarian Resorts. Multicoloured.

3532	1fo. Type **843**	40	10
3533	2fo. Hajduszoboszlo	50	10
3534	5fo. Heviz	1·30	25

844 Ice Dancing

1983. Winter Olympic Games, Sarajevo.

3535	**844**	1fo. multicoloured	25	10
3536	-	1fo. multicoloured	25	10
3537	-	2fo. multicoloured (man lifting girl)	65	10
3538	-	2fo. multicoloured	65	10
3539	-	4fo. multicoloured (man with both arms bent)	1·30	25
3540	-	4fo. multicoloured (man with one arm outstretched)	1·30	25
3541	-	6fo. multicoloured	1·40	50

MS3542 70×70 mm. 20fo. multicoloured (49×39 mm)	6·25	6·25

DESIGNS: Nos. 3536/42, Different ice dancing designs.

845 "Virgin with Six Saints" (Tiepolo)

1984. Paintings Stolen from Museum of Fine Arts, Budapest. Sheet 130×98 mm containing T 845 and similar multicoloured designs.

MS3543 2fo. Type **845**; 2fo. "Esterhazy Madonna" (Raphael); 2fo. "Portrait of Giorgione" (imitator of Giorgione); 2fo. "Portrait of a Woman" (Tintoretto); 2fo. "Pietro Bempo" (Raphael); 2fo. "Portrait of a Man" (Tintoretto); 8fo. "Rest on the Flight into Egypt" (Tiepolo) (47×32 mm)	7·00	7·00

846 Csoma (statue) and Sepulchre, Darjeeling

1984. Birth Bicentenary of Sandor Korosi Csoma (traveller and philologist).

3544	**846**	2fo. multicoloured	65	25

847 "Energy" and Sun

1984. Save Energy Campaign.

3545	**847**	1fo, red and black	25	10

848 Parent and Child

1984. Youth Stamp.

3546	**848**	4fo.+2fo. mult	2·10	2·10

849 40fi. Goya Stamp, 1968

1984. International Stamp Exhibitions. Sheet 125×104 mm containing T 849 and similar vert designs. Multicoloured.

MS3547 4fo. Type **849** ("Espana 84", Madrid); 4fo. 20fi. kangaroo stamp, 1961 ("Ausipex 84", Melbourne); 4fo. 1fo. Schiller stamp, 1959 ("Philatelia '84", Stuttgart)	5·00	5·00

850 Hair Ornaments from Rakamaz

1984. Archaeological Finds.

3548	**850**	1fo. stone and brown	25	10
3549	-	1fo. stone and brown	25	10
3550	-	2fo. stone and brown	50	10
3551	-	2fo. stone and brown	50	10
3552	-	4fo. stone and brown	90	25
3553	-	6fo. stone and brown	1·50	35
3554	-	8fo. stone and brown	2·00	50

DESIGNS: No. 3549, Purse plates from Szolnok-Strazsahalom and Galgocz; 3550, Hair ornaments from Sarospatak; 3551, St. Stephen's sword (Prague) and Attila's sword (Aachen); 3552, Bowl from Ketpo; 3553, Stick handles from Hajdudorog and Szabadattyan; 3554, Saddle-bow from Izsak and bit and stirrups from Muszka.

851 Cracow and Emblem

1984. 25th Session of Permanent Committee of Posts and Telecommunications, Cracow, Poland.

3555	**851**	2fo. multicoloured	65	25

852 "Epiphile dilecta"

1984. Butterflies. Multicoloured.

3556		1fo. Type **852**	30	10
3557		1fo. "Agrias sara"	30	10
3558		2fo. Blue morpho ("Morpho cypris")	65	25
3559		2fo. "Ancyluris formosissima"	65	25
3560		4fo. African monarch	1·30	35
3561		6fo. "Catagramma cynosura"	1·90	60
3562		8fo. Paradise birdwing	2·50	75

No. 3557 is inscribed "Agra sara".

853 "Archer"

1984. Birth Centenary of Zsigmond Kisfaludy Strobl (sculptor).

3563	**853**	2fo. brown and yellow	65	25

854 Hevesi

1984. Birth Centenary of Akos Hevesi (activist in working-class movement).

3564	**854**	2fo. multicoloured	65	25

855 Doves around Map of Hungary

1984. Peace Festival, Pusztavacs.

3565	**855**	2fo. multicoloured	65	25

856 World Map and Airplane

1984. World Aerobatics Championship, Bekescsaba.

3566	**856**	2fo. multicoloured	65	25

857 Four-in-hand

1984. World Team-driving Championships, Szilvasvarad.

3567	**857**	2fo. multicoloured	65	25

858 Conference Emblem

1984. 14th Organization of Socialist Countries' Postal Administrations Conference, Budapest.

3568	**858**	2fo. multicoloured	65	25

859 Four-handled Vase

1984. Stamp Day. Multicoloured.

3569		1fo. Type **859**	40	10
3570		2fo. Platter with flower decoration	90	25
MS3571		80×63 mm. 10fo. Cover with 1874 3k. stamp (44×27 mm)	4·50	4·50

860 "Music crowned by Fame" (fresco, Mor Than)

1984. Reopening of Budapest Opera House. Multicoloured.

3572		1fo. Type **860**	25	10
3573		2fo. Central staircase	65	25
3574		5fo. Auditorium	1·30	50
MS3575		80×65 mm. 20fo. Facade and floor plan (49×39 mm)	6·25	6·25

861 Atrium Hyatt Hotel

1984. Budapest Hotels along the Danube. Multicoloured.

3576		1fo. Type **861**	25	10
3577		2fo. Duna Intercontinental	50	10
3578		4fo. Forum	75	25
3579		4fo. Thermal Hotel, Margaret Island	75	25
3580		5fo. Hilton	1·00	35
3581		8fo. Gellert	1·80	50
MS3582		78×55 mm. 20fo. Hilton (different) (36×25 mm)	6·25	6·25

862 Cep ("Boletus edulis")

1984. Edible Mushrooms. Multicoloured.

3583		1fo. Type **862**	65	20
3584		1fo. Scotch bonnet ("Marasmius orcades")	65	20
3585		2fo. Common morel ("Morchella esculenta")	1·00	20
3586		2fo. Field mushroom ("Agaricus campester")	1·00	20
3587		3fo. Chanterelle ("Cantharellus cibarius")	1·50	35
3588		3fo. Parasol mushroom ("Macrolepiota procera")	1·50	35
3589		4fo. Boot-lace fungus	2·10	60

863 Kato Haman (Labour Movement leader)

1984. Birth Centenaries.

3590	**863**	2fo. brown, gold and black	65	25
3591	-	2fo. brown, gold and black	65	25

DESIGN: No. 3591, Bela Balazs (writer).

864 "Virgin and Child" (small altar, Trencseny)

1984. Christmas.

3592	**864**	1fo. multicoloured	40	10

865 Torah Crown (Buda)

1984. Reopening of Jewish Museum, Budapest. Multicoloured.

3593		1fo. Type **865**	25	10
3594		1fo. Chalice (Moscow)	25	10
3595		2fo. Torah shield (Vienna)	50	10
3596		2fo. Elias chalice (Warsaw)	50	10
3597		4fo. Esrog holder (Augsburg)	75	25
3598		6fo. Candle holder (Warsaw)	1·30	35
3599		8fo. Urn (Pest)	1·80	60

866 Barn Owl

1984. Owls. Multicoloured.

3600		1fo. Type **866**	50	20
3601		1fo. Little owl	50	20
3602		2fo. Tawny owl	90	20
3603		2fo. Long-eared owl	90	20
3604		4fo. Snowy owl	1·40	45
3605		6fo. Ural owl	1·90	70
3606		8fo. Eagle owl	2·50	85

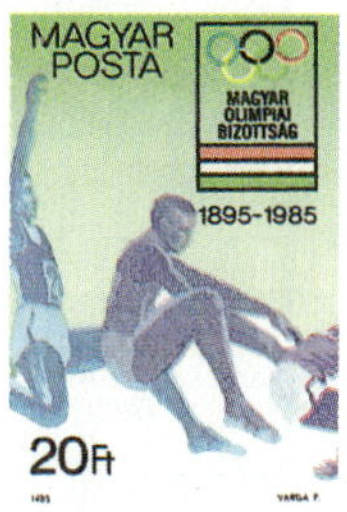

867 Long Jumping and Emblem

1985. 90th Anniv of Hungarian Olympic Committee. Sheet 86×70 mm.

MS3607	**867**	20fo. multicoloured	7·00	7·00

868 Novi Sad Bridge, Yugoslavia

1985. Danube Bridges. Multicoloured.

3608		1fo. Type **868**	25	10
3609		1fo. Baja, Hungary	25	10
3610		2fo. Arpad bridge, Budapest	50	10
3611		2fo. Bratislava, Czechoslovakia	50	10
3612		4fo. Reichsbrucke bridge, Vienna	1·00	25
3613		6fo. Linz, Austria	1·30	50
3614		8fo. Regensburg, West Germany	1·90	60
MS3615		65×80 mm. 20fo. Elizabeth and Chain Bridges, Budapest (49×39 mm)	6·25	6·25

869 Laszlo Rudas

1985. Birth Centenary of Laszlo Rudas (philosopher and socialist).

3616	**869**	2fo. brown, gold & black	65	25

870 Woman and Flowers

1985. International Women's Day.

3617	**870**	2fo. multicoloured	65	25

871 1925 200k. Skiing Stamp

1985. "Olymphilex '85" International Olympic Stamps Exhibition, Lausanne.

3618	**871**	4fo. green, gold and blue	1·30	35
3619	-	5fo. blue, brown and gold	1·40	50

DESIGN: 5fo. 1925 300k. Skating stamp.

872 Liberty Bridge, Liberation Statue and Fireworks

1985. 40th Anniv of Liberation. Sheet 70×95 mm.

MS3620	**872**	20fo. multicoloured	6·25	6·25

873 "Little Red Riding Hood"

1985. Birth Centenary of Jacob Grimm (folklorist).
3621 **873** 4fo.+2fo. mult 1·90 1·90

874 Gyorgy Lukacs

1985. Birth Centenary of Gyorgy Lukacs (philosopher).
3622 **874** 2fo. multicoloured 65 25

875 Title Page

1985. 300th Anniv of Totfalusi Bible.
3623 **875** 2fo. black and gold 65 25

876 Peter Pazmany (founder)

1985. 350th Anniv of Lorand Eotvos University.
3624 **876** 2fo. grey and red 65 60

877 Boxing

1985. 26th European Boxing Championships, Budapest.
3625 **877** 2fo. multicoloured 65 25

878 Women Footballers

1985. International Youth Year. Mult.
3626 1fo. Type **878** 25 10
3627 2fo. Windsurfing 50 10
3628 2fo. Women exercising 50 10
3629 4fo. Karate 1·00 25
3630 4fo. Go-karting 1·00 25
3631 5fo. Hang gliding 1·30 35
3632 6fo. Skate-boarding 1·40 50

879 Monorail Train

1985. "Expo '85" World's Fair, Tsukuba. Mult.
3633 2fo. Type **879** 65 25
3634 4fo. Fuyo Theatre 1·30 35

880 Common Flicker

1985. Birth Bicentenary of John J. Audubon (ornithologist). Multicoloured.
3635 2fo. Type **880** (postage) 90 20
3636 2fo. Bohemian waxwing 90 20
3637 2fo. Pileated woodpecker 90 20
3638 4fo. Northern oriole 1·50 35
3639 4fo. Common flicker (air) 1·50 35
3640 6fo. Common cardinal 2·10 60

881 Nonius XXXVI

1985. Bicentenary of Horsebreeding at Mezohegyes. Multicoloured.
3641 1fo. Type **881** 40 10
3642 2fo. Furioso XXIII 75 10
3643 4fo. Gidran I 1·40 35
3644 4fo. Ramses III 1·40 35
3645 6fo. Krozus I 2·10 50

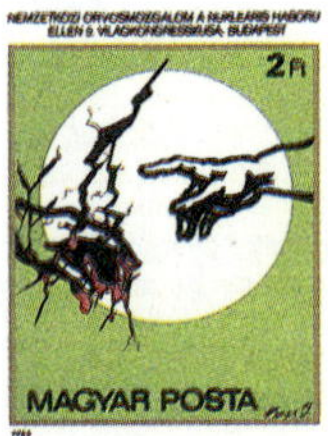

882 Hand pointing to Cracked Earth (Imre Varga)

1985. 5th Congress of International Association of Physicians against Nuclear War, Budapest.
3646 **882** 2fo. multicoloured 65 25

883 Handel, Kettledrum and Horn

1985. Music Year. Multicoloured.
3647 1fo. Type **883** (300th birth anniv) 30 10
3648 2fo. Bach and Thomas Church organ, Leipzig (300th birth anniv) 55 25
3649 4fo. Luigi Cherubini, harp, bass violin and baryton (225th anniv) 90 60
3650 4fo. Chopin and piano (175th birth anniv) 90 60
3651 5fo. Mahler, viola, double horn and kettledrum (125th birth anniv) 1·30 75
3652 6fo. Ferenc Erkel, viola and bass tuba (175th birth anniv) 1·50 1·20

884 Red Square and Emblem

1985. 12th World Youth and Students' Festival, Moscow. Sheet 89×69 mm.
MS3653 **884** 20fo. multicoloured 6·25 6·25

885 Finlandia Palace

1985. 10th Anniv of Helsinki Agreement. Sheet 92×75 mm.
MS3654 **885** 20fo. multicoloured 6·25 6·25

886 Key with Globe as Head

1985. World Tourism Day.
3655 **886** 2fo. multicoloured 65 25

887 Flags on Computer Keyboards

1985. "COMNET '85" Computer Networks Conference, Budapest.
3656 **887** 4fo. multicoloured 90 25

888 Budapest

1985. European Security and Co-operation Conference, Budapest.
MS3657 **888** 20fo. multicoloured 7·50 7·50

889 Water Holder

1985. Stamp Day. Haban Ceramics. Mult.
3658 1fo. Type **889** 40 40
3659 2fo. Tankard with cover 90 90
MS3660 80×60 mm. 10fo. Hexagonal medicine holder 6·25 6·25

890 Italian 1960 5l. Stamp

1985. "Italia '85" International Stamp Exhibition, Rome.
3661 **890** 5fo. multicoloured 1·90 1·90

891 Dove and U.N. Emblem

1985. 40th Anniv of United Nations Organization.
3662 **891** 4fo. turquoise, bl & dp bl 90 25

892 Red Lily

1985. Lily Family. Multicoloured.
3663 1fo. Type **892** 25 10
3664 2fo. Turk's-cap lily 50 10
3665 2fo. Dog's tooth violet 50 10
3666 4fo. Tiger lily 1·00 20
3667 4fo. Snake's-head fritillary 1·00 20
3668 5fo. Day lily 1·30 35
3669 6fo. "Bulbocodium vernum" 1·90 50

893 Carol Singers

1985. Christmas.
3670 **893** 2fo. multicoloured 65 25

894 Istvan Ries

1985. Birth Centenary of Istvan Ries (Minister of Justice).
3671 **894** 2fo. multicoloured 65 25

895 Three Houses under One Roof

1985. S.O.S. Childrens' Village.
3672 **895** 4fo.+2fo. multicoloured 2·10 2·20

896 Fantic "Sprinter", 1984

1985. Centenary of Motor Cycle.

3673	**896**	1fo. black, orange & blue	30	10
3674	-	2fo. black, yellow & blue	50	10
3675	-	2fo. black, green and grey	50	10
3676	-	4fo. multicoloured	1·00	15
3677	-	4fo. black, green and grey	1·00	20
3678	-	5fo. multicoloured	1·30	35
3679	-	6fo. multicoloured	1·90	60

DESIGNS: No. 3674, Harley-Davidson "Duo-Glide", 1960; 3675, Suzuki "Katana GSX", 1983; 3676, BMW "R47", 1927; 3677, Rudge-Whitworth, 1935; 3678, NSU, 1910; 3679, Daimler, 1885.

897 "Ice" Satellite and Dinosaurs

1986. Air. Appearance of Halley's Comet. Multicoloured.

3680	2fo. Type **897**	65	10
3681	2fo. "Vega" satellite and detail of Bayeux Tapestry showing comet	65	10
3682	2fo. "Suisei" satellite and German engraving of 1507	65	10
3683	4fo. "Giotto" satellite and "The Magi" (tapestry after Giotto)	1·30	25
3684	4fo. "Astron" satellite and Virgo, Leo, Corvus, Crater and Hydra constellations	1·30	25
3685	6fo. Space shuttle and Edmond Halley (wrongly inscr "Edmund")	1·90	60

898 Bela Kun

1986. Birth Centenary of Bela Kun (Communist Party leader).

3686	**898**	4fo. multicoloured	90	25

899 "Challenger" (space shuttle)

1986. Challenger Astronauts Commemoration. Sheet 92×79 mm.

MS3687 **899** 20fo. multicoloured	8·25	8·25

900 Guide Dog

1986. The Blind.

3688	**900**	4fo. multicoloured	90	25

901 Running for Ball

1986. World Cup Football Championship, Mexico. Multicoloured.

3689	2fo. Type **901**	65	10
3690	2fo. Heading ball	65	10
3691	4fo. Tackling	1·30	25
3692	4fo. Goalkeeper diving for ball	1·30	25
3693	4fo. Goalkeeper catching ball	1·30	25
3694	6fo. Tackling (different)	1·90	60
MS3695	80×60 mm. 20fo. Team celebrating (40×30 mm)	7·00	7·00

902 Cable Railway

1986. Re-opening of Buda Castle Cable Railway.

3696	**902**	2fo. brown, yell & orge	65	25

903 Rose "Yankee Doodle"

1986. "Ameripex '86" International Stamp Exhibition, Chicago. Sheet 80×100 mm containing T 903 and similar vert designs. Multicoloured.

MS3697 5fo. Type **903**; 5fo. Rose "America"; 10fo. Statue of George Washington, Budapest and exhibition emblem (25×70 mm)	5·75	5·75

904 Japanese and Hungarian Dolls

1986. Hungarian Days in Tokyo.

3698	**904**	4fo. multicoloured	90	25

905 Fay

1986. Birth Bicentenary of Andras Fay (writer, politician and founder of First Hungarian Savings Bank Union).

3699	**905**	4fo. brown & pale brown	90	90

906 Flag and "40"

1986. Youth Stamp. 40th Anniv of Young Pioneers Movement.

3700	**906**	4fo.+2fo. multicoloured	1·90	1·90

907 Ferrari Racing Cars, 1961 and 1985

1986. Centenary of Motor Car. Multicoloured.

3701	2fo. Type **907**	65	10
3702	2fo. Alfa Romeo racing cars, 1932 and 1984	65	10
3703	2fo. Volkswagen "Beetle", 1936, and Porsche "959", 1986	65	10
3704	4fo. Renault "14 CV", 1902, and "5 GT Turbo", 1985	1·30	25
3705	4fo. Fiat "3 1/2", 1899, and "Ritmo", 1985	1·30	25
3706	6fo. Daimler, 1886, and Mercedes-Benz "230 SE", 1986	1·90	60

908 "Wasa" (Swedish ship of the line), 1628

1986. "Stockholmia '86" Int Stamp Exhibition.

3707	**908**	2fo. multicoloured	1·40	1·40

909 Moritz Kaposi (cancer specialist)

1986. 14th International Cancer Congress, Budapest.

3708	**909**	4fo. multicoloured	90	25

910 "Recapture of Buda Castle" (Gyula Benczur) (image scaled to 64% of original size)

1986. 300th Anniv of Recapture of Buda from Turks.

3709	**910**	4fo. multicoloured	90	25

911 "Tranquillity"

1986. Stamp Day. Multicoloured.

3710	2fo. Type **911**	65	65
3711	2fo. "Confidence"	65	65
MS3712	80×60 mm. 10fo. "Hope" (28×49 mm)	5·75	5·75

912 Fragment of 15th-cent Carpet from Anatolia

1986. 5th International Oriental Carpets and Tapestry Conference, Vienna and Budapest.

3713	**912**	4fo. multicoloured	90	25

913 Model of New Theatre

1986. National Theatre, Budapest. Sheet 63×85 mm.

MS3714 **913** 20fo.+10fo. brown, stone and light brown	7·00	7·00

914 Piano and Liszt

1986. 175th Birth Anniv of Franz Liszt (pianist and composer).

3715	**914**	4fo. deep green and green	90	25

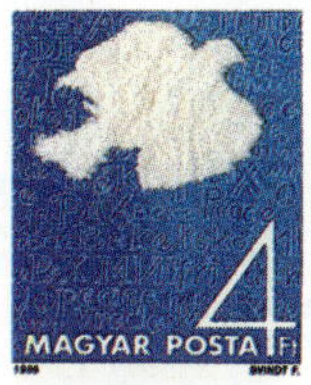

915 Dove

1986. International Peace Year.

3716	**915**	4fo. multicoloured	1·30	1·30

916 Hofburg Palace, Vienna, and Map

1986. European Security and Co-operation Conference Review Meeting, Vienna. Sheet 65×80 mm.

MS3717 **916** 20fo. multicoloured	6·25	6·25

917 Pogany

1986. Birth Centenary of Jozsef Pogany (writer and journalist).

3718	**917**	4fo. multicoloured	90	25

918 Munnich

1986. Birth Centenary of Ferenc Munnich (former Prime Minister).

3719	**918**	4fo. multicoloured	90	25

919 Heads

1986. 12th General Assembly of World Federation of Democratic Youth, Budapest.

3720	**919**	4fo. multicoloured	90	25

920 Apricots ("Kajszi" C.235)

1986. Fruits. Multicoloured.

3721		2fo. Type **920**	65	10
3722		2fo. Cherries ("Good bearer of Erd")	65	10
3723		4fo. Apples ("Jonathan" M.14)	1·30	25
3724		4fo. Raspberries ("Nagymaros")	1·30	25
3725		4fo. Peaches ("Piroska")	1·30	25
3726		6fo. Grapes ("Zalagyongye")	2·50	35

921 Forgach Castle, Szecseny

1986. Castles. Inscr "MAGYAR POSTA".

3727	**921**	2fo. bistre and yellow	30	10
3728	-	3fo. green and light green	40	10
3729	-	4fo. blue and light blue	50	10
3730	-	5fo. red and pink	65	10
3731	-	6fo. brown and orange	75	10
3732	-	8fo. red and orange	1·00	10
3733	-	10fo. brown and ochre	1·00	25
3734	-	20fo. green and yellow	2·00	60
3735	-	30fo. light green and green	2·75	85
3736	-	40fo. blue and light blue	3·25	1·20
3737	-	50fo. deep red and red	4·50	1·50
3738	-	70fo. deep grey and grey	6·25	2·10
3739	-	100fo. violet and lilac	8·25	3·00

DESIGNS: 3fo. Savoya Castle, Rackeve; 4fo. Batthyany Castle, Kormend; 5fo. Szechenyi Castle, Nagycenk; 6fo. Rudnyanszky Castle, Nagyteteny; 8fo. Szapary Castle, Buk; 10fo. Festetics Castle, Keszthely; 20fo. Brunswick Castle, Martonvasar; 30fo. De La Motte Castle, Noszvaj; 40fo. L'Huillier-Coburg Castle, Edeleny; 50fo. Teleki-Degenfeld Castle, Szirak; 70fo. Magochy Castle, Pacin; 100fo. Esterhazy Castle, Fertod.

See also Nos. 3888 and 4045/9.

922 Wild Cat

1986. Protected Animals. Multicoloured.

3740		2fo. Type **922**	75	15
3741		2fo. European otter	75	15
3742		2fo. Stoat	75	15
3743		4fo. Eurasian red squirrel	1·30	25
3744		4fo. East European hedgehog	1·30	25
3745		6fo. European pond turtle	1·90	50

923 St. Stephen I (coronation cloak, 1030)

1986. Kings (1st series).

3746	**923**	2fo. brown, blue and red	50	10
3747	-	2fo. brown, grey and red	50	10
3748	-	4fo. brown, green and red	1·10	25
3749	-	4fo. brown, grey and red	1·10	25
3750	-	6fo. brown, blue and red	1·60	45

DESIGNS: No. 3747, Geza I (enamel portrait on Hungarian crown, 1070); 3748, St. Ladislas I (Gyor Cathedral, 1400); 3749, Bela III (Kalocsa Cathedral statue, 1200); 3750, Bela IV (Jak church statue, 1230).

See also Nos. 3835/7.

924 Death Cap ("Amanita phalloides")

1986. Fungi. Multicoloured.

3751		2fo. Type **924**	50	20
3752		2fo. Fly agaric ("Amanita muscaria")	50	20
3753		2fo. Red-staining inocybe ("Inocybe patouillardi")	50	20
3754		4fo. Olive-wood pleurotus ("Omphalotus olearius")	1·00	45
3755		4fo. Panther cap ("Amanita pantherina")	1·00	45
3756		6fo. Beefsteak morel	1·50	75

925 Banded Gourami

1987. Fishes. Multicoloured.

3757		2fo. Type **925**	50	10
3758		2fo. Thread-finned rainbowfish ("Iriathorina werneri")	50	10
3759		2fo. Zebra mbuna ("Pseudotropheus zebra")	50	10
3760		4fo. Ramirez dwarf cichlid ("Papiliochromis ramirezi")	1·00	35
3761		4fo. Multicoloured lyretail ("Aphyosemion multicolor")	1·00	35
3762		6fo. Bleeding-heart tetra ("Hyphessobrycon erythrostigma")	1·50	50

926 "Sitting Woman"

1987. Birth Centenary of Bela Uitz (painter).

3763	**926**	4fo. multicoloured	75	25

927 Abstract

1987. Birth Centenary of Lajos Kassak (writer and painter).

3764	**927**	4fo. black and red	75	25

928 Flag, Books, Torch and Dove

1987. 30th Anniv of Young Communist League.

3765	**928**	4fo.+2fo. mult	2·00	2·00

929 Hippocrates (medical oath)

1987. Pioneers of Medicine (1st series).

3766	**929**	2fo. brown and blue	50	10
3767	-	4fo. green and black	1·10	25
3768	-	4fo. blue and black	1·10	25
3769	-	4fo. brown and black	1·10	25
3770	-	6fo. brown and black	1·80	45

DESIGNS: No. 3767, Avicenna ("Kanun" book of medical rules); 3768, Ambroise Pare (improved treatment of wounds); 3769, William Harvey (circulation of blood); 3770, Ignac Semmelweis (aseptic treatment of wounds).

See also Nos. 3939/43.

930 Food Jar, Hodmezovasarhely

1987. Neolithic and Copper Age Art. Multicoloured.

3771	**930**	2fo. brown and green	65	10
3772	-	4fo. brown and flesh	1·30	25
3773	-	4fo. brown and pink	1·30	25
3774	-	5fo. brown and green	1·50	45

DESIGNS: No. 3772, Altar, Szeged; 3773, Statue with sickle, Szegvar-Tuzkoves; 3774, Vase with face, Center.

931 King Matthias's Cross

1987. Re-opening of Esztergom Cathedral Treasury. Sheet 64×80 mm.

MS3775	**931** 20fo. multicoloured	5·00	5·00

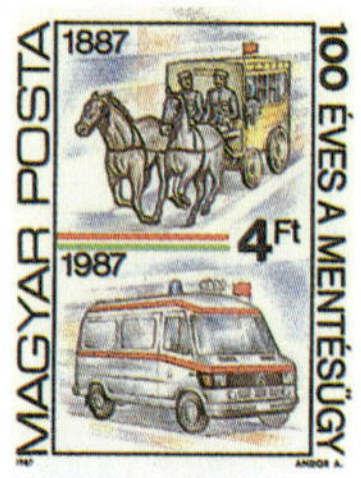

932 Old and Modern Ambulances

1987. Cent of Hungarian First Aid Association.

3776	**932**	4fo. multicoloured	75	25

933 Toronto ("Capex '87")

1987. International Stamp Exhibitions. Mult.

3777		5fo. Type **933**	1·90	1·90
3778		5fo. "Olymphilex 87" building, Rome	1·90	1·90
3779		5fo. "Hafnia 87" building, Copenhagen	1·90	1·90

934 Jozsef Marek

1987. Bicentenary of University of Veterinary Sciences, Budapest.

3780	**934**	4fo. silver, blue and black	75	25

935 Teleki, Route Map and Porters

1987. Cent of Samuel Teleki's African Expedition.

3781	**935**	4fo. multicoloured	75	25

936 Printing Shop (17th-century wood-print, Abraham von Werdt)

1987. 125th Anniv of Hungarian Printing, Paper and Press Workers' Union.

3782	**936**	4fo. brown and stone	75	25

937 James Cook and H.M.S. "Resolution"

1987. Antarctic Exploration. Multicoloured.

3783		2fo. Type **937**	50	20
3784		2fo. Fabian von Bellingshausen and seals	50	20
3785		2fo. Ernest Shackleton and emperor penguins	50	20
3786		4fo. Roald Amundsen and huskies	1·10	35
3787		4fo. Robert F. Scott and "Terra Nova"	1·10	35
3788		6fo. Richard Byrd and Ford Trimotor "Floyd Bennett"	1·50	55
MS3789		86×70 mm. 20fo. Mirnyi Research Station (32×42 mm)	11·50	11·50

938 Old and New Railway Emblems and Institute

1987. Cent of Railway Officers' Training Institute.

3790	**938**	4fo. black and blue	75	25

939 Flowers and Dolphin

1987. Stamp Day. Carvings from Buda Castle.

3791	**939**	2fo. indigo, blue & azure	65	65

3792	-	4fo. olive, green & turq	1·30	1·30
MS3793		68×88 mm. 10fo. agate, grey and lilac	5·00	5·00

DESIGNS: 4fo. King Matthias's arms; 10fo. Capital of Column.

940 Jesse Altar

1987. Gyongyospata Church.

3794	**940**	4fo. multicoloured	2·00	2·00

941 "Orchis purpurea"

1987. Orchids. Multicoloured.

3795	2fo. Type **941**	50	10
3796	2fo. "Cypripedium calceolus"	50	10
3797	4fo. "Ophrys scolopax"	1·00	20
3798	4fo. "Himantoglossum hircinum"	1·00	20
3799	5fo. "Cephalanthera rubra"	1·30	25
3800	6fo. "Epipactis atrorubens"	1·60	35
MS3801	40×60 mm. 20fo. Orchids (24×33 mm)	7·00	7·00

942 Speed Skating

1987. Winter Olympic Games, Calgary. Mult.

3802	2fo. Type **942**	50	10
3803	2fo. Cross-country skiing	50	10
3804	4fo. Biathlon	1·00	20
3805	4fo. Ice hockey	1·00	20
3806	4fo. Four-man bobsleigh	1·00	20
3807	6fo. Ski jumping	1·80	35
MS3808	50×60 mm. 20fo. Slalom (24×41 mm)	6·25	6·25

943 Clasped Hands and Map

1987. U.S.–Soviet Strategic Arms Reduction Talks, Washington. Sheet 78×82 mm.

MS3809 **943**	20fo. multicoloured	6·25	6·25

945 "The White Crane" (Japanese folk tale)

1987. Fairy Tales. Multicoloured.

3816	2fo. Type **945**	65	20
3817	2fo. "The Fox and the Raven" (Aesop)	65	20
3818	4fo. "The Hare and The Tortoise" (Aesop)	1·30	25
3819	4fo. "The Ugly Duckling" (Hans Christian Andersen)	1·30	25
3820	6fo. "The Brave Little Lead Soldier" (Hans Christian Andersen)	1·90	55

946 Zeppelin and Airship LZ-2

1988. 150th Birth Anniv of Ferdinand von Zeppelin (airship pioneer).

3821	**946**	2fo. black and blue	50	20
3822	-	4fo. deep brown & brown	1·30	30
3823	-	4fo. purple and lilac	1·30	30
3824	-	8fo. olive and green	1·90	55

DESIGNS: No. 3822, LZ-4; 3823, "Schwaben"; 3824, "Graf Zeppelin".

947 Skater

1988. World Figure Skating Championships, Budapest. Skaters from 19th-century to date. Multicoloured.

3825	2fo. Type **947**	50	10
3826	2fo. Man wearing hat	50	10
3827	4fo. Woman	1·00	20
3828	4fo. Man in hat and coat	1·00	20
3829	5fo. Woman in modern skating dress	1·10	25
3830	6fo. Pair	1·30	35
MS3831	89×72 mm. 20fo. Pair (different) (32×47 mm)	6·25	6·25

948 Woman's Head

1988. Stamp Day. "Socfilex" International Stamp Exhibition, Kecskemet. Sheet 72×54 mm.

MS3832 **948**	20fo.+10fo. mult	7·50	7·50

949 Monus

1988. Birth Centenary of Illes Monus (newspaper editor).

3833	**949**	4fo. blue, red and black	75	25

950 18th-cent Postmaster's Uniform

1988. Stamp Exhibitions.

MS3834 **950**	4fo. black and stone	2·10	2·10

1988. Kings (2nd series). As T 923.

3835	2fo. brown, green and red	50	10
3836	4fo. brown, blue and red	1·00	25
3837	6fo. brown, violet and red	1·50	35

DESIGNS: 2fo. Karoly I (Charles Robert) (detail of decorated initial from "Illuminated Chronicle", 1358); 4fo. Lajos the Great (relief, St. Simeon's reliquary, Zara, 1380); 6fo. Zsigmond (Sigismund of Luxembourg) (after great seal, 1433).

951 Rowing

1988. Olympic Games, Seoul. Multicoloured.

3838	2fo. Type **951**	50	10
3839	4fo. Hurdling	1·00	35
3840	4fo. Fencing	1·00	35
3841	6fo. Boxing	1·90	60
MS3842	70×80 mm. 20fo. Tennis (31×40 mm)	7·50	7·50

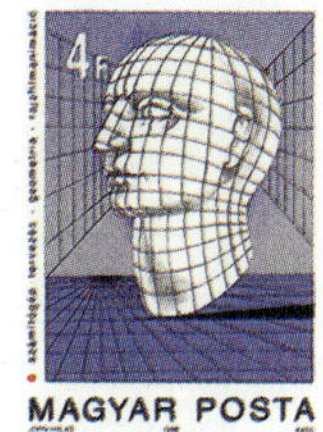

952 Computer Drawing of Head

1988. 6th Anniv of "Dilemma" (first computer-animated film).

3843	**952**	4fo. multicoloured	75	25

953 Card and Emblem

1988. Eurocheque Congress, Budapest.

3844	**953**	4fo. multicoloured	75	25

954 "Santa Maria", 1492

1988. Ships. Multicoloured.

3845	2fo. Type **954**	65	25
3846	2fo. "Mayflower", 1620	65	25
3847	2fo. "Sovereign of the Seas", 1637	65	25
3848	4fo. "Jylland" (steam warship), 1860	1·40	35
3849	6fo. "St. Jupat" (yacht), 1985	2·00	60

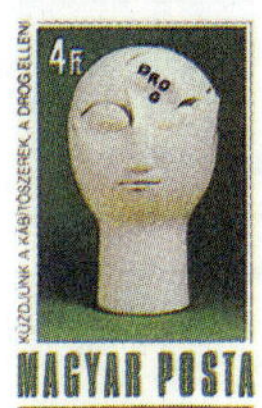

955 Damaged Head

1988. Anti-drugs Campaign.

3850	**955**	4fo. multicoloured	75	25

956 Green-winged Teal ("Anas crecca")

1988. Wild Ducks. Multicoloured.

3851	2fo. Type **956**	55	25
3852	2fo. Common goldeneye ("Bucephula clangula")	55	25
3853	4fo. European wigeon ("Anas penelope")	1·40	35
3854	4fo. Red-crested pochard ("Netta rufina")	1·40	35
3855	6fo. Gadwell	2·10	60
MS3856	90×73 mm. 20fo. Mallard ("Anas platyrhynchos")	6·25	6·25

957 Steam Train

1988. Exhibits in Toy Museum, Kecskemet. Multicoloured.

3857	2fo. Type **957**	65	20
3858	2fo. See-saw	65	20
3859	4fo.+2fo. Pecking chicks	1·90	50
3860	5fo. Johnny Hussar	1·30	35

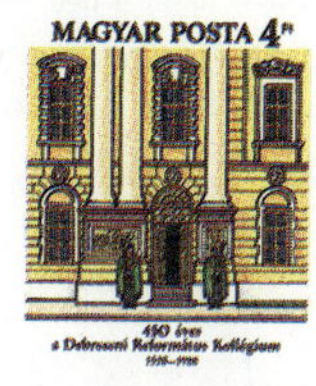

958 Facade

1988. 450th Anniv of Debrecen Calvinist College.

3861	**958**	4fo. multicoloured	75	25

959 Congress Emblem

1988. 58th American Society of Travel Agents Congress, Budapest.

3862	**959**	4fo. multicoloured	75	25

960 Lloyd C.II Biplane

1988. Air. Hungarian Biplanes.

3863	**960**	1fo. green	15	10
3864	-	2fo. purple	25	10
3865	-	4fo. bistre	65	25
3866	-	10fo. blue	1·60	55
3867	-	12fo. red	2·00	60

DESIGNS: 2fo. Hansa Brandenburg C-I; 4fo. UFAG C-I; 10fo. Gerle 13 scout plane; 12fo. WM 13 trainer.

961 Post Official's Collar and Badge

1988. Centenary of Post Office Training School.

3868	**961**	4fo. red, blue and brown	75	25

962 Baross and Postal Savings Bank, Budapest

1988. Stamp Day. 140th Birth Anniv of Gabor Baross (politician). Multicoloured.

3869	2fo. Type **962**	65	60
3870	4fo. Baross with telephone and telegraph equipment	1·30	1·20

MS3871		80×70 mm. 10fo. Baross and East Railway Station, Budapest	5·00	5·00

963 Lengyel

1988. Birth Centenary of Gyula Lengyel (labour movement activist).

3872	963	4fo. multicoloured	75	25

964 Christmas Tree

1988. Christmas.

3873	964	2fo. multicoloured	65	10

965 Richard Adolf Zsigmondy (chemistry, 1925)

1988. Nobel Prize Winners.

3874	965	2fo. deep brown & brown	50	10
3875	-	2fo. deep green and green	50	10
3876	-	2fo. deep brown & brown	50	10
3877	-	4fo. dp mauve & mauve	90	20
3878	-	4fo. green and grey	90	20
3879	-	6fo. brown & light brown	1·40	35

DESIGNS: No. 3875, Robert Barany (medicine, 1914,); 3876, Gyorgy Hevesy (chemistry, 1943); 3877, Albert Szent-Gyorgyi (chemistry, 1937); 3878, Gyorgy Bekesy (medicine, 1961); 3879, Denes Gabor (physics, 1971).

966 Szakasits

1988. Birth Centenary of Arpad Szakasits (President, 1948–50).

3880	966	4fo. multicoloured	75	25

967 Stadium and Emblem

1988. Hungarian Medals at Seoul Olympic Games. Sheet 70×90 mm.

MS3881	967	20fo. multicoloured	7·00	7·00

968 Silver Teapot from Pest, 1846

1988. Metal Work.

3882	968	2fo. blue and brown	75	10
3883	-	2fo. deep brown & brown	75	10
3884	-	4fo. lilac and brown	1·50	35
3885	-	5fo. green and brown	1·90	50

DESIGNS: No. 3883, 18th-century silver pot, Buda; 3884, Silver sugar basin from Pest, 1822; 3885, Pierced cast iron plate from Resicabanya, 1850.

969 Emblem

1989. Foundation of Post and Savings Bank Company.

3886	969	5fo. blue, silver and black	75	25

970 Wallisch

1989. Birth Centenary of Kalman Wallisch (workers' movement activist).

3887	970	3fo. blue and red	65	10

971 Festetics Castle, Keszthely

1989

3888	971	10fo. brown and bistre	1·10	25

972 Athletes

1989. 2nd International Indoor Athletics Championships, Budapest.

3889	972	3fo. multicoloured	65	10

973 Houses of Parliament and Big Ben London

1989. Centenary of Interparliamentary Union. Sheet 78×90 mm containing T 973 and similar vert design. Multicoloured.

MS3890		10fo. Type 973; 10fo. Parliament Building, Budapest	5·75	5·75

974 Gyetvai

1989. Birth Centenary of Janos Gyetvai (journalist).

3891	974	3fo. green and red	65	10

975 "Sky-high Tree" (detail, carpet)

1989. 27th National Youth Stamp Exn, Veszprem.

3892	975	5fo.+2fo. mult	1·90	1·90

976 O Bajan

1989. Bicentenary of Babolina Stud Farm. Mult.

3893		3fo. Type **976**	90	90
3894		3fo. Stud officer	90	90
3895		3fo. Gazal II	90	90

977 Disabled People and "ART '89"

1989. "Art '89" International Festival of Disabled People and their Artist Friends.

3896	977	5fo. multicoloured	75	25

978 Arrangement of Narcissi, Crocuses and Violets

1989. Flower Arrangements. Multicoloured.

3897		2fo. Type **978**	40	10
3898		3fo. Irises, tulips and lilies (horiz)	65	10
3899		3fo. Roses and chrysanthemums	65	10
3900		5fo. Dahlias and lilies (horiz)	1·30	35
3901		10fo. Roses, Chinese lanterns and holly	2·50	60

979 Birds

1989. Bicentenary of French Revolution.

3902	979	5fo. black, red and blue	75	25
MS3903		80×70 mm. **979** 20fo. black, red and blue (49×28 mm)	7·50	7·50

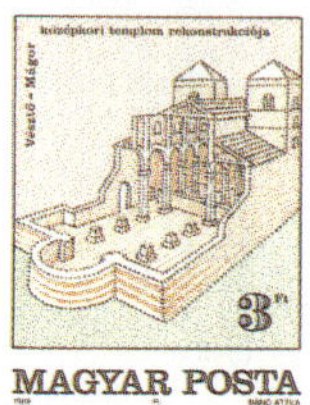

980 Model of Veszto Church

1989. Veszto Church Excavation.

3904	980	3fo. multicoloured	65	10

981 Photographer with Camera

1989. 150th Anniv of Photography.

3905	981	5fo. lt brown, blk & brn	75	25

982 Turistvandi Water-mill

1989. Mills. Multicoloured.

3906		2fo. Type **982**	40	10
3907		3fo. Szarvas horse-driven mill	65	20
3908		5fo. Kiskunhalas windmill	1·00	35
3909		10fo. Shipmill, River Drava	2·30	60

983 Footprint and U.S. Flag

1989. 20th Anniv of First Manned Landing on Moon. Sheet 80×70 mm.

MS3910	983	20fo. multicoloured	5·75	5·75

984 Messenger Glider

1989. "Old Timer" Rally, Budakeszi Airport, and 60th Anniv of Gliding in Hungary. Multicoloured.

3911		3fo. Type **984**	65	25
3912		5fo. Pal glider	1·10	50

985 Sand Lizard

1989. Endangered Reptiles. Multicoloured.

3913		2fo. Type **985**	40	10
3914		3fo. Green lizard	65	15
3915		5fo. Grass snake ("Natrix natrix")	1·10	25
3916		5fo. Orsinis's viper ("Vipera rakosiensis")	1·10	25
3917		10fo. European pond terrapin	2·30	60

986 Competitors

1989. 31st World Modern Pentathlon Championships, Budapest.

3918	986	5fo. multicoloured	75	25

1989. Nos. 3851 and 3853 surch.

3919		3fo. on 2fo. multicoloured	1·60	50
3920		5fo. on 4fo. multicoloured	1·90	85

988 Baradla Cave, Aggtelek

1989. 10th World Speleology Congress, Budapest. Multicoloured.

No.	Description	Unused	Used
3921	3fo. Type **988**	50	10
3922	5fo. Szemlohegy cave, Budapest	90	25
3923	10fo. Anna Cave, Lillafured	1·90	35
3924	12fo. Tapolca cave lake, Miskolctapolca	2·30	60

989 Carriage

1989. World Two-in-Hand Carriage Driving Championship, Balatonfenyves.

No.	Description	Unused	Used
3925 **989**	5fo. multicoloured	1·50	25

990 Zsuzsa Kossuth (War of Independence nurse)

1989. Stamp Day. 125th Anniv of Red Cross Movement.

No.	Description	Unused	Used
3926 **990**	5fo. black, blue and red	90	90
3927 -	10fo. multicoloured	1·90	1·90
MS3928	82×65 mm. 20fo.+10fo. mult	8·25	8·25

DESIGNS: 10fo. Florence Nightingale (nursing pioneer) and decoration. 27×44 mm—20fo. "Battle of Solferini" (Carlo Bossoli).

991 Memorial Statue, Arad

1989. 140th Death Anniv of "Martyrs of Arad". Sheet 110×75 mm.

No.	Description	Unused	Used
MS3929 **991**	20fo.+10fo. mult	8·25	8·25

The surcharge was for the erection of a new statue.

992 Stamp and Miniature Sheets (image scaled to 72% of original size)

1989. Pro Philatelia. Sheet 72×92 mm.

No.	Description	Unused	Used
MS3930 **992**	50fo. multicoloured	15·00	15·00

993 Flowers and Broken Barbed Wire

1989. Dismantling of Electrified Fence on Western Border.

No.	Description	Unused	Used
3931 **993**	5fo. multicoloured	1·00	25

994 "Conquest of Hungary" (Mor Than)

1989. 1100th Anniv of Arpad as Prince of the Magyars.

No.	Description	Unused	Used
3932 **994**	5fo. multicoloured	1·50	25

995 Flight into Egypt

1989. Christmas.

No.	Description	Unused	Used
3933 **995**	3fo. multicoloured	1·30	25

996 Nehru

1989. Birth Centenary of Jawaharlal Nehru (Indian statesman).

No.	Description	Unused	Used
3934 **996**	3fo. brown and stone	1·30	25

997 "Miska" (Dezso Korniss)

1990. Modern Hungarian Paintings. Mult.

No.	Description	Unused	Used
3935	3fo. Type **997**	65	10
3936	5fo. "Sunrise" (Lajos Kassak)	1·30	25
3937	10fo. "Grotesque Burial" (Endre Balint)	2·50	35
3938	12fo. "Remembered Toys" (Tihamer Gyarmathy)	3·00	60

1989. Pioneers of Medicine (2nd series). As T 929.

No.	Description	Unused	Used
3939	3fo. green	75	10
3940	3fo. brown	75	10
3941	4fo. black	1·00	20
3942	6fo. grey	1·50	25
3943	10fo. purple	2·50	60

DESIGNS: No. 3939, Claudius Galenus (anatomist and physiologist); 3940, Paracelsus (pharmacy); 3941, Andreas Vesalius (dissection); 3942, Rudolf Virchow (pathology of cells); 3943, Ivan Petrovich Pavlov (blood circulation, digestion and nervous system).

998 Hands holding Coin

1990. 150th Anniv of Savings Banks in Hungary.

No.	Description	Unused	Used
3944 **998**	5fo. multicoloured	90	25

999 Sewing Machine

1990. 125th Anniv of Singer Sewing Machine.

No.	Description	Unused	Used
3945 **999**	5fo. brown and cinnamon	90	25

1000 Wall Telephone and Jozsefvaros Telephone Exchange

1990. Posts and Telecommunications. Mult.

No.	Description	Unused	Used
3946	3fo. Type **1000**	40	10
3947	5fo. Pillar box and Head Post Office, Budapest	75	10

1001 Northern Bullfinch ("Pyrrhula pyrrhula")

1990. Birds. Multicoloured.

No.	Description	Unused	Used
3960	3fo. Type **1001**	75	25
3961	3fo. River kingfisher ("Alcedo atthis")	75	25
3962	3fo. Syrian woodpecker ("Dendrocopos syriacus")	75	25
3963	5fo. Hoopoe ("Upupa epops")	1·40	35
3964	5fo. European bee eater ("Merops apiaster")	1·40	35
3965	10fo. European roller	2·50	70

1002 "Protea compacta"

1990. African Flowers. Multicoloured.

No.	Description	Unused	Used
3966	3fo. Type **1002**	75	10
3967	3fo. "Leucadendron spissifolium"	75	10
3968	3fo. "Leucadendron tinctum pubibracteolatum"	75	10
3969	5fo. "Protea barbigera"	1·40	25
3970	5fo. "Protea lepidocarpodendron neriifolia"	1·40	25
3971	10fo. "Protea cynaroides"	2·50	60
MS3972	64×82 mm. 20fo. Mixed bouquet (25×36 mm)	8·25	8·25

1003 Sarospatak Teachers' Training School

1990. 28th National Youth Stamp Exhibition, Sarospatak.

No.	Description	Unused	Used
3973 **1003**	8fo.+4fo. mult	2·50	2·50

1004 Janos Hunyadi (regent)

1990. The Hunyadis. Multicoloured.

No.	Description	Unused	Used
3974	5fo. Type **1004**	90	25
3975	5fo. King Matthias I Corvinus	90	25

1005 Penny Black

1990. "Stamp World London 90" International Stamp Exhibition. 150th Anniv of the Penny Black. Sheet 88×60 mm.

No.	Description	Unused	Used
MS3976 **1005**	20fo. multicoloured	7·00	7·00

1006 Gaspar Karoli (statue)

1990. 400th Anniv of Publication of Karoli Bible (first Hungarian translation).

No.	Description	Unused	Used
3977 **1006**	8fo. cream, green & red	2·00	2·00

1007 Footballers

1990. World Cup Football Championship, Italy.

No.	Description	Unused	Used
3978 **1007**	3fo. multicoloured	65	10
3979 -	5fo. multicoloured (ball on ground)	1·10	20
3980 -	5fo. multicoloured (ball in air)	1·10	20
3981 -	8fo. multicoloured (dribbling)	1·80	25
3982 -	8fo. mult (heading ball into goal)	1·80	25
3983 -	10fo. multicoloured	2·30	35
MS3984	95×70 mm. 20fo. mult	7·00	7·00

DESIGNS: Nos. 3979/84, Various footballing scenes.

1008 Hand writing with Quill Pen

1990. 300th Birth Anniv of Kelemen Mikes (writer).

No.	Description	Unused	Used
3985 **1008**	8fo. black and gold	1·50	25

1009 "Weaver" (Noemi Ferenczy)

1990. Birth Centenaries of Noemi and Beni Ferenczy (artists).

3986	**1009**	3fo. multicoloured	1·00	15
3987	-	5fo. black and brown	1·60	20

DESIGN: 5fo. Bronze figure (Beni Ferenczy).

1010 Kazinczy

1990. 159th Death Anniv of Ferenc Kazinczy (writer and language reformer).

3988	**1010**	8fo. multicoloured	1·30	15

1011 Kolcsey (after Anton Einsle)

1990. Birth Bicentenary of Ferenc Kolcsey (composer of national anthem).

3989	**1011**	8fo. multicoloured	1·30	15

1012 "St. Stephen" (carving in Parliament Hall) and Arms

1990. New State Arms.

3990	**1012**	8fo. multicoloured	1·30	15
MS3991 70×90 mm. 20fo. Arms (33×49 mm)			7·00	7·00

1013 Cabernet Franc Grapes, Hajos

1990. Wine Grapes and Regions (1st series). Multicoloured.

3992	3fo. Type **1013**	50	10
3993	5fo. Cabernet Sauvignon, Villany	90	15
3994	8fo. Riesling, Badacsony	1·40	20
3995	8fo. Kadarka, Szekszard	1·40	20
3996	8fo. Leanyka, Eger	1·40	20
3997	10fo. Furmint, Tokaj-Hegyalja	1·90	25

See also Nos. 4363/5, 4436/7, 4521/2, 4596/7, 4686/7, 4895/6 and 5034/6.

1014 "Feast"

1990. Stamp Day. Paintings by Ender Szasz. Multicoloured.

3998	8fo. Type **1014**	1·30	1·30
3999	12fo. "Message"	2·10	2·10
MS4000 70×90 mm. 20fo.+10fo. "Yesterday" (39×44 mm)		7·50	7·50

1015 Tarbosaurus

1990. Prehistoric Animals. Multicoloured.

4001	3fo. Type **1015**	50	10
4002	5fo. Brontosaurus	90	15
4003	5fo. Dimorphodon	1·40	20
4004	5fo. Stegosaurus	1·40	20
4005	8fo. Platybelodon	1·40	20
4006	10fo. Mammoth	1·90	60

1016 Dinosaurs reading

1990. International Literacy Year.

4007	**1016**	10fo. multicoloured	1·90	25

1017 Bird holding Letter

1990. 60th Anniv of Stamp Museum, Budapest.

4008	**1017**	5fo. red and green	90	25

1018 "Great Courier" (detail, Albrecht Durer)

1990. Pro Philatelia. 500th Anniv of Regular European Postal Services. Sheet 90×71 mm.

MS4009 **1018** 50fo. black, red and yellow	9·50	9·50

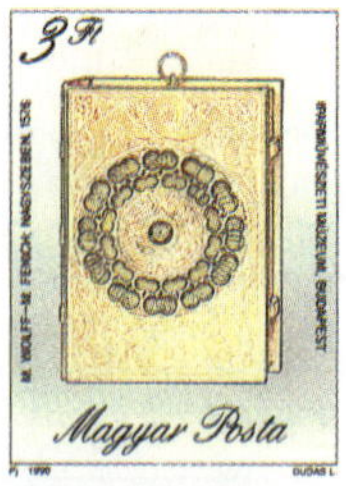

1019 Book-shaped Travelling Clock, by M. Fenich and M. Wolff, 1576

1990. Clocks. Multicoloured.

4010	3fo. Type **1019**	50	10
4011	5fo. Clock by Hans Schmidt, 1643	1·00	15
4012	5fo. Rococo style clock by J. M. Welz, 1790	1·00	15
4013	10fo. Clock by Johann Hillrich, 1814	2·30	75

1020 "Madonna and Child" (Sandro Botticelli)

1990. Christmas.

4014	**1020**	5fo. multicoloured	90	25

1021 Lorand Eotvos (inventor) and Torsion Pendulum

1991. Centenary of Torsion Pendulum.

4015	**1021**	12fo. multicoloured	1·90	25

1022 "Mandevilla splendens"

1991. Flowers of the Americas. Mult.

4016	5fo. Type **1022**	40	10
4017	7fo. "Lobelia cardinalis"	65	15
4018	7fo. Cup and saucer flower	65	15
4019	12fo. "Steriphoma paradoxa"	1·10	25
4020	15fo. Shrimp plant	1·30	75
MS4021 58×80 mm. 20fo. Mixed bouquet (27×43 mm)		6·25	6·25

1023 Post Office, Budapest

1991. Hungarian Full Membership of Council of Europe and Entry into C.E.P.T. (European Posts and Telecommunications Conference). Mult.

4022	5fo. Type **1023**	5·00	5·00
4023	7fo. Post Office, Pecs	5·75	5·75

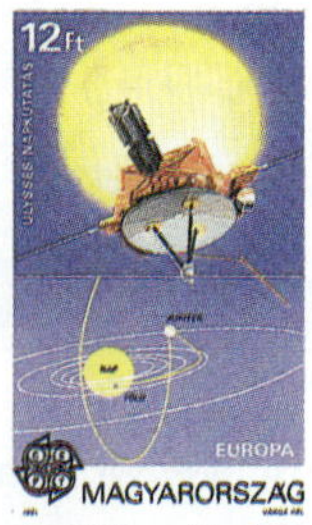

1024 "Ulysses" Jupiter Probe

1991. Europa. Europe in Space. Multicoloured.

4024	12fo. Type **1024**	3·75	2·50
4025	30fo. "Cassini" and "Huygens" (wrongly inscr "Hughes") Saturn probes	8·75	5·00

1025 "Peter and the Wolf" (tapestry, Gabriella Hajnal)

1991. Youth Stamp.

4026	**1025**	12fo.+6fo. mult	1·50	1·50

1026 Gorilla

1991. 125th Anniv of Budapest Zoological and Botanic Gardens. Multicoloured.

4027	7fo. Type **1026**	65	50
4028	12fo. Polar bear	1·00	85
4029	12fo. Rhinoceros	1·00	85
4030	12fo. Keel-billed toucan	1·00	85
4031	20fo. Orchid and glasshouse	1·90	1·60

1027 Teleki

1991. 50th Death Anniv of Count Pal Teleki (Prime Minister, 1920–21 and 1939–41).

4032	**1027**	12fo. brn, cinn & blk	1·50	1·50

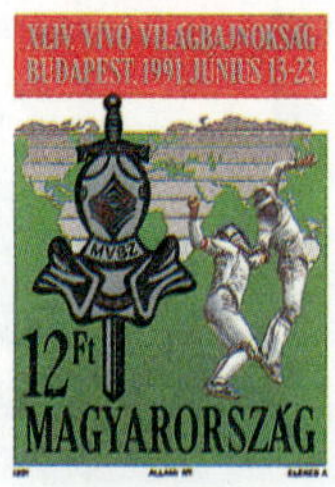

1028 Map, Emblem and Fencers

1991. 44th World Fencing Championships, Budapest.

4033	**1028**	12fo. multicoloured	1·50	1·50

1029 Mariapocs

1991. Visit of Pope John Paul II (1st issue). Shrines to Virgin Mary. Multicoloured.

4034	7fo. Type **1029**	65	50
4035	12fo. Mariagyud	1·00	85
4036	12fo. Celldomolk	1·00	85
4037	12fo. Mariaremete	1·00	85
4038	20fo. Esztergom	1·90	1·60

1030 "Appeggi Landscape" and Marko

1991. Birth Bicent of Karoly Marko (painter).

4039	**1030**	12fo. multicoloured	1·50	1·50

1031 Lilienthal and Monoplane Gliders, 1891

1991. Centenary of First Heavier-than-Air Manned Flight by Otto Lilienthal.

4040	**1031**	7fo. black, ochre & brn	65	50
4041	-	12fo. black, drab & bis	90	75
4042	-	20fo. dp blue, azure & bl	1·50	1·30
4043	-	30fo. black, lilac & vio	2·50	2·10

DESIGNS: 12fo. Wright brothers' Flyer 1, 1903; 20fo. Santos-Dumont's "14 bis", 1906; 30fo. Aladar Zselyi's monoplane, 1910.

1032 Players

1991. Centenary of Basketball.

4044	**1032**	12fo. multicoloured	1·50	1·50

1991. Castles. Inscr "MAGYARORSZAG". As T 921.

4045	7fo. brown and sepia	65	50
4047	12fo. ultramarine and blue	1·00	85
4049	15fo. brown and green	1·00	85

DESIGNS—32×25 mm; 7fo. Esterhazy Castle, Papa; 12fo. Dory Castle, Mihaly, 35×26 mm; 15fo. Festetics Castle, Keszthely.

1033 Pope John Paul II

1991. Papal Visit (2nd issue). Sheet 60×80 mm.

MS4055 **1033** 50fo. black and blue		8·25	8·25

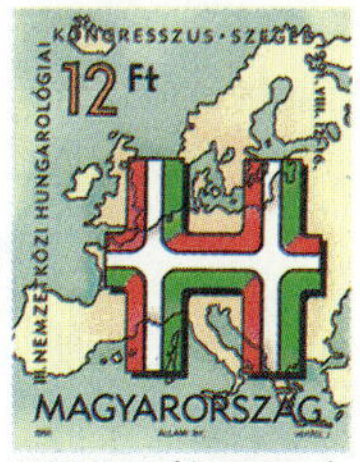

1034 Map of Europe and Congress Emblem

1991. 3rd International Hungarian Philological Society Congress, Szeged.

4056	**1034**	12fo. multicoloured	1·50	1·30

1035 Szechenyi

1991. Birth Bicentenary of Count Istvan Szechenyi (social reformer).

4057	**1035**	12fo. red	1·50	1·30

1036 Mozart as Child

1991. Stamp Day. Death Bicentenary of Wolfgang Amadeus Mozart (composer). Multicoloured.

4058	12fo. Type **1036**	1·30	1·00
4059	20fo. Mozart as youth	2·10	1·80
MS4060	80×61 mm. 30fo.+15fo. Mozart as man (24×36 mm)	7·50	7·50

1037 "Telecom 91"

1991. "Telecom 91" International Telecommunications Exhibition, Geneva.

4061	**1037**	12fo. multicoloured	1·50	1·30

1991. 35th Anniv of 1956 Uprising, No. 4047 optd A FORRADALOM EMLEKERE 1956 1991.

4062	12fo. ultramarine and blue	1·50	1·30

1039 Sebastian Cabot

1991. 500th Anniv (1992) of Discovery of America by Columbus. Multicoloured.

4063	7fo. Type **1039**	65	50
4064	12fo. Amerigo Vespucci	90	75
4065	12fo. Hernan Cortes	90	75
4066	15fo. Ferdinand Magellan	1·30	1·00
4067	20f. Francisco Pizarro	1·90	1·60
MS4068	85×71 mm. 30fo. Columbus (21×33 mm)	4·00	4·00

1040 Arms of Order

1991. Postal Convention with Sovereign Military Order of Malta.

4069	**1040**	12fo. multicoloured	1·50	1·30

1041 "Virgin of Mariapocs"

1991. Christmas. Multicoloured.

4070	7fo. Type **1041**	90	75
4071	12fo. "Virgin of Mariaremete"	1·30	1·00

1042 Flower

1991. Human Rights.

4072	**1042**	12fo. multicoloured	1·50	1·30

1043 Biathlon

1991. Winter Olympic Games, Albertville (1992). Multicoloured.

4073	7fo. Type **1043**	65	50
4074	12fo. Slalom	90	75
4075	15fo. Four-man bobsleigh	1·30	1·00
4076	20fo. Ski jumping	1·50	1·30
4077	30fo. Ice hockey	2·50	2·10
MS4078	73×54 mm. 30fo. Ice skating (pairs) (26×36 mm)	6·25	6·25

1044 1871 25k. Stamp

1991. Pro Philatelia. Sheet 90×71 mm.

MS4079 **1044** 50fo. violet		7·50	7·50

1045 Arms

1992. 350th Anniv of Piarist Order in Hungary.

4080	**1045**	10fo. gold, blue and ultramarine	75	65

1046 Holloko

1992. U.N.E.S.C.O. World Heritage Site.

4081	**1046**	15fo. multicoloured	1·90	1·60

1047 Swimming

1992. Olympic Games, Barcelona. Mult.

4082	7fo. Type **1047**	1·30	1·00
4083	9fo. Cycling	1·90	1·60
4084	10fo. Gymnastics	1·90	1·60
4085	15fo. Running	3·25	2·50

1048 "Indian's Head" Map

1992. "Expo '92" World's Fair, Seville. Fantasy Maps. Multicoloured.

4086	10fo. Type **1048**	1·30	1·00
4087	10fo. Islands, sea monsters and "Santa Maria" forming face	1·30	1·00
4088	15fo. "Conquistador's head" map	1·90	1·60
4089	15fo. Navigation instruments and map forming face	1·90	1·60

1049 Comenius

1992. 400th Birth Anniv of Jan Komensky (Comenius) (educationist).

4090	**1049**	15fo. multicoloured	1·50	1·30

1050 Mindszenty

1992. Birth Centenary of Cardinal Jozsef Mindszenty, Archbishop of Esztergom.

4091	**1050**	15fo. brn, cream & red	1·50	1·30

1051 Statue of Mayan Man

1992. Europa. 500th Anniv of Discovery of America by Columbus. Multicoloured.

4092	15fo. Type **1051**	2·50	1·60
4093	40fo. Statue of Mayan woman	6·25	3·75

1052 "Self-portrait" (Renata Toth)

1992. Youth Stamps. Children's Drawings. Multicoloured.

4094	9fo.+4fo. Type **1052**	90	75
4095	10fo.+4fo. "The Sun Shines for Me" (Sandor Pusoma) (horiz)	90	75
4096	15fo.+4fo. "I will be a Beauty King" (Endre Knipf)	1·30	1·00

1053 Gymnasts and Emblem

1992. European Gymnastics Championships, Budapest.

4097	**1053**	15fo. multicoloured	1·50	1·30

1054 St. Margaret (after J. S. Scott)

1992. 750th Birth Anniv of St. Margaret.

4098	**1054**	15fo. turq, lt bl & bl	1·30	1·00

1055 Saker Falcon

1992. Birds of Prey. Multicoloured.

4099	9fo. Type **1055**	65	50
4100	10fo. Booted eagle	75	65
4101	15fo. Short-toed eagle	1·10	95
4102	40fo. Red kite	2·75	2·30

1056 Wallenberg

1992. 80th Birth Anniv of Raoul Wallenberg (Swedish diplomat).

4103	**1056**	15fo. grey, red and green	1·00	85

1057 Millennium Monument, Budapest

1992. 3rd World Federation of Hungarians Congress, Budapest.

4104	**1057**	15fo. multicoloured	1·00	85

1058 Theodore von Karman (space pioneer, birth centenary (1991))

1992. Anniversaries.

4105	**1058**	15fo. grey, black and deep grey	90	75
4106	-	40fo. grey, black & brn	2·75	2·30

DESIGN: 40fo. Neumann Janos (mathematician, 35th death anniv).

1059 Current Hungarian Post Emblem

1992. Stamp Day."Eurofilex '92" International Postal History Exhibition, Budapest.

4107	**1059**	10fo.+5fo. multicoloured	1·30	1·00
4108	**1059**	15fo.+5fo. multicoloured	1·90	1·60

MS4109 91×66 mm. 50fo.+20fo. brown, cinnamon and black — 5·75 — 5·75

DESIGNS—VERT Hungarian Royal Post emblem, 1867. 39×29 mm—50fo. "Postal Riders" (etching, Ferenc Helbing).

See also No. 4111.

1060 Church of the Holy Family, Barcelona, and Medals

1992. Hungarian Olympic Games (Barcelona) Medal Winners. Sheet 61×80 mm.

MS4110	**1060**	50fo.+20fo. mult	6·25	6·25

1992. As No. 4108 but without premium and commemorative inscription.

4111	15fo. multicoloured	1·40	1·10

1061 Entwined Cables

1992. "Europa Telecom '92" Telecommunications Exhibition, Budapest.

4112	**1061**	15fo. multicoloured	1·00	85

1062 Istvan Bathory (King Stefan I of Poland)

1992. Princes of Transylvania. Multicoloured.

4113	10fo. Type **1062**	65	50
4114	15fo. Istvan Bocskai	90	75
4115	40fo. Gabor Bethlen	3·25	2·50

1063 Pieces on Board

1992. 10th European Chess Team Championship, Debrecen.

4116	**1063**	15fo. multicoloured	2·00	1·70

1064 "Clianthus formosus"

1065 Postal Rider of Prince Ferenc Rakoczi II, 1703–11

1992. Australian Flowers. Multicoloured.

4117	9fo. Type **1064**	65	50
4118	10fo. "Leschenaultia biloba"	90	75
4119	15fo. "Anigosanthos manglesii"	1·30	1·00
4120	40fo. "Comesperma ericinum"	3·00	2·50

MS4121 64×83 mm. 50fo. Mixed flowers (31×41 mm) — 6·25 — 6·25

1065 Postal Rider of Prince Ferenc Rakoczi II, 1703–11

1992. Post Office Uniforms. Multicoloured.

4122	10fo. Type **1065**	90	75
4123	15fo. Postmen, 1874	1·30	1·00

1066 "Holy Family" (iron relief, 1850)

1992. Christmas.

4124	**1066**	15fo. black and blue	1·10	95

1067 "Arachnis flos-aeris"

1993. Asian Flowers. Multicoloured.

4125	10fo. Type **1067**	65	50
4126	10fo. "Dendrobium densiflorium"	65	50
4127	15fo. "Lilium speciosum"	1·30	1·00
4128	15fo. "Meconopsis aculeata"	1·30	1·00

MS4129 64×83 mm. 50fo. Mixed bouquet (31×41 mm) — 7·50 — 7·50

1068 Shield Decoration of Deer

1993. Scythian Remains in Hungary. Mult.

4130	10fo. Type **1068**	90	75
4131	17fo. Gilt-silver embossed deer	1·50	1·30

1069 Single Sculls

1993. Centenary of Rowing Association.

4132	**1069**	17fo. multicoloured	1·50	1·30

1070 Queen Beatrix and King Matthias I Corvinus (detail of Missal) (image scaled to 64% of original size)

1993. King Matthias I Corvinus's "Missale Romanum".

4133	**1070**	15fo. multicoloured	1·80	1·50

MS4134 106×156 mm. 40fo. Illustration from missal (59×39 mm) — 4·50 — 4·50

1071 Animals in Wood

1993. Youth Stamps. Tapestries by Erzsebet Szekeres. Multicoloured.

4135	10fo.+5fo. Type **1071**	1·30	1·00
4136	17fo.+8fo. Animals in tree hiding from dragons	2·10	1·80

1072 Competitors and Globe

1993. World Motocross Championships, Cserenfa.

4137	**1072**	17fo. multicoloured	75	65

1073 Diagram of Solar System and Copernicus

1993. "Polska'93" International Stamp Exn.

4138	**1073**	17fo. multicoloured	75	65

1074 Paks Catholic Church

1993. Europa. Contemporary Art. Architecture by Imre Makovecz. Multicoloured.

4139	17fo. Type **1074**	1·30	1·00
4140	45fo. Hungarian pavilion at "Expo '92" World's Fair, Seville	2·75	2·30

1075 Cauliflower Clavaria

1993. Fungi. Multicoloured.

4141	10fo. Type **1075**	50	40
4142	17fo. Death trumpet	75	65
4143	45fo. Caesar's mushroom	2·50	2·10

1076 "St. Christopher" (Albrecht Durer)

1993. European Year of the Aged.

4144	**1076**	17fo. black, cream and silver	75	65

1077 Class 326 and 424 Steam Locomotives

1993. 125th Anniv of Hungarian Railways.

4145	**1077**	17fo. blue and cobalt	75	65

1078 Rowing Boat approaching Town

1993. 900th Anniv of Mohacs.

4146	**1078**	17fo. brown, cinnamon and red	75	65

1079 Poplar Admiral

1993. Butterflies. Multicoloured.

4147	10fo. Type **1079**	50	40
4148	17fo. "Aricia artaxerxes"	1·00	85
4149	30fo. "Plebejides pylaon"	1·60	1·40

1080 Kalman Latabar

1993. Great Humourists. Multicoloured.

4150	17fo. Type **1080**	90	75
4151	30fo. Charlie Chaplin	1·60	1·40

1081 Ribbon Dove over North-western Europe

1993. 20th Anniv of European Security and Co-operation Conference, Helsinki. Sheet 82×62 mm.

MS4152	**1081** 50fo. multicoloured	3·75	3·75

1082 Solar Panel absorbing Sun's Rays

1993. International Solar Energy Society Congress, Budapest.

4153	**1082**	17fo. multicoloured	75	65

1083 Laszlo Nemeth

1993. Writers. Each blue and azure.

4154	17fo. Type **1083**	90	75
4155	17fo. Dezso Szabo	90	75
4156	17fo. Antal Szerb	90	75

1084 Zoltan Nagy and 1953 20fi. Stamp

1993. Stamp Day. Designers. Multicoloured.

4157	10fo.+5fo. Type **1084**	75	65
4158	17fo.+5fo. Sandor Legrady and 1938 50f. stamp	1·30	1·00
MS4159	56×75 mm. 50fo.+20fo. Ferenc Helbing and 1932 10p. stamp (35×26 mm)	4·50	4·50

1085 Arms

1993. 175th Anniv of Faculty of Agronomics, Pannon Agricultural University, Magyarovar.

4160	**1085**	17fo. multicoloured	1·00	85

1086 "Szent Istvan", 1892

1993. Hungarian Ships. Multicoloured.

4161	10fo. Type **1086**	50	40
4162	30fo. "Szent Istvan" (battleship), 1915	1·80	1·50

1087 Prehistoric Man and Skull (Vertesszolos)

1993. Palaeolithic Remains in Hungary. Mult.

4163	17fo. Type **1087**	90	75
4164	30fo. Men round fire and stone tool (Szeleta Cave, Lillafured)	1·60	1·40

1088 Route-map of Central Europe

1993. Roman Roads. Sheet 80×65 mm.

MS4165	**1088** 50fo. multicoloured	4·50	4·50

1089 "Madonna and Child" (altarpiece by F. A. Hillebrant, Szekestehervar Cathedral)

1993. Christmas.

4166	**1089**	10fo. multicoloured	65	50

1090 Szechenyi Chain Bridge (image scaled to 65% of original size)

1993. "Expo '96" World's Fair, Budapest (1st issue).

4167	**1090**	17fo. dp green & green	75	65
4168	-	30fo. purple and claret	1·40	1·10
4169	-	45fo. dp brown & brown	2·10	1·80

DESIGNS—HORIZ: 30fo. Opera House. VERT: 45fo. Mathias Church.

See also Nos. 4236/8 and 4268/9.

1091 Antall

1993. Jozsef Antall (Prime Minister since 1990) Commemoration.

4170	**1091** 19fo. multicoloured	1·00	85
MS4171	70×50 mm. No. 4170	2·30	2·30

1092 Skiing

1994. Winter Olympic Games, Lillehammer, Norway. Multicoloured.

4172	12fo. Type **1092**	75	65
4173	19fo. Ice hockey	1·10	95

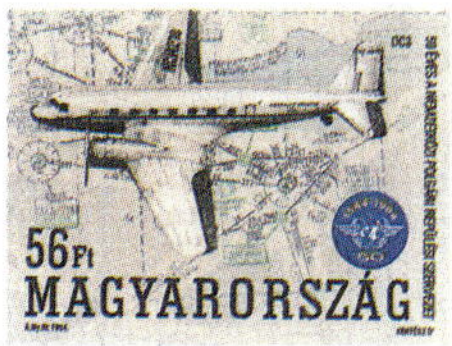

1093 Douglas DC-3

1994. 50th Anniv of I.C.A.O.

4174	**1093**	56fo. multicoloured	2·75	2·30

1094 "Golgotha" (detail, Mihaly Munkacsy)

1994. Easter.

4175	**1094**	12fo. multicoloured	65	50

1095 Mihaly Munkacsy (self-portrait)

1994. Artists' 150th Birth Anniversaries. Multicoloured.

4176	12fo. Gyula Benczur (self-portrait)	65	50
4177	19fo. Type **1095**	90	75

1096 Kossuth

1994. Death Centenary of Lajos Kossuth (Governor of 1849 Republic).

4178	**1096**	19fo. multicoloured	1·00	85

1097 Hen with Chicks

1994. The Great Bustard. Multicoloured.

4179	10fo. Type **1097**	65	50
4180	10fo. Bustards taking off	65	50
4181	10fo. Cock in mating display	65	50
4182	10fo. Hen with chicks (different)	65	50

1098 Bem

1994. Birth Bicent of Jozsef Bem (revolutionary).

4183	**1098**	19fo. multicoloured	1·00	85

1099 Discovery of Franz Josef Land (120th anniv)

1994. Europa. Discoveries. Multicoloured.

4184	19fo. Type **1099**	1·30	1·00
4185	50fo. Mark Aurel Stein and Buddha (expeditions in Asia)	2·50	2·10

1100 "The Little Prince"

1994. Youth Stamp. 50th Anniv of Disappearance of Antoine de Saint-Exupery (writer and pilot).
4186 **1100** 19fo.+5fo. mult 1·30 1·30

1101 Balint Balassi (poet, 400th death)

1994. Writers' Anniversaries.
4187 **1101** 19ft. pink and brown 90 75
4188 - 19ft. stone and grey 90 75
DESIGN: No. 4188, Miklos Josika (novelist, birth bicentenary).

1102 Horsemen

1994. 1100th Anniv (1996) of Magyar Conquest (1st issue). Multicoloured.
4189 19ft. Type **1102** 90 75
4190 19ft. Arpad and standard bearers (58×39 mm) 90 75
4191 19ft. Mounted archer 90 75
Nos. 4189/91 were issued together, se-tenant, forming a composite design of a detail of the painting "in the round" commissioned to celebrate the millenary of the Conquest.
See also Nos. 4240/2 and 4275/7.

1103 Athens Stadium, 1896

1994. Centenary of International Olympic Committee. Multicoloured.
4192 12ft. Olympic medals of 1896 and 1992 40 30
4193 19ft. Type **1103** 75 65
4194 19ft. Ancient Greek athletes, Olympic flag and flame 75 65
4195 35ft. Pierre de Coubertin (founder) 1·40 1·10

1104 Elvis Presley and Players

1994. World Cup Football Championship, U.S.A. American Entertainers. Multicoloured.
4196 19ft. Type **1104** 75 65
4197 19ft. Marilyn Monroe and players 75 65
4198 35ft. John Wayne and players 1·30 1·00

1105 Family

1994. International Year of the Family.
4199 **1105** 19fo. multicoloured 75 65

1106 Summer Snowflake

1994. European Flowers. Multicoloured.
4200 12fo. Type **1106** 50 40
4201 19fo. Common rock-rose 75 65
4202 35fo. "Eryngium alpinum" 1·30 1·00
4203 50fo. Pennycress 1·90 1·60
MS4204 64×83 mm. 100fo. Mixed bouquet (31×40 mm) 5·00 5·00

1107 Heinrich von Stephan (founder) and Emblem

1994. 120th Anniv of Universal Postal Union.
4205 **1107** 19fo. grey, brown & blk 75 65
4206 - 35fo. blue, brown & blk 1·30 1·00
MS4207 98×71 mm. 50fo.+25fo. brown, black and blue (Heinrich von Stephan) (vert); 50fo.+25 fo. brown, black and violet (Gervay Mihaly) (vert) 5·75 5·75
DESIGN: 35fo. Gervay Mihaly (first Director General of Posts) and U.P.U. emblem.

1108 Csik Megye

1994. Traditional Patterns.
4208 1fo. violet and black 15 10
4209 2fo. multicoloured 15 10
4210 3fo. multicoloured 15 10
4210a 5fo. multicoloured 15 10
4211 9fo. multicoloured 20 15
4212 **1108** 11fo. multicoloured 25 20
4213 - 12fo. multicoloured 40 30
4214 - 13fo. multicoloured 40 30
4215 - 14fo. multicoloured 40 30
4216 - 16fo. multicoloured 45 35
4217 - 17fo. black, grey & red 40 30
4218 - 19fo. multicoloured 75 65
4219 - 22fo. multicoloured 75 65
4220 - 24fo. multicoloured 65 50
4220a - 24fo. multicoloured 65 50
4220b - 27fo. multicoloured 75 65
4221 - 32fo. multicoloured 1·00 85
4222 - 35fo. multicoloured 1·30 1·00
4223 - 38fo. multicoloured 1·40 1·10
4224 - 40fo. multicoloured 1·50 1·30
4225 - 50fo. multicoloured 2·50 2·10
4225a - 65fo. black, red and grey 1·30 1·00
4226 - 75fo. multicoloured 1·90 1·60
4226a - 79fo. multicoloured 1·00 85
4227 - 80fo. multicoloured 2·00 1·70
4228 - 90fo. multicoloured 1·90 1·60
4229 - 100fo. multicoloured 1·50 1·30
4229a - 200fo. multicoloured 3·75 3·25
4230 - 300fo. multicoloured 6·25 5·25
4231 - 500fo. multicoloured 10·00 8·25
DESIGNS: 1fo. Torocko; 2fo. Buzsak; 3fo. Vas megye (flowers); 5fo. Rabakoz; 9, 24fo. (4220) Felfold; 12, 27fo. Vas megye (birds); 13, 32fo. Debrecen; 14, 80fo. Sarkoz; 16fo. Csiki-Medence; 17, 35, 65fo. Dunantul; 19, 24fo. (4220a) Kalocsa; 22, 90fo. Heves megye; 300fo. Kalocsa (different); 38, 75fo. Oroshaza; 40fo. Kalotaszeg; 50fo. Szentgal; 79fo. Moldvai csango; 100fo. Szecseny videke; 200fo. Mezokovesd; 500fo. Szolnok megye.

1109 Budapest

1994. Conference of Security and Co-operation in Europe Summit, Budapest. Sheet 92×70 mm.
MS4232 **1109** 100fo. multicoloured 5·00 5·00

1110 Hebrew Tombstone

1994. Holocaust Victims' Commemoration.
4233 **1110** 19fo. multicoloured 1·00 85

1111 "Nativity"

1994. Christmas. Paintings by Pal Molnar. Multicoloured.
4234 12fo. Type **1111** 65 50
4235 35fo. "Flight into Egypt" (31×29 mm) 1·30 1·00

1112 National Museum

1994. "Expo '96" World's Fair, Budapest (2nd issue). Budapest landmarks.
4236 **1112** 19fo. green 75 65
4237 - 19fo. brown 75 65
4238 - 19fo. violet 75 65
DESIGNS: No. 4237, University of Technical Sciences; 4238, Vajdahunyad Castle.

1113 "Ferencz Jozsef I" (paddle-steamer) and "Baross" (container ship)

1995. Cent of Hungarian Shipping Company.
4239 **1113** 22fo. multicoloured 1·00 85

1995. 1100th Anniv (1996) of Magyar Conquest (2nd issue). As T 1102. Multicoloured.
4240 22fo. Ox cart 90 75
4241 22fo. Arpad's consort in ox cart (59×39 mm) 90 75
4242 22fo. Men and pack ox 90 75
Nos. 4240/2 were issued together, se-tenant, forming a composite design of a detail of the painting "in the round" commissioned to celebrate the millenary of the Conquest.

1114 Lamb of God

1995. Easter.
4243 **1114** 14fo. purple and black 75 65

1115 Paddle-steamer

1995. 150th Anniv of Steamer Service on River Tisza (14fo.) and Birth Bicentenary of Pal Vasarhelyi (engineer) (60fo.). Multicoloured.
4244 14fo. Type **1115** 50 40
4245 60fo. Vasarhelyi (after Miklos Barabas) and survey ship 2·10 1·80

1116 Weather Map and Barometer

1995. Anniversaries. Multicoloured.
4246 22fo. Type **1116** (125th anniv of Hungarian Meteorological Service) 1·00 85
4247 22fo. Emblem (50th anniv of F.A.O.) (25×41 mm) 1·00 85
4248 22fo.+10fo. John the Hero (150th anniv of poem by Petofi) (37×45 mm) 1·30 1·00
No. 4248 is the 1995 Youth Stamp.

1117 White Stork and Frog

1995. European Nature Conservation Year. Multicoloured.
4249 14fo. Type **1117** 1·00 85
4250 14fo. Red squirrel 1·00 85
4251 14fo. Blue tit 1·00 85
4252 14fo. Butterfly and hedgehog 1·00 85
Nos. 4249/52 were issued together, se-tenant, forming a composite design.

1118 Allied Flags forming Dove over Map of Europe

1995. Europa. Peace and Freedom.
4253 **1118** 22fo. multicoloured 1·90 1·60

1119 Gymnastics and Ferenc Kemeny (founder)

1995. Centenary of Hungarian Olympic Committee. Multicoloured.
4254 22fo. Type **1119** 90 75
4255 60fo. Throwing the javelin 2·30 1·90
4256 100fo. Fencing 3·75 3·25

1120 Exhibition Emblem

1995. "Olympiafila '95" International Olympic and Sports Stamps Exhibition, Budapest.
4257 **1120** 22fo.+11fo. mult (rings in yellow) 1·40 1·10
4258 **1120** 22fo.+11fo. mult (rings in purple) 1·40 1·10

1121 Saint Ladislas (detail of fresco, Szekelyderzs Castle Chapel)

1995. 900th Death Anniv of St. Ladislas, King of Hungary.
4259 **1121** 22fo. multicoloured 90 75

1122 Almasy

1995. Birth Centenary of Laszlo Almasy (explorer).
4260 **1122** 22fo. multicoloured 1·30 1·00

1123 Museum of Applied Arts, Budapest, and Lechner

1995. 150th Birth Anniv of Odon Lechner (architect).
4261 **1123** 22fo. multicoloured 1·30 1·00

1124 "K XVIII 1923" (Laszlo Moholy-Nagy)

1995. Artists' Birth Centenaries. Multicoloured.
4262 22fo. Type **1124** 1·10 95
4263 22fo. "The Fiddler" (Aurel Bernath) 1·10 95

1125 College Building and Jozsef Eotvos (founder)

1995. Centenary of Eotvos College.
4264 **1125** 60fo. multicoloured 2·50 2·10

1126 Postal Carriage and Map of Postal Routes

1995. Stamp Day. Multicoloured.
4265 22fo. Type **1126** 65 50
4266 40fo. Airplane and route map 1·30 1·00
MS4267 80×61 mm. 100fo.+30fo. Children looking at stamp album (29×44 mm) 5·00 5·00

1995. "Expo '96" World's Fair, Budapest (3rd issue). As T 1112 showing Budapest landmarks.
4268 22fo. grey 75 65
4269 22fo. purple 75 65
DESIGNS: No. 4268, West Railway Station; 4269, Music Hall.

1127 Anniversary Emblem

1995. 50th Anniv of U.N.O.
4270 **1127** 60fo. multicoloured 1·90 1·60

1128 Sparklers

1995. Christmas. Multicoloured.
4271 14fo. Type **1128** 40 30
4272 60fo. Three wise men in stable 1·80 1·50

1129 St Elizabeth bathing Leper

1995. Saint Elizabeth of Hungary.
4273 **1129** 22fo. multicoloured 90 75

1130 Nobel Medals

1995. Centenary of Nobel Trust Fund.
4274 **1130** 100fo. multicoloured 4·00 3·25

1996. 1100th Anniv of Magyar Conquest (3rd issue). As T 1102. Multicoloured.
4275 24fo. Rejoicing crowd 75 65
4276 24fo. Shaman presenting sacrificial white horse (59×39 mm) 75 65
4277 24fo. Bards 75 65
Nos. 4275/7 were issued together, se-tenant, forming a composite design.

1131 Leather Purse

1996. 9th-century Relics from Kares Cemeteries. Multicoloured.
4278 24fo. Type **1131** 75 65
4279 24fo. Gold and silver sabre hilt 75 65

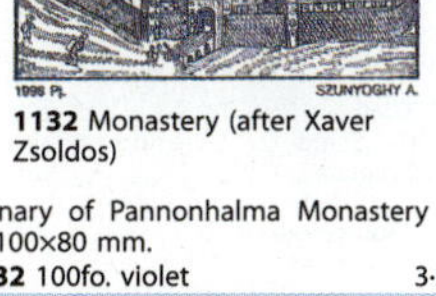

1132 Monastery (after Xaver Zsoldos)

1996. Millenary of Pannonhalma Monastery (1st issue). Sheet 100×80 mm.
MS4280 **1132** 100fo. violet 3·50 3·50
See also Nos. 4290/1 and 4305/6.

1133 Headquarters

1996. Centenary of Journalists' Association.
4281 **1133** 50fo. multicoloured 1·40 1·10

1134 Emblem

1996. Promotion of Hungarian Production.
4282 **1134** 24fo. black, red & green 75 65

1135 Swimming

1996. Centenary of Modern Olympic Games and Olympic Games, Atlanta. Multicoloured.
4283 24fo. Type **1135** 65 50
4284 50fo. Tennis (Csilla Orosz) 1·30 1·00
4285 75fo. Canoeing 1·90 1·60

1996. 1100th Anniv of Magyar Conquest (4th issue). Sheet 150×190 mm containing previous designs. Multicoloured.
MS4286 19fo. ×3 Nos. 4189/91; 22fo. ×3 Nos. 4240/2; 24fo. ×3 Nos. 4275/7 8·25 8·25

1136 First Carriage

1996. Centenary of Budapest Underground Railway.
4287 **1136** 24fo. multicoloured 75 65

1137 Queen Gizella (wife of St. Stephen)

1996. Europa. Famous Women. Hungarian Queens. Multicoloured.
4288 24fo. Type **1137** 1·00 85
4289 75fo. Queen Elisabeth (wife of Francis Joseph I) 2·75 2·30

1138 Triumphal Arch (entrance to Cathedral)

1996. Millenary of Pannonhalma Monastery (2nd issue).
4290 **1138** 17fo. brown 50 35
4291 - 24fo. blue 70 50
DESIGN: 24fo. Monks gathered in cloisters.

1139 Bird and "DRUG"

1996. International Day against Drug Abuse.
4292 **1139** 24fo. multicoloured 85 65

1140 Denes Mihaly (television pioneer)

1996. Inventors. Multicoloured.
4293 24fo. Type **1140** 70 50
4294 50fo. Laszlo Biro and ballpoint pen 1·40 1·00
4295 75fo. Zoltan Bay and Moon radar 2·10 1·60

1141 Laszlo Vitez (puppet)

1996. Youth Stamp. Puppet Festival, Budapest.
4296 **1141** 24fo.+10fo. mult 1·10 85

1142 "Heves", 1846

1996. 150th Anniv of Hungarian Railways. Steam Locomotives. Multicoloured.
4297 17fo. Class 303 55 40
4298 24fo. Class 325 95 70
4299 24fo. Type **1142** 95 70
On No. 4299 the nameplate is inscribed "PEST".

1143 Pyramid

1996. 2nd European Mathematics Congress, Budapest.
4300 **1143** 24fo. multicoloured 95 65

1144 Hungarian Long-horned Wood Beetle ("Ropalopus ungaricus")

1996. "NATUREXPO '96" International Nature Conservation Exhibition, Budapest. Mult.
4301 13fo. Type **1144** 50 35
4302 13fo. Lynx ("Lynx lynx") 50 35
4303 13fo. Siberian iris ("Iris sibirica") 50 35
4304 13fo. Great egret ("Egretta alba") 50 35

1996. Millenary of Pannonhalma Monastery (3rd issue). As T 1138.
4305 17fo. brown 65 45
4306 24fo. green 80 55

DESIGNS: 17fo. Refectory; 24fo. Main library.

1145 Homage to Prince Arpad (from "Vienna Picture Chronicle")

1996. Stamp Day. "Budapest '96" International Stamp Exhibition, Budapest. Mult.

4307 17fo. Type **1145** 65 45

4308 24fo. Prince Arpad on horse-back and soldiers (from "Vienna Picture Chronicle") 80 55

MS4309 92×72 mm. 150fo.+50fo. 1944 1f. Prince Arpad stamp, first page of Deeds of Hungarians and detail of "Compact sealed with Blood" (mural by Bertalan Szekely, Kecskemet Town Hall) 5·50 5·50

1146 1871 10k. Engraved Stamp

1996. World Convention of Hungarian Stamps and Postal History.

4310 **1146** 24fo. multicoloured 80 55

1147 Map and Paddle-steamer "Kisfaludy"

1996. 150th Anniv of Steamer Service on Lake Balaton.

4311 **1147** 17fo. multicoloured 80 55

1148 Mastheads and Demonstration

1996. 40th Anniv of 23 October Uprising. Multicoloured.

4312 13fo. Type **1148** 50 35

4313 16fo. Newspaper, burning flag and motor vehicle 50 35

4314 17fo. Men with rifles and newspaper 65 45

4315 24fo. Newspaper and Imre Nagy (Prime Minister, Oct–Nov 1956) 80 55

MS4316 76×75 mm. 40fo. Imre Nagy and government members (44×29 mm) 2·40 2·40

1149 Atlanta and Medals

1996. Hungarian Medal Winners at Olympic Games. Sheet 85×55 mm.

MS4317 **1149** 150fo. multicoloured 5·50 5·50

1150 "Madonna and Child with Two Angels" (Matteo di Giovanni)

1996. Christmas. Multicoloured.

4318 17fo. Type **1150** 65 45

4319 24fo. "Adoration of the Wise Men" (Salzburg Master) 80 55

1151 List of Years

1996. 50th Anniv of UNICEF.

4320 **1151** 24fo. multicoloured 80 55

1152 Bust, Book, Quill and Shield

1996. Birth Bicentenary of Miklos Wesselenyi (writer).

4321 **1152** 24fo. multicoloured 80 55

1153 Kalman Mikszath and Characters

1997. Writers' Birth Anniversaries. Mult.

4322 27fo. Type **1153** (150th anniv) 80 55

4323 27fo. Aron Tamasi (cent) 80 55

1154 Baranya

1997. Arms. Multicoloured. (a) As T 1154.

4324 27fo. Type **1154** 80 55

4325 27fo. Bacs-Kiskun 80 55

4326 27fo. Bekes 80 55

4327 27fo. Borsod-Abauj-Zemplen 80 55

4328 27fo. Fejer 80 55

4329 27fo. Gyor-Moson-Sopron 80 55

4330 27fo. Heves 80 55

4331 27fo. Jasz-Nagykun-Szolnok 80 55

4332 27fo. Komarom-Esztergom 80 55

4333 27fo. Nograd 80 55

4334 27fo. Pest 80 55

4335 27fo. Somogy 80 55

4336 27fo. Tolna 80 55

4337 27fo. Vas 80 55

4338 27fo. Veszprem 80 55

4339 27fo. Zala 80 55

(b) Size 50×32 mm.

4340 27fo. Hajku-Bihar 80 55

4341 27fo. Budapest 80 55

4342 27fo. Csongrad 80 55

4343 27fo. Szabolcs-Szatmar-Bereg 80 55

MS4344 Four sheets, each 78×125 mm. (a) Nos. 4324/33 and 4340 plus label; (b) Nos. 4328/33; (c) Nos. 4334/9; (d) Nos. 4341/3 Set of 4 sheets 16·00 16·00

1155 Badge, Camp and Sailing

1997. 90th Anniv of Scout Movement.

4345 **1155** 20fo. multicoloured 80 55

1156 Book, Knight and Arany

1997. 150th Anniv of Composition of "Miklos Toldi" by Janos Arany (winning entry in poetry competition).

4346 **1156** 27fo.+10fo. mult 95 65

1157 St. Adalbert

1997. Death Millenary of St. Adalbert (Bishop of Prague).

4347 **1157** 80fo. lilac 2·75 2·00

1158 Emblem and City

1997. World Customs' Union Conference, Budapest.

4348 **1158** 90fo. multicoloured 2·40 1·70

1159 Gemsboks

1997. African Animals. Multicoloured.

4349 16fo. Type **1159** 50 35

4350 20fo. Common zebras 65 45

4351 20fo. Black rhinoceroses 65 45

4352 27fo. Lions 80 55

MS4353 91×64 mm. 90fo. African elephants 4·50 4·50

1160 "The Enchanted Hart"

1997. Europa. Tales and Legends. Mult.

4354 27fo. Type **1160** 95 65

4355 90fo. King St. Stephen oversee-ing burial of Prince Geza (death millenary) 3·00 2·10

1161 Schraetzer ("Gymnocephalus schraetzer")

1997. Fishes. Multicoloured.

4356 20fo. Type **1161** 50 35

4357 20fo. Bullhead "Cottus gobio" 50 35

4358 20fo. Schneider "Alburnoides bipunctatus" 50 35

4359 20fo. Spiny loach ("Cobitis taenia") 50 35

Nos. 4356/9 were issued together, se-tenant, forming a composite design.

1162 St. Jadwiga (after Peter Prokop)

1997. Canonization of Queen Jadwiga of Poland.

4360 **1162** 90fo. multicoloured 2·40 1·70

1163 Janos Selye

1997. Int Congress on Stress, Budapest.

4361 **1163** 90fo. multicoloured 2·40 1·70

1997. No. 4220 surch 60 f.

4362 60fo. on 24fo. multicoloured 1·40 1·00

1997. Wine Grapes and Regions (2nd series). As T 1013. Multicoloured.

4363 27fo. Harslevelu, Gyongyos 65 55

4364 27fo. Nemes Kadarka, Kiskoros 65 55

4365 27fo. Teltfurtu Ezerjo, Mor 65 55

1165 Flower surrounded by Flood Waters

1997. Flood Relief Funds.

4366 **1165** 27fo.+100fo. mult 3·25 2·75

1166 Postman and Csonka Tricycle, 1900

1997. Stamp Day. Multicoloured.

4367 27fo.+5fo. Type **1166** 80 65

4368 55fo.+5fo. Registered letter receiving-machine, 1906 (vert) 1·60 1·30

MS4369 82×68 mm. 90fo.+30fo. Csonka post van, 1905 8·00 8·00

1167 Nativity

1997. Christmas. Multicoloured.

4370 20fo. Type **1167** 50 40

4371 27fo. Adoration of the Wise Men 80 65

1168 Weightlifter

1997. 68th World Weightlifting Championships, Thailand.

4372	**1168**	90fo. multicoloured	2·40	2·00

1169 Skiing

1998. Winter Olympic Games, Nagano, Japan. Multicoloured.

4373	30fo. Type **1169**	65	55
4374	100fo. Snowboarding	2·40	1·80

1170 Szechenyi with Camera

1998. Birth Centenary of Zsigmond Szechenyi (travel writer).

4375	**1170**	60fo. multicoloured	1·70	1·30

1171 Leaf and Lyrics

1998. 175th Anniv of National Hymn by Ferenc Kolcsey.

4376	**1171**	75fo. multicoloured	2·00	1·60

1172 Balint Postas holding Envelope

1998. Introduction of Balint Postas (post mascot). Multicoloured.

4377	23fo. Type **1172**	65	55
4378	24fo. Balint Postas bowing	75	60
4379	30fo. Balint Postas with arms outstretched	85	65
4380	65fo. Balint Postas flying	1·70	1·30

1173 Hearts and Post Box

1998. St. Valentine's Day.

4381	**1173**	24fo. multicoloured	85	65

1174 Szilard

1998. Birth Cent of Leo Szilard (scientist).

4382	**1174**	50fo. multicoloured	1·30	1·10

1175 Sandor Petofi (poet)

1998. 150th Anniv of March Revolution, 1848. Multicoloured.

4383	23fo. Type **1175**	65	55
4384	24fo. Mihaly Tancsics (politician and workers' newspaper editor) and inkwell	75	60
4385	30fo. Lajos Kossuth (Governor of 1849 Republic) and coin	85	65
MS4386	78×65 mm. 150fo.+50fo. Leaders of the Revolution (44×29 mm)	6·75	6·75

1176 "The Resurrection of Christ" (El Greco)

1998. Easter.

4387	-	24fo. red and black	65	55
4388	**1176**	30fo. multicoloured	1·00	80

DESIGN: 27×39 mm—24fo. Dots forming outline of egg.

1177 Vase

1998. Ceramics. Multicoloured.

4389	20fo. Type **1177**	50	40
4390	24fo. Bowl decorated with butterflies (horiz)	60	45
4391	30fo. Spiral vase	65	55
4392	95fo. Bowl with lid (horiz)	2·50	2·00

1178 Postman

1998. Stamp Day. 250th Anniv of Inauguration of Postal Service by Empress Maria Theresa. Multicoloured.

4393	24fo.+10fo. Type **1178**	1·00	80
4394	30fo.+10fo. Mounted courier	1·10	85
MS4395	80×61 mm. 150fo. Horse-drawn post coach	6·00	6·00

1179 American Bison

1998. American Animals. Multicoloured.

4396	23fo. Type **1179**	65	55
4397	24fo. Brown bear	75	60
4398	24fo. Mississippi alligator	75	60
4399	30fo. Ocelot	85	65
MS4400	90×60 mm. 150fo. Marvellous spatule-tail	5·00	5·00

1180 Jendrassik

1998. Birth Centenary of Gyorgy Jendrassik (engineer).

4401	**1180**	100fo. blue	2·75	2·10

1181 Hurdling

1998. European Light Athletics Championships, Budapest. Multicoloured.

4402	24fo. Type **1181**	50	40
4403	65fo. High jumping	1·50	1·20
4404	80fo. Throwing the hammer	2·20	1·70

1182 Canoe

1998. World White-water Canoeing Championships, Szeged.

4405	**1182**	30fo. multicoloured	85	65

1183 Players

1998. World Cup Football Championship, France. Multicoloured.

4406	30fo. Type **1183**	65	55
4407	110fo. Players with ball on ground	2·75	2·10

Nos. 4406/7 were issued together, se-tenant, forming a composite design.

1184 Baross (after Miklos Barabos)

1998. 150th Birth Anniv of Gabor Baross (politician).

4408	**1184**	60fo. multicoloured	1·70	1·30

1185 Signalman and Pioneers in Railway Carriage

1998. 50th Anniv of Budapest Pioneer Railway.

4409	**1185**	24fo. multicoloured	85	65

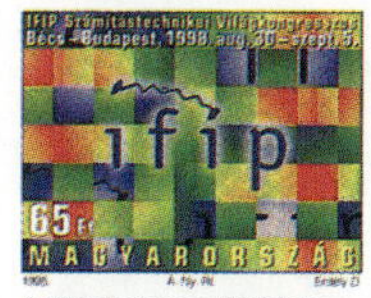

1186 Congress Emblem

1998. World Congress of Computer Technology, Vienna and Budapest.

4410	**1186**	65fo. multicoloured	1·90	1·50

1187 Carved Poles

1998. Europa. National Festivals. Mult.

4411	50fo. Type **1187** (Republic Day)	2·20	1·70
4412	60fo. Carved shield and corn (National Day)	2·75	2·10

1188 Emblem

1998. 60th Anniv of Hungarians Abroad Organization.

4413	**1188**	100fo. multicoloured	3·00	2·30

1189 Hortobagyi National Park

1998. National Parks (1st series). Multicoloured.

4414	24fo. Type **1189**	50	40
4415	70fo. Kiskunsagi National Park	1·90	1·50

See also Nos. 4438/9, 4507/8 and 4559/61.

1190 "Adoration of the Shepherds" (Agnolo Bronzino)

1998. Christmas. Multicoloured.

4416	20fo. Type **1190**	65	55
4417	24fo. "Madonna and Child Enthroned" (Carlo Crivelli) (vert)	75	60

For 24fo. as Type **1190** see No. 4485.

1191 Easter Eggs

1999. Easter. Multicoloured.

4418	27fo. Type **1191**	65	55
4419	32fo. Head of Christ (Ferenc Svindt) (37×52 mm)	85	65

1192 "Self-portrait" (wood carving, Jeno Szervatiusz)

1999. International Year of the Elderly.
4420 **1192** 32fo. multicoloured 85 65

1193 "Novara" (full-rigged ship)

1999. Sailing Ships. Multicoloured.

4421	32fo. Type **1193**		65	55
4422	79fo. "Phoenix" (barge)		1·70	1·30
4423	110fo. "Folyami Vitorlas" (galley)		2·75	2·10

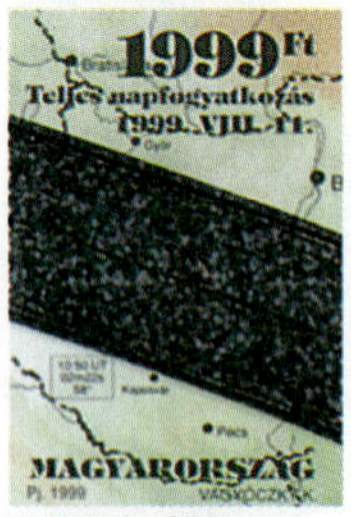

1194 Path of Eclipse

1999. Total Solar Eclipse (11 Aug). Sheet 105×76 mm.
MS4424 **1194** 1999fo. multicoloured 47·00 47·00

1195 Artur Gorgey (commander of Upper Danube)

1999. 150th Anniv of 1848–49 Uprising. Multicoloured.

4425 24fo. Type **1195**	65	55
4426 27fo. Lajos Batthyany (politician)	75	60
4427 32fo. General Jozef Bem	85	65
MS4428 78×65 mm. 100fo. "The Battle of Tapioticske" (detail, Mor Than) (44×27 mm)	3·00	3·00

1196 Scene from "Bobo and the Hare" (animated film)

1999. Youth Stamp.
4429 **1196** 52fo.+25fo. mult 1·70 1·30

1197 Cathedrals within Map and Emblem

1999. 50th Anniv of North Atlantic Treaty Organization.
4430 **1197** 110fo. multicoloured 3·25 2·75

1198 The Five Sports

1999. 5th World Pentathlon Championship, Budapest. Sheet 86×70 mm.
MS4431 **1198** 100fo. multicoloured 3·00 3·00

1199 Papai

1999. 350th Birth Anniv of Ferenc Pariz Papai (scientist, physician and lexicographer).
4432 **1199** 50fo. green and orange 1·00 80

1200 Science Academy, Budapest

1999. World Science Congress, Budapest.
4433 **1200** 65fo. multicoloured 1·20 90

1201 Anniversary Badge on Scroll

1999. Centenary of Ferencvaros Sports Club.
4434 **1201** 100fo. multicoloured 1·90 1·50

1202 Council Flag

1999. 50th Anniv of Council of Europe.
4435 **1202** 50fo. multicoloured 2·50 2·00

1203 Juhfark, Somlo

1999. Wine Grapes and Regions (3rd series). Multicoloured.

4436 24fo. Type **1203**	50	40
4437 27fo. Kekfrankos, Sopron	60	45

1999. Europa. Parks and Gardens. National Parks (2nd series). As T 1189. Multicoloured.

4438 27fo. Aggtelek National Park	2·50	2·00
4439 32fo. Bukk National Park	2·75	2·10

1204 Bengali Tiger

1999. Asian Animals. Multicoloured.

4440 27fo. Type **1204**	85	65
4441 32fo. Giant panda	90	75
4442 52fo. Black leopard	1·30	1·10
4443 79fo. Orang-utan	1·70	1·30
MS4444 78×75 mm. 100fo. Mandarin (49×29 mm)	6·00	6·00

1205 Title Page of Decree

1999. Stamp Day. 250th Anniv of Decree by Empress Maria Theresa establishing Regular Mail Coach Service. Multicoloured.

4445 32fo.+15fo. Type **1205**	1·00	80
4446 52fo.+20fo. Passengers boarding coach and woman with letters	1·30	1·10
MS4447 75×60 mm. 150fo. Horses and mail coach (31×41 mm)	4·25	4·25

1206 Common Poppy

1999. Greetings Stamps. Flowers. Multicoloured.

4448 27fo. Type **1206**	50	40
4449 32fo. Trumpet gentian	85	65

1207 Cukor

1999. Birth Centenary of George Cukor (film director).
4450 **1207** 50fo. multicoloured 1·20 90

1208 U.P.U. Emblem

1999. 125th Anniv of Universal Postal Union. "China '99" International Stamp Exhibition, Peking.
4451 **1208** 32fo. multicoloured 85 65

1209 Woodcut by Samuel Mikoviny (from "Notitia Hungarie" by Matyas Bel)

1999. International Book Fair, Frankfurt.
4452 **1209** 40fo. multicoloured 85 65

1210 High-backed Chair, Szepesseg (17th century)

1999. Antique Furniture.

4453	-	1fo. green and yellow	15	15
4454	-	2fo. green and black	15	15
4455	-	3fo. red and black	15	15
4456	-	4fo. brown	15	15
4457	-	5fo. deep blue and blue	15	15
4458	-	6fo. brown and sepia	15	15
4459	-	7fo. brown and pink	15	15
4460	-	8fo. black and grey	10	10
4460a	-	9fo. violet and maroon	10	10
4461	**1210**	10fo. bistre and black	10	10
4464	-	20fo. green and black	25	20
4467	-	26fo. green and black	35	25
4468	-	29fo. green and black	40	35
4469	-	30fo. mauve and black	50	40
4470	-	31fo. dp mauve and mve	60	45
4470a	-	32fo. pink and red	65	55
4470b	-	33fo. pink and red	75	60
4470c	-	35fo. pink and red	85	65
4471	-	40fo. brown & lt brown	90	75
4472	-	50fo. blue and black	1·00	80
4474	-	60fo. olive and green	1·30	1·10
4475	-	65fo. ochre and brown	1·40	1·10
4476	-	70fo. rose and black	1·50	1·20
4478	-	80fo. grey and black	1·70	1·30
4480	-	90fo. lilac and purple	1·90	1·50
4481	-	100fo. brown and black	2·00	1·60
4482	-	134fo. ochre and brown	3·00	2·40
4483	-	200fo. blue and green	4·25	3·25
4484	-	210fo. green and olive	4·75	3·75
4484a	-	230fo. blue-green and bottle green	5·00	4·00
4484b	-	300fo. red and rosine	6·00	4·50
4484c	-	500fo. blue and cobalt	10·00	8·00
4484d	-	1000fo. olive and bistre	20·00	16·00

DESIGNS—VERT: 1fo. Wooden stool, 1910; 2fo. Heves County wooden chair, 1838; 3fo. 19th-century gilded chair; 4fo. Armchair by Geza Marota; 5fo. Chair by Odon Farago; 6fo. Wooden chair by Marton Kovacs; 7fo. Ornate chair, 1853; 8fo. 19th-century chair; 9fo. 18th-century wooden armchair; 20fo. Armchair by Karoly Lingel, 1915; 26, 31fo. Neo-Gothic chair, 1850; 29fo. Magyargee wooden chair, 1879; 30fo. Armchair by Karoly Nagy, 1935; 32, 33fo. Ornate backed chair, 1890; 35fo. 18th-century carver; 40fo. Ornate chair, 1896; 50fo. Prince Pal Esterhazy's armchair (16th-century); 60fo. Chair, 1840; 65fo. Cane-bottomed ornate armchair, 1920; 70fo. Chair with umbrella-shaped back, 1820; 80fo. High backed chair; 90fo. Upholstered armchair by Lajos Kozma. HORIZ: 100fo. Couch by Lajos Kozma, 1920; 134fo. Double-seated chair, 1900; 200fo. Ornate couch, 1810; 210fo., 230fo. Love seat (1900); 300fo. 18th-century settee; 500fo. Rococo settee, 1880; 1000fo. Vassily chair by Marcel Breuer, 1925.

1211 Three Wise Men (Zsuzsa Demeter)

1999. Christmas. Multicoloured.

4485 24fo. Type **1190**	65	55
4486 27fo. Type **1211**	75	60
4487 32fo. "Madonna and Child" (stained glass window, Miksa Roth) (vert)	85	65

1212 Wigner

1999. 97th Birth Anniv of Jeno Wigner (physicist).
4488 **1212** 32fo. blue 85 65

1213 Paddle-steamer passing under Bridge

1999. 150th Anniv of Chain Bridge, Budapest. Sheet 87×57 mm.
MS4489 **1213** 150fo. blue, red and green 3·25 3·25

1214 Coronation Sceptre

2000. New Millenium.

4490	**1214**	28fo. bistre and purple	50	40
4491	**1214**	30fo. bistre and purple	65	55
4492	-	34fo. multicoloured	75	60
4493	-	36fo. multicoloured	85	65

4494 - 40fo. multicoloured 90 75
DESIGN:—34, 36, 40fo. Millennium flag.

1215 Miklos Kis Misztotfalusi (printer, 350th anniv)

2000. Birth Anniversaries.
4495 **1215** 30fo. grn, stone & brn 85 65
4496 - 40fo. blue, stone & brn 1·20 90
4497 - 50fo. red, stone & brn 1·30 1·10
4498 - 80fo. brown and stone 2·00 1·60
DESIGNS—40fo. Anyos Jedlik (physicist, bicentenary); 50fo. Jeno Kvassay (engineer, 150th anniv); 80fo. Jeno Barcsay (artist, centenary).

1216 Fekete and Animal Characters

2000. Youth Stamp. Birth Centenary of Istvan Fekete (writer).
4499 **1216** 60fo.+30fo. mult 2·20 1·70

1217 Hungarian Cultural Foundation and Exhibition Emblem

2000. "Hunphilex 2000" Stamp Exn, Budapest.
4500 **1217** 200fo.+100fo. mult 6·75 5·25

1218 Mihaly Vorosmarty (poet, bicentenary)

2000. Birth Anniversaries.
4501 **1218** 50fo. green and black 1·00 80
4502 - 50fo. brown and black 1·00 80
4503 - 50fo. green and black 1·00 80
4504 - 50fo. brown and black 1·00 80
4505 - 50fo. green and black 1·00 80
DESIGNS: No. 4502, Mari Jaszai (actress, 150th anniv); 4503, Sandor Marai (writer, centenary); 4504, Lujza Blaha (actress, 150th anniv); 4505, Lorinc Szabo (poet and translator, centenary).

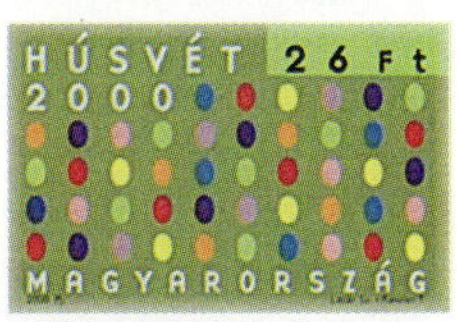

1219 Symbolic Easter Eggs

2000. Easter. Multicoloured.
4506 26fo. Type **1219** 50 40
4507 28fo. Decorated egg (29×31 mm) 60 45

2000. National Parks (3rd series). As T 1189. Mult.
4508 29fo. Ferto-Hansag National Park 65 55
4509 34fo. Duna-Drava National Park 75 60

1220 Airport Building and Lisunov Li-2 Airplane

2000. 50th Anniv of Ferihegy International Airport.
4510 **1220** 136fo. multicoloured 2·50 2·00

1221 Banded Wren

2000. Australian Animals. Multicoloured.
4511 26fo. Type **1221** 60 45
4512 28fo. Opossum 65 55
4513 83fo. Koala 1·70 1·30
4514 90fo. Red kangaroo 1·90 1·50
MS4515 107×70 mm. 110fo. Duck-billed platypus 3·00 3·00

1222 Jigsaw Puzzle

2000. Europa. Multicoloured.
4516 34fo. Type **1222** 2·75 2·10
4517 54fo. "Building Europe" 3·50 2·75

1223 Boat on Corinthian Canal, and Istvan Turr (engineer)

2000. "EXPO 2000" World's Fair, Hanover, Germany.
4518 **1223** 80fo. multicoloured 1·90 1·50

1224 Bisected and Complete 6k. Austrian Empire Stamps

2000. "WIPA 2000" International Stamp Exhibition, Vienna. 150th Anniv of Hungarian Stamps.
4519 **1224** 110fo. multicoloured 2·20 1·70

1225 Queen Gizella I

2000. Stamp Day. Showing decorative figures from Coronation Gown. Multicoloured.
4520 26fo. Type **1225** 50 40
4521 28fo. King Istvan I 60 45

1226 Balatonfured-Csopak

2000. Wine Grapes and Regions (4th series). Mult.
4522 29fo. Type **1226** 50 40

4523 34fo. Aszar-Neszmely 65 55

1227 Evangelical Church, Budapest

2000. Churches. Multicoloured.
4524 30fo. Type **1227** 65 55
4525 30fo. St. Anthony's Friars' Church, Eger 65 55
4526 30fo. Reformed Church, Takos 65 55
4527 30fo. Abbey Church, Jak 65 55

1228 Globe

2000. Millennium. Sheet 120×70 mm.
MS4528 **1228** 2000fo. multicoloured 37·00 37·00

1229 Boeing 767-200

2000. 90th Anniv of Hungarian Aviation.
4529 **1229** 120fo. multicoloured 3·75 3·00

1230 King Laszlo, 1077–95

2000. New Millennium (1st series). Multicoloured.
4530 50fo. Type **1230** 90 70
4531 50fo. Issue of Golden Bull (charter of rights for freemen) by King Andrew II, 1222 90 70
4532 50fo. St. Elizabeth and the Mongol invasion, 1241 90 70
4533 50fo. Reign of King Sigismund, 1395–1437 90 70
4534 50fo. Janos Hunyadi (regent) and Janos Kapisztran 90 70
4535 50fo. Reign of King Matthias, 1458–90 90 70
4536 50fo. The Crucifixion, Miklos Zrinyi (military commander) and Siege of Szigetvas, 1566 90 70
4537 50fo. Horseman, battle scenes and the recapture of Buda Castle and Gyor 90 70
4538 50fo. People outside Church, Transylvania 90 70
4539 50fo. Peter Pazmany (founder) and University, Budapest, 1635 90 70
Nos. 4530/4 and 4535/9 were issued together, se-tenant, forming a composite design.
See also Nos. 4585/**MS**4595.

1231 Detail of Coronation Gown

2000. "HUNPHILEX 2000" International Stamp Exhibition, Budapest. Multicoloured.
MS4540 93×72 mm. 200fo.+100fo. Type **1231** 7·25 7·25

1232 Dohany Utca Synagogue, Budapest

2000. Hungary–Israel Joint Issue.
4541 **1232** 120fo. multicoloured 2·20 1·80

1233 Mary and Jesus leaving Bethlehem

2000. Christmas. Multicoloured.
4542 26fo. Type **1233** 45 35
4543 28fo. Church (27×28 mm) 50 40
4544 29fo. Christmas tree (27×28 mm) 50 40
4545 34fo. Nativity scene on watch face (32×36 mm) 60 50

1234 Emblem and Writing Desk

2000. 50th Anniv of Convention on Human Rights.
4546 **1234** 50fo. multicoloured 1·50 1·20

1235 Rifle Shooting

2000. Olympic Games, Sydney. Multicoloured.
4547 30fo. Type **1235** 45 35
4548 40fo. Weightlifting 75 60
4549 80fo. Gymnastics 1·50 1·20
MS4550 85×63 mm. 120fo. Two-man kayak 3·00 3·00

1236 Eger Castle and Extract from Poem

2001. Youth Stamp. Centenary of Eclipse of the Crescent Moon (poem by Geza Gardonyi).
4551 **1236** 60fo.+30fo. mult 2·00 1·60

1237 Profiles

2001. European Year of Languages.
4552 **1237** 100fo. multicoloured 2·75 2·20

1238 Man blowing Trumpet

2001. Greetings Stamps. Multicoloured.
4553 36fo. Type **1238** 55 45
4554 36fo. Couple dancing 55 45

4555		36fo. Baby in cradle	55	45
4556		36fo. Clown	55	45
4557		36fo. Woman and child	55	45

1239 Ice-skater

2001

4558	**1239**	140fo. multicoloured	2·75	2·20

1240 Easter Eggs and Rabbit

2001. Easter.

4559	**1240**	28fo. multicoloured	95	75

2001. National Parks (4th series). As T 1189. Multicoloured.

4560		28fo. Upper Balaton National Park	60	50
4561		36fo. Koros-Maros National Park	65	55
4562		70fo. Duna-Ipoly National Park	1·30	1·10

1241 Mk 48 Diesel Locomotive, Lillafured State Forest Railway

2001. Light Railways. Multicoloured.

4563		31fo. Type **1241**	60	50
4564		36fo. 490 series steam locomotive, Keeskemet Light Railway	65	55
4565		100fo. 394 series steam locomotive, Szechenyi Railway Museum	2·00	1·60
4566		150fo. C50 diesel locomotive, Csomoder State Forest Railway	2·75	2·20

1242 Emblem and Vegetation

2001. Anniversaries. Multicoloured.

4567		70fo. Type **1242** (50th anniversaries of International Plant Protection Convention and European and Mediterranean Plant Protection Organization)	1·10	85
4568		80fo. Globe, people and emblem (50th anniv of United Nations High Commissioner for Refugees)	1·20	95

1243 Door Inlay, St. Adalbert Basilica

2001. Millenary of Archdiocese of Esztergom.

4569	**1243**	124fo. multicoloured	2·40	1·90

1244 Ringed Seal (*Phoca hispida*)

2001. Animals. Multicoloured.

4570		28fo. Type **1244**	55	45
4571		36fo. Wolf (*Canis lupus*)	65	55
4572		70fo. Herman's tortoise (*Testudo hermanni*)	1·20	95
4573		90fo. River kingfisher (*Alcedo atthis*)	1·60	1·30
MS4574		90×66 mm. 200fo. Red deer males (*Cervus elaphus*)	4·00	4·00

1245 Chest containing Water

2001. Europa. Water Resources. Multicoloured.

4575		36fo. Type **1245**	95	75
4576		90fo. Open globe filled with water	2·40	1·90

1246 1871 1k. Newspaper Stamp

2001. Stamp Day. 130th Anniv of Hungarian Stamps. Multicoloured.

4577		36fo. Type **1246**	65	55
4578		90fo. 1871 3k. stamp	1·50	1·20
MS4579		60×75 mm. 200fo.+40fo. "Pigeon Post" (Miklos Barabas) (39×49 mm)	4·75	4·75

1247 Players

2001. European Water Polo Championship, Budapest.

4580	**1247**	150fo. multicoloured	2·75	2·20

1248 Scout's Hats

2001. 4th European Conference of Former Scouts and Guides, Budapest.

4581	**1248**	150fo. multicoloured	2·75	2·20

1249 Drawing (Aladar Korosfoi-Kriesch)

2001. Art Anniversaries.

4582	**1249**	100fo. blue, mauve and lilac	2·00	1·60
4583	-	150fo. black and blue (49×21 mm)	2·75	2·20

DESIGNS—VERT: 100fo. Type **1249** (centenary of Godollo Artists' Colony). HORIZ: 150fo. Emblems representing different branches of the arts (centenary of FESZEK Club).

1250 Athletics Race

2001. World Youth Athletics Championship, Debrecen.

4584	**1250**	140fo. multicoloured	2·50	2·00

1251 Ferenc Rakovic and Ilona Zrinyi

2001. New Millennium (2nd series). Multicoloured.

4585		50fo. Type **1251**	80	65
4586		50fo. Terezia Maria and royal horse guard	80	65
4587		50fo. Istvan Szechenyi and Chain Bridge	80	65
4588		50fo. Newspaper headline and man on horseback	80	65
4589		50fo. Janos Arany, "The Solitary Cedar" (detail, Tivadar Csontvary Kosztka) and Parliament buildings	80	65
4590		50fo. First World War soldiers and map	80	65
4591		50fo. Mihaly Babits	80	65
4592		50fo. Chain Bridge and Bishop Vilmos Apor	80	65
4593		50fo. Tanks and soldiers (Revolution, 1956) and Zoltan Kodaly (composer)	80	65
4594		50fo. Young children and Millennium flag	80	65
MS4595		105×75 mm. 2001fo. Crown (39×31 mm)	33·00	33·00

1252 Pannonhalma-Sokoroalja

2001. Wine Grapes and Regions (5th series). Multicoloured.

4596		60fo. Type **1252**	1·10	85
4597		70fo. Balatonboglar	1·30	1·10

1253 Common Peacock (30 m mosaic)

2001. Guinness Record Attempt by Hungarian Post Office to Create World's Largest Mosaic from Used Postage Stamps.

4598	**1253**	10fo. multicoloured	40	30

1254 Bridge

2001. Reconstruction of Maria Valeria Bridge, Esztergom–Parkany.

4599	**1254**	36fo. multicoloured	80	65

1255 Angel and Decorations

2001. Christmas.

4600	**1255**	36fo. multicoloured	80	65

1256 1871 2k. Stamp and Emblem

2001. 150th Anniv of Hungarian Stamp Printing.

4601	**1256**	150fo. multicoloured	2·75	2·20

1257 Ice Hockey Player

2002. Winter Olympic Games, Salt Lake City, U.S.A.

4602	**1257**	160fo. multicoloured	3·00	2·40

1258 Soldiers fighting (Defence of Eger Castle)

2002. Youth Stamp. 450th Anniv of War with Ottoman Empire. Sheet 120×68 mm containing T 1258 and similar multicoloured designs.

MS4603		50fo. Type **1258**; 50fo. Istvan Losonczy and Turkish soldiers, Timisoara; 100fo. + 50fo. Soldiers and pages (Battle of Dregely Castle) (39×29 mm)	4·50	4·50

1259 Ordinary "Penny-farthing" Bicycle

2002. History of the Bicycle. Multicoloured.

4604		40fo. Type **1259**	80	65
4605		40fo. Tricycle, 1900s	80	65
4606		40fo. Karoly Iszer (chairman of Budapest Sport Club)	80	65
4607		40fo. Four-man cycle	80	65

1260 Easter Eggs

2002. Easter.

4608	**1260**	30fo. multicoloured	55	45

1261 Libelle

2002. Aviation. Multicoloured.

4609		180fo. Type **1261**	3·00	2·50
4610		190fo. Hungarian Lloyd Aircraft and Engine Factory biplane	3·25	2·75

1262 Lajos Kossuth

2002. Birth Anniversaries. Multicoloured.

4611	33fo. Type **1262** (statesman, bicentenary)	55	45
4612	134fo. Janos Bolyai (mathematician, bicentenary)	2·40	1·90
4613	150fo. Gyula Illyes (poet and writer, centenary)	2·50	2·00

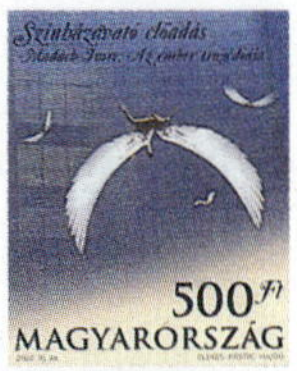

1263 Stage Set for *The Tragedy of Man* (Imre Madach)

2002. Inauguration of New National Theatre, Budapest. Sheet 85×60 mm.

MS4614	**1263** 500fo. multicoloured	8·75	8·75

1264 Parliament Building

2002. Centenary of Inauguration of Parliament Building. Sheet 97×67 mm.

MS4615	**1264** 500fo. multicoloured	8·75	8·75

1265 "S.O.S."

2002. Environmental Protection.

4616	**1265** 158fo. multicoloured	2·75	2·20

1266 Book of Psalms of King David

2002. Bicentenaries of Hungarian National Museum and National Szechenyi Library. Exhibits from the institutions. Multicoloured.

MS4617	150fo. Type **1266**; 150fo. Illumination from the second volume of King Matthias's Book of Rites; 150fo. Civil Guard of Pest Standard, 1848; 150fo. Holy water basin, 1903	10·50	10·50

1267 Deer

2002. Centenary of Halas Lace. Multicoloured.

4618	100fo. Type **1267**	1·90	1·50
4619	110fo. Swan	2·00	1·60
4620	140fo. Couple	2·50	2·00

1268 Wild Cat (*Felis sylvestris*)

2002. Fauna. Multicoloured.

4621	30fo. Type **1268**	55	45
4622	38fo. Crimean bull lizard (*Podarcis taurica*)	65	55
4623	110fo. Jay (*Garrulus glandarius*)	2·00	1·60
4624	160fo. Alpine longhorn beetle (*Rosalia alpina*)	3·00	2·40
MS4625	90×65 mm. 500fo. Sterlet (*Acipenser ruthenus*)	8·75	8·75

1269 Elephant

2002. Europa. Circus.

4626	**1269** 62fo. multicoloured	2·00	1·60

1270 Players

2002. World Cup Football Championship, Japan and South Korea.

4627	**1270** 160fo. multicoloured	3·00	2·40

2002. Greetings Stamps. Designs as Nos. 4448/9 but with change of face value.

4628	30fo. Common poppy	55	45
4629	38fo. Trumpet gentian	65	55

1271 Dog and Kennel (Etesd meg)

2002. Greetings Stamps. Self-adhesive. Multicoloured.

4630	38fo. Type **1271**	65	55
4631	38fo. Washing line (Megszuletem!)	65	55
4632	38fo. Present outside house (Sok boldogsagot!)	65	55
4633	38fo. Sofa and plant (Ontozdmeg...!)	65	55
4634	38fo. Man in room (Ennyire szeretlek!)	65	55

Nos. 4630/4 were issued together, se-tenant, forming a composite design.

1272 "Stone-pelter" (Karoly Ferenczy)

2002. Art. Multicoloured.

4635	62fo. Type **1272**	1·10	85
4636	188fo. "Ballerina" (statue, Ferenc Medgyessy) (vert)	3·50	2·75

1273 Buda Castle

2002. UNESCO World Heritage Sites. Multicoloured.

4637	100fo. Type **1273**	2·00	1·60
4638	150fo. Holloko, Nograd	2·75	2·20
4639	180fo. Aggtelek-Carst Caves (horiz)	3·25	2·75

1274 Facade and Statue

2002. Millenary of Kalocsa Archdiocese.

4640	**1274** 150fo. multicoloured	2·75	2·20

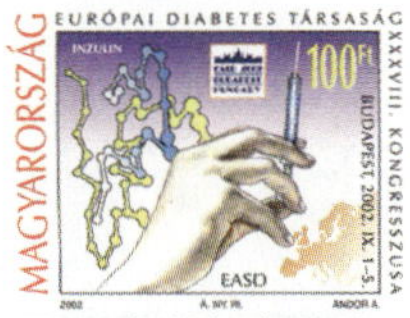

1275 Insulin Molecule, Hand holding Syringe and Map of Europe

2002. Medical Events in 2002. Multicoloured.

4641	100fo. Type **1275** (38th European Diabetes Association Congress)	1·70	1·40
4642	150fo. Arms, arrows and map of Europe (16th European Society of Elbow and Shoulder Surgeons Congress)	2·75	2·20

1276 "Pound Cake Madonna"

2002. 75th Anniv of Stamp Day. Birth Centenary of Margit Kovàacs (ceramicist). Multicoloured.

4643	33fo. Type **1276**	55	45
4644	38fo. "Family Photograph Album"	65	55
MS4645	86×72 mm. 400fo.+200fo. "St. George, The Dragon Slayer" (25×36 mm)	10·00	10·00

1277 "Adoration of the Magi"

2002. Christmas. Paintings by Erzsebet Udvardi. Multicoloured.

4646	30fo. Type **1277**	50	40
4647	38fo. "Bethelem"	65	50

1278 Gymnast

2002. World Gymnastics Championships, Debrecen.

4648	**1278** 160fo. multicoloured	2·50	2·10

1279 Rakoczi Mansion, Tekirdag

2002. Cultural Heritage. Multicoloured.

4649	40fo. Type **1279**	75	60
4650	110fo. Pasha Gazi Kasim Mosque, Pecs	2·00	1·70

Stamps in similar designs were issued by Turkey.

1280 John von Neuman

2003. Birth Anniversaries. Multicoloured.

4651	32fo. Type **1280** (computing pioneer) (centenary)	50	40
4652	40fo. Rezso Soo (botanist) (centenary)	75	60
4653	60fo. Karoly Zipernowsky (electrical engineer) (150th)	1·00	85

1281 Frankenthal Coffee Set

2003. Herend Porcelain. Sheet 138×71 mm containing T 1281 and similar vert designs. Multicoloured.

MS4654	150fo. Type **1281**; 150fo. Blue coffee pot, cup and saucer; 150fo. Tall vase; 150fo. Siang Noir shell bowl and jug	10·00	10·00

1282 Retreating Soldiers

2003. 60th Anniv of Second Royal Hungarian Army's Defeat at the River Don.

4655	**1282** 40fo. multicoloured	75	60

1283 Crucifixion

2003. Easter.

4656	**1283** 32fo. multicoloured	50	40

1284 Title Page

2003. Sport (1st issue). Centenary of "Nemzeti Sport" (sports magazine).

4657	**1284** 150fo. multicoloured	2·50	2·10

See also Nos. 4670 and 4673.

1285 Church

2003. Greetings Stamps. Multicoloured. Self-adhesive.

4658	40fo. Type **1285**	65	50
4659	40fo. Two flowers	65	50
4660	40fo. Flower	65	50
4661	40fo. Decorated eggs	65	50
4662	40fo. Candles in window and Christmas tree	65	50

1286 BMX Cyclist

2003. Youth Stamps. Extreme Sports. Multicoloured.

4663	100fo. Type **1286**	1·80	1·40
4664	100fo. Snowboarding	1·80	1·40
4665	100fo. Parachuting	1·80	1·40
4666	100fo. White water canoeing	2·50	2·10

1287 Rogner Hotel, Heviz

2003. Tourism. Spa Hotels. Multicoloured.

4667	110fo. Type **1287**	1·90	1·60
4668	120fo. Helia Hotel, Budapest	2·10	1·80

1288 Gerle 13 Aircraft, 1933

2003. Hungarian Aviation. Multicoloured.

4669	142fo. Type **1288**	2·50	2·10
4670	160fo. L-2 Roma, 1925	2·75	2·30

1289 *Columbia*

2003. Space Shuttle Columbia Memorial. Sheet 92×72 mm.

MS4671	**1289** 500fo. multicoloured	8·25	8·25

1290 Championship Emblem

2003. Sport (2nd issue). World Division I Ice Hockey Championship, Budapest.

4672	**1290**	110fo. multicoloured	1·90	1·60

1291 Stadium

2003. Sport (3rd issue). Budapest Sports Arena.

4673	**1291**	120fo. multicoloured	2·10	1·80

1292 Hand holding Quill Pen

2003. Signing of Treaty of Accession to the European Union. (1st Issue). Sheet 106×70 mm.

MS4674	**1292** 500fo. multicoloured	9·50	9·50

See also Nos. 4692/3, 4714, 4722 and **MS**4725.

1293 Police Motorcyclist

2003. Police Service.

4675	**1293**	65fo. multicoloured	1·10	95

1294 Statue of Seated Woman (Danubius fountain)

2003. Stamp Day. Multicoloured.

4676	35fo. Type **1294**	65	50
4677	40fo. Statue of seated woman (Danubius fountain) (different)	75	60
MS4678	81×60 mm. 400fo.+100fo. "Calvin Square" (Jozsef Molnar)	8·75	8·75

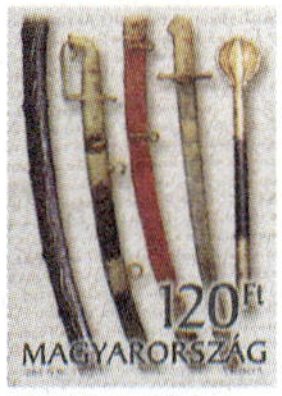

1295 Kuruc Sabre, Sword and Mace

2003. 300th Anniv of Rakoczi's War of Independence. Sheet 121×61 mm containing T 1295 and similar vert designs. Multicoloured.

MS4679	120fo. Type **1295**; 120fo. Coins; 120fo. Old National flag, pipes and drums; 120fo. Pistols and powder horn	8·25	8·25

1296 Steppe Polecat (*Mustela eversmanni*)

2003. Fauna. Multicoloured.

4680	30fo. Type **1296**	65	50
4681	38fo. Short-toed lark (*Calandrella brachydactyla*)	75	60
4682	110fo. European tree frog (*Hyla arborea*)	1·90	1·60
4683	160fo. European weatherfish (*Misgurnus fossilis*)	2·00	1·70
MS4684	90×65 mm. 500fo. Ladybird spider (*Eresus cinnaberinus*) (inscr "cinnabarinus")	8·75	8·75

1297 "Only Posters" (Istvaán Orosz)

2003. Europa. Poster Art.

4685	**1297**	65fo. red, yellow and black	1·90	1·60

1298 Bukkaljai

2003. Wine Grapes and Regions (6th series). Multicoloured.

4686	60fo. Type **1298**	1·00	85
4687	130fo. Balaton-felvideki	2·10	1·80

1299 King Ladislaus and Unknown Queen (image scaled to 46% of original size)

2003. King Ladislaus' Robe (11th-century). Sheet 108×70 mm.

MS4688	**1299** 300fo. multicoloured	5·00	5·00

1300 Bishop Gerard and Angel (sculpture, Imre Varga)

2003. Art. Multicoloured.

4689	32fo. Type **1300**	65	50
4690	60fo. "Roman Bridge at Mostar" (Tivadar Csontvary Kosztka) (horiz)	1·00	85

1301 Crowds and Anniversary Emblem

2003. 50th Anniv of People's Stadium. 50th Anniv of Hungarian Football Team's Victory over England. Sheet 103×68 mm containing T 1301 and similar horiz design. Multicoloured.

MS4691	250fo. Type **1301**; 250fo. Goal and players	8·75	8·75

1302 European Union Emblem as Clock Face

2003. Hungary's Accession to European Union (2nd issue). Multicoloured.

4692	115fo. Type **1302**	2·50	2·10
4693	130fo. As No. 4692 but with clock hands moved forward	3·25	2·50

1303 Fruit and Vegetables

2003. Nutrition.

4694	**1303**	120fo. multicoloured	1·90	1·60

1304 Feet and Cycle Wheel

2003. European Car-free Day.

4695	**1304**	150fo. multicoloured	2·50	2·10

1305 *Dactylorhiza fuchsia sooana*

2003. Birth Centenary of Rezso Soo (botanist).

4696	**1305**	44fo. multicoloured	75	60

1306 The Illuminated Chronicle

2003. Ancient Books. Multicoloured.

4697	44fo. Type **1306**	75	60
4698	44fo. The Book of Zhou Rites	75	60

Stamps of a similar design were issued by Republic of China.

1307 Ferenc Deak

2003. 200th Birth Anniv of Ferenc Deak (politician). Sheet 99×68 mm.

MS4699	**1307** 500fo. multicoloured	8·75	8·75

1308 Reindeer

2003. Christmas. Multicoloured.

4700	35fo. Type **1308**	65	50
4701	44fo. Angels, tree and house	75	60

1309 Globe and Computer Screen

2003. World Science Forum, Budapest. Sheet 87×62 mm.

MS4702	**1309** 500fo. multicoloured	8·75	8·75

1310 Jozsef Bajza

2004. Birth Anniversaries. Multicoloured.

4703	40fo. Balint Balassi (writer) (150th)	65	50
4704	44fo. Type **1310** (writer) (200th)	75	60

4705 80fo. Andras Janos Segner (mathematician) (300th) 1·40 1·10

1311 "Muki" Diesel Engine, Kemence Railway Museum

2004. Light Railways. Multicoloured.
4706 120fo. Type **1311** 2·00 1·70
4707 150fo. "Rezet" steam engine, Cemenc State Forest Railway 2·50 2·10

1312 Masks and Bonfire (Busojaras)

2004. Festivals. Sheet 160×45 mm containing T 1312 and similar horiz designs. Multicoloured.
MS4708 60fo.×4 Type **1312**; Flowers (Viragkarneval); Grapes and wine glass (Borfesztival); Trumpet, scroll and drum (Karnevalok) 4·00 4·00

1313 Puli

2004. Youth Stamps. Dogs. Sheet 140×70 mm containing T 1313 and similar vert designs.
MS4709 100fo. Type **1313**; 100fo. Greyhound; 100fo. Mudi; 100fo.+50fo. Vizsla 7·00 7·00

1314 "e"

2004. European Information Technology Ministerial Conference, Budapest.
4710 40fo. Type **1314** (blue and light blue) 65 50
4711 40fo. "e" (purple and yellow) 65 50
4712 40fo. "e" (orange and pink) 65 50
4713 40fo. "e" (green and red) 65 50

1315 Clock-face

2004. Hungary's Accession to European Union (3rd issue).
4714 **1315** 100fo. multicoloured 2·50 2·10

1316 Athletes

2004. 10th World Indoor Athletics Championship, Budapest.
4715 **1316** 120fo. multicoloured 1·30 1·00

1317 Rabbit and Egg

2004. Easter.
4716 **1317** 48fo. multicoloured 2·00 1·70

1318 Buk Hotel, Bukfurdo

2004. Tourism. Spa Hotels. Multicoloured.
4717 120fo. Type **1318** 2·00 1·70
4718 150fo. Aqua Sol Hotel, Hajdus-zoboszlo 2·50 2·10

1319 St. Martin's Monastery, Pannonia

2004. UNESCO World Heritage Sites. Multicoloured.
4719 150fo. Type **1319** 2·50 2·10
4720 170fo. Tern, cattle and horses, Hortobagy National Park (horiz) 2·75 2·30

1320 Stone inscribed with Star of David

2004. 60th Anniv of Hungarian Holocaust.
4721 **1320** 160fo. multicoloured 2·50 2·10

1321 Clock-face

2004. Hungary's Accession to European Union (4th issue).
4722 **1321** 190fo. multicoloured 4·50 3·50

1322 Twin-handled Vase

2004. 150th Anniv of Zsolnay Porcelain Factory, Pecs. Sheet 138×69 mm containing T 1322 and similar vert designs. Multicoloured.
MS4723 160fo.×4, Type **1322**; Vase surmounted by horseman and small decorative vase; Vase with medieval silk design; "Autumn" mocha set 10·00 10·00

1323 Police Launch

2004. Police Day.
4724 **1323** 48fo. multicoloured 75 60

1324 Stars

2004. Hungary's Accession to European Union (5th issue). Sheet 105×71 mm.
MS4725 **1324** 500fo. multicoloured 8·75 8·75

1325 Embroidered Flowers

2004. Enlargement of European Union.
4726 120fo. Type **1325** 1·90 1·60
4727 150fo. New members' flags and stars 2·50 2·10

1326 Mole Rat (*Nannospalax leucodon*)

2004. Fauna. Multicoloured.
4728 48fo. Type **1326** 75 60
4729 65fo. Bearded tit (*Panurus biarmucus*) 1·00 85
4730 90fo. Snake-eyed skink (*Ablepharus kitaibelii fitzingeri*) 1·50 1·20
4731 120fo. Sturgeon (*Huso huso*) 2·00 1·70
MS4732 90×65 mm. 500fo. *Anthaxia hungarica* 8·25 8·25

1327 "Walls and Doors" (Erzsebet Schaar)

2004. Stamp Day. Art. Multicoloured.
4733 48fo. Type **1327** 75 60
4734 65fo. "Translucent Red Circle" (Tihamer Gyarmathy) 1·00 85
MS4735 71×71 mm. 400fo.+200fo. "Wasp King" (Bela Kondor) (41×32 mm) 9·50 9·50

1328 Hand holding Envelope over Ballot Box

2004. European Elections.
4736 **1328** 150fo. multicoloured 2·50 2·10

1329 People in Countryside

2004. Europa. Holidays.
4737 **1329** 160fo. multicoloured 2·50 2·10

1330 Ball and Turf as Slice of Cake

2004. Centenary of FIFA (Federation Internationale de Football Association).
4738 **1330** 100fo. multicoloured 1·60 1·30

1331 Basilica, Mariazell

2004. Catholics' Day. Sheet 110×160 mm containing T 1331 and similar vert designs. Multicoloured.
MS4739 100fo.×6, Type **1331**; Magna Mater Austriae (Romanesque statue) (Chapel of Grace, Basilica, Mariazell); Madonna (statue); Canopied statue of Mary, Celldomolk; Madonna (painting), Mariazell; Mary of Kiscell, Obuda parish 10·00 10·00

1332 Internet Icons

2004. Information Technology.
4740 **1332** 120fo. multicoloured 1·90 1·60

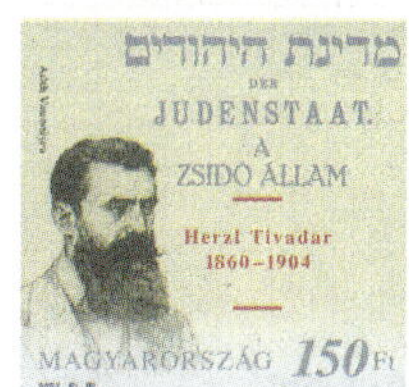

1333 Theodor Herzl

2004. Death Centenary of Theodor Herzl (writer and Zionist pioneer).
4741 **1333** 150fo. multicoloured 2·50 2·10

A stamp of the same design was issued by Israel and Austria.

1334 Rowers

2004. Olympic Games, Athens 2004. Multicoloured.
4742 90fo. Type **1334** 1·50 1·20
4743 130fo. Ball players 2·10 1·80
4744 150fo. Runners 2·50 2·10

1335 Two Dancers

2004. 3rd Folkloriada Festival. Showing folk dancers. Multicoloured.
4745 65fo. Type **1335** 1·10 95
4746 65fo. As No. 4745 with colour change 1·10 95

4747	65fo. Back view of dancer	1·10	95
4748	65fo. As No. 4747 with colour change	1·10	95
4749	65fo. Dancer facing right	1·10	95
4750	65fo. Dancer's skirt	1·10	95
4751	65fo. Back view of dancer facing right	1·10	95
4752	65fo. Two dancers (different)	1·10	95
4753	65fo. Dancer's skirt (different)	1·10	95
4754	65fo. Dancer's feet	1·10	95

1336 Rook and "A sakkjatek tobbnyire"

2004. History of Hungarian Chess. Each stamp either brown and black or flesh and black, the colours alternating to simulate the squares on a chess board (first three words of inscription given).

4755	50fo. Type **1336**	75	60
4756	50fo. "A magyaroknak a"	75	60
4757	50fo. Bishop and "A Magyar tortenelem"	75	60
4758	50fo. King and "A Magyar sakkirodalom"	75	60
4759	50fo. Queen and "A XVIII szazadban"	75	60
4760	50fo. "Az elso magyar"	75	60
4761	50fo. Knight and "Az 1839-ben megalakult"	75	60
4762	50fo. Rook and "A XIX szazad"	75	60
4763	50fo. Pawn and "A Magyar sakkfeladvanyszerzok"	75	60
4764	50fo. Pawn and "Harom, a XIX. szazad"	75	60
4765	50fo. Pawn and "Maroczy Geza 1870"	75	60
4766	50fo. Pawn and "Ket kivalo sakkozonk"	75	60
4767	50fo. Bishop and "A levelezesi sakkozas"	75	60
4768	50fo. Pawn and "A sakkelet megszervezodese"	75	60
4769	50fo. Pawn and "A ferfi orszagos"	75	60
4770	50fo. Pawn and "A II. vilaghaboru utan sokaig"	75	60
4771	50fo. "A noi sakkozas"	75	60
4772	50fo. "1958-ban mar a 10"	75	60
4773	50fo. Knight and "A sakkozok osszefogasanak"	75	60
4774	50fo. "1951-ben indult a"	75	60
4775	50fo. "A XX. szazadnak"	75	60
4776	50fo. "A II. vilaghaboru utan feladvany"	75	60
4777	50fo. "A XX. szazadban"	75	60
4778	50fo. "A XX. szazad"	75	60
4779	50fo. "A vilag sakkeletet"	75	60
4780	50fo. "A ket vilaghaboru kozott"	75	60
4781	50fo. "A haboru utan"	75	60
4782	50fo. "A ferfi sakkolimpian"	75	60
4783	50fo. Pawn and "A nemzetek kozti"	75	60
4784	50fo. "1957-ben a hollandiai"	75	60
4785	50fo. "A noi sakkolimpiakon"	75	60
4786	50fo. "A XIX es XX"	75	60
4787	50fo. "Sakkirodalom nelkul sem"	75	60
4788	50fo. "A XX. Szazad magyar"	75	60
4789	50fo. Bishop and "A szeles sakkozo"	75	60
4790	50fo. "A Magyar Sakkszovetseg"	75	60
4791	50fo. Pawn and "Barcza Gedeon 1911"	75	60
4792	50fo. "Szabo Laszlo 1917."	75	60
4793	50fo. "Portisch Lajos 1937"	75	60
4794	50fo. "Adorjan Andras "1968-ig"	75	60
4795	50fo. "Sax Gyula 1951"	75	60
4796	50fo. "Ribli Zoltan 1951"	75	60
4797	50fo. "Leko peter1979"	75	60
4798	50fo. "Almasi Zoltan 1976"	75	60
4799	50fo. "Bilek Istvan 1932"	75	60
4800	50fo. Knight and "A ket vilaghaboru kozti"	75	60
4801	50fo. "Az olimpiakon tobbszor"	75	60
4802	50fo. "Sok kivalo magyar"	75	60
4803	50fo. Pawn and "Polgar Zsuzsa Budapesten 1969"	75	60
4804	50fo. Pawn and "Polgar Judit Budapesten 1976"	75	60
4805	50fo. Pawn and "Polgar Zsofia 1974"	75	60
4806	50fo. Pawn and "Langos Jozsa 1911"	75	60
4807	50fo. "Veroci Zsuzsa 1949"	75	60
4808	50fo. Pawn and "Ivanka Maria 1950"	75	60
4809	50fo. Pawn and "Madl Ildiko 1969"	75	60
4810	50fo. Pawn and "Orszagos bajnoki cimmel"	75	60
4811	50fo. Rook and "Sakkozasunk a XXI."	75	60
4812	50fo. Knight and "A sakkozassal valo kapcsolat"	75	60
4813	50fo. Bishop and "A magyar sakkazas"	75	60
4814	50fo. King and "Minden osszefoglalo munka"	75	60
4815	50fo. Queen and "A jelen munkaban"	75	60
4816	50fo. "Elek Ferenc 1918—1989"	75	60
4817	50fo. "Katko (Regos) Imre 1904—1948"	75	60
4818	50fo. "grof Pongracz Arnold 1810—1890"	75	60

Nos. 4755/818 were issued in se-tenant sheets of 64 stamps, each stamp bearing an inscription describing part of the history of Hungarian chess. The stamps were arranged to simulate the "Hungarian Defence" opening gambit with the rows marked either 1—8 vertically or a—h horizontally in the margin.

2004. Hungary's Accession to the European Union (6th issue). Sheet 84×72 mm containing horiz designs as T 1302, 1315 and 1321. Multicoloured.

MS4819	100fo.×4, As Nos. 4692/3; As No. 4714; As No. 4722	7·50	7·50

1337 Istvan Bocskai, Swords and Coins

2004. 400th Anniv of Bocskai's War of Independence.

4820	**1337**	120fo. multicoloured	2·00	1·70

1338 INTOSAI Emblem

2004. 28th International Organization of Supreme Audit Institutions (INTOSAI) Conference, Budapest.

4821	**1338**	150fo. multicoloured	2·50	2·10

2004. Christmas (1st issue). Painting by Erzsebet Udvardi. As T 1227. Multicoloured.

4822	48fo. As No. 4647	90	70

1339 Cherub

2004. Christmas (2nd issue). Multicoloured.

4823	48fo. Type **1339**	75	60
4824	48fo. Two cherubs	75	60
4825	48fo. Cherub seated with clasped hands	75	60
4826	48fo. Cherub with left hand raised	75	60
4827	48fo. Cherub facing left	75	60
4828	48fo. Cherub seated looking up	75	60

1340 Biscuits

2004. Christmas (3rd issue). Biscuits. Multicoloured.

4829–4848	48fo.×20 Type **1340** and 19 other different designs showing iced biscuits	7·50	7·50

1341 Green Triangles and Bauble at Right

2004. Christmas (4th issue). Glass Decorations. Multicoloured.

4849	48fo. Type **1341**	75	60
4850	48fo. As No. 4849 but design reversed	75	60
4851	48fo. Bauble at left and blue triangles	75	60
4852	48fo. As No. 4851 but design reversed	75	60
4853	48fo. Bauble at left, red square and green triangles	75	60
4854	48fo. As No. 4853 but design reversed	75	60
4855	48fo. Blue triangle, yellow rectangle, green and blue triangles	75	60
4856	48fo. As No. 4855 but design reversed	75	60
4857	48fo. As Type 1341 but smaller bauble	75	60
4858	48fo. As No. 4857 but with design reversed	75	60

1342 Sandor Csoma (statue), Aurel Stein and Library Hungarian Academy of Science

2004. Hungarian Science. Sandor Korosi Csoma (Tibetan scholar) and Aurel Stein (archaeologist) Commemoration.

4859	**1342**	80fo. multicoloured	1·40	1·10

1343 Pulsatilla and Valley

2004. Natura 2000 (habitat protection).

4860	**1343**	100fo. multicoloured	1·80	1·40

1344 Capricorn

2005. Western Zodiac. Multicoloured.

4861	50fo. Type **1344**	80	65
4862	50fo. Aquarius	80	65
4863	50fo. Pisces	80	65
4864	50fo. Aries	80	65
4865	50fo. Taurus	80	65
4866	50fo. Gemini	80	65
4867	50fo. Cancer	80	65
4868	50fo. Leo	80	65
4869	50fo. Virgo	80	65
4870	50fo. Libra	80	65
4871	50fo. Scorpio	80	65
4872	50fo. Sagittarius	80	65

1345 Seal-point Siamese

2005. Youth Philately. Cats. Sheet 150×50 mm containing T 1345 and similar horiz designs. Multicoloured.

MS4873	100fo. Type **1345**; 100fo. Maine coon; 100fo. White longhair; 100fo.+50fo. Silver tabby	7·50	7·50

The surcharge was for the promotion of philately.

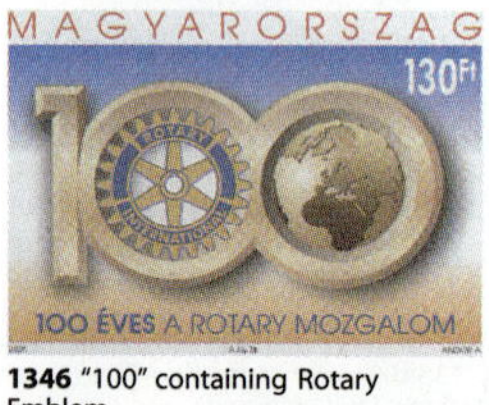

1346 "100" containing Rotary Emblem

2005. Centenary of Rotary International (charitable organization).

4874	**1346**	130fo. multicoloured	2·10	1·80

1347 Rabbit

2005. Easter.

4875	**1347**	50fo. multicoloured	90	70

1348 Weightlifter

2005. Centenary of International Weightlifting Federation.

4876	**1348**	170fo. multicoloured	2·75	2·30

1349 Sandor Iharos

2005. Sandor Iharos (World Champion athlete) Commemoration.

4877	**1349**	90fo. multicoloured	1·50	1·20

1350 Auditorium

2005. Opening of Palace of Arts. Sheet 90×65 mm.

MS4878	**1350**	500fo. multicoloured	8·25	8·25

1351 Figure on Stage

2005. World Theatre Meeting.

4879	**1351**	50fo. multicoloured	90	70

1352 Map and Compass

2005. Corporate Greeting Stamps. Multicoloured.

4880	50fo. Type **1352**	90	70
4881	50fo. Compass at left and map	90	70

1353 Jeno Rejto (writer)

2005. Birth Centenaries. Multicoloured.

4882	90fo. Type **1353**	1·50	1·20
4883	140fo. Attila Jozsef (poet)	2·30	1·90

1354 Police Helicopter

2005. Police Day.

4884	**1354**	85fo. multicoloured	1·40	1·10

1355 "1945", Map and Dove

2005. 60th Anniv of End of World War II.
4885 **1355** 150fo. multicoloured 2·50 2·10

1356 Hungarian Grey Bull

2005. Traditional Farm Breeds. Multicoloured.
4886 50fo. Type **1356** 90 70
4887 70fo. Hungarian spotted cow 1·10 95
4888 100fo. Racka sheep 1·60 1·30
4889 110fo. Cigaja sheep 1·90 1·60
MS4890 90×65 mm. 500fo. Mangalica pigs 8·25 8·25

1357 Chicken Paprika and Dumplings

2005. Europa. Gastronomy. Multicoloured.
4891 160fo. Type **1357** 2·75 2·30
4892 160fo. As No. 4891 but flowers position changed 2·75 2·30
MS4893 132×70 mm. Nos. 4891/2, each×2 11·00 11·00

1358 Pope John Paul II

2005. Pope John Paul II Commemoration. Sheet 110×65 mm.
MS4894 **1358** 500fo. multicoloured 8·25 8·25

1359 Vajdahunyad Castle

2005. Tourism. Budapest. Sheet 150×86 mm containing T 1359 and similar multicoloured designs.
MS4895 100fo.×5, Type **1359**; Saxlehner Palace; Ethnographic museum (horiz); "Reversed Madonna" stamp and printing block (horiz); Sandor Palace (horiz) 8·25 8·25

1360 Jak Church

2005
4896 **1360** 110fo. multicoloured 1·90 1·60

1361 Pintes Grapes, Zala Region

2005. Wine Grapes and Regions (7th series). Multicoloured.
4897 120fo. Type **1361** 2·00 1·70
4898 140fo. Kunleany grapes, Csongrad 2·40 2·00

1362 St. Stephen (statue)

2005. Centenary of St. Stephen's Basilica, Budapest. Sheet 90×67 mm.
MS4899 **1362** 500fo. multicoloured 8·25 8·25

1363 Soyuz 36 Spacecraft

2005. 25th Anniv of Hungarian Cosmonaut Bertalan Farkas' Spaceflight.
4900 **1363** 130fo. multicoloured 2·30 1·90

2005. Stamp Day. Hungarian Formula 1 Grand Prix. Multicoloured.
4901 50fo. Type **1364** 90 70
4901a 50fo. Hungaroring race track 1·00 85
4902 90fo. Car and chequered flag 1·50 1·20
MS4903 80×60 mm. 500fo.+200fo. Hungaroring race track 11·50 11·50

1365 St. Thomas

2005. Holy Crown of Hungary (1st issue). Sheet 90×140 mm containing T 1365 and similar vert designs showing panels from the crown. Multicoloured.
MS4904 80×60 mm. 100fo.×5, Type **1365**; Geza I; Emperor Michael Ducas; Emperor Constantine; Jesus Christ; 500fo. Holy Crown (30×36 mm) 16·00 16·00
See also No. **MS**4971 and **MS**5077.

1366 Post Car

2005. Centenary of First Postal Motor Vehicle.
4905 **1366** 50fo. multicoloured 90 70

1367 Recycling Bins

2005. Waste Management.
4906 **1367** 140fo. multicoloured 2·30 1·90

1368 Wrestlers

2005. World Wrestling Championships, Budapest.
4907 **1368** 150fo. multicoloured 2·40 2·00

1369 Woman

2005. Breast Cancer Awareness Campaign.
4908 **1369** 90fo.+50fo. multicoloured 2·30 1·90
No. 4908 is as Type **2342** of USA. The premium was for the benefit of the National Oncology Institute.

1370 Ferenc Farkas

2005. Birth Centenary of Ferenc Farkas (composer).
4909 **1370** 100fo. multicoloured 1·60 1·30

1371 Emblem

2005. World Science Forum, Budapest.
4910 **1371** 120fo. deep green, green and black 2·00 1·70

1372 Star and Three Wise Men

2005. Christmas (1st issue).
4911 **1372** 50fo. ultramarine and silver 90 70

1373 Candle

2005. Christmas (2nd issue). Multicoloured. Self-adhesive.
4912 50fo. Type **1373** 90 70
4913 50fo. Apple 90 70
4914 50fo. Heart 90 70
4915 50fo. Teddy bear 90 70
Nos. 4912/15 were issued together, se-tenant, forming a composite design.

1374 Pencils as "125"

2005. 125th Anniv of Craft and Design University.
4916 **1374** 90fo. multicoloured 1·50 1·20

1375 Building and Grounds

2005. House of the Future (science museum).
4916a **1375** 100fo. multicoloured 1·80 1·40

1376 Tape Machine and Satellite Dish

2006. 125th Anniv of News Agency.
4916b **1376** 90fo. multicoloured 1·60 1·30

1377 Maps of Italy on Skis

2006. Winter Olympic Games, Turin.
4917 **1377** 200fo. multicoloured 2·50 2·10

1378 4th-Century Chapel and Tomb, Christian Necropolis, Pecs (Sopiane)

2006. World Heritage Sites. Multicoloured.
4918 52fo. Type **1378** 75 60
4919 90fo. Cliffs and town, Ferto-Neusiedler Lake (horiz) 1·40 1·10

1379 Boeing 767-200ER (1993)

2006. Aviation. Multicoloured.
4920 120fo. Type **1379** 1·80 1·40
4921 140fo. Lockheed Sirius 8A (1931) 2·00 1·70

1380 Crucifix

2006. Easter.
4922 **1380** 52fo. multicoloured 75 60

1381 Circle of Stylized Figures and Football

2006. UEFA (Union of European Football Associations) Congress, Budapest.

4923 **1381** 170fo. multicoloured 2·50 2·10

1382 Sandor Legrady

2006. Birth Centenary of Sandor Legrady (artist).

4924 **1382** 75fo. multicoloured 1·10 95

1383

2006. Mrs. Ilona Savsarine-Paulik (Paralympics table tennis champion) Commemoration.

4925 **1383** 185fo. multicoloured 2·75 2·30

1384 Laslo Detre

2006. Birth Centenary of Laslo Detre (astronomer).

4926 **1384** 185fo. multicoloured 3·25 2·50

1385 Transmitter

2006. Wi-Fi (wireless internet connection).

4927 **1385** 240fo. multicoloured 3·50 3·00

1386 Pink Rose

2006. Greetings Stamps (1st issue). Flowers. Multicoloured.

4928 52fo. Type **1386** 75 60
4929 52fo. Cream rose with pink edge 75 60
4930 52fo. Yellow rose 75 60
4931 52fo. Orchid 75 60
4932 52fo. Tulips 75 60
4933 52fo. Gerbera 75 60
4934 52fo. Rose 75 60
4935 52fo. Lily 75 60

See also Nos. 4945/52, 4988/5019 and 5038/72.

1387 Shagya Arab

2006. Hungarian Horses. Multicoloured.

4936 75fo. Type **1387** 1·00 85
4937 90fo. Mezohegyes half-bred 1·30 1·00
4938 140fo. Gidran 2·00 1·70
4939 160fo. Noniusz 2·40 2·00
MS4940 95×70 mm. 200fo.×3, Hucul; Lipizzaner; Kisber half-bred 9·00 9·00

1388 Janos Hunyadi (statue) (Ede Margo)

2006. 550th Anniv of Battle of Belgrade.

4941 **1388** 120fo. multicoloured 1·80 1·40

1389 Ferenc Szisz's Renault Race Car

2006. Youth Welfare. Centenary of Ferenc Szisz's Victory in Inaugural Grand Prix Motor Race.

4942 **1389** 120fo.+50fo. multicoloured 2·50 2·10

1390 Goalkeeper

2006. World Cup Football Championship, Germany.

4943 **1390** 170fo. multicoloured 2·50 2·10

1391 Faces as Flower Petals

2006. Europa. Integration.

4944 **1391** 190fo. multicoloured 3·00 2·40

No. 4944 was issued in sheetlets of four stamps with each stamp rotated at 90 degrees to the previous one, giving a composite design of a flower.

1392 Rings and butterfly

2006. Greetings Stamps (2nd issue). Multicoloured.

4945 52fo. Type **1392** 75 60
4946 52fo. Rose and butterfly 75 60
4947 52fo. Dummy 75 60
4948 52fo. Duck 75 60
4949 52fo. Blue booties 75 60
4950 52fo. Pink booties 75 60
4951 90fo. Orange rose 75 60
4952 90fo. Pink flowers 75 60

1393 George Enescu

2006. Composers' 125th Birth Anniversaries. Multicoloured.

4953 90fo. Type **1393** 1·30 1·00
4954 90fo. Bela Bartok 1·30 1·00

Stamps of a similar design were issued by Romania.

1394 Base Clef as Swan

2006. MISKOLC International Music Festival.

4955 **1394** 190fo. multicoloured 2·75 2·30

1395 Prudence and Temperance (frescos)

2006. Stamp Day. Multicoloured.

4956 52fo. Type **1395** 75 60
4957 52fo. Fortitude and Justice (frescos) 75 60
MS4958 101×71 mm. 400fo.+200fo. Iconostasis, Szentendre Cathedral 8·75 8·75

Nos. 4956/7 were issued together, se-tenant, forming a composite design of "The Four Virtues".

1396 "Madonna and Child with the Infant St John" (Esterhazy Madonna) (Raphael)

2006. Centenary of Museum of Art. Multicoloured.

4959 200fo. Type **1396** 3·00 2·50
4960 200fo. "Mary Magdalene" (El Greco) 3·00 2·50
4961 200fo. Equestrian statue (Leonardo da Vinci) (horiz) 3·00 2·50
4962 200fo. "Three Fishing Boats" (Claude Monet) (horiz) 3·00 2·50

1397 Emblem and Falcon

2006. Border Guards.

4963 **1397** 170fo. multicoloured 2·40 2·10

1398 Diving and Synchronised Swimming

2006. European Swimming Championship, Budapest. Multicoloured.

4964 90fo. Type **1398** 1·30 1·10
4965 180fo. Swimmers in open water 2·50 2·20

1399 "Child with Model Aircraft" (Laszlo Feher)

2006. Art. Multicoloured.

4966 120fo. Type **1399** 1·70 1·40
4967 140fo. "Circle Dance" (sculpture) (Istvan Haraszty) (vert) 1·90 1·70
4968 160fo. "Aequilibrium" (tapestry picture) (Zsuzsa Pereli) (vert) 2·20 1·90

1400 Race Car

2006. 20th Anniv of Hungaroring.

4969 **1400** 75fo. multicoloured 1·10 95

1401 Mandrill

2006. 140th Anniv of Budapest Zoological and Botanical Gardens. Sheet 105×67 mm.

MS4970 **1401** 500fo. multicoloured 7·00 7·00

2006. Holy Crown of Hungary (2nd issue). Sheet 141×104 mm containing vert designs as T 1365 showing panels from the crown. Multicoloured.

MS4971 100fo.×7, John; Andrew; Peter; God the Creator; Paul; Philip; Jacob 10·00 10·00

The stamps of **MS**4971 are arranged in the shape of a cross.

1402 Building Facade

2006. 150th Anniv of Consecration of Esztergom Basilica. Sheet 94×69 mm.

MS4972 **1402** 500fo. multicoloured 7·00 7·00

1403 Flag

2006. 50th Anniv of Uprising. Sheet 90×65 mm.

MS4973 **1403** 500fo. multicoloured 7·00 7·00

1404 The Nativity

2006. Christmas.

4974 **1404** 52fo. multicoloured 70 60

1405 Laszlo Papp (boxing gold medallist)

2006. 50th Anniv of Olympic Games, Melbourne. Sheet 100×65 mm.

MS4975 **1405** 500fo. multicoloured 7·00 7·00

1406 Red Cross and Flag

2006. 125th Anniv of Hungarian Red Cross.

4976 **1406** 100fo. multicoloured 1·40 1·20

1407 Laika

2007. 50th Anniv of Launch of First Man-made Satellite.
4977 **1407** 350fo. multicoloured 4·75 4·75

1408 Boy dousing Girl with Scented Water

2007. Easter.
4978 **1408** 62fo. multicoloured 85 70

1409 Couple

2007. Rural Life.
4979 **1409** 62fo. olive and black 85 70
4980 - 95fo. purple and black 1·30 1·10
4981 - 242fo. green and black 3·50 3·00
DESIGNS: 62fo.Type **1409**; 95fo. Woman with fowl; 242fo. Woman cooking over open fire.

1410 Janos Ferencsik (composer)

2007. Anniversaries.
4982 **1410** 107fo. deep lilac, lilac and blue 1·40 1·20
4983 - 135fo. olive, green and black 1·90 1·70
DESIGNS: 107fo.Type **1410** (birth centenary); 135fo. Count Lajos Batthyany (leader of first independent government) (birth bicentenary).

1411 Arms and Building

2007. 140th Anniv of Customs and Finance Guard.
4984 **1411** 180fo. multicoloured 2·40 2·10

1412 Ferenc Molnar (author)

2007. Centenary of The Boys of Paul Street (novel by Ferenc Molnar). Sheet 121×60 mm containing T 1412 and similar vert designs. Multicoloured.
MS4985 160fo. Type **1412**; 160fo.Nemcsek's certificate; 160fo.+30fo. Boy in red shirt fighting; 160fo.+30fo. Boy in green shirt fighting 9·50 9·50
The stamps and margins of **MS**4985 form a composite design, with the two central 160fo.+30fo. stamps forming a design of two boys fighting with sticks.
The premium was for the benefit for Youth Philately.

1413 John Sigismund, Prince of Transylvania

2007. Anniversaries. Multicoloured.
4986 210fo. Type **1413** (450th anniv of Diet of Torda) 2·75 2·40
4987 230fo. Ferenc Rakoczi II (300th anniv of Diet of Maros-vasarhely) 3·25 2·75

1414 Air Balloons

2007. Greetings Stamps (3rd issue). Graduation. Multicoloured.
4988 (62fo.) Belfold Type **1414** 70 60
4989 (62fo.) Belfold Student holding balloon, table of books and air balloon 70 60
4990 (62fo.) Belfold Mortar board, air balloon and student 70 60
4991 (62fo.) Belfold Three students and air balloon 70 60
4992 (62fo.) Belfold Student in basket of air balloon, student holding balloon and two students standing on books 70 60
4993 (62fo.) Belfold Student carrying portfolio 70 60
4994 (62fo.) Belfold Certificate and students standing on books 70 60
4995 (62fo.) Belfold Certificate enlarged and lower part of student's gown 70 60
4996 (62fo.) Belfold Three students on path 70 60
4997 (62fo.) Belfold Table of books, certificate, path and ink well 70 60
4998 (62fo.) Belfold Two students on path 70 60
4999 (62fo.) Belfold Ink well and three books 70 60
5000 (62fo.) Belfold Student holding magnifier facing right 70 60
5001 (62fo.) Belfold Student holding magnifier facing left 70 60
5002 (62fo.) Belfold Certificate enlarged 70 60
5003 (62fo.) Belfold Student carrying portfolio and table of books 70 60
5004 (62fo.) Belfold Table of books, certificate and smaller inkwell 70 60
5005 (62fo.) Belfold Table of books and certificate enlarged 70 60
5006 (62fo.) Belfold Inkwell and student 70 60
5007 (62fo.) Belfold Certificate and student's upper body 70 60
5008 (62fo.) Belfold Sailor suited arm and hand facing right 70 60
5009 (62fo.) Belfold Elbow, hand and elbow facing right 70 60
5010 (62fo.) Belfold Hand and arm facing right 70 60
5011 (62fo.) Belfold Hand on shoulder facing right 70 60
5012 (62fo.) Belfold Hand on shoulder facing left 70 60
5013 (62fo.) Belfold Hand and arm facing left 70 60
5014 (62fo.) Belfold Elbow, hand and elbow facing left 70 60
5015 (62fo.) Belfold Sailor suited arm and hand facing left 70 60
5016 (62fo.) Belfold Quill, ink bottle and book 70 60
5017 (62fo.) Belfold Certificate and mortar board 70 60
5018 (95fo.) Belfold Elsobbsegi Sailor suited arm 1·20 1·00
5019 (95fo.) Belfold Elsobbsegi Rose, certificate and mortar board 1·20 1·00
Nos. 4988/5017 were for use on domestic mail and were initially sold at 62fo.
Nos. 5018/5019 were for use on priority domestic mail and were initially sold at 95fo.

1415 St. Elisabeth tending the Sick

2007. Stamp Day. Saints' Anniversaries Multicoloured.
5021 62fo. Type **1415** (800th birth anniv) 70 60
5022 95fo. St Elizabeth giving alms 1·20 1·00
MS5023 74×60 mm. 500fo.+200fo. St. Emeric at prayer (birth millenary) (40×31 mm) 8·50 8·50

1416 Komondor

2007. Hungarian Dogs. Multicoloured.
5024 62fo. Type **1416** 80 65
5025 150fo. Transylvanian hound 1·90 1·60
5026 180fo. Kuvasz 2·30 1·90
5027 240fo. Pumi 3·00 2·50
MS5028 90×60 mm. 600fo.Vizla 7·25 7·25

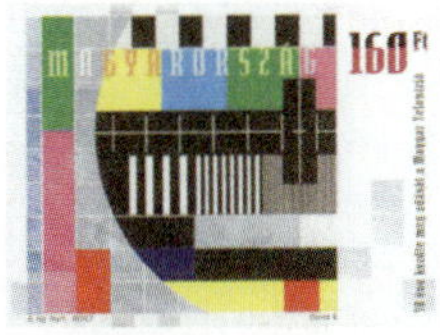

1417 Test Card

2007. 50th Anniv of Television Broadcasting.
5029 **1417** 160fo. multicoloured 2·00 1·70

1418 Scouts canoeing

2007. Europa. Centenary of Scouting. Sheet 104×64 mm containing T 1418 and similar square design. Multicoloured.
MS5030 210fo.×4, Type **1418**×2; Scouts and stone commemorating first camp×2 10·50 10·50
The lower stamps and margins of **MS**5030 share a composite background design.

1419 Helmet and Rope

2007. International Cave Rescue Conference, Aggtelek-Josvafo.
5031 **1419** 200fo. multicoloured 2·50 2·10

1420 Building Facade

2007. Centenary of Academy of Music Building.
5032 **1420** 250fo. multicoloured 3·00 2·50

1421 Mystical Betrothal of St Catherine (c 1490)

2007. 50th Anniv of National Art Gallery. Sheet 170×65 mm containing T 1421 and similar multicoloured designs.
MS5033 150fo.×4, Type **1421**; 'View of Rome' (Karoly Marko the elder (1835)); 'October' (Karoly Ferenczy (1903)); 'Picnic in May' (Pal Szinyei Merse (1873)) (50×35 mm) 7·00 7·00
The three vert stamps of **MS**5030 share a composite background design.

1422 Cirfandli Grapes, Pecs Region

2007. Wine Grapes and Regions (8th series). Multicoloured.
5034 95fo. Type **1422** 1·20 1·00
5035 140fo. Ezerfutu grapes, Etyek-Buda 1·70 1·50
5036 260fo. Zenit grapes, Tolna 3·00 2·50

1423 Emblem and Dog

2007. Border Guards.
5037 **1423** 107fo. multicoloured 1·30 1·10

2007. Greetings Stamps (4th issue). Graduation (5038/57). Door Knockers (5058/67). Budapest (5068/5072). As T 1414. Multicoloured.
5038 (62fo.) Belfold Quill and inkwell 80 65
5039 (62fo.) Belfold Bronze coloured pen with ornate nib 80 65
5040 (62fo.) Belfold Two black pens with gold bands 80 65
5041 (62fo.) Belfold Black pen with gold band and ornate nib 80 65
5042 (62fo.) Belfold Biro facing left 80 65
5043 (62fo.) Belfold Pen top 80 65
5044 (62fo.) Belfold Pen and ink bottle 80 65
5045 (62fo.) Belfold Biro prone 80 65
5046 (62fo.) Belfold Biro facing right 80 65
5048 (62fo.) Belfold Nib and quill pen and feather 80 65
5049 (62fo.) Belfold Black pen and nib 80 65
5050 (62fo.) Belfold Bronze coloured pen with ornate nib prone 80 65
5051 (62fo.) Belfold Nib and quill pen and feather prone facing right 80 65
5052 (62fo.) Belfold Close up of pen top 80 65
5053 (62fo.) Belfold Nib and quill pen and feather prone facing left 80 65
5054 (62fo.) Belfold Ink well, nib and quill 80 65
5055 (62fo.) Belfold Close up of two pens with nibs 80 65
5056 (62fo.) Belfold Top and black pen with gold band 80 65
5057 (62fo.) Belfold Biro in writing position 80 65
5058 (62fo.) Belfold Lion head door knocker on grained door 80 65
5059 (62fo.) Belfold Lion head on peeling turquoise door 80 65
5060 (62fo.) Belfold Bearded man on green streaked door 80 65
5061 (62fo.) Belfold Iron knocker on yellow door 80 65
5062 (62fo.) Belfold Brass lion head on orange brown door 80 65
5063 (62fo.) Belfold Lion head on brown rose door 80 65

5064 (62fo.) Belfold Lion head on blue panelled door 80 65
5065 (62fo.) Belfold Brass door knocker with birds' heads on cream panelled door 80 65
5066 (62fo.) Belfold Horned head with entwined snakes on carved door 80 65
5067 (62fo.) Belfold Filigree door knocker on blue and green streaked door 80 65
5068 (62fo.) Belfold Chain Bridge, Budapest 80 65
5069 (62fo.) Belfold Parliament building, Budapest 80 65
5070 (62fo.) Belfold Millenary Monument, Heroes' Square, Budapest 80 65
5071 (62fo.) Belfold Nagyteteny Castlemuseum, Budapest 80 65
5072 (62fo.) Belfold Fishermen's Bastion, Budapest 80 65

Nos. 5038/5072 were for use on domestic mail and were initially sold at 62fo.

1424 Zoltan Kodaly

2007. 125th Birth Anniv of Zoltan Kodaly (composer).
5073 **1424** 200fo. multicoloured 2·40 2·00

1425 Emblem and Athletes

2007. Centenary of University Sports Federation.
5074 **1425** 360fo. multicoloured 4·25 3·50

1426 Flax Flowers

2007. Flowers. Multicoloured. Self-adhesive.
5075 (230f.) Type **1426** 2·75 2·20
5076 (260f.) Anemone 3·00 2·50

No. 5075 was for use on priority mail within Europe and No. 5076 for use on priority mail outside Europe.

2007. Holy Crown of Hungary (3rd issue). Sheet 90×75 mm containing vert designs as T 1365 showing panels from the crown. Multicoloured.
MS5077 Size 20×26 mm. 300fo.×3, Saint Cosmus; Saint George; Archangel Michael 10·50 10·50

1427 Janos Selye

2007. Second World Conference on Stress, Budapest. Birth Centenary of Janos Selye (researcher into stress and its effects).
5078 **1427** 400fo. multicoloured 4·75 4·00

Nos. 5079/84 have been left for 'Greetings Stamps' (As Nos. 4823/8), issued on 27 September 2007, not yet received.

1428 Emblem

2007. World Science Forum, Budapest.
5085 **1428** 230fo. blue and green 2·75 2·20

1429 Flowers and Houses

2007. Christmas. Multicoloured.
5086 62f. Type **1429** 80 65
5087 62f. Shepherds and the Nativity 80 65
5088 62f. The Magi 80 65

Nos. 5086/8 were issued together, *se-tenant*, forming a composite design of *The Birth of Jesus* (carpet by Erzsebet Szekeres).

2008. Corporate Greeting Stamps. No value expressed. As T 1352. Multicoloured.
5089 (70fo.) Map and compass (As Type **1352**) 95 80
5090 (70fo.) Compass at left and map (As No. 4881) 95 80

Type **1340** is vacant.
Nos. 5089/90 were inscribed 'Belfold' and were for use on domestic mail. They were originally on sale for 70fo.

1431 Eggs

2008. Easter.
5091 **1431** 70f. multicoloured 95 80

1432 King Matthias I and Visegrad Palace

2008. Stamp Day. 550th Anniv of King Matthias I's Reign.
5092 70f. Type **1432** 95 80
5093 100f. King Matthias on horseback, castle and knight 1·30 1·10
MS5094 91×75 mm. 600f.+200f. King Matthias and Queen Beatrix (40×30 mm) 10·50 10·50

1433 Car

2008. Youth Stamps. Transport. Sheet 140×60 mm containing T 1433 and similar vert designs. Multicoloured.
MS5095 150f. Type **1433**; 150f. Ship; 150f.+30f. Train; 150f.+30f. Aircraft 8·75 8·75

The stamps and margins of **MS**5095 form a composite design.

1434 Karoly Knezich

2008. Birth Bicentenary of Karoly Knezich (general).
5096 **1434** 380f. multicoloured 5·00 4·25

1435 Dancer

2008. Hungarian Minorities (1st issue). Roma.
5097 **1435** 260f. multicoloured 3·50 3·00

See also No. 5017.

1436 Water Polo

2008. Olympic Games, Beijing. Designs showing stylized athletes. Multicoloured.
5098 70f. Type **1436** 95 80
5099 100f. Judo 1·30 1·10
5100 170f. Fencing 2·30 1·90

1437 Letter

2008. Europa. The Letter. Sheet 105×65 mm containing T 1437 and similar square design. Multicoloured.
MS5101 100f.×2, Type **1437**×2; 230f.×2, Pen nib×2 8·75 8·75

1438 Hungarian Giant Rabbit

2008. Traditional Farm Breeds. Multicoloured.
5102 145f. Type **1438** 1·90 1·60
5103 150f. Hungarian goat 2·00 1·70
5104 170f. Cikta sheep 2·30 1·90
5105 310f. Hungarian donkey 4·00 3·25
MS5106 90×65 mm. 60f. Water buffalo 8·00 8·00

1439 Dancer

2008. Hungarian Minorities (2nd issue). German.
5107 **1439** 275f. multicolured 3·50 3·00

1440 Crossbill, Lemon Lily and Istvan Chernel (scientist and ornithologist)

2008. Orseg National Park.
5108 **1440** 220f. multicoloured 3·00 2·50

1441 Flags

2008. European Football Championship, Austria and Switzerland.
5109 **1441** 250f. multicloured 3·25 2·75

1442 Cellars and Vineyards

2008. World Heritage Site. Tokaj Wine Region.
5110 **1442** 290f. multicoloured 4·00 3·25

1443 Hand holding Beach Furniture

2008. 10th Anniv of Holiday Vouchers.
5111 **1443** 70f. multicoloured 95 80

1444 Present Giving (Lili Pota)

2008. Civic Responsibilities. Winning Entry in Children's Drawing Competition.
5112 **1444** 100f.+50f. multicoloured 2·00 1·70

1445 Barber

2008. Youth Stamps. PhilaVillage. Multicoloured.
5113 100fo. Type **1445** 1·30 1·10
5114 100fo. Baker (horiz) 1·30 1·10

2008. Youth Stamps. PhilaVillage. As T 1445. Multicoloured.
5115 100fo. Photographer 1·30 1·10
5116 100fo. Optician 1·30 1·10

1446 Chapter Initial Ornamented Letter

2008. 650th Anniv of Illuminated Chronicle (attributed to Nicholas, son of Hertul).
5117 **1446** 400fo. multicoloured 5·25 4·50

2008. Youth Stamps. PhilaVillage. As T 1445. Multicoloured.
5118 100fo. Waiter (vert) 1·30 1·10
5119 100fo. Traffic policeman (horiz) 1·30 1·10

1447 Giraffes and Hippopotamus

2008. 50th Anniv of Debrecen and Veszprem Zoos. Sheet 110×60 mm containing T 1447 and similar horiz design. Multicoloured.
MS5120 260fo.×2, Type **1447**; Camel, lion, zebra and rhinoceros 7·00 7·00

The stamps and margins of **MS**5120 form a composite design.

2008. Holy Crown of Hungary (4th issue). Sheet 90×75 mm containing vert designs as T 1365 showing panels from the crown. Multicoloured.
MS5121 Size 20×26 mm. 300fo.×3, Saint Damian; Saint Demeter; Archangel Gabriel 12·00 12·00

1448 Orchid

2008. Greetings Stamps. Flowers. Multicoloured.

5122 (70fo.) Type **1448** 95 80
5123 (70fo.) Rose 95 80
5124 (70fo.) Lily 95 80
5125 (70fo.) Tulips 95 80
5126 (70fo.) Gerbera 95 80

Nos. 5122/6 were inscribed 'Belfold' and were for use on domestic mail. They were originally on sale for 70f.

2008. Youth Stamps. PhilaVillage. As T 1445. Multicoloured.

5127 100fo. School teacher 1·30 1·10
5128 100fo. Museum guide 1·30 1·10

1449 Miklos Zrinyi

2008. 500th Birth Anniv of Miklos Zrinyi (nationalist leader).

5129 **1449** 190f. multicoloured 2·50 2·10

1450 Archangel Gabriel

2008. 150th Birth Anniv of Gyorgy Zala (sculptor).

5130 **1450** 200f. multicoloured 2·75 2·20

1451 New Synagogue, Szeged

2008. Synagogues. Multicoloured.

5131 200f. Type **1451** 2·75 2·20
5132 250f. Jewish Theological Seminary, Budapest 3·25 2·75

1452 Rabbit

2008. Greetings Stamps. Multicoloured.

5133 (70fo.) Type **1452** 95 80
5134 (70fo.) Lion 95 80
5135 (70fo.) Giraffe 95 80
5136 (70fo.) Cat 95 80
5137 (70fo.) Bear 95 80

Nos. 5133/7 were inscribed 'Belfold' and were for use on domestic mail. They were originally on sale for 70f.

2008. Youth Stamps. PhilaVillage. As T 1445. Multicoloured.

5138 100fo. Station master 1·30 1·10
5139 100fo. Pool life guard 1·30 1·10

1453 The Annunciation

2008. Birth Centenary of Gyorgy Konecsni (artist and stamp designer).

5140 70fo. red 95 80
5141 100fo. blue 1·30 1·10

DESIGNS: 70fo. Type **1453**; 100f. Adoration of the Magi.

1454 Pukas Ferenc

2008. 50th (2002) Anniv of Olympic Games, Helsinki. Sheet 120×70 mm. Phosphor markings.

MS5142 **1454** 60fo. multicoloured 8·00 8·00

1455 Ede Teller

2008. Birth Centenary of Ede Teller (physicist).

5143 **1455** 250fo. multicoloured 3·25 2·75

2008. Youth Stamps. PhilaVillage. As T 1445. Multicoloured.

5144 100fo. Balloon seller (vert) 1·30 1·10
5145 100fo. Postman (horiz) 1·30 1·10

1456 Arms and Building Facade

2008. Bicentenary of Ludovika Academy.

5146 **1456** 300fo. multicoloured 4·00 3·25

1457 *Shepherd's Cross* (Zoltan Reti)

2009. Easter.

5147 **1457** 75fo. multicoloured 1·00 50

1458 Crocus

2009. Endangered Flora. Multicoloured. (a) Ordinary gum. Inscribed 'BELFOLD'.

5148 (75fo.) Type **1458** 1·00 50

(ii) Inscribed 'BELFOLD ELSOBBSEGI'.

5149 (100fo.) Squill 1·50 75

(b) Self-adhesive.

5150 (70fo.) As Type **1458** 1·00 50

Nos. 5148 and 5150 were for use on domestic mail, No. 5149 was for use on domestic prioirty mail.

1459 St. Francis

2009. 800th Anniv of Franciscan Order.

5151 **1459** 100fo. multicoloured 1·50 75

1460 *Bleriot XI* and Cliffs at Dover

2009. Centenary of First Flight across English Channel. Multicoloured.

5152 105fo. Type **1460** 1·50 75
5153 105fo. Louis Bleriot at air display in Hungary 1·50 75

Nos. 5152/3 were printed, se-tenant, in horizontal strips of two stamps surrounding a central label, the whole forming a composite design.

1461 Reactor

2009. 50th Anniv of Research Reactor, Budapest. Sheet 108×70 mm.

MS5154 **1461** 1000fo. multicoloured 9·50 9·50

1462 *Ursus maritimus*(polar Bear)

2009. Preserve Polar Regions and Glaciers. Multicoloured.

5155 75fo. Type **1462** 1·00 50
5156 130fo. *Ovibos moschatus* (muskox) 1·30 65
5157 145fo. *Uncia uncia* (snow leopard) 1·30 65
5158 275fo. *Aptenodytes patagonicus* (king penguins) 5·75 2·75

MS5159 110×75 mm. 260fo.×2, Polar bear and melting ice; *Alopex lagopus* (arctic fox) 5·50 5·50

The stamps and margins of **MS**5159 form a composite design.

1463 Mk 48 Series Diesel Locomotive, Zsuzsi Forest Railway

2009. Railways. Multicoloured.

5160 75fo. Type **1463** 1·00 50
5161 100fo. C 50 series diesel locomotive, Hortobagy Fish Pond Railway 1·50 75
5162 125fo. Type MD 40 diesel locomotive, Nagyborzsony Forest Railway 1·60 80
5163 275fo. *Morgo* steam locomotive, Kiralyret Forest Railway 2·50 1·30

1464 *Three Little Pigs*

2009. Youth Stamps. 150th Birth Anniv of Elek Benedek (writer). Sheet 140×60 mm containing T 1464 and similar vert designs showing author and characters from his books. Multicoloured.

MS5164 100fo. Type **1464**; 100fo. *Diamond Penny*; 100fo.+50fo. Elek Benedek; 100fo.+50fo. *Puss in Boots* 5·50 5·50

The stamps and margins of **MS**5164 form a composite design.

1465 'HAYDN' as Piano Keys

2009. Death Bicentenary of Joseph Haydn (composer).

5165 **1466** 300fo. multicoloured 3·50 1·75

1466 Ferenc Kazinczy

2009. 250th Birth Anniv of Ferenc Kazinczy (writer, language reformist and member of Academy of Science). Sheet 90×65 mm.

MS5166 **1466** 600fo. multicoloured 6·50 6·50

1467 Miklos Radnoti

2009. Birth Centenary of Miklos Radnoti (poet).

5167 **1467** 280fo. multicoloured 2·75 1·40

1468 Galileo Galilei

2009. Europa. Astronomy. Sheet 105×65 mm containing T 1468 and similar square design. Multicoloured.

MS5168 100fo.×2, Type **1468**×2; 230fo.×2, Jupiter and moons×2 6·50 6·50

1469 John Calvin

2009. 500th Birth Anniv of John Calvin (reformer).

5169 **1469** 200fo. multicoloured 2·00 1·00

1470 Donat Banki

2009. 150th Birth Anniv of Donat Banki (engineer and professor).

5170 **1470** 300fo. multicoloured 2·75 1·40

1471 Romanesque Monument and Carvings

2009. Stamp Day. Visegrad Millennary. Multicoloured.

5171		75fo. Type **1471**	1·00	50
5172		100fo. Gothic fountain and tower	1·00	50
MS5173		90×60 mm. 600fo.+200fo. Renaissance courtyard and fountain	7·50	7·50

1472 Virgin and Child (11th–12th century)

2009. 250th Anniv of Finding Ivory Statue of Virgin and Child at Máriabesnyo.

5174	**1472**	200fo. multicoloured	2·00	1·00

1473 St. Stephen and Cathedral, Pecs

2009. Bishopric of Pecs Millenary.

5175	**1473**	100fo. multicoloured	1·00	50

1474 *Hand in Hand* (Zsuzsanna Flora Szabo)

2009. Winning Design in Children's Drawing Competition. Charity Stamp.

5176	**1474**	75fo.+50fo. multicoloured	1·00	1·00

The premium was for the benefit of Krizis Alap (Crisis foundation).

1475

2009. Greetings Stamps. Pecs. Multicoloured.

5177	Belfold Type **1475**	1·00	50
5178	Belfold Calvary Hill	1·00	50
5179	Belfold City Hall	1·00	50
5180	Belfold Cathedral (detail)	1·00	50
5181	Belfold Red building with portico	1·00	50
5182	Belfold Academy of Science	1·00	50
5183	Belfold Synagogue	1·00	50
5184	Belfold Cathedral	1·00	50
5185	Belfold Lion's head door knocker and door handle	1·00	50
5186	Belfold Klimo Library	1·00	50
5187	Belfold National Theatre	1·00	50
5188	Belfold Zsolnay Fountain (base)	1·00	50
5189	Belfold Decorated roof	1·00	50
5190	Belfold Pavement cafe	1·00	50
5191	Belfold Early Christian necropolis	1·00	50
5192	Belfold Decorated gable	1·00	50
5193	Belfold Pasha Gaz Kasim's Mosque	1·00	50
5194	Belfold Barbican	1·00	50
5195	Belfold Jakovali Hassan's Mosque	1·00	50
5196	Belfold Zsolnay Fountain (detail)		

Nos. 5177/96 were inscribed 'Belfold' and were for use on domestic mail. They were originally on sale for 70fo.

1476 '20'

2009. 20th Anniv of Opening of Border between Austria and Hungary.

5197	**1476**	210fo. multicoloured	2·20	1·10

Nos. 5177/96 and Type **1475** are left for Personal Stamps. Pecs, issued on 4 September 2009.

A stamp of a similar design was issued by Austria and Germany.

1477 *Rainbow* (Jozsef Egry)

2009. Art.

5198	**1477**	275fo. multicoloured	2·60	1·30

1478 *Our Lady of the Way* (Masa Feszty)

2009. Christmas.

5199	75fo. multicoloured	1·00	50
5200	100fo. ultramarine and orange-yellow (horiz)	1·00	50

DESIGNS: 75fo. Type **1478**; 100fo. Symbols of Christmas.

1479 'BRAILLE' '200'

2009. Birth Bicentenary of Louis Braille (inventor of Braille writing for the blind).

5201	**1479**	200fo. black and chestnut	2·00	1·00

No. 5201 is embossed with Braille letters.

1480 Decorated Canteen

2009. Hungary–Japan Exchange Year. Multicoloured.

5202	260fo. Type **1480**	2·50	1·30
5203	260fo. Mount Fuji	2·50	1·30
5204	260fo. Plumware pot	2·50	1·30
5205	260fo. Macho embroidery	2·50	1·30
5206	260fo. Elizabeth Bridge	2·50	1·30
5207	260fo. Crane and bamboo embroidery	2·50	1·30

Stamps of a similar design were issued by Japan.

1481 Crystal Ware

2009. The Arts. Crystal.

5208	**1481**	300fo. multicoloured	2·75	1·40

1482 Emblem

2009. World Science Forum, Budapest.

5209	**1482**	100fo. multicoloured	1·00	50

1483 Levi Phila

2009. Philaclub. T 1483 and similar horiz designs showing characters from Philaclub (stamp collecting website for young people). Multicoloured.

5210	20fo. Type **1483**	30	15
5211	20fo. Spotty Mouse	30	15
5212	20fo. Bogi Phila	30	15

EXPRESS LETTER STAMPS

E36

1916. Inscr "MAGYAR KIR. POSTA".

E245	**E36**	2f. olive and red	60	60

1916. Optd KOZTARSASAG.

E301	2f. olive and red	20	45

1919. Inscr "MAGYAR POSTA".

E349	2f. olive and red	60	60

IMPERIAL JOURNAL STAMPS

J1

J2

1868. Imperf.

J3	**J2**	1k. blue	£14000	£9500
J52	**J1**	1k. blue	1·10	55
J53	**J2**	2k. brown	4·25	6·00

No. J3 has the arms at the foot as in Type J **2** but the corner designs differ.

NEWSPAPER STAMPS

N2 St. Stephen's Crown and Posthorn

1871. Posthorn turned to left. Imperf.

N8	**N2**	1k. red on white	£100	47·00

1872. As Type N 2 but with posthorn turned to right. Imperf.

N14	1k. red	20·00	4·75

N4

1874. Imperf.

N64	**N4**	1k. orange	1·30	45

N9

1900. Imperf.

N136	**N9**	(2f.) orange	20	20
N401	**N9**	(10f.) blue	40	40
N402	**N9**	(20f.) purple	40	40

OFFICIAL STAMPS

O44

1921

O428	**O44**	10f. black and purple	65	40
O429	**O44**	20f. black and brown	65	40
O430	**O44**	60f. black and grey	65	40
O431	**O44**	100f. black and red	65	40
O432	**O44**	250f. black and blue	65	40
O433	**O44**	350f. black and blue	65	40
O434	**O44**	500f. black and brown	65	40
O435	**O44**	1000f. black and brown	65	40

1922. Nos. O429/33 surch (No. O439 optd KORONA only).

O436	15k. on 20f. black and brown	50	40
O437	25k. on 60f. black and grey	50	40
O438	150k. on 100f. black and pink	1·30	65
O439	(350)k. on 350f. black and blue	1·50	65
O440	2000k. on 250f. black and blue	2·50	2·50

1922

O441	5k. brown	40	40
O442	10k. brown	40	40
O443	15k. grey	40	40
O444	25k. orange	40	40
O445	50k. red and brown	50	40
O446	100k. red and bistre	50	40
O447	150k. red and green	25	25
O448	300k. red	25	25
O449	350k. red and violet	25	25
O450a	500k. red and orange	2·10	65
O451	600k. red and bistre	1·30	1·30
O452	1000k. red and blue	2·10	1·30
O453	3000k. red and violet	3·25	65
O454	5000k. red and blue	3·25	1·30

PARCEL POST STAMPS

1954. No. 979 surch.

P1398	**153**	1fo.70 on 1fo.40 green	1·90	65
P1399	**153**	2fo. on 1fo.40 green	2·50	65
P1400	**153**	3fo. on 1fo.40 green	1·90	1·90

POSTAGE DUE STAMPS

D9

1903. Inscr "MAGYAR KIR. POSTA". Figures in centre in black.

D91	**D9**	100f. green	1·10	1·60
D170	**D9**	1f. green	65	35
D171	**D9**	2f. green	65	35
D172	**D9**	5f. green	60	35
D173	**D9**	6f. green	1·70	70
D174	**D9**	10f. green	1·70	70
D175	**D9**	12f. green	1·20	35
D176	**D9**	20f. green	60	35
D177	**D9**	50f. green	1·20	35

1915. Surch 20.

D188	**D 9**	20 on 100f. black & grn	1·20	1·70

1915. As Type D 9, but figures in red.

D190	**D9**	1f. green	10	10
D191	**D9**	2f. green	10	10
D192	**D9**	5f. green	70	25
D193	**D9**	6f. green	10	10
D194	**D9**	10f. green	10	10
D195	**D9**	12f. green	10	10
D196	**D9**	15f. green	10	10
D197	**D9**	20f. green	10	10
D198	**D9**	30f. green	10	10
D349	**D9**	40f. green	25	25
D350	**D9**	50f. green	25	25
D351	**D9**	120f. green	25	25
D352	**D9**	200f. green	25	25
D430	**D9**	2k. green	70	95
D431	**D9**	5k. green	50	50
D432	**D9**	50k. green	50	50

1919. Overprinted KOZTARSASAG.

D324	50f. black and green	5·50	5·00
D325	2f. red and green	25	70
D326	3f. red and green	25	70
D327	10f. red and green	25	70
D328	20f. red and green	25	70
D329	40f. red and green	25	70
D330	50f. red and green	25	70

1919. As Type D 9 but inscr "MAGYAR POSTA" and optd with T 37 and MAGYAR TANACS KOZTARSASAG. Figures in black.

D369		2f. green	1·40	1·40
D370		3f. green	1·40	1·40
D371		10f. green	9·50	9·50
D372		20f. green	1·40	1·40
D373		40f. green	1·40	1·40
D374		50f. green	1·40	1·40

1919. As Type D 9, but inscr "MAGYAR POSTA". Figures in Black.

D375		2f. green	30	45
D376		3f. green	30	45
D377		20f. green	30	45
D378		40f. green	30	45
D379		50f. green	30	45

1921. Surch PORTO and value. Inscr "MAGYAR KIR POSTA".

D428	18	100f. on 15f. purple	25	25
D429	18	500f. on 15f. purple	25	25
D433	18	2½k. on 10f. purple	40	40
D434	18	3k. on 15f. purple	40	40
D435	18	9k. on 40f. green	40	40
D436	18	12k. on 60f. green	50	40
D437	18	6k. on 1½k. purple	40	40
D438	18	10k. on 2½k. green	25	25
D439	18	15k. on 1½k. purple	25	25
D440	18	20k. on 2½k. green	25	25
D441	18	25k. on 1½k. purple	25	25
D442	18	30k. on 1½k. purple	25	25
D443	18	40k. on 2½k. green	25	25
D444	18	50k. on 1½k. purple	25	25
D445	18	100k. on 4½k. purple	25	25
D446	18	200k. on 4½k. purple	25	25
D447	18	300k. on 4½k. purple	40	25
D448	18	500k. on 2k. blue	40	25
D449	18	500k. on 3k. brown	40	25
D450	18	1000k. on 2k. blue	40	25
D451	18	1000k. on 3k. brown	50	40
D452	18	2000k. on 2k. blue	65	25
D453	18	2000k. on 3k. brown	1·10	40
D454	18	5000k. on 5k. brown	1·50	75

D61

1926

D479	D61	1f. red	25	15
D480	D61	2f. red	30	25
D481	D61	3f. red	75	75
D482	D61	4f. red	25	25
D483	D61	5f. red	5·00	5·00
D486	D61	16f. red	50	40
D487	D61	32f. red	1·30	65
D489	D61	64f. red	3·75	50
D490	D61	80f. red	5·00	1·50
D509	D61	8f. red	50	25
D510	D61	10f. red	65	25
D512	D61	20f. red	1·30	25
D513	D61	40f. red	1·80	40

1927. Nos. 434/36b surch PORTO and value.

D491	49	1f. on 500k. light green and green	50	50
D492	49	2f. on 1000k. brown and bistre	50	50
D493	49	3f. on 2000k. blue and deep blue	50	65
D494	49	5f. on 5000k. mauve and purple	1·50	1·90
D495	49	10f. on 10000k. purple and red	1·30	1·50

1931. Surch.

D529	D61	4f. on 5 red	1·00	65
D531	D61	10f. on 80f. red	1·30	65
D532	D61	12f. on 50f. red	1·90	1·00
D533	D61	20f. on 32f. red	1·90	1·30
D534	D61	10f. on 16f. red	2·50	2·10

D84

1934

D569	D84	2f. blue	25	10
D570	D84	4f. blue	25	10
D571	D84	6f. blue	25	10
D572	D84	8f. blue	25	15
D573	D84	10f. blue	30	25
D574	D84	12f. blue	40	40
D575	D84	16f. blue	40	40
D576	D84	20f. blue	40	50
D577	D84	40f. blue	1·10	75
D578	D84	80f. blue	1·90	1·00

D115

1941

D684	D115	2f. brown	10	10
D685	D115	3f. brown	10	10
D686	D115	4f. brown	10	10
D687	D115	6f. brown	10	10
D688	D115	8f. brown	10	10
D689	D115	10f. brown	10	10
D690	D115	12f. brown	15	10
D691	D115	16f. brown	20	10
D692	D115	18f. brown	40	25
D693	D115	20f. brown	20	10
D694	D115	24f. brown	25	15
D695	D115	30f. brown	40	25
D696	D115	36f. brown	40	25
D697	D115	40f. brown	25	20
D698	D115	50f. brown	25	20
D699	D115	60f. brown	40	25

1945. Surch 1945 and value. Blue surface-tinted paper.

D825		10f. on 2f. brown	15	15
D826		10f. on 3f. brown	15	15
D827		20f. on 4f. brown	15	15
D828		20f. on 6f. brown	12·00	12·00
D829		20f. on 8f. brown	15	15
D830		40f. on 12f. brown	15	15
D831		40f. on 16f. brown	15	15
D832		40f. on 18f. brown	15	15
D833		60f. on 24f. brown	15	15
D834		80f. on 30f. brown	15	15
D835		90f. on 36f. brown	15	15
D836		1p. on 10f. brown	15	15
D837		1p. on 40f. brown	15	15
D838		2p. on 20f. brown	15	15
D839		2p. on 50f. brown	15	15
D840		2p. on 60f. brown	15	15
D841		10p. on 3f. brown	25	25
D842		12p. on 8f. brown	40	40
D843		20p. on 24f. brown	65	65

D154 Numeral

1946

D984	D154	4f. red and brown	65	15
D985	D154	10f. red and brown	1·50	15
D986	D154	20f. red and brown	65	15
D987	D154	30f. red and brown	65	15
D988	D154	40f. red and brown	1·00	15
D989	D154	50f. red and brown	2·50	75
D990	D154	60f. red and brown	1·50	25
D991	D154	1fo.20 red and brown	2·50	65
D992	D154	2fo. red and brown	3·75	75

1950

D1114		4fi. purple	15	15
D1115		10fi. purple	15	15
D1116		20fi. purple	1·30	15
D1117		30fi. purple	1·30	15
D1118		40fi. purple	65	15
D1119		50fi. purple	1·30	15
D1120		60fi. purple	1·10	15
D1121		1fo.20 purple	1·60	15
D1122		2fo. purple	3·25	25

D201

1951. Fiscal stamps surch with Arms. MAGYAR POSTA PORTO and value.

D1157	D201	8fi. brown	25	25
D1158	D201	10fi. brown	40	40
D1159	D201	12fi. brown	65	65

D215

1951

D1210	D215	4fi. brown	15	15
D1211	D215	6fi. brown	15	15
D1212	D215	8fi. brown	15	15
D1213	D215	10fi. brown	15	15
D1214	D215	14fi. brown	15	15
D1215	D215	20fi. brown	15	15
D1216	D215	30fi. brown	15	15
D1217	D215	40fi. brown	15	15
D1218	D215	50fi. brown	30	15
D1219	D215	60fi. brown	40	15
D1220	D215	1fo.20 brown	50	15
D1221	D215	2fo. brown	90	40

D240

1953. 50th Anniv of 1st Hungarian Postage Due Stamps.

D1305	D240	4fi. black and green	15	15
D1306	D240	6fi. black and green	15	15
D1307	D240	8fi. black and green	15	15
D1308	D240	10fi. black and green	15	15
D1309	D240	12fi. black and green	15	15
D1310	D240	14fi. black and green	15	15
D1311	D240	16fi. black and green	15	15
D1312	D240	20fi. black and green	15	15
D1313	D240	24fi. black and green	15	15
D1314	D240	30fi. black and green	15	15
D1315	D240	36fi. black and green	15	15
D1316	D240	40fi. black and green	20	15
D1317	D240	50fi. black and green	25	15
D1318	D240	60fi. black and green	40	15
D1319	D240	70fi. black and green	40	15
D1320	D240	80fi. black and green	40	15
D1321	D240	1fo.20 black & green	75	15
D1322	D240	2fo. black and green	1·30	15

D282

1958. Forint values are larger (31×22 mm).

D1498	D282	4fi. black and red	15	15
D1499	D282	6fi. black and red	15	15
D1500	D282	8fi. black and red	15	15
D1501	D282	10fi. black and red	15	15
D1502	D282	12fi. black and red	15	15
D1503	D282	14fi. black and red	15	15
D1504	D282	16fi. black and red	15	15
D1505	D282	20fi. black and red	15	15
D1506	D282	24fi. black and red	15	15
D1507	D282	30fi. black and red	15	15
D1508	D282	36fi. black and red	15	15
D1509	D282	40fi. black and red	15	15
D1510	D282	50fi. black and red	15	15
D1511	D282	60fi. black and red	15	15
D1512	D282	70fi. black and red	15	15
D1513	D282	80fi. black and red	15	15
D1514	-	1fo. brown	15	15
D1515	-	1fo.20 brown	15	15
D1516	-	2fo. brown	25	20
D1517	-	4fo. brown	65	25

D587 Money-order Cancelling Machine

1973. Postal Operations.

D2847	D587	20fi. brown and red	10	10
D2848	-	40fi. blue and red	10	10
D2849	-	80fi. violet and red	25	10
D2850	-	1fo. green and red	35	10
D2851	-	1fo.20 green and red	45	10
D2852	-	2fo. violet and red	80	10
D2853	-	3fo. blue and red	1·00	10
D2854	-	4fo. brown and red	1·20	10
D2855	-	8fo. purple and red	1·50	10
D2856	-	10fo. green and red	1·70	10

DESIGNS—As Type D **587**: 40fi. Parcel scales, self-service post office; 80fi. Automatic parcels-registration machine; 1fo. Data-recording machine; 28×22 mm: 1fo. 20, Ilyushin Il-18 mail plane and van; 2fo. Diesel mail train; 3fo. Postman on motor cycle; 4fo. Postman at mailboxes; 8fo. Toshiba automatic sorting machine; 10f. Postman on motor cycle (different).

D944 Foot Messenger

1987. Postal History. Multicoloured.

D3810	1fo. Type D **944**	15	10
D3811	4fo. Post rider	50	10
D3812	6fo. Horse-drawn mail coach	75	10
D3813	8fo. Railway mail carriage	1·00	10
D3814	10fo. Mail van	1·30	10
D3815	20fo. Mail plane	2·50	25

SAVINGS BANK STAMP

B17

1916

B199	B17	10f. purple	60	60

SZEGED

The following issues were made by the Hungarian National Government led by Admiral Horthy, which was set up in Szeged in 1919, then under French occupation, and which later replaced the Communist regime established by Bela Kun.

1919. Stamps of Hungary optd MAGYAR NEMZETI KORMANY Szeged, 1919. or surch. (a) War Charity stamps of 1916.

1	20	10f. (+2f.) red	30	30
2	-	15f. (+2f.) violet	55	55
3	22	40f. (+2f.) lake	1·10	1·60

(b) Harvesters and Parliament Types.

4	18	2f. brown	20	20
5	18	3f. red	20	20
6	18	5f. green	30	30
7	18	6f. blue	8·00	8·00
8	18	15f. violet	30	30
9	18	20f. brown (No. 307)	16·00	27·00
10	18	25f. blue (No. 309)	20	20
11	19	50f. purple	4·25	5·50
12	19	75f. blue	30	30
13	19	80f. green	3·25	3·25
14	19	1k. lake	30	30
15	19	2k. brown	30	30
16	19	3k. grey and violet	30	30
17	19	5k. brown	32·00	38·00
18	19	10k. lilac and brown	32·00	38·00

(c) Nos. 5 and 14 further surch.

19	18	45 on 3f. red	20	20
20	19	10 on 1k. lake	2·20	2·20

(d) Karl and Zita stamps.

21	27	10f. red	30	30
22	27	20f. brown	20	20
23	27	25f. blue	5·50	11·00
24	28	40f. olive	2·20	2·20

The following (Nos. 25/39) are also optd KOZTARSASAG.

(e) War Charity stamp.

25	22	40f. (+2f.) lake	3·25	4·25

(f) Harvesters and Parliament Types.

26	18	3f. red	7·50	9·75
27	18	4f. slate	2·20	2·20
28	18	5f. green	4·25	5·50
29	18	6f. blue	3·25	3·25
30	18	10f. red	4·75	4·75
31	18	20f. brown	16·00	22·00
32	18	20 (f) on 2f. bistre	30	30
33	18	40f. olive	30	30
34	19	3k. grey and violet	16·00	22·00

(g) Karl and Zita stamps.

35	27	10f. red	5·50	5·50
36	27	15f. violet	1·60	1·60
37	27	20f. brown	22·00	22·00
38	27	25f. blue	5·50	5·50
39	28	50f. purple	20	30

EXPRESS LETTER STAMPS

1919. No. E245 optd as above.

E41	E18	2f. olive and red	4·25	4·25

NEWSPAPER STAMP

1919. No. N136 optd MAGYAR NEMZETI KORMANY Szeged, 1919.

N40	N9	(2f.) orange	30	30

POSTAGE DUE STAMPS

D42	D9	2f. red and green	65	65
D43	D9	6f. red and green	2·20	2·20
D44	D9	10f. red and green	65	65
D45	D9	12f. red and green	85	85
D46	D9	20f. red and green	65	65
D47	D9	30f. red and green	2·20	2·20

(b) No. E41 surch PORTO and new value.

D48	**E18**	50f. on 2f. olive and red	65	65
D49	**E18**	100f. on 2f. olive & red	65	65

Pt. 1

HYDERABAD

A state in India. Now uses Indian stamps.

12 pies = 1 anna; 16 annas = 1 rupee.

1

1869

1	**1**	1a. green	19·00	7·50

2

1870

2	**2**	½a. brown	4·00	4·25
3	**2**	2a. green	70·00	50·00

3

1871

13	**3**	½a. brown	2·75	10
13d	**3**	½a. red	2·75	10
14	**3**	1a. purple	9·00	7·00
14b	**3**	1a. brown	1·25	15
14c	**3**	1a. black	2·00	10
15	**3**	2a. green	3·75	15
16b	**3**	3a. brown	3·00	1·50
17b	**3**	4a. grey	5·50	3·25
17c	**3**	4a. green	6·00	2·50
18	**3**	8a. brown	3·50	4·25
19	**3**	12a. blue	4·75	9·00
19a	**3**	12a. green	6·00	6·50

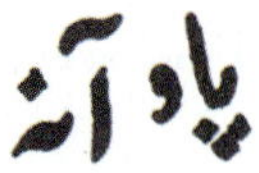

(4)

1898. Surch with T 4.

20	½a. on ½a. brown	50	85

5

1900

21	**5**	¼a. blue	5·50	3·75

6

1905

22	**6**	¼a. blue	3·50	60
23b	**6**	½a. red	4·00	25
26	**6**	1a. red	5·00	10
27cb	**6**	2a. lilac	1·40	10
28b	**6**	3a. orange	1·75	60
29c	**6**	4a. green	1·10	30
30c	**6**	8a. purple	1·25	1·25
31c	**6**	12a. green	7·50	5·00
32d	**6**	¼a. grey	80	10
33	**6**	¼a. purple	2·00	10
34	**6**	½a. green	2·25	10

8 Symbol

9

1915

35	**8**	½a. green	1·10	10
36	**8**	1a. red	2·75	10
37	**9**	1r. yellow	9·00	12·00
58	**8**	½a. red	3·00	75

(10)

1930. Surch as T 10.

38	**6**	4p. on ¼a. grey	90·00	25·00
39	**6**	4p. on ¼a. purple	50	10
40	**8**	8p. on ½a. green	50	10

12 Symbols

13 The Char Minar

1931

41	**12**	4p. black	30	10
42	**12**	8p. green	50	10
43	**13**	1a. brown	50	10
44	-	2a. violet	3·00	10
45	-	4a. blue	1·75	70
46	-	8a. orange	8·00	4·00
47	-	12a. red	9·00	12·00
48	-	1r. yellow	5·50	4·75
59	**12**	6p. red	10·00	8·50
60	**12**	2p. brown	2·50	3·00

DESIGNS—HORIZ (32½x21 mm): 2a. High Court of Justice; 4a. Osman Sagar Reservoir; 12a. Bidar College. VERT: 8a. Entrance to Ajanta Caves; 1r. Victory Tower, Daulatabad.

In No. 59 "POSTAGE" is at foot.

19 Unani General Hospital

1937. Inscr "H.E.H. THE NIZAM'S SILVER JUBILEE".

49	**19**	4p. slate and violet	60	2·25
50	-	8p. slate and brown	1·00	2·25
51	-	1a. slate and yellow	1·40	1·40
52	-	2a. slate and green	1·75	4·50

DESIGNS: 8p. Osmania General Hospital; 1a. Osmania University; 2a. Osmania Jubilee Hall.

23 Family Reunion

1945. Victory Commemoration.

53	**23**	1a. blue	10	10

24 Town Hall

1947. Reformed Legislature.

54	**24**	1a. black	1·60	1·90

25 Power House, Hyderabad

1947. Inscr as in T 25.

55	**25**	1a.4p. green	1·40	2·50
56	-	3a. blue	2·25	4·75
57	-	6a. brown	4·50	20·00

DESIGNS—HORIZ: 3a. Kaktyai Arch, Warangal Fort; 6a. Golkunda Fort.

OFFICIAL STAMPS

(O 1)

1873. Optd with Type O 1.

O1	**1**	1a. green	£110	32·00
O2a	**2**	½a. brown		£750
O3a	**2**	2a. olive		£250

1873. Optd with Type O 1.

O9a	**3**	½a. brown	13·00	3·75
O11	**3**	1a. brown	£170	£100
O12a	**3**	1a. drab	4·00	3·00
O13a	**3**	2a. green	6·50	7·50
O15a	**3**	4a. grey	27·00	26·00
O16b	**3**	8a. brown	65·00	48·00
O17a	**3**	12a. blue	75·00	£110
O19	**3**	1a. black	£100	50
O20e	**3**	3a. brown	8·50	4·00
O20f	**3**	4a. green	£450	8·00
O20h	**3**	12a. green		95·00

1909. Optd as Type O 1, or similar smaller opt.

O21a	**6**	½a. red	£160	25
O31	**6**	1a. red	2·00	15
O32b	**6**	2a. lilac	2·25	1·25
O33b	**6**	3a. orange	25·00	5·00
O34d	**6**	4a. green	4·75	15
O35	**6**	8a. purple	8·50	20
O36	**6**	12a. green	30·00	3·25
O37e	**6**	¼a. grey	2·75	40
O38	**6**	¼a. lilac	3·75	10
O39d	**6**	½a. green	4·50	10
O40	**8**	½a. green	3·50	10
O41e	**8**	1a. red	3·50	10
O54	**8**	½a. red	6·00	7·00

1930. Official stamps surch as T 10.

O42	**6**	4p. on ¼a. grey	£500	20·00
O43	**6**	4p. on ¼a. lilac	2·75	10
O44	**8**	8p. on ½a. green	2·00	10
O45	**6**	8p. on ½a. green	38·00	50·00

1934. Optd as Type O 1 but smaller.

O46	**12**	4p. black	3·50	10
O47	**12**	8p. green	1·50	10
O48	**13**	1a. brown	3·00	10
O49	-	2a. violet (No. 44)	8·50	10
O50	-	4a. blue (No. 45)	4·75	25
O51	-	8a. orange (No. 46)	16·00	70
O52	-	12a. red (No. 47)	16·00	1·75
O53	-	1r. yellow (No. 48)	24·00	2·50
O55	**12**	2p. brown	6·00	10·00
O56	**12**	6p. red	8·00	24·00

Pt. 11

ICELAND

An island lying S.E. of Greenland. An independent state formerly under the Danish sovereign, now a republic.

1873. 96 skilling = 1 riksdaler.
1876. 100 aurar (singular: eyrir) = 1 krona.

1

1873

1	1	2s. blue	£750	£1500
2	1	4s. red	£110	£700
3	1	8s. brown	£225	£800
5	1	3s. grey	£350	£1000
7	1	16s. yellow	85·00	£450

1876

13	5a. blue	£275	£550
18a	20a. mauve	27·00	£375
19	40a. green	80·00	£160
23b	40a. mauve	36·00	30·00
24	50a. red and blue	65·00	70·00
25	100a. purple and brown	60·00	85·00
27	4a. grey and red	14·50	16·00
28	5a. green	3·25	2·20
29a	6a. grey	13·00	14·00
30	10a. red	7·25	2·20
31	16a. brown	60·00	80·00
32a	20a. blue	37·00	28·00
33	25a. blue and brown	23·00	24·00
42	3a. yellow	5·75	16·00

þrír

(6)

1897. Surch as T 6 with figure 3 under word.

38	3 on 5a. green	£425	£350

1897. Surch as T 6.

40	3 on 5a. green	£500	£375

10 King Christian IX

1902

43	10	3a. orange	5·00	2·40
44	10	4a. red and grey	3·50	1·10
45	10	5a. green	23·00	75
46	10	6a. brown	17·00	6·75
47	10	10a. red	5·75	75
48	10	16a. brown	5·00	7·00
49	10	20a. blue	2·00	3·00
50	10	25a. green and brown	2·30	4·00
51	10	40a. mauve	3·50	4·00
52	10	50a. black and grey	4·50	20·00
53	10	1k. brown and blue	6·25	6·75
54	10	2k. blue and brown	25·00	46·00
55	10	5k. grey and brown	£120	£160

1902. Optd I GILDI '02–'03.

65	1	100a. purple and brown	39·00	55·00
67	1	3a. yellow	85	1·40
68	1	4a. grey and red	27·00	41·00
69	1	5a. green	80	5·75
71	1	6a. grey	85	5·75
73	1	10a. red	85	7·00
74	1	16a. brown	17·00	28·00
75	1	20a. blue	75	7·50
77	1	25a. blue and brown	75	12·00
79	1	40a. mauve	75	32·00
80	1	50a. red and blue	3·00	47·00

12 Kings Christian IX and Frederik VIII

1907

81	12	1e. red and green	1·00	75
82	12	3a. brown	3·50	1·10
83	12	4a. red and grey	2·00	1·20
84	12	5a. green	65·00	75
85	12	6a. grey	36·00	2·50
87	12	15a. green and red	5·00	1·10
88	12	16a. brown	6·75	25·00
89	12	20a. blue	6·75	3·50
90	12	25a. green and brown	5·25	7·75
91	12	40a. red	4·50	9·50
92	12	50a. red and grey	5·75	8·25
93	12	1k. brown and blue	18·00	45·00
94	12	2k. green and brown	25·00	55·00
95	12	5k. blue and brown	£170	£225
114	12	10a. red	2·30	1·10

13 Jon Sigurdsson

1911. Birth Centenary of Jon Sigurdsson (historian and Althing member).

96	13	1e. green	2·00	1·00
97	13	3a. brown	3·50	8·25
98	13	4a. blue	1·10	1·20
99	13	6a. grey	8·00	16·00
100	13	15a. violet	9·50	1·10
101	13	25a. orange	20·00	31·00

1912. As T 13, but portrait of King Frederik VIII and "JON SIGURDSSON" omitted.

102	5a. green	23·00	8·25
103	10a. red	23·00	8·25
104	20a. blue	36·00	10·50
105	50a. red	7·50	26·00
106	1k. yellow	25·00	50·00
107	2k. red	23·00	50·00
108	5k. brown	£120	£150

15 King Christian X

1920

116	15	1e. red and green	85	75
117	15	3a. brown	5·50	10·50
119	15	5a. green	1·70	1·20
121	15	8a. brown	8·25	1·40
122	15	10a. red	2·40	6·25
123	15	15a. violet	34·00	75
124	15	20a. blue	2·40	11·00
125	15	25a. green and brown	15·00	1·10
127	15	40a. red	42·00	1·90
128	15	50a. red and grey	£200	6·25
130	15	2k. green and brown	£275	20·00
131	15	5k. blue and brown	65·00	10·00
133	15	10a. green	3·00	1·20
134	15	20a. brown	60·00	1·20
135	15	25a. red	12·00	33·00
136	15	40a. blue	75·00	8·75
184	15	4a. red and grey	2·20	1·40
185	15	6a. grey	2·00	3·00
186	15	7a. green	75	1·10
187	15	10a. brown	£140	95
189	15	30a. green and red	38·00	3·50
191	15	1k. brown and blue	80·00	6·00
193	15	10k. black and green	£375	£150

1921. Various types surch.

137	10	5a. on 16a. brown	3·75	20·00
138	12	5a. on 16a. brown	1·90	5·75
139	15	10a. on 5a. green	8·00	2·40
140	10	20a. on 25a. green & brn	7·25	4·75
141	12	20a. on 25a. green & brn	4·50	5·75
142	10	20a. on 40a. mauve	8·50	14·00
143	12	20a. on 40a. red	11·00	15·00
144	10	30a. on 50a. grey	31·00	26·00
145	10	50a. on 5k. grey & brown	65·00	38·00
146	15	1k. on 40a. blue	£190	30·00
147	13	2k. on 25a. orange	£160	£100
148	-	10k. on 50a. red (No. 105)	£350	£350
149	-	10k. on 1k. yell (No. 106)	£475	£475
150	10	10k. on 2k. black & brn	90·00	23·00
150a	12	10k. on 5k. black & brn	£400	£450

22 Landing Mails at Vik

1925

151	22	7a. green	55·00	5·75
152	-	10a. brown and blue	55·00	70
153	-	20a. red	55·00	70
154	-	35a. blue	90·00	6·50
155	22	50a. brown and green	90·00	1·50

DESIGNS: 10a., 35a. Reykjavik and Esjaberg (mountain); 20a. National Museum, Reykjavik.

1928. Air. Optd with airplane.

156	15	10a. red	1·20	8·75
157	12	50a. purple and grey	75·00	85·00

24 Discovery of Iceland

25 Gyrfalcon

1930. Parliament Millenary Celebration.

158	-	3a. violet and lilac (postage)	2·10	6·75
159	24	5a. blue and grey	2·10	6·75
160	-	7a. green and dp green	2·10	6·75
161	-	10a. purple and mauve	7·00	11·00
162	-	15a. dp blue & blue	2·10	6·75
163	-	20a. red and pink	34·00	47·00
164	-	25a. brown and lt brown	6·25	8·50
165	-	30a. green and grey	4·75	8·50
166	-	35a. blue & ultramarine	5·50	8·50
167	-	40a. red, blue and grey	4·25	8·50
168	-	50a. dp brown and brown	70·00	£100
169	-	1k. green and grey	70·00	£100
170	-	2k. blue and green	90·00	£120
171	-	5k. orange and yellow	42·00	90·00
172	-	10k. lake and red	42·00	90·00
173	25	10a. blue & dp blue (air)	20·00	42·00

DESIGNS—HORIZ: 3a. Parliament House, Reykjavik; 7a. Encampment at Thingvellir; 10a. Arrival of Ingolf Arnarsson; 15a. Naming the Island; 20a. Chieftains riding to the "Althing" (Parliament); 25a. Discovery of Arnarsson's pillar; 30a. View of Thingvellir; 35a. Queen Aud; 40a. National flag; 50a. Proclamation at Thingvellir; 1k. Map of Iceland; 2k. Winter-bound farmstead; 5k. Woman spinning; 10k. Viking sacrifice to Thor.

26 Snaefellsjokull

1930. Air. Parliamentary Millenary Celebration.

174	26	15a. blue and brown	23·00	38·00
175	-	20a. blue and brown	23·00	38·00
176	-	35a. brown and green	45·00	75·00
177	-	50a. blue and green	45·00	75·00
178	-	1k. red and green	45·00	75·00

DESIGNS: 20a. Old Icelandic fishing boat; 35a. Icelandic pony; 50a. The Gullfoss Falls; 1k. Statue of Arnarsson, Reykjavik.

1931. Air. Optd Zeppelin 1931.

179	15	30a. green and red	34·00	£110
180	15	1k. brown and blue	9·00	£110
181	15	2k. green and brown	55·00	£110

29 Gullfoss Falls

1931

195	29	5a. grey	11·50	60
196	29	20a. red	10·00	20
197	29	35a. blue	17·00	8·25
198	29	60a. mauve	11·50	80
199	29	65a. brown	2·30	80
200	29	75a. blue	90·00	23·00

30 Shipwreck and Breeches-buoy

1933. Philanthropic Associations.

201	30	10a.+10a. brown	1·70	4·50
202	-	20a.+20a. red	1·70	4·50
203	30	35a.+25a. blue	1·70	4·50
204	-	50a.+25a. green	1·70	4·50

DESIGNS: 20a. Children gathering flowers; 50a. Aged fisherman and rowing boat.

1933. Air. Balbo Transatlantic Mass Formation Flight. Optd Hopflug Itala 1933.

205	15	1k. brown and blue	£170	£425
206	15	5k. blue and brown	£425	£1000
207	15	10k. black and green	£1100	£2000

32 Avro 504K Biplane over Thingvellir

1934. Air.

208	32	10a. blue	1·90	1·90
209	32	20a. green	4·00	4·25
210a	-	25a. violet	17·00	13·00
211	-	50a. purple	4·50	6·25
212	-	1k. brown	28·00	26·00
213	-	2k. red	11·50	11·00

DESIGNS: 25a., 50a. Monoplane and Aurora Borealis; 1k., 2k. Monoplane over map of Iceland.

33 Dynjandi Falls

1935

214	33	10a. blue	24·00	20
215	-	1k. green	45·00	25

DESIGN—HORIZ: 1k. Mt. Hekla.

35 Matthias Jochumsson

1935. Birth Centenary of M. Jochumsson (poet).

216	35	3a. green	90	2·75
217	35	5a. grey	17·00	95
218	35	7a. green	24·00	1·20
219	35	35a. blue	75	95

36 King Christian X

1937. Silver Jubilee of King Christian X.

220	36	10a. green	2·10	16·00
221	36	30a. brown	2·10	7·25
222	36	40a. red	2·10	7·25

MS223 128½×112 mm. **36** 15a. violet; 25a. red; 50a. blue (sold at 2k.) 42·00 £225

37 The Great Geyser

1938

226	37	15a. purple	5·75	7·75
227	37	20a. red	28·00	25
228	37	35a. blue	85	65
229	-	40a. brown	14·00	21·00
230	-	45a. blue	75	70
231	-	50a. green	27·00	65
232a	-	60a. blue	5·00	6·75
233	-	1k. blue	2·30	25

The frames of the 40a. to 1k. differ from Type **37**.

37b Leif Eiriksson's Statue, Reykjavik

1938. Leif Eiriksson's Day. Sheet 140×100 mm.

MS233b		30a. red (T **37b**), 40a. violet; 60a. green (sold at 2k.)	4·75	24·00

DESIGNS: 40a. Figure from statue; 60a. Part of globe showing Iceland and Vinland (larger).

38 Reykjavik University

1938. 20th Anniv of Independence.

234	**38**	25a. green	5·75	10·50
235	**38**	30a. brown	5·75	10·50
236	**38**	40a. purple	5·75	10·50

1939. Surch 5.

237	**35**	5 on 35a. blue	90	1·00

40 Trylon and Perisphere

1939. New York World's Fair.

238	**40**	20a. red	3·50	4·75
239	-	35a. blue	3·50	6·50
240	-	45a. green	4·25	7·25
241	-	2k. black	50·00	£120

DESIGNS: 35a. Viking longship and route to America; 45a., 2k. Statue of Thorfinn Karlsefni, Reykjavik.

41 Atlantic Cod

42 Icelandic Flag

1939

242a	**41**	1e. blue	40	2·75
243a	-	3a. violet	40	60
244a	**41**	5a. brown	40	30
245	-	7a. green	4·75	6·75
246	**42**	10a. red and blue	2·50	80
247a	-	10a. green	38·00	45
248	-	10a. black	30	25
249	-	12a. green	40	55
250a	**41**	25a. red	27·00	35
251	**41**	25a. brown	35	35
252	-	35a. red	65	25
253	**41**	50a. green	70	25

DESIGN: 3, 7, 10a. (Nos. 247a/8), 12, 35a. Atlantic herring.

43 Statue of Thorfinn Karlsefni

1939

254	**43**	2k. grey	3·50	20
255	**43**	5k. brown	28·00	30
256	**43**	10k. brown	12·00	1·40

1940. New York World's Fair. Optd 1940.

257	**40**	20a. red	7·50	19·00
258	-	35a. blue (No. 239)	7·50	19·00
259	-	45a. green (No. 240)	7·50	19·00
260	-	2k. black (No. 241)	£110	£325

1941. Surch 25.

261	**35**	25a. on 3a. olive	80	95

46 Statue of Snorri Sturluson (O. Vigeland)

1941. 700th Death Anniv of Snorri Sturluson (historian).

262	**46**	25a. red	85	1·30
263	**46**	50a. blue	1·70	3·50
264	**46**	1k. olive	1·70	3·50

47 Jon Sigurdsson (historian and Althing member)

1944. Proclamation of Republic.

265	**47**	10a. grey	45	65
266	**47**	25a. brown	50	65
267	**47**	50a. green	55	65
268	**47**	1k. black	1·00	65
269	**47**	5k. brown	4·25	8·75
270	**47**	10k. brown	46·00	65·00

48 Grumman G-21 Goose Amphibian over Thingvellir

1947. Air.

271	**48**	15a. orange	65	75
272	-	30a. black	65	1·00
273	-	75a. red	65	75
274	-	1k. blue	65	75
275	-	1k.80 blue	12·50	11·00
276	-	2k. brown	1·30	1·60
277	-	2k.50 green	24·00	1·00
278	-	3k. green	1·30	1·90
279	-	3k.30 blue	6·75	5·50

DESIGNS—HORIZ: 30a. Consolidated PBY-5 Catalina flying boat over Isafjordur; 75a. Douglas DC-3 over Eyjafjord; 1k.80, Douglas DC-3 over Snaefellsjokull; 2k.50, Consolidated PBY-5 Catalina over Eiriksjokull; 3k. Douglas DC-4 over Reykjavik; 3k.30, Douglas DC-4 over Oraefajokull. VERT: 1k. Grumman G-21 Goose over Sethisfjordur, Strandatindur; 2k. Consolidated PBY-5 Catalina over Hvalfjordur, Thyrill.

For stamps as Type **48** but without airplane, see Nos. 346/8.

50 Mt. Hekla in Eruption

1948. Inscr "HEKLA 1947".

280	**50**	12a. purple	20	25
281	-	25a. green	1·30	25
282	-	35a. red	40	30
283	**50**	50a. brown	1·70	20
284	-	60a. blue	6·50	3·00
285	-	1k. brown	14·50	60
286	-	10k. violet	41·00	60

DESIGNS—VERT: 35a., 60a. Mt. Hekla in Eruption (different view). HORIZ: 25a., 1k., 10k. Mt. Hekla.

53 Hospital and Child

1949. Red Cross Fund.

287	**53**	10a.+10a. green	65	1·00
288	-	35a.+15a. red	65	1·00
289	-	50a.+25a. brown	75	1·00
290	-	60a.+25a. blue	75	1·10
291	-	75a.+25a. blue	1·10	1·00

DESIGNS: 35a. Nurse and patient; 50a. Nurse arranging patient's bed; 60a. Aged couple; 75a. Freighter and ship's lifeboat.

54 Pony Pack-train

1949. 75th Anniv of U.P.U.

292	**54**	25a. green	40	65
293	-	35a. red	40	65
294	-	60a. blue	55	85
295	-	2k. orange	1·30	1·10

DESIGNS: 35a. Reykjavik; 60a. Map of Iceland; 2k. Almannagja Gorge.

55 "Ingolfur Arnarson" (trawler)

1950

296		5a. brown	20	20
297	**55**	10a. grey	15	25
298	-	20a. brown	20	25
299	**55**	25a. red	20	20
300	-	60a. green	11·50	17·00
301	-	75a. orange	45	35
302	-	90a. red	45	35
303	-	1k. brown	5·00	35
304	**55**	1k.25 purple	23·00	35
305	**55**	1k.50 blue	12·50	35
306	-	2k. violet	21·00	35
307	-	5k. green	34·00	1·20
308	-	25k. black	£150	13·00

DESIGNS—As T **55**: 5, 90a., 2k. Vestmannaeyjar harbour; 20, 75a., 1k. Tractor; 60a., 5k. Flock of sheep; 25k. Parliament Building, Reykjavik (29½×23½ mm).

56 Bishop Jon Arason

1950. 400th Death Anniv of Bishop Arason.

309	**56**	1k.80 red	2·75	2·75
310	**56**	3k.30 green	1·70	2·50

57 Postman, 1776

1951. 175th Anniv of Icelandic Postal Service.

311	**57**	2k. blue	2·50	2·20
312	-	3k. purple	3·25	3·00

DESIGN: 3k. as 2k. but Saab 90 Scandia aeroplane replaces man.

58 President Bjornsson

1952. Death of S. Bjornsson (first President of Iceland).

313	**58**	1k.25 blue	2·20	30
314	**58**	2k.20 green	75	4·25
315	**58**	5k. blue	8·75	1·50
316	**58**	10k. brown	35·00	24·00

1953. Netherlands Flood Relief Fund. Surch Hollandshjalp 1953 + 25.

317	-	75a.+25a. orange (No. 301)	1·30	3·50
318	**55**	1k.25+25a. purple	1·70	3·50

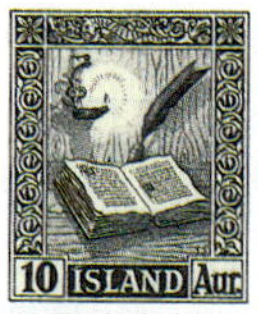

60 "Reykjabok" (Saga of Burnt Njal)

1953

319	**60**	10a. black	20	20
320	-	70a. green	40	30
321	-	1k. red	50	25
322	-	1k.75 blue	23·00	1·10
323	-	10k. brown	10·50	90

DESIGNS: 70a. Hand writing on manuscript; 1k. "Stjorn" (15th century manuscript); 1k.75, Books and candle; 10k. Page from "Skardsbok" (14th century law manuscript).

1954. No. 282 surch 5 AURAR and bars.

324		5a. on 35a. red	40	25

62 Hannes Hafstein

1954. 50th Anniv of Appointment of Hannes Hafstein as First Native Minister of Iceland. Portraits of Hafstein.

325	**62**	1k.25 blue	3·75	35
326	-	2k.45 green	19·00	30·00
327	-	5k. red	19·00	3·75

63 Icelandic Wrestling

1955. Icelandic National Sports.

328	**63**	75a. brown	35	25
329	-	1k.25 blue (Diving)	60	40
330	**63**	1k.50 red	85	25
331	-	1k.75 blue (Diving)	55	25

64 St. Thorlacas

1956. 9th Centenary of Consecration of First Icelandic Bishop and Skalholt Rebuilding Fund. Inscr as in T 64.

332	**64**	75a.+25a. red	35	40
333	-	1k.25+75a. brown	35	40
334	-	1k.75+1k.25 black	90	1·10

DESIGNS—HORIZ: 1k.25, Skalholt Cathedral, 1772. VERT: 1k.75, J. P. Vidalin, Bishop of Skalholt, 1698–1720.

65 Skogafoss

1956. Power Plants and Waterfalls.

335	**65**	15a. blue	25	25
336	-	50a. green	25	25
337	-	60a. brown	2·50	2·75
338	-	1k.50 violet	26·00	20
339	-	2k. brown	1·80	45
340	-	2k.45 black	7·50	7·00
341	-	3k. blue	3·75	75
342	-	5k. green	12·50	1·70

DESIGNS—HORIZ: 50a. Ellidaarvirkjun; 60a. Godafoss; 1k.50, Sogsvirkjun; 2k. Dettifoss; 2k.45, Andakilsarvirkjun; 3k. Laxarvirkjun. VERT: 5k. Gullfoss.

67 Map of Iceland

1956. 50th Anniv of Icelandic Telegraph System.

343	**67**	2k.30 blue	50	85

67a Whooper Swans

1956. Northern Countries' Day.

344	**67a**	1k.50 red	50	75
345	**67a**	1k.75 blue	9·00	9·75

1957. Designs as T 48 but airplane omitted.

346		2k. green	2·50	40
347		3k. blue	2·75	45
348		10k. brown	4·50	55

DESIGNS—HORIZ: 2k. Snaefellsjokull; 3k. Eiriksjokull; 10k. Oraefajokull.

68 Presidential Residence, Bessastadir

1957

349	**68**	25k. black	17·00	3·50

69 Norwegian Spruce

1957. Reafforestation Campaign.

350	**69**	35a. green	20	20
351	-	70a. green	20	20

DESIGN: 70a. Icelandic birch and saplings.

70 Jonas Hallgrimsson

1957. 150th Birth Anniv of Hallgrimsson (poet).

352	**70**	5k. black and green	1·50	55

71 River Beauty

1958. Flowers. Multicoloured.

353		1k. Type **71**	20	20
354		2k.50 Wild pansy	40	35

72 Icelandic Pony

1958

355	**72**	10a. black	20	20
356	**72**	1k. red	40	25
357	**72**	2k.25 brown	55	25

73 Icelandic Flag

1958. 40th Anniv of Icelandic Flag.

358	**73**	3k.50 red and blue	1·30	60
359	**73**	50k. red and blue	6·00	5·00

No. 359 is 23½×26½ mm.

74 Old Government House

1958

360	**74**	1k.50 blue	25	20
361	**74**	2k. green	35	35
362	**74**	3k. red	25	20
363	**74**	4k. brown	65	40

75 Jon Thorkelsson with Children

1959. Death Bicentenary of Jon Thorkelsson (Johannes Thorkillius, Rector of Skalholt).

364	**75**	2k. green	55	55
365	**75**	3k. purple	55	55

76 Vickers Viscount 700 and 1919 Avro 504K Biplane

1959. Air. 40th Anniv of Iceland Civil Aviation.

366	**76**	3k.50 blue	65	60
367	-	4k.05 green	65	80

DESIGN: 4k.05, Douglas DC-4 and Avro 504K aircraft.

77 Atlantic Salmon

1959

368	**77**	25a. blue	20	20
369	-	90a. black and brown	30	30
370	-	2k. black	45	25
371	**77**	5k. green	7·25	95
372	-	25k. violet and yellow	11·50	12·50

DESIGNS—VERT: 90a., 2k. Eiders; 25k. Gyr falcon.

78 "The Outcast" (after Jonsson)

1960. World Refugee Year.

373	**78**	2k.50 brown	25	25
374	**78**	4k.50 blue	90	85

78a Conference Emblem

1960. Europa.

375	**78a**	3k. green	75	55
376	**78a**	5k.50 blue	1·40	1·60

79 Dandelions

1960. Wild Flowers.

377	-	50a. violet, green and myrtle (Campanulas)	20	20
378	-	1k.20 violet, green and brown (Geraniums)	20	20
379	**79**	2k.50 yellow, green & brn	30	20
380	-	3k.50 yellow, green and blue (Buttercup)	35	20

See also Nos. 412/15 and 446/7.

80 Sigurdsson

1961. 150th Birth Anniv of Jon Sigurdsson (historian and Althing member).

381	**80**	50a. red	25	30
382	**80**	3k. blue	1·40	1·10
383	**80**	5k. purple	55	55

81 Reykjavik Harbour

1961. 175th Anniv of Reykjavik.

384	**81**	2k.50 blue and green	55	25
385	**81**	4k.50 blue and violet	75	30

82 Doves

1961. Europa.

386	**82**	5k.50 multicoloured	50	65
387	**82**	6k. multicoloured	50	85

83 B. Sveinsson

1961. 50th Anniv of Iceland University.

388	**83**	1k. brown	25	30
389	-	1k.40 blue	30	30
390	-	10k. green	1·10	85
MS391		99×50 mm. Nos. 388/90. Imperf	1·00	1·20

DESIGNS—VERT: 1k.40, B. M. Olsen (first Vice-chancellor). HORIZ: 10k. University building.

84 Productivity Institute

1962. Icelandic Buildings.

392	**84**	2k.50 blue	35	25
393	-	4k. green	40	25
394	-	6k. brown	60	30

DESIGNS: 4k. Fishing Research Institute; 6k. Agricultural Society's Headquarters.

85 Europa "Tree"

1962. Europa.

395	**85**	5k.50 brown, green & yell	30	25
396	**85**	6k.50 brown, green & yell	55	60

86 Cable Map

1962. Opening of North Atlantic Submarine Telephone Communications.

397	**86**	5k. green, red and lavender	1·00	45
398	**86**	7k. green, red and blue	55	25

87 S. Gudmundsson (scholar and curator)

1963. Centenary of National Museum.

399	**87**	4k. brown and bistre	55	30
400	-	5k.50 brown and olive	45	30

DESIGN: 5k.50, Detail from carving on church door, Valthjofstad.

88 Herring Catch

1963. Freedom from Hunger.

401	**88**	5k. multicoloured	75	35
402	**88**	7k.50 multicoloured	25	25

89 View of Akureyri

1963

403	**89**	3k. green	30	20

90 "Co-operation"

1963. Europa.

404	**90**	6k. yellow, ochre and brown	60	60
405	**90**	7k. yellow, green and blue	60	60

91 Ambulance

1963. Red Cross Centenary.

406	**91**	3k.+50a. multicoloured	70	1·20
407	**91**	3k.50+50a. mult	70	1·20

92 "Gullfoss" (cargo liner)

1964. 50th Anniv of Iceland Steamship Co.

408	**92**	10k. black, purple and blue	1·80	1·40

93 Scout Emblem

1964. Icelandic Boy Scouts Commemoration.

409	**93**	3k.50 multicoloured	60	25
410	**93**	4k.50 multicoloured	60	25

94 Arms of Iceland

1964. 20th Anniv of Icelandic Republic.

411	**94**	25k. multicoloured	2·00	1·70

1964. Wild Flowers. As T 79. Multicoloured.

412	50a. Mountain avens	20	20
413	1k. Glacier buttercup	20	20
414	1k.50 Bogbean	20	20
415	2k. White clover	20	20

95 Europa "Flower"

1964. Europa.

416	**95**	4k.50 turquoise, cream and brown	65	45
417	**95**	9k. sepia, cream and blue	90	70

96 Running

1964. Olympic Games, Tokyo.

418	**96**	10k. black and green	1·00	65

97 Rock Ptarmigan (summer plumage)

1965. Charity stamps.

419	**97**	3k.50+50a. mult	90	1·50
420	-	4k.50+50a. mult	90	1·50

DESIGN: 4k.50, Rock ptarmigan in winter plumage.

98 "Sound Waves"

1965. Centenary of I.T.U.

421	**98**	4k.50 green	75	65
422	**98**	7k.50 blue	25	25

99 Eruption, November 1963

1965. Birth of Surtsey Island. Multicoloured.

423	1k.50 Type **99**	55	55
424	2k. Surtsey in April 1964 (horiz)	55	55
425	3k.50 Surtsey in September 1964 (horiz)	85	65

100 Europa "Sprig"

1965. Europa.

426	**100**	5k. green, brown and ochre	1·70	1·40
427	**100**	8k. green, brown & turq	1·40	1·30

101 E. Benediktsson

1965. 25th Death Anniv of Einar Benediktsson (poet).

428	**101**	10k. brown, black and blue	2·75	3·50

102 Girl in National Costume

1965

429	**102**	100k. multicoloured	7·50	7·00

103 White-tailed Sea Eagle

1966. Multicoloured.

430	20k. Great northern diver	5·00	4·50
431	50k. Type **103**	8·75	8·75

104 Londrangar

1966. Landscapes (1st series). Multicoloured.

432	2k.50 Type **104**	35	30
433	4k. Myvatn	35	30
434	5k. Bulandstindur	60	30
435	6k.50 Dyrholaey	70	30

See also Nos. 465/8.

105 Europa "Ship"

1966. Europa.

436	**105**	7k. turquoise blue and red	2·20	1·80
437	**105**	8k. brown, cream and red	2·20	1·80

106 Society Emblem

1966. 150th Anniv of Icelandic Literary Society.

438	**106**	4k. blue	35	25
439	**106**	10k. red	75	55

107 Cogwheels

1967. Europa.

440	**107**	7k. blue, brown and yellow	2·20	1·40
441	**107**	8k. blue, grey and green	2·20	1·40

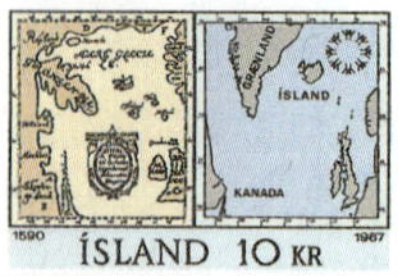

108 Old and New Maps of Iceland

1967. World Fair, Montreal.

442	**108**	10k. multicoloured	50	45

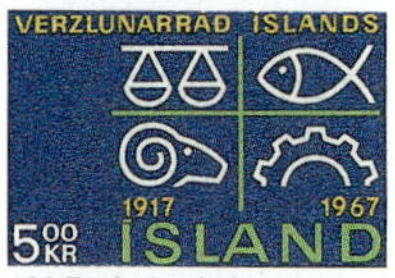

109 Trade Symbols

1967. 50th Anniv of Icelandic Chamber of Commerce.

443	**109**	5k. multicoloured	35	25

110 Nest and Eggs of Ringed Plover

1967. Charity stamps.

444	**110**	4k.+50a. multicoloured	80	1·50
445	-	5k.+50a. multicoloured	80	1·50

DESIGN: 5k. Nest and eggs of rock ptarmigan.

1968. Wild Flowers. As T 79. Multicoloured.

446	50a. Saxifrage	20	20
447	2k.50 Orchid	20	20

111 Europa "Key"

1968. Europa.

448	**111**	9k.50 mauve, black & yell	1·80	1·10
449	**111**	10k. yellow, sepia & green	1·80	1·10

112 Right-hand Traffic

1968. Adoption of Changed Rule of the Road.

450	**112**	4k. brown and yellow	20	20
451	**112**	5k. brown	20	20

113 "Fridriksson and Boy" (statue by S. Olafsson)

1968. Birth Cent of Pastor Fridrik Fridriksson (founder of Icelandic Y.M.C.A. and Y.W.C.A.).

452	**113**	10k. black and blue	50	35

114 Library Interior

1968. 150th Anniv of National Library.

453	**114**	5k. brown and buff	20	20
454	**114**	20k. ultramarine and blue	1·00	95

115 Jon Magnusson (former Prime Minister)

1968. 50th Anniv of Independence.

455	**115**	4k. lake	30	20
456	**115**	50k. sepia	3·50	3·25

116 Viking Ships

1969. 50th Anniv of Northern Countries' Union.

457	**116**	6k.50 red	50	45
458	**116**	10k. blue	50	45

117 Colonnade

1969. Europa.

459	**117**	13k. multicoloured	3·25	2·40
460	**117**	14k.50 multicoloured	1·10	1·00

118 Republican Emblem (after S. Jonsson)

1969. 25th Anniv of Republic.

461	**118**	25k. multicoloured	1·10	75
462	**118**	100k. multicoloured	5·75	5·50

119 Boeing 727 Airliner

1969. 50th Anniv of Icelandic Aviation.

463	**119**	9k.50 ultramarine & blue	50	55
464	-	12k. ultramarine and blue	50	55

DESIGN: 12k. Canadair CL-44-D4 (inscr "Rolls-Royce 400").

120 Snaefellsjokull

1970. Landscapes (2nd series). Multicoloured.

465	1k. Type **120**	20	20
466	4k. Laxfoss and Baula	20	20
467	5k. Hattver (vert)	25	25
468	20k. Fjardagil (vert)	1·40	45

121 First Court Session

1970. 50th Anniv of Icelandic Supreme Court.

469	**121**	6k.50 multicoloured	25	20

122 Part of "Skardsbok" (14th-cent law manuscript)

1970. Icelandic Manuscripts. Multicoloured.

470	5k. Type **122**	25	25
471	15k. Part of preface to "Flateyjarbok"	55	65
472	30k. Illuminated initial from "Flateyjarbok"	1·10	1·10

123 "Flaming Sun"

1970. Europa.

473	**123**	9k. yellow and brown	2·75	1·60
474	**123**	25k. brown and green	3·75	2·75

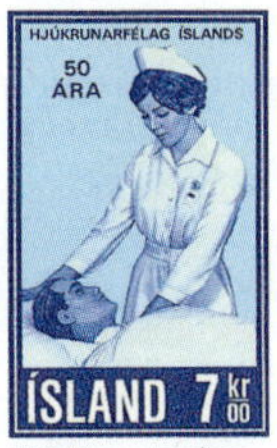

124 Nurse tending Patient

1970. 50th Anniv of Icelandic Nurses Assn.

475	**124**	7k. ultramarine and blue	30	25

125 G. Thomsen

1970. 150th Birth Anniv of Grimur Thomsen (poet).

476	**125**	10k. indigo and blue	55	35

126 "The Halt" (T. B. Thorlaksson)

1970. International Arts Festival, Reykjavik.

477	**126**	50k. multicoloured	1·50	1·30

127 Purple Saxifrage

1970. Nature Conservation Year. Mult.

478	3k. Type **127**	25	20
479	15k. Lakagigar (view)	90	85

128 U.N. Emblem and Map

1970. 25th Anniv of United Nations.

480	**128**	12k. multicoloured	50	45

129 "Flight" (A. Jonsson)

1971. "Help for Refugees".

481	**129**	10k. multicoloured	85	75

130 Europa Chain

1971. Europa.

482	**130**	7k. yellow, red and black	2·50	1·80
483	**130**	15k. yellow, blue and black	3·50	1·60

131 Postgiro Emblem

1971. Inauguration of Postal Giro Service.

484	**131**	5k. blue and light blue	25	20
485	**131**	7k. green and light green	30	25

132 Society Emblem

1971. Centenary of Icelandic Patriotic Society.

486	**132**	30k. lilac and blue	1·10	85
487	-	100k. black and grey	5·50	5·50

DESIGN: 100k. T. Gunnarsson (president and editor).

133 Freezing Plant and Haddock ("Melanogrammus aeglefinus")

1971. Icelandic Fishing Industry. Mult.

488	5k. Type **133**	20	20
489	7k. Landing catch and Atlantic cod ("Gadus morhua")	20	20
490	20k. Canning shrimps and "Pandalus borealis"	85	75

134 Mt. Herdubreid

1972

491	**134**	250k. multicoloured	70	30

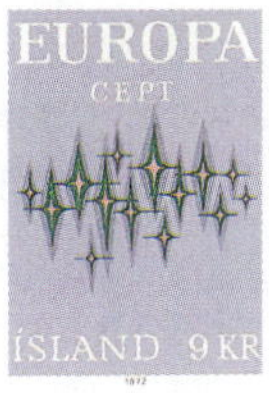

135 "Communications"

1972. Europa.

492	**135**	9k. multicoloured	1·50	75
493	**135**	13k. multicoloured	3·25	1·70

136 "Municipalities"

1972. Centenary of Icelandic Municipal Laws.

494	**136**	16k. multicoloured	25	25

137 World Map on Chessboard

1972. World Chess Championship, Reykjavik.

495	**137**	15k. multicoloured	30	25

138 Tomatoes

1972. Hot-house Plant Cultivation. Mult.

496	8k. Type **138**	20	20
497	12k. Steam source and valve	20	20
498	40k. Rose cultivation	1·10	75

139 Contour Map and Continental Shelf

1972. Iceland's Offshore Claims.

499	**139**	9k. multicoloured	25	25

140 Arctic Tern feeding Young

1972. Charity Stamps.

500	**140**	7k.+1k. multicoloured	55	75
501	**140**	9k.+1k. multicoloured	55	75

141 Europa "Posthorn"

1973. Europa.

502	**141**	13k. multicoloured	4·75	2·20
503	**141**	25k. multicoloured	95	65

142 Postman and 2s. stamp of 1873

1973. Stamp Centenary. Multicoloured.

504	10k. Type **142**	55	30
505	15k. Pony train	35	30
506	20k. "Esja" (mail steamer)	35	30
507	40k. Mail van	35	30
508	80k. Beech Model 18 mail plane	1·10	85

143 "The Nordic House", Reykjavik

1973. Nordic Countries' Postal Co-operation.

509	**143**	9k. multicoloured	40	35
510	**143**	10k. multicoloured	1·10	85

144 Pres. Asgeirsson

1973. 5th Death Anniv of Asgeir Asgeirsson (politician).

511	**144**	13k. red	35	30
512	**144**	15k. blue	30	25

145 Exhibition Emblem

1973. "Islandia 73" Stamp Exhibition. Mult.

513	17k. Type **145**	35	30
514	20k. Exhibition emblem (different)	30	30

146 "The Elements"

1973. Centenary of I.M.O.

515	**146**	50k. multicoloured	80	45

147 "Ingolfur and High-Seat Pillar" (tapestry, J. Briem)

1974. 1100th Anniv of Icelandic Settlement. Multicoloured.

516	10k. Type **147**	25	20
517	13k. "Grimur Geitskor at Thingvellir" (painting) (horiz)	25	30
518	15k. Bishop G. Thorlaksson of Holar	20	20
519	17k. "Snorri Sturluson slaying the King's messenger" (T. Skulason)	30	25
520	20k. Stained glass window from Hallgrimskirkja, Saurbaer	25	20
521	25k. Illuminated "I", from "Flateyjarbok" (manuscript)	30	25
522	30k. "Christ the King" (mosaic altar-piece, Skalholt Cathedral)	75	50
523	40k. 18th-century wood-carving	75	30
524	60k. "Curing the Catch" (concrete relief by S. Olafsson)	1·00	70
525	70k. "Saemunder smiting the Devil Seal" (bronze)	90	60
526	100k. Altar-cloth, Church of Stafafell (horiz)	1·10	85

148 "Horseman" (17th-century wood-carving)

1974. Europa. Sculptures. Multicoloured.

527		13k. Type **148**	50	20
528		20k. "Through the Sound Barrier" (bronze, A. Sveinsson)	1·50	85

149 Purchasing Stamps

1974. Centenary of Universal Postal Union.

529	**149**	17k. brown, blue & yellow	30	25
530	-	20k. brown, blue & green	30	30

DESIGN: 20k. Postman sorting mail.

150 Village with Erupting Volcano in distance

1975. Volcanic Eruption, Heimaey (1973).

531	**150**	20k. multicoloured	35	40
532	**150**	25k. multicoloured	30	30

151 "Autumn Bird" (T. Skullason)

1975. Europa. Paintings. Multicoloured.

533		18k. Type **151**	55	35
534		23k. "Sun Queen" (J. S. Kjarval) (vert.)	1·10	45

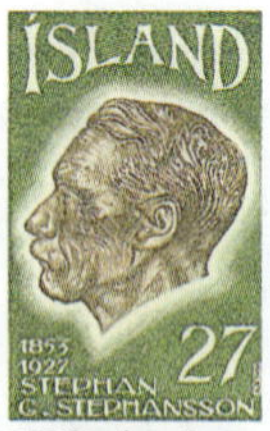

152 Stephan G. Stephansson (poet)

1975. Centenary of Icelandic Settlements in North America.

535	**152**	27k. brown and green	60	30

153 Hallgrimur Petursson (religious poet)

1975. Celebrities.

536	**153**	18k. black and green	20	30
537	-	23k. blue	20	30
538	-	30k. red	30	30
539	-	50k. blue	35	30

PORTRAITS: 23k. Arni Magnusson (historian); 30k. Jon Eiriksson (statesman); 50k. Einar Jonsson (painter and sculptor).

154 Red Cross Flag on Map of Iceland

1975. 50th Anniv of Icelandic Red Cross.

540	**154**	23k. multicoloured	30	25

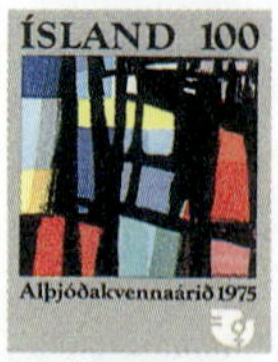

155 "Abstract" (N. Tryggvadottir)

1975. International Women's Year.

541	**155**	100k. multicoloured	1·00	60

156 "Bertel Thorvaldsen" (self-statue)

1975. Centenary of Thorvaldsen Society (Charity organization).

542	**156**	27k. multicoloured	65	30

157 "Forestry"

1975. Reafforestation.

543	**157**	35k. multicoloured	65	30

158 "Landscape" (Asgrimur Jonsson)

1976. Birth Cent of Asgrimur Jonsson (painter).

544	**158**	150k. multicoloured	1·50	1·00

159 Wooden Bowl

1976. Europa. Old Wooden Crafts. Mult.

545		35k. Type **159**	1·10	85
546		45k. Spinning-wheel (vert)	1·10	95

160 Title page of Postal Services Order

1976. Bicent of Icelandic Postal Services.

547	**160**	35k. brown	40	30
548	-	45k. blue	60	45

DESIGN: 45k. Signature appended to Postal Services Order.

161 Iceland 5a. Stamp with Reykjavik Postmark, 1876

1976. Cent of Icelandic Aurar Currency Stamps.

549	**161**	30k. multicoloured	25	20

162 "Workers" and Federation Emblem

1976. 60th Anniv of Icelandic Labour Federation.

550	**162**	100k. multicoloured	85	55

163 Water-lilies

1977. Nordic Countries' Co-operation in Nature Conservation and Environment Protection.

551	**163**	35k. multicoloured	70	45
552	**163**	45k. multicoloured	70	45

164 Ofaerufoss, Eldgja

1977. Europa. Multicoloured.

553		45k. Type **164**	2·75	65
554		85k. Kirkufell from Grundarfjord	2·75	60

165 Harlequin Duck

1977. European Wetlands Campaign.

555	**165**	40k. multicoloured	40	30

166 Co-operative Emblem

1977. 75th Anniv of Federation of Icelandic Co-operative Societies.

556	**166**	60k. blue and light blue	65	40

167 Thermal Spring and Rheumatic Treatment

1977. World Rheumatism Year.

557	**167**	90k. multicoloured	60	40

168 Cairn and Glacier

1977. 50th Anniv of Icelandic Touring Club.

558	**168**	45k. blue	75	50

169 Thorvaldur Thoroddsen (geologist)

1978. Famous Icelanders.

559	**169**	50k. green and brown	30	25
560	-	60k. brown and green	50	55

DESIGN: 60k. Briet Bjarnhedinsdottir (suffragette).

170 Videy Mansion

1978. Europa. Multicoloured.

561		80k. Type **170**	2·30	55
562		120k. Husavik Church (vert.)	2·30	65

171 Dr. A. Johannesson, Junkers W.34 "Island 1" and Junkers F-13 "Island 2"

1978. 50th Anniv of Domestic Flights.

563	**171**	60k. black and blue	30	30
564	-	100k. multicoloured	60	40

DESIGN: 100k. Fokker F.27 Friendship TF-F1K.

172 Skeidara Bridge

1978. Skeidara Bridge.

565	**172**	70k. multicoloured	25	25

173 "Lava Scene near Mt. Hekla" (J. Stefansson)

1978

566	**173**	1000k. multicoloured	3·50	2·50

174 Wreck of "Sargon" and Breeches-buoy

1978. 50th Anniv of National Life-Saving Association of Iceland.

567	**174**	60k. black	25	20

175 "Reykjanesviti" Lighthouse

1978. Centenary of Lighthouses in Iceland.

568	**175**	90k. multicoloured	55	35

176 Halldor Hermannsson

1978. Birth Centenary of Halldor Hermannsson (scholar and librarian).

569	**176**	150k. blue	45	35

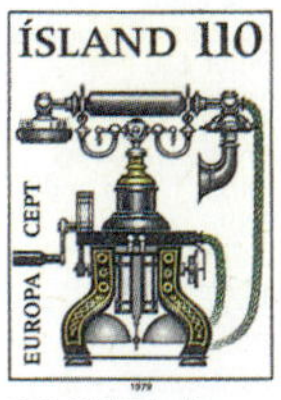

177 Old Telephone

1979. Europa. Multicoloured.

570	110k. Type **177**	2·75	55
571	190k. Posthorn and mailbag	4·25	65

178 Bjarni Thorsteinsson (clergyman and composer)

1979. Famous Icelanders.

572	-	80k. purple	25	25
573	**178**	100k. black	20	20
574	-	120k. red	30	30
575	-	130k. brown	40	45
576	-	170k. red	50	45

DESIGNS: 80k. Ingibjorg H. Bjarnason (headmistress and first female member of Althing); 120k. Petur Gudjohnsen (organist); 130k. Sveinbjorn Sveinbjornson (composer); 170k. Torfhildur Holm (poetess and novelist).

179 Children with Flowers

1979. International Year of the Child.

577	**179**	140k. multicoloured	65	40

180 Icelandic Arms to 1904 and 1904–19

1979. 75th Anniv of Ministry of Iceland.

578	**180**	500k. multicoloured	1·30	85

181 Sigurdsson and I. Einarsdottir

1979. Death Centenaries of Jon Sigurdsson (historian and Althing member) and of his wife, Ingibjorg Einarsdottir.

579	**181**	150k. black	50	40

182 Part of Kringla Leaf (MS of "Heimskringla")

1979. 800th Birth Anniv of Snorri Sturluson (saga writer).

580	**182**	200k. multicoloured	60	40

183 Icelandic Dog

1980. Fauna.

581	**183**	10k. black	15	15
582	-	90k. brown	15	15
583	-	160k. purple	75	35
584	-	170k. black	50	45
585	-	190k. brown	25	25

DESIGNS: 90k. Arctic fox; 160k. Greater redfish; 170k. Atlantic puffins; 190k. Common seal.

184 Jon Sveinsson alias Nonni (writer)

1980. Europa.

586	**184**	140k. pink and black	1·40	55
587	-	250k. pink and black	1·40	65

DESIGN: 250k. Gunnar Gunnarsson (writer).

185 Rowan Berries

1980. Year of the Tree.

588	**185**	120k. multicoloured	35	30

186 Sports Complex, Reykjavik

1980. Olympic Games, Moscow.

589	**186**	300k. turquoise	50	50

187 Embroidered Cushion

1980. Nordic Countries' Postal Co-operation. Multicoloured.

590	150k. Carved and painted cabinet door	55	50
591	180k. Type **187**	80	55

188 University Hospital

1980. 50th Anniv of University Hospital.

592	**188**	200k. multicoloured	45	35

189 Loudspeaker

1980. 50th Anniv of State Broadcasting Service.

593	**189**	400k. multicoloured	80	35

190 Magnus Stephensen (Chief Justice and publisher)

1981. Famous Icelanders.

594	**190**	170a. blue	40	30
595	-	190a. green	45	30

DESIGN: 190a. Finnur Magnusson (writer and Keeper of Privy Archives).

191 Loftur the Sorcerer

1981. Europa. Illustrations of Icelandic legends. Multicoloured.

596	180a. Type **191**	1·40	80
597	220a. Witch wading the deeps off Iceland	1·40	80

192 Winter Wren

1981. Birds.

598	**192**	50a. brown	15	15
599	-	100a. blue	20	15
600	-	200a. black	45	25

DESIGNS: 100a. Golden plover; 200a. Common raven.

193 Human Jigsaw

1981. International Year for Disabled Persons.

601	**193**	200a. multicoloured	25	25

194 Skyggnir Dish Aerial

1981. 75th Anniv of Icelandic Telephone Service.

602	**194**	500a. multicoloured	95	50

195 "Hauling the Line" (Gunnlaugur Scheving)

1981

603	**195**	5000a. multicoloured	5·75	3·50

196 Medieval Driftwood crucifix from Alftamyri

1981. Millenary of Missionary Work in Iceland.

604	**196**	200a. lilac	25	25

197 Leaf-bread (star pattern)

1981. Christmas. Multicoloured.

605	200a. Type **197**	60	50
606	250a. Leaf-bread (tree pattern)	60	50

198 Common Northern Whelk

1982. Shells.

607	**198**	20a. red	20	20
608	-	600a. brown	75	30

DESIGN: 600a. Iceland scallop.

199 Casting Dais Post into Sea (first Iceland settlement, 874)

1982. Europa. Multicoloured.

609	350a. Type **199**	5·25	85
610	450a. Discovery of Vinland (America), 1000	5·25	85

200 Sheep

1982. Domestic Animals.

611	**200**	300a. brown	80	45
612	-	400a. red	35	20
613	-	500a. grey	35	20

DESIGNS: 400a. Cow; 500a. Cat.

201 Co-operative Trading House, Husavik

1982. Centenary of Thingeyjar Co-operative Society.

614	**201**	1000a. black and brown	75	40

202 Horseman

1982. Iceland Ponies and Horsemanship.
615 **202** 700a. multicoloured 45 35

203 Holar

1982. Cent of Holar Agricultural College.
616 **203** 1500a. multicoloured 85 70

204 "Mount Herdubreid" (Isleifur Konradsson)

1982. Year of the Aged.
617 **204** 800a. multicoloured 75 40

205 T. Sveinsdottir

1982. Famous Icelanders. Thorbjorg Sveindsdottir (midwife and founder of Icelandic Women's Association).
618 **205** 900a. brown 50 40

206 Reynistadur Monastery Seal

1982. "Nordia 84" Stamp Exhibition, Reykjavik (1st issue). Sheet 82×80 mm containing T 206 and similar vert design.
MS619 400a. brown and black; 800a. brown and black (sold at 18k.) 5·25 5·25
DESIGN:—800a. Thingeyrar Monastery seal.
See also Nos. **MS**636 and **MS**645.

207 Doves and Opening of "The Night was such a Splendid One"

1982. Christmas. Multicoloured.
620 300a. Type **207** 75 45
621 350a. Bells and close of "The Night was such a Splendid One" (composed by Sigvaldi Kaldalons from poem by E. Sigurdsson) 80 60

208 Marsh Marigold

1983. Flowers. Multicoloured.
622 7k.50 Type **208** 35 25
623 8k. Alpine catchfly 70 45
624 10k. Marsh cinquefoil 1·00 45
625 20k. Water forgetmenot 2·00 85

209 Mount Sulur

1983. Nordic Countries' Postal Co-operation. "Visit the North". Multicoloured.
626 4k.50 Type **209** 80 65
627 5k. Urridafossar Falls 85 70

210 Thermal Area and Heat-exchange Plant

1983. Europa. Multicoloured.
628 5k. Type **210** 19·00 1·10
629 5k.50 Thermal area heating houses 22·00 1·60

211 Stern Trawler

1983. Fishing Industry.
630 **211** 11k. blue 65 60
631 - 13k. blue 1·10 55
DESIGN: 13k. Line fishing.

212 "Laki Craters" (Finnur Jonsson)

1983. Bicentenary of Skafta Eruption.
632 **212** 15k. multicoloured 85 60

213 Skiing

1983. Outdoor Sports. Multicoloured.
633 12k. Type **213** 80 45
634 14k. Jogging 95 55

214 Aircraft and W.C.Y. Emblem

1983. World Communications Year.
635 **214** 30k. multicoloured 1·80 1·10

215 Seal of Bishop Magnus Eyjolfsson

1983. "Nordia 84" Stamp Exhibition, Reykjavik (2nd issue). Sheet 82×80 mm containing T 215 and similar vert design.
MS636 8k. blue and black; 12k. green and black (sold at 30k.) 6·75 6·50
DESIGN: 12k. seal of Bishop Ogmundur Palsson.

216 Virgin Mary and Child

1983. Christmas. Multicoloured.
637 600a. Type **216** 80 45
638 650a. Visitation of the Angel 80 45

217 Pres. Eldjarn

1983. 1st Death Anniv (September) of Kristjan Eldjarn (President, 1968–80).
639 **217** 6k.50 red 80 55
640 **217** 7k. blue 45 25

218 Burnet Rose

1984. Flowers. Multicoloured.
641 6k. Type **218** 60 45
642 25k. Silverweed 1·20 45
See also Nos. 648/9, 657/60 and 717/18.

219 Bridge

1984. Europa. 25th Anniv of European Post and Telecommunications Conference.
643 **219** 6k.50 deep blue and blue 2·40 70
644 **219** 7k.50 dp purple & purple 1·20 75

220 Map of North Atlantic by Abraham Ortelius, 1570

1984. "Nordia 84" Stamp Exhibition, Reykjavik (3rd issue). Sheet 114×76 mm.
MS645 **220** 40k. multicoloured (sold at 60k.) 12·50 12·00

221 Icelandic Flags

1984. 40th Anniv of Republic.
646 **221** 50k. multicoloured 4·75 2·40

222 I.O.G.T. Lodge, Akureyri

1984. Centenary of International Order of Good Templars in Iceland.
647 **222** 10k. green 70 40

1984. Flowers. As T 218. Multicoloured.
648 6k.50 Wild azalea 55 40
649 7k.50 Alpine bearberry 65 65

223 Basalt symbolising Industries

1984. 50th Anniv of Confederation of Icelandic Employers.
650 **223** 30k. multicoloured 1·40 1·00

224 Bjorn Bjarnarson (founder) (after J. P. Wildenradt)

1984. Centenary of National Gallery.
651 **224** 12k. black, brown and green 70 50
652 - 40k. black, green and red 1·90 1·20
DESIGN: 40k. New gallery building.

225 Virgin and Child

1984. Christmas.
653 **225** 600a. blue, lt blue & gold 55 30
654 - 650a. red and gold 70 30
DESIGN: 650a. Angel with Christmas rose.

226 Text from Bible

1984. 400th Anniv of Gudbrand's Bible.
655 **226** 6k.50 red 50 30
656 - 7k.50 purple 45 70
DESIGN: 7k.50, Illustration from Bible.

1985. Flowers. As T 218. Multicoloured.
657 8k. Stone bramble 55 30
658 9k. Rock speedwell 70 30
659 16k. Sea pea 1·90 65
660 17k. Alpine whitlow-grass 70 55

227 Lady playing Langspil

1985. Europa. Music Year. Multicoloured.
661 6k.50 Type **227** 3·25 45
662 7k.50 Man playing Icelandic violin 3·25 1·30

228 Swedish Whitebeam

1985. Centenary of Iceland Horticultural Society.
663 **228** 20k. multicoloured 90 60

229 Girl and I.Y.Y. Emblem

1985. International Youth Year.
664 **229** 25k. multicoloured 1·00 75

230 Common Squid

1985. Marine Life.
665 **230** 7k. purple 35 30
666 - 8k. brown 35 30
667 - 9k. red 75 45
DESIGNS: 8k. Common spider crab; 9k. Sea anemone.

231 Rev. Hannes Stephensen (politician)

1985. Famous Icelanders.
668 **231** 13k. red 55 30
669 - 30k. violet 1·40 70
DESIGN: 30k. Jon Gudmundsson (editor and politician).

232 "Flight Yearning"

1985. Birth Centenary of Johannes Sveinsson Kjarval (artist).
670 **232** 100k. multicoloured 5·00 3·75

233 Snow Scene

1985. Christmas. Multicoloured.
671 8k. Type **233** 70 30
672 9k. Snow scene (different) 70 65

234 Pied Wagtail

1986. Birds. Multicoloured.
673 6k. Type **234** 35 30
674 10k. Pintail 1·30 55
675 12k. Merlin 95 50
676 15k. Razorbill 90 45
See also Nos. 697/700, 720/1, 726/7, 741/2 and 763/4.

235 Skaftafell National Park

1986. Europa. Multicoloured.
677 10k. Type **235** 13·00 1·40
678 12k. Jokulsargljufur National Park 4·50 85

236 Stykkisholmur

1986. Nordic Countries' Postal Co-operation. Twinned Towns. Multicoloured.
679 10k. Type **236** 1·10 60
680 12k. Seydisfjordur 1·10 55

237 Head Office, Reykjavik

1986. Centenary of National Bank. Mult.
681 **237** 13k. green 65 55
682 - 250k. brown 10·00 6·50
DESIGN: 250k. Reverse of first National Bank 5k. note.

238 First Official Seal

1986. Bicentenary of Reykjavik.
683 **238** 10k. red 60 45
684 - 12k. brown 60 45
685 - 13k. green 60 45
686 - 40k. blue 1·50 75
DESIGNS: 12k. "Reykjavik pond, 1856" (illustration from "Journey in the Northern Seas" by Charles Edmond); 13k. Women washing clothes in natural hot water brook, Laugardalur; 40k. City Theatre.

239 Early Telephone Equipment

1986. 80th Anniv of Icelandic Telephone and Telegraph Service. Multicoloured.
687 10k. Type **239** 45 25
688 20k. Modern digital telephone system 1·10 70

240 Hvita River Crossing, 1836 (after Auguste Mayer)

1986. Stamp Day. Sheet 95×67 mm.
MS689 **240** 20k. black (sold at 30k.) 5·00 4·75

241 "Christmas at Peace"

1986. Christmas. Multicoloured.
690 10k. Type **241** 70 35
691 12k. "Christmas Night" 60 35

242 "Svanur" (ketch) anchored off Olafsvik

1987. 300th Anniv of Olafsvik Trading Station.
692 **242** 50k. purple 2·30 1·40

243 Terminal and Boeing 727 Tail

1987. Opening of Leif Eiriksson Terminal, Keflavik Airport.
693 **243** 100k. multicoloured 4·25 1·70

244 Christ carrying Cross

1987. Europa. Stained Glass Windows by Leifur Breidfoerd, Fossvogur Cemetery Chapel. Multicoloured.
694 12k. Type **244** 1·80 70
695 15k. Soldiers and peace dove 3·00 90

245 Rask

1987. Birth Bicentenary of Rasmus Kristjan Rask (philologist).
696 **245** 20k. black 90 65

1987. Birds. As T 234. Multicoloured.
697 13k. Short-eared owl 65 30
698 40k. Redwing 1·70 80
699 70k. Oystercatcher 2·50 1·20
700 90k. Mallard 4·00 2·10

246 Girl Brushing Teeth

1987. Dental Protection.
701 **246** 12k. multicoloured 55 45

247 Vulture

1987. National Guardian Spirits. Each red.
702 13k. Type **247** 70 95
703 13k. Dragon 70 95
704 13k. Bull 70 95
705 13k. Giant 70 95
See also Nos. 713/16, 732 and 743/50.

248 Djupivogur Trading Station, 1836 (after Auguste Mayer)

1987. Stamp Day. Sheet 95×67 mm.
MS706 **248** 30k. black (sold at 45k.) 5·00 5·50

249 Christmas Tree

1987. Christmas. Multicoloured.
707 13k. Type **249** 70 45
708 17k. "Christmas Light" 85 70

250 Steinn Steinarr (poet)

1988. Famous Icelanders. Multicoloured.
709 16k. Type **250** 70 30
710 21k. David Stefansson (writer) 90 55

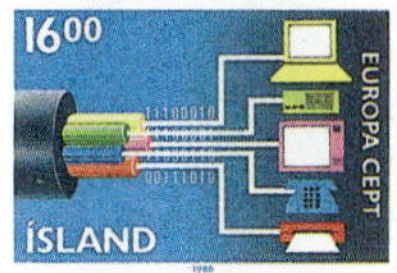

251 Transmission of Messages by Modern Data System

1988. Europa. Communications. Multicoloured.
711 16k. Type **251** 95 45
712 21k. Phone pad and globe within envelope (transmission of letters by facsimile machine) 4·25 1·90

1988. National Guardian Spirit. As Nos. 702/5 but values and colour changed.
713 16k. black (Type **247**) 70 65
714 16k. black (Dragon) 70 65
715 16k. black (Bull) 70 65
716 16k. black (Giant) 70 65

1988. Flowers. As T 218. Multicoloured.
717 10k. Tufted vetch 55 25
718 50k. Wild thyme 2·30 70

252 Handball

1988. Olympic Games, Seoul.
719 **252** 18k. multicoloured 90 45

1988. Birds. As T 234. Multicoloured.
720 5k. Black-tailed godwit 30 20
721 30k. Long-tailed duck 1·40 55

253 "Nupsstadur Farm, Fljotshverfi, 1836" (after Auguste Mayer)

1988. Stamp Day. Sheet 95×67 mm.
MS722 **253** 40k. black (sold at 60k.) 4·50 4·50

254 Mother and Baby

1988. 40th Anniv of W.H.O. "Health for All in 2000".
723 **254** 19k. multicoloured 95 45

255 Fisherman with Haul of Fish

1988. Christmas. Multicoloured.
724 19k. Type **255** 70 40
725 24k. Trawler and buoy 1·10 70

1989. Birds. As T 234. Multicoloured.
726 19k. Red-necked phalarope 70 40
727 100k. Snow buntings 4·50 3·25

256 Peysufot (dress costume)

1989. Nordic Countries' Postal Co-operation. Traditional Costumes. Multicoloured.
728 21k. Type **256** 1·10 60
729 26k. Upphlutur (everyday wear) 1·10 70

257 Children at Seaside

1989. Europa. Childrens' Toys and Games. Multicoloured.
730 21k. Type **257** 6·50 80
731 26k. Girl with hoop and boy with hobby-horse 6·50 80

1989. National Guardian Spirits. As No. 703 but colour and value changed.
732 500k. brown (Dragon) 19·00 11·00

258 Mount Skeggi, Arnarfjord

1989. Landscapes. Multicoloured.
733 35k. Type **258** 1·20 65
734 45k. Namaskard thermal spring 1·20 75
See also Nos. 757/8 and 765/6.

259 College

1989. Cent of Hvanneyri Agricultural College.
735 **259** 50k. multicoloured 1·40 85

260 Seaman throwing Barrels at Whales

1989. Stamp Day. "Nordia 91" Stamp Exhibition, Reykjavik (1st issue). Sheet 114×74 mm containing T 260 and similar vert designs, showing details of the 1539 Carta Marina by Olaus Magnus.
MS736 30k. Type **260**; 30k. Ship harpooning whale; 30k. Sea serpent encircling ship (sold at 130k.) 8·50 8·00
See also Nos. **MS**760 and **MS**771.

261 Stefan Stefansson (co-founder) and Flowers

1989. Centenary of Icelandic Natural History Society. Multicoloured.
737 21k. Type **261** 90 45
738 26k. Bjarni Saemundsson (first Chairman) and Atlantic cod 90 45

262 "Virgin and Child"

1989. Christmas. Multicoloured.
739 21k. Type **262** 90 45
740 26k. "Three Wise Men" 1·00 65

1990. Birds. As T 234. Multicoloured.
741 21k. European wigeons 1·10 45
742 80k. Pink-footed goose and goslings 2·75 1·10

1990. National Guardian Spirits. As Nos. 702/5 but value and colours changed.
743 5k. green (Type **247**) 35 35
744 5k. green (Dragon) 35 35
745 5k. green (Bull) 35 35
746 5k. green (Giant) 35 35
747 21k. blue (Type **247**) 70 70
748 21k. blue (Dragon) 70 70
749 21k. blue (Bull) 70 70
750 21k. blue (Giant) 70 70

263 Gudrun Larusdottir (writer and politician) (after Halldor Petursson)

1990. 110th Birth Anniversaries. Mult.
751 21k. Type **263** 80 45
752 21k. Ragnhildur Petursdottir (women's educationist) (after Asgrimur Jonsson) 80 45

264 Posthouse Street, Reykjavik, Post Office and Old Scales

1990. Europa. Post Office Buildings. Mult.
753 21k. Type **264** 3·75 85
754 40k. Thoenglabakki 4, Reykjavik, Post Office and modern scales 5·25 1·80

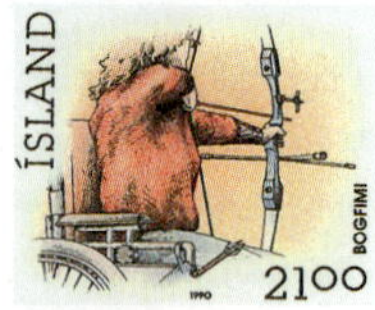

265 Archery

1990. Sport. Multicoloured.
755 21k. Type **265** 80 55
756 21k. Football 80 55

1990. Landscapes. As T 258. Multicoloured.
757 25k. Hvitserkur, Hunafjord 1·10 55
758 200k. Lomagnupur 6·25 2·75

266 Bird, Stars and Map

1990. European Tourism Year.
759 **266** 30k. multicoloured 1·10 80

267 Denmark

1990. Stamp Day. "Nordia 91" Stamp Exhibition, Reykjavik (2nd issue). Sheet 114×74 mm containing T 267 and similar vert designs, showing details of the 1539 Carta Marina by Olaus Magnus.
MS760 40k. Type **267**; 40k. Sweden; 40k. Gotland and sailing ship (sold at 170k.) 9·25 9·00

268 Children around Christmas Tree

1990. Christmas. Multicoloured.
761 25k. Type **268** 1·20 60
762 30k. Carol singers 1·40 75

1991. Birds. As T 234. Multicoloured.
763 25k. Slavonian grebes 1·00 30
764 100k. Northern gannets 4·50 1·30

1991. Landscapes. As T 258. Multicoloured.
765 10k. Mt. Vestrahorn 45 30
766 300k. Kverkfjoll range 9·50 3·75

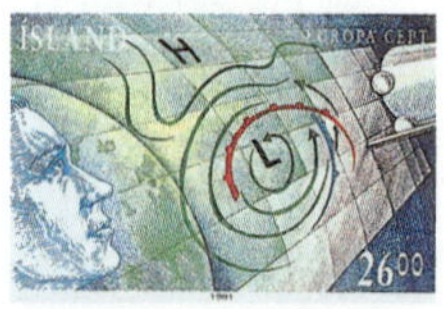

269 Meteorological Information

1991. Europa. Europe in Space. Mult.
767 26k. Type **269** 8·50 1·10
768 47k. Telecommunications satellite 13·50 1·90

270 Jokulsarlon

1991. Nordic Countries' Postal Co-operation. Tourism. Multicoloured.
769 26k. Type **270** 1·40 70
770 31k. Strokkur hot spring 1·50 80

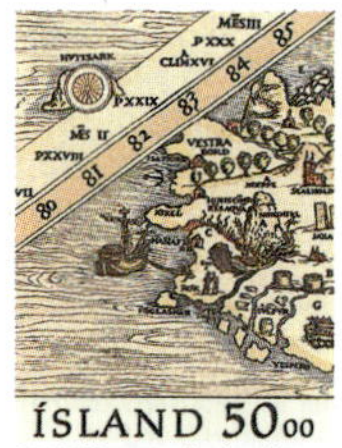

271 Western Iceland

1991. "Nordia 91" Stamp Exhibition (3rd issue). Sheet 114×74 mm containing T 271 and similar vert designs, showing details of the 1539 Carta Marina by Olaus Magnus.
MS771 50k. Type **271**; 50k. Arms and central part of Iceland; 50k. Eastern Iceland, ice floes and compass rose (sold at 215k.) 11·00 10·50

272 Golf

1991. Sports. Multicoloured.
772 26k. Type **272** 90 55
773 26k. Glima (wrestling) 90 55

273 Pall Isolfsson (composer) (after Hans Muller)

1991. Famous Icelanders. Multicoloured.
774 60k. Ragnar Jonsson (founder of Reykjavik College of Music) (after Joannes Kjarval) (horiz) 1·70 1·10
775 70k. Type **273** 2·30 1·60

274 College Building and Student using Sextant

1991. Cent of College of Navigation, Reykjavik.
776 **274** 50k. multicoloured 1·70 90

275 "Soloven" (mail brigantine)

1991. Stamp Day. Ships. Multicoloured.
777 30k. Type **275** 2·75 1·50
778 30k. "Arcturus" (cargo liner) 2·75 1·50
779 30k. "Gullfoss I" (cargo liner) 2·75 1·50
780 30k. "Esja II" (cargo liner) 2·75 1·50

276 "Light of Christmas"

1991. Christmas. Multicoloured.
781 30k. Type **276** 1·00 60
782 35k. Star 1·10 85

277 Skiing

1992. Sport. Multicoloured.

783	30k. Type **277**	1·00	55
784	30k. Volleyball	1·00	55

278 Map and "Santa Maria"

1992. Europa. 500th Anniv of Discovery of America by Columbus. Multicoloured.

785	55k. Map and Viking ship (Leif Eriksson)	6·50	1·60
786	55k. Type **278**	6·50	1·60
MS787	85×67 mm. Nos. 785/6	10·50	9·50

279 Agricultural and Industrial Symbols

1992. 75th Anniv of Iceland Chamber of Commerce (30k.) and 50th Anniv of Icelandic Freezing Plants Corporation (35k.). Multicoloured.

788	30k. Type **279**	1·00	65
789	35k. Trawler and Atlantic cod	1·00	70

280 River Fnjoska Bridge, Skogar

1992. Bridges. Multicoloured.

790	5k. Type **280**	25	20
791	250k. River Olfusa bridge, Selfoss	8·00	5·75

See also Nos. 804/5.

281 Ford "TT", 1920–26

1992. Postal Vehicles. Multicoloured.

792	30k. Type **281**	2·10	1·10
793	30k. Citroen snowmobile, 1929	2·10	1·10
794	30k. Mail/passenger transport car "RE 231", 1933	2·10	1·10
795	30k. Ford bus, 1946	2·10	1·10

282 Face and Candle reflected in Window

1992. Christmas. Multicoloured.

796	30k. Type **282**	1·10	65
797	35k. Full moon	1·10	75

283 Gyr Falcon with Chicks

1992. Endangered Species. The Gyr Falcon. Multicoloured.

798	5k. Type **283**	1·20	30
799	10k. Beating wings	1·40	40
800	20k. Eating	2·00	80
801	35k. On ground	2·50	1·40

284 Handball

1993. Sport. Multicoloured.

802	30k. Type **284**	90	50
803	30k. Running	90	50

1993. Bridges. As T 280. Multicoloured.

804	90k. River Hvita bridge, Ferjukot	3·00	1·60
805	150k. River Jokulsa a Fjollum bridge, Grimsstadir	5·25	3·25

285 The Blue Lagoon, Svartsengi

1993. Nordic Countries' Postal Co-operation. Tourism. Multicoloured.

806	30k. Type **285**	1·00	75
807	35k. Perlan (The Pearl), Reykjavik	1·40	90

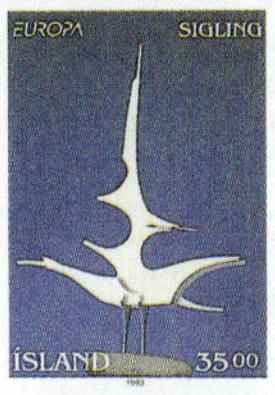

286 "Sailing" (Jon Gunnar Arnason)

1993. Europa. Contemporary Art. Mult.

808	35k. Type **286**	1·70	1·00
809	55k. "Hatching of the Jet" (Magnus Tomasson)	2·75	1·80

287 1933 1k. Balbo Flight Stamp

1993. 60th Anniv of Balbo Transatlantic Mass Formation Flight. Sheet 110×76 mm containing T 287 and similar vert designs. Multicoloured.

MS810	10k. Type **287**; 50k. 1933 5k. Balbo flight stamp; 100k. 1933 10k. Balbo flight stamp (sold at 200k.)	6·75	6·50

288 Junkers "F-13" Seaplane "Sulan" D-483

1993. 65th Anniv of 1st Icelandic Postal Flight. Multicoloured.

811	30k. Type **288**	1·90	75
812	30k. Waco YKS-7 seaplane TF-ORH	1·90	75
813	30k. Grumman G-21 Goose amphibian TF-VK	1·90	75
814	30k. Consolidated PBY-5 Catalina flying boat "Old Peter" TF-TSP	1·90	75

289 Three Wise Men adoring Child

1993. Christmas. Multicoloured.

815	30k. Type **289**	1·00	75
816	35k. Madonna and Child	1·20	95

290 Swimming

1994. Sport. Multicoloured.

817	30k. Type **290**	1·00	45
818	30k. Weightlifting	1·00	45

291 Finger Puppets

1994. International Year of the Family.

819	**291** 40k. multicoloured	1·00	75

292 St. Brendan visiting Iceland

1994. Europa. St. Brendan's Voyages. Multicoloured.

820	35k. Type **292**	1·30	95
821	55k. St. Brendan discovering Faroe Islands	2·00	1·60
MS822	81×76 mm. Nos. 820/1	3·50	3·50

293 Conductor and Instruments

1994. 50th Anniv of Independence. Art and Culture. Multicoloured.

823	30k. Type **293** (44th anniv of Icelandic Symphony Orchestra)	85	45
824	30k. Pottery (55th anniv of College of Arts and Crafts)	85	45
825	30k. Cameraman and actors (16th anniv of National Film Fund)	85	45
826	30k. Ballerina and modern dancers (21st anniv of Icelandic Dance Company)	85	45
827	30k. Theatre masks (44th anniv of Icelandic National Theatre)	85	45

294 Gisli Sveinsson (President of United Althing, 1944)

1994. 50th Anniv of New Constitution.

828	**294** 30k. multicoloured	90	75

295 Sveinn Bjornsson (1944–52)

1994. 50th Anniv of Republic. Presidents. Sheet 118×71 mm containing T 295 and similar vert designs. Multicoloured.

MS829	50k. Type **295**; 50k. Asgeir Asgeirsson (1952–68); 50k. Kristjan Eldjarn (1968–80); 50k. Vigdis Finnbogadottir (1980 onwards)	6·75	6·50

296 Children looking at Stamp Album

1994. Stamp Day. Stamp Collecting. Sheet 120×50 mm containing T 296 and similar square designs. Multicoloured.

MS830	30k. Type **296**; 35k. Magnifying glass over stamps; 100k. Girl and elderly man studying globe (sold at 200k.)	8·50	8·00

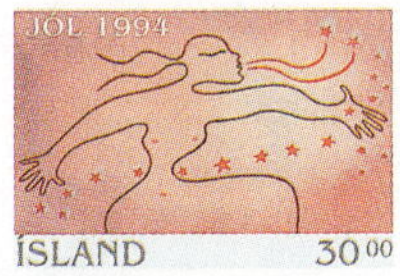

297 Woman and Stars

1994. Christmas. Multicoloured.

831	30k. Type **297**	90	65
832	35k. Man and stars	1·00	75

298 Emblem and Airplane

1994. 50th Anniv of I.C.A.O.

833	**298** 100k. multicoloured	3·25	2·20

299 Flag and Salvation Army Members

1995. Anniversaries. Multicoloured.

834	35k. Type **299** (centenary of Salvation Army in Iceland)	1·00	75
835	90k. Map of fjord (centenary of Seydisfjordur)	2·75	1·60

300 Geyser

1995. 14th World Men's Handball Championship. Multicoloured.

836	35k. Type **300**	1·30	1·80
837	35k. Stadium	1·30	1·80
838	35k. Volcano	1·30	1·80
839	35k. Entrance to fjord	1·30	1·80

301 Laufas

1995. Nordic Countries' Postal Co-operation. Tourism. Multicoloured.

840	30k. Type **301**	1·00	75
841	35k. Fjallsjokull Glacier	1·40	85

302 "Spell-broken" (sculpture, Einar Jonsson)

1995. Europa. Peace and Freedom.
842 **302** 35k. multicoloured 1·20 1·00
843 **302** 55k. multicoloured 2·00 1·50

303 "Laura" (mail ship)

1995. Mail Ships. Multicoloured.
844 30k. Type **303** 1·10 1·00
845 30k. "Dronning Alexandrine" 1·10 1·00
846 30k. "Laxfoss" 1·10 1·00
847 30k. "Godafoss III" 1·10 1·00

304 Redpoll ("Acanthis flammea")

1995. European Nature Conservation Year. Birds. Multicoloured.
848 25k. Type **304** 75 55
849 250k. Common snipe ("Gallinago gallinago") 7·25 6·25

305 Boeing 757

1995. 40th Anniv of Iceland–Luxembourg Air Link.
850 **305** 35k. multicoloured 1·00 85

306 Hraunfossar Waterfalls (left detail)

1995. "Nordia 96" Stamp Exhibition, Reykjavik (1st issue). Sheet 105×65 mm containing T 306 and similar horiz design. Multicoloured.
MS851 10k. Type **306**; 150k. Waterfalls (right detail) (sold at 200k.) 8·00 7·50
The stamps form a composite design.
See also No. **MS**871.

307 Snowman and Snowwoman

1995. Christmas. Multicoloured.
852 30k. Type **307** 90 60
853 35k. Coloured fir trees 1·10 70

308 Anniversary Emblem

1995. 50th Anniv of U.N.O.
854 **308** 100k. multicoloured 2·75 1·80

309 Common Cormorant ("Phalacrocorax carbo")

1996. Birds. Multicoloured.
855 20k. Type **309** 55 45
856 40k. Barrow's goldeneye ("Bucephala islandica") 1·10 95

310 "Seamen in a Boat" (Gunnlaugur Scheving)

1996. Paintings. Multicoloured.
857 100k. Type **310** 2·75 1·50
858 200k. "At the Washing Springs" (Kristin Jonsdottir) 5·00 3·50

311 Halldora Bjarnadottir (founder of women's societies)

1996. Europa. Famous Women. Mult.
859 35k. Type **311** 1·40 1·00
860 55k. Olafia Johannsdottir (women's rights campaigner and temperance worker) 1·70 1·50

312 1931 Buick

1996. Post Buses. Multicoloured.
861 35k. Type **312** 1·10 95
862 35k. 1933 Studebaker 1·10 95
863 35k. 1937 Ford 1·10 95
864 35k. 1946 Reo 1·10 95

313 Running

1996. Olympic Games, Atlanta. Mult.
865 5k. Type **313** 20 15
866 25k. Javelin 70 60
867 45k. Long jumping 1·10 1·10
868 65k. Shot put 1·70 1·60

314 Hospital Ward

1996. Centenary of Order of the Sisters of St. Joseph in Iceland.
869 **314** 65k. black, stone & purple 1·70 1·50

315 School

1996. 150th Anniv of Reykjavik School.
870 **315** 150k. multicoloured 4·00 3·25

316 Godafoss Waterfalls (central detail)

1996. "Nordia 96" Stamp Exhibition, Reykjavik (2nd issue). Sheet 105×65 mm containing T 316 and similar square designs. Multicoloured.
MS871 45k. Type **316**; 65k. Waterfalls (right detail); 90k. Waterfalls (left detail) (sold at 300k.) 8·75 8·25
The stamps form a composite design.

317 Reykjavik Cathedral

1996. Bicentenary of Reykjavik Cathedral.
872 **317** 45k. multicoloured 1·40 1·10

318 "Virgin Mary holding Child Jesus" (ivory figurine)

1996. Christmas. Exhibits from National Museum of Iceland. Multicoloured.
873 35k. Type **318** 1·00 65
874 45k. Pax depicting Nativity 1·50 1·40

319 Red-breasted Merganser ("Mergus serrator")

1997. Ducks. Multicoloured.
875 10k. Type **319** 40 40
876 500k. Green-winged teal ("Anas crecca") 12·50 12·00

320 "Song of Iceland" (Svavar Gudnason)

1997. Paintings. Multicoloured.
877 150k. Type **320** 4·00 3·25
878 200k. "The Harbour" (Thorvaldur Skulason) 5·75 4·25

321 De Havilland D.H.89A Dragon Rapide

1997. Mail Planes. Multicoloured.
879 35k. Type **321** 1·10 80
880 35k. Stinson S.R. 8B Reliant seaplane 1·10 80
881 35k. Douglas DC-3 Dakota 1·10 80
882 35k. De Havilland D.H.C.6 Twin Otter 1·10 80

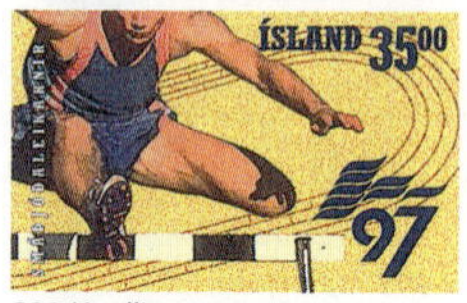

322 Hurdling

1997. 7th European Small States' Games. Multicoloured.
883 35k. Type **322** 1·10 90
884 45k. Sailing 1·50 1·20

323 "The Deacon of Myrka"

1997. Europa. Tales and Legends. Paintings by Asgrimur Jonsson. Multicoloured.
885 45k. Type **323** 1·50 1·30
886 65k. "Surtla at Blalandseyjar" 2·00 1·50

324 Printer's Colour Control and Pieces of Type

1997. Centenary of Formation of Icelandic Printers' Association (now part of Union of Icelandic Graphic Workers).
887 **324** 90k. multicoloured 2·75 2·20

325 Stefania Gudmundsdattir and Idno Theatre

1997. Centenary of Reykjavik Theatre.
888 **325** 100k. multicoloured 2·75 2·40
The actress is shown in the role of the Fairy in "New Year's Night" by Indridi Einarsson.

326 Western Islands Eight-oared Fishing Boat

1997. Stamp Day. Icelandic Boats. Sheet 110×76 mm containing T 326 and similar square designs. Each black, brown and chestnut.
MS889 35k. Type **326**; 65k. Engey six-oared sailing boat, 1912; 100k. Egil (Breidafjordur boat), 1904 (sold at 250k.) 6·25 6·00

327 Wise Men

1997. Christmas. Multicoloured.
890 35k. Type **327** 1·10 95
891 45k. Nativity 1·40 1·10

328 Mounted Mail Carrier

1997. Rural Post.

892	**328**	50k. multicoloured	1·40	1·20

329 Downhill Skiing

1998. Winter Olympic Games, Nagano, Japan. Multicoloured.

893	35k. Type **329**	1·00	85
894	45k. Cross-country skiing	1·50	1·20

330 Sailing Dinghies

1998. Nordic Countries' Postal Co-operation. Sailing. Multicoloured.

895	35k. Type **330**	1·00	85
896	45k. Yachts	1·50	1·10

331 Lumpsucker ("Cyclopterus lumpus")

1998. Fishes (1st series). Multicoloured.

897	5k. Type **331**	20	20
898	10k. Atlantic cod ("Gadus morhua")	25	20
899	60k. Skate ("Raja batis")	1·70	1·60
900	300k. Atlantic wolffish ("Anarhichas lupus")	8·00	7·50
MS901	100×68 mm. Nos. 897/900	10·00	9·75

See also Nos. 913/14, 972/3 and 983/4.

332 Children waving Flags

1998. Europa. National Festivals. National Day. Multicoloured.

902	45k. Type **332**	1·40	1·30
903	65k. Statue of President Jon Sigurdsson and flags	2·10	1·70

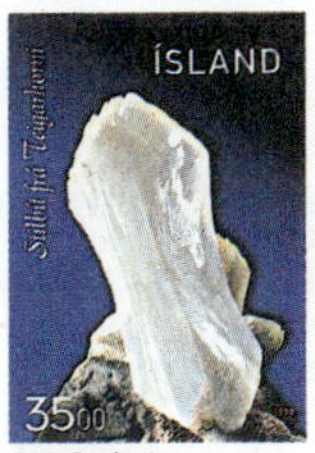

333 Scolecite

1998. Minerals (1st series). Multicoloured.

904	35k. Type **333**	1·00	90
905	45k. Stilbite	1·40	1·10

See also Nos. 933/4.

334 Hospital

1998. Centenary of Founding of Leprosy Hospital, Laugarnes.

906	**334**	70k. multicoloured	1·80	1·60

335 Anniversary Emblem

1998. 125th Anniv of First Iceland Stamps.

907	**335**	35k. multicoloured	1·10	90

336 Peat-cutter

1998. Stamp Day. Agricultural Tools. Sheet 110×76 mm containing T 336 and similar square designs.

MS908	35k. green, black and grey; 65k. ochre, black and grey; 100k. blue, black and grey (sold at 250k.)	7·00	6·75

DESIGNS: 65k. Mower; 100k. Grinder.

337 Cat and Houses (Thelma Ingolfsdottir)

1998. Christmas. Multicoloured.

909	35k. Type **337**	90	80
910	45k. Two angels (Telma Thrastardottir)	1·40	1·10

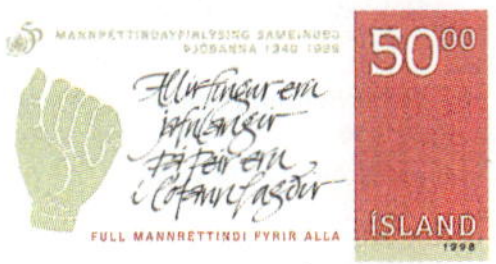

338 Writing and Hand forming Fist

1998. 50th Anniv of Universal Declaration of Human Rights.

911	**338**	50k. black, green and red	1·50	1·40

339 Leifs

1999. Birth Centenary of Jon Leifs (composer).

912	**339**	35k. multicoloured	1·10	95

1999. Fishes (2nd series). As T 331. Multicoloured.

913	35k. Plaice ("Pleuronectes platessa")	1·10	1·00
914	55k. Atlantic herring ("Clupea harengus")	1·60	1·30

340 Killer Whale ("Orcinus orca")

1999. Marine Mammals (1st series). Multicoloured.

915	35k. Type **340**	1·00	80
916	45k. Sperm whale ("Physeter macrocephalus")	1·40	1·10
917	65k. Blue whale ("Balaenoptera musculus")	1·80	1·60
918	85k. Common porpoise ("Phocoena phocoena")	2·30	2·00
MS919	100×80 mm. Nos. 915/19	6·25	6·00

See also Nos. 966/9 and 1000/3.

341 Arnold Jung's Steam Locomotive "Minor", 1892

1999. Transport. Multicoloured.

920	25k. Type **341**	90	85
921	50k. Type **341**	1·40	1·30
922	75k. "Sigurfari" (fishing cutter)	2·30	2·20

342 Dates and Doves

1999. 50th Anniv of Council of Europe.

923	**342**	35k. multicoloured	1·70	1·10

343 Larch Boletes ("Suillus grevillei")

1999. Fungi (1st series). Multicoloured.

924	35k. Type **343**	1·00	75
925	75k. Field mushrooms ("Agaricus campestris")	2·00	1·60

See also Nos. 954/5.

344 Skutustadagigar, Lake Myvatn

1999. Europa. Parks and Gardens. Multicoloured.

926	50k. Type **344**	1·40	1·10
927	75k. Arnarstapi Point	2·00	1·60

345 Wheat ("Land Graedsla")

1999. Nature Conservation. Multicoloured.

928	35k. Type **345**	1·00	90
929	35k. Rainbow and tree within sun ("Loft")	1·00	90
930	35k. Nest with eggs ("Vot Lendis")	1·00	90
931	35k. Tree stump ("Skog Raekt")	1·00	90
932	35k. Fish and birds ("Stlendur")	1·00	90

1999. Minerals (2nd series). As T 333. Mult.

933	40k. Calcite	1·20	1·00
934	50k. Heulandite	1·40	1·20

346 "Facescape" (Erro)

1999. Reykjavik, European Cultural City. Mult.

935	35k. Type **346**	1·10	1·00
936	50k. Cultural symbols	1·50	1·30

347 "Danish Sailing Ship off Drangey" (Carl Baagoe)

1999. Stamp Day. Sheet 110×65 mm.

MS937	**347** 200k. brown and black (sold at 250k.)	7·25	7·00

348 Man cleaning Globe (Jona Greta Gudmundsdottir)

1999. "Stampin' the Future". Winning Entries in Children's International Painting Competition.

938	**348**	35k. multicoloured	1·10	90

349 Goblin (Stiff-legs)

1999. Christmas. Yule Goblins. Multicoloured.

939	35k. Type **349**	1·10	95
940	35k. Leaping over rock (Gully-gawk)	1·10	95
941	35k. With arm raised (Stubby)	1·10	95
942	35k. Licking spoon (Spoon-licker)	1·10	95
943	35k. With hand in cooking pot (Pot-scraper)	1·10	95
944	35k. With finger in mouth (Bowl-licker)	1·10	95
945	35k. Opening door (Door-slammer)	1·10	95
946	35k. Drinking from ladle (Skyr-gobbler)	1·10	95
947	35k. Carrying sausages (Sausage-swiper)	1·10	95
948	35k. Looking through window (Window-peeper)	1·10	95
949	50k. With nose raised (Door-sniffer)	1·40	1·30
950	50k. With leg of meat (Meat-hook)	1·40	1·30
951	50k. With candles (Candle-beggar)	1·40	1·30

350 Embroidered Altar Frontal, Holar Cathedral

2000. Millenary of Christianity in Iceland. Mult.

952	40k. Type **350**	1·10	1·00
MS953	70×46 mm. 40k. Family singing hymns (29×39 mm)	1·00	95

351 Chanterelle (*Cantharellus cibarius*)

2000. Fungi (2nd series). Multicoloured.

954	40k. Type **351**	1·10	95
955	50k. Shaggy ink cap (*Coprinus comatus*)	1·40	1·10

352 Statue of Thorfinn Karlsefni (early settler) and Globe

2000. Millenary of Discovery of the Americas by Leif Eriksson. Multicoloured.

956	40k. Type **352**	1·00	95
957	50k. Viking longship under sail	1·40	1·30
958	75k. Longship on shore	1·80	1·70
959	90k. Leif Eriksson and globe	2·40	2·30
MS960	96×76 mm. Nos. 956/9	6·75	6·50

353 Quill and Profile

2000. New Millennium. Multicoloured.

961	40k. Type **353**	1·10	95
962	50k. Family tree, man and computer chip	1·40	1·10

354 Steam Roller

2000. Transport. Multicoloured.

963	50k. Type **354**	1·40	1·30
964	75k. Fire engine	2·00	1·90

355 "Building Europe"

2000. Europa.

965	**355**	50k. multicoloured	1·70	1·60

2000. Marine Mammals (2nd series). As T 340. Mult.

966	5k. Bottlenose whale (*Hyperoodon ampullatus*)	25	20
967	40k. Atlantic white-sided dolphin (*Lagenorhynchus actus*)	90	95
968	50k. Humpback whale (*Megaptera novaeangliae*)	1·40	1·30
969	75k. Minke whale (*Balaenoptera acutorostrata*)	2·00	1·90

356 Pansy (*Violea x wittrockiana*)

2000. Summer Flowers (1st series). Multicoloured.

970	40k. Type **356**	1·10	95
971	50k. Petunia (*Petunia x hybrida*)	1·30	1·10

See also Nos. 986/7.

2000. Fishes (3rd series). As T 331. Multicoloured.

972	10k. Haddock (*Melanogrammus aeglefinus*)	25	20
973	250k. Capelin (*Mallotus villosus*)	7·25	7·00

357 Dark Marbled Carpet (*Chioroclysta citrata*)

2000. Butterflies. Multicoloured.

974	40k. Type **357**	1·10	95
975	50k. Antler (*Cerapteryx graminis*)	1·40	1·30

358 "Icelandic settlers on the Shore of Lake Winnipeg" (Arni Sigurdsson)

2000. Stamp Day. Sheet 88×73 mm.

MS976	**358** 200k. multicoloured (sold at 250k.)	6·50	6·25

359 Viking Settler's House

2000. Early Dwellings. Multicoloured.

977	45k. Type **359**	1·00	95
978	75k. Viking turf houses, Stong Thjorsardal	1·70	1·60

360 Leppaludi

2000. Christmas. Ogres. Multicoloured.

979	40k. Type **360**	90	90
980	50k. Gryla	1·20	1·10
MS981	105×75 mm. As Nos. 979/80, but 21×36 mm	2·50	2·40

361 Super Puma Helicopter, Fokker 27 Airplane and *Tyr* (ship)

2001. 75th Anniv of Coast Guard Service in Iceland.

982	**361**	20k. multicoloured	90	85

2001. Fishes. As T 331. Multicoloured.

983	55k. Greenland halibut (*Reinhardtius hippogolossides*)	1·20	1·20
984	80k. Saithe (*Pollachius virens*)	1·80	1·70

362 Man's Face, Tents and Emblem

2001. 50th Anniv of United Nations Commissioner for Refugees.

985	**362**	50k. black and brown	1·10	1·10

363 Marigold (*Calendula officinalis*)

2001. Summer Flowers. Multicoloured.

986	55k. Type **363**	1·30	1·20
987	65k. Livingstone daisy (*Dorotheanthus bellidformis*)	1·50	1·40

364 Dog

2001. Icelandic Sheepdogs. Multicoloured.

988	40k. Type **364**	90	85
989	80k. Black and white dog	1·80	1·70

365 Olsen-Jonasson Ognin

2001. Airplanes. Multicoloured.

990	55k. Type **365**	1·20	1·20
991	80k. Klemm KL-25E	1·80	1·70

366 Woman's Head and Waterfall

2001. Europa. Water Resources. Multicoloured.

992	55k. Type **366**	1·30	1·20
993	80k. Cupped hands and wave	1·80	1·70

367 Walking

2001. Horses. Multicoloured.

994	40k. Type **367**	90	85
995	50k. Running walk	1·10	1·10
996	55k. Trotting	1·20	1·20
997	60k. Pacing	1·40	1·30
998	80k. Cantering	1·80	1·70

2001. Domestic Letter Rate. No. 915 optd Bref 50g.

999	(35k.) multicoloured	1·10	1·10

2001. Marine Mammals (3rd series). As T 340. Multicoloured.

1000	5k. Large-beaked dolphin (*Lagenorhynchus albirostris*)	25	20
1001	40k. Fin whale (*Balaenoptera physalus*)	90	85
1002	80k. Sei whale (*Balaenoptera borealis*)	1·80	1·70
1003	100k. Long-finned pilot whale (*Globicephala melas*)	2·30	2·20

369 Grimsey

2001. Islands (1st series). Multicoloured.

1004	40k. Type **369**	90	85
1005	55k. Papey	1·20	1·10

See also Nos. 1031/2, 1061/2 and 1094/5.

370 Esja Mountain

2001. Stamp Day. Sheet 105×48 mm.

MS1006	**370** 250k. multicoloured	6·50	6·25

371 Brautarholt Church, Kjalarnes

2001. Christmas. Multicoloured.

1007	(42k.) Type **371**	1·10	1·10
1008	55k Viomyri Church, Skagafjorour	1·20	1·20

372 Northern Wheatear (*Oenanthe oenanthe*)

2001. Birds (1st series). Multicoloured.

1009	42k. Type **372**	90	85
1010	250k. Ringed plover (*Charadrius hiaticula*)	6·00	5·75

See also Nos. 1036/7,1055/6 and 1092/3.

373 Brown Birch Bolete (*Leccinum scabrum*)

2002. Fungi. Multicoloured. (a) Inscr "Bref 20g".

1011	(42k.) Type **373**	90	85

(b) With face value.

1012	85k. Hedgehog fungus (*Hydnum repandum*)	1·80	1·70

No. 1011 was for use on domestic mail up to 20 grammes.

374 Stanley and 2 h.p. Mollerup Engine

2002. Centenary of First Motorboat in Iceland.

1013	**374**	60k. multicoloured	1·30	1·20

375 Mount Snæfell

2002. International Year of the Mountain. Inscr "Bref 20g".

1014	**375**	(42k.) multicoloured	1·50	1·50

No. 1014 was for use on domestic mail up to 20 grammes.

376 Laxness

2002. Birth Centenary of Halldor Laxness (writer and Nobel Prize winner).

1015	**376**	100k. multicoloured	2·10	2·00
MS1016		75×45 mm. No. 1015	2·10	2·00

377 "Waterfall" (sculpture, Ruri) and Emblem

2002. Nordic Countries' Postal Co-operation. Modern Art. Multicoloured. (a) Inscr "Bref 20g".

1017 (42k.) Type **377** (50th anniv of Nordic Council) 90 85

(b) With face value.

1018 60k. "Tension" (sculpture, Hafsteinn Austmann) and emblem 1·40 1·30

No. 1017 was for use on domestic mail up to 20 grammes.

378 Grotta

2002. Lighthouses. Multicoloured.

1019 60k. Type **378** 1·40 1·30
1020 85k. Kogur 1·90 1·80

379 House and Sesselja Sigmundsdottir

2002. Birth Centenary of Sesselja H. Sigmundsdottir (mental health pioneer and environmentalist).

1021 **379** 45k. multicoloured 1·00 95

380 Trapeze Artists and Clown

2002. Europa. Circus. Multicoloured.

1022 60k. Type **380** 1·40 1·30
1023 85k. Marionette's head and lion leaping through flaming hoop 1·80 1·70

381 Lobelia (*Lobelia erinus*)

2002. Summer Flowers. Multicoloured.

1024 10k. Type **381** 25 20
1025 200k. Cornflower (*Centaurea cyanus*) 4·25 4·00

382 Arctic Charr (*Salvelinus alpinus*)

2002. Fish from Lake Thingvallavatn. Multicoloured. (a) Inscr "Bref 20g".

1026 (45k.) Type **382** 1·10 1·00

(b) Inscr "Bréf 50g".

1027 (55k.) Brown trout (*Salmo trutta*) (vert) 1·40 1·40

(c) With face value.

1028 60k. Arctic charr (*Salvelinus alpinus*) 1·50 1·40
1029 90k. Arctic charr (*Salvelinus alpinus*) 2·10 2·00
1030 200k. Arctic charr (*Salvelinus alpinus*) 4·75 4·75

No. 1026 was for use on domestic mail up to 20 grammes.

No. 1027 was for use on domestic mail up to 50 grammes.

2002. Islands (2nd series). As T 369. Multicoloured.

1031 45k. Vigur 1·00 95
1032 55k. Flatey 1·20 1·10

383 South Street, Reykjavik, and Mount Keilir (volcano)

2002. Stamp Day. Sheet 85×55 mm.

MS1033 **383** 250k. multicoloured 6·25 6·00

384 Bauble, Flags and Gift

2002. Christmas. Multicoloured.

1034 45k. Type **384** 1·00 95
1035 60k. Gifts 1·30 1·20

385 Common Redshank (*Tringa totanus*)

2002. Birds (2nd series). Multicoloured.

1036 50k. Type **385** 1·10 1·00
1037 85k. Grey phalarope (*Phalaropus fulicarius*) 1·80 1·70

386 Modern Policemen

2003. Bicentenary of Icelandic Police Force. Multicoloured.

1038 45k. Type **386** 1·00 95
1039 55k. 1803 policeman 1·20 1·10

387 Annual Phlox (*Phlox drummondii*)

2003. Summer Flowers. Multicoloured.

1040 45k. Type **387** 1·00 95
1041 60k. Treasure flower (*Gazania x hybrida*) 1·30 1·20

388 Bull and Audhumla (mythological cow)

2003. Icelandic Cattle. Multicoloured.

1042 45k. Type **388** 1·00 95
1043 85k. Red-mottled cow 1·90 1·80

389 Map, Crow and Sailing Ship

2003. Nordia 2003 International Stamp Exhibition, Rekjavik. Sheet 86×76 mm.

MS1044 **389** 250k. multicoloured 6·50 6·25

390 *Saefari*

2003. Ferries. Multicoloured.

1045 45k. Type **390** 1·00 95
1046 45k. *Saevar* 1·00 95
1047 60k. *Herjolfur* 1·40 1·30
1048 60k. *Baldur* 1·40 1·30

391 Church

2003. Centenary of Free Church, Reykjavík.

1049 **391** 200k. multicoloured 4·25 4·00

392 Hen and Cockerel

2003. Icelandic Poultry.

1050 **392** 45k. multicoloured 1·00 95

393 Posters

2003. Europa. Poster Art. Multicoloured.

1051 60k. Type **393** 1·40 1·30
1052 85k. Posters (different) 1·80 1·70

394 Friendship (Orn Agustsson)

2006. Winning Entry in Children's Stamp Design Competition.

1053 **394** 45k. multicoloured 1·00 95

395 District Officer and Family

2003. 300th Anniv of First Census.

1054 **395** 60k. multicoloured 1·30 1·20

2003. Birds (3rd series). As T 385. Multicoloured.

1055 70k. Meadow pipit (*Anthus pratensis*) 1·60 1·50
1056 250k. Whimbrel (*Numenius phaeopus*) 5·25 5·00

396 Reindeer (*Rangifer tarandus*)

2003

1057 **396** 45k. multicoloured 1·00 95

397 Barrack converted to House

2003. Stamp Day. Sheet 120×58 mm.

MS1058 **397** 250k. multicoloured 5·25 5·25

398 Girl hanging Baubles on Tree

2003. Christmas. Multicoloured.

1059 45k. Type **398** 1·00 95
1060 60k. Boy lighting candles 1·30 1·20

2003. Islands (3rd series). As T 369.

1061 85k. Heimaey 1·80 1·70
1062 200k. Hrísey 4·25 4·00

399 Marigolds (*Tagetes patula*)

2004. Summer Flowers. Multicoloured.

1063 50k. Type **399** 1·30 1·00
1064 55k. Begonias (*begonia x tuberhybrida*) 1·50 1·20

400 Hannes Hafstein (first minister)

2004. Centenary of Icelandic Home Rule. Multicoloured.

1065 150k. Type **400** 4·00 3·75
MS1066 79×50 mm. No. 1065 4·00 3·75

401 *Coot* (trawler)

2004

1067 **401** 50k. blue and black 1·30 1·10

402 Snorralaug Thermal Pool

2004. Geo-thermal Energy. Multicoloured.

1068 50k. Type **402** 1·40 1·20
1069 55k. Vent, dome and steam (30×48 mm) 1·60 1·40
1070 60k. Pipeline 2·00 1·80
1071 90k. Turbine 3·00 2·75

1072	250k. Map of Iceland, mid Atlantic ridge and clouds (30×48 mm)	6·25	5·75

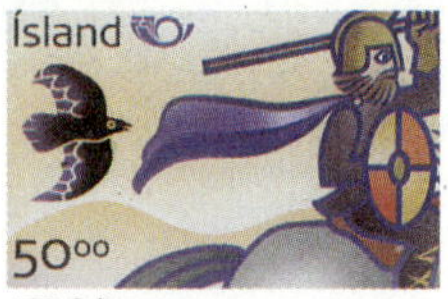

403 Odin

2004. Norse Mythology. Sheet 105×70 mm containing T 403 and similar horiz design (1st issue). Multicoloured.

MS1073	50k. Type **403**; 60k. Sleipnir (Odin's horse)	3·50	3·25

Stamps of a similar theme were issued by Aland Islands, Denmark, Faroe Islands, Finland, Greenland, Norway and Sweden.

See also No. **MS**1137.

404 Ford Fairlane Victoria, 1956

2004. Cars. Multicoloured.

1074	60k. Type **404**	2·00	1·80
1075	60k. Pobeta, 1954	2·00	1·80
1076	85k. Chevrolet Bel Air, 1955	2·75	2·50
1077	85k. Volkswagen, 1952	2·75	2·50

405 Woman reaching into Barrel of Fish

2004. Centenary of Herring Production.

1078	**405**	65k. multicoloured	1·60	1·40

406 Cyclists

2004. Europa. Holidays. Multicoloured.

1079	65k. Type **406**	1·60	1·40
1080	90k. Four-wheel drive vehicles in snow	2·40	2·20

407 Baby and Emblem

2004. Centenary of Hringurinn (women's charitable organization).

1081	**407**	100k. multicoloured	2·50	2·30

408 Hand holding Light Bulb

2004. Centenary of Electrification.

1082	**408**	50k. multicoloured	1·30	1·10

409 Grisette (*Amanita vaginata*)

2004. Fungi. Multicoloured.

1083	50k. Type **409**	1·40	1·20
1084	60k. *Camarophyllus pratensis*	1·60	1·40

410 Cudell (1901)

2004. Centenary of First Motor Car in Iceland.

1085	**410**	100k. black	2·50	2·30

411 Ground Beetle (*Nebria gyllenhali*)

2004. Insects. Multicoloured.

1086	50k. Type **411**	1·60	1·40
1087	70k. White-tailed bumble bee (*Bombus lucorum*)	1·80	1·60

412 Ship and Hospital Building

2004. Centenary of French Hospital, Faskrudsfirdi.

1088	**412**	60k. multicoloured	1·50	1·30

413 Rock, Hvita River, Bruarhlod

2004. Stamp Day. Sheet 85×55 mm.

MS1089	250k. multicoloured	6·50	6·25

414 Ptarmigan in Winter Plumage

2004. Christmas. Multicoloured.

1090	45k. Type **414**	1·30	1·10
1091	65k. Reindeer	1·70	1·50

2004. Birds (4th series). As T 385. Multicoloured.

1092	55k. Sandpiper (*Caladris maritime*)	1·50	1·30
1093	75k. Dunlin (*Caladris alpine*)	2·00	1·80

2005. Islands (4th series). As T 369.

1094	5k. Videy	25	20
1095	90k. Flatey	2·30	2·20

415 Forest

2005. Centenary of Forestation Programme.

1096	**415**	45k. multicoloured	1·30	1·10

416 Brooch (11th-century)

2005. 60th Anniv of Foundation, and Re-opening (2004) of National Museum. Sheet 105×75 mm containing T 416 and similar vert designs. Multicoloured.

MS1097	100k. Type **416**; 150k. Thor (10th-century statue)	7·00	6·75

417 Field Mouse (*Apodemus sylvaticus*)

2005. Mice. Multicoloured.

1098	45k. Type **417**	1·50	1·30
1099	125k. House mouse (*Mus musculus*)	3·50	3·25

418 Rose

2005. Greetings Stamps. Flowers. Multicoloured.

1100	50k. Type **418**	1·60	1·40
1101	50k. Gerbera	1·60	1·40
1102	50k. Zantedeschia	1·60	1·40
1103	70k. Tulip	2·20	2·00

419 *Araneus diadematus*

2005. Insect and Spider. Multicoloured.

1104	50k. Type **419**	1·40	1·20
1105	70k. *Musca domestica*	2·10	1·90

420 *Vorour PH 4*

2005. Old Fishing Boats. Multicoloured.

1106	70k. Type **420**	2·10	1·90
1107	70k. *Karl VE 47*	2·10	1·90
1108	95k. *Sædis IS 67*	2·50	2·30
1109	95k. *Guobjorg NK 74*	2·50	2·30

421 Bridge over Sogid River, Grimsnes

2005. Bridges.

1110	**421**	50k. violet, silver and black	1·60	1·40
1111	-	95k. ultramarine, silver and black	3·00	2·75
1112	-	165k. blue, silver and black	5·00	4·75

DESIGNS: 50k. Type **421**; 95k. Over Lagarfljot river; 165k. Over Jokulsa river, Oxarfjordur.

422 Fish Fillets, Cutlery, Smoked Fish and Water

2005. Europa. Gastronomy. Multicoloured.

1113	70k. Type **422**	1·90	1·60
1114	90k. Cutlery, chillies and fish fillets, smoked fish and flowers	2·50	2·30

423 Fisherman and Red Frances Fly

2005. Salmon Fishing. Multicoloured.

1115	50k. Type **423**	1·50	1·30
1116	60k. Fishing from boat and Laxa Blue fly (vert)	1·70	1·50

424 *Vaccinium uliginosum*

2005. Berries. Multicoloured.

1117	65k. Type **424**	1·80	1·70
1118	90k. *Fragaria vesca*	2·30	2·10

425 Motorcyclist

2005. Centenary of First Motorcycle.

1119	**425**	50k. multicoloured	1·50	1·30

426 Couple dancing

2005. Centenary of Commercial College.

1120	**426**	70k. multicoloured	1·90	1·70

427 Reykjavik

2005. Stamp Day. Sheet 105×55 mm.

MS1121	**427**	200k. multicoloured	6·00	5·75

428 Apple

2005. Christmas.

1122	**428**	50k. vermilion and gold	1·50	1·30
1123	-	70k. green and gold	1·90	1·70

DESIGNS: 50k. Type **428**; 70k. Pine tree.

Nos. 1122/3 were impregnated with the scent of apples and pine, respectively, which was released when rubbed.

429 Greylag (*Anser anser*)

2005. Birds. Multicoloured.
1124 60k. Type **429** 1·80 1·60
1125 105k. Starling (*Sturnus vulgaris*) 2·75 2·50

430 *Dryas octopetala*

2006. National Flower.
1126 **430** 50k. multicoloured 1·50 1·30

431 Record Label, Cadillac, Guitar and Dancers

2006. 50th Anniv of Rock and Roll Music in Iceland.
1127 **431** 60k. multicoloured 1·80 1·60

432 Hands, Dove and Barbed Wire

2006. 50th Anniv of First Refugees.
1128 **432** 70k. multicoloured 2·10 1·90

433 1969 14k.50 Europa Stamp (As Type **117**)

2006. 50th Anniv of Europa Stamps. Sheet 80×49 mm containing T 433 and similar horiz design. Multicoloured.
MS1129 150k.×2, Type **433**; 1968 9k.50 Europa stamp (As Type **111**) 8·25 8·00

434 Camera, Programme and First Cinema

2006. Centenary of Cinema in Iceland. Mult.
1130 50k. Type **434** 2·50 2·30
1131 95k. Faces, projector and tickets 3·00 2·75
1132 160k. Helmeted warrior, clapperboard, popcorn and cameraman 4·25 4·00

435 Landrover (1951)

2006. First Four-wheel Drive Vehicles in Iceland.
1133 70k. Type **435** 1·90 1·90
1134 70k. Willys jeep (1946) 1·90 1·90
1135 90k. Austin Gypsy (1965) 2·75 2·50
1136 90k. Gaz-69 (1955) 2·75 2·50

436 "Mythical Beings" (Johann Briem)

2004. Norse Mythology (2nd issue). Sheet 105×70 mm.
MS1137 **436** 50k. multicoloured 2·50 2·30

Stamps of a similar theme were issued by Aland Islands, Denmark, Faröe Islands, Greenland, Finland, Norway and Sweden.

437 Faxi

2006. Waterfalls. Multicoloured.
1138 55k. Type **437** 1·50 1·30
1139 65k. Oxararfoss (30×48 mm) 1·70 1·50
1140 75k. Glymur (30×48 mm) 1·90 1·70
1141 95k. Hjalparfoss 2·75 2·50
1142 220k. Skeifarfoss 6·00 5·75

438 Enclosed Heart

2006. Europa. Integration. Ordinary or self-adhesive gum.
1143 **438** 75k. scarlet and black 1·90 1·70
1144 - 95k. blue and black (horiz) 2·75 2·50

DESIGNS: No. 1143, Type **438**; 1144, Arrows, one joining from right.

439 Medal and Athlete

2006. 50th Anniv of First Icelandic Olympic Gold Medal.
1147 **439** 55k. multicoloured 1·40 1·30

440 Iceland outlined in Cable

2006. Centenary of Telephony in Iceland.
1148 **440** 65k. multicoloured 1·60 1·40

441 *Empetrum nigrum*

2006. Berries. Multicoloured.
1149 75k. Type **441** 1·80 1·60
1150 130k. *Rubus saxatilis* 3·25 3·00

442 Girdle of Grettir (trophy)

2006. Centenary of Wrestling (Glima) Tournament. Sheet 80×47 mm.
MS1151 **442** 200k. multicoloured 5·00 4·75

443 Angel

2006. Christmas. Multicoloured.
1152 55k. Type **443** 1·50 1·30
1153 75k. Heart 1·80 1·60

No. 1152 also comes self-adhesive.

444 *Dolchiovespula norwegica*

2006. Insects. Multicoloured.
1155 65k. Type **444** 1·70 1·50
1156 110k. *Coccinella undecim-punctata* 2·75 2·50

445 *Xerocomus subtomentosus*

2006. Fungi. Multicoloured.
1157 70k. Type **445** 1·80 1·60
1158 90k. *Kuehneromyces mutablis* 2·50 2·30

446 Emblem

2007. Centenary of Icelandic Women's Society.
1159 **446** 60k. multicoloured 1·60 1·40

447 *Jon foseti*

2007. Centenary of Jon foseti (first Icelandic deep sea trawler).
1160 **447** 65k. multicoloured 1·70 1·50

448 Eruption

2007. 10th Anniv of West Nordic Council. Geothermal Power.
1161 **448** 75k. multicoloured 1·90 1·70

449 Volcano erupting

2007. International Polar Year. Sheet 105×70 mm containing T 449 and similar square design. Multicoloured.
MS1162 75k. Type **449**; 95k. Taking radio echo soundings 3·75 3·50

450 Leaves and Catkins

2007. Centenary of Forestry and Soil Conservation Act. Multicoloured.
1163 10k. Type **450** 20 10
1164 60k. Red leaves 1·60 1·40

451 Figure as Tree

2007. Centenary of National Youth Organization.
1165 **451** 70k. multicoloured 1·80 1·60

452 Face enclosing Script

2007. 125th Anniv of National Archives.
1166 **452** 80k. multicoloured 2·00 1·80

453 *Hamrafell*

2007. Cargo Ships. Multicoloured.
1167 80k. Type **453** 2·00 1·80
1168 80k. *Trollafoss* 2·00 1·80
1169 105k. *Langjokull* 2·50 2·30
1170 105k. *Akranes* 2·50 2·30

454 Breioamerkurjokull

2007. Glaciers. Multicoloured.
1171 5k. Type **453** 10 10
1172 60k. Langjokull (vert) 1·60 1·40
1173 80k. Hofsjokull 2·00 1·80
1174 115k. Snaefellsjokull 3·00 2·75
1175 300k. Oraefajokull (70×30 mm) 7·25 7·00

455 Dunes and Grasses

2007. Centenary of Soil Conservation. (a) No Value expressed. Self-adhesive.

1176	**455**	(60k.) multicoloured	1·60	1·40

(b) Ordinary gum.

1177	(60k.) multicoloured	1·60	1·40

456 Fleur de Lys

2007. Europa. Centenary of Scouting. Multicoloured. Ordinary or self-adhesive gum.

1178	80k. Type **456**	2·00	1·80
1179	105k. Clover leaf	2·75	2·50

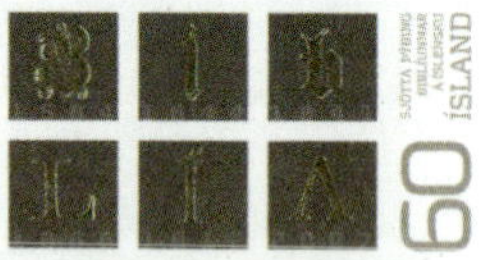

457 'BibLLA' and Dates of Translations

2007. New Translation of the Bible into Icelandic.

1182	**457**	60k. brown and gold	1·50	1·30

458 *Vaccinium myrtillus*

2007. Berries. Multicoloured.

1183	120k. Type **458**	3·00	2·75
1184	145k. *Cornus suecica*	3·25	3·00

459 King Frederick VIII

2007. Centenary of King Frederick VIII's visit to Iceland. Sheet 80×56 mm.

MS1185	250k. brown and gold	6·50	6·25

460 Selfoss Waterfall, Jokulsarglijufur

2007. SEPAC (small European mail services). Multicoloured.

1186	80k. Type **460**	2·10	1·90
1187	105k. Selfoss Waterfall, Jokulsarglijufur (right) (30×27 mm)	3·00	2·75

461 Jonas Hallgrimsson

2007. Birth Centenary of Jonas Hallgrimsson (poet).

1188	**461**	65k. brown	1·80	1·60

462 *Prionocera turcica* (cranefly)

2007. Insects. Multicoloured.

1189	70k. Type **462**	1·90	1·70
1190	190k. *Euceraphis punctipennis* (birch aphid)	5·00	4·75

463 Hospital Facade

2007. Centenary of Psychiatric Hospital, Kleppur.

1191	**463**	80k. multicoloured	2·10	1·90

464 Leaf Bread

2007. Christmas. Multicoloured. Self-adhesive.

1192	60k. Type **464**	1·60	1·40
1193	80k. Leaf bread (different)	2·10	1·90

465 Older Couple

2008. Greetings Stamps. Multicoloured.

1194	65k. Type **465**	1·90	1·70
1195	65k. Mother and child	1·90	1·70
1196	75k. Adolescents	2·10	1·90
1197	85k. Couple about to kiss	2·00	2·00

466 Early Students

2008. Centenary of University of Education.

1198	**466**	85k. multicoloured	2·10	1·90

467 'REFILSAUMUR'

2008. Embroidery. Multicoloured.

1199	65k. Type **467**	1·90	1·70
1200	85k. AUGNSAUMUR	2·10	1·90
1201	110k. KROSSSAUMUR	3·00	2·75

468 Ferguson Tractor TF20

2008. Vintage Agricultural Tools. Multicoloured.

1202	85k. Type **468**	2·10	1·90
1203	85k. IHC Bulldozer	2·10	1·90
1204	110k. Scottish plough (introduced by Torfi Bjarnason's agricultural school)	3·00	2·75
1205	110k. Landbaumotor Lanz (turf killer) (used for leveling hay fields)	1·90	2·75

469 Snaefellsnes (home of 9th-century sorcerer Bardur Snaefellsas)

2008. Norse Mythology. Mythical Places. Sheet 105×70 mm.

MS1206	20k. multicoloured	3·00	2·75

Stamps of a similar theme were issued by Aland Islands, Denmark, Faroe Islands, Greenland, Finland, Norway and Sweden.

470 Proprio Foot (intelligent prosthetic foot)

2008. Icelandic Industrial Design. Multicoloured.

1207	65k. Type **470**	1·70	1·60
1208	120k. Marel *OptiCut* (meat slicer)	2·75	2·50
1209	155k. *Wish* (fly fishing reel)	3·25	3·00
1210	200k. *Gavia* (autonomous underwater vehicle)	4·25	4·00

471 Radiator

2008. Centenary of Geothermal Space Heating.

1211	**471**	75k. multicoloured	1·90	1·80

472 Girl skipping

2008. My Stamp

1212	**472**	50g. (75k.) multicoloured	1·80	1·70

473 Buildings

2008. Centenary of HafnarfJorour.

1213	**473**	80k. multicoloured	1·90	1·80

474 Letter as Paper Boat

2008. Europa. The Letter. Multicoloured. Ordinary or self-adhesve gum.

1214	85k. Type **474**	2·00	1·90
1215	110k. Letter as paper airplane	2·50	2·25

475 Winning Play

2008. Friorik Olafsson—1958 Chess Grandmaster.

1218	**475**	80k. multicoloured	1·80	1·70

476 *por* (coast guard vessel)

2008. 50th Anniv of Extension of Fishery Zone.

1219	**476**	90k. multicoloured	2·00	1·90

477 Algae, Map and Lake Myvatn

2008. Endangered Species. Aegagropila linnaei (lake ball algae).

1220	**477**	140k. multicoloured	3·00	2·75

478 Satellite Image of Iceland

2008. International Year of Planet Earth. Sheet 100×55 mm.

MS1221	multicoloured	4·75	4·50

479 Peace Tower

2008. 1st Anniv of Peace Tower (John Lennon memorial), Videy.

1222	**479**	120k. multicoloured	2·50	2·25

480 Yule Goblin Stiff-Legs

2008. Christmas. Children's Design a Stamp Competition, Winning Designs by Heioar Jokull Hafsteinsson and Konrao K. Pormarr. Multicoloured. Self adhesive.

1223	70k. Type **480**	1·20	1·10
1224	90k. Christmas Cat	1·60	1·50

481 Snow-covered Trees

2008. Centenary of Forestry in Vaglaskogur.

1225	**481**	400k. multicoloured	7·00	6·75

2009. Islands (5th series). As T 369.

1226	75k. Hjorsey	1·20	1·10
1227	90k. Maimey	1·60	1·50

482 *Psychodidae* (Moth Fly)

2009. Insects. Multicoloured.

1228	80k. Type **482**	1·50	1·40
1229	120k. *Gnaphosa lapponum* (field spider)	2·50	2·40

483 Polar Ice

2009. Preserve Polar Regions and Glaciers. Sheet 80×120 mm containing T 483 and similar vert design. Multicoloured.

MS1230	100k. Type **483**; 130k. Iceland	4·50	4·25

484 Hrosshvalur

2009. Legendary Creatures from Folktales. Multicoloured.

1231	80k. Type **484**	2·00	1·90
1232	80k. Skoffin	2·00	1·90
1233	80k. Mushveli	2·00	1·90
1234	80k. Rauokembingur	2·00	1·90
1235	80k. Selamoorir	2·00	1·90
1236	80k. Ofuguggi	2·00	1·90
1237	80k. Saeneyti	2·00	1·90
1238	80k. Skeljaskrimsli	2·00	1·90
1239	80k. Uroarkottur	2·00	1·90
1240	80k. Fjorulalli	2·00	1·90

485 Avro 504K

2009. Civil Aviation. Multicoloured.

1241	90k. Type **485**	2·20	2·10
1242	90k. Waco ZKS-7	2·20	2·10
1243	120k. Boeing 757	3·50	3·25
1244	120k. Fokker 50	3·50	3·25

486 Girl and Water

2009. Centenary of Water Works, Reykjavik.

1245	**486**	10k. multicoloured	1·00	85

487 Athletes

2009. Centenary of Iceland Youth Organization (UMFI) National Sports Tournaments.

1246	**487**	105k. multicoloured	2·40	2·20

488

2009. Europa. Astronomy. Multicoloured. (a) Ordinary or self-adhesive gum.

1247	105k. Type **488**	2·40	2·20
1248	140k. Observatory	3·75	3·25

489 Arch and Gateway

2009. Centenary of Skruour Garden, Dyrafjorour.

1251	**489**	140k. multicoloured	3·75	3·25

490 *Fratercula arctica* (puffin)

2009. Nordia 2009–Nordic Philatelic Exhibition, Reykjavik. Sheet 100×60 mm.

MS1252	multicoloured	4·75	4·75

491 Gathering Sheep from the Hills

2009. Sheep Gathering. Multicoloured.

1253	95k. Type **491**	1·80	1·60
1254	160k. Collection pens (vert)	2·20	2·00

492 Skaftafell

2009. SEPAC (small european mail services). Multicoloured.

1255	120k. Type **492**	2·00	1·80
1256	120k. Skaftafell (right) (30×29 mm)	2·00	1·80

Nos. 1255/6 were printed, se-tenant, each pair forming a composite design of Skaftafell.

493 Heritage Centre

2009. Centenary of National Centre for Cultural Heritage. Sheet 85×57 mm.

MS1257	multicoloured	4·25	4·25

494 *Sermon on the Mount* (detail) (Gudmundur Einarsson)

2009. Christmas. Multicoloured. Self-adhesive.

1258	(70k.) Type **494**	1·70	1·50
1259	120k. *Holy Mother of God* (Finnur Jónsson)	3·50	3·25

495 *Uria lomvia* (Brunnich's guillemot)

2009. Seabirds. Multicoloured.

1260	110k. Type **495**	2·50	2·40
1261	130k. *Larus hyperboreus* (glaucous gull)	3·50	3·25

496 Thingvellir Church

2009. 150th Anniv of Thingvellir Church.

1262	**496**	190k. multicoloured	4·50	4·25

497 *Phoca vitulina* (harbor seal)

2010. Seals. Multicoloured.

1263	5k. Type **497**	75·00	65·00
1264	220k. *Phoca groenlandica* (harp seal)	4·25	4·00

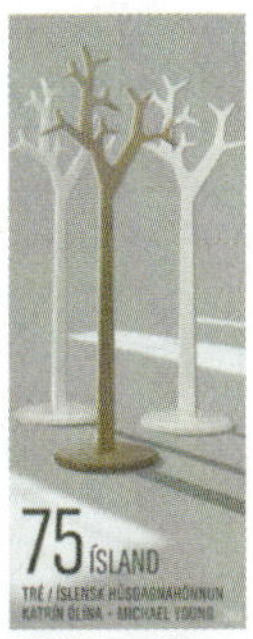

498 Hanger Tree (Katrín Olina Petursdottir and Michael Young)

2010. Icelandic Design. Furniture. Multicoloured.

1265	75k. Type **498**	1·20	1·00
1266	140k. Tango (chair) (Sigurour Gustafsson)	2·00	1·80
1267	155k. MGO 180 dining table (Guorun M. Olafsdottir and Oddgeir Poroarson) (horiz)	2·75	2·50
1268	165k. Dimon sofa (Erla Solveig Oskarsdottir) (horiz)	3·00	2·75

499 Door of Valbjofsstaoir (13th-century)

2010. Icelandic Design. Carving in Wood and Bone. Multicoloured. (a) Ordinary gum.

1269	10k. Type **499**	40	35
1270	(75k.) 17th-century Judge's drinking horn (Brynjolfur Jónsson)	1·20	1·10
1271	200k. *Play in Leaves* (Sigriour Jona Kristjansottir) (vert)	4·25	4·00

(b) Size 32×28 mm. Self-adhesive.

1272	(75k.) As No. 1269 (drinking horn)	1·20	1·10

Nos. 1270 and 1272 were for use on mail within Iceland up to 50 grams.

500 Man pushing Barrel

2010. Norden by the Sea. Life at the Coast. Sheet 105×70 mm containing T 500 and similar vert design. Multicoloured.

MS1273	75k.×2, Type **500**; Women sorting herrings	1·80	1·60

The stamps and margins of **MS**1273 form a composite design.

501 Bjarni riddari GK 1

2010. Trawlers. Multicoloured.

1274	75k. Type **501**	2·20	2·20
1275	75k. *Ingolfur Arnarson RE 201*	2·20	2·20
1276	165k. *Solborg IS 260*	3·75	3·50
1277	165k. *Harobakur EA 3*	3·75	3·50

OFFICIAL STAMPS

1873. As T 1 but inscr "PJON. FRIM." at foot.

O8	4s. green	60·00	£275
O10	8s. mauve	£350	£450

O4

1876

O21b	**O4**	5a. brown	6·50	11·50
O22a	**O4**	10a. blue	49·00	9·50
O23a	**O4**	16a. red	16·00	35·00
O24a	**O4**	20a. green	14·00	23·00
O25	**O4**	50a. mauve	47·00	65·00
O36	**O4**	3a. yellow	10·50	20·00
O37	**O4**	4a. grey	21·00	26·00

1902. As T 10, but inscr "PJONUSTA".

O81	3a. sepia and yellow	2·50	1·90
O82	4a. sepia and green	3·25	1·20
O83	5a. sepia and brown	2·00	2·75
O84	10a. sepia and blue	2·20	2·75
O85	16a. sepia and red	2·30	10·00
O86	20a. sepia and green	11·00	5·75
O87	50a. sepia and mauve	6·00	7·50

1902. Optd I GILDI '02–'03.

O91	16a. red	12·00	43·00
O93	50a. mauve	£425	41·00
O94	3a. yellow	60	1·60
O95	4a. grey	60	1·60
O96	5a. brown	60	1·60
O97	10a. blue	60	1·60
O98	20a. green	60	17·00

1907. As T 12, but inscr "PJONUSTU".

O99	3a. sepia and yellow	5·75	5·75
O100	4a. sepia and green	2·50	6·00
O101	5a. sepia and brown	7·50	2·75
O102	10a. sepia and blue	2·00	2·40

O103		15a. sepia and blue	3·50	6·00
O104		16a. sepia and red	3·00	21·00
O105		20a. sepia and green	9·25	4·25
O106		50a. sepia and mauve	5·00	7·75

1920. As T 15, but inscr "PJONUSTU".

O132		3a. black and yellow	3·00	2·75
O133		4a. black and green	1·10	2·50
O134		5a. black and orange	1·10	1·00
O135		10a. black and blue	3·75	75
O136		15a. black and blue	1·00	1·00
O137		20a. black and green	39·00	3·00
O138		50a. black and violet	34·00	1·20
O139		1k. black and red	34·00	2·30
O140		2k. black and blue	4·50	13·50
O141		5k. black and brown	28·00	40·00

1922. Optd Pjonusta.

O151a	13	2k. red (No. 107)	23·00	42·00
O152	13	5k. brown (No. 108)	£190	£180
O153	15	20a. on 10a. red	19·00	1·60

1930. Parliamentary Commemoratives of 1930 optd Pjonustumerki.

O174	24	3a. violet and lilac (postage)	9·25	24·00
O175	-	5a. blue and grey	9·25	24·00
O176	-	7a. green and dp green	9·25	24·00
O177	-	10a. purple and mauve	9·25	24·00
O178	-	15a. dp blue & blue	9·25	24·00
O179	-	20a. red and pink	9·25	24·00
O180	-	25a. brown & lt brown	9·25	24·00
O181	-	30a. green and grey	9·25	24·00
O182	-	35a. blue & ultramarine	9·25	24·00
O183	-	40a. red, blue and grey	9·25	24·00
O184	-	50a. dp brown & brown	£110	£200
O185	-	1k. green and grey	£110	£200
O186	-	2k. blue and green	£110	£225
O187	-	5k. orange and yellow	£110	£200
O188	-	10k. lake and red	£110	£200
O189	25	10a. blue & dp blue (air)	19·00	80·00

1936. Optd Pjonusta.

O220	15	7a. green	2·30	21·00
O221	15	10a. red	8·00	1·60
O222	12	50a. red and grey	18·00	21·00

Pt. 1

IDAR

A state in Western India. Now uses Indian stamps.

12 pies = 1 anna; 16 annas = 1 rupee.

1 Maharaja Singh Himat

1939

1c	1	½a. green	18·00	27·00

2 Maharaja Singh Himat

1944

3	2	½a. green	3·75	75·00
4	2	1a. violet	3·50	65·00
5	2	2a. blue	3·50	£100
6	2	4a. red	4·00	£110

Pt. 9

IFNI

Spanish enclave on the Atlantic coast of Northern Morocco ceded in 1860.

By an agreement, made effective on 30 June 1969, Ifni was surrendered by Spain to Morocco.

100 centimos = 1 peseta.

1941. Stamps of Spain optd TERRITORIO DE IFNI.

1	181	1c. green (imperf)	6·00	5·25
2	182	2c. brown	6·00	5·25
3	183	5c. brown	85	55
4	183	10c. red	3·25	1·90
5	183	15c. green	75	55
6	196	20c. violet	75	55
7	196	25c. red	75	55
8	196	30c. blue	75	55
9	196	40c. slate	1·20	50
10	196	50c. slate	6·75	1·70
11	196	70c. blue	6·75	4·75
12	196	1PTA. black	6·75	4·75
13	196	2PTAS. brown	80·00	28·00
14	196	4PTAS. red	£250	£140
15	196	10PTS. brown	£800	£375

3 El Santuario

4 Nomad Family

1943

16	A	1c. mauve & brown (postage)	15	15
17	B	2c. blue and green	15	15
18	C	5c. blue and purple	15	15
19	A	15c. green and deep green	15	15
20	B	20c. brown and violet	15	15
21	A	40c. violet and purple	20	20
22	B	45c. red and brown	25	25
23	C	75c. blue and indigo	25	25
24	A	1p. brown and red	1·50	1·50
25	B	3p. green and blue	1·80	1·80
26	C	10p. black and brown	19·00	19·00
27	3	5c. brown and purple (air)	20	20
28	D	25c. brown and green	20	20
29	3	50c. blue and indigo	25	25
30	D	1p. blue and violet	25	25
31	3	1p.40 blue and green	25	25
32	D	2p. brown and purple	1·10	1·10
33	3	5p. violet and brown	1·50	1·50
34	D	6p. green and blue	21·00	21·00
35	4	50c. black and brown	7·50	65

DESIGNS: A, Nomadic shepherds; B, Arab rifleman; C, La Alcazaba; D, Airplane over oasis.

1947. Air. Autogyro type of Spain optd IFNI.

36	195	5c. yellow	2·50	60
37	195	10c. green	2·50	60

1948. Stamps of Spain optd Territorio de Ifni.

39	229	15c. green	3·00	55
41	196	1PTA. black	30	15
45	182	2c. brown (postage)	15	15
46	183	5c. brown	15	15
47	183	10c. red	15	15
48	183	15c. green	15	15
49	196	25c. purple	15	15
50	196	30c. blue	15	15
51	232	40c. brown	15	15
52	232	45c. red	25	25
53	196	50c. grey	25	15
54	232	75c. blue	40	15
55	201	90c. green	40	25
56	201	1p.35 violet	4·25	2·75
57	196	2PTAS. brown	3·00	1·90
58	196	4PTAS. pink	11·00	5·25
59	196	10PTAS. brown	27·00	16·00
60	195	25c. red (air)	45	15
61	195	50c. brown	55	15
62	195	1p. blue	55	15
63	195	2p. green	3·00	60
64	195	4p. blue	8·50	3·25
65	195	10p. violet	11·50	6·75

1949. Stamp Day and 75th Anniv of U.P.U. Spanish stamps optd Territorio de Ifni.

42	240	50c. brown (postage)	2·00	85
43	240	75c. blue	2·00	85
44	240	4p. olive (air)	2·40	85

8 General Franco

1950. Child Welfare.

66	8	50c.+10c. sepia	35	25
67	8	1p.+25c. blue	14·00	5·50
68	8	6p.50+1p.65 green	4·75	2·50

9 Lope Sancho de Valenzuela

1950. Air. Colonial Stamp Day.

69	9	5p. green	1·90	60

10 Woman and Dove

1951. Air. 500th Birth Anniv of Isabella the Catholic.

70	10	5p. red	21·00	6·25

11 General Franco

1951. Gen. Franco's Visit to Ifni.

71	11	50c. orange	30	15
72	11	1p. brown	3·75	90
73	11	5p. green	30·00	8·75

12 Fennec Fox

1951. Colonial Stamp Day.

74	12	5c.+5c. brown	15	15
75	12	10c.+5c. orange	15	15
76	12	60c.+15c. olive	30	15

13 Mother and Child

1952. Child Welfare.

77	13	5c.+5c. brown	15	15
78	13	50c.+10c. black	15	15
79	13	2p.+30c. blue	1·10	40

14 Ferdinand the Catholic

1952. Air. 500th Birth Anniv of Ferdinand the Catholic.

80	14	5p. brown	27·00	5·75

15 Shag

1952. Colonial Stamp Day.

81	15	5c.+5c. brown	20	15
82	15	10c.+5c. red	20	15
83	15	60c.+15c. green	35	20

16

1952. 400th Death Anniv of Leo Africanus (geographer).

84	16	5c. orange	15	15
85	16	35c. green	15	15
86	16	60c. brown	20	15

17 Addra Gazelle and Douglas DC-4 Airliner

1953. Air.

87	17	60c. green	15	15
88	17	1p.20 lake	20	15
89	17	1p.60 brown	25	15
90	17	2p. blue	1·70	20
91	17	4p. myrtle	95	20
92	17	10p. purple	5·25	1·20

18 Musician

1953. Child Welfare. Inscr "PRO INFANCIA 1953".

93	18	5c.+5c. lake	15	15
94	-	10c.+5c. purple	15	15
95	18	15c. olive	15	15
96	-	60c. brown	20	15

DESIGN: 10c., 60c. Two native musicians.

19 Fish and Jellyfish

1953. Colonial Stamp Day. Inscr "DIA DEL SELLO COLONIAL 1953".

97	19	5c.+5c. blue	15	15
98	-	10c.+5c. mauve	15	15
99	19	15c. green	15	15
100	-	60c. brown	35	15

DESIGN: 10, 60c. Dusky grouper and seaweed.

20 Mediterranean Gull

21 Asclepiad

1954

101	**20**	5c. orange	15	15
102	**21**	10c. green	15	15
103	-	25c. red	15	15
104	**20**	35c. green	15	15
105	**21**	40c. purple	15	15
106	-	60c. brown	15	15
107	**20**	1p. brown	8·00	55
108	**21**	1p.25 red	15	15
109	-	2p. blue	15	15
110	**21**	4p.50 green	20	40
111	-	5p. black	34·00	10·50

DESIGN—VERT: 25, 60c., 2, 5p. Cactus.

22 Woman and Child

1954. Child Welfare. Inscr "PRO-INFANCIA 1954".

112	**22**	5c.+5c. orange	15	15
113	-	10c.+5c. mauve	15	15
114	**22**	15c. green	15	15
115	-	60c. brown	20	15

DESIGN: 10c., 60c. Woman and girl.

23 Lobster

1954. Colonial Stamp Day. Inscr "DIA DEL SELLO COLONIAL 1954".

116	**23**	5c.+5c. brown	15	15
117	-	10c.+5c. violet	15	15
118	**23**	15c. green	15	15
119	-	60c. lake	20	15

DESIGN: 10, 60c. Smooth hammerhead.

24 Ploughman and "Justice"

1955. Native Welfare. Inscr "PRO-INDIGENAS 1955".

120	**24**	10c.+5c. purple	15	15
121	-	25c.+10c. lilac	15	15
122	**24**	50c. olive	20	15

DESIGN: 25c. Camel caravan and "Spain".

25 Eurasian Red Squirrel

1955. Colonial Stamp Day.

123	**25**	5c.+5c. brown	15	15
124	-	15c.+5c. bistre	15	15
125	**25**	70c. green	20	15

DESIGN: 15c. Eurasian red squirrel holding nut.

26 "Senecio antheuphorbium"

1956. Child Welfare. Inscr "PRO-INFANCIA 1956".

126	**26**	5c.+5c. green	15	15
127	-	15c.+5c. brown	15	15
128	**26**	20c. green	15	15
129	-	50c. sepia	20	15

DESIGN: 15c., 50c., "Limoniastrum ifniensis".

27 Arms of Sidi-Ifni and Drummer

1956. Colonial Stamp Day. Inscr "DIA DEL SELLO 1956".

130		5c.+5c. sepia	15	15
131	**27**	15c.+5c. brown	15	15
132	-	70c. green	20	15

DESIGNS—VERT: 5c. Arms of Spain and Bohar reedbucks. HORIZ: 70c. Arms of Sidi-Ifni, shepherd and sheep.

28 Feral Rock Pigeons

1957. Child Welfare Fund.

133	**28**	5c.+5c. green and brown	15	15
134	-	15c.+5c. brown & ochre	15	15
135	**28**	70c. brown and green	20	15

DESIGN: 15c. Stock pigeons in flight.

29 Golden Jackal

1957. Colonial Stamp Day. Inscr "DIA DEL SELLO 1957".

136	**29**	10c.+5c. brown & purple	15	15
137	-	15c.+5c. green and brown	15	15
138	**29**	20c. brown and green	20	15
139	-	70c. brown and green	20	15

DESIGN—VERT: 15c., 70c., Head of Golden jackal.

30 Barn Swallows and Arms of Valencia and Sidi-Ifni

1958. "Aid for Valencia".

140	**30**	10c.+5c. brown	15	15
141	-	15c.+10c. brown	15	15
142	-	50c.+10c. brown	20	15

31 Basketball

1958. Child Welfare Fund.

143	**31**	10c.+5c. brown	15	15
144	-	15c.+5c. brown	15	15
145	**31**	20c. green	15	15
146	-	70c. green	20	15

DESIGN: 15, 70c. Cycling.

32 Greater Spotted Dogfish

1958. Colonial Stamp Day.

147	**32**	10c.+5c. red	15	15
148	-	25c.+10c. purple	15	15
149	-	50c.+10c. brown	20	15

DESIGNS—VERT: 25c. Black-chinned guitar-fish. HORIZ: 50c. Fishing boats.

33 Ewe and Lamb

1959. Child Welfare Fund.

150	**33**	10c.+5c. brown	15	15
151	-	15c.+5c. brown	15	15
152	-	20c. turquoise	15	15
153	**33**	70c. green	20	15

DESIGNS—VERT: 15c. Native trader with mule; 20c. Mountain goat.

34 Footballer

1959. Colonial Stamp Day. Inscr "DIA DEL SELLO 1959".

154	**34**	10c.+5c. brown	20	20
155	-	20c.+5c. myrtle	20	20
156	-	50c.+20c. olive	20	20

DESIGNS: 20c. Footballers; 50c. Javelin-thrower.

35 Dromedaries

1960. Child Welfare.

157	**35**	10c.+5c. purple	20	20
158	-	15c.+5c. brown	20	20
159	-	35c. green	20	20
160	**35**	80c. green	20	20

DESIGNS: 15c. Wild boar; 35c. Red-legged partridges.

36 White Stork

1960. Birds.

161	**36**	25c. violet	20	20
162	-	50c. brown	20	20
163	-	75c. purple	20	20
164	**36**	1p. red	20	20
165	-	1p.50 turquoise	20	20
166	-	2p. purple	20	20
167	**36**	3p. blue	45	20
168	-	5p. brown	90	30
169	-	10p. green	3·00	90

BIRDS—HORIZ: 50c., 1p.50, 5p. Eurasian goldfinches. VERT: 75c., 2, 10p. Eurasian skylarks.

37 Church of Santa Cruze del Mar

1960. Stamp Day. Inscr "DIA DEL SELLO 1960".

170	**37**	10c.+5c. brown	20	20
171	-	20c.+5c. green	20	20
172	**37**	30c.+10c. brown	20	20
173	-	50c.+50c. brown	20	20

DESIGN—HORIZ: 20c., 50c. School building.

38 High Jump

1961. Child Welfare. Inscr "PRO-INFANCIA 1961".

174	**38**	10c.+5c. red	20	20
175	-	25c.+10c. violet	20	20
176	**38**	80c.+20c. turquoise	20	20

DESIGN—VERT: 25c. Football.

39

1961. 25th Anniv of General Franco as Head of State.

177	-	25c. grey	20	20
178	**39**	50c. brown	20	20
179	-	70c. green	20	20
180	**39**	1p. red	20	20

DESIGNS—VERT: 25c. Map. HORIZ: 70c. Government Building.

40 Camel and Motor Lorry

1961. Stamp Day. Inscr "DIA DEL SELLO 1961".

181	**40**	10c.+5c. lake	20	20
182	-	25c.+10c. plum	20	20
183	**40**	30c.+10c. brown	20	20
184	-	1p.+10c. orange	20	20

DESIGN: 25c., 1p. Freighter at wharf.

41 Admiral Jofre Tenorio

1962. Child Welfare. Inscr "PRO-INFANCIA 1962".

185	**41**	25c. violet	20	20
186	-	50c. turquoise	20	20
187	**41**	1p. brown	20	20

DESIGN: 50c. C. Fernandez-Duro (historian).

42 Desert Postman

1962. Stamp Day.

188	**42**	15c. blue	20	20
189	-	35c. mauve	20	20
190	**42**	1p. purple	20	20

DESIGN: 35c. Winged letter on hands.

43 "Golden Tower", Seville

1963. Seville Flood Relief.

191	**43**	50c. green	20	20
192	-	1p. brown	20	20

44 Moroccan Copper and Flower

1963. Child Welfare. Inscr "PRO-INFANCIA 1963".

193		25c. blue	20	20
194	**44**	50c. green	20	20
195	-	1p. red	20	20

DESIGN: 25c., 1p. Moroccan orange-tips.

45 Child and Flowers

1963. "For Barcelona".

196	**45**	50c. green	20	20
197	**45**	1p. brown	20	20

46 Beetle ("Steraspis speciosa")

1964. Stamp Day. Inscr "DIA DEL SELLO 1963".

198	**46**	25c. blue	20	20
199	-	50c. olive	20	20
200	**46**	1p. brown	20	20

DESIGN: 50c. Desert locust.

47 Edmi Gazelle

1964. Child Welfare.

201	**47**	25c. violet	20	20
202	-	50c. grey	20	20
203	**47**	1p. red	20	20

DESIGN: 50c. Head of roe deer.

48 Cyclists Racing

1964. Stamp Day.

204	**48**	50c. brown	20	20
205	-	1p. red	20	20
206	**48**	1p.50 green	20	20

DESIGN: 1p. Motor cycle racing.

49 Port Installation, Sidi Ifni

1965. 25th Anniv of End of Spanish Civil War.

207	-	50c. green	20	20
208	-	1p. red	20	20
209	**49**	1p.50 blue	20	20

DESIGNS—VERT: 50c. Ifnian; 1p. "Education" (children in class).

50 "Eugaster fernandezi"

1965. Child Welfare.

210	**50**	50c. purple	20	20
211	-	1p. red ("Halter halteratus")	20	20
212	**50**	1p.50 blue	20	20

51 Arms of Ifni

1965. Stamp Day.

213	-	50c. brown	20	20
214	**51**	1p. red	20	20
215	-	1p.50 blue	20	20

DESIGN—VERT: 50c., 1p.50, Golden Eagle.

52 De Havilland D.H.9C Biplanes

1966. Child Welfare.

216		1p. brown	20	20
217		1p.50 blue	20	20
218	**52**	2p.50 violet	1·10	1·10

DESIGN—VERT: 1p., 1p.50, Douglas DC-8 jetliner over Sidi Ifni.

53 Maid Alice Moth

1966. Stamp Day. Insects.

219	**53**	10c. green and red	20	20
220	-	40c. brown and deep brown	20	20
221	**53**	1p.50 violet and yellow	20	20
222	-	4p. blue and purple	20	20

DESIGN: 40c., 4p. African monarch (butterfly).

54 Coconut Palm

1967. Child Welfare.

223	**54**	10c. green and brown	20	20
224	-	40c. green and brown	20	20
225	**54**	1p.50 turquoise and sepia	20	20
226	-	4p. sepia and brown	20	20

DESIGN: 40c., 4p. Cactus.

55 Bulk Carrier and Floating Crane

1967. Inauguration of Port Ifni.

227	**55**	1p.50 brown and green	20	20

56 Skipper

1967. Stamp Day.

228	**56**	1p. green and blue	20	20
229	-	1p.50 purple and yellow	20	20
230	-	3p.50 red and blue	35	35

FISH—VERT: 1p.50, John Dory, HORIZ: 3p.50, Tub gurnard.

1968. Child Welfare. Signs of the Zodiac. As T 47 of Fernando Poo.

231	1p. mauve on yellow	20	20
232	1p.50 brown on pink	20	20
233	2p.50 violet on yellow	35	35

DESIGNS: 1p., Fishes (Pisces); 1p.50, Ram (Aries); 2p.50, Archer (Sagittarius).

57 Posting Letter

1968. Stamp Day.

234	**57**	1p. black and yellow	20	20
235	-	1p.50 black, plum and blue	20	20
236	-	2p.50 black, blue and green	20	20

DESIGNS: 1p.50, Dove with letter; 2p.50, Magnifying-glass and stamp.

EXPRESS LETTER STAMPS

1943. As T 4, but view of La Alcazaba inscr "URGENTE".

E35	25c. red and green	1·20	1·20

1949. Express Letter stamp of Spain optd Territorio de Ifni.

E66	**E198**	25c. red	20	20

Pt. 1

INDIA

A peninsula in the S. of Asia. Formerly consisted of British India and numerous Native States, some of which issued stamps of their own. Divided in 1947 into the Dominion of India and the Dominion of Pakistan. Now a republic within the British Commonwealth.

1852. 12 pies = 1 anna; 16 annas = 1 rupee.
1957. 100 naye paise = 1 rupee.
1964. 100 paisa = 1 rupee.

1

1852. "Scinde Dawk". Imperf.

S1	1	½a. white	£7500	£1300
S2	1	½a. blue	£20000	£5500
S3	1	½a. red		£14000

3 9 10

1854. Imperf.

1	3	½a. red	£1200	
2	3	½a. blue	95·00	23·00
14	3	1a. red	80·00	55·00
23	9	4a. blue and red	£4000	£325
31	10	2a. green	£130	30·00

11

1855. Perf.

41	11	2a. pink	£750	38·00
46	11	4a. black	£425	5·00
59	11	1a. brown	9·00	1·50
63	11	2a. orange	28·00	2·00
64	11	4a. green	£500	27·00
73	11	8a. red	45·00	7·00
75	11	½a. blue	7·50	1·00

12

1860. Inscr "EAST INDIA POSTAGE". Various frames.

57	12	8p. mauve	15·00	13·00
71	-	4a. green	30·00	3·50
72	-	6a.8p. grey	70·00	27·00
77	-	9p. lilac	19·00	19·00
79	-	1r. grey	65·00	29·00
81	-	6a. brown	8·00	1·50
82	-	12a. brown	12·00	27·00

14

1866. Optd POSTAGE.

66	14	6a. purple	£1000	£140

23

1882. Inscr "INDIA POSTAGE". Various frames.

84	23	½a. green	5·50	10
86	-	9p. red	1·00	2·75
88	-	1a. purple	6·50	30
90	-	1a.6p. brown	1·25	1·50
91	-	2a. blue	4·50	30
94	-	3a. orange	12·00	2·25
96	-	4a. olive	16·00	2·00
97	-	4a.6p. green	30·00	7·00
99	-	8a. mauve	32·00	2·00
100	-	12a. purple on red	8·00	3·50
101	-	1r. grey	24·00	6·00

1891. No. 97 surch 2½ As.

102		2½a. on 4½a. green	5·00	60

37 38

40

1892. As 1882 and some new designs.

103	-	2a.6p. green	4·50	40
106	37	1r. green and red	20·00	2·00
107	38	2r. red and brown	55·00	14·00
108	38	3r. brown and green	45·00	10·00
109	38	5r. blue and violet	60·00	38·00
111	40	3p. red	40	10
112	40	3p. grey	75	1·75
113	23	½a. green	1·60	50
115	-	1a. red	3·50	20
116	-	2a. lilac	6·50	3·25
118	-	2a.6p. blue	5·00	4·50

1898. Surch ¼.

110	23	¼a. on ½a. green	10	50

41 52

1902. As 1882 and 1892, but portrait of King Edward VII (inscribed "INDIA POSTAGE").

119	41	3p. grey	1·00	10
121	-	½a. green	3·00	20
123	-	1a. red	1·75	10
124	-	2a. violet	6·00	40
125	-	2a. mauve	5·50	10
126	-	2a.6p. blue	4·75	60
127	-	3a. orange	4·75	60
128	-	4a. olive	3·00	60
132	-	6a. bistre	15·00	4·50
133	-	8a. purple	8·50	1·00
135	-	12a. purple on red	11·00	2·00
136	-	1r. green and red	6·50	70
139	52	2r. red and brown	60·00	4·00
140	52	3r. brown and green	40·00	24·00
142	52	5r. blue and violet	90·00	35·00
144	52	10r. green and red	£170	32·00
146	52	15r. blue and brown	£225	42·00
147	52	25r. orange and blue	£1100	£1000

1905. No. 121 surch ¼.

148		¼a. on ½a. green	55	10

1906. As Nos. 121 and 123, but inscr "INDIA POSTAGE REVENUE".

149		½a. green	3·00	10
150		1a. red	2·25	10

55 56 57

58 59 60

61 62 63

64 65 66

67 70

71

1911. *Two types of 1½a. brown. Type A as illustrated. Type B inscr "1½ As. ONE AND A HALF ANNAS".

161	57	1a. red	2·75	15
163	58	1½a. brown (A)*	5·00	50
165	58	1½a. brown (B)*	4·75	6·00
166	59	2a. purple	4·00	60
169	59	2a. violet	8·50	70
170	60	2a.6p. blue	2·75	3·00
171	61	2a.6p. blue	2·75	20
173	62	3a. orange	9·00	45
177	64	6a. bistre	4·25	2·00
201	55	3p. grey	30	10
202	56	½a. green	2·25	10
203	57	1a. brown	75	10
204	58	1½a. red (B)*	4·75	10
206	70	2a. purple	3·00	10
207	61	2a.6p. orange	3·50	10
209	62	3a. blue	13·00	10
210	63	4a. olive	1·75	10
211	71	4a. green	6·00	10
212	65	8a. mauve	4·75	10
213	66	12a. red	5·50	30
214	67	1r. brown and green	7·50	45
215	67	2r. red and orange	20·00	80
216	67	5r. blue and violet	40·00	1·25
217	67	10r. green and red	75·00	4·75
218w	67	15r. blue and olive	35·00	32·00
219	67	25r. orange and blue	£150	45·00

See also Nos. 232, etc.

1921. Surch NINE PIES and bar.

192	57	9p. on 1a. red	1·00	30

1922. Surch ¼.

195	56	¼a. on ½a. green	65	35

72 De Havilland Hercules

1929. Air.

220w	72	2a. green	3·00	75
221	72	3a. blue	2·75	2·75
222	72	4a. olive	4·75	1·25
223	72	6a. bistre	2·25	1·00
224	72	8a. purple	5·50	1·00
225	72	12a. red	17·00	7·50

73 Purana Qila

1931. Inauguration of New Delhi.

226	73	¼a. green and orange	3·00	4·50
227	-	½a. violet and green	2·25	40
228	-	1a. mauve and brown	1·25	20
229w	-	2a. green and blue	2·00	3·75
230w	-	3a. brown and red	3·25	2·50
231w	-	1r. violet and green	14·00	40·00

DESIGNS: ½a. War Memorial Arch; 1a. Council House; 2a. Viceroy's House; 3a. Secretariat; 1r. Dominion Columns and Secretariat.

79 80 81

82 83

1932

232	79	½a. green	7·50	10
233	80	9p. green	3·75	10
234	81	1a. brown	4·75	10
235	82	1¼a. mauve	1·00	10
236	70	2a. orange	15·00	4·50
236b	59	2a. orange	3·75	50
237	62	3a. red	12·00	10
238	83	3½a. blue	6·00	20

84 Gateway of India, Bombay

1935. Silver Jubilee.

240w	84	½a. black and green	1·25	15
241w	-	9p. black and green	1·50	20
242w	-	1a. black and brown	3·50	10
243	-	1¼a. black and violet	75	10
244w	-	2½a. black and orange	5·00	1·00
245w	-	3½a. black and blue	4·25	6·50
246	-	8a. black and purple	3·75	3·25

DESIGNS: 9p. Victoria Memorial, Calcutta; 1a. Rameswaram Temple, Madras; 1¼a. Jain Temple, Calcutta; 2½a. Taj Mahal, Agra; 3½a. Golden Temple, Amritsar; 8a. Pagoda in Mandalay.

91 King George VI 92 Dak Runner

100 King George VI

1937

247	91	3p. slate	1·00	10
248	91	½a. brown	7·50	10
249	91	9p. green	8·00	75
250	91	1a. red	1·25	10
251	92	2a. orange	9·50	30
252	-	2a.6p. violet	1·50	20
253	-	3a. green	10·00	30
254	-	3a.6p. blue	7·50	60
255	-	4a. brown	13·00	20
256	-	6a. turquoise	14·00	1·00
257	-	8a. violet	7·50	50
258	-	12a. lake	18·00	1·10
259	100	1r. slate and brown	1·50	15
260	100	2r. purple and brown	9·50	30
261	100	5r. green and blue	35·00	50
262	100	10r. purple and red	25·00	80
263	100	15r. brown and green	£120	75·00
264	100	25r. slate and purple	£170	30·00

DESIGNS—As Type **92**: 2a.6p. Dak bullock cart; 3a. Dak tonga; 3a.6p. Dak camel; 4a. Mail train; 6a. "Strathnaver" (liner); 8a. Mail lorry; 12a. Armstrong Whitworth Ensign 1 mail plane (small head).

100a King George VI 101 King George VI 102 King George VI

1940

265	**100a**	3p. slate	30	10
266	**100a**	½a. purple	1·00	10
267	**100a**	9p. green	1·00	10
268	**100a**	1a. red	1·50	10
269	**101**	1a.3p. brown	1·00	10
269b	**101**	1½a. violet	3·00	30
270	**101**	2a. orange	1·50	10
271	**101**	3a. violet	6·00	30
272	**101**	3½a. blue	1·25	75
273	**102**	4a. brown	1·25	10
274	**102**	6a. turquoise	4·00	10
275	**102**	8a. violet	1·50	30
276	**102**	12a. lake	8·50	1·00
277	-	14a. purple	18·00	2·00

No. 277 is as No. 258, but with large head.

105 "Victory" and King George VI

1946. Victory Commemoration.

278	**105**	9p. green	1·00	1·50
279	**105**	1½a. purple	30	30
280	**105**	3½a. blue	1·00	2·00
281	**105**	12a. red	1·50	1·50

1946. Surch 3 PIES and bars.

282	**101**	3p. on 1a.3p. brown	10	15

DOMINION OF INDIA

303 Douglas DC-4

1947. Independence. Inscr "15TH AUG 1947".

301	-	1½a. green	15	10
302	-	3½a. red, blue and green	2·00	2·25
303	**303**	12a. blue	3·25	2·75

DESIGNS—VERT: 1½a. Asokan capital. HORIZ: 3½a. Indian national flag.

1948. Air. Inauguration of India–U.K. Service. As T 303, but showing Lockheed Constellation flying in opposite direction and inscr "AIR INDIA INTERNATIONAL FIRST FLIGHT 8TH JUNE 1948".

304	12a. black and blue	3·00	3·00

305 Mahatma Gandhi

1948. 1st Anniv of Independence.

305	**305**	1½a. brown	5·50	75
306	**305**	3½a. violet	7·50	3·50
307	**305**	12a. green	10·00	3·50
308	-	10r. brown and lake	£180	85·00

DESIGN—22½x37 mm: 10r. Profile portrait of Mahatma Gandhi.

307 Ajanta Panel **308** Konarak Horse **314** Bhuvanesvara

315 Gol Gumbad, Bijapur

319 Red Fort, Delhi

322 Satrunjaya Temple, Palitana

1949

309	**307**	3p. violet	15	10
310	**308**	6p. brown	25	10
311	-	9p. green	40	10
312	-	1a. blue (A)	60	10
313	-	2a. red	80	10
314	-	3a. orange	1·75	10
315	-	3½a. blue	1·50	5·00
316	**314**	4a. lake	4·25	45
317	**315**	6a. violet	2·25	30
318	-	8a. turquoise	1·75	10
319	-	12a. blue	2·50	30
320	-	1r. violet and green	24·00	10
321	**319**	2r. red and violet	20·00	40
322	-	5r. green and brown	42·00	2·25
323	-	10r. brown and blue	90·00	17·00
324	**322**	15r. brown and red	20·00	28·00
333	-	1a. blue (B)	5·50	10
333b	-	2½a. lake	3·00	3·25
333c	**314**	4a. blue	6·00	10

DESIGNS—As Type **307**: 9p. Trimurti; 1a. Bodhisattva; 2a. Nataraja. As Type **314**: 2½a., 3½a. Bodh Gaya Temple; 3a. Sanchi Stupa, East Gate. As Type **315**: 8a. Kandarya Mahadeva Temple; 12a. Golden Temple, Amritsar. As Type **319**—VERT: 1r. Victory Tower, Chittorgarh; 10r. Qutb Minar, Delhi. HORIZ: 5r. Taj Mahal, Agra.

1 anna: (A) Left arm of statue outstretched. (B) Reversed—right arm outstretched.

323 Globe and Asokan Capital

1949. 75th Anniv of U.P.U.

325	**323**	9p. green	2·75	3·25
326	**323**	2a. red	2·75	3·00
327	**323**	3½a. blue	2·75	3·00
328	**323**	12a. purple	3·75	3·00

REPUBLIC OF INDIA

324 Rejoicing Crowds

1950. Inauguration of Republic.

329	**324**	2a. red	3·75	50
330	-	3½a. blue	5·00	5·50
331	-	4a. violet	5·00	1·25
332	-	12a. purple	6·50	3·00

DESIGNS—VERT: 3½a. Quill, ink-well and verse. HORIZ: 4a. Ear of corn and plough; 12a. Spinning-wheel and cloth.

329 "Stegodon ganesa"

1951. Centenary of Geological Survey.

334	**329**	2a. black and red	3·00	1·25

330 Torch

1951. 1st Asian Games, New Delhi.

335	**330**	2a. purple and orange	1·75	1·00
336	**330**	12a. brown and blue	8·50	2·25

331 Kabir

1952. Indian Saints and Poets.

337	**331**	9p. green	1·25	65
338	-	1a. red (Tulsidas)	1·25	20
339	-	2a. orange (Meera)	3·00	50
340	-	4a. blue (Surdas)	11·00	60
341	-	4½a. mauve (Ghalib)	1·25	1·25
342	-	12a. brown (Tagore)	12·00	1·00

332 Locomotives of 1853 and 1953

1953. Centenary of Indian Railways.

343	**332**	2a. black	2·00	10

333 Mount Everest

1953. Conquest of Mount Everest.

344	**333**	2a. violet	1·50	1·00
345	**333**	14a. brown	7·00	25

334 Telegraph Poles of 1851 and 1951

1953. Centenary of Indian Telegraphs.

346	**334**	2a. green	2·00	10
347	**334**	12a. blue	5·50	40

335 Postal Transport, 1854

1954. Indian Stamp Centenary.

348	**335**	1a. purple	1·25	20
349	-	2a. mauve	65	10
350	-	4a. brown	6·00	1·50
351	-	14a. blue	3·25	40

DESIGNS: 2, 14a. "Airmail"; 4a. Postal transport, 1954.

338 U.N. Emblem and Lotus

1954. U.N. Day.

352	**338**	2a. turquoise	1·00	10

339 Forest Research Institute

1954. 4th World Forestry Congress, Dehra Dun.

353	**339**	2a. blue	65	10

340 Tractor **344** Woman Spinning

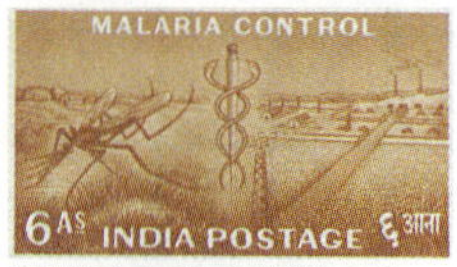

347 "Malaria Control" (Mosquito and Staff of Aesculapius)

1955. Five Year Plan.

354	**340**	3p. mauve	30	10
355	-	6p. violet	30	10
356	-	9p. brown	40	10
357	-	1a. green	45	10
358	**344**	2a. blue	30	10
359	-	3a. green	50	10
360	-	4a. red	50	10
361	**347**	6a. brown	2·25	10
362	-	8a. blue	9·00	10
363	-	10a. turquoise	3·75	2·75
364	-	12a. blue	5·50	10
365	-	14a. green	5·00	60
367	-	1r.2a. grey	2·25	6·00
368	-	1r.8a. purple	11·00	6·00
369	-	2r. mauve	4·50	10
371	-	10r. orange	17·00	4·75
413	-	1r. myrtle	3·75	10
415	-	5r. brown	9·00	50

DESIGNS—As Type **340**: 6p. Power loom; 9p. Bullock-driven well; 1a. Damodar Valley Dam; 4a. Bullocks; 8a. Chittaranjan Locomotive Works; 12a. Hindustan Aircraft Factory, Bangalore; 1r. Telephone engineer; 2r. Rare Earth Factory, Alwaye; 5r. Sindri Fertiliser Factory; 10r. Steel plant. As Type **344**: 3a. Naga woman hand-weaving. As Type **347**: 10a. Marine Drive, Bombay; 14a. Kashmir landscape; 1r.2a. Cape Comorin; 1r.8a. Mt. Kangchenjunga.

358 Bodhi Tree

1956. Buddha Jayanti.

372	**358**	2a. sepia	2·00	10
373	-	14a. orange	5·50	3·75

DESIGN—HORIZ: 14a. Round parasol and Bodhi tree.

360 Lokmanya Bal Gangadhar Tilak

1956. Birth Centenary of Tilak (journalist).

374	**360**	2a. brown	50	10

361 Map of India

1957. Value in naye paise.

375	**361**	1n.p. green	10	10
376	**361**	2n.p. brown	10	10
377	**361**	3n.p. brown	10	10
379	**361**	6n.p. grey	10	10
381	**361**	13n.p. red	1·00	10
402	**361**	5n.p. green	10	10
404	**361**	8n.p. turquoise	1·00	10
405	**361**	10n.p. myrtle	15	10
407	**361**	15n.p. violet	60	10
408	**361**	20n.p. blue	30	10
409	**361**	25n.p. blue	30	10
410	**361**	50n.p. orange	30	10
411	**361**	75n.p. purple	40	10
412	**361**	90n.p. purple	5·50	10

362 The Rani of Jhansi

363 Shrine

1957. Centenary of Indian Mutiny.

386	**362**	15n.p. brown	1·00	10
387	**363**	90n.p. purple	2·00	1·25

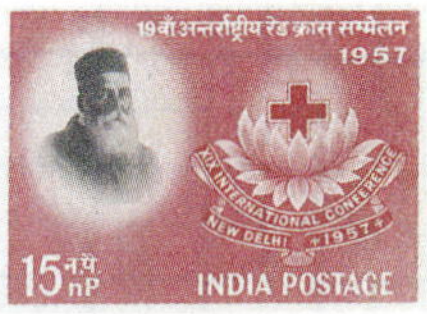

364 Henri Dunant and Conference Emblem

1957. 19th Int Red Cross Conf, New Delhi.

388	**364**	15n.p. grey and red	20	10

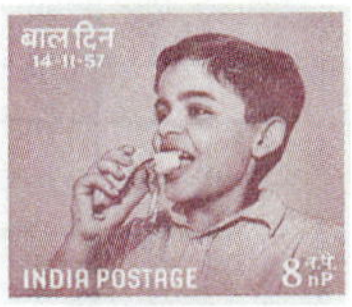

365 "Nutrition"

1957. Children's Day.

389	**365**	8n.p. purple	20	25
390	-	15n.p. turquoise	40	10
391	-	90n.p. brown	50	15

DESIGNS—HORIZ: 15n.p. "Education". VERT: 90n.p. "Recreation".

369 Calcutta University

1957. Centenary of Indian Universities.

392		10n.p. violet	25	60
393	**369**	10n.p. grey	25	60
394	-	10n.p. brown	35	60

DESIGNS—21½×38 mm: No. 392, Bombay University. As Type **369**: No. 394, Madras University.

371 J. N. Tata (founder) and Steel Plant

1958. 50th Anniv of Steel Industry.

395	**371**	15n.p. red	10	10

372 Dr. D. K. Karve

1958. Birth Centenary of Karve (educationist).

396	**372**	15n.p. brown	10	10

373 Westland Wapiti Biplane and Hawker Hunter

1958. Silver Jubilee of Indian Air Force.

397	**373**	15n.p. blue	1·25	25
398	**373**	90n.p. blue	2·00	2·00

375 Bipin Chandra Pal

1958. Birth Centenary of Pal (patriot).

418	**375**	15n.p. green	10	10

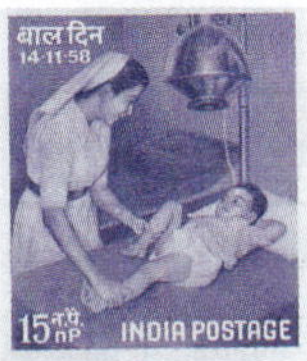

376 Nurse with Child Patient

1958. Children's Day.

419	**376**	15n.p. violet	10	10

377 Jagadish Chandra Bose

1958. Birth Centenary of Bose (botanist).

420	**377**	15n.p. turquoise	20	10

378 Exhibition Gate

1958. India 1958 Exhibition, New Delhi.

421	**378**	15n.p. purple	10	10

379 Sir Jamsetjee Jejeebhoy

1959. Death Centenary of Sir Jamsetjee Jejeebhoy (philanthropist).

422	**379**	15n.p. brown	10	10

380 "The Triumph of Labour" (after Chowdhury)

1959. 40th Anniv of I.L.O.

423	**380**	5n.p. green	10	10

381 Boys awaiting admission to Children's Home

1959. Children's Day.

424	**381**	15n.p. green	10	10

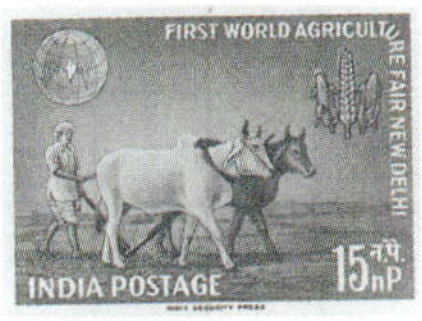

382 "Agriculture"

1959. 1st World Agriculture Fair, New Delhi.

425	**382**	15n.p. grey	30	10

383 Thiruvalluvar (philosopher)

1960. Thiruvalluvar Commemoration.

426	**383**	15n.p. purple	10	10

384 Yaksha pleading with the Cloud (from the "Meghaduta")

385 Shakuntala writing a letter to Dushyanta (from the "Shakuntala")

1960. Kalidasa (poet) Commemoration.

427	**384**	15n.p. grey	65	10
428	**385**	1r.3n.p. yellow and brown	1·60	1·75

386 S. Bharati (poet)

1960. Subramania Bharati Commemoration.

429	**386**	15n.p. blue	10	10

387 Dr. M. Visvesvaraya

1960. Birth Centenary of Dr. M. Visvesvaraya (engineer).

430	**387**	15n.p. brown and red	10	10

388 "Children's Health"

1960. Children's Day.

431	**388**	15n.p. green	10	10

389 Children greeting U.N. Emblem

1960. UNICEF Day.

432	**389**	15n.p. brown and drab	10	10

390 Tyagaraja

1961. 114th Death Anniv of Tyagaraja (musician).

433	**390**	15n.p. blue	10	10

391 "First Aerial Post" Cancellation

392 Air India Boeing 707 Airliner and Humber Sommer Biplane

1961. 50th Anniv of 1st Official Airmail Flight, Allahabad–Naini.

434	**391**	5n.p. olive	1·10	30
435	**392**	15n.p. green and grey	1·10	30
436	-	1r. purple and grey	3·75	2·75

DESIGN—As Type **392**: 1r. H. Pecquet flying Humber Sommer plane, and "Aerial Post" cancellation.

394 Shivaji on Horseback

1961. Chatrapati Shivaji (Maratha ruler) Commemoration.

437	**394**	15n.p. brown and green	80	40

395 Motilal Nehru (politician)

1961. Birth Centenary of Pandit Motilal Nehru.

438	**395**	15n.p. brown and orange	30	10

396 Tagore (poet)

1961. Birth Centenary of Rabindranath Tagore.
439 **396** 15n.p. orange and turquoise 80 40

397 All India Radio Emblem and Transmitting Aerials

1961. Silver Jubilee of All India Radio.
440 **397** 15n.p. blue 10 10

398 Ray

1961. Birth Centenary of Prafulla Chandra Ray (social reformer).
441 **398** 15n.p. grey 10 20

399 Bhatkande

1961. Birth Centenary (1960) of V. N Bhatkande (composer).
442 **399** 15n.p. drab 10 10

400 Child at Lathe

1961. Children's Day.
443 **400** 15n.p. brown 10 20

401 Fair Emblem and Main Gate

1961. Indian Industries Fair, New Delhi.
444 **401** 15n.p. blue and red 10 10

402 Indian Forest

1961. Centenary of Scientific Forestry.
445 **402** 15n.p. green and brown 40 30

403 Pitalkhora: Yaksha

1961. Cent of Indian Archaeological Survey.
446 **403** 15n.p. brown 20 10
447 - 90n.p. olive and brown 1·50 30
DESIGN—HORIZ: 90n.p. Kalibangan seal.

405 M. M. Malaviya

1961. Birth Centenary of Malaviya (educationist).
448 **405** 15n.p. slate 10 20

406 Gauhati Refinery

1962. Inauguration of Gauhati Oil Refinery.
449 **406** 15n.p. blue 40 20

407 Bhikaiji Cama

1962. Birth Centenary of Bhikaiji Cama (patriot).
450 **407** 15n.p. purple 10 10

408 Village Panchayati and Parliament Building

1962. Inauguration of Panchayati System of Local Government.
451 **408** 15n.p. mauve 10 10

409 D. Saraswati (religious reformer)

1962. Dayanard Saraswati Commem.
452 **409** 15n.p. brown 10 10

410 G. S. Vidhyarthi (journalist)

1962. Ganesh Shankar Vidhyarthi Commem.
453 **410** 15n.p. brown 10 10

411 Malaria Eradication Emblem

1962. Malaria Eradication.
454 **411** 15n.p. yellow and lake 10 10

412 Dr. R. Prasad

1962. Retirement of President Dr. Rajendra Prasad.
455 **412** 15n.p. purple 30 20

413 Calcutta High Court

1962. Centenary of Indian High Courts.
456 **413** 15n.p. green 50 20
457 - 15n.p. brown (Madras) 50 20
458 - 15n.p. slate (Bombay) 50 20

416 Ramabai Ranade

1962. Birth Centenary of Ramabai Ranade (social reformer).
459 **416** 15n.p. orange 10 30

417 Indian Rhinoceros

1962. Wild Life Week.
460 **417** 15n.p. brown and turquoise 40 15

418 "Passing the Flag to Youth"

1962. Children's Day.
461 **418** 15n.p. red and green 15 20

419 Human Eye within Lotus Blossom

1962. 19th Int Ophthalmology Congress, New Delhi.
462 **419** 15n.p. brown 20 10

420 S. Ramanujan

1962. 75th Birth Anniv of Srinivasa Ramanujan (mathematician).
463 **420** 15n.p. brown 70 40

421 S. Vivekananda

1963. Birth Cent of Vivekananda (philosopher).
464 **421** 15n.p. brown and olive 40 20

1963. Surch.
465 **385** 1r. on 1r.3n.p. yellow and brown 2·00 10

423 Hands reaching for F.A.O. Emblem

1963. Freedom from Hunger.
466 **423** 15n.p. blue 2·25 30

424 Henri Dunant (founder) and Centenary Emblem

1963. Centenary of Red Cross.
467 **424** 15n.p. red and grey 3·00 40

425 Artillery and Mil Mi-4 Helicopter

1963. Defence Campaign.
468 **425** 15n.p. green 1·25 10
469 - 1r. brown 1·50 65
DESIGN: 1r. Sentry and parachutists.

427 D. Naoroji (parliamentarian)

1963. Dadabhai Naoroji Commemoration.
470 **427** 15n.p. grey 10 10

428 Annie Besant (patriot and theosophist)

1963. Annie Besant Commemoration.

471	**428**	15n.p. green	15	10

No. 471 is incorrectly dated "1837". Mrs. Besant was born in 1847.

1963. Wild Life Preservation. Animal designs as T 417.

472	10n.p. black and orange	1·00	1·50
473	15n.p. brown and green	1·75	60
474	30n.p. slate and ochre	3·00	1·50
475	50n.p. orange and green	3·25	80
476	1r. brown and blue	2·00	50

ANIMALS—As Type **417**: 10n.p. Gaur. 25½×35½ mm: 15n.p. Lesser panda; 30n.p. Indian elephant. 35½×25½ mm: 50n.p. Tiger; 1r. Lion.

434 "School Meals"

1963. Children's Day.

477	**434**	15n.p. bistre	10	10

435 Eleanor Roosevelt at Spinning-wheel

1963. 15th Anniv of Declaration of Human Rights.

478	**435**	15n.p. purple	10	15

436 Dipalakshmi (bronze)

1964. 26th Int Orientalists Congress, New Delhi.

479	**436**	15n.p. blue	20	15

437 Gopabandhu Das (social reformer)

1964. Gopabandhu Das Commemoration.

480	**437**	15n.p. purple	10	10

438 Purandaradasa

1964. 400th Death Anniv of Purandaradasa (composer).

481	**438**	15n.p. brown	15	10

439 S. C. Bose and I.N.A. Badge

1964. 67th Birth Anniv of Subhas Chandra Bose (nationalist).

482	**439**	15n.p. olive	50	20
483	-	55n.p. black, orange & red	50	45

DESIGN: 35n.p. Bose and Indian National Army.

441 Sarojini Naidu

1964. 85th Birth Anniv of Sarojini Naidu (poetess).

484	**441**	15n.p. green and purple	10	10

442 Kasturba Gandhi

1964. 20th Death Anniv of Kasturba Gandhi.

485	**442**	15n.p. brown	10	10

443 Dr. W. M. Haffkine (immunologist)

1964. Haffkine Commemoration.

486	**443**	15n.p. brown on buff	30	10

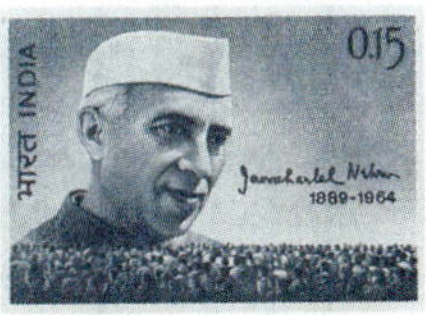

444 Jawaharlal Nehru (statesman)

1964. Nehru Mourning Issue.

487	**444**	15p. slate	10	10

445 Sir Asutosh Mookerjee

1964. Birth Centenary of Sir Asutosh Mookerjee (education reformer).

488	**445**	15p. brown and olive	10	10

446 Sri Aurobindo

1964. 92nd Birth Anniv of Sri Aurobindo (religious teacher).

489	**446**	15p. purple	15	10

447 Raja R. Roy (social reformer)

1964. Raja Rammohun Roy Commemoration.

490	**447**	15n.p. brown	10	10

448 I.S.O. Emblem and Globe

1964. 6th Int Organization for Standardisation General Assembly, Bombay.

491	**448**	15p. red	15	20

449 Jawaharlal Nehru (from 1r. commemorative coin)

1964. Children's Day.

492	**449**	15p. slate	10	10

450 St. Thomas (after statue, Ortona Cathedral, Italy)

1964. St. Thomas Commemoration.

493	**450**	15p. purple	10	30

No. 493 was issued on the occasion of Pope Paul's visit to India.

451 Globe

1964. 22nd International Geological Congress.

494	**451**	15p. green	40	30

452 J. Tata (industrialist)

1965. Jamsetji Tata Commemoration.

495	**452**	15p. dull purple and orange	30	20

453 Lala Lajpat Rai

1965. Birth Centenary of Lala Lajpat Rai (social reformer).

496	**453**	15p. brown	20	10

454 Globe and Congress Emblem

1965. 20th International Chamber of Commerce Congress, New Delhi.

497	**454**	15p. green and red	15	15

455 Freighter "Jalausha" and Visakhapatnam

1965. National Maritime Day.

498	**455**	15p. blue	30	30

456 Abraham Lincoln

1965. Death Centenary of Lincoln.

499	**456**	15p. brown and ochre	15	10

457 I.T.U. Emblem and Symbols

1965. Centenary of I.T.U.

500	**457**	15p. purple	1·00	30

458 "Everlasting Flame"

1965. 1st Death Anniv of Nehru.

501	**458**	15p. red and blue	15	10

459 I.C.Y. Emblem

1965. International Co-operation Year.

502	**459**	15p. green and brown	1·25	1·25

460 Climbers on Summit

1965. Indian Mount Everest Expedition.

503	**460**	15p. purple	45	20

466 Electric Locomotive

475 Dal Lake, Kashmir

1965

504	-	2p. brown	10	1·00
505	-	3p. olive	50	3·50
505a	-	4p. brown	10	3·50
506	-	5p. red	10	10
507	-	6p. black	30	4·00
508	-	8p. brown	30	4·25
509	**466**	10p. blue	40	10
510	-	15p. green	5·50	10
511	-	20p. purple	6·00	10
512	-	30p. sepia	15	10
513	-	40p. purple	15	10
514	-	50p. green	20	10
515	-	60p. grey	35	20
516	-	70p. blue	60	20
517	-	1r. brown and plum	60	10
518	**475**	2r. blue and violet	2·00	10
519	-	5r. violet and brown	2·50	90
520	-	10r. black and green	25·00	80

DESIGNS—VERT (as Type **466**): 2p. Bidri vase; 3p. Brass lamp; 5p. "Family Planning"; 6p. Konarak elephant; 8p. Spotted deer ("Chital"); 30p. Indian dolls; 50p. Mangoes; 60p. Somnath Temple. (as Type **475**): 1r. Woman writing a letter (medieval sculpture). HORIZ (as Type **466**): 4p. Coffee berries; 15p. Plucking tea; 20p. Hindustan Aircraft Industries Ajeet jet fighter; 40p. Calcutta G.P.O.; 70p. Hampi Chariot (sculpture). (As Type **475**): 5r. Bhakra Dam, Punjab; 10r. Atomic reactor, Trombay.

See also Nos. 721/38c.

479 G. B. Pant (statesman)

1965. Govind Ballabh Pant Commemoration.

522	**479**	15p. brown and green	10	20

480 V. Patel

1965. 90th Birth Anniv of Vallabhbhai Patel (statesman).

523	**480**	15p. brown	10	30

481 C. Das

1965. 95th Birth Anniv of Chittaranjan Das (lawyer and patriot).

524	**481**	15p. brown	10	10

482 Vidyapati (poet)

1965. Vidyapati Commemoration.

525	**482**	15p. brown	10	10

483 Sikandra, Agra

1966. Pacific Area Travel Assn Conf, New Delhi.

526	**483**	15p. slate	10	10

484 Soldier, Hindustan Aircraft Industries Ajeet Jet Fighters and Cruiser "Mysore"

1966. Indian Armed Forces.

527	**484**	15p. violet	1·75	75

485 Lal Bahadur Shastri (statesman)

1966. Shastri Mourning Issue.

528	**485**	15p. black	80	10

486 Kambar (poet)

1966. Kambar Commemoration.

529	**486**	15p. green	10	10

487 B. R. Ambedkar

1966. 75th Birth Anniv of Dr. Bhim Rao Ambedkar (lawyer).

530	**487**	15p. purple	10	10

488 Kunwar Singh (patriot)

1966. Kunwar Singh Commemoration.

531	**488**	15p. brown	10	10

489 G. K. Gokhale

1966. Birth Centenary of Gopal Krishna Gokhale (patriot).

532	**489**	15p. purple and yellow	10	10

490 Acharya Dvivedi (poet)

1966. Dvivedi Commemoration.

533	**490**	15p. drab	10	10

491 Maharaja Ranjit Singh (warrior)

1966. Maharaja Ranjit Singh Commemoration.

534	**491**	15p. purple	60	30

492 Homi Bhabha (scientist) and Nuclear Reactor

1966. Dr. Homi Bhabha Commemoration.

535	**492**	15p. purple	15	30

493 A. K. Azad (scholar)

1966. Abul Kalam Azad Commemoration.

536	**493**	15p. blue	15	15

494 Swami Tirtha

1966. 60th Death Anniv of Swami Rama Tirtha (social reformer).

537	**494**	15p. blue	30	30

495 Infant and Dove Emblem

1966. Children's Day.

538	**495**	15p. purple	60	20

496 Allahabad High Court

1966. Centenary of Allahabad High Court.

539	**496**	15p. purple	70	30

497 Indian Family

1966. Family Planning.

540	**497**	15p. brown	15	15

498 Hockey Game

1966. India's Hockey Victory in 5th Asian Games.

541	**498**	15p. blue	1·25	60

499 "Jai Kisan"

1967. 1st Death Anniv of Shastri.

542	**499**	15p. green	30	30

500 Voter and Polling Booth

1967. Indian General Election.

543	**500**	15p. brown	15	15

501 Gurudwara Shrine, Patna

1967. 300th Birth Anniv (1966) of Guru Gobind Singh (Sikh religious leader).

544	**501**	15p. violet	50	15

502 Taj Mahal, Agra

1967. International Tourist Year.

545	**502**	15p. brown and orange	30	15

503 Nandalal Bose and "Garuda"

1967. 1st Death Anniv of Nandalal Bose (painter).

546	**503**	15p. brown	15	15

504 Survey Emblem and Activities

1967. Bicentenary of Survey of India.

547	**504**	15p. lilac	60	40

505 Basaveswara

1967. 800th Anniv of Basaveswara (reformer and statesman).

548 **505** 15p. red 15 15

506 Narsinha Mehta (poet)

1967. Narsinha Mehta Commemoration.

549 **506** 15p. sepia 15 15

507 Maharana Pratap

1967. Maharana Pratap (Rajput leader) Commem.

550 **507** 15p. brown 15 15

508 Narayana Guru

1967. Narayana Guru (philosopher) Commem.

551 **508** 15p. brown 30 20

509 Pres. Radhakrishnan

1967. 75th Birth Anniv of Sarvepalli Radhakrishnan (former President).

552 **509** 15p. red 50 15

510 Martyrs' Memorial, Patna

1967. 25th Anniv of "Quit India" Movement.

553 **510** 15p. lake 15 15

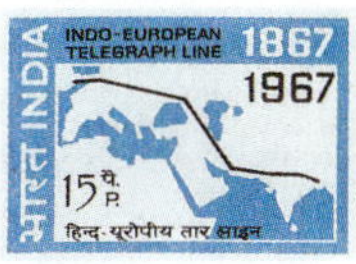

511 Route Map

1967. Centenary of Indo-European Telegraph Service.

554 **511** 15p. black and blue 70 20

512 Wrestling

1967. World Wrestling Championships, New Delhi.

555 **512** 15p. purple and brown 50 20

513 Nehru leading Naga Tribesmen

1967. 4th Anniv of Nagaland as a State of India.

556 **513** 15p. blue 15 15

514 Rashbehari Basu (nationalist)

1967. Rashbehari Basu Commemoration.

557 **514** 15p. purple 15 20

515 Bugle, Badge and Scout Salute

1967. 60th Anniv of Scout Movement in India.

558 **515** 15p. brown 1·00 1·00

516 Men embracing Universe

1968. Human Rights Year.

559 **516** 15p. green 50 30

517 Globe and Book of Tamil

1968. Int Conf and Seminar of Tamil Studies, Madras.

560 **517** 15p. lilac 60 15

518 U.N. Emblem and Transport

1968. United Nations Conference on Trade and Development, New Delhi.

561 **518** 15p. blue 60 15

519 Quill and Bow Symbol

1968. Centenary of "Amrita Bazar Patrika" (newspaper).

562 **519** 15p. sepia and yellow 15 15

520 Maxim Gorky

1968. Birth Centenary of Maxim Gorky.

563 **520** 15p. plum 15 20

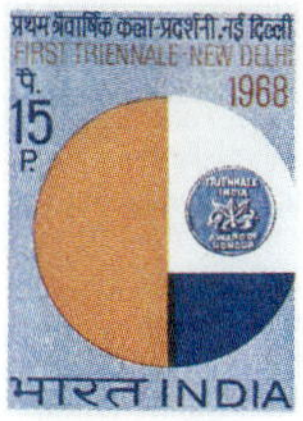

521 Emblem and Medal

1968. 1st Triennale Art Exhibition, New Delhi.

564 **521** 15p. orange, blue & lt blue 30 20

522 Letter-box and "100,000"

1968. Opening of 100,000th Indian Post Office.

565 **522** 20p. red, blue and black 40 15

523 Stalks of Wheat, Agricultural Institute and Production Graph

1968. Wheat Revolution.

566 **523** 20p. green and brown 30 15

524 "Self-portrait"

1968. 30th Death Anniv of Gaganendranath Tagore (painter).

567 **524** 20p. purple and ochre 50 15

525 Lakshminath Bezbaruah

1968. Birth Cent of Lakshminath Bezbaruah (writer).

568 **525** 20p. brown 30 15

526 Athlete's Legs and Olympic Rings

1968. Olympic Games, Mexico.

569 **526** 20p. brown and grey 15 15

570 **526** 1r. sepia and olive 50 15

527 Bhagat Singh and Followers

1968. 61st Birth Anniv of Bhagat Singh (patriot).

571 **527** 20p. brown 1·00 1·00

528 Azad Hind Flag, Swords and Chandra Bose (founder)

1968. 25th Anniv of Azad Hind Government.

572 **528** 20p. blue 1·25 15

529 Sister Nivedita

1968. Birth Cent of Sister Nivedita (social reformer).

573 **529** 20p. green 30 30

530 Marie Curie and Radium Treatment

1968. Birth Centenary of Marie Curie.

574 **530** 20p. lilac 1·40 1·00

531 Map of the World

1968. 21st Int Geographical Congress, New Delhi.

575 **531** 20p. blue 15 15

532 Cochin Synagogue

1968. 400th Anniv of Cochin Synagogue.

576 **532** 20p. blue and red 1·00 40

533 I.N.S. "Nilgiri"

1968. Navy Day.

577 **533** 20p. blue 1·75 40

534 Red-billed Blue Magpie

1968. Birds.

578 **534** 20p. multicoloured 1·25 50

579 - 50p. red, black and green 1·25 1·50

580 - 1r. blue and brown 2·50 1·00

581 - 2r. multicoloured 1·75 1·50

DESIGNS—HORIZ: 50p. Brown-fronted pied woodpecker; 2r. Yellow-backed sunbird. VERT: 1r. Slaty-headed scimitar babbler.

538 Bankim Chandra Chatterjee

1969. 130th Birth Anniv of Chatterjee (writer).
582 **538** 20p. blue 15 20

539 Dr. Bhagavan Das

1969. Birth Centenary of Das (philosopher).
583 **539** 20p. brown 15 40

540 Dr. Martin Luther King

1969. Martin Luther King Commemoration.
584 **540** 20p. brown 60 20

541 Mirza Ghalib and Letter Seal

1969. Death Centenary of Mirza Ghalib (poet).
585 **541** 20p. sepia, red and flesh 15 15

542 Osmania University

1969. 50th Anniv of Osmania University.
586 **542** 20p. green 15 20

543 Rafi Ahmed Kidwai and Lockheed Constellation Mail Plane

1969. 20th Anniv of "All-up" Airmail Scheme.
587 **543** 20p. blue 1·50 30

544 I.L.O. Badge and Emblem

1969. 50th Anniv of Int Labour Organization.
588 **544** 20p. brown 15 20

545 Memorial, and Hands dropping Flowers

1969. 50th Anniv of Jallianwala Bagh Massacre, Amritsar.
589 **545** 20p. red 15 20

546 K. Nageswara Rao Pantulu (journalist)

1969. Kasinadhuni Nageswara Rao Pantulu Commemoration.
590 **546** 20p. brown 15 20

547 Ardaseer Cursetjee Wadia, and Ships

1969. Ardaseer Cursetjee Wadia (ship-builder) Commemoration.
591 **547** 20p. turquoise 75 75

548 Serampore College

1969. 150th Anniv of Serampore College.
592 **548** 20p. plum 15 20

549 Dr. Zakir Husain

1969. President Dr. Zakir Husain Commemoration.
593 **549** 20p. sepia 15 20

550 Laxmanrao Kirloskar

1969. Birth Centenary of Laxmanrao Kirloskar (agriculturist).
594 **550** 20p. black 15 15

551 Gandhi and his Wife

1969. Birth Centenary of Mahatma Gandhi.

595	**551**	20p. brown	70	40
596	-	75p. flesh and drab	1·25	90
597	-	1r. blue	1·25	65
598	-	5r. brown and orange	4·50	6·50

DESIGNS AND SIZES—VERT: 75p. Gandhi's head and shoulders (28×38 mm); 1r. Gandhi walking (woodcut) (20×38 mm). HORIZ: 5r. Gandhi with charkha (36×26 mm).

555 "Ajanta" (bulk carrier) and I.M.C.O. Emblem

1969. 10th Anniv of Inter-Governmental Maritime Consultative Organization.
599 **555** 20p. blue 1·75 40

556 Outline of Parliament Building and Globe

1969. 57th Inter-Parliamentary Conf, New Delhi.
600 **556** 20p. blue 15 20

557 Astronaut walking beside Space Module on Moon

1969. 1st Man on the Moon.
601 **557** 20p. brown 50 30

558 Gurudwara Nankana Sahib (birthplace)

1969. 500th Birth Anniv of Guru Nanak Dev (Sikh religious leader).
602 **558** 20p. violet 30 20

559 Tiger's Head and Hands holding Globe

1969. Int Union for the Conservation of Nature and Natural Resources Conf, New Delhi.
603 **559** 20p. brown and green 75 45

560 Sadhu Vaswani

1969. 90th Birth Anniv of Sadhu Vaswani (educationist).
604 **560** 20p. grey 15 15

561 Thakkar Bapa

1969. Birth Centenary of Thakkar Bapa (humanitarian).
605 **561** 20p. brown 15 20

562 Satellite, Television, Telephone and Globe

1970. 12th Plenary Assembly of Int Radio Consultative Committee.
606 **562** 20p. blue 40 20

563 C. N. Annadurai

1970. 1st Death Anniv of Conjeevaram Natrajan Annadurai (statesman).
607 **563** 20p. purple and blue 30 15

564 M. N. Kishore and Printing Press

1970. 75th Death Anniv of Munshi Newal Kishore (publisher).
608 **564** 20p. lake 15 20

565 Nalanda College

1970. Centenary of Nalanda College.
609 **565** 20p. brown 60 50

566 Swami Shraddhanand (social reformer)

1970. Swami Shraddhanand Commemoration.
610 **566** 20p. brown 75 60

567 Lenin

1970. Birth Centenary of Lenin.
611 **567** 20p. brown and sepia 40 20

568 New U.P.U. H.Q. Building

1970. New U.P.U. Headquarters Building, Berne.
612 **568** 20p. green, grey and black 15 20

569 Sher Shah Suri (15th century ruler)

1970. Sher Shah Suri Commemoration.
613 **569** 20p. green 30 30

570 V. D. Savarkar (patriot) and Cellular Jail, Andaman Islands

1970. Vinayak Damodar Savarkar Commem.
614 **570** 20p. brown 50 30

571 "U N" and Globe

1970. 25th Anniv of United Nations.
615 **571** 20p. blue 40 20

572 Symbol and Workers

1970. Asian Productivity Year.
616 **572** 20p. violet 20 20

573 Dr. Montessori and I.E.Y. Emblem

1970. Birth Centenary of Dr. Maria Montessori (educationist).
617 **573** 20p. purple 30 30

574 J. N. Mukherjee (revolutionary) and Horse

1970. Jatindra Nath Mukherjee Commem.
618 **574** 20p. brown 1·50 30

575 V. S. Srinivasa Sastri

1970. Srinivasa Sastri (educationist) Commemoration.
619 **575** 20p. yellow and purple 30 30

576 I. C. Vidyasagar

1970. 150th Birth Anniv of Iswar Chandra Vidyasagar (educationist).
620 **576** 20p. brown and purple 40 30

577 Maharishi Valmiki

1970. Maharishi Valmiki (ancient author) Commem.
621 **577** 20p. purple 70 30

578 Calcutta Port

1970. Centenary of Calcutta Port Trust.
622 **578** 20p. blue 1·50 70

579 University Building

1970. 50th Anniv of Jamia Millia Islamia University.
623 **579** 20p. green 70 50

580 Jamnalal Bajaj

1970. Jamnalal Bajaj (industrialist) Commemoration.
624 **580** 20p. grey 15 30

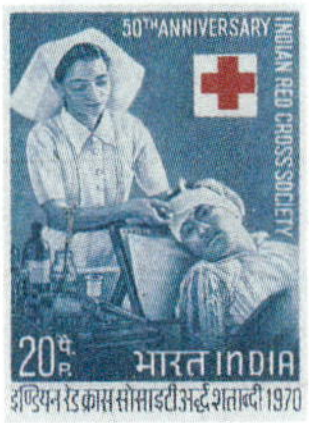

581 Nurse and Patient

1970. 50th Anniv of Indian Red Cross.
625 **581** 20p. red and blue 80 40

582 Sant Namdeo

1970. 700th Birth Anniv of Sant Namdeo (mystic).
626 **582** 20p. orange 15 30

583 Beethoven

1970. Birth Bicentenary of Beethoven.
627 **583** 20p. orange and black 2·50 70

584 Children examining Stamps

1970. Indian National Philatelic Exhibition, New Delhi.
628 **584** 20p. orange and green 50 10
629 - 1r. brown and ochre 2·75 1·00
DESIGN: 1r. Gandhi commemorative through magnifier.

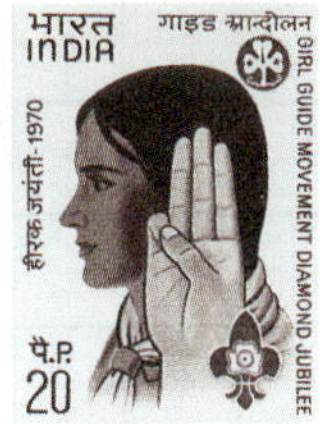

585 Girl Guide

1970. Diamond Jubilee of Girl Guide Movement in India.
630 **585** 20p. purple 60 30

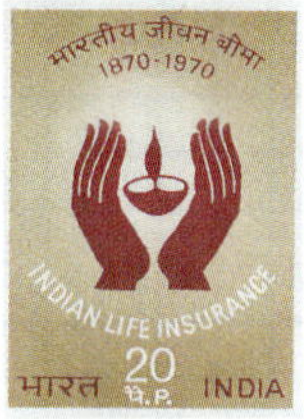

586 Hands and Lamp (emblem)

1971. Centenary of Indian Life Insurance.
631 **586** 20p. brown and red 20 30

587 Vidyapith Building

1971. 50th Anniv of Kashi Vidyapith University.
632 **587** 20p. brown 20 30

588 Sant Ravidas

1971. Sant Ravidas (15th-century mystic) Commemoration.
633 **588** 20p. red 1·00 45

589 C. F. Andrews

1971. Birth Centenary of Charles Freer Andrews (missionary).
634 **589** 20p. brown 35 30

590 Acharya Narendra Deo (scholar)

1971. 15th Death Anniv of Acharya Narendra Deo.
635 **590** 20p. green 15 30

591 Crowd and "100"

1971. Centenary of Decennial Census.
636 **591** 20p. brown and blue 50 30

592 Sri Ramana Maharishi (mystic)

1971. 21st Death Anniv of Ramana Maharishi.
637 **592** 20p. orange and brown 20 30

593 Raja Ravi Varma and "Damayanti and the Swan"

1971. 65th Death Anniv of Ravi Varma (artist).
638 **593** 20p. green 75 50

594 Dadasaheb Phalke and Camera

1971. Birth Centenary of Dadasaheb Phalke (cinematographer).
639 **594** 20p. purple 70 40

595 "Abhisarika" (Tagore)

1971. Birth Centenary of Abanindranath Tagore (painter).
640 **595** 20p. grey, yellow & brown 50 30

596 Swami Virjanand (Vedic scholar)

1971. Swami Virjanand Commemoration.
641 **596** 20p. brown 40 40

597 Cyrus the Great and Procession

1971. 2500th Anniv of Charter of Cyrus the Great.
642 **597** 20p. brown 75 55

598 Globe and Money Box

1971. World Thrift Day.
643 **598** 20p. grey 20 30

599 Ajanta Caves Painting

1971. 25th Anniv of UNESCO.
644 **599** 20p. brown 1·75 1·00

600 "Women at Work" (Geeta Gupta)

1971. Children's Day.
645 **600** 20p. red 20 50

607 Refugees

1971. Obligatory Tax. Refugee Relief. (a) Optd REFUGEE RELIEF in Hindi and English.
646 5p. red (No. 506) 70 10

(b) Optd Refugee Relief.
647 5p. red (No. 506) 3·25 1·50

(c) Optd REFUGEE RELIEF.
649 5p. red (No. 506) 4·00 2·00

(d) Optd Refugee relief.
650c 5p. red (No. 506) 21·00 3·75

(e) Optd Refugee Relief in Hindi and English.
650d 5p. red (No. 506)

(f) Type 607.
651 **607** 5p. red 50 10

From 15 November 1971 until 31 March 1973 the Indian Government levied a 5p. surcharge on all mail, except postcards and newspapers, for the relief of refugees from the former East Pakistan.

608 C. V. Raman (scientist) and Light Graph

1971. 1st Death Anniv of Chandrasekhara Venkata Raman.
652 **608** 20p. orange and brown 50 50

609 Visva Bharati Building and Rabindranath Tagore (founder)

1971. 50th Anniv of Visva Bharati University.
653 **609** 20p. sepia and brown 60 60

610 Cricketers

1971. Indian Cricket Victories.
654 **610** 20p. green, myrtle and sage 2·00 65

611 Map and Satellite

1972. 1st Anniv of Arvi Satellite Earth Station.
655 **611** 20p. purple 45 30

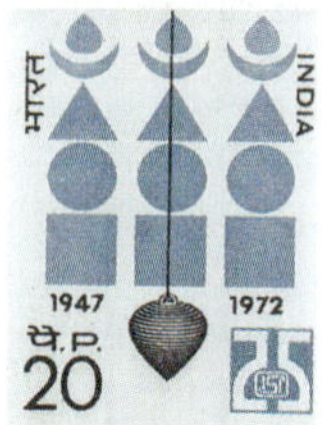

612 Elemental Symbols and Plumb-line

1972. 25th Anniv of Indian Standards Institution.
656 **612** 20p. grey and black 15 50

613 Signal Box Panel

1972. 50th Anniv of Int Railways Union.
657 **613** 20p. multicoloured 1·25 40

614 Hockey-player

1972. Olympic Games, Munich.
658 **614** 20p. violet 2·00 25
659 - 1r.45 green and lake 3·00 2·50
DESIGN: 1r.45, Various sports.

615 Symbol of Sri Aurobindo

1972. Birth Centenary of Sri Aurobindo (religious teacher).
660 **615** 20p. yellow and blue 20 30

616 Celebrating Independence Day in front of Parliament

1972. 25th Anniv of Independence. (1st issue).
661 **616** 20p. multicoloured 1·00 30
See also Nos. 673/4.

617 Inter-Services Crest

1972. Defence Services Commemoration.
662 **617** 20p. multicoloured 70 40

618 V. O. Chidambaran Pillai (trade union leader) and Ship

1972. Birth Cent of V. O. Chidambaran Pillai.
663 **618** 20p. blue and brown 75 40

619 Bhai Vir Singh

1972. Birth Centenary of Bhai Vir Singh (poet).
664 **619** 20p. purple 1·00 40

620 T. Prakasam

1972. Birth Centenary of Tanguturi Prakasam (lawyer).
665 **620** 20p. brown 20 40

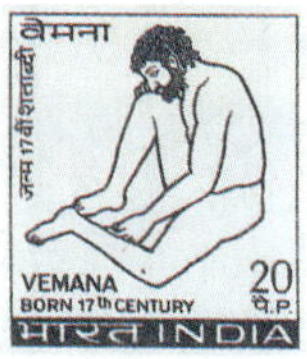

621 Vemana

1972. 300th Birth Anniv of Vemana (poet).
666 **621** 20p. black 20 40

622 Bertrand Russell

1972. Birth Centenary of Bertrand Russell (philosopher).
667 **622** 1r.45 black 3·25 2·75

623 Symbol of "Asia '72"

1972. "Asia '72" (Third Asian International Trade Fair), New Delhi.
668 **623** 20p. black and orange 10 20
669 - 1r.45 orange and black 60 1·75
DESIGN: 1r.45, Hand of Buddha.

624 V. A. Sarabhai and Rocket

1972. 1st Death Anniv of Dr. Vikram A. Sarabhai (scientist).
670 **624** 20p. brown and green 20 40

625 Flag of U.S.S.R. and Kremlin Tower

1972. 50th Anniv of U.S.S.R.
671 **625** 20p. red and yellow 30 60

626 Exhibition Symbol

1973. "Indipex '73" Stamp Exhibition (1st issue).
672 **626** 1r.45 mauve, gold & black 45 1·25
See also No. 701/**MS**704.

627 "Democracy"

1973. 25th Anniv of Independence (2nd issue). Multicoloured.
673 20p. Type **627** 15 15
674 1r.45 Hindustan Aircraft Industries Ajeet jet fighters over India Gate (38×20 mm) 1·40 1·60

628 Sri Ramakrishna Paramahamsa (religious leader)

1973. Sri Ramakrishna Paramahamsa Commem.
675 **628** 20p. brown 70 70

629 Postal Corps Emblem

1973. 1st Anniv of Army Postal Service Corps.
676 **629** 20p. blue and red 40 50

630 Flag and Map of Bangladesh

1973. "Jai Bangla" (Inauguration of 1st Bangladesh Parliament).
677 **630** 20p. multicoloured 15 40

631 Kumaran Asan

1973. Birth Centenary of Kumaran Asan (writer and poet).

678	**631**	20p. brown	20	60

632 Flag and Flames

1973. Homage to Martyrs for Independence.

679	**632**	20p. multicoloured	15	40

633 Dr. Bhim Rao Ambedkar (lawyer)

1973. Ambedkar Commemoration.

680	**633**	20p. green and purple	30	1·25

634 "Radha-Kishangarh" (Nihal Chand)

1973. Indian Miniature Paintings. Multicoloured.

681	20p. Type **634**	30	35
682	50p. "Dance Duet" (Aurangzeb's period)	60	1·50
683	1r. "Lovers on a Camel" (Nasir-ud-din)	80	1·75
684	2r. "Chained Elephant" (Zain-al-Abidin)	1·10	2·50

635 Mount Everest

1973. 15th Anniv of Indian Mountaineering Foundation.

685	**635**	20p. blue	1·00	70

636 Tail of Boeing 747

1973. 25th Anniv of Air-India's International Services.

686	**636**	1r.45 blue and red	4·00	4·00

637 Cross, Church of St. Thomas' Mount, Madras

1973. 19th Death Centenary of St. Thomas.

687	**637**	20p. grey and brown	20	80

638 Michael Madhusudan Dutt (poet–Death Centenary)

1973. Centenaries.

688	**638**	20p. green and brown	1·00	65
689	-	30p. brown	1·25	2·75
690	-	50p. brown	1·50	2·75
691	-	1r. violet and red	1·50	1·50

DESIGNS—HORIZ: 30p. Vishnu Digambar Paluskar (musician, birth cent); 50p. Dr. G. A. Hansen (cent of discovery of leprosy bacillus); 1r. Nicolaus Copernicus (astronomer, 5th birth cent).

639 A. O. Hume

1973. Allan Octavian Hume (founder of Indian National Congress) Commemoration.

692	**639**	20p. grey	20	40

640 Gandhi and Nehru

1973. Gandhi and Nehru Commemoration.

693	**640**	20p. multicoloured	20	40

641 R. C. Dutt

1973. Romesh Chandra Dutt (writer) Commem.

694	**641**	20p. brown	20	40

642 K. S. Ranjitsinhji

1973. K. S. Ranjitsinhji (cricketer) Commemoration.

695	**642**	30p. green	3·50	3·50

643 Vithalbhai Patel

1973. Vithalbhai Patel (lawyer) Commemoration.

696	**643**	50p. brown	30	1·25

644 Sowar of President's Bodyguard

1973. Bicentenary of President's Bodyguard.

697	**644**	20p. multicoloured	1·50	60

645 Interpol Emblem

1973. 50th Anniv of Interpol.

698	**645**	20p. brown	30	40

646 Syed Ahmad Khan (social reformer)

1973. Syed Ahmad Khan Commemoration.

699	**646**	20p. brown	20	1·25

647 "Children at Play" (Bela Raval)

1973. Children's Day.

700	**647**	20p. multicoloured	20	30

648 Indipex Emblem

1973. "Indipex '73" Philatelic Exhibition, New Delhi (2nd issue). Multicoloured.

701	20p. Type **648**	20	30
702	1r. Ceremonial elephant and 1½a. stamp of 1947 (vert)	1·25	1·50
703	2r. Common peafowl (vert)	1·50	3·25
MS704	127×127 mm. Nos. 672 and 701/3. Imperf	4·00	8·00

649 Emblem of National Cadet Corps

1973. 25th Anniv of National Cadet Corps.

705	**649**	20p. multicoloured	20	30

650 C. Rajagopalachari (statesman)

1974. Chakravarti Rajagopalachari Commemoration.

706	**650**	20p. brown	20	50

651 "Sun" Mask

1974. Indian Masks. Multicoloured.

707	20p. Type **651**	15	15
708	50p. "Moon" mask	30	60
709	1r. "Narasimha"	55	80
710	2r. "Ravana" (horiz)	70	1·75
MS711	109×135 mm. Nos. 707/10	2·00	2·50

652 Chhatrapati

1974. 300th Anniv of Coronation of Chhatrapati Shri Shivaji Maharaj (patriot and ruler).

712	**652**	25p. multicoloured	1·00	40

653 Maithili Sharan Gupta (poet)

1974. Indian Personalities (1st series).

713	**653**	25p. brown	15	50
714	-	25p. brown	15	50
715	-	25p. brown	15	50

PORTRAITS: No. 714, Jainarain Vyas (politician and journalist); No. 715, Utkal Gourab Madhusudan Das (social reformer).

654 Kandukuri Veeresalingam (social reformer)

1974. Indian Personalities (2nd series).

716 **654** 25p. brown 25 1·00
717 - 50p. purple 55 2·00
718 - 1r. brown 70 1·75

PORTRAITS: 50p. Tipu Sultan; 1r. Max Mueller (Sanskrit scholar).

655 Kamala Nehru

1974. Kamala Nehru Commemoration.

719 **655** 25p. multicoloured 1·00 1·00

656 W.P.Y. Emblem

1974. World Population Year.

720 **656** 25p. purple and brown 20 30

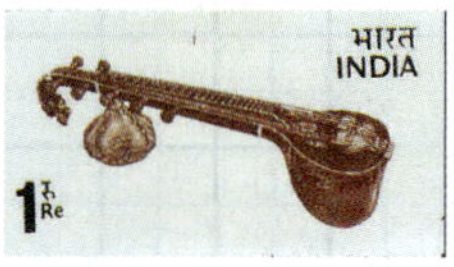

657 Spotted Deer **657a** Sitar

1974. (a) Values expressed with "p" or "Re".

721 - 15p. brown 3·50 1·50
722 **657** 25p. brown 1·50 2·25
723 **657a** 1r. brown and black 2·50 30

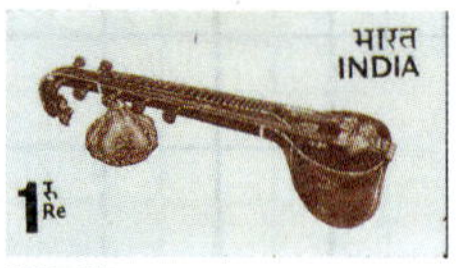

657a Sitar

(b) Values expressed as numerals only.

724 - 2p. brown 1·50 3·00
725 - 5p. red 1·00 10
729 - 10p. blue 1·25 15
730 - 15p. brown 2·00 10
731 - 20p. green 25 10
732 - 25p. brown 8·00 2·75
732b - 30p. brown 4·75 55
733 - 50p. violet 6·50 20
734 - 60p. grey 3·25 1·00
735 **657a** 1r. brown and black 3·25 10
736 - 2r. violet and brown 16·00 40
737 - 5r. violet and brown 3·00 1·25
738d - 10r. grey and green 1·10 1·25

DESIGNS—VERT (as Type **657**): 2p. Bidri vase; 5p. "Family Planning"; 15p. Tiger; 25p. Gandhi; 30p. Indian dolls; 60p. Somnath Temple. HORIZ (as Type **657a**): 10p. Electric locomotive; 20p. Handicrafts toy; 50p. Great egret in flight. (As Type **657a**): 2r. Himalayas; 5r. Bhakra Dam, Punjab; 10r. Atomic reactor, Trombay.

For 30, 35, 50, 60p. and 1r. values as No. 732 see Nos. 968, 979, 1073, 1320 and 1436.

658 President V. Giri

1974. Retirement of President Giri.

739 **658** 25p. multicoloured 15 30

659 U.P.U. Emblem

1974. Centenary of U.P.U.

740 **659** 25p. violet, blue and black 30 10
741 - 1r. multicoloured 50 50
742 - 2r. multicoloured 75 2·00
MS743 – 108×108 mm. Nos. 740/2 2·00 6·50

DESIGNS:—1r. Birds and nest, "Madhubani" style. VERT: 2r. Arrows around globe.

660 Woman Flute-player (sculpture)

1974. Centenary of Mathura Museum.

744 **660** 25p. chestnut and brown 75 1·25
745 - 25p. chestnut and brown 75 1·25

DESIGN: No. 745, Vidyadhara with garland.

661 Nicholas Roerich (medallion by H. Dropsy)

1974. Birth Centenary of Professor Roerich (humanitarian).

746 **661** 1r. green and yellow 65 55

662 Pavapuri Temple

1974. 2,500th Anniv of Bhagwan Mahavira's Attainment of Nirvana.

747 **662** 25p. black 60 20

663 "Cat" (Rajesh Bhatia)

1974. Children's Day.

748 **663** 25p. multicoloured 1·25 70

664 "Indian Dancers" (Amita Shah)

1974. 25th Anniv of UNICEF in India.

749 **664** 25p. multicoloured 55 45

665 Territorial Army Badge

1974. 25th Anniv of Indian Territorial Army.

750 **665** 25p. black, yellow & green 60 40

666 Krishna as Gopal Bal with Cows (Rajasthan painting on cloth)

1974. 19th International Dairy Congress, New Delhi.

751 **666** 25p. purple and brown 40 40

667 Symbols and Child's Face

1974. Help for Retarded Children.

752 **667** 25p. red and black 60 60

668 Marconi

1974. Birth Centenary of Guglielmo Marconi (radio pioneer).

753 **668** 2r. blue 2·50 1·25

669 St. Francis Xavier's Shrine, Goa

1974. St. Francis Xavier Celebration.

754 **669** 25p. multicoloured 15 40

670 Saraswati (Deity of Language and Learning)

1975. World Hindi Convention, Nagpur.

755 **670** 25p. grey and red 50 40

671 Parliament House, New Delhi

1975. 25th Anniv of Republic.

756 **671** 25p. black, silver and blue 75 50

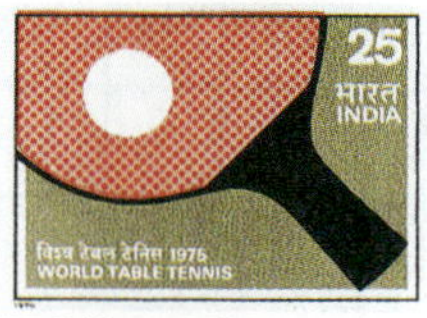

672 Table-tennis Bat

1975. World Table-tennis Championships, Calcutta.

757 **672** 25p. black, red and green 1·00 30

673 "Equality, Development and Peace"

1975. International Women's Year.

758 **673** 25p. multicoloured 85 45

674 Stylized Cannon

1975. Bicent of Indian Army Ordnance Corps.

759 **674** 25p. multicoloured 1·75 75

675 Arya Samaj Emblem

1975. Centenary of Arya Samaj Movement.

760 **675** 25p. red and brown 50 50

676 Saraswati

1975. World Telugu Language Conf, Hyderabad.

761 **676** 25p. black and green 50 30

677 Satellite "Aryabhata"

1975. Launch of First Indian Satellite.

762 **677** 25p. lt blue, blue & purple 1·00 50

678 Blue-winged Pitta

1975. Indian Birds. Multicoloured.

763 25p. Type **678** 75 25
764 50p. Asian black-headed oriole 1·75 2·25
765 1r. Western tragopan (vert) 2·50 2·75
766 2r. Himalayan monal pheasant (vert) 3·25 5·50

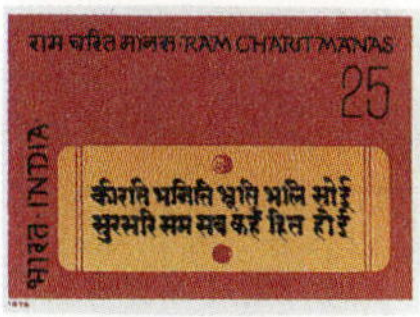

679 Page from "Ramcharitmanas" (manuscript)

1975. 4th Centenary of "Ramcharitmanas" (epic poem by Goswami Tulsidas).
767 **679** 25p. black, yellow and red 1·00 30

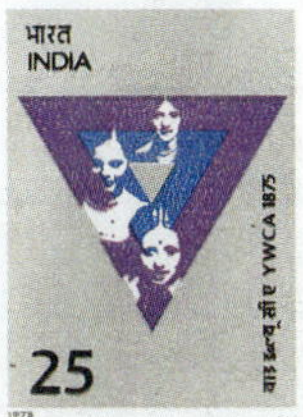

680 Young Women within Y.W.C.A. Badge

1975. Centenary of Indian Y.W.C.A.
768 **680** 25p. multicoloured 75 50

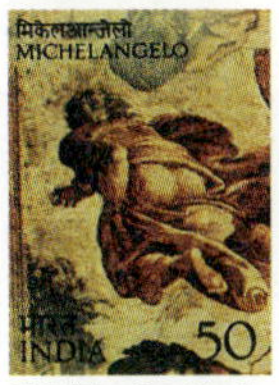

681 "The Creation"

1975. 500th Birth Anniv of Michelangelo. "Creation" Frescoes from Sistine Chapel.
769 **681** 50p. multicoloured 55 90
770 - 50p. multicoloured 55 90
771 - 50p. multicoloured 55 90
772 - 50p. multicoloured 55 90

Nos. 770 and 772 are size 49×34 mm. The four stamps form a composite design.

682 Commission Emblem

1975. 25th Anniv of Int Commission on Irrigation and Drainage.
773 **682** 25p. multicoloured 50 20

683 Stylised Ground Antenna

1975. Inauguration of Satellite Instructional Television Experiment.
774 **683** 25p. multicoloured 50 20

684 St. Arunagirinathar

1975. 600th Birth Anniv of St. Arunagirinathar.
775 **684** 50p. purple and black 1·75 1·25

685 Commemorative Text

1975. Namibia Day.
776 **685** 25p. black and red 50 50

686 Mir Anees (poet)

687 Memorial Temple to Ahilyabai Holkar (ruler)

1975. Indian Celebrities.
777 **686** 25p. green 40 75
778 **687** 25p. brown 40 75

688 Bharata Natyam

1975. Indian Dances. Multicoloured.
779 25p. Type **688** 75 20
780 50p. Orissi 1·10 2·00
781 75p. Kathak 1·40 2·25
782 1r. Kathakali 1·60 1·25
783 1r.50 Kuchipudi 2·50 3·75
784 2r. Manipuri 2·50 3·75

689 Ameer Khusrau

1975. 650th Death Anniv of Ameer Khusrau (poet).
785 **689** 50p. brown and bistre 1·50 2·25

690 V. K. Krishna Menon

1975. 1st Death Anniv of V. K. Krishna Menon (statesman).
786 **690** 25p. green 1·00 1·00

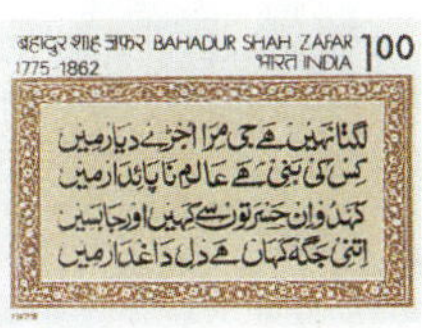

691 Text of Poem

1975. Birth Bicentenary of Emperor Bahadur Shah Zafar.
787 **691** 1r. black, buff and brown 1·75 1·00

692 Sansadiya Soudha, New Delhi

1975. 21st Commonwealth Parliamentary Conference, New Delhi.
788 **692** 2r. green 2·00 3·00

693 V. Patel

1975. Birth Centenary of Vallabhbhai Patel (statesman).
789 **693** 25p. green 15 50

694 N. C. Bardoloi

1975. Birth Centenary of Nabin Chandra Bardoloi (politician).
790 **694** 25p. brown 50 60

695 "Cow" (Sanjay Nathubhai Patel)

1975. Children's Day.
791 **695** 25p. multicoloured 80 80

696 Original Printing Works, Nasik Road

1975. 50th Anniv of India Security Press.
792 **696** 25p. multicoloured 40 40

697 Gurdwara Sisganj (site of martyrdom)

1975. Tercentenary of the Martyrdom of Guru Tegh Bahadur (Sikh leader).
793 **697** 25p. multicoloured 80 80

698 Theosophical Society Emblem

1975. Centenary of Theosophical Society.
794 **698** 25p. multicoloured 60 40

699 Weather Cock

1975. Cent of Indian Meteorological Department.
795 **699** 25p. multicoloured 75 75

700 Early Mail Cart

1975. "Inpex '75" Nat Philatelic Exn, Calcutta.
796 **700** 25p. black and brown 1·00 30
797 - 2r. brown, purple & black 2·50 3·75

DESIGN: 2r. Indian bishop mark, 1775.

701 L. N. Mishra

1976. 1st Death Anniv of Lalit Narayan Mishra (politician).
798 **701** 25p. brown 40 40

702 Tiger

1976. Birth Cent of Jim Corbett (naturalist).
799 **702** 25p. multicoloured 1·00 1·00

703 Painted Storks

1976. Keoladeo Ghana Bird Sanctuary, Bharatpur.
800 **703** 25p. multicoloured 1·00 80

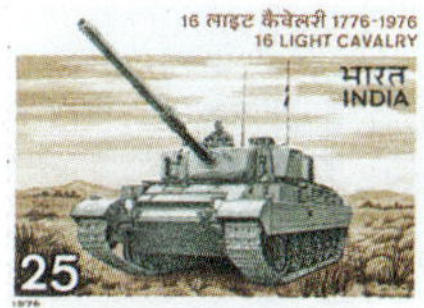

704 Vijayanta Tank

1976. Bicent of 16th Light Cavalry Regiment.
801 **704** 25p. green and brown 1·75 40

705 Alexander Graham Bell

1976. Alexander Graham Bell Commem.
802 **705** 25p. brown and black 1·25 50

706 Muthuswami Dikshitar

1976. Birth Bicentenary of Muthuswami Dikshitar (composer).
803 **706** 25p. violet 70 50

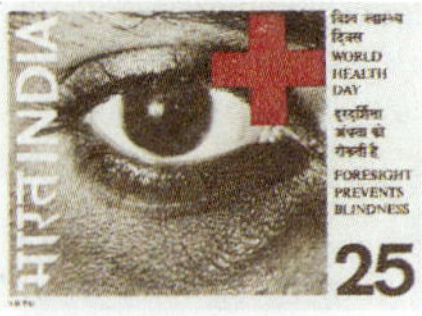

707 Eye and Red Cross

1976. World Health Day. Prevention of Blindness.

804	**707**	25p. brown and red	1·00	60

708 "Industries"

1976. Industrial Development.

805	**708**	25p. multicoloured	30	30

709 Type WDM Diesel Locomotive, 1963

1976. Locomotives. Multicoloured.

806	25p. Type **709**	55	10
807	50p. Rajputara Malwa Railway Class F/1 steam locomotive, 1895	1·50	55
808	1r. Southern Railway Class WP/1 steam locomotive, 1963	2·75	1·25
809	2r. Great Peninsular Railway Class GIP steam locomotive, 1853	3·50	2·50

710 Nehru

1976

810b	**710**	25p. violet	6·00	80
811	-	25p. brown	2·00	30

DESIGN: No. 811, Gandhi.

For these designs in a smaller format see Nos. 732, 968/9, 979/80, 1073/4 and 1320.

713 "Spirit of '76" (Willard)

1976. Bicentenary of American Revolution.

812	**713**	2r.80 multicoloured	1·25	1·25

714 K. Kamaraj (politician)

1976. Kumaraswamy Kamaraj Commemoration.

813	**714**	25p. brown	30	15

715 "Shooting"

1976. Olympic Games, Montreal.

814	**715**	25p. violet and red	30	10
815	-	1r. multicoloured	1·00	90
816	-	1r.50 mauve and black	2·00	3·00
817	-	2r.80 multicoloured	1·75	4·25

DESIGNS: 1r. Shot-put; 1r.50, Hockey; 2r.80, Sprinting.

716 Subhadra Kumari Chauhan (poetess)

1976. S. K. Chauhan Commemoration.

818	**716**	25p. blue	15	50

717 Param Vir Chakra Medal

1976. Param Vir Chakra Commemoration.

819	**717**	25p. multicoloured	15	50

718 University Building, Bombay

1976. 60th Anniv of Shreemati Nathibai Damodar Thackersey Women's University.

820	**718**	25p. violet	40	40

719 Bharatendu Harischandra (writer)

1976. Harischandra Commemoration.

821	**719**	25p. brown	25	40

720 S. C. Chatterji

1976. Birth Centenary of Sarat Chandra Chatterji (writer).

822	**720**	25p. black	25	30

721 Planned Family

1976. Family Planning.

823	**721**	25p. multicoloured	15	40

722 Maharaja Agrasen and Coins

1976. Maharaja Agrasen Commemoration.

824	**722**	25p. brown	40	40

723 Swamp Deer

1976. Indian Wildlife. Multicoloured.

825	25p. Type **723**	65	40
826	50p. Lion	1·50	2·25
827	1r. Leopard (horiz)	1·75	2·25
828	2r. Caracal (horiz)	2·00	3·50

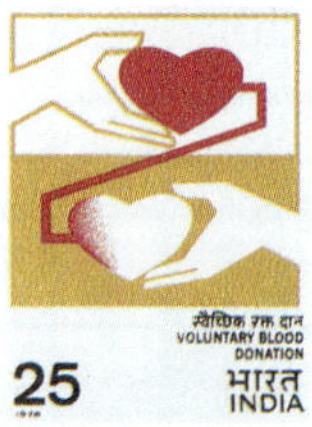

724 Hands holding Hearts

1976. Voluntary Blood Donation.

829	**724**	25p. yellow, red and black	1·25	75

725 Suryakant Tripathi ("Nirala")

1976. 80th Birth Anniv of "Nirala" (poet and novelist).

830	**725**	25p. violet	25	30

726 "Loyal Mongoose" (H. D. Bhatia)

1976. Children's Day.

831	**726**	25p. multicoloured	50	50

727 Hiralal Shastri (social reformer)

1976. Shastri Commemoration.

832	**727**	25p. brown	30	30

728 Dr. Hari Singh Gour (lawyer)

1976. Dr. Hari Singh Gour Commemoration.

833	**728**	25p. purple	40	40

729 Airbus Industrie A300B4

1976. Inauguration of Indian Airlines' Airbus Service.

834	**729**	2r. multicoloured	2·50	2·25

730 Hybrid Coconut Palm

1976. Diamond Jubilee of Coconut Research.

835	**730**	25p. multicoloured	20	30

731 First Stanza of "Vande Mataram"

1976. Centenary of "Vande Mataram" (patriotic song by B. C. Chatterjee).

836	**731**	25p. multicoloured	70	30

732 Globe and Film Strip

1977. 6th International Film Festival of India, New Delhi.

837	**732**	2r. multicoloured	1·10	2·00

733 Seismograph and Crack in Earth's Crust

1977. 6th World Conference on Earthquake Engineering, New Delhi.

838	**733**	2r. lilac	1·00	2·00

734 Tarun Ram Phookun

1977. Birth Cent of Tarun Ram Phookun (politician).
839 **734** 25p. grey 15 30

735 Paramahansa Yogananda

1977. Paramahansa Yogananda (religious leader) Commem.
840 **735** 25p. orange 1·25 1·00

736 Asian Regional Red Cross Emblem

1977. 1st Asian Regional Red Cross Conference, New Delhi.
841 **736** 2r. red, pink and blue 2·00 2·50

737 Fakhruddin Ali Ahmed

1977. Death of President Ahmed.
842 **737** 25p. multicoloured 35 35

738 Emblem of Asian-Oceanic Postal Union

1977. 15th Anniv of Asian–Oceanic Postal Union.
843 **738** 2r. multicoloured 1·10 1·75

739 Narottam Morarjee and "Loyalty" (liner)

1977. Birth Cent of Morarjee (ship owner).
844 **739** 25p. blue 1·00 1·00

740 Makhanlal Chaturvedi (writer and poet)

1977. Chaturvedi Commemoration.
845 **740** 25p. brown 15 50

741 Mahaprabhu Vallabhacharya (philosopher)

1977. Vallabhacharya Commemoration.
846 **741** 1r. brown 30 40

742 Federation Emblem

1977. 50th Anniv of Federation of Indian Chambers of Commerce and Industry.
847 **742** 25p. purple, brown and yellow 15 40

744 "Environment Protection"

1977. World Environment Day.
848 **744** 2r. multicoloured 60 1·25

745 Rajya Sabha Chamber

1977. 25th Anniv of Rajya Sabha (Upper House of Parliament).
849 **745** 25p. multicoloured 15 40

746 Lotus

1977. Indian Flowers. Multicoloured.
850 25p. Type **746** 25 15
851 50p. Rhododendron (vert) 45 1·25
852 1r. Kadamba (vert) 60 1·00
853 2r. Gloriosa lily 90 2·25

747 Berliner Gramophone

1977. Centenary of Sound Recording.
854 **747** 2r. brown and black 1·00 2·00

748 Coomaraswamy and Siva

1977. Birth Centenary of Ananda Kentish Coomaraswamy (art historian).
855 **748** 25p. multicoloured 60 40

749 Ganga Ram and Hospital

1977. 50th Death Anniv of Sir Ganga Ram (social reformer).
856 **749** 25p. purple 30 30

750 Dr. Samuel Hahnemann (founder of homeopathy)

1977. 32nd Int Homeopathic Congress, New Delhi.
857 **750** 2r. black and green 3·50 2·75

751 Ram Manohar Lohia (politician)

1977. Ram Manohar Lohia Commemoration.
858 **751** 25p. brown 50 30

752 Early Punjabi Postman

1977. "Inpex '77" Philatelic Exn, Bangalore.
859 **752** 25p. multicoloured 50 30
860 - 2r. grey and red 2·00 2·75
DESIGN: 2r. "Lion and Palm" essay, 1853.

753 Scarlet "Scinde Dawks" of 1852

1977. "Asiana '77" Philatelic Exn, Bangalore.
861 **753** 1r. multicoloured 1·50 1·00
862 - 3r. blue, orange and black 3·00 4·00
DESIGN: 3r. Foreign mail arriving at Ballard Pier, Bombay, 1927.

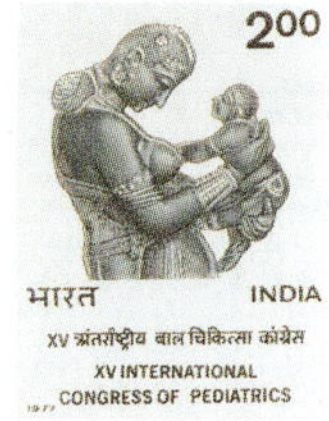

754 "Mother and Child" (Khajuraho sculpture)

1977. 15th Int Congress of Pediatrics, New Delhi.
863 **754** 2r. blue and brown 2·25 2·75

755 Statue of Kittur Rani Channamma, Belgaum

1977. Kittur Rani Channama (ruler) Commem.
864 **755** 25p. green 1·25 1·00

756 Symbolic Sun

1977. Union Public Service Commission.
865 **756** 25p. multicoloured 45 30

757 Ear of Corn

1977. "Agriexpo '77" Agricultural Exhibition, New Delhi.
866 **757** 25p. green 40 40

758 "Cats" (Nikur Dilipbhai Mody)

1977. Children's Day. Multicoloured.
867 25p. Type **758** 50 30
868 1r. "Friends" (Bhavsar Ashish Ramanlal) 2·25 3·00

759 Jotirao Phooley (social reformer)

1977. Indian Personalities.
869 **759** 25p. olive 30 75
870 - 25p. brown 30 75
DESIGN: No. 870, Senapti Bapat (patriot).

760 Diagram of Population Growth

1977. 41st Session of International Statistical Institute, New Delhi.
871 **760** 2r. turquoise and red 60 1·00

761 Kamta Prasad Guru and Vyakarna (Hindi Grammar)

1977. Kamta Prasad Guru (writer) Commem.
872 **761** 25p. brown 20 30

762 Kremlin Tower and Soviet Flag

1977. 60th Anniv of October Revolution.
873 **762** 1r. multicoloured 50 75

763 Climber crossing a Crevice

1978. Conquest of Kanchenjunga (1977). Multicoloured.
874 25p. Type **763** 15 10
875 1r. Indian flag near summit (horiz) 60 90

764 "Shikara" on Lake Dal, Kashmir

1978. 27th Pacific Area Travel Association Conference, New Delhi.
876 **764** 1r. multicoloured 2·00 1·50

765 Children in Library

1978. 3rd World Book Fair, New Delhi.
877 **765** 1r. brown and slate 50 80

766 Mother-Pondicherry

1978. Birth Centenary of Mother-Pondicherry (philosopher).
878 **766** 25p. brown and grey 20 40

767 Wheat and Globe

1978. 5th International Wheat Genetics Symposium, New Delhi.
879 **767** 25p. yellow and turquoise 20 40

768 Nanalal Dalpatram Kavi (poet)

1978. Nanalal Dalpatram Kavi Commemoration.
880 **768** 25p. brown 20 40

769 Surjya Sen (revolutionary)

1978. Surjya Sen Commemoration.
881 **769** 25p. bistre and red 20 30

770 "Two Vaishnavas" (Jamini Roy)

1978. Modern Indian Paintings. Multicoloured.
882 25p. Type **770** 20 30
883 50p. "The Mosque" (Sailoz Mookherjea) 40 1·25
884 1r. "Head" (Rabindranath Tagore) 70 1·50
885 2r. "Hill Women" (Amrita Sher Gil) 90 2·00

771 "Self-portrait" (Rubens)

1978. 400th Birth Anniv of Peter Paul Rubens.
886 **771** 2r. multicoloured 2·00 3·00

772 Charlie Chaplin

1978. Charlie Chaplin Commemoration.
887 **772** 25p. blue and gold 1·50 1·00

773 Deendayal Upadhyaya (politician)

1978. Deendayal Upadhyaya Commemoration.
888 **773** 25p. brown and orange 30 40

774 Syama Prasad Mookerjee

1978. Syama Prasad Mookerjee (politician) Commemoration.
889 **774** 25p. brown 40 50

775 Airavat (mythological elephant), Jain Temple, Gujerat (Kachchh Museum)

1978. Treasures from Indian Museums. Mult.
890 25p. Type **775** 30 30
891 50p. Kalpadruma (magical tree), Besnagar (Indian Museum) 40 1·25
892 1r. Obverse and reverse of Kushan gold coin (National Museum) 55 1·50
893 2r. Dagger and knife of Emperor Jehangir, Mughal (Salar Jung Museum) 75 2·00

776 Krishna and Arjuna in Battle Chariot

1978. Bhagawadgeeta (Divine Song of India) Commemoration.
894 **776** 25p. gold and red 20 30

777 Bethune College

1978. Centenary of Bethune College, Calcutta.
895 **777** 25p. brown and green 20 30

778 E. V. Ramasami

1978. E. V. Ramasami (social reformer) Commemoration.
896 **778** 25p. black 20 20

779 Uday Shankar

1978. Uday Shankar (dancer) Commem.
897 **779** 25p. brown 20 30

780 Leo Tolstoy

1978. 150th Birth Anniv of Leo Tolstoy (writer).
898 **780** 1r. multicoloured 30 30

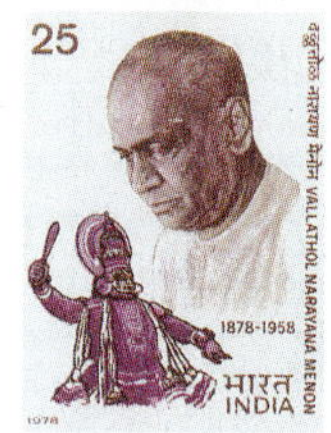

781 Vallathol Narayana Menon

1978. Birth Centenary of Vallathol Narayana Menon (poet).
899 **781** 25p. purple and brown 15 40

782 "Two Friends" (Dinesh Sharma)

1978. Children's Day.
900 **782** 25p. multicoloured 20 40

783 Machine Operator

1978. National Small Industries Fair, New Delhi.
901 **783** 25p. green 20 30

784 Sowars of Skinner's Horse

1978. 175th Anniv of Skinner's Horse (cavalry regiment).
902 **784** 25p. multicoloured 1·25 1·00

785 Mohammad Ali Jauhar

1978. Birth Centenary of Mohammad Ali Jauhar (patriot).

903	**785**	25p. olive	20	40

786 Chakravarti Rajagopalachari

1978. Birth Centenary of Chakravarti Rajagopalachari (first post-independence Governor-General).

904	**786**	25p. brown	20	30

787 Wright Brothers and Flyer I

1978. 75th Anniv of Powered Flight.

905	**787**	1r. violet and yellow	1·00	30

788 Ravenshaw College

1978. Centenary of Ravenshaw College, Cuttack.

906	**788**	25p. red and green	20	30

789 Schubert

1978. 150th Death Anniv of Franz Schubert (composer).

907	**789**	1r. multicoloured	1·75	65

790 Uniforms of 1799, 1901 and 1979 with Badge

1979. 4th Reunion of Punjab Regiment.

908	**790**	25p. multicoloured	1·50	1·00

791 Bhai Parmanand

1979. Bhai Parmanand (scholar) Commemoration.

909	**791**	25p. violet	20	40

792 Gandhi with Young Boy

1979. International Year of the Child.

910	**792**	25p. brown and red	40	30
911	-	1r. brown and orange	60	1·50

DESIGN: 1r. India I.Y.C. emblem.

793 Albert Einstein

1979. Birth Centenary of Albert Einstein (physicist).

912	**793**	1r. blue	1·25	1·25

794 Rajarshi Shahu Chhatrapati

1979. Rajarshi Shahu Chhatrapati (ruler of Kolhapur State, and precursor of social reform in India) Commemoration.

913	**794**	25p. purple	20	40

795 Exhibition Logo

1979. "India '80" International Stamp Exhibition (1st issue).

914	**795**	30p. green and orange	20	40

See also Nos. 942/5 and 955/8.

796 Postcards under Magnifying Glass

1979. Centenary of Indian Postcards.

915	**796**	50p. multicoloured	20	40

797 Raja Mahendra Pratap

1979. Raja Mahendra Pratap (patriot) Commemoration.

916	**797**	30p. green	20	40

798 Hilsa, Pomfret and Prawn

1979

920	-	2p. violet	10	45
921a	**798**	5p. blue	20	10
922a	-	10p. green	1·00	10
923	-	15p. green	30	10
924a	-	20p. red	1·00	10
925a	-	25p. brown	1·00	10
925bb	-	25p. green	1·25	10
926ab	-	30p. green	1·50	10
927	-	35p. purple	1·75	10
928c	-	50p. violet	1·50	10
929b	-	1r. brown	30	10
932a	-	2r. lilac	30	10
933c	-	2r.25 red and green	1·25	20
934	-	2r.80 red and green	2·50	1·50
934ca	-	3r.25 orange and green	50	60
935c	-	5r. red and green	60	40
936b	-	10r. purple and green	50	50

DESIGNS—HORIZ: 2p. Adult education class; 10p. Irrigation canal; 25p. (925a) Chick hatching from egg; 25p. (925bb) Village, wheat and tractor; 30p. Harvesting maize; 50p. Woman dairy farmer, cows and milk bottles. (36×19 mm): 10r. Forest on hillside. VERT (17×20 mm): 15p. Farmer and agricultural symbols; 20p. Mother feeding child; 35p. "Family Welfare". (17×28 mm): 1r. Cotton plant; 2r. Weaving. (20×38 mm): 2r.25, Cashew; 2r.80, Apples; 3r.25, Oranges; 5r. Rubber tapping.

For 75p. in same design as No. 927 see No. 1214.

800 Jatindra Nath Das

1979. 50th Death Anniv of Jatindra Nath Das (revolutionary).

941	**800**	30p. brown	20	60

801 De Havilland Puss Moth

1979. "Air India 80" International Stamp Exhibition (2nd issue). Mail-carrying Aircraft. Multicoloured.

942		30p. Type **801**	50	25
943		50p. Indian Air Force Hindustan Aircraft Industries Chetak helicopter	70	65
944		1r. Indian Airlines Boeing 737 airliner	85	75
945		2r. Air India Boeing 747 airliner	1·10	1·10

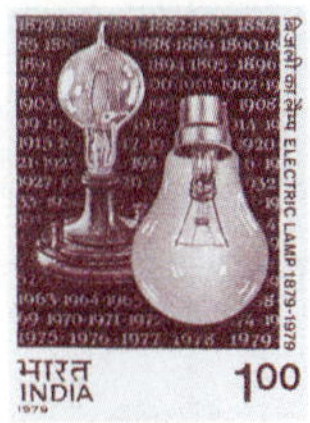

802 Early and Modern Lightbulbs

1979. Centenary of Electric Lightbulb.

946	**802**	1r. purple	20	30

803 Gilgit Record

1979. International Archives Week.

947	**803**	30p. yellow and brown	20	60

804 Hirakud Dam, Orissa

1979. 50th Anniv and 13th Congress of International Commission on Large Dams.

948	**804**	30p. brown and turquoise	20	30

805 Fair Emblem

1979. India International Trade Fair, New Delhi.

949	**805**	1r. black and red	20	30

806 Child learning to Read

1979. International Children's Book Fair, New Delhi.

950	**806**	30p. multicoloured	20	30

807 Dove with Olive Branch and I.A.E.A. Emblem

1979. 23rd International Atomic Energy Agency Conference, New Delhi.

951	**807**	1r. multicoloured	20	45

808 Hindustan Aircraft Industries HAL-26 Pushpak Light Plane and Rohini-1 Glider

1979. Flying and Gliding.

952	**808**	30p. black, brown and blue	1·40	1·00

809 Gurdwara Baoli Sahib Temple, Goindwal, Amritsar District

1979. 500th Birth Anniv of Guru Amar Das (Sikh leader).

953	**809**	30p. multicoloured	40	60

810 Ring of People encircling U.N. Emblem and Cogwheel

1980. 3rd United Nations Industrial Development Organization General Conference, New Delhi.

954	**810**	1r. multicoloured	20	30

811 Army Post Office and Postmarks

1980. "India '80" International Stamp Exhibition (3rd issue).

955 **811** 30p. green 50 30
956 - 50p. brown & deep brown 80 1·25
957 - 1r. red 90 1·00
958 - 2r. brown 90 2·25

DESIGNS: 50p. Money order transfer document, 1879; 1r. Copper prepayment ticket, 1774; 2r. Sir Rowland Hill and birthplace at Kidderminster.

812 Energy Symbols

1980. Institution of Engineers (India) Commem.

959 **812** 30p. gold and blue 20 40

813 Uniforms of 1780 and 1980, Crest and Ribbon

1980. Bicentenary of Madras Sappers.

960 **813** 30p. multicoloured 1·25 1·00

814 Books

1980. 4th World Book Fair, New Delhi.

961 **814** 30p. blue 30 50

815 Bees and Honey-Comb

1980. 2nd International Conference on Agriculture.

962 **815** 1r. bistre and brown 1·50 75

816 Welthy Fisher and Saksharta Nicketan (Literacy House), Lucknow

1980. Welthy Fisher (teacher) Commemoration.

963 **816** 30p. blue 40 40

817 Darul-Uloom, Deoband

1980. Darul-Uloom College Commemoration.

964 **817** 30p. green 30 30

818 Keshub Chunder Sen

1980. Keshub Chunder Sen (religious and social reformer) Commemoration.

965 **818** 30p. brown 50 50

819 Chhatrapati Shivaji Maharaj

1980. 300th Death Anniv of Chhatrapati Shivaji Maharaj (warrior).

966 **819** 30p. multicoloured 40 50

820 Table Tennis

1980. 5th Asian Table Tennis Championships, Calcutta.

967 **820** 30p. purple 50 60

1980. As Nos. 732 and 810, but 17×20 mm in size.

968 30p. brown (Gandhi) 5·50 2·00
969 30p. violet (Nehru) 3·00 75

821 N. M. Joshi

1980. Narayan Malhar Joshi (trade unionist) Commemoration.

970 **821** 30p. mauve 70 40

822 Ulloor S. Parameswara Iyer

1980. Ulloor S. Parameswara Iyer (poet) Commemoration.

971 **822** 30p. purple 70 40

823 S. M. Zamin Ali

1980. Syed Mohammed Zamin Ali (educationist and poet) Commemoration.

972 **823** 30p. green 30 50

824 Helen Keller

1980. Birth Centenary of Helen Keller (campaigner for the handicapped).

973 **824** 30p. black and orange 1·25 55

825 High-jumping

1980. Olympic Games, Moscow. Multicoloured.

974 1r. Type **825** 40 40
975 2r.80 Horse-riding 2·00 3·50

826 Prem Chand

1980. Birth Cent of Prem Chand (novelist).

976 **826** 30p. brown 20 50

827 Mother Teresa and Nobel Peace Prize Medallion

1980. Award of 1979 Nobel Peace Prize to Mother Teresa.

977 **827** 30p. violet 1·50 1·00

828 Lord Mountbatten

1980. Lord Mountbatten Commemoration.

978 **828** 2r.80 multicoloured 3·00 3·50

1980. As Nos. 968/9, but new face value.

979 35p. brown 2·75 70
980 35p. violet 1·25 20

DESIGNS: No. 979, Gandhi; No. 980, Nehru.

829 Scottish Church College, Calcutta

1980. 150th Anniv of Scottish Church College, Calcutta.

981 **829** 35p. lilac 20 30

830 Rajah Annamalai Chettiar

1980. Rajah Annamalai Chettiar (banker and educationist) Commemoration.

982 **830** 35p. lilac 20 30

831 Gandhi marching to Dandi

1980. 50th Anniv of "Dandi March" (Gandhi's defiance of Salt Tax Law).

983 **831** 35p. black, blue and gold 90 1·40
984 - 35p. black, mauve and gold 90 1·40

DESIGN: No. 984, Gandhi picking up handful of salt at Dandi.

832 Jayaprakash Narayan

1980. Jayaprakash Narayan (socialist) Commemoration.

985 **832** 35p. brown 60 70

833 Great Indian Bustard

1980. International Symposium on Bustards, Jaipur.

986 **833** 2r.30 multicoloured 1·00 2·00

834 Arabic Commemorative Inscription

1980. Moslem Year 1400 A.H. Commemoration.

987 **834** 35p. multicoloured 15 30

835 "Girls Dancing" (Pampa Paul)

1980. Children's Day.

988	**835**	35p. multicoloured	1·25	55

836 Dhyan Chand

1980. Dhyan Chand (hockey player). Commemoration.

989	**836**	35p. brown	1·50	1·00

837 Gold Mining

1980. Cent of Kolar Gold Fields, Karnataka.

990	**837**	1r. multicoloured	2·00	30

838 M. A. Ansari

1980. Mukhtayar Ahmad Ansari (medical practitioner and politician) Commemoration.

991	**838**	35p. green	60	50

839 India Government Mint, Bombay

1980. 150th Anniv of India Government Mint, Bombay.

992	**839**	35p. black, blue and silver	20	30

840 Bride from Tamil Nadu

1980. Brides in Traditional Costume. Multicoloured.

993	1r. Type **840**	75	90
994	1r. Rajasthan	75	90
995	1r. Kashmir	75	90
996	1r. Bengal	75	90

841 Mazharul Haque

1981. Mazharul Haque (journalist) Commem.

997	**841**	35p. blue	20	50

842 St. Stephen's College

1981. Centenary of St. Stephen's College, Delhi.

998	**842**	35p. red	20	70

843 Gommateshwara

1981. Millenium of Gommateshwara (statue at Shravanabelgola).

999	**843**	1r. multicoloured	20	30

844 G. V. Mavalankar

1981. 25th Death Anniv of Ganesh Vasudeo Mavalankar (parliamentarian).

1000	**844**	35p. red	20	40

845 Flame of Martyrdom

1981. "Homage to Martyrs".

1001	**845**	35p. multicoloured	20	30

846 Heinrich von Stephan and U.P.U. Emblem

1981. 150th Birth Anniv of Heinrich von Stephan (founder of U.P.U.).

1002	**846**	1r. brown	80	50

847 Disabled Child being helped by Able-bodied Child

1981. International Year for Disabled Persons.

1003	**847**	1r. black and blue	50	30

848 Bhil

1981. Tribes of India. Multicoloured.

1004	1r. Type **848**	50	35
1005	1r. Dandami Maria	50	35
1006	1r. Toda	50	35
1007	1r. Khlamngam Naga	50	35

849 Stylized Trees

1981. Forests Conservation.

1008	**849**	1r. multicoloured	50	30

850 Nilmoni Phukan

1981. Nilmoni Phukan (poet) Commemoration.

1009	**850**	35p. brown	50	65

851 Sanjay Gandhi

1981. 1st Death Anniv of Sanjay Gandhi (politician).

1010	**851**	35p. multicoloured	40	70

852 Launch of "SLV 3" and Diagram of "Rohini"

1981. Launch of "SLV 3" Rocket with "Rohini" Satellite.

1011	**852**	1r. black, pink and blue	30	30

853 Games Logo

1981. Asian Games, New Delhi (1st issue). Multicoloured.

1012	1r. Type **853**	1·00	65
1013	1r. Games emblem and stylized hockey players	1·00	65

See also Nos. 1026, 1033, 1057, 1059 and 1061/6.

854 Flame of the Forest

1981. Flowering Trees. Multicoloured.

1014	35p. Type **854**	55	15
1015	50p. Crateva	1·00	1·00
1016	1r. Golden shower	1·25	50
1017	2r. Bauhinia	1·60	3·00

855 W. F. D. Emblem and Wheat

1981. World Food Day.

1018	**855**	1r. yellow and blue	50	20

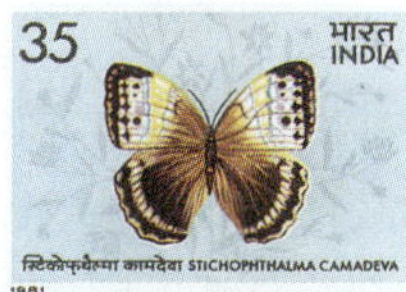

856 "Stichophthalma camadeva"

1981. Butterflies. Multicoloured.

1019	35p. Type **856**	90	20
1020	50p. "Cethosia biblis"	1·75	1·75
1021	1r. "Cyrestis achates" (vert)	2·25	70
1022	2r. "Teinopalpus imperialis" (vert)	2·75	6·00

857 Bellary Raghava

1981. Bellary Raghava (actor) Commemoration.

1023	**857**	35p. green	70	30

858 Regimental Colour

1981. 40th Anniv of Mahar Regiment.

1024	**858**	35p. multicoloured	1·00	30

859 "Toyseller" (Kumari Ruchita Sharma)

1981. Children's Day.

1025	**859**	35p. multicoloured	75	30

860 Rajghat Stadium

1981. Asian Games, New Delhi (2nd issue).
1026 **860** 1r. multicoloured 2·00 30

861 Kashi Prasad Jayasawal and Yaudheya Coin

1981. Birth Centenary of Kashi Prasad Jayasawal (lawyer and historian).
1027 **861** 35p. blue 50 30

862 Indian and P.L.O. Flags, and People

1981. Palestinian Solidarity.
1028 **862** 1r. multicoloured 2·50 40

863 I.N.S. "Taragiri" (frigate)

1981. Indian Navy Day.
1029 **863** 35p. multicoloured 2·25 1·25

864 Henry Heras and Indus Valley Seal

1981. Henry Heras (historian) Commemoration.
1030 **864** 35p. lilac 45 30

865 Map of South-East Asia showing Cable Route

1981. Inauguration of I.O.C.O.M. (Indian Ocean Commonwealth Cable) Submarine Telephone Cable.
1031 **865** 1r. multicoloured 2·50 35

866 Stylized Hockey-players and Championship Emblem

1981. World Cup Hockey Championship, Bombay.
1032 **866** 1r. multicoloured 1·75 30

867 Jawaharlal Nehru Stadium

1981. Asian Games, New Delhi (3rd issue).
1033 **867** 1r. multicoloured 30 20

868 Early and Modern Telephones

1982. Centenary of Telephone Services.
1034 **868** 2r. black, blue and grey 50 50

869 Map of World

1982. International Soil Science Congress, New Delhi.
1035 **869** 1r. multicoloured 30 20

870 Sir J. J. School of Art

1982. 125th Anniv of Sir J. J. School of Art, Bombay.
1036 **870** 35p. multicoloured 20 20

871 "Three Musicians"

1982. Birth Centenary (1981) of Picasso.
1037 **871** 2r.85 multicoloured 2·25 1·10

872 Deer (stone carving), 5th-century A.D.

1982. Festival of India. Ancient Sculpture. Multicoloured.
1038 2r. Type **872** 20 40
1039 3r.05 Kaliya Mardana (bronze statue), 9th-century A.D 35 60

873 Radio Telescope, Ooty

1982. Festival of India. Science and Technology.
1040 **873** 3r.05 multicoloured 35 40

874 Robert Koch and Symbol of Disease

1982. Centenary of Robert Koch's Discovery of Tubercle Bacillus.
1041 **874** 35p. lilac 2·25 1·00

875 Durgabai Deshmukh

1982. 1st Death Anniv of Durgabai Deshmukh (social reformer).
1042 **875** 35p. blue 1·00 1·00

876 Blue Poppy

1982. Himalayan Flowers. Multicoloured.
1043 35p. Type **876** 70 30
1044 1r. Showy inula 1·75 30
1045 2r. Cobra lily 2·25 3·00
1046 2r.85 Brahma kamal 2·75 4·75

877 "Apple" Satellite

1982. 1st Anniv of "Apple" Satellite Launch.
1047 **877** 2r. multicoloured 70 1·25

878 Bidhan Chandra Roy

1982. Birth Centenary of Bidhan Chandra Roy (doctor and politician).
1048 **878** 50p. brown 1·25 1·75

879 "Sagar Samrat" Oil Rig

1982. 25th Anniv of Oil and Natural Gas Commission.
1049 **879** 1r. multicoloured 2·25 75

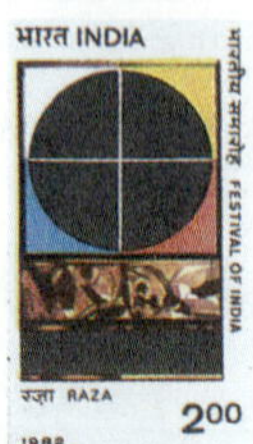

880 "Bindu" (S. H. Raza)

1982. Festival of India. Contemporary Paintings. Multicoloured.
1050 2r. Type **880** 60 50
1051 3r.05 "Between the Spider and the Lamp" (M. F. Hussain) 1·00 1·50

881 Red Deer Stag, Kashmir

1982. Wildlife Conservation.
1052 **881** 2r.85 multicoloured 2·75 2·00

882 Westland Wapiti Biplane and Mikoyan Gurevich MiG-25 Aircraft

1982. 50th Anniv of Indian Air Force.
1053 **882** 1r. multicoloured 6·00 1·75

883 J. Tata with De Havilland Puss Moth

1982. 50th Anniv of Civil Aviation in India.
1054 **883** 3r.25 multicoloured 5·50 2·25

884 Police Patrol

1982. Police Commemoration Day.
1055 **884** 50p. green 60 30

885 Coins and Economic Symbols

1982. Centenary of Post Office Savings Bank.
1056 **885** 50p. brown and light brown 20 20

886 Wrestling Bout

1982. Asian Games, New Delhi (4th issue).
1057 **886** 1r. multicoloured 1·75 30

887 Troposcatter Communication Link

1982. 1st Anniv of Troposcatter Communication Link between India and U.S.S.R.
1058 **887** 3r.05 multicoloured 30 40

888 Arjuna shooting Arrow at Fish

1982. Asian Games, New Delhi (5th issue).

1059	**888**	1r. multicoloured	1·75	30

889 "Mother and Child" (Deepak Sharma)

1982. Children's Day.

1060	**889**	50p. multicoloured	30	30

890 Stylized Cyclists

1982. Asian Games, New Delhi (6th issue). Multicoloured.

1061	50p. Type **890**	15	10
1062	2r. Javelin-throwing	25	30
1063	2r.85 Discus-throwing	30	45
1064	3r.25 Football	40	55

891 "Enterprise" Dinghies Race

1982. Asian Games, New Delhi (7th issue). Multicoloured.

1065	2r. Type **891**	1·25	30
1066	2r.85 Rowing	1·75	70

892 Chetwode Building

1982. 50th Anniv of Indian Military Academy Dehradun.

1067	**892**	50p. multicoloured	30	50

893 Purushottamdas Tandon

1982. Birth Cent of Purushottamdas Tandon (politician).

1068	**893**	50p. brown	30	1·00

894 Darjeeling Himalayan Railway

1982. Cent of Darjeeling Himalayan Railway.

1069	**894**	2r.85 multicoloured	6·50	5·50

895 Vintage Rail Coach and Silhouette of Steam Locomotive

1982. "Inpex 82" Stamp Exhibition. Multicoloured.

1070	50p. Type **895**	1·00	1·00
1071	2r. 1854 ½ anna blue stamp and 1947 3½ anna Independence commem (33×44 mm)	2·50	3·50

896 Antarctic Camp

1983. 1st Indian Antarctic Expedition.

1072	**896**	1r. multicoloured	4·75	2·50

1983. As Nos. 968/9, but with new face value.

1073	50p. brown (Gandhi)	4·50	2·50
1074a	50p. blue (Nehru)	3·25	1·00

897 Roosevelt with Stamp Collection

1983. Birth Centenary of Franklin D. Roosevelt (American statesman).

1075	**897**	3r.25 brown	55	1·25

898 "Siberian Cranes at Bharatpur" (Diane Pierce)

1983. International Crane Workshop, Bharatpur.

1076	**898**	2r.85 multicoloured	3·75	3·75

899 Jat Regiment Uniforms Past and Present

1983. Presentation of Colours to Battalions of the Jat Regiment.

1077	**899**	50p. multicoloured	2·50	2·00

900 Non-aligned Summit Logo

1983. 7th Non-aligned Summit Conference, New Delhi.

1078	**900**	1r. lt brown, brown & blk	20	30
1079	-	2r. multicoloured	30	95

DESIGN: 2r. Nehru.

901 Shore Temple, Mahabalipuram

1983. Commonwealth Day. Multicoloured.

1080	1r. Type **901**	15	30
1081	2r. Gomukh, Gantgotri Glacier	30	1·25

902 Acropolis and Olympic Emblems

1983. Int Olympic Committee Session, New Delhi.

1082	**902**	1r. multicoloured	30	50

903 "St. Francis and Brother Falcon" (statue by Giovanni Collina)

1983. 800th Birth Anniv of St. Francis of Assisi.

1083	**903**	1r. brown	1·25	50

904 Karl Marx and "Das Kapital"

1983. Death Centenary of Karl Marx.

1084	**904**	1r. brown	30	30

905 Darwin and Map of Voyage

1983. Death Centenary (1982) of Charles Darwin (naturalist).

1085	**905**	2r. multicoloured	3·75	3·50

906 Swamp Deer

1983. 50th Anniv of Kanha National Park.

1086	**906**	1r. multicoloured	3·00	1·25

907 Globe and Satellite

1983. World Communications Year.

1087	**907**	1r. multicoloured	75	40

908 Simon Bolivar

1983. Birth Bicentenary of Simon Bolivar (South American statesman).

1088	**908**	2r. multicoloured	2·50	2·25

909 Meera Behn

1983. India's Struggle for Freedom (1st series).

1089	50p. red and green	1·50	2·50
1090	50p. brown, green and red	1·50	2·50
1091	50p. multicoloured	1·50	2·25
1092	50p. brown, green and red	15	50
1093	50p. brown, green and orange	15	50
1094	50p. green, yellow and orange	15	50

DESIGNS—VERT: No. 1089, Type **909**; 1090, Mahadev Desai; 1092, Hemu Kalani (revolutionary); 1093, Acharya Vinoba Bhave (social reformer); 1094, Surendranath Banerjee (political reformer). HORIZ (43×31 mm): No. 1091, Quit India Resolution.

See also Nos. 1119/24, 1144/9, 1191/4, 1230/5, 1287/96 and 1345/9.

910 Ram Nath Chopra

1983. Ram Nath Chopra (pharmacologist) Commemoration.

1095	**910**	50p. red	75	1·50

911 Nanda Devi Mountain

1983. 25th Anniv of Indian Mountaineering Federation.

1096	**911**	2r. multicoloured	2·50	1·25

912 Great Indian Hornbill

1983. Centenary of Natural History Society, Bombay.

1097	**912**	1r. multicoloured	3·75	1·40

913 View of Garden

1983. Rock Garden, Chandigarh.

1098	**913**	1r. multicoloured	2·00	1·25

914 Golden Langur

1983. Indian Wildlife. Monkeys. Multicoloured.

1099	1r. Type **914**	2·50	50
1100	2r. Lion-tailed macaque	3·50	4·50

915 Ghats of Varanasi

1983. 5th General Assembly of World Tourism Organization.

1101	**915**	2r. multicoloured	1·00	1·00

916 Krishna Kanta Handique

1983. Krishna Kanta Handique (scholar).

1102	**916**	50p. blue	30	70

918 Woman and Child (from "Festival" by Kashyap Premsawala)

1983. Children's Day.

1103	**918**	50p. multicoloured	30	50

920 "Udan Khatola", First Indian Hot Air Balloon

1983. Bicentenary of Manned Flight.

1104	1r. Type **920**	1·25	20
1105	2r. Montgolfier balloon	1·75	1·50

921 Tiger

1983. Ten Years of "Project Tiger".

1106	**921**	2r. multicoloured	4·00	4·00

922 Commonwealth Logo

1983. Commonwealth Heads of Government Meeting, New Delhi. Multicoloured.

1107	1r. Type **922**	55	15
1108	2r. Goanese couple, early 19th century	95	85

923 "Pratiksha"

1983. Birth Centenary of Nanda Lal Bose (artist).

1109	**923**	1r. multicoloured	30	30

925 Lancer in Ceremonial Uniform

1984. Bicentenary of 7th Light Cavalry.

1110	**925**	1r. multicoloured	3·75	1·40

926 Troopers in Ceremonial Uniform and Tank

1984. Presentation of Regimental Guidon to the Deccan Horse.

1111	**926**	1r. multicoloured	3·75	1·40

927 Society Building and Sir William Jones (founder)

1984. Bicentenary of Asiatic Society.

1112	**927**	1r. green and purple	30	50

928 Insurance Logo

1984. Centenary of Postal Life Insurance.

1113	**928**	1r. multicoloured	30	30

929 Hawker Siddeley Sea Harrier

1984. President's Review of the Fleet. Multicoloured.

1114	1r. Type **929**	2·00	2·25
1115	1r. "Vikrant" (aircraft carrier)	2·00	2·25
1116	1r. "Vela" (submarine)	2·00	2·25
1117	1r. "Kashin" (destroyer)	2·00	2·25

Nos. 1114/17 were printed together, se-tenant, forming a composite design.

930 I.L.A. Logo and Hemispheres

1984. 12th International Leprosy Congress.

1118	**930**	1r. multicoloured	1·00	55

1984. India's Struggle for Freedom (2nd series). As T 909.

1119	50p. green, lt green & orange	40	1·00
1120	50p. brown, green and orange	40	1·00
1121	50p. multicoloured	1·00	1·25
1122	50p. multicoloured	1·00	1·25
1123	50p. multicoloured	1·00	1·25
1124	50p. multicoloured	1·00	1·25

DESIGNS: No. 1119, Vasudeo Balvant Phadke (revolutionary); 1120, Baba Kanshi Ram (revolutionary); 1121, Tatya Tope; 1122, Nana Sahib; 1123, Begum Hazrat Mahal; 1124, Mangal Pandey.

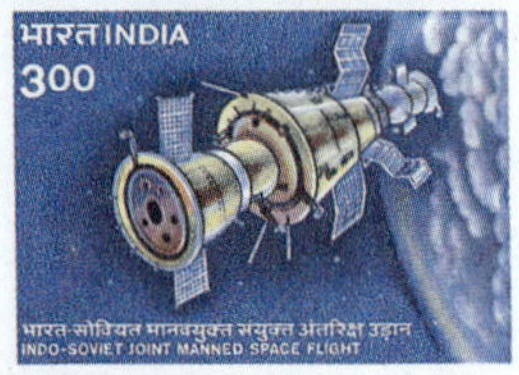

932 "Salyut 7"

1984. Indo-Soviet Manned Space Flight.

1125	**932**	3r. multicoloured	1·00	1·25

935 G. D. Birla

1984. 90th Birth Anniv of G. D. Birla (industrialist).

1126	**935**	50p. brown	75	1·50

936 Basketball

1984. Olympic Games, Los Angeles. Multicoloured.

1127	50p. Type **936**	90	65
1128	1r. High jumping	75	30
1129	2r. Gymnastics (horiz)	1·00	1·50
1130	2r.50 Weightlifting (horiz)	1·25	2·75

937 Gwalior

1984. Forts. Multicoloured.

1131	50p. Type **937**	80	55
1132	1r. Vellore (vert)	1·10	30
1133	1r.50 Simhagad (vert)	2·00	3·00
1134	2r. Jodhpur	2·25	3·25

938 B. V. Paradkar and Newspaper

1984. B. V. Paradkar (journalist) Commemoration.

1135	**938**	50p. brown	75	1·50

939 Dr. D. N. Wadia and Institute of Himalayan Geology, Dehradun

1984. Birth Centenary (1983) of Dr. D. N. Wadia (geologist).

1136	**939**	1r. multicoloured	2·00	55

940 "Herdsman and Cattle in Forest" (H. Kassam)

1984. Children's Day.

1137	**940**	50p. multicoloured	1·00	1·50

941 Indira Gandhi

1984. Prime Minister Indira Gandhi Commemoration (1st issue).

1138	**941**	50p. black, violet & orange	2·50	2·50

See also Nos. 1151, 1167 and 1170.

942 Congress Emblem

1984. 12th World Mining Congress, New Delhi.

1139	**942**	1r. black and yellow	1·75	30

943 Dr. Rajendra Prasad at Desk

1984. Birth Centenary of Dr. Rajendra Prasad (former President).

1140	**943**	50p. multicoloured	1·00	1·50

944 Mrinalini (rose)

1984. Roses. Multicoloured.

1141	1r.50 Type **944**	2·25	2·25
1142	2r. Sugandha	2·50	2·50

945 "Fergusson College" (Gopal Deuskar)

1985. Centenary of Fergusson College, Pune.

1143	**945**	1r. multicoloured	1·00	65

1985. India's Struggle for Freedom (3rd series). As T 909.

1144	50p. brown, green and orange	80	1·25
1145	50p. brown, green and orange	80	1·25
1146	50p. brown, green and orange	80	1·25
1147	50p. brown, green and orange	80	1·25
1148	50p. blue, green and orange	80	1·25

1149 50p. black, green and orange 80 1·25

DESIGNS—VERT: No. 1144, Narhar Vishnu Gadgil (politician); 1145, Jairamdas Doulatram (journalist); 1147, Kakasaheb Kalelkar (author); 1148, Master Tara Singh (politician); 1149, Ravishankar Maharaj (politician). HORIZ: No. 1146, Jatindra and Nellie Sengupta (politicians).

947 Gunner and Howitzer from Mountain Battery

1985. 50th Anniv of Regiment of Artillery.
1150 **947** 1r. multicoloured 4·75 1·50

948 Indira Gandhi making Speech

1985. Indira Gandhi Commemoration (2nd issue).
1151 **948** 2r. multicoloured 4·00 4·00

949 Minicoy Lighthouse

1985. Centenary of Minicoy Lighthouse.
1152 **949** 1r. multicoloured 6·50 1·50

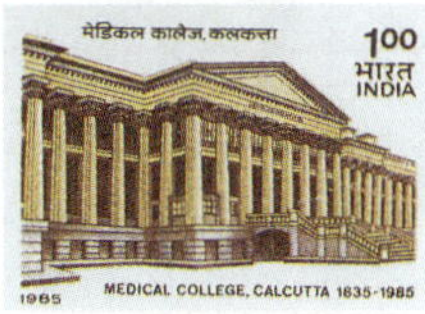

950 Medical College Hospital

1985. 150th Anniv of Medical College, Calcutta.
1153 **950** 1r. yellow, brown & purple 3·50 1·00

951 Medical College, Madras

1985. 150th Anniv of Medical College, Madras.
1154 **951** 1r. light brown and brown 3·50 1·00

952 Riflemen of 1835 and 1985 and Map of North-East India

1985. 150th Anniv of Assam Rifles.
1155 **952** 1r. multicoloured 5·00 1·50

953 Potato Plant

1985. 50th Anniv of Potato Research in India.
1156 **953** 50p. deep brown and brown 1·75 2·00

954 Baba Jassa Singh Ahluwalia

1985. Death Bicentenary (1983) of Baba Jassa Singh Ahluwalia (Sikh leader).
1157 **954** 50p. purple 1·75 2·00

955 St. Xavier's College

1985. 125th Anniv of St. Xavier's College, Calcutta.
1158 **955** 1r. multicoloured 2·00 75

956 White-winged Wood Duck

1985. Wildlife Conservation. White-winged Wood Duck.
1159 **956** 2r. multicoloured 7·00 6·00

957 "Mahara"

1985. Bougainvillea. Multicoloured.
1160 50p. Type **957** 2·00 2·75
1161 1r. "H. B. Singh" 2·25 1·50

958 Yaudheya Copper Coin, c. 200 B.C.

1985. Festival of India (1st issue).
1162 **958** 2r. multicoloured 3·00 2·50

959 Statue of Didarganj Yakshi (deity)

1985. Festival of India (2nd issue).
1163 **959** 1r. multicoloured 1·75 65

962 Swami Haridas

1985. Swami Haridas (philosopher) Commemoration.
1164 **962** 1r. multicoloured 2·00 1·50

963 Stylized Mountain Road

1985. 25th Anniv of Border Roads Organization.
1165 **963** 2r. red, violet and black 2·50 3·50

964 Nehru addressing General Assembly

1985. 40th Anniv of United Nations Organization.
1166 **964** 2r. multicoloured 1·40 1·25

965 Indira Gandhi with Crowd

1985. Indira Gandhi Commemoration (3rd issue).
1167 **965** 2r. brown and black 2·75 3·25

966 Girl using Home Computer

1985. Children's Day.
1168 **966** 50p. multicoloured 1·00 1·25

967 Halley's Comet

1985. 19th General Assembly of International Astronomical Union, New Delhi.
1169 **967** 1r. multicoloured 2·25 1·50

968 Indira Gandhi

1985. Indira Gandhi Commemoration (4th issue).
1170 **968** 3r. multicoloured 3·25 3·50

969 St. Stephen's Hospital

1985. Centenary of St. Stephen's Hospital, Delhi.
1171 **969** 1r. black and brown 1·00 40

971 Map showing Member States

1985. 1st Summit Meeting of South Asian Association for Regional Co-operation, Dhaka, Bangladesh. Multicoloured.
1172 1r. Type **971** 1·75 40
1173 3r. Flags of member nations (44×32 mm) 3·50 4·50

972 Shyama Shastri

1985. Shyama Shastri (composer) Commemoration.
1174 **972** 1r. multicoloured 3·00 1·50

975 Young Runners and Emblem

1985. International Youth Year.
1175 **975** 2r. multicoloured 3·00 1·50

976 Handel and Bach

1985. 300th Birth Annivs of George Frederick Handel and Johann Sebastian Bach (composers).
1176 **976** 5r. multicoloured 5·50 5·50

977 A. O. Hume (founder) and Early Congress Presidents

1985. Centenary of Indian National Congress. Designs showing miniature portraits of Congress Presidents.
1177 **977** 1r. black, orange, green and grey 2·25 2·75
1178 - 1r. black, orange and green 2·25 2·75
1179 - 1r. black, orange and green 2·25 2·75
1180 - 1r. black, orange, green and grey 2·25 2·75

Nos. 1178/80 each show sixteen miniature portraits. The individual stamps can be distinguished by the position of the face value and inscription which are at the top on Nos. 1177/8 and at the foot on Nos. 1179/80. No. 1180 shows a portrait of Prime Minister Rajiv Gandhi in a grey frame at bottom right.

978 Bombay and Duncan Dry Docks, Bombay

1986. 250th Anniv of Naval Dockyard, Bombay.

1181	**978**	2r.50 multicoloured	5·00	5·00

979 Hawa Mahal and Jaipur 1904 2a. Stamp

1986. "INPEX '86" Philatelic Exhibition, Jaipur. Multicoloured.

1182		50p. Type **979**	1·25	1·25
1183		2r. Mobile camel post office, Thar Desert	2·75	3·50

980 I.N.S. "Vikrant" (aircraft carrier)

1986. Completion of 25 Years Service by I.N.S. "Vikrant".

1184	**980**	2r. multicoloured	7·50	7·00

981 Humber Sommer Biplane and Later Mail Planes

1986. 75th Anniv of First Official Airmail Flight, Allahabad–Naini. Multicoloured.

1185		50p. Type **981**	2·25	2·00
1186		3r. Modern Air India Airbus Industries A300 mail plane and Humber Sommer biplane (37×24 mm)	4·75	7·00

982 Triennale Emblem

1986. 6th Triennale Art Exhibition, New Delhi.

1187	**982**	1r. purple, yellow & black	1·50	1·00

983 Chaitanya Mahaprabhu

1986. 500th Birth Anniv of Chaitanya Mahaprabhu (religious leader).

1188	**983**	2r. multicoloured	3·25	3·75

984 Main Building, Mayo College

1986. Mayo College (public school), Ajmer, Commemoration.

1189	**984**	1r. multicoloured	2·00	1·00

985 Two Footballers

1986. World Cup Football Championship, Mexico.

1190	**985**	5r. multicoloured	5·50	5·50

1986. India's Struggle for Freedom (4th series). As T 909.

1191		50p. brown, green and red	1·75	2·25
1192		50p. brown, green and red	1·75	2·25
1193		50p. black, green and orange	1·75	2·25
1194		50p. brown, green and red	1·75	2·25

DESIGNS: No. 1191, Bhim Sen Sachar; 1192, Alluri Seeta Rama Raju; 1193, Sagarmal Gopa; 1194, Veer Surendra Sai.

987 Swami Sivananda

1986. Birth Centenary of Swami Sivananda (spiritual leader).

1195	**987**	2r. multicoloured	3·50	4·25

988 Volleyball

1986. Asian Games, Seoul, South Korea. Multicoloured.

1196		1r.50 Type **988**	2·75	3·00
1197		3r. Hurdling	3·25	4·50

989 Madras G.P.O.

1986. Bicentenary of Madras G.P.O.

1198	**989**	5r. black and red	5·00	5·50

990 Parachutist

1986. 225th Anniv of 8th Battalion of Coast Sepoys (now 1st Battalion Parachute Regiment).

1199	**990**	3r. multicoloured	5·50	5·50

991 Early and Modern Policemen

1986. 125th Anniv of Indian Police. Designs showing early and modern police.

1200	**991**	1r.50 multicoloured	4·00	4·25
1201	-	2r. multicoloured	4·00	4·25

Nos. 1200/1 were printed together, se-tenant, forming a composite design.

992 Hand holding Flower and World Map

1986. International Peace Year.

1202	**992**	5r. multicoloured	4·50	1·75

993 "Girl Rock Climber" (Sujasha Dasgupta)

1986. Children's Day.

1203	**993**	50p. multicoloured	2·25	2·50

994 Windmill

1986. Science and Technology.

1211	-	35p. red	10	10
1212	-	40p. red	10	10
1213	-	60p. green and red	10	10
1214a	-	75p. red	25	10
1215	-	1r. black and red	20	10
1217	-	5r. brown and orange	30	20
1218	-	20r. brown and blue	1·25	60
1219	**994**	50r. black, blue and mauve	2·25	2·25

DESIGNS—20×17 mm: 35p. Family planning. 37×20 mm: 60p. Indian family; 20r. Bio gas. 17×20 mm: 40p. Television set, dish aerial and transmitter; 75p. "Family" (as No. 927). 20×37 mm: 1r. Petrol pump nozzle (Oil conservation); 5r.Solar energy.

995 Growth Monitoring

1986. 40th Anniv of UNICEF. Multicoloured.

1221		50p. Type **995**	2·00	2·00
1222		5r. Immunization	5·00	6·50

996 Tansen

1986. Tansen (musician and composer) Commem.

1223	**996**	1r. multicoloured	2·50	60

997 Indian Elephant

1986. 50th Anniv of Corbett National Park. Multicoloured.

1224		1r. Type **997**	4·00	1·25
1225		2r. Gharial	4·50	6·50

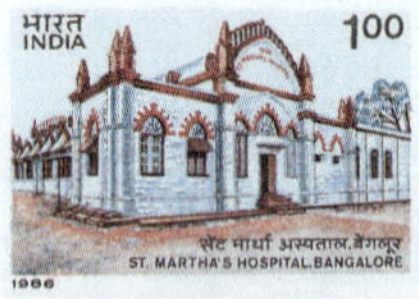

998 St. Martha's Hospital

1986. Centenary of St. Martha's Hospital, Bangalore.

1226	**998**	1r. blue, orange and black	2·50	1·60

999 Yacht "Trishna" and Route Map

1987. Indian Army Round the World Yacht Voyage, 1985–1987.

1227	**999**	6r.50 multicoloured	4·50	5·00

1000 Map of Southern Africa and Logo

1987. Inauguration of AFRICA Fund.

1228	**1000**	6r.50 black	5·50	6·50

1001 Emblem

1987. 29th Congress of International Chamber of Commerce, New Delhi.

1229	**1001**	5r. violet, blue and red	3·75	2·50

1987. India's Struggle for Freedom (5th series). As T 909.

1230		60p. brown, green and orange	2·75	30
1231		60p. violet, green and red	30	30
1232		60p. brown, green and red	30	30
1233		60p. blue, green and orange	30	30
1234		60p. brown, green and red	30	30
1235		60p. brown, green and red	30	30
1236		60p. red, green and orange	30	30

DESIGNS: No. 1230, Hakim Ajmal Khan; No. 1231, Lala Har Dayal; No. 1232, M. N Roy; No. 1233, Tripuraneni Ramaswamy Chowdary; No. 1234, Dr. Kailas Nath Katju; No. 1235, S. Satyamurti; No. 1236, Pandit Hriday Nath Kunzru.

1002 Blast Furnace and Railway Emblem

1987. Cent of South Eastern Railway. Mult.

1237	1r. Type **1002**	40	15
1238	1r.50 Tank locomotive No. 691, 1887 (horiz)	45	35
1239	2r. Electric train on viaduct, 1987	55	60
1240	4r. Steam locomotive, c. 1900 (horiz)	80	1·25

1003 Kalia Bhomora Bridge, Tezpur, Assam

1987. Inauguration of Brahmaputra Bridge.

1241	**1003**	2r. multicoloured	30	40

1004 Madras Christian College

1987. 150th Anniv of Madras Christian College.

1242	**1004**	1r.50 black and red	20	30

1005 Shree Shree Ma Anandamayee

1987. Shree Shree Ma Anandamayee (Hindu spiritual leader) Commemoration.

1243	**1005**	1r. brown	1·00	30

1006 "Rabindranath Tagore" (self-portrait)

1987. Rabindranath Tagore (poet) Commem.

1244	**1006**	2r. multicoloured	40	30

1007 Garwhal Rifles Uniforms of 1887

1987. Centenary of Garwhal Rifles Regiment.

1245	**1007**	1r. multicoloured	75	20

1008 J. Krishnamurti

1987. J. Krishnamurti (philosopher) Commem.

1246	**1008**	60p. brown	1·00	1·25

1009 Regimental Uniforms of 1887

1987. Centenary of 37th Dogra Regt (now 7th Battalion) (1 Dogra), Mechanised Infantry Regt.

1247	**1009**	1r. multicoloured	65	20

1010 Hall of Nations, Pragati Maidan, New Delhi

1987. "India '89" International Stamp Exhibition, New Delhi (1st issue). Multicoloured.

1248	50p. Exhibition logo	10	15
1249	5r. Type **1010**	45	60
MS1250	156×58 mm. Nos. 1248/9 (sold at 8r.)	70	1·00

See also Nos. 1264/8, 1333/4, 1341/2 and 1358/61.

1011 "Sadyah-Snata" Sculpture, Sanghol

1987. Festival of India, U.S.S.R.

1251	**1011**	6r.50 multicoloured	1·00	1·00

1012 Flag and Stylized Birds with "40" in English and Hindi

1987. 40th Anniv of Independence.

1252	**1012**	60p. orange, green & bl	20	20

1013 Sant Harchand Singh Longowal

1987. Sant Harchand Singh Longowal (Sikh leader) Commemoration.

1253	**1013**	1r. multicoloured	1·00	20

1014 Guru Ghasidas

1987. Guru Ghasidas (Hindu leader) Commemoration.

1254	**1014**	60p. red	20	20

1015 Thakur Anukul Chandra

1987. Thakur Anukul Chandra (spiritual leader) Commemoration.

1255	**1015**	1r. multicoloured	1·00	20

1016 University of Allahabad

1987. Centenary of Allahabad University.

1256	**1016**	2r. multicoloured	30	50

1017 Pankha Offering

1987. Phoolwalon Ki Sair Festival, Delhi.

1257	**1017**	2r. multicoloured	30	50

1018 Chhatrasal on Horseback

1987. Chhatrasal (Bundela ruler) Commemoration.

1258	**1018**	60p. brown	30	20

1019 Family and Stylized Houses

1987. International Year of Shelter for the Homeless.

1259	**1019**	5r. multicoloured	50	70

1020 Map of Asia and Logo

1987. Asia Regional Conference of Rotary International.

1260	**1020**	60p. brown and green	15	15
1261	-	6r.50 multicoloured	60	85

DESIGN: 6r.50, Oral polio vaccination.

1021 Blind Boy, Braille Books and Computer

1987. Centenary of Service to Blind.

1262	**1021**	1r. multicoloured	35	15
1263	-	2r. deep blue and blue	65	40

DESIGN: 2r. Eye donation.

1022 Iron Pillar, Delhi

1987. "India '89" International Stamp Exhibition, New Delhi (2nd issue). Delhi Landmarks. Mult.

1264	60p. Type **1022**	20	15
1265	1r.50 India Gate	25	20
1266	5r. Dewan-e-Khas, Red Fort	65	50
1267	6r.50 Old Fort	80	65
MS1268	100×86 mm. Nos. 1264/7 (sold at 15r.)	1·75	2·50

1023 Tyagmurti Goswami Ganeshdutt

1987. Tyagmurti Goswami Ganeshdutt (spiritual leader and social reformer) Commemoration.

1269	**1023**	60p. red	20	20

1024 "My Home" (Siddharth Deshprabha)

1987. Children's Day.

1270	**1024**	60p. multicoloured	30	20

1025 Chinar

1987. Indian Trees. Multicoloured.

1271	**1025**	60p. multicoloured	15	15
1272	-	1r.50 multicoloured	20	20
1273	-	5r. black, green & brown	55	65
1274	-	6r.50 brown, red & green	80	80

DESIGNS—HORIZ: 1r.50, Pipal; 6r.50, Banyan. VERT: 5r. Sal.

1026 Logo (from sculpture "Worker and Woman Peasant" by V. Mukhina)

1987. Festival of U.S.S.R., India.

1275	**1026**	5r. multicoloured	50	50

1027 White Tiger

1987. Wildlife. Multicoloured.

1276	1r. Type **1027**	1·00	15
1277	5r. Snow leopard (horiz)	2·00	85

1028 Execution of Veer Narayan Singh

1987. Veer Narayan Singh (patriot) Commemoration.

1278 **1028** 60p. brown 20 20

1029 Rameshwari Nehru

1987. Rameshwari Nehru (women's rights campaigner) Commemoration.

1279 **1029** 60p. brown 20 20

1030 Father Kuriakose Elias Chavara

1987. Father Kuriakose Elias Chavara (founder of Carmelites of Mary Immaculate) Commemoration.

1280 **1030** 60p. brown 20 20

1031 Dr. Rajah Sir Muthiah Chettiar

1987. Dr. Rajah Sir Muthiah Chettiar (politician) Commemoration.

1281 **1031** 60p. grey 20 20

1032 Golden Temple, Amritsar

1987. 400th Anniv of Golden Temple, Amritsar.

1282 **1032** 60p. multicoloured 75 20

1033 Rukmini Devi and Dancer

1987. Rukmini Devi (Bharatanatyam dance pioneer) Commemoration.

1283 **1033** 60p. red 30 20

1034 Dr. Hiralal

1987. Dr. Hiralal (historian) Commemoration.

1284 **1034** 60p. blue 20 20

1035 Light Frequency Experiment and Bodhi Tree

1988. 75th Session of Indian Science Congress Association.

1285 **1035** 4r. multicoloured 50 60

1036 Rural Patient

1988. 13th Asian Pacific Dental Congress.

1286 **1036** 4r. multicoloured 50 50

1988. India's Struggle for Freedom (6th series). As T 909.

1287	60p. black, green and orange	20	40
1288	60p. brown, green and orange	20	40
1289	60p. red, green and orange	20	40
1290	60p. purple, green and orange	20	40
1291	60p. purple, green and red	20	40
1292	60p. black, green and orange	20	40
1293	60p. lilac, green and red	20	40
1294	60p. deep green, green and red	20	30
1295	60p. brown, green and green	20	30
1296	60p. mauve, green and orange	20	30

DESIGNS: No. 1287, Mohan Lal Sukhadia; 1288, Dr. S. K. Sinha; 1289, Chandra Shekhar Azad; 1290, G. B. Pant; 1291, Dr. Anugrah Narain Singh; 1292, Kuladhor Chaliha; 1293, Shivprasad Gupta; 1294, Sarat Chandra Bose; 1295, Baba Kharak Singh; 1296, Sheikh Mohammad Abdullah.

1037 U Tirot Singh

1988. U Tirot Singh (Khasis leader) Commem.

1297 **1037** 60p. brown 20 20

1038 Early and Modern Regimental Uniforms

1988. Bicentenary of 4th Battalion of the Kumaon Regiment.

1298 **1038** 1r. multicoloured 40 20

1039 Balgandharva

1988. Birth Centenary of Balgandharva (actor).

1299 **1039** 60p. brown 20 20

1040 Soldiers and Infantry Combat Vehicle

1988. Presentation of Colours to Mechanised Infantry Regiment.

1300 **1040** 1r. multicoloured 45 20

1041 B. N. Rau

1988. B. N. Rau (constitutional lawyer) Commemoration.

1301 **1041** 60p. black 20 20

1042 Mohindra Government College

1988. Mohindra Government College, Patiala.

1302 **1042** 1r. mauve 20 20

1043 Dr. D. V. Gundappa

1988. Dr. D. V. Gundappa (scholar) Commem.

1303 **1043** 60p. grey 20 20

1044 Rani Avantibai

1988. Rani Avantibai of Ramgarh Commem.

1304 **1044** 60p. mauve 20 20

1045 "Malayala Manorama" Office, Kottayam

1988. Centenary of "Malayala Manorama" (newspaper).

1305 **1045** 1r. black and blue 20 20

1046 Maharshi Dadhichi

1988. Maharshi Dadhichi (Hindu saint) Commemoration.

1306 **1046** 60p. red 20 20

1047 Mohammad Iqbal

1988. 50th Death Anniv of Mohammad Iqbal (poet).

1307 **1047** 60p. gold and red 20 20

1048 Samarth Ramdas

1988. Samarth Ramdas (Hindu spiritual leader) Commemoration.

1308 **1048** 60p. green 20 20

1049 Swati Tirunal Rama Varma

1988. 175th Birth Anniv of Swati Tirunal Rama Varma (composer).

1309 **1049** 60p. mauve 20 20

1050 Bhaurao Patil and Class

1988. Bhaurao Patil (educationist) Commem.

1310 **1050** 60p. brown 20 20

1051 "Rani Lakshmi Bai" (M. F. Husain)

1988. Martyrs from 1st War of Independence.

1311 **1051** 60p. multicoloured 20 20

1052 Broad Peak

1988. Himalayan Peaks.

1312	**1052**	1r.50 lilac, violet and blue	45	30
1313	-	4r. multicoloured	85	60
1314	-	5r. multicoloured	90	70
1315	-	6r.50 multicoloured	1·10	85

DESIGNS: 4r. K 2 (Godwin Austen); 5r. Kanchenjunga; 6r.50, Nanda Devi.

1053 Child with Grandparents

1988. "Love and Care for Elders".

1316 **1053** 60p. multicoloured 20 20

1054 Victoria Terminus, Bombay

1988. Centenary of Victoria Terminus Station, Bombay.

1317	**1054**	1r. multicoloured	40	20

1055 Lawrence School, Lovedale

1988. 130th Anniv of Lawrence School, Lovedale.

1318	**1055**	1r. brown and green	30	20

1056 Khejri Tree

1988. World Environment Day.

1319	**1056**	60p. multicoloured	20	15

1988. As No. 732, but new face value.

1320		60p. black (Gandhi)	1·75	20

1057 Rani Durgawati

1988. Rani Durgawati (Gondwana ruler) Commemoration.

1322	**1057**	60p. red	20	20

1058 Acharya Shanti Dev

1988. Acharya Shanti Dev (Buddhist scholar) Commemoration.

1323	**1058**	60p. brown	20	20

1059 Y. S. Parmar

1988. Dr. Yashwant Singh Parmar (former Chief Minister of Himachal Pradesh) Commemoration.

1324	**1059**	60p. violet	20	20

1060 Arm pointing at Proclamation in Marathi

1988. 40th Anniv of Independence. Bal Gangadhar Tilak (patriot) Commemoration. Multicoloured.

1325		60p. Type **1060**	20	20
1326		60p. Battle scene	20	20

Nos. 1325/6 were printed together, se-tenant, forming a composite design showing a painting by M. F. Husain.

1061 Durgadas Rathore

1988. 150th Birth Anniv of Durgadas Rathore (Regent of Marwar).

1327	**1061**	60p. brown	20	20

1062 Gopinath Kaviraj

1988. Gopinath Kaviraj (scholar) Commem.

1328	**1062**	60p. brown	20	20

1063 Lotus and Outline Map of India

1988. Hindi Day.

1329	**1063**	60p. red, green & brown	20	20

1064 Indian Olympic Association Logo

1988. "Sports—1988" and Olympic Games, Seoul.

1330	**1064**	60p. purple	35	15
1331	-	5r. multicoloured	3·00	1·00

DESIGN—HORIZ: 5r. Various sports.

1065 Jerdon's Courser

1988. Wildlife Conservation. Jerdon's Courser.

1332	**1065**	1r. multicoloured	2·75	50

1988. "India '89" International Stamp Exhibition, New Delhi (3rd issue). General Post Offices. As T 1022. Multicoloured.

1333		4r. Bangalore G.P.O	50	50
1334		5r. Bombay G.P.O	50	50

1066 "Times of India" Front Page

1988. 150th Anniv of "The Times of India".

1335	**1066**	1r.50 black, gold & yell	20	20

1067 "Maulana Abul Kalam Azad" (K. Hebbar)

1988. Birth Centenary of Maulana Abul Kalam Azad (politician).

1336	**1067**	60p. multicoloured	20	20

1068 Nehru

1988. Birth Centenary (1989) of Jawaharlal Nehru (1st issue).

1337	**1068**	60p. black, orange and green	65	30
1338	-	1r. multicoloured	75	30

DESIGN—VERT: 1r. "Jawaharlal Nehru" (Svetoslav Roerich).

See also No. 1393.

1069 Birsa Munda

1988. Birsa Munda (Munda leader) Commem.

1339	**1069**	60p. brown	20	20

1070 Bhakra Dam

1988. 25th Anniv of Dedication of Bhakra Dam.

1340	**1070**	60p. red	35	70

1071 Dead Letter Office Cancellations of 1886

1988. "India '89" International Stamp Exhibition, New Delhi (4th series). Postal Cancellations.

1341	**1071**	60p. brown, black & red	50	40
1342	-	6r.50 brown and black	1·75	1·40

DESIGN: 6r.50, Allahabad–Cawnpore travelling post office handstamp of 1864.

1072 K. M. Munshi

1988. Birth Centenary (1987) of K. M. Munshi (author and politician).

1343	**1072**	60p. green	20	20

1073 Mannathu Padmanabhan

1989. Mannathu Padmanabhan (social reformer) Commemoration.

1344	**1073**	60p. brown	20	20

1989. India's Struggle for Freedom (7th series). As T 909.

1345		60p. black, green and orange	25	30
1346		60p. orange, green and lilac	25	50
1347		60p. black, green and orange	25	50
1348		60p. brown, green and orange	25	50
1349		60p. brown, green and orange	25	30

DESIGNS: No. 1345, Hare Krishna Mahtab; 1346, Balasaheb Gangadhar Kher; 1347, Raj Kumari Amrit Kaur; 1348, Saifuddin Kitchlew; 1349, Asaf Ali.

1074 Lok Sabha Secretariat

1989. 60th Anniv of Lok Sabha Secretariat (formerly Legislative Assembly Department).

1355	**1074**	60p. green	20	20

1075 Goddess Durga seated on Lion (5th-cent terracotta plaque)

1989. 125th Anniv of Lucknow Museum.

1356	**1075**	60p. deep blue and blue	20	20

1076 Baldev Ramji Mirdha

1989. Birth Centenary of Baldev Ramji Mirdha (nationalist).

1357	**1076**	60p. green	20	20

1077 Girl with Stamp Collection

1989. "India'89" International Stamp Exhibition, New Delhi (5th issue). Philately.

1358	**1077**	60p. yellow, red and blue	15	10
1359	-	1r.50 grey, yellow and black	20	15
1360	-	5r. red and blue	60	50
1361	-	6r.50 black, brown & bl	70	60

DESIGNS: 1r.50, Dawk gharry, c. 1842; 5r. Travancore 1888 2ch. conch shell stamp; 6r.50, Early Indian philatelic magazines.

1078 St. John Bosco and Boy

1989. St. John Bosco (founder of Salesian Brothers) Commemoration.
1362 **1078** 60p. red 20 20

1079 Modern Tank and 19th-century Sowar

1989. 3rd Cavalry Regiment.
1363 **1079** 60p. multicoloured 30 20

1080 Dargah Sharif, Ajmer

1989. Dargah Sharif (Sufi shrine), Ajmer.
1364 **1080** 1r. multicoloured 20 20

1081 Task Force and Indian Naval Ensign

1989. President's Review of the Fleet.
1365 **1081** 6r.50 multicoloured 1·50 1·00

1082 Shaheed Laxman Nayak and Barbed Wire Fence

1989. Shaheed Laxman Nayak Commemoration.
1366 **1082** 60p. brown, grn & orge 20 20

1083 Rao Gopal Singh

1989. Rao Gopal Singh Commemoration.
1367 **1083** 60p. brown 20 20

1084 Sydenham College

1989. 75th Anniv (1988) of Sydenham College, Bombay.
1368 **1084** 60p. black 30 20

1085 Bishnu Ram Medhi

1989. Birth Centenary (1988) of Bishnu Ram Medhi (politician).
1369 **1085** 60p. green, dp grn & red 30 20

1086 Dr. N. S. Hardikar

1989. Birth Centenary of Dr. Narayana Subbarao Hardikar (nationalist).
1370 **1086** 60p. brown 20 20

1087 "Advaita" in Devanagari Script

1989. Sankaracharya (philosopher) Commem.
1371 **1087** 60p. multicoloured 20 20

1088 Gandhi Bhavan, Punjab University

1989. Punjab University, Chandigarh.
1372 **1088** 1r. brown and blue 20 20

1089 Scene from Film "Raja Harischandra"

1989. 75 Years of Indian Cinema.
1373 **1089** 60p. black and yellow 20 20

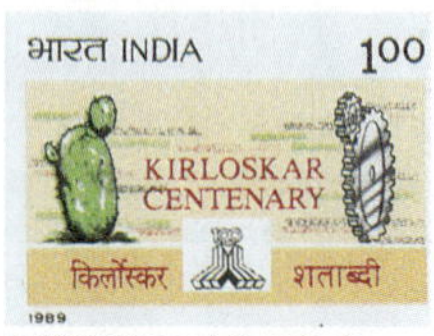

1090 Cactus and Cogwheels

1989. Centenary of Kirloskar Brothers Ltd (engineering group).
1374 **1090** 1r. multicoloured 20 20

1091 Early Class and Modern University Students

1989. Centenary of First D.A.V. College.
1375 **1091** 1r. multicoloured 20 20

1092 Post Office, Dakshin Gangotri Base, Antarctica

1989. Opening of Post Office, Dakshin Gangotri Research Station, Antarctica.
1376 **1092** 1r. multicoloured 1·75 35

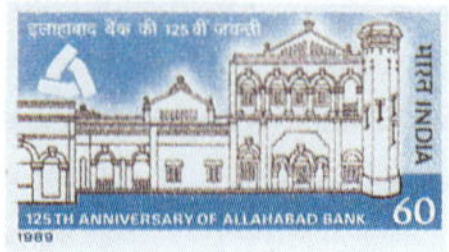

1093 First Allahabad Bank Building

1989. 125th Anniv (1990) of Allahabad Bank.
1377 **1093** 60p. purple and blue 20 20

1094 Nehru inspecting Central Reserve Police, Neemuch, 1954

1989. 50th Anniv of Central Reserve Police Force (formerly Crown Representative's Police).
1378 **1094** 60p. brown 1·50 30

1095 Dairy Cow

1989. Centenary of Military Farms.
1379 **1095** 1r. multicoloured 1·00 30

1096 Mustafa Kemal Ataturk

1989. 50th Death Anniv (1988) of Mustafa Kemal Ataturk (Turkish statesman).
1380 **1096** 5r. multicoloured 1·25 1·00

1097 Dr. S. Radhakrishnan

1989. Birth Centenary (1988) of Dr. Sarvepalli Radhakrishnan (former President).
1381 **1097** 60p. black 20 20

1098 Football Match

1989. Cent of Mohun Bagan Athletic Club.
1382 **1098** 1r. multicoloured 1·75 30

1099 Dr. P. Subbarayan

1989. Birth Centenary of Dr. P. Subbarayan (politician).
1383 **1099** 60p. brown 20 20

1100 Shyamji Krishna Varma

1989. Shyamji Krishna Varma (nationalist) Commemoration.
1384 **1100** 60p. brown, green & red 20 20

1101 Sayajirao Gaekwad III

1989. 50th Death Anniv of Maharaja Sayajirao Gaekwad III of Baroda.
1385 **1101** 60p. grey 20 20

1102 Symbolic Bird with Letter

1989. "Use Pincode" Campaign.
1386 **1102** 60p. multicoloured 75 20

1103 Namakkal Kavignar

1989. Namakkal Kavignar (writer) Commem.
1387 **1103** 60p. black 20 20

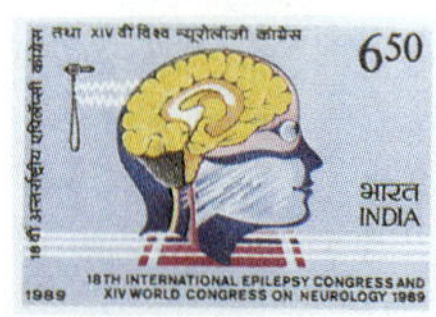

1104 Diagram of Human Brain

1989. 18th International Epilepsy Congress and 14th World Congress on Neurology, New Delhi.
1388 **1104** 6r.50 multicoloured 2·25 75

1105 Pandita Ramabai and Original Sharada Sadan Building

1989. Pandita Ramabai (women's education pioneer) Commemoration.
1389 **1105** 60p. brown 30 20

1106 Releasing Homing Pigeons

1989. Orissa Police Pigeon Post.

1390	**1106**	1r. red	75	30

1107 Acharya Narendra Deo

1989. Birth Centenary of Acharya Narendra Deo (scholar).

1391	**1107**	60p. brown, grn & orge	20	20

1108 Acharya Kripalani

1989. Acharya Kripalani (politician) Commemoration.

1392	**1108**	60p. black, green & red	20	20

1109 Nehru

1989. Birth Cent of Jawaharlal Nehru (2nd issue).

1393	**1109**	1r. brown, deep brown and buff	75	35

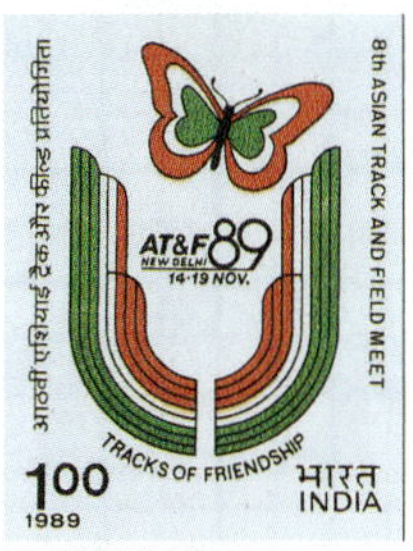

1110 Meeting Logo

1989. 8th Asian Track and Field Meeting, New Delhi.

1394	**1110**	1r. black, orange & grn	30	20

1111 Sir Gurunath Bewoor

1989. Sir Gurunath Bewoor (former Director-General, Posts and Telegraphs) Commemoration.

1395	**1111**	60p. brown	20	20

1112 Balkrishna Sharma Navin

1989. Balkrishna Sharma Navin (politician and poet) Commemoration.

1396	**1112**	60p. black	20	20

1113 Abstract Painting of Houses

1989. Cent of Bombay Art Society (1988).

1397	**1113**	1r. multicoloured	20	20

1114 Lesser Florican

1989. Wildlife Conservation. Lesser Florican.

1398	**1114**	2r. multicoloured	2·00	1·00

1115 Centenary Logo

1989. Centenary of Indian Oil Production.

1399	**1115**	60p. brown	30	20

1116 Dr. M. G. Ramachandran

1990. Dr. M. G. Ramachandran (former Chief Minister of Tamil Nadu) Commemoration.

1400	**1116**	60p. brown	40	20

1117 Volunteers working at Sukhna Lake, Chandigarh

1990. Save Sukhna Lake Campaign.

1401	**1117**	1r. multicoloured	20	20

1118 Gallantry Medals

1990. Presentation of New Colours to Bombay Sappers.

1402	**1118**	60p. multicoloured	1·00	1·50

1119 Indian Chank Shell and Logo

1990. 23rd Annual General Meeting of Asian Development Bank, New Delhi.

1403	**1119**	2r. black, orange & yell	75	30

1120 Penny Black and Envelope

1990. 150th Anniv of the Penny Black.

1404	**1120**	6r. multicoloured	1·25	1·00

1121 Ho Chi-Minh and Vietnamese House

1990. Birth Centenary of Ho Chi-Minh (Vietnamese leader).

1405	**1121**	2r. brown and green	30	30

1122 Chaudhary Charan Singh

1990. 3rd Death Anniv of Chaudhary Charan Singh (former Prime Minister).

1406	**1122**	1r. brown	20	20

1123 Armed Forces' Badge and Map of Sri Lanka

1990. Indian Peace-keeping Operations in Sri Lanka.

1407	**1123**	2r. multicoloured	30	30

1124 Wheat

1990. 60th Anniv of Indian Council of Agricultural Research (1989).

1408	**1124**	2r. black, grn & dp grn	30	30

1125 Khudiram Bose

1990. Khudiram Bose (patriot) Commemoration.

1409	**1125**	1r. orange, green and red	20	20

1126 "Life in India" (Tanya Vorontsova)

1990. Indo–Soviet Friendship. Children's Paintings. Multicoloured.

1410		1r. Type **1126**	1·50	2·25
1411		6r.50 "St. Basil's Cathedral and Kremlin, Moscow" (Sanjay Adhikari)	1·50	2·25

Stamps in similar designs were also issued by U.S.S.R.

1127 K. Kelappan

1990. K. Kelappan (social reformer) Commem.

1412	**1127**	1r. brown	20	20

1128 Girl in Garden

1990. Year of the Girl Child.

1413	**1128**	1r. multicoloured	50	30

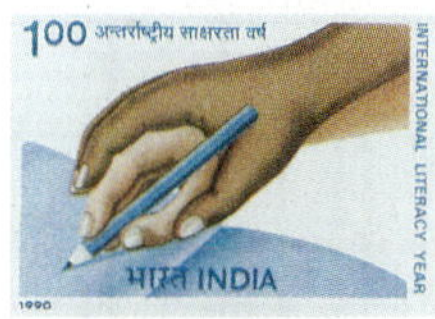

1129 Hand guiding Child's Writing

1990. International Literacy Year.

1414	**1129**	1r. multicoloured	50	30

1130 Woman using Water Pump

1990. Safe Drinking Water Campaign.

1415	**1130**	4r. black, red and green	1·25	1·75

1131 Sunder Lal Sharma

1990. 50th Death Anniv of Sunder Lal Sharma (patriot).
1416 **1131** 60p. red 50 50

1132 Kabbadi

1990. 11th Asian Games, Peking. Mult.
1417 1r. Type **1132** 40 20
1418 4r. Athletics 1·50 2·00
1419 4r. Cycling 1·50 2·00
1420 6r.50 Archery 1·75 2·50

1133 A. K. Gopalan

1990. Ayillyath Kuttiari Gopalan (social reformer) Commemoration.
1421 **1133** 1r. brown 50 30

1134 Gurkha Soldier

1990. 50th Anniv of 3rd and 5th Battalions, 5th Gurkha Rifles.
1422 **1134** 2r. black and brown 1·40 1·60

1135 Suryamall Mishran

1990. 75th Birth Anniv of Suryamall Mishran (poet).
1423 **1135** 2r. brown and orange 50 65

1136 "Doll and Cat" (Subhash Kumar Nagarajan)

1990. Children's Day.
1424 **1136** 1r. multicoloured 60 30

1137 Security Post and Border Guard on Camel

1990. 25th Anniv of Border Security Force.
1425 **1137** 5r. blue, brown & black 1·50 2·00

1138 Hearts and Flowers

1990. Greetings Stamps. Multicoloured.
1426 1r. Type **1138** 20 15
1427 4r. Ceremonial elephants (horiz) 50 80

1139 Bikaner

1990. Cities of India. Multicoloured.
1428 4r. Type **1139** 55 60
1429 5r. Hyderabad 65 75
1430 6r.50 Cuttack 90 1·50

1140 Bhakta Kanakadas and Udipi Temple

1990. Bhakta Kanakadas (mystic and poet) Commemoration.
1431 **1140** 1r. red 55 30

1141 Shaheed Minar Monument

1990. 300th Anniv of Calcutta.
1432 **1141** 1r. multicoloured 30 20
1433 - 6r. black, brown and red 1·25 1·75

DESIGN—HORIZ (44×36 mm): 6r. 18th-century shipping on the Ganges.

1142 Dnyaneshwari (poet) and Manuscript

1990. 700th Anniv of Dnyaneshwari (spiritual epic).
1434 **1142** 2r. multicoloured 30 50

1143 Madan Mohan Malaviya (founder) and University

1991. 75th Anniv of Banaras Hindu University.
1435 **1143** 1r. red 30 20

1991. As No. 732 but new face value.
1436 1r. brown (Gandhi) 20 10

1144 Road Users

1991. International Traffic Safety Conference, New Delhi.
1437 **1144** 6r.50 black, blue and red 1·00 1·50

1145 Exhibition Emblem

1991. 7th Triennale Art Exhibition, New Delhi.
1438 **1145** 6r.50 multicoloured 75 1·00

1146 Jagannath Sunkersett and Central Railways Headquarters

1991. 125th Death Anniv (1990) of Jagannath Sunkersett (educationist and railway pioneer).
1439 **1146** 2r. blue and red 50 60

1147 Tata Memorial Centre

1991. 50th Anniv of Tata Memorial Medical Centre.
1440 **1147** 2r. brown and stone 30 40

1148 River Dolphin

1991. Endangered Marine Mammals.
1441 **1148** 4r. brown, blue and green 1·50 1·50
1442 - 6r.50 multicoloured 2·00 2·50

DESIGN: 6r.50, Sea cow.

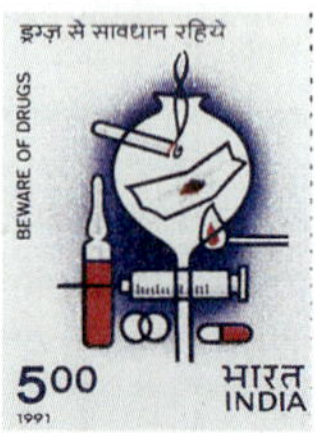

1149 Drugs

1991. International Conference on Drug Abuse, Calcutta.
1443 **1149** 5r. violet and red 1·60 2·00

1150 Hand, Bomb Explosion and Dove

1991. World Peace.
1444 **1150** 6r.50 blk, lt brn & brn 1·00 1·50

1151 Remote Sensing Satellite "IA"

1991. Launch of Indian Remote Sensing Satellite "IA".
1445 **1151** 6r.50 brown and blue 1·00 1·50

1152 Babu Jagjivan Ram

1991. Babu Jagjivan Ram (politician) Commemoration.
1446 **1152** 1r. brown 20 20

1153 Dr. B. R. Ambedkar and Demonstration

1991. Birth Centenary of Dr. Bhimrao Ramji Ambedkar (social reformer).
1447 **1153** 1r. brown and blue 30 20

1154 Valar Dance

1991. Tribal Dances. Multicoloured.
1448 2r.50 Type **1154** 50 40
1449 4r. Kayang 70 80
1450 5r. Hozagiri 80 1·00
1451 6r.50 Velakali 1·00 1·60

1155 Ariyakudi Ramanuja Iyengar and Temples

1991. Ariyakudi Ramanuja Iyengar (singer and composer) Commemoration.
1452 **1155** 2r. brown and green 50 65

1156 Karpoori Thakur

1991. Jan Nayak Karpoori Thakur (politician and social reformer) Commemoration.
1453 **1156** 1r. brown 20 20

1157 Emperor Penguins

1991. 30th Anniv of Antarctic Treaty. Mult.

1454	5r. Type **1157**	1·75	2·00
1455	6r.50 Antarctic map and pair of Adelie penguins	1·75	2·00

Nos. 1454/5 were printed together, se-tenant, forming a composite design.

1158 Rashtrapati Bhavan Building, New Delhi

1991. 60th Anniv of New Delhi. Multicoloured.

1456	5r. Type **1158**	1·40	1·75
1457	6r.50 New Delhi monuments	1·40	1·75

Nos. 1456/7 were printed together, se-tenant, forming a composite design.

1159 Sri Ram Sharma Acharya

1991. Sri Ram Sharma Acharya (social reformer) Commemoration.

1458	**1159**	1r. green and red	20	20

1160 "Shankar awarded Padma Vibhushan" (cartoon)

1991. Keshav Shankar Pillai (cartoonist) Commemoration.

1459	**1160**	4r. brown	1·00	1·50
1460	-	6r.50 lilac	1·40	2·00

DESIGN—VERT: 6r.50, "The Big Show".

1161 Sriprakash and Kashi Vidyapith University

1991. 20th Death Anniv of Sriprakash (politician).

1461	**1161**	2r. brown & light brown	30	30

1162 Gopinath Bardoloi

1991. Birth Centenary (1990) of Gopinath Bardoloi (Assamese politician).

1462	**1162**	1r. lilac	20	20

1163 Rajiv Gandhi

1991. Rajiv Gandhi (Congress Party leader) Commemoration.

1463	**1163**	1r. multicoloured	1·00	70

1164 Muni Mishrimalji and Memorial

1991. Birth Centenary of Muni Mishrimalji (Jain religious leader).

1464	**1164**	1r. brown	30	20

1165 Mahadevi Verma (poetess) and "Varsha"

1991. Hindu Writers.

1465	**1165**	2r. black and blue	50	70
1466	-	2r. black and blue	50	70

DESIGN: No. 1466, Jayshankar Prasad (poet and dramatist) and scene from "Kamayani".

1166 Parliament House and C.P.A. Emblem

1991. 37th Commonwealth Parliamentary Association Conference, New Delhi.

1467	**1166**	6r.50 blue and brown	40	60

1167 Frog

1991. Greetings Stamps.

1468	**1167**	1r. green and red	40	50
1469	-	6r.50 red and green	60	1·00

DESIGN: 6r.50, Symbolic bird carrying flower.

1168 "Cymbidium aloifolium"

1991. Orchids. Multicoloured.

1470	1r. Type **1168**	30	15
1471	2r.50 "Paphiopedilum venustum"	35	35
1472	3r. "Aerides crispum"	40	50
1473	4r. "Cymbidium bicolour"	50	65
1474	5r. "Vanda spathulata"	55	70
1475	6r.50 "Cymbidium devonianum"	70	1·00

1169 Gurkha Soldier in Battle Dress

1991. 90th Anniv of 2nd Battalion, Third Gurkha Rifles.

1476	**1169**	4r. multicoloured	1·50	1·75

1170 Couple on Horse (embroidery)

1991. 3rd Death Anniv of Kamaladevi Chattopadhyaya (founder of All India Handicrafts Board).

1477	**1170**	1r. lake, red and yellow	40	20
1478	-	6r.50 multicoloured	1·50	2·00

DESIGN: 6r.50, Traditional puppet.

1171 Chithira Tirunal and Temple Sculpture

1991. Chithira Tirunal Bala Rama Varma (former Maharaja of Travancore) Commemoration.

1479	**1171**	2r. violet	65	75

1172 "Children in Traditional Costume" (Arpi Snehalbhai Shah)

1991. Children's Day.

1480	**1172**	1r. multicoloured	70	30

1173 Mounted Sowar and Tanks

1991. 70th Anniv (1992) of the 18th Cavalry Regiment.

1481	**1173**	6r.50 multicoloured	2·00	2·50

1174 Kites

1991. India Tourism Year.

1482	**1174**	6r.50 multicoloured	80	1·25

1175 Sports on Bricks

1991. International Conference on Youth Tourism, New Delhi.

1483	**1175**	6r.50 multicoloured	1·10	1·50

1176 "Mozart at Piano" (unfinished painting, J. Lange)

1991. Death Bicentenary of Mozart.

1484	**1176**	6r.50 multicoloured	1·50	2·00

1177 Homeless Family

1991. South Asian Association for Regional Co-operation Year of Shelter.

1485	**1177**	4r. brown and ochre	55	70

1178 People running on Heart

1991. "Run for Your Heart" Marathon, New Delhi.

1486	**1178**	1r. black, grey and red	20	20

1179 "Sidhartha with an Injured Bird" (Asit Kumar Haldar)

1991. Birth Centenary (1990) of Asit Kumar Haldar (artist).

1487	**1179**	2r. yellow, red and black	30	50

1180 Bhujangasana

1991. Yoga Exercises. Multicoloured.

1488	2r. Type **1180**	20	25
1489	5r. Dhanurasana	40	55
1490	6r.50 Ustrasana	50	70
1491	10r. Utthita trikonasana	85	1·25

1181 Y.M.C.A. Logo

1992. Centenary (1991) of National Council of Young Men's Christian Association.

1492	**1181**	1r. red and blue	20	20

1182 Madurai Temple Tower and Hooghly River Bridge

1992. 14th Congress of International Association for Bridge and Structural Engineering, New Delhi.
1493 **1182** 2r. brown, red and blue 1·25 1·50
1494 - 2r. brown, red and blue 1·25 1·50
DESIGN: No. 1494, Gate, Sanchi Stupa and Hall of Nations, New Delhi.

1183 Goat Seal from Harappa Culture, 2500 to 1500 B.C.

1992. 5th International Goat Conference, New Delhi.
1495 **1183** 6r. blue and brown 2·75 2·75

1184 Early 19th-century Letter with Mail Pouch and National Archives Building, New Delhi

1992. Centenary (1991) of National Archives.
1496 **1184** 6r. multicoloured 75 1·00

1185 Krushna Chandra Gajapathi

1992. Krushna Chandra Gajapathi (former Chief Minister of Orissa) Commemoration.
1497 **1185** 1r. lilac 15 15

1186 Vijay Singh Pathik

1992. Vijay Singh Pathik (writer) Commem.
1498 **1186** 1r. brown 15 15

1187 Hang-gliding

1992. Adventure Sports. Multicoloured.
1499 2r. Type **1187** 25 20
1500 4r. Windsurfing 50 60
1501 5r. River rafting 60 75
1502 11r. Skiing 1·25 2·25

1188 Henry Gidney and Anglo-Indians

1992. 50th Death Anniv of Sir Henry Gidney (ophthalmologist).
1503 **1188** 1r. black and blue 1·00 35

1189 Telecommunications Training Centre, Jabalpur

1992. 50th Anniv of Telecommunications Training Centre, Jabalpur.
1504 **1189** 1r. bistre 20 15

1190 Sardar Udham Singh

1992. Sardar Udham Singh (patriot) Commemoration.
1505 **1190** 1r. black and brown 20 15

1191 Men's Discus

1992. Olympic Games, Barcelona. Mult.
1506 1r. Type **1191** 40 10
1507 6r. Women's gymnastics 1·00 1·00
1508 8r. Men's hockey 2·50 2·75
1509 11r. Boxing 2·25 3·00

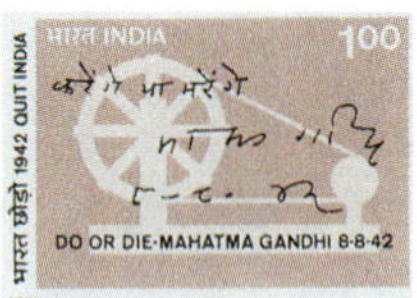

1192 Spinning Wheel Emblem

1992. 50th Anniv of "Quit India" Movement.
1510 **1192** 1r. black and pink 1·75 40
1511 - 2r. black, brown & grey 2·75 3·00
DESIGN: 2r. Mahatma Gandhi and mantra.

1193 Treating Casualty

1992. 50th Anniv of 60th Parachute Field Ambulance.
1512 **1193** 1r. multicoloured 1·25 40

1194 Dr. S. R. Ranganathan and Madras University

1992. Birth Centenary of Shiyali Ramamrita Ranganathan (librarian).
1513 **1194** 1r. blue 1·75 30

1195 "Dev Narayan"

1992. Phad Scroll Paintings from Rajasthan.
1514 **1195** 5r. multicoloured 75 1·25

1196 Hanuman Prasad Poddar

1992. Hanuman Prasad Poddar (editor) Commemoration.
1515 **1196** 1r. green 15 15

1197 Mikoyan Guerevich MiG-29 Fighter and Ilyushin Il-76 Transport

1992. 60th Anniv of Indian Air Force. Mult.
1516 1r. Type **1197** 1·50 1·75
1517 10r. MiG-27 fighter and Westland Wapiti biplane 2·50 2·75

1198 Lighting Candle

1992. 150th Anniv of Sisters of Jesus and Mary's Arrival in India.
1518 **1198** 1r. blue and grey 15 15

1199 "Sun" (Harshit Prashant Patel)

1992. Children's Day.
1519 **1199** 1r. multicoloured 20 15

1200 Yogiji Maharaj

1992. Birth Centenary of Yogiji Maharaj (Hindu reformer).
1520 **1200** 1r. blue 1·75 30

1201 Army Service Corps Transport

1992. Army Service Corps Commemoration.
1521 **1201** 1r. multicoloured 2·00 60

1202 Stephen Smith and Early Rocket Post Covers

1992. Birth Centenary (1991) of Stephen Smith (rocket mail pioneer).
1522 **1202** 11r. multicoloured 1·25 1·75

1203 Electricity Pylons, Farmers and Crops

1992. 25th Anniv of Haryana State.
1523 **1203** 2r. red, dp green & green 15 15

1204 Madanlal Dhingra

1992. Madanlal Dhingra (revolutionary) Commemoration.
1524 **1204** 1r. brown, red and green 30 15

1205 Osprey

1992. Birds of Prey. Multicoloured.
1525 2r. Type **1205** 90 60
1526 6r. Peregrine falcon 1·25 1·10
1527 8r. Lammergeier 1·40 1·75
1528 11r. Golden eagle 1·60 2·00

1206 Pandit Ravishankar Shukla

1992. Pandit Ravishankar Shukla (social reformer) Commemoration.
1529 **1206** 1r. purple 15 15

1207 William Carey

1993. Bicent of William Carey's Appointment as Baptist Missionary to India.
1530 **1207** 6r. multicoloured 1·00 1·50

1208 Fakirmohan Senapati

1993. Fakirmohan Senapati Commemoration.
1531 **1208** 1r. red 40 15

1209 Workers and C.S.I.R emblem

1993. 50th Anniv of Council of Scientific and Industrial Research.
1532 **1209** 1r. purple 40 15

1210 Parachute Drop and Field Gun

1993. 50th Anniv of 9th Parachute Field Artillery Regiment.
1533 **1210** 1r. multicoloured 1·25 30

1211 Westland Wapiti Biplane

1993. 60th Anniv of No. 1 Squadron, Indian Air Force.
1534 **1211** 1r. multicoloured 1·25 30

1212 Rahul Sankrityayan

1993. Birth Centenary of Rahul Sankrityayan (politician).
1535 **1212** 1r. black, cinnamon and brown 20 15

1213 Parliament Building and Emblem

1993. 89th Inter-Parliamentary Union Conference, New Delhi.
1536 **1213** 1r. black 20 15

1214 Neral Matheran Railway Tank Locomotive, 1905

1993. Mountain Locomotives. Multicoloured.
1537 1r. Type **1214** 60 20
1538 6r. Darjeeling and Himalayan Railway, Class B, 1889 1·25 1·25
1539 8r. Nilgiri Hill Railway, 1914 1·40 1·75
1540 11r. Kalka–Simla Railway, 1934 1·90 2·50

1215 Students and College Building

1993. Centenary of Meerut College.
1541 **1215** 1r. black and brown 20 15

1216 Mahalanobis and Office Block

1993. Prasanta Chandra Mahalanobis Commemoration.
1542 **1216** 1r. brown 1·25 20

1217 Bombay Town Hall

1993. Centenary of Bombay Municipal Corporation.
1543 **1217** 2r. multicoloured 20 30

1218 Abdul Ghaffar Khan and Mountainside

1993. Abdul Ghaffar Khan Commemoration.
1544 **1218** 1r. multicoloured 15 15

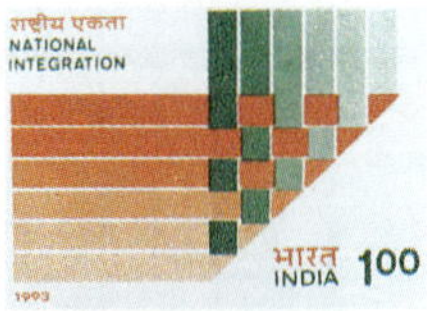

1219 National Integration Emblem

1993. National Integration Campaign.
1545 **1219** 1r. orange and green 15 15

1220 Dadabhai Naoroji and Houses of Parliament, London

1993. Centenary of Dadabhai Naoroji's Election to the House of Commons.
1546 **1220** 6r. multicoloured 75 1·00

1221 Swami Vivekananda and Art Institute, Chicago

1993. Centenary of Swami Vivekananda's Chicago Address.
1547 **1221** 2r. orange and grey 60 60

1222 "Lagerstroemia speciosa"

1993. Flowering Trees.
1548 **1222** 1r. red, green and brown 20 15
1549 - 6r. multicoloured 40 55
1550 - 8r. multicoloured 55 80
1551 - 11r. multicoloured 75 1·25

DESIGNS: 6r. "Cochlospermum religiosum"; 8r. "Erythrina variegata"; 11r. "Thespesia populnea".

1223 College Building and Emblem

1993. 50th Anniv of College of Military Engineering, Pune.
1552 **1223** 2r. multicoloured 20 30

1224 Dr. Dwaram Venkataswamy Naidu playing Violin

1993. Birth Centenary of Dwaram Venkataswamy Naidu (violinist).
1553 **1224** 1r. red 20 20

1225 Children on Elephant

1993. Children's Day.
1554 **1225** 1r. multicoloured 20 20

1226 People with Stress

1993. Heart Care Festival.
1555 **1226** 6r.50 multicoloured 75 1·00

1227 Dr. Kotnis performing Operation

1993. Dr. Dwarkanath Kotnis (surgeon) Commemoration.
1556 **1227** 1r. black 20 20

1228 Tea Symbol

1993. Indian Tea Production.
1557 **1228** 6r. green and red 65 85

1229 Papal Seminary Arms and Building

1993. Centenary of Papal Seminary, Pune.
1558 **1229** 6r. multicoloured 75 1·00

1230 Meghnad Saha and Eclipse of the Sun

1993. Meghnad Saha (astronomer) Commem.
1559 **1230** 1r. blue 50 20

1231 Speedpost Letter and Arrows circling Globe

1993. Inpex '93 National Stamp Exn, Calcutta. Multicoloured.
1560 1r. Type **1231** 20 15
1561 2r. "Custom-house Wharf, Calcutta" (Sir Charles D'Oyly) 55 60

1232 Dinanath Mangeshkar

1993. Dinanath Mangeshkar Commem.
1562 **1232** 1r. red 15 15

1233 Nargis Dutt

1993. Nargis Dutt Commemoration.
1563 **1233** 1r. red 15 15

1234 S. C. Bose inspecting Troops

1993. 50th Anniv of Indian National Army.
1564 **1234** 1r. green, dp grn & red 30 20

1235 Satyendra Nath Bose and Equation

1994. Birth Centenary of Satyendra Nath Bose (scientist).

1565	**1235**	1r. brown	70	25

1236 Dr. Sampurnanand

1994. Dr. Sampurnanand (politician) Commemoration.

1566	**1236**	1r. brown, green and red	15	10

1237 Scene from "Pather Panchali" (image scaled to 71% of original size)

1994. Satyajit Ray (film director) Commemoration. Multicoloured.

1567	6r. Type **1237**	1·75	2·25
1568	11r. Satyajit Ray and Oscar (35×35 mm)	2·00	2·50

1238 Dr. Bhatnagar and University Building

1994. Dr. Shanti Swarup Bhatnagar (scientist) Commemoration.

1569	**1238**	1r. blue	15	10

1239 Prajapita Brahma and Memorial

1994. 25th Death Anniv of Prajapita Brahma (social reformer).

1570	**1239**	1r. lilac and blue	15	10

1240 "Window" (K. Subramanyan)

1994. 8th Triennale Art Exhibition, New Delhi.

1571	**1240**	6r. orange, red and blue	70	80

1241 Agricultural Products and Tea Garden

1994. Centenary of United Planters' Association of Southern India.

1572	**1241**	2r. multicoloured	20	20

1242 Indian Family

1242a Sanchi Stupa

1994

1573	**1242**	75p. brown and red	10	10
1574	-	1r. mauve and green	10	10
1575	-	3r. purple	15	10
1576	**1242a**	5r. brown and green	25	20

DESIGNS (as T **1242**)—HORIZ: 1r. Family outside home. VERT: 3r. Baby and drop of polio vaccine.

1243 Rani Rashmoni on River Bank

1994. Birth Bicentenary of Rani Rashmoni.

1589	**1243**	1r. brown	15	10

1244 Indians releasing Peace Doves

1994. 75th Anniv of Jallianwala Bagh Massacre, Amritsar.

1590	**1244**	1r. black and red	15	10

1245 Chandra Singh Garhwali

1994. 15th Death Anniv of Chandra Singh Garhwali (nationalist).

1591	**1245**	1r. green and orange	15	10

1246 Emblems and National Flag

1994. 75th Anniv of I.L.O.

1592	**1246**	6r. multicoloured	50	65

1247 Silhouette of Drummer and Logo

1994. 50th Anniv of Indian People's Theatre Association.

1593	**1247**	2r. black, green and gold	15	15

1248 Statue of Sepoy

1994. Bicentenary of 4th Battalion, The Madras Regiment.

1594	**1248**	6r.50 multicoloured	1·00	1·25

1249 Institute Building and Emblem

1994. Bicentenary of Institute of Mental Health, Madras.

1595	**1249**	2r. red and blue	15	15

1250 Mahatma Gandhi and Indian Flag

1994. 125th Birth Anniv of Mahatma Gandhi. Multicoloured.

1596	6r. Type **1250**	2·00	2·25
1597	11r. Aspects of Gandhi's life on flag (69×34 mm)	2·25	2·50

Nos. 1596/7 were printed together, se-tenant, forming a composite design.

1251 Symbols of Cancer

1994. 16th International Cancer Congress, New Delhi.

1598	**1251**	6r. multicoloured	75	1·00

1252 Human Resources Emblem

1994. Human Resource Development World Conference, New Delhi.

1599	**1252**	6r. blue, red and azure	65	85

1253 "Me and My Pals" (Namarata Amit Shah)

1994. Children's Day.

1600	**1253**	1r. multicoloured	20	15

1254 Family and Emblem

1994. International Year of the Family.

1601	**1254**	2r. multicoloured	30	20

1255 "Taj Mahal" (illustration from Badsha Nama)

1994. Khuda Bakhsh Oriental Public Library, Patna, Commemoration.

1602	**1255**	6r. multicoloured	4·50	1·25

1256 Grey Teal ("Andaman Teal")

1994. Endangered Water Birds. Multicoloured.

1603	1r. Type **1256**	8·00	2·50
1604	6r. Oriental white stork ("Eastern White Stork")	11·00	5·00
1605	8r. Black-necked crane	11·00	5·50
1606	11r. Pink-headed duck	12·00	7·00

It is reported that Nos. 1603/6 were withdrawn shortly after issue.

1257 J. R. D. Tata and Aspects of Industrial Symbols

1994. J. R. D. Tata (industrialist) Commemoration.

1607	**1257**	2r. multicoloured	50	40

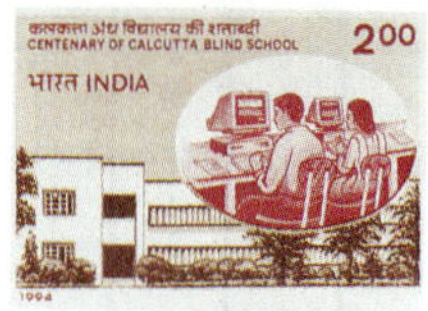

1258 School Building and Computer Class

1994. Centenary of Calcutta Blind School.

1608	**1258**	2r. red, brown and cinnamon	40	25

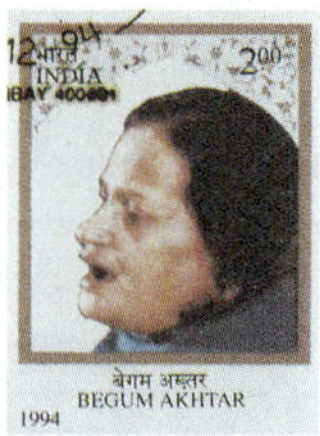

1259 Begum Akhtar

1994. 80th Birth Anniv of Begum Akhtar (singer).

1609	**1259**	2r. multicoloured	6·50	5·00

1260 College Building

1994. 125th Anniv of St. Xavier's College, Bombay.

1610	**1260**	2r. brown and blue	15	15

1261 Cavalryman, Infantryman and Dog Handler

1994. 215th Anniv of Remount Veterinary Corps.

1611	**1261**	6r. multicoloured	2·00	2·00

1262 College Building

1994. Bicentenary of College of Engineering, Guindy, Madras.

1612 **1262** 2r. red, brown and black 15 15

1263 Righthand Ornament of Bronze Stand

1994. Centenary of Baroda Museum.

1613 **1263** 6r. yellow and brown 2·50 2·50

1614 - 11r. yellow and brown 2·50 2·50

DESIGN: 11r. Bronze Rishabhanatha statue of Buddha on stand.

1264 "200" and Aspects of Postal Service (image scaled to 63% of original size)

1994. Bicentenary of Bombay General Post Office.

1615 **1264** 6r. multicoloured 5·00 2·75

1265 Statue of King Rajaraja Chola

1995. 8th International Conference-Seminar of Tamil Studies, Thanjavur.

1616 **1265** 2r. blue, ultramarine and black 3·50 75

1266 Globe and Emblem

1995. 60th Anniv of National Science Academy.

1617 **1266** 6r. multicoloured 65 1·00

1267 Chhotu Ram

1995. Chhotu Ram (social reformer) Commem.

1618 **1267** 1r. brown 1·00 25

1268 Film Reel and Globe

1995. Centenary of Cinema. Multicoloured.

1619 6r. Type **1268** 1·00 1·50

1620 11r. Film reel and early equipment 1·25 1·75

1269 Symbolic Hands and Children

1995. South Asian Association for Regional Cooperation Youth Year.

1621 **1269** 2r. multicoloured 20 20

1270 Prithviraj Kapoor and Mask

1995. 50th Anniv of Prithvi Theatre.

1622 **1270** 2r. multicoloured 3·75 1·00

1271 Field-Marshal Cariappa

1995. Field-Marshal K. Cariappa Commemoration.

1623 **1271** 2r. multicoloured 50 30

1272 Textile Pattern

1995. "TEX-STYLES INDIA '95" Fair, Bombay.

1624 **1272** 2r. brown, buff and red 20 20

1273 Rafi Ahmed Kidwai

1995. Birth Centenary (1994) of Rafi Ahmed Kidwai (politician).

1625 **1273** 1r. brown 15 10

1274 K. L. Saigal, Film Reel and Gramophone

1995. 90th Birth Anniv of K. L. Saigal (singer).

1626 **1274** 5r. brown, grey and black 1·25 1·50

1275 R. S. Ruikar

1995. Birth Centenary of R. S. Ruikar (trade unionist).

1627 **1275** 1r. brown 25 10

1276 Radio Tower, Globe and Dish Aerial

1995. Centenary of Telecommunications.

1628 **1276** 5r. multicoloured 1·50 1·50

1277 Leaves and Symbolic Houses

1995. Delhi Development Authority.

1629 **1277** 2r. multicoloured 30 20

1278 Handshake

1995. 50th Anniv of United Nations. Multicoloured.

1630 1r. Type **1278** 10 10

1631 6r. Work of U.N. Agencies 45 65

1279 Colonnade on Book Cover

1995. Centenary of Bharti Bhawan Library, Allahabad.

1632 **1279** 6r. black, brown and red 55 75

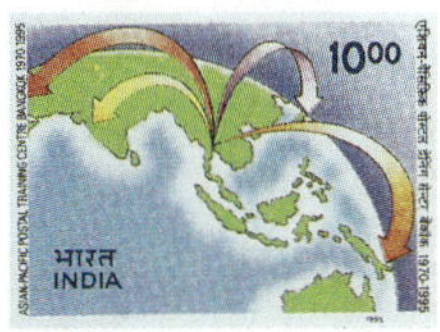

1280 Globe showing South-east Asia

1995. 25th Anniv of Asian-Pacific Postal Training Centre, Bangkok.

1633 **1280** 10r. multicoloured 1·25 1·50

1281 "75" and Taurus Formation Sign

1995. 75th Anniv of Area Army Headquarters, Delhi.

1634 **1281** 2r. multicoloured 65 30

1282 Louis Pasteur in Laboratory (from painting by Edelfelt)

1995. Death Centenary of Louis Pasteur (chemist).

1635 **1282** 5r. black and stone 2·50 1·75

1283 La Martiniere College, Lucknow

1995. 150th Anniv of La Martiniere College, Lucknow.

1636 **1283** 2r. multicoloured 40 30

1284 Gandhi in South Africa

1995. India-South Africa Co-operation. 125th Birth Anniv (1994) of Mahatma Gandhi.

1637 **1284** 1r. red 65 1·00

1638 - 2r. red 65 1·00

MS1639 68×80 mm. Nos. 1637/8 (sold at 8r.) 1·40 2·00

DESIGN: 2r. Gandhi wearing dhoti.

1285 Ears of Grain, "50" and Emblem on Globe

1995. 50th Anniv of F.A.O.

1640 **1285** 5r. multicoloured 1·25 1·50

1286 P. M. Thevar

1995. Pasumpon Muthuramalingam Thevar (social reformer) Commemoration.

1641 **1286** 1r. red 25 10

1287 W. C. Rontgen

1995. 150th Birth Anniv of W. C. Rontgen (discoverer of X-rays).

1642 **1287** 6r. multicoloured 2·25 1·75

1288 Children in Circle

1995. Children's Day.

1643	**1288**	1r. multicoloured	25	10

1289 Sitar

1995. Communal Harmony Campaign.

1644	**1289**	2r. multicoloured	2·25	1·25

1290 Jat War Memorial, Bareilly

1995. Bicentenary of Jat Regiments.

1645	**1290**	5r. multicoloured	2·25	2·00

1291 Men of Rajputana Rifles

1995. 175th Anniv of 5th (Napier's) Battalion, Rajputana Rifles.

1646	**1291**	5r. multicoloured	2·50	2·00

1292 Sant Tukdoji Maharaj and Rural Meeting

1995. Sant Tukdoji Maharaj Commemoration.

1647	**1292**	1r. brown	30	10

Although dated "1993", No. 1647 was not issued until the date quoted above.

1293 Dr. Yellapragada Subbarow

1995. Dr. Yellapragada Subbarow (pharmaceutical scientist) Commemoration.

1648	**1293**	1r. brown	60	15

1294 Pres. Giani Zail Singh

1995. 1st Death Anniv of Pres. Giani Zail Singhn.

1649	**1294**	1r. multicoloured	50	10

1295 Dargah of Ala Hazrat Barelvi

1995. 75th Death Anniv of Ala Hazrat Barelvi (Moslem scholar).

1650	**1295**	1r. multicoloured	50	10

1296 Tata Institute Building

1996. 50th Anniv (1995) of Tata Institute of Fundamental Research.

1651	**1296**	2r. multicoloured	50	20

1297 Kasturba Gandhi

1996. 50th Anniv of the Kasturba Trust.

1652	**1297**	1r. grey, green and red	1·25	30

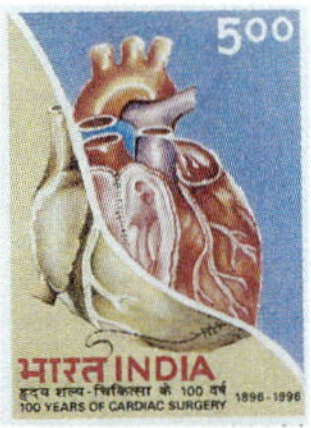

1298 Sectioned Heart

1996. 100 Years of Cardiac Surgery.

1653	**1298**	5r. multicoloured	1·50	1·50

1299 C. K. Nayudu

1996. Cricketers. Multicoloured.

1654	2r. Type **1299**	85	85
1655	2r. Vinoo Mankad	85	85
1656	2r. Deodhar	85	85
1657	2r. Vijay Merchant	85	85

1300 "Vasant" (Spring) (Ragini Basanti)

1996. Miniature Paintings of the Seasons. Multicoloured.

1658	5r. Type **1300**	1·25	1·50
1659	5r. "Greeshma" (Summer) (Jyestha)	1·25	1·50
1660	5r. "Varsha" (Monsoon) (Rag Megh Malbar)	1·25	1·50
1661	5r. "Hernant" (Winter) (Pausha)	1·25	1·50

1301 Kunjilal Dubey

1996. Kunjilal Dubey Commemoration.

1662	**1301**	1r. brown & chocolate	30	10

1302 Morarji Desai

1996. Birth Centenary of Morarji Desai (former Prime Minister) (1st issue).

1663	**1302**	1r. red	40	10

See also No. 1702.

1303 Blood Pheasant

1996. Himalayan Ecology. Multicoloured.

1664	5r. Type **1303**	1·25	1·50
1665	5r. Markhor (goat)	1·25	1·50
1666	5r. "Meconopsis horridula" (Tsher Gnoin) (plant)	1·25	1·50
1667	5r. "Saussurea simpsoniana" (Sunflower)	1·25	1·50
MS1668	175×105 mm. Nos. 1664/7 (sold at 30r.)	4·50	5·50

1304 S.K.C.G. College Building

1996. Centenary of S.K.C.G. College, Gajapati.

1669	**1304**	1r. brown and cream	30	10

1305 Muhammad Ismail Sahib

1996. Birth Centenary of Muhammad Ismail Sahib (Moslem politician).

1670	**1305**	1r. purple	30	10

1306 Modern Stadium and Ancient Athens

1996. Olympic Games, Atlanta. Multicoloured.

1671	5r. Type **1306**	55	65
1672	5r. Hand holding Olympic torch	55	65

1307 Sister Alphonsa

1996. 50th Death Anniv of Sister Alphonsa.

1673	**1307**	1r. black and blue	50	15

1308 "Communications"

1996. 125th Anniv of Videsh Sanchar Nigam Limited (telecommunications company).

1674	**1308**	5r. multicoloured	1·75	1·75

1309 Sir Pherozeshah Mehta

1996. 150th Birth Anniv of Sir Pherozeshah Mehta (politician).

1675	**1309**	1r. blue	30	15

1310 Ahilyabai

1996. Death Bicentenary (1995) of Ahilyabai (ruler of Holkar).

1676	**1310**	2r. brown and deep brown	45	30

1311 Chembai Vaidyanatha Bhagavathar

1996. Birth Centenary of Chembai Vaidyanatha Bhagavathar (musician).

1677	**1311**	1r. brown and green	30	15

1312 Red Junglefowl Cockerel

1996. 20th World Poultry Congress, New Delhi.

1678	**1312**	5r. multicoloured	2·75	2·25

1313 Rani Gaidinliu

1996. Rani Gaidinliu (Naga leader) Commemoration.
1679 **1313** 1r. blue 30 15

1314 Nath Pai

1996. 25th Death Anniv of Nath Pai (politician).
1680 **1314** 1r. blue 30 15

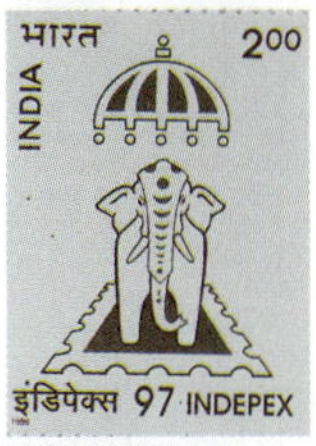

1315 Exhibition Logo

1996. INDEPEX '97 International Stamp Exhibition, New Delhi (1st issue).
1681 **1315** 2r. gold and purple 60 45

See also Nos. 1713/16, 1722/5, 1741/4 and 1758/61.

1316 Historic Steam Locomotives

1996. 25th Anniv of National Rail Museum.
1682 **1316** 5r. multicoloured 2·75 2·25

1317 Jananayak Debeswar Sarmah

1996. Birth Centenary of Jananayak Debeswar Sarmah (politician).
1683 **1317** 2r. brown and deep brown 40 30

1318 Monument and Sikh Sentry

1996. 150th Anniv of Sikh Regiment.
1684 **1318** 5r. multicoloured 2·00 2·00

1319 Dr. Salim Ali

1996. Birth Centenary of Salim Ali (ornithologist). Multicoloured.
1685 8r. Type **1319** 3·00 3·25
1686 11r. Painted storks at nest 3·00 3·25

Nos. 1685/6 were printed together, se-tenant, with the backgrounds forming a composite design.

1320 "Indian Village" (child's painting)

1996. Children's Day.
1687 **1320** 8r. multicoloured 1·25 1·75

1321 Seeds in a Test-tube

1996. 2nd International Crop Science Congress.
1688 **1321** 2r. multicoloured 50 30

1322 Regimental Shrine

1996. Bicentenary of 2nd Battalion, Grenadiers.
1689 **1322** 5r. multicoloured 1·25 1·25

1323 Woman writing

1996. 10th Anniv of South Asian Association for Regional Co-operation (S.A.A.R.C.).
1690 **1323** 11r. multicoloured 1·25 1·75

1324 Abai Konunbaev

1996. 150th Birth Anniv (1995) of Abai Konunbaev (Kazakh poet).
1691 **1324** 5r. chestnut, brown and lilac 1·25 1·50

1325 Buglers in front of Memorial

1996. 25th Anniv of the Liberation of Bangladesh.
1692 **1325** 2r. multicoloured 50 30

1326 Vivekananda Rock Memoria (image scaled to 65% of original size)

1996. 25th Anniv of Vivekananda Rock Memorial, Kanyakumari.
1693 **1326** 5r. multicoloured 2·50 2·25

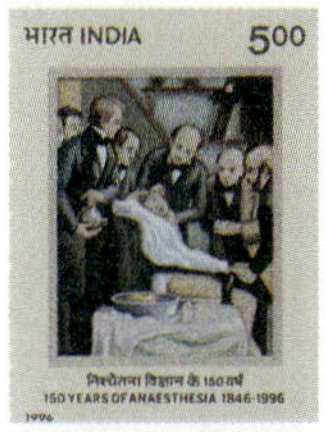

1327 Victorian Doctors performing Operation

1996. 150th Anniv of Anaesthetics.
1694 **1327** 5r. multicoloured 1·75 1·50

1328 Roorkee University Buildings

1997. 150th Anniv of Roorkee University.
1695 **1328** 8r. multicoloured 1·00 1·50

1329 Dr. Vrindavanlal Verma

1997. Dr. Vrindavanlal Verma (writer) Commemoration.
1696 **1329** 2r. red 40 30

1330 Field Post Office

1997. 25th Anniv of Army Postal Service Corps.
1697 **1330** 5r. multicoloured 2·25 1·75

1331 Subhas Chandra Bose

1997. Birth Centenary of Subhas Chandra Bose (nationalist).
1698 **1331** 1r. brown 40 15

1332 Jose Marti

1997. Jose Marti (Cuban writer) Commemoration.
1699 **1332** 11r. black and pink 1·00 1·50

1333 Conference Logo

1997. "Towards Partnership between Men and Women in Politics" Inter-Parliamentary Conference, New Delhi.
1700 **1333** 5r. multicoloured 50 60

1334 St. Andrew's Church

1997. St. Andrew's Church, Egmore, Madras Commemoration.
1701 **1334** 8r. multicoloured 1·00 1·50

1335 Morarji Desai

1997. Birth Centenary of Morarji Desai (former Prime Minister) (2nd issue).
1702 **1335** 1r. brown and deep brown 40 15

1336 Shyam Lal Gupt

1997. Birth Centenary (1996) of Shyam Lal Gupt (social reformer).
1703 **1336** 1r. cinnamon and brown 30 15

1337 Saint Dnyaneshwar

1997. 700th Death Anniv (1996) of Saint Dnyaneshwar.
1704 **1337** 5r. multicoloured 70 80

1338 Parijati Tree

1997. Parijati Tree. Multicoloured.
1705 5r. Type **1338** 1·00 1·25
1706 6r. Parijati flower 1·00 1·25

1339 Monument, Rashtriya Military College

1997. 75th Anniv of Rashtriya Military College, Dehra Dun.

1707 **1339** 2r. multicoloured 1·25 65

1340 Ram Manohar Lohia

1997. Ram Manohar Lohia Commemoration.

1708 **1340** 1r. multicoloured 60 20

1341 Society Centenary Emblem

1997. Centenary of the Philatelic Society of India. Multicoloured.

1709 2r. Type **1341** 65 75

1710 2r. Cover of 1st "Philatelic Journal of India", 1897 65 75

1342 Gyandith Award Winners

1997. Gyandith Award Scheme.

1711 **1342** 2r. multicoloured 40 30

1343 Madhu Limaye

1997. Madhu Limaye Commemoration.

1712 **1343** 2r. green 40 30

1344 Nalanda Monastic University

1997. "INDEPEX '97" International Stamp Exhibition, New Delhi (2nd issue). Buddhist Cultural Sites. Multicoloured.

1713 2r. Type **1344** 25 40

1714 6r. The Bodhi Tree, Bodhgaya 45 60

1715 10r. Stupa and Pillar, Vaishali 60 90

1716 11r. Stupa, Kushinagar 60 90

1345 Pandit Omkarnath Thakur

1997. Birth Centenary of Pandit Omkarnath Thakur (musician).

1717 **1345** 2r. black and blue 1·00 30

1346 Ram Sewak Yadav

1997. Ram Sewak Yadav (politician) Commemoration.

1718 **1346** 2r. brown 40 30

1347 Sibnath Banerjee

1997. Birth Centenary of Sibnath Banerjee (trade unionist).

1719 **1347** 2r. red and purple 40 30

1348 Rukmini Lakshmipathi

1997. Rukmini Lakshmipathi (social reformer) Commemoration.

1720 **1348** 2r. brown 1·50 65

1349 Sri Basaveswara

1997. Sri Basaveswara (reformer and statesman) Commemoration.

1721 **1349** 2r. purple 50 30

1350 Gopalpur-on-Sea Beach

1997. "INDEPEX '97" International Stamp Exhibition, New Delhi (3rd issue). Beaches. Multicoloured.

1722 2r. Type **1350** 40 20

1723 6r. Kovalam 80 65

1724 10r. Anjuna 1·00 1·40

1725 11r. Bogmalo 1·00 1·40

1351 Newspaper Masthead

1997. 50th Anniv of "Swatantra Bharat" (Hindi daily newspaper).

1726 **1351** 2r. multicoloured 40 30

1352 Shah Nawaz Khan, P. K. Sahgal and G. S. Dhillon

1997. I.N.A. Trials Commemoration.

1727 **1352** 2r. multicoloured 40 40

1353 Sir Ronald Ross (bacteriologist)

1997. Centenary of the Discovery of the Malaria Parasite by Sir Ronald Ross.

1728 **1353** 2r. grey 1·50 65

1354 Firaq Gorakhpuri

1997. Birth Centenary (1996) of Firaq Gorakhpuri (poet).

1729 **1354** 2r. brown 40 30

1355 Bhaktivedanta Swami

1997. Birth Centenary (1996) of Bhaktivedanta Swami (philosopher).

1730 **1355** 5r. brown 1·50 1·50

1356 Parachute Regiment Emblem

1997. Bicentenary of 2nd (Maratha) Battalion, Parachute Regiment.

1731 **1356** 2r. multicoloured 1·00 50

1357 Fossil of "Birbalsahnia divyadarshanii"

1997. 50th Anniv of Birbal Sahni Institute of Palaeobotany, Lucknow. Plant Fossils. Multicoloured.

1732 2r. Type **1357** 60 60

1733 2r. "Glossopteris" 60 60

1734 6r. "Pentoxylon" (reconstruction) 1·25 1·25

1735 10r. "Williamsonia sewardiana" (model) 1·75 2·00

1358 Swami Brahmanand

1997. Swami Brahmanand (social reformer) Commemoration.

1736 **1358** 2r. grey and stone 40 30

1359 "Sir William Jones"

1997. 250th Birth Anniv (1996) of Sir William Jones (Sanskrit scholar).

1737 **1359** 4r. multicoloured 50 60

1360 Lawrence School Building and Crest

1997. 150th Anniv of Lawrence School, Sanawar.

1738 **1360** 2r. multicoloured 1·00 45

1361 V. K. Krishna Menon

1997. Birth Centenary (1996) of V. K. Krishna Menon (politician).

1739 **1361** 2r. red 50 30

1362 Policemen and Globe

1997. 66th General Assembly Session of ICPO Interpol.

1740 **1362** 4r. multicoloured 1·00 1·00

1363 Woman from Arunachal Pradesh

1997. "INDEPEX '97" International Stamp Exhibition, New Delhi (4th issue). Women's Costumes. Multicoloured.

1741 2r. Type **1363** 50 20

1742 6r. Gujarat costume 1·10 75

1743 10r. Ladakh costume 1·40 1·60

1744 11r. Kerala costume 1·40 1·60

1364 Students in Meditation, Astachal

1997. Centenary of Scindia School, Gwalior. Multicoloured.

1745	5r. Type **1364**	75	1·00
1746	5r. Gwalior Fort	75	1·00

1365 "Ocimum sanctum"

1997. Medicinal Plants. Multicoloured.

1747	2r. Type **1365**	40	30
1748	5r. "Curcuma longa"	60	70
1749	10r. "Rauvolfia serpentina"	85	1·10
1750	11r. "Aloe barbadensis"	85	1·10

1366 Sant Kavi Sunderdas

1997. 400th Birth Anniv (1996) of Sant Kavi Sunderdas (Hindu theologian).

1751	**1366**	2r. brown	1·50	70

1367 K. Rama Rao

1997. Birth Centenary of K. Rama Rao (parliamentarian and journalist).

1752	**1367**	2r. bistre and brown	1·50	70

1368 Jawaharlal Nehru and Child

1997. Children's Day.

1753	**1368**	2r. multicoloured	60	35

1369 Animals on Globe

1997. World Convention on Reverence for All Life, Pune.

1754	**1369**	4r. multicoloured	1·75	1·50

1370 Hazari Prasad Dwivedi

1997. 90th Birth Anniv of Hazari Prasad Dwivedi (scholar).

1755	**1370**	2r. grey	40	30

1371 Mother Teresa

1997. "INDEPEX '97" International Stamp Exhibition, New Delhi (5th issue). Mother Teresa Commemoration. Sheet 81×68 mm.

MS1756 45r. multicoloured	3·50	3·75

1372 Vallabhbhai Patel and Marchers

1997. 47th Death Anniv of Vallabhbhai Patel (politician).

1757	**1372**	2r. brown	35	30

1373 Head Post Office, Pune

1997. "INDEPEX '97" International Stamp Exhibition, New Delhi (5th issue). Post Office Heritage. Multicoloured.

1758	2r. Type **1373**	20	20
1759	6r. River mail barge	40	50
1760	10r. Jal Cooper (philatelist) and cancellations	70	85
1761	11r. "Hindoostan" (paddle-steamer)	70	85

1374 50th Anniversary Emblem

1997. 50th Anniv of Indian Armed Forces.

1762	**1374**	2r. multicoloured	40	30

1375 Dr. Pattabhi Sitaramayya

1997. Dr. Pattabhi Sitaramayya (politician) Commemoration.

1763	**1375**	2r. brown	65	30

1376 Father Jerome d'Souza and Cathedral

1997. Birth Centenary of Father Jerome d'Souza (academic).

1764	**1376**	2r. brown	40	30

1377 Ram Prasad Bismil and Ashfaqullah Khan

1997. 70th Death Anniv of Ram Prasad Bismil and Ashfaqullah Khan (revolutionaries).

1765	**1377**	2r. brown	30	30

1378 Jail Buildings

1997. Cellular Jail, Port Blair.

1766	**1378**	2r. multicoloured	30	30

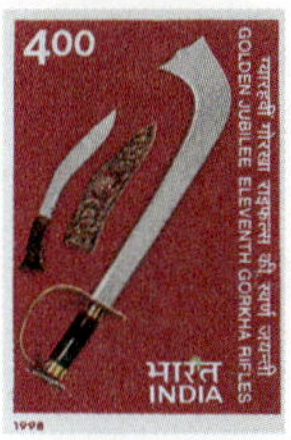

1379 Sword and Kukri

1998. 50th Anniv of 11th Gorkha Rifles.

1767	**1379**	4r. multicoloured	2·25	1·50

1380 Nahar Singh

1998. 140th Death Anniv of Nahar Singh (Sikh leader).

1768	**1380**	2r. purple	40	30

1381 Nanak Singh

1998. Birth Centenary (1997) of Nanak Singh (writer).

1769	**1381**	2r. red	40	30

1382 Rotary International Emblem

1998. Meeting of Rotary International Council on Legislation, Delhi.

1770	**1382**	8r. yellow and blue	75	1·25

1383 Maharana Pratap

1998. 400th Death Anniv of Maharana Pratap (Rajput leader).

1771	**1383**	2r. purple	40	30

1384 V. S. Khandekar

1998. Birth Centenary of V. S. Khandekar (writer).

1772	**1384**	2r. red	40	30

1385 Elephant and Dancers

1998. India Tourism Day.

1773	**1385**	10r. multicoloured	2·25	2·25

1386 Jagdish Chandra Jain

1998. Jagdish Chandra Jain (educationist) Commemoration.

1774	**1386**	2r. brown	40	30

1387 Gandhi as a Young Man and Peasants in Fields

1998. 50th Death Anniv of Mahatma Gandhi. Multicoloured.

1775	2r. Type **1387**	65	75
1776	6r. Woman weaving and Gandhi distributing food	85	95
1777	10r. Gandhi collecting salt	1·10	1·25
1778	11r. Gandhi carrying flag	1·10	1·25

Nos. 1775/8 were printed together, se-tenant, with the backgrounds forming a composite design.

1388 A. Vedaratnam

1998. Birth Centenary (1997) of A. Vedaratnam (social reformer).

1779	**1388**	2r. purple	60	35

1389 Anniversary Emblem

1998. 50th Anniv of Universal Declaration of Human Rights.
1780 **1389** 6r. multicoloured 60 80

1390 Savitribai Phule

1998. Death Centenary (1997) of Savitribai Phule (educational reformer).
1781 **1390** 2r. brown 40 30

1391 Sir Syed Ahmad Khan

1998. Death Centenary of Sir Syed Ahmed Khan (social reformer).
1782 **1391** 2r. brown 55 30

1392 Barren Landscape and Living Forest

1998. 1st Assembly Meeting of Global Environment Facility, Delhi.
1783 **1392** 11r. multicoloured 1·25 1·50

1393 Ramana Maharshi

1998. Ramana Maharshi (religious leader) Commemoration.
1784 **1393** 2r. lilac 40 30

1394 College Arms

1998. 50th Anniv of Defence Services Staff College, Wellington.
1785 **1394** 6r. red 1·10 1·10

1395 Diesel Train on Viaduct (image scaled to 53% of original size)

1998. Completion of Konkan Railway.
1786 **1395** 8r. multicoloured 1·50 1·75

1396 Narayan Ganesh Goray

1998. Narayan Ganesh Goray (social reformer) Commemoration.
1787 **1396** 2r. brown 40 30

1397 Dr. Zakir Husain

1998. Birth Centenary (1997) of Dr. Zakir Husain (former President of India).
1788 **1397** 2r. brown 40 30

1398 Mohammed Abdurahiman Shahib

1998. Mohammed Abdurahiman Shahib (nationalist) Commemoration.
1789 **1398** 2r. brown 40 30

1399 Lokanayak Omeo Kumar Das

1998. Lokanayak Omeo Kumar Das (writer) Commemoration.
1790 **1399** 2r. brown 40 30

1400 Vakkom Abdul Khader, Satyendra Chandra Bardhan and Fouja Singh

1998. Nationalist Martyrs Commemoration.
1791 **1400** 2r. brown and cinnamon 40 30

1401 Bishnu Dey, Tarashankar Bandopadhyay and Ashapurna Devi

1998. Bangla Jnanpith Literary Award Winners Commemoration.
1792 **1401** 2r. brown 40 30

1402 Big Ben, London

1998. 50th Anniv of First Air India International Flight.
1793 5r. Type **1402** 75 85
1794 6r. Lockheed Super Constellation airliner, globe and Gateway of India, Bombay (55×35 mm) 75 85

Nos. 1793/4 were printed together, se-tenant, forming a composite design.

1403 Dr. C. Vijiaraghavachariar

1998. Dr. C. Vijiaraghavachariar (lawyer and social reformer) Commemoration.
1795 **1403** 2r. brown 60 30

1404 Anniversary Logo and Savings Stream

1998. 50th Anniv of National Savings Organization. Multicoloured.
1796 5r. Type **1404** 65 75
1797 6r. Hand dropping coin into jar 65 75

Nos. 1796/7 were printed together, se-tenant, forming a composite design.

1405 Bhagawan Gopinathji

1998. Birth Centenary of Bhagawan Gopinathji (spiritual leader).
1798 **1405** 3r. brown 50 50

1406 Ardeshir and Pirojsha Godrej

1998. Centenary of Godrej (industrial conglomerate).
1799 **1406** 3r. green 50 50

1407 Aruna Asaf Ali

1998. Aruna Asaf Ali (nationalist) Commemoration.
1800 **1407** 3r. brown 50 50

1408 Iswar Chandra Vidyasagar (educationist) and College

1998. 125th Anniv of Vidyasagar College, Calcutta.
1801 **1408** 2r. black 40 30

1409 Shivpujan Sahai

1998. Shivpujan Sahai (writer) Commemoration.
1802 **1409** 2r. brown 40 30

1410 Red Fort, Delhi, and Spinning Wheel

1998. Homage to Martyrs for Independence. Multicoloured.
1803 3r. Type **1410** 50 65
1804 8r. Industrial and scientific development in modern India 1·00 1·25

1411 Gostha Behari Paul

1998. Gostha Paul (footballer) Commemoration.
1805 **1411** 3r. purple 50 50

1412 Youth Hostel and Logo

1998. 50th Anniv of Youth Hostels Association of India.
1806 **1412** 5r. multicoloured 65 65

1413 Uniforms, Badge and Tank

1998. Bicentenary of 4th Battalion, Guards' Brigade (1 Rajput).
1807 **1413** 6r. multicoloured 1·00 80

1414 Bhai Kanhaiyaji

1998. Bhai Kanhaiyaji (Sikh social reformer) Commemoration.
1808 **1414** 2r. red 40 30

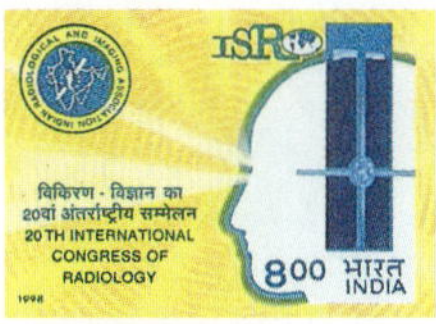

1415 Emblem and Diagram of Head

1998. 20th International Congress of Radiology.
1809 **1415** 8r. multicoloured 1·25 1·40

1416 Dove of Peace and Boy reading Book

1998. 26th International Books for Young People Congress.
1810 **1416** 11r. multicoloured 1·25 1·75

1417 Dr. Tristao Braganza Cunha

1998. Dr. Tristao Braganza Cunha (nationalist) Commemoration.
1811 **1417** 3r. brown 50 50

1418 Janeneta Hijam Irawat Singh

1998. Jananeta Hijam Irawat Singh (social reformer) Commemoration.
1812 **1418** 3r. brown 50 50

1419 Women Aviators and Bi-plane

1998. Indian Women's Participation in Aviation.
1813 **1419** 8r. blue 1·40 1·40

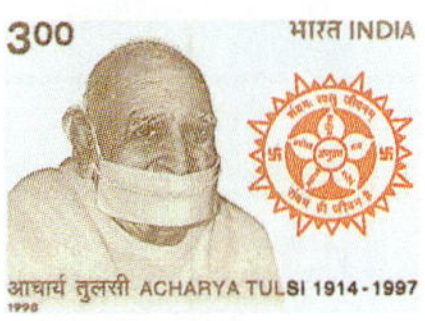

1420 Acharya Tulsi

1998. 1st Death Anniv of Acharya Tulsi (Jain religious leader).
1814 **1420** 3r. brown and orange 50 50

1421 Girl and Bird reading Book

1998. Children's Day.
1815 **1421** 3r. multicoloured 50 50

1422 I.N.S. "Delhi" (destroyer)

1998. Navy Day.
1816 **1422** 3r. multicoloured 1·00 60

1423 Mounted Trumpeter

1998. 225th Anniv of President's Bodyguard.
1817 **1423** 3r. multicoloured 1·00 60

1424 Sir David Sassoon and Library, Bombay

1998. David Sassoon Library and Reading Room Commemoration.
1818 **1424** 3r. ultramarine and blue 50 50

1425 Regimental Arms and Soldier

1998. Bicentenary of 2nd Battalion, Rajput Regiment.
1819 **1425** 3r. multicoloured 1·25 70

1426 Army Postal Service Centre, Kamptee

1998. 50th Anniv of Army Postal Service Training Centre.
1820 **1426** 3r. multicoloured 1·00 60

1427 Connemara Public Library, Madras

1998. Centenary (1996) of Connemara Public Library.
1821 **1427** 3r. brown and ochre 50 50

1428 Neem Tree and Leaves

1998. 50th Anniv of The Indian Pharmaceutical Congress Association.
1822 **1428** 3r. multicoloured 1·00 60

1429 Baba Raghav Das

1998. 40th Death Anniv of Baba Raghav Das (social reformer).
1823 **1429** 2r. violet 40 30

1430 Lt. Indra Lal Roy D.F.C.

1998. Birth Centenary of Indra Lal Roy (First World War pilot).
1824 **1430** 3r. multicoloured 1·00 60

1431 Sant Gadge Baba

1998. Sant Gadge Baba (social reformer) Commemoration.
1825 **1431** 3r. lilac, blue and black 50 50

1432 Rudra Veena (stringed instrument)

1998. Musical Instruments. Multicoloured.
1826 2r. Type **1432** 50 15
1827 6r. Flute 75 50
1828 8r. Pakhawaj (wooden barrel drum) 1·00 1·25
1829 10r. Sarod (stringed instrument) 1·10 1·40

1433 "Chicoreus brunneus" (Murex shell)

1998. Shells. Multicoloured.
1830 3r. Type **1433** 60 60
1831 3r. "Cassis cornuta" (horned helmet) 60 60
1832 3r. "Cypraea staphylaea" (cowrie) 60 60
1833 11r. "Lambis lambis" (common spider conch) 1·50 1·75

1434 Stylized Police Officers

1999. 50th Anniv of Indian Police Service.
1834 **1434** 3r. multicoloured 1·00 60

1435 Modern Weapon Systems

1999. 40th Anniv of Defence Research and Development Organization.
1835 **1435** 10r. multicoloured 1·50 1·60

1436 Issue of "Orunodoi" (Assamese newspaper) for January, 1846

1999. 150th Anniv of Newspapers in Assam.
1836 **1436** 3r. black, yellow and orange 1·00 60

1437 College Building

1999. Centenary of Hindu College, Delhi.
1837 **1437** 3r. blue 50 50

1438 National Defence Academy and Military Equipment

1999. 50th Anniv of National Defence Academy, Khadakwasla.
1838 **1438** 3r. multicoloured 1·40 75

1439 College Building

1999. 175th Anniv of Sanskrit College, Calcutta.
1839 **1439** 3r. brown and ochre 70 45

1440 Patnaik and Tugs

1999. Biju Patnaik (social reformer) Commemoration.
1840 **1440** 3r. brown and green 80 55

1441 Globe and Satellite Dish

1999. 50th Anniv of Press Trust of India.
1841 **1441** 15r. multicoloured 1·10 1·50

1442 "Apsara removing a Thorn from her Foot" (temple statue)

1999. Millenary of the Khajuraho Temples.
1842 **1442** 15r. deep brown, light brown and black 1·10 1·50

1443 Dr. K. B. Hedgewar

1999. Dr. Keshavrao Hedgewar (founder of Rashtriya Swayamsevak Sangha) Commemoration.
1843 **1443** 3r. multicoloured 40 40

1444 Terracotta Model Boat from Lothal, 2200 B.C., and Seal

1999. Maritime Heritage. Multicoloured.
1844 3r. Type **1444** 50 60
1845 3r. Ghurab (sailing ship) of Kanhoji Angre, 1700 50 60

1445 Anandpur Sahib Temple

1999. 300th Anniv of the Khalsa Panth (Sikh Order).
1846 **1445** 3r. multicoloured 1·25 75

1446 Bethune College

1999. 150th Anniv of Bethune Collegiate School, Calcutta.
1847 **1446** 3r. green 40 40

1447 Plane, Satellite and Rocket orbiting Globe

1999. Technology Day.
1848 **1447** 3r. multicoloured 50 50

1448 Mumbai Port

1999. 125th Anniv of Mumbai (Bombay) Port Trust.
1849 **1448** 3r. blue 65 50

1449 Handshake and Airliner

1999. Mizoram Accord (peace agreement) Commemoration.
1850 **1449** 3r. multicoloured 50 50

1450 Gulzarilal Nanda

1999. Birth Centenary of Gulzarilal Nanda (former Prime Minster).
1851 **1450** 3r. multicoloured 40 40

1451 Jijabai and Chatrapati Shivaji

1999. Jijabai (mother of Chatrapati Shivaji (Maratha leader)) Commemoration.
1852 **1451** 3r. purple 40 40

1452 P. S. Kumaraswamy Raja

1999. P. S. Kumaraswamy Raja (politician) Commemoration.
1853 **1452** 3r. brown and blue 40 40

1453 Balai Chand Mukhopadhyay

1999. Birth Centenary of Balai Chand Mukhopadhyay ("Banaphool") (Bengali writer).
1854 **1453** 3r. blue 40 40

1454 River Sindhu, Ladakh

1999. Sindhu Darshan Festival.
1855 **1454** 3r. multicoloured 40 40

1455 Soldier and Young Girl

1999. 50th Anniv of Geneva Conventions.
1856 **1455** 15r. black and red 1·10 1·50

1456 Sardar Ajit Singh

1999. Heroes of Struggle for Freedom.
1857 **1456** 3r. brown and red 30 30
1858 - 3r. brown and blue 30 30
1859 - 3r. blue and red 30 30
1860 - 3r. purple and drab 30 30

DESIGNS: No. 1858, Swami Ramanand Teerth; No. 1859, Vishwambhar Dayalu Tripathi; No. 1860, Swami Keshawanand.

1457 Kalki Krishnamurthy

1999. Birth Centenary of Kalki Krishnamurthy (Tamil writer).
1861 **1457** 3r. grey 40 40

1458 Ramdhari Sinha

1999. Ramdhari Sinha "Dinkar" (poet) Commemoration.
1862 **1458** 3r. brown and blue 40 40

1459 Jhaverchand Kalidas Meghani and Graves

1999. Jhaverchand Kalidas Meghani (writer) Commemoration.
1863 **1459** 3r. red and green 40 40

1460 Rambrikish Benipuri and Statue of Horse

1999. Rambrikish Benipuri (writer and journalist) Commemoration.
1864 **1460** 3r. brown and light brown 40 40

1461 Kazi Nazrul Islam

1999. Birth Centenary of Kazi Nazrul Islam (Bengali poet).
1865 **1461** 3r. sepia and yellow 40 40

1462 Arati Gupta

1999. Arati Gupta (swimmer) Commemoration.
1866 **1462** 3r. multicoloured 40 40

1463 Lionesses

1999. Endangered Species. Asiatic Lion. Mult.
1867 3r. Type **1463** 50 50
1868 3r. Lions and lionesses lying down 50 50
1869 3r. Lioness with cubs 50 50
1870 15r. Two lions 1·25 1·75

1464 A. D. Shroff

1999. A. D. Shroff (economist) Commemoration.
1871 **1464** 3r. green and brown 40 40

1465 A. B. Walawalkar and Map

1999. A. B. Walawalkar (railway engineer) Commemoration.
1872 **1465** 3r. purple 60 45

1466 Chhaganlal K. Parekh and Medical Staff with Child

1999. Chhaganlal K. Parekh (social reformer) Commemoration.
1873 **1466** 3r. blue and brown 40 40

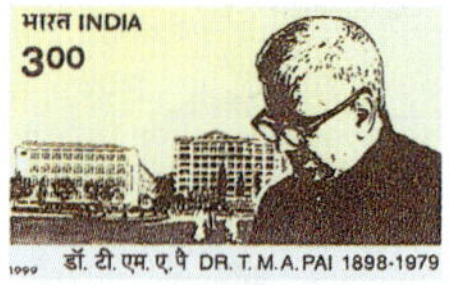

1467 Dr. T. M. A. Pai and Hospital

1999. 20th Death Anniv of Dr. T. M. A. Pai (educator).
1874 **1467** 3r. chocolate and stone 40 40

1468 Chhau Dance Masks

1999. 125th Anniv of Universal Postal Union. Traditional Arts and Crafts. Multicoloured.
1875 3r. Type **1468** 50 50
1876 3r. Elephant and horseman (Rathva wall painting) (vert) 50 50
1877 3r. Man ploughing (Muria ritual collar) 50 50
1878 15r. Angami ornament (vert) 1·50 2·25

1469 Veerapandia Kattabomman

1999. Death Bicentenary of Veerapandia Kattabomman (ruler of Panchalankuruchi).
1879 **1469** 3r. green 40 40

1470 Ustad Allauddin Khan Saheb (sarod player)

1999. Modern Masters of Indian Classical Music. Multicoloured.
1880 3r. Type **1470** 50 50

1881		3r. Musiri Subramania Iyer (singer)	50	50

1471 Brigadier Rajinder Singh

1999. Birth Centenary of Brigadier Rajinder Singh (First recipient of M.V.C. medal).

1882	**1471**	3r. purple	50	50

1472 Elephant and Rhinoceros

1999. Children's Day.

1883	**1472**	3r. multicoloured	50	50

1473 Dam and Pumping Station

1999. Sri Sathya Sai Water Supply Project.

1884	**1473**	3r. multicoloured	1·25	70

1474 Supreme Court, New Delhi

1999. 50th Anniv of Supreme Court of India.

1885	**1474**	3r. multicoloured	40	40

1475 A. Vaidyanatha Iyer and Temple Tower

1999. March of Progress.

1886	**1475**	3r. red	55	55
1887	-	3r. brown and green	55	55
1888	-	3r. buff and black	55	55
1889	-	3r. brown and green	55	55

DESIGNS: No. 1887, Dr. Punjabrao Deshmukh and symbols of agriculture; 1888, Indulal Kanaiyalal Yagnik and newspaper; 1889, Kakkan and machinery.

1476 Aspects of Thermal Power

1999. Centenary of Thermal Power.

1890	**1476**	3r. chocolate and brown	40	40

1477 "Hindustan Times" Front Pages from 1950 and 1999

1999. 75th Anniv of "Hindustan Times" Newspaper.

1891	**1477**	15r. multicoloured	1·40	2·00

1478 Three Faces ("Small Family by Choice")

1999. 50th Anniv of Family Planning Association of India.

1892	**1478**	3r. multicoloured	40	40

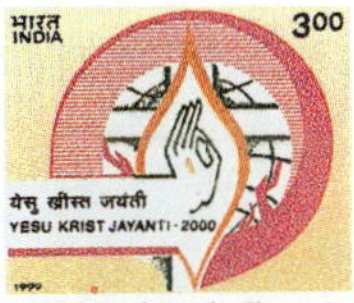

1479 Hand inside Flame in front of Cross

1999. 2000th Birth Anniv of Jesus Christ.

1893	**1479**	3r. multicoloured	75	50

1480 Tabo Monastery and Mountains

1999. New Millennium. Unity in Diversity. Mult.

1894		5r. Type **1480**	90	1·10
1895		10r. Traditional scene	1·00	1·25

1481 Agni II Rocket and Dove

2000. 41st Anniv of Defence Research and Development Organization.

1896	**1481**	3r. multicoloured	65	50

1482 Sunrise

2000. New Millennium.

1897	**1482**	3r. multicoloured	40	40

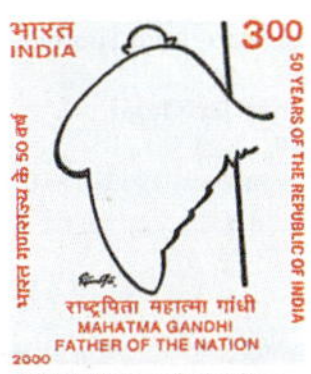

1483 Stylized Outline of Gandhi as Map of India

2000. 50th Anniv of Republic (1st issue).

1898	**1483**	3r. black and red	50	50

1484 Karam Singh and Regimental Badge

2000. 50th Anniv of Republic (2nd issue). Gallantry Award Winners. Multicoloured.

1899		3r. Type **1484**	45	50
1900		3r. Abdul Hamid and armed jeep	45	50
1901		3r. Albert Ekka, hand grenades and knife	45	50
1902		3r. N. J. S. Sekhon and jet fighter	45	50
1903		3r. M. N. Mulla and warship	45	50

1485 Batagur Terrapin

2000. "Millepex 2000" Stamp Exhibition, Bhubaneshwar. Endangered Species. Multicoloured.

1904		3r. Type **1485**	50	65
1905		3r. Olive Ridley turtle	50	65

1486 Balwantrai Mehta

2000. Balwantrai Mehta (former Chief Minister of Gujarot) Commemoration.

1906	**1486**	3r. multicoloured	40	40

1487 Dr. Harekrushna Mahatab

2000. Dr. Harekrushna Mahatab (former Chief Minister of Orissa) Commemoration.

1907	**1487**	3r. multicoloured	40	40

1488 Arun Kumar Chanda

2000. Arun Kumar Chanda (trade union leader) Commemoration.

1908	**1488**	3r. multicoloured	50	40

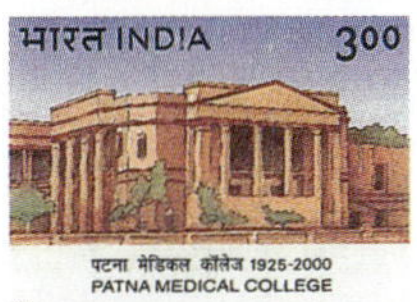

1489 Patna Medical College

2000. 75th Anniv of Patna Medical College.

1909	**1489**	3r. multicoloured	40	40

1490 Dr. Burgula Ramakrishna Rao

2000. Birth Centenary (1999) of Dr. Burgula Ramakrishna Rao (Hyderabad Chief Minister).

1910	**1490**	3r. brown and yellow	40	40

1491 Potti Sriramulu

2000. Potti Sriramulu (Harijan activist) Commemoration.

1911	**1491**	3r. red	40	40

1492 Basawon Sinha

2000. Basawon Sinha (politician) Commemoration.

1912	**1492**	3r. multicoloured	40	40

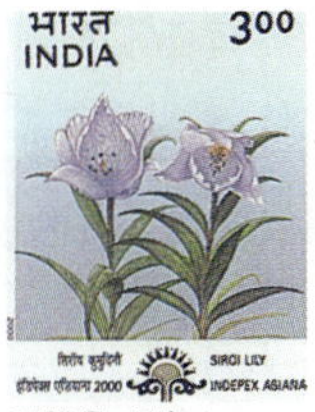

1493 Siroi Lily

2000. "Indepex Asiana 2000" International Stamp Exhibition, Calcutta (1st issue). Flora and Fauna of Manipur and Tripura. Multicoloured.

1913		3r. Type **1493**	55	55
1914		3r. Sangai deer	55	55
1915		3r. Wild guava	55	55
1916		15r. Slow loris	1·40	1·75
MS1917		160×112 mm. Nos. 1913/16	2·75	3·00

See also Nos. 1934/8 and 1966/72.

1494 Maharshi Dayananda Saraswati, Flame and Pages

2000. 125th Anniv of Arya Samaj (philosophical movement).

1918	**1494**	3r. multicoloured	1·25	70

1495 Kankrej Breed

2000. Indigenous Breeds of Cattle. Multicoloured.

1919		3r. Type **1495**	55	55
1920		3r. Kangayam	55	55
1921		3r. Gir	55	55
1922		15r. Hallikar	1·60	2·00

1496 Blackbuck

1497 Leopard Cat

2000. Wildlife.

1923	**1496**	25p. brown	10	10
1924	-	50p. brown	10	10
1925	-	1r. blue	10	10
1925a	-	2r. purple	15	10
1926	-	3r. violet	15	10
1927	-	4r. red	15	15
1928	**1497**	5r. brown and green	15	20
1929	-	10r. orange, brn & grn	25	30
1930	-	15r. red, brn & dp brn	40	45
1931	-	20r. yellow and green	50	55
1932	-	50r. red, brown & blue	1·25	1·40

DESIGNS—VERT (as Type **1496**): 50p. Nilgiri tahr; 1r. Saras crane ("Saras Crane"); 2r. Rose. As Type **1497**: 4r. Painted stork. (19×37 mm): 20r. Amaltaas (plant); 50r. Asiatic paradise flycatcher (bird) ("Paradise Flycatcher"). HORIZ (as Type **1497**): 3r. Smooth Indian otters. (37×19 mm): 10r. Tiger, Sundarban Reserve; 15r. Butterfly.

1498 Railway Locomotive at Dehradoon Station

2000. Centenary of Doon Valley Railway.

1933	**1498**	15r. multicoloured	2·25	2·50

1499 Rose-coloured Starling ("Rosy Pastor")

2000. "Indepex Asiana 2000" International Stamp Exhibition, Calcutta (2nd issue). Migratory Birds. Multicoloured.

1934	3r. Type **1499**	85	85
1935	3r. Garganey ("Garganey Teal")	85	85
1936	3r. Forest wagtail	85	85
1937	3r. White stork	85	85
MS1938	157×114 mm. Nos. 1934/7	3·00	3·00

1500 N. T. Rama Rao

2000. Nandamuri Taraka Rama Rao (former Chief Minister of Andhra Pradesh) Commemoration.

1939	**1500**	3r. multicoloured	40	30

1501 Swami Saraswati

2000. 50th Death Anniv of Swami Sahajanand Saraswati (rural reformer).

1940	**1501**	3r. mauve, brn & stone	60	40

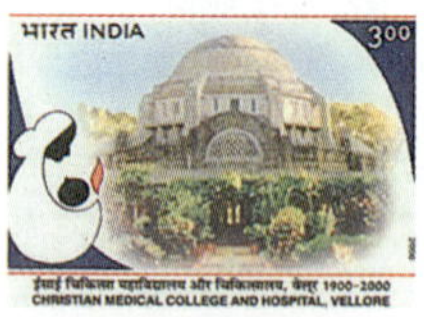

1502 Christian Medical College and Hospital, Vellore

2000. Centenary of Christian Medical College and Hospital, Vellore.

1941	**1502**	3r. multicoloured	60	40

1503 Vijaya Lakshmi Pandit (diplomat)

2000. Social and Political Leaders. Each including the Indian flag. Multicoloured.

1942	3r. Type **1503**	50	50
1943	3r. Bahadur R. Srinivasan (social reformer)	50	50
1944	3r. Jaglal Choudhary (social reformer)	50	50
1945	3r. Radha Gobinda Baruah (social reformer)	50	50

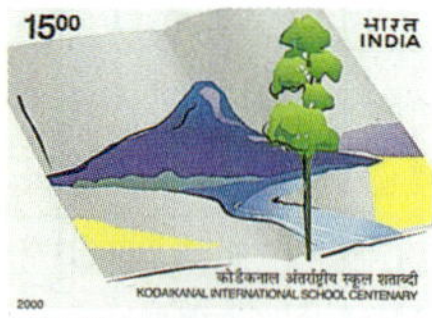

1504 Mountain, River and Tree inside Open Book

2000. Centenary of Kodaikanal International School.

1946	**1504**	15r. multicoloured	1·90	2·25

1505 Discus

2000. Olympic Games, Sydney. Multicoloured.

1947	3r. Type **1505**	35	20
1948	6r. Tennis	55	45
1949	10r. Hockey	55	45
1950	15r. Weightlifting	1·50	2·00

1506 "Oceansat-1"

2000. India's Space Programme. Multicoloured.

1951	3r. Type **1506**	70	70
1952	3r. "Insat 3B" in orbit	70	70
1953	3r. Astronaut with flag, planets and spacecraft (vert)	70	70
1954	3r. Earth and spacecraft (vert)	70	70

Nos. 1953/4 were printed together, se-tenant, with the backgrounds forming a composite design.

1507 Krishna with Gopies (Anmana Devi)

2000. Madhubani-Mithila Paintings. Multicoloured.

1955	3r. Type **1507**	55	55
1956	3r. "Flower Girls" (Nirmala Devi)	55	55
1957	3r. "Ball and Sugriva" (Sanjula) (vert)	55	55
1958	5r. Geometrical pattern with sedan chair at foot (vert)	80	80
1959	10r. Geometrical pattern with elephant at foot (vert)	1·25	1·25

1508 Raj Kumar Shukla

2000. 125th Birth Anniv of Raj Kumar Shukla (social reformer).

1960	**1508**	3r. brown and buff	70	60

1509 Dr. Shanker Dayal Sharma

2000. 1st Death Anniv of Dr. Shanker Dayal Sharma (former President of India).

1961	**1509**	3r. multicoloured	70	60

1510 Subhas Chandra Bose

2000

1962	**1510**	1r. brown	10	10
1963	-	2r. black	10	10
1963a	-	3r. blue	10	10

DESIGNS: 2r. Vallabhbhai Patel. 3r. Dr. B. R. Ambedkar.

1511 "My Best Friend" (Phuhar Uppal)

2000. Children's Day.

1964	**1511**	3r. multicoloured	1·00	70

1512 Maharaja Bijli Pasi

2000. Maharaja Bijli Pasi of Bijnor Commemoration.

1965	**1512**	3r. multicoloured	75	50

1513 Ancient Bead Necklace from Indus Valley

2000. "Indepex Asiana 2000" International Stamp Exhibition, Calcutta (3rd issue). Gems and Jewellery. Multicoloured.

1966	3r. Type **1513**	40	40
1967	3r. Gold necklace from Taxila	40	40
1968	3r. Turban ornament from Sarpech	40	40
1969	3r. Navaratna necklace	40	40
1970	3r. Bridal necklace from South India	40	40
1971	3r. Temple necklace from Rajasthan	40	40
MS1972	162×111 mm. Nos. 1966/7 and 1969/70 (sold at 15r.)	2·00	2·50

1514 17th-century Marakkars Galley

2000. 400th Death Anniv of Admiral Kunjali IV Marakkars.

1973	**1514**	3r. multicoloured	1·25	75

1515 Ustad Hafiz Ali Khan

2000. Ustad Hafiz Ali Khan (musician) Commemoration.

1974	**1515**	3r. multicoloured	75	55

1516 Prithviraj Chauhan, King of Delhi

2000. Historical Personalities. Multicoloured.

1975	3r. Type **1516**	50	50
1976	3r. Raja Bhamashah, Dewan of Mewar	50	50
1977	3r. Rajarshi Bhagyachandra, King of Manipur	50	50
1978	3r. General Zorawar Singh of Kashmir (horiz)	50	50

1517 "St. Aloysius with Children" (painting)

2001. Centenary of Paintings in St. Aloysius College Chapel, Mangalore.

1979	**1517**	15r. multicoloured	1·75	2·00

1518 Sane Guruji (writer)

2001. Personalities. Multicoloured.

1980	3r. Type **1518**	45	50
1981	3r. E. M. S. Namboodiripad (Kerala politician)	45	50
1982	3r. Giani Gurmukh Singh Musafir (Punjab politician)	45	50
1983	3r. Prof. N. G. Ranga (social reformer)	45	50

1519 Sheel Bhadra Yajee

2001. Sheel Bhadra Yajee (patriot) Commemoration.

1984	**1519**	3r. multicoloured	60	50

1520 Jubba Sahni

2001. Personalities. Multicoloured.

1985	3r. Type **1520**	50	50
1986	3r. Yogendra and Baikunth Shukla (patriot)	50	50

1521 Western Railway Building

2001. Western Railway Building, Churchgate, Mumbai.
1987 **1521** 15r. multicoloured 2·50 2·75

1522 Census Emblem

2001. Census of India.
1988 **1522** 3r. multicoloured 75 60

1523 *Tarangini* (cadet ship)

2001. International Fleet Review. Multicoloured.
1989 3r. Type **1523** 40 40
1990 3r. Maratha pal (sailing ship) 40 40
1991 3r. Maratha galbat (sailing ship) 40 40
1992 15r. Fleet Review logo 1·10 1·40

1524 Rocks and Minerals

2001. 150th Anniv of Geological Survey of India.
1993 **1524** 3r. multicoloured 70 60

1525 Soldier in Ceremonial Uniform and Himalaya Patrol

2001. Bicentenary of 4th Battalion, Maratha Light Infantry.
1994 **1525** 3r. multicoloured 1·25 60

1526 Symbols of Jain Teaching

2001. 2600th Birth Anniv of Bhagwan Mahavira (Jain teacher).
1995 **1526** 3r. multicoloured 1·00 60

1527 Yuri Gagarin and Rockets

2001. 40th Anniv of Man's First Space Flight.
1996 **1527** 15r. multicoloured 2·50 2·75

1528 Frederic Chopin

2001. 190th Birth Anniv (2002) of Frederic Chopin (composer).
1997 **1528** 15r. multicoloured 2·50 2·75

1529 Suraj Narain Singh

2001. Suraj Narain Singh (nationalist politician) Commemoration.
1998 **1529** 3r. multicoloured 70 60

1530 B. P. Mandal

2001. B. P. Mandal (former Chief Minister of Bihar) Commemoration.
1999 **1530** 3r. multicoloured 70 60

1531 Samanta Chandra Sekhar, Stars and Gola Yantra (instrument)

2001. Samanta Chandra Sekhar (astronomer) Commemoration.
2000 **1531** 3r. black, vio & grn 1·00 70

1532 "Sant Ravidas" (Phulan Runi)

2001. Sant Ravidas (philosopher-poet) Commem.
2001 **1532** 3r. multicoloured 70 60

1533 Krishna Nath Sarmah

2001. Personalities. Multicoloured.
2002 4r. Type **1533** 60 60
2003 4r. C. Sankaran Nair (lawyer) 60 60
2004 4r. Syama Prasad Mookerjee (politician) 60 60
2005 4r. U Kiang Nongbah (guerilla leader) 60 60

1534 Chandragupta Maurya

2001. Emperor Chandragupta Maurya Commem.
2006 **1534** 4r. multicoloured 70 60

1535 Jhalkari Bai on Horseback

2001. Jhalkari Bai (female warrior from Jhansi) Commemoration.
2007 **1535** 4r. multicoloured 1·00 70

1536 *Fungia horrida* (coral)

2001. Corals. Multicoloured.
2008 4r. Type **1536** 40 40
2009 4r. *Acropora digitifera* 40 40
2010 15r. *Montipora acquituberculata* 90 1·10
2011 45r. *Acropora formosa* 2·40 3·00

1537 Dwarka Prasad Mishra

2001. Birth Centenary of Dwarka Prasad Mishra (former Chief Minister of Madhya Pradesh).
2012 **1537** 4r. black and stone 60 50

1538 Chaudhary Brahmparkash

2001. Chaudhary Brahmparkash (former Chief Minister of Delhi) Commemoration.
2013 **1538** 4r. black and blue 60 50

1539 Revolution Monument, Shaheed Park, Ballia

2001. 60th Anniv (2000) of August Revolution, Ballia.
2014 **1539** 4r. multicoloured 75 60

1540 Jagdev Prasad

2001. Jagdev Prasad (journalist and politician) Commemoration.
2015 **1540** 4r. multicoloured 60 50

1541 Rani Avantibai

2001. Rani Avantibai of Ramgarh Commemoration.
2016 **1541** 4r. multicoloured 1·25 75

1542 Rao Tula Ram

2001. Rao Tula Ram of Rewari (patriot) Commemoration.
2017 **1542** 4r. multicoloured 60 50

1543 Chaudhary Devi Lal

2001. Chaudhary Devi Lal (former Deputy Prime Minister) Commemoration.
2018 **1543** 4r. multicoloured 60 50

1544 Satis Chandra Samanta

2001. Satis Chandra Samanta (West Bengal politician) Commemoration.
2019 **1544** 4r. black and stone 60 50

1545 Sivaji Ganesan

2001. Sivaji Ganesan (Tamil actor) Commemoration.
2020 **1545** 4r. multicoloured 75 60

1546 Gandhi on Salt March

2001. "Mahatma Gandhi—Man of the Millennium". Multicoloured.

2021	4r. Type **1546**	80	80
2022	4r. Mahatma Gandhi	80	80

1547 Bharathidsan (Tamil poet)

2001. Cultural Personalities. Each black, red and stone.

2023	4r. Type **1547**	50	50
2024	4r. Lachhu Maharaj (choreographer)	50	50
2025	4r. Master Mitrasen (writer)	50	50

1548 Jayaprakash Narayan

2001. Birth Centenary (2002) of Jayaprakash Narayan (socialist).

2026	**1548**	4r. multicoloured	75	60

1549 Monkey in Tree and Crocodile

2001. Stories from "Panchatantra" (Indian fables). Multicoloured.

2027	4r. Type **1549**	55	55
2028	4r. Monkey on crocodile's back (29×39 mm)	55	55
2029	4r. Lion and rabbit	55	55
2030	4r. Lion and rabbit at well (29×39 mm)	55	55
2031	4r. Snake attacking crows' eggs	55	55
2032	4r. Snake attacked by villagers (29×39 mm)	55	55
2033	4r. Geese and tortoise talking	55	55
2034	4r. Tortoise flying with geese (29×39 mm)	55	55

1550 Grocer selling Iodized Salt

2001. Global Iodine Deficiency Disorders Day.

2035	**1550**	4r. multicoloured	1·00	70

1551 Thangal Kunju Musaliar

2001. Thangal Kunju Musaliar (industrialist and philanthropist) Commemoration.

2036	**1551**	4r. black and stone	70	60

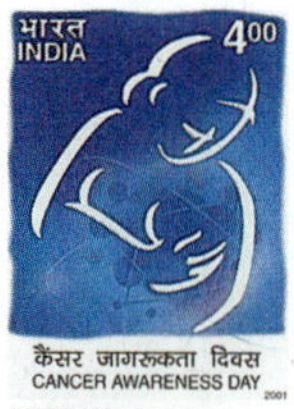

1552 Woman self-examining for Breast Cancer

2001. Cancer Awareness Day.

2037	**1552**	4r. multicoloured	75	60

1553 Maharajah Ranjit Singh

2001. Bicentenary of Ranjit Singh's Coronation as Maharajah of the Punjab.

2038	**1553**	4r. multicoloured	1·00	70

1554 Hands clasped around Globe

2001. Children's Day.

2039	**1554**	4r. multicoloured	75	60

1555 Dr. V. Shantaram and Film Scene

2001. Birth Centenary of Dr. V. Shantaram (film director).

2040	**1555**	4r. multicoloured	75	60

1556 Sobha Singh

2001. Birth Centenary of Sobha Singh (painter).

2041	**1556**	4r. multicoloured	1·00	70

1557 Sun Temple, Konark

2001. Centenary of Conservation at Sun Temple, Konark. Multicoloured.

2042	4r. Type **1557**	75	75
2043	15r. Giant carved wheel, Sun Temple, Konark	1·75	2·00

1558 Handshake above Three Symbolic Figures

2001. International Year of Volunteers.

2044	**1558**	4r. multicoloured	70	60

1559 Raj Kapoor and Film Characters

2001. Raj Kapoor (film actor and director) Commemoration.

2045	**1559**	4r. multicoloured	1·00	70

1560 Digboi Refinery

2001. Centenary of Digboi Oil Refinery, Assam.

2046	**1561**	4r. multicoloured	1·00	70

1561 Flowers, Fireworks and Christmas Tree

2001. Greetings. Multicoloured.

2047	3r. Type **1561**	70	55
2048	4r. Butterflies and flowers	90	70

1562 Vijaya Raje Scindia

2001. Vijaya Raje Scindia (politician and social reformer) Commemoration.

2049	**1562**	4r. multicoloured	70	60

1563 Kedarnath Temple, Uttaranchal

2001. "Inpex-Empirepex 2001" National Stamp Exhibition. Temple Architecture.

2050	**1563**	4r. brown & lt brn	55	55
2051	-	4r. brown & lt brn	55	55
2052	-	4r. brown & lt brn	55	55
2053	-	15r. brown & lt brn	1·50	2·00

DESIGNS: No. 2051, Tryambakeshwar Temple, Maharashtra; 2052, Aundha Nagnath Temple, Maharashtra; 2053, Rameswaram Temple.

1564 Mine Winding Gear and Helmet in Hand

2002. Centenary of Directorate General of Mines Safety.

2054	**1564**	4r. multicoloured	70	50

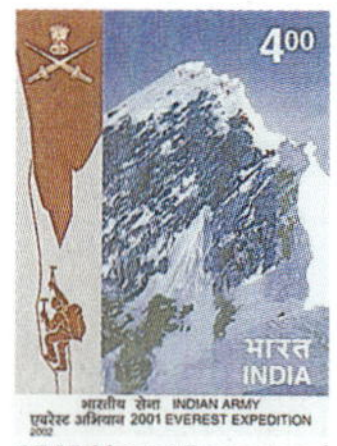

1565 Mount Everest and Climber

2002. Indian Army Expedition to Mt. Everest (2001).

2055	**1565**	4r. multicoloured	1·00	70

1566 Gridhakuta Hills, Rajgir

2002. Bauddha Mahotsav Festival. Multicoloured.

2056	4r. Type **1566**	45	45
2057	4r. Dhamek Stupa, Sarnath	45	45
2058	8r. Mahaparinirvana Temple, Kushinagar	85	95
2059	15r. Mahabodhi Temple, Bodhgaya	1·75	2·00

1567 Cartoon of Boy reading

2002. Year of Books.

2060	**1567**	4r. multicoloured	70	60

1568 Swami Ramanand (mystic)

2002. Swami Ramanand (mystic) Commemoration.

2061	**1568**	4r. multicoloured	70	60

1569 Tank and 19th-century Cannon

2002. Bicentenary of Indian Ordnance Factories.

2062	**1569**	4r. multicoloured	1·25	75

1570 Sido and Kanhu Murmu

2002. Sido and Kanhu Murmu (Santal resistance fighters) Commemoration.

2063	**1570**	4r. multicoloured	1·00	70

1571 First Railway Train, 1853

2002. 150th Anniv of Indian Railways.

2064	**1571**	15r. multicoloured	3·50	3·75
MS2065		112×75 mm. No. 2064	3·50	3·75

1572 Kathakali Dancer (India)

2002. 50th Anniv of Diplomatic Relations between India and Japan. Multicoloured.

2066	15r. Type **1572**	1·75	2·00
2067	15r. Kabuki actor (Japan)	1·75	2·00
MS2068	100×70 mm. Nos. 2066/7	3·50	4·00

1573 Central Hall of Parliament, New Delhi

2002. 50th Anniv of Indian Parliament.

2069	**1573**	4r. gold	75	60

1574 Prabodhankar Thackeray

2002. Prabodhankar Thackeray (writer) Commemoration.

2070	**1574**	4r. black	70	60

1575 Cotton College, Guwahati

2002. Centenary of Cotton College (2001), Assam.

2071	**1575**	4r. purple and green	70	60

1576 P. L. Deshpande

2002. P. L. Deshpande (writer) Commemoration.

2072	**1576**	4r. multicoloured	70	60

1577 Babu Gulabrai

2002. Indian Literary Figures. Multicoloured.

2073	5r. Type **1577**	75	75
2074	5r. Pandit Vyas	75	75

1578 Brajlal Biyani

2002. Brajlal Biyani (journalist and politician) Commemoration.

2075	**1578**	4r. multicoloured	70	60

1579 Sree Thakur Satyananda

2002. Sree Thakur Satyananda Commemoration.

2076	**1579**	5r. multicoloured	70	65

1580 Anna Bhau Sathe

2002. Anna Bhau Sathe (Marathi writer) Commemoration.

2077	**1580**	4r. black and grey	70	60

1581 Anand Rishiji Maharaj

2002. 10th Death Anniv of Anand Rishiji Maharaj (Jain spiritual leader).

2078	**1581**	4r. multicoloured	70	60

1582 Dr. Vithalrao Vikhe Patil

2002. Dr. Vithalrao Vikhe Patil (co-operative movement pioneer) Commemoration.

2079	**1582**	4r. multicoloured	70	60

1583 Sant Tukaram

2002. Sant Tukaram (Marathi poet) Commemoration.

2080	**1583**	4r. multicoloured	1·00	70

1584 Bhaurao Krishnarao Gaikwad

2002. Birth Centenary of Bhaurao Krishnarao Gaikwad (social reformer).

2081	**1584**	4r. multicoloured	70	60

1585 Ayyan Kali

2002. Social Reformers. Multicoloured.

2082	5r. Type **1585**	65	70
2083	5r. Chandraprabha Saikiani	65	70
2084	5r. Gora	65	70

1586 Ananda Nilayam Vimanam, Tirumala

2002. 700th Anniv of Ananda Nilayam Vimanam Temple Tower, Tirumala.

2085	**1586**	15r. multicoloured	2·50	2·75

1587 Kanika Bandopadhyay

2002. Kanika Bandopadhyay (singer) Commemoration.

2086	**1587**	5r. multicoloured	1·00	70

1588 Arya Vaidya Sala, Kottakkal, and Vaidyaratnam Varier (founder)

2002. Centenary of Arya Vaidya Kottakkal Sala (Ayurvedic Medicine), Kottakkal.

2087	**1588**	5r. multicoloured	1·00	1·00

1589 Bhagwan Baba

2002. Bhagwan Baba (mystic and philosopher) Commemoration.

2088	**1589**	5r. multicoloured	1·00	1·00

1590 Bihar Chamber of Commerce Logo

2002. 75th Anniv (2001) of Bihar Chamber of Commerce.

2089	**1590**	4r. multicoloured	80	60

1591 Asiatic Mangrove (*Rhizophora mucronata*)

2002. 8th Session of U.N. Conference on Climate Change, New Delhi. Mangroves. Multicoloured.

2090	5r. Type **1591**	60	60
2091	5r. Mangrove palm (*Nypa fruticans*)	60	60
2092	5r. Burma mangrove (*Bruguiera gymnorrhiza*)	60	60
2093	15r. Mangrove apple (*Sonneratia alba*)	1·75	2·00
MS2094	192×85 mm. Nos. 2090/3	3·25	3·50

1592 Swami Pranavananda

2002. Swami Pranavananda (social reformer) Commemoration.

2095	**159**	5r. multicoloured	1·25	1·25

1593 Vidhan Bhavan (State Assembly Building) and Samadhi (Buddhist Temple), Nagpur

2002. 300th Anniv of Nagpur.

2096	**1593**	5r. multicoloured	1·00	1·25

1594 "Holi Festival" (Aakash Anand)

2002. Children's Day.

2097	**1594**	5r. multicoloured	1·00	1·25

1595 Cane and Bamboo Ware

2002. Handicrafts. Multicoloured.

2098	5r. Type **1595**	75	75
2099	5r. Thewa ware (gold leaf work on coloured glass)	75	75
2100	5r. Patola fabric	75	75
2101	5r. Dhokra ornaments (metal casting)	75	75
MS2102	100×100 mm. Nos. 2098/101	2·75	2·75

1596 Santidev Ghose

2002. Santidev Ghose (classical singer) Commemoration.
2103 **1596** 5r. multicoloured 1·25 1·00

1597 Ajoy Kumar Mukherjee (leader) and Newspaper

2002. 60th Anniv of "National Government" of Tamluk (Tamralipta Jatiya Sarkar). Multicoloured.
2104 5r. Type **1597** 1·00 1·00
2105 5r. Matangini Hazra and demonstration 1·00 1·00

1598 Anglo Bengali Inter College, Allahabad

2002. Anglo-Bengali Inter College, Allahabad.
2106 **1598** 5r. multicoloured 75 60

1599 Gurukula Kangri Vishwavidyalaya University, Hardwar

2002. Gurukula Kangri Vishwavidyalaya University, Hardwar Commemoration.
2107 **1599** 5r. multicoloured 1·00 70

1600 Dhirubhai H. Ambani

2002. Dhirubhai H. Ambani (industrialist) Commemoration.
2108 **1600** 5r. multicoloured 1·00 75

1601 T. T. Krishnamachari

2002. T. T. Krishnamachari (Minister of Commerce and Industry, 1952–56, Finance Minister 1963–5) Commemoration.
2109 **1601** 5r. multicoloured 75 60

1602 Golconda Fort

2002. Forts of Andhra Pradesh. Multicoloured.
2110 5r. Type **1602** 75 75
2111 5r. Palace, Chandragiri Fort 75 75

1603 Hindustan Aircraft Industries HT-2 Trainer, 1951

2003. Centenary of Powered Flight. Aero India 2003. Multicoloured.
2112 5r. Type **1603** 70 70
2113 5r. Hindustan Aircraft Industries Marut ground attack aircraft, 1961 70 70
2114 5r. Hindustan Aircraft Industries LCA light combat aircraft, 2001 70 70
2115 15r. Hindustan Aircraft Industries Dhruv advanced light helicopter 1·90 2·25
MS2116 144×95 mm. Nos. 2112/15 3·50 4·00

1604 Ghantasala

2003. Ghantasala (singer and composer) Commemoration.
2117 **1604** 5r. brown and black 1·00 70

1605 S. L. Kirloskar and Cogwheels

2003. Birth Centenary of S. L. Kirloskar (industrialist).
2118 **1605** 5r. multicoloured 70 60

1606 Kusumagraj

2003. Kusumagraj (Marathi poet) Commemoration.
2119 **1606** 5r. multicoloured 70 60

1607 Sant Eknath

2003. Sant Eknath (saint and poet) Commemoration.
2120 **1607** 5r. multicoloured 70 60

1608 Frank Anthony

2003. 10th Death Anniv of Frank Anthony (politician).
2121 **1608** 5r. multicoloured 70 60

1609 Kakaji Maharaj

2003. Kakaji Maharaj (Swaminarayan spiritual leader and philosopher) Commemoration.
2122 **1609** 5r. multicoloured 70 60

1610 *Commiphora wightii*

2003. Medicinal Plants of India. Multicoloured.
2123 5r. Type **1610** 75 75
2124 5r. *Bacopa monnieri* 75 75
2125 5r. *Emblica officinalis* 75 75
2126 5r. *Withania somnifera* 75 75
MS2127 130×80 mm. Nos. 2123/6 2·75 3·00

1611 Durga Das

2003. Durga Das (journalist and newspaper editor) Commemoration.
2128 **1611** 5r. multicoloured 1·00 75

1612 Kishore Kumar

2003. "Golden Voices of Yesteryear". Multicoloured.
2129 5r. Type **1612** 70 70
2130 5r. Mukesh 70 70
2131 5r. Mohammed Rafi 70 70
2132 5r. Hemant Kumar 70 70
MS2133 89×105 mm. Nos. 2129/32 2·50 2·75

1613 Mt. Everest

2003. 50th Anniv of Ascent of Mount Everest by Edmund Hilary and Tenzing Norgay. Multicoloured.
2134 15r. Type **1613** 2·25 2·50
MS2135 74×97 mm. 15r. As Type **1613** 2·25 2·50

1614 Muktabai

2003. Muktabai (poet) Commemoration.
2136 **1614** 5r. multicoloured 1·00 70

1615 Natesa (12th—Century Bronze from Tanjavur)

2003. Government Museum, Chennai. Multicoloured.
2137 5r. Type **1615** 60 60
2138 5r. Amravati sculpture (medallion) 60 60
2139 15r. Museum Theatre (57×28 mm) 1·50 1·75
MS2140 161×73 mm. Nos. 2137/9 2·50 2·75

No. **MS**2140 is also illustrated with other exhibits from the Government Museum.

1616 Vishwanath Kashinath Rajwade

2003. 140th Birth Anniv of Vishwanath Kashinath Rajwade (historian).
2141 **1616** 5r. lilac 70 60

1617 Bade Ghulam Ali Khan

2003. Bade Ghulam Ali Khan (singer) Commemoration.
2142 **1617** 5r. multicoloured 1·00 70

1618 Three Stylised Children and Rainbow

2003. Autism. Our World of Special Children.
2143 **1618** 5r. multicoloured 1·00 70

1619 Vishal Badri Temple, Badrinath

2003. Temple Architecture. Multicoloured.
2144 5r. Type **1619** 70 70
2145 5r. Mallikarjunaswamy Temple, Srisailam 70 70
2146 5r. Tripureswari Temple, Udaipur 70 70
2147 5r. Jagannath Temple, Puri 70 70

1620 Janardan Swami

2003. 89th Birth Anniv of Janardan Swami (spiritual leader).
2148 **1620** 5r. brown 75 60

1621 Athirapalli Falls

2003. Waterfalls. Multicoloured.

2149	5r. Type **1621**	60	60
2150	5r. Kempty Falls	60	60
2151	5r. Kakolat Falls	60	60
2152	15r. Jog Falls	1·60	1·75
MS2153	134×87 mm. Nos. 2149/52	3·00	3·25

1622 G. Sankara Kurup

2003. Malayalam Jnanpith Literary Award Winners Commemoration. Each black and cream.

2154	5r. Type **1622**	70	70
2155	5r. S. K. Pottekkatt	70	70
2156	5r. Thakazhi Sivasankara Pillai	70	70

1623 Dr. Kota Shivarama Karanth

2003. Dr. Kota Shivarama Karanth (writer and reformer) Commemoration.

2157	**1623**	5r. multicoloured	70	55

1624 Narendra Mohan

2003. First Death Anniv of Narendra Mohan (writer and editor of Dainik Jagran).

2158	**1624**	5r. brown and flesh	70	55

1625 Govindrao Pansare

2003. 90th Birth Anniv of Govindrao Pansare (martyr).

2159	**1625**	5r. multicoloured	70	55

1626 Fish

2003. Greetings Stamps. Multicoloured.

2160	4r. Type **1626**	70	70
2161	4r. Birds	70	70
2162	5r. Butterfly	70	70
2163	5r. Squirrels	70	70

1627 Satellite Dish, Telegraph Key and Mobile Phone

2003. 150th Anniv of Telecommunications.

2164	**1627**	5r. multicoloured	1·00	70

1628 Bengal Engineer Group memorial, Roorkee and Railroad

2003. Bicentenary of the Benegal Sappers and Miners.

2165	**1628**	5r. multicoloured	1·00	80

1629 Steam Locomotive on the Kalka-Shimla Railway

2003. Centenary of the Kalka-Shimla Railway.

2166	**1629**	5r. multicoloured	1·25	1·00

1630 Python

2003. Snakes. Multicoloured.

2167	5r. Type **630**	70	70
2168	5r. Bamboo pit viper	70	70
2169	5r. King cobra	70	70
2170	5r. Gliding Snake	70	70
MS2171	169×123 mm. Nos. 2167/70	2·50	2·50

1631 Children

2003. Children's Day.

2172	**1631**	5r. multicoloured	75	55

1632 Soldiers of the 2 Guards Battalion

2003. 225th Anniv of the 2 Guards (formerly the 1 Grenadiers).

2173	**1632**	5r. green, vermilion and yellow	1·00	80

1633 Harivansh Rai Bachchan

2003. Harivansh Rai Bachchan (poet) Commemoration.

2174	**1633**	5r. black and brown	65	55

1634 Cockerel

2003. Early French and Indian Art. Multicoloured.

2175	22r. Type **1634**	2·25	2·50
2176	22r. Peacock	2·25	2·50
MS2177	116×95 mm. Nos. 2175/6	4·50	5·00

1635 Yashpal

2003. Birth Centenary of Yashpal (revoluntioanry writer).

2178	**1635**	5r. multicoloured	65	55

1636 Cheomseongdae Astronomical Observatory, Gyeongju

2003. 30th Anniv of Diplomatic Relations with South Korea. Multicoloured.

2179	15r. Type **1636**	1·50	1·75
2180	15r. Jantar Mantar astronomical observatory, Jaipur	1·50	1·75

1637 Parliament Building

2003. 200th Session of Rajya Sabha (Council of States).

2181	**1637**	5r. multicoloured	65	55

1638 Mukut Behari Lal Bhargava

2003. Birth Centenary of Mukut Behari Lal Bhargava (politician and lawyer).

2182	**1638**	5r. multicoloured	70	60

1639 Swami Swaroopanandji

2003. Birth Centenary of Swami Swaroopanandji (religious leader).

2183	**1639**	5r. multicoloured	65	55

1640 Actors

2003. 50th Anniv of the Sangeet Natak Akademi. Multicoloured.

2184	5r. Type **1640**	75	75
2185	5r. Dancers	75	75
2186	5r. Musicians	75	75
MS2187	139×82 mm. Nos. 2183/5	2·00	2·00

1641 Lalan Fakir

2003. Folk Music. Multicoloured.

2188	5r. Type **1641**	70	70
2189	5r. Allah Jilai Bai	70	70

1642 Major Somnath Sharma

2003. 80th Birth Anniv of Major Somnath Sharma.

2190	**1642**	5r. multicoloured	60	50

1643 Siddavanahalli Nijalingappa

2003. Siddavanahalli Nijalingappa Commemoration (politician and lawyer).

2191	**1643**	5r. multicoloured	60	50

1644 Chintaman Dwarkanath Deshmukh

2004. Chintaman Dwarkanath Deshmukh (finance expert) Commemoration.

2192	**1644**	5r. multicoloured	60	50

1645 Nani Ardeshir Palkhivala

2004. 2nd Death Anniv of Nani Ardeshir Palkhivala (jurist).

2193	**1645**	5r. multicoloured	75	60

1646 Dr. Bhalchandra Digamber Garware

2004. Birth Centenary (2003) of Dr. Bhalchandra Digamber Garware (industrialist).
2194 **1646** 5r. multicoloured 60 50

1647 Annamacharya

2004. Annamacharya (saint and composer of devotional songs) Commemoration.
2195 **1647** 5r. multicoloured 60 50

1648 9th Battalion of the Madras Regiment, Travancore

2004. Commemoration of the 9th Battalion of the Madras Regiment, Travancore.
2196 **1648** 5r. multicoloured 1·00 80

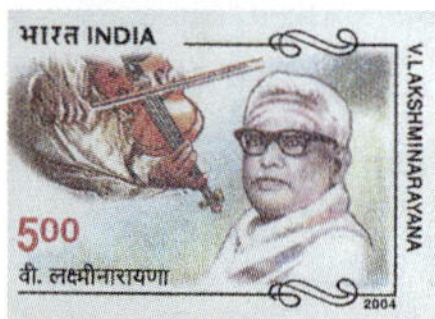

1649 V. Lakshminarayana

2004. V. Lakshminarayana (violinist) Commemoration.
2197 **1649** 5r. multicoloured 1·00 75

1650 INS *Tarangini*

2004. Circumnavigation Voyage of INS Tarangini (three masted barque).
2198 **1650** 5r. multicoloured 1·00 75
MS2199 109×81 mm. No. 2198 1·00 1·00

1651 Illustrated Blocks, Stylised Stairs and Sheaves of Paper

2004. Indian Institute of Social Welfare and Business Management, Kolkata.
2200 **1651** 5r. multicoloured 70 55

1652 Baji Rao Peshwa

2004. Baji Rao Peshwa Commemoration.
2201 **1652** 5r. multicoloured 65 55

1653 Siddhar Swamigal

2004. Birth Centenary of Siddhar Swamigal (spiritual leader).
2202 **1653** 5r. multicoloured 60 50

1654 Indra Chandra Shastri

2004. 92nd Birth Anniv of Indra Chandra Shastri (philosopher).
2203 **1654** 5r. black, deep green and green 60 50

1655 Woodstock School

2004. Woodstock School.
2204 **1655** 5r. multicoloured 60 50

1656 Jyotiprasad Agarwalla

2004. Birth Centenary of Jyotiprasad Agarwalla (2003) (poet and film maker).
2205 **1656** 5r. multicoloured 60 50

1657 P. N. Panicker

2004. Reading Day. Ninth Death Anniv of P. N. Panicker (education reformer).
2206 **1657** 5r. multicoloured 60 50

1658 Nain Singh

2004. The Great Trigonometrical Survey. Multicoloured.
2207 5r. Type **1658** 65 65
2208 5r. Triangles (40×29 mm) 65 65
2209 5r. Radhanath Sikdar 65 65
MS2210 117×75 mm. Nos. 2207/9 1·75 1·90

1659 Aacharya Bhikshu

2004. Aacharya Bhikshu (philosophical writer and social reformer) Commemoration.
2211 **1659** 5r. multicoloured 70 55

1660 Wrestling

2004. Olympic Games, Athens. Multicoloured.
2212 5r. Type **1660** 70 70
2213 5r. Athletics 70 70
2214 15r. Shooting 1·60 1·75
2215 15r. Hockey 1·60 1·75

1661 Kabir (Indian)

2004. Iranian and Indian Poets. T **1661** and similar vert designs. Multicoloured.
2216 15r. Type **1661** 1·25 1·40
2216b 15r. 1·25 1·40
Stamps of the same design were issued by Iran.

1662 Murasoli Maran

2004. 70th Birthday Anniv of Murasoli Maran (writer).
2217 **1662** 5r. multicoloured 60 50

1663 Rajiv Gandhi (President, 1984—89)

2004. 60th Birth Anniv of Rajiv Gandhi and Renewable Energy Day.
2218 **1663** 5r. multicoloured 70 55

1664 S. S. *Vasan*

2004. Birth Centenary of S. S. Vasan (journalist and film producer).
2219 **1664** 5r. multicoloured 60 50

1665 Panini

2004. Panini Sanskrit Grammar (c. 500 BC).
2220 **1665** 5r. multicoloured 60 50

1666 K. Subrahmanyam

2004. Birth Centenary of K. Subrahmanyam (film maker).
2221 **1666** 5r. multicoloured 60 50

1667 M. C. Chagla

2004. M. C. Chagla (Judge) Commemoration.
2222 **1667** 5r. multicoloured 60 50

1668 Shri N. "Tirupur" Kumaran

2004. Birth Centenary of Tirupur Kumaran (revolutionary).
2223 **1668** 5r. multicoloured 60 50

1669 Early Stamp, Mail Ship and Carriage

2004. 150th Anniv of India Post. Multicoloured.
2224 5r. Type **1669** 75 75
2225 5r. Airmail stamp and postal runner 75 75
2226 5r. General Post Office, Calcutta, stamp and pillar box 75 75
2227 5r. Computer terminal and modern postal services 75 75
MS2228 222×114 mm. Nos. 2224/7 2·75 3·00

1670 Neerja Bhanot (Purser, Pan American World Airways)

2004. Winners of the Ashoka Chakra Bravery Award. Multicoloured.
2229 5r. Type **1670** 1·00 1·00
2230 5r. Randhir Prasad Verma (Superintendent of Police) 1·00 1·00

1671 Guru Dutt

2004. 40th Death Anniv of Guru Dutt (film maker).
2231 **1671** 5r. multicoloured 60 50

1672 Indian Soldiers and Peace Dove

2004. Indian Army in UN Peacekeeping Operations.
2232 **1672** 5r. multicoloured 60 60
MS2233 99×99 mm. No. 2232 60 70

1673 Marudhu Pandiar Brothers

2004. Marudhu Pandiar Brothers (anti-colonial leaders and rulers of Sivaganga). Commemoration.
2234 **1673** 5r. multicoloured 60 50

1674 Kites

2004. Greetings Stamps. Multicoloured.
2235 4r. Type **1674** 55 55
2236 4r. Dolls 55 55

1675 Dr. S. Roerich

2004. Birth Centenary of Dr. S. Roerich (artist).
2237 **1675** 5r. multicoloured 60 50

1676 Tenneti Viswanatham

2004. 25th Death Anniv of Tenneti Viswanatham (politician).
2238 **1676** 5r. multicoloured 60 50

1677 Schoolgirls and Rural Village

2004. Children's Day.
2239 **1677** 5r. multicoloured 60 50

1678 Walchand Hirachand

2004. 121st Birth Anniv of Walchand Hirachand (industrialist).
2240 **1678** 5r. multicoloured 60 50

1679 Dula Bhaya Kag

2004. Birth Centenary (2003) of Dula Bhaya Kag (poet and nationalist).
2241 **1679** 5r. multicoloured 60 50

1680 Khas Mahal (image scaled to 51% of original size)

2004. 9th Aga Khan Award for Architecture. Agra Fort. Multicoloured.
2242 15r. Khas Mahal 1·50 2·00
2243 15r. Agrs Fort 1·50 2·00
MS2244 234×105 mm. 15r. Type **1680**; 15r. Agra Fort 3·00 4·00

1681 Bhagat Puran Singh

2004. Birth Centenary of Bhagat Puran Singh (Sikh humanitarian and founder of Pingalwara home for destitute, Amritsar).
2245 **1681** 5r. multicoloured 55 55

1682 Sculpture, Nupilal Memorial Complex, Imphal

2004. Centenary of Nupi Lan ("Women's War") Protest Movement, Manipur.
2246 **1682** 5r. multicoloured 55 55

1683 Natural and Mechanical Symbols of Energy Production

2004. Energy Conservation.
2247 **1683** 5r. multicoloured 55 55

1684 Taj Mahal

2004. Taj Mahal.
2248 **1684** 15r. multicoloured 1·75 2·00
MS2249 98×143 mm. No. 2248 1·75 2·00

1685 Script

2004. 50th Anniv of Sahitya Akademi (literature promotion organization).
2250 **1685** 5r. multicoloured 55 55

1686 Bhaskara Sethupathy

2004. Bhaskara Sethupathy (ruler of Ramanathapuram state, 1889–1903) Commem.
2251 **1686** 5r. multicoloured 55 55

1687 Himalayan Sheep Dog

2005. Indian Breeds of Dogs. Multicoloured.
2252 5r. Type **1687** 60 65
2253 5r. Rampur hound 60 65
2254 5r. Mudhol hound 60 65
2255 15r. Rajapalayam 1·50 1·60
Nos. 2252/3 and 2254/5 were printed together, se-tenant, forming a composite background design.

1688 Padampat Singhania

2005. Birth Centenary of Padampat Singhania (industrialist).
2256 **1688** 5r. multicoloured 55 55

1689 Rotary Emblem and Silhouette of Hands

2005. Centenary of Rotary International.
2257 **1689** 5r. multicoloured 55 55

1690 Krishan Kant

2005. Krishan Kant (Vice-President of India 1997–2002) Commem.
2258 **1690** 5r. multicoloured 55 55

1691 Madhavrao Scindia

2005. Madhavrao Scindia (politician) Commemoration.
2259 **1691** 5r. multicoloured 55 55

1692 Clouded Leopard

2005. Flora and Fauna of North East India. Multicoloured.
2260 5r. Type **1692** 55 55
2261 5r. Dillenia indica 55 55
2262 5r. Mishmi takin 55 55
2263 5r. Pitcher plant 55 55
MS2264 109×100 mm. Nos. 2260/3 2·00 2·00

1693 Einstein and Theory of Relativity

2005. International Year of Physics.
2265 **1693** 5r. multicoloured 55 55

1694 Gandhi leading Dandi March

2005. 75th Anniv of Dandi March. Multicoloured.
2266 5r. Type **1694** 55 55
2267 5r. Gandhi and headline "GREAT MARCH FOR LIBERTY BEGINS" 55 55
2268 5r. Gandhi picking up salt and map showing route 55 55
2269 5r. Gandhi and declaration 55 55
MS2270 125×165 mm. Nos. 2265/9 2·00 2·00
Nos. 2266/9 have lilac backgrounds, but stamps from **MS**2269 have mauve backgrounds.

1695 Soldiers in Early and Modern Uniforms

2005. 300 Years of 15 Punjab (Patiala).
2271 **1695** 5r. multicoloured 55 55

1696 Nehru and Conference Hall

2005. 50th Anniv of Bandung Conference of African and Asian Nations, Bandung, Java, Indonesia.
2272 **1696** 15r. multicoloured 1·25 1·40

1697 Narayan Meghaji Lokhande

2005. Narayan Meghaji Lokhande (campaigner for worker's rights) Commemoration.
2273 **1697** 5r. multicoloured 55 55

1698 Emblem and Symbols of Farming and Industry

2005. Centenary of Co-operative Movement in India.
2274 **1698** 5r. multicoloured 55 55

1699 Family and Bird in Park and Urban Landscape

2005. World Environment Day. Green Cities.
2275 **1699** 5r. multicoloured 55 55

1700 Abdul Qaiyum Ansari

2005. Birth Centenary of Abdul Qaiyum Ansari (nationalist politician).
2276 **1700** 5r. multicoloured 55 55

1701 Dheeran Chinnamalai

2005. Death Bicentenary of Dheeran Chinnamalai (warrior and ruler of Kongu Province).
2277 **1701** 5r. multicoloured 55 55

1702 Seals and Bank Buildings (image scaled to 57% of original size)

2005. Bicentenary of State Bank of India.
2278 **1702** 15r. multicoloured 1·25 1·40

1703 Children planting Flower of Flags

2005. International Day of Peace.
2279 **1703** 5r. multicoloured 55 55

1704 A. M. M. Murugappa Chettiar

2005. 40th Death Anniv of A. M. M. Murugappa Chettiar (industrialist).
2280 **1704** 5r. multicoloured 55 55

1705 Pratap Singh Kairon

2005. 40th Death Anniv of Pratap Singh Kairon (Chief Minister of Punjab, 1956–64).
2281 **1705** 5r. multicoloured 55 55

1706 Dr. T. S. Soundram and Literacy Emblem

2005. Dr. T. S. Soundram (Deputy Minister for Education, 1962) Commemoration.
2282 **1706** 5r. multicoloured 55 55

1707 Victorian Crown Type Letter Box, 1856–7

2005. Letter Boxes. Multicoloured.
2283 5r. Type **1707** 60 60
2284 5r. Hexagonal Penfold letter box, 1866–79 60 60
2285 5r. Two cylindrical letter boxes, from 1879 60 60
2286 5r. Two modern TV type letter boxes 60 60
MS2287 164×118 mm. Nos. 2283/6 2·25 2·25

1708 Kavimani Desiga Vinayagam Pillai

2005. Kavimani Desiga Vinayagam Pillai (Tamil poet) Commemoration.
2288 **1708** 5r. carmine, black and purple 55 55

1709 Vi Kalyanasundarnar

2005. Vi Kalyanasundarnar (nationalist and Tamil scholar) Commemoration.
2289 **1709** 5r. multicoloured 55 55

1710 Ayothidhasa Pandithar

2005. 160th Birth Anniv of Ayothidhasa Pandithar (social reformer).
2290 **1710** 5r. purple 55 55

1711 Prabodh Chandra

2005. Prabodh Chandra (politician) Commemoration.
2291 **1711** 5r. multicoloured 55 55

1712 Festival (Pallavi Majumder)

2005. Children's Day.
2292 **1712** 5r. multicoloured 55 55

1713 Children riding Elephant

2005. 50th Anniv of Children's Film Society.
2293 **1713** 5r. multicoloured 55 55

1714 Map of South Asia and Africa, Ship, Airliner and Buildings

2005. Centenary of PHD Chamber of Commerce and Industry.
2294 **1714** 5r. multicoloured 55 55

1715 Globe

2005. World Summit on the Information Society, Tunis.
2295 **1715** 5r. multicoloured 55 55

1716 Kolkata Police Headquarters

2005. 150th Anniv of Kolkata Police Commissionerate.
2296 **1716** 5r. multicoloured 55 55

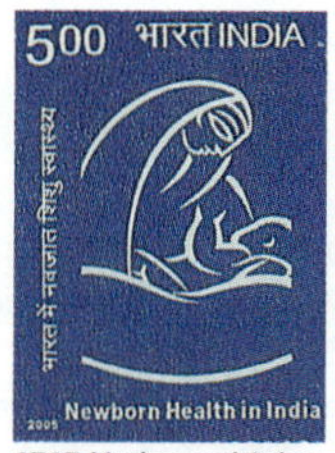

1717 Mother and Baby

2005. Newborn Health.
2297 **1717** 5r. ultramarine 55 55

1718 Jawaharlal Darda

2005. Jawaharlal Darda (founder of Lokmat newspaper) Commemoration.
2298 **1718** 5r. multicoloured 55 55

1719 *Udaygiri*, *Kora* and *Delhi*

2005. Builder's Navy.
2299 **1719** 5r. multicoloured 55 55

1720 M. S. Subbulakshmi

2005. M. S. Subbulakshmi (Carnatic classical singer) Commemoration.
2300 **1720** 5r. multicoloured 55 55

1721 New Railway Carriages

2005. 50th Anniv of Integral Passenger Railway Coach Factory, Chennai.
2301 **1721** 5r. multicoloured 55 55

1722 Students and Jadavpur University

2005. 50th Anniv of Jadavpur University.
2302 **1722** 5r. multicoloured 55 55

1723 Sepecat Jaguar Fighter and Consolidated B-24 Liberator and English Electric Canberra Bombers

2005. 55th Anniv of 16 Squadron Air Force.
2303 **1723** 5r. multicoloured 1·00 70

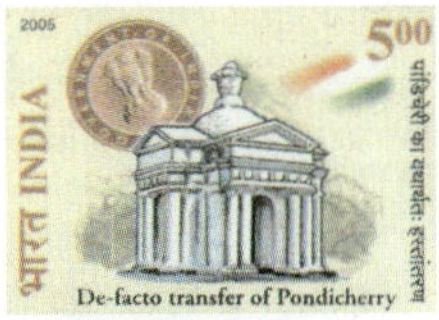

1724 Park Monument, Pondicherry and Seal

2005. 50th Anniv of De Facto Transfer of Pondicherry by the French to India.
2304 **1724** 5r. multicoloured 55 55

1725 Sweet Rice in Clay Pot, Cattle and Crops

2006. Pongal (Tamil harvest festival).
2305 **1725** 5r. multicoloured 55 55

1726 A. V. Meiyappan Chettiar (founder/film director)

2006. 60th Anniv of AVM Studios.
2306 **1726** 5r. multicoloured 55 55

1727 N. M. R. Subbaraman

2006. Birth Centenary of N. M. R. Subbaraman (nationalist and social reformer).
2307 **1727** 5r. multicoloured 55 55

1728 Early Soldier and Cavalcade of the Regiment

2006. 150th Anniv of Third Battalion the Sikh Regiment.
2308 **1728** 5r. multicoloured 1·00 70

1729 INS *Viraat* (aircraft carrier) and BAE Sea Harrier Fighter Plane

2006. President's Review of the Fleet, Visakhapatnam. Multicoloured.
2309 5r. Type **1729** 70 70
2310 5r. Talwar and Brahmaputra class frigates and Sea King helicopter 70 70
2311 5r. Indian Coast Guard offshore patrol ship *Vigraha*, Dornier aircraft and Sandhayak class survey ship 70 70
2312 5r. Sindhughosh and Sishumar class submarines 70 70

1730 Thirumuruga Kiruhananda Variyar

2006. Birth Centenary of Thirumuruga Kiruhananda Variyar (Tamil scholar).
2313 **1730** 5r. purple 55 55

1731 Devaneya Pavanar

2006. 25th Death Anniv of Devaneya Pavanar (Tamil scholar, linguist and author).
2314 **1731** 5r. blue and deep blue 55 55

1732 Dr. U. V. Swaminatha Iyer

2006. 150th Birth Anniv (2005) of Dr. U. V. Swaminatha Iyer (Tamil scholar and researcher).
2315 **1732** 5r. purple 55 55

1733 Tamilavel Umamaheswarar

2006. Tamilavel Umamaheswarar (Tamil scholar) Commemoration.
2316 **1733** 5r. grey and black 55 55

1734 St. Bede's College

2006. Centenary (2004) of St. Bede's College, Shimla.
2317 **1734** 5r. multicoloured 55 55

1735 Gemini Ganesan

2006. Gemini Ganesan (actor) Commemoration.
2318 **1735** 5r. brown, grey and black 55 55

1736 St. John Bosco

2006. Centenary of Don Bosco Salesians in India.
2319 **1736** 5r. multicoloured 55 55

1737 M. Singaravelar

2006. 60th Death Anniv of M. Singaravelar (labour leader and social reformer).
2320 **1737** 5r. multicoloured 55 55

1738 Emblem

2006. World Consumer Rights Day.
2321 **1738** 5r. multicoloured 55 55

1739 Institute Building, Researchers and Crops

2006. Centenary of Indian Agricultural Research Institute, Pusa, New Delhi.
2322 **1739** 5r. multicoloured 55 55

1740 Tank

2006. 50th Anniv of 62 Cavalry (armoured regiment).
2323 **1740** 5r. multicoloured 55 55

1741 . Nati Dance, Himachal Pradesh

2006. Folk Dances. Multicoloured.
2324 15r. Type **1741** 2·00 2·00
2325 15r. Stamna or kouza (pitcher) dance, Cyprus 2·00 2·00
MS2326 146×92 mm. Nos. 2324/5 4·00 4·25

Stamps in similar designs were issued by Cyprus on the same date.

1742 Calcutta Girls' High School

2006. 150th Anniv of Calcutta Girls' High School.
2327 **1742** 5r. multicoloured 55 55

1743 Pannalal Barupal

2006. Pannalal Barupal (social reformer and MP 1952–77) Commemoration.
2328 **1743** 5r. multicoloured 55 55

1744 Kurinji Flowers

2006. Kurinji Flowers (Strobilanthes kunthiranus).
2329 **1744** 15r. multicoloured 1·25 1·40
MS2330 125×84 mm. No. 2329 1·25 1·40

1745 Pond and Tree in Desert

2006. Rainwater Harvesting.
2331 **1745** 5r. multicoloured 55 55

1746 Sri Pratap College, Srinagar

2006. Centenary (2005) of Sri Pratap College, Srinagar.
2332 **1746** 5r. multicoloured 55 55

1747 Entrance to Indraprastha Girls' School

2006. Centenary (2004) of Indraprastha Girls' School, Delhi.
2333 **1747** 5r. multicoloured 55 55

1748 Vellore Fort

2006. Bicentenary of the Vellore Mutiny.
2334 **1748** 5r. multicoloured 55 55

1749 Voorhees College, Vellore

2006. Centenary of Voorhees College, Vellore (2005).
2335 **1749** 5r. multicoloured 55 55

1750 High Court Buildings at Jammu and Srinagar

2006. High Court of Jammu and Kashmir.
2336 **1750** 5r. multicoloured 55 55

1751 Pankaj Kumar Mullick

2006. Birth Centenary of Pankaj Kumar Mullick (singer and composer) (2005).

2337 **1751** 5r. multicoloured 55 55

1752 Oil Well and Offshore Oil Rig

2006. Oil and Natural Gas Corporation Limited.

2338 **1752** 5r. multicoloured 55 55

1753 Ma. Po. Sivagnanam

2006. Birth Centenary of Ma. Po. Sivagnanam (Tamil writer).

2339 **1753** 5r. multicoloured 55 55

1754 University of Madras

2006. 150th Anniv of University of Madras.

2340 **1754** 5r. multicoloured 55 55

1755 L. V. Prasad

2006. L. V. Prasad (film director) Commemoration.

2341 **1755** 5r. multicoloured 55 55

1756 Indian Merchants and Merchant's Chamber Buildings

2006. Centenary (2007) of Indian Merchants' Chamber.

2342 **1756** 5r. multicoloured 55 55

1757 Early 20th-century Bronze Replica of Equestrian Deity Rao Dev from Bastar, Madhya Pradesh

2006. Ancient Art. Multicoloured.

2343 15r. Type **1757** 1·25 1·40

2344 15r. Ancient bronze horse statue, from Murun city, Mongolia 1·25 1·40

MS2345 110×60 mm. Nos. 2343/4 2·50 2·75

Stamps in similar designs were issued by Mongolia.

1758 Greater Adjutant Stork

2006. Endangered Birds of India. Multicoloured.

2346 5r. Type **1758** 55 55

2347 5r. Nilgiri laughing thrush 55 55

2348 5r. Manipur bush-quail 55 55

2349 5r. Lesser florican 55 55

MS2350 109×88 mm. Nos. 2346/9 2·00 2·25

1759 Evolution of Coins in Gwalior Area

2006. Centenary of Madhya Pradesh Chamber of Commerce and Industry, Gwalior.

2351 **1759** 5r. multicoloured 55 55

1760 Bishwanath Roy

2006. Birth Centenary of Bishwanath Roy (MP 1952–77).

2352 **1760** 5r. multicoloured 55 55

1761 G. Varadaraj

2006. 70th Birth Anniv of G. Varadaraj (industrialist and educationist).

2353 **1761** 5r. multicoloured 55 55

1762 Roop Kund

2006. Himalayan Lakes. Multicoloured.

2354 5r. Type **1762** 55 55

2355 5r. Chandra Tal (vert) 55 55

2356 5r. Tsomo Riri 55 55

2357 5r. Sela 55 55

2358 5r. Tsangu 55 55

1763 Lala Deen Dayal and Photographs

2006. Death Centenary of Lala Deen Dayal (pioneer photographer).

2359 **1763** 5r. multicoloured 55 55

1764 Boy Krishna subduing the Serpent Kaliya

2006. Children's Day. Design showing children's paintings by Keval Thakkar and Shivanna Madvi. Multicoloured.

2360 5r. Type **1764** 55 55

2361 5r. Archer 55 55

MS2362 72×133 mm. As Nos. 2360/1 1·10 1·10

1765 "The Tribune" Newspapers

2006. 125th Anniv of "The Tribune" Newspaper.

2363 **1765** 5r. multicoloured 55 55

1766 AIDS Ribbon and Crowd

2006. World AIDS Day.

2364 **1766** 5r. black, scarlet and blue 55 55

1767 Soldier of British Expeditionary Forces in Persia, 1856

2006. 150th Anniv of Indian Army Field Post Offices. Multicoloured.

2365 5r. Type **1767** 55 55

2366 5r. Soldier in desert writing letter 55 55

2367 5r. Soldier reading letter and field post office 55 55

2368 5r. Mail delivery by helicopter to soldiers in Himalayas 55 55

Nos. 2365/8 were printed together, *se-tenant*, in horizontal strips of four stamps

1768 Bartholomaeus Ziegenbalg

2006. 300th Anniv of Arrival of Bartholomaeus Ziegenbalg (first Protestant missionary) in India.

2369 **1768** 5r. multicoloured 55 55

1769 Elephant in Forest (sandalwood carving)

2006. Sandalwood.

2370 **1769** 15r. multicoloured 1·25 1·40

MS2371 100×87 mm. No. 2370 1·25 1·40

Nos. 2370/MS2371 were embossed with sandalwood powder, giving sandalwood fragrance.

1770 Girl Tightrope Walker

2006. "Stop Child Labour". Multicoloured.

2372 5r. Type **1770** 55 55

2373 5r. Boy labourer with hoe 55 55

2374 5r. Boy serving tea 55 55

2375 5r. Boy in fields carrying heavy basket 55 55

1771 Bimal Roy

2007. Bimal Roy (film director) Commemoration.

2376 **1771** 5r. multicoloured 55 55

1772 Batsman and Bowler

2007. 70th Anniv of Tamil Nadu Cricket Association.

2377 **1772** 5r. multicoloured 55 55

1773 "Bhim"

2007. Indian Roses. Multicoloured.

2378 5r. Type **1773** 55 55

2379 15r. "Delhi Princess" 55 55

2380 15r. "Jawahar" 55 55

2381 5r. "Neelam" 55 55

MS2382 87×117 mm. Nos. 2378/81 2·00 2·00

Nos. 2378/MS2382 have a rose fragrance.

1774 Manoharbhai Patel

2007. Birth Centenary (2006) of Manoharbhai Patel (industrialist and educationist).

2383 **1774** 5r. multicoloured 55 55

1775 Elephants at Sonepur Fair, Bihar

2007. Fairs of India. Multicoloured.

2384 5r. Type **1775** 55 55

2385 5r. Pushkar Fair, Rajasthan 55 55

2386 5r. Goa Carnival 55 55

2387 5r. Baul singers at Baul Mela, West Bengal 55 55

MS2388 155×97 mm. Nos. 2384/7 2·00 2·00

1776 Two Women

2007. International Women's Day. Paintings by Joyshree Burman. Multicoloured.

2389	5r. Type **1776**	60	65
2390	5r. Woman holding fan	60	65
2391	15r. Woman holding peacock	1·40	1·50
2392	15r. Woman and temple	1·40	1·50
MS2393	130×76 mm. Nos. 2389/2	3·50	3·75

1777 Raj Narain

2007. 90th Birth Anniv of Raj Narain (Minister of Health 1977–80).

2394	**1777**	5r. grey, red and black	55	55

1778 Mehboob Khan and Scene from *Mother India*

2007. Birth Centenary (2006) of Mehboob Khan (film director).

2395	**1778**	5r. multicoloured	55	55

1779 Dr. R. M. Alagappa Chettiar

2007. 50th Death Anniv of Dr. R. M. Alagappa Chettiar (educationist and industrialist).

2396	**1779**	5r. multicoloured	55	55

1780 Statue of Prince Siddhartha Gautama

2007. 2550 Years of Mahaparinirvana of the Buddha. Multicoloured.

2397	5r. Type **1780**	55	55
2398	5r. Two images of Buddha and stone carving (horiz)	55	55
2399	5r. Stone meditating Buddha head from Sarnath	55	55
2400	5r. Bronze ascetic Buddha from Myanmar	55	55
2401	5r. Bhumisaparsha Buddha holding nectar of immortality in jar	55	55
2402	5r. Dharma Chakra and other Hinayama symbols (horiz)	55	55
MS2403	219×135 mm. Nos. 2397/402	3·00	3·00

1781 Tiger, Sambar and Chital Deer, Bandhavgarh National Park, Madhya Pradesh

2007. National Parks of India. Multicoloured.

2404	5r. Type **1781**	55	55
2405	5r. Gaur and elephants, Bandipur National Park, Karnataka	55	55
2406	5r. Great one-horned rhinoceros, Kaziranga National Park, Assam	55	55
2407	5r. Leopard, deer and sloth bear, Mudumalai National Park	55	55
2408	5r. Elephant, Periyar National Park, Kerala	55	55

1782 Battle at Lucknow

2007. Bicentenary of First War of Independence. Multicoloured.

2409	5r. Type **1782**	60	60
2410	15r. Cavalry and Foot Soldiers in Battle at Kanpur	1·40	1·50
MS2411	150×118 mm. Nos. 2409/10	2·00	2·10

1783 Saint Vallalar

2007. Saint Vallalar (Ramalinga Adigal) Commemoration.

2412	**1783**	5r. multicoloured	55	55

1784 Maraimalai Adigal

2007. Maraimalai Adigal (Tamil scholar) Commemoration.

2413	**1784**	5r. black, yellow and scarlet	55	55

1785 V. G. Suryanarayana Sastriar

2007. Suryanarayana Sastriar (Tamil scholar) Commemoration.

2414	**1785**	5r. multicoloured	55	55

1786 Howrah Bridge, Kolkata

2007. Landmark Bridges of India. Multicoloured.

2415	5r. Type **1786**	55	55
2416	5r. Mahatma Gandhi Setu, Patna	55	55
2417	5r. Pamban Bridge over Palk Strait	55	55
2418	5r. Vidyasagar Setu, Kolkata	55	55
MS2419	150×117 mm. Nos. 2415/18	2·00	2·00

1787 J. P. Naik

2007. Birth Centenary of Dr. J. P. Naik (educationist).

2420	**1787**	5r. cinnamon, black and blue	55	55

1788 Building Facade

2007. 53rd Commonwealth Parliamentary Conference.

2421	**1788**	15r. multicoloured	1·25	1·40

1789 S. D. Burman

2007. Birth Centenary (2006) of Sachin Dev Burman (singer and composer).

2422	**1789**	15r. multicoloured	1·25	1·40

1790 Gandhi expelled from Train, South Africa, 1893

2007. Centenary of Satyagraha. Multicoloured.

2423	5r. Type **1790**	55	55
2424	5r. Gandhi, Indian immigrant in Transvaal and *Indian Opinion* newspaper, 1906	55	55
2425	5r. Gandhi addressing crowd, South Africa, 1906	55	55
2426	5r. Gandhi leading Dandi March, India, 1930	55	55
MS2427	106×112 mm. As Nos. 2423/6	2·00	2·00

1791 Advanced Light Helicopter Dhruv

2007. 75th Anniv of the Indian Air Force. Multicoloured.

2428	5r. Type **1791**	55	55
2429	5r. AWACS (Airborne Warning and Control System) (83×31 mm)	55	55
2430	5r. Westland Wapiti	55	55
2431	15r. IL-78 fighter planes (83×31 mm)	1·40	1·50
MS2432	220×122 mm. Nos. 2428/31	2·75	3·00

1792 Parachutist

2007. 4th CISM Military World Games, Hyderabad and Mumbai.

2433	5r. Type **1792**	55	55
2434	5r. Footballer	55	55
2435	5r. Swimmer	55	55
MS2436	83×130 mm. Nos. 2433/5	1·50	1·50

1793 Maharashtra Police Academy

2007. Centenary of Maharashtra Police Academy.

2437	**1793**	5r. multicoloured	55	55

1794 Children (Swarali V. Bhakare)

2007. Children's Day. 'The Magic of the Night'. Showing children's paintings. Multicoloured.

2438	5r. Type **1794**	55	55
2439	5r. Night fishermen	55	55
MS2440	120×78 mm. Nos. 2438/9	1·10	1·10

1795 Processing Plant ('Biomass Energy')

2007. Renewable Energy. Multicoloured.

2441	5r. Type **1795**	55	55
2442	5r. Small hydropower	55	55
2443	5r. Wind energy (horiz)	55	55
2444	5r. Solar energy (horiz)	55	55
MS2445	123×100 mm. Nos. 2441/4	2·00	2·00

Nos. 2441/4 commemorate the Silver Jubilee of the Ministry of New and Renewable Energy.

1796 Veteran with Medals and Soldiers on Mountainside

2007. 150th Anniv of the Raising of the First Battalion of the Fourth Gorkha Rifles.

2446	**1796**	5r. multicoloured	55	55

1797 Silhouettes

2007. International Day of Disabled Persons.

2447	**1797**	5r. multicoloured	55	55

No. 2447 also has Braille inscriptions.

1798 The Daly College, Indore

2007. 125th Anniv of the Daly College, Indore.
2448 **1798** 5r. multicoloured 55 55

1799 Wilson College, Mumbai

2007. 175th Anniv of Wilson College, Mumbai.
2449 **1799** 5r. multicoloured 55 55

1800 Road leading into Sunset

2007. Greetings Stamps. Multicoloured.
2450 5r. Type **1800** 55 55
2451 5r. Water lily and fish 55 55
2452 5r. Bird in flight 55 55
2453 5r. Human face, flowers and rural houses 55 55
2454 5r. HAPPY NEW YEAR 55 55

1801 S. B. Chavan and Irrigation Project

2007. Shankarrao Bhaurao Chavan (parliamentarian) Commemoration.
2455 **1801** 5r. multicoloured 55 55

1802 Our Lady of Snows Shrine Basilica

2007. 425th Anniv of Our Lady of Snows Shrine Basilica, Tuticorin.
2456 **1802** 5r. multicoloured 55 55

1803 Human Profile and Waves

2007. National Water Year.
2457 **1803** 5r. multicoloured 55 55

1804 Ritwik Ghatak and Film Scene

2007. Ritwik Ghatak (film director) Commemoration.
2458 **1804** 5r. multicoloured 55 55

1805 *Papilio mayo* (Andaman mormon) (male)

2008. Endemic Butterflies of Andaman and Nicobar Islands. Multicoloured.
2459 5r. Type **1805** 55 55
2460 5r. *Papilio mayo* (female) 55 55
2461 5r. *Pachliopta rhodifer* (Andaman club tail) (female) 55 55
2462 5r. *Pachliopta rhodifer* (male) 55 55
MS2463 105×83 mm. Nos. 2459/62 2·00 2·00

1806 Dr. B. P. Pal, Roses and Disease Resistant Wheat

2008. Birth Centenary (2006) of Dr. Benjamin Peary Pal (agricultural scientist).
2464 **1806** 5r. multicoloured 55 55

1807 Dr. D. R. Gadgil

2008. Dr. D. R Gadgil (economist) Commemoration.
2465 **1807** 5r. multicoloured 55 55

1808 Damodaram Sanjeevaiah

2008. 87th Birth Anniv of Damodaram Sanjeevaiah (parliamentarian).
2466 **1808** 5r. multicoloured 55 55

1809 Maharshi Bulusu Sambamurthy

2008. Maharshi Bulusu Sambamurthy (patriot) Commemoration.
2467 **1809** 5r. multicoloured 55 55

1810 Madhubala

2008. 75th Birth Anniv of Madhubala (actress).
2468 **1810** 5r. multicoloured 55 55
MS2469 92×79 mm. No. 2468 55 55

1811 Asrar-Ul-Haq 'Majaaz'

2008. Birth Centenary (2009) of Asrar-Ul-Haq 'Majaaz' (Urdu poet).
2470 **1811** 5r. multicoloured 55 55

1812 Asokan Capitol

2008. Civil Service.
2471 **1812** 5r. multicoloured 1·00 1·00

1813 Steel Production

2008. Centenary of Tata Steel (2007).
2472 **1813** 5r. multicoloured 1·00 1·00

1814 Jasmine

2008. Jasmine. Multicoloured.
2473 5r. Type **1814** 50 50
2474 15r. Close-up of jasmine flowers (horiz) 1·40 1·40
MS2475 107×76 mm. Nos. 2473/4 2·75 2·75
Nos. 2473/**MS**2475 have a jasmine fragrance.

1815 Mosque ('Heritage Restoration')

2008. 30th Anniv of the Aga Khan Foundation. Multicoloured.
2476 5r. Type **1815** 50 50
2477 15r. Foundation projects ('Social Commitment') (67×38 mm) 1·40 1·40
MS2478 130×96 mm. Nos. 2476/7 2·75 2·75

1816 Shirdi Sai Baba

2008. 90th Death Anniv of Saint Shirdi Sai Baba.
2479 **1816** 5r. multicoloured 1·00 1·00

1817 Rajesh Pilot as Pilot and Politician

2008. Rajesh Pilot (Rajeshwar Prasad Singh Vidhudi) (parliamentarian) Commemoration.
2480 **1817** 5r. multicoloured 1·00 1·00

1818 Henning Holck-Larsen

2008. Henning Holck-Larsen (co-founder of Larsen & Toubro engineering firm) Commemoration.
2481 **1818** 5r. multicoloured 1·00 1·00

1819 Madhav Institute of Technology and Science, Gwalior and Sir Jiwaji Rao Scindia (founder)

2008. 50th Anniv of Madhav Institute of Technology and Science, Gwalior.
2482 **1819** 5r. multicoloured 1·00 1·00

1820 Maha Bodhi Temple, Bodh Gaya, India

2008. Temples. Multicoloured.
2483 15r. Type **1820** 1·25 1·25
2484 15r. White Horse Temple, Luoyang, China 1·25 1·25
MS2585 100×100 mm. Nos. 2483/4 3·75 3·75

1821 Soldiers of Nabha Akal Infantry, c. 1757

2008. 250th Anniv of 14 Battalion (Nabha Akal) of Punjab Regiment.
2486 **1821** 5r. multicoloured 1·00 1·00

1822 Damodar Kosambi

2008. Birth Centenary (2007) of Damodar Kosambi (statistician, mathematician and Indologist).
2487 **1822** 5r. multicoloured 1·00 1·00

1823 Aldabra Giant Tortoise

2008. Aldabra Giant Tortoise. Multicoloured.
2488 5r. Type **1823** 50 50
2489 15r. Aldabra giant tortoise (front view) 1·40 1·40
No. **MS**2490 is left for a miniature sheet not yet received.

1824 Olympic Torch and Huanhuan Mascot

2008. Olympic Games, Beijing. Multicoloured.

2491	5r. Type **1824**	30	30
2492	15r. Shooting	1·00	1·00
2493	15r. Archery	1·00	1·00
2494	15r. Boxing	1·00	1·00
MS2495	Nos. 2491/4	4·50	4·50

1825 Dornier Fixed Wing Aircraft

2008. 30th Anniv of Indian Coast Guard. Multicoloured.

2496	5r. Type **1825**	50	50
2497	5r. Advanced light helicopter	50	50
2498	5r. Hovercraft	50	50
2499	5r. Advanced offshore patrol vessel	50	50
MS2500	157×118 mm. Nos. 2496/9	2·75	2·75

1826 Ustad Bismillah Khan playing Shehnai

2008. Ustad Bismillah Khan (shehnai player) Commemoration.

2501	5r. multicoloured	1·00	1·00

1827 Sir Pitti Theagarayar and Weaver

2008. Sir Pitti Theagarayar (founder of Justice Party and Chairman of Madras Municipality 1920–3) Commemoration.

2502	**1827**	5r. multicoloured	1·00	1·00

1828 Dr. C. Natesan

2008. Dr. C. Natesan (founder of Justice Party and co-founder of the Dravidian Movement) Commemoration.

2503	**1828**	5r. multicoloured	1·00	1·00

1829 Dr. T. M. Nair

2008. Dr. Taravat Mahadevan Nair (founder of Justice Party) Commemoration.

2504	**1829**	5r. multicoloured	1·00	1·00

1830 Bijoya Dashami, Kolkata

2008. Festivals of India. Multicoloured.

2505	5r. Type **1830**	50	50
2506	5r. Elephant carrying throne of goddess Chamundeshwari in procession, Dussehra, Mysore	50	50
2507	5r. Lamps ('Happy Deepavali') (vert)	50	50
MS2508	160×110 mm. Nos. 2505/7	1·90	1·90

No. 2505 was incorrectly inscribed 'Dussehra'.

1831 Tiger Mascot Jigr

2008. Third Commonwealth Youth Games, Pune. Multicoloured.

2509	5r. Type **1831**	50	50
2510	5r. Wrestling	50	50
2511	5r. Badminton	50	50
2512	5r. Hurdling	50	50
MS2513	135×99 mm. Nos. 2509/12	2·75	2·75

1832 Rural Post Office

2008. Philately Day.

2514	**1832**	5r. multicoloured	1·00	1·00

A miniature sheet containing the 5r. stamp, No. 1832, was sold for 15r.

1833 Rice Field

2008. Food Safety and Quality Year 2008–9.

2515	**1833**	5r. multicoloured	1·00	1·00

1834 Tiger Mascot Shera

2008. 19th Commonwealth Games, New Delhi (2010).

2516	**1834**	5r. multicoloured	1·00	1·00

A miniature sheet containing the 5r. stamp was sold for 15r.

1835 Girl asleep and Dreaming

2008. Children's Day. 'India of My Dreams'. Designs showing children's paintings by Shanker Dinesh Kamath, Anchal Singh and K. Viswanath. Multicoloured.

2517	5r. Type **1835**	35	35
2518	5r. Group of young people outside church, mosque and temple	35	35
2519	5r. Man, woman and child sat on crescent moon (vert)	35	35
MS2519a	175×127 mm. Nos. 2517/19	2·10	2·10

1836 Saint Alphonsa

2008. Canonisation of St. Alphonsa Muttathupadathu.

2520	**1836**	5r. multicoloured	1·00	1·00

A miniature sheet containing this 5r. stamp was sold for 15r.

1837 B. N. Reddi

2008. Birth Centenary of Bommireddi Narasimha Reddi (film director).

2521	**1837**	5r. multicoloured	1·00	1·00

1838 Standard Chartered Bank Building

2008. 150th Anniv of the Standard Chartered Bank.

2522	**1838**	5r. multicoloured	1·00	1·00

1839 Gasworks

2008. 25th Anniv of GAIL (India) Limited (formerly the Gas Authority of India Limited).

2523	**1839**	5r. multicoloured	1·00	1·00

1840 Joachim and Violet Alva

2008. Birth Centenary of Joachim and Violet Alva (nationalists and journalists).

2524	**1840**	5r. multicoloured	1·00	1·00

1841 Marching Cadets and Cadets abseiling on Training Exercise

2008. 60th Anniv of Sardar Vallabhbhai Patel National Police Academy, Hyderabad. Multicoloured.

2525	5r. Type **1841**	40	40
2526	20r. Statue of Sardar Vallabhbhai Patel	1·75	1·75
MS2527	115×78 mm. Nos. 2525/6	3·25	3·25

1842 St. Joseph's Boys High School

2008. 150th Anniv of St. Joseph's Boys High School, Bangalore.

2528	**1842**	5r. multicoloured	1·00	1·00

1843 Buddhadeva Bose

2008. Birth Centenary of Buddhadeva Bose (writer and educationist).

2529	**1843**	5r. multicoloured	1·00	1·00

1844 Jawaharlal Nehru

1844a Homi Jahangir Baba

2008. 'Builders of Modern India'.

2530	**1844**	25p. black and claret	10	10
2531	–	50p. blue and grey	10	10
2532	–	1r. black, bistre and brown	10	10
2533	–	2r. purple and deep purple	25	25
2534	–	3r. chocolate, purple and mauve	35	35
2535	**1844a**	4r. multicoloured	50	50
2536	–	5r. black and bistre	60	60
2537	–	5r. reddish brown and brown	60	60
2538	–	10r. black and pink	60	60
2538	–	10r. black and pink	60	60
2539	–	15r. black, grey and mauve	1·75	1·75
2540	–	20r. purple, claret and black	28	1·10

DESIGNS—(20×22 mm) No. 2531 E.V. Ramasami;No. 2532 Mahatma Gandhi; No. 2533 Dr. B. R. Ambedkar; No. 2534 Satajit Ray; No. 2536 Indira Gandhi; No. 2537 Rajiv Gandhi; No.2538 10r. C.V. Raman. (20×30 mm)—(as T **1844a**) No. 2538 15r. J.R.D. Tata; No. 2540 Mother Teresa.

No. 2541has been left for addition to this definitive series.

1845 Sunspot and Measurements of Gas Flow

2008. Centenary of the Discovery of the Evershed Effect (the radial flow of gas across the photospheric surface of sunspots).

2542	**1845**	5r. multicoloured	1·00	1·00

1846 Handshake, Map, Warship and Helicopter

2008. Navy Day. 'Reaching Out to Maritime Neighbours'.

2543	**1846**	5r. multicoloured	1·00	1·00

1847 Christmas Star and Sheep

2008. Christmas. Multicoloured.

2544		5r. Type **1847**	50	50
2545		20r. Mary and baby Jesus	1·75	1·75

1848 Dr. Laxmi Mall Singhvi

2008. Dr. Laxmi Mall Singhvi (jurist and constitutional expert) Commemoration.

2546	**1848**	5r. multicoloured	1·00	1·00

1849 Mahatma Gandhi, Abraham Lincoln, Mother Teresa and Martin Luther King

2008. 60th Anniv of the Universal Declaration of Human Rights.

2547	**1849**	5r. multicoloured	1·00	1·00

1850 Indian Institute of Science, Bangalore

2008. Centenary of the Indian Institute of Science, Bangalore. Multicoloured.

2548		5r. Type **1850**	40	40
2549		20r. Scientists and academics including founder Jamsetji Tata and former director C. V. Raman	1·75	1·75
MS2550		130×85 mm. Nos. 2548/9	3·25	3·25

1851 Swami Ranganathananda Maharaj

2008. Birth Centenary of Swami Ranganathananda Maharaj (13th President of Ramakrishna Math and Mission, Kolkata).

2551	**1851**	5r. multicoloured	1·00	1·00

1852 Field Marshal Manekshaw

2008. Field Marshal S. H. F. J. Manekshaw Commemoration.

2552	**1852**	5r. multicoloured	1·00	1·00

1853 T. V. Ramasubbaiyer

2008. Birth Centenary of T. V. Ramasubbaiyer (founder of Tamil newspaper Dinamalar and philanthropist).

2553	**1853**	5r. multicoloured	1·00	1·00

1854 BRAHMOS Missile and Fighter Plane

2008. 10th Anniv of BRAHMOS Supersonic Cruise Missile. Multicoloured.

2554	**1854**	5r. Type **1853**	40	40
2555	**1854**	20r. Warship launching BRAHMOS missile, missiles (on ground) and fighter planes (horiz)	1·75	1·75
MS2556		135×88 mm. Nos. 2554/5	3·25	3·25

1855 Rani Velu Nachchiyar

2008. Rani Velu Nachchiyar (Queen of Sivaganga, 1780–c.1790) Commemoration.

2557	**1855**	5r. multicoloured	1·00	1·00

1856 M. Bhakthavatsalam

2008. M. Bhakthavatsalam (Chief Minister of Madras State 1963–7) Commemoration.

2558	**1856**	5r. multicoloured	1·00	1·00

1857 Thillaiyadi Valliammai

2008. Thillaiyadi Valliammai (anti-Apartheid campaigner in South Africa) Commemoration.

2559	**1857**	5r. multicoloured	1·00	1·00

1858 Sheik Thambi Pavalar

2008. Sheik Thambi Pavalar (Tamil poet) Commemoration.

2560	**1858**	5r. multicoloured	1·00	1·00

1859 A. T. Paneerselvam

2008. A. T. Paneerselvam (Chairman of Indian Banks Association 1997–2000) Commemoration.

2561	**1859**	5r. multicoloured	1·00	1·00

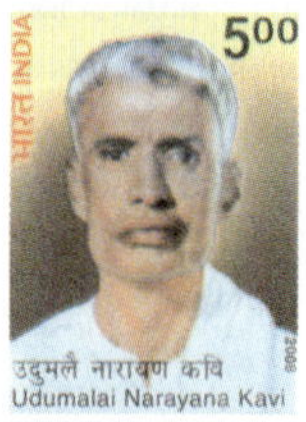

1860 Udumalai Narayana Kavi

2008. Udumalai Narayana Kavi (songwriter) Commemoration.

2562	**1860**	5r. multicoloured	1·00	1·00

1861 Louis Braille and Hands reading Braille

2009. Birth Bicentenary of Louis Braille (inventor of Braille writing for the blind).

2563	**1861**	5r. multicoloured	1·00	1·00

No. 2563 is embossed with Braille characters.

1862 Vaikom Muhammad Basheer

2009. Birth Centenary of Vaikom Muhammad Basheer (Malayalam novelist and short story writer).

2564	**1862**	5r. multicoloured	1·00	1·00

1863 St. Paul's Church, Chennai

2009. 150th Anniv of St. Paul's Church, Chennai.

2565	**1863**	5r. multicoloured	1·00	1·00

1864 Jaisalmer Fort

2009. Heritage Monuments Preservation by INTACH (Indian National Trust for Art and Cultural Heritage). Multicoloured.

2566		5r. Type **1864**	50	50
2567		5r. Mongyu Monastery, Laddakh	50	50
2568		5r. St. Anne Church, Goa	50	50
2569		5r. Qila Mubarak, Patiala	50	50
MS2570		120×76 mm. Nos. 2566/9	50	50

1865 Bishnu Prasad Rabha

2009. Birth Centenary of Bishnu Prasad Rabha (poet, dramatist, musician, dancer and actor).

2571	**1865**	5r. multicoloured	1·00	1·00

1866 Steel Production

2009. 50th Anniv of SAIL (Steel Authority of India).

2572	**1866**	5r. multicoloured	1·00	1·00

1867 Young Girl running

2009. National Girl Child Day.

2573	**1867**	5r. multicoloured	1·00	1·00

1868 Sant Santaji Jagnade Maharaj

2009. Sant Santaji Jagnade Maharaj Commemoration.

2574	**1868**	5r. multicoloured	1·00	1·00

1869 Maha Kavi Magh

2009. Maha Kavi Magh (Sanskrit poet) Commemoration.

2575	**1869**	5r. multicoloured	1·00	1·00

1870 Family under Umbrella

2009. 125th Anniv of Postal Life Insurance.

2576	**1870**	5r. multicoloured	1·00	1·00

1871 Jainacharya Vallabh Suri

2009. Jainacharya Vallabh Suri (Jain monk) Commemoration.
2577 **1871** 5r. multicoloured 1·00 1·00

1872 Harakh Chand Nahata and Mountain Road

2009. Harakh Chand Nahata (entrepreneur, philanthropist and patron of the arts) Commemoration.
2578 **1872** 5r. multicoloured 1·00 1·00

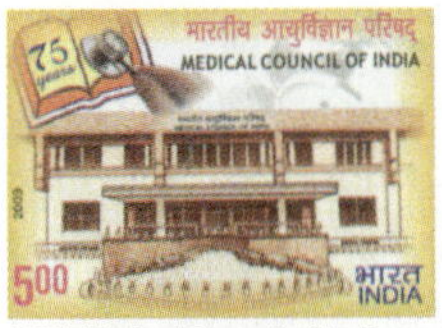

1873 Medical Council of India

2009. 75th Anniv of the Medical Council of India.
2579 **1873** 5r. multicoloured 1·00 1·00

1874 *Pterospermum acerifolium*

2009. Pterospermum acerifolium (flowering tree).
2580 **1874** 5r. multicoloured

1875 Baburao Puleshwar Shedmake

2009. Baburao Puleshwar Shedmake (revolutionary) Commemoration.
2581 **1875** 5r. multicoloured 1·00 1·00

1876 Dr. Krishna Kumar Birla

2009. Dr. Krishna Kumar Birla (industrialist) Commemoration.
2582 **1876** 5r. multicoloured 1·00 1·00

1877 Black Pepper

2009. Spices of India. Multicoloured.
2583 5r. Type **1877** 50 50
2584 5r. Cinnamon 50 50
2585 5r. Cardamom 50 50
2586 5r. Clove 50 50
2587 20r. Turmeric, chilly and coriander 1·75 1·75
MS2588 129×129 mm. Nos. 2583/7 4·75 4·75

1878 R. Sankar

2009. Birth Centenary of R. Sankar (former Minister for Education in Kerala).
2589 **1878** 5r. multicoloured 1·00 1·00

1879 Lifeline Express

2009. Lifeline Express (first modern hospital train).
2590 **1879** 5r. multicoloured 1·00 1·00

1880 Soldier of Madras Regiment

2009. 250th Anniv of Madras Regiment.
2591 **1880** 5r. multicoloured 1·00 1·00

1881 Rev. J. J. M. Nichols Roy

2009. 125th Birth Anniv of Rev. J. J. M. Nichols Roy (tribal leader of Assam).
2592 **1881** 5r. multicoloured 1·00 1·00

1882 Sacred Heart Church

2009. Centenary of Sacred Heart Church, Pudducherry.
2593 **1882** 5r. multicoloured 1·00 1·00

1883 Rampur Raza Library

2009. Rampur Raza Library. Multicoloured.
2594 5r. Type **1883** 50 50
2595 5r. Ram and Laxman with Jatayu (from *Valmiki Ramayana* by Sumer Chand) (vert) 50 50
2596 5r. Madonna holding a book (from Jahangir's album) (vert) 50 50
2597 5r. Illustrated page from *Diwan-i-Hafiz* of Akbar's personal collection (vert) 50 1·00
MS2598 116×145 mm. Nos. 2594/7 2·25 2·25

1884 Petrol Pumps and Oil Refinery

2009. 50th Anniv of Indian Oil Corporation.
2599 **1884** 5r. multicoloured 1·00 1·00

1885 Academy Building

2009. 50th Anniv of Lal Bahadur Shastri National Academy of Administration.
2600 **1885** 5r. multicoloured 1·00 1·00

1886 Ramcharan Agarwal

2009. Ramcharan Agarwal (nationalist) Commemoration.
2601 **1886** 5r. multicoloured 1·00 1·00

1887 The Poet Jayadeva

2009. Jayadeva (Sanskrit poet) and his epic poem Geetagovinda. Designs showing Jayadeva (No. 2602) and incarnations of Vishnu. Multicoloured.
2602 5r. Type **1887** 25 25
2603 5r. Kurma the Tortoise 25 25
2604 5r. Varaaha the Boar 25 25
2605 5r. Matsya the Fish 25 25
2606 5r. Vaamana the Dwarf 25 25
2607 5r. Parasuraama 25 25
2608 5r. Narasimha the Man-lion 25 25
2609 5r. Balaraama 25 25
2610 5r. Buddha 25 25
2611 5r. Raama 25 25
2612 5r. Kalki 25 25
MS2613 160×200 mm. Nos. 2602/12 2·25 2·25

1888 St. Joseph's College, Bangalore

2009. St. Joseph's College, Bangalore.
2614 **1888** 5r. multicoloured 1·00 1·00

1889 Maharshi Patanjali and Symbols of his Work

2009. Maharshi Patanjali (yogi) Commemoration.
2615 **1889** 5r. multicoloured 1·00 1·00

1890 Pingali Venkaiah

2009. Pingali Venkaiah (designer of Indian tricolour) Commemoration.
2616 **1890** 5r. multicoloured 1·00 1·00

1891 Howrah Station

2009. Heritage Railway Stations. Multicoloured.
2617 5r. Type **1891** 50 50
2618 5r. Chennai Central Station 50 50
2619 5r. Mumbai CST Station 50 50
2620 5r. Old Delhi Station 50 50

1892 Uttam Kumar

2009. Uttam Kumar (actor) Commemoration.
2622 **1892** 5r. multicoloured 1·00 1·00

1893 School Building and Statue

2009. Sacred Heart Matriculation Higher Secondary School, Chennai.
2623 **1893** 5r. multicoloured 1·00 1·00

1894 Holy Cross Church

2009. Holy Cross Church, Mapranam.
2624 **1894** 5r. multicoloured 1·00 1·00

1895 Dushyant Kumar

2009. Dushyant Kumar (writer) Commemoration.
2625 **1895** 5r. multicoloured 1·00 1·00

1896 Barbe's Leaf Monkey

2009. Rare Fauna of the North East. Multicoloured.

2626	5r. Type **1896**	50	50
2627	5r. Marbled cat	50	50
2628	5r. Red panda (horiz)	50	50

No. **MS**2629 is left for a miniature sheet not yet received.

1897 Mahatma Gandhi

2009. Mahatma Gandhi and Non Violence.

2630	**1897**	25r. multicoloured	1·00	1·00

1898 Bishop Cotton School and Stained Glass Window

2009. 150th Anniv of Bishop Cotton School, Shimla.

2631	**1898**	5r. multicoloured	1·00	1·00

1899 R. K. Narayan

2009. R. K. Narayan (writer) Commemoration.

2632	**1899**	5r. multicoloured	1·00	1·00

1900 Dineshnandini Dalmia

2009. Dineshnandini Dalmia (Hindi poet and novelist) Commemoration.

2633	**1900**	5r. multicoloured	1·00	1·00

1901 India Post Freighter and Mail Bags

2009. India Post Freighter (aircraft).

2634	**1901**	5r. multicoloured	1·00	1·00

1902 Dilwara Temple, near Mount Abu

2009. Heritage Temples. Multicoloured.

2635	5r. Type **1902**	50	50
2636	5r. Ranakpur Temple, near Sadri	50	50

No. **MS**2637 is left for miniature sheet not yet received.

1903 Maharaja Gulab Singh

2009. Maharaja Gulab Singh (founder of Jammu & Kashmir State) Commemoration.

2638	**1903**	5r. multicoloured	1·00	1·00

1904 Major General Dewan Misri Chand

2009. Major General Dewan Misri Chand (pioneer aviator) Commemoration.

2639	**1904**	5r. multicoloured	1·00	1·00

1905 Old People's Home

2009. Canonization of St. Jeanne Jugan (founder of Order of the Little Sisters of the Poor). T 1905 and similar multicoloured design.

2640	5r. Type **1905**	1·00	
2641	20r. St. Jeanne Jugan (29×32 mm)		

Nos. 2640/1 were printed together, *se-tenant*, in horizontal pairs throughout the sheet, each pair forming a composite design.

1906 Dr. Rajkumar

2009. 80th Birth Anniv of Dr. Rajkumar (actor in Kannada cinema).

2642	**1906**	5r. multicoloured	1·00	1·00

1907 Dr. Mahendra Lal Sircar

2009. Dr. Mahendra Lal Sircar (homeopath) Commemoration.

2643	**1907**	5r. multicoloured	1·00	1·00

1908 Apollo Hospitals

2009. Apollo Hospitals Group.

2644	**1908**	5r. multicoloured	1·00	1·00

1909 Danmal Mathur

2009. Danmal Mathur (pioneer of scout movement in Rajasthan) Commemoration.

2645	**1909**	5r. multicoloured	1·00	1·00

1910 Virchand Raghavji Gandhi

2009. Virchand Raghavji Gandhi (Jain scholar) Commemoration.

2646	**1910**	5r. multicoloured	1·00	1·00

1911 Kathiawari Horses

2009. Indigenous Horses. T 1911 and similar horiz designs. Multicoloured.

2647	5r. Type **1911**	1·00	1·00
2648	5r. Marwari	1·00	1·00
2649	5r. Zanskari	1·00	1·00
2650	5r. Manipuri	1·00	1·00

MS2651 is left for a miniature sheet not yet received.

1912 Rajabhau Khobragade

2009. Rajabhau Khobragade (politician) Commemoration.

2652	**1912**	5r. multicoloured	1·00	1·00

1913 Gaurishanker Dalmia

2009. Gaurishanker Dalmia (magazine publisher) Commemoration.

2653	**1913**	5r. multicoloured	1·00	1·00

1914 Silhouettes and Emblem

2009. 60th Anniv of the Commonwealth.

2654	**1914**	5r. multicoloured	1·00	1·00

1915 Deer drinking from Forest Pool

2009. Children's Day. Showing children's paintings.

2655	5r. Type **1915**	50	50
2656	5r. Tiger	50	50

Nos. 2657/**MS**2658, Type **1916** is left for '25th Anniv of Silent Valley National Park', issued 15 November 2009, not yet received.

1917 Gangetic Dolphin (*Platanista gangetica*)

2009. Dolphin and Whale Shark. Multicoloured.

2659	5r. Type **1917**	50	50
2660	20r. Whale shark (*Rhincodon typus*)	1·75	1·75
MS2661	120×66 mm. Nos. 2657/8	2·25	2·25

Nos. 2659/60 were printed together, se-tenant, forming a composite design.

Similar designs were issued by the Phillippines.

1918 Ganpatrao Govindrao Jadhav

2009. Ganpatrao Govindrao Jadhav (newspaper publisher) Commemoration.

2661	**1918**	5r. multicoloured	1·00	1·00

1919 Tamilnadu Police on Parade

2009. 150th Anniv of Tamilnadu Police.

2663	**1919**	5r. multicoloured	1·00	1·00

1921 Cavalryman of 1809 and Modern Tank

2009. Bicentenary of 2nd Lancers (Gardner's Horse) Regiment.

2669	**1921**	5r. multicoloured	1·00	1·00

Nos. 2664/7, **MS**2668 and T **1920** are left for Greetings stamps issued 1 December 2009, not yet received.

1922 Pupils and School Building

2009. Centenary of Convent of Jesus and Mary School, Ambala Cant.

2670	**1922**	5r. multicoloured	1·00	1·00

1923 Kalamkari

2009. Traditional Indian Textiles. T 1923 and similar vert designs. Multicoloured.

2671	5r. Type **1923**		
2672	5r. Apa Tani weaves	50	50
2673	5r. Kanchipuram silk	50	50
2674	5r. Banaras silk	50	50
MS2675	160×90 mm. Nos. 2671/4	2·25	2·25

1924 Henry Derozio

2009. Birth Bicentenary of Henry Louis Vivian Derozio (poet).

2676	**1924**	5r. black, brown-purple and yellow-ochre	1·00	1·00

1925 Lal Pratap Singh

2009. Lal Pratap Singh (Prince of Kalakankar) Commemoration.

2677	**1925**	5r. multicoloured	1·00	1·00

1926 Penguins

2009. Preserve the Polar Regions and Glaciers. T **1926** and similar horiz design. Multicoloured.

2678	5r. Type **1926**	50	50
2679	5r. Polar bear	50	50

No. **MS**2680 is left for a miniature sheet not yet received.

1927 Venkataramana Bhagvathar

2009. Venkataramana Bhagvathar (composer of Carnatic music) Commemoration.

2681	**1927**	5r. multicoloured	1·00	1·00

1928 Figures forming Triangle

2009. Indian Mathmatical Society.

2682	**1928**	5r. multicoloured	1·00	1·00

1929 Maharaja Surajmal

2009. Maharaja Surajmal (founder of Kingdom of Bharatpur) Commemoration.

2683	**1929**	5r. multicoloured	1·00	1·00

OFFICIAL STAMPS

1866. Optd Service.

O8	**12**	8p. mauve	28·00	60·00
O13	**11**	4a. green	£300	£100
O20	**11**	½a. blue	55·00	50
O23	**11**	1a. brown	60·00	50
O27	**11**	2a. orange	9·00	2·25
O29	-	4a. green (No. 69)	3·25	1·50
O30	**11**	8a. red	3·75	1·50

1866. Fiscal stamp with head of Queen Victoria surch SERVICE TWO ANNAS.

O15	2a. purple	£350	£275

1866. Fiscal stamps optd SERVICE POSTAGE.

O16	2a. purple	£1300	£650
O17	4a. purple	£5500	£1500
O18	8a. purple	£5000	£5000
O19	½a. mauve on lilac	£550	£110

1874. Optd On H. M. S. (Queen Victoria).

O31		½a. blue	17·00	20
O32		1a. brown	19·00	20
O33a		2a. orange	65·00	29·00
O34	-	4a. green (No. 69)	26·00	3·00
O35	**11**	8a. red	9·00	7·00

1883. Queen Victoria stamps of 1882 and 1892 optd On H. M. S.

O37a	**40**	3p. red	20	10
O39	**23**	½a. green	2·75	10
O41	-	1a. purple	1·25	10
O42	-	2a. blue	10·00	60
O44a	-	4a. olive	30·00	50
O46	-	8a. mauve	11·00	50
O48	**37**	1r. green and red	26·00	40
O49	**23**	½a. green	4·00	90
O50	-	1a. red	4·50	10
O51	-	2a. lilac	50·00	1·50

1902. King Edward VII stamps optd On H. M. S.

O54	**41**	3p. grey	2·50	1·00
O56	-	½a. green (No. 122)	1·25	30
O57	-	1a. red (No. 123)	1·00	10
O59	-	2a. lilac	3·25	10
O60	-	4a. olive	17·00	30
O62	-	6a. bistre	1·50	15
O63	-	8a. mauve	6·00	1·00
O65	-	1r. green and red	4·00	80
O68	**52**	2r. red and orange	14·00	1·50
O69	**52**	5r. blue and violet	14·00	1·50
O70	**52**	10r. green and red	38·00	22·00
O71	**52**	15r. blue and olive	95·00	45·00
O72	**52**	25r. orange and blue	£200	75·00

1906. Nos. 149/50 optd On H. M. S.

O66	½a. green	1·25	10
O67	1a. red	2·00	10

1912. King George V stamps optd SERVICE.

O76	**56**	½a. green	50	10
O80	**57**	1a. red	1·00	10
O84	**59**	2a. mauve	1·00	30
O87	**64**	6a. bistre	1·50	3·00
O92	**67**	2r. red and orange	6·00	8·50
O93	**67**	5r. blue and violet	25·00	32·00
O94	**67**	10r. green and red	80·00	65·00
O95	**67**	15r. blue and olive	£140	£140
O96	**67**	25r. orange and blue	£275	£200
O109	**55**	3p. grey	55	10
O111	**57**	1a. brown	20	10
O112	**70**	2a. lilac	30	10
O113	**71**	4a. green	70	20
O115	**65**	8a. mauve	3·50	10
O116	**66**	12a. red	70	2·50
O117	**67**	1r. brown and green	8·50	1·00
O129	**70**	2a. red	3·00	2·50
O132	**63**	4a. olive	2·50	10

1921. No. O81 surch NINE PIES.

O97	**57**	9p. on 1a. red	1·25	1·00

1925. Nos. O70/2 surch in words.

O99	**52**	1r. on 15r. blue and olive	4·25	4·00
O100	**52**	1r. on 25r. orange & blue	24·00	80·00
O101	**52**	2r. on 10r. green and red	3·75	4·25

1925. Nos. O94/6 surch in words.

O102	**67**	1r. on 15r. blue and olive	19·00	75·00
O103	**67**	1r. on 25r. orange & blue	6·50	11·00
O104	**67**	2r. on 10r. green and red	£1400	

1926. No. O62 surch ONE ANNA.

O105	1a. on 6a. bistre	30	30

1926. Surch SERVICE ONE ANNA and two bars.

O106	**58**	1a. on 1½a. brown (A)	20	10
O107	**58**	1a. on 1½a. brown (B)	4·25	4·50
O108	**61**	1a. on 2a.6p. blue	60	80

1932. Optd SERVICE.

O126	**79**	½a. green	2·50	10
O127	**80**	9p. green	30	15
O127b	**81**	1a. brown	3·25	15
O128	**82**	1a.3p. mauve	30	10
O130b	**59**	2a. orange	1·25	10
O131	**61**	2a.6p. orange	50	10

1937. King George VI stamps optd SERVICE.

O135	**91**	½a. brown	17·00	1·00
O136	**91**	9p. green	19·00	1·00
O137	**91**	1a. red	3·50	10
O138	**93**	1r. slate and brown	50	50
O139	**93**	2r. purple and brown	1·75	2·50
O140	**93**	5r. green and blue	7·00	7·50
O141	**93**	10r. purple and red	17·00	11·00

1939. King George V stamp surch SERVICE 1A.

O142	**82**	1a. on 1¼a. mauve	12·00	20

O20 King George VI

1939

O143	**O20**	3p. slate	60	10
O144	**O20**	½a. brown	8·00	10
O144a	**O20**	½a. purple	30	10
O145	**O20**	9p. green	30	10
O146	**O20**	1a. red	30	10
O146a	**O20**	1a.3p. brown	3·75	70
O146b	**O20**	1½a. violet	65	10
O147	**O20**	2a. orange	60	10
O148	**O20**	2½a. violet	1·25	1·25
O149	**O20**	4a. brown	60	10
O150	**O20**	8a. violet	90	30

1948. 1st Anniv of Independence. Optd SERVICE.

O150a	**305**	1½a. brown	55·00	45·00
O150b	**305**	3½a. violet	£1500	£800
O150c	**305**	12a. green	£4500	£2750
O150d	-	10r. brown and red (No. 308)	£32000	

O21 Asokan Capital

1950

O151	**O21**	3p. violet	15	10
O152	**O21**	6p. brown	30	10
O153	**O21**	9p. green	1·25	10
O154	**O21**	1a. blue	1·25	10
O155	**O21**	2a. red	1·75	10
O156	**O21**	3a. red	4·50	2·50
O157	**O21**	4a. purple	7·50	20
O158	**O21**	4a. blue	50	10
O159	**O21**	6a. violet	4·00	2·00
O160	**O21**	8a. brown	2·00	10
O186	-	1r. violet	15	10
O187	-	2r. red	25	10
O188	-	5r. green	40	60
O189	-	10r. brown	90	1·00

The rupee values are larger and with a different frame.

1957. Value in naye paise.

O166	**O21**	2n.p. violet	10	10
O167	**O21**	3n.p. brown	20	10
O168	**O21**	5n.p. green	50	10
O169	**O21**	6n.p. turquoise	40	10
O170	**O21**	13n.p. red	40	10
O175	**O21**	1n.p. slate	10	10
O180	**O21**	10n.p. green	50	50
O182	**O21**	15n.p. violet	10	10
O183	**O21**	20n.p. red	70	10
O184	**O21**	25n.p. blue	10	10
O185	**O21**	50n.p. brown	70	10

O23

1967

O197	**O23**	1r. purple	85	10
O200	**O23**	2p. violet	10	1·00
O201	**O23**	3p. brown	40	1·25
O202	**O23**	5p. green	10	10
O203	**O23**	6p. blue	1·25	1·50
O204	**O23**	10p. green	10	30
O205	**O23**	15p. plum	10	30
O206	**O23**	20p. red	10	30
O207	**O23**	25p. red	18·00	3·75
O208	**O23**	30p. blue	10	60
O209	**O23**	50p. brown	10	60

O25

1971. Obligatory Tax. Refugee Relief. Optd REFUGEE RELIEF in English and Devanagari (No. O210) or in English only (No. O211).

O210		5p. green	75	60
O211		5p. green	1·25	1·00
O213	**O25**	5p. green	30	40

See note below Nos. 646/51.

O26

1976. Designs redrawn showing face-value in figures only and smaller Capital with Hindi motto beneath as Type O 26.

O214	**O26**	2p. blue	20	1·25
O225b	-	2r. red	40	1·50
O226b	-	5r. green	60	2·25
O227	-	10r. red	1·25	3·50
O254	**O26**	5p. green	20	30
O255	**O26**	10p. green	20	30
O256	**O26**	15p. purple	20	30
O257	**O26**	20p. red	20	20
O258	**O26**	25p. red	20	30
O259	**O26**	30p. blue	20	20
O260	**O26**	35p. violet	20	20
O263	**O26**	60p. brown	20	30
O268	**O26**	40p. violet (17×19½ mm)	20	20
O269	**O26**	50p. brown (17×19½ mm)	70	60
O270	**O26**	1r. purple (17×19½ mm)	70	60

The 2, 5 and 10r. values are larger.

O28

1982. As 1977 and 1981 issue but with simulated perforations. Imperf.

O231	**O28**	5p. green	55	1·00
O232	**O28**	10p. green	70	1·00
O233	**O28**	15p. purple	70	1·00
O234	**O28**	20p. red	75	1·00
O235	**O28**	25p. red	1·50	2·00
O236	**O28**	35p. violet	85	65
O237	**O28**	50p. brown	1·50	1·50
O238	**O28**	1r. brown	1·75	1·50
O239	**O28**	2r. red	1·75	4·00
O240	**O28**	5r. green	2·00	5·00
O241	**O28**	10r. brown	2·50	7·00

O27

1998. Redrawn with face value figures in bottom corners. Size 17×19½ mm.

O271	**O27**	2r. red	80	70
O272	**O27**	5r. green	1·25	1·25
O273	**O27**	10r. brown	1·60	1·75

(b) Size 16½×19 mm.

O273b	**O26**	50p. brown	10	10
O274	**O27**	1r. purple	10	10
O275	**O27**	2r. red	10	10
O276	**O27**	3r. orange	10	10
O278	**O27**	5r. green	15	20
O279	**O27**	10r. brown	25	30

Pt. 1

INDIAN CUSTODIAN FORCES IN KOREA

Stamps used by the Indian Forces on custodian duties in Korea in 1953.

12 pies = 1 anna; 16 annas = 1 rupee.

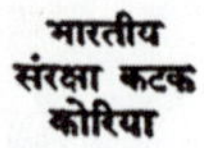

(K1)

1953. Stamps of India (archaeological series) optd with Type K 1.

K1	307	3p. violet	2·25	6·50
K2	308	6p. brown	1·50	6·00
K3	-	9p. green	2·50	4·50
K4	-	1a. blue (B)	1·50	4·50
K5	-	2a. red	1·50	4·50
K6	-	2½a. lake	1·50	4·75
K7	-	3a. salmon	1·50	6·00
K8	314	4a. blue	2·25	4·75
K9	315	6a. violet	10·00	9·00
K10	-	8a. green	2·25	12·00
K11	-	12a. blue	2·25	17·00
K12	-	1r. violet and green	4·50	17·00

Pt. 1

INDIAN EXPEDITIONARY FORCES

Stamps used by Indian Forces during, and after, the War of 1914–18.

12 pies = 1 anna; 16 annas = 1 rupee.

1914. Stamps of India (King George V) optd I. E. F.

E1	55	3p. grey	15	30
E2	56	½a. green	50	30
E3	57	1a. red	1·25	30
E5	59	2a. lilac	1·25	30
E6	61	2a.6p. blue	1·50	3·50
E7	62	3a. orange	1·00	1·50
E8	63	4a. olive	1·00	1·50
E9	65	8a. mauve	1·25	2·50
E11	66	12a. red	2·25	6·00
E13	67	1r. brown and green	2·50	4·00

Pt. 1

INDIAN FORCES IN INDO-CHINA

Stamps used by Indian Forces engaged in the International Commission in Indo-China.

1954. 12 pies = 1 anna; 16 annas = 1 rupee.
1957. 100 naye paise = 1 rupee.
1964. 100 paisa = 1 rupee.

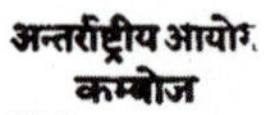

(N 1)

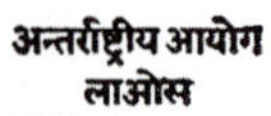

(N 2)

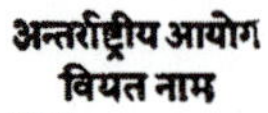

(N 3)

1954. Stamps of India (archaeological series) overprinted.
(a) Optd with Type N 1 for use in Cambodia.

N1	307	3p. violet	2·00	10·00
N2	-	1a. blue (B)	1·00	1·00
N3	-	2a. red	1·00	1·00
N4	-	8a. green	1·50	3·00
N5	-	12a. blue	1·50	3·00

(b) Optd with Type N 2 for use in Laos.

N6	307	3p. violet	2·00	10·00
N7	-	1a. blue (B)	1·00	1·00
N8	-	2a. red	1·00	1·80
N9	-	8a. green	1·50	3·00
N10	-	12a. blue	1·50	3·00

(c) Optd with Type N 3 for use in Vietnam.

N11	307	3p. violet	2·00	9·00
N12	-	1a. blue (B)	1·00	1·00
N13	-	2a. red	1·00	1·00
N14	-	8a. green	1·50	3·00
N15	-	12a. blue	1·50	3·00

1957. Map type of India overprinted. (a) Optd with Type N 1 for use in Cambodia.

N16	361	2n.p. brown	75	30
N17	361	6n.p. grey	50	30
N18	361	13n.p. red	70	40
N19	361	50n.p. orange	2·25	1·25
N20	361	75n.p. purple	2·25	1·25

(b) Optd with Type N 2 for use in Laos.

N21	2n.p. brown	75	30
N22	6n.p. grey	50	30
N23	13n.p. red	70	40
N24	50n.p. orange	2·25	1·25
N25	75n.p. purple	2·25	1·25
N39	3n.p. brown	10	60
N40	5n.p. green	10	15

(c) Optd with Type N 3 for use in Vietnam.

N26	2n.p. brown	75	30
N27	6n.p. grey	50	30
N28	13n.p. red	70	40
N29	50n.p. orange	2·25	1·25
N30	75n.p. purple	2·25	1·25
N43	1n.p. turquoise	10	20
N45	3n.p. brown	10	60
N46	5n.p. green	10	15

1965. Children's Day stamp of India optd ICC for use in Laos and Vietnam.

N49	469	15p. slate	60	4·75

1968. Nos. 504/6, 509/10, 515 and 517/18, of India optd ICC in English and Devanagari, for use in Laos and Vietnam.

N50	-	2p. brown	10	3·75
N51	-	3p. olive	10	3·75
N52	-	5p. red	10	2·00
N53	-	10p. blue	2·25	3·00
N54	467	15p. green	60	3·00
N55	-	60p. grey	35	2·25
N56	-	1r. brown and plum	50	3·00
N57	-	2r. blue and violet	1·25	11·00

Pt. 1

INDIAN U N FORCE IN CONGO

Stamps used by Indian Forces attached to the United Nations Force in Congo.

100 naye paise = 1 rupee.

1962. Map type of India optd U.N. FORCE (INDIA) CONGO.

U1	361	1n.p. turquoise	1·00	4·50
U2	361	2n.p. brown	1·00	1·25
U3	361	5n.p. green	1·00	1·00
U4	361	8n.p. turquoise	1·00	40
U5	361	13n.p. red	1·00	40
U6	361	50n.p. orange	1·00	70

Pt. 1

INDIAN U.N. FORCE IN GAZA (PALESTINE)

Stamps used by Indian Forces attached to the United Nations Force in Gaza.

100 paise = 1 rupee.

1965. Children's Day stamp of India optd UNEF.

G1	449	15p. slate	3·00	8·50

Pt. 6

INDO-CHINA

A French territory in south-east Asia. In 1949 it was split up into the three states of Vietnam, Cambodia and Laos.

1889. 100 centimes = 1 franc.
1918. 100 cents = 1 piastre.

1889. Stamp of French Colonies, "Commerce" type, surch.
(a) INDO-CHINE 1889 5 R-D.

1	J	5 on 35c. black on orange	£110	90·00

(b) INDO-CHINE 89 5 R D.

2	5 on 35c. black on orange	17·00	11·00

1892. "Tablet" key-type inscr "INDO-CHINE" in red (1, 5, 15, 25, 50 (No. 27), 75c., 1f.) or blue (others).

6	D	1c. black on blue	2·20	55
7	D	2c. brown on buff	2·50	2·75
8	D	4c. brown on grey	3·00	3·25
10	D	10c. black on lilac	7·25	1·00
11	D	15c. blue	60·00	55
12	D	20c. red on green	17·00	2·75
13	D	25c. black on pink	32·00	90
14	D	30c. brown on drab	44·00	9·50
15	D	40c. red on yellow	50·00	14·50
16	D	50c. red on pink	55·00	11·00
17	D	75c. brown on orange	42·00	20·00
18	D	1f. green	70·00	24·00
19	D	5f. mauve on lilac	£120	£120
23	D	5c. green	4·25	90
24	D	10c. red	7·75	65
25	D	15c. grey	13·00	45
26	D	25c. blue	48·00	75
27	D	50c. brown on blue	26·00	4·25

1903. Surch.

28	5 on 15c. grey	1·70	1·20
29	15c. on 25c. blue	1·80	75

8 "Grasset" type

1904

30	8	1c. green	20	10
31	8	2c. purple on yellow	75	65
32	8	4c. mauve on blue	35	40
33	8	5c. green	3·00	20
34	8	10c. pink	4·50	30
35	8	15c. brown on blue	2·75	30
36	8	20c. red on green	4·25	55
37	8	25c. blue	20·00	35
38	8	30c. brown on cream	9·25	2·30
39	8	35c. black on yellow	34·00	1·20
40	8	40c. black on grey	8·50	90
41	8	50c. brown	12·00	1·80
42	8	75c. red on orange	50·00	24·00
43	8	1f. green	36·00	2·75
44	8	2f. brown on yellow	65·00	28·00
45	8	5f. violet	£200	£150
46	8	10f. red on green	£200	£150

10 Annamite

11 Cambodian

12 Cambodian

1907

51	10	1c. black and sepia	1·10	30
52	10	2c. black and brown	55	35
53	10	4c. black and blue	1·40	85
54	10	5c. black and green	4·75	30
55	10	10c. black and red	5·25	30
56	10	15c. black and violet	5·00	45
57	11	20c. black and violet	3·75	3·25
58	11	25c. black and blue	12·00	35
59	11	30c. black and brown	18·00	6·75
60	11	35c. black and green	5·25	55
61	11	40c. black and brown	4·50	2·50
62	11	45c. black and orange	17·00	6·50
63	11	50c. black and red	34·00	2·30
64	12	75c. black and orange	14·00	7·25
65	-	1f. black and red	60·00	11·00
66	-	2f. black and green	32·00	36·00
67	-	5f. black and blue	65·00	60·00
68	-	10f. black and violet	£120	£120

DESIGNS—As Type **12**: 1f. Annamites; 2f. Muong; 5f. Laotian; 10f. Cambodian.

1912. Surch in figures.

69	8	05 on 4c. mauve on blue	4·25	11·00
70	8	05 on 15c. brown on blue	90	10
71	8	05 on 30c. brown on cream	45	2·50
72	8	10 on 40c. black on grey	2·00	3·50
73	8	10 on 50c. brown	1·20	2·75
74	8	10 on 75c. red on orange	4·50	7·00

1914. Red Cross. Surch 5c and cross.

76	10	5c.+5c. black and green	55	3·25
77	10	10c.+5c. black and red	45	35
78	10	15c.+5c. black and violet	90	3·25

1918. Nos. 75/6 and 78 further surch in figures and words.

79	4c. on 5c.+5c. blk & grn	4·00	14·00
80	6c. on 10c.+5c. black and red	2·30	12·00
81	8c. on 15c.+5c. blk & vio	17·00	40·00

1919. French stamps of "War Orphans" issue surch INDOCHINE and value in figures and words.

82	23	10c. on 15c.+10c. grey	2·00	4·00
83	23	16c. on 25c.+15c. blue	9·50	11·00
84	-	24c. on 35c.+25c. violet and grey	9·75	26·00
85	-	40c. on 50c.+50c. brown	13·00	50·00
86	26	80c. on 1f.+1f. red	26·00	60·00
87	26	4p. on 5f.+5f. blue & blk	£250	£250

1919. Surch in figures and words.

88	10	⅖c. on 1c. black and sepia	2·75	30
89	10	⅘c. on 2c. black and brown	2·75	1·10
90	10	1⅗c. on 4c. black and blue	5·00	75
91	10	2c. on 5c. black and green	6·50	20
92	10	4c. on 10c. black and red	3·00	30
93	10	6c. on 15c. black and violet	7·75	45
94	11	8c. on 20c. black and violet	8·00	1·40
95	11	10c. on 25c. black and blue	7·25	30
96	11	12c. on 30c. black & brown	9·25	90
97	11	14c. on 35c. black & green	5·75	65
98	11	16c. on 40c. black & brown	6·50	90
99	11	18c. on 45c. black & orange	9·25	2·75
100	11	20c. on 50c. black and red	20·00	90
101	12	30c. on 75c. black & orange	24·00	2·30
102	-	40c. on 1f. black and red	32·00	2·00
103	-	80c. on 2f. black and green	30·00	7·25
104	-	2p. on 5f. black and blue	£110	£110
105	-	4p. on 10f. black and violet	£140	£140

1922. As T 10 and 11 but value in cents or piastres.

115	10	⅒c. red and grey	10	1·70
116	10	⅕c. black and blue	10	20
117	10	⅖c. black and brown	10	90
118	10	⅘c. black and mauve	20	1·00
119	10	1c. black and brown	1·70	10
120	10	2c. black and green	1·10	30
121	10	3c. black and violet	90	50
122	10	4c. black and orange	2·30	20
123	10	5c. black and red	90	10
124	11	6c. black and red	1·90	20
125	11	7c. black and green	3·75	75
126	11	8c. black on lilac	2·30	1·30
127	11	9c. black and yellow	2·30	85
128	11	10c. black and blue	1·40	30
129	11	11c. black and violet	2·50	55
130	11	12c. black and brown	90	20
131	11	15c. black and orange	1·80	65
132	11	20c. black and blue	2·75	90
133	11	40c. black and red	4·00	1·80
134	11	1p. black and green	9·25	17·00
135	11	2p. black & purple on pink	16·00	29·00

22 Ploughman and Tower of Confucius

23 Bay of Along

24 Ruins of Angkor

1927

136	22	⅒c. olive	10	4·25
137	22	⅕c. yellow	35	4·25
138	22	⅖c. blue	35	4·00
139	22	⅘c. brown	1·10	4·50
140	22	1c. orange	1·00	20
141	22	2c. green	1·90	55
142	22	3c. blue	2·30	20
143	22	4c. mauve	2·50	3·50
144	22	5c. violet	2·50	20
145	23	6c. red	2·30	65
146	23	7c. brown	1·40	90
147	23	8c. olive	3·00	2·50
148	23	9c. purple	2·50	2·50
149	23	10c. blue	2·75	45
150	23	11c. orange	2·20	4·25
151	23	12c. grey	2·20	4·25
152	24	15c. brown and red	10·50	11·00
153	24	20c. grey and violet	7·50	85
154	-	25c. mauve and brown	7·75	6·00
155	-	30c. olive and blue	4·25	3·75
156	-	40c. blue and red	8·00	4·50
157	-	50c. grey and green	9·50	2·50
158	-	1p. black, yellow and blue	18·00	7·25
159	-	2p. blue, orange and red	48·00	13·00

DESIGNS—As T **24**: 25, 30c. Wood-carver; 40, 50c. Temple, Thuat-Luong; 1, 2p. Founding of Saigon.

1931. "Colonial Exn" key-types inscr "INDOCHINE" and surch with new value.

160	F	4c. on 50c. mauve	3·50	3·75

161	**G**	6c. on 90c. red	3·25	5·50
162	**H**	10c. on 1f.50 blue	5·50	4·50

33 Junk

36 "Apsara", or dancing Nymph

1931

163	**33**	1/10c. blue	10	2·75
164	**33**	1/5c. red	10	1·20
165	**33**	2/5c. orange	35	6·25
166	**33**	1/2c. brown	10	1·00
167	**33**	4/5c. violet	20	6·75
168	**33**	1c. brown	10	10
169	**33**	2c. green	30	10
170	-	3c. brown	10	10
171	-	3c. green	13·00	65
172	-	4c. blue	2·75	35
173	-	4c. green	2·00	5·00
174	-	4c. yellow	20	1·10
175	-	5c. purple	50	20
176	-	5c. green	1·00	3·50
177	-	6c. red	35	10
178	-	7c. black	60	50
179	-	8c. red	1·10	1·90
180	-	9c. black on yellow	75	75
181	-	10c. blue	1·10	20
182	-	10c. blue on pink	55	30
183	-	15c. brown	9·75	1·20
184	-	15c. blue	55	35
185	-	18c. blue	1·00	3·50
186	-	20c. red	30	10
187	-	21c. green	45	35
188	-	22c. green	1·00	1·30
189	-	25c. purple	3·50	1·00
190	-	25c. blue	1·10	2·20
191	-	30c. brown	75	20
192	**36**	50c. brown	90	10
193	**36**	60c. purple	85	30
194	**36**	70c. blue	80	75
195	**36**	1p. green	75	30
196	**36**	2p. red	75	30

DESIGNS—As Type **33**: 3c. to 9c. Ruins at Angkor; 10c. to 30c. Worker in rice field.

42 Farman F.190 Mail Plane

1933. Air.

197	**42**	1c. brown	10	1·60
198	**42**	2c. green	10	1·20
199	**42**	5c. green	2·20	2·00
200	**42**	10c. brown	90	45
201	**42**	11c. red	2·30	3·25
202	**42**	15c. blue	4·50	1·40
203	**42**	16c. mauve	90	4·25
204	**42**	20c. green	3·00	1·20
205	**42**	30c. brown	90	60
206	**42**	36c. red	4·75	30
207	**42**	37c. green	1·00	20
208	**42**	39c. green	50	3·00
209	**42**	60c. purple	1·50	1·00
210	**42**	66c. green	2·00	1·00
211	**42**	67c. blue	1·10	3·00
212	**42**	69c. blue	45	7·50
213	**42**	1p. black	1·00	10
214	**42**	2p. orange	90	35
215	**42**	5p. violet	3·00	1·20
216	**42**	10p. red	4·50	1·80
217	**42**	20p. green	20·00	12·00
218	**42**	30p. brown	25·00	12·50

44 Emperor Bao Dai of Annam

1936. Issue for Annam.

219	**44**	1c. brown	1·60	2·50
220	**44**	2c. green	1·40	2·50
221	**44**	4c. violet	1·10	1·00
222	**44**	5c. lake	1·30	4·25
223	**44**	10c. red	3·25	4·75
224	**44**	15c. blue	3·00	3·75
225	**44**	20c. red	2·50	6·00
226	**44**	30c. purple	2·30	3·25
227	**44**	50c. green	5·25	5·00
228	**44**	1p. mauve	7·75	7·50
229	**44**	2p. black	9·25	12·00

45 King Sisowath Monivong of Cambodia

1936. Issue for Cambodia.

230	**45**	1c. brown	1·30	2·50
231	**45**	2c. green	1·40	2·75
232	**45**	4c. violet	1·30	2·00
233	**45**	5c. lake	1·40	4·00
234	**45**	10c. red	2·75	4·00
235	**45**	15c. blue	2·50	4·75
236	**45**	20c. red	2·10	4·25
237	**45**	30c. purple	2·75	3·75
238	**45**	50c. green	2·75	3·00
239	**45**	1p. mauve	4·75	3·50
240	**45**	2p. black	3·50	6·25

1937. Int Exn, Paris. As T 58a of Guadeloupe.

241	2c. violet	1·60	2·30
242	3c. green	1·30	2·00
243	4c. red	90	85
244	6c. brown	1·00	45
245	9c. red	1·00	45
246	15c. blue	75	90
MS246a	120×100 mm. 30c. slate-lilac (as T **7**)	10·00	29·00

46 Pres. Doumer

1938. Opening of Trans-Indo-China Railway.

247	**46**	5c. red (postage)	2·00	55
248	**46**	6c. brown	1·60	55
249	**46**	18c. blue	1·60	1·30
250	**46**	37c. orange (air)	55	10

1938. International Anti-cancer Fund. As T 58b of Guadeloupe.

251	18c.+5c. blue	9·25	18·00

1939. New York World's Fair. As T 58c of Guadeloupe.

252	13c. red	75	2·50
253	23c. blue	1·40	2·75

47 Mot Cot Pagoda, Hanoi

1939. San Francisco International Exhibition.

254	**47**	6c. sepia	1·40	1·40
255	**47**	9c. red	75	75
256	**47**	23c. blue	85	2·30
257	**47**	39c. purple	1·80	1·80

1939. 150th Anniv of French Revolution. As T 58d of Guadeloupe.

258	6c.+2c. green & blk (postage)	11·00	23·00
259	7c.+3c. brown and black	11·00	23·00
260	9c.+4c. orange and black	11·00	23·00
261	13c.+10c. red and black	11·00	23·00
262	23c.+20c. blue and black	11·00	23·00
263	39c.+40c. black & orge (air)	25·00	55·00

48 King Sihanouk of Cambodia

1941. Coronation of King of Cambodia. No gum.

264	**48**	1c. orange	1·00	2·30
265	**48**	6c. violet	7·00	9·75
266	**48**	25c. blue	48·00	60·00

49 Processional Elephant

1942. Fetes of Nam-Giao. No gum.

267	**49**	3c. brown	3·00	8·00
268	**49**	6c. red	3·00	7·75

1942. No. 189 surch 10 cents and bars.

269	10c. on 25c. purple	1·80	3·75

51 Hanoi University

1942. University Fund. No gum.

270	**51**	6c.+2c. red	1·10	3·50
271	**51**	15c.+5c. purple	65	3·50

Surch 10c +2 c.

272	10c.+2c. on 6c.+2c. red	45	6·00

53 Marshal Petain

1942. No gum.

273	**53**	1c. brown	65	3·75
274	**53**	3c. brown	1·80	6·50
275	**53**	6c. red	55	1·20
276	**53**	10c. green	1·50	1·60
277	**53**	40c. blue	90	2·50
278	**53**	40c. grey	1·80	1·30

54 Shield and Sword

1942. National Relief Fund. No gum.

279	**54**	6c.+2c. red and blue	1·40	2·30
280	**54**	15c.+5c. black, red & bl	90	1·40

Surch 10c +2 c.

281	10c.+2c. on 6c.+2c. red and blue	55	4·50

55 Emperor Bao Dai of Annam

56 King Sihanouk of Cambodia

57 Empress Nam-Phaong of Annam

58 King Sisavang-Vong of Laos

1942. No gum.

282	**55**	1/2c. purple	75	2·50
283	**56**	1c. purple	85	4·75
284	**58**	1c. brown	80	4·25
285	**55**	6c. red	3·00	1·80
286	**56**	6c. red	45	3·50
287	**57**	6c. red	1·70	1·10
288	**58**	6c. red	90	4·00

59 Saigon Fair

1942. Saigon Fair. No gum.

289	**59**	6c. red	75	2·75

60 Alexandre Yersin

1943. No gum.

290	**60**	6c. red	75	4·25
291	**60**	15c. purple	55	1·30
292	-	15c. purple	55	3·50
293	-	20c. red	75	45
294	-	30c. brown	35	20
295	**60**	$1 green	35	20

DESIGNS—HORIZ: Nos. 292, 294, Alexandre de Rhodes; No. 293, Pigneau de Behaire, Bishop of Adran.

63 Do Huu-Vi

1943. Airmen. No gum.

296	**63**	6c.+2c. red	35	4·00
297	-	6c.+2c. red	75	4·50

Surch 10c +2 c.

298	**63**	10c.+2c. on 6c.+2c. red	45	5·25
299	-	10c.+2c. on 6c.+2c. red	30	2·75

DESIGN—VERT: Nos. 297, 299, Roland Garros.

64 Doudart de Lagree

1943. Sailors. No gum.

300	**64**	1c. brown	20	55
301	**A**	1c. brown	85	1·40

302	B	1c. brown	1·80	2·30
303	B	5c. brown	45	1·10
304	C	6c. red	2·10	1·40
305	D	6c. red	1·10	2·75
306	E	6c. red	40	3·00
307	F	10c. green	85	1·80
308	64	15c. purple	35	3·00
309	F	20c. red	45	1·20
310	64	40c. blue	45	1·00
311	F	1p. green	65	2·75

DESIGNS—HORIZ: A, Francis Garnier; B, La Grandiere; C, Courbet; D, Rigault de Genouilly. VERT: E, Chasseloup Laubat; F, Charner.

66 "Family, Homeland and Labour"

1943. 3rd Anniv of National Revolution. No gum.

312	66	6c. red	55	2·75

67 De Lanessan

1944. Governors. No gum.

313	G	1c. brown	30	4·50
314	67	1c. brown	55	4·00
315	H	2c. mauve	20	2·75
316	J	4c. orange	75	90
317	H	4c. brown	20	30
318	K	5c. purple	55	3·25
319	J	10c. green	75	90
320	H	10c. green	20	2·30
321	K	10c. green	20	1·40
322	G	10c. green	25	90
323	67	15c. purple	1·40	1·70

DESIGNS—HORIZ: G, Van Vollenhoven; J, Auguste Pavie. VERT: H, Paul Doumer; K, Pierre Pasquier.

69 Athlete

1944. Juvenile Sports. No gum.

324	69	10c. purple and yellow	45	75
325	69	50c. red	55	3·25

70 Orleans Cathedral

1944. Martyr Cities. No gum.

326	70	15c.+60c. purple	90	4·50
327	70	40c.+1p.10 blue	90	6·50

1945. As T 149 of France surch INDOCHINE and values.

328	50c.+50c. on 2f. olive	35	7·00
329	1p.+1p. on 2f. brown	35	6·50
330	2p.+2p. on 2f. grey	55	5·75

1946. Air. Victory. As T 63b of Guadeloupe.

331	80c. orange	45	85

1946. Air. From Chad to the Rhine. As T 63c of Guadeloupe.

332	50c. green	90	5·75
333	1p. mauve	90	3·75
334	1p.50 red	90	3·00
335	2p. purple	90	4·75
336	2p.50 blue	90	6·00
337	5p. red	1·40	5·00

1946. Unissued stamps similar to T 24 with portrait of Marshal Petain optd with R F monogram.

338	10c. red	1·00	4·25
339	25c. blue	6·75	8·25

1949. Air. 75th Anniv of U.P.U. As T 39 of French Equatorial Africa.

340	3p. multicoloured	2·75	3·50

OFFICIAL STAMPS

1933. Stamps of 1931 (Nos. 168, etc.) optd SERVICE.

O197	1c. sepia	4·00	30
O198	2c. green	5·75	5·25
O199	3c. brown	3·75	2·50
O200	4c. blue	5·75	2·75
O201	5c. purple	3·25	35
O202	6c. red	3·00	3·50
O203	10c. blue	55	30
O204	15c. sepia	4·75	1·20
O205	20c. red	4·25	55
O206	21c. green	2·75	4·25
O207	25c. purple	2·30	3·00
O208	30c. brown	4·25	2·50
O209	50c. sepia	22·00	5·25
O210	60c. purple	1·00	3·25
O211	1p. green	55·00	11·00
O212	2p. red	18·00	16·00

1934. As T 11 but value in "CENTS" or "PIASTRES" and optd SERVICE.

O219	1c. brown	1·20	1·00
O220	2c. brown	1·40	1·50
O221	3c. green	4·00	2·00
O222	4c. red	3·00	45
O223	5c. orange	2·20	35
O224	6c. red	10·50	17·00
O225	10c. green	6·25	7·75
O226	15c. blue	4·00	2·30
O227	20c. green	6·50	2·30
O228	21c. violet	23·00	28·00
O229	25c. purple	22·00	22·00
O230	30c. violet	5·00	2·50
O231	50c. mauve	18·00	27·00
O232	60c. grey	30·00	34·00
O233	1p. blue	55·00	40·00
O234	2p. red	70·00	65·00

PARCEL POST STAMPS

1891. Stamp of French Colonies, "Commerce" type, optd INDO-CHINE TIMBRE COLIS POSTAUX.

P4	J	10c. black on lilac	28·00	7·00

1898. No. 10 optd Colis Postaux.

P20	D	10c. black on lilac	30·00	60·00

1899. Nos. 10 and 24 optd TIMBRE COLIS POSTAUX.

P21	10c. black on lilac	75·00	50·00
P22	10c. red	70·00	35·00

POSTAGE DUE STAMPS

1904. Postage Due stamps of French Colonies optd with value in figures.

D47	U	5 on 60c. brown on yellow	12·00	11·00
D48	U	5 on 40c. black	60·00	12·00
D49	U	10 on 60c. black	60·00	34·00
D50	U	30 on 60c. black	60·00	25·00

D 13 Annamite Dragon

1908

D69	D13	2c. black	1·30	45
D70	D13	4c. blue	1·30	55
D71	D13	5c. green	1·60	30
D72	D13	10c. red	7·50	30
D73	D13	15c. violet	4·00	9·50
D74	D13	20c. brown	2·20	1·40
D75	D13	30c. olive	3·00	7·00
D76	D13	40c. purple	9·00	12·00
D77	D13	50c. blue	3·75	1·60
D78	D13	60c. yellow	21·00	28·00
D79	D13	1f. grey	30·00	50·00
D80	D13	2f. brown	46·00	40·00
D81	D13	5f. red	65·00	60·00

1919. Surch in figures and words.

D106	D 13	⅘c. on 2c. black	3·00	5·25
D107	D 13	1⅗c. on 4c. blue	2·50	6·00
D108	D 13	2c. on 5c. green	5·50	1·80
D109	D 13	4c. on 10c. red	6·75	35
D110	D 13	6c. on 15c. violet	11·50	3·75
D111	D 13	8c. on 20c. brown	16·00	1·80
D112	D 13	12c. on 30c. green	16·00	3·25
D113	D 13	16c. on 40c. brown	14·50	1·80
D114	D 13	20c. on 50c. blue	30·00	7·25
D115	D 13	24c. on 60c. yellow	4·75	1·40
D116	D 13	40c. on 1f. grey	5·75	3·25
D117	D 13	80c. on 2f. brown	48·00	46·00
D118	D 13	2p. on 5f. red	75·00	60·00

1922. Type D 13, but values in cents or piastres.

D136	⅖c. black	10	1·30
D137	⅘c. black and red	20	3·25
D138	1c. black and yellow	45	45
D139	2c. black and green	1·30	65
D140	3c. black and violet	2·00	1·90
D141	4c. black and orange	1·80	1·30
D142	6c. black and olive	1·80	1·60
D143	8c. black on lilac	1·20	90
D144	10c. black and blue	1·70	1·80
D145	12c. blk & orge on grn	1·90	1·70
D146	20c. black & bl on yell	2·00	3·25
D147	40c. blk & red on grey	1·70	2·30
D148	1p. black & pur on pk	5·50	5·50

D 28 Mot Cot Pagoda Hanoi

D 29 Annamite Dragon

1927

D160	D 28	⅖c. orange and purple	10	2·50
D161	D 28	⅘c. black and violet	10	2·50
D162	D 28	1c. grey and red	75	4·25
D163	D 28	2c. olive and green	1·80	45
D164	D 28	3c. blue and purple	90	4·00
D165	D 28	4c. brown and blue	1·30	85
D166	D 28	6c. red and scarlet	2·75	8·00
D167	D 28	8c. violet and brown	2·30	3·25
D168	D 29	10c. blue	3·50	2·30
D169	D 29	12c. brown	7·75	9·25
D170	D 29	20c. red	4·00	2·50
D171	D 29	40c. green	5·25	8·00
D172	D 29	1p. red	28·00	46·00

D 37

1931. All values from15c. to 50c. are in the same colours.

D197	D 37	⅕c. black & red on yell	10	5·75
D198	D 37	⅖c. black & red on yell	10	4·75
D199	D 37	⅘c. black & red on yell	10	4·75
D200	D 37	1c. black & red on yell	10	2·00
D201	D 37	2c. black & red on yell	10	65
D202	D 37	2,5c. black & red on yell	50	7·25
D203	D 37	3c. black & red on yell	45	7·25
D204	D 37	4c. black & red on yell	30	3·00
D205	D 37	5c. black & red on yell	30	7·25
D206	D 37	6c. black & red on yell	35	1·40
D207	D 37	10c. black & red on yell	35	1·20
D208	D 37	12c. black & red on yell	20	2·30
D209	D 37	14c. black & red on yell	90	7·25
D210	D 37	18c. black & red on yell	75	7·00
D211	D 37	20c. black & red on yell	35	2·30
D212	D 37	50c. black & red on yell	90	5·50
D213	D 37	1p. blue and red on yell	2·75	8·50

D 62

1943

D296	D62	1c. red on yellow	55	7·50
D297	D62	2c. red on yellow	65	7·75
D298	D62	3c. red on yellow	55	7·50
D299	D62	4c. red on yellow	30	7·50
D300	D62	6c. red on yellow	75	5·75
D301	D62	10c. red on yellow	85	6·50
D302	D62	12c. blue on pink	30	7·75
D303	D62	20c. blue on pink	35	5·50
D304	D62	30c. blue on pink	1·40	5·75

Pt. 6, Pt. 17

INDO-CHINESE POST OFFICES IN CHINA

100 centimes = 1 franc.

General Issues

1902. Stamps of Indo-China, "Tablet" key-type, surch CHINE and value in Chinese.

2	D	2c. brown on buff	6·25	10·50
5	D	10c. red	7·50	7·75
6	D	15c. grey	14·50	15·00
11	D	50c. red on pink	95·00	85·00
15	D	1c. black on blue	2·00	1·40
17	D	4c. brown on grey	3·50	5·75
18	D	5c. green	4·00	6·25
20	D	20c. red on green	6·00	9·25
21	D	25c. black on pink	8·50	19·00
22	D	25c. blue	8·00	6·50
23	D	30c. brown on drab	5·00	14·50
24	D	40c. red on yellow	36·00	60·00
25	D	50c. brown on blue	8·25	10·00
26	D	75c. brown on orange	30·00	55·00
27	D	1f. green	50·00	70·00
28	D	5f. mauve on lilac	75·00	£120

1904. Stamps of Indo-China surch CHINE and value in Chinese.

29	8	1c. olive	1·70	1·80
30	8	2c. red on yellow	1·90	1·60
31	8	4c. brown on grey	£750	£650
32	8	5c. green	2·50	1·50
33	8	10c. red	3·00	2·30
34	8	15c. brown on blue	2·00	1·50
36	8	20c. red on green	10·50	32·00
37	8	25c. blue	4·50	8·00
38	8	40c. black on grey	2·50	5·75
39	8	1f. green	£300	£225
40	8	2f. brown on yellow	39·00	55·00
41	8	10f. red on green	£120	£130

Pt. 4, Pt. 21

INDONESIA

An independent republic was proclaimed in Java and Sumatra on 17 August 1945 and lasted until the end of 1948. During this period the Dutch controlled the rest of the Netherlands Indies, renamed "Indonesia" in September 1948. On 27 December 1949 all Indonesia except New Guinea became independent as the United States of Indonesia which, during 1950, amalgamated with the original Indonesian Republic (Java and Sumatra), a single state being proclaimed on 15 August 1950 as the Indonesian Republic. This was within the Netherlands-Indonesian Union which was abolished on 10 August 1954.

100 cents (or sen) = 1 gulden (or rupiah).

A. DUTCH ADMINISTRATION

1948. Stamps of Netherlands Indies optd INDONESIA and bar or bars.

533	81	20c. blue	50	40
535	81	40c. green	50	40
536	81	80c. red	1·30	40
537a	81	1g. violet	1·70	40
538	-	2½g. orange (No. 479)	70·00	13·50
539	81	10g. green	£130	43·00
540	81	25g. orange	£180	80·00
541	81	15c. orange	1·30	40
543	81	25c. green	40	40
544	81	45c. mauve	1·60	1·20
545	81	50c. lake	50	40

86

87 Portal to Tjandi Poentadewa Temple

1949. New Currency.

548A	86	1s. grey	50	35
549A	86	2s. purple	80	35
550A	86	2½s. brown	50	35
551A	86	3s. red	80	35
552A	86	4s. green	80	80
553A	86	5s. blue	50	35
554A	86	7½s. green	80	35
555A	86	10s. mauve	50	35
556A	86	12½s. red	2·50	35
557A	87	15s. red	2·30	80
558A	87	20s. black	1·30	35
559A	87	25s. blue	1·30	35
560A	-	30s. red	1·60	35
561A	-	40s. green	1·60	35
562A	-	45s. purple	3·75	6·25
563A	-	50s. brown	2·10	35
564A	-	60s. brown	2·10	2·50
565A	-	80s. red	5·00	50
566A	-	1r. violet	1·80	35
567A	-	2r. green	8·75	35
568A	-	3r. purple	£130	35
569A	-	5r. brown	90·00	2·50
570A	-	10r. black	£110	2·50
571A	-	25r. brown	1·10	2·50

DESIGNS—As Type **87**: 30 to 45s. Sculpture from Temple at Bedjoening, Bali; 50 to 80s. Minangkabau house, Sumatra; 21×26 mm: 1 to 3r. Toradja house; 5 to 25r. Detail of Temple of Panahan.

89 Globe and Arms of Berne

1949. 75th Anniv of U.P.U.

572	89	15s. red	1·60	50
573	89	25s. blue	1·60	50

B. REPUBLIC, 1945-48

ISSUES FOR JAVA AND MADURA

1945. Stamps of Netherlands Indies optd REPOEBLIK INDONESIA.

J1	46	1c. violet	1·10	1·70
J2	46	2c. purple	4·50	5·50
J3	46	3½c. grey	50·00	55·00
J4	-	2½c. red (No. 462)	1·40	2·30
J5	-	3c. green (No. 463)	1·60	2·30
J6	71	4c. olive	1·60	2·30
J7	71	5c. blue (No. 465)	65·00	75·00
J19	-	2c. red (No. 461)	1·10	2·30

1945. Stamps of Japanese Occupation of Netherlands Indies optd as above.

J8		3½s. red (No. 2)	£275	£375
J9		5s. green (No. 3)	14·00	9·50
J10		3½c. red (No. 5)	38·00	38·00
J11	2	5s. green	45	75
J12	-	10c. blue (No. 7)	30	60
J13	-	20c. olive (No. 8)	55	85
J14	-	40c. purple (No. 9)	90	1·20
J15	4	60c. orange	1·20	1·40
J16	-	80s. brown (No. 11)	11·00	15·00

J5 Bull

1945. Declaration of Independence. Inscr "17 AGOESTOES 1945". Perf or imperf.

J23	J5	10s. (+ 10s.) brown	4·75	6·50
J24	-	20s. (+ 10s.) brown & red	5·75	6·50

DESIGN—VERT: 20s. Bull and Indonesian flag.

J 9 Boat in Storm

1946

J49		5s. blue	75	85
J50		20s. brown	85	1·10
J51	J 9	30s. red	70	2·75

DESIGNS: 5s. Road and mountains; 20s. Soldier on waterfront.

J10 Wayang Puppet

1946

J52	J10	50s. blue	14·00	11·00
J53	-	60s. red	4·25	£140
J54	-	80s. violet	52·00	£400

DESIGNS: 60s. Kris and flag; 80s. Temple.

J13 Buffalo breaking Chains

J14 Bandung, March, 1946

1946. Perf or imperf.

J55b	J13	3s. red	10	40
J56b	J14	5s. blue	30	45
J57	-	10s. black	7·50	10·00
J58	-	15s. purple	9·50	8·00
J59b	-	30s. green	75	75
J60b	-	40s. blue	75	75
J61cb	J 13	50s. black	50	60
J62b	J 14	60s. lilac	1·40	1·70
J63	-	80s. red	2·75	6·00
J64b	-	100s. red	1·20	1·20
J65b	-	200s. lilac	1·10	1·90
J66b	-	500s. red	7·50	7·50
J67b	-	1000s. green	5·75	7·50

DESIGNS—HORIZ: 10, 15s. Soerabaya, November 1945; 30s. Anti-aircraft gunners; 100s. Ambarawa, November 1945; 200s. Wonokromo Dam, Soerabaya; 1000s. Cavalryman. VERT: 40s. Quay at Tandjong Priok; 80s. Airman; 500s. Mass meeting with flags, Djakarta.

1948. Postage Due Stamps of Netherlands Indies surch SEGEL 25 sen PORTO.

J68	D7	25s. on 7½c. orange	14·00	28·00
J69	D7	25s. on 15c. orange	9·50	24·00

Although surcharged for use as postage due stamps the above were employed for ordinary postal use.

J16 "Labour and Transport"

1948. 3rd Anniv of Independence. Imperf.

J70	J16	50s. blue	5·00	6·00
J71	J16	100s. red	7·00	7·00

J18 Flag over Waves

1949. Government's Return to Jogjakarta. Perf or Imperf.

J77b	J18	100s. red	5·00	12·00
J78b	J18	150s. red	8·00	20·00

POSTAGE DUE STAMPS

1948. Nos. J67 and J70/1 optd DENDA, or surch also.

JD72	J16	50s. blue	20·00	
JD73	-	100s. red	20·00	
JD74	-	1r. on 50s. blue (A)	20·00	
JD75	-	1r. on 50s. blue (B)	20·00	
JD76	-	1r. on 1000s. green	20·00	

A. Surcharged "RP 1"; B. Surcharged "1—RP".

ISSUES FOR SUMATRA

1946. Stamps of Netherlands Indies surch Repoeblik Indonesia and value.

S1		15s. on 5c. blue (No. 465)	1·50	1·90
S2	46	20s. on 3½c. grey	7·50	7·50
S3	46	30s. on 1c. violet	7·50	7·50
S4	46	40s. on 2c. purple	25	60
S7	-	50s. on 17½c. orange (No. 431)	55·00	55·00
S9	46	60s. on 2½c. bistre	7·50	5·25
S10	46	80s. on 3c. green	7·50	7·50
S11	-	1r. on 10c. red (No. 429)	6·00	6·00

S9 Ploughing

1946. Freedom Fund.

S17	S9	5s. (+25s.) green	75	2·30
S18	S9	5s. (+25s.) blue	20	1·50
S19	-	15s. (+35s.) red	1·90	3·75
S20	-	15s. (+35s.) blue	20	1·50
S21	-	40s. (+60s.) orange	90	2·30
S22	-	40s. (+60s.) red	75	4·50
S23	-	40s. (+60s.) purple	7·50	24·00
S24	-	40s. (+60s.) brown	12·50	42·00

DESIGNS—VERT: 15s. Soldier and flag; 40s. Oil well and factories, Palembang.

S10 Pres. Sukarno

1946

S25	S10	40s. (+60s.) red	75	5·75

1946. "FONDS KEMERDEKAAN" obliterated by one or two bars.

S27	S9	5s. blue	45·00	£110
S28	-	40s. red (No. S22)	45·00	45·00

1946. As Type S 9 but without "FONDS KEMERDEKAAN". Perf or imperf.

S29	2s. red	45	45·00
S30	2s. brown	2·75	11·50
S31	3s. green	75	4·50
S32	3s. red	3·00	11·50
S33	3s. blue	†	
S34	5s. blue	25	2·75
S35	15s. blue	25	1·50
S36	15s. green	3·00	11·50
S37	40s. brown	30	1·90
S38	40s. blue	15·00	27·00

DESIGNS: 2, 3, 5s. As Type S **9**. 15s. Soldier and flag; 40s. Oil well and factories, Palembang.

1947. Fund for Palembang War Victims. Nos. S18, S20 and S23 optd BPKPP over triple circle.

S39	S9	5s. blue	75·00	90·00
S40	-	15s. blue	75·00	90·00
S41	-	40s. brown	75·00	90·00

S12

1947. Fiscal stamps of Japanese Occupation with blank panels optd in black with prangko N.R.I. and value as in Type S 12.

S42	S 12	0f.50 orange	13·50	30·00
S43	S 12	1f. orange	11·50	23·00
S44	S 12	2f. orange	17·00	30·00
S45	S 12	2f.50 orange	12·00	15·00

1947. No. S25 surch with new value and bars.

S46	50s. on 40s. red	5·00	5·00
S47	1f. on 40s. red	6·75	6·75
S48	1f.50 on 40s. red	4·25	4·25
S49	2f.50 on 40s. red	75	2·30
S50	3f.50 on 40s. red	75	2·30
S51	5f. on 40s. red	75	2·30

1947. Surch with ornament and new value.

S52	30s. on 40s. (No. S28)	60	1·50
S53	50s. on 5s. (No. S34)	6·00	4·50
S54	1f. on 5s. (No. S34)	4·50	4·50
S55	1f.50 on 5s. (No. S34)	6·00	6·00
S56	1r. on 40s. (No. S37)	40	3·00
S57	2r. on 5s. (No. S34)	60	3·00
S59	50s. on 40s. (No. S28)	11·50	15·00
S60	1f. on 40s. (No. S28)	40	1·50
S61	1f.50 on 40s. (No. S28)	3·00	5·25
S62	2f.50 on 40s. (No. S28)	40	1·50
S63	1s. on 15s. (No. S35)	45	1·90
S64	5s. on 3s. (No. S33)	40	1·90
S65	10s. on 15s. red (as Nos. S35/6)	50	1·90
S66	50s. on 3s. (No. S32)	15·00	38·00

1947. No. S56 surch 50.

S58	50(r.) on 1r. on 40s.	45·00	55·00

1947. Air. Surch Pos Udara with ornament and new value.

S67	10r. on 40s. (No. S22)	1·90	2·30
S68	20r. on 5s. (No. S34)	1·10	2·30

1947. Stamps of 1946 (Nos. S 29/37) surch.

S69	10s. on 15s. blue	11·50	11·50
S70	20s. on 15s. blue	11·50	11·50
S71	30s. on 15s. blue	11·50	6·00
S72	1r. on 2s. red	47·00	47·00
S73	2f.50 on 15s. blue	14·00	14·00
S74	5f. on 40s. brown	£225	£170
S75	50s. on 5s. blue	£600	£550
S76	50s. on 15s. blue	£600	£600
S77	0f.50 on 15s. blue	£550	£550
S78	1f. on 5s. blue	£140	£140
S79	1f. on 15s. blue	£275	£375
S80	2f.50 on 5s. blue	£750	£650
S82	2f.50 on 40s. brown	£550	£650
S83	5f. on 15s. blue	£750	£550
S85	2r.50 on 3s. green	19·00	28·00
S87	10r. on 3s. green	70·00	70·00
S88	2r. on 3s. green	33·00	65·00
S89	5r. on 15s. blue	7·00	11·50
S91	20r. on 2s. red	£225	£475
S92	50r. on 15s. blue	£325	£475
S93	100r. on 15s. blue	£110	£110
S94	150r. on 40s. red	£140	£140

No. S94 is surcharged on No. S22 with a pen-stroke through "FONDS KEMERDEKAAN".

(S 23) "O.R.I." = "Oeang Repoeblik Indonesia" (Indonesian Republican Money)

1947. Change of Currency. Various stamps optd with Type S 23. (a) On stamps of Netherlands Indies.

S96	46	3c. green (No. 338)	4·75	6·00
S97	71	4c. olive (No. 464)	7·25	8·00
S98	-	5c. blue (No. 465)	3·50	5·50
S99	S 12	1c. red (No. D226)	8·00	8·50
S100	-	15c. red (No. D448)	6·00	7·25

(b) On stamps of Japanese Occupation of Netherlands Indies.

S101		1c. green (No. 15)	1·10	1·50
S102		2c. green (No. 16)	1·10	1·25
S103		3c. blue (No. 17)	1·10	1·25
S104		3½c. red (No. 18)	1·50	1·90
S105		4c. blue (No. 19)	2·50	3·75
S106		5c. orange (No. 20)	1·50	1·90
S107		10c. blue (No. 21)	6·00	6·75
S108		20c. brown (No. 22)	6·00	6·75
S109	6	30c. purple (No. 23)	1·10	1·10
S110	-	50c. brown (No. 25)	2·20	2·20
S111	-	10c. red (No. 57)	85	1·10
S113	-	25c. green (No. 62)	10·00	12·00
S114	-	30c. brown (No. 63)	8·00	9·00
S115	-	50c. red (No. 66)	10·50	13·00
S116	-	60c. blue (No. 67)	5·50	6·00
S117	-	80c. red (No. 68)	5·50	7·25
S118	-	1g. violet (No. 69)	11·00	12·50

(c) On stamps of Japan.

S119	1s. brown (No. 317)	1·00	1·50
S120	3s. green (No. 319)	1·00	1·50
S121	4s. green (No. 320)	5·00	5·50
S122	6s. orange (No. 322)	1·50	2·00
S123	25s. brn & choc (No. 329)	1·00	1·40
S124	30s. green (No. 330)	2·40	3·50
S125	50s. green & bis (No. 331)	1·00	1·50
S126	1y. brown and chocolate (No. 332)	2·40	3·50

(d) On stamps of Indonesia-Sumatra.

S127	46	20s. on 3½c. grey (No. S2)	6·50	7·50
S128	-	30s. on 1c. violet (No. S3)	6·50	8·00
S129	46	40s. on 2c. purple (No. S4)	3·00	5·00
S132	S 9	5s. green (No. S17)	2·50	4·00
S133	-	5s. blue (No. S18)	90	1·30
S134	-	15s. blue (No. S20)	2·40	4·25
S135	-	40s. red (No. S22)	2·75	3·50
S136	-	2s. red (No. S29)	2·50	3·00
S137	-	3s. green (No. S31)	10·50	10·50
S138	-	3s. red (No. S32)	1·00	1·70
S139	-	5s. blue (No. S34)	75	1·10
S140	-	15s. blue (No. S35)	75	1·10
S141	-	15s. green (No. S36)	3·75	5·50
S142	-	40s. brown (No. S37)	70	1·00
S143	-	1f.50 on 40s. red (No. S48)	6·50	30·00
S144	-	2f.50 on 40s. red (No. S49)	6·25	7·50
S145	-	3f.50 on 40s. red (No. S50)	6·25	7·50
S146	-	30s. on 40s. red (No. S52)	80	1·30
S147	-	1f.50 on 40s. red (No. S61)	6·50	7·50
S148	-	2f.50 on 40s. red (No. S62)	6·25	7·50
S149	-	1s. on 15s. bl (No. S63)	70	1·40
S150	-	10s. on 15s. red (No. S65)	2·40	3·75
S151	-	50s. on 5s. blue (No. S53)	1·80	2·40
S152	-	1f.50 on 5s. blue (No. S55)	5·50	7·25
S153	-	2r. on 5s. blue (No. S57)	1·60	2·50
S154	-	10r. on 40s. red (No. S67)	7·50	10·00

C. UNITED STATES OF INDONESIA

90 Indonesian Flag

1950. Inauguration of United States of Indonesia.

574	90	15s. red (20½×26 mm)	1·10	25
575	90	15s. red (18×23 mm)	6·50	1·10

1950. Stamps of 1949 optd RIS.

579	86	1s. grey	80	65
580	86	2s. purple	1·40	1·80
581	86	2½s. brown	80	65
582	86	3s. red	80	40
583	86	4s. green	80	65
584	86	5s. blue	80	65
585	86	7½s. green	80	65
586	86	10s. mauve	80	60
587	86	12½s. red	1·00	65
588	87	20s. black	24·00	28·00
589	87	25s. blue	80	60

590	-	30s. red	8·25	18·00
591	-	40s. green	80	40
592	-	45s. purple	1·60	1·00
593	-	50s. brown	1·40	85
594	-	60s. brown	7·00	10·50
595	-	80s. red	2·75	1·00
596	-	1r. violet	2·10	45
597	-	2r. green	£350	90·00
598	-	3r. purple	£120	55·00
599	-	5r. brown	49·00	16·00
600	-	10r. black	90·00	35·00
601	-	25r. brown	20·00	13·50

D. INDONESIAN REPUBLIC

94 Indonesian Arms

1950. 5th Anniv of Proclamation of Independence.

602	94	15s. red	2·00	25
603	94	25s. green	2·75	1·10
604	94	1r. sepia	9·75	1·70

95 Maps and Torch

1951. Asiatic Olympic Games, New Delhi.

605	95	5s.+3s. green	10	10
606	95	10s.+5s. blue	10	10
607	95	20s.+5s. red	10	10
608	95	30s.+10s. brown	25	15
609	95	35s.+10s. blue	2·75	2·10

96

97 General Post-Office, Bandung

98 "Spirit of Indonesia"

1951

610	96	1s. grey	40	75
611	96	2s. mauve	40	60
612	96	2½s. brown	5·00	15
613	96	5s. red	40	15
614	96	7½s. green	40	15
615	96	10s. blue	40	15
616	96	15s. violet	40	15
618	96	20s. red	40	15
619	96	25s. green	40	15
620	97	30s. red	10	10
621	97	35s. violet	65	10
622	97	40s. green	10	10
623	97	45s. purple	10	25
624	97	50s. brown	3·00	10
625	98	60s. brown	10	10
626	98	70s. grey	10	10
627	98	75s. blue	10	10
628	98	80s. purple	10	10
629	98	90s. green	10	10

99 President Sukarno

1951

630	99	1r. violet	25	10
631	99	1r.25 orange	1·60	10
632	99	1r.50 brown	25	10
633	99	2r. green	25	10
634	99	2r.50 brown	25	10
635	99	3r. blue	25	10
636	99	4r. green	25	10
637	99	5r. brown	25	10
638	99	6r. mauve	25	10
639	99	10r. grey	25	10
640	99	15r. stone	25	10
641	99	20r. purple	25	10
642	99	25r. red	65	10
643	99	40r. green	80	2·10
644	99	50r. violet	1·10	15

101 Sports Emblem

1951. National Sports Festival.

655	101	5s.+3s. green	35	40
656	101	10s.+5s. blue	35	40
657	101	20s.+5s. orange	35	40
658	101	30s.+10s. sepia	35	40
659	101	35s.+10s. blue	35	1·00

102 Doves

1951. U.N. Day.

660	102	7½s. green	2·75	80
661	102	10s. violet	80	40
662	102	20s. orange	2·00	80
663	102	30s. red	2·75	1·00
664	102	35s. blue	2·75	1·00
665	102	1r. sepia	21·00	3·25

1953. Natural Disasters Relief Fund. Surch 19 53 BENTJANA ALAM +10s.

666	97	35s.+10s. violet	25	15

104 Melati Flowers

1953. Mothers' Day and 25th Anniv of Indonesian Women's Congress.

667	104	50s. green	20·00	55

105 Merapi Volcano in Eruption

1954. Natural Disasters Relief Fund.

668	105	15s.+10s. green	1·10	1·40
669	105	35s.+15s. violet	1·10	1·10
670	105	50s.+25s. red	1·10	1·10
671	105	75s.+25s. blue	1·10	1·10
672	105	1r.+25s. red	1·10	1·10
673	105	2r.+50s. brown	2·75	1·10
674a	105	3r.+1r. green	14·00	7·00
675a	105	5r.+2r.50 brown	16·00	9·75

106 Girls with Musical Instruments

1954. Child Welfare.

676	106	10s.+10s. purple	10	55
677	-	15s.+10s. green	10	65
678	-	35s.+15s. mauve	15	65
679	-	50s.+15s. purple	50	65
680	-	75s.+25s. blue	25	2·50
681	-	1r.+25s. red	35	4·50

DESIGNS: 15s. Menangkabau boy and girl performing Umbrella Dance; 35s. Girls playing "Tjongkak"; 50s. Boy on bamboo stilts; 75s. Ambonese boys playing flutes; 1r. Srimpi dancing girl.

107 Globe and Doves

1955. Asian–African Conference, Bandung.

682	107	15s. black	1·00	65
683	107	35s. brown	1·00	65
684	107	50s. red	3·00	65
685	107	75s. turquoise	1·60	65

108 Semaphore Signaller

1955. National Scout Jamboree.

686	-	15s.+10s. green	15	15
687	108	35s.+15s. blue	15	15
688	-	50s.+25s. red	15	15
689	-	75s.+25s. brown	15	15
690	-	1r.+50s. violet	15	15

DESIGNS: 15s. Indonesian scout badge; 50s. Scouts round campfire; 75s. Scout feeding baby sika deer; 1r. Scout saluting.

109 Proclamation of Independence

1955. 10th Anniv of Independence.

691	109	15s. green	80	65
692	109	35s. blue	80	65
693	109	50s. brown	5·25	40
694	109	75s. purple	1·10	55

110 Postmaster Sukarto

1955. 10th Anniv of Indonesian Post Office.

695	110	15s. brown	80	65
696	110	35s. red	80	65
697	110	50s. blue	6·00	1·50
698	110	75s. green	2·40	65

111 Electors

1955. 1st General Indonesian Elections.

699	111	15s. purple	40	35
700	111	35s. green	55	65
701	111	50s. red	2·00	80
702	111	75s. blue	75	35

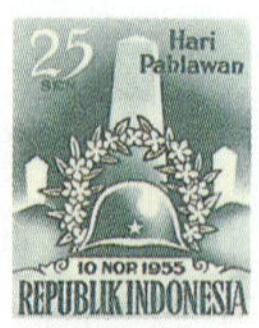

112 Memorial Column, Wreath and Helmet

1955. Heroes' Day.

703	112	25s. green	65	25
704	112	50s. blue	1·60	55
705	112	1r. red	12·00	25

113 Weaving

1956. Blind Relief Fund.

706	113	15s.+10s. green	55	55
707	-	35s.+15s. brown	55	55
708	-	50s.+25s. red	1·20	1·10
709	-	75s.+50s. blue	55	55

DESIGNS—VERT: 35s. Basketwork; 50s. Map reading; 75s. Reading.

114 Torch and Book

1956. Asian and African Students' Conf, Bandung.

710	114	25s. blue	1·00	25
711	114	50s. red	5·00	1·00
712	114	1r. green	2·10	1·00

115 Lesser Malay Chevrotain

1956

713	115	5s. blue	10	10
714	115	10s. brown	10	10
715	115	15s. purple	10	10
716	-	20s. green	10	10
717	-	25s. purple	10	10
718	-	30s. orange	10	10
719	-	35s. blue	10	10
720	-	40s. green	10	10
721	-	45s. purple	1·10	15
722	-	50s. bistre	10	10
723	-	60s. blue	15	10
724	-	70s. red	1·60	25
725	-	75s. sepia	15	10
726	-	80s. red	15	15
727	-	90s. green	15	15

DESIGNS: 20s. to 30s. Hairy-nosed otter; 35s. to 45s. Malayan pangolin; 50s. to 70s. Banteng; 75s. to 90s. Sumatran rhinoceros.

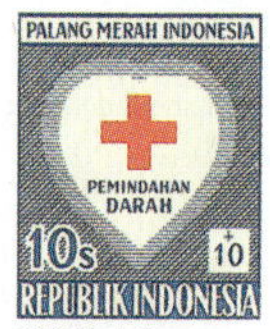

116 Red Cross

1956. Red Cross Fund.

728	116	10s.+10s. red and blue	10	10
729	116	15s.+10s. red & carmine	10	10
730	-	35s.+15s. red and brown	15	15
731	-	50s.+15s. red and green	25	15
732	-	75s.+25s. red & orange	35	25
733	-	1r.+25s. red and violet	50	40

DESIGNS: 35, 50s. Blood transfusion bottle; 75s., 1r. Hands and drop of blood.

117

1956. Bicentenary of Djokjakarta.

734	117	15s. green	1·60	50
735	117	35s. brown	1·60	50
736	117	50s. blue	3·00	80
737	117	75s. purple	3·00	80

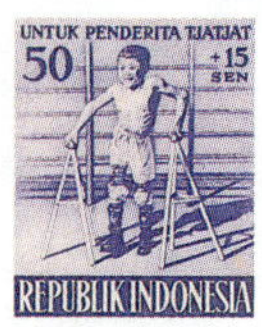

118 Crippled Child

1957. Cripples' Rehabilitation Fund. Inscr "UNTUK PENDERITA TJATJAT".

738	-	10s.+10s. blue	10	10
739	-	15s.+10s. brown	10	10
740	-	35s.+15s. red	10	10
741	118	50s.+15s. violet	25	25
742	-	75s.+25s. green	35	35
743	-	1r.+25s. red	50	50

DESIGNS: 10s. One-legged woman painting cloth; 15s. One-handed artist; 35s. One-handed machinist; 75s. Doctor tending cripple; 1r. Man writing with artificial arm.

119 Telegraph Key and Tape

1957. Centenary of Telegraphs in Indonesia.

744	**119**	10s. red	2·40	50
745	**119**	15s. blue	50	25
746	**119**	25s. black	40	15
747	**119**	50s. red	50	25
748	**119**	75s. green	50	15

120 Two men with Savings-box

1957. Co-operation Day. Inscr "HARI KOOPERASI".

749	**120**	10s. blue	55	40
750	-	15s. red	55	40
751	**120**	50s. green	1·00	65
752	-	1r. violet	1·40	15

DESIGN: 15s., 1r. "Co-operative Prosperity" (hands holding ear of rice and cotton).

121 Kembodja ("Plumeria acuminata")

1957. Various Charity Funds. Floral designs. Multicoloured.

753	10s.+10s. Type **121**	2·10	1·00
754	15s.+10s. Tjempakakuning (michelia)	1·50	1·00
755	35s.+15s. Matahari (sunflower)	1·00	80
756	50s.+15s. Melati (jasmine)	65	65
757	75s.+50s. Larat (orchid)	65	65

122 Convair CV 340 Airliner

1958. National Aviation Day. Inscr "HARI PENERBANGAN NASIONAL 9-4-1958".

758	**122**	10s. brown	15	10
759	-	15s. blue	15	15
760	-	35s. orange	35	25
761	**122**	50s. turquoise	65	40
762	-	75s. slate	1·10	55

DESIGNS: 15s. Hiller "Skeeter" helicopter; 35s. Nurtiano Sikumbang trainer; 75s. De Havilland Vampire jet fighter.

123 "Helping Hands"

1958. Indonesian Orphans Welfare Fund Inscr "ANAK PIATU".

763	**123**	10s.+10s. blue	15	15
764	-	15s.+10s. red	15	15
765	**123**	35s.+15s. green	15	15
766	-	50s.+25s. drab	15	15
767	**123**	75s.+50s. brown	15	15
768	-	1r.+50s. brown	15	15

DESIGN: 15s., 50s., 1r. Girl and boy orphans.

124 Thomas Cup

1958. Indonesian Victory in Thomas Cup World Badminton Championships, Singapore.

769	**124**	25s. red	15	15
770	**124**	50s. orange	15	15
771	**124**	1r. brown	25	15

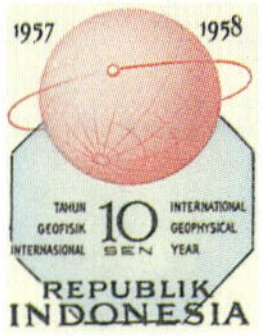

125 Satellite encircling Globe

1958. International Geophysical Year.

785	**125**	10s. pink, green and blue	90	55
786	**125**	15s. drab, violet and grey	25	15
787	**125**	35s. blue, sepia and pink	25	15
788	**125**	50s. brown, blue and drab	25	15
789	**125**	75s. lilac, black and yellow	25	15

126 Racing Cyclist

1958. Tour of Java Cycle Race.

790	**126**	25s. blue	50	25
791	**126**	50s. red	80	25
792	**126**	1r. grey	50	25

127 "Human Rights"

1958. 10th Anniv of Declaration of Human Rights.

793	**127**	10s. sepia	15	15
794	-	15s. brown	15	15
795	-	35s. blue	25	15
796	-	50s. bistre	25	15
797	-	75s. green	25	15

DESIGNS: 15s. Hands grasping "Flame of Freedom"; 35s. Native holding candle; 50s. Family acclaiming "Flame of Freedom"; 75s. "Flame" superimposed on figure "10".

128 Babirusa

1959. Animal Protection Campaign.

798	**128**	10s. sepia and olive	15	15
799	-	15s. sepia and brown	25	25
800	-	20s. sepia and green	35	35
801	-	50s. sepia and brown	50	50
802	-	75s. sepia and red	50	50
803	-	1r. black and turquoise	55	55

ANIMALS: 15s. Anoa (buffalo); 20s. Orang-utan; 50s. Javan rhinoceros; 75s. Komodo lizard; 1r. Malayan tapir.

129 Indonesian Scout Badge

1959. 10th World Scout Jamboree, Manila. Inscr as in T 129. Badges in red.

804	**129**	10s.+5s. bistre	15	15
805	-	15s.+10s. green	25	15
806	**129**	20s.+10s. violet	25	25
807	-	50s.+25s. olive	25	40
808	**129**	75s.+35s. brown	25	40
809	-	1r.+50s. slate	35	40

DESIGN: 15s., 50s., 1r. Scout badge within compass.

130

1959. Re-adoption of 1945 Constitution.

810	**130**	20s. red and blue	15	15
811	**130**	50s. black and red	15	15
812	**130**	75s. red and brown	15	15
813	**130**	1r.50 black and green	25	15

131 Factory and Girder

1959. 11th Colombo Plan Conference, Djakarta.

814	**131**	15s. black and green	15	10
815	-	20s. black and orange	15	10
816	**131**	50s. black and red	15	10
817	-	75s. black and blue	15	10
818	-	1r.15 black and purple	15	10

DESIGNS: 20, 75s. Cogwheel and diesel train; 1r.15, Forms of transport and communications.

132

1960. Indonesian Youth Conference, Bandung. Inscr "1960".

819	**132**	15s.+5s. sepia and bistre	10	25
820	-	20s.+10s. sepia & green	15	25
821	**132**	50s.+25s. purple & blue	15	25
822	-	75s.+35s. green & bis	15	25
823	-	1r.15+50s. black & red	35	25

DESIGNS: 20s., 75s. Test-tubes in frame; 1r.15, Youth wielding manifesto.

133 Refugee Camp

1960. World Refugee Year. Centres in black.

824	**133**	10s. purple	10	15
825	-	15s. ochre	10	15
826	-	20s. brown	10	15
827	**133**	50s. green	15	15
828	-	75s. blue	35	15
829	-	1r.15 red	35	90

DESIGNS: 15s., 75s. Outcast family; 20s., 1r.15, "Care of refugees" (refugee with protecting hands).

134 Tea plants

1960. Agricultural Products.

830		5s. grey	15	10
831		10s. brown	15	10
832		15s. purple	15	10
833		20s. bistre	15	10
834	**134**	25s. green	15	10
835	-	50s. blue	15	10
836	-	75s. red	15	10
837	-	1r.15 red	15	15

DESIGNS: 5s. Oil palm; 10s. Sugar cane; 15s. Coffee plant; 20s. Tobacco plant; 50s. Coconut palm; 75s. Rubber trees; 1r.15, Rice plants.

135 Mosquito

1960. World Health Day.

838	**135**	25s. red	10	10
839	**135**	50s. brown	15	10
840	**135**	75s. green	15	10
841	**135**	3r. orange	40	15

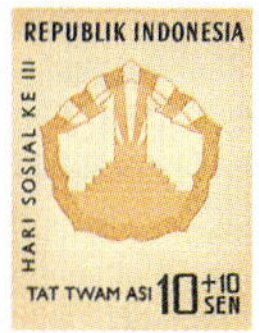

136 Socialist Emblem

1960. 3rd Socialist Day. Inscr as in T 136.

842	**136**	10s.+10s. brown & blk	10	15
843	-	15s.+15s. purple & blk	10	15
844	-	20s.+20s. blue and black	15	15
845	-	50s.+25s. black & brn	15	25
846	-	75s.+25s. black & green	15	25
847	-	3r.+50s. black and red	15	40

DESIGNS: 15s. Emblem similar to Type **136** within plants; 20s. Lotus flower; 50s. Boy and girl; 75s. Ceremonial watering of plant; 3r. Mother with children.

137 Pres. Sukarno and Workers Hoeing

1961. National Development Plan.

848	**137**	75s. black	25	15

1961. Flood Relief Fund. Nos. 832/3 and 836 surch BENTJANA ALAM 1961 and premium.

849	15s.+10s. purple	10	10
850	20s.+15s. brown	10	10
851	75s.+25s. red	10	10

139 Bull Race

1961. Tourist Publicity.

852	-	10s. purple	50	40
853	-	15s. grey	50	40
854	**139**	20s. orange	50	40
855	-	25s. red	50	40
856	-	50s. lake	50	40
857	-	75s. brown	50	40
858	-	1r. green	90	40
859	-	1r.50 bistre	90	40
860	-	2r. blue	1·30	40
861	-	3r. grey	1·30	40

MS862 Three sheets each 140×105 mm containing (a) Nos. 852/3, 859; (b) Nos. 854, 856, 860; (c) Nos. 857/8 and a fourth sheet 105×140 mm. containing Nos. 855, 861 24·00 24·00

DESIGNS: 10s. Ambonese boat; 15s. Tangkuban Perahu crater; 25s. Daja dancer; 50s. Toradja houses; 75s. Balinese temple; 1r. Lake Toba; 1r.50, Bali dancer; 2r. "Buffalo Hole" (gorge); 3r. Borobudur temple.

140 Stadium

1961. Thomas Cup World Badminton Championships.

863	**140**	75s. lilac and blue	10	10
864	**140**	1r. olive and green	15	10
865	**140**	3r. salmon and blue	25	15

141 "United Efforts"

1961. 16th Anniv of Independence.

866	**141**	75s. violet and blue	10	10
867	**141**	1r.50 green and cream	10	10
868	**141**	3r. red and salmon	35	15

142 Sultan Hasanuddin

1961. National Independence Heroes. Portraits in sepia; inscriptions in black.

869	-	20s. olive	10	35
870	**142**	25s. olive	15	35
871	-	30s. violet	15	35
872	-	40s. brown	15	35
873	-	50s. myrtle	15	35
874	-	60s. turquoise	15	35
875	-	75s. brown	90	35
876	-	1r. blue	90	35
877	-	1r.25 green	75	35
878	-	1r.50 green	90	35
879	-	2r. red	75	35
880	-	2r.50 red	90	35
881	-	3r. slate	75	35
882	-	4r. green	75	35
883	-	4r.50 purple	35	35
884	-	5r. red	80	35
885	-	6r. ochre	90	35
886	-	7r.50 blue	1·10	35
887	-	10r. green	75	35
888	-	15r. orange	75	35

PORTRAITS: 20s. Abdul Muis; 30s. Surjopranoto; 40s. Tengku Tjhik Di Tiro; 50s. Teuku Umar; 60s. K. H. Samanhudi; 75s. Capt. Pattimura; 1r. Raden Adjeng Kartini; 1r.25, K. H. Achmad Dahlan; 1r.50, Tuanku Imam Bondjol; 2r. Si Singamangaradja XII; 2r.50, Mohammed Husni Thamrin; 3r. Ki Hadjar Dewantoro; 4r. Gen. Sudirman; 4r.50, Dr. G. S. S. J. Ratulangie; 5r. Pangeran Diponegoro; 6r. Dr. Setyabudi; 7r.50, H. O. S. Tjokroaminoto; 10r. K. H. Agus Salim; 15r. Dr. Soetomo.

143 Census Emblems

1961. 1st Indonesian Census.

889	**143**	75s. purple	25	15

144 Nenas (pineapples)

1961. Charity. Fruits.

890	**144**	20s.+10s. yellow, red and blue	50	40
891	-	75s.+25s. purple, green and slate	75	40
892	-	3r.+1r. red, yell & grn	1·20	1·20

FRUITS: 75s. Manggis; 3r. Rambutan.

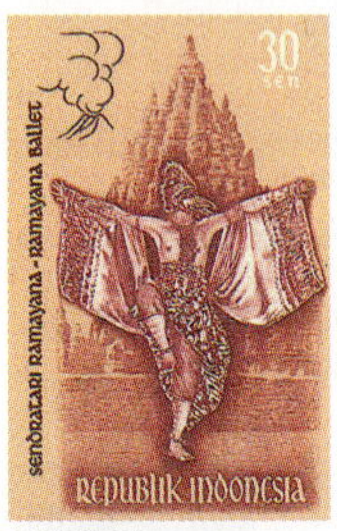

145 Djataju

1962. Ramayana Dancers.

893	**145**	30s. brown and ochre	35	40
894	-	40s. violet and purple	35	40
895	-	1r. purple and green	50	40
896	-	1r.50 green and pink	50	40
897	-	3r. blue and green	1·60	40
898	-	5r. brown and buff	1·40	40

DANCERS: 40s. Hanoman; 1r. Dasamuka; 1r.50, Kidang Kentjana; 3r. Dewi Sinta; 5r. Rama.

146 Aerial View of Mosque

1962. Construction of Istiqlal Mosque.

899	**146**	30s.+20s. blue & yellow	35	25
900	-	40s.+20s. red and yellow	35	25
901	**146**	1r.50+50s. brown & yell	35	25
902	-	3r.+1r. green and yellow	35	25

DESIGN: 40s., 3r. Ground-level view of Mosque.

147 Games Emblem

1962. 4th Asian Games, Djakarta. Inscr as in T 147.

903		10s. green and yellow	15	15
904		15s. brown and ochre	15	15
905		20s. lilac and green	35	25
906		25s. red and green	35	25
907		30s. green and buff	35	15
908		40s. ultramarine and blue	35	15
909		50s. brown and drab	35	35
910		60s. mauve and grey	35	35
911		70s. brown and red	35	35
912		75s. brown and orange	35	15
913		1r. violet and blue	35	35
914	**147**	1r.25 blue and mauve	40	40
915	-	1r.50 red and mauve	1·20	40
916	-	1r.75 red and pink	80	40
917	**147**	2r. brown and green	75	40
918	-	2r.50 blue and green	80	40
919	**147**	3r. black and red	75	40
920	-	4r.50 green and red	75	40
921	**147**	5r. green and bistre	55	40
922	-	6r. red and brown	55	40
923	-	7r.50 brown and pink	55	25
924	-	10r. ultramarine and blue	1·10	55
925	-	15r. violet and light violet	1·20	1·10
926	-	20r. green and bistre	3·00	1·40

DESIGNS—VERT: 10s. Basketball; 20s. Weightlifting; 40s. Throwing the discus; 50s. Diving; 60s. Football; 70s. Press building; 75s. Boxing; 1r. Volleyball; 1r.50, Badminton; 1r.75, Wrestling; 2r.50, Shooting; 4r.50, Hockey; 6r. Water polo; 7r.50, Tennis; 10r. Table tennis; 15r. Cycling; 20r. "Welcome" monument. HORIZ: 15s. Main stadium; 25s. Hotel Indonesia; 30s. Road improvement.

148 Campaign Emblem

1962. Malaria Eradication.

927	**148**	40s. blue and violet	10	10
928	**148**	1r.50 orange and brown	10	10
929	**148**	3r. green and blue	10	10
930	**148**	6r. violet and black	25	15

On the 1r.50 and 6r. the inscription is at top.

149 National Monument

1962. National Monument.

931	**149**	1r.+50c. brown & black	15	15
932	-	1r.50+50c. green & blue	15	15
933	**149**	3r.+1r. mauve and green	25	15
934	-	6r.+1r.50 blue and red	25	15

DESIGN: 1r.50, 6r. Aerial view of Monument.

150 Atomic Symbol

1962. "Science for Development".

935	**150**	1r.50 blue and yellow	15	15
936	**150**	4r.50 red and yellow	25	25
937	**150**	6r. green and yellow	40	25

151 "Phalaenopsis amabilis"

1962. Charity. Orchids. Multicoloured.

938		1r.+50s. "Vanda tricolor" (horiz)	30	15
939		1r.50+50s. Type **151**	35	15
940		3r.+1r. "Dendrobium phalaenopsis"	35	10
941		6r.+1r.50 "Paphiopedilum praestans" (horiz)	25	10

152 West Irian Monument, Djakarta

1963. Construction of West Irian Monument.

942	**152**	1r.+50c. green and red	25	10
943	**152**	1r.50+50c. sepia, black and mauve	15	10
944	**152**	3r.+1r. brown and blue	25	10
945	**152**	6r.+1r.50 bistre & grn	25	15

153 Conference Emblem

1963. 12th Pacific Area Travel Association Conference, Djakarta.

946	**153**	1r. blue and green	15	15
947	-	1r.50 blue and olive	15	15
948	**153**	3r. blue and brown	40	15
949	-	6r. blue and orange	40	15

DESIGNS: 1r.50, Prambanan Temple and Mt. Merapi; 6r. Balinese Meru in Pura Taman Ajun.

154 Rice Sheaves

1963. Freedom from Hunger.

950	**154**	1r. yellow and blue	10	10
951	-	1r.50 blue and green	15	10
952	**154**	3r. yellow and red	15	10
953	-	6r. orange and black	25	15

DESIGN—HORIZ: 1r.50, 6r. Tractor; Nos. 950/1 are inscr "CONTRE LA FAIM"; Nos. 952/3, "FREEDOM FROM HUNGER".

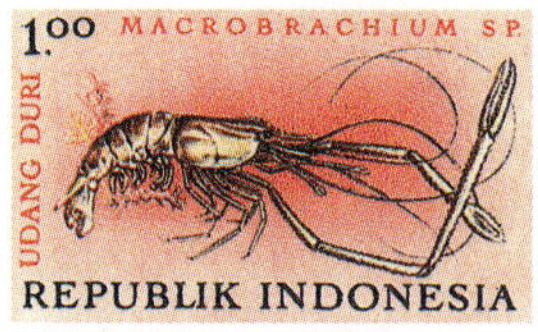

155 Lobster

1963. Marine Life. Multicoloured.

954		1r. Type **155**	35	15
955		1r.50 Kawakawa	35	15
956		3r. River snapper	80	35
957		6r. Chinese pomfret	80	50

156 Conference Emblem

1963. Asian-African Journalists' Conference.

958	**156**	1r. red and blue	15	10
959	-	1r.50 brown and lavender	15	10
960	-	3r. blue, black and olive	40	15
961	-	6r. salmon and black	55	25

DESIGNS—HORIZ: 1r.50, Pen, emblem and map. VERT: 3r. Pen. Globe and broken chain; 6r. Pen severing chain around Globe.

157 Indonesia, from Atjeh to Merauke

1963. Acquisition of West Irian (West New Guinea).

962	**157**	1r.50 orange, red & black	15	10
963	-	4r.50 blue, green & purple	15	15
964	-	6r. brown, yellow & green	80	50

DESIGNS: 4r.50, Parachutist; 6r. Greater bird of paradise.

158 Centenary Emblem

1963. Centenary of Red Cross.

965	**158**	1r. green and red	25	15
966	-	1r.50 red and blue	25	15
967	**158**	3r. grey and red	25	15
968	-	6r. red and bistre	25	15

DESIGN: 1r.50, 6r. Red Cross (inscr in English).

159 Volcano

1963. Bali Volcano Disaster Fund.

969	**159**	4r. (+2r.) red	15	10
970	**159**	6r. (+3r.) green	15	15

160 Bank of Indonesia, Djakarta

1963. National Banking Day.

971	**160**	1r.75 purple and blue	15	15
972	-	4r. green and yellow	15	15
973	**160**	6r. brown and green	15	10
974	-	12r. purple and orange	40	15

DESIGN—VERT: 4r., 12r. Daneswara, God of Prosperity.

161 Athletes with Banners

1963. Games of the New Emerging Forces, Djakarta.

975	**161**	1r.25 sepia and violet	10	10
976	-	1r.75 olive and buff	10	10
977	-	4r. sepia and green	10	10
978	-	6r. sepia and brown	25	15
979	-	10r. sepia and green	25	15
980	-	12r. olive and red	35	15
981	-	25r. ultramarine and blue	50	35
982	-	50r. sepia and red	65	40

DESIGNS: 1r.75, "Pendet" dance; 4r. Conference Hall, Djakarta; 6r. Archery; 10r. Badminton; 12r. Throwing the javelin; 25r. Sailing; 50r. "Ganefo" torch.

162 "Papilio blumei"

1963. Social Day. Butterflies. Multicoloured.

983	1r.75+50s. Type **162**	40	15
984	4r.+1r. "Charaxes dehaani"	40	15
985	6r.+1r.50 Purple-spotted swallowtail	40	15
986	12r.+3r. "Troides amphrysus"	80	40

163 Pres. Sukarno

1964

987	**163**	6r. blue and brown	15	15
988	**163**	12r. purple and bistre	15	15
989	**163**	20r. orange and blue	15	15
990	**163**	30r. blue and orange	15	15
991	**163**	40r. brown and green	15	15
992	**163**	50r. green and red	15	15
993	**163**	75r. red and violet	15	15
994	**163**	100r. brown and grey	15	15
995	**163**	250r. grey and blue	35	15
996	**163**	500r. gold and red	50	35

164 Lorry and Trailer

1964

997	-	1r. purple	15	15
998	**164**	1r.25 brown	15	15
999	-	1r.75 blue	15	15
1000	-	2r. red	15	15
1001	-	2r.50 blue	15	15
1002	-	4r. green	15	15
1003	-	5r. brown	15	15
1004	-	7r.50 green	15	15
1005	-	10r. orange	15	15
1006	-	15r. blue	15	15
1007	-	25r. blue	35	15
1008	-	35r. brown	35	15

DESIGNS—HORIZ: 1r. Ox-cart; 1r.75, "Hadju Agus Salim" (freighter); 2r. Lockheed Electra airliner; 4r. Cycle-postman; 5r. Douglas DC-3 airliner; 7r.50, Teletypist; 10r. Diesel train; 15r. "Sam Ratulangi" (freighter); 25r. Convair Coronado airliner; 35r. Telephone operator. VERT: 2r.50, Buginese sailing boat.

165 Rameses II, Abu Simbel

1964. Nubian Monuments Preservation. Monuments in brown.

1009	**165**	4r. drab	35	15
1010	-	6r. blue	35	15
1011	**165**	12r. pink	35	15
1012	-	18r. green	35	15

DESIGN: 6r., 18r., Trajan's Kiosk, Philae.

166 Various Stamps of Netherlands Indies and Indonesia

1964. Stamp Centenary.

1013	**166**	10r. multicoloured	1·10	15

167 Indonesian Pavilion at Fair

1964. New York World's Fair.

1014	**167**	25r. red, blue and silver	55	40
1015	**167**	50r. red, turquoise & gold	1·40	40

168 Thomas Cup

1964. Thomas Cup World Badminton Championships.

1016	**168**	25r. gold, red and green	25	25
1017	**168**	50r. gold, red and blue	25	25
1018	**168**	75r. gold, red and violet	80	80

169 "Sandjaja" and "Siliwanghi" (destroyers)

1964. Indonesian Navy.

1019	**169**	20r. brown and yellow	40	10
1020	-	30r. black and red	40	10
1021	-	40r. blue and green	80	80

DESIGNS: 30r. "Nanggala" (submarine); 40r. "Matjan Tutul" (torpedo-boat).

170 Pied Fantail

1965. Social Day. Birds.

1022	**170**	4r.+1r. black, lilac and yellow	35	25
1023	-	6r.+1r.50 black, buff and green	35	25
1024	-	12r.+3r. black, blue and olive	55	35
1025	-	20r.+5r. yellow, red and purple	55	40
1026	-	30r.+7r.50 black, slate and mauve	1·00	40

BIRDS: 6r. Zebra dove; 12r. Black drongo; 20r. Black-naped oriole; 30r. Java sparrow.

171 Map and Mosque

1965. Afro-Asian Islamic Conf, Bandung.

1027	**171**	10r. blue and violet	35	10
1028	-	15r. brown and orange	35	10
1029	**171**	25r. green and brown	50	15
1030	-	50r. purple and red	50	50

DESIGN: 15r., 50r. Mosque and handclasp.

172 Scroll in Hand

1965. 10th Anniv of First Afro-Asian Conference, Bandung.

1031	**172**	15r. red and silver	25	10
1032	-	25r. gold, red & turquoise	25	10
1033	**172**	50r. blue and gold	40	15
1034	-	75r. gold, red and lilac	65	65

DESIGN: 25r., 75r. Conference 10th-anniv emblem.

1965. Conf of "New Emerging Forces", Djakarta. T 163 additionally inscr "Conefo". Value, "Conefo" and frame in red; portrait colour given.

1035	1r.+1r. brown	15	10
1036	1r.25+1r.25 red	15	10
1037	1r.75+1r.75 purple	15	10
1038	2r.+2r. green	15	10
1039	2r.50+2r.50 brown	15	10
1040	4r.+3r.50 blue	15	10
1041	6r.+4r. green	15	10
1042	10r.+5r. brown	15	10
1043	12r.+5r.50 orange	15	10
1044	15r.+7r.50 turquoise	15	10
1045	20r.+10r. brown	15	10
1046	25r.+10r. violet	15	10
1047	40r.+15r. purple	15	10
1048	50r.+15r. violet	15	10
1049	100r.+25r. brown	25	15

174 Makara Mask and Rays

1965. Campaign against Cancer.

1050	**174**	20r.+10r. red and blue	25	15
1051	**174**	30r.+15r. blue and red	25	15

175 "Happy Family"

1965. The State's Five Principles and 20th Anniv of Republic.

1052	**175**	10r.+5r. yellow, black and brown	40	25
1053	-	20r.+10r. red, black and yellow	25	25
1054	-	25r.+10r. green, black and red	25	25
1055	-	40r.+15r. black, red and blue	50	25
1056	-	50r.+15r. yellow, black and mauve	50	25

DESIGNS: ("State's Principles"): 20r. "Humanitarianism" (globe and clasped hands); 25r. "Nationalism" (map and garland); 40r. "Democracy" (council meeting); 50r. "Belief in God" (churches and mosques).

177 Samudra Beach Hotel

1965. Tourist Hotels.

1060	**177**	10r.+5r. blue & turq	25	25
1061	-	25r.+10r. violet, black and green	35	35
1062	**177**	40r.+15r. brown, black and blue	40	35
1063	-	80r.+20r. pur & orge	65	35

DESIGN: 25r., 80r. Ambarrukmo Palace Hotel.

178 "Gloriosa superba"

1965. Flowers. Multicoloured, Inscr "1965" and with commas and dashes after figures of value.

1064	30r.+10r. Type **178**	1·00	1·00
1065	40r.+15r. "Hibiscus tiliaceus"	1·00	1·00
1066	80r.+20r. "Impatiens balsamina"	1·00	1·00
1067	100r.+25r. "Lagerstroemia Indica"	1·00	1·00

See also Nos. 1108/1116.

1965. Revalued Currency. Optd '65 Sen. (a) On Nos. 989/94.

1068	**163**	(20)s. on 20r.	15	10
1069	**163**	(30)s. on 30r.	15	15
1070	**163**	(40)s. on 40r.	15	15
1071	**163**	(50)s. on 50r.	15	15
1072	**163**	(75)s. on 75r.	15	2·10
1073	**163**	(100)s. on 100r.	50	15

(b) On Nos. 1005/7.

1074	(10)s. on 10r.	25	10
1075	(15)s. on 15r.	25	10
1076	(25)s. on 25r.	25	10

180 Pres. Sukarno

1966. Revalued Currency. Inscr "1967" (12r.) or "1966" (others). Values and frames turquoise (12r., 25r.) or chocolate (others); portrait and country name in colour given.

1077	**180**	1s. blue	15	10
1078	**180**	3s. olive	15	10
1079	**180**	5s. red	15	10
1080	**180**	8s. turquoise	15	10
1081	**180**	10s. blue	15	10
1082	**180**	15s. black	15	10
1083	**180**	20s. green	15	10
1084	**180**	25s. brown	15	10
1085	**180**	30s. blue	15	10
1086	**180**	40s. brown	15	10
1087	**180**	50s. violet	15	10
1088	**180**	80s. orange	15	10
1089	**180**	1r. green	15	10
1090	**180**	1r.25 brown	15	10
1091	**180**	1r.50 green	15	10
1092	**180**	2r. purple	25	10
1093	**180**	2r.50 slate	25	15
1094	**180**	5r. orange	35	35
1095	**180**	10r. olive	35	15
1096	**180**	12r. orange	35	15
1097	**180**	25r. violet	35	35

1966. Flowers. As T 178 but inscr "1966" and additionally inscr "sen" instead of commas and dashes. Multicoloured.

1108	10s.+5s. "Cassia alata"	1·00	1·00
1109	20s.+5s. "Barleria cristata"	1·00	1·00
1110	30s.+10s. "Ixora coccinea"	1·00	1·00
1111	40s.+10s. "Hibiscus rosa sinensis"	1·00	1·00

MS1112	58×78 mm. No. 1111. Imperf		9·75	2·75

1966. National Disaster Fund. Floral designs as T 178 additionally inscr "BENTJANA ALAM NASIONAL 1966". Multicoloured.

1113		15a.+5s. "Gloriosa superba"	65	65
1114		25a.+5s. "Hibiscus tiliaceus"	65	65
1115		30s.+10s. "Impatiens balsamina"	65	65
1116		80s.+20s. "Lagerstroemia Indica"	65	65

181 Cleaning Ship's Rudder

1966. Maritime Day.

1117	**181**	20s. green and blue	25	10
1118	-	40s. blue and pink	25	10
1119	-	50s. brown and green	25	10
1120	-	1r. multicoloured	25	10
1121	-	1r.50 green and lilac	25	10
1122	-	2r. red and grey	25	15
1123	-	2r.50 red and mauve	25	20
1124	-	3r. black and green	35	15
MS1125		60×78 mm. No. 1124. Imperf	12·00	12·00

DESIGNS: 40s. Anyer Kidul lighthouse; 50s. Fisherman; 1r. Maritime emblem; 1r.50, Madurese sailing boat; 2r. Quayside; 2r.50 Pearl-diving; 3r. Liner in dry-dock.

182 Gen. A. Yani

1966. Victims of Attempted Communist Coup, 1965. Frames and date in blue.

1126	**182**	5r. brown	35	15
1127	**A**	5r. green	35	15
1128	**B**	5r. purple	35	15
1129	**C**	5r. olive	35	15
1130	**D**	5r. grey	35	15
1131	**E**	5r. violet	35	15
1132	**F**	5r. purple	35	15
1133	**G**	5r. green	35	15
1134	**H**	5r. purple	35	15
1135	**I**	5r. orange	35	15

PORTRAITS: A, Lt.-Gen. R. Soeprapto; B, Lt.-Gen. M. Harjono; C, Lt.-Gen. S. Parman; D, Maj.-Gen. D. Pandjaitan; E, Maj.-Gen. S. Siswomihardjo; F, Brig.-Gen. Katamso; G, Col. Soegijono; H, Capt. P. Tendean; I, Insp. K. S. Tubun.

183 Python

1966. Reptiles.

1136	**183**	2r.+25s. brown, green and flesh	15	15
1137	-	3r.+50s. grn, brn & lil	15	15
1138	-	4r.+75s. purple, buff and green	40	15
1139	-	6r.+1r. black, brn & bl	55	15

REPTILES: 3r. Chameleon; 4r. Crocodile; 6r. Green turtle.

184 Tjlempung

1967. Musical Instruments.

1140	**184**	50s. red and black	35	35
1141	-	1r. sepia and red	35	35
1142	-	1r.25 lake and blue	35	35
1143	-	1r.50 green and violet	35	35
1144	-	2r. blue and ochre	35	35
1145	-	2r.50 green and red	35	35
1146	-	3r. green and purple	35	35
1147	-	4r. blue and orange	55	35
1148	-	5r. red and blue	55	35
1149	-	6r. blue and mauve	40	40
1150	-	8r. lake and green	40	40
1151	-	10r. violet and red	40	35
1152	-	12r. green and violet	65	55
1153	-	15r. violet and olive	50	35
1154	-	20r. black and sepia	50	35
1155	-	25r. black and green	60	35

INSTRUMENTS: 1r. Sasando; 1r.25, Foi doa; 1r.50, Kultjapi; 2r. Arababu; 2r.50, Genderang; 3r. Katjapi; 4r. Hape; 5r. Gangsa; 6r. Serunai; 8r. Rebab; 10r. Trompet; 12r. Totobuang; 15r. Tamburn; 20r. Kulintang; 25r. Keledi.

185 Pilot and Mikoyan Gurevich MiG-21 Fighter

1967. Aviation Day. Multicoloured.

1156		2r.50 Type **185**	35	25
1157		4r. Convair Coronado airliner and control tower	35	20
1158		5r. Lockheed C-130 Hercules transport aircraft on tarmac	55	25

186 Thomas Cup and Silhouettes

1967. Thomas Cup World Badminton Championships. Multicoloured.

1159		5r. Type **186**	25	15
1160		12r. Thomas Cup on Globe	50	15

187 Balinese Girl

1967. International Tourist Year.

1161	**187**	12r. multicoloured	1·10	90
MS1162		85×80 mm. No. 1161 (sold at 15r.)	5·00	5·00

188 Heroes Monument

1967. "Heroes of the Revolution". Monument.

1163	**188**	2r.50 brown and green	15	10
1164	-	5r. purple and drab	40	25
1165	-	7r.50 green and pink	40	25

DESIGNS—HORIZ: 5r. Monument and shrine. VERT: 7r.50, Shrine.

190 "Forest Fire"

1967. Paintings by Raden Saleh.

1175	**190**	25r. red and green	40	40
1176	-	50r. purple and red	55	40
MS1177		95×63 mm. No. 1175 (sold at 30r.)	6·25	6·25

PAINTING: 50r. "A Fight to the Death".

191 Flood Victims

1967. National Disaster Fund.

1178	**191**	1r.25+10s. blue & yell	35	35
1179	-	2r.50+25s. blue & yell	35	35
1180	-	4r.+40s. black & orge	35	35
1181	-	5r.+50s. black & orge	35	35
MS1182		95×89 mm. Nos. 1180/1 (sold at 12r.50)	37·00	37·00

DESIGNS: 2r.50, Landslide; 4r. Burning house; 5r. Erupting volcano.

192 Human Rights Emblem

1968. Human Rights Year.

1183	**192**	5r. red, green and blue	20	10
1184	**192**	12r. red, green and drab	20	10

193 Academy Badge

1968. Indonesian Military Academy.

1185	**193**	10r. multicoloured	50	25

194/6 "Sudhana and Manohara at Court of Druma" (relief on wall of Borobudur)

1968. "Save Borobudur Monument".

1186	**194**	2r.50+25s. deep green and green	35	35
1187	**195**	2r.50+25s. deep green and green	35	35
1188	**196**	2r.50+25s. deep green and green	35	35
1189	-	7r.50+75s. green and orange	65	35
MS1190		105×64 mm. Nos. 1186/8 (sold at 12r.50)	37·00	37·00

DESIGN—VERT: 7r.50, Buddhist and statue of Buddha.

197 W.H.O. Emblem and "20"

1968. 20th Anniv of W.H.O.

1191	**197**	2r. purple and yellow	35	25
1192	-	20r. black and green	35	25

DESIGN: 20r. W.H.O. emblem.

198 Diesel Train (1967) and Steam Train (1867)

1968. Centenary (1967) of Indonesian Railways.

1193	**198**	20r. multicoloured	75	25
1194	**198**	30r. multicoloured	1·10	90

199 Scout with Pick

1968. "Wirakarya" Scout Camp.

1195	**199**	5r.+50s. brown & orge	25	15
1196	-	10r.+1r. grey & brown	55	35
1197	-	30r.+3r. brown & grn	90	55

DESIGNS—VERT: 10r. Bugler on hillside. HORIZ: (69×29 mm); 30r. Scouts in camp.

200 Butterfly Dancer

1968. Tourism.

1198	**200**	30r. multicoloured	1·40	1·40
MS1199		84×88 mm. No. 1198 (sold at 35r.)	6·50	6·50

202 Observatory and Stars

1968. 40th Anniv of Bosscha Observatory.

1207	**202**	15r. blue, yellow & black	40	25
1208	-	30r. violet and orange	65	25

DESIGN—VERT: 30r. Observatory on Globe.

203/4 Yachting

1968. Olympic Games, Mexico.

1209		5r. green, brown & black	10	10
1210	**203**	7r.50 blue, yellow & red	25	15
1211	**204**	7r.50 blue, yellow & red	25	15
1212	-	12r. red, blue and yellow	25	10
1213	-	30r. brown, green & orge	50	25
MS1214 95×65 mm. Nos. 1210/11 (sold at 20r.)			7·00	7·00

DESIGNS:—28½×44½ mm: 5r. Weightlifting; 12r. Basketball. 44½×28½ mm: 30r. Dove and Olympic flame.

Nos. 1210/11 were issued together, se-tenant, forming the composite design illustrated.

205 "Eugenia aquea"

1968. Fruits. Multicoloured.

1215	7r.50 Type **205**	35	15
1216	15r. "Carica papaya"	50	25
1217	30r. "Durio zibethinus" (vert)	80	40
MS1218 Two sheets (a) 96×62 mm. No. 1216. (b) 62×96 mm. No. 1217 (sold at 55r. the pair)		10·50	10·50

206 I.L.O. Emblem and part of Globe

1969. 50th Anniv of I.L.O.

1219	**206**	5r. red and green	10	10
1220	-	7r.50 green and orange	15	10
1221	**206**	15r. red and violet	25	15
1222	-	25r. red and turquoise	50	25

DESIGN: 7r.50, 25r. I.L.O. emblem.

207 R. Dewi Sartika

1969. National Independence Heroes.

1223	**207**	15r. green and violet	35	15
1224	-	15r. purple and green	35	15
1225	-	15r. blue and red	35	15
1226	-	15r. ochre and red	35	15
1227	-	15r. sepia and blue	35	15
1228	-	15r. lilac and blue	35	15

PORTRAITS: No. 1224, Tjut Nja Din; 1225, Tjut Nja Meuthia; 1226, Sutan Sjahrir; 1227, Dr. F. L. Tobing; 1228, General G. Subroto.

208 Woman with Flower

1969. Women's Emancipation Campaign.

1229	**208**	20r.+2r. red, yellow and green	65	35

209 Red Cross "Mosaic"

1969. 50th Anniv of League of Red Cross Societies.

1230	**209**	15r. red and green	40	15
1231	-	20r. red and yellow	40	35

DESIGN: 20r. Hands encircling Red Cross.

210 "Planned" Family and Factory

1969. South-East Asia and Oceania Family Planning Conference.

1232	**210**	10r. orange and green	35	15
1233	-	20r. mauve and green	50	25

DESIGN: 20r. "Planned" family and "National Prosperity".

211 Balinese Mask

1969. Tourism in Bali. Multicoloured.

1234	12r. Type **211**	35	25
1235	15r. Girl with offerings	65	35
1236	30r. Cremation rites	65	35
MS1237 96×64 mm. No. 1236 (sold at 35r.)		5·00	5·00

212 "Agriculture"

1969. Five-year Development Plan.

1238	-	5r. blue and green	25	10
1239	**212**	7r.50 yellow and purple	25	10
1240	-	10r. red and blue	25	10
1241	-	12r. red and blue	1·40	65
1242	-	15r. yellow and green	25	10
1243	-	20r. yellow and violet	25	10
1244	-	25r. red and black	25	15
1245	-	30r. black and red	50	15
1246	-	40r. orange and green	55	15
1247	-	50r. brown and orange	1·10	15

DESIGNS: 5r. Religious emblems ("Co-existence"); 10r. Modern family ("Social Welfare"); 12r. Crane and crate ("Overseas Trade"); 15r. Bobbins ("Clothing Industry"); 20r. Children in class ("Education"); 25r. Research worker ("Scientific Research"); 30r. Family and hypodermic syringe ("Health Care"); 40r. Tunas in net ("Fisheries"); 50r. Graph ("Statistics").

213 Dish Aerial

1969. Satellite Communications and Inauguration of Djatiluhur Earth Station. Multicoloured.

1248	15r. Type **213**	40	15
1249	30r. Communications satellite	55	50

214 Vickers Vimy Biplane over Borobudur Temple

1969. 50th Anniv of 1st England–Australia Flight by Ross and Keith Smith.

1253	**214**	75r. purple and red	55	50
1254	-	100r. green and yellow	55	55

DESIGNS: 100r. Vickers Vimy and map of Indonesia.

215 Noble Volute

1969. Sea Shells. Multicoloured.

1255	5r.+50c. Type **215**	55	55
1256	7r.50+50c. Common hairy triton	55	55
1257	10r.+1r. Common spider conch	80	80
1258	15r.+1r.50 Bramble murex	80	80

216 Indonesian Pavilion

1970. "Expo 70" World Fair, Osaka, Japan.

1259	**216**	5r. yellow, green & brn	55	25
1260	-	15r. red, blue and green	75	35
1261	**216**	30r. yellow, blue and red	1·40	55

DESIGN: 15r. Indonesian "Garuda" symbol.

217 Prisoner's Hands and Scales of Justice

1970. "Purification of Justice".

1262	**217**	10r. purple and red	55	35
1263	**217**	15r. purple and green	90	35

218 U.P.U. Monument, Berne

1970. Inauguration of New U.P.U. Headquarters Building, Berne.

1264	**218**	15r. red and green	65	35
1265	-	30r. blue and ochre	1·40	80

DESIGN: 30r. New Headquarters building.

219 Timor Dancers

1970. "Visit Indonesia Year". Traditional Dancers. Multicoloured.

1266	20r. Type **219**	1·10	50
1267	45r. Bali dancers	1·60	80
MS1268 63×97 mm. No. 1267 (sold at 60r.)		8·25	8·25

220 "Productivity" Symbol

1970. Asian Productivity Year.

1269	**220**	5r. red, yellow and green	65	15
1270	**220**	30r. red, yellow and violet	1·40	65

221 Independence Monument

1970. 25th Anniv of Independence.

1271	**221**	40r. violet, purple & blue	16·00	5·00

222 Emblems of Post and Giro, and of Telecommunications

1970. 25th Anniv of Indonesian Post and Telecommunications Services.

1272	**222**	10r. brown, yellow & grn	5·00	25
1273	-	25r. black, yellow & pink	10·50	65

DESIGN: 25r. Telephone dial and P.T.T. worker.

223 U.N. Emblem and Doves

1970. 25th Anniv of United Nations.

1274	**223**	40r. multicoloured	16·00	5·00

224 I.E.Y. Emblem on globe

1970. International Education Year.

1275	**224**	25r. brown, red & yellow	9·75	3·25
1276	-	50r. red, black and blue	20·00	5·00

DESIGNS: 50r. I.E.Y. emblem.

225 "Chrysocoris javanus" (shieldbug)

1970. Insects. Multicoloured.

1277	7r.50+50c. Type **225**	7·00	1·60
1278	15r.+1r.50 "Orthetrum testaceum" (darter)	12·00	8·25
1279	20r.+2r. "Xylocopa flavonigrescens" (carpenter bee)	24·00	5·75

226 Batik handicrafts

1971. "Visit ASEAN (South East Asian Nations Association) Year". Multicoloured.

1280	20r. Type **226**	3·00	1·40
1281	50r. Javanese girl playing angklung (musical instrument) (vert)	4·50	3·75
1282	75r. Wedding group, Minangkabau	11·50	5·25
MS1283 64×97 mm. No. 1281 (sold at 70r.)		55·00	55·00

227 Restoration of Fatahillah Park

1971. 444th Anniv of Djakarta. Multicoloured.

1284	15r. Type **227**	2·50	1·10

1285 65r. Performance at Lenong Theatre 4·50 4·00
1286 80r. Ismail Marzuki Cultural Centre 10·50 3·50
MS1287 121×103 mm. 30r. Djakarta City Hall (sold at 60r.) 26·00 26·00

228 Sita and Rama

1971. International Ramayana Festival.
1288 **228** 30r. multicoloured 2·75 80
1289 - 100r. black, blue and red 4·00 1·80
DESIGN: 100r. Rama.

229 Pigeon with Letter, and Workers

1971. 5th Asian Regional Telecommunications Conf.
1290 **229** 50r. chocolate, brown and buff 2·10 1·00

230 U.P.U. Monument, Berne, and Hemispheres

1971. U.P.U. Day.
1291 **230** 40r. purple, black & blue 2·00 1·00

231 Schoolgirl

1971. 25th Anniv of UNICEF. Mult.
1292 20r. Type **231** 2·75 55
1293 40r. Boy with rice-stalks 4·00 1·10

232 Clown Surgeonfish

1971. Fishes (1st series). Multicoloured.
1294 15r. Type **232** 5·25 1·40
1295 30r. Moorish idol 10·50 3·75
1296 40r. Emperor angelfish 16·00 5·25
See also Nos. 1318/20, 1343/5, 1390/2 and 1423/5.

233 Microwave Tower

1972. 25th Anniv of E.C.A.F.E.
1297 **233** 40r. blue and turquoise 3·50 1·00
1298 - 75r. multicoloured 3·50 1·00
1299 - 100r. multicoloured 5·25 2·10
DESIGNS—VERT: 40r. E.C.A.F.E. emblem. HORIZ: 100r. Irrigation and highways.

234 Human Heart

1972. World Heart Month.
1300 **234** 50r. multicoloured 2·10 80

235 Ancient and Modern Textile Production

1972. 50th Anniv of Textile Technological Institute.
1301 **235** 35r. purple, yellow & orge 2·10 80

236 Children reading Books

1972. International Book Year.
1302 **236** 75r. multicoloured 2·75 1·20

237 "Essa 8" Weather Satellite

1972. Space Exploration.
1303 **237** 35r. brown, violet & blue 2·00 65
1304 - 50r. blue, black and pink 3·75 3·50
1305 - 60r. black, green & brn 6·50 1·10
DESIGNS: 50r. Astronaut on Moon; 60r. Indonesian "Kartika I" rocket.

238 Hotel Indonesia

1972. 10th Anniv of Hotel Indonesia.
1306 **238** 50r. green, pale grn & red 2·50 1·10

239 "Silat" (unarmed combat)

1972. Olympic Games, Munich.
1307 **239** 20r. purple, cobalt & blue 1·40 15
1308 - 35r. violet, brown & mve 1·40 40
1309 - 50r. emer, dp grn & grn 2·75 75
1310 - 75r. rose, purple and pink 2·75 1·80
1311 - 100r. brown, blue & green 5·75 3·00
DESIGNS: 35r. Running; 50r. Diving; 75r. Badminton; 100r. Olympic stadium.

240 Family and Religious Buildings

1972. Family Planning Campaign. Mult.
1312 30r. Type **240** 2·00 65
1313 75r. "Healthy family" 3·75 2·40
1314 80r. "Family of workers" 6·00 3·00

241 Moluccas Dancer

1972. "Art and Culture" (1st series).
1315 **241** 30r. brown, pink & green 2·00 65
1316 - 60r. multicoloured 5·00 2·75
1317 - 100r. bl, brn & cinnamon 7·00 2·75
DESIGNS—VERT: 60r. Couple and Toraja traditional house. HORIZ: 100r. West Irian traditional house.
See also 1336/8, 1373/5 and 1401/3.

1972. Fishes (2nd series). As T 232. Mult.
1318 30r. Triangle butterflyfish 7·00 2·00
1319 50r. Royal angelfish 12·00 3·00
1320 100r. Clown triggerfish 16·00 5·25

242 Thomas Cup and Shuttlecock

1972. Thomas Cup Badminton Championships, Djakarta.
1321 **242** 30r. blue and green 80 25
1322 - 75r. red and green 1·80 50
1323 - 80r. brown and red 3·50 1·00
DESIGNS: 75r. Thomas Cup and Sports Centre; 80r. Thomas Cup and player.

243 Emblem, Anemometer and "Gatotkaca"

1973. I.M.O. and W.M.O. Weather Organization Centenary.
1324 **243** 80r. multicoloured 2·00 80

244 "Health begins at Home"

1973. 25th Anniv of W.H.O.
1325 **244** 80r. blue, orange & green 1·60 80

245 Java Mask

1973. Tourism. Indonesian Folk Masks. Mult.
1326 30r. Type **245** 5·25 90
1327 60r. Kalimantan mask 8·25 3·50
1328 100r. Bali mask 13·00 1·80

246 Savings Bank and Thrift Plant

1973. Two-Year National Savings Drive.
1329 **246** 25r. black, yellow & bis 90 50
1330 - 30r. green, gold & yellow 1·60 50
DESIGN—HORIZ: 30r. Hand and "City" savings bank.

247 Chess

1973. National Sports Week. Multicoloured.
1331 30r. Type **247** 1·60 1·10
1332 60r. Karate 2·75 1·10
1333 75r. Hurdling (horiz) 5·00 90

248 International Policemen

1973. 50th Anniv of Interpol.
1334 **248** 30r. multicoloured 90 35
1335 - 50r. yellow, purple & blk 1·60 65
DESIGN—VERT: 50r. Giant temple guard.

1973. "Art and Culture" (2nd series). Weaving and Fabrics. As T 241. Multicoloured.
1336 60r. Parang Rusak pattern 2·50 2·00
1337 80r. Pagi Sore pattern 5·00 2·10
1338 100r. Merak Ngigel pattern 9·00 3·75

249 "Food Cultivation"

1973. 10th Anniv of World Food Programme.
1339 **249** 30r. multicoloured 2·10 65

250 "Religion"

1973. Family Planning.
1340 **250** 20r. blue, light blue & red 80 40
1341 - 30r. black, yellow & brn 1·60 65
1342 - 60r. black, yellow & grn 3·25 55
DESIGNS: 30r. Teacher and class ("Population Education"); 60r. Family and house ("Health").

1973. Fishes (3rd series). As T 232. Mult.
1343 40r. Powder-blue surgeonfish 1·60 1·10
1344 65r. Melon butterflyfish 6·50 2·00
1345 100r. Blue-ringed angelfish 8·25 3·25

251 Admiral Sudarso and Naval Battle of Arafuru

1974. Naval Day.
1346 **251** 40r. multicoloured 1·80 80

252 Bengkulu Costume

1974. Pacific Area Travel Association Conference, Djakarta. Provincial Costumes. Multicoloured.
1347 5r. Type **252** 16·00 1·10
1348 7r.50 Kalimantan, Timor 8·25 1·10
1349 10r. Kalimantan, Tengah 1·60 80
1350 15r. Jambi 1·60 80
1351 20r. Sulawesi, Tenggara 1·60 80
1352 25r. Nusatenggara, Timor 1·60 80

1353	27r.50 Maluku	1·60	1·60
1354	30r. Lampung	1·60	1·60
1355	35r. Sumatera, Barat	1·60	80
1356	40r. Aceh	1·60	80
1357	45r. Nusatenggara, Barat	4·00	80
1358	50r. Riau	2·40	2·40
1359	55r. Kalimantan, Barat	3·25	80
1360	60r. Sulawesi, Utara	3·25	80
1361	65r. Sulawesi, Tengah	3·25	80
1362	70r. Sumatera, Selatan	3·50	80
1363	75r. Java, Barat	3·50	80
1364	80r. Sumatera, Utara	3·50	80
1365	90r. Yogyakarta	3·75	3·75
1366	95r. Kalimantan, Selatan	3·50	80
1367	100r. Java, Timor	3·50	1·60
1368	120r. Irian, Jaya	6·50	1·10
1369	130r. Java, Tengah	6·50	80
1370	135r. Sulawesi, Selatan	7·25	80
1371	150r. Bali	7·25	80
1372	160r. Djakarta	7·25	1·60

1974. "Art and Culture" (3rd series). Shadow Plays. As T 241. Multicoloured.

1373	40r. Baladewa	3·00	1·30
1374	80r. Kresna	5·25	2·50
1375	100r. Bima	6·50	2·50

254 Pres. Suharto

1974

1376	**254**	40r. brown, green & blk	80	10
1377	**254**	50r. brown, blue & black	2·00	15
1378	**254**	65r. brown, mauve & blk	1·10	65
1379	**254**	75r. brown, yellow & blk	2·00	15
1380	**254**	100r. brown, yellow & blk	2·00	15
1381	**254**	150r. brown, green & blk	2·00	15

See also Nos. 1444/7.

255 "Improvement of Living Standards"

1974. World Population Year.

1382	**255**	65r. multicoloured	1·50	50

256 "Welfare"

1974. Family Planning.

1383	**256**	25r. multicoloured	1·00	40
1384	-	40r. blue, black and green	1·00	40
1385	-	65r. ochre, brown & yell	3·00	40

DESIGNS: 40r. Young couple ("Development"); 65r. Arrows ("Religion").

257 Bicycle Postmen

1974. Centenary of U.P.U.

1386	**257**	20r. brown, yellow & grn	2·50	50
1387	-	40r. brown, orange & bl	2·50	75
1388	-	65r. brown, yellow & blk	2·50	75
1389	-	100r. black, blue and red	2·50	2·00

DESIGNS: 40r. Mail-cart; 65r. Mounted postman; 100r. East Indies galley.

1974. Fishes (4th series). As T 232. Mult.

1390	40r. Sail-finned tang	2·50	50
1391	80r. Blue-girdled angelfish	4·00	2·00
1392	100r. Mandarin fish	6·50	2·40

258 Drilling for Oil

1974. 17th Anniv of Pertamina Oil Complex. Multicoloured.

1393	40r. Type **258**	55	35
1394	75r. Oil refinery	55	35
1395	95r. Control centre (vert)	55	35
1396	100r. Road tanker (vert)	55	35
1397	120r. Fokker Fellowship airliner over storage tank farm (vert)	90	35
1398	130r. Pipelines and tanker (vert)	90	35
1399	150r. Petrochemical storage tanks	90	35
1400	200r. Offshore oil rig	90	35

1975. "Art and Culture" (4th series). As T 241.

1401	50r. silver, red and black	1·50	1·30
1402	75r. silver, green and black	2·40	1·30
1403	100r. yellow, blue and black	4·50	1·30

DESIGNS: 50r. Sumatran spittoon; 75r. Sumatran "sirh" dish; 100r. Kalimantan "sirh" dish.

260 "Donorship"

1975. Blood Donors' Campaign.

1404	**260**	40r. red, yellow and green	1·10	65

261 Measures and Globe

1975. Centenary of Metre Convention.

1405	**261**	65r. blue, red and yellow	2·00	65

262 Women in Public Service

1975. International Women's Year. Mult.

1406	40r. Type **262**	1·60	65
1407	100r. I.W.Y. emblem (21×29 mm)	2·10	65

263 "Dendrobium pakarena"

1975. Tourism. Indonesian Orchids. Mult.

1408	40r. Type **263**	5·00	1·10
1409	70r. "Aeridachnis bogor"	5·00	2·10
1410	85r. "Vanda genta"	9·00	3·25

264 Stupas and Damaged Temple

1975. UNESCO "Save Borobudur Temple" Campaign. Multicoloured.

1411	25r. Type **264**	3·25	80
1412	40r. Buddhist shrines and broken wall	3·75	1·10
1413	65r. Stupas and damaged building (horiz)	7·25	4·50
1414	100r. Buddha and stupas (horiz)	10·50	4·50

265 Battle of Banjarmasin

1975. 30th Anniv of Independence.

1415	**265**	25r. black and yellow	80	50
1416	-	40r. black and red	1·10	50
1417	-	75r. black and red	1·60	1·30
1418	-	100r. black and orange	1·60	1·00

DESIGNS: 40r. Battle of Batua; 75r. battle of Margarana; 100r. Battle of Palembang.

266 "Education"

1975. Family Planning. Multicoloured.

1419	20r. Type **266**	65	15
1420	25r. "Religion"	1·00	25
1421	40r. "Prosperity"	1·60	50

267 Heroes' Monument, Surabaya

1975. 30th Anniv of Independence War.

1422	**267**	100r. red and green	2·40	50

1975. Fishes (5th series). As T 232. Mult.

1423	40r. Twin-spotted wrasse	1·60	50
1424	75r. Saddleback butterflyfish	5·00	1·50
1425	150r. Dusky batfish (vert)	6·50	3·00

269 Thomas Cup

1976. Indonesian Victory in World Badminton Championships. Multicoloured.

1428	20r. Type **269**	1·00	25
1429	40r. Uber cup	1·00	55
1430	100r. Thomas and Uber cups	2·10	55

270 Refugees and New Village

1976. World Human Settlements Day. Mult.

1431	30r. Type **270**	80	15
1432	50r. Old and restored villages	1·50	40
1433	100r. Derelict and rebuilt houses	1·60	40

271 Early and Modern Telephones

1976. Telephone Centenary.

1434	**271**	100r. brown, red & yell	1·30	50

272 Human Eye

1976. World Health Day. Multicoloured.

1435	20r. Type **272**	40	25
1436	40r. Blind man with stick	90	40

273 Main Stadium, Montreal

1976. Olympic Games, Montreal.

1437	**273**	100r. blue	1·30	55

274 Lake Tondano, Sulawesi

1976. Tourism. Multicoloured.

1438	35r. Type **274**	80	40
1439	40r. Lake Kelimutu, Flores	80	40
1440	75r. Lake Maninjau, Sumatra	1·60	50

275 "Light Traffic" Station

1976. Inauguration of Domestic Satellite System.

1441	**275**	20r. multicoloured	80	35
1442	-	50r. black and green	80	35
1443	-	100r. turquoise, bl & vio	1·40	65

DESIGNS: 50r. "Master control" station; 100r. "Palapa" satellite.

1976. As T 254 but with background of wavy lines.

1444	200r. brown, blue and green	8·25	15
1445	300r. brown, red and flesh	2·10	15
1446	400r. brown, green and yellow	4·00	35
1447	500r. brown, red and lilac	5·75	1·00

276 "Vanda Putri Serang"

1976. Orchids. Multicoloured.

1448	25r. "Arachnis flos-aeris"	2·40	1·00
1449	40r. Type **276**	2·40	1·00
1450	100r. "Coelogyne pandurata"	3·50	2·10
MS1451	67×90 mm. No. 1448 (sold at 60r.)	65·00	65·00

277 Stylized Tree

1976. Reafforestation Week.

1452	**277**	20r. green, blue & brown	80	35

278 Kelewang Dagger and Sheath (Timor)

1976. Daggers and Sheaths.

1453	**278**	25r. green, black & brown	1·10	40
1454	-	40r. brown, yellow & orge	1·80	75
1455	-	100r. brown, yellow & grn	2·50	2·10

MS1456 94×64 mm. 40r. No. 1454 (sold at 70r.) 16·00 16·00

DESIGNS: 40r. Mandau dagger and sheath (Borneo); 100r. Rencong dagger and sheath (Aceh).

279 Open Book

1976. Books for Children.

1457	**279**	20r. green, orange & blue	65	25
1458	-	40r. violet, red and yellow	1·30	40

DESIGN: 40r. Children reading book.

280 UNICEF Emblem

1976. 30th Anniv of UNICEF.

1459	**280**	40r. blue, turquoise & vio	1·10	50

281 Ballot Box

1977. Elections.

1460	**281**	40r. blue, yellow and grey	2·10	25
1461	-	75r. blue, yellow and pink	2·40	40
1462	-	100r. bistre, red and black	3·75	1·30

DESIGNS: 75r. Ballot box, factory and produce; 100r. Indonesian arrow.

282 Scout Emblems and Camp

1977. 11th National Scout Jamboree. Mult.

1463	25r. Type **282**	60	35
1464	30r. Emblems, tent and trees	60	35
1465	40r. Emblems, tent and flags	1·40	75

283 Letter and A.O.P.U. Emblem

1977. 15th Anniv of Asian–Oceanic Postal Union. Multicoloured.

1466	65r. Type **283**	80	35
1467	100r. Stylized carrier pigeon	1·40	50

284 Anniversary Emblem

1977. 450th Anniv of Jakarta.

1468	**284**	20r. blue and red	80	40
1469	-	40r. green and blue	80	40
1470	-	100r. blue and turquoise	1·60	80

MS1471 72×96 mm. No. 1470 (sold at 125r.) 9·00 9·00

DESIGNS: 40; 100r. Similar to Type **284** but with emblem and arms differently arranged.

285 Rose

1977. "Amphilex 77" International Stamp Exhibition, Amsterdam.

1472	**285**	100r. red, green and black	1·40	50
1473	-	100r. red, green and black	1·40	50

MS1474 Two sheets (sold at 550r.). (a) 71×95 mm. Nos. 1472/3 each ×2. (b) 72×63 mm. **285** 100r. scarlet, blue and black 20·00 20·00

DESIGN: No. 1473, Envelope.

286 Sports Pictograms

1977. 9th National Sports Week.

1475	**286**	40r. silver, green and red	2·50	1·60
1476	-	50r. silver, blue and red	3·50	1·60
1477	-	100r. gold, black and red	5·75	3·50

DESIGNS: 50; 100r. Similar to Type **286** but with different pictograms.

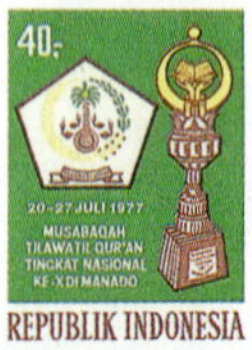

287 Trophy

1977. 10th National Koran Reading Contest.

1478	**287**	40r. brown, green & yell	2·40	50
1479	-	100r. black, yellow & grn	3·00	90

DESIGN: 100r. Emblem.

288 Carrier Pigeon and Map

1977. 10th Anniv of Association of South East Asian Nations. Multicoloured.

1480	25r. Type **288**	50	15
1481	35r. Map of ASEAN members	2·10	65
1482	50r. Transport and flags of ASEAN members	2·10	80

289 Government Officer, Djakarta Region

1977. Economic and Cultural Co-operation with Pakistan.

1483	**289**	25r. brown, gold & green	65	25

290 "Taeniophyllum sp."

1977. Orchids. Multicoloured.

1484	25r. Type **290**	2·40	80
1485	40r. "Phalaenopsis violacea"	2·40	1·60
1486	100r. "Dendrobium spectabile"	5·00	2·40

MS1487 86×71 mm. As No. 1486 but with blue background (sold at 125r.) 11·50 11·50

291 Child and Mosquito

1977. National Health Campaign.

1488	**291**	40r. red, green and black	65	25

292 Proboscis Monkey

1977. Wildlife (1st series). Multicoloured.

1489	20r. Type **292**	80	40
1490	40r. Indian elephant	2·00	80
1491	100r. Tiger	5·25	1·60

MS1492 94×64 mm. As No. 1491 but colours of country name and values reversed (sold at 125r.) 9·75 9·75

See also Nos. 1515/**MS**1518 and 1558/**MS**1561.

293 Hands holding U.N. Emblem

1978. U.N. Conference on Technical Co-operation among Developing Countries.

1493	**293**	100r. blue and ultramarine	1·40	55

294 Mother feeding Baby

1978. Campaign for the Promotion of Breast Feeding.

1494	**294**	40r. green and blue	50	25
1495	-	75r. brown and red	90	40

DESIGN: 75r. Stylised mother and child.

295 Dome of the Rock

1978. Palestine Welfare.

1496	**295**	100r. multicoloured	1·30	50

296 World Cup Emblem

1978. World Cup Football Championship, Argentina.

1497	**296**	40r. green, black and blue	65	25
1498	**296**	100r. mauve, black & bl	1·20	65

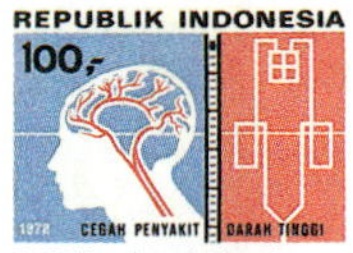

297 Head and Blood Circulation Diagram

1978. World Health Day.

1499	**297**	100r. blue, black and red	1·20	50

298 Leather Puppets

1978. Puppets from Wayang Museum, Djakarta. Multicoloured.

1500	40r. Type **298**	2·40	65
1501	75r. Wooden puppets	2·50	1·30
1502	100r. Actors wearing masks	5·00	2·10

300 Congress Emblem

1978. 27th Congress of World Confederation of Organizations of the Teaching Profession, Djakarta.

1509	**300**	100r. grey	1·00	40

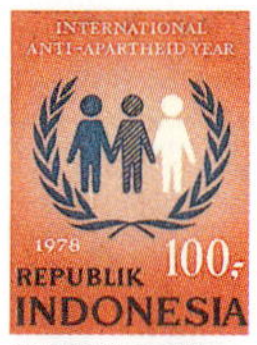

301 I.A.Y. Emblem

1978. International Anti-Apartheid Year.

1510	**301**	100r. blue and red	1·10	40

302 Couple and Tree

1978. 8th World Forestry Congress, Djakarta.

1511	**302**	40r. blue and green	25	15
1512	-	100r. dp green & lt green	1·00	50

DESIGN: 100r. People and trees.

303 Anniversary Emblem

1978. 50th Anniv of Youth Pledge.

1513 **303** 40r. brown and red 65 25
1514 **303** 100r. brown, red and pink 1·00 40

1978. Wildlife (2nd series). As T 292. Mult.

1515 40r. Long-nosed echidna 1·60 40
1516 75r. Sambar 2·40 80
1517 100r. Clouded leopard 4·00 1·20
MS1518 Two sheets (sold at 700r.). (a) 94×63 mm. No. 1517. (b) 115×157 mm. No. 1516 and 1517 ×4 but with colours of inscriptions and value reversed 6·00 6·00

304 "Phalaenopsis sri rejeki"

1978. Orchids. Multicoloured.

1519 40r. Type **304** 1·20 40
1520 75r. "Dendrobium macrophillum" 1·60 65
1521 100r. "Cymbidium fynlaysonianum" 3·25 90
MS1522 63×96 mm. As No. 1521 but with some colours changed (sold at 150r.) 6·00 6·00

306 Douglas DC-3 over Volcano

1979. 30th Anniv of Garuda Indonesian Airways. Multicoloured.

1531 40r. Type **306** 80 35
1532 75r. Douglas DC-9-30 over village 1·00 35
1533 100r. Douglas DC-10 over temple 1·80 1·00

307 Thomas Cup and Badminton Player

1979. Thomas Cup Badminton Championships, Djakarta.

1534 **307** 40r. pink and turquoise 50 50
1535 - 100r. brown and pink 1·00 80
1536 - 100r. brown and pink 1·00 80

DESIGNS: No. 1535, Player on left side of net hitting shuttlecock; 1536, Player on right side of net.

Nos. 1535/6 were issued together, se-tenant, forming a composite design.

308 "Paphiopedilum lowii"

1979. Orchids. Multicoloured.

1537 60r. Type **308** 1·10 35
1538 100r. "Vanda limbata" 1·60 50
1539 125r. "Phalaenopsis gigantea" 2·40 80
MS1540 63×96 mm. No. 1539 (sold at 175r.) 5·00 5·00

See also **MS**1548.

309 Family and Houses

1979. 3rd Five Year Development Plan.

1541 **309** 35r. drab and green 15 10
1542 - 60r. green and blue 25 15
1543 - 100r. brown and blue 50 15
1544 - 125r. brown and green 65 25
1545 - 150r. yellow, orge & red 80 25

DESIGNS: 60r. Pylon, dam and fields; 100r. School and clinic; 125r. Loading produce at factory; 150r. Delivering mail.

310/11 Mrs. R. A. Kartini

1979. Birth Centenary of Mrs. R. A. Kartini (pioneer of women's rights).

1546 **310** 100r. brown and green 80 40
1547 **311** 100r. green and brown 80 40

1979. "Asian–Philatelie '79" International Stamp Exhibition, Dortmund. Sheet 96×119 mm. Multicoloured.

MS1548 250r. Type **308**; 300r. As No. 1538 (sold at 650r.) 8·25 8·25

312 Bureau Emblem

1979. 50th Anniv of International Bureau of Education.

1549 **312** 150r. blue, lt blue & lilac 1·10 40

313 Self Defence

1979. 10th South East Asia Games, Djakarta.

1550 **313** 60r. yellow, black & grn 55 25
1551 - 125r. orange, grey & blue 90 40
1552 - 150r. yellow, black & red 1·30 65

DESIGNS: 125r. Games emblem; 150r. Main stadium, Senayan.

314 Co-operation Emblem

1979. Co-operation Day.

1553 **314** 150r. multicoloured 1·00 35

315 National I.Y.C. Emblem

1979. International Year of the Child.

1554 **315** 60r. black and green 40 15
1555 - 150r. blue and black 1·00 40

DESIGN: 150r. International I.Y.C. emblem.

316 Exhibition Emblem

1979. 3rd World Telecommunications Exhibition, Geneva.

1556 **316** 150r. grey, blue & orange 1·00 50

317 Drug Addict

1979. "End Drug Abuse" Campaign.

1557 **317** 150r. black and pink 1·00 50

1979. Wildlife (3rd series). As T 292. Mult.

1558 60r. Bottle-nosed dolphin 1·10 65
1559 125r. Irrawaddy dolphin 2·75 90
1560 150r. Leatherback turtle 4·50 1·20
MS1561 94×64 mm. 200r. As No. 1560 (sold at 250r.) 8·25 8·25

318 Pinisi Sailing Ship

1980. Djakarta–Amsterdam Spice Race.

1562 **318** 60r. blue 40 15
1563 - 125r. brown 65 40
1564 - 150r. purple 1·50 40
MS1565 64×120 mm. 300r. brown 4·40 4·50

DESIGNS—HORIZ: 125, 300r. Schooner made of leaves. VERT: 150r. Madurese sailing boat.

See also No. **MS**1578.

319 Riding the Rapids

1980. Adventure Sports. Multicoloured.

1566 60r. Type **319** 50 15
1567 125r. Mountaineering (vert) 90 50
1568 150r. Hang gliding 1·30 75
MS1569 62×76 mm. 300r. Type **319** (sold at 350r.) 4·50 4·50

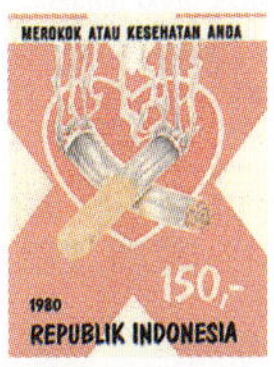

320 Cigarettes and Heart

1980. Anti-smoking Campaign.

1570 **320** 150r. flesh, black and pink 1·00 40

321 Bouquet

1980. 2nd Flower Festival, Jakarta. Mult.

1571 125r. Type **321** 1·50 40
1572 150r. Artificial bouquet 1·80 65

See also No. **MS**1579.

322 Conference Building and Globe

1980. 25th Anniv of First Asian–African Conference, Bandung.

1573 **322** 150r. mauve and gold 1·00 40
MS1574 76×104 mm. **322** 300r. magenta and gold (sold at 350r.) 4·50 4·50

323 Danau Poso Statue

1980. Prehistoric Monuments. Multicoloured.

1575 60r. Type **323** 65 25
1576 125r. Elephant stone, Pasemah Village, South Sumatra 80 50
1577 150r. Taman Bali sarcophagus 1·30 65

1980. "London 1980" International Stamp Exhibition. Two sheets.

MS1578 120×63 mm. 100r. Type **321** 500r. blue 16·00 16·00
MS1579 120×150 mm. 100r. Type **321**; 100r. As No. 1572; 200r. Type **323**; 200r. As No. 1577, each ×2 (sold at 1300r.) 6·50 6·50

324 Discus Thrower

1980. Olympics for the Disabled, Arnhem.

1580 **324** 75r. brown and orange 90 35

325 Draughtsman in Wheelchair

1980. 30th Anniv of Disabled Veterans Corps.

1581 **325** 100r. yellow, blue & blk 90 35

326 President Suharto

1980

1581a **326** 10r. olive and green 1·60 10
1582 **326** 12r.50 green & lt green 35 10
1582a **326** 25r. brown and orange 50 10
1583 **326** 50r. blue and green 35 35
1583a **326** 55r. red and vermilion 50 10
1584 **326** 75r. brown and yellow 75 15
1585a **326** 100r. blue, violet & mve 1·30 35
1586 **326** 200r. brown and orange 2·00 75
1586b **326** 300r. violet, lilac & gold 2·00 25
1586c **326** 400r. grey, pink and gold 2·00 25

Nos. 1585a and 1586 exist dated "1980" or "1981", and Nos. 1582a, 1583a and 1586b/c are dated "1983".

See also Nos. 1830/4.

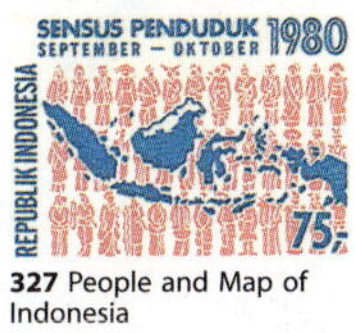

327 People and Map of Indonesia

1980. Population Census.

1587 **327** 75r. blue and pink 40 15

1588	**327**	200r. blue and yellow	1·00	40

328 Ship laying Cable

1980. Inauguration of Singapore–Indonesia Submarine Cable.

1589	**328**	75r. green, dp grn & orge	55	15
1590	**328**	200r. blue, dp bl & orge	1·00	50

329 Immigrants

1980. Indonesian Immigration.

1591	**329**	12r.50 red and green	35	10

330 1946 50s. Stamp

1980. 35th Anniv of Independence.

1592	**330**	75r. cream, black & brn	50	35
1593	-	100r. cream, pur & gold	1·10	40
1594	-	200r. cream, pink and silver	1·50	65

DESIGNS—HORIZ: 100r. 1946 15s. stamp. VERT: 200r. 1946 15s. Freedom Fund stamp.

331 Map of A.O.P.U. Members

1980. 10th Anniv of Asian–Oceanic Postal Union Training School, Bangkok.

1595	**331**	200r. blue, lt blue & turq	1·30	25

332 O.P.E.C. Emblem on Globe

1980. 20th Anniv of Organization of Petroleum Exporting Countries.

1596	**332**	200r. turquoise, bl & red	1·30	35

333 Service Members with Linked Arms

1980. 35th Anniv of Armed Forces. Mult.

1597	75r. Indonesians hailing flag	75	25
1598	200r. Type **333**	1·10	40

334 Pesquet's Parrot

1980. Parrots. Multicoloured.

1599	75r. Type **334**	2·40	75
1600	100r. Chattering lory	2·40	1·50
1601	200r. Rainbow lory	4·00	2·10
MS1602 95×120 mm. 250r. As No. 1601; 350r. Type **334** 400r. As No. 1600		24·00	24·00

335 "Dendrobium insigne"

1980. Orchids. Multicoloured.

1603	75r. Type **335**	1·10	15
1604	100r. "Dendrobium discolor"	1·80	90
1605	200r. "Dendrobium lasianthera"	3·50	65
MS1606 74×104 mm. 250r. As No. 1604; 350r. As No. 1605		16·00	16·00

336 Von Stephan and U.P.U. Emblem

1981. 150th Birth Anniv of Heinrich von Stephan (U.P.U. founder).

1607	**336**	200r. blue and deep blue	1·30	65

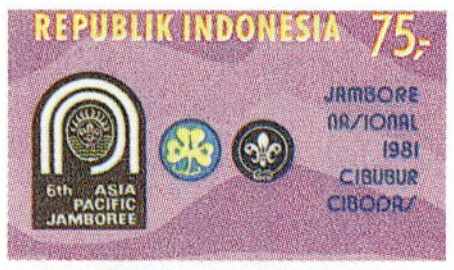

337 Jamboree and Scouting Emblems

1981. 6th Asia–Pacific Scout Jamboree, Cibubur. Multicoloured.

1608	75r. Type **337**	40	35
1609	100r. Scout and Guide map-reading (vert)	1·10	35
1610	200r. Jamboree emblem and tents	1·30	75
MS1611 77×63 mm. 150r. As No. 1609		1·60	1·60

338 Ship (relief carving)

1981. 5th Asian–Oceanic Postal Union Congress, Yogyakarta.

1612	**338**	200r. blue, black & lt bl	1·50	35

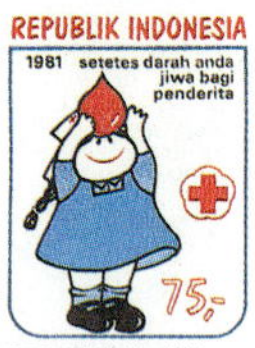

339 Child holding Blood Drop

1981. Blood Donors.

1613	**339**	75r. blue, black and red	50	15
1614	-	100r. red and grey	75	35
1615	-	200r. red, dp blue & blue	1·10	65

DESIGNS: 100r. Hands holding blood drop; 200r. Hands and blood drop.

340 Monuments

1981. International Family Planning Conference.

1616	**340**	200r. pale blue, brn & bl	1·00	40

341 "Song of Sritanjung"

1981. Traditional Balinese Paintings. Mult.

1617	100r. Type **341**	1·10	35
1618	200r. "Song of Sritanjung" (different)	1·60	75
MS1619 96×96 mm. 400r. and 600r. "Birth of the Eagle"		10·50	10·50

Nos. 1617/18 were issued together, se-tenant, forming a composite design.

342 Secretariat Building and Emblem

1981. Inauguration of A.S.E.A.N. Secretariat, Djakarta.

1620	**342**	200r. yellow, orge & pur	1·50	50

343 Uber Cup

1981. International Ladies' Badminton Championships, Tokyo.

1621	**343**	200r. brown, yell & orge	2·40	50

344 "Tree of Life" (relief from Candi Mendut)

1981. World Environment Day.

1622	**344**	75r. bistre, grey and black	75	15
1623	-	200r. bistre, grey & black	1·20	35

DESIGN: 200r. "Yaksha Apacaka".

345 Students reading Koran, Mosque and Emblem

1981. 12th National Koran Reading Contest, Banda Aceh.

1624	**345**	200r. black, red & yellow	1·00	50

346 Blind Man

1981. International Year of Disabled Persons.

1625	**346**	75r. brown, yellow & bis	40	15
1626	-	200r. blue, brown & grn	1·00	50

DESIGN: 200r. Deaf and dumb person.

347 Soekarno-Hatta Monument, Djakarta

1981. Independence Monument.

1627	**347**	200r. blue, yellow & gold	1·50	40

348 Parachute Jumping

1981. National Sports Week, Djakarta.

1628	**348**	75r. red, black and blue	40	15
1629	-	100r. black, blue and red	65	65
1630	-	200r. brown, green & red	1·30	50

DESIGNS—HORIZ: 100r. Scuba diving. VERT: 200r. Horse riding.

349 Food Produce

1981. World Food Day.

1631	**349**	200r. multicoloured	2·40	75

350 Arms of Aceh Special Territory

1981. Provincial Arms (1st series).

1632	**350**	100r. yellow, grn & gold	2·40	75
1633	-	100r. multicoloured	2·40	75
1634	-	100r. multicoloured	2·40	75
1635	-	100r. multicoloured	3·25	1·80
1636	-	100r. multicoloured	10·50	90

DESIGNS: No. 1633, Bali; No. 1634, Bengkulu; No. 1635, Irian Jaya; No. 1636, Djakarta.

See also Nos. 1643/62 and 1710.

351 Salmon-crested Cockatoo

1981. Cockatoos. Multicoloured.

1637	75r. Type **351**	3·75	80
1638	100r. Sulphur-crested cockatoo	4·00	80
1639	200r. Palm cockatoo	6·50	3·00
MS1640 73×64 mm. 150r. As No. 1638; 350r. As No. 1639		18·00	18·00

1982. Provincial Arms (2nd series). As T 350. Multicoloured.

1641	100r. Jambi	1·10	50
1642	100r. Java Barat (West)	1·10	50
1643	100r. Java Tengah (Cent)	1·10	50
1644	100r. Java Timur (East)	1·10	50
1645	100r. Kalimantan Barat (West)	1·10	50
1646	100r. Kalimantan Selatan (South)	1·10	50
1647	100r. Kalimantan Timur (East)	1·10	50
1648	100r. Kalimantan Tengah (Central)	1·10	50
1649	100r. Lampung	1·10	50
1650	100r. Moluccas	75	50
1651	100r. Nusa Tengarra Barat (West)	75	15
1652	100r. Nusa Tengarra Timur (East)	75	15
1653	100r. Riau	75	25
1654	100r. Sulawesi Tengah (Central Celebes)	75	15
1655	100r. Sulawesi Tenggara (South-east Celebes)	75	15
1656	100r. Sulawesi Selatan (South Celebes)	75	25
1657	100r. Sumatera Utara (North Celebes)	90	15
1658	100r. Sumatera Barat (West)	90	15
1659	100r. Sumatera Selatan (South)	75	15
1660	100r. Sumatera Utara (North)	75	15
1661	100r. Yogyakarta	1·80	15
1662	250r. Republic of Indonesia (45×29 mm)	1·00	35

352 Hands enclosing Family

1982. 70th Anniv of Bumiputera Mutual Life Insurance Company.

1663	**352**	75r. yellow, plum & pur	40	15
1664	-	100r. yellow, lt grn & grn	80	35
1665	-	200r. multicoloured	1·10	55

DESIGNS: 100r. Family in countryside; 200r. Hands supporting industrial activities.

353 Helicopter Rescue

1982. 10th Anniv of Search and Rescue Institute.
1666 **353** 250r. multicoloured 1·50 35

354 Houses and Ballot Boxes

1982. General Election. Multicoloured.
1667 75r. Type **354** 40 15
1668 100r. Rural houses and ballot boxes 65 25
1669 200r. Houses and National arms 1·50 65

355 Human Figures, Satellite and Dove

1982. 2nd U.N. Conference on Exploration and Peaceful Uses of Outer Space, Vienna.
1670 **355** 150r. blue, violet & black 75 40
1671 - 250r. green, light green and deep green 1·30 65
DESIGN: 250r. Peace dove and text.

356 Thomas Cup

1982. Thomas Cup Badminton Championship, London.
1672 **356** 250r. multicoloured 1·80 50
MS1673 72×95 mm. No. 1672 ×2 45·00 45·00

357 Footballers

1982. World Cup Football Championship, Spain.
1674 **357** 250r. multicoloured 1·80 50
MS1675 96×72 mm. No. 1674×2 70·00 70·00

358 Taman Siswa Emblem

1982. 60th Anniv of Taman Siswa (educational organization).
1676 **358** 250r. yellow, green & red 1·00 35

359 Flags forming "15"

1982. 15th Anniv of Association of South-East Asian Nations.
1677 **359** 150r. orange, red and blue 1·60 50

360 President Suharto

1982
1678 **360** 110r. red and orange 40 15
1679 **360** 250r. brown and orange 80 15
1680 **360** 275r. green and yellow 1·30 15
Nos. 1678 and 1680 are inscribed "1983".

1982. World Cup Football Championship Result. No. MS1675 optd ITALIA WORLD CHAMPION.
MS1681 96×72 mm. 250r. ×2 mult 70·00 70·00

362 Rothschild's Mynah

1982. 3rd World National Parks Congress, Bali. Multicoloured.
1682 100r. Type **362** 3·25 40
1683 250r. King bird of paradise 5·00 1·20
MS1684 76×104 mm. 500r. Type **362** 14·00 14·00

363 River Bridge

1982. Five Year Plan.
1685 **363** 17r.50 brown and green 50 10

364 Arfak Parotia

1982. Birds of Paradise. Multicoloured.
1686 100r. Type **364** 2·00 40
1687 150r. Twelve-wired bird of paradise 3·25 80
1688 250r. Red bird of paradise 5·00 1·20
MS1689 76×105 mm. 200r. Type **364**; 300r. As No. 1688 20·00 2·00

365 Scouts and Anniversary Emblem

1983. 75th Anniv of Boy Scout Movement.
1690 **365** 250r. blue, green & violet 1·60 35

366 Temple Restoration and Relief

1983. Borobudur Temple.
1691 **366** 100r. green, blue & lt bl 1·60 50
1692 - 150r. lt green, grn & brn 1·60 50
1693 - 250r. black, dp brn & brn 5·25 2·75

MS1694 96×64 mm. 500r. multicoloured 16·00 16·00
DESIGNS—VERT: 150r. Temple and statue. HORIZ: 250, 500r. Silhouette of Temple and seated Buddha.

367 President Suharto

1983
1695 **367** 500r. brown 1·40 35

368 Gas Storage Tanks

1983. 7th International Liquefied Natural Gas Conference, Djarkarta.
1696 **368** 275r. multicoloured 1·40 35

369 Ships and Bird

1983. World Communications Year.
1697 **369** 75r. multicoloured 25 15
1698 - 110r. multicoloured 50 25
1699 - 175r. blue and red 80 40
1700 - 275r. blue, dp blue & red 1·20 65
DESIGNS: 110r. Satellite and receiving station; 175r. Aircraft and dish aerial, 275r. Globe and letter.

370 Man and Woman reading Koran

1983. 13th National Koran Reading Competition.
1701 **370** 275r. yellow, green & blk 1·20 55

371 Eclipse and Map of Indonesia

1983. Total Solar Eclipse.
1702 **371** 110r. brn, dp brn & blk 65 25
1703 - 275r. blue, violet & purple 2·00 40
MS1704 96×64 mm. 500r. blue, violet and purple 14·00 14·00
DESIGN: 275, 500r. Map of Indonesia showing path of eclipse.

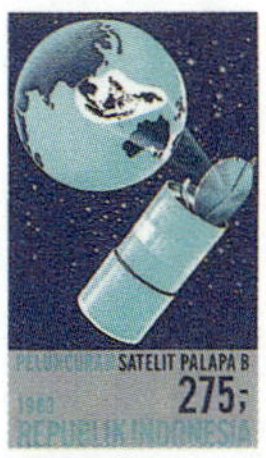

372 Satellite transmitting to Indonesia

1983. Launching of "Palapa B" Communications Satellite.
1705 **372** 275r. green, blue & silver 1·20 55

373 Patient receiving Radiation Treatment

1983. Anti-cancer Campaign.
1706 **373** 55r.+20r. multicoloured 65 40
1707 **373** 75r.+25r. multicoloured 1·10 40

374 Agricultural Produce

1983. Agricultural Census.
1708 **374** 110r. grey, green & black 65 15
1709 - 275r. red, black and green 1·10 25
DESIGN: 275r. Farmer with produce.

1983. Provincial Arms (3rd series). As T 350. Multicoloured.
1710 100r. Timor Timur 1·80 15

375 Traditional Weaving, Pakistan

1983. Indonesia–Pakistan Economic and Cultural Co-operation. Multicoloured.
1711 275r. Type **375** 1·60 75
1712 275r. Traditional weaving, Indonesia 1·60 75

376 Eruption of Krakatoa

1983. Centenary of Krakatoa Volcanic Eruption. Multicoloured.
1713 110r. Type **376** 50 25
1714 275r. Map showing position of Krakatoa 1·60 40

377 Casa-Nurtanio CN-235 Short-haul Passenger Aircraft

1983. Indonesian Aircraft.
1715 **377** 275r. multicoloured 1·20 55

1983. World Communications Year. Opening of Philatelic Museum, Djakarta. Sheet 51×84 mm.
MS1716 500r. As No. 1700 7·00 7·00

378 Tiger Barb

1983. Tropical Fishes. Multicoloured.
1717 110r. Type **378** 2·00 65
1718 175r. Brilliant rasbora 2·00 65
1719 275r. Archerfish 6·00 2·00

1983. "Telecom 83" Exhibition, Geneva. Sheet 75×83 mm. Multicoloured.
MS1720 400r. As No. 1698 8·25 8·25

379 Wilson's Bird of Paradise

1983. Birds of Paradise. Multicoloured.

1721	110r. Type **379**	1·60	40
1722	175r. Black sicklebill	2·40	50
1723	275r. Black-billed sicklebill	3·75	1·10
1724	500r. As No. 1723	5·75	3·00
MS1725	64×95 mm. As No. 1724	20·00	20·00

380 Emblems of Peace and Co-operation

1983. Palestinian Solidarity.

1726	**380**	275r. blue, brown & silver	1·40	35

381 "Stop" Emblem

1984. Anti-poliomyelitis Campaign.

1732	**381**	110r. red, purple and blue	40	15
1733	-	275r. purple, orge & red	1·40	35

DESIGN: 275r. Emblem of Save the Children Fund.

382 Agriculture

1984. 4th Five Year Plan.

1734	**382**	55r. yellow and blue	15	10
1735	-	75r. green and brown	25	15
1736	-	110r. blue and orange	40	25
1737	-	275r. multicoloured	1·10	65

DESIGNS: 75r. Casa-Nurtiano CN-235 airliner (aircraft industry); 110r. Shipbuilding; 275r. Telephone (telecommunications).

383 Manufacturing Plywood

1984. Forestry. Multicoloured.

1738	75r. Type **383**	1·10	15
1739	110r. Seedling	1·10	15
1740	175r. Measuring tree trunk	1·10	40
1741	275r. Transporting trees	1·10	55
MS1742	96×80 mm. Nos. 1740/1	12·00	12·00

384 Children playing with Toys

1984. Children's Day. Multicoloured.

1743	75r.+25r. Type **384**	1·10	15
1744	110r.+25r. Scout camp	65	25
1745	175r.+25r. Children on farm	1·60	40
1746	275r.+25r. Scouts and guides in camp	1·60	50

See also No. **MS**1760.

385 Flags of Member Nations

1984. Association of South-East Asian Nations Meeting, Djakarta.

1747	**385**	275r. multicoloured	1·80	55

386 Pole Vaulting

1984. Olympic Games, Los Angeles. Multicoloured.

1748	75r. Type **386**	50	15
1749	110r. Archery	50	15
1750	175r. Boxing	50	15
1751	250r. Shooting	1·60	50
1752	275r. Weightlifting	2·00	50
1753	325r. Swimming	3·50	25

387 Horse Dance

1984. Art and Culture. Multicoloured.

1754	75r. Type **387**	80	15
1755	110r. "Reog" mask	1·20	25
1756	275r. Lion dance	1·20	65
1757	325r. "Barong" mask	2·75	65

388 Thomas Cup (badminton)

1984. National Sports Day. Multicoloured.

1758	110r. Type **388**	80	25
1759	275r. Keep-fit exercise	1·60	40

1984. "Filacento" International Stamp Exhibition, The Hague. Two sheets.

MS1760	101×101 mm. No. 1746 ×4 plus two labels	18·00	18·00
MS1761	73×64 mm. No. 1757 plus label	45·00	45·00

1984. "Ausipex 84" International Stamp Exhibition, Melbourne. Sheet 101×76 mm.

MS1762	Nos. 1745/6	29·00	29·00

389 Map and Post Code Zones

1984. Introduction of New Post Code Zones.

1763	**389**	110r. blue, brown & orge	50	25
1764	**389**	275r. orange, blue & brn	1·10	65

390 Lauterbach's Bowerbird

1984. Birds. Multicoloured.

1765	75r. Type **390**	2·75	35
1766	110r. Flamed bowerbird	4·00	65
1767	275r. Arfak bird of paradise	5·25	2·40
1768	325r. Superb bird of paradise	5·25	1·60
MS1769	76×105 mm. Nos. 1765 and 1768	26·00	26·00

No. **MS**1769 is inscribed for "Philakorea 1984" International Stamp Exhibition.

391 Flag and Fists

1984. Youth Pledge.

1770	**391**	275r. black and red	1·10	75

392 Boeing 747-200

1984. 40th Anniv of I.C.A.O.

1771	**392**	275r. red, black and blue	1·20	75

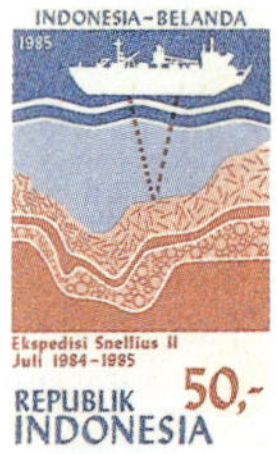

393 "Tyro" and Geological Structure of Seabed

1985. Indonesia–Belanda Expedition.

1772	**393**	50r. blue and brown	65	15
1773	-	100r. blue and purple	1·10	15
1774	-	275r. blue and green	1·20	35

DESIGNS: 100r. "Tyro" (oceanographic survey ship) and map; 275r. "Tyro" and coral reef.

394 Stylized Birds

1985. International Women's Day.

1775	**394**	100r. mauve and red	2·00	65
1776	-	275r. red and brown	3·00	3·00

DESIGN: 275r. Profile silhouettes.

395 Jet Airliner and workers

1985. 4th Five Year Plan.

1777	**395**	75r. red and brown	35	15
1778	-	140r. grey and brown	55	40
1779	-	350r. green and brown	1·50	1·00

DESIGNS: 140r. Children in classroom; 350r. Industrial equipment and buildings.

396 Pres. Suharto

1985

1780	**396**	140r. brown and red	65	15
1781	**396**	350r. mauve and red	1·50	15

397 Conference Building

1985. 30th Anniv of First Asian–African Conference, Bandung.

1786	**397**	350r. multicoloured	1·60	50

398 Globe and Teenagers waving Palm Leaves

1985. International Youth Year.

1787	**398**	75r. yellow, brown & grn	55	15
1788	-	140r. blue, green & mve	1·40	15

DESIGN: 140r. Flower on globe supported by teenagers.

399 Profiles

1985. United Nations Women's Decade.

1789	**399**	55r. brown and green	50	25
1790	-	140r. blue, green & brn	80	25

DESIGN: 140r. Globe and decade emblems.

400 Housing and Hydro-electricity

1985. 40th Anniv of Indonesian Republic.

1791	**400**	140r. green and red	55	15
1792	-	350r. blue, mauve & yell	1·50	35

DESIGN: 350r. Tractor and industrial complex.

401 Sky Diving

1985. National Sports Week, Djakarta. Multicoloured.

1793	55r. Type **401**	35	10
1794	100r. Unarmed combat	80	15
1795	140r. High jumping	80	25
1796	350r. Sailboards (vert)	1·30	50

402 O.P.E.C. Emblem and Globe

1985. 25th Anniv of Organization of Petroleum Exporting Countries.

1797	**402**	40r. blue, mauve & orge	1·00	25

403 Tanker

1985. Centenary of Indonesian Oil Industry. Multicoloured.

1798		140r. Type **403**	50	25
1799		250r. Refinery	90	40
1800		350r. Derrick and rigs	1·30	80

404 Doves, "40" and U.N. Emblem

1985. 40th Anniv of U.N.O. Multicoloured.

1801		140r. Type **404**	50	15
1802		300r. Bombs and green leaves	1·10	40

405 Javan Rhinoceros

1985. Wildlife.

1803	**405**	75r. brown, green & blue	1·00	25
1804	-	150r. brown, orge & grn	1·30	40
1805	-	300r. brown, blue and red	2·50	65

DESIGNS: 150r. Anoa; 300r. Komodo dragon.

406 Emblem

1986. Economic Census. Each orange and violet.

1806		175r. Type **406**	65	25
1807		175r. Symbols of economy	65	25

407 Baby feeding, Powdered Milk, Syringe and Graph

1986. 40th Anniv of UNICEF.

1808	**407**	75r. multicoloured	55	15
1809	-	140r. flesh, brown & pink	90	25

DESIGN: 140r. Vaccinating baby.

408 Industry

1986. 4th Five Year Plan.

1810	**408**	140r. multicoloured	50	15
1811	-	500r. yellow, brown & bl	50	15

DESIGN: 500r. Agriculture.

409 Thomas Cup and Racket

1986. Thomas (men's) and Uber (women's) Cup Badminton Championships, Djakarta.

1812	**409**	55r. black, yellow & blue	65	25
1813	-	150r. red, brown and gold	1·10	25

DESIGN: 150r. Thomas and Uber Cups and shuttlecock.

410 Pinisi Sailing Ship

1986. "Expo 86" World's Fair, Vancouver.

1814	**410**	75r. black, red and yellow	50	15
1815	-	150r. multicoloured	1·00	25
1816	-	300r. silver, red & purple	1·50	35

DESIGNS: 150r. Kentongan village drum and "Palapa" satellite; 300r. Indonesian pavilion emblem.

411 Guides on Parade

1986. National Jamboree. Multicoloured.

1817		100r. Type **411**	35	15
1818		140r. Guides cooking over fire	1·30	35
1819		210r. Scouts consulting map (vert)	1·60	55

412 "86"

1986. Indonesia Air Show.

1820	**412**	350r. multicoloured	1·30	65

413 Tari Legong Kraton

1986. Traditional Dances. Multicoloured.

1821		140r. Type **413**	1·30	15
1822		350r. Tari Barong	2·10	50
1823		500r. Tari Kecak	3·00	55

414 Woman planting

1986. 19th International Society of Sugar Cane Technologists Congress, Djakarta. Multicoloured.

1824		150r. Type **414**	55	15
1825		300r. Cane and sugar spilled from sack	1·40	25

415 Route Map of Cable

1986. Opening of Sea-Me-We Communications Cable.

1826	**415**	140r. green, orange & vio	55	25
1827	-	350r. green, yellow & bl	1·40	55

DESIGN: 350r. Route map of cable (different).

416 Doves, Wheat and Globe

1986. International Peace Year. Each brown, green and black.

1828		350r. Type **416**	1·10	40
1829		500r. Dove with olive twig flying around globe	1·50	15

1986

1830	**326**	50r. deep brown & brown	15	10
1831	**326**	55r. red and pink	35	10
1833	**326**	100r. ultramarine & blue	15	10
1834	**326**	300r. turq, grn & gold	1·00	10
1835	**326**	400r. green, turq & gold	1·30	15

417 Party Emblems and Buildings

1987. General Election.

1840	**417**	75r. blue, yellow & brn	50	10
1841	-	140r. green, orange & yell	50	15
1842	-	350r. blue, yellow & blk	1·30	35

DESIGNS: 140r. Party emblems and arms; 350r. Party emblems, map, wheat and ballot box.

418 Satellite and Globe

1987. Launch of "Palapa B2" Satellite.

1843	**418**	350r. yellow, green & brn	1·00	40
1844	-	500r. multicoloured	1·50	25

DESIGN—VERT: 500r. Rocket and satellite.

419 Boy carving Figures

1987. 4th Five Year Plan.

1845	**419**	140r. brown, yellow & bl	25	15
1846	-	350.r. violet, grn & orge	65	35

DESIGN: 350r. Graph and cattle.

420 Crab and Scanner Unit

1987. 10th Anniv of Indonesian Cancer Foundation.

1847	**420**	350r.+25r. yellow & bl	1·10	50

421 East Kalimantan Couple

1987. Wedding Costumes (1st series). Mult.

1848		140r. Type **421**	1·60	35
1849		350r. Aceh couple	9·75	4·50
1850		400r. East Timor couple	11·50	1·00

See also Nos. 1891/6, 1955/60, 1992/7 and 2010/15.

422 Weightlifting

1987. 14th South-East Asia Games, Djakarta. Designs showing pictograms.

1851	**422**	140r. yellow, red and blue	40	15
1852	-	250r. blue, yellow and red	75	25
1853	-	350r. red, blue and brown	1·10	40

DESIGNS: 250r. Swimming; 350r. Running.

423 Emblems

1987. 460th Anniv of Djakarta and 20th Anniv of Djakarta Fair.

1854	**423**	75r. blue, black & yellow	75	15
1855	-	100r. blue, black & yell	1·40	15

DESIGN—VERT: 100r. Emblems (different).

424 Children reading

1987. Children's Day and National Family Planning Co-ordination Board.

1856	**424**	100r. mauve and orange	40	15
1857	-	250r. yellow and blue	75	15

DESIGN—VERT: 250r. Globe, baby in cupped hands and dropper.

425 Headquarters, Djakarta

1987. 20th Anniv of Association of South-East Asian Nations.

1858	**425**	350r. multicoloured	1·30	50

426 Emblem

1987. 30th Anniv and 7th National Congress of Association of Specialists in Internal Diseases.

1859	**426**	300r. red and blue	1·00	15

427 Mount Bromo and Sand Craters

1987. Tourism. Multicoloured.

1860		140r. Type **427**	50	15
1861		350r. Bedugul Lake, Bali	1·60	55
1862		500r. Sea gardens, Bunaken Island	2·10	25

428 Woman with Broken Chains, Helmet and Pennant flying from Pen

1987. "Woman's Physical Revolution".

1863	**428**	75r. green, red and yellow	35	15
1864	-	100r. green, yellow & red	65	15

DESIGN: 100r. Women with rifles and barbed wire.

429 Giant Gourami

1987. Fishes.

1865	**429**	150r. mauve, yellow & bl	1·60	65
1866	-	200r. mauve, yellow & bl	1·60	35
1867	-	500r. black, yellow & bl	5·00	35

DESIGNS: 200r. Goldfish; 300r. Walking catfish.

430 Soldiers

1988. 31st Anniv of Veterans Legion.

1868	**430**	250r. green and orange	80	15

431 Welder

1988. National Safety and Occupational Health Day.

1869	**431**	350r. blue and green	1·10	50

432 Carved Snake and Frog

1988. 8th Anniv of National Crafts Council.

1870	**432**	120r. blue and brown	65	10
1871	-	350r. blue and brown	1·00	50
1872	-	500r. brown and green	1·60	15

DESIGN: 350r. Cane rocking-chair; 500r. Bamboo goods.

433 Industrial Symbols

1988. 4th Five Year Plan.

1873	**433**	140r. blue and green	25	15
1874	-	400r. purple and red	65	35

DESIGN: 400r. Fishing industry.

434 Indonesian Girls

1988. "Expo 88" World's Fair, Brisbane. Multicoloured.

1875		200r. Type **434**	90	15
1876		300r. Indonesian girl	90	15
1877		350r. Indonesian girl and boy	1·50	65
MS1878		96×95 mm. Nos. 1875/7. Perf or imperf	9·75	9·75

435 Anniversary Emblem

1988. 125th Anniv of Red Cross.

1879	**435**	350r. grey, black and red	1·00	25

436 "Dendrobium none betawi"

1988. Flowers. Multicoloured.

1880		400r. Type **436**	1·60	50
1881		500r. "Dendrobium abang betawi"	1·60	35

437 Running

1988. Olympic Games, Seoul.

1882	**437**	75r. black, brown & gold	50	15
1883	-	100r. black, red and gold	1·10	15
1884	-	200r. black, mve & gold	1·10	50
1885	-	300r. black, green & gold	50	50
1886	-	400r. black, blue and gold	65	40
1887	-	500r. black, blue and gold	3·00	40
MS1888		Two sheets, each 72×96 mm. Perf or imperf. (a) Nos. 1882, 1885 and 1887; (b) Nos. 1883/4 and 1886	36·00	36·00

DESIGNS: 100r. Weightlifting; 200r. Archery; 300r. Table tennis; 400r. Swimming; 500r. Tennis.

438 Figures around Emblem

1988. Centenary of International Women's Council.

1889	**438**	140r. black and blue	65	15

439 Family, Water and Ear of Wheat

1988. National Farmers' and Fishermen's Week.

1890	**439**	350r. stone and red	1·10	50

1988. Wedding Costumes (2nd series). As T 421. Multicoloured.

1891	55r. Sumatera Barat (West)	25	15
1892	75r. Jambi	15	10
1893	100r. Bengkulu	65	10
1894	120r. Lampung	90	10
1895	200r. Moluccas	1·60	15
1896	250r. Nusa Tenggara Timur (East)	2·10	1·10

440 President Suharto

1988

1897	**440**	200r. blue, pink and red	35	15
1898	**440**	700r. mauve, lt grn & grn	1·10	15
1899	**440**	1000r. multicoloured	1·10	15

441 Emblem

1988. 13th Non-Aligned News Agencies Co-ordinating Committee Meeting, Djakarta.

1901	**441**	500r. blue and red	1·20	35

442 Doves and Envelopes

1988. International Correspondence Week.

1902	**442**	140r. blue and red	90	15

1988. "Filacept 88" International Stamp Exhibition, The Hague. Two sheets, each 72×96 mm, each containing design as no. 1630 but colours changed.

MS1903	Two sheets. (a) 200r. 4, black, emerald and rose. (b) 200r. ultramarine, orange and rose plus label	29·00	29·00

443 Means of Transport and Communications

1988. Asian–Pacific Transport and Communications Decade.

1904	**443**	350r. blue and black	1·10	50

444 Al Mashun Mosque, Medan

1988. Tourism. Multicoloured.

1905	250r. Type **444**	55	40
1906	300r. Pagaruyung Palace, Batusangkar	90	35
1907	500r. Keong Emas Theatre, Djakarta	2·10	35
MS1908	96×57 mm. 1000r. As No. 1906. Perf or imperf	18·00	18·00

See also No. **MS**1954.

445 "Papilio gigon"

1988. Butterflies. Multicoloured.

1909	400r. Type **445**	1·50	40
1910	500r. "Graphium androcles"	2·50	55
MS1911	49×93 mm. 1000r. As No. 1910 Perf or imperf	29·00	29·00

446 "Rafflesia sp."

1989. Flowers. Multicoloured.

1916	200r. Type **446**	90	40
1917	1000r. "Amorphophallus titanum"	2·75	40
MS1918	50×103 mm. 1000r. As No. 1917	49·00	49·00

447 "40" and Boeing 747

1989. 40th Anniv of Garuda Airline.

1919	**447**	350r. blue and green	2·00	55

448 Mother and Baby

1989. Endangered Animals. The Orang-utan. Multicoloured.

1920	75r. Type **448**	3·75	1·60
1921	100r. Orang-utan in tree	3·75	75
1922	140r. Mother and baby in trees	3·75	75
1923	500r. Orang-utan	11·50	6·50
MS1924	Two sheets, each 95×125 mm. (a) Nos. 1920/1. (b) Nos. 1922/3	£200	£200

449 Industrial Site

1989. 5th Five Year Plan.

1925	**449**	55r. violet and green	10	10
1926	-	150r. blue and brown	25	15
1927	-	350r. green and orange	55	15

DESIGNS: 150r. Cement works; 350r. Gas plant.

450 Stamp and Map

1989. 125th Anniv of First Netherlands Indies Stamp.

1928	**450**	1000r. green, purple & bl	2·00	15

451 Ki Hadjar Dewantara and Graduate

1989. National Education Day.

1929	**451**	140r. red and purple	55	15
1930	-	300r. violet and green	1·00	35

DESIGN: 300r. Dewantara (founder of Taman Siswa School), pencil and books.

452 Emblem on Map

1989. 10th Anniv of Asia–Pacific Telecommunity.

1931	**452**	350r. purple and green	1·00	75

453 Flag and Cup

1989. Sudirman Cup.

1932	**453**	100r. brown and red	1·60	15

454 Students

1989. Children's Day.

1933	**454**	100r. brown and orange	50	10
1934	-	250r. blue and green	90	25

DESIGN: 250r. Youths exercising.

455 Headquarters

1989. 10th Anniv of Asia–Pacific Integrated Rural Development Centre.

1935	**455**	140r. brown and blue	75	15

456 Skull of "Sangiran 17" and Hunters

1989. Centenary of Palaeoanthropology in Indonesia.

1936	**456**	100r. black and brown	65	10
1937	-	150r. green and red	90	15
1938	-	200r. blue and brown	1·40	35
1939	-	250r. violet and brown	1·60	25
1940	-	300r. green and red	2·00	40
1941	-	350r. blue and brown	2·40	25

DESIGNS—HORIZ: 150r. Skull of "Perning 1" and cavemen; 200r. Skull of "Sangiran 10" and hunter. VERT: 250r. Skull of "Wajak 1"; 300r. Skull of "Sambungmacan 1"; 350r. Skull of "Ngandong 7".

457 Globe and People

1989. Centenary of Interparliamentary Union.

1942	**457**	350r. green and blue	1·00	75

458 Kung Fu

1989. 12th National Games, Djakarta. Mult.

1943		75r. Type **458**	55	15
1944		100r. Tennis	55	15
1945		140r. Judo	55	15
1946		350r. Volleyball	1·60	75
1947		500r. Boxing	2·75	25
1948		1000r. Archery	3·50	65

459 Taman Burung

1989. Tourism. Multicoloured.

1949		120r. Type **459**	75	10
1950		350r. Prangko Museum	1·10	55
1951		500r. Istana Anak-Anak (vert)	2·00	35
MS1952		100×51 mm. 1500r. As No. 1950	11·50	11·50

460 Trophy

1989. Film Industry.

1953	**460**	150r. ochre and brown	1·00	15

1989. "World Stamp Expo '89" International Stamp Exhibition, Washington D.C. Sheet 102×50 mm. containing designs as Nos. 1905/6. Multicoloured.

MS1954		1500r. Type **444**; 2500r. As No. 1906	11·50	11·50

1989. Wedding Costumes (3rd series). As T 421. Multicoloured.

1955		50r. Sumatera Utara (North)	35	10
1956		75r. Sumatera Selatan (South)	35	10
1957		100r. Djakarta	35	10
1958		140r. Sulawesi Utara (North Celebes)	75	15
1959		350r. Sulawesi Tengah (Central Celebes)	1·10	1·10
1960		500r. Sulawesi Selatan (South Celebes)	1·60	55
MS1961		50×102 mm. 1500r. As No. 1958 Perf or imperf	7·00	7·00

461 Worker wearing Safety Belt and Flag

1990. Occupational Safety.

1962	**461**	200r. brown and green	80	15

462 Benteng Marlborough, Bengkulu

1990. Tourism. Multicoloured.

1963		200r. Type **462**	1·00	15
1964		400r. National Museum, Djakarta	1·50	35
1965		500r. Baiturrahman Mosque, Banda Aceh	1·50	50
MS1966		102×51 mm. 1000r. As No. 1964; As No. 1965	9·75	9·75

463 "Mammilaria fragilis"

1990. Plants. Multicoloured.

1967		75r. Type **463**	40	10
1968		1000r. Bonsai of "Gmelina elliptica"	2·00	50
MS1969		105×50 mm. 1500r. As No. 1968	12·00	12·00

464 Tree-felling Equipment

1990. 5th Five Year Plan.

1970	**464**	200r. brown and blue	35	15
1971	-	1000r. black and blue	1·60	1·00

DESIGN: 1000r. Lighthouse and freighter.

465 Arrow pointing to Indonesia

1990. Visit Indonesia Year (1991) (1st issue). Multicoloured.

1972		100r. Type **465**	35	10
1973		500r. Temple	1·30	35

See also Nos. 1998/2000.

1990. "Stamp World London 90" International Stamp exhibition. Sheet 88×52 mm.

MS1974	**465**	5000r. multicoloured	18·00	18·00

466 Battle and Disabled Man using Soldering-iron

1990. 40th Anniv of Disabled Veterans Corp.

1975	**466**	1000r. orange and green	1·50	1·00

467 Player and Goalkeeper

1990. World Cup Football Championship, Italy. Multicoloured.

1976		75r. Type **467**	1·60	1·00
1977		150r. Player tackling	55	10
1978		400r. Players competing for high ball	80	15
MS1979		98×65 mm. 1500r. As No. 1978	9·00	9·00

468 Lampung Bridal Pair

1990. National Stamp exhibition. Sheet 68×95 mm.

MS1980		2000r. multicoloured	7·00	7·00

No. **MS**1980 also bears inscriptions commemorating various stamp exhibition and label for "Stamp World London 90".

469 U.N. Population Award

1990. 20th Anniv of Family Planning Movement.

1981	**469**	60r. brown and red	40	10

470 Figure with Pencil and Open Book

1990. Population Census.

1982	**470**	90r. green and turquoise	55	10

471 Children

1990. Children's Day.

1983	**471**	500r. purple and red	1·10	40

472 Soldier planting Flag

1990. 45th Anniv of Independence. Mult.

1984		200r. Type **472**	65	15
1985		500r. Modern building and roads	1·10	50
MS1986		50×105 mm. 1000r. As No. 1985	8·25	8·25

473 Buildings and Cultural Identities

1990. Indonesia–Pakistan Economic and Cultural Co-operation Organization. Multicoloured.

1987		75r. Type **473**	50	15
1988		400r. Dancer (vert)	1·10	40

474 Emblem

1990. 20th Anniv of Asian–Pacific Postal Training Centre.

1989	**474**	500r. blue & ultramarine	1·00	40

475 Anniversary Emblem

1990. 30th Anniv of Organization of Petroleum Exporting Countries.

1990	**475**	200r. black, grey & orge	80	15

476 Houses

1990. Environmental Health.

1991	**476**	1000r. multicoloured	2·00	35

1990. Wedding Costumes (4th series). As T 421. Multicoloured.

1992		75r. Java Barat (West)	35	10
1993		100r. Java Tengah (Central)	40	10
1994		150r. Yogyakarta	40	10
1995		200r. Java Timur (East)	55	15
1996		400r. Bali	80	40
1997		500r. Nusa Tenggara Barat (West)	90	50

477 Dancer and House

1991. Visit Indonesia Year (2nd issue). Dancers and Traditional Houses. Multicoloured.

1998		200r. Type **477**	1·00	15
1999		500r. House and dancer with saucers	1·40	55
2000		1000r. Dancer and house (different)	2·50	40
MS2001		50×100 mm. 1500r. As Type **477**	14·00	14·00

478 Emblem

1991. 16th National Koran Reading Competition, Yogyakarta.

2002	**478**	200r. green and yellow	80	15

479 Palace of Sultan Ternate, Moluccas

1991. Tourism. Multicoloured.

2003		500r. Type **479**	1·00	25
2004		1000r. Bari House, Palembang	1·60	35
MS2005		100×50 mm. As No. 2004	6·50	6·50

No. **MS**2005 also commemorates Flap Exco Meeting Yogyakarta.

480 Steel Mill

1991. 5th Five Year Plan.

2006	**480**	75r. red and blue	10	10
2007	-	200r. blue and black	25	15

DESIGN—HORIZ: 200r. Computer technology.

481 Damaged Lungs and Cigarette Smoke forming Skull

1991. Anti-smoking Campaign.

2008	**481**	90r. red and black	55	10

482 Hands

1991. 24th Anniv of National Federation for the Welfare of the Mentally Handicapped.

2009	**482**	200r.+25r. black and red	80	25

1991. Wedding Costumes (5th series). As T 421. Multicoloured.

2010	100r. Kalimantan Barat (West)	25	10
2011	200r. Kalimantan Tengah (Central)	80	15
2012	300r. Kalimantan Selatan (South)	50	15
2013	400r. Sulawesi Tenggara (South-east Celebes)	55	25
2014	500r. Riau	80	35
2015	1000r. Irian Jaya	1·00	55

483 Tents

1991. National Boy Scout Jamboree, Cibubur.

2016	**483**	200r. blue, black and red	1·10	15

484 Monument

1991. 42nd Anniv of Return of Republican Government to Djokjakarta.

2017	**484**	200r. green and brown	80	15

485 Temples and Family

1991. Farmers' Week.

2018	**485**	500r. yellow and blue	1·40	15

486 Cells

1991. "chemindo '91" Chemistry Congress, Surabaya.

2019	**486**	400r. red and green	1·00	15

487 Weightlifters

1991. 5th Junior Men's and Fourth Women's Asian Weightlifting Championships, Manado.

2020	**487**	300r. red and black	1·00	15

488 Parachutists

1991. World Parachuting Championships.

2021	**488**	500r. mauve and blue	1·00	15

489 Red Cross and Hands

1991. 46th Anniv of Indonesian Red Cross.

2022	**489**	200r. red and green	80	15

490 Radio Mast

1991. 8th International Amateur Radio Union Region III Conference, Bandung.

2023	**490**	300r. blue and yellow	1·00	15

491 Script and Mosque

1991. Istiqlal Festival, Djakarta.

2024	**491**	200r. black and red	1·00	15

492 Dancer and Inspectors

1991. International Convention on Quality Control Circles, Bali.

2025	**492**	500r. multicoloured	1·20	50

493 Orang-utan

1991. International Conference on Great Apes of the World. The Orang-utan. Multicoloured.

2026	200r. Type **493**	1·00	15
2027	500r. Orang-utan on forest path	1·20	25
2028	1000r. Orang-utan sitting on ground	2·50	55
MS2029	50×100 mm. 2500r. As No. 2028	8·25	8·25

494 Model of Jakarta Post Office

1992. Automation of Postal Service. Mult.

2030	200r. Type **494**	40	15
2031	500r. Sorting machine	80	35

495 "Phalaenopsis ambilis"

1992. Flowers. Multicoloured.

2032	200r. Type **495**	40	15
2033	500r. "Rafflesia arnoldii"	80	35
2034	1000r. "Jasminum sambac"	1·80	40
MS2035	106×50 mm. 2000r. As No. 2034	8·25	8·25

496 Buildings, Ballot Boxes and State Arms

1992. Parliamentary Elections. Mult.

2036	75r. Type **496**	15	10
2037	100r. Ballot boxes and globe	40	10
2038	500r. Ballot boxes and hands holding voting slips	1·00	25

497 Lembah Baliem, Irian Jaya

1992. Visit ASEAN Year. Multicoloured.

2039	300r. Type **497**	65	15
2040	500r. Tanah Lot, Bali	1·00	35
2041	1000r. Lembah Anai, Sumatra Barat	2·10	35
MS2042	100×50 mm. 3000r. As No. 2040	8·25	8·25

498 Road-building

1992. 5th Five Year Plan.

2043	**498**	150r. purple and green	15	15
2044	-	300r. blue and mauve	55	15

DESIGN: 300r. Aircraft.

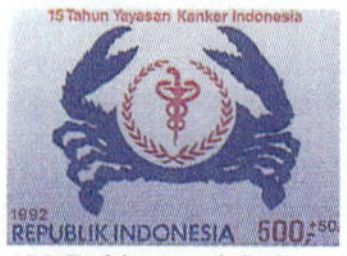

499 Emblem and Crab

1992. 15th Anniv of Indonesian Cancer Foundation.

2045	**499**	200r.+25r. red & brown	40	15
2046	**499**	500r.+50r. red and blue	80	25

500 Weightlifting

1992. Olympic Games, Barcelona. Mult.

2047	75r. Type **500**	25	10
2048	200r. Badminton	35	15
2049	300r. Sports pictograms	65	15
2050	500r. Tennis	80	40
2051	1000r. Archery	2·00	40
MS2052	751×00 mm. 2000r. As No. 2048; 3000r. As No. 2051	9·75	9·75

501 White-crested Laughing Thrush

1992. Birds. Multicoloured.

2053	100r. Type **501**	25	10
2054	200r. Common golden-backed woodpecker	50	15
2055	400r. Rhinoceros hornbill	1·00	50
2056	500r. Amboina king parrot	1·50	55
MS2057	501×00 mm. 3000r. Type **501**	8·25	8·25

502 Busy Street (Tammy Filia)

1992. National Children's Day. Children's paintings. Multicoloured.

2058	75r. Type **502**	10	10
2059	100r. Children with balloons (Cynthia Widiyana Halim)	25	10
2060	200r. Native boats (Dandy Rahmad Adi Kurniawan)	55	15
2061	500r. Girl and bird (Intan Sari Dewi Saputro)	1·40	80

503 Anniversary Emblem

1992. 25th Anniv of Association of South-East Asian Nations. Multicoloured.

2062	200r. Type **503**	40	15
2063	500r. Map and flags of member nations	1·20	40
2064	1000r. "25" and flags	2·40	50

504 Earth and "Palapa B-4" (satellite)

1992. Communications. Multicoloured.

2065	200r. Type **504**	40	15
2066	500r. "Palapa" satellite (16th anniv of launch)	80	40
2067	1000r. Old and modern telephones (modernization of telephone system)	2·00	50

505 Emblem

1992. 10th Non-Aligned Countries Summit, Djakarta. Multicoloured.

2068	200r. Type **505**	35	10
2069	500r. Members' flags and emblem	55	10

506 Ngremo Dance, East Java

1992. Traditional Dances (1st series). Mult.
2070 200r. Type **506** 25 15
2071 500r. Gending Sriwijaya dance, South Sumatra 1·20 1·20
MS2072 50×100 mm. 3000r. Type **506** 7·25 7·25

See also Nos. 2122/5, 2166/73, 2211/15, 2292/6, 2366/71 and 2476/81.

507 Anniversary Emblem

1992. 40th Anniv of International Planned Parenthood Federation.
2073 **507** 200r. blue and green 80 15

508 Antara Building, Djakarta

1992. 55th Anniv of Antara News Agency.
2074 **508** 500r. black and blue 1·00 15

509 Planting Saplings

1992. National Afforestation.
2075 **509** 500r. multicoloured 1·00 25

1993. No. 1831 surch 50r.
2076 **326** 50r. on 55r. red and pink 40 10

511 State Arms and Assembly Building

1993. 10th People's Consultative Assembly. Multicoloured.
2077 300r. Type **511** 40 15
2078 700r. Assembly hall 1·00 25

512 Soldiers and Buildings

1993. 5th Five Year Plan. Multicoloured.
2079 300r. Type **512** 35 35
2080 700r. Workers and arrow 75 75
2081 1000r. Runners 1·10 1·10

513 Swarm of "Ornithoptera goliath"

1993
2082 **513** 1000r. multicoloured 1·60 25

514 Peristiwa Hotel, Yamato, and Adipura Kencana Medal

1993. 700th Anniv of Surabaya (300, 700r.) and "indo tourism 93" (1000r.). Multicoloured.
2083 300r. Type **514** 35 35
2084 700r. Modern city and World Habitat Award, 1992 75 75
2085 1000r. Candi Bajang Ratu (temple) 1·10 1·10

516 Mascot

1993. "indopex'93" Asian Stamp Exhibition, Surabaya. Nos. 2082/5 optd indopex'93 surabaya.
2086 **514** 300r. multicoloured 35 15
2087 - 700r. multicoloured 75 35
2088 **513** 1000r. mult (No. 2082) 2·00 80
2089 - 1000r. mult (No. 2085) 1·30 50
MS2090 **516** 101×50 m. 3500r. multicoloured 5·25 5·25

517 "Jasminum sambac"

1993. Environmental Protection. Mult.
2091 300r. Type **517** 35 15
2092 300r. Moth orchid ("Phalaenopsis amabilis") 35 15
2093 300r. "Rafflesia arnoldi" (flower) 1·30 40
2094 700r. Komodo dragon 1·30 40
2095 700r. Asian bonytongue 1·30 40
2096 700r. Java hawk eagle 1·30 40
MS2097 75×105 mm. 1500r. Type 517; 1500r. As No. 2094 6·00 6·00

Stamps of the same value were issued together, se-tenant, in strips of three stamps, each strip forming a composite design.

518 Scouts making Road

1993. 1st World Community Development Camp, Lebakharjo. Multicoloured.
2098 300r. Type **518** 35 15
2099 700r. Pres. Suharto greeting girl scout 1·00 15

519 President Suharto

1993
2100 **519** 150r. multicoloured 15 15
2101 **519** 300r. multicoloured 35 15
2102 **519** 700r. multicoloured 75 50

On No. 2102 part of the background is a draped flag.

520 "Papilio blumei"

1993. International Butterfly Conference, Ujungpandang.
2103 **520** 700r. multicoloured 1·00 15
MS2104 50×100 mm. **520** 3000r. multicoloured 5·75 5·75

See also **MS**2110.

521 Swimming

1993. "Pon XIII" Sports Week, Djakarta. Multicoloured.
2105 150r. Type **521** 15 15
2106 300r. Cycling 35 35
2107 700r. Mascot 75 75
2108 1000r. High jumping 1·10 1·10
MS2109 51×101 mm. 3500r. As No. 2018 5·25 5·25

1993. "Bangkok 1993" International Stamp Exhibition. Sheet 67×75 mm containing design as T 520 but without top inscription.
MS2110 3000r. multicoloured 6·00 6·00

522 Sigura-Gura Waterfall, North Sumatra

1993. World Tourism Organization Meeting, Bali. Multicoloured.
2111 300r. Type **522** 35 35
2112 700r. Goa Petruk (cave), Central Java 75 75
2113 1000r. Danau Segara Anak (cove), West Nusa Tenggara (horiz) 1·10 1·10
MS2114 71×75 mm. 5000r. Similar design to Type **522** 4·50 4·50

523 General Soedirman

1993. Armed Forces. Each brown, black and red.
2115 300r. Type **523** 35 15
2116 300r. Lt.-Gen. Oerip Soemohardjo 35 15

Nos. 2115/16 were issued together, se-tenant, forming a composite design.

524 "Michelia champaca"

1993. Flora and Fauna. Multicoloured.
2117 300r. Type **524** 75 15
2118 300r. "Cananga adorata" 75 15
2119 300r. Orange-tailed shama ("Copsychus pyrrhopygus") 75 15
2120 300r. Southern grackle ("Gracula religiosa") 75 15

525 Plantation

1993. Resettlement Programme.
2121 **525** 700r. multicoloured 75 75

526 South Sumatran Dancer

1993. Traditional Dances (2nd series). Mult.
2122 300r. Type **526** 55 15
2123 700r. West Kalimantan 1·00 15
2124 1000r. Irian Jaya 1·30 25
MS2125 50×101 mm. 3500r. As No. 2124 5·25 5·25

527 Emblems

1994. International Year of the Family.
2126 **527** 300r. multicoloured 40 15

528 Working Women

1994. 6th Five Year Plan. Multicoloured.
2127 100r. Type **528** 10 10
2128 700r. Graduate and school pupils 75 75
2129 2000r. Doctor, nurse and children 2·10 2·10

529 Netherlands Indies, Japanese Occupation and Indonesia Stamps

1994. 130th Anniv of 1st Netherlands Indies Stamps.
2130 **529** 700r. multicoloured 80 40

530 Ladige's Rainbowfish

1994. Fishes. Multicoloured.
2131 300r. Type **530** 35 15
2132 700r. Boeseman's rainbow fish 90 35
MS2133 103×50 mm. 3500r. As No. 2132 5·00 5·00

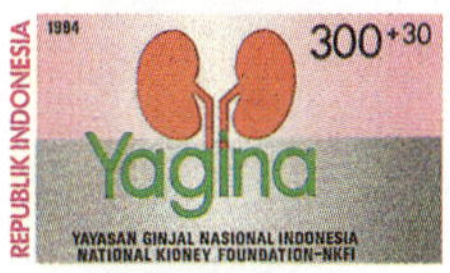
531 Emblem

1994. National Kidney Foundation.
2134 **531** 300r.+30r. mult 50 25

532 Figure, Globe, and Anniversary Emblem

1994. 75th Anniv of International Red Cross Red Crescent Organization.

2135	**532**	300r. black, red and blue	40	15

533 Map and Emblem

1994. Asia–Pacific Ministerial Conference on Women, Djakarta.

2136	**533**	700r. multicoloured	80	35

534 Player

1994. World Cup Football Championship, U.S.A.

2137	**534**	150r. multicoloured	15	10
2138	-	300r. multicoloured	35	15
2139	-	700r. blue, red and black	75	40
2140	-	1000r. multicoloured	1·20	50
MS2141		109×50 mm. 3500r. multi-coloured	5·00	5·00

DESIGNS—VERT: 300r. Striker (mascot). HORIZ: 700r. Emblem; 1000, 3500r. Ball in net .

535 Player and Uber Cup (Women's)

1994. Indonesian Victories in World Team Badminton Championships. Multicoloured.

2142		300r. Type **535**	40	15
2143		300r. Thomas Cup (Men's)	40	15
MS2144		86×92 mm. 1750r. Type **535**; 1750r. As No. 2143	5·00	5·00

Nos. 2142/3 were issued together, se-tenant, forming a composite design.

536 Hand holding Scales

1994. National Commission on Human Rights.

2145	**536**	700r. multicoloured	80	15

1994. "Philakorea 1994" International Stamp Exhibition, Seoul. Sheet 85×91 mm.

MS2146		3500r. multicoloured	5·00	5·00

537 Vase with Bead Cover

1994. Indonesia–Pakistan Economic and Cultural Co-operation Organization. Multicoloured.

2147		300r. Type **537**	25	25
2148		700r. Blue and white vase	65	65

538 Skeleton of Quadruped

1994. Centenary of Bogoriense Zoological Museum. Multicoloured.

2149		700r. Type **538**	80	50
2150		1000r. Outline and skeleton of whale (80×22 mm)	1·10	55
MS2151		123×48 mm. 3500r. As No. 2150	5·00	5·00

539 Mascots

1994. 12th Asian Games, Hiroshima, Japan. Multicoloured.

2152		300r. Type **539**	25	25
2153		700r. Hurdling	65	65

540 Communications and Map

1994. 25th Anniv of Bakosurtanal.

2154	**540**	700r. multicoloured	80	35

541 "Morus macroura"

1994. Flora and Fauna. Multicoloured.

2155		150r. Type **541**	40	15
2156		150r. "Oncosperma tiquillaria"	40	15
2157		150r. "Eucalyptus urophylla"	40	15
2158		150r. Moth orchid ("Phalaenopsis amabilis")	40	15
2159		150r. "Pometia pinnata"	40	15
2160		150r. Great argus pheasant ("Argusianus argus")	40	15
2161		150r. Blue-crowned hanging parrot ("Loriculus pusillus")	40	15
2162		150r. Timor helmeted friarbird ("Philemon buceroides")	40	15
2163		150r. Amboina king parrot ("Alisterus amboinensis")	40	15
2164		150r. Twelve-wired bird of paradise ("Seleucidis melanoleuca")	40	15
MS2165		48×81 mm. 3500r. As No. 2162	5·00	5·00

Nos. 2158 and 2161 are incorrectly inscribed; the correct Latin names are "*Dendrobium phalaenopsis*" and "*Loriculus galgulus*" respectively.

542 Venue

1994. Asia–Pacific Economic Co-operation Summit, Bogor.

2166	**542**	700r. multicoloured	80	25

543 Airplane

1994. 50th Anniv of I.C.A.O.

2167	**543**	700r. multicoloured	80	25

1994. Traditional Dances (3rd series). As T 506. Multicoloured.

2168		150r. Mengaup, Jambi	15	10
2169		300r. Topeng, West Java	25	15
2170		700r. Anging Mamiri, South Sulawesi	65	35
2171		1000r. Pisok, North Sulawesi	90	25
2172		2000r. Bidu, East Nusa Tenggara	1·80	1·00
MS2173		47×87 mm. 3500r. As No. 2169	3·25	3·25

544 Yogyakarta Palace

1995. 20th Anniv of World Tourism Organization. Multicoloured.

2174		300r. Type **544**	25	25
2175		700r. Floating market, Banjarmasin	65	65
2176		1000r. Pasola (equestrian tradition), Sumba	90	90

545 Children, President Suharto and First Lady

1995. "Dedication to the Nation".

2177	**545**	700r. multicoloured	65	65

546 Letter from King of Klungkung, Bali

1995. 6th Five Year Plan. National Letter Writing Campaign. Multicoloured.

2178		300r. Type **546**	25	25
2179		700r. Carrier pigeon (campaign mascot) and letters	65	65

547 "Schizostachyum brachycladum"

1995. 4th International Bamboo Congress, Ubud, Bali. Multicoloured.

2180		300r. Type **547**	25	25
2181		700r. "Dendrocalamus asper"	65	65

548 N250 and National Flag

1995. Inaugural Flight of I.P.T.N. N250 Airliner.

2182	**548**	700r. multicoloured	65	65

549 Anniversary Emblem

1995. 50th Anniv of Indonesian Republic. Multicoloured.

2183		300r. Type **549**	25	25
2184		700r. Boy with national flag	65	65
MS2185		102×48 mm. 2500r. As No. 2184	4·50	4·50

550 Kota Intan Drawbridge

1995. "Jakarta '95" Asian Stamp Exn. Mult.

2186		300r. Type **550**	25	25
2187		700r. Fatahillah Jakarta History Museum	65	65

551 "Dewarutji" (cadet barquentine), Pinisi Sailing Ship and Flag

1995. "Sail Indonesia '95." Tall Ships Race and Fleet Review.

2188	**551**	700r. multicoloured	65	65
MS2189		91×48 mm. 2500r. multi-coloured	4·50	4·50

552 "Mother Love" (Patricia Saerang)

1995. 10th Asia and Pacific Regional Conference of Rehabilitation International, Indonesia.

2190	**552**	700r.+100r. mult	75	75

553 Mushaf Istiqlal (illuminated Islamic text)

1995. Istiqlal Festival.

2191	**553**	700r. multicoloured	65	65

554 P.T.T. Monument

1995. 50th Anniv of Take-over of P.T.T. Headquarters by Republicans.

2192	**554**	700r. multicoloured	65	65

555 Rice

1995. 50th Anniv of F.A.O.

2193	**555**	700r. multicoloured	65	65

556 Flags and Emblem

1995. 50th Anniv of U.N.O. Multicoloured.

2194		300r. Type **556**	25	25
2195		700r. Emblem, Earth and rainbow	65	65

557 "Cyrtostachys renda"

1995. Flora and Fauna. Multicoloured.

2196		150r. Type **557**	15	10
2197		150r. Tiger ("Panthera tigris")	15	10
2198		150r. "Bouea macrophylla"	15	10
2199		150r. Javan rhinoceros ("Rhinoceros sondaicus")	15	10
2200		150r. "Santalum album"	15	10
2201		150r. Komodo dragon ("Varanus komodoensis")	15	10
2202		150r. "Diospyros celebica"	15	10
2203		150r. Maleo fowl ("Macrocephalon maleo")	15	10
2204		150r. "Nephelium ramboutan-ake"	15	10
2205		150r. Malay peacock-pheasant ("Polyplectron schleiermacheri")	15	10
MS2206		48×95 mm. 2500r. as No. 2197	7·75	7·75

558 Yogyakarta Palace

1995. Award of Aga Khan Prize for Architecture to Indonesia. Multicoloured.

2207	300r. Type **558**	25	25
2208	700r. Surakarta Palace	65	65

559 Hill and Postal Carriers

1995. Birth Bicentenary of Sir Rowland Hill (instigator of postal stamps). Multicoloured.

2209	300r. Type **559**	25	25
2210	700r. Hill and Indonesian Postal Service emblem	65	65

1995. Traditional Dances (4th series). As T 506. Multicoloured.

2211	150r. Nguri dance, West Nusa Tenggara	15	15
2212	300r. Muli Betanggai dance, Lampung	25	25
2213	700r. Mutiara dance, Moluccas	65	65
2214	1000r. Gantar dance, East Kalimantan	90	90
MS2215	48×81 mm. 2500r. As No. 2211	3·75	3·75

560 Economic Sectors

1996. Economic Census.

2216	**560**	300r. orange and blue	25	25
2217	-	700r. turquoise & orange	65	65

DESIGN—HORIZ: 700r. Graph of economic activity.

561 Satellite orbiting Earth

1996. Launch of "Palapa-C" Satellite. Mult.

2218	300r. Type **561**	25	25
2219	700r. Satellite orbiting Earth (triangular)	55	55

562 Mixed Flowers

1996. Greetings Stamps. "Happy Holiday". Inscr "Selamat Hari Raya". Multicoloured.

2220	150r. Type **562**	10	10
2221	300r. Mixed flowers (different)	25	25
2222	700r. Mixed flowers (different)	55	55

563 Soemanang Soeriowinoto (Association head, 1946–47 and 1949–50)

1996. 50th Anniv of Indonesian Journalists' Association. Multicoloured.

2223	300r. Type **563**	25	25
2224	700r. Djamaluddin Adinegoro (head of Indonesian Press Bureau Foundation and founder of Academy of Publicity and Publicity Faculty, Padjadjaran University)	55	55

564 Tank firing and Map

1996. 47th Anniv of Return of Republican Government to Djokjakarta. Multicoloured.

2225	700r.+100r. Type **564**	65	65
2226	700r.+100r. Attack on Palace	65	65

Nos. 2225/6 were issued together, se-tenant, forming a composite design.

565 State House, Bandung

1996. "indonesia 96" International Youth Stamp Exhibition, Bandung. Multicoloured.

2227	300r. Type **565**	25	25
2228	700r. Painted parasols	55	55
MS2229	99×73 mm. 1250r. Type **565**; 1250r. As No. 2228	4·00	4·00

566 Indonesian Bear Cuscus

1996. Cuscuses. Multicoloured.

2230	300r. Australian spotted cuscus	25	25
2231	300r. Type **566**	25	25
MS2232	98×81 mm. 1250r. As No. 2230; 1250r. Type **586**	2·10	2·10

Nos. 2230/1 were issued together, se-tenant, forming a composite design.

567 Roses

1996. Greetings Stamps. "Congratulations and Best Wishes". Inscr "Selamat dan Sukses". Multicoloured.

2233	150r. Type **567**	10	10
2234	300r. Orchids	25	25
2235	700r. Chrysanthemums	55	55

568 Students (Y. Edwin Purwanto)

1996. Compulsory Nine Year Education Programme. Winning Entries in Children's Stamp Design Competition. Multicoloured.

2236	150r. Type **568**	10	10
2237	300r. Children in playground (Andi Pradhana)	25	25
2238	700r. Teacher and pupils (Intan Sari Dewi)	55	55

569 Archery

1996. Olympic Games, Atlanta. Mult.

2239	300r. Type **569**	25	25
2240	700r. Weightlifting	55	55
2241	1000r. Badminton	90	90
MS2242	81×48 mm. 2500r. Type **569**	2·10	2·20

中国'96——第9届亚洲国际集邮展览
CHINA'96 — 9th Asian International Philatelic Exhibition
(570)

1996. "China '96" International Stamp Exhibition, Peking. No. MS2232 optd with T 570 in the margin.

MS2243	98×81 mm. 1250r. ×2 multicoloured	5·75	5·75

571 Pres. Suharto and Procession

1996. National Youth Kirab. Multicoloured.

2244	300r. Type **571**	25	25
2245	700r. Pres. Suharto presenting national flag	55	55

572 Nusantara N-2130 Prototype over Soekarno-Hatta Airport

1996. Aviation and Maritime Year. Mult.

2246	300r. Type **572**	25	25
2247	700r. "Palindo Jaya" (inter-island ferry)	55	55

573 Scouts climbing over Rope Ladders

1996. National Scout Jamboree, Djakarta. Multicoloured.

2248	150r. Type **573**	10	10
2249	150r. Scouts on ladder and death slide	10	10
2250	150r. Scouts at base of rope ladders	10	10
2251	150r. Girl scouts constructing wooden apparatus	10	10
2252	150r. Scouts on unicycle and climbing frame	10	10
2253	150r. Girl scouts building fire on campsite	10	10
2254	150r. Soldering metal	10	10
2255	150r. Girl at radio taking notes	10	10

Nos. 2248/55 were issued together, se-tenant, Nos. 2248/51 and 2252/5 forming composite designs.

574 Pinisi Prows and Wave

1996. 50th Anniv of Bank BNI. Multicoloured.

2256	300r. Type **574**	25	25
2257	700r. Pinisi sailing ship	55	55

575 Mother and Child reading (Salt Iodization Programme)

1996. 50th Anniv of UNICEF. Each brown, green and mauve.

2258	300r. Type **575**	25	25
2259	700r. Giving oral vaccine to children (elimination of polio)	55	55
2260	1000r. Children (Children's Rights Convention)	90	90

576 Ibu Tien Suharto

1996. Ibu Suharto (First Lady) Commem.

2261	**576**	700r. multicoloured	55	55
MS2262	47×96 mm. **576**	2500r. multicoloured	2·10	2·10

577 Softball

1996. National Sports Week. Multicoloured.

2263	300r. Type **577**	25	25
2264	700r. Hockey	55	55
2265	1000r. Basketball	90	90

1996. "Istanbul '96" Stamp Exhibition, Turkey. Two sheets, each 94×80 mm. each containing one stamp (62×46 mm) featuring composite designs formerly issued in blocks of four.

MS2266	Two sheets (a) 1250r. As Nos. 2248/51; (b) 1250r. As Nos. 2252/5	1·60	1·60

578 Head of Sumatran Rhinoceros

1996. The Sumatran Rhinoceros ("Dicerorhinus sumatrensis") and the Javan Rhinoceros ("Rhinoceros sondaicus"). Multicoloured.

2267	300r. Type **578**	40	25
2268	300r. Sumatran rhinoceros	40	25
2269	300r. Javan rhinoceros	40	25
2270	300r. Adult and baby Javan rhinoceros	40	25
MS2271	100×47 mm. 1500r. Javan rhinoceros; 1500r. Sumatran rhinoceros	3·75	3·75

579 Flower Arrangement

1996. Greetings Stamps. "Happy New Year". Inscr "Selamat Tahun Baru". Multicoloured.

2272	150r. Type **579**	10	10
2273	300r. Arrangement including red and yellow roses	25	25
2274	700r. Arrangement including white rose and yellow chrysanthemums	55	55

580 Coins and Banknotes

1996. 50th Anniv of Financial Day.

2275	**580**	700r. multicoloured	55	55

581 Sulawesi Hornbill

1996. National Flora and Fauna Day. Mult.

2276	300r. Type **581**	25	25
2277	300r. Irrawaddy dolphin ("Orcaella brevirostris")	25	25
2278	300r. Black-naped oriole ("Oriolus chinensis")	25	25
2279	300r. Sun bear ("Helarctos malayanus")	25	25
2280	300r. Rothschild's mynah ("Leucopsar rothschildi")	25	25
2281	300r. Lontar palms ("Borassus flabellifer")	25	25
2282	300r. Black orchid ("Coelogyne pandurata")	25	25
2283	300r. Michelia ("Michelia alba")	25	25
2284	300r. Giant aroid lily ("Amorphophallus titanum")	25	25
2285	300r. Majegau ("Dysoxylum densiflorum")	25	25
MS2286	Two sheets, each 47×80 mm. (a) 1250r. As No. 2280; (b) 1250r. As No. 2282	1·20	1·20

See also No. **MS**2287.

1996. "Aseanpex '96" International Stamp Exhibition, Manila, Philippines.

MS2287	**581** 2000r. multicoloured	5·00	5·00

582 Somba Opu Fortress

1996. Eastern Region. Multicoloured.
2288 300r. Divers and sea-bed 25 25
2289 700r. Type **582** 55 55

583 School-children at Play

1996. National Movement of Foster Parents. Multicoloured.
2290 150r. Type **583** 15 15
2291 300r. Poor children and photograph of school-child (horiz) 25 25

1996. Traditional Dances (5th series). As T 506. Multicoloured.
2292 150r. Baksa Kembang dance, South Kalimantan 10 10
2293 300r. Ngarojeng dance, Djakarta 25 25
2294 700r. Rampai dance, Aceh 55 55
2295 1000r. Boituka dance, East Timor 90 90
MS2296 46×75 mm. 2000r. As No. 2293 2·00 2·00

584 Dish Aerial and Control Room

1997. Telecommunications Year. Mult.
2297 300r. Type **584** 25 25
2298 700r. Key pad, communications satellite orbiting Earth and woman using telephone 55 55

585 Children shaking Hands ("Happy Birthday")

1997. Greetings Stamps.
2299 **585** 600r. multicoloured 50 50
2300 - 600r. black, brn & mve 50 50
DESIGN: No. 2300, Heart and ribbons ("Best Wishes").

586 Transport, Ballot Boxes and National Flag

1997. General Election. Multicoloured.
2301 300r. Type **586** 25 25
2302 700r. State arms, map, ballot boxes and buildings 55 55
2303 1000r. State arms, ballot boxes, map and city skyline 90 90

1997. "Hong Kong '97" Stamp Exhibition. Sheet 81×47 mm.
MS2304 2000r. As Type **582** but with addition of postmark 2·00 2·00

587 Pres. Suharto and Wahyu Nusantaraaji

1997. Indonesia's 200,000,000th Citizen.
2305 **587** 700r. multicoloured 55 55

588 Children with Stamp Collection

1997. 75th Anniv of Indonesian Philatelic Association. Multicoloured.
2306 300r. Type **588** 25 25
2307 700r. Magnifying glass on 1994 150r. Flora and Fauna stamp 55 55

589 Wage Rudolf Soepratman

1997. Cultural Anniversaries. Multicoloured.
2308 300r. Type **589** (composer of "Indonesia Raya" (national anthem), 60th death anniv (1998)) 25 25
2309 700r. Usmar Ismail (film director, 25th death anniv (1996)) 55 55
2310 1000r. Self-portrait of Affandi (painter, 90th birth anniv) 90 90
MS2311 47×97 mm. As No. 2310 2·00 2·00

590 Picture Jasper

1997. "Indonesia 2000" International Stamp Exn, Bandung (1st issue). Minerals. Multicoloured.
2312 300r. Type **590** 25 25
2313 700r. Chrysocolla 55 55
2314 1000r. Geode 90 90
MS2315 80×47 mm. 2000r. Banded agate 2·00 2·00
See also Nos. 2403/**MS**2407, 2529/**MS**2533 and 2593/**MS**2597.

591 Black-naped Oriole

1997. "Pacific 97" International Stamp Exhibition, San Francisco. Sheet 49×51 mm.
MS2316 **591** 2000r. multicoloured 2·00 2·00

592 Crowd giving Thumbs Up to "No Smoking" Sign

1997. World "No Smoking" Day. Winning Entry in Students' Design Competition.
2317 **592** 1000r. multicoloured 90 90

593 Fishes and Coral Reef

1997. World Environment Day. Mult.
2318 150r. Type **593** 15 15
2319 300r. Rays and other fishes by brain and other corals 25 25
2320 700r. Two coralfishes amongst corals 55 55
MS2321 47×79 mm. 2000r. Coral reef 2·00 2·00

594 Paksi Naga Liman Carriage (built by Pangeran Losari)

1997. 2nd Indonesian Royal Palace Festival, Cirebon. Multicoloured.
2322 300r. Type **594** 25 25
2323 700r. Singa Barong carriage (built by Ki Nataguna), 1549 55 55

595 Venue's Main Gateway

1997. 18th National Koran Reading Contest, Jambi. Multicoloured.
2324 300r. Type **595** 25 25
2325 700r. Al Ikhsaniah Mosque, Olak Kemang, Jambi 55 55

596 Co-operatives Monument, Tasikmalaya

597 Pres. Suharto and Dr. Mohammad Hatta (first vice-president)

1997. 50th Anniv of Co-operatives Movement. Multicoloured.
2326 150r. Type **596** 10 10
2327 150r. Co-operatives Monument, Djakarta 10 10
2328 300r. Child's hand clasping adult's hand 25 25
2329 300r. Figure before globe 25 25
2330 700r. Type **597** 55 55

598 Hands on Globe

1997. 30th Anniv of Association of South-East Asian Nations. Multicoloured.
2331 300r. Type **598** 25 25
2332 700r. Ears of cereals forming "30th" and globe 55 55

599 Games Emblem and Mascot

1997. 19th South-East Asian Games, Djakarta. Multicoloured.
2333 300r. Type **599** 25 25
2334 300r. Torch carrier, flags and emblem 25 25
2335 700r. Running and throwing the discus 55 55
2336 700r. Hurdling and sprinting 55 55

600 Coach, Bus, Java "International Harvester" Bus and Bullock Cart

1997. National Communications Day. Transport Development. Multicoloured.
2337 300r. Type **600** 25 25
2338 300r. Electric, express, diesel and steam railway locomotives 25 25
2339 700r. Container ship, passenger ship, cargo vessel and lette (Madurese sailing boat) 55 55
2340 700r. Seulawah and IPTN CN-235, CN-250 and N-2130 airliners 55 55

601 U.P.U. Monument and Mas Soeharto (first head of Indonesian P.T.T.)

1997. 50th Anniv of Indonesian Membership of U.P.U. Multicoloured.
2341 300r. Type **601** 25 25
2342 700r. Heinrich von Stephan (founder of U.P.U.) and monument 55 55

602 Assembly Emblem and Building

1997. People's Consultative Assembly General Session.
2343 **602** 700r. multicoloured 55 55

603 Village Programme (Army)

1997. Armed Forces Day. Multicoloured.
2344 300r. Type **603** 25 25
2345 300r. Frigates and Jalesveva Jayamahe Monument, Surabaya (Navy) 25 25
2346 300r. "Blue Falcon" acrobatic team (Air Force) 25 25
2347 300r. Rapid Reaction Unit (Police Force) 25 25

604 White Buffalo

1997. "MAKASSAR '97" National Stamp Exhibition, Ujiung Pandeing. Sheet 106×49 mm.
MS2348 **604** 2000r. multicoloured 1·30 1·30

605 Duku Fruit ("Lansium domesticum")

1997. National Flora and Fauna Day. Mult.
2349 300r. Type **605** 25 25
2350 300r. Salacca of Condet ("Salacca zalacca") 25 25

2351 300r. Tengawang tungkul ("Shorea stenoptera") 25 25
2352 300r. Ebony ("Diospyros macrophylla") 25 25
2353 300r. Fibre orchid ("Diplocaulobium utile") 25 25
2354 300r. Belida fish ("Chitala lopis") 25 25
2355 300r. Brahminy kite ("Haliastur indus") 25 25
2356 300r. Helmeted hornbill ("Rhinoplax vigil") 25 25
2357 300r. Timor deer ("Cervus timorensis") 25 25
2358 300r. Anoa ("Bubalus depressicornis") 25 25
MS2359 98×80 mm. 1250r. As No. 2351; 1250r. As No. 2355 1·80 1·80

606 Oil Field

1997. Association of South-east Asian Nations Council on Petroleum Conference, Djakarta. Multicoloured.
2360 300r. Type **606** 25 25
2361 300r. Oil refinery 25 25
2362 300r. "Eka Putra" (oil tanker) 25 25
2363 300r. Petrol tankers 25 25

607 AIDS Ribbon

1997. World AIDS Day.
2364 **607** 700r.+100r. mult 50 50

608 Letter from Foster Son

1997. National Foster Parents Movement.
2365 **608** 700r. multicoloured 50 50

1997. Traditional Dances (6th series). As T 506. Multicoloured.
2366 150r. Mopuputi Cengke dance, Central Sulawesi 10 10
2367 300r. Mandan Talawang Nyai Balau dance, Central Kalimantan 25 25
2368 600r. Gambyong dance, Central Java 40 40
2369 700r. Cawan dance, North Sumatra 50 50
2370 1000r. Legong Keraton dance, Bali 65 65
MS2371 48×79 mm. As No. 2368 1·30 1·30

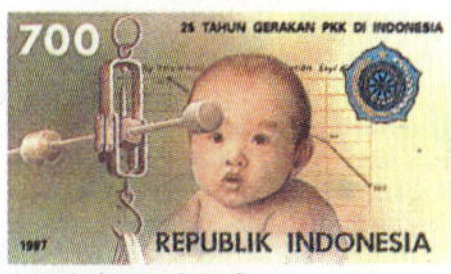

609 Baby and Scales

1997. 25th Anniv of Family Welfare Movement.
2372 **609** 700r. multicoloured 50 50

610 Erau Festival, East Kalimantan

1998. Year of Art and Culture. Festivals. Multicoloured.
2373 300r. Type **610** 10 10
2374 700r. Tabot Festival, Bengkulu 25 25

611 Malin Kundang and his Mother

1998. Folk Tales (1st series). Multicoloured. (a) "Malin Kundang".
2375 300r. Type **611** 10 10
2376 300r. Malin returning home and rejecting mother 10 10
2377 300r. Malin's mother praying to God to curse him 10 10
2378 300r. Malin's ship in storm 10 10
2379 300r. Malin turned to stone 10 10

(b) "Sangkuriang".
2380 300r. Dayang Sumbi weaving 10 10
2381 300r. Dayang Sumbi expelling her son Sanguriang after he killed their dog 10 10
2382 300r. Dayang Sumbi discovering her lover is her son 10 10
2383 300r. Dayang Sumbi creating fake dawn and Sanguriang hurling wooden boat 10 10
2384 300r. Tangkuban Parahu (upturned boat) Mountain 10 10

(c) "Roro Jonggrang".
2385 300r. Pengging people attacking Prambanan people 10 10
2386 300r. Bandung Bondowoso proposing to Roro Jonggrang 10 10
2387 300r. Bandung Bondowoso building temples 10 10
2388 300r. Women banging rice-mothers to prematurely announce dawn 10 10
2389 300r. Prambanan Temple and petrified Roro Jonggrang 10 10

(d) "Tengger".
2390 300r. Roro Anteng and Joko Seger marrying 10 10
2391 300r. Roro and Joko praying to gods for a child 10 10
2392 300r. Volcano erupting 10 10
2393 300r. Raden Kusuma (youngest son) sacrificing himself 10 10
2394 300r. Tengger people giving offerings to volcano 10 10
MS2395 62×64 mm. As No. 2394 65 65

Nos. 2375/94 were issued together, se-tenant, forming a composite design.

See also Nos. 2489/**MS**2509, 2572/**MS**2591, 2679/**MS**2699, 2761/**MS**2781, 2838/**MS**2858, 2942/**MS**2962 and 3000/**MS**3020.

612 Djakarta Palace

1997. Presidential Palaces. Multicoloured.
2396 300r. Type **612** 10 10
2397 300r. Bogor Palace 10 10
2398 300r. Cipanas Palace 10 10
2399 300r. Yogyakarta Palace 10 10
2400 300r. Tampak Siring Palace, Bali 10 10

613 Man and Pregnant Woman

1998. 50th Anniv of W.H.O. Multicoloured.
2401 300r. Type **613** 10 10
2402 700r. Mother and child (horiz) 10 10

1998. "Indonesia 2000" International Stamp Exhibition, Bandung (2nd issue). Minerals. As T 590. Multicoloured.
2403 300r. Chrysopal 10 10
2404 700r. Tektite 15 15
2405 1000r. Amethyst 25 25
MS2406 80×48 mm. 2500r. Petrified wood 40 40
MS2407 Two sheets. (a) 81×48 mm. 2500r. Opal; (b) 118×133 mm. Nos. 2403/5, each ×2, plus stamps as in No. **MS**2406 and **MS**2407a (pair of sheets sold at 35000r.) 80 80

614 Boys playing Football

1998. World Cup Football Championship, France. Multicoloured.
2408 300r. Type **614** 10 10
2409 700r. Boys and goal-posts 15 15
2410 1000r. Boys challenging for ball 25 25
MS2411 87×57 mm. 2500r. As No. 2411 40 40

615 Tropical Rainforest

1998. Environmental Protection. Ecophila Stamp Day. Multicoloured.
2412 700r. Type **615** 15 15
2413 700r. Tropical rainforest (different) 15 15

Nos. 2412/13 were issued together, se-tenant, forming a composite design.

616 Fishing Cat

1998. "Juvalex 98" Youth Stamp Exhibition, Luxembourg. Sheet 48×83 mm.
MS2414 **616** 5000r. multicoloured 65 65

617 School-children and Drug Addict

1998. International Day Against Drug Abuse and Illicit Trafficking. Multicoloured.
2415 700r. Type **617** 15 15
2416 700r. Students campaigning against drugs 15 15

618 Besakih Temple (2/3-size illustration)

1998. Tourism. Multicoloured.
2417 700r. Type **618** 15 15
2418 700r. Taman Ayun Temple (31×23 mm) 15 15
MS2419 77×45 mm. 2500r. Central part of design in Type **618** (41×24 mm) 40 40

619 Tiger

1998. "Singpex 98" Asian Stamp Exhibition, Singapore. Sheet 102×48 mm.
MS2420 5000r. multicoloured 2·75 2·75

620 Cattle Wagon and Truck

1998. Railway Rolling Stock. Multicoloured.
2421 300r. Type **620** 10 10
2422 300r. Truck and goods wagon 10 10
2423 300r. Green and yellow passenger carriages 10 10
2424 300r. Passenger carriage and tender 10 10
2425 300r. Class B50 steam locomotive 10 10
2426 300r. Front half of Class D52 steam locomotive 10 10
2427 300r. Back half of Class D52 steam locomotive with tender 10 10
2428 300r. Passenger carriage with two doors 10 10
2429 300r. Observation car 10 10
2430 300r. Goods wagon 10 10
MS2431 76×48 mm. 2500r. Steam locomotive 50 50

Nos. 2421/30 were issued together, se-tenant, forming a composite design of a train.

621 Pres. Bacharuddin Habibie

1998
2432 **621** 300r. multicoloured 10 10
2433 **621** 700r. multicoloured 15 15
2434 **621** 4500r. multicoloured 90 90
2435 **621** 5000r. multicoloured 1·00 1·00

622 Fencing

1998. 13th Asian Games, Bangkok, Thailand. Multicoloured.
2436 300r. Type **622** 10 10
2437 700r. Taekwondo 15 15
2438 4000r. Kung fu 80 80
MS2439 79×100 mm. Nos. 2436/8 1·00 1·00

623 "Baruna Jaya IV" (research ship)

1998. International Year of the Ocean.
2440 **623** 700r. multicoloured 15 15

624 Javan Kingfisher

1998. 5th Dutch Stamp Dealers' Association Stamp Exhibition, The Hague, Netherlands. Two sheets containing T 624 or similar multicoloured design.
MS2441 Two sheets. (a) 71×46 mm. 5000r. Type **624**; (b) 71×60 mm. 35000r. Javanese wattled lapwing (*Vannelus macropterus*) 9·50 9·50

625 1974 20r. U.P.U. Stamp

1998. World Stamp Day. Multicoloured.
2442 700r. Type **625** 15 15
2443 700r. 1955 15s. Post Office Anniversary stamp 15 15

626 Magpie Goose

1998. Waterfowl (1st series). Multicoloured.
2444 4000r. Type **626** 1·00 1·00
2445 5000r. Spotted whistling duck 1·20 1·20

2446 10000r. Salvadori's duck 2·40 2·40
2447 15000r. Radjah shelduck 3·50 3·50
2448 20000r. White-winged wood duck 5·00 5·00
MS2449 206×115 mm. Nos. 2444/8 13·00 13·00

See also Nos. 2468/**MS**2475 and 2628/9.

627 Djakarta Cathedral

1998. "Italia 98" International Stamp Exhibition, Milan.
MS2450 55×9 mm. **627** 5000r. multicoloured 1·20 1·20

628 State Flag and Jayawijaya Peak

1998. "The Red and White Flag". Multicoloured.
2451 700r. Type **628** 15 15
2452 700r. State flag and Himalayan peak 15 15

629 State Flag

1998. Political Reforms. Multicoloured.
2453 700r. Type **629** 15 15
2454 700r. Dove and State flag 15 15
2455 1000r. Students in front of Parliament building (82×25 mm) 25 25

630 "Stelechocarpus burahol"

1998. Flora and Fauna. Multicoloured.
2456 500r. Type **630** 15 15
2457 500r. Tuberose ("Polianthes tuberosa") 15 15
2458 500r. Four o'clock ("Mirabilis jalapa") 15 15
2459 500r. "Mangifera casturi" 15 15
2460 500r. "Ficus minahassae" 15 15
2461 500r. Zebra dove ("Geopelia striata") 15 15
2462 500r. Red and green junglefowl hybrid ("Gallus varius x G. gallus") 15 15
2463 500r. Indian elephant ("Elephas maximus") 15 15
2464 500r. Proboscis monkey ("Nasalis larvatus") 15 15
2465 500r. Eastern tarsier ("Tarsius spectrum") 15 15
MS2466 Two sheets. (a) 48×80 mm. 2500r. As No. 2457; (b) 48×92 mm. 2500r. As No. 2464 50 50

631 Monument at Blitar and Museum, Bogor

1998. 55th Anniv of Formation of Volunteer National Armed Forces (independence fighters).
2467 **631** 700r.+100r. mult 15 15

632 Australian White-eyed Duck

1998. Waterfowl (2nd series). Multicoloured.
2468 250r. Type **632** 10 10
2469 500r. Pacific black duck 10 10
2470 700r. Grey teal 15 15
2471 1000r. Cotton goose 25 25
2472 1500r. Green pygmy goose 35 35
2473 2500r. Indian whistling duck 50 50
2474 3500r. Wandering whistling duck 75 75
MS2475 45×83 mm. 5000r. Type **632** 1·00 1·00

1998. Traditional Dances (7th series). As T 506. Multicoloured.
2476 300r. Oreng oreng gae dance, Sulawesi Tenggara (South-east Celebes) 10 10
2477 500r. Persembahan dance, Bengkulu 10 10
2478 700r. Kipas (fan) dance, Riau 15 15
2479 1000r. Srimpi dance, Yogyakarta 25 25
2480 2000r. Pasambahan, Sumatera Barat (West) 40 40
MS2481 48×80 mm. 5000r. As No. 2480 1·00 1·00

633 Water Wheel and Power Lines

1999. Year of Creation and Engineering. Multicoloured.
2482 500r. Type **633** 10 10
2483 700r. Water pipe and pipe network in valley 15 15

634 Throwing the Shot

1999. 7th Far East and South Pacific Games for Disabled Persons, Bangkok. Multicoloured.
2484 500r. Type **634** 10 10
2485 500r. Medal and wheelchair 10 10

635 Emblem

1999. 50th Anniv of Garuda Indonesia (state airline). Multicoloured.
2486 500r. Type **635** 10 10
2487 700r. Jet engine 15 15
2488 2000r. Pilot, stewardess and airplane 40 40

1999. Folk Tales (2nd series). As T 611. Multicoloured. (a) "Lake Toba".
2489 500r. Man and yellow fish 15 15
2490 500r. Man proposing to woman 15 15
2491 500r. Woman giving food for father to son Sam and Sam eating it 15 15
2492 500r. Wife turning back into a fish 15 15
2493 500r. Samosir Island and Lake Toba 15 15

(b) "Banjarmasin".
2494 500r. Rebels and contenders to throne 15 15
2495 500r. Local governors crown Prince Samudera 15 15
2496 500r. Tumenggung sends fleet to Samudera's capital, Bandar Masih 15 15
2497 500r. Samudera and Tumenggung meet on board ship 15 15
2498 500r. Ships in Banjarmasin Harbour 15 15

(c) "Buleleng".
2499 500r. I Gusti Gede Paseken leaving with guards for Den Bukit 15 15
2500 500r. Forest giant appearing to I Gusti Gede Paseken 15 15
2501 500r. I Gusti Gede Paseken lifting stranded ship 15 15
2502 500r. I Gusti Gede Paseken arriving before King of Den Bukit 15 15
2503 500r. Procession in kingdom of Buleleng 15 15

(d) "Woiram".
2504 500r. Woiram teaching archery to Woiwallytmang and with wife Donadebu 15 15
2505 500r. Mesan and Mecy looking for shrimps 15 15
2506 500r. Woiram cursing Demontin village 15 15
2507 500r. Woiwallytmang and Mecy clinging to tree trunk 15 15
2508 500r. Woiram's footprints in rock 15 15
MS2509 75×66 mm. 5000r. As No. 2493 1·00 1·00

Nos. 2489/2508 were issued together, se-tenant, forming a composite design.

636 Malang Apple

1999. "Surabaya 99" National Stamp Exhibition. Sheet 78×58 mm.
MS2510 5000r. multicoloured 1·00 1·00

637 Eastern Tarsier

1999. "Australia 99" International Stamp Exhibition, Melbourne. Sheet 60×92 mm.
MS2511 5000r. multicoloured 1·00 1·00

638 "Ascosparassis heinricherii"

1999. Fungi. Multicoloured. (a) T 638 and similar diamond-shaped designs.
2512 500r. Type **638** 10 10
2513 500r. "Mutinus bambusinus" 10 10
2514 500r. "Mycena" sp. 10 10
2515 700r. "Gloephyllum imponens" 15 15
2516 700r. "Microporus xanthopus" 15 15
2517 700r. "Termitomyces eurrhizus" 15 15
2518 1000r. "Boedijnopeziza insititia" 25 25
2519 1000r. "Aseroe rubra" 25 25
2520 1000r. "Calostoma orirubra" 25 25

(b) As Nos. 2512/14 but rectangular designs, size 31×23 mm.
2521 500r. As No. 2513 15 15
2522 500r. As No. 2512 15 15
2523 500r. As No. 2514 15 15

(c) Sheet 62×92 mm.
MS2524 5000r. "Termitomyces eurrhizus" (different) (24½×41 mm) 1·00 1·00

639 Doctor and Patients outside Surgery

1999. Public Health Care Insurance.
2525 **639** 700r. multicoloured 15 15

640 "Dendrobium abang betawi"

1999. "iBRA 99" International Stamp Exhibition, Nuremberg, Germany. Sheet 63×98 mm.
MS2526 5000r. multicoloured 1·40 1·40

641 Y2K "Bug"

1999. Millennium Bug (computer programming fault). Multicoloured.
2527 500r. Type **641** 15 15
2528 500r. Robot exploding 15 15

Nos. 2527/8 were issued together, se-tenant, forming a composite design.

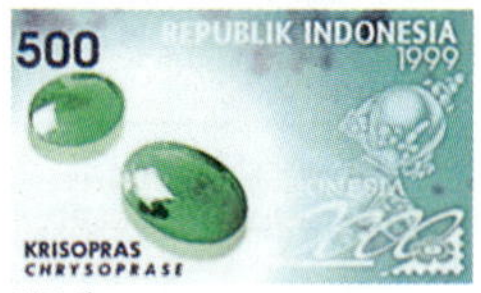

642 Chrysoprase

1999. "Indonesia 2000" International Stamp Exhibition, Bandung (3rd issue). Gemstones. Multicoloured.
2529 500r. Type **642** 15 15
2530 1000r. Smoky quartz 25 25
2531 2000r. Blue opal 55 55
MS2532 80×48 mm. 4000r. Silicified coral 1·00 1·00
MS2533 Two sheets. (a) 80×48 mm. 4000r. Javan jade; (b) 122×160 mm. Nos. 2529 ×4, 2530 ×2, 2531 ×2 plus stamps as in Nos. **MS**2532 and **MS**2533b 3·75 3·75

643 People carrying Banner

1999. General Election. Multicoloured.
2534 1000r. Type **643** 15 10
2535 1000r. Ballot box and map of Indonesia 15 10

Nos. 2534/5 were issued together, se-tenant, forming a composite design.

644 Girl in Blanket and People walking through Water

1999. Environmental Protection. Ecophila Stamp Day. Multicoloured.
2536 500r. Type **644** 15 15
2537 1000r. Boy swimming with duck, plant and berry 40 40

2538 2000r. Elderly woman drinking from jug 80 80

MS2539 79×46 mm. 3000r. As No. 2537 1·20 1·20

645 Prambanan Temple

1999. "Philexfrance 99" International Stamp Exhibition, Paris. Sheet 59×94 mm.
MS2540 5000r. multicoloured 2·00 2·00

646 Nurses helping Children

1999. Red Cross.
2541 **646** 1000r. multicoloured 35 35

647 Frans Kaisiepo (Governor of Irian Jaya, 1964)

1999. National Heroes and Heroines.
2542 **647** 500r. brown & cinnamon 15 15
2543 - 500r. brown & cinnamon 15 15
2544 - 500r. brown & cinnamon 15 15
2545 - 500r. brown & cinnamon 15 15

DESIGNS: No. 2543, Maria Walanda Maramis (founder of "PIKAT" (women's education organization, 1917)); 2544, Dr. W. Z. Johannes (founder of Indonesian Christian Party, 1942); 2545, Martha Christina Tijahahu (revolutionary).

648 Rabbit

1999. "CHINA 99" International Stamp Exhibition, Beijing. Sheet 81×60 mm.
MS2546 5000r. multicoloured 1·60 1·60

649 University Building, 1949

1999. 50th Anniv of Gadjah Mada University, Yogyakarta. Multicoloured.
2547 500r. Type **649** 15 15
2548 1000r. University facade, 1999 40 40

650 Woman painting Parasol

1999. International Year of the Elderly Person.
2549 **650** 500r. multicoloured 15 15

651 Batik Design, Cirebon

1999. Batik Designs. Different Batik designs. Mult.
2550 500r. Type **651** 15 15
2551 500r. Madura 15 15
2552 500r. Yogyakarta 15 15
2553 500r. Jambi 15 15

652 Pillar Box, Postman and Kantoon Post Office (1/2-size illustration)

1999. 125th Anniv of Universal Postal Union. Mult.
2554 500r. Type **652** 15 15
2555 500r. Modern postal building, motorcycle postman and pillar box 15 15
2556 1000r. Pillar box, left-hand side of Kantoon Post Office and postman on horseback (30×31 mm) 80 80
2557 1000r. Motorcycle postman, modern postal building and pillar box (30×31 mm) 80 80

653 Dog and Puppy

1999. Domestic Animals. Multicoloured.
2558 500r. Type **653** 15 15
2559 500r. Cockerel, hen and chick 15 15
2560 500r. Cat 15 15
2561 500r. Rabbits 15 15
2562 1000r. Feral rock pigeon (20×50 mm) 40 40
2563 1000r. Geese and gosling (20×50 mm) 40 40
MS2564 79×47 mm. 4000r. As No. 2561 1·50 1·50

Nos. 2558/9, 2560/1 and 2562/3 respectively were issued together, se-tenant, showing the composite design of a garden.

654 Globe, Diary and Clock Face

1999. New Millennium. Multicoloured.
2565 1000r. Type **654** 40 40
2566 1000r. "2000" and child's face 40 40
MS2567 Two sheets, each 86×57 mm. (a) 20000r. As Type **654**; (b) 20000r. As No. 2566 7·75 7·75

655 Satellite and Fishes

2000. Year of Technology. Multicoloured.
2568 500r. Type **655** 15 15
2569 1000r. Greenhouse and plant 40 40

656 University Campus, Salemba

2000. 50th Anniv of University of Indonesia. Multicoloured.
2570 500r. Type **656** 15 15
2571 1000r. University building, Depok 40 40

2000. Folk Tales (3rd series). As T 611. Multicoloured. (a) "Tapak Tuan".
2572 500r. Dragon finding baby on shore 25 25
2573 500r. Girl meeting other people 25 25
2574 500r. Dragon attacking boat and man 25 25
2575 500r. Man and dragon fighting 25 25
2576 500r. Dead dragon 25 25

(b) "Batu Ballah".
2577 500r. Mak Risah and children 25 25
2578 500r. Children playing 25 25
2579 500r. Mak Risah saddened by her children 25 25
2580 500r. Mak Risah being swallowed by stone 25 25
2581 500r. Mak Risah Rock 25 25

(c) "Sawerigading".
2582 500r. Sariwegading proposing marriage to twin sister 25 25
2583 500r. We Tanriabeng refusing marriage 25 25
2584 500r. Sariwegdaing in stern of boat 25 25
2585 500r. Bow of boat and wedding 25 25
2586 500r. Bulupoloe Mountain 25 25

(d) "7 Putri Kahyangan".
2587 500r. Prince hiding wings and angel weeping 25 25
2588 500r. Prince and angel with their children and angel flying away from Earth 25 25
2589 500r. Prince flying on eagle's back to reclaim wife 25 25
2590 500r. Angel refusing to return to Earth 25 25
2591 500r. Prince wearing magical crown 25 25
MS2592 84×61 mm. 5000r. As No. 2576 2·00 2·00

Nos. 2572/91 were issued together, se-tenant, forming a composite design.

657 Prehnite

2000. "Indonesia 2000" International Stamp Exhibition, Bandung (4th issue). Gemstones. Multicoloured.
2593 500r. Type **657** 25 25
2594 1000r. Chalcedony 40 40
2595 2000r. Volcanic obsidian 75 75
MS2596 80×48 mm. 5000r. Jasperized limestone 2·00 2·00
MS2597 Two sheets. (a) 80×48 mm. 5000r. Copper jasper; (b) 121×156 mm. No. 2593 ×4, 2594 ×2, 2595 ×2 plus stamps as in **MS**2596 and **MS**2597a 3·75 3·75

658 I Brewok (Gun-Gun)

2000. Cartoon Characters. Each black and red.
2598 500r. Type **658** 25 25
2599 500r. "Pak Tuntung" (Basuki) 25 25
2600 500r. "Pak Bei" (Masdi Sunardi) 25 25
2601 500r. "Mang Ohle" (Didin D. Basuni) 25 25
2602 500r. "Panji Koming" (Dwi Koendoro) 25 25

659 Emblem and Weather Chart

2000. 50th Anniv of World Meteorological Organization.
2603 **659** 500r. multicoloured 25 25

660 King Dragon

2000. World Youth Stamp Exhibition and 13th Asian Stamp Exhibition, Bangkok. Sheet 79×49 mm.
MS2604 5000r. multicoloured 1·60 1·60

661 Cycling

2000. 15th National Sports Week. Multicoloured.
2605 500r. Type **661** 50 25
2606 1000r. Canoeing 1·10 40
2607 2000r. High-jumping 2·10 55

662 Coelacanth

2000. "Stamp Show 2000" International Stamp Exhibition, London. Sheet 78×54 mm.
MS2608 5000r. multicoloured 1·60 1·60

663 Red-footed Booby's on Nest

2000. Environmental Protection. Ecophila Stamp Day. Multicoloured.
2609 500r. Type **663** 50 25
2610 1000r. Monkey 1·10 40
2611 2000r. Fishes 2·10 55
MS2612 68×52 mm. 4000r. As No. 2610 1·50 1·50

664 Boxing

2000. Olympic Games, Sydney. Multicoloured.
2613 500r. Type **664** 15 15
2614 500r. Judo 15 15
2615 1000r. Badminton 35 35
2616 1000r. Weightlifting 35 35
2617 2000r. Swimming 65 65
2618 2000r. Running 65 65
MS2619 84×51 mm. 5000r. As No. 2616 1·60 1·60

665 Komodo Dragon

2000. Endangered Species. The Komodo Dragon (Varanus komodoensis). Multicoloured.
2620 500r. Type **665** 40 40
2621 500r. Two dragons fighting 40 40
2622 500r. On branch 40 40
2623 500r. Two dragons walking 40 40
MS2624 101×56 mm. 2500r. As Type **665**; 2500r. As No. 2621 2·75 2·75

666 President Abdurrahman Wahid

2000. President and Vice-President. Multicoloured.

2625	1000r. Type **666**	40	40
2626	1000r. Vice-President Megawati Soekarnoputri	40	40

667 Rhythmic Gymnastics

2000. "Olymphilex 2000" Stamp Exhibition, Sydney. Sheet 52×79 mm.

MS2627	**667** 5000r. multicoloured	2·50	2·50

2000. Waterfowl (3rd series). As T 632. Multicoloured.

2628	800r. Indian whistling duck (*Dendrocygna javanica*)	80	80
2629	900r. Australian white-eyed duck (*Aythya australis*)	1·00	1·00

668 Couple from D. I. Aceh

2000. Regional Costumes. Showing couples wearing traditional costumes from different regions. Multicoloured.

2630	900r. Type **668**	35	35
2631	900r. Jambi	35	35
2632	900r. Banten	35	35
2633	900r. D. I. Yogyakarta	35	35
2634	900r. Kalimantan Tengah	35	35
2635	900r. Sulawesi Tenggara	35	35
2636	900r. Nusa Tenggara Timur	35	35
2637	900r. Sumatera Utara	35	35
2638	900r. Bengkulu	35	35
2639	900r. D. K. I. Jakarta	35	35
2640	900r. Jawa Timur	35	35
2641	900r. Kalimantan Timur	35	35
2642	900r. Sulawesi Selatan	35	35
2643	900r. Maluku	35	35
2644	900r. Sumatera Barat	35	35
2645	900r. Sumatera Selatan	35	35
2646	900r. Jawa Barat	35	35
2647	900r. Kalimantan Barat	35	35
2648	900r. Sulawesi Utara	35	35
2649	900r. Bali	35	35
2650	900r. Maluku Utara	35	35
2651	900r. Riau	35	35
2652	900r. Lampung	35	35
2653	900r. Jawa Tengah	35	35
2654	900r. Kalimantan Selatan	35	35
2655	900r. Sulawesi Tengah	35	35
2656	900r. Nusa Tenggara Barat	35	35
2657	900r. Irian Jaya	35	35

669 Chairil Anwar (poet)

2000. Personalities. Multicoloured.

2658	900r. Type **669**	35	35
2659	900r. Ibu Sud (children's song writer)	35	35
2660	900r. Bing Slamet (entertainer)	35	35
2661	900r. S. Sudjojono (artist)	35	35
2662	900r. I. Ketut Maria (actor)	35	35
MS2663	62×2 mm. 4000r. Chairil Anwar (different) (vert)	1·50	1·50

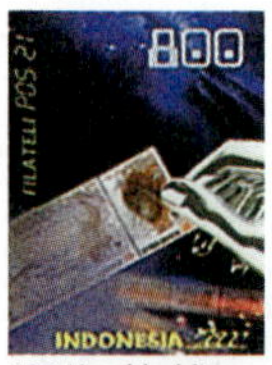

670 Hand holding 1989 500r. Endangered Species Stamp

2000. Communications. Multicoloured.

2664	800r. Type **670**	25	25
2665	900r. Satellite, map, television and letter (horiz)	35	35
2666	1000r. Globe and computer monitor	40	40
2667	4000r. Airplane, globe and computer	1·50	1·50

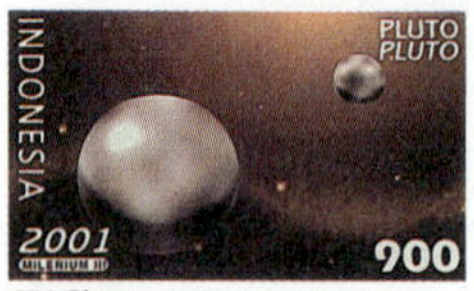

671 Pluto

2001. The Solar System. Multicoloured.

2668	900r. Type **671**	25	25
2669	900r. Neptune	25	25
2670	900r. Uranus	25	25
2671	900r. Saturn	25	25
2672	900r. Jupiter	25	25
2673	900r. Mars	25	25
2674	900r. Earth	25	25
2675	900r. Venus	25	25
2676	900r. Mercury	25	25
2677	900r. Sun	25	25
MS2678	120×71 mm. 5000r. Sun (different)	1·40	1·40

2001. Folk Tales (4th series). As T 611. Multicoloured. (a) "Batang Tuaka".

2679	900r. Two snakes fighting and Tuaka with stone	25	25
2680	900r. Tuaka selling stone to merchant in Tumasik Port	25	25
2681	900r. Tuaka as a successful merchant with his wife	25	25
2682	900r. Mother cursing Tuaka and his wife	25	25
2683	900r. Tuaka and his wife become birds	25	25

(b) "Si Pitung".

2684	900r. Si Pitung and gang stealing money from Dutch sympathizers	25	25
2685	900r. Si Pitung's gang leaving money for villagers	25	25
2686	900r. Dutch ruler fighting Si Pitung	25	25
2687	900r. Villagers mourning dead Si Pitung	25	25
2688	900r. Si Pitung Mosque	25	25

(c) "Terusan Nusa".

2689	900r. Tambing finding and eating dragon's egg	25	25
2690	900r. Tambing turning into dragon	25	25
2691	900r. Dragon (Tambing) eating all the fish in the river	25	25
2692	900r. Tambing dying after eating his own tail	25	25
2693	900r. Empty river	25	25

(d) "Ile Mauraja".

2694	900r. Raja dreaming	25	25
2695	900r. Raja receiving cotton seeds from bearded man	25	25
2696	900r. Raja and wife	25	25
2697	900r. Snake on bed, burning village and snakes causing upheaval of village	25	25
2698	900r. Mountain formed by village	25	25
MS2699	84×61 mm. 5000r. No. 2686	1·40	1·40

Nos. 2679/98 were issued together, se-tenant, forming a composite design.

672 Arsa Wijaya, Bali

2001. Traditional Masks. Showing left (a) or right (b) sides of masks. Multicoloured.

2700	500r. Type **672**	15	15
2701	500r. Arsa Wijaya (b)	15	15
2702	800r. Asmat, Irian Jaya (a)	25	25
2703	800r. Asmat (b)	25	25
2704	800r. Cirebon, Jawa Barat (a)	25	25
2705	800r. Cirebon (b)	25	25
2706	900r. Hudoq, Kalimantan Timur (a)	35	35
2707	900r. Hudoq (b)	35	35
2708	900r. Wayang Wong, Yogyakarta (a)	35	35
2709	900r. Wayang Wong (b)	35	35
MS2710	61× 96 mm. 5000r. No. 2706	1·60	1·60

Nos. 2700/1, 2702/3, 2704/5, 2706/7 and 2708/9 were issued together, se-tenant, each pair forming a composite design.

673 Beduk

2001. Traditional Instruments. Multicoloured.

2711	900r. Type **673**	15	15
2712	900r. Bende (bronze drum)	15	15
2713	900r. Kentongan (percussion)	15	15
2714	900r. Nafiri (horn)	15	15

674 Bouquet

2001. Greetings Stamps. Multicoloured.

2715	800r. Type **674**	15	15
2716	900r. Rose	25	25
2717	1000r. Bouquet of orange roses and leaves	35	35
2718	1500r. Large white flower and dark green leaf	40	40
2719	2000r. Bouquet of yellow flowers with pink bow	55	55
2720	4000r. Amaryllis flower and ribbon	1·20	1·20
2721	5000r. Table decoration and candles	1·50	1·50
2722	10000r. White flower with yellow centre	3·00	3·00

675 Children and Fish (Surayadi)

2001. World Environment Day. Winning entries in Stamp Design Competition (Nos. 2723, 2725). Multicoloured.

2723	800r. Type **675**	25	25
2724	900r. Boys feeding deer	25	25
2725	1000r. Boy swimming with turtle (Lambok Hutabarat)	35	35
MS2726	82×50 mm. 3000r. As No. 2724	90	90

676 Youthful Sukarno wearing Turban

2001. Birth Centenary of Dr. Ahmed Sukarno (Bung Karno) (nationalist leader and first president). Multicoloured.

2727	500r. Type **676**	15	15
2728	800r. As young man wearing collar and tie	25	25
2729	900r. Wearing high-necked jacket	25	25
2730	1000r. Wearing uniform with lapel badges	35	35
MS2731	138×59 mm. 5000r. Giving speech	1·50	1·50

677 Policeman guiding Children across the Road

2001. Indonesian Police Force. Multicoloured.

2732	1000r. Type **677**	35	35
2733	1000r. Helicopter and women police officers giving directions	35	35

678 Scouts raising Flag

2001. National Scout Jamboree, Banyumas, Java. Multicoloured.

2734	1000r. Type **678**	35	35
2735	1000r. Erecting tent	35	35

Nos. 2734/5 were issued together, se-tenant, forming a composite design.

679 Kaki Siapa (blind man's buff)

2001. National Children's Day. Children's Games. Multicoloured.

2736	800r. Type **679**	15	15
2738	900r. Erang Bambu (stilt walking)	25	25
2739	1000r. Dakon (counting game)	25	25
2740	2000r. Kuda Pelepah Pisang (hobby horses)	40	40

680 Sunflower

2001. Philanippon '01 International Stamp Exhibition. Sheet 93×46 mm.

MS2741	**680** 10000r. multicoloured	3·25	3·25

681 Dr. R. Soeharso (founder) and Operating Theatre

2001. 50th Anniv of Dr. R. Soeharso Orthopaedic Hospital.

2742	**681** 1000r. multicoloured	15	15

682 Makasaar Post Office

2001. Post Office Architecture. Showing Post Office building. Multicoloured.

2743	800r. Type **682**	10	10
2744	900r. Bandung	15	15
2745	1000r. Balikpapan	15	15
2746	2000r. Padang	25	25

683 Perahu (boat)

2001. Traditional Transport. Multicoloured.

2747	1000r. Type **683**	15	15
2748	1000r. Becak Dayung (tricycle rickshaw)	15	15
2749	1000r. Andong (horse-drawn taxi)	15	15

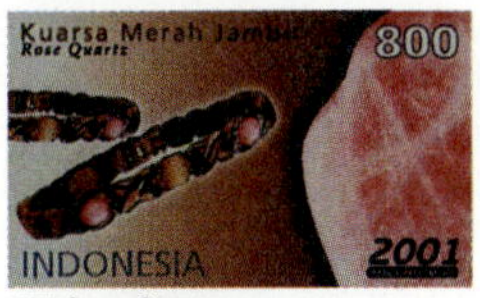

684 Rose Quartz

2001. Gemstones. Multicoloured.

2750	800r. Type **684**	10	10
2751	900r. Brecciated Jasper	15	15
2752	1000r. Malachite	15	15
MS2753	80×47 mm. 5000r. Diamond	1·60	1·60

685 Children encircling Globe

2001. United Nations Year of Dialogue among Civilizations.

2754	**685** 1000r. multicoloured	15	15

686 *Agestrata dehaan*

2001. Insects. Multicoloured.

2755	800r. Type **686**	10	10
2756	900r. *Mormolyce phyllodes*	15	15
2757	1000r. *Batocera rosenbergi*	15	15
2758	1000r. *Chrysochroa buqueti*	15	15
2759	2000r. *Chalcosoma Caucasus*	15	15
MS2760	61×90 mm. 5000r. No. 2759	2·10	2·10

2002. Folk Tales (5th series). As T 611. Multicoloured. (a) Pulau Kembaro, Sumatera Selatan.

2761	1000r. Two women	15	15
2762	1000r. Man and woman	15	15
2763	1000r. Boat sinking	15	15
2764	1000r. Man and woman standing in boat	15	15
2765	1000r. Serpent, boat and bridge	15	15

(b) Nyi Roro Kidul, Jogjakarta.

2766	1000r. Prabu Siliwangi, Dewi Kaita and harem	15	15
2767	1000r. Dewi Kaita and mother changing	15	15
2768	1000r. Cast out of palace	15	15
2769	1000r. Dewi Kaita changing to Nyi Roro Kidul	15	15
2770	1000r. Sea	15	15

(c) Aji Tatin, Kalimantan Timur.

2771	1000r. Palm tree, woman and man with arm outstretched	15	15
2772	1000r. Woman, bird and boat	15	15
2773	1000r. Woman with hand to head	15	15
2774	1000r. Boat breaking	15	15
2775	1000r. Sun and bird	15	15

(d) Danau Tondano, Sulawesi Utara.

2776	1000r. Woman seated	15	15
2777	1000r. Man holding spear	15	15
2778	1000r. Man and woman dressed as man	15	15
2779	1000r. Three men under trees	15	15
2780	1000r. Tree and island	15	15
MS2781	108×61 mm. 5000r. No. 2765	75	75

Nos. 2761/5, 2766/70, 2771/5, 2776/80 respectively were issued together, se-tenant, forming a composite design.

687 Player with Shirt over Head

2002. World Cup Football Championships, Japan and South Korea. Multicoloured.

2782	1000r. Type **687**	15	15
2783	1500r. Players in front of goal	20	20
2784	2000r. Player	25	25
MS2785	52×80 mm. 5000r. No. 2784	75	75

688 Outline of Two Women

2002. 25th Anniv of Cancer Foundation.

2786	**688** 1000r. multicoloured	15	15

689 Aboriginal Man holding Cell Phone

2002. Communications. Multicoloured.

2787	1000r. Type **689**	15	15
2788	1000r. Woman holding hand set	15	15
2789	1000r. Computer, satellite and disc	15	15
2790	1000r. Satellite above globe	15	15

690 *Symphyllia radians*

2002. Marine Life. Ecophila. Multicoloured.

2791	1000r. Type **690**	15	15
2792	1000r. *Charonia tritonis*	15	15
2793	1500r. *Acanthaster planci*	20	20
2794	1500r. Polka dot grouper (*Cromileptes altivelis*)	20	20
2795	2000r. Blue tang (*Paracanthurus hepatus*)	25	25
2796	2000r. *Tridacna gigas*	25	25
MS2797	(a) 97×170 mm. Nos. 2791/5; (b) 60×91 mm. 5000r. No. 2793	1·70	1·70

691 Boy writing and Men dancing

2002. Nanggroe Aceh Province, Darussalam. Multicoloured.

2798	1500r. Type **691**	20	20
2799	3500r. Mosque	45	45

692 Family

2002. National Family Day.

2800	**692** 1000r. multicoloured	15	15

693 Solar Eclipse and Olympiad Emblem

2002. 33rd International Physics Olympiad, Bali. Multicoloured.

2801	1000r. Type **693**	15	15
2802	1000r. Colour spectrum and symbols	15	15

694 Bird-shaped Kite

2002. Layang-Layang. Kite Flying. Multicoloured.

2803	1000r. Type **694**	15	15
2804	1000r. Lion	15	15
2805	1000r. Rhomboid	15	15
2806	1000r. Winged kite	15	15
2807	1000r. Box and glider kites	15	15
MS2808	79×49 mm. 5000r. No. 2803	75	75

Nos. 2803/7 were issued together, se-tenant, forming a composite design.

695 Noni (*Morinda citrifolia*)

2002. Fruit. Multicoloured.

2809	300r. Type **695**	10	10
2810	500r. Mango (*Mangifera indica*)	10	10
2811	1500r. Star fruit (*Averrhoa carambola*)	20	20
2812	3000r. *Durio zibethinus*	40	40

696 Tari Pajaga Dancer, Salawesi Selatan

2002. Philakorea 2002 International Stamp Exhibition, Seoul. Sheet 48×80 mm.

MS2813	**696** 7000r. multicoloured	95	95

697 Mohammad Hatta

2002. Birth Centenary of Mohammad Hatta (first vice-president). Multicoloured.

2814	1000r. Type **697**	20	20
2815	1000r. Wearing high-necked jacket	20	20
2816	1500r. Wearing light jacket and dark tie	20	20
2817	1500r. Wearing light jacket and tie	20	20
MS2818	137×60 mm. 5000r. Wearing light suit and open neck shirt	75	75

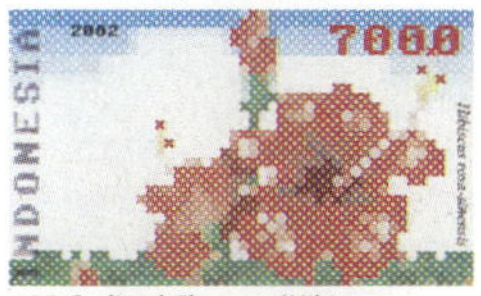

699 Stylised Flowers (*Hibiscus rosa-sinensis*)

2002. Amphilex 2002 International Stamp Exhibition, Amsterdam. Sheet 92×47 mm.

MS2821	7000r. multicoloured	80	80

700 Soldier

2002. Jogja Panfila 2002 International Stamp Exhibition, Jakarta. Sheet 51×85 mm.

MS2822	6000r. multicoloured	80	80

701 "Cat" (Popo Iskander)

2002. Art. Multicoloured.

2823	1000r. (1) Type **701**	10	10
2824	1000r. (2) "Guerrilla Sentry, Seko" (S. Sudjojono)	10	10
2825	1500r. (3) "Women and child" (Hendra Gunawan) (vert)	15	15
2826	1500r. (4) "Gaututkaca, Prigiwa and Prigiwati" (R. Basoeki Abdullah) (vert)	15	15

702 Hagen's Lanzenotter (*Trimeresurus hageni*)

2002. Flora and Fauna. Multicoloured.

2827	1000r. Type **702**	10	10
2828	1000r. *Rafflesia micropylora*	10	10
2829	1500r. Leopard (*Panthera pardus*)	15	15
2830	1500r. *Terminalia catappa*	15	15
2831	2000r. *Papilionanthe hookeriana*	20	20
2832	2000r. Water monitor (*Varanus salvator*)	20	20
MS2833	50×83 mm. 3500r. No. 2829 Perf and Imperf	40	40

Nos. 2827/8, 2829/30 and 2831/2 respectively were issued, together, se-tenant, forming a composite design.

703 Bull

2002. Espana 2002 International Stamp Exhibition, Salamanca. Sheet 83×50 mm.

MS2834	7000r. multicoloured	80	80

704 Buildings, Data Stream and Globe

2002. "LKBN Antara" National News Agency.
2835 **704** 1500r. multicoloured 15 15

705 Party Food

2003. Greeting Stamps. "Happy Birthday".
2836 1500r. Type **705** 15 15
2837 1500r. Birthday cake 15 15

2003. Folk Tales (6th series). As T 611. Multicoloured. (a) "Danau Ranau".
2838 1500r. Man holding golden egg and couple near cooking fire 15 15
2839 1500r. Men, dragon and weeping woman 15 15
2840 1500r. Woman riding dragon 15 15
2841 1500r. Sleeping woman and dragon holding necklace 15 15
2842 1500r. Lake 15 15

Nos. 2838/57 were issued together, se-tenant, forming a composite design.

(b) "Kongga Owose".
2843 1500r. Eagle carrying off cow 15 15
2844 1500r. Eagle attacking villagers 15 15
2845 1500r. Man spearing eagle 15 15
2846 1500r. Eagle, injured man, and villagers 15 15
2847 1500r. Hills, estuary and rocky coastline 15 15

(c) "Putri Gading Cempaku".
2848 1500r. Woman and man wearing tall headdress 15 15
2849 1500r. Man looking back at woman 15 15
2850 1500r. Men with raised arms and distressed woman 15 15
2851 1500r. Man, couple under thatched roof and woman wearing jewelled headdress 15 15
2852 1500r. Birds and sandy coastline 15 15

(d) "Putri Mandalika Nyale".
2853 1500r. King and Princess 15 15
2854 1500r. Princess and suitors bearing gifts 15 15
2855 1500r. Princess and suitors on beach 15 15
2856 1500r. Princess in sea 15 15
2857 1500r. Fishing 15 15
MS2858 106×62 mm. 5000r. No. 2842 55 55

706 Billiard Player

2003. 22nd South East Asian Games, Vietnam. Multicoloured.
2859 1000r. Type **706** 10 10
2860 1500r. Rowers 15 15
2861 2500r. Gymnast 30 30

707 Mount Kerinci

2003. Volcanoes. 50th Anniv of Ascent of Mount Everest (MS2867). Volcanoes. Multicoloured.
2862 500r. Type **708** 10 10
2863 1000r. Merapi 10 10
2864 1000r. Krakatau 10 10
2865 1000r. Tambora 10 10
2866 2000r. Ruang 20 20
MS2867 181×116 mm. Nos. 2862/6, each×2 plus 2 labels 1·20 1·20

708 Moon

2003. Astronomy. Multicoloured.
2868 1000r. Type **708** 10 10
2869 1000r. Earth and Mars 10 10
2870 1000r. Andromeda galaxy 10 10
2871 1500r. Observatory and telescope 15 15
2872 1500r. Observatory, Lembang, Java 15 15
MS2873 116×67 mm. No. 2872 15 15

709 Buildings and Flowers contained in Stylized Banknote (image scaled to 61% of original size)

2003. 50th Anniv of Bank Indonesia. Multicoloured.
2874 1000r. Type **709** 10 10
2875 1500r. Teacher, pens and open books 15 15

710 Sultan Hamengu Buwono IX and Robert Baden-Powell (image scaled to 59% of original size)

2003. Pathfinder Scouts.
2876 **710** 1500r. multicoloured 15 15

711 Pillow Fighting on Pole over Water

2003. Traditional Games. Multicoloured.
2877 1000r. Type **711** 10 10
2878 1000r. Pole climbing 10 10
2879 1500r. Sack racing (horiz) 15 15
2880 1500r. Teams of three racing on planks (horiz) 15 15

712 Dancers

2003. Emmitan Philex 2003 Stamp Exhibition. Seven sheets containing T 712 and similar vert design showing paintings by Srihadi Soedarsono. Multicoloured.
MS2881 107×142 mm. 3000r.×4, Type **712**; Moonlit landscape, each×2 (10th Asean Postal Business Meeting, Surabaya) 70 70
MS2882 Six sheets, each 107×82 mm. Five sheets (a/e) 3000r.×2, Type **712**; Moonlit landscape (each with different margin colours). (f) 107×82 mm Type **712**; Moonlit landscape. Imperf. Set of 6 sheets 1·00 1·00

713 Woman leading Procession (Mome'Ati, Gorontalo)

2003. Tourism. Multicoloured.
2883 1000r. Type **713** 10 10
2884 1000r. Man carried in sedan chair (Jou Uci Sabea, Maluku Utara) 10 10
2885 1500r. Boats (Muang Jong, Bangka Belitung) 15 15
2886 1500r. Seated men (Seba Baduy, Banten) 15 15
MS2887 113×74 mm. No. 2885 15 15

714 Elephant Football, Lampung

2003. Bangkok 2003 International Stamp Exhibition. Sheet 88×25 mm.
MS2888 8000r. multicoloured 90 90

715 Clasped Hands

2003. Greetings Stamps. Multicoloured.
2889 1000r. Type **715** 10 10
2890 1500r. Flag and clasped hands 15 15
2891 1500r. Fish and water lily 15 15
2892 1500r. Sunflower 15 15
2893 1500r. Birds 15 15

716 Anniversary Emblem and Stamps

2003. 75th Anniv of Youth Pledge.
2894 **716** 1500r. multicoloured 15 15

717 *Apis dorsata* (bee)

2003. Flora and Fauna. Multicoloured.
2895 1500r. Type **717** 15 15
2896 1500r. *Freycinetia pseudoinsignis* (flower) 15 15
2897 1500r. *Sia ferox* (grasshopper) 15 15
2898 1500r. *Paphiopedilum mastersianum* (orchid) 15 15
2899 1500r. *Platylomia flavida* (insect) 15 15
2900 1500r. *Osmoxylon palmatum* (plant) 15 15
2901 1500r. *Anaphalis javanica* (flower) 15 15
2902 1500r. *Hierodula vitrea* (mantis) 15 15
2903 1500r. *Saraca declinata* (plant) 15 15
2904 1500r. *Aularches miliaris* (insect) 15 15
2905 1500r. *Butea monosperma* (flower) 15 15
2906 1500r. *Orthetrum testaceum*(dragonfly) 15 15
MS2907 119×74 mm. 3000r.×2, Nos. 2901 and 2906 70 70

718 H. Sutami

2003. Personalities. Each sepia and brown.
2908 2000r. Type **718** (engineer) 20 20
2909 2000r. R. Roosseno (engineer) 20 20
2910 2000r. Martinus Putuhena (architect) 20 20
2911 2000r. Nurtanio Pringgoadisuryo (aviation engineer) 20 20

719 *Styrax benzoin*

2004. Flowers. Multicoloured.
2912 1500r. Type **719** 15 15
2913 1500r. *Kopsia fruticosa* 15 15
2914 1500r. *Impatiens tujuhensis* 15 15
2915 1500r. *Hoya diversifolia* 15 15
2916 1500r. *Etlingera elatior* 15 15
2917 1500r. *Dillenia suffruticosa* 15 15
2918 1500r. *Papilionanthe hookerianum* 15 15
2919 1500r. *Medinilla speciosa* 15 15
2920 1500r. *Costus speciosus* 15 15
2921 1500r. *Melastoma sylvaticum* 15 15
2922 1500r. *Nelumbo nucifera* 15 15
2923 1500r. *Begonia robusta* 15 15
2924 1500r. *Anaphalis longifolia* 15 15
2925 1500r. *Pisonia grandis* 15 15
2926 1500r. *Ixora javanica* 15 15
2927 1500r. *Plumeria acuminate* 15 15
2928 1500r. *Cassia fistula* 15 15
2929 1500r. *Calotropis gigantean* 15 15
2930 1500r. *Dimorphorchis lowii* 15 15
2931 1500r. *Aeschynanthus radicans* 15 15
2932 1500r. *Sonneratia caseolaris* 15 15
2933 1500r. *Rhododendron orbiculatum* 15 15
2934 1500r. *Passiflora edulis* 15 15
2935 1500r. *Pterospermum celebricum* 15 15
2936 1500r. *Quisqualis indica* 15 15
2937 1500r. *Spathiphyllum commutatum* 15 15
2938 1500r. *Lilium longifolium* 15 15
2939 1500r. *Clitoria ternatea* 15 15
2940 1500r. *Pecteilis susannae* 15 15
2941 1500r. *Grammatophyllum speciosum* 15 15

2004. Folk Tales (7th series). As T 611. Multicoloured. (a) "Putri Selaras Pinang Masak".
2942 1500r. Princess 15 15
2943 1500r. Man striking rocks 15 15
2944 1500r. Couple 15 15
2945 1500r. Crowned couple surrounded by cheering crowd 15 15
2946 1500r. Temple 15 15

Nos. 2942/61 were issued together, se-tenant, forming a composite design.

(b) "Tanjung Lesung".
2947 1500r. Woman and sleeping man 15 15
2948 1500r. Man, horse and dog walking and bathing 15 15
2949 1500r. House, knife, man and turtles 15 15
2950 1500r. Couple and men turning into monkeys 15 15
2951 1500r. Monkey in tree 15 15

2004. (c) "Patung Palindo".
2952 1500r. Warrior leading soldiers 15 15
2953 1500r. Battle scene 15 15
2954 1500r. Woman and child, bier, statue and warrior 15 15
2955 1500r. Men toppling statue, fire and battle scene 15 15
2956 1500r. Tilted statue 15 15

(d) "Danae Tolire".
2957 1500r. People carrying plants and seated woman 15 15
2958 1500r. Revelry and drunkenness 15 15
2959 1500r. Woman carrying child running from tidal wave 15 15
2960 1500r. Falling woman 15 15
2961 1500r. Lake and mountain 15 15
MS2962 106× 62 mm. 6000r. No. 2950 70 70

720 Sail Ship (Maritime Museum, Jakarta)

2004. Museums. Multicoloured.
2963 1500r. Type **720** 15 15
2964 1500r. Dinosaur skeleton (National Geological, Bangdung) 15 15
2965 1500r. Metal artefact (Sri Baduga, Bangdung) 15 15

2966 1500r. Early telephone (Telecommunications, Jakarta) 15 15

721 Voters

2004. Elections. Multicoloured.

2967 1500r. Type **721** 15 15
2968 1500r. Voters placing ballots in ballot box 15 15

722 Gedong Bagoes Oka

2004. Famous Women. Multicoloured.

2969 2500r. Type **722** (teacher and religious reformer) 30 30
2970 2500r. Ani Idrus (writer and journalist) 30 30
2971 2500r. Nyonya Meneer (herbal medicine pioneer) 30 30
2972 2500r. Sandiah (Ibu Kasur) (children's campaigner) 30 30

723 Swimming

2004. Olympic Games, Athens 2004. Multicoloured.

2973 2500r. Type **723** 30 30
2974 2500r. High Jump 30 30
2975 2500r. Hurdling 30 30

724 Bird, Porpoise and Boat

2004. Marine Preservation. Multicoloured.

2976 1500r. Type **724** 15 15
2977 1500r. Shark and turtles 15 15
MS2978 103×74 mm. 2500r.×2, Nos. 2976/7 60 60

725 Sambal Udang Terung Pipit Kalimantan Barat

2004. Traditional Food. Multicoloured.

2979 1500r. Type **725** 15 15
2980 1500r. Tinotuan Sulawesi Utara 15 15
2981 1500r. Cajebo Sumatera Barat 15 15
2982 1500r. Kare Rajungan Jawa Timur 15 15

726 Kendaraan Presiden R1 Pertama

2004. Presidential Cars. Multicoloured.

2983 2500r. Type **726** 30 30
2984 2500r. Kendaraan Wakil Presiden R1 Pertama 30 30
MS2985 105×78 mm. Nos. 2983/4 60 60

727 Three Players

2004. Sumsel 2004, Sepaktakraw (ball) Games, Palembang. Multicoloured.

2986 1500r. Type **727** 15 15
2987 1500r. Two players 15 15

728 *Parkia roxburghii*

2004. Flora and Fauna. Multicoloured.

2988 1500r. Type **728** 20 20
2989 1500r. *Heterometrus cynaneus* 20 20
2990 1500r. *Cinnmomun sintoc* (inscr "sintok") 20 20
2991 1500r. *Scolopendra subspinipes* 20 20
2992 1500r. *Alstonia scholaris* 20 20
2993 1550r. *Gryllotalpa hirsute* 20 20
MS2994 120×75 mm. 3000r.×2, Nos. 2988/9 80 80

729 Teacher and Pupils

2004. National Teachers' Day. Multicoloured.

2995 1500r. Type **729** 20 20
2996 1500r. Male teacher and pupils 20 20

730 Dancers ("Setagen Rhythm")

2004. Soerabaija 2004 Stamp Exhibition, Surabaya. Seven sheets containing T 730 and similar horiz designs showing paintings of dancers by Sunaryo. Multicoloured.

MS2997 Three sheets, each 95×94 mm. (a) 5000r. Type **730**; (b) 5000r. "Sebelum Pentas"; (c) 5000r. "Bercinta" 2·00 2·00
MS2998 Three sheets, each 95×94 mm. Imperf. (a) 5000r. Type **730**; (b) 5000r. "Sebelum Pentas"; (c) 5000r. "Bercinta" 2·00 2·00
MS2999 128×128 mm. 5000r.×3, Type **730**; "Sebelum Pentas"; "Bercinta" 2·00 2·00

2005. Folk Tales (8th series). As T 611. Multicoloured. (a) "Lahilote".

3000 1500r. Man and women bathing 20 20
3001 1500r. Woman and man 20 20
3002 1500r. Women 20 20
3003 1500r. Man, woman and child 20 20
3004 1500r. Invisible foot and footprint 20 20

(b) "Kolam Putri".

3005 1500r. Older man and young woman on balcony 20 20
3006 1500r. People arguing 20 20
3007 1500r. Castle, cliff, old man, women and fish 20 20
3008 1500r. Old man and deputation 20 20
3009 1500r. Woman and fish 20 20

(c) "Batu Balai".

3010 1500r. Woman, and man carrying pack 20 20
3011 1500r. Men and ship 20 20
3012 1500r. Couple, small boat and ship 20 20
3013 1500r. Woman begging at couple's feet 20 20
3014 1500r. Rocks and monkey 20 20

(d) "Bulan & Sagu Di Ibuanari".

3015 1500r. Figure with bow 20 20
3016 1500r. Cutting down trees 20 20
3017 1500r. Climbing steps 20 20
3018 1500r. Falling 20 20
3019 1500r. Trees 20 20
MS3020 106×62 mm. 6000r. No. 3008 75 75

Nos. 3000/19 were issued together, se-tenant, each horizontal strip forming a composite design.

731 "50" and Dove (image scaled to 61% of original size)

2005. 50th Anniv of Asia–Africa Conference. Multicoloured.

3021 2500r. Type **731** 30 30
3022 2500r. Dove, globe and faces 30 30
MS3023 120×88 mm. As No. 3021 30 30

732 Face, Map and Flame

2005. National Disaster Fund.

3024 **732** 1500r.+300r. multicoloured 25 25

The premium was for the benefit of victims of 26 December Tsunami disaster.

733 Stork and Mangroves

2005. Environmental Protection. Multicoloured.

3025 1500r. Type **733** 20 20
3026 1500r. Mangrove tree, roots and fish 20 20
MS3027 77×104 mm. As Nos. 3025/6 40 40

Nos. 3025/6 were issued together, se-tenant, forming a composite design.

734 Nine-masted "Treasure Ship"

2005. 600th Anniv of the Voyages of Zheng He (Ma Sanbao).

3028 **734** 2500r. multicoloured 30 30
MS3029 110×65 mm. **734** 2500r. multicoloured 30 30

735 Sayur Tauco

2005. Traditional Foods. Multicoloured.

3030 1500r. Type **735** 20 20
3031 1500r. Soto banjar 20 20
3032 1500r. Nasi timbel 20 20
3033 1500r. Langga roko 20 20

736 Bus, Map and Plug

2005. Energy Conservation. Multicoloured.

3034 1500r. Type **736** 20 20
3035 2000r. Generator, plugs and map 25 25
3036 2500r. Map and car 30 30

737 Ancient Ship (base relief)

2005. Borobudur Ship Expedition (recreating the ancient trading voyages between Indonesia and Africa). Multicoloured.

3037 1500r. Type **737** 20 20
3038 1500r. Reconstructed ship and Buddha head 20 20
MS3039 120×72 mm. As Nos. 3037/8 40 40

738 President Susilo Bambang Yudhoyono

2005. President and Vice-President. Multicoloured.

3040 1500r. Type **738** 20 20
3041 1500r. Vice-President Jusuf Kalla 20 20
3042 2500r. Type **738** 30 30
3043 2500r. Vice-President Jusuf Kalla 30 30
MS3044 122×62 mm. Nos. 3040/1 40 40

739 "Nyawer"

2005. National Philatelic Exhibition, Cilegon. Paintings by Sudjana Kerton. Five sheets containing T 739 and similar horiz designs. Multicoloured.

MS3045 133×102 mm. 5000r. Type **739**; 5000r. "Makan Siang"; 5000r. "Wayang Golek"; 8000r. "Tannah Air Indonesia" 3·00 3·00
MS3046 Four sheets, each 115×75 mm. Imperf. (a) 5000r. "Nyawer". (b) 5000r. "Makan Siang". (c) 5000r. "Wayang Golek". (d) 8000r. "Tannah Air Indonesia" Set of 4 sheets 3·00 3·00

740 *Neophocaena phocaenoides*

2005. Fauna and Flora. Multicoloured.

3047 1500r. Type **740** 20 20
3048 1500r. Dugong dugon 20 20
3049 1500r. *Gelidium latifolium* 20 20
3050 1500r. *Halimeda opuntia* 20 20
MS3051 120×74 mm. 1500r.×2, No. 3047; No. 3049 40 40

2006. Folk Tales (9th series). "Cerita Rakyat". As T 611. Multicoloured.

3052 1500r. Bawang, Merah and Bawang Putih 20 20
3053 1500r. Si Kancil 20 20
3054 1500r. Keong Emas 20 20
3055 1500r. Timun Emas 20 20

MS3056	85×120 mm. Nos. 3052/5	80	80

741 Child and Carriage

2006. Philately Day. Each agate and vermilion (Nos. 3057/70) or multicoloured (Nos. 3071/84).

3057	(1) 1500r. Type **741**	20	20
3058	(2) 1500r. Front wheels and horse	20	20
3059	(3) 1500r. Girl and photos	20	20
3060	(4) 1500r. Kneeling boy and photo of mountains	20	20
3061	(5) 1500r. Seated boy and three photos on floor	20	20
3062	(6) 1500r. Small girl seated	20	20
3063	(7) 1500r. Girl prone	20	20
3064	(8) 1500r. Boy writing	20	20
3065	(9) 1500r. Small boy and crate	20	20
3066	(10) 1500r. Boy making pot	20	20
3067	(11) 1500r. Boy making tall pot	20	20
3068	(12) 1500r. Seated girl and pot with dragons	20	20
3069	(13) 1500r. Small child and decorated pot	20	20
3070	(14) 1500r. Horses	20	20
3071	(15) 1500r. As Type **741**	20	20
3072	(16) 1500r. As No. 3058	20	20
3073	(17) 1500r. As No. 3059	20	20
3074	(18) 1500r. As No. 3060	20	20
3075	(19) 1500r. As No. 3061	20	20
3076	(20) 1500r. As No. 3062	20	20
3077	(21) 1500r. As No. 3063	20	20
3078	(22) 1500r. As No. 3064	20	20
3079	(23) 1500r. As No. 3065	20	20
3080	(24) 1500r. As No. 3066	20	20
3081	(25) 1500r. As No. 3067	20	20
3082	(26) 1500r. As No. 3068	20	20
3083	(27) 1500r. As No. 3069	20	20
3084	(28) 1500r. As No. 3070	20	20

Nos. 3057/8 and 3071/2 were issued in horizontal se-tenant pairs, each pair forming a composite design of horse and carriage.

Nos. 3059/64 and 3073/8 were issued in se-tenant blocks of six stamps, each block forming a composite design of children and floor map.

Nos. 3065/70 and 3079/84 were also issued in se-tenant blocks of six stamps, each block forming a composite design of children and pottery.

742 Emblem, Crowd, Net and Ball

2006. World Cup Football Championship, Germany. Multicoloured. Self-adhesive gum.

3085	(1) 2500r. Type **742**	35	35
3086	(2) 2500r. Emblem, crowd and ball	35	35
3087	(3) 2500r. Ball and trophy	35	35
3088	(4) 2500r. Ball and trophy (different)	35	35

743 Child

2006. Environmental Protection. Multicoloured.

3089	1500r. Type **743**	20	20
3090	1500r. Flowers, lake and butterfly	20	20
MS3091	105×73 mm. As Nos. 3089/90	40	40

744 Pempek

2006. Traditional Foods. Multicoloured.

3092	1500r. Type **744**	20	20
3093	1500r. Ayam Betutu	20	20
3094	1500r. Gudeg	20	20
3095	1500r. Aunu Senebre	20	20

745 Kak Mashudi and Campfire Gathering

2006. National Scout Jamboree. 50th Anniv of Asia—Pacific Region Scouts (3097). Multicoloured.

3096	1500r. Type **745**	20	20
3097	1500r. Scouts as jigsaw puzzle	20	20

746 Sultan Agung

2006. Sultans. Multicoloured.

3098	1500r. Type **746**	20	20
3099	1500r. Ma'moen Al Rasyid Perkasa Alamsyah	20	20
3100	1500r. Hasanuddin	20	20
3101	1500r. Adji Mohammed Parikesit	20	20

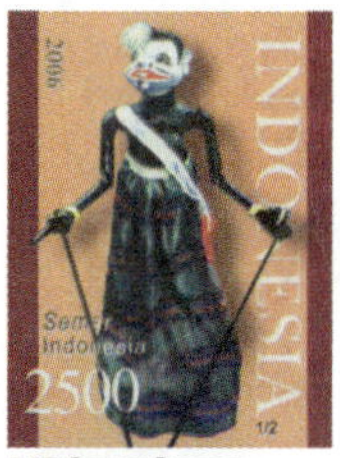

747 Semar Puppet (Wayang Golek traditional theatre), Java

2006. Puppets. Multicoloured.

3102	2500r. Type **747**	20	20
3103	2500r. Gasparko puppet, Slovakia	20	20
MS3104	112×78 mm. As Nos. 3102/3	40	40

Stamps of a similar design were issued by Slovakia.

747a Singer

2006. Eid ul-Fitr (holiday). Sheet 148×174 mm containing T 747a and similar horiz designs. Multicoloured.

MS3104a	1500r.×8, Type **747a** (1); Drummer (5); Older woman greeting young woman (2); Man greeting woman (6); Temple (3); Coach (7); Emblem (4); Rickshaw (8)	1·90	1·90

748 *Melipotes carolae*

2006. Newly Discovered Flora and Fauna. Multicoloured.

3105	1500r. Type **748**	20	20
3106	1500r. *Amblyornis flavifrons*	20	20
3107	1500r. *Licuala arbuscula*	20	20
3108	1500r. *Livistona mamberamoensis*	20	20
MS3109	112×78 mm. 2500r.×2, As Nos. 3106/7	70	70

749 *Panthera pardus*

2006. National Philatelic Exhibition, Bandung 2006. Five sheets, each 123×65 mm containing T 749 and similar horiz design. Multicoloured.

MS3110	2500r.×2, Type **749**; *Bouea macrophylla*	70	70

The stamps and margins of **MS**3110 form a composite design.

750 Rattan Basket, Kalimantan Timur

2006. Crafts. Multicoloured.

3111	1500r. Type **750**	20	20
3112	1500r. Banana leaf pot, Bali	20	20

751 Chinese Zodiac Signs surrounding Lanterns

2007. Chinese Zodiac. Multicoloured.

3113	1500r. vermilion and lemon	20	20
3114	1500r. vermilion and lemon	20	20
MS3115	Two sheets. (a) 90×90 mm. 6000r. multicoloured. (b) 240×174 mm. 2000r.×12, 6000r. vermilion and lemon	14·00	14·00

DESIGNS: No. 3113 Type **751**; 3114 Zodiac surrounding temple gate. **MS**3115a As No. 3114 but with temple gate embossed in gold. **MS**3115b 2000r.×12, Signs of Chinese Zodiac (each 48×32 mm); 6000r. As No. 3114 (96×64 mm). The stamps and margins of No. **MS**3115b form a composite design.

752 Lion Dance (China)

2007. Traditional Dances. Multicoloured.

3116	2500r. Type **752**	35	35
3117	2500r. Dragon dance (Indonesia)	35	35
MS3118	110×77 mm. Nos. 3116/17	70	70

Stamps of a similar design were issued by China.

753 Children writing

2007. Literacy. Multicoloured.

3119	1500r. Type **753**	20	20
3120	1500r. Child and adult	20	20

754 Polar Bear's Forehead and Melting Ice

2007. Environmental Protection. Multicoloured.

3121	1500r. Type **754**	20	20
3122	1500r. Polar bear's lower head and melting ice	20	20
3123	1500r. Burning forest	20	20
3124	1500r. Dead tree	20	20
MS3125	104×74 mm. 2500r.×2, As Nos. 3121/2	70	70

The stamps and margins of **MS**3125 form a composite design of a weeping polar bear and melting ice-flows.

755 Young Footballer and 'SAY NO TO DRUGS'

2007. International Day against Drug Abuse and Trafficking. Multicoloured.

3126	1500r. Type **755**	20	20
3127	1500r. Young guitarist and 'KATAKAN TIDAK PADA NARKOBA'	20	20

756 Roti Cane and Kari Kambing

2007. Traditional Foods. Multicoloured.

3128	1500r. Type **756**	20	20
3129	1500r. Gecok	20	20

757 Emblem

2007. Centenary of Scouting. Multicoloured.

3130	1500r. Type **757**	20	20
3131	1500r. Scout	20	20
3132	2500r. As No. 3131	35	35
3133	2500r. As Type **757**	35	35

758 *Nepenthes mirabilis*

2007. Bangkok 2007 International Stamp Exhibition. Two sheets containing T 758 and similar multicoloured design.

MS3134	104×150 mm. VERT: 1500r.×4, Type **758**×4; HORIZ: 1500r.×4, *Nepenthes ampullaria*×4	3·25	3·25
MS3135	107×69 mm. 2500r. Type **758**; 2500r. *Nepenthes ampullaria*	70	70

759 Fatahillah Museum, Jakarta

2007. Architecture. 40th Anniv of ASEAN (Association of South-east Asian Nations). Multicoloured.

3136	1500r. Type **759**	20	20
3137	2500r. Secretariat Building, Bandar Seri Begawan, Brunei Darussalam	35	35
3138	2500r. National Museum, Cambodia	35	35
3139	2500r. As Type **759**	35	35
3140	2500r. Traditional house, Laos	35	35
3141	2500r. Railway Headquarters Building, Malaysia	35	35
3142	2500r. Yangon Post Office, Union of Myanmar	35	35
3143	2500r. Malacanang Palace, Manila	35	35
3144	2500r. National Museum, Singapore	35	35

3145 2500r. Vimanmek Mansion, Bangkok, Thailand 35 35
3146 2500r. Presidential Palace, Hanoi, Vietnam 35 35

Stamps of a similar design were issued by all member countries.

760 Semarang

2007. Mercusuar. Lighthouses. Multicoloured.
3147 1500r. Type **760** 20 20
3148 1500r. Cikoneng 20 20

761 Tiger and Ram

2007. 50th Anniv of Universitas Padjadjaran. Multicoloured.
3149 1500r. Type **761** 20 20
3150 1500r. People 20 20
3151 1500r. Buildings 20 20
3152 1500r. Symbols of education 20 20

Nos. 3147/8 were issued together, se-tenant, forming a composite design.

762 *Ornithoptera aesacus*

2007. Butterflies. Multicoloured.
3153 1500r. Type **762** 20 20
3154 1500r. *Delias kristianiae* 20 20
3155 1500r. *Ornithoptera croseus* 20 20
3156 1500r. *Troides hypolitus* 20 20
MS3157 116×76 mm. 2500r.×2, As No. 3155; As No. 3154 70 70

2007. Bandung Filex 2007 and Jakarta 2008 International Stamp Exhibitions. Stamps of No. MS3157 surch.
MS3158 5000r.×2, on 2500r.×2 multicoloured 1·30 1·30

764 Ten Pin Bowling

2007. South East Asia Games, Thailand. Multicoloured.
3159 2500r. Type **764** 35 35
3160 2500r. Futsal 35 35
3161 2500r. Hammer throwing 35 35
3162 2500r. Judo 35 35

765 Prime Minister Djuanda Kartadiwidjaja and Symbols of Indonesia

2007. 50th Anniv of Djuanda Declaration. Multicoloured.
3163 1500r. Type **765** 20 20
3164 1500r. Children and islands 20 20
3165 1500r. Djuanda Kartadiwidjaja and archipelago 20 20

766 1600-year-old Inscribed Stone ('Prasasti Tugu')

2008. Jakarta 2008 International Stamp Exhibition. Sheet 123×165 mm containing T 766 and similar horiz designs. Multicoloured.
MS3166 2500r. Type **766**; 2500r. Vishnu (statue) ('Arca Dewa Vishnu'); 2500r. Inscribed stone ('Prasasti Pradrao'); 2500r. Portugis map of Indonesian Archipelago ('Peta Nusantara Zaman Portugis'); 2500r. Covenant document ('Naskah Perjanjian Sund Kelapa'); 2500r. Portugis vessel ('Kapal Bangsa Portugis'); 10000r. Lion flag ('Bendera Singa Ali') and Fatahillah (national hero) (83×25 mm) 3·50 3·50

See also No. **MS**3176, **MS**3195 and **MS**3221.

767 Rat

2008. New Year. Year of the Rat. Multicoloured.
3167 2000r. Type **767** 25 25
3168 2000r. Rat facing left 25 25
3169 2000r. Rat washing paws 25 25

768 Jerry

2008. Chinese New Year. Tom and Jerry (cartoon characters created by William Hanna and Joseph Barbera). Sheet 144×173 mm containing T 768 and similar horiz designs. Multicoloured.
MS3170 1500r.×6, Type **768**; Tom and Chinese characters; Tom and baubles; Jerry and presents; Jerry and lanterns; Tom with clasped fists 1·30 1·30

769 *Casuarius casuarius* (southern cassowary)

2008. Taipei 2008 International Stamp Exhibition. Sheet 128×82 mm containing T 769 and similar vert design. Multicoloured.
MS3171 5000r.×2, Type **769**; *Crinum asiaticum* 60 60

The stamps and margins of **MS**3171 form a composite design.

770 Sailing

2008. Olympic Games, Beijing. Designs showing Barongsai as athlete. Multicoloured.
3172 2500r. Type **770** 35 35
3173 2500r. Football 35 35
3174 2500r. Badminton 35 35
3175 2500r. Weightlifting 35 35

771 Administrative Building ('Istana Pemerintahan')

2008. Jakarta 2008 International Stamp Exhibition (2nd issue). Sheet 123×165 mm containing T 771 and similar horiz designs. Multicoloured.
MS3176 2500r. Type **771**; 2500r. Finance building ('Gedung Keuangan'); 2500r. Puppet and Batavia (Jakarta) battle ('Penyerangan Batavia oleh Sultan Agung'); 2500r. Battle and puppet ('Penyerangan Batavia oleh Sultan Agung'); 2500r. Signatories to the change from Batavia (Netherlands East Indies) to Jakarta (Indonesia) ('Perubahan Batavia Menjadi Jakarta'); 2500r. Signatories to change to Indonesia and arms ('Penyerahan Kekuasaan Indonesia'); 10000r. Troops seizing prince ('Penangkapan Pangeran Jayawikarta oleh Pasukan Banten') (83×25 mm) 3·50 3·50

772 Lake ('Danau Kelimutu')

2008. 50th Anniv of Indonesia—Japan Friendship. Multicoloured.
3177 (1) 2500r. Type **772** 35 35
3178 (2) 2500r. Mount Fuji 35 35
3179 (3) 2500r. Buddhist shrine ('Candi Borobudur') 35 35
3180 (4) 2500r. To-ji temple 35 35
3181 (5) 2500r. *Rafflesia arnoldi* 35 35
3182 (6) 2500r. Cherry blossom 35 35
3183 (7) 2500r. Musical instruments 'Angklung' and 'Gaku-Biwa' 35 35
3184 (8) 2500r. *Scleropages formosus* (horiz) 35 35
3185 (9) 2500r. *Nishiki-goi* (horiz) 35 35
3186 (10) 2500r. ('Danau Kelimutu') 35 35

Stamps of a similar design were issued by Japan.

773 Scout in Wheelchair

2008. Special Needs Education. Multicoloured.
3187 (1) 1500r. Type **773** 20 20
3188 (2) 1500r. Mixed ability Angklung players 20 20
3189 (3) 1500r. Wheelchair racer 20 20

Nos. 3187/9 are embossed with Braille characters.

773a Hand Shake

2008. Visit of President Soekarno to Cuba.
3189a **773a** 1500r. multicoloured 20 20

No. 3189a has 2007 imprint and was printed interspersed with stamps size labels showing Pres. Soekarno and Cuban dignatories.

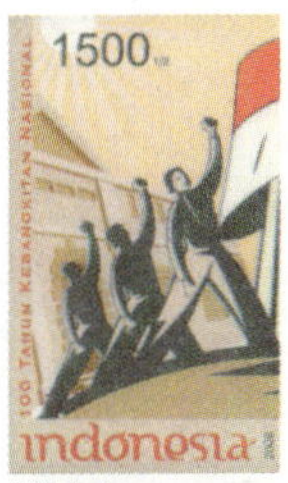

774 Early Demonstrators

2008. Centenary of Nationalism. Multicoloured.
3190 1500r. Type **774** 20 20
3191 1500r. Modern demonstrators 20 20

Nos. 3190/1 were issued together, se-tenant, forming a composite design.

775 Cyclists

2008. Environmental Protection. Multicoloured.
3192 1500r. Type **775** 20 20
3193 1500r. Seedling 20 20

No. 3194 has been left for miniature sheet not yet received.

776 Philatelic Agency, Jakarta ('Kantor Filateli Jakarta')

2008. Jakarta 2008 International Stamp Exhibition (3rd issue). Sheet 123×165 mm containing T 776 and similar horiz designs. Multicoloured.
MS3195 2500r. Type **776**; 2500r. National museum ('Museum Nasional'); 2500r. Roller coaster ('Dunia Fantasi'); 2500r. Recreational park ('Taman Mini Indonesia'); 2500r. Traditional procession ('Wisata Seni & Budaya'); 2500r. Jetski and coastline ('Wisata Bahari'); 10000r. Symbols of Jakarta ('Warna Warni Jakarta') (83×25 mm) 3·50 3·50

777 Mountain Biker

2008. National Games. Multicoloured.
3196 1500r. Type **777** 20 20
3197 1500r. Bodybuilder 20 20
3198 1500r. Steeplechaser 20 20
3199 1500r. Palaran Stadium 20 20

778 Nasi Lemak

2008. Traditional Foods. Multicoloured.
3200 (1) 1500r. Type **778** 20 20
3201 (2) 1500r. Sate Bandeng 20 20
3202 (3) 1500r. Ayam Cincane
3203 (4) 1500r. Kaledo 20 20

779 Bali

2008. Provincial Emblems. Multicoloured.
MS3215 160×250 mm. 2500r.×11, Type **779**; Gorontalo; Jawa Barat; Jawa Tengan; Kalimantan Barat; Maluku; Nanggroe Aceh Darussalam; Papua; Riau; Sulawesi Barat; Sumatera Barat 4·00 4·00

Nos. 3204/14 have been left for sheet stamps not yet received.

781 Welcome Monument, Jakarta

2008. Jakarta 2008–International Stamp Exhibition. Six sheets (numbered 4a/f), each 101×76 mm, containing T 781 and similar horiz designs (4th issue). Multicoloured.

MS3221 5000r. Type **781** — 60 — 60
MS3222 5000r. Airliner leaving Soekarno Hatta International Airport — 60 — 60
MS3223 5000r. Indonesia Stamp Museum — 60 — 60
MS3224 5000r. 1864 10c. stamp (As Type **1**) — 60 — 60
MS3225 5000r. *Haliastur indus* (Brahminy kite) — 60 — 60
MS3226 5000r. Orchestra (80th anniv of Sumpah Pemuda) — 60 — 60

Nos. 3216/20 and T **780** have been left for 'Great Post Road', issued on 27 September 2008, not yet received.

782 Blue Mosque (Sultan Ahmed Mosque, Istanbul)

2008. Indonesia–Turkey Relations. Multicoloured.

3227 2500r. Type **782** — 35 — 35
3228 2500r. Istiqlal Mosque, Jakarta — 35 — 35
3229 2500r. Bosphorus Bridge, Istanbul — 35 — 35
3230 2500r. Barelang Bridge (connecting Batam, Rempang, and Galang), Indonesia — 35 — 35
3231 2500r. Whirling dervishes dancing — 35 — 35
3232 2500r. Saman dance drummers — 35 — 35
3233 2500r. Tulip, Turkey — 35 — 35
3234 2500r. Flame of Irian (*Mucana beneetti*), Indonesia — 35 — 35
3235 2500r. Turkish Van cat — 35 — 35
3236 2500r. *Prionallurus planiceps* (flat-headed cat) — 35 — 35

Stamps of a similar design were issued by Turkey.

783 House

2008. Cat Nyak Dhien Commemoration. Multicoloured.

3237 1500r. Type **783** — 20 — 20
3238 1500r. Cat Nyak Dhien — 20 — 20

Nos. 3237/8 were issue together, se-tenant,r forming a composite design.

784 *Leucopsar rothschildi* (Bali starling), Bali

2008. Provincial Flora and Fauna. Multicoloured.

3239 2500r. Type **784** — 35 — 35
3240 2500r. *Liza dussumieri* (flat-headed cat), Gorontaio — 35 — 35
3241 2500r. *Panthera pardus* (leopard), Jawa Barat — 35 — 35
3242 2500r. *Oriolus chinensis* (black-naped oriole), Jawa Tengah — 35 — 35
3243 2500r. *Rhinoplax vigil* (helmeted hornbill), Kalimantan Barat — 35 — 35
3244 2500r. *Alisterus amboinensis* (Moluccan king parrot), Maluku — 35 — 35
3245 2500r. *Copsychus pyrropygus* (rufous-tailed shama), Nanggroe Aceh Darussalam — 35 — 35
3246 2500r. *Seleucidis melanoleuca* (twelve-wired bird of paradise), Papua — 35 — 35
3247 2500r. *Loriculus galgulus* (blue-crowned hanging parrot), Riau — 35 — 35
3248 2500r. *Aramidopsis plateni* (snoring rail), Sulawesi Barat — 35 — 35
3249 2500r. *Argusianus argus* (great argus), Sumatera Barat — 35 — 35

785 Pulau Batubawaikang, Sulawesi Utaro

2008. Small Outermost Islands. Multicoloured.

3250 1500r. Type **785** — 20 — 20
3251 1500r. Pulau Sebatik, Kalimantan Timur — 20 — 20
3252 1500r. Pulau Bras, Papua — 20 — 20
3253 1500r. Pulau Damar, Kepulaman Riau — 20 — 20

786 Lighthouse and Map

2008. Bicentenary of Great Post Road. Multicoloured.

3254 2500r. Type **786** (1/4) — 35 — 35
3255 2500r. Map and building (2/4) — 35 — 35
3256 2500r. Map and lighthouse (3/4) — 35 — 35
3257 2500r. Letter (4/4) — 35 — 35
MS3258 152×63 mm. 10000r. As Nos. 3254/6 (125×25 mm) — 1·30 — 1·30

Nos. 3254/7 were issued together, se-tenant, forming a composite design.

787 Ox

2009. Chinese New Year. Year of the Ox. Multicoloured.

3259 2000r. Type **787** (1/3) — 25 — 25
3260 2000r. Standing facing left (2/3) — 25 — 25
3261 2000r. Lying facing right (3/3) — 25 — 25
3262 2000r. As Type **787** and symbol — 25 — 25
3263 2000r. As No. 3260 and symbol — 25 — 25
3264 2000r. As No. 3261 and symbol — 25 — 25
3265 81×178 mm. 10000r. Ox and symbol — 1·30 — 1·30

788 Emblem

2009. 50th Anniv of Dies Emas Institut Teknologi Bandung. Multicoloured.

3266 1500r. Type **788** (1/4) — 20 — 20
3267 1500r. Students (2/4) — 20 — 20
3268 1500r. 89 — 20 — 20
3269 1500r. Institute arms (4/4) — 20 — 20

789 Flag of Words

2009. General Elections. Multicoloured.

3270 1500r. Type **789**(1/4) — 20 — 20
3271 1500r. tandai pilihan mu — 20 — 20
3272 1500r. 1 — 20 — 20
3273 1500r. 9 April 2009 — 20 — 20

2009. Preserve Polar Regions and Glaciers. Sheet 162×93 mm containing designs as T 754 and similar horiz design. Multicoloured.

MS3274 2500r.×2, As Type **754**; As No. 3122 — 80 — 80

Type **790** is vacant.

791 Two Oxen

2009. China 2009 International Stamp Exhibition. Sheet 100×67 mm.

MS3275 multicoloured — 1·50 — 1·50

792 Galilean Telescope

2009. International Year of Astronomy. Multicoloured.

3276 2500r. Type **792** (1/3) — 35 — 35
3277 2500r. Emblem (2/3) — 35 — 35
3278 2500r. Galileo Galilei (3/3) — 35 — 35
MS3279 108×70 mm. 5000r.×3, As Nos. 3276/8 — 2·20 — 2·20

Nos. 3276/8 were printed, se-tenant, forming a composite design.

793 Orange Fish

2009. World Ocean Conference and Coral Triangle Initiative Summit, Manado, North Salewesi. Designs showing conference emblems and marine life. Multicoloured.

3280 2500r. Type **793** (1) — 35 — 35
3281 2500r. Anemone and shrimp (2) — 35 — 35
3282 2500r. Fish (3) — 35 — 35
3283 2500r. Coral and underwater craft (4) — 35 — 35
MS3284 108×70 mm. 5000r. Turtle — 80 — 80

794 Polluted and Healthy Environments

2009. Environmental Protection. Winning Designs in National Stamp Design Competition. Multicoloured.

3285 1500r. Type **794** (1/3) — 20 — 20
3286 1500r. Globe, forest, people and factories (2/3) — 20 — 20
3287 1500r. Child holding leaf and parched ground (3/3) — 20 — 20
MS3288 92×61 mm. 5000r. As Type **794** — 80 — 80

795 Statue, Skyline and Bridge, Surabaya

2009. Inauguration of Suramadu Bridge. Multicoloured.

3289 1500r. Type **795** (1/3) — 20 — 20
3290 1500r. Bridge, central span(2/3) — 20 — 20
3291 1500r. Bridge and water buffalo, Madura (3/3) — 20 — 20
MS3292 165×63 mm. 10000r. As Nos. 3289/91 (124×25 mm) — 1·50 — 1·50

Nos. 3289/91 were printed, se-tenant, forming a composite design of the bridge.

The stamp of No. **MS**3292 shows the whole bridge.

796 Ihutilinanga

2009. Traditional Dishes. Multicoloured.

3293 1500r. Type **796** — 20 — 20
3294 1500r. Gulai Balak — 20 — 20
3295 1500r. Sate Tambulinas — 20 — 20
3296 1500r. Sambal Goreng Papai — 20 — 20
3297 1500r. Nasi Uduk — 20 — 20
3298 1500r. Ikan Bobara Kuah Asam — 20 — 20

796a Wrinkled Hornbill (Inscr 'Aceros corrigatus')

2009. Birds. Sheet 162×93 mm containing T 801 and similar multicoloured designs.

MS3298a 2500r.×6, Type **796a**; Red-naped trogon *Harpactes kasumba* (horiz); Rufous-collared kingfisher *Actenoides concretus* (horiz); White-winged duck *Asarcornis scutulata* (horiz); Great argus *Argusianus argus* (horiz); Storm's stork *Ciconia stormi* — 2·20 — 2·20

797 Skipping

2009. National Children's Day. Multicoloured.

3299 1500r. (1) Type **797** — 20 — 20
3300 1500r. (2) Flying kites — 20 — 20
3301 1500r. (3) Hide and seek — 20 — 20
3302 1500r. (4) Cycling — 20 — 20

Nos. 3299/302 were printed, se-tenant, forming a composite design.

798 Fans

2009. Philakorea 2009 International Stamp Exhibition, Seoul. Sheet 106×106 mm.

MS3303 multicoloured — 1·50 — 1·50

799 Banten

2009. Provincial Emblems (2nd series). Multicoloured.

3304 1500r. Type **799** — 20 — 20
3305 1500r. Jawa Timur — 20 — 20
3306 1500r. Kalimantan Tengah — 20 — 20
3307 1500r. Kalimantan Timur — 20 — 20
3308 1500r. Kepulauan Riau — 20 — 20
3309 1500r. Lampung — 20 — 20
3310 1500r. Nusa Tenggara Timur — 20 — 20
3311 1500r. Papua Barat — 20 — 20
3312 1500r. Sulawesi Tengah — 20 — 20
3313 1500r. Sulawesi Tenggara — 20 — 20
3314 1500r. Sumatera Selatan — 20 — 20
MS3315 160×250 mm. 2500r.×11, As Nos. 3304/3314 — 4·00 — 4·00

See also **MS**3215.

(801)

2009. Jipex 2009 International Stamp Exhibition. Birds. Sheet 162×93 mm overprinted as T 801 .

MS3317 2500r.×6, Wrinkled hornbill (Inscr 'Aceros corrigatus'); Red-naped trogon *Harpactes kasumba* (horiz); Rufous-collared kingfisher *Actenoides concretus* (horiz); White-winged duck *Asarcornis scutulata* (horiz); Great argus *Argusianus argus* (horiz); Storm's stork *Ciconia stormi* — 2·20 — 2·20

No. 3516 and Type **800** are left for National Army, issued on 5 October 2009.
No. **MS**3317 is as No. **MS**3298a

802 *Rhinoceros sondaicus* (Javan rhinoceros), Banten

2009. Provincial Flora and Fauna. Multicoloured.

3318	2500r. Type **802**	35	35
3319	2500r. Cockerel, Jawa Timur	35	35
3320	2500r. *Polyplectron schleirmacheri* (Bornean peacock pheasant), Kalimantan Tengah	35	35
3321	2500r. *Orcaella brevirostris* (Irrawaddy dolphin), Kalimantan Timur	35	35
3322	2500r. *Lutjanus sanguineus* (red snapper), Kepulauan Riau	35	35
3323	2500r. *Elephas maximus* (elephant), Lampung	35	35
3324	2500r. *Varanus komodoensis* (Komodo dragon), Nusa Tenggara Timur	35	35
3325	2500r. *Paradisaea rubra* (bird of paradise), Papua Barat	35	35
3326	2500r. *Macrocephalon maleo* (maleo), Sulawesi Tengah	35	35
3327	2500r. *Bubalus depressicornis* (lowland anoa), Sulawesi Tenggara	35	35
3328	2500r. *Notopterus chitala* (clown knifefish), Sumatera Selatan	35	35

EXPRESS LETTER STAMPS

E189 "Garuda" Bird

1967. Inscr "1967".

E1166	**E189**	10r. purple and blue	55	15
E1167	**E189**	15r. purple and orange	1·00	40

1968. As Nos. E1166/7 but dated "1968".

E1202	10r. purple and blue	55	15
E1203	15r. purple & orange	80	25
E1204	20r. purple and yellow	80	25
E1205	30r. purple and green	1·20	50
E1206	40r. purple & lt pur	80	25

1969. As Nos. E1166/7 but dated "1969".

E1250	20r. purple and yellow	40	15
E1251	30r. purple and green	40	15
E1252	40r. purple & lt pur	55	15

POSTAGE DUE STAMPS

1950. Postage Due stamps of Netherlands Indies surch BAJAR PORTO and new value.

D576	2½s. on 50c. (No. D499)	1·00	65
D577	5s. on 100c. (No. D501)	2·75	1·00
D578	10s. on 75c. (No. D500)	5·75	1·40

D100

1951

D645	**D100**	2½s. orange	15	55
D646	**D100**	5s. orange	15	10
D647	**D100**	10s. orange	15	10
D648	**D100**	15s. red	15	15
D649	**D100**	20s. blue	15	15
D650	**D100**	25s. olive	25	15
D651	**D100**	30s. brown	25	25
D652	**D100**	40s. green	25	25
D654	**D100**	1r. green	1·60	1·50
D773	**D100**	15s. orange	25	55
D774	**D100**	20s. orange	25	55
D775	**D100**	25s. orange	25	55
D776	**D100**	30s. orange	25	50
D777	**D100**	50s. orange	1·50	55
D778	**D100**	50s. green	10	10
D779	**D100**	100s. orange	80	55
D780	**D100**	100s. brown	10	10
D781	**D100**	250s. blue	25	10
D782	**D100**	500s. yellow	10	10
D783	**D100**	750s. lilac	25	10
D784	**D100**	1000s. salmon	15	15

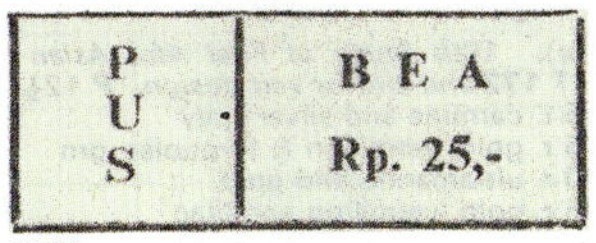

D176

1965. Provisional issue for use on parcels.

D1057	**D176**	25r. black on yellow	15	

1966

D1058	**D100**	50r. red	10	10
D1059	**D100**	100r. lake	15	15

1966. As Type D 100, but with coloured network background incorporating "1966".

D1098	5s. green and yellow	25	25
D1099	10s. red and blue	25	25
D1100	20s. blue and pink	25	25
D1101	30s. sepia and red	25	25
D1102	40s. violet and bistre	25	25
D1103	50s. olive and mauve	25	10
D1104	100s. lake and green	25	10
D1105	200s. green and pink	25	10
D1106	500s. yellow and blue	25	10
D1107	1000s. red and yellow	25	15

1967. As Nos. 1098/1107 but dated "1967".

D1168	50s. green and lilac	15	15
D1169	100s. red and green	15	15
D1170	200s. green and pink	15	15
D1171	500s. brown and blue	50	35
D1172	1000s. mauve and yellow	50	35
D1173	15r. orange and grey	1·00	50
D1174	25r. violet and grey	1·60	1·00

1973. As Type D 100 but inscr "BAYAR PORTO" and dated "1973".

D1320a	25r. violet and grey	1·10	15

1974. As Type D 100 but inscr "BAYAR PORTO" and dated "1974".

D1346	65r. green and yellow	1·80	40
D1347	125r. purple and pink	3·50	1·20

1975. As Type D 100 but inscr "BAYAR PORTO" and dated "1975".

D1401	25r. violet and drab	1·40	90

D268

1976

D1426	**D268**	25r. violet and drab	50	50
D1427	**D268**	65r. green and stone	1·00	1·00

1978. Various stamps surch BAYAR PORTO and value.

D1503	25r. on 1r. sepia and red (No. 1141)	40	40
D1504	50r. on 2r. blue and ochre (No. 1144)	40	40
D1505	100r. on 4r. blue and orange (No. 1147)	80	80
D1506	200r. on 5r. red and blue (No. 1148)	1·60	1·60
D1507	300r. on 10r. violet and red (No. 1151)	2·30	2·30
D1508	400r. on 15r. violet and olive (No. 1153)	2·40	2·40

1978. Nos. 1145 and 1152 surch BAYAR PORTO and value.

D1523	40r. on 2r.50 green and red	1·10	1·10
D1524	40r. on 12r. green and violet	1·10	1·10
D1525	65r. on 2r.50 green and red	1·30	1·30
D1526	65r. on 12r. green and violet	2·30	2·30
D1527	125r. on 2r.50 green & red	75	75
D1528	125r. on 12r. green & violet	1·80	1·80
D1529	150r. on 2r.50 green & red	3·00	3·00
D1530	150r. on 12r. green & violet	75	75

1980. Dated "1980".

D1062	**D 268**	125r. mauve & pink	1·00	75
D1599	**D268**	25r. mauve and drab	15	15
D1600	**D333a**	50r. green and lilac	40	40
D1601	**D333a**	75r. purple and pink	65	65

1981. Dated "1981".

D1641	25r. purple & stone	15	15
D1642	50r. green and lilac	35	35
D1643	75r. purple and pink	50	50
D1644	125r. purple & grn	1·00	1·00

1982. Dated "1982".

D1645	125r. purple & pink	25	15

D333a

1983. Dated "1983".

D1728	200r. lilac and blue	50	15
D1729	300r. green & yell	50	15
D1730	400r. green & buff	75	35
D1731	500r. brown & pink	1·00	50

1984. Dated "1984".

D1772	25r. purple & stone	75	25
D1773	50r. green and lilac	75	35
D1774	500r. deep brown and brown	7·75	1·00

1988. Dated "1988".

D1912	1000r. pur & grey	75	55
D1913	2000r. red & mauve	1·50	1·10
D1914	3000r. red & yellow	2·50	1·60
D1915	5000r. green & blue	4·50	2·10

Pt. 1

INDORE (HOLKAR STATE)

A state in C. India. Now uses Indian stamps.

12 pies = 1 anna; 16 annas = 1 rupee.

1 Maharaja Tukoji Rao Holkar II

1886

2	**1**	½a. mauve	4·50	2·25

2

1889. No gum. Imperf.

4	**2**	½a. black on pink	3·50	3·75

3 Maharaja Shivaji Rao Holkar

1889

5	**3**	¼a. orange	2·00	80
6a	**3**	½a. purple	3·00	15
7	**3**	1a. green	4·00	1·50
8	**3**	2a. red	8·50	2·00

5 Maharaja Tukoji Holkar III

1904

9	**5**	¼a. orange	1·00	10
10	**5**	½a. red	11·00	10
11	**5**	1a. green	2·50	10
12	**5**	2a. brown	17·00	1·00
13	**5**	3a. violet	29·00	7·00
14a	**5**	4a. blue	6·50	1·40

The ¼a. is inscr "HOLKAR".

पाव आना.
(6)

1905. No. 6a. surch as T 6.

15	**3**	¼a. on ½a. purple	8·00	23·00

7 Maharaja Yeshwant Rao Holkar II

1928

16	**7**	¼a. orange	75	20
17	**7**	½a. purple	2·75	10
18	**7**	1a. green	3·50	10
19	**7**	1¼a. green	4·50	1·25
20	**7**	2a. brown	10·00	3·00
21	**7**	2a. green	13·00	2·25
22	**7**	3a. violet	3·00	9·50
23	**7**	3a. blue	20·00	
24	**7**	3½a. violet	7·00	11·00
25	**7**	4a. blue	9·00	5·50
26	**7**	4a. yellow	38·00	2·00
27	**7**	8a. grey	7·50	4·50
28	**7**	8a. orange	30·00	25·00
29	**7**	12a. red	5·00	10·00
30	-	1r. black and blue	10·00	15·00
31	-	2r. black and red	65·00	70·00
32	-	5r. black and brown	£100	£110

The rupee values are larger, 23×28 mm.

1940. Surch diagonally in words.

33		¼a. on 5r. (No. 32)	18·00	1·75
34		½a. on 2r. (No. 31)	26·00	3·25
35	**7**	1a. on 1¼a. green (No. 19)	30·00	80

9 Maharaja Yeshwant Rao Holkar II

1940

36	**9**	¼a. orange	2·25	10
37	**9**	½a. red	4·50	10
38	**9**	1a. green	11·00	10
39	**9**	1¼a. green	17·00	2·25
40	**9**	2a. blue	12·00	1·00
41	**9**	4a. yellow	17·00	13·00
42	-	2r. black and red	15·00	£190
43	-	5r. black and orange	13·00	£275

The rupee values are larger, 23×28 mm.

OFFICIAL STAMPS

1904. Optd SERVICE.

S1	**5**	¼a. orange	1·00	1·25
S2	**5**	½a. red	25	10
S3	**5**	1a. green	15	20
S4	**5**	2a. brown	30	30
S5	**5**	3a. violet	2·50	4·00
S6	**5**	4a. blue	6·00	1·50

Pt. 9

INHAMBANE

A district of Mozambique, which used its own stamps from 1895 to 1920.

1895. 1000 reis = 1 milreis.
1913. 100 centavos = 1 escudo.

1895. 700th Birth Anniv of St. Anthony. Optd CENTENARIO DE S. ANTONIO Inhambane MDCCCXCV. (a) "Embossed" key-type inscr "PROVINCIA DE MOCAMBIQUE".

1	**Q**	5r. black	38·00	28·00
2	**Q**	10r. green	38·00	28·00
3	**Q**	20r. red	55·00	42·00
5	**Q**	40r. brown	55·00	42·00
6	**Q**	50r. blue	55·00	28·00
8	**Q**	200r. violet	75·00	65·00
9	**Q**	300r. orange	75·00	65·00

(b) "Figures" key type inscr "MOCAMBIQUE".

12	**R**	50r. blue	55·00	42·00
13	**R**	80r. green	60·00	49·00
14	**R**	100r. brown on yellow	£200	£200
16	**R**	75r. red	90·00	70·00
17	**R**	150r. red on rose	90·00	70·00

1903. "King Carlos" key type inscr "INHAMBANE".

18	**S**	2½r. grey	40	40
19	**S**	5r. orange	40	40
20	**S**	10r. green	50	45
21	**S**	15r. green	1·30	90
22	**S**	20r. lilac	1·30	90
23	**S**	25r. red	1·30	90
24	**S**	50r. brown	3·00	1·30

25	**S**	65r. blue	14·00	8·00
26	**S**	75r. purple	2·40	1·70
27	**S**	100r. blue on blue	2·40	1·70
28	**S**	115r. brown on pink	5·50	4·75
29	**S**	130r. brown on yellow	5·50	4·75
30	**S**	200r. purple on pink	5·50	4·75
31	**S**	400r. blue on yellow	10·50	6·75
32	**S**	500r. black on blue	15·00	10·00
33	**S**	700r. grey on yellow	24·00	16·00

1905. No. 25 surch 50 REIS and bar.

34	50r. on 65r. blue	4·50	3·25

1911. 1903 issue optd REPUBLICA.

35	2½r. grey	30	30
36	5r. orange	30	30
37	10r. green	40	30
38	15r. green	40	30
39	20r. lilac	75	55
40	25r. red	75	55
41	50r. brown	40	30
42	75r. purple	55	40
43	100r. blue on blue	55	40
44	115r. brown on pink	75	55
45	130r. brown on yellow	1·80	1·30
46	200r. purple on pink	1·10	70
47	400r. blue on yellow	1·80	1·30
48	500r. black on blue	1·90	1·30
49	700r. black on yellow	2·50	1·90

1913. Surch REPUBLICA INHAMBANE and value on "Vasco da Gama" stamps. (a) Portuguese Colonies.

50	¼c. on 2½r. green	1·10	70
51	½c. on 5r. red	1·10	70
52	1c. on 10r. purple	1·10	70
53	2½c. on 25r. green	1·10	70
54	5c. on 50r. blue	1·30	70
55	7½c. on 75r. brown	2·00	1·40
56	10c. on 100r. brown	2·00	1·40
57	15c. on 150r. bistre	2·00	1·80

(b) Macao.

58	¼c. on ½a. green	1·40	1·20
59	½c. on 1a. red	1·40	1·20
60	1c. on 2a. purple	1·40	1·20
61	2½c. on 4a. green	1·40	1·20
62	5c. on 8a. blue	1·40	1·20
63	7½c. on 12a. brown	2·40	1·80
64	10c. on 16a. brown	2·00	90
65	15c. on 24a. bistre	2·00	90

(c) Timor.

66	¼c. on ½a. green	1·40	1·20
67	½c. on 1a. red	1·40	1·20
68	1c. on 2a. purple	1·40	1·20
69	2½c. on 4a. green	1·40	1·20
70	5c. on 8a. blue	1·40	1·20
71	7½c. on 12a. brown	2·40	1·80
72	10c. on 16a. brown	2·00	90
73	15c. on 24a. bistre	2·00	90

1914. No. 34 optd REPUBLICA.

74	50r. on 65r. blue	2·50	1·30

1914. "Ceres" key type inscr "INHAMBANE".

75	**U**	¼c. olive	70	45
76a	**U**	½c. black	2·10	1·60
77	**U**	1c. green	80	45
78	**U**	1½c. brown	80	45
79	**U**	2c. red	80	45
80	**U**	2½c. violet	35	30
81	**U**	5c. blue	50	45
82	**U**	7½c. brown	35	70
83	**U**	8c. grey	1·30	70
84	**U**	10c. red	1·30	90
85	**U**	15c. red	1·70	1·20
86	**U**	20c. green	1·80	1·20
87	**U**	30c. brown on green	2·10	1·30
88	**U**	40c. brown on red	2·10	1·30
89	**U**	50c. orange on pink	4·50	2·30
90	**U**	1e. green on blue	4·50	2·30

Pt. 6

ININI

A territory in French Guiana, in the N.E. of S. America, separately administered from 1930 but reunited with Fr. Guiana in 1946.

100 centimes = 1 franc.

1931. Stamps of French Guiana optd TERRITOIRE DE L'ININI (Type 20) or Territoire de l'ININI (others).

1	**20**	1c. green and lilac	20	7·25
2	**20**	2c. green and red	20	6·50
3	**20**	3c. green and violet	55	8·50
4	**20**	4c. mauve and brown	45	7·75
5	**20**	5c. orange and blue	35	8·25
6	**20**	10c. brown and mauve	15	6·75
7	**20**	15c. orange and brown	15	7·00
8	**20**	20c. green and blue	75	7·50
9	**20**	25c. brown and red	85	8·00
10	**21**	30c. green and deep green	3·50	9·75
11	**21**	30c. brown and green	35	8·50
12	**21**	35c. green and blue	2·75	8·75
13	**21**	40c. grey and brown	65	9·25
14	**21**	45c. green and olive	1·50	8·75
15	**21**	50c. grey and blue	65	7·50
16	**21**	55c. red and blue	3·50	14·50
17	**21**	60c. green and red	65	9·00
18	**21**	65c. green and red	3·00	11·00
19	**21**	70c. green and blue	2·00	9·25
20	**21**	75c. blue and black	5·25	11·00
21	**21**	80c. blue and black	2·10	9·25
22	**21**	90c. red and carmine	4·75	10·50
23	**21**	90c. brown and mauve	2·75	9·25
24	**21**	1f. brown and mauve	23·00	44·00
25	**21**	1f. red	3·50	9·25
26	**21**	1f. blue and black	90	9·25
27	**22**	1f.25 green and brown	3·25	10·00
28	**22**	1f.25 red	2·20	9·25
29	**22**	1f.40 mauve and brown	2·10	9·50
30	**22**	1f.50 light blue and blue	1·00	8·25
31	**22**	1f.60 green and brown	1·30	9·50
32	**22**	1f.75 brown and red	50·00	60·00
33	**22**	1f.75 blue and deep blue	3·00	9·75
34	**22**	2f. red and green	1·00	8·25
35	**22**	2f.25 blue	1·20	10·00
36	**22**	2f.50 brown and red	1·30	10·00
37	**22**	3f. mauve and red	2·20	8·25
38	**22**	5f. green and violet	1·40	8·75
39	**22**	10f. blue and green	1·40	8·75
40	**22**	20f. green and blue	2·00	10·50

1939. New York World's Fair. As T 58c of Guadeloupe.

51	1f.25 red	6·00	19·00
52	2f.25 blue	6·00	19·00

1939. 150th Anniv of French Revolution. As T 58d of Guadeloupe.

53	45c.+25c. green and black	12·00	32·00
54	70c.+30c. brown and black	12·00	32·00
55	90c.+35c. orange and black	12·00	32·00
56	1f.25+1f. red and black	12·00	32·00
57	2f.25+2f. blue and black	12·00	32·00

POSTAGE DUE STAMPS

1932. Postage Due Stamps of French Guiana optd TERRITOIRE DE L'ININI.

D41	**D23**	5c. blue and deep blue	10	6·25
D42	**D23**	10c. blue and brown	45	7·00
D43	**D23**	20c. red and green	45	7·50
D44	**D23**	30c. red and brown	45	7·50
D45	**D23**	50c. brown and mauve	1·70	9·50
D46	**D23**	60c. brown and red	2·00	9·50
D47	**D 24**	1f. brown and blue	2·50	12·00
D48	**D 24**	2f. green and red	3·25	12·50
D49	**D 24**	3f. grey and mauve	4·25	19·00

Pt. 1

IONIAN ISLANDS

A group of islands off the W. coast of Greece, placed under the protection of Gt. Britain in 1815 and ceded to Greece in 1864.

12 pence = 1 shilling; 20 shillings = 1 pound.

1

1859. Imperf.

1	**1**	(½d.) orange	£110	£600
2	**1**	(1d.) blue	28·00	£225
3	**1**	(2d.) red	22·00	£225

Pt. 16

IRAN

A State of W. Asia.

1868. 20 shahis (or chahis) = 1 kran; 10 krans = 1 toman.
1932. 100 dinars = 1 rial.

NOTE.—The word "English" in the descriptive headings to various Persian issues is to be taken as referring to the lettering or figures and not to the language which is often French.

1

1868. Imperf or roul.

1		1(sh.) violet	£200	
1c		1(sh.) grey	£450	
2		2(sh.) green	85·00	
3		4(sh.) blue	£140	
4		8(sh.) red	80·00	
8		8(sh.) green	70·00	42·00
13		1(kr.) yellow	£1200	
15		1(sh.) black	23·00	38·00
16		2(sh.) blue	90·00	55·00
17		4(sh.) red	£190	60·00
18		1kr. red	£375	46·00
19		4kr. yellow	£600	30·00
35		2(sh.) black	£300	£1500
36		4kr. blue	£200	80·00
38		1kr. red on yellow	£1600	80·00
39		1to. bronze on blue	£42000	£5000
40		5kr. violet	£275	75·00
41		5kr. gold	£550	£190

3 Nasred-Din

1876. Perf.

20	3	1(sh.) black and mauve	50·00	12·00
24	3	2(sh.) black and green	16·00	5·00
25	3	5(sh.) black and pink	25·00	4·00
30	3	10(sh.) black and blue	37·00	9·75

4 Nasred-Din

1879. Perf.

45	4	1(sh.) black and red	36·00	6·75
46	4	2(sh.) black and yellow	50·00	4·25
47a	4	5(sh.) black and green	55·00	2·50
48a	4	10(sh.) black and mauve	£325	21·00
49c	4	1(kr.) black and brown	£110	2·30
50c	4	5(kr.) black and blue	46·00	70

5

6

1881

56	5	5c. mauve	25·00	5·25
57a	5	10c. red	25·00	5·00
61a	5	25c. green	£200	10·50
62	6	50c. black, yellow and orange	£325	9·75
63	6	1f. black and blue	80·00	3·50
64	6	5f. black and red	65·00	7·25
65	6	10f. black, yellow and red (30½×36 mm)	£120	12·00
69	6	50c. black	80·00	25·00

1882. As T 5 and 6.

66		5s. green	25·00	1·60
68		10s. black, yellow and orange	49·00	4·00

10

11

1885

70	10	1c. green	12·50	1·20
71	10	2c. red	12·50	1·20
72	10	5c. blue	21·00	80
73	11	10c. brown	12·50	1·20
74	11	1k. grey	29·00	2·10
75	11	5k. purple	£500	29·00

1885. Surch OFFICIEL and value in English and Persian.

76	-	6 on 5s. green (No. 66)	£100	22·00
78	6	12 on 50c. black	£100	22·00
79	-	18 on 10s. (No. 68)	£100	22·00
80	6	1t. on 5f. black and red	£100	22·00
81	-	3 on 5s. green (No. 66)	£100	25·00
83	-	6 on 10s. (No. 68)	£100	25·00
84	6	8 on 50c. black	£100	25·00

13

14

1889

85	13	1c. pink	2·10	40
86	13	2c. blue	2·10	40
87	13	5c. mauve	1·20	40
88	13	7c. brown	8·25	80
89	14	10c. black	1·60	40
90	14	1k. orange	3·00	40
91	14	2k. red	29·00	4·00
92	14	5k. green	21·00	4·00

15

16

1891

93A	15	1c. black	2·10	80
94A	15	2c. brown	2·10	80
95A	15	5c. blue	2·10	25
96B	15	7c. grey	£250	9·75
97A	15	10c. red	2·10	40
98	15	14c. orange	2·10	1·20
99A	16	1k. green	21·00	2·10
100A	16	2k. orange	£550	21·00
101A	16	5k. orange	£650	16·00

17

18

1894

102	17	1c. mauve	80	25
103	17	2c. green	80	25
104	17	5c. blue	80	25
105	17	8c. brown	80	25
106	18	10c. yellow	1·10	80
107	18	16c. pink	21·00	41·00
108	18	1k. pink and yellow	2·50	80
109	18	2k. brown and blue	3·25	1·10
110	18	5k. violet and silver	4·00	1·60
111	18	10k. pink and gold	12·50	8·25
112	18	50k. green and gold	25·00	9·00

See also Nos. 116/24.

1897. Surch in English and Persian in frame.

113	17	5c. on 8c. brown	21·00	3·25
114	18	1k. on 5k. violet and silver	25·00	12·50
115	18	2k. on 5k. violet and silver	41·00	21·00

21 Muzaffered-Din

1898. Chahi values on white or green paper.

116	17	1c. grey	1·20	25
117	17	2c. brown	1·20	25
118	17	3c. purple	1·20	25
119	17	4c. red	1·20	25
120	17	5c. yellow	3·25	25
121	17	8c. orange	3·25	80
123	17	12c. red	2·50	80
124	17	16c. green	5·25	80
125	21	1k. blue	5·00	80
126	21	2k. pink	4·00	1·60
127	21	3k. yellow	4·00	1·60
128	21	4k. grey	4·00	1·60
129	21	5k. green	4·00	1·60
130	21	10k. orange	12·50	6·50
131	21	50k. mauve	25·00	16·00
154	17	10c. blue	4·00	1·60
157	21	1k. red	21·00	8·25
158	21	2k. green	25·00	12·50
159	21	3k. brown	25·00	12·50
160	21	4k. red	25·00	12·50
161	21	5k. brown	25·00	12·50
162	21	10k. blue	£100	12·50
163	21	50k. brown	80·00	12·50

(21a)

1899. Optd with control mark of various scroll devices as T 21a.

132	17	1c. grey	4·00	1·20
133	17	2c. brown	4·00	1·20
134	17	3c. purple	4·00	1·20
135	17	4c. red	4·00	1·20
136	17	5c. yellow	4·00	80
137	17	8c. orange	4·00	1·50
138	17	10c. blue	4·00	80
139	17	12c. red	12·50	1·00
140	17	16c. green	21·00	1·60
141	21	1k. blue	21·00	80
142	21	2k. pink	25·00	2·50
143	21	3k. yellow	25·00	3·00
144	21	4k. grey	25·00	3·00
145	21	5k. green	25·00	3·00
146	21	10k. orange	£100	3·00
147	21	50k. mauve	80·00	6·50

(22)

1900. Optd with T 22 across two stamps.

164	17	1c. grey	29·00	12·50
165	17	2c. brown	37·00	16·00
166	17	3c. purple	60·00	41·00
167	17	4c. red	65·00	41·00
168	17	5c. yellow	16·00	8·25
169	17	10c. blue	£250	80·00
170	17	12c. red	65·00	41·00

Prices quoted in this issue are for pairs.

1901. Surch in various ways in English and Persian.

176		5 on 8c. brown	41·00	2·50
179	21	12c. on 1k. red	80·00	41·00
180	21	5k. on 50k. brown	£160	41·00

(24)

1902. Surch with T 24.

177	17	5c. on 10c. blue	41·00	16·00
178	21	5c. on 1k. red	41·00	16·00

1902. Optd PROVISOIRE 1319 in ornamental frame.

181	17	1c. grey	16·00	1·60
182	17	2c. brown	16·00	1·60
183	17	3c. purple	16·00	1·60
184	17	4c. red	16·00	80
185	17	5c. yellow	33·00	2·50
186	17	8c. orange	49·00	4·00
187	17	10c. blue	41·00	5·00
188	17	12c. red	75·00	10·50
189	17	16c. green	£120	25·00
190	21	1k. red	£600	£500
191	21	2k. green		29·00
192	21	3k. brown		45·00
193	21	4k. red		49·00
194	21	5k. brown		55·00
195	21	10k. blue		55·00
196	21	50k. brown		60·00
197	17	5 on 8c. brown (No. 176)	80·00	41·00
198	21	12c. on 1k. (No. 179)	80·00	41·00
199	21	5k. on 50k. (No. 180)	£160	41·00

28

(29)

1902. Inscr "CHAHIS" or "KRANS" in capital letters. Optd with T 29.

200	28	1c. grey	31·00	2·10
201	28	2c. brown	55·00	2·30
202	28	3c. green	60·00	2·10
203	28	5c. red	31·00	2·10
204	28	10c. yellow	60·00	2·10
205	28	12c. blue	75·00	3·00
206	28	1k. mauve	£110	3·50
207	28	2k. green	£110	7·00
208	28	10k. blue	£130	65·00
209	28	50k. red	£550	£425

1902. Surch 5 KRANS in English and Persian.

210		5k. on 5k. yellow	£140	41·00

1902. Optd PROVISOIRE 1319 in ornamental frame.

211		1c. grey	£120	80·00
212		2c. brown	£120	80·00
213		3c. green	£140	90·00
214		5c. red	80·00	65·00
215		12c. blue	£160	£120

34

1902. Inscr "Chahis" or "Krans" in lower case letters.

227	34	1c. grey	16·00	1·60
228	34	2c. brown	16·00	1·60
229	34	3c. green	16·00	1·60
230	34	5c. red	16·00	80
231	34	10c. yellow	33·00	2·50
232	34	12c. blue	49·00	4·00
233	34	1k. mauve	41·00	5·00
234	34	2k. green	75·00	10·50
235	34	10k. blue	£120	25·00
236	34	50k. red	£600	£500

1902. Surch 5 KRANS without T 29 opt.

237		5k. on 5k. yellow	£140	41·00

1903. Optd PROVISOIRE 1903 and lion in frame, but without Arms opt (T 29).

239	28	1c. grey		11·50
240	28	2c. brown		11·50
241	28	5c. red		7·50
242	28	10c. yellow		23·00
243	28	12c. blue		38·00
244	28	1k. mauve		46·00

38

39 Muzaffered-Din

1903

246	38	1c. lilac	1·60	25
247	38	2c. grey	1·60	25
248	38	3c. green	1·60	25
249	38	5c. red	1·60	25
250	38	10c. brown	2·50	1·20
251	38	12c. blue	3·25	50
252	39	1k. purple	9·75	40
253	39	2k. blue	16·00	1·00
254	39	5k. brown	25·00	1·60
255	39	10k. red	25·00	3·25
256	39	20k. orange	29·00	4·00
257	39	30k. green	49·00	9·75

258	39	50k. green	£325	80·00

See also Nos. 298/303.

1903. Surch in both English and Persian except those marked* which are surch in English only.

272	38	"1 CHAHI" on 3c. green	12·50	8·25
273	38	2c. on 3c. green	12·50	8·25
274	39	12c. on 10k. red	60·00	33·00
275	39	2t. on 50k. green*	£140	80·00
276	39	3t. on 50k. green*	£160	£100
277	38	3c. on 5c. red	16·00	80
278	38	6c. on 10c. brown	16·00	80
279	39	9c. on 1k. purple	29·00	3·25
280	39	2t. on 50k. green	£120	49·00
281	39	3t. on 50k. green	£120	49·00
287	38	"1 CHAI" on 3c. green	29·00	12·50
288	39	1c. on 1k. purple	29·00	12·50
289	39	2c. on 5k. brown	33·00	21·00

50

1906. Optd PROVISOIRE and lion. Imperf. or perf.

292	50	1c. violet	4·00	80
293	50	2c. grey	6·25	4·00
294	50	3c. green	4·00	80
295	50	6c. red	6·25	80
296	50	10c. brown	49·00	37·00
297	50	13c. blue	29·00	8·25

52 Shah Muhammad Ali Mirza

1907

298	38	1ch. violet on blue	1·60	35
299	38	2ch. grey on blue	1·60	35
300	38	3ch. green on blue	1·60	35
301	38	6ch. red on blue	1·60	35
302	38	9ch. yellow on blue	1·60	40
303	38	10ch. sepia on blue	2·50	1·20
305	52	13c. blue	3·25	1·60
306	52	26c. brown	5·00	1·20
307	52	1k. red	4·00	1·60
308	52	2k. green	10·50	1·20
309	52	3k. blue	11·50	80
311	52	4k. ochre	12·50	2·50
312	52	5k. brown	12·50	2·50
313	52	10k. pink	16·00	2·50
314	52	20k. brown	16·00	8·25
315	52	30k. purple	16·00	12·50
316	-	50k. red and gold	80·00	21·00

The 50k. is larger with the head facing the other way.

(54)

1909. Nos. 298/315 optd as T 54. Imperf.

320	38	1ch. on 1ch. violet on blue	£120	80·00
321	38	1ch. on 2ch. grey on blue	£120	80·00
322	38	1ch. on 3ch. green on blue	£120	80·00
323	38	1ch. on 6ch. red on blue	£120	80·00
324	38	1ch. on 9ch. yellow on blue	£120	80·00
325	38	1ch. on 10ch. brown on bl	£120	80·00
326	52	2ch. on 13ch. blue	£120	80·00
327	52	2ch. on 26ch. brown	£120	80·00
328	52	2ch. on 1kr. red	£120	80·00
329	52	2ch. on 2kr. green	£120	80·00
330	52	2ch. on 3kr. blue	£120	80·00
331	52	2ch. on 4kr. yellow	£120	80·00
333	52	2ch. on 5kr. brown	£120	80·00
334	52	2ch. on 10kr. pink	£120	80·00
335	52	2ch. on 20kr. black	£120	80·00
336	52	2ch. on 30kr. purple	£120	80·00

56

1909

337	56	1c. purple and orange	1·60	25
338	56	2c. purple and violet	1·60	25
339	56	3c. purple and green	1·60	25
340	56	6c. purple and red	1·60	25
341	56	9c. purple and grey	2·75	35
342	56	10c. maroon and purple	2·75	35
343	56	13c. purple and blue	5·25	50
344	56	26c. purple and green	5·25	65
345	56	1k. brown, violet and silver	5·25	1·10
346	56	2k. brown, green and silver	21·00	1·10
347	56	3k. brown, grey and silver	21·00	2·10
348	56	4k. brown, blue and silver	25·00	3·25
349	56	5k. sepia, brown and gold	29·00	4·00
350	56	10k. brown, orange and gold	£100	10·50
351	56	20k. brown, green and gold	£120	12·50
352	56	30k. brown, red and gold	£200	15·00

Stamps of this issue offered at very low prices are reprints.

For stamps as Type **56** but with curved inscriptions, see Nos. O836 etc.

57 Ahmed Mirza

1911

361	57	1c. orange and green	65	25
362	57	2c. brown and red	65	25
363	57	3c. green and grey	65	25
364	57	3c. green and brown	65	1·10
365	57	5c. red and brown	1·10	80
366	57	6c. red and grey	1·10	25
367	57	6c. red and green	65	25
368	57	9c. lilac and brown	1·10	25
369	57	10c. brown and red	2·10	25
370	57	12c. blue and green	2·50	25
371	57	13c. blue and violet	12·50	2·10
372	57	24c. green and purple	7·00	25
373	57	26c. green and blue	5·25	25
374	57	1k. red and blue	21·00	7·50
375	57	2k. purple and green	10·50	60
376	57	3k. black and lilac	14·00	60
377	57	4k. black and blue	49·00	16·00
378	57	5k. blue and red	29·00	1·10
379	57	10k. pink and brown	£180	4·00
380	57	20k. buff and brown	£200	8·25
381	57	30k. green and red	£300	9·75

1911. Various stamps optd Relais in English and Persian.

382	56	2ch. purple and violet	80·00	41·00
383	56	3ch. purple and green	80·00	41·00
384	56	6ch. purple and red	80·00	41·00
385	56	13ch. purple and blue	80·00	60·00
386	57	2ch. brown and red	80·00	41·00
387	57	3ch. green and grey	80·00	41·00
388	57	6ch. red and grey	80·00	41·00
388a	57	13ch. blue and violet	£100	60·00

1912. Optd Officiel in English and Persian.

389	1c. orange and green	16·00	2·50
390	2c. brown and red	16·00	2·50
391	3c. green and grey	16·00	2·50
392	6c. red and grey	16·00	2·50
393	9c. lilac and brown	16·00	2·50
394	10c. brown and red	25·00	2·50
395	13c. blue and violet	25·00	4·00
396	26c. green and blue	60·00	5·75
397	1k. red and blue	49·00	8·25
398	2k. purple and green	60·00	8·25
399	3k. black and lilac	80·00	8·25
400	5k. blue and red	£120	12·50
401	10k. pink and brown	£250	25·00
402	20k. buff and brown	£250	25·00
403	30k. green and red	£325	33·00

1914. Surch with new value and 1914 in English and Persian.

412	1c. on 13c. blue and violet	12·50	1·60
413	3c. on 26c. green and blue	12·50	3·25

1915. Surch with new value in frame and 1915 in English and Persian.

414	1c. on 5c. red and brown	12·50	1·60
415b	2c. on 5c. red and brown	12·50	1·60
416	6c. on 12c. blue and green	16·00	1·60

1915. Surch with new value in English and Persian.

417	56	5c. on 1k. (No. 345)	21·00	4·00
418	56	12c. on 13c. (No. 343)	25·00	5·75

(65)

1915. Optd with T 65 ("1333").

419	1c. purple and orange	12·50	2·10
420	2c. purple and violet	12·50	2·10
421	3c. purple and green	12·50	2·10
422	6c. purple and red	12·50	2·10
423	9c. purple and grey	12·50	2·50
424	10c. purple and mauve	41·00	4·00
425	1k. brown, violet and silver	60·00	4·00

66 The Imperial Crown

67 King Darius on his Throne

1915. Coronation of Shah Ahmed.

426	66	1c. blue and red	25	1·60
427	66	2c. red and blue	25	1·60
428	66	3c. green	25	1·60
429	66	5c. red	25	2·10
430	66	6c. red and green	25	1·60
431	66	9c. violet and brown	25	1·60
432	66	10c. brown and green	25	1·60
433	66	12c. blue	25	1·60
434	66	24c. sepia and brown	25	4·00
435	67	1k. black, brown and silver	65	4·00
436	67	2k. red, blue and silver	65	4·00
437	67	3k. brown, lilac and silver	75	4·00
438	67	5k. grey, brown and silver	75	5·75
439	-	1t. black, violet and gold	75	8·25
440	-	2t. brown, green and gold	80	8·25
441	-	3t. red, crimson and gold	80	8·25
442	-	5t. grey, blue and gold	80	8·25

DESIGNS: 1t. to 5t. Gateway of the Palace of Persepolis.

(69)

1915. Optd with T 69 ("1334").

477	56	1k. brown, violet and silver	41·00	16·00
478	56	10k. brown, orange and gold	41·00	16·00
479	56	20k. brown, green and gold	£160	65·00
480	56	30k. brown, red and gold	£160	65·00

1917. Surch with value in English only.

481	57	12c. on 1k. red and blue	£800	£600
482	57	24c. on 1k. red and blue	£500	£325

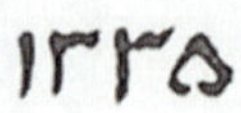

(73)

1917. Optd with T 73 ("1335") or surch also with new value in English and Persian.

483	56	1c. purple and orange	£250	£160
484	56	1c. on 2c. (No. 338)	16·00	2·50
485	56	1c. on 9c. (No. 341)	21·00	3·25
486	56	1c. on 10c. (No. 342)	16·00	2·50
487	56	3c. on 9c. purple and grey	21·00	3·25
488	56	3c. on 26c. (No. 344)	25·00	4·00
489	56	5c. on 13c. (No. 343)	23·00	3·75
490	57	1c. on 10c. brown and red	25·00	1·20
491	57	3c. on 10c. brown and red	25·00	1·20
492	57	5c. on 1k. red and blue	30·00	6·50
493	57	6c. on 10c. brown and red	45·00	15·00
494	57	6c. on 12c. blue and green	49·00	12·50

(78)

1918. Optd with T 78 ("1336").

507	56	2k. brown, green and silver	41·00	8·25

1918. Surch as T 78 and new value in English and Persian.

508	24c. on 4k. (No. 348)	49·00	8·25
509	10k. on 5k. (No. 349)	80·00	12·50

1918. Coronation issue of 1915 optd Novembre 1918 (date also in Persian).

510	67	2k. red, blue and silver	8·25	8·25
511	67	3k. brown, lilac and silver	8·25	8·25
512	67	5k. grey, brown and silver	8·25	8·25
513	-	1t. black, violet and gold	12·50	12·50
514	-	2t. brown, green and gold	12·50	12·50
515	-	3t. red, crimson and gold	12·50	12·50
516	-	5t. grey, blue and gold	12·50	16·00

(82)

1918. Surch as T 82 and new value in English and Persian.

517	57	3c. on 12c. blue and green	33·00	1·20
518	57	6c. on 10c. brown and red	21·00	1·20
519	57	6c. on 1k. red and blue	21·00	1·20

1918. Optd with T 82 ("1337").

520	56	2k. brown, green and silver	80·00	55·00
521	56	3k. brown, grey and silver	49·00	12·50
522	56	4k. brown, blue and silver	80·00	41·00
523	56	5k. sepia, brown and gold	£120	49·00
524	56	10k. brown, orange and gold	£150	49·00
525	56	20k. brown, green and gold	£400	£160
526	56	30k. brown, red and gold	£120	80·00

84 Ahmed Mirza

1919. Type 84 surch Provisoire 1919 and value in English and Persian.

527	84	1c. yellow	12·50	80
528	84	3c. green	12·50	80
529	84	5c. purple	25·00	2·50
530	84	6c. violet	5·00	80
531	84	12c. blue	49·00	8·25

1919. Surch 1919 and value in English and Persian.

532	13	2k. on 5c. mauve	6·25	6·25
533	13	3k. on 5c. mauve	6·25	6·25
534	13	4k. on 5c. mauve	6·25	6·25
535	13	5k. on 5c. mauve	6·25	6·25
536	15	10k. on 10c. red	16·00	16·00
537	15	20k. on 10c. red	16·00	16·00
538	15	30k. on 10c. red	16·00	16·00
539	15	50k. on 14c. orange	16·00	2·50

1921. Surch 6-CHAHIS in English and Persian.

539a	57	6c. on 12c. blue and green	£160	12·50

1921. Coup d'Etat of Reza Khan. Coronation issue of 1915 optd 21. FEV. 1921 in English and Persian.

540	66	3c. green	12·50	
541	66	5c. red	12·50	
542	66	6c. red and green	12·50	
543	66	10c. brown and green	12·50	
544	66	12c. blue	12·50	
545	67	1k. black, brown and silver	16·00	
546	67	2k. red, blue and silver	16·00	
547	67	5k. grey, brown and silver	16·00	
548	-	2t. brown, green and gold	21·00	
549	-	3t. red, crimson and gold	25·00	
550	-	5t. grey, blue and gold	25·00	

1922. Surch with value in English only.

551	57	10c. on 6c. brown & green	£100	33·00
552	57	1k. on 12c. blue and green	£100	33·00

1922. Surcharged with value in English only over BENADERS.

553		10c. on 6c. brown & green	£100	33·00
554		1k. on 12c. blue and green	£100	33·00

1922. Optd CONTROLE 1922 in English and Persian.

555		1c. orange and green	3·25	25
556		2c. brown and red	3·25	25
557		3c. green and grey	3·25	25
558		3c. green and brown	3·50	25
559		5ch. red and brown	60·00	21·00
560		6c. brown and green	4·00	25
561		9c. lilac and brown	4·00	25
562		10c. brown and red	5·00	25
563		12c. blue and green	9·75	10
564		24c. green and purple	12·50	80
565		1k. red and blue	12·50	80
566		2k. purple and green	33·00	80
567		3k. black and lilac	37·00	1·20
568		4k. blue and black	49·00	16·00
569		5k. blue and red	41·00	1·60
570		10k. red and brown	£200	4·00
571		20k. yellow and brown	£200	5·75
572		30k. green and red	£325	8·25

1922. Surch in English and Persian.

573		3c. on 12c. (No. 563)	37·00	1·60
574		6c. on 24c. (No. 564)	37·00	1·60
575		10c. on 20k. (No. 571)	60·00	8·25
576		1k. on 30k. (No. 572)	80·00	12·50

92 Ahmed Mirza

1924

577	**92**	1c. orange	2·75	25
578	**92**	2c. red	2·75	25
579	**92**	3c. brown	2·75	25
580	**92**	6c. sepia	2·75	25
581	**92**	9c. green	5·25	80
582	**92**	10c. violet	5·25	35
583	**92**	12c. red	5·25	40
584	**92**	1k. blue	5·25	1·10
585	**92**	2k. red and blue	5·25	1·60
586	**92**	3k. purple and violet	15·00	1·60
587	**92**	5k. sepia and red	16·00	16·00
588	**92**	10k. violet and sepia	21·00	21·00
589	**92**	20k. sepia and green	25·00	25·00
590	**92**	30k. black and orange	33·00	33·00

1924. Surch p. re. 1924 and value in English and Persian.

591	**84**	1c. brown	2·10	1·10
592	**84**	2c. grey	2·10	1·10
593	**84**	3c. red	2·10	1·10
594	**84**	6c. orange	4·00	1·60

1925. Surch p. re. 1925 and value in English and Persian.

595		2c. green	2·50	50
596		3c. red	2·50	50
597		6c. blue	2·50	50
598		9c. brown	8·25	50
599		10c. grey	16·00	2·50
600		1k. green	33·00	5·75
601		2k. mauve	80·00	21·00

94

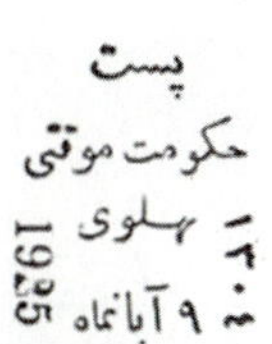

95 "Provisional Pahlavi Government, 31 Oct 1925"

1925. Deposition of Shah Ahmed and Provisional Government of Riza Khan Pahlavi. Fiscal stamps as T 94 (various frames) optd with T 95.

602	**94**	1c. red	5·75	3·25
603	**94**	2c. yellow	5·75	3·25
604	**94**	3c. green	5·75	3·25
605	**94**	5c. grey	25·00	12·50
606	**94**	10c. red	12·50	4·00
607	**94**	1k. blue	12·50	8·25

(96)

1926. Optd with T 96.

608	**92**	1c. orange	2·50	1·20
609	**92**	2c. red	2·50	1·60
610	**92**	3c. brown	3·25	1·20
611	**92**	6c. sepia	60·00	60·00

1926. Optd Regne de Pahlavi 1926 in English and Persian.

612A	**56**	1c. purple and orange	5·75	25
613A	**56**	2c. purple and violet	5·75	25
614A	**56**	3c. purple and green	5·75	25
615A	**56**	6c. purple and red	5·75	25
616A	**56**	9c. purple and grey	5·75	25
617A	**56**	10c. maroon and purple	5·75	40
618A	**56**	13c. purple and blue	12·50	40
619A	**56**	26c. purple and green	25·00	40
620A	**56**	1k. brown, violet and silver	12·50	40
621A	**56**	2k. brown, green and silver	25·00	50
622A	**56**	3k. brown, grey and silver	60·00	50
623A	**56**	4k. brown, blue and silver	£400	8·25
624A	**56**	5k. sepia, brown and gold	£120	7·00
625A	**56**	10k. brown, orange and gold	£325	8·75
626A	**56**	20k. brown, green and gold	£475	9·75
627A	**56**	30k. brown, red and gold	£400	12·50

98 Riza Shah Pahlavi

99 Riza Shah Pahlavi

1926

628	**98**	1c. green	3·25	25
629	**98**	2c. blue	3·25	25
630	**98**	3c. green	3·25	25
631	**98**	6c. red	4·00	25
632	**98**	9c. red	8·25	40
633	**98**	10c. brown	16·00	4·00
634	**98**	12c. orange	16·00	2·50
635	**98**	15c. blue	21·00	1·60
636	**99**	1k. blue	33·00	8·25
637	**99**	2k. mauve	£120	33·00

1927. Air. Optd with airplane and POSTE AERIENNE in English and Persian.

642	**56**	1c. purple and orange	1·60	80
643	**56**	2c. purple and violet	1·60	80
644	**56**	3c. purple and green	1·60	80
645	**56**	6c. purple and red	1·60	80
646	**56**	9c. purple and grey	3·25	80
647	**56**	10c. maroon and purple	5·00	80
648	**56**	13c. purple and blue	6·50	2·10
649	**56**	26c. purple and green	6·50	2·10
650	**56**	1k. brown, violet and silver	6·50	2·10
651	**56**	2k. brown, green and silver	6·50	2·10
652	**56**	3k. brown, grey and silver	21·00	8·25
653	**56**	4k. brown, blue and silver	33·00	12·50
654	**56**	5k. sepia, brown and gold	33·00	8·25
655	**56**	10k. brown, orange and gold	£450	£160
656	**56**	20k. brown, green and gold	£300	£160
657	**56**	30k. brown, red and gold	£300	£160

1928. Air. Fiscal stamps surch with Junkers F-13 airplane, Poste aerien and new value in French and Persian.

657a	**94**	3k. brown	£100	33·00
657b	**94**	5k. brown	25·00	8·25
657c	**94**	1t. violet	25·00	8·25
657d	**94**	2t. green	25·00	8·25
657e	**94**	3t. green	29·00	12·50

102

1929. Air. Fiscal stamps as T 102 (various frames) surch with Junkers F-13 airplane, Poste aerienne and value in French and Persian.

658	**102**	1c. green	80	50
659	**102**	2c. blue	80	25
660	**102**	3c. red	80	25
661	**102**	5c. brown	80	25
662	**102**	10c. green	80	25
663	**102**	1k. violet	1·60	80
664	**102**	2k. orange	4·00	1·60
665	**102**	3k. brown (22×30 mm)	80·00	21·00
666	**102**	5k. brown (22×33 mm)	16·00	4·00
667	**102**	10k. violet (21×31 mm)	21·00	8·25
668	**102**	20k. green (21×31 mm)	25·00	8·25
669	**102**	30k. green (21×31 mm)	33·00	12·50

104 Riza Shah Pahlavi

1929

670	**104**	1c. red and green	1·60	25
671	**104**	2c. blue and red	1·20	25
672	**104**	3c. green and red	1·20	25
673	**104**	6c. green and brown	1·60	25
674	**104**	9c. red and blue	2·50	35
675	**104**	10c. brown and green	3·25	35
676	**104**	12c. violet and black	5·00	40
677	**104**	15c. blue and yellow	5·75	40
678	**104**	24c. lake and olive	5·75	40
679	**104**	1k. black and blue	8·25	1·20
680	**104**	2k. violet and orange	70·00	90
681	**104**	3k. red and green	85·00	90
682	**104**	5k. green and brown	36·00	2·20
683	**104**	1t. red and blue	36·00	4·50
684	**104**	2t. black and red	42·00	27·00
685	-	3t. violet and gold	75·00	30·00

DESIGN: 3t. Shah enthroned (28½×39 mm).

106 Riza Shah Pahlavi and Elburz Mts

1930. Air.

686	**106**	1c. blue and yellow	40	40
687	**106**	2c. black and blue	40	40
688	**106**	3c. violet and olive	40	40
689	**106**	4c. blue and violet	40	40
690	**106**	5c. red and green	40	40
691	**106**	6c. green and red	40	40
692	**106**	8c. violet and grey	40	40
693	**106**	10c. red and blue	40	40
694	**106**	12c. orange and grey	40	40
695	**106**	15c. olive and brown	40	40
696	**106**	1k. red and blue	4·00	2·10
697	**106**	2k. blue and black	4·00	2·10
698	**106**	3k. green and brown	3·50	2·00
699	**106**	5k. black and red	3·75	2·75
700	**106**	1t. purple and orange	18·00	3·50
701	**106**	2t. brown and green	18·00	7·50
702	**106**	3t. green and purple	£130	48·00

107

1931

703	**107**	1c. blue and brown	2·50	25
704	**107**	2c. black and red	2·50	25
705	**107**	3c. brown and mauve	2·50	25
706	**107**	6c. violet and red	2·50	25
707	**107**	9c. red and blue	8·25	40
708	**107**	10c. grey and red	8·25	80
709	**107**	11c. red and blue	20·00	60
710	**107**	12c. mauve and blue	14·00	40
711	**107**	16c. red and black	28·00	90
712	**107**	27c. blue and black	46·00	95
713	**107**	1k. blue and red	40·00	1·20

108 Riza Shah Pahlavi

109

1933. New Currency.

714	**108**	5d. brown	1·20	25
715	**108**	10d. blue	1·20	25
716	**108**	15d. grey	1·20	25
717	**108**	30d. green	1·20	25
718	**108**	45d. blue	1·20	25
719	**108**	50d. mauve	2·10	25
720	**108**	60d. green	3·25	40
721	**108**	75d. brown	5·75	65
722	**108**	90d. red	6·50	80
723	**109**	1r. black and red	16·00	80
724	**109**	1r.20 red and black	18·00	45
725	**109**	1r.50 blue and yellow	22·00	45
726	**109**	2r. brown and blue	28·00	50
727	**109**	3r. green and mauve	36·00	75
728	**109**	5r. red and brown	£180	10·50

110 "Justice"

112 Cement Works, Chah-Abdul-Azim

1935. 10th Anniv of Riza Khan's Advent to Power.

729	**110**	5d. green and brown	1·20	40
730	-	10d. grey and orange	1·20	40
731	-	15d. blue and red	1·60	40
732	-	30d. green and black	1·60	40
733	-	45d. lake and olive	2·50	40
734	**112**	75d. brown and green	4·00	80
735	-	90d. red and blue	18·00	50
736	-	1r. violet and brown	28·00	4·25
737	-	1r.50 blue and purple	40·00	6·50

DESIGNS: 10d. Ruins of Persepolis (40×26 mm); 15d. "Education" (23×33 mm); 30d. De Havilland Tiger Moth biplanes over Teheran Aerodrome (38×25 mm); 45d. Sakhtessar Sanatorium, Mazanderan (40×27 mm); 90d. Gunboat "Palang" (38×24 mm); 1r. Railway bridge over R. Karun (42×29 mm); 1r.50, Post and Customs House, Teheran (42×27 mm).

1935. Optd POSTES IRANIENNES. (a) Stamps of 1929.

738	**104**	1c. red and green	90·00	23·00
739	**104**	2c. blue and red	38·00	30·00
740	**104**	3c. green and red	55·00	38·00
741	**104**	6c. green and brown	38·00	1·50
742	**104**	9c. red and blue	19·00	9·50
743	**104**	1t. red and blue	38·00	3·75
744	**104**	2t. black and red	38·00	30·00
745	-	3t. violet and gold	90·00	49·00

(b) Stamps of 1931.

746	**107**	1c. blue and brown	90·00	30·00
747	**107**	2c. black and red	10·00	4·00
748	**107**	3c. brown and mauve	5·00	4·50
749	**107**	6c. violet and red	22·00	14·00
750	**107**	9c. red and blue	22·00	14·00
751	**107**	11c. red and blue	1·00	15
752	**107**	12c. mauve and blue	65·00	25·00
753	**107**	16c. red and black	16·00	15
754	**107**	27c. blue and black	21·00	15

(c) Stamps of 1933.

755	**108**	5c. brown	90	10
756	**108**	10d. blue	10	10
757	**108**	15d. grey	90	10
758	**108**	30d. green	90	10
759	**108**	45d. blue	90	10

760	108	50d. mauve	1·60	10
761	108	60d. green	2·50	20
762	108	75d. brown	5·25	60
763	108	90d. red	6·00	75
764	109	1r. black and red	15·00	75
765	109	1r.20 red and black	19·00	75
766	109	1r.50 blue and green	23·00	75
767	109	2r. brown and blue	30·00	75
768	109	3r. green and mauve	38·00	1·10
769	109	5r. red and brown	1·90	19·00

1935. Air. Air stamps of 1930 optd Iran.

770	106	1c. blue and yellow	40	40
771	106	2c. black and blue	40	40
772	106	3c. violet and olive	40	40
773	106	4c. blue and violet	40	40
774	106	5c. red and green	40	40
775	106	6c. green and red	40	40
776	106	8c. violet and grey	40	40
777	106	10c. red and blue	40	40
778	106	12c. orange and blue	40	40
779	106	15c. olive and brown	40	40
780	106	1k. red and blue	6·75	5·75
781	106	2k. blue and black	23·00	6·25
782	106	3k. green and brown	4·75	4·50
783	106	5k. black and red	5·00	4·75
784	106	1t. purple and orange	£100	70·00
785	106	2t. brown and green	14·50	10·50
786	106	3t. green and purple	70·00	30·00

116

1935. Rial values are larger, 22×31 mm.

787	116	5d. violet	1·10	25
788	116	10d. purple	1·10	25
789	116	15d. blue	1·10	25
790	116	30d. green	1·50	25
791	116	45d. orange	1·50	25
792	116	50d. brown	1·90	30
793	116	60d. blue	4·50	40
794	116	75d. red	4·50	55
795	116	90d. red	9·00	1·10
796	116	1r. purple	15·00	75
797	116	1r.50 blue	19·00	1·50
798	116	2r. green	30·00	75
799	116	3r. brown	34·00	1·50
800	116	5r. grey	£160	70·00

117 Riza Shah Pahlavi

1936. Rial values are larger, 23×31 mm.

801	117	5d. violet	40	15
802	117	10d. mauve	40	15
803	117	15d. blue	75	25
804	117	30d. green	75	25
805	117	45d. red	90	25
806	117	50d. brown	1·10	25
807	117	60d. brown	1·10	25
808	117	75d. red	1·50	25
809	117	90d. red	1·90	25
810	117	1r. green	11·50	40
811	117	1r.50 blue	11·50	40
812	117	2r. blue	15·00	40
813	117	3r. purple	19·00	75
814	117	5r. green	30·00	90
815	117	10r. blue and brown	£150	15·00

117a

1938. 60th Birthday of Shah. Perf or imperf.

815a	117a	5d. blue	1·10	75
815b	117a	10d. red	1·10	75
815c	117a	30d. blue	1·10	75
815d	117a	60d. brown	1·10	75
815e	117a	90d. red	3·50	1·50
815f	117a	1r. violet	7·50	
815g	117a	1r.50 blue	7·50	3·75
815h	117a	2r. red	7·50	3·75
815i	117a	5r. mauve	30·00	15·00
815j	117a	10r. red	55·00	45·00

118 Riza Shah Pahlavi

1938. Rial values are larger, 23×31 mm.

816	118	5d. violet	40	15
817	118	10d. mauve	40	15
818	118	15d. blue	50	15
819	118	30d. green	50	15
820	118	45d. red	55	15
821	118	50d. brown	90	15
822	118	60d. orange	90	20
823	118	75d. red	1·60	20
824	118	90d. red	2·40	20
825	118	1r. green	7·25	15
826	118	1r.50 blue	9·25	20
827	118	2r. blue	11·50	25
828	118	3r. purple	20·00	35
829	118	5r. green	33·00	60
830	118	10r. blue and brown	£110	8·00

119 Princess Fawzieh and Crown Prince

1939. Royal Wedding.

831	119	5d. brown	20	25
832	119	10d. violet	30	25
833	119	30d. green	70	30
834	119	90d. red	10·00	55
835	119	1r.50 blue	15·00	1·10

120 Railway Bridge over Karun River

123 Mohammed Riza Pahlavi

1942

850	120	5d. violet	1·10	15
851	120	5d. orange	40	15
852	-	10d. mauve	1·10	15
853	-	10d. green	40	15
854	-	20d. violet	1·50	15
855	-	20d. mauve	75	15
856	-	25d. red	19·00	3·75
857	-	25d. violet	3·75	40
858	-	35d. green	1·10	25
859	-	50d. blue	1·90	25
860	-	50d. green	1·10	15
861	-	70d. brown	1·10	30
862	-	75d. purple	9·00	30
863	-	75d. red	7·50	30
864	-	1r. red	7·50	25
865	-	1r. purple	7·50	25
866	-	1r.50 red	7·50	25
867	123	2r. blue	11·50	25
868	-	2r. green	9·00	25
869	-	2r.50 blue	11·50	25
870	-	3r. green	75·00	75
871	-	3r. purple	30·00	30
872	-	5r. green	£140	7·50
873	-	5r. blue	19·00	40
874	123	10r. black and orange	38·00	2·30
875	123	10r. black and brown	15·00	75
876	123	20r. violet and brown	£375	38·00
877	123	20r. black and orange	75·00	3·00
878	123	30r. green and black	£900	38·00
879	123	30r. black and green	34·00	3·75
880	123	50r. red and blue	£110	19·00
881	123	50r. black and purple	38·00	7·50
882	123	100r. black and red	£275	38·00
883	123	200r. black and blue	£275	38·00

DESIGNS—HORIZ: 10d. Vereshk Railway Bridge, N. Iran; 20d. Granary, Ahwaz; 25d. Steam train on Karj Bridge; 50d. Ministry of Justice; 70d. School building. VERT: 35d. Museum; 75d. Side view of museum; 1 to 5r. Full-face portrait of Mohammed Riza Pahlavi.

124 Lion and Bull, Persepolis

1948. Fund to rebuild Avicenna's Tomb at Hamadan (1st issue).

899	124	50d.+25d. green	15	25
900	-	1r.+50d. red	30	40
901	-	2½r.+1¼r. blue	60	55
902	-	5r.+2½r. violet	1·30	1·10
903	-	10r.+5r. purple	2·30	1·50

DESIGNS—VERT: 1r. Persian Warrior, Persepolis. HORIZ: 2½r. Palace of Darius, Persepolis; 5r. Tomb of Cyrus, Pasargades; 10r. King Darius enthroned.

See also Nos. 909/13, 930/4, 939/43 and 1024/28.

126 National Flag

1949. Iran's War Effort.

904	126	25d. multicoloured	1·90	75
905	-	50d. violet	1·90	1·00
906	-	1r.50 red	9·00	1·20
907	-	2r.50 blue	11·50	1·50
908	-	5r. green	38·00	2·40

DESIGNS: 50d. Bandar Shahpur (port); 1r.50, Lorries on winding road; 2r.50, Vereshk Railway Bridge; 5r. Mohammed Riza Pahlavi and map of Iran.

127 King Ardashir II

128 King Ardashir I and Ahura Mazda

1949. Fund to rebuild Avicenna's Tomb (2nd issue).

909	127	50d.+25d. green	95	95
910	-	1r.+50d. red	95	95
911	-	2½r.+1¼r. blue	1·00	1·00
912	-	5r.+2½r. plum	1·50	1·50
913	128	10r.+5r. green	2·00	1·80

DESIGNS—VERT: 1r. King Narses. HORIZ: 2½r. King Shapur I and Emperor Valerian; 5r. Arch of Ctesiphon.

129 Mohammed Riza Pahlavi and Post and Customs House, Teheran

130 Old G.P.O., Teheran

131 Mohammed Riza Pahlavi

1949

914	-	5d. green and red	45	25
915	-	10d. brown and blue	45	25
916	-	20d. blue and violet	45	40
917	-	25d. blue and brown	45	25
918	-	50d. blue and green	90	25
919	-	75d. red and brown	1·70	40
920	-	1r. green and violet	2·30	25
921	-	1r.50 red and green	2·30	25
922	129	2r. brown and red	3·50	40
923	-	2r.50 blue	3·50	40
924	-	3r. orange and blue	4·50	15
925	-	5r. violet and red	7·25	15
926	130	10r. green and red	24·00	55
927	130	20r. red and black	£400	13·00
928	131	30r. blue and brown	43·00	6·75
929	131	50r. blue and red	43·00	6·75

DESIGNS—HORIZ: All show buildings. In the dinar values, portrait is to right of stamp, and in rial values, to left; 5d. Ramsar Hotel, Darband, Caspian Sea; 10d. Zayende River Bridge; 20d. Bank Melli Iran building; 25d. Old Royal Palace, Isfahan; 50d. Chaharbagh School, Isfahan; 75d. Railway Square; 1r. Justice Ministry; 1r.50, Shah Mosque, Teheran; 2r.50, Parliament Building; 3r. The Great Gate, Isfahan; 5r. Isfahan.

132 Tomb of Ali Abarquh

1949. Fund to rebuild Avicenna's Tomb (3rd issue).

930	132	50d.+25d. green	1·10	1·10
931	-	1r.+50d. brown	1·10	1·10
932	-	2½r.+1¼r. blue	1·10	1·10
933	-	5r.+2½r. red	2·30	2·30
934	-	10r.+5r. olive	2·30	2·30

DESIGNS—VERT: 1r. Jami Mosque, Isfahan. HORIZ: 2½r. Tomb tower, Hamadan; 5r. Jami Mosque, Ardistan; 10r. Seljuk coin.

134 Allegory

1950. 75th Anniv of U.P.U.

935		50d. lake	27·00	25·00
936	134	2r.50 blue	33·00	33·00

DESIGN—HORIZ: 50d. Hemispheres and doves.

135 Riza Shah Pahlavi and Mausoleum

1950. Interment of Riza Shah Pahlavi at Shah Abdul Azim.

937	135	50d. brown	13·00	5·25
938	135	2r. black	27·00	7·75

136 Tomb of Baba Afzal, Kashan

1950. Fund to Rebuild Avicenna's Tomb (4th issue).

939	136	50d.+25d. green	1·50	1·50
940	-	1r.+50d. blue	1·50	1·50
941	-	2½r.+1¼r. purple	1·50	1·50
942	-	5r.+2½r. red	2·30	2·30
943	-	10r.+5r. grey	2·30	2·30

DESIGNS—VERT: 1r. Gorgan vase; 2½r. Ghazan Tower, Bistam. HORIZ: 5r. Masjid-i Gawhar Shad Mosque, Meshed; 10r. Niche in wall of Mosque at Rezaieh.

139 Flag and Book

1950. 2nd Economic Conference of Islamic Countries.

944	139	1r.50+1r. multicoloured	22·00	9·25

140 Mohammed Riza Pahlavi in Military School Uniform

1950. Shah's 31st Birthday. Portraits of Shah at different ages, framed as T 140.

945	**140**	25d. black and red	5·75	1·20
946	-	50d. black and orange	5·75	1·20
947	-	75d. black and brown	26·00	6·00
948	-	1r. black and green	15·00	4·50
949	-	2r.50 black and blue	23·00	5·25
950	-	5r. black and red	38·00	7·50

PORTRAITS—Shah in uniform: 50d. Naval cadet; 75d. Boy Scout; 1r. Naval officer; 2r.50, Army officer-cadet; 5r. Army general.

142 Memorial

1950. 4th Anniv of Re-establishment of Control in Azerbaijan.

951		10d.+5d. brown	7·50	3·75
952	**142**	50d.+25d. purple	8·25	3·75
953	-	1r.+50d. purple	17·00	5·00
954	-	1r.50+75d. red and green	17·00	9·75
955	-	2r.50+1r.25 blue	18·00	12·00
956	-	3r.+1r.50 blue	24·00	9·75

DESIGNS—VERT: 10d. Shah and map; 1r.50, Map and battle scene; 2r.50, Shah and flags. HORIZ: 1r. Troops marching; 3r. Cavalry parade.

143 Shah and Queen Soraya

1951. Royal Wedding. T 143 and similar portraits.

959	**143**	5d. purple	5·75	1·10
960	**143**	25d. orange	5·75	1·10
961	**143**	50d. green	7·50	1·50
962	-	1r. brown	7·50	1·50
963	-	1r.50 red	7·50	1·70
964	-	2r.50 blue	7·50	1·70

DESIGNS: 1r. to 2r.50, As T **143** but portraits centrally placed.

144 Farabi

1951. Millenary of Death of Farabi (philosopher).

965	**144**	50d. red	7·50	1·10
966	**144**	2r.50 blue	1·70	1·10

145 Mohammed Riza Pahlavi

146 Mohammed Riza Pahlavi

1951

967	**145**	5d. red	40	25
968	**145**	10d. violet	40	25
969	**145**	20d. sepia	40	25
970	**145**	25d. blue	40	25
971	**145**	50d. green	1·10	25
972	**145**	50d. deep green	23·00	25
973	**145**	75d. red	1·10	25
974	**146**	1r. green	1·10	25
975	**146**	1r. turquoise	1·10	25
976	**146**	1r.50 red	1·70	25
977	**146**	2r. brown	1·70	25
978	**146**	2r.50 blue	1·70	25
979	**146**	3r. orange	5·25	25
980	**146**	5r. green	7·50	40
981	**146**	10r. olive	29·00	30
982	**146**	20r. brown	17·00	90
983	**146**	30r. blue	12·00	1·30
984	**146**	50r. black	31·00	1·80

147 Coran Gate, Shiraz

1951. 600th Death Anniv of Saadi (Muslih-ad-Din) (poet).

985	**147**	25d.+25d. green	3·00	1·70
986	-	50d.+50d. green	3·50	2·00
987	-	1r.50+50d. blue	11·50	6·75

DESIGNS—HORIZ: 50d. Tomb of Saadi. VERT: (as T **144**): 1r.50, Saadi.

150 Shah and Lockheed Super Constellation over Mosque

1952. Air.

988		50d. green	75	25
989	**150**	1r. red	90	25
990	**150**	2r. blue	75	25
991	**150**	3r. sepia	1·10	25
992	**150**	5r. lilac	1·10	25
993	**150**	10r. red	1·90	30
994	**150**	20r. violet	3·00	45
995	**150**	30r. olive	4·50	75
996	**150**	50r. brown	11·50	1·50
997	**150**	100r. sepia	70·00	3·75
998	**150**	200r. green	55·00	7·50

DESIGN: 50d. Shah and Lockheed Super Constellation airplane over Mt. Demavend.

151 Oil Well and Mosque

1953. Discovery of Oil at Qum. (a) Postage.

999	**151**	50d. bistre and green	1·50	25
1000	-	1r. bistre and mauve	1·50	30
1001	**151**	2r.50 bistre and blue	2·30	40
1002	-	5r. bistre and brown	3·75	1·50

(b) Air. With Lockheed Super Constellation airplane.

1003	**151**	3r. bistre and violet	11·50	5·75
1004	-	5r. bistre and brown	23·00	11·50
1005	**151**	10r. bistre and green	30·00	30·00
1006	-	20r. bistre and purple	60·00	60·00

DESIGN: 1r., 5r. (2), 20r. As Type **151** but horiz.

153 Power Station Boiler Plant

1953. 2nd Anniv of Nationalization of Oil Industry.

1007	**153**	50d. green	2·30	40
1008	-	1r. red	2·30	40
1009	-	2r.50 blue	4·50	75
1010	-	5r. orange	4·50	1·10
1011	-	10r. lilac	9·00	1·90

DESIGNS—HORIZ: 1r. Crude oil stabilizer; 5r. Pipe-lines; 10r. View of Abadan. VERT: 2r.50, Super fractionaters.

154 Family and U.N. Emblem

1953. United Nations Day.

1012	**154**	1r. green and turquoise	90	30
1013	**154**	2r.50 blue and light blue	1·70	60

155 Gymnast

1953. Ancient Persian Sports.

1014	**155**	1r. green	3·75	75
1015	-	2r.50 blue	11·50	1·50
1016	-	3r. grey	15·00	1·90
1017	-	5r. ochre	17·00	9·00
1018	-	10r. violet	45·00	3·75

DESIGNS—HORIZ: 2r.50, Archer; 3r. Mountaineers. VERT: 5r. Polo-player (Persian Sports Club Badge); 10r. Lion-hunter.

156 Iranian Roach

157 Machinery

1954. Nationalization of Fishing Industry.

1019	**156**	1r. multicoloured	3·75	75
1020	-	2r.50 multicoloured	23·00	3·00
1021	-	3r. red	11·50	3·75
1022	**157**	5r. green	11·50	4·50
1023	-	10r. multicoloured	38·00	9·00

DESIGNS—HORIZ: As Type **156**: 2r.50, Clupeid; 10r. Sturgeon. As Type **157**: 3r. Refrigeration machinery.

158 Hamadan

159 Avicenna

1954. Fund to Rebuild Avicenna's Tomb (5th issue).

1024	**158**	50d.+25d. green	1·50	1·50
1025	**159**	1r.+½r. brown	1·50	1·50
1026	-	2½r.+1¼r. blue	1·50	1·50
1027	-	5r.+2½r. red	2·30	2·30
1028	-	10r.+5r. olive	3·00	3·00

DESIGNS—VERT: As Type **159**: 2½r. Qabus tower, Gargan. HORIZ: As Type **158**: 5r. Old tomb of Avicenna; 10r. New tomb of Avicenna.

160 Shah in Military Uniform

1954

1029	**160**	5d. brown	20	15
1030	**160**	10d. violet	20	15
1031	**160**	25d. red	20	15
1032	**160**	50d. brown	20	15
1034	-	1r.50 red	45	15
1035	-	2r. brown	65	15
1037	-	3r. green	2·50	20
1038	-	5r. green	5·25	50
1039	-	10r. lilac	11·00	1·00
1040	-	20r. blue	13·50	3·75
1041	-	30r. brown	£150	4·25
1042	-	50r. orange	15·00	2·40
1043	-	100r. violet	£400	29·00
1044	-	200r. yellow	£120	11·00
1062	**160**	5d. violet	60	45
1063	**160**	10d. red	60	25
1064	**160**	25d. brown	60	25
1065	**160**	50d. red	60	25
1066	-	1r. green	60	25
1067	-	1r.50 brown	38·00	3·00
1068	-	2r. green	1·10	25
1069	-	2r.50 blue	1·70	30
1070	-	3r. brown	3·00	25
1071	-	5r. purple	5·25	25
1072	-	10r. blue	9·00	40
1073	-	20r. green	19·00	1·50
1074	-	30r. orange	95·00	15·00
1075	-	50r. brown	70·00	17·00

DESIGN: 1r. to 200r. Shah in naval uniform.

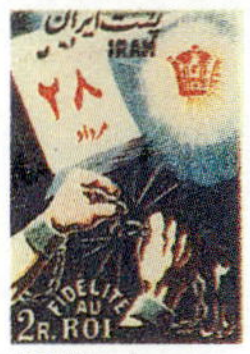

161 Hands breaking Chain

1954. 1st Anniv of Return of Shah. Mult.

1045		2r. Type **161**	3·75	75
1046		3r. Hand holding torch and Iranian flag	6·00	1·50
1047		5r. Man clasping Iranian flag	9·00	2·30

SIZES: 3r. (19½×27½ mm); 5r. (20½×28½ mm).

162 Nurse and Child

1954. U.N. Day.

1048	**162**	2r. orange and purple	2·75	55
1049	**162**	3r. orange and violet	2·00	1·20

163 Felling Trees

1954. 4th World Forestry Congress. Inscr "4eme congres mondial forestier".

1050	**163**	1r. green and brown	14·50	11·00
1051	-	2r.50 blue and green	18·00	13·00
1052	-	5r. brown and lavender	29·00	24·00
1053	-	10r. lake and blue	38·00	33·00

DESIGNS: 2r.50, Man carrying logs; 5r. Man operating circular saw; 10r. Ancient Persian galley.

164

1955. National Costumes.

1054	**164**	1r. multicoloured	4·50	1·50
1055	-	2r. multicoloured	6·00	1·90
1056	-	2r.50 multicoloured	7·50	2·30
1057	-	3r. multicoloured	6·75	2·75
1058	-	5r. multicoloured	15·00	5·00

DESIGNS—2r. Male costume; 2r.50, 3r., 5r. Female costumes.

165 Parliament Building

1955. 50th Anniv of Constitution.

1059		2r. green and purple	1·90	75
1060		3r. blue	7·50	1·50
1061	**165**	5r. orange and green	6·00	3·00

DESIGNS—HORIZ: 2r. Gateway of Parliament Building. VERT: 3r. Winged Statue.

167 U.N. Emblem and Hemispheres

1955. United Nations Day.

1077	**167**	1r. orange and red	1·10	40
1078	**167**	2r.50 light blue and blue	1·10	75

168 Wrestlers

1955. International Success of Iranian Wrestlers.

1079	**168**	2r.50 multicoloured	3·50	1·50

169 Hospital Buildings

1956. Opening of Nemazi Hospital, Shiraz. Multicoloured.

1080	-	50d. (24×33½ mm)	2·30	45
1081	**169**	1r. (36×24½ mm)	3·00	75
1082	-	2r.50 (24×33½ mm)	5·75	2·75
1083	-	5r. (36×23 mm)	12·00	5·25
1084	-	10r. (24×33½ mm)	23·00	7·50

DESIGNS: 50d. Hospital garden; 2r.50, Spear thrower; 5r. Koran gate, Shiraz; 10r. Poet Hafiz and his tomb.

170

1956. 10th Anniv of National Olympic Committee.

1085	**170**	5r. lilac	30·00	15·00

171 Tusi's Tomb, Maragheh

1956. 700th Death Anniv of Nasir ed-Din Tusi, 1201–74 (astronomer and scientist).

1086	**171**	1r. orange	2·75	75
1087	-	2r.50 blue (Astrolabe)	4·50	90
1088	-	5r. lilac and sepia (Portrait)	10·50	1·10

172 Reveille

1956. National Scout Jamboree.

1089	**172**	2r.50 blue & ultramarine	7·50	3·75
1090	-	5r. mauve and lilac	9·00	5·75

DESIGN: 5r. Shah in scout's uniform and badge.

173

1956. World Health Organization.

1091	**173**	6r. mauve	2·30	75

174 U.N. Emblem and Young People

1956. United Nations Day.

1092	**174**	1r. green	1·10	40
1093	-	2r.50 blue and green	1·90	75

DESIGN: 2r.50, U.N. emblem and scales of justice.

175 Telecommunications Centre, Teheran

1956. Centenary of Persian Telegraphs.

1094	**175**	2r.50 green and blue	6·00	2·30
1095	-	6r. mauve and pink	7·50	3·50

DESIGN: 6r. Telegraph poles and mosque.

176 Shah and Pres. Mirza

1956. Visit of President of Pakistan.

1096	**176**	1r. multicoloured	2·30	75

177 Mohammed Riza Pahlavi

1956

1097	**177**	5d. red and rose	55	1·00
1098	**177**	10d. violet and blue	55	1·00
1099	**177**	25d. brown and sepia	75	40
1100	**177**	50d. olive and sepia	75	15
1101	**177**	1r. green and brown	75	25
1102	**177**	1r.50 brown and mauve	75	25
1103	**177**	2r. red and mauve	75	25
1104	**177**	2r.50 blue & ultramarine	40	25
1105	**177**	3r. bistre and brown	1·10	25
1106	**177**	5r. red	1·10	25
1132	**177**	6r. blue and light blue	1·90	25
1133	**177**	10r. turquoise and green	3·00	30
1134	**177**	20r. olive and green	4·50	45
1135	**177**	30r. sepia and blue	7·50	2·30
1136	**177**	50r. brown and sepia	15·00	5·00
1137	**177**	100r. red & bright purple	£150	7·50
1138	**177**	200r. bistre and violet	£110	23·00

178 Mohammed Riza Pahlavi

1956

1107	**178**	6r. mauve and lilac	1·50	25
1108	**178**	10r. green and blue	3·75	25
1109	**178**	20r. blue and green	45·00	40
1110	**178**	30r. orange and red	55·00	7·50
1111	**178**	50r. sage and green	19·00	3·75
1112	**178**	100r. red and purple	£350	30·00
1113	**178**	200r. violet and purple	£150	34·00
1122	**178**	5d. plum and violet	30	2·00
1123	**178**	10d. mauve and purple	30	2·00
1124	**178**	25d. orange and red	60	40
1125	**178**	50d. green and grey	45	25
1126	**178**	1r. turquoise and green	45	25
1127	**178**	1r.50 purple and mauve	60	25
1128	**178**	2r. turquoise and blue	1·90	25
1129	**178**	2r.50 turquoise and blue	1·90	25
1130	**178**	3r. red and rose	1·90	25
1131	**178**	5r. violet and blue	1·90	25

179 Lord Baden-Powell

1957. Birth Centenary of Lord Baden-Powell (founder of Boy Scout movement).

1114	**179**	10r. brown and green	6·00	3·00

180 Steam Express Train and Mosque

1957. Inauguration of Teheran–Meshed Railway. Multicoloured.

1115	2r.50 Track and signal	7·50	1·10
1116	5r. Diesel train and map (horiz)	9·00	1·90
1117	10r. Type **180**	18·00	6·00

181 President Gronchi and Shah

1957. Visit of President of Italy.

1118	**181**	2r. grey, green and red	3·75	90
1119	-	6r. blue, green and red	5·25	1·50

DESIGN: 6r. Plaque and flags between ruins of Persepolis and Colosseum.

183 Queen Soraya and Ramsar Hotel

1957. 6th Medical Congress, Ramsar.

1120	**183**	2r. green and blue	3·00	75

184 Shah and King Faisal II of Iraq

1957. Visit of King of Iraq.

1121	**184**	2r. blue, red and green	3·75	75

185 Globes within Laurel Sprays

1957. Int Cartographical Conf, Teheran.

1140	**185**	10r. multicoloured	6·00	1·50

186 "Flight"

1957. Air. United Nations Day.

1141	**186**	10r. red and mauve	2·30	75
1142	**186**	20r. purple and violet	4·50	90

187 "The Weightlifter"

1957. International Weightlifting Championships.

1143	**187**	10r. blue, green and red	3·75	1·10

188 Radio Mast and Buildings

1958. 30th Anniv of Iranian Broadcasting Service.

1144	**188**	10r. sepia, buff and blue	3·75	1·50

189 Oil Derrick and "Bowl of Flames"

1958. 50th Anniv of Iranian Oil Industry.

1145	**189**	2r. brown, yellow and grey	3·00	75
1146	**189**	10r. brown, yellow & blue	6·00	1·50

190 Exhibition Emblem

1958. Brussels International Exhibition.

1147	**190**	2r.50 red	70	25
1148	**190**	6r. red	1·20	25

191 Steam Train on Viaduct

1958. Inaug of Teheran–Tabriz Railway.

1149	**191**	6r. lilac	15	40
1150	-	8r. green	20	10

DESIGN: 8r. Steam express train and route map.

192 Mohammed Riza Pahlavi

1958

1162	**192**	5d. violet	40	25
1163	**192**	5d. brown	40	25
1164	**192**	10d. red	40	25
1165	**192**	10d. green	40	25
1166	**192**	10d. turquoise	40	25
1167	**192**	25d. red	40	25
1168	**192**	25d. orange	40	25
1169	**192**	50d. blue	40	25
1170	**192**	50d. red	75	40
1171	**192**	1r. green	40	25
1172	**192**	1r. violet	1·10	25
1176	**192**	3r. brown	3·00	25
1177	**192**	6r. blue	3·00	25
1179	**192**	8r. purple	3·75	25

1180	192	8r. brown	3·75	25
1181	192	10r. black	3·75	40
1182	192	14r. blue	3·00	90
1183	192	14r. green	3·75	25
1185	192	20r. green	6·00	60
1186	192	30r. red	7·50	75
1187	192	30r. brown	6·75	40
1188	192	50r. purple	60·00	2·30
1189	192	50r. blue	11·50	75
1190	192	100r. orange	15·00	3·00
1191	192	100r. green	45·00	1·50
1192	192	200r. green	55·00	4·50
1193	192	200r. mauve	£225	9·00
1232	192	2r. brown	3·00	25

193 U.N. Emblem and Map of Persia

1958. United Nations Day.

1194	193	6r. blue and light blue	90	30
1195	193	10r. violet and green	1·50	40

194 Clasped Hands

1958. 10th Anniv of Declaration of Human Rights.

1196	194	6r. brown and chocolate	75	40
1197	194	8r. olive and green	1·10	45

195 Rudagi playing Lyre

1958. 1100th Birth Anniv of Rudagi (poet and musician).

1198	195	2r.50 blue	4·50	90
1199	-	5r. violet	7·50	1·50
1200	195	10r. sepia	19·00	3·00

DESIGN: 5r. Rudagi meditating.

196

1959. Red Cross Commemoration.

1201	196	1r. multicoloured	1·20	60
1202	196	6r. multicoloured	1·80	75

197 Wrestlers

1959. World Wrestling Championships.

1203	197	6r. multicoloured	9·00	2·30

198 Torch of Freedom

1959. United Nations Day.

1204	198	6r. red, brown and bistre	1·10	40

199 Shah and President Khan

1959. Visit of President of Pakistan.

1205	199	6r. multicoloured	5·75	75

200 I.L.O. Emblem

1959. 40th Anniv of I.L.O.

1206	200	1r. blue and light blue	90	40
1207	200	5r. brown and light brown	1·40	55

201 Pahlavi Foundation Bridge, Khorramshahr

1960. Opening of Pahlavi Foundation Bridge, Khorramshahr.

1208	201	1r. blue and brown	1·10	25
1209	-	5r. green and blue	1·90	40

DESIGN: 5r. Close-up view of bridge.

202 "Uprooted Tree and Columns"

1960. World Refugee Year.

1210	202	1r. blue	45	25
1211	-	6r. black and green	60	25

DESIGN: 6r. "Uprooted tree" and columns.

203 Insecticide Sprayer

1960. Anti-Malaria Campaign.

1212		1r. black & red on yellow	1·10	25
1213	203	2r. blue, black & light bl	1·50	40
1214	-	3r. black and red on green	3·00	75

DESIGNS (30×37 mm): 1r., 3r. Different views of mosquito crossed out in red.

204 Polo Player

1960. "Olympic Games Week".

1215	204	1r. purple	85	40
1216	-	6r. violet and blue	2·10	75

DESIGN: 6r. Archer.

205 Shah and King Hussein

1960. Visit of King of Jordan.

1217	205	6r. multicoloured	5·00	75

206 Scout Emblem within Flower

1960. 3rd National Scout Jamboree.

1218	206	1r. green	45	25
1219	-	6r. ochre, sepia and blue	1·00	55

DESIGN: 6r. Scout camp, Persepolis.

207 Shah and Queen Farah

1960. Royal Wedding.

1220	207	1r. green	2·75	40
1221	207	5r. blue	5·00	75

208 UN Emblem

1960. 15th Anniv of U.N.O.

1222	208	6r. sepia, blue and bistre	75	25

209 Shah and Queen Elizabeth II

1961. Visit of Queen Elizabeth II.

1223	209	1r. brown	1·50	40
1224	209	6r. blue	2·30	75

210 Girl playing Pan-pipes

1961. International Music Congress, Teheran.

1225	210	1r. stone and brown	60	40
1226	-	6r. slate	1·40	60

DESIGN—(24×39½ mm): 6r. Safiaddin Anmavi (musician).

211 Royal Family

1961. Birth of Crown Prince.

1227	211	1r. purple	1·90	75
1228	211	6r. blue	5·75	2·30

212 U.N. Emblem and Birds

1961. United Nations Day.

1236	212	2r. red and blue	75	25
1237	212	6r. violet and blue	90	30

213 Tree-planting

1962. Afforestation Week.

1238	213	2r. blue, cream and green	60	25
1239	213	6r. green, blue & ultram	75	30

214 Worker

1962. Workers' Day.

1240	214	2r. multicoloured	60	25
1241	214	6r. multicoloured	90	30

215 Family on Map

1962. Social Insurance.

1242	215	2r. violet, black & yellow	60	25
1243	215	6r. blue, black & lt blue	90	30

216 Sugar Plantation

1962. Sugar Cane Production.

1244	216	2r. green, blue & ultram	60	25
1245	216	6r. blue, cream & ultram	1·00	40

217 Karaj Dam

1962. Inauguration of Karaj Dam.

1246	217	2r. green and brown	1·10	25
1247	217	6r. blue and ultramarine	1·50	40

218 Sefid Rud Dam

1962. Inauguration of Sefid Rud Dam.

1248	**218**	2r. buff, blue and myrtle	1·20	25
1249	-	6r. black, blue and brown	1·50	55

DESIGN: 6r. Distant view of dam.

219 U.N. Emblem

1962. 15th Anniv of UNESCO.

1250	**219**	2r. black, green and red	75	25
1251	**219**	6r. blue, green and red	1·50	40

220 Arrow piercing Mosquito

1962. Malaria Eradication.

1252	**220**	2r. black and green	40	25
1253	-	6r. blue and red	75	25
1254	-	10r. ultramarine and blue	1·50	30

DESIGNS—VERT (29½×34½ mm): 6r. Mosquito and insecticide-sprayer. HORIZ (As Type **220**): 10r. Globe and campaign emblem.

221 Mohammed Riza Pahlavi

222 Shah and Palace of Darius, Persepolis

1962

1255a	**221**	5d. green	90	25
1256	**221**	10d. brown	1·00	55
1257	**221**	25d. blue	1·00	40
1265a	**222**	11r. green	1·40	25
1266a	**222**	14r. violet	1·90	25
1336	**221**	50d. turquoise	75	25
1337	**221**	1r. orange	75	25
1338	**221**	2r. violet	55	25
1339	**221**	5r. brown	3·00	55
1340	**222**	6r. blue	6·00	1·00
1341	**222**	8r. green	3·50	25
1342	**222**	10r. blue	3·00	25
1345	**222**	20r. brown	5·00	1·90
1346	**222**	50r. red	6·00	1·90

223 Oil Pipelines

1962. 2nd Petroleum Symposium of Economic Commission for Asia and the Far East.

1269	**223**	6r. brown and blue	1·20	25
1270	**223**	14r. brown and grey	2·30	45

224 Hippocrates and Avicenna

1962. W.H.O. Medical Congress, Teheran.

1271	**224**	2r. blue, brown and cream	1·90	40
1272	**224**	6r. blue, sage and green	2·30	55

225 New Houses

1962. United Nations Day.

1273	**225**	6r. blue and indigo	1·20	25
1274	-	14r. green and blue	1·70	40

DESIGN—HORIZ: 14r. Laying foundation stone.

226 "Bouquet for the Crown Prince"

1962. Crown Prince's Birthday.

1275	**226**	6r. blue	3·75	75
1276	**226**	14r. green	7·50	1·50

227 Persian Gulf Map

1962. Persian Gulf Seminar.

1277	**227**	6r. blue, pink & pale blue	1·00	25
1278	**227**	14r. blue, flesh and pink	1·50	40

228 Hilton Hotel, Teheran

1963. Opening of Royal Teheran Hilton Hotel.

1279	**228**	6r. blue	2·30	30
1280	**228**	14r. brown	3·75	45

229 Refugees

1963. Earthquake Relief Fund.

1281	**229**	14r.+6r. blue, brn & grn	1·70	75

230 Mohammed Riza Shah Dam

1963. Inaug of Mohammed Riza Shah Dam.

1282	**230**	6r. multicoloured	2·75	30
1283	**230**	14r. multicoloured	4·50	60

231 Worker with Pickaxe

1963. Workers' Day.

1283a	**231**	2r. black and yellow	85	25
1283b	**231**	6r. black and blue	1·50	30

232 Bird and Globe

1963. Freedom from Hunger.

1284	**232**	2r. ultramarine, bl & bis	1·10	25
1285	-	6r. black, bistre and blue	1·70	30
1286	-	14r. bistre and green	2·75	70

DESIGNS: 6r. Globe and ears of wheat (stylized); 14r. Globe encircled by scroll, and campaign emblem.

233 Shah and Scroll

1963. Agrarian Reform Act.

1287	**233**	6r. green and blue	3·75	1·10
1288	**233**	14r. green and yellow	5·75	1·90

234 Shah and King Frederick

1963. Visit of King of Denmark.

1289	**234**	6r. blue and indigo	2·75	55
1290	**234**	14r. brown and sepia	3·75	1·00

235 Flags of Iran and India; Ibn Sina Mosque, Teheran, and Taj Mahal, India

1963. Visit of President Radhakrishnan of India.

1291	**235**	6r. multicoloured	2·75	40
1292	**235**	14r. multicoloured	3·75	75

236 Shahnaz Dam

1963. Inauguration of Shahnaz Dam.

1293	**236**	6r. ultramarine, bl & grn	2·75	40
1294	**236**	14r. green, blue and buff	2·75	60

237 Centenary Emblem

1963. Red Cross Centenary.

1295	**237**	6r. multicoloured	2·75	40
1296	**237**	14r. grey, red and buff	3·50	60

238 Shah and Queen Juliana

1963. Visit of Queen of the Netherlands.

1304	**238**	6r. blue and ultramarine	3·00	40
1305	**238**	14r. green and black	4·50	60

240 Students in Class

1963. Formation of Literacy Teaching Corps.

1306	**240**	6r. multicoloured	3·50	55
1307	**240**	14r. multicoloured	5·00	55

241 Pres. De Gaulle and View of Teheran

1963. Visit of President of France.

1308	**241**	6r. ultramarine and blue	3·50	55
1309	**241**	14r. brown and ochre	4·25	60

242 Plant, Route Map and Emblem

1963. Opening of Chemical Fertilizer Plant, Shiraz.

1310	**242**	6r. black, yellow and red	3·50	55
1311	-	14r. black, blue & yellow	4·25	1·00

DESIGN—HORIZ: 14r. Fertilizer plant and emblem.

243 Pres. Lubke and Shah Mosque, Isfahan

1963. Visit of President of German Federal Republic.

1312	**243**	6r. blue and violet	3·50	55
1313	**243**	14r. brown and grey	4·25	1·00

244 U.N. Emblem

1963. United Nations Day.

1314	**244**	8r. multicoloured	1·90	55

245 Aircraft crossing U.N. Emblem

1963. Iranian Air Force in Congo.

1315	**245**	6r. multicoloured	1·90	55

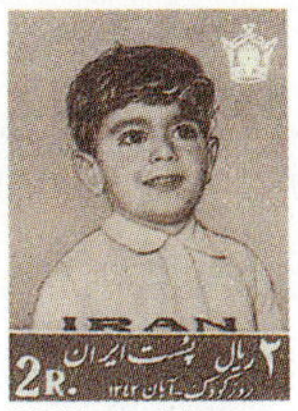

246 Crown Prince Riza

1963. Children's Day.

1316	**246**	2r. brown	1·40	25
1317	**246**	6r. blue	2·40	55

247 Chairman Brezhnev

1963. Visit of Chairman of Soviet Presidium.

1318	**247**	5r. multicoloured	2·40	30
1319	**247**	11r. multicoloured	4·50	60

248 Ataturk's Mausoleum

1963. 25th Death Anniv of Kemal Ataturk.

1320	**248**	4r. brown, grey and green	2·40	25
1321	-	5r. black, red and yellow	2·40	25

DESIGN: 5r. Kemal Ataturk.

249 Scales of Justice and Globe

1963. 15th Anniv of Declaration of Human Rights.

1322	**249**	6r. black, blue and green	1·90	30
1323	**249**	14r. black, cream & brn	2·75	40

250 Mother and Child

1963. Mothers Day.

1324	**250**	2r. multicoloured	1·70	25
1325	**250**	4r. multicoloured	2·40	55

251 Cogwheel and Map

1963. Industrial Development.

1326	**251**	8r. blue, cream & turq	3·00	40

252 Hand with Document (Profit- sharing)

1964. Six-Point Reform Law.

1327	**252**	2r. brown, violet and blue	3·00	10
1328	-	4r. brown and grey	3·00	10
1329	-	6r. multicoloured	3·00	15
1330	-	8r. multicoloured	3·00	1·00
1331	-	10r. red, green & dp grn	3·00	1·20
1332	-	12r. brown and red	6·50	1·50

DESIGNS: 4r. Factory and documents on scales (Sale of Shares to Workers); 6r. Worker on Globe (Education Corps); 8r. Tractor (Land reform); 10r. Trees (Nationalization of forests); 12r. Silhouettes within gateway (Votes for Women).

253 U.N. Emblem

1964. 20th Economic Commission for Asia and the Far East Session, Teheran.

1347	**253**	14r. black and green	2·30	40

254 Blossom

1964. New Year Greetings.

1348	**254**	50d. orange, sepia & grn	40	25
1349	**254**	1r. orange, black and blue	40	25

255 Weather Vane

1964. World Meteorological Day.

1350	**255**	6r. violet and blue	1·10	25

256 "Tourism"

1964. 1st Anniv of Iranian Tourist Organization (INTO).

1351	**256**	6r. green, violet and black	2·00	40
1352	-	11r. orange, brown & blk	2·75	55

DESIGN: 11r. Winged beasts, column and INTO emblem.

257 Rudagi (blind poet)

1964. Opening of Blind Institute.

1353	**257**	6r. blue	1·90	40
1354	**257**	8r. brown	3·50	55

258 Sculptured Head

1964. "7000 Years of Persian Art" Exhibition.

1355	**258**	2r. blue and grey	3·50	1·00
1356	-	4r. ultramarine and blue	7·25	1·40
1357	-	6r. yellow and brown	7·25	1·40
1358	-	10r. green and yellow	9·00	1·40

DESIGNS—HORIZ: 4r. Sumerian war chariot on map. VERT: 6r. Golden cup with lion decorations; 10r. Sculptured head of man.

259 Shah and Emperor Haile Selassie

1964. Visit of Emperor of Ethiopia.

1359	**259**	6r. ultramarine and blue	2·75	40

260 Congress Emblem

1964. 2nd Iranian Dental Assn Congress.

1360	**260**	2r. red, deep blue & blue	1·10	30
1361	-	4r. multicoloured	1·50	40

DESIGN: 4r. "2 IDA" in symbolic form.

261 Bark Beetle under Lens

1964. Inauguration of Plant Parasites and Diseases Research Institute.

1362		2r. brown, red and buff	2·30	25
1363	**261**	6r. indigo, brown & blue	3·00	30

DESIGN: 2r. Microscope, plants and research centre.

262 Plaque

1964. Mehregan Festival.

1364	**262**	8r. red and yellow	1·90	75

263 Eleanor Roosevelt

1964. Eleanor Roosevelt Commemoration.

1365	**263**	10r. blue and violet	1·90	75

264 Clasped Hands and U.N. Emblem

1964. United Nations Day.

1366	**264**	6r. multicoloured	1·10	25
1367	-	14r. red, blue and orange	1·70	40

DESIGN: 14r. U.N. and "Bird" emblems.

265 Gymnast

1964. Olympic Games, Tokyo.

1368	**265**	4r. sepia, turquoise & brn	1·20	40
1369	-	6r. red and blue	1·70	40

DESIGN—Diamond (39×39 mm): 6r. Polo.

266 Crown Prince Riza

1964. Children's Day.

1370	**266**	1r. green and brown	1·10	30
1371	**266**	2r. red and blue	1·90	45
1372	**266**	6r. blue and red	3·00	60

267 Conference and U.N. Emblems

1964. Petro-Chemical Conf and Gas Seminar.

1373	**267**	6r. multicoloured	75	40
1374	**267**	8r. multicoloured	1·50	40

268 Shah and King Baudouin

1964. Visit of King of Belgium.

1375	**268**	6r. black, orange & yell	1·50	40
1376	**268**	8r. black, orange & green	2·30	75

269 Rhazes

1964. 1100th Birth Anniv of Rhazes (Zakariya Ar-Razi, alchemist).

1377	**269**	2r. multicoloured	1·50	40
1378	**269**	6r. multicoloured	2·30	45

270 Shah and King Olav

1965. Visit of King of Norway.

1379	**270**	2r. mauve and purple	1·90	40
1380	**270**	4r. green and olive	2·75	55

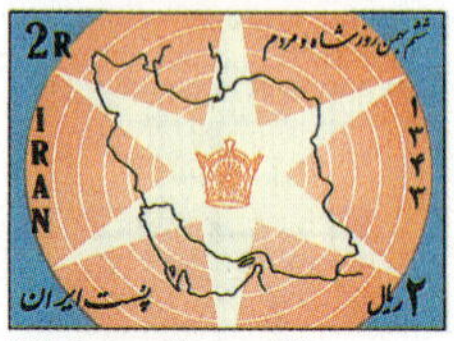

271 Crown, Map and Star

1965. Six-Point Reform Law.

1381	**271**	2r. orange, black and blue	1·10	25

272 Woman and U.N. Emblem

1965. 18th Session of United Nations Commission on Status of Women, Teheran.

1382	**272**	6r. black, blue & lt blue	60	25
1383	**272**	8r. blue, red and light red	90	25

273 Festival Plant

1965. New Year Festival.

1384	**273**	50d. multicoloured	40	25
1385	**273**	1r. multicoloured	40	25

274 Pres. Bourguiba and Minarets

1965. Visit of President of Tunisia.

1386	**274**	4r. multicoloured	1·00	40

275 Map of Oil Pipelines

1965. 14th Anniv of Nationalization of Oil Industry.

1387		6r. multicoloured	1·50	25
1388	**275**	14r. multicoloured	2·30	55

276 I.T.U. Emblem and Symbols

1965. Centenary of I.T.U.

1389	**276**	14r. red and grey	1·20	40

277 I.C.Y. Emblem

1965. International Co-operation Year.

1390	**277**	10r. green and blue	2·30	40

278 Boeing 727-100 and Airline Emblem

1965. Inauguration of Jet Services by Iranian National Airlines.

1391	**278**	14r. multicoloured	2·30	40

279 "Co-operation" (Hands holding Book)

1965. 1st Anniv of Regional Development Co-operation Plan. Multicoloured.

1392	2r. Type **279**	40	25
1393	4r. Globe and flags of Turkey, Iran and Pakistan (40½×24½ mm)	70	25

280 Moot Emblem and Arabesque Pattern

1965. Middle East Rover (Scout) Moot.

1394	**280**	2r. multicoloured	70	25

281 Gateway of Parliament Building

1965. 60th Anniv of Iranian Constitution.

1397	**281**	2r. brown and mauve	40	25

282 Congress Emblem

1965. Iranian Dental Congress.

1398	**282**	6r. blue, mauve and silver	60	25

283 Teacher and Class

1965. World Eradication of Illiteracy Congress, Teheran. Multicoloured.

1399	2r. Type **283**	40	25
1400	5r. Globe showing alphabets (25×30 mm)	40	25
1401	6r. UNESCO emblem and symbols (diamond, 36×36 mm)	75	30
1402	8r. Various scripts (35×23 mm)	75	25
1403	14r. Shah and multi-lingual inscriptions (41×52 mm)	1·50	30

284 Shah Riza Pahlavi

1965. 25th Anniv (actually 24th) of Shah's Accession.

1404	**284**	1r. red and grey	1·50	25
1405	**284**	2r. red and yellow	1·50	40

285 Congress Emblem

1965. 14th Medical Congress.

1406	**285**	5r. ultramarine, bl & gold	55	25

286 President Jonas

1965. Visit of President of Austria.

1407	**286**	6r. blue and brown	1·10	25

287 Plaque

1965. Mehregan Festival.

1408	**287**	4r. multicoloured	60	25

See also No. 1464.

289 U.N. Emblem and "Flowers"

1965. United Nations Day.

1409	**289**	5r. multicoloured	55	25

290 Emblem and "Arches"

1965. Iranian Industrial Exhibition, Teheran.

1410	**290**	3r. multicoloured	55	25

291 Crown Prince Riza

1965. Children's Day.

1411	**291**	2r. chocolate, brn & gold	1·10	45

292 "Weightlifting"

1965. World Weightlifting Championships, Teheran.

1412	**292**	10r. mauve, violet & blue	60	25

293 Open Book

1965. Book Week.

1416	**293**	8r. multicoloured	60	25

294 Shah and King Faisal

1965. Visit of King of Saudi Arabia.

1417	**294**	4r. brown and bistre	1·50	40

295 Scales of Justice

1965. Human Rights Day.

1418	**295**	14r. multicoloured	15	25

296 Tractor (Land Reform)

1966. 3rd Anniv of Shah's White Revolution (Parliamentary Assent to Shah's Reform Plan).

1419	**296**	1r. brown and yellow	25	25
1420	-	2r. green and light green	25	25
1421	-	3r. brown and silver	25	25
1422	-	4r. violet and light violet	40	25
1423	-	5r. lake and red	55	25
1424	-	6r. brown and bistre	75	25
1425	-	7r. ultramarine and blue	75	25
1426	-	8r. ultramarine and blue	1·10	25
1427	-	9r. brown & light brown	1·10	25

DESIGNS: 2r. Trees (Nationalization of Forests); 3r. Cog-wheel emblem (Sale of shares to workers); 4r. Cylinders (Profit-sharing); 5r. Parliament gateway (Votes for Women); 6r. Blackboard and pupils (Education Corps); 7r. Staff of Aesculapius (Medical Corps); 8r. Scales (Justice); 9r. Girders (Construction Corps).

297 Mohammed Riza Pahlavi

1966

1428	**297**	5d. green	25	25
1429	**297**	10d. brown	25	25
1430	**297**	25d. blue	25	25
1431	**297**	50d. turquoise	55	25
1432	**297**	1r. orange	55	25
1433	**297**	2r. violet	40	25
1434	**297**	4r. brown	5·75	75
1435	**297**	5r. sepia	1·00	25
1436	**298**	6r. blue	90	25
1437	**298**	8r. green	90	25
1438	**298**	10r. blue	1·50	25
1439	**298**	11r. green	1·50	25
1440	**298**	14r. violet	2·00	25
1441	**298**	20r. brown	11·50	55
1442	**298**	50r. red	5·00	1·50
1443	**298**	100r. blue	15·00	2·40
1444	**298**	200r. brown	12·00	4·25

299 Nurse taking Oath

1966. Nurses' Day.
1445 **299** 5r. blue and deep blue 55 40
1446 **299** 5r. mauve and red 55 40

300 Narcissus

1966. New Year Festival.
1447 **300** 50d. multicoloured 25 25
1448 **300** 1r. multicoloured 1·50 40
See also Nos. 1530/3.

301 Oil Rigs

1966. Inauguration of Six New Oil Companies in Persian Gulf.
1449 **301** 14r. black, purple & blue 55 15

302 Radar Aerial

1966. C.E.N.T.O. (Iran, Pakistan and Turkey) Telecommunications Organization.
1450 **302** 2r. green 25 25
1451 - 4r. orange and blue 25 25
1452 - 6r. grey and purple 30 25
1453 - 8r. indigo and blue 40 30
1454 - 10r. brown and ochre 55 30
DESIGNS—VERT: 4r. Aerial and radio "waves"; 6r. "CENTO" and emblem; 8r. Emblem and "waves"; 10r. Bowl aerial and "waves".

303 W.H.O. Building

1966. Inaug of W.H.O. Headquarters, Geneva.
1455 **303** 10r. black, blue & yellow 55 30

304 Globe Emblem and Motto

1966. Conference of International Women's Council, Teheran.
1456 **304** 6r. multicoloured 40 30
1457 **304** 8r. multicoloured 55 30

305 UNESCO Emblem

1966. Air. 20th Anniv of UNESCO.
1458 **305** 14r. multicoloured 90 25

306 Ruins of Persepolis, Map and Globe

1966. Int Iranology Congress, Teheran.
1459 **306** 14r. multicoloured 90 40

307 Medical Emblem

1966. 15th Medical Congress, Teheran.
1460 **307** 4r. gold, blue & ultram 40 30

308 Parliament Gateway

1966. 55th Interparliamentary Union Conference, Teheran.
1461 **308** 6r. green, blue and red 25 25
1462 - 8r. green, blue and mauve 40 25
DESIGN: 8r. Senate Building.

309 President Sunay

1966. Visit of President of Turkey.
1463 **309** 6r. brown and violet 40 25

1966. Mehregan Festival. Plaque design similar to T 287 but vert (30×40 mm).
1464 6r. brown and bistre 45 30

310 Farmers

1966. Rural Courts of Justice.
1465 **310** 5r. brown and bistre 1·10 55

311 U.N. Emblem

1966. U.N. Day and 21st Anniv of U.N.O.
1466 **311** 6r. brown and black 40 30

312 Crown Prince

1966. Children's Day.
1467 **312** 1r. blue 60 55
1468 **312** 2r. violet 1·00 55

313 I.W.O. Emblem

1966. Iranian Women's Organization.
1469 **313** 5r. blue, black and gold 30 25

314 Strip of Film

1966. 1st Children's Film Festival, Teheran.
1470 **314** 4r. black, purple & violet 40 25

315 Counting on the Fingers

1966. National Census.
1471 **315** 6r. brown and grey 30 25

316 Cover of Book

1966. Book Week.
1472 **316** 8r. brown, ochre and blue 40 25

317 Riza Shah Pahlavi

1966. Riza Shah Pahlavi Commemoration.
1473 **317** 1r. brown 1·90 40
1474 **317** 1r. blue 1·90 40
1475 - 2r. blue 1·90 40
1476 - 2r. green 1·90 40
Nos. 1475/6 show Riza Shah Pahlavi bare-headed.

318 E.R.O.P.A. Emblem and Map

1966. 4th General Assembly of Public Administrators Organization (E.R.O.P.A.).
1477 **318** 8r. brown and green 45 30

319 Shah with Farmers

1967. 5th Anniv of Land Reform Laws.
1485 **319** 6r. brown, yellow & bis 90 25

320 Torch and Stars

1967. 4th Anniv of Shah's White Revolution.
1486 **320** 2r. multicoloured 1·00 55
1487 - 6r. multicoloured 1·70 55
DESIGN: 6r. Shah acknowledging greetings.

321 Golden "Bull"

1967. Museum Week. Multicoloured.
1488 3r. Type **321** 75 25
1489 5r. Golden "leopard" 1·00 40
1490 8r. Capital with rams' heads 1·30 55

322 Planting a Tree

1967. Tree-planting Week.
1491 **322** 8r. green and brown 30 25

323 Goldfish

1967. New Year Festival.
1492 **323** 1r. blue, red and brown 25 25
1493 - 8r. ultramarine, bl & red 1·10 30
DESIGN—35×27 mm: 8r. Barn swallows.

324 Microscope, Horses and Emblem

1967. 2nd Veterinary Congress.
1494 **324** 5r. red, black and grey 40 25

325 Pres. Arif and Mosques

1967. Visit of President of Iraq.
1495 **325** 6r. green and blue 40 30

326 U.N. Emblem and Fireworks

1967. U.N. Stamp Day.
1496 **326** 5r. multicoloured 40 25

327 Map showing Pipeline Routes

1967. Nationalization of Oil Industry.
1497 **327** 6r. multicoloured 1·00 25

328 Fencing

1967. Int Youth Fencing Championships, Teheran.
1498 **328** 5r. yellow and violet 55 25

329 Shah and King Bhumibol

1967. Visit of King of Thailand.
1499 **329** 6r. brown and light brown 1·10 25

330 Emblem, Old and Young Couples

1967. 15th Anniv of Social Insurance Scheme.
1500 **330** 5r. blue and bistre 30 25

331 Skiing

1967. Olympic Committee Meeting, Teheran.
1501 **331** 3r. brown and black 40 25
1502 - 6r. multicoloured 60 30
1503 - 8r. brown and blue 90 40
DESIGNS: 6r. Olympic "shield"; 8r. Wrestling.

332 "LIONS" and Lions Head

1967. 50th Anniv of Lions International. Mult.
1504 3r. Type **332** 55 25
1505 7r. Lions emblem (36×42 mm) 1·00 25

333 President Stoica

1967. Visit of President of Rumania.
1506 **333** 6r. blue and orange 30 25

334 I.T.Y. Emblem

1967. International Tourist Year.
1507 **334** 3r. blue and red 30 25

335 Iranian Pavilion

1967. World Fair, Montreal.
1508 **335** 4r. red, gold and brown 40 25
1509 **335** 10r. brown, gold and red 55 25

336 First Persian Stamp

1967. Stamp Centenary.
1510 **336** 6r. purple, blue & lt blue 55 25
1511 **336** 8r. purple, myrtle & green 60 25

337 Globe and Schoolchildren

1967. Campaign Against Illiteracy.
1512 **337** 3r. violet and blue 25 25
1513 **337** 5r. brown and yellow 30 25

338 "Musician"

1967. International Musical Education in Oriental Countries Conference, Teheran.
1514 **338** 14r. purple and brown 75 55

339 "Helping Hand"

1967. 1st "S.O.S." Children's Village in Iran.
1515 **339** 8r. brown and yellow 3·00 2·30

340 Winged Ram

1967. 1st Shiraz Arts Festival, Persepolis.
1516 **340** 8r. brown and bistre 60 25

341 U.N. Emblem

1967. United Nations Day.
1517 **341** 6r. blue and bistre 40 25

342 Shah Mohammed Riza Pahlavi and Empress Farah

1967. Coronation of Shah and Empress Farah.
1518 **342** 2r. brown, blue and silver 85 25
1519 **342** 10r. violet, blue and silver 90 55
1520 **342** 14r. multicoloured 2·30 75

343 Crown Prince Riza

1967. Children's Day.
1521 **343** 2r. violet and silver 90 25
1522 **343** 8r. brown and silver 1·20 25

344 Pres. G. Traikov

1967. Visit of President of Bulgaria.
1523 **344** 10r. brown and violet 40 25

345 Scout Emblem and Neckerchiefs

1967. Boy Scouts Co-operation Week.
1524 **345** 8r. brown and green 75 30

346 "Co-operation" (linked hands)

1967. Co-operation Year.
1525 **346** 6r. multicoloured 30 25

347 Shaikh Sabah

1968. Visit of Shaikh of Kuwait.
1526 **347** 10r. green and blue 40 25

348 Shah and Text of Reform Plan

1968. 5th Anniv of Shah's White Revolution.
1527 **348** 2r. green, sepia and flesh 40 25
1528 **348** 8r. violet, green and blue 1·20 25
1529 **348** 14r. brown, blue & mve 1·50 40

1968. New Year Festival. As T 300. Mult.
1530 1r. Almond blossom 25 25
1531 2r. Red tulips 25 25
1532 2r. Yellow tulips 25 25
1533 6r. Festival dancer 75 25

349 Oil Technician and Rig

1968. National Oil Industry.
1534 **349** 14r. black, yellow & green 60 25

350 W.H.O. Emblem

1968. 20th Anniv of W.H.O.
1535 **350** 14r. orange, blue & pur 60 25

351 Ancient Chariot (sculpture)

1968. 5th World Congress of Persian Archaeology and Art, Teheran.
1536 **351** 8r. multicoloured 40 25

352 Shah and King Hassan

1968. Visit of King of Morocco.
1537 **352** 6r. violet and flesh 1·10 25

353 Human Rights Emblem

1968. Human Rights Conference, Teheran.
1538 **353** 8r. red and green 25 25
1539 - 14r. ultramarine and blue 55 25

DESIGN: 14r. As Type **353**, but rearranged, and inscr "INTERNATIONAL CONFERENCE ON HUMAN RIGHTS—TEHERAN 1968".

354 Footballer

1968. Asian Football Cup Finals, Teheran.
1540 **354** 8r. multicoloured 25 25
1541 **354** 10r. multicoloured 55 25

355 Oil Refinery

1968. Inauguration of Teheran Oil Refinery.
1542 **355** 14r. multicoloured 75 25

356 Empress Farah in Guides' Uniform

1968. Iranian Girl Guides "Great Camp".
1543 **356** 4r. blue and purple 1·20 25
1544 **356** 6r. brown and red 2·00 55

357 Mosquito Emblem

1968. 8th International Tropical Medicine and Malaria Congresses, Teheran.
1545 **357** 6r. purple and black 40 25
1546 **357** 14r. green and purple 55 25

358 Allegory of Literacy

1968. World Illiteracy Eradication Campaign Day.
1547 **358** 6r. blue, brown and lilac 30 25
1548 **358** 14r. green, brown & yell 45 25

359 "Horseman" and "Flower"

1968. 2nd Shiraz Arts Festival, Persepolis.
1549 **359** 14r. multicoloured 60 25

360 Police Emblem on Map

1968. Police Day.
1550 **360** 14r. multicoloured 1·00 25

361 Interpol Emblem

1968. 37th Interpol General Assembly.
1551 **361** 10r. purple, black & blue 55 25

362 U.N. Emblem and Dove

1968. United Nations Day.
1552 **362** 14r. ultramarine and blue 75 25

363 Empress Farah

1968. 1st Anniv of Coronation. Mult.
1553 6r. Type **363** 5·25 2·75
1554 8r. Shah Mohammed Riza Pahlavi 6·00 3·75
1555 10r. Family group 7·50 4·50

364 Imperial Crown and Bulls' Heads Capital (festival emblem)

1968. National Festival of Art and Culture, Teheran.
1556 **364** 14r. multicoloured 75 25

365 "Landscape"

1968. Children's Day. Children's Paintings. Multicoloured.
1557 2r. Type **365** 25 25
1558 3r. "Boat and House" (35×29 mm) 25 25
1559 5r. "Flowers" (35×29 mm) 30 25

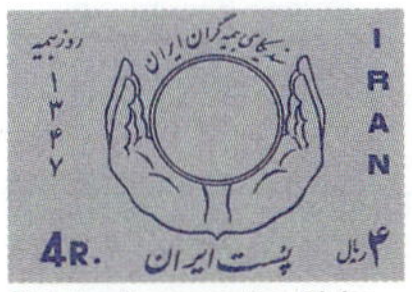

366 Hands supporting Globe

1968. Insurance Day.
1560 **366** 4r. blue and grey 25 25
1561 - 5r. multicoloured 25 25
1562 - 8r. multicoloured 25 25
1563 - 10r. multicoloured 45 25

DESIGNS: 5r. Factory aflame ("Fire risk"); 8r. Urban workers ("Life"); 10r. Insurance Institute emblem and transport ("Travel insurance").

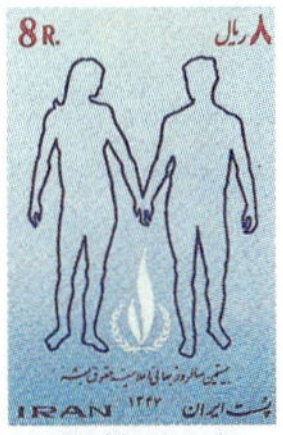

367 Emblem and Human Figures

1968. 20th Anniv of Declaration of Human Rights.
1564 **367** 8r. purple, ultram & bl 30 25

368 Justice, Construction Corps and Medical Corps

1969. 6th Anniv of Shah's White Revolution. Each green, brown and lilac.
1565 2r. Type **368** 1·00 25
1566 4r. Working conditions, civil engineering and irrigation 1·00 25
1567 6r. Land reform, nationalization of forests and sale of shares to workers 1·20 25
1568 8r. Profit-sharing, votes for women and education corps 1·90 25

Nos. 1565/8, each showing symbols of three of the reforms, were issued, se-tenant, forming a composite design of a rosette.

369 Shah Mohammed Riza Pahlavi

1969. 10,000th Day of Shah's Reign.
1569 **369** 6r. brown, red and blue 1·50 25

370 Eurasian Goldfinch

1969. New Year Festival. Multicoloured.
1570 1r. Type **370** 25 25
1571 2r. Common pheasant 45 25
1572 8r. Roses 1·50 25

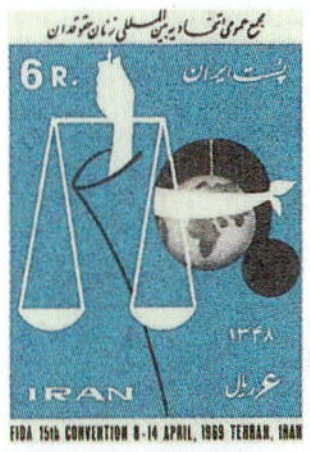

371 Scales of Justice and "Blindfold Globe"

1969. 15th FIDA (Female Jurists) Convention, Teheran.
1573 **371** 6r. black and blue 55 25

372 Symbols of I.L.O.

1969. 50th Anniv of I.L.O.
1574 **372** 10r. violet and blue 55 25

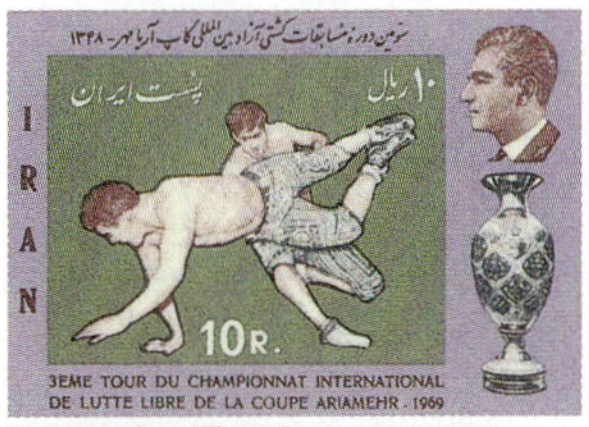

373 Wrestling "Throw"

1969. 3rd Aryamehr Cup International Wrestling Championships.
1575 **373** 10r. multicoloured 1·10 45

374 "Flower and Birds"

1969. World Handicrafts Day.
1576 **374** 10r. multicoloured 75 25

375 Mask and Cord

1969. "Philia 1969". Outdoor Course for Scout Patrol Leaders.

1577	**375**	6r. multicoloured	1·00	25

376 Mughal Miniature (Pakistan)

1969. 5th Anniv of Regional co-operation for Development. Miniatures. Multicoloured.

1578		25r. Type **376**	2·00	55
1579		25r. "Kneeling Figure" (Safavi, Iran)	2·00	55
1580		25r. "Suleiman the Magnificent and Court" (Ottoman, Turkey)	2·00	55

377 Astronauts on Moon

1969. 1st Man on the Moon.

1581	**377**	24r. brown, blue and buff	5·75	1·90

378 "Education" (quotation from Shah's Declaration)

1969. Education Reform Conference.

1582	**378**	10r. red, green and buff	60	25

379 Oil Rig

1969. 10th Anniv of Iranian–Italian Marine Drilling Project.

1583	**379**	8r. multicoloured	1·00	25

380 Festival Emblem

1969. 3rd Shiraz Arts Festival.

1584	**380**	6r. multicoloured	30	25
1585	**380**	8r. multicoloured	40	25

381 Thumb-print and Cross

1969. International Anti-illiteracy Campaign.

1586	**381**	4r. multicoloured	30	25

382 Shah, Persepolis and U.P.U. Emblem (image scaled to 62% of original size)

1969. 16th U.P.U. Congress, Tokyo.

1587	**382**	10r. multicoloured	2·30	55
1588	**382**	14r. multicoloured	2·30	55

383 Fair Emblem

1969. 2nd International Asian Trade Fair, Teheran. Multicoloured.

1589		8r. Type **383**	30	25
1590		14r. As T **383**, but inscr "ASIA 69"	40	25
1591		20r. Emblem and sections of globe (horiz)	55	30

384 "Justice"

1969. Rural Courts of Justice Day.

1592	**384**	8r. brown and green	60	25

385 U.N. Emblem

1969. 25th Anniv of United Nations Day.

1593	**385**	2r. blue and pale blue	40	25

386 Festival Emblem

1969. National Festival of Art and Culture, Teheran.

1594	**386**	2r. multicoloured	60	25

387 "In the Garden"

1969. Children's Week. Children's Drawings. Multicoloured.

1595		1r. Type **387**	25	25
1596		2r. "Three Children" (horiz)	25	25
1597		5r. "Mealtime" (horiz)	55	25

388 Global Emblem

1969. National Association of Parents and Teachers Congress, Teheran.

1598	**388**	8r. brown and blue	40	25

389 Earth Station

1969. Opening of 1st Iranian Satellite Communications Earth Station.

1599	**389**	6r. brown and ochre	40	25

(390)

1969. Air. 50th Anniv of 1st England–Australia Flight. No. 1281 surch as T 390.

1600	**229**	4r. on 14r.+6r.	2·00	60
1601	**229**	10r. on 14r.+6r.	2·00	60
1602	**229**	14r. on 14r.+6r.	2·00	60

391 Mahatma Gandhi

1969. Birth Centenary of Mahatma Gandhi.

1603	**391**	14r. brown and grey	5·25	1·00

392 Globe and Flags

1969. 50th Anniv of League of Red Cross Societies. Multicoloured.

1604		2r. Type **392**	60	25
1605		6r. Red Cross emblems on Globe	90	25

393 Shah and Reform Symbols

1970. 7th Anniv of Shah's White Revolution.

1606	**393**	1r. multicoloured	1·00	40
1607	**393**	2r. multicoloured	1·00	40

394 Pansies

1970. New Year Festival. Multicoloured.

1608		1r. Type **394**	25	25
1609		8r. New Year table (40×26 mm)	1·50	30

395 Nationalization Decree

1970. 20th Anniv of Oil Industry Nationalization. Multicoloured.

1610		2r. Type **395**	1·10	25
1611		4r. Laying pipeline	1·20	30
1612		6r. Part of Kharg Island plant	1·40	40
1613		8r. Ocean terminal, Kharg Island (vert)	1·70	45
1614		10r. Refinery, Teheran	1·90	55

396 "EXPO" Emblem

1970. "EXPO 70" World Fair, Osaka, Japan.

1615	**396**	4r. blue and mauve	30	25
1616	**396**	10r. violet and blue	45	25

397 Dish Aerial and Satellite

1970. Asian Plan Communications Committee Meeting, Teheran.

1617	**397**	14r. multicoloured	75	25

398 New U.P.U. H.Q.

1970. New U.P.U. Headquarters Building, Berne.

1618	**398**	2r. sepia, mauve & green	55	25
1619	**398**	4r. sepia, mauve and lilac	75	25

399 A.P.Y. Emblem

1970. Asian Productivity Year.

1620	**399**	8r. multicoloured	40	25

400 Stork carrying Baby

1970. 50th Anniv of Midwifery School.

1621	**400**	8r. blue and brown	60	25

401 Tomb of Cyrus the Great

1970. 2500th Anniv of Persian Empire (1st issue). Achaemenian Era.

1622	**401**	6r. violet, red and grey	75	25
1623	-	8r. green, black and pink	1·50	55
1624	-	10r. brown, red & yellow	1·90	60
1625	-	14r. brown, black & blue	2·30	1·00

DESIGNS—HORIZ: 10r. Religious ceremony (Median bas-relief); 14r. Achaemenian officers (bas-relief). VERT: 8r. Columns, Palace of Apadana.

See also Nos. 1629/32, 1633/6, 1640/2, 1658/61, 1664/7, 1674/7 and 1679/82.

402 Saiful Malook Lake (Pakistan)

1970. 6th Anniv of Regional Co-operation for Development. Multicoloured.

1626	2r. Type **402**	75	25
1627	2r. Seeyo-Se-Pol Bridge, Isfahan (Iran) (62×46 mm)	75	25
1628	2r. View from Fethiye (Turkey)	75	25

1970. 2500th Anniv of Persian Empire (2nd issue). Achaemenian Era. Designs as T 401.

1629	2r. gold, deep green and green	1·00	40
1630	6r. gold, violet and green	1·20	40
1631	8r. gold, blue and orange	1·70	55
1632	14r. red, black and blue	2·00	1·10

DESIGNS—VERT: 2r. Eagle amulet; 6r. "Lion" goblet; 8r. Winged ibex statue. HORIZ: 14r. Tapestry.

1970. 2500th Anniv of Persian Empire (3rd issue). Coins of Sassanid and Parthian Eras. Designs as T 401. Multicoloured, frames in gold.

1633	1r. Queen Buran dirham	1·00	40
1634	2r. Mithridates I dirham	1·20	40
1635	6r. Shapur I dirham	1·70	45
1636	8r. Ardeshir I dirham	1·70	55

405 Candle and Globe Emblem

1970. World Literacy Day.

1637	**405**	1r. multicoloured	25	25
1638	**405**	2r. multicoloured	25	25

406 Isfahan Tile

1970. International Architects' Congress, Isfahan.

1639	**406**	6r. multicoloured	40	25

1970. 2500th Anniv of Persian Empire (4th issue). Achaemenian and Sassanid Eras. Designs as T 401.

1640	2r. multicoloured	1·20	40
1641	6r. brown, blue and lilac	1·70	55
1642	8r. green, red and lilac	1·70	1·40

DESIGNS—VERT: 2r. Sassanid arch and art. HORIZ: 6r. Archaemenian mounted courier; 8r. Seal of Darius I.

408 Councils Emblem

1970. 1st Congress of Provincial Councils.

1643	**408**	2r. violet and blue	25	25

409 Dove and U.N. Emblem

1970. United Nations Day.

1644	**409**	2r. ultramarine, pur & bl	30	25

410 "1970" and I.A.T.A. Emblem

1970. Air. 26th International Air Transport Association General Meeting, Teheran.

1645	**410**	14r. multicoloured	4·50	55

411 Festival Emblem

1970. National Festival of Art and Culture, Teheran.

1646	**411**	2r. multicoloured	40	25

412 "Goatherd and Goats"

1970. Children's Week. Children's Drawings. Multicoloured.

1647	50d. Type **412**	25	25
1648	1r. "Family picnic"	25	25
1649	2r. "Mosque"	40	25

413 Shah Mohammed Riza Pahlavi

1971. 8th Anniv of Shah's White Revolution.

1650	**413**	2r. multicoloured	2·30	75

414 Common Shelduck

1971. International Wetland and Waterfowl Conference, Ramsar. Multicoloured.

1651	1r. Type **414**	1·10	40
1652	2r. Ruddy shelduck	1·40	60
1653	8r. Greater flamingo (vert)	2·30	75

415 Riza Shah Pahlavi

1971. 50th Anniv of Rise of Pahlavi Dynasty.

1654	**415**	6r. multicoloured	3·50	75

416 Red Junglefowl

1971. New Year Festival. Birds. Multicoloured.

1655	1r. Type **416**	60	25
1656	2r. Barn swallow at nest	1·00	30
1657	6r. Hoopoe	2·75	40

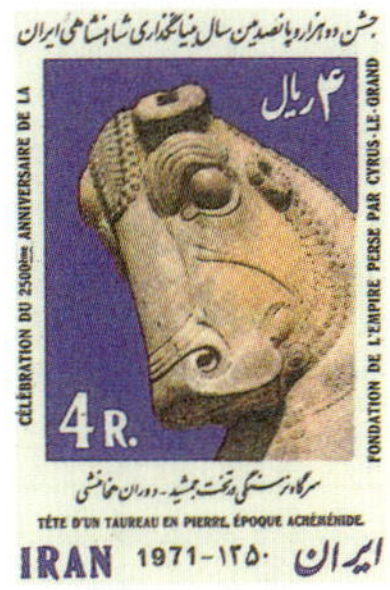

417 Stone Bull's Head, Persepolis

1971. 2500th Anniv of Persian Empire (5th issue). Age of Cyrus the Great. Multicoloured.

1658	4r. Type **417**	1·50	25
1659	5r. Winged lion ornament	1·70	25
1660	6r. Persian Archer (bas-relief)	1·70	55
1661	8r. Imperial audience (bas-relief)	2·30	55

418 Prisoners' Rehabilitation

1971. Rehabilitation Week.

1662	**418**	6r. multicoloured	1·70	25
1663	**418**	8r. multicoloured	3·00	25

1971. 2500th Anniv of Persian Empire (6th issue). Art of Ancient Persia. As T 417.

1664	1r. multicoloured	1·00	25
1665	2r. black and brown	1·50	25
1666	2r. brown, black and purple	1·50	25
1667	10r. black, blue and brown	1·50	25

DESIGNS—VERT: No. 1664, "Harpist" (mosaic); 1667, Bronze head of Parthian prince. HORIZ: No. 1665, "Shapur I hunting" (ornamental plate); 1666, "Investiture of Ardashir I" (bas-relief).

420 Badshahi Mosque, Lahore (Pakistan)

1971. 7th Anniv of Regional Co-operation for Development. Multicoloured.

1668	2r. Type **420**	40	25
1669	2r. Selimiye Mosque, Edirne, Turkey (vert)	40	25
1670	2r. Chaharbagh School, Isfahan (Iran) (vert)	40	25

421 "Shiraz Arts"

1971. 5th Shiraz Arts Festival, Persepolis.

1671	**421**	2r. multicoloured	70	25

422 "Book-reading"

1971. World Literacy Day.

1672	**422**	2r. multicoloured	55	25

423 Kings Abdullah and Hussein II

1971. 50th Anniv of Hashemite Kingdom of Jordan.

1673	**423**	2r. multicoloured	55	25

424 National Steel Foundry

1971. 2500th Anniv of Persian Empire (7th issue). Modern Iran. Multicoloured.

1674	1r. Type **424**	1·00	25
1675	2r. Shahyad Aryamehr Memorial	1·00	40
1676	3r. Senate Building, Teheran	1·00	40
1677	11r. Shah Abbas the Great Dam	2·30	75

425 Ghatur Railway Bridge

1971. Inaug of Iran–Turkey Railway Link.

1678	**425**	2r. multicoloured	1·00	55

426 Shah Mohammed Riza Pahlavi

1971. 2500th Anniv of Persian Empire (8th issue). Pahlavi Era. Multicoloured.

No.	Description	Mint	Used
1679	1r. Type **426**	3·50	1·50
1680	2r. Riza Shah Pahlavi	3·50	1·50
1681	5r. Proclamation tablet of Cyrus the Great (horiz)	3·50	1·50
1682	10r. Pahlavi Crown	5·00	1·50

427 Racial Equality Year Emblem

1971. Racial Equality Year.

No.	Type	Description	Mint	Used
1683	**427**	2r. multicoloured	25	25

428 Shah Mohammed Riza Pahlavi

1971

No.	Type	Description	Mint	Used
1684	**428**	5d. purple	25	25
1685	**428**	10d. red	25	25
1686	**428**	50d. green	25	25
1687	**428**	1r. green	30	25
1688	**428**	2r. brown	30	25
1689	**428**	6r. green	1·10	25
1690	**428**	8r. violet	1·50	1·10
1691	**428**	10r. purple	1·40	30
1692	**428**	11r. green	5·00	1·10
1693	**428**	14r. blue	6·50	55
1694	**428**	20r. mauve	6·00	60
1695	**428**	50r. ochre	5·25	1·20

Nos. 1689/95 are larger, 27×37 mm.
See also Nos. 1715/26b and 1846/50.

429 "Waiters at a Banquet"

1971. Children's Week. Children's Drawings. Multicoloured.

No.	Description	Mint	Used
1696	2r. Type **429**	25	25
1697	2r. "Persepolis Ruins" (vert)	25	25
1698	2r. "Persian Archer" (vert)	25	25

430 UNESCO Emblem

1971. 25th Anniv of UNESCO.

No.	Type	Description	Mint	Used
1699	**430**	6r. blue and purple	40	25

431 Congress Emblem and Livestock

1971. 4th Iranian Veterinary Congress.

No.	Type	Description	Mint	Used
1700	**431**	2r. red, black and grey	40	25

432 I.L.O. Emblem and Globe

1971. 7th Asian International Labour Organization Regional Conference, Teheran.

No.	Type	Description	Mint	Used
1701	**432**	2r. orange, blue and black	40	15

433 Bird feeding Young

1971. 25th Anniv of UNICEF.

No.	Type	Description	Mint	Used
1702	**433**	2r. multicoloured	15	10

434 Shah Mohammed Riza Pahlavi

1972. 9th Anniv of Shah's White Revolution.

No.	Type	Description	Mint	Used
1703	**434**	2r. multicoloured	3·00	1·00
MS1704		80×94 mm. **434** 20r. multicoloured. Imperf	11·50	7·50

435 Chukar Partridge

1972. New Year Festival. Birds. Multicoloured.

No.	Description	Mint	Used
1705	1r. Type **435**	40	25
1706	1r. Pin-tailed sandgrouse	40	25
1707	2r. Swee waxbill and red-cheeked cordon-bleu	2·30	25

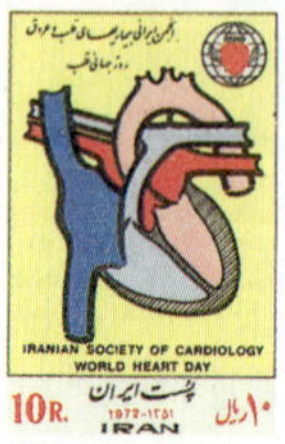

436 Human Heart

1972. World Heart Day.

No.	Type	Description	Mint	Used
1708	**436**	10r. multicoloured	1·70	25

437 Winged Ibex Symbol

1972. International Film Festival, Teheran.

No.	Type	Description	Mint	Used
1709	**437**	6r. gold and blue	75	25
1710	-	8r. multicoloured	1·50	25

DESIGN: 8r. Symbolic spectrum.

438 Scarlet Roses

1972. Roses. Multicoloured.

No.	Description	Mint	Used
1711	1r. Type **438**	30	25
1712	2r. Yellow roses	60	25
1713	5r. Red rose	75	25

1972. As Nos. 1684/95, but with bistre frames and inscriptions.

No.	Type	Description	Mint	Used
1715	**428**	5d. purple	25	25
1716	**428**	10d. brown	25	25
1717	**428**	50d. green	25	25
1718	**428**	1r. green	25	25
1719	**428**	2r. brown	55	25
1720	**428**	6r. green	85	25
1721	**428**	8r. violet	85	25
1722	**428**	10r. purple	1·00	25
1723	**428**	11r. blue	1·40	75
1724	**428**	14r. blue	5·25	60
1725	**428**	20r. mauve	8·25	55
1726	**428**	50r. blue	3·50	1·00
1726a	**428**	100r. violet	5·00	2·00
1726b	**428**	200r. black	10·50	3·50

Nos. 1720/26b are larger, 27×37 mm.

439 "U.I.T." Emblem

1972. World Telecommunications Day.

No.	Type	Description	Mint	Used
1726c	**439**	14r. multicoloured	2·40	55

440 "Fisherman" (Cevat Dereli, Turkey)

1972. 8th Anniv of Regional Co-operation for Development. Paintings. Multicoloured.

No.	Description	Mint	Used
1727	5r. Type **440**	1·40	30
1728	5r. "Iranian Woman" (Behzad, Iran)	1·40	30
1729	5r. "Will and Power" (A. R. Chughtai, Pakistan)	1·40	30

441 Floral Patterns

1972. 6th Shiraz Arts Festival.

No.	Type	Description	Mint	Used
1730	**441**	6r. black, red and green	1·10	25
1731	**441**	8r. black and purple	1·50	25

442 Pens

1972. World Literacy Day.

No.	Type	Description	Mint	Used
1732	**442**	1r. multicoloured	25	25
1733	**442**	2r. multicoloured	40	25

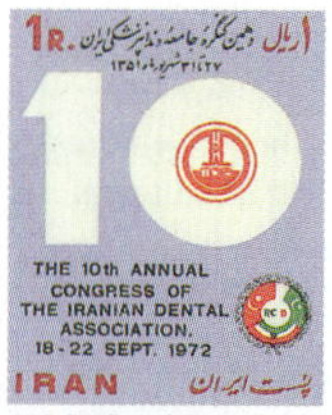

443 "10" and Dental Emblem

1972. 10th Annual Congress of Iranian Dental Association.

No.	Type	Description	Mint	Used
1734	**443**	1r. multicoloured	25	25
1735	**443**	2r. multicoloured	45	25

444 A.B.U. Emblem within "9"

1972. 9th General Assembly of Asian Broadcasting Union, Teheran.

No.	Type	Description	Mint	Used
1736	**444**	6r. multicoloured	75	25
1737	**444**	8r. multicoloured	1·50	25

445 3ch. stamp of 1910 on Cover

1972. World Stamp Day.

No.	Type	Description	Mint	Used
1738	**445**	10r. multicoloured	2·30	25

446 Chess

1972. Olympic Games, Munich. Iranian Sports. Multicoloured.

No.	Description	Mint	Used
1739	1r. Type **446**	2·00	1·50
1740	2r. Hunting	2·00	55
1741	3r. Archery	2·40	55
1742	5r. Horse-racing	2·50	75
1743	6r. Polo	2·75	75
1744	8r. Wrestling	2·75	90
MS1745	177×106 mm. Nos. 1739/44. Imperf	19·00	11·50

447 Communications Emblem

1972. United Nations Day.

No.	Type	Description	Mint	Used
1746	**447**	10r. multicoloured	2·00	25

448 "Children in Garden"

1972. Children's Week. Children's Drawings. Multicoloured.

1747	2r. Type **448**	40	25
1748	2r. "At the Theatre"	75	25
1749	6r. "Children at play" (horiz)	1·40	25

449 Festival Emblem

1972. National Festival of Art and Culture, Teheran.

1750	**449**	10r. multicoloured	5·00	30

450 Family Planning Emblem

1972. Family Planning Campaign.

1751	**450**	1r. multicoloured	25	25
1752	**450**	2r. multicoloured	30	25

451 Scouting Emblem

1972. 20th Anniv of Scouting in Iran.

1753	**451**	2r. multicoloured	55	25

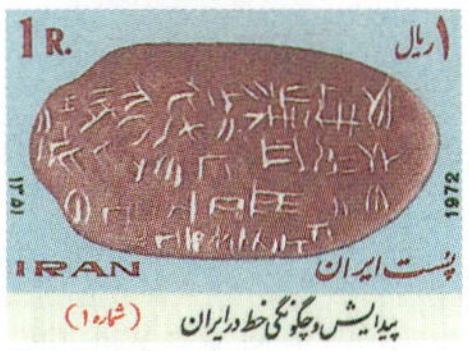

452 Cuneiform Seal

1973. "Origins of Writing" (1st issue). Impressions from ancient seals. Multicoloured. Background colours given.

1754	**452**	1r. blue	60	25
1755	-	1r. yellow	60	25
1756	-	1r. mauve	60	25
1757	-	2r. orange	60	25
1758	-	2r. green	60	25
1759	-	2r. buff	60	25

See also Nos. 1774/9 and 1822/7.

453 Open Books in Space

1973. International Book Year. Multicoloured.

1760	2r. Type **453**	75	25
1761	6r. Illuminated manuscript	1·10	25

454 "Twelve Reforms"

1973. 10th Anniv of Shah's White Revolution. Multicoloured.

1762	1r. Type **454**	25	25
1763	2r. Pyramid of 12 balls	25	25
1764	6r. As Type **454** but size 71×92 mm.	1·70	75
MS1765	71×92 mm. 10r. Design as 2r	2·75	75

455 Long-spined Seabream ("Sparus spinifer")

1973. New Year Festival. Fishes. Multicoloured.

1766	1r. Type **455**	60	25
1767	1r. Purple tang ("Acanthurus sp.")	60	25
1768	2r. Two-banded seabream ("Anisotremus sp.")	90	30
1769	2r. Sergeant major ("Abdufef")	90	30
1770	2r. Black-spotted snapper ("Lutyanus fulniflamma")	90	30

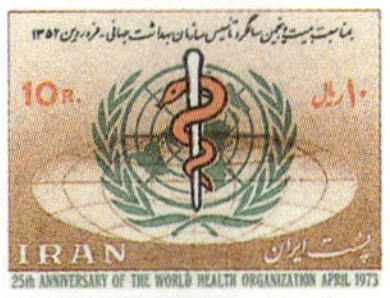

456 W.H.O. Emblem

1973. 25th Anniv of W.H.O.

1771	**456**	10r. multicoloured	1·20	25

457 "Footballers"

1973. 15th Asian Youth Football Tournament, Teheran.

1772	**457**	14r. multicoloured	1·40	25

458 Railway Track encircling Globe

1973. International Railway Conference, Teheran.

1773	**458**	10r. blue, black & mauve	1·20	40

459 Ancient Aryan Script

1973. "Origins of Writing". Multicoloured.

1774	1r. Type **459**	55	25
1775	1r. Achaemenian priest and text	55	25
1776	1r. Kharochtani tablet	55	25
1777	2r. Parthian medallion (Arsacid)	90	25
1778	2r. Parthian coin (Mianeh)	90	25
1779	2r. Gachtak inscribed medallion (Dabireh)	90	25

460 Orchid

1973. Flowers. Multicoloured.

1780	1r. Type **460**	25	25
1781	2r. Hyacinth	55	25
1782	6r. Wild rose	1·20	25

461 Carved Head, Tomb of Antiochus I (Turkey)

1973. 9th Anniv of Regional Co-operation for Development. Multicoloured.

1783	2r. Type **461**	40	25
1784	2r. Statue, Lut excavations (Iran)	40	25
1785	2r. Street in Moenjodaro (Pakistan)	40	25

462 Shah and Oil Installations

1973. Full Independence for Iranian Oil Industry.

1786	**462**	5r. black and blue	1·40	40

463 Soldiers and "Sun"

1973. 20th Anniv of Gen. Zahedi's Uprising.

1787	**463**	2r. multicoloured	30	25

464 Sportswomen and Globe

1973. 7th International Women's Congress on Physical Education and Sport, Teheran.

1788	**464**	2r. multicoloured (blue background)	25	25
1789	**464**	2r. multicoloured (green background)	25	25

465 Festival Poster

1973. 7th Shiraz Arts Festival.

1790	**465**	1r. multicoloured	25	25
1791	**465**	5r. multicoloured	30	25

466 Shahyad Monument and Rainbow

1973. Cent of World Meteorological Organization.

1792	**466**	5r. multicoloured	75	25

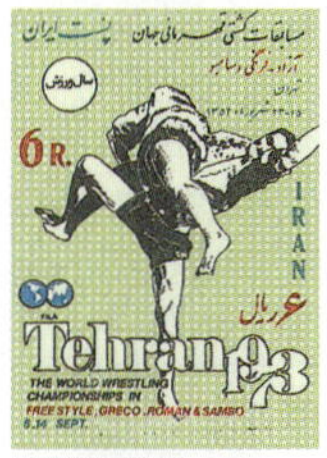

467 Wrestling

1973. World Wrestling Championships, Teheran.

1793	**467**	6r. multicoloured	70	30

468 Alphabetic "Sun"

1973. World Literacy Day.

1794	**468**	2r. multicoloured	25	25

469 Globe wearing Earphones

1973. Int Audio-visual Exhibition, Teheran.

1795	**469**	10r. multicoloured	60	25

470 Al-Biruni

1973. Birth Millenary of Abu al-Rayhan al-Biruni (mathematician and philosopher).

1796	**470**	10r. black and brown	1·10	40

471 C.I.S.M. Badge and Emblem

1973. 25th Anniv of International Military Sports Council (C.I.S.M.).

1797	**471**	8r. multicoloured	60	25

472 Crown Prince Cup

1973. Crown Prince Cup Football Championship.

1798	**472**	2r. brown, black and lilac	40	25

473 Interpol Emblem

1973. 50th Anniv of International Criminal Police Organization (Interpol).

1799	**473**	2r. multicoloured	25	25

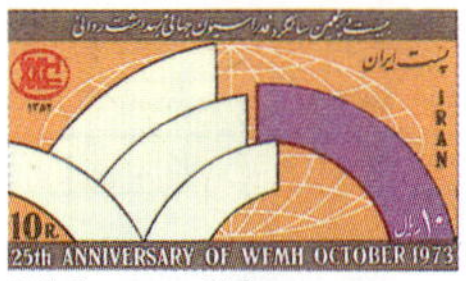

474 Curves on Globe

1973. 25th Anniv of World Mental Health Federation.

1800	**474**	10r. multicoloured	55	25

475 U.P.U. Emblem, Post-horn and Letter

1973. World Post Day.

1801	**475**	6r. orange and blue	55	25

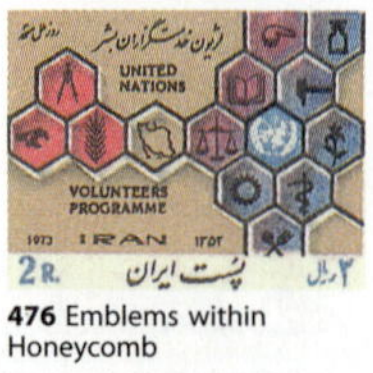

476 Emblems within Honeycomb

1973. 5th Anniv of United Nations Volunteers.

1802	**476**	2r. multicoloured (brown background)	25	25
1803	**476**	2r. multicoloured (green background)	25	25

477 Festival Emblem and "People"

1973. National Festival of Art and Culture, Teheran.

1804	**477**	2r. multicoloured	40	25

478 Bosphorus Bridge

1973. 50th Anniv of Turkish Republic. Mult.

1805	2r. Type **478**	75	25
1806	8r. Meeting of Kemal Ataturk and Reza Shah Pahlavi	1·20	25

479 "House and Garden"

1973. Children's Week. Children's Drawings. Multicoloured.

1807	2r. Type **479**	30	25
1808	2r. "Collecting Fruit"	30	25
1809	2r. "Caravan" (horiz)	30	25

480 Ear of Grain and Cow

1973. 10th Anniv of World Food Programme.

1810	**480**	10r. multicoloured	1·00	25

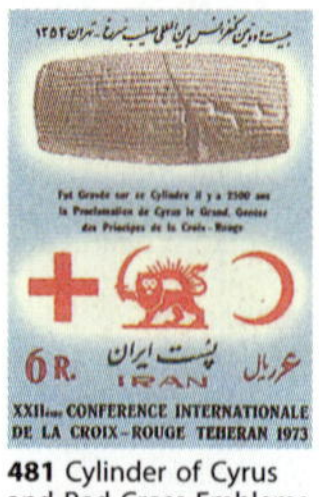

481 Cylinder of Cyrus and Red Cross Emblems

1973. 22nd Int Red Cross Conference, Teheran.

1811	**481**	6r. multicoloured	55	25

482 IATA Emblem

1973. Tourist Managers Congress, Teheran.

1812	**482**	10r. multicoloured	55	25

483 Emblem, Film and Flags

1973. International Film Festival, Teheran.

1813	**483**	2r. multicoloured	25	25

484 Flame Emblem

1973. 25th Anniv of Declaration of Human Rights.

1814	**484**	8r. multicoloured	40	25

485 Harp Emblem

1973. "Art of Music" Festival.

1815	**485**	10r. red, green and black	55	25
1816	-	10r. ultram, bl & pur	55	25

DESIGN: No. 1816, Musical symbols.

486 Reform Symbols

1974. 11th Anniv of Shah's White Revolution. Multicoloured.

1817	1r. Type **486**	25	25
1818	1r. Tractor, factory in cogwheel, women and parliament gate	25	25
1819	2r. Girders, hose and worker	25	25
1820	2r. Rod of Aesculapius, scales and road passing house	25	25
MS1821	76×102 mm. 20r. Symbols from Nos. 1817/20 arranged in four panels. Imperf	3·25	1·20

487 Pir Amooz Ketabaty Script

1974. "Origins of Writing" (3rd issue). Multicoloured.

1822	1r. Din Dabireh Avesta	75	30
1823	1r. Mo Eghely Ketabaty	75	30
1824	1r. Type **487**	75	30
1825	2r. Pir Amooz, Naskh style	75	30
1826	2r. Pir Amooz, decorative	75	30
1827	2r. Pir Amooz, decorative and architectural	75	30

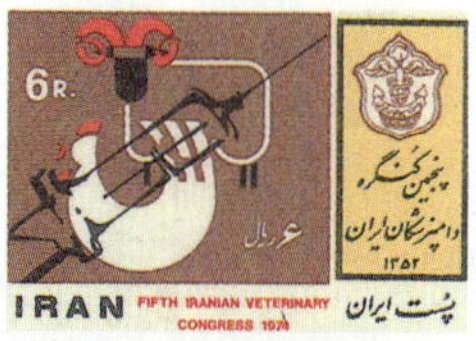

488 Chicken, Cow and Syringe

1974. 5th Iranian Veterinary Congress.

1828	**488**	6r. multicoloured	40	25

490 Scarce Swallowtail

1974. Nawrooz and Spring Festivals. Butterflies. Multicoloured, background colours given.

1841	**490**	1r. mauve	75	25
1842	-	1r. purple	75	25
1843	-	2r. green	1·10	40
1844	-	2r. brown	1·10	40
1845	-	2r. blue	1·10	40

DESIGNS: No. 1842, Swallowtail; 1843, Peacock; 1844, Painted lady; 1845, Cardinal.

1974. As Nos. 1684/95, but colours changed.

1846	**428**	50d. blue and orange	45	25
1847	**428**	1r. blue and green	60	25
1848	**428**	2r. blue and red	85	25
1849	**428**	10r. blue and green	6·00	25
1850	**428**	20r. blue and mauve	3·50	1·10

Nos. 1849/50 are larger, 27×37 mm.

491 Mevlana

1974. 700th Death Anniv of Jalal-udin Mevlana (poet).

1851	**491**	2r. multicoloured	55	25

492 Palace of Forty Columns, Isfahan

1974. 9th Near- and Middle-East Medical Congress, Isfahan.

1852	**492**	10r. multicoloured	55	25

493 Asiatic Wild Ass

1974. International Game and Wild Life Protection Congress, Teheran. Multicoloured.

1853	1r. Type **493**	40	25
1854	2r. Great bustard	55	25
1855	6r. Fawn and fallow deer	1·20	40
1856	8r. Caucasian black grouse	2·00	40

494 Gymnastics

1974. 7th Asian Games, Teheran (1st series). Multicoloured.

1857	1r. Type **494**	55	25
1858	1r. Table tennis	55	25
1859	2r. Boxing	1·00	25
1860	2r. Hurdling	1·00	25
1861	6r. Weightlifting	1·50	25
1862	8r. Handball	2·40	25

See also Nos. 1874/9, 1890/3 and 1909.

495 Lion of St. Mark's

1974. UNESCO "Save Venice" Campaign. Multicoloured.

1863	6r. Type **495**	55	25
1864	8r. Merchants at the Doge's court	1·00	40

496 Chain Link

1974. Farm Co-operatives' Day.

1865	**496**	2r. multicoloured	25	25

497 Shah and Douglas DC-9-80 Super Eighty

1974. Air.

1866	**497**	4r. black and orange	40	25
1867	**497**	10r. black and blue	1·50	25
1868	**497**	12r. black and brown	1·50	40
1869	**497**	14r. black and green	1·70	40
1870	**497**	20r. black and mauve	2·30	55
1871	**497**	50r. black and blue	5·75	1·40

498 De Havilland D.H.9A, 1924

1974. 50th Anniv of Imperial Iranian Air Force. Multicoloured.

1872	10r. Type **498**	1·50	40
1873	10r. McDonnell Douglas F-4D Phantom II fighter of 1974	1·50	40

499 Tennis (men's doubles)

1974. 7th Asian Games, Teheran (2nd series). Multicoloured.

1874	1r. Type **499**	55	25
1875	1r. Swimming	55	25
1876	2r. Wrestling	75	25
1877	2r. Hockey	75	25
1878	4r. Volleyball	1·10	40
1879	10r. Tennis (women's singles)	2·00	55

500 Mazanderan Costume

1974. Regional Costumes. Multicoloured.

1880	2r. Type **500**	1·40	55
1881	2r. Bakhtiari	1·40	55
1882	2r. Turkoman	1·40	55
1883	2r. Ghasgai	1·40	55
1884	2r. Kirmanshah (Kurdistan)	1·40	55
1885	2r. Sanandadj (Kurdistan)	1·40	55

501 Gold Cup

1974. Iranian Football Championships.

1886	**501**	2r. yellow, brown & green	30	25

502 Iranian Carpet

1974. 10th Anniv of Regional Co-operation for Development. Multicoloured.

1887	2r. Pakistani carpet (diamond) centre	45	25
1888	2r. Turkish carpet (striped)	45	25
1889	2r. Type **502**	45	25

503 Rifle-shooting

1974. 7th Asian Games, Teheran (3rd series). Multicoloured.

1890	2r. Type **503**	75	25
1891	2r. Fencing	75	25
1892	2r. Football	75	25
1893	2r. Cycling	75	25

504 Persian King

1974. 8th Shiraz Arts Festival, Persepolis.

1894	**504**	2r. multicoloured	30	25

505 Games Emblem

1974. 7th Asian Games, Tehran (4th issue). Two sheets, each 74×95 mm, containing single stamps as T 505. Multicoloured.

MS1895	(a) 10r. Type **505**; (b) 10r. Plan of Games area	4·50	2·30

506 Petrochemical Works, Khark

1974

1896	**506**	5d. green and brown	30	25
1897	-	10d. orange and brown	30	25
1898	-	50d. green and brown	30	25
1899	-	1r. blue and brown	30	25
1900	-	2r. purple and brown	30	25
1901	-	6r. brown and blue	55	25
1902	-	8r. turquoise and blue	55	25
1903	-	10r. purple and blue	75	40
1904	-	14r. green and blue	13·50	60
1905	-	20r. red and blue	3·50	55
1906	-	50r. violet and blue	4·25	1·10

DESIGNS—As T **506**: 10d. Railway bridge, Ghatur; 50d. Dam, Farahnaz; 1r. Oil Refinery; 2r. Radio telescope. 37×27 mm: 6r. Steelworks, Aryamehr; 8r. Tabriz University; 10r. Shah Abbas Kabir Dam; 14r. Teheran Opera House; 20r. Shahyad Square; 50r. Aryamehr Stadium.

See also Nos. 1939/49.

507 Family within Hands

1974. State Education and Health Services. Multicoloured.

1907	2r. Type **507**	25	25
1908	2r. Children, pen and book within hands	25	25

508 Aryamehr Stadium, Teheran

1974. Seventh Asian Games, Teheran (4th series).

1909	**508**	6r. multicoloured	1·00	25

509 Plan of Hasanlu

1974. 2nd International Architectural Congress, Shiraz.

1910	**509**	8r. multicoloured	40	25

510 Charioteer

1974. Centenary of U.P.U. Multicoloured.

1911	6r. Type **510**	85	40
1912	14r. U.P.U. emblem and letters	1·20	40

511 Road through Park

1974. Opening of Farahabad Park, Teheran. Multicoloured.

1913	1r. Type **511**	25	25
1914	2r. Recreation pavilion	25	25

512 Festival Emblem

1974. National Festival of Art and Culture, Teheran.

1915	**512**	2r. multicoloured	30	25

513 Crown Prince in Aircraft

1974. Air. Crown Prince's Birthday.

1916	**513**	14r. multicoloured	1·10	40

514 Destroyer "Palang"

1974. Navy Day.

1917	**514**	10r. multicoloured	90	25

515 Scarecrow

1974. Children's Week. Children's Drawings. Multicoloured.

1918	2r. Type **515**	25	25
1919	2r. Girl at spinning wheel (horiz)	25	25
1920	2r. New Year picnic (horiz)	25	25

516 Winged Bull Emblem

1974. 3rd International Film Festival, Teheran.

1921	**516**	2r. multicoloured	25	25

517 W.P.Y. Emblem

1974. World Population Year.

1922	**517**	8r. multicoloured	55	25

518 Gold Butterfly Brooch

1974. 14th Wedding Anniv of Shah and Empress Farah. Multicoloured.

1923	6r. Type **518**	45	25
1924	8r. Gold diadem	70	30

519 Angel with Banner

1975. International Women's Year.

1925	**519**	2r. orange, blue and red	25	25

520 Emblems of Agriculture, Industry and the Arts

1975. 12th Anniv of Shah's White Revolution.

1926	**520**	2r. multicoloured	25	25

521 Tourism Year Emblem

1975. South Asia Tourism Year.

1927	**521**	6r. multicoloured	25	25

522 Farabi's Initial

1975. 1100th Birth Anniv of Abu-Nasr al-Farabi (philosopher).

1928	**522**	2r. multicoloured	25	25

523 Ornament

1975. New Year Festival. Multicoloured.

1929	1r. Type **523**	25	25
1930	1r. Blossoms and tree	25	25
1931	1r. Arabesque and patterns	25	25

524 Nasser Khosrov

1975. Birth Millenary of Nasser Khosrov (poet).

1932	**524**	2r. black, red and bistre	25	25

525 Persian Warriors

1975. 70th Anniv of Rotary International. Multicoloured.

1933	2r. Type **525**	1·50	60
1934	10r. Charioteer (horiz)	3·50	90

526 Biochemical Emblem

1975. 5th Biochemical Symposium.

1935	**526**	2r. multicoloured	25	25

527 "Co-operative Peoples"

1975. Co-operatives Day.

1936	**527**	2r. multicoloured	25	25

528 Ancient Signal-beacons

1975. World Telecommunications Day. Mult.

1937	6r. Type **528**	40	25
1938	8r. Telecommunications satellite	55	30

1975. As Nos. 1896/1906 but colours changed.

1939	**506**	5d. orange and turquoise	30	25
1940	-	10d. purple and turquoise	30	25
1941	-	50d. mauve and turquoise	30	25
1942	-	1r. blue and turquoise	30	25
1943	-	2r. brown and turquoise	30	25
1944	-	6r. violet and brown	40	40
1945	-	8r. red and brown	2·00	30
1946	-	10r. green and brown	1·50	25
1947	-	14r. mauve and brown	6·00	25
1948	-	20r. turquoise and brown	3·00	40
1949	-	50r. blue and brown	2·75	75

529 "Iran Air" Boeing 747SP

1975. "Iran Air's" First Teheran–New York Flight.

1950	**529**	10r. multicoloured	60	40

530 Environmental Emblem

1975. World Environment Day.

1951	**530**	6r. multicoloured	30	25

531 Dam and Reservoir

1975. 25th Anniv of International Commission on Irrigation and Drainage.

1952	**531**	10r. multicoloured	40	25

532 Party Emblem

1975. Formation of Resurgence Party.

1953	**532**	2r. multicoloured	25	25

533 Saluting Hand

1975. 2nd National Girl Scout Camp, Teheran.

1954	**533**	2r. multicoloured	25	25

534 Festival Motif

1975. Festival of Tus (honouring poet Firdausi).

1955	**534**	2r. multicoloured	25	25

535 Iranian Tile

1975. 11th Anniv of Regional Co-operation for Development. Multicoloured.

1956	2r. Type **535**	30	25
1957	2r. Pakistani camel-skin vase (vert)	30	25
1958	2r. Turkish porcelain vase (vert)	30	25

536 Parliament Gateway

1975. 70th Anniv of Iranian Constitution.

1959	**536**	10r. multicoloured	40	25

537 Stylized Column

1975. 9th Shiraz Arts Festival.

1960	**537**	8r. multicoloured	55	25

538 Flags over Globe

1975. International Literacy Symposium, Persepolis.

1961	**538**	2r. multicoloured	25	25

539 Stylized Globe

1975. 3rd International Trade Fair, Teheran.

1962	**539**	2r. multicoloured	25	25

540 Envelope on World Map

1975. World Post Day.

1963	**540**	14r. multicoloured	75	25

541 Festival Emblem

1975. National Festival of Art and Culture, Teheran.

1964	**541**	2r. multicoloured	25	25

542 Face within Film

1975. International Festival of Children's Films, Teheran.

1965	**542**	6r. multicoloured	30	25

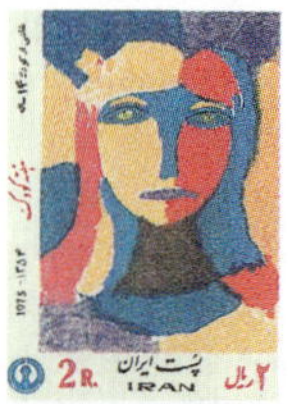

543 "Mother's Face"

1975. Children's Week. Multicoloured.

1966	2r. Type **543**	25	25
1967	2r. "Young Girl"	25	25
1968	2r. "Our House" (horiz)	25	25

544 "Sound Film"

1975. 4th International Film Festival, Teheran.
1969 **544** 8r. multicoloured 45 25

545 Reform Symbols

1976. 13th Anniv of Shah's White Revolution. Multicoloured.
1970 2r. Type **545** 25 25
1971 2r. Symbols representing "People" 25 25
1972 2r. Five reform symbols 25 25

546 Motor Cycle Patrol

1976. Highway Police Day. Multicoloured.
1973 2r. Type **546** 75 30
1974 6r. Bell Model 205 Iroquois police helicopter (horiz) 1·10 45

547 Football Cup

1976. 3rd International Football Cup.
1975 **547** 2r. multicoloured 25 25

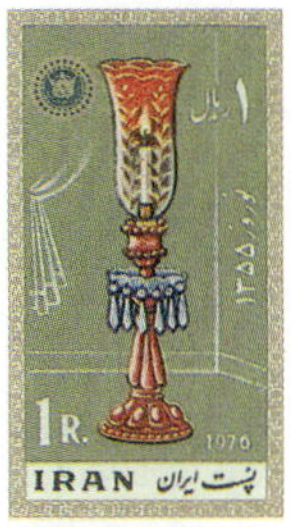

548 Candlestick

1976. New Year. Multicoloured.
1976 1r. Type **548** 25 25
1977 1r. Incense burner 25 25
1978 1r. Rosewater jug 25 25

549 Early and Modern Telephones

1976. Telephone Centenary.
1979 **549** 10r. multicoloured 60 25

550 Human Eye

1976. World Health Day.
1980 **550** 6r. multicoloured 30 10

551 Nurse holding Child

1976. 30th Anniv of Social Services Organization. Multicoloured.
1981 2r. Type **551** 30 25
1982 2r. Workshop apprentices 30 25
1983 2r. Handclasp (help the aged) (vert) 30 25

552 Linked Men on Map

1976. 10th Anniv of Iranian Co-operative Movement.
1984 **552** 2r. multicoloured 30 25

553 Sound Waves and Headphones

1976. World Telecommunications Day.
1985 **553** 14r. multicoloured 55 25

554 "Patriotism"

1976. National Resistance Organization.
1986 **554** 2r. multicoloured 30 25

555 Nasser-Khosrow and Landmarks on Map

1976. Tourism Day and Birth Anniv of Nasser-Khosrow "The Great Iranian Tourist".
1987 **555** 6r. multicoloured 40 25

556 Riza Shah Pahlavi

1976. 12th Anniv of Regional Co-operation for Development. Multicoloured.
1988 2r. Type **556** 45 25
1989 6r. Mohammed Ali Jinnah (Pakistan) 60 25
1990 8r. Kemal Ataturk (Turkey) 75 25

557 Olympic Flame and Emblem

1976. Olympic Games, Montreal.
1991 **557** 14r. multicoloured 75 25

558 Riza Shah Pahlavi in Coronation Dress

1976. 50th Anniv of Pahlavi Dynasty. Mult.
1992 2r. Riza Shah Pahlavi and Mohammed Riza Pahlavi (horiz) 75 30
1993 6r. Type **558** 1·50 40
1994 14r. Mohammed Riza Pahlavi in Coronation dress 2·30 45

559 Festival Emblem

1976. 10th Shiraz Arts Festival.
1995 **559** 10r. multicoloured 55 25

560 Conference Emblem

1976. 10th Asia–Pacific Scout Conference, Teheran.
1996 **560** 2r. multicoloured 25 25

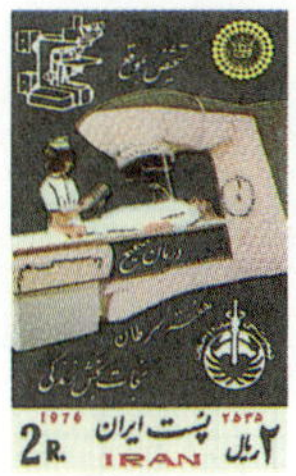

561 Radiation Treatment

1976. Campaign against Cancer.
1997 **561** 2r. multicoloured 30 25

562 Target and Presentation to Policewoman

1976. Police Day.
1998 **562** 2r. multicoloured 30 25

563 Shah in Coronation Dress (image scaled to 74% of original size)

1976. 35th Anniv of Shah's Reign. Sheet 75×100 mm.
MS1999 **563** 20r. multicoloured 6·00 3·75

564 U.P.U. Emblem and Iranian Stamp on Envelope

1976. International Post Day.
2000 **564** 10r. multicoloured 1·00 25

565 Crown Prince presenting Cup

1976. Society of Village Culture Houses.
2001 **565** 6r. multicoloured 30 25

566 Mohammed Riza Pahlavi, Riza Shah Pahlavi and Steam Train

1976. Railway Day.

2002	**566**	8r. multicoloured	2·00	40

567 Festival Emblem

1976. National Festival of Art and Culture, Teheran.

2003	**567**	14r. multicoloured	55	25

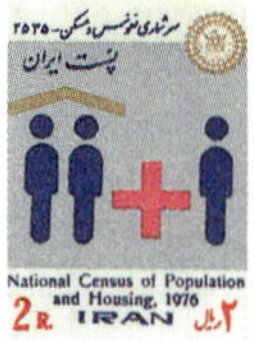

568 Census Symbols

1976. National Census.

2004	**568**	2r. multicoloured	25	25

569 Flowers and Birds

1976. Children's Week. Multicoloured.

2005		2r. Type **569**	40	25
2006		2r. Flowers and bird	40	25
2007		2r. Flowers and butterfly	40	25

570 Mohammed Ali Jinnah (Quaid-i-Azam)

1976. Birth Centenary of Mohammed Ali Jinnah (first Governor-General of Pakistan).

2008	**570**	10r. multicoloured	45	25

571 Tractor (Land reform)

1977. 14th Anniv of Shah's White Revolution. Shah's head and frame in gold.

2009	**571**	5d. green and pink	25	25
2010	-	10d. green and brown	25	25
2011	-	50d. blue and orange	25	25
2012	-	1r. blue and mauve	25	25
2013	-	2r. green and orange	25	25
2014	-	3r. red and blue	40	25
2015	-	5r. lilac and green	40	25
2016	-	6r. purple, brown & black	55	25
2017	-	8r. purple, blue and black	55	25
2018	-	10r. blue, green and black	1·40	25
2019	-	12r. brown, lilac & black	1·10	25
2020	-	14r. red, orange and black	1·40	75
2021	-	20r. orange, grey & black	3·00	55
2022	-	30r. green, blue and black	3·00	60
2023	-	50r. red, yellow and black	4·50	60
2024	-	100r. blue, mauve & blk	4·50	1·10
2025	-	200r. violet, green & blk	9·00	1·90

DESIGNS—21×28 mm: 10d. Trees (Nationalization of forests); 50d. Banknotes (Profit-sharing); 1r. Factory workers (Sale of shares to workers); 2r. Parliament gate (Votes for women); 3r. Teacher and pupils (Education corps); 5r. Doctor examining patient (Medical corps). 36×27 mm: 6r. Bulldozer (Civil engineering); 8r. Scales (Justice); 10r. Dam (Irrigation); 12r. Building site (Construction corps); 14r. Clock and receptionist (Working conditions); 20r. Screen and students (Adult literacy); 30r. Sound waves (Telecommunications); 50r. Students and pupils (Education); 100r. Baby in hands (Child care); 200r. Elderly couple (Care of the aged).

572 Man in Guilan Costume

1977. New Year Festival. Multicoloured.

2026		1r. Type **572**	25	25
2027		2r. Women in Guilan costume	25	25

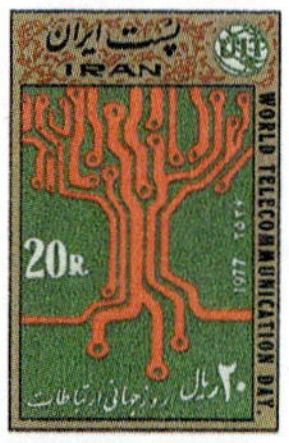

573 Circuit Diagram

1977. World Telecommunications Day.

2028	**573**	20r. multicoloured	90	25

574 Riza Shah Dam

1977. Inauguration of Riza Shah Dam.

2029	**574**	5r. multicoloured	40	25

575 Olympic Rings

1977. Olympic Day.

2030	**575**	14r. multicoloured	70	25

576 Turkish "Human Face" Vase

1977. 13th Anniv of Regional Co-operation for Development. Multicoloured.

2031		5r. Type **576**	30	25
2032		5r. Pakistani toy bullock cart	30	25
2033		5r. Iranian buff earthenware	30	25

577 Flowers on Map of Asia

1977. 2nd Asia–Pacific Jamboree, Nishapur.

2034	**577**	10r. multicoloured	70	25

578 Map and Emblem

1977. 9th Asian Electronics Conference, Teheran.

2035	**578**	3r. multicoloured	25	25

579 "Tree" in Farsi Script

1977. Teachers' Day.

2036	**579**	10r. multicoloured	30	25

580 Globe and Envelope

1977. Centenary of Iran's Admission to U.P.U.

2037	**580**	14r. multicoloured	45	25

581 "Tree and Lions"

1977. Popular Arts Festival.

2038	**581**	5r. multicoloured	40	25

582 Festival Emblem

1977. National Festival of Art and Culture, Teheran.

2039	**582**	20r. multicoloured	60	25

583 "Two Horsemen" (Persian miniature)

1977. Children's Week. Multicoloured.

2040		3r. Type **583**	25	25
2041		3r. "Lover and his mistress"	25	25
2042		3r. "Five people round a bed"	70	70

584 Seminar Emblem

1977. 1st Regional Seminar on Education and Welfare of the Deaf.

2043	**584**	5r. multicoloured	30	25

585 A. M. Iqbal

1977. Birth Centenary of Allama Mohammad Iqbal (Pakistani poet).

2044	**585**	5r. multicoloured	45	25

586 Bronze Head from Nigeria

1977. "Art of Black Africa" Exhibition, Teheran.

2045	**586**	20r. multicoloured	3·00	55

587 Ruins at Persepolis

1978

2059	**587**	1r. brown and gold	30	25
2060	-	2r. green and gold	30	25
2061	-	3r. purple and gold	55	25
2062	-	5r. green and gold	70	25
2063	-	9r. brown and gold	1·40	60
2064	-	10r. blue and gold	4·50	70
2065	-	20r. red and gold	1·70	60
2066	-	25r. blue and gold	19·00	9·00
2067	-	30r. red and gold	2·75	60
2068	-	50r. green and gold	4·50	3·50
2069	-	100r. blue and gold	11·50	9·00
2070	-	200r. violet and gold	15·00	15·00

DESIGNS: 30×23 mm: 2r. Khajou Bridge, Isfahan; 3r. Shah Mosque, Isfahan; 5r. Imam Riza Shrine, Meshed. 35×26 mm: 9r. Warrior frieze, Persepolis; 10r. Djameh Mosque, Isfahan; 20r. Bas-relief, Persepolis; 25r. Shaikh Lotfollah Mosque; 30r. Ruins, Persepolis (different); 50r. Ali Ghapou Palace, Isfahan; 100r. Stone relief, Tagh Bastan; 200r. Relief, Naqsh Rostam.

588 Mohammed Riza Pahlavi

1978. 15th Anniv of Shah's White Revolution.

2071	**588**	20r. multicoloured	3·50	1·00

589 Animals (carpet)

1978. Inauguration of Persian Carpets Museum, Teheran. Multicoloured.

2072	3r. Type **589**	25	25
2073	5r. Court scene	45	25
2074	10r. Floral pattern	60	30

590 Costume of Mazandera Province

1978. New Year Festival. Multicoloured.

2075	3r. Type **590**	25	25
2076	5r. Woman in costume of Mazandera Province	40	25

591 Riza Shah Pahlavi and Crown Prince inspecting Girls' School

1978. Birth Centenary of Riza Shah Pahlavi. Multicoloured.

2077	3r. Type **591**	40	25
2078	5r. Riza Shah Pahlavi and Crown Prince at inauguration of Trans-Iranian Railway	60	30
2079	10r. Riza Shah Pahlavi and Crown Prince at Palace of Persepolis	1·10	40
2080	14r. Shah handing Crown Prince officer's diploma	1·50	60

592 Satellite and Receiving Station

1978. 10th Anniv of Admission to International Telecommunications Union.

2081	**592**	20r. multicoloured	1·00	25

593 Microwave Antenna

1978. World Telecommunications Day.

2082	**593**	15r. multicoloured	60	25

594 Welfare Legion Emblem

1978. 10th Anniv of Universal Welfare Legion.

2083	**594**	10r. multicoloured	60	25

595 Pink Roses

1978. 14th Anniv of Regional Co-operation for Development. Roses. Multicoloured.

2084	5r. Type **595**	55	25
2085	10r. Salmon rose	60	25
2086	15r. Red roses	85	40

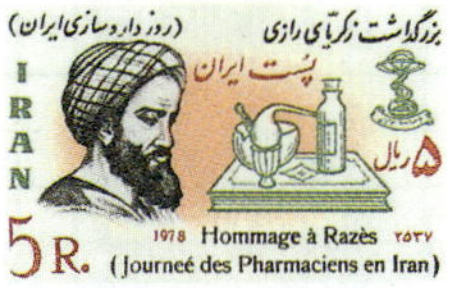

596 Rhazes and Pharmaceutical Equipment

1978. Pharmacists' Day.

2087	**596**	5r. multicoloured	55	25

597 Girl Guides and Aryamehr Arch

1978. 23rd World Girl Guides Conference, Teheran.

2088	**597**	5r. multicoloured	45	25

598 Riza Shah Pahlavi

1978. 50th Anniv of Bank Melli Iran. Mult.

2089	3r. Type **598**	1·20	40
2090	5r. Mohammed Riza Pahlavi	1·50	55

599 Young Girl and Bird

1978. Children's Week.

2091	**599**	3r. multicoloured	75	30

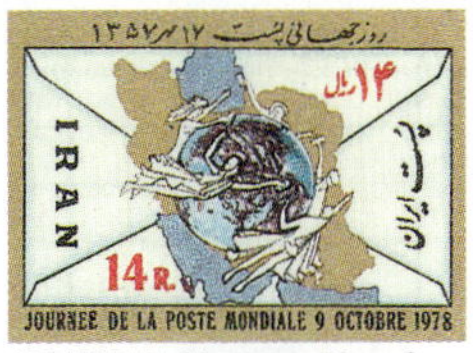

600 U.P.U. Emblem over Map of Iran

1978. World Post Day.

2092	**600**	14r. multicoloured	1·20	40

601 Classroom and Communications Equipment

1978. 50th Anniv of Communications Faculty.

2093	**601**	10r. multicoloured	1·00	40

602 Human Rights Emblem

1978. 30th Anniv of Human Rights Declaration.

2094	**602**	20r. multicoloured	3·00	55

603 Rose

1979. New Year Festival. Multicoloured.

2095	2r. Type **603**	40	25
2096	3r. Man in Khurdistan costume	75	25
2097	5r. Woman in Khurdistan costume	1·10	25

604 Revolutionary Crowd

1979. Islamic Revolution. Multicoloured.

2098	3r. Type **604**	1·50	30
2099	5r. Hands holding flower, gun and torch	1·10	30
2100	10r. Protest march	1·10	55
2101	20r. Bloodied hands releasing dove (vert)	2·40	60

(605)

1979. Designs as T 587 optd with T 605. (a) Nos. 1945/6.

2102	8r. red and brown	3·00	1·00
2103	10r. green and brown	1·50	1·50

(b) Nos. 2063/4, 2068/70 and unissued 15r. and 19r. stamps.

2104	9r. brown and gold	38·00	7·50
2105	10r. turquoise and gold	1·70	1·00
2106	15r. mauve and gold	1·70	1·00
2107	19r. green and gold	1·70	1·00
2108	50r. green and gold	5·00	2·00
2109	100r. blue and gold	7·50	3·00
2110	200r. violet and gold	9·00	6·00

DESIGNS—HORIZ (36×26 mm): 15r. Rock carvings, Naqsh Rostam; 19r. Chehel Sotoon Palace, Isfahan.

606 Tulip formed from "Allah" and "Islamic Republic"

1979. Islamic Republic.

2111	**606**	5r. multicoloured	1·20	40

607 "Iranian Goldsmith" (Kamal el Molk)

1979. 15th Anniv of Regional Co-operation for Development. Paintings. Multicoloured.

2112	5r. Type **607**	3·00	30
2113	5r. "Turkish Harvest" (Namik Ismail)	2·30	30
2114	5r. "Pakistan Village Scene" (Allah Baksh)	2·30	30

608 "Telecom 79"

1979. 3rd World Telecommunications Exhibition, Geneva.

2115	**608**	20r. gold, black and red	6·00	25

609 Tulip rising from Blood of Revolutionary

1979. International Year of the Child. Children's Paintings. Multicoloured.

2116	2r. Type **609**	85	55
2117	3r. Children greeting the rising sun (vert)	1·10	55
2118	5r. Children with banners	1·50	55

610 Persian Rug

1979

2119	**610**	50d. brown and orange	25	25
2120	**610**	1r. blue and light blue	25	25
2121	**610**	2r. red and yellow	25	25
2122	**610**	3r. blue and mauve	25	25
2123	**610**	5r. olive and green	25	25
2124	**610**	10r. black and pink	40	25
2125	**610**	20r. brown and grey	55	25
2126	**610**	50r. violet and grey	1·40	55
2127	**610**	100r. black and green	3·75	1·10
2128	**610**	200r. blue and stone	4·25	2·30

Nos. 2126/8 are larger, 27×37 mm.

611 Globe in Envelope

1979. World Post Day.

2134	**611**	10r. multicoloured	3·00	40

612 Kashani and Astrolabe

1979. 550th Death Anniv of Ghyath-al-din Jamshid Kashani (mathematician and astronomer).

2135	**612**	5r. black and brown	1·50	40

613 Kaaba, Mecca

1980. 1400th Anniv of Hegira (1st issue). Multicoloured.

2136	3r. Type **613**	25	25
2137	5r. Koran and globe (vert)	25	25
2138	10r. Pilgrim and Kaaba	55	25

See also Nos. 2148/51.

614 Flag and Revolutionaries

1980. 1st Anniv of Islamic Revolution. Mult.

2139	1r. Type **614** (28×40 mm)	25	25
2140	3r. Dagger and dripping blood (28×40 mm)	40	25
2141	5r. Open window and rising sun (28×40 mm)	60	30
2432	1r. As No. 2139 but 24×35 mm	25	25
2433	3r. As No. 2140 but 24×36 mm	35	35
2435	5r. As No. 2141 but 24×36 mm	45	45

615 Dehkhoda

1980. Birth Centenary of Dehkhoda (compiler, Iranian encyclopedia).

2142	**615**	10r. multicoloured	30	25

616 Female Costume of East Azerbaijan

1980. New Year Festival. Multicoloured.

2143	3r. Type **616**	25	25
2144	5r. Male costume of East Azerbaijan	25	25

617 M. Mossadegh

1980. Birth Centenary of Dr. Mohammed Mossadegh (statesman).

2145	**617**	20r. multicoloured	60	25

618 Morteza Mottahari

1980. 1st Death Anniv of Prof. Morteza Mottahari.

2146	**618**	10r. black and red	55	25

619 Telephone

1980. World Telecommunications Day.

2147	**619**	20r. black, green and red	55	25

620 Mosque Interior

1980. 1400th Anniv of Hegira (2nd issue). Multicoloured.

2148	50d. Type **620**	25	25
2149	1r. Crowd with banner	25	25
2150	3r. Al-Biruni, Farabi and Avicenna	40	25
2151	5r. Mosque and Kaaba	30	25

621 Dr. Ali Shariati

1980. Dr. Ali Shariati (educator) Commemoration.

2152	**621**	5r. multicoloured	30	25

622 Kaaba and Banner

1980. Birth Anniv of Hazrat Mehdi (Shi'ite Imam).

2153	**622**	5r. green, red and black	30	25

623 Ayatollah Teleghani

1980. Ayatollah Teleghani Commemoration.

2154	**623**	5r. multicoloured	30	25

624 O.P.E.C. Emblem and Globe

1980. 20th Anniv of Organization of Petroleum Exporting Countries. Multicoloured.

2155	5r. Type **624**	30	25
2156	10r. Figures supporting O.P.E.C. emblem	60	25

625 Hands breaking Star of David around Dome of the Rock

1980. "Let us Liberate Jerusalem".

2157	**625**	5r. multicoloured	25	25
2158	**625**	20r. multicoloured	85	25

626 Tulip and Feizieh Theological College

1981. 2nd Anniv of Islamic Revolution. Mult.

2159	3r. Type **626** (dated "1981" at right)	25	25
2160	5r. Tulip (in red), drops of blood and "Martyr" in Persian script	40	25
2161	20r. Open tulip (in red) and crest of Republic	60	25
2434	3r. As No. 2159 but dated at left	35	35
2436	5r. As No. 2160 but orange tulip	45	45
2441	20r. As No. 2161 but orange tulip	70	70

627 Male Costume of Lorestan

1981. New Year Festival. Multicoloured.

2162	5r. Type **627**	25	25
2163	10r. Female costume, Lorestan	30	25

628 I.T.U. and W.H.O. Emblems with Ribbons forming Caduceus

1981. World Telecommunications Day.

2164	**628**	5r. orange, black & green	25	25

630 Militia Training

1981

2165	**630**	50d. black and brown	25	25
2166	-	1r. purple and green	25	25
2167	-	2r. brown and blue	25	25
2168	-	3r. black and green	25	25
2169	-	5r. blue and brown	25	25
2170	-	10r. ultramarine and blue	30	25
2171	-	20r. black and red	60	25
2172	-	50r. black and mauve	1·40	40
2173	-	100r. black and brown	2·30	60
2174	-	200r. blue and black	4·50	1·20

DESIGNS—As Type **630**: 1r. Man and boy at school desk (Literacy campaign); 2r. Digging irrigation ditch. 37×27 mm: 3r. Massed prayers; 20r. Woman with rifle; 50r. Worker at lathe; 100r. Pilgrims around Kaaba. 27×37 mm: 5r. Revolutionary Guards emblem and crowd; 10r. Arabic tapestry; 200r. Niche in Mosque illuminated by sun.

631 Ayatollah Kashani

1981. Birth Centenary of Ayatollah Kashani.

2175	**631**	15r. purple and green	45	25

632 Armed Forces

1981. Islamic Iranian Army.

2176	**632**	5r. multicoloured	40	25

633 Carrier Pigeon flying over Gun Barrels

1981. U.P.U. Day.

2177	**633**	20r. black and blue	55	25

634 Inscription

1981. Millenary of "Nabj al-Blagah" (sacred book).

2178	**634**	25r. green, blue and black	60	25

635 Victims of Bomb at Islamic Party's Headquarters

1981. Iranian Bomb and War Victims, Commemoration.

2179	**635**	3r. black and red	25	25
2180	-	5r. brown & deep brown	25	25
2181	-	10r. multicoloured	25	25

DESIGNS: 5r. President Rajai and Prime Minister Bahomar (bomb victims); 10r. Dr. Chamran (killed in Iran–Iraq War).

636 Ayatollah Tabatabaie

1981. Death Centenary of Ayatollah Ghazi Tabatabaie.

2182	**636**	5r. brown, green and gold	25	25

637 Hand writing on Board

1982. Literacy Campaign.

2183	**637**	5r. blue and gold	25	25

638 Text "God is Great" over Map of Iran

1982. 3rd Anniv of Islamic Revolution. Mult.

2184	5r. Type **638**	25	25
2185	10r. Dove forming tulip	25	25
2186	20r. "God is Great" over Globe	55	25

639 Banner around Globe

1982. Islamic Unity Week.
2187 **639** 25r. multicoloured 1·00 25

640 Manacled Hands reaching towards Christ

1982. Glorification of Christ's Birth.
2188 **640** 20r. multicoloured 55 25

641 Male Costume of Khuzestan

1982. New Year Festival. Multicoloured.
2189 3r. Type **641** 25 25
2190 5r. Female costume of Khuzestan 45 45

642 National Flag

1982. 3rd Anniv of Islamic Republic.
2191 **642** 30r. black, red and green 90 25

643 Ayatollah Sadr

1982. 2nd Death Anniv of Ayatollah Sadr.
2192 **643** 50r. multicoloured 1·00 40

644 Ayatollahs Madani and Dastghib

1982. Ayatollahs Sayed Assadollah Madani and Sayed Abdolhossein Dastghib Commemoration.
2193 **644** 50r. red, black and gold 1·00 40

645 Hand holding Cogwheels

1982. Labour Day.
2194 **645** 100r. multicoloured 2·30 75

646 Geometric Pattern

1982. World Telecommunications Day.
2195 **646** 100r. multicoloured 2·30 75

647 Symbolic Design

1982. Mab'as Festival.
2196 **647** 32r. multicoloured 1·00 40

648 Rifles and Clenched Fist

1982. 19th Anniv of 1963 Islamic Rising.
2197 **648** 20r. black, red and silver 70 30

649 Lieutenant Islambuli

1982. Lieutenant Khaled Islambuli (assassin of Pres. Sadat of Egypt) Commemoration.
2198 **649** 2r. multicoloured 40 25

650 Ayatollah Beheshti

1982. 1st Death Anniv of Ayatollah Mohammed Hossein Beheshti.
2199 **650** 10r. multicoloured 40 25

651 Soldiers, Tanks and Hand holding Banner

1982. Victims of War against Iraq Commemoration.
2200 **651** 5r. multicoloured 25 25

652 Dome of the Rock

1982. World Jerusalem Day.
2201 **652** 1r. multicoloured 25 25

653 Pilgrims around Kaaba

1982. Pilgrimage to Mecca.
2202 **653** 10r. multicoloured 30 25

654 Globe and Letters

1982. World U.P.U. Day.
2203 **654** 30r. multicoloured 75 25

655 Bloodied Hand releasing Dove

1983. 4th Anniv of Islamic Revolution.
2204 **655** 30r. multicoloured (crowd in brown) 75 25
2445 **655** 30r. multicoloured (crowd in orange) 1·00 1·00

656 Casting Vote

1983. 4th Anniv of Islamic Republic.
2205 **656** 10r. red, black and green 30 25

657 "Enlightenment"

1983. Teachers' Day.
2206 **657** 5r. multicoloured 25 25

658 Microwave Antenna and "83"

1983. World Communications Year.
2207 **658** 20r. blue, mauve & brown 60 25

659 Assembly

1983. 1st Session of Islamic Consultative Assembly.
2208 **659** 5r. multicoloured 25 25

660 Doves and Crowd

1983. 20th Anniv of 1963 Islamic Rising.
2209 **660** 10r. multicoloured 30 25

661 Map of Persian Gulf and burning Oil Wells at Nowruz

1983. Ecology Week.
2210 **661** 5r. black, red and blue 55 25

662 Sadooghi

1983. Ayatollah Mohammad Sadooghi Commem.
2211 **662** 20r. black and red 60 25

663 Hands holding Rifle over Dome of the Rock

1983. World Jerusalem Day.
2212 **663** 5r. yellow, brown & blue 25 25

664 Rajai and Bahomar

1983. Government Week (death anniv of Pres. Rajai and Prime Minister Dr. Bahomar).
2213 **664** 3r. orange and blue 25 25

665 Cartridges and Text

1983. War Week.
2214 **665** 5r. green and red 25 25

666 Stamps and Map of Iran around Globe

1983. World U.P.U. Day.
2215 **666** 10r. multicoloured 40 25

667 Esfahani

1983. 4th Death Anniv of Ayatollah Ashrafi Esfahani.
2216 **667** 5r. multicoloured 25 25

668 Mirza Kuchik Khan

1983. Religious and Political Personalities.

2217 - 1r. black and pink 25 25
2218 **668** 2r. black and orange 25 25
2219 - 3r. black and blue 25 25
2220 - 5r. black and red 25 25
2221 - 10r. black and green 30 25
2222 - 20r. black and purple 60 25
2223 - 30r. black and brown 90 30
2224 - 50r. black and blue 1·50 55
2225 - 100r. black and red 2·30 90
2226 - 200r. black and green 4·50 1·50

DESIGNS: 1r. Sheikh Mohammed Khiabani; 3r. Seyd Modjtaba Navab Safavi; 5r. Seyd Jamal-ed-Din Assadabadi; 10r. Seyd Hassah Modaress; 20r. Sheikh Fazel Assad Nouri; 30r. Mirza Mohammed Hossein Naieni; 50r. Sheikh Mohammed Hossein Kashef; 100r. Seyd Hassan Shirazi; 200r. Mirza Reza Kermani.

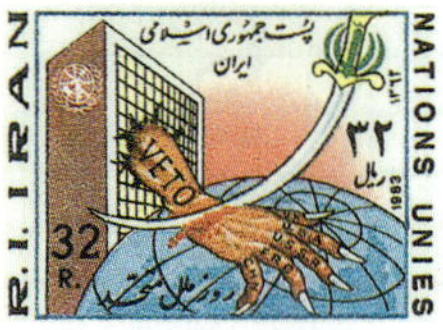

669 Sword severing "Right of Veto" Hand

1983. United Nations Day.
2228 **669** 32r. multicoloured 1·10 40

670 Storming the U.S. Embassy, Hostage and burning American Flag

1983. 4th Anniv of Storming of United States Embassy.
2229 **670** 28r. multicoloured 85 55

671 Avicenna and Globe

1983. International Medical Seminar, Teheran.
2230 **671** 3r. purple and blue 55 25

672 Young and Old Soldiers

1983. Preparation Day.
2231 **672** 20r. green, black and red 60 25

673 Fist with Gun and Dove

1983. Saddam's Crimes Conference.
2232 **673** 5r. black and mauve 25 25

674 Dr. Mohammad Mofatteh

1983. 4th Death Anniv of Dr. Mohammed Mofatteh.
2233 **674** 10r. mauve, black & gold 40 25

675 Light shining on Globe

1983. Mohammed's Birth Anniv.
2234 **675** 5r. blue, brown and green 25 25

676 Tulips and Flag

1984. 5th Anniv of Islamic Revolution.
2235 **676** 10r. multicoloured 75 25

677 Nurse tending Wounded Soldier

1984. Nurses' Day.
2240 **677** 20r. multicoloured 45 25

678 Soldier in Wheelchair

1984. Invalids' Day.
2241 **678** 5r. multicoloured 25 25

679 "Lotus gebelia"

1984. New Year Festival. Flowers. Multicoloured.
2242 3r. Type **679** 25 25
2243 5r. "Tulipa chrysantha" 30 25
2244 10r. "Glycyrrhiza glabra" 45 25
2245 20r. "Matthiola alyssifolia" 90 25

680 Malcolm Little (founder of Union of Moslem Mosques and Organization for African–American Unity)

1984. Struggle Against Racial Discrimination.
2246 **680** 5r. multicoloured 25 25

681 Flag around Globe

1984. 5th Anniv of Islamic Republic.
2247 **681** 5r. multicoloured 25 25

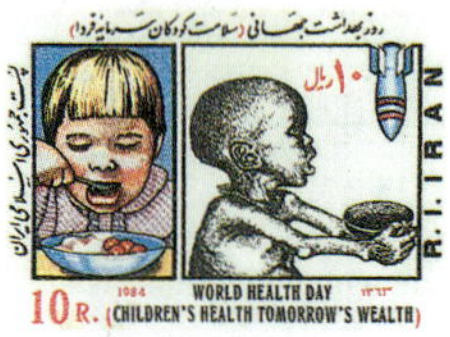

682 Well-fed and Starving Children

1984. World Health Day.
2248 **682** 10r. multicoloured 40 25

683 Harb

1984. 22nd Death Anniv of Sheikh Ragheb Harb.
2249 **683** 5r. black, red and green 25 25

684 Family holding Red Crescent Banner

1984. World Red Cross and Red Crescent Day.
2250 **684** 5r. multicoloured 25 25

685 Transmitter

1984. World Telecommunications Day.
2251 **685** 20r. black, blue and red 60 40

686 Ghotb

1984. 19th Death Anniv of Seyyed Ghotb.
2252 **686** 10r. black, gold & orange 40 25

687 Kaaba and Destruction of Images

1984. Conquest of Mecca.
2253 **687** 5r. multicoloured 25 25

688 Jerusalem, Map of Israel and Koran

1984. World Jerusalem Day (5r.) and Fetr Feast (10r.). Multicoloured.
2254 5r. Type **688** 25 25
2255 10r. Crowd around mosque 40 25

689 Choga Zanbil, Susa

1984. Preservation of Cultural Heritage. Mult.
2256 5r. Type **689** 25 25
2257 5r. Emamzadeh Hossein shrine, Qazvin (Arabic date at left) 25 25
2258 5r. Imam Mosque, Isfahan 25 25
2259 5r. Ark Fortress, Tabriz 25 25
2260 5r. Prophet Daniel's Mausoleum, Susa (with conical tower) 25 25

691 Crowd around Kaaba

1984. Feast of Sacrifices.
2261 **691** 10r. multicoloured 30 25

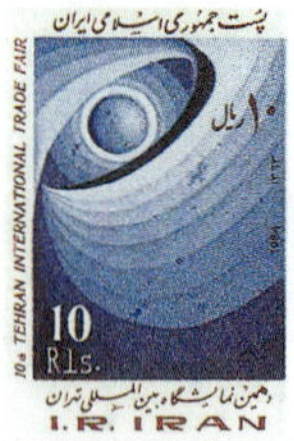

692 Spirit Nebula

1984. 10th International Trade Fair, Teheran.
2262 **692** 10r. blue and red 30 25

693 Rifle and Cartridges on Flower

1984. War Week.
2263 **693** 5r. multicoloured 25 25

694 Stylized Pigeon and U.P.U. Emblem

1984. World Universal Postal Union Day.
2264 **694** 20r. multicoloured 60 40

695 Khomeini

1984. 7th Death Anniv of Haj Seyyed Mostafa Khomeini.
2265 **695** 5r. multicoloured 25 25

696 Tabatabaie

1984. Ghazi Tabatabaie Commemoration.
2266 **696** 5r. black, gold and red 25 25

697 Saadi

1984. 800th Birth Anniv of Saadi (poet) Congress.
2267 **697** 10r. multicoloured 55 25

698 Clasped Hands, Mosque and Koran

1984. Mohammed's Birth Anniv and Unity Week.
2268 **698** 5r. multicoloured 25 25

699 Doves as Petals

1985. 6th Anniv of Islamic Revolution (1st issue).
2269 **699** 40r. multicoloured (tulip emblem in red) 1·10 75
2446 **699** 40r. multicoloured (tulip emblem in mauve) 1·30 1·30

See also No. 2277.

700 Sapling and Forest

1985. Tree Planting Day. Multicoloured.
2270 3r. Type **700** 25 25
2271 5r. Sapling growing near forest 25 25

701 Crown Imperial ("Fritillaria imperialis")

1985. New Year Festival. Multicoloured.
2272 5r. Type **701** 40 25
2273 5r. Pilewort ("Ranunculus ficarioides") 40 25
2274 5r. Saffron crocus ("Crocus sativus") 40 25
2275 5r. "Primula heterochroma" 40 25

702 Procession of Women with Flags

1985. Women's Day and Birth Anniv of Fatima.
2276 **702** 10r. multicoloured 40 25

703 Tulip and Ballot Box

1985. 6th Anniv of Islamic Republic (2nd issue).
2277 **703** 20r. multicoloured 55 30

704 Koran

1985. Mab'as Festival.
2278 **704** 10r. multicoloured 40 25

705 Globe, Chain, Banner, Kaaba and Scales

1985. World Day of the Oppressed.
2279 **705** 5r. multicoloured 25 25

706 I.T.U. Emblem and Telephone Handsets

1985. World Telecommunications Day.
2280 **706** 20r. multicoloured 55 30

707 Soldier saluting and Bridge

1985. Liberation of Khorramshahr.
2281 **707** 5r. multicoloured 25 25

708 Fist, Rifles and Qum Theological College

1985. 22nd Anniv of 1963 Islamic Rising.
2282 **708** 10r. multicoloured 55 25

709 Decorated Plates and Vases

1985. World Handicrafts Day.
2283 **709** 20r. multicoloured 60 40

710 Map of Israel and Dome of the Rock

1985. World Jerusalem Day.
2284 **710** 5r. multicoloured 25 25

711 Arabic Script

1985. Fetr Feast.
2285 **711** 5r. blue, red and black 25 25

712 Organization Emblem

1985. 4th Anniv of Islamic Propagation Organization.
2286 **712** 5r. brown, green & black 25 25

713 Abdolhossein Amini and the Koran

1985. Ayatollah Sheikh Abdolhossein Amini (theologian) Commemoration.
2287 **713** 5r. multicoloured 25 25

714 Pilgrims around Holy Kaaba

1985. Pilgrimage to Mecca.
2288 **714** 10r. multicoloured 40 25

715 Two Swords Pattern

1985. Preservation of Cultural History. Ancient Ceramic Plates from Nishabur. Multicoloured.
2289 5r. Type **715** 25 25
2290 5r. Plate with border of Farsi script 25 25
2291 5r. Stylized bird pattern 25 25
2292 5r. Four leaves and knot pattern 25 25

716 Revolutionaries and Mosque

1985. 50th Anniv of Rising in Goharshad Mosque, Meshed.
2293 **716** 10r. multicoloured 40 25

717 Health Services

1985. Government and People Week. Multicoloured.
2294 5r. Envelope, crane and mechanical digger 25 25
2295 5r. Factory, cogwheel and ear of wheat 25 25
2296 5r. Type **717** 25 25
2297 5r. Literacy campaign emblem on book 25 25

718 Red Tulips dripping Blood

1985. 7th Anniv of "Bloody Friday" Riots.
2298 **718** 10r. multicoloured 40 25

719 O.P.E.C. Emblem and "25"

1985. 25th Anniv of Organization of Petroleum Exporting Countries.
2299 **719** 5r. yellow and brown 25 25
2300 - 5r. blue and green 25 25
DESIGN: No. 2300, O.P.E.C. emblem and world map.

720 Dead Iranian

1985. 5th Anniv of Iran–Iraq War. Multicoloured.
2301 5r. Type **720** 25 25
2302 5r. Dome of mosque and text "Ashura" 25 25
2303 5r. White doves with map of Iran under a hail of bombs 25 25
2304 5r. Oasis and exploding rifle 25 25

721 Symbolic Design

1985. Death Millenary of Ash-Sharif Ar-Radi (writer).
2305 **721** 20r. blue, gold & ultram 60 40

722 Envelopes and Posthorn

1985. World U.P.U. Day.
2306 **722** 20r. multicoloured 60 40

723 Emblem

1985. World Standards Day.
2307 **723** 20r. multicoloured 60 40

724 Seedling and Ear of Wheat in Hand

1985. Agricultural Training and Extension Year.
2308 **724** 5r. multicoloured 25 25

725 Seal of U.S. Embassy

1985. 6th Anniv of Storming of United States Embassy.
2309 **725** 40r. multicoloured 1·40 75

726 Kaaba, Mosque and Clasped Hands

1985. Mohammed's Birth Anniv and Unity Week.
2310 **726** 10r. multicoloured 40 25

727 Rose growing from Pen Nib and Tulip

1985. High Council of Cultural Revolution Anniv.
2311 **727** 5r. multicoloured 25 25

728 Profiles and Symbols of Learning

1985. International Youth Year. Mult.
2312 5r. Type **728** 25 25
2313 5r. Profiles and symbols of war 25 25
2314 5r. Profiles and symbols of industry and agriculture 25 25
2315 5r. Profiles and sports pictograms 25 25

729 Ezzeddin Al-Qassam

1985. 50th Death Anniv of Ezzeddin Al-Qassam.
2316 **729** 20r. brown, red and silver 60 40

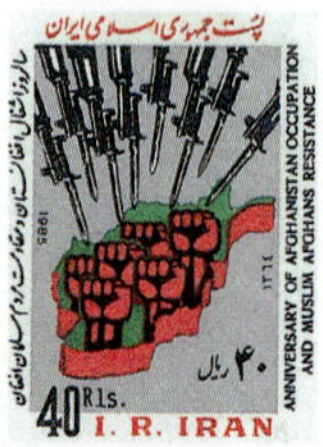

730 Bayonets, Map and Clenched Fists

1985. Afghan Resistance to Occupation.
2317 **730** 40r. multicoloured 1·30 85

731 Mirza Taqi Khan Amir Kabir

1986. 135th Death Anniv of Mirza Taqi Khan Amir Kabir.
2318 **731** 5r. multicoloured 1·20 25

732 Tulips and Crowd destroying Statue

1986. 7th Anniv of Islamic Revolution.
2319 **732** 20r. multicoloured 60 40

733 Sulayman Khater and Dome of the Rock

1986. 40th Death Anniv of Sulayman Khater.
2320 **733** 10r. black, blue and red 40 25

734 Woman, Child and Crowd

1986. Women's Day and Birth Anniv of Fatima.
2321 **734** 10r. multicoloured 40 25

735 "Papaver orientale"

1986. New Year Festival. Flowers. Mult.
2322 5r. Type **735** 30 25
2323 5r. "Anemone coronaria" 30 25
2324 5r. "Papaver bracteatum" 30 25
2325 5r. "Anemone biflora" 30 25

736 Fist and Text

1986. "2000th Day of Sacred Defence" (Iran–Iraq war).
2326 **736** 5r. green and red 25 25

737 Rose, Globe and Coloured Bands

1986. Struggle against Racial Discrimination.
2327 **737** 5r. multicoloured 25 25

738 Iranian Flag and Map

1986. 7th Anniv of Islamic Republic.
2328 **738** 10r. multicoloured 40 25

739 Dome

1986. Mab'as Festival.
2329 **739** 40r. multicoloured 1·20 75

740 Insignia

1986. Army Day.
2330 **740** 5r. multicoloured 25 25

741 Dead Soldier and Wrecked Helicopter

1986. 6th Anniv of United States Landing at Tabas.
2331 **741** 40r. orange, green & blk 1·20 75

742 Text

1986. World Day of the Oppressed. Birth Anniv of Imam Mahdi.
2332 **742** 10r. black, red and gold 40 25

743 Symbolic Design

1986. Teachers' Day.

2333 **743** 5r. multicoloured 25 25

744 Antennae and Radio Waves

1986. World Communications Day.

2334 **744** 20r. black, silver and blue 60 40

745 Soldier and Tanks

1986. International Children's Day.

2335 **745** 15r. multicoloured 45 25

2336 - 15r. black, blue & mauve 45 25

DESIGN: No. 2336, Boy and text.

746 Qum Theological College and Sun Rays

1986. 23rd Anniv of 1963 Islamic Rising.

2337 **746** 10r. multicoloured 40 25

747 Dome of the Rock, Map of Israel and Barbed Wire

1986. World Jerusalem Day.

2338 **747** 10r. multicoloured 40 25

748 Crowd at Prayer

1986. Fetr Festival.

2339 **748** 10r. multicoloured 75 25

749 Baluchi Needle Work

1986. World Handicrafts Day. Multicoloured.

2340 10r. Type **749** 40 30

2341 10r. Master craftswomen at work 40 30

2342 10r. Carpet 40 30

2343 10r. Engraved copper vase 40 30

750 Linked Hands around Map on Globe

1986. Solidarity with South African People.

2344 **750** 10r. multicoloured 40 25

751 Dr. Beheshti, Doves and Explosion

1986. 5th Anniv of Bomb Explosion at Islamic Party Headquarters, Teheran.

2345 **751** 10r. multicoloured 40 25

752 Ayatollah Mohammad Taqi Shirazi and Map

1986. Iraqi Muslim Rising.

2346 **752** 20r. multicoloured 60 40

753 Shrine, Meshed

1986. Birth Anniv of Imam Riza.

2347 **753** 10r. multicoloured 40 25

754 Crowd around Kaaba, Flag and Clenched Fists

1986. Feast of Sacrifices.

2348 **754** 10r. multicoloured 40 25

755 Soltanieh Mosque

1986. Preservation of Cultural Heritage. Mult.

2349 5r. Type **755** 25 25

2350 5r. Mausoleum of Sohel Ben Ali, Astaneh 25 25

2351 5r. Bam fortress 25 25

2352 5r. Gateway of Blue Mosque, Tabriz 25 25

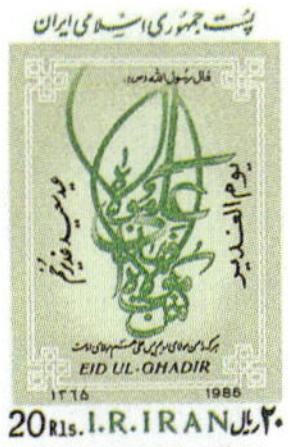

756 "Eid-ul-Ghadir" in Arabic

1986. Ghadir Festival.

2353 **756** 20r. light green, green and black 60 40

757 Graph, Roof and People

1986. Population and Housing Census.

2354 **757** 20r. multicoloured 60 30

758 Missile Boat "Paykan" in Fist below Bombs

1986. 6th Anniv of Iran–Iraq War. Mult.

2355 **758** 10r. blue, black and red 40 25

2356 - 10r. red and black 40 25

2357 - 10r. yellow, black and red 40 25

2358 - 10r. blue, black and red 40 25

2359 - 10r. green, black and red 40 25

DESIGNS: No. 2356, Khorramshar; 2357, Howeizah; 2358, Siege of Abadan; 2359, Susangard.

759 Wrestling

1986. 10th Asian Games, Seoul. Multicoloured.

2360 15r. Type **759** 40 25

2361 15r. Rifle shooting 40 25

760 Bird with Envelopes as Wings on Globe

1986. World Universal Postal Union Day.

2362 **760** 20r. multicoloured 60 40

761 Emblem

1986. 40th Anniv of UNESCO.

2363 **761** 45r. blue, black and red 1·20 70

762 Allameh Tabatabaie

1986. 5th Death Anniv of Allameh Tabatabaie.

2364 **762** 10r. green, gold and black 30 25

763 Sun behind Dome and Minaret

1986. Mohammed's Birth Anniv and Unity Week.

2365 **763** 10r. multicoloured 30 25

764 Militiamen with Flags

1986. "Mobilization of the Oppressed" Week.

2366 **764** 5r. multicoloured 25 25

765 Guerrilla Fighters

1986. Afghan Resistance to Occupation.

2367 **765** 40r. multicoloured 1·20 40

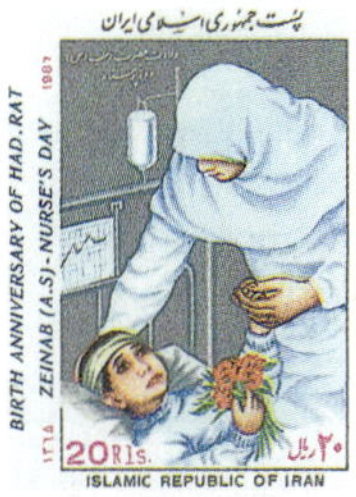

766 Nurse tending Boy

1987. Nurses' Day.

2368 **766** 20r. multicoloured 60 40

767 Emblem and Tulip on Globe

1987. 5th Islamic Theology Conference, Teheran.

2369	**767**	20r. multicoloured	60	40

768 Emblems of Revolution

1987. 8th Anniv of Islamic Revolution.

2370	**768**	20r. multicoloured (38×58 mm)	60	40
2444	**768**	20r. multicoloured (24×37 mm)	70	70

769 Emblem and Crowd

1987. 8th Anniv of Revolutionary Committees.

2371	**769**	10r. yellow, blue and red	30	25

770 Woman and Soldiers

1987. Women's Day and Birth Anniv of Fatima.

2372	**770**	10r. multicoloured	30	25

771 Airbus Industrie A300 Aircraft and Banner around Globe

1987. 25th Anniv of Iranair.

2373	**771**	30r. multicoloured	90	55

772 Ayatollah Naeini

1987. 50th Death Anniv of Ayatollah Mirza Mohammad Hossein Naeini.

2374	**772**	10r. multicoloured	30	25

773 Flag Irises

1987. New Year Festival. Flowers. Mult.

2375	5r. Type **773**	40	25
2376	5r. Tulips	40	25
2377	5r. Dutch irises	40	25
2378	5r. Roses	40	25

774 Arabic Text and Arched Window

1987. Mab'as Festival.

2379	**774**	45r. lt green, grn & gold	1·40	75

775 Flag as Star on Map

1987. 8th Anniv of Islamic Republic.

2380	**775**	20r. multicoloured	60	30

776 Soldiers with Flag

1987. Revolutionary Guards' Day. Birth Anniv of Imam Hossein.

2381	**776**	5r. multicoloured	25	25

777 Emblems on Map and Dome of the Rock

1987. Commemoration of Lebanese Hizbollah Dead.

2382	**777**	10r. red, green and grey	30	25

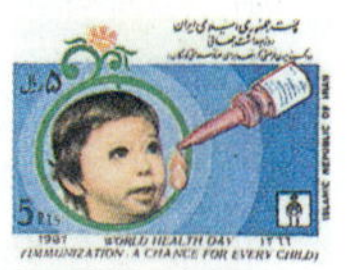

778 Child and Vaccination Dropper

1987. World Health Day. Multicoloured.

2383	3r. Syringe and children	25	25
2384	5r. Type **778**	30	25

779 Stars around Holy Kaaba

1987. World Day of the Oppressed. Birth Anniv of Imam Mahdi.

2385	**779**	20r. multicoloured	60	30

780 Worker with Rifle and Koran, Factory and Cogwheel

1987. International Labour Day.

2386	**780**	5r. multicoloured	25	25

781 Ayatollah Mottahari, Candle and Book

1987. Teachers' Day.

2387	**781**	5r. red, yellow and blue	25	25

782 Map in Telephone Dial

1987. World Telecommunications Day.

2388	**782**	20r. violet and blue	70	30

783 12th-century Ceramic Lidded Pot, Rey

1987. International Museums Day.

2389	**783**	20r. chestnut, brn & grey	60	30
2390	-	20r. brown, black & grn	60	30

DESIGN: No. 2390, Sassanian silver-gilt flower vase.

784 Dove, Globe and Dome of the Rock dripping Blood onto Star

1987. World Jerusalem Day.

2391	**784**	20r. multicoloured	60	30

785 Qum Theological College, Crown and Bayonets

1987. 24th Anniv of 1963 Islamic Rising.

2392	**785**	20r. multicoloured	60	30

786 Blown Glass

1987. World Crafts Day. Multicoloured.

2393	5r. Type **786**	25	25
2394	5r. Khatam marquetry	25	25
2395	5r. Ceramic ware	25	25
2396	5r. Ceramic master-craftsman	25	25

787 Factory, Freighter and Dam

1987. Campaign against Tax Evasion.

2397	**787**	10r. gold, black and silver	40	25

788 Figures in Cupped Hand

1987. Welfare Week.

2398	**788**	15r. multicoloured	45	25

789 Crowd around Mosque

1987. Feast of Sacrifices.

2399	**789**	12r. turquoise, sil & blk	45	25

790 Design from Mosque Tile

1987. Ghadir Festival.

2400	**790**	18r. gold, green and black	55	30

791 Hands clasped over National Emblem

1987. Islamic Banking Week.

2401	**791**	15r. brown, blue and gold	45	25

792 Typical Persian Calligraphy

1987. 1st Iranian Calligraphers' Cultural and Artistic Congress.

2402	**792**	20r. multicoloured	60	30

793 Blood running from Heart as Globe, Mosque and Kaaba

1987. Commemoration of Pilgrims killed at Mecca.

2403	**793**	8r. multicoloured	40	25

794 Toothbrushes as Mouths

1987. 25th Anniv of Iranian Dentists Association.

2404	**794**	10r. multicoloured	40	25

795 Dove with Globe as Eye

1987. International Peace Day.

2405	**795**	20r. bronze and blue	60	30

796 Rifleman and Armed Launch

1987. 7th Anniv of Iran–Iraq War.

2406	**796**	25r. green, blue and black	75	40
2407	-	25r. red, black and blue	75	40

DESIGN: No. 2407, Rifleman and soldiers.

797 Open Book on Crossed Pistols

1987. Police Day.

2408	**797**	10r. multicoloured	30	25

798 People in Cupped Hands

1987. Int Social Security Co-operation Week.

2409	**798**	15r. black, blue and gold	45	25

799 Dove with Envelopes as Tail on Globe

1987. World Post Day. Multicoloured.

2410	15r. Type **799**	45	25
2411	15r. Dr. M. Ghandi (Postal Minister) commemoration	45	25

800 American Flag, Great Seal and Capitol

1987. 6th Anniv of Storming of United States Embassy.

2412	**800**	40r. multicoloured	1·20	60

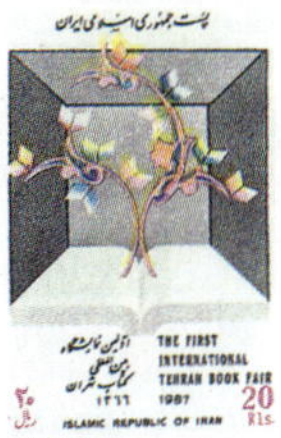

801 Tree growing from Open Book

1987. 1st Teheran Book Fair.

2413	**801**	20r. multicoloured	60	30

802 Clasped Hands

1987. Mohammed's Birth Anniv and Unity Week.

2414	**802**	25r. brown, flesh & green	60	40

803 Ayatollah Modarres

1987. 50th Death Anniv of Ayatollah Seyyed Hassan Modarres.

2415	**803**	10r. brown and ochre	30	25

804 Djameh Mosque, Urmia

1987. Mosques.

2415a	-	1r. orange and silver	10	10
2416	**804**	2r. mauve and silver	15	15
2416a	-	3r. green and silver	10	10
2417	-	5r. red and silver	25	25
2419	-	20r. violet and silver	60	25
2420	-	30r. red and silver	1·20	30
2421	-	40r. blue and silver	1·50	40
2422	-	50r. brown and silver	1·10	60
2423	-	100r. green and silver	1·90	1·10
2594	-	10r. blue and silver	1·10	15
2602	-	200r. black and silver	3·50	2·00
2604	-	500r. green and silver	11·50	5·00

DESIGNS—HORIZ: 1r. Djameh Mosque, Schuschter; 3r. Djameh Mosque, Kerman; 5r. Qazvin; 10r. Veramin; 20r. Saveh; 40r. Shiraz; 100r. Hamadan. VERT: 30r. Natanz; 50r. Isfahan; 200r. Dizful; 500r. Yezd.

805 Open Book, Profiles and Ear of Wheat

1987. Agricultural Training and Extension Week.

2426	**805**	10r. multicoloured	30	25

806 Guerrilla Fighters on Map

1987. Afghan Resistance to Occupation.

2427	**806**	40r. multicoloured	1·10	60

807 Crowd with Banners

1988. 10th Anniv of Qum Uprising.

2428	**807**	20r. multicoloured	60	40

808 Bombs and Pencils

1988. Iranian Schools Victims' Commemoration.

2429	**808**	10r. multicoloured	30	25

809 Takhti and Mountain

1988. Victory of Gholamreza Takhti in World Freestyle Wrestling Championships.

2430	**809**	15r. multicoloured	40	25

810 Woman carrying armed Man

1988. Women's Day and Birth Anniv of Fatima.

2431	**810**	20r. multicoloured	55	30

811 Text

1988. 9th Anniv of Islamic Revolution.

2447	**811**	40r. multicoloured	1·30	1·30

812 Crowd burning Statue

1988. 10th Anniv of Tabriz Uprising.

2448	**812**	25r. multicoloured	55	40

813 Tree in Hand

1988. Tree Day.

2449	**813**	15r. multicoloured	40	30

814 "Anthemis hyalina"

1988. New Year Festival. Flowers. Mult.

2450	10r. Type **814**	30	25
2451	10r. Common mallows	30	25
2452	10r. Violets	30	25
2453	10r. "Echium amaenum"	30	25

815 Hand putting Ballot Paper into Box

1988. 9th Anniv of Islamic Republic.

2454	**815**	20r. multicoloured	60	40

816 Calligraphy

1988. World Day of the Oppressed. Birth Anniv of Imam Mahdi.

2455	**816**	20r. brown and blue	60	40

817 Shahid Mottahari Mosque and Theology School, Teheran

1988. Preservation of Cultural Heritage. Multicoloured.

2456		10r. Type **817**	30	25
2457		10r. Colonnade of Tarikhaneh Mosque, Damghan	30	25
2458		10r. Gateway of Sepahdari Mosque and Theology School, Arak (horiz)	30	25
2459		10r. Agha Bozorg Mosque and Theology School, Kashan (courtyard with pool) (horiz)	30	25

818 Bomb, Gas Cloud and Victims

1988. Halabja Chemical Attack Victims' Commemoration.

2460	**818**	20r. multicoloured	60	40

819 Map, Dome of the Rock and Palestinian

1988. Palestinian "Intifida" Movement. Each brown, red and black.

2461		10r. Type **819**	40	25
2462		10r. Man with rounded beard	40	25
2463		10r. Man wearing crew-necked jumper	40	25
2464		10r. Man with long pointed beard	40	25
2465		10r. Crowd and hand holding stone	40	25

820 Satellite and Telephone Handset

1988. World Telecommunications Day.

2466	**820**	20r. blue and green	60	40

821 Ceramic Vase

1988. International Museum Day. Multicoloured.

2467		10r. Type **821**	30	25
2468		10r. Iran Bastan Museum porch	30	25
2469		10r. 14th-century Tabriz silk rug	30	25
2470		10r. 7th-century B.C. gold ring, Arjan, Behbahan	30	25

822 Miners pushing Coal Truck

1988. Mining Day.

2471	**822**	20r. multicoloured	75	40

823 Children playing by River

1988. International Children's Day.

2472	**823**	10r. multicoloured	40	25

824 Bleeding Dove and Broken Bayonets

1988. 25th Anniv of 1963 Islamic Rising.

2473	**824**	10r. multicoloured	40	25

825 Glim Weaving

1988. World Handicrafts Day. Multicoloured.

2474		10r. Type **825**	30	25
2475		10r. Miniature of horsemen	30	25
2476		10r. Glim weaver (horiz)	30	25
2477		10r. Straw basket (horiz)	30	25

826 Child in Flower

1988. Child Health Campaign.

2478	**826**	20r. blue, green and black	40	25

827 Symbols of Industry and Agriculture

1988. Campaign Against Tax Evasion.

2479	**827**	20r. gold, blue and silver	40	25

828 Balkhi

1988. Allameh Balkhi (Afghan revolutionary writer) Commemoration.

2480	**828**	20r. black, red and silver	40	25

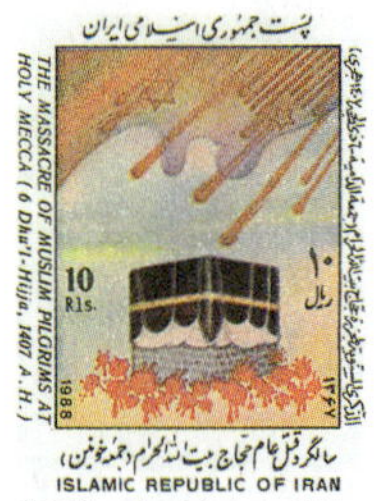

829 Blood raining on Holy Kaaba

1988. 1st Anniv of Death of Mecca Pilgrims. Multicoloured.

2481		10r. Type **829**	25	25
2482		10r. Holy Kaaba and blood-stained robe	25	25

830 Missile hitting Airplane

1988. Destruction of Iranair Passenger Airplane.

2483	**830**	45r. multicoloured	1·10	55

831 Seyyed Ali Andarzgou

1988. 10th Death Anniv of Seyyed Ali Andarzgou (revolutionary).

2484	**831**	20r. blue, black & brown	45	25

832 Central Bank, Teheran

1988. Islamic Banking Week.

2485	**832**	20r. grey, brown and gold	45	25

833 Carrying away Victim

1988. 10th Anniv of "Bloody Friday" Riots.

2486	**833**	25r. green, purple and red	60	40

834 Weightlifting

1988. Olympic Games, Seoul. Multicoloured.

2487		10r. Type **834**	30	25
2488		10r. Men's gymnastics	30	25
2489		10r. Judo	30	25
2490		10r. Football	30	25
2491		10r. Wrestling	30	25

835 Plant

1988. Agricultural Census.

2492	**835**	30r. yellow, black & grn	60	40

836 Iranians and Rifle

1988. 8th Anniv of Iran–Iraq War.

2493	**836**	20r. multicoloured	40	25

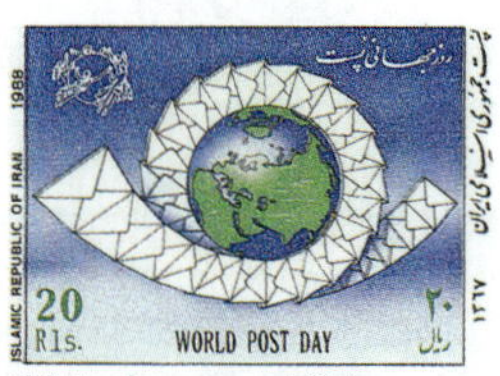

837 Envelopes around Globe

1988. World Post Day.

2494	**837**	20r. green, black and blue	40	25

838 Child's Face and Profiles

1988. Parents' and Teachers' Co-operation Week.

2495	**838**	20r. multicoloured	40	25

839 Clasped Hands and Emblem

1988. Mohammed's Birth Anniv and Unity Week.

2496	**839**	10r. multicoloured	25	25

840 Fist and Shattered Eagle

1988. 7th Anniv of Storming of United States Embassy.

2497	**840**	45r. multicoloured	1·00	55

841 Tree as Umbrella

1988. Insurance Day.

2498	**841**	10r. multicoloured	25	25

842 Tomb of Hafiz

1988. International Hafiz (writer) Congress, Shiraz.

2499	**842**	20r. blue, gold and mauve	55	25

843 Agricultural Symbols on Open Book

1988. Agricultural Training and Extension Week.

2500	**843**	15r. multicoloured	40	25

844 Parvin Etessami (writer)

1988. Iranian Celebrities of Science, Art and Literature. Multicoloured.

2501	10r. Type **844**	30	25
2502	10r. Qaem Maqam Farahani (writer)	30	25
2503	10r. Kamal al-Molk (artist)	30	25
2504	10r. Jalal al-Ahmad (writer)	30	25
2505	10r. Dr. Mohammad Mo'in (writer)	30	25

845 Map and Armed Afghan

1988. Afghan Resistance to Occupation.

2506	**845**	40r. multicoloured	1·00	55

846 Satellite, Envelopes and Dish Aerial

1989. Asian and Pacific Transport and Communications Decade. Multicoloured.

2507	20r. Type **846**	60	40
2508	20r. Air transport	60	40
2509	20r. Road and rail transport	60	40
2510	20r. Shipping	60	40

847 Tulips and Script

1989. Air. 10th Anniv of Islamic Revolution.

2511	**847**	40r. mauve, gold & black	1·00	55
2512	**847**	50r. violet, gold and black	1·30	75

848 Sun illuminating Koran

1989. Mab'as Festival.

2513	**848**	20r. multicoloured	40	30

849 Hands protecting Tree

1989. Tree Day.

2514	**849**	20r. multicoloured	40	30

850 "Cephalanthera kurdica"

1989. New Year Festival. Flowers. Mult.

2515	10r. Type **850**	25	25
2516	10r. "Dactylorhiza romana"	25	25
2517	10r. "Comperia comperiana"	25	25
2518	10r. "Orchis mascula"	25	25

851 Wind Gauge and Wheat

1989. World Meteorological Day. Mult.

2519	20r. Type **851**	45	30
2520	30r. Wind gauge, airplane and weather ship	90	40

852 State Arms

1989. 10th Anniv of Islamic Republic.

2521	**852**	20r. multicoloured	40	30

853 Refinery

1989. Commissioning of First Phase of Abadan Oil Refinery.

2522	**853**	20r. multicoloured	55	30

854 Mottahari

1989. Teachers' Day. 10th Death Anniv of Ayatollah Mottahari.

2523	**854**	20r. multicoloured	40	30

855 Dome of the Rock and Barbed Wire

1989. World Jerusalem Day.

2524	**855**	30r. multicoloured	85	45

856 Satellite, Globe and Dish Aerial

1989. World Telecommunications Day.

2525	**856**	20r. multicoloured	55	30

857 Jar

1989. International Museums Day. 6th-century Gurgan Artefacts.

2526	**857**	20r. yellow, blue & black	45	30
2527	-	20r. blue, black & mauve	45	30

DESIGN: No. 2527, Flagon.

858 Armed Men, Tent and Family with Sheep

1989. Nomads' Day.

2528	**858**	20r. multicoloured	40	25

859 Man engraving Vase

1989. World Crafts Day. Multicoloured.

2529	20r. Type **859**	40	30
2530	20r. Engraved copper vase	40	30
2531	20r. Engraved copper plate (vert)	40	30
2532	20r. Engraved copper wall-hanging (vert)	40	30

860 Khomeini and Crowd

1989. Ayatollah Khomeini Commemoration.

2533	**860**	20r. orange, black and blue (postage)	45	25
2534	-	70r. blk, vio & gold (air)	1·30	75

DESIGN—HORIZ: 70r. Ayatollah Khomeini.

861 Pasteur, Avicenna and Hand holding Quill

1989. "Philexfrance 89" International Stamp Exhibition, Paris. Each black, blue and brown, background colour given.

2535	**861**	30r. blue	60	40
2536	**861**	50r. brown	85	60

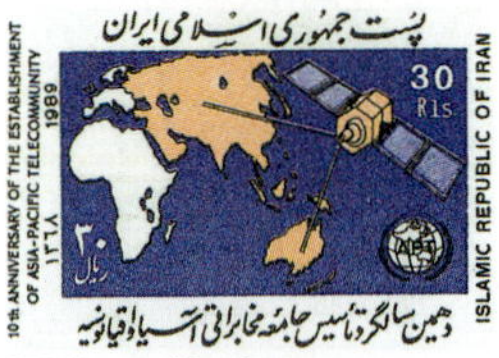

862 Map and Satellite

1989. 10th Anniv of Asia–Pacific Telecommunity.

2537	**862**	30r. orange, black & blue	60	40

863 Araghi

1989. 10th Death Anniv of Mehdi Araghi.

2538	**863**	20r. orange and purple	40	25

864 Shahryar and Monument

1989. Mohammed Hossein Shahryar (poet) Commemoration.

2539	**864**	20r. multicoloured	40	25

865 U.N. Security Council Document

1989. 9th Anniv of Iran–Iraq War.

2540	**865**	20r. multicoloured	40	25

866 Khomeini addressing Crowd

1989. Ayatollah Khomeini.

2541	-	1r. multicoloured	30	25
2542	-	2r. multicoloured	15	15
2543	**866**	3r. multicoloured	30	25
2544	-	5r. multicoloured	30	15
2545	-	10r. multicoloured	70	15
2546	-	20r. multicoloured	40	15
2547	-	30r. multicoloured	60	40
2548	-	40r. multicoloured	75	60
2549	-	50r. multicoloured	90	60
2550	-	70r. multicoloured	1·30	75
2551	-	100r. ultram, bl & grn	1·90	1·10
2552	-	200r. brown, yell & grn	3·50	1·70
2553	-	500r. multicoloured	8·25	4·50
2554	-	1000r. multicoloured	17·00	9·00

DESIGNS: 1r. Rose and courtyard; 2r. Khomeini as young man; 5r. Khomeini going into exile; 10r. Khomeini's return from exile; 20r. Khomeini making speech; 30r. Boy kissing Khomeini; 40r. Ayatollahs; 50r. Khomeini; 70r. Meeting in house; 100r. Arabic inscription; 200r. Microphones and chair; 500r. Qum Mosque and roses; 1000r. Sun's rays.

867 Pigeon carrying Letter

1989. World Post Day.

2561	**867**	20r. multicoloured	40	25

868 Multi-pointed Star in Window Arch

1989. Mohammed's Birth Anniv and Unity Week.

2562	**868**	10r. multicoloured	25	15

869 U.S. Emblem and Crowd in Dove

1989. 8th Anniv of Storming of United States Embassy.

2563	**869**	40r. orange, black & blue	75	45

870 Iranian and Launch with Machine Gun

1989. 10th Anniv of People's Militia.

2564	**870**	10r. multicoloured	40	25

871 Mehdi Elahi Ghomshei

1989. Iranian Celebrities of Science, Art and Literature.

2565	**871**	10r. red, black and gold	25	15
2566	-	10r. green, black and gold	25	15
2567	-	10r. yellow, black & gold	25	15
2568	-	10r. green, black and gold	25	15
2569	-	10r. mauve, black & gold	25	15

DESIGNS: No. 2566, Grand Ayatollah Seyyed Hossein Boroujerdi; 2567, Grand Ayatollah Sheikh Abdulkarim Haeri; 2568, Dr. Abdulazim Gharib; 2569, Seyyed Hossein Mirkhani.

872 Guiding Child's Hand

1990. International Literacy Year.

2570	**872**	20r. multicoloured	40	25

873 Book as Profiles forming Flower

1990. Identity Cards.

2571	**873**	10r. multicoloured	25	15

874 Drinking Vessel

1990. Cultural Heritage.

2572	**874**	20r. black and orange	40	25
2573	-	20r. black and green	40	25

DESIGN: No. 2563, Vase with stem.

875 Crowd

1990. 11th Anniv of Islamic Revolution.

2574	**875**	50r. multicoloured	90	60

876 Emblem

1990. Int Koran Recitation Competition.

2575	**876**	10r. black, blue and green	25	15

877 Soldier in Wheelchair

1990. Invalids' Day.

2576	**877**	10r. multicoloured	25	15

878 Figures encircling Tree

1990. Tree Day.

2577	**878**	20r. multicoloured	40	25

879 "Coronilla varia"

1990. New Year Festival. Flowers. Multicoloured.

2578	10r. Type **879**	25	15
2579	10r. "Astragalus cornucaprae"	25	15
2580	10r. "Astragalus obtusifolius"	25	15
2581	10r. "Astragalus straussii"	25	15

880 Crowd and Ballot Box

1990. 11th Anniv of Islamic Republic.

2582	**880**	30r. multicoloured	60	40

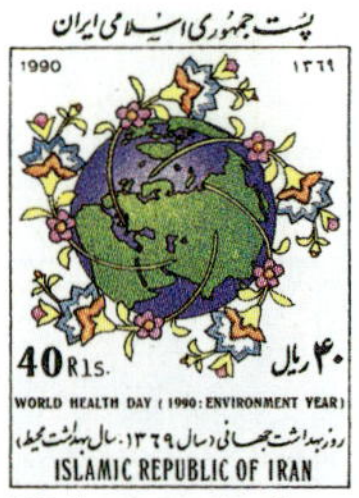

881 Flower growing from Globe

1990. World Health Day.

2583	**881**	40r. multicoloured	75	45

882 Khomeini

1990. 1st Death Anniv of Ayatollah Khomeini.

2584	**882**	50r. multicoloured	1·10	60

883 Turkoman Jewellery

1990. World Handicrafts Day. Multicoloured.

2585	20r. Type **883**	40	25
2586	50r. Gilded-steel bird	90	60

884 Crayons

1990. International Children's Day.

2587	**884**	20r. multicoloured	45	25

885 Seismograph on Map and Red Crescent Camp

1990. Aid for Earthquake Victims.

2588	**885**	100r. multicoloured	1·80	1·10

886 P.O.W. and Roses

1990. Returned Prisoners of War.

2589	**886**	250r. multicoloured	4·50	2·75

887 Ayatollah Khomeini and Dome of the Rock

1990. World Jerusalem Day.

2590	**887**	100r. multicoloured	2·00	1·10

888 Arabic Script

1990. International Congress on Abu-l Kasim Mansur Firdausi (poet). 16 sheets as T 888, each 60× 75 mm. Multicoloured (except T888).

MS2591 16 sheets. (a) 100r. black, gold and silver (Type **888**); (b) Arabic script in cartouches within floral frame; (c) 100r. Arabic script in rectangles; (d) 100r. Portrait of Firdausi; (e) 100r. Statue of Firdausi, Tehran; (f) 100r. Tomb, Tuss; (g) 200r. Shackled man and miners; (h) 200r. Assault on man; (i) 200r. Hunters in forest; (j) 200r. Horesman riding through flames; (k) 200r. Phoenix, boy and archer; (l) 200r. Domestic scene; (m) 200r. White elephant trampling fallen men; (n) 200r. Archer in cage surrounded by birds; (o) 200r. Sleeping archer, demon and horse; (p) 200r. Horesmen greeting each other 70·00 70·00

The 200r. values illustrate Firdausi's works.

889 Flowers, Crowd and Khomeini

1991. 12th Anniv of Islamic Revolution.

2605	**889**	100r. multicoloured	2·00	1·10

890 11th-century Gold Jug

1991. International Museum Day. Multicoloured.

2606	50r. Type **890**	90	60
2607	50r. 14th-century silver-inlaid brass basin	90	60

891 Flowers and Fists

1991. 11th Anniv of Iran–Iraq War.

2608	**891**	100r. multicoloured	1·80	1·10

892 Museum

1991. Inauguration of Post Museum, Teheran.

2609	**892**	200r. brown and black	3·50	25

893 Headset on Globe

1991. World Telecommunications Day (1990).

2610	**893**	50r. multicoloured	90	60

894 "Iris spuria"

1991. New Year Festival. Irises. Multicoloured.

2611	20r. Type **894**	75	45
2612	20r. "Iris lycotis"	40	25
2613	20r. "Iris demawendica"	40	25
2614	20r. "Iris meda"	40	25

895 Map, Dome of the Rock and Hosseini

1991. 10th Death Anniv of Saleh Hosseini.

2615	**895**	30r. red and black	1·00	40

896 Light Beam on Mountains

1991. Mab'as Festival.

2616	**896**	100r. multicoloured	1·80	1·10

897 Revolutionaries

1991. 25th Death Anniv (1990) of Revolutionaries.

2617	**897**	50r. brown and orange	1·10	60

898 Arabic Script

1991. World Day of the Oppressed. Birth Anniv of Mahdi.

2618	**898**	50r. multicoloured	1·20	60

899 Crowd, Flag and Ballot Box

1991. 12th Anniv of Islamic Republic.

2619	**899**	20r. multicoloured	60	25

900 Map and Bayonets

1991. World Jerusalem Day.

2620	**900**	100r. multicoloured	1·80	1·10

901 Mother and Child

1991. Women's Day and Birth Anniv of Fatima.

2621	**901**	50r. multicoloured	90	60

902 Boroujerdi

1991. 30th Death Anniv of Ayatollah Boroujerdi.

2622	**902**	200r. black and green	3·50	2·30

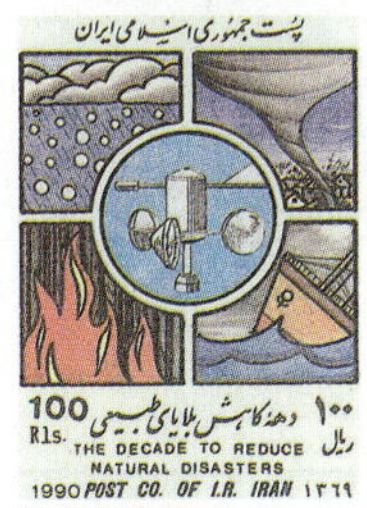

903 Disasters

1991. International Decade for Natural Disaster Reduction.

2623	**903**	100r. multicoloured	2·30	1·30

904 Book, Candle and Dr. Mottahari

1991. Teachers' Day.

2624	**904**	50r. yellow, orange & blk	90	60

906 Mausoleum, Meshed

1991. World Telecommunications Day. "Telecommunications and Safety of Human Life".

2625	**905**	100r. multicoloured	1·80	1·10

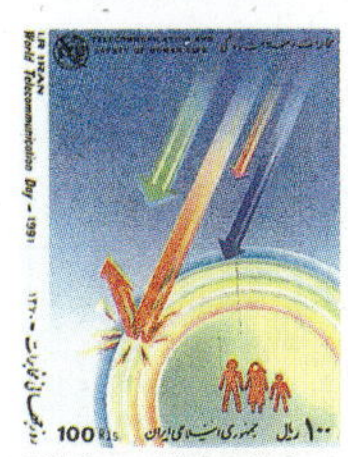

905 Rays striking Globe

1991. Birth Anniv of Imam Riza. Multicoloured.

2626	10r. Type **906**	25	15
2627	30r. Tombstone	60	40

907 Khomeini

1991. 2nd Death Anniv of Ayatollah Khomeini.

2628	**907**	100r. multicoloured	1·80	1·10

908 Karbala Shrine

1991. Iraqi Attack on Shi'ite Shrine, Karbala.

2629	**908**	70r. multicoloured	1·20	75

909 Nisami

1991. 900th Birth Anniv of Nisami (writer) International Congress, Tabris.

2630	**909**	50r. multicoloured	1·00	60

910 Archway

1991. 1330th Death Anniv of Ali ibn Ali Talib (Caliph).

2631	**910**	50r. multicoloured	90	60

911 Hands reaching through Parched Earth to Blood Drop

1991. Blood Donation.

2632	**911**	50r. multicoloured	90	60

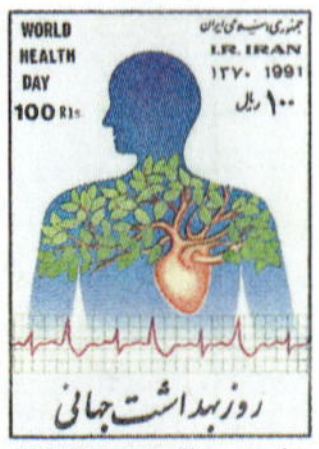

912 Heart as Tree and Cardiograph

1991. World Health Day.

2633	**912**	100r. multicoloured	1·80	1·10

913 Nedjefi

1991. Marashi Nedjefi Commemoration.

2634	**913**	30r. multicoloured	60	40

914 Doves flying from Cage

1991. 1st Anniv of Return of Prisoners of War.

2635	**914**	100r. multicoloured	1·80	1·10

915 Engraved Brassware

1991. World Crafts Day. Multicoloured.

2636	40r. Type **915**	75	45
2637	40r. Gilded samovar	75	45

916 Ayatollah Lari

1991

2638	**916**	30r. multicoloured	60	40

917 Fist and Roses in Cartouche

1991. 11th Anniv of Iran–Iraq War.

2639	**917**	20r. multicoloured	40	25

918 Islamic Symbols

1991. Islamic Unity Week.

2640	**918**	30r. multicoloured	60	40

919 13th-century Kashan Ewer

1991. International Museum Day. Multicoloured.

2641	20r. Type **919**	40	25
2642	40r. 13th-century Kashan ewer with bird's head lip	75	45

920 Gharib

1991. Dr. Mohammed Gharib.

2643	**920**	100r. black and blue	1·80	1·10

921 Banners

1991. Liberation of Khorramshahr.

2644	**921**	30r. multicoloured	70	40

922 Stamped Envelope

1991. World Post Day.

2645	**922**	70r. multicoloured	1·30	75

923 Khaju-Ye Kermani

1991. International Congress on Khaju-Ye Kermani (writer).

2646	**923**	30r. multicoloured	75	40

924 Globe and Seismograph

1991. 1st International Seismology and Earthquake Engineering Conference.

2647	**924**	100r. multicoloured	1·80	1·10

925 Cogwheel, Grain, Tree, Figures and Globe

1991. World Food Day.

2648	**925**	80r. multicoloured	1·40	85

926 Conference Emblem

1991. Palestinian Peoples Conference.

2649	**926**	40r. gold and violet	90	45

927 Green Woodpecker and Flower Decoration

1991. 1st Asian Biennial Exhibition of Children's Book Illustrations.

2650	**927**	100r. multicoloured	2·30	1·10

928 Script and Emblem

1991. Children's Book Fair, Teheran.

2651	**928**	20r. multicoloured	70	25

929 Festival Award

1991. Roshd International Educational Film Festival.

2652	**929**	50r. multicoloured	90	60

930 Meeting Emblem

1991. 7th Ministerial Meeting of Group of 77.

2653	**930**	30r. green and violet	70	40

931 Militia Members

1991. People's Militia Week.

2654	**931**	30r. multicoloured	70	40

932 Child throwing Stone at Star of David

1991. World Children's Day.

2655	**932**	50r. multicoloured	90	60

933 Globe and Doves

1991. World Tourism Day.

2656	**933**	200r. black, mauve & bl	3·50	1·80

934 Emblems

1991. World Standards Day.

2657	**934**	100r. multicoloured	1·80	1·10

935 Trees, Hand, Water and Wheat

1991. Agricultural Training Week.

2658	**935**	70r. multicoloured	1·30	75

936 Araf Hosseini

1992

2659	**936**	50r. multicoloured	90	40

937 Sadegh Ghanji

1992

2660	**937**	50r. multicoloured	90	40

938 Revolutionary Scenes

1992. 13th Anniv of Islamic Revolution. Mult.

2661	30r. Type **938**	75	25
2662	50r. Revolutionary scenes (different)	90	40

939 Members' Flags

1992. Economic Co-operation Organization Summit, Teheran.

2663	**939**	200r. multicoloured	3·25	1·70

940 Seyd Abbas Musawi (Hezbollah Secretary-General) and Dome of the Rock

1992. World Jerusalem Day.

2664	**940**	200r. multicoloured	3·50	1·80

941 Planets, Satellite, Globe and Mobile Dish Aerial

1992. World Meteorological Day.

2665	**941**	100r. multicoloured	1·30	90

942 Badshahi Mosque, Lahore, Pakistan

1992. South and West Asia Postal Union. Multicoloured.

2666	50r. Type **942**	75	45
2667	50r. Imam's Mosque, Isfahan	75	45
2668	50r. St. Sophia's, Istanbul, Turkey	75	45

943 Ayatollah Khomeini Voting

1992. 13th Anniv of Islamic Republic.

2669	**943**	50r. multicoloured	1·20	45

944 Embraer Bandeirante and Crates

1992. Establishment of Postal Air Service.

2670	**944**	60r. multicoloured	1·10	55

945 Hands holding Trees

1992. National Resources Week.

2671	**945**	100r. multicoloured	1·80	90

946 Tulips

1992. New Year Festival. Flowers. Multicoloured.

2672	20r. Type **946**	45	30
2673	20r. Rose	45	30
2674	40r. Orange blossom	75	40
2675	40r. Yellow jasmine	75	40

947 Members' Flags

1992. Economic Co-operation Organization.

2676	**947**	20r. multicoloured	45	30

948 Morse Apparatus

1992. World Telecommunications Day. Mult.

2677	20r. Type **948**	45	30
2678	20r. Telegraph poles and wires	45	30
2679	20r. Old wall and candlestick telephones	45	30
2680	40r. Dish aerials	85	40
2681	40r. Satellite and Earth	85	40

Nos. 2677/81 were issued together, se-tenant, forming a composite design.

949 Sabzevari

1992. Science, Art and Literature. Multicoloured.

2682	50r. Type **949**	75	45
2683	50r. Madjlessi (in turban)	75	45
2684	50r. Arabic script by Mir Emad	75	45
2685	50r. Samani (in fez)	75	45

950 Emblem

1992. 21st Near East Regional Conference Session of F.A.O., Teheran.

2686	**950**	40r. green, blue and black	75	40

951 Globe, Equipment and Charts

1992. International Surveying and Mapping Conf.

2687	**951**	40r. multicoloured	75	40

952 Palm Trees

1992. 2nd Anniv of Unification of Yemen.

2688	**952**	50r. multicoloured	90	45

953 Dome of the Rock, Oasis and Child

1992. World Children's Day.

2689	**953**	50r. multicoloured	90	45

954 Khomeini

1992. 3rd Death Anniv of Ayatollah Khomeini.

2690	**954**	100r. multicoloured	1·50	85

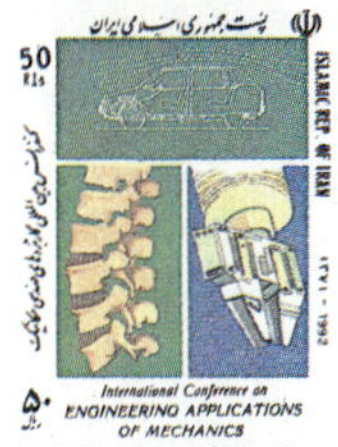

955 Diagram of Wind Tunnel Test, Section of Spine and Robot Hand

1992. International Engineering Applications of Mechanics Conference, Teheran.

2691	**955**	50r. multicoloured	1·10	45

956 Building and Books

1992. Hajia Nosrat Baygom Amin Mo'in (lawyer) Commemoration.

2692	**956**	20r. multicoloured	55	25

957 Emblem and Iranian Flag

1992. 6th Non-aligned News Agencies Pool Conference, Teheran.

2693 **957** 100r. multicoloured 1·40 85

958 ESCAP Emblem

1992. Meeting of Economic and Social Commission for Asia and the Pacific Industry and Technology Ministers.

2694 **958** 100r. green, gold & black 1·40 85

959 Drugs in Hand

1992. World Anti-drugs Day.

2695 **959** 100r. multicoloured 1·40 70

960 Ceramic Bowl, Neyshabour City

1992. International Museum Day. Multicoloured.

2696 40r. Type **960** 75 30

2697 40r. Ceramic vessel, Shahroud City 75 30

961 Khomeini winding Turban

1992. Prayers of Ayatollah Khomeini (1st series). Multicoloured.

2698 50r. Type **961** 90 45

2699 50r. Mosque and Khomeini 90 45

2700 50r. Khomeini 90 45

See also Nos. 2701/2 and 2703.

962 Arabic Script

1992. Prayers of Ayatollah Khomeini (2nd series).

2701 **962** 50r. turquoise and blue 75 40

2702 - 50r. yellow and green 75 40

DESIGN: No. 2702, Arabic script (different).

963 Kaaba

1992. Prayers of Ayatollah Khomeini (3rd series).

2703 **963** 50r. multicoloured 85 40

964 Tanker

1992. 25th Anniv of Iranian Shipping Lines.

2704 **964** 200r. multicoloured 2·75 1·70

965 Arabic Script

1992. Mohammed's Birth Anniv and Unity Week.

2705 **965** 40r. multicoloured 75 30

966 Soldiers and Sun

1992. 12th Anniv of Iran–Iraq War. Multicoloured.

2706 20r. Type **966** 40 15

2707 40r. Soldier on riverbank (horiz) 45 30

967 Patient and Doctor

1992. International History of Medicine in Islam and Iran Congress. Multicoloured.

2708 20r. Type **967** 40 15

2709 40r. Medical instruments 45 30

Nos. 2708/9 were issued together, se-tenant, forming a composite design.

968 Foundry and Steel Products

1992. Steel Industry. Multicoloured.

2710 20r. Type **968** 40 25

2711 70r. Steel products and steel works 85 40

Nos. 2710/11 were issued together, se-tenant, forming a composite design.

969 Isfahan

1992. World Tourism Day. Multicoloured.

2712 20r. Type **969** 40 25

2713 20r. Mazandaran 40 25

2714 30r. Bushehr 55 30

2715 30r. Hormozgan 55 30

970 Map and Flags

1992. International Trade Fair.

2716 **970** 200r. multicoloured 2·75 1·40

971 Early Post Office Service

1992. World Post Day.

2717 **971** 30r. brown and violet 60 40

972 Starving Child and Food Distribution

1992. World Food Day.

2718 **972** 100r. multicoloured 1·50 60

973 Child drawing

1992. International Children's and Youth Photographic Festival.

2719 **973** 40r. multicoloured 75 40

974 Flames and Child's Face

1992. Bosnia and Herzegovina.

2720 **974** 40r. multicoloured 75 40

975 Storming Embassy, Doves and Crow

1992. Multicoloured.

2721 100r. Type **975** (11th anniv of storming of U.S. Embassy) 1·40 60

2722 100r. Soldiers, crows and doves (Students' Day) 1·40 60

2723 100r. Ayatollah Khomeini, crows and doves (13th anniv of Khomeini's return from exile) 1·40 60

Nos. 2721/3 were issued together, se-tenant, forming a composite design.

976 Emblem

1992. 17th Annual Meeting of Islamic Development Bank Board of Governors.

2724 **976** 20r. multicoloured 40 25

977 Flags and Dish Aerials on Maps

1992. Azerbaijan–Iran Telecommunications Co-operation.

2725 **977** 40r. multicoloured 75 40

978 Star

1992. 10th Anniv of Islamic University.

2726 **978** 200r. green & deep green 2·30 1·10

979 Soldiers in Armed Motor Boat

1992. People's Militia Week.

2727 **979** 40r. multicoloured 75 40

980 Shahryar

1992. International Congress on Mohammed Hossein Shahryar (poet).

2728 **980** 80r. multicoloured 90 45

981 "Heaven and Hell"

1992. Women's Day and Birth Anniv of Fatima.

2729 **981** 70r. multicoloured 85 40

982 Oil Derrick

1992. Oil Industry. Multicoloured.

2730 100r. Type **982** 1·10 60

2731 100r. Drilling 1·10 60

983 Arabic Script and Hand holding Pen

1992. Literacy Campaign.

2732	**983**	80r. multicoloured	90	45

984 Ayatollah Mirza Abolhassan Sharani

1993. Celebrities. Multicoloured.

2733	20r. Type **984**	40	25
2734	20r. Prof. Mahmoud Hessabi and formula	40	25
2735	20r. Mohit Tabatabaie and books	40	25
2736	20r. Mehrdad Avesta and Arabic script	40	25

985 Narcissi

1993. Flowers. Multicoloured.

2737	20r. Type **985**	30	25
2738	30r. Blue and yellow irises	45	30
2738a	35r. Tulips	60	40
2739	40r. White irises	30	25
2740	50r. Jasmine	60	40
2741	60r. Viburnum berries	1·10	45
2742	70r. Pansies	1·30	70
2743	75r. Antirrhinums	1·30	70
2745	100r. Martagon lilies	1·10	75
2746	120r. Petunias	1·80	85
2747	150r. Hyacinths	1·50	1·10
2749	200r. Roses	2·30	1·10
2750	500r. Convolvulus	5·25	1·10
2751	1000r. Poppies	10·50	7·25

986 Wings and Koran

1993. Mab'as Festival.

2752	**986**	200r. multicoloured	2·30	1·40

987 Rainbow and Emblem

1993. Programming Day.

2753	**987**	100r. multicoloured	1·70	60

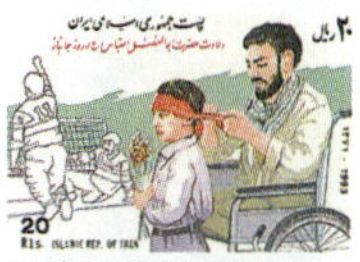

988 Man in Wheelchair tying Girl's Ribbon

1993. Invalids' Day. Multicoloured.

2754	20r. Type **988**	40	25
2755	40r. Medal winner in wheelchair	60	40

Nos. 2754/5 were issued together, se-tenant, forming a composite design.

989 Fatima Mosque, Qom

1993. Preservation of Cultural Heritage. Mult.

2756	40r. Type **989**	60	40
2757	40r. Interior of mosque	60	40

990 Hands reaching towards Sun

1993. World Day of the Oppressed. Birth Anniv of Mahdi.

2758	**990**	60r. multicoloured	75	40

991 National Flag

1993. 14th Anniv of Islamic Revolution. Mult.

2759	20r. Type **991**	85	25
2760	20r. Flag and soldiers	85	25
2761	20r. Guerrillas	85	25
2762	20r. Oil derricks, harvesters and crowd	85	25
2763	20r. Ayatollah Khomeini in motorcade and on arrival in Iran	85	25

Nos. 2759/63 were issued together, se-tenant, forming a composite design.

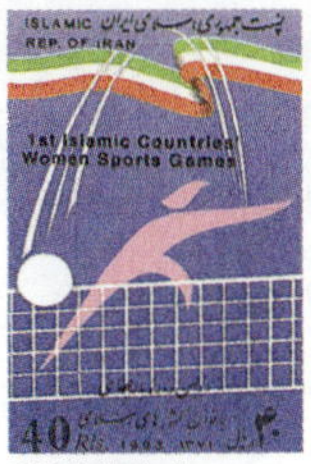

992 Volleyball

1993. 1st Islamic Countries Women's Games. Multicoloured.

2764	40r. Type **992**	90	40
2765	40r. Basketball	90	40
2766	40r. Gold medal	90	40
2767	40r. Swimming	90	40
2768	40r. Running	90	40

Nos. 2764/8 were issued together, se-tenant, forming a compostite design.

993 Ansari

1993. Congress on Sheikh Morteza Ansari.

2769	**993**	40r. multicoloured	50	30

994 World Map as Tree Foliage and Rainbow

1993. Tree Day.

2770	**994**	70r. multicoloured	90	55

995 Burning Tank and Man with Sling

1993. World Jerusalem Day.

2771	**995**	20r. multicoloured	25	15

996 Butterfly and Tulip

1993. New Year Festival. Flowers and Butterflies. Multicoloured.

2772	20r. Type **996**	40	25
2773	20r. Butterfly and narcissus	40	25
2774	40r. Butterfly, tulips and rose	60	40
2775	40r. Butterfly and roses	60	40

997 Grass and Goldfish in Bowl

1993. Fetr Feast.

2776	**997**	100r. multicoloured	2·50	1·40

998 Open Music Book

1993. 14th Anniv of Islamic Republic.

2777	**998**	40r. multicoloured	60	40

999 Door and Landscape

1993. International Birth Millenary of Sheikh Mofeed Congress.

2778	**999**	80r. multicoloured	1·10	60

1000 Emblem

1993. 13th Asian and Pacific Labour Ministers' Conference, Teheran.

2779	**1000**	100r. multicoloured	1·40	75

1001 Globe

1993. Int Congress for Advancement of Science and Technology in Islamic World.

2780	**1001**	50r. multicoloured	90	45

1002 Mirror Box

1993. International Museum Day.

2781	**1002**	40r. multicoloured	75	30

1003 Khomeini

1993. 4th Death Anniv of Ayatollah Khomeini.

2782	**1003**	20r. multicoloured	60	15

1004 Girl on Swing

1993. World Children's Day.

2783	**1004**	50r. multicoloured	85	40

1005 Knitted Socks

1993. World Crafts Day.

2784	**1005**	70r. multicoloured	1·10	55

1006 Family at Window

1993. World Population Day.

2785	**1006**	30r. multicoloured	60	25

1007 Football

1993. Student Games. Multicoloured.

2786	20r. Type **1007**	30	15
2787	40r. Judo and wrestling	75	30
2788	40r. Long jumping, weightlifting, badminton and basketball	75	30

1008 Butterfly and Film Frame

1993. International Children's and Youths' Film Festival, Isfahan.

2789	**1008**	60r. multicoloured	90	45

1009 Postal Messenger

1993. World Post Day.

2790	**1009**	60r. multicoloured	90	45

1010 Stars and Birds

1993. 3rd International Biennial Children's Book Illustrations Exhibition, Teheran. Multicoloured.

2791	30r. Type **1010**	70	30
2792	30r. Moon and girl in boat	70	30
2793	30r. Cherub blowing trumpet	70	30
2794	30r. Trees and clouds	70	30

Nos. 2791/4 were issued together, se-tenant, forming a composite design.

1011 Khaje Nassireddin Tussy

1993. 719th Death Anniv of Khaje Nassireddin Tussy (scientist).

2795	**1011**	30r. multicoloured	60	30

1012 Militia Member

1993. People's Militia Week. Multicoloured.

2796	50r. Type **1012**	75	30
2797	50r. Woman tying headband for Militia member	75	30

1013 Ayatollah Golpayegani

1993. Ayatollah Golpayegani Commem.

2798	**1013**	300r. multicoloured	3·50	1·70

1014 Hopscotch Grid drawn in Blood

1993. Support for Moslems of Bosnia and Herzegovina. Multicoloured.

2799	40r. Type **1014**	90	30
2800	40r. Youth giving "V" sign	90	30
2801	40r. Woman and mosque	90	30

1015 Flags

1994. Invalids' Day and Birthday of Abalfazil el Abbas.

2802	**1015**	80r. multicoloured	1·10	60

1016 Trees and Ploughed Field in Book

1994. Agricultural Week.

2803	**1016**	60r. multicoloured	1·10	60

1017 Electrification of Villages

1994. 15th Anniv of Islamic Revolution. Mult.

2804	40r. Type **1017**	75	45
2805	40r. Ayatollah Khomeini and workers with flag	75	45
2806	40r. Fishing and new roads	75	45
2807	40r. Harvesting wheat and weaving	75	45

Nos. 2804/7 were issued together, se-tenant, forming a composite design.

1018 Dome of the Rock

1994. Congress on Islamic Law.

2808	**1018**	60r. multicoloured	70	40

1019 Doctor, Gymnast, Camera, Paintbrush, Book and Student

1994. Youth Welfare.

2809	**1019**	30r. multicoloured	75	40

1020 Palestinian and Peaceful Scene

1994. World Jerusalem Day.

2810	**1020**	50r. multicoloured	75	40

1021 Black-crowned Night Heron

1994. New Year Festival. Birds. Multicoloured.

2811	40r. Type **1021**	90	45
2812	40r. Eurasian bittern	90	45
2813	40r. Chukar partridges (horiz)	90	45
2814	40r. Common pheasants (horiz)	90	45

1022 Ball and Rectangles

1994. 25th Annual Mathematics Conference.

2815	**1022**	30r. multicoloured	75	40

1023 Book and Roses

1994. 15th Anniv of Islamic Republic.

2816	**1023**	40r. multicoloured	75	40

1024 Child and Roses

1994. World Health Day.

2817	**1024**	100r. multicoloured	1·40	70

1025 Delvari, Cavalrymen and Ship

1994. 80th Death Anniv of Raiss Ali Delvari (revolutionary).

2818	**1025**	50r. multicoloured	75	40

1026 I.Y.F. Emblem

1994. International Year of the Family.

2819	**1026**	50r. multicoloured	60	30

1027 Old Telephone System and Computer Operator

1994. World Telecommunications Day.

2820	**1027**	50r. multicoloured	60	30

1028 Marlik Gold Cup

1994. International Museum Day.

2821	**1028**	40r. multicoloured	60	25

1029 Kufic Enamelled Pot

1994. Cultural Preservation.

2822	**1029**	40r. multicoloured	60	25

1030 Khomeini

1994. 5th Death Anniv of Ayatollah Khomeini.

2823	**1030**	30r. multicoloured	40	25

1031 Motahhari

1994. 15th Death Anniv of Ayatollah Motahhari.

2824	**1031**	30r. multicoloured	40	25

1032 Rose-water Sprinkler

1994. World Crafts Day. Multicoloured.

2825	60r. Type **1032**	70	40
2826	60r. Silk weaving, Khorassan	70	40

1033 Games Emblem

1994. Islamic Countries' University Student Games.

2827	**1033**	60r. multicoloured	60	40

1034 Mosaic and Rose

1994. Mohammed's Birth Anniv and Unity Week.

2828	**1034**	30r. multicoloured	40	25

1035 Cameraman

1994. 14th Anniv of Iran–Iraq War.

2829	**1035**	70r. multicoloured	75	45

1036 Envelope

1994. World Post Day.

2830	**1036**	50r. multicoloured	60	30

1037 Allegory of Woman

1994. Women's Day and Birth Anniv of Fatima.

2831	**1037**	70r. multicoloured	75	45

1038 Soldier

1994. People's Militia Week.

2832	**1038**	30r. multicoloured	40	25

1039 Book

1994. Book Week.

2833	**1039**	40r. multicoloured	45	25

1040 Arms, Map and Town

1994. Support for Moslems of Bosnia and Herzegovina. Multicoloured.

2834	80r. Type **1040**	1·00	55
2835	80r. Commander Adnan (deceased) and family	1·00	55

1041 Araki

1995. 2nd Death Anniv of Grand Ayatollah Mohammad Ali Araki (Shia leader).

2836	**1041**	100r. multicoloured	1·10	60

1042 Arabic Script

1995. World Day of the Oppressed. Birth Anniv of Mahdi.

2837	**1042**	50r. multicoloured	60	30

1043 Flag, Dome and Man

1995. Revolutionaries (1st series). Multicoloured.

2838	50r. Type **1043**	60	30
2839	50r. Man in patterned shirt	60	30
2840	50r. Man with full beard wearing grey shirt	60	30
2841	50r. Man in jacket and sweater looking to right	60	30

See also Nos. 2874/7, 2909/16, 2953/6, 3029/32 and 3034/7.

1044 Crowd, National Flag and Ayatollah Khomeini

1995. 16th Anniv of Islamic Revolution.

2842	**1044**	100r. multicoloured	1·10	60

1045 Dome of the Rock

1995. World Jerusalem Day.

2843	**1045**	100r. multicoloured	1·10	60

1046 Hand holding Tree

1995. Tree Day.

2844	**1046**	50r. multicoloured	60	30

1047 Hyacinths

1995. New Year Festival. Multicoloured.

2845	50r. Type **1047**	70	40
2846	50r. Pansies	70	40
2847	50r. Grass and bow	70	40
2848	50r. Tulips, bow and goldfish bowl	90	55

1048 Diesel Goods Train on Bridge

1995. Inauguration of Bafq–Bandar Abbas Railway.

2849	**1048**	100r. multicoloured	1·10	90

1049 Phoenix rising from Tulips

1995. 16th Anniv of Islamic Republic.

2850	**1049**	100r. multicoloured	1·10	60

1050 Shapes

1995. Press Festival.

2851	**1050**	100r. multicoloured	1·10	60

1051 Khomeini

1995. Ayatollah Ahmad Khomeini Commem.

2852	**1051**	50r. multicoloured	60	30

1052 Arabic Script

1995. Invalids' Day.

2853	**1052**	80r. multicoloured	90	45

1053 Yezd Mosque and Vaziri

1995. Ayatollah Ali Vaziri Commemoration.

2854	**1053**	100r. multicoloured	1·10	60

1054 Telecommunications

1995. World Telecommunications Day.

2855	**1054**	100r. multicoloured	1·10	60

1055 Khomeini

1995. 6th Death Anniv of Ayatollah Khomeini.

2856	**1055**	100r. multicoloured	1·10	60

1056 Immunizing Baby

1995. 50th Anniv of U.N.O. Multicoloured.

2857	100r. Type **1056**	1·10	60
2858	100r. Child laughing	1·10	60
2859	100r. Cereals and world map	1·10	60
2860	100r. Woman reading	1·10	60

1057 Ashtiany

1995. Iqbal Ashtiany (historian) Commem.

2861 **1057** 100r. multicoloured 1·10 60

1058 Dam Workers

1995. Government Week.

2862 **1058** 100r. multicoloured 1·10 60

1059 Man with Gun and Book

1995. People's Militia Week.

2863 **1059** 100r. multicoloured 1·10 60

1060 Envelopes and Globe forming Flower

1995. World Post Day.

2864 **1060** 100r. multicoloured 1·10 60

1061 Cypher

1995. Prophet Mohammed Commemoration.

2865 **1061** 100r. multicoloured 1·10 60

1062 Tondgoyan

1995. M. J. Tondgoyan (oil minister) Commem.

2866 **1062** 100r. multicoloured 1·10 60

1063 Shaghaghi

1996. Fathi Shaghaghi (Islamic Jihad Secretary-General) Commemoration.

2867 **1063** 100r. multicoloured 1·10 60

1064 Crowd, Flowers and Ayatollah Khomeini

1996. 17th Anniv of Islamic Revolution.

2868 **1064** 100r. multicoloured 1·10 60

1065 Dome of the Rock

1996. World Jerusalem Day.

2869 **1065** 100r. multicoloured 1·10 60

1066 Common Cardinal

1996. New Year Festival. Birds. Multicoloured.

2870 100r. Type **1066** 1·70 90

2871 100r. Budgerigar 1·70 90

2872 100r. Golden oriole 1·70 90

2873 100r. European roller 1·70 90

1996. Revolutionaries (2nd series). As T 1043. Multicoloured.

2874 100r. Colonel-pilot Abbas Babaiy 1·10 60

2875 100r. Officer-pilot Ali Akbar Sharoudi 1·10 60

2876 100r. Commandant Mohammad Ebrahim Hemmat 1·00 55

2877 100r. Commandant Mohammad Boroudjerdi 1·10 60

1067 Ayatollah Khomeini, Ballot Box and Crowd

1996. 17th Anniv of Islamic Republic.

2878 **1067** 200r. multicoloured 2·10 1·40

1068 Open Book, Flowers and Birds

1996. International Book Fair, Teheran.

2879 **1068** 85r. multicoloured 1·00 60

1069 Diesel Locomotive in Tunnel, Imam Riza's Shrine, Meshed, and Horses

1996. Meshed–Sarakhs–Tajan International Railway.

2880 **1069** 200r. multicoloured 2·10 1·10

1070 Camel Train and Prisoner tied to Stake

1996. Day of Prisoners of War and Missing in Action.

2881 **1070** 200r. multicoloured 2·30 1·10

1071 Khomeini

1996. 7th Death Anniv of Ayatollah Khomeini.

2882 **1071** 200r. multicoloured 2·30 1·10

1072 Carpet

1996. World Crafts Day.

2883 **1072** 200r. multicoloured 2·30 1·10

1073 Emblem

1996. 3rd Posts and Telecommunications Ministerial Conference, Teheran.

2884 **1073** 200r. multicoloured 2·30 1·10

1074 Zouqeblateyne Mosque

1996. Mohammed's Birth Anniv and Unity Week. Multicoloured.

2885 200r. Type **1074** 2·30 1·10

2886 200r. Tomb of Imam Hossein (dome with flag flying to right) 2·30 1·10

2887 200r. Prophet's Mosque (dome without flag) 2·30 1·10

2888 200r. Tomb of Imam Riza (dome with flag flying to left) 2·30 1·10

2889 200r. Qaba Mosque (with four corner minarets) 2·30 1·10

1075 Teheran Underground

1996. Government Week. Multicoloured.

2890 200r. Type **1075** 2·30 1·10

2891 200r. Ispahan iron works 2·30 1·10

2892 200r. Merchant fleet 2·30 1·10

2893 200r. Bandar-e-Imam oil refinery 2·30 1·10

2894 200r. Boumehen Earth Station 2·30 1·10

1076 Ardabily and Mosque Interior

1996. Allameh Moghaddas Ardabily Commem.

2895 **1076** 200r. multicoloured 2·30 1·10

1077 Artillery Position and Soldier praying

1996. 16th Anniv of Iran–Iraq War.

2896 **1077** 200r. multicoloured 2·30 1·10

1078 Cogs and Equipment

1996. World Standards Day.

2897 **1078** 200r. multicoloured 1·90 1·00

1079 Harvesting and Man working on "Globe" Rick

1996. World Food Summit, Rome.

2898	**1079**	200r. multicoloured	1·90	1·00

1080 Men, Houses and Women

1996. National Population and Housing Census.

2899	**1080**	200r. multicoloured	1·90	1·00

1081 Wrestlers

1996. 2nd World University Wrestling Championship, Teheran.

2900	**1081**	500r. multicoloured	4·50	2·75

1082 Ayatollah Khomeini embracing Youth

1997. 18th Anniv of Islamic Revolution. Mult.

2901	200r. Type **1082**	1·90	1·00
2902	200r. Banner of Khomeini above crowd	1·90	1·00
2903	200r. Khomeini waving	1·90	1·00
2904	200r. Khomeini returning from exile in France	1·90	1·00
2905	200r. Soldiers	1·90	1·00

1083 Hands holding Tree

1997. Tree Day.

2906	**1083**	200r. multicoloured	1·90	1·00

1084 Rainbow and National Flag

1997. 18th Anniv of Islamic Republic.

2907	**1084**	200r. multicoloured	1·90	1·00

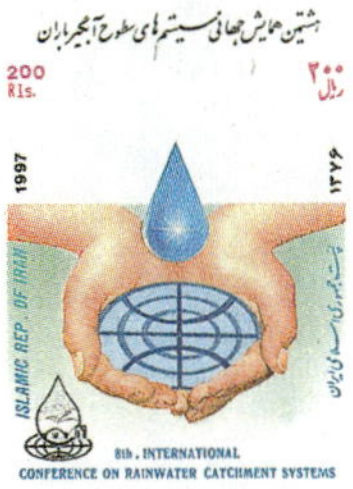

1085 Water Droplet falling to "Globe" Pool in Cupped Hands

1997. 8th International Rainwater Catchment Systems Conference.

2908	**1085**	200r. multicoloured	1·90	1·00

1997. Revolutionaries (3rd series). As T 1043. Multicoloured.

2909	100r. Alireza Mowahhed Danesh (blue flag, white turban)	90	45
2910	100r. Mohammad Reza Dastwareh (orange flag, white turban)	90	45
2911	100r. Abbas Karimi (blue flag, full-face without glasses)	90	45
2912	100r. Nasser Kazemi (orange flag, white vest with red trim)	90	45
2913	100r. Youssef Kolahdouz (blue flag, three-quarter face)	90	45
2914	100r. Yadollah Kolhar (orange flag, full-face)	90	45
2915	100r. Fazlollah Mahallati (blue flag, full-face with glasses)	90	45
2916	100r. Abdollah Meyssami (orange flag, green vest and coat)	90	45

1086 Satellite, Letter, Globe and Computer

1997. Post, Telecommunications and Productivity.

2917	**1086**	200r. multicoloured	1·50	75

1087 Khomeini

1997. 8th Death Anniv of Ayatollah Khomeini.

2918	**1087**	200r. multicoloured	1·50	75

1088 Teheran Underground Railway Map and Tunnel

1997. National Achievements. Multicoloured.

2919	40r. Type **1088**	30	15
2920	50r. Cornfield and silo	40	25
2921	65r. Medals from Student Scientific Olympiads	40	25
2922	70r. Steelworks, Mobarakeh	55	30
2923	100r. Modern communications systems	75	40
2924	130r. Harbour and tanker	60	30
2925	150r. Oil refinery, Bandar Abbas	90	60
2926	200r. Martyr Radja-ee dam	1·20	75
2927	350r. Martyr Radja-ee power station	2·10	1·40
2928	400r. Foreign Ministry building	2·40	1·50
2929	500r. Child receiving oral vaccination	3·00	2·00
2930	650r. Koran Printing House and Koran	3·75	2·75
2931	1000r. Imam Khomeini International Airport, Teheran	60	30
2932	2000r. Tomb of Imam Khomeini, Teheran	5·25	2·75

1089 Flora and Fauna

1997. 10th Anniv of Montreal Protocol (on reduction of use of chlorofluorocarbons).

2933	**1089**	200r. multicoloured	1·20	75

1090 Crowd with Flags and Banners

1997. 17th Anniv of Iran–Iraq War.

2934	**1090**	200r. multicoloured	1·20	75

1091 Allama Mohammad Iqbal (Pakistani poet)

1997. Iranian–Pakistani Culture. Multicoloured.

2935	200r. Type **1091**	1·20	75
2936	200r. Jalal-ad-din Moulana Rumi (Persian mystic)	1·20	75

1092 Airplane, Letters and Computer

1997. World Post Day.

2937	**1092**	200r. multicoloured	1·20	75

1093 Frasheri and Etehemberg Mosque, Tirana

1997. 150th Birth Anniv (1996) of Naim Frasheri (Albanian writer).

2938	**1093**	200r. multicoloured	1·20	75

1094 Calligraphy

1997. 8th Islamic Summit, Teheran. Illustrated pages from the Koran. Each green, gold and red.

2939	300r. Type **1094**	1·80	1·20
2940	300r. Page with rose at bottom left	1·80	1·20
2941	300r. Page with rose on right-hand side	1·80	1·20
2942	300r. Page with rose at top left-hand corner	1·80	1·20
2943	300r. Summit emblem	1·80	1·20

1095 Games Emblem

1997. 2nd Islamic Countries Women's Games, Teheran.

2944	**1095**	200r. multicoloured	1·20	75

1096 Dome of the Rock

1998. World Jerusalem Day.

2945	**1096**	250r. multicoloured	1·50	1·10

1097 State Flags and Poppies

1998. 19th Anniv of Islamic Revolution. Mult.

2946	200r. Type **1097**	1·30	85
2947	200r. Harvesting grain	1·30	85
2948	200r. Soldiers with flags	1·30	85
2949	200r. Crowd with banner of Khomeini	1·30	85
2950	200r. Ayatollah Khomeini	1·30	85

Nos. 2946/50 were issued together, se-tenant, forming a composite design.

1098 Tree and Town

1998. Tree Day.

2951	**1098**	200r. multicoloured	1·30	85

1099 Flower Arrangement and Gifts

1998. New Year Festival.

2952	**1099**	200r. multicoloured	1·30	85

1998. Revolutionaries (4th series). As T 1043. Multicoloured.

2953	100r. Man in open-necked shirt	70	60
2954	100r. Man in vest and jacket (three-quarter face)	70	60
2955	100r. Man in vest and jacket (profile)	70	60
2956	100r. Man in crew-neck jumper and jacket	70	60

1100 M. Shahryar (poet)

1998

2957	**1100**	200r. multicoloured	1·30	1·10

1101 Khomeini

1998. 9th Death Anniv of Ayatollah Khomeini.

2958	**1101**	200r. multicoloured	1·30	1·10

1102 Map and Emblem

1998. 2nd South and West Asia Postal Union Congress.

2959	**1102**	250r. multicoloured	1·50	1·40

1103 Player, Ball and Stadium

1998. World Cup Football Championship, France.

2960	**1103**	500r. multicoloured	3·25	3·00

1104 Globe and Headset

1998. World Telecommunications Day.

2961	**1104**	200r. multicoloured	1·30	1·10

1105 Silver Vessel

1998. World Handicrafts Day.

2962	**1105**	200r. multicoloured	1·30	1·10

1106 State Flag as Dove, Birds and Flowers

1998. 1st Anniv of Presidential Election.

2963	**1106**	200r. multicoloured	1·30	1·20

1107 Khomeini voting

1998. 19th Anniv of Islamic Republic.

2964	**1107**	250r. multicoloured	1·50	1·10

1108 Handshake, Rainbow and Doves

1998. Co-operation Day.

2965	**1108**	250r. multicoloured	1·50	1·40

1109 Arabic Script

1998. "1000th Friday of Public Prayer".

2966	**1109**	250r. blue, gold and black	1·50	1·40

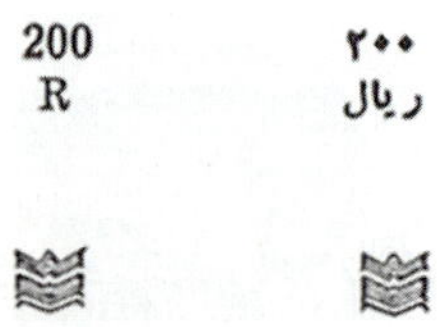

(1110)

1998. Mosques. Nos. 2415a and 2416a surch as T 1110.

2967	**1110**	200r. on 1r. orange and silver	1·20	1·10
2968	**1110**	200r. on 3r. green and silver	1·20	1·10

1111 Globe and Shark's Fin

1998. International Year of the Ocean.

2969	**1111**	250r. multicoloured	1·50	1·40

1112 Arabic Script

1998. Sacred Defence Week.

2970	**1112**	250r. multicoloured	1·50	1·40

1113 Envelope and Clouds as World Map

1998. World Post Day.

2971	**1113**	200r. multicoloured	1·20	1·10

1114 Wrestlers

1998. World Wrestling Championship, Iran.

2972	**1114**	250r. multicoloured	1·40	1·20

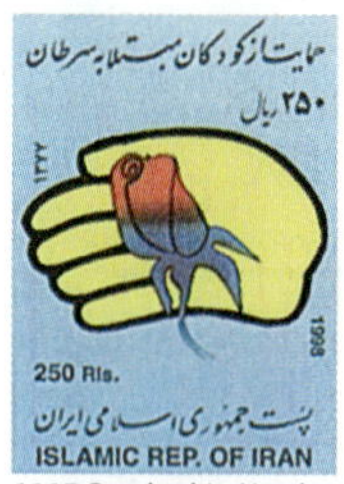

1115 Rosebud in Hand

1998. Children's Cancer Relief.

2973	**1115**	250r. multicoloured	1·10	1·10

1116 Navigation Instrument

1999. Museum Exhibit.

2974	**1116**	250r. multicoloured	1·50	1·40

1117 Khomeini

1999. 20th Anniv of Islamic Revolution.

2975	**1117**	250r. multicoloured	1·30	1·10

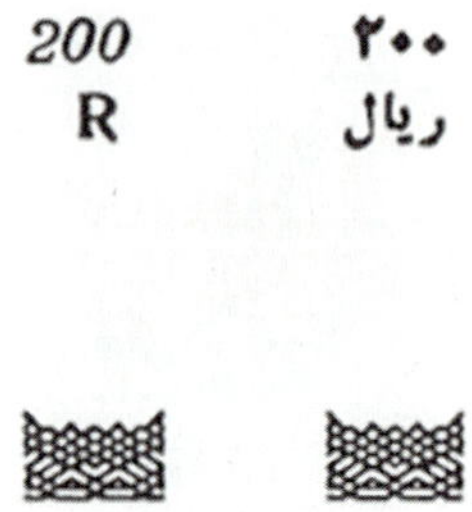

(1118)

1999. Flowers. Nos. 2738/a surch as T 1118.

2976	200r. on 35r. multicoloured	1·10	1·00
2977	900r. on 30r. multicoloured	4·50	4·25

(1119)

1999. International Book Fair, Teheran. No. 2879 surch as T 1119.

2978	250r. on 85r. multicoloured	1·30	1·20

1120 Flag and Emblem

1999. 20th Anniv of Islamic Republic.

2979	**1120**	250r. multicoloured	1·30	1·10

1121 Emblem

1999. Ghadir Khom Religious Festival.

2980	**1121**	250r. multicoloured	1·30	1·20

1122 Harbour

1999. Ayatollah Khomeini Charity Fund. Mult.

2981	250r. Type **1122**	1·20	1·10
2982	250r. Houses	1·20	1·10

1123 Soldier, Tank, Ship and Aircraft

1999. Army Day.

2983	**1123**	250r. multicoloured	1·10	1·00

1124 Sadra al-Din Shirazi

1999. Sadra al-Din Shirazi (philosopher) Commem.

2984	**1124**	250r. multicoloured	1·30	1·20

1125 Khomeini

1999. 10th Death Anniv of Ayatollah Khomeini.

2985	**1125**	250r. multicoloured	1·30	1·20

1126 Parliament Building and Khomeini

1999. 20th Anniv of Iranian Parliament.

2986	**1126**	250r. multicoloured	1·30	1·20

1127 Emblem and Map

1999. Organization of Islamic Conference Interparliamentary Union Congress, Tehran.

2987	**1127**	250r. multicoloured	1·30	1·20

1128 Emblem and Dome

1999. Unity Week.

2988	**1128**	250r. multicoloured	1·10	1·10

1129 Tapestry

1999. World Handicrafts Day.

2989	**1129**	250r. multicoloured	1·10	1·10

1130 River Kingfisher

1999. Birds. Multicoloured.

2990	100r. Hoopoe	1·50	1·40
2991	150r. Type **1130**	75	70
2992	200r. Robin	45	40
2993	250r. Crested lark	1·10	1·10
2994	300r. Red-backed shrike	1·50	1·40
2995	350r. Roller	1·40	1·40
2996	400r. Blue tit	90	85
2997	500r. Bee eater	2·75	2·40
2998	1000r. Redwing	3·75	3·50
2999	2000r. Twite	7·50	7·25
2999a	3000r. Whitethroat	11·50	11·00
2999b	4500r. Collar dove	11·50	11·00

1131 Moon partially covering Sun

1999. Solar Eclipse. Multicoloured.

3000	250r. Type **1131**	1·10	1·10
3001	250r. Moon passing in front of Sun	1·10	1·10
3002	250r. Full solar eclipse	1·10	1·10
3003	250r. Sun appearing from right-hand side of Moon	1·10	1·10
3004	250r. Sun appearing	1·10	1·10

1132 Letters, Globe and Letter Box

1999. 125th Anniv of Universal Postal Union.

3005	**1132**	250r. multicoloured	1·20	1·10

1133 Chinese Girl

1999. International Children's Day. Showing children from different cultures. Multicoloured.

3006	150r. Type **1133**	75	70
3007	150r. Indian girl	75	70
3008	150r. Native American girl	75	70
3009	150r. Arabian boy	75	70
3010	150r. Iranian girl	75	70
3011	150r. Mexican boy	75	70
3012	150r. Eskimo boy	75	70
3013	150r. African girl	75	70
3014	150r. Russian boy	75	70
3015	150r. European girl	75	70

1134 Winged Egg

1999. International Children's Book Illustrations Exhibition. Multicoloured.

3016	250r. Type **1134**	1·20	1·10
3017	250r. Decorated egg	1·20	1·10
3018	250r. Egg decorated with white crescent	1·20	1·10
3019	250r. Egg decorated with flowers	1·20	1·10

1135 Ayatollah Mohammed Taghi

1999. Ayatollah Mohammed Taghi Commemoration.

3020	**1135**	250r. multicoloured	1·20	1·10

1136 Ayatollah Khomeni

2000. 21st Anniv of Islamic Revolution.

3021	**1136**	300r. multicoloured	1·50	1·40

2000. Flowers. Nos. 2741, 2743, 2746 surch 250 R.

3022	250r. on 60r. multicoloured	1·40	1·20
3023	250r. on 75r. multicoloured	1·40	1·20
3024	250r. on 120r. multicoloured	1·40	1·20

1138 Bee Eaters

2000. New Year Festival.

3025	**1138**	300r. multicoloured	2·30	1·50

1139 Inscription

2000. National Archives Day.

3026	**1139**	300r. multicoloured	1·80	1·80

1140 Books, Cogs, Chimneys and Hand holding Torch

2000. 70th Anniv of Science and Technology University.

3027	**1140**	300r. multicoloured	1·70	1·50

1141 Mofatteh and Building

2000. Ayatollah Mofatteh Commemoration.

3028	**1141**	300r. multicoloured	1·70	1·50

1142 Khalil Motahar Nia

2000. Revolutionaries (5th series). Multicoloured.

3029	150r. Type **1142**	1·70	1·50
3030	150r. Haschem Etemadi (pink shirt)	1·70	1·50
3031	150r. Madjid Sepassi (green shirt)	1·70	1·50
3032	150r. Mahmud Sotoudeh (blue T-shirt and shirt)	1·70	1·50

1143 Mother and Baby

2000. International Breast-feeding Week.

3033	**1143**	300r. multicoloured	1·70	1·60

1144 Hadj Reza Habubollahi

2000. Revolutionaries (6th series). Multicoloured.

3034	150r. Type **1144**	85	75
3035	150r. Hassan Agharebparast (shirt with epaulettes)	85	75
3036	150r. Mostafa Ravani Pou (white turban)	85	75
3037	150r. Mohsen Safavi (wearing glasses)	85	75

1145 Books and Educational Symbols

2000. University Anniversary.
3038 **1145** 300r. multicoloured 1·70 1·50

1146 Stylized Bird

2000. 8th Asian-Pacific Postal Union Congress, Tehran.
3039 **1146** 300r. blue, mauve and black 1·70 1·50

1147 Satellite and Dish

2000. International World Space Week. Mult.
3040 500r. Type **1147** 2·00 1·80
3041 500r. Satellite and dish (different) 2·00 1·80

1148 Birds, Flowers and Calligraphy

2001. Eid-ul Ghadir.
3042 **1148** 500r. multicoloured 2·00 1·90

1149 Flowers, Calligraphy and Sun

2001. Year of Imam Ali.
3043 **1149** 500r. multicoloured 2·00 1·90

1150 Red-headed Bunting

2001. New Year Festival. Multicoloured.
3044 300r. Type **1150** 1·20 1·10
3045 300r. Hawfinch (vert) 1·20 1·10

1151 Mosque and Mohamed Al Dorra and Father

2001. Intifada.
3046 **1151** 350r. multicoloured 1·40 1·20

1152 Chaffinch

2001. Belgica 2001 International Stamp Exhibition, Brussels. Multicoloured.
3047 350r. Type **1152** 1·40 1·30
3048 350r. Waxwing 1·40 1·30
3049 350r. Gate to Melli Bagh National Garden (vert) 1·40 1·30

1153 Mount Fuji, Japan

2001. Philanippon '01 International Stamp Exhibition, Tokyo. Multicoloured.
3050 250r. Type **1153** 1·10 90
3051 250r. Mount Damavand, Iran 1·10 90

1154 Flag, Globe and Iranian Buildings

2001. World Tourism Day.
3052 **1154** 500r. multicoloured 2·10 1·90

1155 Police Helicopters and Vehicles

2001. Police Week. Multicoloured.
3053 250r. Type **1155** 1·10 1·00
3054 250r. Flag, boats and Policeman 1·10 1·00

Nos. 3053/4 were issued together, se-tenant, forming a composite design.

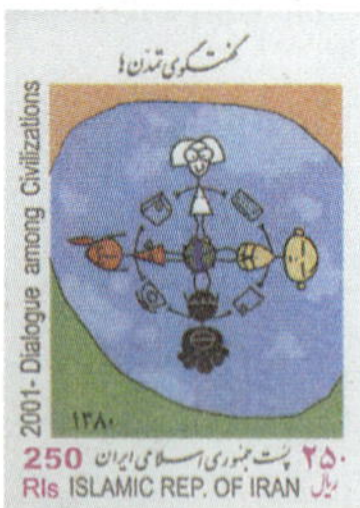

1156 Children encircling Globe

2001. United Nations Year of Dialogue among Civilizations. Multicoloured.
3055 250r. Type **1156** 1·10 90
3056 250r. European and Asian faces (horiz) 1·10 90

1157 Ball and Dove

2001. 3rd Islamic Women's Games, Tehran.
3057 **1157** 250r. multicoloured 1·10 90

1158 Koran and Flowers

2001. Koran.
3058 **1158** 500r. multicoloured 2·10 1·90

1159 P 232 *Tabarza*

2001. Navy Day. Multicoloured.
3059 500r. Type **1159** 2·10 2·00
3060 500r. Frigate 2·10 2·00
3061 500r. Helicopter and hovercraft 2·10 2·00
3062 500r. Submarine 2·10 2·00

1160 Bees on Honeycomb

2001. Bee-keeping.
3063 **1160** 500r. multicoloured 2·10 2·00

1161 Hands enclosing Face

2001. 50th Anniv of United Nations High Commissioner for Refugees.
3064 **1161** 500r. blue, black and mauve 2·10 2·00

1162 Vehicle, Roadways and Bridge

2001. Transportation Day. Multicoloured.
3065 350r. Type **1162** 1·40 1·20
3066 350r. Bridge, vehicles and buildings 1·40 1·20

Nos. 3065/6 were issued together, se-tenant, forming a composite design.

1163 Locomotive

2001. Tehran Subway. Multicoloured.
3067 500r. Type **1163** 1·70 1·50
3068 500r. Locomotive right view 1·70 1·50

1164 Samand Saloon Car

2002. 1st Iranian Manufactured Car. Multicoloured.
3069 500r. Type **1164** 1·50 1·40
3070 500r. Grey car (horiz) 1·50 1·40

1165 Globe as Plant Pot containing Tree

2002. Tree Planting Day.
3071 **1165** 500r. multicoloured 1·50 1·40

1166 Squacco Heron (Ardeola ralloides)

2002. New Year Festival. Multicoloured.
3072 500r. Type **1166** 1·40 1·10
3073 500r. Hoopoe (*Upupa epops*) 1·40 1·10
3074 500r. Blue tit (*Parus caeruleus*) 1·40 1·10
3075 500r. Alexandrine parakeet (*Psittacula eupatria*) 1·40 1·10

1167 Imam Hossein's Wounded Horse returning to Kerbala (image scaled to 50% of original size)

2002. Death of Imam Hossein (grandson of Mohamed). Sheet 99×76 mm. Imperf.
MS3076 **1167** 400r. multicoloured 1·10 1·10

1168 Chestnut Tiger (*Danaus sita*)

2002. Butterflies. Multicoloured.
3077 400r. Type **1168** 1·10 1·00
3078 400r. Comma (*Polygonia c-album*) 1·10 1·00
3079 400r. Blue argus (*Precis orithya*) 1·10 1·00
3080 400r. Painted lady (*Vanessa cardui*) 1·10 1·00
3081 400r. *Papilio maacki* 1·10 1·00

1169 Caspian

2002. Horses. Multicoloured.

3082	400r. Type **1169**	1·10	1·00
3083	400r. Kurd	1·10	1·00
3084	400r. Turkoman	1·10	1·00
3085	400r. Arab	1·10	1·00

1170 *Hyoscyamus muticus*

2002. Philakorea 2002 International Stamp Exhibition, Seoul. Flowers. Multicoloured.

3086	400r. Type **1170**	1·10	1·00
3087	400r. *Fritillaria* ("Frittillaria")	1·10	1·00
3088	400r. *Calotropis procera*	1·10	1·00
3089	400r. *Ranuculus*	1·10	1·00

1171 Ayatollah Khomeini

2002. Birth Centenary of Ayatollah Khomeini.

3090	**1171**	400r. multicoloured	1·00	90

1172 Child and Dome of the Rock

2002. Jerusalem Day.

3091	**1172**	400r. multicoloured	1·00	90

1173 Iranian Decorated Pots

2002. Centenary of Brazil—Iran Diplomatic Relations. Multicoloured.

3092	400r. Type **1173**	1·00	90
3093	400r. Marajoara pots, Brazil	1·00	90

1174 Emblem

2002. 2nd Biennial Exhibition of Contemporary Islamic Painting.

3094	**1174**	400r. multicoloured	1·00	90

1175 Smelting Pot and Mill

2003. 31st Anniv of Esfahan Steel Mill.

3095	**1175**	400r. multicoloured	1·00	90

1176 Grumman F-14A Tomcat

2003. Air Force Day. Multicoloured.

3096	300r. Type **1176**	70	60
3097	400r. Northrop F-5E Tiger II	90	85
3098	500r. F-14A Tomcat and missile carrier	1·10	1·10
3099	600r. Macdonell Douglas F-5E Phantom II	1·40	1·30
3100	700r. Mikoyan Mig-29	1·60	1·60

1177 Urial Sheep (1/2-size illustration)

2003. New Year Festival. Multicoloured.

3101	1000r. Type **1177**	2·30	2·10
3102	1000r. Goitered gazelle male	2·30	2·10
3103	1000r. Goitered gazelle female	2·30	2·10
3104	1000r. Red deer	2·30	2·10

1178 Mosque, Isfahan

2003. Buildings.

3105	400r. Type **1178**	90	75
3106	400r. Bell Tower, Xi'an	90	75

Stamps of the same design were issued by People's Republic of China.

1179 Family enclosed in House of Books

2003. Book, Children and Family.

3107	**1179**	500r. multicoloured	75	70

1180 *Zygaena*

2003. Butterflies. Multicoloured.

3108	100r. Type **1180**	15	15
3109	200r. *Issoria lathonia*	30	30
3110	250r. *Utethesia pulchella*	40	40
3111	300r. *Argynnis paphia*	45	45
3112	500r. *Polygonia egea*	75	75
3113	600r. *Papilio machaon*	90	90
3113a	650r. *Colias aurorina*	90	55
3114	1000r. *Inachis Io*	1·50	1·50
3115	2000r. *Papilio demoleus*	3·00	3·00
3115a	2100r. *Papitio demoleus*	2·75	1·60
3116	3000r. *Euphydryas aurinia*	4·50	4·50
3118	4400r. *Danaus melanippus*	6·25	6·25
3119	5500r. *Colias auriona*	8·00	8·00

1181 Emblem

2003. 50th Anniv of Social Security.

3125	**1181**	600r. multicoloured	75	70

1182 Revolutionaries (1/2-size illustration)

2003

3126	**1182**	600r. multicoloured	90	75

1183 Mohammed Ali Rajai and Arabic Script

2003. Government Week.

3127	**1183**	600r. multicoloured	90	75

1184 Caspian Seal (*Phoca caspia*)

2003. Preservation of the Caspian Sea. Mult.

3128	600r. Type **1184**	90	75
3129	600r. Beluga (*Huso huso*)	90	75
MS3130	130×97 mm. Nos. 3128/9 each×2	3·75	3·75

Stamps of a similar design were issued by Russia.

1185 Hand holding Apple

2003

3131	**1185**	500r. multicoloured	75	70

1186 Computer and Satellite

2003. World Post Day. Multicoloured.

3132	600r. Type **1186**	85	75
3133	600r. Post lorries and airplanes	85	75
3134	600r. Seated man holding letter and lorry	85	75
3135	600r. Post rider and statues	85	75

1187 *Asiatic Cheetah*

2003. Endangered Species. Asiatic Cheetah (Acinonyc jubatus). Multicoloured.

3136	500r. Type **1187**	75	70
3137	500r. Adult and cub	75	70
3138	500r. Two adults	75	70
3139	500r. Adult with open mouth	75	70

1188 Minaret

2003. Fetr Feast.

3140	**1188**	600r. multicoloured	85	75

1189 City Walls

2004. Bam Earthquake. Sheet 136×101 mm containing T 1189 and similar horiz designs. Multicoloured.

MS3141	500r.×4, Type **1189**; Ruins; Medical staff and patients; Rescue workers	3·00	3·00

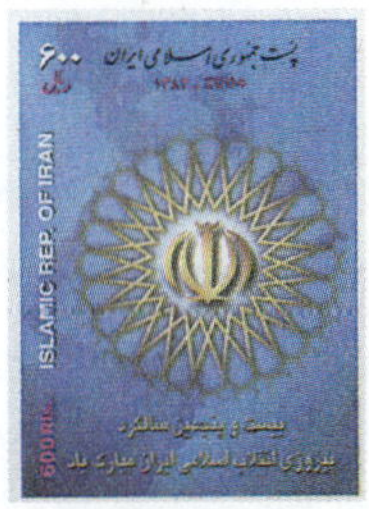

1190 Emblem

2004. 25th Anniv of Republic.

3142	**1190**	600r. multicoloured	90	75

1191 Hossein Rezazadeh (image scaled to 73% of original size)

2004. Hossein Rezazadeh, Champion Weightlifter.

3143	**1191**	1200r. multicoloured	1·80	1·60

1192 Postman and Customer

2004. Obtaining ISO 9001–2000 Certification (quality control).

3144	**1192**	600r. multicoloured	90	75

1193 Goldfish (*Carassius auratus*)

2004. New Year. Ornamental Fish. Multicoloured.

3145	100r. Type **1193**	15	10
3146	200r. *Carrasius auratus* with grey tail	30	25
3147	300r. Guppy (*Poecilia reticulate*)	45	40
3148	400r. Siamese fighting fish (*Betta splendens*)	60	55
3149	500r. *Carassius auratus* large facing left	75	70
3150	600r. *Carassius auratus* with raised fin	90	85

1194 Clown Triggerfish (*Balistoides conspicillum*)

2004. Saltwater Fish. Sheet 137×166 mm containing T 1194 and similar horiz designs. Multicoloured.

MS3151	250r. Type **1194**; 350r. *Acanthurus glaucopareius*; 450r. Lionfish (*Pterois volitans*); 550r. Sail-finned tang (*Zebrasoma veliferum*); 650r. Regal angelfish (*Pygoplites diacanthus*); 750r. Jigsaw triggerfish (*Pseudobalistes fuscus*)	4·50	4·50

1195 National Team Members (2/3-size illustration)
(image scaled to 74% of original size)

2004. Centenary of FIFA (Federation Internationale de Football Association).

3152	**1195**	600r. multicoloured	90	85

1196 Camera, Hand and Page

2004. Reporters Day.

3153	**1196**	650r. multicoloured	60	55

1197 Taekwondo

2004. Olympic Games, Athens. Multicoloured.

3154	650r. Type **1197**	60	45
3155	650r. Weightlifting	60	45
3156	650r. Wrestling	60	45
3157	650r. Judo	60	45

1198 Kabir

2004. Iranian and Indian Poets. Multicoloured.

3158	600r. Type **1198** (Indian)	55	45
3159	600r. Khajeh Shamseddin Mohammad Hafez Shirazi (Hafez) (Iranian)	55	45

Stamps of the same design were issued by India.

1199 Memorial, Hamedan

2004. Avicina International Conference, Bu-Ali Sina University, Hamedan. Multicoloured.

3160	650r. Type **1199**	60	50
3161	650r. Abu Ali al-Husain ibn Abdallah ibn Sina (Avicina) (poet)	60	50

1200 Chacma Baboon (*Papio ursinus*)

2004. World Stamp Collecting Championship, Singapore. Sheet 138×101 mm containing T 1200 and similar horiz designs. Multicoloured.

MS3162	500r.×4, Type **1200**; Chimpanzee (*Pan troglodytes*); Two chimpanzees; Mandrill (*Mandrillus sphinx*)	3·75	3·75

1201 Tabby Shorthair

2004. Cats. Sheet 168×136 mm containing T 1201 and similar vert designs. Multicoloured.

MS3163	500r.×6, Type **1201**; Silver tabby longhair; Bi-colour longhair; Persian; Silver tabby shorthair; Tabby and white shorthair	5·25	5·25

1202 Volleyball Players

2004. Paralympics, Athens.

3164	**1202**	650r. multicoloured	60	55

1203 Airplanes and Missiles

2004. 24th Anniv of Iran–Iraq War.

3165	**1203**	650r. multicoloured	60	55

1204 Emblem

2004. 70th Anniv of Tehran University.

3166	**1204**	650r. multicoloured	60	55

1205 Mullah

2004. Multicoloured.

3167	500r. Type **1205**	45	40
3168	500r. Man with moustache	45	40
3169	500r. Man facing right	45	40
3170	500r. Man facing left	45	40

1206 Damavand Mountain, Iran

2004. Mountains. Multicoloured.

3171	650r. Type **1206**	60	55
3172	650r. Bolivar Peak, Venezuela	60	55

Stamps of a similar design were issued by Venezuela.

1207 Hand

2004. Biennial International Islamic Poster Exhibition. Multicoloured.

3173	500r. Type **1207**	45	40
3174	500r. Bird on nest	45	40
3175	500r. Slingshot	45	40
3176	500r. Moon	45	40

1208 Tomb

2004. Imam Reza Commemoration. Designs showing parts of shrine. Multicoloured.

3177	500r. Type **1208**	45	40
3178	500r. Roof	45	40
3179	500r. Facade	45	40
3180	500r. Doorway	45	40

1209 Ali Daei

2005. Ali Daei (world all-time leading goal scorer in international matches).

3181	**1209**	650r. multicoloured	60	60

1210 Scene from "Where is the Friend's Home" (by Abbas Kiarostami)

2005. Film Museum, Iran. Scenes from Iranian films. Multicoloured.

3182	500r. Type **1210**	45	45
3183	500r. "The Children of Heaven" (by Majid Majidi)	45	45
3184	500r. Museum building	45	45
3185	500r. "The Cow" (Dariush Mehrjui)	45	45

1211 Antonov-140

2005. Aircraft. Multicoloured.

3186	850r. Type **1211**	75	75
3187	850r. Iran-140	75	75

Stamps of a similar design were issued by Ukraine.

1212 Persepolis

2005. World Expo 2005, Aichi, Japan. Sheet 127×99 mm containing T 1212 and similar horiz designs. Multicoloured.

MS3188	650r.×4, Type **1212**; Yazd ventilation wind towers; Desert architecture; Cyrus the Great's Cylinder (First World Charter of Human Rights)	2·30	2·30

1213 Operating Theatre and University Building

2005. 70th Anniv of Tehran University of Medical Sciences.
3189 **1213** 650r. multicoloured 60 60

1214 Officer and Crowd

2005. Police Week.
3190 **1214** 650r. multicoloured 60 60

1215 Rumi and Dervish Dancers

2005. 800th Birth Anniv (2007) of Mevlana Celaleddin (Rumi) (poet and philosopher).
3191 **1215** 650r. multicoloured 60 60

A stamp of a similar design was issued by Syria, Turkey and Afghanistan.

1216 La Granja de San Ildefonso Garden, Segovia

2005. Gardens. Multicoloured.
3192 650r. Type **1216** 60 60
3193 650r. Bagh-e-Shahzadeh, Kerman 60 60

Stamps of a similar design were issued by Spain.

1218 (image scaled to 36% of original size)

2006. Centenary of Constitution Revolution. Sheet 135×102 mm as T 1218. Multicoloured.
MS3195 650r.×4 Type **1218** 6·50 6·50

No. 3194 and Type **1217** have been left for 'Wheat Self-Sufficiency', issued on 4 January 2006, not yet received.

The stamps and margins of **MS**3195 form a composite background design.

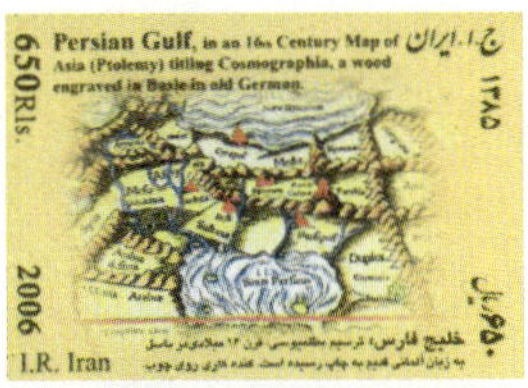
1219 16th-century Map of Persian Gulf

2006. History of Persian Gulf. Maps. Sheet 135×102 mm containing T 1219 and similar horiz designs. Multicoloured.
MS3196 650r.×4 Type **1219**; Persian Sea, 1966; Arab peninsula, 1952; 18th-century map of Persia by Scoteri Motthaei 6·50 6·50

The stamps of **MS**3196 form a composite background design.

1220 Trophy, Players and Emblem

2006. World Cup Football Championship, Germany.
3197 **1220** 650r. multicoloured 1·90 1·90

1221 Abbas Schafi

2006. Personalities. Multicoloured.
3198 650r. Type **1221** 1·70 1·70
3199 650r. Alameh Mohammad Reza Hakimi 1·70 1·70
3200 650r. Mohammad Hossein Gandji 1·70 1·70
3201 650r. Almeh Mohmmad Hassan Amoli 1·70 1·70

1222 Members Flags and Map (image scaled to 73% of original size)

2006. ECO (Economic Cooperation Organization) Postal Authorities Conference, Ankara.
3202 **1222** 650r. multicoloured 1·90 1·90

1223 Parliamentary Association Emblem

2006. General Assembly of Association of Asian Parliaments. Sheet 135×102 mm containing T 1223 and similar horiz designs. Multicoloured.
MS3203 650r.×4 Type **1223**; Dove; Assembly building; Islamic Consultative Assembly emblem 6·75 6·75

The stamps of **MS**3203 form a composite background design.

1224 Flag and Flowers

2006. 27th Anniv of Basji.
3204 **1224** 650r. multicoloured 2·00 2·00

1225 Chehel Sotun Palace

2006. Isfahan. Sheet 135×102 mm containing T 1225 and similar horiz design. Multicoloured.
MS3205 650r.×4 Type **1225**; Imam Mosque; Aliqapu Palace; Khajo Bridge 6·50 6·50

The stamps and margins of **MS**3205 form a composite background design.

1226 Ahmad Kazemi

2007. 1st Death Anniv of Ahmad Kazemi (commander). Multicoloured.
3206 650r. Type **1226** 1·75 1·75
3207 650r. Ahmad Kazemi encircled by other senior officers killed in accident 1·75 1·75

1227 Emblems and Dove (image scaled to 73% of original size)

2007. Nuclear Power.
3208 **1227** 650r. multicoloured 2·00 2·00

1228 Minarets and Dome

2007. Shrine of Lady Fatima Masuma (Fatima al-Masumeh), Qum.
3209 **1228** 650r. multicoloured 2·00 2·00

1229 Dancer

2007. New Year. Multicoloured.
3210 650r. Type **1229** 1·75 1·75
3211 650r. Symbols of New Year 1·75 1·75

1229a Emblem

2007. Communications and Public Relations Day.
3211a **1229a** 650r. multicoloured 1·75 1·75

1230 Persian Gulf

2007
3212 **1230** 300r. multicoloured 1·00 1·00

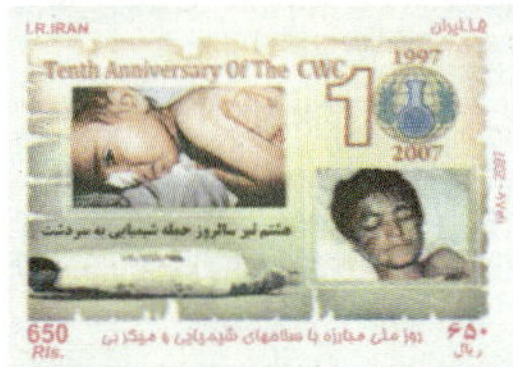
1231 Sick Children

2007. 10th Anniv of Ratification of Chemical Weapons Convention (CWC).
3213 **1231** 650r. multicoloured 2·00 2·00

1232 Emblem

2007. Physics Olympiad, Isfahan.
3214 **1232** 650r. multicoloured 2·00 2·00

2007. As Type 1230.
3214a 4400r. multicoloured 11·25 11·25

1233 K. K. Sarughy

2007. K. K. Sarughy Commemoration.
3215 **1233** 650r. multicoloured 2·00 2·00

1234 Engine

2007. Design and Production of First Iranian Engine.
3216 **1234** 650r. multicoloured 2·00 2·00

1235 Sayyid Musa al-Sadr

2007. Sayyid Musa al-Sadr (Imam Moussa Sadar) (politician and philosopher) Commemoration.

3218	**1235**	650r. multicoloured	2·00	2·00

2007. As Type 1230.

3219	200r. multicoloured	1·00	1·00

1236 Siberian Cranes

2007. Siberian Crane (Grus leucogranus). Multicoloured.

3220	650r. Type **1236**	1·70	1·70
3221	650r. Two cranes (different)	1·70	1·70
3222	650r. Cranes on land	1·70	1·70
3223	650r. Crane preparing to fly	1·70	1·70

1237 Archway

2007. Great Messenger Year (PBUH). Sheet 137×101 mm containing T 1237 and similar horiz designs. Multicoloured.

MS3224 650r.×4, Type **1237**; Script; Coliseum, Rome; Pyramids	6·50	6·50

1238 Posting Letter

2007. World Post Day.

3225	**1238**	650r. multicoloured	2·00	2·00

2007. As Type 1230.

3225a	2100r. multicoloured	5·25	5·25

1239 Jamkaran Mosque, Qum

2007

3226	**1239**	650r. multicoloured	2·00	2·00

2007. As Type 1230.

3226a	650r. multicoloured	2·00	2·00

1240 Swans flying

2007. Anniversary of Prisoners of War Return. Sheet 138×99 mm containing T 1240 and similar horiz designs. Multicoloured.

MS3227 650r.×4, Type **1240**; Cleric; Returnees waving from bus; Motor-cyclists and bus carrying returnees	6·50	6·50

2008. As Type 1230.

3228	5500r. multicoloured	14·00	14·00

2008. As Type 1230.

3229	2000r. multicoloured	3·00	3·00

2008. As Type 1230.

3230	1000r. multicoloured	1·50	1·50

1241 Navvab Safavi

2008. Mojtaba Mir-Lowhi (Navvab Safavi) (founder of Fadayan-e Islam (Iranian Islamic fundamentalist society)) Commemoration.

3231	**1241**	650r. multicoloured	2·00	2·00

1242 Falsafi

2008. Birth Centenary of Mohammad Taqi Falsafi (Falsafi) (preacher).

3232	**1242**	650r. multicoloured	2·00	2·00

1243 Fibre Optic Cable, Satellite and Computer Language (0,1)

2008. Information Technology, Development Infrastructure.

3233	**1243**	650r. multicoloured	2·00	2·00

1244 Mevlana

2008. 800th Birth Anniv of Mawlana Jalal-ad-Din Muhammad Rumi (Mevlana or Rumi) (philosopher and writer).

3234	**1244**	650r. multicoloured	2·00	2·00

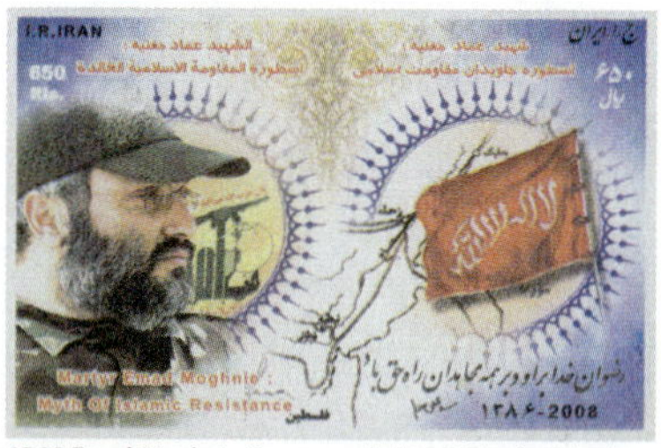

1246 Emad Moghnie (image scaled to 73% of original size)

2008

3236	**1246**	650r. multicoloured	2·00	2·00

No. 3235 and Type **1245** are vacant.

1247 Symbols of New Year

2008. New Year.

3237	**1247**	650r. multicoloured	2·00	2·00

1248 Shrine Complex (Illustration reduced. Actual size 63×24 mm)

2008. H. H. Abdulazim's Holy Shrine (hadith–teller (oral tradition)).

3238	**1248**	650r. multicoloured	2·00	2·00

1249 Fish in Water

2008. Children and Youth Art Festival. Water.

3239	**1249**	650r. multicoloured	2·00	2·00

1250 City and Mountains

2008. Tenth Anniv of Islamic City Councils.

3240	**1250**	650r. multicoloured	2·00	2·00

1250a Sheikh Hashem Ghazvini

2008. Sheikh Hashem Ghazvini Commemoration.

3240a	**1250a**	650r. multicoloured	2·00	2·00

1251 Emblem

2008. 1100th Death Anniv of Thiqat al-Islam Kulayni.

3241	**1251**	650r. multicoloured	2·00	2·00

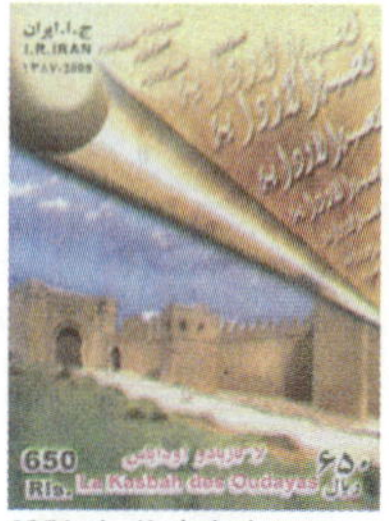

1251a La Kasbah des Oudayas, Morocco and Script

2008. Iran—Morocco Issue. Multicoloured.

3241a	650r. Type **1251a**	2·00	2·00
3241b	650r. Falak Ol Aflak Castle, Iran	2·00	2·00

Stamps of a similar design were issued by Morocco.

2008. As Type 1230.

3242	500r. multicoloured	1·50	1·50

1252 Engraved Copper Cup (Mansour Hafezparast)

2008. World Handicraft Day. Multicoloured.

3243	650r. Type **1252**	2·00	2·00
3244	650r. Mina Vase (Hossein Bagher Esmaili)	2·00	2·00

1253 Javid-al-Asar Motevasselian

2008

3245	**1253**	650r. multicoloured	2·00	2·00

1254 Khan-Tengri Peak, Kyrgyzstan

2008. Mountains. Multicoloured.

3246	650r. Type **1254**	2·00	2·00
3247	650r. Sabalan Peak, Iran	2·00	2·00

Stamps of a similar design were issued by Kyrgyzstan.

1255 17th-century Gold Medallion, Iran

2008. Jewellery. Multicoloured.
3248 650r. Type **1255** 2·00 2·00
3249 650r. 4th/ 5th-century gold buckle, Kazakhstan 2·00 2·00
Stamps of a similar design were issued by Kazakhstan.

2008. As Type 1230.
3250 100r. multicoloured 1·00 1·00

2008. As Type 1230.
3251 400r. multicoloured 1·30 1·30

1255a Symbols of Protest

2008. International Day of Al-Quds (Ghods).
3251a **1255a** 650r. multicoloured 2·00 2·00

1256 Symbols of Post

2008. 20th Anniv of Iran Post Company.
3252 **1256** 1200r. multicoloured 3·75 3·75

1257 Emblem

2008. 80th Anniv of Melli Iran Bank.
3253 **1257** 650r. multicoloured 2·00 2·00

2008. As Type 1230.
3254 250r. multicoloured 2·00 2·00

1257a Emblem

2008. National Day of Exports.
3254a **1257a** 650r. multicoloured 6·00 6·00

1258 M. R. Pourkian

2008. Martyrs.
3255 **1258** 650r. multicoloured 2·00 2·00

1259 Emblem

2008. National Day of Consumers Rights.
3256 **1259** 650r. multicoloured 2·00 2·00

1260 Emblem

2008. 28th Anniv of Security Services.
3257 **1260** 650r. multicoloured 2·00 2·00

1260a Gijack, Badahshon

2008. Musical Instruments. Multicoloured.
3257a 650r. Type **1260a** 6·00 6·00
3257b 650r. Dotar (Inscr 'Dotaar'), Khorasan 6·00 6·00
Stamps of a similar design were issued by Tadjikistan.

1261 Ruins

2008. Zabol.
3258 **1261** 650r. multicoloured 2·00 2·00

1262 Sheikh Kharaghani

2009. Sheikh Abul Hasan Kharaghani Commemoration.
3259 **1262** 650r. multicoloured 2·00 2·00

1263 Crying Woman, Corpse and Flames

2009. Gaza.
3260 **1263** 1200r. multicoloured 3·75 3·75

1264 Ayatollah Khomeini

2009. 30th Anniv of Revolution.
3261 **1264** 650r. multicoloured 2·00 2·00

2009. As Type 1230
3262 3000r. As Type **1230** 8·00 8·00

1265 Abbas Karimi, Reza Cheragi and Mohammed Hemat

2009. Martyrs.
3263 **1265** 650r. multicoloured 2·00 2·00

1266 Launch

2008. 1st Iranian Satellite. Multicoloured.
3264 1300r. Type **1266** 4·00 4·00
3265 1300r. In orbit 4·00 4·00

1267 Emblem growing from Map

2009. 10th Economic Co-operation Organization Conference, Tehran.
3266 **1267** 1300r. multicoloured 4·00 4·00

1268 Symbols of New Year

2009. New Year.
3267 **1268** 1300r. multicoloured 4·00 4·00

1269 Hand holding Apple and Dove

2009. Nurses' Day.
3268 **1269** 1300r. multicoloured 4·00 4·00

1270 Mother and Child

2009. Mothers' Day.
3269 **1270** 1100r. multicoloured 3·50 3·50

1270a (image scaled to 38% of original size)

2009. Trenchless Trench Makers. Sheet 134×103 mm as T 1270a
MS3271a 650r.×4, Type **1270a** 7·50 7·50

1271 *Chaetodontoplus seplentrionalis*

2009. Fish.
3270 **1271** 1000r. multicoloured 3·50 3·50

1272 *Haliaeetus albicilla* (white-tailed eagle)

2009. Raptors. Multicoloured.

3271	2000r. Type **1271**	5·00	5·00
3272	2000r. *Pandion haliaetus* (osprey)	5·00	5·00

Nos. 3271/2 were printed, se-tenant, each pair forming a composite design.

Stamps of a similar design were issued by Portugal.

1273 *Porphyrio porphyrio* (purple swamphen), Flags and *Cyanolimnas cervai* (Zapata rail) (image scaled to 30% of original size)

2009. Convention on Wetlands of International Importance (Ramsar Convention).

3273	**1273**	1500r. multicoloured	2·75	2·75

A stamp of a similar design was issued by Cuba.

1274 *Eretmochelys imbricata*

2009. Conservation of Marine Turtles. Sheet 139×101 containing T 1274 and similar horiz designs. Multicoloured.

MS3274	650r. Type **1274**; 1000r. *Eretmochelys imbricata* (different); 1500r. *Chelonia mydas*; 1850r. *Chelonia mydas* (different)	8·25	8·25

The stamps and margins of No. **MS**3274 form a composite design.

2009. Fish. As T 1271. Multicoloured.

3275	7500r. *Premnas biaculeatus*	15·00	15·00

2009. Fish. As T 1271. Multicoloured.

3276	200r. *Holacanthus ciliaris*	1·00	1·00

1275 Emblem

2009. Book Week.

3277	**1275**	1200r. bright bottle green, deep rose-red and black	3·75	3·75

1276 Document

2009. Rob'e Rashidi Endowment Document.

3278	**1276**	1200r. multicoloured	3·75	3·75

2009. Fish. As T 1271. Multicoloured.

3279	6400r. *Paracanthurus hepatus*	8·75	8·75

1277 Emblem

2009. 60th Anniv of Universal Declaration of Human Rights.

3280	**1277**	1200r. multicoloured	3·75	3·75

2009. Fish. As T 1271. Multicoloured.

3281	500r. *Centropyge bicolor*	1·70	1·70

1278 Soltanieh Dome, Western Zanjan Province, Iran

2009. Cultural Heritage. Multicoloured

3282	2000r. Type **1278**	3·00	3·00
3283	2000r. Al-Markaz Mosque, Makassar City, Indonesia	3·00	3·00

Stamps of a similar design were issued by Indonesia.

1279 Post Van

2010. World Post Day. Multicoloured.

3284	1200r. Type **1279**	3·75	3·75
3285	1200r. Children encircling globe and envelopes as kites	3·75	3·75

Nos. 3284/5 were printed, se-tenant, each pair forming a composite design.

1280 Marveh Sherbini

2010. Martyr.

3286	**1280**	1300r. multicoloured	4·25	4·25

NEWSPAPER POSTAGE DUE STAMPS

1909. Optd Imprimes in English and Persian.

N319	**38**	2ch. grey on blue	26·00	5·25

OFFICIAL STAMPS

1902. Stamp of 1898 surch Service and value in English and Persian.

O224	**21**	5c. on 1k. red	21·00	21·00
O225	**21**	10c. on 1k. red	21·00	21·00
O226	**21**	12c. on 1k. red	25·00	25·00

1903. Stamps of 1903 optd Service.

O259	**38**	1c. lilac	1·60	25
O260	**38**	2c. grey	1·60	25
O261	**38**	3c. green	1·60	25
O262	**38**	5c. red	1·60	25
O263	**38**	10c. brown	3·25	25
O264	**38**	12c. blue	5·00	25
O265	**39**	1k. purple	5·00	80
O266	**39**	2k. blue	5·00	1·30
O267	**39**	5k. brown	12·50	1·60
O268	**39**	10k. red	12·50	2·10
O269	**39**	20k. orange	41·00	5·00
O270	**39**	30k. green	49·00	12·50
O271	**39**	50k. green	£160	65·00

1905. Nos. 275/6 and 280/1 optd Service.

O283	2t. on 50k. green (275)	£100	41·00
O284	3t. on 50k. green (276)	£100	41·00
O285	2t. on 50k. green (280)	£100	41·00
O286	3t. on 50k. green (281)	£100	41·00

(O 57)

1911. Stamps of 1909 optd Service and with Type O57.

O353	**56**	1c. purple and orange	5·75	3·25
O354	**56**	2c. purple and violet	5·75	3·25
O355	**56**	3c. purple and green	5·75	3·25
O356	**56**	6c. purple and red	5·75	3·25
O357	**56**	9c. purple and grey	9·75	6·50
O358	**56**	10c. purple and mauve	9·75	6·50
O359	**56**	1k. brown, violet & silver	2·50	21·00
O360	**56**	2k. brown, green & silver	6·50	49·00

1915. Coronation stamps of 1915 optd SERVICE in English and Persian.

O460	**66**	1c. blue and red	1·80	1·80
O461	**66**	2c. red and blue	1·80	1·80
O462	**66**	3c. green	1·80	1·80
O463	**66**	5c. red	1·80	1·80
O464	**66**	6c. red and green	1·80	1·80
O465	**66**	9c. violet and brown	1·80	1·80
O466	**66**	10c. brown and green	1·80	1·80
O467	**66**	12c. blue	2·10	2·10
O468	**66**	24c. chocolate and brown	3·00	3·00
O469	**67**	1k. black, brown & silver	5·00	5·00
O470	**67**	2k. red, blue and silver	5·25	5·25
O471	-	3k. sepia, lilac and silver	5·25	5·25
O472	**67**	5k. grey, sepia and silver	5·25	5·25
O473	-	1t. black, violet and gold	7·50	7·50
O474	-	2t. brown, green and gold	7·50	7·50
O475	-	3t. red, crimson and gold	9·75	9·75
O476	-	5t. grey, blue and gold	10·50	10·50

O 120

1941

O836	**O120**	5d. violet	3·00	25
O837	**O120**	10d. mauve	3·00	25
O838	**O120**	25d. red	3·00	25
O839	**O120**	50d. black	3·00	25
O840	**O120**	75d. red	4·50	45
O841	**O120**	1r. green	6·00	45
O842	**O120**	1r.50 blue	7·50	1·10
O843	**O120**	2r. blue	9·00	1·10
O844	**O120**	3r. purple	11·50	1·10
O845	**O120**	5r. green	23·00	1·50
O846	**O120**	10r. blue and brown	£225	3·50
O847	**O120**	20r. mauve and blue	£300	11·50
O848	**O120**	30r. green and violet	£375	90·00
O849	**O120**	50r. brown and blue	£750	£150

The rial values are larger (23×30 mm).

O489 Red Lion and Sun Emblem

1974

O1829	**O489**	5d. violet and mauve	25	25
O1830	**O489**	10d. mauve and blue	25	25
O1831	**O489**	50d. orange & green	25	25
O1832	**O489**	1r. blue and gold	30	25
O1833	**O489**	2r. green and orange	55	25
O1834	**O489**	6r. green and yellow	55	25
O1835	**O489**	8r. blue and yellow	70	25
O1836	**O489**	10r. blue and mauve	3·00	25
O1837	**O489**	11r. purple and blue	1·40	25
O1838	**O489**	14r. red and blue	1·40	60
O1839	**O489**	20r. blue and orange	2·40	55
O1840	**O489**	50r. brown and green	6·50	1·70
O2046	**O489**	1r. black and green	25	25
O2047	**O489**	2r. brown and grey	25	25
O2048	**O489**	3r. blue and orange	30	25
O2049	**O489**	5r. green and pink	40	25
O2050	**O489**	6r. black and blue	55	40
O2051	**O489**	8r. red and green	55	40
O2052	**O489**	10r. turquoise & grn	55	25
O2053	**O489**	11r. blue and yellow	1·10	45
O2054	**O489**	14r. green and grey	1·10	45
O2055	**O489**	15r. blue and mauve	2·30	90
O2056	**O489**	20r. purple and yellow	2·30	45
O2057	**O489**	30r. brown & orange	2·75	1·10
O2058	**O489**	50r. black and gold	6·00	1·10

The 6r. to 50r. are larger, 23×37 mm.

PARCEL POST STAMPS

1915. Coronation stamps of 1915 optd COLIS POSTAUX in English and Persian.

P443	**66**	1c. blue and red	2·10	2·10
P444	**66**	2c. red and blue	2·10	2·10
P445	**66**	3c. green	2·10	2·10
P446	**66**	5c. red	2·10	2·10
P447	**66**	6c. red and green	2·10	2·10
P448	**66**	9c. violet and brown	2·10	2·10
P449	**66**	10c. brown and green	2·10	2·10
P450	**66**	12c. blue	2·10	2·10
P451	**66**	24c. chocolate and brown	3·00	3·00
P452	**67**	1k. black, brown & silver	5·00	5·00
P453	**67**	2k. red, blue and silver	5·00	5·00
P454	**67**	3k. sepia, lilac and silver	5·00	5·00
P455	**67**	5k. grey, sepia and silver	5·25	5·25
P456	-	1t. black, violet and gold	7·50	7·50
P457	-	2t. brown, green and gold	7·50	7·50
P458	-	3t. red, crimson and gold	9·75	9·75
P459	-	5t. grey, blue and gold	10·50	10·50

P192

1958

P1151	**P192**	50d. drab	45	25
P1152	**P192**	1r. red	60	25
P1153	**P192**	2r. blue	60	25
P1154	**P192**	3r. myrtle	60	25
P1478	**P192**	5r. violet	3·75	25
P1479	**P192**	10r. brown	3·75	25
P1480	**P192**	20r. orange	6·00	45
P1481	**P192**	30r. mauve	7·50	25
P1482	**P192**	50r. lake	9·00	1·20
P1483	**P192**	100r. yellow	30·00	2·30
P1484	**P192**	200r. green	45·00	5·25

The word "IRAN" with a black frame is printed in reverse on the back of the above stamps and is intended to show through the stamps when attached to parcels.

POSTAL TAX STAMPS

1950. Hospitals Fund.

T1139	**T142a**	50d. red and green	3·00	75
T1396	**T142a**	2r. red and lilac	1·90	55

T142a Red Lion and Sun Emblem (8 lines to each ray)

1976. As T 142a but with five lines to each ray.

T2007	50d. red and green	1·90	25
T2008	2r. red and blue	1·90	1·90

Pt 1., Pt. 19

IRAQ

A country W. of Persia, formerly under Turkish dominion, then under British mandate after the 1914–18 War. An independent kingdom since 1932 until 14 July 1958, when the king was assassinated and a republic proclaimed.

1917. 16 annas = 1 rupee.
1931. 1000 fils = 1 dinar.

1918. Stamps of Turkey (Pictorial issue, Nos. 501/514) surch IRAQ IN BRITISH OCCUPATION and value in Indian currency.

1	¼a. on 5pa. purple	50	1·00
2	½a. on 10pa. green	70	20
3	1a. on 20pa. red	50	10
5	2½a. on 1pi. blue	1·25	1·40
6	3a. on 1½pi. grey and red	1·50	25
7	4a. on 1¾pi. brown and grey	1·50	25
8	6a. on 2pi. black and green	1·60	1·75
9	8a. on 2½pi. green and orange	2·00	1·75
10	12a. on 5pi. lilac	1·75	4·75
11	1r. on 10pi. brown	2·25	1·40
12	2r. on 25pi. green	7·50	2·50
13	5r. on 50pi. red	24·00	27·00
14	10r. on 100pi. blue	85·00	17·00

17		1½a. on 5pa. purple	2·25	1·00

2 Sunni Mosque, Muadhdham

3 Winged Cherub

4 Allegory of Date Palm

1923

41	2	½a. green	1·75	10
42	-	1a. brown	3·75	10
43	3	1½a. red	1·50	10
44	-	2a. buff	2·25	15
45	-	3a. blue	2·25	15
46	-	4a. violet	3·75	30
47	-	6a. blue	1·75	30
48	-	8a. bistre	3·75	30
49	4	1r. brown and green	16·00	1·50
50	2	2r. black	19·00	8·00
51	2	2r. bistre	70·00	3·25
52	-	5r. orange	40·00	13·00
53	-	10r. red	48·00	20·00

DESIGNS—30×24 mm: 1a. Gufas on the Tigris; 2a. Bull from Babylonian wall-sculpture; 6a., 10r. Shiah Mosque, Kadhimain. 34×24 mm: 3a. Arch of Ctesiphon. 24×30 mm: 4, 8a., 5r. Tribal Standard, Dulaim Camel Corps.

10 King Faisal I

1927

78	10	1r. brown	11·00	1·00

11 King Faisal I

12

1931

80	11	½a. green	2·00	30
81	11	1a. brown	1·75	30
82	11	1½a. red	2·00	50
83	11	2a. orange	1·50	10
84	11	3a. blue	1·50	20
85	11	4a. purple	2·00	2·50
86	11	6a. blue	1·75	80
87	11	8a. green	1·75	3·00
88	12	1r. brown	5·00	2·75
89	12	2r. brown	10·00	7·00
90	12	5r. orange	35·00	45·00
91	12	10r. red	95·00	£120
92	10	25r. violet	£950	£1200

1932. Nos. 80/92 and 46 surch in "Fils" or "Dinar".

106	11	2f. on ½a. green	50	10
107	11	3f. on ½a. green	50	10
108	11	4f. on 1a. brown	2·75	25
109	11	5f. on 1a. brown	75	10
110	11	8f. on 1½a. red	50	50
111	11	10f. on 2a. orange	50	10
112	11	15f. on 3a. blue	1·50	1·00
113	11	20f. on 4a. purple	1·75	2·00
114	-	25f. on 4a. violet (No. 46)	3·50	6·00
115	11	30f. on 6a. blue	3·75	60
116	11	40f. on 8a. green	2·75	5·00
117	12	75f. on 1r. brown	3·25	4·75
118	12	100f. on 2r. brown	6·00	4·00
119	12	200f. on 5r. orange	30·00	32·00
120	12	½d. on 10r. red	85·00	£120
121	10	1d. on 25r. violet	£180	£275

1932. As Types 10/12 but value in FILS or DINAR.

138	11	2f. blue	50	20
139	11	3f. green	50	10
140	11	4f. purple	50	10
141	11	5f. green	50	10
142	11	8f. red	1·75	10
143	11	10f. yellow	1·75	10
144	11	15f. blue	1·75	10
145	11	20f. orange	2·75	50
146	11	25f. mauve	3·00	50
147	11	30f. olive	3·00	15
148	11	40f. violet	2·00	1·00
149	12	50f. brown	2·50	20
150	12	75f. blue	6·50	2·75
151	12	100f. green	9·50	70
152	12	200f. red	17·00	3·25
153	10	½d. blue	60·00	55·00
154	10	1d. purple	£140	£140

16 King Ghazi

17

1934

172	16	1f. violet	50	35
173	16	2f. blue	35	35
174	16	3f. green	35	35
175	16	4f. purple	35	35
176	16	5f. green	35	35
177	16	8f. red	60	35
178	16	10f. yellow	70	35
179	16	15f. blue	70	35
180	16	20f. orange	70	35
181	16	25f. mauve	1·40	45
182	16	30f. green	1·10	35
183	16	40f. violet	1·20	35
184	17	50f. brown	3·00	35
185	17	75f. blue	2·40	45
186	17	100f. green	3·50	55
187	17	200f. red	6·00	1·20
188	-	½d. blue	16·00	12·50
189	-	1d. red	70·00	20·00

DESIGN—23×27½ mm: ½, 1d. Portrait as in Types **16/17** but different frame.

19 Mausoleum of Sitt Zubaidah

21 Lion of Babylon

22 Spiral Tower of Samarra

1941

208	19	1f. purple	35	35
209	19	2f. brown	35	35
210	-	3f. green	35	35
211	-	4f. violet	35	35
212	-	5f. red	35	35
213	21	8f. red	85	35
214	21	8f. yellow	35	35
215	21	10f. yellow	16·00	3·25
216	21	10f. red	85	35
217	21	15f. blue	1·40	35
218a	21	15f. black	1·40	55
219	21	20f. black	5·00	65
220	21	20f. blue	70	35
221	22	25f. purple	35	35
222	22	30f. orange	35	35
223b	22	40f. brown	1·40	55
224b	-	50f. blue	3·00	65
225a	-	75f. mauve	1·80	65
226	-	100f. olive	2·10	1·20
227	-	200f. orange	7·25	1·10
228	-	½d. blue	21·00	5·50
229a	-	1d. green	45·00	13·50

DESIGNS—HORIZ: 3f., 4f., 5f. King Faisal's Mausoleum (24×20 mm); ½d., 1d. Mosque of the Golden Dome, Samarra (24×21 mm). VERT: 50f., 75f. as Type **22**, but larger (21×24 mm); 100f., 200f. Oil Wells (20×22 mm).

26 King Faisal II

1942

255	26	1f. brown and violet	40	40
256	26	2f. brown and blue	40	40
257	26	3f. brown and green	40	40
258	26	4f. sepia and brown	40	40
259	26	5f. brown and green	40	40
260	26	6f. brown and red	40	40
261	26	10f. brown and pink	40	40
262	26	12f. brown and green	40	40

27

1948

271	27	1f. blue	60	10
272	27	2f. brown	35	10
273	27	3f. green	35	10
274	27	3f. red	11·50	2·50
275	27	4f. lilac	35	10
276	27	5f. red	35	10
277	27	5f. green	12·00	5·00
278	27	6f. mauve	2·30	15
279	27	8f. brown	5·50	90
280	27	10f. red	50	10
281	27	12f. green	50	10
282	27	14f. green	3·00	35
283	27	15f. black	9·00	2·50
284	27	16f. red	2·75	1·00
285	27	20f. blue	95	15
286	27	25f. purple	1·10	15
287	27	28f. blue	3·00	65
288	27	30f. orange	1·10	15
289	27	40f. brown	2·75	90
290	27	50f. blue	9·00	1·70
291	27	60f. blue	1·80	90
292	27	75f. mauve	1·80	90
293	27	100f. green	7·75	1·70
294	27	200f. orange	6·00	1·70
295	27	½d. blue	16·00	5·50
296	27	1d. green	65·00	21·00
MS297		161×179 mm. Nos. 273, 280, 284 and 292/4. Perf or imperf	£140	£275

The 50f. to 1d. are larger (22½×27½ mm).

29 Vickers Viking "Al Mahfoutha" over Basrah Aerodrome

1949. Air.

330	29	3f. green	35	35
331	-	4f. purple	35	35
332	-	5f. brown	35	35
333	29	10f. red	4·75	1·70
334	-	20f. blue	2·10	80
335	-	35f. orange	2·10	80
336	-	50f. green	3·25	1·30
337	-	100f. violet	8·50	2·75
MS338		235×165 mm. Nos. 330/7	90·00	£110

DESIGNS—As Type **29**: 4, 20f. "Al Mahfoutha" over Kut Barrage; 5, 35f. "Al Mahfoutha" over Faisal II Bridge. 31×22½ mm: 50, 100f. "Al Mahfoutha" over Dhiyala Railway Bridge.

31 King Faisal I and Equestrian Statue

1949. 75th Anniv of U.P.U.

339		20f. blue	3·00	2·00
340	31	40f. orange	4·25	2·00
341	-	50f. violet	10·00	7·25

DESIGNS: 20f. King Ghazi and mounted postman; 50f. King Faisal II, globe and wreath.

32 King Faisal II

1953. Coronation of King Faisal II.

342	32	3f. red	1·40	1·50
343	32	14f. brown	3·00	1·50
344	32	28f. blue	8·50	2·00
MS345		134×138 mm. Nos. 342/4	£120	£325

33

1954

346	33	1f. blue	70	10
347	33	2f. brown	25	10
348	33	3f. lake	25	10
349	33	4f. violet	25	10
350	33	5f. green	35	10
351	33	6f. mauve	35	10
352	33	8f. brown	35	10
353	33	10f. blue	35	10
354	33	15f. black	1·90	1·50
355	33	16f. red	3·00	2·50
356	33	20f. olive	1·40	35
357	33	25f. purple	1·40	10
358	33	30f. red	1·40	10
359	33	40f. brown	1·70	55
360	33	50f. blue	2·20	80
361	33	75f. mauve	3·50	90
362	33	100f. olive	6·75	90
363	33	200f. salmon	11·00	1·90

The 50f. to 200f. are larger (22×28 mm).

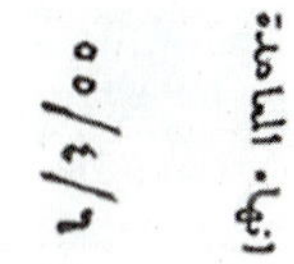

(35)

1955. Abrogation of Anglo-Iraqi Treaty. Optd with T 35.

380		3f. lake	1·30	55
381		10f. blue	1·40	55
382	27	28f. blue	2·40	1·10

36 King Faisal II

1955. 6th Arab Engineers' Conference, Baghdad.

383	36	3f. red	1·10	45
384	36	10f. blue	1·80	65
385	36	28f. blue	2·75	1·70

37 King Faisal II and Globe

1956. 3rd Arab Postal Union Conference, Baghdad.

386	37	3f. red	1·40	65
387	37	10f. blue	1·90	65
388	37	28f. blue	2·75	1·50

38 King Faisal II and Power Loom

1957. Development Week.

389	38	1f. blue and buff	60	20
390	-	3f. multicoloured	60	20
391	-	5f. multicoloured	70	20
392	-	10f. multicoloured	1·10	20
393	-	40f. multicoloured	2·20	90

DESIGNS: 3f. Irrigation dam; 5f. Residential road, Baghdad; 10f. Cement kiln; 40f. Tigris Bridge.

39 King Faisal II and Exhibition Emblem

1957. Agricultural and Industrial Exn, Baghdad.

394	39	10f. brown and cream	1·20	1·20

(40)

1957. Silver Jubilee of Iraqi Red Crescent Society. No. 388 optd with T 40.

395	37	28f. blue	5·50	2·50

41 King Faisal II

1957

396	41	1f. blue	35	55
397	41	2f. brown	35	55
398	41	3f. red	35	55
399	41	4f. violet	35	55
400	41	5f. green	85	85
401	41	6f. red	85	85
402	41	8f. brown	1·70	1·20
403	41	10f. blue	1·70	1·20

42 King Faisal II and Tanks

1958. Army Day.

411	42	8f. grey and green	1·20	1·20
412	-	10f. black and brown	1·60	1·60
413	-	20f. brown and blue	1·60	1·60
414	-	30f. violet and red	2·30	1·80

DESIGNS—As T **42**: King Faisal II and: 10f. Platoon marching; 20f. Mobile artillery unit and De Havilland D.H.112 Venom jet fighters. 22½×27½ mm: 30f. King Faisal II (full-length portrait).

1958. Development Week. As T 38, inscr "1958".

415	3f. green, drab and violet	50	35
416	5f. multicoloured	70	55
417	10f. multicoloured	1·90	1·10

DESIGNS—VERT: 3f. Sugar beet and refining plant. HORIZ: 5f. Building and pastoral scene; 10f. Irrigation dam.

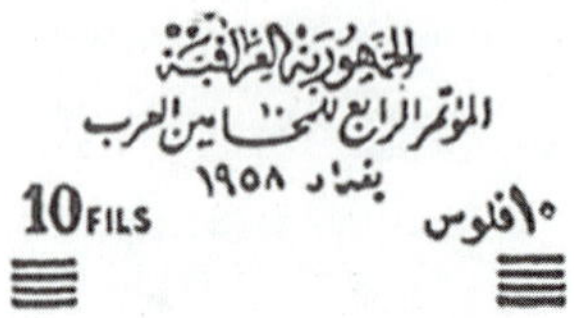

(44)

1958. Optd with T 43. (a) On No. 189.

418	1d. purple	34·00	34·00

(b) On T 27.

418a	1f. blue	43·00	13·50
419	12f. olive	95	35
420	14f. olive	1·20	35
421	16f. red	16·00	4·50
422	28f. blue	1·60	80
423	60f. blue	4·25	80
424	½d. blue	27·00	6·25
425	1d. green	50·00	22·00

(c) On T 33.

426	1f. blue	85	35
427	2f. brown	85	35
428	4f. violet	85	35
429	5f. green	85	35
430	6f. mauve	85	35
431	8f. brown	85	35
432	10f. blue	90	35
433	15f. black	1·20	35
434	16f. red	3·00	65
435	20f. olive	1·40	80
436	25f. purple	95	45
437	30f. red	1·40	45
438	40f. brown	1·40	35
439	50f. blue	6·75	3·75
440	75f. mauve	5·00	1·10
441	100f. olive	6·00	3·75
442	200f. salmon	18·00	7·25

Nos. 439/42 are larger (22×28 mm).

(d) On T 41.

443	1f. blue	4·00	90
444	2f. brown	85	35
445	3f. red	85	35
446	4f. violet	90	35
447	5f. green	85	35
448	6f. red	85	35
449	8f. brown	85	65
450	10f. blue	85	35
451	20f. green	85	35
452	25f. purple	1·80	1·00
453	30f. red	2·10	35
454	40f. brown	5·50	1·90
455	50f. purple	4·00	90
456	75f. green	4·00	1·70
457	100f. orange	5·50	1·70
458	200f. blue	14·50	3·00

Nos. 455/8 are larger (22½×27½ mm).

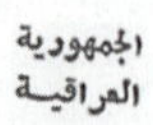

43 "Iraqi Republic"

1958. Arab Lawyers Conf, Baghdad. Surch with T 44.

506	36	10f. on 28f. blue	2·10	1·20

45 Republican Soldier and Flag

1959. Army Day.

507	45	3f. blue	50	20
508	45	10f. olive	95	45
509	45	40f. violet	1·80	90

45a Orange Tree

1959. Afforestation Day.

510	45a	10f. orange and green	95	35

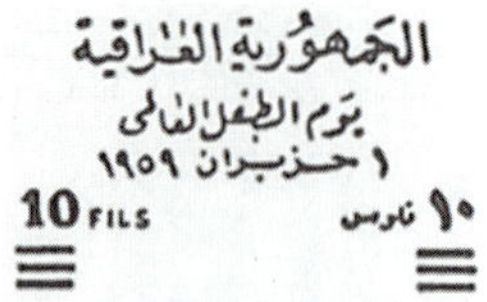

(46)

1959. International Children's Day. Surch with T 46.

511	37	10f. on 28f. blue	1·60	80

47 Worker and Buildings

1959. 1st Anniv of Revolution. Inscr "14TH JULY 1958".

512	47	10f. blue and ochre	70	65
513	-	30f. green and ochre	1·40	90

DESIGN—HORIZ: 30f. Revolutionaries brandishing weapons.

48 Harvesters

1959. Agricultural Reform.

514	48	10f. black and green	70	20

49 Republican Emblem

1959

515	49	1f. multicoloured	25	15
516	49	2f. multicoloured	25	15
517	49	3f. multicoloured	25	15
518	49	4f. multicoloured	25	15
519	49	5f. multicoloured	25	15
520	49	10f. multicoloured	25	15
521	49	15f. multicoloured	70	15
522	49	20f. multicoloured	70	15
523	49	30f. multicoloured	70	35
524	49	40f. multicoloured	1·30	45
525	49	50f. multicoloured	5·00	1·10
526	49	75f. multicoloured	2·10	55
527	49	100f. multicoloured	3·00	1·10
528	49	200f. multicoloured	5·50	1·10
529	49	500f. multicoloured	9·00	3·50
530	49	1d. multicoloured	21·00	9·00

(50)

1959. "Health and Hygiene". Optd with T 50.

531	10f. multicoloured	1·20	65

51 Gen. Kassem and Military Parade

1960. Army Day.

532	51	10f. lake and green	70	70
533	-	16f. red and blue	1·20	90
534	-	30f. olive, brown and buff	1·20	90
535	-	40f. violet and buff	1·70	1·10
536	-	60f. buff, chocolate & brn	2·40	1·30

DESIGNS—Gen. Kassem and: HORIZ: 16f. Infantry on manoeuvres; 60f. Partisans. VERT: 30f. Anti-aircraft gun-crew; 40f. Oilfield guards on parade.

52 Gen. Kassem

1960. Gen. Kassem's Escape from Assassination.

537	52	10f. violet	70	45
538	52	30f. green	1·30	65

53 Al Rasafi (poet)

1960. Al Rasafi Commemoration. Optd 1960 in English and Arabic.

539	53	10l. red	3·50	1·80

See also No 732.

54 Gen. Kassem at Tomb of Unknown Soldier

1960. 2nd Anniv of Revolution.

540	-	6f. gold, olive and orange	85	65
541	54	10f. orange, green and blue	85	65
542	54	16f. orange, violet and blue	1·10	1·10
543	-	18f. gold, blue and orange	1·10	1·10
544	-	30f. gold, brown and orange	1·40	1·20
545	54	60f. orange, sepia and blue	3·00	1·90

DESIGN—VERT: 6f., 18f., 30f. Symbol of Republic.

55 Gen. Kassem, Flag and Troops

1961. Army Day.

546	55	3f. multicoloured	35	15
547	55	6f. multicoloured	35	15
548	55	10f. multicoloured	70	15
549	-	20f. black, yellow and green	85	35
550	-	30f. black, yellow & brown	85	45
551	-	40f. black, yellow and blue	1·20	80

DESIGN: 20, 30, 40f. Kassem and triumphal arch.

56 Gen. Kassem with Children

1961. World Children's Day. Main design brown; background colours given.

558	56	3f. yellow	85	55
559	56	6f. blue	1·20	55
560	56	10f. pink	1·70	55
561	56	30f. lemon	1·70	55
562	56	50f. green	3·00	90

57 Gen. Kassem saluting

1961. 3rd Anniv of Revolution.

563	-	1f. multicoloured	35	10
564	-	3f. multicoloured	35	10
565	57	5f. multicoloured	35	10
566	-	6f. multicoloured	35	10
567	-	10f. multicoloured	50	35
568	57	30f. multicoloured	95	65
569	57	40f. multicoloured	1·20	65
570	-	50f. multicoloured	2·10	1·30
571	-	100f. multicoloured	6·75	3·25

DESIGN: 1, 3, 6, 10, 50, 100f. Gen. Kassem and Iraqi flag.

58 Gen. Kassem and Army Emblem

1962. Army Day.

572		1f. multicoloured	35	35
573		3f. multicoloured	35	35
574		6f. multicoloured	35	35
575	58	10f. black, gold and lilac	60	35
576	58	30f. black, gold and orange	1·20	65
577	58	50f. black, gold and green	2·10	1·30

DESIGN—VERT: 1, 3, 6f. Gen. Kassem saluting and part of speech.

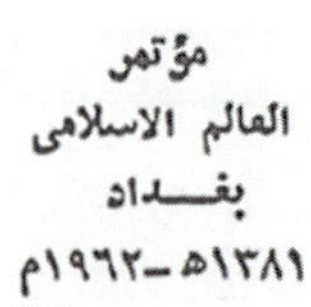

(59)

1962. 5th Islamic Congress. Optd with T 59.

578	49	3f. multicoloured	35	35
579	49	10f. multicoloured	35	35
580	49	30f. multicoloured	1·20	65

60 Gen. Kassem, Flag and Handclasp

1962. 4th Anniv of Revolution. Flag in green and gold.

581	**60**	1f. orange and sepia	10	10
582	**60**	3f. green and sepia	10	10
583	**60**	6f. brown and black	10	10
584	**60**	10f. lilac and sepia	60	55
585	**60**	30f. red and sepia	85	55
586	**60**	50f. grey and sepia	1·70	1·00

61 Fanfare

1962. Millenary of Baghdad. Multicoloured.

603	3f. Type **61**	60	35
604	6f. Al Kindi (philosopher)	60	35
605	10f. Map of old "Round City" of Baghdad	95	45
606	40f. Gen. Kassem and flag	2·75	1·20

62 Republican Emblem

1962. Aerogramme Stamps.

607	**62**	14f. black and green	2·40	85
608	**62**	35f. black and red	3·25	1·30

Nos. 607/8 were originally issued only attached to aerogramme forms covering the old imprinted King Faisal II stamps, but later appeared in sheets.

63 Campaign Emblem

1962. Malaria Eradication.

609	**63**	3f. multicoloured	35	35
610	**63**	10f. multicoloured	85	35
611	**63**	40f. multicoloured	1·40	65

64 Gen. Kassem and Tanks

1963. Army Day.

612	**64**	3f. black and yellow	10	10
613	**64**	5f. sepia and purple	10	10
614	**64**	6f. black and green	10	10
615	**64**	10f. black and blue	35	35
616	**64**	10f. black and pink	35	35
617	**64**	20f. black and blue	85	45
618	**64**	40f. black and mauve	1·40	80
619	**64**	50f. sepia and blue	2·10	1·60

65 Gufas on the Tigris

1963

620	**65**	1f. green	85	35
621	-	2f. violet	85	35
622	**65**	3f. black	85	35
623	-	4f. black and yellow	85	35
624	-	5f. purple and green	95	35
625	-	10f. red	1·30	35
626	-	15f. brown and yellow	2·10	35
627	-	20f. violet	2·20	35
628	-	30f. orange	1·40	45
629	-	40f. green	2·40	35
630	-	50f. brown	10·00	80
631	-	75f. black and green	5·00	55
632	-	100f. purple	5·50	65
633	-	200f. brown	10·00	65
634	-	500f. blue	14·50	3·00
635	-	1d. purple	19·00	5·50

DESIGNS: 2f., 500f. Spiral tower of Samarra; 4f., 15f. Sumerian Harp; 5f., 75f. Republican emblem; 10f., 50f. Lion of Babylon; 20f., 40f. Koranic school of Abbasid period; 30f., 200f. Mosque and minarets; 100f., 1d. Winged bull of Kharsabad.

66 Shepherd with Sheep

1963. Freedom from Hunger.

636	**66**	3f. black and green	35	35
637	-	10f. mauve and brown	85	35
638	-	20f. brown and blue	1·40	90
MS639		175×120 mm. Nos. 636/8 (sold at 50f.)	7·25	7·25

DESIGNS: 10f. Harvester; 20f. Trees.

67 Centenary Emblem

1963. Red Cross Centenary.

640	**67**	3f. violet and red	35	35
641	**67**	10f. blue and red	70	35
642	-	30f. blue and red	1·30	80

DESIGN—HORIZ: 30f. Hospital.

68 Helmet, Rifle and Flag

1964. Army Day.

643	**68**	3f. sepia, green and blue	35	35
644	**68**	10f. sepia, green and pink	70	35
645	**68**	30f. sepia, green and yellow	1·30	80

69 Revolutionaries and Flag

1964. 1st Anniv of 14th Ramadan Revolution. Flag in red, green and black.

646	**69**	10f. violet	70	35
647	**69**	30f. brown	1·30	80
MS648		125×75 mm. Nos. 646/7 in new colours (sold at 50f.)	8·50	6·75

See also No. **MS**746.

70 Shamash (Sun-God) and Hammurabi

1964. 15th Anniv of Declaration of Human Rights.

649	**70**	6f. olive and purple	70	55
650	-	10f. violet and orange	1·30	55
651	**70**	30f. green and blue	2·10	90

DESIGN: 10f. U.N. Emblem and Scales of Justice.

71 Soldier raising Flag on Map of Iraq

1964. 6th Anniv of Revolution.

652	-	3f. orange, grey and black	35	35
653	**71**	10f. red, black and green	35	35
654	**71**	20f. red, black and green	70	35
655	-	30f. orange, grey and black	1·40	80

DESIGN—HORIZ: 3f., 30f. Soldier "protecting" people and factories with outstretched arm.

72 Soldier, Civilians and Star Emblem

1964. 1st Anniv of 18 November Revolution.

656	**72**	5f. orange and brown	50	35
657	**72**	10f. orange and blue	50	35
658	**72**	50f. orange and violet	1·40	55

73 Musician

1964. International Arab Music Conf, Baghdad.

659	**73**	3f. multicoloured	1·30	35
660	**73**	10f. multicoloured	1·30	35
661	**73**	30f. multicoloured	1·80	1·20

74 Conference Emblem and Map

1964. 9th Arab Engineer's Conf, Baghdad.

662	**74**	10f. green and mauve	85	35

75 A.P.U. Emblem

1964. 10th Anniv of Arab Postal Union's Permanent Office.

663	**75**	3f. blue and red	35	15
664	**75**	10f. slate and purple	60	15
665	**75**	30f. blue and orange	1·60	65

76 Soldier, Civilians and Flag

1965. Army Day.

666	**76**	5f. multicoloured	35	15
667	**76**	15f. multicoloured	50	35
668	**76**	30f. multicoloured	1·60	80
MS669		110×83 mm. Stamps similar to No. 668 but without value shown together with stamps-size portrait of Pres. Arif. Imperf. (sold at 60f.)	10·00	10·00

77 Cogwheel and Factory

1965. 1st Arab Ministers of Labour Conf, Baghdad.

670	**77**	10f. multicoloured	70	35

78 Oil Tanker

1965. Inauguration of Deep Sea Terminal for Tankers.

671	**78**	10f. multicoloured	1·30	55

79 Armed Soldier with Flag

1965. 2nd Anniv of 14th Ramadan Revolution.

672	**79**	10f. multicoloured	70	20

80 Tree

1965. Tree Week.

673	**80**	6f. multicoloured	35	35
674	**80**	20f. multicoloured	1·60	35

81 Federation Emblem

1965. Arab Insurance Federation. Sun in gold.

675	**81**	3f. ultramarine and blue	35	35
676	**81**	10f. black and grey	35	35
677	**81**	30f. red and pink	1·30	90

82 Dagger of Deir Yassin, Palestine

1965. Deir Yassin Massacre.

678	**82**	10f. drab and black	1·30	45
679	**82**	20f. brown and blue	2·40	65

83 "Threat of Disease"

1965. World Health Day.

680	**83**	3f. multicoloured	60	35
681	**83**	10f. multicoloured	70	35
682	**83**	20f. multicoloured	1·70	90

84 I.T.U. Emblem and Symbols

1965. Centenary of I.T.U.

683	**84**	10f. multicoloured	95	20
684	**84**	20f. multicoloured	2·10	65
MS685 139×95 mm. Nos. 683/4. Imperf or perf			22·00	17·00

85 Flag and Map

1965. 1st Anniv of Iraq–U.A.R. Pact.

686	**85**	10f. multicoloured	60	20

85a Lamp and Burning Library

1965. Reconstitution of Algiers University Library.

687	**85a**	5f. red, green and black	50	35
688	**85a**	10f. green, red and black	85	35

86 Revolutionary and Flames

1965. 45th Anniv of 1920 Rebellion.

689	**86**	5f. multicoloured	35	20
690	**86**	10f. multicoloured	60	20

87 Mosque

1965. Mohammed's Birthday.

691	**87**	10f. multicoloured	85	80
MS692 110×75 mm. No. 691 (sold at 50f.)			9·00	9·00

88 Factory and Ear of Wheat

1965. 7th Anniv of 14 July Revolution.

693	**88**	10f. multicoloured	60	60

89 I.C.Y. Emblem

1965. Air. International Co-operation Year.

694	**89**	5f. black and brown	85	35
695	**89**	10f. brown and green	1·30	35
696	**89**	30f. black and blue	3·50	1·30

90 Fair Emblem

1965. Baghdad Fair.

697	**90**	10f. multicoloured	50	20

91 Pres. Arif (photo by Studio Jean)

1965. 2nd Anniv of 18 November Revolution.

698	**91**	5f. blue and orange	50	35
699	**91**	10f. sepia and blue	70	35
700	**91**	50f. blue and mauve	3·00	1·10

92 Census Graph

1965. National Census.

701	**92**	3f. black and purple	50	20
702	**92**	5f. red and brown	50	20
703	**92**	15f. bistre and blue	2·20	75

93 Hawker Siddeley Trident 1E Airliner

1965. Air. Inauguration of Hawker Siddeley Trident 1E Aircraft by Iraqi Airways.

704	**93**	5f. multicoloured	50	50
705	**93**	10f. multicoloured	50	50
706	**93**	40f. multicoloured	5·25	1·00

94 Date Palms

1965. 2nd F.A.O. Dates Conference, Baghdad.

707	**94**	3f. multicoloured	50	35
708	**94**	10f. multicoloured	1·20	35
709	**94**	15f. multicoloured	2·20	1·00

95 Army Memorial

1966. 45th Anniv of Army Day.

710	**95**	2f. multicoloured	60	35
711	**95**	5f. multicoloured	60	35
712	**95**	40f. multicoloured	2·40	90

96 "Eagle" and Flag

1966. 3rd Anniv of 14th Ramadan Revolution.

713	**96**	5f. multicoloured	35	35
714	**96**	10f. multicoloured	85	35

96a Arab League Emblem

1966. Arab Publicity Week.

715	**96a**	5f. green, brown & orange	60	20
716	**96a**	15f. blue, purple and olive	60	20

97 Footballers

98x 98 Footballer's Legs, and Iraq Football Union Emblem (1/3-size illustration) (image scaled to 43% of original size)

1966. Arab Football Cup, Baghdad. Mult.

717	2f. Type **97**	60	35
718	5f. Goalkeeper with ball	60	35
719	15f. Type **97**	1·80	90
MS720	116×70 mm. 50f. Type **98**	9·00	11·00

99 Excavator

1966. Labour Day.

721	**99**	15f. multicoloured	35	20
722	**99**	25f. black, silver and red	60	20

100 Queen Nefertari

1966. Nubian Monuments Preservation.

723	**100**	5f. yellow, black and olive	50	35
724	**100**	15f. yellow, brown & blue	50	35
725	-	40f. brown, chestnut & red	2·75	1·90

DESIGN—HORIZ: (41×32 mm): 40f. Rock temples, Abu Simbel.

101 President Arif

1966. 8th Anniv of 14 July Revolution.

726	**101**	5f. multicoloured	50	35
727	**101**	15f. multicoloured	70	35
728	**101**	50f. multicoloured	2·40	1·30

102

1966. Mohammed's Birthday.

729	**102**	5f. multicoloured	25	10
730	**102**	15f. multicoloured	35	10
731	**102**	30f. multicoloured	1·90	1·60

1966. As No. 539 but without opt.

732	**53**	10f. red	12·00	12·00

103 Iraqi Museum, Statue and Window

1966. Inauguration of Iraqi Museum, Baghdad. Multicoloured.

733	15f. Type **103**	1·40	35
734	50f. Gold headdress	2·20	1·00
735	80f. Sumerian head (vert)	4·50	1·50

104 Revolutionaries

1966. 3rd Anniv of 18 November Revolution.

736	**104**	15f. multicoloured	85	65
737	**104**	25f. multicoloured	1·30	1·30

105 "Magic Carpet"

1966. Air. Meeting of Arab International Tourist Union, Baghdad. Multicoloured.

738	2f. White stork emblem (27½×39 mm)	35	35
739	5f. Type **105**	35	35
740	15f. As 2f.	50	50
741	50f. Type **105**	1·90	80

106 UNESCO Emblem

1966. 20th Anniv of UNESCO.

742	**106**	5f. brown, black and blue	25	10
743	**106**	15f. green, black and red	70	35

107 Soldier and Rocket-launchers

1967. Army Day.

744	**107**	15f. ochre, brown & yellow	60	20
745	**107**	20f. ochre, brown and lilac	85	35

1967. 4th Anniv of Revolution of 14th Ramadan. No. MS648 with original inscriptions obliterated "4th" in place of "1st" and sheet value amended to 70fils.

MS746 125×75 mm. Nos. 646/7. Imperf (sold at 70f.)	9·75	9·75

108 Oil Refinery

1967. 6th Arab Petroleum Congress, Baghdad. Multicoloured.

747	5f. Congress emblem (vert)	35	20
748	15f. Type **108**	50	20
749	40f. Congress emblem (vert)	1·10	90
750	50f. Type **108**	2·40	1·20

109 "Spider's Web" Emblem

1967. Hajeer Year (1967).

751	**109**	5f. multicoloured	35	20
752	**109**	15f. multicoloured	50	35

110 Worker holding Cogwheel

1967. Labour Day.

753	**110**	10f. multicoloured	35	10
754	**110**	15f. multicoloured	50	20

111

1967. Mohammed's Birthday.

755	**111**	5f. multicoloured	50	35
756	**111**	15f. multicoloured	60	35

112 Flag and Hands with Clubs

1967. 47th Anniv of 1920 Rebellion.

757	**112**	5f. multicoloured	50	10
758	**112**	15f. multicoloured	70	10

113 Um Qasr Port

1967. 9th Anniv of 14 July Revolution and Inaug of Um Qasr Port. Multicoloured.

759	5f. Type **113**	35	20
760	10f. Freighter at quayside	85	35
761	15f. As 10f.	1·40	35
762	40f. Type **113**	2·75	1·30

114 Costume

1967. Iraqi Costumes.

765	**114**	2f. multicoloured (postage)	35	35
766	-	5f. multicoloured	35	35
767	-	10f. multicoloured	95	35
768	-	15f. multicoloured	1·20	65
769	-	20f. multicoloured	1·60	65
770	-	25f. multicoloured	1·70	80
771	-	30f. multicoloured	2·10	80
772	-	40f. multicoloured (air)	1·80	90
773	-	50f. multicoloured	2·75	1·30
774	-	80f. multicoloured	3·50	1·70

DESIGNS: 5f. to 80f. Different costumes.

115 Pres. Arif and Map

1967. 4th Anniv of 18 November Revolution. Multicoloured.

775	5f. President Arif	50	35
776	15f. Type **115**	1·10	55

116 Ziggurat of Ur

1967. International Tourist Year. Multicoloured.

777	2f. Type **116** (postage)	35	35
778	5f. Statues of Nimroud	35	35
779	10f. Babylon (arch)	60	35
780	15f. Minaret of Mosul (vert)	70	35
781	25f. Arch of Ctesiphon	85	35
782	50f. Statue, Temple of Hatra (vert) (air)	3·75	55
783	80f. Spiral Minaret of Samarra (vert)	4·25	80
784	100f. Adam's Tree (vert)	4·00	1·00
785	200f. Aladdin ("Aladdin's Cave") (vert)	9·00	4·00
786	500f. Golden Mosque of Kadhimain	43·00	25·00

117 Guide Emblem and Saluting Hand

1967. Iraqi Scouts and Guides. Multicoloured.

787	2f. Type **117**	1·80	45
788	5f. Guides by camp-fire	2·20	55
789	10f. Scout emblem and saluting hand	2·40	80
790	15f. Scouts setting up camp	2·40	1·00
MS791 120×48 mm. Nos. 787/90. Imperf (sold at 50f.)		12·00	12·00

118 Soldiers Drilling

1968. Army Day.

792	**118**	5f. brown, green and blue	50	20
793	**118**	15f. indigo, olive and blue	95	35

119 White-cheeked Bulbul

1968. Iraqi Birds. Multicoloured.

794	5f. Type **119**	85	35
795	10f. Hoopoe	1·10	35
796	15f. Jay	1·60	35
797	25f. Peregrine falcon	2·40	55
798	30f. White stork	3·25	55
799	40f. Black partridge	3·75	90
800	50f. Marbled teal	5·25	1·50

120 Battle Scene

1968. 5th Anniv of 14th Ramadan Revolution.

801	**120**	15f. orange, black and blue	4·25	1·10

121 Symbols of "Labour"

1968. Labour Day.

802	**121**	15f. multicoloured	50	35
803	**121**	25f. multicoloured	85	35

122 Football

1968. 23rd International Military Sports Council Football Championship. Multicoloured.

804	2f. Type **122**	50	35
805	5f. Goalkeeper in mid air	50	35
806	15f. Type **122**	60	35
807	25f. As 5f.	3·50	1·00
MS808 59×61 mm. 70f. Championship shield. Imperf		11·00	12·00

123 Soldier with Iraqi Flag

1968. 10th Anniv of 14 July Revolution.

809	**123**	15f. multicoloured	60	20

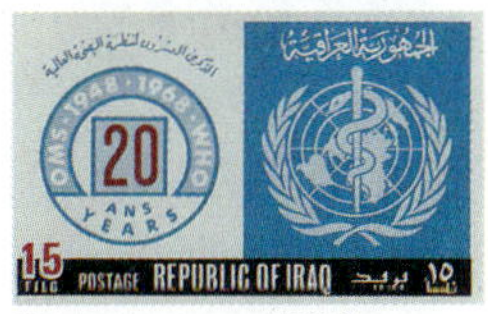

124 Anniversary and W.H.O. Emblems

1968. 20th Anniv of W.H.O.

810	-	5f. multicoloured	35	20
811	-	10f. multicoloured	35	20
812	**124**	15f. red, blue and black	70	20
813	-	25f. red, green and black	95	45

DESIGN—VERT: 5, 10f. Combined anniversary and W.H.O. emblems.

125 Human Rights Emblem

1968. Human Rights Year.

814	**125**	10f. red, yellow and blue	50	35
815	**125**	25f. red, yellow and green	50	35
MS816 55×75 mm. **125** 100f. scarlet, lemon and mauve. Imperf.			7·25	7·25

126 Mother and children

1968. UNICEF Commemoration.

817	**126**	15f. multicoloured	60	35
818	**126**	25f. multicoloured	1·70	45
MS819 56×76 mm. **126** 100f. multicoloured. Imperf			11·00	7·75

127 Army Tanks

1969. Army Day.

820	**127**	25f. multicoloured	4·25	2·00

128 Agricultural Scene

1969. 6th Anniv of 14th Ramadan Revolution.

821	**128**	15f. multicoloured	70	35

129 Mosque and Worshippers

1969. Hajeer Year.

822	**129**	15f. multicoloured	70	70

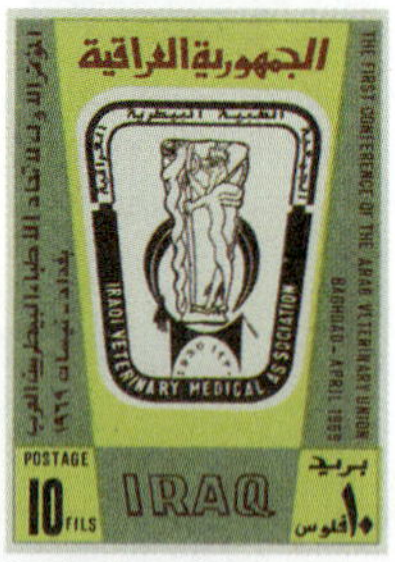

130 Emblem of Iraqi Veterinary Medical Association

1969. 1st Arab Veterinary Union Conf, Baghdad.

823	**130**	10f. multicoloured	85	45
824	**130**	15f. multicoloured	1·30	45

131 Mahseer

1969. Multicoloured. (a) Postage. Fishes.

825	2f. Type **131**	2·10	45
826	3f. Sharpey's barbel	2·20	45
827	10f. Silver pomfret	2·40	45
828	100f. Pike barbel	7·75	4·00

(b) Air. Fauna.

829	2f. Striped hyena	50	35
830	3f. Leopard	50	35
831	5f. Mountain gazelle	50	35
832	10f. Head of Arab horse	60	45
833	200f. Arab horse	14·50	7·75

132 Kaaba, Mecca

1969. Mohammed's Birthday.

834	**132**	15f. multicoloured	85	35

133 I.L.O. Emblem

1969. 50th Anniv of I.L.O.

835	**133**	5f. yellow, blue and black	25	10
836	**133**	15f. yellow, green & black	25	10
837	**133**	50f. yellow, red and black	1·90	1·20
MS838 75×55 mm. **133** 100f. multicoloured. Imperf			7·25	7·25

134 Weightlifting

1969. Olympic Games, Mexico (1968). Mult.

839	3f. Type **134**	70	35
840	5f. High jumping	70	35
841	10f. As Type **134**	85	45
842	35f. As 5f.	1·60	1·10
MS843 91×116 mm. Nos. 839/42. Imperf (sold at 100f.)		13·50	13·50

135 Arms of Iraq and "Industry"

1969. 11th Anniv of 14 July Revolution.

844	**135**	10f. multicoloured	50	35
845	**135**	15f. multicoloured	70	35

136 Rebuilding Roads

1969. Anniv of 17 July Revolution and Inaug of Baghdad International Airport. Mult.

846	10f. Type **136**	70	45
847	15f. Type **136**	70	45
848	20f. Airport building	2·20	55
849	200f. President Bakr (vert)	21·00	10·00

137 Ear of Wheat and Fair Emblem

1969. 6th International Baghdad Fair.

850	**137**	10f. brown, gold and green	85	35
851	**137**	15f. red, gold and blue	1·10	45

138 Floating Crane "Antara"

1969. 50th Anniv of Port of Basra. Mult.

852	15f. Type **138**	60	35
853	20f. Harbour tender "Al-Walid"	85	55
854	30f. Pilot boat "Al-Rashid"	1·30	65
855	35f. Dredger "Hillah"	2·10	1·10
856	50f. Survey ship "Al-Fao"	6·00	3·00

139 Radio Beacon and Outline of Palestine

1969. 10th Anniv of Iraqi News Agency.

857	**139**	15f. multicoloured	1·40	45
858	**139**	50f. multicoloured	3·75	90

140 Emblem, Book and Hands

1969. Campaign Against Illiteracy.

859	**140**	15f. multicoloured	35	20
860	**140**	20f. multicoloured	70	45

141 Ross and Keith Smith's Vickers Vimy Biplane

1969. Air. 50th Anniv of 1st England–Australia Flight.

861	**141**	15f. multicoloured	3·25	1·50
862	**141**	35f. multicoloured	5·00	3·50
MS863 81×100 mm. Nos. 861/2 (sold at 100f.). Imperf			18·00	16·00

142 Newspaper Headline

1969. Centenary of Iraqi Press.

864	**142**	15f. black, orange & yell	70	45

143 Soldier and Map

1970. Army Day.

865	**143**	15f. multicoloured	95	45
866	**143**	20f. multicoloured	1·90	90

144 Iraqis supporting Wall

1970. 7th Anniv of 14th Ramadan Revolution.

867	**144**	10f. multicoloured	25	20
868	**144**	15f. multicoloured	60	20

(145)

1970. New Year ("Nawrooz"). Nos. 891/6 optd with T 145.

869	2f. multicoloured	50	35
870	3f. multicoloured	50	35
871	5f. multicoloured	50	35
872	10f. multicoloured	95	35
873	15f. multicoloured	1·20	35
874	50f. multicoloured	3·25	1·70

146 Map of Arab Countries, and Slogans

1970. 23rd Anniv of Al-Baath Party. Mult.

875	15f. Type **146**	50	35
876	35f. Type **146**	85	65
877	50f. Iraqis acclaiming Party	2·40	90
MS878 115×76 mm. 150f. As 50f. Imperf		14·50	14·50

(147)

1970. Mosul Spring Festival. Nos. 891/6 optd with T 147.

879	2f. multicoloured	70	70
880	3f. multicoloured	70	70
881	5f. multicoloured	70	70
882	10f. multicoloured	70	70
883	15f. multicoloured	1·60	1·10
884	50f. multicoloured	3·50	1·30

148 Iraqis celebrating Labour Day

1970. Labour Day.

885	**148**	10f. multicoloured	50	35
886	**148**	15f. multicoloured	60	45
887	**148**	35f. multicoloured	1·90	90

149 Kaaba, Mecca, Broken Statues and Koran

1970. Mohammed's Birthday.

888	**149**	15f. multicoloured	50	20
889	**149**	20f. multicoloured	50	35

150 Poppies

1970. Spring Festival. Flowers. Multicoloured.

891	2f. Type **150**	60	35
892	3f. Narcissi	60	35
893	5f. Tulip	60	35
894	10f. Carnations	85	45
895	15f. Roses	1·40	65
896	50f. As 10f.	4·25	1·80

1970 ١٩٧٠
عيد الصحافة
(151)

1970. Press Day. No. 864 optd with T 151.

896a	142	15f. black, orange & yell	70	70

152 Revolutionaries

1970. 50th Anniv of Revolution of 1920.

897	152	10f. black and green	25	20
898	152	15f. black and gold	50	20
899	-	35f. black and orange	1·20	55
MS900		119×71 mm. 100f. Designs as Nos. 897 and 899 but without face values. Imperf.	7·25	7·25

DESIGN: 35f. Revolutionary and rising sun.

153 Bomb-burst and Broken Chain

1970. 12th Anniv of 14 July Revolution.

901	153	15f. multicoloured	35	20
902	153	20f. multicoloured	60	20

154 Hands and Map of Iraq

1970. 2nd Anniv of 17 July Revolution.

903	154	15f. multicoloured	35	20
904	154	25f. multicoloured	70	35

155 Pomegranates

1970. Fruits. Multicoloured.

905		3f. Type **155**	50	20
906		5f. Grapefruit	50	20
907		10f. Grapes	50	20
908		15f. Oranges	1·40	45
909		35f. Dates	4·25	2·20

The Latin inscriptions on Nos. 906/7 are transposed.

156 Kaaba, Mecca

1970. Hajeer Year.

910	156	15f. multicoloured	35	20
911	156	25f. multicoloured	70	35

الدورة السابعة

970 – ٩٧٠
(157)

1970. 7th Int Baghdad Fair. Optd with T 157.

912	137	10f. brown, gold and green	4·25	2·20
913	137	15f. red, gold and blue	4·25	2·20

158 Arab League Flag and Map

1970. 25th Anniv of Arab League.

914	158	15f. purple, green and olive	35	10
915	158	35f. red, green and grey	70	55

159 Euphrates Bridge

1970. Air. National Development. Multicoloured.

916		10f. Type **159**	2·40	65
917		15f. Type **159**	3·50	1·60
918		1d. Pres. Bakr and banknotes (37×27 mm)	70·00	28·00

160 I.E.Y. Emblem

1970. International Education Year.

919	160	5f. multicoloured	35	20
920	160	15f. multicoloured	60	35

1970. 25th Anniv of United Nations. No. MS639 optd 1945 UNITED NATIONS 1970 together with other inscriptions and with face values of the stamps in the miniature sheet obliterated.

MS921	175×120 mm. 50f.	9·00	9·00

161 Baghdad Hospital and Society Emblem

1970. 50th Anniv of Iraq Medical Society.

922	161	15f. multicoloured	35	20
923	161	40f. multicoloured	1·60	80

162 Union Emblem

1970. Air. 10th Arab Telecommunications Union Conference, Baghdad.

924	162	15f. multicoloured	35	10
925	162	25f. multicoloured	70	55

163 Sugar Beet

1970. 12th Anniv of Mosul Sugar Refinery. Multicoloured.

926		5f. Type **163**	35	10
927		15f. Sugar refinery (horiz)	60	20
928		30f. Type **163**	2·10	90

164 O.P.E.C. Emblem

1970. 10th Anniv of Organization of Petroleum Exporting Countries (O.P.E.C.).

929	164	10f. blue, bistre and purple	95	45
930	164	40f. blue, bistre and green	3·75	1·60

165 Soldiers, Tank and Aircraft

1971. 50th Anniv of Army Day.

931	165	15f. black, mauve and gold	70	35
932	-	40f. multicoloured	4·00	1·30
MS933		124×91 mm. Nos. 931/2. Imperf (sold at 100f.)	11·50	11·50

DESIGN—42×35 mm: 40f. Soldiers and map of Middle East.

166 "Revolutionary Army"

1971. 8th Anniv of 14th Ramadan Revolution.

934	166	15f. multicoloured	60	35
935	166	40f. multicoloured	1·80	65

167 Pilgrims and Web

1971. Hajeer Year.

936	167	10f. multicoloured	35	20
937	167	15f. multicoloured	60	35

168 Pres. Bakr with Torch

1971. 1st Anniv of 11th March Manifesto.

938	168	15f. multicoloured	95	55
939	168	100f. multicoloured	4·00	1·90

169 Boatman in Marshland

1971. Tourism Week. Multicoloured.

940		5f. Type **169**	60	35
941		10f. Stork over Baghdad	1·10	35
942		15f. Landscape ("Summer Resorts")	1·30	55
943		100f. "Return of Sinbad"	6·75	3·00

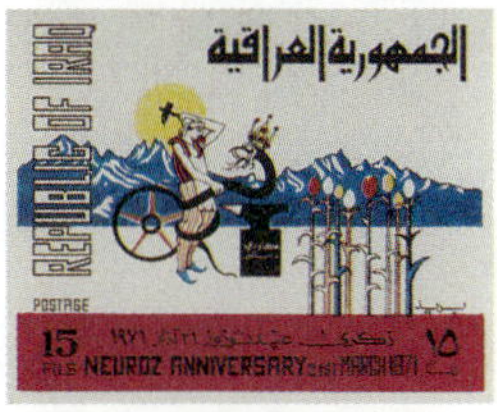

170 Blacksmith taming Serpent

1971. New Year ("Nawrooz").

944	170	15f. multicoloured	1·20	45
945	170	25f. multicoloured	2·30	90

1971. World Meteorological Day. Nos. 780 and 783 optd W.M. DAY 1971 in English and Arabic.

946		15f. multicoloured (postage)	3·75	1·30
947		80f. multicoloured (air)	8·50	5·50

172 Emblem and Workers

1971. 24th Anniv of Al-Baath Party. Mult.

948		15f. Type **172**	1·10	55
949		35f. Type **172**	1·80	1·10
950		250f. As Type **172** but central portion of design only (42×42 mm)	14·50	14·50

On No. 950 the circular centre is also perforated.

مهرجان الربيع
1971
(173)

1971. Mosul Spring Festival. Nos. 765/6 and 770 optd with T 173.

951	114	2f. multicoloured	60	35
952	-	5f. multicoloured	60	45
953	-	25f. multicoloured	2·75	1·20

174 Worker and Farm-girl

1971. Labour Day.

954	174	15f. multicoloured	50	35
955	174	40f. multicoloured	1·80	45

175 Muslim at Prayer

1971. Mohammed's Birthday.

956	175	15f. multicoloured	85	35
957	175	100f. multicoloured	3·00	1·90

176 Revolutionaries, and Hands with Broken Chains

1971. 13th Anniv of 14 July Revolution.

958	**176**	25f. multicoloured	70	35
959	**176**	50f. multicoloured	1·80	80

177 Rising Sun and "Prosperity"

1971. 3rd Anniv of 17 July Revolution.

960	**177**	25f. multicoloured	85	45
961	**177**	70f. multicoloured	2·75	1·00

182 Bank Emblem

1971. 30th Anniv of Rafidain Bank.

989	**182**	10f. multicoloured	70	75
990	**182**	15f. multicoloured	1·20	1·20
991	**182**	25f. multicoloured	2·30	2·30
992	**182**	65f. multicoloured	12·00	10·00
993	**182**	250f. multicoloured	30·00	29·00

Nos. 992/3 are larger, 42×42 mm.

التعداد الزراعي العام

١٩٧١/١٠/١٥

(183)

1971. Agricultural Census. Nos. 905, 908/9 optd with T 183.

994	3f. multicoloured	2·75	2·75
995	15f. multicoloured	2·75	2·75
996	35f. multicoloured	2·75	2·75

184 Football

1971. 4th Pan-Arab Schoolboy Games, Baghdad. Multicoloured.

997	15f. Type **184**	35	35
998	25f. Throwing the discus and running	95	45
999	35f. Table tennis	1·20	1·00
1000	70f. Gymnastics	5·00	1·70
1001	95f. Volleyball and basketball	8·50	3·00
MS1002	195×146 mm. Nos. 997/1001. Imperf (sold at 200f.)	24·00	24·00

70 Fils ●●

يوم الطالب

٢٣ تشرين الثاني

٩٦١ – ٩٧١

٧ فلسا

●●

(185)

1971. Students' Day. Nos. 892/3 surch and 895 optd as T 185.

1003	15f. multicoloured	2·10	45
1004	25f. on 5f. multicoloured	3·25	1·50
1005	70f. on 3f. multicoloured	11·50	3·75

186 Society Emblem

1971. Air. 20th Anniv of Iraqi Philatelic Society.

1006	**186**	25f. multicoloured	1·70	1·20
1007	**186**	70f. multicoloured	5·00	3·00

1971. 25th Anniv of UNICEF. Nos. 817/18 optd 25th Anniversary 971.

1008	**126**	15f. multicoloured	4·00	1·50
1009	**126**	25f. multicoloured	9·75	4·50

188 Schoolchildren on Zebra Crossing

1971. 2nd Traffic Week.

1010	**188**	15f. multicoloured	2·10	1·00
1011	**188**	25f. multicoloured	4·00	1·90

189 A.P.U. Emblem

1971. 25th Anniv of Founding of Arab Postal Union at Sofar Conference.

1012	**189**	25f. brown, yellow & grn	60	35
1013	**189**	70f. red, yellow and blue	2·30	90

190 Racial Equality Year Symbol

1971. Racial Equality Year.

1014	**190**	25f. multicoloured	35	20
1015	**190**	70f. multicoloured	1·40	1·20

191 Soldiers with Flag and Torch

1972. Army Day.

1016	**191**	25f. multicoloured	1·40	80
1017	**191**	70f. multicoloured	5·50	3·00

192 Workers

1972. 9th Anniv of 14th Ramadan Revolution.

1018	**192**	25f. multicoloured	3·00	65
1019	**192**	95f. multicoloured	5·00	3·00

193 Mosque and Crescent

1972. Hajeer Year.

1020	**193**	25f. multicoloured	50	20
1021	**193**	35f. multicoloured	95	55

المؤتمر التاسع للاتحاد الوطني

لطلبة العراق

٢٥ شباط – ٢ آذار / ١٩٧٢

(194)

1972. Air. 9th Iraqi Students' Union Congress. Nos. 916/17 optd with T 194.

1022	**159**	10f. multicoloured	3·00	2·75
1023	**159**	15f. multicoloured	3·00	2·75

195 Dove, Olive Branch and Manifesto

1972. 2nd Anniv of 11 March Manifesto.

1024	**195**	25f. blue, lt blue & black	1·70	45
1025	**195**	70f. purple, mauve & blk	5·00	1·50

196 Observatory and Weather Balloon on Isobar Map

1972. World Meteorological Day.

1026	**196**	25f. multicoloured	2·40	65
1027	**196**	35f. multicoloured	4·25	1·90

197 Cogwheel Emblem

1972. Iraqi Chamber of Commerce.

1028	**197**	25f. multicoloured	70	35
1029	**197**	35f. multicoloured	1·30	55

198 Oil Rig and Flame

1972. Inauguration of North Rumaila Oilfield.

1030	**198**	25f. multicoloured	1·80	35
1031	**198**	35f. multicoloured	2·40	1·20

199 Party Emblem

1972. 25th Anniv of Al Baath Party. Mult.

1032	10f. Type **199**	50	20
1033	25f. Emblem and inscription	1·10	55
1034	35f. Type **199**	1·20	65
1035	70f. As 25f.	3·75	2·75

SIZES—HORIZ: 25f., 70f. 51×27 mm.

200 Mountain Scene

1972. New Year ("Nawrooz").

1036	**200**	25f. mauve, yellow & blue	1·70	35
1037	**200**	70f. brown, yellow & blue	5·50	1·90

201 Congress "Quills" Emblem

1972. 3rd Arab Journalists Congress.

1038	**201**	25f. orange, black & grn	70	20
1039	**201**	35f. blue, black and green	2·40	1·50

202 Federation Emblem

1972. 4th Anniv of Iraqi Women's Federation.

1040	**202**	25f. multicoloured	70	45
1041	**202**	35f. multicoloured	2·40	1·70

204 Hand holding Spanner

1972. Labour Day.

1046	**204**	25f. multicoloured	60	20
1047	**204**	35f. multicoloured	1·10	55

205 Kaaba, Mecca

1972. Mohammed's Birthday.

1048	**205**	25f. black, gold and green	70	20
1049	**205**	35f. black, gold and violet	2·40	1·70

206 Shooting for Goal

1972. Air. 25th International Military Sports Council Football Championship, Baghdad. Multicoloured.

1050	10f. Type **206**	70	35
1051	20f. Players in goalmouth	1·60	35
1052	25f. Type **206**	1·60	35
1053	35f. As 20f.	5·50	1·00
MS1054	77×64 mm. 100f. Olympic and C.I.S.M. emblems. Imperf	24·00	24·00

207 Soldiers and Artillery

1972. 14th Anniv of 14 July Revolution.

1055	**207**	35f. multicoloured	1·20	45
1056	**207**	70f. multicoloured	3·75	1·50

208 "Spirit of Revolution"

1972. 4th Anniv of 17 July Revolution.

1057	**208**	25f. multicoloured	1·60	80
1058	**208**	95f. multicoloured	4·25	3·50

209 Scout Badge and Camp Scene

1972. 10th Jamboree and Conference of Arab Scouts, Mosul.

1059	**209**	20f. multicoloured	3·00	1·50
1060	**209**	25f. multicoloured	4·25	1·70

210 Guide Badge and Camp

1972. 4th Conference and Camp of Arab Guides, Mosul.

1061	**210**	10f. multicoloured	2·10	90
1062	**210**	45f. multicoloured	6·00	1·70

1972 ١٩٧٢

●● 70 Fils ٧٠ ●●

(211)

1972. 3rd Traffic Week. Nos. 1010/11 surch or optd as T 211.

1063	**188**	25f. multicoloured	7·75	3·25
1064	**188**	70f. on 15f. mult	10·00	8·25

مهرجان النخيل
وعيد التمور
١٩٧٢
70 Fils ٧٠

(212)

1972. Festival of Palm Trees and Feast of Dates. Nos. 707 and 709 surch as T 212.

1065	**94**	25f. on 3f. multicoloured	5·00	3·00
1066	**94**	70f. on 15f. multicoloured	13·50	7·75

213 "Strong Man" Statuette

1972. Air. World Body-building Championships and Asian Congress, Baghdad. Multicoloured.

1067	25f. Type **213**	1·80	90
1068	70f. Ancient warriors and modern Strong Man	4·75	3·00

214 Bank Building

1972. 25th Anniv of Central Bank of Iraq.

1069	**214**	25f. multicoloured	1·10	55
1070	**214**	70f. multicoloured	3·25	1·30

216 International Railway Union Emblem

1972. 50th Anniv of Int Railway Union.

1073	**216**	25f. multicoloured	2·20	80
1074	**216**	45f. multicoloured	6·00	4·00

1973. Various "Faisal" definitives with portrait obliterated with 3 bars. (a) 1954 issue.

1075	**33**	10f. blue	4·25	1·30
1076	**33**	15f. black	4·25	1·30
1077	**33**	25f. purple	4·25	1·30

(b) 1957 issue.

1078	**41**	10f. blue	4·25	1·30
1079	**41**	15f. black	4·25	1·30
1080	**41**	25f. purple	4·25	1·30

المؤتمر الدولي
للتاريخ/١٩٧٣

(219)

1973. International History Congress. Nos. 780, 783 and 786 optd with T 219.

1094		15f. multicoloured (postage)	12·00	4·50
1095		80f. multicoloured (air)	24·00	8·25
1096		500f. multicoloured	80·00	80·00

220 Iraqi Oil Workers

1973. 1st Anniv of Nationalization of Iraqi Oil Industry.

1097	**220**	25f. multicoloured	2·75	1·00
1098	**220**	70f. multicoloured	11·50	3·75

221 Harp

1973

1099	**221**	5f. black and orange	25	10
1100	**221**	10f. black and brown	25	10
1101	**221**	20f. black and mauve	35	15
1102	-	25f. black and blue	60	20
1103	-	35f. black and green	70	35
1104	-	45f. black and blue	70	35
1105	-	50f. yellow and green	1·10	35
1106	-	70f. yellow and violet	1·40	65
1107	-	95f. yellow and brown	2·40	1·00

DESIGNS: 25, 35, 45f. Minaret of Mosul; 50, 70, 95f. Statue of a Goddess.

225a Iraqis and Flags

1973. July Festivals.

1122	**225a**	25f. multicoloured	95	45
1123	**225a**	35f. multicoloured	1·90	55

1973. International Journalists' Conference. Nos. 857/8 optd I.O.J. SEPTEMBER 26-29. 1973.

1124	**139**	15f. multicoloured	4·00	4·00
1125	**139**	50f. multicoloured	5·50	5·50

227 Interpol H.Q., Paris

1973. 50th Anniv of International Criminal Police Organization (Interpol).

1126	**227**	25f. multicoloured	1·40	80
1127	**227**	70f. multicoloured	7·25	4·75

228 Flags and Fair Emblems

1973. 10th Baghdad International Fair.

1128	**228**	10f. multicoloured	60	35
1129	**228**	20f. multicoloured	1·10	45
1130	**228**	55f. multicoloured	2·40	1·20

229 W.M.O. Emblem

1973. Cent of World Meteorological Organization.

1148	**229**	25f. black, green & orge	95	20
1149	**229**	35f. black, green & mve	3·00	1·50

230 Arab Flags and Map

1973. 11th Session of Arab States' Civil Aviation Council, Baghdad.

1150	**230**	20f. multicoloured	60	20
1151	**230**	35f. multicoloured	1·90	1·20

المجلس التنفيذي

بغداد/١٩٧٣

(232)

1973. 6th Executive Council Meeting of Arab Postal Union, Baghdad. No. 665 optd with T 232.

1153	**75**	30f. blue and orange	6·75	4·00

233 Human Rights Emblem

1973. 25th Anniv of Declaration of Human Rights.

1154	**233**	25f. multicoloured	35	35
1155	**233**	70f. multicoloured	1·20	65

234 Shield and Military Activities

1974. 50th Anniv of Military College.

1156	**234**	25f. multicoloured	60	35
1157	**234**	35f. multicoloured	2·10	1·30

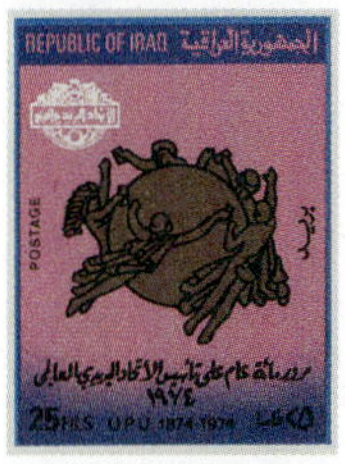

236 U.P.U. Emblem

1974. Centenary of Universal Postal Union.

1159	**236**	25f. multicoloured	1·20	35
1160	**236**	35f. multicoloured	1·20	55
1161	**236**	70f. multicoloured	2·20	1·30

237 Allegory of Nationalization

1974. 2nd Anniv of Nationalization of Iraqi Oil Industry.

1162	**237**	10f. multicoloured	60	20
1163	**237**	25f. multicoloured	1·20	35
1164	**237**	70f. multicoloured	3·50	2·75

238 Festival Theme

1975. July Festivals.

1165	**238**	20f. multicoloured	50	20
1166	**238**	35f. multicoloured	1·40	65

239 National Front Emblem and Heads

1975. 1st Anniv of Progressive National Front.

1167	**239**	20f. multicoloured	85	45
1168	**239**	50f. multicoloured	2·10	1·00

240 Cement Plant

1975. 25th Anniv of Iraqi Cement Industry.

1169	**240**	20f. multicoloured	60	35
1170	**240**	25f. multicoloured	85	45
1171	**240**	70f. multicoloured	1·90	1·50

1975. Surch.

1172	**155**	10f. on 3f. multicoloured	4·75	2·75
1173	-	25f. on 3f. mult (No. 892)	13·50	9·00

242 W.P.Y. Emblem

1975. World Population Year (1974).

1174	**242**	25f. green and blue	85	20
1175	**242**	35f. blue and mauve	1·40	80
1176	**242**	70f. violet and olive	4·25	1·80

243 Festival Emblems

1975. July Festivals.

1177	**243**	5f. multicoloured	35	20
1178	**243**	10f. multicoloured	35	35
1179	**243**	35f. multicoloured	2·40	1·00

244 Map and Emblems

1975. 10th Anniv of Arab Labour Organization.

1180	**244**	25f. multicoloured	70	20
1181	**244**	35f. multicoloured	1·20	80
1182	**244**	45f. multicoloured	1·30	90

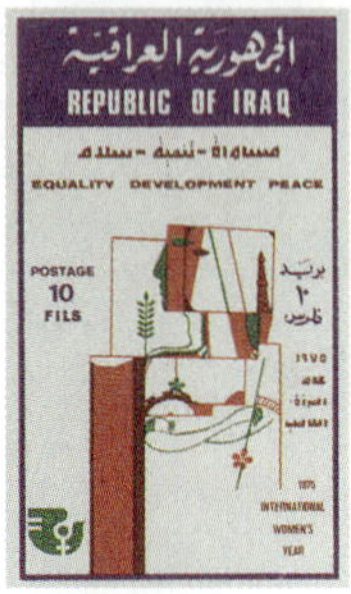

245 "Equality, Development, Peace"

1975. International Women's Year.

1183	**245**	10f. multicoloured	60	35
1184	**245**	35f. multicoloured	1·20	90
1185	**245**	70f. multicoloured	5·00	1·80
MS1186		100×83 mm. 100f. multi-coloured As T **245**, but face value outside design. Imperf	12·00	12·00

246 Diyala Barrage

1975. 25th Anniv of International Commission on Irrigation and Drainage.

1187	**246**	3f. multicoloured	25	10
1188	**246**	25f. multicoloured	95	35
1189	**246**	70f. multicoloured	3·75	1·80

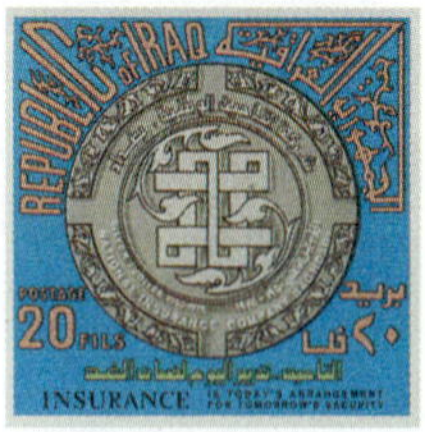

247 Company Seal

1975. 25th Anniv of National Insurance Company, Baghdad.

1190	**247**	20f. multicoloured	1·10	35
1191	**247**	25f. multicoloured	1·30	55
MS1192		71×71 mm. **247** 100f. multi-coloured. Imperf	9·00	9·00

248 Court Musicians

1975. International Music Conference, Baghdad.

1193	**248**	25f. multicoloured	85	35
1194	**248**	45f. multicoloured	2·10	1·20

250 Telecommunications Centre

1975. Opening of Telecommunications Centre.

1203	**250**	5f. multicoloured	25	20
1204	**250**	10f. multicoloured	35	20
1205	**250**	60f. multicoloured	2·40	1·50

251 Diesel Train

1975. 15th Taurus Railway Conference, Baghdad. Multicoloured.

1206		25f. Type **251**	6·75	1·10
1207		30f. Diesel locomotive	10·00	2·20
1208		35f. Tank locomotive and train	13·50	4·50
1209		50f. Steam locomotive	19·00	11·00

252 Goddess (statue)

1976

1210	**252**	5f. multicoloured	10	10
1211	**252**	10f. multicoloured	10	10
1212	**252**	15f. multicoloured	35	10
1213	-	20f. multicoloured	35	15
1214	-	25f. multicoloured	60	20
1215	-	30f. multicoloured	85	20
1216	-	35f. multicoloured	1·10	35
1217	-	50f. multicoloured	1·60	35
1218	-	75f. multicoloured	2·20	80

DESIGNS: 20, 25, 30f. Two females forming column; 35, 50, 75f. Head of bearded man.

253 Soldier and Symbols of Industry and Agriculture

1976. Arab Day.

1219	**253**	5f. multicoloured	25	10
1220	**253**	25f. multicoloured on silver	70	20
1221	**253**	50f. mult on gold	2·10	80

254 Crossed-out Thumbprint

1976. Arab Literacy Day.

1222	**254**	5f. multicoloured	35	35
1223	**254**	15f. multicoloured	60	35
1224	**254**	35f. multicoloured	2·10	1·30

255 Iraq Earth Station

1976. 13th Anniv of Revolution of 14th Ramadan.

1225	**255**	10f. multicoloured	50	35
1226	**255**	25f. multicoloured on silver	1·40	55
1227	**255**	75f. mult on gold	6·00	2·20

256 Early and Modern Telephones

1976. Telephone Centenary.

1228	**256**	35f. multicoloured	1·60	55
1229	**256**	50f. multicoloured	3·25	90
1230	**256**	75f. multicoloured	5·00	1·30

257 Map and Emblem

1976. 20th International Arab Trade Unions Conf.

1231	**257**	5f. mult (postage)	50	20
1232	**257**	10f. multicoloured	50	20
1233	**257**	75f. multicoloured (air)	4·25	1·90

258 Iraqi Family on Map

1976. Police Day.

1234	**258**	5f. multicoloured	25	10
1235	**258**	15f. multicoloured	60	20
1236	**258**	35f. multicoloured	3·00	1·30

259 "Strategy" Pipeline

1976. 4th Anniv of Oil Nationalization.

1237	**259**	25f. multicoloured	2·10	20
1238	**259**	75f. multicoloured	4·75	2·20
MS1239		80×90 mm. 150f. multicol-oured. Imperf	36·00	36·00

DESIGN—35×33 mm.: 150f. President Bakr embracing Prime Minister.

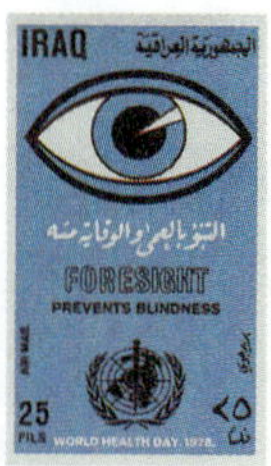

260 Human Eye

1976. Air. World Health Day. "Foresight Prevents Blindness".

1240	**260**	25f. blue and black	50	20
1241	**260**	35f. green and black	70	20

1242	**260**	50f. orange and brown	1·40	80

261 "Agriculture, Industry and Construction"

1976. July Festivals.

1243	**261**	15f. multicoloured	50	35
1244	**261**	35f. multicoloured	1·40	90

262 Basketball

1976. Olympic Games, Montreal. Mult.

1245	25f. Type **262**	60	20
1246	35f. Volleyball	95	65
1247	50f. Wrestling	1·40	1·10
1248	75f. Boxing	2·75	1·80
MS1249	121×91 mm. 100f. Rifle-shooting. Imperf	8·50	8·50

263 Bishop Capucci, Wounded Dove and Map of Palestine

1976. 2nd Anniv of Bishop Capucci's Arrest.

1250	**263**	25f. multicoloured	85	20
1251	**263**	35f. multicoloured	95	45
1252	**263**	75f. multicoloured	3·25	1·70

264 River Kingfisher

1976. Birds. Multicoloured.

1253	5f. Type **264**	3·50	1·00
1254	10f. Turtle dove	3·50	1·00
1255	15f. Pin-tailed sandgrouse	4·25	1·00
1256	25f. Blue rock thrush	7·75	1·20
1257	50f. Purple heron and grey heron	12·00	1·80

See also Nos. O1258/62.

265 Emblem within "15"

1976. 15th Anniv of Iraqi Students' Union.

1263	**265**	30f. multicoloured	85	35
1264	**265**	70f. multicoloured	3·00	1·20

266 Children with Banner

1976. 30th Anniv of UNESCO. "Children's Books". Multicoloured.

1265	10f. Type **266**	35	35
1266	25f. Children in garden	2·75	55
1267	75f. Children with Iraqi flag	4·75	1·70

267 Tanker "Rumaila" and Emblem

1976. 4th Anniv of First Iraqi Oil Tanker and 1st Anniv of Basrah Petroleum Co Nationalization. Multicoloured.

1268	10f. Type **267**	85	35
1269	15f. Type **267**	1·20	45
1270	25f. Oil jetty and installations	2·75	90
1271	50f. As 25f.	3·75	1·60

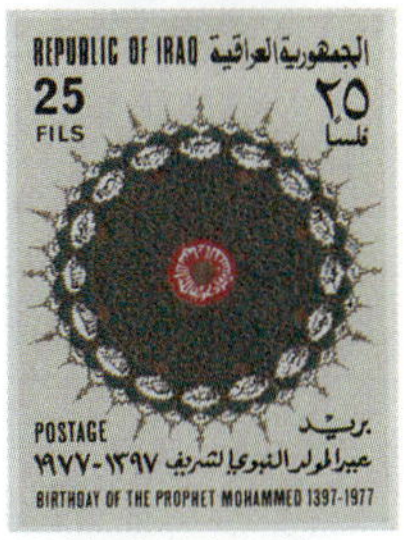

268 Islamic Design with Inscriptions

1977. Birthday of Prophet Mohammed.

1272	**268**	25f. multicoloured	95	35
1273	**268**	35f. multicoloured	1·40	45

269 Dove Emblem

1977. Peace Day.

1274	**269**	25f. multicoloured	50	20
1275	**269**	30f. multicoloured	85	45

270 Dahlia

1977. Flowers. Multicoloured.

1276	5f. Type **270**	35	35
1277	10f. "Lathyrus odoratus"	60	35
1278	35f. "Chrysanthemum coronarium"	1·60	45
1279	50f. "Verbena hybrida"	3·00	90

271 "V" Emblem with Doves

1977. 30th Anniv of Al-Baath Party. Mult.

1280	25f. Type **271**	70	20
1281	75f. Human figures as a flame	2·40	1·30

MS1282	80×60 mm. 100f. Dove with olive-branch. Imperf	7·25	7·25

272 A.P.U. Emblem and Flags

1977. 25th Anniv of Arab Postal Union.

1283	**272**	25f. multicoloured	50	20
1284	**272**	35f. multicoloured	95	55

273 1st May Emblem

1977. Labour Day.

1285	**273**	10f. multicoloured	25	10
1286	**273**	30f. multicoloured	70	20
1287	**273**	35f. multicoloured	95	80

274 First Stage of Lift

1977. 8th Asian Weightlifting Championships, Baghdad. Multicoloured.

1288	25f. Type **274**	1·10	65
1289	75f. Press-up stage of lift	3·00	1·60
MS1290	60×80 mm. 100f. Championships emblem. Imperf	10·00	10·00

275 Dome of the Rock

1977. Palestinian Welfare.

1291	**275**	5f. multicoloured	4·00	65

276 Arabian Garden

1977. Arab Tourism Year. Multicoloured.

1292	5f. Type **276**	35	35
1293	10f. Town view with minarets (horiz)	35	35
1294	30f. Country stream	1·20	35
1295	50f. Oasis (horiz)	3·50	2·20

277 Dove and Ear of Wheat

1977. July Festivals.

1296	**277**	25f. multicoloured	70	20
1297	**277**	30f. multicoloured	95	45

278 Map of Middle East and North Africa

1977. U.N. Conference on Desertification.

1298	**278**	30f. multicoloured	95	55
1299	**278**	70f. multicoloured	3·00	1·10

279 Emblem

1977. Census Day.

1300	**279**	20f. multicoloured	35	20
1301	**279**	30f. multicoloured	95	20
1302	**279**	70f. multicoloured	1·80	1·00

280 Abstract Calligraphic Emblem

1977. Al-Mutanabby Festival.

1303	**280**	25f. multicoloured	35	10
1304	**280**	50f. multicoloured	85	55

281 Kamal Jumblatt and Political Caricatures

1977. Kamal Jumblatt (Lebanese socialist) Commemoration.

1305	**281**	20f. multicoloured	50	35
1306	**281**	30f. multicoloured	70	35
1307	**281**	70f. multicoloured	1·60	80

282 Hajeer Year Emblem

1977. Hajeer Year.

1308	**282**	30f. multicoloured	50	20
1309	**282**	35f. multicoloured	70	35

283 Girl, Boy and National Flag Ribbon

1978. Youth Day.

1310	**283**	10f. multicoloured	25	10
1311	**283**	15f. multicoloured	25	20
1312	**283**	35f. multicoloured	70	45

284 Hand placing Coin in Box

1978. 6th Anniv of Postal Savings Bank.

1313	**284**	15f. multicoloured	50	15
1314	**284**	25f. multicoloured	70	20
1315	**284**	35f. multicoloured	1·30	55

285 Transmitting and Receiving Equipment

1978. 10th World Telecommunications Day and 1st Anniv of Iraqi Microwave Network.

1316	**285**	25f. multicoloured	60	20
1317	**285**	35f. multicoloured	60	20
1318	**285**	75f. multicoloured	1·30	80

286 Map and Flags

1978. 1st Conference of Arabian Gulf Postal Ministers.

1319	**286**	25f. multicoloured	70	20
1320	**286**	35f. multicoloured	1·20	65

287 Silver Coins

1978. Ancient Iraqi Coins.

1321	**287**	1f. black, silver & yellow	20	10
1322	-	2f. black, gold and blue	20	10
1323	-	3f. black, silver & orange	20	10
1324	-	4f. black, gold and green	25	20
1325	-	5f. black, gold and green	3·00	2·75

DESIGNS—HORIZ: 2f. Two gold coins; 3f. Two silver coins; 4f. Two gold coins. VERT: 75f. Gold coin.

288 Flower Emblem

1978. July Festivals.

1326	**288**	25f. multicoloured	50	20
1327	**288**	35f. multicoloured	70	35
MS1328 80×60 mm. 100f. multicoloured (horiz)			7·75	7·75

DESIGN: 100f. Flame and emblem.

289 Nurse, Hospital and Sick Child

1978. Global Eradication of Smallpox.

1329	**289**	25f. multicoloured	35	10
1330	**289**	35f. multicoloured	85	35
1331	**289**	75f. multicoloured	2·40	1·20

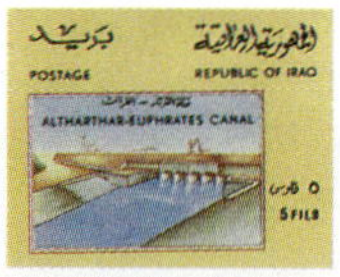

290 Altharthar–Euphrates Canal

1978

1332	**290**	5f. multicoloured	25	20
1333	**290**	10f. multicoloured	25	20
1334	**290**	15f. multicoloured	25	20
1335	**290**	25f. multicoloured	25	20
1336	**290**	35f. multicoloured	50	20
1337	**290**	50f. multicoloured	95	45

See also Nos. O1338/41.

291 I.M.C.O. Emblem

1978. World Maritime Day.

1342	**291**	25f. multicoloured	70	35
1343	**291**	75f. multicoloured	1·80	65

292 Workers in the Countryside

1978. 10th Anniv of People's Work Groups.

1344	**292**	10f. multicoloured	35	20
1345	**292**	25f. multicoloured	70	20
1346	**292**	35f. multicoloured	1·30	80

293 Fair Emblem

1978. Baghdad International Fair.

1347	**293**	25f. multicoloured	25	20
1348	**293**	35f. multicoloured	35	20
1349	**293**	75f. multicoloured	2·30	1·10

294 Map, Rule and Emblem

1978. World Standards Day.

1350	**294**	25f. multicoloured	25	10
1351	**294**	35f. multicoloured	35	20
1352	**294**	75f. multicoloured	2·10	1·10

295 Conference Chamber

1978. 9th Arab Summit Conference, Baghdad.

1353	**295**	25f. multicoloured	35	20
1354	**295**	35f. multicoloured	50	20
1355	**295**	75f. multicoloured	1·60	1·10

296 Congress Emblem

1978. 4th Congress of Association of Thoracic and Cardiovascular Surgeons of Asia.

1356	**296**	25f. multicoloured	50	20
1357	**296**	75f. multicoloured	1·40	90

297 Pilgrims and Kaaba

1978. Pilgrimage to Mecca.

1358	**297**	25f. multicoloured	50	20
1359	**297**	35f. multicoloured	70	35

298 Map and Symbol

1978. U.N. Conference for Technical Co-operation among Developing Countries.

1360	**298**	25f. multicoloured	35	20
1361	**298**	50f. multicoloured	85	35
1362	**298**	75f. multicoloured	1·30	80

299 Hands holding Emblem

1978. International Year to Combat Racism.

1363	**299**	25f. multicoloured	50	20
1364	**299**	50f. multicoloured	95	35
1365	**299**	75f. multicoloured	2·75	80

300 Globe and Human Rights Emblem

1978. 30th Anniv of Declaration of Human Rights.

1366	**300**	25f. multicoloured	60	20
1367	**300**	75f. multicoloured	2·10	1·50

301 Candle and Emblem

1979. Police Day.

1368	**301**	10f. multicoloured	50	35
1369	**301**	25f. multicoloured	50	35
1370	**301**	35f. multicoloured	85	35

302 Open Book, Pencil and Flame

1979. Anniv of Application of Compulsory Education Law.

1371	**302**	15f. multicoloured	25	20
1372	**302**	25f. multicoloured	50	20
1373	**302**	35f. multicoloured	1·20	35

303 School, Teacher and Assyrian Relief

1979. Teachers' Day.

1374	**303**	10f. multicoloured	25	20
1375	**303**	15f. multicoloured	25	20
1376	**303**	50f. multicoloured	1·20	65

304 Clenched Fist, Pencil and Book

1979. National Literacy Campaign.

1377	**304**	15f. multicoloured	35	35
1378	**304**	25f. multicoloured	60	35
1379	**304**	35f. multicoloured	95	35

305 World map, Koran and Symbols of Arab Achievements

1979. The Arabs.

1380	**305**	35f. multicoloured	70	20
1381	**305**	75f. multicoloured	2·10	90

306 Girl playing Flute

1979. Mosul Spring Festival.

1382	**306**	15f. multicoloured	50	35
1383	**306**	25f. multicoloured	70	35
1384	**306**	35f. multicoloured	1·40	55

307 Iraqi Map and Flag with U.P.U. Emblem

1979. 50th Anniv of Admission to Universal Postal Union.

1385	**307**	25f. multicoloured	85	35
1386	**307**	35f. multicoloured	85	35
1387	**307**	75f. multicoloured	2·10	90

308 Championship Emblem with Sea and Sky

1979. 5th Arabian Gulf Football Championship.

1388	**308**	10f. multicoloured	25	20
1389	**308**	15f. multicoloured	50	20
1390	**308**	50f. multicoloured	1·20	65

309 Child with Globe and Candle

1979. International Year of the Child.

1391	**309**	25f. multicoloured	95	45
1392	**309**	75f. multicoloured	2·40	1·50
MS1393 68×80 mm. 100f. multicoloured (vert)			31·00	28·00

DESIGN: 100f. Two children and U.N. emblem.

310 Flower and Branch

1979. July Festivals.

1394	**310**	15f. multicoloured	25	20
1395	**310**	25f. multicoloured	50	20
1396	**310**	35f. multicoloured	70	35

311 Children supporting Globe

1979. 50th Anniv of International Bureau of Education.

1397	**311**	25f. multicoloured	70	35
1398	**311**	50f. multicoloured	1·30	65
1399	**311**	100f. multicoloured	2·20	1·30

312 Jawad Selim (sculptor)

1979. Writers and Artists. Multicoloured.

1400	25f. Type **312**	60	35
1401	25f. S. al-Hosari (philosopher)	60	35
1402	25f. Mustapha Jawad (historian)	60	35

313 The Kaaba, Mecca

1979. Pilgrimage to Mecca.

1403	**313**	25f. multicoloured	60	35
1404	**313**	50f. multicoloured	1·10	45

314 Figure "20" and Globe

1979. 20th Anniv of Iraqi News Agency.

1405	**314**	25f. multicoloured	60	20
1406	**314**	50f. multicoloured	1·30	35
1407	**314**	75f. multicoloured	1·70	55

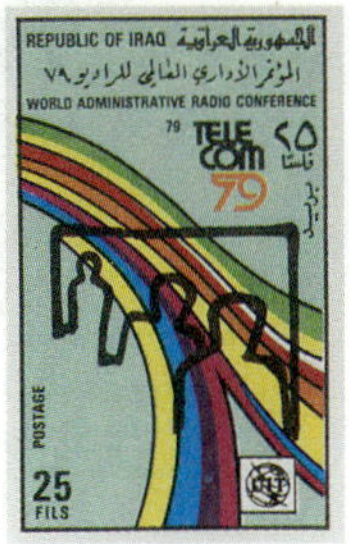

315 Wave Pattern and Television Screen

1979. World Telecommunications Exhibition and Radio Conference, Geneva.

1408	**315**	25f. multicoloured	60	20
1409	**315**	50f. multicoloured	95	45
1410	**315**	75f. multicoloured	1·70	80

316 Clenched Fists and Refugee

1979. Palestinian Solidarity Day.

1411	**316**	25f. multicoloured	1·10	35
1412	**316**	50f. multicoloured	2·10	55
1413	**316**	75f. multicoloured	3·00	1·00

317 Ahmed Hassan Al-Bakir

1979. Inaug of Pres. Saddam Hussain. Mult.

1414	25f. Type **317**	50	35
1415	35f. Pres. Hussain taking the oath	70	35
1416	75f. Type **317**	1·30	55
1417	100f. As No. 1415	5·00	2·75

318 Boy with Violin

1979. Activities of Vanguards (youth organization). Multicoloured.

1418	10f. Type **318**	35	35
1419	15f. Boys on building site	35	35
1420	25f. Boys on assault course and in personal combat	50	35
1421	35f. Vanguards emblem	60	35

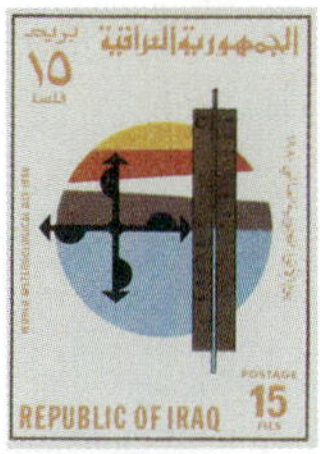

319 Wind-speed Indicator and Thermometer

1980. World Meteorological Day.

1422	**319**	15f. multicoloured	25	20
1423	**319**	25f. multicoloured	35	20
1424	**319**	35f. multicoloured	85	35

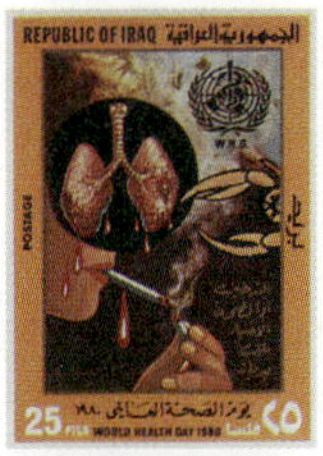

320 Lighting Cigarette and Cancerous Lungs

1980. World Health Day. Anti-smoking Campaign.

1425	**320**	25f. multicoloured	50	35
1426	**320**	35f. multicoloured	60	35
1427	**320**	75f. multicoloured	2·40	65

321 Festivals Emblem

1980. July Festivals.

1428	**321**	25f. multicoloured	50	35
1429	**321**	35f. multicoloured	60	35
MS1430 60×80 mm. 100f. Pres. Hussain (27×44 mm)			7·25	7·25

322 Hurdling

1980. Olympic Games, Moscow. Multicoloured.

1431	15f. Type **322**	35	35
1432	20f. Weightlifting (vert)	60	45
1433	30f. Boxing	1·10	55
1434	35f. Football (vert)	2·10	1·00
MS1435 79×60 mm. 100f. Wrestling (37×29 mm)		12·00	12·00

323 "Rubus sanctus"

1980. Fruit. Multicoloured.

1436	5f. Type **323**	35	20
1437	15f. Peaches	60	20
1438	20f. Pears	85	20
1439	25f. Apples	1·10	20
1440	35f. Plums	1·40	45

324 Conference Emblem and Arabic Text

1980. World Tourism Conference, Manila.

1441	**324**	25f. multicoloured	50	20
1442	**324**	50f. multicoloured	1·10	35
1443	**324**	100f. multicoloured	2·10	1·10

325 A.P.U. Emblem Posthorn and Map

1980. 11th Congress of Arab Postal Union, Baghdad.

1444	**325**	10f. multicoloured	35	35
1445	**325**	30f. multicoloured	60	35
1446	**325**	35f. multicoloured	85	35

326 O.P.E.C. Emblem and Globe

1980. 20th Anniv of Organization of Petroleum Exporting Countries.

1447	**326**	30f. multicoloured	95	35
1448	**326**	75f. multicoloured	2·10	1·00

327 African Monarch

1980. Butterflies. Multicoloured.

1449	10f. Swallowtail	2·20	35
1450	15f. Type **327**	2·75	65
1451	20f. Red admiral	3·50	90
1452	30f. Clouded yellow	6·00	1·50

328 Mosque and Ka'aba

1980. 1400th Anniv of Hegira.

1453	**328**	15f. multicoloured	35	20
1454	**328**	25f. multicoloured	70	20
1455	**328**	35f. multicoloured	85	45

329 Riflemen and Dome of the Rock on Map of Israel

1980. Palestinian Solidarity Day.

1456	**329**	25f. multicoloured	70	20
1457	**329**	35f. multicoloured	1·10	35
1458	**329**	75f. multicoloured	2·20	1·00

330 Soldier and Rocket

1981. 60th Anniv of Army Day.

1459	**330**	5f. multicoloured	35	20
1460	**330**	30f. multicoloured	70	20
1461	**330**	75f. multicoloured	1·90	90

331 "8" and Flags forming Torch

1981. 18th Anniv of 14th Ramadan Revolution.

1462	**331**	15f. multicoloured	35	20
1463	**331**	30f. multicoloured	60	20
1464	**331**	35f. multicoloured	85	35

332 Map of Arab States tied with Ribbon

1981. The Arabs.

1465	**332**	5f. multicoloured	25	20
1466	**332**	25f. multicoloured	60	20
1467	**332**	35f. multicoloured	85	35

333 Pres. Hussain and Modern Military Equipment

1981. Saddam's Battle of Qadisiya.

1468	**333**	30f. multicoloured	60	20
1469	**333**	35f. multicoloured	70	35
1470	**333**	75f. multicoloured	1·30	65
MS1471		80×59 mm. 100f. Pres. Hussain, military equipment and flag (37×29 mm)	6·00	6·00

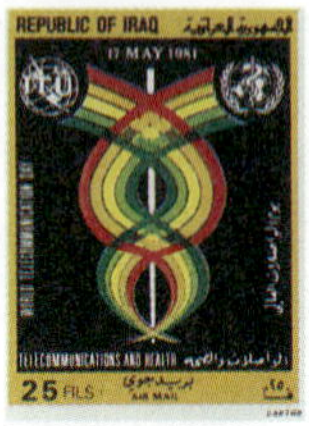

334 I.T.U. and W.H.O. Emblems and Ribbons forming Caduceus

1981. World Telecommunications Day.

1472	**334**	25f. multicoloured	70	35
1473	**334**	50f. multicoloured	1·40	55
1474	**334**	75f. multicoloured	2·40	1·10

335 Mil Mi-24 Helicopters attacking Ground Forces

1981. 50th Anniv of Air Force. Mult.

1475		5f. Type **335** (postage)	25	20
1476		10f. Antonov An-2 biplane trainer	50	20
1477		15f. "SAM-15" missile	60	20
1478		120f. De Havilland Dragon Rapide biplane and Mikoyan Gurevich MiG-21 jet fighters (vert) (air)	5·00	2·75

336 Map and Flower enclosing Ballot Box

1981. 1st Anniv of National Assembly Election.

1479	**336**	30f. multicoloured	60	20
1480	**336**	35f. multicoloured	70	20
1481	**336**	45f. multicoloured	1·20	45

337 Festivals Emblem

1981. July Festivals.

1482	**337**	15f. multicoloured	35	10
1483	**337**	25f. multicoloured	50	20
1484	**337**	35f. multicoloured	85	20

338 Basket Weaver

1981. Popular Industries. Multicoloured.

1485		5f. Type **338**	25	20
1486		30f. Copper worker	70	20
1487		35f. Potter	95	35
1488		50f. Weaver (horiz)	1·20	45

339 Saddam Hussain Gymnasium

1981. Modern Buildings. Multicoloured.

1489		45f. Type **339**	95	35
1490		50f. Palace of Conferences	95	35
1491		120f. As 50f.	2·75	1·80
1492		150f. Type **339**	3·50	2·00

340 Pilgrims

1981. Pilgrimage to Mecca.

1493	**340**	25f. multicoloured	70	15
1494	**340**	45f. multicoloured	1·30	45
1495	**340**	50f. multicoloured	1·30	45

341 Harvesting

1981. World Food Day.

1496	**341**	30f. multicoloured	70	20
1497	**341**	45f. multicoloured	1·30	55
1498	**341**	75f. multicoloured	1·90	1·00

343 Teacher with Deaf Child

1981. International Year of Disabled Persons.

1501	**343**	30f. multicoloured	60	35
1502	**343**	45f. multicoloured	95	45
1503	**343**	75f. multicoloured	1·30	80

344 Medal and Map

1981. Martyr's Day.

1504	**344**	45f. multicoloured	60	45
1505	**344**	50f. multicoloured	70	55
1506	**344**	120f. multicoloured	1·90	1·30

See also Nos. O1507/9.

345 "Ibn Khaldoon" (freighter)

1981. 5th Anniv of United Arab Shipping Company.

1507	**345**	50f. multicoloured	1·60	65
1508	**345**	120f. multicoloured	4·25	2·00

346 Woman and Symbols of Technology

1982. Iraqi Women's Day.

1509	**346**	25f. multicoloured	70	20
1510	**346**	45f. multicoloured	1·20	55
1511	**346**	50f. multicoloured	1·20	65

347 President Hussain, "7" and "Flowers"

1982. 35th Anniv of Al-Baath Party. Mult.

1512		25f. Type **347**	60	20
1513		30f. Rainbow and "7 7 7"	60	20
1514		45f. Type **347**	95	55
1515		50f. As 30f.	95	55
MS1516		99×53 mm. 150f. Pres. Hussain, globe and Arabic "7" (27×39 mm). Imperf	4·75	4·75

348 A.P.U. Emblem and Globe

1982. 30th Anniv of Arab Postal Union.

1517	**348**	25f. multicoloured	70	20
1518	**348**	45f. multicoloured	1·20	45
1519	**348**	50f. multicoloured	1·20	45

349 White Storks

1982. Mosul Spring Festival. Multicoloured.

1520		25f. Type **349**	1·40	20
1521		30f. Doll	85	20
1522		45f. Type **349**	1·40	65
1523		50f. As 30f.	1·30	55

350 World Map, Factories and "1"

1982. Labour Day.

1524	**350**	25f. multicoloured	60	10
1525	**350**	45f. multicoloured	85	45
1526	**350**	50f. multicoloured	95	55

351 Geometric Figure and I.T.U. Problem

1982. World Telecommunications Day.

1527	**351**	5f. multicoloured	20	10
1528	**351**	45f. multicoloured	95	45
1529	**351**	100f. multicoloured	2·20	1·20

352 Oil Gusher

1982. 10th Anniv of Oil Nationalization. Mult.

1530		5f. Type **352**	35	15
1531		25f. Type **352**	70	20
1532		45f. Bronze sculpture of bull and horse flanking couple holding model of oil rig	1·40	55
1533		50f. As 45f.	1·70	55

353 Nuclear Power Emblem and Lion

1982. 1st Anniv of Attack on Iraqi Nuclear Reactor. Multicoloured.

1534		30f. Type **353**	70	35
1535		45f. Bomb aimed at egg	1·20	35
1536		50f. Type **353**	1·30	55
1537		120f. As No. 1535	2·40	1·70

354 Footballers

1982. World Cup Football Championship, Spain. Multicoloured.

1538		5f. Type **354**	60	35
1539		45f. Three footballers	95	45
1540		50f. Type **354**	1·00	55
1541		100f. As 45f.	1·90	1·20
MS1542		85×60 mm. 150f. Two footballers (horiz)	4·25	4·25

355 President Hussain and Fireworks

1982. July Festivals.

1543	**355**	25f. multicoloured	35	20
1544	**355**	45f. multicoloured	85	35
1545	**355**	50f. multicoloured	85	45

356 Green Lizard

1982. Reptiles. Multicoloured.

No.	Description	Mint	Used
1546	25f. Type **356**	2·75	90
1547	30f. Asp	2·75	90
1548	45f. Two green lizards	3·50	1·20
1549	50f. "Natrix tessellata"	3·75	1·80

357 Pandit Nehru (India)

1982. 7th Non-Aligned Countries Conference, Baghdad. Multicoloured.

No.	Description	Mint	Used
1550	50f. Type **357**	1·10	45
1551	50f. Josef Tito (Yugoslavia)	1·10	45
1552	50f. Abdul Nasser (Egypt)	1·10	45
1553	50f. Kwame Nkrumah (Ghana)	1·10	45
1554	100f. President Hussain (Iraq)	2·40	1·20

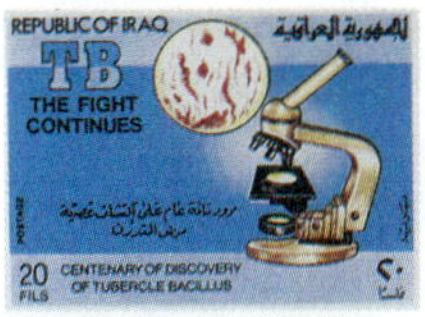

358 Microscope and Bacilli

1982. Cent of Discovery of Tubercule Bacillus.

No.	Type	Description	Mint	Used
1555	**358**	20f. multicoloured	85	20
1556	**358**	50f. multicoloured	1·60	45
1557	**358**	100f. multicoloured	2·75	1·10

359 U.P.U. Building, Berne

1982. U.P.U. Day.

No.	Type	Description	Mint	Used
1561	**359**	5f. multicoloured	25	15
1562	**359**	45f. multicoloured	85	45
1563	**359**	100f. multicoloured	2·20	1·10

360 Drums

1982. Musical Instruments. Multicoloured.

No.	Description	Mint	Used
1564	5f. Type **360**	35	15
1565	10f. Stringed board instrument	35	20
1566	35f. Bowed instruments	1·10	35
1567	100f. Mandolin	3·50	1·20

361 Mosque and Minaret, Mecca

1982. Prophet Mohammed's Birthday. Mult.

No.	Description	Mint	Used
1568	25f. Type **361**	35	20
1569	30f. Courtyard of mosque	50	20
1570	45f. Type **361**	70	45
1571	50f. As No. 1569	85	45

362 Flowers

1982. Flowers. Multicoloured.

No.	Description	Mint	Used
1572	10f. Type **362**	35	20
1573	20f. Flowers (different)	60	20
1574	30f. Type **362**	70	35
1575	40f. As No. 1573	1·20	55
1576	50f. Type **362**	1·40	65
1577	100f. As No. 1573	3·00	1·30

1983. Nos. 1489/51 surch.

No.	Description	Mint	Used
1578	60f. on 50f. Palace of Conferences	1·60	45
1579	70f. on 45f. Type **339**	2·10	65
1580	160f. on 120f. Palace of Conferences	5·00	2·20

364 President Hussain

1983. July Festivals.

No.	Type	Description	Mint	Used
1583	**364**	30f. multicoloured	60	35
1584	**364**	60f. multicoloured	1·30	55
1585	**364**	70f. multicoloured	1·70	80

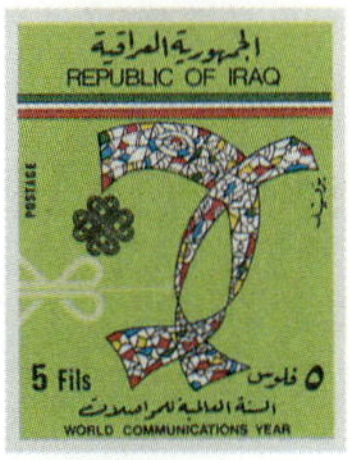

365 Emblem and Interlocked Bands

1983. World Communications Year. Mult.

No.	Description	Mint	Used
1586	5f. Type **365**	20	10
1587	25f. Hexagons of primary colours	35	20
1588	60f. Type **365**	1·30	65
1589	70f. As No. 1587	1·40	80
MS1590	80×60 mm. 200f. Emblem. Imperf	5·00	5·00

366 Horseman and Map

1983. Battle of Thiqar. Multicoloured.

No.	Description	Mint	Used
1591	20f. Type **366**	35	20
1592	50f. Eagle swooping on pyre	95	45
1593	60f. Type **366**	1·20	55
1594	70f. As No. 1592	1·30	65

367 Fair Emblem and Silhouette of Baghdad

1983. Baghdad International Fair.

No.	Type	Description	Mint	Used
1595	**367**	60f. multicoloured	95	55
1596	**367**	70f. multicoloured	1·20	65
1597	**367**	160f. multicoloured	2·75	1·80

368 Pres. Hussain within Figure "9"

1983. 9th Al-Baath Party Congress. Mult.

No.	Description	Mint	Used
1598	30f. Type **368**	50	35
1599	60f. Eagle, torch, map and book	95	55
1600	70f. Type **368**	1·20	65
1601	100f. As No. 1599	1·80	90

369 Fishermen hauling Boat

1983. Paintings. Multicoloured.

No.	Description	Mint	Used
1602	60f. Type **369**	1·70	65
1603	60f. Festive crowd	1·70	65
1604	60f. Hanging decorations	1·70	65
1605	70f. Crowd	1·90	1·00
1606	70f. Bazaar	1·90	1·00

370 Dove and Victim

1983. Massacre of Palestinians in Sabra and Shatila Refugee Camps, Lebanon. Multicoloured.

No.	Description	Mint	Used
1607	10f. Type **370**	35	20
1608	60f. Type **370**	1·30	55
1609	70f. Dove and clasped fist shedding blood and victims	1·60	65
1610	160f. As No. 1609	3·50	1·90

371 Apartment Building

1983. Buildings.

No.	Type	Description	Mint	Used
1611	**371**	60f. lt green, black & grn	95	55
1612	-	70f. purple, black & grey	1·20	65
1613	-	160f. purple, blk & grey	3·00	1·50
1614	**371**	200f. green, black & olive	3·50	1·90

DESIGNS: 70, 160f. Apartment building (different).
See also Nos. O1615/16.

372 President Hussain

1983. 4th Anniv of President Hussain as Party and State Leader.

No.	Type	Description	Mint	Used
1617	**372**	60f. multicoloured	95	45
1618	**372**	70f. multicoloured	1·30	65
1619	**372**	250f. multicoloured	4·25	2·50

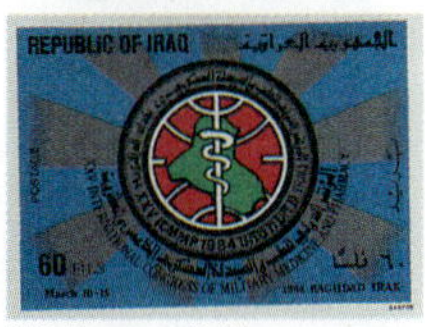

373 Congress Emblem

1984. 25th International Military Medicine and Pharmacy Congress.

No.	Type	Description	Mint	Used
1620	**373**	60f. multicoloured	1·10	55
1621	**373**	70f. multicoloured	1·30	65
1622	**373**	200f. multicoloured	3·50	1·90

374 President Hussain and Flowers

1984. Pres. Saddam Hussain's 47th Birthday. Multicoloured.

No.	Description	Mint	Used
1623	60f. Type **374**	85	45
1624	70f. Pres. Hussain in army uniform	95	55
1625	160f. As No. 1623	2·75	1·80
1626	200f. Type **374**	3·25	2·10
MS1627	81×61 mm. 250f. Pres. Hussain and rose (horiz)	5·00	5·00

375 Boxing

1984. Olympic Games, Los Angeles. Multicoloured.

No.	Description	Mint	Used
1628	50f. Type **375**	95	65
1629	60f. Hurdling, weightlifting and wrestling	1·20	65
1630	70f. Type **375**	1·40	80
1631	100f. As No. 1629	2·10	1·20
MS1632	80×60 mm. 200f. Footballers (30×40 mm)	4·75	4·75

376 Pres. Hussain and Horses' Heads

1984. Battle of Qadisiya. Multicoloured.

No.	Description	Mint	Used
1633	50f. Type **376**	70	45
1634	60f. President Hussain and symbolic representation of battle	95	55
1635	70f. Type **376**	1·10	65
1636	100f. As No. 1634	1·70	90
MS1637	80×60 mm. 200f. Shield and eagle (30×40 mm)	4·75	4·75

377 Flag as Ribbon and Two Domes

1984. Martyr's Day. Multicoloured.

No.	Description	Mint	Used
1638	50f. Type **377**	60	45
1639	60f. Woman holding rifle and medal	85	45
1640	70f. Type **377**	95	55
1641	100f. As No. 1639	1·30	90

378 Text

1985. 5th Anniv of President Hussain's Visit to Al-Mustansiriyah University.

No.	Type	Description	Mint	Used
1646	**378**	60f. red and blue	70	45

1647	**378**	70f. red and green	85	55
1648	**378**	250f. red and black	3·25	1·90

379 Pres. Hussain and Jet Fighters

1985. 54th Anniv of Iraqi Air Force. Mult.

1649	10f. Type **379**	35	10
1650	60f. Fighter airplanes trailing flag and "54" (horiz)	1·70	90
1651	70f. As No. 1650	1·90	90
1652	160f. Type **379**	4·75	2·20
MS1653	80×60 mm. 200f. As No. 1650	6·00	6·00

380 Pres. Hussain within Flower

1985. 48th Birthday of President Saddam Hussain. Multicoloured.

1654	30f. Type **380**	50	35
1655	60f. Pres. Hussain, candle and flowers	85	45
1656	70f. Type **380**	95	55
1657	100f. As No. 1655	1·40	80
MS1658	87×60 mm. 200f. "28", flowers and text	4·25	4·25

381 Graph and Modern Office

1985. Posts and Telecommunications Development. Multicoloured.

1659	20f. Type **381**	50	20
1660	50f. Dish aerial and graph	95	45
1661	60f. Type **381**	95	45
1662	70f. As No. 1660	1·20	65

382 Arms at Crossroads, and Building

1985. Saddam's Battle of Qadisiya. Multicoloured.

1663	10f. Type **382**	25	20
1664	20f. Pres. Hussain and emblem of Al-Baath Party	35	20
1665	60f. Type **382**	1·20	55
1666	70f. As No. 1664	1·30	90
MS1667	80×60 mm. 200f. Peace dove and soldiers (27×43 mm)	4·00	4·00

383 Solar Energy Research Centre

1985

1668	**383**	10f. multicoloured	25	10
1669	**383**	50f. multicoloured	1·20	55
1670	**383**	100f. multicoloured	2·40	1·20

384 Disabled Children

1985. UNICEF Child Survival Campaign. Multicoloured.

1671	10f. Type **384**	15	10
1672	15f. Toddler and baby	25	20
1673	50f. Type **384**	95	45
1674	100f. As No. 1672	1·90	1·10

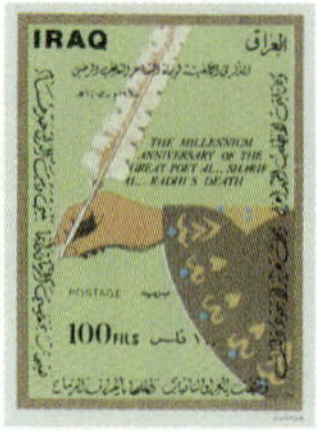

385 Hand holding Quill

1985. Death Millenary of Al-Sharif Al-Radhi (poet).

1675	**385**	10f. multicoloured	35	10
1676	**385**	50f. multicoloured	70	45
1677	**385**	100f. multicoloured	1·60	1·00

386 U.N. Emblem

1985. 40th Anniv of U.N.O.

1678	**386**	10f. multicoloured	20	10
1679	**386**	40f. blue, black & yellow	70	35
1680	**386**	100f. multicoloured	1·80	1·00

387 World Map

1985. Palestinian Solidarity Day.

1681	**387**	10f. multicoloured	35	15
1682	**387**	50f. multicoloured	1·20	55
1683	**387**	100f. multicoloured	2·75	1·20

389 I.Y.Y. Emblem and Soldier with Flag

1985. Martyr's Day.

1684	**388**	10f. multicoloured	25	20
1685	**388**	40f. multicoloured	60	35
1686	**388**	100f. multicoloured	1·70	1·00

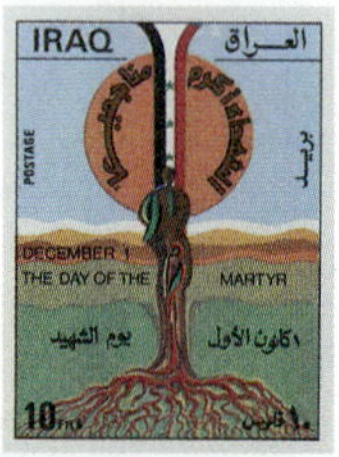

388 Flag, Man and Blood Vessels as Roots

1985. International Youth Year. Multicoloured.

1687	40f. Type **389**	60	35
1688	50f. Young couple, flag and I.Y.Y. emblem	85	45
1689	100f. Type **389**	1·80	1·00
1690	200f. As No. 1688	3·50	2·75

MS1691	80×60 mm. 250f. Cogwheel, flag, rifle and symbols of agriculture, industry and science (29×44 mm)	5·00	5·00

390 Pres. Hussain and Soldier in "6"

1986. Army Day. Multicoloured.

1692	10f. Type **390**	25	20
1693	40f. Pres. Hussain, cogwheel, "6" and missiles (horiz)	85	35
1694	50f. Type **390**	1·10	45
1695	100f. As No. 1693	2·30	1·20
MS1696	80×60 mm. 200f. Pres. Hussain, "6" in star and rifle (51×36 mm)	5·00	5·00

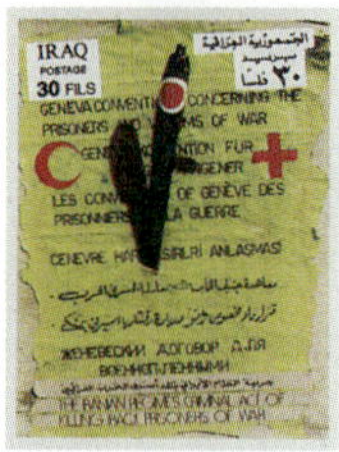

391 Pen as Knife in Sheet of Text

1986. Iraqi Prisoners of War Commemoration. Multicoloured.

1697	30f. Type **391**	50	35
1698	70f. Dove, cherub holding flag and three prisoners	95	55
1699	100f. Type **391**	1·40	90
1700	200f. As No. 1698	3·25	1·80
MS1701	110×80 mm. 250f. As Nos. 1699/1700	5·50	5·50

392 Pres. Hussain with Children

1986. 49th Birthday of President Saddam Hussain. Multicoloured.

1702	30f. Type **392**	60	35
1703	50f. Pres. Hussain and doves holding flag	95	45
1704	100f. Type **392**	1·90	90
1705	150f. As No. 1703	2·75	1·20
MS1706	80×60 mm. 250f. Pres. Hussain, flag and flowers	5·00	5·00

393 Worker, Globe and Cogwheel

1986. Labour Day. Multicoloured.

1707	10f. Type **393**	35	35
1708	40f. Candle in cogwheel	95	35
1709	100f. Type **393**	1·80	90
1710	150f. As No. 1708	2·75	1·20

394 Pres. Hussain and "30 July 17"

1986. July Festivals and 7th Anniv of Pres. Hussain's State Leadership. Multicoloured.

1711	20f. Type **394**	35	20
1712	30f. Pres. Hussain and "17 1986"	50	20
1713	100f. Type **394**	1·60	90
1714	150f. As No. 1712	2·40	1·50
MS1715	80×60 mm. 250f. Pres. Hussain within laurel wreath and text	5·00	5·00

395 Pres. Hussain and Jet Fighter

1986. 55th Anniv of Iraqi Air Force. Multicoloured.

1716	30f. Type **395**	95	35
1717	50f. Pres. Hussain and jet fighters	1·80	45
1718	100f. Type **395**	3·50	1·90
1719	150f. As No. 1717	5·50	2·50
MS1720	80×60 mm. 250f. Air Force Medal. Imperf	6·75	6·75

396 Refinery

1986. Oil Nationalization Day. Multicoloured.

1721	10f. Type **396**	15	10
1722	40f. Derrick and pipeline within flag (vert)	70	20
1723	100f. Type **396**	1·90	1·00
1724	150f. As No. 1722	2·75	1·80

397 Arab Warrior

1986. 1st Battle of Qadisiya. Multicoloured.

1725	20f. Type **397**	50	10
1726	60f. Pres. Hussain and battle scene	1·10	55
1727	70f. Type **397**	1·20	65
1728	100f. As No. 1726	2·10	90

398 Pres. Hussain, Battlefield and Cheering Soldiers

1986. Saadam's Battle of Qadisiya. Mult.

1729	30f. Type **398**	1·20	35
1730	40f. Pres. Hussain within flag "swords" and symbols of ancient and modern warfare (horiz)	1·60	55
1731	100f. Type **398**	3·25	1·60
1732	150f. As No. 1730	5·50	2·20
MS1733	80×60 mm. 250f. Pres. Hussain, soldiers and flag "swords". Imperf	6·00	6·00

399 Pres. Hussain

1986

1734	**399**	30f. multicoloured	85	20
1735	**399**	50f. multicoloured	1·20	35
1736	**399**	100f. multicoloured	2·40	90
1737	**399**	150f. multicoloured	3·25	1·10
1738	**399**	250f. multicoloured	6·00	1·90
1739	**399**	350f. multicoloured	8·50	2·50

401 Women

1986. Iraqi Women's Day. Multicoloured.

1744	30f. Type **401**	60	35
1745	50f. Woman and battle scenes (horiz)	85	45
1746	100f. Type **401**	1·80	1·00
1747	150f. As No. 1745	3·00	1·50

402 Flag and Treble Clef forming Dove

1986. International Peace Year. Multicoloured.

1748	50f. Type **402**	85	35
1749	100f. Globe, dove with flag and hand holding rifle and olive branch	1·60	80
1750	150f. Type **402**	2·30	1·50
1751	250f. As No. 1749	3·25	1·90
MS1752	80×60 mm. 200f. I.P.Y. emblem, flag and dove and fist on map. Imperf	3·25	3·25

403 Freighter "Al Alwah" and Map

1987. 10th Anniv of United Arab Shipping Company. Multicoloured.

1753	50f. Type **403**	70	35
1754	100f. Container ship "Khaled Ibn Al Waleed"	1·40	80
1755	150f. Type **403**	2·30	1·10
1756	250f. As No. 1754	3·50	1·90
MS1757	100×90 mm. 200f."Khaled Ibn Al Waleed" at wharf. Imperf	4·25	4·25

404 Activities on Tree

1987. 40th Anniv of UNICEF. Mult.

1758	20f. Type **404**	35	35
1759	40f. Doves and "40" containing children and UNICEF emblem (horiz)	50	45
1760	90f. Type **404**	1·20	1·10
1761	100f. As No. 1759	1·30	1·20

405 Pres. Hussain in "6"

1987. Army Day. Multicoloured.

1762	20f. Type **405**	35	35
1763	40f. Pres. Hussain and military scenes	50	45
1764	90f. Type **405**	1·20	1·10
1765	100f. As No. 1763	1·30	1·20

406 Torch, Cogwheel, Wheat and Map

1987. 40th Anniv of Al-Baath Party. Mult.

1766	20f. Type **406**	35	35
1767	40f. Pres. Hussain, map and flag as "7"	50	45
1768	90f. Type **406**	1·20	1·10
1769	100f. As No. 1767	1·30	1·20

407 Pres. Hussain

1987. 50th Birthday of President Saddam Hussain. Multicoloured.

1770	20f. Type **407**	35	35
1771	40f. Anniversary dates, flowers and Pres. Hussain	50	45
1772	90f. Type **407**	1·20	1·10
1773	100f. As No. 1771	1·30	1·20

408 Pres. Hussain, Civilians, Soldiers and buried Soldier

1987. July Festivals and 8th Anniv of Pres. Hussain's State Leadership. Multicoloured.

1774	20f. Pres. Hussain and flag (horiz)	35	35
1775	40f. Type **408**	50	45
1776	90f. As No. 1174	1·20	1·10
1777	100f. Type **408**	1·30	1·20

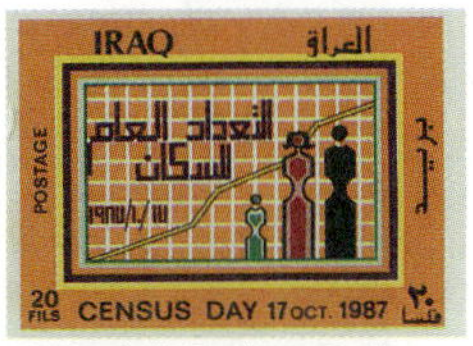

409 Symbolic Family on Graph

1987. Census. Multicoloured.

1778	20f. Type **409**	35	20
1779	30f. People on graph	50	35
1780	50f. As No. 1779	70	35
1781	500f. Type **409**	6·75	4·75

410 Pres. Hussain in "6" and Troops

1988. Army Day. Multicoloured.

1782	20f. Type **410**	35	35
1783	30f. Soldier and medal (horiz)	35	35
1784	50f. Type **410**	70	35
1785	150f. As No. 1783	2·10	80

411 "8" and Pres. Hussain

1988. 18th Anniv of People's Army (1786, 1788) and 25th Anniv of 8th February Revolution (others). Multicoloured.

1786	20f. Type **411**	50	35
1787	30f. Pres. Hussain and eagle on "8" (vert)	60	35
1788	50f. Type **411**	85	45
1789	150f. As No. 1787	2·75	90

412 Flag as "V" and Lyre

1988. Art Day. Multicoloured.

1790	20f. Type **412**	50	35
1791	30f. Pres. Hussain, rifle as torch, clef and dove on film strip	60	45
1792	50f. Type **412**	85	45
1793	100f. As No. 1791	1·70	55
MS1794	60×80 mm. 150f. Musical notes, lute and keyboard. Imperf	3·00	3·00

413 Rally and Ears of Wheat

1988. 41st Anniv of Al-Baath Party. Mult.

1795	20f. Type **413**	50	35
1796	30f. Flowers and "7 April 1947–1988"	60	45
1797	50f. Type **413**	85	45
1798	150f. As No. 1796	2·75	80

414 Emblem

1988. Regional Marine Environment Day. Multicoloured.

1799	20f. Type **414**	60	35
1800	40f. Fishes (horiz)	60	45
1801	90f. Type **414**	1·60	55
1802	100f. As No. 1800	1·70	55

415 Pres. Hussain

1988. 51st Birthday of President Saddam Hussain. Multicoloured.

1803	20f. Type **415**	50	35
1804	30f. Pres. Hussain and hands holding flowers	60	45
1805	50f. Type **415**	85	45
1806	100f. As No. 1804	1·70	65
MS1807	90×100 mm. 150f. Pres. Hussain and flowers within flag as heart. Imperf	2·75	2·75

416 Emblem

1988. 40th Anniv of W.H.O. Multicoloured.

1808	20f. Type **416**	50	35
1809	40f. Red crescent protecting line of people (vert)	60	45
1810	90f. Type **416**	1·60	55
1811	100f. As No. 1809	1·70	55

417 Bomb and Open Book showing School, Child and Wreath

1988. Bilat Al-Shuhada School Bomb Victims. Multicoloured.

1812	20f. Type **417**	50	35
1813	40f. Explosion and girl (horiz)	60	45
1814	90f. Type **417**	1·70	55
1815	100f. As No. 1813	1·70	55
MS1816	80×60 mm. 150f. Child's severed head in clawed hand (49×39 mm)	2·50	2·50

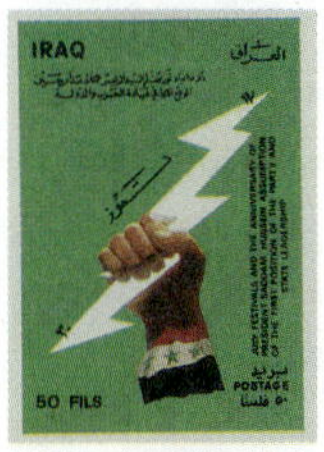

418 Hand holding Flash of Lightning

1988. July Festivals and 9th Anniv of President Hussain's State Leadership. Multicoloured.

1817	50f. Type **418**	85	45
1818	90f. Sun, map and Pres. Hussain	1·60	55
1819	100f. Type **418**	1·70	55
1820	150f. As No. 1818	2·40	65
MS1821	90×70 mm. 250f. Pres. Hussain and flag. Imperf	4·25	4·25

419 Pres. Hussain and al-Sail al-Kabir Miqat

1988. President Hussain's Pilgrimage to Mecca.

1822	**419**	90f. multicoloured	1·60	55
1823	**419**	100f. multicoloured	1·70	80
1824	**419**	150f. multicoloured	2·75	80

420 Mosul

1988. Tourism. Multicoloured.

1825	50f. Type **420**	1·20	35
1826	100f. Basrah	1·80	80
1827	150f. Baghdad (vert)	3·75	1·30

421 Pres. Hussain and Soldiers

1988. "Victorious Iraq".

1828	**421**	50f. multicoloured	6·00	5·50
1829	**421**	100f. multicoloured	11·50	10·50
1830	**421**	150f. multicoloured	17·00	16·00

422 Emblem

1988. Navy Day. Multicoloured.

1831	50f. Type **422**	1·30	45
1832	90f. Missile boats	2·40	65
1833	100f. Type **422**	2·75	80
1834	150f. As No. 1832	3·75	1·20
MS1835 90×70 mm. 250f. Emblem and Pres. Hussain decorating officers. Imperf		7·75	7·75

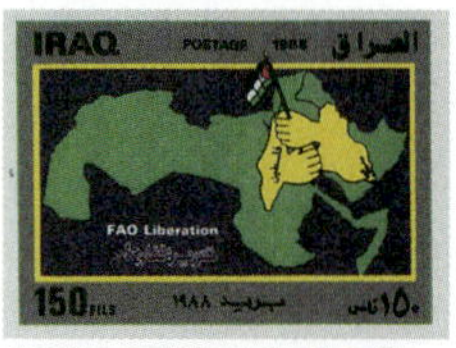

423 Map and Hands holding Flag

1988. Liberation of Fao City.

1836	**423**	100f. multicoloured	2·75	80
1837	**423**	150f. multicoloured	3·75	1·20
MS1838 60× 80 mm. 500f. multicoloured. Imperf			16·00	16·00

DESIGN: 100f. Pres. Hussain and document.

424 Missile Launch from Winged Map

1988. Iraq Missile Research.

1839	**424**	100f. multicoloured	1·70	55
1840	**424**	150f. multicoloured	2·75	90
MS1841 80×60 mm. 500f. multicoloured. Imperf			8·50	8·50

DESIGN: 500f. President Hussain, map and missiles.

425 Boxer and Hodori (mascot)

1988. Olympic Games, Seoul. Multicoloured.

1842	100f. Type **425**	2·75	80
1843	150f. Games emblem	3·75	1·20
MS1844 100×90 mm. 500f. Pres. Hussain presenting football trophy. Imperf		16·00	16·00

426 Dancers and Golden Cow

1988. 2nd Babylon International Festival.

1845	**426**	100f. multicoloured	1·70	55
1846	**426**	150f. multicoloured	2·40	80
MS1847 60×80 mm. 500f. multicoloured. Imperf			8·50	8·50

DESIGN: 500f. Medallion and laurel wreath.

427 Crescent and Camel Train

1988. Mohammed's Birth Anniv.

1848	**427**	100f. multicoloured	1·70	65
1849	**427**	150f. multicoloured	2·40	1·00
1850	**427**	1d. multicoloured	17·00	6·75

428 Hand holding Candle

1988. Martyr's Day.

1851	**428**	100f. multicoloured	1·30	55
1852	**428**	150f. multicoloured	2·40	1·00
1853	**428**	500f. multicoloured	8·50	3·00

انتصر العراق
١٩٨٨/٨/٨

429 "Victory"

1988. Nos. 1738/9 optd with T 429.

1854	**399**	250f. multicoloured	6·00	1·90
1855	**399**	350f. multicoloured	8·50	2·75

430 Family on Pedestrian Crossing

1989. Police Day.

1856	**430**	50f. multicoloured	85	45
1857	**430**	100f. multicoloured	1·70	55
1858	**430**	150f. multicoloured	2·40	1·00

431 Children and Money

1989. Postal Savings Bank. (a) Size 32×32 mm.

1859	**431**	50f. multicoloured	2·20	1·00

(b) Size 24×25 mm. With or without Arabic opt.

1860a	100f. multicoloured	35	35
1861a	150f. multicoloured	50	45

DESIGN: 100, 150f. Motif as Type **431** but with inscriptions differently arranged and inscr "REPUBLIC OF IRAQ".

432 Members' Flags and Leaders

1989. Formation of Arab Co-operation Council (Egypt, Iraq, Jordan and Yemen Arab Republic). Multicoloured.

1862	100f. Type **432**	1·70	55
1863	150f. Leaders in formal pose	2·40	90

433 Dates

1989. 1st Anniv of Liberation of Fao City.

1864	**433**	100f. multicoloured	1·60	55
1865	**433**	150f. multicoloured	2·20	55
MS1866 60×80 mm. 250f. multicoloured. Imperf			3·75	3·75

DESIGN: 250f. Calendar.

434 Pres. Hussain

1989. 52nd Birthday of President Saddam Hussain.

1867	**434**	100f. multicoloured	1·60	55
1868	**434**	150f. multicoloured	2·20	55
MS1869 60×80 mm. 250f. multicoloured. Imperf			3·75	3·75

DESIGN: 250f. Hussain and laurel branches.

435 Khairalla

1989. General Adnan Khairalla Commem.

1870	**435**	50f. multicoloured	1·10	45
1871	**435**	100f. multicoloured	2·10	55
1872	**435**	150f. multicoloured	3·00	1·00

436 Hussain laying Mortar

1989. Completion of Basrah Reconstruction Project.

1873	**436**	100f. multicoloured	2·10	55
1874	**436**	150f. multicoloured	3·00	1·00

437 Crane and Buildings

1989. Start of Reconstruction of Fao City.

1875	**437**	100f. multicoloured	2·10	55
1876	**437**	150f. multicoloured	3·00	1·00

438 "Women"

1989

1877	**438**	100f. multicoloured	1·20	45
1878	**438**	150f. multicoloured	1·80	65
1879	**438**	1d. multicoloured	12·00	4·50
1880	**438**	5d. multicoloured	60·00	19·00

439 Pres. Hussain

1989. July Festivals and 10th Anniv of President Hussain's State Leadership.

1881	**439**	50f. multicoloured	85	45
1882	**439**	100f. multicoloured	1·70	55
1883	**439**	150f. multicoloured	2·75	90

440 Flag and Victory Signs

1989. Victory Day.

1884	**440**	100f. multicoloured	1·70	55
1885	**440**	150f. multicoloured	2·75	90
MS1886 70×90 mm. 250f. multicoloured. Imperf			5·00	5·00

DESIGN: 250f. Hussain, palm, Boeing 737 airliner and container ship "Khawla".

441 Children, Heart and Bride

1989. Iraqi Family.

1887	**441**	50f. multicoloured	1·10	45
1888	**441**	100f. multicoloured	2·10	85
1889	**441**	150f. multicoloured	6·00	2·50

442 Najaf

1989. Tourism. Multicoloured.

1890	100f. Type **442**	2·20	65
1891	100f. Arbil	2·20	65
1892	100f. Marsh Arab punt and Ziggurat of Ur	2·20	65

443 Map and Means of Transport

1989. 5th Session of Arab Ministers of Transport Council, Baghdad. Multicoloured.

1893	50f. Type **443**	1·40	65
1894	100f. Sun, means of transport and map	3·00	90
1895	150f. Means of transport and members' flags (vert)	4·50	1·30

444 City and Pres. Hussain placing Final Stone

1989. Completion of Fao City Reconstruction.

1896	**444**	100f. multicoloured	1·80	55
1897	**444**	150f. multicoloured	2·75	90

445 Anniversary Emblem

1989. 30th Anniv of Iraqi News Agency.

1898	**445**	50f. multicoloured	70	45
1899	**445**	100f. multicoloured	1·40	55
1900	**445**	150f. multicoloured	2·20	90

446 Emblem

1989. 1st Anniv of Declaration of Palestinian State. Multicoloured.

1901	25f. Type **446**	35	35
1902	50f. Crowd of children	85	45
1903	100f. Type **446**	1·70	55
1904	150f. As No. 1902	2·75	80

447 Pansies

1989. Flowers. Multicoloured.

1905	25f. Type **447**	50	45
1906	50f. Antirrhinums	95	45
1907	100f. "Hibiscus trionum"	1·80	55
1908	150f. Mesembryanthemums	3·00	90
MS1909	90×110 mm. As Nos. 1905/8 but larger (26½×36 mm)	11·00	11·00

448 Map and Emblem

1989. Centenary of Interparliamentary Union.

1910	**448**	25f. multicoloured	50	35
1911	**448**	100f. multicoloured	1·70	55
1912	**448**	150f. multicoloured	2·75	90

449 Sun, Flag, Doves and Mosque Domes

1989. Martyr's Day.

1913	**449**	50f. multicoloured	85	45
1914	**449**	100f. multicoloured	1·60	55
1915	**449**	150f. multicoloured	2·20	90

450 Dove, Red Crescent and Pres. Hussain

1989. Iraqi Red Crescent Society.

1916	**450**	100f. multicoloured	85	45
1917	**450**	150f. multicoloured	2·30	90
1918	**450**	500f. multicoloured	7·75	2·75

451 Members' Flags on Map

1990. 1st Anniv of Arab Co-operation Council.

1919	**451**	50f. multicoloured	1·30	65
1920	**451**	100f. multicoloured	3·25	1·20
MS1921		80×60 mm. **451** 250f. multi-coloured. Imperf	9·00	9·00

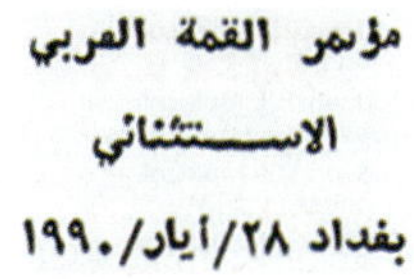

(452)

1990. Arab League Summit Conference, Baghdad. Nos. 1906 and 1908 optd with T 452.

1922	50f. multicoloured	1·40	1·10
1923	150f. multicoloured	4·50	2·75

453 Doves and Flag as Flame

1990. 2nd Anniv of Liberation of Fao City.

1924	**453**	50f. multicoloured	70	65
1925	**453**	100f. multicoloured	1·60	1·50

(454)

1992. No. 1291 surch with T 454.

1927	100f. on 5f. multicoloured	3·50	3·50

455 Children and Currency

1993. Postal Savings.

1928	**455**	100f. multicoloured	35	35
1929	**455**	150f. multicoloured	50	45
1930	**455**	250f. multicoloured	85	80

(456)

1993. No. O1742 surch with T 456.

1931	1d. on 100f. multicoloured	10·00	10·00

(457)

1993. No. 1901 surch with T 457.

1932	10d. on 25f. multicoloured	36·00	36·00

458 Satellite and Receiver

1993. Re-construction. Multicoloured.

1933	250f. Type **458**	95	90
1934	500f. Bridge over Tigris river	1·80	1·70
1935	750f. Power transformers	2·75	2·50
1936	1d. Damaged and restored buildings	3·50	3·25

459 *Ibn Khaldoon* (trading vessel)

1993

1937	**459**	2d. multicoloured	3·00	2·75
1938	**459**	5d. multicoloured	7·75	7·25

(460)

(461)

(461a)

(461b)

(461c)

(461d)

(462)

(462a)

(463)

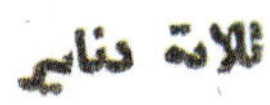
(463a)

(464)

(464a)

(464b)

(464c)

(465)

(466)

(466a)

(467)

1994. No. 1291 surch with T 460/67.

1939	500f. on 5f. multicoloured (T **460**)	2·40	2·40
1940	1d. on 5f. multicoloured (T **461**)	2·40	2·40
1941	1d. on 5f.multicoloured (T **461a**)	3·50	3·50
1942	1d. on 5f. multicoloured (T **461b**)	7·75	7·75
1943	1d. on 5f. multicoloured (T **461c**)	3·50	3·50
1944	1d. on 5f. multicoloured (T **461d**)	3·50	3·50
1945	2d. on 5f. multicoloured (T **462**)	4·25	4·25
1946	2d. on 5f. multicoloured (T **462a**)	4·25	4·25
1947	3d. on 5f. multicoloured (T **463**)	2·40	2·40
1948	3d. on 5f. multicoloured (T **463a**)	2·40	2·40
1950	5d. on 5f. multicoloured (T **464**)	2·40	2·40
1951	5d. on 5f. multicoloured (T **464a**)	3·50	3·50
1952	5d. on 5f. multicoloured (T **464b**)	5·00	5·00
1953	5d. on 5f. multicoloured (T **464c**)	5·00	5·00
1954	10d. on 5f. multicoloured (T **465**)	5·00	5·00
1955	25d. on 5f. multicoloured (T **466**)	10·00	10·00
1957	25d. on 5f. multicoloured (T **466a**)	17·00	17·00
1958	50d. on 5f. multicoloured (T **467**)	34·00	34·00

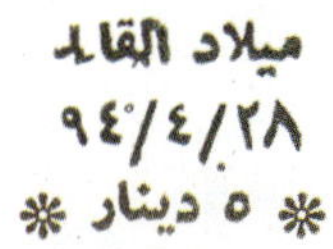

(472)

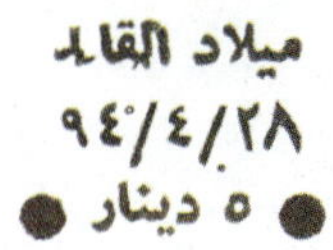

(473)

1994. 57th Birth Anniv of Pres. Hussein. No. 1739 surch with T 472/3.

1967	5d. on 350f. multicoloured (T **472**)	7·25	7·25
1968	5d. on 350f. multicoloured (T **473**)	7·25	7·25

474 Alqaid Bridge

1994

1969	**474**	1d. multicoloured	1·40	1·40
1970	**474**	3d. multicoloured	4·25	4·25

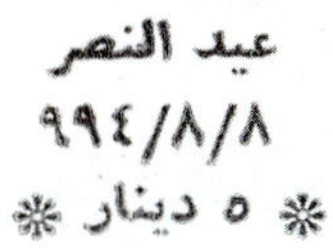

(475)

1994. Victory Day. No. 1739 surch with T 475.

1971	5d. on 350f. multicoloured	5·75	5·75

(476)

1995. 20th Anniv of World Tourism Organization. No. 1878 surch with T 476.

1972	5d. on 150f. multicoloured (Arabic inscription)	4·75	4·75
1973	5d. on 150f. multicoloured (English inscription)	4·75	4·75

477 Baghdad Clock

1995. Multicoloured.
1974 **477** 7d. blue and black 3·00 3·00
MS1975 86×110 mm. 25d. As No. 1974 but with design enlarged. Imperf 14·50 14·50

478 Saddam Tower (television transmitter)

1995
1976 **478** 2d. multicoloured 1·20 1·20
1977 **478** 5d. multicoloured 2·75 2·75

479 Pres. Hussein

1995. 58th Birth Anniv of Pres. Hussein. Two sheets. Imperf.
MS1978 (a) 60×78 mm. 25d. Type **479**; (b) 78×60 mm. 25d. President and child (horiz) Set of 2 sheets 31·00 31·00

480 Woman and River Basin

1995. Completion of "Saddam River" (canal between Iraq and Persian Gulf).
1979 **480** 4d. red and blue 4·50 4·50
1980 **480** 4d. ochre and blue 4·50 4·50
MS1981 106×86m. **480** 25d. multicoloured 16·00 16·00

481 Barbed Wire, Tower, Woman and Child

1995
1982 **481** 10d. blue and red 3·50 3·50
MS1983 85×110 mm. **481** 25d. multicoloured 17·00 17·00

✻ ٢٥ دينار ✻

(482)

1995. No. 1739 surch with T 482.
1984 25d. on 350f. multicoloured 1·40 1·40
1985 250d. on 350f. multicoloured 9·00 9·00
1986 350d. on 350f. multicoloured 22·00 22·00
1987 1000d. on 350f. multicoloured 43·00 43·00

(483)

(484)

(485)

(486)

1995. Nos. 1930 surch as T 483/6.
1988 **483** 50d. on 250f. multicoloured 3·00 3·00
1989 **484** 500d. on 250f. multicoloured 29·00 29·00
1990 **485** 2500d. on 250f. multicoloured £110 90·00
1991 **485** 5000d. on 250f. multicoloured £250 £180

يوم الاستفتاء
١٩٩٥/١٠/١٥
✻ ٢٥ دينار ✻

(487)

Referendum
15/10/1995
✻25 Dinars✻

(488)

1995. Referendum Day. No. 1739 surch with T 487/8.
1992 25d. on 350f. multicoloured 3·50 3·50
1993 25d. on 350f. multicoloured 3·50 3·50

✻ ٢٥ دينار

(489)

1996. No. 1297 surch with T 489 (overprint on overprint).
1994 25d. on 100f. on 5f multicoloured 5·50 5·50

٢٥ دينار

(490)

(490a)

(490b)

1996. Nos. 1859/61 surch with T 490/a/b.
1995 25d. on 100f. multicoloured (T **490**) 1·40 1·40
1996 25d. on 150f. multicoloured (T **490a**) 1·40 1·40
1997 50d. on 50f. multicoloured (T **490b**) (32×32 mm) 3·00 3·00

مائة دينار

(491)

1996. No. O1616 surch with T 491.
1998 100d. on 70f. yellow, black and flesh 6·00 6·00

492 Flag, Doves and Flames

1996. Sheet 86×62 mm. Imperf.
MS1999 100d. multicoloured 13·50 13·50

١٠٠ دينار

(493)

1996. No. 1878 surch with T 493.
2000 100d. on 150f. multicoloured 6·00 6·00

٢٥ دينار

(494)

٥٠ دينار

(495)

1996. Nos. 1989/91 surch with T 494/5 (overprint on overprint).
2001 **494** 25d. on 500d. on 250f. multicoloured 5·50 5·50
2002 **494** 25d. on 5000d. on 250f. multicoloured 5·50 5·50
2003 **495** 50d. on 2500d. on 250f. multicoloured 11·00 11·00

٢٥ دينار (496) خمسون دينارا (497)

1996. Un-issued stamps surch with T 496/7.
2004 **496** 25d. on 10f. multicoloured 42·00 42·00
2005 - 25d. on 25f. multicoloured 2·40 2·40
2006 **497** 50d. on 10f. multicoloured 70·00 70·00
2007 - 50d. on 50f. multicoloured 3·50 3·50
DESIGNS: Nos. 2004/7 School children in classroom.

٥٠ ١٠٠ دينار

(498)

1996. No. 1906 surch with T 498.
2008 100d. on 50f. Antirrhinums 6·75 6·75

٢٥ دينار

(499)

1996. No. 1930 surch with T 499.
2009 25d. on 250f. multicoloured 1·40 1·40

✻ مائة دينار ✻

(500)

1996. No. O1645 surch with T 500.
2010 100d. on 60f. multicoloured 6·25 6·25

مائة دينار ٢٥ دينار

(501)

1996. Nos. 1572/7 surch as T 501/a.
2011 **501** 25d. on 10f. multicoloured 2·30 2·30
2012 **501** 25d. on 30f. multicoloured 2·30 2·30
2013 **501** 25d. on 50f. multicoloured 2·30 2·30
2014 **501a** 100d. on 20f. multicoloured 9·75 9·75
2015 **501a** 100d. on 40f. multicoloured 9·75 9·75
2016 **501a** 100d. on 100f. multicoloured 9·75 9·75

١٠٠ دينار
✻ ✻

(502)

1996. No. 1924 surch with T 502.
2017 100d. on 50f. multicoloured 6·00 6·00

يوم العلم

٢٥ دينار

(503)

1997. No. 1933 surch as T 503.
2018 25d. on 250f. multicoloured 1·40 1·40

504 Geometric Design

1997
2019 **504** 25d. emerald, black and rosine 1·20 1·20
2020 **504** 100d. emerald, blue and vermilion 6·00 6·00

اليوبيل الذهبي
لميلاد الحزب القائد
١٩٩٧
✻ ٢٥ دينار ✻

(505)

1997. 50th Anniv of Baath Party. No. 1920 surch with T 505.
2021 25d. on 100f. multicoloured 2·20 2·20

يوم البريد
١٩٩٧/٤/٢١

✻ ٢٥ دينار ✻

(506)

1997. 45th Anniv of Arab Post Union. No. 1878 surch with T 506.
2022 25d. on 150f. multicoloured 5·00 5·00

507 Pres. Hussein

1997. 2nd Anniv of Referendum.
2023 **507** 25d. multicoloured 1·80 1·80
2024 **507** 100d. multicoloured 7·25 7·25
MS2025 96×81 mm. 250d. President Saddam Hussein and map. Imperf 12·00 12·00

508 Pres. Hussein, Water and Plants

1997. Completion of Al Qaid Water Project. Multicoloured. (a) Sheet stamps. (i) Ordinary gum.
2026 25d. Type **508** 70 70

(ii) Self-adhesive gum.

2027	100d. As No. 2026	3·00	3·00

(b) Miniature Sheets. Ordinary gum.

MS2028 Two sheets. (a) 79×91 mm. 250d. As No. 2026; (b) 75×92 mm. 250d. Pres. Hussein and pipeline Set of 2 sheets 14·50 14·50

509 Saladin and Pres. Hussain

1998. Jerusalem Day. Self-adhesive.

2029	**509**	25d. multicoloured	70	70
2030	**509**	100d. multicoloured	3·00	3·00

MS2031 88×75 mm. **509** 250d. multi-coloured. Imperf 7·25 7·25

510 Zinnias

1998. Kurdish New Year. Two sheets containing T 510 and similar vert design. Imperf.

MS2032 (a) 71×93 mm. 250d. Type **510**; (b) 68×93 mm. 250d. Iris Set of 2 sheets 22·00 22·00

511 Goalkeeper and Players (image scaled to 58% of original size)

1998. World Cup Football Championships, France (1st issue). Two sheets containing T 511 and similar multicoloured design. Imperf.

MS2033 (a) 72×85 mm. 250d. Type **511**; (b) 84×62 mm. 250d. Two players (vert) Set of 2 sheets 17·00 17·00

See also Nos. 2061/2.

512x 512 Emblem (image scaled to 57% of original size)

1998. 25th Anniv of Arab Police Security Chiefs' Conference. Sheet 93×67 mm. Imperf.

MS2034 250d. multicoloured 7·25 7·25

513 *Chamomile recuita*

1998. Flora. Multicoloured. (a) Ordinary gum.

2035	25d. Type **513**	35	35
2036	50d. *Helianthus annuus*	60	60
2037	1000d. *Carduus nutans*	10·00	10·00

(b) Self-adhesive gum.

2038	25d. Type **513**	1·90	1·90

514 Pres. Hussain and Map

1998. Arab Languages Day. Multicoloured.

2039	25d. Type **514**	60	60
2040	100d. Map and emblem	2·30	2·30

515 Mosque Outline, Calligraphy and Dove

1998. Martyrs Day. Multicoloured.

2041	25d. Type **515**	50	50
2042	100d. Calligraphy and banner	1·90	1·90
MS2043	94×74 mm. 250d. Emblem	5·00	5·00

516 *Precis orithya*

1998. Butterflies. Multicoloured.

2044	100d. Type **516**	3·50	3·50
2045	150d. *Anthocharis euphome*	5·50	5·50

517 Ishtar Gate, Babylon

1999. Tower of Babylon and Borsippa Ziggurat Conference. Multicoloured.

2046	25d. Type **517**	50	50
2047	50d. Ishtar Gate (different)	95	95
MS2048	71×90 mm. 250d. Ziggurat, Borsippa	7·25	7·25

518 Tower and Dam

1999. Dams on the Tigris River. Multicoloured.

2049	25d. Type **518**	60	60
2050	100d. Dam, flowers, fruit and pylon	2·30	2·30
MS2051	71×93 mm. 250d. As No. 2050. Imperf	7·25	7·25

519 Pres. Hussain

1999. 62nd Birthday of Pres. Hussain. Multicoloured.

2052	25d. Type **519**	25	25
2053	50d. With flag in background	50	50
2054	150d. With tree in background	1·30	1·30
2055	500d. Wearing uniform facing right	4·50	4·50
2056	1000d. Wearing uniform facing left	9·00	9·00
2057	5000d. Seated with clasped hands (horiz)	46·00	46·00

520 Emblem and Pres. Hussain

1999. Saddamiya al Therthar. Multicoloured.

2058	25d. Type **520**	60	60
2059	100d. Flowers, tower and gateway	2·10	2·10
MS2060	93×71 mm. 250d. Emblem, tower and Pres. Hussain. Imperf	7·25	7·25

521 Two Players

1999. World Cup Football Championships, France (2nd issue). Multicoloured.

2061	25d. Type **521**	95	95
2062	100d. Goalkeeper and players (horiz)	3·50	3·50

522 Bees (*Apis mellifica*)

1999. Apiculture.

2063	**522**	25d. multicoloured	1·20	1·20
2064	**522**	100d. multicoloured	2·75	2·75

523 Dome of the Rock

1999. Jerusalem Day. Multicoloured.

2065	25d. Type **523**	35	35
2066	50d. Dome and map (horiz)	60	60
2067	100d. Dome, flag and shield	1·20	1·20
2068	150d. Dome and Pres. Hussain (horiz)	1·90	1·90
MS2069	93×71 mm. 250d. As No. 2068. Imperf	5·50	5·50

524 Flags and Pres. Hussain

1999. Victory Day. Multicoloured.

2070	25d. Type **524**	60	60
2071	50d. Pres. Hussain and crowd	1·10	1·10
MS2072	93×71 mm. 250d. Eagle's head and Pres. Hussain. Imperf	5·50	5·50

525 Pres. Hussain and Flowers

2000. 63rd Birthday of Pres. Hussain. Multicoloured.

2073	25d. Type **525**	50	50
2074	100d. Pres. Hussain and "28" (horiz)	95	95
MS2075	93×71 mm. 500d. Pres. Hussain wearing coat with fur collar. Imperf	9·75	9·75

526 Men and Women holding Tools (detail)

2000. Nasb al-Hurriyyah (sculpture by Jawad Salim). Multicoloured.

2076	25d. Type **526**	50	50
2077	25d. Women and child carrying corn	50	50
2078	25d. Men and broken fence	50	50
2079	25d. Grieving women	50	50
2080	25d. Men with raised arms	50	50

527 Pres. Hussain

2000. Victory Day. Multicoloured.

2081	25d. Type **527**	95	95
2082	50d. Flag and guns	1·90	1·90
MS2083	72×92 mm. 255d. As No. 2081. Imperf	5·50	5·50

528 Mallards (*Anas platyrhynchos*)

2000. Birds. Multicoloured.

2084	25d. Type **528**	50	50
2085	50d. House sparrow (*Passer domesticus*)	1·10	1·10
2086	100d. Purple swamphen (*Porphyrio porphyrio*)	3·50	3·50
MS2087	92×71 mm. 500d. Goldfinch (*Carduelis carduelis*). Imperf	11·00	11·00

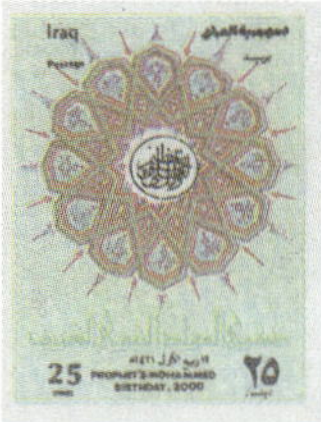

529 Emblem

2000. 430th Birth Anniv of Mohammed. Multicoloured.

2088	25d. Type **529**	85	85
2089	50d. Emblem (different)	1·70	1·70

530 Flag, Pres. Hussain and Voting Cards

2000. 5th Anniv of Referendum. Multicoloured.

2090	25d. Type **530**	35	35
2091	50d. Pres. Hussain wearing uniform (horiz)	85	85
MS2092	93×72 mm. 250d. Pres. Hussain wearing traditional clothes. Imperf	5·50	5·50

531 Emblem

2000. 1200th Anniv of Baytol Hikma.

2093	**531**	50d. multicoloured	60	60
2094	**531**	100d. multicoloured	1·20	1·20

532 Woman carrying Child

2001. 10th Anniv of Al-Amiriyah. Multicoloured.

2095	25d. Type **532**	60	60
2096	50d. National colours and doves	1·20	1·20
MS2097	93×71 mm. 250d. As No. 2095. Imperf	4·25	4·25

533 Inscribed Tablet and Statuette

2001. 5000th Anniv of Writing in Mesopotamia. Multicoloured.

2098	25d. Type **533**	25	25
2099	50d. Sumerian script and figures	60	60
2100	75d. As No. 2098	85	85
2101	100d. As No. 2099	1·10	1·10
2102	150d. Figure wearing skirt (statue)	1·70	1·70
2103	250d. As No. 2102	3·00	3·00

534 Arabic Script as Torch Flame and Crowd

2001. 54th Anniv of Al Baath Party. Multicoloured.

2104	25d. Type **534**	35	35
2105	50d. Michael Aflaq (founder) and Pres. Hussain	60	60
2106	100d. Map of Arab states	1·20	1·20

535 Pres. Hussain

2001. 13th Anniv of Cessation of Hostilities. Multicoloured.

2107	25d. Type **535**	35	35
2108	100d. Pres. Hussain, soldier and map (horiz)	1·20	1·20

536 Pres. Hussain

2001. 64th Birthday of Pres. Hussain. Multicoloured.

2109	25d. Type **536**	25	25
2110	50d. Seated with children (horiz)	50	50
2111	100d. Wearing dark suit (horiz)	95	95
MS2112	90×69 mm. 250d. With children carrying flowers. Imperf	4·75	4·75

537 *Barbus sharpeyi*

2001. Fish. Multicoloured.

2113	25d. Type **537**	35	35
2114	50d. *Barbus esocinus*	70	70
2115	100d. *Barbus xanthopterus*	1·40	1·40
2116	150d. *Pampus argenteus*	2·30	2·30

538 Gazelle (*Gazella subgutturosa*)

2001. Fauna. Multicoloured.

2117	100d. Type **538**	95	95
2118	250d. Hare (*Lepus europaeus*) (vert)	2·40	2·40
2119	500d. Dromedary (*Camelus dromedaries*)	4·75	4·75
MS2120	92×70 mm. 1000d. Horse, gazelle, sheep and camel. Imperf	9·75	9·75

539 Hawk and Flags

2001. 10th Anniv of Um Al Marik.

2121	**539**	25d. multicoloured	25	25
2122	**539**	100d. multicoloured	1·10	1·10

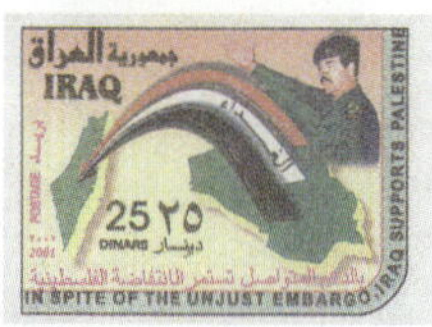

540 National Colours joining Maps of Palestine and Iraq

2001. Al Asqa Intifada. Multicoloured.

2123	25d. Type **540**	35	35
2124	25d. Dome of the Rock, flag and man carrying gun (vert)	35	35
2125	50d. Dome of the Rock, leaves and man with raised arms (vert)	70	70
MS2126	Two sheets, each 89×67 mm. (a) 250d. Mohammed Dorra and father; (b) 250d. Tank and protester. Imperf Set of 2 sheets	6·00	6·00

541 Drilling Rig and Workers

2001. 29th Anniv of Nationalization of Oil Industry. Multicoloured.

2127	25d. Type **541**	35	35
2128	50d. Flaming tower, processing plant and oil	70	70

542 World Map and Footballers

2001. Under 20 Junior World Cup Football Championships, Argentina. Multicoloured.

2129	25d. Type **542**	35	35
2130	50d. Player and trophy (vert)	70	70

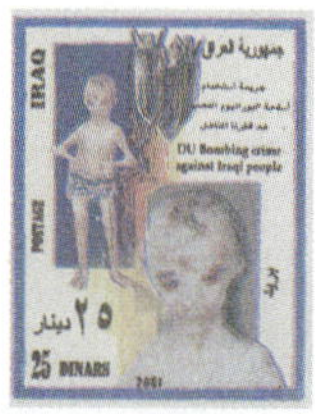

543 Sick Child

2001. 10th Anniv of Gulf War. Multicoloured.

2131	25d. Type **543**	60	60
2132	25d. Woman and children	60	60
2133	50d. Flag and family (horiz)	1·20	1·20
MS2134	70×92 mm. 250d. As No. 2131. Imperf	4·25	4·25

544 Soldiers and Flag

2002. Army Day. Multicoloured.

2135	25d. Type **544**	60	60
2136	50d. Statue of soldiers (vert)	1·20	1·20
2137	100d. Soldier (vert)		
MS2138	70×90 mm. 250d. As No. 2135. Imperf	4·25	4·25

545 Aircraft, Flames and Girl

2002. 11th Anniv of Gulf War.

2139	**545**	100d. multicoloured	1·90	1·90

546 Pres. Hussain wearing Hat

2002. Jerusalem Day.

2140	**546**	25d. multicoloured	35	35
2141	**546**	50d. multicoloured	60	60
2142	**546**	100d. multicoloured	1·20	1·20

547 Flags and Fist

1963. 2002. 39th Anniv of 8 February. Multicoloured.

2143	50d. Type **547**	60	60
2144	100d. Sumerians, Saladin and modern crowd (horiz)	1·20	1·20

548 Aircraft Sights

2002. 11th Anniv of Al-Amiriyah.

2145	**548**	25d. multicoloured	35	35
2146	**548**	50d. multicoloured	60	60

549 Orange Roses

2002. Flowers. Multicoloured.

2147	25d. Type **549**	35	35
2148	50d. Pink and red roses	60	60
2149	150d. Carnations, anemone and narcissi	1·80	1·80
MS2150	73×91 mm. 250d. Bouquet. Imperf	3·50	3·50

550 Web and Mosques

2002. Hajeer New Year. Multicoloured.

2151	25d. Type **550**	35	35
2152	50d. Crescent moon and mosque (vert)	60	60
2153	75d. Web and doves	95	95

551 Envelope

2002. Post Day. Multicoloured.

2154	50d. Type **551**	70	70
2155	100d. Aircraft, ship and train	1·40	1·40
MS2156	70×91 mm. 250d. Envelope and globe. Imperf	5·50	5·50

552 Pres. Hussain as Boy

2002. 65th Birth Anniv of Pres. Hussain. Multicoloured.

2157	25d. Type **552**	35	35
2158	50d. As young man	60	60
2159	75d. With flag at left	95	95
2160	100d. With flag at right	1·20	1·20
MS2161	Two sheets, each 74×91 mm. (a) 250d. Wearing traditional clothes; (b) 250d. Surrounded by flowers. Imperf Set of 2 sheets	7·25	7·25

553 Trophy and Player

2002. World Cup Football Championships, Japan and South Korea. Multicoloured.

2162	50d. Type **553**	60	60
2163	100d. Player chasing ball	1·20	1·20
2164	150d. Player kicking ball	1·80	1·80
MS2165	69×91 mm. 250d. Championship emblem and trophy enclosing players. Imperf	4·75	4·75

554 Soldier, Child and Woman

2002. 2nd Anniv of Al Asqa Intifada.

2166	**554**	5000d. multicoloured	36·00	36·00

555 Sheikh Maruf Mosque

2002. Mosques. Multicoloured.

2167	25d. Type **555**	35	35
2168	50d. Al- Mouiz	70	70
2169	75d. Um Al Marik	1·10	1·10

556 Stylized Eagle, Flag and Pres. Hussain

2002. Victory Day. Multicoloured.

2170	25d. Type **556**	35	35
2171	50d. As No. 2149	60	60
MS2172	70×91 mm. 150d. Eagle's head. Imperf	3·50	3·50

557 Reed Boats and Coracle

2002. Traditional Watercraft. Multicoloured.

2173	150d. Type **557**	1·80	1·80
2174	250d. Galley	3·00	3·00
2175	500d. Sail boat	6·00	6·00

558 Jameel Sidqi Al-Zahawi

2002. Writers. Multicoloured.

2176	25d. Type **558**	35	35
2177	50d. Abdul Musin Al-Qadumi	60	60
2178	75d. Badr Shaker Al-Sayab	95	95
2179	100d. Ma'rouf Al-Rasafi	1·20	1·20
MS2180	71×91 mm. 150d. Badr Shaker Al-Sayab and rose. Imperf	3·50	3·50

559 Hands holding Flowers and Pres. Hussain

2002. Referendum. Multicoloured.

2181	100d. Type **559**	1·20	1·20
2182	150d. Fist and ballot box	1·80	1·80
MS2183	70×92 mm. 250d. As No. 2181. Imperf	3·25	3·25

560 Woman Spinning

2002. Baghdad Day. Multicoloured.

2184	25d. Type **560**	35	35
2185	50d. Street performer and children	60	60
2186	75d. Two women talking (horiz)	95	95
MS2187	91×71 mm. 250d. Musicians. Imperf	6·00	6·00

561 *Oryx leucoryx*

2003. Fauna. Multicoloured.

2188	25d. Type **561**	35	35
2189	50d. *Acinonyx jubatus* (vert)	60	60
2190	75d. *Panthera leo* (vert)	95	95
2191	100d. *Castor fiber*	1·20	1·20
2192	150d. *Equus hemionus*	1·80	1·80
MS2193	69×93 mm. 250d. As No. 2188. Imperf	6·00	6·00

562 Emblem

2003. 10th Anniv of Saddam University.

2194	**562**	50d. multicoloured	60	60
2195	**562**	100d. multicoloured	1·20	1·20

563 Coracle

2004. Transportation. Multicoloured.

2196	50d. Type **563**	50	50
2197	100d. Horse-drawn cab	95	95
2198	250d. Tram	1·60	1·60
2199	500d. Skiff carrying reeds	3·50	3·50
2200	5000d. Camel train. Perf or imperf	26·00	26·00

564 Woman and Flowers

2006. New Year.

2201	**564**	250d. multicoloured	1·60	1·60

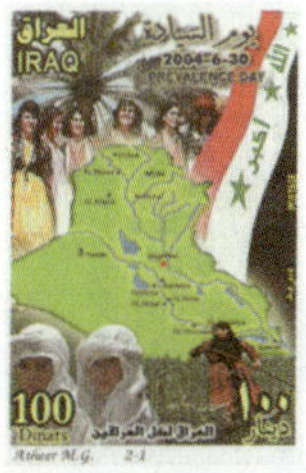

565 Women and Map

2006. Installation of Interim Government, 30 June 2004. Multicoloured.

2202	100d. Type **565**	95	95
2203	250d. Map and hands enclosing sun	3·50	3·50

566 Bust wearing Headdress

2006. Iraqi Civilization. Multicoloured.

2204	100d. Type **566**	95	95
2205	150d. Golden bull	1·40	1·40
2206	200d. Carved bull with human head	1·90	1·90
MS2207	80×61 mm. 250d. Tiled mosaic animals. Imperf	2·40	2·40

567 Football

2006. Olympic Games, Athens (2004). Multicoloured.

2208	100d. Type **567**	95	95
2209	150d. Athletics	1·40	1·40
MS2210	100×70 mm. 500d. Sportsmen. Imperf	2·40	2·40

568 Two Women (Akram Shukri)

2006. Paintings. Multicoloured.

2211	100d. Type **568**	95	95
2212	150d. Abstract (Hafidh Al Duroubi)	1·40	1·40
2213	200d. Horseman (Faiq Hassan)	1·90	1·90
MS2214	88×70 mm. 250d. Abstract (different) Imperf	2·40	2·40

569 *Anemone*

2007. Flowers. Multicoloured. Self-adhesive.

2215	250d. Type **569**	2·40	2·40
2216	750d. *Viola mamola*	7·25	7·25
2217	1000d. *Atropa belladonna*	9·75	9·75
MS2218	88×70 mm. Nos. 2215/17	18·00	18·00

570 *Papilio demodocus*

2007. Butterflies. Multicoloured.

2219	100d. Type **570**	55	55
2220	250d. Inscr 'Precis orithua'	1·20	1·20
2221	500d. Inscr 'Ciotas croceus'	2·30	2·30
MS2222	81×60 mm. 1000d. *Papilio demodocus* (different)	4·25	4·25

572 Rug Maker

2007. Artisans. Multicoloured. Self-adhesive.

2224	250d. Type **572**	1·30	1·30
2225	350d. Blanket maker	1·80	1·80
2226	500d. Basket maker	2·40	2·40
MS2227	106×60 mm. Nos. 2224/6	7·75	7·75

No. 2223 and Type **571** have been left for 'Singers', issued on 23 April 2007, not yet received.

573x 573 Women and Children (Actual size 111×80 mm)

2007. Folklore. Sheet 111×80 mm.

MS2228	multicoloured	4·50	4·50

574 Anniversary Emblem

2007. 65th Anniv (2006) of Rafidain Bank.

2229	**574**	100d. multicoloured	55	55
2230	**574**	150d. multicoloured	90	90
2231	**574**	250d. multicoloured	1·20	1·20
2232	**574**	500d. multicoloured	2·30	2·30

575 Ducks (image scaled to 65% of original size)

2007. Birds. Multicoloured

MS2236 80×83 mm. 1500d. Type **575**. Imperf 7·00 7·00

Nos. 2233/5 have been left for single stamps.

576 Mohammad Alqubanchi (singer)

2007. Theatre Personalities. Multicoloured. Self-adhesive.

(a) Size 30×40 mm.

2237	250d. Type **576**	1·20	1·20
2238	500d. Haqi Al Shibly (theatre manager) (horiz)	2·30	2·30
2239	750d. Nadhum Al Ghazali (singer) (horiz)	3·50	3·50
2240	1000d. Munir Bashir (musician) (horiz)	4·50	4·50

(b) Size 30×42 mm.

2241	250d. As Type **576**	1·30	1·30
2242	500d. As No. 2238 (horiz)	2·40	2·40
2243	700d. As No. 2239 (horiz)	3·50	3·50
2244	1000d. As No. 2240 (horiz)	4·50	4·50

581 Gateway, Female and Animal Statues

2009. Campaign to Regain Iraqi Antiques. Multicoloured.

2253	250d. Type **581**	1·20	1·20
2254	500d. Gateway, two statues and head	2·30	2·30
2255	750d. Gateway, head and plaque	3·50	3·50

It is reported that an imperforate miniature sheet, value 1000d. (Baghdad at Night), two perforated stamps value 250d., 1000d. (Calligraphy) and a imperforated miniature sheet, value 1500d. (Calligraphy), were printed but not issued due to poor printing quality.

Nos. 2245/7 and Type **577** have been left for National Reconciliation, issued on 27 October 2008, not yet received.

Nos. 2248/9 and Type **578** have been left for 50th Anniv of Iraq–China Diplomatic Relations, issued on 28 October 2008, not yet received.

No. 2250 and Type **579** have been left for Poetry, issued on 24 November 2008, not yet received.

Nos. 2251/2 and Type **580** have been left for Graves, issued on 14 December 2008, not yet received.

582 Cooling Towers, Crayfish, Geese and Trees

2009. Environmental Protection.

2256	**582**	1000d. multicoloured	4·50	4·50

583 Boats and Wildfowl

2009. International Campaign to Reclaim Marshes.

2257	**583**	10000d. multicoloured	4·50	4·50

584 Couple

2009. International Children's Day. Children's Paintings. Multicoloured.

2258	50d. Type **584**	35	35
2259	50d. Two girls	35	35
2260	50d. Family	35	35
2261	50d. Mother and daughter	35	35
2262	50d. Three girls	35	35
MS2263	80×60 mm. 500d. Mother cradling baby. Imperf	2·40	2·40

585 Emblem and Goalkeeper

2009. FIFA Confederations Cup, South Africa. Multicoloured.

2264	100d. Type **585**	55	55
2265	250d. Emblem and player	1·20	1·20
2266	500d. Emblem and player with leg extended	2·40	2·40
MS2267	80×80 mm. 750d. Emblem	3·50	5·50

586 Musicians and Seated Men

2009. Tourism Week. Multicoloured.

2268	250d. Type **586**	1·20	1·20
2269	250d. Market, draughtsman and apothecary	1·20	1·20
2270	250d. Women	1·20	1·20
2271	250d. Men working	1·20	1·20
MS2272	90×60 mm. 500d. Horsemen. Imperf	2·40	2·40

Nos. 2268/9 and 2270/1, respectively, were printed, se-tenant, each pair forming a composite design.

587 Emblem

2009. al-Quds—2009 Capital of Arab Culture. Multicoloured.

2273	250d. Type **587**	1·20	1·20
MS2274	60×80 mm. 750d. As Type **587**. Imperf	3·50	3·50

OBLIGATORY TAX

28a King Faisal II

28b

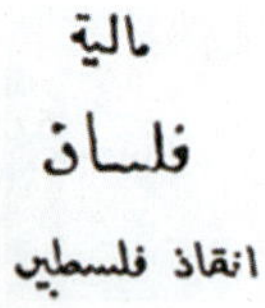

28c "Tax 2 Fils Save Palestine"

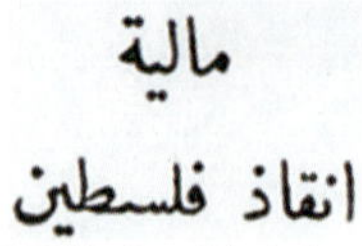

28d "Tax Save Palestine"

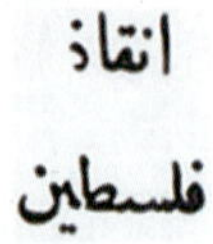

28e "Save Palestine" (size varies)

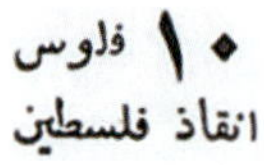

28g "Tax 10 Fils Save Palestine" (size varies)

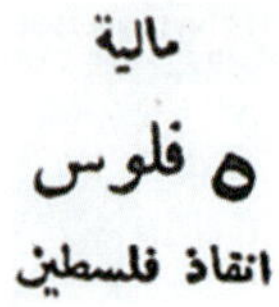

28h "Tax 5 Fils Save Palestine"

1949. Aid for Palestine. (a) Nos. O300 and 278 surch as T 28.

T324	**27**	2f. on 3f. green	36·00	20·00
T325	**27**	2f. on 6f. mauve	48·00	19·00

(b) Nos. O299 and O303 optd as T 28d but smaller.

T326		2f. brown	29·00	12·50
T327		5f. red	60·00	29·00

(c) No. O234 optd with T 28d.

T328	**20**	5f. red	30·00	7·25

(d) Revenue stamp surch in Arabic (="2 Fils Save Palestine") as bottom two lines of T 28c.

T329	**28a**	2f. on 5f. blue	19·00	10·00

(e) Revenue stamps optd with T 28e.

T330		5f. blue	9·75	1·60
T332	**28b**	10f. orange		55·00
T335	**28a**	10f. orange	29·00	12·50

(f) Revenue stamp surch as T 28g.

T336	**28b**	10f. on 20f. green	85·00	36·00

(h) No. 278 surch with T 28h.

T337	**27**	5f. on 6f. mauve	60·00	21·00

113a

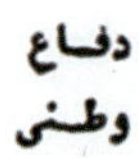

(113b)

1968. Flood Relief.

T763	**113a**	5f. brown	60	35

1968. Defence Fund. Optd with Type 113b.

T764		5f. brown	60	60

(164a)

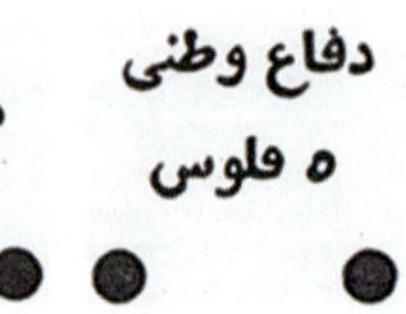

(215)

1970. Obligatory Tax. Defence Fund. Nos. 620 and 625/9 surch with Type T 164a.

T931	**65**	5f. on 1f. green	5·50	6·25
T932	-	5f. on 10f. red	5·50	6·25
T933	-	5f. on 15f. brown & yell	5·50	6·25
T934	-	5f. on 20f. violet	5·50	6·25
T935	-	5f. on 30f. orange	5·50	6·25
T936	-	5f. on 40f. green	5·50	6·25

1973. Obligatory Tax. Defence Fund. Nos. 607/8 surch with Type 215.

T1071	**62**	5f. on 14f. black & grn	9·75	9·75
T1072	**62**	5f. on 35f. black and red	9·75	9·75

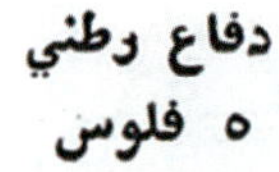

(223)

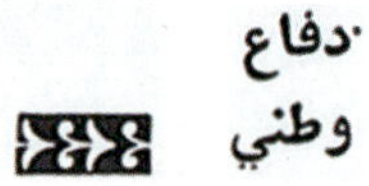

(231)

1973. Nos. 738, 765, 777, 787 and 891 optd similar to Type 215 (No. T1119) or as Type 223 (others).

T1117	-	5f. on 2f. multicoloured	12·00	12·00
T1118	**114**	5f. on 2f. multicoloured	12·00	12·00
T1119	**116**	5f. on 2f. multicoloured	12·00	12·00
T1120	**117**	5f. on 2f. multicoloured	12·00	12·00
T1121	**150**	5f. on 2f. multicoloured	12·00	12·00

1973. No. 1099 optd with Type 231.

T1152	**221**	5f. black and orange	8·50	5·50

235 Soldier

1974. Defence Fund.

T1158	**235**	5f. black, yellow & brn	7·25	4·00

OFFICIAL STAMPS

1920. Issue of 1918 (surch Turkish stamps) optd ON STATE SERVICE.

O20	1a. on 20pa. red	5·00	60
O22	2½a. on 1pi. blue	5·00	5·50
O23	3a. on 1½pi. black and pink	24·00	80
O25	6a. on 2pi. black and green	30·00	7·50
O27	12a. on 5pi. purple	23·00	15·00
O28	1r. on 10pi. brown	30·00	11·00
O29	2r. on 25pi. green	30·00	16·00
O30	5r. on 50pi. red	60·00	45·00
O31	10r. on 100pi. blue	85·00	£110
O33	½a. on 10pa. green	1·00	1·00
O35	1½a. on 5pa. brown	2·75	65
O36	4a. on 1¾pi. brown and blue	2·00	2·50
O38	8a. on 2½pi. green and brown	3·25	2·00

1923. Nos. 41/50 and 52/3 optd ON STATE SERVICE in English only.

O54	**2**	½a. green	1·50	1·75
O55	-	1a. brown	1·75	30
O56	**3**	1½a. red	1·75	3·35
O57	-	2a. buff	2·00	55
O58	-	3a. blue	2·50	1·50
O59	-	4a. violet	4·25	1·75
O60	-	6a. blue	3·75	1·25
O61	-	8a. bistre	4·00	3·50
O62	**4**	1r. brown and green	14·00	3·00
O63	**2**	2r. black	28·00	12·00
O64	-	5r. orange	65·00	38·00
O65	-	10r. red	£120	60·00

1924. Nos. 41/9 and 51/3 optd ON STATE SERVICE in English and Arabic.

O66	**2**	½a. green	1·50	10
O67	-	1a. brown	1·25	10
O68	**3**	1½a. red	1·25	30
O69	-	2a. buff	1·50	10
O70	-	3a. blue	2·00	10
O71	-	4a. violet	4·00	30
O72	-	6a. blue	1·75	20
O73	-	8a. bistre	3·75	35
O74	**4**	1r. brown and green	11·00	2·50
O75	**2**	2r. bistre	38·00	3·75
O76	-	5r. orange	65·00	50·00
O77	-	10r. red	£120	42·00

1927. Optd ON STATE SERVICE in English and Arabic.

O79	**10**	1r. brown	8·00	2·25

1931. Optd ON STATE SERVICE in English and Arabic.

O93	**11**	½a. green	65	2·75
O94	**11**	1a. brown	80	10
O95	**11**	1½a. red	4·50	25·00
O96	**11**	2a. orange	80	10
O97	**11**	3a. blue	85	1·25
O98	**11**	4a. purple	1·00	1·50
O99	**11**	6a. blue	4·75	25·00
O100	**11**	8a. green	4·75	25·00
O101	**12**	1r. brown	16·00	25·00
O102	**12**	2r. brown	26·00	80·00
O103	**12**	5r. orange	42·00	£160
O104	**12**	10r. red	£140	£250
O105	**10**	25r. violet	£950	£1300

1932. Official stamps of 1924 and 1931 surch in "Fils" or "Dinar".

O122	**11**	3f. on ½a. green	5·00	3·50
O123	**11**	4f. on 1a. brown	2·50	10
O124	**11**	5f. on 1a. brown	2·50	10
O125	**4**	8f. on 1½a. red	9·00	50

No.	Type	Description	Unused	Used
O126	11	10f. on 2a. orange	3·50	10
O127	11	15f. on 3a. blue	4·25	5·00
O128	11	20f. on 4a. purple	4·25	4·50
O129	11	25f. on 4a. purple	4·50	2·00
O130	-	30f. on 6a. bl (No. O72)	9·00	1·75
O131	11	40f. on 8a. green	4·00	3·50
O132	12	50f. on 1r. brown	11·00	3·75
O133	12	75f. on 1r. brown	7·50	8·50
O134	2	100f. on 2r. bistre	30·00	3·50
O135	-	200f. on 5r. orange (No. O76)	26·00	26·00
O136	-	½d. on 10r. red (No. 77)	£100	£130
O137	10	1d. on 25r. violet	£190	£325

1932. Issue of 1932 optd ON STATE SERVICE in English and Arabic.

No.	Type	Description	Unused	Used
O155	11	2f. blue	1·50	10
O156	11	3f. green	1·50	10
O157	11	4f. purple	1·50	10
O158	11	5f. green	1·50	10
O159	11	8f. red	1·50	10
O160	11	10f. yellow	2·25	10
O161	11	15f. blue	2·50	10
O162	11	20f. orange	2·50	15
O163	11	25f. mauve	2·50	15
O164	11	30f. olive	3·50	20
O165	11	40f. violet	4·50	30
O166	12	50f. brown	3·25	20
O167	12	75f. blue	2·50	1·00
O168	12	100f. green	11·00	2·00
O169	12	200f. red	22·00	6·50
O170	10	½d. blue	18·00	30·00
O171	10	1d. purple	95·00	£120

1934. Issue of 1934 optd ON STATE SERVICE in English and Arabic.

No.	Type	Description	Unused	Used
O190	16	1f. violet	1·80	65
O191	16	2f. blue	1·80	20
O192	16	3f. green	85	20
O193	16	4f. purple	1·80	20
O194	16	5f. green	1·60	20
O195	16	8f. red	6·00	35
O196	16	10f. yellow	35	20
O197	16	15f. blue	13·50	2·00
O198	16	20f. orange	1·30	20
O199	16	25f. mauve	27·00	7·75
O200	16	30f. green	6·00	35
O201	16	40f. violet	7·75	55
O202	17	50f. brown	1·30	90
O203	17	75f. blue	9·00	1·10
O204	17	100f. green	2·40	1·30
O205	17	200f. red	6·75	3·25
O206	-	½d. blue (No. 188)	17·00	25·00
O207	-	1d. red (No. 189)	65·00	75·00

1941. Issue of 1941 optd ON STATE SERVICE in English and Arabic.

No.	Type	Description	Unused	Used
O230	19	1f. purple	35	20
O231	19	2f. brown	35	20
O232	-	3f. green (No. 210)	35	20
O233	-	4f. violet (No. 211)	35	20
O234	-	5f. red (No. 212)	35	20
O235	21	8f. red	1·20	20
O236	21	8f. yellow	35	20
O237	21	10f. yellow	9·00	55
O238	21	10f. red	95	20
O239	21	15f. blue	9·00	1·00
O240	21	15f. black	1·60	45
O241	21	20f. black	2·75	45
O242	21	20f. blue	85	20
O244	22	25f. purple	1·40	45
O246a	22	30f. orange	60	45
O248a	22	40f. brown	60	35
O249c	-	50f. blue (No. 224)	1·60	90
O250	-	75f. mauve (No. 225)	1·60	35
O251	-	100f. olive (No. 226)	3·25	45
O252	-	200f. orange (No. 227)	4·25	1·10
O253	-	½d. blue (No. 228)	16·00	6·75
O254	-	1d. green (No. 229)	27·00	12·50

1942. Issue of 1942 optd ON STATE SERVICE in English and Arabic.

No.	Type	Description	Unused	Used
O263	26	1f. brown and violet	50	45
O264	26	2f. brown and blue	50	45
O265	26	3f. brown and green	50	45
O266	26	4f. sepia and brown	50	45
O267	26	5f. brown and green	60	55
O268	26	6f. brown and red	60	55
O269	26	10f. brown and pink	85	80
O270	26	12f. brown and green	1·10	1·00

1948. Issue of 1948 optd ON STATE SERVICE in English and Arabic.

No.	Type	Description	Unused	Used
O298	27	1f. blue	25	45
O299	27	2f. brown	25	55
O300	27	3f. green	25	55
O301	27	3f. red	4·25	1·30
O302	27	4f. lilac	25	45
O303	27	5f. red	25	65
O304	27	5f. green	4·75	1·30
O305	27	6f. mauve	25	55
O306	27	8f. brown	25	55
O307	27	10f. red	25	45
O308	27	12f. green	35	45
O309	27	14f. green	2·40	45
O310	27	15f. black	5·50	8·25
O311	27	16f. red	4·25	45
O312	27	20f. blue	35	20
O313	27	25f. purple	35	20
O314	27	28f. blue	1·30	45
O315	27	30f. orange	35	35
O316	27	40f. brown	70	55
O317	27	50f. blue	1·10	45
O318	27	60f. blue	85	35
O319	27	75f. mauve	1·90	35
O320	27	100f. green	1·90	1·30
O321	27	200f. orange	3·00	1·30
O322	27	½d. blue	27·00	20·00
O323	27	1d. green	36·00	42·00

1955. Issue of 1954 optd ON STATE SERVICE in English and Arabic.

No.	Type	Description	Unused	Used
O364	33	1f. blue	20	15
O365	33	2f. brown	20	15
O366	33	3f. lake	20	15
O367	33	4f. violet	35	15
O368	33	5f. green	35	15
O369	33	6f. mauve	35	15
O370	33	8f. brown	35	15
O371	33	10f. blue	35	15
O372	33	16f. red	31·00	31·00
O373	33	20f. olive	60	35
O374	33	25f. purple	3·25	1·50
O375	33	30f. red	1·40	35
O376	33	40f. brown	60	35
O377	-	50f. blue	3·25	1·00
O378	-	60f. purple	21·00	7·25
O379	-	100f. olive	46·00	20·00

No. O378 does not exist without opt.

1958. Issue of 1957 optd ON STATE SERVICE in English and Arabic.

No.	Type	Description	Unused	Used
O404	41	1f. blue	6·00	2·20
O405	41	2f. brown	7·25	4·75
O406	41	3f. red	9·00	3·25
O407	41	4f. violet	11·00	2·20
O408	41	5f. green	6·00	2·20
O409	41	6f. red	6·00	3·25
O410	41	10f. blue	6·00	1·90

1958. Official stamps optd with T 43. (a) Nos. O251/2.

No.	Type	Description	Unused	Used
O459		100f. green		
O459a		200f. orange	13·50	7·25

(b) Nos. O298 etc.

No.	Type	Description	Unused	Used
O460	27	1f. blue	48·00	45·00
O461	27	2f. brown	48·00	45·00
O462	27	3f. green	48·00	45·00
O463	27	3f. red	48·00	45·00
O464	27	4f. lilac	48·00	45·00
O465	27	5f. red	48·00	45·00
O466	27	5f. green	48·00	45·00
O467	27	6f. mauve	48·00	45·00
O468	27	8f. brown	48·00	45·00
O470	27	12f. green	1·40	1·00
O471	27	14f. green	1·70	1·10
O472	27	15f. black	1·20	65
O473	27	16f. red	5·00	2·75
O474	27	25f. purple	4·50	2·75
O475	27	28f. blue	2·75	2·10
O476	27	40f. brown	1·80	1·30
O477	27	60f. blue	6·75	3·25
O478	27	75f. mauve	3·25	2·50
O479	27	200f. orange	3·75	3·25
O480	27	½d. blue	23·00	7·75
O481	27	1d. green	36·00	16·00

(c) Nos. O364 etc.

No.	Type	Description	Unused	Used
O482	33	1f. blue	85	35
O483	33	2f. brown	85	35
O484	33	3f. red	85	35
O485	33	4f. violet	85	35
O486	33	5f. green	90	35
O487	33	6f. mauve	85	55
O488	33	8f. brown	70	35
O489	33	10f. blue	90	35
O490	33	16f. red	10·00	9·00
O491	33	20f. green	85	35
O492	33	25f. purple	85	35
O493	33	30f. red	90	55
O494	33	40f. brown	1·30	55
O495	-	50f. blue	1·30	65
O496	-	60f. purple	1·30	80
O497	-	100f. green	3·00	80

(d) Nos. O404 etc.

No.	Type	Description	Unused	Used
O498	41	1f. blue	35	35
O499	41	2f. brown	35	35
O500	41	3f. red	60	35
O501	41	4f. violet	35	35
O502	41	5f. green	35	35
O503	41	6f. red	35	35
O504	41	8f. brown	85	20
O505	41	10f. blue	95	20

No. O504 does not exist without opt T **43**.

1961. Nos. 515, etc. optd On State Service in English and Arabic.

No.	Type	Description	Unused	Used
O552	49	1f. multicoloured	50	50
O553	49	2f. multicoloured	50	50
O554	49	4f. multicoloured	50	50
O555	49	5f. multicoloured	60	50
O556	49	10f. multicoloured	1·10	80
O557	49	50f. multicoloured	18·00	13·50

1962. Nos. 515, etc. optd ON STATE SERVICE in English and Arabic.

No.	Description	Unused	Used
O587	1f. multicoloured	50	50
O588	2f. multicoloured	50	50
O589	3f. multicoloured	50	50
O590	4f. multicoloured	50	50
O591	5f. multicoloured	50	50
O592	10f. multicoloured	50	50
O593	15f. multicoloured	50	50
O594	20f. multicoloured	50	50
O595	30f. multicoloured	60	50
O596	40f. multicoloured	60	50
O597	50f. multicoloured	70	50
O598	75f. multicoloured	1·20	55
O599	100f. multicoloured	1·30	90
O600	200f. multicoloured	4·75	1·90
O601	500f. multicoloured	17·00	7·75
O602	1d. multicoloured	34·00	16·00

1971. Various stamps optd or surch Official in English and Arabic. (a) Costumes. Nos. 768 and 770/4.

No.	Description	Unused	Used
O962	15f. multicoloured (postage)	2·40	90
O963	25f. multicoloured	16·00	3·75
O964	30f. multicoloured	16·00	3·75
O965	40f. multicoloured (air)	6·75	1·90
O966	50f. multicoloured	8·50	1·90
O967	80f. multicoloured	7·75	1·90

(b) International Tourist Year. Nos. 778 and 780/2.

No.	Description	Unused	Used
O969	5f. multicoloured (postage)	8·50	45
O970	15f. multicoloured	8·50	80
O971	25f. multicoloured	12·00	2·10
O972	50f. multicoloured (air)	7·75	5·00

(c) Birds. No. 798.

No.	Description	Unused	Used
O1178	30f. multicoloured	8·50	5·50

(d) 20th Anniv of W.H.O. Nos. 811/13.

No.	Type	Description	Unused	Used
O973	-	10f. multicoloured	11·50	4·50
O974	124	15f. red, blue and black	11·50	4·50
O975	124	25f. red, green and black	11·50	4·50

(e) Human Rights Year. Nos. 814/15.

No.	Type	Description	Unused	Used
O976	125	10f. red, yellow and blue	7·25	65
O977	125	25f. red, yellow & green	7·25	1·20

126 Mother and children

(f) UNICEF. Nos. 817/18.

No.	Type	Description	Unused	Used
O978	126	15f. multicoloured	7·25	55
O979	126	25f. multicoloured	7·25	1·50

(g) Army Day. No. 820.

No.	Type	Description	Unused	Used
O980	127	25f. multicoloured	16·00	4·50

(h) Fish and Fauna. Nos. 825/7, 829/30 and 832.

No.	Description	Unused	Used
O981	10f. multicoloured (postage)	9·00	5·50
O982	15f. on 3f. multicoloured	9·00	5·50
O983	25f. on 2f. multicoloured	9·00	5·50
O984	10f. multicoloured (air)	9·00	5·50
O985	15f.+3f. multicoloured	9·00	5·50
O986	25f.+2f. multicoloured	9·00	5·50

127 Army Tanks

(i) Fruits. Nos. 906/9.

No.	Description	Unused	Used
O987	5f. multicoloured	7·25	5·00
O988	10f. multicoloured	7·25	5·00
O989	15f. multicoloured	7·25	5·00
O990	35f. multicoloured	7·25	5·00

97 Footballers

(j) Arab Football Cup, Baghdad. No. 717.

No.	Type	Description	Unused	Used
O991	97	2f. multicoloured	8·50	5·50

(k) 50th Anniv of I.L.O. No. 836.

No.	Type	Description	Unused	Used
O992	133	15f. yellow, green & blk	8·50	5·50

1972. Nos. 625/8 optd Official in English and Arabic.

No.	Description	Unused	Used
O1042	10f. red	11·00	11·00
O1043	15f. brown and yellow	11·00	11·00
O1044	20f. violet	11·00	11·00
O1045	30f. orange	11·00	11·00

1973. Various stamps with portrait obliterated by 3 bars. (i) 1948 issue.

No.	Type	Description	Unused	Used
O1081	27	25f. purple (No. O313)	9·00	2·10
O1082	27	50f. blue (No. O317)	9·00	7·75

(ii) 1955 issue.

No.	Type	Description	Unused	Used
O1083	33	25f. purple (No. O374)	9·00	2·10
O1084	-	50f. blue (No. O377)	9·00	7·75

(iii) Similar to 1958 issue (T 41) but size 22½×27½ mm.

No.	Description	Unused	Used
O1085	50f. purple	9·00	7·75

(O218) (size varies)

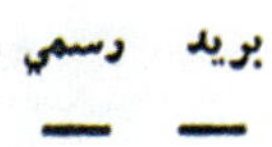

(O237a)

1973. "Faisal" stamps with portrait obliterated. (a) Optd with 3 bars and Type O 218.

No.	Type	Description	Unused	Used
O1086	33	10f. blue	5·50	5·50
O1087	41	15f. black	5·50	5·50

(b) Optd with Type O 218 only.

No.	Type	Description	Unused	Used
O1090	33	15f. black	5·50	1·10
O1091	41	15f. black	5·50	1·10
O1092	33	25f. purple	5·50	1·10
O1093	41	25f. purple	5·50	1·10
O1096	27	25f. purple	21·00	7·75

1973. No. 1097 optd Official in English and Arabic.

No.	Type	Description	Unused	Used
O1099	220	25f. multicoloured	5·50	1·60

1973. Nos. 1099/1107 optd OFFICIAL in English and Arabic.

No.	Type	Description	Unused	Used
O1108	221	5f. black and orange	50	45
O1109	221	10f. black and brown	50	45
O1110	221	20f. black and mauve	85	45
O1111	-	25f. black and blue	1·70	1·70
O1112	-	35f. black and green	1·70	65
O1113	-	45f. black and blue	1·70	80
O1114	-	50f. yellow and green	2·30	90
O1115	-	70f. yellow and violet	2·30	1·20
O1116	-	95f. yellow and brown	3·50	1·60

1973. Various "Faisal" Official stamps optd ON STATE SERVICE in English and Arabic, with portrait obliterated by "leaf" motif similar to that used in Type O 218. (a) 1948 issue.

No.	Type	Description	Unused	Used
O1130a	27	12f. olive	2·30	45
O1131	27	14f. olive	2·30	65
O1132	27	15f. black	2·30	65
O1133	27	16f. red	4·50	1·10
O1134	27	28f. blue	9·00	1·60
O1134a	27	30f. orange	9·00	1·30
O1134b	27	40f. brown	9·00	1·90
O1135	27	60f. blue	9·00	6·75
O1136	27	100f. green	30·00	10·50
O1137	27	½d. blue	80·00	28·00
O1138	27	1d. green	£160	£160

(b) 1955 issue.

No.	Type	Description	Unused	Used
O1139	33	3f. lake	2·30	80
O1140	33	6f. mauve	2·30	80
O1141	33	8f. brown	2·30	80
O1142	33	16f. red	23·00	23·00
O1142a	33	20f. green	2·30	80
O1142b	33	30f. red	2·30	1·30
O1142c	33	40f. brown	2·30	2·30
O1143	-	60f. purple	2·30	2·30
O1144	-	100f. green	41·00	11·00

(c) 1958 issue.

No.	Type	Description	Unused	Used
O1145	41	3f. lake	7·25	1·60
O1146	41	6f. mauve	7·25	1·60
O1147	41	8f. brown	7·25	1·60
O1147a	41	30f. red	7·25	1·60

1974. No. T1158 optd with Type O 237a.

No.	Type	Description	Unused	Used
O1165	235	5f. black, yellow & brn	4·25	4·25

O 249 Eagle Emblem

1975

O1195	**O249**	5f. multicoloured	50	50
O1196	**O249**	10f. multicoloured	50	50
O1197	**O249**	15f. multicoloured	60	60
O1198	**O249**	20f. multicoloured	85	85
O1199	**O249**	25f. multicoloured	1·20	1·20
O1200	**O249**	30f. multicoloured	1·40	1·40
O1201	**O249**	50f. multicoloured	2·30	2·30
O1202	**O249**	100f. multicoloured	4·50	4·50

1976. Nos. 1253/7 additionally inscr "OFFICIAL" in English and Arabic.

O1258	**264**	5f. multicoloured	1·90	1·00
O1259	-	10f. multicoloured	1·90	1·10
O1260	-	15f. multicoloured	1·90	1·10
O1261	-	25f. multicoloured	5·00	1·70
O1262	-	50f. multicoloured	8·50	3·00

1978. As T 290, but additionally inscr "OFFICIAL" in English and Arabic.

O1338	5f. multicoloured	50	50
O1339	10f. multicoloured	50	50
O1340	15f. multicoloured	60	50
O1341	25f. multicoloured	1·20	50

O 342 Entrance to Baghdad University

1981

O1499	**O342**	45f. multicoloured	85	55
O1500	**O342**	50f. multicoloured	95	65

1982. As Nos. 1504/6, additionally inscr "OFFICIAL" in English and Arabic.

O1507	45f. multicoloured	1·90	55
O1508	50f. multicoloured	1·90	65
O1509	120f. multicoloured	4·75	1·70

1983. Nos. O1499/1500 surch.

O1581	60f. on 45f. mult	3·50	65
O1582	70f. on 50f. mult	4·25	1·00

1983. Design as T 371.

O1615	60f. yellow, black and pink	1·20	65
O1616	70f. yellow, black and pink	1·30	90

DESIGN: Nos. O1615/16, Aerial view of building.

1984. Multicoloured.

O1642	20f. Type **377**	50	50
O1643	30f. Type **377**	50	50
O1644	50f. As No. 1639	70	55
O1645	60f. As No. 1639	70	55

O400 Pres. Hussain

1986

O1740	**O400**	30f. multicoloured	85	20
O1741	**O400**	50f. multicoloured	1·20	30
O1742	**O400**	100f. multicoloured	2·30	90
O1743	**O400**	150f. multicoloured	3·00	2·20

Nos. O1740/3 are inscribed "POSTAGE".

Pt. 1

IRELAND

Ireland (Eire) consisting of Ireland less the six counties of Ulster, became the Irish Free State in 1922 and left the British Empire in 1949 when it became an independent republic.

1949. 12 pence = 1 shilling; 20 shillings = 1 pound.
1971. 100 (new) pence = 1 pound (Punt).
2002. 100 cents = 1 euro.

Rialtar
Sealadac
na
hÉireann
1922

(1) "Provisional Government of Ireland, 1922"

1922. Stamps of Great Britain optd with T 1 (date in thin figures and no full point).

1	**105**	½d. green	2·00	40
2	**104**	1d. red	2·50	40
4a	**104**	2½d. blue	1·75	4·00
5	**106**	3d. violet	4·75	5·00
6	**106**	4d. green	6·00	18·00
7	**107**	5d. brown	4·75	8·50
8	**108**	9d. black	13·00	27·00
9	**108**	10d. blue	8·50	48·00
17	**109**	2s.6d. brown	50·00	85·00
19	**109**	5s. red	85·00	£170
21	**109**	10s. blue	£170	£375

On Nos. 17, 19 and 21 the overprint is in four lines instead of five.

Rialtar
Sealadac
na
hÉireann
1922.

(2)

1922. Stamps of Great Britain optd with T 2 (date in thick figures followed by full point).

10	**105**	1½d. brown	2·75	1·25
12	**106**	2d. orange	6·00	50
31	**104**	1d. red	2·75	50
35	**104**	2½d. blue	6·00	24·00
36	**106**	3d. violet	4·00	2·00
37	**106**	4d. green	4·50	7·50
38	**107**	5d. brown	5·50	10·00
39	**107**	6d. purple	8·50	4·25
40	**108**	9d. black	14·00	21·00
41	**108**	9d. green	6·00	42·00
42	**108**	10d. blue	28·00	70·00
43	**108**	1s. brown	11·00	12·00
47	**105**	½d. green	1·00	1·75

Saorstát
Éireann
1922

5 "Irish Free State, 1922"

1922. Stamps of Great Britain optd with T 5.

52		½d. green	2·00	30
53	**104**	1d. red	2·50	50
54	**105**	1½d. brown	3·50	8·50
55	**106**	2d. orange	1·50	1·00
56	**104**	2½d. blue	7·50	10·00
57	**106**	3d. violet	4·25	11·00
58	**106**	4d. green	4·50	9·50
59	**107**	5d. brown	5·50	4·75
60	**107**	6d. purple	3·50	2·00
61	**108**	9d. green	5·50	5·50
62	**108**	10d. blue	21·00	70·00
63	**108**	1s. brown	7·00	11·00
86	**109**	2s.6d. brown	50·00	60·00
87	**109**	5s. red	80·00	£100
88	**109**	10s. blue	£190	£225

6 "Sword of Light"

7 Map of Ireland

8 Arms of Ireland

9 Celtic Cross

1922

71	**6**	½d. green	2·75	90
73	**7**	1½d. purple	2·25	2·50
75	**8**	2½d. brown	4·50	4·25
82	**6**	1s. blue	16·00	4·00
112	**7**	1d. red	30	10
114	**7**	2d. green	30	10
116	**9**	3d. blue (18½×22½ mm)	70	10
117	**8**	4d. blue	55	10
118	**6**	5d. violet (18½×22½ mm)	65	10
119b	**6**	6d. purple	1·25	20
119c	**6**	8d. red	80	1·00
120	**8**	9d. violet	1·50	80
121	**9**	10d. brown	60	80
121b	**9**	11d. red	1·50	3·00
227	**9**	3d. blue (17×21 mm)	40	15
228	**6**	5d. violet (17×21 mm)	30	15

12 Daniel O'Connell

1929. Centenary of Catholic Emancipation.

89	**12**	2d. green	70	45
90	**12**	3d. blue	4·25	9·50
91	**12**	9d. violet	4·25	5·00

13 Shannon Barrage

1930. Completion of Shannon Hydro-electric Scheme.

92	**13**	2d. deep brown	1·25	55

14 Reaper

1931. Bicentenary of Royal Dublin Society.

93	**14**	2d. blue	1·00	30

15 The Cross of Cong

1932. International Eucharistic Congress.

94	**15**	2d. green	2·00	30
95	**15**	3d. blue	3·25	5·00

16 Adoration of the Cross

1933. "Holy Year".

96	**16**	2d. green	2·25	15
97	**16**	3d. blue	3·50	2·50

17 Hurler

1934. 50th Anniv of Gaelic Athletic Assn.

98	**17**	2d. green	1·75	55

18 St. Patrick

1937

123b	**18**	2s.6d. green	1·50	3·25
124ca	**18**	5s. purple	4·00	9·00
125ba	**18**	10s. blue	4·00	16·00

19 Ireland and New Constitution

1937. Constitution Day.

105	**19**	2d. red	2·00	20
106	**19**	3d. blue	5·00	3·75

For similar stamps see Nos. 176/7.

20 Father Mathew

1938. Centenary of Temperance Crusade.

107	**20**	2d. black	2·50	50
108	**20**	3d. blue	12·00	6·50

21 George Washington, American Eagle and Irish Harp

1939. 150th Anniv of U.S. Constitution and Installation of First U.S. President.

109	**21**	2d. red	2·25	1·00
110	**21**	3d. blue	3·25	5·50

1941. 25th Anniv of Easter Rising (1916). (a) Provisional issue. Optd with two lines of Irish characters between the dates "1941" and "1916".

126	**7**	2d. orange	2·00	1·00
127	**9**	3d. blue	25·00	11·00

24 Volunteer and G.P.O., Dublin

(b) Definitive Issue.

128	**24**	2½d. black	3·25	1·25

25 Dr. Douglas Hyde

1943. 50th Anniv of Gaelic League.

129	**25**	½d. green	1·25	70
130	**25**	2½d. purple	2·00	10

26 Sir William Rowan Hamilton

1943. Centenary of Announcement of Discovery of Quaternions.

131	**26**	½d. green	40	70
132	**26**	2½d. brown	2·25	20

27 Bro. Michael O'Clery

1944. Death Tercentenary of Michael O'Clery (Franciscan historian) (commemorating the "Annals of the Four Masters").

133	**27**	½d. green	10	10
134	**27**	1s. brown	1·25	10

28 Edmund Ignatius Rice

1944. Death Centenary of Edmund Rice (founder of Irish Christian Brothers).

135	**28**	2½d. slate	1·75	45

29 "Youth sowing Seeds of Freedom"

1945. Death Centenary of Thomas Davis (founder of Young Ireland Movement).

136	**29**	2½d. blue	1·50	75
137	**29**	6d. purple	6·00	6·00

30 "Country and Homestead"

1946. Birth Centenaries of Michael Davitt and Charles Parnell (land reformers).

138	**30**	2½d. red	2·50	25
139	**30**	3d. blue	3·50	4·25

31 Angel Victor over Rock of Cashel

1948. Air. Inscr "VOX HIBERNIAE".

140	**31**	1d. brown	3·00	4·25
141	-	3d. blue	3·00	3·50
142	-	6d. purple	1·00	2·25
142b	-	8d. lake	7·00	9·00
143	-	1s. green	1·00	2·00
143a	**31**	1s.3d. orange	8·50	1·50
143b	**31**	1s.5d. blue	4·00	2·00

DESIGNS: 3d., 8d. Angel Victor over Lough Derg; 6d. Over Croagh Patrick; 1s. Over Glendalough.

35 Theobald Wolfe Tone

1948. 150th Anniv of Insurrection.

144	**35**	2½d. purple	1·00	10
145	**35**	3d. violet	3·25	4·00

36 Leinster House and Arms of Provinces

1949. International Recognition of Republic.

146	**36**	2½d. brown	1·75	10
147	**36**	3d. blue	6·50	4·25

37 J. C. Mangan

1949. Death Centenary of James Clarence Mangan (poet).

148	**37**	1d. green	1·50	35

38 Statue of St. Peter, Rome

1950. Holy Year.

149	**38**	2½d. violet	1·00	40
150	**38**	3d. blue	8·00	12·00
151	**38**	9d. brown	8·00	12·00

39 Thomas Moore

1952. Death Centenary of Thomas Moore (poet).

152	**39**	2½d. purple	1·00	10
153	**39**	3½d. olive	1·75	4·00

40 Irish Harp

1953. "An Tostal" (Ireland at Home) Festival.

154	**40**	2½d. green	1·75	35
155	**40**	1s.4d. blue	19·00	27·00

41 Robert Emmet

1953. 150th Death Anniv of Emmet (patriot).

156	**41**	3d. green	3·00	15
157	**41**	1s.3d. red	45·00	10·00

42 Madonna and Child (Della Robbia)

1954. Marian Year.

158	**42**	3d. blue	1·00	10
159	**42**	5d. green	2·00	3·25

43 Cardinal Newman (first Rector)

1954. Centenary of Founding of Catholic University of Ireland.

160	**43**	2d. purple	1·50	10
161	**43**	1s.3d. blue	16·00	6·00

44 Statue of Commodore Barry

1956. Barry Commemoration.

162	**44**	3d. lilac	1·00	10
163	**44**	1s.3d. blue	4·50	8·00

45 John Redmond

1957. Birth Centenary of John Redmond (politician).

164	**45**	3d. blue	1·00	10
165	**45**	1s.3d. purple	9·00	15·00

46 Thomas O'Crohan

1957. Birth Cent of Thomas O'Crohan (author).

166	**46**	2d. purple	1·00	15
167	**46**	5d. violet	1·00	4·50

47 Admiral Brown

1957. Death Cent of Admiral William Brown.

168	**47**	3d. blue	3·00	20
169	**47**	1s.3d. red	25·00	16·00

48 "Father Wadding" (Ribera)

1957. Death Tercentenary of Father Luke Wadding (theologian).

170	**48**	3d. blue	2·00	10
171	**48**	1s.3d. lake	15·00	8·50

49 Tom Clarke

1958. Birth Centenary of Thomas J. ("Tom") Clarke (patriot).

172	**49**	3d. green	2·00	10
173	**49**	1s.3d. brown	4·00	11·00

50 Mother Mary Aikenhead

1958. Death Centenary of Mother Mary Aikenhead (foundress of Irish Sisters of Charity).

174	**50**	3d. blue	2·00	10
175	**50**	1s.3d. red	11·00	8·00

1958. 21st Anniv of Irish Constitution.

176	**19**	3d. brown	1·00	10
177	**19**	5d. green	1·50	4·50

51 Arthur Guinness

1959. Bicentenary of Guinness Brewery.

178	**51**	3d. purple	3·00	10
179	**51**	1s.3d. blue	12·00	12·00

52 "The Flight of the Holy Family"

1960. World Refugee Year.

180	**52**	3d. purple	40	10
181	**52**	1s.3d. sepia	60	3·50

53 Conference Emblem

1960. 1st Anniv of Europa.

182	**53**	6d. brown	12·00	3·00
183	**53**	1s.3d. violet	26·00	20·00

54 Dublin Airport, de Havilland Dragon Mk 2 EI-ABI "Iolar" and Boeing 720 EI-ALA

1961. Silver Jubilee of Aer Lingus Airlines.

184	**54**	6d. blue	1·75	3·50
185	**54**	1s.3d. green	2·25	5·00

55 St Patrick

1961. 15th Death Centenary of St. Patrick.

186	**55**	3d. blue	1·00	10
187	**55**	8d. purple	2·75	5·50
188	**55**	1s.3d. green	2·75	1·60

56 John O'Donovan and Edugen O'Curry

1962. Death Centenaries of O'Donovan and O'Curry (scholars).

189	**56**	3d. red	30	10
190	**56**	1s.3d. purple	1·25	2·25

57 Europa "Tree"

1962. Europa.

191	**57**	6d. red	70	1·00
192	**57**	1s.3d. turquoise	80	1·50

58 Campaign Emblem

1963. Freedom from Hunger.

193	**58**	4d. violet	50	10
194	**58**	1s.3d. red	2·75	2·75

59 "Co-operation"

1963. Europa.

195	**59**	6d. red	1·25	75
196	**59**	1s.3d. blue	4·00	3·50

60 Centenary Emblem

1963. Centenary of Red Cross.

197	**60**	4d. red and grey	50	10
198	**60**	1s.3d. red, grey and green	1·50	2·25

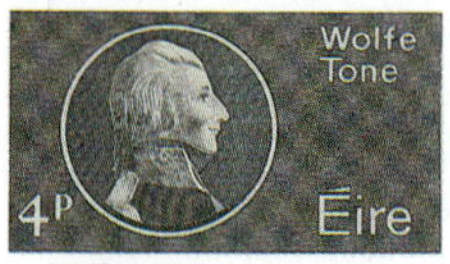

61 Wolfe Tone

1964. Birth Bicentenary of Wolfe Tone (revolutionary).

199	**61**	4d. black	50	10
200	**61**	1s.3d. blue	1·90	2·00

62 Irish Pavilion at Fair

1964. New York World's Fair.

201	**62**	5d. multicoloured	50	10
202	**62**	1s.5d. multicoloured	2·00	2·00

63 Europa "Flower"

1964. Europa.

203	**63**	8d. green and blue	1·50	1·25
204	**63**	1s.5d. brown and orange	7·00	2·75

64 "Waves of Communications"

1965. Centenary of I.T.U.

205	**64**	3d. blue and green	30	10
206	**64**	8d. black and green	1·25	1·60

65 W. B. Yeats (poet)

1965. Birth Centenary of Yeats.

207	**65**	5d. black, brown and green	30	10
208	**65**	1s.5d. black, green & brown	2·25	1·75

66 I.C.Y. Emblem

1965. International Co-operation Year.

209	**66**	3d. blue	60	10
210	**66**	10d. brown	1·00	3·00

67 Europa "Sprig"

1965. Europa.

211	**67**	8d. black and red	1·50	1·00
212	**67**	1s.5d. purple and turquoise	7·00	3·50

68 James Connolly

1966. 50th Anniv of Easter Rising.

213	**68**	3d. black and blue	65	10
214	-	3d. black and bronze	65	10
215	-	5d. black and olive	65	10
216	-	5d. black, orange and green	65	10
217	-	7d. black and brown	65	2·25
218	-	7d. black and green	65	2·25
219	-	1s.5d. black and turquoise	65	1·50
220	-	1s.5d. black and green	65	1·50

DESIGNS: No. 214, Thomas J. Clarke; No. 215, P. H. Pearse; No. 216, "Marching to Freedom"; No. 217, Eamonn Ceannt; No. 218, Sean MacDiarmada; No. 219, Thomas MacDonagh; No. 220, Joseph Plunkett.

76 Roger Casement

1966. 50th Death Anniv of Roger Casement (patriot).

221	**76**	5d. black	15	10
222	**76**	1s. brown	30	50

77 Europa "Ship"

1966. Europa.

223	**77**	7d. green and orange	1·00	40
224	**77**	1s.5d. green and grey	2·00	1·60

78 Interior of Abbey (from lithograph)

1966. 750th Anniv of Ballintubber Abbey.

225	**78**	5d. brown	10	10
226	**78**	1s. black	20	25

79 Cogwheels

1967. Europa.

229	**79**	7d. green, gold and cream	75	40
230	**79**	1s.5d. red, gold and cream	2·25	1·00

80 Maple Leaves

1967. Canadian Centennial.

231	**80**	5d. multicoloured	10	10
232	**80**	1s.5d. multicoloured	20	75

81 Rock of Cashel (from photo by Edwin Smith)

1967. International Tourist Year.

233	**81**	7d. sepia	15	20
234	**81**	10d. blue	15	40

82 1c. Fenian Stamp Essay

1967. Centenary of Fenian Rising.

235	**82**	5d. black and green	10	10
236	-	1s. black and pink	20	30

DESIGN: 1s.24c. Fenian Stamp Essay.

84 Jonathan Swift

1967. 300th Birth Anniv of Jonathan Swift.

237	**84**	3d. black and grey	10	10
238	-	1s.5d. brown and blue	20	30

DESIGN: 1s.5d. Gulliver and Lilliputians.

86 Europa Key

1968. Europa.

239	**86**	7d. red, gold and brown	60	50
240	**86**	1s.5d. blue, gold and brown	90	1·00

87 St Mary's Cathedral, Limerick

1968. 800th Anniv of St. Mary's Cathedral, Limerick.

241	**87**	5d. blue	10	10
242	**87**	10d. green	20	60

88 Countess Markievicz

1968. Birth Centenary of Countess Markievicz (patriot).

243	**88**	3d. black	10	10
244	**88**	1s.5d. indigo and blue	20	20

89 James Connolly

1968. Birth Centenary of James Connolly (patriot).

245	**89**	6d. brown and chocolate	20	75
246	**89**	1s. green, lt green & myrtle	20	10

90 Stylized Dog (brooch)

92 Winged Ox (Symbol of St. Luke)

1968

247	**90**	½d. orange	10	30
248	**90**	1d. green	15	10
249	**90**	2d. ochre	50	10
250	**90**	3d. blue	35	10
251	**90**	4d. red	30	10
252	**90**	5d. green	1·25	75
253	**90**	6d. brown	30	10
254	-	7d. brown and yellow	45	3·75
255	-	8d. brown and chestnut	45	2·25
256	-	9d. blue and green	50	10
257	-	10d. brown and violet	1·50	2·50
258	-	1s. chocolate and brown	40	10
259	-	1s.9d. black and turquoise	4·00	2·75
260	**92**	2s.6d. multicoloured	1·75	30
261	**92**	5s. multicoloured	3·00	3·00
262	-	10s. multicoloured	4·75	4·25

DESIGNS—As Type **90**: 7d., 8d., 9d., 10d., 1s., 1s.9d., Stag. As Type **92**: 10s Eagle (Symbol of St. John The Evangelist).

See also Nos. 287, etc.

94 Human Rights Emblem

1968. Human Rights Year.

263	**94**	5d. yellow, gold and black	15	10
264	**94**	7d. yellow, gold and red	15	40

95 Dail Eireann Assembly

1969. 50th Anniv of Dail Eireann (1st National Parliament).

265	**95**	6d. green	15	10
266	**95**	9d. blue	15	30

96 Colonnade

1969. Europa.

267	**96**	9d. grey, ochre and blue	1·00	1·10
268	**96**	1s.9d. grey, gold and red	1·25	1·40

97 Quadruple I.L.O. Emblems

1969. 50th Anniv of I.L.O.

269	**97**	6d. black and grey	20	10
270	**97**	9d. black and yellow	20	25

98 "The Last Supper and Crucifixion" (Evie Hone Window, Eton Chapel)

1969. Contemporary Irish Art (1st issue).

271	**98**	1s. multicoloured	30	1·50

See also Nos. 280, 306, 317, 329, 362, 375, 398, 408, 452, 470 and 498.

99 Mahatma Gandhi

1969. Birth Centenary of Mahatma Gandhi.

272	**99**	6d. black and green	50	10
273	**99**	1s.9d. black and yellow	75	90

100 Symbolic Bird in Tree

1970. European Conservation Year.

274	**100**	6d. bistre and black	20	10
275	**100**	9d. violet and black	25	80

101 "Flaming Sun"

1970. Europa.

276	**101**	6d. violet and silver	55	10
277	**101**	9d. brown and silver	80	1·25
278	**101**	1s.9d. grey and silver	1·75	2·00

102 "Sailing Boats" (Peter Monamy)

1970. 250th Anniv of Royal Cork Yacht Club.

279	**102**	4d. multicoloured	15	10

103 "Madonna of Eire" (Mainie Jellett)

1970. Contemporary Irish Art (2nd issue).

280	**103**	1s. multicoloured	15	20

104 Thomas MacCurtain

1970. 50th Death Annivs of Irish Patriots.

281	**104**	9d. black, violet and grey	1·00	25
282	-	9d. black, violet and grey	1·00	25
283	**104**	2s.9d. black, blue and grey	1·75	1·50
284	-	2s.9d. black, blue and grey	1·75	1·50

DESIGN: Nos. 282 and 284, Terence MacSwiney.

106 Kevin Barry

1970. 50th Death Anniv of Kevin Barry (patriot).

285	**106**	6d. green	30	10
286	**106**	1s.2d. blue	40	1·10

1971. Decimal Currency. As Nos. 247/62 but with face values in new currency, without "p", and some colours changed.

287	**90**	½p. green	10	10
289	**90**	1½p. red	15	50
291	**90**	2½p. brown	15	10
293	**90**	3½p. orange	25	10
294	**90**	4p. violet	20	10
295	-	5p. brown and olive	1·00	20
296	-	6p. grey and brown	3·50	1·00
297	-	7½p. mauve and brown	50	1·10
299b	**92**	12p. multicoloured	60	1·25
340	**90**	1p. blue	10	10
341	**90**	2p. green	10	10
342	**90**	3p. brown	10	10
344	**90**	5p. green	60	10
346	**90**	6p. grey	20	10
347	-	7p. blue and green	70	35
348	**90**	7p. green	35	10
349	-	8p. brown and deep brown	60	50
350	**90**	8p. brown	30	10
351	-	9p. black and green	70	30
352	**90**	9p. green	30	10
352a	**90**	9½p. red	35	20
353	**92**	10p. multicoloured	1·25	30
354	-	10p. black and lilac	70	10
354a	**90**	10p. mauve	70	10
355	-	11p. black and red	45	30
355a	-	12p. black and green	55	10
355b	**90**	12p. green	30	10
355c	-	13p. brown	40	1·50
356	**92**	15p. multicoloured	55	40
356a	**90**	15p. blue	40	10
356b	-	16p. black and green	40	1·00
356c	**92**	17p. multicoloured	50	1·25
357	**92**	20p. multicoloured	50	15
358	-	50p. multicoloured	1·00	30
359	-	£1 multicoloured	1·75	30
478	**90**	18p. red	45	50
479	**90**	19p. blue	55	1·75
480	**90**	22p. blue	65	10
481	**90**	24p. brown	1·50	1·25
482	**90**	26p. green	1·50	40
483	**90**	29p. mauve	1·75	2·75

DESIGNS—As Type **90**: 5p. (295); 6p. (296); 7p. (347); 7½p., 8p., 9p. (351) 10p. (354), 11p., 12p. (No. 355a), 13p., 16p. Stag. As Type **92**: 50p., £1, Eagle (symbol of St. John the Evangelist).

107 "Europa Chain"

1971. Europa.

302	**107**	4p. brown and green	1·00	10
303	**107**	6p. black and blue	3·75	2·50

108 J. M. Synge

1971. Birth Centenary of J. M. Synge (playwright).

304	**108**	4p. multicoloured	15	10
305	**108**	10p. multicoloured	60	80

109 "An Island Man" (Jack B. Yeats)

1971. Contemporary Irish Art (3rd issue). Birth Centenary of J. B. Yeats (artist).

306	**109**	6p. multicoloured	55	55

110 Racial Harmony Symbol

1971. Racial Equality Year.

307	**110**	4p. red	20	10
308	**110**	10p. black	50	75

111 "Madonna and Child" (statue by J. Hughes)

1971. Christmas.

309	**111**	2½p. black, gold and green	10	10
310	**111**	6p. black, gold and blue	65	65

112 Heart

1972. World Health Day.

311	**112**	2½p. gold and brown	30	15
312	**112**	12p. silver and grey	1·10	1·75

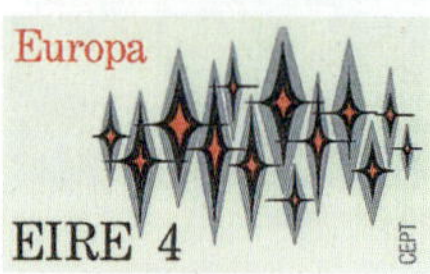

113 "Communications"

1972. Europa.

313	**113**	4p. orange, black and silver	3·50	25
314	**113**	6p. blue, black and silver	9·50	4·75

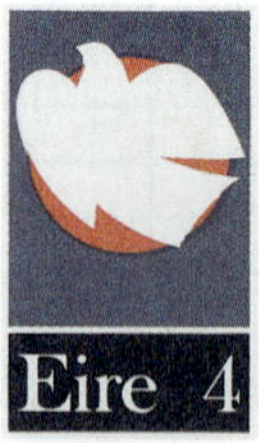

114 Dove and Moon

1972. Patriot Dead 1922–1923.

315	**114**	4p. multicoloured	10	10
316	**114**	6p. yellow, green & dp grn	65	50

115 "Black Lake" (Gerard Dillon)

1972. Contemporary Irish Art (4th issue).

317	**115**	3p. multicoloured	60	35

116 "Horseman" (Carved Slab)

1972. 50th Anniv of Olympic Council of Ireland.

318	**116**	3p. yellow, black and gold	15	10
319	**116**	6p. pink, black and gold	55	60

117 Madonna and Child (from Book of Kells)

1972. Christmas.

320	**117**	2½p. multicoloured	10	10
321	**117**	4p. multicoloured	25	10
322	**117**	12p. multicoloured	1·00	1·00

118 2d. Stamp of 1922

1972. 50th Anniv of 1st Irish Postage Stamp.

323	**118**	6p. grey and green	60	60
MS324		72×104 mm. No. 323×4	5·50	10·00

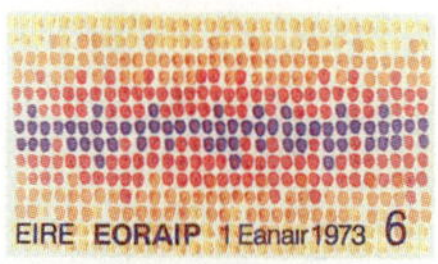

119 Celtic Head Motif

1973. Entry into European Communities.

325	**119**	6p. multicoloured	60	90
326	**119**	12p. multicoloured	80	1·10

120 Europa "Posthorn"

1973. Europa.

327	**120**	4p. blue	1·75	10
328	**120**	6p. black	3·75	3·25

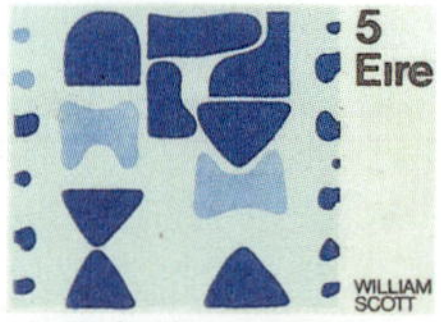

121 "Berlin Blues II" (W. Scott)

1973. Contemporary Irish Art (5th issue).

329	**121**	5p. blue and black	40	30

122 Weather Map

1973. Centenary of I.M.O./W.M.O.

330	**122**	3½p. multicoloured	30	10
331	**122**	12p. multicoloured	1·10	2·00

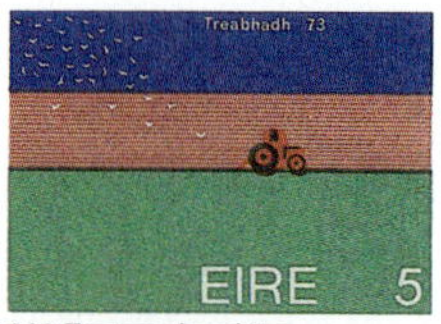

123 Tractor ploughing

1973. World Ploughing Championships, Wellington Bridge.

332	**123**	5p. multicoloured	15	10
333	**123**	7p. multicoloured	1·00	50

124 "Flight into Egypt" (Jan de Cock)

1973. Christmas.

334	**124**	3½p. multicoloured	15	10
335	**124**	12p. multicoloured	1·10	1·50

125 Daunt Island Lightship and "Mary Stanford" (Ballycotton Lifeboat), 1936

1974. 150th Anniv of R.N.L.I.

336	**125**	5p. multicoloured	30	30

126 "Edmund Burke" (statue by J. H. Foley)

1974. Europa.

337	**126**	5p. black and blue	1·50	10
338	**126**	7p. black and green	7·00	2·50

127 "Oliver Goldsmith" (statue by J. H. Foley)

1974. Death Bicentenary of Oliver Goldsmith (writer).

360	**127**	3½p. black and yellow	25	10
361	**127**	12p. black and green	1·25	1·00

128 "Kitchen Table" (Norah McGuiness)

1974. Contemporary Irish Art (6th issue).

362	**128**	5p. multicoloured	35	30

129 Rugby Players

1974. Centenary of Irish Rugby Football.

363	**129**	3½p. green	50	10
364	**129**	12p. multicoloured	2·50	2·75

130 U.P.U. "Postmark"

1974. Centenary of Universal Postal Union.

365	**130**	5p. green and black	25	10
366	**130**	7p. blue and black	35	55

131 "Madonna and Child" (Bellini)

1974. Christmas.

367	**131**	5p. multicoloured	15	10
368	**131**	15p. multicoloured	60	90

132 "Peace"

1975. International Women's Year.

369	**132**	8p. purple and blue	25	75
370	**132**	15p. blue and green	50	1·25

133 "Castletown Hunt" (R. Healy)

1975. Europa.

371	**133**	7p. grey	2·50	15
372	**133**	9p. green	6·50	2·50

134 Putting

1975. Ninth European Amateur Golf Team Championship, Killarney.

373	**134**	6p. multicoloured	75	45
374	-	9p. multicoloured	1·50	1·50

No. 374 is similar to Type **134** but shows a different view of the putting green.

135 "Bird of Prey" (sculpture by Oisin Kelly)

1975. Contemporary Irish Art (7th issue).

375	**135**	15p. brown	75	75

136 Nano Nagle (founder) and Waifs

1975. Bicentenary of Presentation Order of Nuns.

376	**136**	5p. black and blue	20	10
377	**136**	7p. black and brown	30	30

137 Tower of St. Anne's Church, Shandon

1975. European Architectural Heritage Year.

378	**137**	5p. brown	25	10
379	**137**	6p. multicoloured	60	85
380	-	7p. blue	60	10
381	-	9p. multicoloured	65	80

DESIGN: Nos. 380/1, Interior of Holycross Abbey, Co. Tipperary.

138 St. Oliver Plunkett (commemorative medal by Imogen Stuart)

1975. Canonization of Oliver Plunkett.

382	**138**	7p. black	15	10
383	**138**	15p. brown	55	45

139 "Madonna and Child" (Fra Filippo Lippi)

1975. Christmas.

384	**139**	5p. multicoloured	15	10
385	**139**	7p. multicoloured	20	10
386	**139**	10p. multicoloured	75	60

140 James Larkin (from a drawing by Sean O'Sullivan)

1975. Birth Centenary of James Larkin (Trade Union Leader).

387	**140**	7p. green and grey	20	10
388	**140**	11p. brown and yellow	40	55

141 Alexander Graham Bell

1976. Centenary of Telephone.

389	**141**	9p. multicoloured	20	10
390	**141**	15p. multicoloured	45	50

142 1847 Benjamin Franklin Essay

1976. Bicentenary of American Revolution.

391	-	7p. blue, red and silver	20	10
392	-	8p. blue, red and silver	25	1·10
393	**142**	9p. blue, orange and silver	25	10
394	**142**	15p. red, grey and silver	45	75
MS395		95×75 mm. Nos. 391/4	2·75	8·00

DESIGNS: 7p. Thirteen Stars; 8p. Fifty Stars.

143 Spirit Barrel

1976. Europa. Irish Delft. Multicoloured.

396	9p. Type **143**	1·25	20
397	11p. Dish	4·25	1·60

144 "The Lobster Pots, West of Ireland" (Paul Henry)

1976. Contemporary Irish Art (8th issue).

398	**144**	15p. multicoloured	60	60

145 Radio Waves

1976. 50th Anniv of Irish Broadcasting Service.

399	**145**	9p. blue and green	20	10
400	-	11p. brown, red and blue	60	1·00

DESIGN—VERT: 11p. Transmitter, radio waves and globe.

146 "The Nativity" (Lorenzo Monaco)

1976. Christmas.

401	**146**	7p. multicoloured	15	10
402	**146**	9p. multicoloured	15	10
403	**146**	15p. multicoloured	55	55

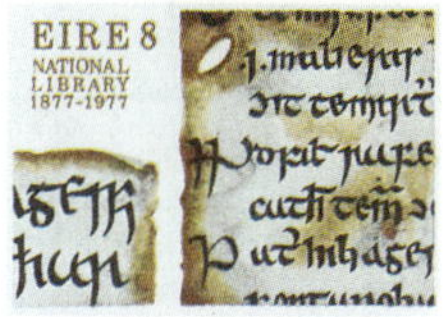

147 16th Century Manuscript

1977. Centenaries of National Library (8p.) and National Museum (10p.). Multicoloured.

404	8p. Type **147**	30	30
405	10p. Prehistoric stone	40	35

148 Ballynahinch, Galway

1977. Europa. Multicoloured.

406	10p. Type **148**	2·00	25
407	12p. Lough Tay, Wicklow	6·00	1·50

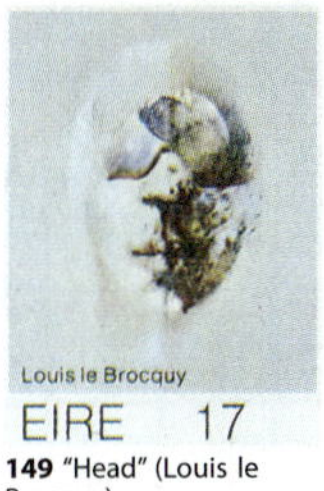

149 "Head" (Louis le Brocquy)

1977. Contemporary Irish Art (9th issue).

408	**149**	17p. multicoloured	55	75

150 Guide and Tents

1977. Scouting and Guiding. Multicoloured.

409	8p. Type **150**	45	10
410	17p. Tent and Scout saluting	95	1·75

151 "The Shanachie" (drawing by Jack B. Yeats)

1977. Anniversaries.

411	**151**	10p. black	35	15
412	-	12p. black	45	1·00

DESIGNS AND EVENTS: 10p. Type **151** (Golden Jubilee of Irish Folklore Society); 12p. The philosopher Eriugena (1100th death anniv).

152 "Electricity" (Golden Jubilee of Electricity Supply Board)

1977. Golden Jubilees.

413	**152**	10p. multicoloured	15	10
414	-	12p. multicoloured	30	1·40
415	-	17p. black and brown	65	35

DESIGNS: 12p. Bulls (from Irish coins) (Agricultural Credit Act); 17p. Greyhound (Greyhound Track Racing).

153 "The Holy Family" (Giorgione)

1977. Christmas.

416	**153**	8p. multicoloured	20	10
417	**153**	10p. multicoloured	20	10
418	**153**	17p. multicoloured	75	1·25

154 Junkers W.33 D-1167 "Bremen" in Flight

1978. 50th Anniv of 1st East–West Transatlantic Flight.

419	**154**	10p. black and blue	20	15
420	**154**	17p. black and brown	35	1·10

155 Spring Gentian

1978. Wild Flowers. Multicoloured.

421		8p. Type **155**	25	40
422		10p. Strawberry tree	25	15
423		11p. Large-flowered Butterwort	25	50
424		17p. St. Dabeoc's Heath	45	2·00

156 Catherine McAuley

1978. Anniversaries and Events. Multicoloured.

425		10p. Type **156** (founder of Sisters of Mercy) (birth bicent)	25	10
426		11p. Doctor performing vaccination (Global Eradication of Smallpox) (horiz)	35	80
427		17p. "Self-portrait" Sir William Orpen (painter) (birth cent)	55	1·10

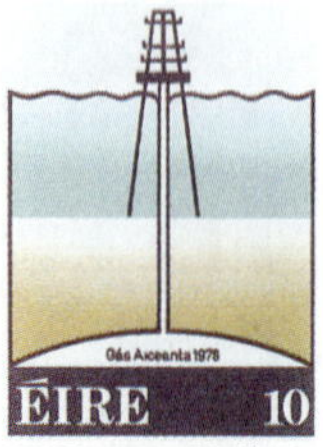

157 Diagram of Drilling Rig

1978. Arrival Onshore of Natural Gas.

428	**157**	10p. multicoloured	30	30

158 Farthing

1978. 50th Anniv of Irish Currency.

429	**158**	8p. black, copper and green	25	20
430	-	10p. black, silver and green	30	10
431	-	11p. black, copper & brn	35	50
432	-	17p. black, silver and blue	65	1·00

DESIGNS: 10p. Florin; 11p. Penny; 17p. Half-crown.

159 "Virgin and Child" (Guercino)

1978. Christmas.

433	**159**	8p. brown, blue and gold	15	10
434	**159**	10p. brown, blue & purple	15	10
435	**159**	17p. brown, blue and green	45	1·40

160 Conolly Folly, Castletown

1978. Europa.

436	**160**	10p. brown	2·25	15
437	-	11p. green	2·25	1·75

DESIGN: 11p. Dromoland Belvedere.

161 Athletes in Cross-country Race

1979. 7th World Cross-country Championships, Limerick. Multicoloured.

438	**161**	8p. multicoloured	20	30

162 "European Communities" (in languages of member nations)

1979. 1st Direct Elections to European Assembly.

439	**162**	10p. green	15	15
440	**162**	11p. violet	15	35

163 Sir Rowland Hill

1979. Death Centenary of Sir Rowland Hill.

441	**163**	17p. black, grey and red	30	60

164 Winter Wren

1979. Birds. Multicoloured.

442		8p. Type **164**	40	80
443		10p. Great crested grebe	40	15
444		11p. White-fronted goose	45	80
445		17p. Peregrine falcon	70	2·00

165 "A Happy Flower" (David Gallagher)

1979. International Year of the Child. Paintings by Children. Multicoloured.

446		10p. Type **165**	20	10
447		11p. "Myself and My Skipping Rope" (Lucy Norman) (vert)	25	60
448		17p. "Swans on a Lake" (Nicola O'Dwyer)	35	85

166 Pope John Paul II

1979. Visit of Pope John Paul II.

449	**166**	12p. multicoloured	30	20

167 Brother with Child

1979. Anniversaries and Events.

450	**167**	9½p. brown and mauve	20	10
451	-	11p. orange, black and blue	20	70
452	-	20p. multicoloured	40	1·40

DESIGNS—VERT: 11p. Windmill and sun (Int Energy Conservation Month). HORIZ: 9½p. Type **167** (Cent of Hospitaller Order of St. John of God in Ireland); 20p. "Seated Figure" (sculpture F. E. McWilliam) (Contemporary Irish Art (10th issue)).

168 Patrick Pearse, "Liberty" and G.P.O., Dublin

1979. Birth Centenary of Patrick Pearse (patriot).

453	**168**	12p. multicoloured	30	15

169 "Madonna and Child" (panel painting from the Domnach Airgid Shrine)

1979. Christmas.

454	**169**	9½p. multicoloured	15	10
455	**169**	20p. multicoloured	30	55

170 Bianconi Long Car, 1836

1979. Europa. Multicoloured.

456		12p. Type **170**	1·50	30
457		13p. Transatlantic cable, Valentia, 1866	2·00	1·40

171 John Baptist de la Salle (founder)

1980. Cent of Arrival of De La Salle Order.

458	**171**	12p. multicoloured	30	30

172 George Bernard Shaw

1980. Europa. Personalities. Multicoloured.

459		12p. Type **172**	1·50	50
460		13p. Oscar Wilde (29×40 mm)	2·50	2·50

173 Stoat

1980. Wildlife. Multicoloured.

461		12p. Type **173**	25	40
462		15p. Arctic hare	25	15
463		16p. Red fox	25	80

464	25p. Red deer	35	1·60
MS465	73×97 mm. Nos. 461/4	1·00	2·75

174 Playing Bodhran and Whistle

1980. Traditional Music and Dance. Mult.

466	12p. Type **174**	15	10
467	15p. Playing Uilleann pipes	20	15
468	25p. Dancing	35	1·10

175 Sean O'Casey

1980. Commemorations.

469	12p. multicoloured	20	10
470	25p. black, buff and brown	35	55

DESIGNS AND COMMEMORATIONS: 12p. Type **175** (playwright) (birth centenary); 25p. "Gold Painting No. 57" (P. Scott) (Contemporary Irish Art (11th issue)).

176 Nativity Scene (painting by Geraldine McNulty)

1980. Christmas.

471	**176**	12p. multicoloured	15	10
472	**176**	15p. multicoloured	20	10
473	**176**	25p. multicoloured	40	1·25

177 Boyle Air-pump, 1659

1981. Irish Science and Technology. Mult.

474	12p. Type **177**	20	10
475	15p. Ferguson tractor, 1936	25	10
476	16p. Parsons turbine, 1884	30	90
477	25p. Holland submarine, 1878	35	1·25

178 "The Legend of the Cock and the Pot"

1981. Europa. Folklore. Paintings by Maria Simonds-Gooding.

491	**178**	18p. black, yellow and red	1·50	10
492	-	19p. black, orange & yellow	3·00	1·50

DESIGN: 19p. "The Angel with the Scales of Judgement".

179 Cycling

1981. 50th Anniv of "An Oige" (Irish Youth Hostel Association). Multicoloured.

493	15p. Type **179**	25	40
494	18p. Hill-walking (horiz)	25	10
495	19p. Mountaineering (horiz)	25	95
496	30p. Rock-climbing	40	95

180 Jeremiah O'Donovan Rossa

1981. 150th Birth Anniv of Jeremiah O'Donovan Rossa (politician).

497	**180**	15p. multicoloured	60	30

181 "Railway Embankment" (W. J. Leech)

1981. Contemporary Irish Art (12th issue).

498	**181**	30p. multicoloured	1·00	70

182 James Hoban and White House

1981. 150th Death Anniv of James Hoban (White House architect).

499	**182**	18p. multicoloured	50	30

183 "Arkle" (steeplechaser)

1981. Famous Irish Horses. Multicoloured.

500	18p. Type **183**	50	1·00
501	18p. "Boomerang" (show-jumper)	50	1·00
502	22p. "King of Diamonds" (Draught horse)	50	30
503	24p. "Ballymoss" (flat-racer)	50	70
504	36p. "Coosheen Finn" (Connemara pony)	60	1·00

184 "Nativity" (F. Barocci)

1981. Christmas.

505	**184**	18p. multicoloured	25	10
506	**184**	22p. multicoloured	30	10
507	**184**	36p. multicoloured	80	1·50

185 Eviction Scene

1981. Anniversaries. Multicoloured.

508	18p. Type **185**	65	25
509	22p. Royal Dublin Society emblem	75	30

ANNIVERSARIES: 18p. Centenary of Land Law (Ireland) Act. 22p. Royal Dublin Society (organization for the advancement of agriculture, industry, art and science), 250th Anniv.

186 Upper Lake, Killarney National Park

1982. 50th Anniv of Killarney National Park. Multicoloured.

510	18p. Type **186**	40	20
511	36p. Eagle's Nest	85	1·60

187 "The Stigmatization of St. Francis" (Sassetta)

1982. Religious Anniversaries.

512	**187**	22p. multicoloured	50	15
513	-	24p. brown	75	85

DESIGNS AND ANNIVERSARIES: 22p. Type **187** (St. Francis of Assisi (founder of Franciscan order) (500th birth anniv); 24p. Francis Makemie (founder of American Presbyterianism) and old Presbyterian Church, Ramelton, Co. Donegal (300th anniv of ordination).

188 The Great Famine, 1845–50

1982. Europa. Historic Events.

514	**188**	26p. black and stone	4·50	50
515	-	29p. multicoloured	6·50	5·00

DESIGN—HORIZ: 29p. The coming of Christianity to Ireland.

189 Padraic O. Conaire (writer) (birth centenary)

1982. Anniversaries of Cultural Figures.

516	**189**	22p. black and blue	25	30
517	-	26p. black and brown	55	30
518	-	29p. black and blue	65	1·75
519	-	44p. black and grey	65	1·60

DESIGNS AND ANNIVERSARIES: 26p. James Joyce (writer) (birth centenary); 29p. John Field (musician) (birth centenary); 44p. Charles Kickham (writer) (death centenary).

190 Porbeagle Shark

1982. Marine Life. Multicoloured.

520	22p. Type **190**	75	1·25
521	22p. Common European oyster	75	1·25
522	26p. Atlantic salmon	90	30
523	29p. Dublin Bay prawn	90	2·25

191 "St. Patrick" (Galway hooker)

1982. Irish Boats. Multicoloured.

524	22p. Type **191**	75	1·25
525	22p. Currach (horiz)	75	1·25
526	26p. "Asgard II" (cadet brigantine) (horiz)	90	30
527	29p. Howth 17 foot yacht	90	2·25

192 "Irish House of Commons" (painting by Francis Wheatley)

1982. Bicentenary of Grattan's Parliament and Birth Centenary of Eamon de Valera. Multicoloured.

528	22p. Type **192**	35	1·25
529	26p. Eamon de Valera (vert)	40	40

193 "Madonna and Child" (sculpture)

1982. Christmas.

530	**193**	22p. multicoloured	30	90
531	**193**	26p. multicoloured	30	35

194 Aughnanure Castle

1983. Irish Architecture.

532	-	1p. blue	10	10
533	-	2p. green	20	10
534	-	3p. black	20	10
535	-	4p. red	20	10
536	-	5p. brown	30	10
537	-	6p. blue	30	15
538	-	7p. green	30	1·00
539	-	10p. black	30	10
540	-	12p. brown	30	1·50
541	**194**	15p. green	45	35
542	**194**	20p. purple	50	45
543	**194**	22p. blue	50	10
544	-	23p. green	85	1·25
544a	-	24p. brown	1·25	35
545	-	26p. black	75	10
545c	-	28p. red	75	45
546	-	29p. green	70	65
547	-	30p. black	70	30
547c	-	32p. brown	2·50	2·75
547d	-	37p. blue	1·00	2·75
547e	-	39p. red	2·50	2·75
548	-	44p. black and grey	1·00	70

548b	-	46p. green and grey	6·50	2·00
549	-	50p. blue and grey	1·75	65
550	-	£1 brown and grey	4·50	3·50
550b	-	£1 blue and grey	5·00	1·25
550c	-	£2 green and black	6·50	5·50
551	-	£5 red and grey	12·00	6·00

DESIGNS—HORIZ: (As T **194**): 1 to 5p. Central Pavilion, Dublin Botanic Gardens; 6 to 12p. Dr. Steevens' Hospital, Dublin; 28 to 37p. St. MacDara's Church. (37×21 mm); 46p., £1 (No. 550) Cahir Castle; 50p., £2 Casino Marino. £5 Central Bus Station, Dublin. VERT: (As T **194**): 23 to 26p., 39p. Cormac's Chapel. (21×37 mm); 44p., £1 (No. 550b) Killarney Cathedral.

195 Ouzel Gallery Goblet

1983. Bicentenaries of Dublin Chamber of Commerce (22p.) and Bank of Ireland (26p.). Multicoloured.

552	22p. Type **195**	30	65
553	26p. Bank of Ireland building (horiz)	35	35

196 Padraig O. Siochfhradha (writer and teacher)

1983. Anniversaries. Multicoloured.

554	26p. Type **196** (birth cent)	50	75
555	29p. Young Boys' Brigade member (centenary)	90	1·50

197 Neolithic Carved Pattern, Newgrange Tomb

1983. Europa.

556	**197**	26p. black and yellow	3·50	50
557	-	29p. black, brown & yellow	8·50	5·50

DESIGN: 29p. Sir William Rowan Hamilton's formulae for the multiplication of quaternions.

198 Kerry Blue Terrier

1983. Irish Dogs. Multicoloured.

558	22p. Type **198**	75	35
559	26p. Irish wolfhound	85	45
560	26p. Irish water spaniel	85	45
561	29p. Irish terrier	1·00	2·25
562	44p. Irish setters	1·40	2·50
MS563	142×80 mm. Nos. 558/62	6·00	8·00

199 Animals (Irish Society for the Prevention of Cruelty to Animals)

1983. Anniversaries and Commemorations.

564	**199**	22p. multicoloured	50	1·00
565	-	22p. multicoloured	50	1·00
566	-	26p. multicoloured	50	60
567	-	26p. multicoloured	50	60
568	-	44p. blue and black	75	2·00

DESIGNS—VERT: No. 565, Sean MacDiarmada (patriot) (birth cent); 567, "St. Vincent de Paul in the Streets of Paris" (150th anniv of Society of St. Vincent de Paul); 568, "Andrew Jackson" (Frank McKelvey) (President of the United States). HORIZ: No. 566, "100" (Centenary of Industrial Credit Company).

200 Postman with Bicycle

1983. World Communications Year. Multicoloured.

569	22p. Type **200**	1·10	75
570	29p. Dish antenna	90	2·00

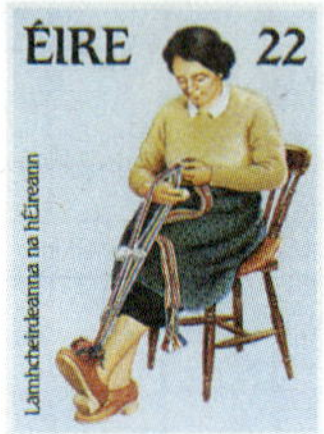

201 Weaving

1983. Irish Handicrafts. Multicoloured.

571	22p. Type **201**	60	50
572	26p. Basket making	60	35
573	29p. Irish crochet	65	1·25
574	44p. Harp making	1·25	2·50

202 "La Natividad" (R. van der Weyden)

1983. Christmas.

575	**202**	22p. multicoloured	40	30
576	**202**	26p. multicoloured	60	30

203 Dublin and Kingstown Railway Steam Locomotive "Princess"

1984. 150th Anniv of Irish Railways. Mult.

577	23p. Type **203**	75	1·25
578	26p. Great Southern Railways steam locomotive "Macha"	75	35
579	29p. Great Northern Railway steam locomotive No. 87 "Kestrel"	85	1·75
580	44p. Two-car electric train Coras Iompair Eireann	1·10	2·25
MS581	129×77 mm. Nos. 577/80	5·50	7·00

204 "Sorbus hibernica"

1984. Irish Trees. Multicoloured.

582	22p. Type **204**	65	70
583	26p. "Taxus baccata fastigiata"	70	30
584	29p. "Salix hibernica"	80	1·75
585	44p. "Betula pubescens"	1·25	2·50

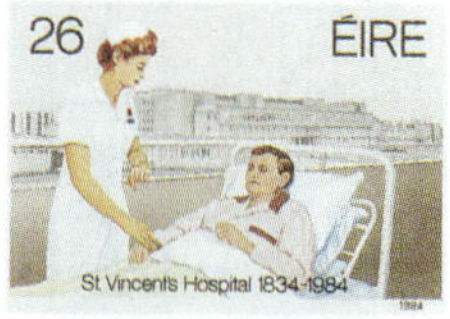

205 St. Vincent's Hospital, Dublin

1984. 150th Anniv of St. Vincent's Hospital and Bicentenary of Royal College of Surgeons. Multicoloured.

586	26p. Type **205**	75	30
587	44p. Royal College and logo	1·25	1·50

206 C.E.P.T. 25th Anniversary Logo

1984. Europa.

588	**206**	26p. blue, dp blue & black	3·00	50
589	**206**	29p. lt green, green & blk	6·00	4·25

207 Flags on Ballot Box

1984. Second Direct Elections to European Assembly.

590	**207**	26p. multicoloured	1·00	70

208 John McCormack

1984. Birth Centenary of John McCormack (tenor).

591	**208**	22p. multicoloured	50	70

209 Hammer-throwing

1984. Olympic Games, Los Angeles.

592	**209**	22p. mauve, black and gold	35	80
593	-	26p. violet, black and gold	40	65
594	-	29p. blue, black and gold	60	1·25

DESIGNS: 26p. Hurdling; 29p. Running.

210 Hurling

1984. Cent of Gaelic Athletic Association. Mult.

595	22p. Type **210**	50	90
596	26p. Irish football (vert)	60	90

211 Galway Mayoral Chain

1984. Anniversaries. Multicoloured.

597	26p. Type **211** (500th anniv of mayoral charter)	35	50
598	44p. St. Brendan (from 15th-cent Bodleian manuscript) (1500th birth anniv) (horiz)	75	1·50

212 Hands passing Letter

1984. Bicentenary of Irish Post Office.

599	**212**	26p. multicoloured	60	70

213 "Virgin and Child" (Sassoferrato)

1984. Christmas. Multicoloured.

600	17p. Christmas star (horiz)	45	80
601	22p. Type **213**	45	1·25
602	26p. Type **213**	65	40

214 "Love" and Heart-shaped Balloon

1985. Greetings Stamps. Multicoloured.

603	22p. Type **214**	50	75
604	26p. Bouquet of hearts and flowers (vert)	60	75

215 Dunsink Observatory (bicentenary)

1985. Anniversaries. Multicoloured.

605	22p. Type **215**	60	50
606	26p. "A Landscape at Tivoli, Cork, with Boats" (Nathaniel Grogan) (800th anniv of City of Cork) (horiz)	60	30
607	37p. Royal Irish Academy (bicentenary)	80	1·75
608	44p. Richard Crosbie's balloon flight (bicentenary of first aeronautic flight by an Irishman)	1·00	1·75

216 "Polyommatus icarus"

1985. Butterflies. Multicoloured.

609	22p. Type **216**	1·50	1·00
610	26p. "Vanessa atalanta"	1·50	70
611	28p. "Gonepteryx rhamni"	1·75	3·00
612	44p. "Eurabyas aurinia"	2·00	3·25

217 Charles Villiers Stanford (composer)

1985. Europa. Irish Composers. Multicoloured.

613	26p. Type **217**	3·50	50
614	37p. Turlough Carolan (composer and lyricist)	8·50	6·00

218 George Frederick Handel

1985. European Music Year. Composers. Mult.

615	22p. Type **218**	1·25	2·50
616	22p. Guiseppe Domenico Scarlatti	1·25	2·50
617	26p. Johann Sebastian Bach	1·50	50

219 U.N. Patrol of Irish Soldiers, Congo, 1960

1985. Anniversaries. Multicoloured.

618	22p. Type **219** (25th anniv of Irish Participation in U.N. Peace-keeping Force)	55	80
619	26p. Thomas Ashe (patriot) (birth cent) (vert)	55	60
620	44p. "Bishop George Berkeley" (James Lathan) (philosopher, 300th birth anniv) (vert)	85	3·00

220 Group of Young People

1985. International Youth Year. Mult.

621	22p. Type **220**	55	50
622	26p. Students and young workers (vert)	55	50

221 Visual Display Unit

1985. Industrial Innovation. Multicoloured.

623	22p. Type **221**	60	75
624	26p. Turf cutting with hand tool and with modern machinery	60	55
625	44p. "The Key Man" (Sean Keating) (150th anniv of Institution of Engineers of Ireland)	1·25	2·50

222 Lighted Candle and Holly

1985. Christmas. Multicoloured.

626	22p. Type **222**	75	65
627	22p. "Virgin and Child in a Landscape" (Adrian van Ijsenbrandt)	1·25	2·25
628	22p. "The Holy Family" (Murillo)	1·25	2·25
629	26p. "The Adoration of the Shepherds" (Louis le Nain) (horiz)	1·25	25

No. 626 was only issued in sheetlets of 16 sold at £3, providing a discount of 52p. off the face value of the stamps.

224 Stylized Love Bird with Letter

1986. Greetings Stamps. Multicoloured.

630	22p. Type **224**	75	90
631	26p. Heart-shaped pillar-box	75	90

225 Hart's Tongue Fern

1986. Ferns. Multicoloured.

632	24p. Type **225**	70	70
633	28p. Rusty-back fern	80	70
634	46p. Killarney fern	1·25	2·10

226 "Harmony between Industry and Nature"

1986. Europa. Protection of the Environment. Multicoloured.

635	28p. Type **226**	8·00	50
636	39p. "Vanessa atalanta" (butterfly) and tractor in field ("Preserve hedgerows") (horiz)	24·00	6·00

227 Boeing 747-200 over Globe showing Aer Lingus Routes

1986. 50th Anniv of Aer Lingus (airline). Multicoloured.

637	28p. Type **227**	1·40	75
638	46p. de Havilland Dragon Mk 2 EI-ABI "Iolar" (first airplane)	1·90	3·00

228 Grand Canal at Robertstown

1986. Irish Waterways. Multicoloured.

639	24p. Type **228**	1·50	1·00
640	28p. Fishing in County Mayo (vert)	1·60	1·00
641	30p. Motor cruiser on Lough Derg	1·75	2·50

229 "Severn" (19th-century paddlesteamer)

1986. 150th Anniv of British and Irish Steam Packet Company. Multicoloured.

642	24p. Type **229**	75	1·00
643	28p. "Leinster" (modern ferry)	85	60

230 Kish Lighthouse and Bell JetRanger III Helicopter

1986. Irish Lighthouses. Multicoloured.

644	24p. Type **230**	1·50	75
645	30p. Fastnet Lighthouse	2·50	2·75

231 J. P. Nannetti (first president) and Linotype Operator (Dublin Council of Trade Unions centenary)

1986. Anniversaries and Commemorations.

646	**231**	24p. multicoloured	60	90
647	-	28p. black and grey	75	80
648	-	28p. multicoloured	75	80
649	-	30p. multicoloured	85	1·00
650	-	46p. multicoloured	1·00	1·75

DESIGNS:—VERT: No. 647, Arthur Griffith (statesman); 649, Clasped hands (International Peace Year). HORIZ: No. 648, Woman surveyor (Women in Society); 650, Peace dove (International Peace Year).

232 William Mulready and his Design for 1840 Envelope

1986. Birth Bicentenaries of William Mulready (artist) (24p.) and Charles Bianconi (originator of Irish mail coach service) (others). Multicoloured.

651	24p. Type **232**	70	70
652	28p. Bianconi car outside Hearns Hotel, Clonmel (vert)	85	55
653	39p. Bianconi car on the road	1·40	1·75

233 "Adoration of the Shepherds" (Francesco Pascucci)

1986. Christmas. Multicoloured.

654	21p. Type **233**	1·10	1·40
655	28p. "Adoration of the Magi" (Frans Francken III) (vert)	65	60

234 "Butterfly and Flowers" (Tara Collins)

1987. Greetings Stamps. Children's Paintings. Multicoloured.

656	24p. Type **234**	75	1·25
657	28p. "Postman on Bicycle delivering Hearts" (Brigid Teehan) (vert)	1·25	1·25

235 Cork Electric Tram

1987. Irish Trams. Multicoloured.

658	24p. Type **235**	65	65
659	28p. Dublin standard tram No. 29	70	85
660	30p. Howth (Great Northern Railway) tram	80	2·00
661	46p. Galway horse tram	1·25	2·25
MS662	131×85 mm. Nos. 658/61	4·50	6·50

236 Ships from Crest (Bicentenary of Waterford Chamber of Commerce)

1987. Anniversaries.

663	**236**	24p. black, blue and green	70	60
664	-	28p. multicoloured	70	60
665	-	30p. multicoloured	70	2·00
666	-	39p. multicoloured	75	1·75

DESIGNS—HORIZ: 28p. Canon John Hayes and symbols of agriculture and development (birth centenary and 50th anniv of Muintir na Tire programme); 39p. Mother Mary Martin and International Missionary Training Hospital, Drogheda (50th anniv of Medical Missionaries of Mary). VERT: 30p. "Calceolaria burbidgei" and College crest (300th anniv of Trinity College Botanic Gardens, Dublin).

237 Bord na Mona Headquarters and "The Turf Cutter" (sculpture, John Behan), Dublin

1987. Europa. Modern Architecture. Mult.

667	28p. Type **237**	4·50	60
668	39p. St. Mary's Church, Cong	8·50	6·50

238 Kerry Cow

1987. Irish Cattle. Multicoloured.

669	24p. Type **238**	80	75
670	28p. Friesian cow and calf	95	60
671	30p. Hereford bullock	1·00	2·25

672		39p. Shorthorn bull	1·10	2·25

239 Fleadh Nua, Ennis

1987. Festivals. Multicoloured.

673		24p. Type **239**	75	70
674		28p. Rose of Tralee International Festival	80	60
675		30p. Wexford Opera Festival (horiz)	1·50	2·00
676		46p. Ballinasloe Horse Fair (horiz)	1·50	2·00

240 Flagon (1637), Arms and Anniversary Ornament (1987) (350th anniv of Dublin Goldsmiths' Company)

1987. Anniversaries and Commemorations.

677	**240**	24p. multicoloured	80	80
678	-	24p. grey and black	80	80
679	-	28p. multicoloured	1·00	60
680	-	46p. multicoloured	1·40	1·10

DESIGNS—VERT: 24p. (No. 678) Cathal Brugha (patriot); 46p. Woman chairing board meeting (Women in Society). HORIZ: 28p. Arms of Ireland and inscription (50th anniv of Constitution).

241 Scenes from "The Twelve Days of Christmas" (carol)

1987. Christmas. Multicoloured.

681		21p. Type **241**	60	1·00
682		24p. The Nativity (detail, late 15th-century Waterford Vestments) (vert)	75	1·00
683		28p. Figures from Neapolitan crib, c. 1850 (vert)	75	80

242 Acrobatic Clowns spelling "LOVE"

1988. Greetings Stamps. Multicoloured.

684		24p. Type **242**	75	60
685		28p. Pillar box and hearts (vert)	75	65

243 "Robert Burke" (Sidney Nolan) and Map of Burke and Wills Expedition Route

1988. Bicent of Australian Settlement. Mult.

686		24p. Type **243**	1·00	60
687		46p. "Eureka Stockade" (mural detail, Sidney Nolan)	1·25	1·75

244 Past and Present Buildings of Dublin

1988. Dublin Millennium.

688	**244**	28p. multicoloured	45	55

245 Showjumping

1988. Olympic Games, Seoul. Multicoloured.

689		28p. Type **245**	1·00	1·40
690		28p. Cycling	1·00	1·40

246 William T. Cosgrave (statesman)

1988. Anniversaries and Events.

691	**246**	24p. grey and black	45	45
692	-	30p. multicoloured	80	1·00
693	-	50p. multicoloured	1·00	1·90

DESIGNS—HORIZ: 30p. Members with casualty and ambulance (50th anniv of Order of Malta Ambulance Corps). VERT: 50p. Barry Fitzgerald (actor) (birth centenary).

247 Air Traffic Controllers and Airbus Industrie A320

1988. Europa. Transport and Communications. Multicoloured.

694		28p. Type **247**	3·00	55
695		39p. Globe with stream of letters from Ireland to Europe	4·00	3·25

248 "Sirius" (paddle-steamer)

1988. Transatlantic Transport Anniversaries. Multicoloured.

696		24p. Type **248** (150th anniv of regular transatlantic steamship services)	1·00	50
697		46p. Short S.20 seaplane "Mercury" G-ADHJ and Short S.21 flying boat G-ADHK "Maia" (Short Mayo composite aircraft) in Foynes Harbour (50th anniv of first commercial transatlantic flight)	1·75	3·00

249 Cottonweed

1988. Endangered Flora of Ireland. Mult.

698		24p. Type **249**	70	55
699		28p. Hart's saxifrage	70	55
700		46p. Purple milk-vetch	1·00	2·75

250 Garda on Duty

1988. Irish Security Forces. Multicoloured.

701		28p. Type **250**	70	1·10
702		28p. Army unit with personnel carrier	70	1·10
703		28p. Navy and Air Corps members with "Eithne" (helicopter patrol vessel)	70	1·10
704		28p. Army and Navy reservists	70	1·10

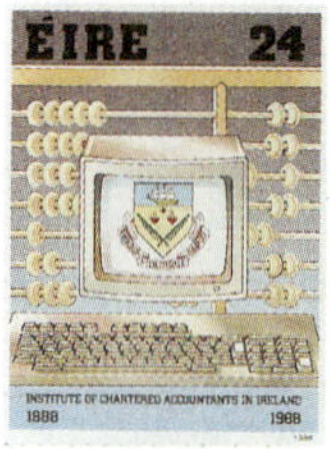

251 Computer and Abacus

1988. Anniversaries. Multicoloured.

705		24p. Type **251** (Institute of Chartered Accountants in Ireland centenary)	40	40
706		46p. "Duquesa Santa Ana" off Donegal (400th anniv of Spanish Armada) (horiz)	1·25	1·25

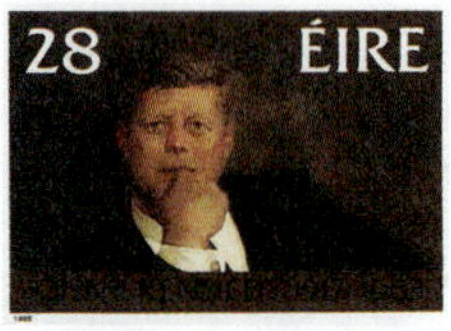

252 "President Kennedy" (James Wyeth)

1988. 25th Death Anniv of John F. Kennedy (American statesman).

707	**252**	28p. multicoloured	1·00	80

253 St. Kevin's Church, Glendalough

1988. Christmas. Multicoloured.

708		21p. Type **253**	80	1·00
709		24p. The Adoration of the Magi	50	60
710		28p. The Flight into Egypt	60	45
711		46p. The Holy Family	1·00	3·00

The designs of Nos. 709/11 are from a 15th-century French Book of Hours.

254 Spring Flowers spelling "Love" in Gaelic

1989. Greetings Stamps. Multicoloured.

712		24p. Type **254**	75	55
713		28p. "The Sonnet" (William Mulready) (vert)	75	55

255 Italian Garden, Garinish Island

1989. National Parks and Gardens. Multicoloured.

714		24p. Type **255**	90	55
715		28p. Lough Veagh, Glenveagh National Park	1·10	55
716		32p. Barnaderg Bay, Connemara National Park	1·25	1·25
717		50p. St. Stephen's Green, Dublin	1·75	1·75

256 "Silver Stream", 1908

1989. Classic Irish Cars. Multicoloured.

718		24p Type **256**	50	55
719		28p Benz "Comfortable", 1898	50	55
720		39p "Thomond", 1929	1·25	1·50
721		46p Chambers' 8 h.p. model, 1905	1·50	1·50

257 Ring-a-ring-a-roses

1989. Europa. Children's Games. Multicoloured.

722		28p. Type **257**	75	75
723		39p. Hopscotch	1·00	2·25

258 Irish Red Cross Flag (50th anniv)

1989. Anniversaries and Events.

724	**258**	24p. red and black	55	60
725	-	28p. blue, black and yellow	1·60	1·10

DESIGN: 28p. Circle of twelve stars (third direct elections to European Parliament).

259 Saints Kilian, Totnan and Colman (from 12th-century German manuscript)

1989. 1300th Death Anniv of Saints Kilian, Totnan and Colman.

726	**259**	28p. multicoloured	55	1·10

260 19th-century Mail Coach passing Cashel

1989. Bicentenary of Irish Mail Coach Service.

727	**260**	28p. multicoloured	1·50	75

261 Crest and 19th-century Dividers (150th anniv of Royal Institute of Architects of Ireland)

1989. Anniversaries and Commemorations.

728	-	24p. grey and black	65	55
729	**261**	28p. multicoloured	65	55
730	-	30p. multicoloured	1·75	2·25
731	-	46p. brown	3·00	2·75

DESIGNS—VERT: 24p. Sean T. O'Kelly (statesman) (drawing by Sean O'Sullivan); 46p. Jawaharlal Nehru (birth centenary). HORIZ: 30p. Margaret Burke-Sheridan (soprano) (portrait by De Gennaro) and scene from "La Boheme" (birth centenary).

262 "NCB Ireland" rounding Cape Horn" (Des Fallon)

1989. First Irish Entry in Whitbread Round the World Yacht Race.

732	**262**	28p. multicoloured	1·50	1·25

263 Willow/Red Grouse

1989. Game Birds. Multicoloured.

733	24p. Type **263**	1·00	55
734	28p. Northern lapwing	1·00	55
735	39p. Eurasian woodcock	1·25	2·25
736	46p. Common pheasant	1·25	2·25
MS737	128×92 mm. Nos. 733/6	5·00	7·00

264 "The Annunciation"

1989. Christmas. Multicoloured.

738	21p. Children decorating crib	75	75
739	24p. Type **264**	75	60
740	28p. "The Nativity"	80	55
741	46p. "The Adoration of the Magi"	1·60	2·50

265 Logo (Ireland's Presidency of the European Communities)

1990. European Events. Multicoloured.

742	30p. Type **265**	1·00	60
743	50p. Logo and outline map of Ireland (European Tourism Year)	2·25	3·00

266 Dropping Messages from Balloon

1990. Greetings Stamps.

744	**266**	26p. multicoloured	1·50	1·25
745	-	30p. red, buff and brown	1·50	1·25

DESIGN: 30p. Heart and "Love" drawn in lipstick.

267 Silver Kite Brooch

1990. Irish Heritage.

746	**267**	1p. black and blue	10	10
747	**267**	2p. black and orange	10	10
748	-	4p. black and violet	15	30
749	-	5p. black and green	20	10
750	-	10p. black and orange	30	25
751	-	20p. black and yellow	50	40
752	-	26p. black and violet	1·50	65
754	-	30p. black and blue	1·25	90
756	-	34p. black and yellow	1·25	1·25
757	-	37p. black and green	1·50	2·00
758	-	38p. black and violet	1·50	2·00
758b	-	40p. black and blue	1·50	1·50
759	-	41p. black and orange	1·50	1·75
760	-	44p. brown and yellow	2·50	2·25
760a	-	45p. black and violet	1·75	2·75
761	-	50p. black and yellow	1·75	1·50
762	-	52p. black and blue	2·75	3·00
763	-	£1 black and yellow	3·25	2·25
764	-	£2 black and green	4·50	3·25
765	-	£5 black and blue	10·00	9·00
809	-	28p. black and orange	1·50	2·25
810	-	32p. black and green	50	80

DESIGNS: 4, 5p. Dunamase food vessel; 26, 28p. Lismore crozier; 34, 37, 38, 40p. Gleninsheen collar; 41, 44p. Silver thistle brooch; 45, 50, 52p. Broighter boat. 22×38 mm: £5 St. Patrick's Bell Shrine. HORIZ: 10p. Derrinboy armlets; 20p. Gold dress fastener; 30p. Enamelled latchet brooch; 32p. Broighter collar. 38×22 mm: £1 Ardagh Chalice; £2 Tara brooch.

For 32p. value as No. 755 but larger, 29×24 mm, and self-adhesive, see No. 823.

268 Posy of Flowers

1990. Greetings Stamps. Multicoloured.

766	26p. Type **268**	2·00	2·50
767	26p. Birthday presents	2·00	2·50
768	30p. Flowers, ribbon and horseshoe	2·00	2·50
769	30p. Balloons	2·00	2·50

269 Player heading Ball

1990. World Cup Football Championship, Italy. Multicoloured.

770	30p. Type **269**	1·75	2·00
771	30p. Tackling	1·75	2·00

270 Battle of the Boyne, 1690

1990. 300th Anniv of the Williamite Wars (1st issue). Multicoloured.

772	30p. Type **270**	1·75	1·75
773	30p. Siege of Limerick, 1690	1·75	1·75

See also Nos. 806/7.

271 1990 Irish Heritage 30p. Stamp and 1840 Postmark

1990. 150th Anniv of the Penny Black. Mult.

774	30p. Type **271**	90	90
775	50p. Definitive stamps of 1922, 1969, 1982 and 1990	1·25	2·25

272 General Post Office, Dublin

1990. Europa Post Office Buildings. Mult.

776	30p. Type **272**	1·25	60
777	41p. Westport Post Office, County Mayo	2·25	3·00

273 Medical Missionary giving Injection

1990. Anniversaries and Events.

778	**273**	26p. multicoloured	80	40
779	-	30p. black	1·00	2·75
780	-	50p. multicoloured	1·00	1·75

DESIGNS—VERT: 30p. Michael Collins (statesman) (birth centenary). HORIZ: 50p. Missionaries working at water pump (Irish missionary service).

274 Narcissus "Foundling" and Japanese Gardens, Tully

1990. Garden Flowers. Multicoloured.

781	26p. Type **274**	60	55
782	30p. "Rosa x hibernica" and Mulahide Castle gardens	70	80
783	41p. Primula "Rowallane Rose" and Rowallane garden	1·40	2·50
784	50p. "Erica erigena" "Irish Dusk" and Palm House, National Botanical Gardens	1·75	2·75

275 "Playboy of the Western World" (John Synge)

1990. Irish Theatre. Multicoloured.

785	30p. Type **275**	1·25	1·75
786	30p. "Juno and the Pay-cock" (Sean O'Casey)	1·25	1·75
787	30p. "The Field" (John Keane)	1·25	1·75
788	30p. "Waiting for Godot" (Samuel Beckett)	1·25	1·75

276 Nativity

1990. Christmas. Multicoloured.

789	26p. Child praying by bed	75	80
790	26p. Type **276**	75	60
791	30p. Madonna and Child	1·25	90
792	50p. Adoration of the Magi	2·25	3·50

277 Hearts in Mail Sack and Postman's Cap

1991. Greetings Stamps. Multicoloured.

793	26p. Type **277**	85	1·00
794	30p. Boy and girl kissing	90	1·00

278 Starley "Rover" Bicycle, 1886

1991. Early Bicycles. Multicoloured.

795	26p. Type **278**	90	60
796	30p. Child's horse tricycle, 1875	1·00	1·00
797	50p. "Penny Farthing", 1871	1·75	2·50
MS798	113×72 mm. Nos. 795/7	3·25	3·75

279 "Cuchulainn" (statue by Oliver Sheppard) and Proclamation

1991. 75th Anniv of Easter Rising.

799	**279**	32p. multicoloured	1·00	1·40

280 Scene from "La Traviata" (50th anniv of Dublin Grand Opera Society)

1991. "Dublin 1991 European City of Culture". Multicoloured.

800	28p. Type **280**	1·00	1·00
801	32p. City Hall and European Community emblem	1·10	1·60
802	44p. St. Patrick's Cathedral (800th anniv)	90	1·60
803	52p. Custom House (bicent) (41×24 mm)	1·00	1·60

281 "Giotto" Spacecraft approaching Halley's Comet

1991. Europa. Europe in Space. Multicoloured.

804	32p. Type **281**	1·00	1·00
805	44p. Hubble Telescope orbiting Earth	1·50	3·00

282 Siege of Athlone

1991. 300th Anniv of the Williamite Wars (2nd issue). Multicoloured.

806	28p. Type **282**	1·25	1·75
807	28p. Generals Ginkel and Sarsfield (signatories of Treaty of Limerick)	1·25	1·75

283 John A. Costello (statesman)

1991. Anniversaries.

811 **283** 28p. black 1·25 70
812 - 32p. multicoloured 1·40 1·00
813 - 52p. multicoloured 1·75 2·50

DESIGNS—VERT: 28p. Type **283** (birth cent) (drawing by Sean O'Sullivan); 32p. "Charles Stewart Parnell" (Sydney Hall) (death cent); HORIZ: 52p. Meeting of United Irishmen.

284 Player on 15th Green, Portmarnock (Walker Cup)

1991. Golf Commemorations. Multicoloured.

814 28p. Type **284** 1·00 75
815 32p. Logo and golfer of 1900 (cent of Golfing Union of Ireland) (vert) 1·25 1·00

285 Wicklow Cheviot

1991. Irish Sheep. Multicoloured.

816 32p. Type **285** 1·00 80
817 38p. Donegal Blackface 1·40 1·75
818 52p. Galway (horiz) 2·00 3·50

286 Boatyard

1991. Fishing Fleet. Multicoloured.

819 28p. Type **286** 70 65
820 32p. Traditional inshore trawlers 80 80
821 44p. Inshore lobster pot boat 1·60 2·50
822 52p. "Veronica" (fish factory ship) 1·90 2·75

1991. As No. 755, but larger, 27×21 mm. Self-adhesive.

823a 32p. black and green 1·00 1·25

287 The Annunciation

1991. Christmas.

827 - 28p. multicoloured 1·00 1·00
828 **287** 28p. blue, green and black 1·00 65
829 - 32p. red and black 1·10 75
830 - 52p. multicoloured 2·00 3·25

DESIGNS: No. 827, Three Kings; No. 829, The Nativity; No. 830, Adoration of the Kings.

288 Multicoloured Heart

1992. Greetings Stamps. Multicoloured.

831 28p. Type **288** 1·00 95
832 32p. "LOVE" at end of rainbow (vert) 1·10 1·10

289 Healthy Family on Apple

1992. "Healthy Living" Campaign.

833 **289** 28p. multicoloured 1·25 1·00

290 Boxing

1992. Olympic Games, Barcelona. Mult.

834 32p. Type **290** 75 90
835 44p. Sailing 1·00 2·25
MS836 130×85 mm. Nos. 834/5×2 4·75 5·00

291 "Mari" (cog) and 14th-century Map

1992. Irish Maritime Heritage. Multicoloured.

837 32p. Type **291** 1·00 90
838 52p. "Ovoca" (trawler) and chart (vert) 1·50 2·75

292 Chamber Logo and Commercial Symbols

1992. Bicentenary of Galway Chamber of Commerce and Industry.

839 **292** 28p. multicoloured 1·00 1·00

293 Cliffs and Cove

1992. Greetings Stamps. Multicoloured.

840 28p. Type **293** 75 1·10
841 28p. Meadow 75 1·10
842 32p. Fuchsia and honeysuckle 75 1·10
843 32p. Lily pond and dragonfly 75 1·10

294 Fleet of Columbus

1992. Europa. 500th Anniv of Discovery of America by Columbus. Multicoloured.

844 32p. Type **294** 1·25 90
845 44p. Columbus landing in the New World 2·00 3·00

295 Irish Immigrants

1992. Irish Immigrants in the Americas. Mult.

846 52p. Type **295** 1·75 1·75
847 52p. Irish soldiers, entertainers and politicians 1·75 1·75

296 Pair of Pine Martens

1992. Endangered Species. Pine Marten. Mult.

848 28p. Type **296** 1·00 70
849 32p. Marten on branch 1·00 80
850 44p. Female with kittens 1·60 1·50
851 52p. Marten catching great tit 2·00 2·50

297 "The Rotunda and New Rooms" (James Malton)

1992. Dublin Anniversaries. Multicoloured.

852 28p. Type **297** 70 65
853 32p. Trinity College Library (27×44 mm) 1·00 1·00
854 44p. "Charlemont House" 1·10 2·00
855 52p. Trinity College main gate (27×44 mm) 1·40 2·25

ANNIVERSARIES: 28, 44p. Bicentenary of Publication of Malton's "Views of Dublin"; 32, 52p. 400th anniv of Founding of Trinity College.

298 European Star and Megalithic Dolmen

1992. Single European Market.

856 **298** 32p. multicoloured 70 80

299 Farm Produce

1992. Irish Agriculture. Multicoloured.

857 32p. Type **299** 1·25 1·25
858 32p. Dairy and beef herds 1·25 1·25
859 32p. Harvesting cereals 1·25 1·25
860 32p. Market gardening 1·25 1·25

Nos. 857/60 were printed together, se-tenant, forming a composite design.

300 "The Annunciation" (from illuminated manuscript)

1992. Christmas. Multicoloured.

861 28p. Congregation entering church 80 65
862 28p. Type **300** 80 65
863 32p. "Adoration of the Shepherds" (Da Empoli) 1·10 1·00
864 52p. "Adoration of the Magi" (Rottenhammer) 1·40 1·50

301 Queen of Hearts

1993. Greetings Stamps. Multicoloured.

865 28p. Type **301** 90 75
866 32p. Hot air balloon trailing hearts (horiz) 1·00 85

302 "Evening at Tangier" (Sir John Lavery)

1993. Irish Impressionist Painters. Multicoloured.

867 28p. Type **302** 70 60
868 32p. "The Goose Girl" (William Leech) 75 65
869 44p. "La Jeune Bretonne" (Roderic O'Conor) (vert) 75 1·75
870 52p. "Lustre Jug" (Walter Osborne) (vert) 80 2·40

303 Bee Orchid

1993. Irish Orchids. Multicoloured.

871 28p. Type **303** 90 60
872 32p. O'Kelly's orchid 1·10 80
873 38p. Dark red helleborine 1·60 2·25
874 52p. Irish lady's tresses 1·90 2·75
MS875 130×71 mm. Nos. 871/4 5·00 6·00

304 "Pears in a Copper Pan" (Hilda van Stockum)

1993. Europa. Contemporary Art. Mult.

876 32p. Type **304** 75 75
877 44p. "Arrieta Orzola" (Tony O'Malley) 1·10 1·10

305 Cultural Activities

1993. Centenary of Conradh Na Gaelige (cultural organization). Multicoloured.

878	32p. Type **305**	85	75
879	52p. Illuminated manuscript cover (vert)	1·50	1·50

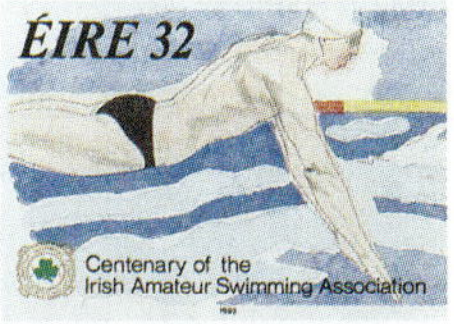

306 Diving

1993. Centenary of Irish Amateur Swimming Association. Multicoloured.

880	32p. Type **306**	1·00	1·50
881	32p. Swimming	1·00	1·50

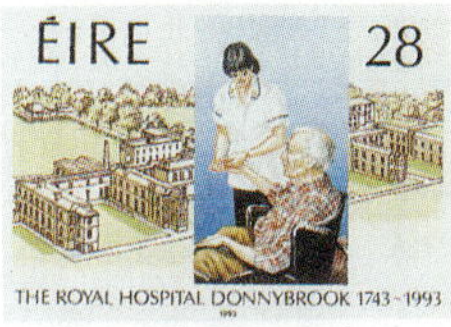

307 Nurse with Patient and Hospital Buildings

1993. Anniversaries and Events. Multicoloured.

882	28p. Type **307** (250th anniv of Royal Hospital, Donnybrook)	1·25	60
883	32p. College building and crest (bicentenary of St. Patrick's College, Carlow) (vert)	80	60
884	44p. Map of Neolithic field system, Ceide (opening of interpretative centre)	1·60	1·40
885	52p. Edward Bunting (musicologist) (150th death anniv) (25×42 mm)	1·75	1·60

308 Great Northern Railways Gardner at Drogheda

1993. Irish Buses. Multicoloured.

886	28p. Type **308**	85	70
887	32p. C.I.E. Leyland Titan at College Green, Dublin	1·00	70
888	52p. Horse-drawn omnibus at Old Baal's Bridge, Limerick	1·75	2·50
889	52p. Char-a-banc at Lady's View, Killarney	1·75	2·50

309 The Annunciation

1993. Christmas. Multicoloured.

890	28p. The flight into Egypt (vert)	80	80
891	28p. Type **309**	80	55
892	32p. Holy Family	90	70
893	52p. Adoration of the shepherds	2·00	2·50

310 Biplane skywriting "Love"

1994. Greetings Stamps. Multicoloured.

894	28p. Type **310**	90	75
895	32p. Couple within heart (vert)	1·00	85

311 Smiling Sun

1994. Greetings Stamps. Multicoloured.

896	32p. Type **311**	1·00	1·25
897	32p. Smiling daisy	1·00	1·25
898	32p. Smiling heart	1·00	1·25
899	32p. Smiling rose	1·00	1·25

1994. "Hong Kong '94" International Stamp Exhibition. Chinese New Year ("Year of the Dog").

MS900	137×74 mm. Nos. 896/8	4·25	5·50

312 Stylized Logo of Macra na Feirme (50th anniv)

1994. Anniversaries and Events.

901	**312**	28p. gold and blue	75	65
902	-	32p. multicoloured	1·25	75
903	-	38p. multicoloured	2·50	2·25
904	-	52p. black, cobalt and blue	2·25	2·50

DESIGNS—38×35 mm: 32p. "The Taking of Christ" (Caravaggio) (loan of painting to National Gallery). 37½×27 mm: 38p. Sir Horace Plunkett with 19th-century milk carts and modern tankers (centenary of Irish Co-operative Organization Society); 52p. Congress emblem (centenary of Irish Congress of Trade Unions).

313 St. Brendan visiting Iceland

1994. Europa. St. Brendan's Voyages. Mult.

905	32p. Type **313**	75	70
906	44p. Discovering Faroe Islands	1·50	2·00
MS907	82×76 mm. Nos. 905/6	2·75	3·75

314 First Meeting of Dail, 1919

1994. Parliamentary Anniversaries. Multicoloured.

908	32p. Type **314** (75th anniv)	90	1·00
909	32p. European Parliament (4th direct elections)	90	1·00

315 Irish and Argentine Footballers

1994. Sporting Anniversaries and Events. Multicoloured.

910	32p. Type **315**	80	1·25
911	32p. Irish and German footballers	80	1·25
912	32p. Irish and Dutch women's hockey match (horiz)	2·00	1·25
913	52p. Irish and English women's hockey match (horiz)	2·25	2·50

ANNIVERSARIES AND EVENTS: Nos. 910/11, World Cup Football Championship, U.S.A.; 912, Women's Hockey World Cup, Dublin; 913, Centenary of Irish Ladies' Hockey Union.

316 "Arctia caja"

1994. Moths. Mult. (a) Size 37×26 mm.

914	28p. Type **316**	65	60
915	32p. "Calamia tridens"	75	70
916	38p. "Saturnia pavonia"	90	1·10
917	52p. "Deilephila elpenor"	1·50	2·00
MS918	120×71 mm. Nos. 914/17	3·50	4·00

(b) Size 34×22 mm. Self-adhesive.

919	32p. "Calamia tridens"	1·25	1·50
920	32p. Type **316**	1·25	1·50
921	32p. "Deilephila elpenor"	1·25	1·50
922	32p. "Saturnia pavonia"	1·25	1·50

317 Statue of Edmund Rice and Class

1994. Anniversaries and Events. Multicoloured.

923	28p. St. Laurence Gate, Drogheda (44×27 mm)	1·50	1·60
924	32p. Type **317**	1·50	1·60
925	32p. Edmund Burke (politician)	1·50	1·60
926	52p. Vickers FB-27 Vimy and map (horiz)	1·50	1·60
927	52p. Eamonn Andrews (broadcaster)	1·50	1·60

ANNIVERSARIES AND EVENTS: No. 923, 800th anniv of Drogheda; 924, 150th death anniv of Edmund Rice (founder of Irish Christian Brothers); 925, 927, The Irish abroad; 926, 75th anniv of Alcock and Brown's first transatlantic flight.

318 George Bernard Shaw (author) and "Pygmalion" Poster

1994. Irish Nobel Prize Winners. Multicoloured.

928	28p. Type **318**	60	90
929	28p. Samuel Beckett (author) and pair of boots	60	90
930	32p. Sean MacBride (human rights campaigner) and peace doves	70	90
931	52p. William Butler Yeats (poet) and poem	1·10	2·00

319 "The Annunciation" (ivory plaque)

1994. Christmas. Multicoloured.

932	28p. Nativity	70	60
933	28p. Type **319**	70	60
934	32p. "Flight into Egypt" (wood carving)	90	70
935	52p. "Nativity" (ivory plaque)	1·40	2·00

320 Tree of Hearts

1995. Greetings Stamps. Multicoloured.

936	32p. Type **320**	1·10	1·25
937	32p. Teddy bear holding balloon	1·10	1·25
938	32p. Clown juggling hearts	1·10	1·25
939	32p. Bouquet of flowers	1·10	1·25

1995. Chinese New Year ("Year of the Pig").

MS940	137×74 mm. Nos. 936, 938/9	4·25	4·25

321 West Clare Railway Steam Locomotive No. 1 "Kilkee" at Kilrush Station

1995. Transport. Narrow Gauge Railways. Mult.

941	28p. Type **321**	85	60
942	32p. County Donegal Railway tank locomotive No. 2 "Blanche" at Donegal Station	1·10	90
943	38p. Cork and Muskerry Railway tank locomotive No. 1 "City of Cork" on Western Road, Cork	1·40	1·75
944	52p. Cavan and Leitrim Railway tank locomotive No. 3 "Lady Edith" on Arigna Tramway	1·90	2·50
MS945	127×83 mm. Nos. 941/4	4·75	5·50

322 English and Irish Rugby Players

1995. World Cup Rugby Championship, South Africa. Multicoloured.

946	32p. Type **322**	1·00	75
947	52p. Australian and Irish players	1·40	1·75
MS948	108×77 mm. £1 Type **322**	3·00	3·50

323 Peace Dove and Skyscrapers

1995. Europa. Peace and Freedom. Mult. (a) Size 38×26 mm. Ordinary gum.

949	32p. Type **323**	85	75
950	44p. Peace dove and map of Europe and North Africa	1·40	2·00

(b) Size 34½×23 mm. Self-adhesive.

951	32p. Type **323**	90	90
952	32p. As No. 950	90	90

324 Soldiers of the Irish Brigade and Memorial Cross

1995. 250th Anniv of Battle of Fontenoy.

953	**324**	32p. multicoloured	1·25	80

325 Irish Brigade, French Army, 1745

1995. Military Uniforms. Multicoloured.

954	28p. Type **325**	70	60
955	32p. Tercio Irlanda, Spanish army in Flanders, 1605	80	75

956	32p. Royal Dublin Fusiliers, 1914	80	75
957	38p. St. Patrick's Battalion, Papal Army, 1860	1·10	1·25
958	52p. 69th Regiment, New York State Militia, 1861	1·60	1·75

326 Guglielmo Marconi and Original Radio Transmitter

1995. Centenary of Radio. Multicoloured.

959	32p. Type **326**	1·50	1·75
960	32p. Traditional radio dial	1·50	1·75

327 Bartholomew Mosse (founder) and Hospital Building

1995. Anniversaries. Multicoloured.

961	28p. Type **327** (250th anniv of Rotunda Hospital)	1·00	70
962	32p. St. Patrick's House, Maynooth College (bicent) (25×41 mm)	80	80
963	32p. Laurel wreath and map of Europe (50th anniv of end of Second World War)	80	80
964	52p. Geological map of Ireland (150th anniv of Geological Survey of Ireland) (32½×32½ mm)	1·25	1·50

328 Natterjack Toad

1995. Reptiles and Amphibians. Multicoloured. (a) Size 40×27 mm. Ordinary gum.

965	32p. Type **328**	1·00	1·25
966	32p. Common lizards	1·00	1·25
967	32p. Smooth newts	1·00	1·25
968	32p. Common frog	1·00	1·25

(b) Size 37×25 mm. Self-adhesive.

969	32p. Type **328**	1·10	1·40
970	32p. Common lizard	1·10	1·40
971	32p. Smooth newts	1·10	1·40
972	32p. Common frog	1·10	1·40

Nos. 965/8 were printed together, se-tenant, with the backgrounds forming a composite design.

329 "Crinum moorei"

1995. Bicentenary of National Botanic Gardens, Glasnevin. Flowers. Multicoloured.

973	32p. Type **329**	1·50	70
974	38p. "Sarracenia x moorei"	1·25	1·10
975	44p. "Solanum crispum" "Glasnevin"	1·50	2·50

330 Anniversary Logo and Irish United Nations Soldier

1995. 50th Anniv of United Nations. Mult.

976	32p. Type **330**	80	70
977	52p. Emblem and "UN"	1·25	1·40

331 "Adoration of the Shepherds" (illuminated manuscript) (Benedotto Bardone)

1995. Christmas. Multicoloured.

978	28p. Adoration of the Magi	1·10	65
979	28p. Type **331**	1·00	65
980	32p. "Adoration of the Magi" (illuminated manuscript) (Bardone)	1·25	70
981	52p. "The Holy Family" (illuminated manuscript) (Bardone)	2·00	2·75

332 Zig and Zag on Heart

1996. Greetings Stamps. Multicoloured.

982	32p. Type **332**	1·25	75
983	32p. Zig and Zag waving	2·50	2·50
984	32p. Zig and Zag in space suits	2·50	2·50
985	32p. Zig and Zag wearing hats	2·50	2·50

1996. Chinese New Year ("Year of the Rat").

MS986	130×74 mm. Nos. 982, 984/5	3·00	3·00

333 Wheelchair Athlete

1996. Olympic and Paralympic Games, Atlanta. Multicoloured.

987	28p. Type **333**	70	65
988	32p. Running	80	80
989	32p. Throwing the discus	80	80
990	32p. Single kayak	80	80

334 Before the Start, Fairyhouse Race Course

1996. Irish Horse Racing. Multicoloured.

991	28p. Type **334**	70	65
992	32p. Steeplechase, Punchestown	80	80
993	32p. On the Flat, The Curragh	80	80
994	38p. Steeplechase, Galway	1·25	1·25
995	52p. After the race, Leopardstown	1·50	1·50

335 Irish and French Coloured Ribbons merging

1996. "L'Imaginaire Irlandais" Festival of Contemporary Irish Arts, France.

996	**335**	32p. multicoloured	80	80

336 Louie Bennett (suffragette)

1996. Europa. Famous Women. (a) Size 40×29 mm. Ordinary gum.

997	**336**	32p. violet	80	70
998	-	44p. green	1·10	1·25

(b) Size 37×25 mm. Self-adhesive.

999	**336**	32p. violet	1·10	1·25
1000	-	32p. green	1·10	1·25

DESIGN: Nos. 998, 1000, Lady Augusta Gregory (playwright).

337 Newgrange Passage Tomb (Boyne Valley World Heritage Site)

1996. Anniversaries and Events.

1001	**337**	28p. brown and black	1·00	60
1002	-	32p. multicoloured	1·10	90

DESIGN: 32p. Children playing (50th anniv of UNICEF.).

1996. "CHINA '96" 9th Asian International Stamp Exhibition, Peking. Sheet 120×95 mm, containing Nos. 992/3.

MS1003	32p. Steeplechase, Punchestown; 32p. On the Flat, The Curragh	11·00	11·00

338 Stanley Woods

1996. Isle of Man Tourist Trophy Motor Cycle Races. Irish Winners. Multicoloured.

1004	32p. Type **338**	80	70
1005	44p. Artie Bell	1·25	1·50
1006	50p. Alec Bennett	1·50	1·75
1007	52p. Joey and Robert Dunlop	1·50	1·75
MS1008	100×70 mm. 50p. As 52p.	1·50	1·75

339 Michael Davitt (founder of The Land League)

1996. Anniversaries and Events. Multicoloured.

1009	28p. Type **339** (150th birth anniv)	80	60
1010	32p. Presidency logo (Ireland's Presidency of European Union) (horiz)	80	70
1011	38p. Thomas McLaughlin (hydro-electric engineer) and Ardnacrusha Power Station (birth centenary) (horiz)	1·25	1·10
1012	52p. Mechanical peat harvester (50th anniv of Bord na Mona) (horiz)	1·75	1·75

340 "Ciara" (coastal patrol vessel)

1996. 50th Anniv of Irish Naval Service. Multicoloured.

1013	32p. Type **340**	80	70
1014	44p. "Cliona" (corvette)	1·40	1·50
1015	52p. "M-1" (motor torpedo boat) (vert)	1·50	1·60

341 Blind Woman with Child

1996. People with Disabilities. Multicoloured.

1016	28p. Type **341**	1·25	1·25
1017	28p. Man in wheelchair playing bowls	1·25	1·25

342 Green-winged Teal

1996. Freshwater Ducks. Multicoloured.

1018	32p. Type **342**	1·00	70
1019	38p. Common shoveler	1·10	1·25
1020	44p. European wigeon	1·25	1·75
1021	52p. Mallard	1·60	2·00
MS1022	127×85 mm. Nos. 1018/21	4·50	5·50

343 "Man of Aran"

1996. Centenary of Irish Cinema. Multicoloured.

1023	32p. Type **343**	85	90
1024	32p. "My Left Foot"	85	90
1025	32p. "The Commitments"	85	90
1026	32p. "The Field"	85	90

344 Visit of the Magi

1996. Christmas. Designs from 16th-century "Book of Hours" (Nos. 1028/30). Multicoloured.

1027	28p. The Holy Family	75	60
1028	28p. Type **344**	60	60
1029	32p. The Annunciation	80	75
1030	52p. The Shepherds receiving new of Christ's birth	1·40	1·60

345 Black-billed Magpie ("Magpie")

1997. Birds. Ordinary gum. Multicoloured. (a) Size 23×26 mm or 26×23 mm.

1031	1p. Type **345**	10	60
1032	2p. Northern gannet ("Gannet") (vert)	15	60
1033	4p. Corn crake (vert)	20	40
1034	5p. Wood pigeon (horiz)	20	60
1035	10p. River kingfisher ("Kingfisher") (vert)	30	80
1036	20p. Northern lapwing ("Lapwing") (vert)	50	70
1037	28p. Blue tit (horiz)	2·00	50
1038	30p. Blackbird (vert)	70	50
1039p	30p. Goldcrest (vert)	70	80
1040	30p. Common stonechat ("Stonechat") (vert)	1·00	1·00
1041	30p. As No. 1036	1·00	1·00
1042	30p. As No. 1032	1·00	1·00
1043	30p. As No. 1033	1·00	1·00
1044	30p. Type **345**	1·00	1·00
1045	30p. As No. 1035	1·00	1·00
1046	30p. Peregrine falcon (vert)	1·00	1·00
1047	30p. Barn owl (vert)	1·00	1·00

1048 30p. European robin ("Robin") (vert) 1·00 1·00
1049 30p. Song thrush (vert) 1·00 1·00
1050 30p. Winter wren ("Wren") (vert) 2·00 2·00
1051 30p. Pied wagtail (vert) 2·00 2·00
1052 30p. Atlantic puffin ("Puffin") (vert) 1·00 1·00
1053 32p. As No. 1048 1·75 55
1054 35p. As No. 1040 1·00 1·00
1055p 40p. Ringed plover (horiz) 1·00 65
1056 44p. As No. 1052 3·00 1·60
1057ac 45p. As No. 1049 1·00 1·00
1058ac 50p. Northern sparrow hawk ("European Sparrow Hawk") (horiz) 1·50 1·00
1059 52p. As No. 1047 3·00 1·50

(b) Size 26×47 mm or 47×26 mm.

1060 £1 White-fronted goose ("Greenland White-fronted Goose") (vert) 2·00 1·60
1061 £2 Northern pintail ("Pintail") (horiz) 3·75 3·50
1062 £5 Common shelduck ("Shel-duck") (vert) 8·50 9·00

(c) Size 17×21 mm or 21×17 mm.

1080 4p. Corn crake 80 1·40
1081a 5p. Wood pigeon 55 75
1082 30p. Blackbird 1·40 1·40
1083 30p. Goldcrest 1·00 1·50
1084 32p. European robin ("Robin") 1·00 1·25
1085 32p. Peregrine falcon 1·50 1·50

(d) Size 24×29 mm. Self-adhesive.

1086 30p. Goldcrest 1·00 1·10
1087 30p. Blackbird 1·00 1·10
1088 32p. Peregrine falcon 2·00 2·50
1089 32p. European robin ("Robin") 2·00 2·50

346 Pair of Doves

1997. Greetings Stamps. Multicoloured.

1100 32p. Type **346** 85 50
1101 32p. Cow jumping over moon 1·10 1·25
1102 32p. Pig going to market 1·10 1·25
1103 32p. Cockerel 1·10 1·25

1997. "HONG KONG '97" International Stamp Exhibition. Chinese New Year ("Year of the Ox").

MS1104 124×74 mm. Nos. 1101/3 2·40 2·40

347 Troops on Parade

1997. 75th Anniv of Irish Free State. Mult.

1105 28p. Page from the "Annals of the Four Masters", quill and 1944 ½d. O'Clery stamp 55 55
1106 32p. Type **347** 60 75
1107 32p. The Dail, national flag and Constitution 60 75
1108 32p. Athlete, footballer and hurling player 60 75
1109 32p. Singer, violinist and bodhran player 60 75
1110 32p. Stained glass window and 1929 9d. O'Connell stamp 60 75
1111 32p. 1923 2d. map stamp and G.P.O., Dublin 60 75
1112 52p. Police personnel and Garda badge 1·00 1·50
1113 52p. The Four Courts and Scales of Justice 1·00 1·50
1114 52p. Currency, blueprint and food-processing plant 1·00 1·50
1115 52p. Books, palette and Seamus Heaney manuscript 1·00 1·50
1116 52p. Air Lingus Boeing 737 and 1965 1s.5d. air stamp 1·00 1·50
MS1117 174×209 mm. As Nos. 1105/16, but each with face value of 32p. 8·50 10·00

348 Grey Seals

1997. Marine Mammals. Multicoloured.

1118 28p. Type **348** 75 60
1119 32p. Bottle-nosed dolphins 85 80
1120 44p. Harbour porpoises (horiz) 1·25 1·40
1121 52p. Killer whale (horiz) 1·40 1·50
MS1122 150×68 mm. As Nos. 1118/21 6·00 6·00

349 Dublin Silver Penny of 997

1997. Millenary of Irish Coinage.

1123 **349** 32p. multicoloured 65 65

350 "The Children of Lir"

1997. Europa. Tales and Legends. Multicoloured. (a) Size 38×28 mm. Ordinary gum.

1124 32p. Type **350** 75 60
1125 44p. Oisin and Niamh 1·10 2·00

(b) Size 36×25 mm. Self-adhesive.

1126 32p. Type **350** 1·50 70
1127 32p. Oisin and Niamh 1·50 70

351 Emigrants waiting to board Ship

1997. 150th Anniv of The Great Famine.

1128 **351** 28p. blue, red and stone 1·00 60
1129 - 32p. orange, blue & stone 1·25 70
1130 - 52p. brown, blue & stone 1·75 2·50

DESIGNS: 32p. Family and dying child; 52p. Irish Society of Friends soup kitchen.

1997. "Pacific '97" International Stamp Exhibition, San Francisco. Sheet 100×70 mm, containing No. 1061. Multicoloured.

MS1131 £2 Pintail (48×26 mm) 4·50 5·50

352 Kate O'Brien (novelist) (birth centenary)

1997. Anniversaries. Multicoloured.

1132 28p. Type **352** 85 1·00
1133 28p. St. Columba crossing to Iona (stained glass window) (1400th death anniv) 85 1·00
1134 32p. "Daniel O'Connell" (J. Haverty) (politician) (150th death anniv) (27×49 mm) 95 70
1135 52p. "John Wesley" (N. Hone) (founder of Methodism) (250th anniv of first visit to Ireland) 1·75 2·50

353 The Baily Lighthouse

1997. Lighthouses. Multicoloured.

1136 32p. Type **353** 1·00 1·00
1137 32p. Tarbert 1·00 1·00
1138 38p. Hookhead (vert) 1·10 1·10
1139d 50p. The Fastnet (vert) 1·10 1·40

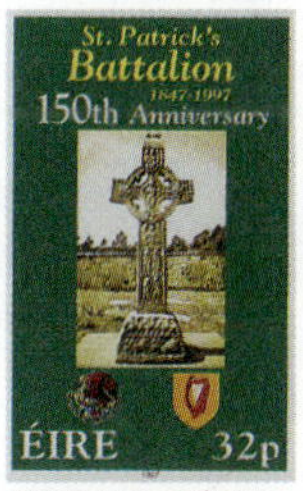

354 Commemorative Cross

1997. Ireland–Mexico Joint Issue. 150th Anniv of Mexican St. Patrick's Battalion.

1140 **354** 32p. multicoloured 55 60

355 Dracula and Bat

1997. Centenary of Publication of Bram Stoker's "Dracula". Multicoloured.

1141 28p. Type **355** 60 55
1142 32p. Dracula and female victim 65 60
1143 38p. Dracula emerging from coffin (horiz) 80 90
1144 52p. Dracula and wolf (horiz) 1·10 1·75
MS1145 150×90 mm. As Nos. 1141/4 3·25 3·75

356 "The Nativity" (Kevin Kelly)

357 Christmas Tree

1997. Christmas. Multicoloured. (a) Stained-glass Windows. Ordinary gum.

1146 28p. Type **356** 70 55
1147 32p. The Nativity (Sarah Purser and A. E. Child) 80 65
1148 52p. The Nativity (A. E. Child) 1·50 1·75

(b) Self-adhesive.

1149 28p. Type **357** 80 80

358 Holding Heart

1998. Greetings Stamps (1st series). Designs based on the "love is ..." cartoon characters of Kim Casali. Multicoloured.

1150 32p. Type **358** 1·10 50
1151 32p. Receiving letter 1·10 1·25
1152 32p. Sitting on log 1·10 1·25
1153 32p. With birthday presents 1·10 1·25

See also Nos. 1173/6.

1998. Chinese New Year ("Year of the Tiger").

MS1154 124×73 mm. Nos. 1151/3 4·50 4·75

359 Lady Mary Heath and Avro Type 581 Avian II over Pyramids

1998. Pioneers of Irish Aviation. Multicoloured.

1155 28p. Type **359** 60 55
1156 32p. Col. James Fitzmaurice and Junkers W.33 "Bremen" over Labrador 65 60
1157 44p. Captain J. P. Saul and Fokker F.VIIa/3m "Southern Cross" 1·25 1·25
1158 52p. Captain Charles Blair and Sikorsky V-S 44 (flying boat) 1·50 1·50

360 Show-jumping

1998. Equestrian Sports. Multicoloured.

1159 30p. Type **360** 90 60
1160 32p. Three-day eventing 95 65
1161 40p. Gymkhana 1·00 1·40
1162 45p. Dressage (vert) 1·00 1·40
MS1163 126×84 mm. Nos. 1159/62 3·50 3·50

361 Figure of "Liberty"

1998. Bicentenary of United Irish Rebellion. Mult.

1164 30p. Type **361** 1·00 1·00
1165 30p. United Irishman 1·00 1·00
1166 30p. French soldiers 1·00 1·00
1167 45p. Wolfe Tone 1·00 1·25
1168 45p. Henry Joy McCracken 1·00 1·25

362 Gathering of the Boats, Kinvara

1998. Europa. Festivals. Multicoloured. (a) Size 39×27 mm.

1169 30p. Type **362** 1·50 80
1170 40p. Puck Fair, Killorglin 1·50 95

(b) Size 34×23 mm. Self-adhesive.

1171 30p. Type **362** 1·50 90
1172 30p. Puck Fair, Killorglin 1·50 90

1998. Greetings Stamps (2nd series). As Nos. 1105/8, but with changed face value. Multicoloured.

1173 30p. As No. 1153 70 95
1174 30p. As No. 1152 70 95
1175 30p. As No. 1151 70 95
1176 30p. Type **358** 70 95

363 Cyclists rounding Bend

1998. Visit of "Tour de France" Cycle Race to Ireland. Multicoloured.

1177 30p. Type **363** 85 85
1178 30p. Two cyclists ascending hill 85 85
1179 30p. "Green jersey" cyclist and other competitor 85 85
1180 30p. "Yellow jersey" (race leader) 85 85

364 Voter and Local Councillors of 1898

1998. Democracy Anniversaries. Multicoloured.

1181	30p. Type **364** (cent of Local Government (Ireland) Act)	60	60
1182	32p. European Union flag and harp symbol (25th anniv of Ireland's entry into European Community)	65	65
1183	35p. Woman voter and suffragettes, 1898 (cent of women's right to vote in local elections)	75	75
1184	45p. Irish Republic flag (50th anniv of Republic of Ireland Act)	1·00	1·25

365 "Asgard II" (cadet brigantine)

1998. "Cutty Sark" International Tall Ships Race, Dublin. Multicoloured. (a) Ordinary gum.

1185	30p. Type **365** (26×38 mm)	70	70
1186	30p. U.S.C.G. "Eagle" (cadet barque) (26×38 mm)	70	70
1187	45p. "Boa Esperanza" (replica caravel) (38×26 mm)	1·00	1·00
1188	£1 "Royalist" (training brigantine) (38×26 mm)	1·90	2·50

(b) Self-adhesive.

1189	30p. "Boa Esperanza" (34×23 mm)	65	85
1190	30p. Type **365** (23×34 mm)	65	85
1191	30p. U.S.C.G. "Eagle" (23×34 mm)	65	85
1192	30p. "Royalist" (34×23 mm)	65	85

366 Ashworth Pillbox (1856)

1998. Irish Postboxes. Multicoloured.

1193	30p. Type **366**	75	1·00
1194	30p. Irish Free State wallbox (1922)	75	1·00
1195	30p. Double pillarbox (1899)	75	1·00
1196	30p. Penfold pillarbox (1866)	75	1·00

367 Mary Immaculate College, Limerick (centenary)

1998. Anniversaries. Multicoloured.

1197	30p. Type **367**	75	60
1198	40p. Newtown School, Waterford (bicent) (vert)	1·00	1·25
1199	45p. Trumpeters (50th anniv of Universal Declaration of Human Rights)	1·10	1·50

1998. "Portugal '98" International Stamp Exhibition, Lisbon. Sheet 101×71 mm, containing design as No. 1187.

MS1200	£2 "Boa Esperanza" (caravel) (horiz)	4·50	5·00

368 Cheetah

1998. Endangered Animals. Multicoloured.

1201	30p. Type **368**	1·40	1·25
1202	30p. Scimitar-horned oryx	1·40	1·25
1203	40p. Golden lion tamarin (vert)	1·40	1·25
1204	45p. Tiger (vert)	1·60	1·50
MS1205	150×90 mm. As Nos. 1201/4	4·25	4·25

369 The Holy Family **370** Choir Boys

1998. Christmas. Mult. (a) Ordinary gum.

1206	30p. Type **369**	70	60
1207	32p. Shepherds	75	65
1208	45p. Three Kings	1·00	1·75

(b) Self-adhesive.

1209	30p. Type **370**	80	80

371 Puppy and Heart

1999. Greetings Stamps. Pets. Multicoloured.

1210	30p. Type **371**	80	50
1211	30p. Kitten and ball of wool	80	1·00
1212	30p. Goldfish	80	1·00
1213	30p. Rabbit with lettuce leaf	80	1·00

1999. Chinese New Year ("Year of the Rabbit").

MS1214	124×74 mm. Nos. 1211/13	3·75	3·75

372 Micheal Mac Liammoir

1999. Irish Actors and Actresses.

1215	**372**	30p. black and brown	65	60
1216	-	45p. black and green	1·00	1·10
1217	-	50p. black and blue	1·00	1·25

DESIGNS: 45p. Siobhan McKenna, 50p. Noel Purcell.

373 Irish Emigrant Ship

1999. Ireland–U.S.A. Joint Issue. Irish Emigration.

1218	**373**	45p. multicoloured	1·25	1·00

374 "Polly Woodside" (barque)

1999. Maritime Heritage. Multicoloured.

1219	30p. Type **374**	55	60
1220	35p. "Ilen" (schooner)	65	70
1221	45p. R.N.L.I. Cromer class lifeboat (horiz)	80	85
1222	£1 "Titanic" (liner) (horiz)	2·00	2·50
MS1223	150×90 mm. No. 1222×2	3·25	4·00

1999. Ireland—Australia Joint Issue. "Polly Woodside" (barque). Sheet 137×72 mm. Multicoloured.

MS1224	45c. Type **603** of Australia; 30p. Type **374** (No. **MS**1224 was sold at 52p. in Ireland)	1·40	1·00

No. **MS**1224 includes the "Australia '99" emblem on the sheet margin and was postally valid in Ireland to the value of 30p.

The same miniature sheet was also available in Australia.

375 Sean Lemass

1999. Birth Centenary of Sean Lemass (politician).

1225	**375**	30p. black and green	1·25	65

376 European Currency Emblem

1999. Introduction of Single European Currency.

1226	**376**	30p. multicoloured	75	65

The face value of No. 1226 is shown in both Irish and euro currency.

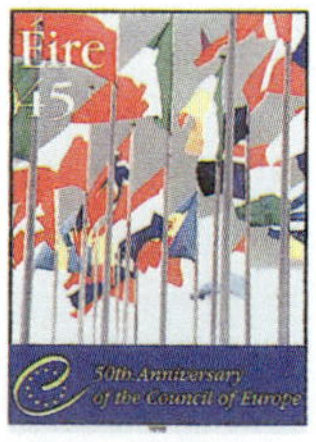

377 European Flags

1999. 50th Anniv of Council of Europe.

1227	**377**	45p. multicoloured	1·00	1·00

378 Whooper Swans, Kilcolman Nature Reserve

1999. Europa. Parks and Gardens. Multicoloured. (a) Size 36×26 mm. Ordinary gum.

1228	30p. Type **378**	90	50
1229	40p. Fallow deer, Phoenix Park	1·00	1·25

(b) Size 34×23 mm. Self-adhesive.

1230	30p. Type **378**	1·50	2·00
1231	30p. Fallow deer, Phoenix Park	1·50	2·00

379 Father James Cullen and St. Francis Xavier Church, Dublin

1999. Centenary of Pioneer Total Abstinence Association.

1232	**379**	32p. brown, bistre and black	75	65

380 Elderly Man and Child using Computer

1999. International Year of Older Persons.

1233	**380**	30p. multicoloured	70	65

381 Postal Van, 1922

1999. 125th Anniv of Universal Postal Union.

1234	**381**	30p. green and deep green	1·40	1·25
1235	-	30p. multicoloured	1·40	1·25

DESIGN: No. 1235, Modern postal lorries.

382 Danno Keeffe

1999. Gaelic Athletic Association "Millennium Football Team". Multicoloured. (a) Size 37×25 mm. Ordinary gum.

1236	30p. Type **382**	65	70
1237	30p. Enda Colleran	65	70
1238	30p. Joe Keohane	65	70
1239	30p. Sean Flanagan	65	70
1240	30p. Sean Murphy	65	70
1241	30p. John Joe Reilly	65	70
1242	30p. Martin O'Connell	65	70
1243	30p. Mick O'Connell	65	70
1244	30p. Tommy Murphy	65	70
1245	30p. Sean O'Neill	65	70
1246	30p. Sean Purcell	65	70
1247	30p. Pat Spillane	65	70
1248	30p. Mikey Sheehy	65	70
1249	30p. Tom Langan	65	70
1250	30p. Kevin Heffernan	65	70

(b) Size 33×23 mm. Self-adhesive.

1251	30p. Type **382**	1·50	2·25
1252	30p. Enda Colleran	65	80
1253	30p. Joe Keohane	1·50	2·25
1254	30p. Sean Flanagan	65	80
1255	30p. Sean Murphy	1·50	2·25
1256	30p. John Joe Reilly	55	60
1257	30p. Martin O'Connell	55	60
1258	30p. Mick O'Connell	1·50	2·25
1259	30p. Tommy Murphy	65	80
1260	30p. Sean O'Neill	55	60
1261	30p. Sean Purcell	65	80
1262	30p. Pat Spillane	65	80
1263	30p. Mikey Sheehy	65	80
1264	30p. Tom Langan	65	80
1265	30p. Kevin Heffernan	55	60

383 Douglas DC-3

1999. Commercial Aviation. Multicoloured.

1266	30p. Type **383**	65	50
1267	32p. Pilatus-Britten BN-2 Norman Islander	75	55
1268	40p. Boeing 707	80	1·40
1269	45p. Lockheed Constellation	90	1·50

384 Mammoth

1999. Extinct Irish Animals. Multicoloured. (a) Size 26×38 mm (vert) or 38×26 mm (horiz). Ordinary gum.

1270	30p. Type **384**	70	70
1271	30p. Giant deer	70	70
1272	45p. Wolves (horiz)	90	1·25
1273	45p. Brown bear (horiz)	90	1·25
MS1274	150×63 mm. Nos. 1270/3	2·50	2·75

(b) Size 33×23 mm (horiz) or 22×34 mm (vert). Self-adhesive.

1275	30p. Brown bear (horiz)	70	85
1276	30p. Type **384**	70	85
1277	30p. Wolves (horiz)	70	85
1278	30p. Giant deer	70	85

385 Holy Family

1999. Christmas. Children's Nativity Plays. Mult. (a) Size 35×25 mm. Ordinary gum.

1279	30p. Type **385**	60	50
1280	32p. Visit of the Shepherds	65	55
1281	45p. Adoration of the Magi	1·25	1·50

(b) Size 16×26 mm. Self-adhesive.

1282	30p. Angel	70	50

386 Grace Kelly (American actress)

1999. New Millennium (1st issue). Famous People of the 20th Century. Multicoloured.

1283	30p. Type **386**	1·75	2·00
1284	30p. Jesse Owens (American athlete)	1·75	2·00
1285	30p. John F. Kennedy (former American President)	1·75	2·00
1286	30p. Mother Teresa (missionary)	1·75	2·00
1287	30p. John McCormack (tenor)	1·75	2·00
1288	30p. Nelson Mandela (South African statesman)	1·75	2·00

See also Nos. 1289/94, 1300/5, 1315/20, 1377/82 and 1383/88.

387 Ruined Castle (Norman Invasion, 1169)

2000. New Millennium (2nd issue). Irish Historic Events. Multicoloured.

1289	30p. Type **387**	1·75	2·00
1290	30p. Flight of the Earls, 1607	1·75	2·00
1291	30p. Opening of Irish Parliament, 1782	1·75	2·00
1292	30p. Eviction (formation of the Land League)	1·75	2·00
1293	30p. First four Irish Prime Ministers (Irish Independence)	1·75	2·00
1294	30p. Irish soldier and personnel carrier (U.N. Peace-keeping)	1·75	2·00

388 Frog Prince

2000. Greetings Stamps. Mythical Creatures. Multicoloured.

1295	30p. Type **388**	1·00	60
1296	30p. Pegasus	1·00	1·25
1297	30p. Unicorn	1·00	1·25
1298	30p. Dragon	1·00	1·25

2000. Chinese New Year ("Year of the Dragon").

MS1299	124×74 mm. Nos. 1296/8	3·00	3·00

389 Revd. Nicholas Callan (electrical scientist)

2000. New Millennium (3rd issue). Discoveries. Multicoloured.

1300	30p. Type **389**	1·75	2·00
1301	30p. Birr Telescope	1·75	2·00
1302	30p. Thomas Edison (inventor of light bulb)	1·75	2·00
1303	30p. Albert Einstein (mathematical physicist)	1·75	2·00
1304	30p. Marie Curie (physicist)	1·75	2·00
1305	30p. Galileo Galilei (astronomer and mathematician)	1·75	2·00

390 "Jeanie Johnston" (emigrant ship)

2000. Completion of "Jeanie Johnston" Replica.

1306	**390**	30p. multicoloured	70	50

391 "Building Europe"

2000. Europa. (a) 25½×36½ mm.

1307	**391**	32p. multicoloured	80	55

(b) 22×34 mm. Self-adhesive.

1308	30p. multicoloured	75	50

DENOMINATION. From No. 1309 to 1465 some Irish stamps are denominated both in Irish pounds and in euros.

392 Oscar Wilde

2000. Death Centenary of Oscar Wilde (writer). Multicoloured.

1309	30p. Type **392**	1·40	1·40
1310	30p. *The Happy Prince*	1·40	1·40
1311	30p. Lady Bracknell from *The Importance of being Earnest*	1·40	1·40
1312	30p. *The Picture of Dorian Gray*	1·40	1·40
MS1313	150×190 mm. £2 Type **392**	3·75	4·00

A further 30p. exists in a design similar to Type **392**, but 29×29 mm, printed in sheets of 20, each stamp having a se-tenant half-stamp size label attached at right inscribed "Oscar". These sheets could be personalized by the addition of a photograph in place of the inscription on the labels. Such stamps are not listed as they were not available at face value, the sheets of 20 containing the "Oscar" labels being sold for £10.

393 Ludwig van Beethoven (German composer)

2000. New Millennium (4th issue). The Arts. Mult.

1315	30p. Type **393**	1·40	1·50
1316	30p. Dame Ninette de Valois (ballet director)	1·40	1·50
1317	30p. James Joyce (author)	1·40	1·50
1318	30p. "Mona Lisa" (Leonardo da Vinci)	1·40	1·50
1319	30p. "Lady Lavery" (Sir John Lavery)	1·40	1·50
1320	30p. William Shakespeare (playwright)	1·40	1·50

394 Running

2000. Olympic Games, Sydney. Multicoloured.

1321	30p. Type **394**	70	70
1322	30p. Javelin throwing	70	70
1323	50p. Long jumping	1·00	1·25
1324	50p. High jumping	1·00	1·25

395 "Space Rocket over Flowers" (Marguerite Nyhan)

2000. "Stampin' the Future" (children's stamp design competition). Multicoloured.

1325	30p. Type **395**	60	50
1326	32p. "Tree, rocket and hands holding globe in '2000'" (Kyle Staunton) (horiz)	70	55
1327	45p. "People holding hands on globe" (Jennifer Branagan) (horiz)	90	1·10
1328	45p. "Colony on Moon" (Diarmuid O'Ceochain) (horiz)	90	1·10

396 Tony Reddin

2000. "Hurling Team of the Millennium". Multicoloured. (a) Size 36×27 mm.

1329	30p. Type **396**	60	70
1330	30p. Bobby Rackard	60	70
1331	30p. Nick O'Donnell	60	70
1332	30p. John Doyle	60	70
1333	30p. Brian Whelahan	60	70
1334	30p. John Keane	60	70
1335	30p. Paddy Phelan	60	70
1336	30p. Lory Meagher	60	70
1337	30p. Jack Lynch	60	70
1338	30p. Jim Langton	60	70
1339	30p. Mick Mackey	60	70
1340	30p. Christy Ring	60	70
1341	30p. Jimmy Doyle	60	70
1342	30p. Ray Cummins	60	70
1343	30p. Eddie Keher	60	70

(b) Size 33×23 mm. Self-adhesive.

1344	30p. Type **396**	75	1·00
1345	30p. Jimmy Doyle	75	1·00
1346	30p. John Doyle	75	1·00
1347	30p. Paddy Phelan	1·25	1·60
1348	30p. Jim Langton	1·25	1·60
1349	30p. Lory Meagher	75	1·00
1350	30p. Eddie Keher	75	1·00
1351	30p. Mick Mackey	75	1·00
1352	30p. Brian Whelahan	75	1·00
1353	30p. John Keane	75	1·00
1354	30p. Bobby Rackard	75	1·00
1355	30p. Nick O'Donnell	75	1·00
1356	30p. Jack Lynch	75	1·00
1357	30p. Ray Cummins	75	1·00
1358	30p. Christy Ring	75	1·00

397 Peacock Butterfly

2000. Butterflies. Multicoloured.

1359	30p. Type **397**	80	50
1360	32p. Small tortoiseshell	85	55
1361	45p. Silver-washed fritillary	1·25	1·75
1362	50p. Orange-tip	1·40	2·50
MS1363	150×90 mm. Nos. 1359/62	3·00	3·00

2000. Military Aviation. Multicoloured. (a) Size 37×26 mm.

1364	30p. Hawker Hurricane Mk IIC	80	80
1365	30p. Bristol F.2B Mk II	80	80
1366	45p. de Havilland DH.115 Vampire T 55	1·10	1·25
1367	45p. Eurocopter S.E. 3160 Alouette III (helicopter)	1·10	1·25

(b) Size 33×22 mm. Self-adhesive.

1368	30p. Bristol F.2B Mk II	70	70
1369	30p. Hawker Hurricane Mk IIC	70	70
1370	30p. de Havilland DH.115 Vampire T.55	70	70
1371	30p. Eurocopter SE. 3160 Alouette III	70	70

398 Tractor ploughing Field

2000. Centenary of An Roinn Talmhaiochta (Department of Agriculture).

1372	**398**	50p. multicoloured	1·00	1·10

399 The Nativity

2000. Christmas. Multicoloured. (a) Size 24×27 mm.

1373	30p. Type **399**	65	50
1374	32p. Three Magi	75	55
1375	45p. Shepherds	1·00	1·25

(b) Size 24×29 mm. Self-adhesive.

1376	30p. Flight into Egypt	80	50

400 Storming the Bastille, Paris, 1789

2000. New Millennium (5th issue). World Events. Multicoloured.

1377	30p. Type **400**	1·75	2·00
1378	30p. Early railway	1·75	2·00
1379	30p. Returning troop ship, 1945	1·75	2·00
1380	30p. Suffragettes	1·75	2·00
1381	30p. Destruction of the Berlin Wall, 1989	1·75	2·00
1382	30p. Internet communications	1·75	2·00

2001. New Millenuim (6th issue). Epic Journeys. As T 400. Multicoloured.

1383	30p. Marco Polo	2·00	2·00
1384	30p. Captain James Cook	2·00	2·00
1385	30p. Burke and Wills expedition crossing Australia, 1860	2·00	2·00
1386	30p. Ernest Shackleton in Antarctica	2·00	2·00
1387	30p. Charles Lindbergh and Ryan NYP Special *Spirit of St. Louis*	2·00	2·00
1388	30p. Astronaut on Moon	2·00	2·00

401 Goldfish

2001. Greetings Stamps. Pets. (a) As Type 401. Mult.

1389	30p. Type **401**	80	50

(b) Designs smaller, 20×30 mm. Self-adhesive.

1390	30p. Lizard	1·00	1·10
1391	30p. Frog	1·00	1·10
1392	30p. Type **401**	1·00	1·10
1393	30p. Snake	1·00	1·10
1394	30p. Tortoise	1·00	1·10

2001. Chinese New Year ("Year of the Snake").

MS1395	124×75 mm. As Nos. 1391 and 1393/4, but larger, 28×39 mm	2·00	2·00

402 Television Presenter and Audience

2001. Irish Broadcasting.

1396	**402**	30p. multicoloured	70	50
1397	-	32p. black, ultramarine and blue	80	55
1398	-	45p. black, brown and orange	1·00	1·10
1399	-	50p. brown, yellow and green	1·00	1·25

DESIGNS: 32p. Radio sports commentators; 45p. Family around radio; 50p. Play on television set.

403 Archbishop Narcissus Marsh and Library Interior

2001. Literary Anniversaries. Multicoloured.

1400	30p. Type **403** (300th anniv of Marsh's Library)	60	50
1401	32p. Book of Common Prayer, 1551 (450th anniv of first book printed in Ireland)	65	1·00

404 Bagpipe Player

2001. 50th Anniv of Comhaltas Ceoltoiri Eireann (cultural organization). Multicoloured.

1402	30p. Type **404**	70	70
1403	30p. Bodhran player	70	70
1404	45p. Young fiddler and Irish dancer (horiz)	1·00	1·25
1405	45p. Flautist and singer (horiz)	1·00	1·25

405 Jordan Formula 1 Racing Car

2001. Irish Motorsport. Multicoloured. (a) As Type 405.

1406	30p. Type **405**	75	50
1407	32p. Hillman Imp on Tulip Rally	80	55
1408	45p. Mini Cooper S on Monte Carlo Rally	1·25	80
1409	£1 Mercedes SSK, winner of 1930 Irish Grand Prix	2·00	2·50
MS1410	150×90 mm. £2 Type **405**	3·75	4·25

(b) Designs smaller, 33½×22½. Self-adhesive.

1411	30p. Type **405**	90	85
1412	30p. Hillman Imp on Tulip Rally	1·10	1·25
1413	30p. Mini Cooper S on Monte Carlo Rally	1·10	1·25
1414	30p. Mercedes SSK, winner of 1930 Irish Grand Prix	1·10	1·25

406 Peter Lalor (leader at Eureka Stockade) and Gold Licence

2001. Irish Heritage in Australia. Multicoloured.

1415	30p. Type **406**	60	60
1416	30p. Ned Kelly (bush ranger) and "Wanted" poster	60	60
1417	45p. Family leaving for Australia and immigrant ship	1·25	1·25
1418	45p. Irish settler and life in gold camp	1·25	1·25
MS1419	150×90 mm. £1 As No. 1416	2·25	2·50

407 Children playing in River

2001. Europa; Water Resources. Multicoloured. (a) Size 36½×26½ mm.

1420	30p. Type **407**	1·25	50
1421	32p. Man fishing	1·50	75

(b) Designs smaller, 33×22 mm. Self-adhesive.

1422	30p. Type **407**	90	90
1423	30p. As 32p	90	90

408 Blackbird

2001. Dual Currency Birds. Vert designs as Nos. 1038, 1050, 1053, 1056/7 and 1060 (some with different face values) showing both Irish currency and euros as in T 408. Multicoloured. (a) Ordinary gum.

1424	30p./38c. Type **408**	90	60
1425	32p./41c. European robin ("Robin")	95	70
1426	35p./44c. Atlantic puffin ("Puffin")	1·10	1·10
1427	40p./51c. Winter wren ("Wren")	1·25	1·25
1428	45p./57c. Song thrush	1·40	1·40
1429	£1/€1.27 White-fronted goose ("Greenland White-fronted Goose") (23×44 mm)	3·00	3·25

(b) Designs as Nos. 1038/9, but 25×30 mm. Self-adhesive.

1430	30p./38c. Type **408**	90	90
1431	30p./38c. Goldcrest	90	90

409 Irish Pikeman

2001. 400th Anniv of Battle of Kinsale. Nine Years War. Multicoloured.

1432	30p. Type **409**	70	70
1433	30p. English cavalry	70	70
1434	32p. Spanish pikeman	80	80
1435	45p. Town of Kinsale	1·10	1·25

410 Ruffian 23 Yachts

2001. Yachts. Multicoloured. (a) Size 26×37½ mm.

1436	30p. Type **410**	70	60
1437	32p. Howth 17 yacht	75	65
1438	45p. 1720 Sportsboat yacht	1·10	1·25
1439	45p. Glen class cruising yacht	1·10	1·25

(b) Self-adhesive. Size 22×34 mm.

1440	30p. Type **410**	70	70
1441	30p. Howth 17 yacht	70	70
1442	30p. Glen class cruising yacht	70	70
1443	30p. 1720 Sportsboat yacht	70	70

411 Padraic Carney (footballer)

2001. Gaelic Athletic Association Hall of Fame 2001 (1st series). Multicoloured. (a) Size 36½×27 mm.

1444	30p. Type **411**	70	70
1445	30p. Frank Cummins (hurler)	70	70
1446	30p. Jack O'Shea (footballer)	70	70
1447	30p. Nicky Rackard (hurler)	70	70

(b) Self-adhesive. Size 33½×22½ mm.

1448	30p. Type **411**	70	70
1449	30p. Frank Cummins (hurler)	70	70
1450	30p. Jack O'Shea (footballer)	70	70
1451	30p. Nicky Rackard (hurler)	70	70

See also Nos. 1550/3.

2001. "Belgica 2001" International Stamp Exhibition, Brussels. No. MS1410 with "Belgica 2001" added to the sheet margin.

MS1452	150×90 mm. £2 Type **405**	4·00	4·25

See also Nos. 1550/3.

412 Blackbird

2001. Birds. Vert designs as Nos. 1038/9, 1048 and 1049, but 24×29 mm, each showing a letter in place of face values as T 412. Multicoloured. Self-adhesive.

1453	(N) Type **412**	1·00	60
1454	(N) Goldcrest	1·00	60
1455	(E) Robin	1·00	55
1456	(W) Song thrush	1·25	1·00

Nos. 1453/6 were intended to cover the changeover period to euros. Nos. 1453/4 were sold for 32p, No. 1455 for 32p. and No. 1456 for 45p.

413 Perch

2001. Freshwater Fish. Multicoloured.

1457	30p. Type **413**	75	50
1458	32p. Arctic charr	80	85
1459	32p. Pike	80	85
1460	45p. Common bream	1·10	1·25

414 "Out of Bounds" (sculpture by Eilis O'Connell)

2001. 50th Anniv of Government Support for Arts.

1461	**414**	50p. multicoloured	1·25	1·40

415 "The Nativity" (Richard King)

2001. Christmas. Paintings by Richard King. Multicoloured. (a) Size 25½×36½ mm.

1462	30p. Type **415**	70	50
1463	32p. "The Annunciation"	75	55
1464	45p. "Presentation in the Temple"	1·10	1·25

(b) Size 25×30 mm. Self-adhesive.

1465	30p. "Madonna and Child"	1·00	50

416 Black-billed Magpie ("Magpie")

2002. New Currency. Birds, as Nos. 1031/62, and new designs, with face values in cents and euros, as T 416. (i) Size 23×26 mm or 26×23 mm.

1466	1c. Type **416**	10	30
1467	2c. Northern gannet ("Gannet")	10	30
1468	3c. Blue tit (horiz)	10	30
1469	4c. Corn crake	10	30
1470	5c. Woodpigeon (horiz)	10	30
1470a	7c. Common stonechat	50	30
1471	10c. River kingfisher ("Kingfisher")	20	30
1472	20c. Northern lapwing ("Lapwing")	35	45
1473	38c. Blackbird	70	55
1474	41c. Chaffinch	70	60
1475	41c. Goldcrest	2·00	2·00
1476	44c. European robin ("Robin")	85	65
1477	47c. Kestrel (horiz)	90	70
1477a	48c. Peregrine falcon	90	70
1477b	48c. Pied wagtail	1·75	1·75
1478	50c. Grey heron (horiz)	90	90
1479	51c. Roseate tern (horiz)	90	75
1480	55c. Oystercatcher (horiz)	1·00	75
1481	57c. Western curlew ("Curlew")	1·00	80
1482	60c. Jay (horiz)	1·00	1·25
1482a	60c. Atlantic puffin	1·25	1·00
1482b	65c. Song thrush	1·25	1·00
1482c	75c. Ringed plover (horiz)	1·50	1·10
1482d	95c. Sparrowhawk (horiz)	2·50	1·40

(ii) Size 47×26 mm or 26×47 mm.

1483	€1 Barnacle goose (horiz)	1·50	1·40
1484	€2 White-fronted goose ("Greenland White-fronted Goose")	3·00	3·00
1485	€5 Northern pintail ("Pintail") (horiz)	7·00	7·00
1486	€10 Common shelduck ("Shelduck")	14·00	15·00

(b) Size 20×23 mm.

1486a	4c. Corncrake	70	1·00
1487	10c. River kingfisher ("Kingfisher")	1·60	2·00
1488	36c. Wren	2·00	2·25
1489	38c. Blackbird	70	70
1490	41c. Chaffinch	70	70
1490a	48c. Peregrine falcon	75	75

(c) Self-adhesive. Size 24×29 mm.

1491	38c. Blackbird	70	70
1492	38c. Goldcrest	70	70
1493	41c. Chaffinch	90	90
1494	41c. Goldcrest	90	90
1495	44c. Robin	95	95
1495b	(–) Peregrine falcon	1·25	1·25
1495c	(–) Pied wagtail	1·25	1·25
1495d	48c. Peregrine falcon	90	90
1495e	48c. Pied wagtail	90	90
1496	50c. Puffin	95	95
1497	57c. Song thrush	1·10	1·10
1497b	60c. Atlantic puffin	1·10	1·10
1497c	65c. Song thrush	1·40	1·40

Nos. 1495b/c were sold for 48c.

417 Reverse of Irish €1 Coin, 2002

2002. Introduction of Euro Currency. Irish Coins.

1506	38c. Type **417**	75	50
1507	41c. Reverse of 50p. coin, 1971–2001	80	60
1508	57c. Reverse of 1d. coin, 1928–71	1·10	1·25

418 Teddy Bear

2002. Greetings Stamps. Toys. Multicoloured. (a) Design 25×37 mm.

1509	38c. Type **418**	70	50

(b) Designs 20×27 mm. Self-adhesive.

1510	38c. Type **418**	80	80
1511	38c. Rag doll	80	80
1512	38c. Rocking horse	80	80
1513	38c. Train	80	80
1514	38c. Wooden blocks	80	80

2002. Chinese New Year ("Year of the Horse").

MS1515	124×74 mm. As Nos. 1511/13, but 25×37 mm	2·25	2·25

419 Around the Camp Fire

2002. 75th Anniv of Scouting Ireland CSI. Multicoloured.

1516	41c. Type **419**	75	75
1517	41c. Setting up camp	75	75
1518	57c. Scouts canoeing	1·10	1·25
1519	57c. Scouts on hill walk	1·10	1·25

420 "Arkle"

2002. 250th Anniv of Steeplechasing in Ireland. Irish Steeplechasers. Multicoloured.

1520	38c. Type **420**	1·00	1·00
1521	38c. "L'Escargot"	1·00	1·00
1522	38c. "Dawn Run"	1·00	1·00
1523	38c. "Istabraq"	1·00	1·00

421 Badger

2002. Irish Mammals. Multicoloured.

1524	41c. Type **421**	75	60
1525	50c. Otter	90	70
1526	57c. Red squirell (vert)	1·10	80
1527	€1 Hedgehog (vert)	1·75	1·90
MS1528	150×67 mm. €5 As 50c.	7·00	7·50

422 Roy Keane

2002. World Cup Football Championship, Japan and Korea (2002). Irish Footballers. Multicoloured. (a) Size 29×40 mm or 40×29 mm.

1529	41c. Packie Bonner (horiz)	1·00	75
1530	41c. Type **422**	1·00	75
1531	41c. Paul McGrath	1·00	75
1532	41c. David O'Leary	1·00	75

(b) Size 25×37 mm or 37×35 mm. Self-adhesive.

1533	41c. Packie Bonner (horiz)	90	90
1534	41c. Type **422**	90	90
1535	41c. Paul McGrath	90	90
1536	41c. David O'Leary	90	90

423 Clown

2002. Europa. Circus. Multicoloured. (a) Size 40×29 mm. Ordinary gum.

1537	41c. Type **423**	70	70
1538	44c. Girl on horse	70	70

(b) Self-adhesive. Size 37×25 mm.

1539	41c. Type **423**	70	70
1540	41c. As No. 1538	70	70

424 Padre Pio

2002. Canonisation of St. Pio de Pietrelcina (Padre Pio).

1541	**424**	41c. multicoloured	75	70

425 Brian Boru leading Army

2002. 1000th Anniv of Declaration of Brian Boru as High King of Ireland. Multicoloured.

1542	41c. Type **425**	75	60
1543	44c. Leading fleet	75	60
1544	57c. Receiving surrender of the O'Neills	90	80
1545	£1 Decreeing primacy of bishopric of Armagh in the Irish Church	1·75	1·90

426 "Before the Start" (J. B. Yeats)

2002. 140th Anniv of National Gallery of Ireland (2004) (1st issue). Paintings. Multicoloured.

1546	41c. Type **426**	70	75
1547	41c. "The Conjuror" (Nathaniel Hone)	70	75
1548	41c. "The Colosseum and Arch of Constantine, Rome" (Giovanni Panini)	70	75
1549	41c. "The Gleaners" (Jules Breton)	70	75

See also Nos. 1606/9 and 1700/3.

2002. Gaelic Athletic Association Hall of Fame 2002 (2nd series). As T 411.

1550	41c. Peter McDermott (footballer)	70	75
1551	41c. Jimmy Smyth (hurler)	70	75
1552	41c. Matt Connor (footballer)	70	75
1553	41c. Seanie Duggan (hurler)	70	75

427 Archbishop Thomas Croke

2002. Death Centenary of Archbishop Croke (first patron of Gaelic Athletic Association).

1554	**427**	44c. multicoloured	80	70

428 U2

2002. Irish Rock Legends. Multicoloured.

1555	41c. Type **428**	1·25	90
1556	41c. Phil Lynott	1·25	90
1557	57c. Van Morrison	1·40	1·50
1558	57c. Rory Gallagher	1·40	1·50
MS1559	Four sheets, each 150×90 mm. (a) €2 Type **428**. (b) €2 No. 1556. (c) €2 No. 1557. (d) €2 No. 1558	12·00	13·00

429 "Adoration of the Magi"

2002. Christmas. Illustrations from "Les Tres Riches Heures du Duc de Berry" (medieval book of hours). Multicoloured. (a) Size 30×41 mm.

1560	41c. Type **429**	70	60
1561	44c. "The Annunciation to the Virgin Mary"	75	60
1562	57c. "The Annunciation to the Shepherds"	1·00	1·10

(b) Size 25×30 mm. Self-adhesive.

1563	41c. "The Nativity"	80	60

430 Labrador Puppies

2003. Greetings Stamps. Baby Animals. Multicoloured. (a) 29×40 mm.

1564	41c. Type **430**	80	65

(b) Designs 24×29 mm. Self-adhesive.

1565	41c. Type **430**	80	80
1566	41c. Chicks	80	80
1567	41c. Kids	80	80
1568	41c. Kittens	80	80
1569	41c. Baby rabbits	80	80

2003. Chinese New Year ("Year of the Goat"). Designs as Nos. 1566/8, but 29×40 mm.

MS1570	124×74 mm. 50c. Chicks; 50c. Kids; 50c. Kittens	3·25	3·50

431 St. Patrick

2003. St. Patrick's Day. Multicoloured. Size 29×40 mm.

1571	41c. Type **431**	80	60
1572	50c. St. Patrick's Day Parade passing St. Patrick's Cathedral, Dublin	95	1·00
1573	57c. St. Patrick's Day Parade, New York	1·10	1·25

(b) Size 25×26 mm. Self-adhesive.

1574	41c. St. Patrick	85	90
1575	50c. St. Patrick's Day Parade passing St. Patrick's Cathedral, Dublin	85	1·00
1576	57c. St. Patrick's Day Parade, New York	95	1·25

432 Seven-spotted Ladybird

2003. Irish Beetles. Multicoloured.

1577	41c. Type **432**	90	60
1578	50c. Great diving beetle	1·00	70
1579	57c. Leaf beetle	1·25	80
1580	€1 Green tiger beetle	2·25	2·50
MS1581	150×68 mm. €2 Type **432**	3·75	4·00

433 Dingle Peninsula ("IRELAND for HOLIDAYS")

2003. Europa. Poster Art. Posters by Paul Henry. Multicoloured.

1582	41c. Type **433**	80	65
1583	57c. Connemara ("IRELAND THIS YEAR")	95	1·10

434 "2003" and EYPD Logo

2003. European Year of People with Disabilities.

1584	**434**	41c. multicoloured	80	65

435 Athletes waving to Crowd

2003. 11th Special Olympics World Summer Games, Dublin. Multicoloured.

1585	41c. Type **435**	75	45
1586	50c. Swimmer	80	60
1587	57c. Athlete on starting block	95	65
1588	€1 Athlete running	2·25	3·25

436 Napier

2003. Centenary of Gordon Bennett Race in Ireland. Racing cars of 1903. Multicoloured. (a) Ordinary gum. Size 39×29 mm.

1589	41c. Type **436**	80	1·00
1590	41c. Mercedes	80	1·00
1591	41c. Mors	80	1·00
1592	41c. Winton	80	1·00

(b) Self-adhesive. Size 36×25 mm.

1593	41c. As No. 1592	80	90
1594	41c. As No. 1591	80	90
1595	41c. As No. 1590	80	90
1596	41c. Type **436**	80	90

437 Henry Ford and Model T Ford, 1908–28

2003. Centenary of the Ford Motor Company.

1597	**437**	41c. multicoloured	80	65

438 Harry Ferguson flying first Irish Monoplane, 1909

2003. Centenary of Powered Flight. Multicoloured.

1598	41c. Type **438**	80	60
1599	50c. Alcock and Brown's Vickers FB.27 Vimy over Galway after first transatlantic flight, 1919	1·10	80
1600	57c. *Wright Flyer I*, 1903	1·25	1·50
1601	57c. Lillian Bland's biplane, 1910	1·25	1·50
MS1602	150×90 mm. €5 As No. 1600	8·50	10·00

439 Robert Emmet

2003. Centenary of Rebellion of 1803. Multicoloured.

1603	41c. Type **439**	80	60
1604	50c. Thomas Russell	1·10	1·10
1605	57c. Anne Devlin	1·40	1·60

2003. 140th Anniv of National Gallery of Ireland (2004) (2nd issue). Paintings. As T 426 but vert. Multicoloured.

1606	48c. "Self-portrait as Timanthes" (James Barry)	1·00	1·25
1607	48c. "Man writing a Letter" (Gabriel Metsu)	1·00	1·25
1608	48c. "Woman reading a Letter" (Gabriel Metsu)	1·00	1·25
1609	48c. "Woman seen from the Back" (Jean-Antoine Watteau)	1·00	1·25

440 Frank O'Connor

2003. Birth Centenary of Frank O'Connor (writer).

1610	**440**	50c. multicoloured	1·00	1·00

441 E. T. S. Walton

2003. Birth Centenary of E. T. S. Walton (Nobel Prize for Physics, 1951).

1611	**441**	57c. cream, black and brown	1·00	1·00

442 Admiral William Brown (founder of the Argentine Navy)

2003. Irish Mariners. Multicoloured. (a) Ordinary gum. Size 40×29 mm.

1612	48c. Type **442**	1·00	1·00
1613	48c. Commodore John Barry (Commanding Officer of US Navy, 1794–1803)	1·00	1·00
1614	57c. Captain Robert Halpin (Commander of cable ship *Great Eastern*)	1·10	1·10
1615	57c. Captain Richard Roberts (captain of *Sirius*, first scheduled passenger steamship London to New York voyage)	1·10	1·10
MS1616	150×90 mm. €5 Commodore John Barry	8·00	8·50

(b) Self-adhesive. Size 36×21 mm.

1617	48c. Commodore John Barry	1·00	1·00
1618	48c. Admiral William Brown	1·00	1·00
1619	48c. Captain Robert Halpin	1·00	1·00
1620	48c. Captain Richard Roberts	1·00	1·00

443 Pope John Paul II

2003. 25th Anniv of the Election of Pope John Paul II. Multicoloured.

1621	48c. Type **443**	1·00	90
1622	50c. Pope in St. Peter's Square, Rome	1·10	95
1623	57c. Making speech at United Nations	1·25	1·10

444 Angel

2003. Christmas. Multicoloured. (a) Ordinary gum.

1624	48c. Flight into Egypt (32×32 mm)	90	80
1625	50c. Type **444**	95	80
1626	57c. Three Kings	1·10	1·25

(b) Self-adhesive. Size 29×24 mm.

1627	48c. Nativity	80	70

445 Boyne Bridge

2004. Ireland's Presidency of European Union.

1628	**445**	48c. multicoloured	1·50	1·00

446 "Monkeys in Love"

2004. Greetings Stamps. Animals. Multicoloured. Ordinary gum. Size 29×39 mm.

1629	48c. Type **446**	1·50	1·25
MS1630	124×74 mm. 60c. Type **446**; 60c. "Jolly Panda"; 60c. "Cute Koalas"	3·50	3·75

(b) Self-adhesive. Size 24×29 mm.

1631	48c. Type **446**	1·00	1·00
1632	48c. "Jolly Panda"	1·00	1·00
1633	48c. "Cute Koalas"	1·00	1·00
1634	48c. "Happy Hippo"	1·00	1·00

447 St. Patrick and Stained Glass Window from Church of the Holy and Undivided Trinity, Magheralin, Co. Down

2004. St. Patrick's Day.

1635	**447**	65c. multicoloured	1·50	1·50

448 Abbey Theatre Logo

2004. Centenary of Abbey Theatre, Dublin.

1636	**448**	48c. multicoloured	1·10	1·10

449 Expedition Members, Dogs and *Endurance* trapped in Ice

2004. 90th Anniv of Shackleton's Antarctic Expedition. Multicoloured.

1637	48c. Type **449**	1·50	1·00
1638	48c. Two crew members, huskies and bow of *Endurance*	1·50	1·00
1639	65c. Crew member looking out of tent	2·25	2·25
1640	65c. Crew members and tented camp on ice	2·25	2·25
MS1641	149×90 mm. €1 As No. 1639; €1 As No. 1640	4·25	4·50

450 Flags, Football and Globe

2004. Centenary of FIFA (Federation Internationale de Football Association).

1642	**450**	60c. multicoloured	1·40	1·40

451 Map of Europe showing Acceding Countries

2004. Enlargement of the European Union.

1643	**451**	65c. multicoloured	2·25	1·40

452 Tufted Duck

2004. Ducks. Multicoloured.

1644	48c. Type **452**	90	70
1645	60c. Red-breasted merganser	1·25	1·25
1646	65c. Gadwall	1·25	1·25
1647	€1 Garganey	1·90	2·00
MS1648	150×90 mm. Nos. 1644/7	4·75	5·00

453 Ross Castle, Co. Kerry

2004. Europa. Holidays. Multicoloured.

1649	48c. Type **453**	90	70
1650	65c. Cliffs of Moher, Co. Clare	1·25	1·50

454 Emblem

2004. 10th Anniv of UN International Year of the Family.

1651	**454**	65c. scarlet, yellow and green	1·25	1·25

455 "Frog" (Daire Lee)

2004. Winning Entries in Children's Painting Competition. Multicoloured.

1652	48c. Type **455**	90	70
1653	60c. "Marmalade Cat" (Cian Colman)	1·25	1·25
1654	65c. "Ralleshin Dipditch" (Daire O'Rourke)	1·25	1·25
1655	€1 "Fish on a Dish" (Ailish Fitzpatrick) (horiz)	1·90	2·00

456 "James Joyce" (Tullio Pericoli)

2004. Centenary of "Leopold Bloom's Adventure" (from Ulysses by James Joyce). Multicoloured.

1656	48c. Type **456**	80	70
1657	65c. James Joyce	1·10	1·40

457 College Entrance

2004. 426th Anniv of Irish College, Paris.

1658	**457**	65c. multicoloured	1·00	1·00

458 LUAS Tram

2004. Introduction of LUAS Tram System, Dublin. Multicoloured.

1659	48c. Type **458**	65	70
1660	48c. People accessing LUAS tram	65	70

459 Javelin Thrower and Olympic Flame

2004. Olympic Games, Athens. Multicoloured.

1661	48c. Type **459**	1·00	70
1662	60c. Discobolus (sculpture, Myron) and Olympic flame	1·40	1·60

460 Two Camogie Players and O'Duffy Cup

2004. Centenary of Camogie (Gaelic game for women). Multicoloured.

1663	48c. Type **460**	95	1·10
1664	48c. Two players and Camogie emblem	95	1·10

461 Common Dog-violet

2004. Wild Flowers. Multicoloured. (a) Ordinary gum. (i) 23×26 mm.

1665	1c. Bloody crane's-bill	10	10
1666	2c. Irish orchid	10	10
1667	3c. Yellow flag	10	10
1668	4c. Type **461**	10	15
1669	5c. Dandelion	10	15
1670	7c. Fly orchid	15	20
1671	10c. Mountain avens	15	20
1672	12c. Autumn gorse	15	20
1673	20c. Thrift	30	35
1674	25c. Common knapweed	35	40
1675	48c. Daisy	65	70
1676	48c. Primrose	65	70
1677	50c. Biting stonecrop	70	75
1678	55c. Large-flowered butterwort	1·20	1·20
1679	60c. Hawthorn	80	85
1680	65c. Bluebell	90	95
1681	75c. Navelwort	1·00	1·10
1682	78c. Black bog-rush	1·80	1·80
1683	82c. Sea aster	1·20	1·30
1684	90c. Viper's bugloss	1·20	1·30
1685	95c. Purple loosestrife	2·20	2·20

(ii) 26×47 mm (€1, €2) or 47×26 mm (others).

1686	€1 Foxglove	1·40	1·50
1687	€2 Lords-and-ladies	2·75	3·00
1688	€5 Dog-rose	6·75	7·00
1689	€10 Spring Gentian	13·50	14·00

(b) Ordinary gum. Size 20×23 mm.

1690	5c. Dandelion	10	10
1691	25c. Common knapweed	55	55
1692	55c. Large-flowered butterwort	1·30	1·30

(d) Size 20×24 mm. Self-adhesive.

1695	-	(N) Large-flowered butterwort	1·75	1·75
1696	-	(N) Blue-eyed grass	1·75	1·75
1696a	-	(N) Yellow-horned poppy	1·75	1·75
1697	-	55c. Large-flowered butterwort	1·70	1·70
1698	-	75c. Navelwort	1·70	1·70
1699	-	78c. Black bog-rush	1·70	1·70
1699b	-	82c. Sea aster	1·80	1·80
1699c	**457**	55c. Large-flowered butterwort	1·70	1·70
1699d	**457**	82c. Sea aster	2·40	2·40

2004. 140th Anniv of National Gallery of Ireland (3rd issue). As T 426. Multicoloured.

1700	48c. "The House Builders" (Walter Osborne)	80	80
1701	48c. "Kitchen Maid with the Supper at Emmaus" (Diego Velazquez)	80	80
1702	48c. "The Lamentation over the Dead Christ" (Nicolas Poussin)	80	80
1703	48c. "The Taking of Christ" (Caravaggio)	80	80

462 William Butler Yeats

2004. Irish Winners of Nobel Prize for Literature. Multicoloured.

1704	(N) Type **462**	75	75
1705	(N) George Bernard Shaw	75	75
1706	(N) Samuel Beckett	75	75
1707	(N) Seamus Heaney	75	75

Nos. 1706 were inscribed "N" and sold for 48c. each. Stamps of similar designs were issued by Sweden.

463 George Fox (Founder of The Society of Friends ("Quakers"))

2004. 350th Anniv of Quakers in Ireland.

1708	**463**	60c. multicoloured	1·00	1·00

464 Patrick Kavanagh

2004. Birth Centenary of Patrick Kavanagh (poet).

1709	**464**	48c. green and dull green	85	75

465 The Holy Family

2004. Christmas. Multicoloured.

1710	48c. Type **465**	85	50
1711	60c. The flight into Egypt	1·10	1·25
1712	65c. The Adoration of the Magi	1·25	1·40

(b) Size 24×29 mm. Self-adhesive.

1713	48c. The Holy Family	1·00	70

466 Lovebirds

2005. Love, Greetings and Chinese New Year of the Rooster. Multicoloured. (a) Ordinary gum.

1714	48c. Type **466**	1·00	1·00
MS1715	130×74 mm. 60c. Rooster; 60c. Type **466**; 60c. Owl	3·00	3·00

(b) Self-adhesive. Designs 30×25 mm.

1716	48c. Rooster	1·00	1·00
1717	48c. Stork	1·00	1·00
1718	48c. Type **466**	1·00	1·00
1719	48c. Owl	1·00	1·00

467 St. Patrick

2005. St. Patrick's Day.

1720	**467**	65c. multicoloured	1·25	1·25

468 "Landscape, Co. Wicklow" (Evie Hone)

2005. Female Artists. Multicoloured.

1721	48c. Type **468**	85	95
1722	48c. "Seabird and Landmarks" (Nano Reid)	85	95
1723	65c. "Three Graces" (Gabriel Hayes) (vert)	1·10	1·25
1724	65c. "Threshing" (Mildred Anne Butler) (vert)	1·10	1·25

469 Statue, City Hall and Churches

2005. Cork–European Capital of Culture 2005. Multicoloured.

1725	48c. Type **469**	80	80
1726	48c. Court House and Shandon Steeple (clock tower)	80	80

Nos. 1725/6 were printed together, se-tenant, forming a composite design showing Patrick's Bridge and a montage of landmark buildings and monuments of the city of Cork.

470 William Rowan Hamilton (birth bicentenary)

2005. UNESCO World Year of Physics. Multicoloured.

1727	48c. Type **470**	85	70
1728	60c. UNESCO Headquarters, Paris, trees and reflections of sunlight	1·10	1·25
1729	65c. Albert Einstein (50th death anniv)	1·25	1·40

471 201 Class Diesel Locomotive pulling "Enterprise Express" Train

2005. 150th Anniv of Dublin–Belfast Railway. Multicoloured.

1730	48c. Type **471**	90	1·00
1731	48c. V Class 3 steam locomotive No. 85, *Merlin*, arriving at Amiens Street (now Connolly) Station, Dublin, c. 1951	90	1·00
1732	60c. Q Class steam locomotive No. 131 crossing Boyne Valley viaduct, Drogheda	1·25	1·40
1733	65c. Modern "Enterprise Express" leaving Belfast Central Station	1·25	1·40
MS1734	150×90 mm. Nos. 1730/3	4·00	4·50

472 Red Deer Stags, Killarney National Park, Ireland

2005. Biosphere Reserves. Multicoloured.

1735	48c. Type **472**	70	70
1736	65c. Saskatoon Berries and Osprey, Waterton Lakes National Park, Alberta, Canada	1·40	1·50
MS1737	150×90 mm. Nos. 1735/6	2·00	2·50

Stamps in similar designs were issued by Canada.

473 Lamb, Cabbage, Carrots and Potato (ingredients of Irish Stew)

2005. Europa. Gastronomy. Multicoloured.

1738	48c. Type **473**	75	70
1739	65c. Oysters	1·00	1·25

474 Small Copper

2005. Butterflies. Multicoloured.

1740	48c. Type **474**	75	70
1741	60c. Green hairstreak	95	90
1742	65c. Painted lady	1·00	1·10
1743	€1 Pearl-bordered fritillary	1·90	2·25
MS1744	150×67 mm. €5 As No. 1742	7·00	8·00

475 *Dunbrody*

2005. Cutty Sark International Tall Ships Race, Waterford. Multicoloured.

1745	48c. Type **475**	85	70
1746	60c. *Tenacious*	1·00	1·10
1747	65c. USCG *Eagle*	1·10	1·25

476 Glendalough, Co. Wicklow

2005. Round Towers of Ireland. Each black.

1748	48c. Type **476**	75	85
1749	48c. Ardmore, Co. Waterford	75	85
1750	48c. Clones, Co. Monaghan	75	85
1751	48c. Kilmacduagh, Co. Galway	75	85

Nos. 1748/51 commemorate the 75th Anniversary of the Monuments of Ireland Act.

477 Bees on Honeycomb

2005. Apimondia 2005 (international bee-keeping conference and exhibition), Dublin.

1752	**477**	65c. multicoloured	1·25	1·25

478 Eamonn Darcy, Christy O'Connor Jnr and Philip Walton holding Ryder Cup

2005. Ireland and the Ryder Cup (golf tournament). Multicoloured.

1753	48c. Type **478**	1·25	1·25
1754	48c. Darren Clarke, Paul McGinley and Padraig Harrington with Ryder Cup	1·25	1·25
1755	60c. Harry Bradshaw, Ronan Rafferty and Christy O'Connor Snr	1·50	1·50
1756	65c. The K Club, Straffan, Co. Kildare (venue of 2006 Ryder Cup)	1·50	1·50

479 Erskine Childers

2005. Birth Centenary of Erskine Childers (President of Ireland 1973–4).

1757	**479**	48c. multicoloured	75	75

480 An Garda Siochana on Overseas Duty

2005. 50th Anniv of Ireland's Membership of United Nations. Multicoloured.

1758	48c. Type **480**	1·00	1·00
1759	48c. Irish Army medical aid in East Timor	1·00	1·00
1760	60c. F. H. Boland (signatory of Ireland's membership), 1955	1·25	1·25
1761	65c. Member of Irish Defence Force in classroom, Lebanon	1·25	1·25

481 "Arthur Griffith" (Leo Whelan) and Title Page of Essay

2005. Centenary of Arthur Griffith's Essays "The Resurrection of Hungary: A Parallel for Ireland".

1762	**481**	48c. multicoloured	75	75

482 Nativity

2005. Christmas. Multicoloured. (a) Ordinary gum.

1763	48c. Type **482**	80	50
1764	60c. Choir of angels with harp	1·10	1·25
1765	65c. Choir of angels with tambourine and trumpet	1·25	1·50

(b) Size 24×29 mm. Self-adhesive.

1766	48c. Type **482**	80	80

483 Patrick Gallagher (founder) and Templecrone Co-operative Store

2006. Centenary of the Templecrone Co-operative Agricultural Society ("The Cope").

1767	**483**	48c. multicoloured	85	85

484 Red Setter and Couple Embracing

2006. Love, Greetings and Chinese New Year of the Dog. Multicoloured. (a) Ordinary gum.

1768	48c. Type **484**	1·00	85
MS1769	130×74 mm. 65c. Two Chinese crested dogs; 65c. As No. 1768.; 65c. Golden labrador	5·00	5·00

(b) Self-adhesive. Size 29×24 mm.

1770	48c. Two Chinese crested dogs	1·00	1·00
1771	48c. Golden Labrador	1·00	1·00
1772	48c. Type **484**	1·00	1·00
1773	48c. Red setter puppy	1·00	1·00

485 "St. Patrick lights the Paschal Fire at Slane" (Sean Keating)

2006. St. Patrick's Day.

1774	**485**	65c. multicoloured	1·25	1·25

486 Sessile Oak ("Quercus petraea")

2006. Trees of Ireland. Multicoloured.

1775	48c. Type **486**	60	85
1776	60c. Yew (*Taxus baccata*)	1·10	1·10
1777	75c. Ash (*Fraxinus excelsior*)	1·40	1·40
1778	€1 Strawberry-tree (*Arbutus unedo*)	1·75	2·00
MS1779	150×90 mm. Nos. 1775/8	6·50	6·50

487 St. Hubert, Church of Ireland, Carnalway, Co. Kildare

2006. 75th Death Anniv of Harry Clarke (stained glass artist).

1780	**487**	48c. multicoloured	1·00	85

488 General Post Office, Dublin

2006. 90th Anniv of the Easter Rising.

1781	**488**	48c. multicoloured	1·00	85

489 Children waving Irish and EU Flags (Katie McMillan)

2006. Europa. Winning Entries in Children's Stamp Design Competition. Multicoloured.

1782	48c. Type **489**	1·25	60
1783	75c. Flags of EU members in flowers (Sarah Naughter)	1·60	2·25

490 EU Flag

2006. 10th Anniv of European Union Flag.

1784	**490**	48c. multicoloured	1·00	85

491 Interior of University Church (Dr. Thomas Ryan)

2006. 150th Anniv of University Church, St. Stephen's Green, Dublin.

1785	**491**	48c. multicoloured	1·00	75

492 Mairtin O Cadhain (Irish language writer) (birth centenary)

2006. Celtic Scholars. Multicoloured.

1786	48c. Type **492**	1·00	1·00
1787	48c. Johann Caspar Zeus (Celtic languages researcher) (birth bicentenary)	1·00	1·00

493 Pebbles and Typewriter Keyboard

2006. 50th Anniv of the Department of the Gaeltacht.

1788	**493**	48c. multicoloured	1·00	75

494 Emblem

2006. 10th Anniv of TG4 (Teilifise Gaeilge 4) Television Channel.

1789	**494**	48c. multicoloured	1·00	75

495 *St. David* (ferry), 1906

2006. Centenary of the Rosslare–Fishguard Ferry Service. Multicoloured.

1790	48c. Type **495**	1·25	1·25
1791	48c. *Stena Lynx* (ferry), 2006	1·25	1·25
MS1792	150×90 mm. Nos. 1790/1	2·50	2·50

496 "The Battle of the Somme (36th Ulster Division)" (J. P. Beadle)

2006. 90th Anniv of the Battle of the Somme.

1793	**496**	75c. multicoloured	2·00	1·75

497 Guide Dog

2006. 30th Anniv of Irish Guide Dogs for the Blind.

1794	**497**	48c. multicoloured	1·40	1·00

498 Golf Ball on Tee

2006. Ryder Cup Golf Tournament, K Club, Straffan, Co. Kildare (1st issue). Multicoloured. (a). Ordinary gum.

1795	48c. Type **498**	1·10	1·10
1796	48c. Golf ball in the rough	1·10	1·10
1797	48c. Golf ball in bunker	1·10	1·10
1798	48c. Golf ball at edge of green	1·10	1·10
MS1799	150×90 mm. Nos. 1795/8	4·25	4·25

See also No. **MS**1808.

(b) Self-adhesive. Size 24×29 mm.

1800	48c. Type **498**	1·00	1·00
1801	48c. As No. 1796	1·00	1·00
1802	48c. As No. 1797	1·00	1·00
1803	48c. As No. 1798	1·00	1·00

499 "Ronnie Delany" (Dr. Thomas Ryan)

2006. 50th Anniv of Ronnie Delany's Gold Medal for 1500 Metres at Olympic Games, Melbourne.

1804	**499**	48c. multicoloured	1·00	75

500 Michael Cusack

2006. Death Centenary of Michael Cusack (founder of Gaelic Athletic Association).

1805 **500** 48c. multicoloured 1·00 75

501 "Michael Davitt" (Sir William Orpen)

2006. Death Centenary of Michael Davitt (founder of Irish National Land League).

1806 **501** 48c. multicoloured 1·00 75

502 RTE National Symphony Orchestra

2006. 25th Anniv of National Concert Hall, Dublin.

1807 **502** 48c. multicoloured 1·00 75

503 Teeing Off

2006. Ryder Cup Golf Tournament, K Club, Straffan, Co. Kildare (2nd issue). Sheet 140×102 mm containing T 503 and similar horiz design. Multicoloured. Self-adhesive.

MS1808 75c. Type **503**; 75c. In bunker 4·00 4·00

504 River Barrow at Graiguenamanagh, Co. Kilkenny

2006. Inland Waterways. Multicoloured.

1809 75c. Type **504** 1·60 1·90

1810 75c. Belturbet Marina, River Erne, Co. Cavan 1·60 1·90

1811 75c. Lock-keepers cottage on Grand Canal, Cornalour, Co. Offaly 1·60 1·90

1812 75c. River Shannon at Meelick Quay 1·60 1·90

505 The Chieftains

2006. Irish Music (1st series). Multicoloured.

1813 48c. Type **505** 1·25 1·00

1814 48c. The Dubliners 1·25 1·00

1815 75c. The Clancy Brothers and Tommy Makem 1·75 2·00

1816 75c. Altan 1·75 2·00

MS1817 150×90 mm. Nos. 1813/16 5·50 5·50

See also Nos. 1919/23.

506 Madonna and Child

507 "The Nativity" (Simon Bening)

2006. Christmas. Multicoloured. (a) Ordinary gum.

1818 48c. Type **506** 1·00 50

1819 75c. Shepherd with lamb 1·75 2·25

(b) Self-adhesive. Size 22×30 mm.

1820 48c. Type **507** 1·00 60

2006. Belgica 2006 International Stamp Exhibition, Brussels. No. MS1817 with Belgica '06 emblem and "16–20 November, 2006" added to the sheet margin.

MS1821 150×90 mm. Nos. 1813/16 5·50 5·50

2006. MonacoPhil 2006 International Stamp Exhibition. No. MS1817 with MonacoPhil 2006 emblem and "1–3 December, 2006" added to the sheet margin.

MS1822 150×90 mm. Nos. 1813/16 5·50 5·50

508 Franciscan and Door to Auditorium of Irish College

2007. 400th Anniv of the Irish Franciscan College, Louvain, Belgium.

1823 **508** 75c. multicoloured 1·75 2·25

509 Father Luke Wadding

2007. 350th Death Anniv of Father Luke Wadding (theologian).

1824 **509** 75c. multicoloured 1·75 2·25

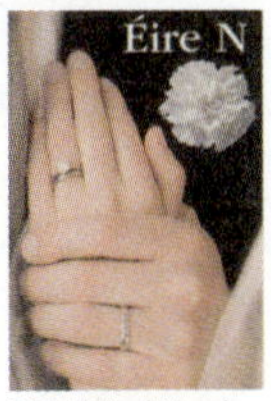

510 Linked Hands

2007. Weddings (1st issue). Chalk-surfaced paper. Self-adhesive.

1825 **510** (N) multicoloured 1·00 70

No. 1825 is inscribed "N" and was sold for 48c. each.

See also Nos. 1862, 1880 and 1929.

511 Cartoon Stamp and Heart

2007. Greetings Stamps. Multicoloured. Self-adhesive.

1826 (48c.) Type **511** 1·00 70

1827 (48c.) Birthday cake 1·00 70

Nos. 1826/7 are inscribed "N" and sold for 48c. each.

512 Two Pigs

2007. Chinese New Year ("Year of the Pig").

1828 **512** 75c. multicoloured 1·75 2·25

MS1829 130×74 mm. 75c.×2 Type **512**; 75c. As Type **512** but green background 5·25 6·75

513 Shamrock

2007. St. Patrick's Day.

1830 **513** 75c. multicoloured 1·75 2·25

514 Hugh O'Neill, Earl of Tyrone

2007. 400th Anniv of the Flight of the Earls. Multicoloured.

1831 48c. Type **514** 1·00 1·00

1832 48c. Rory O'Donnell, Earl of Tyrconnell 1·00 1·00

MS1833 150×90 mm. Nos. 1831/2 2·25 2·25

Nos. 1831/2 were printed together, se-tenant, forming a composite background design showing Lough Swilly and map of Europe.

515 Trim Castle, Co. Meath

2007. Castles. Multicoloured.

1834 55c. Type **515** 1·25 1·25

1835 55c. Dunluce Castle, Co. Antrim 1·25 1·25

1836 55c. Lismore Castle, Co. Waterford 1·25 1·25

1837 55c. Portumna Castle, Co. Galway 1·25 1·25

MS1838 150×90 mm. Nos. 1834/7 5·00 5·00

516 EU Flag, Signatures and Palazzo dei Conservatori, Rome

2007. 50th Anniv of the Treaty of Rome.

1839 **516** 55c. multicoloured 1·25 1·25

517 Girl Scout at Campsite, c. 2007

2007. Europa. Centenary of Scouting. Multicoloured.

1840 55c. Type **517** 1·25 75

1841 78c. Boy scout camping, c. 1907 1·75 2·25

518 Jupiter

2007. The Planets (1st series). Multicoloured.

1842 55c. Type **518** 1·30 1·30

1843 55c. Neptune 1·30 1·30

1844 78c. Saturn 1·80 1·80

1845 78c. Uranus 1·80 1·80

MS1846 150×90 mm. Nos. 1842/5 6·00 6·00

Nos. 1842/3 and 1844/5 were printed together, se-tenant, forming a composite design showing Planet Earth.

519 St. Charles of Mount Argus, Dublin

2007. Canonisation of Blessed Charles of Mount Argus.

1847 **519** 55c. multicoloured 1·25 1·25

520 Anniversary Emblem

2007. 50th Anniv of the IPA (Institute of Public Administration).

1848 **520** 55c. multicoloured 1·25 1·25

521 RTE National Symphony Orchestra

2007. RTE Performing Groups. Multicoloured. Ordinary or self-adhesive gum.

1849 55c. Type **521** 1·25 1·25

1850 55c. RTE Concert Orchestra 1·25 1·25

1851 55c. RTE Vanbrugh Quartet 1·25 1·25

1852 55c. RTE Philharmonic Choir 1·25 1·25

1853 55c. RTE Cor na nOg children's choir 1·25 1·25

522 Society Seal and Gandon Facade of King's Inns Building

2007. 400th Anniv of Revival of the Honourable Society of King's Inns.

1859 **522** 55c. multicoloured 1·25 1·25

523 Bound Books containing Records in Registry of Deeds

2007. 300th Anniv of the Registry of Deeds Act.

1860 **523** 78c. multicoloured 1·75 1·75

524 Girls Choir from Colaiste Iosagain, Co. Dublin

2007. Centenary of the National Anthem.

1861 **524** 55c. multicoloured 1·25 1·25

2007. Weddings (2nd issue). As T 510 but new value. Self-adhesive.

1862 55c. As Type **510** 1·25 1·25

525 *Skuldelev 2* (Viking longship)

2007. Voyage of the Havhingsten fra Glendalough (replica of Viking longship Skuldelev 2) from Denmark to Dublin. Multicoloured.

1863 55c. Type **525** 1·25 1·25
MS1864 150×90 mm. €3 *Havhingsten fra Glendalough* (replica Viking longship) 6·75 6·75

526 Paul O'Connell

2007. Rugby World Cup, France. Multicoloured.

1865 55c. Type **526** 1·30 1·30
1866 78c. Irish players in lineout, Croke Park, 2007 1·80 1·80
MS1867 Two sheets, each 150×90 mm. (a) No. 1865. (b) No. 1866 Set of 2 sheets 3·00 3·00

527 'Fat Cat'

2007. Celtic Cats

1868 55c. Type **527** 1·20 1·20
1869 55c. Celtic Tigress 1·20 1·20
1870 78c. Cool Cats 1·80 1·80
1871 78c. Kilkenny Cat 1·80 1·80
MS1872 150×90 mm. As Nos. 1868/71 but 18×18 mm 6·00 6·00

528 Fr. Joseph Mullooly in 4th-century Basilica, San Clemente, Rome

2007. 150th Anniv of Archaeological Discoveries, San Clemente, Rome.

1873 **528** 55c. multicoloured 1·25 1·25

529 James Fintan Lalor

2007. Birth Bicentenary of James Fintan Lalor (nationalist and journalist).

1874 **529** 55c. multicoloured 1·25 1·25

530 Giant Elk Antlers

2007. 150th Anniv of the Natural History Museum, Dublin.

1875 **530** 55c. multicoloured 1·25 1·25

531 The Presentation in the Temple

2007. Christmas. Multicoloured. (a) Ordinary gum.

1876 55c. Type **531** 1·30 1·30
1877 78c. The Three Magi 2·00 2·00

(b) Self-adhesive. Size 24×29 mm.

1878 55c. The Adoration of the Shepherds 1·30 1·30

532 Charles Wesley (*The Lily Portrait*)

2007. 300th Birth Anniv of Charles Wesley (founder of Methodism and hymn writer).

1879 **532** 78c. multicoloured 1·90 1·90

533 Bride and Groom Embracing

2008. Weddings (3rd issue). Self-adhesive.

1880 **533** 55c. multicoloured 1·40 1·40

534 Rat and Candle

2008. Chinese New Year ('Year of the Rat').

1881 **534** 78c. multicoloured 2·00 2·00
MS1882 130×74 mm. No. 1882×3

535 Liam Whelan and Munich Memorial Clock, Old Trafford, Manchester

2008. 50th Anniv of the Munich Air Disaster.

1883 **535** 55c. multicoloured 1·40 1·40

536 Juggling Frog

2008. Greetings Stamps. Multicoloured. Self-adhesive.

1884 55c. Trumpeting elephant 1·40 1·40
1885 55c. Type **536** 1·40 1·40

537 St. Patrick (line engraving by Leonard Gaultier)

2008. St. Patrick's Day.

1886 **537** 78c. multicoloured 2·00 2·00

No. 1886 is based on a drawing made in 1619 by Thomas Messingham.

538 Logo

2008. European Year of Intercultural Dialogue.

1887 **538** 55c. multicoloured 1·40 1·40

539 *Hugh Lane* (Antonio Mancini)

2008. Centenary of Hugh Lane Gallery, Dublin.

1888 **539** 55c. multicoloured 1·40 1·40

540 *West of Ireland Landscape*

2008. Paul Henry Landscape Paintings. Multicoloured.

1889 55c. Type **540** (signature at left) 1·25 1·25
1890 55c. *West of Ireland Landscape* (rocks in foreground, signature at right) 1·25 1·25
1891 55c. *A Connemara Village* (signature at left) 1·25 1·25
1892 55c. *A Connemara Village* (signature at right) 1·25 1·25

Nos. 1889/92 commemorate the 50th death anniversary of Paul Henry.

541 Logo of Irish League of Credit Unions (ILCU)

2008. 50th Anniv of the Credit Union Movement in Ireland.

1893 **541** 55c. multicoloured 1·40 1·40

542 World Map showing Africa and Asia (Mohammed Rahman)

2008. International Year of Planet Earth. Showing children's plasticine models of Planet Earth. Multicoloured. Self-adhesive.

1894 55c. Type **542** 1·40 1·40
1895 55c. World map showing the Americas and Atlantic Ocean (Conor Reid) 1·40 1·40

543 '50'

2008. 50th Anniv of the Institute of Creative Advertising and Design (ICAD).

1896 **543** 55c. multicoloured 1·50 1·50

544 RMS *Leinster*

2008. 90th Anniv of the Sinking of RMS Leinster.

1897 **544** 55c. multicoloured 1·50 1·50

545 Boy writing Letter

2008. Europa. The Letter. Multicoloured.

1898 55c. Type **545** 1·50 1·50
1899 82c. Girl writing letter 2·00 2·00

546 Aughrim, Co. Wicklow (2007 winner)

2008. 50th Anniv of the Tidy Towns Competition.

1900 **546** 55c. multicoloured 1·50 1·50

547 Lt. Col. McCarthy, Comdt. Higgins, Capt. Lavelle, Comdt. Coughlan and Capt. Henderson

2008. 50th Anniv of the First Irish Defence Forces Mission to the UN.

1901 **547** 55c. multicoloured 1·50 1·50

548 Colm Meaney in *Kings*

2008. Filmed in Ireland

1902 55c. Type **548** 1·50 1·50
1903 55c. Brid Ni Neachtain in *Cre Na Cille* 1·50 1·50
1904 82c. Cillian Murphy in *The Wind that Shakes the Barley* 2·10 2·10
1905 82c. Pat Shortt in *Garage* 2·10 2·10
MS1906 150×90 mm. Nos. 1902/5 7·25 7·25

549 Rowing

2008. Olympic Games, Beijing. Multicoloured.
1907 55c. Type **549** 1·50 1·50
1908 82c. Shot-putt 2·00 2·00
MS1909 150×90 mm. As Nos. 1907/8 optd 'Olympex 2008' 3·50 3·50

550 Parasol (*Macrolepiota procera*)

2008. Fungi. Multicoloured.
1910 55c. Type **550** 1·50 1·50
1911 55c. Orange birch bolete (*Leccinum versipelle*) 1·50 1·50
1912 82c. Pink waxcap (*Hygrocybe calyptriformis*) 2·00 2·00
MS1913 150×67 mm. 95c. Scarlet elfcup (*Sarcoscypha austriaca*) 3·50 3·50

551 HMS *Agamemnon* and USS *Niagra* laying Cable, 1858

2008. 150th Anniv of the First Transatlantic Cable Message.
1914 **551** 82c. multicoloured 2·25 2·25

552 'STATE PENSIOON'

2008. Centenary of the Old Age Pensions Act.
1915 **552** 55c. multicoloured 1·50 1·50

553 Open Books forming Star

2008. Centenary of the National University of Ireland.
1916 **553** 55c. multicoloured 1·50 1·50

554 Padraic Mac Piarais and Cullenswood House, Ranelagh, Dublin, 1908–10

2008. Centenary of Opening of Scoil Eanna (bilingual Irish/English school). Showing founder and school premises.
1917 55c. Type **554** 1·50 1·50
1918 55c. Padraic Mac Piariais and The Hermitage, Rathfarnham, 1910–35 1·50 1·50

555 Planxty

2008. Irish Music (2nd series). Multicoloured.
1919 55c. Type **555** 1·50 1·50
1920 55c. De Dannan 1·50 1·50
1921 82c. Tulla Ceili Band 2·10 2·10
1922 82c. The Bothy Band 2·10 2·10
MS1923 150×90 mm. Nos. 1919/22 7·25 7·25

556 Irish Dancer

2008. Traditional Dances. Multicoloured.
1924 55c. Type **556** 1·50 1·50
MS1925 150×90 mm. No. 1924; 82c. Flamenco dancer 4·00 4·00
Stamps in a similar design were issued by Spain.

557 The Flight into Egypt

2008. Christmas. Multicoloured. (a) Ordinary gum.
1926 55c. Type **557** 1·50 1·50
1927 82c. The Annunciation 2·10 2·10

(b) Self-adhesive. Size 25×30 mm.
1928 55c. Infant Jesus in manger 1·50 1·50

558 Pair of Wedding Rings

2009. Weddings (4th issue). Self-adhesive.
1929 55c. multicoloured 1·60 1·60

559 Eye

2009. Birth Bicentenary of Louis Braille (inventor of Braille writing for the blind).
1930 **559** 55c. black 1·60 1·60
No. 1930 has 'Eire' and '55c' in Braille.

560 Ox

2009. Chinese New Year ('Year of the Ox').
1931 **560** 82c. multicoloured 2·40 2·40
MS1932 130×74 mm. No. 1931×3 7·25 7·25

561 *St. Patrick Climbs Croagh Patrick* (Margaret Clarke)

2009. St. Patrick's Day.
1933 **561** 82c. multicoloured 2·40 2·40

562 Little Girl posting Card, helped by her Father

2009. Greetings Stamps. Multicoloured. Self-adhesive.
1934 55c. Type **562** 1·60 1·60
1935 55c. Girl with opened birthday card and dog 1·60 1·60

563 *Charles Darwin* (pen and ink drawing, Harry Furniss)

2009. Birth Bicentenary of Charles Darwin (naturalist and evolutionary theorist).
1936 **563** 82c. multicoloured 2·40 2·40

564 Scene from *The Playboy of the Western World* (Sean Keating)

2009. Death Centenary of John Millington Synge (writer).
1937 **564** 55c. multicoloured 1·60 1·60

565 *Irish Times* Clock

2009. 150th Anniv of the Irish Times (newspaper).
1938 **565** 55c. multicoloured 1·60 1·60

566 Girl writing Letter

2009. 25th Anniv of An Post. Multicoloured. Self-adhesive. (a) Size 25×30 mm.
1939 55c. Type **566** 1·60 1·60
1940 55c. Girl posting letter 1·60 1·60
1941 55c. Postman emptying pillar box 1·60 1·60
1942 55c. Woman at post office counter 1·60 1·60
1943 55c. An Post van and lorry 1·60 1·60
1944 55c. Flying letters 1·60 1·60
1945 55c. Postman with trolley 1·60 1·60
1946 55c. Postman with mail 1·60 1·60
1947 55c. Seán Kelly cycling team sponsored by An Post 1·60 1·60
1948 55c. G.P.O., Dublin 1·60 1·60

(b) Size 20×24 mm.
1949 55c. As Type **566** 1·60 1·60
1950 55c. As No. 1940 1·60 1·60
1951 55c. As No. 1941
1952 55c. As No. 1942 1·60 1·60
1953 55c. As No. 1943 1·60 1·60
1954 55c. As No. 1944
1955 55c. As No. 1945 1·60 1·60
1956 55c. As No. 1946 1·60 1·60
1957 55c. As No. 1947 1·60 1·60
1958 55c. As No. 1948 1·60 1·60

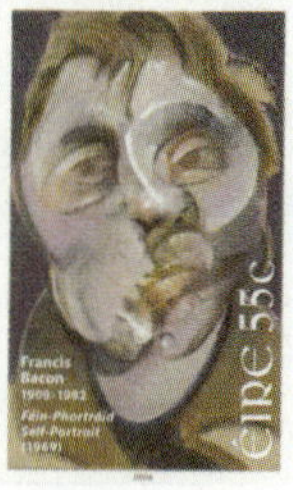

567 *Self-portrait*, 1969

2009. Birth Centenary of Francis Bacon (artist). Multicoloured.
1959 55c. Type **567** 1·60 1·60
MS1960 150×90 mm. 82c. Francis Bacon's studio 2·40 2·40

568 James Larkin (union organiser) addressing Crowd, c. 1908

2009. Centenary of IT&GWU (Irish Transport and General Workers Union).
1961 **568** 55c. multicoloured 1·60 1·60

569 *Green Dragon* (Irish entry)

2009. Volvo Ocean Race. Multicoloured.
1962 55c. Type **569** 1·60 1·60
MS1963 150×90 mm. €3 *Green Dragon* and other yachts (27×47 mm) 8·75 8·75

570 Crab Nebula

2009. Europa. Astronomy. Multicoloured.
1964 55c. Type **570** 1·60 1·60
1965 82c. Brown dwarf 2·40 2·40

571 CEPT Logo, '50', Telephone Dial and Pillar Box

2009. 50th Anniv of CEPT (European Conference of Postal and Telecommunications Administration).
1966 **571** 82c. multicoloured 2·25 2·25

572 'Aberann Conan' (Glen of Imaal terrier)

2009. European Dog Show, Dublin.
1967 **572** 55c. multicoloured 1·50 1·50

573 Castle and St. John's Bridge, Kilkenny City

2009. 400th Anniv of City Status for Kilkenny.
1968 **573** 55c. multicoloured 1·50 1·50

574 Anthony Trollope (from albumen print by Julia Margaret Cameron, 1864)

2009. Anthony Trollope (novelist) Commemoration.
1969 **574** 82c. multicoloured 2·25 2·25

575 *Augustine Birrell* (Sir Leslie Ward)

2009. Centenary of the Birrell Land Act (Irish Land Act).
1970 **575** 82c. multicoloured 2·25 2·25

576 *Wolfgang Amadeus Mozart* (Josef Grassi) and Overture of Opera *Don Giovanni*

2009. Classical Composers. Each showing composer and score . Multicoloured.
1971 55c. Type **576** 1·60 1·60
1972 55c. *George Frideric Handel* (Thomas Hudson, 1736) and last folio from opera *Susanna*, 1748 1·60 1·60
1973 82c. *Joseph Haydn* (John Carl Rossler, 1799) and Symphony No. 95 2·25 2·25
1974 82c. *Frederic Chopin* (Ary Scheffer) and Ballade Number 2 in F 2·25 2·25
MS1975 150×90 mm. Nos. 1971/4 7·50 7·50

577 Arthur Guinness (founder)

2009. 250th Anniv of the Guinness Brewery.
1976 **577** 82c. multicoloured 2·40 2·40

578 'Plantation of Ulster 1609' in Irish

2009. 400th Anniv of the Plantation of Ulster. Multicoloured.
1977 55c. Type **578** 1·60 1·60
1978 55c. 'PLANTATION of ULSTER 1609' in English 1·60 1·60

579 Brian Friel

2009. Modern Irish Playwrights. Multicoloured.
1979 55c. Type **579** 1·60 1·60
1980 55c. Frank McGuinness 1·60 1·60
1981 55c. Tom Murphy 1·60 1·60

580 Irish Bluet (*Coenagrion lunulatum*)

2009. Dragonflies. Multicoloured.
1982 55c. Type **580** 1·60 1·60
1983 55c. Large red damselfly (*Pyrrhosoma nymphula*) 1·60 1·60
1984 82c. Four-spotted chaser (*Libellula quadrimaculata*) (horiz) 2·40 2·40
MS1985 150×65 mm. 95c. Banded demoiselle (*Calopteryx splendens*) (60×26 mm) 2·75 2·75

581 Nativity

2009. Christmas. Illustrations from the Gospel Book, Gamaghiel Monastery, Khizan (1986/7) or the Rosarium of King Philip II of Spain (1988). Multicoloured designs showing illustrations. (a) Ordinary gum.
1986 55c. Type **581** 1·60 1·60
1987 82c. Annunciation 2·40 2·40

(b) Size 25×30 mm. Self-adhesive.
1988 55c. *Virgin and Child* (Simon Bening) 1·60 1·60

The images on Nos. 1986/7 come from the *Gospel Book* from the Monastery of Gamaghiel, Khizan, and on No. 1988 from the Rosarium of Philip II, King of Spain.

582 Dr. Douglas Hyde

2010. 150th Birth Anniv of Douglas Hyde (first President of Ireland 1938–45).
1989 **582** 55c. multicoloured 1·50 1·50

583 Pair of Stylised 'Lovebirds'

2010. Weddings (5th issue). Self-adhesive.
1990 **583** 55c. multicoloured 1·75 1·75

584 Boy Astronaut and Heart

2010. Greetings Stamps. Multicoloured.
1991 55c. Type **584** 1·75 1·75
1992 55c. Girl astronaut riding rocket and birthday cake 1·75 1·75

585 Tiger (18th century Tibetan painting)

2010. Chinese New Year. Year of the Tiger.
1993 **585** 82c. multicoloured 2·25 2·25
MS1994 150×90 mm. No. 1993×3 2·25 2·25

586 St. Patrick (stained glass window, St. Patrick's Cathedral, Co. Armagh)

2010. St. Patrick's Day.
1995 **586** 82c. multicoloured 2·25 2·25

587 Gaisce Symbol and Aras an Uachtarain (President's official residence)

2010. 25th Anniv of Gaisce the President's Award.
1996 **587** 55c. multicoloured 1·60 1·60

588 Women playing Golf, Baking, Exercising and Painting

2010. Centenary of Irish Countrywoman's Association.
1997 **588** 55c. multicoloured 1·50 1·50

589 Monasterboice Cross, Co. Louth

2010. Ireland Series—High Crosses. Each black.
1998 55c. Type **589** 1·50 1·50
1999 55c. Carndonagh Cross, Co. Donegal 1·50 1·50
2000 55c. Drumcliffe Cross, Co. Sligo 1·50 1·50
2001 55c. Ahenny Cross, Co. Tipperary 1·50 1·50

POSTAGE DUE STAMPS

D1

1925

D1	**D1**	½d. green	12·00	16·00
D6	**D1**	1d. red	1·50	70
D7	**D1**	1½d. orange	3·25	8·00
D8	**D1**	2d. green	2·75	70
D9	**D1**	3d. blue	3·50	3·75
D10	**D1**	5d. violet	4·50	3·00
D11a	**D1**	6d. plum	15·00	15·00
D12	**D1**	8d. orange	9·00	13·00
D13	**D1**	10d. purple	8·50	8·50
D14	**D1**	1s. green	8·50	11·00

1971. Decimal Currency. Colours changed.

D15	1p. brown	30	60
D16	1½p. green	40	1·50
D17	3p. stone	60	2·00
D18	4p. orange	60	1·25
D19	5p. blue	60	3·00
D20	7p. yellow	40	3·50
D21	8p. red	40	2·75

D2

1980

D25	**D2**	1p. green	30	70
D26	**D2**	2p. blue	30	70
D27	**D2**	4p. green	40	70
D28	**D2**	6p. flesh	40	80
D29	**D2**	8p. blue	40	85
D30	**D2**	18p. green	75	1·25
D31	**D2**	20p. red	2·25	5·50
D32	**D2**	24p. green	75	2·00
D33	**D2**	30p. violet	3·00	7·50
D34	**D2**	50p. pink	3·75	7·50

D3

1988

D35	**D3**	1p. black, red and yellow	10	60
D36	**D3**	2p. black, red and brown	10	60
D37	**D3**	3p. black, red and purple	15	60
D38	**D3**	4p. black, red and violet	15	60
D39	**D3**	5p. black, red and blue	15	60

D40	D3	17p. black, red and green	40	65
D41	D3	20p. black, red and blue	55	80
D42	D3	24p. black, red and green	60	85
D43	D3	30p. black, red and grey	80	1·25
D44	D3	50p. black, red and grey	1·25	1·75
D45	D3	£1 black, red and brown	1·75	2·25

Pt. 1

ISLE OF MAN

An island in the Irish Sea to the north-west of England. Man became a possession of the English Crown during the Middle Ages, but retains its own Assembly.

Regional issues from 1958 to 1971 are listed at end of "GREAT BRITAIN".

Isle of Man had an independent postal administration from 1973.

100 pence = 1 pound.

5 Castletown

17 Manx Cat

1973. Multicoloured.

12	½p. Type **5**	10	10
13	1p. Port Erin	10	10
14	1½p. Snaefell	10	10
15	2p. Laxey	10	10
16	2½p. Tynwald Hill	10	10
17	3p. Douglas Promenade	10	10
18	3½p. Port St. Mary	10	10
19	4p. Fairy Bridge	10	10
20	4½p. As 2½p.	20	15
21	5p. Peel	15	10
22	5½p. As 3p.	20	15
23	6p. Cregneish	20	15
24	7p. As 2p.	20	15
25	7½p. Ramsey Bay	20	20
26	8p. As 7½p.	25	25
27	9p. Douglas Bay	20	20
28	10p. Type **17**	35	20
29	11p. Monk's Bridge, Ballasalla	35	30
30	13p. Derbyhaven	40	35
31	20p. Manx loaghtyn ram	50	50
32	50p. Manx shearwater	1·00	1·10
33	£1 Viking longship	2·00	2·00

SIZES: Nos. 13/27 and 29/30 as Type **4**; Nos. 31/3 as Type **5**.

23 Viking Landing on Man, A.D. 938

1973. Inauguration of Postal Independence.

34	**23**	15p. multicoloured	35	30

24 No. 1 "Sutherland", 1873

1973. Cent of Steam Railway. Multicoloured.

35	2½p. Type **24**	15	10
36	3p. No. 4 "Caledonia", 1885	15	15
37	7½p. No. 13 "Kissack", 1910	25	25
38	9p. No. 3 "Pender", 1873	25	25

28 Leonard Randles, First Winner, 1923

1973. Golden Jubilee of Manx Grand Prix. Mult.

39	3p. Type **28**	10	15
40	3½p. Alan Holmes, Double Winner, 1957	15	15

30 Princess Anne and Capt. Mark Phillips

1973. Royal Wedding.

41	**30**	25p. multicoloured	45	50

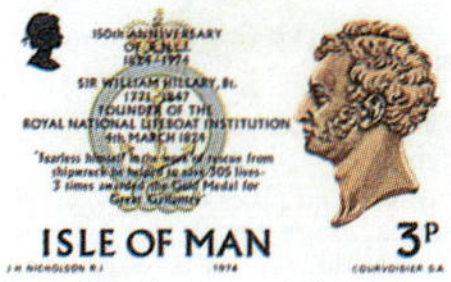

31 Badge, Citation and Sir William Hillary (founder)

1974. 150th Anniv of Royal National Lifeboat Institution. Multicoloured.

42	3p. Type **31**	10	10
43	3½p. Wreck of "St. George", 1830	15	10
44	8p. R.N.L.B. "Manchester and Salford", 1868–87	25	25
45	10p. R.N.L.B. "Osman Gabriel"	30	25

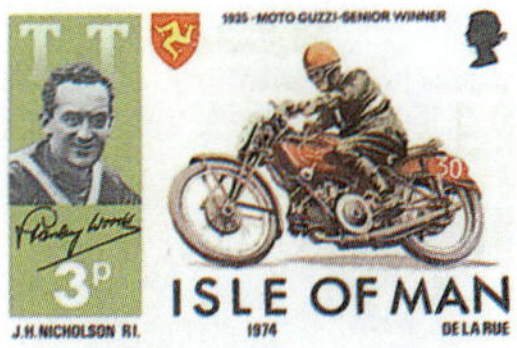

35 Stanley Woods, 1935

1974. Tourist Trophy Motorcycle Races (1st issue). Multicoloured.

46	3p. Type **35**	10	10
47	3½p. Freddy Frith, 1937	10	10
48	8p. Max Deubel and Emil Horner, 1961	25	20
49	10p. Mike Hailwood, 1961	25	20

See also Nos. 63/6.

39 Rushen Abbey and Arms

1974. Historical Anniversaries. Multicoloured.

50	3½p. Type **39**	10	10
51	4½p. Magnus Haraldson rows King Edgar on the Dee	10	10
52	8p. King Magnus and Norse fleet	15	15
53	10p. Bridge at Avignon and bishop's mitre	20	20

COMMEMORATIONS: Nos. 50 and 53, William Russell, Bishop of Sodor and Man, 600th death anniv; Nos. 51/2, 1000th anniv of rule of King Magnus Haraldson.

43 Churchill and Bugler Dunne at Colenso, 1899

1974. Birth Centenary of Sir Winston Churchill. Multicoloured.

54	3½p. Type **43**	10	10
55	4½p. Churchill and Government Buildings, Douglas	10	10
56	8p. Churchill and Manx ack-ack crew	15	15
57	20p. Churchill as Freeman of Douglas	30	25

MS58	121×91 mm. Nos. 54/7	75	75

47 Cabin School and Names of Pioneers

1975. Manx Pioneers in Cleveland, Ohio. Multicoloured.

59	4½p. Type **47**	10	10
60	5½p. Terminal Tower Building, J. Gill and R. Carran	10	10
61	8p. Clague House Museum, and Robert and Margaret Clague	15	15
62	10p. S.S. "William T. Graves" and Thomas Quayle	25	25

51 Tom Sheard, 1923

1975. Tourist Trophy Motor-cycle Races (2nd issue). Multicoloured.

63	5½p. Type **51**	10	10
64	7p. Walter Handley, 1925	15	15
65	10p. Geoff Duke, 1955	15	15
66	12p. Peter Williams, 1973	25	20

55 Sir George Goldie and Birthplace

1975. 50th Death Anniv of Sir George Goldie. Multicoloured.

67	5½p. Type **55**	10	10
68	7p. Goldie and map of Africa (vert)	15	15
69	10p. Goldie as President of Geographical Society (vert)	15	15
70	12p. River scene on the Niger	25	25

59 Title Page of Manx Bible

1975. Christmas and Bicentenary of Manx Bible. Multicoloured.

71	5½p. Type **59**	10	10
72	7p. Rev. Philip Moore and Ballaugh Old Church	15	15
73	11p. Bishop Hildesley and Bishops Court	20	20
74	13p. John Kelly saving Bible manuscript	25	25

63 William Christian listening to Patrick Henry

1976. Bicent of American Independence. Mult.

75	5½p. Type **63**	10	10
76	7p. Conveying the Fincastle Resolutions	15	15
77	13p. Patrick Henry and William Christian	30	30
78	20p. Christian as an Indian fighter	35	35
MS79	153×89 mm. Nos. 75/8	90	1·00

67 First Horse Tram, 1876

1976. Cent of Douglas Horse-Trams. Mult.

80	5½p. Type **67**	10	10
81	7p. "Toast-rack" tram, 1890	15	15
82	11p. Horse-bus, 1895	20	20
83	13p. Royal tram, 1972	25	25

71 Barrose Beaker

1976. Europa. Ceramic Art. Multicoloured.

84	5p. Type **71**	20	10
85	5p. Souvenir teapot	20	10
86	5p. Laxey jug	20	10
87	10p. Cronk Aust food vessel (horiz)	20	10
88	10p. Sansbury bowl (horiz)	20	10
89	10p. Knox urn (horiz)	20	10

77 Diocesan Banner

1976. Christmas and Centenary of Mothers' Union. Multicoloured.

90	6p. Type **77**	10	10
91	7p. Onchan banner	15	15
92	11p. Castletown banner	20	20
93	13p. Ramsey banner	25	25

81 Queen Elizabeth II

1977. Silver Jubilee. Multicoloured.

94	6p. Type **81**	10	10
95	7p. Queen Elizabeth and Prince Philip (vert)	20	20
96	25p. Queen Elizabeth (different)	50	50

84 Carrick Bay from "Tom-the-Dipper"

1977. Europa. Landscapes. Multicoloured.

97	6p. Type **84**	15	15
98	10p. View from Ramsey	25	25

86 F. A. Applebee, 1912

1977. Linked Anniversaries. Multicoloured.

99	6p. Type **86**	15	10
100	7p. St. John's Ambulance Brigade at Governor's Bridge, 1938	15	15
101	11p. Scouts operating the scoreboard	25	25
102	13p. John Williams, 1976	25	30

The events commemorated are: 70th anniv of Manx TT races; 70th anniv of Boy Scouts; Centenary of St. John's Ambulance Brigade.

90 Old Summer House, Mount Morrison, Peel

1977. Bicentenary of First Visit of John Wesley. Multicoloured.

103	6p. Type **90**	15	10
104	7p. Wesley preaching in Castle-town Square	15	15
105	11p. Wesley preaching outside Braddan Church	25	25
106	13p. New Methodist Church, Douglas	25	25

Nos. 104/5 are larger, 38×26 mm.

94 Short Type 184 Seaplane and H.M.S. "Ben-My-Chree", 1915

1978. 60th Anniv of Royal Air Force. Mult.

107	6p. Type **94**	15	10
108	7p. Bristol Scout C and H.M.S. "Vindex", 1915	15	15
109	11p. Boulton Paul P.82 Defiant over Douglas Bay, 1941	25	25
110	13p. SEPECAT Jaguar over Ramsey, 1977	25	25

98 Watch Tower, Langness

1978. Multicoloured.

111	½p. Type **98**	10	10
112	1p. Jurby Church (horiz)	10	10
113	6p. Government Buildings	30	30
114	7p. Tynwald Hill (horiz)	35	35
115	8p. Milner's Tower	25	25
116	9p. Laxey Wheel	35	35
117a	10p. Castle Rushen (horiz)	35	35
118	11p. St. Ninian's Church	40	40
119	12p. Tower of Refuge (horiz)	40	25
120a	13p. St. German's Cathedral (horiz)	30	25
121a	14p. Point of Ayre Lighthouse (horiz)	30	25
122a	15p. Corrin's Tower (horiz)	30	25
123	16p. Douglas Head Lighthouse (horiz)	55	30
124	20p. Fuchsia	50	35
125	25p. Manx cat	65	45
126	50p. Red-billed chough ("Chough")	90	75
127	£1 Viking warrior	1·90	2·00
128	£2 Queen Elizabeth II	3·50	3·50

Nos. 124/7 are larger, 25×31 mm and No. 128, 38×48 mm.

115 Queen Elizabeth in Coronation Regalia

1978. 25th Anniv of Coronation.

132	**115**	25p. multicoloured	50	45

116 Wheel-headed Cross-slab

1978. Europa. Celtic and Norse Crosses. Multicoloured.

133	6p. Type **116**	10	10
134	6p. Celtic wheelcross	10	10
135	6p. Keeil Chiggyrt Stone	10	10
136	11p. Olaf Liotulfson Cross	20	15
137	11p. Odd's and Thorleif's Crosses	20	15
138	11p. Thor Cross	20	15

122 J. K. Ward and Ward Library, Peel

1978. Anniversaries and Events. Multicoloured.

139	6p. Type **122**	10	10
140	7p. Swimmer, cyclist and walker (42×26 mm)	20	15
141	11p. American bald eagle, Manx arms and maple leaf (42×26 mm)	25	25
142	13p. Lumber camp, Three Rivers, Quebec	25	25

ANNIVERSARIES AND EVENTS: 6, 13p. James Kewley Ward (Manx pioneer in Canada) commemoration; 7p. Commonwealth Games, Edmonton; 11p. 50th anniv of North American Manx Association.

126 Hunt the Wren

1978. Christmas.

143	**126**	5p. multicoloured	20	20

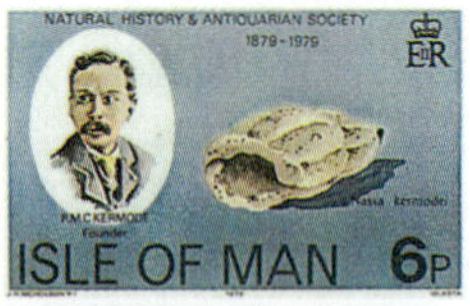

127 P. M. C. Kermode and "Nassa kermodei"

1979. Centenary of Natural History and Antiquarian Society. Multicoloured.

144	6p. Type **127**	10	10
145	7p. Peregrine falcon	25	15
146	11p. Fulmar	25	30
147	13p. "Epitriptus cowini" (fly)	25	35

131 Postman, 1859

1979. Europa. Communications. Multicoloured.

148	6p. Type **131**	15	10
149	11p. Postman, 1979	40	45

133 Viking Longship Emblem

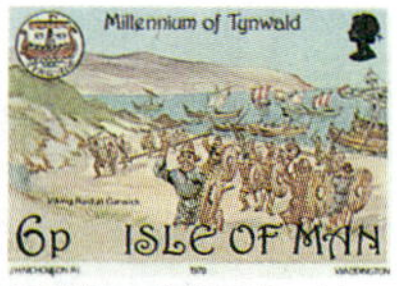

135 Viking Raid at Garwick

1979. Millennium of Tynwald. Multicoloured.

150	3p. Type **133**	10	10
151	4p. "Three Legs of Man" emblem	10	10
152	6p. Type **135**	15	10
153	7p. 10th-century meeting of Tynwald	20	20
154	11p. Tynwald Hill and St. John's Church	25	25
155	13p. Procession to Tynwald Hill	30	30

The 4p. value is as Type **34** and the remainder as Type **35**.

139 Queen and Court on Tynwald Hill

1979. Royal Visit. Multicoloured.

156	7p. Type **139**	15	15
157	13p. Queen and procession from St. John's Church to Tynwald Hill	25	25

141 "Odin's Raven"

1979. Voyage of "Odin's Raven".

158	**141**	15p. multicoloured	45	30

142 John Quilliam seized by the Press Gang

1979. 150th Death Anniv of Captain John Quilliam. Multicoloured.

159	6p. Type **142**	15	15
160	8p. Steering H.M.S. "Victory", Battle of Trafalgar	20	15
161	13p. Captain John Quilliam and H.M.S. "Spencer"	25	25
162	15p. Captain John Quilliam (member of the House of Keys)	30	25

146 Young Girl with Teddybear and Cat

1979. Christmas. Int Year of the Child. Mult.

163	5p. Type **146**	10	10
164	7p. Father Christmas with young children	20	20

148 Conglomerate Arch, Langness

1980. 150th Anniv of Royal Geographical Society. Multicoloured.

165	7p. Type **148**	15	15
166	8p. Braaid Circle	20	20
167	12p. Cashtal-yn-Ard	25	25
168	13p. Volcanic rocks at Scarlett	25	25
169	15p. Sugar-loaf Rock	30	25

153 "Mona's Isle I"

1980. 150th Anniv of Isle of Man Steam Packet Company. Multicoloured.

170	7p. Type **153**	15	15
171	8p. "Douglas I"	20	20
172	11½p. H.M.S. "Mona's Queen II" sinking U-boat	20	25
173	12p. H.M.S. "King Orry III" at surrender of German fleet, 1918	25	25
174	13p. "Ben-My-Chree IV"	35	25
175	15p. "Lady of Mann II"	40	25
MS176	180×125 mm. Nos. 170/5	1·20	1·20

No. **MS**176 was issued to commemorate "London 1980" International Stamp Exhibition.

159 Stained Glass Window, T. E. Brown Room, Manx Museum

1980. Europa. Personalities. Thomas Edward Brown (poet and scholar) Commemoration. Multicoloured.

177	7p. Type **159**	15	15
178	13½p. Clifton College, Bristol	25	25

161 King Olav V and "Norge" (Norwegian royal yacht)

1980. Visit of King Olav of Norway, August 1979.

179	**161**	12p. multicoloured	30	30
MS180		125×157 mm. Nos. 158 and 179	75	75

No. **MS**180 also commemorates the "NORWEX 80" Stamp Exhibition, Oslo.

162 Winter Wren and View of Calf of Man

1980. Christmas and Wildlife Conservation Year. Multicoloured.

181	6p. Type **162**	15	10
182	8p. European robin and view of Port Erin Marine Biological Station	30	35

164 William Kermode and Brig "Robert Quayle", 1819

1980. Kermode Family in Tasmania Commemoration. Multicoloured.

183	7p. Type **164**	15	15
184	9p. "Mona Vale", Van Diemen's Land, 1834	20	20
185	13½p. Ross Bridge, Tasmania	25	25
186	15p. "Mona Vale", Tasmania (completed 1868)	30	25
187	17½p. Robert Quayle Kermode and Parliament Buildings, Tasmania	30	30

169 Peregrine Falcon

1980. Multicoloured.

188	1p. Type **169**	20	20
189	5p. Loaghtyn ram	30	30

171 Luggers passing Red Pier, Douglas

1981. Centenary of Royal National Mission to Deep Sea Fishermen. Multicoloured.

190	8p. Type **171**	15	15
191	9p. Peel Lugger "Wanderer" rescuing survivors from "Lusitania"	20	20
192	18p. Nickeys leaving Port St. Mary	30	30
193	20p. Nobby entering Ramsey Harbour	30	30
194	22p. Nickeys "Sunbeam" and "Zebra" at Port Erin	35	35

176 "Crosh Cuirn" Superstition

1981. Europa. Folklore. Multicoloured.

195	8p. Type **176**	15	10
196	18p. "Bollan Cross" superstition	30	35

178 Lt. Mark Wilks (Royal Manx Fencibles) and Peel Castle

1981. 150th Death Anniv of Colonel Mark Wilks. Multicoloured.

197	8p. Type **178**	20	20
198	20p. Ensign Mark Wilks and Fort St. George, Madras	30	30
199	22p. Governor Mark Wilks and Napoleon, St. Helena	40	35
200	25p. Col. Mark Wilks (Speaker of the House of Keys) and estate, Kirby	45	35

182 Miss Emmeline Goulden (Mrs. Pankhurst) and Mrs. Sophia Jane Goulden

1981. Centenary of Manx Women's Suffrage.

201	**182**	9p. black, grey and stone	20	20

183 Prince Charles and Lady Diana Spencer

1981. Royal Wedding.

202	**183**	9p. black, blue and light blue	15	20
203	**183**	25p. black, blue and pink	75	80
MS204		130×183 mm. Nos. 202/3×2	2·00	2·00

184 Douglas War Memorial, Poppies and Commemorative Inscription

1981. 60th Anniv of The Royal British Legion. Multicoloured.

205	8p. Type **184**	20	20
206	10p. Major Robert Cain (war hero)	25	25
207	18p. Festival of Remembrance, Royal Albert Hall	30	30
208	20p. T.S.S. "Tynwald" at Dunkirk, May 1940 and Supermarine Spitfire	35	35

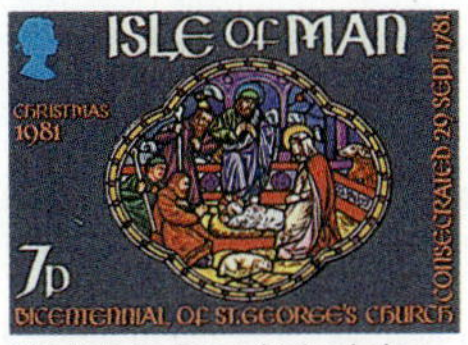

188 Nativity Scene (stained glass window, St. George's Church)

1981. Christmas. Multicoloured.

209	7p. Type **188**	15	15
210	9p. Children from Special School performing nativity play (48×30 mm)	20	20

190 Joseph and William Cunningham (founders of Isle of Man Boy Scout Movement) and Cunningham House Headquarters

1982. 75th Anniv of Boy Scout Movement and 125th Birth Anniv of Lord Baden-Powell. Multicoloured.

211	9p. Type **190**	20	15
212	10p. Baden-Powell visiting Isle of Man, 1911	25	25
213	19½p. Baden-Powell and Scout emblem (40×31 mm)	45	40
214	24p. Scouts and Baden-Powell's last message	50	45
215	29p. Scout salute, handshake, emblem and globe	70	60

195 "The Principals and Duties of Christianity" (Bishop T. Wilson) (first book printed in Manx, 1707)

1982. Europa. Historic Events. Multicoloured.

216	9p. Type **195**	15	10
217	19½p. Landing at Derbyhaven (visit of Thomas, 2nd Earl of Derby, 1507)	40	40

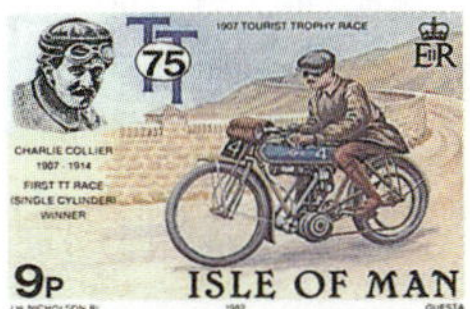

197 Charlie Collier (first TT race (single cylinder) winner) and Tourist Trophy Race, 1907

1982. 75th Anniv of Tourist Trophy Motorcycle Racing. Multicoloured.

218	9p. Type **197**	15	15
219	10p. Freddie Dixon (Sidecar and Junior TT winner) and Junior TT Race, 1927	15	15
220	24p. Jimmie Simpson (TT winner and first to lap at 60, 70 and 80 mph) and Senior TT, 1932	60	55
221	26p. Mike Hailwood (winner of fourteen TT's) and Senior TT, 1961	60	50
222	29p. Jock Taylor (Sidecar TT winner, 1978, 1980 and 1981) and Sidecar TT (with Benga Johansson), 1980	60	60

202 "Mona I"

1982. 150th Anniv of Isle of Man Steam Packet Company Mail Contract. Multicoloured.

223	12p. Type **202**	30	25
224	19½p. "Manx Maid II"	45	45

204 Three Wise Men bearing Gifts

1982. Christmas. Multicoloured.

225	8p. Type **204**	15	15
226	11p. Christmas snow scene (vert)	30	30

206 Princess Diana with Prince William

1982. 21st Birthday of Princess of Wales and Birth of Prince William. Sheet 100×83 mm.

MS227	**206**	50p. multicoloured	1·50	1·50

207 Opening of Salvation Army Citadel, and T. H. Cannell, J.P.

1983. Centenary of Salvation Army in Isle of Man. Multicoloured.

228	10p. Type **207**	20	15
229	12p. Early meeting place and Gen. William Booth	30	25
230	19½p. Salvation Army band	45	45
231	26p. Treating lepers and Lt.-Col. Thomas Bridson	65	60

211 Atlantic Puffins ("Puffins")

227 "Queen Elizabeth II" (Ricardo Macarron)

1983. Sea Birds. Multicoloured.

232	1p. Type **211**	30	30
233	2p. Northern gannets ("Gannets")	30	30
234	5p. Lesser black-backed gulls	60	40
235	8p. Great cormorants ("Cormorants")	60	40
236	10p. Black-legged kittiwakes ("Kittiwakes")	60	35
237	11p. Shags	60	35
238	12p. Grey herons ("Herons")	70	40
239	13p. Herring gulls	70	40
240	14p. Razorbills	70	40
241	15p. Greater black-backed gulls ("Great Black-backed Gulls")	80	50
242	16p. Common shelducks ("Shelducks")	80	50
243	18p. Oystercatchers	80	50
244	20p. Arctic terns	1·00	70
245	25p. Common guillemots ("Guillemots")	1·20	75
246	50p. Common redshank ("Redshanks")	1·70	1·50
247	£1 Mute swans	2·50	2·75
248	£5 Type **227**	8·00	8·50

Nos. 244/7 are larger, 39×26 mm.

228 Design Drawings by Roger Casement for the Great Laxey Wheel (image scaled to 58% of original size)

1983. Europa. The Great Laxey Wheel.

249	**228**	10p. black, blue and buff	25	20
250	-	20½p. multicoloured	50	55

DESIGN: 20½p. Roger Casement and the Great Laxey Wheel.

230 Nick Keig (international yachtsman) and Trimaran "Three Legs of Man III"

1983. 150th Anniv of King William's College. Multicoloured.

251	10p. Type **230**	15	15
252	12p. King William's College, Castletown	20	20
253	28p. Sir William Bragg (winner of Nobel Prize for Physics) and spectrometer	55	55
254	31p. General Sir George White, V.C. and action at Charasiah	65	65

234 New Post Office Headquarters, Douglas

1983. World Communications Year and 10th Anniv of Isle of Man Post Office Authority. Multicoloured.

255	10p. Type **234**	25	25
256	15p. As Type **234** but inscr "POST OFFICE DECENNIUM 1983"	35	40

236 Shepherds

1983. Christmas. Multicoloured.

257	9p. Type **236**	20	20
258	12p. Three Kings	30	30

238 "Manx King" (full-rigged ship)

1984. The Karran Fleet. Multicoloured.

259	10p. Type **238**	20	15
260	13p. "Hope" (barque)	30	20
261	20½p. "Rio Grande" (brig)	45	35
262	28p. "Lady Elizabeth" (barque)	65	50
263	31p. "Sumatra" (barque)	75	65
MS264	103×94 mm. 28p. As No. 262; 31p. "Lady Elizabeth" (as shown on Falkland Islands No. 417) (sold at 60p.)	2·20	1·50

No. **MS**264 was issued to commemorate links between the Isle of Man and the Falkland Islands.

244 C.E.P.T. 25th Anniversary Logo

1984. Europa.

No.	Type	Description	Mint	Used
265	244	10p. orange, brown and light orange	30	25
266	244	20½p. blue, deep blue and light blue	50	50

245 Railway Air Services de Havilland D.H.84 Dragon Mk 2 G-ACXI of Railway Air Service

1984. 50th Anniv of First Official Airmail to the Isle of Man and 40th Anniv of International Civil Aviation Organization. Multicoloured.

No.	Description	Mint	Used
267	11p. Type **245**	35	30
268	13p. West Coast Air Services de Havilland D.H. 86A Dragon Express G-ADJV "Ronaldsway"	40	30
269	26p. B.E.A. Douglas DC-3 G-AGZB	70	65
270	28p. B.E.A. Vickers Viscount 800	70	65
271	31p. Britten-Norman BN-2 Islander G-AXXH of Telair	70	65

250 Window from Glencrutchery House, Douglas

1984. Christmas. Stained-glass Windows. Multicoloured.

No.	Description	Mint	Used
272	10p. Type **250**	20	20
273	13p. Window from Lonan Old Church	40	40

252 William Cain's Birthplace, Ballasalla

1984. William Cain (civic leader, Victoria) Commemoration. Multicoloured.

No.	Description	Mint	Used
274	11p. Type **252**	25	20
275	22p. The "Anna" leaving Liverpool, 1852	50	50
276	28p. Early Australian railway	70	65
277	30p. William Cain as Mayor of Melbourne, and Town Hall	75	65
278	33p. Royal Exhibition Building, Melbourne	70	65

257 Queen Elizabeth II and Commonwealth Parliamentary Association Badge

1984. Links with the Commonwealth. 30th Commonwealth Parliamentary Association Conference. Multicoloured.

No.	Description	Mint	Used
279	14p. Type **257**	35	35
280	33p. Queen Elizabeth II and Manx emblem	65	65

259 Cunningham House Headquarters and Mrs. Willie Cunningham and Mrs. Joseph Cunningham (former Commissioners)

1985. 75th Anniv of Girl Guide Movement. Multicoloured.

No.	Description	Mint	Used
281	11p. Type **259**	30	25
282	14p. Princess Margaret, Isle of Man standard and guides	35	30
283	29p. Lady Olave Baden-Powell opening Guide Headquarters, 1955	70	60
284	31p. Guide uniforms from 1910 to 1985	75	75
285	34p. Guide handclasp, salute and early badge	90	85

264 Score of Manx National Anthem

1985. Europa. European Music Year.

No.	Type	Description	Mint	Used
286	264	12p. black, light brown and brown	30	15
287	-	12p. black, light brown & brown	30	15
288	-	22p. black, light blue & blue	80	25
289	-	22p. black, light blue & blue	80	25

DESIGNS: No. 287, William H. Gill (lyricist); 288, Score of hymn "Crofton"; 289, Dr. John Clague (composer).

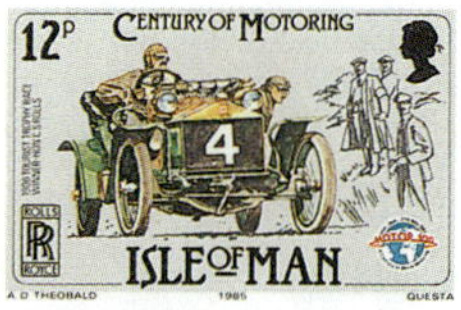

268 Charles Rolls in 20 h.p. Rolls-Royce (1906 Tourist Trophy Race)

1985. Century of Motoring. Multicoloured.

No.	Description	Mint	Used
290	12p. Type **268**	25	15
291	12p. W. Bentley in 3 litre Bentley (1922 Tourist Trophy Race)	25	15
292	14p. F. Gerrard in E.R.A. (1950 British Empire Trophy Race)	25	15
293	14p. Brian Lewis in Alfa Romeo (1934 Mannin Moar Race)	25	15
294	31p. Jaguar "XJ-SC" ("Roads Open" car, 1984 Motor Cycle TT Races)	60	40
295	31p. Tony Pond and Mike Nicholson in Vauxhall "Chevette" (1981 Rothmans International Rally)	60	40

274 Queen Alexandra and Victorian Sergeant with Wife

1985. Centenary of Soldiers', Sailors' and Airmen's Families Association. Association Presidents. Multicoloured.

No.	Description	Mint	Used
296	12p. Type **274**	25	20
297	15p. Queen Mary and Royal Air Force family	35	30
298	29p. Earl Mountbatten and Royal Navy family	65	55
299	34p. Prince Michael of Kent and Royal Marine with parents, 1982	90	85

278 Kirk Maughold (birthplace)

1985. Birth Bicentenary of Lieutenant-General Sir Mark Cubbon (Indian administrator). Mult.

No.	Description	Mint	Used
300	12p. Type **278**	30	25
301	22p. Lieutenant-General Sir Mark Cubbon (vert)	70	65
302	45p. Memorial statue, Bangalore, India (vert)	1·00	95

281 St. Peter's Church, Onchan

1985. Christmas. Manx Churches. Multicoloured.

No.	Description	Mint	Used
303	11p. Type **281**	30	25
304	14p. Royal Chapel of St. John, Tynwald	40	35
305	31p. Bride Parish Church	1·00	90

284 Swimming

1986. Commonwealth Games, Edinburgh. Mult.

No.	Description	Mint	Used
306	12p. Type **284**	20	15
307	15p. Race walking	25	30
308	31p. Rifle-shooting	90	95
309	34p. Cycling	1·00	95

No. 309 also commemorates the 50th anniversary of Manx International Cycling Week.

288 Viking Necklace and Peel Castle

1986. Centenary of Manx Museum. Multicoloured.

No.	Description	Mint	Used
310	12p. Type **288**	20	15
311	15p. Meayll Circle, Rushen	25	20
312	22p. Skeleton of Great Deer and Manx Museum (vert)	65	50
313	26p. Viking longship model (vert)	80	60
314	29p. Open Air Museum, Cregneash	90	60

293 Viking Longship

1986. Manx Heritage Year.

No.	Type	Description	Mint	Used
315	293	2p. multicoloured	40	40
316	-	10p. black, green and grey	35	35

DESIGN: 10p. Celtic cross logo.

295 "Usnea articulata" (lichen) and "Neotinea intacta" (orchid), The Ayres

1986. Europa. Protection of Nature and the Environment. Multicoloured.

No.	Description	Mint	Used
317	12p. Type **295**	30	15
318	12p. Hen harrier, Calf of Man	30	15
319	22p. Manx stoat, Eary Cushlin	60	25
320	22p. "Stenobothus stigmaticus" (grasshopper), St. Michael's Isle	60	25

299 Ellanbane (home of Myles Standish)

1986. "Ameripex '86" International Stamp Exhibition, Chicago. Captain Myles Standish of the "Mayflower". Multicoloured.

No.	Description	Mint	Used
321	12p. Type **299**	20	20
322	15p. "Mayflower" crossing the Atlantic, 1620	25	25
323	31p. Pilgrim Fathers landing at Plymouth, 1620	90	90
324	34p. Captain Myles Standish	95	95
MS325	100×75 mm. Nos. 323/4	2·10	2·10

No. **MS**325 also commemorates the 75th anniversary of the World Manx Association.

303 Prince Andrew in Naval Uniform and Miss Sarah Ferguson

1986. Royal Wedding. Multicoloured.

No.	Description	Mint	Used
326	15p. Type **303**	25	25
327	40p. Engagement photograph	1·50	1·50

305 Prince Philip (from photo by Karsh)

1986. Royal Birthdays. Multicoloured.

No.	Description	Mint	Used
328	15p. Type **305**	30	30
329	15p. Queen Elizabeth II (from photo by Karsh)	30	30
330	34p. Queen Elizabeth and Prince Philip (from photo by Karsh) (48×35 mm)	1·10	1·10

Nos. 328/30 also commemorate "Stockholmia '86" International Stamp Exhibition, Sweden and the 350th anniversary of the Swedish Post Office.

308 European Robins on Globe and "Peace and Goodwill" in Braille

1986. Christmas and International Peace Year. Multicoloured.

No.	Description	Mint	Used
331	11p. Type **308**	30	30
332	14p. Hands releasing peace dove	30	30
333	31p. Clasped hands and "Peace" in sign language	80	80

311 North Quay

1987. Victorian Douglas. Multicoloured.

No.	Description	Mint	Used
334	2p. Type **311**	10	10
335	3p. Old Fishmarket	10	10
336	10p. The Breakwater	25	25
337	15p. Jubilee Clock	30	30
338	31p. Loch Promenade	90	80
339	34p. Beach	1·00	90

317 "The Old Fishmarket and Harbour, Douglas"

1987. Paintings by John Miller Nicholson. Multicoloured.

340	12p. Type **317**	20	20
341	26p. "Red Sails at Douglas"	70	60
342	29p. "The Double Corner, Peel"	90	80
343	34p. "Peel Harbour"	1·00	1·00

321 Sea Terminal, Douglas

1987. Europa. Architecture. Multicoloured.

344	12p. Type **321**	45	15
345	12p. Tower of Refuge, Douglas	45	15
346	22p. Gaiety Theatre, Douglas	65	25
347	22p. Villa Marina, Douglas	65	25

325 Supercharged "BMW" 500cc Motor Cycle, 1939

1987. 80th Anniv of Tourist Trophy Motor Cycle Races. Multicoloured.

348	12p. Type **325**	45	25
349	15p. Manx "Kneeler" Norton 350cc, 1953	50	35
350	29p. MV Agusta 500cc 4, 1956	90	70
351	31p. Guzzi 500cc V8, 1957	90	75
352	34p. Honda 250cc 6, 1967	1·00	90
MS353	150×140 mm. Nos. 348/52	3·00	3·50

Nos. 348/**MS**353 also commemorate the Centenary of the St. John Ambulance Brigade and No. **MS**353 carries the logo of "Capex '87" International Stamp Exhibition, Toronto, on its margin.

330 Fuchsia and Wild Roses

1987. Wild Flowers. Multicoloured.

354	16p. Type **330**	50	30
355	29p. Field scabious and ragwort	90	80
356	31p. Wood anemone and celandine	90	1·00
357	34p. Violets and primroses	1·00	1·20

334 Stirring the Christmas Pudding

1987. Christmas. Victorian Scenes. Multicoloured.

358	12p. Type **334**	40	35
359	15p. Bringing home the Christmas tree	50	55
360	31p. Decorating the Christmas tree	90	90

337 Russell Brookes in Vauxhall "Opel" (Manx Rally winner, 1985)

1988. Motor Sport. Multicoloured.

361	13p. Type **337**	75	35
362	26p. Ari Vatanen in Ford "Escort" (Manx Rally winner, 1976)	1·20	1·20
363	31p. Terry Smith in Repco "March 761" (Hill Climb winner, 1980)	1·40	1·50
364	34p. Nigel Mansell in Williams/Honda (British Grand Prix winner, 1986 and 1987)	1·60	1·70

341 Horse Tram Terminus, Douglas Bay Tramway

356a Queen Elizabeth II taking Salute at Trooping the Colour

1988. Manx Railways and Tramways. Mult.

365	1p. Type **341**	10	10
366	2p. Snaefell Mountain Railway	10	10
367	3p. Marine Drive Tramway	10	10
367c	4p. Douglas Cable Tramway	20	10
368	5p. Douglas Head Incline Railway	20	20
369	10p. Douglas & Laxey Coast Electric Tramway car at Maughold Head	30	30
370	13p. As 4p.	50	50
371	14p. Manx Northern Railway No. 4, "Caledonia", at Gob-y-Deigan	50	50
372	15p. Laxey Mine Railway Lewin locomotive "Ant"	50	50
373	16p. Port Erin Breakwater Tramway locomotive "Henry B. Loch"	50	50
374	17p. Ramsey Harbour Tramway	50	50
375	18p. Locomotive No. 7, "Tynwald", on Foxdale line	55	55
375a	18p. T.P.O. Special leaving Douglas, 3 July 1991	70	70
376	19p. Baldwin Reservoir Tramway steam locomotive No. 1, "Injebreck"	60	60
377	20p. I.M.R. No. 13, "Kissack", near St. Johns	60	60
377a	21p. As 14p.	60	60
377b	23p. Double-deck horse tram, Douglas	80	80
378	25p. I.M.R. No. 12, "Hutchinson", leaving Douglas	60	60
379	50p. Groudle Glen Railway locomotive "Polar Bear"	1·30	1·20
380	£1 I.M.R. No. 11, "Maitland", pulling Royal Train, 1963	2·50	2·50
380a	£2 Type **356a**	5·00	5·00

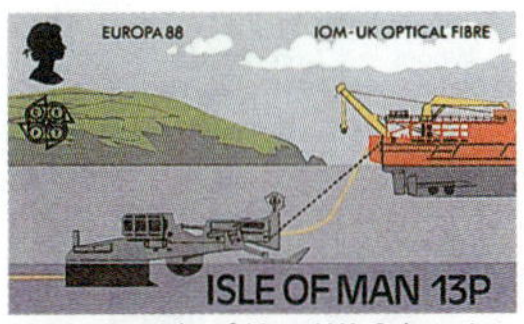

357 Laying Isle of Man–U.K. Submarine Cable

1988. Europa. Transport and Communications. Multicoloured.

381	13p. Type **357**	50	45
382	13p. "Flex Services" (cable ship)	50	45
383	22p. Earth station, Braddan	75	75
384	22p. "INTELSAT 5" satellite	75	75

Nos. 381/2 and 383/4 were each printed together, se-tenant, Nos. 381/2 forming a composite design.

361 "Euterpe" (full-rigged ship) off Ramsey, 1863

1988. Manx Sailing Ships. Multicoloured.

385	16p. Type **361**	45	30
386	29p. "Vixen" (topsail schooner) leaving Peel for Australia, 1853	90	90
387	31p. "Ramsey" (full-rigged ship) off Brisbane, 1870	90	90
388	34p. "Star of India" (formerly "Euterpe") (barque) off San Diego, 1976	1·10	1·10
MS389	110×85 mm. Nos. 385 and 388	1·90	2·00

Nos. 386/7 also commemorate the Bicent of Australian Settlement.

365 "Magellanica"

1988. 50th Anniv of British Fuchsia Society. Multicoloured.

390	13p. Type **365**	40	25
391	16p. "Pink Cloud"	45	35
392	22p. "Leonora"	65	50
393	29p. "Satellite"	90	90
394	31p. "Preston Guild"	1·00	1·00
395	34p. "Thalia"	1·10	1·20

371 Long-eared Owl

1988. Christmas. Manx Birds. Multicoloured.

396	12p. Type **371**	40	30
397	15p. European robin	60	65
398	31p. Grey partridge	1·20	1·20

374 Ginger Cat

1989. Manx Cats. Multicoloured.

399	16p. Type **374**	50	25
400	27p. Black and white cat	90	85
401	30p. Tortoiseshell and white cat	1·20	85
402	40p. Tortoiseshell cat	1·50	1·20

378 Tudric Pewter Clock, c. 1903

1989. 125th Birth Anniv of Archibald Knox (artist and designer). Multicoloured.

403	13p. Type **378**	20	20
404	16p. "Celtic Cross" watercolour	30	25
405	23p. Silver cup and cover 1902–03	50	50
406	32p. Gold and silver brooches from Liberty's Cymric range (horiz)	1·20	1·00
407	35p. Silver jewel box, 1900 (horiz)	1·40	1·00

383 William Bligh and Old Church, Onchan

1989. Bicentenary of the Mutiny on the "Bounty". Multicoloured.

408	13p. Type **383**	30	20
409	16p. Bligh and loyal crew cast adrift	35	30
410	23p. Pitcairn Islands 1989 Settlement Bicentenary 90c., No. 345	1·00	1·00
411	27p. Norfolk Island 1989 Bicentenary 39c., No. 461	1·00	1·00
412	30p. Midshipman Peter Heywood and Tahiti	50	60
413	32p. H.M.S. "Bounty" anchored off Pitcairn Island	50	60
414	35p. Fletcher Christian and Pitcairn Island	50	60
MS415	110×85 mm. Nos. 410/11 and 414	3·75	3·75

390 Skipping and Hopscotch

1989. Europa. Children's Games. Multicoloured.

416	13p. Type **390**	45	50
417	13p. Wheelbarrow, leapfrog and piggyback	45	50
418	23p. Completing model house and blowing bubbles	70	75
419	23p. Girl with doll and doll's house	70	75

Nos. 416/17 and 418/19 were printed together, se-tenant, forming composite designs.

394 Atlantic Puffin

1989. Sea Birds. Multicoloured.

420	13p. Type **394**	55	55
421	13p. Black guillemot	55	55
422	13p. Great cormorant ("Cormorant")	55	55
423	13p. Black-legged kittiwake ("Kittiwake")	55	55

398 Red Cross Cadets learning Resuscitation

1989. 125th Anniv of International Red Cross and Centenary of Noble's Hospital, Isle of Man.

424	**398**	14p. multicoloured	40	30
425	-	17p. grey and red	60	35
426	-	23p. multicoloured	75	85
427	-	30p. multicoloured	1·00	1·10
428	-	35p. multicoloured	1·20	1·20

DESIGNS: 17p. Anniversary logo; 23p. Signing Geneva Convention, 1864; 30p. Red Cross ambulance; 35p. Henri Dunant (founder).

403 Mother with Baby, Jane Crookall Maternity Home

1989. Christmas. 50th Anniv of Jane Crookall Maternity Home and 75th Anniv of St. Ninian's Church, Douglas. Multicoloured.

429	13p. Type **403**	50	45
430	16p. Mother with child	60	60
431	34p. Madonna and Child	1·10	1·20
432	37p. Baptism, St. Ninian's Church	1·20	1·40

407 "The Isle of Man Express going up a Gradient"

1990. Isle of Man Edwardian Postcards. Mult.

433	15p. Type **407**	35	35
434	19p. "A way we have in the Isle of Man"	60	50
435	32p. "Douglas-waiting for the male boat"	1·10	1·10
436	34p. "The last toast rack home, Douglas Parade"	1·50	1·50
437	37p. "The last Isle of Man boat"	1·60	1·60

412 Modern Postman

1990. Europa. Post Office Buildings. Mult.

438	15p. Type **412**	55	20
439	15p. Ramsey Post Office, 1990 (40×26 mm)	55	20
440	24p. Postman, 1890	90	25
441	24p. Douglas Post Office, 1890 (40×26 mm)	90	25

416 Penny Black

1990. 150th Anniv of the Penny Black.

442	**416**	1p. black, buff and gold	15	15
443	-	19p. gold, black and buff	60	50
444	-	32p. multicoloured	1·20	1·10
445	-	34p. multicoloured	1·40	1·10
446	-	37p. multicoloured	1·50	1·10
MS447		100×71 mm. £1 black, gold and buff (50×60 mm)	3·00	3·50

DESIGNS: 19p. Wyon Medal, 1837; 32p. Wyon's stamp essay; 34p. Perkins Bacon engine-turned essay, 1839; 37p. Twopence Blue, 1840; £1 Block of four Penny Black stamps lettered IM-JN.

No. **MS**447 also commemorates "Stamp World London 90" International Stamp Exhibition.

422 Queen Elizabeth the Queen Mother

1990. 90th Birthday of Queen Elizabeth the Queen Mother.

448	**422**	90p. multicoloured	3·00	3·00

423 Hawker Hurricane Mk 1, Bristol Type 142 Blenheim Mk 1, Dornier Do-17 inflames and Home Defence

1990. 50th Anniv of Battle of Britain. Mult.

449	15p. Type **423**	35	20
450	15p. Supermarine Spitfire with Westland Lysander Mk I rescue aircraft and Supermarine Watrus Flying boat	35	20
451	24p. Rearming Hawker Hurricanes Mk I fighters and Supermarine Spitfire	80	25
452	24p. Ops room and scramble	80	25
453	29p. Civil Defence personnel	1·00	30
454	29p. Barrage balloons	1·00	30

429 Churchill with Freedom of Douglas Casket

1990. 25th Death Anniv of Sir Winston Churchill. Multicoloured.

455	19p. Type **429**	45	45
456	32p. Churchill and London blitz	1·00	1·00
457	34p. Churchill and searchlights over Westminster	1·20	1·20
458	37p. Churchill with R.A.F. Hawker Hurricane Mk I fighters	1·20	1·20

433 Boy on Toboggan and Girl posting Letter

1990. Christmas. Multicoloured.

459	14p. Type **433**	40	40
460	18p. Girl on toboggan and skaters	50	50
461	34p. Boy with snowman	1·00	1·00
462	37p. Children throwing snowballs	1·20	1·20
MS463	123×55 mm. As Nos. 459/62, but face values in black	3·00	3·75

437 Henry Bloom Noble and Orphans (Marshall Wane)

1991. Manx Photography.

464	**437**	17p. brown, grey and black	35	35
465	-	21p. brown and ochre	50	50
466	-	26p. brown, stone and black	65	65
467	-	31p. brown, lt brown & blk	90	90
468	-	40p. multicoloured	1·10	1·10

DESIGNS: 21p. Douglas (Frederick frith); 26p. Studio portrait of three children (Hilda Newby); 31p. Castital yn Ard (Christopher Killip); 40p. Peel Castle (Colleen Corlett).

442 Lifeboat "Sir William Hillary", Douglas

1991. Manx Lifeboats. Multicoloured.

469	17p. Type **442**	45	45
470	21p. "Osman Gabriel", Port Erin	55	55
471	26p. "Ann and James Ritchie", Ramsey	90	90
472	31p. "The Gough Ritchie", Port St. Mary	1·20	1·20
473	37p. "John Batstone", Peel	1·40	1·40

No. 469 is inscribed "HILARY" and No. 471 "JAMES & ANN RITCHIE", both in error.

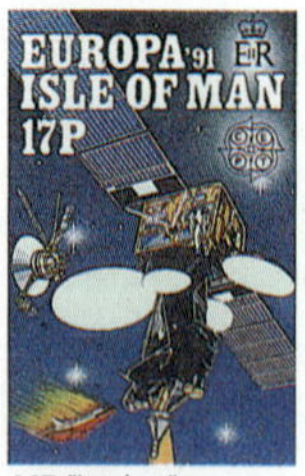

447 "Intelsat" Communications Satellite

1991. Europa. Europe in Space. Multicoloured.

474	17p. Type **447**	70	20
475	17p. "Ariane" rocket launch and fishing boats in Douglas harbour	70	20
476	26p. Weather satellite and space station	1·00	30
477	26p. British Aerospace ATP over Ronaldsway Airport, Manx Radio transmitter and Space shuttle launch	1·00	30

Nos. 474/5 and 476/7 were each printed together, se-tenant, each pair forming a composite design.

451 Oliver Godfrey with Indian 500cc at Start, 1911

1991. 80th Anniv of Tourist Trophy Mountain Course. Multicoloured.

478	17p. Type **451**	50	40
479	21p. Freddie Dixon on Douglas "banking" sidecar, 1923	65	60
480	26p. Bill Ivy on Yamaha 125cc, 1968	80	80
481	31p. Giacomo Agostini on MV Agusta 500cc, 1972	1·20	1·10
482	37p. Joey Dunlop on RVF Honda 750cc, 1985	1·50	1·50
MS483	149×144 mm. Nos. 478/82	4·00	4·00

1991. 9th Conference of Commonwealth Postal Administration, Douglas. Sheet 119×77 mm. Multicoloured.

MS484	Nos. 367c and 377a, each ×2	1·90	2·00

456 Laxey Hand-cart, 1920

1991. Fire Engines. Multicoloured.

485	17p. Type **456**	45	40
486	21p. Horse-drawn steamer, Douglas, 1909	65	65
487	30p. Merryweather "Hatfield" pump, 1936	85	90
488	33p. Dennis "F8" pumping appliance, Peel, 1953	1·20	1·20
489	37p. Volvo turntable ladder, Douglas, 1989	1·40	1·50

461 Mute Swans, Douglas Harbour

1991. Swans. Multicoloured.

490	17p. Type **461**	40	20
491	17p. Black swans, Curraghs Wildlife Park	40	20
492	26p. Whooper swans, Bishop's Dub, Ballaugh	1·10	30
493	26p. Tundra ("Bewick's") swans, Eairy Dam, Foxdale	1·10	30
494	37p. Coscoroba swans, Curraghs Wildlife Park	1·20	40
495	37p. Whooper ("Trumpeter") swans, Curraghs Wildlife Park	1·20	40

The two designs of each value were printed together, se-tenant, forming a composite design.

467 The Three Kings

1991. Christmas. Paper Sculptures. Multicoloured.

496	16p. Type **467**	45	35
497	20p. Mary with manger	65	70
498	26p. Shepherds with sheep	85	85
499	37p. Choir of angels	1·10	1·10

471 North African and Italian Campaigns, 1942–43

1992. 50th Anniv of Parachute Regiment. Mult.

502	23p. Type **471**	70	25
503	23p. D-Day, 1944	70	25
504	28p. Arnhem, 1944	80	30
505	28p. Rhine crossing, 1945	80	30
506	39p. Operations in Near, Middle and Far East, 1945–68	1·20	40
507	39p. Liberation of Falkland Islands. 1982	1·20	40

477 Queen Elizabeth II at Coronation, 1953

1992. 40th Anniv of Accession. Multicoloured.

508	18p. Type **477**	45	40
509	23p. Queen visiting Isle of Man, 1979	60	60
510	28p. Queen in evening dress	70	70
511	33p. Queen visiting Isle of Man, 1989	1·20	1·40
512	39p. Queen arriving for film premiere, 1990	1·40	1·40

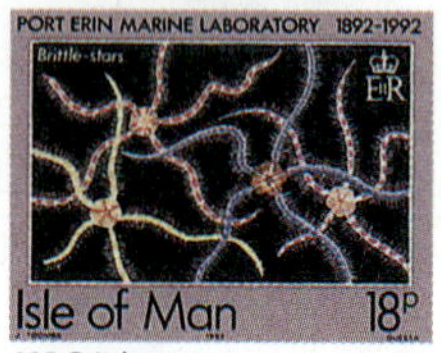

482 Brittle-stars

1992. Centenary of Port Erin Marine Laboratory. Multicoloured.

513	18p. Type **482**	40	35
514	23p. Phytoplankton	60	55
515	28p. Atlantic herring	60	60
516	33p. Great scallop	1·20	1·20
517	39p. Dahlia anemone and delesseria	1·50	1·50

487 The Pilgrim Fathers embarking at Delfshaven

1992. Europa. 500th Anniv of Discovery of America by Columbus. Multicoloured.

518	18p. Type **487**	40	20
519	18p. "Speedwell" leaving Delfshaven	40	30
520	28p. "Mayflower" setting sail for America	75	30
521	28p. "Speedwell" anchored at Dartmouth	75	30

The two designs for each value were printed together, se-tenant, in horizontal pairs forming composite designs.

491 Central Pacific Locomotive "Jupiter", 1869

1992. Construction of the Union Pacific Railroad, 1866–69. Multicoloured.

522	33p. Type **491**	90	35
523	33p. Union Pacific locomotive No. 119, 1869	90	35
524	39p. Union Pacific locomotive No. 844, 1992	1·20	40
525	39p. Union Pacific locomotive No. 3985, 1992	1·20	40
MS526	105×78 mm. £1.50 Golden Spike ceremony, 10 May 1869 (60×50 mm)	3·75	4·50

496 "King Orry V" in Douglas Harbour

1992. Manx Harbours. Multicoloured.

527	18p. Type **496**	45	45
528	23p. Castletown	55	55
529	37p. Port St. Mary	1·20	1·20
530	40p. Ramsey	1·40	1·40

500 "Saint Eloi" in 1972 (image scaled to 44% of original size)

1992. "Genova '92" International Thematic Stamp Exhibition. Sheet 111×68 mm, containing T 500 and similar horiz design. Multicoloured.

MS531	18p. "King Orry V" in 1992 (as in Type **496**); £1 Type **500**	3·25	3·50

501 Stained Glass Window, St. German's Cathedral, Peel

1992. Christmas. Manx Churches. Mult.

532	17p. Type **501**	45	40
533	22p. Reredos, St. Matthew the Apostle Church, Douglas	65	65
534	28p. Stained glass window, St. George's Church, Douglas	80	80
535	37p. Reredos, St. Mary of the Isle Catholic Church, Douglas	95	95
536	40p. Stained glass window, Trinity Methodist Church, Douglas	1·00	1·00

506 Mansell on Lap of Honour, British Grand Prix, 1992

1992. Nigel Mansell's Victory in Formula 1 World Motor Racing Championship. Multicoloured.

537	20p. Type **506**	80	80
538	24p. Mansell in French Grand Prix, 1992	1·00	1·00

508 H.M.S. "Amazon" (frigate)

523a Manx Red Ensign

523b Queen Elizabeth II (hologram)

1993. Ships. Multicoloured.

539	1p. Type **508**	10	10
540	2p. "Fingal" (lighthouse tender)	10	10
541	4p. "Sir Winston Churchill" (cadet schooner)	10	10
542	5p. "Dar Mlodziezy" (full-rigged cadet ship)	10	10
543	20p. "Tynwald I" (paddle-steamer)	40	25
544	21p. "Ben Veg" (freighter)	50	50
545	22p. "Waverley" (paddle-steamer)	50	50
546	23p. Royal Yacht "Britannia"	55	55
547	24p. "Francis Drake" (ketch)	50	35
548	25p. "Royal Viking Sky" (liner)	60	60
549	26p. "Lord Nelson" (cadet barque)	65	65
550	27p. "Europa" (liner)	65	65
551	30p. "Snaefell V" (ferry) leaving Ardrossan	75	75
552	35p. "Seacat" (catamaran ferry)	85	85
553	40p. "Lady of Man I" (ferry) off Ramsey	1·00	90
554	50p. "Mona's Queen II" (paddle ferry) leaving Fleetwood	1·20	1·10
555	£1 "Queen Elizabeth 2" (liner) and "Mona's Queen V" (ferry) off Liverpool	2·50	2·40
556	£2 Type **523a**	3·75	4·00
557	£5 Type **523b**	10·00	12·00

For 4, 20 and 24p. in smaller size, 21×18 mm, see Nos. 687/93.

524 No. 1 Motor Car and No. 13 Trailer at Groudle Glen Hotel

1993. Cent of Manx Electric Railway. Mult.

559	20p. Type **524**	60	60
560	24p. No. 9 Tunnel Car and No. 19 Trailer at Douglas Bay Hotel	90	90
561	28p. No. 19 Motor Car and No. 59 Royal Trailer Special at Douglas Bay	1·00	1·00
562	39p. No. 33 Motor Car, No. 45 Trailer and No. 13 Van at Derby Castle	1·40	1·40

528 "Sir Hall Caine" (statue) (Bryan Kneale)

1993. Europa. Contemporary Art. Works by Bryan Kneale. Multicoloured.

563	20p. Type **528**	40	20
564	20p. "The Brass Bedstead" (painting)	40	20
565	28p. Abstract bronze sculpture	75	30
566	28p. "Polar Bear Skeleton" (drawing)	75	30

532 Graham Oates and Bill Marshall (1933 International Six Day Trial) on Ariel Square Four

1993. Manx Motor Cycling Events. Mult.

567	20p. Type **532**	35	35
568	24p. Sergeant Geoff Duke (1947 Royal Signals Display Team) on Triumph 3T Twin	45	45
569	28p. Denis Parkinson (1953 Senior Manx Grand Prix) on Manx Norton	70	60
570	33p. Richard Swallow (1991 Junior Classic MGP) on Aermacchi	90	90
571	39p. Steve Colley (1992 Scottish Six Day Trial) on Beta Zero	1·00	95
MS572	165×120 mm. Nos. 567/71	4·50	4·50

537 "Inachis io" (Peacock)

1993. Butterflies. Multicoloured.

573	24p. Type **537**	75	65
574	24p. "Argynnis aglaja" (Dark green fritillary)	75	65
575	24p. "Cynthia cardui" (Painted lady)	75	65
576	24p. "Celastrina argiolus" (Holly blue)	75	65
577	24p. "Vanessa atalanta" (Red admiral)	75	65

542 Children decorating Christmas Tree

1993. Christmas. Multicoloured.

578	19p. Type **542**	50	50
579	23p. Girl with snowman	60	60
580	28p. Boy opening presents	70	70
581	39p. Girl with teddy bear	1·10	1·10
582	40p. Children with toboggan	1·10	1·10

547 White-throated Robin

1994. Calf of Man Bird Observatory. Mult.

583	20p. Type **547**	50	20
584	20p. Black-eared wheatear	50	20
585	24p. Goldcrest	80	25
586	24p. Northern oriole	80	25
587	30p. River kingfisher ("King-fisher")	1·00	30
588	30p. Hoopoe	1·00	30
MS589	100×71 mm. £1 Black-billed magpie (51½×61 mm)	3·00	3·50

No. **MS**589 also commemorates the "Hong Kong '94" philatelic exhibition.

554 Gaiety Theatre, Douglas

1994. Manx Tourism Centenary. Multicoloured.

590	24p. Type **554**	65	60
591	24p. Sports	65	60
592	24p. Artist at work and yachts racing	65	60
593	24p. TT Races and British Aerospace Hawk T.1 of Red Arrows display team	65	60
594	24p. Musical instruments	65	60
595	24p. Laxey Wheel and Manx cat	65	60
596	24p. Tower of Refuge, Douglas, with bucket and spade	65	60
597	24p. Cyclist	65	60
598	24p. Tynwald Day and classic car	65	60
599	24p. Santa Mince Pie train, Groudle Glen	65	60

564 "Eubranchus tricolor" (sea slug)

1994. Europa. Discoveries of Edward Forbes (marine biologist). Multicoloured.

600	20p. Type **564**	40	20
601	20p. "Loligo forbesii" (common squid)	40	20
602	20p. Edward Forbes and signature	40	20
603	30p. "Solaster moretonis" (fossil starfish)	75	30
604	30p. "Adamsia carciniopados" (anenome) on hermit crab	75	30
605	30p. "Solaster endeca" (starfish)	75	30

570 Maj-Gen. Bedell Smith and Naval Landing Force including "Ben-my-Chree IV" (ferry)

1994. 50th Anniv of D-Day. Multicoloured.

606	4p. Type **570**	10	10
607	4p. Admiral Ramsay and naval ships including "Victoria" and "Lady of Man" (ferries)	10	10
608	20p. Gen. Montgomery and British landings	50	20
609	20p. Lt-Gen. Dempsey and 2nd Army landings	50	20
610	30p. Air Chief Marshal Leigh-Mallory and U.S. paratroops and aircraft	75	30
611	30p. Air Chief Marshal Tedder and British paratroops and aircraft	75	30
612	41p. Lt-Gen. Bradley and U.S. 1st Army landings	85	45
613	41p. Gen. Eisenhower and American landings	85	45

578 Postman Pat, Jess and Ffinlo at Sea Terminal, Douglas

1994. Postman Pat visits the Isle of Man. Multicoloured.

614	1p. Type **578**	15	15
615	20p. Laxey Wheel	60	60
616	24p. Cregneash	80	80
617	30p. Manx Electric Railway trains	90	90
618	36p. Peel Harbour	1·10	1·10
619	41p. Douglas Promenade	1·20	1·20
MS620	110×85 mm. £1 Postman Pat (25×39 mm)	2·20	2·20

585 Cycling

1994. Centenary of International Olympic Committee. Multicoloured.

621	10p. Type **585**	35	25
622	20p. Downhill skiing	55	50
623	24p. Swimming	70	65
624	35p. Hurdling	95	1·00
625	48p. Centenary logo	1·60	1·80

590 Santa Train to Santon

1994. Christmas. Father Christmas in the Isle of Man. Multicoloured.

626	19p. Type **590**	60	60
627	23p. Father Christmas and Postman Pat on mini tractor, Douglas (vert)	80	80
628	60p. Father Christmas and majorettes in sleigh, Port St. Mary	2·00	2·00

593 Foden Steam Wagon, Highway Board Depot, Douglas

1995. Steam Traction Engines. Multicoloured.

629	20p. Type **593**	55	60
630	24p. Clayton & Shuttleworth and Fowler engines pulling dead whale	60	70

631	30p. Wallis and Steevens engine at Ramsey Harbour	80	85
632	35p. Marshall engine with threshing machine, Ballarhenny	1·10	1·10
633	41p. Marshall convertible steam roller	1·10	1·20

598 Car No. 2 and First Train, 1895

1995. Centenary of Snaefell Mountain Railway. Multicoloured.

634	20p. Type **598**	70	70
635	24p. Car No. 4 in green livery and Car No. 3 in Laxey Valley	80	80
636	35p. Car No. 6 and Car No. 5 in 1971	1·10	1·10
637	42p. Goods Car No. 7 and "Caledonia" steam locomotive pulling construction train	1·20	1·20
MS638	110×87 mm. £1 Passenger car and Argus char-a-banc at Bungalow Hotel (60×37 mm)	3·25	3·25

603 Peace Doves forming Wave and Tower of Refuge, Douglas Bay

1995. Europa. Peace and Freedom. Multicoloured.

639	20p. Type **603**	60	75
640	30p. Peace dove breaking barbed wire	1·00	1·00

605 Spitfire, Tank and Medals

1995. 50th Anniv of End of Second World War. Multicoloured.

641	10p. Type **144**	30	15
642	10p. Hawker Typhoon, anti-aircraft gun and medals	30	15
643	20p. Auro Type **683** Lancaster, H.M.S. "Biter" (escort carrier) and medals	55	25
644	20p. Grumman TBM Avenger aircraft, jungle patrol and medals	55	25
645	24p. Celebrations in Parliament Square	70	25
646	24p. V.E. Day bonfire	70	25
647	40p. Street party	1·10	50
648	40p. King George VI and Queen Elizabeth on Isle of Man in July 1945	1·10	50

613 Reg Parnell in Maserati "4 CLT", 1951

1995. 90th Anniv of Motor Racing on Isle of Man. Multicoloured.

649	20p. Type **613**	65	60
650	24p. Stirling Moss in Frazer Nash, 1951	80	75
651	30p. Richard Seaman in Delage, 1936	90	85
652	36p. Prince Bira in ERA R2B "Romulus", 1937	1·10	1·00
653	41p. Kenelm Guinness in Sunbeam 1, 1914	1·20	1·20
654	42p. Freddie Dixon in Riley, 1934	1·20	1·50
MS655	103×73 mm. £1 John Napier in Arrol Johnston, 1905 (47×58 mm)	3·00	3·00

620 Thomas the Tank Engine and Bertie Bus being Unloaded

1995. 50th Anniv of Thomas the Tank Engine Stories by Revd. Awdry. "Thomas the Tank Engine's Dream". Multicoloured.

656	20p. Type **620**	65	60
657	24p. Mail train	80	75
658	30p. Bertie and engines at Ballasalla	90	85
659	36p. "Viking" the diesel engine, Port Erin	1·10	1·10
660	41p. Thomas and railcar at Snaefell summit	1·20	1·10
661	45p. Engines racing past Laxey Wheel	1·50	1·20

626 "Amanita muscaria"

1995. Fungi. Multicoloured.

662	20p. Type **626**	40	40
663	24p. "Boletus edulis"	50	50
664	30p. "Coprinus disseminatus"	60	60
665	35p. "Pleurotus ostreatus"	75	75
666	45p. "Geastrum triplex"	1·20	1·20
MS667	100×71 mm. £1 Shaggy ink cap and bee orchid (50×59 mm)	3·00	3·00

No. **MS**667 is inscribed "Singapore World Stamp Exhibition 1st–10th September 1995" on the sheet margin.

632 St. Catherine's Church, Port Erin

1995. Christmas. Multicoloured.

668	19p. Type **632**	55	55
669	23p. European robin on holly branch	70	70
670	42p. St. Peter's Church and wild flowers	1·50	1·50
671	50p. Hedgehog hibernating under farm machinery	1·70	1·70

636 Langness Lighthouse

1996. Lighthouses. Multicoloured.

672	20p. Type **636**	50	50
673	24p. Point of Ayre lighthouse (horiz)	60	60
674	30p. Chicken Rock lighthouse	90	90
675	36p. Calf of Man lighthouse (horiz)	1·00	1·00
676	41p. Douglas Head lighthouse	1·10	1·10
677	42p. Maughold Head lighthouse (horiz)	1·20	1·20

642 White Manx Cat and Celtic Interlaced Ribbons

1996. Manx Cats. Multicoloured.

678	20p. Type **642**	50	50
679	24p. Cat and Union Jack ribbons	60	60
680	36p. Cat on rug in German colours, mouse and Brandenburg Gate	90	90
681	42p. Cat, U.S.A. flag and Statue of Liberty	1·10	1·10
682	48p. Cat, map of Australia and kangaroo	1·20	1·20
MS683	100×71 mm. £1.50 Cat with kittens (51×61 mm)	3·50	3·50

See also No. **MS**712.

648 Douglas Borough Arms

1996. Centenary of Douglas Borough. Self-adhesive.

684	**648**	(20p.) multicoloured	70	1·00

1996. Ships. As Nos. 541, 543 and 547, but smaller, 21×18 mm. Multicoloured.

687	4p. "Sir Winston Churchill" (cadet schooner)	20	15
689	20p. "Tynwald I" (paddle-steamer), 1846	60	70
693	24p. "Francis Drake" (ketch)	90	90

The 20p. and 24p. show the positions of the face value and Queen's head reversed.

665 Princess Anne (President, Save the Children Fund) and Children

1996. Europa. Famous Women. Multicoloured.

701	24p. Type **665**	70	75
702	30p. Queen Elizabeth II and people of the Commonwealth	90	1·00

667 Alec Bennett

1996. Tourist Trophy Motorcycle Races. Irish Winners. Multicoloured.

703	20p. Type **667**	50	45
704	24p. Stanley Woods	60	60
705	45p. Artie Bell	90	90
706	60p. Joey and Robert Dunlop	1·40	1·40
MS707	100×70 mm. £1 R.A.F. Red Arrows display team (vert)	3·00	3·00

672 National Poppy Appeal Trophy

1996. 75th Anniv of Royal British Legion. Mult.

708	20p. Type **672**	65	55
709	24p. Manx War Memoial, Braddan	70	60
710	42p. Poppy appeal collection box	1·10	1·20
711	75p. Royal British Legion badge	2·00	2·00

1996. "Capex '96" International Stamp Exhibition, Toronto. No. MS683 additionally inscribed with "CAPEX '96" exhibition logo on sheet margin.

MS712	100×71 mm. £1.50 Cat with kittens (51×61 mm)	6·00	6·50

676 UNICEF Projects in Mexico

1996. 50th Anniv of UNICEF. Multicoloured.

713	24p. Type **676**	50	30
714	24p. Projects in Sri Lanka	50	30
715	30p. Projects in Colombia	60	60
716	30p. Projects in Zambia	60	60
717	42p. Projects in Afghanistan	80	80
718	42p. Projects in Vietnam	80	8

682 Labrador

1996. Dogs. Multicoloured.

719	20p. Type **682**	60	55
720	24p. Border collie	70	65
721	31p. Dalmatian	1·00	90
722	38p. Mongrel	1·10	1·10
723	43p. English setter	1·50	1·50
724	63p. Alsatian	2·00	2·00
MS725	100×71 mm. £1.20 Labrador guide dog and working Border collie (38×50 mm)	3·75	3·75

689 "Snowman and Pine Trees" (David Bennett)

1996. Christmas. Children's Paintings. Multicoloured.

726	19p. Type **689**	55	50
727	23p. "Three-legged Father Christmas" (Louis White)	70	65
728	50p. "Family around Christmas Tree" (Robyn Whelan)	1·60	1·60
729	75p. "Father Christmas in Sleigh" (Claire Bradley)	2·10	2·20

693 Primroses and Cashtyl ny Ard

1997. Spring in Man. Multicoloured.

730	20p. Type **693**	50	50
731	24p. Lochtan sheep and lambs	70	70
732	43p. Daffodils, mallard and ducklings	1·10	1·10
733	63p. Dabchick with young and frog on lily pad	1·60	1·60

697 Barn Owl

1997. Owls. Multicoloured.

734	20p. Type **697**	65	60
735	24p. Short-eared owl	80	75
736	31p. Long-eared owl	1·00	90
737	36p. Little owl	1·20	1·10
738	43p. Snowy owl	1·40	1·50
739	56p. Eurasian tawny owl	1·60	1·70
MS740	100×71 mm. £1.20 Long-eared owl (different) (51×60 mm)	4·00	4·25

No. **MS**740 includes the "HONG KONG '97" International Stamp Exhibition logo on the sheet margin.

704 Moddey Dhoo, Peel Castle

1997. Europa. Tales and Legends. Multicoloured.

741	21p. Type **704**	55	55
742	25p. Fairies in tree and cottage	65	65

743	31p. Fairies at Fairy Bridge	85	85
744	36p. Giant Finn Macooil and Calf of Man	1·10	1·10
745	37p. The Buggane of St. Trinian's	1·10	1·10
746	43p. Fynoderee and farm	1·40	1·40

Nos. 742/3 include the "EUROPA" emblem.

710 Sopwith Tabloid

1997. Manx Aircraft. Multicoloured.

747	21p. Type **710**	30	25
748	21p. Grumman Tiger (1996 Schneider Trophy)	30	25
749	25p. BAe ATP (15th anniv of Manx Airlines)	35	25
750	25p. BAe 146-200 (15th anniv of Manx Airlines)	35	25
751	31p. Boeing 757-200 (largest aircraft to land on Isle of Man)	70	35
752	31p. Farman biplane (1st Manx flight, 1911)	70	35
753	36p. Supermarine Spitfire	75	40
754	36p. Hawker Hurricane	75	40

Nos. 747/8, 749/50, 751/2 and 753/4 respectively were each printed together, se-tenant, the backgrounds forming composite of Isle of Man.

No. 752 is inscribed "EARMAN BIPLANE" in error.

718 14th Hole, Ramsey Golf Club

1997. Golf. Multicoloured.

755	21p. Type **718**	50	50
756	25p. 15th Hole, King Edward Bay Golf and Country Club	60	60
757	43p. 17th Hole, Rowany Golf Club	1·10	1·10
758	50p. 8th Hole, Castletown Golf Links	1·50	1·50
MS759	100×71 mm. £1.30 Golf ball (circular, diameter 39 mm)	3·50	3·50

No. **MS**759 includes the "Pacific '97" International Stamp Exhibition logo on the sheet margin.

1997. Return of Hong Kong to China. Sheet 130×90 mm, containing No. 546. Multicoloured.

MS760	23p. Royal Yacht "Britannia"	1·40	1·60

724 Steve Colley

1997. F.I.M. "Trial de Nations" Motorcycle Team Trials. Multicoloured.

761	21p. Type **724**	55	50
762	25p. Steve Saunders (vert)	65	60
763	37p. Sammy Miller (vert)	1·20	1·00
764	44p. Don Smith	1·50	1·20

728 Angel and Shepherd

1997. Christmas. Multicoloured.

765	20p. Type **728**	65	55
766	24p. Angel and King	75	70
767	63p. The Nativity (54×39 mm)	1·80	1·80

731 Engagement of Princess Elizabeth and Lieut. Philip Mountbatten, 1947

1997. Golden Wedding of Queen Elizabeth and Prince Philip. Multicoloured (except No. 768).

768	50p. Type **731** (brown and gold)	1·00	1·00
769	50p. Wedding photograph, 1947	1·00	1·00
770	50p. At Ascot, 1952	1·00	1·00
771	50p. Golden Wedding photograph, 1997	1·00	1·00
MS772	100×72 mm. £1 Queen Elizabeth and Prince Philip at Peel, 1989 (47×58 mm)	3·00	3·00

738 Shamrock

753 Queen Elizabeth II and Queen Elizabeth the Queen Mother

1998. Flowers. Multicoloured.

773	1p. Bearded iris	10	10
774	2p. Daisy	10	10
775	4p. Type **738**	10	10
776	5p. Silver Jubilee rose	10	15
777	10p. Oriental poppy	20	25
778	20p. Heath spotted orchid	40	30
779	21p. Cushag	40	45
780	22p. Gorse	45	50
781	25p. Princess of Wales rose	50	40
782	26p. Dog rose	50	40
783	30p. Fuchsia "Lady Thumb"	60	60
784	50p. Daffodil	1·00	1·00
785	£1 Spear thistle	2·00	2·00
790	£2.50 Type **753**	5·00	4·75

756 Viking Figurehead

1998. Viking Longships. Multicoloured.

793	21p. Type **756**	55	50
794	25p. Viking longship at sea	75	75
795	31p. Viking longship on beach	90	90
796	75p. Stern of ship	2·20	2·50
MS797	100×71 mm. £1 Viking ship at Peel Castle	3·00	3·00

761 Bottle-nosed Dolphins

1998. UNESCO International Year of the Ocean. Multicoloured.

798	10p. Type **761**	30	30
799	21p. Basking shark	50	50
800	25p. Front view of basking shark	65	65
801	31p. Minke whale	75	75
802	63p. Killer whale and calf	1·60	1·60

766 Locomotive No. 12 "Hutchinson"

1998. 125th Anniv of Isle of Man Steam Railway. Multicoloured.

803	21p. Type **766**	60	50
804	25p. Locomotive No. 10 "G. H. Wood"	70	60
805	31p. Locomotive No. 11 "Maitland"	90	80
806	63p. Locomotive No. 4 "Loch"	1·60	1·60
MS807	119×54 mm. 25p. Pillar box and train at Douglas Station; £1 Locomotive No. 1 "Sutherland"	3·00	3·00

771 Purple Helmets Display Team

1998. Isle of Man T.T. Races and 50th Anniv of Honda (manufacturer). Multicoloured.

808	21p. Type **771**	40	45
809	25p. Joey Dunlop	50	55
810	31p. Dave Molyneux	65	65
811	43p. Naomi Taniguchi	1·00	1·00
812	63p. Mike Hailwood	1·40	1·50

776 Princess Diana wearing Protective Clothing, Angola

1998. Diana, Princess of Wales Commemoration. Multicoloured.

813	25p. Type **776**	50	30
814	25p. Receiving award from United Cerebral Palsy Charity, New York, 1995	50	30
815	25p. With children, South Korea, 1992	50	30
816	25p. Wearing blue jacket, July 1993	50	30

780 Tynwald Day Ceremony

1998. Europa. Festivals. Multicoloured.

817	25p. Type **780**	50	45
818	30p. Traditional dancers, Tynwald Fair	1·10	1·20

782 Father Christmas at North Pole

1998. Christmas. "A Very Special Delivery". Multicoloured.

819	20p. Type **782**	40	30
820	24p. Father Christmas checking list	50	45
821	30p. Flying over Spring Valley sorting office	75	75
822	43p. Passing through Baldrine village	95	95
823	63p. Father Christmas delivering presents	1·40	1·40

787 Large Oval Pillar Box, Kirk Onchan

1999. Local Post Boxes. Multicoloured.

824	10p. Type **787**	25	25
825	20p. Wall box, Ballaterson	45	45
826	21p. King Edward VII pillar box, Laxey Station	50	50
827	25p. Wall box, Spaldrick	85	85
828	44p. Small oval pillar box, Derby Road, Douglas	1·50	1·50
829	63p. Wall box, Baldrine Station	1·75	1·75

793 Cottage, Ballaglass Glen

1999. Europa. Parks and Gardens. Multicoloured.

830	25p. Type **793**	50	50
831	30p. Glen Maye Waterfall	75	80

795 "Ann and James Ritchie", Ramsey

1999. 175th Anniv of Royal National Lifeboat Institution. Multicoloured.

832	21p. Type **795**	50	50
833	25p. "Sir William Hillary", Douglas	55	55
834	37p. "Ruby Clery, Peel"	80	80
835	43p. "Herbert and Edith" (inshore lifeboat), Port Erin	90	90
836	43p. 1974 150th Anniv 8p. stamp	1·00	1·00
837	56p. "Gough Ritchie II", Port St. Mary	1·20	1·20
838	56p. 1991 Manx Lifeboats 21p. stamp	1·50	1·50
MS839	100×70 mm. £1 Sir William Hillary (founder) (37×50 mm)	4·00	4·00

No. **MS**839 includes the "Australia '99" World Stamp Exhibition emblem on the sheet margin.

803 Winter

1999. Centenary of Yn Cheshaght Ghailckagh (Manx Gaelic Society). The Seasons. Multicoloured.

840	22p. Type **803**	60	60
841	26p. Spring	65	65
842	50p. Summer	1·10	1·10
843	63p. Autumn	1·60	1·60

Nos. 840/3 are inscribed "Ellan Vannin", the Manx name for the Isle of Man.

807 Queen Victoria

1999. British Monarchs of the 20th Century. Sheet 170×75 mm, containing T 179 and similar horiz designs. Multicoloured.

MS844	26p. Type **807**; 26p. King Edward VII; 26p. King George V; 26p. King Edward VIII; 26p. King George VI; 26p. Queen Elizabeth II	4·00	4·00

808 Tilling-Stevens Double-deck Bus, 1922

1999. Manx Buses. Multicoloured.

845	22p. Type **808**	50	50
846	26p. Thornycroft BC single-deck, 1928	55	55
847	28p. Cumberland ADC 416 single-deck, 1927	65	65
848	37p. Straker-Squire single-deck, 1914	1·00	1·00
849	38p. Thornycroft A2 single-deck, 1927	1·20	1·20
850	40p. Leyland Lion LT9 single-deck, 1938	1·50	1·50

814 Miss Sophie Rhys-Jones

1999. Royal Wedding. Multicoloured.

851	22p. Type **814**	55	55
852	26p. Leaving St. George's Chapel, Windsor	55	55
853	39p. Prince Edward	80	80
854	44p. Miss Sophie Rhys-Jones and Prince Edward (horiz)	1·10	1·10
855	53p. In landau (horiz)	1·20	1·20

1999. "Philexfrance 99" International Stamp Exhibition, Paris. No. MS807 additionally inscribed with "Philexfrance" exhibition logo on sheet margin.

MS856	119×54 mm. 25p. Pillar box and train at Douglas Station; £1 Locomotive No. 1 "Sutherland"	8·00	8·00

819 St. Luke's Church, Baldwin

1999. Christmas. Churches. Multicoloured.

857	21p. Type **819**	45	45
858	25p. St. Mark's Chapel, Malew	60	60
859	30p. St. German's Parish Church and Cathedral, Peel	70	70
860	64p. Kirk Christ Church, Rushen	1·50	1·50

823 "Massachusetts", 1967

1999. Legends of Music. The Bee Gees (pop group). Designs showing compact discs. Multicoloured.

861	22p. Type **823**	60	50
862	26p. "Words", 1968	70	65
863	29p. "I've Gotta Get a Message to You", 1968	75	75
864	37p. "Ellan Vannin", 1998	90	90
865	38p. "You Win Again", 1987	90	90
866	66p. "Night Fever", 1978	1·50	1·70
MS867	Two sheets, each 119×108 mm. (a) 60p. "Immortality", 1998 (circular, 40 mm diam). (b) 90p. "Stayin' Alive", 1978 (circular, 40 mm diam) Set of 2 sheets	8·00	10·00

831 Sky at Sunset over Calf of Man

1999. New Millennium. Sheet 169×74 mm, containing T 184 and similar vert designs. Multicoloured.

MS868	50p. Type **831**; 50p. Sky at dawn over Maughold Head; £2 Constellations over Man at start of new millennium	8·00	8·00

832 Harrison's Chronometer, 1735, and Map

2000. "The Story of Time". Multicoloured.

869	22p. Type **832**	50	55
870	26p. Daniels' chronometer, 2000, and clock face	55	60
871	29p. Harrison's chronometer, 1767, map and clock	65	70
872	34p. Mudge's chronometer, 1769, and steam locomotives	90	90
873	38p. Arnold's chronometer, 1779, and map of Africa	1·20	1·20
874	44p. Earnshaw's chronometer, 1780, and map of Caribbean	1·50	1·50

838 Duke and Duchess of York on Wedding Day, 1923

2000. "Queen Elizabeth the Queen Mother's Century". Multicoloured (except 26p. and 30p).

875	22p. Type **838**	50	55
876	26p. Queen Elizabeth with Princess Elizabeth, 1940 (brown and black)	55	60
877	30p. King George VI and Queen Elizabeth visiting troops, 1944 (brown and black)	65	70
878	44p. Queen Mother and Queen Elizabeth, 1954	95	80
879	52p. Queen Mother with Prince Charles, 1985	1·00	1·00
880	64p. Queen Mother, 1988	1·10	1·10
MS881	100×70 mm. £1 Queen Mother visiting Isle of Man (74×49 mm)	2·50	2·50

845 Barn Swallow ("Swallow")

2000. Endangered Species. Song Birds. Mult.

882	22p. Type **845**	50	55
883	26p. Spotted flycatcher	55	60
884	64p. Eurasian sky lark ("Sky Lark")	80	80
885	77p. Yellowhammer	1·00	1·00

2000. "The Stamp Show 2000" International Stamp Exhibition, London. As No. MS881, but with "The Stamp Show 2000" multicoloured logo added to the bottom sheet margin.

MS886	100×70 mm. £1 Queen Mother visiting Isle of Man (74×49 mm)	5·00	5·00

849 Lieut. John Quilliam and Admiral Lord Nelson, Battle of Trafalgar

2000. Isle of Man at War. Multicoloured.

887	22p. Type **849**	50	55
888	26p. Ensign Caesar Bacon and Duke of Wellington, Battle of Waterloo	55	60
889	36p. Col. Thomas Leigh Goldie and Earl of Cardigan, Crimea	75	80
890	48p. Bugler John Dunne and Sir Robert Baden Powell, Boer War	1·00	1·10
891	50p. George Kneale and Viscount Kitchener of Khartoum, First World War	1·10	1·20
892	77p. First Officer Alan Watterson and Sir Winston Churchill, Second World War	1·50	1·60
MS893	170×75 mm. 60p. Two Supermarine Spitfires (40×29 mm); 60p. Spitfire on ground (40×29 mm), Battle of Britain	2·75	2·75

856 Prince William as Child

2000. 18th Birthday of Prince William. Sheet 170×75 mm, containing T 189 and similar vert designs. Multicoloured.

MS894	22p. Type **856**; 26p. With Queen Mother; 45p. Prince William; 52p. With Prince Charles and Prince Harry; 56p. Wearing ski-suit	4·50	4·50

857 Ballet Shoes and Painted Ceiling

2000. Centenary of Gaiety Theatre, Douglas. Mult.

895	22p. Type **857**	50	55
896	26p. Comedy mask and box decoration	55	60
897	36p. Drama mask and statue	75	80
898	45p. Pantomime dame with wig and mosaic	95	1·00
899	52p. Opera glasses and decoration	1·10	1·20
900	65p. Top hat with cane and painted ceiling	1·40	1·50

863 Map of Great Britain, Union Jack and Liner

2000. "BT Global Challenge" Round the World Yacht Race. Each showing spinnaker of Isle of Man. Multicoloured.

901	22p. Type **863**	50	55
902	26p. Sydney Opera House, Australian flag and map	55	60
903	36p. New Zealand map and flag	75	80
904	40p. Map of Buenos Aires and waterfront	85	90
905	44p. U.S. flag, map of Boston and harbour	95	1·00
906	65p. South African flag, map and Table Mountain	1·40	1·50

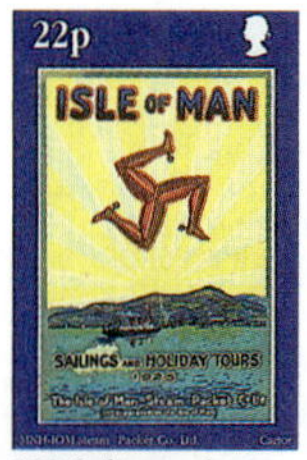

869 Sailing and Holiday Tours Poster, 1925

2000. 170th Anniv of Steam Packet Company. Tourism posters. Multicoloured.

907	22p. Type **869**	50	55
908	26p. "Isle of Man for Happy Holidays"	55	60
909	36p. Woman in swim suit standing on Isle of Man, 1929	75	80
910	45p. Stewardess and ferry	1·50	1·50
911	65p. "Isle of Man for Holidays 1931" and ferry	1·90	2·00

874 Girl with Christingle Candle

2000. Christmas and Europa. Multicoloured.

912	21p. Type **874**	45	50
913	25p. Children dancing around Christmas tree	55	60
914	36p. "Building Europe"	75	80
915	45p. Girl hugging teddy bear	1·50	1·50
916	65p. Children with stars	1·90	2·00

879 Wyon Medal, Penny Black and Queen Victoria

2001. Death Centenary of Queen Victoria. Mult.

917	22p. Type **879**	50	55
918	26p. Great Exhibition medal and Albert Tower, Ramsey	55	60
919	34p. Silver coin and *Great Britain* (early steamship)	75	80
920	39p. Manx coin of 1839, *Oliver Twist* and St. Thomas' Church, Douglas	1·10	1·20
921	40p. Silver coin of 1887, arrival of first train at Vancouver and Jubilee lamp standard	1·10	1·20
922	52p. Silver coin of 1893, Joe Mylchreest at Kimberley diamond mine and Foxdale Clock Tower	1·60	1·70

885 St. Patrick and Snakes (image scaled to 64% of original size)

2001. Chinese New Year ("Year of the Snake"). Sheet 110×85 mm.

MS923	**885** £1 multicoloured	3·00	3·50

No. **MS**923 includes the "Hong Kong 2001" logo on the sheet margin.

886 White-tailed Bumble Bee

2001. Insects. Multicoloured.
924 22p. Type **886** 50 55
925 26p. Seven-spot ladybird 55 60
926 29p. Lesser mottled grasshopper 80 90
927 59p. Manx robber fly 1·50 1·60
928 66p. Elephant hawkmoth 1·90 2·00

891 Letter-carrier, 1805

2001. Postal Uniforms. Multicoloured.
929 22p. Type **891** 50 55
930 26p. Postman, 1859 55 60
931 36p. Postman, 1910 75 80
932 39p. Postman, 1933 1·10 1·20
933 40p. Postman, 1983 1·10 1·20
934 66p. Postman, 2001 1·90 2·00

897 1967–70 Great Britain 1/2d. Machin

2001. 75th Birthday of Queen Elizabeth II. Sheet 170×75 mm, containing T 897 and similar vert designs showing stamps. Multicoloured.
MS935 29p. Type **897**; 34p. 1952–54 Great Britain 6d. Wilding; 37p. 1971 Isle of Man 2½p. Regional; 50p. 1958–68 Isle of Man 4d. Regional 3·75 4·00

898 Joey Dunlop on Rea Yamaha, Parliament Square, 1977 TT Races

2001. Joey Dunlop (motorcycle champion) Commemoration. Each incorporating different portraits. Multicoloured.
936 22p. Type **898** 50 55
937 26p. At Governor's, 1983 TT Races 55 60
938 36p. Leaving Ramsey, 1988 TT Races 75 80
939 45p. On Honda motorbike, 1991 95 1·00
940 65p. On 250cc Honda at Ballaspur, 1999 1·40 1·50
941 77p. On the Mountain 1·60 1·70

904 "The Manx Derby, 1627" (Johnny Jonas)

2001. Horse Racing Paintings. Multicoloured.
942 22p. Type **904** 50 55
943 26p. "Post Haste" (Johnny Jonas) 55 60
944 36p. "Red Rum" (Hamilton-Rennick) 85 80
945 52p. "Hyperion" (Sir Alfred Munnings) 1·50 1·60
946 63p. "Isle of Man" (Johnny Jonas) 1·70 1·70

909 Beef

2001. Europa. Local Dishes prepared by Kevin Woodford. Multicoloured.
947 22p. Type **909** 50 55
948 26p. Queenies with salmon caviar 55 60
949 36p. Seafood 75 80
950 45p. Lamb 1·20 1·20
951 50p. Kipper tart 1·30 1·50
952 66p. Lemon tart with raspberries 1·90 2·00
The 26p. and 36p. show the inscription "EUROPA 2001" at bottom right.

915 Castletown Police Station

2001. The Architecture of Mackay Hugh Bailie Scott. Multicoloured.
953 22p. Type **915** 50 55
954 26p. "Leafield" (semi-detached house) 55 60
955 37p. "The Red House" (Bailie Scott's home) 80 85
956 40p. "Ivydene" (detached house) 1·00 1·10
957 80p. Onchan Village Hall 2·00 2·10
Nos. 953/7 are inscribed "HUGH MACKAY" in error.

2001. "Hafnia 01" International Stamp Exhibition, Denmark. No. MS935 additionally inscr with "Hafnia 01" logo in red on sheet margin.
MS958 170×75 mm. 29p. Type **897**; 34p. 1952–54 Great Britain 6d. Wilding; 37p. 1971 Isle of Man 2½p. Regional; 50p. 1958–68 Isle of Man 4d. Regional 6·50 7·00

920 Royal Refreshments at Glasgow

2001. Golden Jubilee (1st issue). "The Daily Life of the Queen—An Artist's Diary" (paintings by Michael Noakes). Multicoloured.
959 22p. Type **920** 50 55
960 26p. Queen on visit to Lancaster 55 60
961 39p. Queen with labradors, Sandringham 85 90
962 40p. Queen meeting Scottish Korean War veterans 85 90
963 45p. Queen at desk, Sandringham 95 1·00
964 65p. Queen with bouquet, Oxford 1·90 2·00
See also Nos. 970/4.

926 Christmas Tree Wall Decoration

2001. Christmas. Decorations by Isle of Man Floreat Workshop. Multicoloured.
965 21p. Type **926** 45 50
966 25p. Traditional wreath 55 60
967 37p. Table decoration 1·00 1·10
968 45p. Topiary tree 1·20 1·30
969 65p. Contemporary wreath 1·90 2·00

931 "The Coronation, 1953" (Terence Cuneo)

2002. Golden Jubilee (2nd issue). Royal Paintings. Multicoloured.
970 50p. Type **931** 80 60
971 50p. "Queen Elizabeth II as Colonel-in-Chief of Grenadier Guards on Imperial, 1962" (T. Cuneo) 80 60
972 50p. "Queen Elizabeth II in Evening Dress, 1981" (June Mendoza) 80 60
973 50p. "Queen Elizabeth II in Garter Robes, 2000" (Chen Yan Ning) 80 60
974 50p. "The Royal Family in the White Drawing Room, Buckingham Palace" (John Wonnacott) 80 60
MS975 110×85 mm. £1 Sculpture of Queen Elizabeth II by David Cregeen (40×61 mm) 2·00 2·10

937 Cycling

2002. 17th Commonwealth Games, Manchester. Each showing photographic montages. Mult.
976 22p. Type **937** 45 50
977 26p. Running 50 55
978 29p. Javelin and high jump 60 65
979 34p. Swimming 70 75
980 40p. Decathlon 1·00 1·10
981 45p. Wheelchair racing 1·10 1·20

943 "Queen Elizabeth the Queen Mother" (Johnny Jonas)

2002. Queen Elizabeth the Queen Mother Commemoration.
982 **943** £3 multicoloured 6·00 6·25

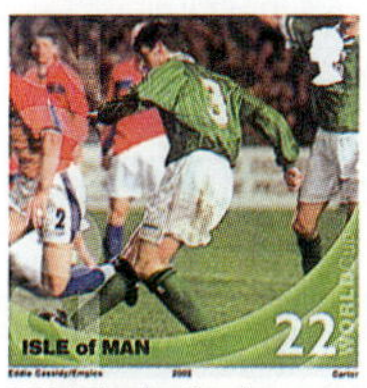

944 Ireland v Czech Republic

2002. World Cup Football Championship, Japan and Korea (2002). Multicoloured.
983 22p. Type **944** 45 50
984 26p. England v Greece 50 55
985 39p. Italy v Belgium 80 85
986 40p. France v Portugal 80 85
987 66p. England v Brazil 1·20 1·40
988 68p. France v Japan 1·40 1·50

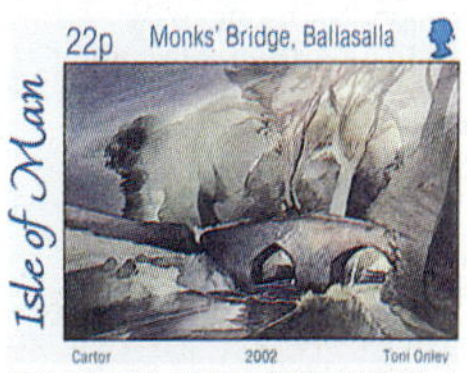

950 "Monk's Bridge, Ballasalla" (Toni Onley)

2002. Watercolours by Toni Onley. Multicoloured.
989 22p. Type **950** 45 50
990 26p. "Laxey" 50 55
991 37p. "Langness Lighthouse" 75 80
992 45p. "King William's College" 1·10 1·20
993 65p. "The Mull Circle and Bradda Head" 1·50 1·60

2002. Golden Jubilee Celebrations. Nos. MS975 additionally inscribed "THE ISLE OF MAN CELEBRATES THE JUBILEE 4th JUNE 2002" in purple on the sheet margin.
MS994 110×85 mm. £1 Sculpture of Queen Elizabeth II by David Cregeen (40×61 mm) 6·50 6·50

955 Magenta Flower on Yellow Background

2002. Memories of the Isle of Man. Multicoloured.
995 22p. Type **955** 45 50
996 26p. Green flower on pink background 50 55
997 29p. Purple flower on green background 60 65
998 52p. Maroon flower on brown background 1·00 1·10
999 63p. Red flower on blue background 1·20 1·40
1000 77p. Orange flower on yellow background 1·50 1·60

961 Manx Milestone (Mrs. B. Trimble)

2002. Photography – The People's Choice. Designs showing competition winners. Multicoloured. Ordinary or self-adhesive gum.
1001 23p. Type **961** 30 25
1002 23p. Plough horses (Miss D. Flint) 30 25
1003 23p. Manx emblem (Ruth Nicholls) 30 25
1004 23p. Loaghtan sheep (Diana Burford) 30 25
1005 23p. Fishing fleet, Port St. Mary (Phil Thomas) 30 25
1006 23p. Peel (Michael Thompson) 30 25
1007 23p. Daffodils (Michael Thompson) 30 25
1008 23p. Millennium sword (Mr. F. K. Smith) 30 25
1009 23p. Peel Castle (Kathy Brown) 30 25
1010 23p. Snaefell Railway (Joan Burgess) 30 25
1011 27p. Laxey Wheel (Kathy Brown) 35 30
1012 27p. Sheep at Druidale (John Hall) 35 30
1013 27p. Carousel at Silverdale (Colin Edwards) 35 30
1014 27p. Grandma (Stephanie Corkhill) 35 30
1015 27p. Manx rock (Ruth Nicholls) 35 30
1016 27p. T.T. riders at Signpost (Neil Brew) 35 30
1017 27p. Groudle Railway (Albert Lowe) 35 30
1018 27p. Royal cascade (Brian Speedie) 35 30
1019 27p. St. Johns (John Hall) 35 30
1020 27p. Niarbyl cottages with poppies (Cathy Galbraith) 35 30

981 Father Christmas

2002. Christmas. Entertainment. Multicoloured.
1041 22p. Type **981** 45 50
1042 26p. Virgin Mary and Jesus 50 55
1043 37p. Clown 75 80
1044 47p. Bandsman playing cymbals 95 1·00
1045 68p. Fairy 1·40 1·50

MS1046	123×55 mm. £1.30 "CHRISTMAS" and festive characters (103×40 mm)	3·00	3·25

The 37p. value includes the "EUROPA" emblem.

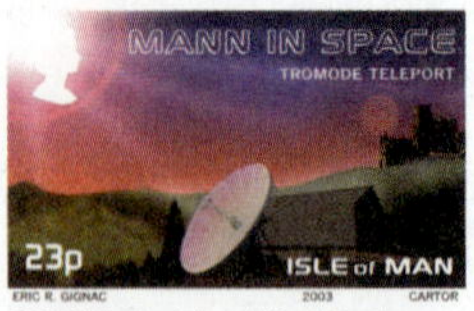

987 Dish Aerial and Peel Castle

2003. Isle of Man Involvement in Space Exploration. Multicoloured.

1047	23p. Type **987**	45	50
1048	23p. Dish aerial, Tromode Teleport	45	50
1049	27p. Camp on Moon and lunar vehicle	55	60
1050	27p. Astronaut exploring lunar surface	55	60
1051	37p. *Sea Launch Odyssey* (marine launch platform)	75	80
1052	37p. *Sea Launch Commander* (assembly command ship)	75	80
1053	42p. Loral Telstar 1 satellite	85	90
1054	42p. Loral Telstar 8 satellite	85	90
MS1055	110×85 mm. 75p. Phobos and American spaceship (30×36 mm); 75p. Mars, astronauts and transfer vehicle (30×36 mm)	4·00	4·00

Nos. 1047/8, 1049/50, 1051/2 and 1053/4 were each printed together, as horizontal se-tenant pairs, in sheets of 8 with enlarged illustrated right margins.

996 Delivery Handcart (1900–45)

2003. Post Office Vehicles. Multicoloured.

1056	23p. Type **996**	45	50
1057	27p. Morris Z van (1942)	55	60
1058	37p. Morris L diesel van (1960s)	1·00	1·10
1059	42p. DI BSA Bantam telegraph delivery motorbikes	1·10	1·20
1060	89p. Ford Escort 55 van	2·20	2·40

1001 Queen Elizabeth II wearing St. Edward's Crown

2003. 50th Anniv of Coronation. Multicoloured.

1061	50p. Type **1001** (26×57 mm)	70	75
1062	50p. The Ring (23×28 mm)	70	75
1063	50p. The Orb (23×28 mm)	70	75
1064	50p. Royal Sceptre and Rod of Equity and Mercy (23×28 mm)	70	75
1065	50p. Queen Elizabeth II wearing Imperial State Crown (26×57 mm)	70	75
1066	50p. State Coach (81×27 mm)	70	75

1007 de Havilland D.H. 83 Fox Moth and Saunders Roe (Saro) Cloud (amphibian)

2003. Centenary of Powered Flight. Each showing two aircraft. Multicoloured.

1067	23p. Type **1007**	45	50
1068	27p. de Havilland D.H. 61 Giant Moth and D.H. 80 Puss Moth	60	60
1069	37p. Avro Type 652 Anson and Boeing B-17 Flying Fortress	70	80
1070	40p. Eurofighter EF-2000 Typhoon and Avro Type **698** Vulcan	70	85
1071	67p. Handley Page Herald and Bristol Wayfarer	80	1·50
1072	89p. Aerospatiale Concorde and projected Airbus Industrie A380	1·20	1·90

1012a Avro Lancaster attacking Mohne Dam (image scaled to 28% of original size)

2003. 60th Anniv of Attack on German Dams by No. 617 ("Dambusters") Squadron. Sheet 170×75 mm.

MS1073	**1012a** £2 multicoloured	4·00	4·25

1013 Prince William

2003. 21st Birthday of Prince William of Wales.

1074	**1013**	42p. black and grey	85	90
1075	-	47p. black and grey	95	1·00
1076	-	52p. black and grey	1·50	1·60
1077	-	68p. black and grey	1·90	2·00

DESIGNS: 47p. to 68p. Showing recent photographs.

2003. Trilaterale Ticino Exhibition, Locarno, Switzerland. No. MS1073 additionally inscr with "Ticino 2003" logo in blue on sheet margin.

MS1078	£2 multicoloured	4·75	4·75

1017 *Manx Gold* (Agatha Christie)

2003. "The Manx Bookshelf". Book covers. Multicoloured.

1079	23p. Type **1017**	45	50
1080	27p. *Quatermass and the Pit* (Nigel Kneale)	55	60
1081	30p. *Flashman at the Charge* (George MacDonald Fraser)	60	65
1082	38p. *The Eternal City* (Hall Caine)	75	80
1083	40p. *Peveril of the Peak* (Sir Walter Scott)	1·00	1·10
1084	53p. *Emma's Secret* (Barbara Taylor Bradford)	1·20	1·30

The 38p. value includes the "EUROPA 2003" emblem.

1023 King Henry VII and Henry Tudor crowned by Sir Thomas Stanley on Bosworth Battlefield

2003. 400th Anniv of End of the Tudor Reign. Multicoloured.

1085	23p. Type **1023**	45	50
1086	27p. King Henry VIII and Manx church (Dissolution of the Monasteries)	55	60
1087	38p. Queen Elizabeth I and globe showing route of Drake's circumnavigation	75	80
1088	40p. King Henry VIII, Cardinal Wolsey and Hampton Court Palace	80	85
1089	47p. Queen Mary I and Tudor rose	95	1·00
1090	67p. Queen Elizabeth I and ships of Spanish Armada	1·40	1·50

1029 Henry Bloom Noble and Orphanage Boys

2003. Centenary of Henry Bloom Noble Trust. Multicoloured.

1091	23p. Type **1029**	40	25
1092	23p. Nurse and Ramsey Cottage Hospital	40	25
1093	23p. Children and Children's Home	40	25
1094	23p. Bathers at Noble's Baths	40	25
1095	23p. Scout and Headquarters	40	25
1096	27p. Noble's Hospital, c. 1912	45	30
1097	27p. Villa Marina	45	30
1098	27p. Noble's Park	45	30
1099	27p. St. Ninian's Church	45	30
1100	27p. Noble's Library	45	30

Nos. 1091/1100 also come self-adhesive.

1039 Boy tying Scarf on Snowman

2003. Christmas. The Snowman by Raymond Briggs. Multicoloured.

1111	22p. Type **1039**	45	50
1112	26p. Snowman (wearing black hat and scarf)	50	55
1113	38p. Boy and Snowman holding hands	75	80
1114	47p. Snowman (wearing brown hat and scarf)	95	1·00
1115	68p. Boy flying with Snowman	1·40	1·50

1044 Aragorn

2003. Making of The Lord of the Rings Film Trilogy: The Return of the King. Multicoloured.

1116	23p. Type **1044**	45	50
1117	27p. Gimli	55	60
1118	30p. Gandalf	60	65
1119	38p. Legolas on horseback	1·00	90
1120	42p. Gollum	1·50	1·00
1121	47p. Frodo and Sam	2·00	2·00
1122	68p. Legolas drawing bow	3·00	3·50
1123	85p. Aragorn on horseback	3·50	3·00
MS1124	120×78 mm. £2 The Ring (44×40 mm)	5·00	5·50

1053 *Maitland* (Simon Hall)

2004. Bicentenary of Running of First Steam Locomotive. Paintings of steam locomotives by named artists. Multicoloured.

1125	23p. Type **1053**	75	75
1126	27p. *Evening Star* (Terence Cuneo)	90	90
1127	40p. *Pen-y-Darren* Tramroad Locomotive (Terence Cuneo)	1·30	1·30
1128	57p. *Duchess of Hamilton* (Craig Tiley)	1·80	1·80
1129	61p. *City of Truro* (B. J. Freeman)	2·00	2·00
1130	90p. *Mallard* (Terence Cuneo)	3·00	3·00

1059 Troops on Landing Craft and Tanks going Ashore

2004. 60th Anniv of D-Day. Multicoloured.

1131	23p. Type **1059**	50	25
1132	23p. Troops leaving landing craft and tanks going ashore	50	25
1133	27p. Troops leaving landing craft	60	30
1134	27p. Landing craft and troops wading ashore	60	30
1135	47p. *Lady of Mann* (ferry used as landing craft carrier)	1·00	50
1136	47p. *Ben-my-Chree* (ferry used as landing craft carrier)	1·00	50
1137	68p. Consolidated B-24 Liberators (bombers) and North American P-51 Mustang (fighter)	1·20	70
1138	68p. Airspeed AS 51 Horsa gliders (troop carriers)	1·20	70
MS1139	170×75 mm. 50p. Winston Churchill; 50p. Troops and aircraft; 50p. Military vehicles on street; 50p. Soldiers with France guidebook	6·50	6·50

Nos. 1131/2, 1133/4, 1135/6 and 1137/8 were each printed together, se-tenant, each pair forming a composite design.

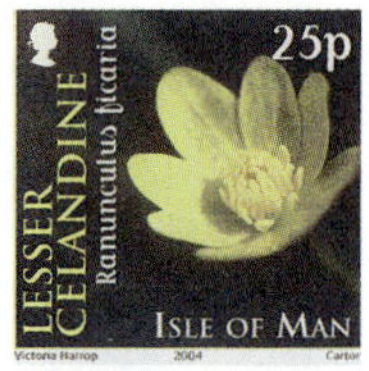

1068 Lesser Celandine

2004. Bicentenary of Royal Horticultural Society. Wild Flowers. Multicoloured.

1140	25p. Type **1068**	85	85
1141	28p. Red campion	95	95
1142	37p. Devil's-bit scabious	1·20	1·20
1143	40p. Northern harebell	1·30	1·30
1144	68p. Wood anemone	2·20	2·20
1145	85p. Common spotted orchid	2·75	2·75

1074 In *No Limit*, 1936

2004. Birth Centenary of George Formby (entertainer). Showing scenes from film No Limit. Multicoloured.

1146	25p. Type **1074**	80	80
1147	28p. Pushing motorcycle	90	90
1148	40p. Riding in TT race	1·30	1·30
1149	43p. With Florence Desmond	1·40	1·40
1150	50p. On motorcycle	1·70	1·70
1151	74p. George Formby in close-up	2·40	2·40

1080 Johnny Weismuller (swimmer), Paris, 1924

2004. Olympic Games, Athens. Olympic Legends. Multicoloured.

1152	25p. Type **1080**	85	85
1153	28p. Jesse Owens (athlete), Berlin, 1936	95	95
1154	43p. John Mark carrying Olympic Flame, London, 1948	1·40	1·40
1155	55p. Fanny Blankers-Koen (sprinter), London, 1948	1·80	1·80
1156	91p. Steve Redgrave and Coxless Four (Gold Medallists), Sydney, 2000	3·00	3·00

1085 Celtic Islanders and Viking Invaders

2004. Manx National Heritage. The Story of Mann. Multicoloured. Ordinary or self-adhesive gum.

1157	(25p.) Type **1085**	50	25
1158	(25p.) Fisherman ("Ships and the Sea")	50	25
1159	(25p.) Miner and Laxey Wheel ("Laxey Miners")	50	25
1160	(25p.) Soldier with Longbow and Castle ("Kings and Lords of Mann")	50	25
1161	(25p.) Woman with Spinning Wheel ("Farmers and Crofters")	50	25
1162	(28p.) Calf of Man	60	30
1163	(28p.) Peel Castle	60	30
1164	(28p.) Laxey Wheel	60	30
1165	(28p.) Castle Rushen	60	30
1166	(28p.) Cregneash	60	30

Nos. 1157/61 and 1167/71 are inscribed "IOM" and were initially sold at 25p. Nos. 1162/6 and 1172/6 are inscribed "UK" and were initially sold at 28p.

1095 Laxey Wheel (image scaled to 40% of original size)

2004. 150th Anniv of the Great Laxey Wheel. Sheet 120×78 mm.

MS1177	£2 multicoloured	6·50	6·50

1096 "Maughold Church"

2004. The Isle of Man Watercolours by Alfred Heaton Cooper. Multicoloured.

1178	25p. Type **1096**	80	80
1179	28p. "Port St. Mary"	90	90
1180	40p. "Ballaugh Old Church"	1·30	1·30
1181	41p. "Douglas Bay (A Midsummer's Night)"	1·30	1·30
1182	43p. "Point of Ayre"	1·40	1·40
1183	74p. "Peel Harbour and Castle"	2·40	2·40

The 28p. and 40p. values include the 'EUROPA 2004' emblem.

2004. Sindelfingen International Stamp Exhibition, Sindelfingen, Germany. No. MS1177 additionally inscribed with "Sindelfingen" logo on the sheet margin.

MS1184	£2 multicoloured	6·50	6·50

1102 Robin on Flower Pot

2004. Robins—Winter's Friends. Multicoloured.

1185	25p. Type **1102**	80	80
1186	28p. Robin at foot of tree	90	90
1187	40p. Robin perched on branch	1·30	1·30
1188	47p. Robin on window ledge	1·50	1·50
1189	68p. Robin on snowy logs	2·30	2·30
MS1190	148×200 mm. Nos. 1185/9	8·50	8·50

1107 Harry Potter (Daniel Radcliffe), Ron Weasley (Rupert Grint) and Hermione Granger (Emma Watson)

2004. "Harry Potter and the Prisoner of Azkaban" (film). Multicoloured.

1191	25p. Type **1107**	80	80
1192	28p. Snowy Owl delivering Owl Post	90	90
1193	39p. Harry Potter and White Stag	1·30	1·30
1194	40p. Hogwarts Express	1·30	1·30
1195	49p. Rubeus Hagrid (Robbie Coltrane)	1·60	1·60
1196	55p. Purple Triple-decker Bus	1·80	1·80
1197	57p. Dementor and Harry Potter flying	1·90	1·90
1198	68p. Harry Potter on the Hippogriff Buckbeak	2·20	2·20

1115 The Nile Campaign

2005. 200th Anniv of the Battle of Trafalgar. Multicoloured.

1199	25p. Type **1115**	50	55
1200	25p. The Battle of Copenhagen	50	55
1201	28p. Emma, Horatia and Nelson	55	60
1202	28p. Band of Brothers	55	60
1203	50p. Prepare for Battle	1·00	1·10
1204	50p. Victory in Sight	1·00	1·10
1205	65p. The Fall of Nelson	1·30	1·40
1206	65p. The Death of Nelson	1·30	1·40
MS1207	170×75 mm. £1 Lieut. John Quilliam and Admiral Lord Nelson (No. 887); £1 Steering HMS *Victory* (No. 160)	4·00	4·25

1124 Two Couples by Waterside

2005. 60th Anniv of the End of World War II. Multicoloured.

1208	26p. Type **1124**	45	30
1209	26p. Group celebrating in the street	45	30
1210	29p. Man trying on hat	50	30
1211	29p. Civil Service personnel	50	30
1212	60p. King George VI and Winston Churchill on balcony of Buckingham Palace	75	70
1213	60p. King George VI and Queen Elizabeth in carriage	75	70
1214	65p. Servicemen	85	70
1215	65p. War graves	85	70
MS1216	170×75 mm. £1 The Manx Regiment; £1 Royal visit, 1945	4·50	4·50

1133 *Mona's Isle* (Samuel Walters)

2005. 175th Anniv of Steam Packet Company. Multicoloured.

1217	26p. Type **1133**	45	30
1218	26p. *Viking* (Norman Wilkinson)	45	30
1219	29p. *King Orry* (Robert Lloyd)	50	30
1220	29p. *Mona's Queen* (Arthur Burgess)	50	30
1221	40p. *Ben-my-Chree* (John Nicholson)	75	45
1222	40p. *King Orry* (Robert Lloyd)	75	45
1223	66p. *Ben-my-Chree* (Robert Lloyd)	1·00	70
1224	66p. *Lady of Mann* (Robert Lloyd)	1·00	70

1141 Bill Ivy and Phil Read

2005. 50th Anniv of Yamaha. Multicoloured.

1225	26p. Type **1141**	50	55
1226	29p. Joey Dunlop and Ray McCullough	60	65
1227	40p. Steve Hislop	80	85
1228	42p. Carl Fogarty	85	90
1229	68p. David Jefferies	1·40	1·50
1230	78p. John McGuinness	1·60	1·70

1147 Paul Harris (founder)

2005. Centenary of Rotary International and Europa. Gastronomy (42p.). Multicoloured.

1231	26p. Type **1147**	50	55
1232	29p. Planting tree, children grouped and child drinking	60	65
1233	40p. Child being immunised and boy with leg braces and crutches	80	85
1234	42p. Food preparations	85	90
1235	64p. Supply truck, children with volunteer and loading cases	1·30	1·40
1236	68p. Child having eye test, group under Rotary banner and family	1·40	1·50

The 42p. value includes the "EUROPA 200" emblem.

1153 Guttin' Herrin'

2005. Time to Remember. Multicoloured. Ordinary or self-adhesive gum.

1237	26p. Type **1153**	45	30
1238	26p. Pickin' spuds	45	30
1239	26p. J. C. Kelly, Master Butcher	45	30
1240	26p. Winkles, Foxdale	45	30
1241	26p. Palace Ballroom	45	30
1242	29p. Land Army	50	30
1243	29p. Farmyard, Glen Maye	50	30
1244	29p. Eva Kane, Summer Season Stars	50	30
1245	29p. Donkey rides	50	30
1246	29p. Alfie Gilmour, "Give us a go Mister!"	50	30

1163 Obelisk in St. Peter's Square (image scaled to 28% of original size)

2005. 20th World Youth Day. Sheet 170×75 mm, containing T 1163 and similar vert design. Multicoloured.

MS1257	42p. Type **1163**; £1.50 St. Peter's Basilica	4·00	4·00

1164 Harry Potter (Daniel Radcliffe)

2005. Harry Potter and the "Goblet of Fire" (film). Multicoloured.

1258	26p. Type **1164**	50	55
1259	29p. Harry Potter, Hermione, Ron Weasley and Goblet of Fire	60	65
1260	33p. Trophy	65	70
1261	64p. Hungarian Horntail Dragon	1·30	1·40
1262	68p. Hogwarts Coat of Arms	1·40	1·50
1263	75p. Murcus, Chieftainess of the Merpeople	1·50	1·60

1170 Arrival of Nelson's funeral procession at St. Paul's Cathedral, London (image scaled to 28% of original size)

2005. Death Bicentenary of Admiral Lord Nelson. Sheet 170×75 mm.

MS1264	£1 Type **1170** together with £1 stamp from Gibraltar No. **MS**1145	4·50	4·50

The same miniature sheet was also issued by Gibraltar.

1171 Mary and Jesus

2005. Christmas. Stained-glass Windows from Manx Churches. Multicoloured.

1265	26p. Type **1171**	50	55
1266	29p. Angel with the Crown of Glory	60	65
1267	42p. Shepherds worshipping Christ Child	85	90
1268	60p. Nativity	1·20	1·30
1269	68p. Three Kings	1·40	1·50

Nos. 1265/7 are from St. German's Cathedral, Peel and Nos. 1268/9 from Kirk Christ, Rushen.

1176 Princess Elizabeth aged Five with Duke and Duchess of York and Princess Margaret, 1931

2006. 80th Birthday of Queen Elizabeth II (1st issue). Multicoloured.

1270	20p. Type **1176**	40	30
1271	20p. Princess Elizabeth wearing ATS uniform, c. 1944	40	30
1272	20p. Queen Elizabeth wearing diadem, 1952	40	30
1273	20p. With Princes Philip, Andrew, Edward, Charles and Princess Anne, 1972	40	30
1274	80p. With Prince Philip at Balmoral on Silver Wedding Anniversary, 1972	1·60	1·00
1275	80p. With regalia in Throne Room, Buckingham Palace, 2001	1·60	1·00
1276	80p. With Prince William on Buckingham Palace balcony	1·60	1·00
1277	80p. With crowd at Aylesbury, Berkshire on Golden Jubilee tour, 2002	1·60	1·00

See also No. **MS**1294.

1184 Jurby Chalice and Jurby Church

2006. Manx Study—Isle of Man Natural History and Antiquarian Society. Multicoloured.

1278	26p. Type **1184**	50	55
1279	29p. Viking period gold pin head and Peel Castle	60	65
1280	64p. Fragment of early Neolithic bowl and Meayll Hill, Rushen	1·30	1·40
1281	68p. Manx stoat and Cronk Sumark late rron age hill fort	1·40	1·50
1282	78p. Hen harrier and South Barrule Hill, Malew	1·60	1·70
1283	97p. Fossil ammonite, Scarlett Point and Castletown	1·90	2·00

1190 Peregrine Falcon

2006. Manx Bird Atlas. Multicoloured. Ordinary or self-adhesive gum.

1284	28p. Type **1190**	55	35
1285	28p. Puffin	55	35
1286	28p. Manx Shearwater	55	35
1287	28p. Chough	55	35
1288	28p. Guillemot	55	35
1289	31p. Whinchat	60	40
1290	31p. Hen harrier	60	40
1291	31p. Goldcrest	60	40
1292	31p. Grey wagtail	60	40
1293	31p. Wren	60	40

1200 Queen Elizabeth II at Tynwald Ceremony, 2003 (image scaled to 40% of original size)

2006. 80th Birthday of Queen Elizabeth II (2nd issue). Sheet 120×78 mm, containing T 1200 and similar vert design. Multicoloured.

MS1294	£1 Type **1200**; £1 Queen in 1972, Manx Cross in background	4·00	4·25

1201 West German Player

2006. World Cup Football Champioship, Germany. 40th Anniv of England's World Cup Victory. Multicoloured.

1295	28p. Type **1201**	55	60
1296	31p. West German team	60	65
1297	44p. Bobby Moore (England captain) with trophy and Alf Ramsey (manager)	90	95
1298	72p. Bobby Moore holding trophy aloft	1·40	1·50
1299	83p. West German players	1·70	1·80
1300	94p. Victorious England team	1·90	2·00

1207 1977 10p. View from Ramsey Stamp (image scaled to 28% of original size)

2006. 50th Anniv of First Europa Stamp. Sheet 170×75 mm containing T 1207 and similar horiz design showing Isle of Man Europa stamps. Multicoloured.

MS1301	42p. Type **1207**; 83p. 1990 15p. Ramsey Post Office Stamp	2·50	2·75

1208 Letitia Tyler (First Lady 1841–2)

2006. Manx Links with Washington. Multicoloured.

1302	28p. Type **1208**	55	60
1303	31p. Joseph Gurney "Czar" Cannon (Speaker of House of Representatives 1903–11)	60	65
1304	45p. Matthew Quay (Civil War hero and Republican Party National Committee chairman)	90	95
1305	50p. Mary Clemmer (19th-century journalist)	1·00	1·10
1306	76p. Ewan Clague (economist)	1·50	1·60
1307	83p. Henry "Marse" Watterson (advisor to Pres. Roosevelt)	1·70	1·80

Nos. 1302/7 were issued to coincide with the Washington 2006 Stamp Exhibition.

1214 Peel P50

2006. Peel Cars. Multicoloured.

1308	28p. Type **1214**	55	60
1309	31p. Trident	60	65
1310	38p. Viking Sport	75	80
1311	41p. BMC GRP Mini	1·00	85
1312	54p. Manxcar	1·50	1·20
1313	94p. P1000	2·00	2·00

1220 "Ewan Christian"

2006. 150th Anniv of National Portrait Gallery, London. Multicoloured.

1314	28p. Type **1220**	55	60
1315	31p. "Dame Agatha Christie" (John Gay)	60	65
1316	38p. "Sir Hall Caine" (Harry Furniss)	75	80
1317	41p. "William Bligh" (John Condé, after John Russell)	80	85
1318	44p. "Lady Maria Callcott" (Sir Thomas Lawrence)	90	95
1319	54p. "John Martin" (Henry Warren)	1·10	1·20
1320	64p. "Sir John Betjeman" (Stephen Hyde)	1·30	1·40
1321	96p. "Sir Edward Elgar" (Herbert Lambert)	1·90	2·00

1228 Christmas Tree and Gifts

2006. Christmas. Trees. Multicoloured. (a) Ordinary gum.

1322	28p. Type **1228**	55	60
1323	31p. Tree with Three Legs of Mann decoration at top	60	65
1324	41p. Tree with four tiers of white decorations	80	85
1325	44p. Monkey-puzzle tree and Three Legs of Mann symbols	90	95
1326	72p. Tree with three tiers of yellow Three Legs of Mann decorations	1·40	1·50
1327	94p. Tree with brown Three Legs of Mann decorations	1·90	2·00

Nos. 1323, 1325 and 1329 include the "EUROPA 2006" emblem.

(b) Size 28×39 mm. Self-adhesive.

1328	28p. Type **1228**	55	60
1329	31p. As No. 1323	60	65

1234 Benjamin Bunny (image scaled to 28% of original size)

2006. "The Tales of Beatrix Potter". Sheet 170×75 mm containing T 1234 and similar multicoloured designs.

MS1330	170×75 mm. 28p. Type **1234**; 50p. Jemima Puddle-duck (horiz); 72p. Peter Rabbit (horiz); 75p. Jeremy Fisher (vert)	4·50	4·75

2006. Belgica '06 International Stamp Exhibition, Brussels. Sheet 148×210 mm Multicoloured.

MS1331	Nos. 1284/93	8·50	10·00

1235 Steve Hislop

2007. Centenary of Isle of Man TT Motor Cycle Races. Multicoloured.

1332	(31p.) Type **1235**	65	50
1333	(31p.) Joey Dunlop (cobalt)	65	50
1334	(31p.) David Jefferies (violet)	65	50
1335	(31p.) Dave Molyneux (black)	65	50
1336	(31p.) John McGuinness (orange)	65	50
1337	(44p.) Stanley Woods (magenta)	85	80
1338	(44p.) Geoff Duke (green)	85	80
1339	(44p.) Bob McIntyre (lilac)	85	80
1340	(44p.) Giacomo Agostini (scarlet)	85	80
1341	(44p.) Mike Hailwood (red)	85	80

Nos. 1332/6 are inscribed "UK" and were sold at 31p. each. Nos. 1337/41 are inscribed "E" and were sold at 44p. each.

1245 Scouts hiking near South Barrule

2007. Centenary of Scouting. Multicoloured.

1342	28p. Type **1245**	65	65
1343	31p. Scout Investiture on Douglas Beach	75	75
1344	44p. Backpacking below Cronk-ny-Arrey-Laa	1·00	1·00
1345	72p. Manx Scouts on parade at St. Johns	1·70	1·70
1346	83p. Sea kayaking off Laxey Beach	2·00	2·00
1347	£1 Manx Scouts operating the TT scoreboard	2·40	2·40
MS1348	135×85 mm. 50p. Two scouts at camp, 1913 (horiz); £1.50 Scout camp with bell tent and open fire, 1913 (42×56 mm)	4·75	4·75

1252 Wedding, 1947

2007. Diamond Wedding of Queen Elizabeth and Prince Philip. Multicoloured.

1349	60p. Type **1252**	1·00	1·00
1350	60p. Queen Elizabeth II and Duke of Edinburgh, c. 1955	1·00	1·00
1351	60p. Queen Elizabeth (wearing pink blouse) and Duke of Edinburgh, c. 1965	1·00	1·00
1352	60p. Queen Elizabeth (wearing red) and Duke of Edinburgh, c. 1977	1·00	1·00
1353	60p. Queen Elizabeth (wearing green dress) and Duke of Edinburgh, c. 1997	1·00	1·00
1354	60p. Queen Elizabeth (wearing pale mauve) and Duke of Edinburgh, c. 2002	1·00	1·00

1258 "Headland, Cornaa"

2007. Watercolour Paintings by Norman Sayle. Multicoloured. (a) Ordinary gum.

1355	28p. Type **1258**	65	65
1356	28p. "Headland, Sound"	65	65
1357	31p. "St Marks Church"	75	75
1358	31p. "Castletown Harbour Moonlight"	75	75
1359	42p. "Bridge House, Castletown"	1·00	1·00
1360	44p. "Winter Sun"	1·00	1·00
1361	65p. "In Ancient Times"	1·50	1·50
1362	75p. "Bracken Mountain"	1·70	1·70

(b) Self-adhesive.

1363	28p. Type **1258**	85	85
1364	28p. As No. 1356	85	85
1365	31p. As No. 1357	95	95
1366	31p. As No. 1358	95	95

1266 King John granting Royal Charter

2007. 800th Anniv of the Royal Charter of Liverpool. Multicoloured.

1367	31p. Type **1266**	70	70
1368	48p. Liverpool Cathedral and Liverpool Metropolitan Cathedral	1·10	1·10
1369	54p. Statue of Capt. Noel Chavasse ("Liverpool war heroes")	1·30	1·30
1370	74p. St. George's Hall	1·70	1·70
1371	80p. Port of Liverpool	1·90	1·90
1372	£1 The Wall of Fame	2·30	2·30

1272 *Susan Constant* and Map showing Voyage from England to Virginia, 1607

2007. 400th Anniv of Jamestown, Virginia, USA. Multicoloured.

1373	28p. Type **1272**	65	65
1374	31p. Capt. Christopher Newport and *Susan Constant*, *God-speed* and *Discovery* on the James River	75	75
1375	44p. James Fort and James River, 1607	1·00	1·00
1376	54p. Algonquin Princess Poca-hontas and Capt. John Smith	1·30	1·30
1377	78p. Jamestown settlement, 1607	1·90	1·90
1378	90p. Powhatan village	2·20	2·20

1278 James Brown (image scaled to 28% of original size)

2007. 800 Years of Trade between Liverpool and the Isle of Man. Sheet 170×75 mm containing T 1278 and similar horiz designs. Multicoloured.

MS1379	25p. Type **1278**; 40p. Joseph Cunningham and holiday camp, c. 1895; 80p. William Gill and first landing stage at Liverpool, c. 1857; 80p. Dalrymple Maitland and "Liverpool Echo" newspaper	5·50	6·00

2007. TT Race Winners. Sheet 180×235 mm.

MS1379a	Nos. 1332/41	11·50	

2007. 21st World Scout Jamboree, Chelmsford, England. No. MS1348 additionally inscr with jamboree emblem on the margin.

MS1380	135×85 mm. 50p. Two scouts at camp, 1913; £1.50 Scout camp with bell tent and open fire, 1913 (42×56 mm)	5·00	5·50

1279 Map by John Speed, 1605

2007. Maps of the Isle of Man. Multicoloured.

1381	28p. Type **1279**	65	65
1382	31p. Map by Captain Greenville Collins, 1693	75	75
1383	44p. Map published by John Drinkwater based on trigo-nometrical survey, 1826	1·10	1·10

1384	48p. Ordnance Survey County series map, 1870	1·10	1·10
1385	75p. Six-inch series map based on National Grid, 1975	1·80	1·80
1386	88p. 1:100,000 map, 2006	2·10	2·10

1285 Captain John Ross and *Victory* trapped in Ice

2007. International Polar Year (1st issue). Voyage of the Victory to the North Pole, 1829–33. Multicoloured.

1387	28p. Type **1285**	65	65
1388	31p. Flares from *Victory* guide returning exploration parties	70	70
1389	55p. *Victory's* crew hunting with Inuit	1·30	1·30
1390	75p. Hunted musk ox	1·80	1·80
1391	90p. Crew on 300 mile trek after abandoning *Victory*	2·10	2·10
1392	117p. Crew in whaleboats rescued by whaler *Isabella*	2·75	2·75

1291 'Ben-my-Chree' Log Cabin, Tagish Lake, British Columbia (image scaled to 28% of original size)

2007. International Polar Year (1291and similar multicoloured designs.

MS1393	50p. Type **1291**; 50p. Graham 'Jimmy' Oates taking motorcycle and sidecar along railroad track to Hudson Bay, 1932 (vert); 75p. Kermode bear (subspecies of Grizzly bear) (vert); 75p. Dog sled and Hudson Bay Post Office, 1931–61	6·00	6·50

1292 Ploughing

2007. European Vintage Ploughing Championships, Isle of Man. Multicoloured.

1394	28p. Type **1292**	65	65
1395	31p. Ploughing with grey tractor	70	70
1396	48p. Horse-drawn plough	1·10	1·10
1397	71p. Hand plough	1·70	1·70
1398	90p. Ploughing with red tractor	2·10	2·10
1399	£1.27 Ploughing with blue tractor	3·00	3·00

No. 1396 is inscr 'sepac'.

1298 Angel playing Trumpet

2007. Christmas. 'Hark the Herald Angels Sing'. Multicoloured. Self-adhesive.

1400	28p. Type **1298**	65	65
1401	31p. Angel playing lute	75	75
1402	69p. Angel wearing crown	1·60	1·60
1403	78p. Angel with harp	1·80	1·80
1404	£1.24 Angel with hands clasped in prayer	3·00	3·00

1303 *Queen Elizabeth 2*

2008. Cunard Ocean Liners. Sheet 170×75 mm.

1405	**1303**	£1 Type **1303**	3·00	3·50
1405a	**1303**	£1 *Queen Mary 2*	3·00	3·50
1405b	**1303**	£1 *Queen Victoria*	3·00	3·50

1306 H.P. 0/400 and Bristol F2B Fighter

2008. 90th Anniv of Royal Air Force. Multicoloured.

1406	31p. Type **1306**	60	60
1407	31p. Avro 504N and Westland Wapiti	60	60
1408	31p. Hawker Hurricane and Short S25 Sunderland	60	60
1409	90p. Gloster Meteor and Westland Whirlwind	1·70	1·70
1410	90p. Hawker Hunter and E.E. Canberra	1·70	1·70
1411	90p. Harrier and Lockheed Hawker Siddeley C-130 Hercules	1·70	1·70

1312 The Pagan Lady of Peel

2008. The Viking Age on the Isle of Man. Multicoloured.

1412	28p. Type **1312**	65	65
1413	31p. Ship burial	75	75
1414	44p. Godred Crovan ('King Orry')	1·00	1·00
1415	54p. Gautr Bjornsson the sculptor	1·30	1·30
1416	69p. Sigurd the dragon slayer	1·60	1·60
1417	£1.24 Coming of Christianity	3·00	3·00

1318 Isle of Man Bank £1 Note, 1956

2008. Bank Notes of the Isle of Man. Multicoloured. (a) Ordinary gum.

1418	30p. Type **1318**	70	70
1419	31p. Isle of Man Govt £10 note, 1972	75	75
1420	44p. Manx Bank (1882–1900) £1 note	1·00	1·00
1421	56p. Isle of Man Govt 50p decimal note, 1969	1·40	1·40
1422	85p. Isle of Man Govt £50 note, 1983	2·00	2·00
1423	114p. Parr's Bank £1 note, 1918	2·75	2·75

(b) Self-adhesive.

1424	30p. As Type **1318**	80	1·00

1324 Archery (image scaled to 28% of original size)

2008. Olympic Games, Beijing. Sheet 170×75 mm containing T 1324 and similar square designs. Multicoloured.

MS1425	1p. Type **1324**; 2p. Showjumping; 3p. Cycling; 94p. Hand holding Olympic torch	2·40	3·00

1325 Cornish Flag

2008. Interceltique. Designs showing flags of Celtic countries. Multicoloured.

1426	20p. Type **1325**	45	45
1427	30p. Isle of Man flag	70	70
1428	31p. Scottish flag	70	70
1429	48p. Breton flag	1·10	1·10
1430	50p. Irish flag	1·20	1·20
1431	56p. Flag of Asturias	1·30	1·30
1432	72p. Welsh flag	1·70	1·70
1433	£1.13 Flag of Galicia	2·75	2·75
MS1434	174×210 mm. Nos. 1426/33	9·75	9·75

Nos. 1428 and 1430 include the 'EUROPA' emblem.

1333 Reg Parnell in Maserati 4CLT

2008. British Motor Racing. Multicoloured.

1435	20p. Type **1333**	45	45
1436	30p. Mike Hawthorn	70	70
1437	70p. Tony Brooks in Vanwall	1·60	1·60
1438	81p. Roy Salvadori in Aston Martin	1·90	1·90
1439	94p. Stirling Moss at Pit Stop	2·20	2·20
1440	£1.22 Jim Clark in Lotus-Climax 25 R4	3·00	3·00
MS1441	170×75 mm. 50p.×6 Aston Martin DB4 GT Zagato, 1961; Ferrari 250 LM, Le Mans, 1965; Ferrari 250 GTO, Goodwood Revival, 1962; Ford GT 40, Goodwood Festival of Speed, 1965; Mercedes-Benz 300 SLR, Mille Miglia Road Race, Italy, 1955; Shelby Cobra, Goodwood Revival, 1964 (all 40×29 mm)	7·00	7·00

1340 Miss M. L. Wood (founder of Manx Music Festival)

2008. New Manx Worthies. Showing characters from book. Multicoloured.

1442	31p. Type **1340**	60	60
1443	31p. Harry Kelly (last native Manx speaker) and cottage at Cregneash Folk Museum	60	60
1444	31p. Sir Frank Gill (telephony and communications engineer) and phone box	60	60
1445	31p. Ramsey Gelling Johnson (second deemster (Manx judge), 1947–54)	60	60
1446	31p. John Nicholson (artist and designer of Manx stamps, currency notes and gold coinage)	60	60
1447	50p. Dr. Dorothy Pantin (Island's first woman doctor and first medical supervisor of Jane Crookall Maternity Home)	1·00	1·00
1448	50p. Richard Costain (founder of construction company)	1·00	1·00
1449	50p. Sir William Percy Cowley (first deemster and Clerk of the Rolls, 1947–58)	1·00	1·00
1450	50p. Revd Fred Cubbon (philanthropist)	1·00	1·00
1451	50p. William Henry Gill (author, musician and collector of Manx folk music)	1·00	1·00

2008. Olympex Olympic Stamp Expo, Beijing. No. MS1425 additionally inscr with 'Beijing 2008' emblem and 'OLYMPEX, THE OLYMPIC EXPO' on the bottom margin.

MS1452	1p. Type **1324**; 2p. Showjumping; 3p. Cycling; 94p. Hand holding Olympic torch	2·40	2·75

2008. Team GB Olympic Cyclists. Sheet 145×208 mm. Multicoloured.

MS1453	3p. Cycling; 94p. Hand holding Olympic torch	2·40	2·75

No. **MS**1453 contains 3p. and 94p. designs as in **MS**1425.

1350 Orange-tip Butterfly (*Anthocharis cardamines*)

2008. A Walk in the Ballaugh Curragh

1454	30p. Type **1350**	70	70
1455	31p Curlew (*Numenius arquata*)	75	75
1456	50p Birch bracket fungus (*Piptoporus betulinus*)	1·20	1·20
1457	70p Large red damselfly (*Pyrrhosoma nymphula*)	1·70	1·70
1458	82p Marsh cinquefoil (*Potentilla palustris*)	1·90	1·90
1459	£1.38 Royal fern (*Osmunda regalis*)	3·25	3·25

1356 Second Lt. Roy F. Corlett, 1916

2008. 90th Anniv of the End of World War I. Manx Soldiers and their Letters Home. Multicoloured.

1460	30p. Type **1356**	70	70
1461	31p. Second Lt. John W. Lewis, 1916	70	70
1462	44p. Pte. Joseph Killey	1·00	1·00
1463	56p. Lt. Col. W. A. W. Crellin, 1917	1·30	1·50
1464	81p. Lance Cpl. Tom Quilliam, 1918	1·90	2·00
1465	94p. Pte. Robert Oates, 1914	2·20	2·50
MS1466	110×70 mm. £2 Manx National War Memorial, St. John's	4·75	5·00

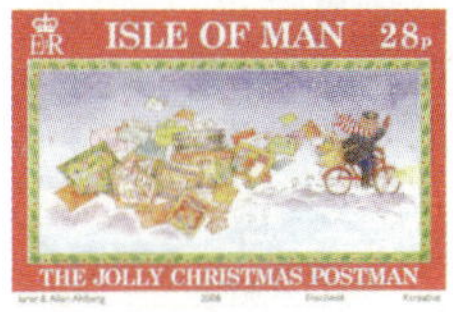

1363 Christmas Cards and Postman on Bicycle

2008. Christmas. Illustrations from The Jolly Christmas Postman by Janet and Allan Ahlberg. T 277 and similar horiz designs. Multicoloured.

1467	28p. Type **1363**	65	65
1468	31p. Postman icing biscuits and giant biscuit tin	75	75
1469	48p. Offering postman mince pies and decorating Christmas tree	1·10	1·10
1470	50p. Postman holding card and Toy Town	1·20	1·20
1471	56p. Postman on bicycle and winter landscape	1·30	1·30
1472	£1.56 Postman relaxing at home	3·50	3·50

1369 Fairey Barracuda II

2009. Centenary of Naval Aviation. Multicoloured.

1473	30p. Type **1369**	70	70
1474	31p. Blackburn Buccaneer S.2	70	70
1475	72p. Fairey Flycatcher	1·75	1·75
1476	85p. EH101 Merlin Helicopter	2·00	2·00
1477	98p. BAe Sea Harrier FRS.1	2·25	2·25
1478	£1.36 Sea Scout SS.24 Airship	3·00	3·00

1375 McClaren Race Car

2009. Lewis Hamilton, Formula One World Champion, 2008. Multicoloured.

1479 30p. Type **1375** 70 70
1480 31p. Celebrating with champagne 70 70
1481 56p. Crossing finishing line 1·25 1·25
1482 85p. Seated in Race Car 2·00 2·00
1483 98p. Race car 2·25 2·25
1484 £1.42 With arms raised in triumph 3·25 3·25

1381 Henry VIII

2009. 500th Anniv of the Accession of King Henry VIII.

1485 50p. Type **1381** 1·25 1·25
1486 50p. Catherine of Aragon 1·25 1·25
1487 50p. Anne Boleyn 1·25 1·25
1488 50p. Jane Seymour 1·25 1·25
1489 50p. Anne of Cleves 1·25 1·25
1490 50p. Catherine Howard 1·25 1·25
1491 50p. Catherine Parr 1·25 1·25
1492 50p. Hampton Court 1·25 1·25

1389 Ballakilley Farm

2009. Mills and Millers. Photographs by Chris Kilip. Multicoloured. (a) Ordinary gum.

1493 32p. Type **1389** 70 70
1494 32p. Grenaby Farm 70 70
1495 33p. Mr. Cubbon 70 70
1496 33p. Glenmoar Mill 70 70
1497 50p. Golden Meadow Mill 1·25 1·25
1498 50p. Bernie Mylcraine 1·25 1·25
1499 78p. Golden Meadow Mill 1·75 1·75
1500 78p. Loughtan Farm 1·75 1·75

(b) Self-adhesive.

1501 32p. multicoloured 70 70
1502 32p. multicoloured 70 70
1503 33p. multicoloured 70 70
1504 33p. multicoloured 70 70

1397 Peonies

2009. China World Stamp Exhibition and Peony Festival, Luoyang. Multicoloured; colour of right-hand border given.

1505 **1397** 10p. multicoloured (gold) 25 25
1506 **1397** 10p. multicoloured (green) 25 25
1507 **1397** 10p. multicoloured (rose) 25 25
1508 **1397** 10p. multicoloured (blue) 25 25
1509 **1397** 10p. multicoloured (mauve) 25 25
1510 **1397** 10p. multicoloured (red) 25 25
1511 **1397** 10p. multicoloured (blue) 25 25
1512 **1397** 10p. multicoloured (yellow) 25 25

1398 Boot Print and *Sunrise over Antares* (Apollo 14 lunar module)

1404 *On the Rim* (John Young and Charlie Duke at North Ray Crater, 1972) (image scaled to 44% of original size)

2009. 40th Anniv of First Manned Moon Landing. Paintings by Alan Bean. Multicoloured.

1513 33p. Type **1398** 1·00 1·00
1514 50p. *Clan MacBean* (Alan Bean) *arrives on the Moon* and *Documenting the Sample* 1·50 1·50
1515 56p. *Pete and Me* (Pete Conrad taking photograph) 1·50 1·50
1516 81p. *Headed for the Last Parking Lot* (Gene Cernan and lunar roving vehicle) 2·00 2·00
1517 105p. *The Eagle* (Apollo 11 lunar module) *is Headed Home* and *In the Beginning* 2·50 2·50
1518 135p. *Ceremony on the Plain at Hadley* and *The Hoer* (Jim Irwin digging trench) 3·00 3·00
MS1519 109×84 mm. **1404** £2.50 multicoloured (vert) 6·00 6·00

1405 Naomi Taniguchi, 1959

2009. 50th Anniv of Honda Motorcycles in World Championship Racing. Multicoloured.

1520 32p. Type **1405** 70 70
1521 33p. Mike Hailwood, 1960s 75 75
1522 56p. Alex George, 1970s 1·25 1·25
1523 62p. Joey Dunlop, 1980s 1·60 1·60
1524 90p. Steve Hislop, 1990s 2·40 2·40
1525 £1.77 John McGuinness, 2000s 3·75 3·75

1411 W. G. Grace at Lord's, 1895; MCC Ashes Trophy and Urn; England v. Australia, Lord's, 2005 (image scaled to 28% of original size)

2009. The Ashes. England v. Australia 2009. Sheet 170×75 mm.

MS1526 £1×3 1411 £1×3 multicoloured 7·00 7·00

1412 Barry, Maurice and Robin Gibb as Boys

2009. 50th Anniv of the Bee Gees (pop group). Multicoloured.

1527 32p. Type **1412** 75 75
1528 33p. *Children of the World* album cover 75 75
1529 50p. *Bee Gees* album cover 1·25 1·25
1530 54p. *Still Waters* album 1·25 1·25
1531 56p. *One Night Only* album 1·25 1·25
1532 62p. *This is Where I Came In* album 1·60 1·60
1533 78p. Bee Gees *Number Ones* ac lbum 1·75 1·75
1534 £1.28 Bee Gees *The Studio Albums* 1967–8 3·00 3·00

2009. 40th Anniv of First Manned Moon Landing (2nd issue). No. MS1519 additionally inscr with '40th anniversary man on the moon' emblem on the bottom right margin.

MS1534a £2.50 *On the Rim* (John Young and Charlie Duke at North Ray Crater, 1972) (Alan Bean) 6·00 6·00

1420 Brown Hare

2009. Country File. Paintings by Jeremy Paul. Multicoloured.

1535 **1420** 32p. 75 75
1536 **1421** 33p. Hedgehogs 75 75
1537 **1422** 54p. Pheasants 1·25 1·25
1538 **1423** 90p. Barn owl 2·40 2·40
1539 **1424** 92p. Cockerel 2·40 2·40
1540 **1425** £1.58 *On the Hill* 3·50 3·50
MS1541 148×210 mm. Nos. 1535/40 11·00 11·00

1426 *Bridge*

2009. Watercolour Paintings by Archibald Knox.

1542 32p. Type **1426** 75 75
1543 33p. *Willows and Blue Mountain* 75 75
1544 56p. *Kew* 1·25 1·25
1545 62p. *Eairy Beg* 1·60 1·60
1546 81p. *Leaning Trees* 1·90 1·90
1547 182p. *Old Laxey* 4·25 4·25

1432 Captain James Teare and SS *Ellan Vannin*; SS *Ellan Vannin* in Ramsey Harbour (image scaled to 28% of original size)

2009. Centenary of Sinking of the SS Ellan Vannin (steam packet). Sheet 170×75 mm.

MS1548 multicoloured 7·00 7·00

1433 Father Christmas putting Present into Stocking

2009. Christmas. Father Christmas. Multicoloured. (a) Ordinary gum.

1549 30p. Type **1433** 70 70
1550 33p. Writing list 75 75
1551 56p. Carrying sack of toys 1·25 1·25
1552 62p. Carrying wrapped present 1·60 1·60
1553 81p. With Archbishop's Staff, Mitre and Robes 1·75 1·75
1554 90p. With Christmas pudding and wine goblet 2·40 2·40

(b) Self-adhesive gum.

1555 30p. As Type **1433** 70 70
1556 30p. Writing list 75 75

1439 Woman walking in Lane

2010. Island Life. Multicoloured. (a) Ordinary gum.

1557 (32p.) Type **1439** 75 75
1558 (32p.) Angler 75 75
1559 (32p.) Yachtsman 75 75
1560 (32p.) Climber 75 75
1561 (33p.) Children riding ponies 75 75
1562 (33p.) Apple picking 75 75
1563 (33p.) Unloading kayak 75 75
1564 (33p.) Motorcyclist 75 75
1565 56p. Children on rocky shore 1·25 1·25
1566 90p. Horses ploughing at Cregneash National Folk Museum 2·40 2·40

(b) Self-adhesive.

1567 (32p.) AS Type **1439** 75 75
1568 (32p.) Angler 75 75
1569 (32p.) Yachtsman 75 75
1570 (32p.) Climber 75 75
1571 (33p.) Children riding ponies 75 75
1572 (33p.) Apple picking 75 75
1573 (33p.) Unloading kayak 75 75
1574 **1446** (33p.) Motorcyclist 75 75

Nos. 1557/60 and 1567/70 were inscribed 'IOM RATE' and sold for 32p. each.

Nos. 1561/4 and 1571/4 were inscribed 'UK RATE' and sold for 33p. each.

1449 Two Rainbows

1457 Manx Guide Leaders (£1.50); Trefoil Guild Members planting Tree, 1985 (£1.50) (image scaled to 28% of original size)

2010. Centenary of Girlguiding. Multicoloured.

1575 32p. Type **1449** 75 75
1576 32p. Company of rainbows and leaders 75 75
1577 33p. Brownies holding badges 75 75
1578 33p. Five brownies 75 75
1579 56p. Girl guide 1·25 1·25
1580 56p. Guides and leaders on parade 1·25 1·25
1581 £1 Senior section members 2·25 2·25
1582 £1 Queen Elizabeth II meeting guide leaders 2·25 2·25
MS1583 170×75 mm. **1457** £1.50×2 7·00 7·00

Nos. 1577 and 1579 include the 'EUROPA' emblem.

1458 Messerschmitt BF109 and Defiant

1464 1981 60th Anniversary of Royal British Legion 20p. Stamp and Ship crowded with Evacuated Troops, Dunkirk, 1940 (£1.50); 1990 50th Anniversary of Battle of Britain Pair of 24p. Stamps and Aircrew running for Planes (£1.50) (image scaled to 28% of original size)

2010. 70th Anniv of the Battle of Britain. Multicoloured.

1584 70p. Type **1458** 1·60 1·60
1585 70p. Spitfire and Messerschmitt BF109 1·60 1·60
1586 70p. Junkers Ju87 and Hurricane 1·60 1·60
1587 70p. Messerschmitt BF110 and Hurricane 1·60 1·60
1588 70p. Blenheim I and Junkers 88 1·60 1·60
1589 70p. Heinkel III and Spitfire 1·60 1·60
MS1590 170×75 mm. **1464** £1.50 multicoloured; £1.50 multicoloured 7·00 7·00

MS1590 also commemorates the 70th anniversary of Operations Dynamo and Ariel (evacuation of troops from Dunkirk).

1465 King George V and Queen Mary at Grand Hall, Douglas, 1920 and Cast of Great Britain 1d. George V Stamp

2010. Centenary of Accession of King George V. Multicoloured.

1591	55p. Type **1465**	1·25	1·25
1592	60p. King George V and Queen Mary, Isle of Man, 1920 and Cape of Good Hope tete-beche pairs of 1861 1d. 'Hope' stamps	1·50	1·50
1593	67p. King George V and Queen Mary arriving at Queen's Pier, Ramsey, 1920 and Great Britain 1910 2d. Tyrian plum stamp	1·60	1·60
1594	96p. King George V and Queen Mary with Nurses, Ramsey, and Oil Rivers Protectorate 1893 20s. on 1s. stamp	2·50	2·50
1595	97p. King George V planting Tree at Bishopscourt, 1920 and George V ½d. green stamp	2·50	2·50
1596	£1.10 King George V and Queen Mary at Castletown and Mauritius 1847 2d. deep blue stamp	3·00	3·00

1471 Model T Speedster, 1915

2010. 50th Anniv of Model T Ford Register. Multicoloured.

1597	35p. Type **1471**	80	80
1598	36p. Model T coupe, 1926	85	85
1599	60p. Model T 7cwt van, 1923	1·50	1·50
1600	74p. Model T town car, 1912	1·75	1·75
1601	97p. Model T charabanc, 1922	2·25	2·25
1602	172p. Model T tourer, 1912	4·00	4·00

POSTAGE DUE STAMPS

D1

1973

D1	**D1**	½p. red, black and yellow	1·50	1·10
D2	**D1**	1p. red, black and brown	50	60
D3	**D1**	2p. red, black and green	15	20
D4	**D1**	3p. red, black and grey	20	20
D5	**D1**	4p. red, black and pink	30	35
D6	**D1**	5p. red, black and blue	30	35
D7	**D1**	10p. red, black and violet	40	40
D8	**D1**	20p. red, black and green	75	60

D2

1975

D9	**D2**	½p. yellow, black and red	10	10
D10	**D2**	1p. brown, black and red	10	10
D11	**D2**	4p. lilac, black and red	10	15
D12	**D2**	7p. blue, black and red	15	20
D13	**D2**	9p. grey, black and red	25	30
D14	**D2**	10p. mauve, blk & red	25	20
D15	**D2**	50p. orange, blk & red	90	90
D16	**D2**	£1 green, black and red	1·50	1·60

D3

1982

D17	**D3**	1p. multicoloured	10	10
D18	**D3**	2p. multicoloured	10	10
D19	**D3**	5p. multicoloured	10	10
D20	**D3**	10p. multicoloured	20	25
D21	**D3**	20p. multicoloured	40	45
D22	**D3**	50p. multicoloured	90	1·10
D23	**D3**	£1 multicoloured	1·60	2·10
D24	**D3**	£2 multicoloured	3·25	4·25

D4

1992

D25	**D4**	£5 multicoloured	8·00	8·50

Pt. 19

ISRAEL

The former British Mandate over Palestine was ended by the partition plan approved by the United Nations General Assembly on 29 November 1947, and on 14 May 1948 the new state of Israel was proclaimed.

1948. 1000 prutot (mils) = 1 Israeli pound.
1960. 100 agorot = 1 Israeli pound.
1980. 100 agorot = 1 shekel.

"**TABS**". All Israeli stamps (except the Postage Dues) exist with descriptive sheet margin attached. These so-called "Tabs" are popular and in some cases scarce. Prices are for stamps without "tab". Separate prices for stamps with "tabs" are given in Stanley Gibbons Catalogue, Part 19 (Middle East).

1 Palm Tree and Baskets with Dates

2 Silver Shekel and Pomegranates

1948. Ancient Jewish Coins. Perf or roul.

1	**1**	3m. orange	1·20	45
2	-	5m. green	1·20	45
3a	-	10m. mauve	7·00	3·50
4	-	15m. red	1·70	45
5	-	20m. blue	3·50	85
6	-	50m. brown	23·00	4·00
7	**2**	250m. green	60·00	23·00
8	**2**	500m. red on buff	£225	£100
9	**2**	1000m. blue on blue (36×24 mm)	£475	£200

DESIGNS ON COINS: 5m. Vine leaf; 10m. Ritual jar; 15m. Bunch of grapes; 20m. Ritual cup; 50m. Tied palm branches and lemon.
See also Nos. 21/6, 40/51 and 90/93.

3 "Flying Scroll" Emblem

1948. Jewish New Year.

10	**3**	3m. brown and blue	95	60
11	**3**	5m. green and blue	95	60
12	**3**	10m. red and blue	1·20	95
13	**3**	20m. blue and light blue	4·75	2·10
14	**3**	65m. brown and red	26·00	11·50

4 Road to Jerusalem

1949. Inauguration of Constituent Assembly.

15	**4**	250pr. brown and grey	3·25	2·50

5 National Flag

1949. Adoption of New National Flag.

16	**5**	20pr. blue	1·50	70

1949. 1st Anniv of Israeli Postage Stamps. Sheet containing stamp similar to T 8 in block of four.

MS16a 75×95 mm. 10pr. claret		£170	95·00

6 Petah Tiqwa Well

1949. 70th Anniv of Founding of Petah Tiqwa.

17	**6**	40pr. brown and green	19·00	3·00

7 Air Force Badge

1949. Jewish New Year.

18	**7**	5pr. blue	1·50	60
19	-	10pr. green	1·50	60
20	-	35pr. brown	11·50	7·00

BADGES: 10pr. Navy; 35pr. Army.

8 Ancient Jewish Coin

1949. 2nd Jewish Coins issue. Inscr at left of 6 or 8 characters.

21	**8**	3pr. grey	25	25
22	-	5pr. violet (as No. 2)	25	25
23	-	10pr. green (as No. 3)	25	25
24	-	15pr. red (as No. 4)	45	25
25	-	30pr. blue	80	45
26	-	50pr. brown (as No. 6)	2·75	95

DESIGN: 30p.r. Ritual vessel.
For designs with larger inscription at left, see Nos. 40/51 and 90/93.

10 Stag and Globe

1950. Israel's Membership and 75th Anniv of U.P.U.

27	**10**	40pr. violet	1·70	95
28	**10**	80pr. red	2·10	1·20

11 Landing of Immigrants

1950. 2nd Anniv of Independence.

29	**11**	20pr. brown	4·75	2·30
30	-	40pr. green	19·00	10·50

DESIGN: 40pr. Line of immigrant ships.

12 Library and Book

1950. 25th Anniv of Founding of Hebrew University, Jerusalem.

31	**12**	100pr. green	70	70

13 Eagle

1950. Air.

32	-	5pr. blue	95	60
33	-	30pr. grey	60	60
34	-	40pr. green	60	60
35	-	50pr. brown	60	60
36	**13**	100pr. red	29·00	19·00
37	-	250pr. blue	3·50	2·30

DESIGNS—VERT: 5pr. Doves pecking grapes; 30pr. Eagle; 40pr. Ostrich; 50pr. Dove. HORIZ: 250pr. Dove with olive branch.

14 Star of David and Fruit

1950. Jewish New Year.

38	**14**	5pr. violet and orange	25	25
39	**14**	15pr. brown and green	1·20	1·20

1950. 3rd Jewish Coins issue. Inscr at left of 13 characters.

40		3pr. grey	25	25
41		5pr. violet	25	25
42		10pr. green	25	25
43		15pr. red	25	25
44		20pr. orange	25	25
45		30pr. blue	25	25
46		35pr. green	80	45
47		40pr. brown	30	30
48		45pr. mauve	30	30
49		50pr. brown	35	30
50		60pr. red	30	30
51		85pr. blue	80	45

DESIGNS ON COINS: 3, 20pr. Palm tree and baskets with dates; 5, 35pr. Vine leaf; 10, 40pr. Ritual jar; 15, 45pr. Bunch of grapes; 30, 60pr. Ritual vessel; 50, 85pr. Tied palm branches and lemon.
For further designs with value at right, see Nos. 90/93.

16 Runner and Track

1950. 3rd Maccabiah (sports meeting).

52	**16**	80pr. green and olive	5·75	3·00

17 "The Negev" (after R. Rubin)

1950. Opening of Post Office at Elat.

53	**17**	500pr. brown & light brown	21·00	14·00

19 Memorial Tablet

1951. 40th Anniv of Founding of Tel Aviv.

54	**19**	40pr. brown	1·00	70

20 "Supporting Israel"

1951. Independence Bonds Campaign.

55	**20**	80pr. red	70	70

21 Metsudat Yesha

1951. 3rd Anniv of State of Israel.

56	**21**	15pr. red	35	35
57	-	40pr. blue (Hakastel)	1·00	1·00

22 Tractor

23 Ploughing and Savings Stamp

1951. 50th Anniv of Jewish National Fund.

58	**22**	15pr. brown	25	25
59	-	25pr. green	25	25
60	**23**	80pr. blue	2·30	1·60

DESIGN—As Type **22**: 25pr. Stylized tree.

24 Dr. T. Herzl

1951. 23rd Zionist Congress.

61	**24**	80pr. green	70	60

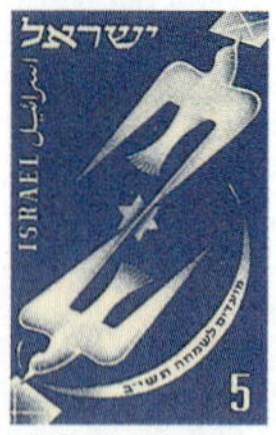
25 Carrier Pigeons

1951. Jewish New Year.

62	**25**	5pr. blue	25	10
63	-	15pr. red	25	10
64	-	40pr. violet	35	35

DESIGNS: 15pr. Woman and dove; 40pr. Scroll of the Law.

26 Menora and Emblems

1952

64a	**26**	1000pr. black and blue	28·00	17·00

26a Haifa Bay, Mt. Carmel and City Seal

1952. Air. National Stamp Exn ("TABA").

64b	-	100pr. blue and black	1·20	80
64c	**26a**	120pr. purple and black	1·60	1·20

DESIGN: 100pr. Haifa Bay and City Seal.

27 Thistle and Yad Mordechai

1952. 4th Anniv of Independence.

65	**27**	30pr. brown and mauve	35	25
66	-	60pr. slate and blue	60	35
67	-	110pr. brown and red	1·20	80

DESIGNS: 60pr. Cornflower and Deganya; 110pr. Anemone and Safed.

28 New York Skyline and Z.O.A. Building

1952. Opening of American Zionist Building, Tel Aviv.

68	**28**	220pr. grey and blue	1·40	70

29 Figs

1952. Jewish New Year.

69	**29**	15pr. yellow and green	45	25

70	-	40pr. yellow, blue and violet	70	45
71	-	110pr. grey and red	1·00	95
72	-	220pr. green, brown & orge	1·50	1·20

FLOWERS: 40pr. Lily ("Rose of Sharon"); 110pr. Dove; 220pr. Nuts.

30 Dr. C. Weizmann (from sketch by R. Errell)

1952. Death of First President.

73	**30**	30pr. blue	35	25
74	**30**	110pr. black	1·00	80

31

1952. 70th Anniv of Bet Yaakov Lechu Venelcha Immigration Organization.

75	**31**	110pr. buff, green and brown	1·00	70

32 Douglas DC-4 Airliner over Tel Aviv Yafo

1953. Air.

76	-	10pr. deep green and green	45	30
77	-	70pr. violet and lilac	45	30
78	-	100pr. deep green and green	45	30
79	-	150pr. brown and orange	45	30
80	-	350pr. red and pink	70	70
81	-	500pr. deep blue and blue	1·50	1·20
81a	-	750pr. deep brown & brown	25	25
82	**32**	1000pr. deep green & green	5·75	4·75
82a	-	3000pr. purple	60	60

DESIGNS—HORIZ: 10pr. Olive tree; 70pr. Sea of Galilee; 100pr. Shaar Hogay on road to Jerusalem; 150pr. Lion Rock, Negev; 350pr. Bay of Elat. VERT: 500pr. Tanour Falls, near Metoulla; 750pr. Lake Hula; 3000pr. Tomb of Meir Baal Haness.

33 Anemones and Arms

1953. 5th Anniv of Independence.

83	**33**	110pr. red, green and blue	60	35

35 Maimonides (philosopher)

1953. 7th Int Congress of History of Science.

84	**35**	110pr. brown	2·00	80

36 Holy Ark, Petah-Tikvah

1953. Jewish New Year.

85	-	20pr. blue	15	15
86	**36**	45pr. red	25	25
87	-	200pr. violet	1·00	70

DESIGNS: 20pr. Holy Ark, Jerusalem; 200pr. Holy Ark, Zefat.

37 Hand holding Globe/Football

1953. 4th Maccabiah.

88	**37**	110pr. brown and blue	70	35

38 Exhibition Emblem

1953. "Conquest of the Desert" Exhibition.

89	**38**	200pr. multicoloured	70	35

39 Ancient Jewish Coin

1954. 4th Jewish Coins issue.

90	**39**	80pr. bistre	15	15
91	-	95pr. green	25	15
92	-	100pr. brown	25	15
93	-	125pr. blue	35	25

DESIGNS ON COINS: 95pr. Wheat; 100pr. Gate; 125pr. Lyre.

40 Gesher and Narcissus

1954. 6th Anniv of Independence.

94		60pr. blue, red and grey	10	10
95	**40**	350pr. brown, yellow & grn	70	45

DESIGN: 60pr. Yehiam and helichrysum.

41 Dr. T. Z. Herzl

1954. 50th Death Anniv of Herzl (founder of World Zionist Movement).

96	**41**	160pr. sepia, buff and blue	60	35

43

1954. Jewish New Year.

97	**43**	25pr. sepia	20	20

44 19th century Mail Coach and P.O.

1954. National Stamp Exhibition.

98	**44**	60pr. black, yellow and blue	10	10
99	-	200pr. black, red and green	60	60

DESIGN: 200pr. Mail van and G.P.O., 1954.

45 Baron Edmond de Rothschild

1954. 20th Death Anniv of De Rothschild (financier).

100	**45**	300pr. turquoise	60	35

46 Lamp of Knowledge

1955. 50th Anniv of Teachers' Association.

101	**46**	250pr. blue	45	35

47 Parachutist and Barbed Wire

1955. Jewish Mobilization during 2nd World War.

102	**47**	120pr. black and turquoise	35	25

48 Menora and Olive Branches

1955. 7th Anniv of Independence.

103	**48**	150pr. orange, black & grn	60	35

49 Immigrants and Ship

1955. 20th Anniv of Youth Immigration Scheme.

104	**49**	5pr. black and blue	10	10
105	-	10pr. black and red	10	10
106	-	25pr. black and green	10	10
107	-	30pr. black and orange	10	10
108	-	60pr. black and violet	10	10
109	-	750pr. black and brown	1·40	80

DESIGNS: 10pr. Immigrants and Douglas DC-3 airplane; 25pr. Boy and calf; 30pr. Girl watering flowers; 60pr. Boy making pottery; 750pr. Boy using theodolite.

50 Musicians playing Timbrel and Cymbals

1955. Jewish New Year.

110	**50**	25pr. green and orange	10	10
111	-	60pr. grey and orange	10	10
112	-	120pr. blue and yellow	10	10
113	-	250pr. brown and orange	45	35

DESIGNS—Musicians playing: 60pr. Ram's horn; 120pr. Tuba; 250pr. Harp.

51 Ambulance

1955. 25th Anniv of Magen David Adom (Jewish Red Cross).

114	**51**	160pr. green, black and red	25	25

52 "Reuben"

1955. Twelve Tribes of Israel.

115A	**52**	10pr. green	10	10
116A	-	20pr. mauve	10	10
117A	-	30pr. blue	10	10
118A	-	40pr. brown	10	10
119A	-	50pr. blue	10	10
120A	-	60pr. bistre	10	10
121A	-	80pr. violet	10	10
122A	-	100pr. red	10	10
123A	-	120pr. olive	20	10
124A	-	180pr. mauve	70	35
125A	-	200pr. green	35	15
126A	-	250pr. grey	45	20

EMBLEMS: 20pr. "Simeon" (castle); 30pr. "Levi" (High Priest's breastplate); 40pr. "Judah" (lion); 50pr. "Dan" (scales); 60pr. "Naphtali" (gazelle); 80pr. "Gad" (tents); 100pr. "Asher" (tree); 120pr. "Issachar" (sun and stars); 180pr. "Zebulun" (ship); 200pr. "Joseph" (sheaf of wheat); 250pr. "Benjamin" (wolf).

53 Professor Einstein

1956. Einstein Commemoration.

127	**53**	350pr. brown	45	35

54 Technion

1956. 30th Anniv of Israel Institute of Technology, Haifa.

128	**54**	350pr. green and black	35	35

55 "Eight Years of Independence"

1956. 8th Anniv of Independence.

129	**55**	150pr. multicoloured	25	15

56 Oranges

1956. 4th International Congress of Mediterranean Citrus Fruit Growers.

130	**56**	300pr. multicoloured	35	35

57 Musican playing Lyre

1956. Jewish New Year. Musicians playing instruments.

131	**57**	30pr. brown and blue	10	10
132	-	50pr. violet and orange	10	10
133	-	150pr. turquoise and orange	20	20

INSTRUMENTS—VERT: 50pr. Sistrum. HORIZ: 150pr. Double oboe.

58 Insignia of "Haganah"

1957. Defence Fund.

134	**58**	80pr.+20pr. green	10	10
135	**58**	150pr.+50pr. red	10	10
136	**58**	350pr.+50pr. blue	20	20

59 Airplane sky-writing Figure "9"

1957. 9th Anniv of Independence.

137	**59**	250pr. black, blue & lt blue	35	25

60 Bezalel Museum and Candelabrum

1957. 50th Anniv of Bezalel Museum, Jerusalem.

138	**60**	400pr. multicoloured	25	25

61 Seal of Tamach and Horse

1957. Jewish New Year. Ancient Hebrew Seals.

139	**61**	50pr. black & brn on blue	10	10
140	-	160pr. black & grn on buff	10	10
141	-	300pr. black & red on pink	20	10

DESIGNS: 160pr. Seal of Shema and lion; 300pr. Seal of Netanyahuv Ne'avadyahu and gazelle.

61a Part of Ancient "Bet Alpha" Synagogue Floor Mosaic (image scaled to 71% of original size)

1957. 1st Israeli International Stamp Exhibition. Sheet containing four triangular stamps, which together form the complete centre-piece of floor mosaic.

MS141a	103×105 mm. 100pr. Type **61a**; 200., 300, 400pr. (similar)	70	70

62 Throwing the Hammer

1958. 25th Anniv of Maccabiah Games.

142	**62**	500pr. red and bistre	35	25

63 Ancient Hebrew Ship

1958. Israel Merchant Marine Commemoration.

143	**63**	10pr. red, blue and brown	10	10
144	-	20pr. brown and green	10	10
145	-	30pr. grey and red	20	10
146	-	1000pr. green and blue	45	45

DESIGNS—As T **63**: 20pr. Immigration ship "Nirit"; 30pr. Freighter "Shomron". 57×22 ½ mm: 1000pr. Liner "Zion".

64 Menora and Olive Branch

1958. 10th Anniv of Independence.

147	**64**	400pr. green, black and gold	35	35

65 Dancing Children forming "10"

1958. 1st World Conference of Jewish Youth, Jerusalem.

148	**65**	200pr. green and orange	35	25

66 Convention Centre, Jerusalem, and Exhibition Emblem

1958. 10th Anniv (of Israel) Exn, Jerusalem.

149	**66**	400pr. orange and lilac on cream	35	35

67 Wheat

1958. Jewish New Year.

150	**67**	50pr. brown and ochre	10	10
151	-	60pr. black and yellow	10	10
152	-	160pr. purple and violet	10	10
153	-	300pr. green and apple	35	35

DESIGNS: 60pr. Barley; 160pr. Grapes; 300pr. Figs.

See also Nos. 166/8.

68 Ancient Stone

1958. 10th Anniv of Declaration of Human Rights.

154	**68**	750pr. black, yellow & blue	45	35

69 Post Office Emblem

1959. 10th Anniv of Israel Postal Services.

155	**69**	60pr. black, red and olive	10	10
156	-	120pr. black, red and olive	20	20
157	-	250pr. black, red and olive	30	20
158	-	500pr. black, red and olive	35	35

DESIGNS—HORIZ: 120pr. Mail van. VERT: 250pr. Radio-telephone equipment; 500pr. "Telex" dial and keyboard.

70 Sholem Aleichem

1959. Birth Cent of Sholem Aleichem (writer).

159	**70**	250pr. brown and green	30	25

71 Tel Aviv

1959. 50th Anniv of Tel Aviv.

160	**71**	120pr. multicoloured	35	25

72 Anemone

1959. 11th Anniv of Independence. Mult.

161	60pr. Type **72**	10	10
162	120pr. Cyclamen	10	10
163	300pr. Narcissus	10	10

See also Nos. 188/9, 211/13 and 257/9.

73 C. N. Bialik

1959. 25th Anniv of Chaim Bialik (poet).

164	**73**	250pr. olive and orange	35	25

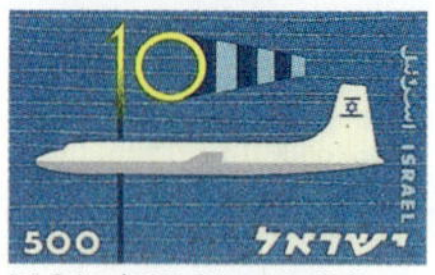

74 Bristol 175 Britannia Airliner and Wind-sock

1959. 10th Anniv of Civil Aviation in Israel.

165	**74**	500pr. multicoloured	45	35

1959. Jewish New Year. As T 67.

166	60pr. red and brown	20	20
167	200pr. green and deep green	35	25
168	350pr. orange and brown	45	35

DESIGNS: 60pr. Pomegranates; 200pr. Olives; 350pr. Dates.

76 E. Ben-Yehuda

1959. Birth Centenary of Ben-Yehuda (pioneer of Hebrew language).

169	**76**	250pr. deep blue and blue	35	35

77 Merhavya Settlement

1959. 50th Anniv of Merhavya and Deganya Settlements. 75th Anniv of Yesud Ha-Maala Settlement.

170	**77**	60pr. green and yellow	10	10
171	-	120pr. brown & light brown	35	25
172	-	180pr. green and blue	60	45

DESIGNS: 120pr. Yesud Ha-Maala; 180pr. Deganya.

78 Ancient Jewish Coin

1960. New currency. Values in black.

173	**78**	1a. bistre on pink	10	10
174	**78**	3a. red on pink	10	10
175	**78**	5a. slate on pink	15	10
176	**78**	6a. green on blue	15	10
176a	**78**	7a. grey on blue	15	10
177	**78**	8a. mauve on blue	15	10
178	**78**	12a. blue on blue	20	10
179	**78**	18a. orange	20	10
180	**78**	25a. blue	30	20
181	**78**	30a. red	35	20
182	**78**	50a. lilac	45	25

79 Tiberias

1960. Air.

183	-	15a. black and lilac	35	25
184	-	20a. black and green	45	35
184a	-	25a. black and orange	70	60
184b	-	30a. black and turquoise	1·20	1·20
184c	-	35a. black and green	1·50	1·20
184d	-	40a. black and lilac	3·00	2·30

184e	-	50a. black and olive	1·20	1·20
185	79	65a. black and blue	3·00	3·00
185a	-	I£1 black and pink	6·50	6·50

DESIGNS—VERT: 15a. Old town, Zefat; 20a. Tower, Ashqelon; 25a. Akko Tower and boats; 30a. View of Haifa from Mt. Carmel. HORIZ: 35a. Ancient synagogue, Capernaum; 40a. Kefar Hittim—Tomb of Jethro; 50a. City walls, Jerusalem. I£1, Old city, Yafo (Jaffa).

80 Operation "Magic Carpet"

1960. World Refugee Year.

186	80	25a. brown	35	35
187	-	50a. green	35	35

DESIGN: 50a. Resettled family.

1960. 12th Anniv of Independence. Flowers as T 72.

188		12a. multicoloured	45	35
189		32a. yellow, green and brown	70	35

DESIGNS: 12a. "Pancratium maritimum"; 32a. "Oenothera drummondi".

81 Atomic Symbol and Reactor Building

1960. Inauguration of Atomic Reactor.

190	81	50a. red, black and blue	1·00	60

83 King Saul

1960. Jewish New Year. Centres multicoloured.

191	83	7a. green	35	25
192	-	25a. brown	70	45
193	-	40a. blue	95	45

DESIGNS: 25a. King David; 40a. King Solomon.

84 Dr. Theodor Herzl

1960. Birth Centenary of Dr. Theodor Herzl (founder of World Zionist Movement).

194	84	25a. sepia and cream	60	60

85 Postal Courier, Prague, 1741

1960. "TAVIV" National Stamp Exhibition, Tel Aviv.

195	85	25a. black and grey	1·90	1·20
MS195a		192×135 mm. No. 195 but in brown and green	46·00	46·00

No. **MS**195a was only sold at the stamp exhibition.

86 Henrietta Szold

1960. Birth Centenary of Henrietta Szold (founder of Youth Immigration Scheme).

196	86	25a. violet and blue	45	35

87 Badges of First Zionist Congress and Jerusalem

1960. 25th Zionist Congress, Jerusalem.

197	87	50a. light and deep blue	1·60	70

88 Ram (Aries)

89 The Twelve Signs

1961. Signs of the Zodiac.

198	88	1a. green	20	10
199	-	2a. red	20	10
200	-	6a. blue	20	10
201	-	7a. brown	20	10
202	-	8a. myrtle	20	10
203	-	10a. orange	20	10
204	-	12a. violet	35	20
205	-	18a. mauve	60	45
206	-	20a. olive	35	25
207	-	25a. purple	60	35
208	-	32a. black	80	65
209	-	50a. turquoise	95	75
210	89	I£1 blue, gold and indigo	2·30	2·00

DESIGNS—As Type **88**: 2a. Bull (Taurus); 6a. Twins (Gemini); 7a. Crab (Cancer); 8a. Lion (Leo); 10a. Virgin (Virgo); 12a. Scales (Libra); 18a. Scorpion (Scorpio); 20a. Archer (Sagittarius); 25a. Goat (Capricorn); 32a. Waterman (Aquarius); 50a. Fishes (Pisces).

1961. 13th Anniv of Independence. Flowers as T 72.

211		7a. yellow, brown and green	25	20
212		12a. green, purple and mauve	45	45
213		32a. red, green and blue	65	50

FLOWERS: 7a. Myrtle; 12a. Squill; 32a. Oleander.

91 Throwing the Javelin

1961. 7th "Hapoel" Sports Association Int Congress, Ramat Gan.

214	91	25a. multicoloured	70	60

92 "A Decade of Israel Bonds"

1961. 10th Anniv of Israel Bond Issue.

215	92	50a. blue	80	70

93 Samson

1961. Jewish New Year. Heroes of Israel. Centres multicoloured.

216	93	7a. red	45	35
217	-	25a. grey	60	45
218	-	40a. lilac	70	60

HEROES: 25a. Yehuda Maceabi; 40a. Bar Kochba.

94 Bet Hamidrash (synagogue), Medzibozh (Russia)

1961. Death Bicentenary of Rabbi Baal Shem Tov (founder of Hassidism movement).

219	94	25a. sepia and yellow	60	45

95 Fir Cone

1961. Afforestation Achievements.

220	95	25a. yellow, black and green	1·30	1·00
221	-	30a. multicoloured	1·40	1·20

DESIGN: 30a. Symbol of afforestation.

96 Musical Instruments

1961. 25th Anniv of Israel Philharmonic Orchestra.

222	96	50a. multicoloured	2·30	2·30

97 Bay of Elat

1962. Air.

223	97	I£3 multicoloured	20·00	15·00

1962. As Nos. 198, 201 and 208 but colours changed and surch.

224	88	3a. on 1a. mauve	20	20
225	-	5a. on 7a. grey	20	20
226	-	30a. on 32a. green	20	20

99 Symbolic Flame

1962. Heroes and Martyrs Day.

227	99	12a. yellow, red and black	45	35
228	-	55a. multicoloured	1·40	1·20

DESIGN: 55a. Nazi "Yellow Star" and candles.

100 Sud Aviation Vatour IIA Bomber

1962. 14th Anniv of Independence.

229	100	12a. blue	85	85
230	-	30a. green	1·50	1·30

DESIGN: 30a. Flight of Vatour IIA bombers.

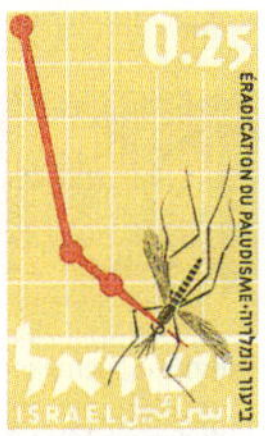

101 Mosquito and Malaria Graph

1962. Malaria Eradication.

231	101	25a. bistre, red and black	60	45

102 Rosh Pinna

1962. 80th Anniv of Rosh Pinna.

232	102	20a. green and yellow	60	45

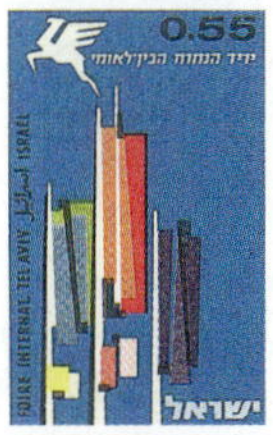

103 Fair Flags

1962. Near East International Fair, Tel Aviv.

233	103	55a. multicoloured	1·00	85

104 "The wolf also shall dwell with the lamb ..."

1962. Jewish New Year. Illustrating quotations from the Book of Isaiah.

234	104	8a. black, red and olive	45	40
235	-	28a. black, purple & olive	1·00	60
236	-	43a. black, orange & olive	1·50	1·20

DESIGNS: 28a. "And the leopard shall lie down with the kid ..."; 43a. "And the suckling child shall play on the hole of the asp ...".

105 Boeing 707 Jetliner

1962. El Al Airline Commemoration.

237	105	55a. indigo, lilac and blue	1·30	1·20
MS237a		195×36 mm. **105** 55a. indigo, lilac and blue (sold at I£1)	4·75	4·75

106 Pennant Coralfish

1962. Red Sea Fish (1st series). Multicoloured.

238		3a. Type **106**	20	20
239		6a. Racoon butterflyfish	20	20
240		8a. Indian Ocean lionfish	35	25
241		12a. Royal angelfish	45	30

See also Nos. 265/8.

107 Symbolic Cogwheels

1962. 25th Anniv of United Jewish Appeal.

242	107	20a. blue, silver and red	70	60

108 J. Korczak (child educator)

1962. Janusz Korczak Commemoration.

243	**108**	30a. sepia and grey	70	60

109 Houbara Bustard

1963. Air. Birds.

244	-	5a. pink, brown and violet	20	15
245	-	20a. turquoise, brn & red	35	25
246	-	28a. black, brown & green	35	25
247	-	30a. multicoloured	35	25
248	-	40a. multicoloured	50	25
249	-	45a. multicoloured	80	60
250	**109**	55a. orange, black & turq	80	60
251	-	70a. bistre, brown & black	95	80
252	-	I£1 orange, black and red	1·00	80
253	-	I£3 multicoloured	3·25	3·25

DESIGNS—HORIZ: 5a. Sinai rosefinch; 20a. White-throated kingfisher; 28a. Mourning wheatear. VERT: 30a. European bee eater; 40a. Graceful prinia; 45a. Palestine sunbird; 70a. Eurasian scops owl; I£1 Purple heron; I£3, White-tailed sea eagle.

110 Bird in the Hand

1963. Freedom from Hunger.

254	**110**	55a. grey and black	1·20	1·20

111 Construction at Daybreak

1963. 25th Anniv of Stockade and Tower Settlements.

255	**111**	12a. brown, black & yell	45	45
256	-	30a. purple, black and blue	70	70

DESIGN: 30a. Settlement at night.

1963. 15th Anniv of Independence. Flowers. As T 72.

257	8a. multicoloured	40	40
258	30a. yellow, rose and pink	1·20	1·20
259	37a. multicoloured	2·00	1·00

FLOWERS: 8a. White lily; 30a. Bristly hollyhock; 37a. Sharon tulip.

112 Compositor

1963. Centenary of Hebrew Press.

260	**112**	12a. purple and buff	1·30	1·00

No. 260 comes in sheets of 16 (4×4) with overall background of replica of front page of first issue of Hebrew newspaper "Halbanon".

113 "And the sun beat upon the head of Jonah ..."

1963. Jewish New Year. Illustrating quotations from the Book of Jonah. Multicoloured.

261	8a. Type **113**	45	45
262	30a. "And there was a mighty tempest in the sea" (horiz)	1·30	1·30
263	55a. "And Jonah was in the belly of the fish" (horiz)	2·40	2·40

114 Hoe clearing Thistles

1963. 80th Anniv of Israeli Agricultural Settlements.

264	**114**	37a. multicoloured	1·20	85

1963. Red Sea Fish (2nd series). As T 106. Multicoloured.

265	2a. Undulate triggerfish	20	20
266	6a. Radial lionfish	30	30
267	8a. Catalufa	40	40
268	12a. Emperor angelfish	60	45

115 "Shalom"

1963. Maiden Voyage of Liner "Shalom".

269	**115**	I£1 blue, turquoise & pur	9·75	7·25

116 "Old Age and Survivors"

1964. 10th Anniv of National Insurance. Multicoloured.

270	12a. Type **116**	1·50	70
271	25a. Nurse and child within hands ("Maternity")	2·40	1·30
272	37a. Family within hand ("Large families")	3·00	1·50
273	50a. Hand with arm and crutch ("Employment injuries")	5·00	2·40

117 Pres. Ben-Zvi

1964. 1st Death Anniv of President Izhak Ben-Zvi.

274	**117**	12a. brown	35	35

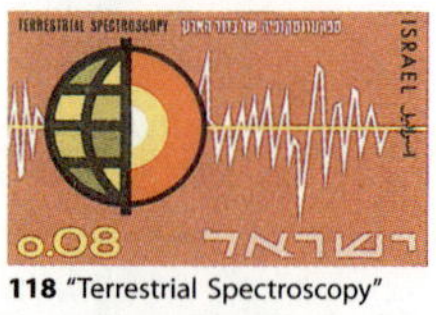

118 "Terrestrial Spectroscopy"

1964. 16th Anniv of Independence. Israel's Contribution to Science. Multicoloured.

275	8a. Type **118**	40	40
276	35a. Macromolecules of living cell	1·20	1·00
277	70a. Electronic computer	2·40	2·10

119 Running

1964. Olympic Games, Tokyo.

278	**119**	8a. black and red	15	15
279	-	12a. black and mauve	25	25
280	-	30a. red, black and blue	30	30
281	-	50a. red, purple and green	45	45

DESIGNS: 12a. Throwing the discus; 30a. Basketball; 50a. Football.

120 3rd Century Glass Vessel

1964. Jewish New Year. Showing glass vessels in Haaretz Museum, Tel Aviv. Multicoloured.

282	8a. Type **120**	15	15
283	35a. 1st-2nd century vessel	45	40
284	70a. 1st century vessel	70	45

121 Congress Emblem

1964. 6th Israel Medical Assn's World Congress.

285	**121**	I£1 multicoloured	1·20	1·00

122 "Exodus" (immigrant ship)

1964. "Year of the Blockade-Runners".

286	**122**	25a. black, blue & turq	45	40

123 Eleanor Roosevelt

1964. 80th Birth Anniv of Eleanor Roosevelt.

287	**123**	70a. purple	60	60

124 Olympics Symbols and Knight

1964. 16th Chess Olympics.

288	**124**	12a. brown	45	30
289	-	70a. green	2·10	1·50

DESIGN: 70a. Olympics symbol and rook.

125 "African–Israeli Friendship"

1964. "TABAI" National Stamp Exn, Haifa.

290	**125**	57a. multicoloured	2·10	1·20
MS290a		125×81 mm. No. 290 (I£1)	2·75	2·75

No. **MS**290a was only sold at the stamp exhibition.

126 Masada

1965. Masada.

291	**126**	25a. green	45	30
292	-	36a. blue	70	45
293	-	I£1 brown	1·00	75

DESIGNS—HORIZ: 36a. "Northern Palace", lower section. VERT: I£l, "Northern Palace" aerial view.

127 Ashdod

1965. Civic Arms (1st series).

294		1a. brown (Lod)	20	20
295		2a. mauve (Qiryat Shmona)	20	20
296		5a. black (Petah Tiqwa)	20	20
297		6a. violet (Nazareth)	20	20
298		8a. orange (Beer Sheva)	20	20
299		10a. green (Bet Shean)	20	20
300		12a. purple (Tiberias)	20	20
301	**127**	15a. green	20	20
302	-	20a. red (Elat)	20	20
303	-	25a. blue (Akko)	40	20
304	-	35a. purple (Dimona)	40	20
305	-	37a. green (Zefat)	1·40	1·20
305a	-	40a. brown (Mizpe Ramon)	60	40
306	-	50a. blue (Rishon Le Zion)	60	40
306a	-	55a. red (Ashqelon)	60	40
307	-	70a. brown (Jerusalem)	1·00	75
307a	-	80a. red (Rosh Pinna)	1·40	1·20
308	-	I£1 green (Tel Aviv-Yafo)	1·20	1·00
309	-	I£3 mauve (Haifa)	1·50	1·40

Nos. 307, 308/9 are 22½×27 mm in size.
See also Nos. 413/24.

128 Fair Emblem

1965. 2nd International Book Fair, Jerusalem.

310	**128**	70a. black, blue and green	45	45

129 Hands reaching for barbed wire

1965. 20th Anniv of Concentration Camps Liberation.

311	**129**	25a. black, yellow and grey	60	45

130 "National Water Supply"

1965. 17th Anniv of Independence.

312	130	37a. brown, dp blue & bl	40	40

131 Potash Works, Sedom

1965. Dead Sea Industrial Development. Mult.

313		12a. Potash Works, Sedom	35	10
314		50a. Type **131**	75	45

The two stamps form one composite design when placed side by side.

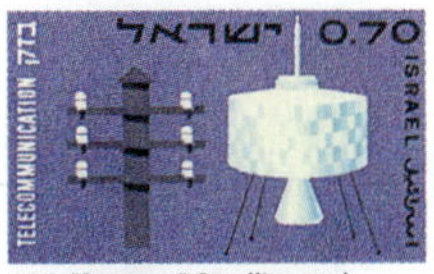

132 "Syncom" Satellite and Telegraph Pole

1965. I.T.U. Centenary.

315	132	70a. violet, black and blue	70	45

133 "Co-operation"

1965. International Co-operation Year.

316	133	36a. multicoloured	45	40

134 "Light"

1965. Jewish New Year. "The Creation". Multicoloured.

317		6a. Type **134**	20	20
318		8a. "Heaven"	20	20
319		12a. "Earth"	20	20
320		25a. "Stars"	40	40
321		35a. "Birds and Beasts"	60	60
322		70a. "Man"	1·00	1·00

135 Foxy Charaxes

1965. Butterflies and Moths. Multicoloured.

323		2a. Type **135**	15	15
324		6a. Southern swallowtail	30	30
325		8a. Oleander hawk moth	30	30
326		12a. Sooty orange-tip	40	40

136 War of Independence Memorial

1966. Memorial Day.

327	136	40a. brown and black	40	40

137 Flags

1966. 18th Anniv of Independence. Mult.

328		12a. Type **137**	10	10
329		30a. Fireworks	15	15
330		80a. Dassault Mirage IIICJ jet fighters and warships	30	30

138 Knesset Building

1966. Inaug of Knesset Building, Jerusalem.

331	138	I£1 blue	85	75

139 Scooter Rider

1966. Road Safety. Multicoloured.

332		2a. Type **139**	10	10
333		5a. Cyclist	10	10
334		10a. Pedestrian on crossing	10	10
335		12a. Child with ball	10	10
336		15a. Motorist in car	20	20

140 Spice Box

1966. Jewish New Year. Religious Ceremonial Objects. Multicoloured.

337		12a. Type **140**	20	20
338		15a. Candlesticks	20	20
339		35a. Kiddush cup	20	20
340		40a. Torah pointer	20	20
341		80a. Hanging lamp	45	45

141 Panther (bronze)

1966. Israel Museum Exhibits. Multicoloured.

342		15a. Type **141**	1·50	1·50
343		30a. Synagogue menora (stone)	2·00	2·00
344		40a. Phoenician sphinx (ivory)	2·40	2·40
345		55a. Earring (gold)	3·00	3·00
346		80a. Miniature capital (gold)	3·50	3·50
347		I£1.15 Drinking horn (gold) (vert)	6·50	6·50

142 Levant Postman and Mail Coach

1966. Stamp Day.

348	142	12a. green and brown	10	10
349	-	15a. mauve, brown & grn	15	15
350	-	40a. blue and mauve	30	30
351	-	I£1 brown and blue	60	45

DESIGNS: 15a. Turkish postman and camels; 40a. Palestine postman and steam locomotive. I£1, Israeli postman and Boeing 707 jetliner.

143 "Fight Cancer and Save Life"

1966. Cancer Research.

352	143	15a. green and red	35	35

144 Akko (Acre)

1967. Ancient Israeli Ports.

353	144	15a. purple	30	15
354	-	40a. green	45	40
355	-	80a. blue	70	60

PORTS: 40a. Caesarea; 80a. Yafo (Jaffa).

145 Book and Crowns

1967. Shulhan Arukh ("Book of Wisdom").

356	145	40a. multicoloured	45	45

146 War of Independence Memorial

1967. Memorial Day.

357	146	55a. silver, blue & turq	60	45

147 Taylorcraft Auster AOP.5 Reconnaissance Plane

1967. Independence Day. Military Aircraft.

358	147	15a. blue and green	20	20
359	-	30a. brown and orange	40	40
360	-	80a. violet and turquoise	60	60

AIRCRAFT: 30a. Dassault Mystere IVA jet fighter; 80a. Dassault Mirage IIICJ jet fighters.

148 Freighter "Dolphin" in Straits of Tiran

1967. Victory in Arab–Israeli War.

361		15a. black, yellow and red	10	10
362	148	40a. green	20	20
363	-	80a. violet	20	20

DESIGNS—VERT: 15a. Sword emblem of "Zahal" (Israeli Defence Forces). HORIZ: 80a. "Wailing Wall", Jerusalem.

149 Law Scroll

1967. Jewish New Year. Scrolls of the Torah (Mosaic Law), and similar designs.

364	149	12a. multicoloured	15	15
365	-	15a. multicoloured	15	15
366	-	35a. multicoloured	30	30
367	-	40a. multicoloured	30	30
368	-	80a. multicoloured	30	30

150 "Welcome to Israel"

1967. International Tourist Year. Each with "Sun" emblem. Multicoloured.

369		30a. Type **150**	20	20
370		40a. "Air hostess"	30	30
371		80a. "Orange" child	30	30

151 Lord Balfour

1967. 50th Anniv of Balfour Declaration.

372	-	15a. green	20	20
373	151	40a. brown	30	30

DESIGN: 15a. Dr. C. Weizmann.

152 Ibex

1967. Israeli Nature Reserves. Multicoloured.

374		12a. Type **152**	10	10
375		18a. Caracal	25	25
376		60a. Dorcas gazelle	40	40

153 Diamond

1968. Air. Israeli Exports.

377	-	10a. multicoloured	15	15
378	-	30a. multicoloured	15	15
379	-	40a. multicoloured	15	15
380	-	50a. multicoloured	40	40
381	-	55a. multicoloured	40	40
382	-	60a. multicoloured	45	40
383	-	80a. multicoloured	45	40
384	-	I£1 multicoloured	70	60
385	-	I£1.50 multicoloured	70	60
386	153	I£3 violet and green	1·20	1·00

DESIGNS: 10a. Draped curtains ("Textiles"); 30a. "Stamps"; 40a. Jar and necklace ("Arts and Crafts"); 50a. Chick and egg ("Chicks"); 55a. Melon, avocado and strawberries ("Fruits"); 60a. Gladioli ("Flowers"); 80a. Telecommunications equipment ("Electronics"). I£1, Atomic equipment ("Isotopes"). I£1.50, Models ("Fashion").

154 Beflagged Football

1968. Pre-Olympic Football Tournament.

387	**154**	80a. multicoloured	40	40

155 "Immigration"

1968. Independence Day. Multicoloured.

388	15a. Type **155**	10	10
389	80a. "Settlement"	30	30

156 Rifles and Helmet

1968. Memorial Day.

390	**156**	55a. multicoloured	35	35

157 Zahal Emblem

1968. Independence Day (Zahal–Israel Defence Forces).

391	**157**	40a. multicoloured	35	35

158 Resistance Fighter (detail from Warsaw Monument)

1968. 25th Anniv of Warsaw Ghetto Rising.

392	**158**	60a. bistre	50	40

159 Moshe Sharett

1968. 27th Zionist Congress, Jerusalem.

393	**159**	I£1 sepia	40	40

160 Candle and Cell Bars

1968. Fallen Freedom Fighters.

394	**160**	80a. black, grey and brown	40	40

161 Jerusalem

1968. Jewish New Year.

395	**161**	12a. multicoloured	20	20
396	-	15a. multicoloured	40	40
397	-	35a. multicoloured	45	45
398	-	40a. multicoloured	60	60
399	-	60a. multicoloured	75	75

DESIGNS: Jerusalem—views of the Old City (12, 15, 35a.) and of the New City (40, 60a.).

162 Scout Badge and Knot

1968. 50th Anniv of Jewish Scout Movement.

400	**162**	30a. multicoloured	25	25

163 "Lions' Gate", Jerusalem (detail)

1968. "Tabira" Stamp Exhibition, Jerusalem.

401	**163**	I£1 brown	35	35
MS402		122×75 mm. No. 401 (sold at I£1.50)	3·50	3·75

164 A. Mapu

1968. Death Cent of Abraham Mapu (writer).

403	**164**	30a. olive	35	25

165 Paralytics playing Basketball

1968. International Games for the Paralysed.

404	**165**	40a. green and light green	35	25

166 Elat

1969. Israeli Ports.

405	**166**	30a. mauve	75	75
406	-	60a. brown (Ashdod)	1·00	1·00
407	-	I£1 green (Haifa)	1·20	1·20

167 "Worker" and I.L.O. Emblem

1969. 50th Anniv of I.L.O.

408	**167**	80a. green and lilac	40	40

168 Israeli Flag at Half-mast

1969. Memorial Day.

409	**168**	55a. gold, blue and violet	40	40

169 Army Tank

1969. Independence Day. Multicoloured.

410	15a. Type **169**	20	20
411	80a. "Elat" (destroyer)	40	40

170 Flaming Torch

1969. 8th Maccabiah.

412	**170**	60a. multicoloured	60	60

171 Arms of Hadera

1969. Civic Arms (2nd series).

413	2a. green (Type **171**)	30	30
414	3a. purple (Herzliyya)	40	40
415	5a. orange (Holon)	45	45
416	15a. red (Bat Yam)	60	60
417	18a. blue (Ramla)	70	70
418	20a. brown (Kefar Sava)	70	70
419	25a. blue (Giv'atayim)	85	85
420	30a. mauve (Rehovot)	40	40
421	40a. violet (Netanya)	1·00	1·00
422	50a. blue (Bene Beraq)	1·50	1·50
423	60a. green (Nahariyya)	1·00	1·00
424	80a. green (Ramat Gan)	2·10	2·10

172 Building the Ark

1969. Jewish New Year, showing scenes from "The Flood". Multicoloured.

425	12a. Type **172**	10	10
426	15a. Animals going aboard	15	15
427	35a. Ark afloat	25	25
428	40a. Dove with olive branch	30	30
429	60a. Ark on Mt. Ararat	30	30

173 "King David" (Chagall)

1969. "King David".

430	**173**	I£3 multicoloured	2·00	2·00

174 Atomic "Plant"

1969. 25th Anniv of Weizmann Institute of Science.

431	**174**	I£1.15 multicoloured	1·50	1·50

175 Dum Palms, Emeq He-Arava

1970. Nature Reserves.

432	**175**	2a. olive	10	10
433	-	3a. blue	10	10
434	-	5a. red	10	10
435	-	6a. green	10	10
436	-	30a. violet	20	20

DESIGNS: 3a. Tahana Waterfall, Nahal Iyon; 5a. Nahal Baraq Canyon, Negev; 6a. Ha-Masreq, Judean Hills; 30a. Soreq Cave, Judean Hills.

176 Immigrant "Aircraft"

1970. 20th Anniv of Operation "Magic Carpet" (Immigration of Yemenite Jews).

437	**176**	30a. multicoloured	40	30

177 Joseph Trumpeldor

1970. 50th Anniv of Defence of Tel Hay.

438	**177**	I£1 violet	1·00	1·00

178 Prime Minister Levi Eshkol

1970. Levi Eshkol Commemoration.

439 **178** 15a. multicoloured 35 35

179 Ze'ev Jabotinsky (commander)

1970. 50th Anniv of Defence of Jerusalem.

440 **179** 80a. green and cream 45 45

180 Camel and Diesel Train

1970. Opening of Dimona–Oron Railway.

441 **180** 80a. multicoloured 1·00 1·00

181 Mania Schochat (author)

1970. 60th Anniv of "Ha-Shomer".

442 **181** 40a. purple and cream 40 40

182 Scene from "The Dybbuk"

1970. 50th Anniv of Habimah National Theatre.

443 **182** I£1 multicoloured 75 75

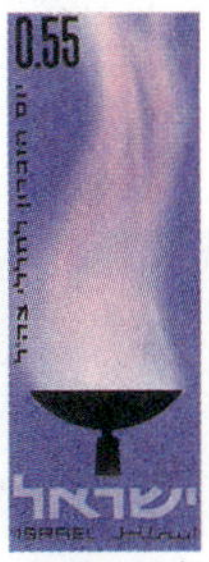

183 Memorial Flame

1970. Memorial Day.

444 **183** 55a. black, red and violet 45 45

184 "Orchis laxifloris"

1970. Independence Day. Israeli Wild Flowers. Multicoloured.

445 12a. Type **184** 30 30
446 15a. "Iris mariae" 45 40
447 80a. "Lupinus pilosus" 75 70

185 C. Netter (founder)

1970. Centenary of Miqwe Yisrael Agricultural College. Multicoloured.

448 40a. Type **185** 70 45
449 80a. College building and gate 1·20 75

186 I.A.I. Arava Transport Airplane

1970. Israeli Aircraft Industry.

450 **186** I£1 silver, violet and blue 60 45

187 Yachts

1970. World "420" Class Sailing Championships. Multicoloured.

451 15a. Type **187** 40 40
452 30a. Yacht with spinnaker 45 40
453 80a. Yachts turning around buoy 70 60

188 Keren Hayesod

1970. 50th Anniv of Keren Hayesod.

454 **188** 40a. multicoloured 40 40

189 Old Synagogue, Cracow

1970. Jewish New Year. Multicoloured.

455 12a. Type **189** 10 10
456 15a. Great Synagogue, Tunis 10 10
457 35a. Portuguese Synagogue, Amsterdam 20 20
458 40a. Great Synagogue, Moscow 20 20
459 60a. Shearith Israel Synagogue, New York 30 30

190 Jewish "Bird" heading for Sun

1970. "Operation Ezra and Nehemiah" (Exodus of Iraqi Jews to Israel).

460 **190** 80a. multicoloured 40 40

191 Mother and Child

1970. 50th Anniv of Women's International Zionist Organization (W.I.Z.O).

461 **191** 80a. yellow, green & silver 70 60

192 Tel Aviv Post Office, 1920

1970. "Tabit" Stamp Exhibition, Tel Aviv, and 50th Anniv of Tel Aviv Post Office.

462 **192** I£1 multicoloured 45 45

MS463 115×70 mm. No. 462 (sold at I£1.50) 3·50 3·50

193 Histadrut Emblem

1970. 50th Anniv of "Histadrut" (General Federation of Labour).

464 **193** 35a. multicoloured 30 30

194 "Landscape with Bridge" (C. Pissaro)

1970. Paintings in Tel Aviv Museum. Mult.

465 85a. "Jewish Wedding" (J. Israels) 30 30
466 I£1 Type **194** 45 45
467 I£2 "Flowers in a Vase" (F. Leger) 75 75

195 "Inn of the Ghosts" (Cameri Theatre)

1971. Israeli Theatre. Multicoloured.

468 50a. Type **195** 40 40
469 50a. "Samson and Delilah" (National Opera Company) 40 40
470 50a. "A Psalm of David" (I.N.B.A.L. Dance Theatre) 40 40

196 Fallow Deer

1971. Nature Reserves. Animals of Biblical Times. Multicoloured.

471 2a. Type **196** 20 20
472 3a. Asiatic wild ass 20 20
473 5a. Arabian oryx 20 20
474 78a. Cheetah 45 20

197 "Haganah" Emblem

1971. Memorial Day.

475 **197** 78a. multicoloured 45 45

198 Jaffa Gate

1971. Independence Day. Gates of Jerusalem (1st series). Multicoloured.

476 15a. Type **198** 45 45
477 18a. New Gate 60 60
478 35a. Damascus Gate 75 75
479 85a. Herod's Gate 1·30 1·30

MS480 93× mm. As Nos. 476/9, but each in 28×28 mm format (sold for I£2) 5·75 5·75

See also 527/**MS**531.

199 Gymnastics

1971. 9th "Hapoel" Games. Multicoloured.

481 50a. Type **199** 30 30
482 50a. Basketball 30 30
483 50a. Running 30 30

200 "... and he wrote upon the tables ..."

1971. Feast of Weeks ("Shavuot"). Illuminated verses from the Bible. Multicoloured.

484 50a. Type **200** 45 45
485 85a. "The first of the firstfruits ..." 70 60
486 I£1. 50 "... and ye shall observe the feast ..." 1·00 85

See also Nos. 488/92.

201 "Sun over the Emeq"

1971. 50th Anniv of Settlements in the "Emeq" (Yezreel Valley).

487 **201** 40a. multicoloured 35 35

1971. Jewish New Year. Feast of the Tabernacles ("Sukkot"). Illuminated Verses from the Bible. As T 200. Multicoloured.

488	15a. "You shall rejoice in your feast"	20	20
489	18a. "You shall dwell in booths ..."	20	20
490	20a. "That I made the people ..."	30	30
491	40a. "... gathered in the produce"	30	30
492	65a. "... I will give you your rains ..."	30	30

202 Kinneret

1971. Landscapes (1st series).

493	-	3a. blue	45	45
494	-	5a. green	30	30
495	-	15a. orange	30	30
496	202	18a. purple	1·70	1·70
497	-	20a. green	1·00	1·00
498	-	22a. blue	2·10	2·10
498a	-	25a. red	45	45
499	-	30a. mauve	40	40
500	-	35a. purple	1·00	1·00
501	-	45a. blue	40	40
502	-	50a. green	60	60
503	-	55a. green	60	60
504	-	65a. brown	1·20	1·20
505	-	70a. red	60	60
505apa	-	80a. blue	5·00	5·00
506	-	88a. blue	2·20	2·20
507	-	95a. red	2·20	2·20
508	-	I£1.10 brown	1·70	1·70
508a	-	I£1.30 blue	1·00	1·00
508b	-	I£1.70 brown	45	45
509pa	-	I£2 brown	3·00	3·00
510a	-	I£10 blue	2·50	2·40
510pa	-	I£3 violet	9·50	9·50

DESIGNS—As T **202**: 3a. Judean desert; 5a. Gan Ha-Shelosha; 15a. Negev desert; 20a. Tel Dan; 22a. Yafo; 25a. Arava; 30a. En Avedat; 35a. Brekhat Ram; 45a. Mt. Hermon; 50a. Rosh Pinna; 55a. Natanya; 65a. Plain of Zebulun; 70a. Engedi; 80a. Beach at Elat; 88a. Akko (Acre); 95a. Hamifratz Hane'Elam; I£1.10, Aqueduct near Acre; I£1.30, Zefat; I£1.70, Nazerat Illit; I£2, Coral Island; I£3, Haifa. 28×27 mm: I£10, Elat.

See also Nos. 682/4a.

203 "Agricultural Research"

1971. 50th Anniv of Volcani Institute of Agricultural Research.

511	203	I£1 multicoloured	45	45

204 Hebrew Text

1971. Educational Development. Multicoloured.

512	15a. Type **204**	20	20
513	18a. Mathematical formulae	20	20
514	20a. Engineering symbols	20	20
515	40a. University degree abbreviations	20	20

205 "The Scribe" (sculpture, B. Schatz)

1972. Jewish Art.

516	205	40a. brown, copper & blk	30	30
517	-	55a. multicoloured	30	30
518	-	70a. multicoloured	45	45
519	-	85a. black and yellow	60	60
520	-	I£1 multicoloured	60	60

DESIGNS—VERT: 55a. "Sarah" (A. Pann); 85a. "Old Jerusalem" (woodcut, J. Steinhardt); I£1; "Resurrection" (A. Kahana). HORIZ: 70a. "Zefat" (M. Shemi).

206 The Flight from Egypt

1972. Passover Feast ("Pesah"). Multicoloured.

521	18a. Type **206**	40	40
522	45a. Baking unleavened bread	45	45
523	95a. "Seder" table	70	70

207 "Let My People Go"

1972. Campaign for Jewish Immigration.

524	207	55a. multicoloured	2·40	2·40

208 Bouquet

1972. Memorial Day.

525	208	55a. multicoloured	40	40

209 Jethro's Tomb

1972. "Nebi Shuaib" (Jethro's Tomb) (Druse shrine).

526	209	55a. multicoloured	40	40

1972. Independence Day. Gates of Jerusalem (2nd series). As T 198. Multicoloured.

527	15a. Lion's Gate	75	60
528	18a. Golden Gate	1·00	70
529	45a. Dung Gate	1·00	75
530	55a. Zion Gate	1·20	85
MS531	93×93 mm. As Nos. 527/530, but each in format 28×28 mm (sold for I£2)	5·75	5·75

210 Ghetto Entrance

1972. 400th Death Anniv of Rabbi Yizhaq Luria ("Ari").

532	210	70a. multicoloured	3·00	3·00

211 Book Year Texts

1972. International Book Year.

533	211	95a. black, red and blue	60	60

212 Dish Aerial

1972. Opening of Satellite Earth Station.

534	212	I£1 multicoloured	40	40

213 Ancona Ark

1972. Jewish New Year. Holy Arks from Italy.

535	213	15a. brown and yellow	20	20
536	-	45a. green, gold & lt green	30	30
537	-	70a. red, blue and yellow	45	45
538	-	95a. purple and gold	70	70

DESIGNS: 45a. Soragna Ark; 70a. Padua Ark; 95a. Reggio Emilia Ark.

214 Menora Emblem

1972. 25th Anniv of State of Israel.

539	214	I£1 blue, purple and silver	30	30

215 Hanukka Lamp (Morocco, 18th–19th century)

1972. Festival of Lights ("Hanukka"). Ceremonial Lamps. Multicoloured.

540	12a. Type **215**	20	20
541	25a. 18th-century Polish lamp	20	20
542	70a. 17th-century German silver lamp	40	40

216 Pendant

1973. Immigration of North African Jews.

543	216	18a. multicoloured	30	30

217 "Horse and Rider"

1973. Children's Drawings. Multicoloured.

544	2a. Type **217**	10	10
545	3a. "Balloon ride" (17×48 mm)	10	10
546	55a. "Party-time"	30	30

218 "Reuben" Window

1973. "Tribes of Israel" Stained-glass Windows by Chagall, Hadassah Synagogue, Jerusalem. Multicoloured.

547	I£1 "Levi"	1·00	1·00
548	I£1 "Simeon"	1·00	1·00
549	I£1 Type **218**	1·00	1·00
550	I£1 "Issachar"	1·00	1·00
551	I£1 "Zebulun"	1·00	1·00
552	I£1 "Judah"	1·00	1·00
553	I£1 "Asher"	1·50	1·50
554	I£1 "Gad"	1·50	1·50
555	I£1 "Dan"	1·50	1·50
556	I£1 "Benjamin"	1·50	1·50
557	I£1 "Joseph"	1·50	1·50
558	I£1 "Naphtali"	1·50	1·50

219 Flame of Remembrance

1973. Memorial Day.

559	219	65a. multicoloured	40	40

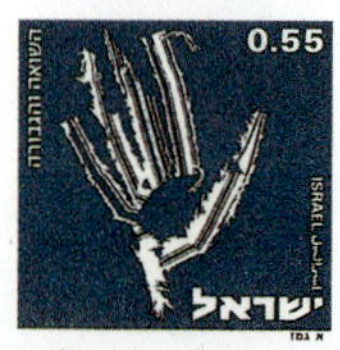

220 Skeletal Hand

1973. Holocaust (Persecution of European Jews 1933–45) Memorial.

560	220	55a. blue	30	30

221 Signatures of Declaration of Independence

1973. Independence Day.

561	**221**	I£1 multicoloured	40	40

MS562 65×147 mm. No. 561 (sold for I£1.50) 1·70 1·70

222 Star of David and Runners

1973. 9th Maccabiah.

563	**222**	I£1.10 multicoloured	30	30

223 Isaiah

1973. Jewish New Year. Prophets of Israel.

564	18a. Type **223**	10	10
565	65a. Jeremiah	15	15
566	I£1.10 Ezekiel	20	20

224 Jews in Boat, and Danish Flag

1973. 30th Anniv of Rescue of Danish Jews.

567	**224**	I£5 black, red and brown	1·20	1·00

225 Institute Emblem and Cogwheel

1973. 50th Anniv of "Technion" Israel Institute of Technology.

568	**225**	I£1.25 multicoloured	30	30

226 Collectors within "Stamp"

1973. "Jerusalem 73" International Stamp Exhibition. Multicoloured.

569	20a. Type **226**	10	10
570	I£1 Collectors within "Stamp" (different)	20	20

MS571 Three sheets, each 121×75 mm. (a) I£1 250m. stamp of 1948; (b) I£2 500m. stamp of 1948; (c) I£3 1000m. stamp of 1948 5·25 5·25

227 Soldier with Prayer Shawl

1974. Memorial Day.

572	**227**	I£1 black and blue	30	30

228 Quill and Bottle of Ink

1974. 50th Anniv of Hebrew Writers' Association.

573	**228**	I£2 black and gold	40	40

229 "Woman in Blue" (M. Kisling)

1974. Jewish Art. Multicoloured.

574	I£1.25 Type **229**	30	30
575	I£2 "Mother and Child" (bronze, C. Orloff)	40	30
576	I£3 "Girl in Blue" (C. Soutine)	40	40

See also Nos. 604/6.

230 Spanner

1974. 50th Anniv of Young Workers' Movement.

577	**230**	25a. multicoloured	20	20

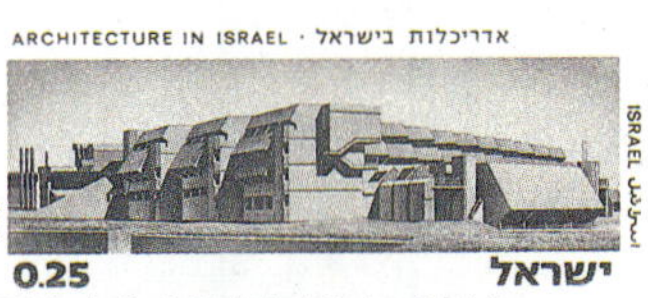

231 Lady Davis Technical Centre, Tel Aviv

1974. "Architecture in Israel" (1st series).

578	**231**	25a. grey	10	10
579	-	60a. blue	20	20
580	-	I£1.45 brown	20	20

DESIGNS: 60a. Elias Sourasky Library, Tel Aviv University. I£1.45, Mivtahim Rest-home, Zikhron Yaaqov.

See also Nos. 596/8.

232 Istanbuli Synagogue

1974. Jewish New Year. Rebuilt Synagogues in Jerusalem's Old City. Multicoloured.

581	25a. Type **232**	10	10
582	70a. Emtzai Synagogue	15	15
583	I£1 Raban Yohanan Ben Zakai Synagogue	20	20

233 Arrows on Globe

1974. Centenary of U.P.U. Multicoloured.

584	25a. Type **233**	15	15
585	I£1.30 Dove "postman" (27×27 mm)	30	30

234 David Ben Gurion (statesman)

1974. Ben Gurion Memorial.

586	**234**	25a. brown	15	15
587	**234**	I£1.30 green	30	30

236 Child with Plant, and Rainbow

1975. Arbour Day. Multicoloured.

588	1a. Type **236**	10	10
589	35a. Bird in tree	10	10
590	I£2 Child with plant and sun	25	25

237 Hebrew University, Jerusalem

1975. 50th Anniv of Hebrew University, Jerusalem.

591	**237**	I£2.50 multicoloured	40	40

238 Welding

1975. "Occupational Safety". Multicoloured.

592	30a. Type **238**	10	10
593	80a. Tractor-driving	15	15
594	I£1.20 Telegraph line maintenance	20	20

239 Harry S. Truman

1975. Truman Commemoration.

595	**239**	I£5 brown	60	60

1975. "Architecture in Israel" (2nd series). As T 231.

596	80a. brown	20	20
597	I£1.30 green	25	25
598	I£1.70 brown	30	30

DESIGNS: 80a. Hebrew University Synagogue, Jerusalem. I£1.30, Museum, Yad Mordechai. I£1.70, City Hotel, Bat Yam.

240 Memorial

1975. Memorial Day.

599	**240**	I£1 red, black and mauve	35	35

241 Text and Poppy

1975. Fallen Soldiers' Memorial.

600	**241**	I£1.45 black, red and grey	35	35

242 Hurdling

1975. 10th Hapoel Games. Multicoloured.

601	25a. Type **242**	20	20
602	I£1.70 Cycling	25	25
603	I£3 Volleyball	30	30

1975. Jewish Art. As T 229. Multicoloured.

604	I£1 "Hanukka" (M. D. Oppenheim)	30	30
605	I£1.40 "The Purim Players" (J. Adler) (horiz)	40	40
606	I£4 "Yom Kippur" (M. Gottlieb)	45	45

243 Old People

1975. Gerontology.

607	**243**	I£1.85 multicoloured	30	30

244 Gideon

1975. Jewish New Year. Judges of Israel. Mult.

608		35a. Type **244**	10	10
609		I£1 Deborah	20	20
610		I£1.40 Jephthah	30	30

245 Zalman Shazar

1975. 1st Death Anniv of Zalman Shazar (President 1963–73).

611	**245**	35a. black and silver	30	30

246 Emblem of Pioneer Women

1975. 50th Anniv of Pioneer Women's Organization.

612	**246**	I£5 multicoloured	35	35

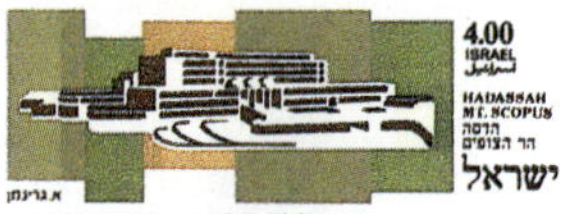

247 New Hospital Buildings

1975. Return of Hadassah Hospital to Mt. Scopus.

613	**247**	I£4 multicoloured	40	40

248 Pratincole

1975. Protected Wild Birds. Multicoloured.

614		I£1.10 Type **248**	30	30
615		I£1.70 Spur-winged plover	40	40
616		I£2 Black-winged stilt	45	45

249 "Air Pollution"

1975. "Environmental Quality". Multicoloured.

617		50a. Type **249**	15	15
618		80a. "Water pollution"	20	20
619		I£1.70 "Noise pollution"	30	30

250 Star of David

1975

620	**250**	75a. blue and red	40	40
621	**250**	I£1.80 blue and grey	45	45
622	**250**	I£1.85 blue and brown	40	40
623	**250**	I£2.45 blue and green	40	40
623a	**250**	I£2.70 blue and mauve	60	60
623b	**250**	I£4.30 blue and red	30	30
624	**250**	I£5.40 blue and bistre	1·20	1·20
625	**250**	I£8 blue and turquoise	85	85

251 Symbolic "Key"

1976. 70th Anniv of Bezalel Academy of Arts and Design, Jerusalem.

626	**251**	I£1.85 multicoloured	40	40

252 "Border Settlements"

1976. Jewish Border Settlements.

627	**252**	I£1.50 multicoloured	40	40

253 "In the days of Ahasuerus ..."

1976. "Purim" Festival. Multicoloured.

628		40a. Type **253**	10	10
629		80a. "He set the royal crown ..."	15	15
630		I£1.60 "Thus shall it be done ..."	20	20
MS631		127×86 mm. Nos. 628/30	95	95

254 Monument to the Fallen

1976. Memorial Day.

632	**254**	I£1.85 multicoloured	40	40

255 "Dancers of Meron" (R. Rubin)

1976. Lag Ba-Omer Festival.

633	**255**	I£1.30 multicoloured	60	45

256 "200" Flag

1976. Bicentenary of American Revolution.

634	**256**	I£4 multicoloured	60	60

257 Diamond ("Industry")

1976. "Netyanya 76" National Stamp Exhibition. Sheet 112×75 mm, containing T 257 and similar vert designs. Multicoloured.

MS635		I£1 Type **257**; I£2 Sailing ("sport"); I£4 Beach umbrella ("tourism")	1·70	1·70

258 High Jump

1976. Olympic Games, Montreal.

636	**258**	I£1.60 black and red	40	40
637	-	I£2.40 black and blue	40	40
638	-	I£4.40 black and mauve	45	45

DESIGNS: I£2.40, Swimming. I£4.40, Gymnastics.

259 Multiple Tent Emblems

1976. Camping.

639	**259**	I£1.60 multicoloured	30	30

260 "Truth"

1976. Jewish New Year. Multicoloured.

640		45a. Type **260**	45	45
641		I£1.50 "Judgement"	45	45
642		I£1.90 "Peace"	45	45

261 Excavated Byzantine House

1976. Archaeology in Jerusalem (1st series). Multicoloured.

643		I£1.30 Type **261**	30	30
644		I£2.40 Arch of 2nd Temple	45	45
645		I£2.80 Staircase to 2nd Temple	60	60

262 Pawn

1976. 22nd Chess Olympiad, Haifa. Mult.

646		I£1.30 Type **262**	60	60
647		I£1.60 Rook	60	60

1976. Archaeology in Jerusalem (2nd series). As T 261. Multicoloured.

648		70a. City Wall, First Temple period	20	20
649		I£5 Omayyad palace	1·00	1·00

263 Clearing Ground

1976. Pioneers.

650	**263**	5a. brown and gold	10	10
651	-	10a. lilac and gold	10	10
652	-	60a. red and gold	15	15
653	-	I£1.40 blue and gold	20	20
654	-	I£1.80 green and gold	20	20

DESIGNS—HORIZ: 10a. Building breakwater. I£1.40, Ploughing. I£1.80, Ditch-clearing. VERT: 60a. Road construction.

264 "Grandfather's Carrot"

1977. Voluntary Service.

655	**264**	I£2.60 multicoloured	45	45

265 "By the Rivers of Babylon"

1977. Drawings of E. M. Lilien.

656	**265**	I£1.70 brown, grey & black	40	35
657	-	I£1.80 black, stone & brn	40	35
658	-	I£2.10 green, lt green & blk	45	45

PAINTINGS—VERT: I£1.80, "Abraham". HORIZ: I£2.10, "May Our Eyes Behold".

266 Jew and Arab shaking Hands

1977. Children's Drawings on Peace. Mult.

659		50a. Type **266**	15	15
660		I£1.40 Arab and Jew holding hands	30	30
661		I£2.70 Peace dove, Jew and Arab	45	45

267 Parachute Troops Memorial

1977. Memorial Day.

662	**267**	I£3.30 multicoloured	65	65

268 Embroidery showing Sabbath Loaves

1977. Sabbath.

663	**268**	I£3 multicoloured	45	45

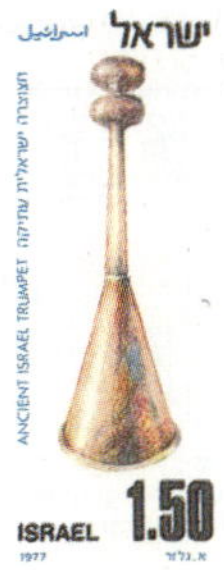

269 Trumpet

1977. Ancient Musical Instruments. Mult.

664	I£1.50 Type **269**	30	30
665	I£2 Lyre	30	30
666	I£5 "Jingle" (cymbals)	35	35

270 Fencing

1977. 10th Maccabiah Games.

667	**270**	I£1 grey, blue and black	30	30
668	-	I£2.50 grey, red and black	35	35
669	-	I£3.50 grey, green & black	45	45

DESIGNS: I£2.50, Putting the shot. I£3.50, Judo.

271 Petah Tiqwa

1977. Centenary of Petah Tiqwa.

670	**271**	I£1.50 multicoloured	35	35

272 American Zionist Emblem

1977. Zionist Organization of America Convention.

671	**272**	I£4 multicoloured	60	60

273 Page of 16th-cent Book "Kohelet Yaakov"

1977. 400th Anniv of Hebrew Printing at Zefat.

672	**273**	I£4 black, gold and red	75	45

274 Sarah

1977. Jewish New Year. Matriarchs of Israel. Multicoloured.

673	70a. Type **274**	10	10
674	I£1.50 Rebekah	15	15
675	I£2 Rachel	30	30
676	I£3 Leah	35	35

See also Nos. 728/30.

275 Police

1977. National Police Force. Multicoloured.

677	I£1 Type **275**	20	20
678	I£1 Civil Guard	20	20
679	I£1 Frontier Guard	20	20

276 Helmet and Model Settlement

1977. "Nahal" Pioneering Fighting Youth.

680	**276**	I£3.50 multicoloured	45	45

277 Accelerator Building, Weizmann Institute

1977. Inauguration of Koffler Accelerator.

681	**277**	I£8 blue and black	80	80

278 Caesarea

1977. Landscapes (2nd series).

682	**278**	10a. blue	95	95
683b	-	I£1 bistre	1·10	1·10
684	-	I£20 green and orange	2·30	2·20
684a	-	I£50 multicoloured	2·75	2·50

DESIGNS—As T **278**: I£1, Arava. 29×27 mm: I£20, Rosh Pinna. 27½×36½ mm: I£50, Soreq Cave.

279 "Mogul" Steam Locomotive, 1892

1977. Railways in the Holy Land. Mult.

685	65a. Type **279**	30	25
686	I£1.50 Steam locomotive	35	35
687	I£2 4-6-0 Class P steam locomotive	35	35
688	I£2.50 Diesel locomotive	45	35
MS689	112×75 mm. Nos. 685/8	2·50	2·50

280 Blood-stained Scallop ("Gloripallium pallium")

1977. Red Sea Shells. Multicoloured.

690	I£2 Type **280**	25	25
691	I£2 Pacific grinning tun ("Malea pomum")	25	25
692	I£2 Isabelle cowrie ("Cypraea isabella")	25	25
693	I£2 Camp Pitar venus ("Lioconcha castrensis")	25	25

281 "The Marriage Parties" (Dutch Ketubah)

1978. Illuminated Jewish Marriage Contracts (Ketubah). Multicoloured.

694	75a. Type **281**	15	15
695	I£3.90 Moroccan Ketubah	35	30
696	I£6 Jerusalem Ketubah	45	40

282 "A Street in Jerusalem" (H. Gliksberg)

1978. Jewish Art.

697	**282**	I£3 multicoloured	30	25
698	-	I£3.80 black, yellow & grey	35	35
699	-	I£4.40 multicoloured	45	45

DESIGNS: I£3.80, "Thistles" (L. Krakauer).I£4.40, "An Alley in Zefat" (M. Levanon).

283 Eliyahu Golomb (leader of Hagana)

1978. Historical Personalities (1st series).

700	**283**	I£2 green and yellow	35	35
701	-	I£2 blue and grey	35	35
702	-	I£2 purple and stone	35	35
703	-	I£2 brown and stone	35	35
704	-	I£2 black and grey	35	35

DESIGNS: No. 701, David Raziel (Irgun commander); 702, Yitzhak Sadeh (nationalist and military commander); 703, Dr. Moshe Sneh (Zionist politician); 704, Abraham Stern (underground fighter).

See also Nos. 721/2, 725/6, 732/3, 738/40, 763/5, 809/11 and 831/3.

284 Children's Flower Paintings (from mural, Petah Tikvah Museum)

1978. Memorial Day.

705	**284**	I£1.50 multicoloured	10	10
706	-	I£1.50 multicoloured	10	10
707	-	I£1.50 multicoloured	10	10
708	-	I£1.50 multicoloured	10	10
709	-	I£1.50 multicoloured	10	10
710	-	I£1.50 multicoloured	10	10
711	-	I£1.50 multicoloured	10	10
712	-	I£1.50 multicoloured	10	10
713	-	I£1.50 multicoloured	10	10
714	-	I£1.50 multicoloured	10	10
715	-	I£1.50 multicoloured	60	45
716	-	I£1.50 multicoloured	60	45
717	-	I£1.50 multicoloured	60	45
718	-	I£1.50 multicoloured	60	45
719	-	I£1.50 multicoloured	60	45

Nos. 705/19 issued together form a composite design, each showing a different portion of the Memorial Wall.

1978. Historical Personalities (2nd series). As T 283.

721	I£2 blue and stone	70	70
722	I£2 brown and grey	70	70

DESIGNS: No. 721, Dr. Chaim Weizmann (first president of Israel); No. 722, Dr. Theodor Herzl (founder of Zionism).

286 Y.M.C.A. Building Jerusalem

1978. Centenary of Jerusalem Y.M.C.A.

723	**286**	I£5.40 multicoloured	60	60

287 Verse of National Anthem

1978. Centenary of Publication of "Hatiqwa" (Jewish National Anthem).

724	**287**	I£8.40 silver, dp blue & bl	75	75

1978. Historical Personalities (3rd series). As T 283.

725	I£2 purple and cream	70	70
726	I£2 green and cream	70	70

DESIGNS: No. 725, Rabbi Ouziel; No. 726, Rabbi Kook.

288 Family Groups

1978. Social Welfare.

727	**288**	I£5.10 multicoloured	60	60

1978. Jewish New Year, Patriarchs of Israel. As T 274. Multicoloured.

728	I£1.10 Abraham	30	30
729	I£5.20 Isaac	35	35
730	I£6.60 Jacob	45	45

289 Star of David, Young Tree and Globe showing U.S.A.

1978. United Jewish Appeal.

731	**289**	I£8.40 multicoloured	75	75

1978. Historical Personalities (4th series). As T 283.

732	I£2 purple and stone	20	20
733	I£2 blue and grey	20	20

DESIGNS: No. 732, David Ben-Gurion (first Prime Minister); No. 733, Ze'ev Jabotinsky (Zionist leader).

290 Shaare Zedek Medical Centre, New and Old Buildings

1978. Opening of New Shaare Zedek Medical Centre, Jerusalem.

734	**290**	I£5.40 multicoloured	20	10

291 Indian Silver and Enamelled Vase

1978. Institute for Islamic Art, Jerusalem. Multicoloured.

735	I£2.40 Type **291**	15	10
736	I£3 13th-century Persian pottery chess rook (elephant with howdah)	30	30
737	I£4 Syrian Mosque lamp	35	35

1978. Historical Personalities (5th series). As T 283.

738	I£2 black and stone	20	20
739	I£2 blue and grey	20	20
740	I£2 black and stone	20	20

DESIGNS: No. 738, Menahem Ussishkin (president of Jewish National Fund); No. 739, Berl Katzenelson (pioneer of Zionist socialism); No. 740, Dr. Max Nordau (journalist).

292 "Iris lortetii"

1978. Wild Irises. Multicoloured.

741	I£1.10 Type **292**	30	30
742	I£5.40 "Iris haynei"	45	45
743	I£8.40 "Iris nazarena"	60	60

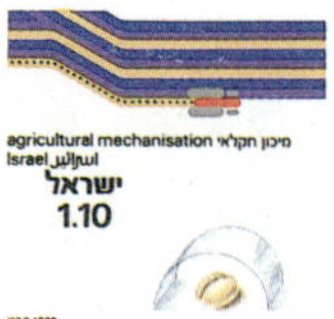

293 Agricultural Mechanization

1979. Technological Achievements. Mult.

744	I£1.10 Type **293**	10	10
745	I£2.40 Sea water desalination	25	15
746	I£4.30 Electronics	25	15
747	I£5 Chemical fertilizers	25	15

294 Jewish Brigade Flag

1979. Yishuv Volunteers serving in Second World War.

748	**294**	I£5.10 yellow, blue & dp bl	60	60

295 "Good from Evil"

1979. "Salute to the Righteous among Nations".

749	**295**	I£5.40 multicoloured	60	60

296 Prayer for Peace in Western Wall

1979. Signing of Egyptian–Israeli Peace Treaty.

750	**296**	I£10 multicoloured	60	60

MS751 119×78 mm. No. 750. Imperf	95	95

297 Naval Memorial, Ashdod

1979. Memorial Day.

752	**297**	I£5.10 multicoloured	45	45

298 Weightlifting

1979. 11th Hapoel Games. Multicoloured.

753	I£1.50 Type **298**	30	25
754	I£6 Tennis	45	45
755	I£11 Gymnastics	75	70

299 "50" and Rotary Emblem

1979. 50th Anniv of Rotary in Israel.

756	**299**	I£7 multicoloured	60	60

300 Rabbi Joshua Ben Hananiah (blacksmith)

1979. Jewish New Year. The "Hazal" (sages and craftsmen). Multicoloured.

757	I£1.80 Type **300**	25	10
758	I£8.50 Rabbi Meir Ba'al Ha-Nes (scribe)	35	25
759	I£13 Rabbi Johanan the Sandal-maker	45	45

301 Tiberias Hot Springs

1979. Health Resorts. Multicoloured.

760	I£8 Type **301**	30	25
761	I£12 Dead Sea Hot Spring	60	60

302 "Searchlight Beam"

1979. 50th Anniv of Jewish Agency.

762	**302**	I£10 blue, grey & turquoise	45	45

1979. Historical Personalities (6th series). As T 283.

763	I£7 purple and grey	30	25
764	I£9 blue	30	25
765	I£13 black and stone	45	45

DESIGNS: I£7, Dr. Arthur Ruppin ("father of Zionist settlement"). I£9, Joseph Trumpeldor (founder of Zion Mule Corps and Jewish Legion). I£13, Aaron Aaronsohn (botanist).

303 Arab and Jew before Jerusalem

1979. Children Paint Jerusalem. Multicoloured.

766	I£1.80 Type **303**	10	10
767	I£4 Jewish, Christian and Muslim citizens of Jerusalem (horiz)	25	15
768	I£5 Worshippers at the Western Wall (horiz)	25	15

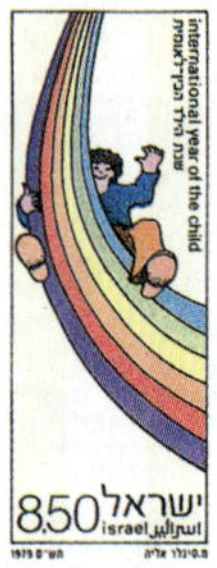

304 Boy sliding down Rainbow

1979. International Year of the Child.

769	**304**	I£8.50 multicoloured	45	45

305 Cog with Star of David

1980. Centenary of Organization for Rehabilitation through Training.

770	**305**	I£13 multicoloured	75	75

306 "Scolymus maculatus"

1980. Thistles. Multicoloured.

771	50a. Type **306**	25	10
772	I£5.50 "Echinops viscosus"	40	30
773	I£8.50 "Cynara syriaca"	45	35

307 "The Road of Courage" Monument

1980. Memorial Day.

774	**307**	I£12 multicoloured	45	45

308 Symbolical Human Figure with Blood-drop

1980. 50th Anniv of Magden David Adom (voluntary medical corps).

775	**308**	I£2.70 red, grey and black	25	15
776	-	I£13 multicoloured	35	35
MS777 124×64 mm. Nos. 775/776 ×2			4·00	4·00

DESIGN: I£13, Mobile intensive care unit and graph.

309 Sabbath Lamp, Netherlands, 18th-century

1980. Jewish New Year. Sabbath Lamps. Multicoloured.

778	I£4.30 Type **309**	15	25
779	I£20 Germany, 18th-century	60	45
780	I£30 Morocco, 19th-century	75	60

310 Yizhak Gruenbrum

1980. 10th Death Anniv of Yizhak Gruenbaum (Zionist and politician).

781	**310**	I£32 brown	1·10	1·10

311 Tree and Flowers

1980. Renewal of Jewish Settlement in Gush Etzion.

782	**311**	I£19 multicoloured	65	65

312 Haifa

1980. "Hafia 80" National Stamp Exhibition. Sheet 100×84 mm containing T 312 and similar vert design showing details of 17th-century engraving of Hafia. Multicoloured.

MS783 2s. Type **312**; 3s. Hafia (different) (sold at 7s.50)	3·50	3·50

313 "Shekel"

1980

784 **313** 5a. green and emerald 35 35
785 **313** 10a. red and mauve 35 35
786 **313** 20a. turquoise and blue 35 35
787 **313** 30a. violet & deep violet 35 35
788 **313** 50a. orange and red 45 35
789a **313** 60a. green and purple 45 35
790 **313** 70a. blue and black 1·10 1·10
791 **313** 90a. violet and brown 1·40 1·40
792 **313** 1s. mauve and green 65 65
793 **313** 1s.10 green and red 60 60
794 **313** 1s.20 blue and red 60 60
795 **313** 2s. green and purple 80 80
796 **313** 2s.80 brown and green 80 80
797a **313** 3s. red and blue 2·30 2·30
798 **313** 3s.20 grey and red 95 80
799b **313** 4s. purple and mauve 1·70 1·70
800 **313** 4s.20 blue and violet 95 80
801a **313** 5s. green and black 95 80
802pa **313** 10s. brown & dp brown 13·50 12·00

314 Golda Meir

1981. Golda Meir (former Prime Minister). Commemoration.
803 **314** 2s.60 purple 60 60

315 Landscape (Anna Ticho)

1981. Paintings of Jerusalem. Multicoloured.
804 50a. Type **315** 25 15
805 1s.50 "View of City" (Joseph Zaritsky) (vert) 45 35
806 2s.50 Landscape (Mordechai Ardon) 60 45

316 Hand putting Coin into Light Bulb

1981. Energy. Multicoloured.
807 2s.60 Type **316** 45 45
808 4s.20 Hand squeezing energy from the sun 65 50

317 A. H. Silver (Zionist)

1981. Historical Personalities (7th series).
809 - 2s. blue 60 60
810 - 2s.80 green 60 60
811 **317** 3s.20 ochre and black 60 60
DESIGNS—As T **283**: 2s. Shmuel Yosef Agnon (writer); 2s.80, Moses Montefiore (Zionist).

318 Biq'at Ha-yarden Memorial

1981. Memorial Day.
812 **318** 1s. multicoloured 35 35

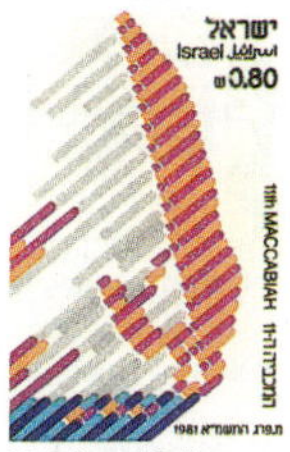

319 Board Sailing

1981. 11th Maccabiah Games. Multicoloured.
813 80a. Type **319** 35 30
814 4s. Basketball 60 50
815 6s. High jump 75 70

320 "Family Tree"

1981. The Jewish Family Heritage.
816 **320** 3s. multicoloured 65 65

321 Moses and the Burning Bush

1981. Jewish New Year. Moses. Multicoloured.
817 70a. Type **321** 15 15
818 1s. Moses and Aaron petitioning Pharoah for Israelites' freedom 30 25
819 3s. Israelites crossing the Red Sea 60 50
820 4s. Moses with the Tablets 65 60

322 "Rosa damascena"

1981. Roses. Multicoloured.
821 90a. Type **322** 25 25
822 3s.50 "Rosa phoenicia" 60 60
823 4s.50 "Rosa hybrida" 75 75

323 Ha-Shiv'a Interchange

1981. Ha-Shiv'a Motorway Interchange.
824 **323** 8s. multicoloured 80 80

324 Balonea Oak

1981. Trees. Multicoloured.
825 3s. Type **324** 45 40
826 3s. Wild strawberry 45 40
827 3s. Judas tree 45 40

325 Elat Stone

1981. Precious Stones. Multicoloured.
828 2s.50 Type **325** 35 25
829 5s.50 Star sapphire 65 60
830 7s. Emerald 80 70

1982. Historical Personalities (8th series). As T 283.
831 7s. multicoloured 75 70
832 8s. brown, stone and black 75 70
833 9s. blue and grey 75 70
DESIGNS: 7s. Perez Bernstein (politician); 8s. Rabbi Arye Levin; 9s. Joseph Gedaliah Klausner (writer, editor and President of Hebrew Language Academy).

327 Child crossing Road

1982. Road Safety.
834 **327** 7s. multicoloured 80 80
MS835 127×79 mm. No. 834 (sold at 10s.) 3·25 3·25

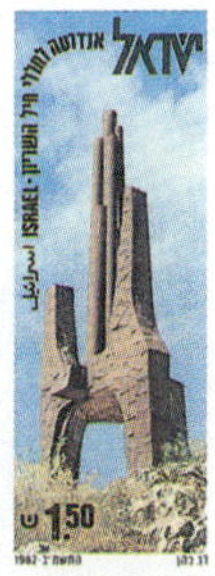

328 Armoured Brigade Memorial, En Zetim

1982. Memorial Day.
836 **328** 1s.50 multicoloured 35 35

329 Landscape (Aryeh Lubin)

1982. Israeli Art. Multicoloured.
837 7s. Type **329** 75 75
838 8s. "Landscape" (Sionah Tagger) (vert) 95 80
839 15s. "Pastorale" (Israel Paldi) 1·60 1·60

330 Emblem and Flowers

1982. 40th Anniv of Gadna (Youth Corps).
840 **330** 5s. multicoloured 1·00 1·00

331 Agricultural Products

1982

841 **331** 40a. blue and green 95 95
842 **331** 80a. blue and mauve 95 95
843 **331** 1s.40 green and red 60 60
844 **331** 6s. mauve and red 1·10 1·10
845 **331** 7s. red and green 45 45
846 **331** 8s. green and red 45 45
847 **331** 9s. green and brown 1·90 1·90
848 **331** 15s. red and green 9·25 9·25
849 **331** 30s. purple and red 4·00 4·00
850 **331** 50s. bistre and red 2·75 2·75
851 **331** 100s. black and green 5·50 5·50
852 **331** 500s. red and black 7·00 7·00

332 Joshua and Israelites setting out for Canaan

1982. Jewish New Year. Joshua. Mult.
860 1s.50 Type **332** 30 25
861 5s.50 Priests carrying Ark of the Covenant over River Jordan 35 35
862 7s.50 The fall of the walls of Jericho 45 40
863 9s.50 The suspension of twilight during the battle against the five kings of Amorite 60 45

333 Rosh Pinna

1982. Centenaries of Rosh Pinna and Rishon Le Zion Settlements. Multicoloured.
864 2s.50 Type **333** 45 45
865 3s.50 Rishon Le Zion 45 45
See also Nos. 868/9, 905/6 and 967.

334 Symbolic Figures on Star of David

1982. 70th Anniv of Hadassah (Women's Zionist Organization of America).
866 **334** 12s. multicoloured 1·10 1·10

335 Branch

1982. No value expressed.
867 **335** (–) brown and orange 60 60

No. 867 was initially sold at 1s.70 but this value was subsequently increased several times.

1982. Centenaries of Zikhron Yaaqov and Mazkeret Batya. As T 333. Multicoloured.

868	6s. Zikhron Yaaqov	75	75
869	9s. Mazkeret Batya	95	95

336 Flower

1982. Council for a Beautiful Israel.

870	**336**	17s. multicoloured	1·40	1·40

1982. Beer Sheva 82" National Stamp Exhibition. Sheet 130×78 mm.

MS871	No. 870 (sold at 25s.)	3·25	3·25

337 Eliahu Bet Tzuri

1982. "Martyrs of the Struggle for Israel's Independence".

872	**337**	3s. grey, black and brown	30	30
873	-	3s. grey, black and olive	30	30
874	-	3s. grey, black and blue	30	30
875	-	3s. grey, black and olive	30	30
876	-	3s. grey, black and brown	30	30
877	-	3s. grey, black and blue	30	30
878	-	3s. grey, black and brown	30	30
879	-	3s. grey, black and olive	30	30
880	-	3s. grey, black and blue	30	30
881	-	3s. grey, black and olive	30	30
882	-	3s. grey, black and brown	30	30
883	-	3s. grey, black and olive	30	30
884	-	3s. grey, black and blue	30	30
885	-	3s. grey, black and brown	30	30
886	-	3s. grey, black and blue	30	30
887	-	3s. grey, black and olive	30	30
888	-	3s. grey, black and blue	30	30
889	-	3s. grey, black and brown	30	30
890	-	3s. grey, black and olive	30	30
891	-	3s. grey, black and brown	30	30

DESIGNS: No. 873, Hannah Szenes; 874, Shlomo Ben Yosef; 875, Yosef Lishanski; 876, Naaman Belkind; 877, Eliezer Kashani; 878, Yechiel Dresner; 879, Dov Gruner; 880, Mordechai Alkachi; 881, Eliahu Hakim; 882, Meir Nakar; 883, Avshalom Haviv; 884, Ya'akov Weiss; 885, Meir Feinstein; 886, Moshe Barazani; 887, Eli Cohen; 888, Samuel Azaar; 889, Dr. Moshe Marzouk; 890, Shalom Salih; 891, Yosef Basri.

338 Honey Bee, Honeycomb and Flowers

1983. Bee-keeping.

892	**338**	30s. multicoloured	2·30	2·30

339 Sweets in Ashtray

1983. Anti-smoking Campaign.

893	**339**	7s. multicoloured	60	60

340 Golan Settlement

1983. Settlements. Multicoloured.

894	8s. Type **340**	75	70
895	15s. Galil settlement	95	95
896	20s. Yehuda and Shomeron settlements	1·10	1·00

341 84th Division "of Steel" Memorial, Besor (Israel Godovitz)

1983. Memorial Day.

897	**341**	3s. multicoloured	45	45

342 Star of David

1983. 35th Anniv of Independence.

898	**342**	25s. multicoloured	2·10	2·10
MS899		120×84 mm. No. 898. Imperf	3·75	3·75

343 Running

1983. 12th Hapoel Games.

900	**343**	6s. multicoloured	60	60

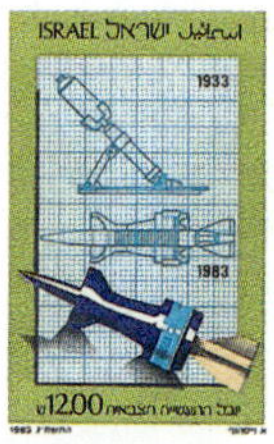

344 Missile and Blueprint

1983. 50th Anniv of Israel Military Industries.

901	**344**	12s. multicoloured	80	80

345 "The Last Way" (Iosef Kuzhovsky)

1983. Babi Yar Massacre.

902	**345**	35s. multicoloured	1·90	1·90

346 Yosef Giazman

1983. 40th Anniv of Warsaw and Vilna Ghettos Uprising. Sheet 120×86 mm containing T 346 and similar square designs. Multicoloured.

MS903	10s. Type **346**; 10s. Commemorative text; 10s. Mordechai Anielewicz (sold at 45s.)	5·00	5·00

347 Raoul Wallenberg

1983. Raoul Wallenberg (Swedish diplomat) Commemoration.

904	**347**	14s. stone and brown	1·40	1·40

1983. Centenary of Yesud Ha-Maala and Nes Ziyyona. As T 333. Multicoloured.

905	11s. Yesud Ha-Maala	75	75
906	13s. Nes Ziyyona	75	75

348 Ohel Moed Synagogue, Tel Aviv

1983. Jewish New Year. Synagogues. Mult.

907	3s. Type **348**	30	30
908	12s. Yeshurun Synagogue, Jerusalem	45	45
909	16s. Ohel Aharon Synagogue, Haifa	80	80
910	20s. Khalaschi Synagogue, Beer Sheva	95	95

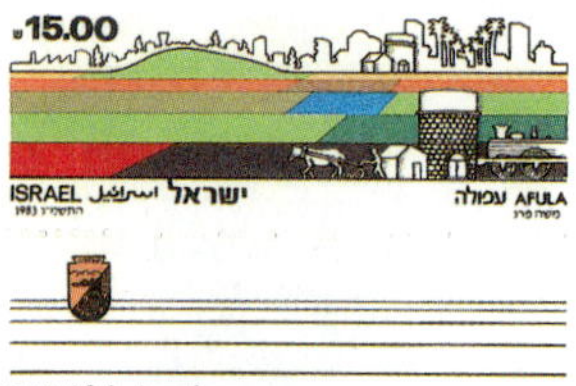

349 Afula Landscape

1983. Afula Urban Centre, Jezreel Valley.

911	**349**	15s. multicoloured	1·00	1·00

350 Promenade, Tel Aviv

1983. "Tel Aviv 83" Stamp Exhibition. Sheet 142×88 mm containing T 350 and similar vert design. Multicoloured.

MS912	30s. Type **350**; 50s. Promenade (sold at 120s.)	10·50	10·50

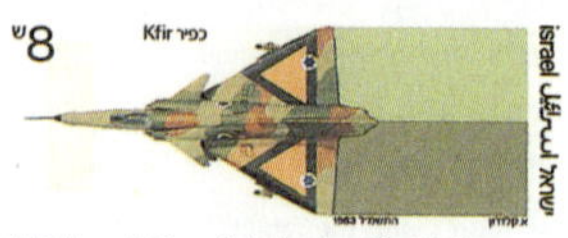

351 Israeli Aircraft Industry Kfir-C2 Jet Fighter

1983. Military Equipment. Multicoloured.

913	8s. Type **351**	30	25
914	18s. "Reshef" (missile vessel)	45	45
915	30s. "Merkava" battle tank	75	70

352 Rabbi Meir Bar-Ilan

1983. 34th Death Anniv of Rabbi Meir Bar-Ilan (Zionist leader).

916	**352**	9s. blue and green	45	45

353 "Aliya" ("immigration")

1983. 50th Anniv of Jewish Immigration from Germany.

917	**353**	14s. red, gold and blue	45	45

354 Michael Halperin

1984. 65th Death Anniv of Michael Halperin (nationalist).

918	**354**	7s. brown, stone & dp brn	35	35

355 Yigal Allon

1984. 4th Death Anniv of Yigal Allon (politician).

919	**355**	15s. blue, green and black	35	35

356 Uri Zvi Grinberg

1984. 3rd Death Anniv of Uri Zvi Grinberg (poet).

920	**356**	16s. brown and red	35	35

357 Hevel Ha-Besor

1984. Settlements. Multicoloured.

921	12s. Type **357**	35	35
922	17s. Arava	45	45
923	40s. Hevel Azza	95	95

358 Alexander Zaid Monument (David Polus)

1984. Sculptures.

924	**358**	15s. stone, black and blue	45	45
925	-	15s. stone, black & brown	45	45
926	-	15s. green, black and grey	45	45

DESIGNS: No. 925, Tel Hay Memorial (Abraham Melnikov); 926, Dov Gruner monument (Chana Orloff).

359 Oliphant House, Dalyat Al Karmil (memorial to Druse Community)

1984. Memorial Day.

927	**359**	10s. multicoloured	30	30

360 Worker with Flag

1984. 50th Anniv of National Labour Federation.

928	**360**	35s. multicoloured	60	60

361 Leon Pinsker

1984. 93rd Death Anniv of Leon Pinsker (Zionist leader).

929	**361**	20s. lilac and purple	35	35

362 Stars and Hearts

1984. 70th Anniv of American Jewish Joint Distribution Committee.

930	**362**	30s. red, blue and black	45	45

363 Dove on Olympic Podium

1984. Olympic Games, Los Angeles.

931	**363**	80s. multicoloured	1·00	1·00
MS932		119×80 mm. **363** 240s. multicoloured	9·25	9·25

364 General Charles Orde Wingate

1984. 40th Death Anniv of Gen. Charles Orde Wingate (military strategist).

933	**364**	20s. grey, black and green	35	35

365 Hannah

1984. Jewish New Year. Women in the Bible. Multicoloured.

934	15s. Type **365**	35	30
935	70s. Ruth	75	70
936	100s. Huldah the prophetess	95	85

366 Nahalal (first Moshav)

1984. Moshavim (Co-operative Workers' Settlements).

937	**366**	80s. multicoloured	80	80

367 David Wolffsohn

1984. 70th Death Anniv of David Wolffsohn (president of Zionist Organization).

938	**367**	150s. brown, blue & black	1·70	1·70

368 "Apartment to Let" (Leah Goldberg, illus Shemuel Katz)

1984. Children's Books. Multicoloured.

939	20s. Type **368**	30	30
940	30s. "Why is the Zebra wearing pyjamas?" (O. Hille, illus Alona Frankel) (28×28 mm)	35	35
941	50s. "Across the Sea" (Haim Nahman Bialik, illus Nahum Gutman)	45	45

369 Bread and Wheat

1984. World Food Day.

942	**369**	200s. multicoloured	1·40	1·40

370 Isaac Herzog

1984. 25th Death Anniv of Isaac Herzog (Israel's first Chief Rabbi).

943	**370**	400s. multicoloured	2·50	2·50

371 Lappet-faced Vulture

1985. Biblical Birds of Prey (1st series). Multicoloured.

944	100s. Type **371**	95	95
945	200s. Bonelli's eagle	1·40	1·40
946	300s. Sooty falcon	2·30	2·30
947	500s. Griffon vulture	3·75	3·75
MS948	120×82 mm. As Nos. 944/7 but smaller (33×23 mm)	14·00	14·00

See also Nos. 1015/**MS**1019.

372 Golani Brigade Monument and Museum

1985. Memorial Day.

949	**372**	50s. multicoloured	45	45

373 Bleriot XI

1985. Aviation in the Holy Land. Mult.

950	50s. Type **373** (landing by Jules Vedrines, 1913)	35	35
951	150s. Short S.17 Kent flying boat "Scipio" (Imperial Airways regular flights via Palestine, 1931–42)	75	75
952	250s. De Havilland D.H.82A Tiger Moth (foundation of Palestine Flying Club, 1934)	1·20	1·20
953	300s. Short S.16 Scion II (international flights by Palestine Airways, 1937–40)	1·40	1·40

374 Zivia and Yitzhak Zuckerman

1985. Zivia and Yitzhak Zuckerman (Polish Jewish freedom fighters) Commemoration.

954	**374**	200s. brown, grey & black	1·10	1·10

375 Nurses tending Patients

1985. 18th International Congress of Nurses.

955	**375**	400s. multicoloured	1·70	1·70

376 Dome of the Rock

1985. "Israphil 85" International Stamp Exhibition, Tel Aviv. Three sheets containing various designs.

MS956	Three sheets. (a) 120×80 mm. 200s. Type **376**; 200s. Western wall; 200s. Church of the Holy Sepulchre; (b) 120×80 mm. 350s. 16th-century relief; 350s. 18th-century relief; 350s. 12–13th century relief (each 25×39 mm); (c) 79×120 mm. 800s. Adam and Eve with serpent (30×30 mm) (sold at 1200s)	24·00	24·00

377 Ark of the Covenant

1985. Jewish New Year. Tabernacle Furnishings. Multicoloured.

957	100s. Type **377**	45	40
958	150s. The table	45	40
959	200s. Candlestick	60	50
960	300s. Incense altar	80	80

378 "Medals"

1985. International Youth Year.

961	**378**	150s. multicoloured	45	45

379 Basketball

1985. 12th Maccabiah Games. Multicoloured.

962	400s. Type **379**	95	95
963	500s. Tennis	1·40	1·20
964	600s. Windsurfing	1·90	1·70

380 Recanati

1985. 40th Death Anniv of Leon Yehuda Racanati (founder of Palestine Discount Bank).

965	**380**	200s. brown, grey and blue	60	60

381 Dizengoff (after J. Steinhardt and M. Sima)

1985. 49th Death Anniv of Meir Dizengoff (founder and Mayor of Tel Aviv).

966	**381**	500s. black, brown & silver	1·70	1·70

1985. Centenary of Gedera. As T 333. Mult.

967	600s. Gedera	1·40	1·40

382 Kibbutz Members

1985. The Kibbutz.

968	**382**	900s. multicoloured	2·20	2·20

383 Dr. Theodor Herzl

1986

969	**383**	1a. blue and red	65	65
970	**383**	2a. blue and green	75	75
971	**383**	3a. blue and bistre	95	95
972	**383**	5a. blue and turquoise	1·10	1·10
973	**383**	10a. blue and orange	1·70	1·70
974a	**383**	20a. blue and purple	7·00	7·00
975a	**383**	30a. blue and yellow	7·00	7·00
976a	**383**	50a. blue and violet	3·75	3·75

384 Corinthian Capital, 1st Century B.C.

1986. Jerusalem Archaeology.

977	-	40a. green, orange & blk	3·25	3·25
978	-	60a. brown, violet & blk	3·25	2·75
979	-	70a. green, brown & blk	3·25	2·75
980	-	80a. purple, bistre & blk	3·75	3·25
981	-	90a. yellow, lilac & black	3·00	2·30
982	**384**	1s. brown, green & black	3·75	3·75
983a	-	2s. blue, green and black	11·50	11·50
984	-	3s. mauve, blue and black	5·50	5·50
987	-	10s. green, blue and black	10·00	10·00

DESIGNS—As T **384**: 40a. Relief, 1st century B.C. (Second Temple); 60a. Byzantine capital, 6th century A.D.; 3s. Archaic Ionic capital, 1st century B.C. (Second Temple). 32×23 mm: 70a. Relief from palace of Umayyid Caliphs, 8th century A.D.; 80a. Crusader capital from Church of Ascension, Mount of Olives, 12–13th centuries; 90a. Relief from Suleiman's Wall, 16th century A.D.; 2s. Insignia of Sayif addin Attaz from Mameluke Academy, 14th century A.D.; 10s. Frieze from burial cave entrance, end of Second Temple period.

385 "Balanophyllia coccinea"

1986. Red Sea Corals. Multicoloured.

991	30a. Type **385**	1·10	1·10
992	40a. "Goniopora"	1·20	1·20
993	50a. "Dendronephthya"	1·40	1·40

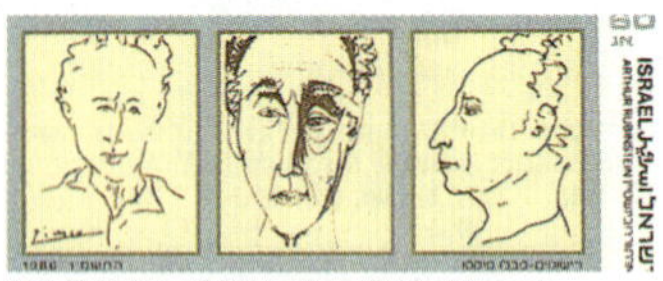

386 Sketches of Rubinstein (Pablo Picasso)

1986. Birth Cent (1987) of Arthur Rubinstein and 5th International Rubinstein Piano Competition.

994	**386**	60a. multicoloured	1·70	1·70

387 Microphone and Map

1986. 50th Anniv of Broadcasting from Jerusalem.

995	**387**	70a. multicoloured	1·40	1·40

388 Negev Bridge Monument, Beer Sheva

1986. Memorial Day.

996	**388**	20a. multicoloured	75	75

389 El-Jazzar Mosque, Akko

1986. Id Al-Fitr (end of Ramadan).

997	**389**	30a. emerald, green & ol	75	75

390 Hebrew Union College, Cincinnati

1986. "Ameripex '86" International Stamp Exhibition, Chicago. Jewish Institutes of Higher Learning. Multicoloured.

998	50a. Type **390**	1·30	1·30
999	50a. Yeshiva University, New York	1·30	1·30
1000	50a. Jewish Theology Seminary, New York	1·30	1·30

MS1001 100×70 mm. 75a. ×3 As Nos. 998/1000 but smaller (35×22 mm) (sold at 3s.) 9·25 9·25

391 Nabi Sabalan's Tomb, Hurfeish

1986. Feast of Nabi Sabalan (Druse feast).

1002	**391**	40a. multicoloured	95	95

392 Graffiti on Wall

1986. Anti-racism Campaign.

1003	**392**	60a. multicoloured	1·50	1·50

393 Sprinzak

1986. Birth Centenary (1985) of Joseph Sprinzak (first Speaker of Knesset).

1004	**393**	80a. blue, green and black	1·50	1·50

394 Airport through Cabin Windows

1986. 50th Anniv of Ben Gurion Airport.

1005	**394**	90a. multicoloured	1·90	1·90

395 Gates of Heaven, with Jerusalem above, opening to Power of Prayer

1986. Jewish New Year. Pages from Worms Mahzor (prayer book). Multicoloured.

1006	20a. Type **395** (prayers for Yom Kippur)	1·10	1·10
1007	40a. Man weighing shekel for Temple (prayer for Sheqalim, first special Sabbath)	1·20	1·20
1008	90a. Roses (illustration of liturgical poem)	1·60	1·60

396 David Ben Gurion

1986. Birth Centenary of David Ben Gurion (Prime Minister, 1948–53 and 1955–63).

1009	**396**	1s. bistre, brown & black	2·00	2·00

397 Map of Holy Land by Gerard de Jode, 1578

1986. "Netanya 86" National Stamp Exhibition. Sheet 126×80 mm.

MS1010 **397** 2s. multicoloured (sold at 3s.) 10·50 10·50

398 Satellite and Isobars over Map

1986. 50th Anniv of Meteorological Service.

1011	**398**	50a. multicoloured	1·40	1·40

399 Basilica of the Annunciation, Nazareth

1986. Christmas.

1012	**399**	70a. multicoloured	2·10	2·10

400 Bronislaw Huberman (violinist and founder)

1986. 50th Anniv of Israel Philharmonic Orchestra.

1013	**400**	1s.50 brown, blk & yell	4·00	4·00
1014	-	1s.50 grey, black & yell	4·00	4·00

DESIGN: No. 1014, Arturo Toscanini (conductor of Orchestra's first concert, 1936).

401 Hume's Owl

1987. Biblical Birds of Prey (2nd series). Owls. Multicoloured.

1015	30a. Desert eagle owl	95	95
1016	40a. Pallid striated scops owl	1·40	1·40
1017	50a. Barn owl	1·90	1·70
1018	80a. Type **401**	3·25	3·00

MS1019 102×82 mm. As Nos. 1015/18 but smaller (31×23 mm) (sold at 3s.) 10·50 10·50

402 Six-Day War Memorial, Ammunition Hill, Jerusalem

1987. Memorial Day.

1020	**402**	30a. multicoloured	1·10	1·10

403 Emblem

1987. 13th Hapoel Games.

1021	**403**	90a. multicoloured	2·20	2·20

404 1952 120pr. "TABA" Stamp

1987. "Hafia 87" National Stamp Exhibition. Sheet 111×77 mm.

MS1022 **404** 2s.70 multicoloured (sold at 4s.) 11·50 11·50

405 Street Cleaner

1987. "A Clean Environment".

1023	**405**	40a. multicoloured	1·10	1·10

406 Saluki

1987. World Dog Show. Dogs of Israeli Origin. Multicoloured.

1024	40a. Type **406**	1·70	1·60
1025	50a. Sloughi	1·70	1·60
1026	2s. Canaan dog	4·00	4·00

407 Radio Operators and Globe

1987. Israel Radio Amateurs.

1027	**407**	2s.50 multicoloured	6·00	6·00

408 Altneuschul Synagogue, Prague

1987. Jewish New Year. Synagogue Models in Museum of the Diaspora, Tel Aviv (1st issue). Multicoloured.

1028		30a. Type **408**	75	75
1029		50a. Main Synagogue, Aleppo, Syria	1·30	1·30
1030		60a. Israelite Temple, Florence	1·70	1·70

See also Nos. 1054/6.

409 Rabbi Amiel

1987. 104th Birth Anniv of Rabbi Moshe Avigdor Amiel (Chief Rabbi of Tel Aviv).

1031	**409**	1s.40 multicoloured	3·50	3·50

410 Family

1987. 75th Anniv of Kupat Holim Health Insurance Institution.

1032	**410**	1s.50 multicoloured	3·50	3·50

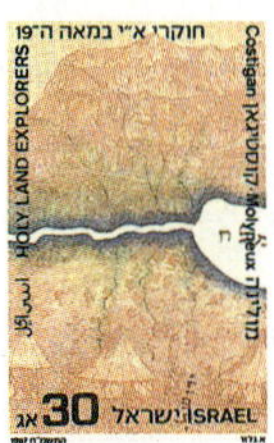

411 Camp (Christopher Costigan, 1835, and Thomas Howard Molyneux, 1847)

1987. Holy Land Explorers. Multicoloured.

1033		30a. Type **411**	1·00	95
1034		50a. Map of River Jordan (William Francis Lynch, 1848)	1·20	1·00
1035		60a. Men in canoe (John MacGregor, 1868–9)	1·60	1·60
MS1036		106×75 mm. 40a. Type **411**; 50a. As No. 1034; 80a. As No. 1035; but each smaller (22×35 mm) (sold at 2s.50)	7·00	7·00

412 Rosen

1987. Birth Centenary of Pinhas Rosen (lawyer and politician).

1037	**412**	80a. multicoloured	1·70	1·70

413 Computers in Industry

1988. Centenary of Israeli Industry. Mult.

1038		10a. Type **413**	65	45
1039		80a. Genetic engineering	2·30	1·70
1040		1s.40 Medical engineering	2·75	1·90

414 Corked Tap

1988. "Save Water".

1041	**414**	40a. multicoloured	1·10	1·10

415 Kangaroos holding Birthday Cake

1988. Bicentenary of Australian Settlement.

1042	**415**	1s. multicoloured	2·75	2·75

416 Sunflower

1988. No value expressed.

1043	**416**	(30a.) green and yellow	1·10	1·10

417 Hebrew Year 5748

1988. Memorial Day.

1044	**417**	40a. multicoloured	1·10	1·10
MS1045		86×70 mm. As No. 1044 but smaller (33×25 mm) (sold at 60a.)	4·75	4·75

418 Anne Frank and House, Amsterdam

1988. 43rd Death Anniv of Anne Frank (concentration camp victim).

1046	**418**	60a. multicoloured	1·90	1·90

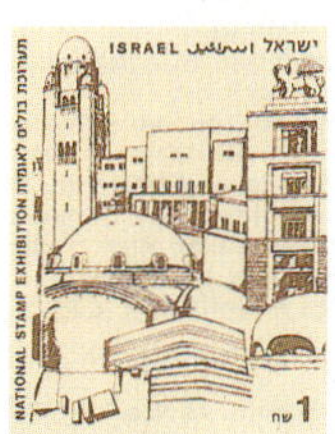

419 Jerusalem

1988. "Independence 40" National Stamp Exhibition, Jerusalem.

1047	**419**	1s. light brown and brown	2·30	2·30
MS1048		68×85 mm. 2s. cinnamon and brown	11·50	11·50

DESIGN. 34×25 mm. 2s. Jerusalem (detail of No. 1047).

420 1963 37a. Kibbutzim Stamp (Settling)

1988. "40th Anniv of Independence" Exhibition, Tel Aviv. Sheet 118×88 mm containing T 420 and similar horiz designs showing stamps. Multicoloured.

MS1049		20a.×9 Type **420**; 1965 50a. Potash Works (Industry); 1956 300pr. Oranges (Agriculture); 1955 25pr. Youth Immigration (Immigrant absorption); 1981 8s. Ha-Shiv'a motorway interchange (Construction); 1964 Cancer Research (Health); 1972 40a. Educational Development (Education) (sold at 2s.40)	11·50	11·50

421 Ein Zin Nature Reserve

1988. Nature Reserves in the Negev. Mult.

1050		40a. Type **421**	1·00	80
1051		60a. She' zaf	1·40	1·30
1052		70a. Ramon	1·60	1·40

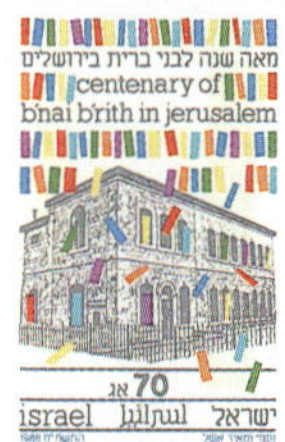

422 Jerusalem Lodge

1988. Centenary of B'nai B'rith in Jerusalem.

1053	**422**	70a. multicoloured	1·60	1·60

1988. Jewish New Year. Synagogue Models in Museum of the Diaspora, Tel Aviv (2nd issue). As T 408. Multicoloured.

1054		35a. 12th-century Kai-Feng Fu Synagogue, China	1·00	1·00
1055		60a. 17th-century Zabludow Synagogue, Poland	1·10	1·10
1056		70a. 18th-century Touro Synagogue, Newport, Rhode Island	1·20	1·20

423 Havivah Reik

1988. Jewish World War II Underground Fighters. Multicoloured.

1057	**423**	40a. multicoloured	95	95
1058	-	1s.65 dp blue, blue & blk	3·75	3·75

DESIGN: 1s.65, Enzo Hayyim Sereni.

424 Dayan

1988. 7th Death Anniv of Moshe Dayan (soldier and politician).

1059	**424**	40a. multicoloured	4·00	4·00

425 Burning Illustration of German Synagogue

1988. 50th Anniv of "Kristallnacht" (Nazi pogrom).

1060	**425**	80a. multicoloured	2·30	2·30

426 Menorah and Soldiers

1988. 74th Anniv of Formation of Jewish Legion.

1061	**426**	2s. dp brown, brn & bis	4·75	4·75

427 Avocado (fruit-growing)

1988. Agricultural Achievements in Israel. Mult.

1062		50a. Type **427**	1·10	1·10
1063		60a. Easter lily (plant breeding)	1·40	1·40
1064		90a. Plants and drip-pipe (irrigation systems)	1·70	1·70

428 Red Sea

1989. Tourism. Multicoloured.

1065		40a. Type **428**	75	75
1066		60a. Dead Sea	95	95
1067		70a. Mediterranean	1·10	1·10
1068		1s.70 Sea of Galilee	2·30	2·30

429 Rabbi Maimon

1989. 114th Birth Anniv of Rabbi Judah Leib Maimon (writer).

1069	**429**	1s.70 multicoloured	3·50	3·50

430 "Rashi" in Rashi Script

1989. 950th Birth Anniv of Rashi (Rabbi Solomon Ben Isaac of Troyes) (scholar).

1070	**430**	4s. cream and brown	7·00	7·00

431 Airforce Memorial, Har Tayassim

1989. Memorial Day.

1071	**431**	50a. multicoloured	95	95

432 Child

1989. 20th Anniv of Israel United Nations Children's Fund National Committee.

1072 **432** 90a. multicoloured 1·70 1·70

433 Games Emblem

1989. 13th Maccabiah Games.

1073 **433** 80a. multicoloured 1·40 1·40

434 Smoira

1989. Birth Centenary (1988) of Moshe Smoira (first President of Israel's Supreme Court).

1074 **434** 90a. blue 2·20 2·20

435 Tree of Liberty

1989. Bicentenary of French Revolution. Sheet 120×80 mm.

MS1075 **435**3s.50 multicoloured 17·00 17·00

436 Garganey

1989. Ducks. Multicoloured.

1076 80a. Type **436** 1·90 1·70

1077 80a. Mallard 1·90 1·70

1078 80a. Green-winged teal ("Teal") 1·90 1·70

1079 80a. Common shelduck ("Shelduck") 1·90 1·70

437 Printed Circuit and Pencil

1989. 13th International Council of Graphic Design Associations Congress.

1080 **437** 1s. multicoloured 2·10 2·10

438 Lion Design (Ukraine, 1921)

1989. Jewish New Year. Paper-cuts. Mult.

1081 50a. Type **438** 75 70

1082 70a. Hand design (Morocco, 1800s) 95 95

1083 80a. Stag design (Germany, 1818) 1·40 1·00

439 Founders of Safa Brurah

1989. Centenaries of Safa Brurah ("Clear Language") and Hebrew Language Committee (precursors of Hebrew Language Council).

1084 **439** 1s. multicoloured 1·70 1·70

440 Rabbi Alkalai

1989. 11th Death Anniv of Rabbi Hai Alkalai (Zionist).

1085 **440** 2s.50 multicoloured 4·00 4·00

441 "Stag"

1989. "Tevel 89" Youth Stamp Exhibition.

1086 **441** 50a. multicoloured 1·70 1·70

442 Postal Authority Emblem

1989. First Stamp Day.

1087 **442** 1s. multicoloured 1·10 1·10

443 "See You Again"

1989. Greetings Stamps. No value expressed. Multicoloured.

1088 (–) Type **443** 3·75 3·50

1089 (–) Patched heart ("With Love") 3·75 3·50

1090 (–) Flower ("Good Luck") 3·75 3·50

See also Nos. 1111/13 and 1128/30.

1989. "World Stamp Expo 89" International Stamp Exhibition, Washington D.C. Sheet 99×64 mm containing design as Nos. 1076/9 but smaller 27×22 mm.

MS1091 80a.×4 multicoloured (sold at 5s.) 11·50 11·50

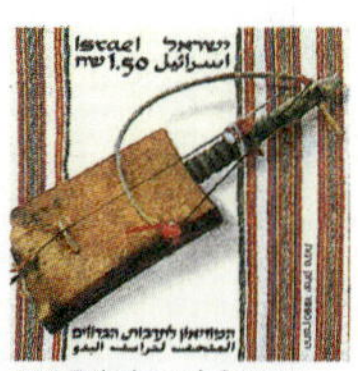

444 Rebab and Carpet

1990. The Bedouin in Israel.

1092 **444** 1s.50 multicoloured 2·20 2·20

445 Traditional Dancing

1990. Circassians in Israel.

1093 **445** 1s.50 multicoloured 2·75 2·75

446 Photograph Album and Orange

1990. Centenary of Rehovot Settlement.

1094 **446** 2s. multicoloured 3·25 3·25

447 Artillery Corps Monument, Zikhron Yaaqov

1990. Memorial Day.

1095 **447** 60a. multicoloured 1·00 1·00

448 Ruins of Gamla, Yehudiyya

1990. Nature Reserves (1st series). Mult.

1096 60a. Type **448** 95 70

1097 80a. Huleh 1·30 80

1098 90a. Mt. Meron 1·50 1·20

See also Nos. 1200/2.

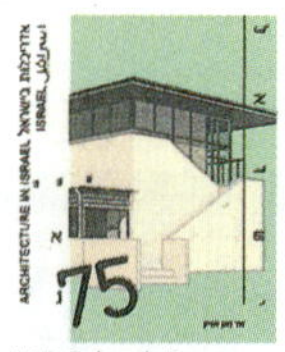

449 School, Deganya Kibbutz (Richard Kauffmann)

1990. Architecture.

1099b 75a. Type **449** 37·00 37·00

1100 1s.10 Dining hall, Tel Yosef Kibbutz (Leopold Krahauer) 1·40 95

1101 1s.20 Engel House, Tel Aviv (Ze'ev Rechter) 1·40 95

1102 1s.40 Weizmann House, Rehovot (Erich Mendelsohn) 1·90 1·10

1103 1s.60 National Institutions Building, Jerusalem (Yohanan Ratner) 1·70 1·40

450 Roads to Jerusalem

1990. "Stamp World London 90" International Stamp Exhibition. Stained Glass Windows by Mordecai Ardon in National and University Library illustrating Book of Isiah. Sheet 151×67 mm containing T **450** and similar vert design. Multicoloured.

MS1110 1s.50 Type **450**; 1s.50 Weapons beaten into ploughshares (sold at 4s.50) 17·00 17·00

1990. Greetings Stamps. As Nos. 1088/90 but with value.

1111 55a. As No. 1090 4·75 4·75

1112a 80a. Type **443** 21·00 21·00

1113a 1s. As No. 1089 35·00 35·00

451 Badges

1990. 70th Anniv of Formation of Hagana (underground military organization).

1114 **451** 1s.50 multicoloured 2·75 2·75

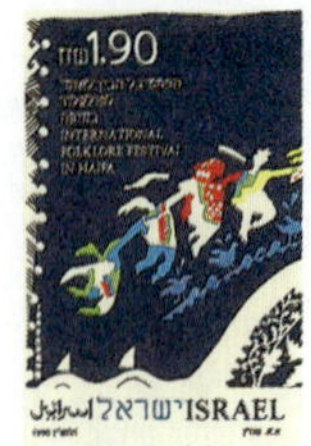

452 Dancers

1990. 8th International Folklore Festival, Haifa. Multicoloured.

1115 1s.90 Type **452** 3·50 3·50

1116 1s.90 Dancers and accordion player 3·50 3·50

Nos. 1115/16 were printed together, se-tenant, forming a composite design.

453 19th-century Austro-Hungarian Spice Box

1990. Jewish New Year. Silver Spice Boxes. Multicoloured.

1117 55a. Type **453** 1·10 80

1118 80a. 19th-century Italian box 1·20 95

1119 1s. German painted and gilt box by Matheus Wolf, 1700 1·40 1·20

454 People forming Star of David

1990. Absorption of Immigrants.

1120 **454** 1s.10 multicoloured 1·70 1·70

455 Ancient and Modern Means of Communication

1990. Electronic Mail.

1121 **455** 1s.20 green, black & yell 1·70 1·70

456 Abraham's well (after 17th-century engraving)

1990. "Beer Sheva 90" National Stamp Exhibition. Sheet 90×86 mm.

MS1122 **456** 3s. multicoloured (sold at 4s.) 8·75 8·75

457 Basketball

1990. Computer Games. Multicoloured.

1123	60a. Type **457**		95	70
1124	60a. Chess		95	70
1125	60a. Racing cars		95	70

458 Tel Aviv-Yafo Post Office and 1948 20m. Stamp

1990. Stamp Day.

1126	**458**	1s.20 multicoloured	3·00	3·00

459 Jabotinsky

1990. 50th Death Anniv of Ze'ev Jabotinsky (Zionist leader).

1127	**459**	1s.90 multicoloured	2·20	2·20

1991. Greetings Stamps. No value expressed. As T 443. Multicoloured.

1128	(–) Birthday cake ("Happy Birthday")	3·50	3·25
1129	(–) Champagne bottle ("Greetings")	3·50	3·25
1130	(–) Envelopes ("Keep in Touch")	3·50	3·25

Nos. 1128/30 were sold at the current inland letter rate.

460 Sarah Aaronsohn (intelligence agent)

1991. Anniversaries. Multicoloured.

1131	1s.30 Type **460** (birth centenary (1990))	1·10	95
1132	1s.30 Rahel Bluwstein (poet, 60th death anniv)	1·10	95
1133	1s.30 Lea Goldberg (writer and translator, 80th birth anniv)	1·10	95

461 Eucalyptus Tree and Hadera

1991. Centenary of Hadera.

1134	**461**	2s.50 multicoloured	2·75	2·75

462 Karate

1991. 14th Hapoel Games. Multicoloured.

1135	60a. Type **462**	1·70	95
1136	90a. Table tennis	95	95
1137	1s.10 Football	1·10	1·00

463 Intelligence Services Memorial, Centre for Special Studies, Tel Aviv

1991. Memorial Day.

1138	**463**	65a. multicoloured	1·00	1·00

464 First (Diesel) Power Station, Tel Aviv

1991. Inauguration of Rutenberg Power Station. Multicoloured.

1139	70a. Type **464**	95	80
1140	90a. Yarden Hydro-electric Station, Naharayim	1·20	1·00
1141	1s.20 Rutenberg coal fired power station, Ashqelon	1·60	1·30

465 Rabbi Shimon Hakham (co-founder) and Armon Building

1991. Centenary (1990) of Bukharim Quarter of Jerusalem.

1142	**465**	2s.10 multicoloured	2·30	2·30

466 Cover bearing Israeli, Palestine and Turkish Stamps

1991. Tel Aviv Postal and Philatelic Museum Project. Sheet 120×89 mm.

MS1143	**466**	3s.40 multicoloured	9·25	9·25

467 Ram's Head and Man blowing Shofar

1991. Festivals. Multicoloured.

1144	65a. Type **467** (Jewish New Year)	75	70
1145	1s. "Penitence Cock", father blessing children and men blowing shofars (Day of Atonement)	1·20	1·00
1146	1s.20 Family in booth (Festival of Tabernacles)	1·30	1·20

468 Front Page of First Edition

1991. 150th Anniv of "Jewish Chronicle" (weekly newspaper).

1147	**468**	1s.50 black, blue and red	1·90	1·90

469 Colonists and Baron Maurice de Hirsch (founder)

1991. Centenary of Jewish Colonization Association.

1148	**469**	1s.60 multicoloured	2·10	2·10

470 "Haifa, 1898" (Gustav Bauernfreind)

1991. "Haifa 91" Israel—Poland Stamp Exhibition. Sheet 104×62 mm.

MS1149	**470**	3s. multicoloured	9·25	9·25

471 Cancelled 1948 5m. Stamp

1991. Stamp Day.

1150	**471**	70a. multicoloured	95	95

472 Rahel Yanait Ben-Zvi (Zionist)

1991. Multicoloured.

1151	1s. Type **472**	1·40	1·20
1152	1s.10 Dona Gracia Nasi (supporter of 16th-century Jewish settlement in Tiberias)	1·50	1·30

473 Runner

1991. Olympic Games, Barcelona.

1153	**473**	1s.10 multicoloured	1·50	1·50

474 Flame and Hebrew Script

1991. 51st Anniv of Lehi (resistance organization).

1154	**474**	1s.50 multicoloured	1·90	1·90

475 Southern Wing of Acre Prison

1991. 60th Anniv of Etzel (resistance organization).

1155	**475**	1s.50 black, red and grey	1·90	1·90

476 Mozart and Score of "Don Giovanni"

1991. Death Bicentenary of Wolfgang Amadeus Mozart (composer).

1156	**476**	2s. multicoloured	3·00	2·50

477 Anemone

1992. No value expressed.

1157	**477**	(–) red and green	2·20	2·20

No. 1157 was sold at the current inland letter rate, initially 75a.

478 Hanna Rovina (actress)

1992. Multicoloured.

1158	80a. Type **478**	1·10	1·10
1159	1s.30 Rivka Guber (teacher and writer)	1·40	1·40

479 Trees

1992. Sea of Galilee. Multicoloured.

1160	85a. Type **479**	2·30	1·90
1161	85a. Sailboard	2·30	1·90
1162	85a. Fishes	2·30	1·90

480 Palmah Emblem

1992. 51st Anniv of Palmah (resistance organization).

1163	**480**	1s.50 gold, blue & mauve	1·90	1·90

481 Samaritans praying on Mount Gerizim

1992. The Samaritans.

1164	**481**	2s.60 multicoloured	3·25	3·25

482 Border Guard Memorial, Eiron Junction (Yechiel Arad)

1992. Memorial Day.

1165 **482** 85a. multicoloured 1·10 1·10

483 Azulai

1992. 186th Death Anniv of Rabbi Hayyim Joseph David Azulai (scholar).

1166 **483** 85a. multicoloured 1·90 1·90

484 Hayyim

1992. 83rd Death Anniv of Rabbi Joseph Hayyim Ben Elijah.

1167 **484** 1s.20 multicoloured 1·90 1·90

485 "Almanach Perpetuum" and Models of Columbus's Ships

1992. 500th Anniv of Discovery of America by Columbus.

1168 **485** 1s.60 multicoloured 2·10 2·10

486 Bedridden Patient and Map

1992. 500th Anniv of Expulsion of Jews from Spain. Sheet 140×71 mm containing T 486 and similar horiz designs showing details of map by Abraham Cresques. Multicoloured.

MS1169 80a. Type **486**; 1s.10 Doctor and map; 1s.40 Writer-philosopher and map 8·25 8·25

487 Diesel Trains, Greasing of Wheels and Blueprint of Baldwin Engine

1992. Centenary of Jaffa–Jerusalem Railway. Mult.

1170 85a. Type **487** 80 70

1171 1s. Scottish steam locomotive, track plan at Lod, electric signalling board at Tel Aviv, semaphore arms and points at Lod 95 80

1172 1s.30 Diesel locomotive, interior and exterior of passenger carriages, Palestine Railways ticket and 1926 timetable 1·20 1·00

1173 1s.60 Diesel train, drawing of facade of Jerusalem station, platform at Lod, Jaffa station in 1900 and points at Bar-Giora station 1·30 1·20

MS1174 140×71 mm. 4 ×50a. As Nos. 1170/3 8·25 8·25

488 Cover of "Or-HaHayyim" ("Light of Life") (Rabbi Hayyim Benatar, 250th (1993) anniv)

1992. Death Anniversaries.

1175 **488** 1s.30 lilac, green & gold 1·20 1·20

1176 - 3s. lilac, green and gold 2·30 2·30

DESIGN: 3s. 19th-century drawing of Bet-El Yeshiva, Jerusalem (Rabbi Shalom Sharabi, 215th anniv).

489 Leopard

1992. Zoo Animals. Multicoloured.

1177 50a. Type **489** 60 45

1178 50a. Indian elephant 60 45

1179 50a. Chimpanzee 60 45

1180 50a. Lion 60 45

490 "Parables" (Yitzhak ben Shlomo ibn Sahula) (1st edition, Brescia, 1491)

1992. Jewish New Year. Centenary of Jewish National and University Library, Jerusalem. Multicoloured.

1181 85a. Type **490** 95 75

1182 1s. Mahzor (prayer book) (15th-century manuscript by Leon ben Yehoshua de Rossi) 1·00 80

1183 1s.20 Draft of translation by Martin Buber of Leviticus 25: 10-13 1·10 1·00

491 Court Building

1992. Inauguration of New Supreme Court Building.

1184 **491** 3s.60 multicoloured 3·75 3·50

492 Wallcreeper

1992. Songbirds. Multicoloured.

1185 10a. Type **492** 30 25

1186 20a. Tristram's grackle 30 25

1187 30a. Pied wagtail ("White") 35 30

1188 50a. Palestine sunbird 45 45

1189 85a. Sinai rosefinch 1·50 50

1190 90a. Barn swallows ("Swallow") 75 40

1191 1s. Trumpeter finches 75 40

1192 1s.30 Graceful prinia ("Graceful Warbler") 95 70

1193 1s.50 Black-eared wheatear 1·10 95

1194 1s.70 White-eyed bulbuls ("Common Bulbul") 1·60 1·30

493 "Judah Released"

1992. 75th Anniv of First All-Hebrew Film. Scenes from films. Multicoloured.

1195 80a. Type **493** (first Hebrew film) 1·40 1·30

1196 2s.70 "Oded the Wanderer" (first Hebrew feature film) 2·10 1·90

1197 3s.50 "This is the Land" (first Hebrew talking film) 2·75 2·30

494 European Community Emblem on Graph

1992. Stamp Day. European Single Market.

1198 **494** 1s.50 multicoloured 1·50 1·50

495 Begin

1993. 1st Death Anniv of Menahem Begin (Prime Minister, 1977–83).

1199 **495** 80a. multicoloured 95 80

1993. Nature Reserves (2nd series). As T 448. Multicoloured.

1200 1s.20 Hof Dor 1·40 95

1201 1s.50 Nahal Ammud 1·20 1·00

1202 1s.70 Nahal Ayun 1·40 1·30

496 Shrine of the Bab

1993. Baha'i World Centre, Haifa.

1203 **496** 3s.50 multicoloured 2·75 2·50

497 Medical Corps Memorial, Carmel, Haifa (Akiva Lomnitz)

1993. Memorial Day.

1204 **497** 80a. multicoloured 80 75

498 "The Eye's Memory"

1993. Illustration of Scientific Concepts. Exhibits from the Israel National Museum of Science, Haifa (Nos. 1205/6) or the Bernard M. Bloomfield Science Museum, Jerusalem (others).

1205 80a. Type **498** 95 80

1206 80a. Colour mixing 95 80

1207 80a. Waves 95 80

1208 80a. Floating balls (principle of lift) 95 80

499 Prisoner

1993. 50th Anniv of Uprisings in the Ghettos and Concentration Camps.

1209 **499** 1s.20 black, yellow & bl 1·20 1·00

500 Hurbat Rabbi Yehuda Hassid Synagogue, Jerusalem

1993. 45th Anniv of Independence.

1210 **500** 3s.60 multicoloured 3·50 3·25

501 Giulio Racah

1993. Physicists. Multicoloured.

1211 80a. Type **501** 80 75

1212 1s.20 Aharon Katchalsky-Katzir 1·10 1·00

502 Family using Crossing (Lior Abohovsky)

1993. Road Safety. Children's Paintings. Mult.

1213 80a. Type **502** 90 80

1214 1s.20 Vehicles and road signs (Elinor Paz) 1·20 1·10

1215 1s.50 Road signals on "man" (Moran Dadush) 1·40 1·20

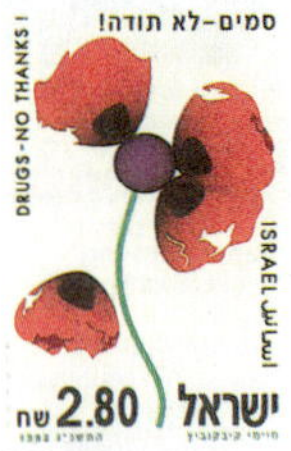

503 Poppy

1993. Anti-drugs Campaign.

1216 **503** 2s.80 multicoloured 2·50 2·50

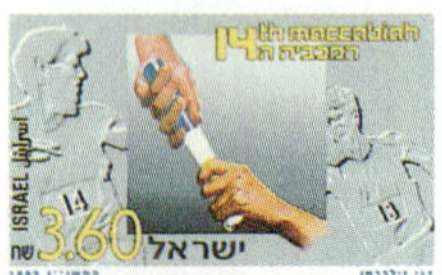

504 Passing Baton

1993. 14th Maccabiah Games.

1217 **504** 3s.60 multicoloured 3·75 3·75

505 Tree

1993. International Day of the Elderly.

1218 **505** 80a. multicoloured 80 75

506 Ear of Wheat

1993. Jewish New Year. Multicoloured.
1219 80a. Type **506** 80 70
1220 1s.20 Grapes 1·10 90
1221 1s.50 Olives 1·60 1·30

507 Environmental Concerns

1993. Environment Year.
1222 **507** 1s.20 multicoloured 1·10 1·00

508 Emblems

1993. 150th Anniv of B'nai B'rith (cultural and social organization).
1223 **508** 1s.50 multicoloured 1·10 1·00

509 "Immigrant Ship" (Marcel Janco)

1993. "Telafila 93" Israel—Rumania Stamp Exhibition, Tel Aviv. Sheet 60×90 mm.
MS1224 **509** 3s.60 multicoloured 7·00 7·00

510 Talmudic Oil Lamp

1993. Festival of Hanukka. Multicoloured.
1225 90a. Type **510** 80 75
1226 1s.30 Hanukka lamp in shape of building 1·20 1·00
1227 2s. "Lighting the Hanukka Lamp" (illustration from the "Rothschild Miscellany") 1·80 1·50

511 Cover of First Issue

1993. Stamp Day. Centenary (1992) of "Miniature World" (children's magazine).
1228 **511** 1s.50 multicoloured 1·50 1·30

512 Yellow-banded Borer ("Chlorophorus varius")

1994. Beetles. Multicoloured.
1229 85a. Type **512** 1·30 1·10
1230 85a. Copper beetle ("Potosia cuprea") 1·30 1·10
1231 85a. Pied ground beetle ("Graphopterus serrator") 1·30 1·10
1232 85a. Seven-spotted ladybird ("Coccinella septempunctata") 1·30 1·10

513 Man carrying Car ("Exercise Regularly")

1994. Health and Well-being. Multicoloured.
1233 85a. Type **513** 80 70
1234 1s.30 Blowing soap bubbles ("Don't Smoke") 1·10 1·00
1235 1s.60 Inspecting food through magnifying glass ("Eat Sensibly") 1·40 1·30

514 Haffkine

1994. 64th Death Anniv of Dr. Mordecai Haffkine (bacteriologist).
1236 **514** 3s.85 multicoloured 3·25 2·75

515 Communications, Electronics and Computer Corps Memorial, Yehud (Claude Grundman)

1994. Memorial Day.
1237 **515** 85a. multicoloured 80 75

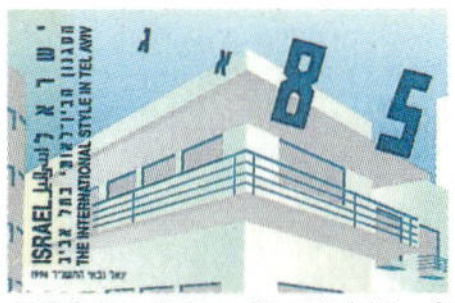

516 Assuta Private Hospital (Yosef Neufeld)

1994. International Style Architecture in Tel Aviv. Each grey, blue and green.
1238 85a. Type **516** 1·00 90
1239 85a. Co-operative workers' housing (flats with separate balconies) (Arieh Sharon) 1·00 90
1240 85a. Citrus House (Karl Rubin) 1·00 90

517 Battered Child

1994. "No to Violence" Campaign.
1241 **517** 3s.85 black and red 2·75 2·50

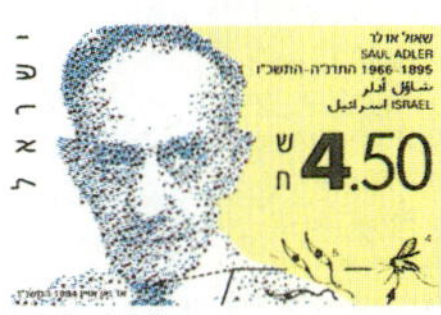

518 Saul Adler

1994. Birth Centenary (1995) of Saul Adler (scientist).
1242 **518** 4s.50 multicoloured 3·00 3·00

519 Inflating Balloon

1994. Ayalon Valley International Hot-Air Balloon Race. Multicoloured.
1243 85a. Type **519** 1·00 90
1244 85a. Balloons in air 1·00 90
1245 85a. Balloon hovering over target (cross on ground) 1·00 90

520 Chemistry Class at Bialystok and Physical Education at Wolyn

1994. 75th Anniv of Tarbut Schools (Hebrew schools in Eastern Europe).
1246 **520** 1s.30 multicoloured 1·00 90

521 Israeli Team at Munich Games, 1972, and National Committee Emblem

1994. Centenary of Int Olympic Committee.
1247 **521** 2s.25 multicoloured 1·60 1·40

522 The Little Prince (book character) and Saint-Exupery

1994. 50th Death Anniv of Antoine de Saint-Exupery (writer and pilot).
1248 **522** 5s. multicoloured 3·50 3·25

523 "Adam and Eve" (Itai Cohen)

1994. Jewish New Year. Entries in the "Children and Young People draw the Bible" exhibition. Multicoloured.
1249 85a. Type **523** 75 65
1250 1s.30 "Jacob's Dream" (Moran Sheinberg) 90 75
1251 1s.60 "Moses in the Bulrushes" (Carmit Crspi) 1·30 1·10
MS1252 65×90 mm. 4s. "Parting of the Red Sea" (Avital Kaisar) (39×50 mm) 4·50 4·50

524 Jewish and Arab Houses merging

1994. Israeli–Palestinian Peace Process.
1253 **524** 90a. multicoloured 1·80 1·60

525 Silicat Brick Factory, Tel Aviv (Fourth Aliya, 1924–28)

1994. Aliyot (immigration of Jews to Israel). Multicoloured.
1254 1s.40 Settlers and booklet distributed in Poland to encourage Jews to settle the Valley of Jezreel (Third Aliya, 1919–23) 80 70
1255 1s.70 Type **525** 1·10 90

526 Road to Peace

1994. Signing of Israel–Jordan Peace Treaty.
1256 **526** 3s.50 multicoloured 2·50 2·30

527 Ford Model "T" Converted Car, 1920s

1994. Public Transport. Multicoloured.
1257 90a. Type **527** 80 70
1258 1s.40 "White Super" bus, 1940s 1·10 90
1259 1s.70 Leyland "Royal Tiger" bus, 1960s 1·30 1·10

528 Hanukka Lamp from Mazagan, Morocco

1994. Festival of Hanukka.
1260 **528** 1s.50 multicoloured 1·20 1·10

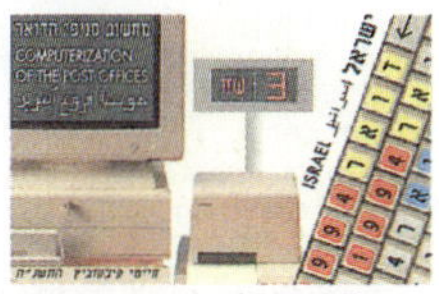

529 Computerized Post Office Counter

1994. Stamp Day. Computerization of the Post Office.
1261 **529** 3s. multicoloured 1·90 1·60

530 Breaking Dreyfus's Sword

1994. Centenary of "The Dreyfus Affair" (conviction for treason of French Army Captain Alfred Dreyfus).
1262 **530** 4s.10 multicoloured 3·00 2·50

531 "Serpentine" (Itzhak Danziger), Yarkon Park, Tel Aviv

1995. Outdoor Sculptures. Multicoloured.
1263 90a. Type **531** 75 80
1264 1s.40 "Stabile" (Alexander Calder), Mount Herzl, Jerusalem 1·10 1·00

1265 1s.70 Hall of Remembrance Gate (David Palombo), Yad Vashem, Jerusalem 1·30 1·10

532 Score from "Schelomo", Solomon (after Dore) and Ernest Bloch

1995. Composers (1st series). Multicoloured.
1266 4s.10 Type **532** 3·00 2·50
1267 4s.10 Score from "Jeremiah", Jeremiah (after Gustave Dore) and Leonard Bernstein 3·00 2·50

See also Nos. 1272/3, 1330 and 1338.

533 Ordnance Corps Memorial, Netanya

1995. Memorial Day.
1268 **533** 1s. multicoloured 90 90

534 Liberation of Dachau Concentration Camp

1995. 50th Anniv of End of Second World War.
1269 **534** 1s. multicoloured 1·30 1·10
MS1270 140×70 mm. 2s.50 As No. 1269 but larger (50×39 mm) 5·00 5·00

535 U.N. Projects

1995. 50th Anniv of U.N.O.
1271 **535** 1s.50 multicoloured 1·60 1·60

1995. Composers (2nd series). As T 532. Multicoloured.
1272 2s.40 Arnold Schoenberg and scene from "Moses and Aaron" 1·90 1·80
1273 2s.40 Darius Milhaud and score and scene from opera "David" 1·90 1·80

536 Soldier teaching Children Hebrew

1995. Jewish Brigade of Second World War. Sheet 95×65 mm.
MS1274 **536** 2s.50 multicoloured 5·00 5·00

537 Canoeist

1995. 15th Hapoel Games.
1275 **537** 1s. multicoloured 2·10 2·10

538 Box Kite and Cody "War" Kite

1995. Kites. Multicoloured.
1276 1s. Type **538** 75 65
1277 1s. Bird-shaped, hexagonal "Tiara" and rhombic "Eddy" kites 75 65
1278 1s. Multiple rhombic and triangular "Deltic" aerobatic kites 75 65

Nos. 1276/8 were printed together, se-tenant, forming a composite design.

539 "Stars in a Bucket" (Anda Amir-Pinkerfeld, illus. Hava Nathan)

1995. Children's Books. Designs illustrating poems. Multicoloured.
1279 1s. Type **539** 90 75
1280 1s.50 "Hurry, Run, Dwarfs" (Miriam Yallan-Stekelis, illus. Tirzah Tanny) 1·30 1·00
1281 1s.80 "Daddy's Big Umbrella" (Levin Kipnis, illus. Pazit Meller-Dushi) 1·40 1·10

540 "Zim Israel" (container ship)

1995. 50th Anniv of Zim Navigation Company.
1282 **540** 4s.40 multicoloured 3·50 3·25

541 Elijah's Chair (German, 1768)

1995. Jewish New Year. Multicoloured.
1283 1s. Type **541** (circumcision) 1·10 90
1284 1s.50 Velvet bag for prayer shawl (Moroccan, 1906) (Bar-Mitzvah) 1·60 1·40
1285 1s.80 Marriage stone (from Bingen Synagogue, Germany, 1700) 1·80 1·50

542 King David playing Harp (mosaic pavement, Gaza Synagogue)

1995. 3000th Anniv of City of David (Jerusalem). Multicoloured.
1286 1s. Type **542** 1·00 90
1287 1s.50 Illustration of Jerusalem from 19th-century map by Rabbi Pinie 1·50 1·30
1288 1s.80 Aerial view of Knesset (parliament) 1·60 1·40

543 "Sheep" (Menashe Kadishman)

1995. 75th Anniv of Veterinary Services.
1289 **543** 4s.40 multicoloured 3·75 3·50

544 Rabin

1995. Yitzhak Rabin (Prime Minister) Commem.
1290 **544** 5s. multicoloured 3·75 3·50

545 Putting out Fire

1995. 70th Anniv of Fire and Rescue Service. Multicoloured.
1291 1s. Type **545** 80 75
1292 1s. Cutting crash victim out of car 80 75

546 Miniature Silver Menorah (Zusia Ejbuszyc)

1995. Festival of Hanukka.
1293 **546** 1s.50 multicoloured 1·30 1·10

547 Flying Model Plane

1995. Stamp Day.
1294 **547** 1s.80 multicoloured 1·30 1·10

548 Film Stars

1995. Centenary of Motion Pictures.
1295 **548** 4s.40 multicoloured 2·75 2·50

The stars depicted are the Marx Brothers, Simone Signoret, Peter Sellers, Danny Kaye and Al Jolson.

549 Illustration from Jerusalem From 19-century Map of Rabbi Pinie

1995. 3000th Anniv of City of David (Jerusalem) (2nd issue) and "Jerusalem 3000" Israeli—European Stamp Exhibition. Sheet 140×70 mm containing T 549 and similar horiz designs. Multicoloured.
MS1296 1s. King David playing Harp (mosaic pavement, Gaza Synagogue); 1s.50 Type **549**; 1s.80 Aerial view of Knesset (Parliament) 7·50 7·50

The stamps in No. **MS**1296 depict the same motifs as No. 1286/8 but with differences in inscriptions.

550 Cycling

1996. Sport. Multicoloured.
1301 1s.05 Type **550** 90 75
1302 1s.10 Show jumping 90 75
1303 1s.80 Water skiing 1·30 1·10
1304 1s.90 Paragliding 1·50 1·20
1305 2s. Volleyball 1·60 1·20
1306 2s.30 Whitewater rafting 1·80 1·30
1307 3s. Bat and ball 1·90 1·40
1308 5s. Archery 2·75 2·40
1309 10s. Abseiling 5·25 4·50

551 "Temple and Walls of Jerusalem"

1996. 3000th Anniv of City of David (Jerusalem) (3rd issue). Third-century Murals from Dura-Europos Synagogue, Syria. Sheet 141×71 mm containing T 551 and similar vert designs. Multicoloured.
MS1310 1s.05 Type **551**; 1s.60, Torah Ark niche; 1s.90 Prophet Samuel anointing David as King 8·75 8·75

552 Cow and Computer

1996. 70th Anniv of Israel Dairy Cattle Breeders' Association.
1311 **552** 4s.65 multicoloured 3·75 3·50

1996. "China 96" International Stamp Exhibition, Peking. Birds. Sheet 128×89 mm containing designs as Nos. 1185/94 but face values and colours changed.
MS1312 30a.×10 multicoloured 13·00 13·00

553 Abraham Shlonsky (poet)

1996. Modern Hebrew Writers. Multicoloured.
1313 40a. Type **553** 40 40
1314 40a. Joseph Brenner (novelist and essayist) 40 40
1315 40a. Judah Gordon (poet) 40 40
1316 40a. Haim Hazaz (novelist) 40 40
1317 40a. Devorah Baron (novelist) 40 40
1318 40a. Yehuda Burla (novelist) 40 40
1319 40a. Micha Berdyczewski (novelist and historian) 40 40
1320 40a. Yaakov Shabtai (novelist) 40 40
1321 40a. Isaac Peretz (novelist) 40 40
1322 40a. Nathan Alterman (poet) 40 40
1323 40a. Saul Tchernichowsky (poet) 40 40
1324 40a. Amir Gilboa (poet) 40 40
1325 40a. Yokheved Bat-Miriam (poet) 40 40
1326 40a. Mendele Sefarim (novelist) 40 40

554 Fallen Policemen Monument, National Police Academy, Kiryat Ata (Yosef Assa)

1996. Memorial Day.
1327 **554** 1s.05 multicoloured 3·75 3·75

555 Circuit Boards

1996. 75th Anniv of Manufacturers' Association.
1328 **555** 1s.05 multicoloured 2·30 2·30

556 Emblem and Old Photographs

1996. Centenary of Metulla.
1329 **556** 1s.90 multicoloured 3·75 3·75

1996. Composers (3rd series). As T 532. Multicoloured.
1330 4s.65 Gustav Mahler, score from "Resurrection Symphony" and creation of light 7·50 7·50

557 Plant growing in Cracked Earth

1996. 50th Anniv of the 11 Negev Settlements.
1331 **557** 1s.05 multicoloured 1·80 1·60

558 Fencing

1996. Olympic Games. Atlanta. Multicoloured.
1332 1s.05 Type **558** 1·50 1·30
1333 1s.60 Pole vaulting 1·80 1·50
1334 1s.90 Wrestling 2·00 1·80

559 Jaffa Orange Tree and Citrus Fruit

1996. Israeli Fruit Production. Multicoloured.
1335 1s.05 Type **559** 1·30 1·10
1336 1s.60 Grape vine, avocado, date, sharon fruit and mango 1·50 1·30
1337 1s.90 Star fruit plant and exotic fruit 1·80 1·60

1996. Composers (4th series). As T 532. Multicoloured.
1338 4s.65 Felix Mendelssohn, Prophet Elijah (after Albrecht Durer) and score from oratorio "Elijah" 4·00 3·75

560 Road Systems

1996. 75th Anniv of Public Works Department.
1339 **560** 1s.05 multicoloured 1·60 1·40

561 New Year

1996. Jewish Festivals. Paintings by Sahar Pick. Multicoloured.
1340 1s.05 Type **561** 1·30 1·10
1341 1s.60 Booth decoration (Festival of Tabernacles) 1·60 1·40
1342 1s.90 Pulpit (Simchat Torah Festival) 1·90 1·60

1996. Centenary of First Zioist Congress, Basel, Switzerland. Multicoloured.
1343 4s.65 Type **562** 4·00 3·50
MS1344 70×97 mm. 5s. Casino, Basel (venue) (39×50 mm) 9·25 9·25

563 Lighted Candles

1996. Festival of Hanukkah. Self-adhesive.
1345 **563** 2s.50 multicoloured 2·10 2·00

564 Bird and Fighter Aircraft

1996. Coexistence between Man and Animals. Multicoloured.
1346 1s.10 Type **564** 1·20 1·00
1347 1s.75 Dog, people and cat 1·40 1·20
1348 2s. Dolphins and diver 1·70 1·50

565 Ahad Ha'am

1996. Centenary of First Edition of "Ha-Shilo'ah" (periodical) and 140th Birth Anniv of Ahad Ha'am (editor and Zionist).
1349 **565** 1s.15 multicoloured 1·30 1·20

566 Shavit Rocket, Earth and "Ofeq-3" (satellite)

1996. Stamp Day. Space Research.
1350 **566** 2s.05 multicoloured 2·30 2·10

567 Equal Opportunities Emblem

1996. Equal Opportunities for Disabled People.
1351 **567** 5s. multicoloured 3·50 3·25

568 Woman, Ethiopia

1997. Traditional Costumes of Jewish Communities Abroad. Multicoloured.
1352 1s.10 Type **568** 1·30 1·20
1353 1s.70 Man, Kurdistan 1·90 1·70
1354 2s. Woman, Salonica 2·30 2·10

569 Alexander Graham Bell demonstrating Telephone

1997. "Hong Kong 97" International Stamp Exhibition. Inventors' 150th Birth Anniversaries. Sheet 90×56 mm containing T 569 and similar vert design.
MS1355 1s.50 Type **569**; 2s. Thomas Edison and lightbulb 6·50 6·50

570 Windmills, Don Quixote and Sancho Panza (Ya'acov Farkas (Ze'ev))

1997. 450th Birth Anniv of Miguel de Cervantes (writer).
1356 **570** 3s. multicoloured 2·30 2·10

571 Logistics Corps Memorial, Hadir

1997. Memorial Day.
1357 **571** 1s.10 multicoloured 1·00 95

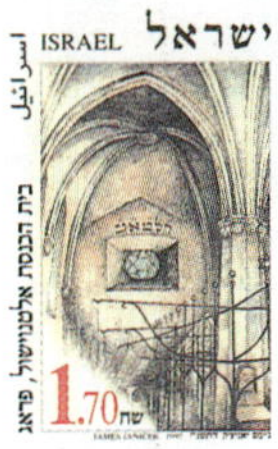

572 Ark of the Torah, Old–New Synagogue (east side)

1997. Jewish Monuments in Prague. Mult.
1358 1s.70 Type **572** 1·70 1·50
1359 1s.70 Grave of Rabbi Loew (chief Rabbi of Prague), Old Jewish Cemetery 1·70 1·50

573 Rabbi Elijah (Mario Sermoneta)

1997. Death Bicentenary of Vilna Gaon (Rabbi Elijah ben Solomon).
1360 **573** 2s. multicoloured 1·50 1·40

574 "Exodus" in Haifa Port

1997. Clandestine Immigration, 1934–48.
1361 **574** 5s. multicoloured 3·00 2·75

575 Ben Ezra Synagogue, Cairo

1997. "Pacific 97" International Stamp Exhibition, San Francisco. Sheet 90×60 mm containing T 575 and similar square design. Multicoloured.
MS1362 2s. Type **575** (centenary of discovery of Cairo Hebrew archives); 3s. Qumran and the Dead Sea, Prof E. Sukenik and Shrine of Dead Sea Scrolls) 6·50 6·50

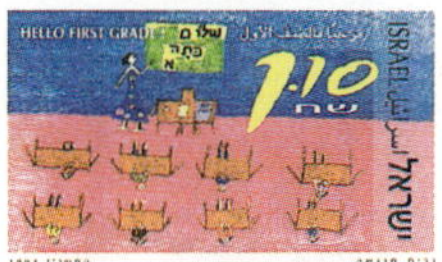

576 Classroom (Navit Mangashsa)

1997. Winning Entry in "Hello First Grade!" Stamp Drawing Competition.
1363 **576** 1s.10 multicoloured 1·20 1·00

577 Drunk Driver

1997. Road Safety. Multicoloured.
1364 1s.10 Type **577** ("Don't Drink and Drive") 1·20 1·00
1365 1s.10 Car sinking in water ("Keep in Lane") 1·20 1·00
1366 1s.10 Car hitting bird ("Keep your Distance") 1·20 1·00

578 Ice Skating

1997. 15th Maccabiah Games.
1367 **578** 5s. multicoloured 4·25 3·50

579 Abraham and Tamarisk Tree

1997. Festival of Sukkot. The Visiting Patriarchs (1st series). Paintings from the Sukkah of Rabbi Loew Immanuel of Szeged, Hungary. Multicoloured.
1368 1s.10 Type **579** 1·00 80
1369 1s.70 Abraham preparing to sacrifice Isaac 1·50 1·10
1370 2s. Jacob dreaming of angels on ladder to heaven 1·90 1·40

See also Nos. 1453/6.

580 Mt. Scopus (Jerusalem) and Choirs

1997. Music and Dance Festivals. Mult.
1371 1s.10 Type **580** (Zimriya World Assembly of Choirs, Hebrew University) 1·20 1·00
1372 2s. Fireworks over Karmiel and dancers (Dance Festival) 1·50 1·40
1373 3s. Zefat and klezmers (Hassidic musicians) (Klezmer Festival) 2·10 1·50

581 "The Night of 29th November" (Ya'acov Eisenscher)

1997. 50th Anniv of U.N. Resolution on Establishment of State of Israel.
1374 **581** 5s. multicoloured 3·00 2·50

582 Sketch by Pushkin of Himself and Onegin

1997. Translation into Hebrew by Arbraham Shlonsky of Eugene Onegin (poem) by Aleksandr Pushkin. Sheet 75×60 mm.

MS1375 **582** 5s. multicoloured		3·75	3·75

583 National Flag and Srulik with Flower

1997. 50th Anniv (1998) of State of Israel. (1st issue). No value expressed. (a) Size 18×23½ mm.

1376	**583**	(–) multicoloured	1·20	95

(b) Size 17½×21½ mm.

1377		(–) multicoloured	1·20	95

See also No. 1395.

584 Norseman Aircraft, Soldier, Missile Corvette and Cannon "Napoleon-Chick"

1997. 50th Anniv of Arrival in Israel of Machal (overseas volunteers) (1377) and Gachal (overseas recruits) (1378). Multicoloured.

1378	1s.15 Type **584**	95	80
1379	1s.80 Infantry soldier and Holocaust survivors	1·20	80

585 Bezalel (spinning-top)

1997. Festival of Hanukka. Museum Exhibits. Multicoloured.

1380	1s.80 Type **585** (Eretz Israel Museum, Tel Aviv)	1·20	1·20
1381	2s.10 Coin of Bar-Kokhba during war against the Romans (Israel Museum, Jerusalem)	1·40	1·00

586 Children leaving Airliner

1997. Chabad Children of Chernobyl Organization (for evacuation of Jewish children from irradiated areas of Europe to Israel).

1382	**586**	2s.10 multicoloured	1·40	1·20

587 Julia Set Fractal

1997. Stamp Day.

1383	**587**	2s.50 multicoloured	1·70	1·50

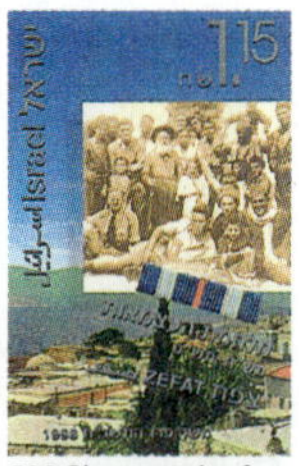

588 Photograph of Soldiers of Palmach Battalion and Civilians (Zefat)

1998. 50th Anniv of War of Independence. Battle Fronts. Multicoloured.

1384	1s.15 Type **588**	95	80
1385	1s.15 "Castel Conquered" (Arieh Navon) superimposed on armoured vehicles (Jerusalem)	95	80
1386	1s.15 Soldiers raising flag (Elat)	95	80
MS1387	140×70 mm. 1s.50, 2s.50, 3s. showing enlarged details of Nos. 1383/5	8·25	8·25

589 Herzog

1998. 80th Birth Anniv of Chaim Herzog (President 1983–93).

1388	**589**	5s.35 multicoloured	3·00	2·75

590 Franz Kafka (writer)

1998. Jewish Contribution to World Culture (1st series). Multicoloured.

1389	90a. Type **590**	70	60
1390	90a. George Gershwin (composer)	70	60
1391	90a. Lev Davidovich Landau (physicist)	70	60
1392	90a. Albert Einstein (physicist and mathematician)	70	60
1393	90a. Leon Blum (writer)	70	60
1394	90a. Elizabeth Rachel Felix (actress)	70	60

See also Nos. 1436/41.

591 Declaration Ceremony, 1948

1998. 50th Anniv of State of Israel (2nd issue).

1395	**591**	1s.15 multicoloured	80	70

592 Olive Branch

1998. Memorial Day.

1396	**592**	1s.15 multicoloured	80	70

593 Swearing In Ceremony in 1948 and Badge entwined with Medal Ribbons

1998. 50th Anniv of Defence Forces.

1397	**593**	5s.35 multicoloured	3·00	2·75

594 Giorgio Perlasca, Aristides de Sousa Mendes, Charles Lutz, Sempo Sugihara and Selahattin Ulkumen (diplomats) (image scaled to 53% of original size)

1998. Holocaust Memorial Day. Righteous Among the Nations (non-Jews who risked their lives to save Jews during the Holocaust).

1398	**594**	6s. multicoloured	4·25	4·25

595 Kitten

1998. Children's Pets. Multicoloured.

1399	60a. Type **595**	60	45
1400	60a. Puppy	60	45
1401	60a. Crimson rosella	60	45
1402	60a. Goldfish	60	45
1403	60a. Hamster	60	45
1404	60a. Rabbit	60	45

Nos. 1399/1404 were issued together in se-tenant sheetlets of six stamps and six triangular labels bearing the emblem of "Israel 98" International Stamp Exhibition, each label with an adjacent stamp completing a square. The complete sheetlet forms a composite design.

596 Srulik at Post Office Counter

1998. Inauguration of Postal and Philatelic Museum, Tel Aviv. Sheet 142×72 mm containing T 596 and similar horiz designs showing illustrations by K. Gardosh. Multicoloured.

MS1405 1s.50 Type **596**; 2s.50 Srulik viewing stamp through magnifying glass; 3s. Srulik posting letter		7·00	7·00

597 Drawing of Temple Entrance

1998. "Israel 98" International Stamp Exhibition, Tel Aviv (1st issue). King Solomon's Temple. Sheet 92×66 mm containing T 597 and similar square design. Multicoloured.

MS1406 2s. Type **597**; 3s. Inscribed ivory pomegranate		5·25	5·25

598 De Havilland D.H.89 Dragon Rapide

1998. Aircraft of War of Independence. Mult.

1407	2s.20 Type **598**	1·20	1·00
1408	2s.20 Supermarine Spitfire	1·20	1·00
1409	2s.20 Boeing B-17 Flying Fortress	1·20	1·00

599 Woman's Head (mosaic from Zippori)

1998. "Israel 98" International Stamp Exhibition, Tel Aviv (2nd issue). Sheet 90×60 mm.

MS1410 **599** 5s. multicoloured		5·25	5·25

600 "Amos" Satellite, Immigration, Grapes, Dove and Lion's Gate, Jerusalem

1998. "Israel Jubilee" Exhibition, Tel Aviv.

1411	**600**	5s.35 multicoloured	2·75	2·30

601 Holding Hands (Nitzan Shupak)

1998. "Living in a World of Mutual Respect" Elementary Education Programme.

1412	**601**	1s.15 multicoloured	70	60

602 Birds (Hechal Yitshak Synagogue, Moshav Yonatan)

1998. Jewish New Year. Synagogue Curtains. Multicoloured.

1413	1s.15 Type **602**	65	50
1414	1s.80 Lions (Ohal Chanah Synagogue, Neve Tsuf)	95	80
1415	2s.20 Leaves (Hatzvi Israel Synagogue, Jerusalem)	1·30	1·00

603 Hebron

1998. Jewish Life in Eretz Israel (1st series). Showing sections from Holy Cities Wall Plaque. Multicoloured.

1416	1s.80 Type **603**	1·00	85
1417	2s.20 Jerusalem	1·30	1·00

See also Nos. 1430/1.

604 State Flag

1998. Self-adhesive.

1418	**604**	1s.15 blue and deep blue	95	80
1419	**604**	2s.15 blue and green	1·40	1·20
1420	**604**	3s.25 blue and mauve	2·10	1·70
1421	**604**	5s.35 blue and yellow	3·50	3·00

605 Hanukka Lamp showing Mattathias (Boris Schatz)

1999. Festival of Hanukka.

1426	**605**	2s.15 multicoloured	1·20	1·20

606 "Hyacinthus orientalis"

1999. Wild Hyacinths. No value expressed.

1427 **606** (1s.15) green and lilac 60 45

607 The Knesset, Menorah and Knesset Stone Wall (des. Danny Karavan)

1999. 50th Anniv of the Knesset (Parliament).

1428 **607** 1s.80 multicoloured 95 80

608 Manuscript

1999. 380th Birth Anniv of Rabbi Shalem Shabazi (Yemeni poet).

1429 **608** 2s.20 multicoloured 1·20 1·00

1999. Jewish Life in Eretz Israel (2nd series). As T 603, showing sections from Holy Cities Wall Plaque. Multicoloured.

1430 1s.15 Zefat 75 65

1431 5s.35 Tiberias 2·50 2·30

609 Part of £1 Share Certificate

1999. Centenary of Jewish Colonial Trust.

1432 **609** 1s.80 multicoloured 95 80

610 Yemeni Woman

1999. Traditional Costumes of Jewish Communities (1st series). Multicoloured.

1433 2s.15 Type **610** 1·20 1·00

1434 3s.25 Woman wearing sari, India 1·60 1·50

See also Nos. 1457/8.

611 Reconstruction of Ship

1999. "Australia 99" International Stamp Exhibition, Melbourne. Excavation of Ancient Ship, Sea of Galilee. Sheet 100×63 mm containing T 611 and similar square design. Multicoloured.

MS1435 3s. Type **611**; 5s. Remains of ship 4·75 4·75

1999. Jewish Contribution to World Culture (2nd series). As T 590. Multicoloured.

1436 90a. Emile Durkheim (sociologist) 60 45

1437 90a. Paul Ehrlich (medical researcher) 60 45

1438 90a. Rosa Luxemburg (revolutionary) 60 45

1439 90a. Norbert Wiener (mathematician) 60 45

1440 90a. Sigmund Freud (psychologist) 60 45

1441 90a. Martin Buber (philosopher) 60 45

612 Memorial to Bedouin Soldiers, Rish Lakish

1999. Memorial Day.

1442 **612** 1s.20 multicoloured 70 60

613 Flags of U.N., Israel and Other States

1999. 50th Anniv of Israel's Admission to United Nations.

1443 **613** 2s.30 multicoloured 1·00 95

614 Holtzberg

1999. 75th Birth Anniv of Simcha Holtzberg.

1444 **614** 2s.50 multicoloured 1·20 1·00

615 "My Favourite Room" (detail)

1999. 50th Death Anniv of James Ensor (artist).

1445 **615** 2s.30 multicoloured 1·20 1·00

616 Ouza the Goose

1999. Lovely Butterfly (children's television programme). Multicoloured.

1446 1s.20 Type **616** 70 60

1447 1s.20 Nooly the chick and Shabi the snail 70 60

1448 1s.20 Batz the tortoise and Pingi the penguin 70 60

617 "Church of the Holy Sepulchre, Jerusalem" (F. Geyer)

1999. Paintings of Christian Pilgrimage Sites. Multicoloured.

1449 3s. Type **617** 1·60 1·50

1450 3s. "Mary's Well, Nazareth" (W. H. Bartlett) 1·60 1·50

1451 3s. "The River Jordan" (E. Finden after A. W. Callcott) 1·60 1·50

618 Illustration from Nehemia Emshel's Manuscript of Musa-Nameh by Shahin (poet)

1999. 205th Death Anniv of Rabbi Or Sharga from Persia.

1452 **618** 5s.60 multicoloured 2·30 2·10

1999. Festival of Sukkot. The Visiting Patriarchs (2nd series). As T 579, showing paintings from the Sukkah of Rabbi Loew Immanuel of Szeged, Hungary. Multicoloured.

1453 1s.20 Joseph interpreting Pharaoh's dreams 75 65

1454 1s.90 Moses and the burning bush 1·00 85

1455 2s.30 Aaron and Holy Ark 1·40 1·20

1456 5s.60 David playing harp 2·50 2·30

1999. Traditional Costumes of Jewish Communities (2nd series). As T 610. Multicoloured.

1457 2s.30 Woman from Seus region, Morocco 1·20 1·00

1458 3s.40 Man from Bukhara 1·70 1·40

619 Family and Part of 1948 250m. Stamp

1999. Stamp Day.

1459 **619** 5s.35 multicoloured 2·30 2·10

620 18th-century Ceramic Urn showing Funeral Procession

1999. Jewish Culture in Slovakia. Multicoloured.

1460 1s.90 Type **620** 95 75

1461 1s.90 18th-century urn showing visit to a sick man 95 75

621 View over Town from Arch of Columns

1999. 50th Anniv of Kiryat Shemona.

1462 **621** 1s.20 multicoloured 70 60

622 "The Street of the Jews in Old Jersusalem" (Ludwig Blum)

1999. 50th Anniv of Proclamation of Jerusalem as Capital.

1463 **622** 3s.40 multicoloured 1·70 1·50

623 Sali

1999. 15th Death Anniv of Admor (Rabbi) Israel Abihssira Sidna "Baba Sali".

1464 **623** 4s.40 multicoloured 2·00 1·70

624 Children and Aliens holding Hands (Renana Barak)

2000. "Stampin' the Future" Children's Painting Competition. Multicoloured.

1465 1s.20 Type **624** 75 65

1466 1s.90 Man and robot (Tal Engelsten) 95 80

1467 2s.30 Futuristic street scene (Asia Aizenshteyn) 1·20 1·00

1468 3s.40 Alien's and child's heads (Ortal Hasid) 1·70 1·50

625 Globe, Joggers and Skiers

2000. Year 2000. Multicoloured.

1469 1s.40 Type **625** (quality of life) 80 70

1470 1s.90 Da Vinci's "Proportion of Man", ear of corn and scientist (biotechnology) 95 80

1471 2s.30 Computer, satellite dish and website address (information technology) 1·20 1·00

1472 2s.80 Moon's surface, astronaut and globe (space research) 1·50 1·20

626 "The Little Mermaid"

2000. 125th Death Anniv of Hans Christian Andersen (writer). Illustrations by Samuel Katz. Multicoloured.

1473 1s.20 Type **626** 75 60

1474 1s.90 "The Emperor's New Clothes" 1·10 95

1475 2s.30 "The Ugly Duckling" 1·40 1·20

627 "All Apostles Church, Capernaum"

2000. Paintings of Christian Pilgrimage Sites (2nd series). Depicting paintings by Zina Roitman. Mult.

1476 1s.40 Type **627** 80 70

1477 1s.90 "St. Andrew's Church, Jerusalem" 1·10 95

1478 2s.30 "The Church of the Visitation, Ein Kerem" 1·40 1·20

628 Fort Shuni (Zina Roitman)

2000. Buildings and Historical Sites.

1479 **628** 2s.30 multicoloured 1·20 1·20

629 King Hussein

2000. King Hussein of Jordan Commemoration.

1480 **629** 4s.40 multicoloured 2·30 2·30

630 Monument to Jewish Volunteers in British Army, Jerusalem

2000. Memorial Day.

1481	**630**	1s.20 multicoloured	85	80

631 Fox yawning

2000. Endangered Species. Blanford's Fox. Mult.

1482	1s.20 Type **631**	70	60
1483	1s.20 Fox watching mourning wheater (bird)	70	60
1484	1s.20 Fox	70	60
1485	1s.20 Three foxes	70	60

632 Mobile Telephone

2000. International Communications Day.

1486	**632**	2s.30 multicoloured	1·00	95

633 Cross, Crescent and Menorah

2000. "The Holy Land".

1487	**633**	3s.40 multicoloured	2·20	2·00

634 Bach (bust) and Manuscript of Juara Chaconne for Violin Solo

2000. 250th Death Anniv of Johann Sebastian Bach (composer).

1488	**634**	5s.60 multicoloured	2·75	2·30

635 Fortified Stone Building (Zina Roitman)

2000. Buildings and Historical Sites.

1489	**635**	1s.20 multicoloured	50	45

636 Couscous

2000. Traditional Foods. Multicoloured.

1490	1s.40 Type **636**	85	70
1491	1s.90 Stuffed carp	1·20	95
1492	2s.30 Falafel	1·50	1·20

637 Olympic Rings and Koala

2000. Olympic Games, Sydney.

1493	**637**	2s.80 multicoloured	1·70	1·50

638 King Hassan II

2000. 1st Death Anniv of King Hassan II of Morocco.

1494	**638**	4s.40 multicoloured	2·30	1·90

639 Young Boy and Girl

2000. Festivals. New Year Cards. Multicoloured.

1495	1s.20 Type **639**	70	60
1496	1s.90 Young woman holding Zionist flag	95	85
1497	2s.30 Man presenting flowers to woman	1·20	95

640 Adam and Eve

2000. Dental Health Campaign.

1498	**640**	2s.20 multicoloured	1·50	1·40

641 Menorah and Interior of Synagogue

2000. Dohany Synagogue, Budapest.

1499	**641**	5s.60 multicoloured	3·50	3·25

642 Revivim Observatory, Negev (Zina Roitman)

2000. Buildings and Historical Sites.

1500	**642**	2s.20 multicoloured	1·30	1·00

643 Struthiomymus running

2000. Dinosaurs. Multicoloured.

1501	2s.20 Type **643**	1·30	1·20
1502	2s.20 Head of Struthiomymus	1·30	1·20
1503	2s.20 Struthiomymus standing by tree	1·30	1·20

644 Robot (*I, Robot*) (Isaac Asimov)

2000. Science Fiction Novels. Multicoloured.

1504	2s.80 Type **644**	1·40	1·10
1505	3s.40 Time travel machine (*The Time Machine*) (H. G. Wells)	1·60	1·30
1506	5s.60 Space rocket (*Journey to the Moon*) (Jules Verne)	2·75	2·20

645 Open Book

2000. Aleppo Codex (earliest known manuscript of the Bible).

1507	**645**	4s.40 multicoloured	2·40	2·20

646 Tof

2001. Hebrew Alphabet. Designs each showing a different Hebrew letter. Multicoloured.

1508	10a. Type **646**	10	10
1509	10a. Shin	10	10
1510	10a. Reish	10	10
1511	10a. Kuf	10	10
1512	10a. Tzadi Kekufa	10	10
1513	10a. Pay Kekufah	10	10
1514	10a. Ayin	10	10
1515	10a. Samech	10	10
1516	10a. Nun	10	10
1517	10a. Mem	10	10
1518	10a. Lamed	10	10
1519	10a. Chof Kefufa	10	10
1520	10a. Yud	10	10
1521	10a. Tes	10	10
1522	10a. Ches	10	10
1523	10a. Zayin	10	10
1524	10a. Vov	10	10
1525	10a. Heh	10	10
1526	10a. Daled	10	10
1527	10a. Gimel	10	10
1528	10a. Beis	10	10
1529	10a. Aleph	10	10
1530	10a. Tzade Peshuta	10	10
1531	10a. Pay Peshuta	10	10
1532	10a. Chof Peshuta	10	10
1533	10a. Mem Stumah	10	10
1534	10a. Vov	10	10
1535	1s. Aleph and Beis	60	45

647 Pupils in front of School (Yavne'el)

2001. Village Centenaries. Multicoloured.

1536	2s.50 Type **647**	1·30	1·00
1537	4s.70 Farmers, horses and cart (Kefar Tavor)	2·30	1·70
1538	5s.90 Cart full of flowers (Menahamiya)	2·75	1·90

648 Segera Spring, Ilaniyya

2001. Buildings and Historical Sites.

1539	**648**	3s.40 multicoloured	2·00	1·70

649 Prairie Gentian

2001. Flowers. Multicoloured.

1540	1s.20 Type **649**	80	65
1541	1s.20 Barberton daisy	80	65
1542	1s.20 Star of Bethlehem	80	65
1543	1s.20 Florists calla	80	65

650 Lesser Kestrel

2001. Endangered Species. Multicoloured.

1544	1s.20 Type **650**	75	60
1545	1s.70 Kuhl's pipstrelle	95	70
1546	2s.10 Roe deer	1·20	80
1547	2s.50 Greek tortoise	1·30	95

651 Jerusalem (detail of ceramic tile, Ze'ev Rabin) (image scaled to 63% of original size)

2001. "Jerusalem 2001" International Stamp Exhibition. Sheet 131×67 mm.

MS1548	**651**	10s. multicoloured	6·50	6·50

652 Monument for the Fallen Nahal Soldiers, Pardes Hanna

2001. Memorial Day.

1549	**652**	1s.20 multicoloured	1·20	1·00

653 Marquise Diamonds

2001. "Belgica 2001" International Stamp Exhibition, Brussels. Diamonds. Sheet 117×70 mm containing T 653 and similar vert designs. Multicoloured.

MS1550 1s.40 Type **653**; 1s.70 Round diamond; 4s.70 Square diamond 7·50 7·50

654 Sha'ar HaGay Inn

2001. Buildings and Historical Sites.

1551	**654**	2s. multicoloured	1·20	95

655 Mausoleum and Terraces

2001. Shrine of the Bab, Haifa.

1552	**655**	3s. multicoloured	2·10	1·40

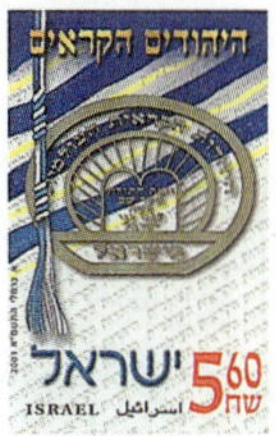

656 Prayer Shawl and Tassel

2001. Karaite Jews.

1553	**656**	5s.60 multicoloured	3·50	2·75

657 Hebron

2001. Ceramic Tiles. Showing tiles from facade of Ahad Ha'am Municipal Boys School, Tel Aviv. Multicoloured.

1554	1s.20 Type **657**	75	60
1555	1s.40 Jaffa	95	70
1556	1s.90 Haifa	1·40	80
1557	2s.30 Tiberias	1·50	95

658 "and me? I want to ride in a hot air balloon" (Eyar Shteiman)

2001. "PHILA NIPPON 01" Intenrational Stamp Exhibition, Tokyo. Winning Entries in Children's Painting Competition. Sheet 120×75 mm containing T 658 and similar vert designs. Multicoloured.

MS1558 1s.20 Type **658**; 1s.40 "I wish I had a kitten" (Rony Schechter-Malve); 2s. "My dream is to be a vet" (Dana Srebrnik); 4s.70 "to swim with dolphins" (Hila Malka) 6·50 6·50

659 Clasped Hands and Hikers

2001. Israeli Council of Youth Movements.

1559	**659**	5s.60 multicoloured	3·75	3·50

660 Soldier and Peace Dove

2001. Festivals. New Year Cards. Multicoloured.

1560	1s.20 Type **660**	95	70
1561	1s.90 Two women	1·40	80
1562	2s.30 Boy carrying flowers	1·50	95

661 Rustaveli

2001. 32nd Anniv of the Translation into Hebrew of The Knight in a Tiger's Skin (poem by Shota Rustaveli).

1563	**661**	3s.40 multicoloured	2·30	2·10

662 Field, Leaves and Sky

2001. Centenary of Jewish National Fund.

1564	**662**	5s.60 multicoloured	3·50	3·00

663 Amichai

2001. 1st Death Anniv of Yehuda Amichai (poet).

1565	**663**	5s.60 multicoloured	2·30	3·00

664 Sunshade on Beach

2001. Coastal Conservation.

1566	**664**	10s. multicoloured	5·75	4·75

665 Flags reflected in Helmet Visor

2001. 1st Israeli Astronaut.

1567	**665**	1s.20 multicoloured	70	60

666 Child Painting (Yaffa Dahan)

2001. 50th Anniv of Association for Rehabilitation of the Handicapped (AKIM).

1568	**666**	2s.20 multicoloured	1·40	1·20

667 "Heinrich Heine" (painting, Moritz Daniel Oppenheim)

2001. 145th Death Anniv of Heinrich Heine (poet and satirist).

1569	**667**	4s.40 multicoloured	3·25	2·75

668 "Israel" in Braille

2001. Centenary of Institute for the Blind, Jerusalem.

1570	**668**	5s.60 multicoloured	3·75	3·25

669 Lily

2002

1571	**669**	1s.20 multicoloured	70	60

670 Hat and Rattle (Adar)

2002. Months of the Year. Multicoloured. Ordinary or self-adhesive gum.

1572	1s.20 Type **670**	70	60
1573	1s.20 Almond twig, flowers and fruit (Shevat)	70	60
1574	1s.20 Grapefruit and anemones (Tevet)	70	60
1575	1s.20 Spinning top and candles (Kislev)	70	60
1576	1s.20 Autumn leaves (Heshvan)	70	60
1577	1s.20 Ram's horn and pomegranates (Tishrei)	70	60
1578	1s.20 Cup, unleavened bread and flowers (Nisan)	70	60
1579	1s.20 Bow, arrows and oleanders (Iyyar)	70	60
1580	1s.20 Sickle and grains (Sivian)	70	60
1581	1s.20 Sunflower and shells (Tammuz)	70	60
1582	1s.20 Couple wearing wedding dress and grapes (Av)	70	60
1583	1s.20 Torah, cotton and figs (Elul)	70	60

671 Field Mushroom

2002. Fungi. Multicoloured.

1596	1s.90 Type **671** (*Agaricus campestri*) (inscr "campester")	1·20	95
1597	2s.20 Fly agaric (*Amanita muscaria*)	1·30	1·00
1598	2s.80 Granulated boletus (*Suillus granulatus*)	1·60	1·40

672 "Ladino" in Rashi Script

2002. Judaic Languages. Multicoloured.

1599	2s.10 Type **671** (Ladino (Judeo-Spanish))	1·40	1·20
1600	2s.10 Peacock (Yiddish)	1·40	1·20

673 Military Police Memorial And Eternal Flame, Bet Lid

2002. Memorial Day.

1601	**673**	1s.20 multicoloured	65	50

674 Heinrich Graetz

2002. Historians. Multicoloured.

1602	2s.20 Type **674**	1·40	1·20
1603	2s.20 Simon Dubnow	1·40	1·20
1604	2s.20 Benzion Dinur	1·40	1·20
1605	2s.20 Yitzhak Baer	1·40	1·20

See also No. 1686/8.

675 King and Torah

2002. Hakel Ceremony.

1606	**675**	4s.70 multicoloured	2·75	2·20

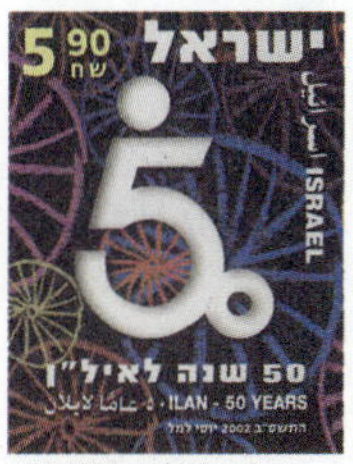

676 "50" and Wheels

2002. 50th Anniv of ILAN (Israel foundation for handicapped children).
1607 **676** 5s.90 multicoloured 3·50 3·00

677 Cable Cars, Menara

2002. Tourism. Cable Cars. Multicoloured.
1608 2s.20 Type **677** 1·20 95
1609 2s.20 Rosh Haniqra 1·20 95
1610 2s.20 Haifa 1·20 95
1611 2s.20 Massada 1·20 95

678 Fish Fossil

2002. Geology. Sheet 115×70 mm containing T 678 and similar vert designs. Multicoloured.
MS1612 2s.20 Type **678**; 3s.40, Copper mineral; 4s.40 Ammonite 6·50 6·50

679 Hatsar Kinneret

2002. Buildings and Historical Sites.
1613 **679** 3s.30 multicoloured 1·50 1·20

680 Rechavam Ze'evy

2002. 1st Death Anniv of Rechavam Ze'evy (Minister for tourism).
1614 **680** 1s.20 multicoloured 80 70

681 Grape Scissors and Grapes

2002. Festivals. Wine. Multicoloured.
1615 1s.20 Type **681** 70 50
1616 1s.90 Cork screw and cork 1·00 70
1617 2s.30 Wine glass and bottle 1·20 80

682 Golden Eagle

2002. Birds of Jordan Valley. Multicoloured.
1618 2s.20 Type **682** 1·30 95
1619 2s.20 Black stork 1·30 95
1620 2s.20 Crane 1·30 95

683 Kadoorie School

2002. Buildings and Historical Sites.
1621 **683** 4s.60 multicoloured 2·30 1·70

684 Baruch Spinoza

2002. 370th Birth Anniv of Baruch (Benedictus) Spinoza.
1622 **684** 5s.90 multicoloured 3·50 3·00

685 Menorah Candlestick

2002
1623 **685** 20a. red 25 10
1624 **685** 30a. brown 25 10
1625 **685** 40a. green 25 10
1626 **685** 50a. olive 25 20
1627 **685** 1s. violet 50 40
1628 **685** 1s.30 blue 65 50

686 Abba Ahimeir

2002. Political Journalists. Multicoloured.
1630 1s.20 Type **686** 70 50
1631 3s.30 Israel Eldad 1·70 1·30
1632 4s.70 Moshe Beilinson 2·50 2·30
1633 5s.90 Rabbi Binyamin (Yehshua Radler-Feldman) 3·50 3·25

687 Marbles

2002. Stamp Day. Children's Toys. Multicoloured.
1634 2s.20 Type **687** 1·20 95
1635 2s.20 Top 1·20 95
1636 2s.20 Five stones 1·20 95
1637 2s.20 Yo-yo 1·20 95

688 Students

2003. Yeshivot Hahesder (college).
1638 **688** 1s.20 multicoloured 70 60

689 "11 September 2001" (Michael Gross)

2003
1639 **689** 2s.30 multicoloured 1·30 95

690 Glider (1902)

2003. Centenary of Powered Flight. Multicoloured.
1640 2s.30 Type **690** 1·00 75
1641 3s.30 Engine and Wright brothers 1·50 1·00
1642 5s.90 Orville Wright flying *Wright Flier* 2·75 1·70

691 Memorial Monument, Mount Herzl

2003
1643 **691** 4s.70 multicoloured 2·40 2·00

692 Burnt-out Vehicle

2003. Memorial Day.
1644 **692** 1s.20 multicoloured 60 45

693 Opened Box

2003. Greetings Stamps (1st issue). Multicoloured.
1645 (1s.20) Type **693** 80 70
1646 (1s.20) Boy and growing heart 80 70
1647 (1s.20) Married couple 80 70
See also Nos. 1655/7.

694 Ya'akov Meridor

2003. 90th Birth Anniv of Ya'akov Meridor (soldier and politician).
1648 **694** 1s.90 multicoloured 85 70

695 Star of David

2003. Holocaust Memorial Day.
1649 **695** 2s.20 multicoloured 1·00 85

696 Ya'akov Dori

2003. 30th Death Anniv of Ya'akov Dori (Chief of Staff 1948—50).
1650 **696** 2s.20 multicoloured 1·00 85

697 Sheikh Ameen Tarif

2003. 10th Death Anniv of Sheikh Ameen Tarif (Druze (religious sect) leader).
1651 **697** 2s.80 multicoloured 1·20 75

698 Soldier

2003. Jewish Immigration from Yemen, 1881.
1652 **698** 3s.30 multicoloured 1·60 1·30

699 Paper Airplane and Computer Circuit Board

2003. 50th Anniv of Israel Aircraft Industries.
1653 **699** 3s.30 multicoloured 1·60 1·30

700 "55"

2003. 55th Anniv of Israel.
1654 **700** 5s.90 multicoloured 3·00 2·50

2003. Greetings Stamps (2nd issue). As T 693. Multicoloured.
1655 (1s.20) Flowers 80 70
1656 (1s.20) Air balloon 80 70
1657 (1s.20) Boy holding teddy bear 80 70

701 Prague Jewish Community Flag (15th-century)

2003. Development of Israel State Flag. Multicoloured.
1658 1s.90 Type **701** 95 75
1659 2s.30 Ness Ziona (Jewish settlement) (1891) 1·00 85
1660 4s.70 Draft design from *Der Judenstaat* (Theodor Herzl) (1896) 2·00 1·40
1661 5s.90 State flag (1948) 2·75 2·20

702 Coast, Ruined Castle and Houses (Atlit)

2003. Village Centenaries. Multicoloured.
1662 3s.30 Type **702** 1·70 1·40
1663 3s.30 Tractor, crops and houses (Givat-Ada) 1·70 1·40
1664 3s.30 Houses and bungalow amongst trees (Kfar-Saba) 1·70 1·40

703 Olives

2003. Olive Oil Production. Multicoloured.

1665	1s.30 Type **703**	70	60
1666	1s.90 Mill stone and wheel	85	70
1667	2s.30 Oil	1·20	80

704 Teddy Bear and Page of Testimony

2003. 50th Anniv of Vad Yashem (Holocaust remembrance organization). Multicoloured.

1668	2s.20 Type **704**	1·10	80
1669	2s.20 Rail tracks and list of forced labourers	1·10	80

705 Deer and flowers (Karakashian-Balian studio, c.1940)

2003. Armenian Ceramics in Jerusalem. Sheet 120×65 mm containing T 705 and similar circular designs showing ceramic patterns. Multicoloured.

MS1670	2s.30 Type **705**; 3s.30 Bird (Stepan Karakshian, c. 1980); 4s.70 Tree of life (Marie Balian, c. 1990)	8·75	8·75

2003. No value expressed. As T 600. Self-adhesive.

1671	**600**	(1s.30) green and lilac	70	60

706 Yehoshua Hankin

2003. 58th Death Anniv of Yehoshua Hankin (Zionist pioneer).

1672	**706**	6s.20 multicoloured	4·00	3·75

707 Boy riding Bicycle

2003. Philately Day. Children and Wheels. Multicoloured.

1673	1s.30 Type **707**	80	60
1674	1s.30 Girl on roller skates	80	60
1675	1s.30 Girl pushing scooter	80	60
1676	1s.30 Boy on skateboard	80	60

708 Leibowitch Family and Administrative Building, Zikhron Ya'akov

2003. 1st and 2nd Aliya (immigration to Eretz Yisrael). Multicoloured.

1677	2s.10 Type **708** (1st Aliya)	1·50	95
1678	6s.20 Young men (2nd Aliya)	3·50	2·30

709 Aharon David Gordon

2003. Personalities. Multicoloured.

1679	3s.30 Type **709** (land purchase pioneer) (81st death anniv)	2·50	1·70
1680	4s.90 Emile Habiby (writer) (82nd death anniv)	3·50	2·50

710 Two-banded Anemonefish (*Amphirion Bicinctus*)

2003. Fish. Multicoloured.

1681	1s.30 Type **710**	70	50
1682	1s.30 Butterfly perch (*Pseudanthias squamipinnis*)	70	50
1683	1s.30 *Pseudochromis fridmani*	70	50
1684	1s.30 Crown butterflyfish (*Chaetodon paucifasciatus*)	70	50
MS1685	118×77 mm. Nos. 1681/4	3·00	3·00

2004. Historians. As T 674. Multicoloured.

1686	2s.40 Emanuel Ringelblum	95	80
1687	3s.70 Jacob Talmon	1·50	1·20
1688	6s.20 Jacob Herzog	2·50	1·80

711 Menachem Begin and Building

2004. Menachem Begin Heritage Centre, Jerusalem.

1689	**711**	2s.50 multicoloured	1·10	85

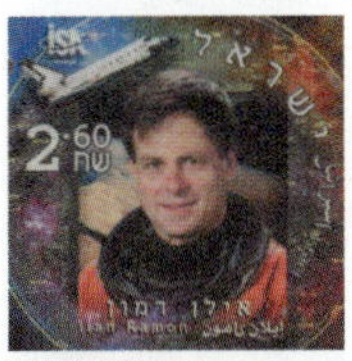

712 Ilan Ramon

2004. 1st Death Anniv of Ilan Ramon (astronaut on Columbia Space Shuttle).

1690	**712**	2s.60 multicoloured	1·10	85

713 Memorial Garden, Mount Herzl

2004. Memorial Day.

1691	**713**	1s.30 multicoloured	55	45

714 Saraya Clock Tower, Safed

2004. Ottoman Clock Towers.

1692	1s.30 Type **714**	45	30
1693	1s.30 Khan El-Umdan, Acre	45	30
1694	1s.30 El-Jarina Mosque, Haifa	45	30
1695	1s.30 Jaffa Gate, Jerusalem	45	30
1696	1s.30 Clock Square, Jaffa	45	30
1697	3s.10 No. 1692	90	55
1698	3s.70 No. 1693	1·10	70
1699	5s.20 No. 1694	1·50	95
1700	5s.50 No. 1695	1·60	1·10
1701	7s. No. 1696	2·00	1·40

715 Football and Israel—USA Match, 1948

2004. Centenary of FIFA (Federation Internationale de Football Association).

1702	**715**	2s.10 multicoloured	75	55

716 Football

2004. 50th Anniv of UEFA (Union of European Football Associations).

1703	**716**	6s.20 multicoloured	2·10	1·90

717 Candlestick, Ornamental Panel and Synagogue Facade

2004. Centenary of the Great Synagogue, Rome. Multicoloured.

1704	2s.10 Type **717**	75	55
1705	2s.10 Synagogue (different)	75	55

Stamps of the same design were issued by Italy.

718 Judo and Israeli Silver Medal (Barcelona, 1992)

2004. Olympic Games 2004, Athens. Multicoloured.

1706	1s.50 Type **718**	55	40
1707	2s.40 Wind surfing and Israeli bronze medal (Atlanta, 1996)	75	55
1708	6s.90 Kayaking and Israeli bronze medal (Sydney, 2000)	2·10	1·50

719 Theodor Herzl

2004. Death Centenary of Theodor Herzl (writer and Zionist pioneer).

1709	**719**	2s.50 multicoloured	85	65

A stamp of the same design was issued by Austria.

720 Anniversary Emblem

2004. 50th Anniv of National Insurance Institute.

1710	**720**	7s. multicoloured	2·30	1·90

721 Ear of Corn

2004. Bread. Multicoloured.

1711	1s.50 Type **721**	60	45
1712	2s.40 Grinding stones	80	60
1713	2s.70 Bread in oven	90	70

722 Building Facade and Test Tubes

2004. Centenary (2005) of Herzliya Hebrew High School.

1714	**722**	2s.20 multicoloured	75	55

723 Parachutist

2004. Children's Adventure Stories. Illustrations from book covers. Multicoloured.

1715	2s.20 Type **723** ("Eight on the Trail of One" by Yemima Avidar-Tchernovitz)	55	40
1716	2s.50 Children and donkey ("Hasamba" by Igal Mossinsohn)	1·00	55
1717	2s.60 Faces ("Our Gang" by Pucho)	1·10	60

724 Building and David Ben-Gurion

2004. Ben-Gurion Heritage Institute.

1718	**724**	2s.50 multicoloured	65	45

725 Airport Buildings

2004. Ben Gurion Airport.

1719	**725**	2s.70 multicoloured	90	65

726 Post Woman and Envelope

2004. Telabul 2004 International Stamp Exhibition, Tel Aviv. Design a Stamp Competition Winner.

1720	**726**	1s.30 multicoloured	45	25

727 Ottoman Period Austrian Mailbox

2004. Stamp Day. Mailboxes. Multicoloured.

1721	2s.10 Type **727**	50	30
1722	2s.20 British Mandate period	55	35
1723	3s.30 Modern	1·70	1·30

728 "20, 50, 100, 200"

2004. 50th Anniv of Bank of Israel.

1724	**728**	6s.20 multicoloured	2·10	1·50

729 Brown Bear

2005. Biblical Animals. Multicoloured.

1725	1s.30 Type **729**	35	25
1726	1s.30 Ostrich	35	25
1727	2s.20 Nile crocodile	65	45
1728	2s.20 Wolf	65	45
MS1729	110×72 mm. 1s.30 No. 1726; 2s.10 Type **729**; 2s.30 No. 1728; 2s.80 No. 1727	4·75	4·75

730 Tunnel and Spoon

2005. Ancient Water Systems. Multicoloured.

1730	2s.10 Type **730** (Hazor) (9th—8th century BC)	55	35
1731	2s.20 Top of shaft (Megiddo) (10th century)	65	45
1732	3s.30 Aqueduct (Caesarea) (BC)	1·70	1·30
1733	6s.20 Tunnel and pool (Hezekiah's Tunnel) (8th century)	2·10	1·50

731 Last of Kin Monument (Micha Ullman)

2005. Memorial Day.

1734	**731**	1s.50 multicoloured	45	30

732 Hebrew Kindergarten, Rishon Le-Zion

2005. Educational Institutions. Multicoloured.

1735	2s.10 Type **732**	55	35
1736	6s.20 Lemel Elementary School, Jerusalem	2·10	1·50

733 University Buildings

2005. 50th Anniv of Bar-Ilan University.

1737	**733**	2s.20 multicoloured	65	45

734 Family and Soldiers

2005. National Reserve Force.

1738	**734**	2s.20 multicoloured	65	45

735 Jewish Partisans

2005. 60th Anniv of End of World War II. Multicoloured.

1739	3s.30 Type **735**	1·20	80
1740	3s.30 Jewish soldiers with Allied Forces	1·20	80

736 Pope John Paul II

2005. Pope John Paul II Commemoration.

1741	**736**	3s.30 multicoloured	1·20	80

737 Emblem

2005. Maccabiah 2005 Sports Festival.

1742	**737**	3s.30 multicoloured	1·20	80

738 Gagea Commutate

2005. No value expressed. Ordinary or self-adhesive gum.

1743	**738**	(1s.30) multicoloured	35	25
1743a	**738**	(1s.50) multicoloured	35	20

739 "Agrippas Street" (Arie Aroch)

2005. Art. Multicoloured.

1744	2s.20 Type **739**	65	45
1745	4s.90 "Tablets of the Covenant" (Moshe Castel)	1·60	1·20
1746	6s.20 "The Rift in Time" (Moshe Kupferman)	2·10	1·50

740 Maimonides as Eagle and Map of Mediterranean

2005. 800th Death Anniv of Maimonides (Rabbi Moses Ben Maimon) (Jewish scholar).

1747	**740**	8s.20 multicoloured	2·75	2·10

741 Sack of Grain (Order of Zeraim)

2005. Mishnah (laws). Multicoloured.

1748	1s.30 Type **741**	35	25
1749	2s.10 Zodiac and wine goblet (Order of Moed)	55	35
1750	2s.30 Two rings (Order of Nashim)	65	50

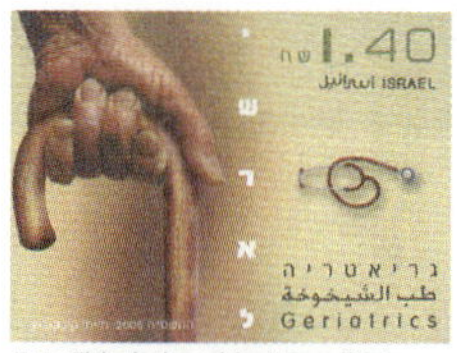

742 Elderly hand holding Stick and Stethoscope (geriatrics)

2005. Medicine. Multicoloured.

1751	1s.40 Type **742**	40	30
1752	2s.20 Wheelchair user and dumb-bell (rehabilitation)	65	45
1753	2s.20 Child holding teddy bear and thermometer (paediatrics)	65	45
1754	6s.20 Bi-coloured face and tablet (mental health)	2·10	1·50

743 Yitzhak Rabin

2005. Yitzhak Rabin Centre.

1755	**743**	2s.20 multicoloured	65	45

744 Albert Einstein

2005. International Year of Physics. Centenary of Publication of "Special Theory of Relativity" by Albert Einstein.

1756	**744**	3s.30 multicoloured	1·20	80

745 Wall

2005. Priestly Blessing.

1757	**745**	6s.20 multicoloured	2·10	1·50

746 Israeli and German Flags

2005. 40th Anniv of Diplomatic Relations with Germany.

1758	**746**	2s.20 multicoloured	65	45

A stamp of the same design was issued by Germany.

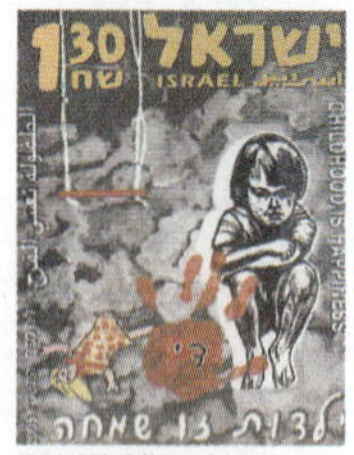

747 "Childhood is Happiness" (Lya Kasif)

2005. International Convention on the Rights of the Child. Winning Designs in Children's Painting Competition. Multicoloured.

1759	1s.30 Type **747**	35	25
1760	1s.30 "A Warm Home" (Menahem Mendel Albo)	35	25
1761	1s.30 "Indifference Hurts" (Irina Rogozinsky)	35	25

748 Moshe Halevy (director)

2005. Theatre Personalities. Multicoloured.

1762	2s.20 Type **748**	65	45
1763	2s.20 Joeseph Millo (actor and director)	65	45
1764	6s.20 Shai K Ophir (Isaiah Goldstein) (actor and director)	2·10	1·50
1765	6s.20 Nissim Aloni (playwright and director)	2·10	1·50

2005. Stamp Day. International Year of Physics. Sheet 84×59 mm.

MS1766	**744**	8s.20 multicoloured	5·00	5·00

749 Symbols of Industry

2005. 85th Anniv of Manufacturers' Association.

1767	**749**	1s.50 multicoloured	45	35

750 Emblem

2006. Inauguration of Israel Post Ltd (1 March 2006).

1768	**750**	1s.50 multicoloured	45	35

751 "Desert Bloom" (Yael Bildner)

2006. Winning Designs in Jewish–American Children's Design-a-Stamp Competition. Multicoloured.

1769	1s.50 Type **751**	45	35
1770	2s.40 "Harmony" (Michela Janower)	70	55
1771	3s.60 "Together in Israel" (Jessica Deautsch)	1·30	90
1772	7s.40 "Colours in Israel" (Marissa Galin)	2·50	1·80

752 Rebbe

2006. Chabad–Lubavitch Chassism (religious movement).

1773	**752**	2s.50 multicoloured	75	60

753 Ezer Weizman

2006. 1st Death Anniv of Ezer Weizman (president 1993–2000).

1774	**753**	7s.40 multicoloured	2·50	1·80

754 Latrun Memorial

2006. Memorial Day.

1775	**754**	1s.50 multicoloured	45	35

755 Aquilegia

2006. Flowers. Multicoloured.

1776	1s.50 Type **755**	45	35
1777	1s.50 Tulip	45	35

756 Uranus

2006. Solar System. Jerusalem 2006 National Stamp Exhibition. Multicoloured. Ordinary or self adhesive gum.

1778	2s.50 Type **756**	75	60
1779	2s.50 Saturn	75	60
1780	2s.50 Jupiter	75	60
1781	2s.50 Neptune and Pluto	75	60
1782	2s.50 Earth and Mars	75	60
1783	2s.50 Mercury and Venus	75	60

757 Symbols of Art and Science

2006. 50th Anniv of Tel Aviv University.

1790	**757**	3s.60 multicoloured	1·30	90

758 Postal Emblem

2006. Israeli Post. Sheet 92×67 mm. Imperf.

MS1791	**758** 5s.90 multicoloured	3·00	3·00

759 Mosaic

2006. 3rd-century Mosaic, Megiddo. Jerusalem 2006 National Stamp Exhibition. Sheet 62×74 mm.

MS1792	**759** 10s. multicoloured	6·00	6·00

760 Jacob Saul Eliachar

2006. Rabbis. Multicoloured.

1793	1s.50 Type **760**	45	35
1794	2s.20 Samuel Salant	65	45
1795	2s.40 Jacob Meir	70	55

761 Moroccan Khamsa

2006. Khamsa (protective amulets). Multicoloured.

1796	1s.50 Type **761**	45	35
1797	2s.50 Tunisian	75	60
1798	7s.40 Iranian	2·50	1·80

762 Rabbis, Children and Star of David

2006. Centenary of Religious Zionist Education.

1799	**762**	3s.60 multicoloured	1·30	90

2006. Mishnah (laws). As T 741. Multicoloured.

1800	1s.50 Bull (Order of Nezikin)	45	35
1801	2s.20 Pigeon (Order of Kodashim)	65	45
1802	2s.40 Hand washing vessel (Order of Tohorot)	70	55

763 Man on Wheel

2006. Centenary of Bezalel Academy of Arts and Design.

1803	**763**	2s.50 emerald	75	60
1804	**763**	2s.50 ultramarine	75	60
1805	**763**	2s.50 orange	75	60

764 Abba Eban

2006. Abba Eban (politician and diplomat) Commemoration.

1806	**764**	7s.30 multicoloured	2·75	2·00

765 *Coriandrum sativum*

2006. Medicinal Plants. Multicoloured.

1807	1s.50 Type **765**	50	40
1808	2s.50 *Micromeria fructicosa*	85	65
1809	3s.30 *Mentha piperita*	1·30	90

766 Oriental Style Fabric, 1882—1948

2006. Fashion in Israel. Designs showing fabric. Multicoloured.

1810	1s.50 Type **766**	50	40
1811	2s.50 Ethnic style, 1948—73	85	65
1812	3s.30 International style, 1973—90	1·30	90
1813	7s.30 Technological style, 1990—2006	2·75	2·20

767 Atlit

2006. Crusader Sites in Israel. Multicoloured.

1814	2s.50 Type **767**	85	65
1815	2s.50 Caesarea	85	65
1816	2s.50 Montfort	85	65
1817	2s.50 Belvoir	85	65

768 Lazarus Ludwig Zamenhof (creator)

2006. 120th Anniv of Esperanto (international constructed language).

1818	**768**	3s.30 multicoloured	1·00	90

769 Ma Pit'om

2007. 40th Anniv of Educational Television. Multicoloured. Ordinary or self-adhesive gum.

1819	2s.50 Type **769**	85	65
1820	2s.50 Krovim	65	65
1821	2s.50 No Secrets	65	65

770 Negev

2007. Development of Negev and Galilee. Multicoloured.

1825	2s.50 Type **770**	85	65
1826	3s.30 Galilee	1·30	90

771 Physical Education in Schools

2007. Physical Education and Sport in Israel. Multicoloured.

1827	2s.90 Type **771**	1·00	80
1828	3s.00 Wingate Institute for Sport	1·10	85
1829	7s.30 Sport for All	2·75	2·20

772 Givati Brigade Memorial

2007. Memorial Day.

1830	**772**	1s.50 multicoloured	50	40

773 Founding Members

2007. 120th Anniv of Neve-Tzedek. Sheet 125×72 mm containing T 773 and similar vert designs. Multicoloured.

MS1831	2s.20 Type **773**; 3s.30 Neve-Tzedek; 5s.80 Intellectuals	6·00	6·00

774 Scouts

2007. Centenary of Scouting.

1832	**774**	2s.50 multicoloured	85	65

775 Sederot (southern Israel)

2007. Urban Development in Israel. Multicoloured.

1833	2s.50 Type **775**	85	65
1834	3s.30 Aqiva (central Israel)	1·30	90
1835	7s.30 Migdal Ha'emeq (northern Israel)	2·75	2·20

776 Circle of Stylized Figures

2007. 40th Anniv of Reunification of Jerusalem.
1836 **776** 1s.50 multicoloured 50 40

777 Figure and Jigsaw

2007. Volunteer Organizations.
1837 **777** 1s.50 multicoloured 50 40

778 Ballet Dancers

2007. Dance. Multicoloured.
1838 2s.20 Type **778** 70 50
1839 2s.20 Ethnic 70 50
1840 2s.20 Folk 70 50
1841 2s.20 Modern 70 50

779 Prison Officers

2007. National Prison Service.
1842 **779** 2s.50 multicoloured 85 65

780 Dining Hall, Knights Hospitaller's Compound, Acre

2007. UNESCO World Heritage Sites. Multicoloured.
1843 3s.30 Type **780** 1·30 90
1844 5s. Zina Dizengoff Circle, Tel Aviv 1·50 1·10
1845 5s.80 Mosaic floor, Western Palace, Masada 2·00 1·50

781 Beach and 'Israel' (in Hebrew)

2007. Personalised Stamp. No value expressed.
1846 **781** (1s.50) multicoloured 50 40

782 Jael (killed Sisera to deliver Israel from the troops of King Jabin.)

2007. Women from the Bible. Multicoloured.
1847 1s.50 Type **782** 50 40
1848 2s.20 Esther (risked her life to save her adoptive father and the Jewish people) 70 50
1849 2s.40 Miriam (sister of Moses) 80 60

783 Horsemen

2007. Centenary of Hashomer (The Watchmen) (early Jewish defence organization).
1850 **783** 3s.30 multicoloured 1·20 90

784 Soldiers and Reservists

2007. National Reserve Force.
1851 **784** 7s.30 multicoloured 2·75 2·20

785 Rabbi Chalom Messas

2007. Rabbi Chalom Messas (Moroccan Jewish Halachic scholar) Commemoration.
1852 **785** 7s.30 multicoloured 2·75 2·20

786 Zina Dizengff Circle (As No. 1844)

2007. Centenary (2009) of Tel Aviv. Sheet 96×70.
MS1853 10s. multicoloured 6·00 6·00

787 Bay Leaves

2007. Herbs. Multicoloured.
1854 1s.55 Type **786** 50 40
1855 2s.25 Wild thyme 75 55

788 Mother and Child

2007. Family Love
1856 1s.55 Type **788** 50 40
1857 2s.25 Brother and sister 70 50
1858 3s.55 Father and child 1·40 1·00

789 Otter, Catfish and Cranes

2007. Hula Nature Reserve. Multicoloured. Ordinary or self-adhesive gum.
1859 2s.25 Type **789** 70 50
1860 2s.25 Terrapins, iris and pelicans 70 50
1861 2s.25 Water buffalo, duck, warbler and jungle cat 70 50

Nos. 1859/61 were issued together, se-tenant, forming a composite design.

790 Dove

2007. Noah's Ark. Sheet 159×93 mm containing T 790 and similar horiz designs. Multicoloured.
MS1865 2s.25×6, Type **790**; Noah, family, Ark and animals; Elephants; Peacocks, bears and tiger; Lions and wolves; Wolf, leopards and kangaroos 6·75 6·75

The stamps and margins of **MS**1865 form a composite design of the Ark and animals on dry land.

791 1927 Western Electric Projector, Pianist and Screen showing *The Jazz Singer*

2007. Stamp Day. Israeli Cinema. Multicoloured.
1866 4s.50 Type **791** 1·50 1·10
1867 4s.60 1937 BTH projector and wide-screen showing *The Robe* 1·50 1·10

792 Rabbi Itzhak Kaduri

2007. Rabbi Itzhak Kaduri Commemoration.
1868 **792** 8s.15 multicoloured 3·00 2·40

793 Israel Rokach

2008. Israel Rokach (mayor of Tel Aviv 1936–1953) Commemoration.
1869 **793** 2s.25 multicoloured 70 50

794 'Shema Servant of Jeroboam' Seal and Tel Hazor ('The Biblical Tels')

2008. World Heritage Sites. Multicoloured.
1870 2s.25 Type **794** 70 50
1871 3s.40 Camel figurine and Nabatean temple ('The Incense Route') 1·30 90

795 Members of Ahuzat-Bayit Association

2008. Ahuzat-Bayit Land Lottery (the founding of Tel Aviv).
1872 **795** 4s.50 multicoloured 1·50 1·20

796 Barbed Wire becoming Flowers

2008. International Holocaust Remembrance Day.
1873 **796** 4s.60 multicoloured 1·50 1·20

797 Symbols of Water

2008. 70th Anniv of Mekorot–National Water System.
1874 **797** 5s.80 multicoloured 2·00 1·50

798 Akiva Weiss

2008. 140th Birth Anniv of Akiva Aryeh Weiss (chairman of Ahuzat–Bayit association).
1875 **798** 8s.15 multicoloured 3·00 2·40

799 Fireworks and Emblem

2008. 60th Anniv of Independence.
1876 **799** 1s.55 multicoloured 50 40

800 Srulik (created by Dosh (cartoonist))

2008. The Israeli. Multicoloured. Ordinary or self-adhesive gum.
1877 (1s.55) Type **800** 50 40

801 Hemerocallis Flower

2008. Memorial Day.

1879	**801**	1s.55 multicoloured	50	40

802 Women and Corn (Paul Kor) (1952)

2008. Independence Day Posters. Multicoloured.

1880	2s.55 Type **802**	85	65
1881	2s.55 Heart as Landscape (Hila Biran) (2006)	85	65
1882	2s.55 Boy watering flowers (Amram Prat) (1965)	85	65
1883	2s.55 Star of David as ship containing immigrants (Assaf Berg) (1989)	85	65
1884	2s.55 Lions supporting tulips as menorah (Kopel Gurwin) (1968)	85	65
1885	2s.55 Landscape with steeples, mosques, synagogues and water towers (Assaf Berg) (1979)	85	65

803 Israeli Flag and World Map as Clasped Hands

2008. 50th Anniv of Export Institute.

1886	**803**	2s.80 multicoloured	1·00	80

804 Rose

2008. Flowers. Multicoloured.

1887	1s.55 Type **804**	50	40
1888	1s.55 *Cyclamen persicum*	50	40

Nos. 1887/8 were impregnated with floral scent.

805 Emblem

2008. 120th Anniv of 'Hatikva' (hope) (song now national anthem). Sheet 140×85 mm.

MS1889 multicoloured	7·25	7·25

806 Girl with Telescope (Israel's 60th) (Daniel Hazan)

2008. 60th Anniv of Independence. Children's Drawings. Multicoloured.

1890	2s.25 Type **806**	70	50
1891	2s.25 Script (Israel is my Home) (Yuval Sulema and Eden Vilker)	70	50
1892	2s.25 House and script (I Love Israel) (Etai Epstein)	70	50

2008. Hula Nature Reserve. Children's self-adhesive stamps. As Type 789. Multicoloured.

1892a	2s.25 As No. 1861 (water buffalo)	70	50
1892b	2s.25 As No. 1859 (otter)	70	50
1892c	2s.25 As No. 1860 (terrapins)	70	50

2008. Noah's Ark. Children's self-adhesive stamps. As Type 790. Multicoloured.

1892d	2s.25 As Type **790**	70	50
1892e	2s.25 Noah, family, Ark and animals	70	50
1892f	2s.25 Elephants	70	50
1892g	2s.25 Peacocks, bears and tiger	70	50
1892h	2s.25 Lions and wolves	70	50
1892i	2s.25 Wolf, leopards and kangaroos	70	50

807 First Concert

2008. Centenary of Tel-Aviv (2009). Sheet 150×85 mm containing T 807 and similar horiz designs showing drawings of Ahuzat Bayit (Tel-Aviv) by Nahum Gutman.

MS1893 3s.50 Type **807**; 4s.50 First Lamp Post; 5s.50 Dr Hisin (physician) riding his donkey	8·50	8·50

808 Circle of Stylized Figures (As Type **776**)

2008. Jerusalem of Gold (song by Naomi Shemer). Sheet 110×70 mm.

MS1894 multicoloured	11·00	11·00

809 Seashore, Neve Dekalim, Greenhouses, Tomatoes and Children

2008. Gush Katif.

1895	**809**	1s.55 multicoloured	50	40

810 Swimming

2008. Olympic Games, Beijing. Multicoloured.

1896	1s.55 Type **810**	50	40
1897	1s.55 Rhythmic gymnastics	50	40
1898	2s.25 Tennis	70	50
1899	2s.25 Sailing, Laser Radial	70	50

811 Capernaum-Tabgha Promenade, Sea of Galilee

2008. Promenades. Multicoloured.

1900	4s.50 Type **811**	1·50	1·10
1901	4s.60 Armon Hanatziv Promenade, Jerusalem	1·50	1·10
1902	8s.15 Rishom Promenade, Netanya	3·00	2·40

812 *Artemisia arborescens*

2008. Herbs. Multicoloured. (a) Ordinary gum.

1903	1s.60 Type **812**	55	45
1904	(2s.90) *Salvia fruticosa*	1·10	85

(b) Size 24×18 mm. Self-adhesive.

1905	(2s.90) As No. 1904	1·10	85

813 Aden

2008. Torah Crowns. Designs showing crowns. Multicoloured.

1906	1s.60 Type **813**	55	45
1907	3s.80 Turkey	1·50	1·10
1908	3s.80 Poland	1·50	1·10

814 Rabbi Samuel Mohilewer

2008. Pioneers of Zionism. Multicoloured.

1909	2s.30 Type **814**	75	55
1910	8s.50 Rabbi Zevi Hirsch Kalischer	3·25	2·50

815 Air France DC3, Envelope and Haifa

2008. 60th Anniv of France—Israel Relations. 60th Anniv of First Flight from Israel to France. Multicoloured.

1911	1s.60 Type **1765**	55	45
1912	3s.80 Paris, envelope and aircraft	1·50	1·10

Stamps of a similar design were issued by France.

816 Families and Calculations

2008. 2008 Census.

1913	**816**	1s.60 multicoloured	55	45

817 Bar Kokhba Letter

2008. Stamp Day. Ancient Letters. Multicoloured.

1914	1s.60 Type **817**	55	45
1915	2s.30 Lachish letter	75	55
1916	8s.50 Letter from Ugarit	3·25	2·50

818 Microphone

2008. 50th (2010) Anniv of Galei Zahal (IDF Broadcasting Service).

1917	**818**	2s.30 multicoloured	75	55

819 Young People enclosed in Frame

2008. Taglit–Birthright Israel (young adults educational tour of Israel).

1918	**819**	5s.60 multicoloured	2·00	1·50

819a Menorah

2009. Menorah. Self-adhesive.

1918a	**819a**	30a. olive-brown	25	15
1918b	**819a**	50a. brown-olive	45	35
1918c	**819a**	1s. deep reddish violet	90	70

See also Nos. 1623 etc.

820 Grapes

2009. Fruit. No Value Expressed. Multicoloured.

1919	(1s.60) Type **820**	55	45
1920	(1s.60) Lemon	55	45
1921	(1s.60) Avocado	55	45
1922	(1s.60) Orange	55	45
1923	(1s.60) Pomegranate	55	45

821 Coastal Scenes

2009. Centenary of Tel Aviv. Multicoloured.

1924	1s.60 Type **821**	55	45
1925	2s.30 White City (World Heritage Site of Bauhaus style buildings)	75	55
1926	3s.80 Parks and gardens	1·50	1·10

822 Mountain Biking

2009. Extreme Sports. Multicloured.

1927	4s.40 Type **822**	1·60	1·30
1928	5s.40 Sky diving	2·00	1·60
1929	5s.60 Surfing	2·30	1·80

2009. Children's Sheets. Eight sheets, each 148×200 mm containing various vert designs.

MS1929a As No. 1645 (open box)	1·00	1·00

MS1929b As No. 1646 (boy growing heart) 1·00 1·00
MS1929c As No. 1655 (flowers) 1·00 1·00
MS1929d As No. 1656 (air balloon) 1·00 1·00
MS1929e As No. 1657 (boy and teddy) 1·00 1·00
MS1929f As No. 1846 (Israel written in sand) 1·00 1·00
MS1929g As No. 1887 (rose) 1·00 1·00
MS1929h As No. 1888 (cyclamen) 1·00 1·00

823 Yossi Banai

2009. Israeli Music. Multicoloured.
1930 1s.60 Type **823** 8·75 6·50
1931 1s.60 Meir Ariel 8·75 6·50
1932 1s.60 Sasha Argov 8·75 6·50
1933 1s.60 Zohar Argov 8·75 6·50
1934 1s.60 Naomi Shemer 8·75 6·50
1935 1s.60 Yair Rosenblum 8·75 6·50
1936 1s.60 Ehud Manor 8·75 6·50
1937 1s.60 Arik Lavie 8·75 6·50
1938 1s.60 Uzi Hitman 8·75 6·50
1939 1s.60 Ofra Hazi 8·75 6·50
1940 1s.60 Moshe Wilensky 8·75 6·50
1941 1s.60 Shoshana Damari 8·75 6·50

Nos. 1930/3 and 1936/9 were printed se-tenant, each strip or pair sharing a composite background design, surrounding a block of four stamp size labels, each showing part of a disc.

824 Jacob's Staff (tool for mapping stars invented by Gersonides)

2009. Astronomy. Multicoloured.
1942 2s.30 Type **824** 1·20 90
1943 3s.80 Gravitational Lensing 2·10 1·60
1944 8s.50 Laser Interferometer Space Antenna 4·75 3·50

825 Memorial Day Badge

2009. Memorial Day.
1945 **825** 1s.60 multicoloured 1·00 75

826 *Berek Joselewicz* (Juliusz Kossak)

2009. Polish Year in Israel. Sheet 70×90 mm.
MS1946 multicoloured 3·25 3·25

827 Heart

2009. Love. No value expressed.
1947 **827** (1s.60) multicoloured 1·60 1·20

No. 1947 was originally on sale for 1s.60.

828 Floating Tourist and Ibex

2009. Dead Sea–Lowest Place on Earth.
1948 **828** 2s.30 multicoloured 1·30 1·00

829 Globe as Kettle

2009. Global Warming. Multicoloured.
1949 2s.30 Type **829** 1·20 90
1950 2s.30 Globe melting in frypan (61×31 mm) 1·20 90
1951 2s.30 Solar powered house 1·20 90

830 Athletes

2009. 18th Maccabiah (games).
1952 **830** 5s.60 multicoloured 3·00 2·30

831 Harpist

2009. 50th Anniv of International Harp Contest, Israel.
1953 **831** 8s.50 multicoloured 4·50 3·25

2009. Menorah. Self-adhesive.
1953a **819a** 40a. slate-green 1·00 1·00

See also Nos. 1623 etc.

832 Honeybee and Flower

2009. Honey. Multicoloured.
1954 1s.60 Type **832** 1·30 1·00
1955 4s.60 Honeycomb 2·20 1·70
1956 6s.70 Pouring honey 3·50 2·50

833 Woman with Dog

2009. Animal Assisted Therapy. Multicoloured. (a) Ordinary gum.
1957 2s.40 Type **833** 1·30 95
1958 2s.40 Girl with dolphin 1·30 95
1959 2s.40 Girl with horse 1·30 95

(b) Self-adhesive.
1960 2s.40 As Type **833** 1·30 95
1961 2s.40 As No. 1958 1·30 95
1962 2s.40 As No. 1959 1·30 95

834 Instant Messaging Software

2009. Virtual Communication. Multicoloured.
1963 2s.40 Type **834** 1·30 95
1964 5s.30 USB flash drive 2·75 1·80
1965 6s.50 Voice over internet protocol 3·75 2·75

835 Child playing Doctor

2009. 75th Anniv of Leumit Health Fund.
1966 **835** 8s.80 multicoloured 4·50 3·75

836 Stage

2009. Death Centenary of Avram Goldfaden (founder of first Yiddish theatre (1876), Iasi, Romania).
1967 **836** 4s..60 multicoloured 2·20 1·70

837 Jaffa

2009. Stamp Day. Lighthouses. Multicoloured.
1968 4s.60 Type **837** 2·20 1·70
1969 6s.70 Tel Aviv 3·75 2·75
1970 8s.80 Ashdod 4·75 3·50

838 Amphora

2009. Marine Archaeology. Multicoloured.
1971 2s.40 Type **838** 80 60
1972 2s.40 Figurines 80 60
1973 3s.60 Weaponry 1·60 1·20
1974 5s. Anchors 2·30 1·80

2009. Fruit. As T 820. No Value Expressed. Multicoloured. Self-adhesive.
1975 (1s.60) As Type **820** 90 65
1976 (1s.60) Lemon (As No. 1920) 90 65
1977 (1s.60) Avocado (As No. 1921) 90 65
1978 (1s.60) Orange (As No. 1922) 90 65
1979 (1s.60) Pomegranate (As No. 1923) 90 65

839 Date Palm and Peppers

2010. 50th Anniv of Settling the Arava.
1980 **839** 1s.60 multicoloured 5·00 3·75

840 *Carduelis carduelis* (gold finch)

2010. Birds. Multicoloured.
1981 2s.40 Type **840** 1·40 1·10
1982 2s.40 *Upupa epops* (hoopoe) (national bird) 1·40 1·10
1983 2s.40 *Prinia gracilis* (graceful prinia) 1·40 1·10

Nos. 1981/3 were printed, se-tenant, forming a composite design.

841 Child and Dove

2010. 50th Anniv of Lions, Israel.
1984 **841** 4s.60 multicoloured 1·00 75

842 Child's and Camp Inmate's Arms

2010. Holocaust Remembrance Day.
1985 **842** 6s.70 multicoloured 3·75 2·75

843 Gymnasts and Students, Alliance School, Tehran, May 1936

2010. 150th Anniv of Alliance Iraelite Universelle.
1986 **843** 8s.80 multicoloured 5·00 3·75

OFFICIAL STAMPS

בול שרות
(O 18)

1951. As Nos. 41 etc, but colours changed. Optd with Type O 18.
O54 5pr. mauve 25 15
O55 15pr. red 25 15
O56 30pr. blue 40 35
O57 40pr. brown 50 35

POSTAGE DUE STAMPS

דמי דאר
(D 3)

1948. As T 1, optd with Type D 3.
D10 **1** 3m. orange on yellow 3·75 2·50
D11 **1** 5m. green on yellow 5·25 4·00
D12 **1** 10m. mauve on yellow 13·00 9·00
D13 **1** 20m. blue on yellow 38·00 30·00
D14 **1** 50m. brown on yellow £140 £110

D9

1949
D27 **D9** 2pr. orange 35 25
D28 **D9** 5pr. violet 60 35
D29 **D9** 10pr. green 60 25
D30 **D9** 20pr. red 70 25
D31 **D9** 30pr. blue 95 45
D32 **D9** 50pr. brown 1·60 1·40

D30

1952

D73	D30	5pr. brown	15	10
D74	D30	10pr. blue	15	10
D75	D30	20pr. purple	30	15
D76	D30	30pr. black	15	10
D77	D30	40pr. green	15	10
D78	D30	50pr. sepia	15	10
D79	D30	60pr. violet	15	10
D80	D30	100pr. red	30	25
D81	D30	250pr. blue	45	25

Pt. 8

ITALIAN COLONIES

100 centesimi = 1 lira

GENERAL ISSUES

1932. As Garibaldi stamps of Italy, but inscr "POSTE COLONIALI ITALIANE".

1	-	10c. green (postage)	3·75	8·50
2	128	20c. red	3·75	7·50
3	-	25c. green	3·75	7·50
4	128	30c. green	3·75	8·50
5	-	50c. red	3·75	7·50
6	-	75c. red	3·75	13·00
7	-	1l.25 blue	3·75	14·00
8	-	1l.75 +25c. blue	8·50	26·00
9	-	2l.55 +50c. sepia	8·50	37·00
10	-	5l.+1l. blue	8·50	47·00
11	130	50c. red (air)	4·75	13·00
12	-	80c. green	4·75	13·00
13	130	1l.+25c. sepia	8·00	27·00
14	-	2l.+50c. sepia	8·00	27·00
15	-	5l.+1l. sepia	8·00	34·00

1932. Dante stamps of Italy (colours changed) optd COLONIE ITALIANE.

18		10c. slate (postage)	1·10	2·10
19		15c. sepia	1·10	2·10
20		20c. green	1·10	2·10
21		25c. green	1·10	2·10
22		30c. brown	1·10	2·10
23		50c. blue	1·10	1·10
24		75c. red	2·10	3·25
25		1l.25 blue	2·10	6·50
26		1l.75 violet	2·10	10·50
27		2l.75 orange	2·10	21·00
28		5l.+2l. olive	2·10	27·00
29	124	10l.+2l.50 blue	2·10	37·00
30	125	50c. slate (air)	2·10	6·50
31	-	1l. blue	2·10	6·50
32	-	3l. green	3·75	13·00
33	-	5l. sepia	3·75	17·00
34	125	7l.70 +2l. red	3·75	27·00
35	-	10l.+2l.50 orange	3·75	32·00
36	127	100l. sepia and green	22·00	85·00

No. 36 is inscribed instead of overprinted.

9 Ploughing

10 Savoia Marchetti S-55X Flying Boat

1933. 50th Anniv of Foundation of Colony of Eritrea.

37	9	10c. brown (postage)	8·00	13·00
38	-	20c. purple	8·00	13·00
39	-	25c. green	8·00	13·00
40	9	50c. violet	8·00	13·00
41	-	75c. red	8·00	17·00
42	-	1l.25 blue	8·00	19·00
43	9	2l.75 red	16·00	27·00
44	-	5l.+2l. green	27·00	55·00
45	-	10l.+2l. brown	27·00	70·00
46	-	50c. brown (air)	8·00	12·00
47	-	1l. black	8·00	12·00
48	10	3l. red	15·00	24·00
49	10	5l. brown	15·00	24·00
50	-	7l.70+2l. green	21·00	48·00
51	10	10l.+2l.50 blue	21·00	48·00
52	-	50l. violet	21·00	49·00

DESIGNS—VERT: (Postage): 20, 75c., 5l. Camel transport; 25c., 1l.25, 10l. Lioness with star on left shoulder (Arms). HORIZ: (Air): 50c., 1l., 7l. 70, Eagle; 50l. Savoia Marchetti S-55X flying boat over map of Eritrea.

11 Agricultural Implements

13 Macchi Castoldi MC-72 Seaplane

1933. 10th Anniv of Fascist March on Rome. (a) Postage.

53	11	5c. orange	8·00	9·50
54	-	25c. green	8·00	9·50
55	-	50c. violet	8·00	9·50
56	11	75c. red	8·00	16·00
57	-	1l.25 blue	8·00	16·00
58	-	1l.75 red	8·00	16·00
59	11	2l.75 blue	8·00	24·00
60	-	5l. black	14·00	28·00
61	-	10l. blue	14·00	37·00
62	-	25l. olive	22·00	48·00

DESIGNS—HORIZ: 50c., 1l.75, 10l. Tractor. VERT: 25c., 1l.25, 5l. Arab and camel; 25l. Soldier.

(b) Air.

63	13	50c. brown	9·50	12·00
64	-	75c. purple	9·50	12·00
65	13	1l. sepia	9·50	12·00
66	-	3l. green	9·50	27·00
67	13	10l. violet	9·50	27·00
68	-	12l. blue	9·50	37·00
69	-	20l. green	19·00	45·00
70	-	50l. blue	29·00	45·00

DESIGNS—HORIZ: 75c., 3, 12l. Savoia Marchetti S-71 airplane. VERT: 20l. Pilot swinging propeller; 50l. Propeller.

15

1934. 15th Milan Exhibition.

71	15	20c. red	1·30	6·50
72	15	30c. green	1·30	6·50
73	15	50c. black	1·30	6·50
74	15	1l.25 blue	1·30	10·50

16 Hailing Marina Fiat MF.5 Flying Boat

1934. Air. Honouring the Duke of the Abruzzi (explorer).

75	16	25l. black	40·00	£150

17 Scoring a Goal

1934. World Football Championship.

76	17	10c. green (postage)	37·00	43·00
77	17	50c. violet	70·00	43·00
78	17	1l.25 blue	70·00	£110
79	-	5l. brown	90·00	£275
80	-	10l. blue	90·00	£275

DESIGN—VERT: 5, 10l. Fascist salute before kick-off.

18 Marina Fiat MF.5 Flying Boat over Stadium

81	18	50c. brown (air)	20·00	43·00
82	18	75c. purple	20·00	43·00
83	-	5l. black	65·00	90·00
84	-	10l. red	65·00	90·00
85	18	15l. red	65·00	90·00
86	-	25l. green	65·00	£190
87	-	50l. green	65·00	£190

DESIGNS—VERT: 5, 10, 25l. "Saving a goal". HORIZ: 50l. Giant football and Marina Fiat MF.5 flying boat.

EXPRESS STAMPS

1932. Air. As Garibaldi stamps of Italy.

E16	E131	2l.25+1l. blk & vio	8·50	27·00
E17	E131	4l.50+1l.50 grn & brn	8·50	37·00

Pt. 8

ITALIAN EAST AFRICA

Italian Empire in East Africa comprising Eritrea, Ethiopia and Italian Somaliland, constituted by Royal Decree of 1 June 1936. Occupied by British Forces 1942–43 (see BRITISH OCCUPATION OF ITALIAN COLONIES (MIDDLE EAST FORCES) in Volume 1).

100 centesimi = 1 lira.

1 Grant's Gazelle

2 R. Nile Statue and Lake Tsana

1938

1	1	2c. red	1·60	1·60
2	A	5c. brown	1·60	10
3	B	7½c. violet	2·10	4·25
4	2	10c. brown	4·25	10
5	C	15c. green	1·60	85
6	B	20c. red	1·60	10
7	D	25c. green	3·25	10
8	1	30c. brown	2·75	1·10
9	A	35c. blue	3·25	8·50
10	B	50c. violet	1·10	10
11	C	75c. red	3·25	65
12	D	1l. green	2·75	10
13	B	1l.25 blue	3·75	60
14	2	1l.75 orange	32·00	10
15	A	2l. red	3·75	65
16	D	2l.55 brown	18·00	29·00
17	1	3l.70 violet	55·00	48·00
18	C	5l. blue	13·00	4·25
19	A	10l. red	18·00	19·00
20	2	20l. green	34·00	32·00

DESIGN—VERT: A, Italian eagle and Lion of Judah; B, Profile of King Emmanuel III; C, Soldier implanting Fascist emblem. HORIZ: D, Shadows on road.

5 Mussolini Monument and Mt. Amba Aradam

1938. Air.

21	E	25c. green	5·25	4·25
22	5	50c. brown	85·00	10
23	F	60c. red	2·75	10·50
24	E	75c. brown	5·25	3·25
25	G	1l. blue	1·60	10
26	5	1l.50 violet	2·75	1·10
27	F	2l. blue	2·75	2·10
28	E	3l. red	4·25	8·50
29	G	5l. brown	34·00	21·00
30	5	10l. purple	13·00	12·00
31	E	25l. blue	32·00	27·00

DESIGNS—HORIZ: E, Savoia Marchetti S-73 airplane, rock sculpture of eagle and Mt. Amba Aradam; F, Savoia Marchetti S-73 airplane over Lake Tsana. VERT: G, Bateleur.

9 Statue of Augustus

1938. Birth Bimillenary of Augustus the Great.

36	9	5c. brown (postage)	1·10	2·10
37	-	10c. red	1·10	1·60
38	9	25c. green	1·10	1·60
39	-	50c. violet	1·10	1·10
40	9	75c. red	1·10	4·25
41	-	1l.25 blue	1·10	10·50

DESIGN: 10c., 50c., 1l.25, Statue of Goddess of Abundance.

10 Eagle and Serpent

42	10	50c. brown (air)	1·60	3·25
43	10	1l. violet	1·60	5·25

11 Ethiopian Canoe

1940. Naples Exhibition.

44	11	5c. brown (postage)	55	1·10
45	-	10c. orange	55	1·10
46	-	25c. green	1·30	2·10
47	11	50c. violet	1·30	1·10
48	-	75c. red	1·30	4·25
49	-	1l.25 blue	1·30	4·25
50	-	2l.+75c. red	1·60	16·00

DESIGNS—VERT: 10c., 75c., 2l. Soldier; 25c., 1l.25, Allegory of Italian Conquest of Ethiopia.

51	50c. grey (air)	1·10	5·25
52	1l. violet	1·10	5·25
53	2l.+75c. blue	1·60	
54	5l.+2l. brown	1·60	

DESIGNS—VERT: 50c., 2l. Savoia Marchetti S-66 flying boat over tractor. HORIZ: 1l., 5l. Savoia Marchetti S.M.83 airplane over city.

15 Hitler and Mussolini

1941. Axis Commemoration.

55	15	5c. yellow (postage)	1·80	
56	15	10c. brown	1·80	
57	15	20c. black	3·25	
58	15	25c. green	3·25	
59	15	50c. purple	3·25	
60	15	75c. red	3·25	
61	15	1l.25 blue	3·25	
62	15	1l. blue (air)	55·00	
63	15	1l. blue	6·50	

In No. 62 the "1 lira" tablet is in the centre; in No. 63 it is in the lower left corner.

EXPRESS LETTER STAMPS

E7 Plough and Native Huts

1938. Air.

E32	E7	2l. blue	5·25	8·50
E33	E7	2l.50 brown	5·25	13·00

E8 King Victor Emmanuel III

1938

E34	E8	1l.25 green	5·25	6·50
E35	E8	2l.50 red (inscr "EXPRESS")	5·25	17·00

POSTAGE DUE STAMPS

1941. Nos. D395/407 of Italy optd A.O.I.

D64	**D141**	5c. brown	1·10	
D65	**D141**	10c. blue	1·10	
D66	**D141**	20c. red	3·25	
D67	**D141**	25c. green	3·25	
D68	**D141**	30c. orange	6·50	
D69	**D141**	40c. brown	6·50	
D70	**D141**	50c. violet	6·50	
D71	**D141**	60c. blue	10·50	
D72	**D142**	1l. orange	27·00	
D73	**D142**	2l. green	27·00	
D74	**D142**	5l. violet	37·00	
D75	**D142**	10l. blue	27·00	
D76	**D142**	20l. red	27·00	

Pt. 3

ITALIAN OCCUPATION OF CEPHALONIA AND ITHACA

Two of the Greek Ionian Islands off the W. coast of Greece, under Italian occupation in 1941.

100 lepta = 1 drachma.

PRICES. Prices are for unsevered pairs. Single stamps from several pairs are worth 1/3 unused and 1/2 used prices.

1941. Stamps of Greece optd ITALIA Occupazione Militare Italiana isole Cefalonia e Itaca across a pair of stamps. (a) On postage stamps of 1937.

1	**86**	5l. blue and brown	28·00	27·00
2	-	10l. brown and blue	28·00	27·00
3	-	20l. green and black	28·00	27·00
4	-	40l. black and green	28·00	27·00
5	-	50l. black and brown	28·00	27·00
6	-	80l. brown and violet	43·00	38·00
7	**89**	1d. green	£325	£190
8	**89a**	1d.50 green	£200	£120
9	-	2d. blue	34·00	43·00
10	-	5d. red	£100	49·00
11	-	6d. brown	£100	49·00
12	-	7d. brown	£100	49·00
13	**89**	8d. blue	£225	£120
14	-	10d. brown	£100	49·00
15	-	15d. green	£200	95·00
16	-	25d. blue	£225	£140
17	**89a**	30d. red	£1000	£600

(b) On air stamps of 1938 and 1935.

18	**D20**	50l. brown (No. 521)	75·00	£190
19	**79**	1d. red	75·00	£110
20	-	2d. blue	28·00	43·00
21	-	5d. mauve	55·00	75·00
22	-	7d. blue	65·00	£110
23	-	25d. red	£325	£375
24	-	30d. green	£400	£475
25	-	50d. mauve	£2000	£2750
26	-	100d. brown	£1000	£1300

(c) On Charity Tax stamps.

27	**D20**	10l. red (No. C498)	34·00	32·00
28	**C96**	10l. red	45·00	32·00
29	**C96**	50l. green (No. C525)	34·00	27·00
30	**C96**	50l. green (No. C554)	£900	£650
31	**C96**	1d. blue (No. C526)	90·00	60·00

Pt. 3

ITALIAN OCCUPATION OF CORFU

One of the Greek Ionian Islands situated off the coast of Albania temporarily occupied by Italy during a dispute with Greece in 1923. For later Occupation Issues see ITALIAN OCCUPATION OF CORFU AND PAXOS below.

100 centesimi = 1 lira.
100 lepta = 1 drachma.

1923. Stamps of Italy optd CORFU.

1	**37**	5c. green	9·50	9·75
2	**37**	10c. red	9·50	9·75
3	**37**	15c. grey	9·50	9·75
4	**41**	20c. orange	9·50	9·75
5	**39**	30c. brown	9·50	9·75
6	**39**	50c. mauve	9·50	9·75
7	**39**	60c. blue	9·50	9·75
8	**34**	1l. brown and green	9·50	9·75

1923. Stamps of Italy surch CORFU and value.

9	**37**	25l. on 10c. red	£100	43·00
10	**39**	60l. on 25c. blue	28·00	
11	**39**	70l. on 30c. brown	28·00	
12	**39**	1d.20 on 50c. mauve	50·00	43·00
13	**34**	2d.40 on 1l. brown & green	50·00	43·00
14	**34**	4d.75 on 2l. green & orange	22·00	

Pt. 3

ITALIAN OCCUPATION OF CORFU AND PAXOS

Greek Ionian Islands occupied by Italy in 1941.

100 lepta = 1 drachma.

1941. Stamps of Greece optd CORFU. (a) On postage stamps of 1937.

1	**86**	5l. blue and brown	6·75	4·25
2	-	10l. brown and blue	3·25	3·25
4	-	20l. green and black	3·25	3·25
5	-	40l. black and green	3·25	3·25
6	-	50l. black and brown	3·25	3·25
7	-	80l. brown and violet	3·25	6·50
8	**89**	1d. green	11·00	16·00
9	**89a**	1d.50 green	11·00	11·00
10	-	2d. blue	8·50	7·50
11	**89**	3d. brown	8·50	7·50
12	-	5d. red	8·50	7·50
13	-	6d. olive	8·50	7·50
14	-	7d. brown	11·00	7·50
15	**89**	8d. blue	28·00	27·00
16	-	10d. brown	£600	£225
17	-	15d. green	31·00	27·00
18	-	25d. blue	22·00	27·00
19	**89a**	30d. red	£100	£110
20	**89**	100d. red	£350	£225

(b) On air stamps of 1938 and 1935.

22	**D20**	50l. brown (No. 521)	12·50	11·00
23	**79**	1d. red	£800	£300
24	**79**	2d. blue	12·50	7·50
25	**79**	5d. mauve	17·00	13·00
26	**79**	7d. blue	17·00	15·00
27	**79**	10d. brown	£900	£425
28	**79**	10d. orange	80·00	49·00
29	**79**	25d. red	£100	65·00
30	**79**	30d. green	£120	90·00
31	**79**	50d. mauve	£120	80·00
32	**79**	100d. brown	£1200	£800

(c) On Charity Tax stamps of 1939.

33	**C96**	10l. red	3·25	6·50
34	**C96**	50l. green	3·25	6·50
35	**C96**	1d. blue	39·00	35·00

(d) On Postage Due stamps of 1902 and 1913.

D36	**D20**	10l. red	4·50	5·50
D37	**D20**	25l. blue	6·75	5·50
D38	**D20**	80l. purple	£1100	£400
D39	**D20**	1d. blue	£1800	£850
D40	**D20**	2d. red	11·00	16·00
D41	**D20**	5d. blue	25·00	27·00
D42	**D20**	10d. green	22·00	27·00
D43	**D20**	15d. brown	25·00	27·00
D44	**D20**	25d. red	25·00	27·00
D45	**D20**	50d. orange	25·00	27·00
D46	**D20**	100d. green	£650	£550

Pt. 3

ITALIAN OCCUPATION OF IONIAN ISLANDS

A group of islands off the W. coast of Greece, placeed under the protection of Gt. Britain in 1815 and ceded to Greece in 1864. Under Italian occupation in 1941. For use in all islands except Kithyra.

100 lepta = 1 drachma.

1941. Stamps of Italy optd ISOLE JONIE. (a) On postage stamps of 1929.

1	**98**	5c. brown	55	2·75
2	-	10c. brown	55	2·75
3	**99**	20c. red	55	2·75
4	-	25c. green	55	2·75
5	**103**	30c. brown	55	2·75
6	**103**	50c. violet	55	2·75
7	-	75c. red	55	2·75
8	-	1l.25 blue	1·10	5·50

(b) On air stamp of 1930.

9	**110**	50c. brown	1·10	6·50

(c) On Postage Due stamps of 1934.

D10	**D141**	10c. blue	1·50	4·25
D11	**D141**	20c. red	1·50	4·25
D12	**D141**	30c. orange	1·50	4·25
D13	**D142**	1l. orange	1·50	4·25

Pt. 8

ITALIAN POST OFFICES IN CHINA

Italian Military Posts in China, including Peking and Tientsin, now closed.

100 centesimi = 1 lira. 100 cents = 1 dollar.

Stamps of Italy overprinted or surcharged.

A. PEKING

1917. Surch PECHINO and value.

1	**37**	2c. on 5c. green	£225	£150
3	**37**	4c. on 10c. pink	£450	£250
4	**41**	6c. on 15c. grey	£900	£550
5	**41**	8c. on 20c. on 15c. grey	£4500	£2500
6	**41**	8c. on 20c. orange	£7500	£2750
7	**39**	20c. on 50c. violet	£46000	£27000
8	**34**	40c. on 1l. brown and green	£180000	£36000

1917. Optd Pechino.

9	**30**	1c. brown	19·00	19·00
10	**31**	2c. brown	19·00	19·00
11	**37**	5c. green	7·50	16·00
12	**37**	10c. pink	7·50	16·00
13	**41**	20c. orange	£170	£150
14	**39**	25c. blue	7·50	19·00
15	**39**	50c. violet	7·50	21·00
16	**34**	1l. brown and green	16·00	34·00
17	**34**	5l. blue and pink	32·00	48·00
18	**34**	10l. green and pink	£190	£400

1918. Surch Pechino and value.

19	**30**	½c. on 1c. brown	£130	£150
20	**31**	1c. on 2c. brown	6·50	14·00
21	**37**	2c. on 5c. green	6·50	14·00
22	**37**	4c. on 10c. pink	6·50	14·00
23	**41**	8c. on 20c. orange	25·00	24·00
25	**39**	20c. on 50c. violet	14·00	24·00
26	**34**	40c. on 1l. brown and green	£225	£275
27	**34**	2 dollari. on 5l. blue and pink	£375	£700
28	**39**	10c. on 25c. blue	6·50	17·00
30	**34**	2 DOLLARI. on 5l. blue and pink	£86000	£65000

EXPRESS LETTER STAMPS

1917. Express Letter stamp optd Pechino or surch 12 CENTS also.

E19	**E41**	30c. blue and pink	13·50	37·00
E28	**E41**	12c. on 30c. bl & pink	80·00	£250

POSTAGE DUE STAMPS

1917. Postage Due stamps optd Pechino.

D19	**D12**	10c. mauve and orange	4·25	14·00
D20	**D12**	20c. mauve and orange	4·25	14·00
D21	**D12**	30c. mauve and orange	4·25	14·00
D22	**D12**	40c. mauve and orange	12·00	17·00

1918. Surch Pechino and value.

D28	4c. on 10c. mve & orge	£86000	£70000
D29	8c. on 20c. mve & orge	27·00	55·00
D30	12c. on 30c. mve & orge	85·00	£140
D31	16c. on 40c. mve & orge	£325	£600

B. TIENTSIN

1917. Surch TIENTSIN and value.

31	**37**	2c. on 5c. green	£450	£375
32	**37**	4c. on 10c. pink	£800	£475
33	**41**	6c. on 15c. grey	£1700	£1200

Prices for the above are for stamps with surcharge inverted.

1917. Optd Tientsin.

34	**30**	1c. brown	14·00	32·00
35	**31**	2c. brown	14·00	32·00
36	**37**	5c. green	7·00	16·00
37	**37**	10c. pink	7·00	16·00
38	**41**	20c. orange	£150	£180
39	**39**	25c. blue	7·00	21·00
40	**39**	50c. violet	7·00	21·00
41	**34**	1l. brown and green	13·00	32·00
42	**34**	5l. blue and pink	19·00	55·00
43	**34**	10l. green and pink	£170	£400

1918. Surch Tientsin and value.

44	**30**	½c. on 1c. brown	£130	£150
45	**31**	1c. on 2c. brown	6·50	14·00
46	**37**	2c. on 5c. green	6·50	14·00
47	**37**	4c. on 10c. pink	6·50	14·00
48	**41**	8c. on 20c. orange	27·00	27·00
49	**39**	10c. on 25c. blue	14·00	27·00
50	**39**	20c. on 50c. violet	14·00	27·00
51	**34**	40c. on 1l. brown and green	£150	£275
52	**34**	2 Dollari. on 5l. blue and pink	£400	£700
54	**34**	2 dollari. on 5l. blue and pink	£11000	£8500

EXPRESS LETTER STAMPS

1917. Express Letter stamp optd Tientsin or surch 12 CENTS also.

E44	**E41**	30c. blue and pink	14·00	37·00
E53	**E41**	12c. on 30c. blue & pink	85·00	£250

POSTAGE DUE STAMPS

1917. Postage Due stamps optd Tientsin.

D44	**D12**	10c. mauve and orange	4·25	14·00
D45	**D12**	20c. mauve and orange	4·25	14·00
D46	**D12**	30c. mauve and orange	4·25	14·00
D47	**D12**	40c. mauve and orange	12·00	14·00

1918. Surch Tientsin and value.

D53	4c. on 10c. mve & orge	£3250	£4750
D54	8c. on 20c. mve & orge	32·00	65·00
D55	12c. on 30c. mve & orge	£120	£150
D56	16c. on 40c. mve & orge	£450	£600

Pt. 8

ITALIAN POST OFFICES IN CRETE

Italian P.O.s in Crete, now closed.

1900. 40 paras = 1 piastre.
1906. 100 centesimi = 1 lira.

Stamps of Italy surcharged or overprinted.

1900. Surch 1 PIASTRA 1.

1	**27**	1pi. on 25c. blue	13·00	75·00

1901. Surch LA CANEA 1 PIASTRA 1.

2	**33**	1pi. on 25c. blue	6·50	16·00

1906. 1901 stamps optd LA CANEA.

3	**30**	1c. brown	2·50	4·25
4	**31**	2c. brown	2·50	4·25
5	**31**	5c. green	3·25	4·25
6	**33**	10c. red	£225	£160
7	**33**	15c. on 20c. orange	4·25	4·25
8	**33**	25c. blue	12·00	16·00
9	**33**	40c. brown	12·00	16·00
10	**33**	45c. green	12·00	16·00
11	**33**	50c. mauve	12·00	16·00
12	**34**	1l. brown and green	70·00	70·00
13	**34**	5l. blue and pink	£325	£325

1907. 1906 stamps optd LA CANEA.

14	**37**	5c. green	2·10	3·25
15	**37**	10c. red	2·10	3·25
16	**41**	15c. black	5·25	5·25
17	**39**	25c. blue	2·10	10·50
18	**39**	40c. brown	34·00	43·00
19	**39**	50c. violet	6·50	10·50

EXPRESS LETTER STAMP

1906. Express Letter stamp optd LA CANEA.

E1	**E35**	25c. red	8·50	24·00

Pt. 8

ITALIAN POST OFFICES IN THE TURKISH EMPIRE

The following were in use in P.O.s in Alexandria, Assab, La Goletta, Massawa, Susa, Tripoli and Tunis and also at Consular post offices at Buenos Aires and Montevideo.

Currency: Italian and Turkish

Stamps of Italy overprinted and surcharged.

A. GENERAL ISSUES.

1874. 1863 type, slightly altered, optd ESTERO.

1	**4**	1c. green	28·00	39·00
2	**5**	2c. brown	33·00	39·00
3	**6**	5c. grey	£1100	42·00
4	**6**	10c. orange	£2250	85·00
5	**10**	20c. blue	£2000	44·00
6	**6**	30c. brown	6·75	28·00
7	**6**	40c. red	6·75	28·00
8	**6**	60c. mauve	17·00	£170
9	**7**	2l. red	£225	£800
10	**6**	10c. blue	£500	30·00
11	**10**	20c. orange	£8000	28·00

1881. 1879 type, slightly altered, optd ESTERO.

12	**12**	5c. green	22·00	22·00
13	**12**	10c. red	12·00	17·00
14	**12**	20c. orange	12·00	17·00
15	**12**	25c. blue	12·00	22·00
16	**12**	50c. mauve	24·00	£110

B. OFFICES IN TURKISH EMPIRE.

(a) Albania

1902. Surch ALBANIA and value.

18	**31**	10pa. on 5c. green	5·25	4·50
19	**33**	35pa. on 20c. orange	8·00	9·00
20	**33**	40pa. on 25c. blue	18·00	9·00
24	**37**	10pa. on 5c. green	50·00	80·00
25	**37**	20pa. on 10c. red	40·00	39·00
26	**33**	80pa. on 50c. mauve	40·00	39·00

1902. Surch with figures of value repeated twice and currency in words thus, 20 Para 20.

21	**31**	10pa. on 5c. green	11·00	4·50

22	**33**	35pa. on 20c. orange	7·00	6·75
23	**33**	40pa. on 25c. blue	36·00	16·00
27	**37**	10pa. on 5c. green	3·50	5·50
28	**37**	20pa. on 10c. red	5·50	5·50
29	**33**	80pa. on 50c. mauve	80·00	60·00

(b) General Offices in Europe and Asia

1908. Surch with figures of value repeated twice and currency in words thus, 30 Para 30.

30	**39**	40pa. on 25c. blue	4·25	4·50
31	**39**	80pa. on 50c. mauve	7·00	5·50
32	**41**	30pa. on 15c. grey	3·25	5·50

EXPRESS LETTER STAMPS

1908. Express Letter stamps surch LEVANTE and new value.

E33	**E35**	1pi. on 25c. red	3·75	5·50
E34	**E41**	60pa. on 30c. blue & red	6·50	7·75

C. INDIVIDUAL OFFICES IN EUROPE AND ASIA.

(a) Constantinople.

1908. Surch in one line with figure of value and currency in words.

40	**37**	10pa. on 5c. green	13·50	18·00
41	**37**	20pa. on 10c. pink	13·50	18·00
43	**39**	1pi. on 25c. blue	13·50	20·00
44	**39**	2pi. on 50c. mauve	90·00	90·00
45	**34**	4pi. on 1l. brown and green	£1200	£1100
46	**34**	20pi. on 5l. blue and pink	£5500	£3250
47	**41**	30pa. on 15c. grey	9·00	11·00

1908. Surch in two lines with figures of value repeated twice and currency in words.

48	**34**	4pi. on 1l. brown and green	65·00	£110
51	**34**	20pi. on 5l. blue and pink	60·00	95·00

1909. Surch Costantinopoli (10pa. to 2pi.) or COSTANTINOPOLI (4 to 40pi.) and value in figures twice repeated and currency in words.

52	**37**	10pa. on 5c. green	2·75	3·25
53	**37**	20pa. on 10c. pink	2·75	3·25
54	**41**	30pa. on 15c. grey	2·75	3·25
55	**39**	1pi. on 25c. blue	2·75	3·25
56	**39**	2pi. on 50c. mauve	3·50	5·50
57	**34**	4pi. on 1l. brown and green	4·50	5·50
58	**34**	20pi. on 5l. blue and pink	70·00	65·00
59	**34**	40pi. on 10l. green and pink	6·75	39·00

1921. Surch with value in figures and currency in words thus, 4 PIASTRE.

60	**37**	1pi. on 5c. green	£170	£425
61	**37**	2pi. on 15c. grey	8·25	17·00
62	**41**	4pi. on 20c. orange	70·00	90·00
63	**39**	5pi. on 25c. blue	70·00	90·00
64	**39**	10pi. on 60c. red	3·25	11·00

1921. Surch with value in figures and currency in words thus, PARA 20.

65	**30**	10pa. on 1c. brown	2·75	4·50
66	**31**	20pa. on 2c. brown	2·75	4·50
67	**37**	30pa. on 5c. green	5·25	7·75
68	**37**	1pi. 20 on 15c. grey	9·00	4·50
69	**41**	3pi. on 20c. orange	11·00	24·00
70	**39**	3pi. 30 on 25c. blue	4·50	4·50
71	**39**	7pi. 20 on 60c. red	7·75	7·75
72	**34**	15pi. on 1l. brown and green	36·00	60·00

1922. Surch COSTANTINOPOLI and value in figures once only after currency in words.

73	**37**	20pa. on 5c. green	20·00	39·00
74	**37**	1pi. 20 on 15c. grey	2·75	4·50
75	**39**	3pi. on 30c. brown	2·75	4·50
76	**39**	3pi. 30 on 40c. brown	2·75	4·50
77	**34**	7pi. 20 on 1l. brown & green	2·75	4·50

1922. Surch Piastre 3,75 in two lines.

78	**39**	3,75pi. on 25c. blue	4·50	4·50

1922. Para values surch in one line thus 30 PARA and piastre values with PIASTRE over new value except Nos. 81, 86, 98 and 99 where the figures of value are above.

79	**31**	30pa. on 2c. brown	3·25	6·75
80	**37**	30pa. on 5c. green	8·25	22·00
81	**41**	1,50pi. on 20c. orange	3·25	6·75
82	**39**	1,50pi. on 25c. blue	3·25	9·00
83	**39**	3,75pi. on 40c. brown	5·50	11·00
84	**39**	4,50pi. on 50c. mauve	12·00	28·00
85	**39**	7,50pi. on 60c. red	11·00	20·00
86	**39**	15pi. on 85c. brown	19·00	39·00
87	**34**	18,75pi. on 1l. brown & grn	11·00	39·00
98	**34**	45pi. on 5l. blue and red	£130	£110
99	**34**	90pi. on 10l. olive and red	£110	£225

1922. Para values surch in two lines and piastre values with PIASTRE under new value.

90	**37**	30pa. on 5c. green	2·75	4·50
91	**37**	1½pi. on 10c. red	2·75	4·50
92	**39**	3pi. on 25c. blue	20·00	9·00
93	**39**	3¾pi. on 40c. brown	4·50	5·50
94	**39**	4½pi. on 50c. mauve	60·00	44·00
95	**39**	7½pi. on 85c. brown	9·75	13·50
96	**34**	7½pi. on 1l. brown and green	11·00	18·00
97	**34**	15pi. on 1l. brown and green	£100	£170

1923. Surch COSTANTINOPOLI and value in figures once only after currency in words.

100	**37**	30pa. on 5c. green	2·75	3·25
101	**39**	1pi. 20 on 25c. blue	2·75	3·25
103	**39**	4pi. 20 on 50c. mauve	2·75	3·25
104	**39**	7pi. 20 on 60c. red	2·75	4·50
105	**39**	15pi. on 85c. brown	2·75	4·50
106	**34**	18pi. 30 on 1l. brown and green	3·25	4·50
107	**34**	45pi. on 5l. blue and pink	5·50	11·00
108	**34**	90pi. on 10l. green & pink	5·50	13·50

EXPRESS LETTER STAMPS

1922. Express Letter stamps surch 15 PIASTRE.

E90	**E41**	15pi. on 1l.20 on 30c. blue and red	33·00	80·00
E100	**E41**	15pi. on 30c. blue and red	£400	£800

1923. Express Letter stamp surch COSTANTINOPOLI 15 PIASTRE.

E109		15pi. on 1l.20 blue and red	9·00	39·00

POSTAGE DUE STAMPS

1922. Postage Due stamps optd Costantinopoli.

D100	**D12**	10c. mauve and orange	75·00	£120
D101	**D12**	30c. mauve and orange	75·00	£120
D102	**D12**	60c. mauve and orange	75·00	£120
D103	**D12**	1l. mauve and blue	75·00	£120
D104	**D12**	2l. mauve and blue	£1400	£2250
D105	**D12**	5l. mauve and blue	£650	£900

Nos. D100/5 bear a control cachet applied over blocks of four so that a quarter of the circle falls in a corner of each stamp.

(b) Durazzo

1909. Surch Durazzo (10pa. to 2pi.) or DURAZZO (4 to 40pi.) and value.

109	**37**	10pa. on 5c. green	1·80	4·50
110	**37**	20pa. on 10c. pink	1·80	4·50
111	**41**	30pa. on 15c. grey	49·00	6·75
112	**39**	1pi. on 25c. blue	2·75	6·75
113	**39**	2pi. on 50c. mauve	2·75	6·75
114	**34**	4pi. on 1l. brown and green	5·25	6·75
115	**34**	20pi. on 5l. blue and pink	£275	£275
116	**34**	40pi. on 10l. green & pink	20·00	£130

1915. No. 111 of Durazzo surch CENT. 20.

116a	**41**	20c. on 30pa. on 15c. grey	6·75	39·00

(c) Janina

1909. Surch Janina (10pa. to 2pi.) or JANINA (4 to 40pi.) and value.

117	**37**	10pa. on 5c. green	2·20	3·25
118	**37**	20pa. on 10c. pink	2·20	3·25
119	**41**	30pa. on 15c. grey	2·20	3·75
120	**39**	1pi. on 25c. blue	2·20	3·75
121	**39**	2pi. on 50c. mauve	2·20	4·50
122	**34**	4pi. on 1l. brown and green	5·25	5·50
123	**34**	20pi. on 5l. blue and pink	£300	£325
124	**34**	40pi. on 10l. green & pink	21·00	£120

(d) Jerusalem

1909. Surch Gerusalemme (10pa. to 2pi.) or GERUSALEMME (4 to 40pi.) and value.

125	**37**	10pa. on 5c. green	10·00	17·00
126	**37**	20pa. on 10c. pink	10·00	17·00
127	**41**	30pa. on 15c. grey	10·00	17·00
128	**39**	1pi. on 25c. blue	10·00	17·00
129	**39**	2pi. on 50c. mauve	27·00	44·00
130	**34**	4pi. on 1l. brown and green	39·00	80·00
131	**34**	20pi. on 5l. blue and pink	£1100	£1000
132	**34**	40pi. on 10l. green & pink	60·00	£450

(e) Salonica

1909. Surch Salonicco (10pa. to 2pi.) or SALONICCO (4 to 40pi.) and value.

133	**37**	10pa. on 5c. green	2·20	3·25
134	**37**	20pa. on 10c. pink	2·20	3·25
135	**41**	30pa. on 15c. grey	3·25	3·25
136	**39**	1pi. on 25c. blue	3·25	3·25
137	**39**	2pi. on 50c. mauve	3·25	3·25
138	**34**	4pi. on 1l. brown and green	5·50	6·75
139	**34**	20pi. on 5l. blue and pink	£550	£550
140	**34**	40pi. on 10l. green & pink	33·00	90·00

(f) Scutari

1909. Surch Scutari di Albania (4pa. to 2pi.) or SCUTARI DI ALBANIA (4 to 40pi.) and value.

141	**31**	4pa. on 2c. brown	3·25	3·75
142	**37**	10pa. on 35c. green	1·30	7·75
143	**37**	20pa. on 10c. pink	1·30	3·25
144	**41**	30pa. on 15c. grey	27·00	3·25
145	**39**	1pi. on 25c. blue	1·30	7·75
146	**39**	2pi. on 50c. mauve	2·20	
147	**34**	4pi. on 1l. brown and green	2·75	
148	**34**	20pi. on 5l. blue and pink	36·00	55·00
149	**34**	40pi. on 10l. green & pink	85·00	£190

1916. No. 144 of Scutari surch CENT. 20.

150	**41**	20c. on 30pa. on 15c. grey	1·20	2·20

(g) Smyrna

1909. Surch Smirne (10pa. to 2pi.) or SMIRNE (4 to 40pi.) and value.

151	**37**	10pa. on 5c. green	1·20	2·20
152	**37**	20pa. on 10c. pink	2·40	4·50
153	**41**	30pa. on 15c. grey	2·40	5·50
154	**39**	1pi. on 25c. blue	3·25	5·50
155	**39**	2pi. on 50c. mauve	3·25	9·00
156	**34**	4pi. on 1l. brown and green	4·00	9·00
157	**34**	20pi. on 5l. blue and pink	£180	£225
158	**34**	40pi. on 10l. green & pink	24·00	44·00

(h) Valona

1909. Surch Valona (10pa. to 2pi.) or VALONA (4 to 40pi.) and value.

159	**37**	10pa. on 5c. green	1·70	3·25
160	**37**	20pa. on 10c. pink	1·70	3·25
161	**41**	30pa. on 15c. grey†	23·00	10·00
162	**39**	1pi. on 25c. blue	3·00	5·50
163	**39**	2pi. on 50c. mauve	3·00	6·75
164	**34**	4pi. on 1l. brown and green	3·25	6·75
165	**34**	20pi. on 5l. blue and pink	55·00	85·00
166	**34**	40pi. on 10l. green & pink	70·00	£180
167	**41**	30pa. on 15c. grey†	6·75	18·00

†On No. 161 the surcharge is **Para**, on No. 167 **PARA**.

1916. No. 167 of Valona surch CENT. 20.

168		20c. on 30pa. on 15c. grey	3·25	22·00

D. OFFICES IN AFRICA.

(a) Benghazi

1901. Surch BENGASI 1 PIASTRA 1.

169	**33**	1pi. on 25c. blue	65·00	£170
170	**39**	1pi. on 25c. blue	65·00	£170

(b) Tripoli

1909. Optd Tripoli di Barberia (1 to 50c.) or TRIPOLI DI BARBERIA (1, 2l.).

171	**30**	1c. brown	6·00	5·25
173	**31**	2c. brown	3·50	5·25
174	**37**	5c. green	£110	14·00
175	**37**	10c. red	4·25	4·25
176	**41**	15c. grey	3·75	8·50
177	**39**	25c. blue	4·25	8·50
178	**39**	40c. brown	8·50	10·50
179	**39**	50c. violet	13·00	13·00
180	**34**	1l. brown and green	£120	£110
181	**34**	5l. blue and pink	47·00	£225

EXPRESS LETTER STAMPS

1909. Express Letter stamps optd TRIPOLI DI BARBERIA.

E182	**E35**	25c. pink	14·00	15·00
E183	**E41**	30c. blue and pink	12·00	21·00

Pt. 8

ITALY

A Republic in S. Europe on the Mediterranean and Adriatic Seas. Originally a kingdom formed by the union of various smaller kingdoms and duchies that issued their own stamps.

1862. 100 centesimi = 1 lira.
2002. 100 cents = 1 euro.

1 King Victor Emmanuel II

1862. Head embossed. Imperf (15c.) or perf (others).

1	1	10c. bistre	£10000	£375
2a	1	20c. blue	26·00	47·00
3	1	40c. red	£350	£225
4a	1	80c. yellow	80·00	£2250
5	1	15c. blue	£100	65·00

For stamps of this type imperf, see Sardinia Nos. 27 etc.

3

1863. Imperf.

7	3	15c. blue	8·50	15·00

4

5

6

7

10

1863. Perf.

8	4	1c. green	10·50	4·75
9	5	2c. brown	37·00	3·25
10	6	5c. grey	£2000	5·25
11	6	10c. brown	£3500	6·50
12	6	15c. blue	£3000	4·25
13	6	30c. brown	15·00	21·00
14	6	40c. red	£6000	9·50
15	6	60c. mauve	32·00	21·00
16	7	2l. red	35·00	£130
20a	10	20c. blue	£900	1·60
21	6	10c. blue	£7500	6·50
22	10	20c. orange	£5000	4·25

1865. Surch C 20 20 C and curved bar.

17	6	20c. on 15c. blue	£850	4·25

1878. Official stamps surch 2 C and wavy bars.

23	O11	2c. on 2c. red	£190	32·00
24	O11	2c. on 5c. red	£225	40·00
25	O11	2c. on 20c. red	£900	5·25
26	O11	2c. on 30c. red	£750	15·00
27	O11	2c. on 1l. red	£650	5·25
28	O11	2c. on 2l. red	£700	12·00
29	O11	2c. on 5l. red	£900	15·00
30	O11	2c. on 10l. red	£650	19·00

12 King Umberto I

1879. Corners vary for each value.

31	12	5c. green	12·00	1·60
32	12	10c. red	£600	2·10
33	12	20c. orange	£550	1·60
34	12	25c. blue	£950	8·50
35	12	30c. brown	£190	£2250
36	12	50c. mauve	27·00	24·00
37	12	2l. orange	65·00	£375

13 Arms of Savoy

14

1889. Figures in four corners. Various frames.

38	13	5c. green	£1000	2·10
39	14	40c. brown	14·00	15·00
40	14	45c. green	£2500	7·50
41	14	60c. mauve	19·00	30·00
42	14	1l. brown and orange	19·00	15·00
43	14	5l. red and green	75·00	£750

1890. Surch Cmi. 2 or Cmi 20.

44	12	2c. on 5c. green	27·00	65·00
45	12	20c. on 30c. brown	£475	12·00
46	12	20c. on 50c. mauve	£600	55·00

1890. Parcel Post stamps surch Valevole per le stampe Cmi. 2 and bars.

47	P13	2c. on 10c. grey	7·50	8·00
48	P13	2c. on 20c. blue	7·50	8·00
49	P13	2c. on 50c. pink	85·00	60·00
50	P13	2c. on 75c. green	7·50	8·00
51	P13	2c. on 1l.25 orange	65·00	43·00
52	P13	2c. on 1l.75 brown	29·00	70·00

21

22

23

24

25

26

27

29

1891

53	21	1c. brown	10·50	6·50
54	22	2c. brown	10·50	5·25
55	23	5c. green	£750	2·75
56	24	5c. green	43·00	2·10
57	25	10c. red	10·50	2·75
58a	26	20c. orange	10·50	2·75
59	27	25c. blue	10·50	1·60
60	27	45c. olive	7·00	3·25
61	29	5l. red and blue	95·00	£225

30

31

33 King Victor Emmanuel III

34 King Victor Emmanuel III

1901. Designs vary.

62	30	1c. brown	1·10	10
63	31	2c. brown	1·10	10
64	31	5c. green	90·00	65
65	33	10c. red	£120	1·40
66	33	20c. orange	21·00	1·40
67	33	25c. blue	£170	3·25
68	33	40c. brown	£800	10·50
69	33	45c. green	12·00	65
70	33	50c. violet	£900	18·00
71	34	1l. brown and green	6·50	65
72	34	5l. blue and pink	36·00	8·50
85	34	10l. green and pink	95·00	25·00

See also Nos. 171s, 181, 185 and 186/7.

1905. Surch C. 15.

73	33	15c. on 20c. orange	95·00	2·75

37

39

41

1906

75	37	5c. green	95	50
76	37	10c. red	1·20	10
77	39	25c. blue	1·60	10
78	39	40c. brown	3·25	10
79	39	50c. violet	1·60	10
90	41	15c. grey	43·00	1·30

See also Nos. 104 etc, 171d/h and 171j/r.

42 Garibaldi

1910. 50th Anniv of Plebiscite in Naples and Sicily.

81	42	5c.(+5c.) green	27·00	32·00
82	42	15c.(+5c.) red	48·00	70·00

43

1910. National Plebiscite of Southern States, 1860.

83	43	5c.(+5c.) pink	£190	£160
84	43	15c.(+5c.) green	£275	£250

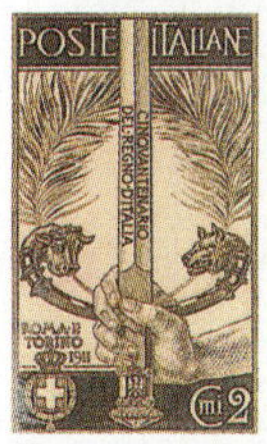

45

46

1911. Jubilee of Italian Kingdom.

86	45	2c.(+3c.) brown	12·00	5·25
87	46	5c.(+5c.) green	17·00	32·00
88	-	10c.(+5c.) red	26·00	48·00
89	-	15c.(+5c.) grey	27·00	75·00

DESIGNS: Symbolic of the Genius of Italy (10c.) and the Glory of Rome (15c.).

50

1912. Re-erection of Campanile of St. Mark, Venice.

91	50	5c. black	8·50	16·00
92	50	15c. brown	41·00	55·00

1913. Surch 2 2.

93	46	2 on 5c. green	2·10	6·50
94	-	2 on 10c. red (No. 88)	2·10	6·50
95	-	2 on 15c. grey (No. 89)	2·10	6·50

53 Banner of United Italy

54 Italian Eagle and Arms of Savoy

1915. Red Cross Society. No. 98 is surch 20.

96	53	10c.+5c. red	3·25	10·50
97	54	15c.+5c. grey	6·50	10·50
98	54	20 on 15c.+5c. grey	10·50	43·00
99	54	20c.+5c. orange	18·00	55·00

1916. Surch CENT. 20.

100	41	20c. on 15c. grey	24·00	1·60

1917. Air. Express Letter stamp optd ESPERIMENTO POSTA AEREA MAGGIO 1917 TORINO=ROMA=ROMA=TORINO.

102	E35	25c. red	20·00	40·00

1917. Air. Express Letter stamp surch IDROVOLANTE NAPOLI-PALERMO NAPOLI 25 CENT 25.

103	E59	25c. on 40c. violet	21·00	48·00

1917

104	37	15c. grey	1·10	65
105	41	20c. orange	5·25	55
106	39	30c. brown	3·00	1·10
107	39	55c. purple	17·00	16·00
108	39	60c. red	3·25	65
109	39	60c. blue	7·00	43·00
110	39	85c. brown	10·50	8·50
111	34	2l. green and orange	32·00	6·50
178	39	20c. orange	2·75	1·30
179	39	20c. green	1·10	30
180	39	20c. purple	2·10	50
181	34	25c. green and light green	2·10	50
182	39	25c. green	10·50	14·00
183	39	30c. grey	3·75	10
184	39	60c. orange	8·50	75
185	34	75c. red and carmine	6·50	50
186	34	1l.25 blue and ultramarine	8·50	50
187	34	2l.50 green and orange	70·00	8·50

See also Nos. 171a/c and 171i.

59 Ancient Seal of Republic of Trieste

1921. Union of Venezia Giulia with Italy.

112	59	15c. red and black	4·25	43·00
113	59	25c. red and blue	4·25	43·00
114	59	40c. red and brown	4·25	43·00

60

1921. 600th Death Anniv of Dante.

115	60	15c. red	5·25	14·00
116	-	25c. green	5·25	14·00
117	-	40c. brown	6·50	15·00

DESIGNS: 25c. Woman with book; 40c. Dante.

62 "Victory"

1921. Victory of 1918.

118	62	5c. green	1·10	2·75
119	62	10c. red	1·10	2·75
120	62	15c. grey	3·25	10·50
121	62	25c. blue	1·10	5·25

1922. 9th Italian Philatelic Congress. Trieste. Optd IX CONGRESSO FILATELICO ITALIANO TRIESTE 1922.

122	37	10c. red	£400	£375
123	37	15c. grey	£250	£275
124	39	25c. blue	£250	£325
125	39	40c. brown	£425	£375

64

1922. 50th Death Anniv of Mazzini.

126	64	25c. purple	6·50	32·00

127	-	40c. purple	27·00	37·00
128	-	80c. blue	6·50	55·00

DESIGNS—VERT: 40c. Mazzini. HORIZ: 80c. Tomb of Mazzini.

66

1923. Tercentenary of Propagation of the Faith.

129	**66**	20c. orange and green	4·25	80·00
130	**66**	30c. orange and red	4·25	80·00
131	**66**	50c. orange and violet	4·25	80·00
132	**66**	1l. orange and blue	4·25	80·00

The portraits and arms in the corners at right vary for each value.

1923. Surch in words and figures. (15c. surch DIECI only).

133	**39**	7½c. on 85c. brown	55	1·70
135	**30**	10c. on 1c. brown	55	45
136	**31**	10c. on 2c. brown	55	45
137	**37**	10c. on 15c. grey	45	55
138	**39**	20c. on 25c. blue	45	55
139	**33**	25c. on 45c. olive	45	55
140	**39**	25c. on 60c. blue	2·10	1·60
141	**39**	30c. on 50c. mauve	55	55
142	**39**	30c. on 55c. purple	75	55
143	**39**	50c. on 40c. brown	3·25	60
144	**39**	50c. on 55c. purple	32·00	15·00
145	**34**	1l.75 on 10l. olive and red	21·00	32·00

73

74

75

1923. 1st Anniv of Fascist March on Rome.

146	**73**	10c. green	4·25	6·50
147	**73**	30c. violet	4·25	6·50
148	**73**	50c. red	6·50	10·50
149	**74**	1l. blue	9·50	10·50
150	**74**	2l. brown	9·50	16·00
151	**75**	5l. black and blue	21·00	65·00

76

1923. Fascist "Black Shirt" Fund.

152	**76**	30c.+30c. brown	37·00	£100
153	**76**	50c.+50c. mauve	37·00	£100
154	**76**	1l.+1l. grey	37·00	£100

77

1923. 50th Death Anniv of A. Manzoni (writer).

155	**77**	10c. black and red	8·50	75·00
156	-	15c. black and green	8·50	75·00
157	-	30c. black	8·50	75·00
158	-	50c. black and brown	8·50	75·00
159	-	1l. black and blue	£110	£325
160	-	5l. black and purple	£750	£2750

DESIGNS: 10c. to 50c. Scenes from Manzoni's "I Promessi Sposi"; 1l. Manzoni's home, Milan; 5l. Portrait of Manzoni.

1924. Victory stamps surch LIRE UNA between stars.

161	**62**	1l. on 5c. green	27·00	£130
162	**62**	1l. on 10c. red	16·00	£130
163	**62**	1l. on 15c. grey	27·00	£130
164	**62**	1l. on 25c. blue	16·00	£130

1924. Trade Propaganda. Optd CROCIERA ITALIANA 1924.

165	**37**	10c. red	2·10	21·00
166	**39**	30c. brown	2·10	21·00
167	**39**	50c. violet	2·10	21·00
168	**39**	60c. blue	10·50	75·00
169	**39**	85c. brown	7·50	75·00
170	**34**	1l. brown and green	65·00	£350
171	**34**	2l. green and orange	55·00	£350

Used on an Italian cruiser which visited South America for trade propaganda.

1924. Previous issues with attached advertising labels (imperf between stamp and label). Colour of label given.

171a	15c. (104) + Columbia (blue)	43·00	43·00
171b	15c. (104) + Bitter Campari (blue)	4·25	19·00
171c	15c. (104) + Cordial Campari (black)	4·25	21·00
171d	25c. (77) + Coen (green)	£250	48·00
171e	25c. (77) + Piperno (brown)	£1600	£750
171f	25c. (77) + Tagliacozzo (brown)	£850	£750
171g	25c. (77) + Abrador (blue)	£120	£110
171h	25c. (77) + Reinach (green)	£100	85·00
171i	30c. (106) + Columbia (green)	34·00	55·00
171j	50c. (79) + Coen (blue)	£1600	85·00
171k	50c. (79) + Columbia (red)	21·00	16·00
171l	50c. (79) + De Montel (blue)	4·25	19·00
171m	50c. (79) + Piperno (green)	£1900	£275
171n	50c. (79) + Reinach (blue)	£225	65·00
171o	50c. (79) + Singer (red)	4·25	8·50
171p	50c. (79) + Tagliacozzo (green)	£2500	£550
171q	50c. (79) + Siero Casali (blue)	21·00	43·00
171r	50c. (79) + Tantal (red)	£400	£120
171s	1l. (71) + Columbia (blue)	£750	£800

81 Church of St. John Lateran

1924. Holy Year (1925).

172	-	20c.+10c. brown & green	3·25	13·00
173	**81**	30c.+15c. brown & choc	3·25	13·00
174	-	50c.+25c. brown & violet	3·25	13·00
175	-	60c.+30c. brown and red	3·25	32·00
176	-	1l.+50c. purple and blue	3·25	32·00
177	-	5l.+2l.50 purple and red	13·00	85·00

DESIGNS: 20c. Church of St. Maria Maggiore; 50c. Church of St. Paul; 60c. St. Peter's; 1l. Pope opening Holy Door; 5l. Pope shutting Holy Door.

82

1925. Royal Jubilee.

188B	**82**	60c. red	1·10	1·10
189B	**82**	1l. blue	2·10	1·10
190A	**82**	1l.25 blue	4·25	2·10

83 Vision of St. Francis

1926. 700th Death Anniv of St. Francis of Assisi.

191	**83**	20c. green	55	1·10
192	-	40c. violet	55	1·10
193	-	60c. red	1·10	1·10
194B	-	30c. black	55	1·10
195B	-	1l.25 blue	1·10	1·10
196	-	5l.+2l.50 brown	14·00	£120

DESIGNS—HORIZ: 40c. St. Damian's Church and Monastery, Assisi; 60c. St. Francis's Monastery, Assisi; 1l.25, Death of St. Francis, from fresco in Church of the Holy Cross, Florence. VERT: 30c., 5l. St. Francis (after Luca della Robbia).

88

1926. Air.

197	**88**	50c. red	4·25	10·50
198	**88**	60c. grey	4·25	10·50
199	**88**	80c. brown and purple	43·00	85·00
200	**88**	1l. blue	8·50	£120
201	**88**	1l.20 brown	19·00	£110
202	**88**	1l.50 orange	19·00	32·00
203	**88**	5l. green	48·00	£110

89 Castle of St. Angelo

1926. 1st National Defence issue.

204	**89**	40c.+20c. black & brown	3·25	7·50
205	-	60c.+30c. brown and red	3·25	7·50
206	-	1l.25+60c. black & grn	3·25	7·50
207	-	5l.+2l.50 black and blue	5·25	15·00

DESIGNS: 60c. Aqueduct of Claudius; 1l.25, Capitol; 5l. Porta del Popolo.

See also Nos. 219/22 and 278/81.

90 Volta

1927. Death Centenary of Volta.

208	**90**	20c. red	1·10	1·10
209	**90**	50c. green	2·10	1·10
210	**90**	60c. purple	4·25	5·25
211	**90**	1l.25 blue	7·50	7·50

91

1927

212	**91**	1l.75 brown	4·75	20
213	**91**	1l.85 black	1·10	1·10
214	**91**	2l.55 red	8·00	10·50
215	**91**	2l.65 purple	8·50	55·00
216	**91**	50c. grey and brown	4·25	45

No. 216 is smaller (17½×21½ mm).

1927. Air. Surch.

217	**88**	50c. on 60c. grey	16·00	55·00
218	**88**	80c. on 1l. blue	43·00	£190

1928. 2nd National Defence issue. As Nos. 204/7.

219	**89**	30c.+10c. black and violet	7·50	27·00
220	-	50c.+20c. black and olive	8·50	27·00
221	-	1l.25+50c. black & blue	27·00	65·00
222	-	5l.+2l. black and red	48·00	£225

92

1928

223	**92**	7½c. brown	4·25	13·00
224	**92**	15c. orange	5·25	25
225	**92**	35c. grey	7·50	12·00
226	**92**	50c. mauve	15·00	10

93 Emmanuele Filiberto

94 Soldier of First World War and Statue

95 Statue, Turin (Maroghetti)

1928. 400th Birth Anniv of Emmanuele Filiberto, Duke of Savoy, and 10th Anniv of Victory in World War.

227a	**93**	20c. blue and brown	2·10	6·50
228a	**93**	25c. green and red	2·10	6·50
229a	**93**	30c. brown and green	4·25	10·50
230	**94**	50c. red and blue	2·10	1·10
231	**94**	75c. red and pink	3·25	5·25
232	**95**	1l.25 black and blue	3·25	5·25
233	**94**	1l.75 green and blue	5·25	16·00
234	**93**	5l. green and mauve	16·00	95·00
235	**94**	10l. black and pink	32·00	£225
236	**95**	20l. green and mauve	70·00	£800

96 King Victor Emmanuel II

1929. 50th Death Anniv of King Victor Emmanuel II. Veterans' Fund.

237	**96**	50c.+10c. green	4·25	8·50

97 Fascist Arms of Italy

98 Romulus, Remus and Wolf

99 Julius Caesar

103 King Victor Emmanuel III

1929. Imperial Series.

238	**97**	2c. orange	65	20
239	**98**	5c. brown	20	20
240	**99**	7½c. violet	20	20
241	-	10c. brown	20	20
242	-	15c. green	20	20
243	**99**	20c. red	20	20
244	-	25c. green	20	20
245	**103**	30c. brown	20	20
246	-	35c. blue	20	20
247	**103**	50c. violet	20	20
248	-	75c. red	20	20
249	**99**	1l. violet	25	20
250	-	1l.25 blue	20	20
251	-	1l.75 orange	20	20
252	-	2l. red	20	20
253	**98**	2l.55 green	20	60
254	**98**	3l.70 violet	25	1·10
255	**98**	5l. red	25	20
256	-	10l. violet	2·10	2·75
257	**99**	20l. green	4·25	13·00
258	-	25l. black	10·50	41·00
259	-	50l. violet	15·00	55·00

DESIGNS—As Type **99**: 10c., 1l.75, 25l. Augustus the Great; 15c., 35c., 2l., 10l. Italia (Woman with castle on her head); 25c., 75c., 1l.25, 50l. Profile of King Victor Emmanuel III.

For stamps as above but without Fascist emblems, see Nos. 633 etc, and for stamps with integral label for armed forces see Nos. 563/74.

104 Bramante Courtyard

1929. 1400th Anniv of Abbey of Montecassino.

260	**104**	20c. orange	1·60	2·10
261	-	25c. green	1·60	2·10
262	-	50c.+10c. brown	2·10	16·00
263	-	75c.+15c. red	3·25	27·00
264	**104**	1l.25+25c. blue	4·25	29·00
265	-	5l.+1l. purple	12·00	85·00
266	-	10l.+2l. green	17·00	£180

DESIGNS—HORIZ: 25c. "Death of St. Benedict" (fresco); 50c. Monks building Abbey; 75c., 5l. Abbey of Montecassino. VERT: 10l. St. Benedict.

109

1930. Marriage of Prince Umberto and Princess Marie Jose.

267	109	20c. orange	1·10	80
268	109	50c.+10c. brown	2·10	4·25
269	109	1l.25+25c. blue	3·25	13·00

110 Pegasus

113

1930. Air.

270	-	25c. green	10	10
271	110	50c. brown	10	10
272	-	75c. brown	10	10
273	-	80c. orange	10	10
274	-	1l. violet	10	10
275	113	2l. blue	10	20
276	110	5l. green	50	45
277	110	10l. red	65	1·10

DESIGNS—As Type **110**: 25c., 80c. Wings; 75c., 1l. Angel.

1930. 3rd National Defence issue. Designs as Nos. 204/7.

278	89	30c.+10c. violet & green	1·10	21·00
279	-	50c.+10c. blue and green	2·10	16·00
280	-	1l.25+30c. green & blue	7·50	48·00
281	-	5l.+1l.50 choc & brn	10·50	£160

114 Ferrucci on Horseback

117 Francesco Ferrucci

1930. 400th Death Anniv of Francesco Ferrucci.

282	114	20c. red (postage)	1·10	1·10
283	-	25c. green	2·10	1·10
284	-	50c. violet	1·10	30
285	-	1l.25 blue	10·50	5·25
286	-	5l.+2l. orange	19·00	£150
287	117	50c. violet (air)	2·10	13·00
288	117	1l. brown	2·10	19·00
289	117	5l.+2l. purple	8·50	£140

DESIGNS—HORIZ: 25c., 50c., 1l.25, Ferrucci assassinated by Maramaldo. VERT: 5l. Ferrucci in helmet.

119 Jupiter sending forth Eagle

1930. Birth Bimillenary of Virgil.

290	-	15c. brown (postage)	1·10	2·10
291	-	20c. orange	1·10	2·10
292	-	25c. green	1·10	2·10
293	-	30c. purple	2·10	4·25
294	-	50c. violet	1·10	1·10
295	-	75c. red	2·10	6·50
296	-	1l.25 blue	2·10	6·50
297	-	5l.+1l.50 brown	65·00	£225
298	-	10l.+2l.50 olive	65·00	£275
299	119	50c. brown (air)	9·50	21·00
300	119	1l. orange	9·50	21·00
301	119	7l.70+1l.30 purple	48·00	£275
302	119	9l.+2l. blue	60·00	£325

DESIGNS (scenes from "Aeneid" or "Georgics"): 15c. Helenus and Anchises; 20c. The passing legions; 25c. Landing of Aeneas; 30c. Earth's bounties; 50c. Harvesting; 75c. Rural life; 1l.25, Aeneas sights Italy; 5l. A shepherd's hut; 10l. Turnus, King of the Rutuli.

120 Savoia Marchetti S-55A Flying Boats

1930. Air. Transatlantic Mass Formation Flight.

303	120	7l.70 blue and brown	£750	£1400

121 St. Antony's Installation as a Franciscan

1931. 700th Death Anniv of St. Antony of Padua.

304	121	20c. purple	3·25	1·60
305	-	25c. green	2·10	1·60
306	-	30c. brown	4·25	2·10
307	-	50c. violet	3·25	1·10
308	-	75c. lake	10·50	10·50
309	-	1l.25 blue	16·00	8·50
310	-	5l.+2l.50 olive	48·00	£190

DESIGNS—HORIZ: 25c. Sermon to the Fishes; 30c. Hermitage of Olivares; 50c. Basilica of the Saint at Padua; 75c. Death of St. Antony; 1l.25, St. Antony liberating prisoners. VERT: 5l. Vision of St. Antony.

123 Tower of the Marzocco

1931. 50th Anniv of Naval Academy, Leghorn.

311	123	20c. red	5·25	2·10
312	-	50c. violet	5·25	1·10
313	-	1l.25 blue	13·00	5·25

DESIGNS—HORIZ: 50c. Cadet ship "Amerigo Vespucci"; 1l.25, Cruiser "Trento".

124 Dante (1265–1321)

125 Leonardo da Vinci's Drawing "Flying Man"

127 Leonardo da Vinci

1932. Dante Alighieri Society. (a) Postage.

314		10c. brown	2·10	2·10
315		15c. green	2·10	2·10
316		20c. red	2·10	1·10
317		25c. green	2·10	1·10
318		30c. brown	3·25	2·10
319		50c. violet	1·10	1·10
320		75c. red	6·50	6·50
321		1l.25 blue	2·10	4·25
322		1l.75 orange	5·25	6·50
323		2l.75 green	21·00	32·00
324		5l.+2l. red	32·00	£160
325	124	10l.+2l.50 olive	43·00	£225

DESIGNS: 10c. Giovanni Boccaccio (writer); 15c. Niccolo Machiavelli (statesman); 20c. Fra Paolo Sarpi (philosopher); 25c. Vittorio Alfieri (poet); 30c. Ugo Foscolo (writer); 50c. Giacomo Leopardi (poet); 75c. Giosue Carducci (poet); 1l.25, Carlo Botta (historian); 1l.75, Torquato Tasso (poet); 2l.75, Francesco Petrarch (poet); 5l. Ludovico Ariosto (poet).

(b) Air.

326	125	50c. brown	2·10	6·50
327	-	1l. violet	3·25	7·50
328	-	3l. red	5·25	27·00
329	-	5l. green	5·25	32·00
330	125	7l.70+2l. blue	7·50	85·00
331	-	10l.+2l.50 grey	10·50	£140
332	127	100l. green and blue	37·00	£450

DESIGN—HORIZ: 1, 3, 5, 10l. Leonardo da Vinci.

128 Garibaldi and Victor Emmanuel

130 Caprera

1932. 50th Death Anniv of Garibaldi.

333	-	10c. blue (postage)	3·25	2·10
334	128	20c. brown	3·25	1·20
335	-	25c. green	3·25	2·10
336	128	30c. orange	3·25	3·25
337	-	50c. violet	2·10	45
338	-	75c. red	16·00	8·50
339	-	1l.25 blue	21·00	5·25
340	-	1l.75+25c. blue	27·00	95·00
341	-	2l.55+50c. brown	27·00	£130
342	-	5l.+1l. lake	27·00	£140

DESIGNS—HORIZ: 10c. Garibaldi's birthplace, Nice; 25c., 50c. "Here we make Italy or die"; 75c. Death of Anita (Garibaldi's wife); 1l.25, Garibaldi's tomb; 1l.75, Quarto Rock. VERT: 2l.55, Garibaldi's statue in Rome; 5l. Garibaldi.

343	130	50c. lake (air)	4·25	8·50
344	-	80c. green	4·25	15·00
345	130	1l.+25c. brown	5·25	32·00
346	-	2l.+50c. blue	6·50	48·00
347	-	5l.+1l. green	9·50	60·00

DESIGNS—VERT: 80c. The Ravenna hut; 2l. Anita; 5l. Garibaldi.

132 Agriculture

1932. 10th Anniv of Fascist March on Rome. (a) Postage.

350	132	5c. sepia	1·10	1·10
351	-	10c. sepia	1·10	1·10
352	-	15c. green	1·10	1·10
353	-	20c. red	1·10	65
354	-	25c. green	1·10	85
355	-	30c. sepia	2·10	3·25
356	-	35c. blue	5·25	10·50
357	-	50c. violet	2·10	20
358	-	60c. brown	5·25	7·50
359	-	75c. red	3·25	4·25
360	-	1l. violet	6·50	6·50
361	-	1l.25 blue	3·25	2·10
362	-	1l.75 orange	7·50	2·10
363	-	2l.55 green	28·00	43·00
364	-	2l.75 green	29·00	43·00
365	-	5l.+2l.50 red	65·00	£300

DESIGNS: 10c. Fascist soldier; 15c. Fascist coastguard; 20c. Italian youth; 25c. Tools forming a shadow of the Fasces; 30c. Religion; 35c. Imperial highways; 50c. Equestrian statue of Mussolini; 60c. Land reclamation; 75c. Colonial expansion; 1l. Marine development; 1l.25, Italians abroad; 1l.75, Sport, 2l.55, Child Welfare; 2l.75. "O.N.D." Recreation; 5l. Caesar's statue.

(b) Air.

366	50c. brown	3·25	10·50
367	75c. brown	9·50	32·00

DESIGNS: 50c. Savoia Marchetti S-55A flying boat over Eagle (front of Air Ministry Building, Rome); 75c. Aerial view of Italian cathedrals.

134 Airship "Graf Zeppelin"

1933. Air. LZ-127 "Graf Zeppelin" issue.

372	134	3l. green and black	10·50	95·00
373	-	5l. brown and green	16·00	£110
374	-	10l. blue and red	16·00	£250
375	-	12l. orange and blue	21·00	£375
376	-	15l. black and brown	21·00	£475
377	-	20l. blue and brown	21·00	£550

DESIGNS (all with airship): 3l. S. Paola Gate and tomb of Consul Caius Cestius; 5l. Appian Way and tomb of Cecilia Metella; 10l. Portion of Mussolini Stadium; 12l. S. Angelo Castle; 15l. Forum Romanum; 20l. Empire Way, Colosseum and Baths of Domitian.

135 Italian Flag / King Victor Emmanuel III / "Flight" (image scaled to 44% of original size)

136 Italian Flag / King Victor Emmanuel III / Rome–Chicago (image scaled to 44% of original size)

1933. Air. Balbo Transatlantic Mass Formation Flight by Savoia Marchetti S-55X Flying Boats.

378	135	5l.25+19l.75 red, green and blue	£170	£2250
379	136	5l.25+44l.75 red, green and blue	£170	£2250

The first part of the illustration in each group is of the Registered Air Express label and has an abbreviation of one of the pilots' names overprinted on it; the second part is the stamp for Ordinary Postage and the third is the actual Air Mail stamp.

137 Athlete

1933. International University Games, Turin.

380	137	10c. brown	55	1·10
381	137	20c. red	55	1·10
382	137	50c. violet	1·10	60
383	137	1l.25 blue	2·10	6·50

138 Dome of St. Peter's

139 St. Peter's and Church of the Holy Sepulchre

1933. "Holy Year". (a) Postage.

384	138	20c. red	3·25	1·10
385	-	25c. green	4·25	2·10
386	-	50c. violet	3·25	1·10
387	138	1l. 25 blue	4·25	6·50
388	-	2l.55+2l.50 black	10·50	£225

DESIGNS: 25, 50c. Angel with Cross; 2l.55, Cross with Doves of Peace.

(b) Air.

389	139	50c.+25c. brown	1·10	16·00
390	139	75c.+50c. purple	3·25	27·00

1934. Air. Rome-Buenos Aires Flight. Surch with airplane, 1934 XII PRIMO VOLO DIRETTO ROMA = BUENOS-AYRES TRIMOTORE "LOMBARDI MAZZOTTI", value and fasces.

391	113	2l. on 2l. yellow	7·50	65·00
392	113	3l. on 2l. green	7·50	£110
393	113	5l. on 2l. red	7·50	£225
394	113	10l. on 2l. violet	7·50	£325

141 Anchor of the "Emmanuele Filiberto"

1934. 10th Anniv of Annexation of Fiume.

395	141	10c. brown (postage)	5·25	4·25
396	141	20c. red	30	1·10
397	-	50c. violet	30	1·10
398	-	1l.25 blue	45	6·50
399	-	1l.75+1l. blue	1·10	37·00
400	-	2l.55+2l. purple	1·10	60·00
401	-	2l.75+2l.50 olive	1·10	60·00

DESIGNS: 50c. Gabriele d'Annunzio; 1l.25, St. Vito's Tower barricaded; 1l.75, Hands supporting crown of historical monuments; 2l.55, Victor Emmanuel III's arrival in the "Brindisi" (cruiser); 2l.75, Galley, gondola and battleship.

402		25c. green (air)	25	4·25
403		50c. brown	25	3·25
404		75c. brown	25	10·50
405		1l.+50c. purple	25	16·00
406		2l.+1l.50 blue	25	24·00
407		3l.+2l. black	1·10	24·00

DESIGNS—Marina Fiat MF.5 flying boat over: 25, 75c. Fiume Harbour; 50c., 1l. War Memorial; 2l. Three Venetian lions; 3l. Roman Wall.

142 Antonio Pacinotti

1934. 75th Anniv of Invention of Pacinotti's Dynamo.

411	**142**	50c. violet	55	60
412	**142**	1l.25 blue	1·10	2·75

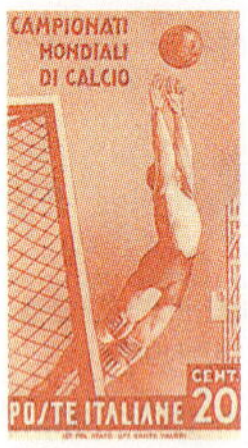

143

1934. World Cup Football Championship, Italy.

413	**143**	20c. red (postage)	10·50	10·50
414	-	25c. green	15·00	3·25
415	-	50c. violet	17·00	1·60
416	-	1l.25 blue	36·00	16·00
417	-	5l.+2l.50 brown	85·00	£400

DESIGNS—VERT: 5l. Players heading the ball. HORIZ: 25c., 50c., 1l.25, Two footballers.

418		50c. red (air)	9·00	21·00
419		75c. blue	9·00	27·00
420		5l.+2l.50 olive	37·00	£225
421		10l.+5l. brown	50·00	£325

DESIGNS—HORIZ: 50c. Marina Fiat MF.5 flying boat over Mussolini Stadium, Turin; 5l. Marina Fiat MF.5 flying boat over Stadium, Rome. VERT: 75c. Savoia Marchetti S-55X flying boat over footballer; 10l. Marina Fiat MF.5 flying boat over Littoral Stadium, Bologna.

145 Luigi Galvani

1934. 1st Int Congress of Electro-radio-biology.

422	**145**	30c. brown on buff	85	1·10
423	**145**	75c. red on pink	1·10	3·25

146 Military Symbol

1934. Military Medal Centenary.

424	**146**	10c. brown (postage)	1·10	2·10
425	-	15c. green	1·10	5·25
426	-	20c. red	1·10	2·10
427	-	25c. green	2·10	2·10
428	-	30c. brown	4·25	8·50
429	-	50c. violet	2·10	1·10
430	-	75c. red	8·50	13·00
431	-	1l.25 blue	9·50	8·50
432	-	1l.75+1l. red	18·00	55·00
433	-	2l.55+2l. purple	20·00	70·00
434	-	2l.75+2l. violet	32·00	75·00

DESIGNS—VERT: 25c. Mountaineers; 1l.75, Cavalry. HORIZ: 15c., 50c. Barbed-wire cutter; 20c. Throwing hand-grenade; 30c. Cripple wielding crutch; 75c. Artillery; 1l.25, Soldiers cheering; 2l.55, Sapper; 2l.75, First Aid.

435		25c. green (air)	2·10	5·25
436		50c. grey	2·10	8·50
437		75c. brown	2·10	10·50
438		80c. blue	2·10	13·00
439		1l.+50c. brown	4·25	34·00
440		2l.+1l. blue	5·25	41·00
441		3l.+2l. black	8·50	48·00

DESIGNS—HORIZ: 25, 80c. Italian "P" Type airship under fire; 50, 75c. Marina Flat MF.5 flying boat and Naval launch; 1l. Caproni Ca 101 airplane and troops in desert; 2l. Pomilio PC type biplane and troops. VERT: 3l. Marina Flat MF.5 flying boat over Unknown soldier's tomb.

148 King Victor Emmanuel III

1934. Air. Rome–Mogadiscio Flight and King's visit to Italian Somaliland.

444	**148**	1l. violet	2·10	35·00
445	**148**	2l. blue	2·10	45·00
446	**148**	4l. brown	5·25	£160
447	**148**	5l. green	5·25	£225
448	**148**	8l. red	24·00	£300
449	**148**	10l. brown	26·00	£375

149 Man with Fasces

1935. University Contests. Inscr "LITTORIALI".

450	**149**	20c. red	1·10	1·10
451	-	30c. brown	3·25	5·25
452	-	50c. violet	1·10	65

DESIGNS: 30c. Eagle and soldier. 50c. Standard-bearer and bayonet attack.

150

1935. National Militia. Inscr "PRO OPERA PREVID. MILIZIA".

453	**150**	20c.+10c. red (postage)	9·50	13·00
454	-	25c.+15c. green	9·50	17·00
455	-	50c.+30c. violet	9·50	24·00
456	-	1l.25+75c. blue	9·50	43·00
457	-	50c.+50c. brown (air)	10·50	37·00

DESIGNS: 25c. Roman standards; 50c. Soldier and cross; 50c.+50c. Wing over Globe; 1l.25, Soldiers and arch.

152 Symbol of Flight

153 Leonardo da Vinci

1935. International Aeronautical Exn, Milan.

458	**152**	20c. red	8·50	2·10
459	**152**	30c. brown	25·00	7·50
460	**153**	50c. violet	32·00	1·10
461	**153**	1l.25 blue	36·00	8·50

154 Vincenzo Bellini

155 "Music"

1935. Death Centenary of Bellini (composer).

462	**154**	20c. red (postage)	6·50	3·25
463	**154**	30c. brown	9·50	10·50
464	**154**	50c. violet	9·50	1·10
465	**154**	1l.25 blue	10·50	13·00
466	-	1l.75+1l. orange	36·00	£150
467	-	2l.75+2l. olive	50·00	£170

DESIGNS—VERT: 2l.75, Bellini's villa. HORIZ: 1l.75, Hands at piano.

468	**155**	25c. brown (air)	2·10	10·50
469	**155**	50c. brown	2·10	5·25
470	**155**	60c. red	5·25	16·00
471	-	1l.+1l. violet	10·50	£110
472	-	5l.+2l. green	18·00	£170

DESIGNS: 1l. Angelic musicians; 5l. Mountain landscape (Bellini's birthplace).

156 "Commerce" and Industrial Map of Italy

1936. 17th Milan Fair. Inscr as in T 156.

473	**156**	20c. red	55	60
474	-	30c. brown	55	1·10
475	-	50c. violet	55	60
476	**156**	1l.25 blue	1·60	3·25

DESIGN—HORIZ: 30c., 50c. Cog-wheel and plough.

157 "Fertility"

1936. 2000th Birth Anniv of Horace.

477	**157**	10c. green (postage)	5·25	1·10
478	-	20c. red	3·25	1·10
479	-	30c. brown	6·50	2·10
480	-	50c. violet	6·50	85
481	-	75c. red	13·00	10·50
482	-	1l.25+1l. blue	30·00	£110
483	-	1l.75+1l. red	37·00	£120
484	-	2l.55+1l. blue	43·00	£160

DESIGNS—HORIZ: 20c., 1l.25, Landscape; 75c. Capitol; 2l.55, Dying gladiator. VERT: 30c. Ajax defying lightning; 50c. Horace; 1l.75, Pan.

485		25c. green (air)	3·25	8·50
486		50c. brown	4·25	8·50
487		60c. red	5·25	16·00
488		1l.+1l. violet	13·00	£130
489		5l.+2l. green	19·00	£190

DESIGNS—HORIZ: 25c. Savoia Marchetti S-55A flying boat; 50c., 1l. Caproni Ca 101 airplane over lake; 60c. Eagle and oak tree; 5l. Rome.

159

160

1937. Child Welfare. Inscr as in T 159/60.

490	**159**	10c. brown (postage)	3·25	1·10
491	**160**	20c. red	3·25	1·10
492	**159**	25c. green	3·25	2·10
493	-	30c. sepia	3·25	3·25
494	**160**	50c. violet	3·25	60
495	-	75c. red	8·50	10·50
496	**160**	1l.25 blue	10·50	10·50
497	-	1l.75+75c. orange	43·00	£120
498	-	2l.75+1l.25 green	30·00	£130
499	**160**	5l.+3l. blue	37·00	£180

DESIGNS—As Type **159**: 30c., 1l.75, Boy between Fasces; 75c., 2l.75, "Bambino" (after della Robbia).

500		25c. green (air)	8·50	10·50
501		50c. brown	8·50	8·50
502		1l. violet	8·50	10·50
503		2l.+1l. blue	13·00	90·00
504		3l.+2l. orange	17·00	£130
505		5l.+3l. red	19·00	£170

DESIGNS—As Type **160**: 25c., 1l., 3l. Little child with rifle. As Type **159**: 50c., 2l., 5l. Children's heads.

163 Naval Memorial

164 Augustus the Great

1937. 2000th Birth Anniv of Augustus the Great.

506	**163**	10c. green (postage)	3·25	1·10
507	-	15c. brown	3·25	1·40
508	-	20c. red	3·25	1·10
509	-	25c. green	3·25	1·10
510	-	30c. brown	3·25	2·10
511	-	50c. violet	3·25	30
512	-	75c. red	5·25	5·25
513	-	1l.25 blue	8·50	6·50
514	-	1l.75+1l. purple	43·00	£120
515	-	2l.55+2l. black	48·00	£130

DESIGNS—VERT: 15c. Military trophies; 20c. Reconstructing temples of Rome; 25c. Census (with reference to birth of Jesus Christ); 30c. Statue of Julius Caesar; 50c. Election of Augustus as Emperor; 75c. Head of Augustus (conquest of Ethiopia); 1l.25, Constructing new fleet; 1l.75, Building Altar of Peace; 2l.55, The Capitol.

516		25c. purple (air)	6·50	10·50
517		50c. brown	6·50	8·50
518		80c. brown	15·00	13·00
519		1l.+1l. blue	34·00	95·00
520	**164**	5l.+1l. violet	45·00	£150

DESIGNS—HORIZ: 25c. "Agriculture"; 50c. Prosperity of the Romans; 80c. Horses of the Sun Chariot; 1l. Staff and map of ancient Roman Empire.

165 Gasparo Spontini (composer)

1937. Famous Italians.

521	**165**	10c. sepia	1·10	1·10
522	-	20c. red	1·10	1·40
523	-	25c. green	1·10	1·10
524	-	30c. brown	1·10	1·10
525	-	50c. violet	1·10	2·10
526	-	75c. red	2·10	65
527	-	1l.25 blue	3·25	5·25
528	**165**	1l.75 orange	3·25	6·50
529	-	2l.55+2l. green	13·00	£120
530	-	2l.75+2l. brown	16·00	£130

DESIGNS: 20c., 2l.55, Antonio Stradivarius (violin maker); 25, 50c. Giacomo Leopardi (poet); 30, 75c., Giovanni Battista Pergolesi (composer); 1l.25, 2l.75, Giotto di Bondone (painter and architect).

166 Marconi

1938. Guglielmo Marconi (telegraphy pioneer) Commemoration.

531	**166**	20c. red	2·10	1·10
532	**166**	50c. violet	1·10	60
533	**166**	1l.25 blue	2·10	4·75

167 Founding of Rome

168 Victor Emmanuel III

1938. 2nd Anniv of Proclamation of Italian Empire.

534	**167**	10c. brown (postage)	2·10	80
535	-	20c. red	2·10	80
536	-	25c. green	2·10	80
537	-	30c. brown	2·10	1·30
538	-	50c. violet	2·10	80
539	-	75c. red	3·25	1·90
540	-	1l.25 blue	6·50	1·90

541	-	1l.75 violet	8·50	2·75
542	-	2l.75 green	21·00	33·00
543	-	5l. red	38·00	41·00

DESIGNS—VERT: 20c. Emperor Augustus; 25c. Dante; 30c. Columbus; 50c. Leonardo da Vinci; 75c. Garibaldi and Victor Emmanuel II; 1l.25, Italian Unknown Warrior's Tomb; 1l.75, "March on Rome"; 2l.75, Wedding ring on map of Ethiopia; 5l. Victor Emmanuel III.

544	**168**	25c. green (air)	3·25	4·50
545	-	50c. brown	3·25	4·50
546	-	1l. violet	4·25	7·00
547	-	2l. blue	5·25	22·00
548	**168**	3l. red	8·50	30·00
549	-	5l. green	9·50	48·00

DESIGNS—HORIZ: 50c., 1l. Dante: 2, 5l. Leonardo da Vinci.

169 Steam Locomotive and ETR 200 Express Train

1939. Centenary of Italian Railways.

550	**169**	20c. red	1·10	45
551	**169**	50c. violet	1·10	45
552	**169**	1l.25 blue	2·10	4·00

170 Hitler and Mussolini

171 Hitler and Mussolini

1941. Italo-German Friendship.

553	**170**	10c. brown	1·10	1·60
554	**170**	20c. orange	1·10	1·60
555	**170**	25c. green	1·10	1·60
556	**171**	50c. violet	2·10	1·60
557	**171**	75c. red	5·25	4·00
558	**171**	1l.25 blue	6·50	7·25

172 Roman Cavalry

1941. 2000th Birth Anniv of Livy (Latin historian).

559	**172**	20c.+10c. red	30	1·30
560	**172**	30c.+15c. brown	30	1·90
561	-	50c.+25c. violet	45	1·90
562	-	1l.25+1l. blue	55	2·40

DESIGN: 50c., 1l.25, Roman legionary.

1942. War Propaganda. Nos. 244/5 and 247 with attached labels (imperf between stamp and label) to encourage war effort.

563	25c. green (Navy)	45	1·30
564	25c. green (Army)	45	1·30
565	25c. green (Air Force)	45	1·30
566	25c. green (Militia)	45	1·30
567	30c. brown (Navy)	45	5·25
568	30c. brown (Army)	45	5·25
569	30c. brown (Air Force)	45	5·25
570	30c. brown (Militia)	45	5·25
571	50c. violet (Navy)	55	1·30
572	50c. violet (Army)	55	1·30
573	50c. violet (Air Force)	55	1·30
574	50c. violet (Militia)	55	1·30

173 Galileo teaching at Padua

1942. Death Tercentenary of Galileo.

575	**173**	10c. red and orange	55	45
576	-	25c. green and olive	55	45
577	-	50c. violet and purple	60	40
578	-	1l.25 blue and grey	60	3·00

DESIGNS: Galileo at Venice (25c.) and at Arcetri, near Florence (1l.25), 50c. Portrait of Galileo.

174 Rossini

1942. 150th Birth Anniv of Rossini (composer).

579		25c. green	20	60
580		30c. brown	20	60
581	**174**	50c. violet	30	60
582	**174**	1l. blue	30	1·60

DESIGN: 25c., 30c. Rossini Monument, Pescaro.

175

1943. Allied Military Government issue.

583	**175**	15c. orange	80	1·20
584	**175**	25c. bistre	80	1·20
585	**175**	30c. grey	80	1·20
586	**175**	50c. violet	80	1·20
587	**175**	60c. yellow	80	1·40
588	**175**	1l. green	80	1·20
589	**175**	2l. red	80	3·00
590	**175**	5l. blue	80	5·50
591	**175**	10l. brown	80	6·75

1943. Allied Military Government issue. Stamps of 1929 optd GOVERNO MILITARE ALLEATO.

592	**99**	20c. red	95	3·00
593	**99**	35c. blue	6·50	20·00
594	**103**	50c. violet	35	1·00

187 Romulus, Remus and Wolf (after Pollaiuolo)

1944

619	**187**	50c. purple	10	2·10

1944. As issue of 1929, but with Fascist emblems removed.

620	**103**	30c. brown	55	25
621	**103**	50c. violet	1·10	2·75
633	-	10c. brown (Augustus the Great)	75	1·10
635	-	50c. violet (Italia)	75	20
636	-	60c. orange (Italia)	75	20
637	**99**	1l. violet	75	20
638	-	2l. red (Italia)	1·30	1·10
640	**99**	20c. red	55	20
641	**103**	60c. green	55	20
643	-	1l.20 brown (Italia)	55	20
645	**98**	5l. red	1·60	20
646	-	10l. violet (Italia)	8·00	7·50

1945. Stamps of Italy surch L. 2,50 (No. 629) and stamps of Italian Social Republic surch POSTE ITALIANE and new value (Nos. 627/8).

627	1l.20 on 20c. red (No. 102)	10	10
628	2l. on 25c. green (No. 103)	15	20
629	2l.50 on 1l.75 orange (No. 251)	15	30

193 "Work, Justice and Family"

195 Planting a Sapling

196 "Peace"

197 "Work, Justice and Family"

1945

647	-	10c. brown	10	10
648	**193**	20c. brown	10	10
649	-	25c. blue	10	20
650	**195**	40c. grey	10	15
651	-	50c. violet	10	15
652	-	60c. green	15	60
653	-	80c. red	10	10
654	**195**	1l. green	20	10
655	-	1l.20 brown	20	50
656	-	2l. brown	20	30
657	-	3l. red	20	10
658	-	4l. red	60	10
659	**193**	5l. blue	4·50	10
660	**195**	6l. violet	11·00	10
661	-	8l. green	6·25	25
662	-	10l. grey	2·00	20
663	**193**	10l. red	41·00	10
664	**195**	15l. blue	16·00	10
665	-	20l. purple	13·00	10
666	**196**	25l. green	34·00	15
667	-	30l. blue	£500	45
668	**196**	50l. purple	14·00	20
669	**197**	100l. red	£550	4·50

DESIGNS: 10, 50, 80c., 8, 10l. (662) Hammer breaking chain ("Freedom"); 25c., 1l.20, 3, 4, 20, 30l. Flaming torch ("Enlightenment"); 60c., 2l. Gardener tying sapling to stake.

198 Clasped Hands and Caproni Campini N-1 Jet

1945. Air.

670	**198**	1l. grey	30	10
671	-	2l. blue	30	10
672	**198**	3l.20 red	45	25
673	-	5l. green	20	15
674	**198**	10l. red	30	15
675	-	25l. blue	15	13·00
676	-	25l. brown	25	10
677	**198**	50l. green	42·00	21·00
678	**198**	50l. violet	25	10

DESIGN: 2, 5, 25l. Barn swallows in flight.

200 Amalfi

1946. Mediaeval Italian Republics.

679	**200**	1l. sepia	20	20
680	-	2l. blue	20	20
681	-	3l. green	20	20
682	-	4l. orange	20	20
683	-	5l. violet	25	20
684	-	10l. red	25	20
685	-	15l. blue	2·40	1·30
686	-	20l. brown	70	45

DESIGNS—VERT: 2l. Lucca; 3l. Siena; 4l. Florence. HORIZ: 5l. Pisa; 10l. Genoa; 15l. Venice; 20l. "The Oath of Pontida".

1947. Air. Surch LIRE 6-.

687	**198**	6l. on 3l.20 orange	45	10

202 Wireless Mast

1947. Air. 50th Anniv of Radio.

688	**202**	6l. violet	20	15
689	-	10l. red	20	15
690	-	20l. orange	1·30	1·10
691	**202**	25l. blue	1·90	1·30
692	-	35l. blue	3·00	2·40
693	-	50l. purple	4·00	3·25

DESIGNS: 10, 35l. Ship's aerial; 20, 50l. Heinkel He 70 Blitz wireless-equipped airplane.

204 Douglas DC-2 over Rome

1948. Air.

911	**204**	100l. green	65	20
912	**204**	300l. mauve	65	30
913	**204**	500l. blue	1·70	1·60
914	**204**	1000l. brown	2·75	2·75

For No. 911 in smaller size see No. 1297.

205 St. Catherine giving her Cloak to a Beggar

206 St. Catherine carrying the Cross

1948. 600th Birth Anniv of St. Catherine of Siena.

698	**205**	3l. blue and green (postage)	20	25
699	-	5l. blue and violet	20	25
700	-	10l. violet and brown	4·50	3·25
701	-	30l. grey and bistre	25·00	21·00
702	**206**	100l. violet and brown (air)	£130	60·00
703	-	200l. blue and bistre	80·00	27·00

DESIGNS—All show St. Catherine. VERT: 5l. Carrying the Cross; 10l. Extending her arms to Italy; 30l. Dictating "The Dialogue" to a Disciple. HORIZ: 200l. Extending her arms to Italy.

207 "Proclamation of New Constitution"

1948. Proclamation of New Constitution.

704	**207**	10l. violet	1·70	1·10
705	**207**	30l. blue	5·50	3·25

208 Rising at Palermo

1948. Centenary of Revolution of 1848.

706	**208**	3l. brown	1·40	70
707	-	4l. purple	1·40	70
708	-	5l. blue	4·50	85
709	-	6l. green	2·75	1·30
710	-	8l. brown	2·50	1·30
711	-	10l. red	4·25	60
712	-	12l. green	16·00	4·25
713	-	15l. black	31·00	3·25
714	-	20l. red	75·00	10·50
715	-	30l. blue	18·00	3·25
716	-	50l. violet	£190	7·50

717	-	100l. blue	£190	27·00

DESIGNS: 4l. Rising at Padua; 5l. Concession of Statute, Turin; 6l. Storming Porta Tosa, Milan; 8l. Proclamation of Venetian Republic; 10l. Defence of Vicenza; 12l. Hero of Curtatone; 15l. Hero of Goito; 20l. Austrian retreat from Bologna; 30l. Fighting at Brescia; 50l. Garibaldi; 100l. Goffredo Mameli (party patriot) on death bed, July 1849.

209 Alpinist and Bassano Bridge

1948. Rebuilding of Bassano Bridge.

718	**209**	15l. green	4·00	2·10

210 Gaetano Donizetti

1948. Death Centenary of Donizetti (composer).

719	**210**	15l. brown	2·75	1·80

211 Exhibition Grounds

1949. 27th Milan Fair.

720	**211**	20l. sepia	17·00	6·00

212

1949. 25th Biennial Art Exhibition. Venice.

721	**212**	5l. red and flesh	1·10	25
722	-	15l. green and cream	7·75	2·75
723	-	20l. brown and buff	13·50	30
724	-	50l. blue and yellow	£110	2·75

DESIGNS: 15l. Clock bell-ringers, St. Mark's Column and Campanile; 20l. Emblem of Venice and "Bucentaur" (state gallery); 50l. Winged lion on St. Mark's Column.

213 Globes and Forms of Transport

1949. 75th Anniv of U.P.U.

725	**213**	50l. blue	£110	10·50

214 Vascello Castle

1949. Centenary of Roman Republic.

726	**214**	100l. brown	£475	£140

215 Worker and Ship

1949. European Recovery Plan.

727	**215**	5l. green	11·00	6·50
728	**215**	15l. violet	50·00	24·00
729	**215**	20l. brown	£120	27·00

216 Statue of Mazzini

1949. Honouring Giuseppe Mazzini (founder of "Young Italy").

730	**216**	20l. black	19·00	6·50

217 V. Alfieri

1949. Birth Bicentenary of Vittorio Alfieri (poet).

731	**217**	20l. brown	13·50	5·25

218 San Giusto Cathedral

1949. 1st Trieste Free Election.

732	**218**	20l. lake	22·00	21·00

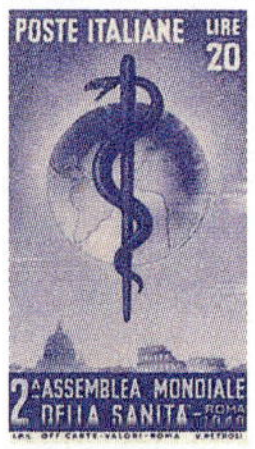

219 Staff of Aesculapius and Globe

1949. 2nd World Health Congress, Rome.

733	**219**	20l. violet	65·00	20·00

220 A. Palladio and Vicenza Basilica

1949. 400th Anniv of Completion of Palladio's Basilica at Vicenza.

734	**220**	20l. violet	22·00	10·50

221 Lorenzo de Medici

1949. 500th Birth Anniv of Lorenzo de Medici "The Magnificent".

735	**221**	20l. blue	19·00	3·75

222 Galleon and Exhibition Buildings

1949. 13th Levant Fair, Bari.

736	**222**	20l. red	13·50	3·75

223 Voltaic Pile

224 Count Alessandro Volta

1949. 150th Anniv of Volta's Discovery of the Electric Cell.

737	**223**	20l. red	11·00	2·75
738	**224**	50l. blue	£170	46·00

225 Holy Trinity Bridge, Florence

1949. Rebuilding of Holy Trinity Bridge, Florence.

739	**225**	20l. green	22·00	3·75

226 Caius Valerius Catullus

1949. Death Bimillenary of Catullus (poet).

740	**226**	20l. blue	22·00	3·75

227 Domenico Cimarosa

1949. Birth Bicentenary of Cimarosa (composer).

741	**227**	20l. violet	19·00	2·75

228 Entrance to Exhibition

1950. 28th Milan Fair.

742	**228**	20l. brown	6·75	2·75

229 Car and Flags

1950. 32nd Int Automobile Exhibition, Turin.

743	**229**	20l. violet	19·00	2·75

230 Statue of Perseus

1950. 5th General UNESCO Conference, Florence.

744	-	20l. green	17·00	2·10
745	**230**	55l. blue	£100	17·00

DESIGN—HORIZ: 20l. Pitti Palace, Florence.

231 St. Peter's Basilica

1950. Holy Year.

746	**231**	20l. violet	17·00	1·10
747	**231**	55l. blue	£140	3·25

232 Gaudenzio Ferrari

1950. Honouring Gaudenzio Ferrari (painter).

748	**232**	20l. green	32·00	3·25

233 Town Hall, Florence, Statue of Columbus and Wireless Mast

1950. International Radio Conf, Florence.

749	**233**	20l. violet	28·00	13·00
750	**233**	55l. blue	£325	£180

234 L. Muratori

1950. Death Bicentenary of Ludovico Muratori (historian).

751	**234**	20l. brown	11·00	2·75

235 Guido D'Arezzo

1950. 9th Death Cent of D'Arezzo (musician).

752	**235**	20l. green	36·00	3·25

236 Galleon

1950. 14th Levant Fair, Bari.

753	**236**	20l. brown	20·00	2·75

237 Marzotto and Rossi

1950. Pioneers of Wool Industry.
754 **237** 20l. blue 6·75 1·80

238 Tobacco Plant and Factory

1950. European Tobacco Conference, Rome.
755 **238** 5l. green and mauve 4·50 2·75
756 - 20l. green and brown 5·50 1·40
757 - 55l. brown and blue £120 30·00
DESIGNS: 20l. Plant; 55l. Girl and plant.

239 Seal of Academy

1950. Bicentenary of Academy of Fine Arts, Venice.
758 **239** 20l. lt brown and brown 9·00 2·75

240 A. Righi

1950. Birth Centenary of Augusto Righi (physicist).
759 **240** 20l. black and buff 9·00 2·75

241 Blacksmith

1950. Provincial Occupations. As T 241.
760 **241** 50c. blue 20 25
762 - 2l. brown 35 25
763 - 5l. black 1·10 15
764 - 6l. brown 35 25
765 - 10l. green 5·50 15
766 - 12l. green 5·50 25
768 - 20l. violet 33·00 15
769 - 25l. brown 6·00 15
770 - 30l. purple 4·50 25
771 - 35l. red 24·00 70
772 - 40l. brown 1·10 25
773 - 50l. violet 50·00 15
774 - 55l. blue 3·25 25
775 - 60l. red 7·75 85
776 - 65l. green 2·20 35
777 - 100l. brown £110 50
778 - 200l. brown 33·00 4·75
881 - 1l. violet 10 10
883 - 15l. blue 1·70 10
DESIGNS: 1l. Motor mechanic; 2l. Stonemason; 5l. Potter; 6l. Girls embroidering and water-carrying; 10l. Weaver; 12l. Fisherman at tiller; 15l. Boat builder; 20l. Fisherman trawling; 25l. Girl packing oranges; 30l. Girl carrying grapes; 35l. Gathering olives; 40l. Carter and wagon; 50l. Shepherd; 55l. Ploughman; 60l. Ox-cart; 65l. Girl harvester; 100l. Women handling maize; 200l. Woodcutter.

242 First Tuscan Stamp

1951. Centenary of First Tuscan Stamp.
779 **242** 20l. red and purple 4·50 1·60
780 **242** 55l. blue and ultramarine 65·00 48·00

243 Car and Flags

1951. 33rd International Motor Show, Turin.
781 **243** 20l. green 24·00 3·75

244 Peace Hall, Rome

1951. Consecration of Hall of Peace, Rome.
782 **244** 20l. violet 17·00 3·75

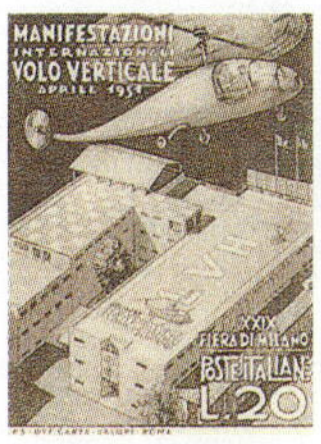

245 Westland W.81 Helicopter over Fair **246** Fair Building

1951. 29th Milan Fair.
783 **245** 20l. brown 22·00 2·75
784 **246** 55l. blue £120 75·00

247 Allegory

1951. 10th International Textile Art and Fashion Exhibition, Turin.
785 **247** 20l. violet 40·00 4·25

248 Columbus disembarking

1951. 500th Birth Anniv of Columbus.
786 **248** 20l. green 33·00 4·25

249 Gymnastics Symbols

1951. Int Gymnastic Festival, Florence.
787 **249** 5l. red and brown 50·00 £450
788 **249** 10l. red and green 50·00 £450
789 **249** 15l. red and blue 50·00 £450

250 Montecassino Abbey restored

1951. Restoration of Montecassino Abbey.
790 **250** 20l. violet 11·00 2·75
791 - 55l. blue £110 65·00
DESIGN: 55l. Abbey in ruins, 1944.

251 Perugino

1951. 500th Birth Anniv of Perugino (painter).
792 **251** 20l. brown and sepia 6·75 4·25

252 Modern Art

1951. Triennial Art Exhibition, Milan.
793 **252** 20l. black and green 13·50 3·25
794 - 55l. pink and blue 65·00 55·00
DESIGN—HORIZ: 55l. Jug and symbols.

253 Cyclist and Globe

1951. World Cycling Championship.
795 **253** 25l. black 20·00 3·75

254 Galleon and Hemispheres

1951. 15th Levant Fair, Bari.
796 **254** 25l. blue 12·00 3·25

255 "Jorio's Daughter"

1951. Birth Centenary of Francesco Paolo Michetti (painter).
797 **255** 25l. brown 11·00 3·25

256 T 1 of Sardinia and Arms of Cagliari

1951. Sardinian Postage Stamp Centenary.
798 **256** 10l. black and sepia 4·00 3·25
799 - 25l. green and red 5·00 2·75
800 - 60l. red and blue 24·00 21·00
DESIGNS: 25l. 20c. stamp and arms of Genoa; 60l. 40c. stamp and arms of Turin.

257 "Industry and Commerce"

1951. 3rd Industrial and Commercial Census.
801 **257** 10l. green 2·20 1·90

258 Census in Ancient Rome

1951. 9th National Census.
802 **258** 25l. black 9·00 1·90

259 G. Verdi and Roncole Church

1951. 50th Death Anniv of Giuseppe Verdi (composer).
803 - 10l. green and purple 5·50 2·75
804 **259** 25l. brown and chocolate 11·00 2·75
805 - 60l. blue and green 75·00 21·00
DESIGNS: 10l. Verdi, Theatre Royal and Cathedral, Parma; 60l. Verdi, La Scala Opera House and Cathedral, Milan.

260 Mountain Forest

1951. Forestry Festival. Inscr "FESTA DEGLI ALBERI".
806 **260** 10l. green and olive 3·25 3·25
807 - 25l. green 11·00 2·10
DESIGN—HORIZ: 25l. Tree and wooded hills.

261 V. Bellini

1952. 150th Birth Anniv of Bellini (composer).
808 **261** 25l. black 6·75 1·60

262 Royal Palace, Caserta

1952. Bicentenary of Construction of Caserta Palace by Vanvitelli.
809 **262** 25l. bistre and green 6·75 1·60

263

1952. 1st Int Sports Stamps Exhibition, Rome.
810 **263** 25l. brown and black 2·75 1·30

264 Motor-boat Pavilion

1952. 30th Milan Fair.
811 **264** 60l. blue 75·00 18·00

265 Leonardo da Vinci

1952. 500th Birth Anniv of Leonardo da Vinci.
812 **265** 25l. orange 65 55
813 - 60l. blue 9·25 8·50
814 **265** 80l. red 26·00 80
DESIGN—(inscr "LEONARDO DA VINCI 1452–1952"): 60l. "The Virgin of the Rocks".

267 Campaniles and First Stamps

1952. Modena and Parma Stamp Centenary.
815 **267** 25l. black and brown 1·70 1·60
816 **267** 60l. indigo and blue 16·00 14·00

268 Hand, Torch and Globe

1952. Overseas Fair, Naples.
817 **268** 25l. blue 3·25 1·30

269 Lion of St. Mark

1952. 26th Biennial Art Exhibition, Venice.
818 **269** 25l. black and cream 4·50 1·30

270 Emblem of Fair

1952. 30th Padua Fair.
819 **270** 25l. red and blue 5·50 1·60

271 San Giusto Cathedral and Flag

1952. 4th Trieste Fair.
820 **271** 25l. green, red and brown 4·50 1·60

272 Caravel and Bari Fair

1952. 16th Levant Fair, Bari.
821 **272** 25l. green 2·00 1·30

273 Girolamo Savonarola

1952. 5th Birth Cent of Savonarola (reformer).
822 **273** 25l. violet 8·25 1·60

274 Savoia Marchetti S.M.95C over Colosseum

1952. 1st Civil Aeronautics Law Conf, Rome.
823 **274** 60l. blue and ultramarine 28·00 27·00

275 Alpine Climbing Equipment

1952. Alpine Troops National Exhibition.
824 **275** 25l. black 1·10 85

276 Army, Navy and Air Force Symbols

277 Sailor, Soldier and Airman

1952. Armed Forces Day.
825 **276** 10l. green 30 10
826 **277** 25l. sepia and brown 85 30
827 - 60l. black and blue 16·00 6·00
DESIGN—As Type **277**: 60l. Airplane, motor torpedo boat and tank.

278 Cardinal Massaia and Map

1952. Centenary of Mission to Ethiopia.
828 **278** 25l. deep brown & brown 2·75 2·40

279 V. Gemito

1952. Birth Centenary of Gemito (sculptor).
829 **279** 25l. brown 1·70 1·10

280 A. Mancini

1952. Birth Centenary of Mancini (painter).
830 **280** 25l. myrtle 1·70 1·10

281

1952. Centenary of Martyrdom of Belfiore.
831 **281** 25l. blue and black 4·00 1·10

282 Antonello da Messina

1953. Antonello Exhibition, Messina.
832 **282** 25l. red 3·25 1·10

283 Cars Racing

1953. 20th "Mille Miglia" Car Race.
833 **283** 25l. violet 1·70 1·10

284 Bee and Medals

1953. Creation of Orders of Meritorious Labour.
834 **284** 25l. violet 1·70 1·10

285 Arcangelo Corelli

1953. Birth Tercentenary of Corelli (composer).
835 **285** 25l. brown 1·70 1·10

286 Coin of Syracuse

1953. (a) Size 17×21 mm.
887 **286** 1l. black 10 10
888 **286** 5l. grey 10 10
889 **286** 6l. brown 10 10
890 **286** 10l. red 10 10
891 **286** 12l. green 10 10
892 **286** 13l. purple 10 10
893 **286** 15l. grey 10 10
894 **286** 20l. brown 10 10
895 **286** 25l. violet 45 10
896 **286** 30l. brown 30 10
897 **286** 35l. red 20 10
898 **286** 40l. mauve 65 10
899 **286** 50l. green 55 10
900 **286** 60l. blue 20 20
901 **286** 70l. green 35 20
902 **286** 80l. brown 35 20
903 **286** 90l. brown 65 20
905 **286** 130l. red and grey 35 25
1008 **286** 100l. brown 35 10
1009 **286** 200l. blue 80 10

(b) Size 22½×28 mm.
846 200l. blue 11·00 65
904 100l. brown 24·00 25
See also Nos. 1202/19b.

287 St. Clare of Assisi

1953. 700th Death Anniv of St. Clare.
847 **287** 25l. red and brown 1·10 75

288 Mountains and Reservoirs

1953. Mountains Festival.
848 **288** 25l. green 2·20 65

289 "Agriculture"

1953. International Agricultural Exn, Rome.
849 **289** 25l. brown 1·70 30
850 **289** 60l. blue 7·75 3·25

290 Rainbow over Atlantic

1953. 4th Anniv of Atlantic Pact.
851 **290** 25l. turquoise and orange 8·25 25
852 **290** 60l. blue and mauve 20·00 4·75

291 L. Signorelli

1953. 500th Birth Anniv of Signorelli (painter).
853 **291** 25l. green and brown 1·30 55

292 A. Bassi

1953. 6th Int Microbiological Congress, Rome.
854 **292** 25l. brown and black 1·10 55

293 Capri

1953. Tourist Series.
855 - 10l. brown and sepia 35 30
856 - 12l. black and blue 55 45
857 - 20l. brown and orange 80 10
858 - 25l. green and blue 2·75 10
859 - 35l. brown and buff 3·25 85
860 **293** 60l. blue and green 6·00 1·10
DESIGNS—VERT: 10l. Siena; 25l. Cortina d'Ampezzo. HORIZ: 12l. Rapallo; 20l. Gardone; 35l. Taormina.

294 Lateran Palace

1954. 25th Anniv of Lateran Treaty.
861 **294** 25l. brown and sepia 80 25
862 **294** 60l. blue and bright blue 5·00 3·75

295 Television Aerial and Screen

1954. Introduction of Television in Italy.
863 **295** 25l. violet 1·90 25
864 **295** 60l. turquoise 9·50 5·25

296 "Everyone Must Contribute to the Public Expense"

1954. "Encouragement to Taxpayers".
865 **296** 25l. violet 2·75 55

297 Vertical Flight Trophy

1954. 1st Experimental Helicopter Mail Flight, Milan–Turin.
866 **297** 25l. green 1·30 75

298 Golden Eagle and Campanile

1954. 10th Anniv of Resistance Movement.
867 **298** 25l. black and brown 60 55

299 A. Catalani

1954. Birth Centenary of Catalani (composer).
868 **299** 25l. green 60 55

300 Marco Polo, Lion of St. Mark, Venice, and Dragon Pillar, Peking

1954. 7th Birth Centenary of Marco Polo.
869 **300** 25l. brown 65 55
870 **300** 60l. green 6·75 6·50

301 Cyclist, Car and Landscape

1954. 60th Anniv of Italian Touring Club.
871 **301** 25l. green and red 80 55

302 "St. Michael the Archangel" (after Guido Reni)

1954. International Police Congress, Rome.
872 **302** 25l. red 55 25
873 **302** 60l. blue 2·20 2·50

303 "Pinocchio"

1954. 64th Death Anniv of Carlo Lorenzini (Collodi) (writer).
874 **303** 25l. red 1·10 55

304 Amerigo Vespucci

1954. 5th Birth Cent of Vespucci (explorer).
875 **304** 25l. purple 65 45
876 **304** 60l. blue 4·00 3·75

305 "Madonna" (Perugino)

1954. Termination of Marian Year.
877 **305** 25l. brown and buff 55 55
878 - 60l. black and cream 2·75 2·75
DESIGN: 60l. Madonna's head (Michelangelo).

306 Silvio Pellico

1955. Death Centenary of Pellico (dramatist).
879 **306** 25l. blue and violet 55 65

308 "The Nation Expects a Faithful Declaration of Your Income"

1955. "Encouragement to Taxpayers".
907 **308** 25l. lilac 2·20 30

309

1955. 4th World Petroleum Congress.
908 **309** 25l. green 55 30
909 - 60l. red 1·30 1·80
DESIGN: 60l. Oil derricks and globe.

310 A. Rosmini

1955. Death Cent of Rosmini (theologian).
910 **310** 25l. brown 1·30 30

311 Girolamo Fracastoro (physician) and Roman Arena, Verona

1955. International Medical Conf, Verona.
915 **311** 25l. brown and black 80 30

312 Basilica of St. Francis

1955. Bicentenary of Elevation of Basilica of St. Francis of Assisi to Papal Chapel.
916 **312** 25l. black and cream 55 30

313 Scholar and Drawing-board

1955. Centenary of "Montani" Institute, Fermo.
917 **313** 25l. green 55 30

314 "The Harvester"

1955. 50th Anniv of Int Agricultural Institute.
918 **314** 25l. brown and red 45 30

315 F.A.O. Building, Rome

1955. 10th Anniv of F.A.O.
919 **315** 60l. violet and black 1·80 1·30

316 G. Matteotti

1955. 70th Birth Anniv of Giacomo Matteotti (politician).
920 **316** 25l. red 1·30 30

317 B. Grassi

1955. 30th Death Anniv of Grassi (biologist).
921 **317** 25l. green 55 30

318 "St. Stephen giving Alms to the Poor"

1955. 5th Death Cent of Fra Angelico (painter).
922 **318** 10l. black and cream 20 20
923 - 25l. blue and cream 35 30
DESIGN—HORIZ: 25l. "St. Lawrence giving goods of the Church to the poor".

319 G. Pascoli

1955. Birth Centenary of Pascoli (poet).
924 **319** 25l. black 55 30

320 G. Mazzini

1955. Air. 150th Birth Anniv of Mazzini (founder of "Young Italy").
925 **320** 100l. green 3·00 1·60

321 "Italia" Ski-jump

1956. 7th Winter Olympic Games, Cortina d'Ampezzo.

926	**321**	10l. green and orange	10	20
927	-	12l. black and yellow	10	30
928	-	25l. purple and orange	45	20
929	-	60l. blue and orange	3·50	3·00

DESIGNS: 12l. Snow Stadium; 25l. Ice Stadium; 60l. Skating Arena, Misurina.

1956. Air. Italian President's Visit to U.S.A. and Canada. Surch 1956 Visita del Presidente della Repubblica negli U.S.A. e nel Canada L. 120.

930	**198**	120l. on 50l. mauve	2·20	2·40

323 Coach and Steam Train

1956. 50th Anniv of Simplon Tunnel.

931	**323**	25l. green	11·00	1·10

324

1956. 10th Anniv of Republic.

932	**324**	10l. grey and blue	30	25
933	**324**	25l. carmine and red	55	25
934	**324**	60l. light blue and blue	6·75	6·50
935	**324**	80l. orange and brown	12·00	70

325 Count Avogadro

1956. Death Centenary of Avogadro (physicist).

936	**325**	25l. black	35	30

326

1956. Europa.

937	**326**	25l. deep green and green	2·20	15
938	**326**	60l. deep blue and blue	14·50	1·40

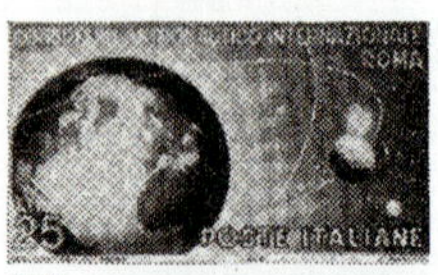

327

1956. Int Astronautical Congress, Rome.

939	**327**	25l. blue	55	30

328 The Globe

1956. 1st Anniv of Admission to U.N.

940	**328**	25l. red and green on pink	35	20
941	**328**	60l. green and red on green	55	30

329 Savings Bank, Books and Certificates

1956. 80th Anniv of Post Office Savings Bank.

942	**329**	25l. blue and slate	35	30

330 Ovid

1957. Birth Bimillenary of Ovid (poet).

943	**330**	25l. black and olive	45	30

331 St. George (after Donatello)

1957

944a	**331**	500l. green	2·75	10
945a	**331**	1000l. red	2·75	30

332 Antonio Canova

1957. Birth Bicentenary of Canova (sculptor).

946	**332**	25l. brown	15	20
947	-	60l. slate	40	65
948	-	80l. blue	45	20

DESIGNS—VERT: 60l. Hercules and Lica. HORIZ: 80l. Pauline Borghese (bust).

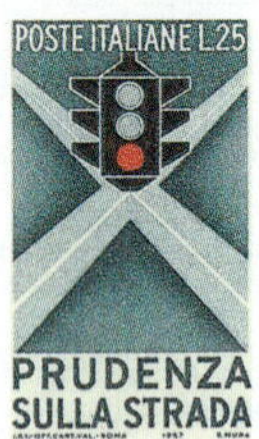

333 Traffic Lights at Crossroads

1957. Road Safety Campaign.

949	**333**	25l. red, black and green	45	30

334 "Europa" Flags

1957. Europa. Flags in national colours.

950	**334**	25l. blue	1·10	10
951	**334**	60l. blue	9·00	1·00

335 Giosue Carducci

1957. 50th Death Anniv of Carducci (poet).

954	**335**	25l. sepia	55	30

336 Filippino Lippi (after self-portrait)

1957. 500th Birth Anniv of Filippino Lippi (painter).

955	**336**	25l. brown	35	30

337 Cicero (bust)

1957. Death Bimillenary of Cicero (statesman).

956	**337**	25l. red	35	30

338 Garibaldi (after M. Lorusso)

1957. 150th Birth Anniv of Garibaldi.

957	**338**	15l. grey	20	15
958	-	110l. lilac	35	20

DESIGN—HORIZ: 110l. Statue of Garibaldi on horseback (after Romanelli).

339 St. Domenico Savio and Youths

1957. Death Centenary of St. Domenico Savio.

959	**339**	15l. black and violet	35	30

340 St. Francis of Paola

1957. 450th Death Anniv of St. Francis of Paola.

960	**340**	25l. black	35	30

341 Dams, Peasant and Map of Sardinia

1958. Inaug of Flumendosa–Mulargia Irrigation Scheme, Sardinia.

961	**341**	25l. turquoise	35	30

342 Statue of the Holy Virgin and Lourdes Basilica

1958. Centenary of Apparition of Virgin Mary at Lourdes.

962	**342**	15l. purple	10	10
963	**342**	60l. blue	30	20

343 "The Constitution"

1958. 10th Anniv of Constitution.

964	**343**	25l. green and brown	10	10
965	-	60l. sepia and blue	10	10
966	-	110l. sepia and brown	10	10

DESIGNS—VERT: 60l. Oak tree with new growth. HORIZ: 110l. Montecitorio Palace, Rome.

344 Exhibition Emblem and Ancient Roman Road

1958. Brussels International Exhibition.

967	**344**	60l. yellow and blue	35	30

345 Rodolfo's Attic ("La Boheme")

1958. Birth Centenary of Puccini (operatic composer).

968	**345**	25l. blue	35	30

346 The Prologue ("I Pagliacci")

1958. Birth Centenary of Leoncavallo (operatic composer).

969	**346**	25l. red and indigo	35	30

347 "Ave Maria" (after Segantini)

1958. Birth Centenary of Giovanni Segantini (painter).

970	**347**	110l. green on cream	55	30

348 "Fattori in his Studio" (self-portrait)

1958. 50th Death Anniv of Giovanni Fattori (painter).

971	**348**	110l. brown	55	35

349 Federal Palace, Brasilia and Arch of Titus, Rome

1958. Visit of Pres. Gronchi to Brazil.

972	**349**	175l. green	80	70

349a "Europa"

1958. Europa.

973	**349a**	25l. blue and red	55	15
974	**349a**	60l. red and blue	1·70	20

350 Naples 1/2 grano stamp of 1858

1958. 1st Naples Postage Stamps Centenary.

975	**350**	25l. brown	10	10
976	-	60l. brown and sepia	10	10

DESIGN: 60l. Naples 1 grano stamp of 1858.

351 "Winged Horse" (sculpture in Sorrento Cathedral)

1958. Visit of Shah of Iran.

977	**351**	25l. sepia and lavender	20	10
978	**351**	60l. blue and pale blue	90	1·10

352 E. Torricelli

1958. 350th Birth Anniv of Evangelista Torricelli (physicist).

979	**352**	25l. red	55	45

353 "Triumphs of Julius Caesar" (after fresco by Mantegna)

1958. 40th Anniv of Victory in World War I.

980	**353**	15l. green	15	10
981	-	25l. slate	15	10
982	-	60l. red	35	20

DESIGNS—HORIZ: 25l. Arms of Trieste, Rome and Trento. VERT: 60l. Memorial bell of Rovereto.

354 Eleonora Duse

1958. Birth Centenary of Eleonora Duse (actress).

983	**354**	25l. blue	35	30

355 "Drama"

1958. 10th Anniv of "Premio Italia" (international contest for radio and television plays).

984	**355**	25l. black, blue and red	10	10
985	-	60l. black and blue	20	20

DESIGN: 60l. "Music" (radio mast and grand piano).

356 Sicily 5gr. stamp of 1859

1959. 1st Sicilian Postage Stamps Centenary.

986		25l. turquoise	10	10
987	**356**	60l. orange	20	20

DESIGN: 25l. Sicily 2gr. stamp of 1859.

357 Capitol, Quirinal Square Obelisk and Dome of St. Peter's

1959. 30th Anniv of Lateran Treaty.

988	**357**	25l. blue	35	30

358 N.A.T.O. Emblem and Map

1959. 10th Anniv of N.A.T.O.

989	**358**	25l. blue and yellow	10	10
990	**358**	60l. blue and green	20	30

359 Arms of Paris and Rome

1959. Rome-Paris Friendship.

991	**359**	15l. red, brown and blue	10	10
992	**359**	25l. red, brown and blue	20	10

360 Olive Branch growing from shattered Tree

1959. Int War Veterans' Assn Convention, Rome.

993	**360**	25l. green	35	30

361 Lord Byron Monument

1959. Unveiling of Lord Byron Monument, Rome.

994	**361**	15l. green	35	30

362 C. Prampolini

1959. Birth Centenary of Camillo Prampolini (politician).

995	**362**	15l. red	9·50	45

363 Quirinal Square Obelisk, Rome

1959. Olympic Games Propaganda. Roman Monuments and Ruins. Inscr "ROMA MCMLX".

996	**363**	15l. sepia and orange	10	10
997	-	25l. sepia and blue	20	20
998	-	35l. sepia and buff	20	20
999	-	60l. sepia and mauve	35	35
1000	-	110l. sepia and yellow	55	20

DESIGNS—VERT: 25l. Tower of City Hall, Quirinal Hill. HORIZ: 35l. Baths of Caracalla; 60l. Arch of Constantine (Colosseum); 110l. Basilica of Massentius.

364 Victor Emmanuel II, Garibaldi, Cavour and Mazzini

1959. Centenary of 2nd War of Independence.

1001	**364**	15l. black	10	10
1002	-	25l. red and brown	10	10
1003	-	35l. violet	20	20
1004	-	60l. blue	20	35
1005	-	110l. lake	45	35

DESIGNS—VERT: 25l. Italian camp after the Battle of Magenta (after painting by Fattori); 110l. Battle of Magenta (after painting by Induno). HORIZ: 35l. Battle of San Fermo (after painting by Trezzini); 60l. Battle of Palestro.

The 25l. is also a Red Cross commemorative.

365 Workers' Monument and I.L.O. Building, Geneva

1959. 40th Anniv of I.L.O.

1006	**365**	25l. violet	10	10
1007	**365**	60l. brown	10	10

366 Romagna 8b. Stamp of 1859

1959. Romagna Postage Stamps Centenary.

1010	**366**	25l. brown and black	10	10
1011	-	60l. green and black	20	20

DESIGN: 60l. Romagna 20b. stamp of 1859.

366a "Europa"

1959. Europa.

1012	**366a**	25l. green	20	20
1013	**366a**	60l. blue	35	35

367

1959. Stamp Day.

1014	**367**	15l. red, black and grey	20	30

368 "The Fire of Borgo" (after Raphael)

1960. World Refugee Year.

1015	**368**	25l. red	20	10
1016	**368**	60l. purple	20	20

369 Garibaldi's Message to Sicilians

1960. Cent of Garibaldi's Expedition to Sicily.

1017	**369**	15l. brown	10	10
1018	-	25l. red	10	10
1019	-	60l. blue	20	20

DESIGNS—VERT: 25l. Garibaldi meeting King Victor Emmanuel II near Naples (after Matania). HORIZ: 60l. Embarkation of volunteers at Quarto, near Genoa (after T. van Elven).

370 "The Discus Thrower" (after Miron)

1960. Olympic Games. Inscr as in T 370.

1020		5l. brown	10	10
1021		10l. blue and orange	10	10
1022		15l. blue	10	10
1023		25l. sepia and lilac	10	10
1024	**370**	35l. red	10	10
1025	-	60l. sepia and green	10	10
1026	-	110l. purple	30	20
1027	-	150l. brown and blue	1·70	1·30
1028	-	200l. green	85	35

DESIGNS—VERT: 5l. Games emblem; 15l. "Starting the Race" (statue); 110l. "Pugilist at rest" (after Apollonius); 200l. "The Apoxiomenos" (after Lisippos). HORIZ: 10l. Olympic Stadium, Rome; 25l. Cycling Stadium, Rome; 60l. Sports Palace, Rome; 150l. Little Sports Palace.

371 Vittorio Bottego (after Ettore Ximenes)

1960. Birth Centenary of Vittorio Bottego (explorer).

1029	**371**	30l. brown	35	30

371a Conference Emblem

1960. Europa.

1030	**371a**	30l. brown and green	20	10
1031	**371a**	70l. orange and blue	20	10

372 Caravaggio

1960. 350th Death Anniv of Caravaggio (painter).

1032	**372**	25l. brown	35	30

373 Coach and Posthorn

1960. Stamp Day.

1033	**373**	15l. sepia and red	35	30

374 Michelangelo

1961. Works of Michelangelo. Frescoes on ceiling of Sistine Chapel. (a) Size 17×20½ mm.

1034	-	1l. black	10	10
1035	-	5l. orange	10	10
1036	-	10l. red	10	10
1037	-	15l. purple	10	10
1038	-	20l. green	10	10
1039	-	25l. brown	10	10
1040	-	30l. purple	10	20
1041	-	40l. red	10	10
1042	-	50l. green	10	10
1043	-	55l. brown	10	30
1044	-	70l. blue	10	10
1045	-	85l. green	10	10
1046	-	90l. mauve	30	50
1047	-	100l. violet	30	10
1048	-	115l. blue	30	30
1049	-	150l. brown	45	20
1050	**374**	200l. blue	65	15

(b) Size 22×26½ mm.

1051	500l. green	5·00	35
1052	1000l. red	3·25	6·75

DESIGNS: 1, 5, 10, 115, 150l. Ignudo (different versions); 15l. Joel; 20l. Libyan Sibyl; 25l. Isaiah; 30l. Erythraean Sibyl; 40l. Daniel; 50l. Delphic Sibyl; 55l. Cumaean Sibyl; 70l. Zachariah; 85l. Jonah; 90l. Jeremiah; 100l. Ezekiel; 500l. Adam; 1000l. Eve.

375 Douglas DC-8 crossing Atlantic Ocean

1961. Visit of President Gronchi to S. America.

1053	**375**	170l. blue (Argentina)	4·50	4·50
1054	**375**	185l. green (Uruguay)	4·50	4·50
1055	**375**	205l. violet (Peru)	13·50	13·50

The countries indicated are shown in deep colours on the map.

376 Pliny the Younger

1961. 19th Birth Cent of Pliny the Younger.

1056	**376**	30l. brown and buff	35	30

377 Ippolito Nievo

1961. Birth Centenary of Ippolito Nievo (poet).

1057	**377**	30l. blue and red	35	30

378 St. Paul in Ship (from 15th-century Bible of Borso d'Este)

1961. 19th Cent of St. Paul's Arrival in Rome.

1058	**378**	30l. multicoloured	20	20
1059	**378**	70l. multicoloured	45	45

379 Cannon and Gaeta Fortress

1961. Cent of Italian Unification and Independence.

1060	**379**	15l. brown and blue	20	10
1061	-	30l. brown and blue	20	20
1062	-	40l. brown and blue	20	45
1063	-	70l. mauve and brown	20	20
1064	-	115l. blue and brown	1·70	20
1065	-	300l. red, brown & green	5·50	5·50

DESIGNS: 30l. Carignano Palace, Turin; 40l. Montecitorio Palace, Rome; 70l. Vecchio Palace, Florence; 115l. Madama Palace, Rome; 300l. Capitals, "Palace of Work", Int. Exn. of Work, Turin.

380 Doves

1961. Europa.

1066	**380**	30l. red	15	10
1067	**380**	70l. green	15	15

381 G. Romagnosi

1961. Birth Bicent of Romagnosi (philosopher).

1068	**381**	30l. green	35	30

382 Imprint of 50c. Provisional Postal Franked Paper of Sardinia, 1819

1961. Stamp Day.

1069	**382**	15l. mauve and black	35	30

383 "The Sweet-burning Lamp" from Pascoli's "La Poesia" (after wood-eng by P. Morbiducci)

1962. 50th Death Anniv of G. Pascoli (poet).

1070	**383**	30l. red	10	10
1071	**383**	70l. blue	10	10

384 Pacinotti's Dynamo (diagram)

1962. 50th Death Anniv of Antonio Pacinotti (physicist).

1072	**384**	30l. black and red	10	10
1073	**384**	70l. black and blue	35	55

385 St. Catherine (after 15th-century woodcut)

1962. 5th Centenary of Canonization of St. Catherine of Siena.

1074	-	30l. violet	10	10
1075	**385**	70l. black and red	55	55

DESIGN: 30l. St. Catherine (after A. Vanni).

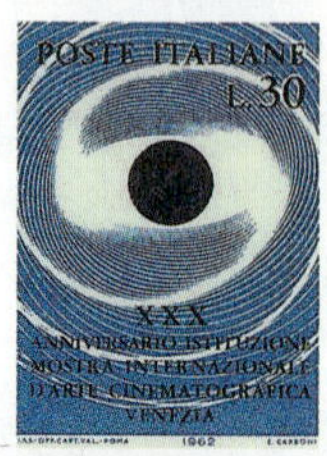

386 Camera Lens

1962. 30th Anniv of International Cinematograph Art Fair. Venice.

1076	**386**	30l. black and blue	10	10
1077	-	70l. black and red	35	55

DESIGN: 70l. Lion of St. Mark.

387 Cyclist being paced

1962. World Cycling Championships.

1078	**387**	30l. black and green	30	10
1079	-	70l. blue and black	30	35
1080	-	300l. black and red	3·00	5·50

DESIGNS: 70l. Cyclists road-racing; 300l. Cyclists on track.

388 Europa "Tree"

1962. Europa.

1081	**388**	30l. red and carmine	60	15
1082	**388**	70l. ultramarine and blue	60	35

389 Balzan Medal

1962. International Balzan Foundation.

1083	**389**	70l. red and green	1·00	45

390 Campaign Emblem

1962. Malaria Eradication.

1084	**390**	30l. violet	10	10
1085	**390**	70l. blue	55	55

391 10c. Stamp of 1862 and 30l. Stamp of 1961

1962. Stamp Day.

1086	**391**	15l. multicoloured	35	30

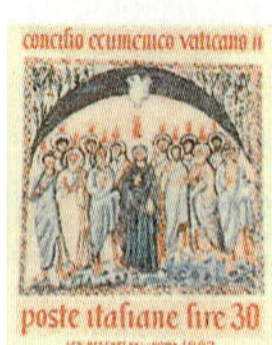

392 "The Pentecost" (from "Codex Syriacus")

1962. Ecumenical Council, Vatican City.

1087	**392**	30l. orange & bl on cream	10	10
1088	**392**	70l. blue & orge on cream	35	35

393 Statue of Cavour (statesman)

1962. Centenary of Court of Accounts.

1089	**393**	30l. green	35	30

394 Pico della Mirandola (scholar)

1963. 5th Birth Cent of G. Pico della Mirandola.

1090	**394**	30l. violet	35	30

395 D'Annunzio

1963. Birth Centenary of Gabriele D'Annunzio (author and soldier).

1091	**395**	30l. green	35	30

396 "Sowing" (bas-relief after G. and N. Pisano)

1963. Freedom from Hunger.

1092	**396**	30l. sepia and red	20	10
1093	-	70l. sepia and blue	35	40

DESIGN: 70l. "Harvesting" (bas-relief after G. and N. Pisano).

397 Monviso, Italian Alps, Ice-axe and Rope

1963. Italian Alpine Club Centenary.

1094	**397**	115l. sepia and blue	35	30

398 "I.N.A." Lighthouse

1963. 50th Anniv of Italian National Insurance Corporation.

1095	**398**	30l. black and green	35	30

399 Posthorn and Globe

1963. Paris Postal Conference Centenary.

1096	**399**	70l. blue and green	35	30

400 Three-dimensional Emblem

1963. Red Cross Centenary.

1097	**400**	30l. red and purple	10	10
1098	**400**	70l. red and blue	55	55

401 "World Tourism"

1963. U.N. Tourism Conference, Rome.

1099	**401**	15l. blue and olive	35	20
1100	**401**	70l. brown and blue	45	45

402 "Co-operation"

1963. Europa.

1101	**402**	30l. brown and red	20	20
1102	**402**	70l. green and brown	65	35

403 "Naples"

1963. 4th Mediterranean Games, Naples. Inscr "NAPOLI 1963".

1103	**403**	15l. ochre and blue	10	10
1104	-	70l. orange and green	20	20

DESIGN: 70l. Greek "Olympic" vase.

404 Mascagni and Costanzi Theatre

1963. 150th Birth Anniv of Verdi (1105) and Birth Centenary of Mascagni (1106) (composers).

1105		30l. brown and green	35	35
1106	**404**	30l. green and brown	35	35

DESIGN: No. 1105, Verdi and La Scala Opera House.

405 G. Belli

1963. Death Centenary of Giuseppe Belli (poet).

1107	**405**	30l. brown	35	30

406 Stamp "Flower"

1963. Stamp Day.

1108	**406**	15l. red and blue	35	30

407 Galileo Galilei

1964. 400th Birth Anniv of Galileo Galilei.

1109	**407**	30l. brown	20	20
1110	**407**	70l. black	35	35

408 Nicodemus (from Michelangelo's "Pieta")

1964. 400th Death Anniv of Michelangelo.

1111	**408**	30l. sepia (postage)	10	10
1112	-	185l. black (air)	55	55

DESIGN: 185l. Michelangelo's "Madonna of Bruges".

410 Carabinieri on Parade

1964. 150th Anniv of Carabinieri (military police).

1113	**410**	30l. red and blue	15	10
1114	-	70l. brown	20	20

DESIGN: 70l. "The Charge at Pastrengo (1848)" (De Albertis).

411 G. Bodoni

1964. 150th Death Anniv (1963) of Giambattista Bodoni (type-designer and printer).

1115	**411**	30l. red	35	30

412 Europa "Flower"

1964. Europa.

1116	**412**	30l. purple	20	15
1117	**412**	70l. blue	45	15

413 European Buildings

1964. 7th European Municipalities' Assembly.

1118	**413**	30l. brown and green	10	10
1119	**413**	70l. brown and blue	30	30
1120	**413**	500l. red	2·20	2·20

414 Victor Emmanuel Monument, Rome

1964. War Veterans' Pilgrimage to Rome.

1121	**414**	30l. brown	15	15
1122	**414**	70l. blue	20	20

415 G. da Verrazzano and Verrazano Narrows Bridge

1964. Opening of Verrazano Narrows Bridge, New York.

1123	**415**	30l. black and brown (postage)	30	30
1124	**415**	130l. black and green (air)	65	30

This American bridge is designated "Verrazano" with one "z".

416 Italian Stamps

1964. Stamp Day.

1125	**416**	15l. brown and bistre	35	30

417 Prisoners of War

1965. 20th Anniv of Resistance.

1126	**417**	10l. black	10	10
1127	-	15l. black, red and green	10	10
1128	-	30l. purple	10	10
1129	-	70l. blue	10	10
1130	-	115l. red	10	10
1131	-	130l. brown, green & red	10	10

DESIGNS—VERT: 15l. Servicemen and casualty ("Liberation Army"); 70l. Alpine soldiers ("Resistance in the mountains"). HORIZ: 30l. Gaunt hands and arms on swastika ("Political and Racial Persecution"); 115l. Patriots with banners ("Resistance in the Towns"); 130l. Ruined building and torn flags ("Martyred Cities").

418 I.T.U. Emblem, Meucci and Marconi

1965. I.T.U. Centenary.

1132	**418**	70l. red and green	35	25

419 "Flying Dutchman" Dinghies

1965. World Sailing Championships, Alassio and Naples.

1133	**419**	30l. black and red	10	10
1134	-	70l. black and blue	10	10
1135	-	500l. black and blue	55	55

DESIGNS—VERT: 70l. "5.5 S.1" class yachts. HORIZ: 500l. "Lightning" dinghies.

420 Mont Blanc and Tunnel

1965. Opening of Mont Blanc Road Tunnel.

1136	**420**	30l. black	30	30

421 A. Tassoni and Episode from his "Secchia Rapita"

1965. 400th Birth Anniv of Alessandro Tassoni (poet).

1137	**421**	40l. multicoloured	30	30

422 Europa "Sprig"

1965. Europa.

1138	**422**	40l. green and orange	15	10
1139	**422**	90l. green and blue	40	20

423 "Hell" (Codex, Vatican Library)

1965. 700th Birth Anniv of Dante.

1140	**423**	40l. multicoloured	20	10
1141	-	90l. multicoloured	20	10
1142	-	130l. multicoloured	20	10
1143	-	500l. green	55	55

DESIGNS—VERT: 90l. "Purgatory" (codex, Marciana Library, Venice); 500l. Head of Dante (bronze, Naples Museum). HORIZ: 130l. "Paradise" (codex, British Museum).

424 House and Savings-bank

1965. Savings Day.

1144	**424**	40l. multicoloured	30	30

425 Douglas DC-6B passing Control-tower

1965. Night Airmail Service.

1145	**425**	40l. red and blue	10	10
1146	-	90l. multicoloured	15	15

DESIGN: 90l. Sud Aviation SE 210 Caravelle jetliner within airmail envelope "border".

426 Map of "Highway to the Sun"

1965. Stamp Day.

1147	**426**	20l. multicoloured	30	30

427 Two-man Bobsleigh

1966. World Bobsleigh Championships, Cortina d'Ampezzo.

1148	**427**	40l. red, blue and grey	10	10
1149	-	90l. violet and blue	15	15

DESIGN: 90l. Four-man bobsleigh.

428 Skier carrying Torch

1966. University Winter Games, Turin.

1150	**428**	40l. black and red	20	10
1151	-	90l. violet and red	20	10
1152	-	500l. brown and red	65	50

DESIGNS—VERT: 90l. Ice skating; 500l. Ice hockey.

429 B. Croce

1966. Birth Centenary of Benedetto Croce (philosopher).

1153	**429**	40l. sepia	35	30

430 Arms of Cities of Venezia

1966. Centenary of Union of Venezia and Italy.

1154	**430**	40l. multicoloured	35	30

431 Pine, Palatine Hill, Rome

1966. "Trees and Flowers". Multicoloured.

1155		20l. Type **431**	10	10
1156		25l. Apples	10	10
1157		40l. Carnations	10	10
1158		50l. Irises	10	10
1159		90l. Anthemis (Golden Marguerite)	10	10
1160		170l. Olive tree, Villa Adriana, Tivoli	10	10
1241		55l. Cypresses (26×35½ mm)	15	10
1242		180l. Broom (26×35½ mm)	30	20

432 "Visit Italy"

1966. Tourist Propaganda.

1161	**432**	20l. multicoloured	35	25

433 Capital "I"

1966. 20th Anniv of Republic.

1162	**433**	40l. multicoloured	10	10
1163	**433**	90l. multicoloured	20	20

434 Battle Scene

1966. Centenary of Battle of Bezzecca.

1164	**434**	90l. olive	35	30

435 "Singing Angels" (from copper panel on altar of St. Antony's Basilica, Padua)

1966. 5th Death Centenary of Donatello.

1165	**435**	40l. multicoloured	35	30

436 Europa "Ship"

1966. Europa.

1166	**436**	40l. violet	20	15
1167	**436**	90l. blue	35	15

437 "Madonna in Maesta" (after Giotto)

1966. Giotto's 700th Birth Anniv.

1168	**437**	40l. multicoloured	35	30

438 Filzi, Battisti, Chiesa and Sauro

1966. 50th Death Annivs of World War I Heroes.

1169	**438**	40l. green and slate	35	30

439 Postal Emblem

1966. Stamp Day.

1170	**439**	20l. multicoloured	30	30

440 Compass and Globe

1967. Centenary of Italian Geographical Society.

1171	**440**	40l. blue and black	35	30

441 Toscanini

1967. Birth Centenary of Arturo Toscanini (orchestral conductor).

1172	**441**	40l. buff and blue	35	30

442 Campidoglio, Rome

1967. 10th Anniv of Rome Treaties.

1173	**442**	40l. brown and black	20	20
1174	**442**	90l. purple and black	20	20

443 Cogwheels

1967. Europa.

1175	**443**	40l. purple and pink	20	15
1176	**443**	90l. blue and cream	35	20

444 Brown Bear (Abruzzo Park)

1967. Italian National Parks. Multicoloured.

1177		20l. Ibex (Gran Paradiso Park) (vert)	10	10
1178		40l. Type **444**	10	10
1179		90l. Red deer stag (Stelvio Park)	20	10
1180		170l. Tree (Circeo Park) (vert)	35	20

445 Monteverdi

1967. 400th Death Anniv of Claudio Monteverdi (composer).

1181	**445**	40l. brown and chestnut	35	30

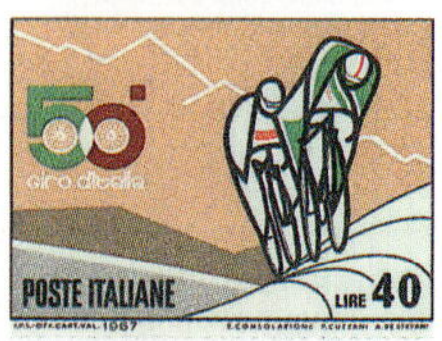

446 Racing Cyclists

1967. 50th Tour of Italy Cycle Race. Designs showing cyclists.

1182	**446**	40l. multicoloured	15	15
1183	-	90l. multicoloured	15	20
1184	-	500l. multicoloured	1·70	95

447 Pirandello and Stage

1967. Birth Centenary of Luigi Pirandello (dramatist).

1185	**447**	40l. multicoloured	35	30

448 Stylized Mask

1967. Two Worlds Festival, Spoleto.

1186	**448**	20l. black and green	15	10
1187	**448**	40l. black and red	20	10

449 Coded Addresses

1967. Introduction of Postal Codes.

1188	**449**	20l. black, blue & yellow	15	10
1189	**449**	25l. black, red and yellow	20	10
1190	**449**	40l. black, purple & yell	15	10
1191	**449**	50l. black, green & yellow	20	10

450 Pomilio PE Type Biplane and Postmark

1967. 50th Anniv of 1st Airmail Stamp.

1192	**450**	40l. black and blue	35	30

451 St. Ivo's Church, Rome

1967. 300th Death Anniv of Francesco Borromini (architect).

1193	**451**	90l. multicoloured	35	30

452 U. Giordano and Music from "Andrea Chenier"

1967. Birth Centenary of Umberto Giordano (composer).

1194	**452**	20l. brown and black	35	30

453 "The Oath of Pontida" (from painting by Adolfo Cao)

1967. 800th Anniv of Oath of Pontida.

1195	**453**	20l. brown	35	30

454 I.T.Y. Emblem

1967. International Tourist Year.

1196	**454**	20l. black, blue and yellow	15	15
1197	**454**	50l. black, blue & orange	20	15

455 Lions Emblem

1967. 50th Anniv of Lions International.

1198	**455**	50l. multicoloured	35	30

456 Sentry

1967. 50th Anniv of Stand on the Piave.

1199	**456**	50l. multicoloured	35	30

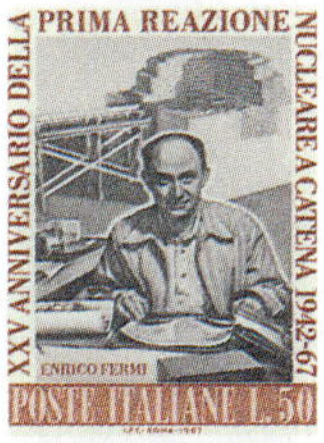

457 E. Fermi (scientist) and Reactor

1967. 25th Anniv of 1st Nuclear Chain Reaction.

1200	**457**	50l. black and brown	35	30

458 Stamp and Dove

1967. Stamp Day.

1201	**458**	25l. multicoloured	35	30

1968. As Nos. 887, etc (1952), size 16×20 mm.

1202	**286**	1l. black	10	10
1203	**286**	5l. slate	10	10
1204	**286**	6l. brown	10	10
1205	**286**	10l. red	10	10
1206	**286**	15l. violet	10	10
1207	**286**	20l. sepia	10	10
1208	**286**	25l. violet	10	10
1209	**286**	30l. brown	10	10
1210	**286**	40l. purple	10	10
1211	**286**	50l. olive	10	10
1212	**286**	55l. violet	10	15
1213	**286**	60l. blue	10	15
1214	**286**	70l. green	10	15
1215	**286**	80l. brown	10	15
1215a	**286**	90l. brown	10	10
1216	**286**	100l. brown	10	10
1216a	**286**	120l. blue and green	10	10
1216b	**286**	125l. purple and brown	55	30
1217	**286**	130l. red and grey	10	10
1217a	**286**	150l. violet	20	10
1217b	**286**	170l. green and brown	45	10
1218	**286**	180l. purple and grey	65	30
1218a	**286**	200l. blue	20	10
1219	**286**	300l. green	65	30
1219a	**286**	350l. orange, red & yell	65	15
1219b	**286**	400l. red	65	15

459 Scouts around Campfire

1968. Italian Boy Scouts.

1220	**459**	50l. multicoloured	50	30

460 Europa "Key"

1968. Europa.

1221	**460**	50l. green and pink	15	15
1222	**460**	90l. brown and blue	30	30

461 "Tending the Sick"

1968. 400th Birth Anniv of Luigi Gonzaga (St. Aloysius).

1223	**461**	25l. violet and brown	35	30

462 Boito and "Mephistopheles"

1968. 50th Death Anniv of Arrigo Boito (composer and librettist).

1224	**462**	50l. multicoloured	35	30

463 F. Baracca and "Aerial Combat" (abstract by G. Balla)

1968. 500th Death Anniv of Francesco Baracca (airman of World War I).

1225	**463**	25l. multicoloured	35	30

464 Giambattista Vico (300th Birth Anniv)

1968. Italian Philosophers' Birth Annivs.

1226	**464**	50l. blue	35	30
1227	-	50l. black	35	30

DESIGN: No. 1227, Tommaso Campanella (400th birth anniv).

465 Cycle Wheel and Stadium

1968. World Road Cycling Championships.

1228	**465**	25l. blue, pink and brown	15	10
1229	-	90l. indigo, red and blue	35	20

DESIGN: 90l. Cyclists and Imola Castle.

466 "St. Mark's Square, Venice" (Canaletto)

1968. Death Bicentenary of Canaletto (painter).

1230	**466**	50l. multicoloured	35	30

467 Rossini

1968. Death Centenary of Gioacchino Rossini (composer).

1231	**467**	50l. red	35	30

468 Mobilization

1968. 50th Anniv of Victory in World War I. Multicoloured.

1232		20l. Type **468**	10	10
1233		25l. Trench warfare	10	10
1234		40l. Naval forces	20	10
1235		50l. Air Force	20	10
1236		90l. Battle of Vittorio Veneto	20	15
1237		180l. Tomb of Unknown Soldier	35	15

469 "Conti Correnti Postali"

1968. 50th Anniv of Postal Cheque Service.

1238	**469**	50l. multicoloured	35	30

470 Tracking Equipment and Buildings

1968. Space Telecommunications Centre, Fucino.

1239	**470**	50l. multicoloured	35	30

471 "Postal Development"

1968. Stamp Day.

1240	**471**	25l. red and yellow	35	30

472 Commemorative Medal

1969. Centenary of State Audit Department.

1243	**472**	50l. black and pink	35	30

473 Colonnade

1969. Europa.

1244 **473** 50l. multicoloured 20 15

1245 **473** 90l. multicoloured 35 20

474 Machiavelli

1969. 500th Birth Anniv of Niccolo Machiavelli (statesman).

1246 **474** 50l. multicoloured 35 30

475 I.L.O. Emblem

1969. 50th Anniv of I.L.O.

1247 **475** 50l. black and green 20 10

1248 **475** 90l. black and red 35 10

476 Postal Emblem

1969. 50th Anniv of Italian Philatelic Federation.

1249 **476** 50l. multicoloured 35 30

477 Sondrio-Tirano Mailcoach of 1903

1969. Stamp Day.

1250 **477** 25l. blue 35 30

478 Skiing

1970. World Skiing Championships, Val Gardena. Multicoloured.

1251 50l. Type **478** 20 15

1252 90l. Dolomites 35 20

479 "Galatea" (detail of fresco by Raphael)

1970. 450th Death Anniv of Raphael. Mult.

1253 20l. Type **479** 20 10

1254 50l. "Madonna of the Goldfinch" 35 10

480 Symbols of Flight

1970. 50th Anniv of Rome–Tokyo Flight by A. Ferrarin.

1255 **480** 50l. multicoloured 20 10

1256 **480** 90l. multicoloured 35 20

481 "Flaming Sun"

1970. Europa.

1257 **481** 50l. yellow and red 20 20

1258 **481** 90l. yellow and green 35 35

482 Erasmo da Narni (from statue by Donatello)

1970. 600th Birth Anniv of Erasmo da Narni "Il Gattamelata" (condottiere).

1259 **482** 50l. green 35 30

483 Running

1970. World University Games, Turin. Mult.

1260 20l. Type **483** 20 10

1261 180l. Swimming 45 30

484 Dr. Montessori and children

1970. Birth Centenary of Dr. Maria Montessori (educationist).

1262 **484** 50l. multicoloured 35 30

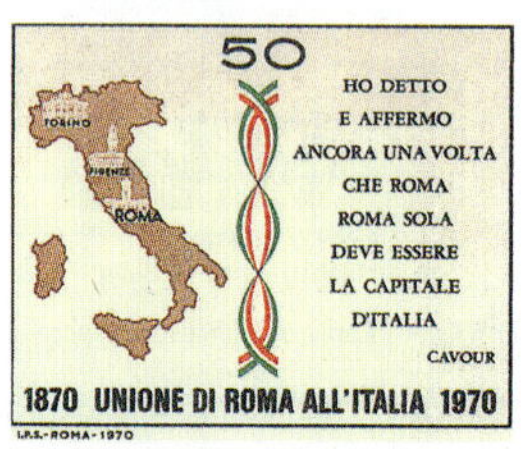

485 Map and Cavour's Declaration

1970. Centenary of Union of Rome and Papal States with Italy.

1263 **485** 50l. multicoloured 35 30

486 Loggia of Campanile, St. Mark's Square, Venice

1970. 400th Death Anniv of Jacopo Tatti, "Il Sansovino" (architect).

1264 **486** 50l. brown 35 30

487 "Garibaldi at Dijon" (engraving)

1970. Centenary of Garibaldi's Participation in Franco-Prussian War.

1265 **487** 20l. grey and blue 20 10

1266 **487** 50l. purple and blue 35 10

488 U.N. Emblem within Tree

1970. 25th Anniv of United Nations.

1267 **488** 25l. green, black & brown 20 15

1268 **488** 90l. yellow, black and blue 45 15

489 Rotary Emblem

1970. 65th Anniv of Rotary International.

1269 **489** 25l. ultramarine, yell & bl 20 10

1270 **489** 90l. ultramarine, yell & bl 35 15

490 Telephone Dial and "Network"

1970. Completion of Telephone Trunk-dialling System.

1271 **490** 25l. green and red 20 15

1272 **490** 90l. blue and red 35 20

491 Urban Complex and Tree

1970. Nature Conservation Year.

1273 **491** 20l. red and green 20 10

1274 **491** 25l. grey and green 35 10

492 Electric Locomotive "Tartaruga"

1970. Stamp Day.

1275 **492** 25l. black 35 30

493 "The Adoration" (F. Lippi)

1970. Christmas. Multicoloured.

1276 25l. Type **493** (postage) 20 30

1277 150l. "The Adoration of the Magi" (Gentile da Fabriano) (44×35 mm) (air) 35 35

494 Saverio Mercadante

1970. Death Centenary of Saverio Mercadante (composer).

1278 **494** 25l. violet and grey 35 30

495 "Mercury" (part of Cellini's "Perseus with the Head of Medusa")

1971. 400th Death Anniv of Benvenuto Cellini (goldsmith and sculptor).

1279 **495** 50l. blue 35 30

496 Bramante's "Little Temple", St. Peter's Montorio, Rome

1971

1280 **496** 50l. black and brown 35 30

497 Adenauer, Schuman and De Gasperi

1971. 20th Anniv of European Coal and Steel Community.

1281 **497** 50l. brown, black & grn 20 15

1282 **497** 90l. brown, black and red 35 20

498 Europa Chain

1971. Europa.

1283 **498** 50l. red 30 15

1284 **498** 90l. purple 50 20

499 Mazzini

1971. 25th Anniv of Republic.

1285 **499** 50l. multicoloured 20 15

1286 **499** 90l. multicoloured 35 20

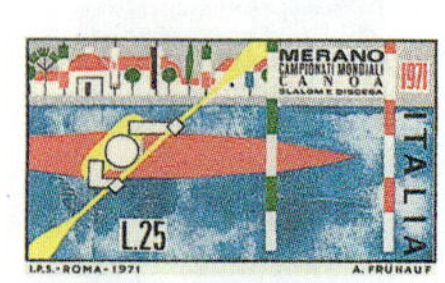

500 Canoeist in Slalom

1971. World Canoeing Slalom and Free Descent Championships, Merano. Multicoloured.

1287 25l. Type **500** 20 10

1288 90l. Canoeist making free descent 35 20

501 Three Sports

1971. Youth Games.
1289 **501** 20l. black, green & brn 10 10
1290 - 50l. black, violet & orge 20 10
DESIGN: 50l. Four other sports.

502 Alitalia Emblem

1971. 25th Anniv of Alitalia State Airline. Multicoloured.
1291 50l. Type **502** 20 10
1292 90l. Emblem and Globe 20 15
1293 150l. Tailplane of Boeing 747 30 20

503 Grazia Deledda

1971. Birth Cent of Grazia Deledda (writer).
1294 **503** 50l. black and brown 35 30

504 Boy in "Savings" Barrel

1971. Postal Savings Bank.
1295 **504** 25l. multicoloured 10 20
1296 **504** 50l. multicoloured 15 15

1971. Air. As No. 911 but smaller, 20×36 mm.
1297 **204** 100l. green 35 30

505 UNICEF Emblem and Paper Dolls

1971. 25th Anniv of UNICEF. Multicoloured.
1301 25l. Type **505** 20 10
1302 90l. Children acclaiming UNICEF emblem 35 20

506 Liner "Tirrenia"

1971. Stamp Day.
1303 **506** 25l. green 35 30

507 "The Nativity"

1971. Christmas. Miniatures from "Matilda's Evangelarium", Nonantola Abbey, Modena. Multicoloured.
1304 25l. Type **507** 20 15
1305 90l. "The Adoration of the Magi" 35 15

508 G. Verga and Sicilian Cart

1972. 50th Death Anniv of Giovanni Verga (writer).
1306 **508** 25l. multicoloured 20 10
1307 **508** 50l. multicoloured 35 10

509 G. Mazzini

1972. Death Cent of Giuseppe Mazzini (statesman).
1308 **509** 25l. green and black 10 10
1309 **509** 90l. grey and black 20 20
1310 **509** 150l. red and black 35 30

510 Stylized Flags

1972. 50th International Fair, Milan.
1311 **510** 25l. green and black 10 10
1312 - 50l. red and black 15 15
1313 - 90l. blue and black 35 20
DESIGNS: 50l. "Windows, stand and pavilions" (abstract); 90l. Abstract general view of Fair.

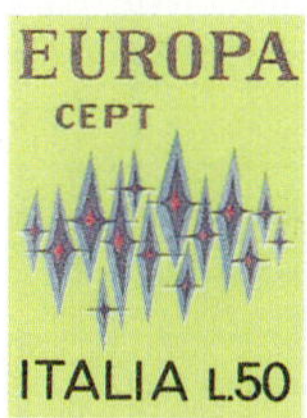

511 "Communications"

1972. Europa.
1314 **511** 50l. multicoloured 55 35
1315 **511** 90l. multicoloured 1·10 45

512 Alpine Soldier

1972. Centenary of Alpine Corps. Multicoloured.
1316 25l. Type **512** 15 15
1317 50l. Soldier's hat 30 20
1318 90l. Soldier and mountains 40 20

513 Brenta Mountains

1972. Centenary of Tridentine Alpinists Society. Multicoloured.
1319 25l. Type **513** 15 10
1320 50l. Alpinist 30 20
1321 180l. Mt. Crozzon 35 35

514 Diagram of Conference Hall

1972. 60th Interparliamentary Union Conference, Rome.
1322 **514** 50l. multicoloured 20 10
1323 **514** 90l. multicoloured 35 15

515 "St. Peter Damiani" (miniature, after G. di Paolo)

1972. 900th Death Anniv of St. Peter Damiani.
1324 **515** 50l. multicoloured 35 30

516 "The Three Graces" (Canova)

1972. 150th Death Anniv of Antonio Canova (sculptor).
1325 **516** 50l. green 35 30

517 Initial and First Verse (Foligno edition)

1972. 500th Anniv of "The Divine Comedy". Multicoloured.
1326 50l. Type **517** 20 10
1327 90l. Initial and first verse (Mantua edition) (vert) 45 15
1328 180l. Initial and first verse ("Jesino" edition) 45 30

518 "Angel"

1972. Christmas. Multicoloured.
1329 20l. Type **518** 10 10
1330 25l. "Holy Child in Crib" (horiz) 20 15
1331 150l. "Angel" (looking to left) 35 40

519 Postal Coach

1972. Stamp Day.
1332 **519** 25l. red 35 30

520 L. B. Alberti (from bronze by M. de Pasti, Louvre)

1972. 500th Death Anniv of Leon B. Alberti (writer and savant).
1333 **520** 50l. blue and yellow 35 30

521 L. Perosi

1972. Birth Centenary of Lorenzo Perosi (composer and priest).
1334 **521** 50l. brown and yellow 20 10
1335 **521** 90l. black and green 35 15

522 Don Orione

1972. Birth Centenary of Don Orione (child-welfare pioneer).
1336 **522** 50l. blue and turquoise 20 10
1337 **522** 90l. green and yellow 35 15

523 Oceanic Survey

1973. Centenary of Military Marine Institute of Hydrography.
1338 **523** 50l. multicoloured 35 30

524 Grand Staircase, Royal Palace, Caserta

1973. Death Bicentenary of Luigi Vanvitelli (architect).
1339 **524** 25l. green 35 30

525 Schiavoni Shore

1973. "Save Venice" Campaign. Multicoloured.
1340 20l. Type **525** 35 15
1341 25l. "The Tetrarchs" (sculpture) (vert) 10 10
1342 50l. "The Triumph of Venice" (V. Carpaccio) 10 10
1343 90l. Bronze horses, St. Mark's Basilica (vert) 20 20
1344 300l. Piazzetta S. Marco 90 65

526 Fair Theme

1973. 75th Int Agricultural Fair, Verona.
1345 **526** 50l. multicoloured 35 30

527 Title-page of "Diverse Figure"

1973. 300th Death Anniv of Salvator Rosa (painter and poet).

1346 **527** 25l. black and orange 35 30

528 Formation of Fiat G-91 PAN Acrobatic Jet Aircraft

1973. 50th Anniv of Military Aviation. Mult.

1349 20l. Type **528** (postage) 20 10

1350 25l. Formation of Savoia Marchetti S-55X flying boats 20 10

1351 50l. Fiat G-91Y jet fighters on patrol 20 10

1352 90l. Fiat CR-32 biplanes performing aerobatics 20 20

1353 180l. Caproni Campini N-1 jet airplane 20 30

1354 150l. Lockheed F-104S Starfighter over Aeronautical Academy, Pozzuoli (air) 35 30

529 Football and Pitch

1973. 75th Anniv of Italian Football Association. Multicoloured.

1355 25l. Type **529** 35 30

1356 90l. Players in goalmouth 80 45

530 A. Manzoni (after F. Hayez)

1973. Death Centenary of Alessandro Manzoni (writer and politician).

1357 **530** 25l. brown and black 35 30

531 Palladio's "Rotunda", Vicenza

1973. Andrea Palladio Commemoration.

1358 **531** 90l. multicoloured 35 30

532 Spring and Cogwheels

1973. 50th Anniv of Italian State Supplies Office.

1359 **532** 50l. multicoloured 35 30

533 Europa "Posthorn"

1973. Europa.

1360 **533** 50l. gold, lilac and yellow 20 15

1361 **533** 90l. gold, green & yellow 35 20

534 "Catcher" and Baseball Field

1973. 1st Intercontinental Baseball Cup. Mult.

1362 25l. Type **534** 20 15

1363 90l. "Striker" and baseball field 35 20

535 Carnival Setting

1973. Viareggio Carnival.

1364 **535** 25l. multicoloured 35 30

536 "Argenta Episode"

1973. 50th Death Anniv of Don Giovanni Minzoni (military chaplain).

1365 **536** 50l. multicoloured 35 30

537 G. Salvemini

1973. Birth Centenary of Gaetano Salvemini (political historian).

1366 **537** 50l. multicoloured 35 30

538 Farnese Palace, Caprorola

1973. 400th Birth Anniv of "Vignola" (Jacopa Barozzi—architect).

1367 **538** 90l. purple and yellow 35 30

539 "St. John the Baptist"

1973. 400th Birth Anniv of Caravaggio (painter).

1368 **539** 25l. black and yellow 35 30

540 Leaning Tower of Pisa

1973. Tourism.

1369 **540** 50l. multicoloured 35 30

541 Botticelli

1973. Italian Painters (1st series).

1370 **541** 50l. brown and red 15 15

1371 - 50l. blue and brown 15 15

1372 - 50l. green and emerald 15 15

1373 - 50l. black and red 15 15

1374 - 50l. brown and blue 15 15

PAINTERS: No. 1371, Piranesi; No. 1372, Veronese; No. 1373, Verrocchio; No. 1374, Tiepolo.

See also Nos. 1392/6, 1456/61, 1495/9 and 1518/22.

542 Immacolatella Fountain, Naples

1973. Italian Fountains (1st series). Mult.

1375 25l. Type **542** 10 10

1376 25l. Trevi Fountain, Rome 10 10

1377 25l. Pretoria Fountain, Palermo 10 10

See also Nos. 1418/20, 1453/5, 1503/5, 1529/31, 1570/2 and 1618/20.

543 "Angels"

1973. Christmas. Sculptures by A. di Duccio.

1378 **543** 20l. black and green 15 10

1379 - 25l. black and blue 15 10

1380 - 150l. black and yellow 20 20

DESIGNS: 25l. "Virgin and Child"; 150l. "Angels" (different).

544 Map and Emblems

1973. 50th Anniv of Italian Rotary.

1381 **544** 50l. blue, green and red 35 30

545 Sud Aviation Super Caravelle 12

1973. Stamp Day.

1382 **545** 25l. blue 35 30

546 Military Medal for Valour

1973. 150th Anniv of Holders of the Gold Medal for Military Valour Organisation.

1383 **546** 50l. multicoloured 35 30

547 Caruso as Duke of Mantua in Verdi's "Rigoletto"

1973. Birth Centenary of Enrico Caruso (operatic tenor).

1384 **547** 50l. red 35 30

548 "Christ crowning King Roger" (Martorana Church, Palermo)

1974. Norman Art in Sicily. Mosaics.

1385 **548** 20l. blue and yellow 10 10

1386 - 50l. red and green 15 10

DESIGN: 50l. "King William offering Church to the Virgin Mary" (Monreale Cathedral).

549 Pres. L. Einaudi

1974. Birth Centenary of Luigi Einaudi (President 1948–55).

1387 **549** 50l. green 20 10

550 G. Marconi in Headphones

1974. Birth Centenary of Guglielmo Marconi (radio pioneer).

1388 **550** 50l. brown and green 20 10

1389 - 90l. multicoloured 35 20

DESIGN: 90l. Marconi and world map.

551 "David" (Bernini)

1974. Europa. Sculptures. Multicoloured.

1390 50l. Type **551** 65 35

1391 90l. "Spirit of Victory" (Michelangelo) 85 35

1974. Italian Painters (2nd series). As T 541.

1392 50l. blue and green 15 10

1393 50l. brown and blue 15 10

1394 50l. black and red 15 10

1395		50l. brown and yellow	15	10
1396		50l. blue and brown	15	10

PORTRAITS: No. 1392, Borromini; No. 1393, Carriera; No. 1394, Giambellino (Giovanni Bellini); No. 1395, Mantegna; No. 1396, Raphael.

552 Guards from Lombardy-Venetia (1848), Sardinian Marines (1815) and Tebro Battalion (1849)

1974. Bicentenary of Italian Excise Guards. Uniforms. Multicoloured.

1397		40l. Sardinian chasseurs, 1774 and 1795, and Royal Fusilier of 1817	15	20
1398		50l. Type **552**	20	20
1399		90l. Lieutenant (1866), Sergeant-major of Marines (1892) and guard (1880)	35	20
1400		180l. Helicopter pilot, naval and alpine guards of 1974	45	45

553 Feather Headdress

1974. 50th Anniv of National Bersaglieri Association. Multicoloured.

1401		40l. Type **553**	15	10
1402		50l. Bersaglieri emblem on rosette	30	10

554 Running

1974. European Athletics Championships, Rome. Multicoloured.

1403		40l. Type **554**	15	10
1404		50l. Pole vaulting	15	10

555 Francesco Petrarch

1974. 600th Death Anniv of Francesco Petrarch (poet and scholar).

1405	**555**	40l. multicoloured	10	10
1406	-	50l. blue, yellow & brown	10	10

DESIGN: 50l. Petrarch at work in his study.

556 Portofino

1974. Tourist Publicity (1st series). Mult.

1407		40l. Type **556**	15	10
1408		40l. Gradara	15	10

See also Nos. 1442/4, 1473/5, 1513/14, 1515/17, 1543/5, 1596/9, 1642/5, 1722/5, 1762/5, 1806/9, 1845/8, 1877/80, 1917/20, 1963/6, 1992/5, 2031/4, 2088/91, 2115/18, 2165/8, 2212/15, 2248/51, 2315/16, 2365/8, 2425/8, 2486/9, 2550/3, 2661/4, 2752/5, 2872/4, 2940/2, 3004/6 and 3158/61.

557 Tommaseo's Statue, Sebenico

1974. Death Centenary of Niccolo Tommaseo (writer).

1409	**557**	50l. green and pink	20	10

558 Giacomo Puccini

1974. 50th Death Anniv of Giacomo Puccini (composer).

1410	**558**	40l. multicoloured	25	15

559 Cover Engraving of Ariosto's "Orlando Furioso"

1974. 500th Birth Anniv of Ludovico Ariosto (poet).

1411	**559**	50l. blue and red	25	10

560 Commemoration Tablet (Quotation from Varrone's "Menippean Satire")

1974. 2000th Death Anniv of Marco Varrone (Varrone Reatino) (author).

1412	**560**	50l. lake, red and yellow	25	10

561 "The Month of October" (detail from 15th-century mural)

1974. 14th International Wine Congress.

1413	**561**	50l. multicoloured	25	10

562 "U.P.U." and Emblem

1974. Centenary of Universal Postal Union. Mult.

1414		50l. Type **562**	15	10
1415		90l. "U.P.U." emblem and letters	35	10

563 "The Triumph of St. Thomas Aquinas" (detail—F. Traini)

1974. 700th Death Anniv of St. Thomas Aquinas.

1416	**563**	50l. multicoloured	25	10

564 Detail of Bas-relief, Ara Pacis

1974. Centenary of Italian Order of Advocates.

1417	**564**	50l. black, green & brown	25	10

1974. Italian Fountains (2nd series). As T 542 Multicoloured.

1418		40l. Oceanus Fountain, Florence	15	20
1419		40l. Neptune Fountain, Bologna	15	20
1420		40l. Maggiore Fountain, Perugia	15	20

565 "The Adoration" (Presepe di Greccio)

1974. Christmas.

1421	**565**	40l. multicoloured	25	10

566 Pulcinella

1974. Children's Comic Characters. Mult.

1422		40l. Type **566**	10	10
1423		50l. Clowns	20	10
1424		90l. Pantaloon from Bisognosi	25	15

567 "God admonishing Adam" (Jacopo della Quercia (sculptor) (1374–1438))

1974. Italian Artists' Anniversaries (1st series).

1425	**567**	90l. violet	20	20
1426	-	90l. multicoloured	20	20

DESIGN: No. 1426, Uffizi Gallery, Florence (Giorgio Vasari (architect and painter) (1511–1574)).

See also Nos. 1445/6, 1480/2, 1523/4, 1564/5, 1593/4, 1699/1700, 1731/2, 1774/5, 1824/5, 1885/6, 1949/50 and 1987.

568 "Angel with Tablet"

1975. Holy Year. Multicoloured.

1427		40l. Type **568**	10	10
1428		50l. Angel with column	10	10
1429		90l. Bridge of the Holy Angels, Rome (49×40 mm)	15	20
1430		150l. Angel with crown of thorns	45	20
1431		180l. Angel with cross	70	30

569 "Pitti Madonna"

1975. 500th Birth Anniv of Michelangelo.

1432	**569**	40l. green	15	10
1433	-	50l. brown	15	10
1434	-	90l. red	15	25

DESIGNS: 50l. Sculptured niche, Vatican Palace; 90l. Detail from fresco "Flood of the Universe" (Sistine Chapel).

570 "The Four Days of Naples" (M. Mazzacurati)

1975. 30th Anniv of Italian Resistance Movement. Resistance Monuments. Multicoloured.

1435		70l. Type **570**	10	10
1436		100l. "Martyrs of the Ardeatine Caves" (F. Coccia)	20	10
1437		150l. "The Resistance Fighters of Cuneo" (U. Mastroianni)	40	25

571 "The Flagellation of Christ" (Caravaggio)

1975. Europa. Paintings. Multicoloured.

1438		100l. Type **571**	70	15
1439		150l. "The Appearance of the Angel to Agar and Ishmael in the Desert" (Tiepolo)	95	25

572 Globe and Emblems

1975. International Women's Year.

1440	**572**	70l. multicoloured	25	10

573 "San Marco III" (satellite) and "Santa Rita" (marine launching pad)

1975. Italian Space Project.

1441	**573**	70l. multicoloured	25	10

1975. Tourist Publicity (2nd series). As T 556. Multicoloured.

1442	150l. Cefalu	35	15
1443	150l. Isola Bella	35	15
1444	150l. Montecatini Terme	35	15

1975. Italian Artists' Annivs (2nd series). As T 567. Multicoloured.

1445	90l. "Flora" (Guido Reni (1575–1642))	20	15
1446	90l. "Artist and Model" (Armando Spadini (1883–1925))	20	15

574 Cover Engraving from Palestrina's "Primo Libro delle Messe"

1975. 450th Birth Anniv of Giovanni Pierluigi da Palestrina (composer).

1447	**574**	100l. purple and brown	40	30

575 Boat in Harbour

1975. Italian Emigration.

1448	**575**	70l. multicoloured	25	30

576 Notoriat Emblem

1975. Centenary of Unification of Italian Laws.

1449	**576**	100l. mauve, stone & blue	25	30

577 Railway Steam Locomotive Driving-wheels

1975. 21st International Railway Congress, Bologna.

1450	**577**	70l. multicoloured	30	30

578 "D'Acquisto's Sacrifice" (Vittorio Pisani)

1975. 32nd Death Anniv of Salvo d'Acquisto (carabiniere who sacrificed himself to save 22 hostages).

1451	**578**	100l. multicoloured	25	30

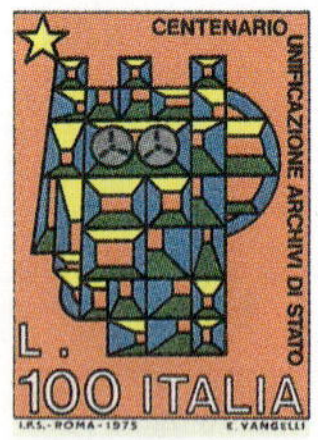

579 Symbolised Head representing Files

1975. Centenary of State Archives Unification.

1452	**579**	100l. multicoloured	25	30

1975. Italian Fountains (3rd series). As T 542. Multicoloured.

1453	70l. Rosello Fountain, Sassari	25	20
1454	70l. 99 Channel Fountain, L'Aquila	25	20
1455	70l. Piazza Fountain, Milan	25	20

1975. Italian Composers. As T 541.

1456	100l. blue, pink and red	25	10
1457	100l. blue, green & deep green	25	10
1458	100l. green, brown & dp brn	25	10
1459	100l. brown, red and lake	25	10
1460	100l. purple, grey and green	25	10
1461	100l. black, lt yellow & yellow	25	10

DESIGNS: No. 1456, Ferruccio Busoni; 1457, Alessandro Scarlatti; 1458, Francesco Cilea; 1459, Antonio Vivaldi; 1460, Franco Alfa; No. 1461, Gaspare Spontini.

581 "Annunciation to the Shepherds"

1975. Christmas. Alatri Cathedral Carvings. Multicoloured.

1462	70l. Type **581**	10	10
1463	100l. "The Nativity"	15	10
1464	150l. "Annunciation to the Kings"	35	25

582 "Children on Horseback"

1975. Stamp Day. Children's Stories. Mult.

1465	70l. Type **582**	10	10
1466	100l. "The Magic Orchard" (vert)	15	10
1467	150l. "Church Procession"	35	25

583 "Boccaccio" (from fresco by A. del Castagno)

1975. 600th Death Anniv of Giovanni Boccaccio. Multicoloured.

1468	100l. Type **583**	15	10
1469	150l. Cover engraving from Boccaccio's "Fiammetta"	25	20

584 Entrance to State Advocate's Office

1976. Centenary of State Advocate's Office.

1470	**584**	150l. multicoloured	35	15

585 "Italia 1976" Emblem

1976. "Italia 76" International Stamp Exhibition, Milan (1st issue).

1471	**585**	150l. red, green and black	25	15
1472	-	180l. multicoloured	25	20

DESIGN: 180l. Exhibition Hall, Milan.

See also Nos. 1487/91.

1976. Tourist Publicity (3rd series). As T 556. Multicoloured.

1473	150l. Fenis Castle, Aosta	30	15
1474	150l. Forio Ischia	30	15
1475	150l. Itria Valley	30	30

586 Majolica Plate

1976. Europa. Italian Crafts. Multicoloured.

1476	150l. Type **586**	75	25
1477	180l. Vase in form of woman's head	1·10	35

587 Republican Flags

1976. 30th Anniv of Republic. Multicoloured.

1478	100l. Type **587**	10	10
1479	150l. Statesmen	30	10

588 "Fortitude" (Giacomo Serpotta) (1656–1732)

1976. Italian Artists' Annivs (3rd series).

1480	**588**	150l. blue	30	15
1481	-	150l. multicoloured	30	15
1482	-	150l. black and red	30	15

DESIGNS: No. 1481, "Woman at Table" (Umberto Boccioni (1882–1916)); 1482, "Gunner's Letter from the Front" (Filippo Tommaso Marinetti (1876–1944)).

589 "The Dragon"

1976. 450th Death Anniv of Vittore Carpaccio (painter).

1483	**589**	150l. red	50	35
1484	-	150l. red	50	35

DESIGN: No. 1484, "St. George".

Nos. 1483/4 form Carpaccio's "St. George and the Dragon".

590 "Flora" (Titian)

1976. 400th Death Anniv of Titian.

1485	**590**	150l. red	40	25

591 St. Francis (13th-century fresco)

1976. 750th Death Anniv of St. Francis of Assisi.

1486	**591**	150l. brown & lt brown	40	15

592 "Cursus Publicus" Post Cart

1976. "Italia 76" International Stamp Exhibition, Milan (2nd issue).

1487	**592**	70l. black, grey and blue	15	10
1488	-	100l. black, grey & yellow	25	15
1489	-	150l. black, grey & brown	40	15
1490	-	200l. multicoloured	55	25
1491	-	400l. multicoloured	70	30

DESIGNS: 100l. Emblem of Royal Sardinian Posts; 150l. 19th-century "Lion's head" letterbox; 200l. Early cancelling machine; 400l. Modern letter-coding machine.

593 Girl with "Protective Umbrella" and Animals

1976. Stamp Day. Nature Protection. Multicoloured.

1492	40l. Type **593**	15	10
1493	100l. "Protective scarf"	20	15
1494	150l. Doctor with bandaged tree	25	20

1976. Italian Painters (3rd series). As T 541.

1495	170l. green, yellow and red	35	10
1496	170l. black, turquoise & green	35	10
1497	170l. black, purple and mauve	35	10
1498	170l. brown, lavender & violet	35	10
1499	170l. black and brown	35	10

DESIGNS: No. 1495, Carlo Dolci; 1496, Lorenzo Ghiberti (sculptor); 1497, Domenico Ghirlandaio; 1498, Giovanni Piazzetta; 1499, "Sassoferrato" (Giovanni Salvi).

594 "The Visit" (S. Lega)

1976. 150th Birth Anniv of Silvestro Lega (painter).

1500	**594**	170l. multicoloured	40	10

595 "Adoration of the Magi" (Bartolo di Fredi)

1976. Christmas. Multicoloured.

1501		70l. Type **595**	20	10
1502		120l. "The Nativity" (Taddao Gaddi)	25	25

1976. Italian Fountains (4th series). As T 542 Multicoloured.

1503	170l. Antique Fountain, Gallipoli	35	15
1504	170l. Erbe Madonna Fountain, Verona	35	15
1505	170l. Fountain of Palazzo Doria, Gerona	35	15

596 Net of Serpents obscuring the Sun

1977. Campaign against Drug Abuse. Mult.

1506	120l. Type **596**	25	15
1507	170l. "Addict" and poppy	30	15

597 Igniting Explosives

1977. 300th Birth Anniv of Pietro Micca (national hero).

1508	**597**	170l. multicoloured	35	25

598 "Globe" and Cross

1977. Salesian Missionaries. Multicoloured.

1509	70l. Type **598**	20	10
1510	120l. St. John Bosco and "United people"	15	10

599 Article 53 of the Italian Constitution

1977. "Encouragement to Taxpayers".

1511	**599**	120l. black, brn & stone	20	15
1512	**599**	170l. black, olive & green	20	15

1977. Europa. As T 556 but with C.E.P.T. emblem. Multicoloured.

1513	170l. Mount Etna	90	25
1514	200l. Castel del Monte	2·20	35

1977. Tourist Publicity (4th series). As T 556. Multicoloured.

1515	170l. Canossa Castle	35	20
1516	170l. Castellana Grotto	35	20
1517	170l. Fermo	35	20

1977. Famous Italians. As T 541.

1518	70l. brown, green & dp green	15	20
1519	70l. black, blue and green	15	20
1520	70l. brown, yellow & lt brown	15	20
1521	70l. blue, pink and red	15	20
1522	70l. black, brown & dp brown	15	20

DESIGNS: No. 1518, Filippo Brunelleschi (architect); 1519, Pietro Aretino (satirist); 1520, Carlo Goldoni (dramatist); 1521, Luigi Cherubini (composer); 1522, Edoardo Bassini (surgeon).

1977. Italian Artists' Anniversaries (4th series). As T 567 Multicoloured.

1523	170l. "Winter" (G. Arcimboldi (c. 1527–93))	40	15
1524	170l. "Justice" (Andrea Delitio (15th century))	40	20

601 Paddle-steamer "Ferdinando Primo"

1977. Italian Ship-building (1st series). Multicoloured.

1525	170l. Type **601**	50	15
1526	170l. Sail corvette "Carracciolo"	50	15
1527	170l. Liner "Saturnia"	50	15
1528	170l. Hydrofoil missile boat "Sparviero"	50	15

See also Nos. 1552/5, 1621/4 and 1691/4.

1977. Italian Fountains (5th series). As T 542. Multicoloured.

1529	120l. Pacassi Fountain, Gorizia	35	35
1530	120l. Fraterna Fountain, Isernia	35	35
1531	120l. Palma Fountain, Palmi	35	35

602 Handball

1977. Stamp Day. "Leisure Time". Multicoloured.

1532	120l. Type **602**	25	10
1533	120l. Catching butterflies	25	10
1534	120l. Kites	25	10

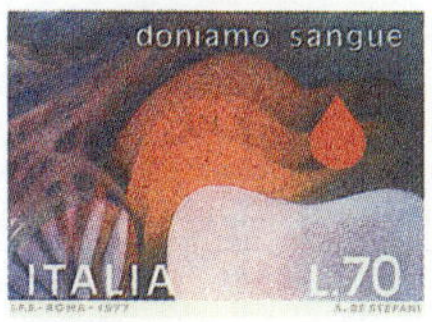

603 "Pulse"

1977. "Give Blood". Multicoloured.

1535	70l. Type **603**	40	15
1536	120l. "Transfusion"	55	15

604 Quintino Sella and 1863 1l. Stamps

1977. 150th Birth Anniv of Quintino Sella (statesman).

1537	**604**	170l. green and brown	35	30

605 Dina Galli

1977. Birth Centenary of Dina Galli (actress).

1538	**605**	170l. multicoloured	40	30

606 "Adoration of the Shepherds" (P. Testa)

1977. Christmas.

1539	**606**	70l. black and green	20	15
1540	-	120l. black and green	25	25

DESIGN: 120l. "The Adoration of the Shepherds" (J. Caraglio).

607 La Scala Opera House

1978. Bicentenary of La Scala Opera House.

1541	170l. Type **607**	40	15
1542	200l. Theatre interior	60	30

1978. Tourist Publicity (5th series). As T 556. Multicoloured.

1543	70l. Gubbio	20	10
1544	200l. Udine	55	15
1545	600l. Paestum	1·10	60

608 Dusky Grouper

1978. Environmental Protection. Mediterranean Fauna. Multicoloured.

1546	170l. Type **608**	70	15
1547	170l. Leathery turtle	70	15
1548	170l. Mediterranean monk seal	70	15
1549	170l. Audouin's gull	70	15

609 Maschio Angioino Castle, Naples

1978. Europa. Multicoloured.

1550	170l. Type **609**	95	35
1551	200l. Pantheon, Rome	1·10	45

1978. Italian Ship-building (2nd series). As T 601. Multicoloured.

1552	170l. Brigantine "Fortuna"	60	25
1553	170l. Cruiser "Benedetto Brin"	60	25
1554	170l. Frigate "Lupo"	60	25
1555	170l. Container ship "Africa"	60	25

610 Matilde Serao (writer)

1978. Famous Italians.

1556	**610**	170l. black and red	35	25
1557	-	170l. brown and blue	35	25
1558	-	170l. blue and pale blue	35	25
1559	-	170l. black and green	35	25
1560	-	170l. brown and green	35	25
1561	-	170l. blue and red	35	25

DESIGNS: No. 1557, Vittorino da Feltre (scientist); No. 1558, Victor Emmanuel II; No. 1559, Pope Pius IX; No. 1560, Marcello Malpighi (biologist); No. 1561, Antonio Meucci (telephone pioneer).

See also Nos. 1600/4.

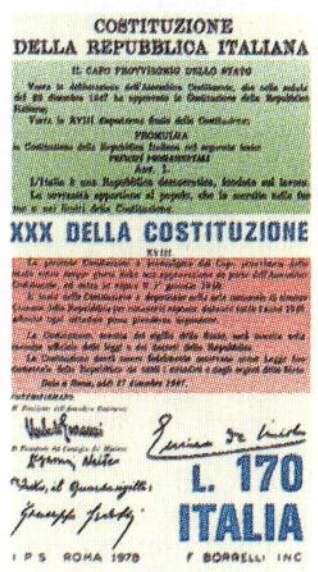

611 First and Last Paragraphs of Constitution

1978. 30th Anniv of Constitution.

1562	**611**	170l. multicoloured	40	30

612 Telephone Wires and Lens

1978. Photographic Information.

1563	**612**	120l. grey, blue and green	25	30

1978. Italian Artists' Annivs (5th series). As T 567. Multicoloured.

1564	170l. "The Ivy" (Tranquillo Cremona, 1837–78)	40	15
1565	520l. "The Cook" (Bernardo Strozzi, 1581–1644)	2·30	80

613 The Holy Shroud of Turin

1978. 400th Anniv of Translation of the Holy Shroud from Savoy to Turin.

1566	**613**	220l. yellow, black & red	75	30

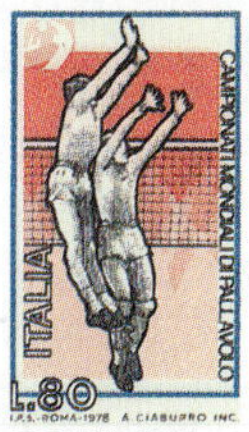

614 Volleyball Players

1978. World Volleyball Championships.

1567	**614**	80l. black, red and blue	20	20
1568	-	120l. black, blue & orge	60	20

DESIGN: 120l. Players with ball.

615 Detail from "St. Peter distributing Ananias's Silver"

1978. 550th Death Anniv of Tommaso Guidi (Masaccio).

1569	**615**	170l. blue	40	10

1978. Italian Fountains (6th series). As T 542. Multicoloured.

1570	120l. Neptune Fountain, Trento	30	20
1571	120l. Fountain of Fortune, Fano	30	20
1572	120l. Cavallina Fountain, Genzano di Lucania	30	20

616 "Madonna and Child" (Giorgione)

1978. Christmas.

1573	**616**	80l. red and brown	20	15
1574	-	120l. multicoloured	25	15

DESIGN—HORIZ (48×27 mm): 120l. "Adoration of the Magi" (Giorgione).

617 "Flowers"

1978. Stamp Day. United Europe. Mult.

1575	120l. Type **617**	25	15
1576	120l. Flags and ribbon	25	15
1577	120l. Figures raising globe inscribed "E"	25	15

618

1978

1578	**618**	1500l. multicoloured	1·40	15
1579	**618**	2000l. multicoloured	3·50	15
1580	**618**	3000l. multicoloured	5·50	15
1581	**618**	4000l. multicoloured	7·50	35
1582	**618**	5000l. multicoloured	9·50	60
1583	**618**	10000l. multicoloured	15·00	90
1584	**618**	20000l. multicoloured	30·00	4·50

619 State Polygraphic Institute

1979. 50th Anniv of State Polygraphic Institute. Multicoloured.

1588	170l. Type **619**	25	15
1589	220l. Printing press	45	30

620 "St. Francis washing the Feet of a Leper" (Maestro di Francesco Bardi)

1979. Leprosy Relief.

1590	**620**	80l. multicoloured	35	15

621 Cyclist carrying Bicycle

1979. World Cyclo-cross Championships.

1591	**621**	170l. multicoloured	25	15
1592	**621**	220l. multicoloured	45	35

1979. Italian Artists' Annivs (6th series). As T 567. Multicoloured.

1593	170l. "Annunciation" (Antonella da Messina c. 1430–79)	35	25
1594	520l. "Field with Haystack" (Ardengo Soffici 1879–1964)	1·10	40

622 Albert Einstein

1979. Birth Centenary of Albert Einstein (physicist).

1595	**622**	120l. purple, grey & bl	30	15

1979. Tourist Publicity (6th series). As T 556. Multicoloured.

1596	70l. Asiago	20	15
1597	90l. Castelsardo, Sardinia	20	15
1598	170l. Orvieto	25	30
1599	220l. Scilla	40	35

1979. Famous Italians. As T 610.

1600	170l. brown, blue and black	30	15
1601	170l. green, yellow and violet	30	15
1602	170l. blue and pink	30	15
1603	170l. brown and ochre	30	15
1604	170l. mauve, brown and green	30	15

DESIGNS: No. 1600, Carlo Maderno (architect); No. 1601, Lazzaro Spallanzani (biologist); No. 1602, Ugo Foscolo (author); No. 1603, Massimo Bontempelli (writer); No. 1604, Francesco Severi (mathematician).

623 Morse Telegraph Apparatus

1979. Europa. Multicoloured.

1605	170l. Type **623**	2·40	35
1606	220l. Carrier pigeon with message tube	2·75	45

624 Flags of Member States forming "E"

1979. First Direct Elections to European Parliament.

1607	**624**	170l. multicoloured	40	15
1608	**624**	220l. multicoloured	35	30

625 Head of Aeneas (bas-relief, Ara Pacis, Rome)

1979. 70th World Rotary Congress, Rome.

1609	**625**	220l. multicoloured	40	30

626 Ball in Basket (poster)

1979. 21st European Basketball Championships.

1610	**626**	80l. multicoloured	25	15
1611	-	120l. lake, black & yellow	35	25

DESIGN: 120l. Two players.

627 "Doctor examining Patient with Stomach Ailment" (woodcut from Giovanni da Cuba's "Hortus Sanitatus")

1979. Prevention of Digestive Illnesses.

1612	**627**	120l. multicoloured	35	25

628 Emblem, Ribbon "3" and Milan Cathedral

1979. Third World Machine Tool Exhibition, Milan.

1613	**628**	170l. multicoloured	45	15
1614	**628**	220l. multicoloured	35	30

629 Ottorino Respighi and Appian Way, Rome

1979. Birth Centenary of Ottorino Respighi (composer).

1615	**629**	120l. multicoloured	35	15

630 Woman with Telephone and Morse Key

1979. 3rd World Telecommunications Exhibition, Geneva.

1616	**630**	170l. black and red	55	15
1617	-	220l. grey and green	40	30

DESIGN: 220l. Woman with early telephone and communications satellite.

1979. Italian Fountains (7th series). As T 542. Multicoloured.

1618	120l. Melograno Fountain, Issogne	40	25
1619	120l. Bollente Fountain, Acqui Terme	40	25
1620	120l. Grand Fountain, Viterbo	40	25

1979. Italian Ship-building (3rd series). As T 601. Multicoloured.

1621	170l. Full-rigged ship "Cosmos"	60	25
1622	170l. Cruiser "Dandolo"	60	25
1623	170l. Ferry "Deledda"	60	25
1624	170l. Submarine "Carlo Fecia di Cossato"	60	25

631 Sir Rowland Hill and Penny Black

1979. Death Centenary of Sir Rowland Hill.

1625	**631**	220l. multicoloured	40	30

632 Christmas Landscape

1979. Christmas.

1626	**632**	120l. multicoloured	35	30

633 Children under Umbrella (Group IIB, Varapodio School)

1979. Stamp Day. International Year of the Child. Drawings by Schoolchildren. Multicoloured.

1627	70l. Children of different races holding hands (L. Carra) (horiz)	15	15
1628	120l. Type **633**	25	25
1629	150l. Children with balloons (V. Fedon) (horiz)	35	25

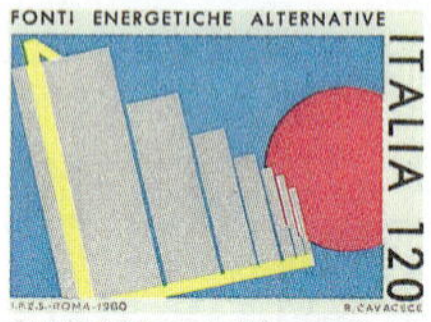

634 Solar Energy (alternative sources)

1980. Energy Conservation. Multicoloured.

1630	120l. Type **634**	20	15
1631	170l. Oil well (reduction of consumption)	35	25

635 "St. Benedict" (detail, fresco by Sodoma in Monastery of Monteoliveto Maggiore)

1980. 1500th Birth Anniv of St. Benedict of Nursia (founder of Benedictine Order).

1632	**635**	220l. blue	40	25

636 Royal Palace, Naples

1980. "Europa 80" International Stamp Exhibition, Naples.

1633	**636**	220l. multicoloured	40	25

637 Antonio Pigafetta (navigator) and "Vitoria"

1980. Europa. Multicoloured.

1634	170l. Type **637**	1·40	30
1635	220l. Antonio lo Surdo (geophysicist)	2·00	45

638 St. Catherine (reliquary bust)

1980. 600th Death Anniv of St. Catherine of Siena.

1636	**638**	170l. multicoloured	40	30

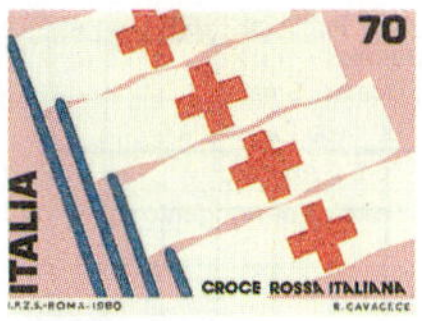

639 Red Cross Flags

1980. 1st International Exhibition of Red Cross Stamps in Italy.

1637	**639**	70l. multicoloured	35	25
1638	**639**	80l. multicoloured	35	25

640 Philae Temples

1980. Italian Work for the World (1st series). Preservation of Philae Temples, Egypt. Multicoloured.

1639	220l. Type **640**	50	15
1640	220l. Right hand view of temples	50	15

Nos. 1639/40 were issued together se-tenant, forming a composite design.

See also Nos. 1720/1, 1758/9, 1780/1, 1830/1, 1865/6 and 1937/40.

641 Footballer

1980. European Football Championship, Italy.

1641	**641**	80l. multicoloured	2·40	2·20

1980. Tourist Publicity (7th series). As T 556. Multicoloured.

1642	80l. Erice	15	30
1643	150l. Ravello	25	25
1644	200l. Roseto degli Abruzzi	45	25
1645	670l. Salsomaggiore Terme	1·40	85

642 "Cosimo I with his Artists" (Vasari)

1980. "Florence and Tuscany of the Medicis in 16th Century Europe" Exhibition. Multicoloured.

1646	170l. Type **642** (ceiling medallion, Palazzo Vecchio, Florence)	30	15
1647	170l. Armillary sphere	30	15

643 Fonte Avellana Monastery

1980. Millenary of Fonte Avellana Monastery.

1648	**643**	200l. dp green, grn & brn	40	50

644 Castel Sant' Angelo, Rome

1980. Castles. (a) Size 22×27 mm.

1649	**644**	5l. blue and red	25	10
1650	-	10l. brown and ochre	25	10
1651	-	20l. brown and blue	25	10
1652	-	30l. orange and blue	25	10
1653	-	40l. brown and blue	25	10
1654	-	50l. multicoloured	25	10
1655	-	60l. green and mauve	25	10
1656	-	70l. multicoloured	25	10
1657	-	80l. multicoloured	25	10
1658	-	90l. multicoloured	25	10
1659	-	100l. multicoloured	25	10
1660	-	120l. blue and pink	25	10
1661	-	150l. violet and brown	35	10
1662	-	170l. black and yellow	80	10
1663	-	180l. blue and pink	1·40	1·20
1664	-	200l. multicoloured	85	10
1665	-	250l. multicoloured	80	10
1666a	-	300l. multicoloured	60	10
1667	-	350l. brown, blue & grn	90	10
1667a	-	380l. multicoloured	80	30
1668	-	400l. blue, green & brn	90	10
1669	-	450l. multicoloured	1·20	10
1670	-	500l. blue, brown & grn	90	10
1670a	-	550l. multicoloured	90	30
1671	-	600l. black and green	1·00	10
1671a	-	650l. multicoloured	1·20	30
1672	-	700l. multicoloured	1·20	10
1673	-	750l. brown, green & bl	1·20	30
1674	-	800l. brown, grn & mve	1·30	15
1675	-	850l. multicoloured	1·40	30
1676	-	900l. multicoloured	1·40	15
1677	-	1000l. multicoloured	1·50	15
1678	-	1400l. brown, blue & vio	2·10	45

(b) Size 16×21 mm.

1679	30l. mauve	30	25
1680b	50l. blue	15	15
1680c	100l. brown	15	15
1681	120l. brown	30	30
1682	170l. violet	30	30
1683	200l. violet and blue	2·00	2·00
1684	300l. light green and green	60	60
1685	400l. brown and green	70	60
1686a	450l. green	75	65
1687	500l. blue	90	70
1687a	600l. green	90	90
1688	650l. mauve	90	90
1689	750l. violet	1·00	1·00
1690	800l. red	1·40	85

DESIGNS: 10l. Sforzesco Castle, Milan; 20l. Castel del Monte, Andria; 30l. (1652), L'Aquila Castle; 30l. (1679), 100l. (1680c), Santa Severa Castle; 40l. Ursino Castle, Catania; 50l. (1654), Rocca di Calascio, L'Aquila; 50l. (1680b), Scilla; 60l. Norman Tower, San Mauro; 70l. Aragonese Castle, Reggio Calabria; 80l. Sabbionara, Avio; 90l. Isola Capo Rizzuto; 100l. (1659), Aragonese Castle, Ischia; 120l. (1660), Estense Castle, Ferrara; 120l. (1681), Lombardia Enna; 150l. Miramare, Trieste; 170l. (1662), Ostia; 170l. (1682), 650l. (1688), Serralunga d'Alba; 180l. Castel Gavone, Finale Ligure; 200l. (1664), Cerro al Volturno; 200l. (1683), Svevo Angioina Fortress, Lucera; 250l. Rocca di Mondavio, Pesaro; 300l. (1666a), Norman Castle, Svevo, Bari; 300l. (1684), 500l. (1687), Norman Castle, Melfi; 350l. Mussomeli; 380l. Rocca di Vignola, Modena; 400l. (1668), Emperor's Castle, Prato; 400l. (1685), 750l. (1689), Venafro; 450l. (1669), Bosa; 450l. (1686a) Piobbico Castle, Pesaro; 500l. (1670), Rovereto; 550l. Rocca Sinibalda; 600l. Scaligero Castle, Sirmione; 650l. (1671a), Montecchio; 700l. Ivrea; 750l. (1673), Rocca di Urbisaglia; 800l. Rocca Maggiore, Assisi; 850l. Castello di Arechi, Salerno; 900l. Castello di Saint-Pierre, Aosta; 1000l. Montagnana, Padua; 1400l. Caldoresco Castle, Vasto.

1980. Italian Ship-building (4th series). As T 601. Multicoloured.

1691	200l. Corvette "Gabbiano"	1·60	30
1692	200l. Destroyer "Audace"	1·60	30
1693	200l. Barque "Italia"	1·60	30
1694	200l. Pipe-layer "Castoro Sei"	1·60	30

645 Filippo Mazzei

1980. 250th Birth Anniv of Filippo Mazzei (writer and American revolutionary).

1695	**645**	320l. multicoloured	80	30

646 Villa Foscari Malcontenta, Venice

1980. Italian Villas (1st series). Multicoloured.

1696	80l. Type **646**	65	35
1697	150l. Barbaro Maser, Treviso	1·20	30
1698	170l. Godi Valmarana, Vicenza	1·40	25

See also Nos. 1737/9, 1770/2, 1811/14, 1853/6, 1893/6 and 1943/7.

1980. Italian Artists Anniversaries (7th series). As T 567. Multicoloured.

1699	520l. "Saint Barbara" (Jacopo Palma, the Elder (1480–1528))	95	65
1700	520l. "Apollo and Daphne" (Gian Lorenzo Bernini (1598–1680))	95	65

647 "Nativity" (Federico Brandani)

1980. Christmas.

1701	**647**	120l. green and brown	40	30

648 "My Town" (Treviso)

1980. Stamp Day. Paintings by Schoolchildren entitled "My Town". Multicoloured.

1702	70l. Type **648**	20	15
1703	120l. Sansepolcro	40	15
1704	170l. Sansepolcro (different)	55	25

649 Daniele Comboni and African Village

1981. 150th Birth Anniv and Death Centenary of Daniele Comboni (missionary).

1705	**649**	80l. brown, indigo and blue	30	30

650 Alcide de Gasperi

1981. Birth Centenary of Alcide de Gasperi (politician).

1706	**650**	200l. green	30	30

651 Landscape outlined by Person in Wheelchair

1981. International Year of Disabled Persons.

1707	**651**	300l. multicoloured	70	30

652 Anemone

1981. Flowers (1st series). Multicoloured.

1708	200l. Type **652**	40	30
1709	200l. Oleander	40	30
1710	200l. Rose	40	30

See also Nos. 1753/5 and 1797/9.

653 Human Chess Game, Marostica

1981. Europa. Multicoloured.

1711	300l. Type **653**	4·00	30
1712	300l. "Il Palio" horse race, Siena	4·00	30

654 St. Rita of Cascia

1981. 600th Birth Anniv of St. Rita of Cascia.

1713	**654**	600l. multicoloured	1·20	60

655 Ciro Menotti

1981. 150th Death Anniv of Ciro Menotti (patriot).

1714	**655**	80l. black and brown	30	30

656 Agusta A.109 Helicopter

1981. Italian Aircraft (1st series). Multicoloured.

1715	200l. Type **656**	55	30
1716	200l. Partenavia P.68B Victor-PART airplane	55	30
1717	200l. Aeritalia G.222 transport	55	30
1718	200l. Aermacchi MB 339 jet trainer	55	30

See also Nos. 1748/51 and 1792/5.

657 Fertile and Barren Soil

1981. Water Conservation.

1719	**657**	80l. multicoloured	35	30

1981. Italian Work for the World (2nd series). As T 640.

1720	300l. blue	70	40
1721	300l. red	70	40

DESIGNS: No. 1720, Sao Simao, Brazil; No. 1721, High Island, Hong Kong.

1981. Tourist Publicity (8th series). As T 556. Multicoloured.

1722	80l. Matera	20	50
1723	150l. Riva del Garda	35	1·20
1724	300l. Santa Teresa di Gallura	75	50
1725	900l. Tarquinia	2·20	90

658 Naval Academy and Badge

1981. Centenary of Naval Academy, Livorno. Multicoloured.

1726	80l. Type **658**		20	10
1727	150l. Aerial view of Academy		40	50
1728	200l. "Amerigo Vespucci" (cadet ship) and sailor using sextant		55	25

659 Spada Palace, Rome, and Decorative Motif from Grand Hall

1981. 150th Anniv of Council of State.

1729	**659**	200l. brown, green & blue	40	30

660 Running

1981. World Cup Light Athletics Championships, Rome.

1730	**660**	300l. multicoloured	80	30

1981. Italian Artists' Annivs (8th series). As T 567. Multicoloured.

1731	200l. "Harbour" (Carlo Carra (1881–1966))		40	35
1732	200l. "Nightfall" (Giuseppe Ugonia (1881–1944))		45	35

661 Riace Bronze

1981. Riace Bronzes (ancient Greek statues). Multicoloured.

1733	200l. Type **661**		70	40
1734	200l. Riace bronze (different)		70	40

662 Virgil (Treviri mosaic)

1981. Death Bimillenary of Virgil (poet).

1735	**662**	600l. multicoloured	1·30	45

663 "Still-life" (Gregorio Sciltian)

1981. World Food Day.

1736	**663**	150l. multicoloured	45	30

1981. Italian Villas (2nd series). As T 646. Multicoloured.

1737	100l. Villa Campolieto, Ercolano	25	25
1738	200l. Villa Cimbrone, Ravello	45	25
1739	300l. Villa Pignatelli, Naples	1·10	35

664 "Adoration of the Magi" (Giovanni da Campione d'Italia)

1981. Christmas.

1740	**664**	200l. dp blue, brown & bl	45	30

665 Pope John XXIII

1981. Birth Centenary of Pope John XXIII.

1741	**665**	200l. multicoloured	80	30

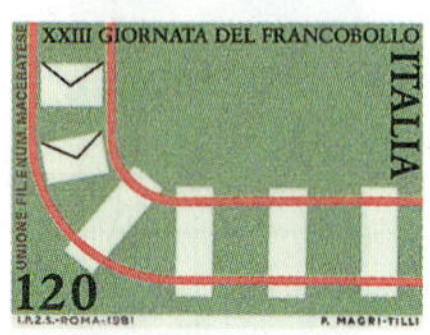

666 Envelopes forming Railway Track

1981. Stamp Day.

1742	**666**	120l. green, red and black	20	50
1743	-	200l. multicoloured	45	65
1744	-	300l. multicoloured	95	30

DESIGNS—VERT: 200l. Caduceus, chest, envelopes and cherub blowing posthorn. HORIZ: 300l. Letter seal.

667 "St. Francis receiving the Stigmata" (Pietro Cavaro)

1982. 800th Birth Anniv of St. Francis of Assisi.

1745	**667**	300l. brown and blue	80	30

668 Paganini (after Ingres)

1982. Birth Bicentenary of Niccolo Paganini (composer and violinist).

1746	**668**	900l. multicoloured	2·10	90

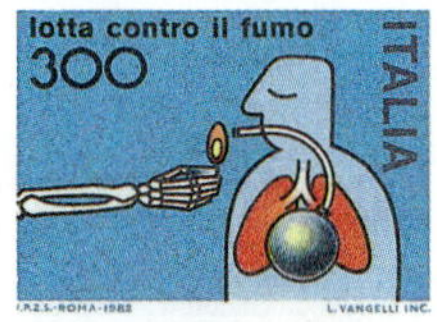

669 Skeletal Hand lighting Cigarette "Bomb"

1982. Anti-smoking Campaign.

1747	**669**	300l. multicoloured	60	30

1982. Italian Aircraft (2nd series). As T 656. Multicoloured.

1748	300l. Panavia (inscr "Aeritalia") MRCA Tornado jet fighter	1·60	65
1749	300l. Savoia SIAI 260 Turbo I-FAIR trainer	1·60	65
1750	300l. Piaggio P-166 DL-3 Turbo I-PIAE	1·60	65
1751	300l. Nardi NH 500 helicopter	1·60	65

670 Church of Santo Spirito o del Vespro, Palermo

1982. 700th Anniv of Sicilian Vespers (uprising).

1752	**670**	120l. red, blue and purple	35	30

1982. Flowers (2nd series). As T 652. Mult.

1753	300l. Camellias	90	90
1754	300l. Carnations	90	90
1755	300l. Cyclamen	90	90

671 Coronation of Charlemagne, 799

1982. Europa.

1756	**671**	200l. brown, black & blue	4·00	1·20
1757	-	450l. multicoloured	4·00	65

DESIGN: 450l. Stars and signatures to Treaty of Rome, 1957.

1982. Italian Work for the World (3rd series). As T 640. Multicoloured.

1758	450l. Radio communication across Red Sea	1·20	30
1759	450l. Automatic letter sorting	1·20	30

672 Garibaldi

1982. Death Centenary of Giuseppe Garibaldi.

1760	**672**	200l. multicoloured	1·10	70

673 Bridge Game, Pisa

1982. Folk Customs (1st series).

1761	**673**	200l. multicoloured	45	35

See also Nos. 1804, 1850, 1875/6, 1914, 1972, 2004, 2028 and 2092.

1982. Tourist Publicity (9th series). As T 556. Multicoloured.

1762	200l. Frasassi Grotto	45	75
1763	200l. Fai della Paganella	45	75
1764	450l. Rodi Garganico	1·40	50
1765	450l. Temples of Agrigento	1·40	50

674 Coxless Four

1982. World Junior Rowing Championships.

1766	**674**	200l. multicoloured	45	35

675 Ducal Palace, Urbino, Montefeltro and Palazzo dei Consoli, Gubbio

1982. 500th Death Anniv of Federico da Montefeltro, Duke of Urbino.

1767	**675**	200l. multicoloured	45	35

676 Footballer holding aloft World Cup

1982. Italy's World Cup Football Victory.

1768	**676**	1000l. multicoloured	2·40	1·20

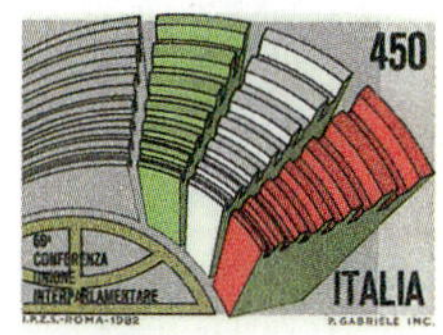

677 Seating Plan

1982. 69th Interparliamentary Union Conference.

1769	**677**	450l. multicoloured	80	30

1982. Italian Villas (3rd series). As T 646. Multicoloured.

1770	150l. Temple of Aesculapius, Villa Borghese, Rome	40	65
1771	250l. Villa D'Este, Tivoli	1·40	35
1772	350l. Villa Lante, Bagnaia, Viterbo	3·00	1·80

678 Francis of Taxis

1982. Commemoration of Establishment of First Public Postal System in Europe.

1773	**678**	300l. red, blue & verm	80	30

1982. Italian Artists' Annivs (9th series). As T 567. Multicoloured.

1774	300l. "Portrait of Antonietta Negroni Prati Morosini as a Child" (Francesco Hayez (1791–1882))	1·00	60
1775	300l. "The Fortuneteller" (Giovanni Piazzetta (1682–1754))	1·00	60

679 Tree, Chair and Bed (Maria di Pastena)

1983. Stamp Day. Timber in Human Life. Drawings by Schoolchildren. Multicoloured.

1776 150l. Type **679** 35 35
1777 250l. Tree with timber products in branches (Lucia Andreoli) 60 35
1778 350l. Forest (Marco Gallea) 80 65

680 Microscope

1983. Cancer Control.

1779 **680** 400l. multicoloured 1·30 40

1983. Italian Work for the World (4th series). Automobile Industry. As T 640. Multicoloured.

1780 400l. Factories on globe 1·20 50
1781 400l. Assembly line 1·20 50

681 Academy Emblem

1983. 400th Anniv of Accademia della Crusca (Florentine Academy of Letters).

1782 **681** 400l. red, brown and blue 95 40

682 Shooting

1983. World Biathlon Championships, Antholz.

1783 **682** 200l. multicoloured 80 40

683 Gabriele Rossetti

1983. Birth Centenary of Gabriele Rossetti (poet).

1784 **683** 300l. blue and brown 80 35

684 Guicciardini (after G. Bugiardini)

1983. 500th Birth Anniv of Francesco Guicciardini (lawyer and diplomat).

1785 **684** 450l. brown 1·10 45

685 Saba and Trieste

1983. Birth Centenary of Umberto Saba (poet).

1786 **685** 600l. multicoloured 1·60 35

686 Pope Pius XII

1983. 25th Death Anniv of Pope Pius XII.

1787 **686** 1400l. blue 3·50 1·50

687 Pope and St. Paul's Basilica

1983. Holy Year. Multicoloured.

1788 250l. Type **687** 70 45
1789 300l. Pope John Paul II and Basilica of Santa Maria Maggiore 80 30
1790 400l. Pope and St. John's Basilica 1·00 25
1791 500l. Pope and St. Peter's Cathedral 1·40 25

1983. Italian Aircraft (3rd series). As T 656. Multicoloured.

1792 400l. Savoia SIAI 211 I-SUE 1·40 65
1793 400l. Agusta A.129 Mangusta helicopter 1·40 65
1794 400l. Caproni C22J glider I-CAVJ 1·40 65
1795 400l. Aeritalia/Aermacchi AM-X jet fighter 1·40 65

688 Launch of Ship

1983. Labour Day.

1796 **688** 1200l. blue 2·75 35

1983. Flowers (3rd series). As T 652. Mult.

1797 200l. Gladiolus 1·10 60
1798 200l. Mimosa 1·10 60
1799 200l. Rhododendron 1·10 60

689 Galileo (after O. Leoni) and Telescope

1983. Europa. Multicoloured.

1800 400l. Type **689** 15·00 1·70
1801 500l. Archimedes (marble bust) and screw 15·00 1·30

690 Moneta and Doves

1983. 150th Birth Anniv of Ernesto Teodoro Moneta (Nobel Peace Prize winner).

1802 **690** 500l. multicoloured 1·10 35

691 Quadriga, Globe and V.D.U.

1983. 3rd International Juridical Information Congress, Rome.

1803 **691** 500l. multicoloured 1·30 35

1983. Folk Customs (2nd series). As T 673. Multicoloured.

1804 300l. Ceri procession, Gubbio 1·10 35

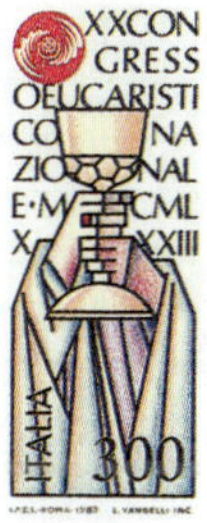

692 Elevation of Host

1983. 20th National Eucharistic Congress, Milan.

1805 **692** 300l. multicoloured 80 35

1983. Tourist Publicity (10th series). As T 556. Multicoloured.

1806 250l. Alghero 95 1·20
1807 300l. Bardonecchia 1·10 1·20
1808 400l. Riccione 1·60 75
1809 500l. Taranto 1·90 50

693 Frescobaldi

1983. 400th Birth Anniv of Girolamo Frescobaldi (composer).

1810 **693** 400l. green, blue & brn 80 35

1983. Italian Villas (4th series). As T 646. Multicoloured.

1811 250l. Villa Fidelia, Spello 1·10 2·40
1812 300l. Villa Imperiale, Pesaro 1·40 30
1813 400l. Michetti Convent, Francavilla al Mare 1·80 25
1814 500l. Villa di Riccia 2·20 25

694 Francesco de Sanctis

1983. Death Centenary of Francesco de Sanctis (writer).

1815 **694** 300l. multicoloured 1·10 35

695 "Madonna of the Chair"

1983. Christmas. 500th Birth Anniv of Raphael (artist). Multicoloured.

1816 250l. Type **695** 35 35
1817 400l. "Sistine Madonna" 75 25
1818 500l. "Madonna of the Candles" 1·90 25

696 Chain of Letters (Roberta Rizzi)

1983. Stamp Day. Drawings by school-children. Multicoloured.

1819 200l. Type **696** 60 50
1820 300l. Space postman delivering letter (Maria Grazia Federico) (vert) 95 35
1821 400l. Steam train leaving envelope and globe (Paolo Bucciarelli) 1·20 30

697 Battered Road Sign

1984. Road Safety. Multicoloured.

1822 300l. Type **697** 80 45
1823 400l. Crashed car and policeman 1·10 60

1984. Italian Artists Anniversaries (10th series). As T 567. Multicoloured.

1824 300l. "Races at Bois de Boulogne" (Giuseppe de Nittis (1846–84)) 1·00 60
1825 400l. "Paul Guillaume" (Amedeo Modigliani (1884–1920)) 1·50 80

698 Maserati "Biturbo"

1984. Italian Motor Industry (1st series). Multicoloured.

1826 450l. Type **698** 2·50 50
1827 450l. Iveco "190.38 Special" lorry 2·50 50
1828 450l. Same Trattori "Galaxy" tractor 2·50 50
1829 450l. Alfa "33" 2·50 50

See also Nos. 1867/70 and 1933/6.

699 Glassblower, Glasses and Jug

1984. Italian Work for the World (5th series). Ceramic and Glass Industries. Multicoloured.

1830 300l. Ceramic plaque and furnace 95 30
1831 300l. Type **699** 95 30

700 European Parliament Building, Strasbourg

1984. Second European Parliament Direct Elections.

1832 **700** 400l. multicoloured 95 70

701 State Forest Corps Hughes 500 Helicopter

1984. Nature Protection. Forests. Multicoloured.

1833 450l. Type **701** 3·50 75
1834 450l. Forest animals and burning cigarette 3·50 75
1835 450l. River and litter 3·50 75
1836 450l. Wildlife and building construction 3·50 75

702 Ministry of Posts and Telecommunications, Rome

1984. "Italia '85" International Stamp Exhibition, Rome (1st issue). Multicoloured.

1837 450l. Type **702** 1·20 30
1838 550l. Appian Way 1·30 30

See also Nos. 1857/9, 1862/4, 1871/3 and 1898/1911.

703 G. di Vittorio, B. Buozzi and A. Grandi

1984. 40th Anniv of Rome Pact (foundation of Italian Trade Unions).

1839	**703**	450l. multicoloured	1·30	60

704 Bridge

1984. Europa. 25th Anniv of European Post and Telecommunications Conference.

1840	**704**	450l. multicoloured	13·50	2·30
1841	**704**	550l. multicoloured	17·00	5·75

705 Symposium Emblem

1984. Int Telecommunications Symposium, Florence.

1842	**705**	550l. multicoloured	1·60	85

706 Horse-race

1984. Centenary of Italian Derby. Multicoloured.

1843	250l. Type **706**	2·00	1·70
1844	400l. Horse-race (different)	3·25	80

1984. Tourist Publicity (11th series). As T 556. Multicoloured.

1845	350l. Campione d'Italia	1·80	2·10
1846	400l. Chianciano Terme	1·90	90
1847	450l. Padula	2·20	90
1848	550l. Syracuse	2·75	1·00

1984. Folk Customs (3rd series). As T 673. Multicoloured.

1850	400l. Procession of Shrine of Santa Rosa, Viterbo	1·20	30

708 Harvester, Thresher and Medieval Fields Map

1984. Peasant Farming. Multicoloured.

1851	250l. Type **708**	65	45
1852	350l. Hand oil press, cart and medieval fields map	90	70

1984. Italian Villas (5th series). As T 646. Multicoloured.

1853	250l. Villa Caristo, Stignano	1·60	1·20
1854	350l. Villa Doria Pamphili, Genoa	2·20	90
1855	400l. Villa Reale, Stupinigi	2·50	1·00
1856	450l. Villa Mellone, Lecce	3·00	1·20

709 Etruscan Bronze of Warrior

1984. "Italia '85" International Stamp Exhibition, Rome (2nd issue). Multicoloured.

1857	550l. Type **709**	1·70	60
1858	550l. Exhibition emblem	1·70	60
1859	550l. Etruscan silver-backed mirror	1·70	60

710 Dish Aerial, Globe and Punched Tape

1985. Information Technology.

1860	**710**	350l. multicoloured	80	45

711 Man helping Old Woman

1985. Problems of Elderly People.

1861	**711**	250l. multicoloured	60	45

712 "Venus in her Chariot" (fresco, Raphael)

1985. "Italia '85" International Stamp Exhibition, Rome (3rd issue). Multicoloured.

1862	600l. Type **712**	1·70	35
1863	600l. Exhibition emblem	1·70	35
1864	600l. Warriors (detail of fresco, Baldassare Peruzzi)	1·70	35

713 Plate, Vase and Pot

1985. Italian Work for the World (6th series). Ceramics. Multicoloured.

1865	600l. Type **713**	1·90	35
1866	600l. Decorated plate	1·90	35

1985. Italian Motor Industry (2nd series). As T 698. Multicoloured.

1867	450l. Fiat "Uno"	4·50	65
1868	450l. Lamborghini "Countach LP500"	4·50	65
1869	450l. Lancia "Thema"	4·50	65
1870	450l. Fiat Abarth "100 Bialbero"	4·50	65

714 St. Mary of Peace Church, Rome

1985. "Italia '85" International Stamp Exhibition, Rome (4th issue). Baroque Art. Multicoloured.

1871	250l. Type **714**	85	50
1872	250l. Exhibition emblem	85	50
1873	250l. Fountain obelisk and Saint Agnes's Church, Rome	85	50

715 Pope Sixtus V

1985. 400th Anniv of Election of Pope Sixtus V.

1874	**715**	1500l. multicoloured	3·50	2·10

1985. Folk Customs (4th series). As T 673. Multicoloured.

1875	250l. March of the Turks, Potenza	1·20	75
1876	350l. Republican regatta, Amalfi	1·70	75

1985. Tourist Publicity (12th series). As T 556. Multicoloured.

1877	350l. Bormio	90	1·20
1878	400l. Castellammare di Stabia	1·30	50
1879	450l. Stromboli	1·60	50
1880	600l. Termoli	4·25	85

716 European Otter

1985. Nature Protection. Multicoloured.

1881	500l. Type **716**	4·25	65
1882	500l. Primulas	4·25	65
1883	500l. Fir tree	4·25	65
1884	500l. Black-winged stilts	4·25	65

1985. Anniversaries of Italian Artists (11th series). As T 567. Multicoloured.

1885	350l. "Madonna" (Giambattista Salvi (1609–85))	1·70	1·30
1886	400l. "The Pride of Work" (Mario Sironi (1885–1961))	2·10	1·10

717 Aureliano Pertile and Giovanni Martinelli (singers)

1985. Europa. Music Year. Multicoloured.

1887	500l. Type **717**	13·00	1·20
1888	600l. Vicenzo Bellini and Johann Sebastian Bach (composers)	17·00	1·70

718 San Salvatore Abbey

1985. 950th Anniv of San Salvatore Abbey, Mt. Amiata.

1889	**718**	450l. multicoloured	1·20	35

719 Cyclists

1985. World Cycling Championships, Bassano del Grappa.

1890	**719**	400l. multicoloured	1·90	45

720 U.N. and Congress Emblems and Globe

1985. 7th United Nations Crime Prevention Congress, Milan.

1891	**720**	600l. multicoloured	1·90	45

721 Profile and Emblem

1985. International Youth Year.

1892	**721**	600l. multicoloured	1·90	45

1985. Villas (6th series). As T 646. Multicoloured.

1893	300l. Villa Nitti, Maratea	1·90	75
1894	400l. Villa Aldrovandi Mazzacorati, Bologna	2·50	30
1895	500l. Villa Santa Maria, Pula	3·00	45
1896	600l. Villa de Mersi, Villazzano	3·75	50

722 State Emblems of Italy and Vatican City and Medallion (Mario Soccorsi)

1985. Ratification of the Modification of 1929 Lateran Concordat.

1897	**722**	400l. multicoloured	1·10	45

723 Parma Town Hall and 1857 25c. Stamp

724 Basel 1845 2½r. Stamp

1985. "Italia '85" International Stamp Exhibition. Rome (5th issue). Multicoloured. (a) As T 723.

1898	300l. Type **723**	70	45
1899	300l. Naples New Castle and 1858 2g. stamp	70	45
1900	300l. Palermo Cathedral and Sicily 1859 ½g. stamp	70	45
1901	300l. Modena Cathedral and 1852 15c. stamp	70	45
1902	300l. Piazzo Navona, Rome, and Papal States 1852 7b. stamp	70	45
1903	300l. Palazzo Vecchio, Florence, and Tuscany 1851 2c. stamp	70	45
1904	300l. Turin and Sardinia 1861 3l. stamp	70	45
1905	300l. Bologna and Romagna 1859 6b. stamp	70	45
1906	300l. Palazzo Litta, Milan, and Lombardy and Venetia 1850 15c. stamp	70	45

(b) As T 724.

1907	500l. Type **724**	3·25	50
1908	500l. Japan 1871 48m. stamp	3·25	50
1909	500l. United States 1847 10c. stamp	3·25	50
1910	500l. Western Australia 1854 1d. stamp	3·25	50
1911	500l. Mauritius 1848 2d. stamp	3·25	50

(c) Sheet 86×56 mm. Imperf.

MS1912	4000l. Sardinia 1851 5c. stamp and Great Britain "Penny Black"	7·50	7·50

725 Skiers

1986. Cross-country Skiing.

1913	**725**	450l. multicoloured	1·20	45

1986. Folk Customs (5th series). As T 673. Multicoloured.

1914	450l. Le Candelore, Catania	1·20	30

726 Amilcare Ponchielli and Scene from "La Gioconda"

1986. Composers. Multicoloured.

1915	2000l. Type **726** (death centenary)	5·25	90
1916	2000l. Giovan Battista Pergolesi (250th death anniv)	5·25	90

727 Acitrezza

1986. Tourist Publicity (13th series). Mult.

1917	350l. Type **727**	1·30	60
1918	450l. Capri	1·70	90
1919	550l. Merano	2·10	35
1920	650l. San Benedetto del Tronto	2·50	65

728 Heart-shaped Tree (life)

1986. Europa. Multicoloured.

1921	650l. Type **728**	8·25	50
1922	650l. Star-shaped tree (poetry)	8·25	50
1923	650l. Butterfly-shaped tree (colour)	8·25	50
1924	650l. Sun-shaped tree (energy)	8·25	50

729 "Eyes"

1986. 25th International Ophthalmology Congress, Rome.

1925	**729**	550l. multicoloured	1·20	30

730 Italian Police

1986. European Police Meeting, Chianciano Terme.

1926	**730**	550l. multicoloured	3·00	1·40
1927	**730**	650l. multicoloured	3·50	1·60

731 Battle Scene

1986. 120th Anniv of Battle of Bezzecca.

1928	**731**	550l. multicoloured	1·60	60

732 Figure with Flag

1986. National Independence Martyrs' Day.

1929	**732**	2000l. multicoloured	5·25	90

733 Bersagliere and Helmets

1986. 150th Anniv of Turin Bersaglieri Corps (alpine troops).

1930	**733**	450l. multicoloured	1·60	50

734 Dish Aerial, Transmitter and "Messages"

1986. Telecommunications.

1931	**734**	350l. multicoloured	80	60

735 Varallo

1986. Holy Mountain of Varallo.

1932	**735**	2000l. green and blue	5·25	90

1986. Italian Motor Industry (3rd series). As T 698. Multicoloured.

1933	450l. Alfa Romeo "AR 8 Turbo"	4·25	1·20
1934	450l. Innocenti "650 SE"	4·25	75
1935	450l. Ferrari "Testarossa"	4·25	75
1936	450l. Fiatallis "FR 10B"	4·25	75

736 Clothes and Woman (fashion)

1986. Italian Work for the World (7th series). Mult.

1937	450l. Type **736**	3·00	50
1938	450l. Man and clothes (fashion)	3·00	50
1939	650l. Olivetti personal computer, keyboard and screen	4·50	50
1940	650l. Breda steam turbine	4·50	50

737 Airplane flying through "40"

1986. 40th Anniv of Alitalia (national airline). Multicoloured.

1941	550l. Type **737**	1·70	30
1942	650l. Airplane and landing lights	2·10	45

1986. Italian Villas (7th series). As T 646. Mult.

1943	350l. Villa Necker, Trieste	1·20	75
1944	350l. Villa Borromeo, Cassana d'Adda	1·20	75
1945	450l. Villa Palagonia, Bagheria	1·40	65
1946	550l. Villa Medicea, Poggio a Caiano	1·80	50
1947	650l. Issogne Castle	2·20	75

738 "Madonna and Child" (bronze sculpture by Donatello)

1986. Christmas.

1948	**738**	450l. bistre	1·20	30

1986. Anniversaries of Italian Artists (12th series). As T 567.

1949	450l. black and orange	2·10	30
1950	550l. multicoloured	3·00	50

DESIGNS: 450l. Drawing of woman (Andrea del Sarto (1486–1531)); 550l. "Daphne at Pavarola" (Felice Casorati (1883–1963)).

739 Lockheed C130 Hercules Transport dropping Squares in National Colours onto Globe

1986. International Peace Year. Multicoloured.

1951	550l. Type **739**	1·70	45
1952	650l. Airplane, Cross and people (commemoration of Italian airmen killed on mission to Kindu, Congo)	2·00	50

740 Engraving 1862 Stamp

1986. Stamp Day. Francesco Maria Matraire (engraver).

1953	**740**	550l. multicoloured	1·90	30

741 Woven Threads (Marzotto Textile Industry)

1987. Italian Industry.

1954	**741**	700l. multicoloured	1·90	90
1955	-	700l. blue and turquoise	1·90	90

DESIGN: No. 1955, Clouds and flame (Italgas Gas Corporation).

742 River Volturno

1987. Nature Protection. Rivers and Lakes. Multicoloured.

1956	500l. Type **742**	3·00	35
1957	500l. Lake Garda	3·00	35
1958	500l. Lake Trasimeno	3·00	35
1959	500l. River Tirso	3·00	35

743 Gramsci

1987. 50th Death Anniv of Antonio Gramsci (politician).

1960	**743**	600l. grey, black and red	2·10	45

744 Church of the Motorway of the Sun, Florence (Giovanni Michelucci)

1987. Europa. Architecture. Multicoloured.

1961	600l. Type **744**	9·00	90
1962	700l. Termini station, Rome (Nervi)	11·50	90

1987. Tourist Publicity (14th series). As T 556. Multicoloured.

1963	380l. Verbania Pallanza	1·40	65
1964	400l. Palmi	1·70	90
1965	500l. Vasto	2·10	65
1966	600l. Villacidro	2·50	65

745 View of Naples on Football

1987. S.S.C. Naples, National Football Champion, 1986–87.

1967	**745**	500l. multicoloured	3·00	1·60

746 "The Absinthe Drinker" (Edgar Degas)

1987. Anti-alcoholism Campaign.

1968	**746**	380l. multicoloured	1·60	60

747 Liguori and Gulf of Naples

1987. Death Bicentenary of St. Alfonso Maria de Liguori (co-founder of Redemptorists).

1969	**747**	400l. multicoloured	1·10	35

748 Emblem and Olympic Stadium, Rome

1987. World Light Athletics Championships, Rome (1970) and "Olymphilex '87" Stamp Exhibition, Rome (1971).

1970	700l. Type **748**	1·60	25
1971	700l. International Olympic Committee building, Foro Italico, Rome	1·60	25

1987. Folk Customs (6th series). As T 673. Multicoloured.

1972	380l. Joust, Foligno	1·20	45

749 Piazza del Popolo, Ascoli Piceno

1987. Piazzas (1st series). Multicoloured.

1973	380l. Type **749**	1·20	65
1974	500l. Piazza Giuseppe Verdi, Palermo	1·40	25
1975	600l. Piazza San Carlo, Turin	1·70	35
1976	700l. Piazza dei Signori, Verona	2·00	65

See also Nos. 2002/3 and 2023/4.

750 "The Adoration in the Manger" (St. Francis's Basilica, Assisi)

1987. Christmas. Frescoes by Giotto. Mult.

1977	500l. Type **750**	1·70	35
1978	600l. "Epiphany" (Scrovegni Chapel, Padua)	2·10	35

751 Battle Scene

1987. 120th Anniv of Battle of Mentana.

1979	**751**	380l. multicoloured	1·60	60

752 "Christ Pantocrator" (mosaic, Monreale Cathedral)

1987. Artistic Heritage. Multicoloured.

1980	500l. Type **752**	2·30	65
1981	500l. San Carlo Theatre, Naples (18th-century engraving)	2·30	65

753 College and 1787 and 1987 Uniforms

1987. Bicentenary of Nunziatella Military Academy, Naples.

1982	**753**	600l. multicoloured	1·90	45

754 Marco de Marchi (philatelist) and Milan Cathedral

1987. Stamp Day.

1983	**754**	500l. multicoloured	2·00	45

755 Man chipping Flints

1988. "Homo aeserniensis".

1984	**755**	500l. multicoloured	1·20	60

756 Lyceum

1988. E.Q. Visconti Lyceum, Rome.

1985	**756**	500l. multicoloured	1·20	45

See also Nos. 2019, 2109 and 2127.

757 Statue, Bosco and Boy

1988. Death Centenary of St. John Bosco (founder of Salesian Brothers).

1986	**757**	500l. multicoloured	1·20	45

1988. Anniversaries of Italian Artists (13th series). As T 567. Multicoloured.

1987	650l. "Archaeologists" (Giorgio de Chirico (1888–1978))	2·50	70

758 15th-Century Soncino Bible

1988. 500th Anniv of First Printing of Bible in Hebrew.

1988	**758**	550l. multicoloured	1·40	45

759 St. Valentine, Epileptics and Wave Patterns

1988. Anti-epilepsy Campaign.

1989	**759**	500l. multicoloured	1·20	60

760 ETR 450 High Speed Train in Station

1988. Europa. Transport and Communications. Multicoloured.

1990	650l. Type **760**	7·25	1·70
1991	750l. Map and keyboard operator (electronic postal systems)	8·25	2·30

1988. Tourist Publicity (15th series). As T 556. Multicoloured.

1992	400l. Castiglione della Pescaia	1·20	90
1993	500l. Lignano Sabbiadoro	1·40	75
1994	650l. St. Domenico's Church, Noto	1·80	90
1995	750l. Vieste	2·20	1·10

761 Golfer on Ball

1988. Golf.

1996	**761**	500l. multicoloured	1·20	35

762 Stadium and Mascot

1988. World Cup Football Championship, Italy (1990) (1st issue).

1997	**762**	3150l. multicoloured	6·25	3·50

See also Nos. 2049 and 2052/87.

763 Milan Cathedral on Football

1988. A. C. Milan. National Football Champion, 1987–88.

1998	**763**	650l. multicoloured	1·10	85

764 Horse's Head

1988. Artistic Heritage. Pergola Bronzes. Multicoloured.

1999	500l. Type **764**	90	60
2000	650l. Bust of woman	1·20	80

765 Student (bas-relief)

1988. 900th Anniv of Bologna University.

2001	**765**	500l. violet	1·20	45

1988. Piazzas (2nd series). As T 749. Mult.

2002	400l. Piazza del Duomo, Pistoia	1·60	75
2003	550l. Piazza del Unita d'Italia, Trieste	2·30	50

1988. Folk Customs (7th series). As T 673. Multicoloured.

2004	500l. Candle procession, Sassari	2·30	45

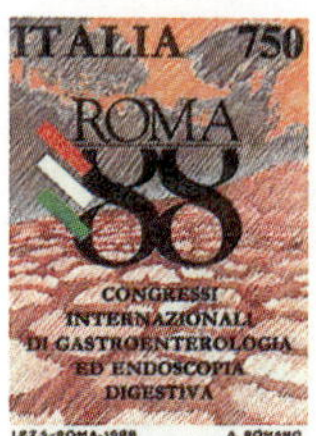

766 Emblem and Appian Way

1988. "Roma 88" Int Gastroenterology and Digestive Endoscopy Congress.

2005	**766**	750l. multicoloured	1·90	60

767 "Ossessione" (Luchino Visconti, 1942)

1988. Italian Films. Scenes from and Advertising Posters of named Films. Multicoloured.

2006	500l. Type **767**	1·40	1·50
2007	650l. "Ladri di Biciclette" (Vittorio de Sica, 1948)	1·80	1·80
2008	2400l. "Roma Citta Aperta" (Roberto Rossellini, 1945)	6·75	1·30
2009	3050l. "Riso Amaro" (Giuseppe de Santis, 1949)	8·75	2·50

768 Bird (aluminium)

1988. Italian Industry. Multicoloured.

2010	750l. Type **768**	1·60	65
2011	750l. Oscilloscope display (electronics)	1·60	65
2012	750l. Banknote engraving, 1986 tourism stamp and medals (60th anniv of State Polygraphic Institute)	1·60	65

769 "Holy Family" (Pasquale Celommi)

1988. Christmas (1st issue).

2013	**769**	650l. multicoloured	2·50	30

See also No. 2015.

770 Borromeo and Plague Victims

1988. 450th Birth Anniv of St. Carlo Borromeo, Archbishop of Milan.

2014	**770**	2400l. multicoloured	5·25	1·30

771 "Nativity" (bas-relief)

1988. Christmas (2nd issue).

2015	**771**	500l. green and brown	2·00	45

772 Edoardo Chiossone (stamp designer) and Japanese 1879 2s. "Koban" Stamp

1988. Stamp Day.

2016	**772**	500l. multicoloured	1·20	45

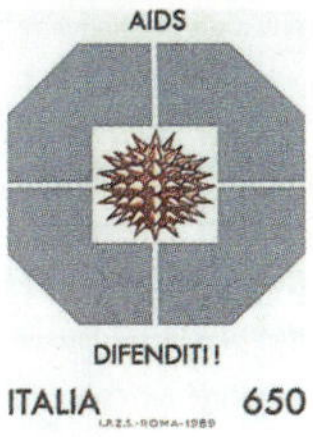

773 AIDS Virus

1989. Anti-AIDS Campaign.

2017	**773**	650l. multicoloured	1·60	25

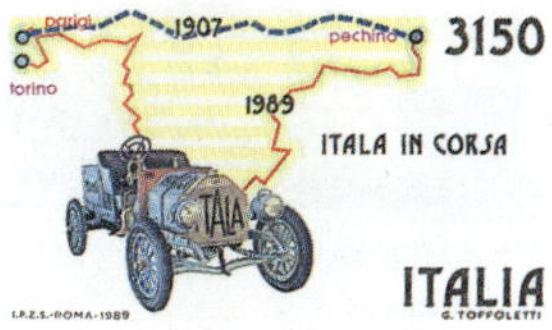

774 1907 Itala Car and Route Map

1989. Re-enactment of 1907 Peking–Paris Car Rally.

2018	**774**	3150l. multicoloured	7·25	4·50

1989. Giuseppe Parini Lyceum, Milan. As T 756.

2019	650l. multicoloured	1·60	45

776 Fresco, Ragione Palace, Padua

1989. Artistic Heritage.

2020	**776**	500l. multicoloured	1·60	75
2021	-	650l. blue	2·00	75

DESIGN: 650l. Crypt, Basilica of St. Nicolas, Bari.

777 Stylized Yachts

1989. World Sailing Championships, Alassio, Naples and Porto Cervo.

2022	**777**	3050l. multicoloured	7·25	2·10

1989. Piazzas (3rd series). As T 749. Mult.

2023	400l. Piazza di Spagna, Rome	1·10	75
2024	400l. Piazza del Duomo, Catanzaro	1·10	75

778 Leap-frog (Luca Rizzello)

1989. Europa. Children's Games. Mult.

2025	500l. Type **778**	4·00	65
2026	650l. Girl dressing up (Serena Forcuti) (vert)	5·25	50
2027	750l. Sack race (Adelise Lahner)	6·00	50

1989. Folk Customs (8th series). As T 673. Multicoloured.

2028	400l. Spello flower paintings	1·10	60

779 Cloisters

1989. Pisa University.

2029	**779**	500l. violet	1·20	50

780 Parliamentary Emblem as Tree on Map

1989. 3rd Direct Elections to European Parliament.

2030	**780**	500l. multicoloured	2·50	45

No. 2030 is also inscribed with the European Currency Unit rate of 0.31 ECU.

1989. Tourist Publicity (16th series). As T 556. Multicoloured.

2031	500l. Grottammare	1·50	85
2032	500l. Spotorno	1·50	85
2033	500l. Pompeii	1·50	85
2034	500l. Giardini Naxos	1·50	85

781 1889 5c. Savoy Arms Stamp

1989. Centenary of Ministry of Posts and Telecommunications. Multicoloured.

2035	500l. Type **781**	1·20	1·80
2036	2400l. Globe within posthorn	6·00	1·80

782 Ball and Club Emblem

1989. Inter Milan, National Football Champion, 1988–89.

2037	**782**	650l. multicoloured	1·20	60

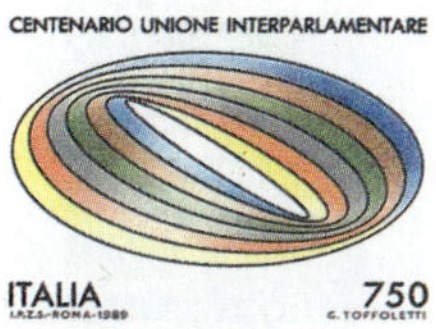

783 Stylized Chamber

1989. Centenary of Interparliamentary Union.

2038	**783**	750l. multicoloured	1·60	45

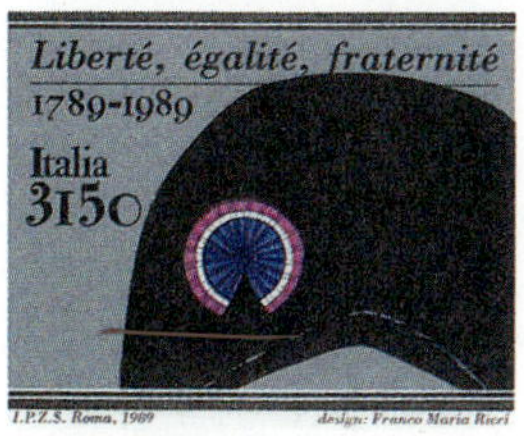

784 Phrygian Cap

1989. Bicentenary of French Revolution.

2039	**784**	3150l. multicoloured	7·00	4·50

785 Corinaldo Wall

1989. Artistic Heritage. 550th Birth Anniv of Francesco di Giorgio Martini (architect).

2040	**785**	500l. multicoloured	1·40	60

786 Chaplin in Film Scenes

1989. Birth Centenary of Charlie Chaplin (film actor and director).

2041	**786**	750l. black and brown	1·90	60

787 "Inauguration of Naples–Portici Line" (left-hand detail, S Fergola)

1989. 150th Anniv of Naples–Portici Railway. Multicoloured.

2042	550l. Type **787**	1·60	30
2043	550l. Right-hand detail	1·60	30

Nos. 2042/3 were printed together, se-tenant, forming a composite design.

788 Castelfidardo, Accordion and Stradella

1989. Italian Industry. Multicoloured.

2044	450l. Type **788**	1·10	65
2045	450l. Books (Arnoldo Mondadori Publishing House)	1·10	65

789 Madonna and Child

1989. Christmas. Details of "Adoration of the Magi" (Correggio). Multicoloured.

2046	500l. Type **789**	1·20	35
2047	500l. Magi	1·20	35

Nos. 2046/7 were printed together, se-tenant, forming a composite design.

790 Emilio Diena (stamp dealer)

1989. Stamp Day.

2048	**790**	500l. black, brown & blue	1·60	45

791 Monument (Mario Ceroli) and Football Pitch

1989. World Cup Football Championship, Italy (1990) (2nd issue).

2049	**791**	450l. multicoloured	1·10	70

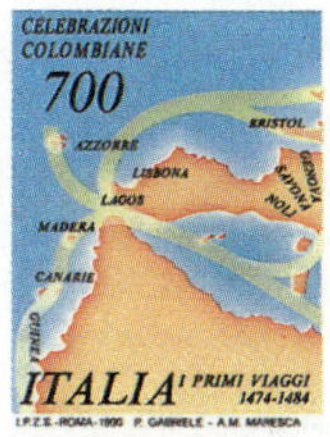

792 Old Map (left half) with Route superimposed

1990. Columbus's First Voyages, 1474–84. Multicoloured.

2050	700l. Type **792**	1·40	35
2051	700l. Right half of map	1·40	35

Nos. 2050/1 were printed together, se-tenant, forming a composite design.

793 Italy

1990. World Cup Football Championship, Italy (3rd issue). Designs showing finalists' emblems or playing venues. Multicoloured.

2052	450l. Type **793**	55	90
2053	450l. U.S.A.	55	90
2054	450l. Olympic Stadium, Rome	55	90
2055	450l. Comunale Stadium, Florence	55	90
2056	450l. Austria	55	90
2057	450l. Czechoslovakia	55	90
2058	600l. Argentina	75	75
2059	600l. U.S.S.R.	75	75
2060	600l. San Paolo Stadium, Naples	75	75
2061	600l. New Stadium, Bari	75	75
2062	600l. Cameroun	75	75
2063	600l. Rumania	75	75
2064	650l. Brazil	85	65
2065	650l. Costa Rica	85	65
2066	650l. Delle Alpi Stadium, Turin	85	65
2067	650l. Ferraris Stadium, Genoa	85	65
2068	650l. Sweden	85	65
2069	650l. Scotland	85	65
2070	700l. United Arab Emirates	90	45
2071	700l. West Germany	90	45
2072	700l. Dall'Ara Stadium, Bologna	90	45
2073	700l. Meazza Stadium, Milan	90	45
2074	700l. Colombia	90	45
2075	700l. Yugoslavia	90	45
2076	800l. Belgium	1·00	75
2077	800l. Uruguay	1·00	75
2078	800l. Bentegodi Stadium, Verona	1·00	75
2079	800l. Friuli Stadium, Udine	1·00	75
2080	800l. South Korea	1·00	75
2081	800l. Spain	1·00	75
2082	1200l. England	1·50	1·10
2083	1200l. Netherlands	1·50	1·10
2084	1200l. Sant'Elia Stadium, Cagliari	1·50	1·10
2085	1200l. La Favorita Stadium, Palermo	1·50	1·10
2086	1200l. Ireland	1·50	1·10
2087	1200l. Egypt	1·50	1·10

See also No. 2104.

1990. Tourist Publicity (17th series). As T 556. Multicoloured.

2088	600l. San Felice Circeo	1·30	65
2089	600l. Castellammare del Golfo	1·30	65
2090	600l. Montepulciano	1·30	65
2091	600l. Sabbioneta	1·30	65

1990. Folk Customs (9th series). As T 673. Multicoloured.

2092	600l. Avelignesi horse race, Merano	1·40	45

794 National Colours

1990. Death Centenary of Aurelio Saffi.

2093	**794**	700l. multicoloured	1·60	45

795 Giovanni Giorgi (inventor)

1990. 55th Anniv of Invention of Giorgi/MKSA System of Electrotechnical Units.

2094 **795** 600l. multicoloured 1·20 45

796 Flags, Globe and Workers (after "The Four States" (Pellizza da Volpedo))

1990. Centenary of Labour Day.

2095 **796** 600l. multicoloured 1·20 35

797 Ball on Map

1990. S. S. C. Naples, National Football Champion, 1989–90.

2096 **797** 700l. multicoloured 1·90 1·20

798 Piazza San Silvestro Post Office, Rome

1990. Europa. Post Office Buildings. Mult.

2097 700l. Type **798** 5·25 50

2098 800l. Fondaco Tedeschi post office, Venice 6·25 50

799 Paisiello

1990. 250th Birth Anniv of Giovanni Paisiello (composer).

2099 **799** 450l. multicoloured 1·10 45

800 Globe, Open Book and Bust of Dante

1990. Centenary of Dante Alighieri Society.

2100 **800** 700l. multicoloured 1·60 35

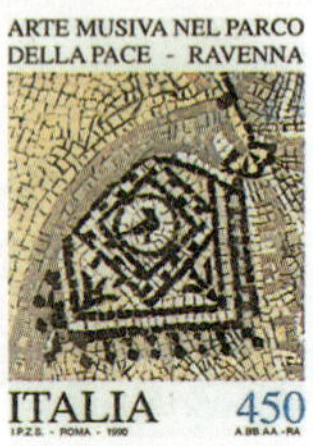

801 Byzantine Mosaic, Ravenna

1990. Artistic Heritage. Multicoloured.

2101 450l. Type **801** 1·00 75

2102 700l. "Christ and Angels" (detail of Rachis altar, Friuli) (Lombard art) 1·60 50

802 Malatestiana Temple, Rimini

1990. 40th Anniv of Malatestiana Religious Music Festival.

2103 **802** 600l. multicoloured 1·40 60

1990. West Germany, Winner of World Cup Football Championship. As No. 2071 but value changed and additionally inscr "CAMPIONE DEL MONDO".

2104 600l. multicoloured 1·90 70

803 "Still Life"

1990. Birth Cent of Giorgio Morandi (painter).

2105 **803** 750l. black 1·90 90

804 Ancient and Modern Wrestlers

1990. World Greco-Roman Wrestling Championships, Rome.

2106 **804** 3200l. multicoloured 6·75 1·30

805 "New Life" (Emidio Vangelli)

1990. Christmas. Multicoloured.

2107 600l. Type **805** 1·40 50

2108 750l. "Adoration of the Shepherds" (fresco by Pellegrino in St. Daniel's Church, Friuli) 1·80 50

806 Catania University

1990

2109 - 600l. multicoloured 1·40 50

2110 **806** 750l. blue and ultramarine 1·80 50

DESIGN—As T **756**: 600l. Bernardino Telesio High School, Cosenza.

807 Corrado Mezzana (stamp designer, self-portrait)

1990. Stamp Day.

2111 **807** 600l. multicoloured 1·60 60

808 Holy Family

1991. "The Living Tableau", Rivisondoli.

2112 **808** 600l. multicoloured 1·40 60

809 Fair Emblem

1991. "EuroFlora '91" Fair, Genoa.

2113 **809** 750l. multicoloured 1·60 35

810 Emblem

1991. 750th Anniv of Siena University.

2114 **810** 750l. gold, black and blue 1·60 35

1991. Tourist Publicity (18th series). As T 556. Multicoloured.

2115 600l. Cagli 1·30 65

2116 600l. La Maddalena 1·30 65

2117 600l. Roccaraso 1·30 65

2118 600l. Sanremo 1·30 65

812 City and Columbus's Fleet

1991. Europa Youth Meeting, Venice.

2119 **811** 750l. multicoloured 1·60 25

No. 2119 is also valued in ECUs (European Currency Unit).

1991. 500th Anniv (1992) of Discovery of America by Christopher Columbus (1st issue). Multicoloured.

2120 750l. Type **812** 1·40 35

2121 750l. Map, Columbus, seal and King and Queen of Spain 1·40 35

Nos. 2120/1 were printed together, se-tenant, forming a composite design.

See also Nos. 2151/4 and **MS**2158.

813 Belli and View of Rome

1991. Birth Bicentenary of Giuseppe Gioachino Belli (poet).

2122 **813** 600l. brown and blue 1·20 35

814 St Gregory's Church, Rome

1991. Artistic Heritage.

2123 **814** 3200l. multicoloured 7·75 1·50

815 "DRS" Satellite

1991. Europa. Europe in Space. Multicoloured.

2124 750l. Type **815** 6·25 90

2125 800l. "Hermes" spaceship and "Columbus" space station 6·50 50

816 Sta Maria Maggiore Church, Lanciano

1991. Artistic Heritage.

2126 **816** 600l. brown 1·20 60

1991. D. A. Azuni Lyceum, Sassari. As T 756.

2127 600l. multicoloured 1·20 60

817 Football and Genoa Lantern

1991. Sampdoria, National Football Champion, 1990–91.

2128 **817** 3000l. multicoloured 6·50 3·50

818 Hands and Ball

1991. Centenary of Basketball.

2129 **818** 500l. multicoloured 1·10 60

819 Children and Butterflies

1991. United Nations Conference on Rights of the Child. Multicoloured.

2130	600l. Type **819**		1·20	15
2131	750l. Child with balloon on man's shoulders		1·60	50

820 "Youth and Gulls" (sculpture, Pericle Fazzini)

1991. Artistic Heritage. Multicoloured.

2132	**820**	600l. yellow, blue & black	1·20	1·20
2133	-	3200l. multicoloured	6·50	1·50

DESIGN: 3200l. Palazzo Esposizioni, Turin (Pier Luigi Nervi (birth centenary)).

821 Winged Sphinx

1991. Egyptian Museum, Turin.

2134	**821**	750l. gold, green & yellow	1·90	35

822 Luigi Galvani (physiologist) and Experimental Equipment

1991. 100 Years of Radio (1st issue).

2135	**822**	750l. multicoloured	2·00	25

Galvani carried out experiments in electricity.

See also Nos. 2148, 2203, 2241 and 2321/2.

823 Mozart at Spinet

1991. Death Bicentenary of Wolfgang Amadeus Mozart (composer).

2136	**823**	800l. multicoloured	2·10	60

824 Bear

1991. Nature Protection. Multicoloured.

2137	500l. Type **824**	1·60	65
2138	500l. Peregrine falcon	1·60	65
2139	500l. Deer	1·60	65
2140	500l. Marine life	1·60	65

825 "The Angel of Life" (Giovanni Segantini)

1991. Christmas.

2141	**825**	600l. multicoloured	1·60	60

826 Giulio and Alberto Bolaffi (stamp catalogue publishers)

1991. Stamp Day.

2142	**826**	750l. multicoloured	1·60	45

827 Signature and National Flag

1991. Birth Cent of Pietro Nenni (politician).

2143	**827**	750l. multicoloured	1·60	60

828 Runners

1992. 22nd European Indoor Light Athletics Championships, Genoa.

2144	**828**	600l. multicoloured	1·30	60

829 Neptune Fountain, Florence

1992. 400th Death Anniv of Bartolomeo Ammannati (architect and sculptor).

2145	**829**	750l. multicoloured	1·60	60

830 Statue of Marchese Alberto V of Este (founder) and University

1992. 600th Anniv (1991) of Ferrara University.

2146	**830**	750l. multicoloured	1·60	60

831 Pediment

1992. Naples University.

2147	**831**	750l. multicoloured	1·60	45

1992. 100 Years of Radio (2nd issue). As T 822. Multicoloured.

2148	750l. Alessandro Volta (physicist) and Voltaic pile	2·20	60

Volta formulated the theory of current electricity and invented an electric battery.

832 Emblem and Venue

1992. "Genova '92" International Thematic Stamp Exhibition (1st issue).

2149	**832**	750l. multicoloured	1·60	25

See also Nos. 2170/5.

833 Medal of Lorenzo (Renato Beradi)

1992. 500th Death Anniv of Lorenzo de Medici, "The Magnificent".

2150	**833**	750l. multicoloured	1·60	60

834 Columbus before Queen Isabella

1992. 500th Anniv of Discovery of America by Columbus (2nd issue). Multicoloured.

2151	500l. Type **834**	1·10	70
2152	500l. Columbus's fleet	1·10	70
2153	500l. Sighting land	1·10	70
2154	500l. Landing in the New World	1·10	70

835 Scenes from Life of St. Maria Filippini (altar, Montefiascone Cathedral)

1992. 300th Anniv of Maestre Pie Filippini Institute.

2155	**835**	750l. multicoloured	1·60	60

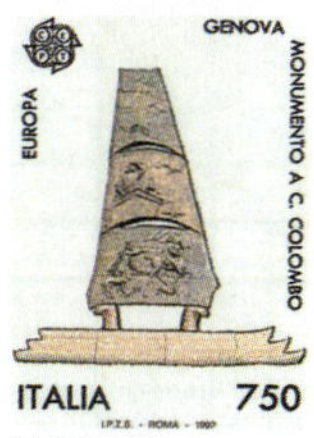

836 Columbus Monument, Genoa (G. Giannetti)

1992. Europa. 500th Anniv of Discovery of America by Columbus. Multicoloured.

2156	750l. Type **836**	5·50	90
2157	850l. Emblem of "Colombo '92" exhibition, Genoa	6·25	65

837 Columbus presenting Natives

1992. 500th Anniv of Discovery of America by Columbus (3rd issue). Six sheets each 113×93 mm containing horiz designs as T 837 reproducing scenes from United States 1893 Columbian Exposition issue.

MS2158 Six sheets (a) 50l. green (Type **837**); 300l. blue (Columbus announcing discovery); 4000l. mauve (Columbus in chains). (b) 100l. lilac (Columbus welcomed at Barcelona); 800l. red (Columbus restored to favour); 3000l. green (Columbus describing third voyage). (c) 200l. blue (Columbus sighting land); 900l. blue (Columbus's fleet); 1500l. red (Queen Isabella pledging jewels). (d) 400l. brown (Columbus soliciting aid of Queen Isabella); 700l. red (Columbus at La Rabida); 1000l. blue (Recall of Columbus). (e) 500l. brown (Landing of Columbus); 600l. green ("Santa Maria"); 2000l. red (Portraits of Queen Isabella and Columbus). (f) 5000l. green ("America", Columbus and "Liberty") Set of 6 sheets 44·00 30·00

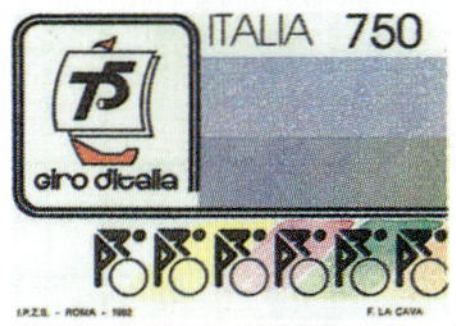

838 Seascape and Cyclists

1992. 75th "Tour of Italy" Cycle Race. Mult.

2159	750l. Type **838**	1·60	50
2160	750l. Mountains and cyclists	1·60	50

Nos. 2159/60 were issued together, se-tenant, forming a composite design.

839 Ball, Team Badge and Stylization of Milan Cathedral

1992. A.C. Milan, National Football Champion, 1991–92.

2161	**839**	750l. green, red and black	1·60	70

840 Viareggio

1992. Seaside Resorts. Multicoloured.

2162	750l. Type **840**	1·60	45
2163	750l. Rimini	1·60	60

841 Nuvolari

1992. Birth Centenary of Tazio Nuvolari (racing driver).

2164	**841**	3200l. multicoloured	7·50	1·60

1992. Tourist Publicity (19th series). As T 556. Multicoloured.

2165	600l. Arcevia	1·50	90
2166	600l. Braies	1·50	90
2167	600l. Maratea	1·50	90
2168	600l. Pantelleria	1·50	90

842 "Adoration of the Shepherds" (detail)

1992. 400th Death Anniv of Jacopo da Ponte (painter).

2169	**842**	750l. multicoloured	1·60	60

843 Columbus's House, Genoa

1992. "Genova '92" International Thematic Stamp Exhibition (2nd issue). Multicoloured.

2170	500l. Type **843**	1·00	50
2171	600l. Departure of Columbus's fleet from Palos, 1492	1·20	35
2172	750l. Route map of Columbus's first voyage	1·50	50
2173	850l. Columbus sighting land	1·80	65
2174	1200l. Columbus landing on San Salvador	2·40	70
2175	3200l. Columbus, "Man" (Leonardo da Vinci), "Fury" (Michelangelo) and Raphael's portrait of Michelangelo	6·75	1·80

844 Woman's Eyes and Mouth

1992. Stamp Day. Ordinary or self-adhesive gum.

2176	**844**	750l. multicoloured	1·60	45

845 Map of Europe and Lions Emblem

1992. 75th Anniv of Lions International and 38th Europa Forum, Genoa.

2178	**845**	3000l. multicoloured	6·75	2·10

846 European Community Emblem and Members' Flags

1992. European Single Market (1st issue).

2179	**846**	600l. multicoloured	1·30	60

See also Nos. 2182/93.

847 Woman with Food Bowl

1992. International Nutrition Conference, Rome.

2180	**847**	500l. multicoloured	1·10	60

848 Caltagirone Crib

1992. Christmas.

2181	**848**	600l. multicoloured	1·50	45

849 Buildings on Flag of Italy

1993. European Single Market (2nd issue). Designs differing in flag of country and language of inscription. Multicoloured.

2182	750l. Type **849**	1·80	50
2183	750l. Belgium	1·80	50
2184	750l. Denmark	1·80	50
2185	750l. France	1·80	50
2186	750l. Germany	1·80	50
2187	750l. Greece	1·80	50
2188	750l. Ireland	1·80	50
2189	750l. Luxembourg	1·80	50
2190	750l. Netherlands	1·80	50
2191	750l. Portugal	1·80	50
2192	750l. United Kingdom	1·80	50
2193	750l. Spain	1·80	50

850 Russian and Italian Alpine Veterans

1993. 50th Anniv Meeting of Veterans of Battle of Nikolayevka.

2194	**850**	600l. multicoloured	1·60	60

851 Mezzettino, Colombina and Arlecchino

1993. Death Bicentenary of Carlo Goldoni (dramatist). Multicoloured.

2195	500l. Type **851**	1·10	80
2196	500l. Arlecchino and portrait of Goldoni	1·10	80

852 "Africa" (mosaic, Roman villa, Piazza Armerina)

1993. Artistic Heritage.

2197	**852**	750l. multicoloured	1·60	60

853 Wedge stopping Heart-shaped Cog

1993. National Health Day. Campaign against Heart Disease.

2198	**853**	750l. multicoloured	1·60	60

854 Tabby

1993. Domestic Cats. Multicoloured.

2199	600l. Type **854**	1·20	65
2200	600l. White Persian	1·20	65
2201	600l. Devon rex (vert)	1·20	65
2202	600l. Maine coon (vert)	1·20	65

1993. 100 Years of Radio (3rd issue). As T 822. Multicoloured.

2203	750l. Temistocle Calzecchi Onesti (physicist) and apparatus for detecting electromagnetic waves	2·00	35

855 "The Piazza"

1993. Death Bicentenary of Francesco Guardi (artist).

2204	**855**	3200l. multicoloured	7·25	2·40

856 Horace

1993. 2000th Death Anniv of Horace (Quintus Horatius Flaccus) (poet).

2205	**856**	600l. multicoloured	1·30	50

857 Cottolengo and Small House of the Divine Providence, Turin

1993. St. Giuseppe Benedetto Cottolengo Commemoration.

2206	**857**	750l. multicoloured	1·60	35

858 "Carousel Horses" (Lino Bianchi Barriviera)

1993. Europa. Contemporary Art. Mult.

2207	750l. Type **858**	2·00	75
2208	850l. "Dynamism of Coloured Shapes" (Gino Severini)	2·40	60

859 Medal (Giuseppe Romagnoli)

1993. 400th Anniv of San Luca National Academy.

2209	**859**	750l. multicoloured	1·60	45

860 Emblem

1993. "Family Fest '93" International Conference, Rome.

2210	**860**	750l. multicoloured	1·60	60

861 Player and Club Badge

1993. Milan, National Football Champion, 1992–93.

2211	**861**	750l. multicoloured	1·60	60

862 Carloforte

1993. Tourist Publicity (20th series). Mult.

2212	600l. Type **862**	1·50	50
2213	600l. Palmanova	1·50	50
2214	600l. Senigallia	1·50	50
2215	600l. Sorrento	1·50	50

See also Nos. 2248/51 and 2315/18.

863 Canoeing

1993. World Canoeing Championships, Trentino.

2216	**863**	750l. multicoloured	1·60	45

864 Observatory

1993. Centenary of Regina Margherita Observatory.

2217	**864**	500l. multicoloured	1·60	50

865 Staircase, St. Salome's Cathedral, Veroli

1993. Artistic Heritage.
2218 **865** 750l. multicoloured 1·60 35

866 Soldier, Boy with Rifle and German Helmet

1993. Second World War 50th Anniversaries (1st issue). Multicoloured.
2219 750l. Type **866** (the Four Days of Naples) 1·60 35
2220 750l. Menorah, people in rail-way truck and Star of David (deportation of Roman Jews) 1·60 35
2221 750l. Seven Cervi brothers (execution) 1·60 35
See also Nos. 2259/61.

867 Carriage

1993. The Taxis Family in Postal History. Multicoloured.
2222 750l. Type **867** 1·50 25
2223 750l. Taxis arms 1·50 25
2224 750l. Gig 1·50 25
2225 750l. 17th-century postal messenger 1·50 25
2226 750l. 18th-century postal messenger 1·50 25

868 Head Office, Rome

1993. Centenary of Bank of Italy. Mult.
2227 750l. Type **868** 4·50 35
2228 1000l. 1000 lire banknote (first note issued by Bank) 6·25 50

869 Colonies Express Letter Stamp Design

1993. Stamp Day. Centenary of First Italian Colonies Stamps.
2229 **869** 600l. red and blue 1·30 45

870 Tableau Vivant, Corchiano

1993. Christmas. Multicoloured.
2230 600l. Type **870** 1·50 65
2231 750l. "The Annunciation" (Piero della Francesca) 1·90 50

871 17th-century Map of Foggia

1993. Treasures from State Archives and Museums (1st series). Multicoloured.
2232 600l. Type **871** (Foggia Archives) 1·30 65
2233 600l. "Concert" (Bartolomeo Manfredi) (Uffizi Gallery, Florence) 1·30 65
2234 750l. View of Siena from 15th-century illuminated manuscript (Siena Archives) (vert) 1·60 30
2235 850l. "The Death of Adonis" (Sebastiano del Piombo) (Uffizi Gallery) 1·80 65
See also Nos. 2266/9, 2306/9 and 2346/9.

872 Ringmaster and Bareback Riders

1994. The Circus. Multicoloured.
2236 600l. Type **872** 1·40 60
2237 750l. Clowns 1·70 35

873 Mother and Child inside House

1994. "The Housewife, a Presence that Counts".
2238 **873** 750l. multicoloured 2·00 30

874 "Bread" (Dario Piazza)

1994. Paintings of Italian Food. Multicoloured.
2239 500l. Type **874** 1·10 75
2240 600l. "Italian Pasta in the World" (Erminia Scaglione) 1·40 50

1994. 100 Years of Radio (4th issue). As T 822. Multicoloured.
2241 750l. Augusto Righi (physicist) and his Hertzian oscillator 2·00 35

875 Boxer

1994. Dogs. Multicoloured.
2242 600l. Type **875** 1·40 50
2243 600l. Dalmatian 1·40 50
2244 600l. Maremma sheepdog 1·40 50
2245 600l. German shepherd 1·40 50

876 "The Risen Christ" (statue)

1994. Procession of "The Risen Christ", Tarquinia.
2246 **876** 750l. multicoloured 2·00 35

877 Pacioli in Study

1994. 500th Anniv of Publication of "Summary of Arithmetic, Geometry, Proportion and Proportionality" by Fra' Luca Pacioli.
2247 **877** 750l. multicoloured 2·00 35

1994. Tourist Publicity (21st series). As T 862. Multicoloured.
2248 600l. Odescalchi Castle, Santa Marinella 1·40 35
2249 600l. St. Michael's Abbey, Monticchio 1·40 35
2250 600l. Orta San Giulio 1·40 50
2251 600l. Cathedral, Messina 1·40 50

878 Kossuth

1994. Death Centenary of Lajos Kossuth (Hungarian statesman).
2252 **878** 3750l. multicoloured 8·00 2·75

879 Women's High-diving

1994. World Water Sports Championships. Multicoloured.
2253 600l. Type **879** 1·30 50
2254 750l. Water polo 1·70 35

880 Club Badge, Football and Colours

1994. Milan, National Football Champion, 1993–94.
2255 **880** 750l. multicoloured 2·10 60

881 Camillo Golgi (cytologist) and Golgi Cells

1994. Europa. Discoveries. Italian Nobel Prize winners. Multicoloured.
2256 750l. Type **881** (medicine, 1906) 2·20 45
2257 850l. Giulio Natta (chemist) and diagram of polymer structure (chemistry, 1963) 2·50 60

882 "Goddess of Caldevigo" (bronze statuette, 5th century B.C.)

1994. "Ancient Peoples of Italy" Archaeological Exhibition, Rimini.
2258 **882** 750l. multicoloured 2·00 35

883 Destruction of Montecassino

1994. Second World War 50th Anniversaries (2nd issue). Multicoloured.
2259 750l. Type **883** 1·80 30
2260 750l. Bound prisoners (Ardeatine Caves Massacre) 1·80 30
2261 750l. Family (Marzabotto Massacre) 1·80 30

884 Washing of Feet

1994. 22nd National Eucharistic Congress, Siena.
2262 **884** 600l. multicoloured 1·60 45

885 "Ariadne, Venus and Bacchus"

1994. Artistic Heritage. 400th Death Anniv of Tintoretto (artist).
2263 **885** 750l. multicoloured 2·00 45

886 "Piazza del Duomo during the Plague, 1630" (attr Cigoli)

1994. 750th Anniv of Arciconfraternita della Misericordia, Florence.
2264 **886** 750l. multicoloured 2·00 30

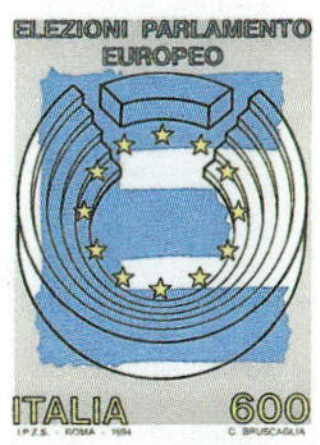

887 "E", European Union Emblem and Parliament

1994. European Parliament Elections.
2265 **887** 600l. multicoloured 1·60 45

1994. Treasures from State Archives and Museums (2nd series). As T 871. Multicoloured.
2266 600l. Frontispiece of notary's register, 1623–24 (Catania Archives) (vert) 1·10 50
2267 600l. "Death of Patroclus" (Attic vase, 5th century B.C.) (Agrigento Archaeological Museum) (vert) 1·10 50
2268 750l. "Galata and his Wife" (statue) (National Roman Museum) (vert) 1·40 25
2269 850l. Civic seal, 1745 (Campobasso Archives) (vert) 1·60 35

888 Olympic Rings and Pierre de Coubertin (founder)

1994. Centenary of Int Olympic Committee.
2270 **888** 850l. multicoloured 2·00 45

889 Vesuvius and "G 7"

1994. Group of Seven (industrialized countries) Summit, Naples.
2271 **889** 600l. blue, ultram & grn 1·30 45

890 Church of the Holy House and "Madonna and Child"

1994. 700th Anniv of Shrine of the Nativity of the Virgin, Loreto.
2272 **890** 500l. multicoloured 1·60 60

891 Pietro Miliani (papermaker) (after Francesco Rosaspina)

1994. Stamp Day. Multicoloured.
2273 600l. Type **891** 1·30 50
2274 750l. Paper and Watermark Museum (former St. Dominic's Monastery), Fabriano 1·60 35

892 Frederick II (sculpture, Bitonto Cathedral)

1994. 800th Birth Anniv of Frederick II, Holy Roman Emperor.
2275 **892** 750l. multicoloured 2·00 30

893 St. Mark's Basilica

1994. 900th Anniv of Dedication of St. Mark's Basilica, Venice.
2276 **893** 750l. multicoloured 2·20 85
MS2277 80×115 mm. No. 2276 together with No. 1491 of San Marino 4·00 3·50

894 "The Annunciation" (Melozzo da Forli)

1994. Christmas. Multicoloured.
2278 600l. Type **894** 1·50 50
2279 750l. "Sacred Conversation" (detail, Lattanzio da Rimini) 3·25 35

895 Club Emblem on Globe

1994. Centenary of Italian Touring Club.
2280 **895** 600l. multicoloured 1·60 45

896 Headquarters, Rome

1994. 75th Anniv of Credit for Businesses and Public Works.
2281 **896** 750l. multicoloured 4·00 35

897 New Emblem

1994. Incorporation of Italian Post. Size 34×26 mm.
2282 - 600l. red and silver 1·80 50
2283 **897** 750l. black, green and red 2·30 35
2284 **897** 750l. red 2·30 35

DESIGN—VERT: 600l. Palazzo Querini Dubois, Venice (restored with Post Office help).

For 750 and 850l. values, size 26×17 mm, see Nos. 2343/4.

898 Gentile

1994. 50th Death Anniv of Giovanni Gentile (philosopher).
2285 **898** 750l. multicoloured 2·10 45

899 Rainbow, Dove, Olive Tree and Flood

1995. For Flood Victims.
2286 **899** 750l.+2250l. mult 9·25 5·75

900 Skater

1995. World Speed Skating Championships, Baselga di Pine.
2287 **900** 750l. multicoloured 2·00 35

901 First Issue of "La Domenica del Corriere"

1995. 50th Death Anniv of Achille Beltrame (painter).
2288 **901** 500l. multicoloured 1·60 60

902 Rice

1995. Italian Food. Multicoloured.
2289 500l. Type **902** 1·40 65
2290 750l. Olives and olive oil 2·00 50

903 Grey Herons

1995. Birds. Multicoloured.
2291 600l. Type **903** 1·40 50
2292 600l. Griffon vultures ("Grifone") 1·40 50
2293 600l. Golden eagles ("Aquila Reale") 1·40 50
2294 600l. White-winged snow finches ("Fringuello Alpino") 1·40 50

904 Anniversary Emblem

1995. 50th Anniv of U.N.O.
2295 **904** 850l. black, blue and gold 2·20 45

905 Detail of Monument (Giuseppe Grande)

1995. Centenary of Monument to the Fallen of the Five Days of Milan (1848 uprising).
2296 **905** 750l. multicoloured 1·60 35

906 Princess Mafalda of Savoy and Concentration Camp

1995. 50th Anniv of End of Second World War. Multicoloured.
2297 750l. Type **906** 1·70 30
2298 750l. DUKW at Anzio 1·70 30
2299 750l. Teresa Gullace and scene of her death 1·70 30
2300 750l. Florence Town Hall and Military Medal 1·70 30
2301 750l. Vittorio Veneto Town Hall and Military Medal 1·70 30
2302 750l. Cagliari Town Hall and Military Medal 1·70 30
2303 750l. Battle of Mount Lungo 1·70 30
2304 750l. Martin B-26 Marauders parachuting supplies in the Balkans 1·70 30
2305 750l. Light cruisers of the Eighth Division in Atlantic 1·70 30

1995. Treasures from State Archives and Museums (3rd series). As T 871. Multicoloured.
2306 500l. Illuminated letter "P" from statute of Pope Innocent III (Rome Archives) (vert) 1·00 65
2307 500l. "Port of Naples" (detail, Bernardo Strozzi) (St. Martin National Museum, Naples) 1·00 65
2308 750l. Illuminated letter "I" showing the Risen Christ from 1481 document (Mantua Archives) (vert) 1·50 35
2309 850l. "Sacred Love and Profane Love" (Titian) (Borghese Museum and Gallery, Rome) 1·80 65

907 Emblem

1995. Centenary of Venice Biennale.
2310 **907** 750l. blue, gold & yellow 1·80 35

908 Santa Croce Basilica, Florence

1995. Artistic Heritage.
2311 **908** 750l. brown 1·80 35

909 Soldiers and Civilians celebrating

1995. Europa. Peace and Freedom. Mult.
2312 750l. Type **909** (50th anniv of end of Second World War in Europe) 2·40 35
2313 850l. Mostar Bridge, (Bosnia) and Council of Europe emblem 2·75 50

910 Players

1995. Centenary of Volleyball.
2314 **910** 750l. blue, orange & grn 2·00 35

1995. Tourist Publicity (22nd series). As T 862. Multicoloured.
2315 750l. Alatri 1·80 35
2316 750l. Nuoro 1·80 35
2317 750l. Susa 1·80 35
2318 750l. Venosa 1·80 35

911 Experiment demonstrating X-rays

1995. Centenary of Discovery of X-rays by Wilhelm Rontgen.
2319 **911** 750l. multicoloured 1·60 35

912 Player and Club Badge

1995. Juventus, National Football Champion, 1994–95.
2320 **912** 750l. multicoloured 2·00 45

913 Villa Griffone (site of Marconi's early experiments)

1995. 100 Years of Radio (5th issue). Centenary of First Radio Transmission. Multicoloured.
2321 750l. Type **913** 1·80 35
2322 850l. Guglielmo Marconi and transmitter (36×21 mm) 2·10 50

914 St. Antony, Holy Basilica (Padua) and Page of Gospel

1995. 800th Birth Anniv of St. Antony of Padua. Multicoloured.
2323 750l. Type **914** 1·80 35
2324 850l. St. Antony holding Child Jesus (painting, Vieira Lusitano) (horiz) 2·10 50

915 Durazzo Pallavicini, Pegli

1995. Public Gardens (1st series). Multicoloured.
2325 750l. Type **915** 1·70 15
2326 750l. Boboli, Florence 1·70 15
2327 750l. Ninfa, Cisterna di Latina 1·70 15
2328 750l. Parco della Reggia, Caserta 1·70 15
See also Nos. 2439/42.

916 Milan Cathedral and Eye (congress emblem)

1995. 10th European Ophthalmological Society Congress, Milan.
2329 **916** 750l. multicoloured 1·60 35

917 "Sailors' Wives"

1995. Birth Centenary of Massimo Campigli (painter).
2330 **917** 750l. multicoloured 2·20 35

918 Dome of Santa Maria del Fiore (Florence), Galileo and Albert Einstein

1995. 14th World Relative Physics Conference, Florence.
2331 **918** 750l. blue, brown & black 1·60 35

919 Rudolph Valentino in "The Son of the Sheik"

1995. Centenary of Motion Pictures.
2332 **919** 750l. black, blue and red 1·70 50
2333 - 750l. multicoloured 1·70 50
2334 - 750l. multicoloured 1·70 50
2335 - 750l. multicoloured 1·70 50
DESIGNS: No. 2333, Toto in "The Gold of Naples"; 2334, Frederico Fellini's "Cabiria Nights"; 2335, Poster (by Massimo Geleng) for "Cinecitta 95" film festival.

920 Wheatfield and Anniversary Emblem

1995. 50th Anniv of F.A.O.
2336 **920** 850l. multicoloured 2·40 45

921 St. Albert's Stone Coffin (detail) and Basilica

1995. 900th Anniversaries of Pontida Basilica and Death of St. Albert of Prezzate.
2337 **921** 1000l. brown and blue 2·20 60

922 Athletes

1995. 1st World Military Games, Rome.
2338 **922** 850l. multicoloured 2·10 45

923 Globe and Means of Communication

1995. 50th Anniv of Ansa News Agency.
2339 **923** 750l. multicoloured 2·00 35

924 Crib (Stefano da Putignano), Polignano Cathedral

1995. Christmas. Multicoloured.
2340 750l. Type **924** 2·75 35
2341 850l. "Adoration of the Wise Men" (detail, Fra Angelico) 3·25 50

925 Renato Mondolfo (philatelist) and Trieste 1949 20l. Stamp

1995. Stamp Day.
2342 **925** 750l. multicoloured 1·60 35

1995. 1st Anniv of Incorporation of Italian Post. Size 26×17 mm.
2343 **897** 750l. red 1·50 15
2344 **897** 850l. black, green and red 1·80 30

926 Collage representing Marinetti's Works

1996. 120th Birth Anniv of Filippo Marinetti (writer and founder of Futurist movement).
2345 **926** 750l. multicoloured 2·00 35

1996. Treasures from State Archives and Museums (4th series). As T 871. Multicoloured.
2346 750l. Arms (Georgofili Academy, Florence) 1·90 35
2347 750l. Illuminated letter showing St. Luke and his ox from Constitution of 1372 (Lucca Archives) (vert) 1·90 35
2348 850l. Inkwells, pen and manuscript of Gabriele d'Annunzio (writer) (Il Vittoriale, Gardone Riviera) 2·20 50
2349 850l. "Life of King Modus and Queen Racio" from 1486 miniature (Turin Archives) 2·20 50

927 "Sarah and the Angel" (fresco, Archbishop's Palace, Udine)

1996. 300th Birth Anniv of Giambattista Tiepolo (painter).
2350 **927** 1000l. multicoloured 2·75 60

928 White Wine

1996. Italian Wine Production. Multicoloured.
2351 500l. Type **928** 1·40 50
2352 750l. Red wine 2·20 35

929 Marco Polo and Palace in the Forbidden City

1996. 700th Anniv (1995) of Marco Polo's Return from Asia and "China '96" International Stamp Exhibition, Peking.
2353 **929** 1250l. multicoloured 3·25 1·50

930 Milan Cathedral (left detail)

1996. "Italia 98" International Stamp Exhibition, Milan (1st issue). Multicoloured.
2354 750l. Type **930** 1·70 35
2355 750l. Cathedral (right detail) 1·70 35
Nos. 2354/5 were issued together, se-tenant, forming a composite design of the Cathedral.
See also Nos. **MS**2412, 2518, 2523, 2528/30 and 2531.

931 Quill pen and Satellite (50th Anniv of National Federation of Italian Press)

1996. Anniversaries.
2356 **931** 750l. multicoloured 2·00 50
2357 - 750l. blue, pink and black 2·00 50
DESIGN—HORIZ: No. 2357, Globe (centenary of "La Gazzetta dello Sport" (newspaper)).

932 Postman and Emblem

1996. International Museum of Postal Images, Belvedere Ostrense.
2358 **932** 500l. multicoloured 1·30 60

933 Uniforms of Different Periods

1996. Centenary of Academy of Excise Guards.

2359	**933**	750l. multicoloured	2·00	35

934 Truck and Route Map

1996. Trans-continental Drive, Rome–New York.

2360	**934**	4650l. multicoloured	10·50	4·75

935 Carina Negrone (pilot) and Biplane

1996. Europa. Famous Women. Multicoloured.

2361	750l. Type **935**	2·20	60
2362	850l. Adelaide Ristori (actress)	2·50	60

936 Fishes, Sea and Coastline from St. Raphael to Genoa

1996. 20th Anniv of Ramoge Agreement on Environmental Protection of the Mediterranean.

2363	**936**	750l. multicoloured	2·00	45

937 Celestino V and Town of Fumone

1996. 700th Death Anniv of Pope Celestino V.

2364	**937**	750l. multicoloured	2·00	35

938 St Anthony's Church, Diano Marina

1996. Tourist Publicity (23rd series). Mult.

2365	750l. Type **938**	1·70	45
2366	750l. Pienza Cathedral	1·70	45
2367	750l. Belltower of St. Michael the Archangel's Church, Monte Sant'Angelo	1·70	45
2368	750l. Prehistoric stone dwelling, Lampedusa	1·70	45

939 Abbey and Relief from 12th-century Ivory Reliquary

1996. 500th Anniv of Reconsecration of Farfa Abbey.

2369	**939**	1000l. black, yell & orge	2·75	70

940 Fair Entrance and Mt. Pellegrino

1996. Mediterranean Fair, Palermo.

2370	**940**	750l. multicoloured	2·00	35

941 State Arms

1996. 50th Anniv of Italian Republic.

2371	**941**	750l. multicoloured	2·00	35

942 Rider and Emblem

1996. 50th Anniv of Production of Vespa Motor Scooters.

2372	**942**	750l. multicoloured	2·75	45

943 Views of Messina and Venice

1996. 40th Anniv of Founding Meetings of European Economic Community, Messina and Venice.

2373	**943**	750l. multicoloured	2·10	45

944 Athlete on Starting Block and 1896 Athletes

1996. Centenary of Modern Olympic Games and Olympic Games, Atlanta. Multicoloured.

2374	500l. Type **944**	1·10	50
2375	750l. Throwing the discus and view of Atlanta (vert)	1·60	65
2376	850l. Gymnast, stadium and basketball player	1·80	50
2377	1250l. 1896 stadium, Athens, and 1996 stadium, Atlanta (vert)	2·75	90

945 "Acanthobrahmaea europaea"

1996. Butterflies. Multicoloured.

2378	750l. Type **945**	2·00	35
2379	750l. "Melanargia arge"	2·00	35
2380	750l. "Papilio hospiton"	2·00	35
2381	750l. "Zygaena rubicundus"	2·00	35

946 "Prima Comunione"

1996. Italian Films (1st series).

2382	**946**	750l. black, red and blue	1·80	50
2383	-	750l. multicoloured	1·80	50
2384	-	750l. multicoloured	1·80	50

DESIGNS: No. 2383, Poster for "Cabiria"; 2384, "Scusate il Ritardo".

See also Nos. 2453/5 and 2528/30.

947 Santa Maria del Fiore

1996. 700th Anniv of Cathedral of Santa Maria del Fiore, Florence.

2385	**947**	750l. blue	2·00	35

948 Player, Shield and Club Badge

1996. Milan, National Football Champion, 1995–96.

2386	**948**	750l. multicoloured	2·75	45

949 Choppy (congress mascot)

1996. 13th International Prehistoric and Protohistoric Sciences Congress.

2387	**949**	850l. multicoloured	2·20	45

950 Games Emblem and Pictograms

1996. Mediterranean Games, Bari (1997).

2388	**950**	750l. multicoloured	2·00	35

951 Fair Entrance

1996. Levant Fair, Bari.

2389	**951**	750l. multicoloured	2·00	35

952 Rejoicing Crowd and Club Badge

1996. Juventus, European Football Champion, 1995–96.

2390	**952**	750l. multicoloured	2·20	45

953 Pertini

1996. Birth Centenary of Alessandro Pertini (President 1978–85).

2391	**953**	750l. multicoloured	2·00	35

954 Montale and Hoopoe

1996. Birth Centenary of Eugenio Montale (poet).

2392	**954**	750l. brown and blue	2·00	35

955 "The Annunciation"

1996. 400th Birth Anniv of Pietro Berrettini da Cortona (artist).

2393	**955**	500l. multicoloured	2·00	60

956 Tex Willer (Galep)

1996. Stamp Collecting. Strip Cartoons. Mult.

2394	750l. Type **956**	2·20	35
2395	850l. Corto Maltese (Hugo Pratt)	2·50	50

957 Vortex and "Stamps"

1996. Stamp Day.

2396	**957**	750l. multicoloured	2·00	35

958 Bell Tower and Former Benedictine Abbey (seat of faculty)

1996. Universities.

2397 **958** 750l. brown 1·60 35
2398 - 750l. blue 1·60 35
2399 - 750l. green 1·60 35

DESIGNS—VERT: No. 2397. Type **958** (centenary of Faculty of Agriculture, Perugia University); 2398, Former St. Matthew's Cathedral (seat of Medical School), Salerno University. HORIZ: No. 2399, Athenaeum, Sassari University.

959 Emblem

1996. World Food Summit, Rome.

2400 **959** 850l. green and black 2·00 45

960 "Madonna of the Quail" (Antonio Pisanello)

1996. Christmas. Multicoloured.

2401 750l. Type **960** 2·30 35
2402 850l. Father Christmas and toys (horiz) 2·75 50

961 "UNESCO" and Globe

1996. 50th Anniversaries of UNESCO and UNICEF.

2403 750l. Type **961** 2·20 35
2404 850l. UNICEF emblem on kite, baby and globe 2·50 50

962 Headquarters, Rome

1996. 70th Anniv of National Statistics Institute.

2405 **962** 750l. multicoloured 2·00 35

963 Bookcase

1996. 50th Anniv of Strega Prize.

2406 **963** 3400l. multicoloured 8·00 2·75

964 Hall of the Tricolour, Reggio Emilia

1997. Bicentenary of First Tricolour (now national flag), Cisalpine Republic.

2407 **964** 750l. multicoloured 1·80 30

965 Tower Blocks and Skier

1997. World Alpine Skiing Championships, Sestriere. Multicoloured.

2408 750l. Type **965** 1·80 50
2409 850l. Olympic colours forming ski run and ski 1·80 50

966 Ferraris, Early Motor and Ferraris National Electrotechnology Institute, Turin

1997. Death Centenary of Galileo Ferraris (physicist).

2410 **966** 750l. multicoloured 1·80 45

967 Loi

1997. 5th Death Anniv of Emanuela Loi (bodyguard killed in Mafia car bombing).

2411 **967** 750l. multicoloured 2·20 45

968 1819 Letter and Handstamps of Italian States

1997. "Italia 98" International Stamp Exhibition, Milan (2nd issue). Sheet 150×80 mm containing T 968 and similar vert designs. Multicoloured.

MS2412 750l. Bologna 1910 cancellation aerogramme from Balboa flight and postcard with 1917 25c. airmail stamp (Aerophilately); 750l. Cancellations used for the signing of the Rome Treaty (forming European Economic Community), Rome Olympic Games and Holy Year, 1952 Leonardo da Vinci 80l. stamp and 1931 inauguration of Milan railway station postcard (Thematic Philately); 750l. Type **968** (Postal History); 750l. "Democratica", Italian stamp catalogue and L'Italia Filatelica (stamp review) (Philatelic Literature) 8·00 3·50

969 Statue of Marcus Aurelius

1997. 40th Anniv of Treaty of Rome (foundation of European Economic Community).

2413 **969** 750l. multicoloured 1·80 45

970 St. Germiniano (after Bartolomeo Schedoni) holding Modena Cathedral

1997. 1600th Death Anniv of St. Germiniano (patron saint of Modena).

2414 **970** 750l. multicoloured 1·80 45

971 "Baptism of St. Ambrose" and "Hand of God recalling him to City"

1997. 1600th Death Anniv of St. Ambrose, Bishop of Milan.

2415 **971** 1000l. multicoloured 2·30 50

The illustrations are taken from reliefs by Volvinio on the Golden Altar in St. Ambrose's Cathedral, Milan.

972 Statue of Minerva, Central Square, Rome University

1997. Universities.

2416 **972** 750l. red 1·80 35
2417 - 750l. blue 1·80 35

DESIGN: No. 2417, Palace of Bo, Padua University.

973 St. Peter's Cathedral and Colosseum within "Wolf suckling Romulus and Remus"

1997. 2750th Anniv of Foundation of Rome.

2418 **973** 850l. multicoloured 2·00 45

974 Pre-Roman Walls, Gela

1997

2419 **974** 750l. multicoloured 1·80 35

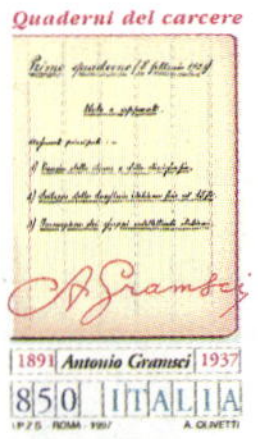

975 First Page of Prison Notebook and Signature

1997. 60th Death Anniv of Antonio Gramsci (politician).

2420 **975** 850l. multicoloured 2·75 45

976 Teracotta Relief and Cloisters

1997. 500th Anniv of Consecration of Pavia Church.

2421 **976** 1000l. multicoloured 2·20 50

977 Shoemaker's Workshop

1997. Europa. Tales and Legends. Mult.

2422 800l. Type **977** ("He who becomes the Property of Others works for his Soup") 1·80 35
2423 900l. Street singer (19th-century copper etching) 2·20 60

978 Detail of 1901 Poster for "Tosca" and Theatre

1997. Centenary of Teatro Massimo, Palermo.

2424 **978** 800l. multicoloured 2·20 30

979 St. Sebastian's Church, Acireale

1997. Tourist Publicity (24th series). Mult.

2425 800l. Type **979** 1·70 35
2426 800l. Cicero and his tomb, Formia 1·70 35
2427 800l. St. Mary of the Assumption, Positano 1·70 35
2428 800l. St. Vitale's Basilica, Ravenna 1·70 35

980 Books and Marble Floor

1997. 10th Book Salon, Turin.

2429 **980** 800l. multicoloured 2·00 35

981 Queen Paola and Castel Sant'Angelo, Rome

1997. 60th Birthday of Queen Paola of Belgium.
2430 **981** 750l. multicoloured 2·00 35

982 Palazzo della Civilta del Lavoro and Fair Pavilions

1997. Rome Fair.
2431 **982** 800l. multicoloured 2·20 35

983 Orvieto Cathedral

1997
2432 **983** 450l. violet 1·10 45

984 Morosini in Via Tasso Prison, 1944

1997. 53rd Death Anniv of Father Giuseppe Morosini.
2433 **984** 800l. multicoloured 2·00 35

985 Player, Club Emblem and Football

1997. Juventus, National Football Champion, 1996–97.
2434 **985** 800l. multicoloured 2·75 40

986 Chamois and "Iris marsica"

1997. 75th Anniv of Abruzzo National Park.
2435 **986** 800l. multicoloured 2·00 35

987 Towers and Fair Complex

1997. Bologna Fair.
2436 **987** 800l. multicoloured 2·00 35

988 Pennant and Ships' Bows

1997. Centenary of Italian Naval League.
2437 **988** 800l. multicoloured 2·00 35

989 Runner, High Jumper and Gymnast

1997. 13th Mediterranean Games, Bari.
2438 **989** 900l. multicoloured 2·20 45

1997. Public Gardens (2nd series). As T 915. Multicoloured.
2439 800l. Orto Botanico, Palermo 1·70 35
2440 800l. Villa Sciarra, Rome 1·70 35
2441 800l. Cavour, Santena 1·70 35
2442 800l. Miramare, Trieste 1·70 35

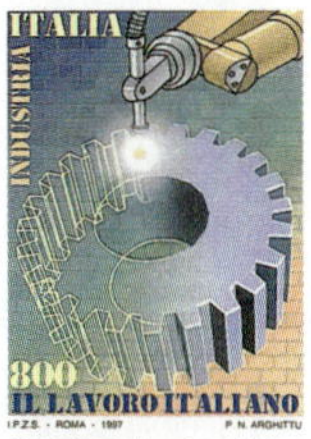

990 Cogwheel and Robot Arm (industry)

1997. Italian Work. Multicoloured.
2443 800l. Type **990** 1·70 35
2444 900l. Cereals, fruit trees, grapes and sun (agriculture) (horiz) 2·00 50

991 Globe and the "Matthew"

1997. 500th Anniv of John Cabot's Discovery of North America.
2445 **991** 1300l. multicoloured 3·25 2·40

992 Verri

1997. Death Bicentenary of Pietro Verri (illuminist).
2446 **992** 3600l. multicoloured 8·00 1·80

993 "Madonna of the Rosary" (Pomarancio il Vecchio)

1997. Painters' Anniversaries. Multicoloured.
2447 450l. Type **993** (400th death anniv) 1·10 35
2448 650l. "The Miracle of Ostia" ((detail, Paolo Uccello) (600th birth anniv)) (26×37 mm) 1·60 65

994 Procession

1997. Varia Festival, Palmi.
2449 **994** 800l. multicoloured 2·00 45

995 Basketball

1997. University Games, Sicily. Multicoloured.
2450 450l. Type **995** 1·10 45
2451 800l. High jumping 1·60 35

996 Rosmini

1997. Birth Bicentenary of Antonio Rosmini (philosopher).
2452 **996** 800l. multicoloured 2·00 30

1997. Italian Films (2nd series). As T 946.
2453 800l. multicoloured 1·80 45
2454 800l. black, blue and red 1·80 45
2455 800l. multicoloured 1·80 45
DESIGNS: No. 2453, Pietro Germi in "Il Ferroviere"; 2454, Anna Magnani in "Mamma Roma"; 2455, Ugo Tognazzi in "Amici Miei".

997 Open Book and Beach, Viareggio

1997. Viareggio-Repaci Prize.
2456 **997** 4000l. multicoloured 8·50 1·70

998 Venue and Bell Tower

1997. International Trade Fair, Bolzano.
2457 **998** 800l. multicoloured 2·00 35

999 Bronze Head (500 BC)

1997. Museum Exhibits. Multicoloured.
2458 450l. Type **999** (National Museum, Reggio Calabria) 1·10 35
2459 650l. "Madonna and Child with Two Vases of Roses" (Ercole de Roberti) (National Picture Gallery, Ferrara) 1·60 65
2460 800l. Miniature of poet Sordello da Goito (Arco Palace Museum, Mantua) 1·90 35
2461 900l. "St. George and the Dragon" (Vitale di Bologna) (National Picture Gallery, Bologna) 2·20 50

1000 Pope Paul VI and Door of Death, St. Peter's Cathedral, Rome

1997. Birth Centenary of Pope Paul VI.
2462 **1000** 4000l. blue 8·75 1·70

1001 Portello Pavilion (venue) and Milan Cathedral

1997. Milan Fair.
2463 **1001** 800l. multicoloured 2·00 45

1002 War-ravaged and Reconstructed Cities

1997. 50th Anniv of European Recovery Programme ("Marshall Plan").
2464 **1002** 800l. multicoloured 2·00 30

1003 Nativity (crib, St Francis's Church, Leonessa)

1997. Christmas. Multicoloured.
2465 800l. Type **1003** 2·30 35
2466 900l. "Nativity" (painting, Sta. Maria Maggiore, Spelo) 2·75 50

1004 Production Plant and Merloni

1997. Birth Centenary of Aristide Merloni (entrepreneur).
2467 **1004** 800l. multicoloured 2·00 35

1005 Cavalcaselle and Drawings

1997. Death Centenary of Giovanni Battista Cavalcaselle (art historian).
2468 **1005** 800l. multicoloured 2·00 35

1006 Magnifying Glass and Fleur-de-lis

1997. Stamp Day.
2469 **1006** 800l. multicoloured 2·00 35

1007 Refugees aboard "Toscana" (steamer)

1997. 50th Anniv of Exodus of Italian Inhabitants from Istria, Fiume and Dalmatia.
2470 **1007** 800l. multicoloured 2·00 35

1008 Arms of State Police and Badge of Traffic Police

1997. 50th Anniv of Traffic Police.
2471 **1008** 800l. multicoloured 2·00 35

1009 Map of Italy in Column and Flag

1998. 50th Anniv of Constitution.
2472 **1009** 800l. black, red & green 2·00 35

1010 "Hercules and the Hydra"

1998. 500th Death Anniv of Antonio del Pollaiolo (painter).
2473 **1010** 800l. multicoloured 2·10 35

1011 Bertolt Brecht

1998. Writers' Birth Centenaries.
2474 **1011** 450l. multicoloured 1·10 50
2475 - 650l. multicoloured 1·50 50
2476 - 800l. multicoloured 1·90 30
2477 - 900l. blue, green & black 2·20 30
DESIGNS—HORIZ: 650l. Federico Garcia Lorca (poet); 800l. Curzio Malaparte. VERT: 900l. Leonida Repaci.

1012 Fair Complex

1998. Verona Fair.
2478 **1012** 800l. multicoloured 2·10 45

1013 Memorial Tablet in Casale Montferrato Synagogue

1998. 150th Anniv of Granting of Full Citizen Rights to Italian Jews.
2479 **1013** 800l. multicoloured 2·10 45

1014 Trombonist

1998. Europa. National Festivals. Mult.
2480 800l. Type **1014** (Umbria Jazz Festival) 1·80 35
2481 900l. Boy holding animal (Giffoni Film Festival) 2·20 50

1015 "The Last Supper"

1998. 500th Anniv of Completion of "The Last Supper" (mural) by Leonardo da Vinci.
2482 **1015** 800l. brown 2·40 45

1016 Costumes designed by Bernardo Buontalenti for First Opera in Florence

1998. Italian Theatre. Multicoloured.
2483 800l. Type **1016** (400th anniv of opera) 2·00 35
2484 800l. Gaetano Donizetti (composer, 150th death anniv) (horiz) 2·00 35

1017 Turin Cathedral and Holy Shroud

1998. 500th Anniv of Turin Cathedral. Display of the Holy Shroud.
2485 **1017** 800l. multicoloured 2·10 35

1018 Otranto Castle

1998. Tourist Publicity (25th series). Mult.
2486 800l. Type **1018** 1·90 35
2487 800l. Mori Fountain and Orsini Tower, Marino 1·90 35
2488 800l. Valfederia Chapel, Livigno 1·90 35
2489 800l. Marciana Marina, Elba 1·90 35

1019 Cagliari Cathedral, Drummer and Fair Building

1998. International Sardinia Fair, Cagliari.
2490 **1019** 800l. multicoloured 2·00 35

1020 "Charge of the Carabinieri at Pastrengo" (Sebastiano de Albertis)

1998. 150th Anniv of Battle of Pastrengo.
2491 **1020** 800l. multicoloured 2·00 35

1021 Flags

1998. Padua Fair.
2492 **1021** 800l. multicoloured 2·00 35

1022 Player and Club Badge

1998. Juventus, National Football Champion, 1997–98.
2493 **1022** 800l. multicoloured 2·20 45

1023 Turin Polytechnic

1998. Universities.
2494 **1023** 800l. blue 2·10 35

1024 Emblem

1998. World Food Programme.
2495 **1024** 900l. multicoloured 2·20 45

1025 Santa Maria de Pesio Carthusian Monastery

1998. Artistic Heritage.
2496 **1025** 800l. multicoloured 2·00 35

1026 Ammonites and Pergola

1998. 4th International "Fossils, Evolution, Ambience" Congress, Pergola.
2497 **1026** 800l. multicoloured 2·00 35

1027 Flag at Half-mast

1998. "The Forces of Order, the Fallen".
2498 **1027** 800l. multicoloured 2·10 35

1028 Endoscope and Globe

1998. 6th World General Endoscopic Surgery Congress, Rome.
2499 **1028** 900l. multicoloured 2·20 35

1029 First Parliamentary Chamber

1998. National Museums. Multicoloured.
2500 800l. Type **1029** (Italian Risorgimento Museum, Turin) 2·00 35
2501 800l. Statue of an ephebus (Athenian youth), Temple of Concord and column of Temple of Vulcan (Regional Archaeology Museum, Agrigento) (vert) 2·00 35
2502 800l. Sculpture by Umberto Boccioni and Palazzo Venier dei Leoni (venue) (Peggy Guggenheim Collection, Venice) 2·00 35

1030 Fair Complex and Basilica

1998. Vicenza Trade Fair.
2503 **1030** 800l. multicoloured 2·10 35

1031 Leopardi (after Luigi Lolli) and Palazzo Leopardi, Recanati

1998. Birth Bicentenary of Giacomo Leopardi (poet).
2504 **1031** 800l. brown and black 2·10 35

1032 Young Etruscan Girl (detail of tomb painting)

1998. Women in Art.

2505	**1032**	100l. black, green & sil	35	25
2506	-	450l. multicoloured	1·50	25
2507	-	650l. multicoloured	2·20	25
2508	-	800l. brown and black	2·75	15
2509	-	1000l. blue, brn & blk	3·50	25

DESIGNS: 450l. Detail of "Herod's Banquet and the Dance of Salome" (fresco by Filippo Lippi in Prato Cathedral); 650l. "Profile of a Woman" (Antonio del Pollaiuolo); 800l. "Lady with a Unicorn" (detail, Raphael); 1000l. "Constanza Buonarelli" (bust by Gian Lorenzo Bernini).

For these designs but with face values in euros added, see Nos. 2537/41.

1033 Pitch, Pitcher and Batter

1998. 33rd World Cup Baseball Championship, Florence.
2510 **1033** 900l. multicoloured 2·20 45

1034 Columbus and Vespucci

1998. 500th Anniversaries of Landing of Christopher Columbus in Venezuela and of Amerigo Vespucci's Explorations.
2511 **1034** 1300l. multicoloured 3·25 1·20

1035 Emblem

1998. 50th International Stamp Fair, Riccione.
2512 **1035** 800l. multicoloured 2·10 45

1036 Mother Teresa and Child

1998. 1st Death Anniv of Mother Teresa (founder of Missionaries of Charity). Multicoloured.

2513	800l. Type **1036**	1·80	35
2514	900l. Mother Teresa (vert)	2·10	45

1037 Father Pio and Monastery Church, San Giovanni Rotondo

1998. 30th Death Anniv of Father Pio da Pietrelcina (Capuchin friar who bore the stigmata).
2515 **1037** 800l. blue 2·20 35

1038 Titus Arch, Rome, and Sicilian Mosaic of Rider

1998. World Equestrian Championships, Rome.
2516 **1038** 4000l. multicoloured 8·50 2·10

1039 Telecommunications College, Rome

1998. Universities.
2517 **1039** 800l. blue 2·00 35

1040 Pope John Paul II and his Message

1998. "Italia 98" International Stamp Exhibition, Milan (3rd issue). Stamp Day.
2518 **1040** 800l. multicoloured 2·75 35

1041 "Giuseppe Garibaldi" (aircraft carrier)

1998. Armed Forces Day. Multicoloured.

2519	800l. Type **1041** (Navy)	2·00	60
2520	800l. Eurofighter EF-2000 Typhoon (75th anniv of Air Force)	2·00	60
2521	800l. Carabiniere (vert)	2·00	45
2522	800l. Battle of El-Alamein at night (Army) (vert)	2·00	45

1042 "Dionysus" (bronze statue)

1998. "Italia 98" International Stamp Exhibition, Milan (4th issue). Art Day.
2523 **1042** 800l. multicoloured 2·00 45

1043 Ferrari competing in Race, 1931

1998. "Italia 98" International Stamp Exhibition, Milan (5th issue). Birth Centenary of Enzo Ferrari (car designer). Sheet 160×110 mm containing T 1043 and similar horiz designs. Multicoloured.
MS2524 800l. Type **1043**; 800l. Formula 1 Ferrari, 1952; 800l. Ferrari GTO, 1963; 800l. Formula 1 Ferrari, 1998 10·50 10·50

1044 Hand releasing Birds

1998. 50th Anniv of Universal Declaration of Human Rights.
2525 **1044** 1400l. multicoloured 4·00 60

1045 Cogwheels and "Proportions of Man" (Leonardo da Vinci)

1998. Europa Day. Ordinary or self-adhesive gum.
2526 **1045** 800l. multicoloured 2·75 30

1998. "Italia 98" International Stamp Exhibition, Milan (6th issue). Cinema Day. As T 946. Multicoloured.

2528	450l. "Ti Conosco Mascherino" (dir. Eduardo de Filippo)	1·80	80
2529	800l. "Fantasmia a Roma" (Antonio Pietrangeli)	3·00	60
2530	900l. "Il Signor Max" (Mario Camerini)	3·50	75

1046 Satellite Dish, Type, Book and "Internet"

1998. "Italia 98" International Stamp Exhibition, Milan (7th issue). Communications Day.
2531 **1046** 800l. multicoloured 2·20 35

1047 Arrows circling Letter

1998. "Italia 98" International Stamp Exhibition, Milan (8th issue). Post Day. Sheet 130×90 mm.
MS2532 **1047** 4000l. multicoloured 10·00 10·50

1048 "Epiphany" (sculpture, St. Mark's Church, Seminara)

1998. Christmas.

2533	**1048**	800l. blue	1·80	35
2534	-	900l. brown	2·20	45

DESIGN—HORIZ: 900l. "Adoration of the Shepherds" (drawing, Giulio Romano).

1049 "Ecstasy of St. Teresa"

1998. 400th Birth Anniv of Gian Lorenzo Bernini (sculptor).
2535 **1049** 900l. multicoloured 2·40 40

1050 Royal Decree and Waldensian Emblem

1998. 150th Anniv of Toleration of the Waldenses (religious sect).
2536 **1050** 800l. multicoloured 2·00 35

DENOMINATION. From No. 2537 Italian stamps are denominated both in lira and in euros. As no coins or notes for the latter were in circulation until 2002, the catalogue continues to use the lira value.

1999. As Nos. 2505/9, but with face value in euros added.

2537	100l. black, green and silver	25	25
2538	450l. multicoloured	1·10	25
2539	650l. multicoloured	1·60	35
2540	800l. brown and black	2·00	25
2541	1000l. blue, brown and black	2·50	25

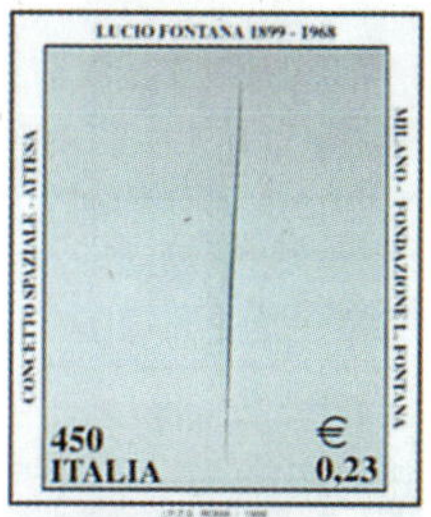

1051 "Space Concept–Wait"

1999. Birth Centenary of Lucio Fontana (artist).
2542 **1051** 450l. blue and black 1·30 45

1052 La Sila National Park, Calabria

1999. Europa. Parks and Gardens. Multicoloured.

2543	800l. Type **1052**	2·30	45
2544	900l. Tuscan Archipelago National Park (horiz)	2·75	45

1053 Holy Door, St. Peter's Cathedral

1999. Holy Year 2000.
2545 **1053** 1400l. multicoloured 3·75 70

1054 St. Egidius's Church, Cellere

1999. Artistic Heritage.
2546 **1054** 800l. brown 2·20 45

1055 Holy Year 2000 and 11th-century Bells

1999. Museums. Multicoloured.
2547 800l. Type **1055** (History of Campanology Museum, Agnone) 2·00 50
2548 800l. "Lake with Swan" (stained glass) (Casina delle Civette Museum, Rome) 2·00 45
2549 800l. Renaissance majolica dish (International Ceramics Museum, Faenza) (vert) 2·00 45

1056 Earth Pyramids, Segonzano

1999. Tourist Publicity (26th series). Multicoloured.
2550 800l. Type **1056** 2·00 45
2551 800l. Marmore Waterfall, Terni 2·00 45
2552 800l. Cathedral, Lecce 2·00 45
2553 800l. Lipari 2·00 45

1057 Audience Chamber

1999. Constitutional Court.
2554 **1057** 800l. multicoloured 2·20 45

1058 Fire Engine at Fire

1999. Fire Brigade.
2555 **1058** 800l. multicoloured 2·20 45

1059 Cadet and Academy

1999. Modena Military Academy.
2556 **1059** 800l. multicoloured 2·20 45

1060 Players and Airplane

1999. 50th Anniv of Death in Aircrash of Grand Turin Football Team. Multicoloured.
2557 800l. Type **1060** 2·00 35
2558 900l. Superga Basilica, club arms and names of victims 2·50 45

1061 Council Seat, Strasbourg

1999. 50th Anniv of Council of Europe.
2559 **1061** 800l. multicoloured 2·20 45

1062 Players and Club Emblem

1999. Milan, National Football Champion, 1998–99.
2560 **1062** 800l. multicoloured 2·40 45

1063 Ballot Box and Parliament Chamber, Strasbourg

1999. 20th Anniv of First Direct Elections to European Parliament.
2561 **1063** 800l. multicoloured 2·20 45

1064 Coppi

1999. 80th Birth Anniv of Fausto Coppi (racing cyclist).
2562 **1064** 800l. multicoloured 2·40 45

1065 "P"

1999. Priority Mail stamp. Self-adhesive.
2563 **1065** 1200l. black and gold 5·25 60
See also Nos. 2591 and 2660.

1066 First Fiat Car (advertising poster)

1999. Centenary of Fiat (motor manufacturer).
2564 **1066** 4800l. multicoloured 10·50 2·40

1067 "Our Lady of the Snow"

1999. Centenary of Erection of Statue of "Our Lady of the Snow" on Mt. Rocciamelone.
2565 **1067** 800l. multicoloured 2·20 45

1068 Pimentel and St. Elmo Castle, Naples

1999. Death Bicentenary of Eleonora de Fonseca Pimentel (writer and revolutionary).
2566 **1068** 800l. multicoloured 2·20 45

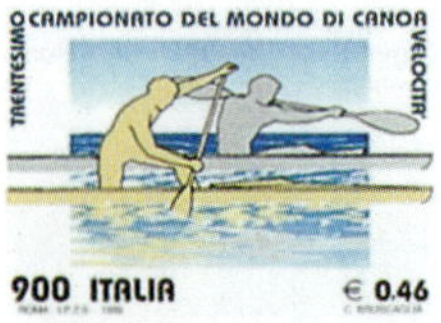

1069 Canoes

1999. 30th World Speed Canoeing Championships.
2567 **1069** 900l. multicoloured 2·40 40

1070 "Goethe in the Rome Countryside" (Johann Tischbein)

1999. 250th Birth Anniv of Johann Wolfgang Goethe (poet and playwright).
2568 **1070** 4000l. multicoloured 9·25 2·30

1071 Cyclist and Stopwatch

1999. World Cycling Championships, Treviso and Verona.
2569 **1071** 1400l. multicoloured 4·00 70

1072 Child with Rucksack

1999. Stamp Day.
2570 **1072** 800l. multicoloured 2·20 35

1073 Architectural Drawing of Basilica

1999. Re-opening of Upper Basilica of St. Francis of Assisi.
2571 **1073** 800l. multicoloured 2·20 45

1074 Parini (after Francesco Rosaspina)

1999. Death Bicentenary of Giuseppe Parini (poet).
2572 **1074** 800l. blue 2·20 45

1075 Volta (bust by Giovan Commolli) and Voltaic Pile

1999. Bicentenary of Invention of Electrochemical Battery by Alessandro Volta.
2573 **1075** 3000l. multicoloured 6·75 1·40

1076 Forms and U.P.U. Emblem

1999. 125th Anniv of Universal Postal Union.
2574 **1076** 900l. multicoloured 2·20 45

1077 Mameli with 1948 and 1949 100l. Stamps

1999. 150th Death Anniv of Goffredo Mameli (poet and patriot) and 150th Anniv of Roman Republic.
2575 **1077** 1500l. multicoloured 3·50 1·70

1078 Man and Town

1999. "The Stamp Our Friend". Multicoloured.
2576 450l. Type **1078** 1·10 40
2577 650l. Campaign emblem 1·60 50
2578 800l. Schoolchildren 2·00 60
2579 1000l. Windmill (toy) 2·50 70

1079 First World War Soldiers (after postcard)

1999. Centenary of Generation of '99.
2580 **1079** 900l. multicoloured 2·40 35

1080 Santa Claus

1999. Christmas. Multicoloured.
2581 800l. Type **1080** 2·20 45
2582 1000l. "Nativity" (Dosso Dossi) 2·75 60

1081 Peutinger Tablet (medieval map showing pilgrim route by C. Celtes and Conrad Peutinger)

1999. Holy Year 2000. Multicoloured.

2583	1000l. Type **1081**		2·50	60
2584	1000l. 18th-century pilgrim's stamp		2·50	60
2585	1000l. 13th-century bas-relief of pilgrims (facade of Fidenza Cathedral)		2·50	60

1082 Urbino State Art Institute

1999. Schools and Universities.

2586	**1082**	450l. black	1·10	60
2587	-	650l. brown	1·60	45

DESIGN: 650l. Pisa High School.

1083 "Leopard bitten by Tarantula"

1999. Birth Centenary of Antonio Ligabue (artist).

2588	**1083**	1000l. multicoloured	2·75	60

1084 Robot's Hand meeting Man's Hand (after Michelangelo)

1999. Year 2000.

2589	**1084**	4800l. multicoloured	10·50	2·75

1085 Child looking at Aspects of Earth

2000. New Millennium. "The Past and the Future". Sheet 110×80 mm containing T 1085 and similar horiz design. Multicoloured.

MS2590 2000l. Type **1085**; 2000l. Astronaut looking at Moon — 10·50 — 9·25

2000. Priority Mail Stamp. As T 1065 but different colour. Self-adhesive.

2591		1200l. black, yellow and gold	5·25	50

1086 Tosca and Scenery

2000. Centenary of the First Performance of Tosca (opera).

2592	**1086**	800l. multicoloured	2·75	45

1087 St. Paul (statue) and Holy Door, St. Peter's Basilica, Rome

2000. Holy Year 2000.

2593	**1087**	1000l. multicoloured	3·00	50

1088 Players

2000. Six Nations Rugby Championship.

2594	**1088**	800l. multicoloured	2·75	45

1089 Painting

2000. 5th Conference on Breast Diseases. Mult.

2595		800l. Type **1089**	2·00	35
2596		1000l. Painting (different)	2·75	60

1090 "Enigma of an Autumn Afternoon"

2000. New Millennium (1st issue). Art and Science. Sheet 111×80 mm containing T 1090 and similar horiz design showing paintings by Giorgio de Chirico. Multicoloured.

MS2597 800l. Type **1090** (art); 800l. "The Inevitable Temple" (science) — 5·25 — 4·50

See also Nos. **MS**2613 and 2623.

1091 Skier and Trophy

2000. World Cup Skiing Championships.

2598	**1091**	4800l. multicoloured	10·50	2·75

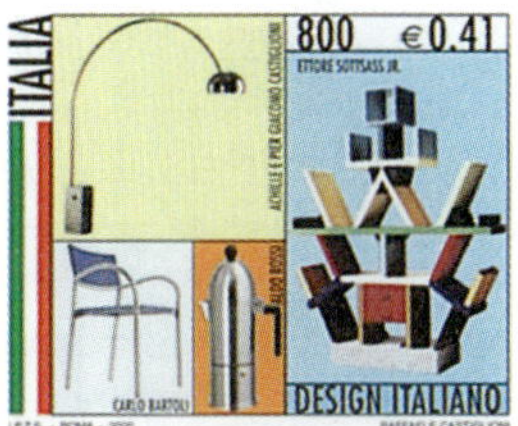

1092 Lamp (Achille and Pier Giacomo Castiglioni), Chair (Carlo Batroli), Coffee Pot (Aldo Rossi) and Bookcase (Ettore Softsass Jr.)

2000. Italian Design. Sheet 154×138 mm containing T 1092 and similar horiz designs. Multicoloured.

MS2599 800l. Type **1092**; 800l. Armchair (Mario Bellini), corkscrew (Alessandro Mendini), table lamp (Vico Magistretti) and suspended lamp (Alberto Meda and Paolo Rizzatto); 800l. Chair (Gio Ponti), bean bag (Gatti Paolini Teodoro), pasta set (Massimo Morozzi) and standard uplighter (Tobia Scarpa); 800l. White standard uplighter (Pietro Chiesa), hostess trolley (Joe Columbo), chair (Cini Boeri and Tomu Katayanagi) and sideboard (Lodovico Acerbis and Giotto Stoppino); 800l. Easy chairs (Gaetano Pesce), chair (Enzo Mari), clothes horse (De Pas d'Urbino Lomazzi) and mobile filing cabinet (Antonio Citterio and Oliver Loew); 800l. Chair (Marco Zanuso), anglepoise lamp (Michele de Lucchi and Giancarlo Fassina), ice bucket (Bruno Munari) and stool (Anna Castelli Ferrieri) — 10·50 — 9·25

1093 "Adoration of the Magi" (Domenico Ghirlandaio)

2000. Holy Year 2000. Multicoloured.

2600		450l. Type **1093**	1·10	35
2601		650l. "Baptism of Christ" (Paolo Caliari Veronese) (vert)	1·60	40
2602		800l. "The Last Supper" (Ghirlandaio) (vert)	1·90	35
2603		1000l. "Regret of Christ's Death" (Giotto di Bondone)	2·40	60
2604		1200l. "The Resurrection" (Piero della Francesca) (vert)	3·00	65

1094 Library and Emblem

2000. 150th Anniv of La Civilta Cattolica Foundation (collection of Church publications).

2605	**1094**	800l. multicoloured	2·75	45

1095 Courtyard

2000. 150th Anniv of St. Joseph's College, Rome.

2606	**1095**	800l. multicoloured	2·75	45

1096 Terre di Franciacorta, Erbrusco

2000. Tourist Publicity (27th series). Multicoloured.

2607		800l. Type **1096**	2·00	45
2608		800l. Dunarobba fossil forest, Avigliano Umbro	2·00	45
2609		800l. View of Ercolano	2·00	45
2610		800l. Beauty Island, Taormina	2·00	45

1097 Cyclist

2000. Centenary of International Cycling Union.

2611	**1097**	1500l. multicoloured	4·00	80

1098 Christ carrying Cross

2000. Papier-mache Figurines, Caltanisetta.

2612	**1098**	800l. multicoloured	2·75	45

1099 Landscape (Gilorgione)

2000. New Millennium (2nd issue). Countryside and City. Sheet 110×80 mm containing T 1099 and similar horiz design. Multicoloured.

MS2613 800l. Type **1099**; 800l. "Perspective of an Ideal Town" (Piero della Francesca) — 5·00 — 3·00

1100 Piccinni

2000. Death Bicentenary of Niccolo Piccinni (composer).

2614	**1100**	4000l. multicoloured	8·00	2·30

1101 "Building Europe"

2000. Europa.

2615	**1101**	800l. multicoloured	3·25	45

1102 Sardinia 1851 5, 20 and 40c. Stamps

2000. Museum of Posts and Telecommunications. Multicoloured.

2616		800l. Type **1102**	2·20	45
2617		800l. Reconstruction of radio and telegraph cabin aboard Elettra (Marconi's steam yacht)	2·20	45

1103 Footballer and Pitch

2000. Lazio, National Football Champion, 1999–2000.

2618	**1103**	800l. multicoloured	2·75	45

1104 Cathedral Facade

2000. 700th Anniv of Monza Cathedral.
2619 **1104** 800l. multicoloured 2·75 45

1105 Globe and Ears of Corn

2000. United Nations World Food Programme.
2620 **1105** 1000l. multicoloured 3·00 60

1106 Statue

2000. Centenary of the Jesus the Redeemer Monument, Nuoro.
2621 **1106** 800l. multicoloured 2·75 45

1107 Bridge, Parana River, Argentina

2000. 120th Anniv of Italian Water Board.
2622 **1107** 800l. multicoloured 2·75 45

1108 Profiles

2000. New Millennium (3rd issue). Technology and Space. Sheet 110×80 mm containing T 1108 and similar horiz design. Multicoloured.
MS2623 800l. Type **1108**; 800l. Symbolic man 4·75 3·00

1109 Child with Ladder to Moon (Giacomo Chiesa)

2000. "Stampin the Future". Winning Entry in Children's International Painting Competition.
2624 **1109** 1000l. multicoloured 3·00 60

1110 Archer

2000. World Archery Championship, Campagna.
2625 **1110** 1500l. multicoloured 3·50 80

1111 Cyclist and Globe

2000. World Junior Cycling Championships.
2626 **1111** 800l. multicoloured 2·75 45

1112 Fair Attractions

2000. Millenary of St. Orso.
2627 **1112** 1000l. multicoloured 3·00 60

1113 "Madonna and Child" (Crivelli)

2000. 570th Birth Anniv of Carlo Crivelli (artist).
2628 **1113** 800l. multicoloured 2·75 45

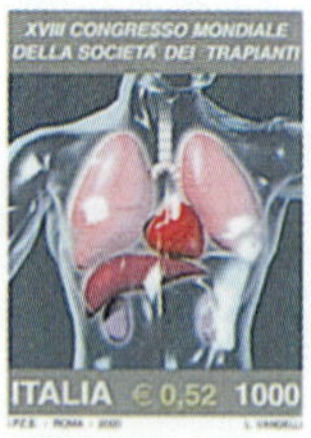

1114 Internal Organs

2000. 18th International Transplantation Society Congress, Rome.
2629 **1114** 1000l. multicoloured 3·00 60

1115 Athlete and Stadium

2000. Olympic Games, Sydney. Multicoloured.
2630 800l. Type **1115** 2·40 35
2631 1000l. "Discus Thrower" (statue) and Sydney Harbour 3·00 60

1116 "War"

2000. New Millennium (4th issue). War and Peace. Frescoes by Taddeo Zuccan. Sheet 110×80 mm containing T 1116 and similar vert design. Multicoloured.
MS2632 800l. Type **1116**; 800l. "Peace" 5·25 3·00

1117 Battle Scene (Jacques Debreville)

2000. Bicentenary of Marengo.
2633 **1117** 800l. multicoloured 2·75 45

1118 Figures in Evening Dress and City Skyline

2000. New Year.
2634 **1118** 800l. multicoloured 2·75 45

1119 Child holding Magnifying Glass

2000. Stamp Day.
2635 **1119** 800l. multicoloured 2·75 45

1120 Monti and Sick Child

2000. Death Centenary of Father Luigi Monti.
2636 **1120** 800l. multicoloured 2·75 45

1121 Salieri

2000. 250th Birth Anniv of Antonio Salieri (composer).
2637 **1121** 4800l. multicoloured 10·00 3·00

1122 Disabled Athletes

2000. Paralympic Games, Sydney.
2638 **1122** 1500l. multicoloured 4·00 80

1123 Emblem, Chaos Model and Globe in Container

2000. World Mathematics Year.
2639 **1123** 800l. multicoloured 2·75 45

1124 Couple and Globe

2000. Volunteers.
2640 **1124** 800l. multicoloured 2·75 45

1125 Quill, Text and Bust of Bruno (Pietro Masulli)

2000. 400th Death Anniv of Giordano Bruno (writer and philosopher).
2641 **1125** 800l. multicoloured 2·75 45

1126 "Madonna of the Rose Garden"

2000. 600th Birth Anniv of Luca della Robbia (artist).
2642 **1126** 800l. multicoloured 2·75 45

1127 Arms of Academy

2000. 250th Anniv of Roveretana degli Agiati Academy.
2643 **1127** 800l. multicoloured 2·75 60

1128 Martino and Map of Europe

2000. Birth Centenary of Gaetano Martino (politician).
2644 **1128** 800l. multicoloured 2·50 60

1129 "Perseus with the Head of Medusa" (bronze statue)

2000. 500th Birth Anniv of Benvenuto Cellini (goldsmith and sculptor).
2645 **1129** 1200l. multicoloured 3·25 1·70

1130 Young Woman

2000. New Millennium (5th series). Meditation and Expression. Sheet 110×80 mm containing T 1130 and similar horiz design. Multicoloured.
MS2646 800l. Type **1130**; 800l. Dancing figures 5·00 3·00

1131 Camerino University

2000. Universities. Each blue.
2647 800l. Type **1131** 2·00 45
2648 1000l. Calabria University 2·75 60

1132 Snowflakes and Globe

2000. Christmas. Multicoloured.
2649 800l. Type **1132** 1·30 45
2650 1000l. Crib, Matera Cathedral 1·60 60

1133 Snowboarding

2001. World Snowboarding Championships, Madonna di Campiglio.
2651 **1133** 1000l. multicoloured 2·75 60

1134 "The Annunciation" (detail, Botticelli)

2001. "Italy in Japan 2001" (cultural and scientific event).
2652 **1134** 1000l. multicoloured 2·50 60

1135 Vincenzo Bellini (composer, birth bicentenary)

2001. Composers' Anniversaries. Sheet 87×180 mm containing T 1135 and similar vert designs. Multicoloured.
MS2653 800l. Type **1135**; 800l. Domenico Cimarosa (death bicentenary); 800l. Gaspare Luigi Pacifico Spontini (150th death anniv); 800l. Giuseppe Verdi (death centenary) 10·00 8·00

1136 St. Rose and Angels (Francesco Podesti di Ancona)

2001. 750th Death Anniv of St. Rose of Viterbo.
2654 **1136** 800l. multicoloured 2·50 35

1137 Racing Car

2001. Ferrari, Formula One Constructor's Championship Winner (2000). Sheet 110×81 mm.
MS2655 **1137** 5000l. multicoloured 11·50 9·25

1138 Abbey of Santa Maria in Sylvis, Sesto al Reghena

2001
2656 **1138** 800l. blue 2·10 45

1139 Lombardy and Venetia 1850 5c. Stamp (151st anniv)

2001. Stamp Anniversaries. Multicoloured.
2657 800l. Type **1139** 2·30 45
2658 800l. Sardinia 1851 5c. stamp (150th anniv) 2·30 45
2659 800l. Tuscany 1851 1q. stamp (150th anniv) 2·30 45

2001. Priority Mail Stamp. As T 1065 but central "P" larger, 12×12 mm. Self-adhesive.
2660 1200l. black, yellow and gold 4·75 60

1140 Bridge, Comacchio

2001. Tourist Publicity (28th series). Multicoloured.
2661 800l. Type **1140** 1·70 45
2662 800l. Diamante 1·70 45
2663 800l. Pioraco 1·70 45
2664 800l. Stintino 1·70 45

1141 Campanula

2001. World Day to Combat Desertification and Drought. Multicoloured.
2665 450l. Type **1141** 95 60
2666 650l. Marmosets 1·40 60
2667 800l. White storks 1·60 45
2668 1000l. Desert and emblem 2·00 70

1142 Map of Italy and Tractors

2001. Confederation General of Italian Agriculture.
2669 **1142** 800l. multicoloured 2·10 45

1143 Castle and Emblem

2001. Millenary of Gorzia City.
2670 **1143** 800l. multicoloured 2·10 45

1144 Water pouring from Vase

2001. Europa. Water Resources.
2671 **1144** 800l. multicoloured 4·00 45

1145 Profiles

2001. European Union.
2672 **1145** 800l. multicoloured 2·00 45

1146 Medals

2001. Centenary of Order of Merit for Labour.
2673 **1146** 800l. multicoloured 2·00 45

1147 Rose and Workers' Silhouettes

2001. National Day for Victims of Industrial Accidents.
2674 **1147** 800l. multicoloured 2·00 45

1148 Child with Stamp and Magnifying Glass (Rita Vergari)

2001. Day for Art and Student Creativity. Multicoloured.
2675 800l. Type **1148** 1·60 45
2676 800l. People standing on rainbow (Lucia Catena) 1·60 45
2677 800l. Painting with eye (Luigi di Cristo) 1·60 45
2678 800l. Colours and profile (Barbara Grilli) 1·60 45

1149 "St. Peter healing with his Shadow"

2001. 600th Birth Anniv of Tommaso de Giovanni di Simone Guidi "Masaccio " (painter).
2679 **1149** 800l. multicoloured 2·00 45

1150 "Madonna and Child" (Piero della Francesca)

2001. 500th Death Anniv of Giovanni della Rovere.
2680 **1150** 800l. multicoloured 2·00 45

1151 Emblem

2001. 50th Anniv of Panathlon International (sports organization).
2681 **1151** 800l. multicoloured 2·00 45

1152 Guaita Tower, Mt. Titano

2001. 1700th Anniv of San Marino.

2682	**1152**	800l. multicoloured	2·00	45

1153 Footballer and Net

2001. A S Roma, National Football Champion, 2000–1.

2683	**1153**	800l. multicoloured	2·75	45

1154 Motorboat and Bell UH1 Iroquois Helicopter

2001. Harbour Master's Office.

2684	**1154**	800l. multicoloured	2·50	45

1155 Quasimodo

2001. Birth Centenary of Salvatore Quasimodo (writer).

2685	**1155**	1500l. multicoloured	3·25	90

1156 Octagonal Hall, Domus Aurea, Rome

2001

2686	**1156**	1000l. brown	16·00	60

1157 Bookcase (Piero Lissoni and Patricia Urquiola) and Chair (Anna Bartolli)

2001. Italian Design. Sheet 155×137 mm containing T 1157 and similar horiz designs. Multicoloured.

MS2687 800l. Type **1157**; 800l. Chair (Monica Graffeo) and table lamp (Rodolfo Dordoni); 800l. Lamp (Ferruccio Laviani) and sofa (Massimo losa Ghini); 800l. Armchair (Anna Gili) and side table (Miki Astori); 800l. Vertical storage unit (Marco Ferreri) and double seat (M. Cananzi and R. Semprini); 800l. Stool (Stefano Giovannoni) and flexible-necked lamp (Massimiliano Datti) 10·00 7·00

1158 "The Fourth State" (detail, Guiseppe Pellizza da Volpedo)

2001

2688	**1158**	1000l. brown	2·75	60

1159 Stone Age Man and Pick

2001. Archaeological Museum, Alto Adige.

2689	**1159**	800l. multicoloured	2·00	45

1160 Schoolchildren

2001. Youth Philately.

2690	**1160**	800l. multicoloured	2·00	45

1161 Fermi

2001. Birth Centenary of Enrico Fermi (physicist).

2691	**1161**	800l. multicoloured	2·00	45

1162 Pavia University

2001. Universities.

2692	**1162**	800l. blue	1·80	45
2693	-	800l. brown	1·80	45
2694	-	800l. turquoise	1·80	45

DESIGNS—VERT: No. 2693 Bari, University. HORIZ: 2694, School of Science, Rome.

1163 Latinas and Messanger

2001. Unione Latina (Romance language speaking countries).

2695	**1163**	800l. black, yellow and blue	2·00	45

1164 Exhibits

2001. National Archaeological Museum, Taranto.

2696	**1164**	1000l. multicoloured	2·50	50

1165 International Fund for Agricultural Development Emblem

2001. World Food Day. Each stamp featuring "The Seed" (sculpture) by Roberto Joppolo. Multicoloured.

2697	800l. Type **1165**	2·20	40
2698	800l. Plants and woman hoeing (50th anniv of Food and Agriculture Organization Summit Conference, Rome) (50×29 mm)	2·20	40
2699	800l. World Food Programme emblem	2·20	40

1166 "Enthroned Christ with Angels" (painting on wood)

2001

2700	**1166**	800l. multicoloured	2·00	45

1167 "Madonna and Child" (painting from triptych)

2001. 500th Anniv of "Madonna and Child, Angels, St. Francis, St. Thomas Aquinas and two Donors" (triptych, Macrino d'Alba).

2701	**1167**	800l. multicoloured	2·00	45

1168 "Dawn of Peace" (collage, San Vito dei Normani Primary School)

2001. Christmas. Multicoloured.

2702	800l. Type **1168**	1·60	45
2703	1000l. "Nativity" (painting, St. Mary Major Basilica)	2·10	60

1169 Fabric

2001. Italian Silk Industry. Sheet 140×92 mm. Self-adhesive gum. Imperf.

MS2704 **1169** 5000l. multicoloured 13·50 9·25

No. **MS**2704 was printed on fabric mounted on silk jacquard. A peel-off plastic backing featured instructions for use. If required, the address could be written in the blank area at the bottom right of the sheet.

2002. Women in Art. As T 1032 but with values expressed in euros.

2705	1c. multicoloured	10	10
2706	2c. multicoloured	10	10
2707	3c. multicoloured	10	10
2708	5c. multicoloured	10	10
2709	10c. multicoloured	15	10
2710	20c. multicoloured	60	15
2711	23c. multicoloured	80	15
2715	41c. brown, grey and black	2·75	15
2716	45c. purple, blue and black	2·75	25
2716a	50c. turquoise, red and black	70	35
2716b	65c. blue and red	90	45
2716c	70c. violet and green	95	45
2717	77c. brown, green and black	2·75	35
2718	85c. purple and black	1·20	60
2719	90c. green and red	1·30	65

DESIGNS: 1c. "Ebe" (detail, painting, Antonia Canova); 2c. Profile (5th-century B.C. coin, Syracuse); 3c. Woman's head (detail from mural, Piero della Francesca); 5c. As No. 2505; 10c. Head (3rd-century B.C. sculpture, "G. Fiorelli" civic museum, Lucera); 20c. Portrait of a Lady (Correggio); 23c. As No. 2506; 41c. As No. 2508; 45c. "Venere di Urbino" (Tiziano Vecellio); 50c. "Portrait of a young girl" (detail, painting, Francesco Mazzola); 65c. "San Giorgio e la Principessa di Trebisonda" (detail by Antonis Pisano); 70c. "Wettuno a Venezia" (detail by Giambattista Foggini, sculpture); 77c. "Spring" (detail, painting, Botticelli); 85c. "Costigiana" (detail, by Vittore (arpaccio)), 90c. "Venere e Marte legati de Amore" (detail, by Paolo Calieri).

1170 "Ducato" (Venetian coin), 1285

2002. European Coins. Multicoloured.

2725	41c. Type **1170**	2·30	45
2726	41c. "Genovino" (Genoa) and "Fiorino" (Florence), 1252	2·30	45
2727	41c. Flags of E.U. forming Euro symbol	2·30	45
2728	41c. 1946 lira coin transforming into euro coin	2·30	45

2002. Priority Mail Stamps. Designs as No. 2660 but with face values in euros only. Multicoloured, background colour given. Self-adhesive gum.

2729	62c. yellow	4·00	35
2730	77c. blue	2·40	80
2731	€1 lavender	2·75	60
2732	€1.24 green	8·00	1·50
2733	€1.86 pink	13·00	2·30
2734	€4.13 lilac	15·00	5·25

1171 Woman's Head and State Arms

2002

2735	**1171**	€1 multicoloured	6·75	9·75
2736	**1171**	€1.24 multicoloured	8·00	90
2737	**1171**	€1.55 multicoloured	10·00	1·20
2738	**1171**	€2.17 multicoloured	13·50	1·40
2738a	**1171**	€2.35 multicoloured	3·25	1·50
2739	**1171**	€2.58 multicoloured	16·00	1·40
2739a	**1171**	€2.80 multicoloured	3·75	1·80
2739b	**1171**	€3 multicoloured	4·00	2·00
2740	**1171**	€3.62 multicoloured	20·00	3·75
2741	**1171**	€6.20 multicoloured	31·00	7·00

1172 Escriva

2002. Birth Centenary of Josemaria Escriva de Balaguer (founder of Opus Dei (religious organization)).

2745	**1172**	41c. multicoloured	2·00	45

1173 Luigi Bocconi and University Building

2002. Centenary of Bocconi University.

2746	**1173**	41c. brown and stone	2·00	45

The University was established with an endowment from Ferinando Bocconi in memory of his son Luigi.

1174 1852 5c. Stamp

2002. 150th Anniv of First Stamp of Parma. Fluorescent paper.
2747 **1174** 41c. multicoloured 2·00 45

1175 Mountain Peak

2002. International Year of Mountains.
2748 **1175** 41c. multicoloured 2·00 45

1176 Emblem and Olympic Rings

2002. Winter Olympic Games, Turin (2006).
2749 **1176** 41c. multicoloured 2·00 35

1177 Queen Elena

2002. 50th Death Anniv of Queen Elena of Savoy.
2750 **1177** 41c.+21c. multicoloured 2·75 1·20

1178 Sculpture (Arnolfo di Cambio)

2002. 700th Death Anniv of Arnolfo di Cambio (sculptor).
2751 **1178** 41c. mauve 2·00 45

1179 Venaria Reale

2002. Tourist Publicity (29th series). Multicoloured.
2752 41c. Type **1179** 1·90 45
2753 41c. Capo d'Orlando 1·90 45
2754 41c. San Gimignano 1·90 45
2755 41c. Sannicandro di Bari 1·90 45

1180 Santa Maria delle Grazie Sanctuary

2002
2756 **1180** 41c. brown 2·00 45

1181 Police Officers, Computer Screen and Patrol Car

2002. 150th Anniv of State Police Force.
2757 **1181** 41c. multicoloured 2·00 45

1182 Ricci and World Map

2002. 450th Birth Anniv of Matteo Rici (missionary).
2758 **1182** 41c. multicoloured 2·00 45

1183 Circus Performers

2002. Europa. Circus.
2759 **1183** 41c. multicoloured 2·75 45

1184 Sailing Ship and Student

2002. Francesco Morosini Naval Military School, Venice.
2760 **1184** 41c. multicoloured 2·00 45

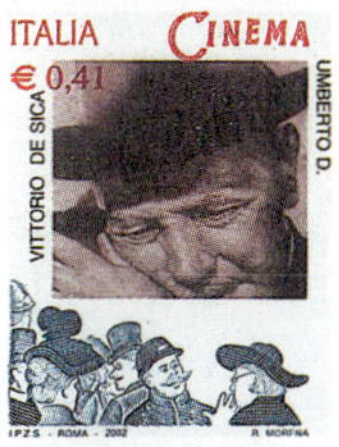

1185 Vittorio de Sica (film director, birth centenary)

2002. Cinema Anniversaries. Multicoloured.
2761 41c. Type **1185** 1·80 45
2762 41c. Text and clouds (birth centenary (1901) of Cesare Zavattini (screen writer)) 1·80 45

1186 Football Player and Emblem

2002. Juventus, National Football Champions, 2001–2002.
2763 **1186** 41c. multicoloured 2·00 45

1187 Falcone and Boresellino

2002. 10th Death Annivs of Giovanni Falcone and Paolo Borsellino (judges).
2764 **1187** 62c. multicoloured 3·25 70

1188 Emblems and Member Flags

2002. Russia's Membership of North Atlantic Treaty Organization (N.A.T.O.).
2765 **1188** 41c. multicoloured 2·00 60

1189 Kayaking

2002. World Kayaking Championship, Valsesia.
2766 **1189** 52c. multicoloured 2·75 45

1190 Modena 1853 1 lira Arms of Este Stamp

2002. 150th Anniv of Modena (Italian State) Stamps.
2767 **1190** 41c. multicoloured 2·00 45

1191 Arms

2002. Italian Military Involvement in Peace Missions.
2768 **1191** 41c. multicoloured 2·00 45

1192 Binda

2002. Birth Centenary of Alfrodo Binda (cyclist).
2769 **1192** 41c. multicoloured 2·00 45

1193 Santo

2002. Canonization of Father Padre Pio Santo.
2770 **1193** 41c. multicoloured 2·00 45

1194 Divisione Acqui (monument, Mario Salazzari)

2002. "Divisione Acqui" (World War II resistance group on Cephalonia).
2771 **1194** 41c. multicoloured 2·75 45

1195 Crucifixion (Arezzo Basilica)

2002
2772 **1195** €2.58 multicoloured 11·50 2·75

1196 Building Facade

2002. Bicentenary of Ministry of Interior.
2773 **1196** 41c. multicoloured 2·00 45

1197 Maria Goretti

2002. Death Centenary of Saint Maria Goretti.
2774 **1197** 41c. multicoloured 2·00 45

1198 Mazarin

2002. 400th Birth Anniv of Cardinal Jules Mazarin (minister to Louis XIV of France).
2775 **1198** 41c. multicoloured 2·00 45

1199 National Colours encircling Globe

2002. "Italians in the World".
2776 **1199** 52c. multicoloured 2·75 60

1200 Monument (Vincenzo Gasperetti)

2002. Monument to the Victims of Massacre at Sant' Anna di Stazzema.
2777 **1200** 41c. multicoloured 2·00 45

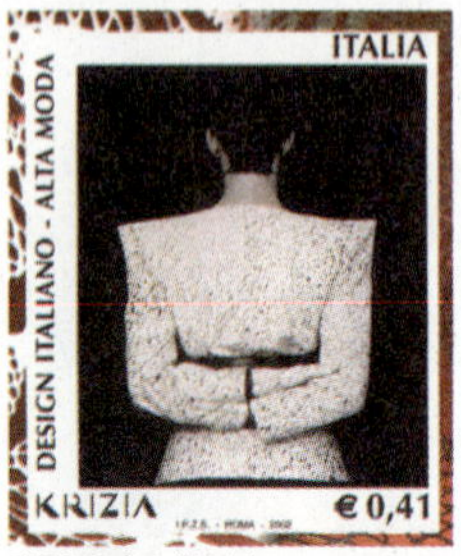

1201 Jacket (Krizia)

2002. Italian Design. Sheet 157×137 mm, containing T 1201 and similar vert designs. Multicoloured.
MS2778 41c. Type **1201**; 41c. Brassiere (Dolce & Gabbana); 41c. Drawing of dress (Gianfranco Ferre); 41c. Drawing of suit (Giorgio Armani); 41c. Dress (Laura Biagiotti); 41c. Shoes (Prada) 12·00 12·00

1202 Cathedral and Tower, Pisa

2002. UNESCO World Heritage Sites. Multicoloured.
2779 41c. Type **1202** 2·30 35
2780 52c. Aeolian Islands 3·00 40
Stamps of a similar design were issued by the United Nations.

1203 Dalla Chiesa

2002. 20th Anniv of Assassination of Carlo Alberto Dalla Chiesa (police chief and prefect of Palermo).
2781 **1203** 41c. multicoloured 2·00 45

1204 Teatro della Concordia, Monte Castello di Vibio, Perugia

2002
2782 **1204** 41c. multicoloured 2·00 45

1205 Yacht

2002. 12th Prada Classic Yacht Challenge, Imperia.
2783 **1205** 41c. multicoloured 2·00 45

1206 Papal States 1852 5b. Stamp

2002. 150th Anniv of First Papal States Stamp.
2784 **1206** 41c. multicoloured 2·00 45

1207 Cross, City Museum, Santa Giulia, Brescia

2002. Museum Exhibits. Multicoloured.
2785 41c. Type **1207** 1·90 45
2786 41c. Busts, Museo Nazionale, Palazzo Altemps, Rome (horiz) 1·90 45

1208 Orchid

2002. Flora and Fauna. Multicoloured.
2787 23c. Type **1208** 80 35
2788 52c. European lynx 1·80 50
2789 77c. Stag beetle 2·75 80

1209 Emblem

2002. World Food Day.
2790 **1209** 41c. multicoloured 2·00 45

1210 Corps Member and Emblem

2002. State Forestry Corps.
2791 **1210** 41c. multicoloured 2·00 45

1211 Gnocchi and Children

2002. Birth Centenary of Carlo Gnocchi (founder of rehabilitation centres for disabled children).
2792 **1211** 41c. multicoloured 2·00 45

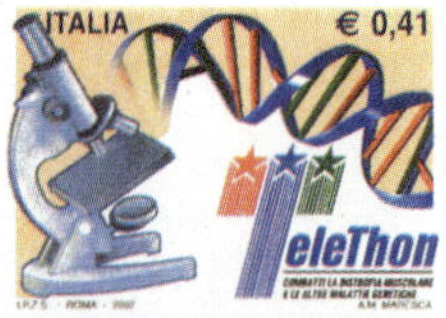

1212 Microscope and Emblem

2002. "Telethon 2002" (campaign to combat muscular dystrophy and genetic disease).
2793 **1212** 41c. multicoloured 2·00 45

1213 The Holy Family

2002. Christmas. Multicoloured.
2794 41c. Type **1213** 7·25 40
2795 62c. Child and Christmas tree 2·00 65

1214 "Nike di Samotracia" (statue) and Athlete

2002. Women in Sport.
2796 **1214** 41c. multicoloured 2·00 45

1215 Flags of Championship Winners and Football

2002. 20th-century World Cup Football Champions. Multicoloured.
2797 52c. Type **1215** 2·50 70
2798 52c. Italian footballer 2·50 70

1216 Magnifying Glass, Stamps and Children

2002. Stamp Day. Philately in Schools.
2799 **1216** 62c. multicoloured 2·00 65

1217 Vittorio Orlando

2002. 50th Death Anniv of Vittorio Emanuele Orlando (politician).
2800 **1217** 41c. multicoloured 2·00 45

1218 Event Emblem

2003. "Tarvisio 2003" (winter sports competition).
2801 **1218** 52c. multicoloured 2·75 50

1219 Family and Scales

2003. The Italian Republic on Stamps.
2802 **1219** 62c. multicoloured 2·75 65

1220 Cyclist carrying Cycle

2003. World Cyclo-cross Championship, Monopoli.
2803 **1220** 41c. multicoloured 1·80 45

1221 Building and Tandem

2003. 150th Anniv (2002) of Fratelli Alinari (photographic company).
2804 **1221** 77c. multicoloured 4·75 80

1222 Jigsaw Puzzle

2003. European Year of the Disabled.
2805 **1222** 41c. multicoloured 1·80 45

1223 Skiers

2003. World Nordic Skiing Championship, Val di Fiemme.
2806 **1223** 41c. multicoloured 1·80 45

1224 Couple, Flower and Emblem

2003. National Civil Service.
2807 **1224** 62c. multicoloured 2·75 65

1225 Knights on Horseback

2003. 500th Anniv of the Barletta Challenge (battle between 13 French and 13 Italian knights).
2808 **1225** 41c. multicoloured 1·80 70

1226 Building Facade

2003. Torquato Tasso Grammar School (gymnasium).
2809 **1226** 41c. multicoloured 1·80 70

1227 "Encounter by the Golden Door" (Giotto)

2003
2810 **1227** 41c. multicoloured 1·80 70

1228 Gian Rinaldo Carli and Building

2003. Gian Rinaldo Carli Grammar School (gymnasium).
2811 **1228** 41c. multicoloured 1·80 70

1229 Academy Emblem

2003. 400th Anniv of "Accademia dei Lincei" (academy of lynxes) (scientific society).
2812 **1229** 41c. multicoloured 1·80 70

1230 Foils and Fencers

2003. World Junior Fencing Championships, Trapani.
2813 **1230** 41c. multicoloured 1·80 70

1231 Sestri Levante

2003. Tourist Publicity (30th series). Multicoloured.
2814 41c. Type **1231** 1·80 70
2815 41c. Lanciano 1·80 70
2816 41c. Procida 1·80 70

1232 Golfer

2003. Centenary of Roma Acquasanta Golf Course.
2817 **1232** 77c. multicoloured 3·50 1·60

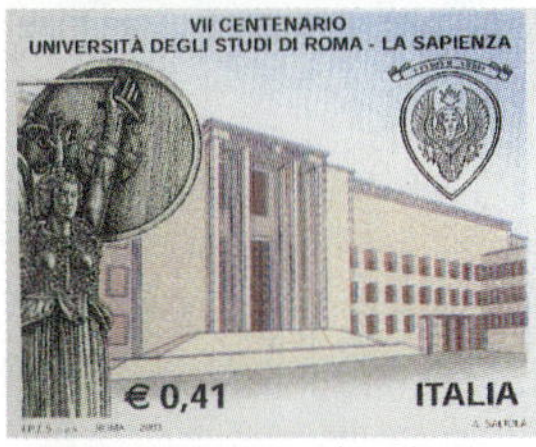

1233 Minerva (statue) and Building Facade

2003. 700th Anniv of La Sapienza University, Rome.
2818 **1233** 41c. multicoloured 2·10 1·00

1234 Pasta

2003. National Pasta Museum, Rome.
2819 **1234** 41c. multicoloured 1·80 85

1235 Guido Carli and University Building

2003. Guido Carli-LUISS (international liberal social studies) University.
2820 **1235** €2.58 multicoloured 8·00 5·25

1236 Woman in Blue Dress

2003. Europa. Poster Art. Posters by Marcello Dudovich. Multicoloured.
2821 41c. Type **1236** 2·20 1·00
2822 52c. Woman in white dress 2·30 1·10

1237 Buildings and Text

2003. 50th Anniv of State Archives.
2823 **1237** 41c. multicoloured 1·70 90

1238 Logo and St. Peter of Verona

2003. Centenary of Veronafil Exhibition.
2824 **1238** 41c. multicoloured 1·70 90

1239 Aldo Moro

2003. 25th Death Anniv of Aldo Moro (politician).
2825 **1239** 62c. multicoloured 2·75 1·40

1240 Antonio Meucci

2003. Antonio Meucci (telephone pioneer) Commemoration. Sheet 90×70 mm.
MS2826 **1240** 52c. multicoloured 2·75 2·20

1241 Padre E. Barsanti and F. Matteucci (motor pioneers)

2003. 150th Anniv of Invention of Internal Combustion Engine.
2827 **1241** 52c. multicoloured 2·40 1·20

1242 Post and Telegraph Building (Angiolo Mazzoni)

2003
2828 **1242** 41c. blue 1·80 1·00

1243 Flags of Italy and European Union

2003. Italian Presidency of the European Union.
2829 **1243** 41c. multicoloured 1·80 1·00

1244 Ezio Vanoni

2003. Birth Centenary of Ezio Vanoni (politician).
2830 **1244** €2.58 multicoloured 11·00 6·50

1245 "The Ascension of Mary"

2003. 300th Birth Anniv of Corrado Giaquinto (artist).
2831 **1245** 77c. multicoloured 3·50 2·10

1246 Eugenio Balzan

2003. 50th Death Anniv of Eugenio Balzan (journalist).
2832 **1246** 41c. multicoloured 1·80 1·00

1247 "Diana and Atteone" (detail, fresco, Sanvitale Castle)

2003. 500th Birth Anniv of Francesco Mazzola (Parmigianino) (artist).
2833 **1247** 41c. multicoloured 1·80 1·00

1248 Player and Club Emblem

2003. Juventus, National Football Champions, 2002–3.
2834 **1248** 41c. multicoloured 1·80 1·00

1249 San Silvestro Abbey, Nonantola

2003
2835 **1249** 41c. multicoloured 1·80 1·00

1250 Mario Calderara

2003. Centenary of First Powered Flight. Italian Aviation. Multicoloured.
2836 52c. Type **1250** (first Italian pilot) 2·40 1·40
2837 52c. Mario Cobianchi (pilot) 2·40 1·40
2838 52c. Gianni Caproni (aircraft designer) 2·40 1·40
2839 52c. Alessandro Marchetti (aircraft designer) 2·40 1·40
MS2840 105×146 mm. Nos. 2836/9 9·75 5·75

1251 Giovanni Giolitti

2003. 75th Death Anniv of Giovanni Giolitti (prime minister 1892–3 and 1903–14).

2841 **1251** 41c. multicoloured 1·80 1·00

1252 "Still Life" (Giorgio Morandi)

2003. Europhalia 2003 Italy Festival. Italian Presidency of European Union. Multicoloured.

2842 41c. Type **1252** 1·80 1·00

2843 52c. Cistalia 202 (1947) 2·40 1·40

Stamps of the same design were issued by Belgium.

1253 Attilio Vallecchi (founder) and "Leonardo"

2003. Centenary of First Publication of "Leonardo". Centenary of Vallecchi Publishing House.

2844 **1253** 41c. multicoloured 1·80 1·00

1254 Family enclosed in Atom Model

2003. The Family.

2845 **1254** 77c. multicoloured 3·50 2·10

1255 "Maesta" (detail) (Duccio di Buoninsegna)

2003. Extension to Metropolitan Opera House, Sienna.

2846 **1255** 41c. multicoloured 1·80 1·00

1256 Vittorio Alfieri

2003. Death Bicentenary of Vittorio Alfieri (writer).

2847 **1256** 41c. multicoloured 1·80 1·00

1257 Ugo La Malfa and Chamber of Deputies Assembly Hall

2003. Birth Centenary of Ugo La Malfa (politician).

2848 **1257** 62c. multicoloured 3·00 1·70

1258 Bernardo Ramazzini and Frontispiece of "De morbis aertifcum diatriba"

2003. 370th Birth Anniv of Bernardo Ramazzini (medical pioneer).

2849 **1258** 41c. multicoloured 1·80 1·00

1259 Building Facade

2003. 120th Anniv of Confediliizia Institute, Rome.

2850 **1259** $2.58 multicoloured 11·50 6·75

1260 "Nativity" (Gian Paolo Cavagna)

2003. Christmas. Multicoloured.

2851 41c. Type **1260** 1·80 1·00

2852 62c. Poinsettia 3·00 1·70

1261 "Forme Grido Viva l'Italia"

2003. 40th Death Anniv of Giacomo Balla (artist). Multicoloured.

2853 41c. Type **1261** 1·80 1·00

2854 52c. "Linee—Forza del Pugno di Boccioni" 2·40 1·40

1262 Pencil and Sharpener

2003. Stamp Day.

2855 **1262** 41c. multicoloured 1·80 1·00

2004. Priority Mail Stamps. Designs as No. 2660. Multicoloured, background colour given. Self-adhesive gum.

2856 60c. orange 2·50 1·50

2856a 62c. yellow 3·00 1·80

2856b 80c. red 3·25 1·90

2856c £1 violet 10·50 6·50

2857 €1.40 green 5·25 3·25

2857a €1.50 grey 5·50 3·25

2858 €2 green 8·00 4·75

2859 €2.20 cannine 8·50 5·25

No. 2856/9 were issued with an attached label inscribed "postaprioritaria Priority Mail".

1263 "50" enclosing Test Screen

2004. 50th Anniv of Television.

2860 **1263** 41c. blue and grey 1·70 1·00

2861 - 62c. multicoloured 2·75 1·70

DESIGN: 62c. "50" enclosed in colour blocks.

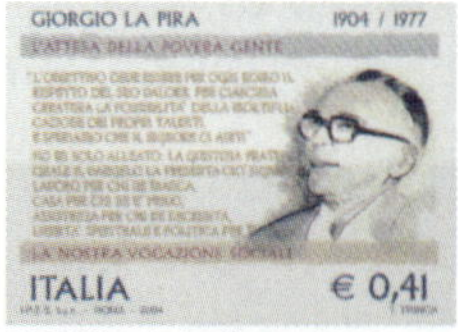

1264 Giorgio La Pira and Script

2004. Birth Centenary of Giorgio La Pira (politician).

2862 **1264** 41c. cinnamon, blue and red 1·70 1·00

1265 Tower, Map and Compass

2004. Genoa–European Capital of Culture, 2004.

2863 **1265** 45c. multicoloured 1·90 1·20

1266 Santa Maria Assunta Church, Pragelato

2004. Winter Olympic Games, Turin (2006) (1st series). Multicoloured.

2864 23c. Type **1266** 90 60

2865 45c. San Pietro Apostolo church, Bardonecchia 1·80 1·20

2866 62c. 28th-century fountain, Sauze d'Oulx 2·40 1·50

2867 65c. Mole Antonelliana, Turin 2·50 1·70

See also Nos. 2926/9.

1267 Petrarch

2004. 700th Birth Anniv of Francesco Petrarca (Petrarch) (poet).

2868 **1267** 45c. multicoloured 1·80 1·20

1268 Mortar, Pestle, Museum Building and Liquorice Sticks

2004. Giorgio Amarelli Liquorice Museum.

2869 **1268** 45c. multicoloured 1·80 1·20

1269 Heart-shaped Seat Belt Buckle and Map covered with Traffic Signs

2004. Road Safety. Multicoloured.

2870 60c. Dashboard and traffic signs (horiz) 2·40 1·50

2871 62c. Type **1269** 2·50 1·70

1270 Vignola

2004. Tourist Publicity (31st series). Multicoloured.

2872 45c. Type **1270** 1·80 1·20

2873 45c. Viterbo 1·80 1·20

2874 45c. Egadi Islands 1·80 1·20

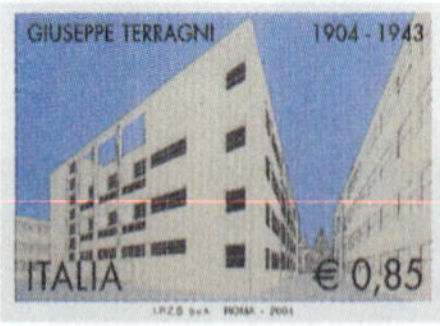

1271 Casa del Fascio

2004. Birth Centenary of Guiseppe Terragni (architect).

2875 **1271** 85c. multicoloured 3·25 2·20

1272 Sakate Temple, Bangkok

2004. Bangkok and Rome. Sheet 140×70 mm containing T 1272 and similar horiz design. Multicoloured.

MS2876 65c.×2, Type **1272**; Colosseum, Rome 5·00 3·25

Stamps of a similar design were issued by Thailand.

1273 St. George and Crowd

2004. 1700th Anniv of Martyrdom of St. George.

2877 **1273** €2.80 multicoloured 11·00 7·00

1274 Case

2004. Europa. Holidays. Multicoloured.

2878 45c. Type **1274** 1·80 1·20

2879 62c. Open case 2·50 1·70

1275 Sheep and Castle, Bologna

2004. Tratturo Magno (drovers' way). Sheet 90×70 mm.

MS2880 **1275** 45c. multicoloured 2·40 1·50

1276 Synagogue Facade

2004. Centenary of the Great Synagogue, Rome. Multicoloured.

2881	60c. Type **1276**	2·40	1·50
2882	62c. Candlestick, ornamental panel and synagogue (vert)	2·50	1·70

Stamps of the same design were issued by Israel.

1277 Football, Player and Emblem

2004. A. C. Milan, National Football Champions, 2004.

2883	**1277**	45c. multicoloured	1·80	1·20

1278 Giacomo Puccini

2004. 50th Anniv of Puccini Festival, Torre del Lago.

2884	**1278**	60c. multicoloured	2·40	1·50

1279 Courtyard and Emblem

2004. 600th Anniv of Turin University.

2885	**1279**	45c. brown	1·80	1·20

1280 Achille Varzi, Motorcycle and Racing Cars

2004. Birth Centenary of Achille Varzi (motorcyclist and racing driver).

2886	**1280**	45c. multicoloured	1·80	1·20

1281 Arms and Policemen

2004. Prison Police.

2887	**1281**	45c. multicoloured	1·80	1·20

1282 Ice Pick and Mountain Peak

2004. 50th Anniv of First Ascent of K2 (mountain).

2888	**1282**	65c. blue, black and ultramarine	2·40	1·50

1283 Statuette and Map

2004. Regions. Multicoloured.

2889	45c. Type **1283** (Abruzzo)	1·80	1·20
2890	45c. Troglodyte settlement and map (Basilicata)	1·80	1·20
2891	45c. Medieval map (Liguria)	1·80	1·20
2892	45c. Roman mosaic (Emilia Romagna)	1·80	1·20

1284 Stained Glass Window

2004. 500th Anniv of the Apparition of Madonna di Tirano.

2893	**1284**	45c. multicoloured	1·80	1·20

1285 St. Nilo and Abbey Buildings

2004. Death Millenary Nilo di Rossano and Millenary of Foundation of Grottaferrata Abbey.

2894	**1285**	45c. multicoloured	1·80	1·20

1286 Map and Stylized Building Façade

2004. Florence State Archive.

2895	**1286**	45c. multicoloured	1·80	1·20

1287 Flower

2004. Lace Making. Self-adhesive. Textile. Imperf.

2896	**1287**	€2.80 blue and cream	11·00	7·00

1288 Hands

2004. 40th Anniv of "Lega del Filo d'Oro" (humanitarian organization for deaf blind people).

2897	**1288**	45c. multicoloured	1·80	1·20

1289 Institute Buildings

2004. Vittorio Emanuele III Technical Institute.

2898	**1289**	45c. multicoloured	1·80	1·20

1290 Luigi Guanella

2004. Luigi Guanella Commemoration (priest and humanitarian).

2899	**1290**	45c. multicoloured	1·80	1·20

1291 Piazza dell'Unita, Trieste

2004. 50th Anniv of Return of Trieste to Italy.

2900	**1291**	45c. multicoloured	1·80	1·20

1292 Emblem

2004. Information and Military Emergency Service.

2901	**1292**	60c. multicoloured	2·40	1·50

1293 Stars and Map of Europe

2004. Constitution of Europe Treaty.

2902	**1293**	62c. multicoloured	2·50	1·70

1294 Nativity

2004. Christmas. Multicoloured.

2903	45c. Type **1294**	1·80	1·20
2904	62c. Decorated tree (vert)	2·50	1·70

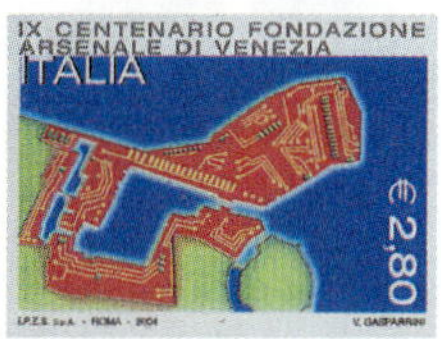

1295 Map of Arsenal

2004. 900th Anniv of Venice Arsenal.

2905	**1295**	€2.80 multicoloured	9·75	6·50

1296 St. Lucia

2004. 1700th Anniv of Martyrdom of St. Lucia.

2906	**1296**	45c. multicoloured	1·80	1·20

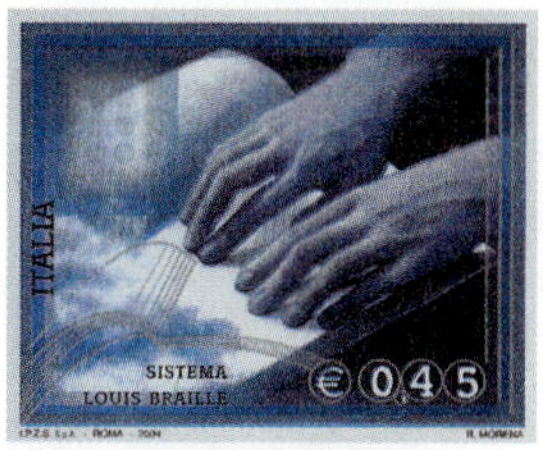

1297 Hands reading Braille

2004. Louis Braille System of Reading and Writing for the Blind.

2907	**1297**	45c. multicoloured	1·80	1·20

No. 2907 was embossed with Braille letters.

1298 Boy holding Stamp

2004. Stamp Day.

2908	**1298**	45c. multicoloured	1·80	1·20

1299 Emblem and Water

2004. 10th "Sport for All" Congress.

2909	**1299**	65c. multicoloured	2·50	1·70

1300 University Building

2004. Libera Universita Maria SS. Assunta (LUMSA) (university), Rome.

2910	**1300**	45c. multicoloured	1·80	1·20

1301 Woman's High-heeled Shoe

2004. Made in Italy. Shoes. Sheet 90×114 mm containing T 1301 and similar vert designs. Multicoloured.

2911-2914	45c.×4 Type **1301**; Man's laced shoe; Man's loafer; Trainers	7·50	2·40

1302 Club Emblem and Italy

2005. Centenary of Automobile Club d'Italia (ACI).
2915 **1302** 45c. multicoloured 1·80 1·20

2005
2916 **1171** €1 multicoloured 4·00 2·50

1303 Luigi Calabresi

2005. Luigi Calabresi (Milanese police officer) Commemoration.
2917 **1303** 45c. multicoloured 1·80 1·20

1304 Refugees

2005. Memorial Day for the Exodus from Istria, Fiume and Dalmazia.
2918 **1304** 45c. multicoloured 1·80 1·20

1305 Emblem

2005. Centenary of Rotary International (charitable organization).
2919 **1305** 65c. ultramarine and yellow 2·50 1·70

1306 Badge and Soldiers

2005. Sassari Brigade.
2920 **1306** 45c. multicoloured 1·80 1·20

1307 "Q"

2005. Quadrennial Exhibition, Rome.
2921 **1307** 45c. multicoloured 1·80 1·20

1308 "Bronzes of Riace" (Greek statues)

2005. Regions. Multicoloured.
2922 45c. Type **1308** (Calabria) 1·80 1·20
2923 45c. Ship (bas relief) and Miramare castle, Trieste (Fruili Venezia Guila) 1·80 1·20
2924 45c. Woman's head (fresco, Pompeii), (Campania) 1·80 1·20
2925 45c. Certosa, Pavia (Lombardy) 1·80 1·20

1309 San Maurizio Church, Pinerolo

2005. Winter Olympic Games, Turin (2006) (2nd series). Multicoloured.
2926 23c. Type **1309** 1·00 65
2927 45c. San Giovanni Battista church, Cesana Torinese, San Sicario 1·80 1·20
2928 60c. Neve and Gliz (Games' mascots) 2·40 1·50
2929 62c. Hotel, Sestriere 2·50 1·70

1310 Pavia (engraving by Gerolamo de Sanctis), Black Hole Diagram, Year Emblem and Feynman Diagram

2005. International Year of Physics.
2930 **1310** 85c. multicoloured 3·25 2·20

1311 Pavilions

2005. Inauguration of Milan International Fair Complex, Pero.
2931 **1311** 45c. multicoloured 1·80 1·20

1312 "100" and Steam

2005. Centenary of State Railways.
2932 **1312** 45c. multicoloured 1·80 1·20

1313 Early and Modern Soldiers

2005. National Army.
2933 **1313** 45c. multicoloured 1·80 1·20

1314 Stars and Grain

2005. Europa. Gastronomy. Multicoloured.
2934 45c. Type **1314** 1·80 1·20
2935 62c. Grapes, wine glass and stars 2·50 1·70

1315 Saint Ignazio

2005. Saint Ignazio of Laconi Commemoration.
2936 **1315** 45c. multicoloured 1·80 1·20

1316 Association Emblem

2005. 60th Anniv of Confcommercio (trade association).
2937 **1316** 60c. silver, steel blue and gold 2·40 1·50

1317 School Building

2005. Tommaso Campanella Grammar School, Reggio Calabria.
2938 **1317** 45c. multicoloured 1·80 1·20

1318 Building Facade

2005. Saint Giuseppe of Copertino Basilica, Osimo.
2939 **1318** 45c. indigo 1·80 1·20

1319 Asolo

2005. Tourist Publicity (32nd series). Multicoloured.
2940 45c. Type **1319** 1·80 1·20
2941 45c. Rocchetta a Volturno 1·80 1·20
2942 45c. Amalfi 1·80 1·20

1320 Gerardo Maiella and St. Gerardo Maiella Church, Materdomini

2005. 250th Death Anniv of Gerardo Maiella (priest).
2943 **1320** 45c. multicoloured 1·80 1·20

1321 Player and Club Emblem

2005. Juventus, National Football Champions, 2004–5.
2944 **1321** 45c. multicoloured 1·80 1·20

1322 Emblems and Map

2005. 20th Anniv of Ratification Italy–Vatican Concordat (abolishing Catholicism as state religion). Multicoloured.
2945 45c. Type **1322** 1·80 1·20
2946 €2.80 Emblems, manuscript and pen 11·00 7·25

Stamps of the same design were issued by Vatican City.

1323 Almerico da Schio and Dirigible

2005. Centenary of First Italian Dirigible.
2947 **1323** €3 multicoloured 12·00 7·75

1324 Mascot and Emblem

2005. European Youth Olympic Festival, Lignano.
2948 **1324** 62c. multicoloured 2·50 1·70

1325 Tunnel containing Flower

2005. International Day against Drugs.
2949 **1325** 45c. multicoloured 1·80 1·20

1326 Emblem

2005. Institute for Marine Security (I.P.SE.MA.).
2950 **1326** 45c. green, ultramarine and silver 1·80 1·20

1327 Leo Longanesi

2005. Birth Centenary of Leo Longanesi (writer and artist).
2951 **1327** 45c. blue 1·80 1·20

1328 Alberto Ascari and Race Car

2005. 50th Death Anniv of Alberto Ascari (World Champion race driver 1952–53).
2952 **1328** €2.80 multicoloured 11·00 7·00

1329 Emblem and Team Aermacchi MB-339 PAN

2005. Frecce Tricolori (Italian Air Force acrobatic display team). Multicoloured.
2953 45c. Type **1329** 1·80 1·20
2954 60c. Aermacchi MB-339 PAN (different) 2·40 1·50

1330 Pietro Savorgnan di Brazza

2005. Death Centenary of Pietro Paolo Savorgnan di Brazza (explorer).
2955 **1330** 45c. multicoloured 1·80 1·20

1331 Guido Gonella

2005. Birth Centenary of Guido Gonella (politician).
2956 **1331** 45c. multicoloured 1·80 1·20

1332 Space Craft and Mars

2005. Mars Exploration Programme. Self-adhesive.
2957 **1332** 80c. multicoloured 3·25 2·10

1333 Raised Arms

2005. 50th Anniv of Intercultura (voluntary service organization).
2958 **1333** 60c. multicoloured 2·40 1·50

1334 Yacht and Trapani Bay

2005. America's Cup Yacht Race, Trapani. Sheet 96×80 mm.
MS2959 **1334** €2.80 multicoloured 11·00 7·25

1335 "F"

2005. Stamp Day.
2960 **1335** 45c. multicoloured 1·80 1·20

1336 Heart as Flower

2005. Italian Organ Donors Association (AIDO).
2961 **1336** 60c. multicoloured 2·40 1·50

1337 Castle

2005. National Association (ANCI).
2962 **1337** 45c. multicoloured 1·80 1·20

1338 "Disputation in the Synagogue" (detail)

2005. Restoration of Frescoes by Filippo Lippi, Prato Cathedral. Multicoloured.
2963 45c. Type **1338** 1·80 1·20
2964 €1.50 "Saint's Funeral" (detail) 6·00 3·75

1339 "The Annunciation" (Beato Angelico)

2005. Christmas. Multicoloured.
2965 45c. Type **1339** 1·80 1·20
2966 62c. Family (vert) 2·50 1·70

1340 Alcide de Gasperi

2005. Alcide de Gasperi (politician) Commemoration.
2967 **1340** 62c. multicoloured 2·50 1·70

1341 "Humanity" Medal

2005. Birth Bicentenary of Giuseppe Mazzini (nationalist).
2968 **1341** 45c. multicoloured 1·80 1·20

1342 Civil Protection Department Emblem

2005. Civil Protection and Italian Red Cross. Multicoloured.
2969 45c. Type **1342** 1·80 1·20
2970 45c. Globe and Red Cross emblem 1·80 1·20

1343 "50" and UN Emblem

2005. 50th Anniv of United Nations Membership.
2971 **1343** 70c. multicoloured 2·75 1·80

1344 Pope John Paul II

2005. Pope John Paul II Commemoration and Election of Pope Benedict XVI. Multicoloured.
2972 45c. Type **1344** 1·80 1·20
2973 65c. Pope Benedict XVI 2·50 1·70

1345 Royal Palace

2005. 60th Anniv of Re-constitution of Caserta Province.
2974 **1345** 45c. multicoloured 1·80 1·20

1346 Stylized Submarine

2005. Re-location of Submarine Enrico Toti to National Museum of Sciences and Technology, Milan.
2975 **1346** 62c. grey and deep grey 2·50 1·70

1347 Egg Timer

2006. Greetings Stamps. 18th Birthday Greetings. Multicoloured, background colour given.
2976 45c. Type **1347** (pink) 1·80 1·20
2977 45c. As No. 2976 (blue) 1·80 1·20

1348 Calciatori (footballers) Sticker Album Emblem

2006. Panini SpA (sticker manufacturer and publisher).
2978 **1348** €2.80 multicoloured 11·00 7·00

1349 First Magazine Cover

2006. 50th Anniv of Quattroruote (motoring magazine founded by G. Mazzochi).
2979 **1349** 62c. multicoloured 2·50 1·70

1350 Alessandro Tassoni State High School, Modena

2006. Schools and Universities.
2980 **1350** 45c. multicoloured 1·80 1·20
2981 - 45c. multicoloured 1·80 1·20
2982 - 45c. multicoloured 1·80 1·20
2983 - 45c. yellow, slate and ultramarine 1·80 1·20

DESIGNS: Type **1350**; No. 2981 Agostino Nifo State High School, Sessa Aurunca; 2982 Ernesto Cairoli State High School, Varese; 2983 Carlo Bo University, Urbino.

1351 Biathlon

2006. Winter Olympic Games, Turin. Each blue, new blue and light blue.
2984 23c. Type **1351** 1·00 65
2985 45c. Figure skating 1·80 1·20
2986 65c. Ice hockey 2·50 1·70
2987 70c. Curling 2·75 1·80
2988 85c. Bob sledding 3·25 2·20
2989 90c. Alpine skiing 3·50 2·30
2990 €1 Olympic flame (detail) 4·00 2·50
2991 €1.30 Luge 5·00 3·25
2992 $1.70 Three medals 6·75 4·25
MS2993 149×102 mm. Nos. 2984/92 29·00 19·00

The stamps and margins of **MS**2993 form a composite design.

1352 1879 5c., 1863 15c., 1901 10c. and 1930 20c. Stamps

2006. Il Regno d'Italia Philatelic Exhibition, Palazzo Montecitorio (chamber of deputies).
2994 **1352** 60c. multicoloured 2·40 1·50

1353 Society Emblem

2006. 80th Anniv of Society for the Preservation of Italian Culture in Dalmatia.
2995 **1353** 45c. blue and vermilion 1·80 1·20

1354 "Camera degli Sposi" (The Wedding Chamber) (Andrea Mantegna)

2006. 500th Death Anniv of Andrea Mantegna (artist).
2996 **1354** 45c. multicoloured 1·80 1·20

1355 Emblem

2006. Centenary of International Congress on Occupational Health. 28th Congress on Occupational Health, Milan.
2997 **1355** 60c.+30c. multicoloured 3·50 2·30

The premium was for the benefit of Breast Cancer charities.

1356 Emblem

2006. Winter Paralympic Games, Turin.
2998 **1356** 60c. multicoloured 2·40 1·50

1357 Ice Cream Seller

2006. Made in Italy. Multicoloured.
2999 60c. Type **1357** 2·40 1·50

3000 €2.80 Marble statue and quarry 11·00 7·00

1358 Football Team with Faces forming Notes

2006. 25th Anniv of National Association of Singers.
3001 **1358** 45c. multicoloured 1·80 1·20

1359 *Cavour* (aircraft carrier)

2006. Navy.
3002 **1359** 60c. multicoloured 2·40 1·50

1360 Swiss and Italian Flags and Tunnel

2006. Centenary of Simplon Tunnel.
3003 **1360** 62c. multicoloured 2·50 1·70

1361 Lake Como

2006. Tourist Publicity (33rd series). Multicoloured.
3004 45c. Type **1361** 1·80 1·20
3005 45c. Marina di Pietrasanta 1·80 1·20
3006 45c. Temple of Serapis, Pozzuoli 1·80 1·20

1362 Three Dimensional Diagram of Mountain Range

2006. Centenary of International Day of Mountains.
3007 **1362** 60c. multicoloured 2·40 1·50

1363 St. Mary Incaldana (icon), Basilica Minore, St. Mary Incaldana, Modragone.

2006. Cultural Heritage.
3008 **1363** 45c. multicoloured 1·80 1·20

1364 Stylized Vote Papers and Ballot Box

2006. 1st Vote cast by Italian Citizens Resident Abroad.
3009 **1364** 62c. multicoloured 2·50 1·70

1365 Palazzo Mentcitorio, Rome and Palazzo Pubblico, San Marino

2006. Le Due Repubbliche (two republics) Philatelic Exhibition. Multicoloured.
3010 62c. Type **1365** 2·50 1·70
MS3011 121×90 mm. 62c.×2, Type **1365**; Type **584** of San Marino 5·00 3·25

No. **MS**3011 is identical to **MS**2084 of San Marino.

1366 Instructor and Pupils

2006. 70th Anniv of Ski School, Cervina.
3012 **1366** 45c. multicoloured 1·80 1·20

1367 "Madonna of Humility" (Gentile da Fabriano), Museo Nazionale di San Matteo, Pisa.

2006. Cultural Heritage.
3013 **1367** €2.80 multicoloured 11·00 7·00

1368 Man at Window (poster) (Raymond Savignac) (1956)

2006. 50th Anniv of "Il Giorno" Newspaper. Photo.
3014 **1368** 45c. multicoloured 1·80 1·20

1369 Court Chamber

2006. 50th Anniv of Constitutional Court.
3015 **1369** 45c. indigo 1·80 1·20

1370 Enrico Mattei

2006. Birth Centenary of Enrico Mattei (entrepreneur).
3016 **1370** 45c. multicoloured 1·80 1·20

1371 Statue (Emanuele Filiberto), Royal Castle, Racconigi (Piedmont)

2006. Regions. Multicoloured.
3017 45c. Type **1371** 1·80 1·20
3018 45c. David (statue) (Michelangelo) and landscape (Tuscany) 1·80 1·20
3019 45c. Sarcophagus of the bride and groom (Sarcofago degli Sposi) and Etruscan necropolis, Cerveteri (Lazio) 1·80 1·20
3020 45c. Basilica of St Nicholas, Bari, outline of Puglia and Tremiti Islands. (Puglia) 1·80 1·20

1372 "La Targa Florio" (Margaret Bradley)

2006. Centenary of Targa Florio (automobile endurance race), Palermo.
3021 **1372** 60c. multicoloured 2·40 1·50

1373 Christopher Columbus

2006. 500th Death Anniv of Christopher Columbus.
3022 **1373** 62c. multicoloured 2·50 1·70

1374 Young People of Many Nations

2006. Europa. Integration. Multicoloured.
3023 45c. Type **1374** 1·80 1·20
3024 62c. Backview 2·50 1·70

1375 Coliseum and Emblem

2006. International Military Sports Council General Meeting, Rome.
3025 **1375** 45c. multicoloured 1·80 1·20

1376 Emblem

2006. International Team Chess Championship, Turin.
3026 **1376** 62c. multicoloured 2·50 1·70

1377 Assembly Chamber and National Colours

2006. 60th Anniv of Elected Constituent Assembly.
3027 **1377** 60c. multicoloured 2·40 1·50

1378 Nilde Iotti (politician)

2006. 60th Anniv of Women's Suffrage.
3028 **1378** 60c. multicoloured 2·40 1·50

1379 Emblem

2006. World Bridge Championship.
3029 **1379** 65c. multicoloured 2·50 1·70

1380 Arms and Map

2006. Test Firing Range, Salto di Quirra (Poligono Interforze del Salto di Quirra (PISQ)), Sardinia.
3030 **1380** 60c. multicoloured 2·40 1·50

1381 Headquarters

2006. Centenary of Guardia di Finanza Cadets Corps and General Headquarters. Multicoloured.
3031 60c. Type **1381** 2·40 1·50
3032 60c. Cadet and building facade (horiz) 2·40 1·50

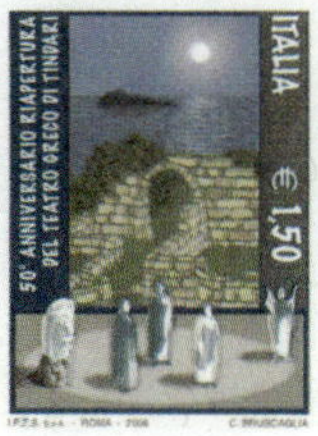

1382 Stage, Walls and Sea

2006. 50th Anniv of Greek Theatre, Tindari.
3033 **1382** €1.50 multicoloured 6·00 3·75

1383 Bridge across Map of Italy

2006. 50th Anniv of Autostrada del Sole.
3034 **1383** 60c. multicoloured 2·40 1·50

1384 Devastation

2006. 26th Anniv of Bombing of Bologna Railway Station.
3035 **1384** 60c. multicoloured 2·40 1·50

1385 Emblem

2006. 40th Anniv of Union of Italian Philatelic Journalists.
3036 **1385** 60c. multicoloured 2·50 1·70

1386 St Gregory

2006. St Gregory Commemoration.
3037 **1386** 60c. multicoloured 2·40 1·50

1387 Flag and Fans

2006. Italy—2006 World Cup Football Champions.
3038 **1387** €1 multicoloured 4·00 2·50

1388 Face and Figure Outlines

2006. Victims of Terrorism.
3039 **1388** 60c. multicoloured 2·40 1·50

1389 Ettore Majorana and Atomic Symbol

2006. Birth Centenary of Ettore Majorana (physicist).
3040 **1389** 60c. multicoloured 2·40 1·50

1390 St Francis Xavier

2006. Saints' Anniversaries. Multicoloured.
3041 60c. Type **1390** (500th birth anniv) 2·40 1·50
3042 60c. St Ignatius Loyola (450th death anniv) 2·40 1·50

1391 Fencers

2006. World Fencing Championship, Turin.
3043 **1391** 65c. multicoloured 2·50 1·70

1392 Boy, Stamps and Globe

2006. Philately Day.
3044 **1392** 60c. multicoloured 2·40 1·50

1393 Blind-folded Woman

2006. 500th Anniv of National Lottery.
3045 **1393** 60c. multicoloured 2·40 1·50

1394 Emblem

2006. National System of Environment Protection.
3046 **1394** 65c. multicoloured 2·50 1·70

1395 Luchino Visconti

2006. Birth Centenary of Luchino Visconti (film maker).
3047 **1395** 60c. multicoloured 2·40 1·50

1396 Dino Buzzati

2006. Birth Centenary of Dino Buzzati (writer).
3048 **1396** 60c. multicoloured 2·40 1·50

1397 "Adoration of the Magi" (Jacopo Bassano)

2006. Christmas.
3049 **1397** 60c. magenta 2·40 1·50
3050 – 65c. multicoloured (vert) 2·50 1·70
DESIGNS: 60c. Type **1397**; 65c. Decorated tree.

1398 Vittoriano Building, Rome and Tomb of the Unknown Warrior

2006. In Memory of the Fallen in Nassiriya.
3051 **1398** 60c. multicoloured 2·40 1·50

1399 St. Evasio Cathedral, Casale Monferrato

2007. Cultural Heritage.
3052 **1399** 60c. cerise 2·40 1·50

1400 Maria Montessori and Children

2007. Centenary of Montessori Nursery Schools.
3053 **1400** 60c. multicoloured 2·40 1·50

1401 Milvio Bridge, River Tiber and Building Facade

2007. 50th Anniv of National School for Public Administration.
3054 **1401** 65c. multicoloured 2·50 1·70

1402 Parma Cathedral and Baptistery

2007. Cultural Heritage.
3055 **1402** 60c. olive 2·40 1·50

1403 Arturo Toscanini

2007. 50th Death Anniv of Arturo Toscanini (conductor).

3056	**1403**	60c. multicoloured	2·40	1·50

1404 "St. Francis of Paola crossing Straits of Medina" (Benedetto Luti)

2007. 500th Death Anniv of St. Francis of Paola.

3057	**1404**	60c. multicoloured	2·40	1·50

1405 "Ferrante Gonzaga triumphing over Envy" (statue, Leone Leoni)

2007. 500th Birth Anniv of Ferrante Gonzaga (soldier).

3058	**1405**	€1 multicoloured	4·00	2·50

1406 Foundation Office

2007. 20th Anniv of Fondazione Antonio Genovesi Salerno.

3059	**1406**	60c. multicoloured	2·40	1·50

1407 Refugees and Map of Sardinia

2007. 60th Anniv of Borgata Giuliana di Fertilia, Alghero (immigration of Italian speaking refugees from Istria and Dalmatia to Sardinia).

3060	**1407**	60c. multicoloured	2·40	1·50

1408 Father Lodovico Acernese

2007. Father Lodovico Acernese (founder of Congregation of the Franciscan Immaculatine Sisters) Commemoration.

3061	**1408**	23c. multicoloured	1·00	65

1409 Giosue Carducci

2007. Death Centenary of Giosue Carducci (1906—Nobel Prize for Literature winner).

3062	**1409**	60c. multicoloured	2·40	1·50

1410 Brescia University

2007

3063	**1410**	60c. multicoloured	2·40	1·50

1411 Stylized Woman and Child

2007. European Year of Equal Opportunities.

3064	**1411**	60c. multicoloured	2·40	1·50

1412 "Scipione Maffel" State High School

2007

3065	**1412**	60c. multicoloured	2·40	1·50

1413 Nicolo Carosio

2007. Birth Centenary of Nicolo Carosio (sports commentator).

3066	**1413**	65c. multicoloured	2·50	1·70

1414 Rialto Bridge and Gondola

2007. Venice–UNESCO World Heritage Site.

3067	**1414**	60c. black	2·40	1·50

1415 Mareccio Castle and Castell del Buonconsiglio (Trentino-Aldo Adige)

2007. Regions. Multicoloured.

3068		60c. Type **1415**	2·40	1·50
3069		60c. Asceli Piceno and "Bronzi Dorati da Cartoceto di Pergola" (statues) (Marche)	2·40	1·50
3070		60c. Orvieto Cathedral and "Annunciation" (mosaic) (Umbria)	2·40	1·50
3071		60c. Beach, flamingo and bronze statue (Sardinia)	2·40	1·50

1416 Circuit Board

2007. International Electro-technical Commission.

3072	**1416**	€1.50 multicoloured	6·00	3·75

1417 '50', Stylized Piazza del Campidoglio and Stars

2007. 50th Anniv of Treaty of Rome. Sheet 120×96 mm containing T 1417 and similar vert design. Multicoloured.

MS3073	60c. Type **1417**; 65c. 'INSIEME', stylized Piazza del Campidoglio and stars	5·00	3·25

The stamps of **MS**3073 form a composite design.

1418 Bishop's Castle, Brunico-Bruneck

2007. Tourist Publicity (34th series). Multicoloured.

3074		60c. Type **1418**	2·40	1·50
3075		60c. Castle, Gaeta	2·40	1·50
3076		60c. Medieval Castle, Massafra	2·40	1·50
3077		60c. Eraclea Minoa Amphitheatre, Cattolica Eraclea	2·40	1·50

1419 Giuseppe di Lampedusa and Il Gattopardo

2007. 50th Death Anniv of Giuseppe Tomasi de Lampedusa (writer).

3078	**1419**	60c. multicoloured	2·40	1·50

1420 Forum

2007. Rome–Capital City.

3079	**1420**	60c. multicoloured	2·40	1·50

1421 Scouts and Canoe

2007. Europa. Centenary of Scouting. Multicoloured.

3080		60c. Type **1421**	2·40	1·50
3081		65c. Scouts and campfire	2·50	1·70
MS3082		97×120 mm. Nos. 3080/1	5·00	3·25

1422 Duccio Galimberti

2007. Birth Centenary of Duccio Galimberti (resistance organiser).

3083	**1422**	60c. multicoloured	2·40	1·50

1423 Statues and Building Facade

2007. 50th Anniv of National Higher School for Economics and Finance.

3084	**1423**	€2.80 multicoloured	11·00	7·00

1424 Director, Camera and Building Facade

2007. 70th Anniv of Cinecitta Film Studios, Rome.

3085	**1424**	65c. multicoloured	2·50	1·70

1425 Polirone Monastery, Mantua

2007. Cultural Heritage.

3086	**1425**	60c. indigo	2·40	1·50

1426 Malatesta Castle, Montefiore

2007. Cultural Heritage.

3087	**1426**	60c. brown	2·40	1·50

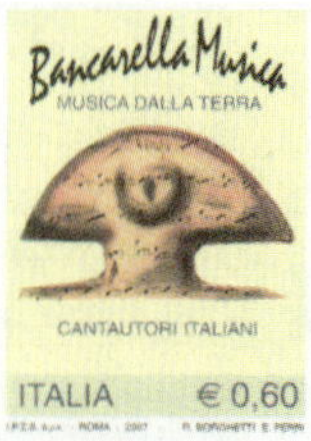

1427 Stele enclosing Musical Score

2007. Folk Music Project.

3088	**1427**	60c. multicoloured	2·40	1·50

1428 Lamborghini Emblem

2007. Made in Italy. Lamborghini Miura.
3089 **1428** 85c. multicoloured 3·25 2·20

1429 Player, Ball and Emblem

2007. Inter Football Club–Series A Champions.
3090 **1429** 60c. multicoloured 2·40 1·50

1430 Chianca Dolmen, Apulia

2007. Cultural Heritage.
3091 **1430** 60c. chestnut 2·40 1·50

1431 Luigi Ganna

2007. 50th Death Anniv of Luigi Ganna (cyclist, winner of first Giro d'Italia–1909).
3092 **1431** 60c. multicoloured 2·40 1·50

1432 Altiero Spinelli

2007. Birth Centenary of Altiero Spinelli (federalist).
3093 **1432** 60c. multicoloured 2·40 1·50

1433 Dancer and Rose Window, Spoleto Cathedral

2007. Festival dei Due Mondi (Festival of the Two Worlds) (annual music and opera festival), Spoleto.
3094 **1433** 60c. multicoloured 2·40 1·50

1434 Basilica, San Vincenzo in Galliano, Cantu

2007. Cultural Heritage. Birch wood. Self-adhesive.
3095 **1434** €2.80 brown 11·00 7·00

No. 3095 was printed on wooden sheets.

1435 Fiat 500

2007. Made in Italy.
3096 **1435** 60c. multicoloured 2·40 1·50

1436 Giuseppe Garibaldi

2007. Birth Bicentenary of Giuseppe Garibaldi (soldier and nationalist).
3097 **1436** 65c. multicoloured 2·50 1·70

1437 Maurizio Poggiali and Tornado Fighter Airplane

2007. 10th Death Anniv of Maurizio Poggiali (poet and pilot).
3098 **1437** 60c. multicoloured 2·40 1·50

1438 Caver, Stalactites, Stalagmites and Bat (club emblem)

2007. Speleological Club of Rome.
3099 **1438** €1.40 multicoloured 5·50 3·50

1439 Primo Carnera

2007. 40th Death Anniv of Primo Carnera (boxer).
3100 **1439** 60c. multicoloured 2·40 1·50

1440 Cloister, 'Marco Foscarini' Boarding School for Classical Studies

2007. Schools. Multicoloured.
3101 60c. Type **1440** 2·40 1·50
3102 60c. S.Pio V 2·40 1·50
3103 60c. Salerno Medical College 2·40 1·50

1441 Donkeys

2007. Italian Protected Donkey Breeds.
3104 **1441** 60c. multicoloured 2·40 1·50

1442 Player

2007. European Senior Women's Basketball Championship.
3105 **1442** 65c. multicoloured 2·50 1·70

1443 Sacra di San Michelle (abbey), Sant'Ambrogio di Torino

2007. Cultural Heritage.
3106 **1443** 60c. Indian red 2·40 1·50

1444 Concetto Marchesi

2007. 50th Death Anniv of Concetto Marchesi (Latin scholar, politician and writer).
3107 **1444** 60c. multicoloured 2·40 1·50

1445 Il Vignola and Scala Regia (royal stairs), Palazzo Farnese, Caprarola

2007. 400th Birth Anniv of Jacopo Barozzi da Vignola (Il Vignola) (architect).
3108 **1445** €2.80 multicoloured 11·00 7·00

1446 Children and Grandparents

2007. Grandparents Day.
3109 **1446** 60c. multicoloured 2·40 1·50

1447 Stamps as Figure

2007. Stamp Day.
3110 **1447** 60c. multicoloured 2·40 1·50

1448 *Cupid and Pscyche* (sculpture)

2007. 250th Birth Anniv of Antonio Canova (artist).
3111 **1448** €1.50 black 6·00 3·75

1449 Beniamino Gigli

2007. Entertainment Personalities' Anniversaries. Sheet 151×100 mm containing T 1449 and similar vert designs. Multicoloured.
MS3112 60c.×3, Type **1449** (tenor) (50th death anniv); Maria Callas (soprano) (30th death anniv); Amedeo Nazzari (actor) (birth centenary) 7·00 4·50

1450 Giuseppe di Vittorio

2007. 50th Death Anniv of Giuseppe di Vittorio (trade unionist and politician).
3113 **1450** 60c. multicoloured 2·40 1·50

1451 Anniversary Emblem

2007. Centenary of Mondadori (publishers).
3114 **1451** 60c. vermilion, black and gold 2·40 1·50

1452 *Madonna and Child* (Giovan Battista Cima Conegliano)

2007. Christmas (1st issue).
3115 **1452** 60c. olive 2·40 1·50

1453 Snow-covered House and Trees

2007. Christmas (2nd issue).
3116 **1453** 65c. multicoloured 2·50 1·70

1454 Soldier carrying Child

2007. Italy's Election as Temporary Member of UN Security Council.
3117 **1454** 85c. multicoloured 3·50 2·30

1455 Maritime and History Museum

2007. Fiume (now Croatian city of Rijeka).
3118 **1455** 65c. multicoloured 2·50 1·70

1456 '60'

2008. 60th Anniv of Constitution.
3119 **1456** 60c. multicoloured 2·50 1·60

1457 Nurses

2008. Centenary of Italian Red Cross Volunteer Nursing Corps.
3120 **1457** 60c. multicoloured 2·50 1·60

1458 Amintore Fanfani

2008. Birth Centenary of Amintore Fanfani (politician).
3121 **1458** €1 multicoloured 4·25 2·75

1459 Building Facade

2008. Bicentenary of Italian Stock Exchange.
3122 **1459** 65c. blue, light blue and brown 2·75 1·80

1460 Typewriter and Factory Building

2008. Centenary of Olivetti Typewriter Factory, Ivrea.
3123 **1460** 60c. multicoloured 2·50 1·60

1461 Villa Reale, Monza

2008. Death Bicentenary of Giuseppe Piermarini (architect).
3124 **1461** €1.40 blue and ultramarine 5·75 3·75

1462 Wheat, Cogwheels, Coin and Villa Lubin (headquarters), Rome

2008. 50th Anniv of National Council of Economics and Labour.
3125 **1462** €1.50 multicoloured 6·25 4·00

1463 Dorando Pietri winning Olympic Marathon, London, 1908

2008. Dorando Pietri (marathon runner) Commemoration.
3126 **1463** 60c. multicoloured 2·50 1·60

1464 Disc and Diver

2008. Nel blu dipinto de blu (song). Sheet 96×79 mm.
MS3127 60c. multicoloured 2·75 1·80

1465 Anna Magnani

2008. Birth Centenary of Anna Magnani (actor).
3128 **1465** 60c. multicoloured 2·50 1·60

1466 Emblem and La Scala Opera House, Milan

2008. Bicentenary of Ricordi Publishing House.
3129 **1466** 60c. black and grey 2·50 1·60

1467 Congress Centre, Rome

2008. Italia 2009 International Festival of Philately. Multicoloured.
3130 60c. Type **1467** 2·50 1·60
3131 65c. Colosseum 2·75 1·80

1468 Building Facade

2008. Carlo Combi High School, Capodistria.
3132 **1468** 60c. multicoloured 2·50 1·60

1469 Edmundo de Amicis

2008. Death Centenary of Edmundo de Amicis (writer).
3133 **1469** 60c. green and black 2·50 1·60

1470 *Self Portrait*

2008. Artistic and Cultural Heritage. Bernadino di Betto (Pintoricchio) (artist) Commemoration.
3134 **1470** 60c. multicoloured 2·50 1·60

1471 Madonna supported by Members of Confraternita di Santa Maria di Loreto

2008. Folklore. Feast of 'La Madonna che scappa in piazza', Sulmona.
3135 **1471** 60c. multicoloured 2·50 1·60

1472 Early Rowers

2008. 120th Anniv of National Rowing Federation.
3136 **1472** 65c. multicoloured 2·75 1·80

1473 *La Conferma della Regola* (from *The Life of Saint Francis* series of paintings by Giotto di Bondone
)

2008. 700th Anniv of the Franciscan Order.
3137 **1473** 60c. multicoloured 2·50 1·60

1474 Imperial Forum

2008. Rome–Capital City.
3138 **1474** 60c. multicoloured 2·50 1·60

1475 Newsletter No. 1

2008. Centenary of National Press Federation.
3139 **1475** 60c. grey and black 2·50 1·60

1476 *The Flight* (bronze statue) (Pasquale Basile) (campaign emblem)

2008. UNESCO International Decade of Education for Sustainable Development.
3140 **1476** €1.40 multicoloured 5·75 3·75

1477 *Giovannino Guareschi* (Arturo Coppola)

2008. Birth Centenary of Giovannino Guareschi (journalist, cartoonist and humorist).
3141 **1477** 60c. multicoloured 2·50 1·60

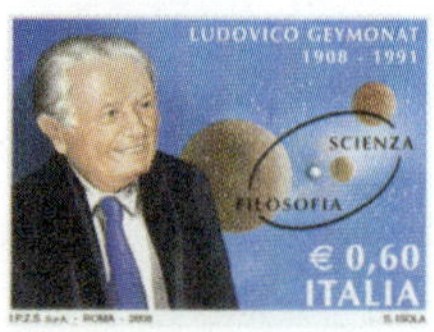

1478 Ludovico Geymonat

2008. Birth Centenary of Ludovico Geymonat (mathematician, historian and philosopher of science).
3142 **1478** 60c. multicoloured 2·50 1·60

1479 Post Box and Envelopes

2008. Europa. The Letter. Multicoloured.
3143 60c. Type **1479** 2·50 1·60
3144 65c. Brown post-box and envelopes 2·75 1·80

1480 Design for Bassano Bridge (Ponte Degli Alpini)

2008. 500th Birth Anniv of Andrea Palladio (architect).
3145 60c. brown, blue and black 2·50 1·60
3146 65c. chestnut and green 2·75 1·80
DESIGNS: 60c. Type **1480**; 65c. Palladian Basilica, Vincenza.

1480a Pope Sixtus V receiving Rule of Order from St Francis

2008. 400th Death Anniv of St Francis Caracciolo (Ascanio Pisquizio) (co-founder of Congregation of Minor Clerks Regular).
3146a **1480a** 60c. multicoloured 2·75 1·80

1481 Savoy Castle, Gressoney Saint Jean and Mount Cervino (Aosta Valley)

2008. Regions. Multicoloured.
3147 60c. Type **1481** 2·75 1·80
3148 60c. *Salome with the Head of John the Baptist* (Titian) and Lagoon City (Veneto) 2·75 1·80
3149 60c. Romanesque Fraterna Fountain, Piazza Celestino V (Molise) 2·75 1·80
3150 60c. Baroque cathedral facade (Sicily) 2·75 1·80

1482 School Building

2008. Guastalla Boarding School.
3151 **1482** 60c. blue 2·75 1·80

1483 Motorcyclist riding Ducati Desmosedici GP7

2008. Ducati Motorcycle.
3152 **1483** 60c. multicoloured 2·75 1·80

1484 Giacomo Puccini

2008. 150th Birth Anniv of Giacomo Puccini.
3153 **1484** €1.50 multicoloured 6·75 4·50

1485 Player wearing Centenary Shirt and Emblem of 16th Victory

2008. Inter–Italian Football Championship 2008–Serie A Winners.
3154 **1485** 60c. multicoloured 2·75 1·80

1486 Torch Relay Runner on Globe

2008. Olympic Games, Beijing. Stylized ceramic plates. Multicoloured.
3155 60c. Type **1486** 2·75 1·80
3156 85c. Greek and Asian athletes 3·75 2·50

1487 Tommaso Landolfi

2008. Birth Centenary of Tommaso Landolfi (writer).
3157 **1487** 60c. multicoloured 2·75 1·80

1488 Dolomite Mountains, Tre Cime di Lavaredo

2008. Tourist Publicity (35th series). Multicoloured.
3158 60c. Type **1488** 2·75 1·80
3159 60c. Mt. Epomeo and port, Casamicciola Terme 2·75 1·80
3160 60c. Medieval tower and Introdacqua village 2·75 1·80
3161 60c. Mamuthones 2·75 1·80

1489 Stigmas and Flowers of *Crocus sativus*

2008. Made in Italy. Zafferano dell'Aquila (saffron from L'Aquila).
3162 **1489** 60c. multicoloured 2·75 1·80

1490 Ingredients

2008. Made in Italy. Spaghetti all'amatriciana Festival.
3163 **1490** 60c. multicoloured 2·75 1·80

1491 Bell Tower, Treviglio

2008. Cultural Heritage.
3164 **1491** 60c. indigo 2·75 1·80

1492 Dante Alighieri High School, Gorizia

2008. Universities and Schools. Multicoloured.
3165 60c. Type **1492** 2·75 1·80
3166 60c. Statue of San Ercolano and griffin (images from official seal), University of Perugia 2·75 1·80

1493 Cesare Pavese and Script

2008. Birth Centenary of Cesare Pavese (writer).
3167 **1493** 65c. black, vermilion and blue 3·00 2·00

1494 *Alberico Gentili* (sculpture by Giuseppe Guastalla)

2008. 400th Birth Anniv of Alberico Gentili (jurist; regius professor of civil law, University of Oxford and one of the first writers on public international law).
3168 **1494** 65c. multicoloured 3·00 2·00

1495 Malatestiana Library, Cesena

2008. Cultural Heritage.
3169 **1495** 60c. black 2·75 1·80

1496 Emblem

2008. Union Cycliste Internationale Road World Championships, Varese.
3170 **1496** 60c. multicoloured 2·75 1·70

1497 Stamps as Map of Italy

2008. Stamp Day.
3171 **1497** 60c. multicoloured 3·25 2·30

1498 Mouth of Truth (1st–century mask, Church of Santa Maria, Rome)

2008. Italia–2009 International Stamp Exhibition. Multicoloured. (a) Ordinary gum.
3172 85c. Type **1498** 4·75 3·25

(b) Self-adhesive.
3173 €2.80 Mouth of Truth 15·00 10·50

1499 Traffic Policeman

2008. Local Police Force.
3174 **1499** 60c. multicoloured 3·25 2·30

1500 *Les Gracques* (sculpture) (Eugene Guillaume)

2008. 2500th Anniv of Roman Republic's People's Tribune.
3175 **1500** 60c. multicoloured 3·25 2·30

1501 *Madonna and Child Enthroned with Two Angels* (Lorenzo di Credi)

2008. Christmas. Multicoloured. (a) Ordinary gum.
3176 60c. Type **1501** 3·25 2·30

(b) Self-adhesive.
3177 €2.80 Wreath 15·00 10·50

1502 Val d' Orcia

2008. World Heritage Sites.
3178 – 60c. green and mauve 3·25 1·70
3179 – €2.80 blue 4·50 2·25
DESIGNS: 60c. Type **1502**; €2.80 Historical Centre, Urbino.

1503 Epicentre

2008. Centenary of Messina Earthquake.
3180 **1503** 60c. multicoloured 3·25 1·70

1504 Cover of First Issue

2008. Centenary of Corriere dei Piccoli (weekly magazine for children).
3181 **1504** 60c. multicoloured 3·25 2·30

1505 Charles Darwin

2009. Birth Bicentenary of Charles Robert Darwin (naturalist and evolutionary theorist).
3182 **1505** 65c. multicoloured 3·50 2·40

1506 Moonlight

2009. Tintarella di Luna (song). Sheet 96×80 mm.
MS3183 multicoloured 3·25 2·30

1507 Father Oreste Benzi, Carlo Valenzi and Vincenzo Muccioli

2009. National Conference on Drugs, Trieste.
3184 **1507** 60c. multicoloured 3·00 2·20

1508 Stamps and Exhibition Visitors (pink background)

2009. Italia 2009–International Stamp Exhibition, Rome. Multicoloured.
3185 60c. Type **1508** 3·00 2·20
3186 €1 Stamps and exhibition visitors (blue-grey background) 5·25 2·50

1509 Rock Engraving, Camonica Valley

2009. Cultural Heritage.
3187 **1509** €2.80 brown 14·50 10·00

1510 Don Primo Mazzolari

2009. 50th Death Anniv of Don Primo Mazzolari (writer and partisan).
3188 **1510** 60c. multicoloured 3·00 2·20

1511 Soldiers

2009. 350th Anniv of Grenadier Corps of Sardinia.
3189 **1511** 60c. multicooured 3·00 2·20

1512 Plazza di Spagna

2009. Rome–Capital City.
3190 **1512** 60c. multicoloured 3·00 2·20

1513 Indro Montanelli and Typewriter

2009. Birth Centenary of Indro Montanelli (journalist).
3191 **1513** 60c. multicoloured 3·00 2·20

1514 Necklace

2009. Made in Italy. 125th Anniv of Bvlgari (jewellery maker).
3192 **1514** 60c. multicoloured 3·00 2·20

1515 Swiss and Italian Flags

2009. Centenary of Italian Chamber of Commerce for Switzerland.
3193 **1515** 60c. multicoloured 3·00 2·20

1516 Division Arms

2009. 40th Anniv of Carabinieri Division for Protection of Cultural Heritage.
3194 **1516** 60c. multicoloured 3·00 2·20

1517 Map and Stylized Athletes

2009. Mediterranean Games.
3195 **1517** 60c. multicoloured 3·00 2·20

1518 European Parliament Headquarters, Strasbourg and Stars

2009. European Parliamentary Elections.
3196 **1518** 60c. multicoloured 3·00 2·20

1519 Italian Galileo Telescope, La Palma, Canary Islands

2009. Europa. Astronomy. Multicoloured.
3197 60c. Type **1519** 3·00 2·20
3198 65c. Satellite *AGILE* and Earth 3·25 2·30

1520 Early Cyclist

2009. Centenary of Giro d'Italia (cycle race).
3199 **1520** 60c. multicoloured 3·00 2·20

1521 Johann von Goethe and Dnate Alighieri (logo)

2009. 50th Anniv of Academy of Italian–German Studies, Merano.
3200 **1521** 60c. multicoloured 3·00 2·20

1522 Alfa Romeo 6C 1500 Gran Sport

2009. Mille Miglia (thousand miles (open-road endurance race which took place from 1927 to 1957)).
3201 **1522** 60c. multicoloured 3·00 2·20

1523 Carrying 'Ingegno' of Sant'Antonio Abate

2009. Festival of Mysteries, Campobasso.
3202 **1523** 60c. multicoloured 3·00 2·20

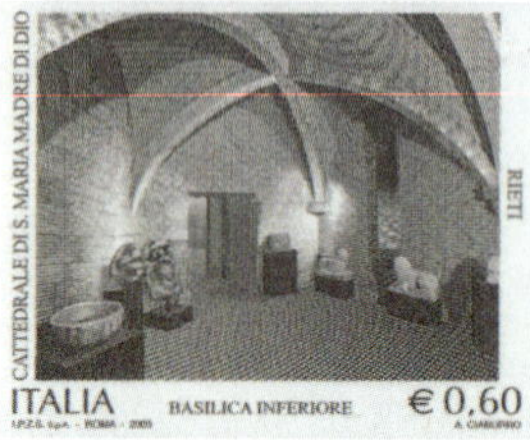

1524 Santa Maria Madre di Dio in Rieti Cathedral

2009. Cultural Heritage.
3203 **1524** 60c. black 2·75 2·10

1525 Giovanni Palatucci

2009. Birth Centenary of Giovanni Palatucci (police chief).
3204 **1525** 60c. multicoloured 2·75 2·10

1526 Gilera VT 317 (reconstruction of first motorbike made by Gilera)

2009. Centenary of Gilera (motorcycle manufacturer).
3205 **1526** 60c. multicoloured 2·75 2·10

1527 1859 1/2g. Stamp of Sicily (As Type 1) and Handstamp

2009. 150th Anniv of First Stamps in Sicily.
3206 **1527** 60c. multicoloured 2·75 1·40

1528 Player

2009. Baseball World Cup. Sheet 80×60 mm.
MS3207 multicoloured 2·75 1·40

1529 Saint John Leonardi

2009. 400th Death Anniv of Saint John Leonardi (San Giovanni Leonardi) (founder of Clerks Regular of the Mother of God of Lucca).

3208	**1529**	60c. multicoloured	2·75	1·40

1530 Player

2009. Italian Football Championship (Inter 2009).

3209	**1530**	60c. multicoloured	2·75	1·40

1531 Ham and San Daniele del Friuli

2009. Made in Italy. San Daniele Ham.

3210	**1531**	60c. multicoloured	2·75	1·40

1532 St. Marks Square

2009. St. Marks Square (SMS) Venice Project

3211	**1532**	60c. black and indigo	2·75	1·40

1533 Envelope

2009. Posta Italiana (Italian Mail). Self adhesive.

3212	**1533**	60c. multicoloured	2·75	1·40
3213	**1533**	€1.40 multicoloured	5·75	2·75
3214	**1533**	€1.50 multicoloured	5·75	2·75
3215	**1533**	€2 multicoloured	8·50	4·00

1534 Women

2009. 65th Anniv of Insurrection of Women of Carrara.

3216	**1534**	€1.50 multicoloured	6·75	3·50

1535 Summit Emblem

2009. G8 Summit, L'Aquila.

3217	**1535**	65c. multicoloured	3·25	1·60

1536 Piazza Sant'Agostino and Ligurian Coast, Verezzi

2009. Tourist Publicity (36th series). Multicoloured.

3218	60c. Type **1536**	75	40
3219	60c. Lighthouse and Port Giglio, Giglio Island	75	40
3220	60c. Headland and typical vegetation, Costa degli Dei–Capo Vaticano	75	40
3221	60c. Narrow lava walls, Alcantara Gorges	75	40

1537 Vintage Advertising Poster

2009. 150th Anniv of La Nazione Newspaper, Florence.

3222	**1537**	60c. multicoloured	3·00	1·50

1538 Freestyle Swimmer

2009. 13th World Aquatics Championships, Italy.

3223	**1538**	€1.50 steel blue	6·75	3·50

1539 Living and Burnt Forest

2009. Measures to Prevent and Fight Fires.

3224	**1539**	60c. multicoloured	3·00	1·50

1540 '30' enclosing Dove

2009. 30th (2010) Meeting for Friendship Among Peoples, Rimini.

3225	**1540**	60c. bright emerald	3·00	1·50

1541 *Ufficiali e tromba dei Cavalleggeri di Montebello* (Antonio Cervi)

2009. 150th Anniv of Lancieri di Montebello Cavalry Regiment.

3226	**1541**	60c. multicoloured	3·00	1·50

1542 *San Gennaro* (Francesco Solimena)

2009. Artistic and Cultural Heritage. Museum of Treasure of San Gennaro, Naples.

3227	**1542**	60c. multicoloured	6·75	3·50

1543 Library and Picture Gallery Building, Milan and *Portrait of a Lady* (Giovanni Ambrogio de Predis)

2009. Artistic and Cultural Heritage. Ambrosian Academy Library and Picture Gallery, Milan.

3228	**1543**	€1.40 black	6·75	3·50

1544 Emilio Alessandrini

2009. 30th Death Anniv of Emilio Alessandrini (magistrate).

3229	**1544**	60c. multicoloured	3·00	1·50

1545 Cross and Map of Europe

2009. Patron Saints of Europe. Sheet 126×126 mm containing T 1545 and similar horiz design. Multicoloured.

MS3230 60c. Type **1545**; 65c. As Type **1545** with colours reversed 3·00 3·00

1546 Early and Modern Front Page

2009. 120th Anniv of L'Union Sarda Newspaper.

3231	**1546**	60c. multicoloured	3·00	1·50

1547 Luigi Sturzo

2009. 50th Death Anniv of Luigi Sturzo (Catholic priest and politician).

3232	**1547**	€1.50 salmon-pink and bistre-brown	7·00	3·50

1548 Norberto Bobbio

2009. Birth Centenary of Norberto Bobbio (philosopher of law and political sciences and historian of political thought).

3233	**1548**	65c. multicoloured	3·00	1·50

1549 Fathers Giovanni Minozzi and Giovanni Semeria

2009. Father Giovanni Semeria and Father Giovanni Minozzi (founders of Opera Nazionale per il Mezzogiorno d'Italia (poverty and war orphans charity)) Commemoration.

3234	**1549**	60c. multicoloured	3·00	1·50

1550 Envelopes surrounding School

2009. Stamp Day.

3235	**1550**	60c. multicoloured	3·00	1·50

1551 Dante and Virgil and Three Wild Beasts (from 15th-century Codex Urbinate Latino 365, Vatican Apostolic Library)

2009. Italia 2009 International Stamp Exhibition, Rome. Italian Language.

3236	**1551**	60c. multicoloured	3·00	1·50

A stamp of a similar design was issued by San Marino and Vatican City.

1552 Gino Bartali (cyclist, twice winner of Giro d'Italia)

2009. Italia 2009. Sports Day. Multicoloured.

3237	60c. Type **1552**	2·25	1·10
3238	65c. Valentino Mazzola (footballer, captain of Grande Torino)	2·25	1·10
3239	€1.40 Michele Alboreto beside a Ferrari F1 156/85 (1997–24 Hours of Le Mans and 2001–12 Hours of Sebring winner)	2·25	1·10

1553 Flags as Pen and Ink

2009. 130th Anniv of Italy–Bulgaria Diplomatic Relations. Sheet 101×71 mm.

MS3240 multicoloured	2·75	2·75

1554 *Coccobill* (Benito Franco Jacovitti)

2009. Italia 2009. Collectors' Day. Italian Comics. Sheet 80×120 mm containing T 1554 and similar horiz designs. Multicoloured.

MS3241 €1×3, Type **1554**; *Diabolik* (Angela and Luciana Giussani); *Lupo Alberto* (Guido Silvestri (Silver))	5·25	5·25

1555 *The Adoration of the Shepherds* (Domenico Piola)

2009. Christmas (1st issue).

3242	**1555**	60c. multicoloured	3·00	1·50

1556 Bauble, Star and Moon

2009. Christmas (2nd issue). Self-adhesive.

3243	**1556**	60c. multicoloured	3·00	1·50

1557 Luciano Pavarotti (tenor)

2009. Italia 2009. Music Day. Multicoloured.

3244	65c. Type **1557**	3·00	1·50
3245	€1 Mino Reitano (singer and actor)	2·00	1·50
3246	€1.50 Nino Rota (musician and composer)	5·50	2·75

1558 Pont du Gard, France

2009. Italia 2009. Europe Day. Multicoloured. Self-adhesive.

3247	65c. Type **1558**	1·50	75
3248	65c. Hadrian's Wall, Great Britain	1·50	75
3249	65c. Odeon of Patras, Greece	1·50	75
3250	65c. Porta Nigra, Trier, Germany	1·50	75
3251	65c. Aqueduct of Segovia, Spain	1·50	75

1559 *Guantanamera* (sculpture) (Giacomo Manzù)

2009. Art. Italian Masters of the 20th Century. Multicoloured.

3252	60c. Type **1559**	3·00	1·50
3253	65c. *The Bear Dance* (Gino Severini)	3·25	1·70
3254	85c. *Donna e Ambiente* (Federico De Pistoris)	3·75	1·90

2009. Posta Italiana (Italian Mail). Self adhesive.

3255	**1533**	€3.30 multicoloured	13·00	7·50

CONCESSIONAL LETTER POST

CL93 Arms of Savoy and Fasces

1928

CL227	**CL93**	10c. blue	3·25	20

CL109 Arms and Fasces

1930

CL267	**CL109**	10c. brown	10	15

1945. No. CL267, surch with Royal Arms (obliterating fasces) and new value.

CL647	40c. on 10c. brown	1·10	1·30

1945. As Type CL 109, but Arms redrawn without fasces.

CL648	10c. brown	55	55
CL649	1l. brown	7·50	3·25

CL201 Italia

1947

CL687	**CL201**	1l. green	1·30	40
CL688	**CL201**	8l. red	36·00	40

CL220 Italia

1948

CL734	**CL220**	15l. violet	£150	20
CL916	**CL220**	20l. violet	30	25
CL917	**CL220**	30l. green	30	25
CL918	**CL220**	35l. brown	30	25
CL919	**CL220**	110l. blue	30	25
CL920	**CL220**	270l. mauve	80	25
CL921	**CL220**	300l. green & pink	65	30
CL922	**CL220**	370l. brown & orge	80	35

CONCESSIONAL PARCEL POST

CP288

1953

CP850	**CP288**	75l. sepia	6·50	50·00
CP851	**CP288**	110l. red	6·50	65·00
CP918	**CP288**	40l. orange	20	55
CP919	**CP288**	50l. blue	20	55
CP920	**CP288**	60l. violet	1·10	3·50
CP921	**CP288**	70l. green	4·50	13·00
CP923	**CP288**	80l. brown	10	10
CP924	**CP288**	90l. lilac	10	10
CP926	**CP288**	110l. yellow	10	10
CP927	**CP288**	120l. green	10	10
CP928	**CP288**	140l. black	20	10
CP929	**CP288**	150l. red	30	35
CP930	**CP288**	180l. red	10	35
CP931	**CP288**	240l. slate	10	35
CP932	**CP288**	500l. brown	55	1·10
CP933	**CP288**	600l. turquoise	55	1·10
CP934	**CP288**	900l. blue	55	1·10

Unused prices are for the complete pair. Used prices are for the left half; right halves are worth more.

CP707

1984

CP1849	**CP707**	3000l. blue and red	4·00	4·00

EXPRESS LETTER STAMPS

E35

1903. For inland letters.

E73	**E35**	25c. red	48·00	1·60
E113	**E35**	50c. red	2·10	2·10
E129	**E35**	60c. red	5·25	1·10
E178	**E35**	70c. red	55	45
E179	**E35**	1l.25 blue	55	10

E41 King Victor Emmanuel III

1908. For foreign letters.

E80	**E41**	30c. blue and pink	1·10	4·25
E180	**E41**	2l. blue and pink	4·25	60·00
E181	**E41**	2l.50 blue and pink	3·25	5·25

E59

1917. Surch 25 and bars.

E112	**E59**	25c. on 40c. violet	37·00	90·00

1921. Surch with new value.

E118	**E41**	L.1.20 on 30c. blue and pink	1·10	19·00
E173	**E41**	L.1.60 on 1l.20 blue and pink	1·60	60·00

1922. Surch in words and figures.

E122	**E35**	60c. on 50c. red	35·00	2·40
E172	**E35**	70c. on 60c. red	1·10	1·10

E131 "Garibaldi" (statue), Savoia Marchetti S-55A Flying Boat and "Anita Garibaldi" (statue)

1932. Air. 50th Death Anniv of Garibaldi.

E348	**E131**	2l.25+1l. violet and red	10·50	60·00
E349	**E131**	4l.50+1l.50 brown and green	10·50	60·00

E132 King Victor Emmanuel III

1932

E350	**E132**	1l.25 green	20	25
E351	**E132**	2l.50 orange	30	4·50

1932. 10th Anniv of March on Rome. As T 132. (a) For inland letters. Inscribed "ESPRESSO".

E368	1l.25 green	2·10	2·10

(b) For foreign letters. Inscribed "EXPRES".

E369	2l.50 orange	6·50	£160

DESIGNS: 1l.25, Roman road; 2l.50, Flags and head of Mussolini.

E133 Savoia Marchetti S-55A Flying Boat

1933. Air.

E370	**E133**	2l. black	10	3·25
E371	**E133**	2l.25 black	4·75	£160

1934. Air. 10th Anniv of Annexation of Fiume. Inscr as in T 141.

E408	2l.+1l.25 blue	1·10	32·00
E409	2l.25+1l.25 green	2·10	27·00
E410	4l.50+2l. red	2·10	27·00

DESIGN: Foundation of Fiume.

1934. Air. Military Medal Centenary. Inscr as in T 146.

E442	2l.+1l.25 brown	6·50	43·00
E443	4l.50+2l. red	10·50	43·00

DESIGN—HORIZ: 2l., 4l.50, Caproni Ca 101 airplane over triumphal arch.

E192 Italia

1945

E647	**E192**	5l. red	30	1·30

E200 Winged Foot of Mercury

1945

E679	**E200**	5l. red	10	10
E680	-	10l. blue	50	55
E681	-	15l. red	5·25	15
E682	**E200**	25l. orange	60·00	10
E683	**E200**	30l. violet	4·25	2·10
E685	-	60l. red	80·00	15
E915	**E200**	50l. purple	10·00	30

DESIGN: 10, 15, 60l. Horse and torch bearer.

E209 Rising at Naples

1948. Centenary of 1848 Revolution.

E718	**E209**	35l. violet	£190	25·00

E341 Etruscan Horses

1958

E961	**E341**	75l. purple	30	10
E1220	**E341**	150l. green	20	10
E1221	**E341**	250l. blue & light blue	35	15
E1222	**E341**	300l. brown & lt brn	40	15

MILITARY POST STAMPS

1943. Stamps of Italy optd P.M. (a) Postage stamps of 1929 (Nos. 239/56).

M583	5c. brown	45	2·10
M584	10c. brown	45	2·10
M585	15c. green	45	2·10
M586	20c. red	45	2·10
M587	25c. green	45	2·10
M588	30c. brown	45	2·10
M589	50c. violet	45	2·10
M590	1l. violet	3·00	16·00
M591	1l.25 blue	45	3·25
M592	1l.75 orange	45	3·25
M593	2l. red	45	3·25
M594	5l. red	45	3·75
M595	10l. violet	45	21·00

(b) Air stamps of 1930 (Nos. 271/7).

M596	50c. brown	45	2·10
M597	1l. violet	45	2·40
M598	2l. blue	45	10·50
M599	5l. green	3·25	14·00
M600	10l. red	3·25	19·00

(c) Air Express stamp of 1933 (No. E370).

M601	2l. black	3·25	27·00

(d) Express Letter stamp of 1932 (No. E350).

M602	1l.25 green	45	16·00

NEWSPAPER STAMPS

N2

1862. Imperf.

N5	**N2**	2c. yellow	60·00	£130

For similar stamps in black, see Sardinia.

OFFICIAL STAMPS

O11

1875

O21	**O11**	2c. red	2·10	4·25
O22	**O11**	5c. red	2·10	4·25
O23	**O11**	20c. red	1·10	2·10
O24	**O11**	30c. red	1·10	3·25
O25	**O11**	1l. red	4·25	13·00
O26	**O11**	2l. red	21·00	37·00
O27	**O11**	5l. red	95·00	£160
O28	**O11**	10l. red	£170	£130

1934. Air. Optd SERVIZIO DI STATO.

O450	**148**	10l. grey	£900	£13000

PARCEL POST STAMPS

P13 King Umberto I

1884. Various frames.

P38	**P13**	10c. grey	£200	£100
P39	**P13**	20c. blue	£375	£180
P40	**P13**	50c. pink	21·00	15·00
P41	**P13**	75c. green	21·00	15·00
P42	**P13**	1l.25 orange	41·00	34·00
P43	**P13**	1l.75 brown	41·00	£140

The left-hand portion of the following parcel post stamps is affixed to the packet-card, the right-hand portion to the receipt. Unused prices are for the complete pair and used prices for the half-stamp. Unsevered stamps in used condition are usually from cancelled-to-order material and are worth more than the half-stamp.

P53

1914

P96	**P53**	5c. brown	1·10	6·50
P97	**P53**	10c. blue	1·10	6·50
P98	**P53**	20c. black	1·10	6·50
P99	**P53**	25c. red	2·10	6·50
P100	**P53**	50c. orange	2·10	19·00
P101	**P53**	1l. violet	2·10	6·50
P102	**P53**	2l. green	5·25	8·50
P103	**P53**	3l. yellow	7·50	21·00
P104	**P53**	4l. grey	16·00	27·00
P105	**P53**	10l. purple	43·00	27·00
P106	**P53**	12l. brown	£150	£300
P107	**P53**	15l. olive	£150	£300
P108	**P53**	20l. purple	£120	£300

1923. Surch with figures on left half and words and figures on right half.

P146	30c. on 5c. brown	1·10	16·00
P147	60c. on 5c. brown	1·10	16·00
P148	1l.50 on 5c. brown	4·25	£110
P149	3l. on 10l. purple	4·25	65·00

P92

1927

P217	**P92**	5c. brown	1·10	2·10
P218	**P92**	10c. blue	1·10	2·10
P219	**P92**	25c. red	1·10	2·10
P220	**P92**	30c. blue	1·10	3·25
P221	**P92**	50c. orange	1·10	2·10
P222	-	60c. red	1·10	3·25
P223	**P92**	1l. violet	1·10	3·25
P224	**P92**	2l. green	1·10	3·25
P225	**P92**	3l. bistre	1·10	7·50
P226	**P92**	4l. black	1·10	7·50
P227	**P92**	10l. purple	3·25	32·00
P228	**P92**	20l. purple	5·25	43·00

The value in the right-hand portion of the 60c. is in figures.

1945. Optd with ornamental device obliterating Fascist emblems in centre.

P647		5c. brown	2·75	2·75
P648		10c. blue	2·75	2·75
P649		25c. red	2·75	2·75
P650		30c. blue	27·00	8·00
P651		50c. orange	2·75	2·75
P652	-	60c. red	2·75	2·75
P653	**P92**	1l. violet	2·75	2·75
P654	**P92**	2l. green	2·75	2·75
P655	**P92**	3l. bistre	2·75	2·75
P656	**P92**	4l. black	2·75	2·75
P657	**P92**	10l. purple	27·00	27·00
P658	**P92**	20l. purple	55·00	55·00

1946. As Type P 92, but without fasces between stamps.

P679	1l. mauve	2·10	55
P680	2l. green	2·10	55
P681	3l. orange	3·25	1·60
P682	4l. black	4·25	1·60
P683	10l. purple	£110	27·00
P684	20l. purple	£160	70·00

P201

1946

P687a	**P201**	25c. blue	10	10
P688	**P201**	50c. brown	60	20
P689	**P201**	1l. brown	60	20
P690	**P201**	2l. blue	1·90	50
P691	**P201**	3l. orange	70	20
P692	**P201**	4l. grey	13·00	4·75
P910	**P201**	5l. purple	10	10
P911	**P201**	10l. violet	10	10
P912	**P201**	20l. purple	10	10
P914	**P201**	40l. violet	10	10
P915	**P201**	50l. red	10	10
P916	**P201**	60l. violet	10	10
P917	**P201**	100l. blue	10	10
P918	**P201**	140l. red	10	10
P919	**P201**	150l. brown	10	10
P920	**P201**	200l. green	10	10
P921	**P201**	280l. yellow	35	20
P922	**P201**	300l. purple	35	20
P923	**P201**	400l. black	55	30
P924	**P201**	500l. brown	1·60	45
P925	**P201**	600l. brown	1·30	55
P926	**P201**	700l. blue	2·20	30
P927	**P201**	800l. orange	2·75	30
P1348	**P201**	30l. purple	20	20

P298

1954

P928a	**P298**	1000l. blue	1·00	75
P929	**P298**	2000l. red and brown	5·00	55

PNEUMATIC POST LETTERS

PE53

1913

PE96	**PE53**	10c. brown	3·25	19·00
PE97	**PE53**	15c. lilac	3·25	24·00
PE98	**PE53**	30c. blue	13·00	£110
PE191	**PE53**	15c. pink	4·25	13·00
PE192	**PE53**	15c. purple	4·25	13·00
PE193	**PE53**	20c. purple	16·00	37·00
PE194	**PE53**	35c. red	19·00	£325
PE195	**PE53**	40c. red	27·00	£225

1924. Surch.

PE165	15c. on 10c. brown	4·25	24·00
PE166	15c. on 20c. purple	10·50	43·00
PE167	20c. on 10c. brown	8·50	40·00
PE168	20c. on 15c. lilac	10·50	24·00
PE169	35c. on 40c. red	21·00	£180
PE170	40c. on 30c. blue	10·50	£160

PE134 Galileo Galilei

1933

PE372	-	15c. purple	30	80
PE373	**PE134**	35c. red	30	80

DESIGN: 15c. Dante Alighieri.

1945. As Type PE 134, but inscr "ITALIA" instead of "REGNO D'ITALIA".

PE679	-	60c. brown (Dante)	55	1·60
PE680	**PE134**	1l.40 blue	55	1·60

PE204 Minerva

1947

PE694	**PE204**	3l. purple	9·00	8·75
PE695	**PE204**	5l. blue	55	15
PE961	**PE204**	10l. red	20	20
PE962	**PE204**	20l. blue	20	20

POSTAGE DUE STAMPS

D3

1863. Imperf.

D6B	**D3**	10c. yellow	£110	£250

FOOTNOTE: Our price for mint stamps is for stamps without gum. Stamps with gum are worth considerably more.

D11

1869. Perf.

D21	**D11**	10c. brown	£4750	65·00

D12

1870

D22	**D12**	1c. mauve and orange	6·50	16·00
D23	**D12**	2c. mauve and orange	17·00	30·00
D24	**D12**	5c. mauve and orange	1·60	1·10
D25	**D12**	10c. mauve and orange	1·60	1·10
D26	**D12**	20c. mauve and orange	16·00	1·10
D27	**D12**	30c. mauve and orange	4·75	1·30
D28	**D12**	40c. mauve and orange	4·75	3·75
D29	**D12**	50c. mauve and orange	4·75	1·10
D30		60c. mauve and orange	£200	4·25
D31		60c. brown and orange	32·00	15·00
D32		1l. brown and blue	£6500	27·00
D33		1l. mauve and blue	27·00	1·60
D34		2l. brown and blue	£6500	43·00
D35		2l. mauve and blue	65·00	6·50
D36		5l. brown and blue	£550	48·00
D37		5l. mauve and blue	£190	32·00
D38		10l. brown and blue	£9000	48·00
D39		10l. mauve and blue	£180	8·50

D13

1884

D40	**D13**	50l. green	95·00	55·00
D41	**D13**	100l. red	75·00	21·00
D73	**D13**	50l. yellow	95·00	55·00
D74	**D13**	100l. blue	75·00	21·00

(D 20)

1890. Surch over numeral as Type D 20.

D47	**D12**	10(c.) on 2c. (D23)	£130	37·00
D48	**D12**	20(c.) on 1c. (D22)	£550	27·00
D49	**D12**	30(c.) on 2c. (D23)	£1700	10·50

D141

D142

1934. With Fascist emblems.

D395	**D141**	5c. brown	55	60
D396	**D141**	10c. blue	55	60
D397	**D141**	20c. red	55	60
D398	**D141**	25c. green	55	60
D399	**D141**	30c. orange	55	60
D400	**D141**	40c. brown	55	3·25
D401	**D141**	50c. violet	55	60
D402	**D141**	60c. blue	55	7·50
D403	**D142**	1l. orange	55	60
D404	**D142**	2l. green	55	60
D405	**D142**	5l. violet	2·10	1·10
D406	**D142**	10l. blue	3·25	4·25
D407	**D142**	20l. red	5·25	15·00

D191

D192

1945. Fascist emblems removed.

D630	**D191**	5c. brown	2·75	2·10
D631	**D191**	10c. blue	75	1·10
D632	**D191**	20c. red	2·75	1·10
D633	**D191**	25c. green	75	1·10
D634	**D191**	30c. orange	75	1·10
D635	**D191**	40c. black	75	1·10
D636	**D191**	50c. violet	75	1·10
D637	**D191**	60c. blue	75	2·10
D639	**D192**	2l. green	75	1·10
D640	**D192**	5l. violet	75	1·10
D641	**D192**	10l. blue	75	1·10
D642	**D192**	20l. red	75	1·10
D685	**D192**	1l. orange	75	10

D201

1947

D690	**D201**	1l. orange	30	10
D691	**D201**	2l. green	65	10
D692	**D201**	3l. red	1·60	2·10
D693	**D201**	4l. brown	1·90	2·10
D695	**D201**	6l. blue	8·00	2·10
D696	**D201**	8l. mauve	30·00	3·25
D698	**D201**	12l. brown	10·50	2·10
D924	**D201**	5l. violet	20	15
D926	**D201**	10l. blue	20	15
D927	**D201**	20l. purple	20	15
D928	**D201**	25l. red	20	15
D929	**D201**	30l. purple	20	15
D930	**D201**	40l. brown	20	15
D931	**D201**	50l. green	20	15
D932	**D201**	100l. orange	20	15
D935	**D201**	500l. red and blue	1·70	55
D936	**D201**	500l. purple and blue	90	30
D937	**D201**	900l. mve, blk & grn	2·00	55
D938	**D201**	1500l. orange & brown	2·40	75

PUBLICITY ENVELOPE STAMPS

1921. Optd B.L.P.

B115	**39**	40c. brown	£110	27·00
B129	**37**	10c. red	£150	£110
B132	**39**	25c. blue	£150	£120
B134	**39**	50c. violet	£750	£750
B135	**39**	60c. red	£2750	£2250
B136	**34**	1l. brown and green	£4250	£2750
B137	**37**	15c. grey	£130	80·00
B138	**41**	20c. orange	£400	£500
B140	**39**	30c. brown	£275	£190
B141	**39**	85c. brown	£350	£500

ITALIAN SOCIAL REPUBLIC

Following the surrender of Italy on 3 September 1943, and his rescue from imprisonment on 12 September, Mussolini proclaimed the Italian Social Republic at Salo on 23 September 1943. From this town on Lake Garda the Republican government administered those parts of Italy, north of the Gustav Line, which were under German occupation.

1944. Stamps of Italy optd G. N. R. (a) Postage. (i) Nos. 239 and 241/59.

1	**98**	5c. brown	3·25	6·50
2	-	10c. brown	3·25	6·50
3	-	15c. green	3·25	6·50
4	**99**	20c. red	3·25	10·50
5	-	25c. green	3·25	6·50
6	**103**	30c. brown	3·25	6·50
7	-	35c. blue	£140	£225
8	**103**	50c. violet	3·25	10·50
9	-	75c. red	3·25	6·50
10	**99**	1l. violet	3·25	6·50
11	-	1l.25 blue	3·25	6·50
12	-	1l.75 red	6·50	37·00
13	-	2l. red	10·50	37·00
14	**98**	2l.55 green	55·00	£275
15	**98**	3l.70 violet	43·00	£190
16	**98**	5l. red	9·50	43·00
17	-	10l. violet	95·00	£350
18	**99**	20l. green	£275	£550
19	-	25l. black	£750	£1700
20	-	50l. violet	£600	£1700

(ii) War Propaganda issue. Nos. 563/74.

21	25c. green (Navy)	8·50	21·00
22	25c. green (Army)	8·50	21·00
23	25c. green (Air Force)	8·50	21·00
24	25c. green (Militia)	8·50	21·00
25	30c. brown (Navy)	8·50	43·00
26	30c. brown (Army)	8·50	43·00
27	30c. brown (Air Force)	8·50	43·00
28	30c. brown (Militia)	8·50	43·00
29	50c. violet (Navy)	8·50	21·00
30	50c. violet (Army)	8·50	21·00
31	50c. violet (Air Force)	8·50	21·00
32	50c. violet (Militia)	8·50	21·00

(b) Air. Nos. 270/7.

33	-	25c. green	16·00	55·00
34	**110**	50c. brown	4·25	10·50
35	-	75c. brown	21·00	75·00
36	-	80c. red	55·00	£160
37	-	1l. violet	4·25	10·50
38	**113**	2l. blue	95·00	£225
39	**110**	5l. green	90·00	£325
40	**110**	10l. red	£1200	£2750

(4)

(5)

1944. Stamps of Italy. (a) Optd with T 4.

57		25c. green (No. 244)	45	2·20
60		75c. red (No. 248)	45	2·75

(b) Optd with T 5.

58	**103**	30c. brown	45	2·20
61	-	1l.25 blue (No. 250)	45	2·75
77	-	50l. violet (No. 259)	£300	£3000

(c) Optd REPUBBLICA SOCIALE ITALIANA.

59	**103**	50c. violet	45	2·10

1944. War Propaganda stamps. Nos. 563/74 optd with T 4 (25c.), T 5 (30c.) or REPUBBLICA SOCIALE ITALIANA (50c.).

64A	25c. green (Navy)	50	2·75
65A	25c. green (Army)	50	2·75
66A	25c. green (Air Force)	50	2·75
67A	25c. green (Militia)	50	2·75
68A	30c. brown (Navy)	50	5·50
69A	30c. brown (Army)	50	5·50
70A	30c. brown (Air Force)	50	5·50
71A	30c. brown (Militia)	50	5·50
72A	50c. violet (Navy)	50	1·70
73A	50c. violet (Army)	50	1·70
74A	50c. violet (Air Force)	50	1·70
75A	50c. violet (Militia)	70	1·70

Prices are for examples overprinted on the stamp part only; items overprinted twice (on stamp and label) are worth more.

10 Loggia dei Mercanti, Bologna

11 Loggia dei Mercanti, Bologna

12 Basilica de St. Lorenzo, Rome

13 Basilica de St. Lorenzo, Rome

1944. Inscr "REPUBBLICA SOCIALE ITALIANA".

102	**10**	20c. red	20	25
103	**12**	25c. green	20	25
106	-	5c. brown	20	30
107	-	10c. brown	20	25
108	**11**	20c. red	20	25
109	**13**	25c. green	20	25
110	-	30c. brown	20	25
111	-	50c. violet	20	25
112	-	75c. red	20	19·00
113	-	1l. violet	20	25
114	-	1l.25 blue	55	13·00
115	-	3l. green	55	55·00

DESIGN: 5c. St. Ciriaco's Church, Ancona; 10c., 1l. Montecassino Abbey; 30c., 75c. Drummer; 50c. Fascist allegory; 1l.25, 3l. St. Mary of Grace, Milan.

17 Bandiera Brothers

1944. Death Centenary of Attilio and Emilio Bandiera (revolutionaries).

117	**17**	25c. green	20	85
118	**17**	1l. violet	20	85
119	**17**	2l.50 red	20	7·00

CONCESSIONAL LETTER POST

Following the surrender of italy on 3 September 1943, and his rescue from imprisonment on 12 September, Mussolini proclaimed the Italian Social Republic at Salo on 23 September 1943. From this town on Lake Garda the Republican government administered those parts of Italy, north of Gustav Line, which were under German Ooccupation.

1944. Concessional Letter Post stamp of Italy optd as T 5 but smaller.

CL76	**CL109**	10c. brown	25	1·10

EXPRESS LETTER STAMPS

1944. Express stamps of Italy optd G. N. R.

E41	**E132**	1l.25 green (postage)	16·00	43·00
E42	**E132**	2l.50 red	£225	£650
E43	**E133**	2l. black (air)	£900	£1400

(E 7)

1944. Express stamps of Italy optd with Type E 7.

E62	**E132**	1l.25 green	45	85
E63	**E132**	2l.50 orange	45	13·00

E16 Palermo Cathedral

1944

E116	**E16**	1l.25 green	20	1·10

PARCEL POST STAMPS

1944. Parcel Post stamps of Italy optd REP. SOC. ITALIANA on left-hand side and Fascist Emblem on right.

P77	**P92**	5c. brown	3·25	37·00
P78	**P92**	10c. blue	3·25	37·00
P79	**P92**	25c. red	3·25	37·00
P80	**P92**	30c. blue	3·25	37·00
P81	**P92**	50c. orange	3·25	37·00
P82	**P92**	60c. red	3·25	£110
P83	**P92**	1l. violet	3·25	37·00
P84	**P92**	2l. green	£325	£1400
P85	**P92**	3l. bistre	6·50	£325
P86	**P92**	4l. black	16·00	£350
P87	**P92**	10l. purple	£140	£1700
P88	**P92**	20l. purple	£375	£2500

The unused and used prices are for unsevered stamps.

POSTAGE DUE STAMPS

1944. Postage Due stamps of Italy optd G. N. R.

D44	**D141**	5c. brown	21·00	60·00
D45	**D141**	10c. blue	21·00	60·00
D46	**D141**	20c. red	21·00	37·00
D47	**D141**	25c. green	21·00	37·00
D48	**D141**	30c. orange	21·00	60·00
D49	**D141**	40c. brown	21·00	37·00
D50	**D141**	50c. violet	75·00	£300
D51	**D141**	60c. blue	£425	£1200
D52	**D142**	1l. orange	32·00	43·00
D53	**D142**	2l. green	43·00	85·00
D54	**D142**	5l. violet	£225	£500
D55	**D142**	10l. blue	£130	£350
D56	**D142**	20l. red	£140	£350

1944. Postage Due stamps of Italy optd with small Fascist emblems.

D89	**D141**	5c. brown	2·10	5·50
D90	**D141**	10c. blue	2·10	5·50
D91	**D141**	20c. red	2·10	5·50
D92	**D141**	25c. green	2·10	5·50
D93	**D141**	30c. orange	2·10	9·50
D94	**D141**	40c. brown	2·10	10·50
D95	**D141**	50c. violet	2·10	4·25
D96	**D141**	60c. blue	10·50	21·00
D97	**D142**	1l. orange	2·10	4·25
D98	**D142**	2l. green	5·25	16·00
D99	**D142**	5l. violet	32·00	£120
D100	**D142**	10l. blue	90·00	£225
D101	**D142**	20l. red	90·00	£225

Pt. 6, Pt. 13

IVORY COAST

A French colony in W. Africa on the Gulf of Guinea, incorporated in French West Africa in 1944. In 1958 it became an autonomous republic within the French Community, and in 1960 it became fully independent.

100 centimes = 1 franc.

1892. "Tablet" key-type inscr "COTE D'IVOIRE" in blue (Nos. 2, 3, 5, 14, 7, 9/11) or red (others).

1	D	1c. black on blue	2·00	3·75
2	D	2c. brown on buff	2·20	2·30
3	D	4c. brown on grey	3·25	3·50
4a	D	5c. green on green	22·00	9·75
5	D	10c. black on lilac	17·00	12·00
6	D	15c. blue	50·00	9·25
7	D	20c. red on green	11·00	17·00
8	D	25c. black on pink	18·00	3·75
9	D	30c. brown on drab	55·00	55·00
10	D	40c. red on yellow	20·00	23·00
11	D	50c. red on pink	55·00	65·00
12	D	75c. brown on yellow	7·75	30·00
13	D	1f. green	60·00	28·00
14	D	10c. red	£110	£120
15	D	15c. grey	4·50	2·75
16	D	25c. blue	38·00	55·00
17	D	50c. brown on blue	17·00	11·00

1904. Surch in figures and bars.

18	0.05 on 30c. brown	80·00	£100
19	0.10 on 75c. brown on yellow	14·00	34·00
20	0.15 on 1f. olive	25·00	36·00

1906. "Faidherbe", "Palms" and "Balay" key-types inscr "COTE D'IVOIRE" in blue (10c., 5f.) or red (others).

22	I	1c. grey	2·50	35
23	I	2c. brown	1·00	90
24	I	4c. brown on blue	55	1·10
25	I	5c. green	3·75	1·20
26	I	10c. pink	7·50	90
27	J	20c. black on blue	5·75	6·00
28	J	25c. blue	3·00	1·80
29	J	30c. brown on pink	11·00	14·50
30	J	35c. black on yellow	7·25	2·30
32	J	45c. brown on green	10·00	13·00
33	J	50c. violet	11·50	17·00
34	J	75c. green on orange	11·00	34·00
35	K	1f. black on blue	34·00	70·00
36	K	2f. blue on pink	50·00	85·00
37	K	5f. red on yellow	80·00	£120

1912. Surch in figures.

38A	D	05 on 15c. grey	1·20	1·50
39A	D	05 on 30c. brown on drab	2·30	8·75
40A	D	10 on 40c. red on yellow	1·10	7·75
41A	D	10 on 50c. brown on blue	2·00	5·50
42A	D	10 on 75c. brown on orange	3·75	13·50

7 River Scene

1913

43	7	1c. violet and purple	20	55
44	7	2c. black and brown	10	1·50
45	7	4c. purple and violet	35	1·70
46	7	5c. green and light green	3·00	1·30
47	7	10c. pink and red	2·30	2·30
48	7	15c. red and orange	1·00	1·20
49	7	20c. grey and black	1·60	1·10
50	7	25c. blue and ultramarine	13·50	4·50
51	7	30c. brown and chocolate	3·25	4·25
52	7	35c. orange and violet	2·30	4·50
53	7	40c. green and grey	2·30	1·40
54	7	45c. brown and red	1·70	2·50
55	7	50c. violet and black	5·50	5·25
56	7	75c. pink and brown	2·00	1·00
57	7	1f. black and yellow	2·00	35
58	7	2f. blue and brown	3·50	1·40
59	7	5f. brown and blue	7·00	6·25
61	7	5c. brown and chocolate	35	80
62	7	10c. green and light green	80	2·10
63	7	10c. pink on blue	50	80
64	7	25c. violet and black	2·50	20
65	7	30c. pink and red	3·00	6·50
66	7	30c. red and blue	35	70
67	7	30c. green and olive	1·20	2·30
68	7	45c. purple and red	8·00	19·00
69	7	50c. blue and ultramarine	1·00	2·50
70	7	50c. blue and green	1·50	30
71	7	60c. violet on pink	1·00	6·50
72	7	65c. green and red	2·10	8·25
73	7	75c. ultramarine and blue	8·00	12·00
74	7	85c. black and purple	1·10	9·25
75	7	90c. carmine and red	11·50	46·00
76	7	1f.10 brown and green	5·75	23·00
77	7	1f.50 blue and light blue	6·50	6·75
78	7	1f.75 mauve and blue	22·00	13·50
79	7	3f. mauve on pink	5·00	2·30

1915. Surch 5c and red cross.

60	10c.+5c. pink and red	1·40	2·75

1934. Surch with new value twice.

80	50 on 45c. purple and red	6·00	7·00
81	50 on 75c. ultramarine & blue	3·50	3·75
82	50 on 90c. pink and red	3·75	3·75
83	60 on 75c. violet on pink	65	90
84	65 on 15c. red and orange	1·40	7·25
85	85 on 75c. pink and brown	1·40	8·00

1922. Surch in figures and bars.

86	25c. on 2f. blue and brown	1·10	7·50
87	25c. on 5f. brown and blue	65	7·75
88	90c. on 75c. pink and red	85	4·50
89	1f.25 on 1f. ultram & blue	30	5·50
90	1f.50 on 1f. blue & light blue	1·40	1·70
91	3f. on 5f. green and red	3·25	6·00
92	10f. on 5f. mauve and red	8·25	38·00
93	20f. on 5f. red and green	11·00	55·00

1931. "Colonial Exhibition" key-types inscr "COTE D'IVOIRE".

94	E	40c. black and green	2·50	6·00
95	F	50c. black and mauve	3·75	8·75
96	G	90c. black and red	1·80	5·25
97	H	1f.50 black and blue	6·00	18·00

1933. Stamps of Upper Volta optd Cote d'Ivoire or surch also.

98	3	2c. brown and violet	35	3·25
99	3	4c. black and yellow	70	3·00
100	3	5c. indigo and blue	1·50	7·00
101	3	10c. blue and pink	2·30	2·30
102	3	15c. brown and blue	1·40	7·25
103	3	20c. brown and green	2·50	3·00
104	-	25c. brown and yellow	2·30	3·25
105	-	30c. deep green and green	2·40	3·75
106	-	45c. brown and blue	10·50	14·00
107	-	65c. indigo and blue	3·50	11·00
108	-	75c. black and violet	3·25	4·75
109	-	90c. red and mauve	3·00	6·50
110	6	1f. brown and green	2·75	4·25
111	-	1f.25 on 40c. black and pink	90	1·20
112	6	1f.50 ultramarine and blue	2·00	1·60
113	-	1f.75 on 50c. black & green	3·25	1·20

12 Baoule Woman

1936

114	12	1c. red	30	3·25
115	12	2c. blue	55	3·50
116	12	3c. green	90	6·25
117	12	4c. brown	70	2·75
118	12	5c. violet	75	1·80
119	12	10c. blue	35	1·60
120	12	15c. red	55	55
121	-	20c. blue	70	1·30
122	-	25c. red	65	85
123	-	30c. green	1·70	3·25
124	-	30c. brown	30	5·75
125	12	35c. green	2·30	4·75
126	-	40c. red	35	65
127	-	45c. brown	1·60	4·25
128	-	45c. green	2·00	7·75
129	-	50c. purple	55	20
130	-	55c. violet	1·80	5·00
131	-	60c. red	2·30	6·25
132	-	65c. brown	1·90	2·50
133	-	70c. brown	1·50	5·75
134	-	75c. violet	1·90	1·70
135	-	80c. brown	1·20	3·25
136	-	90c. red	7·00	16·00
137	-	90c. green	1·00	3·25
138	-	1f. green	3·25	65
139	-	1f. red	3·25	2·50
140	-	1f. violet	1·70	4·00
141	-	1f.25 red	1·70	1·80
142	-	1f.40 blue	1·70	6·25
143	-	1f.50 blue	1·70	1·20
144	-	1f.50 grey	4·50	7·25
145	-	1f.60 brown	1·20	5·75
146	-	1f.75 red	2·50	3·00
147	-	1f.75 blue	2·50	5·00
148	-	2f. blue	1·00	30
149	-	2f.50 blue	1·90	5·00
150	-	2f.50 red	2·00	2·50
151	-	3f. green	1·30	55
152	-	5f. brown	1·10	75
153	-	10f. violet	1·70	85
154	-	20f. red	3·25	3·25

DESIGNS—HORIZ: 20c. to 30c. and 40c. to 55c. Mosque at Bobo-Dioulasso; 60c. to 1f.60, Coastal scene. VERT: 1f.75, to 20f. Comoe Rapids.

12a Commerce

1937. International Exhibition, Paris.

155	12a	20c. violet	1·50	5·25
156	12a	30c. green	90	5·00
157	12a	40c. red	1·00	3·75
158	12a	50c. brown and blue	75	5·00
159	12a	90c. red	90	2·75
160	12a	1f.50 blue	1·60	3·00

MS160a 120×100 mm. 3f. brown (as T 4) 7·25 50·00

16 General Binger

1937. 50th Anniv of Gen. Binger's Exploration.

161	16	65c. brown	45	55

16a Pierra and Marie Curie

1938. International Anti-cancer Fund.

162	16a	1f.75+50c. blue	3·75	17·00

16b

1939. Death Centenary of Rene Caillie (explorer).

163		90c. orange	65	1·50
164	16b	2f. violet	90	1·60
165	16b	2f.25 blue	1·00	2·30

16c

1939. New York World's Fair.

166	16c	1f.25 red	1·40	4·00
167	16c	2f.25 blue	1·50	4·25

16d Storming the Bastille

1939. 150th Anniv of French Revolution.

168	16d	45c.+25c. green and black	7·25	14·50
169	16d	70c.+30c. brown and black	7·25	14·50
170	16d	90c.+35c. orange and black	7·25	14·50
171	16d	1f.25+1f. red and black	7·25	14·50
172	16d	2f.25+2f. blue and black	7·25	14·50

1940. Air.

173	16e	1f.90 blue	50	3·50
174	16e	2f.90 red	1·10	5·00
175	16e	4f.50 green	75	1·50
176	16e	4f.90 olive	85	3·75
177	16e	6f.90 orange	1·00	2·75

16e Twin-engine Airliner over Jungle

1941. National Defence Fund. Surch SECOURS NATIONAL and value.

178	+1f. on 50c. (No. 129)	3·50	5·75
178a	+2f. on 80c. (No. 135)	18·00	40·00
178b	+2f. on 1f.50 (No. 143)	19·00	44·00
178c	+3f. on 2f. (No. 148)	21·00	40·00

16f Pirogue

1942. Marshal Petain issue.

178d	16f	1f. green	75	2·40
178e	16f	2f.50 blue	75	3·00

16g Weighting Baby

1942. Air. Colonial Child Welfare Fund.

178f	–	1f.50+3f.50 green	75	3·75
178g	–	2f.+6f. brown	75	4·50
178h	16g	3f.+9f. red	75	4·00

DESIGNS: 49×28 mm. 1f.50. Maternity Hospital; 2f. Dispensary.

1942. Air Imperial Fortnight.

178i	16h	1f.20+1f.80 blue and red	65	4·50

16h "Vocation"

1942. Air. As T 27 of French Sudan, but inscr "COTE D'IVOIRE".

179	50f. olive and green	2·30	4·00

REPUBLIC

17 African Elephant

1959

180	17	10f. black and green	2·75	1·20
181	17	25f. brown and bistre	1·10	35
182	17	30f. olive and turquoise	1·90	2·30

18 Place Lapalud, Abidjan

1959. Air.

183	**18**	100f. brown, green & choc	4·00	1·40
184	-	200f. brown, myrtle & turq	9·25	5·00
185	-	500f. turquoise, brn & grn	9·50	5·25

DESIGNS: 200f. Houphouet-Boigny railway bridge, Abidjan; 500f. Ayame Barrage.

19 Pres. Houphouet-Boigny

1959. 1st Anniv of Republic.

186	**19**	25f. brown	2·00	1·20

20 Bete Mask

1960. Native Masks.

187	**20**	50c. chocolate and brown	25	4·00
188	-	1f. violet and red	90	2·50
189	-	2f. green and blue	90	2·30
190	-	4f. red and green	1·20	2·75
191	-	5f. brown and red	1·30	1·30
192	-	6f. blue and purple	1·40	2·50
193	-	45f. purple and green	2·75	1·60
194	-	50f. blue and brown	3·25	1·30
195	-	85f. green and red	4·75	3·25

DESIGNS—VERT: MASKS OF: 1f. Guere; 2f. Guere (different type); 45f. Bete (different type); 50f. Gouro; 85f. Gouro (different type). HORIZ: 4f. Baole; 5f. Senoufo; 6f. Senoufo (different type).

1960. 10th Anniv of African Technical Co-operation Commission. As T 4 of Malagasy.

196	25f. violet and turquoise	2·30	1·70

21 Conseil de l'Entente Emblem

1960. 1st Anniv of Conseil de l'Entente.

197	**21**	25f. multicoloured	1·50	2·50

21a "World Peace"

1961. 1st Anniv of Independence.

198	**21a**	25f. black, green & brown	85	50

22 "Thoningia sanguinea"

1961

199	-	5f. red, yellow and green	85	30
200	-	10f. yellow, red and blue	50	30
201	-	15f. purple, green & orange	1·60	50
202	**22**	20f. yellow, red and brown	90	50
203	-	25f. yellow, red and green	90	50
204	-	30f. red, green and black	1·10	75
205	-	70f. yellow, red and green	3·25	1·60
206	-	85f. multicoloured	4·75	1·90

FLOWERS: 5f. "Plumeria rubra"; 10f. "Haemanthus cinnabarinus"; 15f. "Bougainvillea spectabilis"; 25f. "Eulophia cucullata"; 30f. "Newbouldia laevis"; 70f. "Mussaenda erythrophylla"; 85f. "Strophantus sarmentosus".

23 Mail-carriers

1961. Stamp Day.

207	**23**	25f. brown, blue and green	85	65

24 Ayame Dam

1961

208	**24**	25f. sepia, blue and green	85	50

25 Swimming

1961. Abidjan Games. Inscr as in T 25.

209	**25**	5f. sepia, green and blue (postage)	35	10
210	-	20f. brown, green and grey	50	30
211	-	25f. brown, green and blue	85	50
211a	-	100f. blk, red & bl (air)	4·00	2·10

DESIGNS: 20f. Basketball; 25f. Football; 100f. High-jumping.

26 Palms

1962. 17th Session of African Technical Co-operation Commission, Abidjan.

212	**26**	25f. multicoloured	85	50

1962. Air. "Air Afrique" Airline. As T 32 of Mauritania.

213	50f. blue, brown and chestnut	1·60	90

1962. Malaria Eradication. As T 11a Malagasy Republic.

214	25f.+5f. green	1·00	1·00

27 Fort Assinie

1962. Postal Centenary.

215	**27**	85f. multicoloured	2·50	1·50

28 Village, Man Region

1962. Air.

216	-	200f. sepia, purple & green	6·25	2·75
217	**28**	500f. green, purple & black	11·00	5·00

DESIGN—VERT: 200f. Street Scene, Odienne.

28a

1962. 1st Anniv of Union of African and Malagasy.

218	**28a**	30f. red	1·10	95

29 U.N. Headquarters and Emblem

1962. Air. 2nd Anniv of Admission to U.N.

219	**29**	100f. multicoloured	2·40	1·30

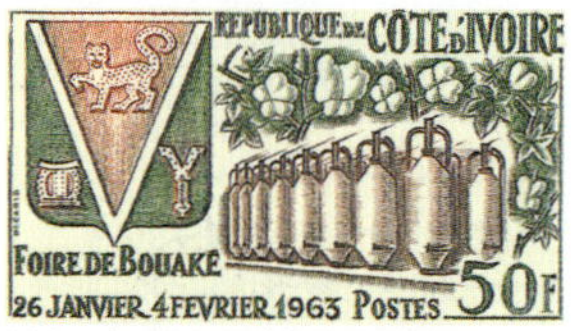

30 Bouake Arms and Cotton Exhibit

1963. Bouake Fair.

220	**30**	50f. sepia, brown and green	90	50

30a

1963. Freedom from Hunger.

221	**30a**	25f.+5f. violet, brown & pur	1·30	1·30

31 Map of Africa

1963. Conference of African Heads of State, Addis Ababa.

222	**31**	30f. green and blue	1·10	95

32 Sassandra Bay

1963. Air.

223	-	50f. green, brown and blue	1·70	60
224	**32**	100f. brown, blue & myrtle	2·75	1·40
225	-	200f. turquoise, grn & brn	5·00	2·40

DESIGNS: 50f. Moosou Bridge; 200f. River Comoe.

1963. Air. African and Malagasian Posts and Telecommunications Union. As T 20a of Malagasy Republic.

226	85f. multicoloured	1·90	1·30

33 Hartebeest

1963. "Tourism and Hunting".

227	-	1f. multicoloured	50	10
228	-	2f. multicoloured	50	30
229	-	4f. multicoloured	45	35
230	-	5f. multicoloured	45	35
231	**33**	10f. brown, green and grey	70	30
232	-	15f. black, green and brown	1·00	50
233	-	20f. brown, green and red	1·40	50
234	-	25f. brown, green & yellow	1·90	75
235	-	45f. purple, green & turq	4·00	1·60
236	-	50f. black, green and brown	5·50	2·10
MS236a		170×100 mm. Nos. 231, 233 and 235/6	27·00	26·00
247	-	5f. green, yellow and brown	70	30
248	-	10f. brown, green & purple	1·80	50
249	-	15f. brown, green & purple	2·75	50

DESIGNS—HORIZ: 1f. Yellow-backed duiker; 4f. Beecroft's hyrax; 5f. (No. 247) African manatee; 10f. (No. 248) Pygmy hippopotamus; 15f. (No. 232) Giant forest hog; 20f. Warthog; 45f. Hunting dogs. VERT: 2f. Potto; 5f. (No. 230) Water chevrotain; 15f. (No. 249) Royal antelope; 25f. Bongo; 50f. Western black and white colobus.

1963. Air. 1st Anniv of "Air Afrique" and "DC-8" Service Inauguration. As T 87 of Mauritania.

237	25f. multicoloured	85	35

34 Scales of Justice, Globe and UNESCO Emblem

1963. 15th Anniv of Declaration of Human Rights.

238	**34**	85f. black, blue and orange	1·70	90

35 Rameses II and Nefertari, Abu Simbel

1964. Air. Nubian Monuments Preservation.

239	**35**	60f. black, brown and red	2·30	1·30

36 Map of Africa

1964. Inter-African National Education Ministers' Conference, Abidjan.
240 **36** 30f. red, green and blue 85 50

37 Weather Balloon

1964. World Meteorological Day.
241 **37** 25f. multicoloured 95 60

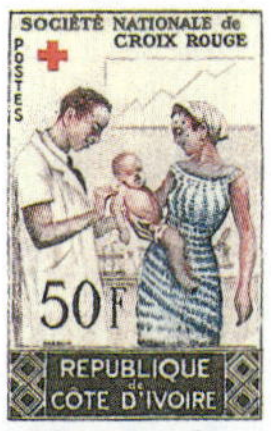

38 Doctor tending Child

1964. National Red Cross Society.
242 **38** 50f. multicoloured 1·50 70

39 Arms of the Ivory Coast

1964. Air.
243 **39** 200f. gold, blue and green 4·25 1·80

40 Globe and Athletes

1964. Olympic Games, Tokyo.
244 **40** 35f. brown, green and violet 1·40 65
245 - 65f. ochre, brown and blue 2·50 1·30
DESIGN—HORIZ: 65f. Wrestling and Globe.

41 Symbolic Tree

1964. 1st Anniv of European–African Convention.
246 **41** 30f. multicoloured 1·00 45

41a "Co-operation"

1964. French, African and Malagasy Co-operation.
250 **41a** 25f. brown, red and green 85 45

42 Pres. Kennedy

1964. Air. Pres. Kennedy Commemoration.
251 **42** 100f. brown and grey 2·75 2·00

43 Korhogo Mail-carriers, 1914

1964. Stamp Day.
252 **43** 85f. sepia, brown and blue 2·40 1·40

44 Pottery

1965. Native Handicrafts.
253 **44** 5f. black, red and green 35 20
254 - 10f. black, purple and green 45 25
255 - 20f. blue, chocolate & brn 80 30
256 - 25f. brown, red and olive 85 50
DESIGNS: 10f. Wood-carving; 20f. Ivory-carving; 25f. Weaving.

45 Mail coming ashore

1965. Stamp Day.
257 **45** 30f. multicoloured 1·00 70

46 I.T.U. Emblem and Symbols

1965. I.T.U. Centenary.
258 **46** 85f. blue, red and green 1·90 1·30

47 Abidjan Railway Station

1965
259 **47** 30f. multicoloured 1·20 70

48 Pres. Houphouet-Boigny and Map

1965. 5th Anniv of Independence.
260 **48** 30f. multicoloured 85 50

49 Hammerkop

1965. Birds.
261 - 1f. green, yellow and violet 55 20
262 - 2f. multicoloured 60 25
263 - 5f. purple, red and olive 85 50
264 **49** 10f. brown, black & purple 85 30
265 - 15f. red, grey and green 1·10 35
266 - 30f. brown, green and lake 1·60 65
267 - 50f. blue, black and brown 3·00 1·00
268 - 75f. red, green and orange 5·50 1·80
269 - 90f. multicoloured 6·00 3·25
BIRDS—HORIZ: 1f. Yellow-bellied green pigeon; 2f. Spur-winged goose; 30f. Namaqua dove; 50f. Lizard buzzard. VERT: 5f. Stone partridge; 15f. White-breasted guineafowl; 75f. Yellow-billed stork; 90f. Latham's francolin.

50 Lieupleu Rope-bridge

1965. Air.
270 **50** 100f. brown, green & lt grn 2·75 1·60
271 - 300f. purple, flesh and blue 7·25 3·75
DESIGN: 300f. Street in Kong.

51 Steam Mail Train, 1906

1966. Stamp Day.
272 **51** 30f. green, black and purple 2·50 1·20

52 "Maternity"

1966. World Festival of Negro Arts, Dakar.
273 **52** 5f. black and green 35 20
274 - 10f. black and violet 50 30
275 - 20f. black and orange 1·60 80
276 - 30f. black and red 2·00 1·00
DESIGNS—CARVED WORK: 10f. Pomade box; 20f. Drums; 30f. "Ancestor".

53 Ivory Hotel

1966. Inauguration of Ivory Hotel.
277 **53** 15f. multicoloured 65 35

54 Tractor Cultivation

1966. 6th Anniv of Independence.
278 **54** 30f. multicoloured 85 55

54a

1966. Air. Inauguration of Douglas DC-8F Air Services.
279 **54a** 30f. grey, black and green 85 50

55 Open-air Class

1966. National School of Administration.
280 **55** 30f. black, blue and lake 85 50

56 Inoculating Cattle

1966. Campaign for Prevention of Cattle Plague.
281 **56** 30f. brown, green and blue 1·00 60

57 UNESCO. "Waves" enveloping "Man"

1966. 20th Anniv of UNESCO.
282 **57** 30f. violet and blue 85 55
283 - 30f. black, brown and blue 85 55
DESIGN: No. 283, Distributing food parcels to children.

58 Bouake Hospital

1966
284 **58** 30f. multicoloured 85 55

59 "Air Afrique" Headquarters

1966. Air.
285 **59** 500f. blue, ochre and green 10·50 4·75

60 Sikorsky S-43 Amphibian (30th anniv)

1967. Stamp Day.
286 **60** 30f. blue, brown & turq 2·75 1·30

61 Cutting Pineapples

1967. Fruits.

287	**61**	20f. purple, brown & green	50	40
288	-	30f. red, brown and green	70	50
289	-	100f. brown, olive and blue	3·00	1·20

DESIGNS: 30f. Cutting palm-nuts; 100f. Cutting bananas.

62 "African Mythology"

1967. 35th Pen Club Int Congress, Abidjan.

290	**62**	30f. black, green and lake	85	55

63 "Improvement of Rural Housing"

1967. 7th Anniv of Independence.

291	**63**	30f. multicoloured	85	40

64 Lions Emblems

1967. 50th Anniv of Lions International.

292	**64**	30f. multicoloured	1·10	65

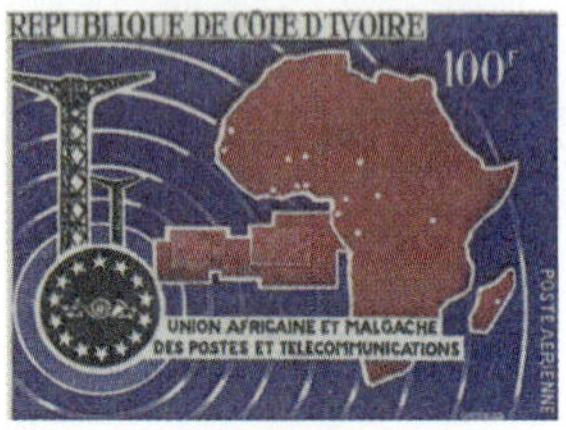

64a

1967. Air. 5th Anniv of U.A.M.P.T.

293	**64a**	100f. red, blue and violet	2·75	1·30

64b

1967. 5th Anniv of West African Monetary Union.

294	**64b**	30f. black, green and mauve	65	35

65 African Man and Woman

1967. 20th Anniv of Recognition Days.

295	**65**	90f. multicoloured	1·90	90

See also No. 342.

66 Senoufo Village

1968. Air.

296	**66**	100f. brown, yellow & green	2·75	1·20
297	-	500f. brown, blue and green	10·50	4·25

DESIGN: 500f. Tiegba lake village.

67 Tabou Radio Station, 1912

1968. Stamp Day.

298	**67**	30f. green, brown & turq	1·00	55

68 Cotton Loom

1968. Industries.

299	-	5f. black, red and green	35	10
300	**68**	10f. brown, green and slate	60	10
301	-	15f. black, blue and red	1·30	70
302	-	20f. blue and purple	95	55
303	-	30f. brown, green and blue	95	70
304	-	50f. black, green and mauve	1·60	90
305	-	70f. chocolate, blue & brn	2·10	1·10
306	-	90f. black, purple and blue	2·75	1·60

DESIGNS—HORIZ: 5f. Palm-oil works; 30f. Flour mills; 50f. Cocoa-butter extraction machine; 90f. Timber sawmill and logs. VERT: 15f. Oil refinery, Abidjan; 20f. Raw cotton and reeling machine; 70f. Soluble-coffee plant.

See also Nos. 335/7.

69 Canoeing

1968. Olympic Games, Mexico.

307	**69**	30f. brown, blue and green	90	45
308	-	100f. purple, ultram & blue	2·40	95

DESIGN: 100f. 100 m sprint.

70 Sacrificial Offering

1968. 8th Anniv of Independence.

309	**70**	30f. multicoloured	85	40

71 Doctor inoculating Patient

1968. 20th Anniv of W.H.O.

310	**71**	30f. chocolate, brown & bl	85	50

72 Impala in Forest

1968. Fauna and Flora Protection.

311	**72**	30f. brown, green and blue	3·50	1·10

73 Museum and Carved Screen

1968. Opening of Abidjan Museum.

312	**73**	30f. brown, red and blue	85	40

74 Human Rights Emblem and "Justice" Totems

1968. Human Rights Year.

313	**74**	30f. orange, purple and blue	85	40

74a "Grand Bassam" (Achalme)

1969. Air. "Philexafrique" Stamp Exhibition, Abidjan, Ivory Coast (1st issue).

314	**74a**	100f. multicoloured.	4·75	4·75

74b Aerial View of San Pedro village and stamp of 1936

1969. Air. "Philexafrique" Stamp Exn, Abidjan, Ivory Coast (2nd issue).

315	**74b**	50f. red, blue and green	2·75	2·75
316	–	100f. blue, brown and orange	4·25	4·25
317	–	200f. slate, blue and brown	6·00	6·00
MS318		161×100 mm. Nos. 315/17	16·00	16·00

DESIGNS—HORIZ: 200f. Chambers of Agriculture and Industry building, Abidjan, and 5f. stamp of 1913. VERT: 100f. Chief's costume and 5f. stamp of 1936.

75 "Ville de Maranhao" (mail steamer) at Grand-Bassam

1969. Stamp Day.

319	**75**	30f. purple, blue and green	1·30	60

76 Ivory Hotel

1969. Opening of Ivory Hotel.

320	**76**	30f. blue, red and green	1·00	50

77 "Man on Horseback" (statuette)

1969. Ivory Coast Art Exn, Vevey, Switzerland.

321	**77**	30f. black, purple and red	1·00	65

78 Hertzian-wave Radio Station, Man

1969. 9th Anniv of Independence.

322	**78**	30f. green, brown and blue	1·00	50

79 Bank Emblem

1969. 5th Anniv of African Development Bank.

323	**79**	30f. brown, green and lake	60	40

80 Arms of Bouake

1969. Coats of Arms.

324	**80**	10f. multicoloured	35	10
325	-	15f. multicoloured	40	20
326	-	30f. black, gold and green	60	20

ARMS: 15f. Abidjan; 30f. Ivory Coast Republic.

See also Nos. 402/3 and 432/6.

81 Game Fishing

1969. Int SKAL Tourist Assn Congress, Abidjan.

327	**81**	30f. blue, purple and violet	2·75	55
328	-	100f. multicoloured	3·50	1·40

DESIGN: 100f. Assinie Holiday Village.

81a

1969. 10th Anniv of Aerial Navigation Security Agency for Africa and Madagascar (A.S.E.C.N.A.).

329	**81a**	30f. red	80	45

82 Man Waterfall

1970. Air.

330	**82**	100f. blue, green and brown	3·00	1·30
331	-	200f. red, green and emerald	3·75	1·60

DESIGN: 200f. Mt. Niangbo.

83 University Hospital Centre, Abidjan

1970. "10 Years of Higher Education".

332	**83**	30f. indigo, green and blue	80	50

84 Telegraphist and Gabriel Dadie (Postal administrator)

1970. Stamp Day.

333	**84**	30f. black, green and red	60	40

85 Abidjan University

1970. 3rd A.U.P.E.L.F. (Association of French Speaking Universities). General Assembly, Abidjan.

334	**85**	30f. purple, green and blue	80	50

86 Safety-match Manufacture

1970. Industrial Expansion.

335	**86**	5f. brown, blue & chocolate	35	30
336	-	20f. red, green and grey	50	30
337	-	50f. brown, blue and green	1·30	40

DESIGNS: 20f. Textile-printing; 50f. Ship-building.

87 Dish Aerial and Television Class

1970. World Telecommunications Day.

338	**87**	40f. green, drab and red	1·00	55

87a

1970. New U.P.U. Headquarters Building, Berne.

339	**87a**	30f. brown, green and purple	1·00	50

88 Wild Life

1970. 25th Anniv of United Nations.

340	**88**	30f. brown, green and blue	2·75	1·30

89 Coffee Plant

1970. 10th Anniv of Independence (1st issue).

341	**89**	30f. green, brown & orange	1·00	50

See also Nos. 344/9.

90 African Man and Woman

1970. 5th P.D.C.I. (Ivory Coast Democratic Party) Congress.

342	**90**	40f. multicoloured	1·00	50

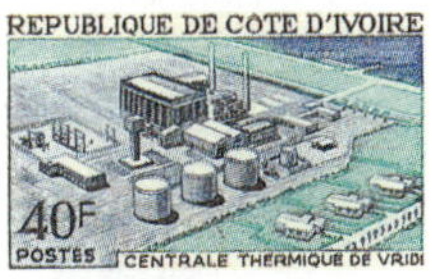

91 Power Station

1970. Thermal Power Plant, Vridi.

343	**91**	40f. brown, blue and green	1·60	45

92 Pres. Houphouet-Boigny and De Gaulle

1970. 10th Anniv of Independence (2nd issue). Embossed on silver (300f. values) or gold foil.

344	300f. Type **92** (postage)	16·00	16·00
345	300f. Ivory Coast Arms	13·00	13·00
346	1000f. Type **92**	46·00	47·00
347	1000f. As No. 345	44·00	44·00
348	300f. Pres. Houphouet-Boigny and African elephants (air)	13·00	13·00
349	1200f. As No. 348	44·00	44·00

93 Mail Bus, 1925

1971. Stamp Day.

350	**93**	40f. purple, green & brown	1·80	50

94 Port of San Pedro

1971. Air.

351	**94**	100f. red, blue and green	1·90	80
352	-	500f. green, blue and brown	10·50	5·00

DESIGN: 500f. African Riviera coastline.

95 Desjardin's Marginella

1971. Marine Life.

353		1f. brown, blue and green	45	10
354		5f. red, lilac and blue	55	35
355		10f. red, blue and green	80	30
356	**95**	15f. brown, purple and blue	95	35
357	-	15f. brown, violet and red	1·30	40
358	-	20f. red and yellow	1·60	45
359	-	20f. lake, purple and red	1·90	65
360	-	25f. brown, black and lake	1·10	25
361	-	35f. red, yellow and green	2·30	80
362	-	40f. brown, blue and green	3·75	1·30
363	-	40f. red, turquoise & brown	2·50	75
364	-	45f. brown, green & emer	4·50	1·70
365	-	50f. green, red and violet	4·50	1·30
366	-	65f. blue, green and brown	3·25	1·60

DESIGNS—HORIZ: 1f. African pelican's-foot; 5f. "Neptunus validus"; 20f. (No. 359) Digitate carrier shell; 25f. Butterfly cone; 40f. (No. 362) Garter cone; 45f. Bubonion conch; 65f. Rat cowrie. VERT: 10f. "Hermodice carunculata"; 15f. (No. 357) Fanel moon; 20f. (No. 358) "Goniaster cuspidatus"; 35f. "Polycheles typhiops"; 40f. (No. 363) African fan scallop; 50f. "Enoplometopus callistas".

96 Telegraph Station, Grand Bassam, 1891

1971. World Telecommunications Day.

367	**96**	100f. brown, green and blue	1·90	85

97 Treichville Swimming Pool

1971. Air.

368	**97**	100f. multicoloured	2·75	95

98 Tool-making

1971. Technical Training and Instruction.

369	**98**	35f. blue, red and green	80	45

99 African Telecommunications Map

1971. Pan-African Telecommunications Network.

370	**99**	45f. yellow, red and purple	80	45

100 Bondoukou Market

1971. 11th Anniv of Independence.

371	**100**	35f. brown, blue and grey (postage)	85	50
372	-	200f. black and blue on gold (air)	4·00	2·20

No. 372 has a similar design to Type **100** but in smaller format, size 38×27 mm.

101 Children of Three Races

1971. Racial Equality Year. Multicoloured.

373	40f. Type **101**	80	30
374	45f. Children around Globe	80	30

101a Headquarters and Ivory Coast Arms

1971. 10th Anniv of U.A.M.P.T.

375	**101a**	100f. multicoloured	1·90	90

U.A.M.P.T. = African and Malagasy Posts and Telecommunications Union.

102 Gaming Table

1971. National Lottery.

376	**102**	35f. multicoloured	1·00	40

103 Technicians working on Power Cables

1971. Electricity Works Centre, Akovai-Santai.

377	**103**	35f. multicoloured	1·50	55

104 Lion of St. Mark's

1972. Air. UNESCO. "Save Venice" Campaign. Multicoloured.

378	100f. Type **104**	3·00	1·40
379	200f. St. Mark's Square	5·25	2·75

105 Cogwheel and Students

1972. Technical Instruction Week.

380	**105**	35f. blue, brown and red	60	45

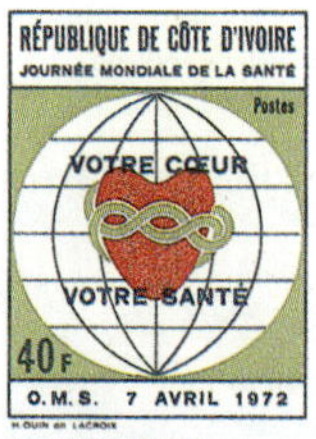

106 Heart Emblem

1972. World Heart Month.
381 106 40f. blue, red and green 80 45

107 Child learning to write

1972. International Book Year.
382 - 35f. brown, orange & grn 60 25
383 107 40f. black, orange & green 85 45
DESIGN—HORIZ: 35f. Students and open book.

108 Gouessesso Tourist Village

1972. Air.
384 108 100f. brown, green & blue 2·75 1·20
385 - 200f. green, brown & blue 4·00 1·60
386 - 500f. brown, bistre & blue 9·75 5·00
DESIGNS: 200f. Jacqueville Lake; 500f. Mosque of Kawara.

109 Regional Postal Training Centre, Abidjan

1972. Stamp Day.
387 109 40f. bistre, green & purple 1·00 50

110 Aerial Mast, Abobo Hertzian Centre

1972. World Telecommunications Day.
388 110 40f. red, blue and green 1·40 50

112 Computer Operator

1972. Development of Information Services.
393 112 40f. blue, brown and green 1·40 50

113 Odienne

1972. 12th Anniv of Independence.
394 113 35f. brown, green and blue 80 50

114 Africans and 500f. Coin

1972. 10th Anniv of West African Monetary Union.
395 114 40f. grey, purple and brown 80 45

115 Diamond and Mine

1972. Development of the Diamond Industry.
396 115 40f. blue, grey and brown 3·00 1·40

116 Lake-dwellings, Bletankoro

1972. Air.
397 116 200f. purple, green & blue 3·75 1·70
398 - 500f. brown, green & blue 10·00 5·00
DESIGN: 500f. Kossou Dam.

117 Louis Pasteur and Institute

1972. Inauguration of Pasteur Institute, Abidjan.
399 117 35f. blue, green and brown 1·00 50

118 Satellite Earth Station

1972. Air. Opening of Satellite Earth Station, Akakro.
400 118 200f. brown, green & blue 4·00 1·60

119 Child pumping Water

1972. "Conserve Water" Campaign.
401 119 35f. black, green and red 1·00 45
See also No. 414.

1973. Coats of Arms. As T 80. Multicoloured.
402 5f. Arms of Daloa 40 10
403 10f. Arms of Gagnoa 40 10
See also Nos. 432/6.

120 Dr. G. A. Hansen

1973. Centenary of Hansen's Identification of Leprosy Bacillus.
404 120 35f. brown, blue & purple 1·00 45

121 Pearly Razorfish

1973. Fishes.
405 - 15f. blue and green 1·20 60
406 - 20f. red and brown 2·20 75
406a - 25f. red and green 3·25 80
406b - 35f. red and green 2·50 1·10
407 121 50f. red, blue and black 3·75 1·40
FISHES: 15f. Grey triggerfish; 20f. West African goatfish; 25f. African hind; 35f. Bigeye.

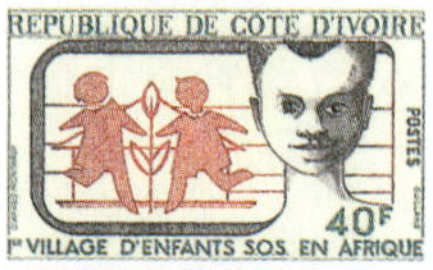

122 Child and Emblem

1973. Establishment of first S.O.S. Children's Village in Africa.
408 122 40f. black, red and green 1·00 60

123 National Assembly Building

1973. 112th Interparliamentary Council Session, Abidjan.
409 123 100f. multicoloured 1·10 50

124 Classroom and Shop

1973. "Commercial Action" Programme.
410 124 40f. multicoloured 60 25

125 "Women's Work"

1973. Technical Instruction for Women.
411 125 35f. multicoloured 80 45

126 Scouts helping with Food Cultivation

1973. 24th World Scouting Congress, Nairobi, Kenya.
412 126 40f. multicoloured 1·00 50

127 Party Headquarters

1973. New Party Headquarters Building, Yamoussokro.
413 127 35f. multicoloured 60 30

128 Children at Dry Pump

1973. Pan-African Drought Relief.
414 128 40f. sepia, brown and red 1·00 40

129 "The Judgment of Solomon" (Nandjui Legue)

1973. Air. 6th World Peace and Justice Conf.
415 129 500f. multicoloured 12·00 5·00

129a

1973. U.A.M.P.T.
416 129a 100f. black, red and violet 1·80 80

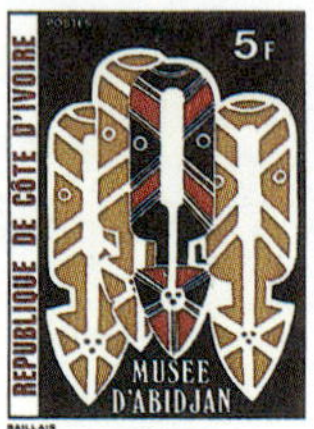

130 "Arrow-heads"

1973. Abidjan Museum.
417 130 5f. black, red and brown 40 20

131 Ivory Coast 1c. Stamp of 1892

1973. Stamp and Post Day.
418 131 40f. black, orange & green 1·00 50

132 Motorway Junction

1973. Motorway Projects. Indenie Interchange, Abidjan.
419 132 35f. black, green and blue 80 45

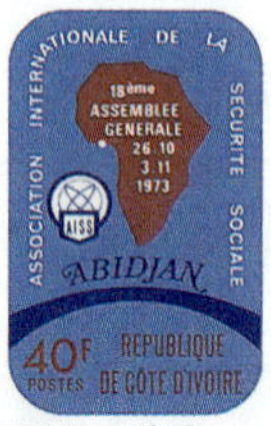

133 Map of Africa and Emblem

1973. 18th General Assembly of International Social Security Association.
420 133 40f. brown, ultram & bl 60 25

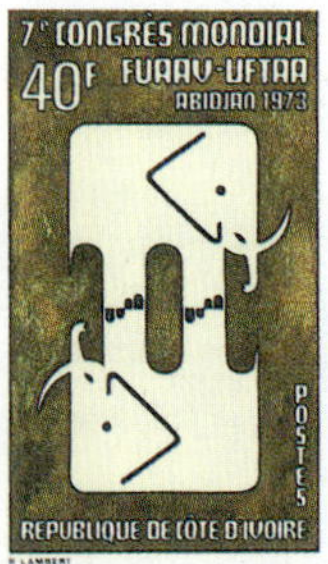

134 "Elephants" Ticket

1973. Travel-Agents Assns' 7th World Congress.

421	**134**	40f. multicoloured	60	25

136 Kong Mosque

1974

426	**136**	35f. brown, blue and green	80	50

137 Grand-Lahou Post Office

1974. Stamp Day.

427	**137**	35f. brown, green and blue	80	50

138 Converging Columns

1974. "Formation Permanente".

428	**138**	35f. multicoloured	60	30

139 Sassandra Bridge

1974. Air.

429	**139**	100f. brown and green	1·80	80
430	**139**	500f. black and green	11·00	3·75

140 Map of Member Countries

1974. 15th Anniv of Conseil de l'Entente.

431	**140**	40f. multicoloured	60	25

141 Arms of Ivory Coast

1974

432	**141**	35f. gold, green and brown	65	10
433	**141**	40f. gold, green and blue	75	10
434	**141**	60f. gold, green and red	80	25
435	**141**	65f. gold, lt green & green	80	25
436	**141**	70f. gold, green and blue	1·00	35

142 View of Factory

1974. Air. Vridi Soap Factory, Abidjan.

437	**142**	200f. multicoloured	3·00	1·50

143 Pres. Houphouet-Boigny

1974

438	**143**	25f. brown, orange & grn	50	25

144 W.P.Y. Emblem

1974. World Population Year.

439	**144**	40f. blue and green	80	25

145 Cotton-picking

1974. Cotton Production (1st series).

440	**145**	50f. multicoloured	1·00	50

See also Nos. 456/7.

146 Pres. Houphouet-Boigny

1974

441	**146**	35f. brown, green & orge	70	10
443	**146**	60f. brown, red and blue	80	35
444	**146**	65f. brown, blue and red	80	35
889	**146**	5f. brown, mauve and red	10	10
890	**146**	10f. brown, blue and green	10	10
891	**146**	20f. lt brown, brown & red	10	10
892	**146**	25f. brown, mauve & blue	30	10
893	**146**	30f. lt brown, brown & red	30	10
894	**146**	40f. brown, orange & grn	35	10
895	**146**	50f. brown, purple and red	45	10
896	**146**	90f. brown, red and purple	75	25
897	**146**	125f. brown, red & purple	1·20	25
898	**146**	155f. brown, blue and lilac	1·20	55

147 U.P.U. Emblem

148 Flag and U.P.U. Emblems

1974. Centenary of U.P.U.

445	**147**	40f. green, blue and brown (postage)	75	25
446	**148**	200f. multicoloured (air)	4·25	2·30
447	**148**	300f. multicoloured	5·25	3·25

149 Raoul Follereau

1974. Follereau (leprosy pioneer) Commem.

448	**149**	35f. red, yellow and green	1·70	70

150 Civic Service Emblem

1974. 14th Anniv of Independence.

449	**150**	35f. multicoloured	60	25

151 Library Building and Students

1975. 1st Anniv of Inauguration of National Library.

450	**151**	40f. multicoloured	60	25

153 Coffee Flower

1975. 52nd International Seedcrushers Association Congress, Abidjan.

451	**152**	40f. black and green	60	25

152 Congress Emblem

1975. Coffee Production. Multicoloured.

452	5f. Type **153**	30	10
453	10f. Coffee-berries	50	25

154 Sassandra Wharf

1975

454	**154**	100f. brown, green & blue	2·00	1·20

155 Postal Sorters

1975. Stamp Day.

455	**155**	40f. multicoloured	1·00	50

156 Cotton Flower

1975. Cotton Production (2nd series). Multicoloured.

456	5f. Type **156**	35	35
457	10f. Cotton bolls	60	35

157 Marie Kore and I.W.Y. Emblem

1975. International Women's Year.

458	**157**	45f. brown, blue and green	80	35

158 Dabou Fort

1975

459	**158**	50f. violet, blue and green	80	50

159 Abidjan Harbour

1975. 25th Anniv of Abidjan Port. Multicoloured.

460	35f. Type **159**	1·00	50
MS461	151×100 mm. 35f. Type **159**; 40f. Grand-Bassam wharf (vert); 100f. Proposed Locodjiro extension	8·75	8·75

160 Cocoa Tree

1975

462	**160**	35f. multicoloured	1·60	50

161 Rural Activities

1975. Promotion of Rural Development.

463	**161**	50f. mauve, violet & black	80	50

162 Railway Bridge over the N'Zi, Dimbokro

1975. 15th Anniv of Independence.

464	**162**	60f. multicoloured	3·50	1·00

164 Baoule Mask

1976. Mothers' Day.

465 **163** 65f. multicoloured 1·70 60

163 "Mother" (statue)

1976. Ivory Coast Art. Multicoloured.

466 20f. Type **164** (postage) 50 25

467 25f. Senoufo statuette 50 30

468 150f. Chief Abron's chair 2·75 1·20

469 200f. Akans royal symbols: fly swatter and panga (air) 4·50 1·80

165 Early and Modern Telephones

1976. Telephone Centenary.

470 **165** 70f. blue, brown and black 1·00 60

166 Effigy, Map and Carrier Pigeon

1976. 20th Anniv of Stamp Day and Ivory Coast Philatelic Club.

471 **166** 65f. multicoloured 80 50

167 "Smiling Trees" and Cat

1976. Nature Protection.

472 **167** 65f. multicoloured 1·00 45

168 Children Reading

1976. Literature for Children.

473 **168** 65f. multicoloured 1·00 50

169 Throwing the Javelin

1976. Olympic Games, Montreal. Multicoloured.

474 60f. Type **169** 85 50

475 65f. Running (horiz) 85 50

170 Mohammed Ali Jinnah

1976. Birth Centenary of Mohammed Ali Jinnah (first Governor-General of Pakistan).

476 **170** 50f. multicoloured 55·00 11·00

171 Cashew-nut

1976

477 **171** 65f. multicoloured 1·70 60

172 Houphouet-Boigny Bridge, Abidjan

1976. 3rd African Roads Conference, Abidjan.

478 **172** 60f. multicoloured 80 45

173 John Paul Jones (after Peale) and detail of "First Salute to the Stars and Stripes" (E. Moran)

1976. Bicentenary of American Revolution. Multicoloured.

479 100f. Type **173** 1·30 25

480 125f. Comte de Rochambeau, grenadier and flag 1·70 45

481 150f. Admiral D'Estaing, French marine and French warships 2·00 50

482 175f. Marquis de Lafayette (after Peale), grenadier and flag 2·00 55

483 200f. Thomas Jefferson (after Peale), militiaman and Declaration of Independence 2·50 70

MS484 101×76 mm. 500f. George Washington (after Stuart), officer and flag 6·25 2·75

174 Independence Motif

1976. 16th Anniv of Independence.

485 **174** 60f. multicoloured 80 50

175 Ife Bronze Mask

1977. 2nd World Festival of Negro Arts, Lagos.

486 **175** 65f. multicoloured 1·00 60

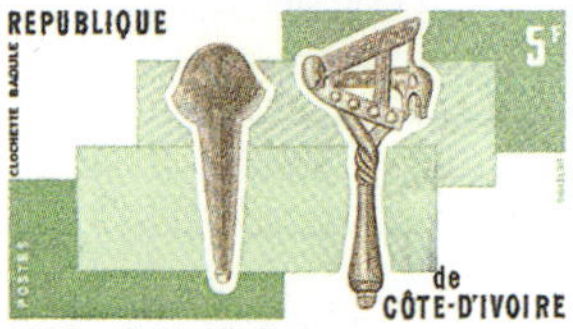

176 Baoule Handbells

1977. Musical Instruments (1st series).

487 **176** 5f. brown and green 30 25

488 - 10f. black and red 30 25

489 - 20f. black and violet 45 25

DESIGNS: 10f. Senoufo xylophone; 20f. Dida tom-tom.

See also Nos. 603/4.

177 Unloading Mail from Douglas DC-8

1977. Stamp Day.

490 **177** 60f. multicoloured 1·00 50

178 "Charaxes jasius epijasius"

1977. Butterflies (1st series). Multicoloured.

491 30f. "Epiphora rectifascia boolana" 3·25 1·70

492 60f. Type **178** 17·00 13·00

493 65f. "Imbrasia arata" 5·50 3·00

494 100f. "Palla decius" 7·75 5·25

See also Nos. 546/9 and 585/7.

179 Tingrela Mosque

1977. Air.

495 **179** 500f. brown, green & blue 6·75 3·75

180 Chateau Sassenage, Grenoble

1977. 10th Anniv of International French Language Council.

496 **180** 100f. multicoloured 1·40 60

181 Wright Brothers and Wright Type A Biplane

1977. History of Flying. Multicoloured.

497 60f. Type **181** 90 35

498 75f. Louis Bleriot crossing English Channel 1·00 25

499 100f. Ross Smith and Vickers Vimy aircraft 1·30 25

500 200f. Charles Lindbergh and "Spirit of St. Louis" 2·75 65

501 300f. Concorde 4·50 1·40

MS502 116×91 mm. 500f. Lindbergh and "Spirit of St. Louis" (different) 6·50 2·40

182 Santos Dumont's "Ville de Paris"

1977. History of the Airship. Multicoloured.

503 60f. Type **182** (air) 80 25

504 65f. Launch of LZ-1 80 25

505 150f. "Schwaben" 1·90 50

506 200f. "Bodensee" 2·75 70

507 300f. "Graf Zeppelin" over Egypt 4·00 1·30

MS508 92×104 mm. 500f. "LZ127" "Graf Zeppelin" over New York (air) 7·00 2·40

183 Congress Emblem

1977. 17th International Congress of Administrative Sciences in Africa.

509 **183** 60f. green and emerald 65 35

184 Pres. Houphouet-Boigny

1977

510 **184** 35f. black, mauve & brown 95 20

511 **184** 40f. black, orange & green 3·50 70

512 **184** 45f. black, green & orange 4·25 95

513 **184** 60f. black, purple & brown 5·00 95

514 **184** 65f. black, orange & green 5·50 1·50

185 Container Ship "Yamoussoukro"

1977. Yamoussoukro Container Port.
515 **185** 65f. multicoloured 2·20 80

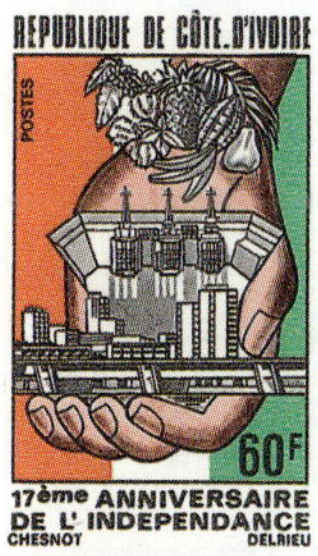

186 Hand holding Symbols of Development **187** "Strophantus hispidus"

1977. 17th Anniv of Independence.
516 **186** 60f. black, orange & green 80 50

1977. Flowers (1st series). Multicoloured.
517 5f. Type **187** 55·00 10·00
518 20f. "Anthurium cultorum" 55·00 10·00
519 60f. "Arachnis flos-aeris" 55·00 5·50
520 65f. "Renanthera storiei" 55·00 5·50

See also Nos. 571/3, 622/5, 678/80, 791c/e, 827a/b and 873e/f.

188 Presidents Giscard d'Estaing and Houphouet-Boigny

1978. Visit of President Giscard d'Estaing of France.
521 **188** 60f. multicoloured 1·00 35
522 **188** 65f. multicoloured 1·00 45
523 **188** 100f. multicoloured 1·70 80
MS524 159×120 mm. 500f. multi-coloured 9·00 9·00

189 "St. George and the Dragon"

1978. 400th Birth Anniv of Peter Paul Rubens (artist). Multicoloured.
525 65f. Type **189** 75 25
526 150f. "Head of a Child" 1·80 60
527 250f. "The Annunciation" 2·75 90
528 300f. "The Birth of Louis XIII" 3·75 1·30
MS529 96×115 mm. 500f. "Madonna and Child" 5·75 2·40

190 Members of the Royal Guard

1978. Images of History.
530 **190** 60f. red, black and blue 1·00 45
531 - 65f. black, blue and red 1·00 45
DESIGN: 65f. Figures of traditional cosmology.

191 Rural Post Office

1978. Stamp Day.
532 **191** 60f. multicoloured 80 50

192 Microwave Antenna

1978. Telecommunications Day.
533 **192** 60f. multicoloured 80 50

193 S. A. Arrhenius and Equipment (Chemistry, 1903)

1978. Nobel Prize Winners. Multicoloured.
534 60f. Type **193** 65 10
535 75f. Jules Bordet (Medicine, 1920) 80 25
536 100f. Andre Gide (Literature, 1947) 1·00 30
537 200f. John Steinbeck (Literature, 1962) 2·00 65
538 300f. UNICEF. (Peace, 1965) 3·50 1·00
MS539 119×81 mm. 500f. Max Planck (physics, 1914) 5·50 1·80

194 Player kicking Ball

1978. World Cup Football Championship, Argentina. Multicoloured.
540 60f. Football and player (horiz) 60 10
541 65f. Type **194** 80 25
542 100f. Football and player (different) (horiz) 1·00 50
543 150f. Goalkeeper (horiz) 1·80 60
544 300f. Football "sun" and player 3·00 95
MS545 102×77 mm. 500f. Football as globe showing South America 5·50 1·80

1978. Butterflies (2nd series). As T 178. Multicoloured.
546 60f. "Miniodes discolor" 3·00 90
547 65f. "Charaxes lactetinctus" 3·00 90
548 100f. "Papilio zalmoxis" 4·75 1·70
549 200f. "Papilio antimachus" 7·50 3·25

195 Banded Cricket

1978. Insects (1st series). Multicoloured.
550 10f. Type **195** 70 30
551 20f. "Nepa cinerea" (water scorpion) 1·10 40
552 60f. Horned tree-hopper 2·20 80
553 65f. "Goliathus cassicus" (beetle) 3·25 1·00

See also Nos. 600/2.

196 Passengers in Train

1978. Educational Television. Multicoloured.
554 60f. Figures emerging from television screen 75 30
555 65f. Type **196** 75 30

197 "Astragale" (oil exploration ship)

1978. 1st Anniv of Discovery of Oil in Ivory Coast. Multicoloured.
556 60f. Type **197** 1·30 45
557 65f. Ram, map of Ivory Coast and gold goblets 1·30 45
MS558 89×110 mm. 500f. Ram, map of Ivory Coast and President holding goblets 10·50 10·50

1978. Air. "Philexafrique" Stamp Exhibition, Gabon (1st issue) and International Stamp Fair, Essen, West Germany. As T 203a of Mauritania. Multicoloured.
559 100f. Common pheasant and Bavaria 1849 1k. stamp 3·50 2·40
560 100f. African elephant and Ivory Coast 1965 90f. stamp 3·50 2·40

See also Nos. 588/9.

198 National Assembly Building, Paris

1978. Centenary of Paris U.P.U. Congress.
561 **198** 200f. multicoloured 1·90 80

199 African with Ballot Box **200** Ribbon of Flags

1978. 18th Anniv of Independence.
562 **199** 60f. multicoloured 1·00 50

1978. Technical Co-operation among Developing Countries. Multicoloured.
563 60f. Type **200** 80 30
564 65f. Ribbon of flags forming arrows 80 30

201 Ploughing

1979. Agriculture.
565 **201** 100f. multicoloured 1·50 50

202 King Hassan and Pres Houphouet-Boigny

1979. Visit of King Hassan of Morocco.
566 **202** 60f. multicoloured 2·20 75
567 **202** 65f. multicoloured 3·50 1·10
568 **202** 500f. multicoloured 17·00 7·25

203 Isis

1979. UNESCO. Campaign for Preservation of Nubian Monuments.
569 **203** 200f. silver, green & turq 2·30 1·20
570 - 500f. gold, brown & orge 5·50 3·00
DESIGN: 500f. Gold medal.

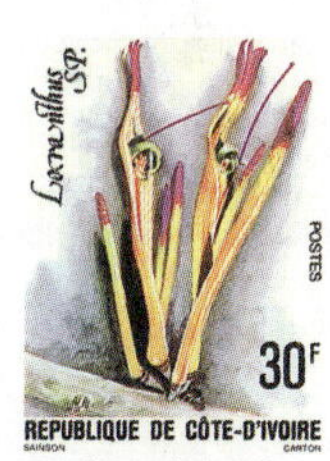

204 "Loranthus sp."

1979. Flowers (2nd series). Mult.
571 30f. Type **204** 90 50
572 60f. "Vanda josephine" 1·30 60
573 65f. "Renanthera storiei" 1·60 80

205 Sable Antelopes

1979. Endangered Animals (1st series). Mult.
574 5f. Type **205** 50 30
575 20f. Yellow-backed duiker 80 45
576 50f. Pygmy hippopotamus 1·50 40
577 60f. Aardvark 2·75 1·00

See also Nos. 613/18.

206 Children and Globe

1979. International Year of the Child. Mult.
578 60f. Type **206** 60 35
579 65f. Child on dove 75 45
580 100f. Type **206** 1·30 80
581 500f. As 65f. 5·25 3·00

207 Travelling Post Office

1979. Stamp Day.

582	207	60f. multicoloured	1·00	30

208 Korhogo Cathedral

1979. 75th Anniv of Arrival of Holy Fathers.

583	208	60f. multicoloured	80	45

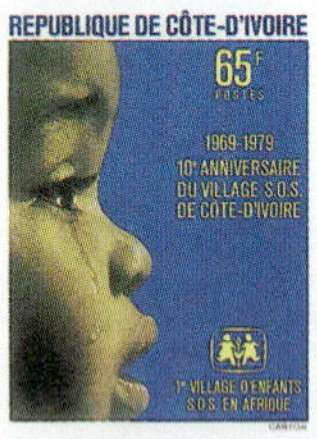

209 Crying Child

1979. 10th Anniv of S.O.S. Children's Village.

584	209	65f. multicoloured	80	50

210 "Euphaedra xypete"

1979. Butterflies (3rd series). Multicoloured.

585		60f. Type **210**	1·80	60
586		65f. "Pseudacraea bois duvali"	2·00	65
587		70f. "Auchenisa schausi"	3·00	90

211 Carved Figure and Antelope

1979. "Philexafrique", Stamp Exhibition, Gabon (2nd issue).

588	211	70f. multicoloured	2·50	2·00
589	-	70f. green, turquoise & red	2·50	2·00

DESIGN: No. 589, U.P.U. emblem, antenna, ship and truck.

212 Astronaut Greeting Boy

1979. 10th Anniv of Moon Landing. Mult.

590		60f. Type **212**	95	60
591		65f. Trajectory between Earth and Moon (horiz)	95	60
592		70f. Type **212**	1·50	75
593		150f. As 65f.	2·75	1·80

213 A4 Pacific (4-6-2) Locomotive and Great Britain £1 stamp, 1878

1979. Death Centenary of Sir Rowland Hill. Multicoloured.

594		60f. Type **213**	55	20
595		75f. Steam locomotive and Ivory Coast 45c. stamp, 1936	75	25
596		100f. Diesel locomotive No. 105, U.S.A. and Hawaiian 13c. "missionary" stamp, 1852	1·30	45
597		150f. Steam locomotive No. 1, Japan and Japanese 20s. stamp, 1872	1·50	50
598		300f. Class BB 15000 electric locomotive, France and French 15c. stamp, 1850	3·00	85
MS599		105×78 mm. 500f. Locomotive, Concorde and Ivory Coast 35c. stamp, 1936	7·25	2·40

214 "Delta sp."

1979. Insects (2nd series). Mult.

600		30f. Type **214**	6·00	2·00
601		60f. "Mantis religiosa" (vert)	9·50	3·00
602		65f. "Locusta migratorius"	10·50	3·00

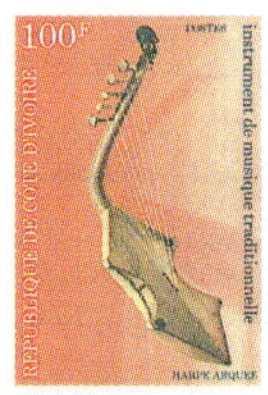

215 Harp

1979. Musical Instruments (2nd series). Mult.

603		100f. Type **215**	30·00	9·50
604		150f. Senoufo funeral horns	40·00	14·00

216 "Telecom 79"

1979. 3rd World Telecommunications Exhibition, Geneva.

605	216	60f. grey, orange and blue	80	35

217 Carved Head

1979. Culture Days.

606	217	65f. multicoloured	80	30

218 Boxing

1979. Pre-Olympic Year. Multicoloured.

607		60f. Type **218**	60	25
608		65f. Running	70	25
609		100f. Football	1·20	45
610		150f. Cycling	1·50	60
611		300f. Wrestling	3·00	1·00
MS612		117×85 mm. 500f. Gymnastics (horse)	5·50	1·70

See also Nos. 642/**MS**646.

219 Jentink's Duiker

1979. Endangered Animals (2nd series). Multicoloured.

613		40f. Type **219**	1·80	25
614		60f. Olive colobus	2·00	45
615		75f. African manatees	2·75	45
616		100f. Temminck's giant squirrel	4·00	65
617		150f. Pygmy hippopotamus	5·75	85
618		300f. Chimpanzee	10·50	1·80

220 Raoul Follereau and Institute

1979. Raoul Follereau d'Adzope Institute.

619	220	60f. multicoloured	1·30	50

221 Post, Adze and Plant

1979. 19th Anniv of Independence.

620	221	60f. multicoloured	1·00	25

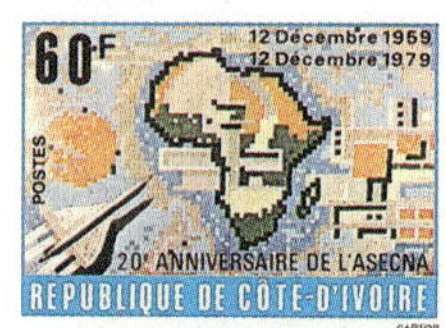

222 Concorde and Map of Africa

1979. 20th Anniv of ASECNA (African Air Safety Organization).

621	222	60f. multicoloured	80	30

222a Coelancanth

1979. Fishes (1st series). Multicoloured.

621a		60f. Lionfish	£120	7·75
621b		65f. Type **222a**	£120	7·75

See also Nos. 629/31 and 666/8.

223 "Clerodendron thomsonae"

1980. Flowers (3rd series). Multicoloured.

622		5f. Type **223**	10	10
623		10f. "La Boule de Feu" (horiz)	30	10
624		50f. "Costus incanusiamus"	85	25
625		60f. "Ficus elastica"	95	30

224 Elephant, Map and Rotary Emblem

1980. 75th Anniv of Rotary International.

626	224	65f. multicoloured	80	35

225 Seal

1980. International Archives Day.

627	225	65f. multicoloured	80	50

226 Boys with Stamp Album

1980. Stamp Day.

628	226	65f. brown and turquoise	1·00	25

1980. Fishes (2nd series). As T 222a. Multicoloured.

629		60f. Emperor snapper	2·75	60
630		65f. Guinean fingerfish (vert)	2·75	95
631		100f. Banded gourami	3·50	1·30

228 Missionary and Church, Aboisso

1980. 75th Anniv of Settlement of Holy Fathers at Aboisso.

632	228	60f. multicoloured	1·00	50

229 Hands protecting Child from Cigarettes

1980. Anti-Smoking Campaign.

633	229	60f. multicoloured	1·00	25

230 Pope John-Paul II and President Houphouet-Boigny

1980. Papal Visit.

634	230	65f. yellow, brn & dp brn	2·30	90

231 "Le Belier" Express Train, Abidjan–Bouake

1980. Railways. Multicoloured.

635	60f. Type **231**	75	25
636	65f. Abidjan Station, 1904	75	45
637	100f. Steam train, 1908	1·30	60
638	150f. Steam goods train, 1940	1·80	90

232 Headquarters Building, Dakar

1980. 1st Anniv of West African Central Bank.

639	232	60f. multicoloured	80	45

233 Cobra

1980. Animals. Multicoloured.

640	60f. Type **233**	1·40	35
641	150f. Toad	3·25	1·20

234 Gymnastics

235 World Tourism Conference Emblem

1980. Air. Olympic Games, Moscow. Multicoloured.

642	75f. Type **234**	95	25
643	150f. Ring exercise	1·60	45
644	250f. Vaulting horse (horiz)	2·75	80
645	350f. Bar exercise	3·75	1·30
MS646	106×80 mm. 500f. Floor exercise (horiz)	5·00	1·70

1980. Tourism. Multicoloured.

647	60f. Village scene	60	35
648	65f. Type **235**	60	25

1980. Insects (3rd series). As T 214. Mult.

649	60f. "Ugada limbata" (25×35 mm)	3·50	1·60
650	60f. "Forticula auricularia" (36×26 mm)	1·60	1·00
651	65f. "Mantis religiosa" (26×32 mm)	3·50	1·60
652	200f. Grasshopper (35×25 mm)	6·00	2·50

236 Hands breaking Chains, Map and President

1980. President Houphouet-Boigny's 75th Birthday.

653	236	60f. mult (postage)	1·30	55
654	-	65f. multicoloured	1·50	65
655	-	70f. multicoloured	1·80	85
656	236	150f. multicoloured	4·00	2·10
657	-	300f. multicoloured	7·00	3·50
658	-	2000f. silver (air)	20·00	20·00
659	-	3000f. gold	31·00	31·00

DESIGNS—SQUARE: 70f. Presidential speech on map in national colours. HORIZ (44×29 mm): 65f., 300f. President and symbols of progress. VERT (35×45 mm): 2000f., 3000f. President Houphouet-Boigny.

237 Map of Ivory Coast

1980. 7th P.D.C.I.–R.D.A. Congress.

660	237	60f. green, orange & black	80	25
661	237	65f. green, orange & black	80	25

238 "Sotra" (ferry)

1980. New Lagoon Transport.

662	238	60f. multicoloured	1·00	50

239 Abidjan

1980. 20th Anniv of Independence.

663	239	60f. multicoloured	80	25

240 Conference Emblem

1980. 5th General Conference of African Universities Association, Yamoussoukro.

664	240	60f. multicoloured	80	35

241 Map of Africa and Posthorn

1980. 5th Anniv of African Posts and Telecommunications Union.

665	241	150f. multicoloured	1·50	50

241a Red-billed Dwarf Hornbill

1980. Birds. Multicoloured.

665a	60f. Superb starling	80·00	4·75
665b	65f. Type **241a**	80·00	4·75
665c	65f. South African crowned crane	80·00	4·75
665d	100f. Saddle-bill stork	80·00	14·50

242 Rio Grande Cichlid

1981. Fishes (3rd series). Multicoloured.

666	60f. Type **242**	90	55
667	65f. Red-tailed black shark	90	55
668	200f. Green pufferfish	2·75	1·50

243 Post Office, Grand Lahou

1981. Stamp Day.

669	243	60f. multicoloured	80	25

244 Mask

1981. 25th Anniv of Ivory Coast Philatelic Club.

670	244	65f. black, lt brown & brn	80	25

245 Red Cross Aircraft, Satellite and Globe (Telecommunications and Health)

1981. World Telecommunications Day.

671	245	30f. multicoloured	35	10
672	245	60f. multicoloured	90	35

246 "Viking" landing on Mars

1981. Conquest of Space. Multicoloured.

673	60f. Type **246**	60	20
674	75f. Space Shuttle on launch pad	80	25
675	125f. Space Shuttle erecting experiment	1·30	55
676	300f. Space Shuttle performing experiment	2·75	1·30
MS677	103×78 mm. 500f. Space Shuttles constructing framework in space	5·50	1·70

1981. Flowers (4th series). Multicoloured.

678	50f. Type **247**	1·50	55
679	60f. Sugar cane flowers	2·10	80
680	100f. "Heliconia ivoirea"	3·00	1·40

See also Nos. 791c/e, 827a/b and 873e/f.

248 Prince Charles, Lady Diana Spencer and Coach

1981. Royal Wedding.

681	248	80f. multicoloured	80	25
682	-	100f. multicoloured	1·00	45
683	-	125f. multicoloured	1·30	60
MS684		104×80 mm. 500f. multicoloured	5·25	1·80

DESIGNS: 100f. to 500f. Showing Prince Charles, Lady Diana Spencer and coaches.

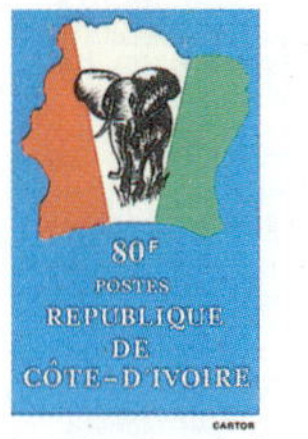

249 Map formed of Flag

1981

684a	249	5f. multicoloured	10	10
684aa	249	10f. multicoloured	30	10
684ab	249	20f. multicoloured	35	10
684b	249	25f. multicoloured	30	10
684c	249	30f. multicoloured	35	10
684ca	249	35f. multicoloured	45	10
684d	249	40f. multicoloured	50	10
684e	249	50f. multicoloured	50	10
685	249	80f. multicoloured	75	25
686	249	100f. multicoloured	1·00	50
687	249	125f. multicoloured	1·30	60

250 Goalkeeper

1981. World Cup Football Championship, Spain (1982). Multicoloured.

688	70f. Type **250**	60	25
689	80f. Saving a goal	80	50
690	100f. Diving for ball (vert)	1·00	55
691	150f. Goalmouth scene	1·50	85
692	350f. Fighting for ball (vert)	3·50	1·60
MS693	103×78 mm. 500f. Goalmouth scene	5·25	3·75

251 Association Emblem

1981. West Africa Rice Development Association.

694	251	80f. multicoloured	1·00	35

252 Post Office

1981. Stamp Day.

695	252	70f. multicoloured	60	25
696	252	80f. multicoloured	75	45
697	252	100f. multicoloured	95	50

253 Hands with and without Fruit, and F.A.O. Emblem

1981. World Food Day.

698	253	100f. multicoloured	1·00	50

254 Felice Nazarro

1981. 75th Anniv of French Grand Prix Motor Race. Multicoloured.

699	15f. Type **254**	30	10
700	40f. Jim Clark	50	25
701	80f. Fiat, 1907	1·00	50
702	100f. Auto Union, 1936	1·30	60
703	125f. Ferrari, 1961	1·50	75
MS704	121×95 mm. 500f. Monaco Grand Prix, 1933	6·25	2·30

255 Symbols of Economic Growth

1981. 21st Anniv of Independence.

705	**255**	50f. multicoloured	50	25
706	**255**	80f. multicoloured	80	50

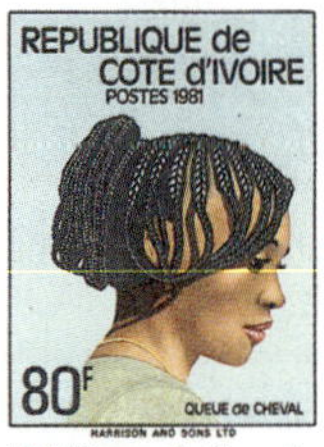

256 "Queue de Cheval"

1982. Hairstyles. Multicoloured.

707	80f. Type **256**	1·30	60
708	100f. "Belier"	2·10	85
709	125f. "Cheri regarde mon visage"	2·75	1·10

257 Bingerville Post Office, 1902

1982. Stamp Day.

710	**257**	100f. multicoloured	1·00	50

258 Rotary Emblem on Map of Africa

1982. Rotary International Conference, Abidjan.

711	**258**	100f. blue and gold	1·00	55

259 George Washington

1982. Celebrities' Anniversaries. Multicoloured.

712	80f. Type **259** (250th birth anniv)	80	30
713	100f. Auguste Piccard (20th death anniv)	1·00	50
714	350f. Goethe (150th death anniv)	3·50	1·30
715	450f. Princess of Wales (21st birthday)	4·25	1·70
MS716	80×104 mm. 500f. Princess of Wales (different)	4·50	1·90

260 Hexagonal Pattern and Telephone

1982. World Telecommunications Day.

717	**260**	80f. multicoloured	80	30

261 Presidents Mitterand and Houphouet-Boigny

1982. Visit of President Mitterand of France.

718	**261**	100f. multicoloured	1·40	60

262 Dr. Koch, Bacillus and Microscope

1982. Cent of Discovery of Tubercle Bacillus.

719	**262**	30f. multicoloured	50	25
720	**262**	80f. multicoloured	1·30	70

263 Scouts in Dinghy

1982. 75th Anniv of Boy Scout Movement. Multicoloured.

721	80f. Type **263**	80	25
722	100f. Dinghy (horiz)	1·30	35
723	150f. Leaning into wind	1·50	60
724	350f. Hauling sail	3·50	1·20
MS725	65×81 mm. 500f. Yachts	5·75	1·80

264 Aerial View of Coastline

1982. 10th Anniv of U.N. Environmental Programme.

726	**264**	40f. multicoloured	50	25
727	**264**	80f. multicoloured	90	50

265 Congress Emblem

1982. First League of Ivory Coast Secretaries Congress, Abidjan.

728	**265**	80f. multicoloured	80	30
729	**265**	100f. multicoloured	1·00	45

247 "Amorphophallus sp."

1982. Birth of Prince William of Wales. Nos. 681/MS684 optd NAISSANCE ROYALE 1982.

730	**247**	80f. multicoloured	85	35
731	-	100f. multicoloured	1·00	50
732	-	125f. multicoloured	1·20	60
MS733		104×80 mm. 500f. multicoloured	4·50	4·50

267 "Child with Dove"

1982. Picasso Paintings. Multicoloured.

734	80f. Type **267**	75	35
735	100f. "Self-portrait"	1·10	35
736	185f. "Les Demoiselles d'Avignon"	2·50	60
737	350f. "The Dream"	4·25	1·20
738	500f. "La Colombe de l'Avenir" (horiz)	6·00	1·70

268 Post Office Counter, Abidjan 17

1982. World U.P.U. Day. Multicoloured.

739	80f. Type **268**	95	45
740	100f. Postel 2001 Building, Abidjan (vert)	1·20	45
741	350f. Counter clerks at Abidjan 17 Post Office	3·50	1·40
742	500f. Exterior and interior views of Postel 2001 (48×36 mm)	5·00	2·20

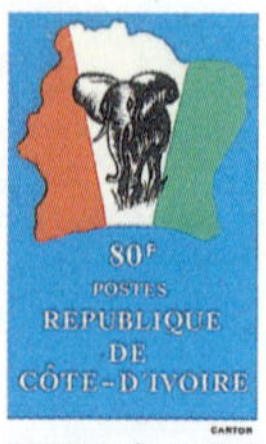

249 Map formed of Flag

1982. World Cup Football Championship Results. Nos. 688/92 optd.

743	70f. Type **249**	60	25
744	80f. Saving a goal	80	50
745	100f. Diving for ball (vert)	1·00	50
746	150f. Goalmouth scene	1·50	85
747	350f. Fighting for ball (vert)	3·50	1·60
MS748	103×78 mm. 500f. Goalmouth scene	5·25	5·25

DESIGNS: 70f. **1966 VAINQUEUR GRAND-BRETAGNE**; 80f. **1970 VAINQUEUR BRESIL** 100f. **1974 VAINQUEUR ALLEMAGNE** (REA) (vert); 150f. **1978 VAINQUEUR ARGENTINE**; 350f. **1982. VAINQUEUR ITALIE** (vert); 500f. **ITALI-ALLEMAGNE (RFA) 3 1**.

270 President Houphouet-Boigny with Farming Implements and Agricultural Produce

1982. 22nd Anniv of Independence.

749	**270**	100f. multicoloured	1·00	50

271 Emblem and Map of Member Countries

1982. 20th Anniv of West African Monetary Union.

750	**271**	100f. brown, blue & dp bl	1·00	55

272 Man Waterfall

1982. Landscapes. Multicoloured.

751	80f. Type **272**	11·00	1·20
752	80f. Wooded savanna	14·50	65
753	500f. Type **272**	39·00	5·50

273 Child and S.O.S. Village

274 Long-tailed Pangolin

1983. S.O.S. Children's Village.

754	**273**	125f. multicoloured	1·40	60

274 Long-tailed Pangolin

1983. Animals. Multicoloured.

755	35f. Type **274**	50	25
756	90f. Bush pig (horiz)	1·00	45
757	100f. Eastern black-and-white colobus	1·30	50
758	125f. African buffalo (horiz)	1·40	60

275 Post Office, Grand Bassam, 1903

1983. Stamp Day.

759	**275**	100f. multicoloured	1·00	50

276 Montgolfier Balloon, 1783

1983. Bicentenary of Manned Flight. Mult.

760	100f. Type **276**	1·00	35
761	125f. Charles's hydrogen balloon, 1783	1·40	45
762	150f. Balloon "Armand Barbes" (Paris siege post, 1870) (horiz)	1·70	55
763	350f. Balloon "Double Eagle II" over Atlantic	4·25	1·20
764	500f. Advertising airship (horiz)	6·25	1·80

277 "Descent from the Cross"

1983. Easter. Multicoloured.

765	100f. Type **277**	1·00	25
766	125f. "The Resurrection of Christ" (horiz)	1·20	45
767	350f. "The Raising of the Cross" (horiz)	3·25	1·10
768	400f. "The Piercing of the Lance"	4·00	1·30
769	500f. "Descent from the Cross"	4·50	1·60

278 Safe containing U.N. Emblem

1983. 25th Anniv of U.N. Economic Commission for Africa.

770	**278**	100f. multicoloured	1·00	50

279 African Fish Eagle

1983. Birds. Multicoloured.

771	100f. Type **279**	1·50	60
772	125f. Grey parrot (horiz)	2·00	55
773	150f. Violet turaco (horiz)	3·00	85

280 Swimming

1983. Air. Pre-Olympic Year. Multicoloured.

774	100f. Type **280**	95	30
775	125f. Diving	1·20	50
776	350f. Backstroke	3·25	1·20
777	400f. Butterfly stroke	3·75	1·40
MS778	116×90 mm. 500f. water polo	5·75	1·80

281 Forest destroyed by Fire

1983. Ecology in Action. Multicoloured.

779	25f. Type **281**	60	35
780	100f. Animals running from fire	1·70	70
781	125f. Protected animals	2·30	95

282 Flali Dance

1983. Traditional Dances. Multicoloured.

782	50f. Type **282**	45	25
783	100f. Mask dance	95	45
784	125f. Stilt dance	1·40	50

283 Hotel Ivoire

1983. 20th Anniv of Hotel Ivoire, Abidjan.

785	**283**	100f. multicoloured	1·00	50

284 Rally Car and Route

1983. World and African Car Rally Championships.

786	**284**	100f. multicoloured	1·30	60

285 "Christ and St. Peter"

1983. Christmas. Paintings by Raphael. Mult.

787	100f. Type **285**	1·00	40
788	125f. Study for St. Joseph	1·30	55
789	350f. "Virgin of the House of Orleans"	3·50	1·30
790	500f. "Virgin of the Blue Diadem"	4·50	1·70

286 President Houphouet-Boigny

1983. 23rd Anniv of Independence.

791	**286**	100f. multicoloured	1·00	50

286a Telegraphist, Dish Aerial and National Postal Sorting Centre

1983. World Communications Year. Mult.

791a	100f. Cable-laying, Postel 2001 building, Abidjan, and telephonists	75·00	4·75
791b	125f. Type **286a**	75·00	6·50

1983. Flowers (5th series). As T 247. Multicoloured.

791c	100f. Pineapple flowers	£200	
791d	125f. "Heliconia rostrata"	49·00	12·00
791e	150f. "Rose de Porcelaine"	49·00	12·00

287 Arrow piercing Television Screen

1984. First Audio-Visual Forum.

792	**287**	100f. black and green	1·00	50

288 Competition Emblem

1984. Africa Cup Football Competition.

793	**288**	100f. multicoloured	95	45
794	-	200f. orange, green & blk	1·80	85

DESIGN: 200f. Maps of Africa and Ivory Coast shaking hands.

289 Spider

1984. Multicoloured.

795	100f. Type **289**	1·70	70
796	125f. "Polistes gallicus" (wasp)	2·00	95

290 Abidjan Post Office, 1934

1984. Stamp Day.

797	**290**	100f. multicoloured	1·00	45

291 Swimming

1984. Air. Olympic Games, Los Angeles. Multicoloured.

798	100f. Type **291**	1·00	30
799	125f. Cross-country	1·30	45
800	185f. Pistol shooting	1·70	55
801	350f. Fencing	3·50	1·10
MS802	104×80 mm. 500f. Equestrian	6·00	1·80

292 Lions Club Badge

1984. 3rd Lions Multi District 403 Convention. Multicoloured.

803	100f. Type **292**	1·00	50
804	125f. As Type **292** but with badge at right	1·50	75

293 Telecommunications Stations on Map of Ivory Coast

1984. World Telecommunications Day.

805	**293**	100f. multicoloured	1·10	50

294 Flags, Agriculture and Symbols of Unity and Growth

1984. 25th Anniv of Council of Unity.

806	**294**	100f. multicoloured	95	45
807	**294**	125f. multicoloured	1·30	50

295 First Government House, Grand-Bassam

1984. Old Buildings (1st series). Multicoloured.

808	100f. Type **295**	1·00	45
809	125f. Palace of Justice, Grand-Bassam	1·30	50

See also Nos. 873a/c.

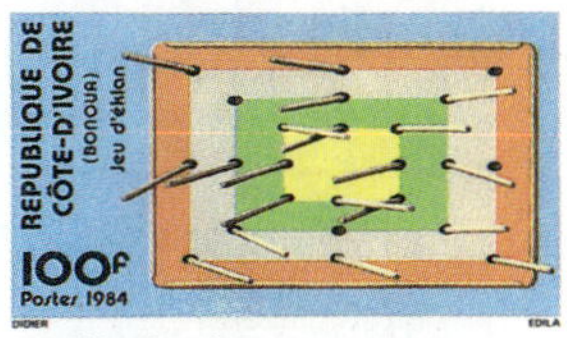

296 Eklan Board

1984. Eklan. Multicoloured.

810	100f. Type **296**	1·30	40
811	125f. Two Eklan players	1·30	60

297 "La Gazelle" Express Train, Abidjan–Ouagadougou

1984. Transport. Multicoloured. (a) Locomotives.

812	100f. Type **297**	1·20	40
813	125f. Steam locomotive, 1931, France	1·80	50
814	350f. Type 10 steam locomotive, Belgium	4·25	1·20
815	500f. Class GT2 Mallet steam locomotive	6·00	1·70

(b) Ships.

816	100f. Container Ship	1·00	35
817	125f. Cargo liner	1·30	50
818	350f. "Queen Mary" (liner)	3·75	1·10

819 500f. "France" (liner) 6·00 1·60

298 Envelope, Map and Symbols of Postal Service

1984. Stamp Day.
820 **298** 100f. multicoloured 1·30 55

299 Emblem

1984. 10th Anniv of West African Economic Community.
821 **299** 100f. multicoloured 95 50

300 Book Cover

1984. 90th Anniv (1982) of Ivory Coast Postage Stamps.
822 **300** 125f. multicoloured 1·30 85

301 Map Outline, People and Flag

1984. 24th Anniv of Independence.
823 **301** 100f. multicoloured 95 50

302 G. Tiacoh (400 m silver)

1984. Air. Olympic Games Medallists. Mult.
824 100f. Type **302** 1·10 25
825 150f. C. Lewis (100 and 200 m gold) 1·60 45
826 200f. A. Babers (400 m gold) 2·20 80
827 500f. J. Cruz (800 m gold) 4·75 1·50

1984. Flowers (6th series). As T 247. Mult.
827a 100f. "Allamanda cathartica" 55·00 12·00
827b 125f. Baobab flowers 55·00 12·00

302a Serval

1984. Animals. Multicoloured.
827c 100f. Bushbuck 49·00 12·00
827d 150f. Type **302a** 49·00 12·00

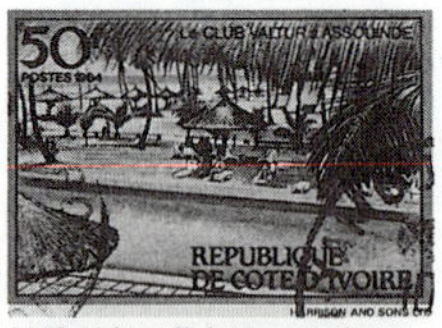

302b Valtur Club, Assouinde

1984
827e 50f. Type **302b** 43·00 7·75
827f 100f. Azagni Canal 43·00 8·75

303 "Virgin and Child" (Correggio)

1985. Air. Christmas. Multicoloured.
828 100f. Type **303** 1·10 50
829 200f. "Virgin and Child" (Andrea del Sarto) 2·10 90
830 400f. "Virgin and Child" (Jacopo Bellini) 4·00 1·90

Nos. 829/30 are wrongly inscribed "Le Correge" (Correggio).

304 Map, Hands, Emblem and Dove

1985. African Conference of Rotary International, Abidjan.
831 **304** 100f. multicoloured 1·00 50
832 **304** 125f. multicoloured 1·20 55

305 "Le Babou" (Dan costume)

1985. Traditional Costumes. Multicoloured.
833 90f. Type **305** 1·30 40
834 100f. Avikam post-natal dress 1·30 60

305a Hadada Ibis

1985. Birds. Multicoloured.
834a 25f. Marabou stork £120 15·00
834b 100f. African jacana £120 15·00
834c 350f. Type **305a** £120 15·00

306 River Steamer "Adjame"

1985. Stamp Day.
835 **306** 100f. multicoloured 1·60 80

308 Emblem

1985. 7th Conference of District 18 of Zonta International, Abidjan.
836 **308** 125f. multicoloured 1·20 45

309 Airplane, Van and Industrial Landscape

1985. "Philexafrique" Stamp Exhibition, Lome, Togo (1st issue). Multicoloured.
837 200f. Type **309** 2·30 1·60
838 200f. Sports and agriculture 2·30 1·60

See also Nos. 864/5.

310 Red-breasted Mergansers

1985. Air. Birth Bicentenary of John J. Audubon (ornithologist). Multicoloured.
839 100f. Type **310** 1·00 50
840 150f. American white pelican (vert) 1·60 70
841 200f. American wood stork (vert) 2·75 90
842 350f. Velvet scoters 3·75 1·60

311 Chemical Plant, Senegal

1985. 20th Anniv of African Development Bank.
843 100f. Type **311** 1·00 40
844 125f. Tree seedlings, Gambia 1·30 60

312 Profiles within Map and IYY Emblem

1985. International Youth Year.
845 **312** 125f. multicoloured 1·20 60

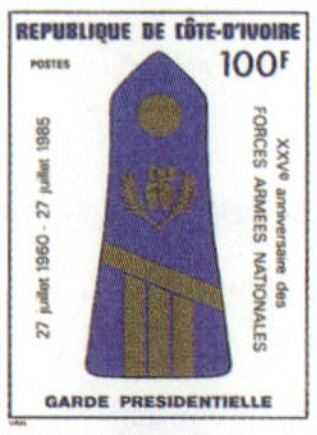

313 Presidential Guard Shoulder Flash

1985. 25th Anniv of National Armed Forces.
846 **313** 100f. gold and purple 95 40
847 - 100f. gold and blue 95 40
848 - 125f. gold and black 1·30 60
849 - 200f. gold and brown 2·20 85
850 - 350f. silver and blue 3·25 1·50

DESIGNS: Shoulder flashes of—No. 847, F.A.N.C.I. (army); 848, Air Force; 849, Navy; 850, Gendarmerie.

314 Ivory Coast Arms

1985. Postal Convention with Sovereign Military Order of Malta. Multicoloured.
851 125f. Type **314** 1·20 60
852 350f. Sovereign Military Order of Malta arms 3·25 1·90

315 Footballers

1985. World Cup Football Championship, Mexico. Multicoloured.
853 100f. Type **315** 95 40
854 150f. Footballers (different) 1·30 65
855 200f. Footballers (different) 1·70 80
856 350f. Footballers (different) 3·50 1·40
MS857 106×82 mm. 500f. Footballers (different) 4·50 1·70

316 Pope and Abidjan Cathedral

1985. Visit of Pope John Paul II.
858 **316** 100f. multicoloured 1·60 80

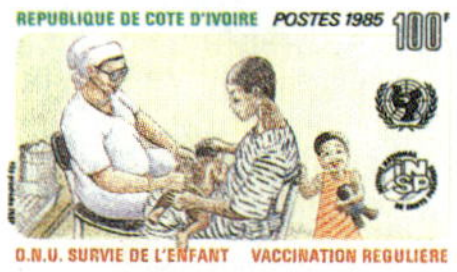

317 Vaccinating Baby

1985. UNICEF Child Survival Campaign. Multicoloured.
859 100f. Type **317** 95 50
860 100f. Mother breast-feeding baby while child plays 95 50
861 100f. Mother spoon-feeding child 95 50
862 100f. Mother giving child a drink (oral rehydration) 95 50

318 Rainbow, U.N. Emblem and Joined Hands

1985. 40th Anniv of U.N.O. and 25th Anniv of Ivory Coast Membership.
863 **318** 100f. multicoloured 95 40

319 Footballers and Children with Injured Animal

1985. Air. "Philexafrique" International Stamp Exhibition, Lome, Togo (2nd issue). Mult.
864 250f. Type **319** 3·50 2·20
865 250f. Dish aerial, rocket and container ship 3·50 2·20

320 City Skyline

1985. "Expo 85" World's Fair, Tsukuba, Japan.

866	**320**	125f. multicoloured	1·30	55

321 Young Duiker

1985. World Wildlife Fund. Banded Duiker. Multicoloured.

867	50f. Type **321**	2·50	40
868	60f. Duiker in front of bushes	3·75	60
869	75f. Two duikers	6·25	1·00
870	100f. Duiker (different)	8·25	1·50

322 Children on Open Ground

1985. "Return to the Earth".

871	**322**	125f. multicoloured	1·30	55

323 Woman spinning Cotton

1985. Rural Handicrafts. Multicoloured.

872	125f. Type **323**	1·30	55
873	155f. Man painting on cotton cloth	1·70	75

323a Samatiguila Mosque

1985. Old Buildings (2nd series). Multicoloured.

873a	100f. Bondoukou Market	29·00	8·00
873b	125f. Type **323a**	29·00	8·00
873c	200f. Samory House, Bondoukou	29·00	8·00

1985. Flowers (7th series). As T 247. Mult.

873d	100f. "Amorphophallus staudtii"	32·00	9·50
873e	125f. Crinum	32·00	9·50
873f	200f. "Triphyophyllum peltotum"	32·00	9·50

324 Edmond Halley and Computer Picture of Comet

1986. Air. Appearance of Halley's Comet. Multicoloured.

874	125f. Type **324**	1·20	45
875	155f. Sir William Herschel and Uranus	1·50	65
876	190f. Space telescope and comet	1·70	80
877	350f. "MS T-5" space probe and comet	3·25	1·40
878	440f. "Skylab" and Kohoutek's comet	3·75	1·80

325 "Millettia takou"

1986. Plants. Multicoloured.

879	40f. "Omphalocarpum elatum"	45	20
880	50f. "Momordica charantia"	55	25
881	125f. Type **325**	1·30	65
882	200f. "Costus afer"	2·00	1·00

326 Vase from We

1986. Traditional Kitchenware and Tools. Multicoloured.

883	20f. Type **326**	20	10
884	30f. Baoule vase	30	10
885	90f. Baoule dish	1·00	35
886	125f. Dan knife (vert)	1·30	50
887	440f. Baoule pottery jug (vert)	4·25	2·00

327 Institute Building

1986. 10th Anniv of Institute for Higher Technical and Professional Education.

888	**327**	125f. multicoloured	1·30	55

329 Cable Ship "Stephan", 1910

1986. Stamp Day.

899	**329**	125f. multicoloured	1·70	55

330 Footballers

1986. Air. World Cup Football Championship, Mexico.

900	**330**	90f. multicoloured	80	35
901	-	125f. multicoloured	1·30	45
902	-	155f. multicoloured	1·50	65
903	-	440f. multicoloured	4·00	1·80
904	-	500f. multicoloured	4·50	2·10

MS905	104×83 mm. 600f. multicoloured	5·50	2·00

DESIGNS: 125f. to 600f. Different football scenes.

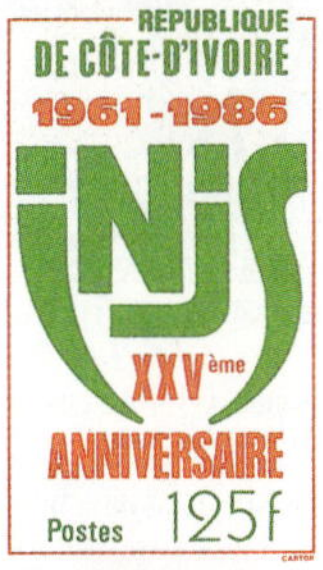

331 Emblem

1986. 25th Anniv of National Youth and Sports Institute.

906	**331**	125f. green and orange	1·30	55

332 Endlicher's Bichir

1986. Fishes. Multicoloured.

907	5f. Type **332**	15	15
908	125f. Daget's squeaker	1·30	70
909	150f. West African lung-fish	1·70	80
910	155f. Ivory Coast squeaker	1·80	80
911	440f. Electric catfish	5·00	2·30

333 Sacred Tom-tom

1986. Enthronement of King of the Agni. Multicoloured.

912	50f. Type **333**	45	45
913	350f. King being carried	3·50	2·00
914	440f. King and his Court	4·50	2·75

334 Baoule Village, Aoulo

1986. Rural Dwellings (1st series). Multicoloured.

915	125f. Type **334**	1·20	60
916	155f. Avikam village, Eva	1·50	85
917	350f. Lobi village, Soukala	3·25	1·80

See also Nos. 938/9, 990 and 1012.

336 Rocky Coastline

1986

921	**335**	50f. red	45	20
924	**335**	125f. green	1·30	30
926	**335**	155f. red	1·50	30
927	**335**	195f. blue	1·80	30

335 Ivory Coast Arms

1986. Coastal Landscapes. Multicoloured.

930	125f. Type **336**	1·50	80
931	155f. Sandy beach	2·00	1·00

337 Fishery Lake

1986. Oceanographic Research Centre. Mult.

932	125f. Type **337**	1·20	60
933	155f. Fishermen hauling in net	1·50	85

338 Pres. Houphouet-Boigny, Rainbow and Dove

1986. International Peace Year.

934	**338**	155f. multicoloured	1·50	75

339 Bull

1986. Research and Development. Mult.

935	125f. Type **339**	1·60	90
936	155f. Rice (IDSA 6)	1·60	90

340 Pres. Houphouet-Boigny and Symbols of Development

1986. 26th Anniv of Independence.

937	**340**	155f. multicoloured	1·50	75

341 Guesseple Dan Village

1987. Rural Dwellings (2nd series). Mult.

938	190f. Type **341**	2·00	1·20
939	550f. M'Bagui Senoufo village	5·50	3·00

342 Postman, 1918

1987. Stamp Day.

940	**342**	155f. multicoloured	1·50	85

343 Elephant and Cockerel

1987. 25th Anniv of French–Ivory Coast Cultural Friendship. Jean Mermoz College. Multicoloured.

941	40f. Type **343**	45	25
942	155f. Children's faces in dove	1·50	70

344 Child running to Adult

1987. World Red Cross Day.

943	**344**	195f.+5f. multicoloured	2·30	1·80

345 "Soling" Class Yachts

1987. Air. Olympic Games, Seoul (1988) (1st issue). Sailing. Multicoloured.

944	155f. Type **345**	1·50	65
945	195f. Windsurfers	2·00	80
946	250f. "470" class dinghies	2·75	95
947	550f. Windsurfer	5·50	2·20
MS948	104×80 mm. 650f. "470" class yachts (51×30 mm)	7·25	2·50

See also Nos. 959/**MS**963.

346 "Excavations" (Krah N'Guessan)

1987. Paintings. Multicoloured.

949	195f. Type **346**	2·00	1·20
950	500f. "Ceremonial Cortege" (Santoni Gerard)	4·50	3·00

347 Airplane and Van

1987. World Post Day. International Express Post.

951	**347**	155f. multicoloured	1·50	1·00
952	**347**	195f. multicoloured	1·80	1·20

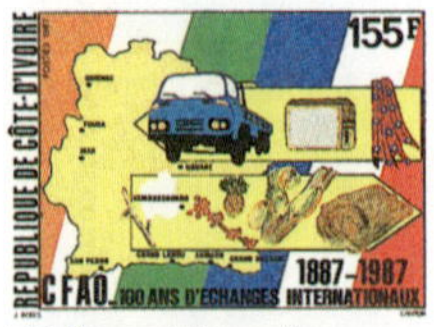

348 Map and Forms of Communication

1987. 100 Years of International Mail and Communications Exchanges.

953	**348**	155f. multicoloured	1·50	85

349 Tower Block reflecting Symbols of Progress

1987. 27th Anniv of Independence.

954	**349**	155f. multicoloured	1·50	85

350 Baby in Aloe Plant on Map

1988. Lions International. "For the Life of a Child".

955	**350**	155f. multicoloured	1·50	85

351 Bereby Post Office, 1900

1988. Stamp Day.

956	**351**	155f. multicoloured	1·50	80

352 Heart

1988. 15th Francophone Cardiological Congress, Abidjan.

957	**352**	195f. red and black	2·30	1·50

353 Man working Soil

1988. 10th Anniv of International Agricultural Development Fund.

958	**353**	195f. multicoloured	2·00	1·00

354 Gymnastics (rings)

1988. Air. Olympic Games, Seoul (2nd issue). Multicoloured.

959	100f. Type **354**	95	45
960	155f. Women's handball	1·50	65
961	195f. Boxing	2·00	90
962	500f. Gymnastics (parallel bar)	4·50	2·00
MS963	102×78 mm. 500f. Gymnastics (fixed bar) (51×39 mm)	10·00	2·40

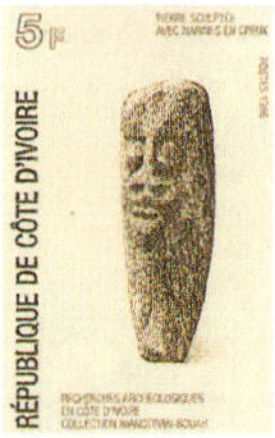

355 Stone Sculpture with Deep Nostrils

1988. Archaeological Research. Stone Sculptures from Niangoran-Bouah Collection.

964	**355**	5f. brown and flesh	10	10
965	-	10f. brown and green	10	10
966	-	30f. brown and green	30	10
967	-	155f. brown and yellow	1·60	80
968	-	195f. brown and green	2·40	1·00

DESIGNS: 10f. Sculpture with full lips; 30f. Sculpture with large nose; 155f. Sculpture with triangular mouth; 195f. Sculpture with sunken eyes.

356 Healthy Youth and Drug Addict

1988. 1st International Drug Abuse and Illegal Trafficking Day.

969	**356**	155f. multicoloured	1·50	1·00

357 "The Couple" (K. J. Houra)

1988. Paintings by Local Artists. Multicoloured.

970	20f. Type **357**	30	10
971	30f. "The Canary of Gentleness" (Monne Bou) (horiz)	30	10
972	150f. "The Eternal Dancer" (Monne Bou)	1·40	80
973	155f. "The Termite Hill" (Mathilde Moro)	1·50	85
974	195f. "The Sun of Independence" (Michel Kodjo)	2·00	1·00

358 Emblem

1988. 25th Anniv of Organization of African Unity.

975	**358**	195f.+5f. multicoloured	1·80	1·70

359 Collector with Album

1988. World Post Day.

976	**359**	155f. multicoloured	1·50	85

360 Emblem

1988. 28th Anniv of Independence. Forestry Year. Multicoloured.

977	40f. Type **360**	50	25
978	155f. "To each his tree"	1·90	85
979	155f. "Stop fires"	1·90	90

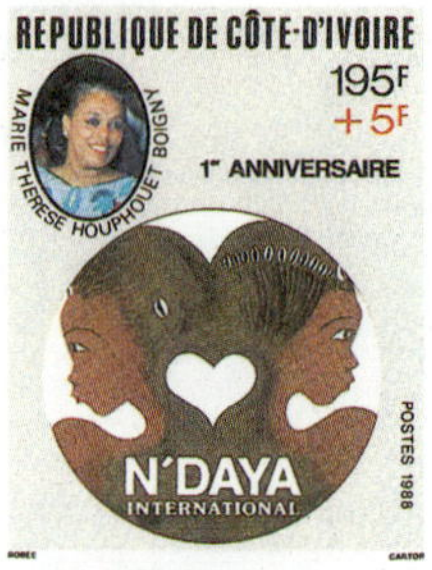

361 Marie Therese Houphouet-Boigny and Emblem

1988. 1st Anniv of N'Daya International.

980	**361**	195f.+5f. multicoloured	2·10	1·90

362 Money Cowries and Bones

1989. History of Money (1st series).

981	**362**	50f. multicoloured	80	25
982	-	195f. black, grey and blue	2·30	1·20

DESIGN: 195f. Bank of Senegal notes.

See also Nos. 1004/5, 1019/21 and 1053.

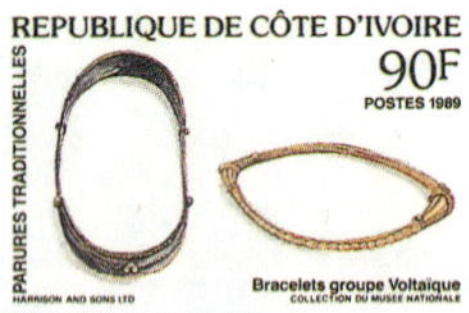

363 Voltaic Bracelets

1989. Traditional Jewellery. Multicoloured.

983	90f. Type **363**	1·00	60
984	155f. Dan ankle bracelets	1·80	1·20

364 Stamp used as Money

365 "Old Man and Child"

1989. Stamp Day.

985	**364**	155f. multicoloured	1·70	95

1989. Carvings by Christian Lattier. Mult.

986	40f. Type **365**	45	25
987	155f. "Saxophone Player"	1·80	95
988	550f. "Panther" (horiz)	5·00	2·75

366 Map and Tractor

1989. 30th Anniv of Council of Unity.

989	**366**	75f. multicoloured	1·00	45

367 Sirikukube Dan

1989. Rural Dwellings (3rd series).

990	**367**	155f. multicoloured	1·50	85

368 Congress Venue and Pres. Houphouet-Boigny

1989. International Peace Congress, Yamoussoukro.

991	**368**	195f. multicoloured	1·80	95

369 Map and King holding Court

1989. Anniversaries. Multicoloured.

992 200f. Type **369** (279th anniv of accession of King Sekou Watara of Kong) 3·00 1·80

993 200f. Bastille and detail of Declaration of Rights of Man (bicentenary of French Revolution) 3·00 1·80

370 Nile Monitor

1989. Reptiles. Multicoloured.

994 25f. Type **370** 30 15

995 100f. Nile crocodile 1·30 80

371 Globe and Emblem

1989. World Post Day.

996 **371** 195f. multicoloured 1·80 85

372 Telephone Kiosks and Mail Boxes

1989. 30th Anniv of West African Posts and Telecommunications Association.

997 **372** 155f. multicoloured 1·50 85

373 Milan

1989. Air. World Cup Football Championship (1990) Preliminary Rounds. Multicoloured.

998 195f. Type **373** 2·00 75

999 300f. Genoa 2·75 1·10

1000 450f. Turin 3·75 1·70

1001 550f. Bologna 5·50 1·90

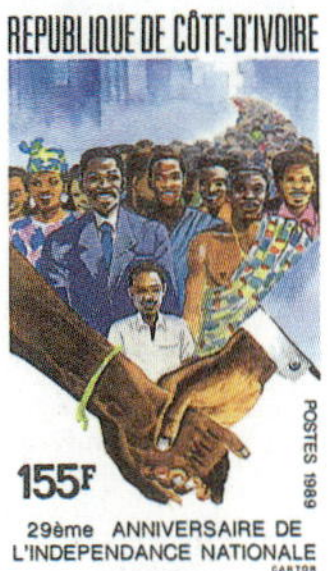

374 Crowd and Handclasp

1989. 29th Anniv of Independence.

1002 **374** 155f. multicoloured 1·50 80

375 Emblem

1990. 10th Anniv of Pan-African Postal Union.

1003 **375** 155f. multicoloured 1·40 75

376 West African Bank 25f. Banknote

1990. History of Money (2nd series).

1004 **376** 155f. black and green 1·50 80

1005 - 195f. black and orange 2·30 1·20

DESIGN: 195f. Banknotes, 1917–44.

See also Nos. 1019/21 and 1053.

377 "Afrique" (steam packet)

1990. Stamp Day.

1006 **377** 155f. multicoloured 1·80 85

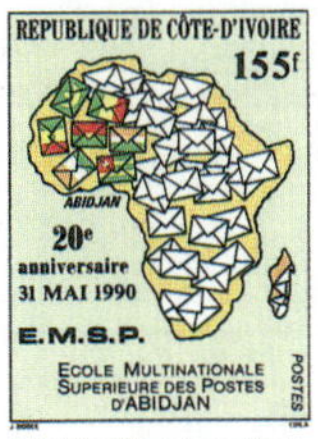

378 Envelopes on Map

1990. 20th Anniv of Multinational Postal Training School, Abidjan.

1007 **378** 155f. multicoloured 1·50 75

379 Footballers

1990. Air. World Cup Football Championship, Italy. Designs showing match scenes. Multicoloured.

1008 155f. Type **379** 1·50 55

1009 195f. Brazil v. West Germany 2·00 75

1010 500f. England v. Russia 4·50 1·90

1011 600f. England v. Netherlands 6·25 2·30

1990. Rural Dwellings (4th series). As T 367. Multicoloured.

1012 155f. Malinke village 1·40 55

380 Teacher writing Letters on Blackboard

1990. International Literacy Year.

1013 **380** 195f. multicoloured 1·80 85

381 Cathedral

1990. Consecration of Our Lady of Peace Cathedral, Yamoussoukro. Multicoloured.

1014 155f. Type **381** 1·50 80

1015 195f. Aerial view 2·30 1·20

382 Pres. Houphouet-Boigny and Pope

1990. 3rd Visit of Pope John Paul II.

1016 **382** 500f. multicoloured 5·00 2·75

383 Postman delivering to Village

1990. World Stamp Day.

1017 **383** 195f. multicoloured 3·25 1·60

384 Modern Building and Road Network

1990. 30th Anniv of Independence.

1018 **384** 155f. multicoloured 1·60 85

1991. History of Money (3rd series). As T 376.

1019 40f. black and yellow 45 25

1020 155f. black and green 1·50 85

1021 195f. black and mauve 2·00 1·30

DESIGNS: 40, 155f. West African Bank 100f. and 5f. notes, 1942; 195f. Issuing Institute for French West Africa and Togo 50f. and 500f. notes.

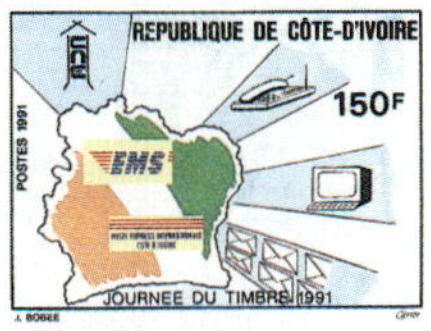

385 Communications

1991. Stamp Day. Multicoloured.

1022 150f. Type **385** 1·40 50

386 Suzanne Lenglen

1991. Centenary of French Open Tennis Championships. Tennis players. Multicoloured.

1023 200f. Type **386** 2·00 1·50

1024 200f. Helen Wills Moody 2·00 1·50

1025 200f. Simone Mathieu 2·00 1·50

1026 200f. Maureen Connolly 2·00 1·50

1027 200f. Francoise Durr 2·00 1·50

1028 200f. Margaret Court 2·00 1·50

1029 200f. Chris Evert 2·00 1·50

1030 200f. Martina Navratilova 2·00 1·50

1031 200f. Steffi Graf 2·00 1·50

1032 200f. Henri Cochet 2·00 1·50

1033 200f. Rene Lacoste 2·00 1·50

1034 200f. Jean Borotra 2·00 1·50

1035 200f. Donald Budge 2·00 1·50

1036 200f. Marcel Bernard 2·00 1·50

1037 200f. Ken Rosewall 2·00 1·50

1038 200f. Rod Laver 2·00 1·50

1039 200f. Bjorn Borg 2·00 1·50

1040 200f. Yannick Noah 2·00 1·50

387 "Europe"

1991. Steam Packets. Multicoloured.

1041 50f. Type **387** 50 25

1042 550f. "Asie" 5·00 3·00

1991. Various stamps surch.

1043 - 150f. on 155f. mult (987) 1·50 45

1044 **367** 150f. on 155f. mult 1·50 45

1045 - 150f. on 155f. black and green (1020) 1·50 60

1046 - 200f. on 195f. black and mauve (1021) 2·00 80

389 Post and Savings Society's Emblem and Letter-box

1991. World Post Day. Multicoloured.

1047 50f. Type **389** 50 25

1048 100f. S.I.P.E. emblem and globe 95 50

390 We Drum

1991. Drums.

1049 **390** 5f. purple and lilac 10 10

1050 - 25f. red and pink 25 10

1051 - 150f. green and turquoise 1·60 1·00

1052 - 200f. green and brown 1·90 1·40

DESIGNS: 25f. Krou drum, Soubre; 150f. Nafana drum, Sinematiau; 200f. Akye drum, Alepe.

1991. History of Money (4th series). As T 376.

1053 100f. black and mauve 1·00 65

DESIGN: 100f. French West Africa and Togo banknotes.

391 Government Buildings

1991. 31st Anniv of Independence.

1054 **391** 150f. multicoloured 1·60 70

392 Orchid

1991. Orchids.

1055	**392**	150f. mauve, green & blk	1·50	45
1056	-	200f. red, emerald & grn	2·00	80

DESIGNS—HORIZ: 200f. Different orchid.

393 Footballer and Cup

1992. Ivory Coast Victory in African Nations Football Cup Championship, Senegal. Mult.

1057	20f. Type **393**	1·00	85
1058	150f. Elephants supporting cup with their trunks (vert)	1·60	1·30

394 African Civet

1992. Animals in Abidjan Zoo.

1059	**394**	5f. brown, red and green	10	10
1060	-	40f. brown, green & orge	45	10
1061	-	150f. brown, green & red	1·80	75
1062	-	500f. brown, grn & ochre	4·75	3·00

DESIGNS: 40f. African palm civet; 150f. Bongo; 500f. Leopard.

395 World Map

1992. World Post Day.

1063	**395**	150f. blue and black	1·40	80

396 1892 "Tablet" and 1962 Postal Centenary Stamps

1992. Stamp Day. Centenary of First Ivory Coast Stamps. Multicoloured.

1064	150f. Type **396**	1·50	95
1065	150f. 1961 Independence and 1991 World Post Day stamps	1·50	95
MS1066	290×104 mm. As Nos. 1064/5 but each size 78×45 mm	35·00	33·00

397 Tomb Entrance

1992. Tourism, Funerary Monuments.

1067	**397**	5f. red, green and blue	10	10
1068	-	50f. brown, green & blue	60	25
1069	-	150f. brown, blue & green	1·50	80
1070	-	400f. green, blue and red	3·75	1·80

DESIGNS (tombs): 50f. Angels, lions and figures; 150f. Drummer, angel, sentry and animals; 400f. Angels, figures and tree.

398 Dove, Flag and Head of Statue of Liberty

1992. 32nd Anniv of Independence. Mult.

1071	30f. Type **398**	35	35
1072	150f. Crowd waving flags, Statue of Liberty and map	1·70	80

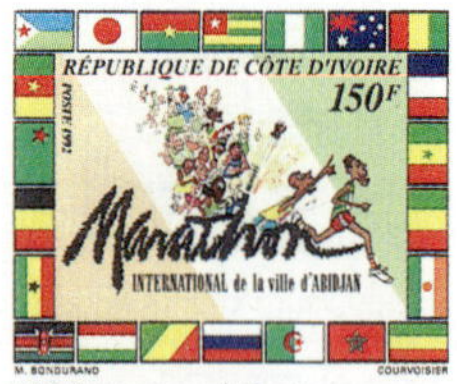

399 Runners and Flags

1992. International Marathon. Multicoloured.

1073	150f. Type **399**	1·20	50
1074	200f. Runners and landmarks	2·00	70

400 Emblem and Map

1992. 1st Anniv of Ity Gold Mine.

1075	**400**	200f. multicoloured	2·00	75

400a Dent de Man

1992. Tourist Sites. Multicoloured.

1075a	10f. Hotel complex
1075b	25f. Type **400a**
1075c	100f. Holiday village (horiz)
1075d	200f. Tourist map

400b Building and Emblem

1992. 1st World Conference on Environmental Protection. Multicoloured.

1075e	150f. Tree (vert)
1075f	200f. Type **400b**

401 Girl with Stockbook and Collectors swapping Stamp

402 "Argemone mexicana"

1993. Stamp Day. Youth Philately. Multicoloured.

1076	50f. Type **401**	50	25
1077	50f. Girl pointing at stamps	50	25
1078	150f. Boy perusing album and girls viewing exhibition display	1·70	80

1993. Medicinal Plants. Multicoloured.

1079	5f. Type **402**	25	10
1080	20f. "Hibiscus esculentus"	30	10
1081	200f. "Cassia alata"	2·20	1·30

403 Presidential Decree establishing Colony

1993. Centenary of Ivory Coast.

1082	**403**	25f. black and green	30	10
1083	-	100f. blue and black	1·10	65
1084	-	500f. black and brown	5·00	3·00

DESIGNS: 100f. Louis Binger (first Governor) and Felix Houphouet-Boigny (President); 500f. Factory.

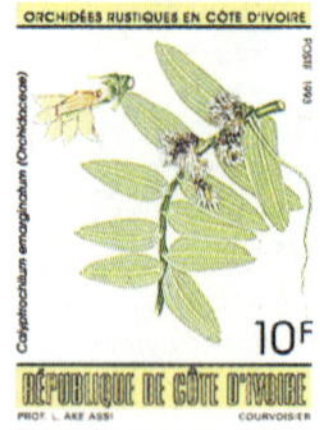

404 "Calyptrochilum emarginatum"

1993. Orchids. Multicoloured.

1085	10f. Type **404**	10	10
1086	50f. "Plectrelminthus caudathus"	45	25
1087	150f. "Eulophia guineensis"	1·50	95

405 Heading Ball

1993. World Cup Football Championship, U.S.A. (1994). Multicoloured.

1088	150f. Type **405**	1·00	45
1089	200f. Players jumping	2·00	80
1090	300f. Player dribbling ball past opponent	2·75	1·80
1091	400f. Ball ricocheting off players	3·75	2·30

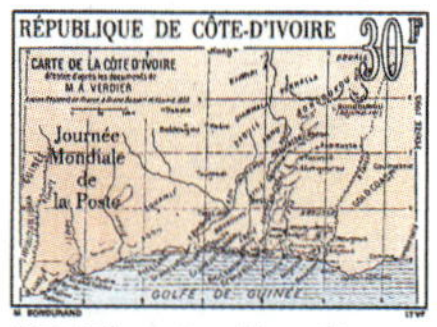

406 19th-century Map of Ivory Coast

1993. World Post Day.

1092	**406**	30f. red, black and blue	45	30
1093	-	200f. multicoloured	2·00	1·30

DESIGN: 200f. Bouake post office.

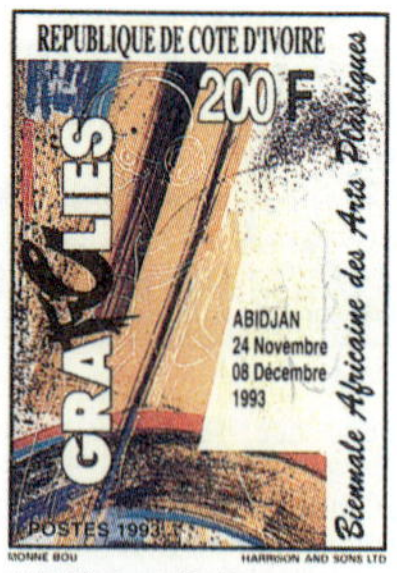

407 Abstract Design

1993. African Plastic Arts Biennale, Abidjan.

1094	**407**	200f. multicoloured	1·30	70

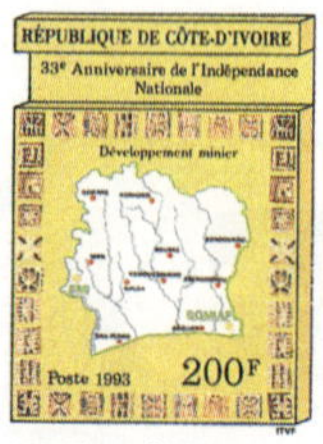

408 Map of Mining Centre

1993. 33rd Anniv of Independence.

1095	**408**	200f. multicoloured	2·00	95

409 Boigny and Modern Developments

1994. Felix Houphouet-Boigny (President, 1960–93) Commemoration. Multicoloured.

1096	150f. Type **409**	80	25
1097	150f. Boigny, tractor, ploughing with oxen and container ship	80	25
1098	150f. Boigny and Our Lady of the Peace Cathedral, Yamoussoukro	80	25
1099	200f. Type **409**	1·10	45
1100	200f. As No. 1097	1·10	45
1101	200f. As No. 1098	1·10	45
MS1102	195×81 mm. 500f. Type **409**; 500f. As No. 1097; 500f. As No. 1098	9·00	9·00

410 Raoul Follereau and Globe

1994. 50th Anniv (1992) of World Anti-leprosy Campaign.

1103	**410**	150f. multicoloured	1·10	50

411 Globe, Satellites and Flags

1994. 1st Meeting of Regional African Satellite Communications Organization Board of Directors, Abidjan.

1104	**411**	150f. multicoloured	80	40

412 Country-woman with Basket on Back

1994. Multicoloured, colour of frame given.

1105	**412**	5f. orange	10	10
1106	**412**	25f. blue	10	10
1107	**412**	30f. bistre	10	10
1108	**412**	40f. green	10	10
1109	**412**	50f. brown	20	10
1110	**412**	75f. purple	35	10
1111	**412**	150f. green	75	45
1112	**412**	180f. purple	95	35
1115	**412**	280f. grey	1·30	65
1116	**412**	300f. violet	1·40	75

413 "Christ"

1994. Stained Glass Windows by Pierre Fakhoury from Our Lady of Peace Cathedral, Yamoussoukro. Multicoloured.

1120	25f. Type **413**	25	10
1121	150f. "The Fisher of Men"	1·00	60
1122	200f. "Madonna and Child"	1·20	80
MS1123	103×85 mm. 600f. Our Lady of Peace Cathedral, Yamoussoukro (28×42 mm)	4·50	4·50

414 Modern Developments

1994. 34th Anniv of Independence. The Family.

1124	**414**	150f. multicoloured	80	45

415 Green Mamba

1995. Snakes. Multicoloured.

1125	10f. Royal python	10	10
1126	20f. Green bush snake	10	10
1127	100f. Type **415**	50	25
1128	180f. Common puff adder	1·10	65
1129	500f. Rhinoceros viper	2·40	1·50

416 Women collecting Water

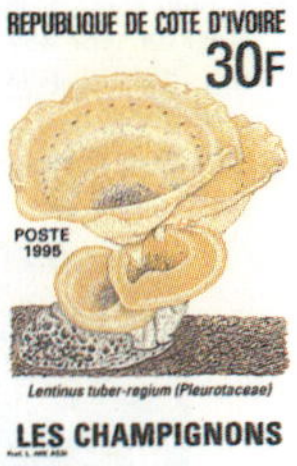

417 "Lentinus tuberregium"

1995. 50th Anniversaries. Multicoloured.

1130	100f. Type **416** (F.A.O.)	70	25
1131	280f. Dove on globe (U.N.O.)	1·90	70

1995. Fungi. Multicoloured.

1132	30f. Type **417**	45	25
1133	50f. Chinese mushroom	80	70
1134	180f. "Dictyophora indusiata"	2·40	95
1135	250f. Termite mushroom	2·75	1·90

418 Laboratory Worker and Pasteur

1995. Death Centenary of Louis Pasteur (chemist).

1136	**418**	280f. multicoloured	1·50	80

419 GSR Emblem on Butterfly Wing

1995. School Philatelic Clubs. Multicoloured.

1137	50f. Type **419**	45	25
1138	180f. LBP emblem on butterfly wing	1·40	75

420 Palla

1995. Butterflies. Multicoloured.

1139	180f. Type **420**	2·10	75
1140	280f. Mocker swallowtail	3·00	1·00
1141	550f. Emperor swallowtail	4·25	1·70

421 Motor Vehicles and Handcart

1996. Abidjan Transport. Multicoloured.

1142	180f. Type **421**	1·10	60
1143	280f. Catching bus	1·60	95

422 African Bonytongue

1996. Fishes. Multicoloured.

1144	50f. Type **422**	30	25
1145	180f. Western grunter	1·00	60
1146	700f. Guinean butter catfish	4·00	2·30

423 "Cyrtorchis arcuata"

424 Boxing

1996. Flowers. Multicoloured.

1147	40f. Type **423**	25	25
1148	100f. "Eulophia horsfalii"	65	35
1149	180f. "Eulophidium maculatum"	1·40	95
1150	200f. "Ansellia africana"	1·50	85

1996. Centenary of Modern Olympic Games and Olympic Games, Atlanta. Multicoloured.

1151	200f. Type **424**	1·10	60
1152	280f. Running	1·60	1·00
1153	400f. Long jumping	2·20	1·30
1154	500f. National Olympic Committee arms and pictograms	2·75	1·80

425 Huntsmens' Sticks, Birifor

1996. Ceremonial Sticks.

1155	**425**	180f. black and green	1·10	60
1156	-	200f. black and orange	1·10	70
1157	-	280f. black and lilac	1·60	1·00

DESIGNS: 200f. Lobi chief's stick from Bindam; 280f. Lobi chief's stick from Gboberi.

426 Sacred Lotus

1997. Water Plants. Multicoloured.

1158	50f. Type **426**	30	25
1159	180f. White lotus	1·10	60
1160	280f. Cape Blue water-lily	1·60	1·00
1161	700f. White water-lily	4·00	2·40

427 Pres. Houphouet-Boigny and Cathedral

1997. Our Lady of Peace Cathedral, Yamoussoukro. Multicoloured.

1162	180f. Type **427**	1·10	80
1163	200f. Interior of church	1·10	80
1164	280f. Pope John Paul II and elevated view of cathedral	1·60	1·00

428 Pearl Necklace

1997. Traditional Necklaces. Each lilac and black.

1165	50f. Type **428**	30	25
1166	100f. Necklace of small pearls	55	45
1167	180f. Broken necklace of pearls	1·10	70

429 Stone Head

1997. Stone Heads from Gohitafla. Multicoloured.

1168	100f. Type **429**	55	25
1169	180f. Stone head (full-face)	1·10	70
1170	500f. Stone head (side-view)	2·75	1·50

430 Pulley

1997. Wooden Weaving Tools.

1171	**430**	180f. multicoloured	1·10	50
1172	-	280f. black, grn & dp grn	1·60	75
1173	-	300f. black, bl & ultram	1·60	75

DESIGNS—VERT: 280f. Combing frame. HORIZ: 300f. Shuttle.

431 Manatees

1997. Endangered Species. Multicoloured.

1174	180f. Type **431**	1·60	95
1175	280f. Jentink's duiker	1·60	95
1176	400f. Waterbuck	2·20	1·30

432 Goalkeeper

1998. World Cup Football Championship, France. Multicoloured.

1177	180f. Type **432**	1·10	65
1178	280f. Player composed of flags of competing nations (vert)	1·60	90
1179	400f. Match scene showing trajectory of ball	2·20	1·30
1180	500f. Players and ball as mascot (vert)	2·75	1·30

433 "Agaricus bingensis"

1998. Fungi. Multicoloured.

1181	50f. Type **433**	55	35
1182	180f. "Lactarius gymnocarpus"	1·30	95
1183	280f. "Termitomyces letestui"	2·10	1·30

434 "Hutchinsonia barbata"

1998. Plants. Multicoloured.

1184	40f. Type **434**	35	10
1185	100f. "Synsepalum aubrevillei"	75	50
1186	180f. "Cola lorougnonis"	1·10	70

435 Tapa Woman

1998. Traditional Costumes. Multicoloured.

1187	180f. Type **435**	1·10	60
1188	280f. Raphia woman	1·60	90

436 Steam Locomotive, South Africa, 1918

1999. Railways of Africa. Multicoloured.

1189	180f. Type **436**	1·10	65
1190	280f. Beyer Peacock 15th Class Garratt type steam locomotive, 1925 (wrongly inscr "Garret")	1·60	1·00

MS1191 110×80 mm. 500f. Cecil Rhodes 3·00 3·00

437 Man carrying Parcel

1999. 40th Anniv of Rural Development Council.

1192	**437**	180f.+20f. mult	1·10	75

438 Emblem and Carved Heads

1999. 125th Anniv of Universal Postal Union. Multicoloured.

1193	180f.+20f. Type **438**	1·10	65
1194	280f. Emblem and forms of transport	1·60	1·00

439 African Elephants

1999. "PHILEX FRANCE '99" International Stamp Exhibition, Paris. Animals in Abidjan Zoo. Mult.

1195	180f.+20f. Type **439**	1·50	1·10
1196	250f. African buffaloes	1·50	1·10
1197	280f. Chimpanzees	1·70	1·10
1198	400f. Savanna monkey	2·30	1·60

440 *Ancistrochilus rothschildianus*

1999. Flowers. Multicoloured.

1199	100f. Type **440**	55	35
1200	180f.+20f. *Brachycorythis pubescens*	1·60	1·10
1201	200f. *Bulbophyllum barbigerum*	1·60	1·10
1202	280f. *Habenaria macrandra*	1·80	1·10

441 Rock and Trees

1999. Rock Formations, Ahouakro. Multicoloured.

1203	180f.+20f. Type **441**	1·30	65
1204	280f. Two rocks	1·60	95
1205	400f. Large rock (vert)	2·20	1·40

442 France 1849 20c. Ceres Stamp

1999. 150th Anniv of First French Stamp.

1206	**442**	280f. multicoloured	2·00	1·20

443 African Golden Oriole (*Oriolus auratus*)

1999. Birds. Multicoloured.

1207	50f. Type **443**	35	25
1208	180f.+20f. Variable sunbird (*Nectarinia venusta*)	1·30	95
1209	280f. Madagascar green pigeon (*Treron australis*)	2·00	1·20
1210	300f. Grey parrot (*Psittacus erithacus*)	2·00	1·20

444 Wahrindi (*Synodontis schall*)

1999. Fishes. Multicoloured.

1211	100f. Type **444**	65	35
1212	180f.+20f. Gunther's krib (*Chromidotilapia guntheri*)	1·30	95
1213	280f. Grass-eater perch (*Distichodus rostratus*)	2·00	1·20

445 School Children and "EDUCATION"

1999. New Millennium. Multicoloured.

1214	100f. Type **445**	55	30
1215	180f.+20f. Fruit and "AGRICULTURE"	1·10	65
1216	200f. Factory and "INDUSTRIE"	1·10	65
1217	250f. Computer and "INFORMATIQUE"	1·40	85
1218	280f. Dove and "PAIX"	1·40	90
1219	400f. Mask and "CULTURE"	1·60	1·30

446 Wambele

2000. Traditional Masks. Multicoloured.

1220	50f. Type **446**	30	25
1221	180f.+20f. Dje	1·10	70
1222	400f. Korobla (vert)	2·00	1·30

447 *Blighia sapida*

2000. Native Plants. Multicoloured.

1223	30f. Type **447**	25	20
1224	180f.+20f. *Ricinodendron heudelotti*	1·20	75
1225	300f. *Telfaira occidentalis*	1·50	1·00
1226	400f. *Napoleonaea vogelii*	2·00	1·40

448 Pres. Robert Guei, Map, Elephant and Dove

2000. 40th Anniv of Independence.

1227	**448**	180f.+20f. mult	1·10	80
1228	**448**	400f. multicoloured	2·20	1·40

449 Cacao

2000

1229	**449**	5f. multicoloured	10	10
1230	**449**	10f. multicoloured	10	10
1231	**449**	20f. multicoloured	10	10
1232	**449**	25f. multicoloured	10	10
1233	**449**	30f. multicoloured	10	10
1234	**449**	40f. multicoloured	15	15
1235	**449**	50f. multicoloured	20	15
1236	**449**	100f. multicoloured	45	15
1237	**449**	180f.+20f. mult	85	30
1238	**449**	300f. multicoloured	1·30	50
1239	**449**	350f. multicoloured	1·50	50
1240	**449**	400f. multicoloured	1·70	50
1241	**449**	600f. multicoloured	2·50	75

450 Emblem

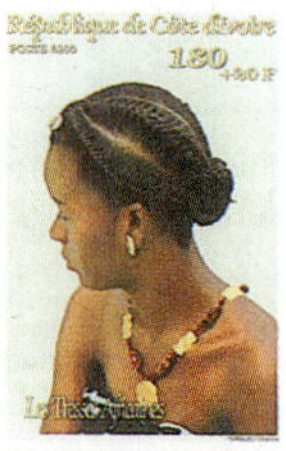

452 Braided Hairstyle

451 Football

2000. 30th Anniv of National Lottery.

1242	**450**	180f.+20f. mult	1·10	80
1243	**450**	400f. multicoloured	2·20	1·60

2000. Olympic Games, Sydney. Multicoloured.

1244	180f.+20f. Type **451**	1·10	70
1245	400f. Kangaroo holding rugby ball and Sydney Opera House	2·20	1·50
1246	600f. Athletics	3·25	2·10
1247	750f. Olympic stadium and bird	4·25	3·00

2000. Hairstyles. Multicoloured.

1248	180f.+20f. Type **452**	1·10	70
1249	300f. Braid in hair	1·60	1·10
1250	400f. Twisted hair on head	2·20	1·50
1251	500f. Braided into loops	2·75	1·70

453 Mandela

2000. 10th Anniv of Release of Nelson Mandela.

1252	**453**	300f. multicoloured	1·60	1·10

454 "Queen Pokou"

2000. Statues. Multicoloured.

1253	180f.+20f. Type **454**	1·10	75
1254	400f. "Akwaba"	2·20	1·40
1255	600f. "Invocation of the Spirits"	3·25	2·10

455 Refugees

2000. 50th Anniv of United Nations Commissioner for Refugees.

1256	**455**	400f. multicoloured	2·20	1·60

456 Buffalo

2001. Abokouamekro National Park. Multicoloured.

1257	50f. Type **456**	35	20
1258	100f. Rhinoceros and calf	55	30
1259	180f.+20f. Rhinoceros	1·10	80
1260	400f.+20f. Buffalo under trees	2·50	1·40

457 Carved Wooden Poles

2001. Exhibits in National Museum, Abidjan. Multicoloured.

1261	100f. Type **457**	45	10
1262	180f.+20f. Blolo Bian	85	35
1263	300f.+20f. Botoumo	1·40	60
1264	400f.+20f. Odi Oka	1·80	80

458 Maps and Flag

2001. 41st Anniv of Independence.

1265	**458**	180f.+20f. multicoloured	90	85

459 Player heading Ball

2001. World Cup Football Championship (2002), Japan and South Korea. Multicoloured.

1266	180f.+20f. Type **459**	95	70
1267	400f.+20f. Players legs	1·50	1·20
1268	600f.+20f. Players tackling	3·00	2·10
1269	700f. Players tackling	3·25	2·40

460 Children encircling Globe

2001. United Nations Year of Dialogue among Civilisations.

1270	**460**	400f.+20f. multicoloured	1·80	1·70

461 National Flag

2001. 1st Anniv of Second Republic.

1271	**461**	180f.+20f. multicoloured	90	85

462 Cloth

2001. Traditional Crafts. Korhogo Cloth. Multicoloured.

1272	100f. Type **462**	45	10
1273	180f.+20f. Animals and birds	95	35
1274	400f.+20f. Man decorating cloth (vert)	1·90	80

463 Emblem, Map of Africa and Dancers

2001. 23rd UPU Congress (2004), Abidjan.

1275	**463**	180f.+20f. multicoloured	90	35
1276	**463**	400f.+20f. multicoloured (26×37 mm)	1·90	80
1277	**463**	600f.+20f. multicoloured (36×49 mm)	2·75	1·10

464 Heart enclosing Couple and Cupid

2002. St. Valentine's Day. Self-adhesive.

1278	**464**	180f.+20f. multicoloured	95	35

465 Airplane, Flags and Globe

2002. 40th Anniv of Jean Mermoz International College. Multicoloured.

1279	180f.+20f. Type **465**	90	35
1280	400f.+20f. As No. 1279 but with title banner changed	1·90	75

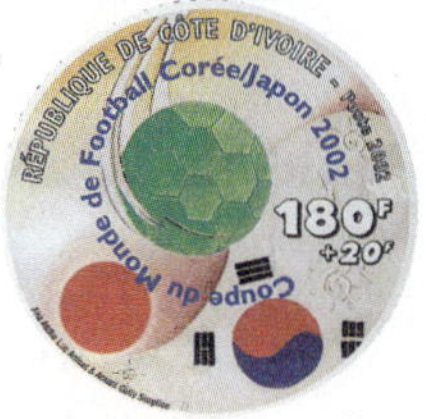

466 Football and Emblems

2002. World Cup Football Championships, Japan and South Korea. Multicoloured.

1281	180f.+20f. Type **466**	1·00	35
1282	300f.+20f. Players tackling (36×28 mm)	1·70	55
1283	400f.+20f. As No. 1281 but with colours changed	2·20	75
1284	600f.+20f. Trophy enclosing two players (28×36 mm)	3·25	1·10
MS1285	96×96 mm (circular) 500f. No. 1283	2·50	2·50

467 Elephants

2002. Decentralization.

1286	**467**	400f.+20f. multicoloured	1·90	75

468 Flags and Palace de Culture Building

2003. 20th Anniv of Ivory Coast—People's Republic of China Diplomatic Relations.

1288	**468**	180f. multicoloured	80	25
1289	**468**	400f. multicoloured	1·80	75
1290	**468**	650f. multicoloured	3·00	1·20

469 Alingue Bia

2003. Carved Columns, Museum of Civilization. Multicoloured.

1291	20f. Type **469**	10	10
1292	100f. Lalie	45	20
1293	180f.+20f. Tre Ni Tre	85	35
1294	300f.+20f. Golikple-Kple	1·40	55

470 People pointing to AIDS Virus (image scaled to 67% of original size)

2003. Anti-AIDS Campaign. Multicoloured.

1295	180f.+20f. Type **470**	90	30
1296	400f.+20f. Combating virus (38×38 mm) (circular)	1·80	70

MILITARY FRANK STAMP

MF59

1967. No value indicated.

MF1	**MF59**	(–) multicoloured	2·75	2·75

OFFICIAL STAMPS

O135 Arms of Ivory Coast

1973. No value indicated. Multicoloured. Background colours given.

O422	**O135**	(–) green and turquoise	65	25
O423	**O135**	(–) yellow and orange	1·00	50
O424	**O135**	(–) pink and mauve	1·40	80
O425	**O135**	(–) violet and blue	3·75	1·60

Nos. O422/5 represent the following face values. No. O422, 35f. No. O423, 75f. No. O424, 100f. No. O425, 250f.

PARCEL POST STAMPS

1903. Postage Due stamps of French Colonies optd. (a) Cote d'Ivoire COLIS Postaux.

P18	**U**	50c. purple	55·00	65·00
P20	**U**	1f. pink on buff	60·00	55·00

(b) Colis Postaux.

P19	50c. purple	£3250	£3250
P21	1f. pink on buff	£3250	£3250

(c) Cote d'Ivoire Colis Postaux.

P22	50c. purple	£140	£140
P23	1f. pink on buff	£100	£110

1903. Postage Due stamps of French Colonies surch. (a) Cote d'Ivoire Colis Postaux and new value.

P24	50c. on 15c. green	30·00	19·00
P25	50c. on 60c. brown on buff	60·00	55·00
P26	1f. on 5c. blue	24·00	26·00
P27	1f. on 10c. brown	29·00	40·00
P30	4f. on 60c. brown on buff	£130	£130

(b) Colis Postaux Cote d'Ivoire and new value.

P28	4f. on 15c. green	£130	£130
P29	4f. on 30c. pink	£130	£130
P35	4f. on 5c. blue	£250	£250
P36	8f. on 15c. green	£250	£250

1904. Postage Due stamps of French Colonies optd. (a) C. P. Cote d'Ivoire.

P31	50c. purple	42·00	70·00
P32	1f. pink on buff	24·00	65·00

(b) Cote d'Ivoire C.P.

P33	50c. purple	55·00	55·00
P34	1f. pink on buff	65·00	65·00

1905. Postage Due stamps of French Colonies surch Cote d'Ivoire C. P. and new value.

P39	2f. on 1f. pink on buff	£225	£225
P40	4f. on 1f. pink on buff	£225	£225
P41	8f. on 1f. pink on buff	£500	£550

POSTAGE DUE STAMPS

1906. "Natives" key-type inscr "COTE D'IVOIRE".

D38	**L**	5c. green	1·40	90
D39	**L**	10c. purple	1·20	1·40
D40	**L**	15c. blue on blue	3·50	2·30
D41	**L**	20c. black on yellow	2·00	2·75
D42	**L**	30c. red on cream	6·50	6·75
D43	**L**	50c. violet	2·75	5·50
D44	**L**	60c. black on buff	7·25	60·00
D45	**L**	1f. black on pink	18·00	55·00

1915. "Figure" key-type inscr "COTE D'IVOIRE".

D60	**M**	5c. green	10	4·00
D61	**M**	10c. red	10	1·60
D62	**M**	15c. grey	10	2·50
D63	**M**	20c. brown	35	4·75
D64	**M**	30c. blue	20	4·75
D65	**M**	50c. black	20	5·00
D66	**M**	60c. orange	45	5·50
D67	**M**	1f. violet	55	6·00

1927. Surch in figures.

D94	"2 F." on 1f. purple	45	7·00
D95	"3 F." on 1f. brown	45	7·50

D21 Guere Mask

1960. Values in black.

D196	**D21**	1f. violet	1·10	5·50
D197	**D21**	2f. green	1·10	5·50
D198	**D21**	5f. yellow	1·30	5·75
D199	**D21**	10f. blue	1·50	6·50
D200	**D21**	20f. mauve	2·00	13·00

D30 Mask

1962

D220	**D30**	1f. blue and orange	15	15
D221	-	2f. red and black	30	25
D222	-	5f. green and red	40	40
D223	-	10f. purple and green	80	80
D224	-	20f. black and violet	1·40	1·40

DESIGNS: 2f. to 20f. Various native masks from Bingerville Art School.

D70 Baoule Weight

1968. Designs showing different types of weights.

D309	**D70**	5f. multicoloured	15	15
D310	-	10f. multicoloured	30	25
D311	-	15f. multicoloured	80	80
D312	-	20f. multicoloured	1·00	95
D313	-	30f. multicoloured	1·50	1·40

D111 "Animal" Weight

1972. Gold Weights and Measures.

D389	**D111**	20f. brown and violet	95	90
D390	-	40f. brown and red	1·30	1·30
D391	-	50f. purple and orange	2·00	1·90
D392	-	100f. brown and green	3·75	3·50

DESIGNS: 40f. "Dagger"; 50f. "Bird"; 100f. "Triangle".

APPENDIX

The following stamps have either been issued in excess of postal needs, or have not been available to the public in reasonable quantities at face value. Such stamps may later be given full listings if there is evidence of regular postal use. Miniature sheets and imperforate stamps are excluded from this listing.

2005

Otters.250f.; 400f.; 650f.; 1000f.
Football World Cup, Germany, 2006. 3000f. x 2
Olympic Games, Beijing, 2008. 3000f. x 2
Death Centenary of Jules Verne. 3000f. x 4
Michael Schumacher-Formula I World Champion 3000f. x 2

Pt. 1

JAIPUR

A state of Rajasthan, India. Now uses Indian stamps.

12 pies = 1 anna; 16 annas = 1 rupee.

2 Chariot of the Sun God, Surya

1904

3	**2**	½a. blue	3·50	7·50
4	**2**	1a. red	6·00	15·00
5	**2**	2a. green	7·00	16·00

3 Chariot of the Sun God, Surya

1904

9	**3**	¼a. olive	1·25	1·50
10a	**3**	½a. blue	1·75	60
11a	**3**	1a. red	4·00	60
12	**3**	2a. green	5·50	2·00
13	**3**	4a. brown	9·00	2·50
14	**3**	8a. violet	5·50	2·75
15a	**3**	1r. yellow	27·00	16·00

This set was issued engraved in 1904 and surface-printed in 1913.

4 Chariot of the Sun God, Surya

1911. No gum.

17	**4**	¼a. olive	30	1·50
18	**4**	½a. blue	30	1·50
20	**4**	1a. red	50	1·50
21a	**4**	2a. green	2·00	7·00

३ आना

(5)

1926. Surch with T 5.

32	**3**	3a. on 8a. violet	2·50	4·00
33	**3**	3a. on 1r. yellow	3·00	7·50

6 Chariot of the Sun God, Surya

7 Maharaja Sawai Man Singh II

1931. Investiture of Maharaja. Centres in black.

40	**6**	¼a. red	3·50	3·25
41	**7**	½a. violet	50	20
42	-	1a. blue	11·00	11·00
43	-	2a. orange	9·50	10·00
44	-	2½a. red	32·00	60·00
45	-	3a. green	21·00	45·00
46	-	4a. green	21·00	60·00
47	-	6a. blue	6·00	55·00
48	-	8a. brown	20·00	£100
49	-	1r. olive	48·00	£375
50	-	2r. green	55·00	£425
51	-	5r. purple	65·00	£475
58	**7**	¼a. red	50	50
59	**7**	¾a. red	9·00	4·75

60	7	1a. blue	11·00	5·50
61	7	2a. orange	11·00	6·00
62	7	2½a. red	5·00	3·50
63	7	3a. green	4·00	80
64	7	4a. green	55·00	£180
65	7	6a. blue	8·00	35·00
66	7	8a. brown	32·00	£150
67	7	1r. bistre	20·00	£200

DESIGNS—VERT: 1a. (No. 42), Elephant and banner; 2a. (No. 43), Sowar in armour; 2½a. (No. 44), Common peafowl; 8a. (No. 48), Sireh-Deorhi Gate. HORIZ: 3a. (No. 45), Bullock carriage; 4a. (No. 46), Elephant carriage; 6a. (No. 47), Albert Museum; 1r. (No. 49), Chandra Mahal; 2r. Amber Palace; 5r. Maharajas Sawai Jai Singh and Man Singh.

1932. As T 7, but inscr "POSTAGE & REVENUE". Portrait in black.

52	1a. blue	3·50	2·25
53	2a. brown	5·00	2·75
54	4a. green	4·50	14·00
55	8a. brown	6·00	19·00
56	1r. bistre	27·00	£140
57	2r. green	£100	£550

1936. Nos. 57 and 51 surch One Rupee.

68	1r. on 2r. green	10·00	£130
69	1r. on 5r. purple	12·00	95·00

1938. No. 41 surch in native characters.

70	7	¼a. on ½a. violet	16·00	19·00

21 Maharaja and Amber Palace

1947. Silver Jubilee of Maharaja's Accession to the Throne. Inscr as in T 21.

71	21	¼a. brown and green	2·00	5·50
72	-	½a. green and violet	50	4·50
73	-	¾a. black and red	2·25	7·50
74	-	1a. brown and blue	1·00	4·75
75	-	2a. violet and red	1·00	5·00
76	-	3a. green and black	2·25	8·50
77	-	4a. blue and brown	1·00	5·00
78	-	8a. red and brown	1·00	6·00
79	-	1r. purple and green	3·50	55·00

DESIGNS: ½a. Palace Gate; ¾a. Map of Jaipur; 1a. Observatory; 2a. Wind Palace; 3a. Coat of Arms; 4a. Amber Fort Gate; 8a. Chariot of the Sun; 1r. Maharaja's portrait between State flags.

1947. No. 41 surch 3 PIES and bars.

80	7	3p. on ½a. violet	19·00	30·00

OFFICIAL STAMPS

1929. Optd SERVICE. No gum (except for No. O6a).

O1a	3	¼a. bistre	3·25	2·75
O2	3	½a. blue	1·75	20
O3c	3	1a. red	2·50	50
O5	3	2a. green	2·50	40
O6a	3	4a. brown (with gum)	2·50	1·75
O7	3	8a. violet	17·00	60·00
O8	3	1r. orange	38·00	£425

1931. Stamps of 1931–32 optd SERVICE.

O13	7	½a. violet	30	10
O14	-	1a. blue (No. 42)	£300	4·00
O15	-	2a. orange (No. 43)	4·50	5·50
O16	-	4a. green (No. 46)	60·00	48·00
O18	-	1a. blue (No. 52)	5·00	15
O19	-	2a. brown (No. 53)	7·00	15
O20	-	4a. green (No. 54)	£375	13·00
O21	-	8a. brown (No. 55)	13·00	1·25
O22	-	1r. bistre (No. 56)	35·00	30·00
O23	7	¼a. red	40	10
O24	7	¾a. red	1·75	50
O25	7	1a. blue	5·50	30
O26	7	2a. orange	4·50	2·25
O27	7	2½a. red	12·00	£110
O28	7	4a. green	7·00	7·50
O29	7	8a. brown	4·50	8·50
O30	7	1r. bistre	40·00	

1932. No. O5 surch in native characters.

O17	3	½a. on 2a. green	£180	3·00

1947. Official stamps surch.

O32	7	9p. on 1a. blue	3·75	3·00
O33	7	3p. on ½a. violet	4·75	12·00

1948. No. O13 surch in native characters.

O34	3	¾a. on ½a. violet	15·00	16·00

For later issues see **RAJASTHAN**.

Pt. 1

JAMAICA

An island in the W. Indies. Part of the Br. Caribbean Federation from 3 January 1958, until 6 August 1962 when Jamaica became an independent state within the Commonwealth.

1860. 12 pence = 1 shilling; 20 shillings = 1 pound.
1969. 100 cents = 1 dollar.

8

1860. Portrait as T 8. Various frames.

7	8	½d. red	16·00	3·50
8	8	1d. blue	80·00	75
9	8	2d. red	85·00	70
11	8	4d. orange	£225	11·00
16a	8	½d. green	1·00	10
18a	8	1d. red	55·00	60
20a	8	2d. grey	95·00	65
21a	8	3d. green	2·50	1·75
22b	8	4d. brown	2·00	35
23a	8	6d. yellow	4·00	3·50
24	8	1s. brown	7·00	6·00
25	8	2s. red	27·00	24·00
26	8	5s. lilac	65·00	85·00
52a	8	6d. lilac	10·00	24·00

See also Nos. 47a etc.

11

1889

27	11	1d. purple and mauve	6·00	20
28a	11	2d. green	14·00	6·00
29	11	2½d. purple and blue	5·50	50

1890. No. 22a surch TWO PENCE HALF-PENNY.

30	8	2½d. on 4d. orange	30·00	13·00

13 Llandovery Falls, Jamaica

1900

31	13	1d. red	6·50	20
32	13	1d. black and red	6·00	20

14 Arms of Jamaica

1903

33	14	½d. grey and green	1·50	30
34	14	1d. grey and red	3·00	10
35	14	2½d. grey and blue	5·50	30
36	14	5d. grey and yellow	15·00	23·00
42	14	2½d. blue	3·75	1·25
44	14	6d. purple	13·00	15·00
45	14	5s. grey and violet	48·00	50·00

16

1906

38b	16	½d. green	3·00	20
40	16	1d. red	1·50	10

1908. Queen Victoria portraits as 1860.

47a	3d. purple on yellow	2·00	1·50
49	4d. black on yellow	8·50	55·00
50	4d. red on yellow	1·50	6·50
54	1s. black on green	7·00	8·50
56	2s. purple on blue	8·50	3·50

17

1911

57	17	2d. grey	4·75	13·00

1912. As T 17, but King George V.

58	1d. red	1·50	10
59	1½d. orange	1·00	60
60	2d. grey	2·00	1·75
61	2½d. blue	1·50	15
62	3d. purple on yellow	50	45
63	4d. black and red on yellow	50	3·50
64a	6d. purple and mauve	1·00	1·00
65	1s. black on green	2·25	2·00
66	2s. purple and blue on blue	18·00	26·00
67	5s. green and red on yellow	80·00	95·00
89a	½d. green	1·75	10

1916. Optd WAR STAMP. in one line (with full point).

68	16	½d. green	10	35
69a	-	3d. purple on yellow (62)	1·00	19·00

See also Nos. 76/77a.

1916. Optd WAR STAMP. in two lines.

73	16	½d. green	1·00	30
74	-	1½d. orange (No. 59)	20	10
75	-	3d. purple on yellow (No. 62)	1·00	1·40

1919. Optd WAR STAMP in one line (no full point).

76	15	½d. green	20	15
77b	-	3d. purple on yell (No. 62)	4·50	1·25

23 Jamaica Exhibition, 1891

24 Arawak Woman preparing Cassava

27 Return of War Contingent, 1919

34

1919

79	24	1d. red and orange (A)*	1·75	1·25
81	-	2d. blue and green	1·00	4·00
82a	27	2½d. blue	1·50	1·75
91a	23	½d. green and olive	30	50
92	24	1d. red and orange (B)*	1·50	10
93	-	1½d. green	1·75	45
96a	-	3d. green and blue	1·25	15
97	-	4d. brown and green	1·00	30
98a	-	6d. black and blue	12·00	1·50
99a	-	1s. orange	1·75	65
100	-	2s. blue and brown	3·25	65
101	-	3s. violet and orange	13·00	9·00
102c	-	5s. blue and bistre	30·00	22·00
103	34	10s. green	55·00	70·00

DESIGNS—HORIZ (41½×26 mm): 1½d. War Contingent embarking, 1915; 6d. Port Royal, 1853. (27×22 mm): 3d. Landing of Columbus, 1494. VERT (22×29 mm): 2d. King's House, Spanish Town; 4d. Cathedral, Spanish Town. (25×30 mm): 1s. Statue of Queen Victoria, Kingston; 2s. Admiral Rodney Memorial, Spanish Town; 3s. Sir Charles Metcalfe Monument; 5s. Jamaican scenery.

*Two types of the 1d. (A) Without and (B) with "POSTAGE & REVENUE" at foot.

37

1923. Child Welfare. Designs as T 37.

104	37	½d.+½d. black and green	75	5·50
105	-	1d.+½d. black and red	1·90	10·00
106	-	2½d.+½d. black and blue	14·00	18·00

41

1929. Various frames.

108	41	1d. red	7·50	20
109	41	1½d. brown	4·50	15
110	41	9d. maroon	5·50	1·00

43 Coco Palms at Don Christopher's Cove

45 Priestman's River, Portland

1932

111	43	2d. black and green	28·00	3·25
112	-	2½d. turquoise and blue	6·00	1·50
113	45	6d. black and purple	28·00	3·50

DESIGN—As T 43: 2½d. Wag Water River, St. Andrew.

1935. Silver Jubilee. As T 14a of Kenya, Uganda and Tanganyika.

114	1d. blue and red	50	15
115	1½d. blue and black	60	1·50
116	6d. green and blue	10·00	19·00
117	1s. grey and purple	6·50	12·00

1937. Coronation. As T 14b of Kenya, Uganda and Tanganyika.

118	1d. red	30	15
119	1½d. grey	65	30
120	2½d. blue	1·00	70

46 King George VI

47 Coco Palms at Don Christopher's Cove

48 Bananas

52 Bamboo Walk

1938

121	46	½d. green	1·75	10
121b	46	½d. orange	1·25	30
122	46	1d. red	1·25	10
122a	46	1d. green	2·00	10
123	46	1½d. brown	1·25	10
124d	47	2d. black and green	1·25	10
125	-	2½d. green and blue	6·00	2·25
126	48	3d. blue and green	1·00	1·50
126b	48	3d. green and blue	3·50	1·25
126c	48	3d. green and red	4·25	30
127	-	4d. brown and green	70	10
128a	-	6d. black and purple	2·25	10
129	-	9d. red	1·00	50
130	-	1s. green and brown	9·50	20
131	52	2s. blue and brown	29·00	1·00
132ba	-	5s. blue and brown	7·50	3·00
133a	-	£1 brown and violet	50·00	35·00
133aa	-	10s. green	17·00	7·00

DESIGNS—As Type **47**: 2½d. Wag Water River, St. Andrew. As Type **48**: 4d. Citrus grove; 9d. Kingston Harbour; 1s. Sugar industry; £1 Tobacco growing and cigar making. As previous issues, but with portrait of King George VI: 6d. As Type **45**; 5s. As No. 102c; 10s. As Type **34**.

54 Courthouse, Falmouth

56 Institute of Jamaica

1945. New Constitution.

134	**54**	1½d. brown	20	30
135a	-	2d. green	30	50
136	**56**	3d. blue	20	50
137	-	4½d. black	30	30
138	-	2s. brown	50	50
139	-	5s. blue	2·25	1·00
140	**56**	10s. green	2·25	2·25

DESIGNS—VERT (as Type **54**): 2s. "Labour and Learning". HORIZ (as Type **54**): 2d. Kings Charles II and George VI. (As Type **56**): 4½d. House of Assembly; 5s. Scroll, flag and King George VI.

59a Houses of Parliament, London

1946. Victory.

141a	**59a**	1½d. brown	30	4·00
142a	**59a**	3d. blue	30	6·50

59b King George VI and Queen Elizabeth

59c

1948. Silver Wedding.

143	**59b**	1½d. brown	30	10
144	**59c**	£1 red	28·00	75·00

59d Hermes, Globe and forms of Transport

59e Hemispheres, Jet-powered Vickers Viking Airliner and Steamer

59f Hermes and Globe

59g U.P.U. Monument

1949. U.P.U.

145	**59d**	1½d. brown	20	15
146	**59e**	2d. green	1·25	4·75
147	**59f**	3d. blue	50	1·50
148	**59g**	6d. purple	50	2·50

59h University Arms

59i Princess Alice

1951. Inauguration of B.W.I. University College.

149	**59h**	2d. black and brown	30	50
150	**59i**	6d. black and purple	45	30

60 Scout Badge and Map of Caribbean

61 Scout Badge and Map of Jamaica

1952. 1st Caribbean Scout Jamboree.

151	**60**	2d. blue, green and black	30	10
152	**61**	6d. green, red and black	70	60

61a Queen Elizabeth II

1953. Coronation.

153	**61a**	2d. black and green	1·50	10

1953. Royal Visit. As T 47 but with portrait of Queen Elizabeth II and inscr "ROYAL VISIT 1953".

154	2d. black and green	55	10

63 H.M.S. "Britannia" (ship of the line) at Port Royal

1955. Tercentenary Issue.

155	**63**	2d. black and green	85	10
156	-	2½d. black and blue	15	35
157	-	3d. black and claret	15	30
158	-	6d. black and red	30	20

DESIGNS: 2½d. Old Montego Bay; 3d. Old Kingston; 6d. Proclamation of Abolition of Slavery, 1838.

67 Coconut Palms

75 Blue Mountain Peak

71 Mahoe

79 Arms of Jamaica

1956

159	**67**	½d. black and red	10	10
160	-	1d. black and green	10	10
161	-	2d. black and red	10	10
162	-	2½d. black and blue	75	50
163	**71**	3d. green and brown	20	10
164	-	4d. green and blue	20	10
165	-	5d. red and green	20	2·50
166	-	6d. black and red	2·50	10
167	**75**	8d. blue and orange	1·00	10
168	-	1s. green and blue	1·00	10
169	-	1s.6d. blue and purple	80	10
170	-	2s. blue and green	11·00	3·00
171	**79**	3s. black and blue	2·00	3·00
172	-	5s. black and red	4·00	6·50
173	-	10s. black and green	30·00	21·00
174	-	£1 black and purple	30·00	21·00

DESIGNS—As Type **67**: 1d. Sugar cane; 2d. Pineapples; 2½d. Bananas. As Type **71**: 4d. Bread-fruit; 5d. Ackee; 6d. Streamertail. As Type **75**: 1s. Royal Botanic Gardens, Hope; 1s.6d. Rafting on the Rio Grande; 2s. Fort Charles. As Type **79** but vert: 10s., £1 Arms without portrait.

80a Federation Map

1958. British Caribbean Federation.

175	**80a**	2d. green	60	10
176	**80a**	5d. blue	1·10	3·50
177	**80a**	6d. red	1·10	40

81 Bristol Britannia 312 flying over "City of Berlin", 1860

83 1s. Stamps of 1860 and 1956

1960. Centenary of Jamaica Postage Stamps.

178	**81**	2d. blue and purple	55	10
179	-	6d. red and olive	55	50
180	**83**	1s. brown, green and blue	55	55

DESIGN—As Type **81**: 6d. Postal mule-cart and motor-van.

1962. Independence. (a) Nos. 159/74 optd INDEPENDENCE and 1962 (3d. to 2s.) or 1962 1962 (others).

182	-	1d. black and green	10	10
183	-	2½d. black and blue	10	1·00
184	**75**	3d. green and brown	10	10
185	-	5d. red and olive	20	60
186	-	6d. black and red	2·50	10
187	**76**	8d. blue and orange	20	10
188	-	1s. green and blue	20	10
189	-	2s. blue and olive	1·00	1·50
190	**77**	3s. black and blue	1·00	1·50
191	-	10s. black and green	3·25	4·25
192	-	£1 black and purple	3·25	5·50
205	**74**	½d. black and red	10	15

86 Military Bugler and Map

(b) As T 86 inscr "INDEPENDENCE".

193	**86**	2d. multicoloured	2·00	10
194	**86**	4d. multicoloured	1·25	10
195	-	1s.6d. black and red	5·00	85
196	-	5s. multicoloured	7·50	4·00

DESIGNS: 1s.6d. Gordon House and banner; 5s. Map, factories and fruit.

89 Kingston Seal, Weightlifting, Boxing, Football and Cycling

1962. 9th Central American and Caribbean Games, Kingston.

197	**89**	1d. sepia and red	20	10
198	-	6d. sepia and blue	20	10
199	-	8d. sepia and bistre	20	10
200	-	2s. multicoloured	30	90

DESIGNS: 6d. Diver, sailing, swimming and water polo; 8d. Javelin, discus, pole-vault, hurdles and relay-racing; 2s. Kingston coat of arms and athlete.

93 Farmer and Crops

1963. Freedom from Hunger.

201	**93**	1d. multicoloured	25	10
202	**93**	8d. multicoloured	1·00	60

94 Red Cross Emblem

1963. Cent of Red Cross.

203	**94**	2d. red and black	15	10
204	**94**	1s.6d. red and blue	50	1·50

95 Carole Joan Crawford ("Miss World 1963")

1964. "Miss World 1963" Commem.

214	**95**	3d. multicoloured	10	10
215	**95**	1s. multicoloured	15	10
216	**95**	1s.6d. multicoloured	20	50

MS216a 153×101 mm. Nos. 214/16. Imperf 1·10 2·75

96 "Lignum vitae"

103 Gypsum Industry

1964

217	**96**	1d. blue, green and brown	10	10
218	-	1½d. multicoloured	15	10
219	-	2d. red, yellow and green	15	10
220	-	2½d. multicoloured	1·00	60
221	-	3d. yellow, black & green	15	10
222	-	4d. ochre and violet	50	10
223	-	6d. multicoloured	2·25	10
224	-	8d. multicoloured	2·50	1·50
225	**103**	9d. blue and bistre	1·50	10
226	-	1s. black and brown	20	10
227	-	1s.6d. black, blue & buff	4·00	15
228	-	2s. brown, black and blue	2·75	15
229b	-	3s. blue and green	35	65
230	-	5s. black, ochre and blue	1·25	1·00
231	-	10s. multicoloured	1·25	1·25
232	-	£1 multicoloured	2·00	1·00

DESIGNS—HORIZ (As T **96**): 1½d. Ackee (fruit); 2½d. Land shells; 3d. National flag over Jamaica; 4d. Antillean murex (sea shell); 6d. "Papilio homerus" (butterfly); 8d. Streamertail. VERT (As T **96**): 2d. Blue Mahoe (tree). HORIZ (As T **103**): 1s. National Stadium; 1s.6d. Palisadoes International Airport; 2s. Bauxite mining; 3s. Blue marlin (sport fishing); 5s. Exploration of sunken city, Port Royal; £1 Queen Elizabeth II and national flag. VERT (As T **96**): 10s. Arms of Jamaica.

114 Scout Badge and Alligator

1964. 6th Inter-American Scout Conf, Kingston.

233		3d. red, black and pink	10	10
234		8d. blue, olive and black	15	25
235	**114**	1s. gold, blue and light blue	20	45

DESIGNS—VERT (25½×30 mm): 3d. Scout belt; 8d. Globe, scout hat and scarf.

115 Gordon House, Kingston

1964. 10th Commonwealth Parliamentary Conference, Kingston.

236	115	3d. black and green	10	10
237	-	6d. black and red	30	10
238	-	1s.6d. black and blue	50	30

DESIGNS: 6d. Headquarters House, Kingston; 1s.6d. House of Assembly, Spanish Town.

118 Eleanor Roosevelt

1964. 16th Anniv of Declaration of Human Rights.

239	118	1s. black, red and green	10	10

119 Guides' Emblem on Map

1965. Golden Jubilee of Jamaica Girl Guides' Association. Inscr "1915–1965".

240	119	3d. yellow, green and black	10	10
241	-	1s. yellow, black and green	20	40

DESIGN—TRIANGULAR (61½×30½ mm): 1s. Guide emblems.

121 Uniform Cap

1965. Centenary of Salvation Army. Mult.

242	3d. Type **121**	25	10
243	1s.6d. Flag-bearer and drummer (vert)	50	50

123 Paul Bogle, William Gordon and Morant Bay Court House

1965. Centenary of Morant Bay Rebellion.

244	123	3d. brown, blue and black	10	10
245	123	1s.6d. brown, green & blk	20	10
246	123	3s. brown, red and black	30	75

124 Abeng-blower, "Telstar", Morse Key and I.T.U. Emblem

1965. Centenary of I.T.U.

247	124	1s. black, slate and red	40	20

1966. Royal Visit. Nos. 221, 223, 226/7 optd ROYAL VISIT MARCH 1966.

248	3d. yellow, black and green	15	10
249	6d. multicoloured	1·75	30
250	1s. black and brown	55	10
251	1s.6d. black, blue and buff	2·00	2·00

126 Sir Winston Churchill

1966. Churchill Commemoration.

252	126	6d. black and green	65	30
253	126	1s. brown and blue	85	80

127 Statue of Athlete and Flags

1966. 8th British Empire and Commonwealth Games.

254	127	3d. multicoloured	10	10
255	-	6d. multicoloured	40	10
256	-	1s. multicoloured	10	10
257	-	3s. gold and blue	35	45
MS258		128×103 mm. Nos. 254/7. Imperf	4·00	8·00

DESIGNS: 6d. Racing cyclists; 1s. National Stadium, Kingston; 3s. Games emblem.

131 Bolivar's Statue and Flags of Jamaica and Venezuela

1966. 150th Anniv of "Jamaica Letter".

259	131	8d. multicoloured	20	10

132 Jamaican Pavilion

1967. World Fair, Montreal.

260	132	6d. multicoloured	10	15
261	132	1s. multicoloured	10	15

133 Sir Donald Sangster (Prime Minister)

1967. Sangster Memorial Issue.

262	133	3d. multicoloured	10	10
263	133	1s.6d. multicoloured	20	20

134 Traffic Duty

1967. Centenary of Constabulary Force. Mult.

264	3d. Type **134**	40	10
265	1s. Personnel of the Force (56½×20½ mm)	40	10
266	1s.6d. Badge and Constables of 1867 and 1967	50	75

1968. M.C.C.'s West Indies Tour. As Nos. 445/7 of Guyana.

267	6d. multicoloured	50	65
268	6d. multicoloured	50	65
269	6d. multicoloured	50	65

137 Sir Alexander and Lady Bustamante

1968. Labour Day.

270	137	3d. red and black	10	15
271	137	1s. olive and black	10	15

138 Human Rights Emblem over Map of Jamaica

1968. Human Rights Year. Multicoloured.

272	3d. Type **138**	10	10
273	1s. Hands cupping Human Rights emblem	10	10
274	3s. Jamaican holding "Human Rights"	30	90

141 I.L.O. Emblem

1969. 50th Anniv of I.L.O.

275	141	6d. yellow and brown	10	10
276	141	3s. green and brown	30	30

142 Nurse and Children being Weighed and Measured

1969. 20th Anniv of W.H.O. Multicoloured.

277	6d. Type **142**	10	15
278	1s. Malaria eradication (horiz)	10	15
279	3s. Trainee nurse	20	1·25

1969. Decimal Currency. Nos. 217, 219, 221/3 and 225/32 surch C-DAY 8th September 1969 and value.

280	95	1c. on 1d. blue, grn & brn	10	10
281	-	2c. on 2d. red, yellow & grn	10	10
282	-	3c. on 3d. yellow, black and green	10	10
283	-	4c. on 4d. ochre and violet	1·25	10
284	-	5c. on 6d. multicoloured	1·25	10
285	103	8c. on 9d. blue and bistre	10	10
286	-	10c. on 1s. black & brown	10	10
287	-	15c. on 1s.6d. black, blue and buff	50	90
288	-	20c. on 2s. brown, blk & bl	1·50	1·50
289	-	30c. on 3s. blue & green	2·00	3·00
290	-	50c. on 5s. black, ochre and blue	1·25	3·00
291	-	$1 on 10s. multicoloured	1·25	6·50
292	-	$2 on £1 multicoloured	1·50	6·50

146 "The Adoration of the Kings" (detail, Foppa)

1969. Christmas. Paintings. Multicoloured.

293	2c. Type **146**	20	40
294	5c. "Madonna, Child and St. John" (Raphael)	25	40
295	8c. "The Adoration of the Kings" (detail, Dosso Dossi)	25	40

149 Half Penny, 1869

1969. Centenary of 1st Jamaican Coins.

296	149	3c. silver, black and mauve	15	25
297	-	15c. silver, black and green	10	10

DESIGN: 15c. One penny, 1869.

151 George William Gordon

1970. National Heroes. Multicoloured; background colours given.

298	151	1c. mauve	10	10
299	-	3c. blue	10	10
300	-	5c. grey	10	10
301	-	10c. red	15	10
302	-	15c. green	30	25

PORTRAITS: 3c. Sir Alexander Bustamante; 5c. Norman Manley; 10c. Marcus Garvey; 15c. Paul Bogle.

156 "Christ appearing to St. Peter" (Carracci)

1970. Easter. Centres multicoloured; frame colours given.

303	156	3c. red	10	10
304	-	10c. green	10	10
305	-	20c. grey	20	60

DESIGNS: 10c. "Christ Crucified" (Antonello); 20c. Easter lily.

1970. No. 219 surch 2c.

306	2c. on 2d. red, yellow & green	20	20

160 "Lignum vitae"

1970. Decimal Currency. Designs as Nos. 217, 219, 221/23, 225/32, but with values inscr as T 160 in new currency.

307	160	1c. blue, green and brown	75	2·00
308	-	2c. red, yell & grn (as 2d.)	30	10
309	-	3c. yell, blk & grn (as 3d.)	50	1·00
310	-	4c. ochre and violet (as 4d.)	2·75	30
311	-	5c. multicoloured (as 6d.)	3·00	65
312	103	8c. blue and yellow	2·25	10
313	-	10c. black & brown (as 1s.)	60	20
314	-	15c. black, blue and buff (as 1s.6d.)	2·75	3·00
315	-	20c. brown, black and blue (as 2s.)	1·25	3·00
316	-	30c. blue and green (as 3s.)	4·00	6·50
317	-	50c. black, ochre and blue (as 5s.)	1·25	3·75
318	-	$1 multicoloured (as 10s.)	1·00	5·50
319	-	$2 multicoloured (as £1)	1·25	4·00

161 Cable Ship "Dacia"

1970. Centenary of Telegraph Service.

320	**161**	3c. yellow, black and red	15	10
321	-	10c. black and green	20	10
322	-	50c. multicoloured	50	1·00

DESIGNS: 10c. Bright's cable gear aboard "Dacia"; 50c. Morse key and chart.

164 Bananas, Citrus, Sugar-Cane and Tobacco

1970. 75th Anniv of Jamaican Agricultural Society.

323	**164**	2c. multicoloured	25	60
324	**164**	10c. multicoloured	45	10

165 Locomotive "Projector" (1845)

1970. 125th Anniv of Jamaican Railways.

325	3c. Type **165**	30	10
326	15c. Steam locomotive No. 54 (1944)	65	30
327	50c. Diesel locomotive No. 102 (1967)	1·25	1·75

168 Church of St. Jago de la Vega

1971. Centenary of Disestablishment of Church of England in Jamaica.

328	**168**	3c. multicoloured	10	10
329	**168**	10c. multicoloured	10	10
330	**168**	20c. multicoloured	30	30
331	-	30c. multicoloured	30	1·25

DESIGN: 30c. Emblem of Church of England in Jamaica.

169 Henry Morgan and Ships

1971. Pirates and Buccaneers. Multicoloured.

332	3c. Type **169**	75	10
333	15c. Mary Read, Anne Bonny and trial pamphlet	1·00	15
334	30c. Pirate schooner attacking merchantman	1·75	1·25

170 1s. Stamp of 1919 with Frame Inverted

1971. Tercentenary of Post Office.

335	-	3c. black and brown	15	20
336	-	5c. black and green	20	20
337	-	8c. black and violet	20	10
338	-	10c. brown, black and blue	20	10
339	-	20c. multicoloured	35	45
340	**170**	50c. brown, black and grey	50	2·00

DESIGNS—HORIZ: 3c. Drummer packet letter, 1705; 5c. Pre-stamp inland letter, 1793; 8c. Harbour St. P.O., Kingston, 1820; 10c. Modern stamp and cancellation; 20c. British stamps used in Jamaica, 1859.

171 Satellite and Dish Aerial

1972. Opening of Jamaican Earth Satellite Station.

341	**171**	3c. multicoloured	15	10
342	**171**	15c. multicoloured	30	15
343	**171**	50c. multicoloured	65	1·25

172 Causeway, Kingston Harbour

1972. Multicoloured.

344	1c. Pimento (vert)	10	10
345	2c. Red ginger (vert)	10	10
346	3c. Bauxite Industry	10	10
347	4c. Type **172**	10	10
348	5c. Oil refinery	10	10
349	6c. Senate Building, University of the West Indies	10	10
350	8c. National Stadium	30	10
351	9c. Devon House	10	10
352	10c. Air Jamaica Hostess and Vickers VC-10	20	10
353	15c. Old Iron Bridge, Spanish Town (vert)	2·00	10
354	20c. College of Arts, Science and Technology	30	15
355	30c. Dunn's River Falls (vert)	65	15
356	50c. River rafting	1·75	40
357	$1 Jamaica House	75	1·50
358	$2 Kings House	1·00	1·50

Designs for 8c. to $2 are larger, 35×27 or 27×35 mm.

1972. 10th Anniv of Independence Nos. 346, 352 and 356 optd TENTH ANNIVERSARY INDEPENDENCE 1962–1972.

359	3c. multicoloured	30	30
360	10c. multicoloured	30	10
361	50c. multicoloured	75	2·25

175 Arms of Kingston

1972. Centenary of Kingston as Capital.

362	**175**	5c. multicoloured	15	10
363	**175**	30c. multicoloured	35	35
364	-	50c. multicoloured	60	2·25

DESIGN—HORIZ: 50c. design similar to Type **175**.

176 Mongoose on Map

1973. Centenary of Introduction of the Small Indian Mongoose.

365	**176**	8c. green, yellow and black	15	10
366	-	40c. dp blue, blue & black	35	65
367	-	60c. pink, salmon & black	60	1·25
MS368		165×95 mm. Nos. 365/7	1·10	4·00

DESIGNS: 40c. Mongoose and rat; 60c. Mongoose and chicken.

177 "Euphorbia punicea"

1973. Flora. Multicoloured.

369	1c. Type **177**	10	30
370	6c. "Hylocereus triangularis"	15	20
371	9c. "Columnea argentea"	15	20
372	15c. "Portlandia grandiflora"	25	20
373	30c. "Samyda pubescens"	40	60
374	50c. "Cordia sebestena"	60	1·40

178 "Broughtonia sanguinea"

1973. Orchids. Multicoloured.

375	5c. Type **178**	40	10
376	10c. "Arpophyllum jamaicense" (vert)	50	10
377	20c. "Oncidium pulchellum" (vert)	1·00	25
378	$1 "Brassia maculata"	2·50	3·25
MS379	161×95 mm. Nos. 375/8	4·00	5·50

179 "Mary", 1808–15

1974. Mail Packet Boats. Multicoloured.

380	5c. Type **179**	75	10
381	10c. "Queensbury", 1814–27	75	10
382	15c. "Sheldrake", 1829–34	1·00	40
383	50c. "Thames I", 1842	2·00	2·50
MS384	133×159 mm. Nos. 380/3 (sold at 90c.)	2·75	5·00

180 "Journeys"

1974. National Dance Theatre Company. Mult.

385	5c. Type **180**	10	10
386	10c. "Jamaican Promenade"	10	10
387	30c. "Jamaican Promenade" (different)	30	30
388	50c. "Misa Criolla"	50	80
MS389	161×102 mm. Nos. 385/8 (sold at $1)	1·50	2·50

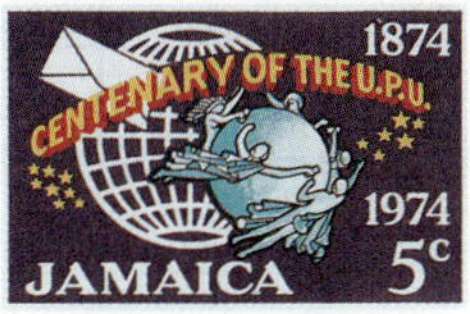

181 U.P.U. Emblem and Globe

1974. Centenary of U.P.U.

390	**181**	5c. multicoloured	10	10
391	**181**	9c. multicoloured	10	10
392	**181**	50c. multicoloured	35	80

182 Senate Building and Sir Hugh Wooding

1975. 25th Anniv of University of West Indies. Mult.

393	5c. Type **182**	10	10
394	10c. University Chapel and Princess Alice	10	10
395	30c. Type **182**	20	25
396	50c. As 10c.	35	60

183 Commonwealth Symbol

1975. Heads of Commonwealth Conf. Mult.

397	5c. Type **183**	10	10
398	10c. Jamaican coat of arms	10	10
399	30c. Dove of Peace	15	30
400	50c. Jamaican flag	30	2·25

184 Jamaican Kite Swallowtail

1975. Butterflies (1st series), showing the family "Papilionidae". Multicoloured.

401	10c. Type **184**	55	20
402	20c. Orange swallowtail ("Papilo thoas")	1·10	1·10
403	25c. False androyeus swallow-tail ("Papilo thersites")	1·25	2·00
404	30c. Homerus swallowtail ("Papilo homerus")	1·40	2·75
MS405	134×179 mm. Nos. 401/4 (sold at 95c.)	5·50	7·50

See also Nos. 429/32 and 443/6.

185 Koo Koo or Actor Boy

1975. Christmas. Belisario prints of "John Canoe" Festival (1st series). Multicoloured.

406	8c. Type **185**	15	10
407	10c. Red Set-girls	15	10
408	20c. French Set-girls	50	20
409	50c. Jaw-bone or House John Canoe	95	2·50

MS410 138×141 mm. Nos. 406/9 (sold at $1)		1·75	3·50

See also Nos. 421/3.

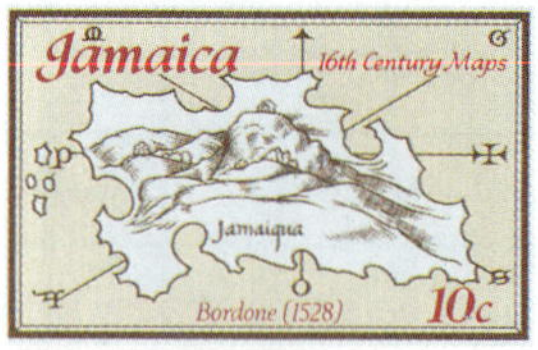

186 Bordone Map, 1528

1976. 16th Century Maps of Jamaica.

411	186	10c. brown, lt brown & red	25	10
412	-	20c. multicoloured	45	25
413	-	30c. multicoloured	70	85
414	-	50c. multicoloured	95	2·75

DESIGNS: 20c. Porcacchi map, 1576; 30c. De Bry map, 1594; 50c. Langenes map, 1598.

See also Nos. 425/8.

187 Olympic Rings

1976. Olympic Games, Montreal.

415	187	10c. multicoloured	15	10
416	187	20c. multicoloured	30	20
417	187a	25c. multicoloured	30	25
418	187a	50c. multicoloured	45	2·25

187a Map of the Caribbean

1976. West Indian Victory in World Cricket Cup.

419	10c. Type **187a**	50	50
420	25c. Prudential Cup	75	1·75

1976. Christmas. Belisario Prints (2nd series). As T 185. Multicoloured.

421	10c. Queen of the Set-girls	10	10
422	20c. Band of the Jaw-bone John Canoe	25	10
423	50c. Koo Koo (actor-boy)	45	2·00
MS424	110×140 mm. Nos. 421/3 (sold at 90c.)	70	2·00

1977. 17th Cent Maps of Jamaica. As T 186.

425	9c. multicoloured	30	40
426	10c. red, brown and buff	30	10
427	25c. black, blue and light blue	70	60
428	40c. black, blue and green	80	2·25

DESIGNS: 9c. Hickeringill map, 1661; 10c. Ogilby map, 1671; 25c. Visscher map, 1680; 40c. Thornton map, 1689.

1977. Butterflies (2nd series). As T 184. Mult.

429	10c. False barred sulphur ("Eurema elathea")	35	10
430	20c. Bronze wing ("Dynamine egaea")	75	55
431	25c. Jamaican harlequin ("Chlosyne pantoni")	1·00	1·50
432	40c. Mimic ("Hypolimnas misippus")	1·50	5·00
MS433	139×120 mm. Nos. 429/32 (sold at $1.05)	4·50	7·00

188 Map, Scout Emblem and Streamertail

1977. Sixth Caribbean Scout Jamboree, Jamaica.

434	188	10c. multicoloured	65	10
435	188	20c. multicoloured	1·00	25
436	188	25c. multicoloured	1·00	35
437	188	50c. multicoloured	1·50	1·75

189 Trumpeter

1977. 50th Anniv of Jamaica Military Band. Mult.

438	9c. Type **189**	15	10
439	10c. Clarinet players and oboe player	15	10
440	20c. Two kettle drummers and clarinetist (vert)	40	35
441	25c. Double-bass player and trumpeter (vert)	55	65
MS442	120×137 mm. Nos. 438/41 (sold at 75c.)	2·50	4·50

1978. Butterflies (3rd series). As T 184. Multicoloured.

443	10c. Jamaican hairstreak ("Callophrys crethona")	50	10
444	20c. Malachite ("Siproeta stelenes")	85	20
445	25c. Common long-tailed skipper ("Urbanus proteus")	95	65
446	50c. Troglodyte ("Anaea troglodyta")	2·00	3·25
MS447	100×125 mm. Nos. 443/6 (sold at $1.15)	4·50	6·00

190 Half-figure with Canopy

1978. Arawak Artefacts (1st series).

448	190	10c. brown, yellow & black	10	10
449	-	20c. brown, mauve & black	15	10
450	-	50c. brown, green & black	35	35
MS451		135×90 mm. Nos. 448/50 (sold at 90c.)	60	1·25

DESIGNS: 20c. Standing figure; 50c. Birdman.

See also Nos. 479/83.

191 Norman Manley (statue)

1978. 24th Commonwealth Parliamentary Conference. Multicoloured.

452	10c. Type **191**	15	10
453	20c. Sir Alexander Bustamante (statue)	25	15
454	25c. City of Kingston Crest	35	20
455	40c. Gordon House Chamber, House of Representatives	35	65

192 Band and Banner

1978. Christmas. Centenary of Salvation Army. Multicoloured.

456	10c. Type **192**	30	10
457	20c. Trumpeter	35	20
458	25c. Banner	35	30
459	50c. William Booth (founder)	60	2·00

193 "Negro Aroused" (sculpture by Edna Manley)

1978. International Anti-Apartheid Year.

460	193	10c. multicoloured	30	20

194 Tennis, Montego Bay

1979. Multicoloured.

461	1c. Type **194**	70	75
462	2c. Golf, Tryall, Hanover	2·25	2·75
463	4c. Horse riding, Negril Beach	50	2·25
464	5c. Old waterwheel, Tryall, Hanover	1·25	30
465	6c. Fern Gully, Ocho Rios	1·50	2·50
466	7c. Dunn's River Falls, Ocho Rios	50	30
467	8c. Jamaican tody	1·00	1·25
468	10c. Jamaican mango	1·00	20
469	12c. Yellow-billed amazon	1·00	2·00
470	15c. Streamertail	1·00	30
471	35c. White-chinned thrush	1·50	30
472	50c. Jamaican woodpecker	1·75	30
473	65c. Rafting, Martha Brae Trelawny	1·75	2·75
474	75c. Blue Marlin fleet, Port Antonio	2·00	2·25
475	$1 Scuba diving, Ocho Rios	2·00	2·25
476	$2 Sailing boats, Montego Bay	2·00	65
477	$5 Arms and map of Jamaica (37×27 mm)	1·00	1·75

1979. 10th Anniv of Air Jamaica. No. 352 optd TENTH ANNIVERSARY AIR JAMAICA 1st APRIL 1979.

478	10c. multicoloured	50	50

197 Grinding Stone, c. 400 B.C.

1979. Arawak Artefacts (2nd series). Multicoloured.

479	5c. Type **197**	10	10
480	10c. Stone implements, c. 500 B.C. (horiz)	10	10
481	20c. Cooking pot, c. 300 A.D. (horiz)	10	15
482	25c. Serving boat, c. 300 A.D. (horiz)	10	20
483	50c. Storage jar fragment, c. 300 A.D.	25	60

198 1962 1s.6d. Independence Commemorative Stamp

1979. Death Centenary of Sir Rowland Hill.

484	198	10c. black, brown and red	15	10
485	-	20c. yellow and brown	15	15
486	-	25c. mauve and blue	20	20
487	-	50c. multicoloured	25	70
MS488		146×94 mm. No. 485 (sold at 30c.)	30	85

DESIGNS: 20c. 1920 1s. with frame inverted; 25c. 1860 6d. stamp; 50c. 1968 3d. Human Rights Year commemorative.

199 Group of Children

1979. Christmas. International Year of the Child. Multicoloured.

489	10c. Type **199**	10	10
490	20c. Doll (vert)	10	10
491	25c. "The Family" (painting by child)	15	15
492	50c. "House on the Hill" (painting by child)	25	40

200 Date Tree Hall, 1886 (original home of Institute)

1980. Centenary of Institute of Jamaica. Mult.

493	5c. Type **200**	10	10
494	15c. Institute building, 1980	15	10
495	35c. Microfilm reader (vert)	25	20
496	50c. Hawksbill turtle and green turtle	45	85
497	75c. Jamaican owl (vert)	1·75	3·00

201 Don Quarrie (200 m, 1976)

1980. Olympic Games, Moscow. Jamaican Olympic Gold Medal Winners. Multicoloured.

498	15c. Type **201**	40	15
499	35c. Arthur Wint (4×400 m Relay, 1952)	45	80
500	35c. Leslie Laing (4×400 m Relay, 1952)	45	80
501	35c. Herbert McKenley (4×400 m Relay, 1952)	45	80
502	35c. George Rhoden (4×400 m, 1952)	45	80

202 Parish Church

1980. Christmas. Churches (1st series). Multicoloured.

503	15c. Type **202**	10	10
504	20c. Coke Memorial Church	10	10
505	25c. Church of the Redeemer	15	10
506	$5 Holy Trinity Cathedral	1·00	2·00
MS507	120×139 mm. Nos. 503/6 (sold at $5.70)	1·25	3·25

See also No. 537/9 and 570/2.

203 Blood Cup Sponge

1981. Marine Life (1st series). Multicoloured.

508	20c. Type **203**	15	10
509	45c. Tube sponge (horiz)	25	35
510	60c. Black coral	35	45
511	75c. Tyre reef (horiz)	40	75

See also Nos. 541/5.

204 Brown's Hutia (or Indian Coney)

1981. Brown's Hutia (or Indian Coney).

512	20c. Hutia facing right	15	30
513	20c. Type **204**	15	30
514	20c. Hutia facing left and eating	15	30
515	20c. Hutia family	15	30

205 White Orchid

1981. Royal Wedding. Multicoloured.

516	20c. Type **205**	10	10
517	45c. Royal Coach	10	10
518	60c. Prince Charles and Lady Diana Spencer	25	20
519	$5 St. James' Palace	70	85
MS520	98×85 mm. No. 519	1·00	1·75

206 Blind Man at Work

1981. International Year for Disabled Persons. Multicoloured.

521	20c. Type **206**	20	15
522	45c. Painting with the mouth	40	40
523	60c. Deaf student communicating with sign language	50	75
524	$1.50 Basketball players	2·25	2·50

207 W.F.D. Emblem on 1964 11/2d. Definitive

1981. World Food Day. Stamps on Stamps.

525	**207**	20c. multicoloured	45	15
526	-	45c. black, red and orange	80	40
527	-	$2 black, blue and green	2·25	1·40
528	-	$4 black, green and brown	3·25	2·50

DESIGNS—VERT (As T **207**): 45c. 1922 1d. value. HORIZ (40×26 mm): $2 As 1938 3d. but with W.F.D. emblem replacing King's head; $4 As 1938 1s. but with W.F.D. emblem replacing King's head.

208 "Survival" (song title)

1981. Bob Marley (musician) Commemoration. Song Titles. Multicoloured.

529	1c. Type **208**	70	1·10
530	2c. "Exodus"	70	1·10
531	3c. "Is this Love"	70	1·10
532	15c. "Coming in from the Cold"	3·25	30
533	20c. "Positive Vibration"	3·25	30
534	60c. "War"	4·00	3·00
535	$3 "Could you be Loved"	6·50	12·00
MS536	134×110 mm. $5.25 Bob Marley	8·50	4·75

No. 533 is incorrectly inscribed "OSITIVE VIBRATION".

209 Webb Memorial Baptist Church

1981. Christmas. Churches (2nd series). Multicoloured.

537	10c. Type **209**	10	10
538	45c. Church of God in Jamaica	30	15
539	$5 Bryce United Church	1·75	2·50
MS540	120×168 mm. Nos. 537/9	3·50	3·50

210 Gorgonian Coral

1982. Marine Life (2nd series). Multicoloured.

541	20c. Type **210**	45	10
542	45c. Hard sponge and diver (horiz)	65	25
543	60c. American manatee (horiz)	90	55
544	75c. Plume worm (horiz)	1·00	65
545	$3 Coral banded shrimp (horiz)	2·50	1·75

211 Cub Scout

1982. 75th Anniv of Boy Scout Movement. Mult.

546	20c. Type **211**	50	15
547	45c. Scout camp	85	40
548	60c. "Out of Many, One People"	1·10	90
549	$2 Lord Baden-Powell	1·75	2·50
MS550	80×130 mm. Nos. 546/9	5·00	6·00

212 "Lignum vitae" (national flower)

1982. 21st Birthday of Princess of Wales.

551	20c. Type **212**	35	20
552	45c. Carriage ride	50	35
553	60c. Wedding	70	60
554	75c. "Saxifraga longifolia"	1·25	2·75
555	$2 Princess of Wales	1·60	3·00
556	$3 "Viola gracilis major"	1·60	3·50
MS557	106×75 mm. $5 Honeymoon photograph	1·40	2·50

1982. Birth of Prince William of Wales. Nos. 551/6 optd ROYAL BABY 21.6.82.

558	20c. Type **212**	20	20
559	45c. Carriage ride	30	35
560	60c. Wedding	40	60
561	75c. "Saxifraga longifolia"	70	2·25
562	$2 Princess of Wales	75	2·75
563	$3 "Viola gracilis major"	1·00	2·50
MS564	106×75 mm. $5 Honeymoon photograph	1·50	3·50

213 Prey Captured

1982. Jamaican Birds (1st series). Jamaican Lizard Cuckoo. Multicoloured.

565	$1 Type **213**	1·40	1·60
566	$1 Searching for prey	1·40	1·60
567	$1 Calling prior to prey search	1·40	1·60
568	$1 Adult landing	1·40	1·60
569	$1 Adult flying in	1·40	1·60

See also Nos. 642/5 and 707/10.

1982. Christmas. Churches (3rd series). As T 209. Multicoloured.

570	20c. United Pentecostal Church	70	10
571	45c. Disciples of Christ Church	1·25	25
572	75c. Open Bible Church	2·00	3·75

214 Queen Elizabeth II

1983. Royal Visit. Multicoloured.

573	$2 Type **214**	3·00	3·50
574	$3 Coat of arms	4·00	6·00

215 Folk Dancing

1983. Commonwealth Day. Multicoloured.

575	20c. Type **215**	15	15
576	45c. Bauxite mining	35	35
577	75c. World map showing position of Jamaica	45	45
578	$2 Coat of arms and family	60	1·40

216 General Cargo Ship at Wharf

1983. 25th Anniv of International Maritime Organization. Multicoloured.

579	15c. Type **216**	75	30
580	20c. "Veendam" (cruise liner) at Kingston	1·00	40
581	45c. "Astronomer" (container ship) entering port	1·75	85
582	$1 Tanker passing International Seabed Headquarters Building	2·75	5·00

217 Norman Manley and Sir Alexander Bustamante

1983. 21st Anniv of Independence.

583	**217**	15c. multicoloured	15	50
584	**217**	20c. multicoloured	15	60
585	**217**	45c. multicoloured	30	85

218 Ship-to-Shore Radio

1983. World Communications Year. Multicoloured.

586	20c. Type **218**	90	15
587	45c. Postal services	1·75	40
588	75c. Telephone communications	1·90	3·50
589	$1 T.V. via satellite	2·00	4·00

219 "Racing at Caymanas" (Sidney McLaren)

1983. Christmas. Paintings. Multicoloured.

590	15c. Type **219**	15	10
591	20c. "Seated Figures" (Karl Parboosingh)	15	10
592	75c. "The Petitioner" (Henry Daley) (vert)	50	65
593	$2 "Banana Plantation" (John Dunkley) (vert)	1·25	4·00

220 Sir Alexander Bustamante

1984. Birth Centenary of Sir Alexander Bustamante. Multicoloured.

594	20c. Type **220**	90	1·60
595	20c. Birthplace, Blenheim	90	1·60

221 De Havilland Gipsy Moth Seaplane

1984. Seaplanes and Flying Boats. Multicoloured.

596	25c. Type **221**	1·50	20
597	55c. Consolidated Commodore flying boat	2·00	85
598	$1.50 Sikorsky S-38A flying boat	3·25	4·00
599	$3 Sikorsky S-40 flying boat "American Clipper"	4·00	6·00

222 Cycling

1984. Olympic Games, Los Angeles. Multicoloured.

600	25c. Type **222**	2·00	50
601	55c. Relay running	60	30
602	$1.50 Start of race	1·75	4·50
603	$3 Finish of race	2·25	5·00
MS604	135×105 mm. Nos. 600/3 (sold at $5.40)	7·50	8·50

1984. Nos. 465 and 469 surch.

605	5c. on 6c. Fern Gully, Ocho Rios	15	40
606	10c. on 12c. Yellow-billed amazon	1·10	60

224 Head of Jamaican Boa Snake

1984. Endangered Species. Jamaican Boa Snake. Multicoloured.

607	25c. Type **224**	6·00	40
608	55c. Boa snake on branch over tree	7·00	80
609	70c. Snake with young	8·00	4·00
610	$1 Snake on log	9·00	5·00
MS611	133×97 mm. As Nos. 607/10 but without W.W.F. emblem (sold at $2.60)	6·00	7·00

225 Locomotive "Enterprise" (1845)

1984. Railway Locomotives (1st series). Mult.

612	25c. Type **225**	1·50	30
613	55c. Tank locomotive (1880)	1·75	70
614	$1.50 Kitson-Meyer tank locomotive (1904)	2·75	3·00
615	$3 Super-heated locomotive No. 40 (1916)	4·00	5·50

See also Nos. 634/7.

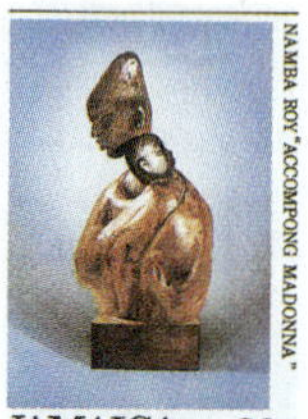

226 "Accompong Madonna" (Namba Roy)

1984. Christmas. Sculptures. Multicoloured.

616	20c. Type **226**	30	10
617	25c. "Head" (Alvin Marriott)	35	10
618	55c. "Moon" (Edna Manley)	80	65
619	$1.50 "All Women are Five Women" (Mallica Reynolds (Kapo))	1·90	4·00

227 Brown Pelicans flying

1985. Birth Bicentenary of John J. Audubon (ornithologist). Brown Pelican. Multicoloured.

620	20c. Type **227**	1·00	20
621	55c. Diving for fish	1·50	40
622	$2 Young pelican taking food from adult	2·50	3·25
623	$5 "Brown Pelican" (John J. Audubon)	3·75	6·50
MS624	100×100 mm. Nos. 620/3 (sold at $7.85)	6·00	8·00

228 The Queen Mother at Belfast University

1985. Life and Times of Queen Elizabeth the Queen Mother. Multicoloured.

625	25c. With photograph album, 1963	50	10
626	55c. With Prince Charles at Garter Ceremony, Windsor Castle, 1983	70	15
627	$1.50 Type **228**	1·25	1·75
628	$3 With Prince Henry at his christening (from photo by Lord Snowdon)	2·25	3·25
MS629	91×74 mm. $5 With the Queen, Prince Philip and Princess Anne at Ascot	2·75	1·75

229 Maps and Emblems

1985. International Youth Year and 5th Pan-American Scout Jamboree.

630	**229**	25c. multicoloured	1·50	10
631	**229**	55c. multicoloured	1·75	25
632	**229**	70c. multicoloured	2·00	1·50
633	**229**	$4 multicoloured	4·00	10·00

1985. Railway Locomotives (2nd series). As T 225. Multicoloured.

634	25c. Baldwin steam locomotive No. 16	1·25	30
635	55c. Rogers locomotive	1·75	35
636	$1.50 Locomotive "Projector", 1845	2·75	3·50
637	$4 Diesel locomotive No. 102	3·75	6·50

230 "The Old Settlement" (Ralph Campbell)

1985. Christmas. Jamaican Paintings. Mult.

638	20c. Type **230**	10	10
639	55c. "The Vendor" (Albert Huie) (vert)	15	15
640	75c. "Road Menders" (Gaston Tabois)	20	35
641	$4 "Woman, must I not be about my Father's business?" (Carl Abrahams) (vert)	1·10	2·25

1986. Jamaican Birds (2nd series). As T 213. Multicoloured.

642	25c. Chestnut-bellied cuckoo	50	10
643	55c. Jamaican becard	65	30
644	$1.50 White-eyed thrush	85	2·00
645	$5 Rufous-tailed flycatcher	1·75	4·75

230a Princess Elizabeth and Princess Margaret, 1939

1986. 60th Birthday of Queen Elizabeth II. Multicoloured.

646	20c. Type **230a**	35	10
647	25c. With Prince Charles and Prince Andrew, 1962	35	10
648	70c. Queen visiting War Memorial, Montego Bay, 1983	40	30
649	$3 On state visit to Luxembourg, 1976	60	1·50
650	$5 At Crown Agents Head Office, London, 1983	75	2·25

231 Bustamante Children's Hospital

1986. "Ameripex '86" International Stamp Exhibition, Chicago. Multicoloured.

651	25c. Type **231**	70	15
652	55c. Air Jamaica Boeing 737 airliner and map of holiday resorts	2·25	40
653	$3 Norman Manley Law School	1·25	4·00
654	$5 Bauxite and agricultural exports	7·50	9·50
MS655	85×106 mm. Nos. 651/4 (sold at $8.90)	10·50	12·00

231a Prince Andrew and Miss Sarah Ferguson, Ascot, 1985

1986. Royal Wedding. Multicoloured.

656	20c. Type **231a**	15	10
657	$5 Prince Andrew making speech, Fredericton, Canada, 1985	1·00	1·90

232 Richard "Shrimpy" Clarke

1986. Jamaican Boxing Champions. Multicoloured.

658	45c. Type **232**	20	15
659	70c. Michael McCallum	30	30
660	$2 Trevor Berbick	70	1·75
661	$4 Richard "Shrimpy" Clarke, Michael McCallum and Trevor Berbick	1·25	3·00

1986. Nos. 472/3 surch.

662	5c. on 50c. Jamaican woodpecker	3·00	3·00
663	10c. on 65c. Rafting, Martha Brae Trelawny	1·75	2·50

234 "Heliconia wagneriana"

1986. Christmas. Flowers (1st series). Mult.

664	20c. Type **234**	10	10
665	25c. "Heliconia psittacorum" (horiz)	10	10
666	55c. "Heliconia rostrata"	20	30
667	$5 "Strelitzia reginae" (horiz)	1·60	5·00

See also Nos. 703/6 and 739/42.

235 Crown Cone

1987. Sea Shells. Multicoloured.

668	35c. Type **235**	45	15
669	75c. Measled cowrie	65	60
670	$1 Atlantic trumpet triton	75	90
671	$5 Rooster-tail conch	1·50	4·50

236 Norman Manley

237 Arms of Jamaica

1987. Portraits.

672A	**236**	1c. red and pink	10	75
673A	**236**	2c. red and pink	10	75
674A	**236**	3c. green and stone	10	75
675A	**236**	4c. green & light green	10	75
676A	**236**	5c. blue and grey	30	40
677A	**236**	6c. blue and grey	20	75
678A	**236**	7c. violet and mauve	50	75
679A	**236**	8c. mauve and pink	20	10
680A	**236**	9c. sepia and brown	50	10
681aB	-	10c. red and pink	20	30
682A	-	20c. orange and flesh	20	30
683A	-	30c. green & light green	40	10
684B	-	40c. deep green & green	60	50
685A	-	50c. green and grey	30	40
685cB	-	55c. bistre and cream	75	40
686A	-	60c. blue and light blue	30	20
687A	-	70c. violet & light violet	30	20
688A	-	80c. violet and lilac	50	30
689A	-	90c. brown & lt brown	60	75
690A	**237**	$1 brown and cream	30	20
690cB	**237**	$1.10 brown and cream	70	40
691AB	**237**	$2 orange and cream	1·00	70
692aB	**237**	$5 green and stone	65	80
693A	**237**	$10 blue and azure	70	1·75
693cB	**237**	$25 violet and lilac	1·50	1·75
693dB	**237**	$50 mauve and lilac	2·50	3·00

DESIGN: 10c. to 90c. Sir Alexander Bustamante.

The 5, 20, 40, 50, 90c. and $1 exist with or without imprint date at foot.

238 Jamaican Flag and Coast at Sunset

1987. 25th Anniv of Independence. Multicoloured.

694	55c. Type **238**	1·50	60
695	70c. Jamaican flag and inscription (horiz)	1·50	2·75

239 Marcus Garvey

1987. Birth Centenary of Marcus Garvey (founder of Universal Negro Improvement Association). Each black, green and yellow.

696	25c. Type **239**	1·25	2·00
697	25c. Statue of Marcus Garvey	1·25	2·00

240 Salvation Army School for the Blind

1987. Cent of Salvation Army in Jamaica. Mult.

698	25c. Type **240**	1·50	30
699	55c. Col. Mary Booth and Bramwell Booth Memorial Hall	1·50	30
700	$3 Welfare Service lorry, 1929	4·75	5·50
701	$5 Col. Abram Davey and S.S. "Alene", 1887	6·00	8·50
MS702	100×80 mm. Nos. 698/701 (sold at $8.90)	15·00	15·00

1987. Christmas. Flowers (2nd series). As T 234. Multicoloured.

703	20c. Hibiscus hybrid	15	10
704	25c. "Hibiscus elatus"	15	10
705	$4 "Hibiscus cannabinus"	2·00	3·75
706	$5 "Hibiscus rosasinensis"	2·25	3·75

1988. Jamaican Birds (3rd series). As T 213. Multicoloured.

707	45c. Chestnut-bellied cuckoo, black-billed amazon and Jamaican euphonia	1·75	2·50
708	45c. Black-billed amazon, jamaican white-eyed vireo, rufous-throated solitaire and yellow elaenia	1·75	2·50
709	$5 Snowy plover, little blue heron and great blue heron (white phase)	4·25	5·50
710	$5 Black-necked stilt, snowy egret, snowy plover and black-crowned night heron	4·25	5·50

The two designs of each value were printed together, se-tenant, each pair forming a composite design.

243 Blue Whales

1988. Marine Mammals. Multicoloured.

711	20c. Type **243**	2·00	70
712	25c. Gervais's whales	2·00	70
713	55c. Killer whales	3·00	80
714	$5 Common dolphins	5·00	10·00

243a Jackie Hendriks

1988. West Indian Cricket. Each showing portrait, cricket equipment and early belt buckle. Multicoloured.

715	25c. Type **243a**	1·50	40
716	55c. George Headley	1·60	40
717	$2 Michael Holding	3·50	3·00
718	$3 R. K. Nunes	3·75	4·75
719	$4 Allan Rae	4·00	5·00

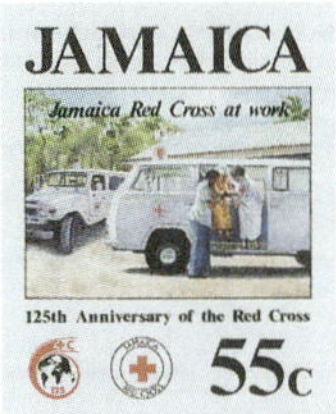

244 Jamaican Red Cross Workers with Ambulance

1988. 125th Anniv of Int Red Cross. Mult.

720	55c. Type **244**	75	30
721	$5 Henri Dunant (founder) in field hospital	2·75	4·25

245 Boxing

1988. Olympic Games, Seoul. Multicoloured.

722	25c. Type **245**	40	10
723	45c. Cycling	2·50	70
724	$4 Athletics	2·50	3·25
725	$5 Hurdling	2·50	3·25
MS726	127×87 mm. Nos. 722/5 (sold at $9.90)	7·00	7·00

246 Bobsled Team Members and Logo

1988. Jamaican Olympic Bobsled Team. Mult.

727	25c. Type **246**	50	1·25
728	25c. Two-man bobsled	50	1·25
729	$5 Bobsled team members (different) and logo	2·50	4·00
730	$5 Four-man bobsled	2·50	4·00

1988. Hurricane Gilbert Relief Fund. Nos. 722/5 surch + 25c HURRICANE GILBERT RELIEF FUND.

731	25c.+25c. Type **245**	10	20
732	45c.+45c. Cycling	20	30
733	$4+$4 Athletics	1·10	2·25
734	$5+$5 Hurdling	1·10	2·50

248 Nurses and Firemen

1988. Year of the Worker. Multicoloured.

735	25c. Type **248**	2·00	30
736	55c. Woodcarver	45	30
737	$3 Textile workers	1·00	3·00
738	$5 Workers on fish farm	1·25	3·50

1988. Christmas. Flowers (3rd series). As T 234. Multicoloured.

739	25c. "Euphorbia pulcherrima"	70	10
740	55c. "Spathodea campanulata" (horiz)	85	15
741	$3 "Hylocereus triangularis"	2·00	2·00
742	$4 "Broughtonia sanguinea" (horiz)	2·00	2·00

249 Old York Castle School

1989. Bicent of Methodist Church in Jamaica.

743	**249**	25c. black and blue	30	10
744	-	45c. black and red	35	10
745	-	$5 black and green	3·00	5·50

DESIGNS: 45c. Revd. Thomas Coke and Parade Chapel, Kingston; $5 Father Hugh Sherlock and St. John's Church.

250 "Syntomidopsis variegata"

1989. Jamaican Moths (1st series). Multicoloured.

746	25c. Type **250**	50	10
747	55c. "Himantoides perkinsae"	80	30
748	$3 "Arctia nigriplaga"	1·50	3·50
749	$5 "Sthenognatha toddi"	1·90	4·25

See also Nos. 758/61 and 790/3.

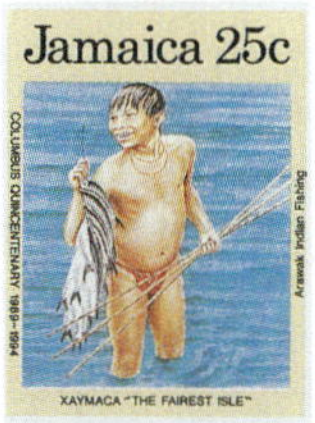

251 Arawak Fisherman with Catch

1989. 500th Anniv (1992) of Discovery of America by Columbus (1st issue). Multicoloured.

750	25c. Type **251**	20	10
751	70c. Arawak man smoking	45	30
752	$5 King Ferdinand and Queen Isabella inspecting caravels	3·25	4·50
753	$10 Columbus with chart	6·50	9·50
MS754	150×200 mm. Nos. 750/3 (sold at $16.15)	17·00	17·00

See also Nos. 774/7 and 802/7.

252 Girl Guide

1990. 75th Anniv of Girl Guide Movement in Jamaica. Multicoloured.

755	45c. Type **252**	1·50	30
756	55c. Guide leader	1·50	30
757	$5 Brownie, guide and ranger	6·00	9·00

1990. Jamaican Moths (2nd series). As T 250. Multicoloured.

758	25c. "Eunomia rubripunctata"	85	35
759	55c. "Perigonia jamaicensis"	1·25	35
760	$4 "Uraga haemorrhoa"	2·50	4·50
761	$5 "Empyreuma pugione"	2·50	4·50

1990. "EXPO '90" International Garden and Greenery Exhibition, Osaka. Nos. 758/61 optd EXPO '90 and logo.

762	25c. "Eunomia rubripunctata"	85	35
763	55c. "Perigonia jamaicensis"	1·25	35
764	$4 "Uraga haemorrhoa"	2·50	4·50
765	$5 "Empyreuma pugione"	2·50	4·50

254 Teaching English

1990. International Literacy Year. Mult.

766	55c. Type **254**	75	25
767	$5 Teaching maths	4·75	6·50

255 "To the Market"

1990. Christmas. Children's Paintings. Mult.

768	20c. Type **255**	60	10
769	25c. "House and Garden"	60	10
770	55c. "Jack and Jill"	80	15
771	70c. "Market"	1·00	40
772	$1.50 "Lonely"	1·75	3·50
773	$5 "Market Woman" (vert)	3·50	7·00

256 Map of First Voyage, 1492

1990. 500th Anniv (1992) of Discovery of America by Columbus (2nd issue). Multicoloured.

774	25c. Type **256**	1·50	40
775	45c. Map of second voyage, 1493	1·75	40
776	$5 Map of third voyage, 1498	5·50	6·00
777	$10 Map of fourth voyage, 1502	8·00	10·00
MS778	126×99 mm. 25, 45c., $5, $10 Composite map of Caribbean showing routes of voyages	15·00	17·00
MS779	148×207 mm. Nos. 774/7. Imperf	17·00	19·00

257 Weather Balloon, Dish Aerial and Map of Jamaica

1991. 11th World Meteorological Congress, Kingston.

780	**257**	50c. multicoloured	50	20
781	**257**	$10 multicoloured	6·50	9·50

258 Bust of Mary Seacole

1991. International Council of Nurses Meeting of National Representatives.

782	**258**	50c. multicoloured	85	30
783	-	$1.10 multicoloured	1·75	2·25
MS784		89×60 mm. $8 agate, brown and ochre (sold at $8.20)	3·75	7·50

DESIGNS: $1.10 Mary Seacole House; $8 Hospital at Scutari, 1854.

259 Jamaican Iguana

1991. 50th Anniv of Natural History Society of Jamaica. Jamaican Iguana. Multicoloured.

785	$1.10 Type **259**	80	1·00
786	$1.10 Head of iguana looking right	80	1·00
787	$1.10 Iguana climbing	80	1·00
788	$1.10 Iguana on rock looking left	80	1·00
789	$1.10 Close-up of iguana's head	80	1·00

1991. Jamaican Moths (3rd series). As T 250. Multicoloured.

790	50c. "Urania sloanus"	65	20
791	$1.10 "Phoenicoprocta jamaicensis"	90	60
792	$1.40 "Horama grotei"	1·10	90
793	$8 "Amplypterus gannascus"	3·25	6·00

1991. "Phila Nippon '91" International Stamp Exhibition, Tokyo. Nos. 790/3 optd PHILA NIPPON 91 and emblem.

794	50c. "Urania sloanus"	1·00	20
795	$1.10 "Phoenicoprocta jamaicensis"	1·40	65
796	$1.40 "Horama grotei"	1·50	1·00
797	$8 "Amplypterus gannascus"	5·00	8·00

261 "Doctor Bird"

1991. Christmas. Children's Paintings. Mult.

798	50c. Type **261**	80	10
799	$1.10 "Road scene"	1·25	25
800	$5 "Children and house"	4·00	3·50
801	$10 "Cows grazing"	7·00	9·00

262 Indians threatening Ships

1991. 500th Anniv (1992) of Discovery of America by Columbus (3rd issue). Multicoloured.

802	50c. Type **262**	65	15
803	$1.10 Spaniards setting dog on Indians	75	30
804	$1.40 Indian with gift of pineapple	75	30
805	$25 Columbus describes Jamaica with crumpled paper	8·50	12·00
MS806	125×102 mm. Nos. 802/5 (sold at $28.20)	9·00	12·00
MS807	210×150 mm. Nos. 802/5. Imperf	10·00	12·00

263 Compasses and Square Symbol

1992. 250th Anniv of First Provisional Grand Master of English Freemasonry in Jamaica. Multicoloured.

808	50c. Type **263**	70	30
809	$1.10 Symbol in stained glass window	90	40
810	$1.40 Compasses and square on book	90	40
811	$25 Eye in triangle symbol	9·00	12·00
MS812	140×80 mm. Nos. 808/11 (sold at $28.50)	15·00	16·00

264 Ship in Flooded Street

1992. 300th Anniv of Destruction of Port Royal. Multicoloured.

813	50c. Type **264**	55	40
814	$1.10 Church tower falling	70	45
815	$1.40 Houses collapsing	70	45
816	$25 Inhabitants falling into fissure	9·00	12·00
MS817	116×75 mm. $5 Contemporary broadsheet of earthquake	7·00	8·00

265 Credit Union Symbol

1992. 50th Anniv of Credit Union Movement.

818	**265**	50c. blue, emerald & green	1·00	50
819	-	$1.40 multicoloured	1·75	1·75

DESIGN: $1.40, O'Hare Hall.

266 Jamaican Flag and Beach Scene

1992. 30th Anniv of Independence.

820	**266**	50c. multicoloured	10	10
821	**266**	$1.10 multicoloured	20	20
822	**266**	$25 multicoloured	2·75	6·00

267 "Rainbow" (Cecil Baugh)

1993. Art Ceramics and Pottery. Multicoloured.

823	50c. Type **267**	20	10
824	$1.10 "Yabba Pot" (Louisa Jones)	30	20
825	$1.40 "Sculptured Vase" (Gene Pearson)	30	20
826	$25 "Lidded Form" (Norma Harrack)	4·50	6·50

268 Girls' Brigade Parade

1993. Centenary of Girls' Brigade. Mult.

827	50c. Type **268**	90	50
828	$1.10 Brigade members	1·00	1·10

269 Cadet, Armoured Car and Emblem

1993. 50th Anniv of Jamaica Combined Cadet Force. Multicoloured.

829	50c. Type **269**	40	20
830	$1.10 Cadet and Britten Norman Islander aircraft (horiz)	60	40
831	$1.40 Cadet and patrol boats	60	40
832	$3 Cadet and emblem (horiz)	80	2·00

270 Constant Spring Golf Course

1993. Golf Courses. Multicoloured.

833	50c. Type **270**	45	10
834	$1.10 Type **270**	65	20
835	$1.40 Half Moon	70	20
836	$2 As $1.40	1·00	90
837	$3 Jamaica Jamaica	1·10	1·25
838	$10 As $3	2·50	3·50
MS839	66×71 mm. $25 Tryall (vert) (sold at $28)	5·75	6·00

271 Norman Manley

1994. Birth Centenary of Norman Manley.

840	**271**	$25 multicoloured	2·00	2·75
841	**271**	$50 multicoloured	2·50	4·25

1994. "Hong Kong '94" International Stamp Exhibition. No. MS839 optd HONG KONG '94 and emblem.

MS842	66×71 mm. $25 Tryall	6·00	6·50

273 Flags of Great Britain and Jamaica

1994. Royal Visit. Multicoloured.

843	$1.10 Type **273**	65	10
844	$1.40 Royal Yacht "Britannia"	1·50	30
845	$25 Queen Elizabeth II	3·00	4·00
846	$50 Queen Elizabeth and Prince Philip	5·00	8·00

274 Douglas DC-9

1994. 25th Anniv of Air Jamaica. Mult.

847	50c. Type **274**	35	25
848	$1.10 Douglas DC-8	35	25
849	$5 Boeing 727	75	75
850	$50 Airbus A300	3·50	6·50

275 Giant Swallowtail

1994. Giant Swallowtail Butterfly Conservation. Multicoloured.

851	50c. Type **275**	40	25
852	$1.10 With wings closed	40	25
853	$10 On flower	1·60	2·25
854	$25 With wings spread	2·75	5·00
MS855	56×61 mm. $50 Pair of butterflies	5·50	7·00

276 "Royal Botanical Gardens" (Sidney McLaren)

1994. Tourism. Multicoloured.

856	50c. Type **276**	55	20
857	$1.10 Blue Mountains	85	30
858	$5 Tourist in hammock and water sports	3·00	3·75
MS859	105×80 mm. $25 Carolina parakeets; $25 Silhouetted scuba diver; $25 Carolina parakeet and foliage; $25 Tourist raft	6·00	7·50

277 Jamaican Red Poll Calf

1994. Jamaican Red Poll Cattle. Multicoloured.

860	50c. Type **277**	10	10
861	$1.10 Red Poll heifer	10	10
862	$25 Red Poll cow	1·25	2·25
863	$50 Red Poll bull	2·50	4·50

278 Refuse Collectors

1994. Christmas. Children's Paintings. Multicoloured.

864	50c. Type **278**	10	10
865	90c. Hospital ward	10	10
866	$1.10 House	10	10
867	$50 Landscape	3·75	6·00

279 Jamaican Band- tailed Pigeon ("Ring- tailed Pigeon")

1995. Jamaican Wild Birds. Multicoloured.

868	50c. Type **279**	65	40
869	90c. Yellow-billed amazon ("Yellow-billed parrot")	80	40
870	$1.10 Black-billed amazon ("Black-billed parrot")	80	40
871	$50 Jamaican owl ("Brown owl")	5·50	7·00
MS872	47×62 mm. $50 Streamertail	4·75	7·00

For No. **MS**872 additionally inscribed for "Singapore '95" see No. **MS**888.

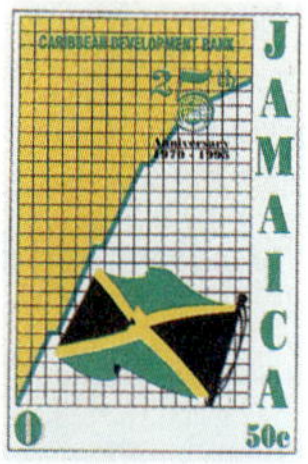

280 Graph, National Flag and Logo

1995. 25th Anniv of Caribbean Development Bank.

873	**280**	50c. green, black and yellow	10	10
874	**280**	$1 green, black and yellow	10	10
875	-	$1.10 multicoloured	10	25
876	-	$50 multicoloured	2·75	5·50

DESIGNS—HORIZ: $1.10, Industry, agriculture and commerce; $50 Jamaican currency.

281 "Song of Freedom"

1995. 50th Birth Anniv of Bob Marley (reggae singer). Record covers. Multicoloured.

877	50c. Type **281**	40	15
878	$1.10 "Fire"	55	20
879	$1.40 "Time will Tell"	60	25
880	$3 "Natural Mystic"	1·10	1·00
881	$10 "Live at Lyceum"	2·00	3·00
MS882	105×57 mm. $100 "Legend"	8·00	9·00

282 Queen Elizabeth the Queen Mother

1995. 95th Birthday of Queen Elizabeth the Queen Mother. Sheet 81×95 mm.

MS883	**282** $75 multicoloured	4·50	5·50

283 Michael Manley

1995. Recipients of the Order of the Caribbean Community. Multicoloured.

884	50c. Type **283**	15	15
885	$1.10 Sir Alister McIntyre	20	10
886	$1.40 Justice P. Telford Georges	20	10
887	$50 Dame Nita Barrow	6·50	8·50

1995. "Singapore '95" International Stamp Exhibition. No. MS872 additionally inscr with exhibition emblem on sheet margin.

MS888	47×62 mm. $50 Streamertail	3·75	5·00

284 Dish Aerial and Landrover, Balkans

1995. 50th Anniv of United Nations. Multicoloured.

889	50c. Type **284**	30	20
890	$1.10 Antonov An-32 aircraft, Balkans	55	25
891	$3 Bedford articulated road tanker, Balkans	70	90
892	$5 Fairchild C-119 Flying Boxcar, Korea	80	1·40
MS893	100×70 mm. $50 U.N.T.A.G. vehicles, Namibia	2·25	3·50

285 Landing of Indian Immigrants

1996. 150th Anniv of Indian Immigration to Jamaica. Multicoloured.

894	$2.50 Type **285**	25	15
895	$10 Indian musicians and traditional dancers	75	1·25

286 Jamaican Flag and UNICEF Emblem

1996. 50th Anniv of UNICEF.

896	**286**	$2.50 multicoloured	65	20
897	**286**	$8 multicoloured	1·25	1·25
898	**286**	$10 multicoloured	1·25	1·50

287 Brown's Hutia

1996. Endangered Species. Brown's Hutia ("Jamaican Hutia"). Multicoloured.

899	$2.50 Type **287**	15	10
900	$10 Hutia on rock	50	65

901	$12.50 Female with young	60	1·00
902	$25 Head of hutia	1·25	2·25

288 High Altar, Church of St. Thomas the Apostle

1997. 300th Anniv of Kingston Parish Church. Multicoloured.

903	$2 Type **288**	35	10
904	$8 Church of St. Thomas the Apostle	1·10	80
905	$12.50 "The Angel" (wood carving by Edna Manley) (vert)	1·75	2·25
MS906	106×76 mm. $60 St. Thomas the Apostle at sunset (42×56 mm)	3·50	4·50

No. 903 is inscribed "ALTER" in error.

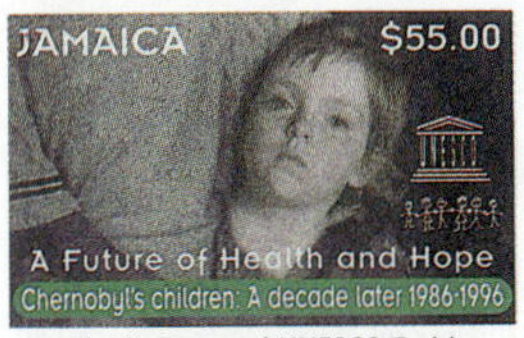

289 Child's Face and UNESCO Emblem

1998. 10th Anniv of Chernobyl Nuclear Disaster.

907	**289**	$55 multicoloured	3·25	3·75

289a Map of Caribbean

1997. 50th Anniv of Caribbean Integration Movement and 18th CARICOM Heads of Government Conference. Multicoloured.

907a	$2.50 Type **289a**	5·50	5·50
907b	$8 Coastal scenery	6·50	2·25
907c	$10 As $8	7·00	2·25

290 "Coelia triptera"

1997. Orchids. Multicoloured.

908A	$1 Type **290**	20	30
909A	$2 "Oncidium pulchellum" (horiz)	30	30
910A	$2.50 "Oncidium triquetium"	30	20
911A	$3 "Broughtonia negrilensis"	40	30
912A	$4.50 "Oncidium gauntlettii" (horiz)	50	40
913A	$5 "Encyclia fragans" (horiz)	50	30
914A	$8 "Broughtonia sanguinea" (horiz)	80	30
915A	$12 "Phaius tankervilleae"	1·00	60
916B	$25 "Cochleanthes flabelliformis" (horiz)	1·75	2·00
917A	$50 "Broughtonia sanguinea" (three varieties) (horiz)	1·40	1·50

291 Diana, Princess of Wales

1998. Diana, Princess of Wales Commemoration. Multicoloured.

918	$20 Type **291**	1·00	1·25
MS919	70×100 mm. $80 Princess Diana and Mother Teresa (42×55 mm)	4·50	5·50

292 University Chapel, Mona

1998. 50th Anniv of University of West Indies. Multicoloured.

920	$8 Type **292**	40	40
921	$10 Philip Sherlock Centre for Creative Arts, Mona	40	40
922	$50 University arms (vert)	2·25	3·75

293 Flags of Jamaica and CARICOM

1998. 25th Anniv of Caribbean Community.

923	**293**	$30 multicoloured	2·50	2·50

294 Jamaican Footballer

1998. World Cup Football Championship, France. Multicoloured.

924	$10 Type **294**	65	40
925	$25 Jamaican team (horiz)	1·50	1·50
926	$100 As $25	5·00	7·00

295 Coral Reef

1998. Christmas. International Year of the Ocean. Multicoloured.

927	$10 Type **295**	1·00	40
928	$30 Fishing boats, Negril	2·50	1·25
929	$50 Black spiny sea urchin	3·50	4·00
930	$100 Composite design as Nos. 927/9 (22×41 mm)	7·00	10·00

296 Michael Collins (astronaut)

1999. 30th Anniv of First Manned Landing on Moon. Multicoloured.

931	$7 Type **296**	40	25
932	$10 Service module docking with lunar module	50	40
933	$25 Buzz Aldrin on Moon's surface	1·00	1·40
934	$30 Command module in Earth orbit	1·10	1·50
MS935	90×80 mm. $100 Earth as seen from Moon (circular, 40 mm diam)	3·50	4·75

297 Lesley Ann Masterton and Fong-Yee (polo)

1999. Jamaican Sporting Personalities. Mult.

936	$5 Type **297**	75	35
937	$10 Lawrence Rowe, Collie Smith and Alfred Valentine (cricket)	1·25	55
938	$20 Vivalyn Latty-Scott (women's cricket) (vert)	1·75	1·25
939	$25 Lindy Delapenha (football) (vert)	1·75	1·25
940	$30 Joy Grant-Charles (netball) (vert)	1·75	1·75
941	$50 Percy Hayles, Gerald Gray and Bunny Grant (boxing)	1·90	4·00
MS942	110×90 mm. $100 Lindy Delapenha and Joy Grant-Charles (56×42 mm)	4·50	6·00

298 "Spey" (mail ship), 1891

1999. 125th Anniv of Universal Postal Union. Multicoloured.

943	$7 Type **298**	1·00	30
944	$10 "Jamaica Planter" (mail ship), 1936	1·25	50
945	$25 Lockheed Constellation (aircraft), 1950	2·25	2·75
946	$30 Airbus A-310 (aircraft), 1999	2·25	3·00

299 Airbus A-310

1999. 30th Anniv of Air Jamaica. Multicoloured.

947	$10 Type **299**	1·25	50
948	$25 A-320	2·00	2·25
949	$30 A-340	2·25	2·50

300 Shih Tzu

1999. Dogs. Multicoloured.

950	$7 Type **300**	1·25	65
951	$10 German shepherd	1·50	65
952	$30 Doberman pinscher	3·25	3·75

301 Nelson Mandela Park

1999. Parks and Gardens. Multicoloured.

953	$7 Type **301**	40	35
954	$10 St. William Grant Park	50	35
955	$25 Seaview Park	1·25	1·50
956	$30 Holruth Park	1·50	2·00

302 "The Prophet" (sculpture)

2000. Birth Centenary of Edna Manley (artist). Multicoloured.

957	$10 Type **302**	45	35
958	$25 "Horse of the Morning"	1·10	90
959	$30 "The Angel"	1·40	1·25
960	$100 Edna Manley	4·50	7·50
MS961	128×159 mm. Nos. 957/60	7·00	10·00

303 Lennox Lewis

2000. Lennox Lewis, World Heavyweight Boxing Champion. Multicoloured.

962	$10 Holding W.B.C. Championship belt	30	45
963	$10 In ring with right arm raised	30	45
964	$10 Holding W.B.C. belt above head	30	45
965	$25 Taking punch on chin	75	1·00
966	$25 Type **303**	75	1·00
967	$25 In corner	75	1·00
968	$30 With W.B.C. belt after fight	95	1·10
969	$30 Holding all four belts	95	1·10
970	$30 With belts in front of skyscraper	95	1·10

304 Ferrari Racing Car 125 S, 1947

2000. Birth Centenary (1998) of Enzo Ferrari (car designer). Racing cars. Multicoloured.

971	$10 Type **304**	60	70
972	$10 375 F1, 1950	60	70
973	$10 312 F1, 1966	60	70
974	$25 DINO 166 P, 1965	1·10	1·50
975	$25 312 P, 1971	1·10	1·50
976	$25 F1 90, 1990	1·10	1·50

305 Queen Elizabeth the Queen Mother

2000. Queen Elizabeth the Queen Mother's 100th Birthday. Multicoloured, background colours given.

977	**305**	$10 lavender	70	35
978	-	$25 green	90	90
979	-	$30 mauve	1·60	1·40
980	-	$50 blue	2·50	4·00

DESIGNS: $25 to $50, Various recent photographs.

306 "The Runner", Jamaican Flag and Olympic Rings

2000. Olympic Games, Sydney. Each showing "The Runner" (sculpture by Alvin Marriot), Jamaican flag and Olympic Rings. Multicoloured.

981	$10 Type **306**	80	35
982	$25 Head and shoulders	1·40	90
983	$30 With flag at top (vert)	1·75	1·40
984	$50 With flag in centre (vert)	2·75	4·00

307 Bull Thatch Palm

2000. Native Trees. Multicoloured.

985	$10 Type **307**	80	35
986	$25 Blue mahoe	1·75	1·25
987	$30 Silk cotton	2·00	1·75

No.	Description		
988	$50 Yellow poui	3·00	5·00
MS989	112×70 mm. $100 Lignum Vitae (horiz)	7·50	8·50

308 "Madonna and Child" (Osmond Watson)

2000. Christmas. Jamaican Religious Paintings. Multicoloured.

No.	Description		
990	$10 Type **308**	55	35
991	$20 "Boy in the Temple" (Carl Abrahams) (horiz)	90	90
992	$25 "Ascension" (Carl Abrahams)	1·10	1·10
993	$30 "Jah Lives" (Osmond Watson)	1·25	1·40

309 Children of the Commonwealth

2001. 25th Anniv of Commonwealth Day.

No.	Type	Description		
994	**309**	$30 multicoloured	1·50	1·75

310 Andrew Mowatt (founder)

2001. Centenary of Jamaica Burial Scheme Society.

No.	Type	Description		
995	**310**	$15 multicoloured	1·25	1·25

311 "Falmouth Market" (lithograph)

2001. Birth Bicentenary of Adolphe Duperly (pioneer photographer). Multicoloured.

No.	Description		
996	$15 Type **311**	1·00	50
997	$40 "Ferry Inn, Spanish Town Road" (lithograph)	2·25	2·25
998	$45 "Coke Chapel, Kingston" (lithograph)	2·25	2·25
999	$60 "King Street, Kingston" (lithograph)	3·00	3·50
MS1000	103×170 mm. Nos. 996/9	9·00	10·00

312 Poinsettia in Church Window

2001. Christmas.

No.	Type	Description		
1001	**312**	$15 multicoloured	1·00	50
1002	**312**	$30 multicoloured	2·00	1·40
1003	**312**	$40 multicoloured	2·25	2·25

2002. Golden Jubilee. As T 219 of Falkland Islands.

No.	Description		
1004	$15 agate, blue and gold	1·00	50
1005	$40 multicoloured	2·25	2·25
1006	$45 black, blue and gold	2·25	2·25
1007	$60 multicoloured	3·00	3·50
MS1008	162×95 mm. Nos. 1004/7 and $30 multicoloured	8·00	8·50

DESIGNS—HORIZ: $15 Princess Elizabeth in orchard, 1941; $40 Queen Elizabeth wearing pearls and striped dress; $45 Queen Elizabeth in evening dress, 1953; $60 Queen Elizabeth visiting Gloucester, 1995. VERT (38×51 mm): $30 Queen Elizabeth after Annigoni.

Designs as Nos. 1004/7 in No. **MS**1008 omit the gold frame around each stamp and the "Golden Jubilee 1952–2002" inscription.

313 Queen Elizabeth and Jamaican Royal Standard

2002. Royal Visit. Multicoloured.

No.	Description		
1009	$15 Type **313**	1·00	50
1010	$45 Queen Elizabeth in evening dress and Jamaican coat of arms	2·50	2·75

314 Sir Philip Sherlock

2002. Birth Centenary of Sir Philip Sherlock (historian).

No.	Type	Description		
1011	**314**	$40 mauve, magenta and blue	1·50	1·60

315 Female Dancers

2002. 40th Anniv of National Dance Theatre Company.

No.	Type	Description		
1012	**315**	$15 multicoloured	1·25	1·00

316 P.A.H.O. Centenary Logo

2002. Centenary of Pan American Health Organization.

No.	Type	Description		
1013	**316**	$40 multicoloured	2·25	1·75

317 "Masquerade" (Osmond Watson)

2002. Christmas. Local Works of Art. Multicoloured.

No.	Description		
1014	$15 Type **317**	1·00	45
1015	$40 "John Canoe in Guanaboa Vale" (Gaston Tabois) (horiz)	2·00	1·50
1016	$45 "Mother and Child" (carving by Kapo)	2·00	1·75
1017	$60 "Hills of Papine" (carving by Edna Manley) (horiz)	2·75	2·75

318 Dancers

2002. 40th Anniv of Independence. Multicoloured.

No.	Description		
1018	$15 Type **318**	1·00	45
1019	$40 Independence Day celebrations	2·25	1·75
1020	$60 Welder and fish processing worker	3·50	4·50

319 Kingston in Early 1800s

2002. Bicentenary of Kingston. Multicoloured.

No.	Description		
1021	$15 Type **319**	1·00	1·25
1022	$15 Wharf and statue of Queen Victoria, early 1900s	1·00	1·25
1023	$15 Horse-drawn cab, early 1900s, and modern street scene	1·00	1·25

Nos. 1021/3 were printed together, se-tenant, as horizontal strips of 3 throughout the sheet, forming a montage.

320 Queen Elizabeth II in St. Edward's Chair flanked by Bishops of Durham and Bath & Wells

2003. 50th Anniv of Coronation. Multicoloured.

No.	Description		
1024	$15 Type **320**	1·00	45
1025	$45 Coronation Coach in procession	2·50	3·00
MS1026	95×115 mm. $50 As $45; $100 As Type **320**	6·00	7·50

Nos. 1024/5 have scarlet frame; stamps from **MS**1026 have no frame and country name in mauve panel.

321 "30" as Key

2003. 30th Anniv of CARICOM.

No.	Type	Description		
1027	**321**	$40 multicoloured	2·25	2·00

322 Jamaican Stripe-headed Tanager

2003. Bird Life International. (1st series). Jamaican Birds. Multicoloured.

No.	Description		
1028	$15 Type **322**	1·25	65
1029	$40 Crested quail dove (horiz)	2·00	1·75
1030	$45 Jamaican tody (horiz)	2·00	1·75
1031	$60 Blue mountain vireo	2·75	3·50
MS1032	175×80 mm. $30 Jamaican blackbird nestlings (34×30 mm); $30 Searching for food in bromeliad (30×34 mm); $30 Singing from perch (30×34 mm); $30 Singing from perch (34×30 mm); $30 With insect in beak (34×30 mm)	8·50	9·00

See also Nos. 1040/9.

323 Sailing ships and Map of Kingston Harbour

2003. Maritime History. Multicoloured.

No.	Description		
1033	$40 Type **323**	2·25	2·25
1034	$40 Passengers on cruise ship and sailing ships	2·25	2·25
1035	$40 *Sugar Refiner* (cargo ship)	2·25	2·25

Nos. 1033/5 were printed together, se-tenant, forming a composite design.

324 Baby Jesus

2003. Christmas. Multicoloured.

No.	Description		
1036	$15 Type **324**	85	35
1037	$30 Close-up of Baby Jesus	1·60	65
1038	$60 Holy Family	2·75	3·25

325 Toussaint L'Ouverture

2004. Bicentenary of Haitian Revolution.

No.	Type	Description		
1039	**325**	$40 multicoloured	2·25	1·75

326 Yellow-billed Amazon

2004. Bird Life International (2nd series). Caribbean Endemic Birds Festival. Multicoloured.

No.	Description		
1040	$10 Type **326**	90	90
1041	$10 Jamaican oriole	90	90
1042	$10 Orangequit	90	90
1043	$10 Yellow-shouldered grassquit	90	90
1044	$10 Jamaican woodpecker	90	90
1045	$10 Streamertail ("Red-billed Streamertail")	90	90
1046	$10 Jamaican mango	90	90
1047	$10 White-eyed thrush	90	90
1048	$10 Jamaican lizard cuckoo	90	90
1049	$10 Arrow-headed warbler	90	90

327 Water Lilies

2004. World Environment Day. Sheet 195×85 mm containing T 327 and similar horiz designs. Multicoloured.

No.	Description		
MS1050	$10 Type **327**; $10 Hawksbill turtle; $10 Tube sponge; $10 Man in canoe, Parottee pond; $40 Vase sponge and Star coral; $40 Sea fan and black and white crinoid; $40 Glassy sweeper; $40 Giant sea anemone	6·00	7·00

328 Hurdling

2004. Olympic Games, Athens. Multicoloured.

1051	$30 Type **328**	1·00	65
1052	$60 Running	2·00	1·75
1053	$70 Swimming	2·00	1·90
1054	$90 Badminton and shooting	2·75	3·50

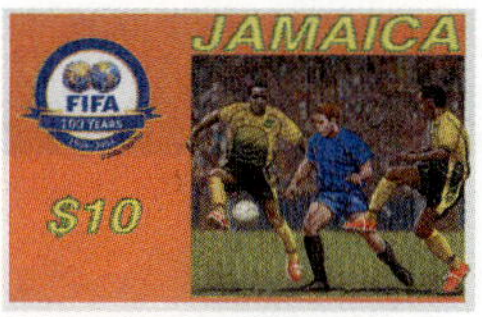

329 Two Jamaican Players and Opponent (blue strip)

2004. Centenary of FIFA (Federation Internationale de Football Association). Multicoloured.

1055	$10 Type **329**	55	30
1056	$30 Two Jamaican players and opponent (white top)	1·25	70
1057	$45 Two Jamaican players and opponent (blue top)	1·75	1·50
1058	$50 Two Jamaican players and opponent (white strip)	1·75	2·50

330 Ambassador John Pringle and Round Hill Hotel

2004. Centenary of the Jamaica Hotel Law. Multicoloured.

MS1059	152×114 mm. $40 Type **330** (bottom left panel in pink or blue, three of each)	8·00	9·00
MS1060	152×114 mm. $40 Abe Issa and Tower Isle Hotel; $40 John Issa and Tower Isle Hotel (both with bottom right panels in green, light green or carmine, two of each)	8·00	9·00
MS1061	152×114 mm. $40 Ralph Lauren and Doctors Cave Beach, Montego Bay (with left-hand panel in dark blue, blue or azure, two of each)	8·00	9·00

331 White Sorrel

2004. Christmas.

1062	**331**	$10 multicoloured	65	20
1063	-	$20 multicoloured	1·25	40
1064	-	$50 multicoloured (horiz)	2·75	2·75
1065	-	$60 multicoloured (horiz)	2·75	2·75

DESIGNS: $20 to $60 All showing white sorrel.

332 Mary Morris Knibb and Mizpah Moravian Church

2004. 250th Anniv of the Moravian Church in Jamaica. Multicoloured.

1066	90c. Type **332**	10	40
1067	$10 Reverend W. O'Meally and Mizpah Moravian Church	65	30
1068	$50 Bishop S. U. Hastings and Redeemer Moravian Church	3·25	3·50

333 Ackee, Lychee and Pak Choy

2005. 150th Anniv of Chinese Population in Jamaica. Multicoloured.

1069	$30 Type **333**	1·25	60
1070	$60 Old Chinatown	2·50	2·00
1071	$90 Entrance to Chinese Benevolent Association Headquarters, Kingston	4·00	4·50

334 Rose Hall Great House, St James

2005. Buildings (1st series). Multicoloured. (a) Ordinary gum.

1072	90c. Type **334**	10	20
1073	$5 Holy Trinity Cathedral	20	20
1074	$30 Atrium of the National Commercial Bank, New Kingston	1·10	90
1075	$60 The Court House, Falmouth	2·25	2·50

(b) Self-adhesive.

1076	$5 Holy Trinity Cathedral	20	30
1077	$30 As No. 1074	1·10	1·10
1078	$60 As No. 1075	2·25	2·75

See also Nos. 1105/12.

335 CEPT Emblem

2005. 50th Anniv of the European Philatelic Corporation (Europa). Each showing the CEPT emblem, each with a different colour "stamp frame". Multicoloured.

1079	$60 Type **335**	1·60	1·25
1080	$70 Yellow frame	1·75	1·75
1081	$100 Blue frame	2·50	3·50
MS1082	120×70 mm. Nos. 1079/81	5·25	6·00

336 Gun Captain holding Powder Cartridge

2005. Bicentenary of the Battle of Trafalgar (1st issue). Multicoloured.

1083	$20 Type **336**	1·00	70
1084	$30 Admiral Nelson (vert)	1·40	75
1085	$50 British 12 Pounder cannon	1·60	1·25
1086	$60 HMS *Africa* (vert)	2·25	1·75
1087	$70 HMS *Leviathan* (vert)	2·40	2·50
1088	$90 HMS *Victory*	3·00	4·00
MS1089	120×79 mm. $200 HMS *Africa* at Port Royal (44×44 mm)	8·00	9·00

No. 1088 contains traces of powdered wood from HMS *Victory*. See also Nos. 1092/4.

337 Rotary Emblem

2005. Centenary of Rotary International.

1090	**337**	$30 multicoloured	1·50	1·50

338 Pope John Paul II

2005. Pope John Paul II Commemoration.

1091	**338**	$30 multicoloured	1·50	1·50

339 HMS *Victory*

2005. Bicentenary of the Battle of Trafalgar (2nd issue). Multicoloured.

1092	$50 Type **339**	1·75	1·10
1093	$90 Ships engaged in battle (horiz)	3·00	3·25
1094	$100 Admiral Lord Nelson	3·00	3·25

340 Mary Seacole and Herbal Remedies and Medicines

2005. Birth Bicentenary of Mary Seacole (nursing pioneer). Multicoloured.

1095	$30 Type **340**	80	55
1096	$50 Mary Seacole and Seacole Hall, Mona Campus, University of the West Indies	1·25	1·10
1097	$60 Mary Seacole and Crimean War soldiers, 1854–6	1·75	1·40
1098	$70 Mary Seacole and her British Crimean, Turkish Medjidie, French Legion of Honour and Jamaican Order of Merit medals	1·75	2·00

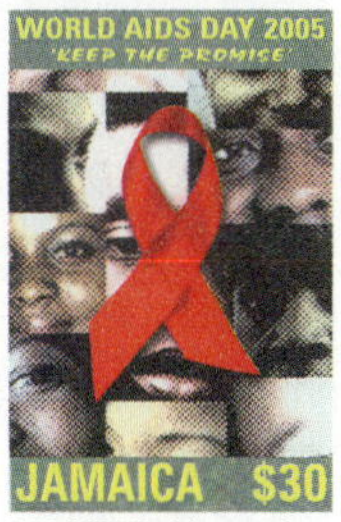

341 AIDS Emblem and Montage of Faces

2005. World AIDS Day.

1099	**341**	$30 multicoloured	1·00	1·00

342 Poinsettia Flowers and Star

2005. Christmas. Multicoloured (background colours given).

1100	**342**	$20 claret and scarlet	70	40
1101	**342**	$30 violet and scarlet	95	55
1102	**342**	$50 scarlet and emerald	1·50	1·00
1103	**342**	$80 green and scarlet	2·50	3·25

343 Jessie Ripoll (Mother Claver) (founder)

2005. 125th Anniv of Alpha.

1104	**343**	$30 multicoloured	75	75

2006. Buildings (2nd series). As T 334. Multicoloured. Ordinary or self-adhesive gum.

1105	$10 Courthouse, Morant Bay	45	30
1106	$15 Spanish Town Square, St. Catherine	65	40
1107	$20 Mico College	80	50
1108	$25 Jamaica College	90	60
1109	$50 Devon House, St. Andrew	1·75	1·25
1110	$70 Ward Theatre	2·25	2·50
1111	$90 Vale Royal, St. Andrew	2·75	3·00
1112	$100 Falmouth Post Office	2·75	3·00

344 Nestlings

2006. Endangered Species. Black-billed Amazon (Amazona agilis). Square designs. Multicoloured.

1121	$5 Type **344**	65	50
1122	$10 In close-up	85	50
1123	$30 In captivity	2·25	1·75
1124	$50 Pair in native forest	3·00	3·50

345 *Blakea trinervia* (cup and saucer)

2006. Christmas. Flowers. Multicoloured.

1125	$20 Type **345**	1·25	70
1126	$30 *Guaiacum officinale* (Lignum Vitae)	1·75	90
1127	$50 *Neocogniauxia monophylla* (vert)	2·25	1·75
1128	$60 *Dendrophylax funalis* (ghost orchid) (vert)	2·50	3·00

346 Courtney Walsh (fast bowler 1984–2001)

2007. ICC Cricket World Cup. Multicoloured.

1129	$30 Type **346**	1·75	1·10
1130	$30 Collie Smith (cricketer 1955–9)	1·75	1·10
1131	$40 New Sabina Park Stadium, Kingston (horiz)	1·90	1·25
1132	$50 Type **346**	2·25	1·75
1133	$60 Trelawny Multi-purpose Sports Complex (horiz)	2·50	3·00
MS1134	118×92 mm. $200 ICC Cricket World Cup trophy	8·50	9·00

347 Emblem

2007. Bicentenary of the Abolition of the Transatlantic Trade in Africans.

1135	**347**	$30 multicoloured	1·00	75

348 Scout and Jamaican Flag

2007. Centenary of Scouting. Multicoloured.

1136	$5 Type **348**	35	25
1137	$10 Early Jamaican scouts	50	25
1138	$30 Scout leaders	1·25	75
1139	$70 Scouts with Jamaican flag	2·75	3·50
MS1140	90×65 mm. $50 Scout parade (vert); $100 Lord Baden-Powell (vert)	4·00	4·50

349 *Tolumnia triquetra*

2007. 'The Christmas Collection 2007'. Flowers. Multicoloured.

1141	$20 Type **349**	80	35
1142	$30 *Broughtonia negrilensis* (horiz)	1·25	50
1143	$50 *Broughtonia sanguinea* (horiz)	2·00	1·50
1144	$60 *Spathelia sorbifolia*	2·25	2·50

350 Asafa Powell

2008. Olympic Games, Beijing. Designs showing athletes. Multicoloured.

1145	$20 Type **350**	75	40
1146	$30 Aleen Bailey and Veronica Campbell-Brown	1·25	1·40
1147	$30 Sherone Simpson and Tayna Lawrence	1·25	1·40
1148	$60 Veronica Campbell-Brown	2·50	2·75

Nos. 1146/7 were printed together, se-tenant, forming a composite design showing athletes with medals.

351 Anniversary Emblem

2008. 50th Anniv of University of Technology, Jamaica.

1149	**351**	$30 multicoloured	1·00	65
MS1150		95×70 mm. **351** $30 multi-coloured	1·00	1·25

352 Keyboard

2008. Centenary of ABRSM (Associated Board of the Royal Schools of Music) Examinations in Jamaica. Multicoloured.

1151	$30 Type **352**	1·25	60
1152	$70 Violin	2·50	3·00

353 Fern Fronds

2008. Christmas. Ferns. Multicoloured.

1153	$20 Type **353**	80	50
1154	$30 Curled single fern leaf	1·25	60
1155	$50 Close-up of fern frond	2·00	1·50
1156	$60 Fern frond	2·25	2·50

354 George Headley

2009. Birth Centenary of George Headley (cricketer). Multicoloured.

1157	$10 Type **354**	25	15
1158	$30 George Headley at wicket	75	50
1159	$200 Statue of George Headley	4·25	4·00
MS1160	110×95 mm. $250 Statue of George Headley at Sabina Park, Kingston (42×56 mm)	5·50	5·50

355 Angel and Two Children

2009. Christmas. Multicoloured.

1161	$20 Type **355**	70	50
1162	$30 Madonna and infant Jesus	75	50
1163	$50 Madonna (horiz)	1·50	1·10

OFFICIAL STAMPS

1890. Optd OFFICIAL.

O3	**8**	½d. green	10·00	1·75
O4	**11**	1d. red	7·50	1·25
O5	**11**	2d. grey	16·00	1·25

Pt. 1

JAMMU AND KASHMIR

A state in the extreme N. of India.

12 pies = 1 anna; 16 annas = 1 rupee.

1

1866. Imperf.

8	**1**	4a. red	£110	£160
15	**1**	1a. black	£350	
16	**1**	4a. black	£325	
19	**1**	4a. blue	£250	
20	**1**	½a. green	£140	£325
21	**1**	1a. green	£140	£350
24	**1**	1a. yellow	£1100	
25	**1**	4a. yellow	£650	
26	**1**	½a. red	42·00	70·00
27	**1**	1a. red	55·00	£225
34	**1**	1a. blue	45·00	£350
37	**1**	4a. green	£170	
41	**1**	½a. black	38·00	75·00
44	**1**	½a. blue	70·00	£350
48	**1**	½a. yellow	£170	

Prices for the circular stamps (Nos. 5/48) are for cut-square examples. Cut-to-shape examples are worth from 10% to 20% of these prices, according to condition.

4

1867

55	**4**	1a. blue	£1000	£475
58	**4**	½a. blue	£275	£130
60	**4**	½a. red	10·00	5·50
61	**4**	1a. red	24·00	15·00
64	**4**	½a. orange	£150	£170
65	**4**	1a. orange	£3500	£2000
68	**4**	½a. green	£2750	£1400
69	**4**	1a. green	£4000	£2250
69a	**4**	½a. black	£180	£225
69b	**4**	1a. black	£3000	£2000

The characters denoting the value are in the upper part of the inner circle and contains three ½a. and one 1a. values.

8 (1/4a.)

1867. Imperf.

90	**8**	¼a. black	5·50	5·50
91	**8**	½a. blue	6·00	2·50
93	**8**	1a. blue	£4750	£2000
94	**8**	1a. orange	18·00	14·00
97	**8**	2a. yellow	24·00	26·00
99	**8**	4a. green	60·00	55·00
101	**8**	8a. red	65·00	55·00

12 (1/4a.)

1878. Imperf or perf.

105	**12**	½a. violet	21·00	18·00
106	**12**	1a. mauve	30·00	32·00
108	**12**	2a. violet	38·00	38·00
110	**12**	2a. blue	80·00	80·00
125	**12**	¼a. red	4·75	5·50
126	**12**	½a. red	1·50	1·50
127	**12**	1a. red	3·25	4·25
128	**12**	2a. red	4·00	6·00
129	**12**	4a. red	14·00	13·00
130	**12**	8a. red	15·00	15·00
130a	**12**	¼a. blue	£1000	£650
131	**12**	¼a. orange	16·00	20·00
132	**12**	½a. orange	26·00	19·00
133	**12**	1a. orange	29·00	18·00
134	**12**	2a. orange	22·00	18·00
135	**12**	4a. orange	55·00	65·00
136	**12**	8a. orange	85·00	90·00
139	**12**	⅛a. yellow	2·00	2·50
142	**12**	¼a. brown	1·75	1·00
143	**12**	½a. blue	10·00	
148	**12**	1a. grey	1·50	1·50
150	**12**	1a. green	1·50	1·50
152	**12**	2a. red on yellow	3·50	1·50
153	**12**	2a. red on green	4·75	5·00
156	**12**	4a. green	4·75	4·75
159	**12**	8a. blue	11·00	12·00
161a	**12**	8a. lilac	11·00	25·00

OFFICIAL STAMPS

1878. Imperf or perf.

O6	¼a. black	2·25	2·50
O7	½a. black	15	1·00
O8	1a. black	50	1·50
O9	2a. black	30	45
O10	4a. black	1·75	2·25
O11	8a. black	3·00	1·25

Pt. 18

JAPAN

An empire of E. Asia, consisting of numerous islands.

1871. 100 mon = 1 sen.
1872. 10 rin = 1 sen; 100 sen = 1 yen.

1 (48 mon)

1871. Imperf.

1	1	48m. brown	£250	£375
3	1	100m. blue	£225	£300
5	1	200m. red	£375	£325
15b	1	500m. green	£550	£550

1872. Perf.

17		½s. brown	90·00	£130
19		1s. blue	£325	£325
21		2s. red	£475	£500
22		5s. green	£650	£650

5

12

1872. Various sizes. Design details differ.

34	5	½s. brown	20·00	25·00
35	5	1s. blue	80·00	46·00
36	5	2s. red	£170	60·00
46	5	4s. red	£140	33·00
57	12	6s. brown	£180	75·00
58	5	10s. green	£160	65·00
59	5	20s. violet	£325	£100
60	5	30s. black	£375	£100
66	5	½s. grey	24·00	22·00
67	5	1s. brown	38·00	24·00
68	5	4s. green	£140	30·00
69	12	6s. orange	£110	27·00
70	5	10s. blue	£190	30·00
71	5	20s. red	£150	21·00
72	5	30s. violet	£190	70·00
74	5	2s. yellow	£120	16·00
75	12	5s. green	£200	£110

13 Bean Goose

1875

61	13	12s. red	£375	£160
62	-	15s. lilac (Pied Wagtail)	£375	£160
63	-	45s. red (Northern Goshawk)	£475	£190

20

21

22

23

24

1876

77	20	1s. black	45·00	5·00
78	20	1s. brown	15·00	2·00
79	20	2s. grey	90·00	12·50
82a	20	4s. blue	50·00	6·25
83b	21	5s. brown	55·00	2·00
86d	21	10s. blue	50·00	2·50
87e	21	12s. red	£225	£170
88	22	15s. green	£150	12·50
89	22	20s. blue	£160	£150
90	22	30s. mauve	£250	£110
95	20	3s. orange	75·00	30·00
102f	20	2s. violet	70·00	2·50
103	20	4s. green	50·00	5·00
104	21	6s. orange	£190	90·00
105	21	8s. brown	37·00	3·00
111	22	45s. red	£500	£600
112	22	50s. red	£225	17·00
113c	20	1s. green	15·00	1·20
114f	20	2s. red	22·00	1·00
115g	21	5s. blue	32·00	2·00
116	20	5r. grey	3·50	30
117	20	3s. red	25·00	1·00
118h	20	4s. bistre	17·00	75
119	21	8s. violet	37·00	3·00
120h	21	10s. brown	25·00	75
121h	22	15s. violet	60·00	1·00
122h	22	20s. orange	75·00	3·00
123h	23	25s. green	£110	3·00
124h	22	50s. brown	£120	6·00
125h	24	1y. red	£150	6·00

25 Imperial Crest and Cranes

1894. Emperor's Silver Wedding.

126	25	2s. red	37·00	3·50
127	25	5s. blue	50·00	15·00

26 Prince Kitashirakawa

27 Prince Arisugawa

1896. China War.

128	26	2s. red	32·00	4·00
129	27	2s. red	32·00	4·00
130	26	5s. blue	75·00	4·00
131	27	5s. blue	75·00	4·00

Both 2s. have an oval medallion, and both 5s. a circular one.

28

29

30

31

32 Empress Jingu

1899

132	28	5r. grey	14·00	15·00
133	28	½s. grey	7·50	25
134	28	1s. brown	10·00	25
135b	28	1½s. blue	30·00	1·20
136	28	1½s. violet	22·00	60
137	28	2s. green	20·00	25
138	28	3s. purple	20·00	30
139	28	3s. red	25·00	25
140	28	4s. red	20·00	2·50
141	28	5s. yellow	30·00	30
142	29	6s. red	50·00	5·00
143	29	8s. olive	65·00	6·00
144	29	10s. blue	25·00	25
145	29	15s. violet	25·00	35
146	29	20s. orange	50·00	30
147	30	25s. green	£110	1·50
148	30	50s. brown	£110	2·00
149	31	1y. red	£150	2·50
183	32	5y. green	£600	6·00
184	32	10y. violet	£900	10·00

33 Rice Cakes used at Japanese Weddings

1900. Prince Imperial Wedding.

152	33	3s. red	36·00	1·10

34 Symbols of Korea and Japan

1905. Amalgamation of Japanese and Korean Postal Services.

153	34	3s. red	£130	23·00

35 Gun and Japanese Flag

1906. Triumphal Military Review of Russo-Japanese War.

154	35	1½s. blue	55·00	7·00
155	35	3s. red	£110	29·00

36

37

38

1914

167e	36	½s. brown	5·00	25
168e	36	1s. orange	6·50	25
170e	36	2s. green	9·00	25
172e	37	4s. red	25·00	2·50
174e	37	6s. brown	40·00	7·50
175e	37	8s. grey	32·00	22·00
176e	37	10s. blue	22·00	25
178e	37	20s. red	£130	2·00
179e	37	25s. olive	22·00	2·50
180e	38	30s. brown	35·00	1·50
181e	38	50s. brown	50·00	2·20
232	36	1½s. blue	6·50	25
236	37	13s. brown	14·00	35
238	38	30s. orange and green	40·00	60
239	38	50s. brown and blue	17·00	90
298	36	3s. red	3·00	45
300	37	5s. violet	11·00	30
302	37	7s. orange	14·00	30
309	38	1y. green and brown	£150	1·10

40 Ceremonial Cap

42 Hall of Ceremony

1915. Emperor's Coronation.

185	40	1½s. grey and red	4·00	85
186	-	3s. violet and brown	5·25	1·20
187	42	4s. red	23·00	15·00
188	42	10s. blue	55·00	25·00

DESIGN—As T **40**: 3s. Imperial throne.

43 Mandarin Duck

44 "Kammuri" (ceremonial headband)

1916. Investiture of Prince Hirohito as Heir Apparent.

189	43	1½s. green, red and yellow	4·25	1·60
190	43	3s. red and yellow	8·00	1·90
191	44	10s. blue	£950	£400

45 Dove of Peace

46 Dove of Peace

1919. Restoration of Peace.

192	45	1½s. brown	3·50	1·40
193	46	3s. green	4·75	2·20
194	45	4s. red	11·50	7·00
195	46	10s. blue	34·00	20·00

1919. Air. 1st Tokyo–Osaka Airmail Service. Optd with airplane.

196	36	1½s. blue	£375	£150
197	36	3s. red	£650	£450

48 7th-century Censor

1920. First Census.

198	48	1½s. purple	8·25	6·00
199	48	3s. red	9·50	6·00

49 Meiji Shrine

1920. Dedication of Meiji (Emperor Mutsuhito) Shrine.

200	49	1½s. violet	4·00	2·00
201	49	3s. red	4·00	2·00

50 Postal and National Flags

51 Dept. of Communications, Tokyo

1921. 50th Anniv of Japanese Post.

202	50	1½s. red and green	3·25	1·90
203	51	3s. brown	4·50	2·50
204	50	4s. red and pink	55·00	44·00
205	51	10s. blue	£300	£200

52 Warships "Katori" and "Kashima"

1921. Return of Crown Prince from European Tour.

206	52	1½s. violet	4·00	2·20
207	52	3s. olive	3·50	2·20
208	52	4s. red	48·00	33·00
209	52	10s. blue	70·00	40·00

53 Mt. Fuji and Sika Deer

1922

211	53	8s. red	34·00	9·75
266	53	4s. orange	15·00	55
267	53	8s. green	22·00	35
268	53	20s. purple	95·00	55
293	53	4s. green	4·50	1·10
303	53	8s. bistre	19·00	2·20
305	53	20s. blue	22·00	70

54 Mt. Niitaka

1923. Crown Prince's visit to Taiwan.

213	54	1½s. yellow	20·00	23·00
214	54	3s. violet	25·00	12·50

55

56

1923. Imperf.

215	55	½s. grey	4·75	5·00
216	55	1½s. blue	7·25	2·20
217	55	2s. brown	8·25	2·20
218	55	3s. red	3·75	1·40
219	55	4s. green	38·00	34·00
220	55	5s. violet	19·00	2·20
221	55	8s. red	55·00	44·00
222	56	10s. brown	50·00	2·20
223	56	20s. blue	80·00	2·75

58 Empress Jingu

1924

224	58	5y. green	£300	4·50
225	58	10y. violet	£475	3·25

59 Cranes

60 Phoenix

1925. Imperial Silver Wedding.

226	59	1½s. purple	2·20	1·70
227a	60	3s. brown and silver	4·00	3·50
228	59	8s. red	32·00	23·00
229b	60	20s. green and silver	70·00	60·00

61a Yomei Gate, Tosho Shrine, Nikko

1926

241	-	2s. green	3·00	15
242	61a	6s. red	14·00	50
243	-	10s. blue	14·00	15
304	-	10s. red	12·50	30

DESIGNS: 2s. Mt. Fuji; 10s. Nagoya Castle.

62 Baron Maeshima

63 Globe

1927. 50th Anniv of Membership of U.P.U.

244	62	1½s. purple	3·75	2·20
245	62	3s. olive	5·00	2·20
246	63	6s. red	90·00	65·00
247	63	10s. blue	£130	65·00

64 Phoenix

65 Ceremonial Shrines

1928. Emperor's Enthronement.

248	64	1½s. green on yellow	1·00	90
249	65	3s. purple on yellow	1·00	85
250	64	6s. red on yellow	5·50	3·25
251	65	10s. blue on yellow	5·75	4·00

66 Shrine of Ise

1929. 58th Vicennial Removal of Shrine of Ise.

255	66	1½s. violet	2·20	1·60
256	66	3s. red	2·75	2·20

67 Nakajima-built Fokker F.VIIb/3m over Lake Ashi, Hakone

1929. Air.

257	67	8½s. brown	65·00	50·00
258	67	9½s. red	17·00	11·00
259	67	16½s. green	20·00	20·00
260	67	18s. blue	19·00	8·25
261	67	33s. black	55·00	11·00

68 Map of Japan

1930. 3rd Census.

262	68	1½s. purple	3·75	1·90
263	68	3s. red	4·25	2·40

Although Type **68** is inscr "Second Census", this was actually the third census.

69 Meiji Shrine

1930. 10th Anniv of Meiji Shrine Dedication.

264	69	1½s. green	2·75	2·20
265	69	3s. orange	4·00	2·75

1934. Air. Establishment of Communications Commemoration Day. Sheet containing Nos. 258/61.

MS271	110×100 mm	£1300	£1800

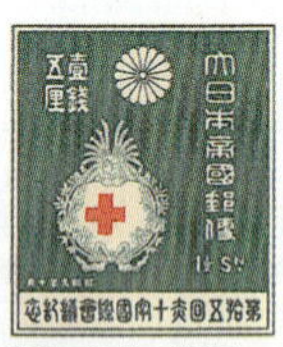

70 Insignia of Red Cross Society

1934. 15th Int Red Cross Conference, Tokyo.

272	70	1½s. green	2·30	1·80
273	-	3s. violet	2·75	3·00
274	70	6s. red	13·50	13·00
275	-	10s. blue	16·00	12·50

DESIGN—HORIZ: 3s.; 10s. Red Cross Society Buildings, Tokyo.

72 Cruiser "Hiyei" and Pagoda, Liaoyang

73 Akasaka Palace, Tokyo

1935. Visit of Emperor of Manchukuo.

276	72	1½s. green	1·80	1·60
277	73	3s. brown	3·00	1·80
278	72	6s. red	10·50	8·75
279	73	10s. blue	14·00	11·00

74 Mt. Fuji (after Kazan Watanabe)

1935. New Year's Greetings.

280	74	1½s. red	18·00	35

75c Mt. Fuji from Mishima

1936. Fuji-Hakone National Park.

281	-	1½s. brown	4·00	6·75
282	-	3s. green	7·25	11·50
283	-	6s. red	16·00	22·00
284	75c	10s. blue	18·00	25·00

DESIGNS: Mt. Fuji (1½s.); from Lake Ashi (3s.); from Lake Kawaguchi (6s.).

76 Dove of Peace

77 Shinto Shrine Port Arthur

1936. 30 Years of Occupation of Kwantung.

285	76	1½s. violet	18·00	22·00
286	77	3s. brown	22·00	27·00
287	-	10s. green	£200	£250

DESIGN—HORIZ: 10s. Govt. House, Kwantung.

78 Imperial Diet

1936. Inauguration of New Houses of the Imperial Diet, Tokyo.

288	78	1½s. green	2·00	2·00
289	-	3s. purple	2·30	2·30
290	-	6s. red	7·75	8·75
291	78	10s. blue	15·00	11·00

DESIGN: 3, 6s. Grand Staircase.

80 Wedded Rocks, Futami Bay

1936. New Year's Greetings.

292	80	1½s. red	8·00	35

82 Goshuinsen (16th-cent trading ship)

83 General Nogi

84 Lake Taisho, Kamikochi

85 Mitsubishi B5N1 and Map

86 Kamatari Fujiwara

87 Plum Tree

1937. Imperf or perf (424), perf (others). Without gum (424), with or without gum (392, 394, 396), with gum (others).

313	82	½s. violet	1·30	80
314	-	1s. brown	3·50	70
316	-	3s. green	1·00	10
317	-	4s. green	1·30	10
318	84	5s. blue	2·30	10
319	-	6s. orange	4·75	2·10
320	-	7s. green	1·20	45
321	-	8s. violet	1·50	60
322	-	10s. red	7·00	20
323	85	12s. blue	1·00	1·00
324	-	14s. red and brown	1·30	45
325	-	20s. blue	1·60	10
326	-	25s. light brown and brown	1·20	30
327	-	30s. blue	3·50	20
328	-	50s. green and bistre	1·60	20
329	-	1y. light brown and brown	6·25	80
331	87	10y. purple	32·00	1·60
392b	83	2s. red	65	60
394	83	3s. brown	1·10	15
396	-	5s. purple	40	20
398	-	7s. red	1·20	50
424	86	5y. green	6·25	80

DESIGNS: 1s. Rice harvesting; 3s. Hydro-electric Power Station; 4, 5s. (No. 396), 7s. (No. 398), Admiral Togo; 6s. Garambi Lighthouse, Taiwan; 7s. (No. 320), Diamond Mountains, Korea; 8s. Meiji Shrine; 10s. Yomei Gate, Tosho Shrine, Nikko; 14s. Inner Gate, Kasuga Shrine; 20s. Mt. Fuji and cherry blossom; 25s. Horyu Temple; 30s. Torii, Itsukushima Shrine at Miyajima; 50s. Temple of Golden Pavilion, Kyoto; 1y. Great Buddha, Kamakura.

88 Nakajima-built Douglas DC-2 Airliner

1937. Aerodrome Fund.

336	88	2s.+2s. red	2·75	1·80
337	88	3s.+2s. violet	2·75	2·10
338	88	4s.+2s. green	3·50	1·90

89 New Year's Emblem

1937. New Year's Greetings.

339	89	2s. red	13·00	20

90 Nantai Volcano

92 Shinkyo Bridge

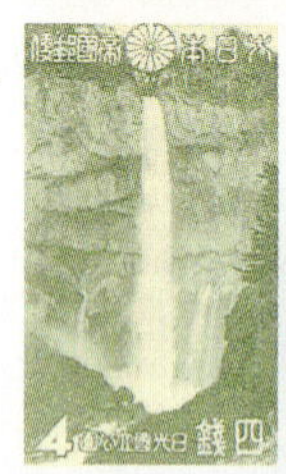

91 Kegon Falls

93 Hiuchi Volcano

1938. Nikko National Park.

340	90	2s. orange	80	95
341	91	4s. green	80	95
342	92	10s. red	9·50	8·25
343	93	20s. blue	9·75	8·50

MS344	128×182 mm. Nos. 340/3 (sold at 50s.)	70·00	80·00

94 Daisen Volcano and Meadow

95 Yashima Plateau and Estuary

96 Abuto Kwannon Shrine

97 Tomo Bay

1939. Daisen and Setonaikai National Parks.

345	**94**	2s. brown	60	80
346	**95**	4s. green	5·00	2·75
347	**96**	10s. red	10·00	10·50
348	**97**	20s. blue	10·00	10·50
MS349 127×180 mm. Nos. 345/8 (sold at 50s.)			44·00	50·00

98 Mt. Kuju and Village

99 Naka Volcano

100 Naka Crater

101 Volcanic Cones of Mt. Aso

1939. Aso National Park.

350	**98**	2s. brown	60	1·10
351	**99**	4s. green	3·50	6·50
352	**100**	10s. red	23·00	27·00
353	**101**	20s. blue	33·00	22·00
MS354 127×181 mm. Nos. 350/3 (sold at 50s.)			£140	£160

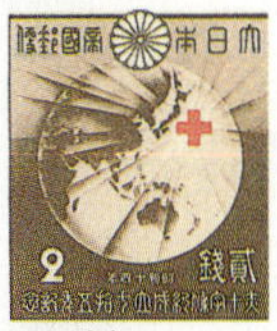

102 Globe

1939. 75th Anniv of Membership of International Red Cross Union.

355	**102**	2s. brown	1·90	2·00
356	-	4s. green	2·20	2·50
357	**102**	10s. red	12·50	15·00
358	-	20s. blue	12·50	15·00

DESIGN: 4s., 20s. Count Tsunetami Sano.

104 Golden Bird

105 Mt. Takachiho

106 Sake Jar and Ayu

107 Kashiwara Shrine

1940. 2600th Anniv of Japanese Empire.

359	**104**	2s. orange	1·10	1·60
360	**105**	4s. green	55	85
361	**106**	10s. red	5·25	7·75
362	**107**	20s. blue	1·60	2·50

108 Mt. Hokuchin

109 Mt. Asahi

110 Sounkyo Gorge, Kobako

111 Tokachi Range

1940. Daisetsu-zan National Park.

363	**108**	2s. brown	60	1·10
364	**109**	4s. green	3·25	5·50
365	**110**	10s. red	10·50	11·50
366	**111**	20s. blue	13·00	11·50
MS367 127×181 mm. Nos. 363/6 (sold at 50s.)			£300	£325

112 Mt. Shimmoe

113 Takachiho Peak

114 Kirishima Shrine

115 Lake Roku-Kwannon

1940. Kirishima National Park, Kyushu.

368	**112**	2s. brown	60	1·10
369	**113**	4s. green	1·30	2·20
370	**114**	10s. red	9·75	11·50
371	**115**	20s. blue	12·50	11·50
MS372 127×181 mm. Nos. 368/71 (sold at 50s.)			£300	£375

116 Ceremonial Shrine (after Y. Araka)

117 "Loyalty and Filial Piety"

1940. 50th Anniv of Promulgation of Imperial Re-script on Education.

373	**116**	2s. violet	1·10	1·90
374	**117**	4s. green	1·50	2·40

118 Mt. Daiton

119 Central Peak, Mt. Niitaka

120 Buddhist Temple, Mt. Kwannon

121 View of Mt. Niitaka

1941. Daiton and Niitaka-Arisan National Parks.

375	**118**	2s. brown	1·30	1·30
376	**119**	4s. green	2·75	2·75
377	**120**	10s. red	8·25	10·00
378	**121**	20s. blue	11·50	11·50
MS379 128×182 mm. Nos. 375/8 (sold at 90s. together with No. **MS**384)			£130	£150

122 Seisui Precipice, East Taiwan Coast

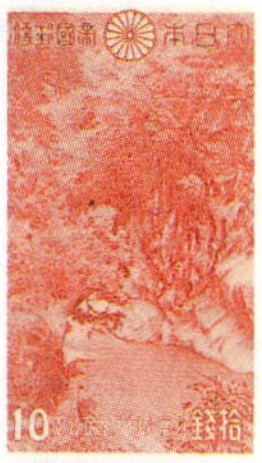

124 Taroko Gorge, Taiwan

123 Mt. Tsugitaka

125 Mt. Taroko, Source of R. Takkiri

1941. Tsugitaka and Taroko National Parks.

380	**122**	2s. brown	1·30	1·30
381	**123**	4s. green	2·75	2·75
382	**124**	10s. red	8·25	9·75
383	**125**	20s. blue	11·50	13·50
MS384 128×182 mm. Nos. 380/3 (sold at 90s. together with No. **MS**379)			£100	95·00

シンガポール 陥落

+1

(126)

1942. Surrender of Singapore. Surch as T 126.

385	**83**	2s.+1s. red	1·10	2·00
386	-	4s.+2s. green (No. 317)	1·10	2·00

127 Kenkoku Shrine

129 Orchids and Crest of Manchukuo

1942. 10th Anniv of Establishment of Manchukuo.

387	**127**	2s. brown	55	85
388	-	5s. olive	85	1·30
389	**127**	10s. red	1·90	3·75
390	**129**	20s. blue	4·00	5·75

DESIGN—VERT: 5s. Boys of Japan and Manchukuo.

130 Girl War-worker

135 "The Enemy will Surrender"

140 Garambi Lighthouse, Taiwan

141 Garambi Lighthouse, Taiwan

1942. Imperf (418/19, 421), imperf or perf (400, 420), perf (others). With or without gum (398, 420), without gum (400, 418/19, 421), with gum (others).

391	**130**	1s. brown	15	15
393	-	2s. green	80	80
395	-	4s. green	30	30
397	-	6s. blue	65	65
399	-	10s. red and pink	95	10
400	**135**	10s. grey	5·25	5·25
401	-	15s. blue	4·00	2·30
402	-	17s. violet	1·20	25
404	-	27s. red	1·20	1·10
405	-	30s. green	4·00	2·00
406	**140**	40s. purple	1·60	15
407	**141**	40s. purple	2·40	2·10
418	**135**	10s. blue	45·00	
419	-	10s. orange	60	35
420	-	20s. blue	80	30
421	-	30s. blue	2·20	70

DESIGNS: 2s. Shipbuilding; 4s. Hyuga Monument and Mt. Fuji; 6s. War-worker; 10s. (No. 399) Palms and map of Greater East Asia; 10s. (No. 419); 20s. Mt. Fuji; 15s. Airman; 17s., 27s. Yasukuni Shrine; 30s. (2) Myajima Shrine.

142 Class C59 Steam Locomotive No. 28

1942. 70th Anniv of First National Railway.

408	**142**	5s. green	3·75	6·00

143 Tanks in action at Bataan

1942. 1st Anniv of Declaration of War.

409	**143**	2s.+1s. brown	1·60	2·75
410	-	5s.+2s. blue	2·40	3·75

DESIGN: 5s. Attack on Pearl Harbor.

144 Yasukuni Shrine

1944. 75th Anniv of Yasukuni Shrine.

411	**144**	7s. green	80	1·30

145 Kwantung Shrine and Map of Kwantung Peninsula

1944. Dedication of Kwantung Shrine.

412	145	3s. brown	3·75	11·50
413	145	7s. grey	4·00	11·50

146 Sun and Cherry Blossom

149 Torii of Yasukuni Shrine

1945. Imperf or perf and with or without gum (422), imperf without gum (others).

415	146	3s. red	50	40
416	-	5s. green	40	30
422	-	50s. brown	85	30
423	149	1y. olive	1·90	95

DESIGNS: 5s. Sunrise and Kawasaki Ki-61 Hien fighter; 50s. Coal miners.

150 Pagoda of Horyu Temple, Nara

153 Kiyomizu Temple, Kyoto

154 Noh Mask

1946. Imperf or perf (30s., 50, 100y.), imperf (others). With or without gum (30s., 5, 50, 100y.), without gum (others).

426	-	15s. green	60	55
427	150	30s. violet	1·00	30
428a	-	1y. blue	1·70	30
429	-	1y.30 bistre	4·50	1·40
430	-	1y.50 grey	4·00	80
431	153	2y. red	3·25	30
432	-	5y. mauve	10·50	1·10
433b	154	50y. brown	£100	1·50
434a	-	100y. purple	£100	1·30

DESIGNS: 15s. Baron H. Maeshima; 1y. Mt. Fuji, after Hokusai; 1y.30, Snow and white-fronted geese (after Hokusai); 1y.50, Kintai Bridge, Iwakuni; 5y. Veil-tailed goldfish; 100y. Plum tree.

For 30s., 1y.20, 4y. and 10y. as Nos. 427, 429 and 434a but with Japanese characters reading in reverse order, see Nos. 441, 445/6 and 449.

156 Mediaeval Postman's Bell

157 Baron Maeshima

1946. 75th Anniv of Government Postal Service.

436	156	15s. orange	6·00	6·00
437	157	30s. green	8·00	8·00
438	-	50s. red	4·00	4·00
439	-	1y. blue	4·00	4·00
MS440 183×125 mm. Nos. 436/9 (sold at 3y.). Imperf. No gum.			£170	£190

DESIGNS—As Type **156**: 50s. First Japanese Postage Stamp; 1y. Symbols of communication.

160

161 Baron Maeshima

163 National Art

1947. As issues of 1946 but with Japanese characters in reverse order and new designs. Imperf without gum (449), perf with gum (others).

441	150	30s. violet	6·00	6·00
442	160	35s. green	95	65
443	-	45s. mauve	1·40	1·20
444	161	1y. brown	5·00	75
445	150	1y.20 green	2·50	70
446	-	4y. blue (as No. 429)	6·75	30
447	-	5y. blue	10·00	20
448	163	10y. violet	11·00	15
449	-	10y. purple (as No. 434a)	46·00	2·10

DESIGNS—VERT: 45s. Numeral; 5y. Whaling.

For similar designs, but without the chrysanthemum emblem, see Nos. 467/70.

164 Mother and Child

165 Roses and Wisteria

1947. Inauguration of New Constitution.

451	164	50s. red	65	70
452	165	1y. blue	95	90
MS453 128×180 mm. Nos. 451/2 (sold at 3y.). Imperf. No gum			10·50	12·00

1947. "Know Your Stamps" Exhibition, Tokyo, 1947. May Sheet containing No. 445 in block of fifteen.

MS454 237×76 mm (sold at 18y.)	£200	£180

166 National Products

1947. Re-opening of Private Foreign Trade.

455	166	1y.20 brown	4·00	2·10
456	166	4y. blue	8·00	2·75

1947. "Know Your Stamps" Exhibition, Kyoto, August 1947. Sheet containing No. 431 in block of five. Imperf. No gum.

MS457 115×69 mm (sold at 10y.)	33·00	38·00

167 Lily of the Valley

1947. Relief of Ex-convicts Day.

458	167	2y. green	6·50	3·25

1947. 75th Anniv of Japanese Railway Service. Imperf. No gum.

MS459 115×72 mm. 168 4y. blue (sold at 5y.)	23·00	23·00

169 Hurdling

1947. 2nd National Athletic Meeting. Kanazawa. Each mauve.

460	1y.20 Type 169	13·00	12·00
461	1y.20 Diving	13·00	12·00
462	1y.20 Throwing the discus	13·00	12·00
463	1y.20 Volleyball	13·00	12·00

1947. Philatelic Week. Sheet containing No. 428a in strip of five. No gum.

MS464 114×71 mm	5·50	6·75

170

1947. Community Chest.

465	170	1y.20+80s. red	2·00	1·80

1947. Philatelic Exhibition, Sapporo, November 1947. Sheet containing No. 422 in block of five. Imperf. No gum.

MS466 114×71 mm. (sold at 2y.50)	18·00	20·00

172 Kiyomizu Temple, Kyoto

173 National Art

1948. Designs without chrysanthemum.

467	-	1y.50 blue	4·50	65
468	172	2y. red	12·00	30
469	-	3y.80 brown	12·00	7·75
470	173	10y. violet	23·00	25

DESIGNS: 1y.50, 3y.80, Numeral types.

1948. Philatelic Exhibition, Osaka. Sheet containing No. 432 twice with two Japanese characters in centre below stamps. Imperf. No gum.

MS472 114×71 mm	18·00	22·00

1948. Philatelic Exhibition, Nagoya. Sheet as last but three Japanese characters in centre below stamps.

MS473 114×71 mm	21·00	23·00

174 Stylized Tree

1948. Encouragement of Afforestation.

474	174	1y.20 green	1·60	1·60

1948. Philatelic Exhibition, Mishima, April, 1948. Sheet No. MS473 optd at top, bottom and sides with Japanese characters and flowers in green.

MS475 114×71 mm	£110	46·00

1948. Death Centenary of Hokusai Katsushika (painter). Sheet No. MS464 optd at top and bottom with Japanese characters in purple.

MS476 114×71 mm	37·00	28·00

175 Sampans, Seto Inland Sea

1948. Sheets Commemorating Various Exhibitions. Each sheet contains two stamps as T 175 (2y. red), with coloured borders and inscriptions. Imperf. No gum.

(a) Communications Exhibition, Tokyo, April 27 to May 4 1948.

MS477 113×71 mm. Green border	21·00	11·50

(b) Newspaper and Postage Stamp Exhibition, Aomori City.

MS478 113×71 mm. Blue border	28·00	20·00

(c) Communications Exhibition, Fukushima.

MS479 113×71 mm. Turquoise	28·00	20·00

176 Boy and Girl reading

1948. Re-organization of Educational System.

480	176	1y.20 red	1·60	1·40

177 Horse Race

1948. 25th Anniv of Japanese Horse Racing Laws.

481	177	5y. brown	3·50	2·00

178 Swimmer

1948. 3rd National Athletic Meeting, Yawata.

482	178	5y. blue	4·75	2·40

179 Distillery Towers

1948. 10th Anniv of Govt. Alcohol Monopoly.

483	179	5y. brown	4·50	2·75

1948. Philatelic Exhibition, Kumamoto. Sheet containing two copies of Nos. 467 and 469. Imperf. Nogum.

MS484 114×71 mm	46·00	38·00

180 Nurse

181 Varied Tit Feeding Young

1948. Red Cross and Community Chest.

485	180	5y.+2y.50 red	12·50	12·50
486	181	5y.+2y.50 green	12·50	12·50
MS487 128×90 mm. T 181 (both 5y.+5y.). Imperf. No gum			95·00	80·00

182 Farm Girl

183 Harpooning

184 Miner

185 Girl plucking Tea

186 Girl Printer

187 Mill Girl

188 Mt. Hodaka

189 Tree Planting

190 Postman

191 Blast-Furnace

192 Constructing Class C62 Steam Locomotive

1948

488	182	2y. green and light green	3·25	10
489	183	3y. turquoise	7·75	20
490	184	5y. bistre	18·00	1·50
491	185	5y. green	60·00	8·00
492	186	6y. orange	12·00	15
493	184	8y. brown	13·00	10
494	187	15y. blue	4·75	20
495	188	16y. blue	12·50	6·50
496	189	20y. green	50·00	20
497	190	30y. blue	60·00	20
506	191	100y. red	£650	1·40
507	192	500y. blue	£550	1·60

1948. Philatelic Exhibition, Nagano. Sheet comprising No. 494. Imperf. No gum.

MS508 114×71 mm	60·00	44·00

193 Baseball

1948. 3rd National Athletic Meeting, Fukuoke.

509	193	5y. green	13·50	6·75
510	-	5y. green (bicycle race)	13·50	6·75
511	-	5y. green (sprinter)	13·50	6·75
512	-	5y. green (high jumper)	13·50	6·75

1948. Commemorating the Shikoku Travelling Philatelic Exhibition, November 1948. Sheet containing two copies of No. 490. Imperf. No gum.

MS513 115×72 mm	70·00	55·00

194 "Beauty Looking Back" (Moronobu Hishikawa)

1948. Philatelic Week.

514	**194**	5y. brown	95·00	49·00

1948. Postal Service Exhibition, Kanazawa and Takaoka. Sheet containing No. 514. Imperf. No gum.

MS515 71×115 mm.	65·00	39·00

195 Girl playing with Shuttlecock

1948. New Year's Greetings.

516	**195**	2y. red	6·50	6·00

196 Skater

197 Ski Jumper

1949. 4th National Athletic Meeting. (a) Suwa City.

517	**196**	5y. violet	3·75	2·30

(b) Sapporo, Hokkaido.

518	**197**	5y. blue	4·50	2·30

198 "Koan Maru" (ferry) in Beppu Harbour

1949

519	**198**	2y. blue and red	1·60	1·20
520	**198**	5y. blue and green	6·75	1·70

199 Exhibition Grounds

1949. Foreign Trade Fair, Yokohama. Perf or imperf.

521	**199**	5y. red	4·25	2·75

200 Seto Inland Sea

1949. Matsuyama, Okayama and Takamatsu Exhibitions.

522	**200**	10y. red (Matsuyama)	37·00	23·00
523	**200**	10y. pink (Okayama)	30·00	21·00
524	**200**	10y. claret (Takamatsu)	55·00	26·00

201 Stylized Trees

1949. Encouragement of Afforestation.

525	**201**	5y. green	12·50	2·40

202 Shishi-Iwa (Lion Rock)

203 Mt. Omine

204 Doro-Hatcho River Pool

205 Hashikui-Iwa

1949. Yoshino-Kumano National Park.

526	**202**	2y. brown	1·70	1·00
527	**203**	5y. green	5·50	1·60
528	**204**	10y. red	21·00	12·00
529	**205**	16y. blue	10·00	5·50

MS530 126×182 mm. Nos. 526/9. No gum. (sold at 40y.)	50·00	37·00

206 Boy

1949. Children's Day.

531	**206**	5y. purple and buff	7·50	2·40

1949. Children's Exhibition, Inuyama. Sheet containing No. 531 in block of ten. Imperf.

MS532 143×90 mm.	£400	£375

207 Radio Mast

1949. Electrical Communications Week. Sheet containing T 207.

MS533 71×108 mm. 20y. blue	£140	£120

208 Observatory Tower

1949. 75th Anniv of Central Meteorological Observatory, Tokyo.

534	**208**	8y. green	4·50	2·20

209 Radio Mast, Pigeon and Globe

1949. Establishment of Joint Ministries of Postal and Electrical Communications.

535	**209**	8y. blue	4·50	2·20

210 Park in Autumn

211 Park in Spring

212 Park in Summer

213 Park in Winter

1949. Fuji-Hakone National Park.

536	**210**	2y. brown	4·50	1·10
537	**211**	8y. green	4·75	1·60
538	**212**	14y. red	2·20	65
539	**213**	24y. blue	7·50	80

MS540 127×180 mm. Nos. 536/9 (sold at 55y.)	47·00	47·00

214 Woman holding Rose

1949. Establishment of Memorial City at Hiroshima.

541	**214**	8y. brown	10·50	2·75

215 Doves

1949. Establishment of International Cultural City at Nagasaki.

542	**215**	8y. green	6·25	2·75

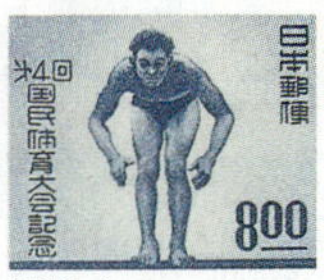

216 Swimmer

1949. 4th National Athletic Meeting, Yokohama.

543	**216**	8y. blue	5·25	2·10

217 Boy Scout

1949. 1st National Scout Jamboree, Tokyo.

544	**217**	8y. brown	8·75	2·75

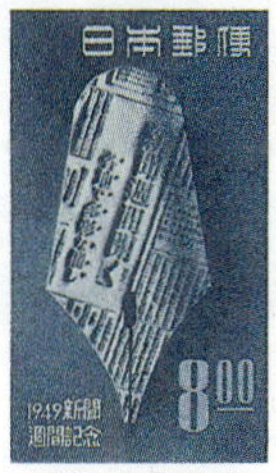

218 Symbolical of Writing and Printing

1949. Press Week.

545	**218**	8y. blue	6·75	2·75

219 Map of Japan and Letters

220 Globe and Forms of Transport

1949. 75th Anniv of U.P.U.

546	**219**	2y. green	3·50	2·10
547	**220**	8y. red	4·50	2·10
548	**219**	14y. red	12·50	9·00
549	**220**	24y. blue	17·00	10·00

MS550 115×70 mm. Nos. 546/7. Imperf. No gum	5·75	6·75

221 Throwing the Javelin

1949. 4th National Athletic Meeting, Tokyo. Each brown.

551	8y. Type **221**	8·50	3·50
552	8y. Dinghy sailing	8·50	3·50
553	8y. Relay racing	8·50	3·50
554	8y. Tennis	8·50	3·50

222 Telescope

1949. 50th Anniv of Establishment of Latitude Observatory, Mizusawa.

555	**222**	8y. green	4·75	2·10

223 "Moon and Brent Geese" (after Hiroshige)

1949. Postal Week.

556	**223**	8y. violet	£140	50·00

224 Dr. H. Noguchi A B C D E F G H I J K L M N O P Q R

1949. Various portraits as illustrated, in frame as T 224.

557	A	8y. green	11·50	1·40
558	B	8y. green	4·75	1·40
559	C	8y. green	4·75	1·40
560	D	8y. green	4·50	1·40
561	E	8y. violet	12·50	4·50
562	F	8y. purple	4·50	1·40
563	G	8y. green	11·50	2·75
564	H	8y. violet	11·50	2·75
565	I	8y. red	18·00	2·75
566	J	8y. red	30·00	3·00
567	K	8y. brown	18·00	3·00
568	L	8y. blue	14·00	3·00
569	M	10y. green	60·00	5·50
570	N	10y. purple	12·50	1·80
571	O	10y. red	4·50	1·60
572	P	10y. grey	6·00	1·60
573	Q	10y. brown	5·50	1·60
574	R	10y. blue	6·00	1·60

PORTRAITS: A, Hideyo Noguchi (bacteriologist); B, Y. Fukuzawa (educationist); C, Soseki Natsume (novelist); D, Shoyo Tsubouchi (dramatist); E, Danjuro Ichikawa (actor); F, Jo Niijima (religious leader); G, Hogai Kano (painter); H, Kanzo Uchimura (religious leader); I, Mme. Higuchi (author); J, Ogai Mori (doctor); K, S. Masaoka (poet); L, S. Hishida (painter); M, A. Nishi (scholar); N, K. Ume (lawyer); O, H. Kimura (astrophysicist); P, I. Nitobe (statesman); Q, T. Torada (physicist); R, Tenshin Okakura (writer).

225 Green Pheasant and Pampas Grass

1950. Air.

575	225	16y. grey	41·00	27·00
576	225	34y. purple	70·00	24·00
577	225	59y. red	95·00	17·00
578	225	103y. orange	65·00	21·00
579	225	144y. olive	70·00	30·00

226 Tiger (after Maruyama Okyo)

1950. New Year's Greetings.

580	226	2y. red	9·75	2·75

227 Microphones of 1925 and 1950

1950. 25th Anniv of Japanese Broadcasting System.

582	227	8y. blue	4·50	2·10

228 Dove

1950. 1st Anniv of Joint Ministries of Postal and Electrical Communications.

583	228	8y. green	4·25	1·60

229 Lake Akan and Mt. O-Akani

230 Lake Kutcharo

231 Mt. Akan-Fuji

232 Lake Mashu

1950. Akan National Park.

584	229	2y. brown	1·60	1·20
585	230	8y. green	3·25	1·80
586	231	14y. red	15·00	6·75
587	232	24y. blue	16·00	7·75
MS588 127×181 mm. Nos. 584/7 (sold at 55y.)			50·00	49·00

233 Gymnast on Rings

1950. 5th National Athletic Meeting.

589	233	8y. red	32·00	17·00
590	-	8y. red (Pole vaulting)	32·00	17·00
591	-	8y. red (Football)	32·00	17·00
592	-	8y. red (Horse jumping)	32·00	17·00

234 Tahoto Pagoda, Ishiyama Temple

235 Baron Maeshima

236 Long-tailed Cock

237 Kannon Bosatsu (detail of wall painting, Horyu Temple)

238 Himeji Castle

239 Phoenix Temple, Uji

240 Buddhisattva Statue, Chugu Temple

1950. With noughts for sen after value.

593	234	80s. red	2·30	2·10
594	235	1y. brown	3·00	45
595	236	5y. green and brown	6·75	20
596	237	10y. lake and mauve	13·50	15
597	238	14y. brown	55·00	44·00
598	239	24y. blue	44·00	23·00
599	240	50y. brown	£160	1·00

For designs without noughts see Nos. 653 etc and for designs additionally inscr "NIPPON" see Nos. 1041/59.

1950. Miniature sheets, each 76×50 mm and each containing one of stamps from the above issue.

MS600	80s. carmine	10·50	14·00
MS601	14y.brown	75·00	85·00
MS602	24y. blue	47·00	60·00
MS603	50y. brown	£300	£350

241 Girl and Rabbit

1951. New Year's Greetings.

604	241	2y. red	8·00	1·10

For 50y. in this design dated "1999" see No. 2565.

242 Skiing, Mt. Zao

1951. Tourist Issue. Mt. Zao.

606	242	8y. olive	18·00	3·75
607	-	24y. blue	20·00	8·75

DESIGN—HORIZ: 24y. Two skiers on Mt. Zao.

243 Nihon-Daira

244 Mt. Fuji from Nihon Daira

1951. Tourist Issue. Nihon-Daira.

608	243	8y. green	18·00	3·75
609	244	24y. blue	£130	35·00

1951. 80th Anniv of Japanese Postal Service. Sheet containing No. 594 in block of four.

MS610	86×64 mm	25·00	22·00

245 Child's Head

1951. Children's Charter.

611	245	8y. brown	30·00	4·50

246 Hot Springs, Owaki Valley

247 Lake Ashi

1951. Tourist Issue. Hakone Spa.

612	246	8y. brown	11·00	3·00
613	247	24y. blue	9·25	4·50

248 Senju Waterfall

249 Ninai Waterfall

1951. Tourist Issue. Akame Waterfalls.

614	248	8y. green	13·00	3·00
615	249	24y. blue	12·00	4·50

250 Waka-no-Ura

251 Tomo-ga-Shima

1951. Tourist Issue. Coastal Resorts.

616	250	8y. brown	9·25	3·00
617	251	24y. blue	8·75	4·50

252 Oirase River

253 Lake Towada

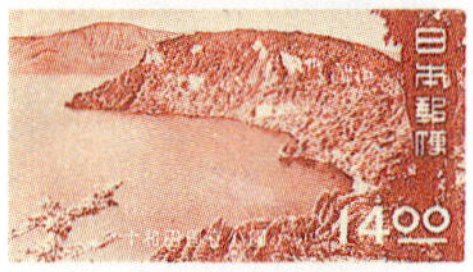

254 View from Kankodai

255 Hakkoda Mountains

1951. Towada National Park.

618	252	2y. brown	3·00	1·10
619	253	8y. green	11·00	1·60
620	254	14y. red	12·50	6·75
621	255	24y. blue	14·00	7·75
MS622 128×182 mm. Nos. 618/21 (sold at 55y.)			47·00	47·00

256 Uji River

257 Uji Bridge

1951. Tourist Issue. Uji River.

623	256	8y. brown	9·75	3·00
624	257	24y. blue	9·00	4·50

258 Douglas DC-4 Airliner over Horyuji Pagoda

259 Douglas DC-4 Airliner and Mt. Tate

1951. Air. With noughts for sen after numerals of value.

625	258	15y. violet	5·75	4·50
626	258	20y. blue	38·00	2·75
627	258	25y. green	37·00	50
628	258	30y. red	29·00	45
629	258	40y. black	9·75	50

630	**259**	55y. blue	£250	46·00
631	**259**	75y. red	£180	25·00
632	**259**	80y. mauve	37·00	5·75
633	**259**	85y. black	60·00	21·00
634	**259**	125y. brown	20·00	5·75
635	**259**	160y. green	46·00	6·25

For similar designs, but without noughts after numerals of value, see Nos. 671/81.

260 Chrysanthemum

261 Japanese Flag

1951. Peace Treaty.

636	**260**	2y. brown	2·75	1·40
637	**261**	8y. red and blue	8·00	3·75
638	**260**	24y. green	25·00	8·75

262 Oura Catholic Church, Nagasaki

263 Gateway, Sofuku Temple

1951. Tourist Issue. Nagasaki.

639	**262**	8y. red	13·00	3·00
640	**263**	24y. blue	9·75	4·50

264 Lake Marunuma

265 Lake Sugenuma

1951. Tourist Issue.

641	**264**	8y. purple	17·00	2·75
642	**265**	24y. green	8·25	4·50

266 Shosenkyo Valley

267 Nagatoro Bridge

1951. Tourist Issue. Shosenkyo.

643	**266**	8y. red	12·50	3·00
644	**267**	24y. blue	13·50	4·50

268 Putting the Shot

1951. 6th National Athletic Meeting.

645	**268**	2y. brown	4·50	2·50
646	-	2y. blue (Hockey)	4·50	2·50

269 Noh Mask

1952. New Year's Greetings.

647	**269**	5y. red	14·00	1·10

270 Ship's Davit and Southern Cross

1952. 75th Anniv of U.P.U. Membership.

649	**270**	5y. violet	7·75	1·80
650	-	10y. green	20·00	4·50

DESIGN: 10y. Earth and Ursa Major. Inscr "1952".

271 Red Cross and Lily

1952. 75th Anniv of Japanese Red Cross.

651	**271**	5y. red	6·00	2·00
652	-	10y. green and red (Nurse)	14·00	4·00

272 Akita Dog

273 Small Cuckoo

274 Tahoto Pagoda, Ishiyama Temple

275 Mandarins

276 Japanese Serow

277 Chuson Temple

278 Veil-tailed Goldfish

279 Yomei Gate, Tosho Shrine, Nikko

280 "Marimo" (water plant) and Sockeye Salmon

281 Great Purple

282 Fishing with Japanese Cormorants

283 "Bridge and Irises" (from lacquered box)

1952. Without noughts after numerals of value.

653	**235**	1y. brown	55	10
654	**272**	2y. black	10	10
655	**273**	3y. turquoise	15	10
656	**274**	4y. purple and red	2·50	10
657	**275**	5y. brown and blue	15	10
658	**276**	8y. brown and light brown	10	10
659	**237**	10y. red and mauve	5·50	10
660	**238**	14y. green	7·50	2·40
661	**277**	20y. green	1·50	10
662	**239**	24y. violet	18·00	4·50
663	**239**	30y. purple	43·00	80
664	**278**	35y. orange	12·00	10
665	**279**	45y. blue	5·25	10
666	**240**	50y. brown	6·50	10
667	**280**	55y. green, black and blue	18·00	80
668	**281**	75y. multicoloured	9·75	80
669	**282**	100y. red	35·00	10
670	**283**	500y. purple	85·00	15

For 1, 2, 3, 50, 55 and 75y. in same designs, but inscr "NIPPON", see Nos. 1041, 1582a, 1226, 1058/60, 1232 and 1064.

1952. Air. As Nos. 625/35 but without noughts after numerals of value.

671	**258**	15y. violet	2·10	95
672	**258**	20y. blue	60·00	1·30
673	**258**	25y. green	1·20	10
674	**258**	30y. red	4·50	10
675	**258**	40y. black	5·50	25
676	**259**	55y. blue	90·00	6·75
677	**259**	75y. red	£160	16·00
678	**259**	80y. mauve	£120	4·50
679	**259**	85y. black	5·00	2·75
680	**259**	125y. brown	10·00	3·75
681	**259**	160y. green	43·00	4·50

284 Mt. Yari

285 Kurobe Valley

286 Mt. Shirouma

287 Mt. Norikura

1952. Chubu-Sangaku National Park.

682	**284**	5y. brown	7·00	1·20
683	**285**	10y. green	33·00	4·00
684	**286**	14y. red	8·50	7·75
685	**287**	24y. blue	14·00	7·75
MS686		129×182 mm. Nos. 682/5 but imperf. No gum (sold at 60y.)	£130	£120

288 Central Hall

1952. 75th Anniv of Tokyo University.

687	**288**	10y. green	21·00	3·50

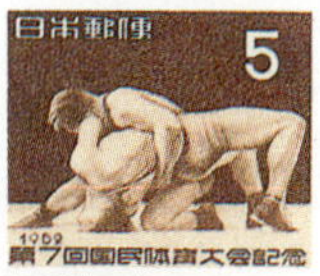

289 Wrestlers

1952. 7th National Athletic Meeting.

688	-	5y. blue (Mountaineer)	8·00	2·40
689	**289**	5y. brown	8·00	2·40

290 Mt. Azuma-Kofuji

291 Mt. Asahi

292 Mt. Bandai

293 Mt. Gessan

1952. Bandai-Asahi National Park.

690	**290**	5y. brown	5·50	1·00
691	**291**	10y. olive	17·00	2·75
692	**292**	14y. red	6·75	4·50
693	**293**	24y. blue	14·00	7·50
MS694		128×181 mm. Nos. 690/3 but imperf. No gum (sold at 60y.)	£150	95·00

294 "Kirin" and Chrysanthemums

295 Flag of Crown Prince

1952. Investiture of Crown Prince Akihito.

695	**294**	5y. orange and brown	3·00	1·20
696	**294**	10y. orange and green	3·00	2·50
697	**295**	24y. blue	18·00	8·75
MS698		130×130 mm. Nos. 695/7. Imperf. No gum (sold at 50y.)	£120	£350

296 Dancing Doll

1953. New Year's Greetings.

699	**296**	5y. red	9·50	1·10

297 First Japanese Electric Lamp

1953. 75th Anniv of Electric Lamp in Japan.

701	**297**	10y. brown	9·00	3·00

299 Kintai Bridge

1953. Tourist Issue. Kintai Bridge.

702	-	10y. brown	9·25	3·00
703	**299**	24y. blue	8·50	4·50

DESIGN—VERT: 10y. Kintai Bridge (after Hiroshige).

300 Lake Shikotsu (1/2-size illustration)

301 Mt. Yotei (1/2-size illustration)

1953. Shikotsu-Toya National Park.

704	**300**	5y. blue	2·75	80
705	**301**	10y. green	8·75	1·60
MS706		148×105 mm. Nos. 704/5 but imperf. No gum (sold at 20y.)	50·00	47·00

302 Great Buddha, Kamakura

1953. Air.

707	**302**	70y. brown	4·00	15
708	**302**	80y. blue	5·75	15
709	**302**	115y. olive	2·75	20
710	**302**	145y. turquoise	18·00	2·10

303 Wedded Rocks, Futami Bay (1/2-size illustration)

304 Nakiri Coast (1/2-size illustration)

1953. Ise Shima National Park.

711	**303**	5y. red	2·50	80
712	**304**	10y. blue	5·50	1·60

MS713 148×105 mm. Nos. 711/2 but imperf. No gum (sold at 2y.) 39·00 21·00

305 "Ho-o" (Happy Phoenix)

1953. Return of Crown Prince from Overseas Tour.

714	**305**	5y. lake	4·25	1·60
715	-	10y. blue	7·50	2·75

DESIGN: 10y. Manchurian crane in flight.

306 Judo

1953. 8th National Athletic Meeting, Matsuyama.

716	**306**	5y. green	7·25	2·10
717	-	5y. black	7·25	2·10

DESIGN: 5y. Rugby footballers.

307 Tokyo Observatory

1953. 75th Anniv of Tokyo Observatory.

718	**307**	10y. blue	13·00	3·00

308 Mt. Unzen (1/2-size illustration)

309 Mt. Unzen (1/2-size illustration)

1953. Unzen National Park.

719	**308**	5y. red	2·75	80
720	**309**	10y. blue	6·00	1·60

MS721 148×105 mm. Nos. 719/20 but imperf. No gum (sold at 20y.) 39·00 21·00

310 Wooden Horse

1953. New Year's Greetings.

722	**310**	5y. red	7·25	80

311 Ice Skaters

1954. World Speed Skating Championships, Sapporo.

724	**311**	10y. blue	6·50	2·75

312

1954. International Trade Fair, Osaka.

725	**312**	10y. red	5·50	2·10

313 Wrestlers

1954. Int Free-style Wrestling Championship.

726	**313**	10y. green	4·50	2·00

314 Mt. Asama (1/2-size illustration)

315 Mt. Tanigawa (1/2-size illustration)

1954. Jo-Shin-Etsu Kogen National Park.

727	**314**	5y. sepia	3·00	80
728	**315**	10y. turquoise	5·50	1·60

MS729 148×108 mm. Nos. 727/8 but imperf. No gum (sold at 20y.) 39·00 21·00

316 Archery

1954. 9th National Athletic Meeting, Sapporo.

730	**316**	5y. green	6·25	2·00
731	-	5y. brown (Table tennis)	6·25	2·00

317 Telegraph Table

1954. 75th Anniv of Japan's Membership of I.T.U.

732	**317**	5y. purple	2·75	1·30
733	-	10y. blue	7·50	2·30

DESIGN—HORIZ: 10y. I.T.U. Monument.

1954. Philatelic Week. Sheet 150×50 mm containing ten of No. 659 (arranged as one row of 6 and one row of 4 (with printed label at each end).

MS734 10y. lake and mauve £200 £190

318 Tumbler

1954. New Year's Greetings.

735	**318**	5y. red and black	7·25	80

319 Tama Gorge

320 Chichibu Mountains

1955. Chichibu-Tama National Park.

737	**319**	5y. blue	2·00	80
738	**320**	10y. lake	2·50	1·10

MS739 148×105 mm. Nos. 737/8 but imperf. No gum (sold at 20y.) 39·00 21·00

321 Paper Carp

1955. 15th International Chamber of Commerce Congress, Tokyo.

740	**321**	10y. multicoloured	7·25	2·40

322 Bentenzaki Peninsula

323 Jodoga Beach

1955. Rikuchu-Kaigan National Park.

741	**322**	5y. green	1·70	65
742	**323**	10y. red	2·50	1·10

MS743 147×104 mm. Nos. 741/2 but imperf. No gum (sold a20y.) 37·00 21·00

324 Gymnastics

1955. 10th National Athletic Meeting, Kanagawa.

744	**324**	5y. red	4·00	1·60
745	-	5y. blue (Running)	4·00	1·60

325 "Girl Playing Glass Flute" (Utamaro)

1955. Philatelic Week.

746	**325**	10y. multicoloured	16·00	12·00

326 "Kokeshi" Dolls

1955. New Year's Greetings.

747	**326**	5y. green and red	2·75	40

327 Table Tennis

1956. World Table Tennis Championships.

749	**327**	10y. brown	2·00	1·10

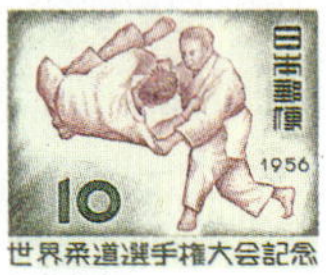
328 Judo

1956. World Judo Championships.

750	**328**	10y. purple and green	2·20	1·10

329 Children and Paper Carps

1956. International Children's Day.

751	**329**	5y. black and blue	1·70	80

330 Osezaki Lighthouse (1/2-size illustration)

331 Kujuku Island (1/2-size illustration)

1956. 25th Anniv of National Park Law. Saikai National Park.

752	**330**	5y. brown	1·30	65
753	**331**	10y. indigo and blue	1·70	1·10

MS754 147×104 mm. Nos. 752/3 but imperf. No gum (sold at 20y.) 31·00 20·00

332 Imperial Palace, and Modern Buildings

1956. 5th Centenary of Tokyo.

755	**332**	10y. purple	2·75	1·20

333 Sakuma Dam

1956. Completion of Sakuma Dam.

756	**333**	10y. blue	2·75	1·20

334 Basketball

1956. 11th National Athletic Meeting, Kobe.

757	**334**	5y. green	1·60	80
758	-	5y. purple (Long jumping)	1·60	80

335 Ebizo Ichikawa (actor) (after Sharaku)

1956. Philatelic Week.

759	**335**	10y. black, orange and grey	13·50	9·75

336 Mt. Manaslu and Mountaineer

1956. Conquest of Mt. Manaslu.

760	**336**	10y. multicoloured	4·50	2·40

337 View of Yui (after Hiroshige) and Type EF 58 Electric Locomotive No. 4

1956. Electrification of Tokaido Railway Line.

761	**337**	10y. black, green & brown	7·25	2·40

338 Cogwheel, Valve and Freighter "Nissyo Maru"

1956. Floating Machinery Fair.

762	**338**	10y. blue	1·10	1·00

339 Whale (float)

1956. New Year's Greetings.

763	**339**	5y. multicoloured	1·70	30

340 U.N.O. Emblem

1957. 1st Anniv of Japan's Admission into U.N.

765	**340**	10y. red and blue	1·00	80

341 I.G.Y. Emblem, Emperor Penguin and Antarctic Research Vessel "Soya"

1957. International Geophysical Year.

766	**341**	10y. blue, yellow and black	1·00	65

342 Atomic Reactor

1957. Completion of Atomic Reactor at Tokai-Mura.

767	**342**	10y. violet	60	30

343 Gymnast

1957. 12th National Athletic Meeting, Shizuoka.

768	**343**	5y. blue	55	35
769	-	5y. red (Boxing)	55	35

344 "Girl Bouncing Ball" (after Harunobu)

1957. Philatelic Week.

770	**344**	10y. multicoloured	2·10	2·40

345 Ogochi Dam

1957. Completion of Ogochi Dam.

771	**345**	10y. blue	50	40

346 Japan's First Blast Furnace and Modern Plant

1957. Centenary of Japanese Iron Industry.

772	**346**	10y. purple and orange	35	30

347 "Inu-hariko" (toy dog)

1957. New Year's Greetings.

773	**347**	5y. multicoloured	35	30

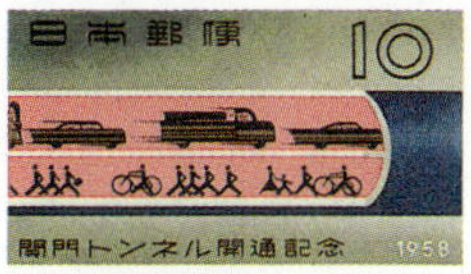
348 Kan-Mon Tunnel

1958. Opening of Kan-Mon Undersea Tunnel.

775	**348**	10y. multicoloured	50	25

349 "Lady returning from Bath-house" (after Kiyonaga)

1958. Philatelic Week.

776	**349**	10y. multicoloured	80	25

350 Statue of Ii Naosuke, "Powhattan" (1858 paddle-steamer) and Modern Liner

1958. Centenary of Opening of Ports to Traders.

777	**350**	10y. red and blue	40	25

351 National Stadium, Tokyo

1958. 3rd Asian Games, Tokyo. Inscr as in T 351. Multicoloured.

778	5y. Type **351**	25	20
779	10y. Flame and Games emblem	50	40
780	14y. Runner breasting tape	40	30
781	24y. High-diver	50	40

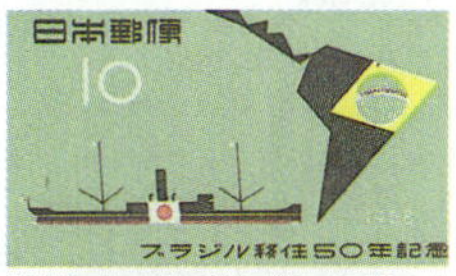
352 Emigration Ship "Kasato Maru" and South American Map

1958. 50th Anniv of Japanese Emigration to Brazil.

782	**352**	10y. multicoloured	40	20

353 Dado-Okesa Dancer on Sado Island

354 Mt. Yahiko and Echigo Plain

1958. Sado-Yahiko Quasi-National Park.

783	**353**	10y. multicoloured	1·10	40
784	**354**	10y. multicoloured	1·30	60

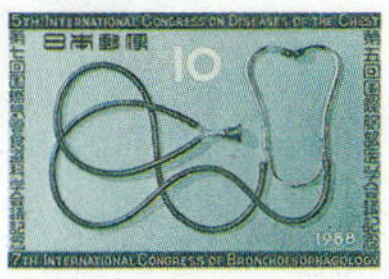
355 Stethoscope

1958. International Congresses of Chest Diseases and Bronchoesophagology, Tokyo.

785	**355**	10y. turquoise	40	25

356 "Old Kyoto Bridge" (after Hiroshige)

1958. International Correspondence Week.

786	**356**	24y. multicoloured	3·50	90

The design is taken from the series of 53 woodcuts, showing stages of the Tokaido Road. Others from this series are shown on Nos. 810, 836, 878 and 908.

357 Badminton Player

1958. 13th National Athletic Meeting, Toyama.

787	**357**	5y. purple	45	25
788	-	5y. blue (Weightlifting)	45	25

358 Yukichi Fukuzawa (founder) and Keio University

1958. Centenary of Keio University.

789	**358**	10y. red	50	25

359 Children Skipping across Globe

1958. International Child and Social Welfare Conferences, Tokyo.

790	**359**	10y. green	50	25

360 "Flame of Freedom"

1958. 10th Anniv of Declaration of Human Rights.

791	**360**	10y. multicoloured	45	25

361 Ebisu with Madai Seabream (toy)

1958. New Year's Greetings.

792	**361**	5y. multicoloured	65	20

362 Map of Kojima Bay and Tractor

1959. Completion of Kojima Bay Reclamation Project.

794	**362**	10y. purple and ochre	40	25

363 Karst Plateau

364 Akiyoshi Cavern

1959. Akiyoshidai Quasi-National Parks.

795	**363**	10y. multicoloured	2·00	25
796	**364**	10y. multicoloured	3·50	25

365 Map of Asia

1959. Asian Congress Commemorating 2500th Anniv of Buddha's Death.

797	**365**	10y. red	50	25

366 Crown Prince Akihito and Princess Michiko

1959. Imperial Wedding.

798	-	5y. violet and purple	35	15
799	**366**	10y. purple and brown	90	25
800	-	20y. sepia and brown	1·20	25
801	**366**	30y. deep green and green	3·75	35

MS802 127×88 mm. Nos. 798/9 but imperf. No gum (sold at 20y.) 7·00 5·25

DESIGN: 5, 20y. Ceremonial fan.

367 "Ladies reading poems" (from "Ukiyo Genji" after Eishi)

1959. Philatelic Week.

803	**367**	10y. multicoloured	4·75	2·00

368 Graduated Glass and Scales

1959. Ratification of Adoption of Metric System in Japan.

804	**368**	10y. sepia and blue	40	15

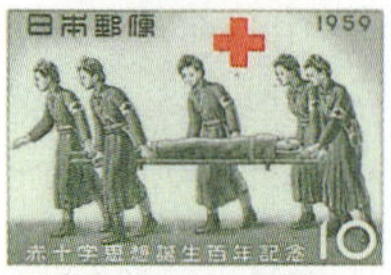

369 Stretcher-party with Casualty

1959. Red Cross.

805	**369**	10y. red and green	50	15

370 Mt. Fuji from Lake Motosu

1959. National Parks Day.

806	**370**	10y. green, purple and blue	80	15

371 Ao Caves, Yabakei

372 Japanese Cormorant with Hita and Mt. Hiko background

1959. Yaba-Hita-Hikosan Quasi-National Parks.

807	**371**	10y. multicoloured	1·40	40
808	**372**	10y. multicoloured	1·40	40

373 Nagoya and Golden Dolphin

1959. 350th Anniv of Nagoya.

809	**373**	10y. gold, black and blue	1·10	15

374 "Kuwana" (after Hiroshige)

1959. International Correspondence Week.

810	**374**	30y. multicoloured	12·00	1·60

375 Flying Manchurian Crane and I.A.T.A. Emblem

1959. 15th International Air Transport Association Meeting, Tokyo.

811	**375**	10y. blue	80	40

376 Throwing the Hammer

1959. 14th National Athletic Meeting, Tokyo.

812	**376**	5y. blue	1·00	30
813	-	5y. brown (Fencer)	1·00	30

377 Open Book showing portrait of Shoin Yoshida

1959. Death Centenary of Shoin Yoshida (educator) and National Parents/Teachers Assn Convention.

814	**377**	10y. brown	70	30

378 Halves of Globe

1959. 15th Session of Contracting Parties to G.A.T.T.

815	**378**	10y. brown	70	30

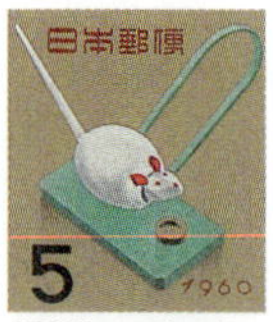

379 Rice-eating Rat of Kanazawa (toy)

1959. New Year's Greetings.

816	**379**	5y. multicoloured	1·80	25

380 Yukio Ozaki and Clock Tower Memorial Hall

1960. Completion of Ozaki Memorial Hall, Tokyo.

818	**380**	10y. purple and brown	70	30

381 Deer

1960. 1250th Anniv of Transfer of Capital to Nara.

819	**381**	10y. olive	90	30

382 Godaido Temple, Matsushima

383 Bridge of Heaven (sandbank), Miyazu Bay

384 Miyajima from the Sea

1960. "Scenic Trio".

820	**382**	10y. turquoise and brown	2·20	60
821	**383**	10y. green and blue	3·00	60
822	**384**	10y. green and violet	3·00	60

385 Takeshima-Gamagori Causeway

1960. Mikawa Bay Quasi-National Park.

823	**385**	10y. multicoloured	1·25	20

386 "Ise" (from Satake picture scroll "Thirty-six Immortal Poets")

1960. Philatelic Week.

824	**386**	10y. black, red and brown	4·50	2·75

387 "Kanrin Maru" (barque) crossing the Pacific

1960. Centenary of Japanese–American Treaty.

825	**387**	10y. sepia and green	80	30
826	-	30y. black and red	2·20	45

DESIGN: 30y. Pres. Buchanan receiving Japanese mission.

388 Japanese Crested Ibis

1960. 12th Int Bird Preservation Congress, Tokyo.

827	**388**	10y. red, pink and grey	90	45

389 Radio Waves around Globe

1960. 25th Anniv of Japanese Overseas Broadcasting Service, "Radio Japan".

828	**389**	10y. red	70	30

390 Abashiri Flower Gardens

1960. Abashiri Quasi-National Park.

829	**390**	10y. multicoloured	1·70	45

391 Cape Ashizuri

1960. Ashizuri Quasi-National Park.

830	**391**	10y. multicoloured	1·70	45

392 Rainbow linking Hawaii and Japan

1960. 75th Anniv of Japanese Emigration to Hawaii.

831	**392**	10y. multicoloured	1·10	30

393 Douglas DC-8 and Farman H.F.III Biplane

1960. 50th Anniv of Japanese Aviation.

832	**393**	10y. brown and grey	80	30

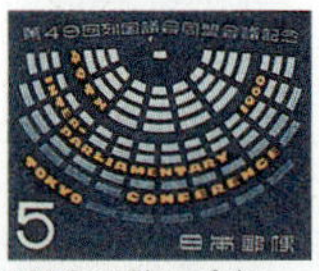

394 Seat Plan of the Diet

1960. 49th Inter-Parliamentary Union Conference. Inscr "49TH INTER-PARLIAMENTARY CONFERENCE TOKYO 1960".

833	**394**	5y. orange and blue	70	25
834	-	10y. brown and blue	1·00	30

DESIGN: 10y. "Clear Day with Southern Breeze" (from "36 Views of Mt. Fuji" by Hokusai Katsushika).

1960. Visit of Crown Prince Akihito and Princess Michiko to the United States. Sheet containing Nos. 825/6.
MS835 120×76 mm 39·00 31·00

395 "Kambara" (after Hiroshige)

1960. International Correspondence Week.
836 **395** 30y. multicoloured 25·00 5·50

396 Okayama Observatory

1960. Opening of Okayama Astrophysical Observatory.
837 **396** 10y. violet 1·10 25

397 "Kendo" (Japanese fencing)

1960. 15th National Athletic Meeting, Kumamoto.
838 **397** 5y. blue 80 30
839 - 5y. purple (Vaulting) 80 30

398 Lieut. Shirase and Map of Antarctica

1960. 50th Anniv of 1st Japanese Antarctic Expedition.
840 **398** 10y. black and brown 1·10 25

399 Red Beko and Golden Bekokko (Japanese toys)

1960. New Year's Greetings.
841 **399** 5y. multicoloured 1·10 25

400 Diet Building and Stars

1960. 70th Anniv of Diet.
843 **400** 5y. violet and black 70 25
844 - 10y. red 1·00 25
DESIGN: 10y. Opening ceremony of first session of Diet.

401 Narcissus

1961. Japanese Flowers. Flowers in natural colours. Background colours given.
845 10y. purple (T **401**) 6·00 1·10
846 10y. brown (Plum blossom) 2·50 1·10
847 10y. bistre (Camellia) 1·80 1·10
848 10y. grey (Cherry blossom) 1·80 1·10
849 10y. sepia (Peony) 1·40 1·00
850 10y. grey (Iris) 75 85
851 10y. turquoise (Lily) 60 50
852 10y. blue (Morning glory) 60 50
853 10y. sage (Bellflower) 60 50
854 10y. orange (Gentian) 60 50
855 10y. blue (Chrysanthemum) 60 50
856 10y. slate (Camellia) 60 50

402 Pearl-divers at Shirahama

1961. Minami-Boso Quasi-National Park.
857 **402** 10y. multicoloured 1·00 30

403 Hirase's Slit Shell

404 Nanten

405 Cherry Blossoms

406 Engaku Temple

407 Yomei Gate, Tosho Shrine, Nikko

408 Noh Mask

409 Copper Pheasant

410 "The Wind God"

411 Manchurian Cranes

412 "Kalavinka" (legendary bird)

1961
858 **403** 4y. red and brown 15 10
859 **404** 6y. red and green 15 10
860 **405** 10y. mauve and purple 35 10
861 **406** 30y. violet 6·25 10
862 **407** 40y. red 7·50 10
863 **408** 70y. black and ochre 3·00 10
864 **409** 80y. brown and red 1·50 10
865 **410** 90y. green 42·00 30
866 **411** 100y. grey, black and pink 15·00 10
867 **412** 120y. violet 14·50 75
For 70, 80, 90, 100, and 120y. in different colours and additionally inscr "NIPPON" see Nos. 1065/6, 1068, 1234/6 and 1238.

413 Baron Maeshima

1961. 90th Anniv of Japanese Postal Service.
868 **413** 10y. green and black 2·00 25

414 "Dancing Girl" (from 17th-century screen)

1961. Philatelic Week.
869 **414** 10y. multicoloured 2·00 1·60

415 Lake Biwa

1961. Lake Biwa Quasi-National Park.
870 **415** 10y. multicoloured 1·10 30

416 Rotary Emblem and "Peoples of the World"

1961. 52nd Rotary International Convention.
871 **416** 10y. orange and black 50 25

417 "Benefits Irrigation"

1961. Inauguration of Aichi Irrigation Scheme.
872 **417** 10y. blue and purple 50 30

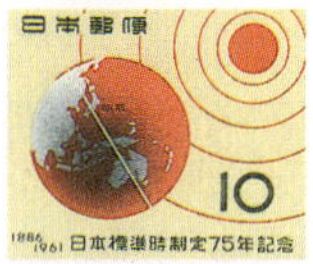
418 Globe showing Longitude 135° E. and Sun

1961. 75th Anniv of Japanese Standard Time.
873 **418** 10y. red, black and ochre 70 25

419 Parasol Dancer, Tottori Beach

1961. San'in Kaigan Quasi-National Park.
874 **419** 10y. multicoloured 1·40 30

420 Komagatake Volcano

1961. Onuma Quasi-National Park.
875 **420** 10y. multicoloured 1·40 30

421 Gymnast

1961. 16th National Athletic Meeting, Akita.
876 **421** 5y. green 80 30
877 - 5y. blue (Rowing) 80 30

422 "Hakone" (after Hiroshige)

1961. International Correspondence Week.
878 **422** 30y. multicoloured 9·75 6·25

423 Throwing the Javelin

1961. Olympic Games, Tokyo, 1964 (1st issue).
879 **423** 5y.+5y. brown 1·30 1·60
880 - 5y.+5y. green 1·30 1·60
881 - 5y.+5y. red 1·30 1·60
DESIGNS: No. 880, Wrestling; 881, Diver (Woman).
See also Nos. 899/901, 909/11, 935/7, 949/52, 969/72 and 981/5.

424 Library and Book

1961. Opening of National Diet Library.
882 **424** 10y. blue and gold 50 30

425 Tiger (Izumo toy)

1961. New Year's Greetings.
883 **425** 5y. multicoloured 90 10

426 Mt. Fuji from Lake Aishi

427 Minokake-Iwa, Irozaki

428 Mt. Fuji from Mitsutoge

429 Mt. Fuji from Osezaki

1962. Fuji-Hakone-Izu National Park.
885 **426** 5y. green 1·00 30
886 **427** 5y. blue 90 30
887 **428** 10y. brown 1·40 45
888 **429** 10y. black 1·80 55

430 Omishima Island

1962. Kitanagato-Kaigan Quasi-National Park.
889 **430** 10y. multicoloured 80 30

431 Doll Festival

1962. National Festivals. Multicoloured.

890		10y. Type **431**	1·70	60
891		10y. Children and decorated tree ("Star Festival")	60	30
892		10y. Three children ("Seven-Five-Three Festival")	60	30
893		10y. Children throwing beans ("Spring Festival")	50	30

432 "Dancer" (after N. Kano)

1962. Philatelic Week.

894	**432**	10y. multicoloured	2·00	1·60

433 Sakurajima Volcano

1962. Kinkowan Quasi-National Park.

895	**433**	10y. multicoloured	60	30

434 Mount Kongo

1962. Kongo-Ikoma Quasi-National Park.

896	**434**	10y. multicoloured	60	30

435 Suigo View

1962. Suigo Quasi-National Park.

897	**435**	10y. multicoloured	80	30

436 "Hakucho" (swan) Express Train emerging from Tunnel

1962. Opening of Hokuriku Railway Tunnel.

898	**436**	10y. brown	3·00	40

1962. Olympic Games, Tokyo, 1964 (2nd issue). Sports. As T 423.

899		5y.+5y. red	80	1·10
900		5y.+5y. green	80	1·10
901		5y.+5y. purple	80	1·10

SPORTS: No. 899 Judo; 900, Water-polo; 901, Gymnastics (female).

437 Scout's Hat on Map

1962. Asian Scout Jamboree, Mt. Fuji.

902	**437**	10y. black, bistre and red	40	30

438 Mt. Shibutsu and Ozegahara Swamp

439 Smoking Summit of Mt. Chausu, Nasu

440 Lake Chuzenji and Mt. Nantai

441 Senryu-kyo Narrows, Shiobara

1962. Nikko National Park.

903	**438**	5y. turquoise	40	25
904	**439**	5y. lake	40	25
905	**440**	10y. purple	60	25
906	**441**	10y. olive	60	25

442 Wakato Suspension Bridge

1962. Opening of Wakato Suspension Bridge.

907	**442**	10y. red	1·10	45

443 "Nihonbashi" (after Hiroshige)

1962. International Correspondence Week.

908	**443**	40y. multicoloured	8·25	5·50

1962. Olympic Games, Tokyo, 1964 (3rd issue). Sports. As T 423.

909		5y.+5y. green	70	55
910		5y.+5y. lilac	70	55
911		5y.+5y. red	70	55

SPORTS: No. 909, Basketball; 910, Rowing; 911, Fencing.

444 Rifle-shooting

1962. 17th National Athletic Meeting, Okayama.

912	**444**	5y. purple	40	30
913	-	5y. blue	40	30

DESIGN: No. 913, Softball.

445 Hare-bell (Nogomi toy)

1962. New Year's Greetings.

914	**445**	5y. multicoloured	60	10

For 50y. in this design dated "1999" see No. 2566.

446 Mt. Ishizuchi and Kamega Forest

1963. Ishizuchi Quasi-National Park.

916	**446**	10y. multicoloured	50	30

447 "Five Towns"

1963. Amalgamation of Five Towns as Kita-Kyushu.

917	**447**	10y. brown	40	25

448 Frosted Foliage, Fugen Peak

449 Amakusa Islands and Mt. Unzen

1963. Unzen-Amakusa National Park.

918	**448**	5y. blue	40	25
919	**449**	10y. red	40	25

450 Midorigaike (Green Pond)

451 Hakusan Mountains

1963. Hakusan National Park.

920	**450**	5y. brown	30	25
921	**451**	10y. green	30	25

452 Great Rocks, Keya

1963. Genkai Quasi-National Park.

922	**452**	10y. multicoloured	50	10

453 Globe and Emblem

1963. Freedom from Hunger.

923	**453**	10y. green	40	25

454 "Portrait of Heihachiro Honda" (anon-Yedo period)

1963. Philatelic Week.

924	**454**	10y. multicoloured	1·20	70

455 Centenary Emblem and World Map

1963. Centenary of Red Cross.

925	**455**	10y. multicoloured	40	25

456 Globe and Leaf

1963. 5th International Irrigation and Drainage Commission Congress, Toyko.

926	**456**	10y. blue	40	25

457 Mt. Ito, Asahi Range

458 Mt. Bandai across Lake Hibara

1963. Bandai-Asahi National Park.

927	**457**	5y. green	40	30
928	**458**	10y. brown	50	30

459 Purple Jay

1963. Japanese Birds. Multicoloured.

929		10y. Type **459**	1·20	70
930		10y. Rock ptarmigan	60	30
931		10y. Eastern turtle dove	60	30
932		10y. White stork	60	30
933		10y. Japanese bush warbler	60	30
934		10y. Siberian meadow bunting	60	30

1963. Olympic Games, Tokyo, 1964 (4th issue). Sports. As T 423.

935		5y.+5y. blue	60	30
936		5y.+5y. brown	60	30
937		5y.+5y. brown	60	30

SPORTS: No. 935, Dinghy sailing; 936, Boxing; 937, Volleyball.

460 Road Junction, Ritto, Shiga

1963. Opening of Nagoya–Kobe Expressway.

938	**460**	10y. green, black & orange	40	10

461 Girl Scout and Flag

1963. Asian Girl Scout Camp, Nagano.

939	**461**	10y. multicoloured	40	25

462 Mt. Washiu

463 Whirlpool at Naruto

1963. Seto Inland Sea National Park.

940	**462**	5y. brown	40	25
941	**463**	10y. green	50	25

464 Lake Shikaribetsu

465 Mt. Kurodake

1963. Daisetsuzan National Park.

942	**464**	5y. blue	40	25
943	**465**	10y. purple	50	25

466 Antenna

1963. 14th International Scientific Radio Union Conference, Tokyo.

944	**466**	10y. multicoloured	40	25

467 "Great Wave off Kanagawa" (from "36 Views of Mt. Fuji" by Hokusai Katsushika)

1963. International Correspondence Week.

945	**467**	40y. multicoloured	6·75	2·30

The design is taken from the series of 36 woodcuts showing Mt. Fuji. Others from this series are shown as Nos. 989, 1010, 1075, 1100, 1140 and 1185.

468 Athletes

1963. "Pre-Olympic" Athletic Meeting, Tokyo.

946	**468**	10y. multicoloured	40	25

469 Wrestling

1963. 18th National Athletic Meeting, Yamaguchi.

947	**469**	5y. brown	40	25
948	-	5y. green	40	25

DESIGN: No. 948, Free-style gymnastics.

1963. Olympic Games, Tokyo, 1964 (5th issue). Sports. As T 423.

949	5y.+5y. blue	50	25
950	5y.+5y. olive	50	25
951	5y.+5y. black	50	25
952	5y.+5y. purple	50	25

SPORTS: No. 949, Cycling; 950, Show jumping; 951, Hockey; 952, Pistol-shooting.

470 Hachijo Island

1963. Izu Islands Quasi-National Park.

953	**470**	10y. multicoloured	50	25

471 Kai and Iwai Dragon Toys

1963. New Year's Greetings.

954	**471**	5y. multicoloured	60	25

472 Wakasa Bay

1964. Wakasa Bay Quasi-National Park.

956	**472**	10y. multicoloured	50	25

473 View from Horikiri Pass and Agave Plant

1964. Nichinan-Kaigan Quasi-National Park.

957	**473**	10y. multicoloured	50	25

474 Uji Bridge

475 View of Toba

1964. Ise-Shima National Park.

958	**474**	5y. brown	40	25
959	**475**	10y. purple	50	45

476 Festival Float and Mt. Norikura (Tokayama Festival)

477 "Yamaboko" Shrine (Gion Festival)

478 Warriors on Horseback (Soma Horse Festival)

479 Festival Scene (Chichibu Festival)

1964. Regional Festivals.

960	**476**	10y. multicoloured	40	25
961	**477**	10y. multicoloured	40	25
962	**478**	10y. multicoloured	40	15
963	**479**	10y. multicoloured	50	15

480 Prince Niou playing for Lady Nakanokimi (detail of Takayoshi "Yadorigi" scroll illustrating "Tale of Genji" by Lady Murasaki)

1964. Philatelic Week.

964	**480**	10y. multicoloured	60	30

481 Himeji Castle

1964. Rebuilding of Himeji Castle.

965	**481**	10y. brown	50	30

482 Handball

1964. 19th National Athletic Meeting, Niigata.

966	**482**	5y. green	40	25
967	-	5y. red (Gymnastics)	40	25

483 Cross-section of Cable

1964. Opening of Japan–U.S. Submarine Telephone Cable.

968	**483**	10y. multicoloured	40	25

1964. Olympic Games, Tokyo (6th issue). Sports. As T 423.

969	5y.+5y. violet	50	25
970	5y.+5y. blue	50	25
971	5y.+5y. lake	50	25
972	5y.+5y. olive	50	25

SPORTS: No. 969, Modern pentathlon; 970, Canoeing; 971, Football; 972, Weightlifting.

484 Nihonbashi Bridge

1964. Opening of Tokyo Expressway.

973	**484**	10y. green, silver and black	40	25

1964. Olympic Games, Tokyo (12th issue). Set of six miniature sheets each 135×60 mm containing stamps as indicated below.

MS974 Nos. 879/81	9·25	9·75
MS975 Nos. 899/901	6·00	6·75
MS976 Nos. 909/11	4·50	5·00
MS977 Nos. 935/7	11·00	12·00
MS978 Nos. 949/52	11·00	12·00
MS979 Nos. 969/72	11·00	12·00

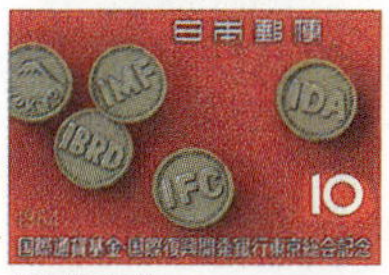

485 "Coins"

1964. Int Monetary Fund Convention, Tokyo.

980	**485**	10y. gold and red	40	25

486 Olympic Flame

1964. Olympic Games, Tokyo (7th issue). Inscr "1964". Multicoloured.

981	5y. Type **486**	30	25
982	10y. Main stadium (horiz)	40	25
983	30y. Fencing hall (horiz)	80	30
984	40y. Indoor stadium (horiz)	1·00	30
985	50y. Komazawa hall (horiz)	1·10	30
MS986	93×144 mm. Nos. 981/5	6·00	6·25

487 "Agriculture"

1964. Reclamation of Hachirogata Lagoon.

987	**487**	10y. gold and purple	60	25

488 "Hikari" (light) Express Train

1964. Inauguration of Tokyo–Osaka Shinkansen Railway Line.

988	**488**	10y. blue and black	90	15

489 "Tokaido Highway" (from "36 Views of Mt. Fuji" by Hokusai Katsushika)

1964. International Correspondence Week.

989	**489**	40y. multicoloured	2·00	60

490 Straw Snake

1964. New Year's Greetings.

990	**490**	5y. multicoloured	50	25

491 Mt. Daisen and Akamatsu Pond

492 Jodo-ga-Ura (Paradise Islands) of Oki

1965. Daisen-Oki National Park.

992	**491**	5y. blue	30	25
993	**492**	10y. brown	40	25

493 Niseko-Annupuri Mountains

1965. Niseko Shakotan Otaru Quasi-National Park.
994 **493** 10y. multicoloured 40 25

494 Radar Station

1965. Completion of Meteorological Radar Station, Mt. Fuji.
995 **494** 10y. multicoloured 40 25

495 Kiyotsu Gorge

496 Mt. Myoko across Lake Nojiri

1965. Jo-Shin-Etsu Kogen National Park.
996 **495** 5y. brown 30 25
997 **496** 10y. purple 40 25

497 Postal Museum

1965. Inauguration of Postal Museum, Ote-machi, Tokyo, and Stamp Exhibition.
998 **497** 10y. green 40 15

498 "The Prelude" (after Shoen Uyemura)

1965. Philatelic Week.
999 **498** 10y. multicoloured 50 25

499 Children at Play

1965. Inaug of National Children's Gardens.
1000 **499** 10y. multicoloured 50 10

500 Tree within "Leaf"

1965. Reafforestation.
1001 **500** 10y. multicoloured 40 25

501 Globe and Symbols

1965. Centenary of I.T.U.
1002 **501** 10y. multicoloured 40 25

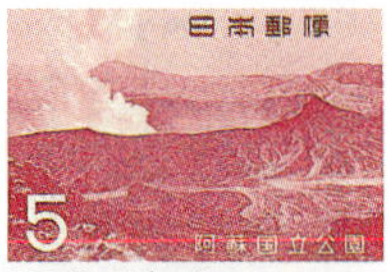
502 Mt. Naka Crater

503 Aso Peaks

1965. Aso National Park.
1003 **502** 5y. red 30 25
1004 **503** 10y. green 40 25

504 I.C.Y. Emblem and Doves

1965. International Co-operation Year.
1005 **504** 40y. multicoloured 90 10

505 "Meiji Maru" (cadet ship) and Japanese Gulls

1965. 25th Maritime Day.
1006 **505** 10y. multicoloured 60 25

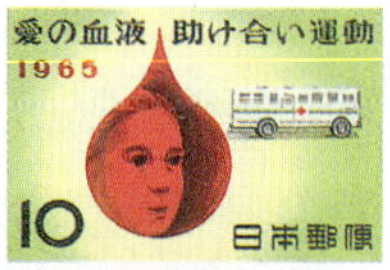
506 "Blood Donation"

1965. Campaign for Blood Donors.
1007 **506** 10y. multicoloured 40 25

507 Atomic Power Station, Tokyo

1965. 9th International Atomic Energy Authority Conference, Tokyo.
1008 **507** 10y. multicoloured 40 25

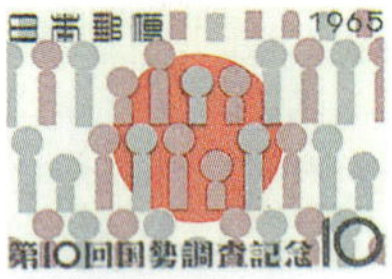
508 "Population"

1965. 10th National Census.
1009 **508** 10y. multicoloured 40 25

509 "Water at Misaka" (from "36 Views of Mt. Fuji" by Hokusai Katsushika)

1965. International Correspondence Week.
1010 **509** 40y. multicoloured 1·30 70

510 Emblems and Plan of Diet

1965. 75th Anniv of National Suffrage.
1011 **510** 10y. multicoloured 40 25

511 Walking

1965. 20th National Athletic Meeting, Gifu.
1012 **511** 5y. green 40 30
1013 - 5y. brown (Gymnastics) 40 30

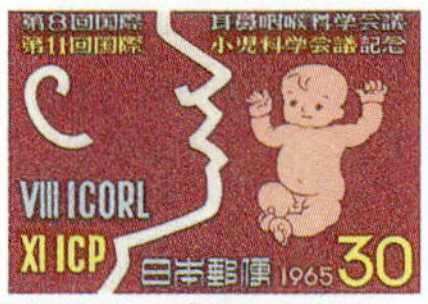
512 Outline of Face, and Baby

1965. International Conferences of Otology, Rhinology and Laryngology (ICORL) and Pediatrics (ICP), Tokyo.
1014 **512** 30y. multicoloured 70 25

513 Mt. Iwo

514 Mt. Rausu

1965. Shiretoko National Park.
1015 **513** 5y. turquoise 30 25
1016 **514** 10y. blue 40 25

515 Antarctic Map, Research Vessel "Fuji" and Aurora Australis

1965. Antarctic Expedition of 1965.
1017 **515** 10y. multicoloured 50 10

516 "Straw Horse"

1965. New Year's Greetings.
1018 **516** 5y. multicoloured 60 30

517 Telephone Switchboard (1890) and Modern Dial

1965. 75th Anniv of Japanese Telephone Service.
1020 **517** 10y. multicoloured 40 25

518 Spiny Lobster

1966. Fishery Products. Multicoloured.
1021 10y. Type **518** 40 15
1022 10y. Golden carp 40 15
1023 10y. Madai seabream 40 15
1024 10y. Skipjack tuna 40 15
1025 10y. Ayu 40 15
1026 15y. Japanese eel 50 15
1027 15y. Chub mackerel 50 15
1028 15y. Chum salmon 50 15
1029 15y. Buri 80 15
1030 15y. Tiger pufferfish 80 25
1031 15y. Japanese common squid 1·00 30
1032 15y. Horned turban (shellfish) 1·40 30

NIPPON. From this point onwards all stamps are additionally inscribed "NIPPON".

519 Pleasure Garden, Mito

519a Pleasure Garden and Manchurian Cranes, Okayama

519b Kerokuen Garden, Kanazawa

1966. Famous Japanese Gardens.
1033 **519** 10y. green, black & gold 40 10
1034 **519a** 15y. black, red and blue 50 10
1035 **519b** 15y. black, green & sil 50 10

520 Crater of Mt. Zao

1966. Zao Quasi-National Park.
1036 **520** 10y. multicoloured 40 25

521 Muroto Cape

522 Senba Cliffs, Anan

1966. Muroto-Anan Kaigan Quasi-National Park.
1037 **521** 10y. multicoloured 40 25
1038 **522** 10y. multicoloured 40 25

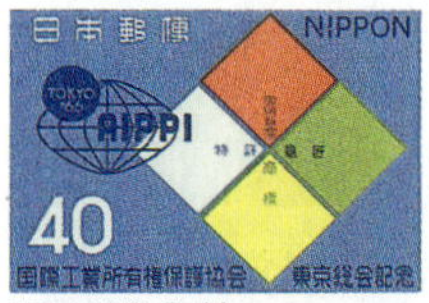
523 A.I.P.P.I. Emblem

1966. General Assembly of Int Association for Protection of Industrial Property (A.I.P.P.I.).
1039 **523** 40y. multicoloured 1·20 25

524 "Butterflies" (after T. Fujishima)

1966. Philatelic Week.
1040 **524** 10y. multicoloured 90 30

525 Goldfish

526 Chrysanthemums

527 Fuji (wisteria)

528 Hydrangea

529 Golden Hall, Chuson Temple

530 "Watasenia scintillans" (squid)

531 Yomei Gate, Tosho Shrine, Nikko

532 Mizubasho

533 Konponchudo Hall, Enryaku Temple

534 Ancient Clay Horse

535 Garden of Katsura Palace

536 Onjo Bosatsu (relief from bronze lantern, Todai Temple)

537 Kongo-Rikishi Statue, Todai Temple Nara

1966. Inscr "NIPPON".

1041	**235**	1y. bistre	15	10
1047	**525**	7y. orange and green	25	20
1049	**526**	15y. yellow and blue	1·80	20
1050	**526**	15y. yellow and blue	35	20
1052	**527**	20y. green and violet	2·10	20
1053	**528**	25y. blue and green	80	10
1054	**529**	30y. gold and blue	1·30	15
1055	**530**	35y. black, brown & blue	2·50	20
1056	**531**	40y. green and brown	80	10
1057	**532**	45y. multicoloured	80	20
1058	**240**	50y. red	12·50	20
1059	**240**	50y. mauve	1·10	20
1060	**280**	55y. green, black and blue	1·20	10
1061	**533**	60y. green	1·30	20
1062	**534**	65y. brown	20·00	20
1063	**534**	65y. orange	1·40	20
1064	**281**	75y. multicoloured	1·40	20
1065	**410**	90y. brown and gold	2·75	20
1066	**411**	100y. grey, black and red	2·00	10
1067	**535**	110y. brown	2·00	20
1068	**412**	120y. red	3·50	20
1069	**536**	200y. green	7·25	20
1070	**537**	500y. purple	8·00	25

No. 1050 is as T **526** but with white figures of value.
See also Nos. 1226/49.

538 U.N. and UNESCO Emblems

1966. 20th Anniv of UNESCO.

1071	**538**	15y. multicoloured	40	25

539 Pacific Ocean

1966. 11th Pacific Science Congress, Tokyo.

1072	**539**	15y. multicoloured	40	25

540 Amakusa Bridges

1966. Completion of Amakusa Bridges.

1073	**540**	15y. multicoloured	40	25

541 Family and Emblem

1966. 50th Anniv of Post Office Life Insurance Office.

1074	**541**	15y. multicoloured	40	25

542 "Sekiya on the Sumida" (from "36 Views of Mt. Fuji" by Hokusai Katsushika)

1966. International Correspondence Week.

1075	**542**	50y. multicoloured	2·20	85

543 Rotary Cobalt Radiator

1966. 9th. International Cancer Congress, Tokyo.

1076	**543**	7y.+3y. black & orge	30	25
1077	-	15y.+5y. multicoloured	40	25

DESIGN—VERT: 15y. Detection by X-rays.

544 Triple Jump

1966. 21st National Athletic Meeting, Oita.

1078	**544**	7y. red	40	25
1079	-	7y. blue (Clay-pigeon shooting)	40	25

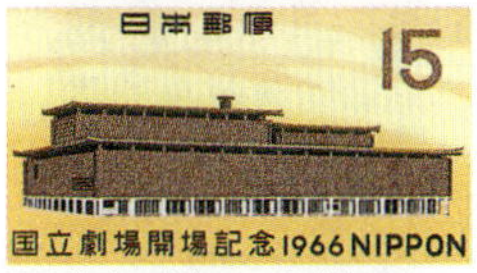

545 National Theatre Building

1966. Inauguration of Japanese National Theatre. Multicoloured.

1080		15y. Type **545**	40	25
1081		25y. "Kabuki" performance (48×33½ mm)	1·10	40
1082		50y. "Bunraku" puppet act (33½×48 mm)	1·30	60

546 Rice Year Emblem

1966. International Rice Year.

1083	**546**	15y. black, ochre and red	40	25

547 Ittobori Sheep (sculpture)

1966. New Year's Greetings.

1084	**547**	7y. multicoloured	60	30

548 Satellite "Intelsat 2", Earth and Moon

1967. Inauguration of International Commercial Satellite Communications in Japan.

1086	**548**	15y. brown and blue	40	10

549 Douglas DC-8 and Flight Route

1967. Inauguration of Round-the-World Air Service.

1087	**549**	15y. multicoloured	40	10

550 Literature Museum

1967. Opening of Japanese Modern Literature Museum, Meguro-ku, Tokyo.

1088	**550**	15y. multicoloured	40	25

551 "Lakeside" (after S. Kuroda)

1967. Philatelic Week.

1089	**551**	15y. multicoloured	50	30

552 Port of Kobe

1967. 5th International Association of Ports and Harbours Congress, Tokyo.

1090	**552**	50y. multicoloured	1·30	40

553 Emblem of Welfare Service

1967. 50th Anniv of Welfare Commissioner Service.

1091	**553**	15y. gold and agate	50	10

554 Pedestrian Road Crossing

1967. 20th Anniv of Road Safety Campaign.

1092	**554**	15y. multicoloured	40	25

555 Mts. Kita and Koma

556 Mts. Akashi, Hijiri and Higashi

1967. Southern Alps National Park.

1093	**555**	7y. blue	30	10
1094	**556**	15y. purple	40	10

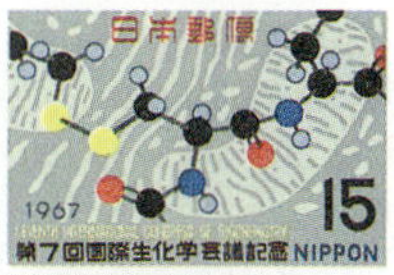

557 Protein Molecules

1967. 7th Int Biochemistry Congress, Tokyo.

1095	**557**	15y. multicoloured	40	25

558 Gymnast

1967. "Universiade 1967" (Sports Meeting), Tokyo. Multicoloured.

1096		15y. Type **558**	40	25
1097		50y. Universiade "U" emblem (25×35½ mm)	1·30	40

559 Paper Lantern

560 Mt. Fuji (after T. Yokoyama)

1967. International Tourist Year.

1098	**559**	15y. multicoloured	60	30
1099	**560**	50y. multicoloured	2·40	1·70

561 "Kajikazawa in Kai Province" (from "36 Views of Mt. Fuji" by Hokusai Katsushika)

1967. International Correspondence Week.

1100	**561**	50y. multicoloured	3·00	80

562 Athlete

1967. 22nd National Athletic Meeting, Saitama.

1101	**562**	15y. multicoloured	1·00	30

563 Buddha, Koryu Temple, Kyoto

564 Kudara Kannon (Budda), Horyu Temple, Nara

565 Horyu Temple, Nara

1967. National Treasures. Asuka Period.

1102	**563**	15y. multicoloured	60	40
1103	**564**	15y. multicoloured	60	40
1104	**565**	50y. multicoloured	2·50	1·00

See also Nos. 1113/15, 1120/2, 1134/6, 1152/4, 1170/2 and 1177/80.

566 Motor Expressway

1967. 13th World Road Congress, Tokyo.

1105	**566**	50y. multicoloured	1·30	30

567 Mt. Kumotori

568 Lake Chichibu

1967. Chichibu-Tama National Park.

1106	**567**	7y. olive	30	10
1107	**568**	15y. violet	40	10

569 "Noborizaru" (Miyazaki toy)

1967. New Year's Greetings.

1108	**569**	7y. multicoloured	60	30

570 Mt. Sobo

571 Takachiho Gorge

1967. Sobo-Katamuki Quasi-National Park.

1110	**570**	15y. multicoloured	40	10
1111	**571**	15y. multicoloured	40	10

572 Boy and Girl and Cruise Liner "Sakura Maru"

1968. Youth Goodwill Cruise to mark Meiji Centenary.

1112	**572**	15y. violet, yellow & blue	30	10

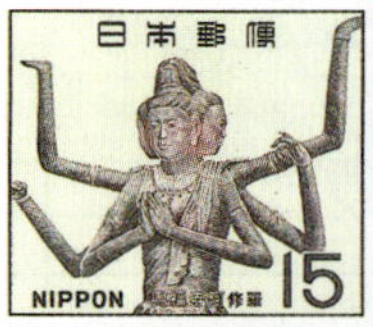

573 Asura Statue, Kofuku Temple, Nara

574 Gakko Bosatsu, Todai Temple, Nara

575 Srimaha devi (painting), Yakushi Temple, Nara

1968. National Treasures. Nara Period (710–784).

1113	**573**	15y. multicoloured	50	30
1114	**574**	15y. multicoloured	60	30
1115	**575**	50y. multicoloured	2·20	1·40

576 Mt. Yatsugatake and Cattle

577 Mt. Tateshina and Lake

1968. Yatsugatake-Chushin Kogen Quasi-National Park.

1116	**576**	15y. multicoloured	50	30
1117	**577**	15y. multicoloured	50	30

578 "Dancer in a Garden" (after Bakusen Tsuchida)

1968. Philatelic Week.

1118	**578**	15y. multicoloured	80	30

579 View of Rishiri Island from Rebun Island

1968. Rishiri-Rebun Quasi-National Park.

1119	**579**	15y. multicoloured	40	25

580 Lacquer Casket

582 "Fugen Bosatsu" (painting of Bodishattva Samantabhadva)

581 "The Origin of Shigisan" (painting in Chogo-sonshi Temple)

1968. National Treasures. Heinan Period (794–1185).

1120	**580**	15y. multicoloured	50	40
1121	**581**	15y. multicoloured	60	40
1122	**582**	50y. multicoloured	4·75	2·00

583 Centenary Tower and Star

1968. Hokkaido Centenary.

1123	**583**	15y. multicoloured	40	25

584 Biro Trees and Pacific Sunrise

1968. Return of Ogasawara Islands to Japan.

1124	**584**	15y. multicoloured	40	25

585 "Map of Japan" in Figures

1968. Postal Codes Campaign.

1125	**585**	7y. red, brown & grn (I)	1·50	30
1126	-	7y. red, brown & grn (II)	1·50	30
1127	**585**	15y. mauve, vio & bl (I)	1·50	30
1128	-	15y. mauve, vio & bl (II)	1·50	30

(II) Inscr reading "Postal code also on your address" measures 12 mm.

586 River Kiso

587 Inuyama Castle and View

1968. Hida-Kisogawa Quasi-National Park.

1129	**586**	15y. multicoloured	40	10
1130	**587**	15y. multicoloured	40	10

588 Federation Emblem and "Sun"

1968. Int Youth Hostel Conference, Tokyo.

1131	**588**	15y. multicoloured	40	25

589 Humans forming Emblem

590 Baseball "Pitcher"

1968. 50th All-Japan High School Baseball Championships, Koshi-en, Tokyo.

1132	**589**	15y. multicoloured	1·20	40
1133	**590**	15y. multicoloured	1·20	40

591 "Minamoto Yoritomo" (Jingo Temple Collection)

593 Red-braided Armour (Kasuga Grand Shrine Collection)

592 Emperor Nijo escaping from Black Palace (from "Tale of Heiji" picture scroll)

1968. National Treasures. Kamakura Period (1185–1334).

1134	**591**	15y. multicoloured	60	40
1135	**592**	15y. multicoloured	60	40
1136	**593**	50y. multicoloured	3·00	1·60

594 Mt. Iwate

595 Lake Towada

1968. Towada-Hachimantai National Park.

1137	**594**	7y. brown	30	10
1138	**595**	15y. green	40	10

596 Gymnastics

1968. 23rd National Athletic Meeting.

1139	**596**	15y. multicoloured	50	30

597 "Fujimihara in Owari Province" (from "36 Views of Mt. Fuji" by Hokusai Katsushika)

1968. International Correspondence Week.

1140	**597**	50y. multicoloured	1·90	95

598 Centenary Emblem and Sail Warship "Shohei Maru", 1868

599 "Arrival of the Imperial Carriage in Tokyo" (after Tomone Kobori)

1968. Centenary of Meiji Era.

1141	**598**	15y. multicoloured	40	25
1142	**599**	15y. multicoloured	40	25

600 Old and New Kannonzaki Lighthouses

1968. Centenary of Japanese Lighthouses.

1143	**600**	15y. multicoloured	50	10

601 Ryo's Dancer and State Hall

1968. Completion of Imperial Palace.

1144	**601**	15y. multicoloured	60	30

602 Mt. Takachiho

603 Mt. Motobu, Yaku Island

1968. Kirishima-Yaku National Park.

1145	**602**	7y. violet	60	30
1146	**603**	15y. orange	60	30

604 "Niwatori" (Yamagata toy)

1968. New Year's Greetings.

1147	**604**	7y. multicoloured	60	30

605 Human Rights Emblem and Dancers

1968. Human Rights Year.

1149	**605**	50y. multicoloured	1·10	30

606 Siberian Chipmunk with Nuts

1968. Savings Promotion.

1150	**606**	15y. sepia and green	70	25

607 Coastal Scenery

1969. Echizen-Kaga-Kaigan Quasi-National Park.

1151	**607**	15y. multicoloured	60	30

608 Silver Pavilion, Jisho Temple, Kyoto

609 Pagoda, Anraku Temple, Nagano

610 "Winter Landscape" (Sesshu)

1969. National Treasures. Muromachi Period.

1152	**608**	15y. multicoloured	50	30
1153	**609**	15y. multicoloured	50	30
1154	**610**	50y. multicoloured	2·20	1·40

611 Mt. Chokai, from Tobishima

1969. Chokai Quasi-National Park.

1155	**611**	15y. multicoloured	50	10

612 "Expo" Emblem and Globe

613 "Cherry Blossom" (from mural Chichakuin Temple, Kyoto)

1969. "EXPO 70" World Fair, Osaka (1st issue).

1156	**612**	15y.+5y. mult	60	45
1157	**613**	50y.+10y. mult	1·60	1·20

See also Nos. 1193/**MS**1196 and 1200/**MS**1203.

614 Mt. Koya from Jinnogamine

615 Mt. Gomadan and Rhododendrons

1969. Koya-Ryujin Quasi-National Park.

1158	**614**	15y. multicoloured	40	25
1159	**615**	15y. multicoloured	40	25

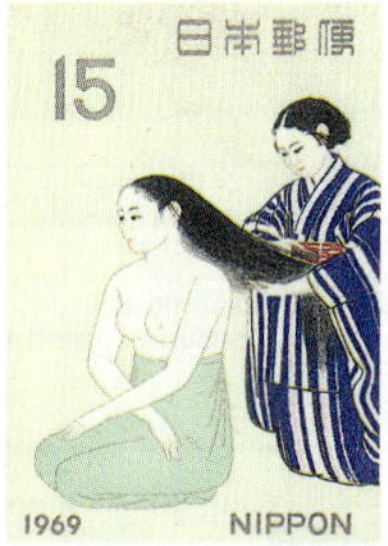

616 "Hair" (Kokei Kobayashi)

1969. Philatelic Week.

1160	**616**	15y. multicoloured	60	40

617 Woman and Child crossing "Roads"

1969. Road Safety Campaign.

1161	**617**	15y. green, blue and red	40	25

618 Sakawagawa Bridge

1969. Completion of Tokyo–Nagoya Expressway.

1162	**618**	15y. multicoloured	50	30

619 Museum Building

1969. Opening of National Museum of Modern Art, Tokyo.

1163	**619**	15y. multicoloured	40	25

620 Nuclear-powered Freighter "Mutsu" and Atomic Symbol

1969. Launching of Japan's 1st Nuclear Ship "Mutsu".

1164	**620**	15y. multicoloured	50	10

621 Cable Ship "KDD Maru" and Map

1969. Opening of Japanese Ocean Cable.

1165	**621**	15y. multicoloured	50	10

622 Symbol and Cards

1969. Postal Codes Campaign.

1166	**622**	7y. red and green	30	25
1167	-	15y. red and blue	80	25

DESIGN: 15y. Symbol, postbox and code numbers.

624 Lions Emblem and Rose

1969. 52nd Lions Int Convention, Tokyo.

1168	**624**	15y. multicoloured	60	30

625 Hotoke-ga-ura (coast)

1969. Shimokita-Hanto Quasi-National Park.

1169	**625**	15y. multicoloured	60	30

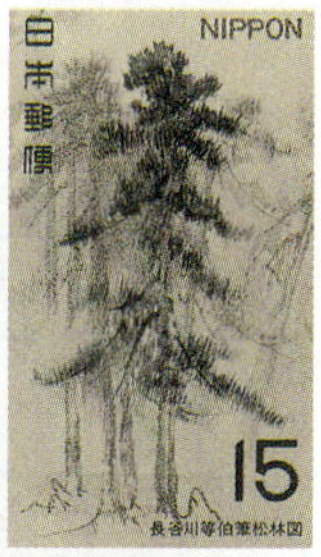

626 Himeji Castle, Hyogo Prefecture

627 "Pinewoods" (T. Hasegawa)

628 "The Japanese Cypress" (artist unknown)

1969. National Treasures. Momoyama Period.

1170	**626**	15y. multicoloured	60	30
1171	**627**	15y. black and drab	60	30
1172	**628**	50y. multicoloured	1·10	55

629 Harano-fudo Waterfalls

630 Mt. Nagisan

1969. Hyonosen-Ushiroyama-Nagisan Quasi-National Park.

1173	**629**	15y. multicoloured	40	25
1174	**630**	15y. multicoloured	40	25

631 Mt. O-akan

632 Mt. Iwo

1969. Akan National Park.

1175	**631**	7y. blue	30	25
1176	**632**	15y. sepia	40	25

633 "Choben" (T. Ikeno)

634 "The Red-plum Tree" (K. Ogata)

635 "The White-plum Tree" (K. Ogata)

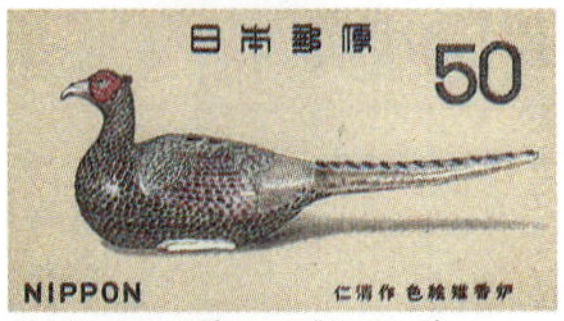
636 "Japanese Pheasant" Incense-burner (after Ninsei)

1969. National Treasures. Edo Period.

1177	**633**	15y. multicoloured	60	45
1178	**634**	15y. multicoloured	60	45
1179	**635**	15y. multicoloured	60	45
1180	**636**	50y. multicoloured	2·40	1·40

637 Globe and Doves

638 "Woman Reading a Letter" (Utamaro Kitagawa)

639 "Reading a Letter" (Harunobu Suzuki)

640 "Miyako Dennai" (Sharaku Toshusai)

1969. 16th U.P.U. Congress, Tokyo.

1181	**637**	15y. multicoloured	40	25
1182	**638**	30y. multicoloured	1·00	80
1183	**639**	50y. multicoloured	1·60	95
1184	**640**	60y. multicoloured	1·60	95

641 "Mishima Pass" (from "36 Views of Mt. Fuji" by Hokusai Katsushika)

1969. International Correspondence Week.

1185	**641**	50y. multicoloured	1·30	80

642 Rugby Football

1969. 24th National Athletic Meeting.

1186	**642**	15y. multicoloured	60	30

643 Cape Kitayama

644 Goishi Coast

1969. Rikuchu-Kaigan National Park.

1187	**643**	7y. blue	30	25
1188	**644**	15y. red and salmon	40	25

645 Worker in Safety Helmet

1969. 50th Anniv of I.L.O.

1189	**645**	15y. multicoloured	40	30

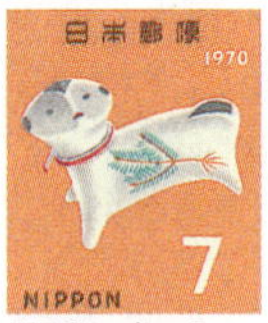
646 Guardian Dog, Hokkeji Temple

1969. New Year's Greetings.

1190	**646**	7y. multicoloured	60	30

647 Peasants, Tsushima Island

1970. Iki-Tsushima Quasi-National Park.

1192	**647**	15y. multicoloured	50	10

648 View of Fair and Firework Display

1970. "EXPO 70" World Fair, Osaka (2nd issue). Multicoloured.

1193	7y. Type **648**	30	25
1194	15y. Earth and cherry blossom garland	30	25
1195	50y. "Irises" (Korin Ogata) (48×33 mm)	50	25
MS1196	144×93 mm. Nos. 1193/5	3·50	3·75

651 "Woman with Drum" (Saburosuke Okada)

1970. Philatelic Week.

1197	**651**	15y. multicoloured	40	25

652 Cherry Blossom, Mt. Yoshino

653 Waterfall, Nachi

1970. Yoshino-Kumano National Park.

1198	**652**	7y. black and pink	30	25
1199	**653**	15y. dp green, green & bl	40	25

654 Kanto (lantern) Festival

655 Japanese Pavilions

656 "Flowers of Autumn" (detail, Hoitsu Sakai)

1970. "EXPO 70" World Fair, Osaka (3rd issue).

1200	**654**	7y. multicoloured	30	25
1201	**655**	15y. multicoloured	30	25
1202	**656**	50y. multicoloured	80	45
MS1203		144×93 mm. Nos. 1200/2	2·50	2·50

657 Houses and Code Symbol

1970. Postal Codes Campaign.

1204	**657**	7y. violet and green	40	10
1205	**657**	15y. purple and blue	60	10

658 Utaemon Nakamura VI as Hanako in "Musume Dojoji"

659 Danjuro Ichikawa XI as Sukeroku in "Sukeroku"

660 "Kanjincho"

1970. Japanese Theatre "Kabuki".

1206	**658**	15y. multicoloured	30	25
1207	**659**	15y. multicoloured	30	25
1208	**660**	50y. multicoloured	1·00	40

See also Nos. 1250/2, 1284/6 and 1300/2.

661 Girl Scout saluting

1970. 50th Anniv of Japanese Girl Scouts.

1209	**661**	15y. multicoloured	50	10

662 Festival Drummer and Kinoura Coastline

663 Mt. Tate from Himi Shore

1970. Noto-Hanto Quasi-National Park.

1210	**662**	15y. multicoloured	40	25
1211	**663**	15y. multicoloured	40	25

664 "Sunflower" and U.N. Emblem

1970. 4th U.N. Congress on Prevention of Crime and Treatment of Offenders, Kyoto.

1212	**664**	15y. multicoloured	40	25

665 Mt. Myogi

666 Mt. Arafune

1970. Myogi-Arafune-Sakukuogen Quasi-National Park.

1213	**665**	15y. multicoloured	40	25
1214	**666**	15y. multicoloured	40	25

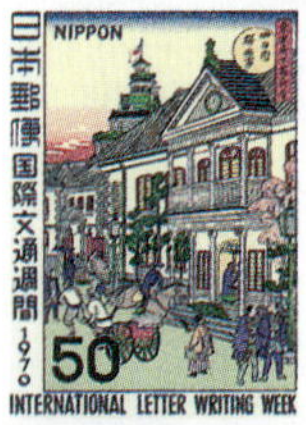
667 "Tokyo Post Office" (woodcut, Hiroshige III)

1970. International Correspondence Week.

1215	**667**	50y. multicoloured	1·10	40

668 Show Jumping, Mt. Iwate and Paulownia Flowers

1970. 25th National Athletic Meeting, Iwate.

1216	**668**	15y. multicoloured	60	30

669 "Hodogaya Stage" (print, Hiroshige III)

1970. Centenary of Telegraph Service.

1217	**669**	15y. multicoloured	60	30

670 U.N. Emblem within "Tree"

1970. 25th Anniv of U.N.O. Multicoloured.

1218	15y. Type **670**	40	25
1219	50y. U.N. emblem, New York H.Q. and flags	1·00	30

672 Competition Emblem

1970. 19th International Vocational Training Competition, Chiba City.

1220	**672**	15y. multicoloured	40	25

673 Diet Building and Doves

1970. 80th Anniv of Japanese Diet.

1221	**673**	15y. multicoloured	60	30

674 "Wild Boar" (folk-handicraft)

1970. New Year's Greetings.

1222	**674**	7y. multicoloured	60	30

675 Ski Jumping

1971. Winter Olympic Games, Sapporo (1972) (1st issue). Multicoloured.

1224	15y.+5y. Type **675**	50	40
1225	15y.+5y. Ice-hockey (horiz)	50	20

See also Nos. 1280/**MS**1283.

677 Mute Swan

678 Sika Deer

679 "Allomyrina dichotomus"

680 "Pine Tree" (T. Kano)

682 Golden Eagle

684 "Ho-o" (Phoenix), Byodoin Temple, Uji

692 Statue of Kissho, Joruri Temple

1971. Inscr "NIPPON".

1226	**273**	3y. green	30	10
1227	**677**	5y. blue	20	10
1228	**678**	10y. brown and green	20	10
1229	**679**	12y. brown	35	10
1230	**680**	20y. brown and green	35	15
1231	**528**	25y. blue and green	40	15
1232	**240**	50y. green	90	10
1233	-	60y. green and yellow	1·10	15
1234	**408**	70y. black and orange	1·40	15
1235	**409**	80y. brown and red	1·40	15
1236	**410**	90y. brown and orange	1·80	15
1237	**682**	90y. black and red	1·80	10
1238	**412**	120y. brown and green	1·70	10
1239	-	140y. purple and mauve	2·40	15
1240	**684**	150y. turquoise & green	3·00	10
1240a	**684**	150y. brown and red	2·75	15
1241	-	200y. red	3·75	10
1242	-	200y. brown	3·25	10
1243	-	200y. red	1·80	10
1244	-	250y. blue	3·25	15
1245	-	300y. blue	5·00	15
1246	-	350y. brown	5·00	15
1247	-	400y. red	5·50	15
1248	-	500y. green	4·25	10
1249	**692**	1000y. multicoloured	11·00	60
MS1249a		51×102 mm. No. 1249	15·00	13·00

DESIGNS: 60y. Narcissi; 140y. Noh mask of aged man; 200y. (No. 1241), Onjo Bosatsu (relief), Todai Temple; 200y. (Nos. 1242/3), Warrior (statuette); 250y. Komainu (guardian dog), Katori Shrine; 300y. Buddha, Kofuku Temple; 350y. Goddess of Mercy, Yaluski Temple, Nara; 400y. Tentoki (demon); 500y. Buddhist deity.

No. 1231 is Type **528**, redrawn. The inscription and face value are smaller, but the main difference is in the position of the leaves. On No. 1053 they touch the left edge of the design, but on No. 1231 they are completely clear of it.

No. 1241 is as Type **536** but smaller, 18×22 mm.

For 210y. as Nos. 1242/3 and 360y. as No. 1246, see Nos. 1600 and 1604.

693 "Gen-jo-raku"

694 "Ko-cho"

695 "Tai-hei-raku"

1971. Japanese Theatre "Gagaku".

1250	**693**	15y. multicoloured	30	25
1251	**694**	15y. multicoloured	30	25
1252	**695**	50y. multicoloured	1·00	40

696 Voter and Diet Building

1971. 25th Anniv of Women's Suffrage.

1253	**696**	15y. multicoloured	40	30

697 Pine Trees and Maple Leaves

1971. National Afforestation Campaign.

1254	**697**	7y. black, violet & green	30	10

698 "Tsukiji-akashicho" (K. Kaburagi)

1971. Philatelic Week.

1255	**698**	15y. multicoloured	40	25

699 "Posting a Letter" (K. Dogishi)

700 "Postman" (K. Kasai)

701 "Railway Post Office" (S. Onozaki)

1971. Centenary of Japanese Postal Services.

1256	**699**	15y. multicoloured	40	10
1257	**700**	15y. black and brown	40	10
1258	**701**	15y. multicoloured	40	10

702 Great Tit

1971. 25th Bird Week.

1259	**702**	15y. multicoloured	50	10

703 Adelie Penguins

1971. 10th Anniv of Antarctic Treaty.

1260	**703**	15y. multicoloured	1·00	30

704 Goto-Wakamatsu-Seto

705 Kuzyuku-shima

1971. Saikai National Park.

1261	**704**	7y. green	40	30
1262	**705**	15y. brown	40	30

706 Postal Code Numerals

1971. Postal Code Campaign.

1263	**706**	7y. red and green	30	10
1264	**706**	15y. red and blue	50	25

707 Scout Bugler

1971. 13th World Scout Jamboree, Asagiri.

1265	**707**	15y. multicoloured	50	10

708 Rose Emblem

1971. 50th Anniv of Family Conciliation System.

1266	**708**	15y. multicoloured	40	30

709 "Tokyo Horse Tram" (Yoshimura)

1971. International Correspondence Week.

1267	**709**	50y. multicoloured	1·10	25

710 Emperor's Standard

1971. European Tour by Emperor Hirohito and Empress Nagako. Multicoloured.

1268	15y. Type **710**	40	30
1269	15y. "Beyond the Sea" (drawing by Empress Nagako)	40	30
MS1270	141×111 mm. Nos. 1268/9. Imperf	2·00	1·60

712 Tennis

1971. 26th National Athletic Meeting.

1271	**712**	15y. multicoloured	40	30

713 Child's Face and "100"

1971. Centenary of National Family Registration System.

1272	**713**	15y. multicoloured	40	30

714 "Dragon" (G. Hashimoto)

1971. Centenary of Government Printing Works, Tokyo. Multicoloured.

1273	15y. Type **714**	50	25
1274	15y. "Tiger" (from same drawing as above)	50	25

716 Mt. Yotei from Lake Toya

717 Mt. Showa-Shinzan

1971. Shikotsu-Toya National Park.

1275	**716**	7y. green and olive	30	25
1276	**717**	15y. blue and brown	40	25

718 Takarabune ("Treasure Ship")

1971. New Year's Greetings.

1277	**718**	7y. multicoloured	30	25
1278	**718**	10y. multicoloured	40	25

719 Skiing

1972. Winter Olympic Games, Sapporo (2nd issue). Multicoloured.

1280	20y. Type **719**	40	25
1281	20y. Bobsleighing	40	25
1282	50y. Figure skating (pair) (52×36 mm)	90	30
MS1283	145×94 mm. Nos. 1280/2	2·00	1·60

722 "Kumagai-jinya"

723 "Nozaki-mura"

724 "Awa-no-Naruto"

1972. Japanese Theatre. "Banraku" Puppet Theatre.

1284	**722**	20y. multicoloured	30	25
1285	**723**	20y. multicoloured	30	25
1286	**724**	50y. multicoloured	1·00	40

725 "Hikari" Express Train

1972. Centenary of Japanese Railways (1st issue) and Opening of Sanyo Shinkansen Line.

1287	**725**	20y. multicoloured	50	10

See also Nos. 1305/6.

727 Fishing, Taishakukyo Valley

726 Hiba Mountains

1972. Hiba-Dogo-Taishaku Quasi-National Park.

1288	**726**	20y. multicoloured	40	25
1289	**727**	20y. multicoloured	40	25

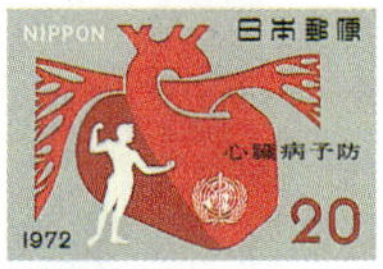
728 Adult with Human Heart

1972. World Heart Month.

1290	**728**	20y. multicoloured	40	30

729 "Rising Balloon" (Gakuryo Nakamura)

1972. Philatelic Week.

1291	**729**	20y. multicoloured	40	30

730 Courtesy Gate, Shuri

1972. Return of Ryukyu Islands to Japan.

1292	**730**	20y. multicoloured	40	30

731 Japanese Camellia

1972. National Afforrestation Campaign.

1293	**731**	20y. yellow blue & green	40	30

732 Mt. Kurikoma and Kokeshi Doll

733 Naruko-kyo Gorge and Kokeshi Doll

1972. Kurikoma Quasi-National Park.

1294	**732**	20y. multicoloured	40	30
1295	**733**	20y. multicoloured	40	30

734 Envelope and Code Symbol

1972. Postal Codes Campaign (5th issue).

1296	**734**	10y. black, purple & blue	30	10
1297	-	20y. red and green	30	10

DESIGN: 20y. Mail-box and code symbol.

736 Mt. Hodaka

737 Mt. Tate

1972. Chubu Sangaku National Park.

1298	**736**	10y. violet and mauve	40	30
1299	**737**	20y. blue and brown	40	30

738 "Tamura"

739 "Aoi-no-ue"

740 "Hagoromo"

1972. Japanese Theatre. "Noh".

1300	**738**	20y. multicoloured	30	25
1301	**739**	20y. multicoloured	30	25
1302	**740**	50y. multicoloured	1·00	40

741 "Profiles of Schoolchildren"

1972. Centenary of Japanese Educational System.

1303	**741**	20y. multicoloured	40	30

742 "Eitai Bridge" (Hiroshige III)

1972. International Correspondence Week.

1304	**742**	50y. multicoloured	1·00	25

743 "Inauguration of Railway Service" (Hiroshige III)

1972. Centenary of Japanese Railways (2nd issue). Multicoloured.

1305	20y. Type **743**	70	10
1306	20y. Class C-62 steam locomotive No. 2	70	10

745 Kendo (Japanese Fencing)

1972. 27th National Athletic Meeting, Kagoshima.

1307	**745**	10y. multicoloured	40	30

746 Scout and Cub

1972. 50th Anniv of Japanese Boy Scouts.

1308	**746**	20y. multicoloured	50	10

747 "Harbour and Bund, Yokohama" (Hiroshige III)

1972. Centenary of Japanese Customs Service.

1309	**747**	20y. multicoloured	50	10

748 "Plum Blossoms" Plate (K. Ogata)

1972. New Year's Greetings.

1310	**748**	10y. multicoloured	40	25

749 Mt. Tsurugi

750 River Yoshino, Oboke Valley

1973. Tsurugi-San Quasi-National Park.

1312	**749**	20y. multicoloured	40	25
1313	**750**	20y. multicoloured	40	25

751 Mt. Takao

752 Minoo Falls and Japanese Macaques

1973. Meiji-no-mori Quasi-National Park.

1314	**751**	20y. multicoloured	50	10
1315	**752**	20y. multicoloured	50	10

753 "Dragon" (East Wall)

754 "Male Figures" (East Wall)

755 "Female Figures" (West Wall)

1973. Asuka Archaeological Conservation Fund. Takamatsuzuka Kofun Tomb Murals.

1316	**753**	20y.+5y. multicoloured	40	30
1317	**754**	20y.+5y. multicoloured	40	30
1318	**755**	50y.+10y. multicoloured	1·30	1·00

756 Phoenix Tree

1973. National Afforestation Campaign.

1319	**756**	20y. multicoloured	40	30

757 "Sumiyoshimode" (R. Kishida)

1973. Philatelic Week.

1320	**757**	20y. multicoloured	50	30

758 Mt. Kama

759 Rock Outcrops, Mt. Haguro

1973. Suzuka Quasi-National Park.

1321	**758**	20y. multicoloured	40	30
1322	**759**	20y. multicoloured	40	30

760 Chichi-jima Island Beach

761 Coral Reef, Minami-jimi Island

1973. Ogasawara Islands National Park.

1323	**760**	10y. blue	30	10
1324	**761**	20y. purple	40	10

762 Postal Code Symbol and Tree

1973. Postal Codes Campaign.

1325	**762**	10y. gold and green	30	10
1326	-	20y. lilac, red and blue	40	10

DESIGN: 20y. Postman and symbol.

765 Waterfall, Sandan-kyo Gorge

764 Mt. Shinnyu

1973. Nishi-Chugoku-Sanchi Quasi-National Park.

1327	**764**	20y. multicoloured	40	30
1328	**765**	20y. multicoloured	40	30

766 Valley of River Tenryu

767 Oriental Scops Owl and Woodland Path, Mt. Horaiji

1973. Tenryu-Okumikowa Quasi-National Park.

1329	**766**	20y. multicoloured	70	10
1330	**767**	20y. blue, green and silver	70	10

768 "Cock" (J. Ito)

1973. International Correspondence Week.

1331	**768**	50y. multicoloured	1·20	10

769 Sprinting

1973. 28th National Athletic Meeting. Chiba.

1332	**769**	10y. multicoloured	40	30

770 Kan-Mon Bridge

1973. Opening of Kan-Mon Suspension Bridge.

1333	**770**	20y. multicoloured	50	10

771 Hanasaka-jijii and his Dog

772 Hanasaka-jijii finds the Gold

773 Hanasaka-jijii and Tree in Blossom

1973. Japanese Folk Tales (1st series). "Hanasaki-jijii".

1334	**771**	20y. multicoloured	40	15
1335	**772**	20y. multicoloured	40	15
1336	**773**	20y. multicoloured	40	15

See also Nos. 1342/4, 1352/4, 1358/60, 1362/4, 1378/80 and 1387/9.

774 Lantern

1973. New Year's Greetings.

1337	**774**	10y. multicoloured	30	10

775 Niju-bashi Bridge

1974. Imperial Golden Wedding. Mult.

1339	20y. Type **775**	40	30
1340	20y. Imperial Palace	40	30
MS1341	145×89 mm. Nos. 1339/40	1·60	1·20

777 "The Crane Damsel"

1974. Japanese Folk Tales (2nd series). "Tsuru-Nyobo". Multicoloured.

1342	20y. Type **777**	40	10
1343	20y. Manchurian Crane "weaving"	40	10
1344	20y. Manchurian Cranes in flight	40	10

780 "A Reefy Coast" (Hyakusui Hirafuku)

1974. International Ocean Exposition, Okinawa (1975) (1st issue).

1345	**780**	20y.+5y. multicoloured	50	40

See also Nos. 1401/3.

781 Marudu Falls

782 Seascape

1974. Iriomote National Park.

1346	**781**	20y. multicoloured	50	10
1347	**782**	20y. multicoloured	50	10

783 Iriomote Cat

1974. Nature Conservation (1st series).

1348	**783**	20y. multicoloured	50	25

See also Nos. 1356, 1361, 1372, 1377, 1381, 1405, 1419, 1422, 1430, 1433/4, 1449, 1457, 1469, 1470, 1475, 1490, 1497 and 1502.

784 "Finger" (Shinsui Ito)

1974. Philatelic Week.

1349	**784**	20y. multicoloured	40	30

785 Nambu Red Pine

1974. National Afforestation Campaign.

1350	**785**	20y. multicoloured	40	30

786 Supreme Court Building

1974. Completion of Supreme Court Building, Tokyo.

1351	**786**	20y. brown	40	30

787 "Sailing in a Wooden Bowl"

788 "Conquering the Goblins"

789 "Wielding the Little Magic Mallet"

1974. Japanese Folk Tales (3rd series). "The Dwarf".

1352	**787**	20y. multicoloured	40	30
1353	**788**	20y. multicoloured	40	30
1354	**789**	20y. multicoloured	40	30

790 "Uniform Rivalry" (detail after Kunimasa Baido)

1974. Centenary of Japanese Police System.

1355	**790**	20y. multicoloured	40	30

1974. Nature Conservation (2nd series). As T 783. Multicoloured.

1356 20y. European otter ("Lutra lutra") 50 25

792 World Blood Donation

1974. International Red Cross Day.

1357 **792** 20y. multicoloured 50 10

793 "Discovery of Kaguya Hime"

795 "The Ascent to Heaven"

794 "Kaguya Hime as Young Woman"

1974. Japanese Folk Tales (4th series). "Kaguya Hime".

1358 **793** 20y. multicoloured 40 30
1359 **794** 20y. multicoloured 40 30
1360 **795** 20y. multicoloured 40 30

1974. Nature Conservation (3rd series). As T 783. Multicoloured.

1361 20y. Ryukyu rabbit ("Pentalagus furnessi") 50 25

797 Old Men in front of Yahata Shrine

798 Old Man dancing with Demons

799 Old Man with Two Warts

1974. Japanese Folk Tales (5th series). "Kobutori-Jiisan".

1362 **797** 20y. multicoloured 40 30
1363 **798** 20y. multicoloured 40 30
1364 **799** 20y. multicoloured 40 30

800 Map of World

1974. 61st Inter-Parliamentary Union Congress, Tokyo. Multicoloured.

1365 20y. Type **800** 30 10
1366 50y. "Aizen"—Mandarins in pond (Kawabata) (48×33 mm) 90 25

802 "Pine and Northern Goshawk" (detail, Sesson)

1974. International Correspondence Week.

1367 **802** 50y. brown and purple 1·00 25

803 U.P.U. Emblem

1974. Centenary of U.P.U. Multicoloured.

1368 20y. Type **803** 40 10
1369 50y. "Tending a Cow" (fan-painting—Sotatsu Tawaraya) (50×29 mm) 90 25

805 Footballers

1974. 29th National Athletic Meeting.

1370 **805** 10y. multicoloured 40 30

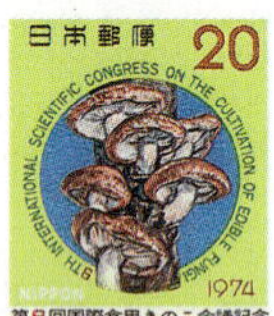

806 Shii-take Mushrooms

1974. 9th International Scientific Congress on Cultivation of Edible Fungi.

1371 **806** 20y. multicoloured 50 10

1974. Nature Conservation (4th series). As T 783. Multicoloured.

1372 20y. Bonin Islands flying fox ("Pteropus pselaphon") 80 30

808 Class D51 Locomotive

809 Class C57 Locomotive

1974. Railway Steam Locomotives (1st series).

1373 **808** 20y. multicoloured 65 10
1374 **809** 20y. multicoloured 65 10

See also Nos. 1382/3, 1385/6, 1395/6 and 1398/9.

810 "Kugikakushi" (ornamental nail-covering) in the form of a daffodil

1974. New Year's Greetings.

1375 **810** 10y. multicoloured 40 25

1975. Nature Conservation (5th series). As T 783. Multicoloured.

1377 20y. Short-tailed albatrosses ("Diomedea albatrus") (vert) 1·00 10

812 Taro releasing Tortoise

813 Sea-God's Palace

814 Taro and Pandora's Box

1975. Japanese Folk Tales (6th series). "Urashima Taro".

1378 **812** 20y. multicoloured 40 10
1379 **813** 20y. multicoloured 40 10
1380 **814** 20y. multicoloured 40 10

1975. Nature Conservation (6th series). As T 783. Multicoloured.

1381 20y. Manchurian cranes ("Grus japonensis") (vert) 1·00 25

816 Class C58 Locomotive

817 Class D52 Locomotive

1975. Railway Steam Locomotives (2nd series).

1382 **816** 20y. multicoloured 80 25
1383 **817** 20y. multicoloured 80 25

818 "Sight and Hearing" (Shiko Munakata)

1975. 50th Anniv of Japanese Broadcasting Corporation.

1384 **818** 20y. multicoloured 40 25

819 Class 8620 Locomotive No. 68622

820 Class C11 Locomotive

1975. Railway Steam Locomotives (3rd series).

1385 **819** 20y. multicoloured 80 25
1386 **820** 20y. multicoloured 80 25

821 Old Man feeding Mouse

822 Old Man holding Mouse's Tail

823 Mice giving Feast to Old Man

1975. Japanese Folk Tales (7th series). "Nezumi No Jodo".

1387 **821** 20y. multicoloured 40 25
1388 **822** 20y. multicoloured 40 25
1389 **823** 20y. multicoloured 40 25

824/5 Matsuura Screen

1975. Philatelic Week.

1390 **824** 20y. multicoloured 40 25
1391 **825** 20y. multicoloured 40 25

Nos. 1390/1 were issued together, se-tenant, forming the composite design shown.

827 Oil Rigs

1975. 9th World Petroleum Congress, Tokyo.

1394 **827** 20y. multicoloured 40 25

828 Class 9600 Locomotive No. 69820

829 Class C51 Locomotive No. 225

1975. Railway Steam Locomotives (4th series).

1395 **828** 20y. multicoloured 80 25
1396 **829** 20y. multicoloured 80 25

830 Plantation

1975. National Land Afforestation Campaign.

1397 **830** 20y. multicoloured 40 25

831 Class 7100 Locomotive "Benkei", 1880

832 Class 150 Locomotive, 1872

1975. Railway Steam Locomotives (5th series).

1398	**831**	20y. black and buff	80	25
1399	**832**	20y. black and yellow	80	25

833 Woman's Head and I.W.Y. Emblem

1975. International Women's Year.

1400	**833**	20y. multicoloured	40	25

834 Okinawa Dance

1975. International Ocean Exposition, Okinawa (2nd issue). Multicoloured.

1401	20y. Type **834**	40	25
1402	30y. Bingata textile pattern	60	25
1403	50y. "Aquapolis and Globe" emblem (48×34 mm)	90	30
MS1404	144×94 mm. Nos. 1401/3	2·00	1·60

1975. Nature Conservation (7th series). As T 783. Multicoloured.

1405	20y. Bonin Island honey-eater ("Apalopteron familiare")	1·00	25

838 Kentoshisen (7th–9th centuries)

839 Kenminsen (7th–9th centuries)

1975. Japanese Ships (1st series).

1406	**838**	20y. red	70	25
1407	**839**	20y. brown	70	25

See also Nos. 1409/10, 1420/1, 1423/4, 1428/9 and 1431/2.

840 Apple

1975. Centenary of Apple Cultivation in Japan.

1408	**840**	20y. multicoloured	40	25

841 Goshuin-sen (16th-century trading ship)

842 "Tenchi-maru" (state barge), 1630

1975. Japanese Ships (2nd series).

1409	**841**	20y. green	70	25
1410	**842**	20y. blue	70	25

843 "Green Peafowl" (after K. Ogata)

1975. International Correspondence Week.

1411	**843**	50y. multicoloured	1·20	30

844 United States Flag

1975. American Tour by Emperor Hirohito and Empress Nagako. Multicoloured.

1412	20y. Type **844**	40	25
1413	20y. Japanese flag	40	25
MS1414	146×93 mm. Nos. 1412/3	1·90	1·50

846 Savings Box

1975. Centenary of Japanese Post Office Savings Bank.

1415	**846**	20y. multicoloured	40	25

847 Weightlifting

1975. 30th National Athletic Meeting.

1416	**847**	10y. multicoloured	40	25

848 "Tatsu- guruma" (toy)

1975. New Year's Greetings.

1417	**848**	10y. multicoloured	60	25

1976. Nature Conservation (8th series). As T 783. Multicoloured.

1419	50y. Ryukyu robin ("Erithacus komadori")	1·20	25

850 Sengoku-bune (fishing boat)

851 "Shohei Maru" (sail warship)

1976. Japanese Ships (3rd series).

1420	**850**	50y. blue	1·00	25
1421	**851**	50y. violet	1·00	25

1976. Nature Conservation (9th series). As T 783. Multicoloured.

1422	50y. Tortoise ("Goemyda spengleri")	1·00	10

853 "Taisei Maru" (cadet ship)

854 "Tenyo Maru" (liner)

1976. Japanese Ships (4th series).

1423	**853**	50y. black	1·00	25
1424	**854**	50y. brown	1·00	25

855 Section of Hikone Folding Screen

1976. Philatelic Week. Multicoloured.

1425	50y. Type **855**	70	25
1426	50y. Similar to Type **855**	70	25

NOTE: The two stamps form a composite design of the "Hikone Folding Screen".

857 Cedar Forest, Plum Blossom, and Mt. Tsukuba

1976. National Land Afforestation Campaign.

1427	**857**	50y. multicoloured	70	10

858 "Asama Maru" (liner)

859 "Kinai Maru" (cargo liner)

1976. Japanese Ships (5th series).

1428	**858**	50y. green	1·00	25
1429	**859**	50y. brown	1·00	25

1976. Nature Conservation (10th series). As T 783. Multicoloured.

1430	50y. Green tree frog ("Racophorus arboreus") (vert)	1·10	25

861 "Kamakura Maru" (container ship)

862 "Nissei Maru" (oil tanker)

1976. Japanese Ships (6th series).

1431	**861**	50y. blue	1·00	25
1432	**862**	50y. blue	1·00	25

1976. Nature Conservation (11th and 12th series). As T 783. Multicoloured.

1433	50y. Tokyo bitterling ("Tanakia tanago")	1·10	25
1434	50y. Three-spined sticklebacks ("Gasterosteus aculeatus")	1·10	25

865 "Kite and Rooks" (detail, Yosa Buson)

1976. International Correspondence Week.

1435	**865**	100y. multicoloured	1·90	25

866 Gymnastics

1976. 31st National Athletic Meeting.

1436	**866**	20y. multicoloured	40	25

867 "KDD Maru" (cable ship) laying cable

1976. Opening of Sino-Japanese Cable.

1437	**867**	50y. multicoloured	1·00	25

868 Man-zai-raku (classical dance)

1976. Golden Jubilee of Emperor's Accession.

1438	**868**	50y. multicoloured	70	25
1439	-	50y. red, gold and black	70	25
MS1440		144×93 mm. Nos. 1438/9	1·90	1·50

DESIGN: No. 2439, Coronation coach.

870 Children at First Kindergarten

1976. Centenary of First Kindergarten. Tokyo.

1441	**870**	50y. multicoloured	70	25

871 Family Group

1976. 50th Anniv (1977) of Health Insurance System.
1442 **871** 50y. multicoloured 70 25

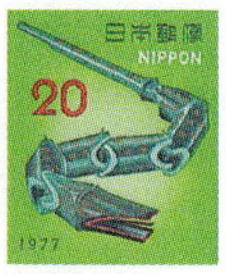

872 Bamboo Snake

1976. New Year's Greetings.
1443 **872** 20y. multicoloured 50 25

873 East Pagoda, Yakushi Temple

1976. National Treasures (1st series). Mult.
1445 50y. Type **873** 1·20 30
1446 100y. Deva King, Todai Temple (33×48 mm) 2·20 45

See also Nos. 1447/8, 1452/3, 1463/4, 1471/2, 1480/1 and 1486/9.

875 Golden Pavilion, Toshodai Temple

1977. National Treasures (2nd series). Mult.
1447 50y. Type **875** 1·20 30
1448 100y. Illustration from "Heike Nokyo Sutra" (33×48 mm) 2·40 45

1977. Nature Conservation (13th series). As T 783. Multicoloured.
1449 50y. Horseshoe crabs ("Tachypleus tridentatus") 1·00 10

878 Figure Skating

879 Figure Skating

1977. World Figure Skating Championships, Tokyo.
1450 **878** 50y. multicoloured 70 25
1451 **879** 50y. multicoloured 70 25

880 Detail of Picture Scroll (attr. Toba Sojo Kakuyu)

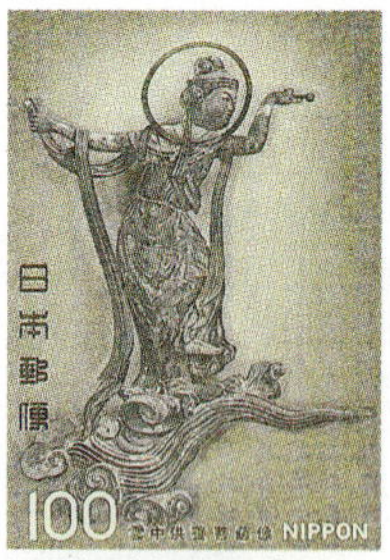

881 Wood Carving of Buddhist Saint (attr. Jocho) Byodoin Temple, Uji

1977. National Treasures (3rd series).
1452 **880** 50y. multicoloured 80 25
1453 **881** 100y. dp brn, brn & grn 2·00 30

882 Forest in Sunshine

1977. National Land Afforestation Campaign.
1454 **882** 50y. multicoloured 1·00 10

883/4 "Women" Weavers (part)

1977. Philatelic Week.
1455 **883** 50y. multicoloured 70 25
1456 **884** 50y. multicoloured 70 25

Nos. 1455/6 were issued in se-tenant pairs, forming a composite design.

1977. Nature Conservation (14th series). As T 783. Multicoloured.
1457 50y. Mikado swallowtail ("Graphium doson") (vert) 1·00 25

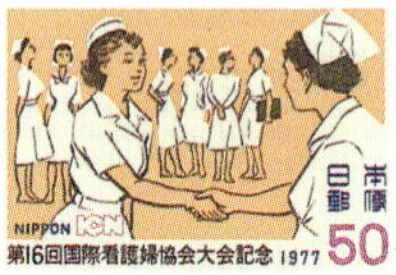

886 Nurses

1977. 16th Congress of the International Council of Nurses.
1458 **886** 50y. multicoloured 70 25

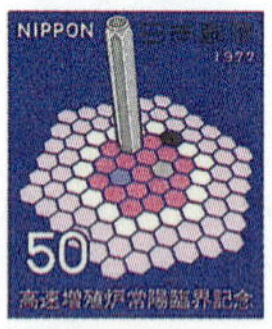

887 Central Part of Nuclear Reactor

1977. Reaching of Critical Mass by Joyo Fast-Breeder Reactor, Oarai Town.
1459 **887** 50y. multicoloured 70 25

888 Carrier Pigeons and Mail Box with U.P.U. Emblem

889 U.P.U. Emblem and World Map

1977. Centenary of Japan's Admission to U.P.U.
1460 **888** 50y. multicoloured 70 25
1461 **889** 100y. multicoloured 1·80 30
MS1462 144×93 mm. Nos. 1460/1 2·40 1·90

890 Illustration from "Picture Scroll of Lady Murasaki's Diary"

891 Statue of Seitaka Doji

1977. National Treasures (4th series).
1463 **890** 50y. multicoloured 70 25
1464 **891** 100y. brown, deep brown and light brown 1·80 30

892 Green Cross (safety emblem) and Workmen

1977. National Safety Week. Multicoloured.
1465 50y. Type **892** 1·10 25
1466 50y. Worker and high-rise building 1·10 25
1467 50y. Unloading freight 1·10 25
1468 50y. Machine-worker 1·10 25

1977. Nature Conservation (15th series). As T 783. Multicoloured.
1469 50y. Firefly ("Luciola cruciata") 1·00 10

1977. Nature Conservation (16th series). As T 783. Multicoloured.
1470 50y. Cicada ("Euterpnosia chibensis") 1·00 10

898 Drawing of Han Shan by Kao

899 Matsumoto Castle

1977. National Treasures (5th series).
1471 **898** 50y. multicoloured 70 25
1472 **899** 100y. multicoloured 1·80 30

900 Map and Child on Telephone

1977. Opening of Okinawa–Luzon–Hong Kong Submarine Cable.
1473 **900** 50y. multicoloured 70 10

901 Surgeon

1977. 27th Congress of International Society of Surgeons.
1474 **901** 50y. multicoloured 70 15

1977. Nature Conservation (17th series). As T 783. Multicoloured.
1475 50y. Dragonfly ("Boninthemis insularis") (vert) 1·00 25

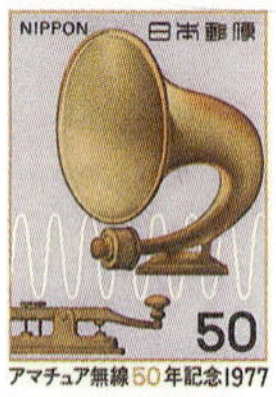

903 Horn-shaped Speaker and Telegraph Key

1977. 50th Anniv of Amateur Radio League.
1476 **903** 50y. multicoloured 70 10

904 Racing Cyclist and Mt. Iwaki

1977. 32nd National Athletic Meeting.
1477 **904** 20y. multicoloured 40 30

905 "Kacho-zu" (Nobuharu Hasegawa)

1977. International Correspondence Week.
1478 **905** 100y. multicoloured 2·00 25

906 Long-necked Dinosaur and Museum

1977. Centenary of National Science Museum.
1479 **906** 50y. multicoloured 2·00 30

907 Detail, Folding Screen, Chishakuin Temple, Kyoto

908 Kiyomizu-dera Temple

1977. National Treasures (6th series).
1480 **907** 50y. multicoloured 70 25
1481 **908** 100y. brown, green & bl 1·70 30

909 Toy Horse

1977. New Year's Greetings.
1482 **909** 20y. multicoloured 50 10

910 Underground Train, 1927

911 Underground Train No. 1101, 1977

1977. 50th Anniv of Japanese Underground Railway.
1484 **910** 50y. multicoloured 1·00 25
1485 **911** 50y. multicoloured 1·00 25

912 Genji's Carriage at Sumiyoshi Shrine (scene on folding screen (Sotatsu Tawaraya) from "Tale of Genji" by Lady Murasaki)

913 Inkstone Case (Koetsu Honami)

1978. National Treasures (7th series).
1486 **912** 50y. multicoloured 70 25
1487 **913** 100y. multicoloured 1·70 30

914 "Noryozu" (Morikage Kusumi)

915 Yomei Gate, Tosho Shrine, Nikko

1978. National Treasures (8th series).
1488 **914** 50y. multicoloured 70 25
1489 **915** 100y. multicoloured 1·70 30

916 "Primula sieboldi"

1978. Nature Conservation (18th series).
1490 **916** 50y. multicoloured 90 25

917 Seated Woman With Flower (hanging scroll)

918 Dancing Woman (hanging scroll)

1978. Philatelic Week. "Kanbun Bijinzu" Genre Paintings.
1491 **917** 50y. multicoloured 70 30
1492 **918** 50y. multicoloured 70 30

919 Rotary Emblem and Mt. Fuji (from "36 Views of Mt. Fuji" by Hokusai Katsushita)

1978. Rotary International Convention, Tokyo.
1493 **919** 50y. multicoloured 1·00 10

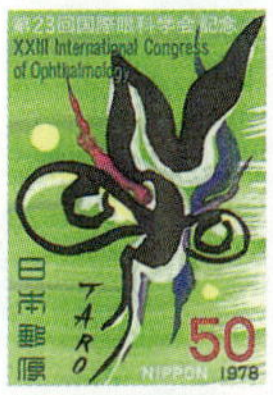
920 Congress Emblem

1978. 23rd Int Ophthalmological Congress.
1494 **920** 50y. multicoloured 70 10

921 Passenger Terminal Buildings

1978. Opening of Narita Airport, Tokyo.
1495 **921** 50y. multicoloured 80 10

922 Cape Ashizuri, Rainbow and Cedar Trees

1978. National Afforestation Campaign.
1496 **922** 50y. multicoloured 70 10

923 "Pinguicula ramosa"

1978. Nature Conservation (19th series).
1497 **923** 50y. multicoloured 90 25

924 "Karashishi" (attr. Sotatsu Tawaraya) and Lions Emblem

1978. 61st Lions International Convention, Tokyo.
1498 **924** 50y. multicoloured 1·00 10

925/6 "Grand Champion Raigoyo Hidenoyama in the Ring" (Toyokuni III)

927 "Drum Tower of Ekoin Temple, Ryogoku" (Hiroshige)

1978. Sumo (Japanese Wrestling) Pictures (1st series).
1499 **925** 50y. multicoloured 70 30
1500 **926** 50y. multicoloured 70 30
1501 **927** 50y. multicoloured 70 30

Nos. 1499/500 were issued together, se-tenant, forming the composite design illustrated.

See also Nos. 1505/7, 1513/15, 1519/21 and 1523/5.

928 "Dicentra peregrina"

1978. Nature Conservation (20th series).
1502 **928** 50y. multicoloured 90 25

929 Keep Fit Exercise

1978. 50th Anniv of Radio Gymnastic Exercises.
1503 **929** 50y. multicoloured 1·60 10

930 Chamber of Commerce and Industry Building and Centenary Emblem

1978. Centenary of 1st Chambers of Commerce, Tokyo and Osaka.
1504 **930** 50y. multicoloured 70 10

931/2 "Dohyoiri" wrestlers Tanikaze and Onogawa (Shunsho Katsukawa)

933 "Jinmaku versus Raiden" (Shunnei Katsukawa)

1978. Sumo Pictures (2nd series).
1505 **931** 50y. multicoloured 70 30
1506 **932** 50y. multicoloured 70 30
1507 **933** 50y. multicoloured 70 30

Nos. 1505/6 were issued together se-tenant, forming the composite design illustrated.

934 Statues on Tokyo Securities Exchange Building

1978. Centenary of Tokyo and Osaka Stock Exchanges.
1508 **934** 50y. brown, purple & grn 70 10

935 Copper Pheasant (detail of door painting attr. Sanraku Kano)

1978. International Correspondence Week.
1509 **935** 100y. multicoloured 2·50 25

936 Mt. Yari and Softball Players

1978. 33rd National Athletic Meeting.
1510 **936** 20y. multicoloured 40 30

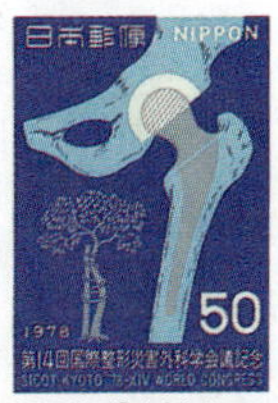
937 Artificial Joint

1978. 14th Congress of International Society of Orthopaedic and Traumatic Surgeons, Kyoto.
1511 **937** 50y. blue, ultram & silver 70 15

938 Refracting Telescope and Stars

1978. Centenary of Tokyo Astronomical Observatory.

1512	**938**	50y. multicoloured	70	10

939/40 "The then Heroic Champion's Sumo Wrestling" (detail, Toyokuni III)

941 "Children's Charming Sumo Play" (Utamaro Kitagawa)

1978. Sumo Pictures (3rd series).

1513	**939**	50y. multicoloured	70	30
1514	**940**	50y. multicoloured	70	30
1515	**941**	50y. multicoloured	70	30

Nos. 1513/14 were issued together se-tenant, forming the composite design Illustrated.

942 Sheep Bell (folk toy)

1978. New Year's Greetings.

1516	**942**	20y. multicoloured	50	10

943 Family and Human Rights Emblem

1978. 30th Anniv of Declaration of Human Rights.

1518	**943**	50y. multicoloured	70	10

944/5 "Great Sumo Wrestlers crossing Ryogoku Bridge" (Toyokuni III)

946 "Yumitori Ceremony at Grand Fund-raising Tournament" (Kunisada II)

1979. Sumo Pictures. (4th series).

1519	**944**	50y. multicoloured	70	30
1520	**945**	50y. multicoloured	70	30
1521	**946**	50y. multicoloured	70	30

Nos. 1519/20 were issued together se-tenant, forming the composite design illustrated.

947 Hands protecting Children

1979. Education for the Handicapped.

1522	**947**	50y. multicoloured	70	25

948/9 "Takekuma versus Iwamigata" (Kuniyoshi Utagawa)

950 "Daidozan's Dohyoiri" (Sharaku Toshusai)

1979. Sumo Pictures (5th series).

1523	**948**	50y. multicoloured	70	30
1524	**949**	50y. multicoloured	70	30
1525	**950**	50y. multicoloured	70	30

Nos. 1523/4 were issued together se-tenant, forming the composite design illustrated.

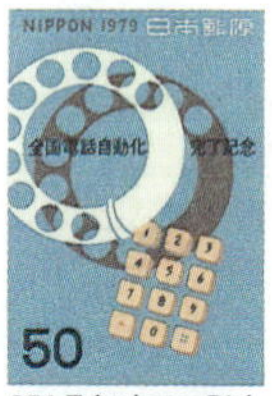

951 Telephone Dial and Pushbuttons

1979. Telephone Automation Completion.

1526	**951**	50y. multicoloured	70	10

952 Drawing by Leonardo da Vinci

1979. Centenary of Western Medicine in Japan.

1527	**952**	50y. multicoloured	70	10

953 "Standing Beauties" (Kaigetsudo School)

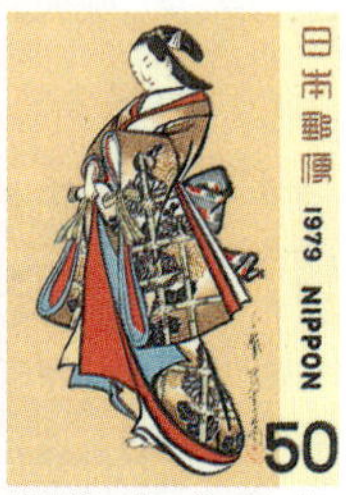

954 "Standing Beauties" (Kaigetsudo School)

1979. Philatelic Week.

1528	**953**	50y. multicoloured	70	25
1529	**954**	50y. multicoloured	70	25

955 Mt. Horaiji and Maple Leaves

1979. National Afforestation Campaign.

1530	**955**	50y. multicoloured	70	10

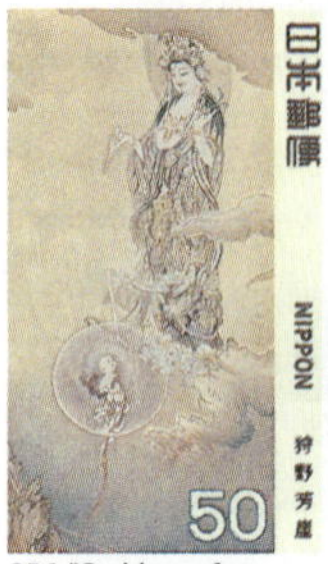

956 "Goddess of Maternal Mercy" (Kano Hogai)

957 "The Princess of the Sea God" (Aoki Shigeru)

1979. Modern Japanese Art (1st series).

1531	**956**	50y. multicoloured	90	25
1532	**957**	50y. multicoloured	80	25

See also Nos. 1533/4. 1544/5, 1550/1, 1558/9, 1567/8, 1574/5, 1610/11, 1618/19, 1628/9, 1650/1, 1656/7, 1675/6, 1689/90, 1693/4 and 1697/8.

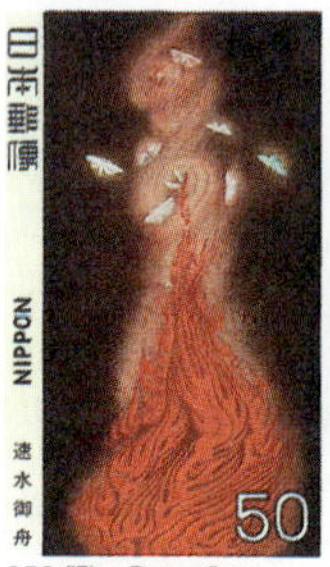

958 "Fire Dance" (Gyosha Hayami)

959 "Leaning Figure" (Tetsugoro Yorozu)

1979. Modern Japanese Art (2nd series).

1533	**958**	50y. multicoloured	1·20	25
1534	**959**	50y. multicoloured	1·20	25

960 Quarantine Officers

1979. Centenary of Quarantine System.

1535	**960**	50y. multicoloured	1·00	10

961 Girl with Letter

962 Hakata Doll

1979. Letter writing Day.

1536	**961**	20y. multicoloured	40	25
1537	**962**	50y. multicoloured	70	25

963 Baseball Pitcher and Ball

1979. 50th National Inter-City Amateur Baseball Tournament.

1538	**963**	50y. multicoloured	70	15

964 Girl collecting Stars

965 Boy catching Toy Insects

1979. International Year of the Child.

1539	**964**	50y. multicoloured	1·00	15
1540	**965**	50y. multicoloured	1·00	15
MS1541		144×93 mm. Nos. 1539/40	2·40	1·90

966 "The Moon over the Castle Ruins" (Bansui Doi and Rentaro Taki)

967 "Evening Glow" (Uko Nakamura and Shin Kusakawa)

1979. Japanese Songs (1st series).

1542	**966**	50y. multicoloured	70	25
1543	**967**	50y. multicoloured	70	25

See also Nos. 1552/3, 1556/7, 1561/2, 1565/6, 1572/3, 1580/1, 1616/17 and 1620/1.

968 "Black Cat" (Shunso Hishida)

969 "Kinyo" (Sotaro Yasui)

1979. Modern Japanese Art (3rd series).

1544	**968**	50y. multicoloured	1·10	25
1545	**969**	50y. multicoloured	1·10	25

970 "Steep Mountains and the Dark Dale" (Okyo Maruyama)

1979. International Correspondence Week.

1546	**970**	100y. multicoloured	2·50	25

971 Long Distance Runner

1979. 34th National Athletic Meeting, Miyazaki.

1547	**971**	20y. multicoloured	70	10

972 "ITU" and Globe

1979. Centenary of Admission to International Telecommunications Union.
1548 **972** 50y. multicoloured 70 10

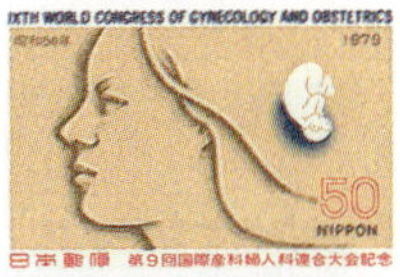

973 Woman and Embryo

1979. 9th International Obstetrics and Gynaecology Convention, Tokyo.
1549 **973** 50y. multicoloured 70 25

974 "Nude" (Kagaku Murakami)

975 "Harvest" (Asai Chu)

1979. Modern Japanese Art (4th series).
1550 **974** 50y. multicoloured 70 25
1551 **975** 50y. multicoloured 50 10

976 "Maple Leaves" (Tatsuyuki Takano and Teiichi Okano)
977 "Birthplace" (Tatsuyuki Takano and Teiichi Okano)

1979. Japanese Songs (2nd series).
1552 **976** 50y. multicoloured 50 10
1553 **977** 50y. multicoloured 50 10

978 "Happy Monkeys" (folk toy)

1979. New Year's Greeting.
1554 **978** 20y. multicoloured 50 10

979 "Winter Scene" (anon)

980 "Mount Fuji" (anon)

1980. Japanese Songs (3rd series).
1556 **979** 50y. multicoloured 1·00 25
1557 **980** 50y. multicoloured 1·00 25

981 "Salmon" (Yuichi Takahashi)
982 "Hall of the Supreme Buddha" (Kokei Kobayashi)

1980. Modern Japanese Art (5th series).
1558 **981** 50y. multicoloured 1·20 25
1559 **982** 50y. multicoloured 1·20 25

983 Scales

1980. Centenary of Government Auditing Bureau.
1560 **983** 50y. multicoloured 70 10

984 "Spring Brook" (Tatsuyuki Takano and Teiichi Okano)

985 "Cherry Blossoms" (anon)

1980. Japanese Songs (4th series).
1561 **984** 50y. multicoloured 70 25
1562 **985** 50y. multicoloured 70 25

986 "Scenes of Outdoor Play in Spring" (Sukenobu Nishikawa)
987 "Scenes of Outdoor Play in Spring" (Sukenobu Nishikawa)

1980. Philatelic Week.
1563 **986** 50y. multicoloured 70 25
1564 **987** 50y. multicoloured 70 25

988 "Sea" (Ryuha Hayashi and Takeshi Inoue)
989 "Misty Moonlight Night" (Tatsuyuki Takano and Teiichi Okano)

1980. Japanese Songs (5th series).
1565 **988** 50y. multicoloured 70 25
1566 **989** 50y. multicoloured 70 25

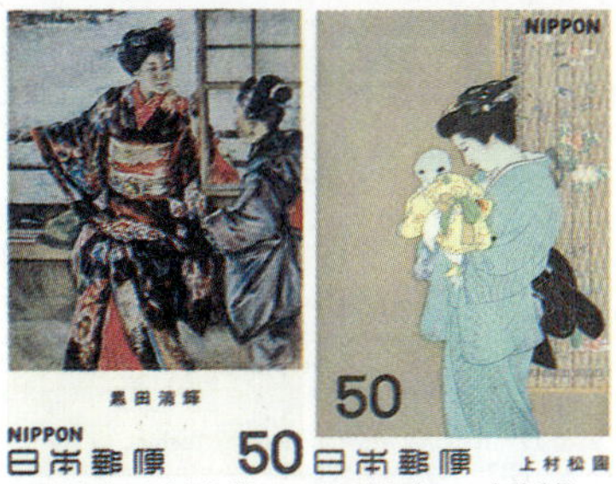

990 "Maiko Girls" (Seiki Kuroda)
991 "Mother and Child" (Shoen Uemura)

1980. Modern Japanese Art (6th series).
1567 **990** 50y. multicoloured 70 25
1568 **991** 50y. multicoloured 70 25

992 "Nippon Maru I"

1980. 50th Anniv of Training Cadet Ships "Nippon Maru I" and "Kaio Maru".
1569 **992** 50y. multicoloured 1·20 10

993 Mount Gozaisho and Cedars

1980. National Afforestation Campaign.
1570 **993** 50y. multicoloured 80 30

994 "Acrobatic Performances on a Ladder at New Year's Parade of Yayosu Fire Brigades" (Hiroshige III)

1980. Centenary of Fire Fighting System.
1571 **994** 50y. multicoloured 80 30

995 "The Sun" (Tatsuyuki Takano and Teiichi Okano)
996 "Memories of Summer" (Shoko Ema and Yoshinao Nakata)

1980. Japanese Songs (6th series).
1572 **995** 50y. multicoloured 80 25
1573 **996** 50y. multicoloured 80 25

997 "Black Fan" (Takeji Fujishima)
998 "The Dance 'Are Yudachi ni'" (Seiho Takeuchi)

1980. Modern Japanese Art (7th series).
1574 **997** 50y. multicoloured 80 25
1575 **998** 50y. multicoloured 80 25

999 Teddy Bear holding Letter
1000 Knotted Letter

1980. Letter Writing Day.
1576 **999** 20y. multicoloured 50 30
1577 **1000** 50y. multicoloured 1·00 25

1001 "Luehdorfia japonica"

1980. 16th International Congress of Entomology, Kyoto.
1578 **1001** 50y. multicoloured 90 30

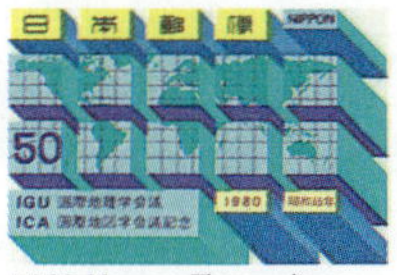

1002 Map on Three- dimensional Graph

1980. 24th International Geographical Congress and 10th International Cartographic Conference, Tokyo.
1579 **1002** 50y. multicoloured 80 30

1003 "Red Dragonfly" (Rofu Miki and Kosaku Yamada)
1004 "Song by the Sea" (Kokui Hayashi and Tamezo Narita)

1980. Japanese Songs (7th series).
1580 **1003** 50y. multicoloured 80 25
1581 **1004** 50y. multicoloured 80 25

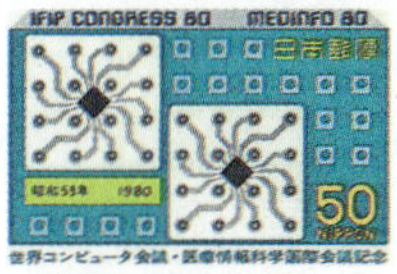

1005 Integrated Circuit

1980. 8th World Computer Congress and Third World Conference on Medical Informatics, Tokyo.
1582 **1005** 50y. multicoloured 80 30

1006 Akita Dog
1007 Adonis
1008 Lily

1009 Camellia
1010 Small Cabbage Whites on Rape Blossom
1011 Japanese Babylonia

1012 Noble Scallops
1013 Flowering Cherry
1014 Hanging Bell, Byodoin Temple, Uji

1015 Yoka Star Shell

1016 Precious Wentletrap

1017 Flautist, Horyu Temple

1018 Deer (from lacquer writing box)

1019 Mirror with Figures

1020 Heart-shaped Earthen Figurine

1021 Silver Crane, Kasuga Taisha Shrine, Nara

1022 Miroku Bosatsu, Horyu Temple

1023 Dainichi Buddha, Chuson Temple

1024 Keiki Doji, Kongobu Temple

1025 Komoku Ten, Todai Temple, Nara

1026 Lady Maya, Horyu Temple

1027 Tea Jar with Wisteria Decoration (Ninsei Nonomura)

1028 Miroku Bosatsu

1980. 41y. and 62y. perf or imperf (self-adhesive), others perf.

1582a	**1006**	2y. blue	10	10
1583	**1007**	10y. yellow, grn & brn	20	15
1584	**1008**	20y. yellow, blue & grn	30	15
1585	**1009**	30y. multicoloured	55	20
1586	**1010**	40y. multicoloured	50	15
1587	**1011**	40y. multicoloured	85	25
1588	**1012**	41y. multicoloured	70	20
1589	**1013**	50y. multicoloured	80	15
1590	**1014**	60y. green and black	70	10
1591	**1015**	60y. multicoloured	1·00	10
1592	**1016**	62y. multicoloured	1·10	20
1593	**1017**	70y. blue and yellow	1·30	30
1594	**1018**	70y. yellow, black & bl	80	15
1594a	**1018**	72y. yellow, black & bl	80	15
1595	**1019**	80y. green and black	1·50	10
1596	**1020**	90y. yellow, blk & grn	1·60	10
1597	**1021**	100y. black, blue and ultramarine	90	10
1598	**1022**	170y. purple and bistre	2·00	15
1599	**1022**	175y. brown, grn & bis	1·90	15
1600	-	210y. orange and lilac (as No. 1242)	2·30	15
1601	**1023**	260y. brown and red	3·00	15
1602	**1024**	300y. brown	3·50	10
1603	**1025**	310y. brown and violet	3·50	10
1604	-	360y. purple and pink (as No. 1246)	4·00	25
1605	**1026**	410y. orange and blue	6·50	30
1606	**1027**	410y. multicoloured	6·75	20
1607	**1028**	600y. yellow, purple and lilac	7·00	15

1031 "Manchurian Cranes" (door painting, Motooki Watanabe)

1980. International Correspondence Week.

1608	**1031**	100y. multicoloured	1·90	30

1032 Archery and Mt. Nantai

1980. 35th National Athletic Meeting, Tochigi.

1609	**1032**	20y. multicoloured	40	25

1033 "Woman" (sculpture, Morie Ogiwara)

1034 "Woman of the Kurofune-ya" (Yumeji Takehisa)

1980. Modern Japanese Art (8th series).

1610	**1033**	50y. multicoloured	80	25
1611	**1034**	50y. multicoloured	80	25

1035 "Energy"

1980. 35th World Congress of Junior Chambers of Commerce, Osaka.

1612	**1035**	50y. multicoloured	80	30

1036 Diet Building and Doves

1980. 90th Anniv of Japanese Diet.

1613	**1036**	50y. multicoloured	1·00	10

1037 Toy Rooster

1980. New Year's Greetings.

1614	**1037**	20y. multicoloured	50	10

1038 "Komori-Uta" (nursery song)

1039 "Coconut" (Toson Shimazaki and Toraji Ohaka)

1981. Japanese Songs (8th series).

1616	**1038**	60y. multicoloured	80	25
1617	**1039**	60y. multicoloured	80	25

1040 "Power Station in the Snow" (Shiskanosuke Oka)

1041 "Nukada-no-Okimi of Asuka in Spring" (Yukihiko Yasuda)

1981. Modern Japanese Art (9th series).

1618	**1040**	60y. multicoloured	1·10	30
1619	**1041**	60y. multicoloured	1·10	30

1042 "Spring has Come" (Tatsuyuki Takano and Teiichi Okano)

1043 "Cherry Blossoms" (Hagoromo Takeshima and Rentaro Taki)

1981. Japanese Songs (9th series).

1620	**1042**	60y. multicoloured	1·10	25
1621	**1043**	60y. multicoloured	1·10	25

1044 Port Island and Exposition Emblem

1981. Kobe Port Island Exposition, Kobe City.

1622	**1044**	60y. multicoloured	1·00	30

1045 Cereal, Tree and Fish on "100"

1981. Centenary of Agricultural, Forestry and Fishery Promotion.

1623	**1045**	60y. multicoloured	1·20	10

1046/7 "Yugao" (Lady of the Evening Roses) and Genji

1981. Philatelic Week. Details of Harunobu Suzuki's Illustrations of "Tale of Genji" by Lady Murasaki.

1624	**1046**	60y. multicoloured	1·00	30
1625	**1047**	60y. multicoloured	1·00	30

Nos. 1624/5 were issued together, se-tenant, forming a composite design.

1048 Pagodas at Nara and Double Cherry Blossom

1981. National Afforestation Campaign.

1626	**1048**	60y. multicoloured	1·00	30

1049 Container Ship and Crane

1981. 12th International Port and Harbour Association Conference.

1627	**1049**	60y. multicoloured	1·00	10

1050 "N's Family" (Narashinge Koide)

1051 "Bamboo Shoots" (Heihachiro Fukuda)

1981. Modern Japanese Art (10th series).

1628	**1050**	60y. multicoloured	80	25
1629	**1051**	60y. multicoloured	80	25

1052 Stylized Debris Barriers

1981. Centenary of Land Erosion Control.

1630	**1052**	60y. multicoloured	1·00	25

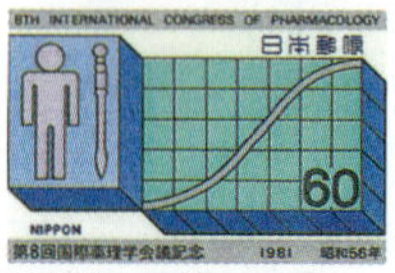
1053 Human Figure and Dose Response Chart

1981. 8th International Congress of Pharmacology, Tokyo.

1631	**1053**	60y. multicoloured	1·00	30

1054 Girl writing Letter

1055 Boy with Pencil and Stamp

1981. Letter Writing Day.

1632	**1054**	40y. multicoloured	70	30
1633	**1055**	60y. multicoloured	1·00	25

1056 Japanese Crested Ibis

1981. 50th Anniv of National Parks.

1634	**1056**	60y. multicoloured	1·10	30

1057 Electric Plug and dripping Tap

1058 Energy Recycling

1981. Energy Conservation.

1635	**1057**	40y. dp blue, lilac & bl	80	30
1636	**1058**	60y. multicoloured	1·20	25

1059 Oura Cathedral, Nagasaki

1060 Hyokei Hall, Tokyo

1981. Modern Western-style Architecture (1st series).

1637	**1059**	60y. multicoloured	1·00	30
1638	**1060**	60y. multicoloured	1·00	30

See also Nos. 1648/9, 1654/5, 1658/9, 1669/70, 1680/1, 1695/6, 1705/6, 1710/11 and 1732/3.

1061 Bluebird and I.Y.D.P. Emblem

1981. International Year of Disabled Persons.

1639	**1061**	60y.+10y. mult	1·20	30

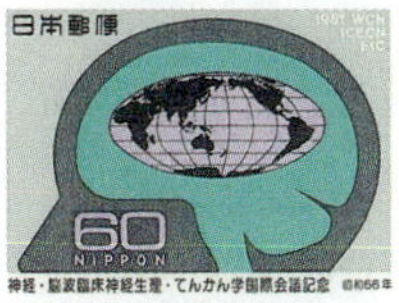

1062 Globe in Brain

1981. International Neurological Conferences, Kyoto.

1640	**1062**	60y. multicoloured	80	10

1063 Convention Emblem

1981. International Federation of Postal, Telegram and Telephone Workers' Unions World Convention, Tokyo.

1641	**1063**	60y. multicoloured	1·00	30

1064 "Eastern Turtle Doves" (Sanraku Kano)

1981. International Correspondence Week.

1642	**1064**	130y. multicoloured	2·50	30

1065 48m. Stamp 1871

1981. "Philatokyo '81" International Stamp Exhibition, Tokyo. Multicoloured, frame colour of stamp within design given.

1643	**1065**	60y. brown	90	30
1644	-	60y. blue	90	30
1645	-	60y. red	90	30
1646	-	60y. green	90	30

DESIGNS: No. 1644, 100m. stamp, 1871; 1645, 200m. stamp, 1871; 1646, 500m. stamp, 1871.

1069 Badminton and Lake Biwa

1981. 36th National Athletic Meeting, Shiga.

1647	**1069**	40y. multicoloured	70	25

1070 Former Kaichi School Matsumoto

1071 Doshisha Chapel, Kyoto

1981. Modern Western-style Architecture (2nd series).

1648	**1070**	60y. multicoloured	1·00	30
1649	**1071**	60y. multicoloured	1·00	30

1072 "Portrait of Reiko" (Ryusei Kishida)

1073 "Ichiyo" (Kiyokata Kaburagi)

1981. Modern Japanese Art (11th series).

1650	**1072**	60y. multicoloured	80	30
1651	**1073**	60y. multicoloured	80	30

1074 Clay Dog (folk toy)

1981. New Year's Greetings.

1652	**1074**	40y. multicoloured	70	10

1075 St John's Church, Inuyama

1076 Military Exercise Hall, Sapporo Agricultural School

1982. Modern Western-style Architecture (3rd series).

1654	**1075**	60y. multicoloured	1·00	30
1655	**1076**	60y. multicoloured	1·00	30

1077 "Yoritomo in a Cave" (Seison Maeda)

1078 "Posters on a Terrace" (Yuzo Saeki)

1982. Modern Japanese Art (12th series).

1656	**1077**	60y. multicoloured	80	30
1657	**1078**	60y. multicoloured	80	30

1079 Bank of Japan, Kyoto Branch (now museum)

1080 Saiseikan Hospital, Yamagata

1982. Modern Western-style Architecture (4th series).

1658	**1079**	60y. multicoloured	1·00	30
1659	**1080**	60y. multicoloured	1·00	30

1081 Gorilla and Greater Flamingo

1982. Ueno Zoo. Centenary. Multicoloured.

1660	60y. Type **1081**	90	25
1661	60y. Lion and king penguins	90	25
1662	60y. Giant panda and Indian elephants	90	25
1663	60y. Giraffe and common zebras	90	25

1085/6 "Enjoying Snow Landscape of Matsuchi-yama" (Torii Kiyonaga)

1982. Philatelic Week.

1664	**1085**	60y. multicoloured	90	30
1665	**1086**	60y. multicoloured	90	30

Nos. 1664/5 were issued together se-tenant forming the composite design illustrated.

1087 Lion

1982. 10th Anniv of Return of Okinawa (Ryukyu Islands).

1666	**1087**	60y. multicoloured	90	25

1088 Arbor Festival Emblem and Blue and White Fly-catcher

1982. National Afforestation Campaign.

1667	**1088**	60y. multicoloured	1·20	25

1089 Noh Mask

1982. 16th World Dermatology Congress, Tokyo.

1668	**1089**	60y. multicoloured	90	25

1090 Divine Gate of Oyama Shrine, Kanazawa

1091 Former Iwasaki Mansion, Taito-ku, Tokyo (now Training Institute)

1982. Modern Western-style Architecture (5th series).

1669	**1090**	60y. multicoloured	90	25
1670	**1091**	60y. multicoloured	90	25

1092 Class 1290 Locomotive "Zenko", 1881

1093 "Yamabiko" (echo) Express Train

1982. Opening of Tohoku-Shinkansen Railway Line.

1671	**1092**	60y. multicoloured	1·10	25
1672	**1093**	60y. multicoloured	1·10	25

1094 Gull and Balloon with Letter

1095 Bird carrying Letter to Fairy

1982. Letter Writing Day.

1673	**1094**	40y. multicoloured	90	30
1674	**1095**	60y. multicoloured	1·30	25

1096 "Garment Patterned with Irises" (Saburosuke Okada)

1097 "Buddhisattva Kannon on Potalaka Island" (Tessai Tomioka)

1982. Modern Japanese Art (13th series).

1675	**1096**	40y. multicoloured	90	25
1676	**1097**	60y. multicoloured	90	25

1098 Wreath (condolences)

1099 Folded Paper Crane (congratulations)

1100 Pine, Plum and Bamboo Blossom (congratulations)

1982. Special Correspondence Stamps.

1677	**1098**	60y. multicoloured	1·20	30
1678	**1099**	60y. multicoloured	1·20	30
1679	**1100**	70y. multicoloured	1·40	30

For other values see Nos. 1722/3, 2013/16 and 2289/92.

1101 Hokkaido Prefectural Building, Sapporo

1102 Saigo Tsugumichi Mansion, Meguro (now in Inuyama)

1982. Modern Western-style Architecture (6th series).

1680	**1101**	60y. multicoloured	1·40	40
1681	**1102**	60y. multicoloured	1·40	40

1103 16th-century Portuguese Galleon and World Map

1982. 400th Anniv of Christian Boys' Delegation to Europe.

1682	**1103**	60y. multicoloured	1·20	25

1104 "T'ien T'an in the Clouds" (Ryuzaburo Umehara)

1982. 10th Anniv of Restoration of Diplomatic Relations with China.

1683	**1104**	60y. multicoloured	1·00	30

1105 Table Tennis and Monument of the Meet

1982. 37th National Athletic Meeting, Matsue.

1684	**1105**	40y. multicoloured	70	30

1106 "Amusement" (wooden doll by Goyo Hirata)

1982. International Correspondence Week.

1685	**1106**	130y. multicoloured	1·90	30

1107 "Bank of Japan near Eitaibashi in Snow" (Yasuji Inoue)

1982. Centenary of Central Bank System.

1686	**1107**	60y. multicoloured	1·00	30

1108 "Asahi" (rising sun) Express Train

1109 ED 16 Electric Locomotive No. 8

1982. Opening of Joetsu–Shinkansen Railway Line.

1687	**1108**	60y. multicoloured	1·10	25
1688	**1109**	60y. multicoloured	1·10	25

1110 "Srimhadevi" (Shiko Munakata)

1111 "Saltimbanque" (Seiji Togo)

1982. Modern Japanese Art (14th series).

1689	**1110**	60y. multicoloured	90	25
1690	**1111**	60y. multicoloured	90	25

1112 "Kintaro on a Wild Boar" (clay Tsutsumi doll)

1982. New Year Greetings.

1691	**1112**	40y. multicoloured	70	25

1113 "Snowstorm" (Shinsui Ito)

1114 "Spiraea and Calla in a Perrian Vase" (Zenzaburo Kojima)

1983. Modern Japanese Art (15th series).

1692	**1113**	60y. multicoloured	75	10
1693	**1114**	60y. multicoloured	90	25

1115 Fujimura Memorial Hall, Kofu (formerly Mutsuzawa School)

1116 Porch of Sakuranomiya Public Hall, Osaka

1983. Modern Western-style Architecture (7th series).

1695	**1115**	60y. multicoloured	90	25
1696	**1116**	60y. multicoloured	90	25

1117 "Selflessness" (Taikan Yokoyama)

1118 "Aged Monkey" (wood carving, Koun Takamura)

1983. Modern Japanese Art (16th series).

1697	**1117**	60y. multicoloured	1·00	30
1698	**1118**	60y. multicoloured	1·00	30

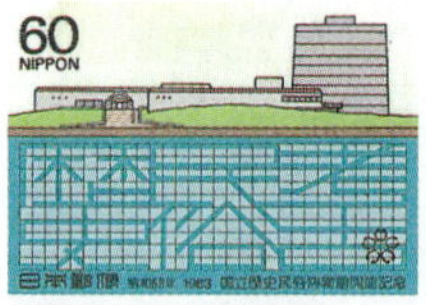

1119 Museum and Japanese Characters representing History, Folklore and Antiquity

1983. Opening of National Museum of History and Folklore.

1699	**1119**	60y. multicoloured	1·00	30

1120/1 "Women working in the Kitchen" (Utamaro Kitagawa)

1983. Philatelic Week.

1700	**1120**	60y. multicoloured	1·00	30
1701	**1121**	60y. multicoloured	1·00	30

Nos. 1695/6 were issued together, se-tenant, forming the composite design illustrated.

1122 "Hiba arborvitae", Japanese Black Fritillary and Hakusan Mountains

1983. National Afforestation Campaign.

1702	**1122**	60y. multicoloured	1·00	30

1123 Colt and Racehorse

1983. 50th Nippon Derby.

1703	**1123**	60y. multicoloured	1·20	25

1124 Rabbit and Empty Can

1983. Islands Clean-up Campaign.

1704	**1124**	60y. multicoloured	1·20	25

1125 Hohei-kan House (Wedding Hall), Sapporo

1126 Glover House, Nagasaki

1983. Modern Western-style Architecture (8th series).

1705	**1125**	60y. multicoloured	90	25
1706	**1126**	60y. multicoloured	90	25

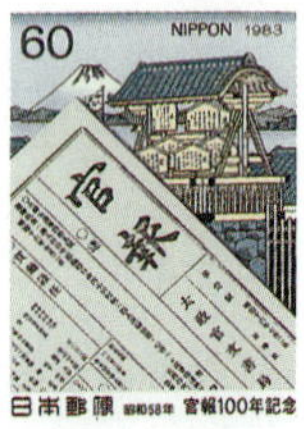

1127 First Issue and Nihonbashi Bulletin Board

1983. Centenary of "Government Journal".

1707	**1127**	60y. multicoloured	1·00	30

1128 Boy with Letter

1129 Fairy with Letter

1983. Letter Writing Day.

1708	**1128**	40y. multicoloured	70	30
1709	**1129**	60y. multicoloured	1·00	25

1130 59th Bank, Hirosaki

1131 Auditorium of Gakushuin Elementary School (now in Narita)

1983. Modern Western-style Architecture (9th series).
1710 **1130** 60y. multicoloured 90 25
1711 **1131** 60y. multicoloured 90 25

1132 Theatre and Noh Player

1983. Opening of National Noh Theatre, Tokyo.
1712 **1132** 60y. multicoloured 1·00 30

1133 Okinawa Rail

1983. Endangered Birds (1st series). Multicoloured.
1713 60y. Type **1133** 1·50 30
1714 60y. Blakiston's fish owl ("Ketupa blakistoni") (horiz) 1·50 30
See also Nos. 1724/5, 1729/30, 1735/6 and 1742/3.

1135 "Chi-kyu" (paper doll by Juzo Kagoshima)

1983. International Correspondence Week.
1715 **1135** 130y. multicoloured 1·90 40

1136 Naginata Player and Myogi Mountains

1983. 38th National Athletic Meeting, Gumman.
1716 **1136** 40y. multicoloured 70 30

1137 Ferris Wheel

1138 Children supporting Globe

1983. World Communications Year.
1717 **1137** 60y. multicoloured 1·00 30
1718 **1138** 60y. multicoloured 1·00 30

1139 Park and Monument

1983. Opening of Showa Memorial National Park.
1719 **1139** 60y. multicoloured 1·00 25

1140 Congress Emblem and Mouth Mirror

1983. 71st World Dental Congress, Tokyo.
1720 **1140** 60y. multicoloured 1·00 30

1141 "Shirase"

1983. Maiden Voyage of Antarctic Research Ship "Shirase".
1721 **1141** 60y. multicoloured 2·50 25

1983. Special Correspondence Stamps.
1722 **1098** 40y. multicoloured 80 30
1723 **1099** 40y. multicoloured 80 30

1983. Endangered Birds (2nd series). As T 1133. Multicoloured.
1724 60y. Pryer's woodpecker ("Sapheopipo noguchii") 1·40 25
1725 60y. Canada goose ("Branta canadensis leucopareia") (horiz) 1·40 25

1144 "Mouse riding a Small Hammer" (folk toy)

1983. New Year's Greetings.
1726 **1144** 40y. multicoloured 70 25

1145 Human Rights Emblem

1983. 35th Anniv of Declaration of Human Rights.
1728 **1145** 60y. multicoloured 70 25

1984. Endangered Birds (3rd series). As T 1133. Multicoloured.
1729 60y. Japanese marsh warbler ("Megalurus pryeri pryeri") (horiz) 1·00 30
1730 60y. Crested serpent eagle ("Spilornis cheela perplexus") 1·50 25

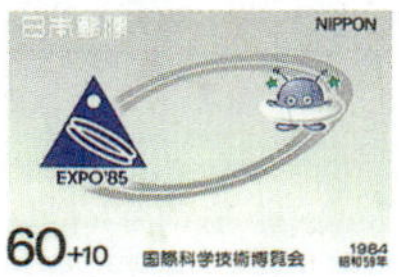
1148 Exhibition Emblem and Mascot

1984. "Expo '85" International Science and Technology Exhibition, Tsukuba (1985).
1731 **1148** 60y.+10y. mult 1·50 25

1149 Bank of Japan Head Office

1150 Hunter House, Kobe

1984. Modern Western-style Architecture (10th series).
1732 **1149** 60y. multicoloured 90 25
1733 **1150** 60y. multicoloured 90 25

1151 Japanese-style Cake and Bamboo Tea Whisk

1984. 20th Confectionery Fair, Tokyo.
1734 **1151** 60y. multicoloured 1·00 30

1984. Endangered Birds (4th series). As T 1133. Multicoloured.
1735 60y. Black wood pigeon ("Columba janthina nitens") 1·50 25
1736 60y. Spotted greenshank ("Tringa guttifer") (horiz) 1·50 25

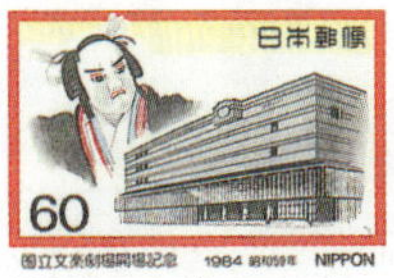
1154 Bunraku Puppet and Theatre

1984. Opening of National Bunraku Theatre, Osaka.
1737 **1154** 60y. multicoloured 1·40 40

1155 "Otani Oniji as Edobeh" (Toshusai Sharaku)

1156 "Iwai Hanshiro IV as Shigenoi" (Toshusai Sharaku)

1984. Philatelic Week.
1738 **1155** 60y. multicoloured 1·00 30
1739 **1156** 60y. multicoloured 1·00 30

1157 Kaikozu Tree and Sakura Volcano

1984. National Afforestation Campaign.
1740 **1157** 60y. multicoloured 1·00 30

1158 "Himawari" Weather Satellite and Chart

1984. Centenary of National Weather Forecasts.
1741 **1158** 60y. multicoloured 1·00 25

1984. Endangered Birds (5th series). As T 1133. Multicoloured.
1742 60y. White-backed woodpecker ("Dendrocopos leucotos owstoni") (horiz) 1·50 25
1743 60y. Peregrine falcon ("Falco peregrinus fruitii") 1·50 25

1161 Doves

1984. Federation of UNESCO Clubs and Associations World Congress, Sendai.
1744 **1161** 60y. multicoloured 1·20 25

1162 Birds in Tree

1163 Bird and Flowers

1984. Letter Writing Day.
1745 **1162** 40y. multicoloured 90 30
1746 **1163** 60y. multicoloured 1·30 25

1164 "Fire and Wind" (Motomi Hagimoto)

1165 "Bonds" (Noboru Kanda)

1984. Disaster Prevention Week.
1747 **1164** 40y. multicoloured 70 30
1748 **1165** 60y. black and yellow 1·00 25

1166 "Leontopodium fauriei"

1984. Alpine Plants (1st series). Multicoloured.
1749 60y. Type **1166** 1·00 30
1750 60y. "Lagotis glauca" (horiz) 1·00 30
See also Nos. 1752/3, 1769/70, 1775/6, 1802/3, 1813/14 and 1827/8.

1168 Basho's Crossroads, Sendai

1984. 6th International Virology Congress, Sendai.
1751 **1168** 60y. multicoloured 90 25

1984. Alpine Plants (2nd series). As T 1166. Multicoloured.
1752 60y. Globe flower ("Trollius riederianus") 1·00 30
1753 60y. "Primula cuneifolia" 1·00 30

1171 Logo

1984. Electronic Mail.
1754 **1171** 500y. multicoloured 14·50 6·25

1172 "Serenity" (doll by Ryujo Hori)

1984. International Correspondence Week.

1755 **1172** 130y. multicoloured 1·90 30

1173 Silver Pavilion, Jisho Temple

1984. 17th International Internal Medicine Congress, Kyoto City.

1756 **1173** 60y. multicoloured 90 25

1174 Hockey and East Pagoda of Yakushi Temple

1984. 39th National Athletic Meeting, Nara.

1757 **1174** 40y. multicoloured 70 30

1175 Birds in Tree

1176 Flowers

1177 Chrysanthemums Design

1178 Leaf and Bird Design

1984. Traditional Crafts (1st series). Kutani Porcelain Plates and Nishijin Silk Weavings.

1758 **1175** 60y. multicoloured 90 25
1759 **1176** 60y. multicoloured 90 25
1760 **1177** 60y. multicoloured 90 25
1761 **1178** 60y. multicoloured 90 25

See also Nos. 1771/4, 1787/90, 1795/8, 1805/8, 1820/3 and 1829/32.

1179 Eiji Sawamura (pitcher)

1984. 50th Anniv of Japan Tokyo Baseball Club. Multicoloured.

1762 60y. Type **1179** 90 25
1763 60y. Masaru Kageura (striker) 90 25
1764 60y. Ball, birds and Matsutaro Shoriki (founder) 90 25

1182 Workers' Profiles and Symbols

1984. Centenary of Technical Education.

1765 **1182** 60y. multicoloured 1·20 25

1183 Bamboo Ox (Sakushu folk toy)

1984. New Year's Greetings.

1766 **1183** 40y. multicoloured 1·10 30

1984. Endangered Birds (6th series). Sheet 93×120 mm. As Nos. 1714 and 1743.

MS1768 60y. blue (as No. 1714); 60y. purple (as No. 1730); 60y. black (as No. 1743) 6·00 4·00

1984. Alpine Plants (3rd series). As T 1166. Multicoloured.

1769 60y. "Rhododendron aureum" 1·00 30
1770 60y. "Oxytropis nigrescens" (horiz) 1·00 30

1186 Dolls

1187 Doll with Cat

1188 Bird and Flower Design

1189 Birds and Chrysanthemums Design

1985. Traditional Crafts (2nd series). Edo Kimekomi Dolls and Okinawa Bingata Cloth.

1771 **1186** 60y. multicoloured 1·00 30
1772 **1187** 60y. multicoloured 1·00 30
1773 **1188** 60y. multicoloured 1·00 30
1774 **1189** 60y. multicoloured 1·00 30

1985. Alpine Plants (4th series). As T 1166. Multicoloured.

1775 60y. "Dryas octopetala" (horiz) 1·00 30
1776 60y. "Draba japonica" 1·00 30

1192 Theme Pavilion and Symbol Tower

1985. "EXPO '85" World Fair, Tsukuba. Multicoloured.

1777 40y. Type **1192** 80 30
1778 60y. Geometric city 90 30
MS1779 144×93 mm. Nos. 1777/8 3·25 2·50

1194 University Buildings, Chiba City, and Transmitter

1985. Inauguration of University of the Air.

1780 **1194** 60y. multicoloured 1·00 25

1195 Aerial and Communication Lines

1985. Privatization of Nippon Telegraph and Telephone Corporation.

1781 **1195** 60y. multicoloured 1·00 25

1196 Map of Japan (after Teixeira's Map in Ortelius's "Atlas", 1595)

1985. World Import Fair, Nagoya.

1782 **1196** 60y. multicoloured 1·20 25

1197 Korekiyo Takahashi (proposer of Patent Laws)

1985. Centenary of Industrial Patents System.

1783 **1197** 60y. multicoloured 90 25

1198 "Winter in the North" (Yumeji Takehisa)

1199 "Toward the Morning Light" (Yumeji Takehisa)

1985. Philatelic Week.

1784 **1198** 60y. multicoloured 90 30
1785 **1199** 60y. multicoloured 90 30

1200 Mt. Aso and Gentian

1985. National Afforestation Campaign.

1786 **1200** 60y. multicoloured 1·20 25

1201 Hawk

1202 Ducks

1203 Bowl

1204 Plate

1985. Traditional Crafts (3rd series). Yew Wood Carvings and Arita Porcelain.

1787 **1201** 60y. multicoloured 1·00 30
1788 **1202** 60y. multicoloured 1·00 30
1789 **1203** 60y. multicoloured 1·00 30
1790 **1204** 60y. multicoloured 1·00 30

1205/6 "Cherry Trees at Night" (Taikan Yokoyama)

1985. 50th Anniv of Radio Japan (overseas broadcasting station).

1791 **1205** 60y. multicoloured 1·00 30
1792 **1206** 60y. multicoloured 1·00 30

Nos. 1791/2 were issued together, se-tenant, forming the composite design illustrated.

1207 Maeshima and "Tokyo Post Office" (Hiroshige III)

1985. 150th Birth Anniv of Baron Hisoka Maeshima (first Postmaster-General).

1793 **1207** 60y. multicoloured 90 25

1208 Bridge

1985. Opening of Great Naruto Bridge.

1794 **1208** 60y. multicoloured 90 25

1209 Weaving

1210 Weaving

1211 Dish

1212 Panel

1985. Traditional Crafts (4th series). Ojiya Linen Weavings and Kamakura Lacquered Wood Carvings.

1795 **1209** 60y. multicoloured 90 30
1796 **1210** 60y. multicoloured 90 30
1797 **1211** 60y. multicoloured 90 30
1798 **1212** 60y. multicoloured 90 30

1213 Silhouette of Laurel and Couple

1985. International Youth Year.

1799 **1213** 60y. multicoloured 90 25

1214 Owl with Letter

1215 Girl holding Bird, Letter and Cat

1985. Letter Writing Day.

1800 **1214** 40y. multicoloured 70 30
1801 **1215** 60y. multicoloured 1·00 30

1985. Alpine Plants (5th series). As T 1166. Multicoloured.

1802	60y. Gentian ("Gentiana nipponica")	1·00	30
1803	60y. "Callianthemum insigne"	1·00	30

1218 Logo

1985. Electronic Mail.

1804	**1218**	500y. multicoloured	9·25	95

1219 Noh Theatre Actor

1220 Mother with Child

1221 Tea Kettle with Fish Design

1222 Tea Kettle

1985. Traditional Crafts (5th series). Hakata Clay Figurines and Nambu Iron Ware.

1805	**1219**	60y. multicoloured	90	30
1806	**1220**	60y. multicoloured	90	30
1807	**1221**	60y. multicoloured	90	30
1808	**1222**	60y. multicoloured	90	30

1223 Hideki Yukawa (physicist) and Meson Field

1985. 50th Anniv of Yukawa's Meson Theory.

1809	**1223**	60y. multicoloured	90	25

1224 Gymnasts

1985. University Games, Kobe.

1810	**1224**	60y. multicoloured	90	25

1225 Competitor filing Test Piece

1985. 28th International Vocational Training Competition, Osaka.

1811	**1225**	40y. multicoloured	80	30

1226 "Hibiscus syriacus" (national flower of S. Korea)

1985. 20th Anniv of Japan–South Korea Diplomatic Relations.

1812	**1226**	60y. multicoloured	1·00	30

1985. Alpine Plants (6th series). As T 1166. Multicoloured.

1813	60y. "Viola crassa" (horiz)	1·00	30
1814	60y. "Campanula chamissonis"	1·00	30

1229 Tunnels and Section through Mt. Tanigawa

1985. Opening of North-bound Kan-Etsu Tunnel.

1815	**1229**	60y. multicoloured	90	25

1230 "Seisen" (doll by Goyo Hirata)

1985. International Correspondence Week.

1816	**1230**	130y. multicoloured	1·90	30

1231 Youth helping African Farmer

1985. 20th Anniv of Japanese Overseas Co-operation Volunteers.

1817	**1231**	60y. multicoloured	90	25

1232 Honey Bee on Strawberry Blossom

1985. 30th International Bee-keeping Congress, Nagoya.

1818	**1232**	60y. multicoloured	1·20	25

1233 Handball Player and Mt. Daisen

1985. 40th Int Athletic Meeting, Tottori.

1819	**1233**	40y. multicoloured	1·10	40

1234 Table

1235 Bowl

1236 Lantern on Column

1237 Lantern

1985. Traditional Crafts (6th series). Wajima Lacquerware and Izumo Sandstone Lanterns.

1820	**1234**	60y. multicoloured	90	30
1821	**1235**	60y. multicoloured	90	30
1822	**1236**	60y. multicoloured	90	30
1823	**1237**	60y. multicoloured	90	30

1238 Osaka Papier-mache Tiger

1985. New Year's Greetings.

1824	**1238**	40y. multicoloured	70	25

1239 Cabinet Emblem and Official Seal

1985. Cent of Cabinet System of Government.

1826	**1239**	60y. multicoloured	90	25

1986. Alpine Plants (7th series). As T 1166. Multicoloured.

1827	60y. "Diapensia lapponica"	1·00	30
1828	60y. "Pedicularis apodochila"	1·00	30

1242 Fan with Tree Design

1243 Fan with Flower Design

1244 Flask with Fish Pattern

1245 Tea Caddy

1986. Traditional Craft (7th series). Kyoto Fans and Tobe Porcelain.

1829	**1242**	60y. multicoloured	90	30
1830	**1243**	60y. multicoloured	90	30
1831	**1244**	60y. multicoloured	90	30
1832	**1245**	60y. multicoloured	90	30

1246 Gothic Style Finial and "Golden Norm"

1986. Centenary of Architecture Institute, Shiba, Tokyo.

1833	**1246**	60y. multicoloured	1·00	30

1247 Standing Lady

1248 Seated Lady

1986. Philatelic Week. Details of "South of Hateruma" by Kaigetsu Kikuchi.

1834	**1247**	60y. multicoloured	1·00	30
1835	**1248**	60y. multicoloured	1·00	30

1249 Phoenix and Enthronement Hall, Kyoto Palace

1250 Imperial Palace Ridge Decoration

1986. 60th Anniv of Emperor Hirohito's Accession.

1836	**1249**	60y. multicoloured	1·00	30
1837	**1250**	60y. multicoloured	1·00	30
MS1838		144×93 mm. Nos. 1836/7	2·50	1·90

1251 "Mt. Fuji in Early Morning" (Yukihiko Yasuda)

1986. 12th Economic Summit of Industrialized Countries, Tokyo.

1839	**1251**	60y. multicoloured	1·00	30

1252 Bull-headed Shrike in Reeds

1986. National Afforestation Campaign.

1840	**1252**	60y. multicoloured	1·20	25

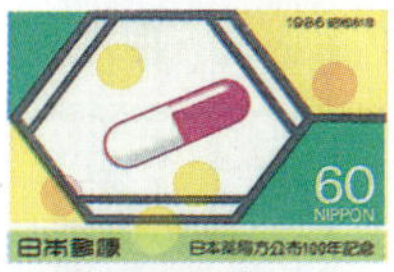

1253 Capsule, Tablets and Structure of Toluene

1986. Centenary of Japanese Pharmacopoeia.

1841	**1253**	60y. multicoloured	90	25

1254 Map and Clock

1986. Centenary of Japanese Standard Time.

1842	**1254**	60y. multicoloured	1·00	30

1255 Bird on Chair and Letter on Table

1986. Letter Writing Day. Multicoloured.

1843	40y. Type **1255**	90	25
1844	60y. Girl holding rabbit and letter	1·30	25

1257 Yataro Iwasaki, Makoto Kondo and Cadet Ship "Nippon Maru II"

1986. 110th Anniv of Merchant Navy Education.

1846	**1257**	60y. multicoloured	1·20	25

1258 Asian Apollo ("Parnassius eversmanni")

1986. Insects (1st series). Multicoloured.

1847 60y. Type **1258** 1·50 30
1848 60y. Shieldbug ("Poecilocoris lewisi") 1·50 30
1849 60y. Longhorn beetle ("Rosalia batesi") 1·50 30
1850 60y. "Epiophlebia superstes" 1·50 30

See also Nos. 1854/7, 1861/4, 1869/72, 1878/**MS**1882 and 1911/12.

1262 "Folkways in Twelve Months" (detail, Shunsho Katsukawa)

1986. 52nd International Federation of Library Associations General Conference, Tokyo.

1851 **1262** 60y. multicoloured 1·00 30

1263 Electron Microscope

1986. 11th International Electron Microscopy Congress, Kyoto.

1852 **1263** 60y. multicoloured 1·00 30

1264 Couple and Conference Emblem

1986. 23rd International Social Welfare Conference, Tokyo.

1853 **1264** 60y. multicoloured 1·00 30

1986. Insects (2nd series). As T 1258. Mult.

1854 60y. Dragonflies ("Sympetrum pedemonatanum") 1·50 30
1855 60y. Weevil ("Damaster blaptoides") 1·50 30
1856 60y. Stag beetle ("Dorcus hopei") 1·50 30
1857 60y. Wonderful hair-streak ("Thermozephyrus ataxus") 1·50 30

1269 "Ohmori Miyage" (shiso doll, Juzoh Kagoshima)

1986. International Correspondence Week.

1858 **1269** 130y. multicoloured 2·00 30

1270 Gymnast and Mt. Fuji

1986. 41st National Athletic Meeting, Yamanashi.

1859 **1270** 40y. multicoloured 70 25

1271 "Flowers in Autumn and Girl in Rakuhoku"

1986. 5th World Ikebana Convention, Kyoto.

1860 **1271** 60y. multicoloured 1·00 30

1986. Insects (3rd series). As T 1258. Mult.

1861 60y. "Elcysma westwoodii" (moth) 1·50 30
1862 60y. "Rhyothemis variegata" 1·50 30
1863 60y. Cicada ("Tibicen japonicus") 1·50 30
1864 60y. "Chrysochroa holstii" 1·50 30

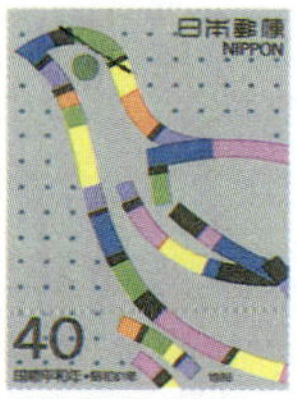

1276 Stylized Dove

1986. International Peace Year. Mult.

1865 40y. Type **1276** 70 30
1866 60y. Circle of children (horiz) 1·00 30

1278 "Rabbits making Rice Cake" (Nagoya clay model)

1986. New Year's Greetings.

1867 **1278** 40y. multicoloured 1·10 40

For 50y. in this design dated "1999" see No. 2567.

1987. Insects (4th series). As T 1258. Mult.

1869 60y. "Cheirotonus jambar" 1·50 30
1870 60y. Chestnut tiger ("Parantica sita") 1·50 30
1871 60y. "Anotogaster sieboldii" 1·50 30
1872 60y. Stag beetle ("Lucanus maculifemoratus") 1·50 30

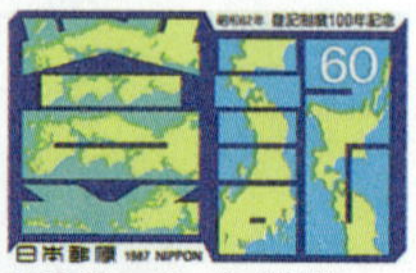

1283 Characters for "Toki" (Registry) and Map

1987. Centenary of Land Registration.

1873 **1283** 60y. multicoloured 1·00 30

1284 Basho Matsuo (after Haritsu Ogawa)

1285 "Departing Spring" (Senju)

1286 Kegon Falls

1287 "Sunlight" (Toshu Shrine)

1987. "Narrow Road to a Far Province" (travel diary) by Basho Matsuo (1st series).

1874 **1284** 60y. multicoloured 1·00 30
1875 **1285** 60y. multicoloured 1·00 30
1876 **1286** 60y. multicoloured 1·00 30
1877 **1287** 60y. multicoloured 1·00 30

In this series, each pair of stamps (except Nos. 1874/5) illustrates one "haiku" (17-syllable poem) from the diary. The full text of the "haiku" is printed on one stamp and given in calligraphy on the other with appropriate illustrations. Each "haiku" was written at a particular point in the journey (given in brackets in the caption to the second stamp of each pair).

See also Nos. 1896/9, 1906/9, 1925/8, 1932/5, 1945/8, 1962/5, 1973/6, 1982/5 and 2000/3.

1987. Insects (5th series). As T 1258. Mult.

1878 60y. Owl-fly ("Ascaraphus ramburi") 1·50 30
1879 60y. Cockchafer ("Polyphylla laticollis") 1·50 30
1880 60y. Leaf butterfly ("Kallima inachus") 1·50 30
1881 60y. "Calopteryx cornelia" 1·50 30

MS1882 143×93 mm. multicoloured. 40y. Orange-tip ("Anthocaris cardamines"); 40y. Great purple ("Sasakia charonda"); 60y. Asian apollo ("Parnassius eversmanni"); 60y. Chestnut tiger ("Parantica sita") 5·50 4·25

1294 Wind Orchid

1295 Lobster-root

1987. 12th International Orchid Conference, Tokyo.

1883 **1294** 60y. multicoloured 1·00 30
1884 **1295** 60y. multicoloured 1·00 30

1296 Early Mail Sorting Carriage

1987. Ending of Railway Mail Carriage Contracts.

1885 60y. Type **1296** 1·20 30
1886 60y. Loading mail sacks (detail of scroll painting by Beisen Kubota) 1·20 30

1298 Class 860 Tank Locomotive No. 137, 1893

1987. Privatization of Japan Railways. Mult.

1887 60y. Type **1298** 1·10 25
1888 60y. Maglev MLU 002 1·10 25

1300 Nudibranchs

1987. Centenary of Marine Biology Studies in Japan.

1889 **1300** 60y. multicoloured 1·00 30

1301 "Woman with a Comb"

1987. Philatelic Week. Paintings by Goyo Hashiguchi. Multicoloured.

1890 60y. Type **1301** 1·00 30
1891 60y. "Woman putting on make-up" 1·00 30

1303 Map and Emblem

1987. 20th Annual General Meeting of Asian Development Bank.

1892 **1303** 60y. multicoloured 1·00 30

1304 Black-billed Magpie and Forested Coastline

1987. National Afforestation Campaign.

1893 **1304** 60y. multicoloured 1·00 30

1305 Yatsuhashi Gold Lacquer and Nacre Inkstone Case (Kohrin Ogata)

1306 Hikone Castle

1987. National Treasures (1st series).

1894 **1305** 60y. multicoloured 1·00 40
1895 **1306** 110y. multicoloured 1·80 55

See also Nos. 1900/1, 1929/30, 1949/50, 1968/9, 1980/1, 2006/7 and 2017/18.

1307 European Cuckoo

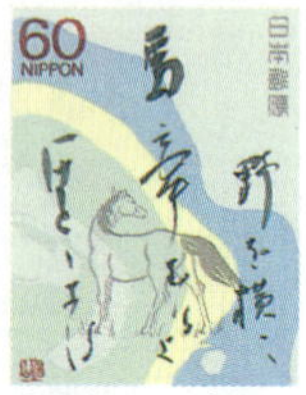

1308 Horse and River (Nasu)

1309 "In the Shade of the Willow"

1310 Paddy Field (Ashino)

1987. "Narrow Road to a Far Province" by Basho Matsuo (2nd series).

1896 **1307** 60y. multicoloured 1·50 30
1897 **1308** 60y. multicoloured 1·50 30
1898 **1309** 60y. multicoloured 1·50 30
1899 **1310** 60y. multicoloured 1·50 30

1311 Golden Turtle Reliquary for Buddha's Ashes (Tashodai Temple)

1312 Inuyama Castle

1987. National Treasures (2nd series). Multicoloured.

1900	**1311**	60y. multicoloured	1·00	40
1901	**1312**	110y. multicoloured	1·80	55

1313 Flowers in Envelope

1987. Letter Writing Day. Multicoloured.

1902	40y. Type **1313**	90	30
1903	60y. Elephant holding letter in trunk	1·30	45

1315 Flood Barrier across Rivers

1987. Centenary of Modern Flood Control of Rivers Kiso, Nagara and Ibi.

1905	**1315**	60y. multicoloured	1·00	25

1316 Chestnut Blossoms

1317 Chestnut Leaves (Sukagawa)

1318 Transplanting Rice

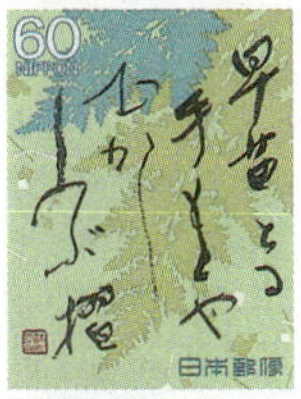

1319 Fern Leaves ("Dyeing Stone", Shinobu)

1987. "Narrow Road to a Far Province" by Basho Matsuo (3rd series).

1906	**1316**	60y. multicoloured	1·00	30
1907	**1317**	60y. multicoloured	1·00	30
1908	**1318**	60y. multicoloured	1·00	30
1909	**1319**	60y. multicoloured	1·00	30

1320 Temple of Emerald Buddha and Cherry Blossom

1987. Centenary of Japan–Thailand Friendship Treaty.

1910	**1320**	60y. multicoloured	1·00	30

1987. Insects (6th series). As T 1258. Mult.

1911	40y. Orange-tip ("Anthocaris cardamines")	2·00	1·60
1912	40y. Great purple ("Sasakia charonda")	2·00	1·60

1321 "Gensho Kanto" (Ryujo Hori)

1987. International Correspondence Week. Multicoloured.

1913	130y. Type **1321**	2·00	40
1914	150y. "Utage-no-Hana" (Goyo Hirata)	2·20	45

1323 "Three Beauties" (detail, Toyokuni Utagawa)

1987. 13th International Certified Public Accountants Congress, Tokyo.

1915	**1323**	60y. multicoloured	1·00	30

1324 Lion's Head Public Water Tap

1987. Centenary of Yokohama Waterworks.

1916	**1324**	60y. multicoloured	1·00	30

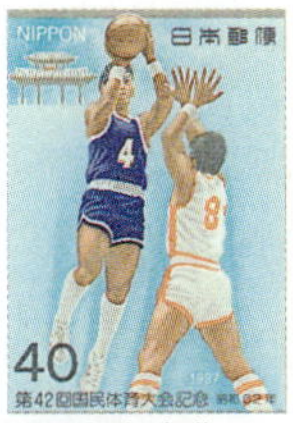

1325 Basketball Players and Shuri Gate, Naha

1987. 42nd National Athletic Meeting, Okinawa.

1917	**1325**	40y. multicoloured	30	25

1326 Playing Card with Queen holding Bird and King smoking

1987. 6th International Smoking and Health Conference, Tokyo.

1918	**1326**	60y. multicoloured	1·00	30

1327 Dish Aerial, Kashima Station

1987. International Telecommunications Conference, Tokyo.

1919	**1327**	60y. multicoloured	1·00	25

1328 Nijo Castle

1987. World Historic Cities Conference, Kyoto.

1920	**1328**	60y. multicoloured	1·00	30

1329 "Family in Tree" (Takahiro Nagahama)

1987. International Year of Shelter for the Homeless. Multicoloured.

1921	40y. Type **1329**	90	30
1922	60y. "Houses" (Yoko Sasaki)	1·30	25

1331 Kurashiki Papier-mache Dragon

1987. New Year's Greetings.

1923	**1331**	40y. multicoloured	70	25

1332 Sweet Flags

1333 Sweet Flags and Birds (Sendai)

1334 "Recollecting the Past"

1335 "Summer Grasses" (Hiraizumi)

1988. "Narrow Road to a Far Province" by Basho Matsuo (4th series).

1925	**1332**	60y. multicoloured	1·00	30
1926	**1333**	60y. multicoloured	1·00	30
1927	**1334**	60y. multicoloured	1·00	30
1928	**1335**	60y. multicoloured	1·00	30

1336 Kongo Samma-in Pagoda, Mt. Koya

1337 Ekoh-Doji, Kongobu Temple

1988. National Treasures (3rd series).

1929	**1336**	60y. multicoloured	1·00	40
1930	**1337**	110y. multicoloured	1·80	55

1338 Class ED 79 Locomotive "Sea of Japan" leaving Tunnel and Map

1988. Opening of Seikan (Aomori–Hakodate) Railway Tunnel.

1931	**1338**	60y. multicoloured	1·20	25

1339 Safflower

1340 Willow Trees (Obanazawa)

1341 Risshaku (or Mountain) Temple

1342 Pine Trees (Risshaku Temple)

1988. "Narrow Road to a Far Province" by Basho Matsuo (5th series).

1932	**1339**	60y. multicoloured	1·00	40
1933	**1340**	60y. multicoloured	1·00	40
1934	**1341**	60y. multicoloured	1·00	40
1935	**1342**	60y. multicoloured	1·00	40

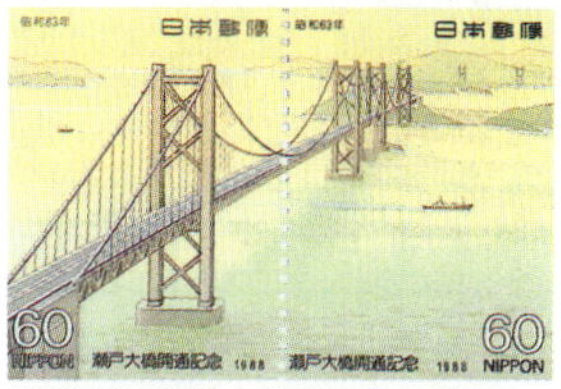

1343/4 South Bisan Section from Kagawa Side

1345/6 Shimotsui Section from Okayama Side

1988. Opening of Seto Great Road and Rail Bridge.

1936	**1343**	60y. multicoloured	1·40	40
1937	**1344**	60y. multicoloured	1·40	40
1938	**1345**	60y. multicoloured	1·40	40
1939	**1346**	60y. multicoloured	1·40	40

Nos. 1936/7 and 1938/9 were printed together, se-tenant, each pair forming the composite design illustrated.

1347 "Long Undergarment" (Kotondo Torii)

1988. Philatelic Week. Multicoloured.

1940	60y. Type **1347**	1·40	40
1941	60y. "Kimono Sash" (Kotondo Torii)	1·40	40

1349 Detail of Biwa Plectrum Guard

1988. "Silk Road" Exhibition. Nara.

1943	**1349**	60y. multicoloured	1·40	45

1350 Yashima, Small Cuckoo and Olive Tree

1988. National Afforestation Campaign.

1944 **1350** 60y. multicoloured 1·50 45

1351 River Mogami

1352 Irises in the Rain (Oishida)

1353 Moon Mountain

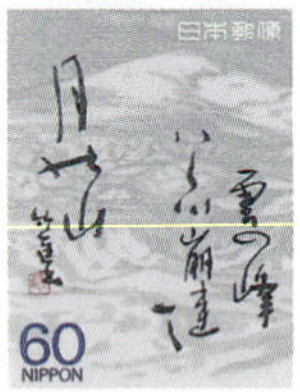

1354 Moon Mountain (Gassan)

1988. "Narrow Road to a Far Province" by Basho Matsuo (6th series).

1945 **1351** 60y. multicoloured 1·00 30

1946 **1352** 60y. multicoloured 1·00 30

1947 **1353** 60y. multicoloured 1·00 30

1948 **1354** 60y. multicoloured 1·00 30

1355 Morodo Shrine, Itsukushima

1356 Kozakura-gawa Braided Armour

1988. National Treasures (4th series).

1949 **1355** 60y. multicoloured 1·00 30

1950 **1356** 100y. multicoloured 1·70 40

1357 Mt. Sakura

1988. International Conference on Volcanoes, Kagoshima.

1951 **1357** 60y. multicoloured 1·00 30

1358 Cat with Letter

1988. Letter Writing Day. Multicoloured.

1952 40y. Type **1358** 90 30

1953 40y. Crab with letter (34×25 mm) 1·20 40

1954 60y. Fairy with letter 1·40 40

1955 60y. Girl and letter (25×32 mm) 90 30

Nos. 1952 and 1954 exist both perforated with ordinary gum and imperforate with self-adhesive gum.

1362 Ohana (Kinosuke puppet, Japan)

1988. International Puppetry Festival, Nagoya, Iida and Tokyo. Multicoloured.

1956 60y. Type **1362** 90 25

1957 60y. Stick puppet of girl (Czechoslovakia) 90 25

1958 60y. Shadow puppet (China) 90 25

1959 60y. Knight (Italy) 90 25

1366 Peonies

1988. 10th Anniv of Japanese–Chinese Treaty of Peace and Friendship. Multicoloured.

1960 60y. Type **1366** 1·50 25

1961 60y. Ton-ton (giant panda) 1·50 25

1368 Mimosa Flowers

1369 Lagoon and Grass (Kisagata)

1370 Rough Sea

1371 Waves (Ichiburi)

1988. "Narrow Road to a Far Province" by Basho Matsuo (7th series).

1962 **1368** 60y. multicoloured 1·00 30

1963 **1369** 60y. multicoloured 1·00 30

1964 **1370** 60y. multicoloured 1·00 30

1965 **1371** 60y. multicoloured 1·00 30

1372 Nagoya and Egg

1988. 18th International Poultry Congress, Nagoya.

1966 **1372** 60y. multicoloured 1·00 30

1373 Globe and "Rehabilitation" in Braille

1988. 16th Rehabilitation International World Congress, Tokyo.

1967 **1373** 60y. multicoloured 90 25

1374 Nakatsuhime-no-mikoto, Yakushi Temple

1375 Murou Temple

1988. National Treasures (5th series).

1968 **1374** 60y. multicoloured 1·00 30

1969 **1375** 100y. multicoloured 1·70 40

1376 "Kimesaburo Iwai as Chiyo" (Kunimasa Utagawa)

1988. International Correspondence Week. Mult.

1970 80y. Type **1376** 1·10 40

1971 120y. "Komazo Ichikawa III as Ganryu Sasaki" (Toyokuni Utagawa) 1·80 40

1378 Gymnast and Temple of the Golden Pavilion

1988. 43rd National Athletic Meeting, Kyoto.

1972 **1378** 40y. multicoloured 60 25

1379 Rice

1380 Ariso Sea (Kurikara Pass)

1381 Sun

1382 "Autumn Wind and Sun" (Kanazawa)

1988. "Narrow Road to a Far Province" by Basho Matsuo (8th series).

1973 **1379** 60y. multicoloured 1·00 30

1974 **1380** 60y. multicoloured 1·00 30

1975 **1381** 60y. multicoloured 1·00 30

1976 **1382** 60y. multicoloured 1·00 30

1383 Mexican State Arms

1988. Centenary of Japan–Mexico Friendship and Trade Treaty.

1977 **1383** 60y. multicoloured 1·00 40

1384 Snake (Shimotsuke clay bell)

1988. New Year's Greetings.

1978 **1384** 40y. multicoloured 1·00 25

1385 Figures on Globe

1988. 40th Anniv of Declaration of Human Rights.

1979 **1385** 60y. multicoloured 90 25

1386 Gold-plated Silver Pot with Hunting Design, Todai Temple

1387 Bronze Figure of Yakushi (Buddha of Medicine), Horyu Temple

1989. National Treasures (6th series).

1980 **1386** 60y. multicoloured 1·00 30

1981 **1387** 100y. multicoloured 1·70 40

1388 Nata Temple

1389 Pampas Grass (Natadera)

1390 Moonlight, Kehi Shrine

1391 Moon and Pine Trees (Tsuruga)

1989. "Narrow Road to a Far Province" by Basho Matsuo (9th series).

1982 **1388** 60y. multicoloured 1·00 30

1983 **1389** 60y. multicoloured 1·00 30

1984 **1390** 60y. multicoloured 1·00 30

1985 **1391** 60y. multicoloured 1·00 30

1989. Letter Writing Day (1988).

1986 40y. As Type **1354** 1·10 85

1987 60y. As No. 1954 1·40 1·10

1989. Narrow Road to a Far Province by Basho Matsuo (10th series). Ten sheets, each 112×72 mm.

MS1988 10 sheets. (a) Nos. 1874/5; (b) Nos. 1876/7; (c) Nos. 1896/7; (d) Nos. 1898/9; (e) Nos. 1906/7; (f) Nos. 1908/9; (g) Nos. 1925/6; (h) Nos. 1927/8; (i) Nos. 1932/3; (j) Nos. 1934/5 29·00 23·00

1392 Globe and Exhibition Site

1989. "Fukuoka '89" Asian–Pacific Exhibition, Fukuoka.

1989	**1392**	60y. multicoloured	1·00	25
1996	**1392**	62y. multicoloured	1·00	45

1393 "Russian Ladies sight-seeing at Port" (detail, Yoshitora) and Art Gallery

1989. "Space and Children" Exhibition, Yokohama.

1990	**1393**	60y. multicoloured	90	25
1997	**1393**	62y. multicoloured	90	45

1394 Bonsai Japanese White Pine

1989. World Bonsai Convention, Omiya.

1993	**1394**	62y. multicoloured	90	25

1395 Lute-player

1989. Philatelic Week. Details of "Awa Dance" (painting) by Tsunetomi Kitano. Multicoloured.

1994	62y. Type **1395**	90	25
1995	62y. Dancer	90	25

1397 "Dutch East Indiaman entering Harbour" (Nagasaki woodblock print)

1989. "Holland Festival '89".

1998	**1397**	62y. multicoloured	1·00	25

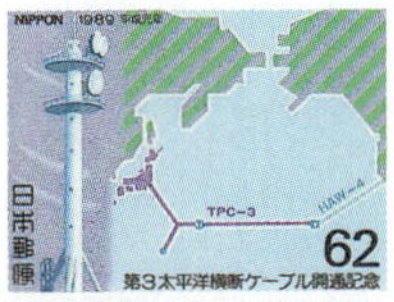

1398 Chikura Communication Tower and Cable Route

1989. Opening of 3rd Trans-Pacific Submarine Telephone Cable (Japan–Hawaii).

1999	**1398**	62y. multicoloured	1·40	30

1399 Beach in Autumn

1400 Bush Clover (Ironohama)

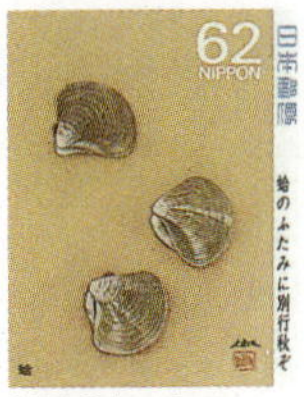

1401 Poker-drop Venuses

1402 Wedded Rocks, Futami Bay (Ohgaki)

1989. "Narrow Road to a Far Province" by Basho Matsuo (11th series).

2000	**1399**	62y. multicoloured	1·00	30
2001	**1400**	62y. multicoloured	1·00	30
2002	**1401**	62y. multicoloured	1·00	30
2003	**1402**	62y. multicoloured	1·00	30

1403 Mt. Tsurugi, Lime and Bay Trees

1989. National Afforestation Campaign.

2004	**1403**	62y. multicoloured	90	25

1404 Children in Bird and Flower "Balloon"

1989. International Garden and Greenery Exposition, Osaka (1990) (1st issue).

2005	**1404**	62y.+10y. mult	1·50	30

See also Nos. 2035/6.

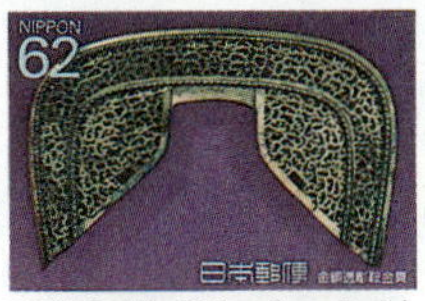

1405 Saddle Fitting from Burial Mound, Konda

1406 "Beetle Wings" Zushi, Horyu Temple

1989. National Treasures (7th series).

2006	**1405**	62y. multicoloured	90	25
2007	**1406**	100y. multicoloured	1·60	30

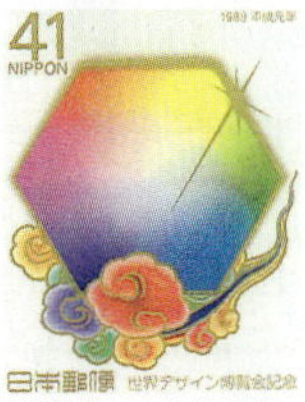

1407 "Crystal of Light and Auspicious Clouds"

1989. World Design Exposition, Nagoya. Multicoloured.

2008	41y. Type **1407**	60	25
2009	62y. "design"	90	25

1409 Bird as Vase holding Envelope

1989. Letter Writing Day. Multicoloured.

2010	41y. Type **1409**	70	45
2011	62y. Mother Rabbit reading letter	1·90	1·50

1989. Narrow Road to a Far Province by Basho Matsuo (12th series). Ten sheets, each 112×72 mm.

MS2012 10 sheets. (a) Nos. 1945/6; (b) Nos. 1947/8; (c) Nos. 1963/4; (d) Nos. 1965/6; (e) Nos. 1973/4; (f) Nos. 1975/6; (g) Nos. 1982/3; (h) Nos. 1984/5; (i) Nos. 2000/2001; (j) Nos. 2002/3 — 29·00 — 23·00

1989. Special Correspondence Stamps.

2013	**1098**	41y. multicoloured	60	30
2014	**1099**	41y. multicoloured	90	30
2015	**1099**	62y. multicoloured	1·00	30
2016	**1100**	72y. multicoloured	1·20	30

1411 Gold Stamp

1412 Bronze Mirror

1989. National Treasures (8th series).

2017	**1411**	62y. multicoloured	90	25
2018	**1412**	100y. multicoloured	1·60	30

1413 Bouquet of Orchids and Stephanotis

1989. 6th Interflora World Congress, Tokyo.

2019	**1413**	62y. multicoloured	90	60

1414 Wheelchair Race

1989. Far East and South Pacific Games for the Disabled, Kobe.

2020	**1414**	62y. multicoloured	90	60

1415 Narrators and Drummers

1989. "Europalia 89 Japan" Festival, Belgium. Details of "Okuni Theatre" (painting on folding screen). Multicoloured.

2021	62y. Type **1415**	90	25
2022	70y. Okuni (actress)	1·00	30

1417 New Emperor and Kaoru playing Go ("Yadorigi" scroll)

1989. International Correspondence Week. Details of Takayoshi Picture Scrolls illustrating "Tale of Genji" by Lady Murasaki. Multicoloured.

2023	80y. Type **1417**	1·00	30
2024	120y. Yugao's granddaughters playing Go ("Takekawa scroll")	1·80	45

1419 Ear of Rice and Paddy Field

1989. 7th Asian/African Conference of Int Irrigation and Drainage Commission.

2025	**1419**	62y. multicoloured	90	25

1420 Shinzan (first winner of all five major races)

1989. 100th Tenno Sho Horse Race.

2026	**1420**	62y. multicoloured	1·00	30

1421 Hot-air Balloons

1989. 9th Hot Air Balloon World Championship, Saga City.

2027	**1421**	62y. multicoloured	1·00	25

1422 Conductor

1989. 50th Anniv of Japanese Copyright Control Act.

2028	**1422**	62y. multicoloured	90	25

1423 Yawata Wooden Horse

1989. New Year's Greetings.

2029	**1423**	41y. multicoloured	1·00	25

1424 Hamamatsu Papier-mache Horse

1989. New Year Lottery Stamp.

2030	**1424**	62y. multicoloured	1·00	60

Each stamp carries a lottery number.

1425 Type 10000

1990. Electric Railway Locomotives (1st series).

2031	**1425**	62y. purple, lilac & grn	1·10	25
2032	-	62y. multicoloured	1·10	25

DESIGN: No. 2032, Type EF 58 No. 38, 1946.
See also Nos. 2033/4, 2039/40, 2089/90 and 2101/2.

1990. Electric Railway Locomotives (2nd series). As T 1425. Multicoloured.

2033	62y. Type ED 40 No. 12, 1919	1·10	25
2034	62y. Type EH 10 No. 8, 1954	1·10	25

1429 Fairies on Flower

1990. "Expo 90" International Garden and Greenery Exposition, Osaka. Multicoloured.

2035	41y.+4y. Type **1429**	70	55
2036	62y. Bicycle under tree	1·00	30

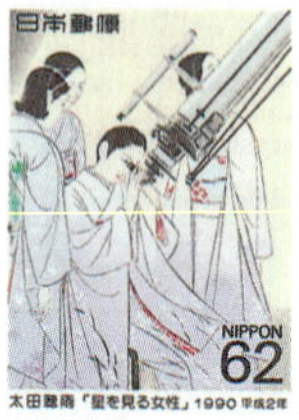

1431 "Women gazing at the Stars" (Chou Ohta)

1990. Philatelic Week.

2037	**1431** 62y. multicoloured	80	30
MS2038	60×77 mm. No. 2037	2·00	1·60

1990. Electric Railway Locomotives (3rd series). As T 1425. Multicoloured.

2039	62y. Type EF 53, 1932	1·10	25
2040	62y. Type ED 70, 1957	1·10	25

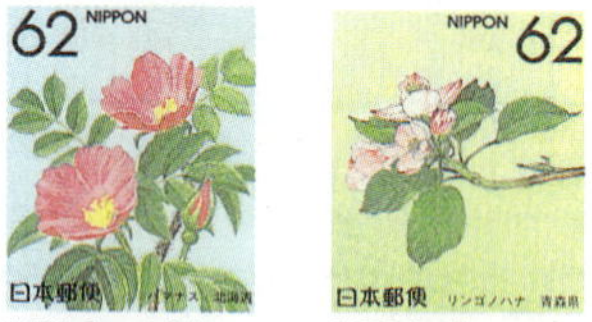

1434 Sweet Briar (Hokkaido)
1435 Apple Blossom (Aomori)

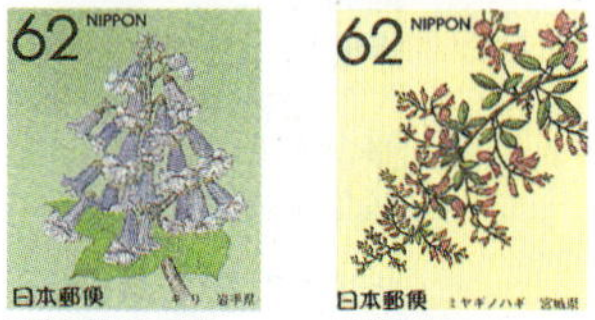

1436 "Paulownia tomentosa" (Iwate)
1437 Japanese Bush Clover (Miyagi)

1438 Butterbur Flower (Akita)
1439 Safflower (Yamagata)

1440 Rhododendron (Fukushima)
1441 Rose (Ibaraki)

1442 Yashio Azalea (Tochigi)
1443 Japanese Azalea (Gunma)

1444 Primrose (Saitama)
1445 Rape (Chiba)

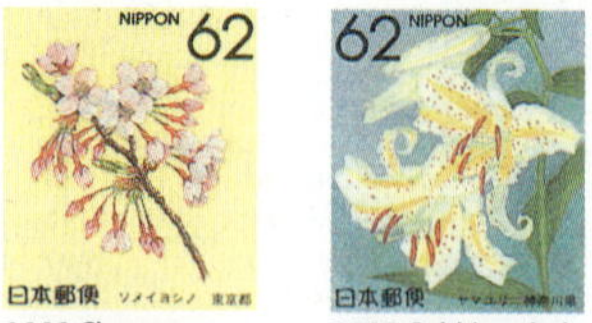

1446 Cherry Blossom (Yamanashi)
1447 Gold-banded Lily (Kanagawa)

1448 Cherry Blossom (Tokyo)
1449 Gentian (Nagano)

1450 Tulip (Niigata)
1451 Tulip (Toyama)

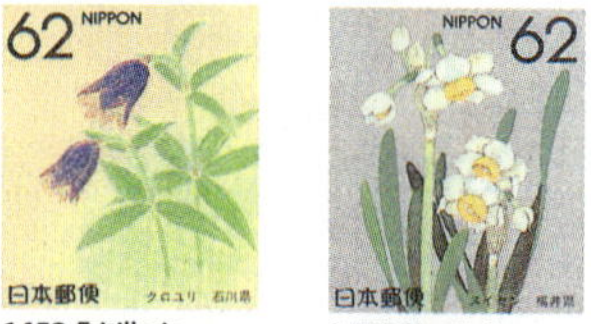

1452 Fritillaria (Ishikawa)
1453 Narcissi (Fukui)

1454 Chinese Milk Vetch (Gifu)
1455 Azalea (Shizuoka)

1456 Rabbit-ear Iris (Aichi)
1457 Iris (Mie)

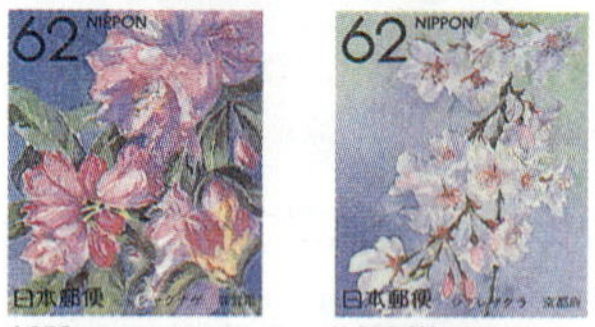

1458 Rhododendron (Shiga)
1459 Weeping Cherry Blossom (Kyoto)

1460 Japanese Apricot and Primrose (Osaka)
1461 Marguerites (Hyogo)

1462 Double Cherry Blossom (Nara)
1463 Japanese Apricot (Wakayama)

1464 Pear Blossom (Tottori)
1465 Peony (Shimane)

1466 Peach Blossom (Okayama)
1467 Japanese Maple (Hiroshima)

1468 Summer Orange Blossom (Yamaguchi)
1469 Sudachi Orange Blossom (Tokushima)

1470 Olive Blossom (Kagawa)
1471 Mandarin Orange Blossom (Ehime)

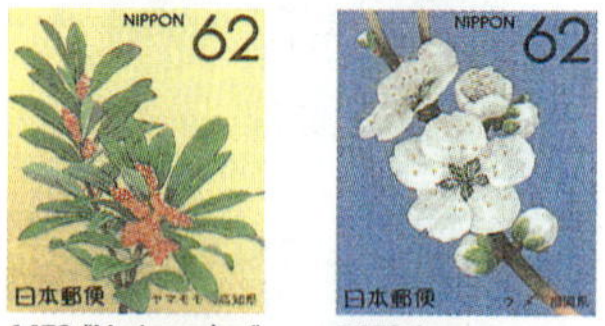

1472 "Myrica rubra" (Kochi)
1473 Japanese Apricot (Fukuoka)

1474 Laurel (Saga)
1475 Unzen Azalea (Nagasaki)

1476 Gentian (Kumamoto)
1477 Japanese Apricot (Oita)

1478 Crinum (Miyazaki)
1479 Rhododendron (Kagoshima)

1480 Coral Tree (Okinawa)

1990. Prefecture Flowers.

2041	**1434**	62y. multicoloured	2·50	1·90
2042	**1435**	62y. multicoloured	80	60
2043	**1436**	62y. multicoloured	80	60
2044	**1437**	62y. multicoloured	80	60
2045	**1438**	62y. multicoloured	80	60
2046	**1439**	62y. multicoloured	80	60
2047	**1440**	62y. multicoloured	80	60
2048	**1441**	62y. multicoloured	80	60
2049	**1442**	62y. multicoloured	80	60
2050	**1443**	62y. multicoloured	80	60
2051	**1444**	62y. multicoloured	80	60
2052	**1445**	62y. multicoloured	80	60
2053	**1446**	62y. multicoloured	80	60
2054	**1447**	62y. multicoloured	80	60
2055	**1448**	62y. multicoloured	80	60
2056	**1449**	62y. multicoloured	2·50	1·90
2057	**1450**	62y. multicoloured	80	60
2058	**1451**	62y. multicoloured	80	60
2059	**1452**	62y. multicoloured	80	60
2060	**1453**	62y. multicoloured	80	60
2061	**1454**	62y. multicoloured	1·00	80
2062	**1455**	62y. multicoloured	1·30	1·00
2063	**1456**	62y. multicoloured	80	60
2064	**1457**	62y. multicoloured	80	60
2065	**1458**	62y. multicoloured	2·00	1·60
2066	**1459**	62y. multicoloured	2·00	1·60
2067	**1460**	62y. multicoloured	80	60
2068	**1461**	62y. multicoloured	80	60
2069	**1462**	62y. multicoloured	1·30	1·00
2070	**1463**	62y. multicoloured	1·00	80
2071	**1464**	62y. multicoloured	80	60
2072	**1465**	62y. multicoloured	80	60
2073	**1466**	62y. multicoloured	80	60
2074	**1467**	62y. multicoloured	80	60
2075	**1468**	62y. multicoloured	80	60
2076	**1469**	62y. multicoloured	1·00	80
2077	**1470**	62y. multicoloured	3·25	2·50
2078	**1471**	62y. multicoloured	1·60	1·20
2079	**1472**	62y. multicoloured	1·30	1·00
2080	**1473**	62y. multicoloured	80	60
2081	**1474**	62y. multicoloured	80	60
2082	**1475**	62y. multicoloured	80	60
2083	**1476**	62y. multicoloured	80	60
2084	**1477**	62y. multicoloured	80	60
2085	**1478**	62y. multicoloured	80	60
2086	**1479**	62y. multicoloured	80	60
2087	**1480**	62y. multicoloured	80	60

1481 Mt. Unzen and Unzen Azalea

1990. National Afforestation Campaign.

2088	**1481** 62y. multicoloured	80	30

1990. Electric Railway Locomotives (4th series). As T 1425. Multicoloured.

2089	62y. Type EF 55, 1936	1·10	25
2090	62y. Type ED 61 No. 13, 1958	1·10	25

1484 Fritillary on Thistle

1990. Winning Entries in Postage Stamp Design Contest. Multicoloured.

2091	62y. Type **1484**	1·40	25
2092	70y. "Communication"	1·60	30

1486 17th-century Ottoman Tile

1990. Century of Japan–Turkey Friendship.
2093 **1486** 62y. multicoloured 80 30

1487/91 Folding Screen (image scaled to 45% of original size)

1492 "Ponies" (Kayo Yamaguchi)

1990. The Horse in Culture (1st series).
2094 **1487** 62y. multicoloured 1·50 25
2095 **1488** 62y. multicoloured 1·50 25
2096 **1489** 62y. multicoloured 1·50 25
2097 **1490** 62y. multicoloured 1·50 25
2098 **1491** 62y. multicoloured 1·50 25
2099 **1492** 62y. multicoloured 1·50 25

Nos. 2094/8 were printed together, se-tenant, forming a composite design showing a 17th-century folding screen painting.

See also Nos. 2106/8, 2113/14, 2132/4 and 2135/6.

1493 Emblem and Landscape

1990. 38th International Youth Hostel Federation Congress. Muikamachi and Kashiwazaki.
2100 **1493** 62y. multicoloured 90 30

1990. Electric Railway Locomotives (5th series). As T 1425. Multicoloured.
2101 62y. Type ED 57, 1941 1·10 25
2102 62y. Type EF 30 Nos. 3 and 6, 1961 1·10 25

1496 Bluebird and Heart

1497 Fairy on Horse

1990. Letter Writing Day.
2103 **1496** 41y. multicoloured 70 30
2104 **1497** 62y. multicoloured 1·00 25
MS2105 72×93 mm. No. 2104 1·50 1·20

For similar design to No. 2104, see No. 2157.

1500 "A Horse" (Suisho Nishiyama)

1990. The Horse in Culture (2nd series). Multicoloured.
2106 62y. 16th-century lacquered saddle 1·50 25
2107 62y. 16th-century lacquered stirrups 1·50 25
2108 62y. Type **1500** 1·50 25

1501 Origami Polyhedron

1990. Int Mathematicians Congress, Kyoto.
2109 **1501** 62y. multicoloured 80 30

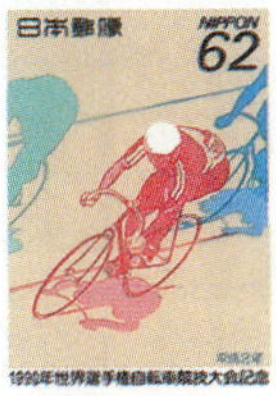

1502 Track Race

1990. World Cycling Championships. Maebashi and Tochigi Prefecture.
2110 **1502** 62y. multicoloured 80 30

1503 Ogai Mori (translator) and Passage from Goethe's "Faust"

1990. 8th International Association for Germanic Studies Congress, Tokyo.
2111 **1503** 62y. blue, yellow & brn 80 30

1504 "Ji" (character) and Rosetta Stone

1990. International Literacy Year.
2112 **1504** 62y. multicoloured 80 30

1505 "Kurabeuma Race" (detail of Kimono)

1506 "Kettei" (Shodo Sasaki)

1990. The Horse in Culture (3rd series).
2113 **1505** 62y. multicoloured 80 30
2114 **1506** 62y. multicoloured 80 30

1507 Peaceful Landscape

1990. International Decade for Natural Disaster Reduction Conference, Yokohama.
2115 **1507** 62y. multicoloured 80 30

1508 Animals at Dance

1990. International Correspondence Week. Details from "Choju-jinbutsu-giga" Picture Scroll. Multicoloured.
2116 80y. Type **1508** 1·20 40
2117 120y. Dancing frogs 1·80 40

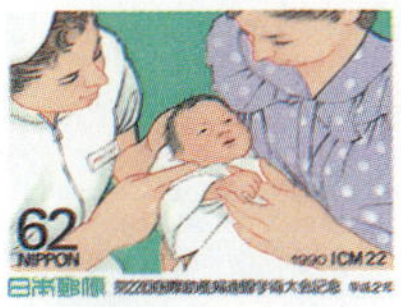

1510 Midwife, Mother and Baby

1990. 22nd International Confederation of Midwives Congress, Kobe City.
2118 **1510** 62y. multicoloured 80 40

1511 "Letter Bearer" (detail, Harunobu Suiendo)

1990. "Phila Nippon '91" International Stamp Exhibition, Tokyo (1st issue).
2119 **1511** 100y. multicoloured 1·40 45
MS2120 94×90 mm. No. 2119 2·00 1·60

See also. Nos. 2170/**MS**2171.

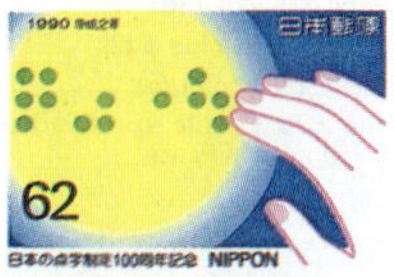

1512 Hand reading Braille

1990. Centenary of Japanese Braille.
2121 **1512** 62y. multicoloured 80 30

1513 "Justice" (Supreme Court bronze statue, Katsuzo Entsuba)

1990. Centenary of Modern Judiciary System.
2122 **1513** 62y. multicoloured 80 30

1514 Chinese Phoenix (detail from dais of Emperor's enthronement seat)

1990. Enthronement of Emperor. Multicoloured.
2123 62y. Type **1514** 1·00 30
2124 62y. Pattern from robe of Manzai Raku dancers 1·00 30
MS2125 144×93 mm. Nos. 2123/4 3·00 2·30

1516 Stained Glass Window (Diet building)

1990. Centenary of Diet.
2126 **1516** 62y. multicoloured 80 30

1517 Sheep (Nogomi ceramic bell)

1990. New Year's Greetings.
2127 **1517** 41y. multicoloured 1·00 25

1519 Tsuneishi-Hariko Papier-mache Ram

1990. New Year Lottery Stamps. Multicoloured.
2128 41y. Sheep (Tosa ceramic bell) 70 55
2129 62y. Type **1519** 1·00 80

Each stamp carries a lottery number.

1520 Dr. Nishina and Radio Isotope

1990. Birth Centenary of Dr. Yoshio Nishina (physicist) and 50th Anniv of First Japanese Cyclotron (radio isotope generator).
2130 **1520** 62y. multicoloured 80 30

1521 "Lady using Telephone" (Senseki Nakamura)

1990. Centenary of Telephone Service in Japan.
2131 **1521** 62y. multicoloured 80 30

1522/3 Horse-drawn Post Carriages (details of scroll painting by Beisen Kubota)

1524 Inkstone Case (Korin Ogata)

1991. The Horse in Culture (4th series).
2132 **1522** 62y. multicoloured 1·00 30
2133 **1523** 62y. multicoloured 1·00 30
2134 **1524** 62y. multicoloured 1·00 30

Nos. 2132/3 were issued together, se-tenant, forming the composite design illustrated.

1525 "Spring Warmth" (Kogetsu Saigo)

1526 "Senju in Musashi Province" (from "36 Views of Mt. Fuji" by Hokusai Katsushika)

1991. The Horse in Culture (5th series).

2135	**1525**	62y. multicoloured	80	30
2136	**1526**	62y. multicoloured	80	30

1527 Figure Skating

1991. Winter Universiade, Sapporo and Furano. Multicoloured.

2137	41y. Type **1527**	80	40
2138	62y. Short-track speed skating (horiz)	90	40

1529 Bouquet

1991. New Postal Life Insurance System.

2139	**1529**	62y. multicoloured	80	60

1530 "Glory of the Earth" (Komei Bekki)

1991. "Ceramic World Shigaraki '91" Exn.

2140	**1530**	62y. multicoloured	80	30

1531 "Beauty looking Back" (Moronobu Hishikawa)

1991. Philatelic Week. 120th Anniv of First Japanese Stamps.

2141	62y. Type **1531**	90	30
2142	62y. "The Prelude" (Shuho Yamakawa)	90	30
MS2143	93×77 mm. Nos. 2141/2	2·50	2·00

1533 Weeping Cherry Blossom and Phoenix Hall, Byodoin Temple

1991. National Afforestation Campaign.

2144	**1533**	41y. multicoloured	60	30

1534 Early Leveller and Standard Datum Repository, Tokyo

1991. Centenary of Standard Datum of Levelling.

2145	**1534**	62y. multicoloured	80	30

1535 Flowers

1991. Winning Entries in Postage Stamp Design Contest.

2146	**1535**	41y. multicoloured	60	30
2147	-	62y. multicoloured	80	30
2148	-	70y. brown, blue & blk	1·10	30
2149	-	100y. multicoloured	1·60	40

DESIGNS—HORIZ: 62y. Couple in traditional dress; 100y. Butterfly. VERT: 70y. "World Peace".

1539 Japanese Snipe ("Gallinago hardwickii")

1991. Water Birds (1st series). Multicoloured.

2150	62y. Type **1539**	1·50	80
2151	62y. Brown booby ("Sula leucogaster")	1·50	80

See also Nos. 2162/3, 2179/80, 2184/5, 2198/9, 2241/2, 2247/8 and 2251/2.

1541 Kikugoro Onoe VI in Title Role of "Spirit of the Lion"

1542 Utaemon Nakamura VI as Princess Yaegaki in "24 Examples of Filial Piety"

1991. Kabuki Theatre (1st series).

2152	**1541**	62y. green, gold & black	1·00	30
2153	**1542**	100y. multicoloured	1·70	40

See also Nos. 2164/5, 2172/3, 2181/2, 2186/7 and 2190/1.

1543 "Solidarity" in Sign Language and Congress Emblem

1991. 11th World Federation of the Deaf International Congress, Tokyo.

2154	**1543**	62y.+10y. mult	1·00	30

The premium was assigned to programmes for helping the deaf.

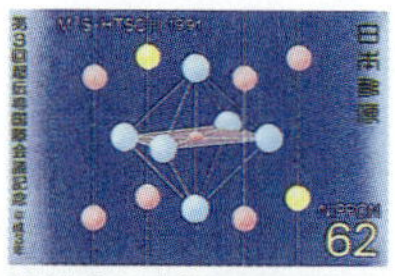

1544 Crystal Structure

1991. International Conf on Materials and Mechanism of Superconductivity, Kanazawa.

2155	**1544**	62y. multicoloured	80	30

1545 Girl sitting on Morning Glory

1546 Fairy on Horse

1991. Letter Writing Day.

2156	**1545**	41y. multicoloured	70	30
2157	**1546**	62y. multicoloured	1·00	30
MS2158		72×93 mm. No. 2157	1·10	85

For design similar to No. 2157 but with central motif drawn larger, see No. 2104.

1547 High Jumping

1991. 3rd World Athletics Championships, Tokyo. Multicoloured.

2159	41y. Type **1547**	60	30
2160	62y. Putting the shot	80	30

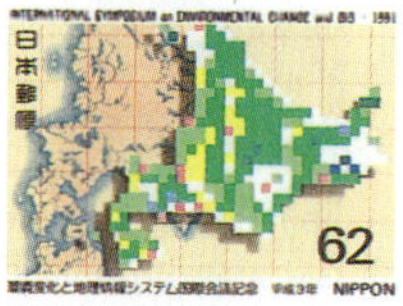

1549 Map and Computer Image of Hokkaido

1991. International Symposium on Environmental Change and Geographic Information Systems, Asahikawa, Hokkaido.

2161	**1549**	62y. multicoloured	80	30

1991. Water Birds (2nd series). As T 1539. Multicoloured.

2162	62y. Japanese gull ("Larus crassirostris")	1·50	80
2163	62y. Little grebe ("Podiceps ruficollis")	1·50	80

1552 Koshiro Matsumoto VII as Benkei in "The Subscription List"

1553 Danjuro Ichikawa XI as Danjo in "Tweezers"

1991. Kabuki Theatre (2nd series).

2164	**1552**	62y. black, grey & gold	1·00	30
2165	**1553**	100y. multicoloured	1·70	40

1554 Nobles watching burning Oten Gate

1991. International Correspondence Week. Details from Ban Dainagon Picture Scrolls by Mitsunaga Tokiwa. Multicoloured.

2166	80y. Type **1554**	1·00	30
2167	120y. Arrest of Yoshio Tomo (arsonist)	1·60	45

1556 "Clear Day with Southern Breeze" (from "36 Views of Mt. Fuji" by Hokusai Katsushika) and Seismographic Wave

1991. Earthquake and Natural Disaster Countermeasures Conference. Tokyo.

2168	**1556**	62y. multicoloured	85	30

1557 Tea Utensils and Flower

1991. 800th Anniv of Introduction of Green Tea into Japan.

2169	**1557**	62y. multicoloured	85	30

1558 "Saucy Girl" (from "A Selection of Beautiful Women" by Kunisada Utagawa)

1991. "Phila Nippon '91" International Stamp Exhibition, Tokyo (2nd issue).

2170	**1558**	62y. multicoloured	95	30
MS2171		93×77 mm. No. 2170 ×2	2·00	2·00

1559 Baigyoku Nakamura III as the Ogiya Courtesan Yugiri in "Yoshida-ya"

1560 Ganjiro Nakamura III as Jihei Kamiya in "Shinju-Ten no Amijima"

1991. Kabuki Theatre (3rd series). Works by Chikamatsu Monzaemon.

2172	**1559**	62y. black, pur & gold	1·00	30
2173	**1560**	100y. multicoloured	1·80	40

1561 Boy building Toy Town

1991. 30th Anniv of Administrative Councillors System.

2174	**1561**	62y. multicoloured	85	25

1562 Ishikawa Papier-mache Monkey

1991. New Year's Greetings. Multicoloured.

2175	41y. Type **1562**	65	30
2176	62y. Obata monkey	85	30

1565 Obata Monkey

1991. New Year Lottery Stamps. Multicoloured.

2177		41y.+3y. Ishikawa papier-mache monkey	85	60
2178		62y.+3y. Type **1565**	1·20	85

Each stamp carries a lottery number.

1992. Water Birds (3rd series). As T 1539. Multicoloured.

2179		62y. Tufted puffin ("Lunda cirrhata")	1·60	70
2180		62y. Hooded cranes ("Grus monacha")	1·60	70

1568 Kichiemon Nakamura I as Jiro Naozane Kumagai in "Chronicle of Two Boys in Battle of Ichinotani" by Munesuke Namiki

1569 Nizaemon Kataoka XIII as Old Man in "Kotobuki Shiki Sambaso"

1992. Kabuki Theatre (4th series).

2181	**1568**	62y. multicoloured	1·00	30
2182	**1569**	100y. multicoloured	1·80	40

1570 Orchid and Chimpanzees

1992. 8th Conference of Parties to Convention on International Trade in Endangered Species, Kyoto City.

2183	**1570**	62y. multicoloured	1·30	40

1992. Water Birds (4th series). As T 1539. Multicoloured.

2184		62y. Whooper swan ("Cygnus cygnus")	1·60	35
2185		62y. Painted-snipe ("Rostratula benghalensis")	1·50	35

1573 Enjaku Jitsukawa II as Ishikawa-Geomon in "Two-Storey Gate—Pawlonia" by Gohei Namiki

1574 Hakuo Matsumoto I as Oishi-Kuranosuke in "Loyal Retainers in Genroku" by Seika Mayama

1992. Kabuki Theatre (5th series).

2186	**1573**	62y. multicoloured	1·00	35
2187	**1574**	100y. multicoloured	1·80	40

1575 "Flowers on Chair" (Hoshun Yamaguchi)

1992. Philatelic Week.

2188	**1575**	62y. multicoloured	85	35

1576 Shuri Castle

1992. 20th Anniv of Return of Okinawa (Ryukyu Islands).

2189	**1576**	62y. multicoloured	1·30	25

1577 Baiko Onoe VII as the Wisteria Maiden

1578 Shoroku Onoe II as Goro Soga and Kanzaburo Nakamura XVII as Juro Soga in "Kotobuki-Soga-taimen"

1992. Kabuki Theatre (6th series).

2190	**1577**	62y. multicoloured	1·00	35
2191	**1578**	100y. multicoloured	1·80	40

1579 "ADEOS" Observation Satellite

1992. International Space Year. Multicoloured.

2192		62y. Type **1579**	85	25
2193		62y. "BS-3" broadcasting satellite and space station	85	25

Nos. 2192/3 were printed together, se-tenant, forming a composite design.

1581 Bird delivering Letter to Flower

1992. Letter Writing Day. Multicoloured.

2194		41y. Type **1581**	75	25
2195		62y. Bird delivering letter to dog	1·00	60
MS2196		76×93 mm. No. 2195	3·25	2·75

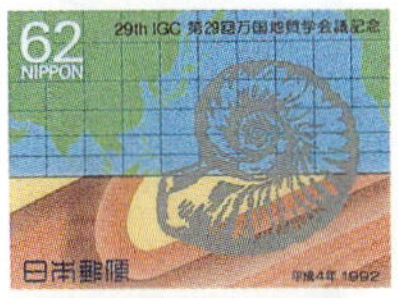

1583 Ammonite, Map and Stratigraphic Plan

1992. 29th Int Geological Congress, Kyoto.

2197	**1583**	62y. multicoloured	85	40

1992. Water Birds (5th series). As T 1539. Multicoloured.

2198		62y. White-faced shearwater ("Calonectris leucomelas")	1·60	60
2199		62y. Ruddy kingfisher ("Halcyon coromanda")	1·60	60

1586 Canoeing

1992. 47th National Athletic Meeting, Yamagata.

2200	**1586**	41y. multicoloured	75	25

1587 Japanese Jar (Ninsei Nonomura)

1588 Chinese Vase (Tang dynasty)

1992. 20th Anniv of Restoration of Diplomatic Relations with China.

2201	**1587**	62y. multicoloured	85	35
2202	**1588**	62y. multicoloured	85	35

1589 Nobles arriving at Taiken Gate

1590 Fujiwarano Nobuyori giving Audience

1992. International Correspondence Week. Details from "Tale of Heiji" Shinzei Picture Scroll.

2203	**1589**	80y. multicoloured	1·20	35
2204	**1590**	120y. multicoloured	1·90	35

1591 "Friends" (Tomoko Komoto)

1992. 3rd Stamp Design Competition Winners. Multicoloured.

2205		62y. Type **1591**	85	35
2206		70y. "Gaiety on Christmas Night" (Brat Anca)	95	35

1593 "Kyo" Ideograph, Mt. Fuji, Sun and Waves

1992. 30th International Co-operative Alliance Congress, Tokyo.

2207	**1593**	62y. multicoloured	85	35

1594 Takakazu Seki (mathematician, 350th birth)

1595 Akiko Yosano (poet, 50th death)

1992. Anniversaries.

2208	**1594**	62y. multicoloured	1·10	35
2209	**1595**	62y. multicoloured	1·10	35

1596 Certified Public Tax Accountants' Assn Emblem

1992. 50th Anniv of Tax Accountants Law.

2210	**1596**	62y. multicoloured	85	35

1597 Papier-mache and Clay Cock

1992. New Year's Greetings. Multicoloured.

2211		41y. Type **1597**	75	35
2212		62y. Tsuyazaki clay cock on drum	1·10	35

1600 Tsuyazaki Clay Cock on Drum

1992. New Year Lottery Stamps. Multicoloured.

2213		41y.+3y. Papier-mache and clay cock	85	70
2214		62y.+3y. Type **1600**	1·20	95

Each stamp carries a lottery number.

1601 "Orthetrum albistylum" (dragonfly)

1601a "Oxycetonia jucunda" (beetle)

1602 Mikado Swallowtail

1603 Ladybirds

1603a Honey Bee

1603b "Lycaena phleas" (copper butterfly)

1604 Mandarin

1605 Japanese White-Eye

1606 Eastern Turtle Dove

1606a Great Tit

1607 Varied Tit

1608 Greater Pied Kingfisher

1609 Pacific Black Duck

1609a Little Ringed Plover

1609b Bull-headed Shrike

1610 Northern Bullfinch

1610a Masked Hawfinch

1610b Jay

1611 Orchids

1612 Wild Pink

1613 Adder's Tongue Lily

1614 Day- flowers

1615 Iris

1616 Violets

1617 Praying Mantis, Chrysanthemums and Hibiscus (after Hatsu Sakai)

1618 "Pine and Hawk" (Sesson Shukei)

1992

2215	**1601**	9y. yellow, black & bl	20	20
2215a	**1601a**	10y. multicoloured	20	20
2216	**1602**	15y. brown, light green and green	30	25
2217	**1603**	18y. green, grey and red	65	55
2217a	**1603a**	20y. multicoloured	45	20
2217b	**1603b**	30y. multicoloured	75	35
2218	**1604**	41y. orge, dp bl & bl	95	25
2219	**1605**	50y. yellow, bl & blk	1·60	55
2220	**1606**	62y. orge, dp bl & bl	1·10	45
2220a	**1606a**	70y. multicoloured	1·20	45
2221	**1607**	72y. orange, bl & grn	2·40	95
2222	**1608**	80y. blue, stone and green	2·50	55
2223	**1609**	90y. brown, yell & bl	3·00	60
2223a	**1609a**	110y. multicoloured	2·20	70
2223b	**1609b**	120y. multicoloured	2·75	95
2224	**1610**	130y. multicoloured	2·40	45
2224a	**1610a**	140y. multicoloured	3·25	1·10
2224b	**1610b**	160y. multicoloured	3·75	1·10
2225	**1611**	190y. multicoloured	3·50	70
2226	**1612**	270y. multicoloured	5·50	90
2227	**1613**	350y. mauve, lilac and green	7·00	1·20
2228	**1614**	390y. multicoloured	7·50	80
2229	**1615**	420y. violet, light green and green	8·75	1·40
2230	**1616**	430y. multicoloured	8·00	1·60
2231	**1617**	700y. multicoloured	13·00	5·25
2232	**1618**	1000y. multicoloured	15·00	5·25

The 41, 50, 62 and 80y. also exist imperforate with self-adhesive gum.

1993. Water Birds (6th series). As T 1539. Multicoloured.

2241	62y. River kingfisher ("Alcedo atthis")	1·80	45
2242	62y. Cattle egret ("Bubulcus ibis")	1·80	45

1623 Super Giant Slalom

1993. World Alpine Skiing Championships, Shizukuishi (nr. Morioka). Multicoloured.

2243	41y. Type **1623**	75	35
2244	62y. Downhill	1·10	35

1625 Poppies (after Hochu Nakamura)

1993. Seasonal Flowers (1st series). Multicoloured.

2245	41y. Type **1625**	1·10	45
2246	62y. Cherry Blossoms (after Haitsu Sakai) (25×35 mm)	1·70	45

See also Nos. 2258/9, 2269/70 and 2287/8.

1993. Water Birds (7th series). As T 1539. Multicoloured.

2247	62y. White-fronted geese ("Anser albifrons")	1·80	45
2248	62y. Japanese white-naped cranes ("Grus vipio")	1·80	45

No. 2247 is wrongly inscribed "Ansner".

1629 "In the Studio" (Nanpu Katayama)

1993. Philatelic Week.

2249	**1629**	62y. multicoloured	95	35

1630 Coral Trees and Reef, Minnajima Island

1993. National Afforestation Campaign.

2250	**1630**	41y. multicoloured	1·20	45

1993. Water Birds (8th series). As T 1539. Multicoloured.

2251	62y. Baikal teal ("Anas formosa")	1·30	1·10
2252	62y. White-tailed sea eagle ("Haliaeetus albicilla")	1·30	1·10

1635 "Mandarin Duck in Nest" and "Gardenia in Nest"

1993. Wedding of Crown Prince Naruhito and Masako Owada. Multicoloured.

2253	62y. "Mandarin Duck in Nest" (pattern of groom's jacket) (vert)	1·10	45
2254	62y. "Gardenia in Nest" (pattern of bride's robe) (vert)	1·10	45
2255	70y. Type **1635**	1·20	45

1636 Manchurian Crane with Chicks

1993. 5th Meeting of Ramsar Convention for the Preservation of Wetlands, Kushiro (Hokkaido).

2256	62y. Type **1636**	1·10	45
2257	62y. Head of Manchurian crane	1·10	45

1993. Seasonal Flowers (2nd series) As T 1615. Multicoloured.

2258	41y. Lily (after Kiitsu Suzuki)	75	25
2259	62y. Thistle (after Shiko Watan-abe) (25×35 mm)	1·10	45

1640 Stylized Ideographs for "Commercial Registration"

1993. Centenary of Commercial Registration System.

2260	**1640**	62y. multicoloured	1·10	45

1641 Puppy reading Letter under Tree

1993. Letter Writing Day. Multicoloured.

2261	41y. Type **1641**	95	35
2262	62y. Man pointing at flying letter (23×27 mm)	1·30	45
MS2263	72×93 mm. No. 2262	1·40	1·10

1643 Heart, Clouds and Flowers

1993. World Federation for Mental Health Congress, Chiba City.

2264	**1643**	62y. multicoloured	1·10	45

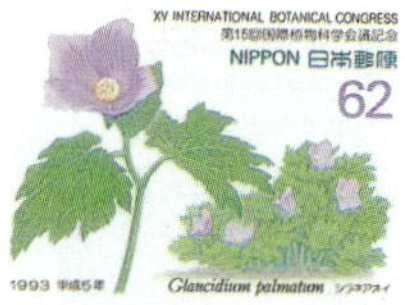

1644 "Glaucidium palmatum"

1993. 15th International Botanical Congress, Yokohama. Multicoloured.

2265	62y. Type **1644**	1·10	45
2266	62y. "Sciadopitys verticillata"	1·10	45

1646 Swimming

1993. 48th National Athletic Meeting, Kagawa Prefecture. Multicoloured.

2267	41y. Type **1646**	85	35
2268	41y. Karate	85	35

1993. Seasonal Flowers (3rd series). As T 1615. Multicoloured.

2269	41y. "Chinese Bell-flowers" (Korin Ogata)	75	25
2270	62y. Chrysanthemums (detail of "Cranes and Plants in Spring and Autumn", Kiitsu Suzuki) (25×35 mm)	1·20	45

1650 "Arrival of Portuguese" (folding screen)

1993. 450th Anniv of First Portuguese Visit to Japan. Multicoloured.

2271	62y. Type **1650**	1·10	45
2272	62y. Jesuit mother-of-pearl inlaid host box	1·10	45

1652 Ki no Tsurayuki (Agetatami Scrolls)

1993. International Correspondence Week. Picture Scrolls of the Thirty-six Immortal Poets.

2273	80y. Type **1652**	1·40	55
2274	120y. Kodai no Kimi (Satake Scrolls)	2·10	80

1654 Sprinter

1993. 10th International Veterans' Athletic Championships, Miyazaki.

2275	**1654**	62y. multicoloured	1·10	45

1655 Prince Naruhito and Princess Masako

1993. Wedding of Crown Prince Naruhito and Masako Owada (2nd issue). Sheet 90×93 mm.

MS2276	62y. multicoloured	2·40	1·90

1656 Toson Shimazaki (writer, 50th death)

1993. Anniversaries. Multicoloured.

2277	62y. Type **1656**	1·10	45
2278	62y. Umetaro Suzuki (scientist, 50th death)	1·10	45
2279	62y. Kazan Watanabe (after Chinzan Tsubaki) (artist, birth bicentenary)	1·10	45

1659 Shibahara Clay Dog

1993. New Year's Greetings. Multicoloured.

2280	41y. Type **1659**	95	35
2281	62y. Kosen clay tosa dog	1·10	45

1662 Kosen Clay Tosa Dog

1993. New Year Lottery Stamps. Multicoloured.

2282	41y. Shibahara clay dog	1·10	90
2283	62y. Type **1662**	1·20	95

1663 Rice Flowers

1993. Centenary of Agricultural Research Centre, Nishigahara.

2284	**1663**	62y. multicoloured	1·10	45

1664 Man and Bird (Soichiro Asaba)

1993. 45th Anniv of Declaration of Human Rights. Stamp design contest winning entries.

2285	62y. Type **1664**	1·10	45
2286	70y. Symbols (Armand Clotagatilde)	1·20	45

1994. Seasonal Flowers (4th series). As T 1625. Multicoloured.

2287	50y. Plum Blossom (after Korin Ogata)	85	35
2288	80y. Winter Camellia (after Hoitsu Sakai) (26×35 mm)	1·40	60

1994. Special Correspondence Stamps. As Nos. 1677/9 but values changed.

2289	**1098**	50y. multicoloured	1·50	45
2290	**1099**	50y. multicoloured	85	35
2291	**1099**	80y. multicoloured	1·40	60
2292	**1100**	90y. multicoloured	1·60	60

1668 Ladies' Figure Skating

1994. World Figure Skating Championships, Chiba City. Multicoloured.

2293	50y. Type **1668**	85	35
2294	50y. Ice dancing	85	35
2295	80y. Men's figure skating	1·40	60
2296	80y. Pairs figure skating	1·40	60

1672 "Irises" (Heihachiro Fukuda)

1994. Philatelic Week.

2297	**1672**	80y. multicoloured	2·40	60

1673 "Love" (Chieko Kitajima)

1994. International Year of the Family. Winning Entries in Stamp Design Contest. Multicoloured.

2298	50y. Type **1673**	1·20	35
2299	50y. "Happiness Flower" (Shigenobu Nagaishi)	1·20	35
2300	80y. "Family flowering at Home" (Junichi Mineta)	3·75	1·30
2301	80y. "Family in Flight" (Soichiro Asaba)	1·70	60

1677 White Stork, Marguerites and Camphor Tree

1994. National Afforestation Campaign.

2302	**1677**	50y. multicoloured	1·50	60

1678 Houses by the Waterside

1994. International Conference on Reduction of Natural Disasters, Yokohama.

2303	**1678**	80y. multicoloured	1·40	60

1679 Pylon and Monju Building

1994. Achievement of Initial Criticality (self-sustaining reaction) in Monju Nuclear Fast Breeder Reactor, Tsuruga.

2304	**1679**	80y. multicoloured	2·40	60

1680 Wildlife

1994. Environment Day.

2305	**1680**	80y. multicoloured	2·40	60

1681 Envelope "Ship" and Man

1994. Letter Writing Day. Multicoloured.

2306	50y. Type **1681**	1·10	35
2307	80y. Giraffe carrying envelope	1·40	60
MS2308	72×93 mm. No. 2307	1·50	1·20

1683 Emblem in Eye

1994. 10th Int AIDS Conference, Yokohama.

2309	**1683**	80y. multicoloured	1·40	60

1684 Baron Maeshima (Postal Minister) and 1871 48 mon "Dragon" Stamp

1994. History of Stamps (1st series). First Japanese Issue. Multicoloured, frame colour of "Dragon" stamp given.

2310	**1684**	80y. brown	1·40	60
2311	-	80y. blue	1·40	60
2312	-	80y. red	1·40	60
2313	-	80y. green	1·40	60

DESIGNS: No. 2311, 100mon "Dragon" stamp; 2312, 200mon "Dragon" stamp; 2313, 500mon "Dragon" stamp.

The central portion of the stamp portrayed varies according to value.

See also Nos. 2339/42, 2345/6, 2363/4, 2382/5 and 2416/19.

1685/6 Airport and Boeing 747 bearing Airport Code

1994. Opening of Kansai International Airport, Osaka. Multicoloured.

2314	80y. Type **1685**	1·40	60
2315	80y. Type **1686**	1·40	60
2316	80y. Airplane approaching Airport	1·40	60

Nos. 2314/15 form the composite design shown.

1688 Dish Aerial and Satellite

1994. I.T.U. Plenipotentiary Conference, Kyoto.

2317	**1688**	80y. multicoloured	1·40	55

1689 Kickball

1994. 12th Asian Games, Hiroshima. Mult.

2318	50y. Type **1689**	85	35
2319	80y. Steeplechase	1·40	55
2320	80y. Synchronized swimming	1·40	55

1692 Sugoroku

1994. International Correspondence Week. Details of "House of Entertainment" (folding screen). Multicoloured.

2321	90y. Type **1692**	1·60	60
2322	110y. Shogi	1·90	80
2323	130y. Go	2·20	90

1695 Handball

1994. 49th National Athletic Meeting, Aichi.

2324	**1695**	50y. multicoloured	85	35

1696 Michio Miyagi (composer)

1994. Birth Anniversaries. Multicoloured.

2325	80y. Type **1696**	1·40	55
2326	80y. Gyoshu Hayami (painter) and "Moths"	1·40	55

1698 Fujiwara no Michinaga and Insulin Crystals

1994. 15th International Diabetes Federation Congress, Kobe.

2327	**1698**	80y. multicoloured	1·40	55

Fujiwara no Michinaga (966–1028) was the earliest known Japanese diabetic.

1699/1703 "Viewing Maple Leaves at Takao" (folding screen, Hideyori Kano) (image scaled to 45% of original size)

1704 "Yokuryuchi Pool, Shugakuin Imperial Villa" (Kenji Kawai)

1705 "Rock Garden, Ryoan Temple" (Eizo Kato)

1994. 1200th Anniv of Kyoto. Paintings.

2328	**1699**	80y. multicoloured	1·40	55
2329	**1700**	80y. multicoloured	1·40	55
2330	**1701**	80y. multicoloured	1·40	55
2331	**1702**	80y. multicoloured	1·40	55
2332	**1703**	80y. multicoloured	1·40	55
2333	**1704**	80y. multicoloured	1·40	55
2334	**1705**	80y. multicoloured	1·40	55

Nos. 2328/32 were issued together, se-tenant, forming the composite design illustrated.

1706 Izumo Papier-mache Boar

1994. New Year's Greetings. Multicoloured.

2335	50y. Type **1706**	85	35
2336	80y. Boar (Takayama soft toy)	1·40	55

1709 Boar (Takayama soft toy)

1994. New Year's Greetings. Lottery Stamps. Multicoloured.

2337	50y.+3y. Izumo Papier-mache boar	95	35
2338	80y.+3y. Type **1709**	1·50	60

Each stamp carries a lottery number.

1710 5r. Stamp and Eduardo Chiossone (designer)

1994. History of Stamps (2nd series). "Koban" issue of 1876–88. Multicoloured, colour of featured stamp given.

2339	**1710**	80y. grey	1·40	55
2340	-	80y. brown	1·40	55
2341	-	80y. red	1·40	55
2342	-	80y. blue	1·40	55

FEATURED STAMPS: No. 2340, 1s. stamp (Type **20**); 2341, 12s. stamp (Type **21**); 2342, 20s. stamp (Type **22**).

1711 Himeji Castle Tower

1712 "Himeji Castle" (Masami Takahashi)

1994. World Heritage Sites (1st series).

2343	**1711**	80y. multicoloured	1·40	55
2344	**1712**	80y. multicoloured	1·40	55

See also Nos. 2347/8, 2373/4 and 2400/1.

1713 2s. Stamp and Postal Delivery by Hand-drawn Cart

1995. History of Stamps (3rd series). 1894 Emperor's Silver Wedding issue and paintings by Shinsai Shibata. Multicoloured.

2345	80y. Type **1713**	1·40	55
2346	80y. 5s. stamp and postal delivery by horse-drawn carriage	1·40	55

1715 "Kannon Bosatsu" (wall painting, Kondo Hall)

1716 Kondo Hall, Horyu Temple

1995. World Heritage Sites (2nd series). Multicoloured.

2347	**1715**	80y. multicoloured	1·40	55
2348	**1716**	110y. multicoloured	1·90	80

1717 Emblem and National Flowers

1995. Centenary of Japan–Brazil Treaty of Friendship. Multicoloured.

2349	80y. Type **1717**	1·40	55
2350	80y. Emblem and sports	1·40	55

1719 Unebi and Nijo Mountains and Tile from Palace

1720 "Remembering Times Past" (Saburosuke Okada)

1995. 1300th Anniv of Fujiwara Palace, Kashihara.

2351	**1719**	50y. multicoloured	85	35
2352	**1720**	80y. multicoloured	1·40	55

1721 "Dissection" (Seison Maeda)

1995. Modern Anatomy Education.

2353	**1721**	80y. multicoloured	1·40	55

1722 "National Census" and "16"

1995. 16th National Census.

2354	**1722**	80y. multicoloured	1·40	55

1723 Volunteer teaching Bangladeshi Woman to Read

1995. 30th Anniv of Japanese Overseas Co-operation Volunteers Service.

2355	**1723**	80y. multicoloured	1·40	55

1724 "Visitor to Art Studio" (Keika Kanashima)

1995. Philatelic Week.

2356	**1724**	80y.+20y. mult	1·80	1·50

The premium was for the Osaka/Kobe and Awaji earthquake victims' fund.

1725 Auspicious Clouds

1726 Reeds (mourning)

1727 Water Lily (mourning)

1728 Cloud, "Wind" and Pine Bark Pattern

1729 "Daphniphyllum macropodum"

1995. Special Correspondence Stamps.

2357	**1725**	50y. multicoloured	85	35
2358	**1726**	50y. multicoloured	1·20	35
2359	**1727**	80y. multicoloured	1·70	55
2360	**1728**	80y. multicoloured	1·40	55
2361	**1729**	90y. multicoloured	1·60	60

1730 Maple and Shrine Island, Akiteline

1995. National Afforestation Campaign.

2362	**1730**	50y. multicoloured	85	35

1731 81/2s. Stamp and First Airmail Flight from Osaka to Tokyo

1995. History of Stamps (4th series). 1929 First Airmail issue. Multicoloured.

2363	110y. Type **1731**	1·90	80
2364	110y. 18s. stamp and loading freight onto airplane	1·90	80

1733 Hearts forming Flower

1995. Greetings Stamps. Mult. Self-adhesive.

2365	80y. Type **1733**	1·40	55
2366	80y. Child with balloon	1·40	55
2367	80y. Flower and pencil	1·40	55
2368	80y. Star, sun and moon	1·40	55
2369	80y. Child with dog	1·40	55

1738 Postman

1995. Letter Writing Day. Multicoloured.

2370	50y. Type **1738**	85	35
2371	80y. Ostrich	1·40	55
MS2372	72×93 mm. No. 2371	1·50	1·20

1740 Cedar

1995. World Heritage Sites (3rd series). Yaku Island. Multicoloured.

2373	80y. Type **1740**	1·40	55
2374	80y. Sika deer	1·40	55

1742 "Friends, One and All" (Yuki Ogawa)

1743 Atomic Bomb Dome, Hiroshima (Nobuya Nagata)

1744 "Light of Peace" (Nobuo Suenaga)

1995. 50th Anniv of End of Second World War. Stamp Design Contest Winners.

2375	**1742**	50y. multicoloured	85	35
2376	**1743**	80y. multicoloured	1·40	55
2377	**1744**	80y. multicoloured	1·40	55

1745 Marathon Runners

1995. 18th International University Games, Fukuoka.

2378	**1745**	80y. multicoloured	1·40	55

1746 Radio-controlled Aircraft

1995. World Aeromodel Championships, Kasaoka. Multicoloured.

2379	50y. Type **1746**	85	35
2380	80y. Radio-controlled helicopter	1·40	55

1748 Horse, Cow and Labrador

1995. World Veterinary Congress, Yokohama.

2381	**1748**	80y. multicoloured	1·40	1·10

1749 5y. Stamp and Cherub and Tokyo Mailbox

1995. History of Stamps (5th series). Industries issue of 1948–49. Multicoloured.

2382	80y. Type **1749**	1·30	55
2383	80y. 50y. stamp and mail van	1·30	55
2384	80y. 90y. stamp and mail van	1·30	55
2385	80y. 10y. stamp and cherub on Tokyo mailbox	1·30	55

1753 Judo (Makuhari, Chiba)

1995. World Sports Championships. Mult.

2386	80y. Type **1753**	1·30	55
2387	80y. Gymnastics (Sabae, Fukui)	1·30	55

1755 Shell Matching Game (from "New Year's Amusements")

1995. International Correspondence Week. Details of paintings on folding screens. Multicoloured.

2388	90y. Type **1755**	1·40	1·10
2389	110y. Battledore and Shuttlecock (from "Twelve Months")	1·70	1·40
2390	130y. Playing Cards (from "Matsuura Folding Screen")	2·10	1·70

1758 Cyclists

1995. 50th Anniv of National Athletic Meeting, Fukushima.

2391	**1758**	50y. multicoloured	95	45

1759 Patchwortk Hearts (Tomoko Suzuki)

1995. 50th Anniversaries of U.N.O. (2392) and UNESCO (2393). Multicoloured.

2392	80y. Type **1759**	1·30	1·10
2393	80y. Children with Heart Balloon (Yukino Ikeda)	1·30	1·10

1761 Tadataka Ino (cartographer, 250th birth)

1995. Anniversaries. Multicoloured.

2394	80y. Type **1761**	1·30	55
2395	80y. Kitaro Nishida (philosopher, 50th death)	1·30	55

1763 Tsutsumi Clay Rat on Cayenne Pepper

1995. New Year's Greetings. Multicoloured.

2396	50y. Type **1763**	75	25
2397	80y. Satsuma papier-mache rat in rice store	1·30	55

1766 Satsuma Papier-mache Rat in Rice Store

1995. New Year's Lottery Stamps. Multicoloured.

2398	50y.+3y. Tsutsumi clay rat on turnip	1·10	90
2399	80y.+3y. Type **1766**	1·50	1·20

Each stamp carries a lottery number.

1767 Beech Forest

1995. World Heritage Sites (4th series). Shirakami Mountains. Multicoloured.

2400	80y. Type **1767**	1·30	55
2401	80y. Black woodpecker	1·30	55

1769 Obi Material showing Choson Dynasty Boxes (Keisuke Serizawa)

1995. 30th Anniv of Resumption of Japan–Korea Diplomatic Relations.

2402	**1769**	80y. multicoloured	1·30	55

1770 Siebold

1996. Birth Bicentenary of Philipp Franz von Siebold (physician and Japanologist).

2403	**1770**	80y. multicoloured	1·40	55

1771 Twined Ropes

1996. 50th Anniv of Labour Relations Commissions.

2404	**1771**	80y. multicoloured	1·20	45

1772 Turtle and Crane

1996. Senior Citizens.

2405	**1772**	80y. multicoloured	1·20	45

1773 Driving to Diet for Promulgation of Constitution, 1946

1774 Signing San Francisco Peace Treaty, 1951

1775 Return of Okinawa, 1972

1996. 50 Post-war Years (1st series).

2406	**1773**	80y. mauve, lilac & gold	2·20	1·10
2407	**1774**	80y. dp grn, grn & gold	2·20	1·10
2408	**1775**	80y. indigo, blue and gold	2·20	1·10

See also Nos. 2420/1, 2429/30, 2443/4 and 2449/54.

1776 Woman and Diet Building

1996. 50th Anniv of Women's Suffrage.

2409	**1776**	80y. multicoloured	1·20	45

1777 "Window" (Yukihiko Yasuda)

1996. Philatelic Week.

2410	**1777**	80y. multicoloured	1·20	45

1778 Mother and Child

1996. 50th Anniv of UNICEF.

2411	**1778**	80y. multicoloured	1·50	55

1779 Children and Sun

1996. Child Welfare Week.

2412	**1779**	80y. multicoloured	1·50	55

1780 Narcissus Flycatcher

1996. Bird Week. Multicoloured.

2413	80y. Type **1780**	1·30	55
2414	80y. Binoculars and bird feeding nestlings	1·30	55

1782 Cherry Blossom and Tokyo Buildings

1996. National Afforestation Campaign.

2415	**1782**	50y. multicoloured	95	45

1783 1991 Design

1784 1949 Design

1996. History of Stamps (6th series). Philatelic Week Issues.

2416	**1783**	80y. brown, ochre and lilac	1·20	45
2417	**1783**	80y. multicoloured	1·20	45
2418	**1784**	80y. deep lilac and lilac	1·20	45
2419	**1784**	80y. multicoloured	1·20	45

1785 Olympic Flame (Olympic Games, Tokyo, 1964)

1786 Sun Tower ("EXPO 70" World Fair, Osaka)

1996. 50 Post-war Years (2nd series).

2420	**1785**	80y. multicoloured	1·50	45
2421	**1786**	80y. multicoloured	1·50	45

1787/8 "Oirase no Keiryu" (Chikkyo Ono)

1996. Centenary of Modern River Control Systems.

2422	**1787**	80y. multicoloured	1·30	1·10
2423	**1788**	80y. multicoloured	1·30	1·10

Nos. 2422/3 were issued together, se-tenant, forming the composite design illustrated.

1789 Emblem

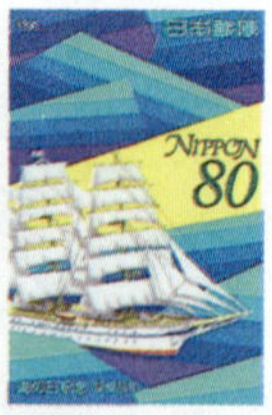

1790 "Nippon Maru II" (cadet ship)

1996. Marine Day.

2424	**1789**	50y. multicoloured	95	45
2425	**1790**	80y. multicoloured	1·30	45

1791 Cat

1996. Letter Writing Day. Multicoloured.

2426	50y. Type **1791**	95	80
2427	80y. Toy horse	1·30	1·10
MS2428	72×93 mm. No. 2427	1·50	1·20

1793 "Hikari" Express Train and Motorway

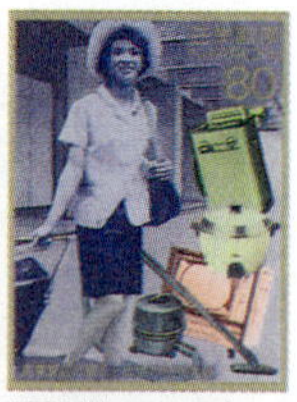

1794 Woman and Modern Appliances

1996. 50 Post-war Years (3rd series). Modern Life.

2429	**1793**	80y. multicoloured	1·50	1·20
2430	**1794**	80y. multicoloured	1·50	1·20

1795 Kenji Miyazawa (writer, centenary)

1996. Birth Anniversaries. Multicoloured.

2431	80y. Type **1795**	1·50	1·20
2432	80y. Hokiichi Hanawa (scholar and editor, 250th)	1·50	1·20

1797 Archer

1996. 51st National Athletic Meeting, Hiroshima.

2433	**1797**	50y. multicoloured	85	70

1798 Paper-chain People around Red Feather (donor pin)

1996. 50th Anniv of Community Chest.

2434	**1798**	80y. multicoloured	1·50	1·20

1799 Piano Keys and Double Clef

1996. International Music Day.

2435	**1799**	80y. multicoloured	1·50	1·20

1800 "Water Mill in Onden"

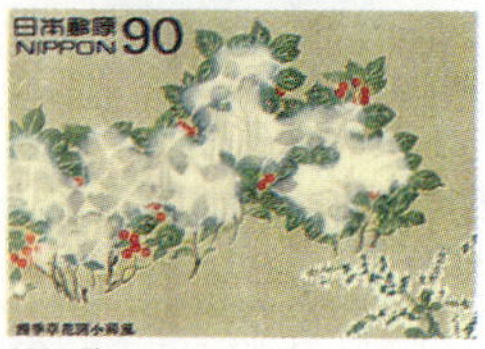

1801 Flowers

1803 Flowers

1805 Flowers

1996. International Correspondence Week. Paintings from "36 Views of Mt. Fuji" by Hokusai Katsushika (2436, 2438, 2440) and details of paintings on folding screen by Kohrin Ogata (others).

2436	**1800**	90y. multicoloured	1·30	1·10
2437	**1801**	90y. multicoloured	1·30	1·10
2438	-	110y. multicoloured	1·80	1·50
2439	**1803**	110y. multicoloured	1·80	1·50
2440	-	130y. multicoloured	2·10	1·70
2441	**1805**	130y. multicoloured	2·10	1·70

DESIGNS—As T **1800**: No. 2438, "Fine Day with a South Wind"; 2440, "Lake in Sosyu Hakone".

1806 Congress Emblem and Squirrel

1996. 18th Int Savings Banks Congress, Tokyo.

2442	**1806**	80y. multicoloured	1·50	1·20

1807 Mobile Telephone, Fibre-optic Cable and Communications Satellite

1808 Satellite Photograph of Earth

1996. 50 Post-war Years (4th series). Telecommunications and Environmental Protection.

2443	**1807**	80y. multicoloured	1·50	1·20
2444	**1808**	80y. multicoloured	1·50	1·20

1809 Okinawa Papier-mache Fighting Bull

1996. New Year's Greetings. Multicoloured.

2445	50y. Type **1809**	95	80
2446	80y. Child on bull (Takamatsu wedding doll)	1·40	1·10

1812 Child on Bull (Takamatus Wedding Doll)

1996. New Year Lottery Stamps. Multicoloured.

2447	50y.+3y. Okinawa papier-mache fighting bull	1·10	90
2448	80y.+3y. Type **1812**	1·50	1·20

Each stamp carries a lottery number.

1813 Yujiro Ishihara (actor) as Youth

1814 Ishihara smoking Pipe

1815 Hibari Misora (actress' and singer) in "Kanashiki Kuchibue"

1816 Misora singing

1817 Osamu Tezuka (cartoonist) and Cartoon Characters

1818 Self-portrait and Astroboy

1997. 50 Post-war Years (5th series). Entertainers.

2449	**1813**	80y. black, brn & gold	1·20	45
2450	**1814**	80y. multicoloured	1·20	45
2451	**1815**	80y. black, blue & gold	1·20	45
2452	**1816**	80y. multicoloured	1·20	45
2453	**1817**	80y. multicoloured	1·20	45
2454	**1818**	80y. multicoloured	1·20	45

1819 Emblem

1997. Winter Olympic Games, Nagano (1998). Multicoloured.

2455	80y.+10y. Type **1819**	1·60	1·30
2456	80y.+10y. Snowlets (mascots)	1·60	1·30

1821 "Daigo" (Togyu Okumura)

1997. Philatelic Week.

2457	**1821**	80y. multicoloured	1·50	60

1822 Main Court Room

1997. 50th Anniv of Supreme Court.

2458	**1822**	80y. multicoloured	1·50	60

1823 Parachutist

1824 Waving to Mechanical Doll

1825 Stamp Lover

1826 Helicopter Postman

1827 With Love Letter

1997. Greetings Stamps. Doraemon (cartoon character). Self-adhesive gum.

2459	**1823**	80y. multicoloured	1·30	90
2460	**1824**	80y. multicoloured	1·30	90
2461	**1825**	80y. multicoloured	1·30	90
2462	**1826**	80y. multicoloured	1·30	90
2463	**1827**	80y. multicoloured	1·30	90

1828 Mexican Mythological Figures (Luis Nishizawa)

1997. Centenary of Japanese Emigration to Mexico.

2464	**1828**	80y. multicoloured	1·50	60

1829 Zao Crater Lake and Bush Clover

1997. National Afforestation Campaign.

2465	**1829**	50y. multicoloured	85	35

1830 House's Seal and Diet Building

1997. 50th Anniv of House of Councillors.

2466	**1830**	80y. multicoloured	1·50	60

1831 "Happy Balloon" (Orville Isaac)

1832 "Bird Friends" (Haruka Kumiya)

1833 "Message from Rainbow Forest" (Anna Romanovskaya)

1834 "Greetings" (Yumi Kiryu)

1997. Letter Writing Day.

2467	**1831**	50y. multicoloured	95	80
2468	**1832**	70y. multicoloured	1·20	95
2469	**1833**	80y. multicoloured	1·40	1·10
2470	**1834**	90y. multicoloured	1·50	1·20
MS2471		72×93 mm. No. 2469	1·80	1·30

1835 Bird with Letter and Owl on Blackboard

1997. 50th Anniv of High School Part-time and Correspondence Courses.

2472	**1835**	50y. multicoloured	85	35

1836 Stylized Worker

1997. 50th Anniv of Labour Standards Law.

2473	**1836**	80y. multicoloured	1·50	60

1837 Pacific Ocean and Mt. Osorno (after Hokusai Katsushika)

1997. Centenary of Japan–Chile Relations.

2474	**1837**	80y. multicoloured	1·50	60

1838 Mopi (mascot) and Synchronized Swimmers

1997. 52nd National Athletic Meeting, Osaka.

2475	**1838**	50y. multicoloured	85	35

1839 "Hodogaya" (from "53 Stations of Tokaido")

1840 Woodpecker and Flower

1842 Foliage

1844 Snow-covered Tree

1997. International Correspondence Week. Paintings by Hiroshige Ando (Nos. 2476, 2478, 2480) and details from "The Four Seasons" by Hoitsu Sakai (others). Multicoloured.

2476	90y. Type **1839**	1·40	60
2477	90y. Type **1840**	1·40	60
2478	110y. "Kameyama" (from "53 Stations of Tokaido")	1·70	70
2479	110y. Type **1842**	1·70	70
2480	130y. "Snow View from Sumida River Revetment" (from "Edo Scenic Sites: Snow, Moon and Flower")	2·10	90
2481	130y. Type **1844**	2·10	90

1845 Auditorium, Takeru (opera character) and Ballerina

1997. Inaug of New National Theatre, Tokyo.

2482	**1845**	80y. multicoloured	1·50	60

1846 "Iihi Tabidachi" (Shinji Tanimura)

1847 "Tsuki no Sabaku" (Masao Kato and Suguru Sasaki)

1997. Favourite Songs (1st series).

2483	**1846**	50y. multicoloured	95	45
2484	**1847**	80y. multicoloured	1·40	60

See also Nos. 2497/8, 2499/2500, 2522/3, 2527/8, 2531/2, 2558/9, 2568/9 and 2578/9.

1848 Rohan Kouda (writer, 130th anniv)

1997. Birth Anniversaries. Multicoloured.

2485	80y. Type **1848**	1·50	60
2486	80y. Hiroshige Ando (after Toyo Kuni III) (painter, bicentenary)	1·50	60

1850 Miharu Hariko Paper Tiger

1997. New Year's Greetings. Multicoloured.

2487	50y. Type **1850**	95	80
2488	80y. Hakata Hariko paper tiger	1·40	1·10

1853 Hakata Hariko Paper Tiger

1997. New Year Lottery Stamps. Multicoloured.

2489	50y.+3y. Miharu Hariko paper tiger	1·10	90
2490	80y.+3y. Type **1853**	1·50	1·20

Each stamp carries a lottery number.

1854 "Yotsutake, Ryukyu Dance" (Taiji Hamada)

1997. 25th Anniv of Return of Okinawa (Ryukyu Islands).

2491	**1854**	80y. multicoloured	1·50	60

1855 Former Shibuya House, Yamagata

1856 Tomizawa House

1997. Traditional Houses (1st series).

2492	**1855**	80y. multicoloured	1·50	60
2493	**1856**	80y. multicoloured	1·50	60

See also Nos. 2513/14, 2529/30, 2539/40 and 2570/2.

1857 "Mother Sea" (Bokunen Naka)

1858 "Mother Earth" (Bokunen Naka)

1997. United Nations Framework Convention on Climate Change, Kyoto.

2494	**1857**	80y. multicoloured	1·50	60
2495	**1858**	80y. multicoloured	1·50	60

1859 Drying Harvested Rice

1997. 50th Anniv of Agricultural Insurance System.

2496	**1859**	80y. multicoloured	1·50	60

1860 "Sunayama" (Hakushu Kitahara and Shinpei Nakayama)

1861 "Jingle Bells" (Shoji Miyazawa and J. Pierpont)

1997. Favourite Songs (2nd series).

2497	**1860**	50y. multicoloured	95	45
2498	**1861**	80y. multicoloured	1·40	60

1862 "Shabondama" (Ujo Noguchi and Shinpei Nakayama)

1863 "Kitaguni no Haru" (Haku Ide and Minoru Endo)

1998. Favourite Songs (3rd series).

2499	**1862**	50y. multicoloured	95	45
2500	**1863**	80y. multicoloured	1·40	60

1864 Hollyhock

1998. Winter Paralympics, Nagano. Mult.

2501	50y. Type **1864**	1·40	60
2502	80y. Ice sledge hockey	1·70	70

1866 Miyama Gentian ("Gentiana nipponica")

1871 Snow-boarding

1998. Winter Olympic Games, Nagano. Mult.

2503	50y. Type **1866**	95	80
2504	50y. Marsh marigold ("Caltha palustris")	95	80
2505	50y. Black lily ("Fritillaria camtschaensis")	95	80
2506	50y. Peony ("Paeonia japonica")	95	80
2507	50y. Adder's tongue lily ("Erythronium japonicum")	95	80
2508	80y. Type **1871**	1·30	1·10
2509	80y. Curling	1·30	1·10
2510	80y. Speed skating	1·30	1·10
2511	80y. Cross-country skiing	1·30	1·10
2512	80y. Alpine skiing	1·30	1·10

1876 Former Baba House, Nagano

1877 Naka House

1998. Traditional Houses (2nd series).

2513	**1876**	80y. multicoloured	1·50	60
2514	**1877**	80y. multicoloured	1·50	60

1878 Fireman and Ambulance

1879 Fireman and Fire Engine

1998. 50th Anniv of Japanese Fire Service.

2515	**1878**	80y. multicoloured	1·50	60
2516	**1879**	80y. multicoloured	1·50	60

The firemen in the designs are taken from paintings of actors by Kunichika Toyohara.

1880 Puppy

1998. Greetings Stamps. Self-adhesive. Mult.

2517	80y. Type **1880**	1·20	95
2518	80y. Kitten	1·20	95
2519	80y. Budgerigars	1·20	95
2520	80y. Pansies	1·20	95
2521	80y. Rabbit	1·20	95

1885 "Medaka-no-Gakko" (Shigeru Chaki and Yoshinao Nakada)

1886 "Aoi Sanmyaku" (Yaso Saijo and Ryoichi Hattori)

1998. Favourite Songs (4th series).

2522	**1885**	50y. multicoloured	95	45
2523	**1886**	80y. multicoloured	1·40	60

1887 "Poppies" (Kokei Kobayashi)

1998. Philatelic Week.

2524	**1887**	80y. multicoloured	1·50	60

1888 "Liberty Leading the People" (Eugene Delacroix)

1998. Year of France in Japan.

2525	**1888**	110y. multicoloured	1·80	1·10

1889 Trout and Japanese Azalea

1998. National Afforestation Campaign.

2526	**1889**	50y. multicoloured	85	35

1890 "Wild Roses" (Sakufu Kondo and Franz Schubert)

1891 "Hill abloom with Tangerine Flowers" (Minoru Uminuma and Shogo Kato)

1998. Favourite Songs (5th series).

2527	**1890**	50y. multicoloured	95	45
2528	**1891**	80y. multicoloured	1·40	60

1892 Kowata Residence, Shinji

1893 Kamihaga Residence, Uchiko

1998. Traditional Houses (3rd series).

2529	**1892**	80y. multicoloured	1·50	60
2530	**1893**	80y. multicoloured	1·50	60

1894 "This Road" (Hakusyu Kitahara and Kousaku Yamada)

1895 "I'm a Boy of the Sea" (anon)

1998. Favourite Songs (6th series).

2531	**1894**	50y. multicoloured	95	45
2532	**1895**	80y. multicoloured	1·40	60

1896 Boy writing

1998. Letter Writing Day. Multicoloured.

2533	50y. Type **1896**	95	45
2534	50y. Girl with letter	95	45
2535	80y. Girl holding pen	1·50	60
2536	80y. Boy holding pen	1·50	60
2537	80y. Boy and girl reading letters (horiz)	1·50	60
MS2538	93×72 mm. No. 2537	1·80	1·50

1901 Kamio Residence, Oita

1902 Nakamura Residence, Okinawa

1998. Traditional Houses (4th series).

2539	**1901**	80y. multicoloured	1·50	60
2540	**1902**	80y. multicoloured	1·50	60

1903 FJ Class Dinghy Racing

1998. 53rd National Athletic Meeting, Kanagawa.

2541	**1903**	50y. multicoloured	85	35

1904 "Sketch of Maple Leaf" (detail)

1905 "Parakeet in Oak Tree"

1907 "Coloured Chicken in Snow-laden Bamboo"

1909 "Parakeet in Rose Bush"

1998. International Correspondence Week. Paintings by Shakuchu Ito. Multicoloured.

2542	90y. Type **1904**	1·50	1·20
2543	90y. Type **1905**	1·50	1·20
2544	110y. "Drake and Duck in Snow" (detail)	1·80	1·50
2545	110y. Type **1907**	1·80	1·50
2546	130y. "Butterfly in the Peonies" (detail)	2·10	1·70
2547	130y. Type **1909**	2·10	1·70

1910 Serving

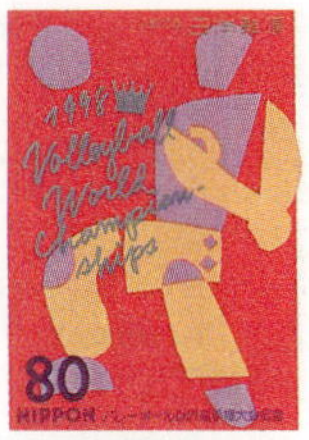

1911 Receiving

1912 Set and Attack

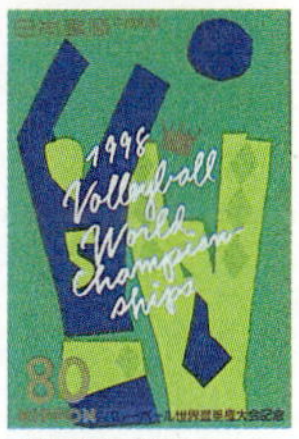

1913 Blocking

1998. World Volleyball Championships, Japan.

2548	**1910**	80y. multicoloured	1·50	60
2549	**1911**	80y. multicoloured	1·50	60
2550	**1912**	80y. multicoloured	1·50	60
2551	**1913**	80y. multicoloured	1·50	60

1914 Bakin Takizawa (writer, 150th death anniv)

1915 Yoshie Fujiwara (opera singer, birth centenary)

1998. Anniversaries.

2552	**1914**	80y. multicoloured	1·50	60
2553	**1915**	80y. multicoloured	1·50	60

1916 Sahara Papier-mache Rabbit making Rice Cake

1998. New Year's Greetings. Multicoloured.

2554	50y. Type **1916**	95	45
2555	80y. Yamagata papier-mache rabbit on ball	1·40	60

1919 Yamagata Papier-mache Rabbit on Ball

1998. New Year's Lottery Stamps. Multicoloured.

2556	50y.+3y. Sahara papier-mache rabbit making rice cake	1·10	90
2557	50y.+3y. Type **1919**	1·50	1·20

Each stamp carries a lottery number.

1920 "The Apple Song" (Hachiro Sato and Tadashi Manjome)

1921 "The Toy Cha-Cha-Cha" (Akiyuki Nasaka and Osamu Yoshioka)

1998. Favourite Songs (7th series).

2558	**1920**	50y. multicoloured	95	45
2559	**1921**	80y. multicoloured	1·40	60

1922 Tango Dancers (Goro Sasaki)

1998. Centenary of Friendship Treaty between Japan and Argentina.

2560	**1922**	80y. multicoloured	1·50	60

1923 "Family" (Chakou Wiam)

1924 "Heart Tree" (Atsuko Niizato)

1925 "Hito" (Shozo Somekawa)

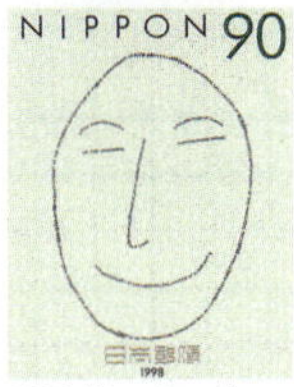

1926 "Happiness" (Mary Carmel Mulloor)

1998. 50th Anniv of Universal Declaration of Human Rights.

2561	**1923**	50y. multicoloured	95	45
2562	**1924**	70y. multicoloured	1·30	55
2563	**1925**	80y. multicoloured	1·40	60
2564	**1926**	90y. multicoloured	1·70	70

1998. 50th Anniv of New Year's Greetings Stamps. Previous issues now dated "1999".

2565	**241**	50y. mauve	95	45
2566	**445**	50y. multicoloured	95	45
2567	**1278**	50y. multicoloured	95	45

1927 "Flowing like a River" (Yasushi1 Akimoto and Akira Mitake)

1928 "Song of the Four Seasons" (Toyohisa Araki)

1999. Favourite Songs (8th series).

2568	**1927**	50y. multicoloured	1·20	55
2569	**1928**	80y. multicoloured	1·80	80

1929 Iwase Residence, Nishi-Akao

1930/1 Ogimachi Houses, Shirakawa (1/2-size illustration) (image scaled to 70% of original size)

1999. Traditional Houses (5th series).

2570	**1929**	80y. multicoloured	1·50	60
2571	**1930**	80y. multicoloured	1·50	60
2572	**1931**	80y. multicoloured	1·50	60

Nos. 2571/2 were issued together, se-tenant, forming the composite design illustrated.

1932 "The Kaen-daiko Drum" (Shinsho Kokontei V)

1933 "Toku the Boatman" (Bunraku Katsura VIII)

1934 "Mr. Kobee, the Faultfinder" (Ensho Sanyutei VI)

1935 "Time Noodles" (Kosan Yanagiya V)

1936 "Once in a Hundred Years" (Beicho Katsura III)

1999. Comic Stories.

2573	**1932**	80y. multicoloured	1·30	90
2574	**1933**	80y. multicoloured	1·30	90
2575	**1934**	80y. multicoloured	1·30	90
2576	**1935**	80y. multicoloured	1·30	90
2577	**1936**	80y. multicoloured	1·30	90

1937 "Sukiyaki" (Rokusuke Ei and Hachidai Nakamura)

1938 "Early Spring" (Kazumasa Yoshimaru and Akira Nakada)

1999. Favourite Songs (9th series).

2578	**1937**	50y. multicoloured	95	45
2579	**1938**	80y. multicoloured	1·50	60

1939 Kitten

1999. Greetings Stamps. Mult. Self-adhesive.

2580	80y. Type **1939**	1·50	90
2581	80y. Roses	1·50	90
2582	80y. Puppy (47×37 mm)	1·50	90
2583	80y. Brown rabbit	1·50	90
2584	80y. Grey and white rabbit (41×38 mm)	1·50	90

1944 Body Parts and Staff of Asclepius

1999. 25th General Assembly of Japan Medical Congress.

2585	**1944**	80y. multicoloured	1·70	60

1945/6 "Hare playing on the field in Spring" (Insho Domoto)

1999. Philatelic Week.

2586	**1945**	80y. multicoloured	1·50	60
2587	**1946**	80y. multicoloured	1·50	60

Nos. 2586/7 were issued together, se-tenant, forming the composite design illustrated.

1947 Nazca Lines, Llama and Machu Picchu Ruins

1999. 100 Years of Japanese Emigration to Peru.

2588	**1947**	80y. multicoloured	1·50	60

1948 Amagi Alpine Rose and Mount Fuji

1999. National Afforestation Campaign.

2589	**1948**	50y. multicoloured	1·10	70

1949 Tholos, Delphi

1999. Centenary of Japan–Greece Treaty of Commerce and Navigation.

2590	**1949**	80y. multicoloured	1·50	60

1950 Demon Dancer (Ouro Carnival), Lake Titicaca and Andean Condor

1999. 100 Years of Japanese Emigration to Bolivia.

2591	**1950**	80y. multicoloured	1·50	60

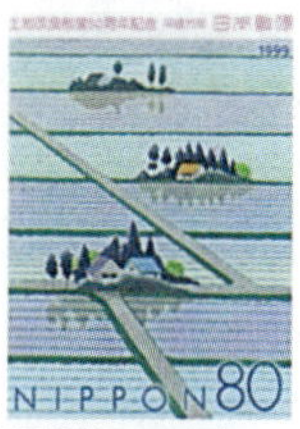

1951 Houses and Paddy Fields

1999. 50th Anniv of Land Improvement Law.

2592	**1951**	80y. multicoloured	1·50	60

1952 "Hill where Camellias Bloom" (detail of statue, Naoki Tominaga) and "Hope" (detail of stained glass window, Louis Fransen)

1999. 50th Anniv of Family Court.

2593	**1952**	80y. multicoloured	1·50	60

1953 Primroses

1999. 50th Anniv of Rehabilitation Support Programme.

2594	**1953**	80y. multicoloured	1·50	60

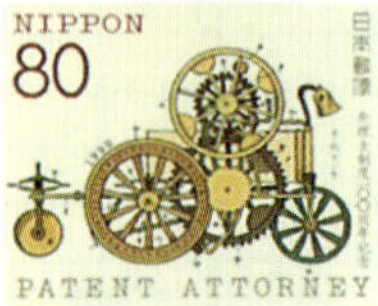
1954 Rickshaw, 1899

1999. Centenary of Patent Attorney System.

2595	**1954**	80y. multicoloured	1·50	60

1955 Masaakira Tomii, Kenjiro Ume and Nobushige Hozumi (drafters)

1999. Centenaries of Civil (1998) and Commercial (1999) Laws.

2596	**1955**	80y. multicoloured	1·50	60

1956 Sayo-chan, Saku-chan and Ken-chan (originator, developer and inspector) (Takashi Yanase)

1999. Centenary of Japanese Copyright System.

2597	**1956**	80y. multicoloured	1·50	60

1957 Children and Envelope

1999. Letter Writing Day. 50th Anniv of Japanese Association of Pen Friend Clubs.

2598	**1957**	50y. multicoloured	1·10	70
2599	-	50y. multicoloured	1·10	70
2600	-	50y. multicoloured	1·10	70
2601	-	50y. multicoloured	1·10	70
2602	-	80y. blue, black & yell	1·50	95
2603	-	80y. multicoloured	1·50	95
2604	-	80y. black, blue & yell	1·50	95
2605	-	80y. black, red & yellow	1·50	95
2606	-	80y. multicoloured	1·50	95
2607	-	80y. black, yellow & bl	1·50	95
2608	-	80y. multicoloured	1·50	95
2609	-	80y. black and red	1·50	95
2610	-	80y. black, yellow & grn	1·50	95
2611	-	80y. green, black & yell	1·50	95

DESIGNS: As T **1957**—No. 2599, Bear and crayon; 2600, Girl with pen; 2601, Clown jumping from envelope; 2604, Boy and star; 2606, Miffie and Barbara; 2610, Girl with letter. 52×27 mm—2602, Giraffes. 35×27 mm—2603, Kite. 29×29 mm—2605, Girl with pencil; 2609, Girl; 2611, Ducklings. 38×38 mm—2607, Boy playing trumpet. 27×36 mm—2608, Girl playing cello.

1971 Doves and Hearts

1999. Greetings Stamps.

2613	50y. Type **1971**	95	60
2614	80y. Japanese character	1·50	1·10
2615	90y. Manchurian crane and leaves	1·70	1·30

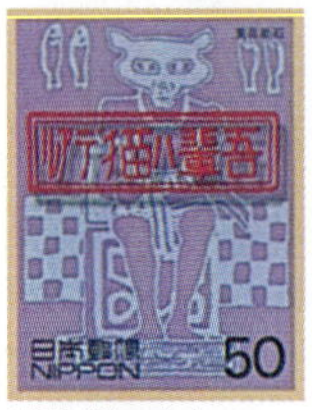
1974 "Wagahai wa Neko de Aru" (novel by Natsume Soseki)

1976 Yosano Akiko (poet)

1978 Tram, Tokyo, 1903

1980 "Haikara" (western-style fashion)

1982 Moving Casualties, Russo–Japanese War, 1904–05

1999. The Twentieth Century (1st series). The 1900s. Multicoloured.

2616	50y. Type **1974**	1·30	95
2617	50y. "Bochan" (novel by Natsume Soseki)	1·30	95
2618	80y. Type **1976**	1·50	1·10
2619	80y. Denkikan Cinema, Asakusa	1·50	1·10
2620	80y. Type **1978**	1·50	1·10
2621	80y. Kawakami Otojirou and Sadayakko (actor couple)	1·50	1·10
2622	80y. Type **1980**	1·50	1·10
2623	80y. Sumo wrestlers (opening of Sumo Ring, Ryogoku, Tokyo, 1909)	1·50	1·10
2624	80y. Type **1982**	1·50	1·10
2625	80y. Military hospital, Russo–Japanese War	1·50	1·10

See also Nos. 2627/36, 2664/53, 2677/86, 2687/96, 2697/2706, 2707/16, 2717/26, 2739/48, 2759/68, 2771/80, 2798/807, 2808/17, 2819/28, 2832/41, 2850/59 and 2861/70.

1984 Golfer and Gentian

1999. 54th National Sports Festival, Kumamoto.

2626	**1984**	50y. multicoloured	1·10	60

1985/6 Biplane "Kaishiki No. 1" and Airship "Yamadashiki No. 1" (first Japanese built aircraft)

1987 Children singing (School Song Book, 1910)

1989 Dr. Noguchi Hideyo (discovery of Oroya Fever germ, 1926)

1991 Kanaguri Shizo and Mishima Yahiko at Opening Parade, Olympic Games, Stockholm, 1912

1993 Matsui Sumako as Kachucha in "Resurrection" (play by Shimamura Hogetsu), 1914

1999. The Twentieth Century (2nd series). Multicoloured.

2627	50y. Type **1985**	1·30	95
2628	50y. Type **1986**	1·30	95
2629	80y. Type **1987**	1·50	1·10
2630	80y. Explorer and dog (Shirase Antarctic Expedition, 1910)	1·50	1·10
2631	80y. Type **1989**	1·50	1·10
2632	80y. Wolf (extinction of indigenous wolves, 1905)	1·50	1·10
2633	80y. Type **1991**	1·50	1·10
2634	80y. Dancers (formation of Takarazuka Musical Company, 1913)	1·50	1·10
2635	80y. Type **1993**	1·50	1·10
2636	80y. Mother and children (first sale of milk caramel in Japan, 1913)	1·50	1·10

Nos. 2627/8 were issued together, se-tenant forming the composite design illustrated.

1995 Stork on Elephant

1999. International Year of the Elderly.

2637	**1995**	80y. multicoloured	1·50	80

1996 "Sea Route in Kazusa Area" (from "36 Views of Mt. Fuji" by Hokusai Katsushika)

1998 "Rain beneath the Mountain Top" (from "36 Views of Mt. Fuji")

1999 "Chrysanthemums and a Horsefly"

2000 "Under the Fukagawa Mannen Bridge" (from "36 Views of Mt. Fuji")

1999. International Correspondence Week. 125th Anniv of Universal Postal Union. Multicoloured.

2638	90y. Type **1996**	1·60	95
2639	90y. "Confederate Roses and a Sparrow"	1·60	95
2640	110y. Type **1998**	2·20	1·10
2641	110y. Type **1999**	2·20	1·10
2642	130y. Type **2000**	2·40	1·30
2643	130y. "Peonies and a Butterfly"	2·40	1·30

2002 Couple in Junk (Takehisa Yumeji)

2004/5 Inauguration of Tokyo Railway Station, 1914

2006 Navy Cadets (Start of First World War, 1914)

2008 Akutagawa Ryunosuke and Title Page of Rashomon (first book of poetry, published 1915)

2010 Yoshino Sakuzo (political scientist) (Taisho Democracy)

1999. The Twentieth Century (3rd series). Mult.

2644	50y. Type **2002**	1·30	95
2645	50y. Takehisa Yumeji (artist)	1·30	95
2646	80y. Type **2004**	1·50	1·10
2647	80y. Type **2005**	1·50	1·10
2648	80y. Type **2006**	1·50	1·10
2649	80y. "Yohatsu" (western-style hair)	1·50	1·10
2650	80y. Type **2008**	1·50	1·10
2651	80y. Princess and Clouds (postal life assurance, 1916)	1·50	1·10
2652	80y. Type **2010**	1·50	1·10
2653	80y. Farmers (rice riots, 1918)	1·50	1·10

Nos. 2646/7 were issued together, se-tenant, forming the composite design illustrated.

2012 Yokohama Bay Stars Mascot (Central League)

2013 Chunichi Dragon Mascot (Central League)

2014 Seibu Lions Mascot (Pacific League)

2015 Nippon Ham Fighters Mascot (Pacific League)

2016 Yomiuri Giants Mascot (Central League)

2017 Yakult Swallows Mascot (Central League)

2018 Orix Blue Wave Mascot (Pacific League)

2019 Fukuoka Daiei Hawks Mascot (Pacific League)

2020 Hiroshima Toyo Carp Mascot (Central League)

2021 Hanshin Tigers Mascot (Central League)

2022 Kintetsu Buffaloes Mascot (Pacific League)

2023 Chiba Lotte Marines Mascot (Pacific League)

1999. Professional Japanese Baseball Clubs. Self-adhesive.

2654	**2012**	80y. multicoloured	1·50	1·10
2655	**2013**	80y. multicoloured	1·50	1·10
2656	**2014**	80y. multicoloured	1·50	1·10
2657	**2015**	80y. multicoloured	1·50	1·10
2658	**2016**	80y. multicoloured	1·50	1·10
2659	**2017**	80y. multicoloured	1·50	1·10
2660	**2018**	80y. multicoloured	1·50	1·10
2661	**2019**	80y. multicoloured	1·50	1·10
2662	**2020**	80y. multicoloured	1·50	1·10
2663	**2021**	80y. multicoloured	1·50	1·10
2664	**2022**	80y. multicoloured	1·50	1·10
2665	**2023**	80y. multicoloured	1·50	1·10

2024 Rainbow, Buildings and Mt. Fuji

1999. 50th Anniv of Japanese Science Council.

2666	**2024**	80y. multicoloured	1·50	95

2025 Katsushika Hokusai (artist, 150th death anniv)

2026 Uemera Shoen (artist, 50th death anniv)

2027 Kawabata Yasunari (author, birth centenary)

1999. Anniversaries.

2667	**2025**	80y. multicoloured	1·50	95
2668	**2026**	80y. multicoloured	1·50	95
2669	**2027**	80y. multicoloured	1·50	95

2028 Paulownia and Bamboo Embroidery (Manzairaku costume)

1999. 10th Anniv of Accession of Emperor Akihito. Multicoloured.

2670	80y. Type **2028**	1·00	20
2671	80y. Chinese phoenix embroidery (Engiraku costume)	1·60	1·10
MS2672	144×93 mm. As Nos. 2670/1	3·50	3·00

2030 Karatsuyama ningyo Folk Toy

1999. New Year's Greetings. Multicoloured.

2673	50y. Type **2030**	1·30	80
2674	80y. Tsuneishihariko doll	2·10	1·10

2033 Tsuneishihariko Doll

1999. New Year's Lottery Stamps. Multicoloured.

2675	50y.+3y. Karatsuyama ningyo folk toy	1·20	95
2676	80y.+3y. Type **2033**	1·80	1·50

Each stamp carries a lottery number.

2034 Onoe Matsunosuke (silent film star, 1925)

2035 Bandoh Tsumasaburo (silent film star, 1925)

2036 Runners (first Hakone relay marathon, 1920)

2038 Ruined Building (Great Kanto earthquake, 1923)

2040 Adventures of Sho-chan (comic illustrated by Katsuichi Kabashima, 1923)

2042 Baseball Players (opening of Koshien Stadium, 1924)

1999. The Twentieth Century (4th series). Mult.

2677	50y. Type **2034**	1·30	95
2678	50y. Type **2035**	1·30	95
2679	80y. Type **2036**	1·50	1·10
2680	80y. Gramophone (*Gondola Song*, 1920)	1·50	1·10
2681	80y. Type **2038**	1·50	1·10
2682	80y. Easygoing Dad (comic strip character by Yutaka Aso, 1923)	1·50	1·10
2683	80y. Type **2040**	1·50	1·10
2684	80y. Manchurian crane (protected species, 1924)	1·50	1·10
2685	80y. Type **2042**	1·50	1·10
2686	80y. Couple wearing western-style clothes	1·50	1·10

2044 Underground Train (opening of Tokyo Underground, 1927)

2046 Arashi Chozaburo in Title Role (*Kurama Tengu* (film), 1927)

2048 Tsuruta Yoshiyuki (swimmer) (Gold Medal winner, Olympic Games, Amsterdam, 1928)

2050 2nd August Track and Field Programme (Olympic Games, Amsterdam)

2052 Man (emergence of cafes for social gatherings)

2000. The Twentieth Century (5th series). Mult.

2687	50y. Type **2044**	1·30	95
2688	50y. Platform (opening of Tokyo Underground)	1·30	95
2689	80y. Type **2046**	1·50	1·10
2690	80y. Man doing gymnastics (first radio broadcast of gymnastic exercises, 1928)	1·50	1·10
2691	80y. Type **2048**	1·50	1·10
2692	80y. Oda Mikio (athlete) (Gold medal winner, Olympic Games, Amsterdam)	1·50	1·10
2693	80y. Type **2050**	1·50	1·10
2694	80y. Hitomi Kinue (athlete) (Silver medal winner, Olympic Games, Amsterdam)	1·50	1·10
2695	80y. Type **2052**	1·50	1·10
2696	80y. Cover of Horoki (novel by Hayashi Fumiko)	1·50	1·10

2054/5 Datsun Model 10, 1932 and Toyota Model AA, 1936 (mass production of domestic cars)

2056 Eruption of Mt. Asama, 1929

2058 Couple wearing Western Clothes (importing of western fashion)

2060 Kabutoyama (winner of first Japanese Derby, 1932)

2062 Woman (release of *Longing for Your Shadow* (song by Koga Masao), 1931)

2000. The Twentieth Century (6th series). Mult.

2697	50y. Type **2054**	1·30	95
2698	50y. Type **2055**	1·30	95
2699	80y. Type **2056**	1·50	1·10
2700	80y. Kobayashi Takiji (author) (*Crab Cannery Ship* published in *War Banner* paper) (25×32 mm)	1·50	1·10
2701	80y. Type **2058**	1·50	1·10
2702	80y. Kuro (comic strip character by Tagawa Suiha, 1931) (27×33 mm)	1·50	1·10
2703	80y. Type **2060**	1·50	1·10
2704	80y. Matsumidori (winner of 14th Derby) (27×33 mm)	1·50	1·10
2705	80y. Type **2062**	1·50	1·10
2706	80y. Prime Minister's Residence (assassinations of Prime Minister Tsuyoshi Inukai, 1932, and of Finance Minister Takahashi Korekiyo and Lord Keeper of the Privy Seal Saito Makoto, 1936) (25×35 mm)	1·50	1·10

Nos. 2697/8 were issued together, se-tenant, forming the composite design illustrated.

2064/5 D51 Steam Locomotive, 1936

2066 Otsuki Fumihiko (first edition of Daigenkai (dictionary compiled by Otsuki Fumihiko and Otsuki Joden), 1932)

2071 Chuken Hachiko and Statue (erection of statue of Chuken Hachiko, Shikuya Station, 1934)

2069/70 Players (formation of Tokyo Baseball Club, 1934)

2000. The Twentieth Century (7th series). Mult.

2707	50y. Type **2064**	1·30	95
2708	50y. Type **2065**	1·30	95
2709	80y. Type **2066**	1·50	1·10
2710	80y. Woman (release of *Tokyo Ondo* (song by Nakayama Shimpei), 1933) (25×33 mm)	1·50	1·10
2711	80y. Enomoto Kenichi (actor) (25×33 mm)	1·50	1·10
2712	80y. Type **2069**	1·50	1·10
2713	80y. Type **2070**	1·50	1·10
2714	80y. Type **2071**	1·50	1·10
2715	80y. Yoshikawa Eiji (author) (*Miyamoto* (story) first published in 1935) (27×33 mm)	1·50	1·10
2716	80y. Silver-banded black pigeon (declared extinct, 1936) (27×33 mm)	1·50	1·10

Nos. 2707/8 and 2712/13 respectively were issued together, se-tenant, forming the composite design illustrated.

2074/5 Mitsubishi Twin-engined Transport and Ki-15 Prototype Type 97 *Kamikaze* Airplanes

2076 Helen Keller's First Visit to Japan, 1937

2078 Yamamoto Yuzo (author) (*Robo No Ishi* (novel) first published in 1937)

2080 Yokozuna Futabayama (sumo wrestler) (victory in 69 consecutive matches, 1936–39)

2082 Birds (release of *Dareka Kokyo wo Omowazaru* (song by Koga Masao))

2000. The Twentieth Century (8th series). Mult.

2717	50y. Type **2074**	1·30	95
2718	50y. Type **2075**	1·30	95
2719	80y. Type **2076**	1·50	1·10
2720	80y. Woman with bag and civilian in national uniform (wartime clothing, 1937–40) (25×33 mm)	1·50	1·10
2721	80y. Type **2078**	1·50	1·10
2722	80y. Tanaka Kinuyo and Uehara Ken (actors) in *Aizenkatsura* (film), 1938 (25×33 mm)	1·50	1·10
2723	80y. Type **2080**	1·50	1·10
2724	80y. Sawamura Eiji (baseball player) (27×33 mm)	1·50	1·10
2725	80y. Type **2082**	1·50	1·10
2726	80y. Woodblock carving (Munakata Shiko) (25×34 mm)	1·50	1·10

Nos. 2717/18 were issued together, se-tenant, forming the composite design illustrated.

2084/5 Children and Flowers

2086/7 Faces and Building

2088 Girl as Butterfly with Book

2089 Two Faces and Building

2000. Children's Book Day.

2727	**2084**	80y. multicoloured	1·60	1·10
2728	**2085**	80y. multicoloured	1·60	1·10
2729	**2086**	80y. multicoloured	1·60	1·10
2730	**2087**	80y. multicoloured	1·60	1·10
2731	**2088**	80y. multicoloured	1·60	1·10
2732	**2089**	80y. multicoloured	1·60	1·10

Nos. 2727/8 and 2929/30 respectively were issued together, se-tenant, forming the composite designs illustrated.

2090 Hanaoka Seisyu (surgeon) and Korean Morning Glory

2000. Cent of Japanese Surgical Society Congress.

2733	**2090**	80y. multicoloured	1·80	1·10

2091/2 *Liefde* (17th-century merchant ship), Dutchman and Nagasaki

2000. 400th Anniv of Japan–Netherlands Cultural Relations.

2734	**2091**	80y. multicoloured	1·80	1·10
2735	**2092**	80y. multicoloured	1·80	1·10

Nos. 2734/5 were issued together, se-tenant, forming a composite design.

2093/4 "Ryukozu" (Hashimoto Gaho) (image scaled to 74% of original size)

2000. Philatelic Week.

2736	**2093**	80y. multicoloured	1·80	1·10
2737	**2094**	80y. multicoloured	1·80	1·10

Nos. 2736/7 were issued together, se-tenant, forming the composite design illustrated.

2095 Japanese White-eye, Plum Tree and Kuju Mountain Range

2000. National Afforestation Campaign.

2738	**2095**	50y. multicoloured	1·10	60

2096 Golden Bat (comic strip character by Suzuki Ichiro)

2098 Vice-Consul Sugihara Chiune (issued visas to Jews from Consulate in Lithuania), 1940

2100 Airplane over Pearl Harbor (outbreak of Second World War in the Pacific, 1941)

2102 Mt. Showashin- zan (formed by volcanic activity of Mt. Usu, 1944)

2104 Statue (atomic bomb on Nagasaki, 9 August 1945)

2000. The Twentieth Century (9th series). Mult.

2739	50y. Type **2096**	1·60	1·10
2740	50y. Golden Bat (27×36 mm)	1·60	1·10
2741	80y. Type **2098**	1·80	1·30
2742	80y. Children (Kokumin Gakko school system, 1941) (25×33 mm)	1·80	1·30
2743	80y. Type **2100**	1·80	1·30
2744	80y. Takamura Kotaro (poet) (*Dotei* (collected poems) awarded First Imperial Art Academy Prize, 1942) (26×35 mm)	1·80	1·30
2745	80y. Type **2102**	1·80	1·30
2746	80y. Damaged buildings (atomic bomb on Hiroshima, 6 August 1945) (27×33 mm)	1·80	1·30
2747	80y. Type **2104**	1·80	1·30
2748	80y. Lieut-General Umezu, Chief of the Imperial General Staff signing Surrender (end of Second World War, 1945)	1·80	1·30

2106 Bean Goose

2109 "Girl playing Glass Flute" (Kitagawa Utamaro)

2111 Roses and Pansies

2113 Girl with Pen and Boy with Letter

2000. "Phila Nippon '01" International Stamp Exhibition, Tokyo. Multicoloured. Self-adhesive.

2749	80y. Type **2106**	1·80	1·30
2750	80y. White wagtail (25×34 mm)	1·80	1·30
2751	80y. Northern goshawk (25×35 mm)	1·80	1·30
2752	80y. Type **2109**	1·80	1·30
2753	80y. Ichikawa Ebizo (actor) (Toshusai Sharaku) (25×48 mm)	1·80	1·30
2754	80y. Type **2111**	1·80	1·30
2755	80y. Puppy and kitten (24×42 mm)	1·80	1·30
2756	80y. Type **2113**	1·80	1·30
2757	80y. Children and letter (31×43 mm)	1·80	1·30
2758	80y. Girl with letter and boy with pen (31×40 mm)	1·80	1·30

2116 Astro Boy (comic strip character by Tezuka Osamu, 1951) on cover of *Shonen* (magazine), July, 1951

2118 Cover of Music Score and Apples (release of *Song of Apples* (song by Sato Hachiro and Manjoume Tadashi), 1945)

2120 Mother and Child (promulgation of new constitution, 1947)

2122 Dr. Yukawa Hideki and Atoms (winner of Nobel Prize for Physics, 1949)

2124 Kishi Keiko and Sata Keiji (actors) in *Kimino Na Wa* (film), 1953

2000. The Twentieth Century (10th series). Mult.

No.	Type	Description	Mint	Used
2759		50y. Type **2116**	1·60	1·10
2760		50y. Astro Boy from cover of *Shonen*, August, 1961 (26×36 mm)	1·60	1·10
2761		80y. Type **2118**	1·80	1·30
2762		80y. Sazae San (comic strip by Hasegawa Machiko) (25×34 mm)	1·80	1·30
2763		80y. Type **2120**	1·80	1·30
2764		80y. Trophy (new world records set by Furuhashi Hironoshin (swimmer), 1949) (25×34 mm)	1·80	1·30
2765		80y. Type **2122**	1·80	1·30
2766		80y. Championship flag (first radio broadcast of Kohaku Uta Gassen (singing competition), 1951) (25×34 mm)	1·80	1·30
2767		80y. Type **2124**	1·80	1·30
2768		80y. Tsuboi Sakae (author) and cover illustration by Morita Motoko from first edition of *Nijyu-Yon No* Hitomi (novel) (25×34 mm)	1·80	1·30

2126 Flowers

2127 Flowers and Sea

2000. Kyushu–Okinawa Summit.

No.	Type	Description	Mint	Used
2769	**2126**	80y. multicoloured	1·80	1·30
2770	**2127**	80y. multicoloured	1·80	1·30

2128 Tokyo Tower Entrance Ticket, 1958

2131/2 Kurosawa Akira (film director) and Scene from *Seven Samurai*, 1954

2133 Rikidozan (wrestler) and Championship Belt

2136 Prince Shotoku (issue of 10,000 yen banknote, 1958)

2000. The Twentieth Century (11th series).

No.	Type	Description	Mint	Used
2771	**2128**	50y. multicoloured	1·60	1·10
2772	-	50y. multicoloured (27×35 mm)	1·60	1·10
2773	-	80y. multicoloured (25×35 mm)	1·80	1·30
2774	**2131**	80y. multicoloured	1·80	1·30
2775	**2132**	80y. multicoloured	1·80	1·30
2776	**2133**	80y. multicoloured	1·80	1·30
2777	-	80y. multicoloured (28×36 mm)	1·80	1·30
2778	-	80y. multicoloured (25×33 mm)	1·80	1·30
2779	**2136**	80y. brown and stone	1·80	1·30
2780	-	80y. multicoloured (25×33 mm)	1·80	1·30

DESIGNS: No. 2772, Tokyo Tower (construction completed in 1958); 2773, Early radio and television sets (regular television broadcasts, 1953); 2777, Rikidozan; 2778, *Godzilla* (release of film, 1954); 2780, Influence of Taiyozoku Fashion on Youth Culture (release of *Taiyo No Kisetsu* (film), 1956).

Nos. 2774/5 were issued together, se-tenant, forming the composite design illustrated.

2138/9 Sunflowers

2000. 50th Anniv of Crime Prevention Campaign.

No.	Type	Description	Mint	Used
2781	**2138**	80y. multicoloured	1·80	1·30
2782	**2139**	80y. multicoloured	1·80	1·30

Nos. 2781/2 were issued together, se-tenant, forming the composite design.

2140 Girl with Pen

2000. Letter Writing Day. Multicoloured.

No.	Type	Description	Mint	Used
2783		50y. Type **2140**	1·70	1·20
2784		50y. House and birds (25×33 mm)	1·70	1·20
2785		50y. Clown and envelope (25×33 mm)	1·70	1·20
2786		50y. Boy with dog (25×33 mm)	1·70	1·20
2787		80y. Girl and dog in balloon basket (27×36 mm)	2·10	1·50
2788		80y. Apple tree (30×30 mm)	2·10	1·50
2789		80y. Parrots holding letter (22×34 mm)	2·10	1·50
2790		80y. Bicycle (28×40 mm)	2·10	1·50
2791		80y. Girl and boy holding dove (29×35 mm)	2·10	1·50
2792		80y. Girl, letter and hedgehog (27×40 mm)	2·10	1·50
2793		80y. Girl playing harp (28×35 mm)	2·10	1·50
2794		80y. Boy playing recorder (27×35 mm)	2·10	1·50
2795		80y. Boy playing cello (23×39 mm)	2·10	1·50
2796		80y. Boy carrying pen (27×36 mm)	2·10	1·50
MS2797		72×93 mm. Nos. 2784 and 2791	3·25	2·75

2154/5 Taro and Giro (left at Showa Base, 1958)

2156 Commemorative Cake Box (marriage of Prince Akihito, 1959)

2158 Stars and Music Score (release of *Sukiyaki* (song by Ei Rokusuke and Nakamura Hachidai), 1960)

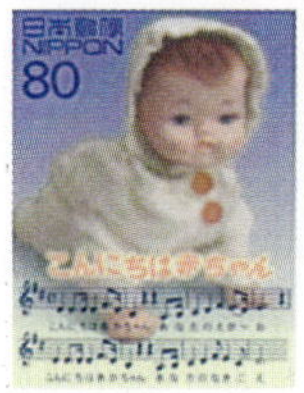

2160 Doll and Music Score (release of *Hello, My Baby* (song by Ei Rokusuke and Nakamura Hachidai)), 1963

2162 Official Poster of Olympic Games, Tokyo, 1964

2000. The Twentieth Century (12th series). Mult.

No.	Type	Description	Mint	Used
2798		50y. Type **2154**	1·80	1·30
2799		50y. Type **2155**	1·80	1·30
2800		80y. Type **2156**	2·10	1·50
2801		80y. Meteorological chart showing the Isewan typhoon, 1959 (25×33 mm)	2·10	1·50
2802		80y. Type **2158**	2·10	1·50
2803		80y. Shiba Ryotaro (author) (serialization of *Ryomaga Yuku* (novel)), 1962 (25×33 mm)	2·10	1·50
2804		80y. Type **2160**	2·10	1·50
2805		80y. Tokyo–Osaka High Speed Bullet Train Service, 1964 (25×33 mm)	2·10	1·50
2806		80y. Type **2162**	2·10	1·50
2807		80y. Official poster of Olympic Games, Tokyo (28×36 mm)	2·10	1·50

Nos. 2798/9 were issused together, se-tenant, forming the composite design illustrated.

2164/5 Characters from *Hyokkori Hyotan-jima* (launch of children's television programme, 1964)

2166 Television, Car and Air Conditioning Unit, 1960

2168 Baltan (character from *Ultraman*)

2170 Kawabata Yasunari and Oe Kenzaburo (winners of the Nobel Prize for Literature)

2172 Tower of the Sun (sculpture, Okamoto Taro) (World's Fair, Osaka, 1970)

2000. The Twentieth Century (13th series). Mult.

No.	Type	Description	Mint	Used
2808		50y. Type **2164**	1·80	1·30
2809		50y. Type **2165**	1·80	1·30
2810		80y. Type **2166**	2·10	1·50
2811		80y. Ultraman (launch of *Ultraman* (television series), 1966) (27×33 mm)	2·10	1·50
2812		80y. Type **2168**	2·10	1·50
2813		80y. Guitars (formation of pop bands following 1966 tour by The Beatles) (25×33 mm)	2·10	1·50
2814		80y. Type **2170**	2·10	1·50
2815		80y. Atsumi Taro (actor) in *Otokowa Tsuraiyo* (film) (25×34 mm)	2·10	1·50
2816		80y. Type **2172**	2·10	1·50
2817		80y. Youths and music score (release of *Children Who Didn't Know the War* (song), by Kitayama Osamu and Sugita Jiro, 1971) (25×33 mm)	2·10	1·50

Nos. 2808/9 were issued together, se-tenant, forming the composite design illustrated.

2174 Naruse Jinzo (founder of Women's University), Yoshioka Yayoi (founder of Women's Medical College, Tokyo) and Tsuda Umeko (founder of Tsuda College)

2000. Centenary of Private Higher Education for Women.

No.	Type	Description	Mint	Used
2818	**2174**	80y. multicoloured	2·10	1·30

2175 Oh Sadaharu (baseball player) swinging Bat, 1964

2177 Wall Painting (discovery of wall paintings at Takamatsu Zuka, 1972)

2179 Pandas (gift from China to Japan, 1972)

2181 Lady Oscar (character from *Belubara*, 1972) (cartoon by Ikeda Riyoko)

2183 Cliffs and Music Score (release of *Erimo Misaki* (song) by Okamoto Osami and Yoshida Takuro, 1974)

2000. The Twentieth Century (14th series). Multicoloured.

No.	Type	Description	Mint	Used
2819		50y. Type **2175**	1·80	1·30
2820		50y. Nagashima Shigeo (baseball player) running, 1962	1·80	1·30
2821		80y. Type **2177**	2·10	1·50
2822		80y. Wall painting (from Takamatsu Zuka)	2·10	1·50
2823		80y. Type **2179**	2·10	1·50
2824		80y. Shureimon Gate (return to Japan of administrative rights over Okinawa, 1972)	2·10	1·50
2825		80y. Type **2181**	2·10	1·50
2826		80y. Ozawa Seiji (conductor)	2·10	1·50
2827		80y. Type **2183**	2·10	1·50
2828		80y. Futuristic space shuttle (cartoon series *Uchu Senkan Yamato* by Matsumoto Reiji, 1974)	2·10	1·50

2185 "Okabe"

2000. International Correspondence Week. Paintings from "53 Stations of the Tokaido" by Ando Hiroshige. Multicoloured.

No.	Type	Description	Mint	Used
2829		90y. Type **2185**	2·20	1·60
2830		110y. "Maisaka"	2·75	2·20
2831		130y. "Okazaki"	3·25	2·50

2188 Gundam (cartoon character) (launch of *Kidosenshi Gundam*, television programme, 1979)

2190 Guitar and Music Score (release of *Jidai* (song by Nakajima Miyuki), 1975)

2192 Microphones and Musical Notes (introduction of Karaoke, 1977)

2194 Alien Space Ship and Music Score (release of *UFO* (song by Aku Yu and Tokura Shunichi), 1979)

2196 Keyboard and Musical Notes (popularity of synthesizer music, 1970s)

2000. The Twentieth Century (15th series). Multicoloured.

2832	50y. Type **2188**	1·80	1·30
2833	50y. Amuro (cartoon character from *Kidosenshi Gundam*)	1·80	1·30
2834	80y. Type **2190**	2·10	1·50
2835	80y. Fish and music score (release of *Oyoge! Taiyaki-kun* (song by Takada Hiroo and Sase Juichi), 1975)	2·10	1·50
2836	80y. Type **2192**	2·10	1·50
2837	80y. Flowers and music score (release of *Cosmos* (song by Sada Masashi), 1977)	2·10	1·50
2838	80y. Type **2194**	2·10	1·50
2839	80y. People crossing field (launch of *San Nen B Gumi Kinpachi Sensi* (television series), 1979)	2·10	1·50
2840	80y. Type **2196**	2·10	1·50
2841	80y. Woman and snow-covered house (launch of *Oshine* (television drama), 1983)	2·10	1·50

2198 Nagaoka Hantaro (physicist, 50th death anniv) and Atomic Models

2199 Nakaya Ukichiro (physicist, birth centenary) and Snow Crystal

2200 Nakamura Teijo (haiku poet, birth centenary) and Text

2000. Anniversaries.

2842	**2198**	80y. multicoloured	2·10	1·50
2843	**2199**	80y. multicoloured	2·10	1·50
2844	**2200**	80y. multicoloured	2·10	1·50

2201 Jindaiji (snake-shaped clay bell)

2000. New Year's Greetings. Multicoloured.

2845	50y. Type **2201**	1·30	90
2846	80y. Sasano (carved wooden toy snake)	2·10	1·50

2204 Sasano (carved wooden toy snake)

2000. New Year's Lottery Stamps. Multicoloured.

2847	50y.+3y. Jindaiji (snake-shaped clay bell)	1·40	1·20
2848	80y.+3y. Type **2204**	2·20	1·80

Each stamp carries a lottery number.

2205/6 Characters from *Go! Anpanman* (launch of children's television programme, 1988)

2207 Trains on Trial and Inaugural Runs (opening of Seikan Tunnel, 1988)

2209 Rebuilt Watchtower (excavation of ruins at Yoshinogari Iseki, 1989)

2211/12 "J-Boy" (mascot) and Football (Inception of J-League Football, 1993)

2213 "Tonkomeisya" (detail of painting, Hirayama Ikuo) (World Heritage Site, 1987)

2000. The Twentieth Century (16th series). Multicoloured.

2849	50y. Type **2205**	1·80	1·30
2850	50y. Type **2206**	1·80	1·30
2851	80y. Type **2207**	2·10	1·50
2852	80y Halley's Comet (first appearance for 76 years, 1986)	2·10	1·50
2853	80y. Type **2209**	2·10	1·50
2854	80y. Misora Hibari (singer) (recipient of National Medal of Honor, 1989)	2·10	1·50
2855	80y. Type **2211**	2·10	1·50
2856	80y. Type **2212**	2·10	1·50
2857	80y. Type **2213**	2·10	1·50
2858	80y. "Ikarugano Sato Cyoyo Horyuji" (detail of painting, Hirayama Ikuo) (World Heritage Site, 1998)	2·10	1·50

Nos. 2849/50 and 2855/6 were respectively issued together, se-tenant, forming the composite design illustrated.

2215 Central Tower and Mosaic Marble Floors (detail)

2000. 110th Anniv of Diet (Japanese Parliament).

2859	**2215**	80y. multicoloured	2·10	1·50

2216 Emblem, Nagano Olympic Games, 1998

2218 Crown Prince Noruhito and Princess Masako (wedding, 1993)

2220 Lap-top Computer and Mobile Phone (increased use of wireless telecommunications)

2222 Doi Takao (Japanese astronaut) outside Spaceship

2224 "Mother Earth" (Bokunan Naka) (United Nations Framework Convention on Climate Change, Kyoto, 1997)

2000. The Twentieth Century (17th series). Multicoloured.

2860	50y. Type **2216**	1·80	1·30
2861	50y. "Snowlets" (Nagano Olympic mascots)	1·80	1·30
2862	80y. Type **2218**	2·10	1·50
2863	80y. Phoenix, map of Hanshin-Awaji and collapsed bridge (Hanshin-Awaji earthquake, 1995)	2·10	1·50
2864	80y. Type **2220**	2·10	1·50
2865	80y. Launch of space shuttle *Endeavor* (inclusion of first Japanese astronaut on N.A.S.A. mission, 1992)	2·10	1·50
2866	80y. Type **2222**	2·10	1·50
2867	80y. Footballer (Japanese participation in World Cup Football Championship, France, 1998)	2·10	1·50
2868	80y. Type **2224**	2·10	1·50
2869	80y. Official poster of Nagano Olympic Games	2·10	1·50

2226/7 Manchurian Cranes (*"Grus japonensis"*, Matazo Kayama)

2001. "Internet Expo 2001 Japan" (virtual Internet fair).

2870	**2226**	80y. multicoloured	1·70	1·40
2871	**2227**	80y. multicoloured	1·70	1·40

Nos. 2870/1 were issued together, se-tenant, forming a composite design.

2228 Heliotrope, Flax and Emblem

2001. United Nations Year of Volunteers.

2872	**2228**	80y. multicoloured	1·70	1·40

2229 "Gyoseishoshi" (Japanese calligraphy) and Computer

2001. 50th Anniv of Gyoseishoshi Lawyer System (specialist administrative lawyers).

2873	**2229**	80y. multicoloured	1·70	1·40

2230 Shinkyo Bridge, Futarasan Shrine

2231 Main Sanctuary, Futarasan Shrine

2232 Karamon Gate, Toshugu Shrine

2233 Kirin (mythical winged horse) (painting), Toshugu Shrine

2234 Wind God (statue), Rinnoji Temple

2235 Thunder God (statue), Rinnoji Temple

2236 Peacock, Toshugu Shrine

2237 Sleeping Cat, Toshugu Shrine

2238/9 Rinnoji Temple

2001. World Heritage Sites (1st series). Shrines and Temples, Nikko.

2874	**2230**	80y. multicoloured	1·70	1·40
2875	**2231**	80y. multicoloured	1·70	1·40
2876	**2232**	80y. multicoloured	1·70	1·40
2877	**2233**	80y. multicoloured	1·70	1·40
2878	**2234**	80y. multicoloured	1·70	1·40
2879	**2235**	80y. multicoloured	1·70	1·40
2880	**2236**	80y. multicoloured	1·70	1·40
2881	**2237**	80y. multicoloured	1·70	1·40
2882	**2238**	80y. multicoloured	1·70	1·40
2883	**2239**	80y. multicoloured	1·70	1·40

Nos. 2883/4 were issued together, se-tenant, forming the composite design illustrated.

See also Nos. 2887/96, 2906/15, 2960/9, 2985/94, 2997/3006, 3020/9, 3045/54, 3060/9, 3083/92 and 3107/16.

2240 Emblem

2241 "The Annunciation" (detail, Botticelli)

2242 "The Annunciation" (detail, Botticelli)

2001. "Italy in Japan 2001" (cultural and scientific event).

2884	**2240**	80y. multicoloured	1·70	1·40
2885	**2241**	110y. multicoloured	2·40	1·90
2886	**2242**	110y. multicoloured	2·40	1·90

Nos. 2885/6 were issued together in se-tenant pairs featuring two separate panels of the painting.

2243/4 Marodo Shrine

2245 Main Sanctuary

2246 Lion Dog (statue)

2247 Marodo Shrine and Pagoda

2248 Traditional Dance Mask

2249 Horse (statue)

2250 Buildings

2251 Treasure Pagoda

2252 Oomoto Shrine

2001. World Heritage Sites (2nd series). Itsukushima Shrine.

2887	**2243**	80y. multicoloured	1·70	1·40
2888	**2244**	80y. multicoloured	1·70	1·40
2889	**2245**	80y. multicoloured	1·70	1·40
2890	**2246**	80y. multicoloured	1·70	1·40
2891	**2247**	80y. multicoloured	1·70	1·40
2892	**2248**	80y. multicoloured	1·70	1·40
2893	**2249**	80y. multicoloured	1·70	1·40
2894	**2250**	80y. multicoloured	1·70	1·40
2895	**2251**	80y. multicoloured	1·70	1·40
2896	**2252**	80y. multicoloured	1·70	1·40

Nos. 2888/9 were issued together, se-tenant, forming the composite design illustrated.

2253 Emblem

2001. Centenary of Japanese Dermatological Association. Multicoloured, colour of triangle beneath face value given.

2897	**2253**	80y. pink	1·70	1·40
2898	**2253**	80y. flesh	1·70	1·40
2899	**2253**	80y. yellow	1·70	1·40
2900	**2253**	80y. green	1·70	1·40
2901	**2253**	80y. blue	1·70	1·40

2254 Woman posting Letter (Nakamura Senseki)

2001. Philatelic Week. Centenary of Red Cylindrical Letter Boxes (designed by Taraya Takashhichi and Nakamura Koji).

2902	**2254**	80y. multicoloured	1·70	1·40

2255 "Ato, Nik and Kaz" (mascots)

2256 "Kaz"

2257 "Nik"

2001. World Cup Football Championship, Japan and South Korea (2002).

2903	**2255**	80y.+10y. mult	2·20	1·80
2904	**2256**	80y.+10y. mult	2·20	1·80
2905	**2257**	80y.+10y. mult	2·20	1·80

2258 Hosodono, Maidono and Tsuchinoya Halls, Kamowakeikazuchi Shrine

2259 Roman Gate, Kamowakeikazazuchi Shrine

2260 East Main Hall, Kamomioya Shrine

2261 Guardian Dog (statue), Kamomioya Shrine

2262 Pagoda and South Great Gate, Toji Temple

2263 Fukuu Joju Nyorai (statue), Toji Temple

2264 Pagoda and West Gate, Kiyomizudera Temple

2265 Main Hall, Kiyomizudera Temple

2266 "Nyorin Kannon" (painting), Toji Temple

2267 Daiitoku Myoo (statue), Toji Temple

2001. World Heritage (3rd series). Temples and Shrines, Kyoto.

2906	**2258**	80y. multicoloured	1·70	1·40
2907	**2259**	80y. multicoloured	1·70	1·40
2908	**2260**	80y. multicoloured	1·70	1·40
2909	**2261**	80y. multicoloured	1·70	1·40
2910	**2262**	80y. multicoloured	1·70	1·40
2911	**2263**	80y. multicoloured	1·70	1·40
2912	**2264**	80y. multicoloured	1·70	1·40
2913	**2265**	80y. multicoloured	1·70	1·40
2914	**2266**	80y. multicoloured	1·70	1·40
2915	**2267**	80y. multicoloured	1·70	1·40

2268 Flowers and Pigeons

2001. 50th Anniv of Membership of United Nations Educational, Scientific and Cultural Organization.

2916	**2268**	80y. multicoloured	1·70	1·40

2269 Swimming

2001. 9th International Swimming Federation Championships, Fukuoka. Multicoloured.

2917	**2269**	80y. Type **2269**	1·70	1·40
2918	**2270**	80y. Synchronized swimming	1·70	1·40
2919	**2271**	80y. Diving	1·70	1·40
2920	**2272**	80y. Water polo	1·70	1·40

Nos. 2917/20 were issued together, se-tenant, the backgrounds forming a composite design.

2273 Rabbits

2001. Letter Writing Day. Multicoloured.

2921	50y. Type **2273**	1·30	1·10
2922	50y. Girl and pencil (28×36 mm)	1·30	1·10
2923	50y. Boy holding envelope (28×36 mm)	1·30	1·10
2924	50y. Girl with ribbons (28×36 mm)	1·30	1·10
2925	80y. Bird in tree (30×30 mm)	1·70	1·40
2926	80y. Girl holding rabbit (27×36 mm)	1·70	1·40
2927	80y. Boy holding pen (27×36 mm)	1·70	1·40
2928	80y. Girl with envelope and dog (27×26 mm)	1·70	1·40
2929	80y. Girl and flowers (27×36 mm)	1·70	1·40
2930	80y. Flowers and bird with envelope (30×30 mm)	1·70	1·40
2931	80y. Birds and roof (27×36 mm)	1·70	1·40
2932	80y. Rabbit and flowers (22×33 mm)	1·70	1·40
2933	80y. Boy and rabbit (27×33 mm)	1·70	1·40
2934	80y. Chicks, hen and pig (27×39 mm)	1·70	1·40
MS2935	72×93 mm. Nos. 2923 and 2932	3·25	3·00

2287 "Ootani Oniji as Edobei" (Toshusai Sharaku)

2288 "Iwai Hanshiro IV as Shigenoi" (Toshusai Shakuru)

2289 "Sakata Hangoro as Fujikwa Mizuemon" (Toshusai Shakuru)

2290 "Segawa Kikunojo as Oshizu, Tanabe Bunzo's Wife" (Toshusai Shakuru)

2291 "Ichikawa Omezo as Yakko Ippei" (Toshusai Shakuru)

2292 "Beauty looking Back" (Hishikawa Moronobu)

2293 "Girl playing Glass Flute" (Kitagawa Utamaro)

2294 "Fuzoku Higashino Nishiki, returning from the Bath-house in the Rain" (Torii Kiyonaga)

2295 "Iwai Kumesaburo as Chiyo" (Utagawa Kunimasa)

2296 "Ichikawa Komazo III as Sasaski Ganryu" (Utagawa Toyokuni)

2297 "Iwai Hanshiro IV as Shigenoi" (Toshusai Shakuru)

2298 "Ootani Oniji as Edobei" (Toshusai Shakuru)

2299 Mandarin Duck

2300 Japanese White-Eye

2301 Girl and Boy holding Envelopes

2302 "Iwai Kumesaburo as Chiyo" (Utagawa Kunimasa)

2303 "Ichikawa Komazo III as Sasaki Ganryu" (Utagawa Toyokuni)

2304 Eastern Turtle Dove

2305 Greater Pied Kingfisher

2306 1871 48m. Stamp

2001. "PHILA NIPPON '01" International Stamp Exhibition, Tokyo. (a) Ordinary gum.

2936	**2287**	50y. multicoloured	1·40	1·10
2937	**2288**	50y. multicoloured	1·40	1·10
2938	**2289**	50y. multicoloured	1·40	1·10
2939	**2290**	50y. multicoloured	1·40	1·10
2940	**2291**	50y. multicoloured	1·40	1·10
2941	**2292**	80y. multicoloured	1·70	1·40
2942	**2293**	80y. multicoloured	1·70	1·40
2943	**2294**	80y. multicoloured	1·70	1·40
2944	**2295**	80y. multicoloured	1·70	1·40
2945	**2296**	80y. multicoloured	1·70	1·40

(b) Self-adhesive gum.

2946	**2297**	50y. multicoloured	1·50	1·20
2947	**2298**	50y. multicoloured	1·50	1·20
2948	**2299**	50y. multicoloured	1·50	1·20
2949	**2300**	50y. multicoloured	1·50	1·20
2950	**2301**	50y. multicoloured	1·50	1·20
2951	**2302**	80y. multicoloured	1·80	1·50
2952	**2303**	80y. multicoloured	1·80	1·50
2953	**2304**	80y. multicoloured	1·80	1·50
2954	**2305**	80y. multicoloured	1·80	1·50
2955	**2306**	80y. multicoloured	1·80	1·50

2307 Fly Casting and Discus

2001. 6th World Games, Akita. Multicoloured.

2956	50y. Type **2307**	1·30	1·10
2957	50y. Aerobics and billiards	1·30	1·10
2958	80y. Water skiing and life saving	1·70	1·40
2959	80y. Tug of war and body building	1·70	1·40

2311 Konpon Chudo Hall, Enryakuji Temple

2312 Eternal Flame, Enryakuji Temple

2313 Ninai-do Hall, Enryakuji Temple

2316 Pagoda, Daigoji Temple

2314/15 Sanbo-in Temple Garden, Daigoji Temple

2317 Palace, Ninnaji Temple

2318 Pagoda, Ninnaji Temple

2319 Phoenix Hall, Byodoin Temple

2320 Bodhisattva floating on Clouds (statue), Byodoin Temple

2001. World Heritage (4th series). Temples, Kyoto.

2960	**2311**	80y. multicoloured	1·70	1·40
2961	**2312**	80y. multicoloured	1·70	1·40
2962	**2313**	80y. multicoloured	1·70	1·40
2963	**2314**	80y. multicoloured	1·70	1·40
2964	**2315**	80y. multicoloured	1·70	1·40
2965	**2316**	80y. multicoloured	1·70	1·40
2966	**2317**	80y. multicoloured	1·70	1·40
2967	**2318**	80y. multicoloured	1·70	1·40
2968	**2319**	80y. multicoloured	1·70	1·40
2969	**2320**	80y. multicoloured	1·70	1·40

Nos. 2963/4 were issued together, se-tenant, forming the composite design illustrated.

2321 War Memorial Opera House and Flowers

2001. 50th Anniv of San Francisco Peace Treaty.

2970	**2321**	80y. multicoloured	2·20	1·80

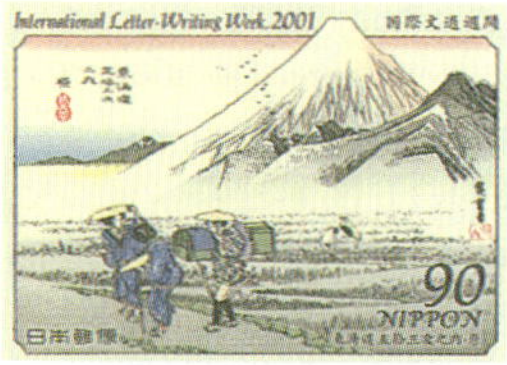

2322 "Hara"

2001. International Correspondence Week. Paintings from "53 Stations of Tokaido" by Ando Hiroshige. Multicoloured.

2971	90y. Type **2322**	2·50	2·00
2972	110y. "Oiso"	3·00	2·40
2973	130y. "Sakanoshita"	3·25	2·75

2325 Boy with Birds and Insects

2001. "Let's Keep our Towns Safe" (national community safety campaign). Multicoloured.

2974	80y. Type **2325**	1·80	1·50
2975	80y. Girl with bird and animals	1·80	1·50

2327 Man catching Disc

2001. 1st National Sports Games for the Disabled, Sendai City and Miyagi-gun. Multicoloured.

2976	80y. Type **2327**	1·80	1·50
2977	80y. Wheelchair race	1·80	1·50

2329 Norinaga Motoori (writer and scholar, death bicentenary)

2330 Gidayu Takemoto (jojuri chanter and puppeteer, 350th birth) and Illustration from "Sonezaki Shinju"

2001. Anniversaries.

2978	**2329**	80y. multicoloured	1·80	1·50
2979	**2330**	80y. multicoloured	1·80	1·50

2331 Horse carrying Rice

2001. New Years Greeting's. Multicoloured.

2980	50y. Type **2331**	1·30	1·10
2981	80y. Red horse of Kira	1·70	1·40

2334 Red Horse of Kira (sedge handicraft)

2001. New Year's Lottery Stamps. Multicoloured.

2982	50y.+3y. Horse carrying rice	1·40	1·10
2983	80y.+3y. Type **2334**	1·80	1·50

Each stamp carries a lottery number.

2335 Television Camera, Television Set and Radio Microphone

2001. 50th Anniv of Commercial Broadcasting.

2984	**2335**	80y. multicoloured	1·70	1·40

2336 Ujikami Shrine

2337 Kaeru Mata (main shrine), Ujikami Shrine

2338 Path to Kozanji Temple

2339 Sekisuiin, Kozanji Temple

2340 Kasumijima Garden, Saihoji Temple

2341 Kojokan Garden, Saihoji Temple

2342/3 Garden, Tenryuji Temple

2344 Golden Temple, Rokuonji Temple

2345 Golden Temple in Winter

2001. World Heritage (5th series). Temples and Shrines, Kyoto.

2985	**2336**	80y. multicoloured	1·70	1·40
2986	**2337**	80y. multicoloured	1·70	1·40
2987	**2338**	80y. multicoloured	1·70	1·40
2988	**2339**	80y. multicoloured	1·70	1·40
2989	**2340**	80y. multicoloured	1·70	1·40
2990	**2341**	80y. multicoloured	1·70	1·40
2991	**2342**	80y. multicoloured	1·70	1·40
2992	**2343**	80y. multicoloured	1·70	1·40
2993	**2344**	80y. multicoloured	1·70	1·40
2994	**2345**	80y. multicoloured	1·70	1·40

Nos. 2985/94 were issued together in sheetlets of ten stamps, Nos. 2991/2 forming the composite design illustrated, with descriptions of each stamp in Japanese in the illustrated margin.

2346 Upraised Hand

2002. 50th Anniv of Legal Aid System.

2995	**2346**	80y. multicoloured	1·70	1·40

2347 Horse-shaped Fiddle Head

2002. 30th Anniv of Japan—Mongolia Diplomatic Relations.

2996	**2347**	80y. multicoloured	1·70	1·40

2348 Silver Pavilion in Snow, Jishoji Temple

2349 Silver Pavilion

2350 Hojo Garden, Ryoanji Temple

2351 Hojo Garden in Winter

2352 Karamon Gate, Honganji Temple

2353 Hiunkaku, Honganji Temple

2354 Shoin, Honganji Temple

2355 Ninomaru Palace, Nijo Castle

2356 Hawk on Pine (detail, painting), Nijo Castle

2357 Hawk on Pine (detail)

2002. World Heritage (6th series). Temples, Kyoto.

2997	**2348**	80y. multicoloured	1·70	1·40
2998	**2349**	80y. multicoloured	1·70	1·40
2999	**2350**	80y. multicoloured	1·70	1·40
3000	**2351**	80y. multicoloured	1·70	1·40
3001	**2352**	80y. multicoloured	1·70	1·40
3002	**2353**	80y. multicoloured	1·70	1·40
3003	**2354**	80y. multicoloured	1·70	1·40
3004	**2355**	80y. multicoloured	1·70	1·40
3005	**2356**	80y. multicoloured	1·70	1·40
3006	**2357**	80y. multicoloured	1·70	1·40

2358 Bell and Mythical Lion-dog

2002. 50th Anniv of Japan Lions (charitable organization).

3007	**2358**	80y. multicoloured	1·60	1·30

2359 Men's Singles Skater

2002. World Figure Skating Championships, Nagano. Multicoloured.

3008	80y. Type **2359**	1·60	1·30
3009	80y. Pairs skaters	1·60	1·30

2361 Taj Mahal, India

2362 Artefact and Ruins, Moenjodaro, Pakistan

2363 Sigiriya, Sri Lanka

2364 Terracotta Panel and Ruins, Paharpur, Bangladesh

2002. 50th Anniv of Japan–South East Asia Diplomatic Relations.

3010	**2361**	80y. multicoloured	1·60	1·30
3011	**2362**	80y. multicoloured	1·60	1·30
3012	**2363**	80y. multicoloured	1·60	1·30
3013	**2364**	80y. multicoloured	1·60	1·30

2365 Two Horsemen

2002. Philately Week. (Kamo folding screen). Multicoloured.

3014	80y. Type **2365**	1·60	1·30
3015	80y. Horseman and spectator	1·60	1·30

2367 *Hikawa-Maru* (passenger ship)

2002. 50th Anniv of Japan–U.S.A. Fulbright Exchange Programme.

3016	**2367**	80y. multicoloured	1·60	1·30

2368 Ship and Irises

2002. 30th Anniv of Return of Okinawa.

3017	**2368**	80y. multicoloured	1·60	1·30

2369 Stylized Football Pitch

2002. World Cup Football Championships, Japan and South Korea. Multicoloured.

3018	80y. Type **2369**	1·60	1·30
3019	80y. FIFA World Cup Trophy	1·60	1·30

2371 Great Buddha Hall, Todaiji Temple

2372 Southern Gate, Todaiji Temple

2373 Great Buddha (detail), Todaiji Temple

2374 Virupaksu (statue), Todaiji Temple

2375 Lotus Hall, Todaiji Temple

2376 Five-storied Pagoda, Kofukuji Temple

2377 Northern Octagonal Hall, Kofukuji Temple

2378 Ashura (statue), Kofukuji Temple

2379 Buddha Head, Kofukuji Temple

2380 Ryutoki Demon (statue), Kofukuji Temple

2002. World Heritage (7th series). Temples, Nara.

3020	**2371**	80y. multicoloured	1·60	1·30
3021	**2372**	80y. multicoloured	1·60	1·30
3022	**2373**	80y. multicoloured	1·60	1·30
3023	**2374**	80y. multicoloured	1·60	1·30
3024	**2375**	80y. multicoloured	1·60	1·30
3025	**2376**	80y. multicoloured	1·60	1·30
3026	**2377**	80y. multicoloured	1·60	1·30
3027	**2378**	80y. multicoloured	1·60	1·30
3028	**2379**	80y. multicoloured	1·60	1·30
3029	**2380**	80y. multicoloured	1·60	1·30

Nos. 3020/9 were issued in sheetlets of ten stamps, with descriptions of each stamp in Japanese in the illustrated margin.

2381 Girl carrying Envelope

2002. National Letter Writing Day.

3030	**2381**	50y. multicoloured	1·20	95
3031	-	50y. multicoloured	1·20	95
3032	-	50y. multicoloured	1·20	95
3033	-	50y. multicoloured	1·20	95
3034	-	80y. multicoloured	1·60	1·30
3035	-	80y. lemon, black and blue	1·60	1·30
3036	-	80y. multicoloured	1·60	1·30
3037	-	80y. multicoloured	1·60	1·30

3038	-	80y. multicoloured	1·60	1·30
3039	-	80y. multicoloured	1·60	1·30
3040	-	80y. multicoloured	1·60	1·30
3041	-	80y. multicoloured	1·60	1·30
3042	-	80y. multicoloured	1·60	1·30
3043	-	80y. multicoloured	1·60	1·30
MS3044 72×94 mm. Nos. 3031 and 3040			3·25	3·00

DESIGNS: No. 2383, House and flowers (28×34 mm); 2384, Young boy and fence (25×34 mm); 2385, Ladybird and caterpillar (28×25 mm); 2386, Farmer and sheep (30×25 mm); 2387, Cow (32×25 mm); 2388, Girl and flowers (30×41 mm); 2389, Boy with football (22×35 mm); 2390, Girl carrying Tennis racquet (22×35 mm); 2391, Mother and child (28×36 mm); 2392, Man riding bicycle (28×36 mm); 2393, Girl and vase (27×27 mm); 2394, Van and car (27×27 mm).

2395 Covered Passageway, Kasuga Taisha Shrine

2396 Middle Gate, Kasuga Taisha Shrine

2397 Deer, Kasuga-yama Forest

2398 Zen Meditation Hall, Gango-ji Temple

2399 Pagoda, Gango-ji Temple

2400 East and West Pagodas, Yakushi-ji Temple

2401 Buddha of Healing, Yakushi-ji Temple

2402 Golden Hall, Toshodai-ji Temple

2403 Standing Image of the Thousand Handed Goddess of Mercy, Toshodai-ji Temple

2404 Suzakumon Gate, Heijo Imperial Palace

2002. World Heritage (8th series). Temples.

3045	**2395**	80y. multicoloured	1·60	1·30
3046	**2396**	80y. multicoloured	1·60	1·30
3047	**2397**	80y. multicoloured	1·60	1·30
3048	**2398**	80y. multicoloured	1·60	1·30
3049	**2399**	80y. multicoloured	1·60	1·30
3050	**2400**	80y. multicoloured	1·60	1·30
3051	**2401**	80y. multicoloured	1·60	1·30
3052	**2402**	80y. multicoloured	1·60	1·30
3053	**2403**	80y. multicoloured	1·60	1·30
3054	**2404**	80y. multicoloured	1·60	1·30

Nos. 3045/54 were issued in sheetlets of ten stamps, with descriptions of each stamp in Japanese in the illustrated margin.

2405 Stylized Human and Flowers

2002. 12th World Psychiatry Congress.

3055	**2405**	80y. multicoloured	1·60	1·30

2406 Basketball Players

2002. World Wheelchair Basketball Championship, Japan.

3056	**2406**	80y. multicoloured	1·60	1·30

2407 Boeing 777 and Douglas DC-7

2002. 50th Anniv of Japanese Civil Aviation.

3057	**2407**	80y. multicoloured	1·60	1·30

2408 "Shitoka" (Denj Lin)

2409 "Generyucho" (Wang Chuan Feng)

2002. 30th Anniv of Japan–China Diplomatic Relations.

3058	**2408**	80y. multicoloured	1·60	1·30
3059	**2409**	80y. multicoloured	1·60	1·30

2410/11 Houses, Ogimachi, Shirakawa-Mura

2412 House and Flowers, Ogimachi

2413 Houses, Ogimachi

2414 Houses covered in Snow, Ogimachi

2415 Aerial View, Ainokura, Taira-Mura

2416 House, Ainokura

2417 Houses, Ainokura

2418 House, Ainokura

2419 House covered in Snow, Ainokura

2002. World Heritage (9th series). Ogimachi and Ainokura Communitites.

3060	**2410**	80y. multicoloured	1·60	1·30
3061	**2411**	80y. multicoloured	1·60	1·30
3062	**2412**	80y. multicoloured	1·60	1·30
3063	**2413**	80y. multicoloured	1·60	1·30
3064	**2414**	80y. multicoloured	1·60	1·30
3065	**2415**	80y. multicoloured	1·60	1·30
3066	**2416**	80y. multicoloured	1·60	1·30
3067	**2417**	80y. multicoloured	1·60	1·30
3068	**2418**	80y. multicoloured	1·60	1·30
3069	**2419**	80y. multicoloured	1·60	1·30

Nos. 3060/9 were issued in sheetlets of ten stamps, Nos. 3060/1 forming the composite design illustrated, with descriptions of each stamp in Japanese in the illustrated margin.

2420 Naval Ships and Flags

2002. Fleet Review.

3070	**2420**	80y. multicoloured	1·60	1·30

2421 "Yui"

2002. International Correspondence Week. Paintings from "53 Stations of Tokaido" by Ando Hiroshige. Multicoloured.

3071	90y. Type **2421**	1·80	1·50
3072	110y. "Shono"	2·40	2·00
3073	130y. "Tozuka"	2·75	2·40

2424 Stylized People

2002. Asian and Pacific Decade of Disabled Persons Conference.

3074	**2424**	80y. multicoloured	1·60	1·30

2425 Masaoka Shiki (writer, death centenary)

2426 "Three Women" (Torii Kiyonaga (artist, 250th birth))

2427 Tanakadate Aikitu (geophysicist, 50th death)

2002. Anniversaries.

3075	**2425**	80y. multicoloured	1·60	1·30
3076	**2426**	80y. multicoloured	1·60	1·30
3077	**2427**	80y. multicoloured	1·60	1·30

2428 Sheep (earthenware Dorei figure)

2002. New Year's Greetings. Multicoloured.

3078	50y. Type **2428**	1·30	1·10
3079	80y. Sheep with Gem (Edo folk toy)	1·60	1·30

2430 Sheep holding Fan (Aizunakayugawa doll)

2002. New Year Lottery Stamps. Multicoloured.

3081	50y.+3y. Type **2430**	1·40	1·10
3082	80y.+3y. Sheep (Oku Hariko doll)	1·70	1·40

Each stamp carries a lottery number.

2432 Stone Lion, Shou Dynasty Royal Mausoleum

2433 Stone Gate, Sonohyan'utaki Sanctuary

2434 Cherry Blossom, Nakijinjou castle

2435 Stone Gate, Zakimijou Castle

2436 Katsurenjou Castle Walls

2437 Second Citadel, Nakagusukujou Castle

2438 "Kankaimon", Shurijou Castle Gate

2439 Main Hall, Shurijou Castle

2440 "Shikina'en" (royal garden)

2441 Seifautaki Sanctuary

2002. World Heritage (10th series).

3083	**2432**	80y. multicoloured	1·60	1·30
3084	**2433**	80y. multicoloured	1·60	1·30
3085	**2434**	80y. multicoloured	1·60	1·30
3086	**2435**	80y. multicoloured	1·60	1·30
3087	**2436**	80y. multicoloured	1·60	1·30
3088	**2437**	80y. multicoloured	1·60	1·30
3089	**2438**	80y. multicoloured	1·60	1·30
3090	**2439**	80y. multicoloured	1·60	1·30
3091	**2440**	80y. multicoloured	1·60	1·30
3092	**2441**	80y. multicoloured	1·60	1·30

2442 Kabuki Screen showing Izumo no Okuni in Costume

2443 Actors from "Shibaraku" and "Tsuchigumo"

2003. 400th Anniv of First Kabuki Theatre Performance.

3093	**2442**	80y. multicoloured	1·70	1·40
3094	**2443**	80y. multicoloured	1·70	1·40

2444 Television Company Emblem and Street Television Set

2003. 50th Anniv of Japanese Television. Multicoloured.

3095	80y. Type **2444**	1·70	1·40
3096	80y. "Hyokkori Hyotan-Jima" (puppet) and early television set	1·70	1·40

2446 Heart

2003. Greetings Stamps. Multicoloured. Self-adhesive.

3097	80y. Type **2446**	1·70	1·40
3098	80y. Dog wearing party clothes	1·70	1·40
3099	80y. Snowman	1·70	1·40
3100	80y. Bird on cake	1·70	1·40
3101	80y. Cranes and turtle	1·70	1·40
3102	80y. Roses	1·70	1·40
3103	80y. Reindeer	1·70	1·40
3104	80y. Cat	1·70	1·40
3105	80y. Cats in car	1·70	1·40
3106	80y. Cherry blossom	1·70	1·40

2456 Genbaku Dome (atomic bomb memorial)

2003. World Heritage (11th series). Peace Stamp Design Competition Winners. Multicoloured.

3107	80y. Type **2456**	1·70	1·40
3108	80y. Hiroshima Prefectural Hall	1·70	1·40
3109	80y. "La Paix" (Jean-Paul Veret LeMarinier)	1·70	1·40
3110	80y. "Taika" (peace) (Pakalkaite Joskaude)	1·70	1·40
3111	80y. "Universal Shrine of Peace" (Issac M. Oriville)	1·70	1·40
3112	80y. "A Prayer for Peace" (Keiji Sugita)	1·70	1·40
3113	80y. "The Radiance of Life" (Shigenobu Nagaishi)	1·70	1·40
3114	80y. "An Encounter" (Natsuki Nakatani)	1·70	1·40
3115	80y. Rainbow-coloured Dove" (Makoto Oooka)	1·70	1·40
3116	80y. "Rabbit" (Shiho Kobayashi)	1·70	1·40

2466 Posuton

2003. Postal Services Mascots. Self-adhesive. Multicoloured.

3117	50y. Aichan	1·60	1·30
3118	50y. Kanchan boy	1·60	1·30
3118a	50y. Posuton	1·60	1·30
3118b	50y. Yuchan	1·60	1·30
3119	50y. Kanchan girl	1·60	1·30
3120	50y. Posuton	1·60	1·30
3121	80y. Type **2466**	1·60	1·30
3122	80y. Aichan	1·60	1·30
3123	80y. Kanchan girl	1·60	1·30
3124	80y. Posuton	1·60	1·30
3125	80y. Yuchan	1·60	1·30
3126	80y. Kanchan boy	1·60	1·30

2476 Yellow Flower

2003. Inauguration of Japan Post (public postal corporation). Designs from "Birds and Flowers of the Four Seasons" (folding screen by Sakai Hoitsu). Multicoloured. Self-adhesive.

3127	80y. Type **2476**	1·70	1·40
3128	80y. Primula	1·70	1·40
3129	80y. Violets and quince	1·70	1·40
3130	80y. Horsetail	1·70	1·40
3131	80y. White wisteria	1·70	1·40
3132	80y. Flowering cherry and swallow	1·70	1·40
3133	80y. Hydrangea	1·70	1·40
3134	80y. Magnolia	1·70	1·40
3135	80y. Water lily and moorhen	1·70	1·40
3136	80y. Peonies and butterfly	1·70	1·40

2486 Tree and Sheep

2003. Philately Week. (Batik folding screen).

3137	**2486**	80y. multicoloured	1·70	1·40

2487 Map of Edo (folding screen)

2003. 400th Anniv of Edo Shogunate (1st issue). Multicoloured.

3138	80y. Type **2487**	1·70	1·40
3139	80y. Hon-maru (fresco, Edo Castle)	1·70	1·40
3140	80y. Domarugusoku Helmet and Armour	1·70	1·40
3141	80y. Hatsune maki-e Lacquer Box(detail)	1·70	1·40
3142	80y. 24 91 "Chujo" (Noh mask)	1·70	1·40

See also Nos. 3143/8 and 3159/64.

2492 "Nihonbashi Bridge" ("53 Stations of Tokaido")

2003. 400th Anniv of Edo Shogunate (2nd issue). Multicoloured.

3143	80y. Type **2492**	1·50	1·20
3144	80y. Fireman's Haori (coat)	1·50	1·20
3145	80y. "Beauty Spots in Edo" (folding screen)	1·50	1·20
3146	80y. Kyoho-Bina Girl Doll	1·50	1·20
3147	80y. Kyoho-Bina Boy Doll	1·50	1·20
3148	80y. Danjuro Ichikawa (actor) as Goro Takenuki	1·50	1·20

2498 Omar Ali Saifuddien Mosque,

2499 Angkor Wat, Cambodia Brunei Darussalam

2500 Borobudur Temple, Indonesia

2501 That Luang, Laos

2502 Sultan Abdul Samad Building, Malaysia

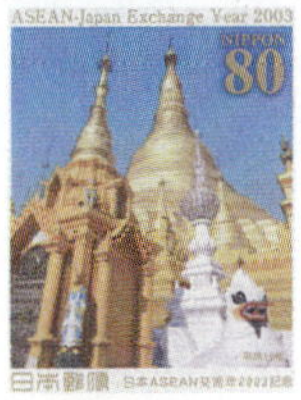

2503 Shwedagon Pagoda, Myanmar

2504 Rice Terraces, Cordilleras, Philippines

2505 Merlion (legendary beast), Singapore

2506 Wat Phra Kaeo, Thailand

2507 Van Mieu, Vietnam

2003. ASEAN—Japan Exchange Year (Association of Southeast Asian Nations and Japan co-operation).

3149	**2498**	80y. multicoloured	1·70	1·40
3150	**2499**	80y. multicoloured	1·70	1·40
3151	**2500**	80y. multicoloured	1·70	1·40
3152	**2501**	80y. multicoloured	1·70	1·40
3153	**2502**	80y. multicoloured	1·70	1·40
3154	**2503**	80y. multicoloured	1·70	1·40
3155	**2504**	80y. multicoloured	1·70	1·40
3156	**2505**	80y. multicoloured	1·70	1·40
3157	**2506**	80y. multicoloured	1·70	1·40
3158	**2507**	80y. multicoloured	1·70	1·40

2508/9 *Powhatan*

2003. 400th Anniv of Edo Shogunate (3rd issue). Multicoloured.

3159	80y. Type **2508**	1·70	1·40
3160	80y. Type **2509**	1·70	1·40
3161	80y. Bakumatsu Fusoku Zukan (detail, screen)	1·70	1·40
3162	80y. Dutch East India Company plate	1·70	1·40
3163	80y. European Woman (detail, painting)	1·70	1·40
3164	80y. Wind-up Clock (Hisahige Tanaka)	1·70	1·40

2514 Bear playing Guitar (281/2×36 mm)

2003. Letter Writing Day. Multicoloured.

3165	50y. Type **2514**	1·40	1·10
3166	50y. Monkey (28½×36 mm)	1·40	1·10
3167	50y. Crocodile playing Accordion (28½×36)	1·40	1·10
3168	50y. Cat holding Camera and Envelope (28½×36 mm)	1·40	1·10
3169	80y. Hippo holding Flowers (29×40 mm)	1·70	1·40
3170	80y. Parrot (28×37 mm)	1·70	1·40
3171	80y. Owl (30×30 mm)	1·70	1·40
3172	80y. Seated Bear holding Envelope (28×40 mm)	1·70	1·40
3173	80y. Elephant (28×37 mm)	1·70	1·40
3174	80y. Giraffe (29×40 mm)	1·70	1·40
3175	80y. Rabbit holding Envelope and Flowers (41×24 mm)	1·70	1·40
3176	80y. Lion carrying Lantern (28×37 mm)	1·70	1·40
3177	80y. Goat holding Envelope (28×37 mm)	1·70	1·40
3178	80y. Gorilla (28×37)	1·70	1·40
MS3179	72×94 mm. Nos. 3170 and 3165	4·25	4·00

2528 "Kawaski"

2529 "Miya"

2530 "Otsu"

2003. International Correspondence Week. Paintings from "53 Stations of Tokaido" by Ando Hiroshige.

3180	**2528**	90y. multicoloured	2·10	1·80
3181	**2529**	110y. multicoloured	2·40	2·00
3182	**2530**	130y. multicoloured	2·75	2·40

2531 Byakko (White Tiger of the West)

2003. Cultural Heritage. Wall Paintings, Kitora Tumulus, Nara Prefecture. Multicoloured.

3183	80y.+10y. Type **2532**	1·60	1·30
3184	80y.+10y. Suzaku (Red Bird of the South)	1·60	1·30

2533 Mokichi Saito (writer, 150th death)

2534 Shibasaburo Kitasato (scientist, 150th birth)

2003. Anniversaries.

3185	**2533**	80y. multicoloured	1·70	1·40
3186	**2534**	80y. multicoloured	1·70	1·40

2535 Flowers and Butterflies, Amami Forest (painting, Isson Tanaka)

2003. 50th Anniv of Return of Amami Islands to Japan.

3187	**2535**	80y. multicoloured	1·70	1·40

2536 Monkey (Iyo Ittobori wood carving)

2003. New Year's Greetings. Multicoloured.

3188	50y. Type **2536**	1·30	1·10
3189	80y. The Successful Monkey (Edo folk toy)	1·60	1·30

2539 The Successful Monkey (Edo folk toy)

2003. New Year Lottery Stamps. Multicoloured.

3191	50y.+3y. Monkey (Iyo Ittobori wood carving)	1·40	1·10
3192	80y.+3y. Type **2539**	1·70	1·40

Each stamp carries a lottery number.

2540 Tetsuwan Atom (flying down)

2003. Science, Technology and Animation (1st issue). Multicoloured.

3193	80y. Type **2540**	1·80	1·50
3194	80y. Tetsuwan Atom (with raised arm)	1·80	1·50
3195	80y. Tetsuwan Atom (upside down)	1·80	1·50
3196	80y. Yumihiki Doji (Edo mechanical doll)	1·80	1·50
3197	80y. Nagaoka Hantaro (physicist)	1·80	1·50
3198	80y. H-II Rocket	1·80	1·50
3199	80y. Morph 3 Robot	1·80	1·50
3200	80y. Tetsuwan Atom (flying up)	1·80	1·50

See also Nos. 3202/8; 3224/31; 3232/9, 3264/71, 3286/93 and 3305/12.

2548 Super Jetter 1

2549 Wadokei (clock)

2550 Otomo-go (vintage car)

2551 KAZ (modern car)

2552 Stratospheric Balloon

2553 Super Jetter

2554 Super Jetter 3

2555 Super Jetter 4

2004. Science, Technology and Animation (2nd issue).

3201	**2548**	80y. multicoloured	1·80	1·50
3202	**2549**	80y. multicoloured	1·80	1·50
3203	**2550**	80y. multicoloured	1·80	1·50
3204	**2551**	80y. multicoloured	1·80	1·50
3205	**2552**	80y. multicoloured	1·80	1·50
3206	**2553**	80y. multicoloured	1·80	1·50
3207	**2554**	80y. multicoloured	1·80	1·50
3208	**2555**	80y. multicoloured	1·80	1·50

2556 Hello Kitty **2557** Hello Kitty

2558 Hello Kitty **2559** Hello Kitty

2560 Hello Kitty **2561** Hello Kitty

2562 Hello Kitty **2563** Hello Kitty

2564 Hello Kitty **2565** Hello Kitty

2566 Hello Kitty

2567 Hello Kitty

2568 Hello Kitty

2569 Hello Kitty

2570 Hello Kitty

2004. Greetings Stamps. Hello Kitty. Self-adhesive.

3209	**2556**	50y. multicoloured	1·30	1·10
3210	**2557**	50y. multicoloured	1·30	1·10
3211	**2558**	50y. multicoloured	1·30	1·10
3212	**2559**	50y. multicoloured	1·30	1·10
3213	**2560**	50y. multicoloured	1·30	1·10
3214	**2561**	50y. multicoloured	1·30	1·10
3215	**2562**	50y. multicoloured	1·30	1·10
3216	**2563**	50y. multicoloured	1·30	1·10
3217	**2564**	50y. multicoloured	1·30	1·10
3218	**2565**	50y. multicoloured	1·30	1·10
3219	**2566**	80y. multicoloured	1·80	1·50
3220	**2567**	80y. multicoloured	1·80	1·50
3221	**2568**	80y. multicoloured	1·80	1·50
3222	**2569**	80y. multicoloured	1·80	1·50
3223	**2570**	80y. multicoloured	1·80	1·50

2571 Marvellous Melmo 1

2572 Hanaoka Seishu

2573 Wooden Microscope

2574 Takamine Jokichi

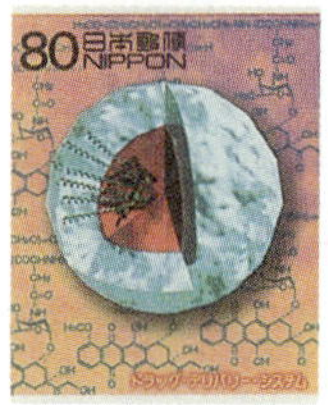

2575 Drug Delivery System

2576 Marvellous Melmo 2

2577 Marvellous Melmo 3

2578 Marvellous Melmo 4

2004. Science, Technology and Animation (3rd issue).

3224	**2571**	80y. multicoloured	1·80	1·50
3225	**2572**	80y. multicoloured	1·80	1·50
3226	**2573**	80y. multicoloured	1·80	1·50
3227	**2574**	80y. multicoloured	1·80	1·50
3228	**2575**	80y. multicoloured	1·80	1·50
3229	**2576**	80y. multicoloured	1·80	1·50
3230	**2577**	80y. multicoloured	1·80	1·50
3231	**2578**	80y. multicoloured	1·80	1·50

2579 Kagaku Ninja-Tai Gatchman 1

2580 Perpetual Motion Machine

2581 OHSUMI (satellite) 2502 Conducting Polymer

2583 Eye (Tissue/Organ Reproductive Medicine)

2584 Kagaku Ninja-Tai Gatchman 2

2585 Kagaku Ninja-Tai Gatchman 3

2586 Kagaku Ninja-Tai Gatchman 4

2004. Science, Technology and Animation (4th issue).

3232	**2579**	80y. multicoloured	1·80	1·50
3233	**2580**	80y. multicoloured	1·80	1·50
3234	**2581**	80y. multicoloured	1·80	1·50
3235	**2582**	80y. multicoloured	1·80	1·50
3236	**2583**	80y. multicoloured	1·80	1·50
3237	**2584**	80y. multicoloured	1·80	1·50
3238	**2585**	80y. multicoloured	1·80	1·50
3239	**2586**	80y. multicoloured	1·80	1·50

2587 Morizo and Kiccoro (official mascots) in Orbit

2005. EXPO 2005 World Exhibition, Aichi, Japan. Multicoloured.

3240	80y.+10y. Type **2587**	1·90	1·60
3241	80y.+10y. Morizo and Kiccoro holding hands	1·90	1·60

2589 "Uchuno sakura gohiki no saru zu" (Mori Sosen)

2004. Philately Week.

3242	**2589**	80y. multicoloured	1·80	1·50

2590 *Ten Point* and *Tosho Boy* (22nd Arima Memorial Stakes)

2004. 50th of Japan Racing Association. Multicoloured.

3243	80y. Type **2590**	1·80	1·50
3244	80y. *Narita Brian* (61st Tokyo Yushun (Japanese Derby))	1·80	1·50

2592 Police Car

2004. 50th Anniv of Police Law. Multicoloured.

3245	80y. Type **2592**	1·80	1·50
3246	80y. Police motorcyclist	1·80	1·50

Nos. 3245/6 were issued together, se-tenant, forming a composite design.

2594 Donkichi holding Pencil

2003. Letter Writing Day. Multicoloured.

3247	50y. Type **2594**	1·30	1·10
3248	50y. Hime (25×33 mm)	1·30	1·10
3249	50y. Shochan (25×33 mm)	1·30	1·10
3250	50y. Owl (33×36 mm)	1·30	1·10
3251	80y. Pigeon carrying envelope (33×34 mm)	1·80	1·50
3252	80y. Squirrel with wings (33×36 mm)	1·80	1·50
3253	80y. Stork (30×30 mm)	1·80	1·50
3254	80y. Hime with wings (27×36 mm)	1·80	1·50
3255	80y. Donkichi (27×37 mm)	1·80	1·50
3256	80y. Kuriko (27×37 mm)	1·80	1·50
3257	80y. Goddess (28×40 mm)	1·80	1·50
3258	80y. Shochan with wings (28×36 mm)	1·80	1·50
3259	80y. Squirrel holding envelope and flowers (28×29 mm)	1·80	1·50
3260	80y. Rabbit (30×30 mm)	1·80	1·50
MS3261	72×94 mm. Nos. 3247 and 3256	3·25	3·00

2608 Athens 2004 Emblem

2004. Olympic Games, Athens. Multicoloured.

3262	80y. Type **2608**	1·60	1·30
3263	80y. Olympic Rings, Flame and Olympia Ruins	1·60	1·30

2610 Majinga Z 4

2611 Model Steam Engine

2612 KS Steel

2613 Shinkai 6500

2614 Fuel Cell

2615 Majinga Z 1

2616 Majinga Z 2

2617 Majinga Z 3

2004. Science, Technology and Animation (5th issue).

3264	**2610**	80y. multicoloured	1·70	1·40
3265	**2611**	80y. multicoloured	1·70	1·40
3266	**2612**	80y. multicoloured	1·70	1·40
3267	**2613**	80y. multicoloured	1·70	1·40
3268	**2614**	80y. multicoloured	1·70	1·40
3269	**2615**	80y. multicoloured	1·70	1·40
3270	**2616**	80y. multicoloured	1·70	1·40
3271	**2617**	80y. multicoloured	1·70	1·40

2618 *Mount Fuji* (Frederic Harris)

2004. 150th Anniv of America—Japan Relations. Multicoloured.

3272	80y. Type **2618**	1·70	1·40
3273	80y. Cafe (Yasuo Kuniyoshi)	1·70	1·40

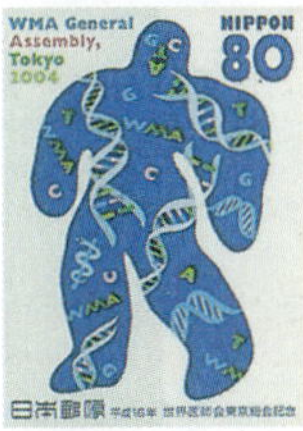
2620 Medical Symbols as Figure

2004. World Medical Association (WMA) General Assembly, Tokyo.

3274	**2620**	80y. multicoloured	1·70	1·40

2621 "Hirarsukai"

2004. International Correspondence Week. Paintings from "53 Stations of Tokaido" by Utagawa Hiroshige. Multicoloured.

3275	90y. Type **2621**	1·90	1·60
3276	110y. "Yokkaichi"	2·50	2·10
3277	130y. "Tsuchiyama"	3·00	2·50

2624 Lafcadio Hearn (Koizumi Yakumo) (writer) (death centenary)

2004. Anniversaries. Multicoloured.

3278	80y. Type **2624**	1·60	1·30
3279	80y. Isamu Noguchi (sculptor) (birth centenary)	1·60	1·30
3280	80y. Koga Masao (composer) (birth centenary)	1·60	1·30

2627 Rooster (Hita-Dorei (clay bell))

2004. New Year's Greetings.

3281	50y. Type **2627**	1·10	90
3282	80y. Rooster (Shimotsuke-Dorei (clay bell))	1·60	1·30

2630 Rooster (Shimotsuke-Dorei (clay bell))

2004. New Year Lottery Stamps. Multicoloured.

3284	50y.+3y. Rooster (Hita-Dorei (clay bell))	1·20	95
3285	80y.+3y. Type **2630**	1·70	1·40

Each stamp carries a lottery number.

2631 Doraemon 4

2632 Hiraga Gennai

2633 Mechanical "netsuke"

2634 Television Set

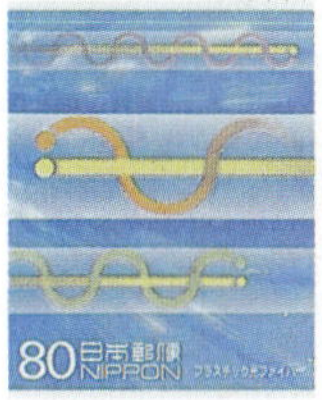
2635 Plastic Optical Fibre (POF)

2636 Doraemon 1

2637 Doraemon 2

2638 Doraemon 3

2004. Science, Technology and Animation (6th issue). Multicoloured.

3286	**2631**	80y. multicoloured	1·60	1·30
3287	**2632**	80y. multicoloured	1·60	1·30
3288	**2633**	80y. multicoloured	1·60	1·30
3289	**2634**	80y. multicoloured	1·60	1·30
3290	**2635**	80y. multicoloured	1·60	1·30
3291	**2636**	80y. multicoloured	1·60	1·30
3292	**2637**	80y. multicoloured	1·60	1·30
3293	**2638**	80y. multicoloured	1·60	1·30

2639 "tori" (Tensho style) (Toda Teizan)

2640 "tori" (Kinbun style) (Seki Masato)

2641 "tori" (Kinbun style) (Onchi Shunyou)

2642 "tori" (Tensho style) (Funamoto Hou'un)

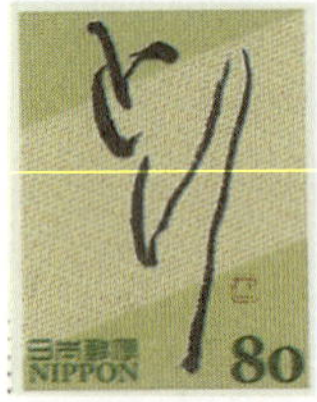
2643 "tori" (Kana style) (Koyama Yasuko)

2644 "tori" (Sousho style) (Watanabe Kan'ou)

2645 "tori" (Kobun style) (Inamuru un'dou)

2646 "tori" (Reisho style) (Oono Kouken)

2647 "tori" (Kokotsumoji style) (Oohira Santou)

2648 "tori" (Kobun style) (Noguchi Hakutei)

2004. Greetings Stamps. Eto Calligraphy.

3294	**2639**	80y. multicoloured	1·60	1·30
3295	**2640**	80y. multicoloured	1·60	1·30
3296	**2641**	80y. multicoloured	1·60	1·30
3297	**2642**	80y. multicoloured	1·60	1·30
3298	**2643**	80y. multicoloured	1·60	1·30
3299	**2644**	80y. multicoloured	1·60	1·30
3300	**2645**	80y. multicoloured	1·60	1·30
3301	**2646**	80y. multicoloured	1·60	1·30
3302	**2647**	80y. multicoloured	1·60	1·30
3303	**2648**	80y. multicoloured	1·60	1·30

2649 "Nangicho" (bird of suffering)

2005. International Conference on Disaster Reduction.

3304	**2649**	80y. multicoloured	1·60	1·30

2650 Douglas 747 and Flowers

2005. Opening of Chubu International Airport.

3304a	**2650**	80y. multicoloured	1·60	1·30

2651 Time Bokan 1

2652 Circular Loom (invented by Toyoda Sakichi)

2653 Shinkansen (bullet train)

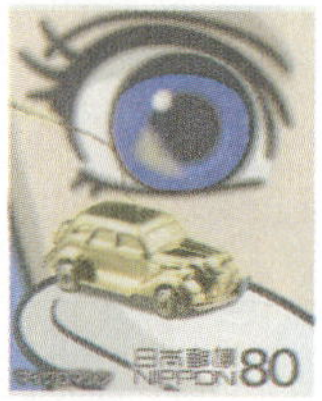
2654 Micro-machine

2655 International Space Station

2656 Time Bokan 2

2657 Time Bokan 3

2658 Time Bokan 4

2005. Science, Technology and Animation (7th issue).

3305	**2651**	80y. multicoloured	1·60	1·30
3306	**2652**	80y. multicoloured	1·60	1·30
3307	**2653**	80y. multicoloured	1·60	1·30
3308	**2654**	80y. multicoloured	1·60	1·30
3309	**2655**	80y. multicoloured	1·60	1·30
3310	**2656**	80y. multicoloured	1·60	1·30
3311	**2657**	80y. multicoloured	1·60	1·30
3312	**2658**	80y. multicoloured	1·60	1·30

2659/60 Mammoth and Globe

2005. EXPO 2005, World Exposition, Aichi.

3313	**2659**	80c. multicoloured	1·60	1·30
3314	**2660**	80c. multicoloured	1·60	1·30

Nos. 3313/14 were issued together, *se-tenant*, forming a composite design.

2661 Daikei-shiyu-zu (giant hen and rooster)

2005. Philately Week.

3315	**2661**	80c. multicoloured	1·60	1·30

2662 Children

2005. Centenary of Rotary International.

3316	**2662**	80c. multicoloured	1·60	1·30

2663 Mt. Hodakadake
2664 *Anemone narcissiflora*

2665 Mt. Yarigatake
2666 *Aquilegia flabellate*

2005. Centenary of Japanese Alpine Club.

3317	**2663**	50c. multicoloured	1·30	1·10
3318	**2664**	50c. multicoloured	1·30	1·10
3319	**2665**	50c. multicoloured	1·30	1·10
3320	**2666**	50c. multicoloured	1·30	1·10

2667 Rayquaza
2668 Gonbe

2669 Pikachu

2670 Rizadon

2671 Mew

2005. Heroes and Heroines of Animation (1st issue). Pocket Monsters.

3321	**2667**	50y. multicoloured	1·30	1·10
3322	**2668**	50y. multicoloured	1·30	1·10
3323	**2669**	80y. multicoloured	1·60	1·30
3324	**2670**	80y. multicoloured	1·60	1·30
3325	**2671**	80y. multicoloured	1·60	1·30

See also Nos. 3341/50, 3389/98, 3404/13, 3536/45, 3572/81 and 3692/3701.

2672 Squirrel holding Nut

2005. Letter Writing Day. Multicoloured.

3326	50y. Type **2672**	1·30	1·10
3327	50y. Rabbit	1·30	1·10
3328	50y. Owl	1·30	1·10
3329	50y. Kuriko carrying envelope	1·30	1·10
3330	80y. Pigeon carrying envelope	1·60	1·30
3331	80y. Donkichi	1·60	1·30
3332	80y. Castle	1·60	1·30
3333	80y. Shochan	1·60	1·30
3334	80y. White rabbit	1·60	1·30
3335	80y. Kuriko	1·60	1·30
3336	80y. Hime	1·60	1·30
3337	80y. Violet	1·60	1·30
3338	80y. Squirrel	1·60	1·30
3339	80y. Fox	1·60	1·30
MS3340	72×94 mm. Nos. 3327 and 3333	3·00	2·75

2686 Gundum W

2687 Hiiro

2688 Freedom Gundum and Kira Yamato

2689 Justice Gundum and Arthrun Zala

2690 Amuro Ray

2691 Gundum

2692 Zaku

2693 Char Aznable

2694 Kamille

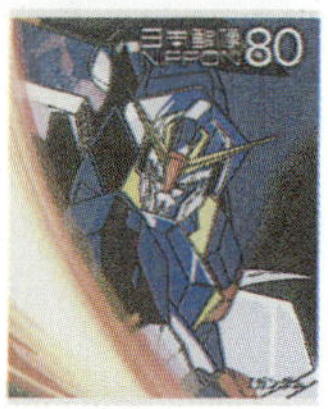
2695 Z Gundum

2005. Heroes and Heroines of Animation (2nd issue). Mobile Suit Gundum.

3341	**2686**	50y. multicoloured	1·20	95
3342	**2687**	50y. multicoloured	1·20	95
3343	**2688**	80y. multicoloured	1·60	1·30
3344	**2689**	80y. multicoloured	1·60	1·30
3345	**2690**	80y. multicoloured	1·60	1·30
3346	**2691**	80y. multicoloured	1·60	1·30
3347	**2692**	80y. multicoloured	1·60	1·30
3348	**2693**	80y. multicoloured	1·60	1·30

3349	**2694**	80y. multicoloured	1·60	1·30
3350	**2695**	80y. multicoloured	1·60	1·30

Nos. 3341/2, Nos. 3343/4, Nos. 3345/6, Nos. 3347/8 and Nos. 3349/50, respectively, were issued together, se-tenant, forming a composite design.

2696 Ono No Komachi (poet) (painting) (Tosa Mitsuoki)

2697 Fujiwara no Teika (poet) (painting) (Kano Tanyu)

2005. Literary Anniversaries.

3351	**2696**	80y. multicoloured (1100th anniv of Kokinshu)	1·60	1·30
3352	**2697**	80y. multicoloured (800th anniv of Shinkokinshu)	1·60	1·30

2698/9 Globe, Satellite and Rocket

2005. International Astronautical Congress, Fukuoka.

3353	**2698**	80y. multicoloured	1·60	1·30
3354	**2699**	80y. multicoloured	1·60	1·30

Nos. 3353/4 were issued together, se-tenant, forming a composite design.

2700 "Mariko"

2701 "Minakuchi"

2702 "Shinagawa"

2005. International Correspondence Week. Paintings from "53 Stations of Tokaido" by Utagawa Hiroshige.

3355	**2700**	90y. multicoloured	1·70	1·40
3356	**2701**	110y. multicoloured	1·90	1·60
3357	**2702**	130y. multicoloured	2·20	1·80

2703 Cyclamen (Arai Sonoko)

2005. Greetings Stamps. Self-adhesive.

3358	50y. Type **2703**	1·20	95
3359	50y. Flower Fairy (Nagata Moe)	1·20	95
3360	50y. Bear (Sugita Yutaka)	1·20	95
3361	50y. Gorilla (Murakami Tsutomu)	1·20	95
3362	50y. Snowman (Koide Masaki)	1·20	95
3363	80y. Father Christmas (Koide Masaki) (27×38 mm)	1·60	1·30
3364	80y. Poinsettias and Candle (Arai Sonoko) (27×38 mm)	1·60	1·30
3365	80y. Angel, Presents and Tree (Nagata Moe) (27×38 mm)	1·60	1·30
3366	80y. Hamster (Sugita Yutaka) (27×38 mm)	1·60	1·30
3367	80y. Cat (Murakami Tsutomu) (27×38 mm)	1·60	1·30

2713 Akita Dog

2005. New Year's Greetings. Multicoloured.

3368	50y. Type **2713**	1·20	95
3369	80y. Dog (Sadowara (clay))	1·60	1·30
MS3370	94×72 mm. Nos. 3368/9	2·75	2·40

2716 Dog (Sadowara (clay))

2005. New Year Lottery Stamps. Multicoloured.

3371	50y.+3y. Akita Dog	1·30	1·10
3372	80y.+3y. Type **2716**	1·70	1·40

Each stamp carries a lottery number.

2717 "inu" (Tensho style) (Ooi Kintei)

2718 "inu" (Kinbun style) (Takagiwa Suihou)

2719 "inu" (pictograph) (Kaneko Takyoshi)

2720 "inu" (phonetic letters) (Yonemoto Ikkou)

2721 "inu" (Tensho style) (Kishimoto Tarou)

2722 "inu" (Tensho style in half moon) (Tsujimoto Daiwun)

2723 "inu" (symbolic characters) (Seki Masato)

2724 "inu" (semi-cursive style) (Tanaka Touwun)

2725 "inu" (semi-cursive style) (Katou Shoudou)

2726 "inu" (Koukotsumoji style) (Kobayashi Hougyu)

2005. Greetings Stamps. Eto Calligraphy.

3373	**2717**	80y. multicoloured	1·60	1·30
3374	**2718**	80y. multicoloured	1·60	1·30
3375	**2719**	80y. multicoloured	1·60	1·30
3376	**2720**	80y. multicoloured	1·60	1·30
3377	**2721**	80y. multicoloured	1·60	1·30
3378	**2722**	80y. multicoloured	1·60	1·30
3379	**2723**	80y. multicoloured	1·60	1·30
3380	**2724**	80y. multicoloured	1·60	1·30
3381	**2725**	80y. multicoloured	1·60	1·30
3382	**2726**	80y. multicoloured	1·60	1·30

2727 Beethoven

2005. Germany in Japan. Multicoloured.

3383	80y. Type **2727**	1·60	1·30
3384	80y. Karl Benz driving Benz Patent Motorwagen, 1886	1·60	1·30
3385	80y. Male Japanese musician (Meissen)	1·60	1·30
3386	80y. Female Japanese musician (Meissen)	1·60	1·30
3387	80y. Equestrian acrobat (Meissen)	1·60	1·30
3388	80y. Harlequin (Meissen)	1·60	1·30

2733/4 Tetsuro and Maetel

2735/6 Claire and The Conductor

2737/8 Freija and Maetel and Tetsuro and Moriki Yutaka

2739/40 Emeraldas and Count Mecha and Herlock

2741/2 Maetel and Galaxy Express 999

2006. Heroes and Heroines of Animation (3rd issue). Galaxy Express 999.

3389	**2733**	80y. multicoloured	1·60	1·30
3390	**2734**	80y. multicoloured	1·60	1·30
3391	**2735**	80y. multicoloured	1·60	1·30
3392	**2736**	80y. multicoloured	1·60	1·30
3393	**2737**	80y. multicoloured	1·60	1·30
3394	**2738**	80y. multicoloured	1·60	1·30
3395	**2739**	80y. multicoloured	1·60	1·30
3396	**2740**	80y. multicoloured	1·60	1·30
3397	**2741**	80y. multicoloured	1·60	1·30
3398	**2742**	80y. multicoloured	1·60	1·30

Nos. 3389/90, 3391/2, 3393/4, 3395/6 and 3397/8, respectively, were issued together, se-tenant, each pair forming a composite design.

2743 Rabbit and Bird (Hirosawa Yo)

2006. International Exchanges and Friendship. Winning Entries in Design a Stamp Competition. Multicoloured.

3399	80y. Type **2743**	1·60	1·30
3400	80y. Children kissing (Ogasawara Maki)	1·60	1·30
3401	80y. Bears exchanging Fish (Mori Kiyotaka)	1·60	1·30
3402	80y. Dog and bear (Kobayashi Ryota)	1·60	1·30
3403	80y. Animals on globe (Takanami Suzuka)	1·60	1·30

2748/9 Shrunken Detective and Detective Conan

2750/1 Shin'ichi and Conan and Ran

2752/3 Doctor Agasa and Ayumi and Mitsuhiko and Genta

2754/5 Haibara Ai and Conan

2756/7 Mysterious Thief Kid and Shin'ichi and Conan

2006. Heroes and Heroines of Animation (4th issue). Detective Conan.

3404	**2748**	80y. multicoloured	1·60	1·30
3405	**2749**	80y. multicoloured	1·60	1·30
3406	**2750**	80y. multicoloured	1·60	1·30
3407	**2751**	80y. multicoloured	1·60	1·30
3408	**2752**	80y. multicoloured	1·60	1·30
3409	**2753**	80y. multicoloured	1·60	1·30
3410	**2754**	80y. multicoloured	1·60	1·30
3411	**2755**	80y. multicoloured	1·60	1·30
3412	**2756**	80y. multicoloured	1·60	1·30
3413	**2757**	80y. multicoloured	1·60	1·30

Nos. 3404/5, 3406/7, 3408/9, 3410/11 and 3412/13 respectively, were issued together, se-tenant, each pair forming a composite design.

2758 Morning Glory

2006. Philatelic Week. Paintings by Maruyama Oukyo. Multicoloured.

3414	80y. Type **2758**	1·50	1·20
3415	80y. Puppies	1·50	1·20

2760 Australian Flag and Uluru (Ayers Rock)

2006. Japan—Australia Exchange Year—2006. Multicoloured.

3416	80y. Type **2760**	1·50	1·20
3417	80y. Kangaroo	1·50	1·20
3418	80y. Sydney Opera House	1·50	1·20
3419	80y. Flag and Sydney Opera House	1·50	1·20
3420	80y. Fish (Great Barrier Reef)	1·50	1·20
3421	80y. Heart Reef	1·50	1·20
3422	80y. Golden wattle	1·50	1·20
3423	80y. Bottle bush	1·50	1·20
3424	80y. Koalas	1·50	1·20
3425	80y. Kookabura	1·50	1·20

Nos. 3416/17 3418/19 and 3424/5 respectively were issued together, se-tenant, forming composite designs.

2770/1 Kumano Hongu-taisha Shrine

2772 Nachinoootaki Waterfall

2773 Kumano Hongu-taisha Shrine

2774 Fire Festival, Nachi

2775 Nyoirin-dou Main Hall, Seigantoji Temple

2776 Kongobuji Temple Gate

2777 Kongaradouji (wooden statue), Kongobuji Temple

2778 Zaou-dou Main Hall, Kinpusenji Temple

2779 Zaou-gongen (wooden statue), Kinpusenji Temple

2006. World Heritage.

3426	**2770**	80y. multicoloured	1·50	1·20
3427	**2771**	80y. multicoloured	1·50	1·20
3428	**2772**	80y. multicoloured	1·50	1·20
3429	**2773**	80y. multicoloured	1·50	1·20
3430	**2774**	80y. multicoloured	1·50	1·20
3431	**2775**	80y. multicoloured	1·50	1·20
3432	**2776**	80y. multicoloured	1·50	1·20
3433	**2777**	80y. multicoloured	1·50	1·20
3434	**2778**	80y. multicoloured	1·50	1·20
3435	**2779**	80y. multicoloured	1·50	1·20

2780 Fairy on Flower

2006. Greetings Stamps. Multicoloured. Self-adhesive.

3436	50y. Type **2780** (23×27 mm)	1·10	90
3437	50y. Church bell (23×27 mm)	1·10	90
3438	50y. Bouquet (23×27 mm)	1·10	90
3439	50y. Dolphin (23×27 mm)	1·10	90
3440	50y. Humming bird (23×27 mm)	1·10	90
3441	80y. Pink orchid (23×27 mm)	1·50	1·20
3442	80y. Fairy and flowers (25×37 mm)	1·50	1·20
3443	80y. Oranges and blossom (25×37 mm)	1·50	1·20
3444	80y. Parrot (25×37 mm)	1·50	1·20
3445	80y. Orange flowers (25×37 mm)	1·50	1·20

2790 "Iseno-taifu" (Koyama Yasuko)

2791 "Goptokudaijino-sadaijin" (Mitsuoka Keiso)

2792 "Ooshikouchi-no-mitsune" (Miyazaki Shikou)

2793 "Yamabeno-akahito" (Matsumoto Eiko)

2794 "Suouno-naishi" (Miyake Soushu)

2795 "Double Cherry Blossoms" (Koyama Yasuko)

2796 "Iseno-taifu" (Koyama Yasuko)

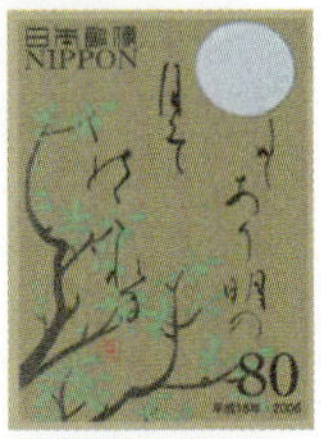

2797 "A Wan Morning Moon" (Mitsuoka Keiso)

2798 "Goptokudaijino-sadaijin" (Mitsuoka Keiso)

2799 "White Chrysanthemums" (Miyazaki Shikou)

2800 "Ooshikouchino-mitsune" (Miyazaki Shikou)

2801 "Mt. Fuji" (Matsumoto Eiko)

2802 "Yamabeno-akahito" (Matsumoto Eiko)

2803 "Spring Night" (Miyake Soushu)

2804 "Suouno-naishi" (Miyake Soushu)

2006. Letter Writing Day. Multicoloured. Sizes Nos. 3446/50 25x30 mm. and Nos. 3451/60 28x39 mm.

3446	**2790**	50y. multicoloured	1·10	90
3447	**2791**	50y. multicoloured	1·10	90
3448	**2792**	50y. multicoloured	1·10	90
3449	**2793**	50y. multicoloured	1·10	90
3450	**2794**	50y. multicoloured	1·10	90
3451	**2795**	80y. multicoloured	1·50	1·20
3452	**2796**	80y. multicoloured	1·50	1·20
3453	**2797**	80y. multicoloured	1·50	1·20
3454	**2798**	80y. multicoloured	1·50	1·20
3455	**2799**	80y. multicoloured	1·50	1·20
3456	**2800**	80y. multicoloured	1·50	1·20
3457	**2801**	80y. multicoloured	1·50	1·20
3458	**2802**	80y. multicoloured	1·50	1·20
3459	**2803**	80y. multicoloured	1·50	1·20
3460	**2804**	80y. multicoloured	1·50	1·20

2805 World and Flowers

2006. Letter Writing Week. 50th Anniv of Accession to United Nations. Multicoloured.

3461	90y. Type **2805**	1·70	1·40
3462	110y. World, mountain and flowers	1·90	1·60

2807 Vanda "Miss Joaquim"

2808 Mokara "Lion's Gold"

2809 Vanda "Mimi Palmer"

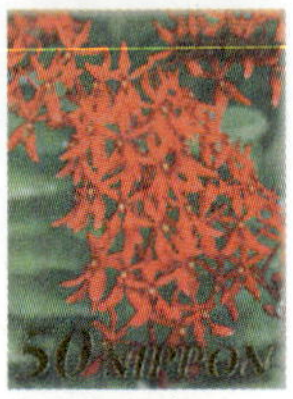

2810 Renanthera Singaporean

2811 Heron and Hollyhocks (detail) ("Flowers and Birds of Four Seasons") (Sakai Hoitsu)

2812 Iris and Moorhen (detail) ("Flowers and Birds of Four Seasons") (Sakai Hoitsu)

2006. Greetings Stamps. 40th Anniv of Japan—Singapore Diplomatic Relations. Self-adhesive.

3463	**2808**	50y. multicoloured	1·10	90
3464	**2810**	50y. multicoloured	1·10	90
3465	**2807**	80y. multicoloured	1·50	1·20
3466	**2809**	80y. multicoloured	1·50	1·20
3467	**2811**	90y. multicoloured	1·70	1·40
3468	**2812**	110y. multicoloured	1·90	1·60

Stamps of a similar design were issued by Singapore.

2813 "Tange Sazen"

2814 "Carmen Comes Home"

2815 "Ugetsu Monogatari"

2816 "Tokyo Story"

2817 "Seven Samurai" **2818** "A Night in Hawaii"

2819 "Unknown" **2820** "Guitar o Motta Wataridori"

2821 "Miyamoto Musashi" **2822** "Kyupora no Aru Machi"

2823 "Sailor-fuku to Kikanju" **2824** "Otoko wa Tsuraiyo"

2825 "Kamata Koshin-kyoku" **2826** "Yomigaeru Kinro"

2827 "MacArthur's Children" **2828** "HANA-BI"

2829 "Paradise Lost" **2830** "Gamera"

2831 "Twilight Samurai" **2832** "Godzilla"

2006. Japanese Cinema.

3469	**2813**	80y. multicoloured	1·50	1·20
3470	**2814**	80y. multicoloured	1·50	1·20
3471	**2815**	80y. multicoloured	1·50	1·20
3472	**2816**	80y. multicoloured	1·50	1·20
3473	**2817**	80y. multicoloured	1·50	1·20
3474	**2818**	80y. multicoloured	1·50	1·20
3475	**2819**	80y. multicoloured	1·50	1·20
3476	**2820**	80y. multicoloured	1·50	1·20
3477	**2821**	80y. multicoloured	1·50	1·20
3478	**2822**	80y. multicoloured	1·50	1·20
3479	**2823**	80y. multicoloured	1·50	1·20
3480	**2824**	80y. multicoloured	1·50	1·20
3481	**2825**	80y. multicoloured	1·50	1·20
3482	**2826**	80y. multicoloured	1·50	1·20
3483	**2827**	80y. multicoloured	1·50	1·20
3484	**2828**	80y. multicoloured	1·50	1·20
3485	**2829**	80y. multicoloured	1·50	1·20
3486	**2830**	80y. multicoloured	1·50	1·20
3487	**2831**	80y. multicoloured	1·50	1·20
3488	**2832**	80y. multicoloured	1·50	1·20

2833 Autumn Flowers and Ox Cart **2834** Autumn Flowers and Ox Cart

2006. 50th Anniv of International Ikebana Convention.

3489	**2833**	80y. multicoloured	1·50	1·20
3490	**2834**	80y. multicoloured	1·50	1·20

2835 Treasured Boar

2006. New Year's Greetings. Multicoloured.

3491	50y. Type **2835**	1·10	90
3492	80y. Zodiac boar	1·50	1·20

2838 Zodiac Boar

2006. New Year Lottery Stamps. Multicoloured.

3494	50y.+3y. Treasured boar	1·20	95
3495	80y.+3y. Type **2838**	1·60	1·30

Each stamp carries a lottery number.

2839 Squirrel (Sugita Yutaka)

2006. Greetings Stamps. Multicoloured. Self-adhesive.

3496	50y. Type **2839**	1·10	90
3497	50y. Bell (Arai Sonoko)	1·10	90
3498	50y. Clown (Nagata Moe)	1·10	90
3499	50y. Polar bear (Watanabe Hiroshi)	1·10	90
3500	50y. Bear Santa Claus (Murakami Tsutomu)	1·10	90
3501	80y. Cat Santa Claus (Murakami Tsutomu)	1·50	1·20
3502	80y. Cyclamen (Nagata Moe)	1·50	1·20
3503	80y. Snowman (Koide Masaki)	1·50	1·20
3504	80y. Reindeer (Watanabe Hiroshi)	1·50	1·20
3505	80y. Wreath (Arai Sonoko)	1·50	1·20

2849 Semi-cursive Style (Minagawa Gashu) **2850** Kinbun Style (Usuda Tousen)

2851 Reisho Style (Hayashi Shouen) **2852** Former Japanese Cursive (Yamazaki Kyouko)

2853 Kinbun Style (Sugano Seihou) **2854** Kinbun Style (Seki Masato)

2855 Inscribed on Kanae (Youhida Seiso) **2856** Kinbun Style (Nakano Hokumei)

2857 Tensho Style (Sadamasa Shoutou) **2858** Reisho Style (Kamigori Aichiku)

2006. Greetings Stamps. Eto Calligraphy.

3506	**2849**	80y. multicoloured	1·50	1·20
3507	**2850**	80y. multicoloured	1·50	1·20
3508	**2851**	80y. multicoloured	1·50	1·20
3509	**2852**	80y. multicoloured	1·50	1·20
3510	**2853**	80y. multicoloured	1·50	1·20
3511	**2854**	80y. multicoloured	1·50	1·20
3512	**2855**	80y. multicoloured	1·50	1·20
3513	**2856**	80y. multicoloured	1·50	1·20
3514	**2857**	80y. multicoloured	1·50	1·20
3515	**2858**	80y. multicoloured	1·50	1·20

2859/60 Research Ship and Pilatus PC-6 Turbo Porter Research Airplane

2861/2 Penguins

2863/4 Research Ship and Penguins and Penguins

2865/6 Sled Dog and Sled Dog standing

2867/8 Ship and Scientist and Tracked Vehicle

2869 Tracked Vehicle **2870** Research Airplane

2871 Research Ship and Sled Team **2872** Seal

2873 Penguin **2874** Two Penguins

2875 Sled Dog

2876 Penguin Chicks

2877 Penguin and Chick

2878 Sled Dog

2007. 50th Anniversary of the Japanese Antarctic Research Expedition. Ordinary gum.

3516	**2859**	80y. multicoloured	1·50	1·20
3517	**2860**	80y. multicoloured	1·50	1·20
3518	**2861**	80y. multicoloured	1·50	1·20
3519	**2862**	80y. multicoloured	1·50	1·20
3520	**2863**	80y. multicoloured	1·50	1·20
3521	**2864**	80y. multicoloured	1·50	1·20
3522	**2865**	80y. multicoloured	1·50	1·20
3523	**2866**	80y. multicoloured	1·50	1·20
3524	**2867**	80y. multicoloured	1·50	1·20
3525	**2868**	80y. multicoloured	1·50	1·20

(b) Self-adhesive.

3526	**2869**	80y. multicoloured	1·60	1·30
3527	**2870**	80y. multicoloured	1·60	1·30
3528	**2871**	80y. multicoloured	1·60	1·30
3529	**2872**	80y. multicoloured	1·60	1·30
3530	**2873**	80y. multicoloured	1·60	1·30
3531	**2874**	80y. multicoloured	1·60	1·30
3532	**2875**	80y. multicoloured	1·60	1·30
3533	**2876**	80y. multicoloured	1·60	1·30
3534	**2877**	80y. multicoloured	1·60	1·30
3535	**2878**	80y. multicoloured	1·60	1·30

Nos. 3516/17, 3518/19, 3520/1, 3522/3 and 3524/5 respectively were issued together, se-tenant, each pair forming a composite design.

Nos. 3526/35 were issued together forming a composite design.

2879/80 Evangelion Unit 01 and Ikari Shinji

2881/2 Ayanami Rei and Evangelion Unit 00

2883/4 Soryu Asuka Langley and Evangelion Unit 02

2885/6 Ayanami Rei and Soryu Asuka Langley and Katsuragi Misato

2887/8 Nagisa Kaworu and Sachiel, the Third Angel

2007. Heroes and Heroines of Animation (5th issue). Neon Genesis Evangelion.

3536	**2879**	80y. multicoloured	1·50	1·20
3537	**2880**	80y. multicoloured	1·50	1·20
3538	**2881**	80y. multicoloured	1·50	1·20
3539	**2882**	80y. multicoloured	1·50	1·20
3540	**2883**	80y. multicoloured	1·50	1·20
3541	**2884**	80y. multicoloured	1·50	1·20
3542	**2885**	80y. multicoloured	1·50	1·20
3543	**2886**	80y. multicoloured	1·50	1·20
3544	**2887**	80y. multicoloured	1·50	1·20
3545	**2888**	80y. multicoloured	1·50	1·20

Nos. 3536/7, 3538/9, 3540/1, 3542/3 and 3544/5, respectively, were issued together, se-tenant, forming a composite design.

2889 Honden, Yoshino Mikumari Shrine

2890 Romon Soshoku, Yoshino Mikumari Shrine

2891 Omine-Okugake-Michi

2892 Honden, Kumano Hayatama-taisha Shrine

2893 Honden, Kumano Hayatama-taisha Shrine

2894 Kumano-Fusum-ino-Okami-Zazo, Kumano Hayatama-taisha Shrine

2895 Kumano Sankei-Michi Nakahechi

2896 Statue, Kumano Sankei-Michi Nakahechi

2897 Tahoto, Kongo-Sanmaiin Temple

2898 Kyozo, Kongo-Sanmaiin Temple

2007. World Heritage.

3546	**2889**	80y. multicoloured	1·50	1·20
3547	**2890**	80y. multicoloured	1·50	1·20
3548	**2891**	80y. multicoloured	1·50	1·20
3549	**2892**	80y. multicoloured	1·50	1·20
3550	**2893**	80y. multicoloured	1·50	1·20
3551	**2894**	80y. multicoloured	1·50	1·20
3552	**2895**	80y. multicoloured	1·50	1·20
3553	**2896**	80y. multicoloured	1·50	1·20
3554	**2897**	80y. multicoloured	1·50	1·20
3555	**2898**	80y. multicoloured	1·50	1·20

2899 Running Boar ((detail) 'Inoshishi-Zu')

2007. Philately Week. Paintings by Mori Ippo. Multicoloured.

3556	80y. Type **2899**	1·30	85
3557	80y. Sparrow ((detail) 'Sakura-Ni-suzume-Zu')	1·30	85
3558	80y. Cherry Tree ((detail) 'Sakura-Ni-suzume-Zu')	1·30	85
3559	80y. Flock of Birds ((detail) 'Guncho')	1·30	85
3560	80y. Great Tits ((detail) 'Hagi-Ni-Shijukara-Zu')	1·30	85
3561	80y. Sleeping Boar ((detail) 'Inoshishi-Zu')	1·30	85

2905 Taj Mahal

2007. Japan–India Friendship Year. Multicoloured.

3562	80y. Type **2905**	1·30	85
3563	80y. Camels	1·30	85
3564	80y. Bengal Tiger	1·30	85
3565	80y. Peacock	1·30	85
3566	80y. Buddhist Monastery, Sanchi	1·30	85
3567	80y. Goddess (statue), Sanchi	1·30	85
3568	80y. Woman ((detail) Indian miniature painting)	1·30	85
3569	80y. Woman ((detail) Indian calico print)	1·30	85
3570	80y. Bharat Natyam	1·30	85
3571	80y. Kathakali	1·30	85

2915/6 Conan and Lana

2917/8 Lana and Conan (different)

2919/20 Monsley and Lepka

2921/2 Jimsy, Umaso and Dyce

2923/4 Dr. Lao and Grandpa

2007. Heroes and Heroines of Animation (6th issue). Future Boy Conan.

3572	**2915**	80y. multicoloured	1·30	85
3573	**2916**	80y. multicoloured	1·30	85
3574	**2907**	80y. multicoloured	1·30	85
3575	**2918**	80y. multicoloured	1·30	85
3576	**2919**	80y. multicoloured	1·30	85
3577	**2920**	80y. multicoloured	1·30	85
3578	**2921**	80y. multicoloured	1·30	85
3579	**2922**	80y. multicoloured	1·30	85
3580	**2923**	80y. multicoloured	1·30	85
3581	**2924**	80y. multicoloured	1·30	85

Nos. 3572/3, 3574/5, 3576/7, 3578/9 and 3580/1 were issued together, se-tenant, forming a composite design.

2925/6 Lake and Mountains and Lake and Mountains (different)

2007. World Heritage. Shiretoko. Multicoloured.

3582	80y. Type **2925**	1·30	85
3583	80y. Type **2926**	1·30	85
3584	80y. Blakiston's fish owl	1·30	85
3585	80y. Sea ice and Mount Rausu	1·30	85
3586	80y. Chishima cherry blossom	1·30	85
3587	80y. Brown bear	1·30	85
3588	80y. Harbour seal	1·30	85
3589	80y. Yezo deer	1·30	85
3590	80y. Sea eagle	1·30	85
3591	80y. *Viola kitmiana*	1·30	85

Nos. 3582/3 were issued together, in se-tenant pairs, forming a composite design.

2935 Kino Tsurayuki

2936 Empress Jito

2937 Sarumaru Dayu

2938 Minamotono Kanemasa

2939 Nijoinno Sanuki

2940 Plum Blossom

2941 Kino Tsurayuki

2942 Mount Kagu

2943 Empress Jito

2944 Deer

2945 Sarumaru Dayu

2946 Plovers

2947 Minamotono Kanemasa

2948 Stone in Sea

2949 Nijoinno Sanuki

2007. Letter Writing Day.

3592	**2935**	50y. multicoloured	1·30	85
3593	**2936**	50y. multicoloured	1·30	85
3594	**2937**	50y. multicoloured	1·30	85
3595	**2938**	50y. multicoloured	1·30	85
3596	**2939**	50y. multicoloured	1·30	85
3597	**2940**	80y. multicoloured	1·30	85
3598	**2941**	80y. multicoloured	1·30	85
3599	**2942**	80y. multicoloured	1·30	85
3600	**2943**	80y. multicoloured	1·30	85
3601	**2944**	80y. multicoloured	1·30	85
3602	**2945**	80y. multicoloured	1·30	85
3603	**2946**	80y. multicoloured	1·30	85
3604	**2947**	80y. multicoloured	1·30	85
3605	**2948**	80y. multicoloured	1·30	85
3606	**2949**	80y. multicoloured	1·30	85

2950 Tamesue Dai

2951 Ikeda Kumiko

2952 Kanemaru Yuzo

2953 Suetsugu Shingo

2954 Fukushi Kayoko

2955 Naito Masato

2956 Daigo Naoyuki

2957 Narisako Kenji

2958 Sawano Daichi

2959 Murofushi Koji

2007. International Association of Athletics Federations' World Championships, Osaka.

3607	**2950**	80y. multicoloured	1·30	85
3608	**2951**	80y. multicoloured	1·30	85
3609	**2952**	80y. multicoloured	1·30	85
3610	**2953**	80y. multicoloured	1·30	85
3611	**2954**	80y. multicoloured	1·30	85
3612	**2955**	80y. multicoloured	1·30	85
3613	**2956**	80y. multicoloured	1·30	85
3614	**2957**	80y. multicoloured	1·30	85
3615	**2958**	80y. multicoloured	1·30	85
3616	**2959**	80y. multicoloured	1·30	85

2960 Maple Leaves and Bamboo

2961 Cherry Blossoms

2962 Ratchaphruek Flower

2963 *Rhynchostylis gigantean*

2964 Elephant

2965 Flower

2966 Thai Dancer

2967 Wat Phra Keo

2968 Elephant (Toshogu Shrine)

2969 Elephant (Toshogu Shrine)

2007. 120th Anniv of Japan—Thailand Diplomatic Relations. Self-adhesive.

3617	**2960**	80y. multicoloured	1·30	85
3618	**2961**	80y. multicoloured	1·30	85
3619	**2962**	80y. multicoloured	1·30	85
3620	**2963**	80y. multicoloured	1·30	85
3621	**2964**	80y. multicoloured	1·30	85
3622	**2965**	80y. multicoloured	1·30	85
3623	**2966**	80y. multicoloured	1·30	85
3624	**2967**	80y. multicoloured	1·30	85
3625	**2968**	80y. multicoloured	1·30	85
3626	**2969**	80y. multicoloured	1·30	85

2970 *Hodogaya*

2007. International Correspondence Week. Paintings from 53 Stations of Tokaido by Utagawa Hiroshige. Multicoloured.

3627	90y. Type **2970**	1·40	90
3628	110y. *Arai*	1·50	1·00
3629	130y. *Kusatsu*	1·70	1·10

2973 Maejima Hisoka (founder of modern post office)

2007. Establishment of Japan Post Corporation. Multicoloured.

3630	80y. Type **2973**	1·30	85
3631	80y. Early Post Office	1·30	85
3632	80y. Mail cart	1·30	85
3633	80y. Early customers	1·30	85
3634	80y. Early customers queuing	1·30	85
3635	80y.18 71 100mon Stamp (As Type **2**)	1·30	85
3636	80y. Sunflower	1·30	85
3637	80y. Leaves and blossom	1·30	85
3638	80y. Chrysanthemums	1·30	85
3639	80y. Maple leaves	1·30	85
3640	80y. Maple leaves (different)	1·30	85
3641	80y. Roses	1·30	85
3642	80y. Bird and flowers	1·30	85
3643	80y. Peonies	1·30	85
3644	80y. Irises	1·30	85
3645	80y. Hydrangeas	1·30	85

2989 Computer Programming

2990 Computer Programming

2991 Plastering

2992 Plastering

2993 Cooking

2994 Cooking

2995 Flower Arranging

2996 Flower Arranging

2997 Metal Worker and Car

2998 Metal Worker

2007. International Skills Festival.

3646	**2989**	80y. multicoloured	1·30	85
3647	**2990**	80y. multicoloured	1·30	85
3648	**2991**	80y. multicoloured	1·30	85
3649	**2992**	80y. multicoloured	1·30	85
3650	**2993**	80y. multicoloured	1·30	85
3651	**2994**	80y. multicoloured	1·30	85
3652	**2995**	80y. multicoloured	1·30	85
3653	**2996**	80y. multicoloured	1·30	85
3654	**2997**	80y. multicoloured	1·30	85
3655	**2998**	80y. multicoloured	1·30	85

2999 Two Rats sitting on Straw Bag

2007. New Year's Greetings. Multicoloured.

3656	50y. Type **2999**	60	10
3657	50y. Rat ('Junishi Shofuku Dorei')	60	10

3002 Rat ('Junishi Shofuku Dorei') ('Fukutoku Junishi Dorei')

2007. New Year Lottery Stamps. Multicoloured.

3658	50y.+3y. Two Rats sitting on Straw Bag ('Fukutoku Junishi Dorei')	60	10
3659	80y.+3y. Type **3002**	1·30	85

Each stamp carries a lottery number.

3003 '08 NEW YEAR'

2007. New Year 2008.

3660	**3003**	50y. multicoloured	70	10
3661	**3003**	50y. multicoloured	70	10

3004 Church (Tsutomu Murakami)

2007. Greetings Stamps. Multicoloured. Self-adhesive.

3662	50y. Type **3004**	60	10
3663	50y. Swans (Moe Nagata)	60	10
3664	50y. Santa Claus (Tsutomu Murakami)	60	10
3665	50y. Flowers (Sonoko Arai)	60	10
3666	50y. Kitten (Ken Kuroi)	60	10
3667	80y. Santa Claus and Reindeer (Murakami Tsutomu)	1·30	85
3668	80y. Hellebore (Nagata Moe)	1·30	85
3669	80y. Snowman	1·30	85
3670	80y. Strawberries	1·30	85
3671	80y. Snowman	1·30	85

Nos. 3662/6 are 29×29 mm. and Nos. 3667/71 are 27×33 mm.

3014 'Rat' Kinbun Style (Seki Masato)

3015 'Rat' Reisho Style (Dairaku Kasersu)

3016 'Boshi' Reisho Style (Goto Chiskusei)

3017 'Rat' (Ishitobi Hakuko)

3018 'Rat' Sosho Style (Yahagi Shunkei)

3019 'Rat' Shoden Style (Yoshikawa Juichi)

3020 'Rat' Tensho Style (Hatsumi Kazuo)

3021 'Ne' Kana Style (Uchiyama Reiko)

3022 'Rat' Zhou Dynasty (Mizushima Sanyo)

3023 'Rat' Kinbun Style (Nakagawa Kyoji)

2007. Greetings Stamps. Eto Calligraphy.

3672	**3014**	80y. multicoloured	1·30	85
3673	**3015**	80y. multicoloured	1·30	85
3674	**3016**	80y. multicoloured	1·30	85
3675	**3017**	80y. multicoloured	1·30	85
3676	**3018**	80y. multicoloured	1·30	85
3677	**3019**	80y. multicoloured	1·30	85
3678	**3020**	80y. multicoloured	1·30	85
3679	**3021**	80y. multicoloured	1·30	85
3680	**3022**	80y. multicoloured	1·30	85
3681	**3023**	80y. multicoloured	1·30	85

3024 Mount Fuji

3025 Mount Fuji in Spring

3026 Mount Fuji in Summer

3027 Mount Fuji in Autumn

3028 Mount Fuji in Winter

3029 Bamboo Grove

3030 Somei-Yoshino Cherry Blossom

3031 *Hydrangea macrophylla*

3032 Maple Leaves

3033 Narcissus

2008. Yokoso! Japan Weeks (experiencing Japan).

3682	**3024**	80y. multicoloured	1·30	85
3683	**3025**	80y. multicoloured	1·30	85
3684	**3026**	80y. multicoloured	1·30	85
3685	**3027**	80y. multicoloured	1·30	85
3686	**3028**	80y. multicoloured	1·30	85
3687	**3029**	80y. multicoloured	1·30	85
3688	**3030**	80y. multicoloured	1·30	85
3689	**3031**	80y. multicoloured	1·30	85
3690	**3032**	80y. multicoloured	1·30	85
3691	**3033**	80y. multicoloured	1·30	85

3034/5 Hanasaka Jisan

3036/7 Kaguya Hime

3038/9 Kasajizo

3040/1 Momotaro

3042/3 Tsuru no Ongaeshi

2008. Heroes and Heroines of Animation (7th issue). Manga Nippon Mukashi Banashi.

3692	**3034**	80y. multicoloured	1·30	85
3693	**3035**	80y. multicoloured	1·30	85
3694	**3036**	80y. multicoloured	1·30	85
3695	**3037**	80y. multicoloured	1·30	85
3696	**3038**	80y. multicoloured	1·30	85
3697	**3039**	80y. multicoloured	1·30	85
3698	**3040**	80y. multicoloured	1·30	85
3699	**3041**	80y. multicoloured	1·30	85
3700	**3042**	80y. multicoloured	1·30	85
3701	**3043**	80y. multicoloured	1·30	85

Nos. 3692/3, 3694/5, 3696/7, 3698/9 and 3700/1, respectively, were issued together, se-tenant, each pair forming a composite design.

3044/5 Sun and Saturn

3046/7 Galaxy and *Suzaku* X-Ray Astronomy Satellite

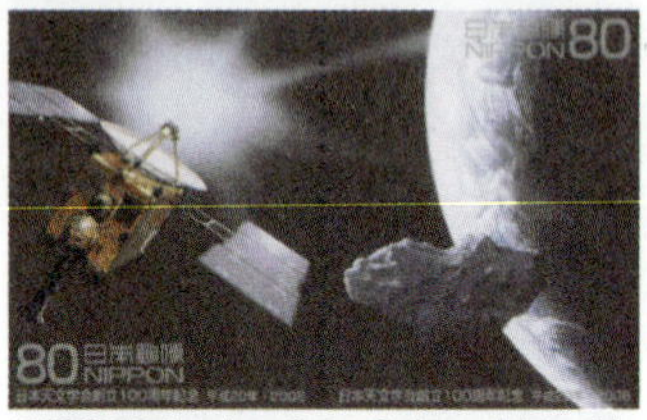

3048/3049 *Hayabusa* Space Probe and Asteroid and Earth

3050/3051 National Astronomical Observatory Subaru Telescope and Galaxy

3052/3053 Mars and National Astronomical Observatory Nobeyama 45 mm Radio Telescope

2008. Centenary of National Astronomical Society.

3702	**3044**	80y. multicoloured	1·30	85
3703	**3045**	80y. multicoloured	1·30	85
3704	**3046**	80y. multicoloured	1·30	85
3705	**3047**	80y. multicoloured	1·30	85
3706	**3048**	80y. multicoloured	1·30	85
3707	**3049**	80y. multicoloured	1·30	85
3708	**3050**	80y. multicoloured	1·30	85
3709	**3051**	80y. multicoloured	1·30	85
3710	**3052**	80y. multicoloured	1·30	85
3711	**3053**	80y. multicoloured	1·30	85

Nos. 3702/3, 3704/5, 3706/7, 3708/9 and 3710/11, respectively, were issued together, se-tenant. each pair forming a composite design.

3054 Bird Cherry

2008. Philately Week. Multicoloured.

3712	80y. Type **3054**	1·40	90
3713	80y. Peony and butterfly	1·40	90
3714	80y. Egrets	1·40	90
3715	80y. Grapes and rat	1·40	90
3716	80y. Seabirds	1·40	90

3059 Boats

2008. Hometowns. Multicoloured.

3717	80y. Type **3059**	1·40	90
3718	80y. Bus stop	1·40	90
3719	80y. Fishing	1·40	90
3720	80y. Railway	1·40	90
3721	80y. Beach	1·40	90
3722	80y. Jetty and boats	1·40	90
3723	80y. Children	1·40	90
3724	80y. Waterside houses	1·40	90
3725	80y. Postal delivery	1·40	90
3726	80y. Railway station	1·40	90

3069/3070 Hideyo Noguchi (bacteriologist), Microscope and Map of Africa

2008. 80th Death Anniv of Hideyo Noguchi. Hideyo Noguchi Africa Prize.

3727	**3069**	80y. multicoloured	1·40	90
3728	**3070**	80y. multicoloured	1·40	90

Nos. 3727/8 were issued together se-tenant forming a composite design.

3071/3072 Visa Stamp, Beans and Migrant Ship

3073/3074 Christ the Redeemer and Rio de Janeiro Port

3075/3076 Iguazu Falls

3077/3078 Salvador Historical Buildings

3079/3080 Brazilian Morpho and Toucan

2008. Japan—Brazil Exchange Year.

3729	**3071**	80y. multicoloured	1·40	90
3730	**3072**	80y. multicoloured	1·40	90
3731	**3073**	80y. multicoloured	1·40	90
3732	**3074**	80y. multicoloured	1·40	90
3733	**3075**	80y. multicoloured	1·40	90
3734	**3076**	80y. multicoloured	1·40	90
3735	**3077**	80y. multicoloured	1·40	90
3736	**3078**	80y. multicoloured	1·40	90
3737	**3079**	80y. multicoloured	1·40	90
3738	**3080**	80y. multicoloured	1·40	90

3081 Anne Shirley

3082 Anne's House

3083/3084 Mathew Cuthbert and Anne

3085/3086 Anne and Diana Barry

3087/3088 Teenage Anne and Gilbert Blythe

3089/3090 Mathew, Anne and Marilla Cuthbert

2008. International Correspondence Week. Centenary of Anne of Green Gables (written by Lucy Maud Montgomery).

3739	**3081**	80y. multicoloured (38×28 mm)	1·40	90
3740	**3082**	80y. multicoloured (38×28 mm)	1·40	90
3741	**3083**	80y. multicoloured (29×36 mm)	1·40	90
3742	**3084**	80y. multicoloured (29×36 mm)	1·40	90
3743	**3085**	80y. multicoloured (29×36 mm)	1·40	90
3744	**3086**	80y. multicoloured (29×36 mm)	1·40	90
3745	**3087**	80y. multicoloured (29×36 mm)	1·40	90
3746	**3088**	80y. multicoloured (29×36 mm)	1·40	90
3747	**3089**	80y. multicoloured (29×36 mm)	1·40	90
3748	**3090**	80y. multicoloured (29×36 mm)	1·40	90

Nos. 3741/2, 3743/4, 3745/6 and 3747/8, respectively, were issued together, se-tenant, each pair forming a composite design.

Stamps of a similar design to Nos. 3739/40 were issued by Canada.

3091 Keri Lake

3092 Mount Fuji

3093 Buddhist Shrine, Borobudur

3094 To-ji Temple

3095 *Rafflesia arnoldi*

3096 Cherry Blossom

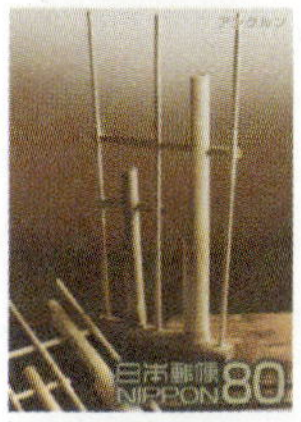

3097 Angklung (Musical instrument)

3098 Gaku-Biwa (Musical instrument)

3099 *Scleropages formosus* (horiz)

3100 *Nishiki-goi* (horiz)

2008. 50th Anniv of Japan—Indonesia Friendship.

3749	**3091**	80y. multicoloured	1·40	90
3750	**3092**	80y. multicoloured	1·40	90
3751	**3093**	80y. multicoloured	1·40	90
3752	**3094**	80y. multicoloured	1·40	90
3753	**3095**	80y. multicoloured	1·40	90
3754	**3096**	80y. multicoloured	1·40	90
3755	**3097**	80y. multicoloured	1·40	90
3756	**3098**	80y. multicoloured	1·40	90
3757	**3099**	80y. multicoloured (38×28 mm)	1·40	90
3758	**3100**	80y. multicoloured (38×28 mm)	1·40	90

Stamps of a similar design were issued by Indonesia.

3101 Cranes

2008. 60th Anniv of Local Government, Hokkaido. Multicoloured.

3759	**3101**	80y. Type **3101**	1·40	90
3760	**3101**	80y. Goryokaku Fort-multicoloured (28×34 mm)	1·40	90
3761	**3101**	80y. Autumn Landscape (28×34 mm)	1·40	90
3762	**3101**	80y. *Clione limacina* (sea angel) (28×34 mm)	1·40	90
3763	**3101**	80y. Canal (28×34 mm)	1·40	90

3106 Mt. Yotei

3107 Shiraneaoi Flowers

3108 Peak

3109 Squirrel

3110 Toya Lake

3111 Blossom

3112 Fukidashi Park

3113 Rowan Berries

3114 Lake and Peak

3115 Fox Cub

2008. G8 Summit, Hokkaido.

3764	**3106**	80y. multicoloured	1·40	90
3765	**3107**	80y. multicoloured	1·40	90
3766	**3108**	80y. multicoloured	1·40	90
3767	**3109**	80y. multicoloured	1·40	90
3768	**3110**	80y. multicoloured	1·40	90
3769	**3111**	80y. multicoloured	1·40	90
3770	**3112**	80y. multicoloured	1·40	90
3771	**3113**	80y. multicoloured	1·40	90
3772	**3114**	80y. multicoloured	1·40	90
3773	**3115**	80y. multicoloured	1·40	90

3116 Murasaki Shikibu

3117 Fujiwara

3118 Murasaki Shikibu

3119 Tsutomu Hiroshi Dainagon

3120 Murasaki Shikibu

3121/3122 Moon, Cloud and Murasaki Shikibu

3123/3124 Twigs and Fujiwara

3125/3126 Cliff, Tree and Murasaki Shikibu

3127/3128 Waterfall and Tsutomu Hiroshi Dainagon

3129/3130 Trees and Murasaki Shikibu

2008. Letter Writing Day.

3774	**3116**	50y. multicoloured (25×30 mm)	85	60
3775	**3117**	50y. multicoloured (25×30 mm)	85	60
3776	**3118**	50y. multicoloured (25×30 mm)	85	60
3777	**3119**	50y. multicoloured (25×30 mm)	85	60
3778	**3120**	50y. multicoloured (25×30 mm)	85	60
3779	**3121**	80y. multicoloured (28×38 mm)	1·40	90
3780	**3122**	80y. multicoloured (28×38 mm)	1·40	90
3781	**3123**	80y. multicoloured (28×38 mm)	1·40	90
3782	**3124**	80y. multicoloured (28×38 mm)	1·40	90
3783	**3125**	80y. multicoloured (28×38 mm)	1·40	90
3784	**3126**	80y. multicoloured (28×38 mm)	1·40	90
3785	**3127**	80y. multicoloured (28×38 mm)	1·40	90
3786	**3128**	80y. multicoloured (28×38 mm)	1·40	90
3787	**3129**	80y. multicoloured (28×38 mm)	1·40	90
3788	**3130**	80y. multicoloured (28×38 mm)	1·40	90

3131/3132 Dear Daniel and Hello Kitty

3133/3134 Hello Kitty and Dear Daniel

3135/3136 Dear Daniel and Hello Kitty

3137/3138 Hello Kitty and Dear Daniel

3139/3140 Dear Daniel and Hello Kitty

3141 Hello Kitty and Dear Daniel

3142 Hello Kitty

3143 Hello Kitty

3144 Dear Daniel

3145 Dear Daniel and Hello Kitty

3146 Hello Kitty

3147 Hello Kitty

3148 Dear Daniel

3149 Hello Kitty and Dear Daniel

3150 Hello Kitty

2008. Greetings Stamps. Hello Kitty. Self adhesive.

3789	**3131**	50y. multicoloured (28×28 mm)	85	60
3790	**3132**	50y. multicoloured (28×28)	85	60
3791	**3133**	50y. multicoloured (28×28 mm)	85	60
3792	**3134**	50y. multicoloured (28×28 mm)	85	60
3793	**3135**	50y. multicoloured (28×28 mm)	85	60
3794	**3136**	50y. multicoloured (28×28 mm)	85	60
3795	**3137**	50y. multicoloured (28×28 mm)	85	50
3796	**3138**	50y. multicoloured (28×28 mm)	85	60
3797	**3139**	50y. multicoloured (28×28 mm)	85	60
3798	**3140**	50y. multicoloured (28×28 mm)	85	60
3799	**3141**	80y. multicoloured (45×28 mm)	1·40	90
3800	**3142**	80y. multicoloured (45×28 mm)	1·40	90
3801	**3143**	80y. multicoloured (45×28 mm)	1·40	90
3802	**3144**	80y. multicoloured (45×28 mm)	1·40	90
3803	**3145**	80y. multicoloured (45×28 mm)	1·40	90
3804	**3146**	80y. multicoloured (34×34 mm (circular))	1·40	90
3805	**3147**	80y. multicoloured (34×34 mm (circular))	1·40	90
3806	**3148**	80y. multicoloured (34×34 mm (circular))	1·40	90
3807	**3149**	80y. multicoloured (34×34 mm (circular))	1·40	90
3808	**3150**	80y. multicoloured (40×28 mm (oval))	1·40	90

Nos. 3789/90, 3791/2, 3793/4, 3795/6 and 3797/8 were issued together, se-tenant, each pair forming a composite design.

3151/3152 Woman (Utamaro Kitagawa) and *One Hundred Views of Edo* (Hiroshige Utagawa)

3153/3154 *One Hundred Views of Edo* (Hiroshige Utagawa) and Man

3155/3156 Woman (Utamaro Kitagawa) and *One Hundred Views of Edo* (Hiroshige Utagawa)

3157/3158 *One Hundred Views of Edo* (Hiroshige Utagawa) and Man

3159/3160 Woman (Utamaro Kitagawa) and *One Hundred Views of Edo* (Hiroshige Utagawa)

2008. Paintings.

3809	**3151**	80y. multicoloured	1·40	90
3810	**3152**	80y. multicoloured	1·40	90
3811	**3153**	80y. multicoloured	1·40	90
3812	**3154**	80y. multicoloured	1·40	90
3813	**3155**	80y. multicoloured	1·40	90
3814	**3156**	80y. multicoloured	1·40	90
3815	**3157**	80y. multicoloured	1·40	90
3816	**3158**	80y. multicoloured	1·40	90
3817	**3159**	80y. multicoloured	1·40	90
3818	**3160**	80y. multicoloured	1·40	90

3161 Temple of Heaven

3162 Huangshan Lingfeng Peak

3163 Painting, Dunhuang Caves

3164 Horyuji Pagoda

3165/3166 Mandarin Ducks

3167 *Water Fish Seasons* (plum blossom, Spring)

3168 *Water Fish Seasons* (water lily, Summer)

3169 *Water Fish Seasons* (leaves, Autumn)

3170 *Water Fish Seasons* (daffodils, Winter)

2008. 30th Anniv of Japan—China Treaty.

3819	**3161**	80y. multicoloured	1·40	90
3820	**3162**	80y. multicoloured	1·40	90
3821	**3163**	80y. multicoloured	1·40	90
3822	**3164**	80y. multicoloured	1·40	90
3823	**3165**	80y. multicoloured	1·40	90
3824	**3166**	80y. multicoloured	1·40	90
3825	**3167**	80y. multicoloured	1·40	90
3826	**3168**	80y. multicoloured	1·40	90
3827	**3169**	80y. multicoloured	1·40	90
3828	**3170**	80y. multicoloured	1·40	90

Nos. 3823/4 were issued together, se-tenant, the pair forming a composite design.

3171/2 Ingram and Noa Izumi

3173/4 Isao Ohta and Ingram 2

3175/6 Shinobu Nagumo and Ingram 3

3177/8 Type Zero and Asuma Shinohara

3179/80 Ingram and Two Division

2008. Heroes and Heroines of Animation (8th issue). Patlabor, The Mobile Police.

3829	**3171**	80y. multicoloured	1·40	90
3830	**3172**	80y. multicoloured	1·40	90
3831	**3173**	80y. multicoloured	1·40	90
3832	**3174**	80y. multicoloured		
3833	**3175**	80y. multicoloured	1·40	90
3834	**3176**	80y. multicoloured	1·40	90
3835	**3177**	80y. multicoloured	1·40	90
3836	**3178**	80y. multicoloured	1·40	90
3837	**3179**	80y. multicoloured	1·40	90
3838	**3180**	80y. multicoloured	1·40	90

Nos. 3829/30, 3831/2, 3833/4, 3835/6 and 3837/8, respectively, were issued together, se-tenant, each pair forming a composite design.

3181 Statues and Temple

2008. Tourism. Arashiyama and Sagano, Kyoto. Multicoloured.

3839	80y. Type **3181**	1·40	90
3840	80y. Gateway	1·40	90
3841	80y. Autumn colour	1·40	90
3842	80y. Grove in autumn	1·40	90
3843	80y. Boddhisattvas	1·40	90
3844	80y. Small Temple	1·40	90
3845	80y. Pagoda	1·40	90
3846	80y. Sagano train	1·40	90
3847	80y. Hozu River boat tour	1·40	90
3848	80y. Togetsukyo Bridge	1·40	90

3191 Houses

2008. Hometowns. Multicoloured.

3849	80y. Type **3191**	1·40	90
3850	80y. Wedding	1·40	90
3851	80y. Lake	1·40	90
3852	80y. Planting	1·40	90
3853	80y. Gardening	1·40	90
3854	80y. Boats on lake	1·40	90
3855	80y. Crops, farm and forest	1·40	90
3856	80y. Weeding, buildings and train	1·40	90
3857	80y. Roadside stall	1·40	90
3858	80y. River valley	1·40	90

3201 Musicians

3202 Seated Group

3203 Cradling Child

3204 Man and Woman

3205 Woman reading

3206 Serenade

3207 Man and Woman behind Decorated Screens

3208 Women

3209 Woman and Two Men

3210 Woman cradling Child

2008. Tale of Genji (Murasaki Shikibu) (11th century).

3859	**3201**	80y. multicoloured	1·80	1·30
3860	**3202**	80y. multicoloured	1·80	1·30
3861	**3203**	80y. multicoloured	1·80	1·30
3862	**3204**	80y. multicoloured	1·80	1·30
3863	**3205**	80y. multicoloured	1·80	1·30
3864	**3206**	80y. multicoloured	1·80	1·30
3865	**3207**	80y. multicoloured	1·80	1·30
3866	**3208**	80y. multicoloured	1·80	1·30
3867	**3209**	80y. multicoloured	1·80	1·30
3868	**3210**	80y. multicoloured	1·80	1·30

3211/12 Kiyomizu Temple

3213/14 Flowers

3215/16 Kodaiji Temple

3217 Steps

3218 Pagoda

3219 Maiko (apprentice Geisha)

3220 Waterside

2008. Tourism. Kiyomizu-dera and Gion, Kyoto.

3869	**3211**	80y. multicoloured	1·80	1·30
3870	**3212**	80y. multicoloured	1·80	1·30
3871	**3213**	80y. multicoloured	1·80	1·30
3872	**3214**	80y. multicoloured	1·80	1·30
3873	**3215**	80y. multicoloured	1·80	1·30
3874	**3216**	80y. multicoloured	1·80	1·30
3875	**3217**	80y. multicoloured	1·80	1·30
3876	**3218**	80y. multicoloured	1·80	1·30
3877	**3219**	80y. multicoloured	1·80	1·30
3878	**3220**	80y. multicoloured	1·80	1·30

Nos. 3869/70, 3871/2 and 3873/4, respectively, were issued together,se-tenant, each pair forming a composite design.

3221 Kanagawa

3222 Mishima

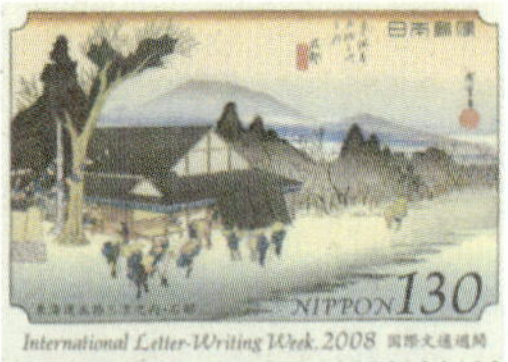
3223 Ishibe

2008. International Correspondence Week. 53 Stations of Tokaido by Utagawa Hiroshige.

3879	**3221**	90y. multicoloured	2·40	1·70
3880	**3222**	110y. multicoloured	2·40	1·70
3881	**3223**	130y. multicoloured	2·40	1·70

3224 Early Map showing Japan

2008. World Heritage. Iwami Ginzan Silver Mine. Multicoloured.

3882	80y. Type **3224**	1·40	90
3883	80y. Ryugenji Mabu Mine shaft	1·40	90
3884	80y. Smelting plant ruins	1·40	90
3885	80y. Dragon (shrine fresco)	1·40	90
3886	80y. Bridge and shrine	1·40	90
3887	80y. Omori Ginzan District	1·40	90
3888	80y. Silver-plated dog	1·40	90
3889	80y. Kumagai house	1·40	90
3890	80y. Payment token	1·40	90
3891	80y. Naito house	1·40	90

3234 *Tales of Genji* (detail)

2008. 60th Anniv of Local Government, Kyoto. Multicoloured.

3892	80y. Type **3234**	2·20	1·60
3893	80y. Cherry blossom	2·20	1·60
3894	80y. Thatched house, Nantan	2·20	1·60
3895	80y. Pagoda	2·20	1·60
3896	80y. Amanohashidate	2·20	1·60

3238a

2008. New Year 2009.

3896a	**3238a**	50y. multicoloured	85	60
3896b	**3238a**	50y. multicoloured	85	60

3239 Ox

2008. New Year's Greetings. Multicoloured.

3897	50y. Type 3239	85	60
3898	80y. Figure seated on Ox	1·40	90

3242 Figure seated on Ox

2008. New Year Lottery Stamps. Multicoloured.

3899	50y.+3y. Ox	1·00	70
3900	80y.+3y. Type **3234**	1·60	1·10

Each stamp carries a lottery number.

3243 Train

2008. Hometowns. Multicoloured.

3901	80y. Type **3243**	1·40	90
3902	80y. Snow-covered farm	1·40	90
3903	80y. Seaside station	1·40	90
3904	80y. Bridge and waterwheel	1·40	90
3905	80y. Horse pulling timber	1·40	90
3906	80y. Mail delivery	1·40	90
3907	80y. Families in snow	1·40	90
3908	80y. Family on path	1·40	90
3909	80y. Hillside houses	1·40	90
3910	80y. Snow-covered building	1·40	90

3253/4 Yukichi Fukuzawa and Arms

3255/6 Campus Buildings

3257/8 Rugby and Baseball

3259/60 Stained Glass Window

3261/2 Stained Glass Window

2008. 150th Anniv of Keio University.

3911	**3253**	80y. multicoloured	2·20	1·60
3912	**3254**	80y. multicoloured	2·20	1·60
3913	**3255**	80y. multicoloured	2·20	1·60
3914	**3256**	80y. multicoloured	2·20	1·60
3915	**3257**	80y. multicoloured	2·20	1·60
3916	**3258**	80y. multicoloured	2·20	1·60
3917	**3259**	80y. multicoloured	2·20	1·60
3918	**3260**	80y. multicoloured	2·20	1·60
3919	**3261**	80y. multicoloured	2·20	1·60
3920	**3262**	80y. multicoloured	2·20	1·60

Nos. 3911/12, 3913/14, 3915/16, respectively, were issued together, se-tenan, each pair forming a composite design.

Nos. 3917/18 and 3919/20, were issued together, se-tenant pairs, each pair forming a composite design and the block of four forming a design of the stained glass window.

3263 Ox

3264 Ox

3265 Ox

3266 Ox

3267 Ox

3268 Ox

3269 Ox

3270 Ox

3271 Ox

3272 Ox

2008. Greetings Stamps. Eto Calligraphy. Year of the Ox.

3921	**3263**	80y. multicoloured	2·20	1·60
3922	**3264**	80y. multicoloured	2·20	1·60
3923	**3265**	80y. multicoloured	2·20	1·60
3924	**3266**	80y. multicoloured	2·20	1·60
3925	**3267**	80y. multicoloured	2·20	1·60
3926	**3268**	80y. multicoloured	2·20	1·60
3927	**3269**	80y. multicoloured	2·20	1·60
3928	**3270**	80y. multicoloured	2·20	1·60
3929	**3271**	80y. multicoloured	2·20	1·60
3930	**3272**	80y. multicoloured	2·20	1·60

3273/4 Blast Furnace, Chimney and Conveyor Belt

2008. 150th Anniv of Iron and Steel Industry. Multicoloured.

3931	80y. Type **3273**	2·20	1·60
3932	80y. Type **3274**	2·20	1·60
3933	80y. Aira	2·20	1·60
3934	80y. Aira (different)	2·20	1·60
3935	80y. Stylized furnace	2·20	1·60
3936	80y. Processing plant	2·20	1·60

3279 Santa

2008. Greetings Stamps. Multicoloured.Self-adhesive.

3937	50y. Type **3279**	1·40	90
3938	50y. Stylized Bell (Hoshiyama Rika)	1·40	90
3939	50y. Two Kittens (Kuroi Ken)	1·40	90
3940	50y. Bears and Parcel (Moe Nagata)	1·40	90
3941	50y. Chick (Arai Sonoko)	1·40	90
3942	80y. Two Kittens (Kuroi Ken)	1·80	1·30
3943	80y. Child as Santa (Moe Nagata)	1·80	1·30
3944	80y. Bouquet (Arai Sonoko)	1·80	1·30
3945	80y. Santa	1·80	1·30
3946	80y. Fruit and Flowers (Arai Sonoko)	1·80	1·30

3289 Silver Token

2008. Tourism. Okinawa. Multicoloured.

3947	80y. Type **3289**	1·40	90
3948	80y. Coast line (28×34 mm)	1·40	90
3949	80y. Pagoda (28×34 mm)	1·40	90
3950	80y. Bridge, Tsuwano(28×34 mm)	1·40	90

3951	80y. Dotaku (ritual bell) (28×34 mm)	1·40	90

3294/5 Shurijo Castle

3296/7 Ryukyu Dancers

3298 Mamoru Rei Gate

3299 Water Clock

3300 Parkland

3301 Kaneshiro

3302/3 Statue and Monorail

2009. Tourism Okinawa (1st issue).

3952	**3294**	80y. multicoloured	1·40	90
3953	**3295**	80y. multicoloured	1·40	90
3954	**3296**	80y. multicoloured	1·40	90
3955	**3297**	80y. multicoloured	1·40	90
3956	**3298**	80y. multicoloured	1·40	90
3957	**3299**	80y. multicoloured	1·40	90
3958	**3300**	80y. multicoloured	1·40	90
3959	**3301**	80y. multicoloured	1·40	90
3960	**3302**	80y. multicoloured	1·40	90
3961	**3303**	80y. multicoloured	1·40	90

Nos. 3952/3, 3954/5 and 3960/1, respectively, were printed, se-tenant, each pair forming a composite design.

3304/5 Statue and Flower

3306/7 Churaumi Aquarium

3308/9 Churaumi Aquarium

3310 Steps and Blossom, Nakizin Castle

3311 Okinawa Rail (*Gallirallus okinawae*)

3312 Cliffs

3313 Mangroves

2009. Tourism Okinawa (2nd issue).

3962	**3304**	80y. multicoloured	1·40	90
3963	**3305**	80y. multicoloured	1·40	90
3964	**3306**	80y. multicoloured	1·40	90
3965	**3307**	80y. multicoloured	1·40	90
3966	**3308**	80y. multicoloured	1·40	90
3967	**3309**	80y. multicoloured	1·40	90
3968	**3310**	80y. multicoloured	1·40	90
3969	**3311**	80y. multicoloured	1·40	90
3970	**3312**	80y. multicoloured	1·40	90
3971	**3313**	80y. multicoloured	1·40	90

3314/15 GeGeGe no Kitaro and Medama-oyaji

3316/17 Kitaro

3318/19 Villains

3320/1 Kitaro and Neko Musume

3322/3 Kitaro and Yokai

2009. Heroes and Heroines of Animation (9th issue). GeGeGe no Kitaro.

3972	**3314**	80y. multicoloured	1·40	90
3973	**3315**	80y. multicoloured	1·40	90
3974	**3316**	80y. multicoloured	1·40	90
3975	**3317**	80y. multicoloured	1·40	90
3976	**3318**	80y. multicoloured	1·40	90
3977	**3319**	80y. multicoloured	1·40	90
3978	**3320**	80y. multicoloured	1·40	90
3979	**3321**	80y. multicoloured	1·40	90
3980	**3322**	80y. multicoloured	1·40	90
3981	**3323**	80y. multicoloured	1·40	90

Nos. 3972/3, 3974/5, 3976/7, 3978/9 and 3980/1, respectively, were printed se-tenant, each pair forming a composite design.

3324 Hillside Houses and Cultivation

2009. Hometowns. Multicoloured.

3982	80y. Type **3324**	1·40	90
3983	80y. Planting rice	1·40	90
3984	80y. House and pennants	1·40	90
3985	80y. Rape Flowers and Cloche	1·40	90
3986	80y. Crops and family	1·40	90
3987	80y. Watermill	1·40	90
3988	80y. Women and barns	1·40	90
3989	80y. School children, conversation and train	1·40	90
3990	80y. Older woman and children	1·40	90
3991	80y. Post Office	1·40	90

3334 Temple

3335 Statue

3336 Statue, Kofukuji Temple

3337 Nara Museum

3338/9 Kasuga Shrine

3340 Deer

3341 Building

3342/3 Lake and Blossom

2009. Tourism. Nara.

3992	**3334**	80y. multicoloured	1·40	90
3993	**3335**	80y. multicoloured	1·40	90
3994	**3336**	80y. multicoloured	1·40	90
3995	**3337**	80y. multicoloured	1·40	90
3996	**3338**	80y. multicoloured	1·40	90
3997	**3339**	80y. multicoloured	1·40	90
3998	**3340**	80y. multicoloured	1·40	90
3999	**3341**	80y. multicoloured	1·40	90
4000	**3342**	80y. multicoloured	1·40	90
4001	**3343**	80y. multicoloured	1·40	90

Nos. 39996/7 and 4000/1, respectively, were printed se-tenant, each pair forming a composite designs.

3344

3345

3346

3347

3348

3349

3350

3351

3352

3353

3354

3355

3356

3357

3358

3359

3360

3361

3362

3363

2009. 50th Anniv of Comics for Boys (1st issue). Weekly Shonen Sunday (4002/11). Weekly Shonen Magazine (4012/21).

4002	**3344**	80y. multicoloured	1·80	1·20
4003	**3345**	80y. multicoloured	1·80	1·20
4004	**3346**	80y. multicoloured	1·80	1·20
4005	**3347**	80y. multicoloured	1·80	1·20
4006	**3348**	80y. multicoloured	1·80	1·20
4007	**3349**	80y. multicoloured	1·80	1·20
4008	**3350**	80y. multicoloured	1·80	1·20
4009	**3351**	80y. multicoloured	1·80	1·20
4010	**3352**	80y. multicoloured	1·80	1·20
4011	**3353**	80y. multicoloured	1·80	1·20
4012	**3354**	80y. multicoloured	1·80	1·20
4013	**3355**	80y. multicoloured	1·80	1·20
4014	**3356**	80y. multicoloured	1·80	1·20
4015	**3357**	80y. multicoloured	1·80	1·20
4016	**3358**	80y. multicoloured	1·80	1·20
4017	**3359**	80y. multicoloured	1·80	1·20
4018	**3360**	80y. multicoloured	1·80	1·20
4019	**3361**	80y. multicoloured	1·80	1·20
4020	**3362**	80y. multicoloured	1·80	1·20
4021	**3363**	80y. multicoloured	1·80	1·20

3364 Fan

3365 Bonbonieru

2009. 50th Wedding Anniv of Emperor Akihito and Empress Michiko.

4022	**3364**	80y. multicoloured	1·80	1·20
4023	**3365**	80y. multicoloured	1·80	1·20
MS4024 135×112 mm. 80y.×2, Type **3364**; Type **3365**			3·25	3·25

3366/7 Conan, Young Detectives and Dr. Agasa

3368/9 Shinich Kudo and Ayumi Yoshida

3370/1 Conan and Gin

3372/3 Conan and Ayumi Yoshida

3374/5 Kaito Kid and Conan

2009. Heroes and Heroines of Animation (10th issue). Detective Conan.

4025	**3366**	80y. multicoloured	1·70	1·10
4026	**3367**	80y. multicoloured	1·70	1·10
4027	**3368**	80y. multicoloured	1·70	1·10
4028	**3369**	80y. multicoloured	1·70	1·10
4029	**3370**	80y. multicoloured	1·70	1·10
4030	**3371**	80y. multicoloured	1·70	1·10
4031	**3372**	80y. multicoloured	1·70	1·10
4032	**3373**	80y. multicoloured	1·70	1·10
4033	**3374**	80y. multicoloured	1·70	1·10
4034	**3375**	80y. multicoloured	1·70	1·10

3376 Peonies (pink and red)

3377 Peonies (grey, blue and pink)

3378/9 Peonies (pale pink) (image scaled to 74% of original size)

3380/1 Peonies (single white, central pink)

2009. Stamp Week.

4035	**3376**	80y. multicoloured	1·70	1·10
4036	**3377**	80y. multicoloured	1·70	1·10
4037	**3378**	80y. multicoloured	1·70	1·10
4038	**3379**	80y. multicoloured	1·70	1·10
4039	**3380**	80y. multicoloured	1·70	1·10
4040	**3381**	80y. multicoloured	1·70	1·10

Nos. 4037/8 and 4039/40 were printed, se-tenant, each pair forming a composite design.

3382 Henry Dunant (founder) and Nobel Peace Prize Certificate

2009. 150th Anniv of Henry Dunant's Experience at Battle of Solferino (Austro–Sardinian War) (which led to start of Red Cross movement). Multicoloured.

4041	80y. Type **3382**	1·80	1·20
4042	80y. Early Red Cross poster	1·80	1·20

3384 Kamikochi

2009. Tourism. Nagano. Multicoloured.

4043	80y. Type **3384**	4·00	2·50
4044	80y. Rape field (28×34 mm)	4·00	2·50
4045	80y. Pagoda (28×34 mm)	4·00	2·50
4046	80y. Pagodas and azaleas (28×34 mm)	4·00	2·50
4047	80y. Statue (28×34 mm)	4·00	2·50

3389 Emblem

2009. Inauguration of Lay Judge Trials. Multicoloured.

4048	80y. Type **3389**	4·25	2·50
4049	80y. Birds on scales	4·25	2·50

3391

3392

3393

3394

3395

3396

3397

3398

3399

3400

3401

3402

3403

3404

3405

3406

3407

3408

3409

3410

2009. 50th Anniv of Comics for Boys (2nd issue). Weekly Shonen Sunday (4050/9). Weekly Shonen Magazine (4060/9). .

4050	**3391**	80y. multicoloured	1·80	1·20
4051	**3392**	80y. multicoloured	1·80	1·20
4052	**3393**	80y. multicoloured	1·80	1·20
4053	**3394**	80y. multicoloured	1·80	1·20
4054	**3395**	80y. multicoloured	1·80	1·20
4055	**3396**	80y. multicoloured	1·80	1·20
4056	**3397**	80y. multicoloured	1·80	1·20
4057	**3398**	80y. multicoloured	1·80	1·20
4058	**3399**	80y. multicoloured	1·80	1·20
4059	**3400**	80y. multicoloured	1·80	1·20
4060	**3401**	80y. multicoloured	1·80	1·20
4061	**3402**	80y. multicoloured	1·80	1·20
4062	**3403**	80y. multicoloured	1·80	1·20
4063	**3404**	80y. multicoloured	1·80	1·20
4064	**3405**	80y. multicoloured	1·80	1·20
4065	**3406**	80y. multicoloured	1·80	1·20
4066	**3407**	80y. multicoloured	1·80	1·20
4067	**3408**	80y. multicoloured	1·80	1·20
4068	**3409**	80y. multicoloured	1·80	1·20
4069	**3410**	80y. multicoloured	1·80	1·20

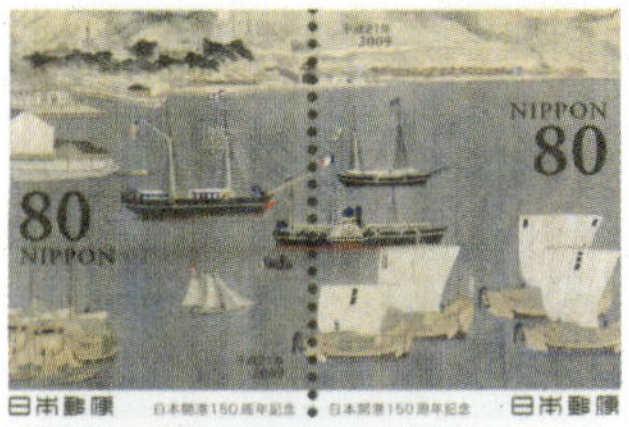

3411/12 Early View of Nagasaki Harbour

3413/14 Modern Nagasaki Harbour at Night

3415/16 Stylised Boats (early and modern)

3421/2 Early Yokohama Harbour

3423/4 Modern Yokohama by Night

3429/30 Early Hakodate Harbour

3431/2 Modern Hakodate by Night

2009. 150th Anniv of Opening of Japan Ports to Foreign Visitors. Multicoloured.

4070	80y. Type **3411**	1·80	1·20
4071	80y. Type **3412**	1·80	1·20
4072	80y. Type **3413**	1·80	1·20
4073	80y. Type **3414**	1·80	1·20
4074	80y. Type **3415**	1·80	1·20
4075	80y. Type **3416**	1·80	1·20
4076	80y. Nagasaki at night	1·80	1·20
4077	80y. Oura Cathedral	1·80	1·20
4078	80y. Megami Bridge	1·80	1·20
4079	80y. Clover Park and Nagaski Port	1·80	1·20
4080	80y. Type **3421**	1·80	1·20
4081	80y. Type **3422**	1·80	1·20
4082	80y. Type **3423**	1·80	1·20
4083	80y. Type **3424**	1·80	1·20
4084	80y. Yokonhama Bay Bridge	1·80	1·20
4085	80y. Memorial Hall	1·80	1·20
4086	80y. *Nippon Maru*(sail ship)	1·80	1·20
4087	80y. Passenger ship terminal	1·80	1·20
4088	80y. Type **3429**	1·80	1·20
4089	80y. Type **3430**	1·80	1·20
4090	80y. Type **3431**	1·80	1·20
4091	80y. Type **3432**	1·80	1·20
4092	80y. Hachiman-zaka Slope and Hakodate	1·80	1·20
4093	80y. Orthodox Church, Hakodate	1·80	1·20
4094	80y. Old Pier	1·80	1·20
4095	80y. Hakodate Park and Port	1·80	1·20

3437 Flowering Cherry (Edohigan)

3438 *Zelkova serrata* (Keyaki)

3439 Red Pine

3440 Japanese Bird Cherry

3441 *Magnolia kobus* (Kita Kobushi)

3442 Camellia (Yukibata Tsubaki)

3443 Horse Chestnut (Buckeye)

3444 Japanese Flowering Dogwood (Yamaboushi)

3445/6 Narcissae

2009. 60th National Planting Festival. Re-afforestation Programme.

4096	**3437**	50y. multicoloured	1·10	95
4097	**3438**	50y. multicoloured	1·10	95
4098	**3439**	50y. multicoloured	1·10	95
4099	**3440**	50y. multicoloured	1·10	95
4100	**3441**	50y. multicoloured	1·10	95
4101	**3442**	50y. multicoloured	1·10	95
4102	**3443**	50y. multicoloured	1·10	95
4103	**3444**	50y. multicoloured	1·10	95
4104	**3445**	50y. multicoloured	1·10	95
4105	**3446**	50y. multicoloured	1·10	95

3447 Flowers in the Rain, Gunma

2009. Hometowns. Multicoloured.

4106	80y. Type **3447**	1·80	1·20
4107	80y. Potato flowers, Hokkaido	1·80	1·20
4108	80y. Family amongst alpine flowers, Nagano	1·80	1·20
4109	80y. Terraced gardens, Yamaguchi	1·80	1·20
4110	80y. Mother, child and woman working in gardens, Hyogo	1·80	1·20
4111	80y. House, woman and child on Precipitous Path, Miyazaki	1·80	1·20
4112	80y. Rural post office, Okinawa	1·80	1·20
4113	80y. Lotus flowers and house, Ishikawa	1·80	1·20
4114	80y. Women picking flowers, Chiba	1·80	1·20
4115	80y. Peach orchard, Yamanashi	1·80	1·20

3457 Polar Bears

2009. International Polar Year. Preserve Polar Regions and Glaciers. Sheet 80×120 mm containing T 3457 and similar vert designs. Multicoloured. Self-adhesive.

MS4116 80y.×4, Type **3457**; Seal; Arctic fox; Penguin 7·25 7·25

3458 Crested Ibis, Sado-ga-shima Island

2009. Tourism. Niigata. Multicoloured.

4117	80y. Type **3458**	1·80	1·20
4118	80y. Cherry blossom, Takada (28×34 mm)	1·80	1·20
4119	80y. Fireworks, Nagaoka (28×34 mm)	1·80	1·20
4120	80y. Newt pond (28×34 mm)	1·80	1·20
4121	80y. Snow festival, Tokamachi (28×34 mm)	1·80	1·20

3463 Statue, Kongobuji Temple

2009

4122	**3463**	300y. multicoloured	7·25	7·25

No. 4122 was for use on recorded delivery letters.

3464 Ono No Komachi

3465 Junii letaks

3466 Minstrel Jakuren Hoshi

3467 Sakanoue no Korenori

3468 Daini no Sanmi

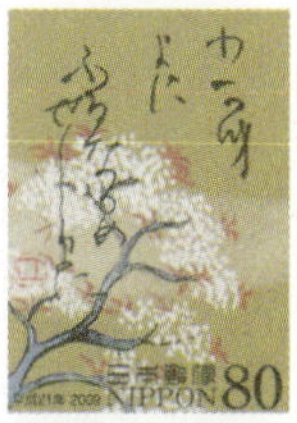

3469 Blossom Tree

3470 Ono No Komachi

3471 Branches

3472 Junii letaka

3473 Green Twigs

3474 Minstrel Jakuren Hoshi

3475 Dead Trees

3476 Sakanoue no Korenori

3477 Leaves

3478 Daini no Sanmi

2009. Letter Writing Day.

4123	**3464**	50y. multicoloured	1·80	1·20
4124	**3465**	50y. multicoloured	1·80	1·20
4125	**3466**	50y. multicoloured	1·80	1·20
4126	**3467**	50y. multicoloured	1·80	1·20
4127	**3468**	50y. multicoloured	1·80	1·20
4128	**3469**	80y. multicoloured (28×38 mm)	1·80	1·20
4129	**3470**	80y. multicoloured (28×38 mm)	1·80	1·20
4130	**3471**	80y. multicoloured (28×38 mm)	1·80	1·20
4131	**3472**	80y. multicoloured (28×38 mm)	1·80	1·20
4132	**3473**	80y. multicoloured (28×38 mm)	1·80	1·20
4133	**3474**	80y. multicoloured (28×38 mm)	1·80	1·20
4134	**3475**	80y. multicoloured (28×38 mm)	1·80	1·20
4135	**3476**	80y. multicoloured (28×38 mm)	1·80	1·20
4136	**3477**	80y. multicoloured (28×38 mm)	1·80	1·20
4137	**3478**	80y. multicoloured (28×38 mm)	1·80	1·20

3479 *Suwa Bluff, Nippori* (Utagawa Hiroshige)

3480 *Pensive Love* (Kitagawa Utamaro-ga)

3481 *Otani Tokuji as yakko Sodesuke* (Toshusai Sharaku)

3482 *Kumano Junisha Shrine* (Utagawa Hiroshige)

3483 *Moon Promontory* (Utagawa Hiroshige)

3484 *Woman reading Letter* (Kitagawa Utamaro-ga)

3485 *Nakajima Wadaemon as Bodara Chozaemon and Nakamura Konozo as funayado Kanagawa no Gon* (Toshusai Sharaku)

3486 *Pagoda, Zojo Temple, Akabane* (Utagawa Hiroshige)

3487 *Clear Weather after Snowfall at Japan Bridge* (Utagawa Hiroshige)

3488 *Kamekichi of Sodegaura* (Kitagawa Utamaro-ga)

2009. Edo Ukiyo-e. Paintings.

4138	**3479**	80y. multicoloured	1·80	1·20
4139	**3480**	80y. multicoloured	1·80	1·20
4140	**3481**	80y. multicoloured	1·80	1·20
4141	**3482**	80y. multicoloured	1·80	1·20
4142	**3483**	80y. multicoloured	1·80	1·20
4143	**3484**	80y. multicoloured	1·80	1·20
4144	**3485**	80y. multicoloured	1·80	1·20
4145	**3486**	80y. multicoloured	1·80	1·20
4146	**3487**	80y. multicoloured	1·80	1·20
4147	**3488**	80y. multicoloured	1·80	1·20

3493/3494 Asuka Village, Takaichi District

3495/3496 Tachibana-dera Temple

3497 Stone Fountains, Asuka Historical Museum, Sekinjinzo

3498 Stone Age burial Mound

3499/3500 Tanzan Shrine

3501/3502 Founding of Tonomine (illustrated scroll)

2009. Tourism. Nara.

4152	**3493**	80y. multicoloured	1·80	1·20
4153	**3494**	80y. multicoloured	1·80	1·20
4154	**3495**	80y. multicoloured	1·80	1·20
4155	**3496**	80y. multicoloured	1·80	1·20
4156	**3497**	80y. multicoloured	1·80	1·20
4157	**3498**	80y. multicoloured	1·80	1·20
4158	**3499**	80y. multicoloured	1·80	1·20
4159	**3500**	80y. multicoloured	1·80	1·20
4160	**3501**	80y. multicoloured	1·80	1·20
4161	**3502**	80y. multicoloured	1·80	1·20

Nos. 4148/51 and Types **3489/92** are vacant.

Nos. 4152/3, 4154/5, 4158/9 and 4160/1, respectively, were printed, se-tenant, each pair forming a composite design.

3503 Lanterns and Script (Masoka Shiki)

2009. Haiku (poetry) in Matsuyama. Multicoloured.

4162	50y. Type **3503**	1·10	75
4163	50y. Rooftops and script (Masoka Shiki)	1·10	75
4164	50y. Mountain and script (Kyoshi Takahama)	1·10	75
4165	50y. Building facade and script (Natsumi Soseki)	1·10	75
4166	50y. Cherry blossom and script (Kawahigashi Hekigoto)	1·10	75

3508 Popii

3509 Miru

3510 Rabu

3511 Bibian

3512 Koto

3513 Ramu

3514 Momo

3515 Moko

3516 Momonatsu

3517 Sakura

2009. 60th Anniv of Be Kind to Animals Week. Drawings of Winning Photographs in Anniversary Competition

4167	**3508**	50y.+5y. multicoloured	1·10	75
4168	**3509**	50y.+5y. multicoloured	1·10	75
4169	**3510**	50y.+5y. multicoloured	1·10	75
4170	**3511**	50y.+5y. multicoloured		
4171	**3512**	50y.+5y. multicoloured	1·10	75
4172	**3513**	50y.+5y. multicoloured	1·10	75
4173	**3514**	50y.+5y. multicoloured		
4174	**3515**	50y.+5y. multicoloured	1·10	75
4175	**3516**	50y.+5y. multicoloured	1·10	75
4176	**3517**	50y.+5y. multicoloured	1·10	75

3518 Stadium

2009. 64th National Sports Festival. Multicoloured.

4177	50y. Type **3518**	1·10	75
4178	50y. Basketball	1·10	75
4179	50y. Boxing	1·10	75

No. 4180 and Type **3521** are left for stamp not yet received.

3522 Procession, Nagasaki

2009. Hometowns. Multicoloured.

4181	80y. Type **3522**	1·80	1·20
4182	80y. Weeding and harvesting, Satsuma	1·80	1·20
4183	80y. Carp streamers, Iwakura	1·80	1·20
4184	80y. Procession through snow, Waga-gun	1·80	1·20
4185	80y. Deer dance, Ehime	1·80	1·20
4186	80y. Crowd, Naniwa-ku	1·80	1·20
4187	80y. Dancers and family, Akumi District	1·80	1·20
4188	80y. Procession, Wakayama	1·80	1·20
4189	80y. Women floating fFlowers in river, Tottori	1·80	1·20
4190	80y. Eating outside, Tano-gun	1·80	1·20

3532 Fujisawa

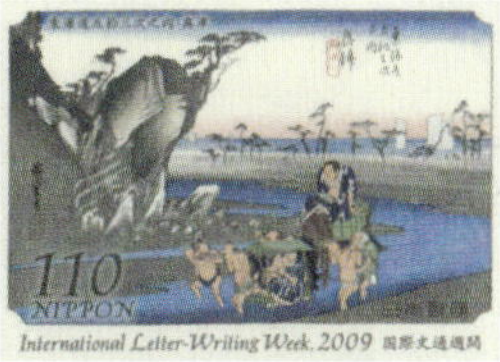

3533 Okitsu

3534 Chiryu

2009. International Correspondence Week. 53 Stations of Tokaido by Utagawa Hiroshige.

4191	**3532**	90y. multicoloured	1·80	1·20
4192	**3533**	110y. multicoloured	2·00	1·30
4193	**3534**	130y. multicoloured	2·50	1·70

3535 *Frege Bardach* **3536** *Autumn*

3537/8 Kunsthistorisches Museum, Vienna and Empress Elizabeth of Austria

3539/40 Merck Monastery

3541/2 Mozart and Salzburg

3543/4 Hallstat

2009. Austria–Japan Year.

4194	**3535**	80y. multicoloured	1·80	1·20
4195	**3536**	80y. multicoloured	1·80	1·20
4196	**3537**	80y. multicoloured	1·80	1·20
4197	**3538**	80y. multicoloured	1·80	1·20
4198	**3539**	80y. multicoloured	1·80	1·20
4199	**3540**	80y. multicoloured	1·80	1·20
4200	**3541**	80y. multicoloured	1·80	1·20
4201	**3542**	80y. multicoloured	1·80	1·20
4202	**3543**	80y. multicoloured	1·80	1·20
4203	**3544**	80y. multicoloured	1·80	1·20

Nos. 4196/7, 4198/9, 4200/1 and 4202/3 were printed, se-tenant, each pair forming a composite design.

3545 Decorated Canteen

3548/9 Hungarian Parliament Building

3553/4 Porcelain Statue and Vase

2009. Hungary–Japan Exchange Year. Multicoloured.

4204		80y. Type **3545**		
4205		80y. Mount Fuji	1·80	1·20
4206		80y. Plumware pot	1·80	1·20
4207		80y. Type **3548**	1·80	1·20
4208		80y. Type **3549**	1·80	1·20
4209		80y. Macho embroidery	1·80	1·20
4210	**3551**	80y. Elizabeth Bridge	1·80	1·20
4211	**3552**	80y. Crane and bamboo embroidery	1·80	1·20
4212	**3553**	80y. Type **3553**	1·80	1·20
4213	**3553**	80y. Type **3554**	1·80	1·20

Nos. 4207/8 and 4212/13 were printed, se-tenant, each pair forming a composite design.

3555/6 Naruto Uzumaki and Sasuke Uchiha

3557/8 Sakura Haruno and Kakashi Hatake

3559/60 Cy and Shikamaru Nara

3561/2 Deidara and Madara Uchiha

3563/4 Jiraiya and Hokage 4

2009. Heroes and Heroines of Animation (11th issue). Naruto.

4214	**3555**	80y. multicoloured	1·80	1·20
4215	**3556**	80y. multicoloured	1·80	1·20
4216	**3557**	80y. multicoloured	1·80	1·20
4217	**3558**	80y. multicoloured	1·80	1·20
4218	**3559**	80y. multicoloured	1·80	1·20
4219	**3560**	80y. multicoloured	1·80	1·20
4220	**3561**	80y. multicoloured	1·80	1·20
4221	**3562**	80y. multicoloured	1·80	1·20
4222	**3563**	80y. multicoloured	1·80	1·20
4223	**3564**	80y. multicoloured	1·80	1·20

3565 H-II Rocket and Mount Tsukuba

2009. Tourism. Ibaraki. Multicoloured.

4224	80y. Type **3565**	1·80	1·20
4225	80y. Fukuroda waterfall	1·80	1·20
4226	80y. Tokugawa Mitsukuni	1·80	1·20
4227	80y. Fishing trawl on Lake Kasumigaura	1·80	1·20
4228	80y. Fireworks	1·80	1·20

3570 Orange Tiger, Shizuoka

2009. New Year's Greetings. Multicoloured.

4229	50y. Type **3570**	1·10	75
4230	80y. Yellow tiger, Kaga	1·80	1·20

3573 Yellow Tiger, Kaga

2009. New Year Lottery Stamps. Multicoloured.

4231	50y.+3y. Orange tiger, Shizuoka	1·10	75
4232	80y.+3y. Type **3573**	1·80	1·20

Each stamp carries a lottery number.

3574 Phoenix

3575 Green Kirin

3576 Blue Kirin

2009. 20th (2010) Anniv of Enthronement of Emperor Akihito.

4233	**3574**	80y. multicoloured	1·80	1·20
4234	**3575**	80y. multicoloured	1·80	1·20
4235	**3576**	80y. multicoloured	1·80	1·20
MS4236		135×112 mm. 80y.×2 Nos. 4234/5	5·50	5·50

3577 Tiger (cursive) **3578** Tiger (clerical script)

3579 Tiger (Western Zhou period) **3580** Tiger

3581 Tiger (Kana hiriga-na) **3582** Tiger (hieroglyph)

3583 Tiger (Zhou dynasty) **3584** Tiger (Geng cursive)

3585 Tiger **3586** Tiger

2009. Greetings Stamps. Calligraphy. Year of the Tiger.

4237	**3577**	80y. multicoloured	1·80	1·20
4238	**3578**	80y. multicoloured	1·80	1·20
4239	**3579**	80y. multicoloured	1·80	1·20
4240	**3580**	80y. multicoloured	1·80	1·20
4241	**3581**	80y. multicoloured	1·80	1·20
4242	**3582**	80y. multicoloured	1·80	1·20
4243	**3583**	80y. multicoloured	1·80	1·20
4244	**3584**	80y. multicoloured	1·80	1·20
4245	**3585**	80y. multicoloured	1·80	1·20
4246	**3586**	80y. multicoloured		

3587 Girl with Apple (As Finland No. 1982) (Minna Immonen)

2009. Winter Greetings Stamps. Multicoloured. Self-adhesive.

4247	50y. Type **3587**	1·10	75
4248	50y. Snowman (Masami Koide) (26×35 mm)	1·10	75
4249	50y. Angel carrying toys (Moe Nagata) (26×35 mm)	1·10	75
4250	50y. Wreath surrounding apple (Arai Sonoko) (26×35 mm)	1·10	75
4251	50y. Sad and happy (Reich Karoly (children's book illustrator)) (35×26 mm)	1·10	75
4252	80y. Wreath (As Finland Type **852**) (Minna Immonen) (26×35 mm)	1·10	75
4253	80y. Santa playing fiddle (Masami Koide) (26×35 mm)	1·10	75
4254	80y. Lamplight (Arai Sonoko) (26×35 mm)	1·10	75
4255	80y. Angel (Moe Nagata) (26×35 mm)	1·10	75
4256	80y. Decorated fir twig (Reich Karoly) (26×35 mm)	1·10	75

MILITARY FRANK STAMPS

軍
事

(M 36)

1910. No. 139 optd with Type M 36.

M156b **28**	3s. red	£275	65·00

1913. No. 298 optd with Type M 36.

M185e **36**	3s. red	40·00	25·00

1921. No. 37 of Japanese Post Offices in China optd with Type M 36.

M202	3s. red	£9500	£4500

PREFECTURE STAMPS

Prefecture stamps were often issued both as perforated stamps within sheets with an outer margin, and as panes of ten with three margins imperforate and a selvage at one end. Single stamps from these panes will have one side or two adjacent sides imperforate, depending on position.

In several cases stamps were issued by more than one Prefecture on the same day, for the convenience of collectors, these are listed under each Prefecture for which they were issued.

AICHI

1 Fish and Nagoya Castle

1989

1	**1**	62y. multicoloured	1·50	80

1990. Flowers.

2	62y. As Type **1456** of Japan	1·20	80

2 Owl and Mount Horaiji

1992

3	**2**	62y. multicoloured	1·50	90

3 Horse-shaped Float

1996. Nagoya Festival. Multicoloured.

4	80y. Type **3**	2·10	1·40
5	80y. Two floats	2·10	1·40

4 *Satou Ichiei* (painting by Fujii Tokio)

1999. Birth Centenary of Satou Ichiei (poet). Multicoloured.

6	80y. Type **4**	2·10	1·40
7	80y. *Beautiful Yamato* (painting by Munakata Shikou)	2·10	1·40

5 Willow and Frog

2000

8	**5**	80y. multicoloured	2·75	1·90

6 Roadway, Oohashi Bridge

2001. Automobile City. Multicoloured.

9	50y. Type **6**	1·60	1·10
10	50y. Tokyo stadium	1·60	1·10

7 Roses

2007. Flowers. Multicoloured.

11	50y. Type **7**	1·60	1·10
12	50y. Chrysanthemums	1·60	1·10
13	50y. Orchids	1·60	1·10
14	50y. Cyclamen	1·60	1·10

8 Iris

2007. Flowers and Scenery of Tokai. Multicoloured.

15	80y. Type **8**	2·50	1·70
16	80y. Gassho-zukuri houses and vetch flowers	2·50	1·70
17	80y. Lily and Nagoya Castle	2·50	1·70
18	80y. Iris and Couple rock	2·50	1·70
19	80y. Azalea and coastline, Jogasaki	2·50	1·70

Nos. 15-19 were also issued by Gifu, Mie and Shizuoka on 2 April 2007.

9-10 *Fuji* (Antarctic research ship) and Hibiscus

2007. Nagoya Port. Multicoloured.

20	80y. Type **9**	2·50	1·70
21	80y. Type **10**	2·50	1·70
22	80y. Dolphin and azalea	2·50	1·70
23	80y. Two dolphins and azaleas	2·50	1·70
24	80y. Meiko Triton bridge and double chrysanthemum	2·50	1·70
25	80y. Meiko Triton bridge and single chrysanthemum	2·50	1·70
26	80y. Pink flowers and fireworks	2·50	1·70
27	80y. Sailing ship and fireworks	2·50	1·70
28	80y. Azaleas and port, left	2·50	1·70
29	80y. Azaleas and port, right	2·50	1·70

Nos. 20-1, 22-3, 24-5, 26-7 and 28-9 were issued together, se-tenant, each pair forming a composite design.

AKITA

1990. Flowers.

1	62y. As Type **1438** of Japan	1·20	80

1 Fireworks

1990. Omagari Firework Festival.

2	**1**	62y. multicoloured	1·30	80

2 Coastline, Nyudo-zaki

1993

3	**2**	41y. multicoloured	1·20	70

3 Kanto Festival

1997

4	**3**	80y. multicoloured	2·10	1·40

4 Snow-covered Samurai Houses, Kakunodate

1999

5	**4**	80y. multicoloured	2·20	1·50

5 Trees and River

2000. Cherry Trees. Multicoloured.

6	80y. Type **5**	2·50	1·70
7	80y. Tree, central, Iwate	2·50	1·70
8	80y. Group of trees, Fukishima	2·50	1·70
9	80y. Tree, left, Miyagi	2·50	1·70
10	80y. Cherry blossom, Aomori	2·50	1·70
11	80y. Group of trees with spreading branches, Yamagata	2·50	1·70

Nos. 6-11 were also issued by Yamagata, Iwate, Miyagi, Aomori and Fukushima.

6 Kujuku Island

2000

12	**6**	80y. multicoloured	2·75	1·80

7 Igloo with Dog and Children

2001. Kamakura Igloo.

13	**7**	80y. multicoloured	2·50	1·70

8 Butterbur Flower

2004. Prefectural Flowers. Multicoloured.

14	50y. Type **8**	1·60	1·10
15	50y. Paulownia (Iwate)	1·60	1·10
16	50y. Japanese bush clover (Miyagi)	1·60	1·10
17	50y. Apple blossom (Aomori)	1·60	1·10
18	50y. Safflower (Yamagata)	1·60	1·10
19	50y. Alpine rose (*Rhododendron ferrugineum*) (Fukushima)	1·60	1·10

Nos. 14-19 were also issued by Yamagata, Iwate, Miyagi, Aomori and Fukushima.

9 Kanto Festival

2004. 400th Anniv of Akita City. Multicoloured.

20	50y. Type **9**	1·60	1·10
21	50y. Namahage (new year's eve demon costume)	1·60	1·10

Nos. 20-1 were issued together, se-tenant, forming a composite design.

10 Kanto Matsuri (Akita)

2006. Festivals of Tohuku. Multicoloured.

22	80y. Type **10**	2·10	1·40
23	80y. Nebuta Matsuri (Aomori)	2·10	1·40
24	80y. Hanagasa Matsuri (Yamagata)	2·10	1·40
25	80y. Sendai Tanabata Matsuri (Miyagi)	2·10	1·40

Nos. 22-5 were also issued by Aomori, Yamagata, and Miyagi.

11 Oga Penisula and Pinks

2007. North Eastern Scenery. Multicoloured.

26	80y. Type **11**	2·50	1·70
27	80y. Oirase stream	2·50	1·70
28	80y. Hirosaki Castle	2·50	1·70

29 80y. Chusonji Temple 2·50 1·70
30 80y. Rocks and lily (sukashiyuri) 2·50 1·70
31 80y. Matsushima island and rape flowers 2·50 1·70
32 80y. Dicentra and water filled crater 2·50 1·70
33 80y. Lily (nikkoukisuge) and mountain 2·50 1·70
34 80y. Skunk cabbage flowers, Oze National Park 2·50 1·70
35 80y. Safflower 2·50 1·70

Nos. 26-35 were also issued by Aomori, Fukushima, Iwate, Miyagi and Yamagata on 2 July 2007.

12 Rugby Players

2007. National Sports Festival.
36 **12** 50y. multicoloured 1·60 1·10

13-14 Flower Meadows

2008. National Re-afforestation Campaign. Multicoloured.
37 50y. Type **13** 1·60 1·10
38 50y. Type **14** 1·60 1·10
39 50y. Pink flower, left 1·60 1·10
40 50y. Pink flowers, right 1·60 1·10
41 50y. Maples in Autumn, left 1·60 1·10
42 50y. Maples, right 1·60 1·10
43 50y. Woods in Autumn, left 1·60 1·10
44 50y. Woods, right 1·60 1·10
45 50y. Flowers and rocks 1·60 1·10
46 50y. Waterfall 1·60 1·10

Nos. 37-8, 39-40, 41-2, 43-4 and 45-6 were issued togerther, se-tenant, each pair forming a composite design.

15 Fuki (*Petasites japonicus*)

2008. Prefectural Flowers. Multicoloured.
47 50y. Narcissus (Fukui) 1·60 1·10
48 50y. Pink plum blossom (Wakayama)
49 50y. Type **15** 1·60 1·10
50 50y. White plum blossom (Fukuoka) 1·60 1·10
51 50y. Weeping cherry blossom (Kyoto) 1·60 1·10
52 80y. Narcissus (Fukui) 2·50 1·70
53 80y. White plum blossom (Wakayama) 2·50 1·70
54 80y. Fuki (*Petasites japonicus*) (Akita) 2·50 1·70
55 80y. Pink plum blossom (Fukuoka) 2·50 1·70
56 80y. Weeping cherry blossom (Kyoto) 2·50 1·70

AOMORI

1 Apples

1990
1 **1** 62y. multicoloured 1·30 60

1990
2 62y. As Type **1435** of Japan 1·20 80

2 Rapids, Oirase

1993
3 **2** 62y. multicoloured 1·50 1·00

3 Nebuta Festival

1996
4 **3** 80y. multicoloured 2·10 1·40

1998
5 **1** 80y. multicoloured 2·10 1·40

4 Shirakami Mountains

1999
6 **4** 80y. multicoloured 2·10 1·40

5 Cherry Blossom

2000. Cherry Trees. Multicoloured.
7 80y. Type **5** 2·50 1·70
8 80y. Tree, central, Iwate 2·50 1·70
9 80y. Group of trees, Fukishima 2·50 1·70
10 80y. Tree, left, Miyagi 2·50 1·70
11 80y. Trees and river, Akita 2·50 1·75
12 80y. Group of trees with spreading branches, Yamagata 2·50 1·70

Nos. 7-12 were also issued by Yamagata, Iwate, Miyagi, Akita and Fukushima.

6 Mount Iwaki and Apples

2002
13 **6** 80y. multicoloured 2·20 1·50

7 Speed Skater and Ski Jumper

2003. Winter Asian Games, Aomori.
14 **7** 50y. multicoloured 1·60 1·10

8 Apple Blossom (Aomori)

2004. Prefecture Flowers. Multicoloured.
15 50y. Type **8** 1·60 1·10
16 50y. Paulownia (Iwate) 1·60 1·10
17 50y. Japanese bush clover (Miyagi) 1·60 1·10
18 50y. Butterbur flower (Akita) 1·60 1·10
19 50y. Safflower (Yamagata) 1·60 1·10
20 50y. Alpine rose (*Rhododendron ferrugineum*) (Fukushima) 1·60 1·10

Nos. 15-20 were also issued by Yamagata, Iwate, Miyagi, Akita and Fukushima.

9 Apples (Aomori)

2005. Fruits of Tohoku. Multicoloured.
21 50y. Type **9** 1·60 1·10
22 50y. Apple (Iwate) 1·60 1·10
23 50y. Cherry (Yamagata) 1·60 1·10
24 50y. Peach (Fukushima) 1·60 1·10

Nos. 21-4 were also issued by Yamagata, Iwate and Fukushima.

10 Nebuta Matsuri (Aomori)

2006. Festivals of Tohuku. Multicoloured.
25 80y. Type **10** 2·20 1·50
26 80y. Kanto Matsuri (Akita) 2·20 1·50
27 80y. Hanagasa Matsuri (Yamagata) 2·20 1·50
28 80y. Sendai Tanabata Matsuri (Miyagi) 2·20 1·50

Nos. 25-8 were also issued by Akita, Yamagata, and Miyagi.

11 Oirase Stream

2007. North Eastern Scenery. Multicoloured.
29 80y. Type **11** 2·50 1·70
30 80y. Hirosaki Castle 2·50 1·70
31 80y. Chusonji Temple 2·50 1·70
32 80y. Rocks and lily (sukashiyuri) 2·50 1·70
33 80y. Matsushima island and rape flowers 2·50 1·70
34 80y. Dicentra and water filled crater 2·50 1·70
35 80y. Oga penisula and pinks 2·50 1·70
36 80y. Lily (nikkoukisuge) and mountain 2·50 1·70
37 80y. Skunk cabbage flowers, Oze National Park 2·50 1·70
38 80y. Safflower 2·50 1·70

Nos. 29-38 were also issued by Akita, Fukushima, Iwate, Miyagi and Yamagata on 2 July 2007.

CHIBA

1 Raccoons

1989
1 **1** 62y. multicoloured 1·30 60

1990
2 62y. As Type **1445** of Japan 1·20 80

2 Woods in Autumn

1993
3 **2** 41y. multicoloured 1·30 90

3 Cows

1995. Holstein Show.
4 **3** 80y. multicoloured 1·80 1·20

4 Tunnel Entrance

1997. Tokyo-Wan Aqualine. Multicoloured.
5 80y. Type **4** 1·80 1·20
6 80y. Tunnel entrance (different) 1·80 1·20

Nos. 5-6 were also issued by Kanagawa.

5 Ooga Lotus Blossom

1999
7 **5** 80y. multicoloured 2·10 1·40

6 Flowers, Trees and Children floating on Bubbles

2003. National Afforestation Campaign.
8 **6** 50y. multicoloured 1·60 1·10

7 Rose and Mount Tsukubasan

2004. Flowers of Kanto (1st issue). Multicoloured.
9 50y. Type **7** 1·60 1·10
10 50y. Yoshi azalea and Lake Chuzenjiko 1·60 1·10
11 50y. Japanese azalea and Mt. Akagisan 1·60 1·10
12 50y. Primrose and Tajimagahara native primrose field 1·60 1·10
13 50y. Rape blossom and Nojimazaki lighthouse 1·60 1·10

Nos. 9-13 were also issued by Tochigi, Saitama, Gunma and Ibaraki.
See also Nos. 14-18.

8 Sunflowers at Hana-hotaru (Chiba)

2005. Flowers of Kanto (2nd issue). Multicoloured.
14 50y. Type **8** 1·60 1·10
15 50y. Nikko-kisuge (Nikko day lily) and Kirifuri Heights (Tochigi) 1·60 1·10
16 50y. Azaleas, Tsutsujigaoka Park (Gunma) 1·60 1·10
17 50y. Bush clover, Kairakuen garden (Ibaraki) 1·60 1·10

18 50y. Allspice flowers and Mt. Bukousan (Saitama) 1·60 1·10

Nos. 14-18 were also issued by Gunma, Saitama, Tochigi and Ibaraki.

Nos. 19-23 and Type **9** have been left for 'Fruits of Kanto', issued on 1 September 2006, not yet received.

10 Rape Flowers

11 Rape Flowers

2009. Prefectural Flowers. Multicoloured.

24 50y. Peach blossom (Okayama) 1·70 1·30
25 50y. Type **10** (Chiba) 1·70 1·30
26 50y. Plum blossom and primula (Osaka) 1·70 1·30
27 50y. Bayberry (Kochi) 1·70 1·30
28 50y. Ume blossom (*Prunus mume* var. bungo) (Oita) 1·70 1·30
29 80y. Peach blossom (Okayama) (different) 2·75 1·70
30 80y. Type **11** (Chiba) 2·75 1·70
31 80y. Plum blossom and primula (Osaka) (different) 2·75 1·70
32 80y. Bayberry (Kochi) (different) 2·75 1·70
33 80y. Ume blossom (*Prunus mume* var. bungo) (Oita) (different) 2·75 1·70

Stamps of the same design were issued by Kochi, Oita, Okayama and Osaka on 1 Dec 2009.

EHIME

1 Building Facade

1989. Dogo Spa.

1 **1** 62y. multicoloured 1·30 90

1990

2 62y. As Type **1471** of Japan 2·40 1·60

2 Kurushima Strait

1992

3 **2** 62y. multicoloured 2·50 1·70

3 Nishiumi Marine Park

1996

4 **3** 80y. multicoloured 1·60 1·10

1999. Dogo Spa.

5 **1** 80y. multicoloured 2·10 1·40

4 Pagoda and Bridge

1999. Shimanami Highway and Bridges. Mult.

6 80y. Type **4** 1·80 1·20
7 80y. Islands 1·80 1·20
8 80y. Single span bridge 1·80 1·20
9 80y. Bridge pier at right 1·80 1·20
10 80y. Roadway and pier 1·80 1·20
11 80y. Ships 1·80 1·20
12 80y. Suspension wires and bridge 1·80 1·20
13 80y. Aerial view of bridge 1·80 1·20
14 80y. Suspension bridge from below 1·80 1·20
15 80y. Semi-circular bridge 1·80 1·20

Nos. 6-15 were also issued by Hiroshima.

5 Uwajima Castle

2000

16 **5** 80y. multicoloured 2·50 1·70

6 Masaoka Shiki and Matsuyama Castle

2001. Death Centenary (2002) of Masaoka Shiki (haiku poet). Multicoloured.

17 50y. Type **6** 1·60 1·10
18 50y. *Bocchasn* locomotive and Dogo Spa 1·60 1·10

7 Mikan (mandarin oranges) and Sata-misaki Promontory (Ehime)

2002. Multicoloured.

19 50y. Type **7** 1·50 1·00
20 50y. Sudachi (sour citrus fruit) and Mt. Tsurugisan (Tokushima) 1·50 1·00
21 50y. Yamamomo (bayberry) and Tengu highland (Kochi) 1·50 1·00
22 50y. Olive and Shodoshima island (Kagawa) 1·50 1·00

Nos. 19-22 were also issued by Tokushima, Kochi and Kagawa.

8 Zizouji Temple

2005. Cultural Heritage. Shizuoka Temples. Multicoloured.

23 80y. Type **8** 2·50 1·70
24 80y. Seated Buddha, Anrakuji Temple 2·50 1·70
25 80y. Inscribed belfry gateway, Jurakuji Temple 2·50 1·70
26 80y. Double roofed gateway, Kumadaniji Temple 2·50 1·70
27 80y. Pagoda, Yakuoji Temple 2·50 1·70
28 80y. Statues, ramp, lanterns and pagoda, Hotsumisakiji Temple 2·50 1·70
29 80y. Gateway and long steep steps, Shinjouji Temple 2·50 1·70
30 80y. Path, gateway, steps and main temple, Kongochoji Temple 2·50 1·70
31 80y. Buddha seated on peacock, Ryukoji Temple 2·50 1·70
32 80y. Bell and autumn colour, Butsumokuji Temple 2·50 1·70
33 80y. Dragon, Meisekiji Temple 2·50 1·70
34 80y. Steps and many roofed buildings, Daihouji Temple 2·50 1·70
35 80y. Carved decorative gable, Kokubunji Temple 2·50 1·70
36 80y. Leafless tree and snow-covered building, Yokomineji Temple 2·50 1·70
37 80y. Buddha, Kouonji Temple 2·50 1·70
38 80y. Courtyard and building, Houjuji Temple 2·50 1·70
39 80y. Inscribed pillars and gateway, Douryuji Temple 2·50 1·70
40 80y. Wall mounted statues, Goushouji Temple 2·50 1·70
41 80y. Eagle surmounting gateway, Tennouji Temple 2·50 1·70
42 80y. Courtyard with stone lined path and building, Kokubunji Temple 2·50 1·70

Nos. 23-42 were also issued by Tokushima, Kochi and Kagawa.

9 Hourinji Temple

2006. Cultural Heritage. Shizuoka Temples. Mult.

43 80y. Type **9** 2·50 1·70
44 80y. Kirihata-ji (statue), Kirihata Temple 2·50 1·70
45 80y. Cherry blossom and building, Fujiidera Temple 2·50 1·70
46 80y. Snow-covered pagoda and temple, Shozanji Temple 2·50 1·70
47 80y. Wide path, inscribed pillar and gateway, Konomineji Temple 2·50 1·70
48 80y. Decorative carved roof boss and bell, Dainichiji Temple 2·50 1·70
49 80y. Cherry blossom and grass edged path, Kokubunji Temple 2·50 1·70
50 80y. Cherry blossom and statue, Zenrakuji Temple 2·50 1·70
51 80y. Cliff face and temple building, Iwayaji Temple 2·50 1·70
52 80y. Decorated footprints, Joururiji Temple 2·50 1·70
53 80y. Spot-lighted statues, Yasakaji Temple 2·50 1·70
54 80y. Lantern, tree, path, gateway and inscribed pillar, Sairinji Temple 2·50 1·70
55 80y. Temple buildings through hole in rock, Kichijoji Temple 2·50 1·70
56 80y. Cherry blossom and roofs, Maegamiji Temple 2·50 1·70
57 80y. Carving with dragon and phoenix, Sankakuji Temple 2·50 1·70
58 80y. Snow-covered roofs and trees, Unbenji Temple 2·50 1·70
59 80y. Wide path, pilgrim and gateway, Shiromineji Temple 2·50 1·70
60 80y. Row of statues, Negoroji Temple 2·50 1·70
61 80y. Lantern, courtyard and building, Ichinomiyaji Temple 2·50 1·70
62 80y. Animal statues and building, Yashimaji Temple 2·50 1·70

Nos. 43-62 were also issued by Tokushima, Kochi and Kagawa.

10 Statue

2008. Cultural Heritage. Temples. Ehime Multicoloured.

63 80y. Type **10** 2·50 1·70
64 80y. Gateway 2·50 1·70
65 80y. Square, shrub and main hall 2·50 1·70
66 80y. Trees, temple roof and hill 2·50 1·70
67 80y. Bell tower gate 2·50 1·70
68 80y. Bamboo temple 2·50 1·70
69 80y. Statues, pathway and temple 2·50 1·70
70 80y. Paved path and entrance 2·50 1·70
71 80y. Buddha 2·50 1·70
72 80y. Decorated ceiling and bell 2·50 1·70
73 80y. Temple lit from below 2·50 1·70
74 80y. Paved path, steps and temple 2·50 1·70
75 80y. Guardian statue 2·50 1·70
76 80y. Gateway 2·50 1·70
77 80y. Carved ceiling and bell 2·50 1·70
78 80y. Pagoda and temple at night 2·50 1·70
79 80y. Temple and mountains 2·50 1·70
80 80y. Pilgrims entering gateway 2·50 1·70
81 80y. Pilgrims and temple 2·50 1·70
82 80y. Temple, banners and mountains 2·50 1·70
83 80y. Well 2·50 1·70
84 80y. Kobo Daishi (statue) 2·50 1·70
85 80y. Buddha 2·50 1·70
86 80y. Three roofed pagoda 2·50 1·70
87 80y. Pilgrims, steps and gateway 2·50 1·70
88 80y. Demon 2·50 1·70
90 80y. Rock statues 2·50 1·70
91 80y. Bodhisattva 2·50 1·70
92 80y. Cave and temple at night 2·50 1·70
93 80y. Kobo Daishi (painting) 2·50 1·70

Nos. 63-93 were also issued by Tokushima, Kagawa and Kochi on 1 August 2007.

FUKUI

1990. Flowers.

1 62y. As Type **1453** of Japan 1·20 80

1 Girl wearing Glasses

1991

2 **1** 62y. multicoloured 1·50 90

2 Beach and Trees, Kehi-no-matsubara

1994

3 **2** 50y. multicoloured 1·50 1·00

3 Murasaki Shikibu (novelist and poet)

1996

4 **3** 80y. multicoloured 2·10 1·40

4 Dinosaur

1999. Dinosaurs. Multicoloured.

5 80y. Type **4** 1·50 1·00
6 80y. Raptors 2·10 1·40

Nos. 5-6 were issued together, se-tenant, forming a composite design.

5 Zuwai (snow) Crab

1999. Multicoloured.

7 80y. Type **5** 2·10 1·40
8 80y. Cliffs, Tojinbo 2·10 1·40

6 Narcissi Blooms

2001. Narcissi. Multicoloured.

9 50y. Type **6** 1·60 1·10
10 80y. Flowers and cliffs 2·50 1·70

7 Tulip

2005. Flowers of Hokuriku. Multicoloured.

11 50y. Type **7** 1·60 1·10

12	50y. Hydrangea	1·60	1·10
13	50y. Rhododendron	1·60	1·10
14	50y. Lily	1·60	1·10

Nos. 11-14 were also issued by Toyama and Ishikawa.

8 'Love, Love'

2006. Maruoka Castle. Multicoloured.

15	80y. Type **8**	2·10	1·40
16	80y. Castle roof, pink sky and hills	2·10	1·40
17	80y. Castle roof, blue sky and clouds	2·10	1·40
18	80y. Castle roof, orange sky and sun	2·10	1·40
19	80y. Castle roof, blue sky and moon	2·10	1·40

9 Narcissus

2008. Prefectural Flowers. Multicoloured.

20	50y. Type **9**	1·60	1·10
21	50y. Pink plum blossom (Wakayama)	1·60	1·10
22	50y. Fuki (*Petasites japonicus*) (Akita)	1·60	1·10
23	50y. White plum blossom (Fukuoka)	1·60	1·10
24	50y. Weeping cherry blossom (Kyoto)	1·60	1·10
25	80y. Narcissus (Fukui)	2·50	1·70
26	80y. White plum blossom (Wakayama)	2·50	1·70
27	80y. Fuki (*Petasites japonicus*) (Akita)	2·50	1·70
28	80y. Pink plum blossom (Fukuoka)	2·50	1·70
29	80y. Weeping cherry blossom (Kyoto)	2·50	1·70

FUKUOKA

1990

1	62y. As Type **1473** of Japan	1·20	80

1 Hurdler

1990. 45th National Athletics Meet.

2	**1**	62y. multicoloured	1·20	80

2 Songbird and Lake

1992. Afforestation. Photo.

3	**2**	41y. multicoloured	90	60

3 Kurodabushi

1992

4	**3**	62y. multicoloured	1·20	80

4 Fort and Map

1997. Multicoloured.

5	80y. Type **4**	1·80	1·20
6	80y. Early rail way and map	1·80	1·20
7	80y. Interchange and map	1·80	1·20
8	80y. Building and map	1·80	1·20

Nos. 5-8 were issued together, se-tenant, forming a composite design.

Nos. 5-8 were also issued by Nagasaki and Saga.

5 Hakata Gion Festival

1999

9	**5**	80y. multicoloured	2·10	1·40

6 Hakata Doll

2000

10	**6**	80y. multicoloured	2·75	1·90

7 Ooe Kouwaka-mai Dance

2001

11	**7**	80y. multicoloured	2·40	1·60

8 Kitakyushu Expo-Festival

2001

12	**8**	80y. multicoloured	2·20	1·60

9 Ume Blossom and Dazaifu-Tenmangu

2005. Flowers and Scenery of Kyushu (1st series). Multicoloured.

13	50y. Type **9**	1·60	1·10
14	50y. Sakura (cherry blossoms) and Kanmon bridge (Fukuoka)	1·60	1·10
15	50y. Kusunohana (camphor blossoms) and Ariake Sea (Saga)	1·60	1·10
16	50y. Unzen-Tsutsuji (azaleas) and Mt. Fugendake (Nagasaki)	1·60	1·10
17	50y. Tulips and Huis Ten Bosch (Nagasaki)	1·60	1·10
18	50y. Rindou (gentians) and Mt. Aso (Kumamoto)	1·60	1·10
19	50y. Ume blossoms and Mt. Takasaki (Ooita)	1·60	1·10
20	50y. Hamayu (crinums) and Nichinan beach (Miyazaki)	1·60	1·10
21	50y. Miyama-Kirishima (azaleas) and Kirishima mountains (Kagoshima)	1·60	1·10
22	50y. Hibiscus and Adan (screw-pine) (Kagoshima)	1·60	1·10

See also Nos. 23-32.

Nos. 13-22 were also issued by Saga, Nagasaki, Kumamoto, Oita, Miyazaki and Kagoshima.

10 Daffodils and Shrine (Fukuoka) Nokonoshima Island (Fukuoka)

2006. Flowers and Scenery of Kyushu (2nd series). Multicoloured.

23	80y. Type **10**	2·40	1·60
24	80y. Chinese bellflowers and Hiraodai (Fukuoka)	2·40	1·60
25	80y. Hydrangeas and Mikaeri-notaki fall (Saga)	2·40	1·60
26	80y. Cosmos and Kujukushima islands (Nagasaki)	2·40	1·60
27	80y. Camellias and the five bridges of Amakusa (Kumamoto)	2·40	1·60
28	80y. Purple flowers and Mt. Aso (Kumamoto)	2·40	1·60
29	80y. Primroses and Mt. Yu-fudake (Oita)	2·40	1·60
30	80y. Lavender and Kujurenzan (Oita)	2·40	1·60
31	80y. Poppies and Mt. Hinamori-dake (Miyazaki)	2·40	1·60
32	80y. Field of yellow flowers and Mt. Kaimondake (Kagoshima)	2·40	1·60

Nos. 23-32 were also issued by Saga, Nagasaki, Kumamoto, Oita, Miyazaki and Kagoshima.

11-12 Procession

2008. Tanabata Festival. Multicoloured.

33	50y. Type **11**	1·60	1·10
34	50y. Type **12**	1·60	1·10
35	50y. Lanterns, left	1·60	1·10
36	50y. Lanterns, right	1·60	1·10
37	50y. Procession and roofs, left	1·60	1·10
38	50y. Procession and roofs, right	1·60	1·10
39	50y. Dancers, left	1·60	1·10
40	50y. Dancers, right	1·60	1·10
41	50y. Drummers, left	1·60	1·10
42	50y. Drummers, right	1·60	1·10

Nos. 33-4, 35-6, 37-8, 39-40 and 41-2 were issued together, setenant, each pair forming a composite design.

Nos. 78-87 were also issued by Tokushima, Okinawa, Miyagi and Tokyo on 1 August 2008.

13 White Plum Blossom

2008. Prefectural Flowers. Multicoloured.

43	50y. Narcissus (Fukui)	1·60	1·10
44	50y. Pink plum blossom (Wakayama)	1·60	1·10
45	50y. Fuki (*Petasites japonicus*) (Akita)	1·60	1·10
46	50y. Type **13**	1·60	1·10
47	50y. Weeping cherry blossom (Kyoto)	1·60	1·10
48	80y. Narcissus (Fukui)	2·50	1·70
49	80y. White plum blossom (Wakayama)	2·50	1·70
50	80y. Fuki (*Petasites japonicus*) (Akita)	2·50	1·70
51	80y. Pink plum blossom (Fukuoka)	2·50	1·70
52	80y. Weeping cherry blossom (Kyoto)	2·50	1·70

FUKUSHIMA

1990. Flowers.

1	62y. As Type **1440** of Japan	1·20	80

1 Peaches

1990

2	**1**	62y. multicoloured	1·20	80

2 Peony

1996. Peonies of Sukagawa.

3	**2**	80y. multicoloured	1·80	1·20

3 Streamers

1999. Summer Festivals. Multicoloured.

4	80y. Type **3**	2·10	1·40
5	80y. Festival goers and banners	2·10	1·40

Nos. 4-5 were issued together, *se-tenant*, forming a composite design.

Nos. 4-5 were also issued by Miyagi.

4 Kiku-ningyo (chrysanthemum petal doll)

1999

6	**4**	80y. multicoloured	2·10	1·40

5 Group of Trees

2000. Cherry Trees. Multicoloured.

7	80y. Type **5**	2·50	1·70
8	80y. Tree, central, Iwate	2·50	1·70
9	80y. Group of trees, Yamagata (different)	2·50	1·70
10	80y. Tree, left, Miyagi	2·50	1·70
11	80y. Cherry blossom, Aomori	2·50	1·70
12	80y. Trees and river, Akita	2·50	1·70

Nos. 7-12 were also issued by Yamagata, Iwate, Miyagi, Akita and Aomori.

6 Festival Goers

2000. Hata Festival, Kohata.

13	**6**	80y. multicoloured	2·75	1·80

7 Mount. Bandaisan and Dream Flying Machine

2001. Fukushima Expo.

14	**7**	80y. multicoloured	2·40	1·60

8 Boardwalk through Marshland, Ozegahara

2002. Oze. Multicoloured.

15	50y. Type **8**	1·50	1·00
16	50y. Day lilies, Ohe-shitsugen	1·50	1·00

9 Tsurugajo Castle and Persimmons

2003

17	**9**	80y. multicoloured	1·40	1·60

10 Alpine Rose (*Rhododendron ferrugineum*) (Fukushima)

2004. Prefectural Flowers. Multicoloured.

18	50y. Type **10**	1·60	1·10
19	50y. Paulownia (Iwate)	1·60	1·10
20	50y. Japanese bush clover (Miyagi)	1·60	1·10
21	50y. Butterbur flower (Akita)	1·60	1·10
22	50y. Safflower (Yamagata)	1·60	1·10
23	50y. Apple blossom (Aomori)	1·60	1·10

Nos. 18-23 were also issued by Yamagata, Iwate, Miyagi, Aomori and Akita.

11 Peach (Fukushima)

2005. Fruits of Tohoku. Multicoloured.

24	50y. Type **11**	1·60	1·10
25	50y. Apple (Iwate)	1·60	1·10
26	50y. Cherry (Yamagata)	1·60	1·10
27	50y. Apples (Aomori)	1·60	1·10

Nos. 24-7 were also issued by Aomori, Iwate and Fukushima.

12 Skunk Cabbage Flowers, Oze National Park

2007. North Eastern Scenery. Multicoloured.

28	80y. Type **12**	2·50	1·70
29	80y. Oirase stream	2·50	1·70
30	80y. Hirosaki Castle	2·50	1·70
31	80y. Chusonji Temple	2·50	1·70
32	80y. Rocks and lily (sukashiyuri)	2·50	1·70
33	80y. Matsushima island and rape flowers	2·50	1·70
34	80y. Dicentra and water filled crater	2·50	1·70
35	80y. Oga penisula and pinks	2·50	1·70
36	80y. Lily (nikkoukisuge) and mountain	2·50	1·70
37	80y. Safflower	2·50	1·70

Nos. 28-37 were also issued by Akita, Aomori, Iwate, Miyagi and Yamagata on 2 July 2007.

13 Nemotoshakunage (*Rhododendron brachycarpum*)

2008. Flowers. Multicoloured.

38	50y. Type **13**	1·60	1·10
39	50y. Lily	1·60	1·10
40	50y. Sweet briar	1·60	1·10
41	50y. Safflower	1·60	1·10
42	50y. Gentian	1·60	1·10
43	80y. Lily (25×35 mm)	2·50	1·70
44	80y. Sweet briar (25×35 mm)	2·50	1·70
45	80y. Rhodedendron (25×35 mm)	2·50	1·70
46	80y. Safflower (25×35 mm)	2·50	1·70
47	80y. Gentian (25×35 mm)	2·50	1·70

Nos. 38-47 were also issued by Hokkaido, Kanagawa, Nagano and Yamagata on 1 July 2008.

GIFU

1990. Flowers.

1	62y. As Type **1454** of Japan	1·50	1·00

1 Bridge at Spring Festival

1990. Takayama. Multicoloured.

2	62y. Type **1**	1·50	60
3	62y. Ptarmigans	1·50	60
4	62y. Lantern and procession	1·50	60
5	62y. Houses in snow	1·50	60

2 Flowers

1995

6	**2**	80y. multicoloured	1·90	1·30

3 Bridge at Spring Festival (As Type **1**)

1995. Hida. Multicoloured.

7	80y. Type **3**	1·80	60
8	80y. Ptarmigans (As No. 3)	1·80	60
9	80y. Lantern and procession (As No. 4)	1·80	60
10	80y. Houses in snow (As No. 5)	1·80	60

Nos. 7-10 differ from Nos. 2-5 both in the face value and an inscription 'Beautiful Hida' situated along the lower edge of the stamps.

4 Okaisho-Daiko (ritual drum)

1998

11	**4**	80y. multicoloured	2·10	1·40

5 Ancient Cherry Tree

1999

12	**5**	80y. multicoloured	2·10	1·40

6 Tanigumi-Odori Folk Dance

2001. Tradition and Nature of Ibi. Multicoloured.

13	50y. Type **6**	1·60	1·10
14	50y. Persimmons, Fuyugaki	1·60	1·10

7 Gujou-odori Dance

2002

15	**7**	50y. multicoloured	1·80	1·20

8 Cormorant Fishing

2003. Cormorant Fishing on Nagaragawa River and Gifu Castle. Multicoloured.

16	50y. Type **8**	1·60	1·10
17	50y. Gifu Castle1	60	1·10

Nos. 16-17 were issued together, se-tenant, forming a composite design.

9 Milk Vetch, Mount Norikuradake and Gifucho Butterflies

2006. National Afforestation Campaign.

18	**9**	50y. multicoloured	1·60	1·10

10 Gassho-zukuri Houses and Vetch Flowers

2007. Flowers and Scenry of Tokai. Multicoloured.

19	80y. Type **10**	2·50	1·70
20	80y. Iris	2·50	1·70
21	80y. Lily and Nagoya Castle	2·50	1·70
22	80y. Iris and Couple Rock	2·50	1·70
23	80y. Azalea and coastline, Jogasaki	2·50	1·70

Nos. 19-23 were also issued by Aichi, Mie and Shizuoka on 2 April 2007.

11 Women dancing

2009. Gujo Odori Dance Festival. Multicoloured.

24	50y. Type **11**	1·70	1·30
25	50y. Men dancing	1·70	1·30

Nos. 24-5 were printed se-tenant, each pair forming a composite design.

12 Float, Spring Festival

2009. Takayama Spring and Autumn Festivals. Multicoloured.

26	50y. Type **12**	1·70	1·30
27	50y. Float at night, Autumn Festival	1·70	1·30

GUNMA

1990. Flowers.

1	62y. As Type **1443** of Japan	1·20	80

1 Tortoise and the Hare

1991

2	**1**	62y. multicoloured	1·50	90

2 Waterfall

1994

3	**2**	80y. multicoloured	1·90	1·10

3 River, Tree and Mountain, Oze

1998. Multicoloured.

4	80y. Type **3**	2·10	1·40
5	80y. Trees in autumn	2·10	1·40

4 Flints

1999

6	**4** 80y. multicoloured	2·10	1·40

5 Railway Bridge

2000. Railways. Multicoloured.

7	50y. Type **5**	1·60	1·10
8	50y. Railway buildings	1·60	1·10

6 Azuma Rhododendron and Tanigawa Mountain

2002. Mount Tanigawadake. Multicoloured.

9	50y. Type **6**	2·20	1·50
10	50y. Ichi-no kurasawa in autumn	2·20	1·50

7 Yoshi Azalea and Lake Chuzenjiko

2004. Flowers of Kanto (1st issue). Multicoloured.

11	50y. Type **7**	1·60	1·10
12	50y. Rose and Mount Tsukubasan	1·60	1·10
13	50y. Japanese azalea and Mt. Akagisan	1·60	1·10
14	50y. Primrose and Tajimagahara native primrose field	1·60	1·10
15	50y. Rape blossom and Nojimazaki lighthouse	1·60	1·10

Nos. 11-15 were also issued by Tochigi, Saitama, Gunma and Ibaraki.

See also Nos. 16-20.

8 Azaleas, Tsutsujigaoka Park (Gunma)

2005. Flowers of Kanto (2nd issue). Multicoloured.

16	50y. Type **8**	1·60	1·10
17	50y. Nikko-kisuge (Nikko day lily) and Kirifuri Heights (Tochigi)	1·60	1·10
18	50y. Sunflowers at Hana-hotaru (Chiba)	1·60	1·10
19	50y. Bush clover, Kairakuen garden (Ibaraki)	1·60	1·10
20	50y. Allspice flowers and Mt. Bukousan (Saitama)	1·60	1·10

Nos. 16-20 were also issued by Tochigi, Saitama, Chiba and Ibaraki.

Nos. 21-5 and Type **9** have been left for 'Fruits of Kanto', issued on 1 September 2006, not yet received.

HIROSHIMA

1 Junk and Islands

1989. Setonikai. Multicoloured.

1	62y. Type **1**	1·30	1·60
2	62y. Islands and building	1·30	1·60

Nos. 1-2 were issued together, se-tenant, forming a composite design.

2 Drummer

1990

3	62y. As Type **1467** of Japan	1·20	80

1993. Hana-taue.

4	**2** 62y. multicoloured	1·50	80

3 Gateway in Water

1998. Inland Sea. Multicoloured.

5	80y. Type **3**	2·10	1·40
6	80y. Roadway and bridge	2·10	1·40

Nos. 5-6 were issued together, se-tenant, forming a composite design.

4 Ibara Railway

1999

7	**4** 80y. multicoloured	2·10	1·40

No. 7 was also issued by Okayama.

5 Islands

1999. Shimanami Highway and Bridges. Mult.

8	80y. Type **5**	1·80	1·20
9	80y. Pagoda and Bridge	1·80	1·20
10	80y. Single span bridge	1·80	1·20
11	80y. Bridge pier at right	1·80	1·20
12	80y. Roadway and pier	1·80	1·20
13	80y. Ships	1·80	1·20
14	80y. Suspension wires and bridge	1·80	1·20
15	80y. Aerial view of bridge	1·80	1·20
16	80y. Suspension bridge from below	1·80	1·20
17	80y. Semi-circular bridge	1·80	1·20

Nos. 8-17 were also issued by Ehime.

6 Momiji (maple leaves) and Itsukushima Shrine Gate

2000. Multicoloured.

18	50y. Type **6**	1·50	1·00
19	50y. Nijisseikinashi (Japanese pear tree) and Tottori dune	1·50	1·00
20	50y. Botan (peonies) and Izumo-taisha Shrine	1·50	1·00
21	50y. Momonohana (peach blossoms) and traditional houses in Kurashiki	1·50	1·00
22	50y. Natsumikan (summer-orange blossoms) and the sea	1·50	1·00

Nos. 18-22 were also issued by Tottori, Shimane, Okayama and Yamaguchi.

7 Nukui Dam

2002. Northern Hiroshima. Multicoloured.

23	80y. Type **7**	2·20	1·50
24	80y. On-bashi Bridge	2·20	1·50

8 Cenotaph for Atomic Bomb Victims (Memorial Monument for Hiroshima)

2005. Peace Memorial Park. Multicoloured.

25	50y. Type **8**	1·60	1·10
26	50y. Peace Memorial Museum	1·60	1·10

9 Maple Leaves and Miyajima Shrine (Hiroshima)

2006. Flowers of Chugoku. Multicoloured.

27	50y. Type **9**	1·60	1·10
28	50y. Tree peonies and Hinomisaki Lighthouse (Shimane)	1·60	1·10
29	50y. Peach blossoms and Seto-oohashi bridge (Okayama)	1·60	1·10
30	50y. Pear blossom and Yumigahama beach (Tottori)	1·60	1·10
31	50y. Chinese citron blossom and Oomijima island (Yamaguchi)	1·60	1·10

Nos. 27-31 were also issued by Tottori, Shimane, Okayama and Yamaguchi.

10 Ducks swimming

2007. Birds. Multicoloured.

32	80y. Type **10**	2·50	1·70
33	80y. Swans	2·50	1·70
34	80y. Pheasants	2·50	1·70
35	80y. Mandarin ducks	2·50	1·70
36	80y. Cranes	2·50	1·70

Nos. 32-36 were also issued by Okayama, Shimane, Tottori and Yamaguchi on 1 May 2007.

11 Maple

12 Maple

2009. Prefectural Flowers. Multicoloured.

36	50y. Gentian (Kumamoto)	1·70	1·30
37	50y. Wild chrysanthemum (Hyogo)	1·70	1·30
38	50y. Bush clover blossom (Miyagi)	1·70	1·30
39	50y. Fritillary (*Fritillaria camschatcensis*) (Ishikawa)	1·70	1·30
40	50y. Type **11** (Hiroshima)	1·70	1·30
41	80y. Gentian (Kumamoto) (different)	2·75	1·70
42	80y. Wild chrysanthemum (Hyogo) (different)	2·75	1·70
43	80y. Bush clover blossom (Miyagi) (different)	2·75	1·70
44	80y. Fritillary (*Fritillaria camschatcensis*) (Ishikawa) (different)	2·75	1·70
45	80y. Type **12** (Hiroshima)	2·75	1·70

Stamps of the same design were issued by Hyogo, Ishikawa, Kumamoto and Miyagi on 1 July 2009.

HOKKAIDO

1 Building Facade

1989. Prefectural Government.

1	**1** 62y. multicoloured	1·50	80

2 Runner

1989. 44th National Athletic Meet.

2	**2** 62y. multicoloured	1·30	60

3 Ice Hockey Players

1990. 2nd Asian Winter Games.

3	**3** 62y. multicoloured	1·20	85

1990. Flowers.

4	62y. As Type **1434** of Japan	3·75	2·50

4 Cranes

1990

5	**4** 62y. multicoloured	1·50	80

5 Lily of the Valley

1991. Flora. Multicoloured.

6	62y. Type **5**	1·20	80
7	62y. Pink lilac	1·20	80
8	62y. Lilies	1·20	80
9	62y. Rowan berries in snow	1·20	80

6 Foxes

1992

10	**6** 62y. multicoloured	1·50	70

7 Largha Seals

1993

11	**7**	62y. multicoloured	1·30	90

8 Stag, Ezo-shika

1994

12	**8**	50y. multicoloured	1·50	70

9 Chipmunks, Ezoshimarisu

1995

13	**9**	80y. multicoloured	1·90	1·30

10 Lady's Slipper Orchid

1995

14	**10**	80y. multicoloured	1·90	1·30

11 Kurione (sea angel)

1996

15	**11**	80y. multicoloured	1·80	1·20

12 Roses

1996

16	**12**	80y. multicoloured	2·10	1·40

13 Flowers

1997. Ezo-murasakitsutsuji.

17	**13**	80y. multicoloured	2·10	1·40

14 Stoat

1997. Hokkaido Ermine.

18	**14**	50y. multicoloured	1·30	90

15 Snow-covered Berries

1998. Flora. Multicoloured.

19	80y. Type **15**	1·80	1·20
20	80y. Pink blossom	1·80	1·20

16 Ice-flows

1999. Land of Snow (1st series). Multicoloured.

21	50y. Type **16**	1·20	80
22	50y. Cranes	1·20	80
23	80y. Snowflake	1·20	80
24	80y. Snowman	1·20	80

See also Nos. 42-5.

1999. Flora. Multicoloured.

25	80y. Lily (As Type **5**)	2·10	1·40
26	80y. Pink lilac (As No. 7)	2·10	1·40
27	80y. Lilies (As No. 8)	2·10	1·40
28	80y. Rowan berries in snow (As No. 9)	2·10	1·40

17 Lavender Field

1999. Northern Paradise (1st series). Multicoloured.

29	50y. Type **17**	1·60	1·10
30	80y. Cornfield	2·40	1·60

See also Nos. 46-9.

1999. Fauna. Multicoloured.

31	80y. Foxes (As Type **6**)	2·10	1·40
32	80y. Largha seals (As Type **7**)	2·10	1·40

18 Eagle

1999. Birds. Multicoloured.

33	50y. Type **18**	1·30	90
34	50y. Puffin	1·30	90
35	50y. Owl	1·30	90
36	50y. Crane	1·30	90

19 Sweet Corn

1999. Vegetables and Children. Multicoloured.

37	50y. Type **19**	1·50	1·00
38	50y. Potatoes	1·50	1·00
39	50y. Asparagus	1·50	1·00
40	50y. Squash	1·50	1·00

20 Sleigh

1999. Santa Claus.

41	**20**	80y. multicoloured	2·20	1·50

21 Nusamai Bridge

2000. Land of Snow (2nd series). Multicoloured.

42	80y. Type **21**	2·40	1·60
43	80y. Otaru canal	2·40	1·60
44	80y. Sapporo clock tower	2·40	1·60
45	80y. Orthodox Church, Hakodate	2·40	1·60

22 Potato Field and Barn

2000. Northern Paradise (2nd series). Multicoloured.

46	50y. Type **22**	1·60	1·10
47	50y. Barn and potato field	1·60	1·10
48	80y.+20y. Houses and hay field	3·25	2·20
49	80y.+20y. Hay field and barns	3·25	2·20

Nos. 48-95, each carry a premium for the aid of victims of the eruption of Mt. Usu and were on sale at all Japanese Post Offices.

23 Sable

2001. Ezo Sable.

50	**23**	80y. multicoloured	2·40	1·60

24 Orchid

2001. Flowers of Hokkaido (1st series). Mult.

51	50y. Type **24**	1·50	1·00
52	50y. *Papaver fauriei*	1·50	1·00

See also Nos. 63-6.

25 Poplar Avenue

2001. Northern Landscape. Multicoloured.

53	80y. Type **25**	2·40	1·60
54	80y. Statue of Dr. William Clark (founder of Sapporo Agricultural College), Hitsujigaoka Hill	2·40	1·60

26 Ezo Flying Squirrels

2002

55	**26**	80y. multicoloured	2·20	1·50

27 Tulip Field and Windmill

2002. Colouring the North. Multicoloured.

56	80y. Type **27**	2·20	1·50
57	80y. Sunflowers and field showing name of 'Hokuryu' (town)	2·20	1·50

28 Ainu Design

2003. Cultural and Natural Heritage. Multicoloured.

58	80y. Type **28**	2·40	1·60
59	80y. Lake Mashuko	2·40	1·60

29 Kiritappu Wetland

2004. Cultural and Natural Heritage. Multicoloured.

60	80y. Type **29**	2·50	1·70
61	80y. Wakka Primeval Garden	2·50	1·70

30 Sea Ice, *Garinko-go 2* (ice-breaker) and Steller's Sea Eagle

2004

62	**30**	80y. multicoloured	2·50	1·70

31 Sweetbrier

2005. Flowers of Hokkaido (2nd series). Mult.

63	50y. Type **31**	1·60	1·10
64	50y. Lavender	1·60	1·10
65	50y. Yellow flowers	1·60	1·10
66	50y. Lily of the valley	1·60	1·10

32 Sweetbrier and former Shana Post Office

2005. Northern Hokkaido. Multicoloured.

67	80y. Type **32**	2·50	1·70
68	80y. Sea otter	2·50	1·70
69	80y. Cherry blossom	2·50	1·70
70	80y. Tufted puffin	2·50	1·70

Nos. 67-70 were issued together, se-tenant, forming a composite background design.

33 Fox

2005. Animals of Northern Hokkaido. Mult.

71	50y. Type **33**	1·60	1·10
72	50y. Bear and cub	1·60	1·10
73	50y. Squirrel	1·60	1·10
74	50y. Owl	1·60	1·10

34 Cranes

2007. Fauna. Multicoloured.

75	80y. Type **34**	2·50	1·70
76	80y. Rabbits (ezoyukiusagi)	2·50	1·70
77	80y. Flying squirrels (ezo-momonga)	2·50	1·70
78	80y. Yezo deer	2·50	1·70
79	80y. Harbour seals	2·50	1·70

35 Sweet Briar Flowers

2007. National Re-Afforestation Programme.

80	**35**	50y. multicoloured	1·60	1·10

36 Sweet Briar

2008. Flowers. Multicoloured.

81	50y. Type **36**	1·60	1·10
82	50y. Lily	1·60	1·10
83	50y. Nemotoshakunage (*Rhododendron brachycarpum*)	1·60	1·10
84	50y. Safflower	1·60	1·10
85	50y. Gentian	1·60	1·10
86	80y. Lily (25×35 mm)	2·50	1·70
87	80y. Sweet briar (25×35 mm)	2·50	1·70
88	80y. Rhodedendron (25×35 mm)	2·50	1·70
89	80y. Safflower (25×35 mm)	2·50	1·70
90	80y. Gentian (25×35 mm)	2·50	1·70

Nos. 81-90 were also issued by Fukushima, Kanagawa, Nagano and Yamagata on 1 July 2008.

HYOGO

1990. Flowers.

1	62y. As Type **1461** of Japan	1·20	80

1 Weathervane, Kobe

1991

2	**1**	62y. multicoloured	1·50	90

2 Stork and Tower, Shinkoro

1994

3	**2**	50y. multicoloured	1·50	1·00

3 Bridge

1998. Kobe-Awaji-Naruto Expressway. Mult.

4	80y. Type **3**	2·10	1·40
5	80y. Bridge (different)	2·10	1·40

Nos. 4-5 were also issued by Tokushima.

4 Kobe Luminarie (light festival)

1998. (1st series).

6	**4**	80y. multicoloured	2·10	1·40

See also Nos. 14-15.

5 Child as Bee and Flower

2000. Multicoloured.

7	50y. Type **5**	1·50	1·00
8	80y. Child as fairy and flowers (26×36 mm)	2·40	1·60

6 Pandas

2001. Multicoloured.

9	50y. Type **6**	2·10	1·40
10	80y. Night scene, Kobe	2·40	1·60

7 Takarazuka Revue

2001. Takarazuka. Multicoloured.

11	80y. Type **7**	2·40	1·60
12	80y. Violets	2·40	1·60

8 Fairy riding Stork

2005. Re-introduction of the Oriental White Stork.

13	**8**	80y. multicoloured	2·50	1·70

9 Frontone (arched facade)

2005. Kobe Luminarie (2nd series). Multicoloured.

14	50y. Type **9**	1·60	1·10
15	50y. Spalliera (wide facade)	1·60	1·10

10 Nozigiku (wild chrysanthemums) (Hyogo)

2006. Flowers of Kinki. Multicoloured.

16	50y. Yae-zakura (double cherry blossoms) (Nara)	1·60	1·10
17	50y. Type **10**	1·60	1·10
18	50y. Shakunage (rhododendron) (Shiga)	1·60	1·10
19	50y. Ume blossoms (Wakayama)	1·60	1·10
20	50y. Sakuraso (primrose) (Osaka)	1·60	1·10
21	50y. Shidare-zakura (weeping cherry) (Kyoto)	1·60	1·10

Nos. 16-21 were also issued by Osaka, Nara, Shiga, Wakayama and Kyoto.

12 Himeji Castle

2007. Castles in Kinki Region. Multicoloured.

23	50y. Type **12**	1·60	1·10
24	50y. Koriyama	1·60	1·10
25	50y. Hikone	1·60	1·10
26	50y. Osaka	1·60	1·10
27	50y. Wakayama	1·60	1·10

No. 22 and Type **11** have been left for 'National Athletics Meet', issued on 1 September 2006, not yet received.

Nos. 23-7 were also issued by Nara, Osaka, Shiga and Wakayama on 1 June 2007.

13 Wild Chrysanthemum

14 Wild Chrysanthemum

2009. Prefectural Flowers. Multicoloured.

28	50y. Gentian (Kumamoto)	1·70	1·30
29	50y. Type 13 (Hyogo)	1·70	1·30
30	50y. Bush clover blossom (Miyagi)	1·70	1·30
31	50y. Fritillary (*Fritillaria camschatcensis*) (Ishikawa)	1·70	1·30
32	50y. Maple (Hiroshima)	1·70	1·30
33	80y. Gentian (Kumamoto) (different)	2·75	1·70
34	80y. Type **14** (Hyogo)	2·75	1·70
35	80y. Bush clover blossom (Miyagi) (different)	2·75	1·70
36	80y. Fritillary (*Fritillaria camschatcensis*) (Ishikawa) (different)	2·75	1·70
37	80y. Maple (Hiroshima) (different)	2·75	1·70

Stamps of the same design were issued by Hiroshima, Ishikawa, Kumamoto and Miyagi on 1 July 2009..

IBARAKI

1990. Flowers.

1	62y. As Type **1441** of Japan	1·20	80

1 Young Crows

1990

2	**1**	62y. multicoloured	1·50	80

2 Fukuroda-no-taki Waterfall

1993

3	**2**	62y. multicoloured	1·50	1·00

3 Yacht, Lake Kasumigaura

1997

4	**3**	80y. multicoloured	2·10	1·40

4 Koubuntei Pavilion and Ume Blossoms (Spring)

2001. Kairakuen Garden. Multicoloured.

5	50y. Type **4**	1·50	1·00
6	50y. Chumon Gate (summer)	1·50	1·00
7	50y. Togyokusen spring (autumn)	1·50	1·00
8	50y. Lake and Koubuntei pavilion (winter)	1·50	1·00

5 Mount Tsukuba, Itako (blind shaman)

2003

9	**5**	80y. multicoloured	2·40	1·60

6 Japanese Azalea and Mount and Iris Flowers Akagisan

2004. Flowers of Kanto (1st issue). Multicoloured.

10	50y. Type **6**	1·60	1·10
11	50y. Yoshi azalea and Lake Chuzenjiko	1·60	1·10
12	50y. Rose and Mount Tsuku-basan	1·60	1·10
13	50y. Primrose and Tajimagahara native primrose field	1·60	1·10
14	50y. Rape blossom and Nojima-zaki lighthouse	1·60	1·10

Nos. 10-14 were also issued by Tochigi, Saitama, Chiba and Gunma.

See also Nos. 16-20.

7 Iris Flowers, Mount Tsukuba and Lake Kasumigaura

2005. National Afforestation Campaign.

15	7	50y. multicoloured	1·60	1·10

8 Bush Clover, Kairakuen Garden (Ibaraki)

2005. Flowers of Kanto (2nd issue). Multicoloured.

16	50y. Type **8**	1·60	1·10
17	50y. Nikko-kisuge (Nikko day lily) and Kirifuri Heights (Tochigi)	1·60	1·10
18	50y. Sunflowers at Hana-hotaru (Chiba)	1·60	1·10
19	50y. Azaleas, Tsutsujigaoka Park (Gunma)	1·60	1·10
20	50y. Allspice flowers and Mt. Bukousan (Saitama)	1·60	1·10

Nos. 16-20 were also issued by Tochigi, Saitama, Chiba and Gunma.

Nos. 21-25 and Type **9** have been left for 'Fruits of Kanto', issued on 1 September 2006, not yet received.

ISHIKAWA

1 Bell Tower

1989. Kenroku-en.

1	1	62y. multicoloured	1·30	60

1990

2	62y. As Type **1452** of Japan	1·20	80

2 Child in Pearl Shell

1991. 46th National Athletic Meet.

3	2	41y. multicoloured	1·50	70

3 Bridge, Nanao-wan

1993

4	3	62y. multicoloured	1·50	1·00

4 Kanazawa-jo Castle

1995

5	4	80y. multicoloured	1·90	1·30

5 Mount Hakusan

1998

6	5	50y. multicoloured	1·30	90

6 Cherry Tree and Kaiseki Pagoda

1999. Kenrokuen Garden. Multicoloured.

7	80y. Type **6**	2·10	1·40
8	80y. Fountain	2·10	1·40
9	80y. Kinjo Reitaku well	2·10	1·40
10	80y. Snow-covered Kotoji Stone Lantern	2·10	1·40

7 Festival Goers and Banners

1999. Noto Kiriko Festival.

11	7	80y. multicoloured	2·10	1·40

8 Samurai Warrior and Kaga Gold Lacquer Designs

2001

12	8	80y. multicoloured	2·40	1·60

9 *Adenophora triphylla var. hakusanensis*

2002. Alpine Flora of Mount Hakusan. Mult.

13	50y. Type **9**	1·60	1·10
14	50y. *Fritillaria camtschatcensis* and Mt. Betsusan	1·60	1·10
15	50y. *Geranium yesoense var. nipponicum* and Mt. Gozen-gamine	1·60	1·10
16	50y. *Anemone narcissiflora* and Mt. Gozengamine	1·60	1·10

10 Fukada Kyuya and Mount Hakusan and Mount Betsusan

2003. Birth Centenary of Fukada Kyuya (mountaineer and writer).

17	10	80y. multicoloured	2·40	1·60

11 Morning Glory Flowers and Script

2003. 300th Birth Anniv of Chiyojo (haiku poet). Multicoloured.

18	50y. Type **11**	2·40	1·60
19	50y. Chiyojo	2·40	1·60

Nos. 18-19 were issued together, se-tenant, forming a composite design.

12 Hydrangea

2005. Flowers of Hokuriku. Multicoloured.

20	50y. Type **12**	1·60	1·10
21	50y. Tulip	1·60	1·10
22	50y. Rhododendron	1·60	1·10
23	50y. Lily	1·60	1·10

Nos. 20-3 were also issued by Toyama and Fukui.

13 Fritillary (*Fritillaria camschatcensis*)

14 Fritillary (*Fritillaria camschatcensis*)

2009. Prefectural Flowers. Multicoloured.

24	50y. Gentian (Kumamoto)	1·70	1·30
25	50y. Wild chrysanthemum (Hyogo)	1·70	1·30
26	50y. Bush clover blossom (Miyagi)	1·70	1·30
27	50y. Type **13** (Ishikawa)	1·70	1·30
28	50y. Maple (Hiroshima)	1·70	1·30
29	80y. Gentian (Kumamoto) (different)	2·75	1·70
30	80y. Wild chrysanthemum (Hyogo) (different)	2·75	1·70
31	80y. Bush clover blossom (Miyagi) (different)	2·75	1·70
32	80y. Type **14** (Ishikawa)	2·75	1·70
33	80y. Maple (Hiroshima) (different)	2·75	1·70

Stamps of the same design were issued by Hyogo, Hiroshima, Kumamoto and Miyagi on 1 July 2009.

IWATE

1990

1	62y. As Type **1436** of Japan	1·20	80

1 Iwate Mountain

1991

2	1	62y. multicoloured	1·30	90

2 Coastline, Rikuchu

1992

3	2	62y. multicoloured	1·50	90

3 Caravan and Mount Iwate

1998

4	3	80y. multicoloured	2·10	1·40

4 Gentian

1999

5	4	80y. multicoloured	1·80	1·20

5 Cherry Tree

2000. Cherry Trees. Multicoloured.

6	80y. Type **5**	2·50	1·70
7	80y. Group of trees with spreading branches, Yamagata	2·50	1·70
8	80y. Group of trees, Fukishima	2·50	1·70
9	80y. Tree, left, Miyagi	2·50	1·70
10	80y. Cherry blossom, Aomori	2·50	1·70
11	80y. Trees and river, Akitan	2·50	1·70

Nos. 6-11 were also by Yamagata, Aomori, Miyagi, Akita and Fukushima.

6 Chusonji Temple

2000

12	6	80y. multicoloured	2·75	1·90

7 Paulownia (Iwate)

2004. Prefectural Flowers. Multicoloured.

13	50y. Type **7**	1·60	1·10
14	50y. Apple blossom (Aomori)	1·60	1·10
15	50y. Japanese bush clover (Miyagi)	1·60	1·10
16	50y. Butterbur flower (Akita)	1·60	1·10
17	50y. Safflower (Yamagata)	1·60	1·10
18	50y. Alpine rose (*Rhododendron ferrugineum*) (Fukushima)	1·60	1·10

Nos. 13-18 were also issued by Yamagata, Aomori, Miyagi, Akita and Fukushima.

8 Apple (Iwate)

2005. Fruits of Tohoku. Multicoloured.

19	50y. Type **8**	1·60	1·10
20	50y. Apples (Aomori)	1·60	1·10
21	50y. Cherry (Yamagata)	1·60	1·10
22	50y. Peach (Fukushima)	1·60	1·10

Nos. 19-22 were also issued by Yamagata, Iwate and Fukushima.

9 Chusonji Temple

2007. North Eastern Scenery. Multicoloured.

23	80y. Type **9**	2·50	1·70
24	80y. Oirase stream	2·50	1·70
25	80y. Hirosaki Castle	2·50	1·70
26	80y. Rocks and lily (sukashiyuri)	2·50	1·70
27	80y. Matsushima island and rape flowers	2·50	1·70
28	80y. Dicentra and water filled crater	2·50	1·70
29	80y. Oga penisula and pinks	2·50	1·70
30	80y. Lily (nikkoukisuge) and mountain	2·50	1·70
31	80y. Skunk cabbage flowers, Oze National Park	2·50	1·70
32	80y. Safflower	2·50	1·70

Nos. 23-32 were also issued by Akita, Aomori, Fukushima, Miyagi and Yamagata on 2 July 2007.

KAGAWA

1990

1	62y. As Type **1470** of Japan	4·75	3·25

1 Archer on Horseback

1991. Yashima.

2	**1**	62y. multicoloured	1·20	80

2 Peace Statues

1993

3	**2**	62y. multicoloured	1·50	1·00

3 Marugame Castle

1997

4	**3**	80y. multicoloured	2·10	1·40

4 Seto-Ohashi Bridges

1998

5	**4**	80y. multicoloured	2·10	1·40

5 Ritsurin Park

1999

6	**5**	80y. multicoloured	2·10	1·40

6 Olive and Shodoshima Island (Kagawa)

2002. Multicoloured.

7	50y. Type **6**	1·50	1·00
8	50y. Sudachi (sour citrus fruit) and Mt. Tsurugisan (Tokushima)	1·50	1·00
9	50y. Yamamomo (bayberry) and Tengu highland (Kochi)	1·50	1·00
10	50y. Mikan (mandarin oranges) and Sata-misaki Promontory (Ehime)	1·50	1·00

Nos. 7-10 were also issued by Ehime, Kochi and Tokushima.

7 Kompira-Ohshibai Theatre and Mount Zouzusan

2003. Former Kompira-Ohshibai Theatre.

11	**7**	80y. multicoloured	2·40	1·60

2005. Cultural Heritage. Shizuoka Temples. Multicoloured.

12	80y. As Type **8** of Ehime	2·50	1·70
13	80y. Seated Buddha, Anrakuji Temple	2·50	1·70
14	80y. Inscribed belfry gateway, Jurakuji Temple	2·50	1·70
15	80y. Double roofed gateway, Kumadaniji Temple	2·50	1·70
16	80y. Pagoda, Yakuoji Temple	2·50	1·70
17	80y. Statues, ramp, lanterns and pagoda, Hotsumisakiji Temple	2·50	1·70
18	80y. Gateway and long steep steps, Shinjouji Temple	2·50	1·70
19	80y. Path, gateway, steps and main temple, Kongochoji Temple	2·50	1·70
20	80y. Buddha seated on peacock, Ryukoji Temple	2·50	1·70
21	80y. Bell and autumn colour, Butsumokuji Temple	2·50	1·70
22	80y. Dragon, Meisekiji Temple	2·50	1·70
23	80y. Steps and many roofed buildings, Daihouji Temple	2·50	1·70
24	80y. Carved decorative gable, Kokubunji Temple	2·50	1·70
25	80y. Leafless tree and snow-covered building, Yokomineji Temple	2·50	1·70
26	80y. Buddha, Kouonji Temple	2·50	1·70
27	80y. Courtyard and building, Houjuji Temple	2·50	1·70
28	80y. Inscribed pillars and gateway, Douryuji Temple	2·50	1·70
29	80y. Wall mounted statues, Goushouji Temple	2·50	1·70
30	80y. Eagle surmounting gateway, Tennouji Temple	2·50	1·70
31	80y. Courtyard with stone lined path and building, Kokubunji Temple	2·50	1·70

Nos. 12-31 were also issued by Ehime, Kochi and Tokushima.

2006. Cultural Heritage. Temples. Multicoloured.

32	80y. As Type **9** of Ehime	2·50	1·70
33	80y. Kirihata-ji (statue), Kirihata Temple	2·50	1·70
34	80y. Cherry blossom and building, Fujiidera Temple	2·50	1·70
35	80y. Snow-covered pagoda and temple, Shozanji Temple	2·50	1·70
36	80y. Wide path, inscribed pillar and gateway, Konomineji Temple	2·50	1·70
37	80y. Decorative carved roof boss and bell, Dainichiji Temple	2·50	1·70
38	80y. Cherry blossom and grass edged path, Kokubunji Temple	2·50	1·70
39	80y. Cherry blossom and statue, Zenrakuji Temple	2·50	1·70
40	80y. Cliff face and temple building, Iwayaji Temple	2·50	1·70
41	80y. Decorated footprints, Joururiji Temple	2·50	1·70
42	80y. Spot-lighted statues, Yasakaji Temple	2·50	1·70
43	80y. Lantern, tree, path, gateway and inscribed pillar, Sairinji Temple	2·50	1·70
44	80y. Temple buildings through hole in rock, Kichijoji Temple	2·50	1·70
45	80y. Cherry blossom and roofs, Maegamiji Temple	2·50	1·70
46	80y. Carving with dragon and phoenix, Sankakuji Temple	2·50	1·70
47	80y. Snow-covered roofs and trees, Unbenji Temple	2·50	1·70
48	80y. Wide path, pilgrim and gateway, Shiromineji Temple	2·50	1·70
49	80y. Row of statues, Negoroji Temple	2·50	1·70
50	80y. Lantern, courtyard and building, Ichinomiyaji Temple	2·50	1·70
51	80y. Animal statues and building, Yashimaji Temple	2·50	1·70

Nos. 32-51 were also issued by Tokushima, Kochi and Ehime.

2007. Cultural Heritage. Temples. As T 10of Ehime Multicoloured.

52	80y. Type **10**	2·50	1·70
53	80y. Gateway	2·50	1·70
54	80y. Square, shrub and main hall	2·50	1·70
55	80y. Trees, temple roof and hill	2·50	1·70
56	80y. Bell tower gate	2·50	1·70
57	80y. Bamboo temple	2·50	1·70
58	80y. Statues, pathway and temple	2·50	1·70
59	80y. Paved path and entrance	2·50	1·70
60	80y. Buddha	2·50	1·70
61	80y. Decorated ceiling and bell	2·50	1·70
62	80y. Temple lit from below	2·50	1·70
63	80y. Paved path, steps and temple	2·50	1·70
64	80y. Guardian statue	2·50	1·70
65	80y. Gateway	2·50	1·70
66	80y. Carved ceiling and bell	2·50	1·70
67	80y. Pagoda and temple at night	2·50	1·70
68	80y. Temple and mountains	2·50	1·70
69	80y. Pilgrims entering gateway	2·50	1·70
70	80y. Pilgrims and temple	2·50	1·70
71	80y. Temple, banners and mountains	2·50	1·70
72	80y. Well	2·50	1·70
73	80y. Kobo Daishi (statue)	2·50	1·70
74	80y. Buddha	2·50	1·70
75	80y. Three roofed pagoda	2·50	1·70
76	80y. Pilgrims, steps and gateway	2·50	1·70
77	80y. Demon	2·50	1·70
78	80y. Rock statues	2·50	1·70
79	80y. Bodhisattva	2·50	1·70
80	80y. Cave and temple at night	2·50	1·70
81	80y. Kobo Daishi (painting)	2·50	1·70

Nos. 52-81 were also issued by Ehime, Tokushima and Kochi on 1 August 2007.

KAGOSHIMA

1990. Flowers.

1	62y. As Type **1479** of Japan	1·20	80

1 Mount Sakurajima

1990

2	**1**	62y. multicoloured	1·30	80

2 Festival Goers, Ohara

1993

3	**2**	41y. multicoloured	1·30	90

3 Satsuma Ware Bowl

1998. 400th Satsuma-Yaki Festival. Multicoloured.

4	80y. Type **3**	2·10	1·40
5	80y. Vase	2·10	1·40

4 Cycle Ball and Sunset Bridge, Kaseda (for bicycles only)

2001

6	**4**	80y. multicoloured	2·50	1·70

5 Tsubame (800 Series Shinkansen)

2004. Inauguration of Kyushu-Shinkansen Line–Tsubame (high-speed rail line).

7	**5**	50y. multicoloured	1·60	1·10

6 Miyama-Kirishima (azaleas) and Kirishima and Mount Sakurajima mountains (Kagoshima)

2005. Flowers and Scenery of Kyushu (1st series). Multicoloured.

8	50y. Ume Blossom and Dazaifu-Tenmangu Shrine (Fukuoka)	1·60	1·10
9	50y. Sakura (cherry blossoms) and Kanmon bridge (Fukuoka)	1·60	1·10
10	50y. Kusunohana (camphor blossoms) and Ariake Sea (Saga)	1·60	1·10
11	50y. Unzen-Tsutsuji (azaleas) and Mt. Fugendake (Nagasaki)	1·60	1·10
12	50y. Tulips and Huis Ten Bosch (Nagasaki)	1·60	1·10
13	50y. Rindou (gentians) and Mt. Aso (Kumamoto)	1·60	1·10
14	50y. Ume blossoms and Mt. Takasaki (Ooita)	1·60	1·10
15	50y. Hamayu (crinums) and Nichinan beach (Miyazaki)	1·60	1·10
16	50y. Type **6**	1·60	1·10
17	50y. Hibiscus and Adan (screw-pine) (Kagoshima)	1·60	1·10

Nos. 8-17 were also issued by Fukuoka, Nagasaki, Saga, Miyazaki, Kumamoto and Oita.

7 Field of yellow flowers and Mt. Kaimondake (Kagoshima)

2006. Flowers and Scenery of Kyushu (2nd series). Multicoloured.

18	80y. Daffodils and Nokonoshima Island (Fukuoka)	2·50	1·70
19	80y. Chinese bellflowers and Hiraodai (Fukuoka)	2·50	1·70

20	80y. Hydrangeas and Mikaeri-notaki fall (Saga)	2·50	1·70
21	80y. Cosmos and Kujukushima islands (Nagasaki)	2·50	1·70
22	80y. Camellias and the five bridges of Amakusa (Kumamoto)	2·50	1·70
23	80y. Purple flowers and Mt. Aso (Kumamoto)	2·50	1·70
24	80y. Primroses and Mt. Yu-fudake (Oita)	2·50	1·70
25	80y. Lavender and Kujurenzan (Oita)	2·50	1·70
26	80y. Poppies and Mt. Hinamori-dake (Miyazaki)	2·50	1·70
27	80y. Type **7**	2·50	1·70

Nos. 18-27 were also issued by Fukuoka, Nagasaki, Saga, Kumamoto, Oita and Miyazaki.

KANAGAWA

1 Doll

1989

1	**1**	62y. multicoloured	

1990. Flowers.

2	62y. As Type **1447** of Japan	1·30	90

2 Shasui Waterfall (Shasui-no-taki)

1992

3	**2**	62y. multicoloured	1·20	80

3 Flowers, Sengokubara Marsh

1996

4	**3**	80y. multicoloured	2·10	1·40

4 Tunnel Entrance

1997. Tokyo-Wan Aqualine. Multicoloured.

5	80y. Type **4**	1·80	1·20
6	80y. Tunnel entrance (different)	1·80	1·20

Nos. 5-6 were also issued by Chiba.

5 Minamoto no Yoritomo

1999

7	**5**	80y. multicoloured	2·10	1·40

6 Decorated Bamboo Banners

2000. Hiratsuka Tanabata Festival. Multicoloured.

8	50y. Type **6**	1·50	1·00
9	50y. Father and child	1·50	1·00

7 Castle and Chrysanthemums

2000. Odwara Castle. Multicoloured.

10	50y. Type **7**	1·80	1·20
11	50y. Blossom, gate and castle	1·80	1·20

8 Ship in Dock

2002. Yokohama, Port Town. Multicoloured.

12	50y. Type **8**	1·50	1·00
13	50y. Port, ship and woman in Victorian dress	1·50	1·00

9 Rose and Buildings at Night, 21 Area

2004. Tourism. Multicoloured.

14	50y. Type **9**	1·60	1·10
15	50y. Lily, Kanagawa Prefectural Government, Yokohama Customs, and Yokohama Memorial Museum buildings	1·60	1·10
16	50y. Wisterias and Enoshima Island	1·60	1·10
17	50y. Hydrangea and Lake Ashinoko, Hakone	1·60	1·10

10 Azaleas, Eboshi-iwa and Minato-Mirai Mount Fuji

2004. Flowers. Multicoloured.

18	80y. Type **10**	2·10	1·40
19	80y. Daffodils and avenue of pines, Sakawagawa river	2·10	1·40
20	80y. Pinks and Tanzawa mountains	2·10	1·40
21	80y. Balloon flowers and Mt. Fuji	2·10	1·40

11 Lily

2008. Flowers. Multicoloured.

22	50y. Type **11**	1·60	1·10
23	50y. Sweet briar	1·60	1·10
24	50y. Nemotoshakunage (*Rhododendron brachycarpum*)	1·60	1·10
25	50y. Safflower	1·60	1·10
26	50y. Gentian	1·60	1·10
27	80y. Lily (25×35 mm)	2·50	1·70
28	80y. Sweet briar (25×35 mm)	2·50	1·70
29	80y. Rhodedendron (25×35 mm)	2·50	1·70
30	80y. Safflower (25×35 mm)	2·50	1·70
31	80y. Gentian (25×35 mm)	2·50	1·70

Nos. 22-31 were also issued by Fukushima, Hokkaido, Nagano and Yamagata on 1 July 2008.

12 Standard Bearers and Dancers

2008. Hokone Procession Festival. Multicoloured.

32	50y. Type **11**	1·70	1·30
33	50y. Three men	1·70	1·30

Nos. 32-3 were printed se-tenant, each pair forming a composite design..

KOCHI

1990

1	62y. As Type **1472** of Japan	1·90	1·30

1 Man and Child riding on Whale

1991

2	**1**	62y. multicoloured	1·80	80

2 Lighthouse

1995

3	**2**	80y. multicoloured	1·90	1·30

3 Cliff-top Teahouse and Gateway, Katsura Beach

1999. Sakamoto Ryoma (warrior and naval pioneer). Multicoloured.

4	80y. Type **3**	2·20	1·50
5	80y. Whale tail, telescope and Sakamoto Ryoma	2·20	1·50

4 Kochi Castle

2001. Kochi Castle and Sunday Market. Mult.

6	80y. Type **4**	2·40	1·60
7	80y. Sunday market	2·40	1·60

5 Yamamomo (bayberry) and Tengu Highland (Kochi)

2002. Multicoloured.

8	50y. Type **5**	1·50	1·00
9	50y. Sudachi (sour citrus fruit) and Mt. Tsurugisan (Tokushima)	1·50	1·00
10	50y. Mikan (mandarin oranges) and Sata-misaki Promontory (Ehime)	1·50	1·00
11	50y. Olive and Shodoshima island (Kagawa)	1·50	1·00

Nos. 8-11 were also issued by Ehime, Tokushima and Kagawa.

6 Runners

2002. 57th National Athletic Meet.

12	**6**	50y. multicoloured	1·60	1·10

2005. Cultural Heritage. Shizuoka Temples. Multicoloured.

13	80y. As Type **8** of Ehime	2·50	1·70
14	80y. Seated Buddha, Anrakuji Temple	2·50	1·70
15	80y. Inscribed belfry gateway, Jurakuji Temple	2·50	1·70
16	80y. Double roofed gateway, Kumadaniji Temple	2·50	1·70
17	80y. Pagoda, Yakuoji Temple	2·50	1·70
18	80y. Statues, ramp, lanterns and pagoda, Hotsumisakiji Temple	2·50	1·70
19	80y. Gateway and long steep steps, Shinjouji Temple	2·50	1·70
20	80y. Path, gateway, steps and main temple, Kongochoji Temple	2·50	1·70
21	80y. Buddha seated on peacock, Ryukoji Temple	2·50	1·70
22	80y. Bell and autumn colour, Butsumokuji Temple	2·50	1·70
23	80y. Dragon, Meisekiji Temple	2·50	1·70
24	80y. Steps and many roofed buildings, Daihouji Temple	2·50	1·70
25	80y. Carved decorative gable, Kokubunji Temple	2·50	1·70
26	80y. Leafless tree and snow-covered building, Yokomineji Temple	2·50	1·70
27	80y. Buddha, Kouonji Temple	2·50	1·70
28	80y. Courtyard and building, Houjuji Temple	2·50	1·70
29	80y. Inscribed pillars and gateway, Douryuji Temple	2·50	1·70
30	80y. Wall mounted statues, Goushouji Temple	2·50	1·70
31	80y. Eagle surmounting gateway, Tennouji Temple	2·50	1·70
32	80y. Courtyard with stone lined path and building, Kokubunji Temple	2·50	1·70

Nos. 13-32 were also issued by Ehime, Tokushima and Kagawa.

2006. Cultural Heritage. Temples. Multicoloured.

33	80y. As Type **9** of Ehime	2·50	1·70
34	80y. Kirihata-ji (statue), Kirihata Temple	2·50	1·70
35	80y. Cherry blossom and building, Fujiidera Temple2	50	1·70
36	80y. Snow-covered pagoda and temple, Shozanji Temple	2·50	1·70
37	80y. Wide path, inscribed pillar and gateway, Konomineji Temple	2·50	1·70
38	80y. Decorative carved roof boss and bell, Dainichiji Temple	2·50	1·70
39	80y. Cherry blossom and grass edged path, Kokubunji Temple	2·50	1·70
40	80y. Cherry blossom and statue, Zenrakuji Temple	2·50	1·70
41	80y. Cliff face and temple building, Iwayaji Temple	2·50	1·70
42	80y. Decorated footprints, Joururiji Temple	2·50	1·70
43	80y. Spot-lighted statues, Yasakaji Temple	2·50	1·70
44	80y. Lantern, tree, path, gateway and inscribed pillar, Sairinji Temple	2·50	1·70
45	80y. Temple buildings through hole in rock, Kichijoji Temple	2·50	1·70

46 80y. Cherry blossom and roofs, Maegamiji Temple 2·50 1·70
47 80y. Carving with dragon and phoenix, Sankakuji Temple 2·50 1·70
48 80y. Snow-covered roofs and trees, Unbenji Temple 2·50 1·70
49 80y. Wide path, pilgrim and gateway, Shiromineji Temple 2·50 1·70
50 80y. Row of statues, Negoroji Temple 2·50 1·70
51 80y. Lantern, courtyard and building, Ichinomiyaji Temple 2·50 1·70
52 80y. Animal statues and building, Yashimaji Temple 2·50 1·70

Nos. 33-52 were also issued by Tokushima, Ehimei and Kagawa.

2007. Cultural Heritage. Temples. As T 10 of Ehime. Multicoloured.
53 80y. Type **10** 2·50 1·70
54 80y. Gateway 2·50 1·70
55 80y. Square, shrub and main hall 2·50 1·70
56 80y. Trees, temple roof and hill 2·50 1·70
57 80y. Bell tower gate 2·50 1·70
58 80y. Bamboo temple 2·50 1·70
59 80y. Statues, pathway and temple 2·50 1·70
60 80y. Paved path and entrance 2·50 1·70
61 80y. Buddha 2·50 1·70
62 80y. Decorated ceiling and bell 2·50 1·70
63 80y. Temple lit from below 2·50 1·70
64 80y. Paved path, steps and temple 2·50 1·70
65 80y. Guardian statue 2·50 1·70
66 80y. Gateway 2·50 1·70
67 80y. Carved ceiling and bell 2·50 1·70
68 80y. Pagoda and temple at night 2·50 1·70
69 80y. Temple and mountains 2·50 1·70
70 80y. Pilgrims entering gateway 2·50 1·70
71 80y. Pilgrims and temple 2·50 1·70
72 80y. Temple, banners and mountains 2·50 1·70
73 80y. Well 2·50 1·70
74 80y. Kobo Daishi (statue) 2·50 1·70
75 80y. Buddha 2·50 1·70
76 80y. Three roofed pagoda 2·50 1·70
77 80y. Pilgrims, steps and gateway 2·50 1·70
78 80y. Demon 2·50 1·70
79 80y. Rock statues 2·50 1·70
80 80y. Bodhisattva 2·50 1·70
81 80y. Cave and temple at night 2·50 1·70
82 80y. Kobo Daishi (painting) 2·50 1·70

Nos. 53-82 were also issued by Ehime, Kagawa and Tokushima on 1 August 2007.

7 Bayberry

8 Bayberry

2009. Prefectural Flowers. Multicoloured.
83 50y. Peach blossom (Okayama) 1·70 1·30
84 50y. Rape flowers (Chiba) 1·70 1·30
85 50y. Plum blossom and primula (Osaka) 1·70 1·30
86 50y. Type **7** (Kochi) 1·70 1·30
87 50y. Ume blossom (*Prunus mume* var. bungo) (Oita) 1·70 1·30
88 80y. Peach blossom (Okayama) (different) 2·75 1·70
89 80y. Rape flowers (Chiba) (different) 2·75 1·70
90 80y. Plum blossom and primula (Osaka) (different) 2·75 1·70
91 80y. Type **8** (Kochi) 2·75 1·70
92 80y. Ume blossom (*Prunus mume* var. bungo) (Oita) (different) 2·75 1·70

Stamps of the same design were issued by Chiba, Oita, Okayama and Osaka on 1 Dec 2009..

KUMAMOTO

1 Kumamoto Castle

1989
1 **1** 62y. multicoloured 1·30 60

1990. Flowers.
2 62y. As Type **1476** of Japan 1·20 80

2 Aqueduct discharging Water, Tsujun-kyo

1991
3 **2** 62y. multicoloured 1·50 90

3 Boy

1996. Ushibuka-haiya Festival.
4 **3** 80y. multicoloured 1·80 1·20

4 Globe and Ball

1997. World Men's Handball Championship.
5 **4** 50y. multicoloured 2·10 1·40

5 Traditional Fishing Boat

1999
6 **5** 80y. multicoloured 2·10 1·40

6 Yachiyoza Theatre

2002
7 **6** 80y. multicoloured 2·20 1·50

7 Rindou (gentians) and Mt. Aso (Kumamoto)

8 Camellias and Five Bridges of Amakusa (Kumamoto)

2005. Flowers and Scenery of Kyushu (1st series). Multicoloured.
8 50y. Ume Blossom and Dazaifu-Tenmangu Shrine (Fukuoka) 1·60 1·10
9 50y. Sakura (cherry blossoms) and Kanmon bridge (Fukuoka) 1·60 1·10
10 50y. Kusunohana (camphor blossoms) and Ariake Sea (Saga) 1·60 1·10
11 50y. Unzen-Tsutsuji (azaleas) and Mt. Fugendake (Nagasaki) 1·60 1·10
12 50y. Tulips and Huis Ten Bosch (Nagasaki)
13 50y. Type **7** 1·60 1·10
14 50y. Ume blossoms and Mt. Takasaki (Ooita) 1·60 1·10
15 50y. Hamayu (crinums) and Nichinan beach (Miyazaki) 1·60 1·10
16 50y. Miyama-Kirishima (azaleas) and Kirishima mountains (Kagoshima) 1·60 1·10
17 50y. Hibiscus and Adan (screw-pine) (Kagoshima) 1·60 1·10

Nos. 8-17 were also issued by Fukuoka, Nagasaki, Saga, Miyazaki, Oita and Kagoshima.

2006. Flowers and Scenery of Kyushu (2nd series). Multicoloured.
18 80y. Daffodils and Nokonoshima Island (Fukuoka) 2·20 1·50
19 80y. Chinese bellflowers and Hiraodai (Fukuoka) 2·20 1·50
20 80y. Hydrangeas and Mikaeri-notaki fall (Saga) 2·20 1·50
21 80y. Cosmos and Kujukushima islands (Nagasaki) 2·20 1·50
22 80y. Type **8** 2·20 1·50
23 80y. Purple flowers and Mt. Aso (Kumamoto) 2·20 1·50
24 80y. Primroses and Mt. Yufudake (Oita) 2·20 1·50
25 80y. Lavender and Kujurenzan (Oita) 2·20 1·50
26 80y. Poppies and Mt. Hinamori-dake (Miyazaki) 2·20 1·50
27 80y. Field of yellow flowers and Mt. Kaimondake (Kagoshima) 2·20 1·50

Nos. 18-27 were also issued by Fukuoka, Nagasaki, Saga, Oita, Miyazaki and Kagoshima.

9 Tower and Cherry Blossom

2007. 400th Anniv of Kumamoto Castle. Multicoloured.
28 80y. Type **9** 2·50 1·70
29 80y. Castle and lawn 2·50 1·70
30 80y. Castle in autumn 2·50 1·70
31 80y. Castle in snow 2·50 1·70
32 80y. Roof tops 2·50 1·70

10 Gentian

11 Gentian

2009. Prefectural Flowers. Multicoloured.
32 50y. Type **10** (Kumamoto) 1·70 1·30
33 50y. Wild chrysanthemum (Hyogo) 1·70 1·30
34 50y. Bush clover blossom (Miyagi) 1·70 1·30
35 50y. Fritillary (*Fritillaria camschatcensis*) (Ishikawa) 1·70 1·30
36 50y. Maple (Hiroshima) 1·70 1·30
37 80y. Type **11** (Kumamoto) 2·75 1·70
38 80y. Wild chrysanthemum (Hyogo) (different) 2·75 1·70
39 80y. Bush clover blossom (Miyagi) (different) 2·75 1·70
40 80y. Fritillary (*Fritillaria camschatcensis*) (Ishikawa) (different) 2·75 1·70
41 80y. Maple (Hiroshima) (different) 2·75 1·70

Stamps of the same design were issued by Hyogo, Ishikawa, Hiroshima and Miyagi on 1 July 2009.

KYOTO

1990. Flowers.
1 62y. As Type **1459** of Japan 3·00 2·00

1 Maiko (apprentice geisha)

1990
2 **1** 62y. multicoloured 1·20 80

2 Ushiwaka-maru (Aikido master)

1995
3 **2** 80y. multicoloured 1·90 1·30

3 Kyoto University

1997
4 **3** 80y. multicoloured 2·10 1·40

4 Hiyoshi Dam

1998
5 **4** 80y. multicoloured 2·10 1·40

5 Amanohashidate Sand Bar

1999
6 **5** 80y. multicoloured 2·10 1·40

6 Cherry Blossoms, Maruyama Park (spring)

2000. Four Seasons. Multicoloured.
7 80y. Type **6** 2·75 1·90
8 80y. Kamogawa river (summer) 2·75 1·90
9 80y. Togetsukyo bridge, Arashiyama (autumn) 2·75 1·90
10 80y. Cedar forest, Kitayama (winter) 2·75 1·90

7 Carriage decorated with Japanese Wisteria

2003. Traditional Events in Kyoto. Multicoloured.
11 50y. Type **7** 1·60 1·10
12 50y. Gion-masturi (festival float) 1·60 1·10
13 50y. Okuribi (fire to send off spirits at Mt. Nyoig) 1·60 1·10
14 50y. Jidai-matsuri (royal carriage) 1·60 1·10

8 Shidare-zakura (weeping cherry) Aoi-matsuri Festival (Kyoto)

2006. Flowers of Kinki. Multicoloured.

15	50y. Type **8**	1·60	1·10
16	50y. Sakuraso (primrose) (Osaka)	1·60	1·10
17	50y. Yae-zakura (double cherry blossoms) (Nara)	1·60	1·10
18	50y. Nozigiku (wild chrysanthemums) (Hyogo)	1·60	1·10
19	50y. Shakunage (rhododendron) (Shiga)	1·60	1·10
20	50y. Ume blossoms (Wakayama)	1·60	1·10

Nos. 15-20 were also issued by Osaka, Nara, Shiga, Wakayama and Hyogo.

9 Weeping Cherry Blossom

2008. Prefectural Flowers. Multicoloured.

21	50y. Narcissus (Fukui)	1·60	1·10
22	50y. Pink plum blossom (Wakayama)	1·60	1·10
23	50y. Fuki (*Petasites japonicus*) (Akita)	1·60	1·10
24	50y. White plum blossom (Fukuoka)	1·60	1·10
25	50y. Type **9**	1·60	1·10
26	80y. Narcissus (Fukui)	2·50	1·70
27	80y. White plum blossom (Wakayama)	2·50	1·70
28	80y. Fuki (*Petasites japonicus*) (Akita)	2·50	1·70
29	80y. Pink plum blossom (Fukuoka)	2·50	1·70
30	80y. Weeping cherry blossom (Kyoto)	2·50	1·70

MIE

1990. Flowers.

1	62y. As Type **1457** of Japan	1·20	80

1 Ninja

1991

2	**1**	62y. multicoloured	1·50	90

2 Meoto-iwa (wedded rocks) and Plovers, Futami-ga-ura

1994

3	**2**	80y. multicoloured	1·90	1·30

3 Hamayu (crinum) Blossom

1996. Multicoloured.

4	80y. Type **3**	1·80	1·20
5	80y. Ama divers	1·80	1·20

4 Trees and Mountains

1999. Kumano Old Path. Multicoloured.

6	80y. Type **4**	2·10	1·40
7	80y. Trees and shoreline	2·10	1·40
8	80y. Pathway	2·10	1·40
9	80y. Scree	2·10	1·40

5 Free Fall

2000. World Parachuting Championships. Mult.

10	80y. Type **5**	2·75	1·90
11	80y. Parachutist	2·75	1·90

Nos. 10-11 were issued together, se-tenant, forming a composite design.

6 Matsuo Basho (haiku poet) and Iga-ueno Castle

2002. Iga-Ueno. Multicoloured.

12	80y. Type **6**	2·20	1·50
13	80y. Iga-Ueno castle and Haisei-den hall	2·20	1·50

Nos. 12-13 were issued together, se-tenant, forming a composite design.

7 Ozu Yasujiro and Mitchell Camera

2003. Birth Centenary of Ozu Yasujiro (film director).

14	**7**	80y. multicoloured	2·20	1·50

8 Iris and Couple Rock

2007. Flowers and Scenry of Tokai. Multicoloured.

15	80y. Type **8**	2·50	1·70
16	80y. Iris	2·50	1·70
17	80y. Gasshó-zukuri houses and vetch flowers	2·50	1·70
18	80y. Lily and Nagoya Castle	2·50	1·70
19	80y. Azalea and coastline, Jogasaki	2·50	1·70

Nos. 15-19 were also issued by Aichi, Gifu and Shizuoka on 2 April 2007.

MIYAGI

1990. Flowers.

1	62y. As Type **1437** of Japan	1·20	80

1 Swans

1990

2	**1**	62y. multicoloured	1·50	80

2 Coastline, Matsushima

1994

3	**2**	80y. multicoloured	1·30	80

3 Zalkova (Japanese elm) Trees

1995

4	**3**	50y. multicoloured	1·30	80

4 Festival Goers and Banners

1999. Summer Festivals. Multicoloured.

5	80y. Type **4**	2·10	1·40
6	80y. Streamers	2·10	1·40

Nos. 5-6 were issued together, se-tenant, forming a composite design.

Nos. 5/6 were also issued by Fukishima.

5 Cherry Tree

2000. Cherry Trees. Multicoloured.

7	80y. Type **5**	2·50	1·70
8	80y. Group of trees with spreading branches, Yamagata	2·50	1·70
9	80y. Group of trees, Fukishima	2·50	1·70
10	80y. Tree, central, Iwate	2·50	1·70
11	80y. Cherry blossom, Aomori	2·50	1·70
12	80y. Trees and river, Akita	2·50	1·70

Nos. 7-12 were also issued by Yamagata, Iwate, Aomori, Akita and Fukushima.

6 Float and Festival Dancers

2001. 400th Anniv of Sendai.

13	**6**	80y. multicoloured	2·50	1·70

7 Volleyball Players and Bush Clover

2001. 56th National Athletic Meet.

14	**7**	50y. multicoloured	2·10	1·40

8 Japanese Bush Clover (Miyagi)

2004. Prefectural Flowers. Multicoloured.

15	50y. Type **8**	1·60	1·10
16	50y. Apple blossom (Aomori)	1·60	1·10
17	50y. Paulownia (Iwate)	1·60	1·10
18	50y. Butterbur flower (Akita)	1·60	1·10
19	50y. Safflower (Yamagata)	1·60	1·10
20	50y. Alpine rose (*Rhododendron ferrugineum*) (Fukushima)	1·60	1·10

Nos. 15-20 were also issued by Yamagata, Aomori, Miyagi, Iwate and Fukushima.

8 Sendai Tanabata Matsuri (Miyagi)

2006. Festivals of Tohuku. Multicoloured.

21	80y. Type **9**	2·50	1·70
22	80y. Kanto Matsuri (Akita)	2·50	1·70
23	80y. Hanagasa Matsuri (Yamagata)	2·50	1·70
24	80y. Nebuta Matsuri (Aomori)	2·50	1·70

Nos. 21-4 were also issued by Akita, Aomori, and Yamagata.

10 Matsushima Island and Rape Flowers

2007. North Eastern Scenery. Multicoloured.

25	80y. Type **10**	2·50	1·70
26	80y. Oirase stream	2·50	1·70
27	80y. Hirosaki Castle	2·50	1·70
28	80y. Chusonji Temple	2·50	1·70
29	80y. Rocks and lily (sukashiyuri)	2·50	1·70
30	80y. Dicentra and water filled crater	2·50	1·70
31	80y. Oga penisula and pinks	2·50	1·70
32	80y. Lily (nikkoukisuge) and mountain	2·50	1·70
33	80y. Skunk cabbage flowers, Oze National Park	2·50	1·70
34	80y. Safflower	2·50	1·70

Nos. 25-34 were also issued by Akita, Aomori, Fukushima, Iwate and Yamaguchi on 2 July 2007.

11-12 Lanterns

2008. Tanabata Festival. Multicoloured.

35	50y. Type **11**	1·60	1·10
36	50y. Type **12**	1·60	1·10
37	50y. Procession and roofs, left	1·60	1·10
38	50y. Procession and roofs, right	1·60	1·10
39	50y. Dancers, left	1·60	1·10
40	50y. Dancers, right		
41	50y. Procession, left	1·60	1·10
42	50y. Procession, right	1·60	1·10

43	50y. Drummers, left	1·60	1·10
44	50y. Drummers, right	1·60	1·10

Nos. 35-6, 37-8, 39-40, 41-2 and 43-4 were issued together, se-tenant, each pair forming a composite design.
Nos. 35-44 were also issued by Tokushima, Okinawa, Tokyo and Fukuoka on 1 August 2008.

13 Bush Clover Blossom

14 Bush Clover Blossom

2009. Prefectural Flowers. Multicoloured.

44	50y. Gentian (Kumamoto)	1·70	1·30
45	50y. Wild chrysanthemum (Hyogo)	1·70	1·30
46	50y. Type **13** (Miyagi)	1·70	1·30
47	50y. Fritillary (*Fritillaria camschatcensis*) (Ishikawa)	1·70	1·30
48	50y. Maple (Hiroshima)	1·70	1·30
49	80y. Gentian (Kumamoto) (different)	2·75	1·70
50	80y. Wild chrysanthemum (Hyogo) (different)	2·75	1·70
51	80y. Type **14** (Miyagi)	2·75	1·70
52	80y. Fritillary (*Fritillaria camschatcensis*) (Ishikawa) (different)	2·75	1·70
53	80y. Maple (Hiroshima) (different)	2·75	1·70

Stamps of the same design were issued by Hyogo, Ishikawa, Kumamoto and Hiroshima on 1 July 2009.

MIYAZAKI

1990. Flowers.

1	62y. As Type **1478** of Japan	1·20	80

1 Horses and Coastline, Toi-misaki

1991

2	**1**	62y. multicoloured	2·10	1·40

2 Drummer

1996. Shimozuru Usudaiko Odori.

3	**2**	80y. multicoloured	2·10	1·40

3 Nichinan Taihei Dance

1999. Obi Town. Multicoloured.

4	80y. Type **3**	2·10	1·40
5	80y. Building and statue	2·10	1·40

4 Sekino'o-taki Waterfall

2000. Landscapes. Multicoloured.

6	80y. Type **4**	2·75	1·80
7	80y. Kirishima volcano	2·75	1·80

Nos. 6-7 were issued together, se-tenant, forming a composite design.

5 Noh Theatre

2003. Nobeoka–City of Noh. Multicoloured.

8	80y. Type **5**	2·40	1·60
9	80y. Tenkaichi Takigi-Noh (traditional dance)	2·40	1·60

6 Flowering Tree and Mountains

2004. National Afforestation Campaign.

10	**6**	50y. multicoloured	1·60	1·10

7 Hamayu (crinums) and Nichinan Beach (Miyazaki)

2005. Flowers and Scenery of Kyushu (1st series). Multicoloured.

11	50y. Type **7**	1·60	1·10
12	50y. Sakura (cherry blossoms) and Kanmon bridge (Fukuoka)	1·60	1·10
13	50y. Kusunohana (camphor blossoms) and Ariake Sea (Saga)	1·60	1·10
14	50y. Unzen-Tsutsuji (azaleas) and Mt. Fugendake (Nagasaki)	1·60	1·10
15	50y. Tulips and Huis Ten Bosch (Nagasaki)	1·60	1·10
16	50y. Rindou (gentians) and Mt. Aso (Kumamoto)	1·60	1·10
17	50y. Ume blossoms and Mt. Takasaki (Oita)	1·60	1·10
18	50y. Ume blossom and Dazaifu-Tenmangu Shrine (Fukuoka)	1·60	1·10
19	50y. Miyama-Kirishima (azaleas) and Kirishima mountains (Kagoshima)	1·60	1·10
20	50y. Hibiscus and Adan (screw-pine) (Kagoshima)	1·60	1·10

Nos. 11-20 were also issued by Fukuoka, Nagasaki, Saga, Oita, Kumamoto and Kagoshima.

8 Poppies and Mt. Hinamoridake (Miyazaki)

2006. Flowers and Scenery of Kyushu (2nd series). Multicoloured.

21	80y. Daffodils and Nokonoshima Island (Fukuoka)	2·40	1·60
22	80y. Chinese bellflowers and Hiraodai (Fukuoka)	2·40	1·60
23	80y. Hydrangeas and Mikaerinotaki fall (Saga)	2·40	1·60
24	80y. Cosmos and Kujukushima islands (Nagasaki)	2·40	1·60
25	80y. Camellias and the five bridges of Amakusa (Kumamoto)	2·40	1·60
26	80y. Purple flowers and Mt. Aso (Kumamoto)	2·40	1·60
27	80y. Primroses and Mt. Yufudake (Oita)	2·40	1·60
28	80y. Lavender and Kujurenzan (Oita)	2·40	1·60
29	80y. Type **8**	2·40	1·60
30	80y. Field of yellow flowers and Mt. Kaimondake (Kagoshima)	2·40	1·60

Nos. 21-30 were also issued by Fukuoka, Nagasaki, Saga, Kumamoto, Oita and Kagoshima.

NAGANO

1 Monkeys

1989

1	**1**	62y. multicoloured	1·50	80

1990. Flowers.

2	62y. As Type **1449** of Japan	3·75	2·50

2 Tsumago Inn

1990. Inns.

3	**2**	62y. ochre and brown	1·50	80
4	-	62y. yellow and brown	1·50	80

DESIGNS: No. 3 Type **2**; No. 4 Magome.

3 Matsumoto-jo Castle

1993

5	**3**	62y. multicoloured	1·50	1·00

4 Building, Kashiwabara

1994

6	**4**	80y. multicoloured	1·90	1·10

5 Conductor and Orchestra

1996. Saito Kinen Festival.

7	**5**	80y. multicoloured	2·10	1·40

6 Campanula Flowers

1996. Rindo.

8	**6**	80y. multicoloured	2·10	1·40

7 Jomon's Venus

1998

9	**7**	80y. multicoloured	2·10	1·40

8 Horse Rider

1998. Puppetry Festival. Multicoloured.

10	50y. Type **8**	1·30	90
11	50y. Bird and man	1·30	90

Nos. 10-11 were issued together, se-tenant, forming a composite design.

9 Kiso Observatory, Tokyo University

1999

12	**9**	80y. multicoloured	2·10	1·40

10 Matsumoto Castle

1999

13	**10**	80y. multicoloured	2·10	1·40

1999. Inns. As T 2.

14	62y. ochre and brown	2·10	1·40
15	62y. yellow and brown	2·10	1·40

DESIGNS: No. 14 Tsumago (As Type **2**); No. 15 Magome (As No. 4).

1999

16	**1**	80y. multicoloured	2·10	1·40

11 Cherry Blossom

2000

17	**11**	80y. multicoloured	2·40	1·60

12 Azumino

2000

18	**12**	80y. multicoloured	2·40	1·60

13 Fishing and Score

2000. Shinano-no-kuni (prefecture song). Multicoloured.

19	50y. Type **13**	1·60	1·10
20	50y. Autumnal trees, bridge and score	1·60	1·10

14 Zenkoji Temple

2001. Nagano Homeland. Multicoloured.

21	50y. Type **14**	2·50	1·70
22	50y. Mt. Iizunayama and apple blossoms	2·50	1·70

Nos. 21-2 were issued together, se-tenant, forming a composite design.

15 Dog's Tooth Violet Hakuba Mountains (Chushin area)

2003. Flora. Multicoloured.

23	50y. Type **15**	1·60	1·10
24	50y. Skunk cabbage and Okususobana-shizen'en (Hokushin area)	1·60	1·10
25	50y. Lilies and Mt. Kirigamine (Nanshin area)	1·60	1·10
26	50y. Cosmos and Cosmos highway (Toshin area)	1·60	1·10

16 Apple Blossom

2005. Flora. Multicoloured.

27	50y. Type **16**	1·60	1·10
28	50y. Renge-tsutsuji (renge azalea)	1·60	1·10
29	50y. Suzuran (lily of the valley)	1·60	1·10
30	50y. Rindou (gentian)	1·60	1·10

17 Mountains of Echigo

2006. Nature of Shin'etsu. Multicoloured.

31	80y. Type **17**	2·10	1·40
32	80y. Sankayou (*Diphylleia cymosa*)	2·10	1·40
33	80y. Mt. Asamayama	2·10	1·40
34	80y. Sakurasou (*Primula sieboldii*)	2·10	1·40

Nos. 31-4 were also issued by Niigata.

18 Gentian

2008. Flowers. Multicoloured.

35	50y. Type **18**	1·60	1·10
36	50y. Lily	1·60	1·10
37	50y. Sweet briar	1·60	1·10
38	50y. Nemotoshakunage (*Rhododendron brachycarpum*)	1·60	1·10
39	50y. Safflower	1·60	1·10
40	80y. Lily (25×35 mm)	2·50	1·70
41	80y. Sweet briar (25×35 mm)	2·50	1·70
42	80y. Rhodedendron (25×35 mm)	2·50	1·70
43	80y. Safflower (25×35 mm)	2·50	1·70
44	80y. Gentian (25×35 mm)	2·50	1·70

Nos. 35-44 were also issued by Fukushima, Hokkaido, Kanagawa and Yamagata on 1 July 2008.

NAGASAKI

1990. Flowers.

1	62y. As Type **1475** of Japan	1·20	80

1 Ship and Gateway

1990. Journey Expo.

2	**1**	62y. multicoloured	1·20	80

2 Dragon Dance, Kunci Festival

1994

3	**2**	62y. multicoloured	1·90	1·30

1997. Fukuoka. Multicoloured.

4	80y. Fukuoka Type **4**	1·80	1·20
5	80y. Early rail way and map	1·80	1·20
6	80y. Interchange and map	1·80	1·20
7	80y. Building and map	1·80	1·20

Nos. 4-7 were issued together, se-tenant, forming a composite design.

Nos. 4-7 were also issued by Saga and Fukuoka.

3 Mount Heisei Shinzan

1998

8	**3**	80y. multicoloured	2·10	1·40

4 Dejima (artificial island)

1999

9	**4**	80y. multicoloured	2·10	1·40

5 Former Alt House and Part of Former Ringer House

2002. Glover Garden (home of Thomas Blake Glover (industrialist)). Multicoloured.

10	50y. Type **5**	1·50	1·00
11	50y. Part of former Ringer House and former Glover House	1·50	1·00

Nos. 10-11 were issued together, se-tenant, forming a composite design.

6 Tulips and Huis Ten Bosch (Nagasaki)

2005. Flowers and Scenery of Kyushu. Mult.

12	50y. Type **6**	1·60	1·10
13	50y. Sakura (cherry blossoms) and Kanmon bridge (Fukuoka)	1·60	1·10
14	50y. Kusunohana (camphor blossoms) and Ariake Sea (Saga)	1·60	1·10
15	50y. Unzen-Tsutsuji (azaleas) and Mt. Fugendake (Nagasaki)	1·60	1·10
16	50y. Ume Blossom and Dazaifu-Tenmangu Shrine (Fukuoka)	1·60	1·10
17	5y. Rindou (gentians) and Mt. Aso (Kumamoto)	1·60	1·10
18	50y. Ume blossoms and Mt. Takasaki (Ooita)	1·60	1·10
19	50y. Hamayu (crinums) and Nichinan beach (Miyazaki)	1·60	1·10
20	50y. Miyama-Kirishima (azaleas) and Kirishima mountains (Kagoshima)	1·60	1·10
21	50y. Hibiscus and Adan (screw-pine) (Kagoshima)	1·60	1·10

Nos. 12-21 were also issued by Fukuoka, Saga, Kumamoto, Oita, Miyazaki and Kagoshima.

7 Cosmos and Kujukushima islands (Nagasaki)

2006. Flowers and Scenery of Kyushu (2nd series). Multicoloured.

22	80y. Daffodils and Nokonoshima Island (Fukuoka)	2·10	1·40
23	80y. Chinese bellflowers and Hiraodai (Fukuoka)	2·10	1·40
24	80y. Hydrangeas and Mikaerinotaki fall (Saga)	2·10	1·40
25	80y. Type **7**	2·10	1·40
26	80y. Camellias and the five bridges of Amakusa (Kumamoto)	2·10	1·40
27	80y. Purple flowers and Mt. Aso (Kumamoto)	2·10	1·40
28	80y. Primroses and Mt. Yufudake (Oita)	2·10	1·40
29	80y. Lavender and Kujurenzan (Oita)	2·10	1·40
30	80y. Poppies and Mt. Hinamoridake (Miyazaki)	2·10	1·40
31	80y. Field of yellow flowers and Mt. Kaimondake (Kagoshima)	2·10	1·40

Nos. 22-31 were also issued by Fukuoka, Miyasaki, Saga, Kumamoto, Oita and Kagoshima.

NARA

1990. Flowers.

1	62y. As Type **1462** of Japan	3·00	2·00

1 Mountain, Temple and Building

1991. Yoshino. Multicoloured.

2	62y. Type **1**	1·50	1·00
3	62y. Blossom	1·50	1·00

1995. Yoshino. Multicoloured.

4	80y. Mountain, temple and building (As Type **1**)	1·80	80
5	80y. Blossom (As No. 3)	1·80	80

2 Grass burning, Mount Wakakusa

1996

6	**2**	50y. multicoloured	1·30	80

3 Birds and Landscape

1999. Asuka. Multicoloured.

7	80y. Type **3**	2·10	1·40
8	80y. Kofun (megalithic tomb)	2·10	1·40

4 Murouji's Five-Storied Pagoda and Rhododendrons

2004. National Heritage.

9	**4**	80y. multicoloured	2·50	1·70

5 Yae-zakura (double cherry blossoms) (Nara)

2006. Flowers of Kinki. Multicoloured.

10	50y. Type **5**	1·30	80
11	50y. Nozigiku (wild chrysanthemums) (Hyogo)	1·30	80
12	50y. Shakunage (rhododendron) (Shiga)	1·30	80
13	50y. Ume blossoms (Wakayama)	1·30	80
14	50y. Sakuraso (primrose) (Osaka)	1·30	80
15	50y. Shidare-zakura (weeping cherry) (Kyoto)	1·30	80

Nos. 10-15 were also issued by Osaka, Hyogo, Shiga, Wakayama and Kyoto.

6 Koriyama Castle

2007. Castles in Kinki Region. Multicoloured.

16	50y. Type **6**	1·60	1·10
17	50y. Hikone	1·60	1·10
18	50y. Himeji	1·60	1·10
19	50y. Osaka	1·60	1·10
20	50y. Wakayama	1·60	1·10

Nos. 16-20 were also issued by Hyogo, Osaka, Shiga and Wakayama on 1 June 2007.

7 Yaezakura Cherry Blossom

2009. Prefectural Flowers. Multicoloured.

21	50y. Somei Yoshino cherry blossom (Tokyo)	1·60	1·10

22	50y. Yashio tsutsuji (*Rhododendron albrechtii*) (Tochigi)	1·60	1·10
23	50y. Tulips (Niigata)	1·60	1·10
24	50y. Rhododendron (*Rhododendron japonicum*) (Shiga)	1·60	1·10
25	50y. Type **7** (Nara)	1·60	1·10
26	80y. Somei Yoshino cherry blossom (Tokyo)	2·50	1·70
27	80y. Yashio tsutsuji (*Rhododendron albrechtii*) (Tochigi)	2·50	1·70
28	80y. Tulips (Niigata)	2·50	1·70
29	80y. Rhododendron (*Rhododendron japonicum*) (Shiga)	2·50	1·70
30	80y. Yaezakura cherry blossom (Nara)	2·50	1·70

Stamps of the same design were issued by Tokyo, Niigata, Shiga, and Tochigi on 2 February 2009.

NIIGATA

1 Prefecture Hall

1989

1	1	62y. multicoloured	1·30	70

1990. Flowers.

2	62y. As Type **1450** of Japan	1·20	80

2 Koi Carp

1991

3	2	62y. multicoloured	1·80	70

3 Gogo-an (Ryokon's hermit hut)

1992

4	3	41y. multicoloured	1·20	80

4 Soma Gyofu (poet)

1995

5	4	80y. multicoloured	1·90	1·30

5 Hanayome

1997. Seto no Hanayome (The Inland Sea Bride).

6	5	50y. multicoloured	1·30	90

6 Snow-covered Buildings

1999. Snow Festival.

7	6	80y. multicoloured	2·10	1·40

7 Kites

1999. Kite Battle, Shirone. Multicoloured.

8	80y. Type **7**	2·10	1·40
9	80y. Kites (different)	2·10	1·40

Nos. 8-9 were issued together, se-tenant, forming a composite design.

8 Two Ibis

1999. Toki (ibis (prefecture official bird)). Multicoloured.

10	80y. Type **8**	2·10	1·40
11	80y. Ibis in flight	2·10	1·40

9 Cherry Blossoms, Takada Castle at Night

2001

12	9	80y. multicoloured	2·40	1·60

10 Fireworks

2001. Grand Firework Festival, Nagaoka. Multicoloured.

13	50y. Type **10**	1·50	1·00
14	50y. Fireworks (different)	1·50	1·00

Nos. 13-14 were issued together, se-tenant, forming a composite design.

11 Camellias and Kamoyama Kouen Park (Chu'etsu area)

2002. Flowers of Echigo. Multicoloured.

15	50y. Type **11**	1·50	1·00
16	50y. Daylily and Oonogame (Sado area)	1·50	1·00
17	50y. Iris and Ijimino Kouen Park (Ka'etsu area)	1·50	1·00
18	50y. *Shortia soldanelloides* and Mt. Myoukousan (Joetsu area)	1·50	1·00

2006. Nature of Shin'etsu. Nagano. Multicoloured.

19	80y. As Type **17** of Nagano	2·10	1·40
20	80y. Sankayou (*Diphylleia cymosa*)	2·10	1·40
21	80y. Mt. Asamayama	2·10	1·20
22	80y. Sakurasou (*Primula sieboldii*)	2·10	1·40

Nos. 9-22 were also issued by Nagano.

12 Tulips

2007. Flora. Multicoloured.

23	80y. Type **12**	2·50	1·70
24	80y. Rice	2·50	1·70
25	80y. Pear 'Le Lectier'	2·50	1·70
26	80y. Primula	2·50	1·70
27	80y. Iris	2·50	1·70

13 Tulips (Niigata)

2009. Prefectural Flowers. Multicoloured.

28	50y. Somei Yoshino cherry blossom (Tokyo)	1·60	1·10
29	50y. Yashio tsutsuji (*Rhododendron albrechtii*) (Tochigi)	1·60	1·10
30	50y. Type **13**	1·60	1·10
31	50y. Rhododendron (*Rhododendron japonicum*) (Shiga)	1·60	1·10
32	50y. Yaezakura Cherry Blossom (Nara)	1·60	1·10
33	80y. Somei Yoshino cherry blossom (Tokyo)	2·50	1·70
34	80y. Yashio tsutsuji (*Rhododendron albrechtii*) (Tochigi)	2·50	1·70
35	80y. Tulips (Niigata)	2·50	1·70
36	80y. Rhododendron (*Rhododendron japonicum*) (Shiga)	2·50	1·70
37	80y. Yaezakura cherry blossom (Nara)	2·50	1·70

Stamps of the same design were issued by Nara, Tokyo, Shiga, and Tochigi on 2 February 2009.

OITA

1 Monkey

1989

1	1	62y. multicoloured	1·50	80

1990

2	62y. As Type **1477** of Japan	1·50	80

2 Tsurusaki Dancers

1992

3	2	62y. multicoloured	1·20	80

3 Gion Festival, Hita

1998

4	3	50y. multicoloured	1·30	90

4 Cliffs

1999. Blue Tunnels. Multicoloured.

5	80y. Type **4**	2·10	1·40
6	80y. Tunnel	2·10	1·40

5 International Wheelchair Marathon

2000

7	5	80y. multicoloured	2·75	1·90

6 Ume Blossoms and Mount Takasaki (Ooita)

2005. Flowers and Scenery of Kyushu. Mult.

8	50y. Type **6**	1·60	1·10
9	50y. Sakura (cherry blossoms) and Kanmon bridge (Fukuoka)	1·60	1·10
10	50y. Kusunohana (camphor blossoms) and Ariake Sea (Saga)	1·60	1·10
11	50y. Unzen-Tsutsuji (azaleas) and Mt. Fugendake (Nagasaki)	1·60	1·10
12	50y. Tulips and Huis Ten Bosch (Nagasaki)	1·60	1·10
13	50y. Rindou (gentians) and Mt. Aso (Kumamoto)	1·60	1·10
14	50y. Ume blossom and Dazaifu-Tenmangu Shrine (Fukuoka)	1·60	1·10
15	50y. Hamayu (crinums) and Nichinan beach (Miyazaki)	1·60	1·10
16	50y. Miyama-Kirishima (azaleas) and Kirishima mountains (Kagoshima)	1·60	1·10
17	50y. Hibiscus and Adan (screw-pine) (Kagoshima)	1·60	1·10

Nos. 8-17 were also issued by Fukuoka, Nagasaki, Saga, Miyazaki, Kumamoto and Kagoshima.

7 Primroses and Mt. Yufudake (Oita)

2006. Flowers and Scenery of Kyushu (2nd series). Multicoloured.

18	80y. Daffodils and Nokonoshima Island (Fukuoka)	2·10	1·40
19	80y. Chinese bellflowers and Hiraodai (Fukuoka)	2·10	1·40
20	80y. Hydrangeas and Mikaerinotaki fall (Saga)	2·10	1·40
21	80y. Cosmos and Kujukushima islands (Nagasaki)	2·10	1·40
22	80y. Camellias and the five bridges of Amakusa (Kumamoto)	2·10	1·40
23	80y. Purple flowers and Mt. Aso (Kumamoto)	2·10	1·40
24	80y. Type **7**	2·10	1·40
25	80y. Lavender and Kujurenzan (Oita)	2·10	1·40
26	80y. Poppies and Mt. Hinamoridake (Miyazaki)	2·10	1·40
27	80y. Field of yellow flowers and Mt. Kaimondake (Kagoshima)	2·10	1·40

Nos. 18-27 were also issued by Fukuoka, Nagasaki, Saga, Kumamoto, Miyazaki and Kagoshima.

8 Oita Sports Stadium

2008. 63rd National Sports Meet. Multicoloured.

28	50y. Type **8**	1·60	1·10
29	50y. Fencing	1·60	1·10
30	50y. Athletics		
31	50y. Canoeing	1·60	1·10

9 Ume blossom (*Prunus mume* var. bungo)

10 Ume blossom (*Prunus mume* var. bungo)

2009. Prefectural Flowers. Multicoloured.

32	50y. Peach blossom (Okayama)	1·70	1·30
33	50y. Rape flowers (Chiba)	1·70	1·30
34	50y. Plum blossom and primula (Osaka)	1·70	1·30
35	50y. Bayberry (Kochi)	1·70	1·30
36	50y. Type **9** (Oita)	1·70	1·30
37	80y. Peach blossom (Okayama) (different)	2·75	1·70
38	80y. Rape flowers (Chiba) (different)	2·75	1·70
39	80y. Plum blossom and primula (Osaka) (different)	2·75	1·70
40	80y. Bayberry (Kochi) (different)	2·75	1·70
41	80y. Type **10** (Oita)	2·75	1·70

Stamps of the same design were issued by Chiba, Kochi, Okayama and Osaka on 1 Dec 2009.

OKAYAMA

1990. Flowers.

1	62y. As Type **1466** of Japan	1·20	80

1 Pot with Lid

1991. Bizen Ware. Multicoloured.

2	62y. Type **1**	1·20	80
3	62y. Red glazed pot	1·20	80

2 Calligrapher

1995. Niimi-no-sho Festival.

3a	**2**	80y. multicoloured	2·10	1·40

3 Castle

1997. 400th Anniv of Okayama Castle.

4	**3**	80y. multicoloured	2·10	1·40

1999

5	80y. As Type **4** of Hiroshima	2·10	1·40

No. 5 was also issued by Hiroshima.

4 Kurashiki District

1999

6	**4**	80y. multicoloured	2·10	1·40

5 Cranes and Ume Blossom

2000. 300th Anniv of Korkuen Garden. Mult.

7	80y. Type **5**	2·40	1·60
8	80y. Kayou-no-ike pond	2·40	1·60
9	80y. Yuishinzan mound	2·40	1·60
10	80y. Cranes flying over frozen stream	2·40	1·60

6 Momonohana (peach blossoms) and Traditional Houses, Kurashiki

2000. Multicoloured.

11	50y. Type **6**	1·50	1·00
12	50y. Natsumikan (summer-orange blossoms) and sea	1·50	1·00
13	50y. Nijisseikinashi (Japanese pear tree) and Tottori dune	1·50	1·00
14	50y. Botan (peonies) and Izumo-taisha Shrine	1·50	1·00
15	50y. Momiji (maple leaves) and Itsukushima Shrine Gate	1·50	1·00

Nos. 11-15 were also issued by Yamaguchi, Shimane, Tottori and Hiroshima.

7 Cherry Blossom, Hiikawa River

2002. Multicoloured.

16	50y. Type **7**	1·50	1·00
17	50y. Pagoda, Bicchu-Kokubunji Temple	1·50	1·00

Nos. 16-17 were also issued by Shimane.

8 Main Hall, Kibitsu-jinja Shrine and Southern Zuijin Gate

2003. Kibitsu Shrine.

18	**8**	80y. multicoloured	2·40	1·60

9 Runner and Momotaro Stadium

2005. 60th National Athletic Meet.

19	**9**	50y. multicoloured	1·60	1·10

10 Peach Blossoms and Seto-oohashi Bridge (Okayama)

2006. Flowers of Chugoku. Multicoloured.

20	50y. Type **10**	1·50	1·00
21	50y. Tree peonies and Hinomisaki Lighthouse (Shimane)	1·50	1·00
22	50y. Pear blossom and Yumigahama beach (Tottori)	1·50	1·00
23	50y. Maple leaves and Miyajima shrine (Hiroshima)	1·50	1·00
24	50y. Chinese citron blossom and Oomijima island (Yamaguchi)	1·50	1·00

Nos. 20-4 were also issued by Tottori, Shimane, Hiroshima, and Yamaguchi.

11 Pheasants

2007. Birds. Multicoloured.

25	80y. Type **11**	2·50	1·70
26	80y. Mandarin ducks	2·50	1·70
27	80y. Swans	2·50	1·70
28	80y. Ducks swimming	2·50	1·70
29	80y. Cranes	2·50	1·70

Nos. 25-9 were also issued by Hiroshima, Shimane, Tottori and Yamaguchi on 1 May 2007.

12 Peach Blossom

13 Peach Blossom

2009. Prefectural Flowers. Multicoloured.

30	50y. Type **12** (Okayama)	1·70	1·10
31	50y. Rape flowers (Chiba)	1·70	1·10
32	50y. Plum blossom and primula (Osaka)	1·70	1·10
33	50y. Bayberry (Kochi)	1·70	1·10
34	50y. Ume blossom (*Prunus mume* var. bungo) (Oita)	1·70	1·10
35	80y. Type **13** (Okayama)	2·75	1·70
36	80y. Rape flowers (Chiba) (different)	2·75	1·70
37	80y. Plum blossom and primula (Osaka) (different)		
38	80y. Bayberry (Kochi) (different)	2·75	1·70
39	80y. Ume blossom (*Prunus mume* var. bungo) (Oita) (different)	2·75	1·70

Stamps of the same design were issued by Chiba, Kochi, Oita and Osaka on 1 Dec 2009.

OKINAWA

1 Temple, Shurei-no-mon

1989

1	**1**	62y. multicoloured	1·30	80

1990. Flowers.

2	62y. As Type **1480** of Japan	1·30	80

2 Ryukyu Dancer

1990

3	**2**	62y. multicoloured	1·20	80

3 Black Pearls

1991

4	**3**	41y. multicoloured	1·50	70

4 Boat Race

1992. Naha Ha-ree.

5	**4**	62y. multicoloured	1·20	80

5 Tug of War

1994

6	**5**	50y. multicoloured	1·20	80

6 Eisa Drummers

1995

7	**6**	80y. multicoloured	1·90	1·30

7 Temple and Dragon

1996. Shurijo.

8	**7**	80y. multicoloured	2·10	1·40

8 Pineapples

1997. Fruit. Multicoloured.

9	50y. Type **8**	1·30	90
10	50y. Mangoes	1·30	90

9 Shanshin (three stringed instrument)

1998

11	**9**	80y. multicoloured	2·10	1·40

3 Ryukyu Island 5 sen Stamp (Type **1**)

1998. 50th Anniv of Okinawa Stamps. Multd.

12	80y. Type **10**	2·10	1·40
13	80y. Ryukyu Island 5c. stamp (Type **218**)	2·10	1·40

11 Woman

1999. 125th Anniv of Post. Multicoloured.

14	80y. Type **11**	2·10	1·40
15	80y. Masks	2·10	1·40

12 Ryukyu Dancers

1999

16	**12**	80y. multicoloured	2·10	1·40

13 Boat, Fishers and Iejima Tatchu Rock

1999

17	**13**	80y. multicoloured	2·10	1·40

14 Royal Family Country Villa and Bridge

1999. Shikina-en Gardens. Multicoloured.

18	50y. Type **14**	1·50	1·00
19	50y. Tea house and bridge	1·50	1·00

Nos. 18-19 were issued together, se-tenant, forming a composite design.

15 Abaca Cloth (Tamanaha Yukou)

2000

20	**15**	50y. multicoloured	1·80	1·20

16 Bankoku Shinryokan Conference Centre

2000

21	**16**	80y. multicoloured	2·75	1·80

17 Memorial and Flowers

2001

22	**17**	80y. multicoloured	2·40	1·60

18 Taiwan Cherry and Iejima Island

2002. Flowers. Multicoloured.

23	50y. Type **18**	1·50	1·00
24	50y. Hibiscus and Kaichu-douro highway	1·50	1·00
25	50y. Bougainvillea and traditional house, Tsuboya	1·50	1·00
26	50y. Lilies and Higashi-hennazaki	1·50	1·00
27	50y. Seishika flowers and Seishika bridge	1·50	1·00

19 Monorail, Shurijo Castle, and Coral Tree Flowers

2003. Okinawa Urban Monorail. Multicoloured.

28	50y. Type **19**	1·60	1·10
29	50y. Monorail, Naha Airport, and hibiscus	1·60	1·10

20 Dancer and Theatre Building

2005. Ryukyuan Dance and National Theatre Okinawa.

30	**20**	50y. multicoloured	1·60	1·10

21 Goya (bitter melon)

2005

31	**21**	50y. multicoloured	1·60	1·10

22 Whale Shark

2007. Sea Fauna. Multicoloured.

32	80y. Type **22**	2·50	1·70
33	80y. Angelfish	2·50	1·70
34	80y. Clownfish	2·50	1·70
35	80y. Blue damselfish	2·50	1·70
36	80y. Manta ray	2·50	1·70

Nos. 32-6 were issued together, se-tenant, each strip forming a composite design.

23-24 Drummers, left

2008. Tanabata Festival. Multicoloured.

37	50y. Type **23**	1·60	1·10
38	50y. Type **24**	1·60	1·10
39	50y. Lanterns, left	1·60	1·10
40	50y. Lanterns, right	1·60	1·10
41	50y. Procession and roofs, left	1·60	1·10
42	50y. Procession and roofs, right	1·60	1·10
43	50y. Dancers, left	1·60	1·10
44	50y. Dancers, right	1·60	1·10
45	50y. Procession, left	1·60	1·10
46	50y. Procession, right	1·60	1·10

Nos. 37-8, 39-40, 41-2, 43-4 and 45-6 were issued together, se-tenant, each pair forming a composite design.

Nos. 37-46 were also issued by Tokushima, Tokyo, Miyagi and Fukuoka on 1 August 2008.

OSAKA

1 Faces

1989. Bunraku.

1	**1**	62y. multicoloured	1·30	70

1990

2	62y. As Type **1460** of Japan	1·20	80

2 Symbols of Business

1992. Business Park.

3	**2**	41y. multicoloured	1·00	50

3 Danjiri Festival

1995

4	**3**	80y. multicoloured	1·90	1·30

4 Gymnast

1999

5	**4**	80y. multicoloured	2·10	1·40

5 Performers and Puppets

2000. World Performing Arts Festival.

6	**5**	80y. multicoloured	2·75	1·80

6 Thunder God playing Table Tennis

2001. Sports. Multicoloured.

7	50y. Type **6**	1·50	1·00
8	50y. Wind God playing table tennis	1·50	1·00
9	50y. Bowling	1·50	1·00
10	50y. Taekwondo	1·50	1·00

7 Namdaemun, Seoul and Doton-bori, Osaka

2001. 14th General Assembly of World Trade Organization. Multicoloured.

11	80y. Type **7**	2·40	1·60
12	80y. Bunraku actors, Japan and Nong-ak drummers, Korea	2·40	1·60

8 Osaka Dome and Lion (part of railing, Naniwabashi bridge)

2002. 85th Lions Clubs International Convention.

13	**8**	80y. multicoloured	2·20	1·50

9 Scouts and Osaka Castle

2002. 23rd Asia-Pacific Scout Jamboree.

14	**9**	80y. multicoloured	1·80	1·20

10 Rotary Emblem and Irises

2004. Rotary International Convention, Osaka.

15	**10**	80y. multicoloured	2·50	1·70

11 Sakuraso (primrose) (Osaka)

2006. Flowers of Kinki. Multicoloured.

No.	Description	Mint	Used
16	50y. Type **11**	1·50	1·00
17	50y. Shidare-zakura (weeping cherry) (Kyoto)	1·50	1·00
18	50y. Yae-zakura (double cherry blossoms) (Nara)	1·50	1·00
19	50y. Nozigiku (wild chrysanthemums) (Hyogo)	1·50	1·00
20	50y. Shakunage (rhododendron) (Shiga)	1·50	1·00
21	50y. Ume blossoms (Wakayama)	1·50	1·00

Nos. 16-21 were also issued by Hyogo, Nara, Shiga, Wakayama and Kyoto.

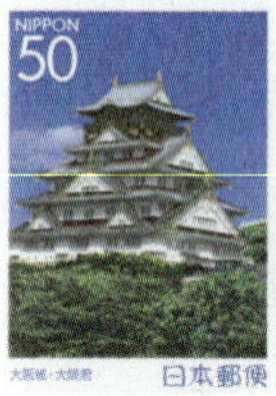

12 Osaka Castle

2007. Castles in Kinki Region. Multicoloured.

No.	Description	Mint	Used
22	50y. Type **12**	1·60	1·10
23	50y. Koriyama	1·60	1·10
24	50y. Hikone	1·60	1·10
25	50y. Himeji	1·60	1·10
26	50y. Wakayama	1·60	1·10

Nos. 22-6 were also issued by Hyogo, Nara, Shiga and Wakayama on 1 June 2007.

13 Plum Blossom and Primula

14 Plum Blossom and Primula

2009. Prefectural Flowers. Multicoloured.

No.	Description	Mint	Used
27	50y. Peach blossom (Okayama)	1·70	1·30
28	50y. Rape flowers (Chiba)	1·70	1·30
29	50y. Type **13** (Osaka)	1·70	1·30
30	50y. Bayberry (Kochi)	1·70	1·30
31	50y. Ume blossom (*Prunus mume* var. bungo) (Oita)	1·70	1·30
32	80y. Peach blossom (Okayama) (different)	2·75	1·70
33	80y. Rape flowers (Chiba) (different)	2·75	1·70
34	80y. Type **14** (Osaka)	2·75	1·70
35	80y. Bayberry (Kochi) (different)	2·75	1·70
36	80y. Ume blossom (*Prunus mume* var. bungo) (Oita) (different)	2·75	1·70

Stamps of the same design were issued by Chiba, Kochi, Oita and Okayama on 1 Dec 2009.

SAGA

1990

No.	Type	Description	Mint	Used
1		62y. As Type **1474** of Japan	1·20	80

1 Yoshinogari Historical Park

1991

No.	Type	Description	Mint	Used
2	**1**	62y. multicoloured	1·20	80

2 Karatsu-Kunchi

1995

No.	Type	Description	Mint	Used
3	**2**	80y. multicoloured	1·90	1·30

3 Vase

1996. World Ceramic Exhibition.

No.	Type	Description	Mint	Used
4	**3**	80y. multicoloured	1·80	1·20

1997. Multicoloured.

No.	Description	Mint	Used
5	80y. As Type **4** of Fukuoka	1·80	1·20
6	80y. Early rail way and map	1·80	1·20
7	80y. Interchange and map	1·80	1·20
8	80y. Building and map	1·80	1·20

Nos. 5-8 were issued together, se-tenant, forming a composite design.

Nos. 5-8 were also issued by Nagasaki and Fukuoka.

4 Yoshinogari Historical Park

1999

No.	Type	Description	Mint	Used
9	**4**	80y. multicoloured	2·20	1·50

5 Child in Air Balloon

2000. International Balloon Festival.

No.	Type	Description	Mint	Used
10	**5**	80y. multicoloured	2·75	1·90

6 Iroe Komainu (lion dog) and 'Sometsuke Arita Sarayama-shokunin-zukushi-ezu oozara' (blue and white ceramic ware depicting ceramic workers)

2003. Imari-Arita Ceramics.

No.	Type	Description	Mint	Used
11	**6**	80y. multicoloured	2·40	1·60

7 Kusunohana (camphor blossoms) and Ariake Sea (Saga)

2005. Multicoloured.

No.	Description	Mint	Used
12	50y. Type **7**	1·60	1·10
13	50y. Sakura (cherry blossoms) and Kanmon bridge (Fukuoka)	1·60	1·10
14	50y. Ume Blossom and Dazaifu-Tenmangu Shrine (Fukuoka)	1·60	1·10
15	50y. Unzen-Tsutsuji (azaleas) and Mt. Fugendake (Nagasaki)	1·60	1·10
16	50y. Tulips and Huis Ten Bosch (Nagasaki)	1·60	1·10
17	50y. Rindou (gentians) and Mt. Aso (Kumamoto)	1·60	1·10
18	50y. Ume blossoms and Mt. Takasaki (Ooita)	1·60	1·10
19	50y. Hamayu (crinums) and Nichinan beach (Miyazaki)	1·60	1·10
20	50y. Miyama-Kirishima (azaleas) and Kirishima mountains (Kagoshima)	1·60	1·10
21	50y. Hibiscus and Adan (screw-pine) (Kagoshima)	1·60	1·10

Nos. 12-21 were also issued by Fukuoka, Nagasaki, Kumamoto, Oita, Miyazaki and Kagoshima.

8 Hydrangeas and Mikaerinotaki Falls (Saga)

2006. Flowers and Scenery of Kyushu (2nd series). Multicoloured.

No.	Description	Mint	Used
22	80y. Daffodils and Nokonoshima Island (Fukuoka)	2·40	1·60
23	80y. Chinese bellflowers and Hiraodai (Fukuoka)	2·40	1·60
24	80y. Type **8**	2·40	1·60
25	80y. Cosmos and Kujukushima islands (Nagasaki)	2·40	1·60
26	80y. Camellias and the five bridges of Amakusa (Kumamoto)	2·40	1·60
27	80y. Purple flowers and Mt. Aso (Kumamoto)	2·40	1·60
28	80y. Primroses and Mt. Yufudake (Oita)	2·40	1·60
29	80y. Lavender and Kujurenzan (Oita)	2·40	1·60
30	80y. Poppies and Mt. Hinamoridake (Miyazaki)	2·40	1·60
31	80y. Field of yellow flowers and Mt. Kaimondake (Kagoshima)	2·40	1·60

Nos. 22-31 were also issued by Fukuoka, Nagasaki, Kumamoto, Oita, Miyazaki and Kagoshima.

SAITAMA

1990

No.	Type	Description	Mint	Used
1		62y. As Type **1444** of Japan	1·20	80

1 Stylized Children

1990. Toryanse (children's song).

No.	Type	Description	Mint	Used
2	**1**	62y. multicoloured	1·20	80

2 Kuroyama-santaki Waterfalls

1995

No.	Type	Description	Mint	Used
3	**2**	80y. multicoloured	1·90	1·30

3 Hozoji Pond

1997

No.	Type	Description	Mint	Used
4	**3**	50y. multicoloured	1·80	1·20

4 Collared Doves and Walkers

1997. Walking Festival.

No.	Type	Description	Mint	Used
5	**4**	80y. multicoloured	2·10	1·40

5 Dove and Buildings

2000. New Urban Centre. Multicoloured.

No.	Description	Mint	Used
6	50y. Type **5**	1·50	1·00
7	50y. Buildings and flowers	1·50	1·00

Nos. 6-7 were issued together, se-tenant, forming a composite design.

6 Yatai and Fireworks

2000. Night Festival, Chichibu. Multicoloured.

No.	Description	Mint	Used
8	80y. Type **6**	2·75	1·90
9	80y. Kasahoko	2·75	1·90

7 Bonsai Tree

2002

No.	Type	Description	Mint	Used
10	**7**	80y. multicoloured	2·20	1·50

8 Primrose and Tajimagahara Primrose Field

2004. Flowers of Kanto (1st issue). Multicoloured.

No.	Description	Mint	Used
11	50y. Type **8**	1·60	1·10
12	50y. Yoshi azalea and Lake Chuzenjiko	1·60	1·10
13	50y. Japanese azalea and Mt. Akagisan	1·60	1·10
14	50y. Rose and Mount Tsukubasan	1·60	1·10
15	50y. Rape blossom and Nojimazaki lighthouse	1·60	1·10

See also Nos. 17-21.

Nos. 11-15 were also issued by Tochigi, Chiba, Gunma and Ibaraki.

9 Gymnast

2004. National Athletic Meet.

No.	Type	Description	Mint	Used
16	**9**	50y. multicoloured	1·60	1·10

10 Allspice Flowers and Mount Bukousan (Saitama)

2005. Flowers of Kanto (2nd issue). Multicoloured.

17 50y. Type **10** 1·60 1·10
18 50y. Nikko-kisuge (Nikko day lily) and Kirifuri Heights (Tochigi) 1·60 1·10
19 50y. Sunflowers at Hana-hotaru (Chiba) 1·60 1·10
20 50y. Bush clover, Kairakuen garden (Ibaraki) 1·60 1·10
21 50y. Azaleas, Tsutsujigaoka Park (Gunma) 1·60 1·10

Nos. 17-21 were also issued by Gunma, Tochigi, Chiba and Ibaraki.

Nos. 22-26 and Type **11** have been left for 'Fruits of Kanto', issued on 1 September 2006, not yet received.

SHIGA

1 Figurine

1989. Shigaraki Ware.

1 **1** 62y. multicoloured 1·30 60

1990. Flowers.

2 62y. As Type **1458** of Japan 3·00 2·00

2 Yachts, Lake Biwa

1993

3 **2** 62y. multicoloured 1·50 1·00

3 Temmple

1996. Mount Hiei.

4 **3** 80y. multicoloured 2·10 1·40

4 Trout and Rhododendron

2001. 9th International Conference on the Conservation and Management of Lakes.

5 **4** 50y. multicoloured 1·60 1·10

5 Shakunage (rhododendron) (Shiga)

2006. Flowers of Kinki. Multicoloured.

6 50y. Yae-zakura (double cherry blossoms) (Nara) 1·60 1·10
7 50y. Nozigiku (wild chrysanthemums) (Hyogo) 1·60 1·10
8 50y. Type **5** 1·60 1·10
9 50y. Ume blossoms (Wakayama) 1·60 1·10
10 50y. Sakuraso (primrose) (Osaka) 1·60 1·10
11 50y. Shidare-zakura (weeping cherry) (Kyoto) 1·50 1·10

Nos. 6-11 were also issued by Osaka, Hyogo, Nara, Wakayama and Kyoto.

6 Hikone Castle

2007. Castles in Kinki Region. Multicoloured. Photo.

12 50y. Type **6** 1·60 1·10
13 50y. Koriyama 1·60 1·10
14 50y. Himeji 1·60 1·10
15 50y. Osaka 1·60 1·10
16 50y. Wakayama 1·60 1·10

Nos. 12-16 were also issued by Hyogo, Nara, Osaka and Wakayama on 1 June 2007.

SHIMANE

1990. Flowers.

1 62y. As Type **1465** of Japan 1·20 80

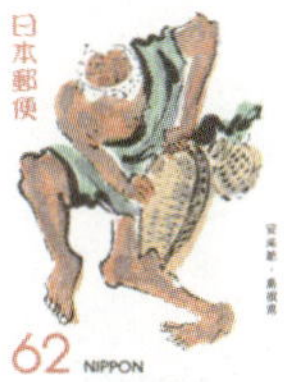

1 Yasukibushi Dancer

1990

2 **1** 62y. multicoloured 1·20 80

2 Izumo-no-Okuni (dancer and founder Kubuki theatre)

1994

3 **2** 80y. multicoloured 1·90 1·10

3 Railway Bridge, Tsuwano

1999. Multicoloured.

4 80y. Type **3** 2·10 1·40
5 80y. Street, Hagi 2·10 1·40

Nos. 4-5 were also issued by Yamaguchi.

4 Botan (peonies) and Izumo-taisha Shrine

2000. Multicoloured.

6 50y. Type **4** 1·50 1·00
7 50y. Natsumikan (summer-orange blossoms) and sea 1·50 1·00
8 50y. Nijisseikinashi (Japanese pear tree) and Tottori dune 1·50 1·00
9 50y. Momonohana (peach blossoms) and traditional houses in Kurashiki 1·50 1·00
10 50y. Momiji (maple leaves) and Itsukushima Shrine Gate 1·50 1·00

Nos. 6-10 were also issued by Yamaguchi, Shimane, Okayama and Hiroshima.

5 Matsue Castle and Cherry Blossoms

2001. Matsue Castle and Tea Ceremony Culture. Multicoloured.

11 80y. Type **5** 2·40 1·60
12 80y. Meimei-an teahouse and camellias 2·40 1·60

6 Pagoda, Bicchu-Kokubunji Temple

2002. Multicoloured.

13 50y. Type **6** 1·50 1·00
14 50y. Cherry Blossom, Hiikawa River 1·50 1·00

Nos. 13-14 were also issued by Okayama.

7 Tree Peonies and Hinomisaki Lighthouse (Shimane)

2006. Flowers of Chugoku. Multicoloured.

15 50y. Type **7** 1·50 1·00
16 50y. Pear blossom and Yumigahama Beach (Tottori) 1·50 1·00
17 50y. Peach blossoms and Seto-oohashi bridge (Okayama) 1·50 1·00
18 50y. Maple leaves and Miyajima shrine (Hiroshima) 1·50 1·00
19 50y. Chinese citron blossom and Oomijima island (Yamaguchi) 1·50 1·00

Nos. 15-19 were also issued by Tottori, Okayama, Hiroshima and Yamaguchi.

8 Swans

2007. Birds. Multicoloured.

20 80y. Type **8** 2·50 1·70
21 80y. Mandarin ducks 2·50 1·70
22 80y. Pheasants 2·50 1·70
23 80y. Ducks swimming 2·50 1·70
24 80y. Cranes 2·50 1·70

Nos. 20-24 were also issued by Hiroshima, Okayama, Tottori and Yamaguchi on 1 May 2007.

SHIZUOKA

1990. Flowers.

1 62y. As Type **1455** of Japan 3·00 2·00

1 Tea Gatherer

1990

2 **1** 62y. multicoloured 1·20 50

2 Magpie and Mount Fuji

1993

3 **2** 41y. multicoloured 1·30 90

3 Tea Pickers

1997

4 **3** 50y. multicoloured 1·30 90

4 Cattle and Mount Fuji

1997. Mount Fuji. Multicoloured.

5 80y. Type **4** 2·10 1·40
6 80y. Mount Fuji at dusk 2·10 1·40

5 Softball Players

1998

7 **5** 80y. multicoloured 2·10 1·40

6 Shimizu Port

1999

8 **6** 80y. multicoloured 2·10 1·40

7 Atami-baien Ume Orchard

2000. Izu. Multicoloured.

9 50y. Type **7** 1·80 1·20
10 50y. Kawazu-nanadaru waterfalls and statues 1·80 1·20

8 Palace Festival Float

2001. Hamamatsu Festival. Multicoloured.

11 80y. Type **8** 2·50 1·70
12 80y. Kite match 2·50 1·70

9 Football Players, Mount Fuji and Azaleas

2003. National Athletic Meet.

13	**9**	50y. multicoloured	1·60	1·10

10 Gerbera

2004. Flora. Multicoloured.

14	80y. Type **10**	2·50	1·70
15	80y. Carnations	2·50	1·70
16	80y. Roses	2·50	1·70
17	80y. Prairie gentian	2·50	1·70

11 Ryozenji Temple

2004. Cultural Heritage. Temples (1st series). Multicoloured.

18	80y. Type **11**	2·50	1·70
19	80y. Bells encircling tree, Gokurakuji Temple	2·50	1·70
20	80y. Courtyard, Konsenji Temple	2·50	1·70
21	80y. Row of statues, Dainichiji Temple	2·50	1·70
22	80y. Roofs, statue and pagoda, Tatsueji Temple	2·50	1·70
23	80y. Veranda and pagoda, Kakurinji Temple	2·50	1·70
24	80y. Trees at night, Tairyuji Temple	2·50	1·70
25	80y. Shrine and steps, Byou-douji Temple	2·50	1·70
26	80y. Decorated panels, Iwamo-toji Temple	2·50	1·70
27	80y. Stone turtle, Kongoufukuji Temple	2·50	1·70
28	80y. Plants, stone lantern and monks, Enkouji Temple	2·50	1·70
29	80y. Steps and gateway, Kanji-zaiji Temple	2·50	1·70
30	80y. Interior, Nankoubou Temple	2·50	1·70
31	80y. Pebbles and roofs, Taizanji Temple	2·50	1·70
32	80y. Autumn leaves and statue, Eifukuji Temple	2·50	1·70
33	80y. God (Bishamon)(statue), Sennyuji Temple	2·50	1·70
34	80y. Trees, bell and pathway, Shusshakaji Temple	2·50	1·70
35	80y. Wide path, tree, steps and gateway, Kouyamaji Temple	2·50	1·70
36	80y. Metal staff, Zentsuji Temple	2·50	1·70
37	80y. Courtyard, Kouzouji Temple	2·50	1·70

12 Silvereye Butterfly and Kawazu Cherry Blossoms

2006. Cherry Blossom. Multicoloured.

38	50y. Type **12**	1·60	1·10
39	50y. Blossom	1·60	1·10

13 Azalea and Coastline, Jogasaki

2007. Flowers and Scenery of Tokai. Multicoloured.

40	80y. Type **13**	2·50	1·70
41	80y. Iris	2·50	1·70
42	80y. Gassho-zukuri houses and vetch flowers	2·50	1·70
43	80y. Lily and Nagoya Castle	2·50	1·70
44	80y. Iris and Couple Rock	2·50	1·70

Nos. 40-4 were also issued by Aichi, Gifu and Mie on 2 April 2007.

TOCHIGI

1990. Flowers.

1	62y. As Type **1442** of Japan	1·20	80

1 Walkers in Countryside

1991

2	**1**	62y. multicoloured	1·20	80

2 Kirifuri-no-taki Waterfall

1995

3	**2**	50y. multicoloured	1·30	80

3 Mountain and Lake

1999. Lake Chuzenji. Multicoloured.

4	80y. Type **3**	2·10	1·40
5	80y. Autumn leaves and lake	2·10	1·40

4 Ashikaga School

2001. Ashikaga School. Multicoloured.

6	50y. Type **4**	2·10	1·40
7	80y. Gate, Ashikaga School	2·10	1·40

5 Rape Blossom and Nojimazaki Lighthouse

2004. Flowers of Kanto (1st issue). Multicoloured.

8	50y. Type **5**	1·60	1·10
9	50y. Yoshi azalea and Lake Chuzenjiko	1·60	1·10
10	50y. Japanese azalea and Mt. Akagisan	1·60	1·10
11	50y. Primrose and Tajimagahara native primrose field	1·60	1·10
12	50y. Rose and Mount Tsuku-basan	1·60	1·10

See also Nos. 13-17.

Nos. 8-12 were also issued by Tochigi, Saitama, Gunma and Ibaraki.

6 Nikko-kisuge (Nikko day lily) and Kirifuri Heights (Tochigi)

2005. Flowers of Kanto (2nd issue). Multicoloured.

13	50y. Type **6**	1·60	1·10
14	50y. Azaleas, Tsutsujigaoka Park (Gunma)	1·60	1·10
15	50y. Sunflowers at Hana-hotaru (Chiba)	1·60	1·10
16	50y. Bush clover, Kairakuen garden (Ibaraki)	1·60	1·10
17	50y. Allspice flowers and Mt. Bukousan (Saitama)	1·60	1·10

Nos. 13-17 were also issued by Gunma, Saitama, Chiba and Ibaraki.

8 Yashio tsutsuji (*Rhododendron albrechtii*)

2009. Prefectural Flowers. Multicoloured.

23	50y. Somei Yoshino cherry blossom (Tokyo)	1·60	1·10
24	50y. Type **8** (Tochigi)	1·60	1·10
25	50y. Tulips (Niigata)	1·60	1·10
26	50y. Rhododendron (*Rhododendron japonicum*) (Shiga)	1·60	1·10
27	50y. Yaezakura cherry blossom (Nara)	1·60	1·10
28	80y. Somei Yoshino cherry blossom (Tokyo)	2·50	1·70
29	80y. Yashio tsutsuji (*Rhododendron albrechtii*) (Tochigi)	2·50	1·70
30	80y. Tulips (Niigata)	2·50	1·70
31	80y. Rhododendron (*Rhododendron japonicum*) (Shiga)	2·50	1·70
32	80y. Yaezakura cherry blossom (Nara)	2·50	1·70

Nos. 18-22 and Type No. **7**have been left for 'Fruits of Kanto', issued on 1 September 206, not yet received.

Stamps of the same design were issued by Nara, Niigata, Shiga, and Tokyo on 2 February 2009.

TOKUSHIMA

1990

1	62y. As Type **1469** of Japan	1·50	1·00

1 Puppet (head and shoulders)

1991

2	**1**	62y. multicoloured	1·30	70

2 Awa-odori Dancers

1994

3	**2**	50y. multicoloured	1·50	1·00

3 Bridge

1998. Kobe-Awaji-Naruto Expressway. Multicoloured.

4	80y. Type **3**	2·10	1·10
5	80y. Bridge (different)	2·10	1·40

Nos. 4-5 were also issued by Hyogo.

4 Awa-odori Dancers

2000

6	**4**	80y. multicoloured		

5 Sudachi (sour citrus fruit) and Mt. Tsurugisan (Tokushima)

2002. Multicoloured.

7	50y. Type **5**	1·50	1·00
8	50y. Mikan (mandarin oranges) and Sata-misaki Promontory (Ehime)	1·50	1·00
9	50y. Yamamomo (bayberry) and Tengu highland (Kochi)	1·50	1·00
10	50y. Olive and Shodoshima island (Kagawa)	1·50	1·00

Nos. 7-10 were also issued by Ehime, Kochi and Kagawa.

2005. Cultural Heritage. Shizuoka Temples. Multicoloured.

11	80y. As Type **8** of Ehime	2·50	1·70
12	80y. Seated Buddha, Anrakuji Temple	2·50	1·70
13	80y. Inscribed belfry gateway, Jurakuji Temple	2·50	1·70
14	80y. Double roofed gateway, Kumadaniji Temple	2·50	1·70
15	80y. Pagoda, Yakuoji Temple	2·50	1·70
16	80y. Statues, ramp, lanterns and pagoda, Hotsumisakiji Temple	2·50	1·70
17	80y. Gateway and long steep steps, Shinjouji Temple	2·50	1·70
18	80y. Path, gateway, steps and main temple, Kongochoji Temple	2·50	1·70
19	80y. Buddha seated on peacock, Ryukoji Temple	2·50	1·70
20	80y. Bell and autumn colour, Butsumokuji Temple	2·50	1·70
21	80y. Dragon, Meisekiji Temple	2·50	1·70
22	80y. Steps and many roofed buildings, Daihouji Temple	2·50	1·70
23	80y. Carved decorative gable, Kokubunji Temple	2·50	1·70
24	80y. Leafless tree and snow-covered building, Yokomineji Temple	2·50	1·70
25	80y. Buddha, Kouonji Temple	2·50	1·70
26	80y. Courtyard and building, Houjuji Temple	2·50	1·70
27	80y. Inscribed pillars and gateway, Douryuji Temple	2·50	1·70
28	80y. Wall mounted statues, Goushouji Temple	2·50	1·70
29	80y. Eagle surmounting gateway, Tennouji Temple	2·50	1·70
30	80y. Courtyard with stone lined path and building, Kokubunji Temple	2·50	1·70

Nos. 11-30 were also issued by Ehime, Kochi and Kagawa.

2006. Cultural Heritage. Temples. Multicoloured.

31	80y. As Type **9** of Ehime	2·50	1·70
32	80y. Kirihata-ji (statue), Kirihata Temple	2·50	1·70
33	80y. Cherry blossom and building, Fujiidera Temple	2·50	1·70
34	80y. Snow-covered pagoda and temple, Shozanji Temple	2·50	1·70

35	80y. Wide path, inscribed pillar and gateway, Konomineji Temple	2·50	1·70
36	80y. Decorative carved roof boss and bell, Dainichiji Temple	2·50	1·70
37	80y. Cherry blossom and grass edged path, Kokubunji Temple	2·50	1·70
38	80y. Cherry blossom and statue, Zenrakuji Temple	2·50	1·70
39	80y. Cliff face and temple building, Iwayaji Temple	2·50	1·70
40	80y. Decorated footprints, Joururiji Temple	2·50	1·70
41	80y. Spot-lighted statues, Yasakaji Temple	2·50	1·70
42	80y. Lantern, tree, path, gateway and inscribed pillar, Sairinji Temple	2·50	1·70
43	80y. Temple buildings through hole in rock, Kichijoji Temple	2·50	1·70
44	80y. Cherry blossom and roofs, Maegamiji Temple	2·50	1·70
45	80y. Carving with dragon and phoenix, Sankakuji Temple	2·50	1·70
46	80y. Snow-covered roofs and trees, Unbenji Temple	2·50	1·70
47	80y. Wide path, pilgrim and gateway, Shiromineji Temple	2·50	1·70
48	80y. Row of statues, Negoroji Temple	2·50	1·70
49	80y. Lantern, courtyard and building, Ichinomiyaji Temple	2·50	1·70
50	80y. Animal statues and building, Yashimaji Temple	2·50	1·70

Nos. 31-50 were also issued by Ehime, Kochi and Kagawa.

2007. Cultural Heritage. Temples. As T 10 of Ehime. Multicoloured.

51	80y. Type **10**	2·50	1·70
52	80y. Gateway	2·50	1·70
53	80y. Square, shrub and main hall	2·50	1·70
54	80y. Trees, temple roof and hill	2·50	1·70
55	80y. Bell tower gate	2·50	1·70
56	80y. Bamboo temple	2·50	1·70
57	80y. Statues, pathway and temple	2·50	1·70
58	80y. Paved path and entrance	2·50	1·70
59	80y. Buddha	2·50	1·70
60	80y. Decorated ceiling and bell	2·50	1·70
61	80y. Temple lit from below	2·50	1·70
62	80y. Paved path, steps and temple	2·50	1·70
63	80y. Guardian statue	2·50	1·70
64	80y. Gateway	2·50	1·70
65	80y. Carved ceiling and bell	2·50	1·70
66	80y. Pagoda and temple at night	2·50	1·70
67	80y. Temple and mountains	2·50	1·70
68	80y. Pilgrims entering gateway	2·50	1·70
69	80y. Pilgrims and temple	2·50	1·70
70	80y. Temple, banners and mountains	2·50	1·70
71	80y. Well	2·50	1·70
72	80y. Kobo Daishi (statue)	2·50	1·70
73	80y. Buddha	2·50	1·70
74	80y. Three roofed pagoda	2·50	1·70
75	80y. Pilgrims, steps and gateway		
76	80y. Demon	2·50	1·70
77	80y. Rock statues	2·50	1·70
78	80y. Bodhisattva	2·50	1·70
79	80y. Cave and temple at night	2·50	1·70
80	80y. Kobo Daishi (painting)	2·50	1·70

Nos. 51-80 were also issued by Ehime, Kagawa and Kochi on 1 August 2007.

6-7 Dancers, left

2008. Tanabata Festival. Multicoloured.

81	50y. Type **6**	1·60	1·50
82	50y. Type **7**	1·60	1·50
83	50y. Lanterns, left	1·60	1·50
84	50y. Lanterns, right		
85	50y. Procession and roofs, left	1·60	1·50
86	50y. Procession and roofs, right	1·60	1·50
87	50y. Procession, left	1·60	1·50
88	50y. Procession, right	1·60	1·50
89	50y. Drummers, left	1·60	1·50
90	50y. Drummers, right	1·60	1·50

Nos. 81-2, 83-4, 85-6, 87-8 and 89-90 were issued together,se-tenant, each pair forming a composite design.

Nos. 81-90 were also issued by Tokyo, Okinawa, Miyagi and Fukuoka on 1 August 2008.

TOKYO

1 Station Building

2 Shin-Tokyo Post Office

1989. Tokyo Station.

1	**1**	62y. multicoloured	1·30	70

1990

2	62y. As Type **1448** of Japan	1·20	80

2 Shin-Tokyo Post Office

1990

3	**2**	62y. multicoloured	1·50	80

3 Fringed Orchids

1991

4	**3**	41y. multicoloured	1·30	80

4 Blossom and Forest, Mount Takao-san

1993

5	**4**	62y. multicoloured	1·50	1·00

5 Rainbow Bridge

1994

6	**5**	50y. multicoloured	1·90	1·30

6 Akamon

1995

7	**6**	50y. multicoloured	1·20	70

7 Kaminarimon Gate

1996

8	**7**	80y. multicoloured	2·10	1·40

8

9

10

11

12

1997. Places of Interest.

9	**8**	80y. multicoloured	1·80	1·20
10	**9**	80y. multicoloured	1·80	1·20
11	**10**	80y. multicoloured	1·80	1·20
12	**11**	80y. multicoloured	1·80	1·20
13	**12**	80y. multicoloured	1·80	1·20

13 Gateway

1998. Business Show.

14	**13**	80y. multicoloured	1·80	1·20

14 Tama Monorail

1998

15	**14**	80y. multicoloured	2·10	1·40

15 Orchid

1999. Multicoloured.

16	80y. Type **15**	2·10	1·40
17	80y. Pink orchid	2·10	1·40

16 Fireworks and Bridge

1999. Sumidagawa River Firework Display. Mult.

18	80y. Type **16**	2·10	1·40
19	80y. Fireworks and bridge (different)	2·10	1·40
20	80y. Pink morning glory blossom	2·10	1·40

Nos. 18-19 were issued together, se-tenant, forming a composite design.

17 Whales

2000. Tourism. Multicoloured.

21	50y. Type **17**	1·50	1·00
22	50y. Mother and child	1·50	1·00
23	50y. Sanja-matsuri festival	1·50	1·00
24	50y. Family and gingko trees	1·50	1·00
25	50y. Odaiba-kaihin park at night	1·50	1·00

18 Cosmos Flowers

2000. Seasonal Splendours (1st series). Multicoloured.

26	50y. Type **18**	1·50	1·00
27	50y. Roses	1·50	1·00
28	50y. Bird of Paradise flowers	1·50	1·00
29	50y. Camellias	1·50	1·00
30	50y. Freesias	1·50	1·00

See also Nos. 34-8, 43-6, 47-50, 51-4 and 55-8.

19 Children and Ducks

2000

31	**19**	80y. multicoloured	2·75	1·90

20 Shinjuku, New Centre of Tokyo

2000. Greetings from Tokyo. Multicoloured.

32	80y.+20y. Type **20**	3·50	2·40
33	80y.+20y. Tokyo at night	3·50	2·40

The premium was for the victims of eruptions and earthquakes.

21 Cherry Blossom

2001. Seasonal Splendours (2nd series). Mult.

34	50y. Type **21**	1·60	1·10
35	50y. Hydrangea	1·60	1·10
36	50y. Salvia	1·60	1·10
37	50y. Chrysanthemums	1·60	1·10
38	50y. Camellias	1·60	1·10

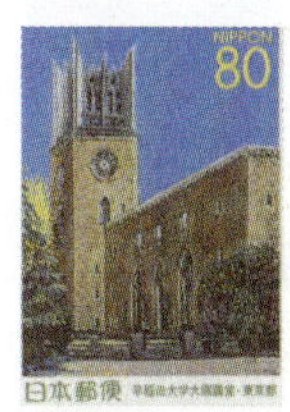
22 Okuma Auditorium and Clock Tower

2001

39	**22**	80y. multicoloured	2·50	1·70

23 Tokyo Millenario (festival of lights)

2001

40	**23**	80y. multicoloured	2·40	1·60

24 Morning Glory Fair

2002. Fairs and Markets. Multicoloured.

41	80y. Type **24**	2·20	1·50
42	80y. Hozuki (ground cherry) fair	2·50	1·50

25 Azaleas

2002. Seasonal Splendours (3rd series). Mult.

43	50y. Type **25**	1·50	1·00
44	50y. Lily	1·50	1·00
45	50y. Crape myrtle	1·50	1·00
46	50y. *Gingko biloba* (maidenhair tree)	1·50	1·00

26 Ume Blossom

2003. Seasonal Splendours (4th series). Mult.

47	50y. Type **26**	1·60	1·10
48	50y. Wisteria	1·60	1·10
49	50y. Irises	1·60	1·10
50	50y. Tea blossom	1·60	1·10

27 Magnolia Blossom

2004. Seasonal Splendours (5th series). Mult.

51	50y. Type **27**	1·60	1·10
52	50y. Azalea	1·60	1·10
53	50y. *Anemone flaccida*	1·60	1·10
54	50y. Bush clover	1·60	1·10

28 Ebine Orchid

2005. Seasonal Splendours (6th series). Mult.

55	50y. Type **28**	1·60	1·10
56	50y. Crinum	1·60	1·10
57	50y. Kerria blossom	1·60	1·10
58	50y. Azalea	1·60	1·10

29 Cherry Blossom

2006. Seasonal Splendours (7th series). Multicoloured.

59	80y. Type **29**	2·50	1·70
60	80y. Roses and Asakasa Palace	2·50	1·70
61	80y. Cosmos, Shouwas Kinen Park	2·50	1·70
62	80y. Apricot blossom and Yushima Tenjin Shrine	2·50	1·70

30 Tokyo Tower and Winter Sweet

2007. Tourism. Multicoloured.

63	80y. Type **30**	2·50	1·70
64	80y. Bridge	2·50	1·70
65	80y. Jingu gardens and osmanthus flowers	2·50	1·70
66	80y. Lake and gentians	2·50	1·70
67	80y. Bridge with lamps, Nihonbashi	2·50	1·70

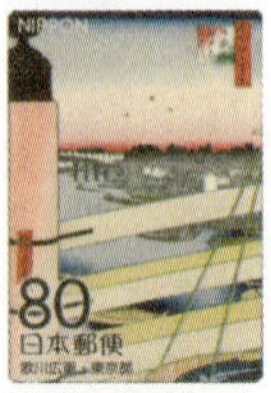

31 *Nihonbashi and Edobashi Bridges ((100 Famous Views of Edo))* (Hiroshige Utagawa)

2007. Ukiyoe Festival 2007. Multicoloured.

68	80y. Type **31**	2·50	1·70
69	80y. *Takashima Ohisa* (Utamaro Kitagawa)	2·50	1·70
70	80y. *Ichikawa Yaozo III as Tanabe Bunzo* (Toshusai Sharaku)	2·50	1·70
71	80y. *Iris Garden at Horikiri (100 Famous Views of Edo)* (Utagawa Hiroshige)	2·50	1·70
72	80y. *Asakusa Kinryuzan (100 Famous Views of Edo)* (Utagawa Hiroshige)	2·50	1·70
73	80y. *Sugatami Shichinin Kesho* (Kitagawa Utamaro)	2·50	1·70
74	80y. *Arashi Ryuzou II as Ishibe Kinkichi* (Toshusai Sharaku)	2·50	1·70
75	80y. *Suidobashi Surugadai (100 Famous Views of Edo)* (Utagawa Hiroshige)	2·50	1·70
76	80y. *The Moon Pine at Ueno (100 Famous Views of Edo)* (Utagawa Hiroshige)	2·50	1·70
77	80y. *Courtesan Hanaogi of the Ogiya* (Kitagawa Utamaro)	2·50	1·70

32-33 Procession and Roofs

2008. Tanabata Festival. Multicoloured.

78	50y. Type **32**	1·60	1·50
79	50y. Type **33**	1·60	1·50
80	50y. Lanterns, left	1·60	1·50
81	50y. Lanterns, right	1·60	1·50
82	50y. Dancers, left	1·60	1·50
83	50y. Dancers, right	1·60	1·50
84	50y. Procession, left	1·60	1·50
85	50y. Procession, right	1·60	1·50
86	50y. Drummers, left	1·60	1·50
87	50y. Drummers, right	1·60	1·50

Nos. 78-9, 80-1, 82-3, 84-5 and 86-7 were issued together, se-tenant, each pair forming a composite design.

Nos. 78-87 were also issued by Tokushima, Okinawa, Miyagi and Fukuoka on 1 August 2008.

34 Somei Yoshino Cherry Blossom

2009. Prefectural Flowers. Multicoloured.

88	50y. Type **34** (Tokyo)	1·60	1·50
89	50y. Yashio tsutsuji (*Rhododendron albrechtii*) (Tochigi)	1·60	1·50
90	50y. Tulips (Niigata)		
91	50y. Rhododendron (*Rhododendron japonicum*) (Shiga)	1·60	1·50
92	50y. Yaezakura cherry blossom (Nara)	1·60	1·50
93	80y. Somei Yoshino cherry blossom (Tokyo)	2·50	1·70
94	80y. Yashio tsutsuji (*Rhododendron albrechtii*) (Tochigi)	2·50	1·70
95	80y. Tulips (Niigata)	2·50	1·70
96	80y. Rhododendron (*Rhododendron japonicum*) (Shiga)	2·50	1·70
97	80y. Yaezakura cherry blossom (Nara)	2·50	1·70

Stamps of the same design were issued by Nara, Niigata, Shiga, and Tochigi on 2 February 2009.

35 Shrine carried through Water

2009. Fukagawa Hachiman Festival. Multicoloured.

98	50y. Type 35	1·70	1·30
99	50y. Shrine, water throwing and temple	1·70	1·30

Nos.98-9 were printed, se-tenant, each pair forming a composite design.

TOTTORI

1990

1	62y. As Type **1464** of Japan	1·20	80

1 Fruit

1991

2	**1**	62y. multicoloured	1·20	80

2 Shanshan Festival

1996

3	**2**	80y. multicoloured	2·10	1·40

3 Ship

1997. Tottori Expo.

4	**3**	80y. multicoloured	2·10	1·40

4 Nijisseikinashi (Japanese pear tree) and Dune

2000. Multicoloured.

5	50y. Type **4**	1·50	1·00
6	50y. Natsumikan (summer-orange blossoms) and sea	1·50	1·00
7	50y. Botan (peonies) and Izumo-taisha Shrine	1·50	1·00
8	50y. Momonohana (peach blossoms) and traditional houses in Kurashiki	1·50	1·00
9	50y. Momiji (maple leaves) and Itsukushima Shrine Gate	1·50	1·00

Nos. 5-9 were also issued by Yamaguchi, Shimane, Okayama and Hiroshima.

5 Uradome Coast and Snow Crab

2001. Homeland Tottori. Multicoloured.

10	50y. Type **5**	1·60	1·10
11	50y. Dunes	1·60	1·10
12	50y. Paper Hina dolls in river	1·60	1·10
13	50y. Mt. Daisen	1·60	1·10
14	80y. Nageiredo Hall	2·75	1·80
15	80y. Mukibanda Palaeolithic site	2·75	1·80

6 Flower Dome, Flowers and Mount Daisen

2004. Hana-Kairou Flower Park.

16	**6**	80y. multicoloured	2·50	1·70

7 Pear Blossom and Yumigahama Beach (Tottori)

2006. Flowers of Chugoku. Multicoloured.

17	50y. Type **7**	1·60	1·10
18	50y. Tree peonies and Hinomisaki Lighthouse (Shimane)	1·60	1·10
19	50y. Peach blossoms and Setooohashi bridge (Okayama)	1·60	1·10
20	50y. Maple leaves and Miyajima shrine (Hiroshima)	1·60	1·10
21	50y. Chinese citron blossom and Oomijima island (Yamaguchi)	1·60	1·10

Nos. 17-21 were also issued by Shimane, Okayama, Hiroshima, and Yamaguchi.

8 Mandarin Ducks

2007. Birds. Multicoloured.

22	80y. Type **8**	2·50	1·70
23	80y. Swans	2·50	1·70
24	80y. Pheasants	2·50	1·70
25	80y. Ducks swimming	2·50	1·70
26	80y. Cranes	2·50	1·70

Nos. 22-6 were also issued by Hiroshima, Okayama, Shimane and Yamaguchi on 1 May 2007.

TOYAMA

1 Waterfall

1990. Shomyo-no-taki.

1	**1**	62y. multicoloured	1·20	80

1990. Flowers.

2	62y. As Type **1451** of Japan	1·20	80

2 Mount Tateyama

1992

3	**2**	62y. multicoloured	1·50	90

3 Bridge and Waterfall, Kurobe-kyokoku

1994

4	**3**	80y. multicoloured	1·90	1·10

4 Woman Dancer

1997. Owara Kaze no Bon. Multicoloured.

5	80y. Type **4**	1·80	1·20
6	80y. Male dancer	1·80	1·20

Nos. 5-6 were issued together, se-tenant, forming a composite design.

5 Firefly Squids

1999

7	**5**	80y. multicoloured	2·10	1·40

6 Dancer

1999

8	**6**	80y. multicoloured	2·10	1·40

7 Tateyama Mountain Range and Tulip Field

2000. Multicoloured.

9	50y. Type **7**	1·50	1·00
10	80y. Tulips	2·50	1·70

8 Badminton Player

2000. 55th National Athletic Meet.

11	**8**	50y. multicoloured	1·80	1·20

9 Sanmon Gate, Zuiryuji Temple

2004. Zuiryuji Temple.

12	**9**	80y. multicoloured	2·50	1·70

10 Child Dancers

2004. Owara Dance, Bon Festival of Wind II. Multicoloured.

13	50y. Type **10**	1·60	1·10
14	50y. Women dancers	1·60	1·10
15	50y. Men dancers	1·60	1·10
16	50y. Musicians	1·60	1·10

Nos. 13-16 were issued together, se-tenant, forming a composite design.

11 Rhododendron

2005. Flowers of Hokuriku. Multicoloured.

17	50y. Type **11**	1·60	1·10
18	50y. Hydrangea	1·60	1·10
19	50y. Tulip	1·60	1·10
20	50y. Lily	1·60	1·10

Nos. 17-20 were also issued by Ishikawa and Fukui.

12 Bon Dancers

2007. Owara Kaze no Bon. Multicoloured.

21	80y. Type**12**	2·50	1·70
22	80y. Dancers and screen	2·50	1·70
23	80y. Child performers	2·50	1·70
24	80y. Dancers woman at left		
25	80y. Dancers and moon	2·50	1·70

WAKAYAMA

1990. Flowers.

1	62y. As Type **1463** of Japan	1·50	1·00

1 Kumano Path

1990

2	**1**	62y. multicoloured	1·20	80

2 Yachts, Waka-no-ura

1994

3	**2**	80y. multicoloured	1·90	1·20

1998

4	80y. multicoloured	2·10	1·40

3 Waterfall

1999. Southern Kii Penisula. Multicoloured.

5	80y. Type **3**	2·10	1·40
6	80y. Island at sunset	2·10	1·40

Nos. 5-6 were issued together, se-tenant, forming a composite design.

4 Mount Koya

1999. Koyasan Temples. Multicoloured.

7	80y. Type **4**	2·10	1·40
8	80y. Statue	2·10	1·40

5 Azaleas, Wakayama Marina City, and Wakaura Bay

2002

9	**5**	80y. multicoloured	2·20	1·50

6 Shakunage (rhododendron) (Shiga)

2006. Flowers of Kinki. Multicoloured.

10	50y. Yae-zakura (double cherry blossoms) (Nara)	1·60	1·10
11	50y. Nozigiku (wild chrysanthemums) (Hyogo)	1·60	1·10
12	50y. Type **6**	1·60	1·10
13	50y. Ume blossoms (Wakayama)	1·60	1·10
14	50y. Sakuraso (primrose) (Osaka)	1·60	1·10
15	50y. Shidare-zakura (weeping cherry) (Kyoto)	1·60	1·10

Nos. 10-15 were also issued by Osaka, Nara, Shiga, Hyogo and Kyoto.

7 Wakayama Castle

2007. Castles in Kinki Region. Multicoloured.

16	50y. Type **7**	1·60	1·50
17	50y. Koriyama	1·60	1·50
18	50y. Hikone	1·60	1·50
19	50y. Himeji	1·60	1·50
20	50y. Osaka	1·60	1·50

Nos. 16-20 were also issued by Hyogo, Nara, Osaka and Shiga on 1 June 2007.

8 Pink Plum Blossom

2008. Prefectural Flowers. Multicoloured.

21	50y. Narcissus (Fukui)	1·60	1·50
22	50y. Type **8**	1·60	1·50
23	50y. Fuki (*Petasites japonicus*) (Akita)	1·60	1·50
24	50y. White plum blossom (Fukuoka)	1·60	1·50
25	50y. Weeping cherry blossom (Kyoto)	1·60	1·50
26	80y. Narcissus (Fukui)	2·50	1·70
27	80y. White plum blossom (Wakayama)	2·50	1·70
28	80y. Fuki (*Petasites japonicus*) (Akita)	2·50	1·70
29	80y. Pink plum blossom (Fukuoka)	2·50	1·70
30	80y. Weeping cherry blossom (Kyoto)	2·50	1·70

YAMAGATA

1 Cherries

1989

1	**1**	62y. multicoloured	1·50	80

1990. Flowers.

2	62y. As Type **1439** of Japan	1·20	80

2 Trees in Autumn, Yama-dera

1995

3	**2**	80y. multicoloured	1·90	1·00

3 Dancers, Hanagasa Festival

1998

4	**3**	50y. multicoloured	1·30	90

1999

5	**1**	80y. multicoloured	2·10	1·40

4 Group of Trees

2000. Cherry Trees. Multicoloured.

6	80y. Type **4**	2·50	1·70
7	80y. Tree, central, Iwate	2·50	1·70
8	80y. Group of trees, Fukishima	2·50	1·70
9	80y. Tree, left, Miyagi	2·50	1·70
10	80y. Cherry blossom, Aomori	2·50	1·70
11	80y. Trees and river, Akita	2·50	1·70

Nos. 6-11 were also issued by Aomori, Iwate, Miyagi, Akita and Fukush.

5 Safflowers, Mogamigawa River, and Mount Gassan

2002. National Afforestation Campaign.

12	**5**	50y. multicoloured	1·60	1·10

6 Safflower (Yamagata)

2004. Prefectural Flowers. Multicoloured.

13	50y. Type **6**	1·60	1·10
14	50y. Apple blossom (Aomori)	1·60	1·10
15	50y. Paulownia (Iwate)	1·60	1·10
16	50y. Butterbur flower (Akita)	1·60	1·10
17	50y. Japanese bush clover (Miyagi)	1·60	1·10
18	50y. Alpine rose (*Rhododendron ferrugineum*) (Fukushima)	1·60	1·10

Nos. 13-18 were also issued by Yamagata, Aomori, Miyagi, Iwate and Fukushima.

7 Cherry (Yamagata)

2005. Fruits of Tohoku. Multicoloured.

19	50y. Type **7**	1·60	1·10
20	50y. Apple (Iwate)	1·60	1·10
21	50y. Apples (Aomori)	1·60	1·10
22	50y. Peach (Fukushima)	1·60	1·10

Nos. 19-22 were also issued by Aomori, Iwate and Fukushima.

8 Hanagasa Matsuri (Yamagata)

2006. Festivals of Tohuku. Multicoloured.

25	80y. Type **8**	2·50	1·70
26	80y. Kanto Matsuri (Akita)	2·50	1·70
27	80y. Nebuta Matsuri (Aomori)	2·50	1·70
28	80y. Sendai Tanabata Matsuri (Miyagi)	2·50	1·70

Nos. 25-8 were also issued by Akita, Aomori, and Miyagi.

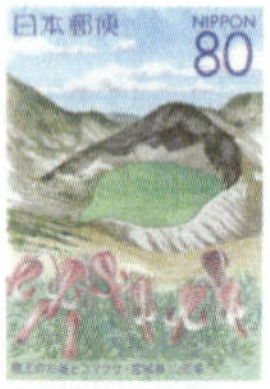

9 Dicentra and Water Filled Crater

2007. North Eastern Scenery. Multicoloured.

29	80y. Type **9**	2·50	1·70
30	80y. Oirase stream	2·50	1·70
31	80y. Hirosaki Castle	2·50	1·70
32	80y. Chusonji Temple	2·50	1·70
33	80y. Rocks and lily (sukashiyuri)	2·50	1·70
34	80y. Matsushima island and rape flowers	2·50	1·70
35	80y. Oga penisula and pinks	2·50	1·70
36	80y. Lily (nikkoukisuge) and mountain	2·50	1·70
37	80y. Skunk Cabbage Flowers, Oze National Park	2·50	1·70
38	80y. Safflower	2·50	1·70

Nos. 29-38 were also issued by Akita, Aomori, Fukushima, Iwate and Miyagi on 2 July 2007.

10 Safflower

2008. Flowers. Multicoloured.

39	50y. Type **10**	1·60	1·70
40	50y. Lily	1·60	1·10
41	50y. Sweet briar	1·60	1·10
42	50y. Nemotoshakunage (*Rhododendron brachycarpum*)	1·60	1·10
43	50y. Gentian	1·60	1·10
44	80y. Lily (25×35 mm)	2·50	1·70
45	80y. Sweet briar (25×35 mm)	2·50	1·70
46	80y. Rhododendron (25×35 mm)	2·50	1·70
47	80y. Safflower (25×35 mm)	2·50	1·70
48	80y. Gentian (25×35 mm)	2·50	1·70

Nos. 39-48 were also issued by Fukushima, Hokkaido, Kanagawa and Nagano on 1 July 2008.

YAMAGUCHI

1 Bird-shaped Lanterns

1989

1	**1** 62y. multicoloured	1·30	70

1990

2	62y. As Type **1468** of Japan	1·20	80

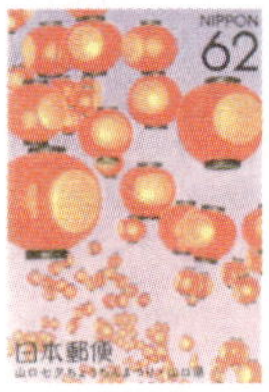

2 Lanterns

1992. Lantern Festival.

3	**2** 62y. multicoloured	1·20	80

3 Street, Hagi

1999. Multicoloured.

4	80y. Type3	2·10	1·40
5	80y. Railway bridge, Tsuwano	2·10	1·40

Nos. 4-5 were also issued by Shimane.

4 Natsumikan (summer-orange blossoms) and Sea

2000. Multicoloured.

6	50y. Type **4**	1·50	1·00
7	50y. Nijisseikinashi (Japanese pear tree) and Tottori dune	1·50	1·00
8	50y. Botan (peonies) and Izumo-taisha Shrine	1·50	1·00
9	50y. Momonohana (peach blossoms) and traditional houses in Kurashiki	1·50	1·00
10	50y. Momiji (maple leaves) and Itsukushima Shrine Gate	1·50	1·00

Nos. 6-10 were also issued by Tottori, Shimane, Okayama and Hiroshima.

5 Kintaikyo Bridge

2000

11	**5** 80y. multicoloured	2·75	1·90

6 Aji Wild Ducks

2001. Japan EXPO, Yamaguchi. Multicoloured.

12	50y. Type **6**	1·60	1·10
13	80y. Yamaguchi Kirara band and EXPO site	2·50	1·70

7 Kaikyo-Messe Tower, Shimonoseki and Blue Whale

2002. International Whaling Commission.

14	**7** 80y. multicoloured	2·20	1·50

8 Kaneko Misuzu

2003. Birth Centenary of Kaneko Misuzu (poet). Multicoloured.

15	80y. Type **8**	2·40	1·60
16	80y. Tairyo	2·40	1·60

Nos. 15-16 were issued together, se-tenant, forming a composite design.

9 Lord Mouri Takachika's Procession

2003. 400th Anniv of Hagi City. Multicoloured.

17	80y. Type **9**	2·50	1·70
18	80y. Lord Mouri Takachika's procession (different)	2·50	1·70

Nos. 17-18 were issued together, se-tenant, forming a composite design.

10 Chinese Citron Blossom and Oomijima Island (Yamaguchi)

2006. Flowers of Chugoku. Multicoloured.

19	50y. Type **10**	1·60	1·10
20	50y. Tree peonies and Hinomisaki Lighthouse (Shimane)	1·60	1·10
21	50y. Peach blossoms and Seto-oohashi bridge (Okayama)	1·60	1·10
22	50y. Maple leaves and Miyajima shrine (Hiroshima)	1·60	1·10
23	50y. Pear blossom and Yumigahama Beach (Tottori)	1·60	1·10

Nos. 19-23 were also issued by Tottori, Shimane, Okayama and Hiroshima.

11 Cranes

2007. Birds. Multicoloured.

24	80y. Type **8**	2·50	1·70
25	80y. Mandarin ducks	2·50	1·70
26	80y. Swans	2·50	1·70
27	80y. Pheasants	2·50	1·70
28	80y. Ducks swimming	2·50	1·70

Nos. 22-28 were also issued by Hiroshima, Okayama, Shimane, Tottori on 1 May 2007.

YAMANSHI

1990

1	62y. As Type **1446** of Japan	1·20	80

1 Bride

1991

2	**1** 62y. multicoloured	1·20	80

2 Waterfall

1996. Shosenkyo Gorge.

3	**2** 50y. multicoloured	1·30	90

3 Leaves, Lake and Mountain

1999. Five Lakes, Fuji. Multicoloured.

4	80y. Type **3**	2·10	1·40
5	80y. Cherry blossom, lake and mountain	2·10	1·40
6	80y. Flower, lake, forest and mountain	2·10	1·40
7	80y. Shoreline, lake, jetty forest and mountain	2·10	1·40
8	80y. Trees, lake, hills and mountain	2·10	1·40

4 Symbols of Yamanashi, Mount Fuji and Jewellry

2001

9	**4** 80y. multicoloured	2·40	1·60

5 Butterfly and Mount Mizugakisan, Azuma-Shakunage

2001. National Reforestation Campaign.

10	**5** 50y. multicoloured	1·60	1·10

6 Peach Blossom and Shirane-sanzan Mountains (Kyoto area)

2001. Yamanashi Scenery. Multicoloured.

11	50y. Type **6**	1·50	1·00
12	50y. Iris and Mt. Kitadake (Kyochu area)	1·50	1·00
13	50y. Horses and Mt. Yatsuga-take (Kyohoku area)	1·50	1·00
14	50y. Snow-covered houses and Oshino-hakkai ponds (Gunn-nai area)	1·50	1·00
15	50y. Cherry blossom, Minobu (Kyonan area)	1·50	1·00

7 Sunflower and Mount Yatsugatake

2005. Flowers of Yamanashi. Multicoloured.

16	80y. Type **7**	2·50	1·70
17	80y. Gentian and Mt. Kitadake, Southern Japanese Alps	2·50	1·70
18	80y. Evening primrose and Mt. Fuji	2·50	1·70
19	80y. Lady's slipper and Mt. Fuji	2·50	1·70

8 Cherry Tree

2007. Yamanashi Scenery. Multicoloured.

20	80y. Type **8**	2·50	1·70
21	80y. Grapes and vineyard	2·50	1·70
22	80y. Azalea	2·50	1·70
23	80y. Lavender and Mt Fuji	2·50	1·70
24	80y. Peaches and blossom	2·50	1·70

JAPANESE TAIWAN (FORMOSA)

From 1895 to 1045 Taiwan was part of the Japanese Empire, using the stamps of Japan. During 1945 American naval and air forces disrupted communications between Taiwan and Japan. The following were issued when supplies of Japanese stamps ran short.

1 Numeral and Chrysanthemum

1945. Imperf.

J1	1	3s. red	26·00	25·00
J2	1	5s. green	24·00	20·00
J3	1	10s. blue	35·00	32·00

Pt. 17

JAPANESE OCCUPATION OF CHINA

Japanese troops occupied Canton in 1938 and by 1945 had overrun much of Kwangtung province. Unoverprinted stamps of China were used until the following stamps were issued.

100 cents = 1 dollar.

I. KWANGTUNG

1 "Special for Kwantung"

1942. Stamps of China optd with T 1.

1	-	1c. orange (411)	1·90	2·40
2	77	1c. orange	2·40	3·75
3	58	2c. green	7·00	7·00
4	72	3c. red	2·75	2·75
5	77	5c. green	2·40	3·75
7	72	8c. olive	2·75	2·75
8	77	8c. green	2·75	3·75
9	72	10c. green	2·75	3·00
11	77	10c. emerald	3·25	3·25
12	72	16c. brown	4·75	5·25
13	72	17c. green	3·25	3·00
14	-	20c. blue (519)	3·25	3·75
15	72	30c. red	3·75	2·75
16	77	30c. red	3·25	3·75
17	72	50c. blue	3·75	7·75
18	77	50c. blue	3·25	3·75
19	72	$1 sepia and brown	7·25	9·25
20	72	$2 brown and blue	7·75	9·25
21	72	$5 green and red	7·00	8·50
22	72	$10 violet and green	15·00	20·00
23	72	$20 blue and purple	7·00	9·25

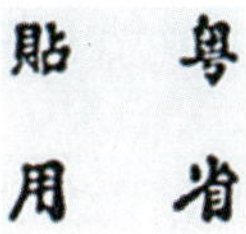

(2)

1942. Stamps of China optd with T 2. (a) On 1938 issue.

24	2c. green	65	70
25	3c. red	65	70
26	5c. green	65	1·00
28	8c. green	75	1·00
29	10c. green	1·00	1·20
30	16c. brown	1·20	1·20
31	25c. blue	1·20	2·75
32	30c. red	1·10	2·40
33	50c. blue	2·20	2·75
35	$1 brown and red	8·25	8·50
37	$2 brown and blue	7·50	8·00
39	$5 green and red	10·00	12·00
40	$10 violet and green	15·00	20·00
42	$20 blue and purple	14·00	20·00

(b) On 1941 issue.

44	77	2c. blue	50	50
45	77	5c. green	50	50
46	77	8c. orange	55	50
47	77	8c. green	55	90
48	77	10c. green	65	65
49	77	17c. green	1·00	1·00
50	77	25c. purple	1·00	1·00
51	77	30c. red	1·00	1·10
52	77	50c. blue	1·00	1·10
53	77	$1 black and brown	4·75	7·75
54	77	$2 black and blue	6·00	8·50
55	77	$5 black and red	4·75	4·75
56	77	$10 black and green	8·50	12·50
57	77	$20 black and purple	10·50	13·00

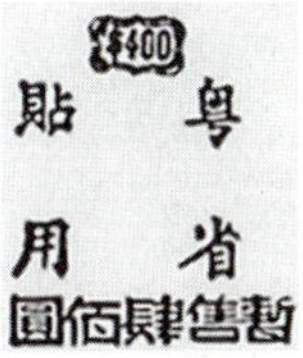

(3)

1945. Canton provisionals. Surch as T 3.

58	72	$200 on 10c. green (No. 29)	£120	75·00
59	72	$400 on 8c. olive (No. 28)	£120	75·00

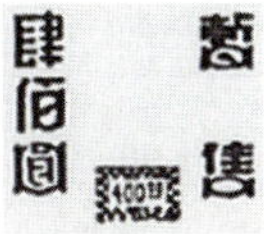

(4)

1945. Swatow provisional. No. 508 of China surch with T 4.

60	$400 on 1c. orange	£700	£600

POSTAGE DUE STAMPS

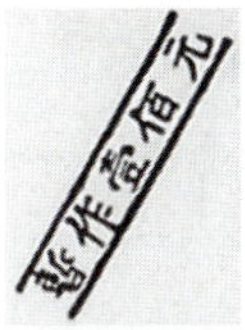

(D 3)

1945. Postage Due stamp of China surch with Type D 3.

D58	D62	$100 on $2 orange	£700	£650

II. MENGKIANG (INNER MONGOLIA)

The autonomous area of Mengkiang ("the Mongolian Borderlands"), consisting of Suiyuan, South Chahar and North Shansi, was established by the Japanese in November, 1937.

For the first issue in 1941 see the note at the beginning of III North China.

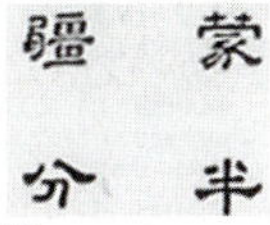

(3)

1942. Stamps of China optd "Mengkiang" and surch half original value at T 3.

68	58	10c. on 20c. blue	35·00	35·00
69	72	1c. on 2c. green	2·20	1·30
72	72	4c. on 8c. green	70	70
73	72	5c. on 10c. green	1·10	70
75	72	15c. on 30c. red	5·25	7·25
77	72	25c. on 50c. blue	7·75	8·75
82	72	$1 on $2 brown and blue	12·50	12·50
84	72	$10 on $20 blue and purple	75·00	90·00
86	-	½c. on 1c. orange (411)	30	50
87	60	2c. on 4c. lilac	4·25	4·25
88	-	10c. on 20c. blue (519)	6·25	6·25
93	58	1c. on 2c. green	7·75	13·00
94	58	2c. on 4c. green	55	70
95	72	8c. on 16c. brown	1·80	2·50
96	72	50c. on $1 sepia and brown	12·50	12·50
98	72	$5 on $10 violet and green	70·00	70·00
99	-	5c. on 10c. purple (515)	4·50	8·00
100	-	10c. on 20c. red (418)	5·25	8·00
101	-	15c. on 30c. purple (542)	2·00	3·00
102	-	20c. on 40c. orange (524)	8·00	8·75
103	-	25c. on 50c. green (525)	2·20	4·50

4 Dragon Pillar, Peking

1943. 5th Anniv of Establishment of Mengkiang Post and Telegraph Service.

104	4	4c. orange	1·30	2·00
105	4	8c. blue	1·40	2·00

5 Miners

1943. 2nd Anniv of War in East Asia.

106	5	4c. green	1·30	2·00
107	5	8c. red	1·40	2·00

6 Stylized Horse

7 Prince Yun

1943. 1st Anniv of Federation of Autonomous Governments of Mongolian Provinces.

108	6	3c. red	1·10	2·00
109	7	8c. blue	1·10	2·00

8 Blast Furnace

1944. Productivity Campaign.

110	8	8c. brown	1·30	3·00

1945. Stamps of China optd "Mengkiang" as top characters in T 3.

111	58	2c. green	10·50	8·75
112	58	4c. green	18·00	13·00
113	58	5c. green	11·00	11·00
114	72	$1 sepia and brown	3·00	3·75
115	72	$2 brown and blue	12·50	12·50
116	72	$5 green and red	44·00	44·00
117	-	1c. orange (411)	90	90
118	-	8c. orange (514)	85	85
119	-	10c. purple (515)	30	40
120	-	20c. red (418)	1·90	2·50
121	-	30c. red (542)	40	1·30
122	-	40c. orange (524)	45	45
123	-	50c. green (525)	8·00	8·75

(10)

1945. Stamps of China optd "Mengkiang" (as T 3 of North China) and surch as T 10.

124B	60	10c. on ½c. sepia	3·75	4·50
126B	-	10c. on 1c. orange (411)	1·00	1·20
130B	72	50c. on 2c. olive	1·10	1·70
131B	60	50c. on 4c. lilac	90	1·10
132B	72	50c. on 5c. olive	75	1·50
135	58	50c. on 2c. olive	3·00	3·00
136	58	50c. on 4c. green	4·50	4·50
137	58	50c. on 5c. green	45	45
138	-	$1 on 8c. orange (514)	35	1·90

III. NORTH CHINA

The Japanese conquered North China in 1937 and formed a puppet Government in Peking.

Type **2** of Meng Kiang and **B** to **J** are the six "district" overprints comprising North China (including Mengkiang) and a detailed list of the overprints on the stamps of China is given in the Stanley Gibbons' Catalogue, Part 17 (China).

In 1942 stamps of China overprinted with Types **B** to **J** were further overprinted with Type **1** (to commemorate the Fall of Singapore) or with Type **2** (to commemorate the tenth Anniversary of Manchukuo). These stamps are also listed in the Stanley Gibbons' Catalogue Part 17 (China).

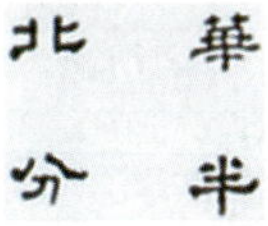

(3)

2x (**2** of Meng Kiang "Mengkiang")

B (**B.** "Honan")

D (**D.** "Hopeh")

E (**E.** "Shansi")

H (**H.** "Shantung")

J (**J.** "Supeh")

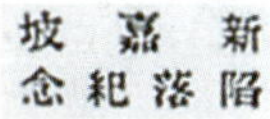

(1)

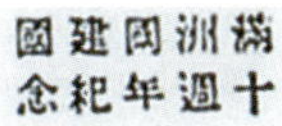

(2)

1942. Stamps of China optd "Hwa Pei" (= North China) and surch half original value at T 3.

88	72	1c. on 2c. olive	45	30
91	72	4c. on 8c. olive	55	50
92	72	5c. on 10c. green	55	45
96	72	15c. on 30c. red	1·30	1·10
98	72	25c. on 50c. blue	1·80	1·50
109	72	$10 on $20 blue and purple	44·00	47·00
111	-	½c. on 1c. orange (No. 411)	30	20
114	-	1c. on 2c. blue (No. 509)	1·50	1·50
116	60	2c. on 4c. lilac	90	70
120	-	5c. on 10c. pur (No. 515)	2·40	2·50
122	-	10c. on 20c. blue (No. 519)	3·25	65
128	58	1c. on 2c. olive	35	20
129	58	2c. on 4c. green	85	20
130	72	8c. on 16c. olive	35	30
131	72	50c. on $1 brown and red	4·25	3·00
132	72	$1 on $2 brown and blue	5·25	3·00
133	72	$5 on $10 violet and green	21·00	21·00
134	-	4c. on 8c. orange (No. 514)	60	30
135	-	10c. on 20c. lake (No. 418)	1·50	1·30
136	-	15c. on 30c. purple (No. 542)	65	70
137	-	20c. on 40c. orge (No. 542)	1·90	30
138	-	25c. on 50c. grn (No. 525)	1·70	1·30

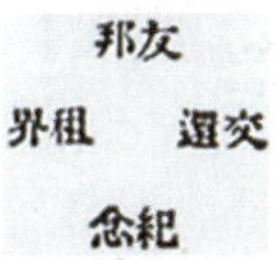

(4)

Return to China of Foreign Concessions. Optd with T 4.

39	58	2c. on 4c. green (No. 129)	30	90
140	72	4c. on 8c. olive (No. 91)	1·30	1·50
141	72	8c. on 16c. olive (No. 130)	1·30	1·80

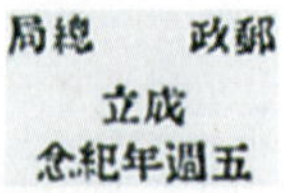

(5)

1943. 5th Anniv of Directorate-General of Posts for North China. Optd with T 5.

142	58	2c. on 4c. green (No. 129)	40	70
143	72	4c. on 8c. olive (No. 91)	40	95
144	72	8c. on 16c. olive (No. 130)	45	70

1943. Stamps of China optd "Hwa Pei" as top characters in T 3.

145		10c. green	45	40
153	58	2c. olive	30	50
154	58	4c. green	30	1·30
155	58	5c. green	55	65
156	72	9c. olive	40	55
157	72	16c. olive	30	50
158	72	18c. olive	30	40
159	72	$1 brown and red	3·75	1·10
160	72	$2 brown and blue	2·10	90
161	72	$5 green and red	4·50	6·25
162	72	$10 violet and green	8·00	8·00
163	72	$20 blue and purple	9·00	11·00
164	-	1c. orange (No. 411)	30	20
165	-	10c. purple (No. 515)	35	65
166	-	20c. lake (No. 418)	45	55
167	-	30c. red (as No. 542)	40	40
168	-	40c. orange (No. 524)	40	65
169	-	50c. green (No. 525)	1·10	1·10

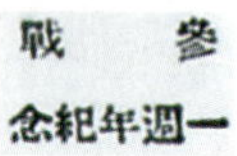

(6)

1944. 1st Anniv of Declaration of War on Allies by Japanese-controlled Nanking Govt. Optd with T 6.

170	58	4c. green (No. 154)	1·80	1·70
171	72	10c. green (No. 149)	1·80	1·70

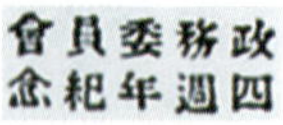

(7)

1944. 4th Anniv of North China Political Council. Optd with T 7.

172		9c. olive (No. 156)	90	1·30
173		18c. olive (No. 158)	90	2·50
174	-	50c. green (No. 169)	5·25	6·25
175	72	$1 brown and red (No. 159)	1·90	2·50

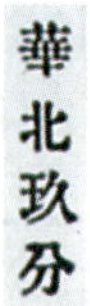

(8)

1944. Stamps of Japanese Occupation of Shanghai and Nanking optd "Hwa Pei" and surch as T 8.

176	5	9c. on 50c. orange	1·20	1·50
177	5	18c. on $1 green	1·30	1·90
178	6	36c. on $2 blue	1·50	1·90
179	6	90c. on $5 red	1·90	2·10

(9)

1944. 6th Anniv of Directorate-General of Posts for North China. Optd with T 9.

180	72	9c. olive (No. 156)	85	1·30
181	72	18c. olive (No. 158)	85	2·50
182	-	50c. green (No. 169)	1·30	1·90
183	72	$1 brown and red (No. 159)	3·00	3·50

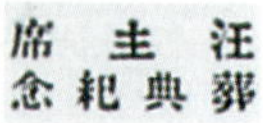

(10)

1944. Death of Wang Ching-wei. Optd with T 10.

184	-	20c. lake (No. 166)	2·50	3·00
185	-	50c. green (No. 169)	2·50	3·00
186	72	$1 brown and red (No. 159)	5·25	6·00
187	72	$2 brown and blue (No. 160)	1·50	1·50

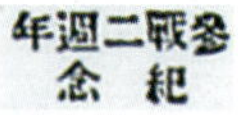

(11)

1945. 2nd Anniv of Declaration of War on Allies by Nanking Govt. Optd with T 11.

188	-	20c. lake (No. 166)	2·50	3·50
189	-	50c. green (No. 169)	8·00	8·00
190	72	$1 brown and red (No. 159)	2·75	3·00
191	72	$2 brown and blue (No. 160)	1·90	1·80

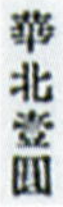

(12)

1945. Stamps of Japanese Occupation of Shanghai and Nanking surch as T 12.

192	7	50c. on $3 orange	55	70
193	7	$1 on $6 blue	55	70

13 Dragon Pillar

14 Long Bridge

15 Imperial City Tower

16 Marble Boat, Summer Palace

1945. 5th Anniv of Establishment of North China Political Council. Views of Peking.

194	13	$1 yellow	1·30	1·30
195	14	$2 blue	30	1·30
196	15	$5 red	90	65
197	16	$10 green	45	1·00

17

1945. Optd "Hwa Pei" as top characters in T 3.

198	17	$1 brown	30	20
199	17	$2 blue	1·00	20
200	17	$5 red	2·10	2·10
201	17	$10 green	2·10	65
202	17	$20 purple	2·10	1·50
203	17	$50 brown	44·00	50·00

18 Wutai Mountain, Shansi

19 Kaifeng Iron Pagoda, Honan

20 International Bridge, Tientsin

21 Taishan Mountain, Shantung

22 G.P.O., Peking

1945. 7th Anniv of Directorate-General of Posts for North China.

204	18	$5 green	30	90
205	19	$10 brown	65	90
206	20	$20 purple	50	1·30
207	21	$30 grey	75	1·30
208	22	$50 red	2·10	2·50

IV. NANKING AND SHANGHAI

The Japanese captured Shanghai and Nanking in 1937 and Hankow in 1938. During the same year Nanking was made the seat of Japanese-controlled administration for the Yangtse Basin. The stamps listed below were used in parts of Anhwei, Southern Kiangsu, Chekiang, Hupeh, Kiangsi, Hunan and Fukien.

N.B. With the exception of Nos. 114 to 119 the following are all surcharged on stamps of China.

(1)

1941. Air. Surch as T 1.

1	61	10s. on 50c. brown	45	1·70
2	61	18s. on 90c. olive	40	2·20
4	61	20s. on $1 green	60	2·50
5	61	25s. on 90c. olive	35	1·80
6	61	35s. on $2 brown	35	1·70
7	61	60s. on 35s. on $2 brn (No. 6)	20	2·75

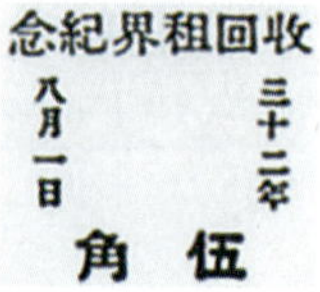

(2)

1943. Return to China of Shanghai Concessions. Surch as T 2.

8	72	25c. on 5c. green	1·30	1·30
9	77	50c. on 8c. orange	1·30	1·30
10	72	$1 on 16c. olive	1·30	1·30
11	77	$2 on 50c. blue	1·30	1·30

1943. As No. 422 but colour changed. Issued at Shanghai.

12	72	15c. brown	15·00	28·00

(3)

(4)

1943. Stamps of China and No. 12 above surch as T 3 (cent values) or T 4 (dollar values). (a) On T 58.

13	58	$6 on 5c. green	85	1·90
14	58	$20 on 15c. red	95	1·40
15	58	$500 on 15c. green	1·00	1·50
17	58	$1000 on 20c. blue	3·00	3·00
18	58	$1000 on 25c. blue	3·00	3·00

(b) On Martyrs issue (as T 60).

88	60	$7.50 on ½c. sepia	1·30	2·50
89	-	$15 on 1c. orange	35	1·30
91	-	$30 on 2c. blue	1·20	1·80
93	-	$200 on 1c. orange	30	70
94	-	$200 on 8c. orange	70	1·20

(c) On T 72.

19	72	25c. on 5c. green	2·10	3·50
20	72	30c. on 2c. green	65	1·70
21	72	50c. on 3c. red	30	35
22	72	50c. on 5c. green	30	30
23	72	50c. on 8c. green	65	1·20
24	72	$1 on 8c. green	30	20
26	72	$1 on 15c. brown	55	65
27	72	$1.30 on 16c. brown	30	75
28	72	$1.50 on 3c. red	30	45
30	72	$2 on 10c. green	30	35
31	72	$3 on 15c. brown	30	35
32	72	$4 on 16c. brown	45	30
33	72	$5 on 15c. brown	30	30
38	72	$6 on 10c. green	30	55
39	72	$10 on 10c. green	30	35
40	72	$10 on 16c. brown	55	30
41	72	$20 on 3c. red	30	45
42	72	$20 on 15c. red	1·20	2·50
43	72	$20 on 15c. brown	45	45
45	72	$100 on 3c. red	55	45
46	72	$500 on 8c. green	2·50	5·00
47	72	$500 on 10c. green	2·50	3·75
48	72	$500 on 15c. red	2·75	2·50
49	72	$500 on 15c. brown	2·50	2·75
50	72	$500 on 16c. brown	2·00	4·50
51	72	$1000 on 25c. blue	2·30	4·50
54	72	$1.70 on 30c. red	75	1·50
55	72	$2 on 5c. green	45	1·30
56	72	$2 on $1 sepia and brown	2·75	2·50
59	72	$3 on 8c. green	55	55
61	72	$6 on 5c. green	45	55
62	72	$6 on 8c. green	40	70
64	72	$20 on $2 brown and blue	1·30	1·30
65	72	$50 on 30c. red	85	90
66	72	$50 on 50c. blue	70	70
67	72	$50 on $5 green and red	1·00	1·00
68	72	$50 on $20 blue and purple	2·10	2·50
75	72	$1000 on 50c. blue	2·00	2·75
76	72	$1000 on $2 brown and blue	2·50	8·75
77	72	$2000 on $5 green and red	2·00	3·00
83	72	$100 on $10 violet and green	45	65
84	72	$200 on $20 blue and purple	55	65
86	72	$1000 on 30c. red	3·00	3·50
87a	72	$5000 on $10 violet & green	11·00	13·00

(d) On T 77.

95	77	5c. on ½c. sepia	35	1·10
96	77	10c. on 1c. orange	35	90
97	77	20c. on 1c. orange	35	75
98	77	40c. on 5c. green	35	85
99	77	$5 on 5c. green	35	40
100	77	$10 on 10c. green	35	40
101	77	$50 on ½c. sepia	35	40
102	77	$50 on 1c. orange	40	45
103	77	$50 on 17c. olive	40	45
104	77	$200 on 5c. green	65	65
105	77	$200 on 8c. green	60	60
106	77	$200 on 8c. orange	65	75
107	77	$500 on $5 black and red	1·30	2·00
108	77	$1000 on 1c. orange	1·10	2·10
109	77	$1000 on 25c. purple	1·20	1·80
110	77	$1000 on 30c. red	1·40	2·20
111	77	$1000 on $2 black and blue	1·90	1·90
112	77	$1000 on $10 black & green	1·20	1·80
113	77	$2000 on $5 black and red	1·40	1·90

5 Wheat and Cotton Flower **6** Purple Mountain, Nanking

1944. 4th Anniv of Establishment of Chinese Puppet Government at Nanking.

114	5	50c. orange	60	70
115	5	$1 green	60	70
116	6	$2 blue	60	75
117	6	$5 red	60	75

7 Map of Shanghai and Foreign Concessions

1944. 1st Anniv of Return to China of Shanghai Foreign Concessions.

118	7	$3 orange	95	70
119	7	$6 blue	40	70

1945. 5th Anniv of Establishment of Chinese Puppet Government at Nanking. Surch as T 4.

124	5	$15 on 50c. orange	60	1·30
125	5	$30 on $1 green	60	1·30
126	6	$60 on $2 blue	60	1·30
127	6	$200 on $5 red	60	1·30

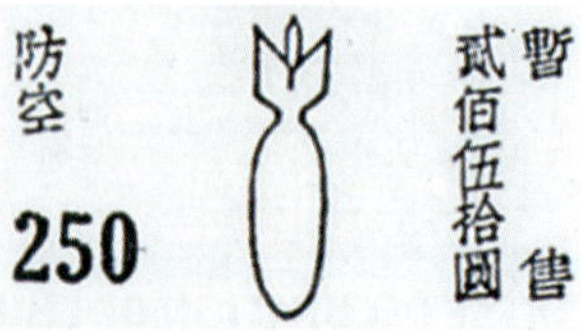

(9)

1945. Air Raid Precautions Propaganda. Air stamps surch as T 9.

128	61	$150 on 15c. green	60	1·00
129	61	$250 on 25c. orange	60	1·00
130	61	$600 on 60c. blue	60	1·00
131	61	$1000 on $1 green	60	1·00

POSTAEG DUE STAMPS

(D 8)

1945. Postage Due stamps surch as Type D 8.

D120	**D62**	$1 on 2c. orange	65	1·80
D121	**D62**	$2 on 5c. orange	65	1·70
D122	**D62**	$5 on 10c. orange	65	1·70
D123	**D62**	$10 on 20c. orange	65	1·50

Pt. 4

JAPANESE OCCUPATION OF NETHERLANDS INDIES

The Japanese occupied the Netherlands Indies from March 1942 to 1945.

100 sen (cents) = 1 rupee (gulden).

I. JAVA

1 Eastern Asia

1943. 1st Anniv of Japanese Occupation of Java.

1	**1**	2s. brown	5·50	4·75
2	-	3½s. red	5·50	4·75
3	-	5s. green	7·75	4·75
4	-	10s. blue	21·00	5·50

DESIGNS: 3½s. Farmer ploughing ricefield; 5s. Mt. Soemer; 10s. Bantam Bay.

2 Native soldier

1943. Savings Campaign.

5	**2**	3½c. red	45·00	13·50
6	**2**	10c. blue	65·00	7·75

3 Wayang puppet

5 Bird of Vishnu and Mt. Soemer

1943. Designs with rectangular panel of characters as at foot of T 3 and 5.

7	-	3½c. red	4·00	2·50
8	**3**	5c. green	4·00	2·50
9	-	10c. blue	4·00	2·50
10	-	20c. olive	4·00	2·50
11	-	40c. purple	4·50	2·50
12	**5**	60c. orange	5·50	4·50
13	-	80c. brown	10·50	5·50
14	-	1r. violet	28·00	6·75

DESIGNS—As Type **3**: 3½c. Native head; 10c. Boroboudur Temple; 20c. Map of Java; 40c. Seated dancer and Temple. As Type **5**: 80c. Ploughing with oxen; 1r. Terraced ricefields.

II. SUMATRA

6 Lake Toba

1943. Designs with rectangular panel characters as at foot of T 6.

15		1c. olive	2·75	2·00
16		2c. green	2·75	2·00
17		3c. blue	2·75	2·00
18		3½c. red	5·00	2·00
19		4c. blue	3·50	2·00
20		5c. orange	2·75	1·50
21		10c. blue	6·75	1·50
22		20c. brown	3·50	1·50
23	**6**	30c. purple	4·00	2·75
24	**6**	40c. brown	4·50	3·00
25	-	50c. bistre	11·00	4·50
26	-	1r. violet	55·00	7·25

DESIGNS: 1c. to 3c. Batak house; 3½c. to 5c. Minangkabau house; 10c., 20c. Ploughing with oxen; 50c., 1r. Carabao Canyon (20×28 mm).

(7)

1944. Various stamps optd with T 7. (a) On Netherlands Indies stamps of 1933.

27A	**46**	3½c. grey	1·10	2·50
34A	**47**	42½c. yellow	55·00	75·00
35A	**47**	50c. blue	26·00	36·00
36A	**47**	2g.50 purple	£450	£600
37A	**46**	1c. violet	90	2·00
38A	**46**	2c. purple	90	2·00
39A	**46**	2½c. bistre	90	2·00
40A	**46**	3c. green	36·00	50·00
42B	**47**	15c. blue	2·50	7·75
43B	**47**	20c. purple	1·20	2·00
44B	**47**	25c. green	2·50	4·00
45A	**47**	30c. blue	27·00	36·00
46B	**47**	35c. violet	2·50	4·00
47B	**47**	40c. green	4·50	4·50
48A	**47**	2g. green	£750	£850
49B	**47**	5g. bistre	25·00	65·00
50B	**67**	10c. red	1·30	2·10

(b) On Nos. 429/44 of Netherlands Indies.

28A	-	10c. red	12·50	18·00
43A	-	20c. mauve	20·00	36·00
44A	-	25c. green	5·50	8·25
52B	-	15c. blue	2·50	3·75
53B	-	17½c. orange	2·20	3·75
56B	-	30c. brown	1·70	3·25
57A	-	35c. purple	27·00	14·50
58B	-	40c. green	2·50	5·25
59B	-	50c. red	4·00	4·50
60B	-	60c. blue	3·75	5·50
61B	-	80c. red	4·50	6·25
62B	-	1g. violet	5·50	7·75
63B	-	2g. green	4·75	7·25
64A	-	5g. brown	£300	£475
65A	-	10g. green	47·00	75·00
66A	**68**	25g. orange	£550	£650

(c) On Nos. 463/6 of Netherlands Indies.

66	-	3c. green	1·10	2·75
67	**71**	4c. green	1·10	2·75
68	-	5c. blue	1·10	2·75
69	-	7½c. violet	1·10	2·75

(d) On Nos. 506 and 509 of Netherlands.

70	**94**	5c. green	13·50	17·00
71	**94**	12½c. blue	6·75	14·50

III. JAPANESE NAVAL CONTROL AREA

(9)

1942. Various stamps optd with T 9. (a) On Netherlands Indies stamps of 1933.

83	**46**	4c. green	33·00	55·00
84	**46**	5c. blue	13·50	20·00
86	**47**	30c. blue	55·00	55·00
88	**47**	50c. blue	75·00	£100
89	**46**	1c. violet	5·50	21·00
90	**46**	2c. purple	1·10	4·75
91	**46**	2½c. bistre	1·10	4·75
92	**46**	3c. green	1·00	4·75
95	**47**	10c. red	65·00	85·00
96	**47**	15c. blue	12·50	19·00
97	**47**	20c. purple	1·30	4·75
98	**47**	25c. green	5·50	11·00
100	**47**	35c. violet	1·30	5·00
101	**47**	40c. green	1·30	5·00
102	**47**	80c. red	£275	£400
103	**47**	1g. violet		
104	**47**	2g. green		
105	**47**	5g. bistre		

(b) On Nos. 270 and 360 of Netherlands Indies.

106	**48**	30c. blue	£300	£450
107	-	5c. blue	1·30	4·75

(c) On Nos. 429/44 of Netherlands Indies.

108		10c. red	4·00	5·25
110		15c. blue	4·25	20·00
111		17½c. orange	1·50	5·50
112		20c. mauve	28·00	44·00
113		25c. green	37·00	55·00
114		30c. brown	5·25	13·50
115		35c. purple	60·00	75·00
116		40c. green	25·00	35·00
117		50c. red	13·00	14·50
118		60c. blue	6·25	11·00
119		80c. red	10·50	19·00
120		1g. violet	7·25	14·50
121		2g. green	55·00	90·00
122		5g. brown		
123	**68**	25g. orange		

(d) On Nos. 462/6 of Netherlands Indies.

124	-	2½c. purple	6·25	10·00
125	-	3c. green	2·75	5·00
126	**71**	4c. green	4·00	4·75
127	-	5c. blue	8·00	19·00
128	-	7½c. violet	1·10	5·25

(e) On Nos. 506 and 509 of Netherlands.

129	**94**	5c. green		
130	**94**	12½c. blue		

1943. Air. Nos. 89 and 91 surch.

148	**46**	"f. 2" on 1c. violet	17·00	27·00
151	**46**	"f. 8.50" on 2½c. bistre	55·00	90·00

10 Japanese Flag and Palms

11 Mt. Fuji, Flag and Bird

1943

152	**10**	2c. brown	1·10	55·00
153	**10**	3c. green	1·10	55·00
154	**10**	3½c. orange	2·00	55·00
155	**10**	5c. blue	1·10	27·00
156	**10**	10c. red	1·10	27·00
157	**10**	15c. blue	1·20	27·00
158	**10**	20c. violet	1·20	27·00
159	**11**	25c. orange	4·50	27·00
160	**11**	30c. blue	5·25	31·00
161	**11**	50c. green	11·00	33·00
162	**11**	1g. purple	55·00	45·00

POSTAGE DUE STAMPS

1942. Netherlands Indies Postage Due stamps of 1913 and 1937 optd with T 9.

D132	2½c. orange	2·00	4·75
D133	3½c. orange	4·50	9·25
D134	5c. orange	2·50	4·75
D135	7½c. orange	2·50	4·75
D136	10c. orange	1·90	4·75
D137	20c. orange	2·50	4·75
D138	20c. on 37½c. orange	65·00	£100
D139	25c. orange	2·00	4·75
D140	30c. orange	5·00	11·00
D142	1c. orange	9·00	18·00
D144	15c. orange	2·50	4·50
D146	40c. orange	2·30	5·25
D147	1g. blue	7·25	13·50

Pt. 22

JAPANESE OCCUPATION OF PHILIPPINES

100 centavos or sentimos = 1 peso.

1942. Stamps of Philippines optd with bars or surch also.

J1	**104**	2c. green	25	45
J2	-	12c. black (No. 529)	2·75	2·75
J3	-	16c. blue (No. 530)	6·75	6·25
J4a	-	5c. on 6c. brn (No. 526)	25	85
J5	-	16c. on 30c. red (No. 505)	1·40	1·80
J6	-	50c. on 1p. black and orange (No. 534)	5·50	5·25
J7	-	1p. on 4p. black and blue (No. 508)	£100	£110

1942. No. 460 of Philippines surch CONGRATULATIONS FALL OF BATAAN AND CORREGIDOR 1942 2.

J8	2c. on 4c. green	5·75	5·75

J 4 Agricultural Produce

1942. Red Cross Fund.

J9	**J4**	2c.+1c. violet	5·75	2·75
J10	**J4**	5c.+1c. green	5·75	2·75
J11	**J4**	16c.+2c. orange	£190	80·00

1942. 1st Anniv of "Greater East Asia War". No. 460 of Philippines surch with native characters, 12-8-1942 and 5.

J12	5c. on 4c. green	2·30	2·30

1943. 1st Anniv of Philippine Executive Commission. Nos. 566 and 569 of Philippines surch with native characters, 1-23-43 and value.

J13	**105**	2c. on 8c. red	1·40	1·80
J14	**105**	5c. on 1p. sepia	1·80	2·30

J 7 Nipa Hut

J 9 Mt. Mayon and Mt. Fuji

1943

J15	**J7**	1c. orange	80	80
J16	-	2c. green	80	80
J17	**J7**	4c. green	80	80
J18	**J9**	5c. brown	80	1·40
J19	-	6c. red	80	1·00
J20	**J9**	10c. blue	80	1·00
J21	-	12c. blue	1·40	1·70
J22	-	16c. brown	80	80
J23	**J7**	20c. purple	1·50	1·70
J24	**J9**	21c. violet	1·00	1·40
J25	-	25c. brown	1·10	80
J26	**J9**	1p. red	9·00	2·75
J27	-	2p. purple	23·00	6·75
J28	-	5p. olive	32·00	11·00

DESIGNS—VERT: 2, 6, 25c. Rice planter; 12, 16c., 2, 5p. Morro vinta (sailing canoe).

J 11 Map of Manila Bay

1943. 1st Anniv of Fall of Bataan and Corregidor.

J29	**J11**	2c. red	1·90	1·90
J30	**J11**	5c. green	1·90	1·90

1943. 350th Anniv of Printing in the Philippines. No. 531 of Philippines surch Limbagan 1593–1943 and value.

J31	12c. on 20c. bistre	1·90	1·90

J 13 Filipino Girl

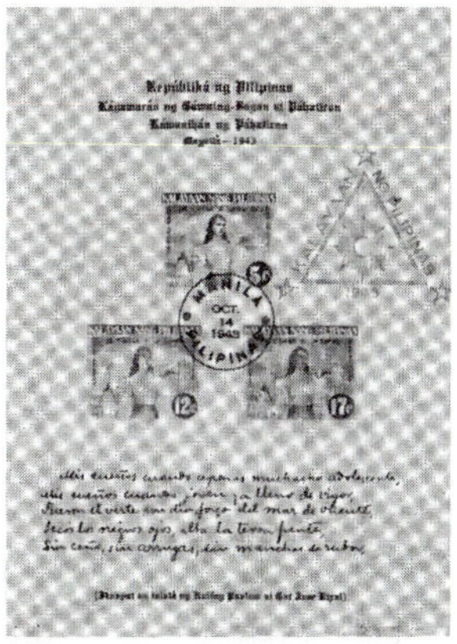

J 14

1943. Japanese Declaration of the "Independence of the Philippines". Imperf or perf. (a).

J32B	**J13**	5c. blue	1·90	1·90
J33B	**J13**	12c. orange	1·90	1·90
J34B	**J13**	17c. red	1·90	1·90

(b) Miniature sheet, 127×177 mm containing Nos. J32/4.

MSJ35	(sold at 2p.50)	£110	28·00

1943. Luzon Flood Relief. Surch BAHA 1943 + and premium.

J36	-	12c.+21c. blue (No. J21)	90	1·90
J37	**J7**	20c.+36c. purple	90	1·90
J38	**J9**	21c.+40c. violet	90	1·90

J 17 Rev. Jose Burgos

J 19 (image scaled to 49% of original size)

1944. National Heroes. Imperf or perf. (a).

J39B	-	5c. blue (Rizal)	2·75	1·50
J40B	**J17**	12c. red	2·75	1·50
J41B	-	17c. orange (Mabini)	2·75	1·50

(b) Miniature sheet 101×143 mm containing Nos. J39/41. Without gum.

MSJ42 (sold at 1p.)		4·50	7·50

1944. 2nd Anniv of Fall of Bataan and Corregidor. Nos. 567/8 of Philippines surch REPUBLIKA NG PILIPINAS 5-7-44 and value.

J43	**105**	5c. on 20c. blue	2·50	3·50
J44	**105**	12c. on 60c. green	3·50	4·50

J 24 Jose P. Laurel

1945. 1st Anniv of Republican Government. Imperf.

J45	**J24**	5s. brown	90	2·75
J46	**J24**	7s. green	90	2·75
J47	**J24**	20s. blue	90	2·75

POSTAGE DUE STAMPS

1942. Postage Due stamp of Philippines surch 3 CVOS. 3 and bar.

JD9	**D51**	3c. on 4c. red	28·00	23·00

OFFICIAL STAMPS

1943. Stamps of Philippines optd variously with bars, (K.P.) and Japanese characters or surch also.

JO29	**104**	2c. green (No. 563)	90	2·00
JO30	-	5c. on 6c. brown (No. 526)	1·90	2·30
JO32	-	16c. on 30c. red (No. 505)	5·75	8·00

1944. No. 526 of Philippines surch 5 REPUBLIKA NG PILIPINAS (K.P.) and four bars.

JO45	5c. on 6c. brown	1·90	2·75

1944. Official stamp of Philippines (No. 531 optd O.B.), further optd Pilipinas REPUBLIKA K.P. and bars.

JO46	20c. bistre	4·00	5·75

1944. Air stamp of Philippines optd REPUBLIKA NG PILIPINAS (K.P.) and two bars.

JO47	**105**	1p. sepia	9·75	11·50

Pt. 17

JAPANESE POST OFFICES IN CHINA

Post Offices at Shanghai and other Treaty Ports operated between 1876 and 1922.

10 rin = 1 sen; 100 sen = 1 yen.

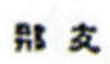

(1)

1900. Stamps of Japan, 1899, optd with T 1.

1	**28**	5r. grey	7·00	5·75
2	**28**	½s. grey	5·75	2·30
3	**28**	1s. brown	7·50	2·10
4	**28**	1½s. blue	17·00	5·25
5	**28**	1½s. violet	8·50	1·70
6	**28**	2s. green	8·50	1·70
7	**28**	3s. purple	10·50	2·10
8	**28**	3s. red	7·00	1·50
9	**28**	4s. red	10·50	2·75
10	**28**	5s. yellow	21·00	2·75
11	**29**	6s. red	23·00	22·00
12	**29**	8s. green	15·00	15·00
13	**29**	10s. blue	15·00	1·50
14	**29**	15s. purple	33·00	2·30
15	**29**	20s. orange	28·00	1·60
16	**30**	25s. green	55·00	8·50
17	**30**	50s. brown	55·00	3·00
18	**31**	1y. red	£110	3·50
19	**32**	5y. green	£650	80·00
20	**32**	10y. violet	£1100	£150

1900. Imperial Wedding issue of Japan optd with T 1.

21	**33**	3s. red	55·00	34·00

1913. Stamps of Japan, 1913, optd with T 1.

33	**36**	½s. brown	5·25	2·75
34	**36**	1s. orange	5·75	2·75
35	**36**	1½s. blue	6·50	2·30
36	**36**	2s. green	7·50	2·10
37	**36**	3s. red	5·75	1·50
38	**37**	4s. red	17·00	8·50
39	**37**	5s. violet	30·00	20·00
40	**37**	6s. brown	38·00	34·00
41	**37**	8s. grey	42·00	42·00
42	**37**	10s. blue	21·00	2·75
43	**37**	20s. red	55·00	8·50
44	**37**	25s. olive	70·00	10·50
45	**38**	30s. brown	£110	55·00
46	**38**	50s. brown	£130	55·00
47	**38**	1y. green and brown	£170	13·00
48	**38**	5y. green	£2250	£750
49	**38**	10y. violet	£4500	£2500

Pt. 18

JAPANESE POST OFFICE IN KOREA

10 rin = 1 sen; 100 sen = 1 yen.

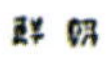

(1)

1900. Stamps of Japan, 1899, optd with T 1.

1	**28**	5r. grey	18·00	15·00
2	**28**	1s. brown	22·00	10·50
3a	**28**	1½s. blue	£300	£180
4	**28**	2s. green	32·00	21·00
5	**28**	3s. purple	21·00	8·00
6	**28**	4s. red	£100	50·00
7	**28**	5s. yellow	90·00	33·00
8	**29**	8s. green	£350	£225
9	**29**	10s. blue	44·00	7·50
10	**29**	15s. purple	£110	10·50
11	**29**	20s. orange	£110	8·00
12	**30**	25s. green	£325	80·00
13	**30**	50s. brown	£200	27·00
14	**31**	1y. red	£550	16·00

1900. Wedding of Prince Imperial. No. 152 of Japan optd with T 1.

15	**33**	3s. red	£130	41·00

Pt. 1

JASDAN

A state of India. Now uses Indian Stamps.

12 pies = 1 anna; 16 annas = 1 rupee.

1 Sun

1942

4	**1**	1a. green	21·00	£200

Index